BC 01/17

D1345932

938403145

THE OXFORD NAMES COMPANION

THE OXFORD
NAMES
COMPANION

Patrick Hanks · Flavia Hodges

A.D. Mills · Adrian Room

OXFORD

UNIVERSITY PRESS

OXFORD
UNIVERSITY PRESS

Great Clarendon Street, Oxford OX2 6DP

Oxford University Press is a department of the University of Oxford.
It furthers the University's objective of excellence in research, scholarship,
and education by publishing worldwide in

Oxford New York

Auckland Bangkok Buenos Aires Cape Town Chennai
Dar es Salaam Delhi Hong Kong Istanbul Karachi Kolkata
Kuala Lumpur Madrid Melbourne Mexico City Mumbai Nairobi
São Paulo Shanghai Singapore Taipei Tokyo Toronto

with an associated company in Berlin

Oxford is a registered trade mark of Oxford University Press
in the UK and in certain other countries

Published in the United States
by Oxford University Press Inc., New York

British Library Cataloguing in Publication Data
Data available

Library of Congress Cataloging in Publication Data
Data available

ISBN 0–19–860561–7

3 5 7 9 10 8 6 4 2

Typeset in Pondicherry, India, by
Alliance Interactive Technology

Printed and bound in Slovenia by
Delo tiskarna d.d., Lubljana
by arrangement with Preševnova družba d.d., Ljubljana

CONTENTS

INTRODUCTION

PATRICK HANKS

An Unparalleled Flowering of Name Studies

The 1990s witnessed an unparalleled growth and flowering of names studies in all their different aspects throughout the world, including areas that had previously been neglected, such as computational analysis of surname distribution. As the new millennium begins, onomastics, the study of names, promises to be the single discipline that does most to bring together technical academic study with general public involvement.

The English Place-Names Society is more active than ever in its 80th year, while the more general (and more recently founded) Society for Names Studies in Britain and Ireland goes from strength to strength. Local history societies, family history societies, and one-name study groups are equally active and growing in number. Similar societies around the world, many of them quite new, are forums for the study of names in other languages, population migration, and the naming of places. In January 2002 the Public Record Office went live with the 1901 British census on line. Public interest was so great that the computers could not bear the volume of traffic and crashed, so that the whole site had to be rebuilt with improved bandwidth, firewalls, and load balancing to cope with the huge demand.

Names are not only of interest to historians and genealogists. Geneticists now study the correlation between inherited genetic characteristics of individuals and people who have the same surname. A standard exercise in first-year university statistics courses is to predict the growth and demise of surnames within a population, given standard assumptions about birth, marriage, child-bearing, and death. Names studies contribute to our understanding of linguistics and language change, while links between names and cultural history are studied by cultural historians. Developers of online lexicons report that over 70% of the items held in their databases are names (business names and product names as well as personal names and place-names). The percentage continues to grow, while the number of vocabulary words remains fairly static. Words are counted in hundreds of thousands, but names are counted in millions.

Names studies involve a great variety of different activities in different disciplines, including computational analysis of medieval archives, migration records, and other documents, with direct relevance and interest to ordinary people as individual bearers of surnames. Most significantly of all, the wealth of data that is rapidly becoming available on the Internet can sometimes enable researchers to accomplish in a few hours tasks that previously took days or even weeks of patient labour in libraries, public record offices, and other archive collections. In this, we are witnesses to the start of an unstoppable revolution. New records, new data, and new websites become available online every day. The number of web pages that can be searched is growing exponentially, and in no area is growth of online resources more dramatic than names studies.

The need now is not only to encourage students to take up onomastics as an academic discipline but also for academically trained experts to make their expertise available, through conferences, meetings of local societies, online discussion forums, and other means, to the wider, untrained, but increasingly large and enthusiastic public. Even a casual glance through the multitude of genealogical forums and websites that have sprung up in the past few years produces two striking impressions: the extraordinarily high level of public interest in the study of names and the extraordinarily wide disparity in levels of knowledge and expertise. Literally millions of people throughout the world now study the history of their family, their name, and the local history of the place in which they live. Cyndi's List—a US-based inventory of online resources for students of genealogy and family names—boasts no less than 15,000 visitors a day. Some web documents are extremely well researched and lay out clearly the whole history of a family, the names of its members, and its linguistic origins. In other cases, researchers hardly get beyond identifying their paternal grandfather before issuing a cry for help or perpetuating a myth. Their enthusiasm needs channelling by expert advice and guidance.

English and Welsh Place-Names

The oldest and (until recently) the most active area of scholarly study of names concerns place-names. It has long been recognized that detailed study of the names of places brings an important perspective to history. The serious academic study of place-names began among medievalists, because the geographical and historical record of names can supplement other historical evidence, sometimes in unexpected ways.

Studying the past through place-names is a highly technical business. The English Place-Name Society was founded in 1923 to promote a county-by-survey study of English place-names. More than one volume is devoted to each county. Lincolnshire, for example, is expected to take 29 volumes. More than 75 volumes have been published so far, and a dozen more are in progress. Place-name scholars collect spellings of place-names (including the names of old places that have since been lost) from charters, court records, and other ancient documents. They study the relationship between names, vocabulary words, and physical geography.

Not only counties, towns, and villages, but also names of individual houses and farms, roads, streets, and fields are collected, especially if they are of any antiquity. Microtoponyms (names of small places) can be especially important in studying family names of local origin: some families took their name, not from a village or larger settlement, but from an individual farm or house in which they lived. Cf. **Blakeway**, from a farm near Much Wenlock in Shropshire, or **Copplestone**, from a minor locality in Colebrook, Devon.

An important development in place-name studies in Britain has been clearer recognition of the range of medieval languages required for satisfactory scholarship. Eighty years ago, the focus was on Old English and Old Norse. Many medieval records are, of course, in Latin and Anglo-Norman French, but the influence of these languages on the actual naming of places is rare. (Exceptions are in some cases cosmetic, as in the case of the Old English place-name *Fulepet* 'foul pit', which was renamed *Beaumont* 'beautiful hill' in Anglo-Norman French by its 12th-century Norman landlord.) The legacy of the Welsh-speaking inhabitants of England in pre-Anglo-Saxon times is now more widely appreciated. Scholars have always recognized that many English river names are of Celtic origin, but this now extends to some habitational and other names. In the words of Professor Richard Coates, 'Whereas the older tendency was to try to explain the most difficult names as English, it is now normal to experiment with full Celtic solutions.'

The Situation in Scotland

Not only in England and Wales, but also in southern and central Scotland, place-names of Welsh origin are important. The 'Strathclyde Britons' in particular, were a Welsh-speaking people of the early Middle Ages, living in southwest Scotland, with their capital in Dumbarton, sandwiched between the Gaelic-speaking kingdom of Dalriada in the west and the Anglo-Saxons of Northumbria and Edinburgh in the east. Welsh was probably spoken in rural districts of southern Scotland at least until the 14th century, possibly later. The Scottish surname **Galbraith** refers to these people: it is from a Gaelic term meaning 'the British [i.e. Welsh-speaking] stranger'. The place name **Fintry** (Stirlingshire) means 'the white house', not in Gaelic but in Welsh. Scottish place-names are at least as complex as those in England, but their study is much less far advanced. A Scottish Place-Name Society was founded in 1996 and the work of systematically collecting early records is just beginning. The complex interactions among Old English, Old Norse, Gaelic, and Welsh, have been studied on the basis of available evidence by scholars such as Nicolaisen, but there is now an urgent need for the energetic and systematic collection and evaluation of early place-name evidence.

Much the same is true of Scottish surnames. The history of the most famous Gaelic clan names of the Highlands and Islands has, in most cases, been studied and recorded from oral tradition as well as ancient documents; but a great deal of work remains to be done on other Scottish surnames. G. F. Black's heroic efforts, published in New York in 1947, were but a start. Many Scottish surnames are nicknames and occupational names from Older Scots. Others are habitational names from towns, old baronies, and other place-names in Scotland. Some important Scottish surnames are of Norman French and English local origin, as a result of developments in the 12th century. King David I of Scotland (ruled 1124–53) spent his formative years at the English court of Henry I. From 1107 he ruled Cumbria, Strathclyde, and parts of Lothian, under his brother, King Alexander I of Scotland. In 1113 he married the powerful and influential Matilda, Countess of Huntingdon, daughter of the Earl of Northumberland. In 1124 (somewhat unexpectedly, three elder brothers having pre-deceased him), he came to the throne of Scotland, bringing with him a retinue of Anglo-Norman barons and their retainers, and set about a vigorous programme of modernization and bureaucratic reform on the Anglo-Norman model. The influence of these events, not only on Scottish history and Scottish

society, but also on the development of Scottish surnames, should not be underesti-
mated. The Anglo-Norman surnames of Scotland are not all traceable to the reign of
David I, but many of them are, and in other cases the possible connection is a question for research.

Names Studies in Ireland

Mention of Gaelic brings us to Ireland. Here, the story is very different. The main
task for Irish onomasticians, both in place-names and surnames, has been to rediscover the original Irish Gaelic forms of names that have been altered, sometimes
dramatically, under English influence. From the 17th century to the early 20th, the
Gaelic language was proscribed by the English administration. Indeed, Irish people
themselves sometimes went to considerable lengths to disguise the Gaelic origins of
their surnames. The traditional prefix *Mac* 'son of' was very often dropped, but in
some cases left a trace, so that, for example, **Mac Fhilib** 'son of Philip' gave rise to
the surname **Killip** (*Fh-*, the lenited form of *F-*, being silent in Gaelic). This was then
in some cases further disguised as **Caleb**, as if it were of Biblical origin. Now, it is
fashionable for Irish people (even those who speak no Gaelic) to rediscover and in
some cases re-adopt the Gaelic names of their forebears.

Similar tales may be told of Irish place-names. That English **Crusheen** corresponds to Gaelic **Croisín** 'little cross' seems straightforward enough, but the relationship between **Ravensdale** and **Gleann na bhFiach** (terms with the same
meaning referring to the same place, in County Louth) is not obvious to non-Gaelic
speakers. A great deal has been accomplished in Irish onomastics, and the general
lines for most names are now probably as clear as they ever will be. The work of the
Ordnance Survey of Ireland on place-names parallels the achievements of Edward
MacLysaght on family names. In both areas, a framework has been established,
enabling more detailed studies to proceed with confidence.

In Northern Ireland, the situation is more complex due to the substantial influx of
Scottish and English population in the 17th century. The Northern Ireland place
name project was founded in 1987 and is achieving results that have aroused considerable public interest in the community. Excellent dictionaries of surnames in
northern Ireland are also now available.

Surnames and First names

The great difference between the study of place-names and that of personal names is
that places stay put, while personal names (or rather their bearers) move around. It is
possible to inspect a place today and draw certain conclusions about its naming in the
6th or 7th century. But the original bearer of a surname is very rarely known at all.
Even if he were, we cannot go and look at him to decide whether he was black-haired
(Old English *blaec*, modern English surname **Blake**) or blond (Anglo-Norman
French **bla(n)c**, modern English surname **Blake!**)

Within the two fields, other differences emerge, too. Surnames are, on the whole,
of much more recent origin than place-names. The student of the origins of English
surnames must be proficient in the Middle English and Anglo-Norman French of the

12th to 14th centuries. The student of the origins of English place-names must be proficient in the Old English of the 7th to 10th centuries.

Surnames encapsulate late medieval occupations (*Smith, Baker, Fletcher, Fuller, Wright,* etc.), nicknames (*long, short, black, grey*), and pet names (*Hopkins, Dickson, Harris*). Traditional forenames reach back across the millennia to Biblical Hebrew (*David, Adam, Job, Zillah*) or into the mists of prehistoric Germanic or Celtic culture (*William, Richard, Robert; Kevin, Neil, Brigid*).

Forenames are chosen; surnames and place-names are imposed. The inventory of common surnames is very large; the inventory of common forenames is very small. New forenames are created often (especially nowadays, when the ties of tradition are in decline) with reference to popular culture; surnames are inherited and many people do not give much thought to their surname.

The inventory of place-names is almost completely static, and the inventory of surnames only slightly less so. People may change their surname, and foreign surnames may be brought into a community from another culture, but it is most unusual to invent a new surname. The student of modern forenames, on the other hand, is trying to hit a moving target: new forenames are frequently invented. Indeed, in certain communities, for example among Black Americans, it is customary to invent an entirely new forenames for a child, especially a female child, a forename that no other child has ever borne (*Condoleezza, Shanayaqua, Latashita*). However, there is an irony in this, in that the norms of phonology impose certain constraints and preferences on the form of the invented name, so that often enough creativity runs out and several families end up inventing the same name independently.

The Geography of Surnames

For many years, surnames studies were neglected (in part, no doubt, because of the instability and inaccessibility of the data), while place-name studies were the carefully guarded specialist preserve of medievalists. In recent years these two strands have started to interact. Computational studies reveal that, even in the late 20th century, when so many people move home so often, a surname may still be strongly associated with a particular locality. Indeed, over half the surnames in Britain still have a statistically significant association with a particular locality, despite all the scattering of population that has taken place since the Industrial Revolution began two hundred years ago. Certainly, people move, but often they do not move very far. In Britain, a surname may be associated with the locality in which it originated (as has been demonstrated time and again in the case of surnames of local origin such as **Armitage**, **Clee**, **Dunwoodie**, **Oxenham**, and **Rockley**), or it may reflect early migration, as in the case of the surname **Rootham**, which originated in Kent but is now associated with Bedfordshire. More puzzling are the surnames which appear to have been widespread in medieval times, but which are now strongly localized. Here, some sort of 'funnelling' process appears to have taken place, according to which a surname thrived in one locality, but died out in others. The association between a surname and a locality may actually strengthen as time goes by, although of course in most cases the tendency is for it to weaken.

The nature of these associations has not yet been properly studied and evaluated. A full picture is only just beginning to emerge. The relationship between surnames and geography will not be fully understood until medieval pipe rolls, 17th-century prot-estation returns, hearth tax returns, 19th-century censuses and civil registration re-cords, and other surviving past records are all fully available in machine-readable form for computational and statistical analysis.

A particularly fascinating area for future study is the evaluation of surname evi-dence for lost place-names, for example **Addicott** (Somerset or Devon), **Beardsley** (Nottinghamshire), **Coatsworth** (Durham). Are these surnames really from place-names, as their form suggests? If so, where were these lost places? Are they genuinely lost places, or are they alternative forms of the names of places that exist today? Or are they so small that they have been overlooked hitherto? What can old records tell us about the early bearers of these names? Where exactly did they live, and what was their social status and occupation? What was their religious affiliation, and how did this change from generation to generation? One or two scattered examples may pro-vide little or no reliable evidence for a hypothesis, but geodemographic cluster an-alysis of large-scale records is extremely revealing. Some very striking results have already been achieved in the mapping of surname distribution, and as old records become available this process will continue.

Surnames are much more variable than place-names, and often certainty is an impossible goal. The nature of the evidence requires statistical analysis, with probabilistic conclusions. Some English and Scottish names now survive in North America, Australia, and elsewhere even though they have almost or completely died out at home, so studies need always to have a global perspective. An example is **Throckmorton**, a surname derived from a place name in Worcestershire. Sir Nich-olas Throgmorton, a leading Tudor banker, gave his name to a street in London; in Tudor times the family seat was at Coughton Court, a magnificent house in Warwickshire, on the Worcestershire border. The surname has thrived in America, but is now rare in Britain. The genealogy has been extensively studied, and is in-structive for a number of reasons. The earliest forebearer who has been traced by genealogists in direct linear ascent is Robert Throgmorton (born about 1353 in Fladbury, Worcestershire), but the surname was already established before that date: Reaney and Wilson report *Adam de Throkemerton* appearing in 1221 at Wor-cester Assizes. In Tudor times, successive generations of the family bore sons pro-lifically (a tendency dramatically reversed in later years), and in the 17th century a John Throckmorton (a 12th generation descendent of 1353 Robert) went to North America, along with several 13th and 14th generation descendants. This also reminds us that generations get out of step. There is, typically, an increasing spread across time of a single generation of distant cousins. For example, among the 14th gener-ation members of this family (taking 1353 Robert as generation 1), the oldest was born in 1589, while the youngest was born over a hundred years later, in 1696. The history of this family also reminds how rapidly things may change: within a couple of generations a family may go from great wealth, power, and prestige to comparative ordinariness or even hard times and poverty, or they may achieve new prosperity on a new continent.

Computers and Names Studies

Traditionally, names studies are pursued in libraries and record offices. The Public Record Office at Kew, for example, is the national archive of England, Wales and the United Kingdom, collecting and preserving the records of central government (such as tax returns) and the law courts. Given patience and persistence, it is sometimes possible to track down quite detailed traces of past individuals. The records span an unbroken period from the 11th century to the present day.

However, pursuing studies in such archives is slow and wearisome, and until recently it has been literally impossible to understand the broader picture of surname history and distribution, because the data was intractable. That situation is now changing. Future surname dictionaries will emulate vocabulary dictionaries in attempting to 'say something about everything' or at least something about every name above a certain specified frequency. Future one-name studies will take account of the relative stability and shifts in geographical distribution of the name. No longer will surname dictionaries propose an Anglo-Scandinavian origin for surnames that are known to be associated with Gloucestershire (a county untouched by Scandinavian settlement); no longer will researchers have to be satisfied with a few scattered examples garnered from selected records when trying to determine the distribution of a surname in times past. Surname studies will be informed by statistics about historical and geographical distribution. Researchers will be able to fire up, at the click of a button, maps of the present-day distribution of a surname and compare them with its distribution in previous centuries. They will be able to zero in on whatever information is on record about the occupation, wealth, lawsuits, criminal activities, and social status of all known bearers of a particular surname, and construct hypotheses about the changing role of this or that family in local and national society, migration, colonization, etc. The very absence of older records for a surname, if it is now frequent will be contrastively suggestive for surname detectives: a name that is frequent now but is sparse in the records of the past must either have been rare then (the modern frequency perhaps being accounted for by a series of large families of male offspring), or it may have been borne by generations of unremarkable middle- and lower-class, law-abiding citizens, probably not very literate, who minded their own business, meddled little in the affairs of others, and left little trace of their sojourn on this earth behind them. At present we do not have the data that enables us to propose hypotheses of this sort for many individual surnames, but it is surely coming. When it comes, it can be linked to GIS (Geographical Information Systems) based projects such as the proposed Social Historical Atlas of Great Britain, with mutual benefits. The new developments that allow us to dream of such things are, in short, the first fruits of what will be a steady flow of large-scale source materials in machine-readable form. Thanks largely to the efforts of the Church of Jesus Christ of Latter-Day Saints (LDS, popularly called the Mormons), together with member of the Federation of Family History Societies, the UK 1881 census is now available on CD-Rom.

The Mormons' strong beliefs in the family and their inclusion of deceased family members in their rituals have long prompted them to collect and make publicly available records of human beings of the past, collected world wide from parish registers, civil registration records, censuses, and other sources. The LDS International Genealogical Index (IGI) is rightly regarded as indispensable by family historians and students of surnames. The IGI can be consulted free of charge, instantly, online, from home, via the Internet. The GUI (graphic user interface) has been beautifully organized, to enable access by name and by country. The IGI is part of an LDS website called Familysearch.com, which, at the time of writing, holds the names of over 200 million individuals.

At present, the IGI is strongly biased towards the English-speaking world, and researchers must constantly bear in mind the 'failure to find fallacy'. Failure to find Greek or Turkish records of a name in past centuries via Familysearch does not mean that the name is not Greek or Turkish: it may mean only that the relevant records are not available or have not yet been collected. Presumably the long-term goal of Familysearch is to incorporate into the database all surviving records of all human beings who have ever lived: many, many billions of records. As that goal moves nearer to fulfilment, we need to make statistical adjustments to compensate for the relative wealth or paucity of evidence in particular regions and particular periods in time, in relation to known facts about the size of population in those places at that time. But now, right now, the emphasis is on collecting data. Evaluating it comes later.

March 2002

ACKNOWLEDGEMENTS

The Publishers and Authors are very grateful to the following who gave their time and expertise to the respective sections of the Companion text.

Where a date is given, this is the year in which the text was first published. The academic affiliations are those held by the individuals at that time.

Surnames 1988

Professor Morton Benson for lending a list of Croatian surnames

Professor Tomás de Bhaldraithe, Professor of Irish Dialectology, University College, Dublin

Mr Tom Bonington, Slavonic Cataloguing Section, Birmingham University Library

Mrs Ela Bullon for her help with Polish sources

Professor G. F. Cushing, Professor of Hungarian, School of Slavonic and Eastern European Studies, University of London

Mr Ian A. Fraser, School of Scottish Studies, University of Edinburgh

Dr Margaret Gelling, Reader: English Place-Name Studies, University of Birmingham

Dr David L. Gold, The Jewish Family Name File, Association for the Study of Jewish Languages, University of Haifa, Israel

Mr M. J. de K. Holman, Department of Russian Studies, University of Leeds

Dr Hywel Wyn Owen, Director, Clwyd Place-Name Council; Y Coleg Normal, Bangor, Wales

Mr O. J. Padel, Institute of Cornish Studies (University of Exeter), Redruth, Cornwall

Derek Palgrave, chairman of the Guild of One-Name Studies

Mrs Ewa Radziminska-Kazmierczak Łódź Medical Academy, Łódź, Poland

Dr Veronica Smart, Centre for Advanced Historical Studies, University of St Andrews, Scotland

Dr G. C. Stone, Fellow of Hertford College, Oxford

Mr C. J. Wells, Fellow and Tutor in Medieval German, St Edmund Hall, Oxford

Dr Geoffrey West, Hispanic Section, The British Library

First Names 1990

Professor Tomás de Bhaldraithe, Royal Irish Academy

Ronald Black, Lecturer in Celtic, University of Edinburgh

P. S Falla, Editor, Oxford-Russian Dictionary

Docent Lena Peterson, University of Uppsala

Professor Emeritus Gwynedd Pierce, University of Wales College of Cardiff

Dr Joseph A. Rief, Bar-Ilan University

Place-Names

English place-names 1991 First Edition and 1998 Second Edition

Professor Kenneth Cameron and Mr Victor Watts, respectively past and present Honorary Directors of the English Place-Name Society for permission to quote from the county surveys published by the Society.

E. Ekwall's monumental *Concise Oxford Dictionary of English Place-Names* was a indispensable source.

Irish place-names 2001-02

Dr Kay Muhr, Department of Celtic Studies, School of Languages, Queen's University, Belfast

Scottish place-names 2001-02

Professor W. F. H. Nicolaisen, Honorary Research Professor, Department of English, University of Aberdeen and former President of the International Council of Onomastic Sciences

Welsh place-names 2001-02

Professor Hywel Wyn Owen, Department of Communication and Media, University of Wales, Bangor

The Welsh place-name entries are heavily indebted to Professor Wyn Owen's *A Pocket Guide: The Place-Names of Wales* (University of Wales Press, 1998)

A DICTIONARY OF
SURNAMES

PATRICK HANKS · FLAVIA HODGES

INTRODUCTION

Organization of Entries

The names in the dictionary are listed in 'nested' groups under a main entry. Where there are several names in a group, the choice of main entry is made on a variety of criteria such as comparative present-day frequency, historical priority, and etymological simplicity. Simple forms, that is, those having no overt diminutive, patronymic, or other morphemes, are usually preferred as main entries, and within each main entry the nested groups consist of variants, diminutives, patronymics, and so on, subdivided according to language. The spelling selected for the main entry is normally the one that is most common now as a surname. Other spellings of what is basically the same name are listed as variants. Preference has been given to English names when selecting a form for the main entry. Where there is no English name in a group, or where the English members of the group are comparatively rare, the main entry form is from one of the other languages of Europe, generally the one in which the name is most prominent.

Each entry explains the linguistic origins of each surname, together with peculiarities of its history, current distribution, and other relevant facts. In many cases, more than one origin is postulated. There is a tendency for uncommon surnames to assimilate to more common ones, which partly underlies the phenomenon of multiple origin.

TYPOLOGY OF SURNAMES

Monogenetic and Polygenetic

How many different types of surname are there? One important distinction already mentioned is between *monogenetic* surnames and *polygenetic* surnames. Monogenetic surnames are those which have a single origin, often being derived from just one original bearer or family of bearers at one particular place and time. Most polygenetic surnames were coined independently in many different places. *Smith*, *Brown*, and *Newton* are classic examples of English polygenetic surnames.

It is not normally possible to identify the original bearer of a monogenetic surname, but it is sometimes possible to postulate that a name must be monogenetic on the basis of its distribution. Thus *Asquith* and *Auty*, the one a local name and the other from a Norse personal name, are both so strongly identified with West Yorkshire that the chances of their being monogenetic must be rated very high. However, whether present-day bearers of the surname *Asquith* are all descended from a single individual, or whether there are several lines stretching back to different individuals all from the village of *Askwith*, is another matter for family-history research rather than for a dictionary of surnames, and it may well be that, as in many questions arising about surnames, not enough evidence survives to give a definitive answer. However, it is also certainly the case that much evidence remains to be discovered and evaluated.

Classification by Type of Origin

Broadly, surnames are conventionally divided into a small number of types according to their origin. Cottle distinguishes just four broad types: those based on patronymics, those derived from local names, those from occupational names, and those from nicknames. We use a fuller classification, but Cottle's four types can be clearly seen underlying them.

Patronymic Surnames

The oldest and most pervasive type of surname is that derived from a given name. Two main strands in the origins of given names may be singled out: vernacular naming traditions and religious naming traditions. In vernacular naming traditions, names were originally composed of vocabulary elements in the local language, and no doubt bestowed for their auspicious connotations (e.g. *Raymond* is derived from elements meaning 'counsel' and 'protection'). In religious naming traditions, names were bestowed in honour of a cult figure. Leaving aside for the moment Jewish naming traditions, it is obvious that the most powerful religious influence on naming in Europe has been the Christian Church. There is hardly a country in Europe that does not have surnames derived from forms of *Peter*, *Paul*, and the other saints, apostles, and missionaries. It comes as something of a surprise, therefore, to note that in many countries, especially in northern

Europe, baptismal names honouring Christian saints and biblical figures were a fairly recent introduction at the time when the bulk of surnames were taking shape. These Christian names were in competition with the older and better-established vernacular naming traditions, for example the Germanic names in use at the time of Charlemagne (742–814).

Surnames derived from ancient Germanic personal names have cognates in many languages. The court of Charlemagne was Christian and Latin-speaking, but the vernacular was the Frankish dialect of Old High German, and the personal names in use were Germanic and vernacular. These personal names were adopted in many parts of northwest Europe, especially among the ruling classes. They were in use among the Normans; hence, many common English and French names such as *Richard*, *Robert*, and *William* (*Guillanume*) are of Germanic origin and have cognates in other European languages.

Some Germanic personal names such as *Siegfried* also have Slavonic derivatives, but on the whole the Slavs had their own inventory of personal names. In western Slavonic-speaking areas (in particular, in Poland and Czechoslovakia), native Slavonic names have given rise to surnames. In Russia, on the other hand, vernacular Slavonic names were proscribed as given names by the Orthodox Church in favour of those honouring Christian saints. For this reason, Russian patronymic surnames are mostly derived from saints' names rather than vernacular Slavonic names.

The most basic type of surname derived from a patronymic—that is, from a person's father's given name—simply presents the father's name as a distinguishing epithet placed either before (as in the case of Hungarian) or more usually after the bearer's own given name. Surnames of this type are found in almost all European languages, but in most of them they are rather, or considerably, less common than names formed with explicitly patronymic endings.

The range of affixes which have been utilized with a patronymic function is very wide. Some are prefixes (Gaelic *mac*, Welsh *ap*, *ab*, Norman French *fitz*, Italian *fi-*), but more are suffixes. These were for the most part originally adjectival or possessive in function (English *-s*, North German *-ing* and *-er*, Rumanian *-esco*, Russian *-ov*), or else result from a more or less reduced form of a phrase meaning 'son of' (English *-son*, Danish/Norwegian *-sen*, Swedish *-son*).

In such cases the surname was almost always originally patronymic in function, although the reference seems occasionally to have been to a grandfather or more distant relative, and in some early examples women are known to have acquired the given name of their husbands as a distinguishing epithet: it may be that some hereditary surnames are derived from this use.

In this category also belong surnames that are derived from shortened or familiar forms of given names, pet forms, and forms with diminutive suffixes. In the Middle Ages such forms were in common use, often almost to the exclusion of the official baptismal form, hence the frequency of such common English surnames as *Hobson* and *Dobson*, based on popular forms of the baptismal name *Robert*, or the equally common North and central European derivatives of *Hans*, a German pet form of *Johannes* John, or the great profusion of Italian surnames derived from diminutive forms of given names.

Metronymic Surnames

Much less common than patronymics, with no more than a handful of surviving examples in the majority of European languages, are metronymics, derived from the name of the first bearer's mother. Since European society has been patriarchal throughout the historical period, it has naturally been the given name of the male head of the household that has been handed on as a distinguishing name to successive generations of sons (and daughters, until their marriage). The few exceptions (e.g. *Catlin*, *Marguerite*, *Dye*) seem to be derived from the names of women who were either widows for the greater part of their adult lives, or else heiresses in their own right. Because such instances are so rare in medieval records, it has been possible in a few cases to pinpoint the individual whose given name has been preserved in this way.

However, Jewish naming practice differs from that of the rest of Europe in this respect, since metronymics are far from uncommon among Ashkenazim (e.g. *Dvorkin* (see DVORIN), *Sorkin* (see SORIN), *Rifkin*). There are several probable reasons for this, which cannot at present be ranked in importance due to the lack of statistical data: (a) before, during, and after the surname period, Ashkenazic Jews have frequently used nicknames, many of them consisting of a parent's given name plus Yiddish possessive *-s*; many of the nicknames containing the mother's given name presumably gave rise to metronymic family names; (b) in other cases, these nicknames consist of the spouse's given name plus Yiddish possessive -*s*, hence men could have taken these nicknames as family names; (c) it is probable that children of deserted mothers (or widows) took family names based on the mother's given name. In connection with (b), we may note a class of surnames which seems to exist only among Ashkenazic Jews (and no other Jews or non-Jews), indicating explicitly the husband of the woman named, for example *Esterman* ('Esther' + 'husband'). In other cases, we cannot tell whether Ashkenazic family names belong in this category or not: *Roseman(n)*, for instance, might be one of these names (cf. the Yiddish female given name *Royze* Rose) or it might be merely an ornamental name. *Perlman* is even more complicated: it could be one of these names (cf. the Yiddish female given name *Perl* Pearl); it might be an ornamental name; or it might indicate someone who dealt in pearls (though this last possibility is the least likely because the relative high frequency of the name clashes with the small number of Ashkenazic Jews who dealt in pearls).

Other Derivatives of Given Names
A few surnames in various languages illustrate some other relationship between the first bearer of the surname and the bearer of a given name incorporated in it: employment (e.g. *Bateman*; see BATE), connection by marriage (e.g. *Watmough*), or residence in the same dwelling (e.g. *Anttila*).

Surnames from Kin Terms
A small group of surnames, but with representatives in most European languages, identifies the bearer by his family relationship (e.g. *Oade*, *Neame*, *Ayer*), presumably to some well-known local figure, simply by mentioning the kinship term.

Local Names
Surnames derived from placenames may be divided into two broad categories: *topographic* names and *habitation* names. These terms have been used throughout this work in preference to the traditional but vaguer term 'local name'. Topographic names are derived from general descriptive references to someone who lived near a physical feature such as an oak tree, a hill, a stream, or a church. Habitation names are derived from pre-existing names denoting towns, villages, farmsteads, or other named habitations. Other classes of local names include those derived from the names of rivers, individual houses

with signs on them, regions, and whole countries. As a general rule, the further someone had travelled from his place of origin, the broader the designation. Someone who stayed at home might be known by the name of his farm or locality in the parish; someone who moved to another town might be known by the name of his village; while someone who moved to another county could acquire the name of the county or region from which he originated.

Habitation Names
It is sometimes difficult, especially in the case of multiple-element names (in England usually a defining adjective plus a generic noun), to be precise about whether a surname is derived from an identifying topographic phrase such as '(at) the broad ford' or '(by) the red hill' or from an established placename such as *Bradford* or *Redhill*. It is also sometimes possible that what has been thought of as a topographic name is in fact a habitation name from some minor, unidentified place now lost.

Polish names ending in -*owski* have consistently been identified in this dictionary as habitation names, in spite of the fact that it has by no means always been possible to identify relevant places named with the base forms in -*ów* or -*owo*. Others may wish to pursue this task. Place-names with meanings such as 'oak-tree locality' or 'woody area' were clearly numerous in Poland. (In the case of Jewish surnames, the ending -*owski* does not normally indicate a habitation name, but has merely been borrowed as an appropriate surname ending to be attached to formations of several different classes. To some extent, this process was probably going on in Polish even earlier: much further research is needed on individual names before the threads can be properly disentangled in each case.)

Topographic Names
It has already been mentioned that topographic names are those that refer to physical features such as trees, forests, hills, streams, and marshes, as well as to man-made structures such as churches, city walls, and castles.

Surnames derived from the proper names of geographical features such as rivers have also been classed here as topographic rather than habitation names, since they refer to a geographic location rather than to a particular named settlement.

Some surnames that are ostensibly topographic, such as *Hall* and *Monkhouse*, are in fact occupational, for they originally denoted someone who was employed at such a place: for example, at a great house or monastery.

Regional and Ethnic Names

Another category of local surnames comprises those denoting origin in a particular region or country. These tended to be acquired when someone migrated a considerable distance from his original home, so that a specific habitation name would have been meaningless to his new neighbours, and he would be known simply as coming 'from the East', or 'from Devon', or 'from France'. Many of these names have the form of adjectives (e.g. *French*, *Dench*, *Walsh*); others are in the form of nouns denoting a person (e.g. *Fleming*, *Moravec*). It is possible that in some cases these were originally nicknames bestowed in line with the imagined character traits associated with the inhabitants of the region or country concerned, rather than denoting actual nationality. Someone called 'French' may actually have been French, or he may have adopted sophisticated or even affected mannerisms and tastes popularly associated with French people and culture. In other cases, such names denoted some trading or other connection with a remote place, as is the case with some Ashkenazic Jewish surnames of this type.

House Names

Another category of local names is the 'house name', referring to a distinctive sign attached to mark out a house before the days of numbered streets and addresses. A number of early surnames have been documented as having this origin, and several old Jewish surnames are derived from the names of houses in the Jewish quarter of Frankfurt-am-Main, for example *Rothschild*. However, the importance of this category of surname has sometimes been exaggerated, and many names that have been so explained are in fact nicknames of uncertain significance, or, in the case of Jewish surnames, ornamental names.

Occupational Names

There are many types of surname that are explicitly occupational, in that they refer directly to the particular trade or occupation followed by the first bearer. Buried within this dictionary lies an inventory of the common trades of medieval Europe. These occupations can be divided into classes such as agricultural (e.g. *Sheppard*, *Bouvier*), manufacturing (e.g. *Smith*, *Glover*), retail (e.g. *Menger*, *Kuptsov*), and so on.

They can also be classified according to linguistic criteria. The most basic type of occupational name is represented by words straightforwardly denoting the activity involved, whether as a primary derivative of a verbal root (e.g. *Webb*, *Hunt*) or formed by means of an agent suffix attached to a verb (e.g. *Baker*, *Tissier*) or to a noun (e.g. *Potter*, *Töpfer*). Some occupational names are derived from a noun plus an agent noun from a verb (e.g. *Leadbetter*, *Eisenhauer*, and the more lexicalized *Schuster* and *Stellmacher*).

Another type of surname refers to a calling by metonymy, naming the principal object associated with that activity, whether tool (e.g. *Pick*, *Nadel*) or product (e.g. *Pain*, *Maslov*).

Particularly in the case of Ashkenazic Jewish surnames, occupational names may have attached to them the explicit suffix *-man(n)* (e.g. *Federman*, *Hirshman*). This is also occasionally the case with German (*-mann*) and English (*-man*) occupational names (e.g. *Habermann*, *Zimmermann*, *Milman*).

Another group is similar in form to one type of surname derived from nicknames (see below), but semantically it clearly belongs in the category of occupational names. Members of this group consist of a verb-stem plus a noun, describing the typical action and object involved in the trade of the person concerned, sometimes in a humorous way (e.g. *Catchpole* for a bailiff; *Knatchbull*, *Tueboeuf*, and *Mazzabue* for slaughterers).

In the Middle Ages, people, at least among the Christian population, did not pursue specialized occupations exclusively to the extent that we do today. Smiths, millers, and wrights were indeed specialists, but even they would normally have their own smallholding for growing crops and keeping a few animals. Other members of society who acquired occupational names would concentrate some but not all of their energies on the particular occupation.

Others were instead simply designated as the servant of some person of higher social status. This is the source, for example, of the English surnames *Maidment* and *Parsons*, and of many English surnames with *-man* added to a given name or even, in a few cases, to a surname. Many surnames ostensibly denoting high rank or descent from someone of high rank, such as *Abbott* and *Squire*, probably have this origin (see the section below on status names).

Surnames from Nicknames

Surnames having a derivation from nicknames form the broadest and most miscellaneous class of surnames. To a large extent this is a catch-all category, encompassing many different types of origin. The most typical classes refer adjectivally to the general physical aspect of the person concerned (e.g. *Blake, Hoch, Tolstoy*), or to his character (e.g. *Stern, Fromm, Smirnyagin*). Others point, with an adjective and noun, to some particular physical feature (e.g. *Whitehead, Białowąs*). Many nicknames refer unambiguously to some physical deformity (e.g. *Cripwell, Baube*), while others may be presumed to allude to it (e.g. *Hand, Daum*). Others probably make reference to a favoured article or style of clothing (e.g. *Boot, Cope*).

Many surnames derived from the names of animals and birds were originally nicknames, referring to appearance or character, from the attributes traditionally assigned to animals. In the Middle Ages anthropomorphic ideas were held about the characters of other living creatures, based more or less closely on their observed habits, and these associations were reflected and reinforced by large bodies of folk tales featuring animals behaving as humans. The nickname *Fox* (*Goupil, Lysenko*) would thus be given to a cunning person, *Lamb* to a gentle and inoffensive one. In other cases, surnames derived from words denoting animals are of anecdotal origin (see next paragraph).

Anecdotal Surnames

A large group of surnames derived from a particular kind of nickname arose as the result of some now irrecoverable incident or exploit that involved the bearer. In studies of modern nicknames borne by individuals within a community, this type is found to be common, but it is also apparent that the reason for the nickname, which may only ever have been known to a few people, is quickly forgotten, whereas the name itself may continue to have wide and enduring currency. It is fruitless to try to guess now at the events that lay behind the acquisition of nicknames such as *Death* and *Leggatt* in past centuries.

'Imperative' Surnames

Another group of anecdotal surnames consists of a small but disproportionately fascinating number of nicknames composed of a verb-stem plus a noun (e.g. *Shakespeare*). These apparently commemorate either a characteristic action (e.g. *Wagstaff*) or a particular incident (e.g. *Tiplady*). A further source of interest is that many of them may be obscene.

Seasonal Surnames

Also related to such 'incident' names are those names that refer to a season (e.g. *Winter, Lenz*), month (e.g. *May, Davout*), or day of the week (e.g. *Freitag*). It has been suggested that these names refer to the time of birth, baptism, or conversion. In the cases of more recently acquired surnames, in particular Jewish names, reference is sometimes to the time of official registration of the name. Certainly surnames derived from the names of various Christian festivals (e.g. *Christmas, Toussaint, Santoro*) seem to have been acquired in this way. But the seasonal names may also have referred to a 'frosty' or 'sunny' character, while the medieval day names may have referred to feudal service owed on a particular day of the week. No explanation offered for either Christian or Jewish names in this group has been proven conclusively.

Status Names

One group of surnames, dealt with by some writers as 'occupational names' and by others as 'nicknames', we have labelled as a separate category—status names. These for the most part denote a particular role in medieval society (e.g. *Bachelor, Franklin, Knight, Squire*). It must be remembered, though, that there are names that are ostensibly status names (e.g. *King, Prince, Duke, Earl, Bishop*), which are of comparatively exalted status, so that present-day bearers are most unlikely to be descended from a holder of the rank in question. In most cases the name was probably originally borne by a servant of the dignitary mentioned, in other cases it may have been given as an 'incident name' to someone who had acted such a role in a pageant or other festivities, or else mockingly to someone who behaved in a lordly manner. Jewish names of this type (e.g. *Kaiser, Graf, Herzog*) are probably all ornamental only.

Ornamental and Arbitrary Names

A category of surname not found in most European languages and apparently confined to communities where the adoption of surnames was late and enforced rather than organic, is the ornamental or arbitrary coinage.

Variants, Diminutives, Augmentatives, and Pejoratives

Finally, brief mention must be made of the common classes of surnames that are derived from base forms of personal names and nicknames, and occasionally from occupational names. In this dictionary these are generally listed under the base form following an appropriate heading. Diminutives include surnames that are formed from vocabulary words with a hypocoristic suffix (e.g. Czech *Sedláček* 'little farmer', Italian *Scarsello* 'little miser') and those that are derived from pet forms of given names or nicknames (e.g. English *Jess* and *Jessel* from *Joseph*, *Russell* from *Rouse* 'red-head'). In addition, there are names that are explicitly patronymic in form, derived from pet forms of given names (e.g. English *Jesson* from *Jess*, *Robson* from a diminutive of *Robert*). As a general definition, a diminutive is a pet form, which has hypocoristic force. In practice, it has not always been possible to differentiate between a diminutive and a simple variant. The Flemish name *Gorick* is a case in point: it is a derivative of a Flemish form of the Greek name *Geōrgios* 'George', but it is not clear from the available evidence whether it is hypocoristic. More often than

not, however, diminutives are distinguished by specifically diminutive suffixes, of which Italian has a particularly rich and productive set. Russian and Polish are not far behind, while diminutives of one kind and another are also found in most other European languages. They are much rarer in Spanish surnames, which do not boast the wide variety of derivative forms found in most other European languages.

Augmentatives are much rarer. They mean 'big', whereas diminutives mean 'little'. Typical augmentative endings are Italian *-oni* and *-one*, and French *-at*. Czech *-ec* also has augmentative force.

The other class of derivative surname to be mentioned here is the pejorative, where an ending that originally had an insulting or derogatory force has been added to a word or given name to form a surname. Typical pejorative endings are Italian *-azzi* and *-acci* and French *-ard* and *-aud*.

ABBREVIATIONS

Aberdeens.	Aberdeenshire	Gaul.	Gaulish
acc.	accusative	Gen.	Genesis
adj.	adjective	gen.	genitive
ANF	Anglo-Norman French	Ger.	German
art.	article	Gk	Greek
aug.	augmentative	Gloucs.	Gloucestershire
Ayrs.	Ayrshire	Gmc	Germanic
Banffs.	Banffshire	Hants	Hampshire
Beds.	Bedfordshire	Hebr.	Hebrew
Beloruss.	Belorussian	Herefords.	Herefordshire
Berks.	Berkshire	Herts.	Hertfordshire
Berwicks.	Berwickshire	Hung.	Hungarian
Bret.	Breton	Hunts.	Huntingdonshire
Brit.	British	Ir.	Irish
Bucks.	Buckinghamshire	It.	Italian
Bulg.	Bulgarian	Jer.	Jeremiah
Cambs.	Cambridgeshire	Josh.	Joshua
Cat.	Catalan	Judg.	Judges
Celt.	Celtic	Kincardines.	Kincardineshire
Ches.	Cheshire	L	Latin
Chron.	Chronicles	Lanarks.	Lanarkshire
class.	classical	Lancs.	Lancashire
Conn.	Connecticut (U.S.A.)	Leics.	Leicestershire
Corn.	Cornish	LGk	Late Greek
cpd	compound	Lincs.	Lincolnshire
Cumb.	Cumbria/Cumberland	lit.	literally
Dan.	Danish/Daniel (context)	LL	Late Latin
dat.	dative	masc.	masculine
def.	definite	Mass.	Massachusetts (U.S.A.)
Denbighs.	Denbighshire	Matt.	Matthew
Derbys.	Derbyshire	MD	Maryland (U.S.A.)
deriv.	derivative	MDu.	Middle Dutch
dial.	dialect	ME	Middle English
dim.	diminutive	med.	medieval
Du.	Dutch	metr.	metronymic
Eng.	English	MHG	Middle High German
Exod.	Exodus	MLG	Middle Low German
fem.	feminine	mod.	modern
fl.	*floruit*, flourished	n.	noun
Flem.	Flemish	Neh.	Nehemiah
Flints.	Flintshire	neut.	neuter
Fr.	French	nom.	nominative
freq.	frequentative	Northants	Northamptonshire
Fris.	Frisian	Northumb.	Northumberland
Gael.	Gaelic	Norw.	Norwegian
		Notts.	Nottinghamshire

Num.	Numbers	Pol.	Polish
O	Old (with various languages)	Port.	Portuguese
OBret.	Old Breton	pres.	present
OBulg.	Old Bulgarian	Prov.	Provençal
OCat.	Old Catalan	Ps.	Psalm(s)
OCorn.	Old Cornish	Renfrews.	Renfrewshire
OCzech	Old Czech	Rev.	Revelation
ODa.	Old Danish	Roxburghs.	Roxburghshire
OE	Old English	Rum.	Rumanian
OED	*Oxford English Dictionary*	Russ.	Russian
OF	Old French	Sam.	Samuel
OFris.	Old Frisian	Sc.	Scots
OHG	Old High German	sc.	scilicet, namely
OIcel.	Old Icelandic	Shrops.	Shropshire
OIr.	Old Irish	sing.	singular
OIt.	Old Italian	Skt	Sanskrit
ON	Old Norse	Slav.	Slavonic
ONF	Old Northern French	Sp.	Spanish
OProv.	Old Provençal	Staffs.	Staffordshire
OSax.	Old Saxon	Stirlings.	Stirlingshire
OSlav.	Old Slavonic	Swed.	Swedish
OSp.	Old Spanish	Ukr.	Ukrainian
OSwed.	Old Swedish	var.	variant
OW	Old Welsh	vocab.	vocabulary
Oxon.	Oxfordshire	W	West/Welsh (context)
part.	participle	Warwicks.	Warwickshire
patr.	patronymic	Wigtons.	Wigtonshire
Pebbles.	Peebleshire	Wilts.	Wiltshire
pej.	pejorative	Worcs.	Worcestershire
Pembrokes.	Pembrokeshire	Yid.	Yiddish
Perths.	Perthshire	Yorks.	Yorkshire
pl.	plural	*	hypothetical form

A

Aagaard *see* ÅGÅRD

Aalbers *see* ALBERT

Aalto Finnish: ornamental name from Finn. *aalto* wave. This is one of many Finn. surnames selected from vocab. words denoting natural phenomena of the landscape and sea at the time when surnames were being adopted in Sweden and Finland during the 18th and 19th cents.
Var.: **Aaltonen**.

Aaron Jewish: from the Hebr. given name *Aharon*, borne by the brother of Moses, who was the first high priest of the Israelites (Exod. 4: 14). The traditional derivation is from Hebr. *har-on* 'mountain of strength', but it is more probably of Egyptian origin, like MOSES, with a meaning no longer recoverable. In some countries *Aaron* was also a Gentile given name, and so not all occurrences of the surname and its derivs. are Jewish.
Vars.: **Aron** (esp. Fr.); **Agron(ski)** (Russ.); **Aharoni** (Israeli).
Patrs.: **A(a)rons**, **A(a)ronso(h)n** (Ashkenazic); **Aronov(ich)**, **Aronoff**, **Aronow(icz)**, **Arunowicz**, **Aronowitz**, **Aronovitz**, **Aronin** (E Ashkenazic); **Arnow(icz)**, **Arnowitz** (from the E Yid. form *Arn*); **Ben-Aharon** (Israeli).
Patrs. (from dims.): **Areles** (Ashkenazic); **Arkow**, **Arkin** (E Ashkenazic).
Cpds: **Aronstam** ('stock of Aaron'); **Aronstein** ('rock of Aaron', ornamental elaboration).

Aartsen *see* ARNOLD

Abadam *see* ADAM

Abajo Spanish: topographic name for someone who lived downhill or downstream from the main settlement, from Sp. *abajo* below (a development, not attested before the 15th cent., of OSp. *baxo*, from LL *bassus*; cf. BASS). Cf. ARRIBA.

Abascal Spanish (possibly of Basque origin; cf. ABASOLO): local name composed of the elements *abas* priest + *kale* street (cf. ABBÉ and CALLE).

Abasolo Basque: topographic name for someone who lived by or on a patch of land in the ownership of the church, from *abas* priest (a Romance borrowing; cf. ABBÉ) + *solo* meadow.

Abatelli *see* ABBÉ

Abb *see* ALBERT

Abbé French: from OF *abe(t)*, *abed* priest, member of the clergy (see ABBOTT), perhaps a nickname for a sanctimonious person or an occupational name for someone employed in the household of a priest. The Scots cogn.

Abbie in at least one case was an occupational name, borne by a family who provided hereditary lay abbots.
Vars.: **Labbé** (with fused def. art.); **Labbey** (Burgundy); **Labbez** (N France).
Dims.: It.: **Ab(b)atini**, **Ab(b)atelli**, **Ab(b)atucci**; **Labadini**; **Badini**, **Vatini**.
Patrs.: It.: **Dell'Ab(b)ate**, **Degli Ab(b)ati**.

Abbey English: topographic name for someone living by an abbey or occupational name for someone working in one, from ME *abbeye*, *abbaye* (OF *abeie*, LL *abbātia* abbey, priest's house, a deriv. of Gk *abbas*; see ABBOTT).
Vars.: **Abb(a)y**, **Abbe**; **Abdey**, **Abdie** (derived directly, not via OF, from the L term).

Abbondi Italian: from the personal name *Abbondio* (L *Abundius*, from LL *abundus*, class. L *abundans*, copious, abundant (literally, 'overflowing')). This was the name of a 5th-cent. bishop, patron saint of Como. The surname is particularly common around Lake Como and in Ticino canton, Switzerland.
Vars.: **Abondi**, **Ab(b)ondio**.

Abbott English: occupational name for someone employed in the household of an abbot, or perhaps a nickname for a sanctimonious person thought to resemble an abbot, from ME *abbott*, OE *abbod*, reinforced by OF *abe(t)* priest; see ABBÉ. Both the OE and the OF term are from LL, Gk *abbas*, *abbatis* priest, from Aramaic *aba* father). The ostensible celibacy of the clergy makes it unlikely that the surname is an occupational one for a cleric, but cf. *Abbie* at ABBÉ.
Vars.: **Abbot**, **Abbet**.
Patrs.: Ir., Sc.: **McNab(b)**, **McNabo**, **Monaboe** (Gael. **Mac an Aba(dh)**).

Abbs *see* ABEL

Abbühl *see* BÜHLER

Abdey *see* ABBEY

Abear *see* BEER

Abeke *see* ALBERT

Abel 1. English, French, and Dano-Norwegian: from the Hebr. given name *Hevel*, which is of uncertain origin; the traditional derivation is from Hebr. *hevel* breath, vigour, used also in the figurative sense 'vanity', 'worthlessness'. This name was borne by the son of Adam who was murdered by his brother Cain (Gen. 4: 1–8), and was popular as a given name in Christendom during the Middle Ages, when there was a cult of suffering innocence which Abel represented. **2.** German: dim. of ALBERT.

Vars. (of 1): Eng.: **Abell**, **Able**. Fr.: **Abeau**.

Dims. (of 1): Eng.: **Ablett**, **Ablitt** (chiefly E Anglia); **Ablott**; **Hablot**.

Patrs. (from 1): Eng.: ABELSON. Dan., Norw.: **Abels**.

Patr. (from 1) (dim.): Eng.: **Abbs** (chiefly Norfolk).

Abella Catalan: **1.** nickname for a small and active person, or metonymic occupational name for a bee-keeper, from Cat. *abella* bee (LL *apicula*, dim. of class. L *apis*). **2.** habitation name from places so called in the provinces of Lérida and Barcelona. The name is of uncertain etymology, and may be akin to that of *Avelia* in Italy, normally considered to be of Etruscan origin.

Vars. (of 2): **Abellan**, **Abellà**.

Dims. (of 1): Prov.: **Abeilhé**, **Abeilhon**, **Abeilhou**.

Abelló Catalan: of uncertain origin. It may be akin to ABELLA, but is also possibly from the L personal name *Abellio*, gen. *Abelliōnis*, which seems to have originally denoted a god worshipped in the Pyrenean region in Roman times, and is of opaque etymology.

Abelson **1.** English: patr. from the given name ABEL. **2.** Jewish (Ashkenazic): patr. from *Abele*, a dim. of the Yid. given name *Abe*, from Aramaic *aba* father (cf. ABBOTT).

Vars. (of 1): **Ableson**. (Of 2): **Abeles**, **Abells**; **Abelov(itz)**, **Abelevitz**, **Abilowitz** (E Ashkenazic).

Abendroth German (nickname) and Jewish (Ashkenazic, ornamental name): from Ger. *Abendrot* sunset (OHG *ābintrōto*, from *ābint* evening + *rōt* red). As a Ger. nickname it may have been applied to a large man, in allusion to the giant *Abendrot*, the subject of several medieval folk tales. As a Jewish name it was chosen as an ornamental name; cf. MORGENSTERN.

Abensperg Austrian: habitation name from a place in Carinthia, so called from OHG *ābint* evening + *berg* hill, probably because the hill is to the W of the town and the sun sinks behind it in the evening.

Aberbach *see* AUERBACH

Abercrombie Scots: habitation name from a place in Fife (earlier *Abarcrumbach*), so called from Brittonic *aber* confluence + a river name containing the element *crom* crooked + the local suffix *-ach*.

Var.: **Abercromby**.

Åberg Swedish: ornamental name composed of the elements *å*, *aa* river + *berg* hill.

Var.: **Oberg** (an Anglicized spelling found in the U.S.).

Abernethy Scots: habitation name from a place near Perth, so called from Brittonic *aber* confluence + a river name possibly akin to Gael. *neithich* water sprite.

Var.: **Abernathy**.

Abhamon *see* HAMMOND

Abhervé *see* HARVEY

Abilowitz *see* ABELSON

Abivon *see* IVE

Abken *see* ALBERT

Able *see* ABEL

Ableson *see* ABELSON

Ablewhite *see* APPLETHWAITE

Äbli *see* ALBERT

Abondi *see* ABBONDI

Abonville French: habitation name from a place in Eure-et-Loir, Normandy, so called from the Gmc personal name *Abbo* (of uncertain origin, perhaps akin to Gothic *aba* man) + OF *ville* settlement, village (see VILLE).

Vars.: **(D')Aboville**.

Abraham Jewish, English, French, German, Dutch, etc.: from the Hebr. personal name *Avraham*, borne by the first of the Jewish patriarchs, founder of the Jewish people (Gen. 11–25). The name is explained in Gen. 17: 5 as being derived from Hebr. *av hamon goyim* 'father of a multitude of nations'. It was commonly used as a given name among Christians in the Middle Ages, and has always been a popular Jewish given name.

Vars.: **Abram** (but for Eng. see also ADBURGHAM). Ger.: BRAHM. Jewish: **Abrahm**, **Abrahamer**; **Avra(h)am**, **Avra(h)m**, **Abramski**, **Abramsky** (E Ashkenazic); **Abra(ha)mi**, **Abrahamy**, **Avrahami**, **Avra(ha)my** (Israeli).

Dims.: Jewish: **Abramcik**. Prov.: **Abramin**. It.: **Abramino**. Ukr., Beloruss.: **Abramchik**, **Avramchik**.

Patrs.: Eng.: **Abra(ha)ms(on)**. It.: **D'Abramo**. Ger.: **Abrami** (Latinized). Low Ger.: **Abra(h)ms**, **Abramsen**; **Brahms**. Flem., Du.: **Abrahams**; **Bra(h)ams**. Norw., Dan.: **Abrahamsen**, **Bramsen**. Swed.: **Abrahamsson**. Jewish: **Abra(ha)ms**; **Abrahamso(h)n**, **Abra(h)mson**, **Abramzon**, **Bramson**; **Abrah(a)mov**, **Abramov**, **Abra(ha)mof(f)**, **Abramow**, **Abrahamovich**, **Abramowitz**, **Abra(ha)mowicz**, **Abramowitch**, **Abramovitz**, **Abramovicz**, **Abramovitch**, **Abramovic(h)**, **Abramowsky**, **Avra(ha)mov**, **Avrahamof(f)**, **Avramow**, **Avramovich**, **Avramovitz**, **Avramovsky** (E Ashkenazic); **Abra(h)movici** (Rum. spelling); **Abrahamian**, **Avra(ha)mian**, **Aprahamian** (among Iranian Jews). Russ.: **Abramov**, **Avramov**; **Ibraimov** (from *Ibrahim*, an Arabic form of the name used in Turkic (Moslem) areas). Ukr., Beloruss.: **Abramovich**. Pol.: **Abramowicz**. Croatian: **Abramović**, **Avramović**.

Patrs. (from dims.): Jewish: **Abrashkin**. Russ.: **Avrashkov**, **Avras(h)in**.

Abram *see* ADBURGHAM

Abreu Portuguese: from the Gmc (Visigothic) personal name *Avredo*, probably composed of the elements *alb*, *alv* elf + *rēd* counsel (cf. ALFRED). The name was borne by a 7th-cent. Hispanic bishop.

Abry French: habitation name for someone living in a rudimentary dwelling, from OF *abri* shelter, refuge (from OF *abrier* to put under covers, keep dry, from L *apricāre* to dry in the sun).

Var.: **Abric**.

Absalom English: from the Hebr. personal name *Avshalom*, composed of the elements *av* father + *shalom* peace. This was the name of the third son of King David, who rebelled against him and was eventually killed, to the great grief of his father (2 Sam.: 15–18). The story was a favourite one in medieval England and elsewhere, and the given name was in use among Christians in spite of the omen. The actual circumstances in which Absalom met his death, with his long hair getting caught in a tree as he was fleeing in his chariot, led to the use of the name as a nickname for a man with a fine head of hair, and the surname may also have originated from this use.

Vars.: Eng.: **Absolom**, **Absolon**, **Aspelon**, **Asplen**, **Asplin(g)**; **Ashplant** (altered by folk etymology, as if from *ash* + *plant*).

Patrs.: Gael.: MCAUSLAN. Russ.: **Avesalomov** (a clerical name adopted by priests). Jewish: **Abs(h)alomov**.

Abstreiter German: habitation name from a place in Bavaria called *Abstreit*, a metathesized deriv. of Late MHG *abtes* abbot's + *reut* clearing. Folk etymology, however, makes it appear to be derived from Ger. *abstreiten* to dispute, repudiate, deny.

Var.: **Absreuter** (*Absreuten* is the name of a place in Württemberg of the same origin).

Acard see ACHARD

Accard see ACHARD

Accorsi see BONACCORSO

Ace English: from the ONF given name *Ace*, *Asse*, which is from a Frankish personal name *A(t)zo*, a hypocoristic form of any of the various Gmc cpd names with a first element *adal* noble (see ADEL).

Var.: **Aze**.

Dims.: Eng.: **As(t)let(t)**, **As(t)lin(g)**, **Ashlin**, ASHLING. Fr.: **Ascelin**, **Asselin(eau)**. It.: **Azzini**, **Azzol(in)i**.

Aug.: It.: **Azzoni**.

Patrs.: Ger.: **Atzen**. It.: **D'Azzi**.

Acedo Spanish: nickname for a brusque or stern person, from OSp. *açedo* harsh (LL *acētus* bitter, from *acētum* vinegar).

Aceituno Spanish: topographic name for someone who lived near an olive tree or in an olive grove, from Sp. *aceituno* olive tree (a deriv. of *aceite* (olive) oil, from Arabic *zait*).

Acero Spanish: nickname for an inflexible person, or metonymic occupational name for a maker of steel objects, from Sp. *acero* steel (LL *(ferrum) aciārium*, a deriv. of *acies* blade, point of a sword, from *acer* sharp, keen).

Acevedo Spanish: topographic name for someone who lived in a place overgrown with holly bushes, from a collective of OSp. *azevo* holly (L *acrifolium*; cf. GRIFFOUL).

Acha Spanish form of Basque **Atxa**: topographic name for someone who lived near an outcrop of rock or a large boulder, from Basque *atx* rock, crag + the def. art. *-a*.

Achard English (Norman) and French: from the ANF personal name *Aschard*, a cogn. of ECKHARDT.

Vars.: Eng.: **Achert**, **Ashard**, **Hatchard**. Fr.: **Achart**, **Ac(c)ard**, **Acquard**, **Acquart**.

Patr.: It.: **D'Accardo**.

Achatz German: from the L given name *Achātius*, probably a deriv. of *achātes* agate (of Gk origin). The name was borne by a 4th-cent. Byzantine saint, numbered among the '14 Holy Helpers' and honoured chiefly in Bavaria.

Vars.: **Agatz**, **Agotz**.

Acheson see ADAM

Achrameev see BARTHOLOMEW

Achten see AGGIS

Achtermann Low German: habitation name for someone whose home was at the back of a settlement, from MLG *achter* behind (cogn. with Eng. *after*, which has been specialized in a temporal sense) + *mann* man.

Vars.: **Echtermann**; **Achterling**, **Echterling**.

Ackary see ZACHARY

Acker English, German, and Jewish (Ashkenazic): topographic name for someone who lived by a plot of cultivated land, from ME *acker* field (OE *æcer*) or from Ger. *Acker* field, agriculture (OHG *ackar*).

Vars.: Eng.: **Aker**, **A(c)kers**, **Acre(s)**, **Akker(s)**, **Akess**. Jewish: **Aker**.

Cpds (ornamental): Swed.: **Åkerberg** ('field hill'); **Åkerblom** ('field flower'); **Åkerlind** ('field lime-tree'); **Åkerlund** ('field grove'); **Åkerstedt** ('field homestead'); **Åkerström** ('field river').

Ackerman 1. English and Jewish (Ashkenazic): topographic name, var. of ACKER. 2. English: status name under the feudal system for a bond tenant who was employed as a ploughman for a manor. On many manors there were separate tenements held by 'acremen' in return for ploughing service.

Vars.: **Akerman**, **Acreman**.

Acket see HACKETT

Ackland English: 1. habitation name from *Acland* Barton in Landkey, Devon, earlier *Ackelane* (13th cent.), deriving from the OE personal name *Acca* + OE *lane* lane. Acca is probably a derivative of *āc* oak, with connotations of strength and reliability. 2. habitation name from any of various minor places so called from OE *āc* oak + *land* land. 3. habitation name from *Acklam* in Yorks., so called from OE *āc* oak + *lēum* dat. pl. of *lēah* wood, clearing.

Var.: **Acland**.

Ackroyd English: topographic name, most common in W Yorks., given originally to someone who lived in a clearing in an oak wood, from Northern ME *ake* oak (OE *āc*) + *royd* clearing (OE *rod*).

Vars.: **Acroyd**, **Ak(e)royd**, **Aykroyd**, **Akred**, **Ecroyd**.

Acland see ACKLAND

Acosta Spanish (probably of Portuguese origin): topographic name for someone who lived on a hillside or near the coast, from a misdivision of Port. *Da Costa* (see COSTE) into *(D')Acosta*.

A'Court see COURT

Acquard see ACHARD

Acre see ACKER

Acreman see ACKERMAN

Acroyd see ACKROYD

Ács Hungarian: occupational name for a worker in wood, from *ács* carpenter.

Acton English: habitation name from one of the places so called in Shrops. and adjacent counties, most of which get their name from OE *āc* oak + *tūn* enclosure, settlement. A few may have a first element that represents the OE personal name *Acca* (see ACKLAND).

Adair *see* EDGAR

Adam English, French, Catalan, Italian, German, Flemish/Dutch, Polish, and Jewish (Ashkenazic): from the Hebr. personal name *Adam*, which was borne, according to Genesis, by the first man. It is of uncertain etymology; it is often said to be from Hebr. *adama* earth; cf. the Gk legend that Zeus fashioned the first human beings from earth. It was very popular as a given name among non-Jews throughout Europe in the Middle Ages.

Vars.: It.: **Adami**; **Dami** (an aphetic form). Pol.: **Adamski** (with the surname suffix *-ski*; see BARANOWSKI). Jewish: **Adamski**, **Adamsky** (E Ashkenazic).

Low Ger.: **Dehm**.

Dims.: Eng.: **Adnett**, **Adnitt**, **Ade**; **Ad(de)kin**, **Atkin**; **Ai(t)kin**, **Aitken** (chiefly Scots); **Ai(c)ken** (chiefly N Ireland); **Adcock** (esp. E Midlands), **Atcock**, **Hadcock**; **Ad(d)ie**, **Ad(d)(e)y**, **Adye**; **Haddy** (Devon and Cornwall). Fr.: **Adanet**, **Ad(e)net**, **Adné**, **Ad(e)not**. It.: **Adamini**, **Adamol(l)i**; **Dametti**. Low Ger.: **Dahmke**. Pol.: **Adamek**; **Adamczyk** (also Jewish). Czech: **Adamík**, **Adámek**. Ukr.: **Adamik**.

Augs.: Pol.: **Adamiec**. Czech: **Adamec**.

Patrs.: Eng.: **Ad(d)ams**, **Adhams**; **Adamson**. Welsh: **Abadam**; **Baddams**. Ir., Sc.: **McAdam** (Gael. **Mac Adaim**). Ir.: **MEGAW**. It.: **D'Adamo**; **D'Adda**. Sp.: **Adanez**. Dan., Norw.: **Adamsen**. Swed.: **Adamsson**. Pol.: **Adamowicz**, **Adamiak**. Jewish: **Adams**; **Adamov(itch)**, **Adamovitz**, **Adamowitz**, **Adamovicz** (E Ashkenazic). Croatian: **Adam(ov)ić**. Beloruss.: **Adamovich**. Gk: **Adamou**, **Adamides**.

Patrs. (from dims.): Eng.: **Ades**, **Addess**; **Addis** (chiefly N Ireland); **Adkins**, **Hadkins**, **At(t)kins**; **Adcocks**; **Adeson**, **Addison**; **At(t)kinson**; **Ai(t)chison** (chiefly Scots); **A(t)cheson** (chiefly N Ireland). Sc.: **McAd(d)ie**, **McCad(d)ie**, **Ked(d)ie**, **Keddy**, **Kiddie**, **Kiddy** (Gael. **Mac Adaidh**). Pol.: **Adamkiewicz**.

'Servant of A. (dim.)': Eng.: **Addyman**.

Habitation names: Pol.: **Adamczewski**. Czech: **Adamovský**.

Adar *see* ODER

Adburgham English: habitation name from a place near Manchester (now *Abram*), named from the gen. case of the OE female personal name *Ēadburg* (composed of the elements *ēad* prosperity + *burh, burg* fort) + OE *hām* homestead.

Var.: **Abram** (chiefly common in Lancs., but may nevertheless also be derived from ABRAHAM).

Adcock *see* ADAM

Addams *see* ADAM

Adde *see* ADEL

Adderley English (W Midlands): habitation name from places in Staffs. and Shrops., both so called from OE personal names + OE *lēah* wood, clearing. The Staffs. Adderley contains *Ealdrēd* (see ALDRITT 2); the Shrops. placename contains a fem. personal name, perhaps *Ealdþrȳð*.

Addington English: habitation name from any of various places in Bucks., Kent, Northants, and Surrey, so called from OE *Eaddingtūn* or *Æddingtūn* 'settlement (OE *tūn*) associated with *Eadda* (or *Æddi*)'.

Addionisio *see* DENNIS

Ade *see* ADAM

A'Deane *see* DEAN

Adeane *see* DEAN

Adel 1. German: short form of any of the numerous Gmc cpd personal names with the first element *adal* noble; cf. e.g. ALBERT. **2.** Jewish (Ashkenazic): ornamental name from Ger. *Adel* nobility; cf. EDEL.

Var. (of 2): **Adelman**.

Dims. (of 1): Ger.: **Adde**. Low Ger.: **Adelmann**. Fris.: **Adema**. Patrs. (from 1): Ger.: **Adelung**. Low Ger.: **Aden**. Fris.: **Adena**.

Cpds (ornamental): Jewish: **Adelbaum** ('noble tree'), **Adelsberg** ('noble hill'), **Adelsburg** ('noble city'), **Adelstein**, **Edelstein** ('precious stone').

Adeline *see* ALLIS

Adell Catalan: **1.** cogn. of ADEL 1. **2.** from the L personal name *Atīlius*, an old Roman family name of uncertain origin.

Dim.: **Dalí**.

Adenauer German: habitation name from *Adenau*, a village in the Rhineland. The first element is a river name, *Adana*, of uncertain origin; the second is probably MHG *ou(we)* marshy ground (mod. Ger. *Aue*, cogn. with OE *ēg*; see NYE).

Adger *see* EDGAR

Adhams *see* ADAM

Adie *see* ADAM

Adkin *see* ADAM

Adlard *see* ALLARD

Adler German (nickname) and Jewish (Ashkenazic, ornamental name): from Ger. *Adler* eagle (MHG *adelar*, a cpd of *adal* noble (see ADEL 1) + *ar* eagle (var. of *arn*, cogn. with OE *(e)arn*; cf. EARNSHAW)). Nobility is an attribute of the eagle in most European cultures, it being considered king of the birds.

Vars.: Jewish: **Adlerman**; **Adlar** (Israeli).

Cpds (probably ornamental coinages, but perhaps also habitation names from places so called): Jewish: **Adlerstein** ('eagle rock'), **Adlerberg** ('eagle hill').

Adlington English: habitation name from places so called in Ches. (*Edulvinton* in Domesday Book) and in Lancs. (*Adelventon*). Both get their names from OE *Ēadwulfingtūn*, 'settlement associated with *Ēadwulf*', a personal name composed of the elements *ēad* wealth, prosperity + *wulf* wolf.

Adné *see* ADAM

Adolf German: from the Gmc personal name *Adalwulf*, composed of the elements *adal* noble + *wulf* wolf. This was a common given name until the Second World War and was, for example, a dynastic name in the noble houses of Holstein and Nassau.

Dims.: It.: **Adolfino**.

Patrs.: Low Ger.: **A(h)lfs**; **Adolfsen**. Swed.: **Adolfsson**.

Adorno Italian: from a medieval given name, meaning 'gifted' (L *adornātus*, past part. of *adornāre* to decorate, adorn), bestowed by fond parents as a good omen.

Dim.: **Adornetti**.

Adrados Spanish: habitation name from any of various places so called, for example in the provinces of Segovia and León. The placename is of uncertain derivation, possibly from LL *hederātus*, an adj. deriv. of class. L *hedera* ivy.

Adrian English, French, German, and Dano-Norwegian: from the L personal name *(H)adriānus*, originally an ethnic name referring to someone who came from the Adriatic Sea (L *Adria*, possibly akin to *ater* black). It was adopted as a cognomen by the emperor who was among other things responsible for the construction of Hadrian's Wall across the North of England. It was also borne by several minor saints, in particular an early martyr at Nicomedia (d. *c.*304) who is the patron saint of soldiers, butchers, and (in Flanders and Switzerland) smiths. There was also an English St Adrian (d. 710), born in N Africa; he was abbot of St Augustine's, Canterbury, and his cult enjoyed a brief vogue after the supposed discovery of his remains in 1091. Later, the name was adopted by several popes, including the only pope of English birth, Nicholas Breakspear, who reigned as Adrian IV (1154–9).

Var.: Fr.: **Adrien**.

Dims.: It.: **Arianello**, **Arianetto**.

Patrs.: Flem.: **Adriaens**. Du.: **Adriaans(z)**, **Adriaanse(n)**.
Russ.: **Adrianov**.

Patr. (dim.): Russ.: **Adriyashev**.

Adshead English: habitation name from an unidentified place, probably in Lancs., the origin of which would be OE *Æddeshēafod* 'headland of *Æddi*' (cf. ADDINGTON).

Ady *see* ADAM

Aebrechts *see* ALBERT

Aegten *see* AGGIS

Aeles *see* ALLIS

Aelion Jewish (Sefardic): ornamental name from Hebr. *haelyon* 'the One on High', i.e. God.

Afanasyev Russian: patr. from the given name *Afanasi* (Gk *Athanasios* 'immortal', from *a-* not + *thanasios* mortal, a deriv. of *thanatos* death). The name owes its currency to the cult, especially popular in the Eastern Church, of St Athanasius (*c.*297–373), bishop of Alexandria, one of the most influential of the fathers of the Christian Church.

Var.: **Afanasov**.

Dims. (patrs.): Russ.: **Afonchikov**, **Afonyushkin**, **Afonichev**, **Afonchin**; **Fon(k)in**, **Funikov**. Croatian: **Atanacković**, **Tanasković**.

Dims. (not patrs.): Ukr., Beloruss.: **Panasik**, **Panchenko**.

Affery *see* AUBREY

Affleck *see* AUCHINLECK

Afonchikov *see* AFANASYEV

Afremov *see* YEFREMOV

Agace French: **1.** nickname for someone supposedly resembling a magpie, such as a chattering or nagging person, from OF *agache, agasse* magpie (of Gmc origin; cf. OHG *agaza*). **2.** cogn. of AGGIS.

Vars. (of 1): **Agasse**, **Lagasse**; **Agache**, **Lagache** (Normandy, Picardy); **Ageasse**, **Ajasse**; **Ayasse**.

Dims. (of 1): Fr.: **Agassis**, **Agassiz** (Switzerland). It.: **Agazzini**; **Gazzini**, **Gazzola**.

Agapov Russian: patr. from the given name *Agap* (Gk *Agapios*, a deriv. of *agapē* spiritual love). This name was borne by various early saints, most notably one martyred at Caesarea in Palestine in AD 306.

Vars.: **Agapyev**, **Agapeev**; **Gapeev**.

Agar *see* EDGAR

Ågård Danish: habitation name from any of various minor places so called from the elements *å* river + *gård* enclosure, yard.

Var.: **Aagaard**.

Agas *see* AGGIS

Agate English: topographic name from someone who lived by a gate; the first syllable represents the fused ME preposition *a, o*, in origin a var. of the Eng. vocab. word *on*, reinforced by ANF *a* (L *ad*).

Agatestein Jewish (Ashkenazic): Anglicized form of an ornamental name composed of a Yid. element meaning 'agate' (cf. ACHATZ) + the ornamental suffix *-stein* stone.

Agatz *see* ACHATZ

Ageasse *see* AGACE

Ager *see* EDGAR

Agethen *see* AGGIS

Aggis English: from the medieval female given name *Agace*, a vernacular form of the name (L *Agatha*, Gk *Agathē*, from Gk *agathos* good) borne by a 3rd-cent. Sicilian martyr.

Vars.: **Agiss**, **Ag(g)as(s)**; **Haggis**.

Dims.: Eng.: **Agget(t)**. It.: **Agatiello** (Naples); **Agatini**.

Aug.: It.: **Agatoni**.

Patrs.: Ger.: **Agethen**; **Eit(h)ner**, **Eidtner**, **Eythner**. Flem.: **Aegten**, **Achten**. It.: **D'Agata**, **Dell'Agata** (Sicily).

Aghini *see* ECK

Agiss *see* AGGIS

Agneesen *see* ANNIS

Agnew **1.** English (Norman): nickname for a meek or pious person, from OF *agnel, agneau* lamb (LL *agnellus*, dim. of class. L *agnus*). **2.** English (Norman): habitation name from *Agneaux* in La Manche, the etymology of which is uncertain; it was probably assimilated by folk etymology to Fr. *agneau* lamb from some unknown Gaul. original. **3.** Irish: stressed on the second syllable, this is an Anglicized form of Gael. **Ó Gnímh** 'descendant of *Gníomh*', a byname meaning 'Action', 'Activity'. The Ó

Gnímh family held the hereditary office of poet to a branch of the O'Neills and to the Macdonalds.

Dims. (of 1): It.: **Agnellini**, **Agnellotti**, **Agnelutti**.

Patrs. (of 1): Fr.: **Delagneau**. It.: **D'Agn(i)ello**.

Agnoletti *see* ANGEL

Agosti Italian: from the medieval given name *Agosto* (L *Augustus*, from *augere* to increase, become greater). Originally a title used by the Roman emperors after accession, the name was popular also among early Christians, who read into it the implication that the bearer had become greater by being baptized. The month of *August* was so called after the first Emperor Augustus, and occasionally the given name was bestowed because of some association with the month; cf. DAVOUT.

Var.: **Agusto**.

Augs.: It.: **Agostoni**, **Agustoni**.

Patr.: Swed.: **Augustsson**.

Agostinetti *see* AUSTIN

Agotz *see* ACHATZ

Agricola German: Latinization of any of various names meaning 'farmer', esp. ACKERMAN and BAUER.

Agrifoul *see* GRIFFOUL

Agron *see* AARON

Aguado Spanish: topographic name, metonymic nickname, or metonymic occupational name, from Sp. *aguado* water, a deriv. of *agua* (L *aqua*). It may have denoted a water seller, an abstemious person who drank only water, or someone who lived by a spring. Cf. BOILEAU and DRINKWATER.

Agudo Spanish: nickname for a clever or witty person, from Sp. *agudo* sharp, astute (L *acūtus* sharp, past part. of *acuere* to sharpen).

Agüero Spanish: **1.** habitation name from places so called in the provinces of Huesca and Santander. These probably get their name from LL *(vīcus) aquārius* well-watered (settlement). **2.** from the given name or nickname *Agüero* (good) omen' (L *augurium*), bestowed on a child in the hope that it would bring him luck.

Aguilar Spanish and Catalan: habitation name from any of numerous places so called, from L *aquilāre* haunt of eagles (a deriv. of *aquila*; see EAGLE). It is also found as a Jewish (Sefardic) name, in which case it is probably ornamental.

Var.: **Aguilera** (from L *aquilāria*).

Aguillaume *see* WILLIAM

Aguiló Catalan: of uncertain origin, probably from the L personal name *Aquilo*, gen. *Aquilōnis*, 'North (wind)' (a deriv. of *aquila* EAGLE or *aqua* water).

Aguinaga Spanish form of Basque **Aginaga**: topographic name for someone who lived near a group of yew trees, from Basque *(h)agin* yew + the collective suffix *-aga*.

Aguirre Spanish form of Basque **Agirre**: topographic name for someone who lived in a prominent position in a village, from Basque *ager, agir* plainly visible, conspicuous. This is also used as the first element of a large number

of topographic names referring to conspicuous geographical features, such as **Aguirrezabal(a)** 'conspicuous open space'.

It is also possible that this term (with the fused OF preposition *de*) is the origin of *Daguerre*, a place in the parish of Saint-Martin-de-Seignaux, Landes, which has given rise to the surname borne by the inventor of photography, Louis Jacques Mandé **Daguerre** (1789–1851).

Agulló Catalan: habitation name from a place near Àger, apparently so called from the L personal name *Aculeo*, gen. *Aculeōnis*, a deriv. of *aculeus* sting, point.

Agusto *see* AGOSTI

Agutter English: topographic name for someone living by a watercourse or drainage channel, from ME *a* (cf. AGATE) + *gutter* (ANF *goutiere*, LL *guttāria*, from *gutta* drop).

Aharoni *see* AARON

Ahern Irish: Anglicized form of Gael. Ó hEachthighearna 'descendant of *Eachthighearna*', a personal name composed of the elements *each* horse (see KEOGH) + *tighearna* master, lord (see TIERNEY). The name is most common in SW Ireland.

Vars.: **Ahe(a)rne**, HEARNE.

Ahl **1.** German: nickname for a 'slippery' individual or metonymic occupational name for an eel fisher, from MHG, OHG *āl* eel. **2.** Low German: cogn. of ADEL. **3.** Swedish: ornamental name from Swed. *a(h)l* ALDER.

Vars. (of 3): **Ahlman**, **A(h)lsén**; **A(h)lenius** (Latinized).

Cpds (ornamental, from 3): Swed.: **Ahlberg** ('alder hill'); **Ahlbom** ('alder tree'); **Ahlborg** ('alder town'); **A(h)lfors** ('alder waterfall'); **A(h)lgren** ('alder branch'); **Ahlmark** ('alder territory'); **Ahlqvist** ('alder twig'); **Ahlstedt** ('alder homestead'); **Ahlström** ('alder river').

Ahlers *see* ALLARD

Ahlfors *see* AHL

Ahlfs *see* ADOLF

Ahmel *see* AMERY

Ahonen Finnish: ornamental name from Finn. *aho* glade + the gen. suffix *-nen*, perhaps adopted in some cases as a topographic surname by someone who lived in a glade in the forest.

Ahrén Swedish: status name for a tenant farmer, from Swed. *arende* leasehold, tenancy.

Var.: **Arrhenius** (a Latinized form).

Ahrendsen *see* ARNOLD

Åhs Swedish: ornamental name from Swed. *ås* ridge, perhaps in some cases adopted as a topographic surname by someone living on a ridge. This is one of the many surnames taken from words denoting features of the natural landscape when surnames were adopted in Sweden during the 18th and 19th cents.

Var.: **Åsell**.

Cpds: **Å(h)sberg** ('ridge hill'); **Åslund** ('ridge grove'); **Åstrand** ('ridge shore').

Aichele *see* OAK

Aichison *see* ADAM

Aides *see* EDEL

Aiello Italian: habitation name from any of the many places in S Italy so called, from LL *agellus*, dim. of L *ager* field.
Vars.: **D'Aiello**, **(D')Ajello**; **D'Azeglio** (Piedmont); **Gelli** (Tuscany); **Zelli** (Lombardy).

Aigner *see* EIGNER

Aigrefeuille *see* GRIFFOUL

Aihel *see* OAK

Aiken *see* ADAM

Aikman *see* OAK

Aillier French: occupational name for a seller of garlic, OF *aillier* (L *alliārius*, a deriv. of *allium* garlic).

Ailmer *see* AYLMER

Ailward *see* AYLWARD

Ailwyn *see* ALWYN

Aimer *see* AYLMER

Aimetti *see* HAMMOND

Ainger English (Norman) and French: from the Gmc personal name *Ansger*, composed of the elements *ans-* god + *ger, gar* spear.
Vars.: Eng.: **Ang(i)er**, **Angear**, **Aunger**. Fr.: **Anger**; **Anquier** (Normandy, Picardy); **Ansquer** (Brittany).

Ainhorn *see* EINHORN

Ainscough English: habitation name from a lost place in Lancs. The second element of the name is clearly ON *skógr* wood; the first may be ON *einn* alone, solitary (a cogn. of OE *ān*, mod. E *one*), with the meaning 'wood standing alone'.
Var.: **Ainscow**.

Ainslie Scots: apparently a habitation name, from an unidentified place. The surname is found chiefly in the border regions of Scotland and Northumb. It may be that the placename source should be sought in this area, or the surname may have been brought in from elsewhere. If the name came from the South, it may derive from one of several places so named in the Midlands, such as *Ansley* in Warwicks. or *Annesley* in Notts. (The former is from OE *ānsetl* hermitage + *lēah* wood, clearing; the latter is apparently from the gen. case of a byname derived from OE *ān* solitary (see AINSCOUGH) + *lēah*.)
Vars.: **Ainsley**, **Aynsley** (more common south of the border); **Ainslee**.

Ainstein *see* EINSTEIN

Ainsworth English: habitation name from a place near Manchester, so called from the gen. case of the OE personal name *Ǣgen* (a short form of the rare cpd names with the first element *ǣgen* own) + OE *worð* enclosure (see WORTH). The surname is most common in Lancs.

Air *see* AYER

Airey English: habitation name from some minor place in N England named *Eyrará* 'gravel-bank stream', for example *Aira* Beck and *Aira* Force near Ullswater in Cumbria.
Var.: **Airy**.

Aisenberg *see* EISEN

Aish *see* ASH

Aiskew *see* ASKEW

Aiskowitz *see* ISAAC

Aïstov Russian: patr. from the nickname *Aïst* 'Stork', used for a tall thin man with long legs.

Aitchison *see* ADAM

Aizen *see* EISEN

Aizenshtat *see* EISENSTADT

Aizic *see* ISAAC

Aizlewood *see* HAZELWOOD

Ajam *see* JOHN

Ajasse *see* AGACE

Ajean *see* JOHN

Ajello *see* AIELLO

Ajsenberg *see* EISEN

Ajsik *see* ISAAC

Ajzen *see* EISEN

Ajzenstadt *see* EISENSTADT

Aker *see* ACKER

Akerman *see* ACKERMAN

Akeroyd *see* ACKROYD

Akhmatov Russian: patr. of Turkic origin, from the Arabic given name *Ahmed, Ahmad* 'most praiseworthy one', borne by Muslims in honour of the son of the prophet Muhammad.

Akimakin *see* JOACHIM

Akker *see* ACKER

Akred *see* ACKROYD

Aksyonov Russian: patr. from the given name *Aksyon* (Gk *Auxentios*, from *auxein* to increase, magnify). This name was borne by a 4th-cent. saint of Mopsuestia in Cilicia and a 5th-cent. Syrian hermit, both much revered in the Orthodox Church.
Vars.: **Aks(y)anov**, **A(v)ksentyev**, **Aksentsev**, **Aksentsov**, **Aksyutin**.

Alabarbe *see* BARBE

Alabaster English: alteration (by folk etymology) of ANF *arblaster* crossbowman (OF *arbalestier*, LL *arcuballistārius*, from *arcuballista*, a cpd of *arcus* bow + *ballista* catapult, ballista). The term was not only an occupational name for a soldier trained to use one of these weapons, but also denoted a category of feudal tenant in sergeantry, originally, no doubt, one who provided armed service with a crossbow.

Vars.: **Arblaster**, **Albisser**.

Aladerne Provençal: topographic name for someone living near a patch of buckthorn, OProv. *aladerne* (LL *alaterna*). In medieval France this shrub was regarded as a symbol of righteousness, and this fact suggests that in some cases the surname may have originally been a nickname for a righteous person.

Vars.: **Daladerne** (Roussillon); **Daladier** (Vaucluse).

Álamo Spanish: topographic name for someone who lived near a poplar tree or poplar grove, from Sp. *álamo* poplar (of uncertain etymology, probably from L *(populus) alba* white poplar, crossed with Celt. *elmos* poplar).

Collective: **Alameda**.

Alan *see* ALLEN

Alarcón Spanish: habitation name from places so called in the provinces of Cuenca and Córdoba, which are of uncertain etymology.

Alard *see* ALLARD

Alaric French: from a Gmc personal name composed of the elements *ala* all, entire + *rīc* power.

Vars.: **Alari**, **Alric**; **Hal(l)ary**; **Aury**, **Auric**.

Alastar *see* ALEXANDER

Alauze French: nickname for a cheerful person, always singing, from OF *alauze* skylark (L *alauda*).

Alaway *see* ALLOWAY

Alayrac French: habitation name from *Alairac* in Aude, *Aleyrac* in Drôme, or *Alleyrac* in Haute-Loire, all apparently so called from the Gallo-Roman personal name *Alarius* (of uncertain origin) + the local suffix *-ācum*.

Var.: **D'Alayrac**.

Alba Spanish and Italian: habitation name from any of the numerous places so called. The meaning of the placename is unknown; the coincidence in form with L *alba* (fem.) white is probably no more than coincidental. It may be of Ligurian origin (compare *Alba Longa*, the name of the oldest Latin town).

Albalat *see* VALLAT

Alban English, French, German, and Swedish: from the given name *Alban* (L *Albānus*, originally an ethnic name from the many places in Italy and elsewhere called ALBA). In England the given name was bestowed chiefly in honour of St Alban, the first British martyr (3rd or 4th cent.); it is now most common in E Anglia.

Vars.: Eng.: **Al(l)bon**, **Allbond**, **Allbone**, **Al(l)born**. Fr.: **Albain**, **Auba(i)n**. Ger.: **Albohn**.

Dims.: Fr.: **Aubanel**. It.: **Albanelli**. Cat.: **Albanell**.

Albaret French: topographic name for someone who lived by a poplar grove, OF *albaret* (LL *albarētum*, collective of *(populus) alba* white poplar (see ÁLAMO), influenced by *arborētum*, a collective of *arbor* tree).

Vars.: **Albarède**; **Auvray**.

Albarracín Spanish: habitation name from a place in the province of Teruel, originally named as 'the land of *Razīn*', from the Arabic def. art. *al* + *barr* land + the personal name *Razīn*. During the 11th cent. this place constituted a small independent kingdom in Muslim Spain.

Albarrán Spanish: nickname for a newcomer to an area, from Sp. *albarrán* stranger (from the Arabic def. art. *al* + *barrani* foreign, a deriv. of *barr* land).

Albee English: habitation name from *Alby* in Norfolk or *Ailby* in Lincs., both of which are derived from the ON personal name *Ali* (a short form of the various cpd personal names with the first element *all* all) + ON *býr* farm, settlement.

Var.: **Alby**.

Albeisser *see* ALTBÜSSER

Alberdi Basque: topographic name, apparently from *arb(el)* slate + *erdi* centre, middle; the first element has undergone metathesis under the influence of the second.

Albert English, Low German, French, Catalan, and Hungarian: from a Gmc personal name (*Albrecht* in mod. Ger.), composed of the elements *adal* noble + *berht* bright, famous. This was one of the most common Gmc given names, and was borne by various medieval princes, military leaders, and great churchmen, notably St Albert of Prague (Czech name VOJTĚCH, Latin name *Adalbertus*), a Bohemian prince who died a martyr in 997 attempting to convert the Prussians to Christianity; St Albert the Great (?1193–1280), Aristotelian theologian and tutor of Thomas Aquinas; and Albert the Bear (1100–70), Margrave of Brandenburg.

Vars.: Eng.: **Al(l)bright** (altered by folk etymology); **Aubert** (Norman). Low Ger.: **Aber(t)**, **Allebrach**. Fr.: **Auber(t)**, **Aubé**, **Aubey**.

Dims.: Fr.: **Aubertin**, **Auberty**, **Auberton**; **Aub(e)lin**, **Aub(e)let**. Prov.: **Alberty**. It.: **Albertini**, **Albert(in)elli**, **Albertol(l)i**, **Albertotti**, **Albertocci**, **Albertuzzi**; **Libertini**, **Libertucci**. Ger.: ABEL; **Ap(p)el** (Franconia; see also APPLE); **Opel** (Saxony); **Elbel**, **Etzel** (U.S. **Edsel**) (Bavaria); **Abe(r)le**, **Abe(r)li(n)**, **Oberlin**, **Äbli** (Switzerland). Low Ger.: **Abb**, **Ab(b)eke**. Fris.: **Ab(b)ema**.

Aug.: It.: **Albertoni**.

Pej.: It.: **Albertazzi**.

Patrs.: Eng.: **Alberts**. Fr.: **D'Albert**. It.: **D'Alberti**, **De Albertis**; **De Liberto**. Ger.: **Alberding**, **Allerding**, **Albrink**. Low Ger.: **Albers**. Fris.: **Alpers**. Flem.: **Aebrechts**, **Olbrechts**. Du.: **Alberts**, **A(a)lbers**. Norw., Dan.: **Albrechtsen**, **Albertsen**. Pol.: **Olbrychtowicz**.

Patrs. (from dims.): Low Ger.: **Abbing**, **Ab(b)en**; **Ab(e)ken**, **Abeking**.

Albin English, French, and German (Austrian): from the given name *Albin*, (L *Albīnus*, a deriv. of *albus* white; cf. ALBAN). This was the name of several minor early Christian saints, including St Aubin, bishop of Angers (d. *c*.554). The popularity of the given name was also influenced, esp. in Austria, by the Gmc given name *Albuin*, composed of the elements *alb* elf + *win* friend. This was the name of the Lombard leader (d. 572) who made himself king of N Italy, and also of a bishop of Brixen (Bressanone) in S Tyrol who has been confused with St Aubin, mentioned above.

Vars.: Eng.: **Aubin**, **Obin**. Fr.: **Alby**; **Aubin**, **Auby**. Ger.: **Albien**.

Dims.: Fr.: **Albinet**, **Aubinet**, **Aubineau**. It.: **Albinelli**, **Albinetti**, **Albinotti**, **Albinuzzi**.

Aug.: It.: **Albinoni**.

Patr.: Eng.: **Albinson**.

Habitation name: Pol.: **Albinowski**.

Albiol Catalan: habitation name from a place in Tarragona, so called from the L personal name *Albiōlus*, a dim. of *Albius* (from *albus* white).

Albisser *see* ALABASTER

Albrook *see* HOLBROOK

Albuquerque Spanish: habitation name from *Alburquerque* in the province of Badajoz, so called from L *alba* white (fem.) + *quercus* oak. Although of Sp. origin, this surname is now much more common in Portugal.

Albutt English (W Midlands): from the Gmc personal name *Albodo*, composed of the elements *adal* noble + *bodo* messenger, which was introduced into England by the Normans.

Var.: **Allbutt**.

Alcaide Spanish: occupational name for the military governor of a castle or city, Sp. *alcaide* (from the Arabic def. art. *al* + *qā'id* captain, governor, a deriv. of *qāda* to lead). The word, first attested in the 11th cent., is still in use in Spain today.

Alcalá Spanish: habitation name from any of the numerous fortified villages named during the Moorish occupation of Spain with the Arabic def. art. *al* + *qalá* fortress, castle.

Alcalde Spanish: occupational name for a judge, OSp. *alcalde* (from the Arabic def. art. *al* + *qādī* judge, pres. part. of *qadā* to resolve, decide). In mod. Sp. the word means 'mayor', but this sense does not seem to have developed before the 15th cent., and is probably too late to be reflected in the surname.

Alcántara Spanish: habitation name from any of various places, for example in the provinces of Cáceres, Cadiz, and Valencia, so called from the Arabic def. art. *al* + *qántara* arch, bridge. The dim. **Alcantarilla** is still in use in Spain as a vocab. word.

Alcaraz Spanish: habitation name from a place in the province of Albacete, so called from the Arabic def. art. *al* + *karaz* cherry tree.

Alcázar Spanish: habitation name from any of the numerous places, for example in the provinces of Ciudad Real, Cuenca, and Granada, so called from Sp. *alcázar* citadel, palace (from the Arabic def. art. *al* + *qasr* fortress, itself a borrowing of L *castrum*; cf. CASTRO).

Alcocer Spanish: habitation name from any of various places, for example in the provinces of Alicante and Guadalajara, so called from the Arabic def. art. *al* + *qusayr* small palace (a dim. of *qasr*; cf. ALCÁZAR).

Alcock English: from a dim., with ME -*cok* (see COCK 1), of various given names beginning with *Al*-, notably *Alan* (see ALLEN), ALBAN, ALBERT, and ALEXANDER.

Vars.: **Allcock**, **Alecock**, **Aucock**, **Awcock**, **Alcoe**, ALCOTT.

Patr.: **Al(l)cox**.

Alcolea Spanish: habitation name from any of the numerous places so called from the Arabic def. art. *al* + *qulay'a* fort.

Alcott English: 1. habitation name for someone living in an old cottage, from OE *(e)ald* old + *cot* cottage (see COATES). 2. var. of ALCOCK, in some cases the result of deliberate alteration because of the obscene connotations that could, from the 18th cent., be read into that name.

Vars.: **Allcott**, **Allcoat**, **Aucott**, **Aucutt**.

Aldakov *see* YEVDOKIMOV

Aldar *see* ADLER

Alday Spanish form of Basque **Aldai**: habitation name from a place in the province of Biscay, so called from Basque *alde* region, area + the suffix -*i*.

Aldea Spanish: habitation name from any of the numerous places so called from Sp. *aldea* village (from the Arabic def. art. *al* + *dái'a* village, countryside).

Aldecoa Basque: apparently a local name composed of the elements *alde* region, area (cf. ALDAY) + the gen. suffix -*ko* + the def. art. -*a*.

Alden English: 1. from the ME personal name *Aldine*, OE *Ealdwine*, composed of the elements *eald* old + *wine* friend. 2. var. of HALDANE. 3. German: see OLD.

Vars.: **Aldin(e)**, **Auden**, **Olden**. (Of 1 only): ALWYN.

Alder English: 1. from one of two OE personal names, *Ealdhere* or *Æðelhere*, composed of the elements *eald* old or *æðel* noble + *here* army. 2. topographic name for someone living near an alder tree (OE *alor*).

Vars. (of 2): NALDER, ALDERMAN.

Patrs. (of 1): Eng.: **Alders**, **Alderson**.

Alderdice *see* ALLARDYCE

Alderman English: 1. title of office, from OE *ealdorman* elder. In Anglo-Saxon England an alderman was a functionary appointed by the king to administer justice in a shire, and to lead the local militia into battle when needed; in the later Middle Ages the term came to be used to denote the governor of a guild. 2. var. of ALDER 2.

Alderton English: habitation name from any of various places so called. Those in Suffolk and Shrops. (*Alretuna* in Domesday Book) get the name from OE *alra*, gen. pl. of *alor* alder + *tūn* enclosure, settlement (cf. ALLERTON). Those in Gloucs., Northants, and Wilts. (*Aldri(n)tone* in Domesday Book) derive from OE *Ealdheringtūn* 'settlement associated with *Ealdhere*' (cf. ALDER 1). The one in Essex contains a different personal name, perhaps the fem. name *Æðelwaru*, composed of the elements *æðel* noble + *waru* defence.

Aldobrandi Italian: 1. from a Gmc (Langobardic) personal name composed of the elements *ald* old + *brand* (flaming) sword. **2.** in the Tuscan dialect, in which initial *I*-regularly became *A*-, it may represent a version of HILDEBRAND.

Vars.: **Aldovrandi**; **Aldrovandi** (Emilia); **Drovandi** (Liguria).

Dim.: **Aldobrandini**.

Aldous 1. English: from the ME fem. given name *Aldus*, a pet form of any of the numerous OE personal names (borne by both sexes) with a first element *(e)ald* old. **2.** Scots: habitation name from a place in Strathclyde (Renfrewshire), named as OE *eald* old + *hūs* house. (The Gael. etymology that has been suggested, from *alld* burn + *fhuathais* goblin, spectre, is less than plausible.)

Vars. (of 1): **Aldus**, **Al(l)dis(s)**, **Audis**, **Oldis**. (Of 2, or by folk etymology from 1): **Aldhouse**.

Dims. (of 1): It.: **Aldini**, **Audin(ucc)i**.

Aldritt English (chiefly Sussex): **1.** from the ME personal name *Aldred*, which represents a coalescence of two OE personal names: *Ealdrǣd*, composed of the elements *eald* old + *rǣd* counsel, and *Æðelrǣd* (Ethelred), from *æðel* noble + *rǣd*. **2.** topographic name for someone who lived by an alder grove, ME *aldrett*, a deriv. of ALDER.

Vars.: **Audritt**, **Aldred**, **Al(l)red**; **Eldrett**, **Eldritt**, **Eldred**.

Alecock *see* ALCOCK

Alegret *see* ALLEGRI

Alen *see* ALLIS

Alenius *see* AHL

Alévêque *see* BISHOP

Alexander English: from the given name *Alexander*, which in various spellings was popular in the Middle Ages throughout Europe. An aphetic form (see SANDER) was also common, while in Slav. languages most of the dims. are indistinguishable from those of Russ. *Aleksei*, Pol. *Olek* (see ALEXIS). The name *Alexander* is from Gk *Alexandros*, which probably originally meant 'defender of men', from Gk *alexein* to defend + *anēr*, gen. *andros*, man. This was a byname of Paris, son of King Priam of Troy, in Homer's *Iliad*, but its popularity in the Middle Ages was largely due to the Macedonian conqueror, Alexander the Great (356–323 BC)—or rather to the hero of the mythical versions of his exploits which gained currency in the 'Alexander Romances'. The name was also borne by various early Christian saints, including a patriarch of Alexandria (AD *c*.250–326), who was venerated for condemning the Arian heresy.

Vars.: **Elesander**, **Elshenar**, **Alshioner**; **Alastar** (Scotland; from *Alasdair*, the Gael. form of the given name).

Dims.: It.: **Alessandrelli**, **Alessandretti**, **Alessandrini**, **Alessandrucci**; **Lissandrini**; **Lisciardelli** (Sicily). Czech: **Lešek**, **Lexa**. Ukr.: **Olenchenko**, **Lenchenko**.

Augs.: It.: **Alessandrone**.

Patrs.: Sc., Ir.: **McAl(l)aster**, **McAl(l)ister**, **McAlester**, **McCallister** (Gael. **Mac Alastair**). Manx: **Callister**. It.: **D'Alessandro**. Rum.: **Alexandrescu**. Dan., Norw.: **Alexandersen**. Swed.: **Alexandersson**. Pol.: **Aleksandrowicz**. Russ.: **Aleksan(dr)ov**. Ukr., Beloruss.: **Aleksandrovich**. Bulg.: **Aleksandrov**, **Aleksandrev**. Croatian: **Aleksić**. Jewish (E Ashkenazic): **Aleksandrovich**, **Alexandrowicz**. Gk: **Alexandrou**.

Patrs. (from dims.): Ir.: **McElistrum**, **McElistrim** (Gael. **Mac Alastraim**; common in Co. Kerry). Russ.: **Aleksankov**,

Aleksankin; **Aleksakhin**, **Aleksashin**; **Alenov**, **Alenin**, **Alyonov**, **Alen(n)ikov**, **Alenshev**, **Alentyev**, **Alenichev**, **Alenchikov**, **Olenov**, **Olenin**, **Olyonov**, **Olen(n)ikov**, **Olenichev**, **Olenchikov**; LENIN.

'Son of the wife of A.': Russ.: **Aleksandrikhin**.

Alexis French: from the given name *Alexis*, ultimately from Gk *alexios* helping, defending. The name owed its popularity in the Middle Ages to St Alexi(u)s, a shadowy figure about whom many legends grew up. The historical St Alexis appears to have been a religious figure venerated as a 'man of God' who lived in the 4th–5th cent. in Edessa (a centre of early Christianity in Syria). His cult was also popular in the Eastern Church, which accounts for the frequency of the Russ. given name *Aleks(e)i* (dim. *Alyosha*).

Dims.: Pol.: **Olczyk**, **Oleszczuk**. Beloruss.: **Alekseichik**, **Lyosik**.

Patrs.: It.: **D'Ales(s)io**, **D'Alesco**. Pol.: **Olech(n)owicz**, **Olkowicz**; **Oleksiak**. Beloruss.: **Aleksich**. Russ.: **Alekseev**. Georgian: **Aleksidze**.

Patrs. (from dims.): Pol.: **Oleszkiewicz**; **Ol(esz)czak**. Russ.: **Alekhov**, **Aleshkov**, **Aleshintsev**, **Alyokhin**, **Alyoshin**, **Alosh(i)kin**, **Aloshechkin**, **Alyukin**, **Alyushin**, **Alyutin**, **Alesin**, **Olekhov**, **Olyosh(k)in**, **Oleshunin**, **Olyunin**, LYOKHIN.

Habitation name: Pol.: **Oleksiński**.

Alfaro Spanish: habitation name from a place in the province of Logroño, apparently so called from the Arabic def. art. *al* + OSp. *faro* beacon (from LL *farus*, Gk *pharos*).

Alfonso Spanish: from a Gmc personal name, *Adafuns* (composed of the elements *adal* noble + *funs* ready). This was especially popular among the Visigoths and Langobards, and was later taken by a number of kings of Spain.

Var.: **Alonso**.

Dims.: It.: **Alfonsetti**, **Alfonsini**.

Augs.: It.: **Alfonsoni**; **Fonzone**.

Alford English: habitation name from any of various places so called, three in particular: one in Surrey (recorded as *Aldeford* in the 14th cent.), from OE *eald* old + *ford* FORD; one in Somerset (*Aldedeford* in Domesday Book), of which the first element, according to Ekwall, is the OE female personal name *Ealdgȳð*, composed of the elements *eald* old + *gȳð* battle; and one in Lincs. (*Alforde* in Domesday Book), of which the first element is probably either OE *alor* ALDER or *(e)alh* temple, shrine. There is also a place of the same name in the former county of Aberdeen (now part of Grampian region), which may lie behind some Scots examples of the surname.

Var.: **Allford**.

Alfors *see* AHL

Alfred English: from the ME personal name *Alvred*, *Alured*, OE *Ælfrēd*, composed of the elements *ælf* elf + *rēd* counsel. This owed its popularity as a given name in England chiefly to the fame of the W Saxon king Alfred the Great (849–99), who defeated the Danes, keeping them out of Wessex, and whose court was a great centre of learning and culture. The Fr. form given below is derived from a Continental Gmc cogn.

Vars.: **Al(l)ured** (with vocalization of the consonant in the Latinized spelling *Alvredus*).

Patrs.: Eng.: **Alfreds**, **Alfredson**. Swed.: **Alfredsson**.

Alfrey see AUBREY

Alfs see ADOLF

Alger English: from the ME personal name *Alger*, in which several names of different origins, both Continental Gmc (through the Normans) and OE, have fallen together. The final element of all of them is *gar, ger* spear (cf. GORE 1 and GARLICK). The first element is generally *alb* elf, but may also be *adal* noble or *ald* old. The Norman French forms have also absorbed OE cogns. beginning in *Ælf-* and *Æðel-*. In regions that were under Scandinavian influence the name is normally derived from the ON cogn. *Álfgeirr* 'elf spear'.

Vars.: **Algar, Auger; Elgar, Elger**.

Dims.: Fr.: **Augereau, Augeron**.

Algren see AHL

Alguacil Spanish: occupational name for the governor of a region or for an officer of justice, Sp. *alguacil* (from the Arabic def. art. *al* + *wazir* vizier, official, originally 'porter').

Aliaga Spanish: topographic name for someone who lived on a patch of land overgrown with gorse, Sp. *aliaga, aulaga* (of uncertain, probably pre-Roman, origin). The surname is now most common in Catalonia, especially in the provinces of Valencia, Alicante, and Barcelona, but it seems to have originated in Aragon.

Aliman see ALMAN

Alimov see OLIMPIEV

Aline see ALLIS

Aliot see ELLIS

Alison Scots: **1.** dim. or metr. from the ME female name *Alise, Alice* (from an ONF contracted form of Gmc *Adalhaidis (Adelaide)*, composed of the elements *adal* noble + *haid* kind, sort). **2.** patr. from the ME male name ELLIS, or else from a short form of ALLEN or ALEXANDER (cf. ALCOCK).

Var.: **Allison**.

Allamand see ALMAN

Allard English (Norman) and French: from an OF personal name, *Adelard*, composed of the Gmc elements *adal* noble + *hard* hardy, brave, strong. The ANF form *Alard* has probably absorbed the OE names *Ælfheard* and *Æðelheard*.

Vars.: Eng.: **Adlard, Allart, Aylard, Ellard, Ellert, Hallard; Hallet(t)** (mainly Somerset and Devon). Fr.: **Alard**.

Patrs.: Low Ger.: **Ahlers, Aller(t)s**.

Allardyce Scots: habitation name from *Allardice* in the former county of Kincardines. This is of uncertain origin (the first element is probably ME *aller* alder, OE *alor*). The traditional pronunciation of the name is /'ɛərdɪs/.

Vars.: **Allardice, Allardes; Alderdice** (N Ireland); **Ardes**.

Allbon see ALBAN

Allbright see ALBERT

Allbutt see ALBUTT

Allcoat see ALCOTT

Allcock see ALCOCK

Alldis see ALDOUS

Alleaume French: from an OF version of the Gmc personal name *Adalhelm*, composed of the elements *adal* noble + *helm* protection, helmet.

Vars.: **Alliaume, Allem**.

Allegri Italian: nickname from It. *allegro* quick, lively, cheerful (L *alacer*, gen. *alacris*), which was also used occasionally as a given name in the Middle Ages.

Dims.: It.: **Allegretti, Allegrini, Allegrucci**. Fr.: **Allégret**. Cat.: **Alegret**.

Aug.: It.: **Allegroni**.

Derivs. (from abstract nouns meaning 'cheerfulness'): It.: **Allegria; Allegrezza**. Cat., Port.: **Alegria**. Sp.: **Alegría**.

Allemandet see ALMAN

Allen 1. English and Scots: from a Celt. personal name of great antiquity and obscurity. In England the given name is now usually spelt *Alan*, the surname *Allen* or (esp. in Scotland) *Allan*. Various suggestions have been put forward regarding its origin; most probably it originally meant 'little rock' (Gael. *ailín*, dim. of *ail* rock). The present-day frequency of the surname in England and Ireland is accounted for by the popularity of the given name among Bret. followers of William the Conqueror, by whom it was imported first to Britain and then to Ireland. St *Alan(us)* was a 5th-cent. bishop of Quimper about whom nothing factual is known, but who was a cult figure in medieval Brittany. Another St *Al(l)an* was a Corn. or Bret. saint of the 6th cent., to whom a church in Cornwall is dedicated. **2.** Low German, Danish, and Swedish (**Allén**): probably from a Gmc personal name rather than a borrowing from Breton. The most likely source would be *Alle*, a Low Ger. short form of any of various Gmc cpd personal names with the first element *adal* noble (cf. ADEL).

Vars. (of 1): **Al(l)an, Alleyne, Allin(e)**.

Patrs. (from 1): Eng.: ALLIS; **Allenson, Allanson, Alli(n)son, Hallison; FitzAlan**. Sc.: **McAllan, McAline, McEllen, McElane, McKellan, McKellen** (Gael. **Mac Ailín, Mac Aileáin**).

'Descendant of A.': Ir.: **O'Hallyn, Hallin** (Gael. **Ó hAilín**).

Allenby English: habitation name from *Allonby* or *Ellonby*, both in Cumb. and both being late (post-Conquest) formations from the personal name *Alein*, from ANF *aguillon* goad, spur + Northern ME *by* farm, settlement (ON *býr*).

Allende Spanish: habitation name for someone who lived some distance from the main settlement, or whose home was beyond some particular landmark, from OSp. *allende* (from) yonder, beyond (a cpd of *allá* (L *illāc* there) + *ende* (L *inde* thence)).

Allerton English: habitation name from any of several places so called. Allerton on Merseyside, Chapel Allerton in W Yorks, and most of the others in W Yorks. are so called from OE *alra*, gen. pl. of *alor* alder + *tūn* enclosure, settlement; cf. ALDERTON. Chapel Allerton in Somerset (*Allwarditone* in Domesday Book) and Allerton Mauleverer in W Yorks. (*Alvertone* in Domesday Book) were originally named in OE as the settlements of

Ælfweard 'elf guardian' and *Ælfhere* 'elf army' respectively.

Allfield *see* OLDFIELD

Allford *see* ALFORD

Allilaire *see* HILARY

Allimant *see* ALMAN

Alliot *see* ELLIS

Allis English: **1.** contracted form of *Allins*, patr. of ALLEN. **2.** from the ME, OF female given name *Alis*, a contracted form of the Gmc personal name *Adalhaid(is)*, composed of the elements *adal* noble + *haid* kind, sort. A modern revival of the uncontracted form is *Adelaide*. The given name *Alice (Alis)* and its dim. ALISON were very popular throughout the Middle Ages. It was the name of the wife of the emperor Otto the Great, St Adelaide (or Alice; d. 999); it was also the name of the goose in medieval beast tales. It fell out of use in the 16th–17th cents., being revived again in the 19th.

Vars.: **Alliss, Alis, Hallis**. (Of 2 only): **Alise**.

Dims. (of 2): Eng.: **Allott, Allatt** (both chiefly common in Yorks.). Fr.: **Al(l)ine, Allot**; **Adeline**.

Metrs. (from 2): Flem.: **Al(is)en, Aeles**; **Leyten**. Ger.: **Al(i)scher, Altscher, Alschner**.

Allison *see* ALISON

Allmers *see* AYLMER

Alloway 1. English: from the OE personal name *Æðelwīg*, composed of the elements *æðel* noble + *wīg* battle. **2.** Scots: habitation name from any of several places called *Alloway, Alloa*, or *Alva*, e.g. *Alloway* in the former county of Ayrshire. All are so named from Gael. *allmhagh* rocky plain.

Vars.: **Aloway, Al(l)(a)way, Elloway, Halloway, Hallaway**.

Allred *see* ALDRITT

Allsop English (chiefly Midlands): habitation name from *Alsop* in Derbys., named in OE as *Ælleshop* 'valley (see HOPE) of *Ælli*'.

Vars.: **Allsopp, Alsop(p), Allsep(p)**; **Elsop, Elsip**.

Allston *see* ALSTON

Allured *see* ALFRED

Allvey *see* ALVEY

Allward *see* AYLWARD

Allwood *see* ELLWOOD

Allwyn *see* ALWYN

Almagro Spanish: habitation name from a place in the province of Ciudad Real, so called from the Arabic def. art. *al* + *mágra* red clay.

Alman 1. English: ethnic name for someone from Germany, from ANF *aleman* German or *alemayne* Germany (LL *Alemannus* and *Alemannia*, from a Gmc tribal name, probably meaning simply 'all the men'). In some cases the reference may have been to the Norman region of *Allemagne*, to the south of Caen, which was probably so

named from Gmc settlers there. **2.** Jewish (Ashkenazic): surname taken by a widower, Hebr. *alman*.

Vars. (of 1): **Allman, Al(l)mann, Aliman, Allmen, Almon; Al(l)mand, Allamand, Allimant, Al(l)ment**, ALMOND (the excrescent dental was common after a final -*n*; cf. *Dayman* at DAY).

Dims.: (of 1): Fr.: **Allemandet, Allemandou**.

Patr. (from 1): Rum.: **Alimanesco** (usually referring to people of Swiss origin).

Almazán Spanish: habitation name from a place in the province of Soria, so called from the Arabic def. art. *al* + *mazan* fortified (place).

Almazov Russian: patr. from the nickname *Almaz* 'Diamond', perhaps denoting a jeweller, or more likely bestowed as an affectionate indication of worth. The word derives from Gk *adamas* (from *a-* not + *damān* to conquer, i.e. 'the unconquerable', with reference to its hardness) via Arabic, where the first syllable was assimilated to the def. art. *al*.

Almberg *see* ELM

Almeida Portuguese: habitation name from any of the numerous places, including a town in the province of Beira Baixa, so called from the Arabic def. art. *al* + *mâ'ida* plateau, (low) hill.

Almendro Spanish: topographic name for someone who lived near an almond tree or in an almond grove, from Sp. *almendro* almond (L *amygdalus*, from Gk; the first syllable has been assimilated to the form of the Arabic def. art. *al*). Cf. MANDEL. There are various places named with this word, for example in the province of Huelva, and they may also have contributed to the surname as habitation names.

Var.: **Almendros** (pl.; the name of a place in Cuenca).

Almers *see* AYLMER

Almgren *see* ELM

Almirall Catalan: occupational name for a local dignitary, Cat. *almirall* (from Arabic *'amīr* ruler + *a'ālī* high, with later assimilation of the first syllable to the form of the Arabic def. art. *al*).

Almond English: **1.** var. of ALMAN. **2.** from the OE personal name *Æðelmund*, composed of the elements *æðel* noble + *mund* protection. There is no evidence of any connection with the almond nut or tree (cf. ALMENDRO).

Alonso *see* ALFONSO

Alós Catalan: habitation name from any of various places so called. The placename is of pre-Roman origin and unknown meaning.

Var.: **Alòs**.

Aloshechkin *see* ALEXIS

Alov Russian: patr. from the nickname *Aly* 'Crimson', a word taken from some Turkic language. It seems unlikely that the nickname referred to complexion or hair colour; more probably, it indicated a predilection for dressing in flamboyant colours.

Aloway *see* ALLOWAY

Alper *see* HEILBRONN

Alpers *see* ALBERT

Alpert 1. Frisian: var. of ALBERT. 2. Jewish (Ashkenazic): of uncertain origin, probably a var. of HEILBRONN.

Vars.: **Alper**. (Of 2 only): **Halper**.

Alphege *see* ELPHICK

Alpin Scots and Irish: apparently from the ancient Celt. personal name *Alpin*, of unknown etymology, which was borne by Pictish kings.

Vars.: **Alpine**; **Elfin**.

Patrs.: Sc.: **MacAlpin(e)** (Gael. **Mac Ailpín**).

'Descendant of A.': Ir.: **(O')Halpin**, **(O')Halpen**, **Halpen(n)y**, HALFPENNY (Gael. **Ó hAilpín**).

Alred *see* ALDRITT

Alric *see* ALARIC

Alscher *see* ALLIS

Alsén *see* AHL

Alshioner *see* ALEXANDER

Alsop *see* ALLSOP

Alstead *see* HALSTEAD

Alston English: 1. from the ME personal name *Alstan*, representing a coalescence of various OE personal names composed of the elements *æðel* noble, *ælf* elf, *(e)ald* old, or *(e)alh* shrine, temple + *stān* stone. 2. habitation name from any of various places called *Alston* (in Lancs., Devon, and Somerset) or *Alstone* (in Gloucs. and Staffs.). These are variously the settlements (OE *tūn*) of bearers of the OE personal names *Ælfwine* ('elf friend'), *Ælfsige* ('elf victory'), *Æðelnoð* ('noble daring'), and *Ælfrēd* ('elf counsel'). Alston in Cumb. is a ME placename, *Aldenstune*, from the ON personal name *Alden* (from *Halfdan*; see HALDANE) + *tune* settlement.

Vars.: **Alstone**, **Allston(e)**, EDLESTONE.

Altbach *see* OLD

Altbüsser German: occupational name for a cobbler or shoemender, from MHG *alt* old (OHG *alt*) + an agent deriv. of *buessen* to mend, improve (OHG *buossan*).

Vars.: **Albeisser** (S Germany and Switzerland); **Albiez**.

Altés Catalan: habitation name from a place in the province of Lérida, recorded in the 12th cent. in the form *Autés*. The name is of uncertain origin, according to Corominas from Basque *othaitz* 'full of gorse' (from *ote* gorse + the suffix of plurality *-i(t)z*).

Alton English: habitation name from any of various places so called. Those in Hants, Dorset, and Wilts. are at the sources of the rivers Wey, Piddle, and Avon respectively, and derive their names from OE *æwiell* spring, source + *tūn* enclosure, settlement. Alton in Derbys. and Alton Grange in Leics. seem to have had as their first element OE *(e)ald* old. Other examples derive from various OE personal names; one in Staffs. was the settlement of *Ælfa* (a short form of any of the various cpd personal names with the first element *ælf* elf), one in Wilts. belonged to *Ælla*, and one in Worcs., recorded as *Eanulfintun* in 1023, to

Ēanwulf (from an element of obscure origin + OE *wulf* wolf).

Altscher *see* ALLIS

Altschul Jewish (Ashkenazic): from Yid. *alt* old (MHG *alt*) + *shul* synagogue (MHG *schul* school); the reason for adoption of the surname is unclear.

Var.: **Altschul(l)er**, **Altshuler**.

Altufyev *see* YEVTIKHIEV

Alty *see* AUTY

Aluard *see* AYLWARD

Alured *see* ALFRED

Álvaro Spanish and Portuguese: from a Gmc (Visigothic) personal name, probably composed of the elements *all* all + *wēr* true.

Var.: Sp.: **Alvar**.

Patrs.: Sp.: **Álvarez**. Port.: **Álvares**, **Alves**.

Alven *see* ALWYN

Alverichs *see* AUBREY

Alvey English: from the ME given name *Alfwy*, OE *Ælfwīg*, composed of the elements *ælf* elf + *wīg* battle. The surname is most common in Notts.

Vars.: **Alvy**, **Allvey**; **Elphey**, **Elv(e)y**.

Alway *see* ALLOWAY

Alwyn English: from the ME personal names *Al(f)win*, *Elwin*, representing a coalescence of various OE personal names: *Ælfwine* (composed of the elements *ælf* elf + *wine* friend), *Æðelwine* ('noble friend'), and *Ealdwine* ('old friend'). In some cases it may even be from the female name *Ælfwynn*, composed of the elements *ælf* elf + *wynn* joy.

Vars.: **Ailwyn**, **A(y)lwen**, **A(y)lwin**, **Allwyn**; **Elwyn**, **Elwin**, **Alvin**, **Alven**; **Elvin** (chiefly Norfolk).

Alyokhin *see* ALEXIS

Alyonov *see* ALEXANDER

Amadei Italian: from the given name *Amadeo*, which was coined in the early Middle Ages from the elements *ama* love + *Deo* God. This was the name of two 12th-cent. Burgundian nobles (father and son) who became Cistercian monks, and their fame may have contributed to the subsequent popularity of the given name.

Vars.: **Amade**, **Amadi**, **Amaddei**, **Amad(d)io**, **Amedei**; **Amod(d)eo**, **Amod(d)io**; **Mad(d)ei**.

Dim.: It.: **Amadini**.

Amalfi Italian: habitation name from the seaport of this name on the rocky coast south of Naples.

Vars.: **Malfi**; **Malfitano**, **Amalfitano**.

Amand French and English: from the given name *Amand* (L *Amandus* 'Lovable', from *amāre* to love), which was borne by a number of early Christian churchmen (abbots and bishops) in France and elsewhere, including a 5th-cent. bishop of Bordeaux, and a 7th-cent. bishop of Maastricht known as 'the apostle of the Netherlands'.

Vars.: Eng.: **Aman(n)**, **Amman**.

Amann see AMMANN

Amant French: from the given name *Amans* (L *Amans*, gen. *Amantis*, 'Loving', pres. part. of *amāre* to love), bestowed on children with reference to spiritual love. In some cases it may also have been a nickname for a philanderer, and the It. patr. forms may refer obliquely to birth out of wedlock (cf. AMOR).

Dim.: It.: **Amantino**.

Patrs.: It.: **D'Amante, Damanti**.

Amar see AYLMER

Amaral Portuguese: habitation name from any of the numerous minor places so called. They are of uncertain etymology, probably from Port. *amaral* a kind of black grape (from L *amārus* bitter); alternatively a connection has been suggested with a collective deriv. of Sp. *maro, amaro* catthyme (L *marum*, influenced by Sp. *amargo* bitter).

Amatore Italian: from a medieval given name (L *Amātor* 'Lover' (i.e. of God), from *amāre* to love). The personal name was borne by several early Christian saints, most famously a hermit in Roman Gaul who founded the shrine of Our Lady of Rocamadour in Provence, which was a popular place of pilgrimage in the Middle Ages. The Sp. cogn. *Amador* owed its popularity as a given name chiefly to a 9th-cent. saint martyred at Cordoba by the Moors, while in Portugal many churches are dedicated to a local saint of this name, of uncertain date. A Fr. cogn. is noticeably absent, probably suppressed because of the pej. connotations of the vocab. word *amateur*, with which it would have been identical in form.

Vars.: **Amatori, Amadore**.

Dims.: It.: **Amadorucci, Amadoruzzi**.

Amatucci see AMEY

Ambihl see BÜHLER

Ambler English: 1. occupational name for an enameller, ANF *amayler* (OF *esmailler*, from OF *esmail* enamel, a word of Gmc origin akin to mod. Eng. *smelt*). The -*b*- is intrusive. 2. from ME *ambler* walker (via OF from L *ambulāre* to walk), of uncertain application. The term was used of the slowest gait of a horse or mule, and the surname may have been an occupational name for a stablekeeper or a nickname for a person with an ambling gait.

Ambridge English: of uncertain origin, in form ostensibly a habitation name from some unidentified place so called. If this is correct, the second element is OE *brycg* BRIDGE; the first is obscure. However, the name is more likely to be an alteration by folk etymology of AMBROSE.

Ambrose English: from a medieval given name (L *Ambrosius*, from Gk *ambrosios* immortal), which owes its popularity largely to the fame of St Ambrose (*c*.340–97), one of the four 'Latin Fathers of the Church', who was the teacher of St Augustine.

Dims.: Fr.: **Ambroisin, Ambresin; Brosset** (Belgium). It.: **Ambrosini, Ambrogini, Ambrosetti, Ambrogetti, Ambrosoli, Ambrogioli, Ambrogelli, Ambrogiotti, Brosini, Brog(g)ini, Brosetti, Brogetti, Brosoli, Brogelli, Brogiotti, Brusin** (Venetia). Ger.: **Brösel**. Low Ger.: **Broseke, Bröseke**. Flem.: **Broseman**. Ger. (of Slav. origin): **Bros(ch)ke, Broschek;**

Pros(ch)ke, Pros(ch)ek. Czech: **Brožek**. Pol.: **Ambrozik; Jambrozek; Brożek**.

Augs.: It.: **Ambrosoni, Ambrogioni; Brogioni**.

Patrs.: Sc., Ir.: **McCambridge** (Gael. **Mac Ambróis**). It.: **D'Ambrosi(o), D'Ambrogi(o), De Ambrosi(s)**. Flem.: **Brosenius** (Latinized). Pol.: **Ambrożewicz; Ambroziak**.

Patrs. (from dims.): Pol.: **Broszkiewicz; Jamrowicz**.

Amedei see AMADEI

Amend see ENDE

Amery English: from a Gmc personal name composed of the elements *amal* bravery, vigour + *rīc* power, introduced into England by the Normans. In OF the given name has a profusion of different forms *(Amalri(c), Aumari(c), Amauri, Emaurri, Haimeri, Ymeri*, etc.) and several of these are reflected in vars. of the surname.

Vars.: **Amory; Emery, Emory, Emary; Ember(r)y, Embr(e)y, Embur(e)y; Emeric(k); Im(b)ery, Im(b)rie, Imbrey, Imray** (Scotland and Northumb.); **Hemery, Hembr(e)y**.

Dims.: Ger.: **Emmel, Emmlein**. Low Ger.: **Ahmel(mann), Ehm(e)cke**.

Patr.: Eng.: **Emerson**.

Patrs. (from dim.): Low Ger.: **Ahmels; Ameling, Amelung, Ahmling**.

Ames see AMIS

Amey English (Norman): from the OF given name *Amé* (L *Amātus* 'Beloved', past part. of *amāre* to love).

Vars.: **Amy, Amie**.

Dims.: It.: **Amatucci, Amatulli**.

Patrs.: Eng.: AMIS. It.: **D'Amato**.

Amezaga Basque: topographic name for someone who lived by an oak tree or in an oak wood, from *ametz* oak + the local suffix -*aga*.

Amherst English: habitation name from *Amhurst* Hill in Pembury, Kent which is found as *Hemhurst* in 1250, and probably derives its name from OE *hem* boundary + *hyrst* wooded hill (see HURST).

Amie see AMEY

Amiranda see MIRANDA

Amis English (Norman): from the OF given name or nickname *Amis* (oblique case *Ami*) 'Friend' (L *amīcus*, a deriv. of *amāre* to love).

Vars.: **Amiss, Am(i)es**.

Dims.: Fr.: **Ami(gu)et, Amiot, Amyot, Amiel**. It.: **Amicelli, Amicino, Amighini, Ami(gh)etti, Amigotti**. Cat.: **Amigó**.

Augs.: It.: **Amiconi, Ami(g)oni**.

Pej.: Fr.: **Amiard**.

Patrs.: Eng.: **Am(i)son**. It.: **D'Amico, D'Amici; De Amicis**.

Amman see AMAND

Ammann German: occupational name for an administrative official or head of a community owing allegiance to a feudal superior, from an assimilated form of *Amtmann* (MHG *ambet(man)*, from OHG *ampacht* retainer). The surname is most common in S Germany and Switzerland.

Var.: **Amann**.

Ammon see AMOND

Amo Spanish: occupational name or nickname from Sp. *amo* tutor, guardian, master (a masc. form of *ama* nurse, LL *amma*, probably in origin a nursery word).

Amoddeo see AMADEI

Amond N English: from a Scandinavian personal name (OIcel. *Ogmundr*, OSwed. *Aghmund*, mod. Dan. *Amund*), composed of the Gmc elements *agi* awe (or possibly *ag* point; cf. ACHARD) + *mund* protection. See also HAMMOND.

Vars.: **Am(m)on**.

Patrs.: Eng.: **Ammonds**. Norw., Dan.: **Amundsen**.

Amoore see MOORE

Amor Spanish, French, and English: from the medieval nickname or given name *Amor* (L *amor* love), which was popular in Spain, Italy, and France, and introduced into England by the Normans. There was a St Amor, of obscure history and unknown date, whose relics were preserved and venerated at the village of St Amour in Burgundy. The Ger. forms owe their origin to an 8th-cent. evangelist who founded the monastery of *Amorbach* in Franconia and a 9th-cent. Belgian saint who was sometimes confused with him. It is also possible that in some cases the surname arose from a nickname for a lovable person or a philanderer, or for someone who had played the part of Love (personified) in a pageant or mystery play.

Vars.: Sp.: **Amores**. Fr., Eng.: **Amour**.

Dims.: It.: **Amor(i)elli**, **Amoretti**, **Amorini**.

Patrs. (often suggesting illegitimate origin): It.: **D(ell)'Amore**.

Amorim Portuguese: habitation name from places in the provinces of Oporto and Aveiro, so called from L *Amorīni (villa)* (settlement) of *Amorīnus'*, a deriv. of AMOR.

Amort see ORT

Amory see AMERY

Amos 1. Jewish: from the Hebr. given name *Amos* 'Borne (by God)'. This was the name of a prophet of the 8th cent. BC, whose oracles are recorded in the Book of Amos. 2. English (SE England): probably a var. of AMIS. The given name *Amos* is not found among non-Jews before the Reformation, and so the English surname is unlikely to be derived from it.

Patr. (from 1): **Ben-Amos** (Israeli).

Amoureux French: nickname for a philanderer or an affectionate man, from OF *amoureux* loving, amorous (L *amorōsus*, a deriv. of *amor* love).

Var.: **Lamoureux** (with fused def. art.).

Dims.: It.: **Amoroselli**, **Amorosini**.

Amphlet see FLEET

Amschel Jewish (Ashkenazic): from the Yid. male given name *An(t)shl*, ultimately from L *angelus* angel.

Vars.: **Amszel** (a Polish spelling), AMSEL, **Anchel** (a Fr. spelling), ANCEL.

Patr.: **Antzilewitz** (E Ashkenazic).

Amsel 1. German: from MHG *amsel* blackbird (OHG *ams(a)la*), in various applications; a habitation name for someone who lived in a house with a sign bearing a picture of this bird, a metonymic occupational name for a bird catcher, or a nickname for someone thought to resemble a blackbird in some way. 2. Jewish: var. of AMSCHEL.

Amsler Jewish (Ashkenazic): habitation name from *Amsle*, Yid. name of *Namstau* in Silesia.

Var.: **Amschler**.

Amson see AMIS

Amsterdam, van Dutch (largely Jewish): habitation name from the city in N Holland, so called from being originally built round a dam on the river *Amstel*. Many Jews settled in Amsterdam after being expelled from Spain and Portugal in the late 16th cent., and they helped to make it a centre of the diamond-cutting trade. Before the First World War approximately 10 per cent of the population of Amsterdam was Jewish.

Vars.: Jewish: **Amsterdam(er)**; **Amsterdamski** (E Ashkenazic).

Amszel see AMSCHEL

Amundsen see AMOND, HAMMOND

Amy see AMEY

Amyot see AMIS

Anacleto Portuguese: from a given name (Gk *Anaklētos* 'Invoked', a deriv. of *anakalein* to call on) supposedly borne by the third pope, also known as *Anenklētos* 'Irreproachable'.

Anastasijević see ANSTICE

Anaya Spanish form of Basque **Anaia**: from *anai* brother + the def. art. *-a*, which was used in the Middle Ages both as a byname and as a personal name.

Ancel 1. French: occupational name for a domestic servant, OF *ancel(e)* (L *ancilla* serving maid). 2. Jewish (Ashkenazic): var. of AMSCHEL.

Vars. (of 1): **Ancelle** (fem.); **Anceau(x)**, **Anseau(x)**, **Ansiau**; **Lancel**.

Dims. (of 1): **Ancel(l)in**, **Anselin**, **Ancel(l)et**, **Anselet**, **Ancelot**, **Anselot**.

Patr. (from 2): **Ancelevitch**.

Anchel see AMSCHEL

Andelman see HANDLER

Anderton English: habitation name from either of two places, in Ches. and Lancs., so called from the OE personal name *Ēanrēd* (composed of the elements *ēan*, of uncertain origin, + *rēd* counsel) + *tūn* enclosure, settlement.

Andjelić see ANGEL

Andrade Portuguese: of uncertain origin. There are various minor places so called, for example near Coimbra, Estremoz, Figueira da Foz, and Penafiel, but the placename is probably derived from the surname, rather than the other way about. The surname may derive from the Gk personal name *Andras* (a short form of various cpd names with the first element *anēr*, gen. *andros*, man) by way of the LL acc. form *Andradem*. The surname is also relatively common in Spain.

Andrew English: from the name (Gk *Andreas*, a deriv. of *andreios* manly, from *anēr*, gen. *andros*, man, male) by which the first of Jesus Christ's disciples is known, in various local forms, throughout Christendom. (It is presumably a Gk translation of a lost Aramaic name.) The disciple is the patron saint of Scotland, and there is a legend that his relics were brought to Scotland in the 4th cent. by a certain St Regulus. He is also the patron saint of Russia. The name was also popular in Eastern Europe (Czech *Ondřej*, Pol. *Andrzej*, *Jędrej*), and in Pol. there has been some confusion with derivs. of *Henryk* (see HENRY).

Var. (aphetic): DREW.

Port.: **André**. It.: **Andrei, Andrea, Andri(a); Dr(e)i**. Rum.: **Andrei**. Ger.: **Andre(a)s, Anders(ch), Enders; Endres, Entre(i)s** (Bavaria). Low Ger.: **Dreus, Drees**. Flem., Du.: **Andries; Dries, Drees**. Swed.: **Andre(e)**. Ger. (of Slav. origin): **Andrasch, Hantusch, Jendrusch; Wandrey, Fandrey**. Czech: **Andrejs, Andrys; Ondruš, Ondřich, Ondra, Ondrák, Vondra, Vondrák, Vondrys**. Pol.: **Andrzej; Jędrzej; Jendrys, Jędrys, Jędrych, Jędruch, Indruch, Jędras, Jędryka**. Hung.: **Andor, András(sy)**. Gk: **Andreas**.

Dims.: Eng.: **Dand(y), Dandie; Tandy** (W Midlands); **Tancock**. Fr.: **Andrin; Andrivel, Andriveaux, Andrivot**. It.: **Andr(e)elli, Andr(e)etti, Andr(e)ini; Andr(e)ol(l)i, Andriol(l)i, Andr(e)oletti, Andrioletti, Andreotti, Andreutti, Andreucci, Andreuzzi, Andriuzzi; Andino; Dreini, Dreossi, Drioli, Driussi, Driuzzi, Driutti**. Ger.: **Anderl, Enderl(e), Enderlein; Enterl(e), Enterlein** (Bavaria). Ger. (of Slav. origin): **Andrich, Andrick, Angrick; Androck, Angrock; Andrag, Antrag, Antrack; Handri(c)k, Handrek, Handro(c)k; Gandrich; Wandrach, Wandrack, Wandrich; Vondrach; Fandrich; Wanderschek, Wondraschek**. Czech: **Andrýsek, Andrík; Ondráček, Ondrášek, Ondr(o)ušek, Ondřiček, Vondráček, Von(dr)ášek, Vondruška**. Pol.: **Jędrzejczyk, Jędraszczyk, Jędraszek, Jędrasik, Jędrysik**. Ukr.: **Andryushchenko, Andrichuk, Andrichak, Andrusyak**. Beloruss.: **Androsik, Andreichik**.

Augs.: Fr.: **Andrat**. It.: **Andreone, Andrioni; Dreoni**.

Pejs.: Fr.: **Andraud, Andrault**. It.: **Andreacci(o), Andreazzi; Dreassi**.

Patrs.: Eng.: **Andrew(e)s, Andress, Andriss; Anderson, Enderson**. Sc.: **McAndrew; Kendrew** (now common in W Yorks.). It.: **D'Andrea, De Andreis**. Ger.: **Anderer; Andresser, Endresser** (Austria). Low Ger.: **Drees(s)en, Driessen; Drewing**. Flem.: **Driesen**. Du.: **Andriesse(n)**. Norw., Dan.: **Andersen, Andresen, Andrea(s)sen**. Swed.: **Andersson, Andreasson; Andrén**. Pol.: **Jędrzejewicz, Jędrachowicz; Andrzejak, Andrysiak; Russ.: **Andreev**. Lithuanian: **Andriulis**. Croatian: **Andr(ejev)ić**. Gk: **Andreou**.

Patrs. (from dims.): Gael.: **Mac Aindrín**. Eng.: **Dan(di)son**. Ger.: **Endler** (Bavaria). Pol.: **Jędrzejkiewicz, Jędrzaszkiewicz; Andrzejczak, Andryszczak, Jędrzejczak**. Russ.: **Andryushin, Andryunin, Andrusov**.

'Son of the servant of A.': Sc., Ir.: **Gillanders** (Gael. **Mac Gille Andrais** (Sc.), **Mac Giolla Aindréis** (Ir.)).

Habitation names: Pol.: **Andrzejewski, Andrzejowski, Jędrzéjewski, Jędrychowski**.

Andrewartha Cornish: habitation name from *Trewartha* in St Agnes parish (formerly called *Andrewartha*, from the def. art. *an* + *dre*, a mutated form of *tre* village + *wartha* higher).

Angear see AINGER

Angel English and French: nickname from ME, OF *angel* angel (L *angelus*, from Gk *angelos* messenger; cf. ENGEL), denoting a person of angelic temperament or appearance,

or one who had played the part of an angel in a mystery play or pageant. It was also occasionally used as a given name, especially on the Continent.

Vars.: Eng.: **Angell**. Fr.: **Ange(au)**.

Dims.: Fr.: **Angelet, Angelot, Angelin**. It.: **Angelini, Angiolini; Angeletti, Angioletti, Agnoletti, Angioletti; Angelozzi, Agnolozzi; Angelillo, Angiolillo; Angioli, Angiuli**.

Augs.: It.: **Angioni, Angheloni, Agnoloni**.

Patrs.: It.: **D'Angelo, De Angelis; D'Agnolo, Dell'Agnol**. Russ.: **Angelov** (adopted by priests). Croatian: **Andjelić**. Gk: **Angelopoulos**.

Patr. (from a dim.): Croatian: **Andjelković**.

Angilbert see ENGELBERT

Anglade Provençal: topographic name for someone who lived on a remote nook of land, from OProv. *anglade* corner, recess (LL *ang(u)lāta*, a deriv. of *angulus*; see ANGLE).

Angle English: topographic name for someone who lived on an odd corner of land, from ME, OF *angle* (L *angulus* angle, corner).

Var.: NANGLE.

Angless see ENGLISH

Angold see OSGOOD

Angove see GOUGH

Angrick see ANDREW

Ångström see ENG

Anguera Catalan: topographic name for someone who lived on the banks of the river *Anguera*, in the province of Tarragona. The name is of uncertain etymology, perhaps related to L *angustiae* narrows, strait, gorge (from *angustus* narrow).

Angus Scots and Irish: from the Gael. personal name *Aonghus*, composed of the elements *aon* one + *ghus* choice. It was borne by a famous but shadowy 8th-cent. Pictish king, said to be the son of Daghda, the chief god of the Irish, and Boann, who gave her name to the river Boyne. This king gave his name to the county (now part of Tayside) called *Angus*, and many Scots have received it as a given name in his honour. Some examples of the surname may also be regional names from this source.

Vars.: INNES; **Nish**. See also MCGUINNESS, HENNESSY, and MCNEICE.

Angwin 1. English (Norman): regional name from OF *angevin* man from *Anjou*, a province of France which was ruled by a count as an independent territory from the 10th cent. until it became a property of the English Crown for fifty years at the end of the 12th cent. 2. Cornish: nickname for someone with fair hair or a pale complexion, from Corn. *an* def. art. + *gwyn* white, fair.

Aniceto Portuguese: from a medieval given name (L *Anicētus*, Gk *Anikētos* 'Invincible', the name of a 2nd-cent. pope).

Anketell see ASHKETTLE

Annas see ANNIS

Anne English: 1. var. of HANNA. 2. habitation name from *Ann* in Hants, which is so called from an old stream name, probably a Brit. cogn. of W *on* ash tree.

Annion *see* ONION

Annis English: from a ME vernacular form of the female given name *Agnes* (ultimately from Gk *hagnos* pure, chaste, but early associated by folk etymology with L *agnus* lamb, a symbol of Christ). The name was borne by an early Christian saint, a twelve-year-old Roman girl who was martyred for her Christian belief in the time of Diocletian.

Vars.: **Agnes(s)**; **Anness**, **Annas**.

Dims.: Eng.: **Annott**, **Annatt**; **Annett** (chiefly N Ireland). It.: **Agnesetti**, **Agnesini**.

Metrs.: Eng.: **Annison**. It.: **D'Agnese**. Ger.: **Agneter**. Low Ger.: **Agnesen**, **Ne(e)sen**. Flem.: **Agneesen(s)**, **Niesen**.

Metr. (from a dim.): Eng.: **Annets**.

Anouilh S French: said by Dauzat to be from a Roussillonese dial. term meaning 'slowworm', and hence a nickname for a lethargic or sluggish person.

Anquetin *see* ASHKETTLE

Anquier *see* AINGER

Anseau *see* ANCEL

Ansell English (chiefly E Anglia): from a Gmc personal name composed of the elements *ans*- god + *helm* protection, helmet. This was a distinctively Langobardic name, and was common in Italy. Among its bearers were several famous medieval churchmen. It was brought to France and England by St Anselm (*c.*1033–1109), known as the father of Scholasticism. He was born in Aosta, joined the Benedictine order at Bec in Normandy, and in 1093 became archbishop of Canterbury.

Vars.: **Anshell**, **Ansill**, **Hansel(l)**, **Hansill**, **Hancell**.

Dims.: Eng.: **Anslyn**. Fr.: **Ansermet**. It.: **Anselmini**; **Selmini**. Ger.: **Ansle**, **Ansli**, **Ensle**, **Ensli(n)**, **Esslin**. Low Ger.: **Anselmann**.

Anslow English: habitation name from a place in Staffs., so called from the OE female name *Ēanswīð* + *lēah* wood, clearing.

Ansquer *see* AINGER

Anstey English: habitation name from any of the dozen places in England called *Anstey* or *Ansty*, from OE *ānstiga*, a cpd of *ān* one + *stīg* path, used of a short stretch of road forking at both ends. The surname is found principally in Somerset and the W Country.

Vars.: **Anstie**, **Ansty**.

Anstice English: from the ME male given name *Ansta(y)se* (L *Anastasius*, from Gk *anastasis* resurrection) or the fem. *Anastasie* (L *Anastasia*).

Vars.: **Anstis(s)**, **Ansteys**.

Dim.: It.: **Stassino**.

Patrs.: It.: **D'Anastasio**. Flem., Du.: **Stassen** (see also STACE).

Croatian: **Anastasijević**; **Nastić**. Gk: **Anastasiou**.

Anstruther Scottish: habitation name from a place in Fife, which is sometimes said to get its name from Gael. *an* the + *sruthar* stream, but which is more probably de-

rived from ON *engi* meadow + an unattested word *struðr, which would be a cogn. of OE *strōd* marshy land overgrown with brushwood. The pronunciation is usually /ˈænstrə/ or /ˈeɪnstrə/.

Antell *see* ASHKETTLE

Anthony English: from the given name so spelled, which, with its cogns. and derivs., is one of the commonest European given names. It is derived from L *Antōnius*, an ancient Roman family name of unknown etymology. The most famous member of the family was the soldier and triumvir Mark Antony (*Marcus Antonius*, *c.*83–30 BC). The spelling with -*h*-, which first appears in Eng. in the 16th cent. and in Fr. (*Anthoine*) at about the same time, is due to the erroneous belief that the name derives from Gk *anthos* flower.

The popularity of the given name in Christendom is largely due to the cult of the Egyptian hermit St Antony (AD 251–356), who in his old age gathered a community of hermits around him, and for that reason is regarded by some as the founder of monasticism. It was further increased by the fame of St Antony of Padua (1195–1231), who has always enjoyed a great popular cult, and is believed to help people find lost things.

Aphetic forms of the given name are common in most European languages (Eng. *Tony*, Fr. *Toine*, It. *Tonio*, Low Ger. *Thon*, etc.), and these have given rise to their own sets of surnames (see TONEY).

Vars.: **Antony**, **Ant(h)oney**.

Dims.: Fr.: **Antoinet**. It.: **Antonell(in)i**, **Antognelli**, **Anton(i)etti**, **Antognetti**, **Anton(i)utti**, **Antonucci**, **Antoniotti**, **Antognozzi**, **Antonioli**, **Antognoli**. Pol.: **Antonczyk**, **Antosik**, **Antoszczyk**; **Jadczyk**. Ukr.: **Anton(ch)ik**, **Antuk**.

Augs.: Fr.: **Anto(i)nat**, **Antonas**. It.: **Antonioni**, **Antognoni**.

Pejs.: It.: **Antonacci**, **Anton(i)azzi**, **Antognazzi**.

Patrs.: Sp.: **Antúnez**. Port.: **Antunes**. It.: **D'Antoni(o)**, **D'Antuoni**, **De Antoni**, **Di Antonio**, **Degli Antoni**. Rum.: **Antonescu**. Low Ger.: **Ant(h)oni)es**. Flem.: **Antoons**. Dan., Norw.: **Ant(h)onsen**. Swed.: **Antonsson**. Russ.: **Antonov** (popular form); **Antonyev** (learned form). Ukr.: **Antonich**. Croatian: **Antonijević**, **Antonović**, **Antić**. Pol.: **Antonowicz**, **Antoniewicz**; **Antoniak**. Hung.: **Antalffy**. Gk: **Antoniou**, **Antonopoulos**, **Antoniades**.

Patrs. (from dims.): Russ.: **Anton(n)ikov**; **Antoshin**, **Antushev**, **Antyshev**, **Antyukhin**. Pol.: **Antczak**; **Jadczak**.

Habitation name: Pol.: **Antoniewski**, **Antoszewski**, **Antowski**.

Antifeev *see* YEVTIKHIEV

Antipov Russian: patr. from the given name *Antip* (Gk *Antipas*, a short form of *Antipatēr*, from the elements *anti* equal to, like + *patēr* father). It was adopted as a baptismal name in the Eastern Church in honour of St Antipas of Pergamum, first bishop of that city, who was martyred in about AD 90, and who is referred to in the book of Revelation (2: 13) as the 'faithful witness'.

Vars.: **Antipyev**, **Antipin**.

Antonini Italian: 1. dim. of ANTHONY. 2. from the L personal name *Antōnīnus*, a deriv. of *Antōnius* (see ANTHONY), which was borne by several Roman emperors, starting with Antoninus Pius (AD 138–61), and by various early saints, including a 2nd-cent. converted executioner of Christians.

Vars.: **Antognini**, **Antongini**.

Antrack see ANDREW

Antrobus English: habitation name from a place in Ches., recorded in Domesday Book as *Entrebus*, apparently from the ON personal name *Eindriði, Andriði* (which is of doubtful etymology) + ON *buski* shrub, bush, thicket.

Anttila Finnish: topographic name for someone who lived at the house of a bearer of the given name *Antti* (Finnish equivalent of ANDREW), with the local suffix *-la*.

Antuñano Basque: habitation name from some minor place so called, from L *Antōniānus (fundus)* (farm, estate) of *Antōnius*; see ANTHONY.

Antzilewitz see AMSCHEL

Anyan see ONION

Aoustin see AUSTIN

Aparicio Spanish: from a given name bestowed on children born on the Feast of the Epiphany (6 January), from Sp. *aparición* appearance, manifestation (LL *apparitio*, gen. *apparitiōnis*, from *appārēre* to come into view).
Var.: **París**.

Apel see ALBERT

Apelbaum see APPLE

Apelbe see APPLEBY

Apfelbaum see APPLE

Appel see ALBERT

Apple English: from ME *appel* (OE *æppel*) apple, acquired as a surname in any of various senses. It may originally have been used as a topographic name for someone living by a prominent apple tree or apple orchard; a metonymic occupational name for a grower or seller of apples; or a nickname for someone supposed to resemble an apple in some way, e.g. in having bright red cheeks. The economic importance in medieval N Europe of apples, as a fruit which could be grown in a cold climate and would keep for use throughout the winter, is hard to appreciate in these days of easy imports of southern fruits.
Cpds: Swed. (ornamental): **Appelberg** ('apple hill'), **Appelgren** ('apple branch'), **Appelkvist** ('apple twig'). Ger.: **Apfelbaum** ('apple tree'). Low Ger.: **Appel(bohm)**. Du.: **Appelboom**. Jewish: **Ap(p)elbaum**, **Applebaum**, **Ap(p)elbo(i)m**, **Epelbaum** ('apple tree', ornamental or topographic); **Apfelberg**, **Appelberg** ('apple hill', ornamental); **Ap(p)elblat** ('apple leaf', ornamental); **Apeloig** ('apple eye', ornamental, with Yid. *oyg*); **Apfelschnitt** ('apple slice'. ornamental).

Appleby N English: habitation name from any of various places, for example in Leics., Lincs. (Humberside), and Cumb., so called from ON *apall* APPLE + *býr* farm, settlement.
Vars.: **Applebey**, **Applebe(e)**, **Apelbe**.

Applegarth N English and Scots: topographic name for someone who lived by an apple orchard, Northern ME *applegarth* (from ON *apall* APPLE + *garðr* enclosure, orchard), or habitation name from a place so named, for example in Cumb. and N and E Yorks., as well as in the former county of Dumfries.
Vars.: **Applegath**, **Applegate**. See also APPLEYARD.

Applethwaite English: habitation name from one of the places in Cumb. so called, from ON *apall* APPLE + *þveit* meadow (see THWAITE).
Vars.: **Applewh(a)ite**, **Ablewhite**.

Appleton English: habitation name from any of the many places, for example in Ches., Oxon., and N Yorks., so called from OE *æppeltūn* orchard (a cpd of *æppel* APPLE + *tūn* enclosure, settlement).
Var.: **Napleton** (from OE *æt þæm æppeltūne* 'at the orchard', ME *atten Appleton*).

Appleyard N English: topographic name for someone who lived by an apple orchard, ME *appleyard* (from OE *æppel* APPLE + *geard* enclosure, orchard; an Anglicized form of APPLEGARTH, replacing the native APPLETON) or at a place so named, of which the most significant source of surnames is in W Yorks.

Apps English: from ME *apse*, OE *æps, æspe* aspen, usually no doubt a topographic name for someone who lived near an aspen tree, but occasionally perhaps a nickname for a timorous person, with reference to the trembling leaves of the tree.
Vars.: **Aps**, **Happs**; **Apsey** (Somerset); **Aspey** (Lancs.; metathesized); **Asp**; **Epps**, **Hesp(e)**.
Cpd: Swed.: **Asplund** ('aspen grove').

Aprahamian see ABRAHAM

April English: from the month of April (OF *avril*, L *aprīlis (mensis)*, apparently a deriv. of *aperīre* to open, with reference to the opening of buds and flowers in the spring). This was used as a given name for someone born, baptized, or officially registered in April, or having some other connection with the month.
Vars.: **Avril**, **Averill**. See also EVERILL.
Dim.: Fr.: **Avrillon**.

Aps see APPS

Apt Jewish (E Ashkenazic): habitation name from *Apt*, Yid. name of *Opatów* in the province of Kielce, Poland, so called from Pol. *opactwo* abbey.
Vars.: **Apter(man)**; **Opatowski**, **Opatowsky**, **Opatovsky** (from the Pol. name of the town).

Aquilini see EAGLE

Aragón Spanish: ethnic name from *Aragón* in NE Spain, which was an independent kingdom from 1035 to the 14th cent. There are various speculations about the etymology of the name, but the true origin is probably irrecoverable. The royal house of *Aragón* was descended from Ramiro I of Aragon (reigned 1035–63), illegitimate son of Sancho III of Navarre.
Vars.: **Aragonés**, **Aragoneses**.

Aramburu Spanish form of Basque **Aranburu**: topographic name for someone who lived at the upper end of a valley or in the principal settlement in a valley, from Basque *aran* valley (see ARANA) + *buru* head, summit.
Var.: **Arampuru** (Fr.).

Arana Basque: topographic name for someone who lived in a valley, from *aran* valley + the def. art. *-a*.
Var.: **Aran** (Fr.).

Aranda Spanish: habitation name from any of various places, for example in the provinces of Burgos and Saragossa. The placename may be from L *aranda* arable land (from the gerundive of *arāre* to plough), or from the Celt. elements *are-randa* near, next to the frontier, or from a deriv. of Basque *aran* valley (cf. ARANA).

Aranguren Basque: topographic name for someone who lived at the end of a valley, from Basque *aran* valley (see ARANA) + *guren* edge, border. There are places named with these elements in the provinces of Biscay and Navarre, and these may also be partial sources of the surname.

Aranzello *see* NARANJO

Araújo Portuguese: habitation name from any of various minor places so called, for example in Coimbra, Elvas, Estremoz, Lisbon, Moncorvo, Monsão, Serpa, Setúbal, and Villa Verde. The surname is also relatively common in Spain in the form **Araujo**.

Arbatov Russian: habitation name from an area of Moscow called the *Arbat*, with the addition of the usual surname ending *-ov* (formally a patr.). The origin of the placename is not clear. It is traditionally said to be derived from *arba* cart, but this is probably the result of folk etymology; it is more probably taken from some word in a Turkic language (cf. Khirgiz *yrabat* large building).

Arbaud *see* HERBAUD

Arber *see* HARBER

Arblaster *see* ALABASTER

Arbós Catalan: topographic name for someone who lived by a strawberry tree or arbutus, Cat. *arboç* (LL *arbuteus*, from class. L *arbutus*, apparently a deriv. of *arbor* tree). In part it may derive from a place in the province of Tarragona called *L'Arbós*, from this word.

Arbuckle Scots: habitation name from a place in the parish of Airdrie, in the former county of Lanarks., so called from Gael. *àrd an buachaille* 'height of the shepherd'.
Vars.: **Arnbuckle**; **Ironbuckle** (by English folk etymology).

Arbus Jewish (E Ashkenazic): of uncertain origin, probably connected either with Yid. *arbes* pea or with Russ. *arbuz* watermelon (see ARBUZOV).
Vars.: **Arbuss**, **Arbuz**, **Arbusman**.

Arbuthnot Scots: habitation name from *Arbuthnott*, south of Aberdeen, earlier *Aberbuthnot*. The place is so called from Brittonic *aber* confluence + a stream name (*Buadhnat* in Gael.) from a dim. of *bothen* virtuous; that is, it was regarded as a holy stream with the power to heal wounds or sickness.
Var.: **Arbuthnott**.

Arbuzov Russian: patr. from the nickname *Arbuz* 'Watermelon' (ultimately from Persian *khärbuze* melon), perhaps referring to a grower or enthusiastic eater of the fruit. The word was also used as a term of endearment.

Arcas Spanish: **1.** occupational name for a cabinet-maker, from the vocab. word *arca* chest, coffer (from L *arcēre* to shut in, enclose). **2.** nickname for a broad-chested individual, from the same word applied to the part of the body in a sense development paralleled by Eng. *chest*. **3.** topographic name from the same word used in any of various senses. In Galicia it was used of a dolmen, in Astorga of a millstone, from the supposedly box-like appearance of these objects.

Arce Spanish: **1.** topographic name for someone who lived by a prominent maple tree, Sp. *arce* (metathesized from L *acer*, gen. *aceris*). **2.** habitation name from places in the provinces of Santander and Navarre, whose names represent a Castilianized spelling of Basque *artze* stony place (from *arri* stone + the suffix of abundance *-tz(e)*).

Archdale English and Irish: ostensibly a habitation name from ME *arch* (of a bridge; see ARCO) + *dale* valley (see DALE). However, no place with this name exists, and the surname is more likely to be a garbling of some Gaelic or possibly Scandinavian original.

Archer English and French: occupational name for a bowman, from ME *archere*, OF *arch(i)er* (L *arc(u)ārius*, from *arcus* bow; see ARCO).
Vars.: Fr.: **Archier**, **LARCHER**; **Arquier** (Normandy, Picardy).

Archibald English and Scots: from a Norman given name, recorded in the form *Archambault*, composed of the Gmc elements *ercan* precious + *bald* bold, daring. The surname is chiefly common in Scotland, where it had been used as an Anglicized form of GILLESPIE, for reasons that are unclear.
Vars.: **Archibould**, **Archbo(u)ld**, **Archbald**, **Archbell**, **Archbutt**. Fr.: **Archimb(e)aud**, **Archambault**. Du.: **Arkenbout**.

Arco Italian and Spanish: **1.** metonymic occupational name for a bowman or a maker of bows, from It., Sp. *arco* bow (L *arcus*); cf. ARCHER. **2.** topographic name for someone who lived by the arch of a bridge or aqueduct, from the same word used in an architectural sense.
Vars.: It.: **Archi**, **D(ell)'Arco**. Sp.: **Arcos**.
Dims.: It.: **Archetto**, **Archetti**, **Archini**, **Arcucci**. Fr.: **Arquet**, **Arquin**.
Augs.: It.: **Arcone**, **Arconi**.

Arct *see* ARZT

Arden English: regional name from the Forest of *Arden* in Warwicks. or from *Arden* in N Yorks. Both placenames are probably linguistically identical with the forest of the *Ardennes* in France and Belgium, and are derived from a Celtic word meaning 'high'.

Ardes *see* ALLARDYCE

Arding *see* HARDING

Ardley English: habitation name from any of several places. *Ardley* in Oxon. and *Ardeley* in Herts. are so called from an OE personal name, *Eardwulf* (composed of the elements *eard* native land + *wulf* wolf) or a short form, *Earda*, + *lēah* wood, clearing. *Eardley* End in Staffs. is from OE *eard* dwelling place + *lēah*; *Ardleigh* in Essex may have the same origin, or it may have *erð* ploughed land as a first element.
Vars.: **Ardleigh**; **Eardley** (Staffs).

Ardouin French: from a Gmc personal name, *Hardwin*, composed of the elements *hard* hardy, brave, strong + *win* friend.

Vars.: **Hardo(u)in**.

Ardura Spanish: nickname, apparently for a careworn individual, from Sp. *ardura* difficulty, trouble, anxiety (LL *ardūra*, from *arduus* steep, difficult).

Areles *see* AARON

Arellano Spanish: habitation name from a place in the province of Navarre, so called from LL *Aurēliānus (fundus)* (farm, estate) of *Aurēlius*', a personal name possibly derived from L *aurum* gold.

Arenas Spanish: habitation name from any of the numerous places so called, from the pl. (collective) form of Sp. *arena* sand (L *(h)arēna*).

Dims.: Sp.: **Arenillas**. It.: **Arenella, Aren(i)ello**.

Ares Spanish: of uncertain etymology. It is generally assumed to derive from a medieval personal name that is probably of Gmc origin.

Aresti Basque: topographic name for someone who lived by an oak wood, from *areitz* oak tree + the suffix of abundance *-di* (*-ti* after a sibilant).

Arévalo Spanish: habitation name from places in the provinces of Ávila and Soria. The placename is of uncertain etymology, possibly from Celt. *are-valon* 'near, next to the wall, fence'.

Argemí Catalan: from the Gmc (Gothic) personal name *Argimir*, composed of the elements *harjis* army + *meri, mari* famous.

Argent 1. French and English (Norman): from OF *argent* silver (L *argentum*). This was probably most commonly a nickname for someone with silvery grey hair, but it may also have been originally an occupational name for a worker in the metal or a topographic name for someone who lived near a silver mine. There are several French towns and villages called *Argent* (e.g. in Cher) because silver was mined there, and the surname may also derive from any of these. **2.** French: habitation name from either of the places, in Aude and Basses-Alpes, called *Argens*, from the LL personal name *Argenteus* or *Argentius* 'Silvery'.

Vars.: Eng.: **Hargent, Largent**.

Argüello Spanish: habitation name from any of various minor places so called, from OSp. *arboleo* well-wooded (LL *arboleus*, for class. L *arboreus*, a deriv. of *arbor* tree).

Argyle Scots: regional name from *Argyll*, a district in SW Scotland, so called from Gael. *oirthir Ghaidheal* 'coast of the Gaels'.

Arianello *see* ADRIAN

Arias Spanish and Jewish (Sefardic): of uncertain origin. The Spanish name has been explained as a patronymic, either from the medieval personal name ARES, which is probably of Gmc origin, or else from a medieval personal name *Aria* or *Arius*, which is probably of Romance origin.

Arillotta *see* GRILL

Ariñó Catalan: topographic name for someone who lived by a sloe tree, Cat. *aranyó* (of Celt. origin).

Ariza Spanish: habitation name from a place in the province of Saragossa, so called from an Arabic term for a possession or holding.

Arkenbout *see* ARCHIBALD

Arkhipov Russian: patr. from the given name *Arkhip* (Gk *Arkhippos*, composed of the elements *arkh-* rule + *hippos* horse). The name was borne by a 1st-cent. companion of St Paul, traditionally regarded as the first bishop of Colossae.

Var.: **Arkhipyev**.

Arkin *see* AARON

Arkle English: from the ON personal name *Arnkell*, composed of the elements *arn* eagle + *ketil* cauldron, helmet, or helmeted warrior. The surname is found chiefly in N England, where Scandinavian influence was strongest, and is most common in Northumb.

Vars.: **Arkley**; **Arkill, Arkell** (the two latter are now chiefly W Midlands).

Arkwright English: occupational name for a maker of chests, from ME, OF *arc* chest, ark (see ARCAS) + ME *wrytte* maker, craftsman (see WRIGHT). The surname is most common in Lancs.

Vars.: **Atrick; Hartwright, Hartrick, Hattrick**.

Arling *see* HARLING

Arlott English: nickname from ME, OF *(h)arlot, herlot* vagabond, rascal (of obscure origin). The vocab. word also denoted an itinerant entertainer, also a male servant, so it may in some instances have been originally an occupational name. The sense referring to a woman of easy sexual availability is not recorded before the 15th cent., and is unlikely to have contributed to the surname.

Var.: **Arlot**.

Patr.: Prov.: **Darlot**.

Armandin *see* HERMANN

Armengol Catalan: from a Gmc personal name composed of the element *ermin* (see ARMIN) + the tribal name *Gaut* (see JOCELYN).

Var.: **Armengou**.

Armer English: occupational name for a maker of arms, ANF *armer* (OF *armier*, L *armārius*, a deriv. of *arma* arms).

Var.: **Larmer** (with fused ANF def. art.). See also ARMOUR.

Armetriding English: habitation name from *Armetridding*, a minor place in the parish of Leyland, Lancs., so called from ME *ermit, armit* hermit + *rid(d)ing* clearing.

Var.: **Armetrading**.

Armgardt *see* ERMGARD

Armin English and French: from the ME, OF given name *Armin, Ermin*, derived from the Gmc element *ermin*. This seems to have been the name, of unknown etymology, of an ancient Gmc god, but in later times it was also used in various cpd names with the meaning 'whole', 'entire' (cf.

ARMENGOL and MENÉNDEZ). For the change of *Er-* to *Ar-*, cf. MARCHANT.

Var.: **Ermin**.

Dim.: Fr.: **Arminot**.

Patrs.: Eng.: **Arminson, Arm(i)son; Armes** (Norfolk).

Armistead 1. English: topographic name for someone who lived by a hermit's cell, from ME *(h)ermite* hermit (see ARMITAGE) + *stede* place (see STEAD 1). 2. Anglicized form of **Darmstädter**, a habitation name from *Darmstadt* in Hesse, W Germany.

Var. (of 1): **Armstead**.

Armitage English: topographic name for someone who lived by a hermitage (ME, OF *(h)ermitage*, a deriv. of OF *(h)ermite* hermit, LL *erēmīta*, Gk *erēmītēs*, from *erēmos* solitary), or habitation name from some place so named.

Vars.: **Armytage, Hermitage**.

Armor *see* ARMOUR

Armour English and Scots: metonymic occupational name for a maker of arms and armour, from ME, OF *armure* (LL *armātūra*, a deriv. of *arma* arms), used of offensive weapons as well as defensive clothing. The ending of the vocab. word and surname has been assimilated to the agent suffix *-o(u)r*, and there has been some confusion with ARMER.

Vars.: **Armor; Larmo(u)r** (with fused ANF def. art.).

Armstrong N English and S Scots: nickname from ME *arm* + *strong*, i.e. with strong arms.

Var.: **Strongitharm**.

Arnbuckle *see* ARBUCKLE

Arndell *see* ARUNDEL

Ärnli *see* ARNOLD

Arnold English: 1. from a Norman personal name composed of the Gmc elements *arn* eagle + *wald* rule. 2. habitation name from one of the two places, in Notts. and Humberside, named with the OE elements *earn* eagle + *halh* nook, hollow (see HALE 1). The name of both places has been assimilated to the given name from earlier *Ernehale, Arnhale*. 3. Jewish (Ashkenazic): of uncertain origin.

Vars.: (of 1): **Arnhold, Arnould, Arnout, Arnoll, Arnald, Arnaud, Arnall, Arnell, Arnull,** ARNOTT, **Arnatt, Arnull; Harnott, Harnett, Hornet(t)**.

Dims. (of 1): Fr.: **Arnaudet, Arnaudin, Arnaudon, Arnaudot**. Prov.: **Arnaldy, Arnaudy, Arnauduc** (Gascony). Ger.: **Arni, Erni, Ärnli** (Switzerland). Low Ger.: **Arn(ec)ke, Ernke**.

Patrs. (from 1): Eng.: **Arnison, Arn(a)son**. Basque: **Arnáiz, Arnáez**. Low Ger.: **Arnhol(t)z, Ar(n)tz(en), Ahrens, Ahrendsen**. Flem.: **Arents**. Du.: **Aren(d)s; Arendse(n), Aartsen**. Norw., Dan.: **Arndtsen**.

Arnott 1. English: var. of ARNOLD. 2. Scots: habitation name from *Arnot* near Kinross, probably so called from Gael. *ornacht* barley.

Var.: **Arnot**.

Arnou French: from the Gmc personal name *Arnwulf*, composed of the elements *arn* eagle + *wulf* wolf.

Vars.: **Arnoux, Arnoul(f)**.

Arnow *see* AARON

Aron *see* AARON

Aronde *see* HIRON

Aróstegui Spanish form of Basque **Arostegi** or **Aroztegi**: habitation name for someone who lived near a house occupied by the village smith or carpenter, from Basque *arotz* smith, carpenter + the suffix *-tegi* house of.

Arquet *see* ARCO

Arrandale *see* ARUNDEL

Arranz Spanish: of unclear etymology. It is seemingly derived from a personal name, since the same element occurs also in the cpd surnames **Antoranz, Estebaranz**, and **Gilarranz**. The unusual final consonantal combination *-nz* is found also in the surnames *Herranz* (see FERNANDO) and *Sanz* (see SANCHO).

Arregui Spanish form of Basque **Arregi**: topographic name for someone who lived in a stony place, from Basque *arri* stone + the local suffix *-egi*, or for someone who lived by a rocky incline, from *arri* stone + *egi* slope.

Arrhenius *see* AHRÉN

Arriba Spanish: topographic name for someone who lived uphill or upstream from the main settlement, from Sp. *arriba* above, upstream (from LL *ad* at, towards + *ripa* riverbank). Compare ABAJO. There are various places, for example in the provinces of Lugo and Navarre, named with this word, and the surname may also be a habitation name from any of these.

Var.: **Arribas**.

Arrichiello *see* HENRY

Arriero Spanish: occupational name for a driver of mules and other pack animals, Sp. *arriero* (from *arrear* to drive animals, a deriv. of the interjection *(h)arre*, found also in Prov. and It. dialects, used to urge animals on).

Arrieta Basque: topographic name for someone who lived on a patch of stony soil, from *arri* stone + the collective suffix *-eta*. There are several places so named, for example in the provinces of Álava, Biscay, and Navarre, and they may all have contributed to the surname.

Var.: **Arriola** (with a local suffix).

Arrington English: 1. var. of HARRINGTON. 2. habitation name from a place in Cambs., so called from OE *Earningatūn* 'settlement (OE *tūn*) of the people of *Earn(a)*', a byname meaning 'Eagle'.

Arrizabalaga Basque: topographic name for someone who lived near a patch of open stony ground, from *arri* stone + *zabal* broad, wide + the local suffix *-aga*.

Arrowsmith English: occupational name for a maker of iron arrowheads, from OE *arwe* arrow + *smið* SMITH. The surname is most common in N England and the Midlands.

Vars.: **Arsmith, Harrowsmith, Harrismith**.

Arroyo Spanish: topographic name for someone who lived near a stream or irrigation channel, from Sp. *arroyo* watercourse (of pre-Roman origin).

Arrufat Catalan: nickname for someone with a wizened or wrinkled face or a habitually dishevelled appearance, from the past. part. of *arrufar* to crease, crumple (of uncertain origin).

Arscott English: habitation name from a place in Shrops., first recorded in the 13th cent. in the form *Ardescot(e)*. The first element probably represents a shortened form of the gen. case of a cpd OE personal name such as *Æðelrǣd* ('noble counsel') or *Ēadrǣd* ('prosperity counsel'); the second is OE *cot* hut, cottage (see COATES).

Arsenyev Russian: patr. from the given name *Arseni* (Gk *Arsenios* 'virile, masculine'). This was the name of several minor early Christian saints, but owes its currency mainly to St Arsenius the Great (d. *c*.449), who was tutor to the sons of the Emperor Theodosius, Honorius and Arcadius, who divided the Roman Empire between them.

Arsmith *see* ARROWSMITH

Artaud French: from the Gmc personal name *Hartwald*, composed of the elements *hard* hardy, brave, strong + *wald* rule.

Vars.: **Arthaud**, **Arthault**; **Hartaud**.

Arteaga Basque: topographic name for someone who lived by a holm oak, from *arte* holm oak + the local suffix *-aga*. There are several places in the province of Biscay named with these elements, all of which may have contributed to the surname.

Arteche Spanish form of Basque **Artetxe**: topographic name for someone who lived in a house on a patch of empty land, from Basque *arte* (intervening) space, middle + *etxe* house.

Artelt *see* ORT

Arthur English and French: from the Celt. personal name *Arthur*, which is of obscure and disputed etymology; it may possibly be derived from some early cogn. of Gael. *art*, W *arth* bear (cf. CARTON). It has been continuously in use as a given name in Britain since the early Middle Ages, owing its popularity to the legendary exploits of King Arthur and his Round Table, which gave rise to a prolific literature in many W European languages, starting with Welsh. Virtually nothing is known of the historical figure who lies behind the legends beyond the fact that he was probably a Brit. leader in the 6th cent. who fought victorious battles against the Saxon invaders. The name has absorbed the Scandinavian name *Arnðórr*, which comes from *arn* eagle + *Þorr* the name of the god of thunder.

Vars.: Fr.: **Art(h)us**, **Arthuys**.

Dims.: Fr.: **T(h)urel**, **T(h)ureau**, **T(h)uret**, **T(h)urin**, **T(h)uron**, **T(h)urot**. It.: **Artusino**.

Patrs.: Eng.: **Arthurs** (chiefly N Ireland). Sc., Ir.: **McArthur**, **McArtair**, **McAirter**, **McCa(i)rtair**, **McCarter** (Gael. **Mac Artair**). Manx: CARTER.

Artiga Catalan: topographic name for someone who lived on a patch of land newly broken up, Cat. *artiga* (of uncertain, possibly Celt. origin). There are places in the provinces of Biscay and Barcelona named with the pl. form of this word, and both may have contributed to the surname.

Vars.: **Artigas**, **Artigues**.

Artz *see* ARNOLD

Arundel English: **1.** habitation name from a place in W Sussex, seat of the Duke of Norfolk, which perhaps gets its name from OE *hārhune* hoarhound (from *hār* grey + *hūne* an earlier name of the same plant, of obscure origin) + *dell* valley. **2.** nickname (Norman) for someone supposedly resembling a swallow in some way, from OF *arondel*, dim. of *arond* swallow (L *hirundo*, confused with *(h)arundo* reed).

Vars.: **Ar(u)ndell**, **Ar(r)undale**, **Arrandale**.

Arunowicz *see* AARON

Arvidsson Swedish: patr. from the popular Nordic given name *Arvid*, composed of the elements represented by ON *are* eagle + *við* wide.

Arzt German and Jewish (Ashkenazic): occupational name for a physician, Ger. *Arzt* (MHG *arzet*, OHG *arzāt*, derived via LL *arciāter* from Gk *archiatros* chief physician, a cpd of *arch-* chief, principal + *iatros* physician). This word became the usual OHG term for a physician during the Carolingian period, gradually supplanting the earlier Gmc word (represented by MHG *lāchener*; cf. LEACH 1).

Var.: Jewish: **Arct** (Pol. spelling).

Asam *see* ERASMUS

Åsberg *see* ÅHS

Asbury English: habitation name of uncertain origin; the place from which it is derived has not been identified. The second element is clearly OE *burh* fortified town (see BURKE); the first may be ASH, EAST, or the OE personal name *Æsc* 'Spear'. The name is chiefly common in the W Midlands.

Asby *see* ASHBY

Ascelin *see* ACE

Ascensão Portuguese: from a given name bestowed on someone born on the Feast of the Ascension of Christ (LL *ascensio*, gen. *ascensiōnis*, for class. L *ascensus*).

Asch *see* ASH

Ascham English: habitation name from any of several places called *Askham*. Those in Notts. and N Yorks. get the name from OE *æsc* ASH + *hām* homestead, while the one in Cumb. is from OE *æscum*, the dat. pl. of *æsc*, originally used after a preposition.

Vars.: **Ask(h)am**.

Ascher *see* ASHER

Aschew *see* ASKEW

Ascot English: habitation name from places in Berks. and Oxon., so called from OE *ēast* EAST + *cot* hut, cottage (see COATES).

Var.: **Ascott**.

Ascroft *see* ASHCROFT

Åsell *see* ÅHS

Ash 1. English: topographic name for someone who lived near a prominent ash tree, OE *æsc* ash, or habitation name from some minor place so named. **2.** Jewish (Ashkenazic):

acronym from Yid. *AltSHul* (see ALTSCHUL) or *AyznSHtot* (see EISENSTADT).

Vars. (of 1): **Ashe** (now chiefly Irish); **Asch(e)**, **Aish**, **Aysh**, **Esh**; ASHMAN, ASHER; DASH, NASH, RASH, TASH. (Of 2): **Asch**.

Cpd (of 1): Swed.: **Asklund** ('ash grove').

Ashall English: probably a habitation name from an unidentified place so called, from OE *æsc* ASH + *hall* HALL or *hall* nook, recess (see HALE 1). The surname is most common in Lancs.

Ashard *see* ACHARD

Ashburnham English: habitation name from the village of *Ashburnham* in Sussex, which gets its name from the local stream, the *Ashburn* (from OE *æsc* ASH + *burna* stream; see BOURNE) + OE *hām* homestead.

Var.: **Esburnham**.

Ashby English: habitation name from any of the numerous places so called from ON *askr* ASH + *býr* farm, settlement. It is possible that in some cases the first element is the ON personal name *Aski*, a short form of the various cpd personal names with the first element *ask-* ash, spear (spear shafts were generally made of ash wood).

Vars.: **Ashbey**, **Ashbee**; **Asby**.

Ashcroft English: habitation name from any of various places so called from OE *æsc* ASH + *croft* paddock, enclosure (see CROFT).

Var.: **Ascroft**.

Ashdown English: regional name from either of two places: the *Ashdown* Forest in E Sussex, and *Ashdown*, which was until the 18th cent. the name of the Berkshire Downs. It is impossible to say whether the first part of these names is the tree-name *æsc* ASH or a personal name identical in form, from *æsc* in the sense 'spear'.

Ashenden English: topographic name for someone who lived by a valley in which ash trees grew, from OE *æscen* ashen (a deriv. of *æsc* ASH) + *denu* valley (see DEAN), or from a place named with these words, such as *Ashington* in Northumb.

Asher **1.** English: topographic name, a var. of ASH. **2.** Jewish: from the Hebr. given name *Asher* 'Blessed'.

Vars. (of 2): **Ascher**; **Asser** (among Sefardic Jews in Holland); **Asheri**, **Ashery** (Israeli; formed with the Hebr. suffix *-i*). See also OSHER and USHER.

Patrs. (from 2): **As(c)herov**, **Asheroff**, **Asherovi(t)ch** (E Ashkenazic).

Ashfield English (W Midlands): habitation name from any of several places so called, for example in Shrops. The placename is from OE *æsc* ASH + *feld* pasture, open country (see FIELD).

Ashford English: habitation name from any of several places so called. Those in Devon, Derbys., Essex, Shrops., and Surrey get their name from OE *æsc* ASH + *ford* FORD. One in Kent, however, is a collapsed form of *æsc-scēatford*, the middle element being OE *scēat* copse (see SKEAT). One in Middlesex is first recorded in 969 in the form *Ecelesford*, where the first element perhaps represents the gen. case of an OE personal name **Eccel*, dim. of *Ecca*,

a short form of any of the OE personal names containing the first element *ecg* edge (of a sword).

Ashkenazi Jewish: name for an Ashkenazic (Yiddish-speaking) Jew who had settled in an area where non-Ashkenazic Jews were in the majority. *Ashkenaz* is a biblical placename (Gen. 10: 3, Jer. 51: 27), etymologically related to Gk *Skythia* Scythia. However, since the 9th cent. AD, if not earlier, it has been applied to Germany, probably because of its phonological similarity to Ger. *Sachsen* Saxony.

Vars.: **Ashkenazy**, **Ashkenasi**, **Ashkenasy**, **Ashkinazi**, **Ashkinazy**, **Ashkynazi**, **Ashkanazy**, **Aszkenazy**, **Aszkinazy**, **Askenazi**, **Askenazy**, **Askenasi**, **Askenasy**, **Askinazi**, **Askinazy**, **Aski(e)nasy**, **Askanazi**; **Ashkenaz**, **Ashkenas**, **Ashkinas**, **Ashkinos**, **Aszkenas**, **Askenas(e)**, **Askinas**; **Eskenazi** (reflecting a Sefardic pronunciation); **Ashkinadze** (with the ending changed to resemble the Georgian patr. suffix *-adze*); **Schinasi** (an It. form).

Ashkettle English: from the ON personal name *Ásketill*, composed of the elements *óss*, *áss* god + *ketill* kettle, sacrificial cauldron.

Vars.: **Askel**, **Haskel(l)**, **Ax(t)ell**; **Astell**, **Astill** (see also ASTLE); **Ankettle**, **Anketell**, **Ankill**, **Antill**, **Antell** (Norman).

Dims.: Eng.: **Askin**, **Ashken**, **Haskin(g)**, **Astin**, **Hastin**; **Ankin**, **Antin**. Fr. (Norman): **Anquetin**, **Lanquetin**, **Lanctin**.

Patrs.: Sc., Ir.: **McAsgill**, **McAskill**, **McCaskell**, **McCaskil(l)**, **McKaskil(l)** (Gael. *Mac Asgaill*). Manx: **Castell**, **Caistel**. Low Ger.: **Eschels**, **Eschelsen**. Norw., Dan.: **Axelsen**. Swed.: **Axelsson**.

Patrs. (from dims.): Eng.: **Askins**, **Haskin(g)s**, **Astins**, **Hastins**. Sc., Ir.: **McAskie**, **McCaskie** (Gael. *Mac Ascaidh*).

Ashley English: habitation name from any of the numerous places in S and Midland England so called, from OE *æsc* ASH + *lēah* wood, clearing.

Ashlin *see* ACE

Ashling **1.** from a Norman given name, a dim. of ACE. **2.** habitation name from the villages of E and W Ashling in Sussex, probably so called from OE *æscelingas* 'people of *æscel*' (a hypocoristic deriv. of the personal name *æsc*; see ASHDOWN).

Ashman English: **1.** topographic name, a var. of ASH. **2.** from the ME given name *Asheman*, OE *æscmann*, probably originally a byname from *æscman* seaman, pirate (a cpd of OE *æsc* (boat made of) ash + *mann* man. There is no evidence that the OE word *æscmann* survived into ME, but if it did this surname could also have been an occupational name for a seaman. Nor is there any evidence that *æscmann* was an occupational name for a spearman, even though this is inherently plausible since *æsc* was also used in OE to mean 'spear'.

Ashmole English: of unknown origin. It may represent a lost habitation name, derived perhaps from an OE personal name *æschelm* (composed of the elements *æsc* ash, spear + *helm* protection, helmet) + *holh* hollow, depression.

Ashmore English: habitation name from any of several minor places, so called from OE *æsc* ASH + *mōr* marsh, fen (see MOORE 1). In the case of *Ashmore* in Dorset, however, the early forms suggest that the second element is probably OE *mere* lake or *(ge)mære* boundary.

Ashplant *see* ABSALOM

Ashton English: habitation name from any of the numerous places so called, esp. *Ashton* under Lyne near Manchester. Most get the name from OE *æsc* ASH + *tūn* enclosure, settlement, but a few have been assimilated to this form from different sources. One in Devon was originally named as the settlement of *æschere*, an OE personal name composed of the elements *æsc* ash, spear + *here* army; one in Herts. was the settlement of *ælli* and one in Northants represents the OE dat. pl. *æscum*, originally used after a preposition.

Ashurst English: habitation name from any of various places, so called from OE *æsc* ASH + *hyrst* wooded hill (see HURST). The most significant of these are in Kent and Sussex, but the surname is found chiefly in Lancs., where it probably derives from *Ashurst* Beacon, near Wigan.

Ashwell English: habitation name from any of various places, for example in Essex, Herts., and Leics., so called from OE *æsc* ASH + *well(a)* spring, stream (see WELL).

Ashwood English: topographic name for somebody who lived by an ash wood, or habitation name from a minor place so called, from OE *æsc* ASH + *wudu* WOOD.

Ashworth English: habitation name from any of various places, in Lancs. and elsewhere, so called from OE *æsc* ASH + *worð* enclosure (see WORTH). The surname is still especially common in Lancs.

Asipenko *see* JOSEPH

Askam *see* ASCHAM

Askanazi *see* ASHKENAZI

Askel *see* ASHKETTLE

Askew N English: habitation name from a place, such as *Aiskew* in N Yorks., named with the ON elements *eiki* OAK + *skógr* wood (see SHAW). The surname is found in ME as *Akeskeugh*.
Vars.: **Aiskew, Aschew, A(y)scough, Askey, Haskew, Haskey**.

Asklund *see* ASH

Askwith *see* ASQUITH

Aslam *see* HASLAM

Aslet *see* ACE

Åslund *see* ÅHS

Asmall *see* ASPINALL

Asmes *see* ERASMUS

Asp *see* APPS

Aspden English: habitation name from a minor place in Lancs., between Accrington and Blackburn, so called from OE *æspe* aspen + *denu* valley.

Aspelon *see* ABSALOM

Aspig *see* GILLESPIE

Aspinall English: (S Lancs. and W Yorks.): habitation name from *Aspinwall* or *Asmall*, a minor place in the parish of Ormskirk, Lancs., so called from OE *æspen* of the aspen, trembling poplar + *wæll(a)* spring, stream (see WALL 2 and WELL). According to McKinley, there may have been some confusion with the earlier surname *Aspinhalgh* (which has a second element from OE *halh* nook, recess; see HALE 1).
Vars.: **Aspinal, Aspinell, Aspinwall, Haspineall, Asmall**.

Asplen *see* ABSALOM

Asquith English (Yorks): habitation name from *Askwith* in N Yorks., so called from ON *ask* ASH + *viðr* WOOD.
Var.: **Askwith**.

Assard *see* HASARD

Asselin *see* ACE

Asser *see* ASHER

Assmann *see* ERASMUS

Ast *see* NAST

Astachov *see* OSTAPOV

Astell *see* ASHKETTLE

Astle English: **1.** var. of ASTLEY 1. **2.** habitation name from a place in Ches., so called from OE *(e)ast* EAST + *hyll* HILL.
Vars.: **Astles**; **Astell, Astill** (chiefly Notts.; see also ASHKETTLE).

Astlet *see* ACE

Astley English: habitation name from a place in Warwicks., so called from OE *(ē)ast* EAST + *lēah* wood, clearing. There are several other places in W and NW England of this name, but the surname is particularly associated with the one in Warwicks. See also ASTLE.

Astman *see* EASTMAN

Aston English: **1.** habitation name from any of a large number of places. Most are so called from OE *(ē)ast* EAST + *tūn* enclosure, settlement, but in a few cases the first element is from OE *æsc* ash (cf. ASHTON). **2.** from some OE personal name such as *Æðelstān*, and so a var. of EDLESTONE or ALSTON 1. **3.** topographic name for someone who lived by a conspicuous STONE, with fusion of the ME preposition *at*.

Astor Provençal: nickname for someone with a fancied resemblance to a bird of prey, from OProv. *astur* goshawk (LL *auceptor*, from class. L *accipiter* hawk, crossed with *auceps* fowler, from *avis* bird + *capere* to catch).
Dim.: It.: **Astorini**.

Åstrand *see* ÅHS

Astruc Provençal (also Jewish): from the medieval given name *Astruc*, a deriv. of L *astrum* star, bestowed in the sense 'born under a lucky star', 'fortunate', 'blessed'.
Vars.: Fr.: **Astrug, Stroux**. Jewish (Ashkenazic): **Stroic(h), Stroo(c)k, Stra(c)k**.

Asum *see* ERASMUS

Asunción Spanish: nickname for someone born on 15 August, the Feast of the Assumption (OSp. *asumpción*, LL *assumptio*, gen. *assumptiōnis*, from *assumere* to take up). It may also reflect a given name bestowed with reference to the Marian title *Nuestra Señora de la Asunción* 'Our Lady of the Assumption'.

Aszkenas *see* ASHKENAZI

Atack *see* OAK

Atanackovič *see* AFANASYEV

Atberry *see* BURY

Atcheson *see* ADAM

Atfield *see* FIELD

Atheis *see* HAYES

Atherden *see* DEAN

Atherfold *see* FOLD

Atherlee *see* LEE

Athersmith *see* SMYTHE

Atherton English: habitation name from a place near Manchester, so called from the OE personal name *Æðelhere* (composed of the elements *æðel* noble + *here* army) + *tūn* enclosure, settlement.

Athey English: topographic name for someone who lived by an enclosure, from ME *at* at (OE *æt*) + *hay, hey* enclosure (see HAY 1).
Vars.: **Athy**, **Atty**.

Athill English: topographic name for someone who lived by a hill, from ME *at* + HILL.
Vars.: **Atthill**; **Athell**; **At(t)rill**, **Attrell** (from ME *atter hill*; cf. RYE (1 and 2)).

Athoke *see* HOOK

Athol Scots: habitation name from the district of *Athol* in Glen Garry, seat of the Dukes of Atholl, recorded in the 8th cent. as *Athfhoithle*. Watson interprets this as meaning 'new Ireland', from Gael. *ath* new, re- + the personal name *Fhotla* or *Fodla*, of uncertain origin, borne by one of the seven sons of the legendary king Cruithne and eponymous for Ireland.

Athorn *see* HORN

Athowe *see* ATTOE

Atkey *see* KAY

Atkin *see* ADAM

Atlas Jewish (Ashkenazic): **1.** ornamental name from Ger. *Atlas*, Pol. *atlas* satin (ultimately from an Arabic word meaning 'smooth'), and possibly also a metonymic occupational name for a maker or seller of articles made of satin. **2.** acrostic name from Hebr. *Ach Tov Leyisrael Sela* 'truly, God is good to Israel', the opening words of Psalm 73.
Vars.: **Atlasz** (Hung. spelling); **Atlasman**; **Atlasovitch**, **Atlasovitz**, **Atlasovicz**, **Atlasowich** (patr. in form, but there is no Jewish given name *Atlas*); **Atlasberg** ('satin hill', an ornamental name).

Atlay *see* LEE

Atmore *see* MOORE

Atrakhovich *see* TROFIMOV

Atrick *see* ARKWRIGHT

Atrill *see* ATHILL

Attack *see* OAK

Attale *see* HALE

Attaway *see* WAY

Attenborough English: habitation name for someone who lived 'at the manor house', from ME *atten* at the (cf. NYE) + *burh* manor house (see BERRY 1 and BURY).
Vars.: **Attenbrough**, **Attenb(ur)ow**, **Attenbarrow**.

Atterbury *see* BURY

Atteridge *see* RIDGE

Attfield *see* FIELD

Atthill *see* ATHILL

Attick *see* WICK

Attkins *see* ADAM

Attle *see* LEE

Attoe English: topographic name for someone who lived by a hill or ridge, from ME *at* + *hoe* (cf. HOE and HUFF).
Vars.: **Atto**, **At(t)howe**.

Attride *see* READ

Attwell English: topographic name for someone who lived by a spring or stream, from ME *at* + WELL.
Vars.: **At(te)well**, **Attawell**, **Twell(s)**; **At(t)will**, **Atte(r)will**, **Attiwill**; **At(t)wool**, **Attwooll**.

Attwood English: topographic name for someone who lived by a wood, from ME *at* + WOOD.
Var.: **Atwood**.

Atty *see* ATHEY

Attyea *see* YEO

Atwell *see* ATTWELL

Atwood *see* ATTWOOD

Atzen *see* ACE

Aubain *see* ALBAN

Aubé *see* ALBERT

Aubel *see* BEAU

Aubin *see* ALBIN

Aubreton *see* BRETT

Aubrey English: from the ME, OF given name *Aubri*, derived from the Gmc personal name *Alberic*, composed of the elements *alb* elf + *rīc* power. Some of the vars. listed below probably absorbed OE *Ælfrīc* (composed of the elements *ælf* elf + *rīc* kingdom). They seem also to have absorbed the much rarer female name *Albreda*, composed of the Gmc elements *alb* + *rēd* counsel (cf. ALFRED). Both

Alberic and *Albreda* were introduced into England by the Normans.

Vars.: **Aubr(a)y**, **Aubery**, **Aubury**, **Obray**; **Alfr(e)y**, **Affery**, **Avery**, **Avory**.

Prov.: **Albéric**, **Albaric**, **Alfaric**. Cat.: **Alberic(h)**. It.: **Alb(e)rici**, **Alberig(h)i**, **Albrigi(o)**, **Albrisi(o)**, **Albriz(z)i**. Ger.: **Albrich**.

Dims.: Fr.: **Aubriet**, **Aubryet**, **Aubriot**.

Patrs.: Eng.: **Averies**. Low Ger.: **Alverichs**.

Aubrun *see* BROWN

Aucelli *see* UCCELLO

Auchamp *see* CHAMP

Auchinleck Scots: habitation name from places in the former counties of Ayrs. or Angus called *Auchinleck* or (in a contracted form) *Affleck*, from Gael. *achadh na leac* 'field of the flat stones', i.e. tombstones.

Var.: **Affleck**.

Auclerc *see* CLARK

Aucoc *see* COCK

Aucock *see* ALCOCK

Aucott *see* ALCOTT

Aucourt *see* COURT

Aude *see* OLD

Auden *see* ALDEN

Audenis *see* DENNIS

Audini *see* ALDOUS

Audley English: habitation name from a place in Staffs., so called from the OE female name *Ealdgȳð* (composed of the elements *eald* old + *gȳð* battle) + OE *lēah* wood, clearing.

Audrey *see* AWDREY

Audritt *see* ALDRITT

Audsley English: habitation name from an unidentified place (probably in Yorks., where the surname is most common), so called from the gen. case of an OE personal name with the first element *(e)ald* old + OE *lēah* wood, clearing.

Auduc *see* DUKE

Auerbach Jewish (Ashkenazic): habitation name from any of several places in S Germany so called, usually taken as being from *Aurochs* (a kind of wild bull, now extinct) + *bach* stream.

Vars.: **Auerbacher**; **O(h)rbach** (associated by folk etymology with Ger. *Ohr* ear); **Awerbach**, **Averbach**, **Aberbach**, **Averback**, **Aberback**, **Awerbuch**, **Averb(o)uch**, **Aberbuch**; **Averbuj** (a Sp. spelling).

Aufaure *see* FÈVRE

Augagneux *see* GAGNEUX

Augello *see* UCCELLO

Auger *see* ALGER

Augras *see* GRASS

Augros *see* GROSS

Augustin *see* AUSTIN

Augustsson *see* AGOSTI

Aujean *see* JOHN

Auld *see* OLD

Auler *see* EULER

Aumaître *see* MASTER

Aumarchand *see* MARCHANT

Aumas *see* MAS

Aumasson *see* MASON

Aumerle *see* MERLE

Aumeunier *see* MILLER

Aumoine *see* MONK

Aumonier French: nickname for a beggar, from an agent deriv. of OF *aumone* alms (ultimately from Gk *eleēmosynē* mercy; the word acquired a concrete monetary sense in LL).

Var.: **Laumonier** (with fused def. art.).

Aunger *see* AINGER

Aupetit *see* PETTIT

Aupol *see* PAUL

Auric *see* ALARIC

Auriol *see* ORIOL

Aurousseau *see* RUSSELL

Auroux *see* ROUSE

Aurrecoechea Spanish form of Basque **Aurrekoetxea**: habitation name for someone who lived in a house situated in front of its fellows, from Basque *aurre* front + the gen. particle *ko* + *etxe* house + the def. art. *-a*.

Ausielli *see* UCCELLO

Austerlitz German and Jewish: habitation name from a town in Moravia, called *Austerlitz* in Ger. (*Slavkov* in Czech). In 1805 this was the site of a battle in which Napoleon defeated the armies of Austria and Russia.

Austin English and French: from the ME, OF given name *Austin*, the vernacular form of L *Augustīnus* (a deriv. of *Augustus*; see AGOSTI). This was an extremely common given name in every part of W Europe during the Middle Ages, owing its popularity chiefly to St Augustine of Hippo (354–430), whose influence on Christianity is generally considered to be second only to that of St Paul. Various religious orders came to be formed following rules named in his honour, including the 'Austin canons', established in the 11th cent., and the 'Austin friars', a mendicant order dating from the 13th cent. The popularity of the name in England was further increased by the fact that it was borne by St Augustine of Canterbury (d. *c*.605), an It. Benedictine monk known as 'the Apostle of the English', who brought Christianity to England in 597 and founded the see of Canterbury.

Vars.: Eng.: **Austen, Auston; Augustin(e)** (a learned form). Fr.: **Augustin** (a learned form); **Gustin; Aoustin; Autin, Outin**.

Dims.: It.: **Augustinello, Agostinetti**. Low Ger.: **Stienke**. Flem.: **Tienke** (see also MARTIN).

Aug.: It.: **Agostinone**.

Patrs.: Eng.: **Austins**. Gael.: COSTAIN. It.: **De Agostini, Dell'Agostino**. Low Ger.: **Stienes, Stinnes, Stienen**. Pol.: **August(yn)owicz, Augustyniak**.

Patr. (from a dim.): Flem.: **Tienken**.

Habitation names: Pol.: **Augustowski, Gustowski, Augustyński**.

Autessier *see* TISSIER

Autin *see* AUSTIN

Auty English (Yorks): from the ON personal name *Auti*, a short form of the various cpd personal names with the first element *auð* riches, prosperity (cf. OADE).

Var.: **Alty**.

Avann *see* FENN

Avans *see* EVAN

Avdakov *see* YEVDOKIMOV

Aveline *see* EVELYN

Avenel *see* AVOINE

Averbach *see* AUERBACH

Averies *see* AUBREY

Averill *see* APRIL

Avesalomov *see* ABSALOM

Aveyard English: habitation name from some minor place, presumably in Yorks., where the surname is most common. The second element is clearly OE *geard* enclosure; the first is probably a personal name such as OE *Afa*, of uncertain origin.

Avigdor Jewish: from a given name. This originated in the Hebr. phrase *avi-Gedor* 'father of Gedor', which occurs in 1 Chron. 4: 4, 18, and was used as a given name under the influence of VICTOR.

Vars.: **Vigdor, Wigdor, Figdor** (aphetic forms); **Vigder, Wigder** (Yid. forms).

Dims.: **Vigdorchik, Wigdorchik, Wigdorczik** (E Ashkenazic).

Patrs.: **D'Avigdor; Vigderson** (Ashkenazic); **Vigdorovitch, Vigderovitsch, Vigdorowitz, Vigdorowicz, Wigdorowicz** (E Ashkenazic).

Avila Spanish: habitation name from the city and province so called. The former is extremely ancient, reputedly founded by the Phoenicians, and its name, first found in the L forms *Avela* and *Abulia*, is of quite uncertain meaning.

Vars.: **Dávila, Avilés**.

Avilin *see* BABEL

Avis English: from the ME, OF given name *Avice* (L *Avitius* (fem. *Avitia*), of uncertain origin, perhaps an adaptation of a Gmc or Celt. name).

Patr.: **Avison**.

Avksentyev *see* AKSYONOV

Avnet Jewish (Ashkenazic): name assumed by a member of the priestly caste, from Yid., Hebr. *avnet* girdle worn by priests.

Avogadro N Italian: regional var. of the occupational term *avocato* adviser, counsellor (L *advocātus*, past part. of *advocāre* to call on). In the Middle Ages the term was not restricted to lawyers but was applied to various functionaries and officials (cf. VOGT).

Vars.: **Avogaro, Avvocato**.

Avoine French: metonymic occupational name for a grower or seller of oats, from OF *avoine* oats (L *avēna*).

Vars.: **Avenne; Lavoin(n)e, Lavenne** (with fused def. art.); **Davei(s)ne, D(el)avenne** (with fused preposition *de*); **Avenier, Lavenier** (agent nouns).

Dims.: Fr.: **Avenel, Avenet, Avenol**.

Avory *see* AUBREY

Avraam *see* ABRAHAM

Avril *see* APRIL

Avseev *see* EUSÉBIO

Avtukhov *see* YEVTIKHIEV

Avvocato *see* AVOGADRO

Awcock *see* ALCOCK

Awdrey English: from the ME female given name *Aldreda*, recorded in Domesday Book, apparently from OE *Æðelþrýð*, composed of the elements *æðel* noble + *þrýð* strength. This was fairly common from the earliest times, and its popularity was increased in the Christian era by the fame of St Etheldreda (d. 679), queen of Northumbria and founder of the convent at Ely.

Vars.: **Audrey, Awdry**.

Awerbach *see* AUERBACH

Axell *see* ASHKETTLE

Axtell *see* ASHKETTLE

Ayasse *see* AGACE

Ayckbourn N English: habitation name from a place, not now identifiable, deriving its name from ON *eiki* Oak + OE *burna* stream (see BOURNE).

Ayer 1. English: nickname for a man who was well known to be the heir to a title or fortune, from ME *eir, eyr* heir (OF *(h)eir*, from L *hērēs*). 2. Scots: habitation name from the city of *Ayr* in SW Scotland, so called from ON *eyrr* tongue of land, gravelly bank.

Vars.: **Ayr(e), Air**. (Of 1 only): **Eyer, Eyre, Hayer, Heyer**.

Patrs. (of 1): **Ayers, Ayres, Ayris, E(a)yr(e)s, Eyers**.

Aykroyd *see* ACKROYD

Aylard *see* ALLARD

Ayler *see* AILLIER

Ayliff English: 1. from the ME female given name *Ayleve, Aylgive*, OE *Æðelgifu*, composed of the elements *æðel* noble + *gifu* gift, which was borne by a daughter of King Alfred the Great, who became abbess of Shaftesbury.

2. from the ON byname *Eilífr*, which is composed of the elements *ei* always + *lífr* life.

Vars.: **Ayliffe**, **Ellif(f)**.

Ayling English: from the OE word *æðeling* prince, a deriv. of *æðel* noble. This word was commonly used as a byname among Anglo-Saxons before and after the Norman Conquest, and was in use for a time as a personal name. The surname derives from this use rather than from a nickname; still less does it denote descent from noble Anglo-Saxon blood.

Vars.: **Aylen**, **Aylin**.

Aylmer 1. English: from the ME given name *Ailmar*, OE *Æðelmǣr*, composed of the elements *æðel* noble + *mǣr* famous, which was reinforced after the Conquest by the introduction of OF *Ailmer*, from a Continental cogn. **2.** Scots: apparently a habitation name. Emmed *de Ailmer* and Roger *de Almere* are recorded in Selkirk in 1296. The latter individual is recorded also as *de Aylemer* and *de Alnmer*, but the place from which he derived his name has not been identified. The *de* may be purely honorific, and the origin as in 1.

Vars.: **Ailmer**, **Aylmore**. (Of 1 only): **Elmer**, **Elmar**; **Aymer**, **Aimer**, **Amar**.

Patrs.: Eng.: **Elmers**, **Aimers**. It.: **D'Ameri(o)**, **Damero**. Low Ger.: **Al(l)mers**.

Aylward English: from a common Gmc personal name, found in OE as *Æðelweard*, composed of the elements *adal* noble + *ward* guard.

Vars.: **Ailward**, **Allward**; **Aluard**.

Aylwen *see* ALWYN

Aymer *see* AYLMER

Aymonic *see* HAMMOND

Aynsley *see* AINSLIE

Ayo Spanish: **1.** apparently a name for someone who was the guardian of an orphan in a community, from Sp. *ayo* tutor, guardian, a masc. form of *aya* nurse (L *avia* grandmother). **2.** The surname is common in Bilbao in the Basque country, and it is possible that it was adopted as a Castilian form of the Basque surname **Aia** or **Aya**, a topographic name from Basque *ai* slope + the def. art. *-a*.

Ayr *see* AYER

Ayscough *see* ASKEW

Aysh *see* ASH

Aysik *see* ISAAC

Ayson *see* MCKAY

Ayuso Spanish: topographic name for someone who lived in the lower part of a settlement, from Sp. *ayuso* (down) below (LL *ad* at + *jūsum*, *jōsum*, from class. L *deorsum* downwards).

Azarian *see* LAZAR

Azcárate Spanish form of Basque **Azkarate**: topographic name for someone who lived by a pass between high rocks, from Basque *aitz, atx* rock, crag + *gara* high + *ate* pass, defile.

Azcona Spanish form of Basque **Azkona**: nickname for someone who resembled a badger in some way, from Basque *azkon* badger + the def. art. *-a*.

Azcorra Spanish form of Basque **Azkorra**: nickname from the adj. *azkor* forgetful + the def. art. *-a*. The adj. also has the meaning 'lively, animated' in the dialect of Biscay and 'shy, unsociable' in the Guipúzcoa dialect; either of these senses could also have contributed to the origin of the surname.

Azcue Spanish form of Basque **Azkue**: topographic name for someone who lived near a rock or crag, from Basque *aitz, atx* rock, crag + the local suffix *-qu(n)e*.

Aze *see* ACE

Aznar Spanish: from a medieval given name, L *Asinārius*. This is probably composed of the Gmc elements *ans* god + *hari, heri* army, but to have been altered as the result of folk etymological association with an agent deriv. of L *asinus* ass, donkey.

Azzini *see* ACE

B

Baack *see* BAUD

Baamonde Spanish (of Galician origin): habitation name from a place in the province of Lugo, so called from L *Badamundi (fundus)* (farm) of *Badamundus*', a Gmc personal name composed of the elements *bad* (cf. BADE) + *mund* protection.

Vars.: **Bahamonde**, **Vaamonde**.

Baanders *see* BANNERMAN

Baarmann *see* BERMANN

Baas Low German and Dutch: nickname or occupational name from MLG *baas* master, overseer, boss.

Var.: **Baasch**.

Babb English (chiefly Devon): Reaney suggests that this is from the medieval female given name *Babb*, a pet form of *Barbara* (see BARBARY), or a nickname meaning 'baby', from ME *bab(e)*. However, a more probable source is the OE personal name *Babba*, found in several placenames, including *Babbacombe* in Devon and BABINGTON in Somerset. This is of uncertain origin, perhaps a nursery name from a child's babbling.

Dims.: **Bab(b)itt**, **Babet**, **Babot**, **Babcock**.

Patr.: **Babbs**.

Babel 1. Jewish (Ashkenazic): surname chosen as a symbol of exile, from Hebr. *Bavel* Babylon (from the Assyrian elements *bāb* gate + *ilu* god). The Jewish people were held in captivity in Babylon from 597 to about 538 BC. **2.** French: from a medieval given name bestowed in honour of St *Babylas*, a 3rd-cent. Christian patriarch of Antioch. His name is of uncertain origin; it is conceivably an ethnic name ultimately derived from the city of Babylon.

Var. (of 1): **Bavel**; **Babli**, **Bably**, **Bavli**, **Bavly**, **Bawli**, **Bawly** (Israeli habitation names). (Of 2): **Babeau**.

Dims. (of 2): **Bab(e)let**, **Bab(e)lon**, **Bab(e)lin**.

Patrs. (from 2): Russ.: **Vavilov**, **Vavilin**; **Avilov**, **Avilin**.

Baber English: surname common in Somerset, for which no satisfactory etymology has been proposed.

Babeuf French: occupational nickname for a slaughterman, from OF *bat(tre)* to hit, strike (LL *battuere*; cf. BATAILLE) + *boef*, *buef* bull (L *bōs*, gen. *bovis*).

Babin Russian: metr. or patr. from *Baba* 'Grandmother', 'Old Woman' (originally a nursery word), either meaning son of an old woman or a nickname denoting a fussy old man.

Dims.: Russ.: **Bab(ush)kin**, **Babukhin** (patrs.). Ukr.: **Babenko**.

Habitation name: Pol.: **Babiński**.

Babington English: habitation name from a place so called in Somerset or from *Bavington* in Northumb. Both are named from OE *Babbingtūn* 'settlement (OE *tūn*) associated with *Babba*' (see BABB). The latter was

the original home of the family of the historian Thomas Babington Macaulay (1800–59).

Bacchus 1. English: var. of BACKHOUSE. **2.** French: nickname for a heavy drinker, from *Bacchus*, the Greek and Roman god of wine, whose cult and name are probably of Oriental origin.

Bach 1. German and English: topographic name for someone who lived by a stream, from MHG *bach* or ME *bache* (OHG *bah*; OE *bæce*, *bece*). **2.** German and Low German: occupational name for a BAKER. **3.** Polish and Czech: dim. of SEBASTIAN. **4.** Jewish (Ashkenazic): acronymic surname from the initial letters of the Hebr. phrase *ben chayim* 'son of life'; cf. HYAM. **5.** Catalan: topographic name for someone who lived in a sunless spot, from an aphetic form of Cat. *obac* dark, shady (L *opācus*).

Vars. (of 1): Eng.: **Bache** (chiefly W Midlands); **Batch**, **Ba(i)sh**; BACK. Ger.: **Bacher**, **Bachmann**; **Pach(er)**, **Pachmann** (Bavaria). Low Ger.: **Beck**, **Becker**, **Beckmann**, **Bee(c)ke(r)**, **Becken**; **Torbeck**, **Terbeck**. Flem.: **Bee(c)k**, **Beckx**, **Verbeke**, **Van der Beken**. Du.: **Beek**, **Van (der) Beek**, **Verbeek**, **Terbeek**, **Beekman**. (Of 4): **Bacher**, **Bachman(n)**. (Of 5): Cat.: **Bachs**, **Ubach**.

Dims. (of 3): Pol.: **Baszek**, **Baszniak**. Czech: **Bašek**.

Patr. (from a dim. of 3): Pol.: **Baszkiewicz**.

Habitation name (from 3): Pol.: **Bachański**.

Bacha *see* BARTHOLOMEW

Bacharach Jewish (Ashkenazic): habitation name from a town on the Rhine near Koblenz, recorded in the earliest L documents as *Bacaraca*. The placename seems to be the same as that of *Baccarat* in the Vosges and is of Celt. origin but unknown meaning.

Vars.: **Bach(e)rach**, **Bach(e)rich**, **Bacherig**.

Bachelor English: status name for a young knight or novice at arms, ME, OF *bacheler* (med. L *baccalārius*, of unknown origin). The word had already been extended to mean (young) unmarried man' by the 14th cent., but it is unlikely that many bearers of the surname derive it from the word in that sense.

Vars.: **Batchel(l)or**, **Ba(t)chel(l)er**, **Batcheldor**, **Batchelder**, **Backler**.

Dims.: Fr.: **Bachelet**, **Bachelin**, **Bachelot**.

Pej.: Fr.: **Bachelard**.

Bacher *see* BAKER

Bachofen German: habitation or occupational name, ostensibly meaning 'bake-oven' and therefore perhaps denoting a baker. The second element is probably MHG *ofen* oven (OHG *ovan*), but the var. **Bachof** suggests that the name could in fact be a habitation name from MHG *bach* stream (see BACH 1) + the dat. pl. case (originally used after a preposition) of MHG *hof* court (see HOFER).

Vars.: **Backof(en)**.

Bächtold *see* BERTHOLD

Back 1. English: nickname for someone with a hunched back or some other noticeable peculiarity of the back or spine, from ME *bakke* back (OE *bæc*). **2.** topographic name for someone who lived on a hill or ridge (from the same OE word as in 1), or at the rear of a settlement (this last sense being the meaning of the Scand. cogn). **3.** English: from the OE personal name *Bacca*, which was still in use in the 12th cent. It is of uncertain origin, but may have been a byname in the same sense as 1. **4.** English: nickname from ME *bakke* bat (apparently of Scand. origin), from some fancied resemblance to the animal. **5.** Swedish: cogn. of BANKS.

Vars. (of 2): **Backer**, **Backman** (topographic names, most common in N England). (Of 5): **Backman**.

Patrs. (from 3): Eng.: **Backs**, **Bax**.

Bäcker *see* BAKER

Backhouse English: habitation name for someone who lived at a bakery, or occupational name for someone employed in one, from OE *bæchūs* bakehouse (from *bacan* to bake + *hūs* house).

Vars.: **Bakehouse**, **Backouse**, **Backus**, BACCHUS.

Bäcklund *see* BECK

Backlund *see* BANKS

Bacon 1. English: metonymic occupational name for a preparer and seller of cured pork, from ME, OF *bacun*, *bacon* bacon, ham (of Gmc origin, akin to BACK 1). **2.** English: from the Gmc personal name *Bac(c)o*, *Bahho*, from the root *bag-* to fight. The name was relatively common among the Normans in the form *Bacus*, of which the oblique case was *Bacon*. **3.** Jewish (Ashkenazic): origin unknown.

Var. (of 2): BAGGE.

Dims. (of 2): Eng.: **Baggett**, **Bag(g)ot(t)**, **Bagehot**. Fr.: **Baqu(e)lin**.

Patrs. (from 2): Eng.: **Bagges**. Dan.: **Baggesen**.

Bączyk *see* BĄK

Badanes Jewish (E Ashkenazic): metr. from the Yid. female given name *Badane* (from Czech *Bohdana*, a fem. form of *Bohdan*; see BOGDANOV).

Vars.: **Bodanis**, **Bodanoff**; **Bodankin** (from a dim. form).

Badaud 1. French: from a Gmc personal name composed of the elements *badu* battle + *wald* rule. **2.** Provençal: nickname for a stupid or naïve individual, an open-mouthed idiot, from OProv. *badar* to open (LL *batāre*; cf. BADIER) + the pej. suffix *au(l)d*.

Var.: **Badault**.

Dims. (of 2): Prov.: **Bad(i)ou**, **Badoc(he)**, **Badolle**.

Baddams *see* ADAM

Baddeley English: habitation name from a place in Staffs., the OE name of which was *Baddingléah*, i.e. 'wood or clearing (OE *léah*) associated with *Badda*' (see BADE).

Bade English: probably from a ME survival of the OE personal name *Bad(d)a*, which is of uncertain origin, per-

haps a short form of the various cpd names with the first element *beadu* battle.

Dims.: **Badcock** (chiefly Devon); **Badcoe**.

Badeke *see* BOTHA

Bader 1. German and Jewish (Ashkenazic): occupational name for an attendant in a public bath house, from an agent deriv. of Ger. *Bad* bath (MHG *bat*, OHG *bad*). In former times, such attendants undertook a variety of functions, including blood-letting and hair-cutting. **2.** Provençal: var. of BADIER.

Vars. (of 1): **Bäder**, **Beder**; **Peder**.

Badger English (W Midlands): **1.** habitation name from a place in Shrops., probably so called from the OE personal name *Bæcg* (a deriv. of *Bacga*, attested but of uncertain origin) + OE *ofer* ridge. **2.** occupational name for a maker of bags (see BAGGE 1) or for a pedlar who carried his wares about with him in a bag. It is unlikely that the surname has anything to do with the animal (see BROCK 2), which was not known by this name until the 16th cent.

Patr. (from 2): **Badgers**.

Badham English: habitation name from some minor place (probably in the W Midlands, where the surname is commonest), so called from the OE personal name *Bēada* (a short form of the various cpd names with the first element *beadu* battle) + OE *hām* homestead. Reaney, however, derives it from *Abadam*, a Welsh patr. of ADAM.

Badier Provençal: occupational name for a janitor, from OProv. *badar* to open (cf. BADAUD 2).

Vars.: BADER, **Badé**; **Badaire**.

Badini *see* ABBÉ

Badman English: in spite of appearances, this is probably not a nickname for a reprobate, but an occupational name for the servant of someone called *Badd* or BATT.

Badner Jewish: of uncertain origin, possibly a var. of *Bodner* (see BÜTTNER), or a habitation name from any of various places in Germany called *Baden* 'Baths'.

Badrick *see* BETTERIDGE

Baeck *see* BECK

Baena Spanish: habitation name from a place in the province of Córdoba, so called from L *Badiāna (villa)* 'settlement of *Badius*', a byname meaning 'Reddish' (see BAY).

Baert *see* BARTHOLOMEW

Baeta Portuguese: metonymic occupational name for a maker or seller of baize and flannelette, or a nickname for a habitual wearer of the material, Port. *baeta* (OF *bayette*, a dim. of BAY, from its normal colour).

Baeten *see* BÉATRICE

Báez *see* PELAYO

Baeza Spanish: habitation name from a place in the province of Jaén, apparently so called from L *Vīvātia (villa)* 'settlement of *Vīvātius*'.

Baffin *see* BAUGHAN

Bagehot *see* BACON

Baggat *see* BATHGATE

Bagge English: **1.** metonymic occupational name for a maker of bags and sacks of various kinds, including wallets and purses, from ME *bagge* bag (of uncertain origin). **2.** from the Gmc personal name *Bac(c)o, Bahho*; see BACON 1.

Vars.: **Bagg**, **Bage**.

Bagiński Polish: topographic name from *bagno* marsh + *-ski* suffix of local surnames (see BARANOWSKI).

Var.: **Bagieński**.

Bagley English: habitation name from any of the places so called, mainly in Berks., Shrops., Somerset, and W Yorks. These get their names either from the OE personal name *Bacga* (cf. BADGER) + OE *lēah* wood, clearing or from an OE word for a 'bag-shaped' animal + *lēah*.

Vars.: **Baguley** (a place in Ches.), **Bagguley**; **Baggaley**, **Baggall(a)y**, **Baggarley**.

Bagliardi *see* BAILEY

Bagnacci *see* BAIN

Bagnall English: habitation name from a place in Staffs., so called from the OE personal name *Badeca, Baduca* (from a short form of the various cpd names with the first element *beadu* battle) + OE *halh* nook, recess (see HALE) or *holt* wood (see HOLT).

Vars.: **Bagnell**, **Bagenal**, **Bagnold**.

Bagratian Armenian: patr. from the personal name *Bagratuni*. In AD 806 Ashot Bagratuni 'the Carnivorous' was chosen as Prince of Armenia, and he established a line of Bagratid emperors, who ruled the country until the 11th cent. Prince Pyotr Ivanovich Bagration (1765–1812), a distinguished Russian general at the time of the Napoleonic Wars, was descended from this line.

Vars.: **Bagration**, **Bagradian**.

Bagshaw English: habitation name from a place in Derbys. The first element of the placename is probably the OE personal name *Bacga* (cf. BADGER), the second is OE *sceaga* wood, copse.

Var.: **Bagshawe**.

Bahamonde *see* BAAMONDE

Bahlke *see* BAUD

Bahring *see* BEAR

Bahrmann *see* BERMANN

Bai *see* BAY

Baião Portuguese: habitation name from a place in the region of Oporto, so called from L *Badiānus (fundus)* 'farm, estate of *Badius*' (cf. BAENA).

Baiard *see* BAYARD

Baibakov Russian: patr. from the nickname *Baibak* 'Steppe-Marmot' (of Turkic origin). The animal was reputedly sluggish, and so the nickname was frequently used for a lazy person.

Baier *see* BAYER

Baiker *see* BAKER, PAUKER

Bailey English: **1.** occupational name for a steward or official (or occasionally perhaps an ironic nickname for an officious person), from ME *bail(l)i* (OF *baillis*, oblique case *bailif*, from LL *bāiulīvus*, a deriv. of *bāiulus* carrier, porter). The word survives in Scotland as *bailie*, the title of a municipal magistrate, and elsewhere as *bailiff*, which in England denotes an officer who serves writs and summonses and ensures that court orders are carried out. **2.** topographic name for someone who lived in a district by the outermost wall of a castle, ME *bail(l)y, baile* (apparently from OF *bail(le)* enclosure, a deriv. of *bailer* to enclose, of unknown origin). The situation is complicated by the fact that this name, originally denoting a particular part of a castle, sometimes became a placename in its own right: some bearers of the name undoubtedly derive it from the Old Bailey in London, which formed part of the early medieval outer wall of the city. **3.** habitation name from *Bailey* in Lancs., so called from OE *bēg* berry + *lēah* wood, clearing. Examples of the name derived from this source occur in the surrounding area from the 13th cent.

Vars.: **Baillie** (chiefly Scots); **Bailie** (chiefly N Irish); **Baily**, **Bayl(e)y**, **Baylay**. (Of 1 only): **Bail(l)if(f)**, **Bayliff(e)**, **Baylis(s)**, **Bayless**, **Bailess**. (Of 2 only): **Bail(e)(s)**, **Bale(s)**, **Bayl(e)(s)**.

Dims. (of 1): Fr.: **Baillivet**. (Of 2): Fr.: **Bail(l)et**, **Baylet**, **Beylet**, **Baillot**, **Baylot**, **Beylot**. Prov.: **Bailloux**, **Bailloud**. It.: **Baglietti**, **Baglini**.

Augs. (of 1): It.: **Baglione**, **Bailone**.

Pejs. (of 1): Fr.: **Baillaud**. It.: **Bagliardi**.

Bailin *see* BEILIN

Bain **1.** Scots: nickname for a fair-haired person, from Gael. *bàn* white, fair. **2.** N English: nickname meaning 'bone', probably bestowed on an exceptionally tall, lean man, from OE *bān* bone. In Northern ME *-ā-* was preserved, whereas in Southern dialects (which later became standard), it was changed to *-ō-*. **3.** N English: nickname for a hospitable person, from Northern ME *beyn, bayn* welcoming, friendly (ON *beinn* straight, direct). **4.** English and French: metonymic occupational name for an attendant at a public bath house (cf. BADER 1), from ME, OF *baine* bath (L *balnea*, originally a neut. pl., later treated as fem. sing.).

Vars.: **Baine**, **Bayne**. (Of 1 only): **Bawn**, **Baun**.

Dims. (of 4): It.: **Bagnu(o)lo**, **Bagnoli**. Sp.: **Banuelos**.

Augs. (of 4): It.: **Bagnone**. Sp.: **Bañón**.

Pej. (of 4): It.: **Bagnacci**.

Bainbridge English: habitation name from a place in N Yorks., so called from the river *Bain* on which it stands (which is from ON *beinn* straight; cf. BAIN 3) + OE *brycg* BRIDGE.

Baines **1.** Scots and N English: nickname meaning 'bones' (cf. BAIN 2). **2.** Welsh: patr. (*ab Einws*), from the given name *Einws*, a dim. of *Ennion* 'Anvil'.

Vars.: **Baynes**, **Bains**, **Banes**.

Baird *see* BARD

Bairnsfather N English and Scots: nickname for the father or alleged father of an illegitimate child, from the gen. case of Northern ME *bairn* child (see BARNES 2) + *father* (OE *fæder*, reinforced by ON *faðir*). It has also been suggested that the name is a remodelling by folk etymology of the ON personal name *Barnvarðr*, composed of the elements *barn* warrior, hero + *varðr* guard.

Vars.: **Ba(r)n(s)father**.

Bairstow English: habitation name from *Bairstow* in W Yorks., probably so called from OE *beger* berry + *stōw* place. The surname is still most common in Yorks.

Vars.: **Barstow**, **Ba(i)stow**.

Baise *see* BASS

Baish *see* BACH

Baitson *see* BATE

Bajard *see* BAYARD

Bajol *see* BAY

Bąk Polish: probably a nickname for an irritating individual, from Pol. *bąk* horsefly (also meaning 'bittern').

Dim.: **Bączyk**.

Habitation name: Pol.: **Bąkowski**.

Bakehouse *see* BACKHOUSE

Baker English: occupational name, from ME *bakere*, OE *bæcere*, a deriv. of *bacan* to bake. It may have been used for someone whose special task in the kitchen of a great house or castle was the baking of bread, but since most humbler households did their own baking in the Middle Ages, it may also have referred to the owner of a communal oven used by the whole village. The right to be in charge of this and exact money or loaves in return for its use was in many parts of the country a hereditary feudal privilege; cf. MILLER. Less often the surname may have been acquired by someone noted for baking particularly fine bread or by a baker of pottery or bricks.

Vars.: Eng.: **Baiker**, **Bacher**; **Baxter** (originally a fem. form; common esp. in E Anglia).

Patr.: Flem, Du.: **Beckers**.

Equivs. (not cogn.): Fr.: BOULANGER, FOURNIER. Ger.: PFISTER. Pol.: KOŁACZ, PIEKARSKI. Russ.: KHLEBNIKOV. Hung.: LISZT.

Bakewell English: habitation name from the town in Derbys., so called from the OE personal name *Badeca*, *Baduca* (from a short form of the various cpd personal names with the first element *beadu* battle) + OE *well(a)* spring, stream (see WELL).

Bakhrushin *see* BARTHOLOMEW

Baklanov Russian: patr. from the nickname *Baklan* 'Cormorant', presumably denoting a rapacious or greedy person (cf. the mod. Eng. use of the term *gannet*).

Bakunin Russian: patr. from the nickname *Bakuna*, a deriv. of *bakat* to chatter, gossip; cf. BALAKIREV.

Var.: **Bakulin**.

Bal French: **1.** nickname, a deriv. of OF *baller* to move, shake, dance (LL *ballāre*, from Gk *ballein* to throw). The original meaning of the surname is by no means clear, as the verb had a wide variety of uses in OF. The most plausible of the many possible origins are that it was given in some cases to a musician, in others to a good dancer. **2.** from the Gmc personal name *Ballo*, which is of uncertain origin and meaning, but may represent an assimilated form

of *Baldo*, a short form of various personal names containing the element *bald* bold.

Vars. (of 1): **Bal(l)and** (from the pres. part.), **Bal(l)a(n)dier** (an agent deriv. of the last).

Dims.: **Bal(l)et**, **Bal(l)ot**, **Bal(l)on**. Prov.: **Bal(l)ou**.

Balaam English: habitation name from *Baylham* in Suffolk, recorded in Domesday Book as *Beleham*, and apparently deriving its name from OE **bēgel* bend + *hām* homestead or *hamm* water meadow. The spelling has been affected by folk etymological association with the biblical character who was converted to the Israelite cause by his talking ass (Num. 22–3).

Var.: **Ballaam**.

Balaguer Catalan: habitation name from a place in the province of Lérida, of uncertain etymology. It is possibly a deriv. of the regional term *bàlec* broom (perhaps of Celt. origin).

Var.: **Balagué**.

Balakirev Russian: patr. from the nickname *Balakir* 'Chatterer', a deriv. of *bal(irov)at* to chatter (of imitative origin; cf BAKUNIN). This is also the root of the name of the musical instrument the *balalaika*.

Balañá Catalan: habitation name from *Balenyà* in the province of Barcelona. The placename is of uncertain origin, but may be from LL *Valēniāna (villa)* 'settlement of *Valēnius*', a personal name probably related to VALENTE.

Balanesco *see* BLANC

Balat *see* VALLAT

Balbaud *see* BAUBE

Balboa *see* VALBUENA

Balcells Catalan: topographic name from the pl. form of a dim. of Cat. *balç* precipice (L *balteus* belt; the transferred sense apparently derives from the notion of the cliffs encircling the mountain).

Var.: **Balsells**.

Balch English: **1.** from ME *balch*, *belch* balk, beam (OE *bælc*, *balca*). This is either a habitation name for someone who lived in a house with a roof-beam rather than in a simple hut (cf. BELCHEM), or a nickname for a man built like a tree trunk, i.e. one of stocky, heavy build. **2.** nickname from ME *balche*, *belche* swelling (OE *bælc(e)*). This was probably chiefly given in the sense 'swelling pride', 'overweening arrogance', but it can also mean 'eructation', 'belch' and may therefore in some cases have been acquired by a man given to belching.

Vars.: **Baulch**, **Belch**, **Belk**; **Boakes**; **Ba(u)lcher**, BELCHER.

Dim.: **Balchin**.

Balcombe English: habitation name from a place in Sussex, which is so called from OE *bealu* evil, calamity + *cumb* valley (see COOMBE).

Bald *see* BALL

Baldacchi *see* BAUD

Balderston English: habitation name from either of two places in Lancs. called *Balderston(e)*, deriving their names from the gen. case of the OE personal name *Bealdhere* (composed of the elements *beald* bold, brave + *here* army) + OE *tūn* enclosure, settlement. A place of the same name and etymology in the former county of W Lothian may be the source of some examples of the surname in Scotland.

Vars.: **Balderstone**, **Bo(u)lderstone**.

Baldock English: habitation name from a place in Herts., first so called in the 12th cent. by the Knights Templar, who held the manor there. It was named in commemoration of the city of *Baghdad*, known in ME, OF as *Baldac*; its Arabic etymology is said to be 'city of *Dat*', the personal name of a dervish.

Var.: **Baldick**.

Baldry English: from a Gmc personal name composed of the elements *bald* bold, brave + *rīc* power. This may have been present in OE in the form **Bealdrīc*, but it was re-introduced by the Normans as *Baldri, Baudri*, and it is from these forms that the surname is derived. The name is now found chiefly in E Anglia.

Vars.: **Baldrey**, **Baudr(e)y**; **Boldry**, **Boldero(e)**, **Boldra**, **Bowdery**; **Baldrick**, **Baudrick**.

Patr.: Flem.: **Bouderickx**.

Baldwin 1. English: from a Gmc personal name composed of the elements *bald* bold, brave + *wine* friend, which was extremely popular among the Normans and in Flanders in the early Middle Ages. It was the given name of the Crusader who in 1100 became the first Christian king of Jerusalem, and of four more Crusader kings of Jerusalem. It was also borne by Baldwin, Count of Flanders (1172–1205), leader of the Fourth Crusade, who became first Latin Emperor of Constantinople (1204). 2. Irish: surname adopted by bearers of the Gael. name **Ó Maolagáin** (see MILLIGAN), as a result of an association of the first element with Eng. *bald* hairless.

Ger.: **Baldewein**, **Ballwe(i)n**, **Bol(l)wahn**, **Bollwagen**. Flem., Du.: **Baudewijn**, **Bou(de)wijn**, **Bouwen**, **Bauwen**.

Patrs.: Low Ger.: **Bauwens**. Flem., Du.: **Baudewijns**, **Boudewijns**, **Bauwens**.

Bale *see* BAILEY

Balfe Irish: Anglicized form of Gael. *Balbh* 'Stammering', 'Dumb', itself probably a translation of a Norman family name of similar meaning (see for example BAUBE).

Patrs. (from dims.): **(O')Balivan** (Gael. **Ó Balbháin**).

Balfour 1. Scots: habitation name from any of several places in the Highlands, so called from Gael. *bail(e)* village, farm, house + *pùir*, gen. case of *pór* pasture, grass (lenited to *phùir* in certain contexts). The second element is akin to W *pawr* pasture. The principal family bearing this name derive it from lands in the parish of Markinch, Fife. According to the traditional pronunciation the accent falls on the second syllable, but these days it is found more commonly on the first. 2. Jewish (Israeli): surname (and male given name) adopted in the 20th cent. in commemoration of the Balfour Declaration of 2 November 1917, in which the British foreign secretary Arthur James Balfour (1848–1930) pledged support for the establishment of a Jewish homeland in Palestine.

Balkwill English: habitation name from some minor place (probably in Devon, where the surname is most common),

presumably so called from OE *balca* beam (see BALCH 1) + *wiell(a)* spring, stream (see WELL). The reference is probably to a place where a tree trunk had been placed across a stream as a primitive foot-bridge.

Ball English: 1. nickname for a short, fat person, from ME *bal(le)* ball (ON *böllr*). In some cases it may have referred to a bald man, from the same word used in the sense of a (round) hairless patch on the skull; mod. Eng. *bald* is from ME *ballede*, from *bal(le)* + *-ede*, i.e., 'having a *balle*'. 2. topographic name for someone who lived on or by a knoll or rounded hill, from the same ME word, *bal(le)*, used in this sense. 3. from the ON personal name *Balle*, apparently derived from *bal* torture, pain (see also BAL 2).

Vars. (of 1): **Balle**; **Bald** (Scots). (Of 2): **Baller**.

Pej. (of 1): Eng.: **Ballard** (a nickname).

Patrs. (from 3): Eng.: **Balls**. Dan.: **Balling**.

Ballantyne Scots: apparently a habitation name from *Bellenden* in the former counties of Roxburghs and Selkirk, probably so called from Gael. *baile an deadhain* farmstead of the dean.

Vars.: **Ballantine**, **Ballintyne**, **Ballintine**; **Ballentine**, **Ballendine** (N Ireland).

Ballaster English: occupational name for a maker of crossbows or a soldier armed with a crossbow, from an agent deriv. of ME, OF *baleste* crossbow (L *ballista* (military) catapult, ultimately from Gk *ballein* to throw; cf. BAL 1). During the Middle Ages the Sp. and Port. cogns. came to be used as the title of a minister who slept in a room adjoining his master's, originally as a kind of bodyguard, and also of various other court officials involved in royal ceremonial.

Vars.: **Bal(le)ster**, **Ballister**.

Dims.: It.: **Balestrelli**, **Balestrini**.

Pejs.: It.: **Balestrazzi**, **Balestracci**, **Balestrassi**.

Ballin *see* HAYLING

Ballinger *see* BERINGER

Balliol English and Scots (Norman): habitation name from *Bailleul*-en-Vimeu in Picardy, or from one of the numerous other places called *Bailleul* in N France, all of which are probably named from a deriv. of OF *baille* fortification; see BAILEY 2.

Var.: **Baliol**.

Balme 1. Provençal: topographic name for someone who lived by a cave, OProv. *baume* (of Celt. origin), or habitation name from one of the various minor places named with this word. 2. French: metonymic occupational name for a seller of perfumes and spices, from OF *balme* ointment; see BALMER 1.

Vars. (of 1): **Balma**, **Baume**, **Barme**; **Balmadier**, **Baum(ad)ier**.

Dim. (of 1): **Balmette**.

Aug. (of 1): **Baumat**.

Balmer 1. English: occupational name for a seller of spices and perfumes, from an agent deriv. of ME, OF *basme*, *balme*, *ba(u)me* balm, ointment (L *balsamum* aromatic resin, from Gk, and probably ultimately of Oriental origin). There is insufficient evidence to justify the speculation that the term meant an embalmer. 2. German:

habitation name from one of the places in Switzerland and Baden called *Balm*, which almost certainly get their names from a Celt. word meaning 'cave', as in BALME 1.

Balmforth *see* BAMFORD

Balogh Hungarian: nickname for a left-handed person, from *balog* left, left-handed, clumsy.

Var.: **Balog** (common in the U.S.).

Balser 1. German: var. of BALTHASAR. 2. Jewish (E Ashkenazic): habitation name, an altered form of *Belzer*, native or inhabitant of a town called *Belz*, of which there are two: one in the Ukraine and the other in Galicia.

Balthasar German and French: from the Babylonian personal names *Balthazar* and *Belshazzar*, which were originally distinct but by medieval times had come to be regarded as vars. of a single name. The first is from Aramaic *Balshatzar*, Babylonian *Baal tas-assar* 'may Baal preserve his life', the second from Babylonian *Baal sharuzzur* 'may Baal protect the king'. The second of these was borne by the Chaldean king for whom Daniel interpreted the writing on the wall (Dan. 5); the main reason for the popularity of the first in medieval Italy and Germany was that, according to legend, it was the name of one of the three Magi from the East who attended Christ's birth. His supposed relics were venerated at first in Milan, but after 1164 in Cologne, where they had been taken by Rainald of Dassel.

Vars.: Ger.: **Bal(t)zer**, BALSER; **Ba(l)thas**, **Baltus**, **Baldus**, **Baltes**, **Baldes**, **Bal(t)z**, **Bals**. Fr.: **Balthasard**, **Balthazar(d)**.

Dims.: Ger.: **Balzel**; **Balzl** (Bavaria); **Bälzle** (Swabia); **Balzli** (Switzerland). Pol.: **Balcerek**. Czech: **Balcárek**, **Balek**, **Balík**. It.: **Baldasserini**, **Baldisserotto**; **Balzarini**, **Balzarotti**; **Saretti**, **Serett(in)i**, **Sarotti**, **Serotti**.

Augs.: It.: **Baldasseroni**, **Seroni**.

Patrs.: Norw., Dan.: **Baltzersen**. Pol.: **Balcewicz**. Armenian: **Bogdass(ar)ian**, **Bogdikian**.

Baltrushaitis *see* BARTHOLOMEW

Balzac French: of uncertain origin, perhaps from a Basque nickname *baltsa* 'the black one', with the spelling altered by association with the common placename element *-ac* (from the Gallo-Roman local suffix *-ācum*).

Bälzle *see* BALTHASAR

Bamber English: habitation name from *Bamber* Bridge in Lancs., originally *Bimme*'s bridge', from a ME personal name of uncertain origin.

Bamberger Jewish (Ashkenazic): habitation name from the city of *Bamberg* in Bavaria (formerly in Upper Franconia). Between 1007 and 1702 it was the capital of a powerful ecclesiastical state, and in the 15th cent. the bishops of Bamberg were raised to princely rank.

Var.: **Vámbéry** (Magyarized form, borne by Hungarian Jews).

Bambrough English: habitation name from the town of *Bamburgh* in Northumb., which is mentioned in the form *Bebbanburg* by the Venerable Bede, according to whom it was called after a certain queen *Bebbe* + OE *burh* fort. The surname is still most common in Northumb.

Bamford English: habitation name from any of various places (the two main ones being in Derbys. and Lancs.) so called from OE *bēam* tree, plank + *ford* FORD, i.e. a

ford that could be crossed by means of a tree trunk or plank bridge by those who wished to keep their feet dry.

Vars.: **Bampford**, **Bam(p)forth**; **Balmforth** (with intrusive *-l-*).

Bampfylde English: habitation name from *Bampfylde* Lodge in Poltimore, Devon, recorded in 1306 as *Benefeld*, 'open land where beans are grown'. See BANFIELD.

Bampton English: habitation name from any of various places so called. Those in Cumb. and Oxon. are so called from OE *bēam* tree, plank + *tūn* enclosure, settlement, although the exact sense of the cpd is not clear. A further example in Devon represents a contracted form of OE *bæðhēmatūn* 'settlement of the dwellers by a bath, hot spring'.

Banasevich *see* BENNETT

Banbury English: habitation name from the town in Oxon., so called from an OE personal name *Ban(n)a* (apparently a byname meaning 'Felon', 'Murderer') + OE *burh* fort.

Bancroft English: habitation name from any of various minor places so called, from OE *bēan* beans (a collective sing.) + *croft* paddock, smallholding (see CROFT).

Var.: **Bencroft** (a place in Northants).

Band German and Jewish (Ashkenazic): metonymic occupational name for someone who made the wooden hoops with which wooden barrels were fastened together, from Ger. *Band* hoop, band (MHG *bant*, OHG *band*, a deriv. of *bindan* to bind; cf. BINDER).

Vars.: Ger.: **Bandt**, **Bande**. Jewish: **Bandman(n)**, **Bandelman**, **Bandler**, **Bandner**.

Dims.: Ger.: **Bandel**, **Bandle**. Jewish: **Bandel**.

Banes *see* BAINES

Banfather *see* BAIRNSFATHER

Banfield English: habitation name from an unidentified place, evidently so called from OE *bēan* beans (collective sing.) + *feld* field, land converted to arable use. The place may well be identical with Bampfylde Lodge in Devon (see BAMPFYLDE).

Var.: **Benfield**.

Bang Danish: nickname for a timid person, from Dan. *bang* fearful, nervous (from the ON prefix *bí* + *angr* grief, sorrow).

Banham English: habitation name from a place in Norfolk, so called from OE *bēan* beans (a collective sing.) + *hām* homestead. The surname is still much more common in Norfolk than elsewhere.

Bankhead English: topographic name for someone who lived at the top of a bank or hill; see BANKS 1. The name is now found mainly in N Ireland, where it is probably a habitation name of Scots origin. There are several minor places in Scotland so called, but the most likely source of the surname is one on the border between the parishes of Kilmarnock and Dreghorn in the former county of Ayrs. (now part of Strathclyde region).

Bańkowski Polish: of uncertain origin, probably a deriv. of *bańka* meaning 'bulging vessel', used as a nickname for a fat man. *Bańka* is not actually attested in this meaning, but the related word *bania* is.

Banks 1. English and Scots: topographic name for someone who lived on the slope of a hillside or by a riverbank, from Northern ME *bank(e)* (of Scand. origin; cf. ON *bakke*). The final *-s* may occasionally represent a plural form, but it is most commonly an arbitrary addition made after the main period of surname formation, perhaps under the influence of patr. forms with a possessive *-s*. **2.** Irish: Anglicized form of Gael. **Ó Bruacháin** 'descendant of *Bruachán*', a byname for a large-bellied person. The Eng. form was chosen because of a mistaken association of the Gael. name with *bruach* boundary.

Vars. (of 1): **Bankes**, **Bangs**; **Banker**. (Of 2): **O'Bro(g)han**.

Cpds (ornamental, from a cogn. of 1): Swed.: **Backlund** ('bank grove'); **Backström** ('bank river').

Bannan Irish: Anglicized form of Gael. **Ó Banáin**, 'descendant of *Banán*', a personal name representing a dim. of *ban* white.

Vars.: **O'Bannan**, **(O')Bannion**, **(O')Bynnan**, **(O')Banane**, **Banan**, **Bannon**, **Banin**, **Banim**.

Bannerman Scots: occupational name for a standard bearer, from ANF *banere* flag, ensign (OF *baniere*, LL *bandāria*, a deriv. of *bandum*, of Gmc origin) + ME *man* (OE *mann*).

Patr.: Du.: **Baanders**.

Bannister English: metonymic occupational name for a basket weaver, from ANF *banastre* basket (the result of a LL cross between Gaul. *benna* and Gk *kanastron*). The word is not used of a stair rail before the 17th cent., too late to have given rise to a surname.

Vars.: **Banister**, **Bannester**.

Bañón see BAIN

Bantele see PANTALEONE

Bantzer see PANZER

Banuelos see BAIN

Banwell English: habitation name from a place in Somerset, so called from the OE byname *Ban(n)a* (see BANBURY) + OE *well(a)* stream.

Banyard English: metathesized form of a Gmc personal name introduced by the Normans in the form *Baynard*. The first element is of uncertain origin, but may be akin to ON *beinn* straight (cf. BAIN 3); the second is *hard* brave, hardy, strong, a common element in Gmc names.

Vars.: **Bunyard**, **Baynard**.

Baptiste French: from a medieval given name, derived from the distinguishing epithet of St John the Baptist, who baptized people, including Christ Himself, in the river Jordan (Mark 1: 9), and was later beheaded by Herod. The name is from L *Baptista* (Gk *baptistēs*, a deriv. of *baptein* to dip, wash).

Var.: **Batisse**.

Dims.: It.: **Bat(t)istelli**, **Bat(t)istetti**, **Bat(t)istini**, **Bat(t)istuzzi**, **Bat(t)istucci**, **Bat(t)istotti**.

Augs.: It.: **Bat(t)istoni**, **Tittoni**.

Patrs.: It.: **Di Bat(t)ista**.

Baquelin see BACON

Bar see BARD

Barabino Italian: nickname for a ruffian, from a dim. of the Aramaic personal name *Bar-abas* 'son of *Aba*', a byname meaning 'father'. This was the name borne by the thief whose life was demanded by the crowd in Jerusalem in preference to that of Jesus (Matt. 27: 15–21). The surname is especially common in Liguria, in and around Genoa.

Baradulin see BORODIN

Baragwanath Cornish: metonymic occupational name for a baker of fancy loaves, from Corn. *bara* bread + *gwaneth* wheat, or a nickname for someone who would eat only wheat bread; everyday loaves were made of coarser rye or barley. Cf. WHITBREAD.

Var.: **Baragwaneth**.

Barahona Spanish: habitation name from places in the provinces of Segovia and Soria, of uncertain etymology (the first element possibly LL *vara* fence; cf. BARAJAS).

Barajas Spanish: habitation name from places in the provinces of Cuenca and Madrid; the latter is now the site of an international airport. The placename is of uncertain origin, but may be from LL *varālia* fencing, a deriv. of *vara* fence (of Celt. origin).

Baranda Spanish: habitation name from a place in the province of Burgos. Many different explanations of the origin of the placename have been offered, but none is convincing and the etymology remains uncertain.

Baranov Russian: patr. from the nickname *Baran* 'Ram', which was given either to a forceful or lusty man or else to a shepherd.

Dims.: Beloruss.: **Baranchik**. Pol.: **Baraniek**. Czech: **Béránek**. Jewish: **Baranchuk**.

Baranowski Polish and Jewish (E Ashkenazic): habitation name from a place named with Pol. *baran* ram, + the possessive suffix *-ów* (a common placename element), with the addition of the suffix of surnames *-ski* (a standard adj. ending in Polish, cognate with Eng. *-ish*). In surnames *-ski* originally indicated association with a place, but soon came to be regarded as equivalent to Fr. *de* or Ger. *von*, and so indicative of gentry status. In many but by no means all cases, the bearer was indeed lord of the estate or manor to which the name referred. Later, the suffix came to be used much more widely to form surnames, being attached indiscriminately to given names (as *Adamski*), nicknames, and occupational names (as *Bednarski*), as well as to habitation names. Baranowski is therefore probably a habitation name in origin, but in some cases it may be no more than an elaboration of a nickname, *Baran*, meaning 'Ram' (see BARANOV).

The suffix *-ski* is also found as an ending of Russ. surnames, but these are generally of Pol. origin or formed under Pol. influence. The Czech cogn. suffix *-ský* is very much less common, and tends to be more strictly associated with habitation names. *-ski* is also found as a suffix of E Ashkenazic Jewish surnames. By the time most Jews on Polish territory were acquiring family names, in the late 18th and early 19th cents., it was already very widely used as a general surname suffix. In Jewish surnames, therefore, it is found attached to several different kinds of stems, including some of non-Slavic origin, as in the E Ashkenazic surname *Kohansky* (see COHEN). In English-speaking countries, most Jews bearing surnames with this suffix spell it *-sky*.

Vars.: Jewish: **Baranovski**, **Baranovsky**.

Barbary 1. English: from the female given name *Barbara*, which was borne by an enormously popular but almost certainly non-existent saint, who according to legend was imprisoned in a tower and later put to death by her own father for refusing to recant her Christian beliefs. The name comes from a fem. form of L *barbarus*, Gk *barbaros* foreign(er) (originally an onomatopoeic word formed in imitation of the unintelligible babbling of non-Greeks). **2.** Provençal: from a dim. of OProv. *barbare* foreigner, barbarian; see above. In particular it came to be used for a Moor or *Berber* from the *Barbary* Coast in N Africa, and hence was applied to a man of swarthy appearance or uncouth habits.

Vars. (of 1): Eng.: **Barbara**; **Barbery** (Cornwall). (Of 2): Prov.: **Barbarin**, **Barbarou(x)**.

Dims. (of 1): Eng.: BABB. It. **Barbarelli**, **Barbarino**, **Barbarotto**, **Barbarulo**.

Pejs. (of 1): It.: **Barbarac(c)i**.

Metrs. (from 1): Russ.: **Varvarin**; **Varvarinski** (clerical).

Metrs. (from 1 (dim.)): Russ.: **Varvarkin**, **Varyushin**.

Barbe French: **1.** nickname for someone with a beard, OF *barbe* (L *barba*). **2.** from a pet form of the given name *Barbara*; see BARBARY.

Vars. (of 1): **Barbé**, **Barbu(t)**; **Alabarbe**.

Dims. (of 1): Fr.: **Barbet**, **Barbin**, **Barby**, **Barbot**, **Barbon**. It.: **Barbella**, **Barb(ol)ini**, **Barbetti**, **Barbucci**, **Barbuzzi**. Sp.: **Barbadillo**.

Augs. (of 1): Fr.: **Barbas**, **Barb(u)at**. It.: **Barbone**.

Pej. (of 1): It.: **Barbacci**.

Patr. (from 1): Rum.: **Barbulesco**.

Barber 1. English: occupational name for a barber (ANF *barber*, OF *barbier*, from LL *barbārius*, a deriv. of *barba* beard; see BARBE 1), who in the Middle Ages was a person who not only cut hair and shaved beards, but also practised surgery and pulled teeth. **2.** Jewish (Ashkenazic): of uncertain origin. Since the name is found in areas where English influence is highly unlikely, it cannot always, if ever, be an Anglicization of some semantically equivalent Jewish surname. Possibly it is an acronymic surname from Hebr. *bar-* 'son of ...', with a male given name beginning with *B-* (cf. BROCK).

Var. (of 1): **Barbour** (Scots and N Irish).

Dims. (of 1): Fr.: **Barbereau**, **Barberet**, **Barberon**, **Barberot**. It.: **Barberini**, **Barbarolli**.

Patrs. From 1): It.: **De Barb(i)eri**, **De Barberis**. Du.: **Barbiers**.

Barberà Catalan: habitation name from a place in the province of Tarragona, so called from LL *Barbariānum* 'place of *Barbarius*', a deriv. of *Barbarus* (see BARBARY).

Vars.: **Barbarà**, **Barberàn**.

Barbosa Portuguese: topographic name for someone who lived on a piece of land overgrown with leafy vegetation, from LL *barbōsa (terra)* 'bearded' land (cf. BARBE 1).

Barcan *see* COHEN

Barceló Catalan: habitation name from *Barcelona*, the principal city of Catalonia. The placename is of uncertain, certainly pre-Roman, origin. The settlement was established by the Carthaginians, and according to tradition it was named from the Carthaginian ruling house of *Barca*; the L form was *Barcino, Barcilo*.

Bárcena Spanish: habitation name from any of various places, for example in the provinces of Biscay, Burgos, León, Oviedo, Palencia, and Santander, so called from a pre-Roman topographical element **bargina*, descriptive of an area of cultivated land.

Vars.: **Bárcenas**; **Barcina** (a place in Burgos).

Dim.: **Barcenilla** (places in Burgos, Palencia, and Santander).

Barclay English and Scots: habitation name from *Berkeley* in Gloucs., or possibly in a few cases from another place similarly named, e.g. *Berkely* in Somerset. The placename is derived from OE *be(o)rc* BIRCH + *lēah* wood, clearing. For the change of *-er-* to *-ar-* in ME, cf. MARCHANT. The surname is particularly common in Scotland, whither it was brought by a Berkeley from Gloucs. in the 12th cent.; Walter *de Berchelai* or *Berkelai* was Chamberlain of Scotland in 1165.

Vars.: **Berk(e)ley**; **Barkley** (N Ireland).

Barco Spanish: **1.** metonymic occupational name for a boatman or ferryman, from Sp. *barco* boat (L *barca*). **2.** habitation name from any of various places, for example in the provinces of Avila and Orense, called *(El) Barco*. These are of uncertain etymology, possibly from the Celt. element *berg, barg* height, eminence. The name could also be related to the N Italian dial. term *barco* haystack, hayloft (possibly of pre-Roman origin). In this case the name may have been given originally to a hill shaped like a haystack.

Var. (of 1): **Barquero**.

Bar-Cohen *see* COHEN

Barcroft English: habitation name from a place so called from OE *bere* barley + *croft* paddock, smallholding. For the change of *-er-* to *-ar-* in ME, cf. MARCHANT.

Bard 1. Scots: occupational name from Gael. *bàrd* poet, minstrel, singer. **2.** Scots: perhaps a habitation name, to judge from the earliest forms—Henry *de Barde* and Richard *de Baard*—but no suitable place has been identified, and *de* occasionally occurs, either by analogy or by mistake, for *le*. **3.** French: from the Gmc personal name *Bardo*, a short form of any of the rare cpd names with the first element *bard*, perhaps from *barta* axe. **4.** French: habitation name from any of the several minor places called *Bar(d)*, from the Gaul. element *barro* height, hill (cf. BARR 3). **5.** French: metonymic occupational name for someone who used a handcart or barrow in his work, from OF *bard* barrow (of uncertain origin, possibly akin to a Gmc element meaning 'carry, bear'). Dims. of this vocab. word were also used to denote beasts of burden, and so the surname may have originated as an occupational name for a driver of pack animals or as a nickname for an overworked servant. **6.** French: from OF *bart* mud, clay (LL *barrum*, apparently of Celt. origin), in which case it is either a topographic name for someone living in a muddy area or an occupational name for a builder or bricklayer. **7.** Jewish (Ashkenazic): possibly an acronymic surname from Hebr. *bar*- 'son of...', with a male given name beginning with *D*-, such as *David* (cf. BROCK). However, it is more likely to be a nickname for someone with a luxurious beard, from a blend of Ger. *Bart* and Yid. *bord*, both meaning 'beard'.

Vars.: **Bar(t)**. (Of 3 only): **Bardon** (oblique case).

Dims. (of 3): Fr.: **Bardonneau**, **Bardonnet**. It.: **Bardell(in)i**, **Bardetti**, **Bardotti**, **Barducci**; **Pardelli**, **Pardini**, **Parducci** (Liguria). (Of 5): **Bardet**, **Bardot**, **Bardy**, **Bardinet**, **Bardinot**, **Bardineau**, **Bardinon**.

Augs. (of 3): It.: **Bard(i)oni**.

Pejs. (of 3): It.: **Bardacci**, **Bardazzi**.

Patrs. (from 1): Sc.: **Baird** (Gael. **Mac an Baird**). Ir.: **McAward**, **McWard**, **Quard**, **Ward** (Gael. **Mac an Bhaird**).

Collectives (of 6): Port.: **Barreto**, **Barradas**.

Bar-Dayan *see* DAYAN

Barde Provençal: metonymic occupational name for someone who made and sold spades, or used them in his work, from OProv. *barda* spade (which probably derives from It., and ultimately from Arabic *barda'a*).

Barden English: habitation name from places in N and W Yorks., so called from OE *bere* barley (or the derived adj. *beren*) + *denu* valley (see DEAN 1).

Bardsley English: habitation name from a place in Lancs., so called from the gen. case of the OE personal name *Beornrēd* (composed of the elements *beorn* young warrior + *rēd* counsel, advice) + OE *lēah* wood, clearing. There may have been some confusion with BEARDSLEY.

Bardwell English: habitation name from a place in Suffolk, so called from the OE byname *Bearda* (a deriv. of *beard* BEARD; cf. BEARDSLEY) + OE *well(a)* spring, stream (see WELL). An alternative possibility is that the first element may be from a dissimilated form of OE *bre(o)rd* brim, bank.

Vars.: **Beardwell**, **Bardell**.

Barelli *see* BEAR

Barenbaum *see* BIRNBAUM

Barends *see* BERNARD

Bärenreiter German: habitation name from the village of *Bernreut* in Bavaria, so called from MHG *brennen* to burn + *reut* clearing, i.e. a clearing made by burning trees. The name has been assimilated by folk etymology to Ger. 'bear rider' (from *Bär* bear + *reiten* to ride), which is a name given to the star Alkor in the Great Bear constellation.

Vars.: **Bernreut(h)**, **Bernreith**.

Barff *see* BARROW

Barfield English: 1. habitation name, probably from *Bardfield* in Essex, so called from OE *byrde* riverbank + *feld* cultivated land; the name is still most common in N Essex. 2. topographic name for someone who lived by an area where barley was cultivated, from ME *berefeld*.

Barfoot English: nickname for someone who was in the habit of going about his business unshod, from OE *bær* bare, naked + *fōt* foot. It may have referred to a peasant unable to afford even the simplest type of footwear, or to

someone who went barefoot as a religious penance. Black, however, is convinced that as a Scots surname it is 'doubtless of local origin'.

Var.: **Barefoot**.

Bargalló Catalan: topographic name for someone who lived by a fan palm or palmetto, a tropical plant that grows on the Mediterranean coast and on the Balearic islands. The word has been derived from L *barba Jovis* 'Jupiter's beard', but is far more likely to come from Mozarabic *(a)bregalyon*, ultimately from LL *africānio*, gen. *africāniōnis*, a deriv. of *Africa*, the original home of the plant.

Barge English and French: metonymic occupational name for a boatman or mariner, from ME, OF *barge* boat, barge (L *barca*).

Vars.: Eng.: **Bargeman**. Fr.: **Barque**.

Dims.: Fr.: **Bargeton**, **Barjon**, **Barjou**, **Barjot**.

Barham English: habitation name from any of the various places so called. Most, for example those in Cambs. and Suffolk, are so called from OE *beorg* hill (see BERG) + *hām* homestead. The one in Kent, however, gets its first element from the OE byname *Biora*, *Beora* (a deriv. of *bera* BEAR).

Vars.: **Bareham**, **Barhams**, **Barhem(s)**, **Barhims**.

Baril French: metonymic occupational name for a cooper, or a nickname for a rotund man, from OF *baril* barrel (of uncertain origin, perhaps a deriv. of *bar(r)e* bar; cf. BARR 1, 2).

Vars.: **Barial**, **Barral**, **Barrau(d)**, **Barrau(l)t**, **Bar(r)aux**; **Barill(i)er**, **Barralier**, **Barrailler** (occupational names).

Dims.: Fr.: **Bar(il)let**, **Bar(il)lot**, **Bar(r)illon**, **Barlon**. It.: **Bar(i)letti**, **Bariglietti**, **Barletta**, **Barilini**, **Barilotti**, **Barilucci**.

Augs.: It.: **Barilone**, **Bariglione**.

Barish Jewish (Ashkenazic): acronymic surname from a Hebrew-Aramaic patr. phrase *Bar Rabi SHelomo, SHemuel, SHimon, SHimshon*, etc., i.e. 'son of (rabbi) SALOMON, SAMUEL, SIMON, SAMSON', or some other male given name beginning with SH-. Cf. BROCK.

Vars.: **B(a)rasch**, **Barash**, **Brosch**, **Brisch**.

Barizeret *see* BASIL

Barker English: 1. occupational name for a tanner of leather, from ME *bark(en)* to tan (from the *bark* of a tree, which was used in the process; the word is of Scand. origin, and is probably cogn. with OE *be(o)rc*, a byform of *bi(e)rce* BIRCH). 2. occupational name for a shepherd, ANF *bercher* (LL *berbicārius*, from *berbex*, gen. *berbicis*, ram). With the change of -*ar*- to -*er*- in ME, this became indistinguishable from the preceding name.

Dims. (of 2): Fr.: **Bergeret**, **Bergerot**, **Bergeron**, **Berger(onn)eau**. Prov.: **Bergerioux**.

Barley English: 1. habitation name from any of various places so called. Those in Lancs. and W Yorks. get the name from OE *bār* wild boar or *bær* barley + *lēah* wood, clearing. A place of the same name in Herts. has as its first element the OE byname *Be(o)ra* (from *bera* BEAR). 2. metonymic occupational name for a grower or seller of barley, from OE *bærlic*, originally an adj. deriv. of *bær* barley (a byform of *bere*; cf. BARCROFT and BARDEN).

Vars.: **Barlee**. (Of 2 only): **Barleyman**.

Barling *see* BURLING

Barlow English: habitation name from any of several places so called, esp. those in Lancs. and W Yorks. The former gets its name from OE *bere* barley + *hlāw* hill; the latter probably has as its first element the derived adj. *beren* or the cpd *bere-ærn* barn. There is also a place of this name in Derbys., so called from OE *bār* boar or *bær* barley + *lēah* wood, clearing, and one in Shrops., which is from *bær* barley + *lēah*.

Barme *see* BALME

Barnaby English: **1.** from the ME vernacular form of the given name *Barnabas*, borne by the companion of St Paul (Acts 4: 36). This is of Aramaic origin, from *Bar-nabia* 'son of *Nabia*', a personal name perhaps meaning 'confession'. **2.** habitation name from a place in N Yorks., so called from the OE personal name *Beornwald* (composed of the elements *beorn* young warrior + *wald* rule) + ON *býr* settlement.

Vars.: **Barnabe(e)**, **Barneby**.

Dims. (of 1): It.: **Barna**, **Barn(in)i**, **Barnabucci**.

Barnacle *see* COYNE

Barnaud *see* BERAUD

Barnes **1.** English: topographic name or occupational name for someone who lived or worked at a barn, from the gen. case or pl. of ME *barn* barn, granary (OE *bern*, originally a cpd of *bere* barley + *ærn* house, building). The placename *Barnes* (on the Surrey bank of the Thames in W London) has the same origin, and some bearers may be members of families hailing from there. **2.** English: name borne by the son or servant of a *barne*, a term used in the early Middle Ages for a member of the upper classes, although its precise meaning is not clear (it derives from OE *beorn*/ON *barn* young warrior, akin to the Gmc element *ber(an)* BEAR). Barne was also occasionally used as a given name (from an OE/ON byname), and some examples of the surname may derive from this use. **3.** Irish: Anglicized form of Gael. **Ó Bearáin** 'descendant of *Bearán*', a byname meaning 'Spear'. **4.** Jewish: probably a var. of PARNES.

Vars. (of 1 and 2): **Barne**, **Barns**. (Of 3): BARRINGTON. (Of 4): **Barness**.

Barnet English: **1.** habitation name from any of the numerous places, for example in N London, so called from OE *bærnet* place cleared by burning (a deriv. of *bærnan* to burn, set light to). **2.** from a medieval given name, a var. of BERNARD or cogn. of BERAUD.

Var.: **Barnett**.

Barnfather *see* BAIRNSFATHER

Barnfield English: habitation name from some minor place (probably in the W Midlands, where the name is commonest) so called, probably from OE *bern* barn (see BARNES 1) + *feld* pasture, open country (see FIELD).

Barnsley English: habitation name from any of the several places so called, notably one in W Yorks. (from the

gen. case of the OE byname *Beorn* 'Warrior' + OE *lēah* wood, clearing) and one in Gloucs. (from the gen. case of the OE personal name *Beornmōd* ('warrior spirit') + *lēah*). The surname is common in the Birmingham area as well as in W Yorks.

Barnum English: **1.** habitation name from one of the various places, for example in Norfolk, Suffolk, and W Sussex, called *Barnham*. They are probably all so called from the OE byname *Beorn(a)* (see BARNES 2) + OE *hām* homestead. **2.** topographic or occupational name for someone who lived or worked at a group of barns, from the dat. pl. of OE *bern* (see BARNES 1).

Var. (of 1): **Barnham**.

Barnwell English: habitation name from a place so called; there is one in Cambs. and another in Northants. The former derives its name from OE *beorna* warriors' + *well(a)* stream; the latter from OE *byrgen* burial mound, barrow + *well(a)*.

Var.: **Barnewall**.

Baron **1.** English and French: from the title of nobility, ME, OF *baron*, *barun* (of Gmc origin; cf. BARNES 2). As a surname it is unlikely to be a status name denoting a person of rank. The great baronial families of Europe had distinctive surnames of their own. However, 'baron' in Scotland denoted a member of a class of minor landowners who had a certain degree of jurisdiction over the local populace, and the title was also awarded to certain freemen of the cities of London and York and of the Cinque Ports; either of these uses might be the source of a surname. Far more commonly, however, the surname is derived from an OF personal name *Baro* (oblique case *Baron*), or else referred to service in a baronial household or was acquired as a nickname by a peasant who had ideas above his station. **2.** Irish: Anglicized form of Gael. *Ó Bearáin*; see BARNES. **3.** Jewish: of uncertain origin, possibly a var. of *Baran* (see BARANOV), or from the Hebrew-Aramaic patr. phrase *bar-Aharon* 'son of AARON', or an ornamental name meaning 'baron'. In Israel the surname is often interpreted, by folk etymology, as being from *Bar-On* 'Son of Strength'.

Var. (of 1 and 2): **Barron**.

Dims. (of 1): Fr.: **Baronnet**. It.: **Barontini**, **Baroncini**, **Baroncelli**.

Barr **1.** Scots and N Irish: habitation name from any of the many places in SW Scotland that get their names from Gael. *barr* height, hill, or from a Brit. cognate. **2.** English: topographic name for someone who lived by a gateway or barrier, from ME, OF *barre* bar, obstruction (of obscure origin, possibly akin to the Celt. element *barr* height and therefore cogn. with 1). **3.** English (Norman): habitation name from *Barre*-en-Ouche in Eure or *Barre*-de-Semilly in Manche. These places derive their names from the same word as in 2. **4.** English: metonymic occupational name for a maker of bars, or nickname for a tall, thin man, from special applications of the ME, OF word *barre*. **5.** English: habitation name from any of various places, as for example Great *Barr* in the W Midlands, named with the Celt. element *barro* height, hill (cf. BRYAN). This is also the origin of various Fr. placenames, as for example *Barre* in Lozère (cf. BARD 4). **6.** Irish: see BARRY 6.

Dims. (of 2 and 3): Fr.: **Barret, Barrel(le), Bar(r)eau, Barrelet, Barrot.** Prov.: **Baradel, Baradeau.** Sp.: **Bar(r)ella.**

Augs. (of 2 and 3): Prov.: **Baradas, Baradat.**

Barraclough English (mainly Yorks.): habitation name from *Barrowclough* near Halifax in W Yorks., so called from OE *bearu* grove (see BARROW 1) + *clōh* ravine (see CLOUGH).

Vars.: **Barrowclough; Barrowcliff(e)** (Notts.); **Barnaclough, Berecloth, Berrycloth.**

Barragán Spanish: **1.** nickname for a strong or brave man, from Sp. *barragán* young man, warrior (of uncertain origin, probably a deriv. of a Gmc element; cf. BARNES 2). **2.** metonymic occupational name for a maker or seller of a kind of material, Sp. *barragán* (from Arabic *barrakân*).

Barranco Spanish: habitation name from any of various minor places, for example in the province of Alicante, named with the topographical term *barranco* ravine, gorge (of pre-Roman origin).

Barré French: from the past part. of OF *barrer*, a deriv. of *barre* bar (see BARR 2). Both verb and noun had a large number of senses in OF and it is not certain what the original meaning of the name was. It may sometimes have been a topographic name for a person who lived in a place that was naturally cut off or particularly well fortified, but in most cases it was more probably a nickname meaning 'striped', referring to a habitual wearer of striped clothing or possibly to someone with a noticeable birthmark. In the Middle Ages the term was applied to the Carmelite Friars, who wore habits striped in black, yellow, and white, but in view of the celibacy of the clergy it is unlikely that this is the origin of many instances of the name, unless as a nickname for someone supposedly resembling a Carmelite in some way.

Barrena Basque: topographic name for someone who lived in a dip or hollow or at the bottom of a slope, from *barren* lowest point + the def. art. *-a*.

Barrenechea Spanish form of Basque **Barrenetxea**: topographic name for someone who lived in a house in a dip or hollow or at the bottom of a slope, from Basque *barren* lowest point + *etxe* house + the def. art. *-a*.

Barrera Spanish: **1.** topographic name for someone who lived near a gate or fence, from Sp. *barrera* barrier (a deriv. of BARR 2). **2.** topographic name for someone who lived by a clay-pit, Sp. *barrera, barrero* (a deriv. of *barro* mud, clay; cf. BARROS 1 and BARD 6).

Barrett English: **1.** from a Gmc personal name introduced into England by the Normans; see BERNARD and BERAUD. **2.** nickname for a quarrelsome or deceitful person, from ME *bar(r)et(t)e, bar(r)at* trouble, strife, deception, cheating (OF *barat* commerce, dealings, a deriv. of *barater* to barter, haggle, LL *prattāre*, from Gk *prattein* to do, practise). It is possible that the original sense of *barat* survived unrecorded into ME as a word for a market trader; the It. cogns. have this sense. **3.** nickname or metonymic occupa-

tional name from OF *barette* cap, bonnet (LL *birrum* hood, cowl, of Celt. origin).

Vars.: **Barret, Barrat(t), Barritt.**

Dims. (of 2): Fr.: **Baratin, Baraton, Barateau.** Prov.: **Baratoux.** It.: **Barattini, Barattucci.**

Aug. (of 2): **Barattoni.**

Barriga Spanish: nickname for someone with a large belly, from Sp. *barriga* belly, paunch. The word may be BARIL, and may originally have had the same sense, but this is not evidenced in the Middle Ages and is unlikely to lie behind the surname.

Barrington **1.** English: habitation name from any of several places of this name. The one in Gloucs. is so called from OE *Beorningtún* 'settlement (OE *tún*) associated with *Beorn*' (see BARNES 2); the one in Somerset was probably named as the 'settlement associated with **Bāra*'; the one in Cambs. gets its first element from the gen. case of the personal name **Bāra*. **2.** Irish: Anglicized form of Gael. *Ó Bearáin*; see BARNES 3.

Barrio Spanish: topographic name for someone who lived on the outskirts of a town, from Sp. *barrio* outlying region (Arabic *barr* suburb, dependent village).

Var.: **Barrios.**

Barros Spanish: **1.** topographic name for someone who lived on a patch of muddy land or clay soil; cf. BARD 6. **2.** nickname for someone with a birthmark or a spotty complexion, from Sp. *barro* spot, mark (LL *varus*).

Barrow English: **1.** topographic name for someone who lived by a grove, OE *bearo, bearu* (dat. *bear(o)we, bearuwe*), or habitation name from any of the numerous places named with this word, in Ches., Derbys., Gloucs., Lancs., Leics., Lincs., Shrops., Suffolk, and Somerset. **2.** topographic name for someone who lived by a hill or burial mound, OE *beorg* (dat. *beorge*, ME *berwe, barwe*; cf. BERG), or habitation name from either of the places named with this word, near Leicester and in Somerset. **3.** habitation name from *Barrow* in Furness, Cumb., which gets its name from Celt. *barro-*, here meaning 'promontory'.

Vars.: (of 1 and 2): **Barrows, Barrass; Berrow** (W Midlands). (Of 2 only): **Bar(u)gh, Barff** (pronounced /bɑːf/; cf. *Barff* Hill in E Yorks. and *Barugh* in N Yorks.).

Barrowman see BURKMAN

Barry **1.** English and French: topographic name from ANF *barri* rampart, later a suburb outside the rampart of a town (a word of uncertain origin, perhaps a technical term derived from Sp. BARRIO). **2.** Scots: habitation name from any of various places, esp. one in the former county of Angus, probably so called from Gael. *borrach* rough grassy hill. **3.** Welsh: patr. from HARRY, the medieval Eng. vernacular form of HENRY, preceded by W *ap* 'son of'. **4.** Welsh: habitation name from any of various places so called from W *barr* summit. **5.** Irish: Anglicized form of Gael. *Ó Beargha* 'descendant of *Beargh*', a byname meaning 'Robber'. **6.** Irish: Anglicized form of Gael. *Ó Báire* 'descendant of *Báire*', a short form of various personal names.

Vars. (of 1): Fr.: **Barri, Dubarry.** (Of 2): Sc.: **Barrie.**

Dims. (of 1): Fr.: **Barriol, Barrion.**

Barsham *see* BASHAM

Barski Polish: **1.** from *barć* wild honey bees' nest + *-ski* suffix of local surnames (see BARANOWSKI). It is therefore either a topographic name or an occupational name for a forester officially empowered to collect wild honey. **2.** from a much reduced form of the given name *Bartłomiej* BARTHOLOMEW + *-ski*.

Barstow *see* BAIRSTOW

Barsukov Russian: patr. from the nickname *Barsuk* 'Badger' (of Turkic origin).

Bart *see* BARTHOLOMEW

Bartels *see* BERTHOLD

Barthe French: topographic name for someone who lived on a piece of land overgrown with bushes or scrub, OF *barthe* (apparently of Gaul. origin).

Vars.: **Barte**, **Labart(h)e**; **Barthès**.

Dims.: **Bart(h)et**.

Augs.: **Bart(h)as**.

Bartholomew **1.** English: from a medieval given name, which is from the Aramaic patr. *bar-Talmay* 'son of *Talmay*', a given name meaning 'having many furrows', i.e. rich in land. As a given name in Christian Europe, it derived its popularity from the apostle St Bartholomew (Matt. 10: 3), the patron saint of tanners, vintners, and butlers, about whom virtually nothing is known. **2.** Irish: Anglicized form of *Mac Pharthaláin*; see McFARLANE.

Var.: **Bartlam** (Midlands).

Dims.: Eng.: **Bartlet(t)**, **Bartleet**; **Bart(le)**, **Barty**, **Bartie**; BATE; BATT. Fr.: **Bert(h)elémot**; **Bart(h)ol(in)**, **Bert(h)olin**; **Bart(h)el(et)**, **Bert(h)el(et)**; **Bart(h)ot**, **Bert(h)ot**, **Bart(h)od**. It.: **Bartolomeotti**, **Bartolomucci**, **Bartol(in)i**, **Bartal(in)i**, **Bartoletti**, **Bartaletti**, **Bartolozzi**, **Bartalucci**; **Bartelli**, **Bartocci**, **Bartozzi**; **Vartoli** (Calabria); **Bortol(i)**, **Bartul**, **Bortoletti**, **Bortolotti**, **Bortolozzi**, **Bortolini**, **Bortolutti**, **Bortoluzzi**, **Bortolussi** (Venetia); **Tolomelli**, **Tolumello**; **Tolotti**, **Tolossi**, **Tolussi**. Ger.: **Bart(h)(el)**, **Bartl** (see also BEARD). Du., Flem.: **Ba(e)rt**; **Bartolijn**, **Bartoleyn**. Ger. (of Slav. origin): **Bartke**, **Bartek**; **Bach(ur)a**, **Bachnik**. Czech: **Bartošek**, **Bartušek**, **Bartůnek**. Pol.: **Bartłomiejczyk**, **Bartoszek**, **Bartosik**. Hung.: **Bartók**, **Bertók**.

Augs.: Fr.: **Bart(h)olat**. It.: **Bartolomeoni**; **Bartaloni**, **Bortoloni**; **Toloni**.

Pejs.: It.: **Bartolomeazzi**, **Bartolacci**, **Bortolazzi**, **Meazzi**, **Miazzi**.

Patrs.: It.: **Di Bartolom(m)eo**; **Di Meo**, **(De) Meis**. Pol.: **Bartoszewicz**; **Bartosiak**. Russ.: **Varfolomeev**, **Varfalameev**, **Vachrameev**, **Bachrameev**, **Achrameev**, **Achromov**, **Folomeev**, **Falameev**. Lithuanian: **Baltrushaitis**.

Patrs. (from dims.): Eng.: **Barson**. It.: **Di Bartoli**. Ger.: **Bart(h)els**. Low Ger.: **Bar(e)t(z)(en)**. Du., Flem.: **Ba(e)rts**; **Bartens**; **Mees(s)en(s)**, **Meuwissen**. Russ.: **Vakhrushev**, **Vakhrushkov**, **Vakhrushin**, **Bakhrush(k)in**; **Vakh(l)ov**, **Vakh(o)nin**; **Folomin**, **Folomkin**, **Folonin**; **Cholomin**, **Chalonin**. Beloruss.: **Bartoshevich**, **Butrimovich**. Pol.: **Bartkiewicz**; **Bartłomieczak**, **Bartczak**. Croatian: **Bartolić**.

Habitation names: Pol.: **Bartoszewski**, **Bartos(z)iński**; **Bar(sz)czewski**, **Barczyński**; **Bartkowiak**.

Bartley English: habitation name from a place in Hants so called, or from *Bartley* Green in the W Midlands, both of which derive their name from OE *be(o)rc* birch + *lēah* wood, clearing; cf. BARCLAY.

Barton **1.** English: habitation name from any of the numerous places so called from OE *bere* or *bær* barley + *tūn* enclosure, settlement, i.e. an outlying grange. Cf. BARWICK. **2.** U.S.: Anglicization of Czech *Bartoň*, a form of BARTHOLOMEW.

Var. (of 1): **Barten**.

Bartram *see* BERTRAM

Baruch Jewish: from the Hebr. male given name *Baruch* 'blessed', 'fortunate'. This was borne by a disciple of Jeremiah, who is the supposed author of one of the books of the Apocrypha.

Var.: **Barukh**.

Patrs.: **Baruchso(h)n**; **Boruchson** (from Yid. *Borekh*); **Boro(k)hov**, **Borochov**, **Boru(c)hov**, **Borochovski**, **Borochowski**, **Borochovi(t)ch**, **Borochovitz**, **Borohovich** (E Ashkenazic).

Barwell English: habitation name from a place in Leics., so called from OE *bār* wild boar + *well(a)* spring, stream (see WELL).

Barwick English: habitation name from any of various places, chiefly in Norfolk, Somerset, and W Yorks., so called from OE *bere* barley + *wīc* outlying farm, i.e. a granary lying some distance away from the main village. Cf. BARTON.

Vars.: **Barrick**, **Berwick**, **Berrick**, **Borwick**.

Baryła Polish: from Pol. *baryl* barrel, applied either as a metonymic occupational name for a cooper or as a nickname for a fat man.

Var.: **Barylski** (with surname suffix *-ski*; see BARANOWSKI).

Baryshnikov Russian: patr. from the nickname *Baryshnik* 'Lucky man' (a deriv. of *barysh* profit, gain).

Basch Jewish: acronymic surname from the Hebr. patr. phrases *Ben SHelomo, SHemuel, SHimon,* or *SHimshon*. See BARISH; see also BROCK.

Bascou *see* VASCO

Bašek *see* BACH

Bäseke *see* BASIL

Bash *see* BACH

Basham English: habitation name of uncertain origin. It may be from places in Norfolk and Suffolk called *Barsham*, from the gen. case of the OE byname *Bār* 'wild boar' + OE *hām* homestead.

Vars.: **Bassham**, **Barsham**.

Bashford English (W Midlands): habitation name from one of the several places called *Basford*, esp. the one in Staffs. There are others in Ches. and Notts. All are named from a personal name + OE *ford* FORD. The first element in the Staffs. place is *Beorcol*, in the Notts. place *Basa*, and in the Ches. place probably ON *Barkr*.

Vars.: **Bas(s)ford**.

Basil English and French: from a medieval given name spelled thus, ultimately from Gk *Basileios* 'Royal', the name borne by a 4th-cent. bishop of Caesarea in Cappadocia, regarded as one of the four Fathers of the Eastern Church; he wrote important theological works and established a rule for religious orders of monks. In some cases the surname also comes from the fem. form of the given name, ME, OF *Basil(l)(i)e*. St Basilla (d. AD 304) was a Roman maiden who according to legend chose death rather than marry a pagan. Various other saints are also known under these and cogn. names; the popularity of *Vasili* as a Russ. given name is largely due to the fact that this was the Church name of St Vladimir (956–1015), Prince of Kiev, who was chiefly responsible for the introduction of Christianity to Russia.

Vars.: Eng.: **Bassil(l)**, **Bazell(e)**; **Baz(e)ley**, **Basel(e)y** (from the fem. form). Fr.: **Bazil(l)e**.

Dims.: Fr.: Bazin, **Basin**, **Basillon**. Prov.: **Barizeret**. It.: **Basilotta**; **Basezzi**; **Beggini**. Low Ger.: **Bäseke**, **Beseke**. Pol.: **Wasielczyk**. Ukr.: **Vas(s)il(ch)enko**, **Vashchenko**, **Vasilik**, **Vasilechko**. Beloruss.: **Bazylets**, **Vasilchenko**, **Vasilyonok**.

Aug.: It.: **Basilone**.

Patrs.: Russ.: **Vasilyev(ski)**, **Vasil(man)ov**. Ukr.: **Vasilevich**. Beloruss.: **Bazilev**, **Basilevich**, **Vasilevich**. Bulg.: **Vasiliev**. Croatian: **Vasil(jev)ić**, **Vasić**, **Vasović**. Pol.: **Wasi(e)lewicz**, **Wasiela**. Rum.: **Vasiescu**. Georgian: **Bassilashvili**. Armenian: **Vassilian**.

Patrs. (from dims.): Pol.: **Wasylkiewicz**. Russ.: **Vasilishchev**, **Vasil(chi)kov**, **Vasiltsov**; **Vasenkov**, **Vasi(sh)chev**, **Vasentsov**, **Vasyaev**, **Vasyukhichev**, **Vasyukhnov**, **Vasyuchov**, **Vasyukov**, **Vasyun(k)in**, **Vasyu(sh)khin**, **Vasyunichev**, **Vasyut(n)in**, **Vasyutochkin**, **Vasyutichev**; **Vaskov**, **Vasnetsov**, **Vasnev**, **Vasechkin**, **Vasenin**, **Vasyagin**, **Vasyanin**, **Vasyatkin**, **Vas(k)in**.

Habitation name: Pol.: **Wasi(e)lewski**, **Bazylewski**.

Baskerville English (Norman): habitation name from *Boscherville* in Eure, Normandy, so called from ONF *boschet* copse, thicket (a dim. of Bois) + *ville* settlement, town (see VILLE). The name is now found chiefly in Devon.

Vars.: **Baskwell**, **Baskerful**, **Baskerfield**, **Basketfield**, **Basterfield**, **Pasterfield**, **Pesterfield**.

Baskin Jewish (E Ashkenazic): metr. from the Yid. female given name *Basye*, from Hebr. *Batya* 'daughter of God'; cf. PESHIN.

Var.: **Baskind** (for the excrescent *-d*, see SÜSSKIND).

Bason see BATE

Basquet see VASCO

Bass 1. English: nickname for a short man, from ME, OF *bas(se)* low, short (L *bassus* thickset, i.e. wide as opposed to tall, itself used as a family name in the Republican period). In the later Middle Ages the word was also used metaphorically to mean 'of humble origin', but apparently without contemptuous overtones, and in some cases this may have given rise to the surname. 2. English: nickname for a person supposedly resembling a fish or metonymic occupational name for a fish-seller, from *bass* the fish, OE *bæs*. 3. Scots: habitation name from a place in the former county of Aberdeen (now part of Grampian region), apparently so called from Gael. *bathais* forehead, front. Andrew *de Bas* is

recorded as a juror in 1206. 4. Jewish (Ashkenazic): of unknown origin.

Vars.: **Ba(i)se**, **Basse**.

Dims. (of 1): Eng.: **Basset(t)**. Fr.: **Basset**, **Bassot**. It.: **Bassini**, **Bassetti**, **Bassotti**, **Bassoli**, **Bassolino**.

Aug. (of 1): It.: **Bassone**.

Patrs. (from 1): It.: **(De) Bassis**.

Bast see SEBASTIAN

Bastable English (W Midlands): of uncertain origin; possibly, as Reaney suggests, a habitation name from *Barnstaple* in Devon or *Barstable* Hall in Essex, both from OE *beard* + *stapol* post, and so meaning 'bearded post', apparently referring to a post with something resembling a beard attached to it. However, the traceable distribution of the name casts doubt on Reaney's suggestion.

Bastard English and French: nickname for an illegitimate child, ME, OF *bastard* (of uncertain origin, probably a pej. from *bast* pack saddle (L *bastum*), i.e. a child conceived on a makeshift couch rather than in the marriage bed). The surname was formerly far more common than now, when the vocab. word *bastard* has become a general term of abuse, so that many former bearers of it have changed their names.

Vars.: Fr. **(Le) Bâtard**.

Dims.: Fr.: **Bastardeau**, **Bâtardeau**; **Bastardon**.

Basterra Basque: topographic name for someone who lived by a boundary, or on the edge of a settlement or the corner of a street, from *bazter* border, edge, corner + the def. art. *-a*.

Basterrechea Spanish form of Basque **Basterretxea**: topographic name for someone who lived in a house by a boundary or on a corner, from Basque *bazter* border, edge, corner + *etxe* house + the def. art. *-a*.

Bastide Provençal: habitation name from OProv. *bastide* building (LL *bastīta*, fem. sing. or neut. pl. past part. of *bastīre* to build, of Gmc origin). The term was used in particular of a number of small fortified villages that were established in the 13th and 14th cents. and inhabited by free citizens.

Vars.: **(La) Bastie**, **(La) Bâtie**, **Labastida**.

Dim.: Prov.: **Bastidon**.

Bastow see BAIRSTOW

Bataille French: nickname for a combative person, or topographic name for someone who lived at a place remembered as the site of a military engagement, from OF *bat(t)aille* battle (a fem. noun from the LL neut. pl. *battālia* military exercises, a deriv. of *batt(u)ere* to beat, strike, probably of Gmc origin).

Vars.: **Battaille**; **Bat(t)aill(i)er** (an agent noun).

Port.: **Batalha**.

Dims.: Fr.: **Bat(t)aillon**. It.: **Batta(gl)ini**, **Battai(gl)ioli**.

Augs.: It.: **Battai(gl)ioni**.

Pejs.: Fr.: **Bat(t)aillard**.

Bâtard see BASTARD

Batch see BACH

Batchelder see BACHELOR

Bate English and Scots: **1.** from the ME given name *Bat(t)e*, a pet form of BARTHOLOMEW. **2.** metonymic occupational name for a boatman, from OE *bāt* boat; for the Northern ME retention of *-ā-*, cf. ROPER.

Vars. (of 2): **Boatte**; **Boater** (see also BOWATER); **Boatman**, **Bottman**.

Dims. (of 1): **Batey** (Northumb.); **Batie** (Scots); BEATTY.

Patrs. (from 1): **Bates**; **Bateson**, **Baitson**, **Beatson**; **Bason**.

'Servant of B. (1)': **Bateman**.

Bath English: habitation name from the town in Somerset, site of sumptuous, but in the Middle Ages ruined, Roman baths. The place is named from OE *bæð* bath. In some cases the surname may have originated as a metonymic occupational name for an attendant at a public bath house; cf. BADER 1 and BAIN 4.

Bathas *see* BALTHASAR

Bathgate Scots: habitation name from a town in W Lothian, recorded *c*.1160 as *Batchet*, and probably derived from Brittonic *bat* boar + *cēd* wood.

Var.: **Baggat**.

Bathurst English: habitation name from a place in the parish of Warbleton, Sussex, so called from the OE personal name *Bada* (a short form of the various cpd names with the first element *beadu* battle) + OE *hyrst* wooded hill (see HURST).

Bâtie *see* BASTIDE

Batisse *see* BAPTISTE

Batley English: habitation name from a place in W Yorks., so called from the OE personal name *Bata* (see BATT 2) + OE *lēah* wood, clearing.

Batram *see* BERTRAM

Batrick *see* BETTERIDGE

Batsford English: habitation name from a place in Gloucs., so called from the gen. case of the OE personal name *Bæcci* (of uncertain origin) + OE *ōra* shore, slope. In some cases it may come from the much smaller place of the same name in the parish of Warbleton, Sussex, where the first element would seem to be a personal name, *Bætel*, and the second OE *ford* FORD. There has undoubtedly been some confusion with BATTISFORD.

Batt 1. English: like BATE, a deriv. of the ME given name *Batte*, a pet form of BARTHOLOMEW. **2.** English: possibly from a ME survival of an OE personal name or byname *Bata*, of uncertain origin and meaning, but perhaps akin to *batt* cudgel and so, as a byname, given to a thickset man or a belligerent one. **3.** English: topographic name of uncertain meaning. That it is a topographic name seems clear from examples such as Walter *atte Batte* (Somerset 1327), but the term in question is in doubt. A connection has been suggested with OE *bāt* boat, but this would normally give ME *bote* in S England and *bate* in N England (cf. BATE 2). The surname is most common in Sussex. **4.** German: from a medieval given name (L *Beātus* 'Blessed'), bestowed in

honour of the apostle who was reputed to have brought Christianity to Switzerland and S Germany.

Dims. (of 1 and 2): Eng.: **Battin(g)**, **Batten**, **Bat(t)on**; **Batty(e)** (chiefly Yorks.); **Battie** (chiefly Scots); **Baty** (Northumb.); **Batcock**. (Of 4): Low Ger.: **Battmann**.

Patrs. (from 1 and 2): Eng.: **Batts**; **Batson**, **Batt(e)son**.

'Servant of B. (1 and 2)': Eng.: **Batman**, BADMAN.

Battersby English: habitation name from a place in N Yorks., so called from the gen. case of the ON personal name *Boðvarr* (composed of the elements *boð* messenger + *var* guard) + ON *býr* settlement.

Battiati *see* VATTIATO

Battigne *see* BEATON

Battisford English: habitation name from a place in Suffolk, recorded in Domesday Book as *Beteforda* and *Betesfort*, from (the gen. case of) the OE personal name *Bætti* or *Betti* (of uncertain origin) + OE *ford* FORD. See also BATSFORD.

Battle English: habitation name from a place named as having been the site of a battle, e.g. *Battle* in Sussex, site of the Battle of Hastings.

Var.: **Battell**. Cf. BATAILLE.

Battu French: **1.** nickname for a mistreated servant, from OF *battu*, past part. of *battre* to beat, strike (LL *batt(u)ere*; see BATAILLE). **2.** topographic name for someone living by a beaten track, from the same word as in 1.

Vars.: **Batu**, **Bat(t)ut**.

Baube French: nickname for someone with a speech defect, from OF *baube* stuttering, stammering (L *balbus*, itself used as a Roman family name).

Var.: **Baubier**.

Dims.: Fr.: **Baubet**, **Baubot**; **Bauberon**. Prov.: **Balbet**.

Pejs.: Fr.: **Baubault**, **Baubard**. Prov.: **Balbaud**.

Bauch German: nickname for a greedy or fat person, from Ger. *Bauch* belly, paunch (MHG *būch*, OHG *būh*).

Dim.: Ger.: **Bäuchle**, **Beuchel**.

Bauche French: topographic name for someone who lived on a patch of clay soil, or possibly denoting a house built of wattle and daub, from OF *bauche* clay (of Gaul. origin).

Dims.: **B(e)auchet**.

Baud French: **1.** from the Gmc personal name *Baldo*, a short form of the various cpd names with the first element *bald* bold. **2.** nickname for a lively person, from OF *baud* joyful, abandoned (of Gmc origin—see above—but with an altered sense).

Vars.: **Baude**, **Bault**.

Dims. (of 1): Fr.: BAUDEL, **Baud(in)et**, **Baudon**, **Baudin(ot)**; **Baudesson**, **Bod(es)son**, **Baudichon**, **Bodechon**; **Baudic** (Brittany). Prov.: **Baudou(x)**, **Baudy**. It.: **Baldin(ott)i**, **Baldelli**, **Baldetti**, **Balducci**, **Baldocci**; **Baudino**, **Baudinelli**, **Bauducc(i)o**. Eng.: **Bawcock**, **Bawcutt**, **Baucutt**; **Bowcocl**, **Bo(o)cock** (Yorks. and Lancs.); **Bowcutt**. Low Ger.: **Böldeke**,

Bö(h)lke, Ba(h)lke; Bohlje; Bo(h)lmann, Bahlmann, Bolzmann. Fris.: **Bolesma, Baack, Baake, Backe.**

Augs. (of 1): It.: **Baldoni, Baudone.**

Pejs. (of 1): It.: **Baldazzi, Baldassi, Baldacchi, Baldacco; Baudacci, Baudassi, Baudasso.**

Patr. (from 1): It.: **Di Baudi.** Sp.: **Val(a)déz.** Port.: **Valdes.** Eng.: **Balding, Bo(u)lding, Boulting.** Ger.: **Baldung, Bölting.** Low Ger.: **Bahls, Bo(h)l(en)s, Bolzen, Bo(h)lsen, Boolsen, Böhling.** Flem., Du.: **Baudts, Bouts.**

Patrs. (from 1) (dim.): Fris.: **Backen.**

Baudel French: **1.** dim. of BAUD 1. **2.** nickname for a stubborn or stupid person or occupational name for a pack driver, from OF *baudel* mule, donkey, pack animal (of uncertain origin, perhaps the same as in 1).

Vars.: **Baudeau.** (of 2 only) **Baudelier** (an agent noun).

Dims.: **Baudelot; Baudeloche, Baudeloque.**

Baudelaire French: of uncertain origin. It may be a Prov. cogn. of *Baudelier* (see BAUDEL), but more probably it is from OF *badelaire* cutlass (of unknown origin), and so a metonymic occupational name for a maker of these weapons or a nickname for a swordsman or armed robber.

Var.: **Bazelaire.**

Baudewijns *see* BALDWIN

Baudier French: from a Gmc personal name composed of the elements *bald* bold, brave + *hari, heri* army or *gar, ger* spear.

Var.: **Baudié.**

Dims.: Fr.: **Baudereau, Baud(e)ron, Baudrin.**

Baudrey *see* BALDRY

Bauer German and Jewish (Ashkenazic): status name for a peasant or nickname meaning 'neighbour, fellow citizen', from Ger. *Bauer*, MHG *(ge)būr* (OHG *gibūro*). The MHG word denoted an occupier of a *būr*, a small dwelling or building (cf. OE *būr*, mod. Eng. *bower*). This word later fell together with MHG *būwære* (OHG *būāri*), an agent noun from OHG *būan* to cultivate, later also (at first in Low Ger. dialects) to build. The Ger. surname thus had two possible senses: 'peasant' and 'neighbour, fellow citizen'. The precise meaning of the Jewish surname, which is of later formation, is unclear.

Vars.: Ger.: **Pauer** (Bavaria, Austria); **Gebühr; Baumann.** Jewish: **Bauman(n).**

Dims.: Ger.: **Bäuerle, Beuerle.**

Patrs.: Low Ger.: **Bührs, Bu(h)rs.** Du.: **Boer(man)s, Boering; Boumans.**

Baugh Welsh: nickname for a small or short man, from W *bach* little.

Baughan 1. Welsh: dim. of BAUGH, from W *bychan*, hypocoristic form of *bach* little. **2.** English: of uncertain origin. The earliest home of the surname seems to have been in Great Rollright in Oxon.; it may well be that all present-day bearers descend from a single family in this area, possibly of Welsh immigrants.

Vars.: **Baugh(e)n, Baugham, Baffin, Boffin.** (Of 1 only): VAUGHAN.

Baulch *see* BALCH

Baum 1. German: topographic name for someone who lived by a tree that was particularly noticeable in some respect, from Ger. *Baum* tree (MHG, OHG *boum*), or else a nickname for a particularly tall person. **2.** Jewish (Ashkenazic): possibly a topographic name as in 1, or an ornamental name from Ger. *Baum* tree, or a short form of any of the many ornamental surnames containing this word as a final element, for example *Feigenbaum* (see FEIGE) and *Mandelbaum* (see MANDEL).

Vars. (of 1): **Baumer(t), Bäum(l)er.**

Baumadier *see* BALME

Baumgarten German and Jewish (Ashkenazic): topographic or occupational name for someone who owned or lived by an orchard or was employed in one, from Ger. *Baumgarten* orchard, MHG *boumgarte* (a cpd of OHG *boum* tree + *garto* enclosure). There are also several villages named with this word, and so in some cases the surname may have originated as a habitation name from one of these.

Vars.: Ger.: **Baumgart(e); Baumgartner.** Jewish: **Baumgart, Baumgard; Baumgartner.**

Baun *see* BAIN

Baustian *see* SEBASTIAN

Bavel *see* BABEL

Baverel *see* BAYER

Baverstock English: habitation name from a place in Wilts., which is so called from the gen. case of the OE personal name *Babba* (of uncertain origin, possibly a nursery name) + OE *stoc* farm (see STOKE).

Bavridge *see* BEVERIDGE

Bawcock *see* BAUD

Bawdon *see* BOWDEN

Bawli *see* BABEL

Bawn *see* BAIN

Bax *see* BACK

Baxendale English (Lancs.): habitation name, probably from *Baxenden* near Accrington. This means 'bakestone valley', from OE *bæcstān* bakestone (a flat stone on which bread was baked) + *denu* valley. ME *dale* was sometimes substituted for OE *denu* in northern placenames.

Baxter *see* BAKER

Bay English and French: nickname for someone with chestnut or auburn hair, from ME, OF *bay, bai* reddish-brown (L *badius*, used originally of horses).

Var.: Fr.: **Bai.**

Dims.: Fr.: **Bayet.** Prov.: **Bayol, Bajol(et), Bayoux.**

Pej.: Fr.: BAYARD.

Patrs.: Eng.: **Bay(e)s.**

Bayard English and French: **1.** nickname for a reckless person, from ME, OF *baiard, baiart* foolhardy (the name—a deriv. of *baie* reddish-brown (see BAY)—of the magnificent but reckless horse given to Renaud by Charlemagne, according to numerous medieval romances).

2. metonymic occupational name for a carrier, from ME, OF *baiard, baiart* hand barrow, open cart (apparently a deriv. of OF *baier* to open; cf. BADAUD 2 and BADIER).

Vars.: Fr.: **Baiard**, **Bayart**, **Bajard**.

Baybutt English (Lancs.): of uncertain origin, possibly from *Baitebuk*, an occupational nickname for a goatherd, composed of the elements *baite(n)* to feed (ON *beita*, causative of *bíta* to bite) + *buk* BUCK, which is found in Lancs. in the 14th cent.

Bayer German and Jewish (Ashkenazic): regional name for someone from from *Bavaria*, Ger. *Bayern*. This region of S Germany derives its name from that of the Celt. tribe of the *Boii* who once inhabited this area as well as Bohemia (cf. BÖHM); in the 6th cent. AD they were displaced by a Gmc people, a branch of the Marcomanni, who took the name *Boioarii* or *Baiuoarii*.

Vars.: **Baier**, **Beier**, **Beyer**.

Dims.: Ger.: **Bayerle(in)**, **Beierle(in)**. Fr.: **Baverel**; **Baverey** (E France); **Baverez** (N and NE France).

Bayfield English: habitation name from a place in Norfolk, so called from the OE personal name *Bǣga* (of uncertain origin) + OE *feld* pasture, open country.

Bayford English: habitation name from a place in Herts., so called from the OE personal name *Bǣga* (cf. BAYFIELD) + OE *ford* FORD.

Bayl *see* BAILEY

Baynard *see* BANYARD

Bayne *see* BAIN

Baynes *see* BAINES

Bazelaire *see* BAUDELAIRE

Bazeley *see* BASIL

Bazin **1.** French: dim. of BASIL. **2.** French: metonymic occupational name for a maker or seller of *bombasin*, a kind of cheap cotton cloth. The word was popularly supposed to be a cpd of *bon* good + *basin*, and so lost its imagined first element, but in fact it comes whole from LL *bombacīnum*, a deriv. of Gk *bombyx* silk-(worm). **3.** Jewish: of unknown origin.

Vars. (of 1 and 2): **Bazy**. (Of 3): **Bazini**.

Dims. (of 1 and 2): **Bazinet**, **Bazenet**.

Beach *see* BEECH

Beadle English: occupational name for a medieval court official, from ME *bedele* (OE *bydel*, reinforced by OF *bedel*). The word is of Gmc origin, and akin to OE *béodan* to bid, command and OHG *bodo* messenger (see BOTHA). In the Middle Ages a beadle in England and France was a junior official of a court of justice, responsible for acting as an usher in a court, carrying the mace in processions in front of a justice, delivering official notices, making proclamations (as a sort of town crier), and so on. By Shakespeare's day a beadle was a sort of village constable, appointed by the parish to keep order.

Vars.: Eng.: **Beadel(l)**, **Be(e)dle**; **Beddall**, **Bed(d)ell**; **Biddle**, **Biddell**; **Buddle**, **Buddell**.

Patrs.: Eng.: **Beadles**, **Biddles**, **Buddles**.

Beake English (Somerset): probably a nickname for someone with a prominent nose, from ME *beke* beak of a bird (OF *bec*, LL *beccus*, of Gaul. origin). Although this word is not recorded in the transferred sense 'human nose' until Florio (1598), it was probably in colloquial use somewhat earlier. Cf. BECK 2 and BECKETT 1.

Beal English: **1.** Norman nickname for a handsome man, from OF *bel* fair, lovely (see BEAU). **2.** habitation name from places so called in Northumb. and W Yorks. The former of these (*Behil* in early records) comes from OE *bēo* bee + *hyll* HILL; the latter (*Begale* in Domesday Book) is from OE *bēag* ring (or a derived personal name **Beaga*) + *halh* nook, recess (see HALE 1).

Vars.: **Beal(l)e**, **Beel**.

Patrs. (from 1): **Beal(l)(e)s**, **Beels**, **Beal(e)son**.

Béal French: topographic name for someone who lived by a millrace, from the Lyonnaise dial. term *béal, bezale, bedale* (of Gaul. origin).

Vars.: **Bezal**, **Bezault**, **Bedal**, **Bedau**, **Betau**; **Biez**, **Bié**, **(Du) Bief**.

Beaman *see* BEEMAN

Beamish English and Irish (Norman): habitation name from *Beaumais*-sur-Dire in Calvados, Normandy, or *Beaumetz* in Somme and Pas-de-Calais; in the last *département* there are three different places of the same name, distinguished as Beaumetz-lès-Aire, Beaumetz-lès-Cambrai, and Beaumetz-lès-Loges. These are from OF *beu* fair, lovely (see BEAU) + *més* dwelling (cf. MAS). Beamish in Co. Durham is a Norman Fr. placename of the same origin, first mentioned in the 13th cent.; it is possible that a few bearers take their name from this place.

Vars.: **Beam(e)s**, **Beamiss**.

Bean **1.** English: metonymic occupational name for a grower or seller of beans, from OE *bēan* beans (a collective sing.). Occasionally it may also have been a nickname for a man regarded as of little importance. **2.** English: nickname for a pleasant person, from ME *bēne* friendly, amiable (of unknown origin, with apparently no connection with BAIN 3 or BON). **3.** Scots: Anglicized form of the Gael. personal name *Beathán*, a dim. of *be(a)tha* life.

Dim. (of 1): Du.: **Boontje**.

Patrs. (from 3): Scot.: **McBean**, **McBain**, **McBayne** (Gael. **Mac Beathain**); **McVain** (Gael. **Mac Bheathain**).

Beanland English (Yorks.): habitation name from an unidentified place named as the place where beans were grown, from OE *bēan* (see BEAN 1) + *land* land, both of which are common formative elements in Eng. placenames.

Bear English: **1.** from the ME nickname *Bere* 'Bear' (OE *bera*, which is also found as a byname), or possibly from a personal name derived from a short form of the various Gmc cpd names with this first element (cf. e.g. BERNARD). The bear has generally been regarded with a mixture of fear and amusement, due to its strength and unpredictable temper on the one hand and its clumsy gait on the other. Both these qualities are no doubt reflected in the nickname. Throughout the Middle Ages the bear was a familiar figure in popular entertainments such as bear baiting and dancing bears. **2.** habitation name, var. of BEER 1.

Dims. (of 1): Ger.: **Beerli** (Switzerland). Fr.: **Béronneau**. It.: **Barell(in)i**, **Barett(in)o**, **Barini**, **Barotti**, **Barocci**, **Barutti**, **Barucci**, **Baruzzi**, **Barusso**.

Patrs. (from 1): Low Ger.: **Ba(h)ring**, **Be(h)ring**, **Bö(h)rnsen**.

Du.: **Beers**. Dan., Norw.: **Bjørnsen**. Swed.: **Björnsson**. Jewish: **Berso(h)n**, **Berzon**.

Patrs. (from dims. of 1): Jewish (E Ashkenazic): **Berkovich**, **Berkowicz**, **Berkovitz**.

Beard English: **1.** nickname for a wearer of a beard (ME, OE *beard*). To be clean-shaven was the norm in non-Jewish communities in NW Europe from the 12th to the 16th cent., the crucial period for surname formation. There is placename and other evidence that this word was used as a byname in the OE period, when beards were the norm; in this period the byname would have referred to a large or noticeable beard. **2.** habitation name from a place in Derbys., which derives its name by dissimilation from OE *brerd* brim, bank.

Patrs. (from 1): **Beards** (W Midlands).

Beardmore English: apparently a habitation name from some lost place (probably in Staffs., where the surname is overwhelmingly common), so called from the OE byname *Beard* BEARD' + OE *mōr* marsh, fen (see MOORE 1). A less plausible possibility is that it originally referred to a relative (see MAW 2) of someone with the byname *Beard*.

Var.: **Bearsmore**.

Beardsley English: habitation name, from an unidentified place (probably in Notts., where the surname is overwhelmingly common), apparently so called from the gen. case of the OE byname *Beard* BEARD' + OE *lēah* wood, clearing.

Beardsworth English (Lancs.): habitation name, from *Beardsworth*, the former name of *Beardwood* in Lancs., which was so called from the gen. case of the OE byname *Beard* BEARD' + OE *worð* homestead (see WORTH).

Var.: **Beardwood** (from the later name of the same place).

Beardwell *see* BARDWELL

Beare *see* BEER

Bearman English: occupational name for a keeper of a dancing bear or one who kept bears for baiting; see BEAR 1. See also BERMAN 1.

Beasley English: habitation name from *Beesley* in Lancs., perhaps a cpd of OE *bēos* bent grass + OE *lēah* wood, clearing. The name is now common in the W Midlands and elsewhere, as well as in Lancs.

Vars.: **Beazley**, **Beesley**, **Beazleigh**, **Beisley**.

Beaston *see* BEESTON

Beaton English and Scots: **1.** Norman habitation name from *Béthune* in Pas-de-Calais, Picardy, recorded in the 8th cent. in the L form *Bitunia*, probably an adj. (with *villa* understood; see VILLE) derived from the oblique form of a Gmc personal name *Betto*, a hypocoristic formation (cf. BETTENCOURT). **2.** from the medieval given name *Be(a)ton*, apparently a dim. from a short form of BÉATRICE and (in Scotland) of BARTHOLOMEW.

Vars.: **Beeton**, **Beaten**, **Betton**. (Of 1 only): **Batti(g)ne** (the name of an ancient Hants and Sussex family).

Béatrice French: from a medieval female given name borne in honour of a 4th-cent. saint, martyred together with her brothers Simplicius and Faustinus. Her name was originally *Viātrix* 'Traveller' (a fem. form of *viātor*, from *via* way; the name was adopted by early Christians in reference to the journey through life, and Christ's description of Himself as 'the way, the life, and the truth'); it was later altered as a result of folk etymological association with L *bēatus* blessed.

Vars.: **Béatrix**, **Biétrix**.

Dims.: Fr.: **Biétron**, **Beltrine**. Eng.: BEATON.

Metrs. (from dims.): Flem.: **Behets**, **Baeten**.

Beatson *see* BATE

Beatty **1.** Scots and N Irish: from the given name *B(e)atie*, a dim. from a short form of BARTHOLOMEW; cf. BATE 1. **2.** Irish: Anglicized form of the Gael. occupational term *biadhtach* hospitaller; cf. McVITIE.

Vars. (of 1): **Beattey**, **Beat(e)y**, **Beattie**.

Beau French: nickname for a handsome man (perhaps also ironically for an ugly one), from OF *beu*, *bel* fair, lovely (LL *bellus*). Fr. and It. forms such as *Labelle* and *La Bella* were in part ironical nicknames for an effeminate man. Without the article, they are more likely to represent a metronymic; the fem. form of the adj. was in common use as a medieval female given name.

Vars.: **Lebeau**, **(Le) Bel**, **Lebbel(l)**; **Labelle**; **Belle**.

Dims.: Fr.: **Bel(l)et**, **Bel(l)on**, **Bel(l)ot**, **Beluchot**. It.: **Bellini**, **Bellino**, **Bellel(l)i**, **Bellett(in)i**, **Bellotti**, **Bellozzi**, **Bellocci**, **Bellutti**, **Belluzzi**, **Bellucci(o)**, **Belloli**. Cat.: **Belló**.

Augs.: Fr.: **Bellat**. It.: **Belloni**.

Pejs.: It.: **Bellacci**, **Bellazzi**.

Patrs.: Fr.: **Aubel**. Eng.: **Bewson**. It.: **Di Bello**, **Del Bello**, **De Bei**, **De Belli(s)**; **Belleschi**, **Belluschi**.

Patr. (from a dim.): Flem.: **Belleken**.

Metr.: It.: **Della Bella**.

Beauchamp English (Norman) and French: habitation name from any of several places in France, for example in the *départements* of Manche and Somme, that get their names from OF *beu*, *bel* fair, lovely (see BEAU) + *champ(s)* field, plain (see CHAMP). In Eng. the surname is generally pronounced /'bi:tʃəm/.

Vars.: Eng.: **Beacham(p)**, **Beecham**; **Beacom** (N Irish); **Belchamp**, BELCHEM.

Beauclerk English (Norman): nickname meaning 'fair clerk', used either of a handsome priest or of one who wrote with a fair hand, from OF *beu*, *bel* fair, lovely (see BEAU) + *clerc* clerk, cleric (see CLARK).

Beaufort English (Norman) and French: habitation name from various places in France, for example in the *départements* of Nord, Somme, and Pas-de-Calais, so called from OF *beu*, *bel* fair, lovely (see BEAU) + *fort* fortress, stronghold (see FORT 1).

Var.: **Belfort**.

Beaulieu French: habitation name from any of the extremely numerous places in France named from OF *beu, bel* fair, lovely (see BEAU) + *lieu* place, location (L *locus*). The name is occasionally also found in England; it is then either a Norman name from one of the French places just mentioned or derives from an English placename of the same origin, *Beaulieu* (pronounced /'bju:lɪ/) in Hants, seat of the Montagu family.

Var.: **Beaulieux**.

Beauman *see* BOWMAN

Beaumarchais French: habitation name from any of several places named from OF *beu, bel* fair, lovely (see BEAU) + *marchais* marsh, swamp (a word of Gaul. origin). This is the name of several villages in N France, for example in the parishes of Pleudihen (Côtes-du-Nord), Cintray (Eure), Cloyes (Eure-et-Loir), Autrèche (Indre-et-Loire), Othis (Seine-et-Marne), and Bretignolles (Vendée).

Vars.: **Beaumarchaix**, **Beaumarcheix**.

Beaumont 1. English (Norman) and French: habitation name from any of the five places in Normandy or several others elsewhere in France so named. The placename comes from OF *beu, bel* fair, lovely (see BEAU) + *mont* hill (see MONT). There are also places in England so named under Norman influence (in Cumb., Lancs., and Essex, the last of which changed its name in the 11th cent. from *Fulepet* 'foul pit' to *Bealmont* 'beautiful hill'); these may also have given rise to surnames. The surname is now widespread throughout England, but most common in Yorks. 2. Welsh: Anglicized form of a patr. from the given name EDMOND.

Vars. (of 1): Eng.: **Beamont**, **Beamond**, **Bea(u)ment**, **Bea(u)mant**, **Beamand**, **Bem(m)and**; **Beauman**, BEEMAN; **Belmont**.

Beauregard French: 1. habitation name from any of various places, for example in Ain, Dordogne, Drôme, Lot, and Puy-de-Dôme, so called from OF *beu, bel* fair, lovely (see BEAU) + *regard* aspect, outlook (a deriv. of *regarder* to look at, watch, from *g(u)arder* to watch, guard; see WARD 1), with reference to their handsome site; cf. BEAVER 1. 2. nickname for someone of a pleasant appearance, from the same elements as above.

Beaurepaire French: habitation name from any of various places, for example in Isère, Nord, Oise, Saône-et-Loire, Seine-Maritime, and Vendée, so called from OF *beu, bel* fair, lovely (see BEAU) + *repaire* retreat (a deriv. of *repair(i)er* to retreat, LL *repatriāre* return to one's country, from *patria* native land).

Beaushaw *see* BELCHER

Beausire *see* BOWSER

Beaver English: 1. Norman habitation name from any of several places in France called *Beauvoir*, for example in Manche, Somme, and Seine-Maritime, or from *Belvoir* in Leics. All of these get their names from OF *beu, bel* fair, lovely (see BEAU) + *veïr, voir* to see (L *vidēre*), i.e. a place with a fine view. 2. nickname from ME *bevere*, OE

beofor beaver, possibly referring to a hard worker, or from some other fancied resemblance to the animal.

Vars.: **Beever(s)** (Yorks.); **Biever**, **Be(e)vor**, **Bevar**, **Bevir**. (Of 1 only): **Belvoir**; **Belvedere**.

Beavin *see* BEVIN

Beavis English (Norman): 1. nickname from OF *bel fi(l)z*, a term of affectionate address, from *beu, bel* fair, lovely (see BEAU) + *filz, fi(t)z* son (L *filius*). The mod. Fr. sense 'son-in-law' is not attested before 1468, and only gradually ousted *filiâtre* (LL *filiaster*), so that it is not likely that this sense lies behind any examples of the surname. 2. habitation name from *Beauvais* in Oise (which derives its name from that of the Gaul. tribe recorded in L sources as the *Bellovaci*), or from various other places in N France called *Beauvois* (LL *bellum visum* lovely sight; cf. BEAVER 1).

Vars.: **Be(a)ves**, **Be(e)vis(s)**, **Bovis**.

Bebbington English: habitation name from *Bebington* in Ches., so called from OE *Bebbingtūn* 'settlement (OE *tūn*) associated with Bebbe', a personal name borne by both men and women and of uncertain origin, perhaps a nursery word.

Bécard *see* BECK

Becerra Spanish: nickname, probably for a high-spirited individual, from Sp. *becerra* young cow, heifer (of uncertain origin, perhaps akin to L *ibex*, gen. *ibicis*, chamois, mountain goat, an equally high-spirited creature). It may also have been a metonymic occupational name for a cowherd.

Vars.: **Becerro**; **Becerril** (an adj. deriv.).

Becher 1. German: metonymic occupational name for a turner of wooden vessels, from Ger. *Becher* cup, mug (MHG *becher*, OHG *behhari*, L *bicārium*, from Gk *bikos* pot, pitcher). 2. German: occupational name for someone who worked with pitch, for example in making vessels watertight, from an agent deriv. of MHG *bech, pech* pitch (cf. PECHER 1). 3. Jewish (Ashkenazic): of uncertain origin, perhaps derived as in 1 or 2 above. 4. English: topographic name, var. of BEECH.

Becherini *see* BUTCHER

Bechor Jewish (Sefardic): from the Judezmo male given name *Bexor* (from Hebr. *Bechor* 'First-born'), given to a first-born son. The Jewish surnames **Bechar** and **Behar** may be related to *Bechor*, but this is not certain.

Bechstein German: probably a topographic name for someone who lived near an outcrop of pitchstone, a smooth shiny black type of quartz, MHG *pechstein*.

Var.: **Pechstein**.

Bechtloff *see* BERTOLF

Bechtold *see* BERTHOLD

Beck 1. English: topographic name for someone who lived beside a stream, from Northern ME *bekke* stream (ON *bekkr*). 2. English (Norman): habitation name from any of the various places in N France, for example *Bec Hellouin* in Eure, which get their name from ONF *bec*, from the same ON root as in 1. 3. English: var. of BEAKE. 4. English: metonymic occupational name for a maker, seller, or user of a mattock or pickaxe, OE *becca*. In some cases the name may represent a survival of an OE byname derived from this word; cf. BECKFORD and BECKHAM. **5.** German and Jewish (Ashkenazic): occupational surname, cogn. of BAKER, from Ger. dial. *Beck*, W Yid. *bek*, both meaning 'baker'. Some Jewish bearers of the name claim that it is an acronym of Hebr. *ben-kedoshim* 'son of martyrs', i.e. a name taken by one whose parents had been martyred for being Jews. **6.** Low German: cogn. of BACH.

Vars. (of 1): **Becke, Beckman.** (Of 5): Ger.: **Becke, Baeck; Böck** (Bavaria); **Beckmann.** Jewish: BEK, **Be(c)kman.**

Dims. (of 3): Eng.: BECKETT. Fr.: **Béchet, Bécher(eau), Bécherel(le); Becquet, Béquet, Becquereau, Becquerel; Béchillon; Becquelin.**

Pejs. (of 3): Fr.: **Béc(h)ard.**

Patr. (from 3): Eng.: **Bexon** (Notts.).

Cpds (ornamental, from a cogn. 1): Swed.: **Bäcklund** ('stream grove'); **Bäckström** ('stream river', a tautological formation).

Becken *see* BACH

Beckers *see* BAKER

Beckett English: **1.** dim. of BECK 3 or, more rarely, of BECK 1. **2.** habitation name from places so called in Berks. and Devon; the former is named from OE *bēo* bee + *cot* cottage, shelter (see COATES); the latter has as its first element the OE personal name *Bicca* (apparently from *becca* pickaxe, mattock; see BECK 4).

Var.: **Becket.**

Beckford English: habitation name from a place in Gloucs., so called from the OE byname *Becca* (see BECK 4) + OE *ford* FORD.

Beckham English: habitation name from a place in Norfolk, so called from the OE byname *Becca* (see BECK 4) + OE *hām* homestead.

Beckles English: habitation name from *Beccles* in Norfolk, which Ekwall derives from OE *bec(e)*, *bæce* stream + *lǣs* meadow.

Beckley English: habitation name from any of the various places, in Kent, Oxon., and Sussex, so called from the OE byname *Becca* (see BECK 4) + OE *lēah* wood, clearing.

Beckwith English: habitation name from a place in W Yorks., so called from OE *bēc(e)* BEECH + ON *viðr* WOOD (replacing the cogn. OE *widu*, *wudu*).

Bedal *see* BÉAL

Beddall *see* BEADLE

Beddard *see* EDWARD

Beddow Welsh: from the personal name *Bedo*, a dim. form of *Meredydd*; see MEREDITH.

Vars.: **Beddoe, Bedo; Eddow** (a back-formation, as if from a patr. with the prefix *ap*).

Patrs.: **Beddow(e)s, Beddoes, Beddis, Eddowes, Edess.**

Bede *see* BENNETT

Beder *see* BADER

Bedford English: habitation name from the county town of Beds., or a smaller place of the same name in Lancs.

Both are so called from the OE personal name *Bēda* (apparently a deriv. of *bēd* prayer) + OE *ford* FORD. The name is now very common in Yorks. as well as Beds.

Bedingfeld English: habitation name from a place in Suffolk, so called from OE *Bēdingafeld* FIELD of the people of *Bēda*' (cf. BEDFORD).

Bedmond *see* EDMOND

Bednarz Polish and Jewish (E Ashkenazic): occupational name for a cooper, Pol. *bednarz*.

Vars.: **Bednarski** (with surname suffix -*ski*; see BARANOWSKI); **Bednarsh** (U.S.). Jewish: **Bednarsky.**

Dims.: Pol.: **Bednarek, Bednarczyk.** Czech: **Bednařík.**

Patr.: Pol.: **Bednarowicz.**

Bednyakov Russian: patr. from the nickname *Bednyak* 'Pauper' (a deriv. of *bedny* poor).

Bedrosian *see* PETER

Bedwell English: habitation name from any of various minor places, e.g. in Herts., named with the OE elements *byde(n)* tub + *well(a)* spring, stream (see WELL).

Vars.: **Bid(d)well** (from *Bidwell* in Herts.); **Bidewell.**

Bedwinek Polish: dim. of Pol. *bedwin* pedlar, a borrowing via Ger. of OF *beduin* wanderer, nomad (a word picked up by Crusaders from Arabic *badāwi* (sing. *badwi*) Bedouins, desert dwellers, a deriv. of *badw* desert).

Bedworth English (W Midlands): habitation name from a place in Warwicks., so called from the OE personal name *Bēda* (cf. BEDFORD) + OE *worð* homestead (see WORTH).

Bee English: probably a nickname for an energetic or active person, from the insect, ME *be*, OE *bēo*, which has long been taken as the type of a busy worker. Cf. BEEMAN 2.

Beeby English: habitation name from a place in Leics., so called from OE *bēo* bee + ON *býr* settlement, village.

Beech English: **1.** topographic name for someone who lived by a stream, ME *beche* (OE *bece*, a byform of *bæce*; cf. BACH 1). **2.** topographic name for someone who lived by a beech tree or beech wood, from ME *beche* beech tree (OE *bēce*). For Continental cogns., see at BUCH and BUKOWSKI.

Vars.: **Beach, Beecher,** BECHER, **Beech(a)man.**

Beecham *see* BEAUCHAMP

Beechey English: habitation name from some minor place named as an enclosure by a beech wood, from ME *beche* beech (see BEECH 2) + *heie, haie* enclosure (see HAY 1).

Beeck *see* BACH

Beecroft English: habitation name from some minor place named as the place where bees were kept, from OE *bēo* bee + *croft* paddock, smallholding.

Beedle *see* BEADLE

Beel *see* BEAL

Beeman English: **1.** var. of BEAUMONT. **2.** occupational name for a beekeeper, from OE *bēo* bee + *mann* man.

Vars.: **Be(a)man.**

Beentjes see BENNETT

Beer 1. English (W Country): habitation name from any of the forty or so places in SW England called *Beer(e)* and *Bear(e)*. Most of these derive their names from the W Saxon dat. case, *beara*, of OE *bearu* grove, wood (the standard OE dat. *bearwe* being preserved in BARROW). Some may be from OE *bēr* swine pasture. **2.** Low German: cogn. of BEAR.
Vars. (of 1): **Be(e)re**, **Beare**, BEAR; **Abear(e)** (with fusion of the preposition *at*).

Beerli see BEAR

Beesley see BEASLEY

Beeston English: habitation name from any of the various places so called. Most of them, for example those in Beds., Norfolk, Notts., and W Yorks., get the name from OE *bēos* rough grass + *tūn* enclosure, settlement. However, the one in Ches. probably gets it from OE *byge* trade, commerce + *stān* stone, meaning 'rock where a market was held'. A few other *Beestons* have different derivations.
Var.: **Beaston**.

Beetham English: habitation name from a place in Cumbria (formerly N Lancs.), recorded in Domesday Book as *Biedun*, the origin of which, according to Ekwall, is the dat. pl. of ON *bióðr* table, in the transferred sense 'flat land'. The surname is still most common in Lancs.
Var.: **Betham**.

Beethoven Low German, Flemish, and Dutch: habitation name from some minor place named as the yard used for the cultivation of root crops, from MLG, MDu. *bete* beet + *hoven* dat. pl. (originally used after a preposition such as *van* of) of MLG, MDu. *hov* yard, court (cf. HOFER).

Beeton see BEATON

Beever see BEAVER

Beevis see BEAVIS

Bégard see BÈGUE

Begg Scots and N Irish: nickname or byname for a small man, from Gael. *beag* small.
Var.: BIGG.
Patrs.: **Beggs** (chiefly N Irish), **Biggs**.
'Descendant of the small man': Ir.: **Beggan**, **Beggin** (Gael. *Ó Beagáin*).

Beggini see BASIL

Begley Irish: Anglicized form of Gael. **Ó Beaglaoich** 'descendant of *Beaglaoch*', a personal name composed of the elements *beag* small + *laoch* hero.

Begnudelli see BENVENUTI

Bègue French: nickname for someone afflicted with a stammer, a deriv. of OF *beguer* to stammer (from MLG *beggen* to chatter). In the 12th cent. in Liège a priest called *Lambert le Begue* (Lambert the Stammerer) founded a Christian sisterhood whose members followed an austere rule of life; they came to be known as the *Béguines*. A century later an order of lay brothers modelled on this sisterhood was founded in Flanders, called the *Beghards*. Both

these orders have contributed to the Fr. vars. of this surname, doubtless as a result of some fancied resemblance to the religious, rather than by way of direct descent.
Vars.: **Lebègue**; **Bég(o)uin**, **Bégin**, **Béguen**; **Bég(h)ard** (pej. in form, though not necessarily in meaning).
Dims.: Fr.: **Bégon**, **Béguet**, **Bégot**.

Behaim see BÖHM

Behan Irish: Anglicized form of Gael. **Ó Beachain** 'descendant of *Beachán*', a personal name from a dim. of *beach* bee.

Behenna Cornish: of unknown origin. It is first found, in the form *Behennow*, in 1525.

Behets see BÉATRICE

Behn see BENNETT

Behrends see BERNARD

Behring see BEAR

Behrman see BERMANN

Beier see BAYER

Beilin Jewish (E Ashkenazic): metr. from the Yid. female given name *Beyle* (from the Czech given name *Běla*, which a blend of Czech *běl* white (cf. Pol. BIAŁAS) and L or It. *bella* beautiful), with the Slav. suffix *-in*.
Vars.: **Belin**, **Bailin** (E Ashkenazic); **Beiles**, **Beilis(s)** (Ashkenazic, with the Yid. possessive *-s* ending); **Beli(n)son** (Ashkenazic).

Beillard see BÉLIER

Beimbrinke see BRINK

Bein see BENNETT

Beirne see BYRNE

Beisley see BEASLEY

Bejarano Spanish and Jewish (Sefardic): habitation name for someone from the town of *Béjar* in the province of Salamanca. The placename is of pre-Roman origin and unknown meaning; the original form seems to have been *Bigerra*.
Vars.: Jewish: **Bejerano**, **Bidjerano**.

Bek 1. Polish: nickname for a stupid person or one with a bleating voice, from Pol. *bek* baa. **2.** Jewish (Ashkenazic): generally a var. of BECK 5, but in some cases the derivation may be the same as that of the Pol. name in 1 above. **3.** Danish: var. of *Bekker*; see BECHER.

Bekman see BECK

Bel see BEAU

Belch see BALCH

Belchamp see BEAUCHAMP

Belchem English: **1.** var. of BEAUCHAMP. **2.** habitation name from a group of villages in Essex now called *Belchamp*. This name has been altered so that it appears to be derived from OF *bel* fair, lovely (see BEAU) + *champ(s)* field (see CHAMP), but in fact the ME name was *Balc-ham*, from OE *bælc, balca* roof beam + *hām* homestead, i.e. homestead with a prominent roof beam.

Vars.: **Belcham**, **Bel(l)sham**.

Belcher English: **1.** (Norman) nickname from OF *beu, bel* fair, lovely + *chere* face, countenance (LL *cara*, from Gk *kara* head). Although it originally meant 'face', the word *chere* later came to mean also 'demeanour', 'disposition' (hence Eng. *cheer*), and the nickname may thus also have denoted a person of pleasant, cheerful disposition. There has been some confusion with BOWSER. **2.** var. of BALCH.

Vars. (of 1): **Belshaw**, **Be(a)ushaw**, **Bewshaw**, **Bewshea**, **Beuscher**, **Beushire**, **Bowsher**.

Belenger *see* BERINGER

Belfort *see* BEAUFORT

Belgrave English: habitation name from a place in Leics., recorded in Domesday Book as *Merdegrave*. The original name derived from OE *mearð* marten + *grāf* grove, but after the Norman Conquest the first element was taken to be OF *merde* dung, filth (L *merda*), and changed to OF *beu, bel* fair, lovely, to remove the unpleasant association. A mid-12th-cent. writer refers to the place as *Merthegrave, nunc* (now) *Belegrava*.

Belham English (Norman): nickname from OF *beu, bel* fair, lovely (see BEAU) + *homme* man (L *homo*).

Vars.: **Bell(h)am**.

Belić *see* BIAŁAS

Bélier French: nickname from OF *belier* ram (MDu. *belhamel* belled sheep, i.e. the leader of the flock). The nickname no doubt refers in many cases to sexual prowess, but since *belier* also means 'battering ram', it may sometimes have been applied to a man of powerful build.

Dims.: **Béliot**, **Belin**, **Belisson**.

Pejs.: **Béliard**, **Beillard**.

Belin *see* BEILIN

Belkin **1.** Russian: patr. from the nickname *Belka* 'Squirrel' (a deriv. of *bely* white, referring to the animal's white stomach). **2.** Jewish (E Ashkenazic): metr. from *Beylke*, pet form of the Yid. female given name *Beyle* (see BEILIN), with the Slav. suffix *-in*. In some cases the Jewish name may have the same derivation as the Russian name in 1 above.

Vars.: (of 2): **Belkind** (for the excrescent *-d*, see SÜSSKIND); **Belkis** (with the Yid. possessive ending *-s*).

Bell **1.** English: from the ME, OE vocab. word *belle* bell, in various applications; most probably a metonymic occupational name for a bellringer or bellfounder, or a habitation name for someone living 'at the bell' (as attested by 14th-cent. forms such as *John atte Belle*). This indicates either residence by an actual bell (e.g. a town's bell in a belltower, centrally placed to summon meetings, sound the alarm, etc.) or 'at the sign of the bell', i.e. a house or inn sign. However, surnames derived from house and inn signs are rare in English. **2.** English and Scots: from the medieval given name *Bel*. As a man's name this is from OF *beu, bel* handsome (see BEAU), which was also used as a nickname. As a female name it represents a short form of *Isobel*, a form of *Elizabeth*. **3.** Scots: Anglicized form of Gael. **Mac**

Giolla Mhaoil 'son of the servant of the devotee'; see MULLEN 1. **4.** Jewish (Ashkenazic): Anglicization of one or more like-sounding Jewish surnames.

Vars. (of 1): **Beller**, **Bel(l)man**. (Of 3): **(Mc)Gilveil**.

Bellam *see* BELHAM

Bellamy Irish (Norman) and French: literal or ironic nickname meaning 'fine friend', from OF *beu, bel* fair, handsome (see BEAU) + *ami* friend (L *amīcus*).

Var.: Fr.: **Belami**.

Bellay French: habitation name from any of the numerous places that derive their names from LL *betullētum* birch grove (a deriv. of *betullus* birch; see BOUL).

Vars.: **Du Bellay**, **Belloy**.

Bellew English (Norman): habitation name from any of the various places in N France named with the OF elements *beu, bel* lovely (see BEAU) + *ewe* water (L *aqua*).

Bellhouse English: habitation name for someone who lived by a belltower; see BELL 1. The surname is largely confined to Yorks.

Var.: **Bellas**.

Bellido Spanish: nickname for a handsome person, from Sp. *bellido* beautiful, handsome (LL *bellitus*, perhaps the result of a cross between *bellus* (see BEAU) and the term of endearment *mellitus* 'honey'). Bellido was also used in the Middle Ages as a given name, and this may lie behind some examples of the surname.

Bellingham English: habitation name from places in Kent and Northumb. The former is so called from OE *Beringhām* 'homestead (OE *hām*) associated with *Be(o)ra*', a byname meaning BEAR'; the latter seems to have been originally named as the 'homestead of the dwellers at the bell', from OE *belle* used in a transferred sense of a bell-shaped hill.

Bellis *see* ELLIS

Bellsyer *see* BOWSER

Bellwood English: apparently a habitation name from a place named with OE *wudu* WOOD as second element. This may be *Belwood* in Lincs. (of which the first element is obscure), but the surname is most common in Yorks. and identification cannot be made with any certainty.

Belmont *see* BEAUMONT

Belton **1.** English: habitation name from any of various places so called, for example in Leics., Lincs., and Suffolk. The first element, *bel*, is of uncertain origin; the second is OE *tūn* enclosure, settlement. **2.** Irish: see WELDON.

Beltramelli *see* BERTRAM

Beltrine *see* BÉATRICE

Belvedere *see* BEAVER

Beman *see* BEEMAN

Bemand *see* BEAUMONT

Ben-Aharon *see* AARON

Ben-Amos *see* AMOS

Benard *see* BERNARD

Benavente Spanish: habitation name from places in the provinces of Badajoz, Huesca, and Zamora, so called from L *Beneventum*. The L placename seems to mean 'welcome' (from *bene* well + *ventum*, past part. of *venīre* to come), but this is probably a folk etymological distortion of an earlier name.

Benavides Spanish: patr. from the common medieval given name *Ben Avid*, of Arabic origin, from *ibn Abd* 'son of the servant (of God)'.

Benbow English: occupational nickname for an archer, from ME *bend(en)* to bend (OE *bendan*) + *bowe* bow (OE *boga*).

Bench English (W Midlands): of uncertain origin. It is perhaps a topographic name for someone who lived by a bank or raised piece of ground, ME *benche* (from OE *benc* bench). However, this transferred sense of the word is not well attested, and some other sense of the word may be in question; perhaps one who sat on a bench in a hall, i.e. a retainer.

Bencroft *see* BANCROFT

Ben-Dayan *see* DAYAN

Bendy *see* PARRY

Benedict *see* BENNETT

Benfield *see* BANFIELD

Benger *see* BERINGER

Bengoa Basque: topographic name for someone who lived at the lower end of a village, from *be(e)ngo* furthest down + the def. art. *-a*.

Bengoechea Spanish form of Basque **Bengoetxea**: habitation name from a house situated at the lower end of a village, from *be(e)ngo* furthest down + *etxe* house + the def. art. *-a*.

Benham 1. English: habitation name from a group of villages in Berks., so called from the OE personal name **Benna* (of uncertain origin) + OE *hamm* river-meadow. 2. Scots: habitation name from *Benholm* in the former county of Angus (now part of Tayside region) in which the final element is Northern ME *holm* island, dry land in a fen (see HOLME).

Benjamin Jewish, English, and French: from the Hebr. male given name *Binyamin* 'Son of the South'. In the Book of Genesis, it is treated as meaning 'Son of the Right Hand'. The two senses are connected, since in Hebr. the south is thought of as the right-hand side of a person who is facing east. Benjamin was the youngest and favourite son of Jacob and supposed progenitor of one of the twelve tribes of Israel (Gen. 35: 16–18; 42: 4). It is also a rare Eng. and Fr. surname, for although the given name was not common among Gentiles in the Middle Ages, its use was sanctioned by virtue of having been borne by a saint martyred in Persia in about AD 424. In some cases in medieval Europe it was also applied as a byname or nickname to the youngest

(and beloved) son of a large family; this is the sense of the mod. Fr. vocab. word *benjamin*.

Vars.: Jewish: **Benyamin**, **Binyamin**; **Benjamini**, **Benjaminy**, **Benyamini**, **Binyamini**, **Biniamini** (Israeli, with the Hebr. ending *-i*).

Dims.: Fr.: (aphetic); **Jaminet**, **Jaminot**.

Patrs.: Jewish: **Benjaminov**, **Benjaminowitsch**, **Benyaminov**, **Binyaminov(ich)**, **Biniaminovitz**. Beloruss.: **Benyaminov**. Du.: **Benjamins**, **Benjamens**.

Patrs. (from the Russ. dim. *Velya*): Russ.: **Velyashev**, **Velyushin**, **Velekhov**, **Velikhov**, **Velyugin**.

Benn English (chiefly Yorks.): from the ME given name *Benne*, which is in part a short form of *Benedict* (see BENNETT), in part a form of the ON personal name *Bjorn* 'Bearcub, Warrior'.

Dims.: **Benney** (Devon and Cornwall); **Bennie** (Scots).

Patrs.: **Benn(i)s**, BENSON.

Patr. (from a dim.): Sc.: **Benzies** (pronounced /'bɛnjtz/).

Bennett English: from the medieval given name *Benedict* (L *Benedictus* 'Blessed'). This owed its popularity in the Middle Ages chiefly to St Benedict (*c*.480–550), who founded the Benedictine order of monks at Monte Cassino and wrote a monastic rule that formed a model for all subsequent rules. No doubt the meaning of the L word also contributed to its popularity as a given name, especially in Romance countries. In the 12th cent. the L form of the name is found in England alongside versions derived from the OF form *Beneit*, *Benoit*, which was common among the Normans.

Vars.: **Bennet**; **Benedict**, **Ben(ne)dick** (Sc.).

Dims.: Eng.: BENN. Corn.: **Bennetto**. Fr.: **Beneteau**, **Benoîton**. It.: **Bene(de)ttini**, **Benet(t)elli**, **Benet(t)ollo**, **Benini**. Ger.: **Ben(t)z** (see also **Berthold**). Low Ger.: **Bente**, **Benn(e)**, **Behn(e)**, **Bein(e)**, **Beyn(e)**; **Behn(e)(c)ke**, **Bein(c)ke**, **Beynke**, **Benck**. Fris.: **Be(n)tje**, **Be(n)tke**. Du.: **Betjeman**. Dan.: **Bennike**. Czech: **Bendík**. Pol.: **Banasik**, **Banaszczyk**. Lithuanian: **Benduhn**. Hung.: **Bede**, **Benkö**.

Patrs.: Eng.: **Bennet(t)s** (chiefly Devon and Cornwall). It.: **De Benedetti**; **De Benedictis**, **De Benedetti** (S Italy). Sp.: **Benítez**. Flem., Du.: BENTINCK. Low Ger.: **Bendix(en)**, **Bentsen**, **Bentzen**. Norw., Dan.: **Ben(g)tsen**, **Bend(t)sen**, **Bennedsen**, **Bentzen**, **Ben(g)tson**. Swed.: **Benediktsson**, **Bengtsson**. Russ.: **Venediktov**, **Vedeniktov**, **Vedentyev**, **Vedenisov**, **Vedeneev**, **Videneev**, **Vidineev** (metathesized versions, in part associated by folk etymology with Russ. *videt* to see). Beloruss.: **Benediktovich**. Pol.: **Benedyktowicz**. Jewish (E Ashkenazic): **Beinosovitch**.

Patrs. (from dims.): Sp.: **Benítez**. Low Ger.: **Benes**, **Bennen**; **Behn(e)(c)ken**, **Bein(c)ken**, **Beynken**. Fris.: **Be(n)tje(n)s**. Du.: **Beentjes**, **Bennink**. Pol.: **Banaszkiewicz**; **Banasiak**. Jewish (E Ashkenazic): **Banishevitz**. Russ.: **Vedeshkin**, **Vedyashkin**, **Vedekhov**, **Vedikhov**, **Vedekhin**, **Vedyaev**, **Vedyasov**, **Vedishchev**, **Vedenyakin**, **Vedenyapin**, **Vidyapin**, **Vedenichev**. Beloruss.: **Beneshevich**, **Banasevich**.

Habitation name (from a dim.): Pol.: **Banaszewski**.

Ben-Sasson *see* SASON

Benson 1. English: patr. from the medieval given name *Benne* (see BENN). 2. English: habitation name from a place in Oxon., so called from OE *Benesingtūn* 'settlement (OE *tūn*) associated with *Banesa*', a personal name of obscure origin, perhaps a deriv. of *Bana* 'slayer'. 3. Jewish (E Ashkenazic): shortened form of **Besenson**, which is of uncertain origin.

Var.: **Benn(i)son**.

Benstead English: habitation name from any of various places, such as *Banstead* in Surrey (*Benestede* in Domesday Book), named with the OE elements *bēan* beans (a collective sing.) + *stede* place.

Var.: **Bensted**.

Bent English: topographic name for someone who lived on a patch of land with bent grass, rushes, or reeds (OE *beonet*, a collective sing.) growing on it.

Bentele *see* PANTALEONE

Benthall English: habitation name from a place in Shrops., so called from OE *beonet* bent grass + *halh* nook, recess (see HALE 1).

Vars.: **Bentall**, **Bendall**, **Bendell**, **Bendle**.

Bentham English: habitation name from any of various places, for example in W Yorks., so called from OE *beonet* bent grass (see BENT) + *hām* homestead.

Bentinck English and Dutch: patr. (formed with the Gmc suffix *-ing*) from the Du. given name *Bent*, a contracted form of *Benedict* (cf. BENNETT).

Var.: **Benting**.

Bentley English: habitation name from any of various places, the chief of which are in Derbys., Essex, Hants, Shrops., Staffs., Suffolk, Warwicks., Worcs., and E and W Yorks., so called from OE *beonet* bent grass (see BENT) + *lēah* wood, clearing.

Benton English: habitation name, apparently from a pair of villages in Northumb., so called from OE *bēan* beans (a collective sing.) or *beonet* bent grass (see BENT) + *tūn* enclosure, settlement. However, the name is now most frequent in the W Midlands, so it may be that a place of the same name in that area should be sought as its origin.

Bentz *see* BENNETT, BERTHOLD

Benveniste Italian and Jewish (non-Ashkenazic): nickname from the expression *benveniste* 'welcome' (L *bene venistis* you have arrived well; cf. BENVENUTI).

Vars.: Jewish: **Benvenisti**, **Benvenisty**, **Benvenishte**, **Benveneste**.

Benvenuti Italian: from the medieval given name *Benvenuto* 'Welcome' (from OIt. *bene* well + *venuto* arrived, past part. of *venire* to come, arrive). Generally it was applied to a long-awaited and much-desired child.

Vars.: **Benvegnu**; **Venut(t)i**; **Nuti**, **Gnuti**, **Gnudi**.

Dims.: **Venutelli**, **Vignudelli**, **Begnudelli**, **Vignodolli**, **Vignudini**; **Nutini**.

Béquet *see* BECK

Béránek *see* BARANOV

Beraud French: from the Gmc personal name *Ber(n)wald*, composed of the elements *ber(n)* bear + *wald* rule. There

has been some confusion between this name and the more common BERNARD; see BARRETT.

Vars.: **Béraud**, **Berau(l)t**, **Bérault**, **Braud**, **Brault**; **Bernaud**, **Barnaud**.

Dims.: Fr.: **Braudel**, **Braudey**. It.: **Beraldini**.

Berchthold *see* BERTHOLD

Berdyaev Russian: from the Tatar nickname *Berdi* 'he has given' (from *bermak* to give), with assimilation to the normal Russ. patr. ending *-ev*. The name was originally borne by a Tatar noble family; the Russianized form was adopted with the loss of Tatar independence in the 16th cent.

Vars.: **Berdiev**, **Berdyev**.

Bere *see* BEER

Berebaum *see* BIRNBAUM

Berecloth *see* BARRACLOUGH

Beresford English: habitation name from a place in the parish of Alstonfield, N Staffs., so called from the gen. case of the OE byname *Beofor* 'Beaver' + OE *ford* FORD.

Vars.: **Berresford**, **Ber(r)isford**.

Bereznikov Russian: patr. from the topographic term *Bereznik* 'dweller by birch trees' (from *beryoza* birch; cogn. with Pol. *brzoza* birch tree, *brzezina* birch forest). The word is ultimately cogn. with Eng. BIRCH and probably also with *bright*, the reference originally being to the distinctive white bark of the tree.

Vars.: **Berezin**, **Berezov**.

Dims.: Ukr.: **Berezko**. Beloruss.: **Beryozkin** (patr.). Pol.: **Brzózka**.

Habitation names: Pol.: **Brzeziński** (from places called *Brzezie* and *Brzeziny*); **Brzozowski**.

Berg 1. German and Swedish: topographic name for someone who lived on or by a hill or mountain (OHG *berg*, ON *bjarg*). As a Swedish surname it is often an ornamental name, one of the many formed by more or less arbitrary selection of vocab. words referring to natural phenomena. **2.** Jewish (Ashkenazic): possibly a topographic name as in 1, or an ornamental name from Ger. *Berg* or Yid. *berg* hill, or a short form of any of the many ornamental surnames containing this word as a final element, for example *Schönberg* (see SCHÖN) and *Goldberg* (see GOLD).

Vars. (of 1): Ger.: **Berger**, **Bergmann**. Swed.: **Bergman**, **Bergén**, **Berg(l)in**.

Cpds (of 1, ornamental): Swed.: **Berg(en)dahl** ('hill valley'); **Berggren** ('hill branch'); **Bergholm** ('hill island'); **Berglind** ('hill lime'); **Berglöf** ('hill leaf'); **Berglund** ('hill grove'); **Bergqvist** ('hill twig'); **Bergstedt** ('hill homestead'); **Bergsten** ('hill stone'); **Bergstrand** ('hill shore'); **Bergström** ('hill river'); **Bergvall** ('hill slope').

Berge French: **1.** topographic name for someone who lived on a steep bank, from OF *berge* bank (apparently of Gaul. origin). **2.** hypercorrected var. of BARGE.

Var. (of 1): **Delbergue**.

Dims. (of 1): **Bergeau**, **Bergeon**.

Bergeest *see* GEEST

Bergereau *see* BARKER

Bergès *see* VERDIER

Bergin 1. Irish: Anglicized form of Gael. **Ó Beirgin** or **Ó Meirgin**, a shortened version of **Ó hAimheirgin** 'descendant of *Aimheirgin*', a common personal name in early Irish mythology and historical tales, perhaps composed of the elements *amhra* wonderful + *gin* birth. **2.** Swedish: var. of BERG.

Vars. (of 1): **Berrigan**; **Mergin**.

Bergogne *see* BOURGOIN

Bering *see* BEAR

Beringer English (Norman): from the OF given name *Berenger*. This is in origin a Gmc personal name, composed of the elements *ber(n)* bear + *ger, gar* spear, and owed its popularity in part to the fact that it was the name of one of the characters in the Charlemagne romances.

Vars.: **Berringer**, **Bellinger**, **Bel(l)enger**; **Ballinger** (chiefly W Midlands); **Bell(h)anger** (altered by folk etymology); **Ben(nin)ger**.

Berisford *see* BERESFORD

Berkeley *see* BARCLAY

Berkenblit *see* BIRCH

Berkhout Dutch: topographic name for someone who lived by a birch wood, from MDu. *berke* BIRCH + *holt* wood (see HOLT).

Berkutov Russian: patr. from the nickname *Berkut* 'Golden Eagle' (a borrowing from a Turkic language).

Berlanczyk *see* BRILLANT

Berle French: apparently from OF *berle* water parsnip, an aquatic plant (of Celt. origin, cf. W *berur*, Gael. *biorar* watercress). The reasons why this word should have given rise to a surname are not clear; perhaps it was an occupational name for a grower of the plant.

Var.: **Berlier** (which has the form of an occupational name).

Dims.: **Berl(i)et**, **Berlot**, **Berlioz**.

Berlin Jewish (Ashkenazic) and German: habitation name from the city of *Berlin*, former capital of Germany, now of the German Democratic Republic. This city takes its name from a Wendish word meaning 'river rake', a scaffold of beams built over a river to prevent logs from jamming; the river in question is the Spree. Folk etymology, however, has put a bear into the arms of the city, as if the name were derived from *Bärlin*, a dim. of *Bär* bear. The German name is also found in the Hamburg area, where it may be derived from the village of the same name, but uncertain etymology, in Holstein.

Vars.: **Berliner**; **Berlinski**, **Berlinsky** (E Ashkenazic).

Berman 1. English: occupational name for a porter, ME *berman* (OE *bǣrmann*, from *beran* to carry + *mann* man). **2.** English: possibly from a ME given name, *Ber(e)man*, which may be derived from OE *Beornmund*, composed of the elements *beorn* young man, warrior + *mund* protection. **3.** Anglicized form of BERMANN (1–3). **4.** Jewish (Ashkenazic): var. of BERMANN 4.

Patr. (from 1): Sp.: **Bermúdez**.

Bermann 1. German: occupational name for someone exhibiting a bear; see BEARMAN. **2.** German: occupational name for a swineherd, from MHG, OHG *bēr* boar + *man* man. **3.** Low German: pet form of any of the various medieval given names derived from Gmc cpd names with the first element *ber(n)* bear (cf., e.g., BERNARD and BERAUD). **4.** Jewish (Ashkenazic): either an elaboration of the Yid. male given name *Ber* 'Bear' or else an ornamental name referring to the bear.

Vars. (of 1): **Permann** (Bavaria). (Of 2): **Behrmann**, **Bahrmann**, **Baarmann**. (Of 4): BERMAN: **Behrman(n)**.

Bermejo Spanish: nickname for a man with red hair or a ruddy complexion, from Sp. *bermejo* red, ruddy (LL *vermiculus*, from *vermis* worm, since a red dye was obtained from the bodies of worms).

Bermingham *see* BIRMINGHAM

Bermitter *see* PERMENTER

Bernard English, French, Polish, and Czech: from the Gmc given name *Bernhard*, composed of the elements *ber(n)* bear + *hard* brave, hardy, strong. This was brought to England by the Normans, reinforcing OE *Beornheard*. The popularity of the given name among the Normans in the centuries immediately following the Conquest was greatly increased by virtue of its having been borne by St Bernard of Clairvaux (*c*.1090–1153), founder and abbot of the Cistercian monastery at Clairvaux, and in Holland and N Germany it vied with ARNOLD as the most popular given name during the 13th and 14th cents. Another sanctified bearer of the name was St Bernard of Menthon (923–1008), founder of Alpine hospices and patron saint of mountaineers, whose cult accounts for the frequency of the name in Alpine regions.

Vars.: Eng.: **Barnard**. Fr.: **Barnard**, **Bénard**; **Besnard** (hypercorrected); **Benard** (Belg.). Pol.: **Biernat**, **Biernacki**, **Bernadzki**. Czech: **Ber(n)**, **Berán**.

Dims.: Eng.: BARNET. Fr.: **Bernardeau**, **Bénardeau**, **Besnardeau**; **Berna(r)det** (fem. **Berna(r)dette**), **Bernadé**; **Bernet** (fem. **Bernette**), **Berney**; **Berna(r)dot** (fem. **Berna(r)dotte**), **Bernot**; **Bernardin**, **Bernardy**, **Berna(r)don**, **Berna(r)dou(x)**, **Bernon**; **Bernol(l)et**, **Nollet**, **Nolleau**, **Nolot**, **Nolin**. It.: **Bern(ard)ini**, **Bernard(in)elli**, **Bern(ard)otti**, **Bernetti**, **Bernocchi**, **Bernucci**, **Bernuzzi**. Sp., Port.: **Bernardino**. Ger.: **Betz** (see also BERTHOLD); **Berni**, **Bernli(n)** (Switzerland). Czech: **Bernášek**; **Beránek**, **Berka**.

Augs.: Fr.: **Bernat**. It.: **Bernardoni**, **Nardoni**.

Patrs.: Sp.: **Bernárdez**, **Bernáldez**. Port.: **Bernardes**. It.: **Di Bernardo**, **De Bernardi(s)**; **Bernardeschi**. Low Ger.: **Baren(d)ts(en)**, **Behren(d)s(en)**, **Ber(e)ns**; **Bernhardi** (Latinized). Du.: **Behrens**, **Berends(en)**, **Berndsen**, **Baren(d)s**, **Barense(n)**. Dan., Norw.: **Bern(d)tssen**. Swed.: **Bernhardsson**, **Bern(d)tsson**. Pol.: **Biernatowicz**, **Bernakiewicz**; **Bernaciak**.

Berne *see* BYRNE

Berner 1. English: from the Norman given name *Bernier*, which is of Gmc origin, being composed of the elements *ber(n)* bear + *hari, heri* army. **2.** English: occupational name for a burner of lime or charcoal, from OE *beornan* to burn. This may also have occasionally denoted someone who baked bricks or distilled spirits, or who carried out some other manufacturing process involving burning. **3.** English: occupational name for a keeper of hounds, from ONF *bern(i)er*, *brenier* (a deriv. of *bren, bran* bran (of

Gaul. origin), on which the dogs were fed). **4.** English: habitation name or topographic name, a var. of BARNES 1 or BOURNE. **5.** Jewish (Ashkenazic): of unknown origin.

Var. (of 2 and 3): BRENNER.

Dims. (of 1): Fr.: **Berneret** (fem. **Bernerette**); **Berneron**, **Bernerin**, **Bernelin**.

Patr. (from 1): Eng.: **Berners**.

Berney *see* BURNEY

Bernreith *see* BÄRENREITER

Bernstein 1. Jewish (Ashkenazic): ornamental name from Ger. *Bernstein* amber (from MLG *bernen* to burn + *stēn* stone; i.e. it was thought to be created by burning, although it is in fact fossilized pine resin). **2.** German: habitation name from a place so called, of which there is one in Bavaria and another in what used to be E Prussia (now the town of *Pełczyce* in NW Poland; see PEŁCZYŃSKI). Both of these probably get their Ger. names from the notion of a 'burnt stone', for example in brick making, rather than from 'amber'.

Vars. (of 1): Jewish: **Bernshtein**, **Berens(h)tein**; **Bernstejn**, **Berensztejn** (Pol. spellings); **Bor(e)nstein**, **Bor(e)nshtein**, **Bor(e)nshtain**, **Borenstain**, **Bor(e)nsztein** (mixed Pol.-Ger. spellings); BURNS, BURSTIN.

Béronneau *see* BEAR

Berrick *see* BARWICK

Berridge *see* BEVERIDGE

Berriman *see* BURY

Berrocal Spanish: topographic name for someone who lived on a patch of stony ground, Sp. *berrocal* (a deriv. of *berrueco* rock, crag, a word of uncertain, probably Celt., origin).

Berrow *see* BARROW

Berry 1. English: topographic name or habitation name, a var. of BURY. **2.** Irish (Galway and Mayo): Anglicized form of Gael. *Ó Beargha*; see BARRY 6. **3.** French: regional name for someone from *Berry*, a former province of central France, so called from L *Boiriācum*, apparently a deriv. of a Gaul. personal name, *Boirius* or *Barius*.

Vars. (of 3): Fr.: **Berrier**, **Berryer**, **Berruer**, **Berrue(i)x**.

Bert French, English, and (rarely) German: from the Gmc personal name *Berto*, a short form of the various cpd personal names with the first element *berht* bright, famous (cf. e.g. BERTHIER, BERTHOLD, BERTOLF, and BERTRAM). See also BURT.

Dims.: N Eng.: **Bertie**. Fr.: **Berton** (also from the oblique case), **Bert(h)oneau**, **Bertet**, **Bert(h)elin**, **Bert(h)elot**, **Bertil(l)on**, **Bert(h)ilet**. It.: **Bert(or)elli**, **Bertin(ett)i**, **Bertinotti**; **Bertucc(ell)i**, **Bertuccini**, **Bertuccioli**; **Bertozzi**, **Bertuzzi**, **Bertocc(h)(in)i**; **Pertini**, **Pertotti** (N Italy). Cat.: **Bert(h)elin**, **Bertolin**. Ger.: **Bert(h)el**; **Bertl** (Franconia). Low Ger.: **Beth(k)e**, **Bethmann**.

Aug.: It.: **Bertoni**.

Pejs.: It.: **Bertacco**, **Bertacchi**.

Patrs.: It.: **Bertenghi**, **Bertinghi**.

Patrs. (from dims.): Ger.: **Bert(h)els**, **Berlitz**.

Bertel *see* BARTHOLOMEW

Berthier French: from the Gmc personal name *Berther*, composed of the elements *berht* bright, famous + *heri, hari* army.

Var.: **Bertier**.

Dims.: Fr.: **Bert(h)eron**, **Bertron**. Prov.: **Bert(h)erou(x)**, **Bertrou**. It.: **Bertarini**.

Berthold German: from the Gmc personal name *Bertwald*, composed of the elements *berht* bright, famous + *wald* rule.

Vars.: **Berchthold**, **Bergdolt** (Bavaria); **Perthold** (Austria); **Bächtold**, **Bechtold** (Switzerland).

Dims.: Ger.: **Ben(t)z** (Bavaria, Austria; see also BENNETT); **Betz** (see also BERNARD). Fr.: **Bert(h)audet**, **Bet(h)audé**. It.: **Bertoletti**, **Bertolini**, **Bertolucci**, **Bertoluzzi**.

Patrs.: Low Ger.: **Bart(h)els**; **Bartholdy** (Latinized). Swed.: **Bertilsson**.

Bertolet *see* BERTOLF

Bertolf German: from the Gmc personal name *Bertolf*, composed of the elements *berht* bright, famous + *wolf* wolf.

Vars.: **Bertleff**; **Bechtolf**, **Bechtloff** (Switzerland).

Dims.: Fr.: **Bert(h)o(u)let**, **Bert(h)ollet**.

Aug.: Fr.: **Bert(h)olat**.

Bertram English, French, and German: from the Gmc personal name *Bertram*, composed of the elements *berht* bright, famous + *hrabn* raven. The raven was the bird of Odin, king of the gods, in Gmc mythology. The given name was common in France throughout the Middle Ages, where its popularity was increased by the fame of the troubadour Bertrand de Born (?1140–?1214). The spelling *Bertrand* is Fr., coined by folk etymology under the influence of the pres. part. ending -*and*, -*ant*. The name was brought to England by the Normans in the forms *Bertran(d)*, *Bertram*, and *Bartram*.

Vars.: Eng.: **Bartram**, **Bart(t)rum**; **Ba(t)tram**, **Batterham**, **Borthram**, **Buttrum**, **Bertrand**. Fr.: **Bertran(d)**, **Bétran**. Low Ger.: **Berterman** (Schleswig).

Dims.: Fr.: **Bertran(d)et**, **Bertrandot**, **Bertrandeau**, **Bertrandon**. Prov.: **Bertaneu**. It.: **Beltramelli**, **Beltrametti**, **Beltramini**; **Bertamini**.

Patrs.: Low Ger.: **Tra(h)ms**.

Bertwistle *see* BIRTWISTLE

Berzal Spanish: topographic name for someone who lived by a cabbage patch, Sp. *berzal* (a deriv. of *berza* cabbage, from LL *viridia* cabbage, 'greens', neut. pl. of *viridis* green).

Bès Provençal: topographic name for someone who lived by a birch tree or in a birch wood, from OProv. *bès* birch (LL *bettius*, of Gaul. origin).

Vars.: **Bex**, **Bez**; **Besse**.

Dims.: **Besseau**, **Besset**, **Bessey**; **Bezou(t)**.

Collectives: **Bessière(s)**, **Besseire**, **Besseyre**, **Bessède**.

Besançon French: habitation name from the town in the *département* of Doubs, which apparently gets its name from a Celtiberian element *ves* mountain + suffix -*unt*, with a further (L) suffix -*io* (gen. -*iōnis*). In folk etymology there has been some association with OF *bison* the (European) bison, which animal appears in the arms of the city.

Var.: **Bezançon**.

Besant English: from ME *besant*, the name of a gold coin (via OF from L *(nummus) byzantius*, so called because it was first minted at Byzantium). The surname arose as a metonymic occupational name for a coiner or else a nickname for a man rich in cash. A certain Lefwin Besant is recorded in London in 1168 as a moneyer.

Vars.: **Bessant**, **Bessent**, **Bez(z)ant**.

Beschoren *see* PSCHORR

Beseke *see* BASIL

Besgen *see* SEBASTIAN

Besnard *see* BERNARD

Besse *see* BÈS

Bessell English or Welsh: of uncertain origin, possibly a var. of BISSELL. The name apparently occurs in the placename *Bessels Leigh*, in Berks., the manor of which was held by Petrus *Besyles* in 1412.

Bessemer English: **1.** occupational name for a maker of brooms, from an agent deriv. of ME *besem* broom (OE *bes(e)ma*). **2.** altered form of Fr. *Bassemer*; see below.

Besser German: occupational name for a collector of fines, from an agent deriv. of MHG *buoz(e)* fine, reparation (OHG *buoz(a)*).

Var.: **Besserer**.

Besson Provençal: nickname for one of a pair of twins, from OProv. *besson* twin (a deriv. of OF, L *bis* twice).

Var.: **Bessou**.

Dims.: Prov.: **Bessonet**, **Bessoneau**.

Aug.: Prov.: **Bessonat**.

Pej.: Prov.: **Bessonaud**.

Best 1. English and French: from ME, OF *beste* animal, beast (L *bestia*). This was applied as a surname in two ways: as a metonymic occupational name for someone who looked after beasts—i.e. a herdsman—and as a nickname for someone thought to resemble an animal—i.e. a violent, uncouth, or stupid man. It is unlikely that the name is derived from *best*, OE *betst*, superlative of *good*. **2.** German: topographic name for someone who lived by the river *Beste*, a tributary of the Trave, or habitation name from any of various villages called *Besten*, said by Bahlow to be named from a MLG word for poor soil. **3.** German: short form of SEBASTIAN.

Vars.: **Beste**. (Of 1 only): Eng.: **Bester**, **Bestar**, **Best(i)man** (in the sense 'herdsman'). Fr.: **Best(e)au(x)**, **Bétiau** (in the sense 'brutal', from OF *best(i)al*). Port.: **Bicha**.

Dims. (of 1): Fr.: **Bestel(le)**. (Of 3): Ger.: **Bestel**.

Beswick English: habitation name from places in Lancs. and N Yorks., the second element of which is clearly OE *wīc* outlying (dairy) farm (see WICK). The first element of the Lancs. name may be an OE personal name *Bēac*; that of the Yorks. name is possibly *Besi*.

Var.: **Bestwick**.

Betau *see* BÉAL

Betaudé *see* BERTHOLD

Betham *see* BEETHAM

Bethe *see* BERT

Bethell 1. English: from a medieval dim. of *Beth*, short form of the female name *Elizabeth* (cf. BELL 2 and LILLY). **2.** Welsh: patr. (*ab Ithel*) from the given name *Ithael* 'bountiful lord'; cf. IDLE and JEKYLL.

Vars. (of 2): **Bithell** (now chiefly Lancs.); **Bythell**, BISSELL; see also BESSELL.

Bétiau *see* BEST

Betje *see* BENNETT

Bétran *see* BERTRAM

Bett English: from a medieval given name, a short form of *Bartholomew*, *Beatrice*, or *Elizabeth*.

Patrs./Metrs.: **Bett(i)s(on)**, **Bettenson**.

Bettencourt French: habitation name from any of various places so called, with minor variations in spelling, of which the main one is in Somme. They get their name from a Gmc personal name *Betto* (of uncertain origin, probably an assimilated form of *Berto*; see BERT) + OF *court* farm(yard) (see COURT 1). The name is now very frequent in Portugal, where it first occurs in the 14th cent.

Var.: **Betancourt**.

Betteridge English: from the OE personal name *Beaduric*, composed of the elements *beadu* battle + *rīc* power.

Vars.: **Bettridge**, **Betteriss**, **Bat(t)rick**, **Badrick**, **Badrock**.

Betton *see* BEATON

Betz *see* BERNARD

Beuchel *see* BAUCH

Beuerle *see* BAUER

Beuscher *see* BELCHER

Beuvin *see* BEVIN

Bevan Welsh: patr. from EVAN, with fused patr. prefix *ap*, *ab*.

Vars.: **Bevans**, BEVIN.

Bevar *see* BEAVER

Beveridge English and Scots: probably from ME *beverage* drink (OF *bevrage*, from *beivre* to drink, L *bibere*). The term was used in particular of a drink bought by a purchaser to seal a bargain, and the surname may have been acquired as a nickname in this context. Reaney adduces evidence to suggest that the nickname may have been bestowed on a man who made a practice of getting free drinks by entering into bargains which he did not keep. The name is more common in Scotland than in England.

Vars.: **Bavridge**; **Berridge** (Midlands).

Beverley English: habitation name from a place in E Yorks. (now Humberside), the name of which contains OE *beofor* beaver, combined with a second element that may mean 'stream'.

Var.: **Beverly**.

Beves see BEAVIS

Bevin 1. English (Norman): nickname for a wine drinker, from OF *bei(vre)*, *boi(vre)* to drink (L *bībere*) + *vin* wine (L *vīnum*). **2.** Welsh: var. of BEVAN, patr. from EVAN.

Vars.: (of 1): **Beavin**, **Bivin**, **Bivan**.

Dim. (of 1): Fr.: **Boivinet**.

Patrs. (probably mostly of 1): Eng.: **Be(a)vins**, **Bevens**, **Bivins**, **Bivens**, **Bivans**, **Beavans**, **Bavens**, **Bavins**, **Beevens**.

Bevington English (SW Midlands): habitation name from one of the places so called, in Warwicks. and Gloucs. The placename means 'Bēofa's settlement', from the OE personal name *Bēofa* + OE *tūn* settlement.

Bewes 1. English (Norman): habitation name from *Bayeux* in Calvados, which gets its name from being the seat of a Gaul. tribe recorded in L sources as the *Ba(d)iocasses*. **2.** Welsh: patr. from the given name HUGH, with the addition of the Welsh prefix *ab*, *ap*, and (tautologically) the Eng. suffix *-s*.

Vars.: BEWS. (Of 2 only): **Bew**, **Bugh**; PUGH.

Bewick English: habitation name from a place in Northumb., so called from OE *bēo* bee + *wīc* outlying farm; apparently originally a station for the production of honey. There is another place of the same name in N Yorks.

Vars.: **Bewicke**, **Bowick**; **Buick** (N Ireland).

Bewley see BEAULIEU

Bewshaw see BELCHER

Bewson see BEAU

Bex see BÈS

Bexon see BECK

Beyer see BAYER

Beylet see BAILEY

Beyn see BENNETT

Beynon see ONION

Bez see BÈS

Bezal see BÉAL

Bezançon see BESANÇON

Bezant see BESANT

Bezděk Czech: apparently from the adverb *bezděky* involuntarily, unintentionally. The application as a surname is not clear, but it may be a nickname from some lost anecdote. On the other hand there are several placenames in Bohemia formed with this element, and although the surname is not a habitation name in form, it may nevertheless be derived from one of these. Moldanová cites a certain Jan *Bezděcký* from *Bezděčí Hora*, recorded in 1576.

Bezobrazov Russian: patr. from the nickname *Bezobrazny* 'Ugly', from *bez* without + *obraz* shape, form, beauty.

Bezuidenhout Dutch: topographic name from MDu. *bezuiden* on the south side (from *zuid* south) + *hout* forest (see HOLT).

Biagelli see BLAISE

Białas Polish: nickname or byname for a fair-haired person, from Pol. *biał-* white, fair, blond + *-as* masc. suffix.

Var.: **Biela**.

Dims.: Pol.: **Białasik**, **Białczyk**, **Białek**. Czech: **Bělík**, **Bílek**. Ukr.: **Bilko**. Beloruss.: **Belyak**. Jewish (E Ashkenazic): **Bialik**, **Bielak**; **Bialovchik**.

Patrs.: Pol.: **Białasiewicz**, **Bilewicz**, **Bielak**. Croatian: **B(i)jelić**, **Belić**. Russ.: **Belyaev**. Beloruss.: **Belov** (Anglicized **Beloff**). Jewish: **Bialovitch**, **Bialovitz**, **Bialowitz**, **Bialowice**.

Patrs. (from dims.): Polish: **Bilczak**. Russ.: **Belyanchikov**. Jewish: **Bialkovitz**, **Bialkovits**, **Bilkowitz**.

Habitation names: Pol.: **Białasiński**, **Białkowski**.

Biale Jewish (E Ashkenazic): habitation name from any of various places in E Europe named in Yid. as *Byale*, from a Slav. element meaning 'white' (cf. BIAŁAS, BIELSKI).

Vars.: **Biali**, **Bialy**, **Bialo**; **Bialer**, **Bieler**.

Biale see VITALE

Bialecki see BIELSKI

Bialistock Jewish (E Ashkenazic): habitation name from the Polish city of *Białystok*, which is so named from Pol. *biały* white + *stok* hillside.

Vars.: **Bialistocki**, **Bialistotzki**, **Bialistotzky**, **Bialystocky**, **Bialostocki**, **Bialostocky**, **Bialostotzky**, **Bialostotsky**, **Bialostozki**, **Bialostatzki**, **Bielostocki**.

Białobrzeski Polish: habitation name from the city of *Białobrzegi*, which is so named from Pol. *biało-* white + *brzeg* shore, riverbank.

Białoskórski Polish: from *białoskóra* white leather, probably an occupational name for a leather worker.

Białowąs Polish: nickname for someone with a white moustache, from Pol. *biało-* white + *wąs* moustache.

Bianchetti see BLANC

Biard French: from the Gmc personal name *Bighard*, composed of the elements *big*, of uncertain meaning + *hard* brave, hardy, strong.

Vars.: **Bihard**, **Bicard**, **Bigard**.

Dims.: Fr.: **Biardeau**, **Biardot**.

Bibby English: from the medieval female given name *Bibbe*, a dim. of *Isabel* (see HIBBS). In this form the surname is most common in Lancs.

Var.: **Bibb** (chiefly W Midlands).

Bicard see BIARD

Bicha see BEST

Bichet French: from OF *bichet* measure for grain (a word related to mod. Eng. *beaker* and *pitcher*; all derive ultimately from Gk *bīkos*, a type of vase). The surname was probably first applied as a metonymic occupational name for an official corn-measurer or perhaps a maker of such measures.

Bichl see BÜHLER

Bick 1. English: of uncertain origin, perhaps from the OE personal name *Bicca* (cf. BECKETT 2). **2.** Jewish (E Ashkenazic): German or English spelling of E Yid. *bik*, Pol. *byk*, or

Russ. *byk*, all meaning 'ox' or 'bull'. This may be one of the many Jewish ornamental names taken from the animal kingdom, or it may represent an unflattering nickname bestowed by a non-Jewish government official, or it may be taken from a nickname.

Vars. (of 2): **Byk**; **Bykoff**; **Bikovski, Bikovsky, Bykovski**.

Dims. (of 2): Jewish: **Bickel**. Czech: **Býček**.

Habitation name (related to 2): Pol.: **Bykowski**.

Bicker English: 1. occupational name for a beekeeper, ME *bīker* (OE *bēocere*). Bees were important in medieval England because their honey provided the only means of sweetening food, and was also useful in preserving. 2. habitation name from a place in Lincs., so called from ON *býr* farm, settlement + *kjarr* wet ground, brushwood (see KERR).

Var.: **Bikker**.

Patr. (from 1): **Bickers**.

Bickerdike English: habitation name from some place (probably in Yorks., where the surname is commonest), perhaps meaning 'disputed ditch', from ME *biker* to quarrel (of unknown origin) + *dik* dyke, ditch (ON *díki*, OE *dīc*).

Bickerstaff English: habitation name from a minor place in the parish of Ormskirk, Lancs. so called from OE *bēocere* beekeeper (see BICKER 1) + *stæð* landing place.

Vars.: **Bickerstaffe, Biggerstaff, Bick(er)steth**.

Bickerton English: habitation name from any of the various places (for example in Ches., Northumb., and W Yorks.) so called from OE *bēocere* beekeeper (see BICKER 1) + *tūn* enclosure, settlement. The name is common in Staffs.

Bickford English: habitation name from a place so named from the OE personal name *Bicca* (cf. BECKETT 2) + OE *ford* FORD. There is one such place in Staffs., but the surname is more common in Devon, where it is derived from *Bickford* Town in Plympton St Mary parish.

Bickley English: habitation name from one of the places called *Bickley* in Worcs., Ches., or Kent or *Bickleigh* in Devon, all of which are possibly so called from an OE personal name *Bicca* (cf. BECKETT 2) + OE *lēah* wood, clearing. The first element could alternatively be a word meaning 'bee's nest'.

Var.: **Bickle** (chiefly Devon).

Bicknell English: habitation name from *Bickenhall* in Somerset, so called from the OE personal name *Bicca* (cf. BECKETT 2) + OE *hyll* HILL or *h(e)all* HALL.

Vars.: **Bignell, Bignall, Bignold**.

Bidaway see WAY

Biddell see BEADLE

Biddlecombe English: habitation name from *Bittiscombe* in Somerset, which is recorded in 1180 in the form *Bitelescumba*, and apparently comes from the OE personal name *Bitel*, a deriv. of the attested name *Bita* (of unknown origin) + OE *cumb* valley (see COOMBE).

Biddulph English (Midlands): habitation name from a place in Staffs., recorded as *Bidolf* in Domesday Book.

This gets its name from OE *bī* beside + **dylf* digging (a putative deriv. of *delfan* to dig), i.e. a mine or quarry.

Biddwell see BEDWELL

Bider see BIEDERMANN

Bidjerano see BEJARANO

Bie see BEE

Biedermann 1. German: nickname from Ger. *Biedermann* honest man, a cpd of MHG *biderbe* honourable (OHG *biderbi*) + *mann* man (OHG *man*). Associated with it is the surname **Biedermeier** (see MAYER), adopted in 1853 by a group of German humorists as the name of a fictitious writer, Gottlob Biedermeier, satirized as an unimaginative bourgeois philistine. The name came to be used to refer to the stolid style of furnishing and decoration that was popular in mid-19th-cent. Germany. 2. Jewish (Ashkenazic): surname adopted because of its honorific meaning, from mod. Ger. *bieder* honest, upright + -*mann*.

Vars. (of 2): **Bi(e)der(man)**.

Biegel see BÜHLER

Biela see BIAŁAS

Bieler see BIALE

Bielostocki see BIALISTOCK

Bielski Polish and Jewish (Ashkenazic): 1. habitation name from any of the many places in E Europe whose name incorporates the Slav. element *byel*- white (mod. Pol. *biały*; cf. BIAŁAS) + the surname suffix -*ski* (see BARANOWSKI). 2. nickname for a fair-haired person, var. of BIAŁAS. See also BIALE.

Vars.: Pol.: **Bielecki, Bialecki; Bieliński, Bielawski; Bilski** (E Pol. and Ukr.). Jewish: **Bilski, Bialski, Bielecki, Bielicki, Biletzki, Bialecky; Bi(e)linski, Bi(e)linsky, Bielensky, Bialinski**.

Bien Jewish (Ashkenazic): ornamental name from Yid. *bin* bee, Ger. *Biene*, or metonymic occupational name for a beekeeper.

Vars.: **Bin, Biener, Binman**.

Cpds: **Binenbaum** ('bee tree'); **Binenfeld** ('bee field'); **Binenkopf** ('bee head', an unflattering name probably assigned by a non-Jewish government official); **Bi(e)nstein** ('bee stone').

Bienstock Jewish (Ashkenazic): name taken by a beekeeper, from Yid. *binshtok* beehive.

Vars.: **Bins(h)to(c)k; Bi(e)nenstock, Binens(h)tok** (from mod. Ger. *Bienenstock*).

Bier German and Jewish (Ashkenazic): metonymic occupational name for a brewer of beer, mod. Ger. *Bier*, Yid. *bir* (MHG *bier*, OHG *bior*, from LL *biber*, a deriv. of *bibere* to drink).

Vars.: Ger.: **Biermann**. Jewish: **Bierman(n)**.

Bierbaum see BIRNBAUM

Biernacki see BERNARD

Biers see BYERS

Biétrix see BÉATRICE

Biever see BEAVER

Biez see BÉAL

Bigard see BIARD

Bigaud French: from the Gmc personal name *Bigwald*, composed of the elements *big* (see BIARD) + *wald* rule.

Vars.: **Bigau(l)t**.

Bigg 1. English (chiefly Birmingham): nickname from ME *bigge* large, strong, stout (apparently of ON origin). In the case of Laurentia *atte Bigge* (Somerset 1327), however, the name appears to be local; if so, the meaning is not certain, but there may be some connection with BIGGIN. **2.** Scots and N Irish: var. of BEGG.

Biggerstaff see BICKERSTAFF

Biggin English: habitation name from any of the various places in England named from Northern ME *bigging* building (from ON). This word came to denote especially an outbuilding, and is still used in and around Northumb. and Cumb.

Vars.: **Biggin(g)s**.

Biggs see BEGG

Biglietti see WILLIAM

Bignall see BICKNELL

Bignon French: apparently a dim. of OF *bigne* bruise, swelling (of unknown origin). The term was used in the Middle Ages as a nickname for someone who held his head on one side; the connection may be that this was perceived as the result of a beating. See also BUNYAN.

Aug.: **Bignat**.

Pejs.: **Bignau(l)d**.

Bigot French: originally a contemptuous nickname, of unknown origin, applied to the Normans by the French. The sense 'excessively religious individual' did not arise until the 15th cent., after the general period of surname formation. Roger *Bigod* was one of William the Conqueror's chief advisers.

Dim.: **Bigotteau**.

Bigrave see BYGRAVE

Bihard see BIARD

Bijelić see BIAŁAS

Bikker see BICKER

Bikovski see BICK

Bilbao Basque: habitation name from the city in the province of Biscay, which was founded in the 13th cent. on the site of an ancient settlement. The placename is of uncertain origin; it probably contains the element *ibai* river.

Biłczak see BIAŁAS

Bilek see BIAŁAS

Biles English: topographic name for someone who lived on a promontory or elevation, from OE *bil(e)*, literally the bill or beak of a bird, but also used in a transferred sense.

Var.: **Byles**.

Biletzki see BIELSKI

Bill 1. English and German: from a Gmc personal name, either a short form of cpd names such as BILLARD and BILLAUD, or else a byname *Bill(a)*, from OE *bil* sword, halberd (or a Continental cogn.). *Bill* was not used as a short form of WILLIAM during the Middle Ages. **2.** English: metonymic occupational name for a maker of pruning hooks and similar implements, from ME *bill* (from OE *bil* sword, with the meaning shifted to a more peaceful agricultural application).

Var. (of 2): **Biller**.

Patrs. (from 1): Eng.: **Bill(e)s**, **Billson**, **Billing(s)**. Ger.: **Billung**.

Billard French: from the Gmc personal name *Bilhard*, composed of the elements *bil* sword + *hard* brave, hardy, strong. The spelling has been influenced by OF *bille* piece of wood, stick (cf. BILLET 2).

Var.: **Bilard**.

Dim.: **Billardon**.

Patr.: Ger.: **Bilharz**.

Billaud French: from the Gmc personal name *Bilwald*, composed of the elements *bil* sword + *wald* rule, with the spelling influenced by *bille*, as in BILLARD.

Vars.: **Billau(l)t**.

Dims.: **Billaudet**, **Billaudel**.

Billet French: **1.** aphetic var. of *Robillet*, itself a dim. of ROBERT. **2.** metonymic occupational name for a carpenter, from a dim. of OF *bille* piece of wood, stick (of Gaul. origin). **3.** metonymic occupational name for a secretary, from a dim. of OF *bulle* letter (L *bulla* round object, seal, applied to the seal on papal missives and so to the documents themselves). However, this sense of *billet* did not become established until the 15th cent., rather late for surname formation.

Billingham English: habitation name from a place so called. The surname is found chiefly in the NW Midlands (Staffs.), but the only place of this name recorded by Ekwall is in Co. Durham, deriving its name from OE *Billingahām* 'homestead (OE *hām*) of the people of *Billa*' (see BILL 1). The distribution of this name, together with evidence from other names (for example the two following) suggests that it may be derived from a lost place in Staffs. or nearby.

Billingsley English: habitation name from a place so called in Shrops., which derives from OE *Billingeslēah*, probably 'clearing (OE *lēah*) near a sword-shaped hill' (see BILL).

Billington English: habitation name from places in Lancs. and Staffs. (and possibly Beds.). The first of these is first recorded in 1196 as *Billinduna* 'sword-shaped hill' (see BILL), the second in Domesday Book as *Belintone* 'settlement (OE *tūn*) of *Billa*'. The place in Lancs. is apparently the most important source of the surname, which to this day is found in large numbers in Preston and Liverpool.

Billo see JACOB

Billon French: **1.** aphetic var. of *Robillon*, itself a dim. of ROBERT. **2.** metonymic occupational name for a coiner, from OF *billon* ingot of precious metal. This word is actually a specialized application of a dim. of *bille* stick; see BILLET 2 In S France it may be a metonymic occupational name for an assayer of weights and measures, from OProv. *bilhon* weight. **3.** habitation name from *Billom* in Puy-de-Dôme, earlier *Billomaco*. This is of obscure etymology; it may be from a Gaul. personal name *Billios* or a doubtfully attested word *bilio* sacred tree + the Gaul. placename element *magos* plain.

Var.: **Billion**.

Billsborough English: habitation name from *Bilsborrow* in Lancs., near Preston, so called from the gen. case of the OE personal name *Bill* (see BILL 1) + OE *burh* fortified manor (see BURY).

Var.: **Bilsborrow**.

Bilt Low German: topographic name for someone who lived on a hillock or mound, MLG *bilte, bulte*.

Bilton English: habitation name from places in Northumb. and Yorks., so called from the OE personal name *Billa* (see BILL 1) + OE *tūn* enclosure, settlement. There is a Bilton in Warwicks., of which the first element is probably OE *beolone* henbane, but this place does not seem to have yielded any surviving surnames.

Bilz *see* PILZ

Bimpson *see* BINN

Bin *see* BIEN

Binchy Irish: of uncertain origin, apparently introduced to Ireland from England in the 17th cent.; there may be some connection with BINKS, or it may ultimately derive from a Norman habitation name. The Ir. surname is almost exclusively confined to Co. Cork, and has been Gaelicized as **Binnse**.

Binder German and Jewish (Ashkenazic): one of the many occupational names for a cooper or barrel maker, from Ger. *Binder*, an agent deriv. of *binden* to bind (OHG *bintan*). Less often the same word is used to denote a book binder. The surname is found principally in S Germany and Switzerland; see also BÖTTCHER, BÜTTNER, and SCHÄFFLER.

Var.: Jewish: **Binderman**.

Cpds: Ger. **Büddenbinder** (with *Büdde, Bütte* cask, wine flask); **Fassbinder** (with *Fass* barrel). Jewish: **Fassbinder**; **Buchbinder** ('book binder', Anglicized **Bookbinder**); **Einbinder** (from Yid. *aynbinder* book binder).

Binenshtok *see* BIENSTOCK

Bines Jewish (Ashkenazic): metr. from the Yid. female given name *Bine* (from Yid. *bin* bee, used as a translation of the Hebr. female given name *Devora* 'Deborah', the literal meaning of which is 'bee'; cf. DVORIN). However, *Bine* is often folk-etymologized as being from the Hebr. noun *bina* understanding.

Var. (E Ashkenazic): **Binovitch**.

Metr. (from a dim.): **Binkin** (from the dim. female given name *Binke*).

Bing 1. English: of uncertain origin. The most plausible suggestion is that it derives from an unattested OE clan name **Binningas*, a deriv. of the attested *Binna* (see BINN). **2.** Jewish (Ashkenazic): habitation name from

Bing, Yid. name of the Ger. town of *Bingen* in the Rhineland.

Vars. (of 1): **Byng**; **Binning**.

Bingham English: habitation name from a place in Notts., so called from OE *Binningas* descendants of *Binna* (see BING 1) or an OE word cogn. with ON *bingr* stall, manger + OE *hām* homestead.

Biniamini *see* BENJAMIN

Binks N English: topographic name for someone living at a *bink*, a northern dial. term for a flat raised bank of earth or a shelf of flat stone suitable for sitting on. The word is a northern form of mod. Eng. *bench*.

Var.: **Binch** (Notts.).

Binn English: **1.** from a ME given name, *Binne*, OE *Binna* (of uncertain origin). **2.** topographic name for someone who lived by an open manger or stall or in a hollow place so named, from OE *binn* manger, bin. It may also have been a metonymic occupational name for a maker of mangers.

Patrs. (from 1): **Binns** (chiefly Yorks.); **Bim(p)son** (Lancs.).

Binney 1. English: topographic name for someone who lived on land surrounded by a bend in a river, from OE *binnan ēa* 'within the river'. **2.** Scots: habitation name from *Binney* or *Binniehill* near Falkirk, so called from Gael. *beinn* hill + the local suffix *-ach*.

Var. (of 2): **Binnie**.

Biondelli *see* BLUNT

Biram *see* BYRON

Birch English: topographic name for someone who lived by a birch tree or in a birch wood, from OE *birce* birch.

Vars.: **Burch**, **Byrch**; **Birk(s)**, **Burk** (northern forms).

Dim.: Ger.: **Birkle**, **Bürcklin**; **Pirkl**.

Cpds (ornamental): Swed.: **Björklund** ('birch grove'); **Björkqvist** ('birch twig'). Jewish: **Berkenblit** ('birch blossom'); **Birkenfeld**, **Berkenfeld** ('birch field'); **Birchental**, **Birkental** ('birch valley').

Birchall English: habitation name from a lost place in the parish of Eccles, Lancs., possibly so called from OE *birce* BIRCH + *hall* HALL or *halh* nook, recess (see HALE 1), or else from OE **bircel* group of birches.

Var.: **Burchall**.

Bircham English: habitation name from a group of villages in Norfolk, so called from OE *brēc* land newly broken up for cultivation + *hām* homestead.

Bird 1. English: from ME *bird, brid* nestling, young bird (OE *bridd*), applied as a nickname or perhaps occasionally as a metonymic occupational name for a bird catcher. The metathesized form is first found in the Northumb. dial. of ME, but the surname is more common in the Midlands and South. It may possibly also be derived from ME *burde* maiden, girl, applied as a mocking nickname. **2.** Irish: see HENEGHAN. **3.** Jewish: trans. of various Ashkenazic surnames meaning 'Bird', as for example VOGEL.

Vars. (of 1): **Byrd**, **Burd**; **Bride** (but see also KILBRIDE).

Dim. (of 1): **Burdekin**.

Birdsall English: habitation name from a place in N Yorks., near Malton, so called from the gen. case of the OE byname *Bridd* BIRD' + OE *halh* nook, recess (see HALE 1). The surname is still largely confined to Yorks.

Birkbeck English: habitation name from a minor place named after the river in Cumb. on which it stands. This derives its name from ON *birki* BIRCH + *bekkr* stream (see BECK 1).

Var.: **Birbeck**.

Birkby English: habitation name from one of the places in N and W Yorks. so called, originally known as *Bretteby* 'settlement (ON *býr*) of the Britons', later assimilated to Northern ME *birke* BIRCH. The surname is still largely confined to Yorks.

Birkdale English: habitation name from a place in Lancs., so called from ON *birki* BIRCH + *dalr* valley (see DALE).

Var.: **Brickdale**.

Birkenshaw *see* BURKINSHAW

Birkett N English: topographic name for someone who lived by a grove of birch trees, from OE *bircett*, *byrcett*, a deriv. of *birce* BIRCH. There has been some confusion with BURKETT.

Vars.: **Birchett**, **Burchett** (S Eng. forms); **Brickett** (a metathesized form).

Birkin *see* BURKIN

Birkle *see* BURKETT

Birling *see* BURLING

Birmingham English: habitation name from the city in the W Midlands. In Domesday Book the name is already found as *Bermingeham*, but it seems likely that it was originally *Beornmundingahām* 'homestead (OE *hām*) of the people of *Beornmund*', a personal name composed of the elements *beorn* young man, warrior + *mund* protection.

Var.: **Bermingham** (this spelling now found chiefly in Ireland).

Birnbaum German and Jewish (Ashkenazic): topographic name for someone who lived by a pear tree, from Ger. *Birnbaum* pear tree, from Ger. *Birn(e)* pear (MHG *bir*) + *Baum* tree (MHG *boum*). As a Jewish name, it is largely ornamental.

Vars.: Ger.: **Bi(e)rbaum**; **Pirpamer** (Austria, Tyrol). Jewish (Ashkenazic, largely ornamental): **Birn**, **Bir(en)baum**, **Bir(e)nboim**, **Birnboym**, **Birnboum**, **Berebaum**, **Barenbaum**, **Barenboim** (also in part from the sign of house no. 187 in the Jewish quarter of Frankfurt-am-Main, and the name of a place outside Poznań).
Cpds (ornamental): Jewish: **Bir(e)nbach** ('pear stream'); **Bir(e)nberg**, **Bernberg** ('pear hill'); **Birenblat** ('pear leaf'); **Ber(e)nblum** ('pear flower'); **Bir(e)ndorf** ('pear village'); **Birnfeld**, **Ber(e)nfeld** ('pear field'); **Birnholz**, **Berenhol(t)z**, **Berenholl(t)z**, **Birenholc**, **Berenholc**, **Barenhol(t)z**, **Barnholz** ('pear wood'); **Birnstein** ('pear stone'); **Birnstock** ('pear trunk'); **Bir(e)nzweig**, **Birenzwaig**, **Birencwaig**, **Birencwajg**, **Birencvaig**, **Birencweig** ('pear twig').

Birnie Scots: habitation name from a place in the former county of Morays. (now part of Grampian region), recorded in the 13th cent. as *Brennach*, probably from Gael. *braonach* damp place.

Var.: **Birney**.

Biró Hungarian: occupational name for a judge, Hung. *bíró*.

Var.: **Bíró**.

Biron 1. French: habitation name from any of the places so called, in Charente-Maritime, Dordogne, and Basses-Pyrénées. The L form of the name is *Biriācum*, apparently from a Gaul. personal name *Birius* (of unknown origin) + the local suffix -*ācum*. 2. English: var. of BYRON.

Birt *see* BURT

Birtwistle English (Lancs.): habitation name from a now depopulated hamlet near Padiham, Lancs., so called from ME *bird* young bird, nestling (OE *bridd*; see BIRD) + *twissel* fork (i.e. stream-junction; OE *twisla*).

Vars.: **Birtwhistle**, **Bertwistle**, **Burtwistle**; **Birdwhistell**.

Bisconti *see* VISCONTE

Bisdomini *see* VISDOMINI

Bish *see* BUSH

Bishop English: from ME *biscop*, OE *bisc(e)op*, which comes via L from Gk *episkopos* overseer (from *epi* on, over + *skopein* to look). The Gk word was adopted early in the Christian era as a title for an overseer of a local community of Christians, and has yielded cogns. in every European language: Fr. *évêque*, It. *vescovo*, Sp. *obispo*, Russ. *yepiskop*, Ger. *Bischof*, etc. The word came to be applied as a surname for a variety of reasons, among them service in the household of a bishop, supposed resemblance in bearing or appearance to a bishop, and selection as the 'boy bishop' on St Nicholas's Day.

Var.: **Bisp** (Bristol).
Dims.: Fr.: **Evéquot** (Switzerland). Prov.: **Piscot**. It.: **Vescovini**; **Piscop(i)ello**, **Piscotti**, **Pisculli**. Czech.: **Biskupek**.
Pejs.: Fr.: **Véquaud**, **Vécard**.
Patrs.: Ir.: **McAnaspie** (Gael. **Mac an Easpuig**). Fr.: **Alévêque**. Pol.: **Biskupiak**. Russ.: **Yepiskopov**.

Bishton English (W Midlands): habitation name from any of the various places in Staffs., Shrops., etc., so called. All of them derive their names from OE *Biscopestūn* 'manor (OE *tūn* settlement) of the bishop'.

Bismarck German: habitation name from the place near Altmark in Magdeburg, recorded *c*.1200 in the form *Biscopesmark*, from its situation on the boundary (see MARK 2) of a bishopric.

Bispham English (Lancs.): habitation name from one of two places in Lancs, so called from OE *Biscopeshām* 'manor (OE *hām* homestead) of the bishop'.

Biss English: nickname for someone with an unhealthy complexion or who habitually dressed in particularly drab garments, from ME, OF *bis* dingy, murky (of Gmc origin).

Dims.: Eng.: **Bisset(t)** (Scots); BISSELL. Fr.: **Biset**, **Bizet**, **Bisot**, **Bizot**. It.: **Bisetti**, **Biselli**, **Bisini**.
Pejs.: Fr.: **Bisard**, **Bizard**.

Bissell 1. English: metonymic occupational name for a corn merchant or factor, one who measured corn, from ME *buyscel*, *busshell*, *bysshell* bushel, measure of corn (OF *boissel*, *buissel*, of Gaul. origin). The name may also have been applied to a maker of vessels designed to hold or measure out a bushel. **2.** English: dim. of Biss. **3.** Welsh: var. of Bethell; cf. Bessell.

Vars. (of 1): **Bissill**, **Bishell**; **Bushell**, **Bushill**, **Bussel**; **Boshell**, **Bossel**.

Dim. (of 1): Fr.: **Boisselet**.

Aug. (of 1): Fr.: **Boisselat**.

Pejs. (of 1): Fr.: **Bois(s)ard**.

Bissex see Isaac

Bisson see Buisson

Bitelli see Vito

Bithell see Bethell

Bittcher see Böttcher

Bittner see Büttner

Bivan see Bevin

Bizard see Biss

Bjelić see Białas

Björklund see Birch

Björnsson see Bear

Blache S French: topographic name for someone who lived by an oak grove, originating in the SE Fr. dial. word *blache* oak plantation (said to be of Gaulish origin), originally a plantation of young trees of any kind.

Vars.: Prov.: **Blach(i)er**, **Blachère**.

Dim.: Prov.: **Blachon**.

Aug.: Prov.: **Blacas**.

Blacher see Blech

Black 1. English and Scots: from ME *blak(e)* black (OE *blæc*, *blac*), a nickname given from the earliest times to a swarthy or dark-haired man. The nickname may have been given for other reasons too: Tengvik records the case (1080) of a certain *Wlfricus Niger* (Wulfric the Black), who received the nickname after blackening his face with charcoal to go undetected at night among his enemies. **2.** English and Scots: from OE *blāc* pale, fair, i.e. precisely the opposite meaning to 1, and a var. of Blake 2. *Blake* and *Black* are found more or less interchangeably in many surnames and placename elements. **3.** English: var. of Blanc as a Norman name. The pronunciation of the nasalized vowel gave considerable difficulty to Eng. speakers, and its quality was often ignored. **4.** Scots and Irish: trans. of various names from Gael. *dubh* black; see Duff. **5.** Jewish: trans. of various names meaning 'black', for example Schwarz.

Vars.: **Blacke**; Bleach; **Blackman**, **Blackmon**, **Blakeman**; **Blagg**.

Dims.: Blackett, Blackie.

Blackall English: habitation name from any of various minor places so called from OE *blæc* Black, dark + *hall* hall, manor (see Hall) or *halh* nook, recess (see Hale 1).

Vars.: **Blackhall** (chiefly Scots); **Blackale**.

Blackburn English: habitation name from any of various places, but especially the one in Lancs., so called from OE *blæc* Black, dark + *burna* stream (see Bourne). The sur-

name is mainly found in N England; the second element, *burna*, is characteristically northern.

Vars.: **Blackburne**, **Blackbourn(e)**.

Blacker English: occupational name for a bleacher of textiles, from ME *blāken* to bleach or whiten, from OE *blāc* white, pale (see Blake 2). The name might also plausibly be derived as an agent noun from *blæc* Black, but it is not clear to what occupation or activity this would refer.

Var.: Bleacher.

Blackett English: **1.** dim. of Black. **2.** nickname for a person with dark hair, or topographic name for someone who lived by a dark headland, from ME *blak(e)* Black + *heved* head (OE *hēafod*).

Blackford English: habitation name from any of various places, e.g. in Somerset, so called from OE *blæc* Black, dark + *ford* Ford.

Blackham English: habitation name from some place so called, presumably deriving its name from OE *blæc* Black (or the OE personal name *Blaca*) + *hām* homestead. Reaney associates the name with *Blakenham* in Suffolk, but at the present day the name is found mainly in the W Midlands.

Blackhurst English: habitation name from some minor place so called, possibly in Lancs., where the surname is chiefly found. This would be derived from OE *blæc* Black, dark + *hyrst* wooded hill (see Hurst).

Blackie Scots: **1.** dim. of Black. **2.** nickname for a person with beautiful dark eyes or one who was reputed to have the power of casting the evil eye on someone, from ME *blak(e)* Black + *ie* eye (OE *ē(a)ge*).

Vars.: **Blaikie**; **Blakey** (Northumb.).

Blackledge English: habitation name from *Blacklache* near Leyland, Lancs., so called from OE *blæc* Black, dark + *læc(e)* boggy stream.

Blacklock N English: nickname for someone with dark hair, ME *blakelok*, from OE *blæc* Black, dark + *locc* (lock of) hair. Reaney comments that although *blake* might mean either 'dark' or 'fair' (see Blake), the meaning 'dark hair' is the most probable since this name contrasts with Whitlock.

Blackmore English: habitation name from any of various places so called from OE *blæc* Black, dark + *mōr* moor, marsh (see Moore 1) or *mere* lake (see Delamare). The former is the second element of *Blackmore* in Essex, Wilts., and Worcs., as well as *Blackmoor* in Dorset; the latter is the second element of *Blackmore* in Herts. and *Blackmoor* in Hants, the early forms of which are *Blachemere*, *Blakemere*.

Vars.: **Blackmoor**, **Blakemore**.

Blackshaw English: habitation name from a place in W Yorks., so called from OE *blæc* Black, dark + *sceaga* copse, thicket (see Shaw).

Blacksmith see Smith

Blackwell English: habitation name from any of various places, for example in Cumb., Derbys., Co. Durham, Warwicks., and Worcs., named from OE *blæc* Black, dark + *wæll(a)*, *well(a)* spring, stream (see WALL 2 and WELL).

Var.: **Blackwall**.

Blackwood English and Scots: habitation name from various places, for example in Yorks., Dumfries, and Strathclyde, so called from OE *blæc* BLACK, dark + *wudu* WOOD.

Blades English: **1.** metonymic occupational name for a cutler, from the pl. or gen. sing. of ME *blade* cutting edge, sword (OE *blæd*). **2.** habitation name from a place of uncertain location and etymology. Its status as a habitation name is deduced from early forms cited by Reaney, such as Alan *de Bladis* (Leics. 1230), Hugh *de Bladis* (Staffs. 1258), and William *de Blades* (Yorks. 1301).

Vars.: **Blaydes**. (Of 1 only): **Blade(r)**; **Bladesmith** (see SMITH).

Blagoveshchenski Russian: from *blagoveshchenie* (Feast of the) Annunciation, the Christian festival on 25 March in commemoration of the annunciation to the Virgin Mary of the impending birth of Christ, from *blago*-good (cf. BLÁHA) + *veshchenie* announcement, a calque of Gk *euangelismos*, from *eu*- good + *angelismos* announcement. The word came to be used as a surname in two ways; as a habitation name from various places in Russia called *Blagoveshchensk* on account of having a church dedicated to the Annunciation, but more commonly as a byname adopted by Orthodox priests in honour of this festival.

Bláha Czech: **1.** nickname for a good man, from the vocab. word *blahý* good (now meaning 'happy, fortunate'). **2.** short form of one of the Czech personal names, principally *Blahoslav* and *Blahomil*, that contain *blaho*- good as a first element. **3.** altered short from of the Czech given name *Blažej* BLAISE.

Vars.: **Blahák, Blahuta, Blaheň**.

Dims.: **Blaháček, Blahušek**.

Patr. (cogn. of 2): Croatian: **Blagojević**.

Blain Scots: **1.** Anglicized form of the Gael. personal name *Bláán*, a dim. of *blá* yellow. This was the name of an early Celt. saint. **2.** (also N English) nickname for a person suffering from boils, from ME *blain* blister, pustule (OE *blegen*).

Var.: **Blaine**.

Patr. (from 1): **McBlain**.

Blair Scots and N Irish: habitation name from one of the numerous places so called, from Gael. *blár* (gen. *bláir*) plain, field, esp. a battlefield.

Blaisdale *see* BLEASDALE

Blaise French: from the medieval given name *Blaise* (L *Blasius*). This is an old Roman family name, orig. a byname for someone with some defect, either of speech or gait (cf. L *blaesus* stammering and Gk *blaisos* bowlegged). It was borne by a Christian saint martyred in Armenia in 316, whose cult achieved wide popularity, in particular as the patron saint of carders by virtue of the fact that he was

'carded' to death, i.e. his flesh was scraped off in small pieces with metal combs.

Var.: **Blais**.

Dims.: Fr.: **Blaison, Blaisot; Blazin; Bla(i)zot**. It.: **Blasini, Biasini, Biagini, Blasetti, Biasetti, Biag(g)etti, Biag(g)elli, Biasioli, Biag(g)ioli, Biasotti, Biag(g)iotti**. Ger.: **Blasl; Bläsli, Blesli** (Switzerland). Low Ger.: **Bläsgen, Bläske**. Ger. (of Slav. origin): **Blaschek, Blaschke, Plaschke, Bluschke, Bloschke**. Czech: **Blažek** (from the Czech form of the given name, *Blažej*), BLÁHA. Pol.: **Błaszczyk; Błasik, Błażek** (from the Pol. form of the given name, *Błazej*). Ukr.: **Vlasyuk; Vlasenko** (also Beloruss.).

Augs.: It.: **Blasoni, Biasioni, Biag(g)ioni**.

Patrs.: It.: **De Blase, De Blasi(o), De Blasiis; De Biasi(o), Di Biasi(o); De Biag(g)i, Di Biagio**. Ger.: **Bläsing, Blesing; Plessing**. Russ.: **Vlasov, Vlasyev, Vlasin**. Beloruss.: **Blazhevich**. Pol.: **Błażewicz; Błasiak**. Croatian: **Blaž(ev)ič**.

Patrs. (from dims.): Russ.: **Vlasenkov**. Pol.: **Błaszkiewicz; Błaszczak**.

Habitation names: Pol.: **Błaż(ej)ewski, Błażyński; Błaszczyński** (from a dim.).

Blajman *see* BLEI

Blake 1. English: var. of BLACK 1, meaning 'swarthy' or 'dark-haired', from a byform of the OE adj. *blæc, blac* black, with change of vowel length. **2.** English: nickname from OE *blāc* wan, pale, white, fair. In ME the two words *blac* and *blāc*, with opposite meanings, fell together as ME *blake*. In the absence of independent evidence as to whether the person referred to was dark or fair, it is now impossible to tell which sense was originally meant. **3.** Irish: Anglicized form of Gael. **Ó Bláthmhaic** 'descendant of *Bláthmhac*', a personal name from *bláth* flower, blossom, fame, prosperity + *mac* son. In part, however, the Irish name is derived from OE *blæc* dark, swarthy, as in 1 above. Many bearers are descended from Richard Caddell, nicknamed *le blac*, sheriff of Connaught in the early 14th cent. The Eng. name has been Gaelicized **de Bláca**.

Vars. (of 1 and 2): **Blaik** (Scots and N Eng.). (Of 3): **Blowick**.

Blakeley English and Scots: habitation name from some place called *Blakeley* or *Blackley* (e.g. in Greater Manchester, but probably also somewhere in Scotland), from OE *blæc* BLACK, dark + *lēah* wood, clearing.

Vars.: **Blackley** (Scots); **Blakely** (N Ireland).

Blakeway English (W Midlands): habitation name, probably from *Blakeway* Farm near Much Wenlock, Shrops. The placename is derived from OE *blæc* BLACK, dark + *weg* road, path, way.

Blamire N English: of uncertain origin, possibly a habitation name from a place named with the ON elements *blár* dark + *myrr* swamp, marsh. The place *Blamires* in W Yorks. probably takes its name from the surname rather than vice versa.

Vars.: **Blaymire, Blamore, Blamires**.

Blanc 1. French: nickname for a man with white or fair hair or a pale complexion, from OF *blanc* white (of Gmc origin, cf. OHG *blanc* bright, shining, white, beautiful).

2. Jewish (Ashkenazic): probably an ornamental name from mod. Ger. *blank* bright, shiny.

Vars.: (of 1): **Leblanc**; **Blanche**, **Blanque** (fem. forms; also a female given name). (Of 2): **Blank**, **Blank(i)er**.

Dims.: Fr.: **Blanchet(eau)**, **Blanch(et)on**, **Blanchonnet**, **Blanchot**. Prov.: **Blanquet**, **Blancot**, **Blanqui**. It.: **Bianchetti**, **Bianchin(ott)i**, **Biancucci**, **Biancol(in)i**, **Biancotti**.

Aug.: It.: **Bianconi**.

Pej.: Fr.: BLANCHARD.

Patrs.: Eng.: **Blanks**. It.: **De Bianchi**, **Del Bianco**. Rum.: **Balanesco**.

Blanchard French and English: **1.** pej. of BLANC. **2.** from a Gmc personal name composed of the elements *blanc* shining, white, beautiful + *hard* brave, hardy, strong.

Var.: Fr.: **Blancard**.

Patrs. (from 2): Low Ger.: **Blanka(e)rts**, **Blankertz**.

Blanchflower English: nickname from OF *blanche* (fem.) white (see BLANC) + *flour* FLOWER. Presumably the nickname was originally given ironically to a man of effeminate appearance.

Var.: **Branchflower**.

Bland English: habitation name from a place so called in W Yorks., the etymology of which is uncertain. Possibly it is from OE *(ge)bland* storm, commotion (from *blandan* to blend, mingle), with reference to its exposed situation. The mod. Eng. adjective *bland* did not come into English (from Latin) until the 15th cent., and is therefore unlikely to have given rise to surnames.

Blandford English: habitation name from *Blandford Forum* and other places called *Blandford* in Dorset (*Bleneford* in Domesday Book). The etymology of this is uncertain; Ekwall derives it from OE *blǣgna ford* ford of the gudgeons, from the gen. pl. of *blǣge* gudgeon.

Blaney Irish (of Welsh origin): topographic name from W *blaenau*, pl. of *blaen* point, tip, end, i.e. uplands, or remote region, or upper reaches of a river.

Blanton Ostensibly an Eng. habitation name, but no satisfactory origin has been proposed. There are several bearers in Los Angeles; the name may well represent an Anglicized form of a foreign original.

Bläsgen see BLAISE

Blass see BLOSS

Blatch see BLEACH

Blatcher see BLEACHER

Blatchford English (chiefly Devon): habitation name from *Blatchford* in Sourton, Devon, which is probably derived from the OE personal name *Blæcca* + OE *ford* FORD.

Blatherwick English (E Midlands): habitation name from *Blatherwycke* in Northants. The second element of the placename is clearly OE *wīc* outlying settlement (see WICK); the first, Ekwall suggests, may be 'a worn-down form of OE *blæcþorn*' blackthorn.

Blatt Jewish (Ashkenazic): from Ger. *Blatt*, Yid. *blat* leaf, normally a shortened form of one of the cpds with this

second element, adopted as ornamental surnames in the 18th and 19th cents.

Vars.: **Blat**; **Bleterman** (from Yid. *bleter* or Ger. *Blätter*, both meaning 'leaves').

Blau German: from Ger. *blau* blue (MHG *bla*, OHG *blāo*), a nickname with various senses—a person who habitually wore blue clothes, a person with blue eyes, a sickly or pale person, a person with a bluish complexion resulting from poor circulation, etc. **2.** Jewish (Ashkenazic): ornamental name, one of the many such Ashkenazic surnames taken from names of colours.

Vars.: Ger.: **Blauer(t)** (Bavaria); **Plab(st)** (Bavaria, Austria). Jewish: **Blauer**.

Dim.: Eng.: BLEWETT.

Cpds (ornamental unless otherwise stated): Jewish: **Blaufarb** ('blue colour'); **Blaufeder** ('blue feather'); **Blaufeld** ('blue field'); **Blaugrund** ('blue ground'); **Blaukopf** ('blue head'); **Blauschild** ('blue shield', topographic name from a house marked with a blue shield); BLAUSTEIN; **Blauweiss** ('blue white', a reference to the blue and white colours of the prayer shawl, which was to become the model for the flag of the State of Israel); **Blauzwirn** ('blue thread').

Blaustein Jewish (Ashkenazic): ornamental name from Ger. *blau* blue (MHG *blā*) + *Stein* stone, i.e. lapis lazuli.

Vars.: **Blausztein**, **Blausztain**; **Blus(h)tein**, **Blusztein**, **Blusztejn**, **Blusztain**, **Bluehstein**, **Bloustein**, **Bloustine**, **Bluvstein**, **Blovstein**, **Blowstein** (in part from the Yid. cogn. *bloyshteyn*); **Bluestein** (partly Anglicized); **Bluestone** (fully Anglicized).

Blay see BLISS

Bleach English: var. of BLAKE 2, from the W Saxon form of OE *blǣc*, *blāc*, in which the final palatal consonant /c/ was affricated to /tʃ/ rather than retracted to velar /k/ as in other dialects.

Var.: **Blatch**.

Bleacher English: occupational name for someone who was responsible for bleaching newly woven cloth; cf. BLACKER and BLEACH.

Var.: **Blatcher**.

Bleasby English: habitation name from one of the places in Lincs. and Notts. so called from the ON byname *Blesi* (from *blesi* blaze, white spot) + ON *býr* settlement, village.

Bleasdale English (Cumb. and Lancs.): habitation name from a place in the Lake District, so called from the ON byname *Blesi* (cf. BLEASBY), or from the same word used in the sense of a white spot on a hillside, + ON *dalr* valley.

Vars.: **Blaisdale**, **Blaisdell**.

Blech German and Jewish (Ashkenazic): generally a metonymic occupational name from Ger. *Blech* tin, Yid. *blekh* (MHG *blech* sheet metal, OHG *bleh*), denoting a worker in tin or other metal. The Ger. word also acquired the sense 'cheap rubbish', and it is therefore possible that the Ger. surname was sometimes bestowed as a derogatory nickname.

Vars.: Ger.: **Blech(n)er**, **Blechler**; **Blechschmidt** (see SMITH). Jewish: **Blechmann** (U.S. **Blechman**); **Blacher** (reflecting a central Yid. pronunciation of Yid. *blekher* tinsmith).

Bledsoe English: habitation name from *Bledisloe* in Gloucs., recorded in Domesday Book as *Bliteslav*, and apparently derived from OE *Blīðeshlāw* 'hill (see LAW 2) of *Blīð*', a byname meaning 'cheerful' (see BLIGH 1).

Blei Jewish (Ashkenazic): ornamental name from Ger. *Blei*, Yid. *blay* lead.

Vars.: **Bleiman(n)**; **Blajman** (Pol. spelling).

Cpds: **Bleiberg** ('lead hill', ornamental name); **Bleifeder** (apparently from Ger. *Bleifeder* lead pencil, unless the elements are to be interpreted literally as 'lead feather', in which case the reasons for its adoption as a surname are unknown); **Blajwajs** (Pol. spelling, apparently from Ger. *Bleiweiss* 'white lead, ceruse', reason for adoption unknown).

Blenkinsopp English: habitation name from a place in Northumb., of obscure etymology. A certain John *Blenkynson* is recorded in 1553 as a freeman of the city of York, and this suggests that there may have been a ME given name *Blenkyn* (perhaps from OE *Blenca). The placename may consist of the gen. case of this + ME, OE *hop* valley (see HOPE).

Var.: **Blenkinsop**.

Blennerhasset English: habitation name from a place in Cumb., so called from an old Brit. name composed of the elements *blaen* hill, top + *dre* farm, settlement, with the addition of a later ON name composed of the elements *hey* hay + *sætr* shieling, shelter.

Blériot French: nickname meaning 'badger' or metonymic occupational name for a badger hunter, from OF *bleriot, blereau* badger (of Celt. origin, related to OF *bler* having a white blaze on the forehead, Gael. *blar*).

Vars.: **Bléreau**, **Blériau**.

Blesing *see* BLAISE

Blessed English: nickname for a fortunate individual, from ME *(i)blescede, blissed* blessed (from OE *blētsian* to bless). The word also appears to have been in use in the Middle Ages as a female given name, and some cases of the surname may be derived from this.

Vars.: **Blissett**, **Blest**.

Bleterman *see* BLATT

Blevin Welsh: from the given name *Ble(i)ddyn*, originally a byname meaning 'Wolf Cub', from *blaidd* wolf + the dim. suffix *-yn*. *Blaidd* was often used in Medieval Welsh as a term for a hero, and sometimes for a cruel man or for an enemy who feigned friendship.

Var.: **Blethyn**.

Patrs.: **Blevins**; **Ple(a)vin(s)**, **Pleven**, **Pleaden** (the last 3 from *ap Blethyn* son of Blethyn).

Blewett English: nickname for a habitual wearer of blue clothes or for someone with blue eyes, from ME *bluet* blue woollen cloth or *bleuet* cornflower. Both are from OF *bleuet*, dim. of *bleu* blue (of Gmc origin; see BLAU). The surname is now common chiefly in Devon and Cornwall.

Vars.: **Blewitt**, **Bl(o)uet**.

Blick 1. English: var. of BLUCK. 2. Jewish (Ashkenazic): of uncertain origin; possibly from Yid. *blik* look, and based on some now irrecoverable anecdote.

Bligh 1. English: nickname for a cheerful person, from OE *blīðe* merry, cheerful. 2. Irish: Anglicized from of **Ó Blighe** 'descendant of *Blighe*', a personal name probably derived from the ON byname *Blígr* (from *blígja* to gaze). 3. Cornish: nickname from Corn. *blyth* wolf (cf. BLEVIN).

Vars.: **Bly(e)**; BLYTHE. (Of 3 only): **Blight**.

Blinov Russian: patr. apparently derived from the nickname *Blin*, from *blin* a type of pancake (ultimately connected with *molot* to mill or grind; cf. MOLOTOV). It is not clear what significance the nickname had, unless it was an occupational name.

Bliss 1. English: nickname for a cheerful individual, from ME *blisse* joy, OE *blīðs*; cf. BLIGH 1. 2. English (Norman): habitation name from the village of *Blay* in Calvados, recorded in 1077 in the form *Bleis* and of unknown origin. The village of *Stoke Bliss* in Worcs. was named after a Norman family *de Blez*, recorded several times in the county from the 13th cent. 3. Welsh: patr. from ELLIS. 4. Jewish: of unknown origin. 5. U.S.: Anglicized form of Ger. **Blitz(er)** lightning (MHG *blicze*), presumably a nickname for a fast mover.

Var. (of 2): **Blay**.

Blissett *see* BLESSED

Blitstein *see* BLÜTHNER

Block 1. German: from Ger. *Block* block of wood, stocks (MHG *bloch*, OHG *bloh*). The surname apparently originated as a nickname for a large, lumpish man, or perhaps as a nickname for a persistent lawbreaker who found himself often in the stocks. 2. Jewish: Anglicized form of *Bloch* (see VLACH).

Vars. (of 1): **Blockmann**. (Of 2): **Blok**.

Dim. (of 1): Ger.: **Blöcklin**.

Blokhin Russian: patr. from the nickname *Blokha* 'Flea', used for a small and light person, or else for someone who was infested with fleas.

Dim.: Ukr.: **Bloshchenko**.

Blomberg *see* BLUM

Blondeau *see* BLUNT

Błonski Polish: topographic name for someone living by a meadow, from OPol. *błonie* meadow + *-ski* suffix of local surnames.

Blood 1. English: apparently from OE *blōd* blood, but with what significance is not clear. In ME the word was in use as a metonymic occupational term for a physician, i.e. one who let blood, and also as an affectionate term of address for a blood relative. 2. Welsh: of uncertain origin, possibly a patr. (with prefix *ap, ab*) from the given name LLOYD.

Bloom 1. Jewish (Ashkenazic): Anglicized spelling of BLUM. 2. English: metonymic occupational name for an iron worker, from ME *blome* ingot of iron (OE *blōma*). The mod. Eng. word *bloom* flower came into Eng. from ON in the 13th cent., but probably did not give rise to any surnames.

Vars. (of 2): Eng.: **Blo(o)mer**, **Blumer**.

Bloomenson *see* BLUMENSOHN

Bloomfield 1. Jewish (Ashkenazic): Anglicized form of Yid. *Blumfeld* (see BLUM). 2. English (Norman): habitation name from *Blonville*-sur-Mer in Calvados. The first element is probably an ON personal name; the second is OF *ville* settlement (see VILLE).

Vars.: **Blom(e)field**.

Bloomingdale Jewish (Ashkenazic): Anglicized form of Ger. *Blument(h)al* or Du. *Bloemendaal*, both of which are ornamental names composed of elements meaning 'flower valley'; cf. BLUM and DALE.

Bloschke *see* BLAISE

Bloshchenko *see* BLOKHIN

Bloss German: 1. nickname for a simple person, from MHG *blōz* simple, straightforward (MLG *bloot*; cf. mod. Ger. *bloss* only). 2. nickname for a pale person, from Ger. *blass* pale, wan (MHG *blas* weak, insignificant). 3. cogn. of Fr. BLAISE.

Var. (of 2 and 3): **Blass**.

Blouet *see* BLEWETT

Bloustein *see* BLAUSTEIN

Blower 1. English: from ME *blōwere* (OE *blāwere*, a deriv. of *blāwan* to blow; for the change in the vowel, cf. ROPER). The name was applied chiefly to someone who operated a bellows, either as a blacksmith's assistant or to provide wind for a church organ. In other cases it was applied to someone who blew a horn, i.e. a huntsman or a player of the musical instrument. 2. Welsh: patr. (with prefix *ap, ab*) from the given name *Llywerch*; see FLOWER.

Vars.: **Blow**; **Bloor(e)** (Midlands).

Patrs. (from 1): **Blowers** (E Anglia); **Blow(e)s**.

Blowick *see* BLAKE

Bloxham English: habitation name from *Bloxham* in Oxon. and *Bloxholm* in Lincs., both of which are recorded in Domesday Book as *Blockesham*, apparently from an unrecorded OE byname **Blocc* (presumably referring to a large, ungainly fellow; cf. BLOCK 1) + OE *hām* homestead.

Vars.: **Bloxam**; **Bloxsom(e)**.

Bloyd *see* LLOYD

Blücher German: from a place of this name, of Slav. origin, near Boizenburg on the Elbe.

Bluck English: of unknown origin; possibly a var. of BLACK, BLAKE, or BLOGG, with alteration of the vowel.

Var.: **BLICK**.

Blud *see* LLOYD

Bluehstein *see* BLAUSTEIN

Bluet *see* BLEWETT

Blum Jewish (Ashkenazic): ornamental name from Yid. *blum* flower (Ger. *Blume*).

Vars.: **Blume**, **Bluhm**, BLOOM.

Dims.: Jewish: **Blü(h)mke**.

Cpds (ornamental): Jewish: **Blum(en)berg**, **Blumberger** ('flower hill'; partly Anglicized as **Bloomberg**); **Blumenfarb** ('flower colour'); **Blum(en)feld(t)** (Anglicized as BLOOMFIELD and **Blumenfield**); **Blumenfrucht** ('flower fruit'); **Blumenkopf**

('flower head'); **Blumenkran(t)z**, **Blumenkranc** ('flower garland'; the second form is a Pol. spelling); **Blumenkrohn** ('flower crown'); **Blumrosen** ('flower roses'); **Blum(en)stein**, **Blumensztajn** ('flower stone'; the second form is a Pol. spelling); **Blument(h)al** ('flower valley'; see BLOOMINGDALE); **Blumenzweig** ('flower twig'). Swed.: **Blomberg** ('flower hill'); **Blomdahl** ('flower valley'); **Blomgren** ('flower branch'); **Blomqvist** ('flower twig'); **Blomstedt** ('flower homestead'); **Blomstrand** ('flower shore'); **Blomström** ('flower river').

Blumensohn Jewish (Ashkenazic): metr. from the Yidd. female given name *Blume* 'Flower'.

Vars.: **Bloomenson**; **Blumovitz** (E Ashkenazic); **Blumkin(d)** (from the dim. given name *Blumke*; for the excrescent *-d*, see SÜSSKIND), **Blumkine**.

Blunden English: of uncertain origin, perhaps a nickname for someone with grizzled hair, from OE *blonden-, blandan-feax* (a cpd of *blandan* to mix, blend + *feax* hair).

Blunt English: 1. nickname for someone with fair hair or a light complexion, from ANF *blunt* blond (OF *blund, blond*, of Gmc origin, perhaps akin to BLUNDEN). 2. nickname for a stupid person, from ME *blunt, blont* dull (prob. from OE *blinnan* to stop, cease or ON *blundr* sleepy, dozing).

Vars.: **Blund**, **Blount**.

Dims. (of 1): Eng.: **Blundell** (chiefly Lancs.). Fr.: **Blondel**, **Blond(el)eau**, **Blondiau(x)**, **Blondot**, **Blondet**, **Blondin**, **Blondy**, **Blondeix**. It.: **Biondell(in)i**, **Blondell(in)i**, **Biondetti**.

Bluntschli Swiss: nickname in the Alemannic dialect of German for a fat man, from MHG *blunsen* to swell up.

Vars.: **Pluntsch**, **Plunz** (also Bavarian).

Bluschke *see* BLAISE

Blüthner German: occupational name for a flower seller (cf. Silesian dialect *Blütnerei* flower shop), from Ger. *Blüte* bloom, flower head (MHG, OHG *bluot*).

Cpds (ornamental): **Blutreich** ('blossom-rich'); **Blut(h)stein**, **Blitstein** ('blossom stone').

Bly *see* BLIGH

Blythe English: 1. var. of BLIGH. 2. habitation name from any of several places, esp. the one in Northumb., named from OE *blīðe* merry, cheerful, probably on account of their pleasant situation, or from a nearby river, which would have been so named by reason of its merry chattering sound.

Vars.: **Blyth**, **Blyde**.

Boada Catalan: of uncertain origin, probably a habitation name from some place named from med. L *bouada* a measure of land equivalent to the amount that a team of oxen could plough in a day (from L *bōs*, gen. *bovis*, ox), or else from med. L *buada* silo, underground grain store (probably from L *volvita* vault).

Boakes *see* BALCH

Boal *see* BOWLER

Boarder English: 1. topographic name for someone who lived in a plank-built cottage, from OE *bord* board, plank of wood. 2. topographic name for someone who lived at the edge of a village or by some other boundary, from ME *border* (OF *bordure* edge, ultimately cogn. with OE *bord*, by way of the sense 'side of a ship').

Vars. (of 1): **Boardman** (chiefly Lancs.); **Bord(i)er**; **Board**, **Boord**.

Dims. (of 1): Prov.: **Bourdet**, **Bordey**; **Lebo(u)rdais**; **Bo(u)rdillon**, **Bo(u)rdillot**, **Bo(u)rdel(le)**, **Bourdelin**. Cat.: **Bordils**, **Bordiu**.

Augs. (of 1): Fr.: **Bo(u)rdas(se)**.

Boarer *see* BOWER

Boas Jewish and English: from the Hebr. male given name *Boaz* (of uncertain etymology), which, in the Bible, was borne by Ruth's rich kinsman who later became her husband. Boaz was occasionally used as a given name by Christians in Britain, and this seems to have given rise to a surname, which in the 18th cent. is found as far apart as St Ives in Cornwall and Dundee in Scotland.

Vars.: Jewish (Ashkenazic): **Boaz**, **Boazi** (with the Hebr. suffix *-i*). Eng. (Cornwall): **Boase**, **Boays**.

Patr.: Jewish (Ashkenazic): **Boasson**.

Boast English: nickname for a boastful man, from ME *bōst* bragging, vainglory (of uncertain origin; cf. Bos).

Var.: **Boost**.

Boater *see* BATE, BOWATER

Boberg *see* BOMAN

Bobo 1. Spanish: nickname for a sufferer from a speech defect, from Sp. *bobo* stammering (L *balbus*, which was also a Roman family name). 2. Jewish: of unknown origin.

Bobrov 1. Russian: patr. from the nickname *Bobr* 'Beaver'. The Russ. and the Eng. words are probably both ultimately cogn. with the Eng. vocab. word *brown*, referring to the brown colouring of the animal. 2. Jewish (E Ashkenazic): ornamental name from Russ. *bobr* beaver, one of the many Jewish ornamental names taken from words for animals.

Vars.: Jewish: **Bobroff**; **Bobrovsky**, **Bobrow(sky)**; **Bobrovitz(ki)**; **Bober(man)**.

Habitation name: Pol.: **Bobrowski**.

Bocca Italian: nickname for a talkative or indiscreet person, an orator, or a person with a large or deformed mouth, from It. *bocca* mouth (L *bucca* cheek).

Vars.: **Bocchi**; **Bucchi**, **Bucco**, **Bucca** (S Italy).

Dims.: It.: **Bocchetta**, **Bocchini**, **Boccucci**, **Boccuzzi**, **Boccotti**, **Buccello**, **Buccolini**.

Aug.: It.: **Boccone**.

Pejs.: It.: **Boccacci(o)**, **Boccaccia**.

Boccanegra Italian: nickname from *bocca* mouth (see BOCCA) + *negra* (fem.) black (see NOIR), referring to a foul-mouthed or abusive person.

Boček Czech: 1. nickname for an illegitimate child, from the vocab. word *boček*, dim. of *bok* side. 2. from a dim. of the OSlav. personal name *Bok*, which is apparently from *bok* side, and may well have denoted illegitimacy as in 1 above.

Var.: **Bočko**.

Bocheński Polish: occupational nickname for a baker, from Pol. *bochen* loaf + *-ski* suffix of surnames (see BARANOWSKI).

Bocian 1. Polish: nickname for a tall, gangling individual, from Pol. *bocian* stork. 2. Jewish (E Ashkenazic): ornamental name from Pol. *bocian* stork.

Habitation name: Pol.: **Bocianowski**.

Böck *see* BECK

Bockett *see* BURKETT

Böckler German: occupational name for a shield-bearer, from an agent deriv. of MHG *buckel* shield (boss) (LL *buccula*, dim. of *bucca* (distended) cheek, mouth; see BOCCA).

Bocock *see* BAUD

Bocquel *see* BUCK

Boczek Polish: apparently from Pol. *boczek* side, which also means 'bacon'. The application of this word as a surname is not clear; unlike the Czech cogn. BOČEK, the Pol. word does not mean 'illegitimate'. However, the surname is common in Silesia, and may perhaps be the result of influence from across the Czech border. Alternatively, it could be a metonymic occupational name for a supplier of bacon.

Habitation name: Pol. and Jewish (E Ashkenazic): **Boczkowski**.

Bodanis *see* BADANES

Bodas Spanish: nickname from *bodas* wedding (L *vōta* (marriage) vows, pl. of *vōtum*, from *vōvēre* to vow). The reasons for its adoption as a surname are probably anecdotal.

Boddington English: habitation name from either of the places so called in Gloucs. and Northants. The former is recorded in Domesday Book as *Botin(g)ton* 'settlement (OE *tūn*) associated with *Bōta*' (see BOTT), the latter as *Botendone* 'hill (OE *dūn*) of *Bōta*'.

Bodechon *see* BAUD

Bodega *see* BÖTTCHER

Bodeke *see* BOTHA

Bodfish English: of uncertain origin; possibly from ME *butte* flounder, flatfish + *fissche* fish, given either as a nickname or as an occupational name for a fishmonger.

Var.: **Botfish**.

Bodle *see* BOODLE

Bodley English: habitation name, possibly from *Budleigh* in Devon (*Bodelie* in Domesday Book), so called from OE *budda* beetle (or the same word used as a byname) + *lēah* wood, clearing. However, the surname is more common in the W Midlands than in Devon, and it may be that a Midland origin should be sought.

Vars.: **Bodleigh**, **Budleigh**.

Bodner 1. German: topographic name for someone who dwelt in a valley bottom, from a deriv. of Ger. *Boden* floor, bottom (MHG *bodem*, OHG *bodam*). 2. Jewish (Ashkenazic): occupational name for a cooper, from Yid. *bodner* cooper; see BÜTTNER, BONDAR.

Vars. (of 1): **Bothner**; **Bodmer** (esp. from *Bodmen* in Switzerland near Zurich).

Bodros Hungarian: nickname for a man with curly hair, from Hung. *bodros* curly, frizzy.

Body English: 1. nickname from ME *body*, OE *bodig* body, trunk, presumably denoting a corpulent individual. In ME the word was also used in the sense 'individual', 'person'; cf. GOODBODY. 2. occupational name for a messenger, ME *bode* (OE *boda*; cf. BOTHA), with the spelling altered to preserve a disyllabic pronunciation. This development can be clearly traced in Sussex.

Vars.: **Boddy**, **Bod(d)ie**, **Bodey**.

Boehm *see* BÖHM

Boeing *see* BOYE

Boering *see* BAUER

Boeter *see* BOWATER

Boeuf French: 1. nickname for a powerfully built man, from OF *boeuf* bull (L *bōs*, gen. *bovis*). In some cases it may have been originally a metonymic occupational name for a herdsman; cf. BOUVIER.

Vars.: **Leboeuf**; **Boey**, **Boez**.

Dims.: Fr.: **Bouvel(et)**, **Bouv(el)ot**, **Bouvon**, **Bou(v)et**. It.: **Bo(v)elli**, **Bo(v)etto**, **Bovino**, **Bovoli**; **Buini**; **Voiello** (Sicily, Campania).

Patrs.: It.: **Dal Bo**, **Del Bue**.

Boffin *see* BAUGHAN

Bofill Catalan: nickname from the elements *bo* good + *fill* son; cf. BEAVIS. It seems also to have been used as a given name in the early Middle Ages (the Latinized form *Bonofilio* appearing in Cat. territory in the 10th cent.), and this may also be a partial source of the surname.

Bogatov Russian: patr. from the nickname *Bogaty* 'Rich' (of disputed etymology, perhaps akin to *Bog* God, in the sense of being favoured by God; cf. L *divus* divine, *dives* rich).

Dim.: Czech: **Boháček**.

Bogdanov Russian, Bulgarian, Croatian, and Jewish (E Ashkenazic): patr. from the Slav. personal name *Bogdan* (fem. *Bogdana*), composed of the elements *Bog* God + *dan* gift. It was not a Christian name sanctioned by the Orthodox Church, but was common as a familiar vernacular name, usually representing an equivalent of the baptismal *Feodor* (Gk *Theodoros* 'gift of God'; see TUDOR) or *Feodot* (Gk *Theodotos* 'given by God'). Among the Orthodox it was sometimes used to denote an illegitimate child or foundling. The Jewish surname represents an adoption of one of the Slav. form.

Vars.: Croatian: **Bogdanović**. Jewish: **Bogdanski**, **Bogdanowitch**.

Dims. (not patrs.): Ukr.: **Bohdanchik**, **Bohdanets**.

Bogdassarian *see* BALTHASAR

Boggis English: probably a nickname from ME *boggish* boastful, haughty (of unknown origin, perhaps akin to the Gmc elements *bag* and *bug*, with the literal meaning

'swollen', 'puffed up'). The name (in the forms *Boge(y)s*, *Boga(y)s*) is found in the 12th cent. in Yorks. and E Anglia, and also around Bordeaux, which had trading links with E Anglia.

Vars.: **Bogg(er)s**.

Bøgh *see* BUCH

Boghan *see* BOWEN

Bogie Scots: habitation name from a place in Fife, first recorded as *Bolgyne*. The mod. Gael. name is *Srath* (valley) *Bhalgaidgh*. The origin of the placename is uncertain. Watson suggests a connection with Gael. *bolg* bag, sack, in the sense 'bag-shaped pool'.

Bogle Scots and N Irish: nickname for a person of frightening appearance, from older Scots *bogill* hobgoblin, bogy (of uncertain origin, probably Gael.).

Bogosian *see* PAUL

Bogren *see* BOMAN

Bogusławski Polish: from the given name *Bogusław* (composed of the Slav. elements *Bog* God + *slav* glory) + -*ski* suffix of surnames (see BARANOWSKI).

Dims.: Pol.: **Bogus(z)**, **Bogucki**. Czech: **Boušek**, **Bouška** (from the Czech dim. personal name *Bohuša*).

Patrs.: Croatian: **Bogosavljević**. Jewish (E Ashkenazic, adoptions of the non-Jewish surname): **Bogoslawicz**, **Bogoslavitz**.

Boháček *see* BOGATOV

Bohane *see* BOWEN

Bohdanchik *see* BOGDANOV

Bohden *see* BOTHA

Böhe *see* BOYE

Bohlens *see* BAUD

Bohlin *see* BOMAN

Böhling *see* BAUD

Böhm German: ethnic name for a native or inhabitant of Bohemia (the Czech part of Czechoslavakia), from *Böhmen* Ger. name of Bohemia (MHG *Böheim*, *Bēheim*). This derives its name from the tribal name *Baii* + *heim* homeland; the *Baii* were a tribe, probably Celtic, who inhabited the region in the 1st cent. AD and were gradually displaced by Slav. settlers up to the 5th cent. The same tribe also gave their name to *Bavaria* (see BAYER). Bohemia was an independent Slav. kingdom from the 7th cent. to 1526, when it fell to the Habsburgs. In 1627 it was formally declared a Habsburg Crown Land. It did not gain independence until 1918, after the defeat of Austria-Hungary in the First World War.

Vars.: **Böhme**, **Boehm(e)**; **Behm**, **Beha(i)m**; **Böhmig**, **Böhmisch**; **Bömak**.

Bohnhoff *see* BONHOFF

Böhrnsen *see* BEAR

Bohun *see* BOON

Boice *see* BOYCE

Boie *see* BOYE

Boieldieu French: nickname for someone who made frequent use of the OF oath *boyau Dieu* 'God's bowels' (from *bo(i)el* entrails, LL *botellus* + *Dieu* God; see DIOS). The surname is most common in the Rouen area.

Boileau French: nickname for a teetotaller, from OF *boi(re)* to drink (L *bibere*) + the def. art. *l'* (L *illa* that) + *eau* water (L *aqua*). Cf. DRINKWATER.

Var.: **Boilleau**

Boin *see* BOUDIN

Bois French: topographic name for someone living or working in a wood, from OF *bois* wood (LL *bosci*, pl. of *boscus* shrub, undergrowth, of Gmc origin; cf. OHG *busc*, Ger. *Busch*, Eng. *bush*). See also BUSH and BOISSIER.

Vars.: **Dubois**, **Desbois**; **Bos**, **Bost**, **Dubos(t)** (central France).

Dims.: Fr.: **Boisot**, **Boisin**, **Bo(u)squet**, **Boschet**, **Boschot**. It.: **Boschini**, **Boschetti**, **Boschetto**, **Boschello**, **Boschini**, **Boscolo**. Cat.: **Busquet(s)**.

Boisard *see* BISSELL

Boissier French: occupational name for a forester and, subsequently, for a carpenter or joiner, an OF agent noun from *bois* wood (see BOIS).

Var. (in the sense 'forester'): **Bosquier** (Normandy).

Dims.: Fr.: **Boissereau**. Prov.: **Bouscarel**, **Bouscayrol**. It.: **Boscarello**, **Bosca(r)ino**, **Busca(r)ino**; **Boscariolo**, **Boscaroli**, **Boscherini**.

Boisson *see* BUISSON

Boissy French: habitation name from any of numerous places so called in N and NW France. These in Roman times were called *Bucciācum* or *Buxeācum* and get their names either from a Gallo-Roman personal name *Buccius, Buttius* (of obscure origin) + the local suffix *-ācum*, or from L *buxus* box (the shrub; see Box) + *-ācum*.

Var.: **Bussy**.

Boiteux French: nickname for someone with a limp, OF *boisteux*, from *boiste* box (L *buxus*, Gk *pyxis* container, from *pyxos* box wood, of which boxes used to be made). The nickname arose because the limp was thought to be caused by the leg fitting incorrectly into the 'box' of the pelvis.

Vars.: **Boiteau**, **Boitel**.

Boivinet *see* BEVIN

Boje *see* BOYE

Bolag *see* POLAK

Bolam English (mainly Northumb.): habitation name from *Bolam* in Northumb. or Co. Durham, or from *Bolham* in Notts. These placenames could derive from the dat. pl. (*bolum*) of either of two unattested OE words, **bola* tree-trunk (cf. ON *bolr*, mod. Eng. *bole*) or **bol* rounded hill (cf. MLG *bolle* round object).

Bolan *see* HAYLING

Boland 1. English: habitation name from any of various places such as *Bowland* in Lancs. and W Yorks., *Bowlands* in E Yorks., and *Bolland* in Devon. All of them are probably named with OE *boga* bow (in the sense of a bend in a river) + *land* land. 2. Irish: Anglicized form of Gael. Ó

Beólláin 'descendant of *Beóllán*', an old Ir. name of uncertain origin.

Vars.: **Bolland(s)**, **Bowland(s)**.

Bolaños Spanish: habitation name from any of various places, for example in the provinces of Valladolid and Ciudad Real, so called from the pl. of Sp. *bolaño* boulder.

Bold 1. English: nickname from ME *bold* courageous, daring (OE *b(e)ald*, cogn. with OHG *bald*). In some cases it may derive from an OE personal name; see BAUD 1. 2. English: habitation name for someone who lived or worked at a particular house, from OE *bold*, the typical W Midland and NW form of OE *bōðl, bōtl* dwelling house, hall. 3. English: habitation name for someone from *Bold* in Lancs., which gets its name from OE *bold* dwelling, as in 2 above. The surname is especially frequent in Lancs. 4. German: cogn. of BAUD.

Vars. (of 1–3): **Bou(l)d**, BOLT. (Of 2 only): BOOTLE, BOODLE.

Boldero *see* BALDRY

Bolderstone *see* BALDERSTON

Bolding *see* BAUD

Bole *see* BOYLE

Boler *see* BOWLER

Bolesławski Polish: from the given name *Bolesław* (composed of the Slav. elements *bole* greater + *slav* glory) + *-ski* suffix of surnames (see BARANOWSKI).

Dims.: Pol.: **Bolek**. Czech: **Boleček**.

Boleyn *see* BULLEN

Bolger 1. English: occupational name for a leather worker, from ME, OF *boulgier*, agent deriv. of OF *boulge* leather bag, wallet (ME *bulge*, LL *bulga*, a word probably of Gaul. origin). 2. Irish: Anglicized form of Gael. Ó **Bolguidhir** 'descendant of *Bolgodhar*', a personal name composed of the elements *bolg* belly + *odhar* yellow, sallow.

Vars.: **B(o)ulger**, **Bolgar**, **Boulsher**.

Bolin *see* BOMAN

Bolingbroke English: habitation name from a place in Lincs., recorded in Domesday Book as *Bolinbroc*, from OE *Bulingbrōc* 'brook associated with *Bul(l)a*' (see BULL).

Bolino *see* JACOB

Bolitho Cornish: habitation name from one of two places in Cornwall, so called from Cornish *bos, bod* dwelling + a personal name of uncertain form.

Bolívar Spanish form of Basque **Bolibar**: habitation name from a place in the province of Biscay, so called from Basque *bolu* mill + *ibar* meadow, riverbank.

Bölke *see* BAUD

Bolognese Italian: habitation name for someone from the city of *Bologna* in N Italy. In early classical times this was an independent Tuscan town called *Felsina*, but was renamed *Bonōnia* (perhaps a deriv. of *bonus* good; see BON) when it became a Roman colony in 190 BC. See also BULLEN.

Var.: **Bologna**.

Bolshakov Russian: patr. from the nickname or familiar name *Bolshak* 'Big One', from *bolshoi* big (see BOLSHOV). This was often used as a familiar name to distinguish between two sons bearing the same given name. It was also a nickname for a large man. Compare MENSHIKOV.

Bolshov Russian: patr. from the adj. *bolshoi* big, normally referring simply to physical size (cf. BOLSHAKOV).

Bolster *see* POLSTER

Bolt English (chiefly W Country): **1.** occupational name for a bolter or sifter of flour, from the ME verb *bo(u)lt* (OF *beluter*, of Gmc origin). **2.** from ME *bolt* bolt, bar (OE *bolt* arrow; cf. the *bolt* shot from a crossbow). In part this may have originated as a nickname or byname for a short but powerfully built person (cf. ON *Boltr* in the same sense), in part as a metonymic occupational name for a maker of bolts. **3.** var. of BOLD.

Vars.: **Boult**, **Bo(u)lter**.

Boltflower English: occupational nickname for a miller or sifter of flour, from ME *boult* to sift (see BOLT 1) + *flour*, *flower* flour (see FLOWER).

Vars.: **Boultflower**, **Bo(u)tflower**, **Bough(t)flower**.

Bolton English: habitation name from any of the numerous places in N England, esp. the one in Lancs., so called from OE *bōðl* dwelling, house (see BOLD 2) + *tūn* enclosure, settlement.

Var.: **Boulton**.

Boltwood English: habitation name from an unidentified minor place, so called from the OE byname *Bolt* (see BOLT 2) + *wudu* WOOD.

Bolwell English (W Country): of uncertain origin, perhaps a habitation name from an unidentified place named with the OE elements *bol* trunk, plank + *well(a)* spring, stream, i.e. the site of a primitive bridge. On the other hand, it may be an Anglicized form of the Norman habitation name *de Bolville*, which is recorded in Somerset in the 13th cent.

Bömak *see* BÖHM

Boman Swedish: topographic name for someone who lived on an outlying homestead, from Swed. *bo* dwelling, farm (ON *bú*) + *man* man (ON *maðr*). In some cases this may have been arbitrarily adopted as an ornamental name by people who had no connection with any outlying farm or homestead. **2.** English: variant of BOWMAN

Vars.: **Bohman**; **Bo(h)lin**.

Cpds (ornamental): **Boberg** ('farm hill'); **Bogren** ('farm branch'); **Bolinder** ('dweller by the farm lime tree'); **Boqvist** ('farm twig'); **Boström** ('farm river').

Bompard Provençal: nickname meaning 'good companion', from OProv. *bon* good (see BON) + *par* equal, fellow (see PEAR 2).

Bomphrey *see* HUMPHREY

Bomptan *see* BONTEMPS

Bon French: **1.** generally an approbatory (or ironic) nickname, from OF *bon* good (L *bonus*). **2.** occasionally from the L personal name *Bonus* (likewise meaning 'Good'), which was borne by a minor 3rd-cent. Christian saint, martyred at Rome with eleven companions under the Emperor Vespasian. It was adopted as a given name partly in his honour and partly because of the transparently well-omened meaning.

Vars.: **Lebon**; **Bonne**, **Labonne** (fem.).

Dims.: Fr.: **Bon(n)in**, **Bonnineau**, **Bon(n)ot**, BONNET. Prov.: **Bounin**, **Bouniol**. Port.: **Bonito** (in the sense 'pretty'). It.: **Bonelli**, **Boniello**, **Bonini**, **Bonucci**, **Bonuccello**, **Bonioli**, **Bon(i)otti**; **Bonito**, **Boniello** (S Italy); **Bonutti** (Venetia).

Augs.: Fr.: **Bonnat**. It.: **Bononi**.

Pejs.: Fr.: **Bon(n)ard**, **Bonnaud**. Prov.: **Bounaud**. It.: **Bonacci(o)**, **Bonazzi**, **Bonassi**; see also FIBONACCI.

Patrs.: It.: **De Bono**, **Di B(u)ono**, **De Boni(s)**, **Del B(u)ono**; **De Vuono** (S Italy).

Bonaccorso Italian: from a medieval given name, composed of the elements *bono* good (see BON) + *accorso* aid (LL *accursus*, from *adcurrere* to aid, lit. run up); cf. BONAIUTO.

Vars.: **Bonacorso**, **Bonac(c)orsi**, **Bonac(c)urso**; **Accorso**, **Accorsi**, **Accurs(i)o**; **Corso**, **Corsi**.

Dims.: **Corsini**, **Corsell(in)i**, **Corsello**, **Corsetti**.

Patrs.: **D'Accorso**, **D'Accurs(i)o**, **Del Corso**.

Bonagente Italian: nickname for someone who came from a well-respected family, perhaps someone suspected of being the illegitimate offspring of a noble house; from *bona* (fem.) good (see BON) + *gente* family (L *gens*, gen. *gentis*).

Bonaiuto Italian: from a given name that was relatively frequent in the Middle Ages. Composed of the elements *bono* good (see BON) + *aiuto* help, aid (LL *adiutus*, from *adiuvāre* to help), it was bestowed in the hope that the son so named would grow up to be a support to the family.

Bonally Scots (now rare): of uncertain origin. According to Black, it is from a placename, *Bonaly* near Edinburgh or *Banaley* (now lost) in Fife, which are of obscure origin. According to Reaney, it is more probably from *bonaillie*, a catch phrase used with a toast drunk on parting, from OF *bon* good (see BON) + *aller* to go (from L *ambulāre* to walk), in which case it would have arisen as a nickname for one who made frequent use of this expression.

Vars.: **Bonallo**, **Bon(n)ella**, **Bonello**.

Bonaparte Italian: from It. *bona* (fem.) good (see BON) + *parte* part, portion, place, party (L *pars*, gen. *partis*). The origin of application of this expression as a surname is uncertain, but it is claimed that it arose in the politics of early medieval Florence, where one party on the governing council described itself as the 'good party' (*buona parte*). The name has also been adopted as a Jewish surname.

Var.: **Buonaparte**.

Bonar **1.** English and Scots: nickname from ME *boner(e)*, *bonour* gentle, courteous, handsome (OF *bonnaire*, from the phrase *de bon(ne) aire* of good bearing or appearance, from which also comes mod. Eng. *debonair*). **2.** Irish (Donegal): trans. of Gael. **Ó Cnáimhsighe** 'descendant of *Cnáimhseach*', a byname meaning 'Mid-wife'. The word seems to be a deriv. of *cnámh* bone (with the fem. ending *-seach*), but if so the reason for this is not clear.

Vars.: **Bonnar**, **Bon(n)er**.

Dim. (of 1): It.: **Bonarelli**.

Bonchrétien French: nickname for a notably pious individual, or ironically for a notorious reprobate, from OF *bon* good (see BON) + *chrétien* CHRISTIAN.

Var.: **Bonchrestien**.

Bond English: status name for a peasant farmer or husbandman, ME *bonde* (OE *bonda, bunda*, reinforced by ON *bónde, bóndi*). The ON word was also in use as a personal name, and this has given rise to other Eng. and Scandinavian surnames alongside those originating as status names. The status of the peasant farmer fluctuated considerably during the Middle Ages; moreover, the underlying Gmc word is of disputed origin and meaning. *OED* connects it with OE *būan* to dwell, via the pres. part. *būende* dweller. However, it is more likely that the word is ultimately akin to *bindan* to bind: the Proto-Gmc word **bonda* probably signified a member of a band or tribe bound together by loyalty to their chief. Among Gmc peoples who settled to an agricultural life, the term came to signify a farmer holding lands from, and bound by loyalty to, a lord; from this developed the sense of a free landholder as opposed to a serf. In England after the Norman Conquest the word sank in status and became associated with the notion of bound servitude, whereas in Scandinavia *bonde* means simply 'farmer', with no such derogatory overtones.

Vars.: **Bonde**, **Bound**; **Bound(e)y**; **Bund(e)y**.

Patrs.: Eng.: **Bo(u)nds**. Norw., Dan.: **Bondesen**, **Bonnesen**.

Bondar Ukrainian: occupational name for a cooper, Ukr. *bondar*, metathesized cogn. of Pol. BEDNARZ, Ger. BÜTTNER.

Patrs.: Belorussian: **Bondarovich**. Jewish: **Bonderow**, **Bonderoff**, **Bonderefsky**.

Bondiou Provençal: nickname from OProv. *bon* good (see BON) + *diou* God (L *deus*), presumably denoting a frequent user of this oath.

Var.: **Bondivenne**.

Bone English: 1. nickname, of Norman origin, meaning 'good', from OF *bon* good (see BON). 2. nickname for a thin, bony individual; see BAIN 2.

Vars. (of 1): **Bonn**, **Bunn**; BOON.

Bonehill English: habitation name from a place in Staffs. (*Bolenhull* in early records), probably so called from the gen. case of OE *bula* bull(ock) (or the same word used as a personal name) + OE *hyll* HILL.

Bonenfant French: nickname, probably slightly mocking in tone, from *bon* good (see BON) + *enfant* child (see INFANTE).

Bones *see* BUNIN

Bonfield English (Norman): habitation name, altered by folk etymology, from any one of three places in Normandy called *Bonneville*, from OF *bonne* (fem.) good (see BON) + *ville* settlement (see VILLE).

Var.: **Bondfield**.

Bongars French: nickname for a trusted servant, from *bon* good (see BON) + *gars* servant, lad (see GARS).

Var.: **Bongard**.

Bongi *see* BUDGEN

Bonham English: 1. generally an alteration of OF *bon homme* (L *bonus homo*). This had two senses relevant to surname formation; partly it had the literal meaning 'good man', and partly it came to mean 'peasant farmer'. 2. habitation name from an unidentified place, of which the second element is OE *hām* homestead, or possibly *hamm* water meadow, while the first may be a personal name (OE *Buna*), of unknown etymology.

Dims. (of 1): Fr.: **Bonhommet**, **Bonzoumet**.

Bonheur French: from OF *bonne* (fem.) good (see BON) + *heure* moment, time (from L *hōra* hour), probably a given name for a child whose birth was felt to be a happy or lucky moment, e.g. one born to parents long childless. The mod. Fr. sense 'happiness' is a more recent development, and is unlikely to underlie any instances of the surname.

Var.: **Bonheure**.

Bonhoff German: habitation name from a place near Siegburg in Westphalia or from any of several other minor localities in the same area. The second element is OHG *hof* court, yard (see HOFER); the first is of unknown origin (Bahlow regards it as one of many pre-Gmc terms denoting a marshy locality, but it is equally plausibly a personal name, perhaps cognate with OE *Buna* (cf. BONHAM 2)).

Vars.: **Bonhöffer**; **Bohnhoff**.

Boniface English and French: from the medieval given name *Boniface* (L *Bonifatius*, from *bonum* good + *fātum* fate, destiny). In LL *-ti-* and *-ci-* came to be pronounced identically; the name was thus often respelled *Bonifacius* and assigned the meaning 'doer of good deeds', derived by folk etymology from L *facere* to do. Bonifatius was the name of the Roman military governor of N Africa in 422–32, who was a friend of St Augustine, and it was also borne by various early Christian saints, notably St Boniface (*c*.675–754), who was born in Devon and martyred in Friesland after evangelical work among Ger. tribes. It was also adopted by nine popes. The given name was always more popular in Italy (in its various cogn. forms; see below) than elsewhere; the original sense 'well fated' remained transparent in It., so the name was often bestowed there for the sake of the good omen.

Vars.: Eng.: **Bonniface**, **Bonifas**.

Dims.: It.: **Bonifacino**; **Fazzini**, **Fazzioli**, **Fazzuoli**, **Fassini**, **Fassioli**, **Fac(c)ini**, **Faccioli**, **Facciotti**. Hung.: **Bónis**.

Augs.: It.: **Fassone**, **Faccione**.

Patrs.: It.: **De Fazio**, **Di Fazio**, **De Facci**. Du.: **Faasen**.

Bonilla Spanish: habitation name from places in the provinces of Ávila and Cuenca, so called from LL *balnella*, pl. of *balnellum*, a dim. of class. L *balneum* bath (cf. BAIN 4).

Bonjour French: nickname from OF *bon* good (see BON) + *jorn, jour* day (LL *diurnum*, a deriv. of class. L *diēs*), presumably denoting someone who made frequent use of this salutation. The It. and Sp. cogns. were also occasionally used as given names in the Middle Ages, bestowed on a child as an expression of the parent's satisfaction at the birth, or for the sake of a good omen.

Bonnefoi French: nickname from Fr. *bonne* (fem.) good (see BON) + *foi* faith (L *fidēs*), presumably denoting someone who made frequent use of this oath.

Bonner *see* POYNER

Bonnet French: 1. nickname from a dim. of BON. 2. from the L personal name *Bonītus*, a deriv. of *bonus* good (see BON). This name was borne by a 7th-cent. saint from the Auvergne, in whose honour it enjoyed considerable popularity there and elsewhere in France throughout the Middle Ages. 3. metonymic occupational name for a milliner, or nickname for a wearer of unusual headgear, from OF *bon(n)et* bonnet, hat. This word is found in med. L as *abonnis*, but is of unknown origin.
Vars. (chiefly of 2): **Bonet**; **Bon(n)ay**, **Bon(n)ey** (E France); **Bon(n)ex** (central France); **Bon(n)ez** (N France).
Dims.: Fr. (chiefly of 2): **Bonnet(a)in**, **Bonneteau**, **Bonneton**, **Bonnetot**.
Pej. (of 3): Fr.: **Bonnetaud**.
Patr. (from 2): Fr.: **Dubonnet**.

Bonnevie French: nickname for someone who enjoyed life, a glutton or womanizer or simply someone who enjoyed prosperity, from OF *bonne* (fem.) good (see BON) + *vi(th)e* life (L *vīta*). In some cases the It. and Port. cogns. may derive from a given name bestowed on a child for the sake of the good omen.

Bonney English (chiefly Lancs.): nickname for a handsome person, esp. a large or well-built one, from N dial. *bonnie* fine, beautiful (still a common Scots word; apparently a dim. of OF *bon* good, although the development is not clear).

Bonnington English: habitation name from any of various places of this name in Kent, Northumb., and Scotland, from OE *Buningtūn* 'settlement (OE *tūn*) associated with *Buna*'; cf. BONHAM 2.

Bonomo Italian: 1. nickname meaning 'good man', a cogn. of BONHAM 1. 2. occupational name for various elected officials, for example in 12th-cent. Florence, who bore this title.
Dims.: **Bonomelli**, **Bonometti**, **Bonomini**, **Bonomolo**.
Aug.: **Bonomone**.

Bonser English: nickname from OF *bon sire* good sir, given either to a fine gentleman (perhaps ironically), or to someone who made frequent use of this term of address. The surname is now found chiefly in Notts.

Bontein *see* BUNTING

Bontemps French: nickname for a person of cheerful disposition, from OF *bon* good (see BON) + *temps* weather (L *tempus* time, season). Cf. MERRYWEATHER.
Vars.: **Bontant**, **Bomptan**.
Dim.: It.: **Bontempelli**.

Bonthuys Dutch: from residence in a brightly coloured or in a half-timbered house. MDu. *bont*, MLG *bunt* means either 'black-and-white', 'piebald', or 'gaily coloured'.

MHG *bunt* means 'black-and-white' or 'grey-and-white' and is applied particularly to furs; the regular MHG word for 'brightly coloured' is *vēch*. The most plausible explanation for the origin for the name is therefore 'one living in a black-and-white house'.

Bonvoisin French: nickname for a neighbourly person, from OF *bon* good (see BON) + *voisin* neighbour (L *vīcīnus*, a deriv. of *vīcus* neighbourhood, village).

Boocock *see* BAUD

Boodle English: topographic name for someone who lived or worked at a particular large house, from OE *bōðl*, *bōtl* dwelling house, hall, or habitation name for someone who came from a place named with this element, such as *Buddle* in Fordingbridge, Hants, *Buddle* in Niton, Isle of Wight, or *Buddle* Oak in Halse, Somerset.
Vars.: **Buddle**; **Buttle**; **Bodle**, **Boydell** (Sussex, probably from *Bodle* Street near Hailsham); BOOTLE, BOLD.

Boohan *see* BOWEN

Bookbinder *see* BINDER

Booker English: 1. occupational name for someone concerned with books, generally as a scribe or binder, from ME *boker*, OE *bōcere*, agent deriv. of *bōc* book. 2. occupational name for a bleacher of cloth, from ME *bouken* to bleach, steep in lye (from MLG, MDu. *būken*). See also BOWKER 2.

Bool *see* BULL

Boon 1. English (Norman): var. of BONE 1. 2. English (Norman): habitation name from *Bohon* in La Manche, of obscure etymology. 3. Dutch: cogn. of BEAN 1.
Vars. (of 1 and 2): **Boone** (the more common U.S. spelling); **Bown(e)**. (Of 2 only): **Bohun**.

Boontje *see* BEAN

Boord *see* BOARDER

Boorer *see* BOWER

Boorne *see* BOURNE

Boosey 1. English: topographic name for someone who lived by a cattle stall, and so in effect an occupational name for a cowherd, from ME *bōs(e)* cattle stall (from OE *bōsig*, reinforced by the cogn. MLG *bōs*). 2. Scots: habitation name from *Balhousie* in Fife, earlier *Balwolsy*, probably from Gael. *baile a'choille* farmstead of the wood.
Vars.: **Boosie**, **Bousie**.

Boost *see* BOAST

Boot 1. English: metonymic occupational name for a maker or seller of boots, from ME, OF *bote* (of unknown origin). 2. Dutch: cogn. of BATE 2.
Var. (of 1): **Boote**.

Booth N English: topographic name for someone who lived in a small hut or bothy (ME *bōth(e)*), esp. a cowman or shepherd. The word is of Scandinavian origin (cf. ODa. *bōth*, OIcel. *būð*), and was used to denote various kinds of temporary shelter, typically a cowshed or a herdsman's hut. The surname is still today more common in N England, where Scandinavian influence was more marked, and in Scotland, where the word was borrowed into Gael. as *both(an)*.

Vars.: **Boothe**; **Boothman**.

Boothby English: habitation name from a group of villages in Lincs., so called from Northern ME *bōth(e)* hut, shed (see BOOTH) + *by* farm, settlement (ON *býr*).

Boothroyd English: habitation name from a place in W Yorks., so called from Northern ME *bōth(e)* hut, shed (see BOOTH) + *royd* clearing (see RHODES).

Bootle English: habitation name from places in Lancs. and Cumb., so called from OE *bōtl* dwelling, large house (see BOODLE, BOLD 2).

Bopf *see* POPP

Boquel *see* BUCK

Boqvist *see* BOMAN

Borbón *see* BOURBON

Borchers *see* BURKETT

Bordasse *see* BOARDER

Bordeaux French: habitation name from the city in Gironde, apparently so called from Old Aquitanian roots of obscure significance, *burd* and *gala*.

Borden English: habitation name from a place in Kent, perhaps so called from OE *bār* boar + *denn* (swine) pasture. Alternatively the first element may be OE *bord* board (cf. BOARDER 1) or a Gmc element meaning 'elevation', 'hill' (cf. BOREHAM).

Boreham English: habitation name from any of three places so called, in Essex, Herts., and Sussex. The surname is most common in Essex. In each case early forms point clearly to an OE first element **bor*, which is not independently attested, but may be akin to OHG *bor* upper chamber and OE *borlice* excellently, with some such sense as 'elevation', 'hill'. The second element is OE *hām* homestead.

Borel *see* BOURREL

Borenshtain *see* BERNSTEIN

Borer *see* BOWER

Boret *see* BURRETT

Borgazzo *see* BURKE

Borgeest *see* GEEST

Borger *see* BURGER

Borges Catalan and Portuguese: habitation name from a place in the province of Tarragona, N Spain, of uncertain etymology. It may represent a pl. form of BORJA, or else it may be of pre-Roman origin, cogn. with the Fr. placename *Bourges*.

Borghesetti *see* BURGESS

Borgne French: nickname for a person with only one eye or with a squint, from OF *borgne* squinting, of unknown origin.

Vars.: **Borne**, **Lebor(g)ne**.

Dims.: **Bor(g)net**, **Bor(g)not** (E France). Prov.: **Borgn(i)ol**.

Pej.: **Bornard** (E France).

Borisov Russian: patr. from the common given name *Boris*. The etymology of this is uncertain. It may be a shortening of an OSlav. personal name, *Boroslav*, from *bor* struggle, conflict + *slav* glory, but more probably it is an alteration of the OBulg. personal name *Bogoris*, borne by the King of the Bulgars (sometimes known as Boris) who was converted to Christianity in 864. This is a byname from Turkic *bogori* small. *Boris* is one of the very few names of non Byzantine origin admitted as a baptismal name in the Orthodox Church, largely because of the popular cult of St Boris (d. 1010), patron saint of Moscow (whose baptismal name was ROMAN). The surname has also occasionally been adopted by Jews.

Var.: **Borisovich**.

Dims. (patrs.): Russ.: **Borin**, **Bori(sh)chev**.

Borja Spanish: habitation name from a place in the province of Saragossa, so called from Arabic *borğ, borj* tower.

Borkowski Polish and Jewish (E Ashkenazic): habitation name from any of several places called *Borków* (so named from Pol. *bór* pine forest + *-ek* dim. suffix + *-ów* possessive suffix forming placenames), with the addition of the suffix of local surnames *-ski* (see BARANOWSKI).

Var.: **Borek**.

Borland Scots: habitation name from any of several places called *Bor(e)land* or *Bordland*, which get their names from ME or OE *bord* board, table + *land* land, i.e. land which supplied the lord's table, in other words 'home farm'.

Var.: **Boreland**.

Borley English: habitation name from *Borley* in Essex or *Boreley* in Worcs., both so called from OE *bār* (wild) boar (cf. BORDEN) + *lēah* wood, clearing.

Var.: **Boreley**.

Bormann *see* BOURNE

Börnsen *see* BEAR

Borochov *see* BARUCH

Borodin Russian: patr. from the nickname *Boroda* 'BEARD' (the two words are ultimately cogn.). In E Europe cleanshavenness was in fashion from the 12th to 16th cents., except among Jews, so bearded men stood out as exceptional. Among Jewish men, on the other hand, beards were the norm, and someone who was beardles stood out, hence the E Ashkenazic surname **Bezborodko** 'Beardless'.

Dims. (patrs.): Russ.: **Borodulin**, **Baradulin**. Beloruss.: **Baradzeya**.

Boronat Catalan: from a dissimilated form of the medieval given name *Bonanat* (L *bonā (horā) nātus* born in a good hour; cf. BONHEUR), bestowed on a child as a good omen. It may also in part have been a nickname for a lucky individual.

Borowski Polish and Jewish (E Ashkenazic): habitation name from a place named from Pol. *bór* pine forest + *-ów* possessive suffix, with the adition of *-ski* suffix of local surnames (see BARANOWSKI). The Pol. word *borowik* means 'forest mushroom', and in some cases surnames of this group may derive from it. In the case of Jewish instances of these surnames, the origin is generally ornamental.

Vars.: Pol.: **Borowicki**, **Borowiński**; **Borecki**, **Borucki**; **Burski**; **Borowiec**, **Borowicz** (patr. in form). Jewish: **Borovski**, **Borovsky**, **Borowsky**. See also BORKOWSKI.

Borrego Spanish: nickname for a simpleton or a gentle person, or metonymic occupational name for a shepherd, from Sp. *borrego* lamb (LL *burrēcus*, a deriv. of *burra* lambswool).

Var.: **Borreguero** (an agent deriv.).

Borroman *see* BURKMAN

Borromeo Italian: nickname for a pious person who had made the pilgrimage to Rome, or an amiable man who bore the given name *Romeo*, from *bono* good (see BON) + *Romeo* ROMAN.

Var.: **Borromei**.

Borrow *see* BURROWS

Borthram *see* BERTRAM

Borthwick Scots: habitation name from a place near Hawick in S Scotland, where a family of this name held Borthwick Castle since the 14th cent. The placename comes from OE *bord* board, table + *wīc* outlying village, dairy farm (see WICK). For the sense, compare BORLAND.

Bortolazzi *see* BARTHOLOMEW

Borton *see* BURTON

Borwick *see* BARWICK

Bos French: **1.** var. of BOIS. **2.** from a Gmc personal name, *Boso*, derived from an element meaning 'audacious'; cf. MHG *boese*, MLG *bōse* reckless, daring (mod. Ger. *böse* naughty).

Vars. (of 2, from the oblique case of the Gmc word): **Boson**, **Bo(u)zon**.

Dims. (of 2): Fr.: **Bosonnet**, **Bozounet**. It.: **Boselli**, **Bosetti**, **Bosin(ell)i**, **Bosotti**, **Bosutti**.

Aug. (of 2): It.: **Bosone**.

Bosanquet **1.** Cornish: habitation name from *Bosanketh*, so called from Corn. *bos, bod* dwelling + a personal name of uncertain form. **2.** English, of Huguenot origin: nickname for a short person, from the S French dial. term *bouzanquet* dwarf.

Boscaino *see* BOISSIER

Boscawen Cornish: habitation name from any of three places, two near St Buryan and the other near Helston, so called from Corn. *bos, bod* dwelling + *scawen* elder tree (cf. Bret. *scaven*, W *ysgawen*).

Boschello *see* BOIS

Böschgen *see* BUSH

Boshell *see* BISSELL

Bossard French: **1.** from a Gmc personal name composed of the elements *bos* audacious (see BOS 2) + *hard* hardy, brave. **2.** nickname for a hunchback, from OF *bosse* hump, hunched back (of unknown origin) + the pej. suffix *-ard*.

Dim.: Prov.: **Boussardon**.

Bosse *see* BURKETT

Bossut French: nickname for a hunchback, from OF *bossu* hunchbacked (a deriv. of *bosse* lump, hump; cf. BOSSARD 2).

Vars.: **Bossé**, **Bosseux**; **Bosse**.

Dim.: Fr.: **Bosuet**.

Aug.: Fr.: **Bossuat**.

Bostock English: habitation name from *Bostock* in Ches. (*Botestoch* in Domesday Book), so called from the OE personal name *Bōta* (see BOTT) + OE *stoc* place (see STOKE).

Boston English: habitation name from the place in Lincs., the name of which means 'Bōtwulf's stone'. This has been considered to refer to St Botulf, and to be the site of the monastery that he built in the 7th cent., but it is more likely that the Bōtwulf of the placename was an ordinary landowner, and that the association with the saint was a later development because of the name.

Boström *see* BOMAN

Boswell English and Scots (Norman): habitation name from *Beuzeville* in Seine Maritime, which gets its name from OF *Beuze* (a personal name probably of Gmc origin; cf. BOS 2) + *ville* settlement (see VILLE). The final element has been altered as a result of association with the common placename ending *-well* 'spring', 'stream'.

Var.: **Boswall**.

Bosworth English: habitation name from Market *Bosworth* in Leics., so called from an OE personal name *Bōsa* (cf. BOS 2) + OE *worð* enclosure (see WORTH). Husbands Bosworth is a different name in origin (*Bareswordе* in Domesday Book), from OE *bār* boar + *worð*.

Botas Spanish: **1.** metonymic occupational name for a maker of leather bottles for wine, or a maker of wine casks, called *botas* in OSp. (from LL *but(t)is*; see also BÜTTNER and BUTLER). **2.** metonymic occupational name for a maker of boots, or nickname for a wearer of boots, at a time when the majority of the population had more primitive footwear. The vocab. word for all of these was *botas*, which is of uncertain origin; it has been suggested that it is the same word as in 1, since both boots and bottles were normally made of leather, but it is more probably of separate origin.

Var.: **Boto**.

Dim.: **Botija**.

Bote Spanish: **1.** metonymic occupational name for a potter, from Sp. *bote* vase, pot (of unknown origin, perhaps akin to Eng. *pot*; see POTTER). **2.** nickname for a forceful or pugnacious individual, from Sp. *bote* blow, thrust (a deriv. of *botar* to hit, strike, apparently of Gmc origin and cogn. with mod. Eng. *beat*, OE *bēatan*).

Botelho Portuguese: metonymic occupational name for a gatherer of kelp or seaweed, Port. *botelho*.

Boter *see* BOWATER

Botfish *see* BODFISH

Botflower *see* BOLTFLOWER

Botha Frisian: from an OFris. personal name *Botho* 'Messenger' (OHG *Boto, Bodo*, from Gmc **buð* to announce). See also BOTT and BOUDON.
Dims.: Fris.: **Botje, Botma.** Low Ger.: **Bodeke, Badeke.**
Patrs.: Low Ger.: **Bo(h)den, Baden(ius), Bading.**

Bothner *see* BODNER

Bothwell Scots and N Irish: habitation name from a place in the former county of Lanarks. (now part of Strathclyde region), so called from ME *bōth(e)* (see BOOTH) + *well(a)* spring, stream (see WELL).

Botler *see* BUTLER

Bott English: apparently from an OE personal name, of uncertain form and origin. It may be a cogn. of BOTHA, or it may be akin to BUTT. Forms such as Walter *le botte* (Oxon. 1279) seem to point to a nickname, perhaps from OF *bot* but, cask, or the homonymous *bot* toad; cf. BOTTRELL.
Patr.: **Botting.**

Böttcher German: one of several occupational names for a cooper, Ger. *Böttcher*, from MHG *botecher, bötticher, bütticher*, an agent deriv. of *botige, butche* wine barrel (OHG *potega, poteche*, via L *apotēca* from Gk *apothēkē* wine cellar, store room). Böttcher was the term regularly used for a cooper in N and E Germany. See also BINDER, BÜTTNER, and SCHÄFFLER.
Vars.: **Bötticher, Böttger, Bötjer, Bittcher.**

Botticelli *see* JACOB

Bottman *see* BATE

Bottom N English: topographic name for someone who lived in a broad valley, from OE *botm* valley bottom.
Vars.: **Bottoms, Bottams, Botham.**
Cpds.: Eng.: HIGGINBOTTOM; LONGBOTTOM; SHUFFLEBOTTOM; SIDEBOTTOM; WINTERBOTTOM.

Bottomley English (Yorks. and Lancs.): habitation name from a place in W Yorks., so called from OE *botm* broad valley (see BOTTOM) + *lēah* wood, clearing.

Bottrell English (Norman): probably a habitation name from *Les Bottereaux* in Eure, Normandy, apparently so named from being infested with toads. The placename is recorded in the late 12th cent. in the L form *Boterelli*, from a dim. of OF *bot* toad (of Gmc origin, perhaps akin to a root meaning 'to swell, puff up'; cf. BUTT 1). It has also been suggested that the name originated as a Norman nickname, from ONF *bottereau* toad, or as an occupational name for a worker in a buttery, ME *butterer*.
Vars.: **Botterell, Bott(e)rill; Butteriss.**

Bouch *see* BUDGE

Boucher *see* BUTCHER

Boud *see* BOLD

Bouda *see* BUZEK

Bouderickx *see* BALDRY

Boudet 1. French: dim. of BOUDON. 2. Provençal: aphetic form of Prov. *néboudet* great-nephew, dim. of *nébout* nephew (L *nepos*, gen. *nepōtis*, nephew, grandson).

Boudewijns *see* BALDWIN

Boudin French: 1. dim. of BOUDON. 2. metonymic occupational name for a maker of black pudding and sausages, or nickname for a rotund individual, from OF *boudin* black pudding (cogn. with ME *poding* pudding, LG *pudden* sausage, probably from a Gmc root meaning 'to bulge'; cf. BOTT, BOTTRELL, and BUTT 1).
Vars.: **Boudy, Bo(u)in.** (Of 2 only): **Boudinier** (an agent noun).
Dims.: Fr.: **Bo(ud)ineau, Boudinot.**

Boudon French: from the OF oblique case of the Gmc personal name *Bodo* 'Messenger', 'Herald' (see BOTHA).
Var.: BOUTON.
Dims.: BOUDET, BOUDIN, **Boudot, Boudeau.**

Boudts *see* RUMBOLD

Bouet *see* BOEUF

Bouffard French: nickname for a glutton, a pej. from OF *bouffer* to stuff oneself, earlier to puff out the cheeks (a word probably of imitative origin).
Vars.: **Boufard, Bouffaud.**

Bougan *see* BOWEN

Bough (pronounced /bɒf/ or /baʊ/): 1. English and Irish: var. of Bow. 2. English: from a Norman form of OF *boeuf* bull. See BOEUF.

Boughflower *see* BOLTFLOWER

Boughton English: habitation name from any of the numerous places so called. Those in Cambs. (formerly Hunts.). Lincs., Norfolk, Northants, and Notts. get their first element from the OE byname *Bucca* (see BUCK 1); those in Ches. and Kent get the name from OE *bōc* beech (a byform of *bēce*; see BEECH 2) + *tūn* enclosure, settlement.

Bouille French: 1. topographic name for someone who lived by a marsh, OF *bouille* (a deriv. of *boue* mud, of Celt. origin). 2. topographic name for someone who lived by a birch grove, from the OF dial. term *bouille* (from LL *betul(l)ia*, a deriv. of *bettius* birch; cf. BOUL 1 and BÈS).
Var.: **Delbouille.**
Dims.: **Bouillet(te), Bouillé, Bouillot, Bouillon.**
Aug.: **Bouillat.**
Pej.: **Bouillard.**

Boul French: 1. topographic name for someone who lived by a birch tree, OF *boul* (LL *bettulus*, a dim. of *bettius*; see BÈS). The mod. Fr. term *bouleau* is a further dim. of this. 2. nickname for a short, rotund man, from OF *boule* ball (L *bulla*; cf. BILLET 3).
Vars.: **Boul(l)e.**
Dims.: **Boul(l)et, Bouley, Boulez, Bouleau, Boul(l)ot.**
Collectives (of 1): **(Du) Boulay, (Du) Bouloy, Boulais, Boulois;** BOUILLE.

Boulanger French: occupational name for a baker, originally the man responsible for dividing the dough into *boules* (balls). The name is comparatively late in origin (12th cent.) and replaced the older FOURNIER only in N France.

Boulderstone *see* BALDERSTON

Boulding *see* BAUD

Boule *see* BOWLER

Boulger *see* BOLGER

Boullen *see* BULLEN

Boult *see* BOLT

Boultby English: habitation name from a place presumably so called from the ON personal name *Boltr* (see BOLT 2) + ON *býr* settlement. There is a *Boltby* in N Yorks. However, the surname is more common in the E Midlands.

Boulton *see* BOLTON

Boumans *see* BAUER

Boumphrey *see* HUMPHREY

Bounaud *see* BON

Bound *see* BOND

Bouquet *see* BUCK

Bour *see* BOWER

Bourbon French: habitation name from a village in Allier, site of the (now ruined) castle of *Bourbon*, or from another place so called, e.g. one in Saône-et-Loire. The placename is of uncertain origin, according to Dauzat derived from a 'Celt. and pre-Celt.' element **borb-* describing a well or hot spring. Many bearers of the surname claim a connection with the former Fr. royal family, but the name is also derived from residence in these villages and from the *Bourbonnais*, a former province in central France around Bourbon in Allier.

Vars.: **Bourbonnais**, **Bourbonneux**. Sp.: **Borbón**.

Bourdas *see* BOARDER

Boure French: nickname for someone who habitually dressed in brown, or metonymic occupational name for a worker in the wool trade, from OF *b(o)ure*, a type of coarse reddish-brown woollen cloth with long hairs (LL *burra* coarse untreated wool).

Var.: **Bure**.

Bourgat *see* BURKE

Bourgoin French: regional name for someone from Burgundy (OF *Bourgogne*), a region of E France having Dijon as its centre. The area was invaded by the *Burgundii*, a Gmc tribe from whom it takes its name, in AD *c*.480. The duchy of Burgundy, created in 877 by Charles II, King of the West Franks, was extremely powerful in the later Middle Ages, esp. under Philip the Bold (1342–1404; duke from 1363).

Vars.: **Bourgouin**, **Bergoin**; **Bourgogne**, **Bergogne**; **Bourguignon**, **Bergo(u)gnon**, **Bergougnan**, **Bergougnou(x)**.

Bourne English: topographic name for someone who lived beside a stream, e.g. Richard *atte Bourne* (Sussex 1327), or

habitation name from a place named from being beside a stream. The OE word *burna*, *burne* spring, stream, was replaced as the general word for a stream in S dialects by OE *brōc* (see BROOK) and came to be restricted in meaning to a stream flowing only intermittently, esp. in winter (cf. WINTERBORNE). A large area of Kent by the Little Stow river was once called *Bourn*, but this is unlikely to be the origin for most bearers of the surname, which is established in the W Midlands and Staffs. rather than the South-East.

Vars.: **Bourn**, **Burn(e)**; **BURNS**; **Born(e)** (see also BORGNE), **Boorne**; **Burner**, **Bo(u)rner**. See also BROWN.

Cpd (ornamental): Swed.: **Brunnberg** ('well hill').

Bourrel French: **1.** from a dim. of BOURE. The word had many senses in OF, among them 'cushion', 'harness', 'collar', 'crest', and 'headdress'; the surname could have been used for a maker, seller, or habitual wearer of any of these. **2.** occupational name for a judicial torturer, OF *bourreau*, from *bourrer* to maltreat, torture, lit. to card wool, a deriv. of BOURE. It may also be an occupational name for a wool carder, but the corresponding vocab. word in OF does not seem to be recorded in this sense.

Vars.: **Bourreau**, **Bor(r)el**.

Boursier French: occupational name for a maker of purses and leather wallets, from an agent deriv. of OF *bourse* purse (LL *bursa*, whence also OE *purs*; see PURSER).

Vars.: **Bourcier**; **Bourse**.

Dims.: **Bourseret**, **Bourseron**, **Bourserot**, **Boursereau**; **Bourset**, **Boursin**, **Bours(ill)on**; **Bourzec** (Brittany).

Bourstin *see* BURSTIN

Bourton *see* BURTON

Bouscarel *see* BOISSIER

Boušek *see* BOGUSŁAWSKI

Bousfield English: habitation name from a hamlet of this name near Orton in Cumb. The surname was first recorded there as *Busfeld* in 1342. The first element may be from ON *buskr* bush, shrub, or it may represent a reduced form of the gen. case of some ON or OE personal name; the second is probably OE *feld* pasture, open country.

Bousie *see* BOOSEY

Bousquet *see* BOIS

Boussardon *see* BOSSARD

Bouton French: **1.** var. of BOUDON. **2.** nickname for someone with a prominent wart, carbuncle, or boil, from OF *bo(u)ton* knob, lump, excrescence (from *bo(u)ter* to thrust or strike; cf. BUTLIN). **3.** metonymic occupational name for a maker or seller of buttons, from OF *bo(u)ton*, the same word as in 2, specialized to mean 'button'.

Vars. (of 3): **Bouton(n)ier**.

Dims.: Fr.: **Boutonnet**, **Boutonneau**.

Bouts *see* BAUD

Bouverie French: topographic name for someone who lived by a cowshed or occupational name for someone who worked in one, from OF *boverie* stable for oxen (LL *bovāria*; cf. BOUVIER).

Vars.: **Boverie, Bovary, Bouv(e)ry.**

Bouvier French: occupational name for a herdsman, OF *bouvier* (LL *bovārius*, a deriv. of *bōs*, gen. *bovis*, ox; cf. BOEUF).

Var.: **Bovier.**

Dims.: Fr.: **Bouv(e)ret, Bouv(e)ron.**

Bouzic *see* BOX

Bouzon *see* BOS

Bovary *see* BOUVERIE

Bovelli *see* BOEUF

Bovier *see* BOUVIER

Bovill English (Norman): habitation name from *Bouville* in Seine Maritime, recorded in 1212 as *Bovilla*, apparently from a Gmc personal name *Bolo* (of uncertain origin) + L *villa* settlement (see VILLE), or less probably from either of two places named *Beuville* in Calvados, so called from the Gmc personal name *Bodo* (see BOTHA and BOUDON) + *ville*.

Vars.: **Boville, Bovell.**

Bovingdon English: habitation name from a place in Herts., so called from the OE phrase *būfan dūne* on, upon the hill (see DOWN 1). The surname may also have arisen as a topographic name from the same phrase used independently. There has probably also been some confusion with BOVINGTON.

Vars.: BOWDEN, **Bowton, Bufton.**

Bovington English: habitation name from a place in Dorset, so called from OE *Bōfingtūn* 'settlement (OE *tūn*) associated with *Bōfa*', a personal name of uncertain origin. There is also likely to have been confusion with BOVINGDON, and it may also be a topographic name for someone living 'above the (main) settlement', OE *būfan tūne*.

Bovis *see* BEAVIS

Bow 1. English: metonymic occupational name for a maker or seller of bows, from ME *bow* (OE *boga*, from *būgan* to bend). Before the invention of gunpowder, the bow was an important long-range weapon for shooting game as well as in warfare. *Boga* is also found as a personal name in OE, and it is possible that this survived into ME and so may lie behind the surname. 2. English: topographic name for someone living near a bridge, e.g. Richard *atte Bowe, boga* having acquired the sense 'arch', 'vault', 'span (of a bridge)' from a supposed resemblance of the arch to a drawn bow. 3. Irish: Anglicized form of Gael. Ó Buadhaigh 'descendant of *Buadhach*', a personal name meaning 'Victorious'. (The Brit. name *Boudicca* or *Boadicea*, borne by the Queen of the Iceni who in AD 62 led a revolt against the Roman occupation of her country, is a cogn.)

Vars.: **Bowe** (chiefly Irish), BOWES; BOUGH.

Bowater English: topographic name for someone who lived on a bank above an expanse of water, from ME *buven* above (OE *būfan*) + *water* (OE *wæter*); cf. the much less common **Bowbrick** 'above the BROOK'. The surname is most common in Staffs.

Vars.: **Bo(e)ter; Boater** (see also BATE).

Bowcock *see* BAUD

Bowcott English: habitation name from some minor place (probably in Worcs., where the surname is most common), perhaps so called from OE *boga* arched bridge (see BOW 2) + *cot* cottage, dwelling (see COATES).

Bowden 1. English: habitation name from a place so called. The places called *Bowden* in Devon and Derbys., and *Bowdon* in Ches., get their names from OE *boga* Bow + *dūn* hill (see DOWN 1), i.e. hill shaped like a bow; one in Leics. (*Bugedone* in Domesday Book) comes, according to Ekwall, from the OE personal name *Būga* (masc.) or *Bucge* (fem.) + *dūn*. There are also Scots places of this name, and it is possible that these derive from Gael. *both an duin* 'house on the hill', but there are comparatively few bearers of the surname *Bowden* north of the Border. The surname is found most frequently in Lancs. and in the W Country; in Devon and Cornwall there has been some confusion with the Norman given name BALDWIN. 2. English: topographic name for someone who lived at the top of a hill, from the OE phrase *būfan dūne* above the hill; cf. BOWATER and see also BOVINGDON. 3. Irish: Anglicized form of Gael. Ó Buadáin 'descendant of *Buadán*', an OIr. personal name cogn. with *Buadach* (see BOW 3).

Vars.: **Bowdon, Bawdon.**

Bowdery *see* BALDRY

Bowditch English: habitation name, possibly from OE *boga* bow + *dīc* ditch, i.e. a bow-shaped water channel. There is a place of this name in Devon, however, which is derived from the OE phrase *būfan dīce* above the ditch; cf. BOWATER.

Var.: **Bowdidge.**

Bowell 1. English (Norman): habitation name from *Bouelles* in Seine Maritime, so called from ONF *boelle* enclosure, dwelling (of Gmc origin; cf. BOMAN and BOWER 1). 2. Welsh: patr. from the given name HOWELL, with fusion of the patr. element *ap, ab*.

Vars.: **Bowells, Bowle(s)** (but see also BOWLER).

Bowen 1. Welsh: patr. from the given name OWEN, with fusion of the patr. element *ap, ab*. 2. Irish: Anglicized form of Gael. Ó Buadhacháin 'descendant of *Buadachán*', a dim. of *Buadach* (see BOW 3).

Vars. (of 2): **Boohan, Bohane, (O')Boug(h)an, (O')Boghan.**

Bowen *see* OWEN

Bower English: 1. topographic name for someone who lived in a small cottage or occupational name for a house servant (cf. CHAMBERS), from OE *būr* bower, cottage, inner room (cf. BAUER). 2. habitation name from places in Essex and Somerset named *Bower(s)*, from the OE word mentioned in 1 above. 3. var. of BOW (1 and 2).

Vars. (of 1 and 2): **Bowers, Bour; Bow(e)rer, Bo(o)rer, Boarer, Bowra(h); Bowerman, Bo(o)rman; Bow(e)ring.**

Bowes 1. N English: habitation name from *Bowes* (formerly in N Yorks., now in Co. Durham), or from some other place so called, the name being derived from ME *boges* arches of a bridge (see Bow 2). **2.** Irish: Anglicized form of Gael. *Ó Buadhaigh*; see Bow 3.

Bowick *see* BEWICK

Bowie Irish and Scots: nickname from Gael. *buidhe* yellow, fair-haired.

Bowker English (chiefly Manchester): **1.** var. of BUTCHER. **2.** occupational name for someone whose job was to steep cotton or linen in alkali before bleaching it, from an agent deriv. of ME *bouken* to wash (from MDu.; cf. BOOKER 2).

Bowland *see* BOLAND

Bowler English (chiefly Notts.): nickname for a heavy drinker (ME *boller*, from OE *bolla* bowl, drinking vessel + the agent suffix *-er*), or occupational name for a maker or seller of bowls. Medieval bowls were made of wood as well as of earthenware.
Vars.: **Bo(a)ler**, **Bowller**; **Bowle(s)**, **Boule(s)**; **Boal** (N Ireland).

Bowley English: habitation name from a place so called from OE *bula* BULL (perhaps a byname) + *lēah* wood, clearing. There is one such in Herefords. near Leominster, but the surname is most common in Notts.

Bowman English: **1.** occupational name for an archer, from OE *boga* bow + *mann* man. This name seems to be generally distinguished from BOWYER, which denoted a maker or seller of the articles. It is possible that in some cases the surname referred originally to someone who untangled wool with a bow. This process seems to have originated in Italy, but became quite common in England in the 13th cent. The vibrating string of a bow was worked into a pile of tangled wool, where its rapid vibrations separated the fibres, while still leaving them sufficiently entwined to produce a fine, soft yarn when spun. **2.** in America, sometimes an Anglicized form of Ger. and Du. *Baumann* (see BAUER).
Vars. (of 1): **Boman**; **Beauman** (see also BEAUMONT).

Bown *see* BOON

Bowser English (Norman): nickname from the term of address *beu sire* fine sir. The nickname would have been acquired by someone who used the phrase very frequently.
Vars.: **Beausire**, **Bellsyer**, **Belshire**, BELCHER.

Bowsher *see* BELCHER

Bowton *see* BOVINGDON

Bowyer English: occupational name for a maker or seller of bows (see BOW 1), rather than an archer (cf. BOWMAN 1).

Box English: from ME, OE *box* box tree (L *buxus*, from Gk *pyxos*), in any of a number of possible applications. It may have been a topographic name for someone who lived by a box thicket, or a habitation name from one of the places called *Box*, in Gloucs., Herts., and Wilts. Box wood is very hard and because of this it was used to make a variety of tools; the name may therefore also have been a metonymic occupational name for a worker in the wood. In some cases it may even have been a nickname for a person with pale or yellow skin, for example as

the result of jaundice, with reference to the colour of box wood.
Var.: **Boxer**.
Ger.: BUCHS.
Dims.: Fr.: BUISSON; **Bouzic**, **Bouzit** (Brittany). Cat.: **Buxó**.
Collective: Fr.: **Bussière**.

Boxall English: habitation name from a lost hamlet near Kirford, Sussex, called *Boxholte*, from OE *box* Box + *holt* wood (see HOLT). The surname has been found in the surrounding area since the 14th cent.
Vars.: **Boxhall**, **Boxell**.

Boyce 1. English: topographic name for someone who lived by a wood, from OF *bois* wood (see BOIS). **2.** English: patr. from the ME nickname *boy* lad, servant (a word of disputed origin, probably from a MLG form of OSax. *bodo* messenger, servant (see BOTHA), the dental being regularly lost between vowels). In some cases it may derive from an OE personal name *Boia* or a Continental Gmc cogn. of this, both being of uncertain origin. Examples such as Aluuinus *Boi* (Domesday Book) and Ivo *le Boye* (Lincs. 1232) support the view that it was a byname or even an occupational name; examples such as *Stephanus filius Boie* (Northumb. 1202) suggest that it was in use as a personal name in the ME period, while the placename *Boyland* in Norfolk is evidence for its use as an OE personal name. **3.** Irish: Anglicized form of Gael. *Ó Buadhaigh*; see BOW 3.
Vars. (of 1 and 2): **Boy(e)s** (chiefly Yorks.); **Boice**, **Boise**, **Boyse**. (Of 2 only): **Boyson**.

Boycott English: habitation name from places in Bucks., Worcs., and Shrops., so called from the OE personal name *Boia* (see BOYE) + OE *cot* shelter, cottage (see COATES).

Boyd Scots and Irish: of uncertain origin, perhaps from the island of Bute in the Firth of Clyde, Gael. *Bód* (gen. case *Bóid*).
Vars.: **Boyde**, **Boyda**.

Boydell *see* BOODLE

Boye Low German and Danish: from a Gmc personal name, *Boio* or *Bogo*, of uncertain origin. It may represent a var. of BOTHA, with the regular Low Ger. loss of the dental between vowels, but a cogn. name appears to have existed in OE (see BOYCE, BOYCOTT and BOYTON), where this feature does not occur. *Boje* is still in use as a given name in Friesland. See also SAINTE-BEUVE.
Vars.: **Boje**, **Boie**. Low Ger.: **Böhe**. Dan.: **Bøje**.
Dims.: Low Ger.: **Boyk(e)**. Eng.: **Boykin**.
Patrs.: Low Ger.: **Boysen**, **Boyens**, **Bojens**, **Boeing**. Dan.: **Boysen**, **Boisen**, **Boj(e)sen**, **Boesen**. Eng.: BOYCE.

Boyle 1. Irish: Anglicized form of Gael. **Ó Baoighill** 'descendant of *Baoigheall*', a personal name of uncertain meaning, perhaps from *baoth* rash + *geall* pledge. **2.** Irish (Norman): apparently an altered form of *Binville*; see below. **3.** Scots (Norman): habitation name from *Boyville* near Caen, so called from the Gmc personal name *Boio* (see BOYE) + OF *ville* settlement (see VILLE).
Vars.: **Boyles**, **Bole**. (Of 1 only): **O'Boyle**.

Boyton English: habitation name from any of various places, for example in Cornwall, Essex, Suffolk, and

Wilts., so called from the OE personal name **Boia* (see
BOYCE 2) + OE *tūn* enclosure, settlement.

Bozon *see* BOS

Braams *see* ABRAHAM

Brabazon English (Norman): ostensibly an ethnic name,
from ONF *brabançon*, for a native of *Brabant* (see BRAB-
HAM), but by the 13th cent., if not before, an occupational
name for a mercenary, specifically a member of one of the
more or less independent marauding bands of mercenaries,
noted for their lawlessness and cruelty, who originated in
Brabant but in the course of time accepted recruits from
almost anywhere.

Var.: **Brobson**.

Brabham English: altered form (by association with habitation names ending in *-ham*) of an ethnic name for someone from the duchy of *Brabant*, in what is now Belgium
and the S Netherlands. See also BRABAZON.

Vars.: **Brab(b)an(t)**, **Brab(b)en**, **Brab(b)in**, **Brab(b)on**,
Brab(b)yn; **Brab(i)ner**, **Brebner**; **BREMNER**.

Brace English: 1. metonymic occupational name for a
maker or seller of armour, specifically armour designed
to protect the upper arms, ME *brace* (from OF *brace*
(two) arms, L *bracchia*, pl. of *bracchium* arm). 2. metonymic occupational name for a maker of breeches, or nickname meaning 'Breeches', from OE *brēc*.

Var.: **Brass** (Northumb.).

Bracegirdle English (Lancs.): metonymic occupational
name for a maker of belts for holding up the breeches,
from OE *brēc* breeches (see BRACE 2) + *gyrdel* belt, girdle.

Bracewell N English: habitation name from a place in W
Yorks., so called from the gen. case of the ON personal
name *Breiðr* 'Broad' (which possibly replaced earlier OE
Brægd 'Trick') + OE *well(a)* spring, stream (see WELL).

Brach English: 1. topographic name for someone who
lived by any of the various pieces of land that were
named from the time when they were first cultivated,
from OE *brēc* newly cultivated land (a deriv. of *brecan*
to break, i.e. land broken by the plough); cf. Ger.
Brachland land ploughed and then left to lie fallow, Du.
braak (adj.) fallow. 2. var. of BRACK.

Vars. (of 1): **Bre(a)ch**, **Britch**; **Bra(t)cher**, **Bre(a)cher**, **Britcher**.

Brack German and English: metonymic occupational
name for a master of hunting dogs or nickname for one
thought to resemble a hunting dog, MHG *bracke* (OHG
bracho). The cognate ME word was derived via OF *brachez*
(pl. of *brachet*, dim. of **brache*), the sing. form being re-
created by back-formation from the OF pl.

Vars.: Ger.: **Prack** (Bavaria). Eng.: BRACH; **Brackner**.

Dims.: Ger.: **Präckl** (Bavaria). Eng.: **Bracket**, **Brachet**. Fr.:
Brachet, **Braquet**; **Braconnet**, **Braconnot**.

Bracken Irish: Anglicized form of Gael. **Ó Breacáin**
'descendant of *Breacán*', a personal name from a dim. of
breac speckled, spotted. This name was borne by a 6th-
cent. saint who lived at Ballyconnel, Co. Cavan, and was
famous as a healer; in his honour is named St Bricin's Military Hospital, Dublin.

Vars.: **(O')Brackan**, **(O')Breckan**.

Brackenridge Scots: habitation name from *Brackenrig* in
the former county of Lanarks. (now part of Strathclyde
region), probably so called from Northern ME *braken*
bracken (ON *brækni*) + *rigg* ridge (ON *hryggr*).

Vars.: **Breckenridge**, **Brekonridge**.

Brackley English: habitation name from a place in Northants, so called from the OE personal name *Bracc(a)* (perhaps akin to BRACK) + OE *lēah* wood, clearing.

Brackpool English: apparently a habitation name from an
unidentified place. *Brapool* Barn in Patcham, Sussex, has
been suggested, but this may derive from the surname rather than vice versa. The first element is probably the OE
personal name *Bracca* (although it is tempting to link it
with MDu. *brac*, the source of Mod. Eng. *brackish*); the
second is fairly clearly OE *pōl* pool, pond.

Bradbrook English: habitation name from some minor
place so called from OE *brād* broad + *brōc* stream.

Vars.: **Braybrook(e)** (from a place in Northants, in which the first
element is from ON *breiðr* broad, a cogn. of *brād*).

Bradbury English: habitation name from one of the minor
places so called, in several counties, all first recorded fairly
late. The etymology is generally OE *brād* broad + *burh* fort
(see BURY), but *Bradbury* in Co. Durham is recorded in
OE as *Brydbyrig*, the first element probably being OE *bred*
board. This is probably also the first element in *Bradbury*,
Ches.

Vars.: **Bradber(r)y**.

Braddock English: topographic name for someone living
by a notable broad oak, from OE *brād* broad + *āc* oak, or
habitation name from a minor place so named. The only
modern village with this name is *Braddock* in Cornwall
(*Brodehoc* in Domesday Book, later *Brethok*, *Brothok*),
the name of which is probably of Celt. origin; it is unlikely
to be the source of the surname. The Eng. phrase was certainly used in forming placenames, e.g. Hatfield *Broad Oak*
in Essex.

Braddon English: habitation name from the *Braddons*, a
range of heights in S Devon, on the north side of Torquay,
so called from OE *brād* broad + *dūn* hill.

Brade *see* BROAD

Braden Irish: Anglicized form of Gael. **Ó Bradáin** 'descendant of *Bradán*', a personal name meaning 'Salmon'.

Vars.: **Braiden**, **(O')Bradane**, **(O')Bradden**, SALMON, FISHER.

Bradfield English: habitation name from any of the places
so called in Berks., Devon, Essex, Suffolk, S Yorks., and
elsewhere, from OE *brād* broad + *feld* pasture, open country (see FIELD).

Var.: **Broadfield** (places in Herefords. and Herts.).

Bradford English: habitation name from any of the many
places, large and small, so called; in particular the city in W
Yorks, which was originally a wool town. There are others
in Derbys., Devon, Dorset, Greater Manchester, Norfolk,
Somerset, and elsewhere. They all take their names from
OE *brād* broad + *ford* FORD.

Vars.: **Bradforth**, **Braidford**.

Bradić *see* BROTHER

Bradley 1. English and Scots: habitation name from one of the many places so called, from OE *brād* broad + *lēah* wood, clearing. Places named with these elements are found in every part of England and also in Scotland. **2.** Irish: Anglicized form of Gael. *Ó Brolcháin*; see BROLLY.

Vars. (of 1): **Bradly, Bratl(e)y, Bradlaugh, Broad(e)ly.**

Bradman English: nickname from OE *brād* broad (in this case, well built) + *mann* man. See also BROAD.

Var.: **Braidman.**

Bradshaw English: habitation name from one of the places so named, from OE *brād* broad + *sceaga* thicket (see SHAW). There are places so called in Lancs., W Yorks., and elsewhere. The surname is widely distributed, but most frequent in Lancs.

Vars.: **Brayshaw** (chiefly W Yorks.); **Brashaw, Brayshay.**

Bradstreet English: topographic name for someone living by a Roman road or other great highway, from OE *brād* broad + *strǣt* highway (see STREET).

Bradwell English: habitation name from a place so called, of which there are examples in Bucks., Derbys., Essex, Somerset, Suffolk, and elsewhere. The name is from OE *brād* broad + *well(a)* spring, stream (see WELL).

Brady 1. Irish: Anglicized form of Gael. *Ó Brádaigh* 'descendant of *Brádach*', a byname the meaning of which is not clear. It is unlikely to be connected with Gael. *bradach* thieving, dishonest, which has a short first vowel. **2.** English: nickname for a person with large or wide-set eyes, from OE *brād* broad + *eage* eye. **3.** English: habitation name from some place known as 'broad island', from OE *brād* broad + *ēg* island. **4.** English: topographic name for someone who lived by a broad enclosure, from OE *brād* broad + *(ge)hæg* enclosure (see HAY 1).

Vars.: **Bradey, Bradie, Bready.** (Of 1 only): **O'Brady.** (Of 2–4): **Broady, Broadie.**

Dims. (of 1): **O'Bradaghan; (O')Braddigan, (O')Brodigan, Bradekin, Bradican** (Gael. *Ó Bradacháin*).

Braga Portuguese: habitation name from a city in N Portugal, so called from L *Bracāria*, a deriv. of the Celt. tribal name *Bracari*. This is apparently from *bracae* trousers, leggings, breeches (cf. BRACE 2), but it may alternatively derive from Celt. *berg, barg* height, eminence.

Bragg English: nickname for a cheerful or lively person, from ME *bragge* lively, gay, active (of unknown origin).

Braham *see* BREAM

Brahm 1. German and Jewish: aphetic var. of ABRAHAM. **2.** German: topographic name for someone who lived by a bramble thicket, from MHG *brāme* blackberry, bramble (OHG *brāmo*).

Var. (of 1): Jewish: **Braham.**

Patr. (from 1): **Brahms.**

Braille French: of uncertain origin. It is possibly from the OF verb *brailler* to squabble (LL *bragulāre*, apparently of Celt. origin), and hence a nickname for a quarrelsome individual, or alternatively it may be a metonymic occupational name for a winnower, from the OF dial. term *braile* harvest.

Brailsford English: habitation name from a place in Derbys., so called from OE **brægels*, a metathesized form of *bærgels*, itself a byform of *byrgels* tumulus, barrow + *ford* FORD. The name is still found chiefly in the E Midlands, esp. in Nottingham.

Vars.: **Brel(lis)ford.**

Brain Irish and Scots: Anglicized form of Gael. **Mac an Bhreitheamhan** 'son of the judge', from *breitheamh* judge (see BREW 2).

Vars.: **Braine, Brayne, Brohoon.**

Patrs.: **McBrayne, McBrehon, McBrohoon, McVrehoune, McEbrehowne, McEvrehune, McAbreham, McAbrahams.**

Braines Jewish (Ashkenazic): metr. from the Yid. female given name *Brayne*, a back-formation from *Brayndl*, itself a dim. of Yid. *broyn* brown.

Vars.: **Breines; Brainin** (E Ashkenazic).

Braitbart *see* BREIT

Braithwaite N English: habitation name from any of the places in Cumb. and Yorks. named from ON *breiðr* broad + *þveit* clearing (see THWAITE).

Var.: **Braithwait.**

Brake English: topographic name for someone who lived by a clump of bushes or by a patch of bracken. *Brake* thicket and *brake* bracken were homonyms in ME. The first is from OE *bracu*; the second is by folk etymology from northern ME *braken* (from ON *brakni*), *-en* being taken as a pl. ending. After the words had fallen together, their senses also became confused.

Bramall English: habitation name from one of the places, in Ches. and Sheffield, named as a sheltered spot with broom (gorse) growing in it, from OE *brōm* broom + *halh* nook, recess (see HALE 1). There may also have been some confusion with BRAMWELL.

Vars.: **Brammall, Bramhall, Bramah, Brammer, Bramble, Brummell.**

Bramley English: habitation name from any of various places (in Derbys., Hants, Surrey, Yorks., and elsewhere), so called from OE *brōm* broom, gorse + *lēah* clearing, wood. The surname is found chiefly in Yorks., Notts., and Derbys.

Var.: **BROMLEY.**

Brampton English: habitation name from any of the various places, found in every part of England, so called from OE *brōm* broom, gorse + *tūn* enclosure, settlement.

Bramwell English: habitation name from one or more unidentified minor places, so called from OE *brōm* broom, gorse + *well(a)* spring, stream (see WELL). The surname is distributed fairly evenly throughout England. See also BRAMALL.

Branch English: from ME, OF *branche* branch (LL *branca* foot, paw), the application of which as a surname is not clear. In America it has been adopted as a translation of any of the numerous Swed. surnames containing the element *gren* branch, and likewise of Finn. HAARLA.

Dims.: Fr.: **Branchet, Branquet.**

Branchflower *see* BLANCHFLOWER

Brand 1. English, French, and German: from the Gmc (esp. Langobardic) personal name *Brando*, a short form of the various cpd personal names containing the element *brand* sword (a deriv. of *brinnan* to flash), of which the best known is HILDEBRAND. There is placename evidence for *Brant(a)* as an OE personal name, and in ME and ONF it is found as *Brand*, but was probably introduced to both from Norse; *Brandr* is a common ON personal name. **2.** German: topographic name for someone who lived in an area that had been cleared by fire, MHG *brant* (from *brennen* to burn, causative of *brinnan*).

Vars. (of 1): Eng.: **Braund** (Devon); **Brant** (W Midlands). Fr.: BRANDON. (Of 1 and 2): Ger.: **Bran(d)t** (also Jewish).

Dims. (of 1): Ger.: **Brandel**, **Brändel**, **Brändle**, **Brantl**; **Brendel** (also Jewish); **Prantl** (Bavaria); **Brändli** (Switzerland). Low Ger.: **Brendeke**, **Brenneke**. Fris.: **Brandsma**. Fr.: **Brandin**. It.: **Brand(ol)ini**, **Brandino**; **Prandin(i)** (N Italy).

Augs. (of 1): It.: **Brandoni**, **Brandone**; **Prandoni**, **Prantoni** (N Italy).

Pejs. (of 1): It.: **Brandacci**, **Brandassi**.

Patrs. (from 1): Eng.: **Braunds**; **Branson**, **Bransom**; **Bramson** (see also ABRAHAM); BRANSTON. Ger.: **Brand(t)s**, **Brandes**. Du.: **Brands(en)**.

Brandejs Czech: habitation name from the town of *Brandýs*, on the Labe (Elbe) some 20 km. north of Prague, called *Brandeis* in German.

Brandon 1. English: habitation name from any of various places so called, found in Co. Durham, Northumb., Norfolk, Suffolk, Warwicks., and elsewhere. Most of these get the name from OE *brōm* broom, gorse + *dūn* hill. One in Lincs., however, may be named from the river *Brant*, on which it stands, whose name is derived by Ekwall from OE *brant* steep, presumably with reference to its steep banks. **2.** French: var. of BRAND, from the OF oblique case of the name.

Brandwain see BRONFMAN

Brangwyn English or Welsh: perhaps from the W female given name *Branwen* (composed of the elements *bran* raven + *gwen* fair). Brangwain is the name of Isolde's companion in the Tristan legend; Branwen, daughter of Llyr, was a legendary Welsh heroine.

Var.: **Brangwin**.

Braniff Irish: Anglicized form of Gael. Ó Branduibh 'descendant of *Brandubh*', a personal name composed of the elements *bran* raven + *dubh* black.

Brannan see BRENNAN

Brannick Irish: Anglicized form of the Gael. ethnic name or nickname *Breathnach* Briton (*Breithneach* in Donegal and Ulster).

Vars.: **Bran(n)agh**, **Brennach**, **Brawnick**.

Brannigan Irish: Anglicized form of Gael. Ó Branagáin 'descendant of *Branagán*', a personal name from a dim. of *bran* raven (cf. BYRNE).

Vars.: **O'Brannigan**, **(O')Branigan**, **(O')Branagan**, **Brankin**.

Branston English: **1.** habitation name from any of various places, such as *Branston* in Leics., Lincs., and Staffs., *Braunston* in Leics. and Northants, *Brandeston* in Suffolk, or *Brandiston* in Norfolk, all of which get their name from

the gen. case of the OE personal name *Brant* (see BRAND 1) + OE *tūn* enclosure, settlement. **2.** altered form of *Branson*; see BRAND 1.

Brasch see BARISH

Brash Scots: probably a nickname for an impetuous person, from the N Eng. dial. term *brasche* rash, impetuous (associated with *brasche* assault, attack, a word of imitative origin).

Brasher English: **1.** occupational name, of Norman origin, for a brewer, from OF *brasser* to brew (LL *braciāre*, a deriv. of *braces* malt, of Gaul. origin). **2.** occupational name for a worker in brass, from OE *bræsian* to cast in brass (a deriv. of *bræs* brass).

Vars. (of 1): **Braisher**, **Bracer**, **Brasseur**. (Of 2): **Brasier**, **Bra(i)zier**.

Brassington English: habitation name from a place in Derbys., which Ekwall suggests is derived from OE *Brantstīgtūn* 'enclosure (*tūn*) by the steep (*brant*) path (*stīg*)'. *Brandsigingtūn* 'settlement associated with *Brandsige*' is more likely. *Brandsige*, composed of the elements *brand* sword + *sige* victory, is not attested as an OE personal name, but seems plausible.

Bratt English (W Midlands): of uncertain origin, possibly a nickname for an unruly child, or somebody who behaved like one, though this sense of *brat* is not recorded by *OED* before the 16th cent. Alternatively, it may be derived from the older word *brat(te)* apron, pinafore (of Celt. origin), as a nickname for someone who habitually wore one.

Braud see BERAUD

Braude see BRODSKI

Brauers see BREWER

Braunfeld see BROWN

Braunschweig German and Jewish (Ashkenazic): habitation name from the city in Saxony known in Eng. as *Brunswick*. This derives its name from the gen. case of the Gmc personal name *Bruno* (see BROWN), borne by the Duke of Saxony who founded the city in 861 + OHG *wīch* dwelling place (see WICK).

Braunstein Jewish (Ashkenazic): ornamental surname, composed of the Ger. elements *braun* BROWN + *stein* STONE.

Vars.: **Brons(h)tein**, **Bronstien**; **Brons(z)tejn** (Pol. spelling); **Brownstein** (partly Anglicized); **Brownstone** (fully Anglicized).

Bravo Spanish and Portuguese: nickname for a cruel or fierce-tempered man, from Sp., Port. *bravo* fierce, violent (probably from L *barbarus* barbarian, ruffian; cf. BARBARY). The sense 'courageous', 'brave' did not emerge until the 16th cent., and is therefore too late to be reflected in the surname.

Dim.: It.: **Bravetti**.

Pej.: Fr.: **Bravard**.

Brawley see BROLLY

Braxton English: habitation name from an unidentified place, so called from the gen. case of the OE personal name *Bracc* (cf. BRACKLEY) + OE *tūn* enclosure, settlement.

Bray English: habitation name from places in Berks. and Devon. The former is probably so called from OF *bray* marsh (cf. BRIARD), the latter from the Corn. element *bre* hill.

Brazil Irish: Anglicized form of Gael. **Ó Breasail** 'descendant of *Breasal*', a byname meaning 'Strife'. The accent is on the first syllable.

Vars.: **Brassill, (O')Breassell**.

Dims.: **(O')Breslane, Breslin** (Gael. **Ó Breisle(á)in**).

Breach *see* BRACH

Bready *see* BRADY

Breakspear English: nickname for a successful warrior or participant in a joust, from ME *brek(en)* to break (OE *brecan*) + *sper(e)* spear (OE *spere*).

Var.: **Brakspear**.

Breakwell English: apparently a habitation name from some unidentified minor place (probably in the W Midlands, where the surname is commonest). The etymology is unclear. The second element is almost certainly OE *well(a)* spring, stream (see WELL), but the first cannot be established without placename evidence.

Var.: **Breakell** (Lancs.).

Bream English: **1.** habitation name from *Braham* or *Bramham* in E Yorks., both of which derive their name from OE *brōm* broom, gorse + *hām* homestead. **2.** habitation name from *Brantham* in Suffolk, so called from the OE personal name *Brant* (see BRAND 1) + *hām* homestead. **3.** nickname for a fierce or energetic person, from ME *brem(e)*, *brim(me)* fierce, vigorous (apparently from OE *brēme* famous, noble, although the semantic development is unclear).

Vars. (of 1): **Braham(e), Bra(i)me, Brayham; Bramham**. (Of 2): **Brantham**. (Of 3): **Breem, BRIM**.

Brear English (Yorks.): **1.** topographic name for someone who lived by a briar patch, ME *brere* (OE *brēr, brǣr*). **2.** nickname for a prickly, difficult individual, from the same word as in 1, applied in a transferred sense.

Var.: **Brier(s), Bryer(s), Briar(s)**.

Brearley *see* BRIERLEY

Breassell *see* BRAZIL

Brebner *see* BRABHAM

Brecht *see* ALBERT

Breckan *see* BRACKEN

Breckenridge *see* BRACKENRIDGE

Breddy English (Bristol): of uncertain origin, possibly a habitation name from Long or Little *Bredy* in Dorset, so called from their situation on the river *Bride*, which apparently bears a Brit. name akin to W *brydio* to boil.

Breed English: habitation name from any of various minor places, e.g. *Brede* in Sussex, named with OE *brǣdu* breadth, broad place (a deriv. of *brād* broad).

Vars.: **Bre(e)de, Breeds; Breeder**.

Breedon English: habitation name from *Breedon* in Leics. or *Bredon* in S Worcs., which are so called from the Brit. term *bre* hill + the tautologous OE addition *dūn* (see DOWN).

Var.: **Bredon**.

Breen Irish: Anglicized form of Gael. **Ó Braoin** 'descendant of *Braon*', a byname meaning 'Moisture', 'Drop'.

Vars.: **O'Breen, O'Brean; O'Bruen; Brewin** (Liverpool).

Breeze 1. English: nickname for an irritating person, from ME *breeze* gadfly (OE *brēosa*). **2.** Welsh: patr. from RHYS.

Var.: **Breese**.

Bregman Jewish (Ashkenazic): topographic name for someone who lived near a river or stream, from E Yid. *breg* shore, bank, coast (from Pol. *brzeg*) + *-man*.

Breines *see* BRAINES

Breinl *see* BROWN

Breit German: nickname for a stout or fat person, from Ger. *breit* BROAD.

Var.: **Breitmann**.

Cpds: Jewish: **Breitbart, Braitbart, Breitbard, Brajtbard** ('broad beard', a nickname); **Breitholz** ('broad wood', ornamental name); **Breitstein** ('broad stone', ornamental or topographic name).

Brejcha Czech: of uncertain origin, perhaps an altered form of the OCzech personal name *Brixí*, or a topographic name for someone who lived by a ford (from Czech dial. *brejchat se* to wade, ford a stream).

Brelford *see* BRAILSFORD

Bremner Scots: regional name for someone from *Brabant* in the Low Countries, from earlier Scots *Brebner*, *Brabanare*, native or inhabitant of Brabant (see BRABHAM).

Vars.: **Brimner, Brymner**.

Brenchley English: habitation name from a place in Kent, so called from an OE personal name *Brænci* (of uncertain history) + OE *lēah* wood, clearing.

Brendeke *see* BRAND

Brennach *see* BRANNICK

Brennan Irish: Anglicized form of Gael. **Ó Braonáin** 'descendant of *Braonán*', a personal name from a dim. of *braon* moisture, drop; cf. BREEN.

Vars.: **O'Brennan, (O')Brenane, (O')Brinan(e), Brannan; BRENNAND**.

Brennand English (Lancs.): according to Reaney a nickname for someone whose hand had been scarred by burning, as a punishment or in trial by ordeal rather than by accident, from ME *brent* burnt (past part. of *brennen* to burn) + *hand* hand; this is clearly the meaning in the case of Matilda *Brendhand*, recorded in Cambs. in 1295. Reaney ascribes the origin of forms such as *Brenhand* (N Yorks. 1229) to a nickname for the official who carried out the harsh punishment. Independent evidence for the existence of an official so named is not, however, forthcoming. The mod. surname may be no more than a var. of BRENNAN.

Vars.: **Burnand**.

Brenner 1. German and Jewish (Ashkenazic): from Ger. *Brenner*, literally 'burner', an agent deriv. of Ger. *brennen* to burn, in various applications. Often it is an occupational name for a distiller of spirits. In the case of the non-Jewish surname, it may also refer to a charcoal burner or to someone who cleared forests by burning. 2. English: metathesized var. of BERNER.

Vars.: Jewish: **Brener**, **Brenman**.

Brent English: 1. topographic name for someone who lived by a piece of ground that had been cleared by fire, from ME *brent*, past part. of *brennen* to burn. 2. habitation name from one of the places in Devon and Somerset so called from OE *brant* steep, or from an earlier Celt. (Brit.) word meaning 'hill', 'high place'. 3. byname or nickname for a criminal who had been branded; cf. Henry *Brendcheke* ('burned cheek'), recorded in Northumb. in 1279.

Vars.: **Brend**, **Brunt**. (Of 1 only): **Brind** (a place in Humberside).

Brentnall English: of uncertain origin, possibly a habitation name from some place (probably in Notts., where the surname is most common) so called from the gen. case of the OE personal name **Branta* (see BRAND 1) + *halh* nook, recess (see HALE 1).

Brenton English (Devon): habitation name from *Brenton* near Exminster, probably named in OE as *Brȳningtūn* 'settlement (OE *tūn*) associated with *Brȳni*' (see BRYNING), and therefore identical with BRINGTON.

Brereton English: habitation name from places so called in Ches. and Staffs. The former gets its name from OE *brǣr*, *brēr* briar (see BREAR) + *tūn* enclosure, settlement; the latter originally had as its final element OE *dūn* hill (see DOWN 1).

Breslane *see* BRAZIL

Breslau Jewish (Ashkenazic): from the Ger. name, *Breslau*, of the city of *Wrocław* in Poland (see WROCŁAWSKI), which for a long time was part of Germany.

Vars.: **Bres(s)lauer**; **Breslaw(ski)**, **Breslav(ski)**; **Breslow**; **Bres(s)ler** (from the Yid. name of the city, *Bresle*).

Bresset *see* BRICE

Bressington English (chiefly Bristol): habitation name from an unidentified place so called, probably originally *Brīosingtūn* 'settlement (OE *tūn*) associated with *Brīosa*', a byname meaning 'Gadfly' (see BREEZE 1).

Bretécher French: occupational name for a maker of a kind of wooden fortification, or topographic name for a dweller by such a fortification, from OF *bretesche*, med. L *britisca*, which also means 'British'. The connection, if any, between these two meanings is not clear.

Var.: **Labretesche**.

Bretherick English: habitation name from some minor place (probably in Yorks., where the surname is most common) so called from ON *brœðr* or OE *breðra* (see BRETHERTON) + OE *wīc* village, outlying farm (see WICK).

Bretherton English: habitation name from *Bretherton* in Lancs., which gets its name from ON *brœðr* (gen. sing.) of the brother or OE *breðra* (gen. pl.) of the brothers + OE *tūn*

enclosure, settlement. The surname is still most common in Lancs.

Brett English and French: ethnic name for a Breton, from OF *bret* (oblique case *breton*). The Bretons were Celt.-speakers driven from SW England to NW France in the 6th cent. AD by Anglo-Saxon invaders; some of them reinvaded England in the 11th cent. as part of the army of William the Conqueror. In France and among Normans, Bretons had a reputation for stupidity, and in some cases this name and its vars. and cogns. may have originated as derogatory nicknames. The Eng. surname is most common in E Anglia, where many Bretons settled after the Conquest. In Scotland it may also denote a member of one of the Celt.-speaking peoples of Strathclyde, who were known as *Bryttas* or *Brettas* well into the 13th cent.

Vars.: Eng.: **Britt**; **Breton** (Scotland), BRETTON, BRITTAIN. Fr.: **Bret**, **Lebret**; **Breton**, **Lebreton**; **Bretonnier**, **Bretegnier**; **Bretagne**, **Bretange**.

Dims.: Eng.: **Brettell**, **Brettle**, **Brittle** (W Midlands). Fr.: **Bretel**, **Breteau**, **Brethiot**, **Brétillon**; **Breton(n)el** (see BRUDENELL), **Bretonneau**.

Pej.: Fr.: **Bretaud**.

Patrs.: Fr.: **Aubreton**, **Laubreton**. Sc.: **McBratney**, **McBratnie** (Gael. **Mac an Bhreatnaich**, an old Galloway surname).

Bretton English: 1. var. of BRETT, from the OF oblique case. 2. habitation name from Monk and West *Bretton* in W Yorks., or *Bretton* in Derbys. These are so called either from OE *brēc* broken (i.e. newly cultivated) land (cf. BRACH 1) + *tūn* enclosure, settlement or from *Brettatūn* 'settlement of Britons'. The surname is most common in the area around Barnsley, and also in Leeds.

Breuel *see* BRÜHL

Breuil French: topographic name from OF *breuil* marshy woodland (LL *brogilum*, of Gaul. origin). In Fr. the term later came to mean 'enclosed woodland' and then 'cleared woodland', and both these senses may also be reflected in the surname.

Vars.: **Breuilh**, **Bruel**, **Bre(i)l**; **Dubreuil**, **Dubrule**.

Dims.: **Breu(il)let**, **Breuillon**, **Breuillot**.

Aug.: **Breuillat**.

Pejs.: **Breuillaud**, **Breuillard**.

Brew 1. Irish: Anglicized form of Gael. **Ó Brughadha** 'descendant of *Brughaidh*', a byname meaning 'Farmer'. 2. Manx: Anglicized form of the Gael. occupational term *breitheamh* judge; see BRAIN.

Patr. (from 2): **McBreive**.

Brewer English: 1. occupational name for a brewer of beer or ale, from OE *brēowan* to brew. The name in this form is found chiefly in the W Country. 2. Norman habitation name, a var. of Fr. BRUYÈRE, from a place in Calvados.

Vars. (of 1): **Brewster**, BRUSTER (the *-ster* suffix originally denoted fem. gender, but by the 13th cent. the term was used indiscriminately for male and female brewers).

Patrs. (from 1): Low Ger.: **Brauers**, **Breuers**. Flem., Du.: **Brouwers**, **Broyers**.

Equivs. (not cogn.): Pol.: PIWOWARSKI. Czech: PATOČKA.

Brewis English (chiefly Northumb.): 1. Norman habitation name from *Briouse* in Orne, which probably gets its name from a Gaul. word meaning 'muddy'; cf. BREUIL. **2.** occupational name for someone who worked in a brewery, from ME *brewhus* (a cpd of OE *brēow(an)* to brew + *hūs* house, building).

Brezhnev Russian: of uncertain origin. It is perhaps from the Ukr. nickname *Berezhny* 'Careful', 'Cautious', with the addition of the Russ. patr. ending, or a contracted form of the topographic name BEREZNIKOV.

Brian *see* BRYAN

Briar *see* BREAR

Briard French: habitation name for someone from any of several places called *Brie*, of varied origins. In most cases the name comes from Gaul. *briga* height, hill (cf. BRYAN), but the places so called in Aisne and Ille-et-Villaine get their names from OF *brai* mud (of Gaul. origin). Brie in the *département* of Somme probably represents Gaul. *briva* bridge.

Vars.: **Briaud**, **Briault**; **Brie**, **Debrie**.

Bric French: **1.** derogatory nickname from OF *bric* foolish, idle (of unknown origin). **2.** metonymic occupational name for a bird catcher, from OF *bric, brit, bret* snare (from Gmc *bredan* to snare).

Vars.: **Bri(cq)**, **Bry**.

Dim.: **Bricon**.

Pejs.: **Bricard**, **Bricaud**, **Bricault**.

Brice 1. English and French: from a personal name, probably of Celt. origin (Latinized as *Britius*), which was borne by a 5th-cent. saint who succeeded St Martin as bishop of Tours. It consequently had a certain currency in France in the early Middle Ages and in England after the Norman Conquest. **2.** Jewish (Ashkenazic): Anglicization of **Briess**, a Jewish family name of unknown origin.

Vars.: Eng.: **Bryce** (chiefly Scots). Fr.: **Bris(se)**, **Brés**, **Brix**.

Dims.: Fr.: **Bresset**, **Bresson**, **Bressot**, **Brisset**, **Brisson(neau)**, **Brissot**. Ger.: **Brixle**.

Pejs.: Fr.: **Brissaud**, **Brissard**.

Patrs.: Eng.: **Bryceson**, BRYSON.

Brickdale *see* BIRKDALE

Brickett *see* BIRKETT

Bride *see* BIRD

Bridge English: topographic name for someone who lived near a bridge or metonymic occupational name for a bridge keeper, from ME *brigge*, OE *brycg* bridge, cogn. with MHG *brucke*, OHG *brucca*. Building and maintaining bridges was one of the three main feudal obligations, along with bearing arms and maintaining fortifications. The cost of building a bridge was often defrayed by charging a toll, the surname thus being acquired by the toll gatherer. The form *Bridge* (without the -*s*) is most common in Lancs. The -*s* in the form *Bridges* generally represents the gen. case, but may occasionally be a pl.; in some cases this name denoted someone from the Flem. city of *Bruges* (*Brugge*), meaning 'bridges', which had extensive trading links with England in the Middle Ages.

The Ger. cogns. generally have the same meaning as the Eng.; in addition, there are several Ger. villages called *Brügge(n)* and the Low Ger. surname in some cases indi-

cates origin from one of these. The word *Brückner* denoted a road maker as well as a bridge builder.

Vars.: **Bridge(n)s**; **Brigg(s)** (N English and Scots, from ON *bryggja*); BURGE; **Bridger**; **Bridg(e)man**; **Brigman**.

Cpds: Jewish (ornamental elaborations): **Bruckstein** ('bridge stone'); **Bruckent(h)al** ('bridge valley').

Bridgewater English: habitation name from *Bridgwater* in Somerset (or possibly from some other place with a prominent bridge); the water which the bridge at Bridgwater crosses is the river Parrett, but the placename actually derives from *Brigewaltier*, i.e. 'Walter's bridge', after Walter de Dowai, the 12th-cent. owner. The surname has become common in Birmingham.

Var.: **Bridgwater**.

Bridle English: **1.** metonymic occupational name for a maker of bridles for horses, from OE *brīdel* bridle. **2.** habitation name from some minor place called *Brid(e)well*, e.g. *Bridwell* in Uffculme, Devon, or *Bridewell* Springs in Westbury, Wilts. These two get the name from OE *brȳd* 'bride' + *well(a)* spring (perhaps a spring associated with a fertility cult). There may be other places so called with different derivations, e.g. from OE *bridd* nestling, young bird (see BIRD) or from St *Bride* (see KILBRIDE). There has probably also been some confusion with BRIGHTWELL.

Vars.: **Bridel(l)**. (Of 2 only): **Bridewell**.

Bridson *see* KILBRIDE

Brien *see* BRYAN

Brière *see* BRUYÈRE

Brierley English: habitation name from any of the places called *Brierl(e)y*, in the W Midlands, W and S Yorks., and elsewhere, all of which get their names from OE *brǣr* briar + *lēah* clearing.

Vars.: **Brierly**, **Brearley**, **Briarl(e)y**.

Brigden N English: of uncertain origin, possibly a habitation name from some lost place named with OE *brycg* BRIDGE + *denu* valley.

Brigginshaw *see* BURKINSHAW

Bright English: **1.** from a ME nickname or given name, meaning 'bright', 'fair', 'pretty', from OE *beorht* bright, shining. **2.** from a short form of any of several OE personal names of which *beorht* was the first element, such as *Beorhthelm* 'bright helmet'; cf. BERT.

Var.: **Brightman**.

Brighton English: habitation name from *Breighton* in Humberside on the river Derwent. This place gets its name from OE *brycg* BRIDGE + *tūn* enclosure, settlement. The surname is unlikely to derive from *Brighton* in Sussex, which was known as *Brighthelmestone* until the end of the 18th cent.

Var.: **Brighten**.

Brightwell English: habitation name from any of various places, for example in Berks., Oxon., and Suffolk, so called from OE *beorht* bright, clear + *well(a)* spring, stream. See also BRIDLE.

Brill 1. Low German and Dutch: habitation name from a place in E Friesland, of uncertain etymology. It may be akin to the fish name *brill*. **2.** Jewish (Ashkenazic): acronymic surname from Hebr. *bar-* 'son of ...', with a male given name beginning with *L-*. Cf. BROCK.

Vars. (of 1): Du.: **Brilleman**. (Of 2): **Bril**.

Brillant Jewish (Ashkenazic): ornamental name from Ger. *Brillant* diamond of the finest cut (from Fr. *brillant*, pres. part. of *briller* to shine, glitter), or from the Pol. cogn. *brylant*, which has the same meaning, or from the Yid. cogn. *brilyant* which has a more general meaning, 'diamond, jewel'. Cf. DIAMOND and JAGLOM.

Vars.: **Brilant**, **Bril(l)iant**; **Berland** (metathesized, and with excrescent -d under the influence of Yid. *land* or Ger. *Land* country). Dim.: Jewish (E Ashkenazic): **Berlanczyk**.

Brim 1. English: var of BREAM 3. **2.** Jewish (Ashkenazic): of unknown origin, possibly an acronymic surname from Hebr. *bar-* 'son of ...', with a male given name beginning with *M-*. Cf. BROCK.

Var. (of 1): **Brimm**.

Brimner *see* BREMNER

Brinan *see* BRENNAN

Brind *see* BRENT

Brindle English: habitation name from a place in Lancs., so called from OE *burna* stream (see BOURNE) + *hyll* HILL. The surname is still largely restricted to Lancs.

Brindley English (chiefly Ches., Staffs., and S Lancs.): habitation name from a place in Ches., so called from OE *berned* burnt (see BRENT 1) + *lēah* wood, clearing.

Brington English: habitation name from places in Cambs. (formerly Hunts.) and Northants, so called from OE *Brȳningtūn* 'settlement (OE *tūn*) associated with *Brȳni*' (see BRYNING).

Brink 1. Low German, Dutch, and Danish: topographic name for someone who lived by a pasture, from MLG *brinc* meadow, pasture, esp. a raised meadow in low-lying marshland. **2.** Jewish (Ashkenazic): of unknown origin, possibly an acronymic surname from Hebr. *bar-* 'son of...', with a male given name beginning with *K-*. Cf. BROCK.

Vars. (of 1): Low Ger.: **Brinck**, **Brinken**; **Brin(c)kmann**; **Tenbrin(c)k**, **Tombrin(c)k** (Germanized **Zumbrink**); **Beimbrinke**. Du.: **(Ten) Brink**, **Van de(n) Brin(ć)k**, **Brin(c)kman**. Dan.: **Brinck**, **Brinch**. (Of 2): **Brinkmann**.

Brinkley English: habitation name from a place in Cambs., apparently so called from the OE personal name *Brynca* (of uncertain origin) + OE *lēah* wood, clearing.

Brinton English: habitation name from a place so called, perhaps the one in Norfolk, which has the same origin as BRINGTON.

Brion French: habitation name from any of several places so called. Most of them apparently derive from the Gaul. element *briga* height, hill (cf. BRYAN) + the suffix *-o(n)*. A few are more plausibly derived from Gaul. *berria* plain, with the same suffix. The Sp. placename (examples in the provinces of Logroño and La Coruña) and surname **Briones** is of similar origin.

Brisard French: nickname for a clumsy person, from OF *bris(er)* to break (of Celt. origin) + the pej. suffix *-ard*.

Brisbane English: nickname from OF *bris(er)* to break + OE *bān* bone. The sense of this hybrid name is not entirely clear; it may have been used for someone crippled by a broken bone or, more probably, for a violent man who broke other people's bones.

Brisch *see* BARISH

Briscoe N English: habitation name from any of various places so called. *Briscoe* in Cumb. is so called from ON *Bretaskógr* 'wood of the (Strathclyde) Britons' (cf. BRETT), whereas *Brisco* in Cumb. and *Briscoe* in N Yorks. are so called from ON *birki* BIRCH + *skógr*.

Vars.: **Brisco**, **Briskey**; **Brisker** (see also BRISK).

Brisk Jewish (E Ashkenazic): habitation name from *Brisk*, the Yid. name of two Polish cities (Brześć Litewski, now Brest Litovsk in the Soviet Union, and Brześć Kujawski). See also BRZESKI.

Vars.: **Brisker** (from Yid. *Brisker* native or inhabitant of Brisk); **Briskman**, **Briskin**.

Bristow English: habitation name from the city of *Bristol*, so called from OE *brycg* BRIDGE + *stōw* assembly place. The final *-l* of the modern form is due to a regional pronunciation.

Vars.: **Bristowe**, **Bristo(e)**, **Brister**.

Britch *see* BRACH

Brito Portuguese: habitation name from a place in the province of Minho, or from any of the numerous other minor places with the same name, which is of uncertain origin.

Britt *see* BRETT

Brittain English: **1.** national or ethnic name for a Briton or Breton; see BRETT. **2.** surname adopted by recent immigrants to Britain as a token of their new patriotism.

Vars.: **Brittan**; **Britton** (very common around Bristol); **Britten**, **Brittin** (Northants); **Brittner**, **Britnor**, **Bruttner**.

Broad English: nickname for a stout or fat person, from ME *brode*, OE *brād*. The surname **Brading** (i.e. 'son of Broad') suggests that OE **Brāda* and ME *Brade* may have been in use as personal names. For the Northern ME retention of *-ā*, cf. ROPER.

Vars.: **Brade**; **Braid** (Scots); BRADMAN.

Broadbent N English: habitation name from a minor place in Lancs., near Oldham, so called from OE *brād* BROAD + *beonet* bent grass (see BENT).

Broadely *see* BRADLEY

Broadfield *see* BRADFIELD

Broadhead English (Yorks.): nickname for someone with a wide forehead or large head, from ME *brōd* BROAD + *heved* head (OE *hēafod*).

Broadhurst English: habitation name from a minor place so called, perhaps *Broadhurst* Manor Farm in Horsted Keynes, Sussex. The placename is from OE *brād* BROAD + *hyrst* wooded hill (see HURST).

Broadie *see* BRADY

Broben *see* ROBIN

Brobson *see* BRABAZON

Broc French: **1.** nickname, probably for a person with a prickly temperament, from OF *broc* point, spur (of Gaul. origin). The word has many other meanings—a pointed weapon for stabbing, a deer's antler, a needle, a spit, a jug with a pointed handle, spiny vegetation, etc.—and any or all of these senses may also have contributed to the surname, which may also have been originally an occupational or topographic name. **2.** nickname meaning 'badger', from Bret. *broc'h* (see BROCK 2).

Vars. (of 1): **Broche, Bro(c)que; Broch(i)er, Broquier** (these last being occupational names for makers of pointed objects of some kind).

Dims. (of 1): Fr.: **Brochet, Bro(c)quet, Brochon, Brochot.**
Pejs. (of 1): Fr.: **Broc(h)ard, Broc(h)art.**

Brock 1. English and Low Ger.: var. and cogn. of BROOK. **2.** English: nickname for a person supposedly resembling a badger, ME *broc(k)* (OE *brocc*, of Celt. origin; cf. Welsh *broch*, Corn. *brogh*, Ir. *bruic*). In the Middle Ages badgers were regarded as unpleasant creatures. **3.** Jewish (Ashkenazic): probably an acronymic surname from Hebr. *bar-* 'son of...', with a male given name beginning with *K-*. Many Jewish surnames beginning with *Br-* and *Bar-* are probably of acronymic origin, but without detailed evidence from family histories it is impossible to specify the given name from which each is derived.

Vars. (of 1): Eng.: **Brockman.** Low Ger.: **Bröcker, Brockmann, Tombrock.** (Of 3): **Brok, Brockman(n); Brockmon.**
Dim. (of 2): Scot: **Brockie.**

Brockenshaw *see* BURKINSHAW

Brockhole English: habitation name from an unidentified minor place named from ME *broc(k)* badger (see BROCK 2) + *hole* hole, hollow (see HOLE). See also BROCKWELL.

Brocklebank English: habitation name from a place in Cumb., near Wigton, apparently so called from a bank of earth that was a favourite haunt of badgers; cf. BROCKHOLE and BANKS.

Brocklehurst English (Lancs.): habitation name from a place near Accrington, apparently so called from a wooded hill that was a favourite haunt of badgers; cf. BROCKHOLE and HURST.

Brocklesby English (Lancs.): habitation name from a place in Lincs., so called from the ON byname *Bróklauss* 'Breechless' + ON *býr* farm, settlement.

Brockwell English: probably a var. of BROCKHOLE. OE *Brocchol* is known to have developed into *Brockwell* in at least one instance, in Derbys. Both Brockwell Park in London and Brockwell Farm in Bucks. are of comparatively recent origin, probably deriving their names from the surname rather than vice versa.

Broders *see* BROTHER

Brodie 1. Scots: habitation name from *Brodie* Castle on the coast between Nairn and Forres. The placename is probably from Gael. *brothach* muddy place rather than

bruthach steep place. **2.** Jewish (E Ashkenazic): Anglicized spelling of *Brodi*; see BRODSKI.

Brodigan *see* BRADY

Brodski 1. Jewish (Ashkenazic) and Polish: habitation name from *Brod* in Moravia or *Brody* in the Ukraine, which were important centres of Jewish life up to the time of Hitler. Both places get their names from the Slav. element *brod* ford, Pol. *bród*. **2.** Polish: nickname for a bearded man, a cogn. of BORODIN.

Vars. (of 1): Jewish: **Brodsky; Broda, Brodi, Brody,** BRODIE; **Broida, Broide, Broido; Braude** (W. Ashkenazic); **Brode(r), Brod(t), Brodman.** (Of 1 and 2): Pol.: **Brodowski, Brodziński.**
Patrs. (from 1): Jewish: **Broderson, Broderzon.**

Bröers *see* BROTHER

Brogan Irish: Anglicized form of Gael. **Ó Brógáin** 'descendant of *Brógán*', a personal name apparently derived from a dim. of *bróg* shoe.

Vars.: **O'Brognan(e).**

Brogden English (Yorks.): habitation name from *Brogden* in W Yorks., so called from OE *brōc* BROOK + *denu* valley (see DEAN 1).

Brogelli *see* AMBROSE

Brohoon *see* BRAIN

Broksch *see* PROKOP

Brolin Swedish: topographic name for someone who lived by a bridge, from Swed. *bro* bridge + the local suffix *-lin*.
Vars.: **Brohlin; Broman.**
Cpds (ornamental): **Broberg** ('bridge hill'); **Broström** ('bridge river').

Brolly Irish: Anglicized form of Gael. **Ó Brólaigh** 'descendant of *Brolach*', a personal name possibly derived from *brollach* breast.
Var.: **Brawley.**
Dims.: **(O')Brollaghan,** BRADLEY (Gael. **Ó Brolcháin**).

Bromage English: habitation name from any of the various places called *Bromwich* (West Bromwich, Castle Bromwich, Little Bromwich) in the W Midlands, to which area the surname and its vars. are still largely confined. The placename is from OE *brōm* broom, gorse + *wīc* dairy farm (see WICK).
Vars.: **Bromwich, Bromidge, Brommage.**

Bromberg Jewish (Ashkenazic): from the Ger. name of the city of *Bydgoszcz* in Poland, from *Brom(beere)* bramble (OHG *brāma*) + *berg* hill.
Var.: **Bromberger.**

Bromley English: habitation name from any of the many places called *Bromley* in Essex, Herts., Kent, Greater London, Greater Manchester, Staffs., and elsewhere. All are probably named with OE *brōm* broom + *lēah* wood, clearing.
Vars.: **Bromiley, Bromilow,** BRAMLEY.

Broms Swedish: nickname for an irritating person, from *broms* gadfly, horsefly; cf. BREEZE 1.

Bronfman Jewish (Ashkenazic): occupational name for a distiller, from Yid. *bronfn* brandy (cf. Ger. *Brantwein*) + *man* man.

Vars.: **Bronfmann**; **Bronfin**; **Brandwein(man)**, **Brandwain(man)**, **Brandwin**; **Brandweinhendler** ('brandy seller').

Broniewski Polish: habitation name from a place named with a short form of various cpd Slav. personal names with the first element *broń* weapon, armour, protection, such as *Bronisław* (lit. 'weapon (i.e. defender) of glory'), with the addition of the surname suffix -*ski* (see BARANOWSKI).

Dims.: **Bronisz** (directly from the given name); **Broniszewski** (habitation name).

Bronowski Polish and Jewish (E Ashkenazic): of uncertain origin, apparently a habitation name from some place called *Bronów* or *Bronowo*, perhaps named with the same element as BRONIEWSKI.

Bronshtein *see* BRAUNSTEIN

Bronson English: patr. from the nickname BROWN. In Lancs. it may sometimes derive from the surname BROWN; formation of surnames ending in -*son* from existing surnames was a relatively common phenomenon in NW England.

Vars. (of 1): **Brownson**, **Brunson**.

Brontë *see* PRUNTY

Brook English: topographic name for someone who lived by a brook or stream, from OE *brōc* brook or, by extension, water meadow. 'Water meadow' or 'marsh' is the regular meaning of the Low Ger. cogn. *brook* (Du. *broek*; Ger. *Bruch*, OHG *bruoh*). The Eng. spelling *Brooke* preserves a trace of the OE dat. sing. case, originally used after a preposition (e.g. 'at the brook'), and forms in -*(e)s* preserve a gen. (i.e. 'of the brook'). Both nom. and dat. sing. forms are widely distributed throughout England, but especially common in W and S Yorks.; the gen. var. *Brook(e)s*, on the other hand, has a much more even distribution. Brooks is also borne by Ashkenazic Jews, presumably as an Anglicization of one or more like-sounding Jewish surnames.

Vars.: **Brooke**, **Brook(e)s**, **Broke**, BROCK, **Bruck**; **Brooker**, **Brucker**; **Brookman**; **Brooking** (Devon).

Brookfield English: habitation name from a minor place (probably in Lancs., where the surname is commonest) so called, from OE *brōc* BROOK + *feld* pasture, open country (see FIELD).

Brooksbank English (Yorks.): habitation name from a minor place named from ME *brokes*, gen. of *broke* BROOK + *bank* bank (see BANKS). There are places with this name in Bradfield and Agbrigg, W Yorks.

Brooksby English: habitation name from a place in Leics., recorded in Domesday Book as *Brochesbi*. This may contain a Scandinavian personal name *Brók* + ON *býr* farm, settlement, but it is also possible that the first element is OE *brōc* BROOK, or its Dan. cogn.

Var.: **Bruxby**.

Broom English: habitation name from a place named *Broom(e)* or *Brome*, from OE *brōm* broom, gorse. There

are such places in Beds., Co. Durham, Norfolk, Shrops., Suffolk, Worcs., and elsewhere.

Vars.: **Bro(o)me**.

Broomfield English: habitation name from one of the places named from OE *brōm* broom, gorse + *feld* open country, e.g. *Broomfield* in Essex, Kent, and Somerset, or *Bromfield* in Cumb. and Shrops.

Var.: **Bromfield**.

Broomhall English: habitation name from a place so called, probably the one in Ches., which takes its name from OE *brōm* broom, gorse + *halh* nook, hollow—i.e. 'hollow with gorse growing in it'; cf. BRAMALL.

Broomhead English (chiefly S Yorks.): habitation name from *Broomhead* Hall, near Penistone, so called from OE *brōmig* overgrown with broom + *hēafod* headland.

Brophy Irish: Anglicized form of Gael. Ó Bróithe 'descendant of *Bróth*', a personal name or byname of unknown origin.

Var.: **Broy**.

Brosch *see* BARISH

Brosnahan Irish: Anglicized form of Gael. Ó Brosnacháin 'descendant of *Brosnachán*', a personal name derived from *Brosne*, a town and river in Co. Kerry.

Var.: **Brosnan**.

Brosse French: topographic name for someone who lived in a scrubby area of country, from OF *broce* brushwood, scrub (LL *bruscia*). Occasionally it may be a metonymic occupational name for a brush maker, from the same OF word in the transferred sense 'brush'.

Vars.: **Brouss**, **Brosses**, **Labro(u)sse**, **De(la)bro(u)sse**; **Brossier** (an occupational name).

Dims.: Fr.: **Brousset**, **Broussot**, **Brousseau**, **Brouss(el)oux**; **Brosset** (see also AMBROSE); **Brossollet**, **Brossolette**.

Pejs.: Fr.: **Bro(u)ssard**.

Broster *see* BRUSTER

Brother 1. English: from a byname occasionally used for a younger son, i.e. the brother (OE *brōðor*) of someone important, or for a guild member, esp. a fellow guild member (*brother* being used in this sense in ME). 2. English and Irish: from the cogn. ON *Bróðir*, which was in use as a personal name, originally for a younger son. In Ireland Ó Bruadair (Anglicized as **Brothers**) is an ancient Donegal sept name: it has also been derived, probably wrongly, from Gael. *bruadar* dream, reverie.

Dim.: Fris.: **Broersma**.

Patrs.: Low Ger.: **Broders(en)**; **Bröers**. Flem., Du.: **Broeders**; **Broeren**, **Broerse(n)**. Dan.: **Brodersen**. Jewish: **Bruderso(h)n** (reasons for adoption as a surname not clear). Croatian: **Bradić**.

Patr. (from a dim.): Du.: **Broertjes**.

Brotherstone Scots: habitation name from a place so called in Midlothian, or from another in Berwicks. The Midlothian place is first recorded in 1153 as *Brothirstanys*, and is either from the ON personal name *Bróðir* 'Brother' + the pl. of OE *stān* stone, or means 'twin stones'.

Var.: **Brotherston**.

Brouard French: nickname for a poor man or a miser, one who could or would only eat gruel, from OF *breu, brou* broth, thin soup, gruel (of Gmc origin; cf. Ger. *Brühe*) + the pej. suffix -*ard*.

Dim.: **Brouardel**.

Brough English: habitation name from any of the various places, of which there are several in Yorks. and Derbys. as well as elsewhere, so called from OE *burh* fortress (see also BERRY, BURY, and BURKE). In most cases these are the sites of Roman fortifications. The name is widely distributed, but most common in Staffs. The pronunciation is usually / brʌf/.

Vars.: **Brugh**, **Bruff**.

Brougham English: habitation name from *Brougham* in Cumb., so called from OE *burh* fortress (see BURKE) + *hām* homestead. The pronunciation is /bru:m/.

Broughton English: habitation name from any of the many places in all parts of England so called. The first element is variously OE *brōc* BROOK, *burh* fortress (see BURKE), or *beorg* hill, mound (see BARROW); the second is in all cases OE *tūn* enclosure, settlement.

Brouwers *see* BREWER

Brown English: generally a nickname, ME *brun, le brun*, from OE *brūn* or OF *brun* (both of Gmc origin; cf. OHG *brūn*), referring to the colour of the hair, complexion, or clothing. It may occasionally be from a personal name, OE *Brūn* or ON *Brúni*, with the same origin. *Brun-* was also a Gmc name-forming element; some instances of OE *Brūn* may therefore be short forms of cpd names such as *Brungar, Brunwine*, etc. The Ger. cogns. are associated with the much more common Continental personal name *Bruno*, which was borne by the Dukes of Saxony, among others, from the 10th cent. or before. It was also the name of several medieval German and Italian saints, including the founder of the Carthusian order (1030–1101), who was born in Cologne.

Brown also occurs as an Anglicization of the Jewish names listed below, including compounds, and of names in other langs. meaning 'Brown'.

Vars.: **Browne**, **Broun(e)**.

Dims.: Eng.: **Brunet**, **Brownett**, **Burnet(t)**, **Burnell**. Ger.: **Bräunle(in)**, **Breinl(ein)**; **Praundl(in)** (Bavaria). Low Ger.: **Bru(h)nke**, **Brü(h)nicke**; **Brüntje**. Fris.: **Bruinsma**. Fr.: **Brunet(on)**, **Brunel**, **Bruneau**, **Brunon**, **Brunot**; **Brugnot** (Switzerland). It.: **Brunetti**, **Brunelli**, **Brunini**, **Brunotti**. Cat.: **Brunet**.

Aug.: It.: **Brunone**.

Patrs.: Eng.: BRONSON. Ger.: **Brauns**. Low Ger.: **Bru(h)ns(en)**. Fris.: **Bruins**. Flem.: **Br(u)yns**. Du.: **Bruns**. Fr.: **Aubrun**.

Rum.: **Brunesco**.

Patrs. (from dims.): Low Ger.: **Brüntjen**. Du.: **Bruyntjes**. It.: **Brunelleschi**.

Cpds (ornamental): Jewish: **Braunfeld** ('brown field', Anglicized as **Brownfield**); **Braunroth** ('brownish red'); **Braunstein** ('brown stone', Anglicized as **Brownstein**); **Braunthal** ('brown valley').

Brownhill 1. English: habitation name from any of various places, for example in Yorks., Ches., and Staffs., so called from OE *brūn* BROWN + *hyll* HILL. 2. Jewish: Anglicization of some unidentified Jewish surname.

Vars.: **Brownell**, **Brownill**, **Brownhall**.

Browning English: from the ME and OE personal name *Brūning*, originally a patr. from the byname *Brūn* (see BROWN).

Var.: **Brunning**.

Dan.: **Breuning**.

Patrs.: Eng.: **Brownings**. Ger.: **Brünings**. Flem.: **Bruyninckx**. Fris.: **Bruninga**.

Brownridge English: habitation name from an unidentified place so called from OE *brūn* brown + *hrycg* ridge. The surname is commonest in Yorks., but the placename *Brownrigg* is common in Cumb.; two of the places so called are earlier recorded as *Brownridge*.

Brownsmith *see* SMITH

Broxholme English: habitation name from a place in Lincs., recorded already in this form in Domesday Book, from the gen. case of ODan. *brōk* marsh + ON *holmr* island, dry land in a fen (see HOLME 2). The surname is still largely confined to Lincs., with smaller concentrations in the nearby areas of Derbys., Notts., and S Yorks.

Bruce Scots and English (Norman): habitation name from a place in Normandy, whose identification has been much disputed. Traditionally it is derived from *Brix* near Cherbourg, but *Le Brus* in Calvados and *Briouze* in Orne have also been proposed as candidates. If the last is correct, the name is identical with BREWIS 1.

Bruck *see* BROOK

Bruckental *see* BRIDGE

Bruckisch *see* PROKOP

Brudenell English (Norman): ethnic name for a Breton, or nickname, probably with derogatory overtones, meaning 'little Breton', from ONF *Bretonnel*, dim. of *Bret* Breton (see BRETT). Among the followers of William the Conqueror were many Bretons, ancestors of the bearers of this name among them.

Brudersohn *see* BROTHER

Bruel *see* BREUIL

Bruff *see* BROUGH

Brugnot *see* BROWN

Brühl 1. German; topographic name for someone who lived by a water meadow, MHG *brüel* (OHG *bruil*, a cogn. of Fr. BREUIL). 2. German and Jewish (Ashkenazic): habitation name from the town of *Brühl* in Germany.

Vars. (of 1): **Breuel**. (Of 2): **Brühler**.

Brûlé French: topographic name for someone living in a place cleared for use by burning, from OF *brusle* burnt, past part. of *brusler* to burn (probably a blend of LL *ustulāre* (OF *usler*) with a Gmc verb **brōjan*). Some instances of the name may derive from the same word used with reference to disfigurement by burning, either accidentally or as a medieval ordeal or punishment (cf. BRENT 3).

Vars.: **Bruley**, **Bruslé**.

Dims.: **Brulot**, **Brul(l)on**, **Brulin**.

Pej.: **Brulard**.

Brummell see BRAMALL

Bruninga see BROWNING

Brunnberg see BOURNE

Brunson see BRONSON

Brunt see BRENT

Brunton N English and Scots: habitation name from either of two places in Northumb. so called from OE *burna* stream (see BOURNE) + *tūn* enclosure, settlement.

Brunty see PRUNTY

Brush English: of uncertain origin. It may be a nickname for someone thought to resemble a brush (ME *brusche*, from OF *brosse*; see BROSSE) or a metonymic occupational name for a brush maker. It could also be from a related word, *brusche* cut wood, branches lopped off trees (OF *brousse*, cogn. with *brosse*), as a metonymic occupational name for a forester or woodcutter.
Var.: **Brusch**.

Brusin see AMBROSE

Bruster English: 1. var. of *Brewster* (see BREWER). 2. occupational name for an embroiderer or embroideress, ME *broudestere* (from OF *brouder* to embroider, of Gmc origin). The suffix *-ster(e)* was originally feminine, but by the ME period was being used interchangeably for both men and women in words like *Brewster* (see BREWER) and *Baxter* (see BAKER), and in some regions such as E Anglia was the standard occupational suffix for men as well as women. However, there is no evidence that men did very much embroidery.
Var.: **Broster**.

Bruton English: habitation name from a place so called in Somerset, 'settlement (OE *tūn*) on the river *Brue*'. The river name is derived from a Brit. element cogn. with W *bryw* brisk, vigorous.
Var.: **Brueton**.

Bruttner see BRITTAIN

Bruxby see BROOKSBY

Bruyère French: topographic name for someone who lived in a place where heather grew, from OF *bruyere* heather (LL *brucāria*, from Gaul. **bruko*), or habitation name from one of the places in France (e.g. in Calvados) deriving their names from this word.
Vars.: **Labruyère**, **Delabruyère**; **Bruère**; **Brug(i)ère**, **Brug(i)er**; **Brière**, **Brierre**, **Delabrierre**.
Dims.: **Brugerolle(s)**, **Brugeron**.

Bry see BRIC

Bryan English: from the Celt. personal name *Brian*, which apparently contains the element *bre-* hill, probably with the transferred sense 'eminence'. Breton bearers of this name were among the Normans who invaded England in 1066, and they went on to invade and settle in Ireland in the 12th cent., where the name mingled with a native Irish version of it, borne in particular by one of the greatest of Irish septs, descendants of Brian Boru, who rose to the high kingship of Ireland in 1002. This native Ir. name had

also been borrowed by Vikings, who introduced it independently in NW England before the Norman Conquest.
Vars.: **Brian**, **Brien**; **Bryant**, **Briant** (with excrescent *-t*).
Dim.: Fr.: **Briandet**.
Patrs.: Ir.: **Bryans** (N Ireland); **McBrien** (Gael. **Mac Briain**).
'Descendant of B.': Ir.: **O'Brien** (one of the commonest surnames in Ireland), **O'Brian**, **O'Bryan** (Gael. **Ó Briain**).

Bryce see BRICE

Brydson see KILBRIDE

Bryer see BREAR

Brymner see BREMNER

Bryning English: from a ME, OE personal name, *Bryning*, a patr. from the OE personal name *Brȳni* (from OE *bryne* fire, flame). The latter is found as a placename element; cf. e.g. BRINGTON.

Bryns see BROWN

Bryson 1. English: patr. from the given name BRICE. 2. Irish: Anglicized form of Gael. **Ó Briosáin**, an altered version of *Ó Muirgheasáin* (see MORRISSEY).

Brzeski Polish: 1. habitation name from the town of *Brzeg*, which gets its name from Pol. *brzeg* shore, bank, coast. 2. habitation name from one of the towns named *Brześć* (cogn. with Pol. *brzost* elm; see also BRISK).

Brzeziński see BEREZNIKOV

Bubb English: of uncertain origin, possibly from an OE personal name, *Bubba*; this is attested in placenames, but there is no evidence of its survival into the ME period. The surname may also be from an unrelated nursery word, i.e. a nickname meaning 'baby', but there is no evidence of a ME vocab. word with *-u-* with this meaning.

Bube German: nickname meaning 'boy', MHG *buobe* (originally a nursery word). The word was also used to denote a menial servant.
Var.: **Bueb**.
Dims.: **Bübelin**; **Buberl** (Bavaria).

Bucca see BOCCA

Buch German: topographic name for someone who lived by a beech tree or beech wood, Ger. *Buche* (MHG *buohe*; cf. BEECH).
Vars.: **Bucher(t)**, **Büch(n)er**, **Buchmann**, **Büchmann**; **Puchner** (Bavaria).
Cpds: Jewish (topographic or ornamental): **Buchhol(t)z** ('beech wood'; also a Ger. habitation name); **Buchwald** ('beech forest').

Buchan Scots: regional name from any of various districts so called, principally that north of Aberdeen, although there is an obsolete barony of *Buchquane* in Strathore, Fife, a settlement called *Buchan* in Kirkcudbright, and a hill so called near Minnigaff in Dumfries and Galloway. There may be others. The derivation is probably from a Brit. word meaning 'cow' (cf. W *buwch*), or from the cogn. Gael. *baogh* cow + the dim. suffix *-an*.

Buchanan Scots: habitation name from a place near Loch Lomond, so called from Gael. *buth* house + *chanain* of the canon.

Buchbinder *see* BINDER

Buche *see* BUDGE

Büchelmann *see* BÜHLER

Bucher *see* BUTCHER

Buchs German: topographic name for someone who lived by a box thicket, Ger. *Buchs* (MHG *buhs*; cf. BOX).

Vars.: **Buchsbaum**, **Bux(baum)**; **Puxbaum** (Austria).

Buck 1. English: nickname for a man with some fancied resemblance to a he-goat (OE *bucc(a)*). OE *Bucca* is found as a personal name, as is ON *Bukkr, Bukki*. Names such as *Walter le Buk* (Somerset 1243) seem to be nicknames, but it is not clear what quality was alluded to: lechery, sturdiness, or something else. **2.** English: topographic name for someone who lived near a prominent beech tree, as *Peter atte Buk* (Suffolk 1327), from OE *bōc* BEECH. **3.** German: from a given name, a short form of *Burkhardt* (see BURKETT). **4.** Low German and Danish: cogn. of BAUCH.

Dims. (of 1): Ger.: **Böcklin**. Fr.: **Bo(c)quet, Bouquet, Bo(c)quel**.

Buckett *see* BURKETT

Buckingham English: habitation name from the town of this name, or perhaps in some cases from the county of which it was the county town. The placename comes from OE *Buccingahamm* 'water meadow (OE *hamm*) of the people of *Bucc(a)*' (see BUCK 1).

Buckland English: habitation name from any of the many places so called in S England (nine in Devon alone), which get their names from OE *bōc* book + *land* land, i.e. land held by right of a written charter, as opposed to *folcland*, land held by right of custom.

Buckle English: **1.** metonymic occupational name for a maker of buckles, from ME *bokel* buckle (OF *bocle*, from L *buccula* cheek strap of a helmet, dim. of *bucca* cheek). **2.** metonymic occupational name for a maker of shields; see BÖCKLER.

Vars.: **Buckell, Buckler**; **Buckles**.

Buckley 1. English: habitation name from any of the minor places so called, most of which are from OE *bucc(a)* he-goat (see BUCK 1) + *lēah* clearing, wood. Several instances of *Buckley* and *Buckleigh* in Devon derive from *boga* Bow + *clif* cliff, however. It is also possible that in some cases the surname derives from the contracted local pronunciation of *Bulkeley*, Ches., so called from OE *bulluc* bullock + *lēah*. **2.** Irish: Anglicized form of Gael. Ó Buachalla 'descendant of *Buachaill*', a byname meaning 'Cowherd' or 'Servant'.

Vars. (of 1): **Buckleigh**. (Of 2): **O'Boughelly, (O')Buhilly**.

Buckman English: **1.** occupational name for a goatherd, ME *bukkeman*, from OE *bucca* he-goat (see BUCK 1) + *mann* man. **2.** occupational name for a scholar or scribe, ME *bocman*, from OE *bōc* book + *mann* man. **3.** possibly also a habitation name representing a contracted pronunciation of BUCKINGHAM; cf. *Deadman* from DEBENHAM.

Buckmaster English: ostensibly an occupational name meaning 'master of the goats', but in fact a habitation name from *Buckminster* in Leics., which gets its name from the OE byname *Bucc(a)* (see BUCK 1) + OE *mynster* monastery (L *monastērium*).

Var.: **Buckminster**.

Bucknell English: habitation name from places called *Bucknell* in Oxon. and Shrops. or *Bucknall* in Lincs. and Somerset. The first element in all these is the OE byname *Bucc(a)* (see BUCK 1); the second element is *hyll* HILL in the first two, *healh* nook, hollow (see HALE 1) in the latter two.

Var.: **Bucknall**.

Buckston *see* BUXTON

Buczak *see* BUKOWSKI

Buda *see* BUZEK

Budd English: from an OE byname, *Budde*, which was applied to a thickset or plump person, for reasons that are now obscure. By the ME period it had become a common personal name, with derivs. showing hypocoristic suffixes, *Budecok* and *Budekin*. Reaney, however, derives the name from OE *budda* beetle.

Dim.: **Budcock**.

Patrs.: **Budds**; **Budding**.

Budde *see* BÜTTNER

Buddell *see* BEADLE

Büddenbinder *see* BINDER

Buddenbrock German: habitation name from a place in Westphalia, so called from a MLG personal name *Budde* (probably cognate with OE *Budde*; see BUDD) + MLG *brock* water meadow, marsh (see BROOK).

Vars.: **Buddenbrook(s)**.

Buddle *see* BEADLE, BOODLE

Budge 1. English: nickname from ANF *buge* mouth (LL *bucca*; see BOCCA), applied either to someone with a large or misshapen mouth or to someone who made excessive use of his mouth, i.e. a garrulous or indiscreet person or a glutton. The word is also recorded in ME in the sense 'victuals supplied for retainers on a military campaign', and the surname may therefore also have arisen as a metonymic occupational name for a medieval quartermaster. **2.** Welsh: var. of BEWES. **3.** Scots: surname found in Caithness and Orkney, of uncertain origin.

Vars. (of 1): **Bouch, Buche**.

Budgen English: nickname from the ANF phrase *bon Jean* 'good JOHN'.

Var.: **Budgeon**.

Dims.: It.: **Bong(in)i, Bongino**.

Budgett *see* BURKETT

Budleigh *see* BODLEY

Bueb *see* BUBE

Bufton *see* BOVINGDON

Bugg English: **1.** from the ON byname *Buggi* 'Fat man'. **2.** nickname for an uncouth or weird man, from ME *bugge* hobgoblin, scarecrow (perhaps from W *bwg* ghost); cf. BOGLE.

Bugh *see* BEWES

Buhilly *see* BUCKLEY

Buhl German: 1. nickname for a relative (i.e. a member of an important family who was not the head of it), from MHG *buole* kinsman (OHG *buolo*, also used as a personal name). 2. nickname for a lover or the (illegitimate) child of a lover, from the same word in the later sense 'paramour', 'lover', 'mistress'.

Var.: **Buhle**.

Bühler German: topographic name for someone who lived on a hillside, from Ger. *Büh(e)l* hill (Swiss, Austrian, and S German dialects; OHG *buhil*), or habitation name from a place so called, e.g. *Bühl* in Baden.

Vars.: **Büh(e)l**, **Bühlmann**, **Biehlmann**; **Ambihl**, **Ambihl**, **Abbühl**, **Zumbühl**, **Zumbichl** (chiefly Swiss, with assimilated preposition); **Biehler**, **Biegler**, **Bichler**, **Bichl**, **Biegel** (chiefly Bavarian); **Pichl(er)**, **Pigler**, **Piller**, **Pillmann** (chiefly Austrian); **Büchler**, **Büchelmann** (but see also BEECH).

Buhrs *see* BAUER

Buick *see* BEWICK

Buini *see* BOEUF

Buisson French: topographic name for someone who lived in an area of scrub land or by a prominent clump of bushes, from OF *buisson* bush, scrub (a dim. of *bois* wood; see BOIS and also BUSH).

Vars.: **Dubuisson**; **Boisson**; **Bisson** (Normandy).

Dims.: Fr.: **Buissonnet**, **Boissonet**.

Collective: Fr. **Buissonnière**.

Buitrago Spanish: habitation name from places in the provinces of Madrid and Soria, so called from the LL personal name *Vulturius* (a deriv. of *vultur* vulture) + the local suffix *-ācum*.

Bukowski Polish and Jewish (E Ashkenazic): topographic name for someone who lived in a beech wood or by a beech tree, Pol. *buk* (see BEECH 2). Jewish instances of this group of names are generally, if not always, ornamental.

Vars.: Pol.: **Buczkowski**, **Bukowiecki**; **Buczyński**. Jewish: **Bukowsky**, **Bukovski**; **Bukovitz**.

Dims.: Pol.: **Buczek**, **Buczak**. Jewish: **Buczko**.

Bulgakov Russian: patr. from the nickname *Bulgak* 'Restless', 'Troublesome' (of Turkic origin).

Var.: **Bulganin**.

Bulger *see* BOLGER

Bull English: nickname for a large, aggressive, bull-like man, from ME *bul(l)e*, *bol(l)e*. Occasionally, the name may denote a keeper of a bull (cf. BULMAN), while the form *Simon atte Bole* (London 1377) suggests that in addition this may be derived from a house or inn sign. *Bula* is not attested as an OE word except by the existence of placenames such as BULMER and *Bulwick* (see BULLICK), where it may in some cases represent a personal name. Nevertheless the vocab. word may well have been in use long before it occurs in surviving records: the deriv. *bulluca* BULLOCK is attested in OE. The fact that it gave rise to

surnames that are of mainly S English distribution suggests that in the ME period it was established in S England as a vocab. word, and makes it unlikely that it is a Norse borrowing.

Vars.: **Bulle**; **Bool(e)**.

Dims.: Eng.: BULLOCK; **Bullcock**.

Bullen English: habitation name from the French Channel port of *Boulogne*, recorded in L sources both as *Gessoriācum* and as *Bonōnia*. The latter name is clearly the source of the modern placename. It is ostensibly a deriv. of L *bonus* good (cf. BOLOGNESE), but may in fact come from a Gaul. element **bona* foundation. Boulogne has long been a major trading port between England and France.

Vars.: **Bulleyn**, **Bullon**, **Bullin**, **Bullan(t)**, **Bullent**; **Boullen**, **Boullin**; **Bollen**, **Boleyn**.

Buller 1. English: occupational name for a scribe or copyist, from an agent deriv. of ME, OF *bulle* letter, document (cf. BILLET 3). 2. English (Norman): habitation name from a place in Normandy that has not been identified. If it is *Bouillé*, and so identical with BULLEY 1, the *-er(s)* may have arisen by analogy with other Norman placenames in *-ière(s)*; cf. e.g. FERRERS and VILLIERS. 3. German: nickname for a man with a loud voice, from an agent deriv. of MHG *bullen* to roar (of imitative origin).

Vars. (of 1): Eng.: **Bullar**. (Of 2): Eng.: **Bullers**.

Bulley English: 1. Norman habitation name from any of the several places in Normandy called *Bouillé* or *Bully*, from a Gaul. personal name of uncertain form and meaning + the local suffix *-ācum*. 2. habitation name from *Bulleigh* in Devon or *Bulley* in Gloucs., both of which get their names from OE *bula* BULL (perhaps a byname) + *lēah* wood, clearing.

Var.: **Bully**.

Bullick English: habitation name, perhaps from *Bolwick* in Norfolk or *Bulwick* in Northants, which are so called from OE *bula* BULL (perhaps a byname) + *wīc* outlying settlement (see WICK). The surname is now found mainly in N Ireland.

Bullock English: nickname for an exuberant young man, from ME *bullok* bullock, referring to a young steer rather than a castrated one (OE *bulluca*, dim. of *bula* BULL).

Bulman English (chiefly Northumb.): occupational name for the keeper of a bull, from ME *bule* BULL + *man* man.

Var.: **Bullman**.

Bulmer English: habitation name from a place in Essex, recorded in Domesday Book as *Bulenemera*, from OE *bulena*, gen. pl. of *bula* BULL + *mere* lake (cf. DELAMARE).

Bulstrode English: habitation name from a place in Bucks., so called from OE *burh* fortress, town + *strōd* brushwood, or from one in Herts., which is from OE *bula* BULL + *strōd*.

Bumpas English: nickname, of Norman origin, for someone who was a swift walker, from OF *bon* good (see BON) + *pas* pace (L *passus*). It may also have been a local name, with the second element used in the sense 'passageway'. Cf. MALPAS.

Bumphries *see* HUMPHREY

Bunbury English: habitation name from *Bunbury* near Nantwich, Ches., so called from the OE personal name *Buna* (of uncertain origin) + OE *burh* fortress.

Bunch English: nickname for a hunchback, from ME *bunche* hump, swelling (of unknown origin).
Var.: **Bunche**.

Buncombe English: habitation name from an unidentified place, probably named as a valley with reeds growing in it, from OE *bune* reed + *cumb* valley (see COOMBE).
Var.: **Bunkum**.

Bundey *see* BOND

Bunin 1. Jewish (E Ashkenazic): metr. from a southern Yid. pronunciation of the Yid. female given name *Bone*, from It. *Bona* 'Good' (see BON), with the addition of the Slav. suffix *-in*. 2. Russian: patr. from the nickname *Buna* (from *bunet* to drone), referring to a haughty or boring person.
Vars. (of 1): **Bunis**; **Bones**, **Bonis** (from a NE Yid. pronunciation);
Metr. (from a dim. of 1): **Bunkin** (from the S Yid. dim. given name *Bunke*).

Bunker English: nickname, of Norman origin, for a reliable or good-hearted person, from OF *bon* good (see BON) + *cuer* heart (L *cor*; cf. COEUR).

Bunn *see* BONE

Bunner *see* POYNER

Bunnett English: of uncertain origin, probably a var. of *Bonnett*; see BONNET. This form is recorded in Suffolk in the early years of the 17th cent.
Var.: **Bunnyt**.

Bunney English (now chiefly Devon): of uncertain origin, possibly a nickname, as Reaney suggests, for someone having a prominent lump or swelling, from ME *bunny* swelling, bunion (see BUNYAN). It is also possibly a topographic name from the SW Eng. dial. word *bunny* ravine.

Bunter S English: occupational name for a sifter of flour, from an agent deriv. of ME *bont(en)*, *bunt(en)* to sieve, sift (of uncertain origin, possibly akin to BOLT 1).

Bunting English: nickname from the bird so called. The word is attested from at least the 13th cent., and may be the first element in the placename *Buntingford*, recorded a century earlier. It is of unknown origin; it is possibly a deriv. of a Gmc element meaning 'short and thick', cf. BUNZ.
Vars.: **Buntin(e)**, **Bunten**, **Bunton**, **Buntain**, **Bontein**, **Bontine**.

Bunyan English: nickname for someone disfigured by a lump or hump, from a dim. of OF *bugne* swelling, protuberance. The term *bugnon* was also applied to a kind of puffed-up fruit tart, and so the surname may also have been a metonymic occupational name for a baker of these.
Vars.: **Bunyon**, **Bunnion**.

Bunyard *see* BANYARD

Bunz German: nickname for a fat man, from the Alemannic (Swiss) dialect word *bunz* little barrel (perhaps ultimately from L *punctio* stamp, i.e. a barrel stamped with a seal of approval).
Dims.: **Bünzli** (Switzerland). Jewish (Ashkenazic): **Bunzel**.

Buonaparte *see* BONAPARTE

Buonarroti Italian: from the medieval (chiefly Tuscan) given name *Buonarroto*, composed of the elements *buona* (fem.) good (see BON) + *arrota* gain, increase (from the verb *arrogare*, L *adrogāre* to appropriate, acquire). The name was used to denote a child whose birth provided a welcome addition to the family.

Buonsangue Italian: nickname for an illegitimate child suspected of being of noble parentage, from OIt. *buon(o)* good (see BON) + *sangue* blood (L *sanguis*).

Burbage English: habitation name from places in Wilts., Derbys., and Leics., so called from OE *burh* fort (see BURKE) + *bæc* hill, ridge (see BACK 1).
Vars.: **Burbidge**.

Burch *see* BIRCH

Burchall *see* BIRCHALL

Burchett *see* BIRKETT

Burchfield English: habitation name from some minor place named with the OE elements *birce* BIRCH + *feld* pasture, open country (see FIELD).

Bürcklin *see* BIRCH

Burd *see* BIRD

Burda Czech: 1. nickname for a large, loutish fellow, Czech *burda*. 2. dim. of BURIAN.
Var.: **Burdák**.

Burdon English (chiefly W Country): 1. Norman, from the OF personal name *Burdo* (oblique case *Burdon*), probably of Gmc origin, but uncertain meaning. 2. nickname for a pilgrim or one who carried a pilgrim's staff (ME, OF *bourdon*, of uncertain origin, probably from LL *burdo*, gen. *burdōnis*, mule, pack animal, with later extension to mean 'support'). 3. habitation name from places in W Yorks and Co. Durham, so called from OE *burh* fortress (see BURKE) + *dūn* hill (see DOWN 1). Another Burdon in Co. Durham means 'valley with a byre', from *bȳre* byre + *denu* valley.
Var.: **Burden**.

Bure *see* BOURE

Burford English: habitation name from places in Oxon. and Shrops., so called from OE *burh* fortress (see BURKE) + *ford* FORD.

Burge English (chiefly Somerset and Dorset): 1. var. of BRIDGE, OE *brycg*, with metathesis of *u* and *r*, as exemplified in several placenames of this origin in various parts of S England. 2. var. of BURKE.

Burgemeister German: status name for the mayor or chief magistrate of a town, from Ger. *Bürgemeister*, a cpd of MHG *burc* town (see BURKE) + *meister* MASTER.

Burger German, Dutch/Flemish, and English: status name for a freeman of a town, esp. one who was a member of its governing council, a deriv. of MHG *burc*, ME *burg* (fortified) town (see BURKE). There is a difficulty with the

Eng. name, in that it is found occasionally as a surname from the 13th cent. onwards, but is not recorded as a vocab. word until the 16th cent., when it was apparently borrowed from Ger. The usual Eng. term was the OF word *burgeis* BURGESS. This name also occurs as a Jewish surname, but the reasons for its adoption are uncertain.

Vars.: Ger.: **Bürger**. Flem., Du.: **De Burg(h)er**; **Borger**. Eng.: **Burgher**, **Burker**. Jewish: **Burg(mann)**.

Patrs.: Low Ger.: **Borgers**; **Bürgers** (Rhineland). Du., Flem.: **Burgers**, **Borgers**.

Burgess English: from ME *burge(i)s*, OF *burgeis* inhabitant and (usually) freeman of a (fortified) town (see BURKE), esp. one with municipal rights and duties. Burgesses generally had tenure of land or buildings from a landlord by *burgage* (L *burgāgium*). In medieval England burgage involved the payment of a fixed money rent (as opposed to payment in kind); in Scotland it involved payment in service, guarding the town. The *-eis* ending is from L *-ēnsis* (mod. Eng. *-ese* as in *Chinese*). Compare BURGER.

Vars.: **Burges**, **Burgis(s)**.

Dims.: It.: **Borghesetti**, **Borghesini**.

Burian Czech: from an OSlav. personal name, which appears to derive originally from the Russ. or Pol. word *bury* grizzly (a borrowing from Turkish, *bur* chestnut, applied to horses; not found in Czech as a vocab. word) + *Jan* JOHN.

Dims.: **Buriánek**, **Burýšek**; **Bureš**, BURDA.

Burke English: topographic name from ME *burc*, *burk* fort, from OE *burh* or (via OF) OHG *burg*, the common Gmc word for a fortification. In the Middle Ages any sizeable habitation had to be fortified, but in England the term *burc* came to be specialized to denote the site of a prehistoric hill fort, while its doublet *burig*, *borough* denoted a fortified manor house or fortified town (see BURY).

Vars.: **Bourke**; **Burgh** (the name of places in Cumb., W Yorks., Lincs., and Norfolk, as well as Suffolk), **De Burgh**; **Brough**, **Burge**.

Dims.: Fr.: **Bourgel**, **Bourget**, **Bourgey**, **Bourquet**; **Dubourquet**. It.: **Borghetti**, **Borghini**, **Borgotti**.

Augs.: Fr.: **Bourg(e)at**, **Bourgeas**. It.: **Borgoni**.

Pej.: It.: **Borgazzo**.

Cpd (ornamental): Swed.: **Borgström** ('town river').

Burkett English: from an OE personal name, *Burgheard*, composed of the elements *burh*, *burg* fort (see BURKE) + *heard* hardy, brave, strong. The name was reintroduced into ME by the Normans in the forms *Bou(r)chart*, *Bocard*; hence many of the variants. In the form *Burkhard* it was a very popular medieval Ger. name. There has been considerable confusion between this Eng. surname and BIRKETT.

Vars.: **Burkitt**, **Burkart**, **Borkett**, **Bockett**, **Buckett**; **Burchett**, **Burchatt**, **Burchard**, **Butchard**, **Budgett**.

Dims.: Ger.: BUCK, **Bürk(el)**; **Birkle** (Württemberg); **Bürkli**, **Busse**, **Bosse** (S Germany, Switzerland).

Patrs.: Low Ger.: **Borchers**; **Borcherding**.

Burkin 1. English: habitation name from the parish of *Birkin* in W Yorks., so called from OE *bircen* birch grove (originally an adj. deriv. of *birce* BIRCH). 2. Jewish (Ashkenazic): of unknown origin.

Var. (of 1): **Birkin**.

Burkinshaw English (Yorks.): habitation name from *Birkenshaw* near Wakefield in W Yorks., so called from OE *bircen*, an adj. deriv. of *birce* BIRCH + *sceaga* copse (see SHAW).

Vars.: **Birkenshaw**, **Burtenshaw**, **Birtenshaw**, **Brigginshaw**, **Bro(c)kenshaw**.

Burkman English: from ME *burghman*, *borughman* (OE *burhmann*) inhabitant of a (fortified) town (see BURKE), esp. one holding land or buildings by *burgage* (see BURGESS).

Vars.: **Burman**; **Borro(w)man**, **Barrowman**, **Barryman**.

Burley English: habitation name from any of various places, for example in Derbys., Leics., Shrops., and W Yorks., so called from OE *burh* fort (see BURY) + *lēah* wood, clearing.

Var.: **Burleigh**.

Burling English: apparently an OE patr. in *-ing* from a personal name that has not been certainly identified, possibly a dim. of *Burgheard* (see BURKETT), **Byrgla* (suggested by Ekwall as underlying *Birlingham* in Worcs.), or **Bærla* (from OE *bār* boar, suggested by Ekwall as underlying *Birling* in Kent and *Barling* in Essex).

Vars.: **Birling**, **Barling**.

Burn see BOURNE

Burnand see BRENNAND

Burnell see BROWN

Burney 1. English (Norman): habitation name from *Bernay* in Eure, Normandy, so called from a Gaul. personal name *Brenno* (cf. BRYAN) + the local suffix *-ācum*, or from *Berney* in Norfolk, which apparently gets its name from Ralph *de Bernai* (Domesday Book), a Norman who received grants of land there. 2. Irish: Anglicized form of the personal name *Biorna*, a Gael. form of ON *Bjarni* (from *björn* bearcub, warrior; cf. BARNES 2).

Vars. (of 1): **Berney**, **Burnie**.

Patrs. (from 2): **McBurney**, **McBirney** (Gael. **Mac Biorna**).

Burnham English: habitation name from any of several places so called. Those in Bucks. (Burnham Beeches), Norfolk (various villages), and Essex (Burnham-on-Crouch) get the name from OE *burna* stream (see BOURNE) + *hām* homestead. In the case of Burnham-on-Sea in Somerset, however, the second element is OE *hamm* water meadow. Burnham in Lincs. is so called from *brunnum*, dat. pl. of ON *brunnr* spring, originally used after a preposition, i.e. (at) the springs'.

Burnley English (Lancs. and Yorks.): habitation name from *Burnley* in Lancs., so called from OE *burna* stream (see BOURNE) + *lēah* wood, clearing.

Burns 1. Scots and N English: topographic name for someone who lived by a stream or streams, from the ME nom. pl. or gen. sing. of *burn* (see BOURNE). 2. Scots: topographic name or habitation name from the ME elements *burn* stream + *house* house. 3. Irish: Anglicized form of Gael. *Ó Broin*; see BYRNE. 4. Jewish (Ashkenazic): Anglicized and shortened form of BERNSTEIN.

Vars. (of 2): **Burnhouse**, **Burness**.

Burnside Scots and N Irish: topographic name for someone living beside a burn or stream or habitation name from one of the places so called, of which the most significant is near Dalry, in the former county of Ayrs.

Burr English: of uncertain origin. Reaney explains this as a nickname for a person who is difficult to shake off, from ME *bur(r)* bur (seed-head that sticks to clothing). There is a problem with this explanation, in that *Burre* occurs as a surname or byname as early as 1185, whereas the vocab. word is not recorded by *OED* until the 14th cent. Reaney says, 'This sense may well be older'. The surname could be a var. of BURKE, but the loss of the final consonant would be hard to explain. Another possibility is derivation from OE *būr* small dwelling or building (mod. Eng. *bower*; cf. Ger. BAUER), but there are phonological difficulties here too.

Burrett English: **1.** from the ME given name *Burret*, OE *Burgrǣd*, composed of the elements *burh, burg* fortress, stronghold + *rǣd* counsel. **2.** nickname for someone with thick and dishevelled hair, from ME *b(o)urre* coarse woollen cloth (cf. BOURE) + *heved* head (OE *hēafod*).

Vars.: **Borrett**, **Boret**, **Borritt**.

Burridge English: **1.** habitation name from any of three places in Devon so called from OE *burh* fort (see BURKE) + *hrycg* ridge. **2.** from the ME given name *Burrich*, OE *Burgrīc*, composed of the elements *burh, burg* fortress, stronghold + *rīc* power.

Var.: **Burrage**.

Burrows English: topographic name (with locative gen. -*s*) for someone who lived by a hill or tumulus (OE *beorg*, a cogn. of OHG *berg* hill, mountain; see BERG). However, the name has become inextricably confused with derivs. of OE *burh* fort (see BURKE and BURY). (Reaney suggests a further derivation from OE *būr* BOWER + *hūs* house.)

Vars.: **Burrowes**, **Burrough(e)s**, **Burris**; **Burrow** (Yorks. and Lancs.); **Burrough**, **Borrow(s)**.

Burs *see* BAUER

Burski *see* BOROWSKI

Burstin Jewish (E Ashkenazic): from Yid. *burshtin* amber, which is from Pol. *bursztyn*, which in turn is from Ger. *Bernstein* (see BERNSTEIN).

Vars.: Jewish: **Burshtin**, **Burshtyn**, **Burs(z)tyn**; **Burs(h)tein**, **Burs(h)tain**, **Burszt(e)in**, **Bursztejn** (showing influence of Ger. -*stein*); **Bursten**, **Bourstin** (Anglicized).

Burt English (common in SW England): probably a var. of BERT, from the OE byform *Byrht* of *Be(o)rht*.

Var.: **Birt**.

Burton English: habitation name from a placename that is very common in Midland and Northern England. The derivation is generally from OE *burh* fort (see BURKE) + *tūn* enclosure, settlement.

Vars.: **Bo(u)rton**.

Burtwistle *see* BIRTWISTLE

Bury English: habitation name or topographic name, ultimately from the dat. case, *byrig*, of OE *burh* fortified place (see BURKE), originally used after a preposition (e.g. Rich-

ard *atte Bery*). As inflections were lost in ME, derivs. of the OE dat. replaced the OE nom., the word taking forms such as *biri, berie*, and *burie*. In ME this word acquired two different senses, both of which have given rise to surnames. In late OE and early ME it denoted a fortified manor house; and the surname was used for someone who lived near a manor house or as an occupational name for someone employed in a manor house. The word also came to denote a fortified town, and is therefore a habitation name from any of various places so named. From this sense developed the mod. Eng. word *borough*. The surname *Bury* is especially common in Lancs., where it is no doubt mainly if not exclusively a habitation name from the town of this name, but may also be from various other, less important, places similarly named.

Vars.: BERRY; **Berryman**, **Berriman** (chiefly Devon); **At(ter)bury**, **Atberry** (with fused preposition; cf. ATTENBOROUGH).

Burzyński Polish: habitation name from a place called *Burzyn*, which apparently gets its name from Pol. *burza* tempest, storm.

Busby English: habitation name from a place in N Yorks., recorded in Domesday Book as *Buschebi*, from ON *buski* bush, shrub (see BUSH) + *býr* homestead, village, or from some other place so called. The surname is now most common in the W Midlands.

Buscaino *see* BOISSIER

Büschgen *see* BUSH

Bušek *see* BUZEK

Bush 1. English: topographic name for someone who lived by a thicket of bushes, from ME *bush(e)* bush (probably from ON *Buski*, or an unrecorded OE *busc*). The surname may also be from ON *Buski* used as an personal name. **2.** Jewish (Ashkenazic): Anglicized form of Ger. *Busch*, which was adopted by some Jews in allusion to the story of the burning bush from which God spoke to Moses (Exod. 3: 2–4).

Vars.: Eng.: **Bish**, **Bysh**, **Bysshe** (from a hypothetical OE word *(ge)bysce* bushy area, thicket).

Dims.: Low Ger.: **Büschgen**, **Böschgen**.

Bushby English: habitation name from a place so called, or a var. of BUSBY. There is a *Bushby* in the parish of Thurnby, Leics., named from the ON personal name *Butr* (see BUTT 1) + ON *býr* homestead, village. Derivation has also been proposed from *Bushbury* in Staffs., recorded in Domesday Book as *Biscopesberie*, i.e. the manor (see BURY) of the BISHOP. However, neither of these Midland origins is supported by the early distribution of the surname, which is Northern; it is first recorded in Cumb. From the 16th cent. it has been found in three main groups: in Cumb., Northumb., and N Yorks.; in Beds.; and in Sussex.

Var.: **Bushbye**.

Bushell *see* BISSELL

Busquet *see* BOIS

Buss English: metonymic occupational name for a cooper or else a nickname for a rotund, fat man, from ME, OF *busse* cask, barrel (of unknown origin). The word was also used in ME of a type of ship, and the surname may perhaps have been given to someone who sailed in one. The by-name seems to occur already in Domesday Book, where a Siward *Buss*, and a John and Richard *Buss* are recorded at Brasted in Kent.

Var.: **Busse**.

Busse *see* BURKETT, BUSSE

Bussey English: Norman habitation name from any of several places in Normandy: *Boucé* in Orne, from which came Robert *de Buci* mentioned in Domesday Book, *Boucey* (Manche), or *Bucy*-le-Long (Aisne). All of these places get their names from a L personal name *Buccius* (presumably a deriv. of *bucca* mouth; cf. BOCCA) + the local suffix *-ācum*.

Bussière *see* BOX

Bussy *see* BOISSY

Bustamante Spanish: habitation name from a lost place, so called from LL *bustum Amantii* 'pasture (see BUSTO) of *Amantius*', a personal name derived from LL *Amans*, gen. *Amantis*, 'Loving'.

Busto Spanish: habitation name from any of various minor places in W Spain, so called from LL *bustum* pasture for oxen or bullocks (a deriv. of *bos* ox, gen. *bovis*; cf. BOEUF and BOUVIER).

Var.: **Bustos**.

Dim.: **Bustillos**.

Butchard *see* BURKETT

Butcher English: occupational name for a butcher or slaughterer, ME *bo(u)cher* (OF *bouchier*, a deriv. of *bouc* ram; cf. BUCK 1).

Vars.: **Bucher**, **Bou(t)cher**; BOWKER, **Boucker**.

Dims.: Fr.: **Bouchereau**, **Boucherot**, **Boucheron**. It.: **Becherini**.

Aug.: It.: **Becheroni**.

Patr.: It.: **Del Beccaro**.

Equivs. (not cogn.): Sp.: CARNICERO. Ger.: METZGER. Pol.: RZEŹNIK. Russ.: MYASNIKOV.

Butler English and Irish: occupational name for a wine steward, usually the chief servant of a medieval household, from ANF *butuiller* (OF *bouteillier*, L *buticulārius*, from *buticula* bottle, dim. of *but(t)is* cask; cf. BOTAS). In the large households of royalty and the most powerful nobility, the title frequently denoted an officer of high rank and responsibility, only nominally concerned with the supply of wine. The name has also been adopted as a Jewish surname, for reasons that are not clear.

Vars.: **Botler** (though this may also be derived from ME *boteler* maker of (leather) bottles, from ME *botel*, OF *bouteille*); **Bottle**, **Bottell**, **Buttle**.

Butlin English: apparently from ME *Butevilain* (recorded in Norfolk in 1130 and elsewhere), which is either a compounded byname, BUTT the peasant', or a nickname meaning 'strike the peasant', from ANF *but(er)* to strike (of Gmc origin) + *vilain* peasant, bondsman (see VILLAIN). The surname is now found chiefly in the E Midlands.

Butrimovich *see* BARTHOLOMEW

Butt English: 1. from a ME personal name, *But(t)*, of unknown origin, perhaps originally a nickname meaning 'short and stumpy', and akin to late ME *butt* thick end, stump, buttock (of Gmc origin). ME *but(te)* was also a vocab. word denoting various types of salt fish, originally a fish with a blunt head. The surname may sometimes have been acquired by a seller of salt fish. 2. topographic name for someone who lived near a place used for archery practice, from ME *but* mark for archery, target, goal (from OF *but* aim, target; of unknown origin).

Patrs. (from 1): **Butts**; **Butson** (common in Devon and Cornwall from the 17th cent. onwards); **Butting**.

Butter English: 1. nickname for someone with some fancied resemblance to a bittern, perhaps in the booming quality of the voice, from ME, OF *butor* bittern (of obscure etymology). 2. metonymic occupational name for a dairyman or seller of butter, from OE *butere* butter (from L *būtyrum*, Gk *boutyron*, a cpd of *bous* cow + *tyron* cheese).

Var. (of 2): **Butterman**.

Patr. (from 1): Eng.: BUTTERS.

Butterfield English: topographic name, common in the Bradford and Leeds area, for someone who lived by a pasture for cattle or at a dairy farm, or habitation name from a place so called (of which there is one in W Yorks.), from OE *butere* butter (see BUTTER 2) + *feld* pasture, open country (see FIELD).

Butteriss English: 1. var. of BOTTRELL (according to Reaney). 2. occupational name for a servant working in a wine cellar, ANF *boterie* (LL *botāria*, a deriv. of *bota* cask), with the ME gen. ending -*s*.

Vars.: **Buttriss**, **Buttress**, **Buttrice**, BUTTERS, **Buttrey**.

Butteriss *see* BOTTRELL

Butters English: 1. patr. from BUTTER 1. 2. var. of BUTTERISS.

Butterworth English (Lancs. and Yorks.): habitation name from places in Lancs. (near Rochdale) and in W Yorks. Both are so called from OE *butere* butter (see BUTTER 2) + *worð* enclosure (see WORTH). The surname is recorded from an early date in each of these two places; it probably arose independently in each.

Buttle *see* BOODLE

Büttner German: one of several occupational names for a cooper or barrel-maker, Ger. *Büttner*, agent deriv. of MHG *büte(n)* cask, wine barrel (OHG *butin*, prob. via LL from Gk *butinē* chamber pot; cf. BOTAS and BUTLER). This name is more common in eastern German-speaking regions. The vocab. word was taken into Czech (as *bednář*), Pol. (as *bednarz*), and Ukr. (in the metathesized form *bondar*). See also BINDER, BÖTTCHER, SCHÄFFLER.

Vars.: **Bittner**; **Pittner** (Bavaria). Low Ger.: **Budde**.

Buttrum *see* BERTRAM

Bux *see* BUCHS

Buxó *see* BOX

Buxtehude German: habitation name from a town so called SW of Hamburg, which apparently gets its name (earlier *Bucstede*) from a Gmc personal name, *Bucc* (see Buck 1) + MLG *stede* homestead, place (see Stead 1).

Buxton English: **1.** habitation name from *Buxton* in Derbys., which in ME was called *Buchestanes, Bucstones* (i.e. 'bowing stones', from ME *b(o)ugen*, OE *būgan* to bow + *stanes* stones). It probably gets its name from logan stones in the vicinity. (Logan stones are boulders so poised that they rocked at a touch.) **2.** less commonly, a habitation name from *Buxton* in Norfolk, which gets its name from the gen. case of the OE personal name *Bucc* (see Buck 1) + OE *tūn* settlement, enclosure.

Vars.: **Buckston(e)**.

Buy *see* Bye

Buzek Czech: from a dim. of the Czech personal name *Budislav*, composed of the elements *budi-* to awaken, inspire + *slav* glory, or of any other personal name containing *budi-* as the first element.

Vars.: **Bouzek, Bušek; B(o)uda, Budek, Budík, Budil**.

Byatt English: topographic name for someone who lived near a gate, from ME *by* by, beside (OE *bī*) + *yat(e)* gate (OE *geat*).

Býček *see* Bick

Bye English: topographic name for someone who lived near a bend in a river, from OE *byge* bend (a deriv. of *būgan*; cf. Buxton 1).

Vars.: **By, Buy(e)**.

Byers N English and Scots: topographic name for someone who lived by a cattleshed, ME, OE *bȳre*, or habitation name from a place so named, e.g. *Byers* Green in Co. Durham or *Byres* near Edinburgh.

Vars.: **Byres, Biers**.

Byfield English: **1.** habitation name from a place, for example in Northants, so called from OE *byge* bend (see Bye) + *feld* pasture, open country. **2.** topographic name for someone who lived near a patch of open land, from ME *by* by, beside (OE *bī*) + *fe(i)ld(e)* open country.

Byford English: **1.** habitation name from a place so named from OE *byge* bend (see Bye) + *ford* Ford. There is one such on the Wye near Hereford. **2.** topographic name for someone who lived by a ford, from ME *by* by, beside (OE *bī*) + *ford*. The surname is found chiefly in Essex.

Bygrave English: topographic name for someone whose home was by a (defensive) ditch or dike, from ME *by* by, beside (OE *bī*) + *grave* ditch (OE **grafa*, a deriv. of *grafan* to dig), or a habitation name from *Bygrave* in Herts.

Vars.: **Bygraves, Bigrave(s)**.

Bykoff *see* Bick

Byles *see* Biles

Byng *see* Bing

Bynnan *see* Bannan

Byrch *see* Birch

Byrd *see* Bird

Byres *see* Byers

Byrne Irish: Anglicized form of Gael. **Ó Broin** 'descendant of *Bran*', a personal name probably from *bran* raven. Bran was the name of a son of the King of Leinster, who died at Cologne in 1052.

Vars.: **O'Byrne, (O')Be(i)rne, Byrnes**, Burns.

Byron English: from OE *bȳrum* 'at the cattle sheds', dat. pl. of *bȳre* byre, and thus a topographic name for one living at such a place or occupational name for one employed there, a cowman. This name and its vars. *Biron* and *Biram*, have occasionally been adopted as Jewish surnames, presumably as Anglicizations of Jewish names that cannot now be identified.

Vars.: **Biron, Byran, Byrom, Byram, Biram**.

Bysh *see* Bush

Bythell *see* Bethell

Bytheway English: topographic name for one whose home was beside a main highway, from the ME phrase *bi the weie*. The surname is found mainly in the W Midlands.

Bythway *see* Way

Bywater **1.** English: topographic name for someone living by a lake or river, from ME *by* by, beside (OE *bī*) + *water* water (OE *wæter*). **2.** Irish: translation of *Ó Srutháin* (see Strohane).

Var.: **Bywaters**.

Byway *see* Way

Bywood *see* Wood

C

Ca *see* CASA

Cabaço Portuguese: nickname for a fat man or a heavy drinker, from Port. *cabaço* gourd (cogn. with Sp. *calabaza*, of uncertain, probably pre-Roman, origin).

Cabane Provençal: topographic name for someone who lived in a rough or temporary dwelling, from OProv. *cabane* hut, cabin (LL *capanna*, apparently of Celt. or Gmc origin). There are a number of places in France named with this word (and its vars. and derivs.), and the surname may also be a habitation name from any of these.
Vars.: **Caban(ne)**; **Chaban(n)e(s)** (Limoges, Auvergne); **Chavan(n)e(s)** (Poitou); **Cabanès**, **Cabanais**; **Cabanié**, **Chabanier**, **Chebanier**.
Dims.: Prov.: **Cabanel**, **Chavanel**, **Chavaneau**; **Chabanet**, **Chabaneix**; **Cabanot**; **C(h)abanon**, **Chavenon**. Sp.: **Cabanillas**, **Cavanillas**.
Augs.: Prov.: **Chabanas**, **Chabanat**.

Cabello Spanish: nickname for a man with a particularly luxuriant growth of hair (or perhaps ironically for a bald man), from Sp. *cabello* hair (L *capillus*, a collective noun).
Var.: **Cabellos**.

Cabestany Catalan: topographic name for someone who lived at the head of a lake, from Cat. *cap* head, top (see CAP) + *estany* lake, pond. There is a place named with these elements in Rousillon, S France, which may be a partial source of the surname.
Var.: **Cavestany**.

Cabeza Spanish: habitation name from any of the numerous minor places so called from LL *capitia* head (a deriv. of class. L *caput*; cf. CAP), a frequent term for a small hill. In some case it may also have been a nickname for someone with a large or deformed head.
Vars.: **Cabezas**; **Cabezudo** (a nickname).
Dim.: Sp.: **Cabezuelo**.
Aug.: Sp.: **Cabezón**.

Cabiron *see* CHEEVER

Cabiten *see* CAPITAINE

Cable English: metonymic occupational name for a maker of rope, especially the type of stout rope used in maritime applications, from ANF *cable* cable (LL *capulum* halter, of Arabic origin, but associated by folk etymology with L *capere* to take, seize).
Var.: **Cabel**.

Cabot French: nickname for someone with a large head, or metonymic occupational name for a fisherman, from OF *cabot* miller's thumb, *Cottus gobio* (OProv. *cabotz*, from LL *capōceus*, a deriv. of *caput* head; cf. CAP).
Dim.: Fr.: **Cabotin**.

Cabotto *see* JACOB

Cabrera Spanish: habitation name from any of various minor places so called from LL *caprāria* 'place of goats' (a deriv. of *caper* goat; cf. CHEEVER).

Cacci *see* JACK

Cáceres Spanish: habitation name from a city in W Spain, whose name apparently derives, via Arabic *Al-Cazires*, from L *castra Cereris* 'town of *Ceres*', the Roman goddess of agricultural prosperity, who had a temple there.

Cadbury English: habitation name from places in Somerset and Devon, so called from the OE personal name *Cada* (see CADE 1) + OE *burh* fortress, town (see BURY), here referring to prehistoric hill-forts.

Caddock 1. Welsh: from the OW personal name *Cadoc*, which is possibly a dim. of the Celt. element reflected in W *cad* battle (cf. CADELL), or else a pet form of *Cadfael*. 2. English: nickname for a frail or infirm person or a sufferer from epilepsy, from ME, OF *caduc* (LL *cadūcus*, a deriv. of *cadere* to fall).
Var. (of 1): **Caddick** (chiefly W Midlands).
Dims. (of 1): **Cadwgan**, **Cadogan**; DUGGAN.

Cade English: 1. from a ME given name, *Cade*, a survival of the OE personal name or byname *Cada*, which is apparently from a Gmc root meaning 'lump', 'swelling'; it may have been applied to a fat person. 2. metonymic occupational name for a cooper, from ME, OF *cade* cask, barrel (of Gmc origin, probably akin to the root mentioned in 1). 3. nickname for a gentle or inoffensive person, from ME *cade* domestic animal, pet (of unknown origin).
Var.: **Cadd**.
'Servant of C.': **Cadman**.

Cadel Provençal: 1. nickname for a playful person, from OProv. *cadel* puppy (L *catulus*). 2. status name for a chieftain or village elder, OProv. *capdel* (LL *capitelum*, a dim. of *caput*; see CAP).

Cadell British: from an OW personal name derived from the Celt. element reflected in W *cad* battle. The surname is found in Scotland and Ireland, and also in Wales where the given name was popular in the Middle Ages as a result of the fame of Cadell ab Urien, a 7th-cent. saint who founded the chapel of Llangadell 'church of Cadell', in Glamorgan.
Vars.: **Caddel(l)**, **Cattell**, **Cadle**.

Cadena Catalan and Spanish: metonymic occupational name for a maker of chains, or perhaps for a gaoler, from Sp. *cadena* chain (L *catēna*). The sing. *Cadena* is rare as a surname in Castile, but frequent in Catalonia; the pl. **Cadenas** occurs in both regions but is more frequent in the former.

Cadge *see* CAGE

Cadillac French: habitation name from a place in Gironde, so called from the Gallo-Roman personal name *Catilius* (probably a Latinized form of a Celt. deriv. of the element *cad* battle; cf. CADELL) + the local suffix -*ācum*.
Vars.: **Cadilhac**; **Cadilhon**, **Cadilhou** ('man from C.').

Cadiou 1. Provençal: nickname from a favourite oath, OProv. *cap* head (see CAP) + *Diou* God (L *deus*). 2. N French: from a Bret. personal name, a dim. formation from the Celt. element *cad* battle (cf. CADELL).
Vars.: **Cadioux**, **Cadio(t)**. (Of 1 only): **Cadéo**, **Cadieu**.

Cadwallader Welsh: from a given name composed of the elements *cad* battle + *gwaladr* leader.

Cadwell see CALDWELL

Caff see CHAFF

Cafferky see McCAFFERTY

Caffin see COFFIN

Caffyn see KYFFIN

Cagan see COHEN

Cage English: metonymic occupational name for a maker and seller of small cages for animals or birds, or a keeper of the large public cage in which petty criminals were confined for short periods of imprisonment. The name is from ME, OF *cage* cage, enclosure (L *cavea* container, cave, from *cavus* hollow; cf. CAVE 1).
Vars.: **Cadge**; **Ca(i)ger**.
Dims.: Fr.: **Cajet**, **Cajot**, **Cajel(ot)**. Prov.: **Caujol(le)**.

Cagliari see CALLEGARO

Cagney Irish: Anglicized form of Gael. **Ó Caingnigh** 'descendant of *Caingneach*', a personal name meaning 'Pleader', or a byname for a contentious person.

Cahalan see CALLAN

Cahan see COHEN

Cahane see KEANE

Caherny see CARNEY

Cahill Irish: Anglicized form of Gael. **Ó Cathail** 'descendant of *Cathal*', a personal name composed of the proto-Celt. elements *cad* battle + *valos* powerful, mighty.
Var.: **O'Cahill**.

Cahouet see CHOUAN

Cahy see MULCAHY

Caiger see CAGE

Cail French: 1. nickname for a timid or stupid person, or metonymic occupational name for a catcher of quails, from OF *caille* quail (L *quaccula*; cf. QUAIL 1). 2. in Normandy and Picardy, normally a topographic name for someone who lived on a patch of stony soil, from ONF *cail(ou)* pebble, stone (of Celt. origin). 3. in S France, a metonymic

occupational name for a dairy worker, from OProv. *cail* curds (L *coagulum*, from *coagulāre* to congeal).
Vars.: **Caill**. (Of 1 only): **Lacaille**. (Of 2 and 3): **Caillier**. (Of 3 only): **Couaillier**.
Dims. (of 1): **Caillette**. (Of 2): **Cailloux**, **Caillouet**; **Chaillou(x)**, **Chaillouet**, **Chaillot**, **Chaillet**. (Of 3): **Calhau**; **Caill(i)ot**, **Caill(e)aux**, **Cailleteau**, **Cailleton**, **Caillotin**; **Couaillet**.
Augs.: Fr.: **Caill(i)at**.
Pej.: Fr.: **Caillard**.

Cain English: 1. nickname for a tall, thin man, from ME, OF *cane* cane, reed (L *canna*). It is also possibly a topographic name for someone who lived in a damp area overgrown with reeds, or a metonymic occupational name for someone who gathered reeds, which were widely used in the Middle Ages as a floor covering and for weaving small baskets. 2. Norman habitation name from the town of *Caen* in Calvados, Normandy, named with the Gaul. elements *catu* battle + *magos* field, plain. 3. Manx: var. of COYNE 2 and 3.
Vars.: **Ca(i)ne**, **Kain(e)**, **Ka(y)ne**; see also KEYNES.
Dims. (of 1): Cat.: **Cañellas**. Port.: **Canelas**.
Collectives (of 1): Fr.: **CANET**. Sp.: **Cañada(s)**, **Cañete**, **Cañizares**.

Caines see KEYNES

Caird Scots: occupational name from Gael. *ceard* craftsman, tinker.
Patrs.: **McNecaird**, **McNokerd**, **McNakard** (Gael. **Mac na Ceardadh**).

Cairnduff Scots and N Irish: habitation name from a minor place named as the 'black cairn', from Gael. *carn* (see CAIRNS) + *dubh* black (see DUFF). Most examples probably derive from the lands of *Carnduff* in the old lordship of Avondale.
Var.: **Carnduff**.

Cairns Scots: topographic name for someone who lived by a cairn, i.e. a pile of stones raised as a boundary marker or a memorial, from Gael. *carn* cairn. The surname comes mainly, if not exclusively, from lands in the parish of Mid-Calder, Lothian.
Vars.: **Carn(e)s**, CARNE.

Caistel see ASHKETTLE

Cajel see CAGE

Cakebread English: metonymic occupational name for a baker who specialized in fancy breads, from ME *cake* flat loaf made from fine flour (ON *kaka*) + *bread* bread (OE *brēad*).

Calabria Italian: regional name for someone from the region of this name in SW Italy. The surname and its vars. may also in part have been originally nicknames, for in the Trentine dialect the Calabrians are a byword for craft and guile, in the Abruzzi for high living, and in Naples for coarse boorishness.
Vars.: **Calabri**, **Calabro**; **Calabresi**, **Calabrese**.

Calado Portuguese: nickname for a silent or reserved person, from Port. *calado*, past part. of *calar* to be silent (LL *callāre*, from Gk).

Calamel *see* CHALLAMEL

Calatayud Spanish: habitation name from a place in the province of Saragossa, so called from Arabic *qala(t)* fortress, castle (see ALCALÁ) + the personal name *Ayub* (an Arabic form of JOB).

Caldas Portuguese: habitation name from any of various minor places so called, from Port. *caldas*, fem. pl. form of *caldo* hot (L *calidus*, from *calēre* to be hot). Some word such as *fontes* springs or *águas* waters has been lost.

Caldbeck *see* COLBECK

Calder 1. Scots: habitation name from any of the various places called *Calder*, *Caldor*, or *Cawdor*. Calder in Thurso is recorded in the early 13th cent. in the form *Kalfadal* and gets its name from ON *kalf* calf + *dalr* valley. The others are of more problematic origin; they seem to derive from river names, perhaps the same as in 2 below, or from ON *kaldr* cold (cf. CALDICOTT), or from Gael. *call* hazel + *dobhar* water. 2. English: habitation name from *Calder* in Cumb., named from the river on which it stands. This is probably a Brit. name, from ancestors of W *caled* hard, harsh, violent + *dwfr* water, stream.

Vars.: **Caulder**, **Cau(l)dor**, **Caldor**.

Calderon English, French, and Jewish (Sefardic): metonymic occupational name for a tinker or maker of large cooking vessels, from OF *cauderon* cauldron (L *caldārium* hot bath).

Vars.: Eng.: **Cauldron**, **Cowdron**, **Coldron**. Fr.: **Chaudron**, **Codron**. Jewish: **Kalderon**.

Prov.: **Caldairou(x)**, **Caldayrou(x)**, **Caldeyroux**. It.: **Calderone**, **Calterone**, **Caldroni**; **Caldaro**.

Dims.: Fr.: **Chaudret**, **Chaudrelle**; **Jodrellec** (Brittany). It.: **Calderonello**.

Calderwood Scots: habitation name from a place in the former county of Lanarks. (now part of Strathclyde region), so called from the river name CALDER + ME *wood* WOOD.

Caldicott English: habitation name from any of the numerous places (in Beds., Berks., Cambs., Ches., Northants, Warwicks., and elsewhere), mostly spelled *Caldecote*, which get their names from OE *c(e)ald* cold + *cot* cottage, dwelling (see COATES). It has been suggested that the OE expression *calde cot* denoted an unattended shelter for wayfarers, although in fact some places with this name were of considerable status by 1086, when they appear in Domesday Book. The surname is most common in the W Midlands. Some examples of the contracted forms listed below may come from *Calcutt* in Wilts., *Collacott(s)* in Devon, or a lost *Calcot* in Berks., in all of which the first element apparently comes from the OE personal name *Cola* (see COLE 2) or the vocab. word *col* (char)coal, in which case the meaning would be something like 'coalshed'.

Vars.: **Caldicot**, **Caldecot(t)**, **Caldecourt**, **Callicot**, **Cal(l)cott**, **Calcut(t)**, **Caulcutt**, **Caulkett**, **Cawcutt**, **Corcut**, **Corkett**, **Corkitt**, **Coldicott**, **Colicot**, **Collacott(t)**, **Collecott**, **Collicutt**, **Colcot(t)**, **Colcutt(t)**, **Colkett**, **Colocott**, **Chaldcott**, **Chalcott**.

Caldwell English, Scots, and N Irish: habitation name from any of several places in England and Scotland, variously spelled, that get their names from OE *c(e)ald* cold +

well(a) spring, stream (see WELL). Caldwell in N Yorks. is one major source of the surname; Caldwell in the former county of Renfrews. in Scotland (now part of Strathclyde region) another.

Vars.: **Calwell**, **Cau(l)dwell**, **Caudell**, **Caudle**, **Cawdell**; **Cowdell**; **Cadwell**, **Cardwell**, **Cou(l)dwell**, **Chadwell**, **Cholwell**.

Calendri Italian: nickname from the lark, OIt. *calendra* (L *calendula*). The bird was noted for its fine voice and early rising, but was also widely believed to be very stupid, so that in a number of cases the nickname may have denoted a vague or credulous man (cf. ALAUZE).

Var.: **Calendra**.

Dims.: It.: **Calandrino**, **Calandrini**. Prov.: **Calandreau**, **Calendreau**.

Pej.: Prov.: **Calandraud**.

Calero Spanish: occupational name for a quarryman or a lime-burner, Sp. *calero*, an agent deriv. of *cal* lime, chalk (L *calx*; cf. CHAUSSÉE).

Caley *see* CAYLEY

Calf English: from the ON personal name *Kalfr*, originally a byname meaning 'Calf', or possibly from OE *calf*, Anglian form of *cealf* calf, used either as a nickname or as a metonymic occupational name for someone who was responsible for tending calves.

Var.: **Callf**.

Dims.: Ger.: **Kälble**, **Kelble** (Swabian).

Calhau *see* CAIL

Calhoun *see* COLQUHOUN

Calladine English (Notts.): of unknown origin. It is conceivably a var. of CARWARDINE.

Callaghan Irish: Anglicized form of Gael. Ó Ceallacháin 'descendant of *Ceallachán*', a dim. of the personal name *Ceallach* 'Contention', 'Strife'. This name was borne by a 10th-cent. king of Munster, from whom many present-day bearers of the surname claim descent.

Vars.: **O'Calla(g)han**, **Callahan**, **Calligan**, **(O')Kelaghan**, **Kealahan**.

Callan 1. Irish: Anglicized form of Gael. Ó Cathaláin 'descendant of *Cathalán*', a personal name representing a dim. of *Cathal*; see CAHILL. 2. Scots: Anglicized form of Gael. **Mac Ailin**, patr. from an old Gael. personal name derived from *ail* rock; cf. ALLEN.

Vars.: **Callen**, **Callin**. (Of 1 only): **Cahalan(e)**. (Of 2 only): **McCallan**.

Callander 1. English: occupational name for a person who gave a smooth finish to freshly woven cloth by passing it between heavy rollers to compress the weave. The Eng. term for such a worker, *calander*, is from OF *calandrier*, *calandreur*, from the verb *calandrer*. The origin of this verb is by no means certain, but it seems likely that it comes from LL **colendrāre*, a deriv. of **colendra* roller (Gk *kylindros*, from *kylindesthai* to roll; the fem. gender of the L word could have arisen by confusion with *columna* column). 2. Scots: habitation name from either of two places so called, near Falkirk and Perth. The original form and meaning of both placenames is unclear, but it is certain that they were once distinct, later falling together through the accident of having the same lords—the Livingstones, Earls of Linlithgow.

Vars.: **Cal(l)endar**, **Callender**.

Calle Spanish: topographic name for someone who lived beside a narrow path or a cattle track, Sp. *calle* (L *callis*). In mod. Sp. this is the normal word for a street, but at the time when surnames were being formed it referred to something rather more modest.

Var.: **Calles**.

Dims.: **Calleja(s)**, **Callejo**.

Callegaro Italian: occupational name for a maker of footwear and leggings, from an agent deriv. of It. *callega* shoe (L *caliga* military boot).

Vars.: **Callegari**, **Calegari**; **Cal(l)igari**, **Calgari**, **Cal(li)garo**, **Cal(l)iari**, **Cagliari**, **Calligher**, **Callegher** (Venetia); **Galliga(r)i** (Tuscany); **Cal(l)(i)eri**, **Caliero**, **Callero**, **Caglieri**, **Cagliero** (NW Italy).

Dims.: **Callegarin(i)**, **Cagliarotti**, **Callierotti**, **Callierotti**.

Patrs.: **Cal(le)garis**, **Caligaris**, **Caglieris**.

Callery *see* MCILWRAITH

Callister *see* ALEXANDER

Callot French: metonymic occupational name for a hatter, or nickname for a man given to wearing unusual headgear, from OF *callot*, a dim. of OF *cale* hat, head-dress (a word for which various more or less fanciful etymologies have been suggested).

Vars.: **Calot**, **Cal(l)et**, **Calon**.

Callow 1. English: habitation name from any of several places so called, esp. in Derbys. Most get their names from OE *calu* bare, bald (i.e. bald-topped hill), often with the addition of *hlāw* hill. In some cases, e.g. the places by Wirksworth and by Hathersage, Derbys., the etymology is OE *cald* cold + *hlāw*. Calow by Chesterfield is from *calu* + *healh* nook (see HALE). 2. English: of uncertain origin, introduced into England via Sussex from Bordeaux in the mid-13th cent., and subsequently established in Norfolk. It may be a var. of CALLOWAY, but could equally well be from the Dutch or Flemish nickname *de Caluwe* 'the bald one' (see KAHL), which could have been taken to Bordeaux by Dutch or Flemish traders. 3. Manx: Anglicized form of Gael. **Mac Caolaidhe**, a patr. from the personal name *Caoladhe*, a deriv. of *caol* slender, comely.

Vars.: **Callowe**, **Calow(e)**, **Caloe**. (Of 3 only): CAYLEY.

Calloway English (Norman): habitation name from *Caillouet*-Orgeville in Eure, so called from a collective of ONF *cail(ou)* pebble (see CAIL 2).

Vars.: **Callaway**, **Calway**, **Kellaway**, **Kel(le)way**.

Callum *see* COLEMAN

Calmel *see* CHAUME

Calnan Irish: Anglicized form of Gael. **Ó Callanáin** 'descendant of *Callanán*', a personal name of uncertain origin.

Vars.: **Callanan**, **Callinan**.

Calver English: habitation name from *Calver* in Derbys., so called from OE *c(e)alf* CALF + *ofer* ridge. There may have been some confusion with CALVERT and absorption by CARVER.

Calverley English: habitation name from *Calverley* in W Yorks., so called from OE *c(e)alfra*, gen. pl. of *c(e)alf* CALF + *lēah* wood, clearing; or from *Calverleigh* in Devon, so called from OE *calu(w)* bare, bald (see CALLOW 1) + *wudu* wood + *lēah*.

Calvert English: occupational name for a tender of cattle, from ME *calfhirde*, from OE (Anglian) *calf* CALF + *hierde* herdsman (see HEARD). The surname is now most common in N and NE England and in N Ireland.

Vars.: **Calverd**, **Calvard**.

Calzetta *see* CHAUSSE

Camacho Spanish: of uncertain origin. The surname seems to have originated in Andalusia and is now also very common in Portugal. It was probably originally a nickname for a lame or bowlegged person, and is probably akin to the Celt. element *camb-* bent (cf. CAMPBELL).

Camarillo *see* CHAMBERS

Camber English: occupational name from an agent deriv. of OE *camb* comb, referring perhaps to a maker or seller of combs, or to someone who used them in disentangling wool or flax. This was an alternative process to carding, and caused the wool fibres to lie more or less parallel to one another, so that the cloth produced had a hard, smooth finish without nap.

Vars.: **Cammer**; **Com(b)er** (see also COOMBE); **Lecomber**; **Camb**; **Kember**; **Kempster** (in origin a fem. form).

Cambet *see* GAMBE

Camden English: of uncertain origin, possibly a habitation name from Chipping *Campden* and Broad *Campden* in Gloucs., although the loss of the *-p-* is not easily explained. These derive their names from OE *campas* enclosure (from L *campus* plain) + *denu* valley (see DEAN 1).

Var.: **Cambden**.

Camel 1. English and French: nickname from the animal, ANF *came(i)l* (L *camēlus*, from Gk *kamēlos*, ultimately of Semitic origin; cf. Hebr. *gamal*). The surname may originally have denoted a clumsy or ill-tempered person. It may also be a house name for someone who lived at a house with a sign depicting a camel. 2. English: from an assimilated pronunciation of CAMPBELL.

Vars.: **Cam(m)ell**.

Cpds (ornamental, perhaps associated with the clothing trade): Jewish (Ashkenazic): **Kamelgarn** ('mohair', literally 'camel yarn'); **Kamelhar**, **Kamelhor** ('camlet' (a type of fabric), lit. 'camel hair'); **Kamelhorn** ('camel horn', ornamental).

Cameron Scots: 1. as a Highland clan name it represents a nickname from Gael. *cam* crooked, bent + *sròn* nose. 2. in the Lowlands it is normally a habitation name from any of various places so called, all of which show early forms such as *Cambrun*, and seem to be named from Gael. *cam* crooked, bent + *brun* hill (cf. BRYAN).

Camidge *see* GAMAGE

Camilo Portuguese: from the medieval given name *Camilo* (L *Camillus*, a Roman family name of Etruscan origin).

Caminel *see* CHEMIN

Camões Portuguese: habitation name for someone from *Camós* in Galicia, which is of uncertain etymology.
Var.: **Camoens**.

Camoletto *see* JAMES

Camoys English (Norman): nickname from ME, ONF *cammus*, *camois* snub-nosed (OF *camus*, of obscure origin). Some early forms, such as Stephen *de Cameis* (Northants 1200) and Matillis *de Camois* (Surrey 1205) point to origin as a habitation name, but derivation from *Campeaux* in Calvados, Normandy, which has been proposed, is far from certain. The *de* in these instances may be purely honorific.
Vars.: **Cammis(h)**, **Camis**, **Cam(o)us**, **Keemish**, **Kemmis**.
Dims.: Fr.: **Camuset**, **Camuzet**, **Camuseau**, **Camuzeau**. It.: **Camozzini**.
Augs.: Fr.: **Camus(s)at**, **Camuzat**.
Pej.: Fr.: **Camard**.

Camp *see* CHAMP

Campbell Scots: nickname from Gael. *cam* crooked, bent + *beul* mouth. This nickname was first borne by Gillespie Ó Duibhne, who lived at the beginning of the 13th cent. and was the founder of the clan Campbell. The surname was often rendered in L documents as *de bello campo* 'of the fair field', which led to the name sometimes being retranslated into Norman French as BEAUCHAMP.
Vars.: **Cambell**, **Camble**; see also CAMEL.

Campion English (Norman) and French: **1.** occupational name for a professional champion, esp. as an agent employed to represent one of the parties in a trial by combat, a method of settling disputes current in the Middle Ages. The word comes from ANF *campion*, *campiun* (LL *campio*, gen. *campiōnis*, a deriv. of *campus* plain, field of battle). **2.** habitation name from *Compiègne* in Oise, Picardy, so called from L *compendium* shortcut, abridgement (a deriv. of *compendere* to weigh together).
Var. (of 1): **Champion**.
Dim. (of 1): Fr.: **Championnet**.

Campling English: metonymic occupational name for a maker or seller of camel-hair cloth, or perhaps a nickname for a wearer, from ANF *camelin* (L *camēlīnus*, a deriv. of *camēlus* CAMEL).
Var.: **Camplin**.

Cañada *see* CAIN

Canaletto *see* CHENAL

Canally *see* McNALLY

Canavan Irish: Anglicized form of Gael. Ó **Ceanndubháin** 'descendant of *Ceanndubhán*', a byname meaning 'little black-headed one', from *ceann* head + *dubh* black + the dim. suffix *-án*.
Vars.: **Cannavan**, **Kinavan**, **O'Can(n)avan**, **O'Cannovane**, **O'Kennavain**. See also WHITEHEAD.

Cancellor *see* CHANCELLOR

Candelario Spanish: nickname from the Catholic feast of the Purification of the Virgin, given perhaps to someone born on this day of the year (2 February) or having some other association with it. The name derives from L *candela* candle (cf. CHANDLER), since on this day candles were blessed by a priest and then lit to invoke the protection of the Virgin Mary (cf. the English word for this feast day, *Candlemas*).

Cândido Portuguese: nickname for someone with white hair, from Port. *cândido* (shining) white (L *candidus*, a deriv. of *candēre* to be white). In Port. the word also came to mean 'innocent', 'simple', and the surname may in many cases originally have had this sense.

Candish *see* CAVENDISH

Candlish *see* McCANDLESS

Cane *see* CAIN

Cañellas *see* CAIN

Canet 1. French: metonymic occupational name for a maker or seller of jugs, from OF *canet* jug, pitcher (apparently a dim. of *canne* reed, and not related to OE *canna* can). **2.** French: nickname from a dim. of OF *can* duck (of uncertain, possibly imitative, origin). **3.** Provençal and Catalan: habitation name from any of various places so called. Most seem to get their names from L *can(n)ētum*, a collective of *canna* reed (cf. CAIN 1), but in a few cases the name may go back to a pre-Roman element *kan-* height, hill.

Canham English: habitation name representing a contracted form of *Cavenham*, Suffolk, so called from the gen. case of the OE byname *Cāfa* 'Bold', 'Active' (cf. CAVENDISH) + OE *hām* homestead.

Cann English: habitation name from a place in Dorset, so called from OE *canna* can, used in a transferred sense of a deep valley. Alternatively, it may be a topographic name from the same word used elsewhere in SW England.
Var.: **Canner**.

Canning 1. English: habitation name from a place in Wilts. called *Cannings*, apparently from OE *Caningas* 'people of *Cana*', a byname of uncertain origin. **2.** Irish: var. of CANNON 2.

Cannon 1. English: nickname from ME *canun* canon, a clergyman living with others in a clergy house (ONF *canonie*, *canoine* (from LL *canōnicus*, a deriv. of *canōn* rule, discipline, from Gk *kanōn* rule, measure), which completely absorbed the OE form *canonic* from the same L source). Most early bearers of the name were serfs who perhaps gained the name from a certain dignity of bearing, or as the result of a now irrecoverable anecdote. **2.** Irish: Anglicized form of Gael. Ó **Canáin** 'descendant of *Canán*', a personal name derived from *cana* wolf-cub. **3.** Manx and Irish: Anglicized form of Gael. **Mac Canannáin** 'son of *Canannán*', a personal name of uncertain origin, perhaps a double dim. of *cana*.
Vars. (of 1): **Canon**, **Cannan**, **Canaan**; CHANNON. (Of 2): **(O')Cannan**, **O'Cannon**, CANNING. (Of 3): **McCanon**.

Canny *see* McCANN

Caño Spanish: topographic name for someone who lived near an underground passage or cave, Sp. *caño* (of uncertain origin; probably derived from L *canna* reed (cf. CAIN 1), although the semantic development is not clear).

Canova see CASANOVA

Cant English and Scots: metonymic occupational name for a singer in a chantry, or nickname for a person who sang a lot, from ONF *cant* song (OF *chant*; cf. CHANSON).

Vars.: **Caunt** (chiefly E Midlands); **Chant**; **C(h)anter**, **Cantor** (see also KANTOR).

Dims.: **Canty**, **Cantie** (Scotland).

Cantalejo Spanish: habitation name from a place in the province of Segovia, so called from Sp. *cantal* rocky place (see CANTO) + the dim. or pej. suffix *-ejo*.

Cantarero Spanish: occupational name for a potter, Sp. *cantarero*, an agent deriv. of *cántaro* jug, pitcher (LL *cantarus*, from Gk *kanthēros*).

Cantellow English (Norman): habitation name from any of a number of places in Normandy, such as *Canteleu* in Seine-Maritime or *Canteloup* in Calvados, so called from ONF *cante(r)* to sing (L *cantāre*, freq. of *canere*) + *lou*, *leu* wolf (L *lupus*) or the fem. *loup* (L *lupa*; cf. LOVE 2). These appear originally to have been grimly humorous names denoting settlements where the wolves could be heard howling in the uncleared woods around the settlement; cf. CHANTERAINE.

Vars.: **Cantel(l)o**, **Cantlow**.

Canter see KANTOR

Canto Spanish and Portuguese: 1. topographic name for someone who lived on a patch of stony ground or near a quarry, or metonymic occupational name for a quarryman or mason, from Sp., Port. *canto* stone (of uncertain, probably pre-Roman, origin). 2. topographic name for someone who lived on the corner of a street, Sp., Port. *canto* (L *cantus*, rim, edge (of a wheel)).

Vars.: **Cantos**. (Of 1 only): **Cantera** (habitation name); **Cantero** (occupational name).

Cantó Catalan: 1. topographic name for someone who lived on the corner of a street, a cogn. of CANTO 2. 2. from a medieval given name of uncertain origin; it appears in the L form *Cantonus* in early Hispanic inscriptions.

Cantwell English: apparently a habitation name from an unidentified place, perhaps so called from the OE personal name *Cant(a) + well(a)* spring, stream (see WELL). The surname is fairly common in Ireland as well as England.

Var.: **Cantle**.

Canudet see CHENU

Cap Provençal: nickname for a person with something distinctive about his head, from OProv. *cap* head (L *caput*). The word was often used in the metaphorical sense 'chief', 'principal', and the surname may also have denoted a leader or a village elder. In some cases it may also be a topographic name from the same word used in the sense of a promontory or headland.

Augs.: It.: **Capone**, **Caponi** (S Italy, esp. Naples; see also CAPON).

Pejs.: Fr.: **Capard**, **Capart**. It.: **Capasso**, **Capaccio**.

Capain see CHAPLIN

Caparròs Catalan: nickname for a person with a small head or limited intellect, from Cat. *cap* head (see CAP) + *arròs* (grain of) rice.

Capdevielle Provençal: topographic name for someone who lived at the top of a village, from OProv. *cap* head (see CAP) + *de* of (L *de* from) + *vi(e)lle* village, settlement (see VILLE).

Vars.: **Capdeville**, **Chefdeville**, **Chédeville**, **Chavialle**, **Duchefdelaville**.

Cape see CHAPE

Capel see CHAPPELL

Capinetti see JACOB

Capitaine French: status name from OF *capitaine* captain (LL *capitāneus* head, chief, principal, from *caput* head; cf. CAP). This title was used in various senses, for example of the master of a boat and as an official rank in the army.

Vars.: **Capita(i)n**, **Capitand**, **Capiten**, **Cabiten**.

Dims.: It.: **Capitanelli**, **Capitanucci**; **Capitanin** (Venetia).

Caplan see KAPLAN

Capon English and French: nickname from ME, OE *capun* capon, castrated cock (L *capo*, gen. *capōnis*), referring to a cuckold, or else a metonymic occupational name for someone who was engaged in raising poultry.

Vars.: **Cappon**. Fr. only: **Chap(p)on**; **Capou**.

Dims.: Fr.: **Chap(p)oneau**, **Chap(p)onet**.

Patrs.: Flem., Du.: **Cap(p)oens**, **Capuyns**.

Capper English: occupational name for a maker of caps and hats, or nickname for a wearer of some kind of noticeable headgear, from an agent deriv. of ME *cappe* cap, headgear (OE *cæp*, reinforced by ONF *cape*; cf. CHAPE).

Vars.: **Capp**, **Cape**.

Patrs.: **Capps**, **Capes**.

Capretti see CHEEVER

Capron English (Norman) and French: nickname for someone who wore a particularly distinctive head-dress, from ONF *caprun*; a dim. of *cape* (cf. CHAPE).

Vars.: Fr.: **Caperon**, **Chap(e)ron**; **Capronnier** (occupational name for a maker of headgear).

Capstick English (Lancs. and Yorks.): apparently an occupational nickname for a woodcutter, from OF *coupe(r)* to cut (from *coup* cut, blow, LL *colaphus* blow, punch, from Gk) + ME *stikke* (OE *sticca*) stick or *stake* (OE *staca*) pin, stake. Cf. TALBOYS.

Vars.: **Capstack**, **Capstake**, **Copestake**, **Copestick**.

Captal see CHEPTEL

Capus see CHAPUIS

Carballo Spanish: topographic name for someone who lived by a conspicuous oak tree or in an oak wood, from the dial. term *carvallo* oak. This is also the name of several villages in Galicia and Asturias, and so the surname may also be a habitation name from any of these.

Vars.: **Caraballo**, **Carbajo**.

Collectives: Sp.: **Car(a)bajal**, **Car(a)vajal(es)**; **Carballedo**, **Carballeda**. Port.: **Carvalhal**; **Carvalheira**.

Carberry 1. Scots: habitation name from a place in the parish of Inveresk, Lothian, first recorded in the form *Crebarrin*, from Gael. *craobh* tree + *barran* hedge. **2.** Irish: Anglicized form of Gael. **Ó Cairbre** and **Mac Cairbre** 'descendant' and 'son of *Cairbre*', a byname perhaps meaning 'Charioteer'.

Vars. (of 2): **Carb(e)ry**.

Carbonell English (Norman), French, and Catalan: nickname for a man with dark hair or swarthy complexion, from a dim. of ANF, OF, OCat. *carbon* charcoal (L *carbo*, gen. *carbōnis*).

Vars.: Eng.: **Charbonell**, **Shrapnel**. Fr.: **Carbon(n)el**, **Carboneau**; **Charbonel**, **Charbonneau(x)**; **Cherbonneau** (a hypercorrected form); **Charbonnet**. Cat.: **Carbó**.

Carceller Catalan: occupational name for a gaoler (LL *carcellārius*, a deriv. of *carcer* gaol).

Carcopino Italian: habitation name from a place in Sarrola, Corsica, apparently so called from *carcare* to load (LL *carricāre*, from *carricus* waggon; cf. CARRIER) + *pino* pine tree (L *pīnus*), although the exact meaning of this compound is not clear. The surname is also relatively common in France.

Card English: metonymic occupational name for someone who carded wool, from ME, OF *card(e)* instrument for untangling wool (OProv. *carda*, a deriv. of *cardar* to card, from L *cārere*, an ultimate cogn. of Eng. *shear*, crossed with *card(e)* thistle; cf. CARDING).

Vars.: **Carde**; **Carder**.

Cárdenas Spanish: habitation name from places in the provinces of Almería and Logroño, so called from the fem. pl. form of Sp. *cárdeno* blue or blueish purple (LL *cardinus*, from *carduus* thistle; cf. CARDING). Presumably the noun *tierras* 'lands' is to be understood, and the reference is to land covered with bluish plants, e.g. thistles themselves or vines.

Cardet *see* CIARDO

Cardew Cornish and English: habitation name ·from places so called in the parishes of Trevalga and Warbstow, Cornwall, and in Cumb. All are of Celt. origin, from the elements *ker* fort (cf. W *caer*) + *du* dark, black.

Vars.: **Carthew** (from places in the parishes of St Issey, St Austell, Wendron, and Madron, Cornwall, which show a mutated form (*dhu*) of the adj.), **Cardy**.

Cardinal English and French: nickname from ME, OF *cardinal* cardinal, the church dignitary (L *cardinālis*, originally an adj. meaning 'crucial', 'vital', from *cardo*, gen. *cardinis*, door-hinge). The surname could perhaps also have denoted a servant who worked in a cardinal's household, but far more often it was bestowed on someone who habitually dressed in red or who had played the part of a cardinal in a pageant, or on one who acted in a lordly and patronizing manner, like a prince of the Church.

Vars.: Eng.: **Cardinall**, **Cardnell**, CARNELL. Fr.: **Cardinau(x)**, **Cardenal**.

Dim.: It.: **Cardinaletti**.

Patr.: Du.: **Cardinaels**.

Carding English: topographic name for someone who lived on a patch of land overgrown with thistles, from

ONF *cardon* thistle (a dim. of *carde*, from L *carduus*). It may also have been an occupational name for someone involved in the carding of wool, originally carried out with thistles and teasels; perhaps also a nickname for a prickly and unapproachable person.

Vars.: **Carden** (see also CARWARDINE), **Cardon**.

Dims.: Fr.: **Chardon(n)et**, **Chardonnot**, **Chardenot**, **Chardon(n)el**, **Chardon(n)eau**.

Collectives: Fr.: **Chardonnay**, **Chardonnière**.

Cardona Catalan: habitation name from a place in the province of Barcelona. Its name dates from the pre-Roman period and probably has the same origin as that of *Cortona* in Italy, but the meaning is unknown.

Cardwell *see* CALDWELL

Careaga Spanish form of Basque **Kareaga**: topographic name for someone who lived on a patch of chalk soil, from Basque *kare* chalk, limestone + the local suffix *-aga*.

Carette *see* CHARRETTE

Carew Welsh: habitation name from any of various minor places in Wales, so called from W *caer* fort + *rhiw* hill, slope, or just possibly from *caerau*, pl. of *caer* fort. It is also possible that the surname in some cases may derive from the cogn. Corn. *kerrow* (pl. of *ker*), which occurs seven times as a placename in Cornwall.

Var.: CAREY.

Carey 1. Welsh and Cornish: var. of CAREW. **2.** English: habitation name from one of the minor places in Devon and Somerset so called from their situation on a river of this name, apparently from the Celt. root *car-* love, liking (cf. CRADDOCK), and meaning perhaps 'pleasant stream'. The same element is probably also to be seen in the Fr. river names *Cher* and *Chiers*, as well as the *Car* in Wales. **3.** English (Norman): habitation name from the manor of *Carrey*, near Lisieux, Normandy, of uncertain etymology. **4.** Irish: Anglicized form of Gael. **Ó Ciardha** 'descendant of *Ciardha*', a personal name derived from *ciar* dark, black.

Vars.: **Cary(e)**. (Of 4 only): **Keary**, **Keery**.

Cargill Scots: habitation name from a place near Stanley on the Tay, apparently originally named as 'fort of the pledge', from ancient Brit. cogns. of OW *kaer* fort (cf. CARDEW) + *geall*, gen. *gill*, pledge, wager, tryst. The placename thus apparently commemorates some otherwise forgotten incident.

Caritat Provençal: nickname for a kindly person, from OProv. *caritat* love, kindness, charity (L *cāritās*, gen. *cāritātis*, from *cārus* dear, beloved, a distant cogn. of the Celt. element mentioned in CAREY 2 above).

Carl *see* CHARLES

Carless English (chiefly W Midlands): nickname for a carefree person, from OE *carlēas* (a cpd of *caru* grief, care + *lēas* free from, without).

Vars.: **Careless**; **Corless** (Lancs.); **Curless**.

Carlier *see* CHARLIER

Carlin 1. Irish (now also common in Scotland): Anglicized form of Gael. **Ó Cearbhalláin** 'descendant of *Cearbhallán*', a dim of the personal name *Cearbhall*; see

CARROLL. **2.** Jewish (E Ashkenazic): Anglicized spelling of KARLIN. **3.** French: dim. of CHARLES.

Vars. (of 1): **Carolan**, CARLTON, CHARLTON.

Carliner *see* KARLIN

Carlisle English: habitation name from the city in Cumb., in whose name Brit. *ker* fort (cf. CARDEW) has been compounded with the Romano-British name of the settlement, *Luguvalium*. The surname is now very common in N Ireland.

Vars.: **Carlile**, **Carlill**, **Carlyle**.

Carlton 1. English: habitation name from any of various places so called, from ON *karl* common man, peasant + OE *tūn* settlement; cf. CHARLTON 1. The places with *C-* rather than *Ch-* are in areas of Scandinavian settlement, mostly in N England. **2.** Irish: var. of CARLIN 1.

Var.: **Carleton**.

Carlyon Cornish: habitation name from any of three places in Cornwall so called, in St Minver and Kea parishes. The first element is Brit. *ker* fort; the second could represent the plural of Corn. *legh* slab.

Carman 1. English: from an ON personal name *Kar(l)maðr* (acc. *Kar(l)mann*), composed of the elements *karl* male, man (cf. CHARLES) + *maðr* man, person. **2.** English and Flemish: occupational name for a carter, from ANF, MLG *car* cart (LL *carrus*; cf. CARRIER) + ME, MLG *man* man.

Var. (of 2): Flem.: **Carreman**.

Patr. (from 2): Flem.: **Carmans**.

Carmichael Scots: habitation name from *Carmichael* in the former county of Lanarks. (now part of Strathclyde region), from Brit. *ker* fort (cf. CARDEW) + the personal name MICHAEL.

Carmo Portuguese: from the medieval given name *Carmo*, from the Marian title *Maria do Carmo* 'Mary of Mt Carmel'. The epithet refers to a mountain range in the Holy Land extending southward from Haifa, and probably derived from Hebr. *kerem-el* God's vineyard. The range came to be inhabited by hermits in the early Christian centuries, and at the time of the Crusades they grew in number, becoming the order of Carmelite friars. The cult of Our Lady of Mt Carmel, their patron, was instituted in the 14th cent.

Related name: Jewish: **Karmeli** (Israeli, with the Hebr. ending *-i*).

Carmody Irish: Anglicized form of Gael. **Ó Cearmada** 'descendant of *Cearmaid*', a personal name of uncertain origin.

Carmona Spanish (now also very common in Portugal): habitation name from places in the provinces of Santander and (more famously) Seville. The placename is of pre-Roman origin and uncertain meaning.

Carmoy *see* CHARME

Carnduff *see* CAIRNDUFF

Carne 1. Cornish: cogn. of CAIRNS. **2.** French: Norman and Picard form of CHARME.

Vars. (of 2): **Carme**, **Ducarne**, **Ducarme**.

Carné French: nickname for a thin man or alternatively for a fat one. The surname derives from the OF past part. of the verb *charner* (Norman, Picard, and Prov. *carner*), from *c(h)ar* flesh, meat (L *caro*, gen. *carnis*). The verb was used in a variety of contradictory senses, as for example to strip flesh from the bone or to feed animals with meat, and it is from this that the ambiguity of the nickname arises.

Vars.: **Carnu(s)**, **Charnu(t)**.

Carnegie Scots: habitation name from a place near Carmyllie in the former county of Angus (now part of Tayside region), so called from Gael. *cathair an eige* fort at the gap or nick.

Var.: **Carnegy**.

Carnell English: **1.** apparently an occupational name for a crossbowman who specialized in fighting from the battlements of castles, from ANF *carnel* battlement, embrasure (a metathesized form of *crenel*, LL *crenellus*, a dim. of *crēna* notch; for the change of *-er-* to *-ar-* cf. MARCHANT). **2.** contracted form of CARBONELL or CARDINAL.

Vars.: **Carnall**. (Of 1 only): **Crenel(l)**.

Carnero Spanish: nickname for a forceful or lusty person, or metonymic occupational name for a keeper of rams, from Sp. *carnero* ram (a deriv. of *carne* meat, flesh (cf. CARNÉ), since the animal was reared for its meat rather than its wool).

Carnes *see* CAIRNS

Carnevali Italian: nickname from It. *carnevale* festival (from *carnelevare* fast, lit. removal of meat, from L *caro*, gen. *carnis*, meat (cf. CARNÉ) + *levāre* to lift, remove; it was the normal practice to have a riotous carnival before a period of solemn fast such as Lent, and this gradually acquired a greater significance than the fast itself and usurped the meaning of the word). The nickname may have denoted someone born at the time of a carnival, or someone of a particularly festive spirit. In mod. It. a *carnevale* is normally a fat, awkward, stupid fellow, but in the Bolognese dialect it is used less unkindly of a corpulent and jovial person.

Vars.: **Carnevale**, **Carnavale**, **Carnovali**, **Carnovale**; **Carlevari**, **Carlvaro**, **Carleveri** (N Italy); **Carlavara** (Venetia).

Dims.: **Carnevalini**, **Carlevarini**, **Carlevarino**.

Carney Irish: Anglicized form of Gael. **Ó Catharnaigh** 'descendant of *Catharnach*', a byname meaning 'Warlike'.

Vars.: **(O')Caherny**, **O'Carney**.

Carnicero Spanish: occupational name for a butcher, Sp. *carnicero* (LL *carnicārius*, an agent deriv. of *carniceus*, itself an adj. deriv. of *caro*, gen. *carnis*, meat, flesh; cf. CARNÉ).

Caro Italian and Spanish: nickname from It., Sp. *caro* dear, beloved (L *carus*).

Vars.: It.: **Cari**; **Li Cari** (S Italy).

Dims.: It.: **Carello**, **Carelli**; **Carillo** (S Italy); **Caretti**; **Carino**, **Carini**; **Carucci(o)**, **Carrocci**; **Carricchio** (S Italy); **Carollo**, **Carullo**, **Carulli** (S Italy); **Carotti**.

Augs.: It.: **Caroni**, **Carone**. Sp.: **Carazo**.

Patrs.: It.: **De Caro**, **Di Caro** (S Italy).

Caron French: from a personal name of Gaul. origin, represented in L records in the form *Caraunus* and probably derived from the Celt. element *car* to love (cf. CAREY 2 and CRADDOCK). This name was borne by a 5th-cent. Bret. saint who lived at Chartres and was murdered by robbers; his legend led to its widespread use as a given name during the Middle Ages.

Var.: **Chéron**.

Dims.: **Caronet**; **Cheronnet**, **Cheroneau**.

Carpenter English: occupational name for a worker in wood, ANF *carpentier* (LL *carpentārius* cartwright, from *carpentum* cart, a word of Gaul. origin related to *carrum*; cf. CARRIER).

Dims.: Fr.: **Charpent(e)reau**.

Equivs. (not cogn.): French: CHAPUIS; BOISSIER. Ger.: ZIMMERMANN. Polish: CIEŚLAK (q.v. for other Slav. words). Russ.: PLOTNIK. Hung.: ÁCS.

Carpio 1. Spanish: habitation name from any of the various minor places in the area of Salamanca named with the regional term *carpio* hill (of uncertain origin). 2. Italian: nickname for someone thought to resemble a carp in some way, from It. *carpio(ne)* carp (of Gmc origin; cf. KARPOV 2).

Carr 1. N English and Scots: var. of KERR. 2. Irish: Anglicized form of Gael. **Ó Carra** 'descendant of *Carra*', a byname meaning 'Spear'. 3. Irish: Anglicized form of Gael. **Mac Giolla Chathair** 'son of the servant of *Cathar*', a personal name derived from *cath* battle.

Carrasco Spanish and Portuguese: topographic name for someone who lived by a holm-oak or in a wood of the trees, from Sp. *carrasco, carrasca* (from L *cerrus*, itself apparently representing a pre-Roman word native to the peninsula).

Dims.: **Carrasquillo**, **Carrasquilla**. Cat.: **Carrascó**.

Collective: Sp.: **Carrascal**.

Carré French: nickname for a squat, thickset man, from OF *carré* square (L *quadrātus*, past part. of *quadrāre* to form a square, from *quadr-* four).

Vars.: **Carrey**, **Carrez**; **Le Carré**.

Carrelet see QUARRELL

Carriage see KENDRICK

Carrick see CRAIG

Carrier English and French: occupational name for someone who transported goods, from ME, OF *car(r)ier* (LL *carrārius*, a deriv. of *carrum* cart, waggon, of Gaul. origin; cf. CARMAN, CARTER, and also CARPENTER).

Vars.: Eng.: **Carryer**. Fr.: **Carrié**, **Carriez**, **Quarrier**, **Charrier**, **Chareour**; **Carrec** (Brittany).

Dims.: It.: **Carraretto**, **Carrarini**, **Carraroli**.

Carrière French: topographic name for someone who lived on a fairly major thoroughfare, originally a road passable by vehicles as well as pedestrians (from LL *carrāria (via)*, a deriv. of *carrum* cart; cf. CARRIER).

Vars.: **Carrère**, **Charrière**, **Charraire**, **Charrayre**, **Charreyre**.

Dim.: Fr.: **Charreyron**.

Carrigy see MCCARRICK

Carrillo Spanish: nickname for a person with some peculiarity of the cheek or jaw, Sp. *carrillo*. The word is attested since the 13th cent., but its etymology is uncertain. It appears to be a dim. of *carro* cart, wagon, and it has been suggested that the reference is to the movements of the jaw in chewing. The surname may also have denoted originally a bold or shameless person; for the semantic development cf. CHEEK.

Carrington English and Scots: habitation name from any of the places so called, in Ches., Lincs., and Lothian. The one in Lincs. is probably 'settlement (OE *tūn*) of *Cora*'s people'; those in Ches. and Lothian seem to be 'settlement associated with *Cāra*'.

Carrión Spanish: habitation name from any of the various places, for example in the provinces of Ciudad Real, Palencia, Seville, and Valladolid, so called.

Carrizo Spanish: topographic name for someone who lived on a patch of ground thickly grown with reeds, from Sp. *carrizo* rush, sedge (LL *cariceum*, in origin an adj. deriv. of class. L *carex*, gen. *caricis*). In some cases it may alternatively represent a nickname for a tall, thin person.

Collective: Sp.: **Carracedo**.

Carroll Irish: Anglicized form of the Gael. personal name *Cearbhall*. This is of uncertain origin, perhaps originally a byname for a butcher or a fierce warrior, from *cearbh* hacking.

Vars.: **Carrol**, CARVILL.

Patrs.: **McCarroll**, **McCarvill**, **McKarrill** (Gael. **Mac Cearbhaill**). 'Descendant of C.': **O'Carro(wi)ll**, **O'Carvill**, **O'Carwell** (Gael. **Ó Cearbhaill**).

Carron see CHARRON

Carruthers Scots: habitation name from a place near Ecclefechan in Dumfries, locally pronounced /'krɪdɛrz/. The name is first recorded in 1334 in the form *Carrothres*, and then more clearly in *c*.1350 as *Caer Ruther*, and derives from Brit. *ker* fort (cf. CARDEW) + a personal name probably composed of elements meaning 'red' + 'king', 'ruler'.

Vars.: **Car(r)others**; **Crothers** (see also CROWTHER); **Carradice**, **Carrodus**, **Cardis**, **Cardus**, **Crowdace**, **Cruddace**, **Cruddas**, **Caruth**.

Carslake English: apparently a habitation name from a lost place, perhaps named from OE *cærse* (water)cress + *lacu* stream (see LAKE). For the semantics, cf. CRESWELL.

Vars.: **Caslake**, **Karslake**, **Ke(r)slake**.

Carson Scots: of uncertain origin, probably a habitation name. The surname is now prominent in N Ireland.

Vars.: **Corson**, **Corsan** (see also CURZON).

Carstairs Scots: habitation name from a place in the former county of Lanarks., recorded in 1170 in the form *Casteltarres* and apparently named from ME *castel* CASTLE + a personal name *Tarra*, of uncertain origin.

Carstens see CHRISTIAN

Carter 1. English: occupational name for a transporter of goods, from ME *carter*, from ANF *car(e)tier*, a deriv. of OF *caret*, dim. of *car* cart (LL *carrum*, cf. CARRIER). The OF word coalesced with an earlier ME word *cart(e)* cart, which is from either ON *kartr* or OE *cræt*, both of which, like the LL word, were probably originally derived from Celtic). **2.** Manx: var. of *McArthur*; see Arthur.

Var.: **Charter**.

Dims.: Fr.: **Cart(e)ron, Cart(e)ret**.

Cartledge English: habitation name from a place in Derbys., so called from ON *kartr* rocky ground + OE *læcc* boggy stream.

Var.: **Cartlidge**.

Cartmell English (Cumb. and Lancs.): habitation name from *Cartmel* in Cumb. (formerly N Lancs.), the site of a famous priory, inland from Cartmel Sands. The placename is derived from ON *kartr* rocky ground + *melr* sandbank.

Var.: **Cartmill**.

Carton *see* McCartney

Cartwright English: occupational name for a maker of carts, from ME *cart* (apparently a metathesized form of OE *cræt*, or a borrowing of the cogn. ON *kartr*; cf. Carter) + Wright. The surname is attested from the late 13th cent., although the vocab. word does not occur before the 15th cent.

Var.: **Kortwright**.

Carus English: habitation name from a dwelling named as the 'house on wet ground' or 'house by the brushwood', from ME *kerr* wet ground or brushwood (ON *kjarr*; see Kerr) + *h(o)us* house (OE *hūs*).

Vars.: **Carass, Carras, Caress, Car(r)iss**.

Caruso Italian: nickname from It. *caruso* close-cropped. This word was also used in the more general sense 'boy', 'lad', since in the Middle Ages young men of fashion sometimes wore their hair much shorter than was the prevailing style (cf. Tous). In the Girgenti area of Sicily the term was an occupational one for a worker in the sulphur pits, since such workers apparently were required to wear their hair short.

Vars.: **Carusi(o), Carosi(o)**.

Dims.: **Carusello, Caruselli, Caros(i)ello, Caroselli**.

Augs.: **Carusone, Carosoni**.

Carver English: **1.** occupational name for a carver of wood or a sculptor of stone, from an agent deriv. of ME *kerve(n)* to cut, carve (OE *ceorfan*). **2.** occupational name for a ploughman, ANF *caruier* (LL *carrucārius*, a deriv. of *carruca* cart, plough—a word from the same group as *carrum* and *carpentum*, cf. Carrier and Carpenter; in Ger. the word has been borrowed in a different sense, see Karch).

Carvill 1. English and Irish (Norman): habitation name from places in Calvados and Seine-Maritime called *Carville*, from the Scandinavian personal name *Kare* + OF Ville settlement. **2.** Irish: var. of Carroll.

Vars.: **Carville, Carvell**.

Carwardine English: habitation name from *Carden* in Ches., which is recorded in the mid-13th cent. in the form *Kawrdin* and in the early 14th as *Cawardyn*; it is probably named from OE *carr* rock + *worðign* enclosure (see Worthy).

Var.: **Carden** (see also Carding).

Casa Italian and Spanish: habitation name from It., Sp. *casa* house (L *casa* hut, cottage, cabin). It perhaps originally denoted the occupier of the most distinguished house in the village.

Vars.: It.: Case, **Caso**; Ca (N Italy); **Della Casa, Dalla Casa, Dalla C(h)a, Da C(h)a, Dacca**. Sp.: **Casas; Casero** ('tenant').

Dims.: It.: **Casella, Casello, Caselli; Casel** (Venetia); **Casi(e)llo, Casol(l)a** (Naples); **Casetta, Caset(ti); Casina, Casine, Casino, Casini; Casotti**. Prov.: **C(h)azelle(s), Chézelle(s), C(h)azot(te), C(h)azet(te), Casin, Cazin**. Sp.: **Casillas**. Cat.: **Casellas**.

Augs.: It.: **Casone, Casoni** (Lombardy); **Cason** (Venetia).

Pejs.: It.: **Casacc(h)ia, Casacci(o), Casassa, Casazza**.

Casado Spanish: nickname for a married man, the head of his own household, from Sp. *casado*, past part. of *casar* to marry (a deriv. of Casa house).

Casale Italian: topographic name for someone who lived in a hut or small cottage, OIt. *casale* (LL *casāle*, a deriv. of Casa house), or habitation name from any of the various places named with this word, most notably a town in Piedmont.

Vars.: **Casal(i); Casalaro, Casalari**.

Dims.: It.: **Casaletto, Casaletti; Casalin(i), Casalino** (Venetia); **Casagli(a)** (Tuscany). Prov.: **Cazalet, Cazalin**.

Augs.: It. **Casalone, Casaloni**.

Casanova Italian, Spanish, and Catalan: habitation name for someone who lived in a newly built house, from Romance derivs. of L *casa* house (see Casa) + *nova* (fem.) new.

Vars.: It.: **Canova**. Sp.: **Casanueva**. Cat.: **Casanovas, Cànovas**.

Casaril *see* Cheeseman

Casaubon Provençal: habitation name for someone who lived in an impressive or well-built house, from OProv. *casal* cottage (see Casale) + Bon good.

Var.: **Cazaubon**.

Case 1. English: metonymic occupational name for a maker of boxes or chests, from ANF *cas(s)e* case, container (L *capsa*, a deriv. of *capere* to hold, contain). **2.** Provençal: cogn. of Casa. **3.** Italian: metonymic occupational name for a maker or seller of cheese; see Cheeseman.

Vars.: (of 1): **Cash**, Cashman.

Casement Manx: Anglicized form of Gael. *Mac Easmuinn*; see Osmond.

Casewell *see* Creswell

Casey Irish: Anglicized form of Gael. **Ó Cathasaigh** 'descendant of *Cathasach*', a byname meaning 'Vigilant' or 'Noisy'.

Var.: **O'Casey**.

Casheen *see* McCashin

Cashman 1. English: var. of Case. **2.** Irish: Anglicized form of Gael. *Ó Ciosáin*; see Kissane. **3.** Jewish (Ashkenazic): of unknown origin.

Var. (of 3): **Kashman**.

Cashmore English: apparently a habitation name from *Cashmoor* in Dorset, which is probably so called from OE *cærse* cress + *mōr* fen, marsh (see Moore 1). The surname is now most frequent in Birmingham.

Caslake *see* CARSLAKE

Caspary *see* KASPAR

Cass English: from the medieval female given name *Cass*, a short form of *Cassandra*. This was the name (of uncertain, possibly non-Gk, origin) of an ill-fated Trojan prophetess of classical legend, condemned to foretell the future but never be believed; her story was well known and widely popular in medieval England.
Dim.: **Cassie** (Scotland).
Metr.: **Casson** (N England).

Cassagne Provençal: topographic name for someone who lived by an oak tree or in an oak wood, from OProv. *cassagne* oak (LL *cassanea (arbor)*, a deriv. of *cassanos*; see CASSE 1).
Vars.: **Cassaigne**, **Cassan**, **Chassa(i)gne**, **Chasseigne**, **Chassa(i)ng**, **Chassin**, **Chassan(t)**; **Lac(h)assagne**.
Dims.: **C(h)assagnol**, **Cassagnou**, **Cassagnau**, **Cassignol**.
Aug.: **Chassinat**.
Collective: **Cassagnade**.

Cassard French: apparently a nickname for a clumsy person, from OF *casse(r)* to break, smash (L *quassāre* to shake violently, freq. of *quatere* to shake), with the addition of the pej. suffix *-ard*.
Var.: **Cassart**.

Casse French: **1.** topographic name for someone who lived by an oak tree or in an oak wood, from OF *casse* oak (LL *cassanos*, of Celt. origin; cf. CASSAGNE). **2.** metonymic occupational name for a maker of ladles, from OF *casse* ladle (OProv. *cassa*, LL *cattia*, from Gk *kyathion*, dim. of *kyathos* cup).
Vars. (of 1): **Cassé**, **Casses**; **Delcasse**, **Delcassé**, **Ducasse**.
Dims. (of 1): **Cassin**, **Casset**. It.: **Cassini**.

Cassegrain French: apparently an occupational nickname for a miller, from OF *casse(r)* to break (see CASSARD) + *grain* grain, corn (L *grānum*).

Cassens *see* CHRISTIAN

Cassidy Irish: Anglicized form of Gael. **Ó Caiside** 'descendant of *Caiside*', a byname from *cas* curly(-headed).
Vars.: **Cassedy**, **Kassidy**, **Casserl(e)y**; **O'Cassidy**, **O'Cahsedy**.

Castan French: topographic name for someone who lived by a (horse-)chestnut tree, OF *castan(h)* (L *castanea*, from Gk). The surname may also perhaps have been originally a nickname for someone of chestnut or auburn colouring.
Vars.: **C(h)astaing**, **Chastan(g)**, **Chastand**, **Chat(a)in**; **C(h)astagnier**, **Châtai(g)nier**, **Chatenier**, **Castanié**, **Castagné**.
Dims.: Fr.: **Casta(i)gnet**, **C(h)astanet**, **Chastenet**, **Châtenet**, **Chataignon**, **Châtaignoux**, **Chataigneaux**. It.: **Castagnetta**, **Castagnetto**, **Catagnetti**; **Castagnotto**; **Castagnoli** (Liguria).
Augs.: It.: **Castagnone**. Sp.: **Castañón**.
Pej.: It.: **Castagnasso**.
Collectives: Fr.: **Châtenay**. It.: **Castagneto**. Sp.: **Castañeda**.
Port.: **Catanheira**.

Castejón Spanish: habitation name from any of the numerous places so called, from LL *castellio*, gen. *castelliōnis*, fortified town or village (a deriv. of *castellum*; see CASTLE).

Castel-Branco Portuguese: habitation name from a place so called, from Port. *castelo* CASTLE + *branco* white (see BLANC).
Var.: **Castelo-Branco**.

Castelarin *see* CHÂTELIER

Castell *see* ASHKETTLE

Castellan English (Norman): occupational name for the governor or constable of a castle, or the warder of a prison, from ANF *castelain* (L *castellānus*, a deriv. of *castellum* CASTLE).
Vars.: **Castellain**, **Castelein**, **Castling**, **Chatelain**.

Castelnau Provençal: topographic name for someone living by a castle of relatively recent construction at the time when the surname was formed, from OProv. *castel* CASTLE + *nau* new (L *novus*), or habitation name from a place so named.

Castelvieil Provençal: topographic name for someone who lived by an ancient castle, from OProv. *castel* CASTLE + *vieil* old, or habitation name from a place so named.

Castille French: regional name for someone from *Castille*, the Fr. name of Sp. *Castilla*. An independent kingdom between the 10th and 15th cents., it formed the largest power in the Iberian peninsula. The name derives from the many castles in the region.

Castle English: topographic name from ANF *castel* castle, fortified building or set of buildings, especially the residence of a feudal lord (LL *castellum*, a dim. of *castrum* fort; see CASTRO). The name would also have denoted a servant who lived and worked at such a place. The LL word was used occasionally (as, for example, in the Vulgate translation of the Bible) in the sense 'village', 'settlement', and this use had already been borrowed into OE, but was almost entirely restricted to scriptural contexts, and died out in the face of the competing sense introduced from France.
Vars.: **Castles**, **Castell(s)**; **Cassel(l)(s)** (perhaps largely from the place in the *département* of Nord so named); **Kestle**, **Kestell** (Cornwall); **Castleman**.
Dims.: Fr.: **Castelot**, **Châtelot**, **Châtelet**. Prov.: **Castillon**, **Castillou**; **Casterot**, **Casterou** (Gascony). It.: **Castelletti**, **Castelletto**, **Castellini**, **Castellino**, **Castellucci(o)**, **Castelluzzi**, **Castelluzzo**, **Castellotti**, **Castellotto**. Sp.: **Castillejo**. Cat.: **Castellet**.
Augs.: It.: **Castellone** (Lombardy). Sp.: **Castillón**.
Pejs.: It.: **Castellacci(o)**, **Castellazzi**, **Castellazzo**.

Castro Italian, Spanish, Portuguese, and Jewish (Sefardic): topographic name for someone living by a castle or walled town, from It., Sp., Port. *castro* (L *castrum* legionary camp), or habitation name from a place named with this element.
Vars.: It.: **Castri**, **Lo Cast(r)o**, **Licastri**, **De Castri(s)**.
Dim.: Sp.: **Castrillo**.

Catagnetti *see* CASTAN

Catalán Spanish: regional name for someone from Catalonia (Sp. *Cataluña*), apparently so called from a pre-

Roman tribal name, which is of unknown origin and meaning.

Dim.: It.: **Catalanotti**.

Catan *see* KATAN

Catchpole English (chiefly E Anglia): occupational name for a bailiff, originally one empowered to seize poultry and other livestock in case of default on debts or taxes. The name comes from ANF *cachepol*, a cpd of *cache(r)* to chase, pursue (OF *chace(r)*, L *captāre* to snatch at, freq. of *capere* to take, seize) + *pol* fowl (L *pullus* young animal or bird; cf. PULLEN).

Vars.: **Catchpo(o)l**, **Catchpoole**, **Catchpoule**.

Cater English: occupational name for the buyer of provisions for a large household, from an aphetic form of ANF *acatour* (LL *acceptātor*, agent deriv. of *acceptāre* to accept, freq. of *accipere* to receive). Mod. Eng. *caterer* results from the addition of a second agent suffix to the word.

Vars.: **Cator**; **Chater**, **Chaytor**.

Cates English: apparently a patr. from the ON byname *Káti* (from *káti* boy). (*Kate* was not in use as a short form of *Catherine* during the Middle Ages.)

Var.: **Kates**.

Catesby English: habitation name from a place in Northants, so called from the common ON byname *Káti* (see CATES) + ON *býr* settlement, village.

Cathcart Scots: habitation name from a place near Glasgow, the second element of which clearly refers to the river *Cart*, on which it stands. This river name is extremely ancient, probably of pre-Celtic origin; Nicolaisen connects it with IE *kov-* hard, stony. The first element ostensibly commorates a battle (Brit. *cad* or Gael. *cath*; cf. CADELL). However, the earliest recorded spelling of the placename is *Kerkert* (1158), which suggests derivation from Brit. *ker* fort (cf. CARDEW).

Catlin English: from the medieval female given name *Cat(e)lin(e)*, ANF form of *Catherine*. This is of obscure origin and etymology, being first attested in the form *Aikaterina* but later affected by folk etymological associations with Gk *katharos* pure. It was borne by numerous early Christian saints, and was popular throughout the Middle Ages.

Vars.: **Cattlin**, **Catling**.

Dims.: Eng.: CATT, CATTON, CATON, **Catten**; **Cattell** (chiefly W Midlands). Fr.: **Cathelineau**, **Catherinet**; **Cat(he)ron**; **Cat(he)rou(x)**; **Cat(h)elet**, **Cat(h)elon**, **Cat(h)elot**; **Cat(h)eau**, **Cat(h)et**, **Cat(t)in**, **Catineau**, CATON, **Catillon**. It.: **Cat(t)era**, **Cattaruccia**, **Cataruzza**, **Cattarossi**, **Cattarulla**; **Cat(t)a**, **Cat(t)e**, **Cattini**, **Cattozzo**, **Cattuzza**. Ger.: **Triene**. Flem.: **Kate**, **Trine**. Ukr.: **Katerinyuk**.

Augs.: Fr.: **Cathelat**, **Catenat**, **Catinat**.

Pejs.: Fr.: **Catheraud**, **Catinaud**.

Metrs.: Russ.: **Yekaterinin**, **Katerinin**, **Katerinov**. Ukr.: **Katerinich**.

Metrs. (from dims.): Ger.: **Trienen**, **Treinen**. Russ.: **Katynin**, **Katyush(k)in**. Ukr.: **Katrin**, **Katr(ev)ich**.

Caton 1. English: habitation name from places in Derbys. and Lancs. The former is probably so called from the OE personal name or byname *Cada* (see CADE 1) + OE *tūn*

enclosure, settlement; the latter derives its first element from the ON byname *Káti* (see CATES). 2. English and French: dim. of CATLIN.

Dims. (of 2): Fr.: **Cat(t)onnet**, **Catonné**, **Catenot**, **Cathenod**.

Catt English: 1. nickname from the animal, ME, OE *catte* cat, reinforced by ONF *cat* (OHG *kazza*; LL *cattus* is probably from this, rather than vice versa). The word is found in similar forms in most European languages from very early times (e.g. Gael. *cath*, Slav. *kotu*). Domestic cats were unknown in Europe in classical times, where weasels fulfilled many of their functions, for example in hunting rodents. When they were introduced into S Europe, apparently in the 1st cent. AD, they were known to the Romans by the Gk name *ailouros* 'wavy tail'. They seem to have come from Egypt, where they were regarded as sacred animals. 2. from a medieval female given name, a short form of CATLIN.

Vars.: **Chatt**, **Katte**.

Dims. (of 1): It.: **Gattin(ell)i**, **Gattullo**. Czech: **Koťátko**; **Kotík**, **Kotek**; **Kocourek**. Pol., Jewish (E Ashkenazic): **Kotek**.

Aug. (of 1): It.: **Gattone**.

Patrs. (from 1): Flem., Du.: **Cats**, **Kats**. Pol.: **Kotowicz**, **Kotkiewicz** (from the dim.). Russ., Bulg.: **Kotev**.

Habitation names: Pol., Jewish (E Ashkenazic): **Kotowski** (in some cases no doubt from the city of *Kotovsk*, now in the Ukraine); **Kotkowski**; **Kociszewski**.

Cattell *see* CADELL

Catterall English: habitation name from a place in Lancs., of uncertain etymology, perhaps from the gen. case of ON *kottr* cat + *hali* tail, referring to a long, thin piece of land. The surname is common in Lancs., and almost unknown elsewhere.

Vars.: **Cattrall**, **Catt(e)rell**, **Catterill**, **Catt(e)roll**, **Cath(e)rall**.

Cattermole English: of uncertain origin. It is confined mainly to E Anglia and London, and may be a Low German importation.

Var.: **Cattermoul**.

Catton English: 1. habitation name from any of the various places so called, for example in Derbys., Norfolk, and N Yorks., all apparently from an OE byname *Catta* 'Cat' (see CATT 1) or ON *Káti* 'Boy' (see CATES) + OE *tūn* enclosure, settlement. 2. dim. of CATLIN.

Caublance *see* KOBLENZ

Cauce *see* CHAUSSE

Cauchie *see* CHAUSSÉE

Caudell *see* CALDWELL

Caudor *see* CALDER

Cauffin *see* COFFIN

Caughey Irish: (pronounced /ˈkahi/) 1. Anglicized form of Gael. **Mac Eachaidh**, patr. from the byname *Eachaidh* 'Horseman' (a deriv. of *each* horse; cf. KEOGH). 2. Anglicized form of Gael. *Ó Maolchathaigh*; see MULCAHY.

Vars. (of 1): **McCaughey**, **McCah(e)y**, **McGaughey**, **McGaughie**, **McGauhy**, **McGuggy**, **McGah(e)y**, **Megahey**, **(Mc)Gaffey**.

Caujol *see* CAGE

Caulcutt *see* CALDICOTT

Cauldron *see* CALDERON

Caulfield English: apparently a habitation name from an unidentified minor place, perhaps so called from OE *c(e)ald* cold + *feld* pasture, open country (see FIELD).
Var.: **Cauldfield**.

Caumont French: habitation name from any of various places called *C(h)aumont*, for the most part clearly so named from OF *c(h)auf* bald, bare (see CHAFF) + *mont* hill (see MONT). In a few cases the first element may originally have been Gaul. *calm* plateau (see CHAUME 1).
Vars.: **Chaumont**, **Chomont**.

Caunce *see* CHANCE

Caunt *see* CANT

Causer *see* CHAUCER

Causey English (Norman): topographic name for someone who lived by a causeway, ME *caucey* (from ONF *cauciée*; see CHAUSSÉE); the ending of the vocab. word was in time assimilated by folk etymology to ME *way* (OE *weg* path).
Var.: **Cawsey**.

Causton *see* CAWSTON

Cavalcanti Italian: occupational nickname for a horseman or knight, from It. *cavalcante*, pres. part. of *cavalcar* to ride on horseback (LL *caballicāre*, from *caballus* horse; cf. CAVALLO and CHEVALIER).

Cavallo Italian: metonymic occupational name for a man in charge of horses, perhaps also a nickname for someone supposedly resembling a horse, from It. *cavallo* horse (LL *caballus*).
Vars.: **Cavalli(o)**.
Dims.: It.: **Cavallin(i)**, **Cavallino**, **Cavaletti**, **Cavaletto**, **Cavalotti**, **Cavalotto**, **Cavallucci(o)**, **Cavaluzzi**. Fr.: **Chevaleau**, **Cheval(l)et**, **Chevalley**, **Chevalin**, **Chevalon**.
Aug.: It.: **Cavallone**.
Pejs.: It.: **Caval(l)acci**. Fr.: **Cheval(l)ard**.

Cavan *see* KEEFE

Cavanagh *see* KAVANAGH

Cavanillas *see* CABANE

Cavaretta *see* CHEEVER

Cave 1. English: habitation name from a place in Humberside, apparently so called from a river name derived from OE *cāf* swift. 2. English (Norman): var. of CHAFF. 3. French: metonymic occupational name for someone employed in or in charge of the wine cellars of a great house, from OF *cave* cave, cellar (L *cavea*, a derivative of *cavus* hollow; see also CAGE). 4. French: topographic name for someone who lived in or near a cave, from the same word as in 3 in an older sense.
Vars. (of 1 and 2): **Kave**. (Of 3 and 4): **Lacave**; **Cavier**.
Dims. (of 3 and 4): Fr.: **Cavel**, **Caveau**, **Cavin**, **Cavy**.

Cavell *see* CHAFF

Cavendish English: habitation name from a place in Suffolk, so called from an OE byname *Cāfna* 'Bold', 'Daring' + OE *edisc* enclosed pasture.
Var.: **Candish** (a contracted form).

Cavenett English: of uncertain origin, probably from a Fr. nickname for a bald man, from a double dim. (*-in* + *-et*) of *cave* (see CHAFF).

Cavero Spanish: 1. in Aragon and Navarre, a status name for a knight, or nickname meaning 'knight'. The word is either a deriv. of *cabo* head, chief (see CAP) or else a contracted form of *cabellero* (see CHEVALIER). 2. in the province of Álava, an occupational name for a digger of ditches, from an agent deriv. of *cavar* to dig, excavate (L *cavāre*, from *cavus* hollow; cf. CAVE 3).

Cavestany *see* CABESTANY

Cavill English: habitation name from *Cavil(le)* in E Yorks. The placename is from OE *cā* jackdaw (see COE) + *feld* pasture, open country (see FIELD).

Cavolini *see* JACOB

Cawcutt *see* CALDICOTT

Cawdell *see* CALDWELL

Cawker *see* CHALK

Cawley *see* McAULAY

Cawood English (Yorks. and Lancs.): habitation name from places in N Yorks. and Lancs., both so called from OE *cā* jackdaw (see COE) + *wudu* WOOD.

Cawsey *see* CAUSEY

Cawston English: habitation name from places in Norfolk and Warwicks., so called from the gen. case of the ON byname *Kalfr* 'Calf' + OE *tūn* enclosure, settlement.
Var.: **Causton**.

Cawthorn English: habitation name from *Cawthorn* in N Yorks. or *Cawthorne* in W Yorks., both so called from OE *c(e)ald* cold + *þorn* thorn bush.
Var.: **Cawthorne**.

Caxton English: habitation name from a place in Cambs., so called from the gen. case of the ON byname *Kakkr* (apparently a deriv. of *kokkr* lump) + OE *tūn* enclosure, settlement.

Cayley 1. English (Norman): habitation name from places in Eure and Seine-Maritime called *Cailly*, from a Gallo-Roman personal name *Callius* + the local suffix *-ācum*. 2. English: habitation name from a minor place in the parish of Winwick, Lancs., so called from OE *cā* jackdaw (see COE) + *lēah* wood, clearing. 3. Manx: Anglicized form of Gael. *Mac Caolaidhe*; see CALLOW.
Vars.: **Cal(l)ey**, **Callie**, **Ka(y)ley**.

Cazalet *see* CASALE

Cazaubon *see* CASAUBON

Cazelle *see* CASA

Cea Spanish: habitation name from places in the provinces of León and Orense. The placename is first found in the form *Cegia*, and it is probably related to CEJA 2.

Cebolla Spanish: **1.** metonymic occupational name for a grower or seller of onions, from Sp. *cebolla* onion (from LL *cēpulla*, dim. of class. L *cēpa*; the Ger. name ZWIEBEL is a cogn.). **2.** habitation name from a place in the province of Valencia, originally named with the Arabic element *jubayla* small hill (which underlies the placename *Gibraltar*), but altered by folk etymology to *Cebolla* 'onion'.

Var. (of 1): **Cebollas**, **Cebollero**.

Cebrián Spanish: from the medieval given name *Cebrián* (L *Cypriānus*, originally an ethnic name for an inhabitant of *Cyprus*, Gk *Kypros*). The name was borne by a 3rd-cent. bishop of Carthage, and by another saint, probably legendary, whose cult was suppressed by the Holy See in 1969.

Vars.: **Cipran(o)**.

Cecchetelli *see* FRANCIS

Čech Czech: name meaning 'Czech', used in particular to distinguish a native or inhabitant of Bohemia (Czech *Čechy*) from Slovaks, Moravians, and other ethnic groups. The word itself is of unknown but vigorously disputed etymology.

Patrs.: Pol.: **Czechowicz**. Russ.: **Chekhov**.

Habitation name: Pol., Jewish (Ashkenazic): **Czechowski**.

Cecil Welsh: from the OW personal name *Seisyllt*, apparently a mutilated form of the L name *Sextilius*, a deriv. of *Sextus* 'Sixth' (from *sex* six; cf. SIX). The spelling has, however, been modified as a result of folk etymological association with the L name *C(a)ecilius*, a deriv. of *caecus* blind.

Vars.: **Saycell**, **Seisill**.

Ceder 1. Jewish (Ashkenazic): ornamental name from Yid. *tseder* cedar or Ger. *Zeder* (from L *cedrus*, from Gk). **2.** Swedish: ornamental name from Swed. *ceder*, of the same origin as 1.

Vars.: Jewish: **Tseder**, **Zeder(baum)**; **Cederbaum**, **Cederboim** (Pol. spellings).

Cpds (ornamental): Swed.: **Cederberg** ('cedar hill'); **Cederblad** ('cedar leaf'); **Ced(er)gren** ('cedar branch'); **Cederholm** ('cedar island'); **Cederlund** ('cedar grove'); **Ced(er)löf**, **Ced(er)löv** ('cedar leaf'); **Cederquist** ('cedar twig'); **Cederstrand** ('cedar shore'); **Cederström** ('cedar river'); **Ced(er)wall** ('cedar pasture').

Ceeley *see* SEALEY

Cefariello *see* CIFARO

Cegielski Polish: topographic name for someone who lived by a brickworks, or occupational name for one who worked in one, from Pol. *cegielna* brickworks.

Var.: **Cegiełkowski**.

Ceiley *see* SEALEY

Ceitlin *see* ZEITLIN

Ceja Spanish: **1.** nickname for someone particularly noted for his beetling brows, from Sp. *ceja* eyebrow (LL *cilium*, which in class. L meant 'eyelid', a deriv. of the root *cel-* hide, conceal). **2.** topographic name for someone who lived on the brow of a hill, from the same word used in this transferred sense.

Celada Spanish: habitation name from any of various places, for example in the provinces of Burgos, Córdoba,

Palencia, and Santander, so called from Sp. *celada* place of concealment (for hunters), ambuscade (LL *celāta*, a deriv. of *celāre* to hide, conceal).

Celaya Spanish form of Basque **Zelaia**: topographic name for someone who lived by a patch of pastureland, from Basque *zelai* field, meadow + the def. art. *-a*.

Var.: **Zelaya**.

Celle French: habitation name from any of the numerous places so called from having once been the site of a hermit's cell, OF *celle* (L *cella* (small) room, a deriv. of the root *cel-* hide, conceal). The Sp. cogn. *Cela* denoted a granary or storehouse, and the surname may have been acquired as a metonymic occupational name by an official responsible for receiving produce into the lord's granary. See also SELLER 3.

Var.: **Celles**.

Dims.: It.: **Celletti**, **Cellin(i)**, **Cellucci**, **Cellotto**.

Augs.: It.: **Cellon(i)**.

Cellier *see* SELLER

Celon *see* MICHAEL

Cely *see* SEALEY

Centeno Spanish: metonymic occupational name for someone who grew or sold rye, or topographic name for someone who lived by a field given over to the cultivation of this crop, from Sp. *centeno* rye (LL *centēnum*, a deriv. of *centum* hundred, so called as the plant was supposed to be capable of producing a hundred grains on each stalk).

Center *see* ZEHENDER

Cenzon *see* VINCENT

Cepeda Spanish: topographic name for somebody who lived on a patch of land that had been cleared of trees, leaving only stumps behind, from Sp. *cepeda*, a collective of *cepo* base of a tree trunk (from L *cippus* pillar).

Cercott *see* CIRCUIT

Cerda Spanish: apparently a nickname for someone with a prominent tuft of hair, from Sp. *cerda* bristle, hair (LL *cirra*, for class. L *cirrus*; the form may have been influenced by the now obsolete *seda* bristle, L *saeta*). One of the sons of King Alfonso X (1221–84) was known as Fernando *de la Cerda*.

Cerf 1. French: nickname from the stag, OF *cerf* (L *cervus*), given with reference to the presumed lustiness of the creature, or conversely to the horns supposed to be a sign of a cuckold (see HORN 4). **2.** Jewish: surname adopted because of the connection of the deer with the Hebr. given name *Naftali*; cf. HIRSCH 2.

Var. (of 1): **Lecerf**.

Dims. (of 1): Fr.: **Cerfon**. It.: **Cervini**.

Aug. (of 1): It.: **Cervoni**.

Cérié *see* CERISIER

Cerisier French: topographic name for someone who lived near a cherry tree or who owned a cherry orchard, from OF *cerisier* cherry tree (LL *cerasārius*, a deriv. of *cerasus* cherry, from Gk).

Vars.: **Cérié, Serier(s), Seriés, Serieys, Serieyx.**

Dims.: It.: **Cersini, Ceresoli, Ceresolo, Ceras(u)ola, Cerasoli, Cerisola.**

Collectives: It.: **Cereseto.** Sp.: **Cereceda.**

Cerlin see SORIN

Čermák Czech: nickname meaning literally 'redstart', the name of a common European songbird. The Czech word was also used as a euphemism for the devil, and this no doubt affected its use as a nickname.

Cernin see SATURNIN

Černohlávek see CHERNYAKOV

Cerqueira Portuguese: habitation name from a place near Braga, so called from LL *quercāria* oak grove (a deriv. of *quercus* oak).

Cerro Spanish: topographic name for someone who lived on or by a hill or ridge, Sp. *cerro* (from L *cirrus* bristle, hair (cf. CERDA); the transfer of meaning seems to be due to the fact that the L word was used in particular of the hairs along the spinal ridge of an animal).

Dim.: **Cerrillo.**

Cervantes Spanish: of uncertain origin and meaning. Most probably it is a patr. from a medieval given name *Servanto*, arising as the result of a cross between L *serviens*, gen. *servientis*, 'servant (of the Lord)' and *servandus* 'he who shall be saved'. There seems to have been some further confusion in the spelling with Sp. *ciervo* stag (cf. CERF).

Červenka see CZERWIŃSKI

Cervera Spanish: habitation name from any of numerous places so called, from LL *cervāria* 'place of stags' (a deriv. of *cervus* stag; see CERF).

Dim.: Cat.: **Cerveró.**

Cervini see CERF

Cesare Italian: from the given name *Cesare*, from the famous Roman family name *Caesar*. This was associated by folk etymology in classical times with L *caesaries* head of hair, but is in fact probably of Etruscan origin, perhaps ultimately a cogn. of CHARLES. After the spectacular success of Julius Caesar the name was adopted by his imperial successors, and eventually came to be taken as a generic title. As such it has been adopted into most European languages (see KAISER).

Vars.: **Cesaro, Cesar(i).**

Dims.: It.: **Cesarin(i), Cesarelli, Cesarotti.**

Augs.: It.: **Cesaroni, Cesarone.**

Patrs.: It.: **De Cesare, Di Cesare, De Cesaris.**

Cesarić see KAISER

Ceschelli see FRANCIS

Céspedes Spanish: topographic name for someone who lived on a patch of peat soil, from the pl. of Sp. *cesped* peat, turf (L *caespes*, gen. *caespitis*). In some cases it may originally have been a metonymic occupational name for someone who cut and sold turf.

Ceyssen see FRANCIS

Cézanne French: habitation name from a place in Upper Piémont, apparently so called from the L personal name *Caetius* + the local suffix *-ānum*.

Chabanas see CABANE

Chabroullet see CHEVREUIL

Chacón Spanish: of uncertain meaning. It may have been a nickname for a noisy, jolly person, from a word of imitative origin. The element *chac-* is used in other Sp. words descriptive of the noise of musical instruments or of convulsive laughter, as for example *chacota* and *chacona*.

Chadash see CHODOSH

Chaderton see CHATTERTON

Chadwell see CALDWELL

Chadwick English: habitation name from any of various places so called, in Lancs., Warwicks., and two in Worcs. One of the latter and the one in Warwicks. are named as being the dairy farm (OE *wīc*, see WICK) of *Ceadel*. The other Worcs. place and the one in Lancs. are named as *Ceadda's* dairy farm'. *Ceadda* is the name of an Anglo-Saxon bishop, St Chad.

Vars.: **Chadwyck, Chaddock, Chattock; Shadwick, Shaddick, Shaddock, Shattock.**

Chaff English (Norman): nickname for a bald man, from OF *chauf* bald (L *calvus*; cf. CALLOW). *Calvus* was a Roman family name, originally a byname, and was still occasionally used as a given name in Italy in the Middle Ages, so that in some cases the It. cogns. may derive from this source.

Vars.: **Chaffe, Chave; Caff,** CAVE (from Norman forms).

Dims.: Eng.: **Chaffin, Chafen, Chauvin; Cavell.** Fr.: **Chalvet, Chauvet, Cho(u)vet, Charvet; Chauveau, Choveau, Chauvel(et), Chovel, Chauvelin, Chauvelon, Chauvelot; Chalvin, Chauvin(eau), Chauvenet, Cho(u)vin, Chevin, Charvin; Chalvon, Chalv(e)ron, Chauvon, Chauv(e)ron, Chauvillon.**

It.: **Calvino, Calvini, Calvelli, Calvello, Calv(i)etti, Calvillo.**

Cat.: **Calvet, Calvó.**

Aug.: Fr.: **Chauvat.**

Pej.: Fr.: **Chauvard.**

Chagal see SEGAL

Chagas Portuguese: religious byname from the pl. form of Port. *chaga* wound (L *plāga* blow), with reference to the wounds of Christ.

Chagne see CHÊNE

Chaifetz see HEIFETZ

Chaillet see CAIL

Chaim see HYAM

Chait Jewish (Ashkenazic): occupational name for a tailor, Yid. *khayet* (from Hebr. *chayat*). In Anglophone countries the name is often given the spelling pronunciation /tʃeɪt/, as opposed to the original /ˈxajət/.

Vars.: **Khait**, **Khaet**; **Chayat**, **Chajat** (from the Hebr. form; the latter is a Pol. spelling); **Hayat**, **Hyat(t)** (see also HIGHET).

Dims.: **Chaitchik**, **Chajczyk**, **Chajczuk** (E Ashkenazic).

Patrs.: **Chaitin**, **Chaitow(itz)**, **Khaitovich** (E Ashkenazic).

Chajat *see* CHAIT

Chalcot *see* CALDICOTT

Chalk English: topographic name for someone who lived on a patch of chalk soil, or habitation name from any of the various places named from OE *cealc(e)* chalk, as for example *Chalk* in Kent or *Chalke* in Wilts.

Vars.: **Chalke**, **Chaulk**; **Chalker**, **Cawker**, **Kalker** (in part occupational names from OE *(ge)cealcian* to chalk, whitewash).

Chalkley English: habitation name from an unidentified place (probably in S England, where the surname is commonest and where chalk hills abound), apparently so called from OE *cealc* chalk + *lēah* wood, clearing.

Challamel French: probably a metonymic occupational name for a gatherer of reeds or a thatcher, from a dim. of OF *c(h)al(l)ame* reed (L *calamus*).

Vars.: **C(h)alamel(le)**, **Charameau**, **Chalamet**, **Chalumeau**, **Charamon**.

Challenor English: occupational name for a maker or seller of blankets, from an agent deriv. of ME *chaloun* blanket, coverlet. The articles were named from being first and most notably produced in the town of *Châlons*-sur-Marne, so called from having been the seat of a Gaul. tribe recorded in L sources as *Catalauni*.

Vars.: **Challen(d)er**, **Challinor**, **Chal(l)oner**, **Chawner**, **Channer**; **Challen(s)**, **Challin**.

Challis English (Norman): habitation name from *Eschalles* in Pas-de-Calais, which gets its name from the pl. form of OF *eschelle* ladder (L *scala*).

Vars.: **Challiss**, **Chal(l)ice**, **Challace**, **Challes**.

Chalmers Scots: var. of CHAMBERS. The -*l*- was originally an orthographic device to indicate the length of the vowel after assimilation of -*mb*- to -*m(m)*-.

Chalonin *see* BARTHOLOMEW

Chaloupek Czech: status name for a poor farmer living in a cottage (Czech *chalupa*), esp. one with very little land attached to it. A *chalupník* had even less land than a small-holder (ZAHRADNÍK).

Var.: **Chal(o)upník**.

Habitation names: **Chalupa**, **Chaloupka**.

Chamberlain English: occupational name from ANF *c(h)ambrelain*, *cambrelanc*, *cambrelen(c)* chamberlain (of Gmc origin, cf. OHG *kemerlinc*, from *kamer*, *chamara* chamber, room (L *camera*; see CHAMBERS) + the suffix -*(l)ing*). This was originally the name of an official in charge of the private chambers of his master, later a title of high rank (for similar increases in dignity, see BUTLER, MARSHALL, SCHENKE, SENESCHAL, and STEWART). The Italian

cogn. *camerlengo* was used of the manager of a pontifical court.

Vars.: **Chamberlaine**, **Chamberlayne**, **Chamberlen**, **Chamberlin**, **Champerlen**.

Chambers English: occupational name for someone who was employed in the private living quarters of his master, rather than in the public halls of the manor. The name represents a gen. or pl. form of ME, OF *cha(u)mbre* chamber, room (L *camera*), and is synonymous in origin with CHAMBERLAIN, but as that office rose in the social scale, this term remained reserved for more humble servants of the bedchamber.

Var.: CHALMERS.

Dims.: Fr.: **Cambron**, **Cambran(d)**, **Cambrin**, **Cambret(te)**, **Cambrillon**. It.: **Camerino**. Sp.: **Camarillo**. Port.: **Camarin(h)o**.

Aug.: Fr.: **Chambras**.

Chambet *see* GAMBE

Chambly *see* CHOLMONDELEY

Chamizo Spanish: **1.** topographic name for someone who lived in a thatched cottage, Sp. *chamizo* (from *chamiza* dried straw, of Galician/Port. origin, from *chama* flame, L *flamma*). **2.** nickname for someone with dark hair or a swarthy complexion, from *chamizo* soot, half-burned wood (likewise from *chama* flame).

Chamorro Spanish: nickname for a clean-shaven or closely cropped man. The word is first attested in the mid-14th cent. and is of unknown origin, possibly a survival of a pre-Roman word with cogns. in Basque. In the Middle Ages it was applied as an ethnic nickname to the Portuguese, who wore their hair short in contrast with the Castilian custom of allowing it to attain its natural length.

Champ French: topographic name for someone who lived in or near a field or expanse of open country, or else in the countryside as opposed to a town, from OF *champ* field, open land (L *campus* plain, expanse of flat land).

Vars.: **Camp** (Normandy, Picardy); **C(h)amps**; **Dec(h)amp**, **Delcamp**, **Duc(h)amp**, **Desc(h)amps**, **Decamps**; **Auchamp**.

Dims.: Fr.: **Champeau(x)**, **Champel**, **Champon(net)**, **Champot**, **Champet**, **Champeix**. It.: **Campetti**, **Campolo**, **Campoli**, **Campino**. Sp.: **Campillo**.

Augs.: It.: **Campone**, **Camponi**.

Pejs.: It.: **Campacci(o)**, **Campasso**, **Campassi**, **Campazzo**, **Campazzi**.

Champion *see* CAMPION

Champney English: regional name for someone from *Champagne* in France, from ANF *champeneis*, a deriv. of OF *Champagne* (L *Campānia*, from *campus* plain, flat land; see CHAMP). This is also the name of various villages in France, and in a few cases the Fr. cogns. may derive from one of these. Rarely the name may also have referred in general terms to a dweller in the countryside rather than a town.

Vars.: **Champneys** (usually pronounced /ˈtʃæniːz/); **Champness**, **Champniss**; **Champain**.

Champouillon French: apparently a habitation name from some minor place so called from OF CHAMP field + *pouillon* bug (a dim. of *pou* flea, L *pūlex*).

Var.: **Champollion**.

Chance English: nickname for an inveterate gambler, or perhaps for someone who had survived an accident by a remarkable piece of luck, from ANF *chea(u)nce* (good) fortune (a deriv. of *cheoir* to fall (out), L *cadere*).

Vars.: **C(h)aunce**.

Chancellor English and Scots: occupational name for a secretary or administrative official, from ANF *c(h)ancelier* (LL *cancellārius* usher of a law court, from *cancelli* lattice, grating dividing the court officials from the general public). The King's Chancellor was one of the highest officials in the land, but the term was also used to describe the holder of a variety of offices in the medieval world, such as the secretary or record keeper in a minor manorial household. In some cases, however, the name is found referring to people in very humble circumstances, including serfs, who are unlikely to have been chancellors or descended from chancellors, in any sense of the word. This suggests origin as a nickname.

Var.: **Cancellor**.

Chandler English: occupational name for a maker and seller of candles, ME *cha(u)ndeler* (OF *chandelier*, LL *candēlārius*, a deriv. of *candēla* candle, from *candēre* to be bright). While a medieval chandler no doubt made and sold other articles beside candles, the extended sense of mod. Eng. *chandler* does not occur until the 16th cent. The name may also, more rarely, have denoted someone who was responsible for the lighting arrangements in a large house, or else one who owed rent in the form of wax or candles.

Var.: **Chantler**.

Chandlish see MCCANDLESS

Chaneles see HANNA

Channon English (chiefly W Country): var. of CANNON 1, taken from the central French form *chanun*, as opposed to the Norman *canun*.

Chanson French: **1.** nickname for a man with a fine voice or fond of singing at his work, from OF *chanson* song (LL *cantio*, gen. *cantiōnis* singing, song, a deriv. of *cantāre* to sing, replacing class. L *cantus*; cf. CANT). **2.** occupational name for a cup-bearer, from an aphetic form of OF *échanson*, a word of Gmc origin (see SCHENKE).

Chant see CANT

Chanteraine French: habitation name from a place in the Vosges, so called from OF *chante(r)* to sing (L *cantāre*, freq. of *canere*) + *raine* frog (L *rāna*), a humorous name for a marshy locality where the frogs could be heard croaking.

Vars.: **Chantraine, Chantreine, Chanterenne**.

Chanudet see CHENU

Chapaev Russian: patr. from a nickname derived from either of two homonymous verbs *chapat* to snatch, seize and *chapat* to swing, waver (both are of uncertain, but apparently distinct, origin).

Chape French: from OF *chape* hooded cloak, cape, hood, or hat (LL *cappa*, *cāpa*, perhaps a deriv. of *caput* head; see CAP), applied as a metonymic occupational name for a maker of either cloaks or hats, or as a nickname for a ha-

bitual wearer of a distinctive cloak or hat. The two L byforms, *cappa* and *cāpa*, were borrowed into OE as *cæppe* and *cāp* respectively, becoming mod. Eng. *cap* and *cope* (see CAPPER and COPE), with later semantic differentiation. Mod. Eng. *cape* could in part represent a N English development of OE *cāp* (cf. ROPER), but more probably it was reintroduced, with yet another distinction in meaning, from Provence in the 16th cent.

Vars.: **Chappe; Cape** (Normandy, Picardy); **Chapu(t)** (nicknames); **Chapier, Caper(s)** (occupational names).

Ger.: **Kappe; Käppner, Keppner** (occupational). Pol.: **Kapelusz**.

Dims.: Fr.: **Chapet, Chapé, C(h)apez, Chapey; Chapel(et), Chapeau, C(h)aplot, Chapleteau; Capelon, Capot; Chapel(l)ier** (occupational). It.: **Cappini** ('small cape'); **Cappell(in)i** ('hat'), **Capp(i)ello, Cappilli, Cap(p)elletti, Cappellut(t)i, Cap(p)ellozzi; Capelli, Capello** (S Italy; see also CABELLO); **Cap(p)ellaro, Cap(p)ellari, Cappell(i)eri** (occupational); **Cappuza** ('hood'), **Cap(p)ucc(in)i, Copozzi** (Emilia); **Capucciaro** (occupational); COPPOLA. Sp.: **Capote** ('cape'); **Capellero** ('hat'; occupational). Cat.: **Capel(l); Capeller, Capellé.** Ger.: **Käppel(e)** ('cape'), **Keppel; Kep(p)ler** (occupational). Bulg.: **Shápka.** Jewish: **Keppel, Kep(p)ler** (Ashkenazic, occupational for a cloak maker); **Kapelushnik** (E Ashkenazic, occupational for a hat maker).

Chaperon see CAPRON

Chapiro see SHAPIRO

Chaplin **1.** English and French: occupational name for a clergyman, or perhaps for the servant of one, from ME, OF *chapelain* chantry priest, a priest endowed to sing mass daily on behalf of the souls of the dead (LL *capellānus*, a deriv. of *capella*; see CHAPPELL). **2.** Russian: patr. from the nickname *Chaplya* 'Heron', 'Stork' (Pol. *czapla*), referring to a man with long, thin legs or perhaps one who was shy and easily frightened.

Vars. (of 1): Eng.: **Chaplain, Chapling, Chaperlin(g), Cap(e)len, Cap(e)lin, Capeling.** Fr.: **Chapel(a)in, Chaplain; Cap(el)ain, Capelan, Capéran; Lechapelain, Lecap(e)lain.** See also KAPLAN. (Of 2): Russ.: **Tsaplin.**

Dims. (of 2): Pol.: **Czapnik.** Czech: **Čapek.**

Habitation names (from 2): Pol.: **Czapliński, Czaplicki.**

Chapman English: occupational name for a merchant or trader, ME *chapman*, OE *cēapmann*, a cpd of *cēap* barter, bagain, price, property + *mann* man.

Vars.: **Chipman** (from W Saxon *cȳp(e)mann*); **Chapper, Chipper, Cheeper** (from the OE verb *cē(a)pan, cȳpan*); COPEMAN.

Patrs.: Du.: **Koo(p)mans.** Flem.: **Coo(p)mans.** Finn.: **Kauppinen.**

Chapon see CAPON

Chappell English: topographic name for someone who lived close to a chapel, or occupational name for someone employed in one. The name comes from ME, OF *chapel(l)e* chapel (LL *capella*, originally a dim. of *cāpa* hood, cloak (see CHAPE), but later transferred to the sense 'chapel', 'sanctuary', with reference to the shrine at Tours where the cloak of St MARTIN was preserved as a relic).

Vars.: **Chappel(le), Chapell; Chapple** (W Country); **Cap(p)el(l), Capelle** (from Norman forms); **Capewell** (chiefly Midlands).

Chaptal see CHEPTEL

Chapuis French: occupational name for a carpenter or joiner, a deriv. of OF *chapuiser* to cut, trim (LL *cappulāre*, of uncertain origin).

Vars.: **C(h)apus**.

Dims.: **Chapu(i)set**, **Chapuzet**, **Chapu(i)sot**, **Chapuzot**, **Chapuiseau**.

Aug.: **Chapuisat**.

Charbonel *see* CARBONELL

Chardel *see* CIARDO

Chardenot *see* CARDING

Chareour *see* CARRIER

Charles 1. French, Welsh, and English: from the Gmc personal name *Carl* 'Man' (which was Latinized as *Carolus*). In France the given name was popular from an early date, due to the fame of the Emperor *Charlemagne* (?742–814; Latin name *Carolus Magnus*, i.e. Charles the Great). The OF form *Charles* was briefly introduced to England by the Normans, but was rare during the main period of surname formation. It was introduced more successfully to Scotland in the 16th cent. by the Stuarts, who had strong ties with France, and was brought by them to England in the 17th cent. Its frequency as a Welsh surname is attributable to the late date of Welsh surname formation. The Ger. cogn., *Karl*, is rare or unknown as a surname, probably because the given name was not in use among the general population in German-speaking countries in the Middle Ages, but was restricted to the nobility. OE *Ceorl* 'peasant' is also found as a byname, but the resulting ME form, *Charl*, with a patr. in *-s*, if it existed at all, would have been absorbed by the French form introduced by the Normans. English vars. pronounced with initial /k-/ for the most part reflect the cogn. ON personal name *Karl, Karli*. 2. English: patr. from an occupational name or status name for a peasant farmer, ME *charl, cherl*, OE *ceorl* peasant (see CHARLTON).

Vars.: Eng.: **Carl(e)**, **Karl(e)**. (Of 1 only): Fr.: **Charle**; **Charlon** (oblique case); **Carle** (Normandy, Picardy); **Chasle(s)** (Beauce).

Dims. (of 1): Fr.: **C(h)arlet**, **Charley**, **Charlin**, **Charlon**, **Charlo(t)**; CARLIN. It.: **Carletti**, **Carletto**, **Carlin(i)**, **Carlin(o)**, **Carlucci(o)**, **Carluzzi**, **Carlotti**, **Carlotto**, **Carlozzi**. Czech: **Karlík**, **Karlíček**. Pol.: **Karolczyk**.

Augs. (of 1): It.: **Carlon(i)**, **Carlone**.

Patrs. (from 1): Eng.: **Charleston** (with intrusive *-t-*, cf. JOHNSTON 2; the various places called *Charleston* are all of too recent origin to have given rise to surnames). Sc.: **McCarlish** (Gael. **Mac Carlais**). It.: **De Carlo**, **De Carli**, **Di Carlo**, **De Caroli(s)**. Flem., Du.: **Carlens**. Dan., Norw.: **Karlsen**, **Carlsen**. Swed.: **Karlsson**, **Carlsson**. Pol.: **Karłowicz**; **Karolak**, **Karolczak**.

Habitation names (from 1): Pol.: **Karolewski**, **Karłowski**. Czech: **Karlovský**.

Charlesworth English: habitation name from a place in Derbys., recorded in Domesday Book as *Cheuenesuurde* and in the 13th cent. as *Chauelisworth*. The name apparently comes from the gen. case of an OE byname derived from *ceafl* jaw + OE *worð* enclosure (see WORTH), but the first element has suffered from late folk etymological association with the given name CHARLES.

Charlier French: occupational name for a cartwright, from OF *charrelier*, a deriv. of *charrel* cart (dim. of *char*, LL *carrum*; cf. CARRIER).

Var.: **Carlier** (Norman, Picard).

Charlton 1. English: habitation name from any of the numerous places so called in every part of England, from OE *Ceorlatūn* 'settlement (OE *tūn*) of the peasants'. OE *ceorl* denoted originally a free peasant of the lowest rank, later (but probably already before the Norman conquest) a tenant in pure villeinage, a serf or bondsman. 2. Irish: var. of CARLIN 1.

Vars.: **Charleton**, CHORLTON, CARLTON.

Charme French: topographic name for someone who lived by a conspicuous hornbeam (witch elm) or group of such trees, from OF *charme* (L *carpīnus*).

Vars.: **Charmes**, **Charne**, CARNE; **Decharme**, **Ducharme**, **Ducharne**.

Dims.: Fr.: **Charmet**, **Charmey**. It.: **Carpinelli**, **Carpanelli**, **Carpenetti**, **Carpanini**.

Aug.: It.: **Carpanoni**.

Collectives: Fr.: **C(h)armoy**, **Charmay**, **Carnoy**, **Charpenay**. It.: **Carpineto**, **Carpineti**, **Carpaneto**, **Carpeneto**, **Carpeneti**.

Charnes *see* CHERNYAKOV

Charnley English (Lancs.): apparently a habitation name from an unidentified place so called, possibly from the same element as in CHARNOCK with the addition of OE *lēah* wood, clearing.

Charnock English (Lancs.): habitation name from *Charnock* Richard or Heath *Charnock* in S Lancs., so called from a Brit. deriv. of a placename element cogn. with W *carn* stone (see CAIRNS).

Charnu *see* CARNÉ

Charpentereau *see* CARPENTER

Charraire *see* CARRIÈRE

Charrette French: from OF *char(r)ette* cart, a dim. of *char(re)* (LL *carrum* (neut.) and *carra* (fem., originally neut. pl.), of Celt. origin). This may have been acquired as a metonymic occupational name for a user or maker of carts (see CARTER, CARTWRIGHT), or perhaps as a nickname for someone who owned a wheeled vehicle in an area where asses or mules were the usual means of transport.

Vars.: **C(h)arette**.

Charrington *see* CHERRINGTON

Charron French: metonymic occupational name for a maker of carts, from OF *charron* cart (L *carro*, gen. *carrōnis*, a deriv. of *carrum* cart; cf. CARMAN).

Vars.: **Carron** (Normandy; see also CARON); **Charrondier**, **Charrandier** (with added agent suffix).

Chart English: habitation name from any of various places named with OE *ce(a)rt* rough heathland, as for example *Chart* in Kent and Surrey or *Churt* in Surrey, or possibly a topographic name from the same word used independently.

Var.: **Chard** (a place in Somerset).

Charter see CARTER

Charteris 1. Scots and English: Norman habitation name from the Fr. town of *Chartres*, so called from having been the seat of a Gaul. tribe whose name is recorded in L sources in the form *Carnutes*. **2.** English: habitation name from *Chatteris* in Cambs., which is of uncertain etymology, possibly the 'ridge (OE *hrycg*) of *Ceatta*', a personal name of uncertain origin (cf. CHATFIELD).
Vars. (of 1): **Charters**, **Chatres**. (Of 2): **Chatter(i)s**.

Chase English: apparently a metonymic occupational name for a huntsman, or rather a nickname for an exceptionally skilled huntsman, from ME *chase* hunt (OF *chasse*, from *chasser* to hunt, chase, L *captāre*; cf. CATCHPOLE).
Var.: **Chace**.

Chaskelovic see EZEKIEL

Chassagne see CASSAGNE

Chastagnier see CASTAN

Chaster see CHESTER

Chateaubriand French: habitation name from a place in Loire-Inférieure, so named from being the seat (OF *chasteau*; see CASTLE) of a Bret. proprietor bearing a personal name meaning 'Eminence' (see BRYAN).

Chatelain see CASTELLAN

Châtelet see CASTLE

Châtelier French: habitation name any of the numerous places named from OF *chastelier* small castle, minor fort (L *castellāre*, a deriv. of *castellum* castle; cf. CASALE from CASA and VILLIERS from VILLE).
Vars.: **Chatellier**, **Duchâtelier**, **Duchatellier**.
Dims.: It.: **Castel(l)arin(i)**.

Chater see CATER

Chatfield English: habitation name from an unidentified place, apparently so called from the OE personal name *Ceatta* (probably a var. of *Catta*; see CATT 1) + OE *feld* pasture, open country (see FIELD).

Chatham English: habitation name from the place so called in Kent (or possibly from *Chatham* Green in Essex). These places appear in Domesday Book as *Ceteham* and *Cetham* respectively, and Ekwall derives the first part from a Brit. element *ceto-* forest (cf. W *coed*); the second is OE *hām* homestead. See also CHEETHAM.

Chatt see CATT

Chattaway English: habitation name from an unidentified place (probably in the W Midlands, where the surname is commonest), apparently so called from the OE personal name *Ceatta* (cf. CHATFIELD) + OE *weg* path, way.

Chatterley English: habitation name from a place in Staffs., so called from a first element *chader-* (probably a Brit. word meaning 'chair', used of a commanding hill; cf. CHATTERTON) + OE *lēah* wood, clearing.

Chatterton English: habitation name from *Chadderton* in Lancs., which was recorded in 1224 in the form *Chaterton*. The first element may preserve a Brit. term which became

W *cadair* chair, used in placenames to denote a commanding hill; the second is OE *tūn* enclosure, settlement.
Var.: **Chaderton**.

Chatto Scots: habitation name from a place in the former county of Roxburghs. (now part of Borders region), of uncertain, possibly Gael., etymology. The surname is now rare in SE Scotland.

Chatwin see CHETWYND

Chaucer English: occupational name for a maker of leggings; see CHAUSSE.
Vars.: **Chauser**; **Causer** (W Midlands).

Chaudrelle see CALDERON

Chaume French: **1.** topographic name for someone who lived on a high treeless plateau, from the OF dial. term *chaume* plateau (of apparently Gaul. origin). **2.** topographic name for someone who lived by a patch of fallow land, from OF *chaume* hay stubble (L *calamus* reed; cf. CHALLAMEL).
Vars.: **Chaulme(s)**; **Lachaume**; **Delachaume**; **Chaumier**, **Chaumié**.
Dims.: Fr.: **Chaumel**, **Chomel**, **Chaumet(te)**, **Chomet(te)**, **Chaumeix**, **Chaumeil**, **Chaumot**, **Chaumillon**, **Chaumeton**.
Prov.: **Calmette**, **Calmel(s)**.
Aug.: Fr.: **Chaumat**.

Chaumont see CAUMONT

Chausse French: metonymic occupational name for a maker of shoes or leggings, or nickname for a wearer of distinctive ones, from OF *chausse* footwear or leggings (LL *calcia*, for class. L *calceus* sandal, shoe, a deriv. of *calx*, gen. *calcis*, heel). In medieval Europe this term was used very widely, and denoted boots, shoes, leggings, leg armour, gaiters, hose, breeches, pantaloons, and so on; its modern descendants include Fr. *chaussures* shoes and *chaussettes* socks.
Vars.: **Cauce** (Normandy, Picardy); **Chaussier** (occupational); **Chaussé** (nickname).
Dims.: Fr.: **Chausson**; **Chaussec**, **Chossec** (Brittany). It.: **Calzetta**, **Calzette**, **Calzetti**.
Pej.: Fr.: **Chausard**.

Chaussée French: topographic name for someone who lived by a paved road, Fr. *chaussée*, a relatively rare feature of the medieval countryside. *Chaussée* is from L *(via) calciāta* 'limed (way)', from *calx* chalk, limestone, gen. *calcis*. This word has also named a number of Fr. villages, and the surname may be a habitation name from one of these.
Vars.: **Lachaussée**, **Delachaussée**; **Cauchie**, **Cauchy**, **Delcauchie** (Normandy, Picardy).

Chaustov see FAUST

Chavalier see CHEVALIER

Chavane see CABANE

Chavarría see ECHEVERRÍA

Chaves Portuguese: habitation name from a place in the province of Tras-os-Montes, so called from L *(aquis) Flaviis*, the abl. case, originally used after a preposition, of *aquae Flaviae* 'waters of *Flavius*'. The place was the site of sulphurous springs with supposedly health-giving properties, around which a settlement was founded in the 1st cent. AD by the Emperor Vespasian.

Chavialle *see* CAPDEVIELLE

Chavkin *see* KHAVKE

Chazan Jewish (Ashkenazic): occupational name for a cantor in a synagogue, Hebr. *chazan*.
Vars.: **Chasan**, **Haz(z)an**, **Khazan**, **Kazan**; **Chason** (reflecting an Ashkenazic pronunciation of the Hebr. word); **Chazen**, **Chasen**, **Chasin** (reflecting Yid. *khazn*).
Patrs.: **Chazanow**, **Chazanoff**, **Chasanoff**, **Chas(i)noff**, **Khazanov(ich)**, **Kazanov(ich)**, **Kazanowitz**, **K(h)azanovski** (E Ashkenazic); **Chasins** (with Yid. possessive -*s*).

Chazelle *see* CASA

Cheadle English: habitation name from *Cheadle* in Ches. and Staffs. Ekwall explains the name as being from the Brit. element *ceto-* wood, with the tautologous addition of OE *lēah* wood, clearing (cf. CHETWODE).
Var.: **Chettle**.

Cheater English: occupational name for an escheator, the official in charge of supervising the reversion of property to the feudal lord in the absence of legal heirs. The name comes from ME *chetour*, an aphetic form of ANF *eschetour* (a deriv. of *eschete* lot, from *eschoir* to fall to the lot of, L *excadere* to fall out; cf. CHANCE); the opportunities for dubious dealing implicit in the post led to the later sense of the verb *cheat*.
Var.: **Chetter**.

Chebanier *see* CABANE

Checchetelli *see* FRANCIS

Checkley English: habitation name from any of the places so called, in Ches., Herefords., and Staffs. The last two are probably *Ceacca*'s clearing (OE *lēah*)'; the Ches. name is *Ceaddica*'s clearing', from a deriv. of the same personal name.

Cheek English: nickname for someone with some deformity or scar in the region of the cheek or jawbone, ME *cheeke* (OE *cē(a)ce*).
Vars.: **Che(e)ke**, **Cheak(e)**.

Cheeld *see* CHILD

Cheeper *see* CHAPMAN

Cheesbrough English: probably a habitation name from an unidentified place, apparently so called from OE *cis* gravel + *burh* fortress, town. A place in Northumb., now *Cheeseburn*, is recorded in 1286 as *Cheseburgh*; a place now called *Chirbury* in Hodnet parish, Shrops., is spelled *Ches(e)bury* in 1291–5. Either of these may be the source of this surname, which, however, is now found most commonly in Yorks.

Cheeseman English: occupational name for a maker or seller of cheese, from OE *cȳse*, *cēse* cheese (L *cāseus*) + *mann* man.
Vars.: **Cheesman**, **Ches(e)man**, **Cheasman**, **Chi(e)sman**, **Chessman**, **Chismon**; **Cheese**, **Chiese**; **Cheese(w)right**, **Che(e)swright**, **Chesswright**, **Cherrett**, **Cherritt** (see WRIGHT).
Dims.: Fr.: **Chazereau**. It.: **Casarin(i)**, **Casarino**, **Casaroli**, **Casiroli**, **Casaril(e)**.
Patrs.: Flem.: **Caesmans**. Du.: **Kaesmans**, **Kaesmakers**.

Cheetham English: habitation name from a place in Lancs., apparently so called from the Brit. element *ceto-* wood + OE *hām* homestead; cf. CHATHAM.
Vars.: **Cheatham**.

Cheever English: nickname for a stubborn person, or metonymic occupational name for a goatherd, from ANF *chivere*, *chevre* goat (L *capra* nanny goat).
Dims.: Fr.: **Chevrel**, **Chevreau**, **Chevret**, **Chevrey**, **Cheuret**, **Chevr(et)ot**, **Chevrill(on)**. Prov.: **Crabet(te)**, **Crabot**; **Cabiron**, **Cabrit**. Eng.: **Cheverell**, **Cheverall**, **Cheverill**, **Chiv(e)rall**, **Chiverell**. It.: **Caprin(i)**, **Caprino**, **Capretti**, **Capr(i)otti**, **Capruzzi**, **La Capruccia**; **Cavrini**, **Cavrotti**, **Cavrulli**, **Cavaretta**; **Cravetti**, **Cravetta**, **Cravino**, **Cravin(i)**, **Cravotta**, **Craviotto**; **Crapulli**. Port.: **Cabrita**.
Aug.: It.: **Caproni**.
Patrs.: Eng.: **Che(e)vers**; **Chivers**.

Chefdeville *see* CAPDEVIELLE

Chefetz *see* HEIFETZ

Chegwin Cornish: habitation name from the elements *chy* house + *gwyn* white (see GWYN).
Var.: **Chegwyn**.

Chekhov *see* ČECH

Chelazzi *see* MICHAEL

Chemin French: topographic name for someone who lived near a thoroughfare, from OF *chemin* path, way (LL *camminus*, of apparently Celt. origin).
Vars.: **Duchemin**; **Quemin**, **Quémin**, **Duquemin** (Normandy).
Dims.: Fr.: **Cheminel**, **Chemineau**. Prov.: **Caminel**.

Chenal French: topographic name for someone who lived near an irrigation channel, from OF *chenal* channel, pipe (LL *canālis*, a deriv. of *canna* reed; cf. CAIN 1).
Vars.: **Chenau(d)**, **Chenault**, **Chenaux**; **Lachenal**, **Lachenaud**, **Delachenal**.
Dims.: It.: **Canaletto**, **Canalini**.

Chêne French: topographic name for someone who lived near a conspicuous oak tree, or in an oak forest, from OF *chesne* oak (LL *caxinus*, a var. of *cassanus* (see CASSE 1 and CASSAGNE), influenced by *fraxinus* ash). The surname may perhaps occasionally also have been a nickname for a man with a 'heart of oak'.
Vars.: **Chesne**, **Cha(i)gne**; **Lechêne**, **Lechesne**; **Dechêne**, **Dechesne**; **Duchêne**, **Duchesne**; **Chénier**, **Chesnier**. See also QUÊNE.
Dims.: Fr.: **Chénel**, **Chesnel**, **Chéneau**, **Chesneau**, **Chénet**, **Chesnet**, **Chesné**, **Chénot**, **Chesnot**, **Chênelot**; **Chagneaux**, **Chagnon**, **Chagnoux**, **Chagnot**, **Chagnol**.
Collectives: Fr.: **Chênai(s)**, **Chesnais**, **Che(s)nay**, **Chénois**, **Chênoy**, **Chesnoy**, **Duchenois**, **Duchenoy**, **Chénière(s)**, **Chesnière**. Eng.: **Che(y)ney**, **Cha(i)ney**, **Cheenay**, **Chesnay**,

Chesnoy (from various places in France so named); **Chenery**, **Chin(n)ery** (Suffolk).

Chenevier French: occupational name for a cultivator of hemp, from an agent deriv. of OF *cheneve* (L *cannabis*, from Gk; said to be ultimately from Scythian). The tough fibres found in the stem of this plant were long used in the manufacture of ropes and canvas.
Var.: **Chennevier**.

Chenoweth Cornish: habitation name from the elements *chy* house + *noweth* new.
Var.: **Chynoweth**.

Chenu French: nickname for an old man or someone with prematurely white hair, from OF *chenu* white-haired (LL *cānūtus*, for class. L *cānus*). The word also acquired the sense 'prudent', 'judicious', through association with the wisdom and experience of old age.
Var.: **Quenu** (Normandy).
Dims.: Fr.: **Chenu(d)eau**, **Chenuet**, **Chenuil**; **Chanudet**.
Prov.: **Canu(d)et**, **(Le) Canuel**.

Cheptel French: topographic name for someone who lived near an enclosure for livestock, from OF *cheptel* pen, fold (L *capitālia*, a deriv. of *caput*, gen. *capitis*, head (of cattle)), or occupational name for someone who worked in such an enclosure, tending the animals.
Vars.: **Chétel**, **Cheteau**; **Cheftel** (Normandy); **Chatal** (Brittany).
Prov.: **Captal**; **Chaptal**, **Chateau** (Massif Central).

Cherbonneau *see* CARBONELL

Cherntsov Russian: patr. from the occupational term (or nickname) *chernets* monk (a deriv. of *cherny* black; see CHERNYAKOV).
Vars.: **Chentsov**, **Cheltzov**.

Chernyakov Russian: patr. from the nickname *Chernyak* 'Black(-haired)' or 'Dark(-skinned) one' (from *cherny* black; Pol. *czarny*, Czech *černý*).
Vars.: **Chernakov**, **Chernyakin**, **Chernyagin**, **Chernigin**, **Chern(ya)ev**, **Chernyshyov**, **Chernishev**, **Chernukhin**, **Chernyatin**, **Chernavin**; **Chernov**; **Chernyshevski** (a clergy name formed by the addition of the suffix *-ski* to an existing surname).
Dims.: Beloruss.: **Chernyonok**. Ukr.: **Chernenko**. Pol.: **Czernik**, **Czernek**. Ger. (of Slav. origin): **Scharnke**, **Tscharnke**, **Tschernke**, **Zarn(c)ke**, **Zörneke**.
Patrs.: Jewish: **Tshernichov**, **Tshernichow**; **Chernichowsky**, **Tchernichovsky**, **Czernichowski**. Croatian: **Crnković**.
Metrs.: Jewish (from the E Yid. female given name *Tsharne* or *Tsherne*): **Charnes**, **Czernas**, **Czernin**, **Chernov**, **Czernov**; **Czerninski**, **Czarninski**, **Chernovsky**, **Czerniawski**.
Metrs. (from a dim.): Jewish: **Charnylas**, **Czarnylas**, **Czernilov**; **Czarnolewski**.
Cpds: Jewish: **Chernobelski**, **Czernobilski** ('black-white'); **Charnobroda**, **Czarnobroda** ('black beard'); **Czarnoczapka** ('black cap'); **Chernomorski**, **Chernomorsky** (from the Black Sea, Russ. *Chernoe More*, with the addition of the general surname ending *-ski*). Czech: **Černohlávek** ('black-haired man').

Cheroneau *see* CARON

Cherrington English: habitation name from any of various places called *Cherington* or *Cherrington*. *Cherrington* in Shrops. may mean 'settlement by a river bend', but others

(*Cherington* in Gloucs. and *Cherrington* in Warwicks.) are 'church settlement', from OE *cyrice* church + *tūn* settlement. Places called *Cheriton* in Devon, Hants., Kent, and Somerset also have this last etymology.
Vars.: **Charrington**; **Cheriton**.

Cherry English: topographic name for someone who lived by a cherry tree, or metonymic occupational name for a grower and seller of cherries, from ME *cheri(e)* (a back-formation from ANF *cherise* (see CERISIER), taken as a pl.).
Vars.: **Cherrie**; **Cherryman**, **Cherriman**.

Cheseldine English: apparently a habitation name from an unidentified place in Lincs., perhaps so called from OE *ceosel* gravel + *denu* valley (see DEAN 1).

Cheshire English: regional name for someone from the county of Cheshire in NW England, the name of which is recorded in Domesday Book as *Cestrescire*, a cpd of the county town CHESTER + OE *scīr* district, division.
Vars.: **Chesshire**, **Chesshyre**, **Cheshir**, **Chesher**, **Chesser**, **Chessor**.

Chester English: habitation name from the county town of CHESHIRE, or from any of the various smaller places so called from OE *ceaster* Roman fort (L *castra* legionary camp).
Vars.: **Chaster**, **Chesters**.

Chesterton English: habitation name from any of the various places, for example in Cambs., Gloucs., Oxon., Staffs., and Warwicks., so called from OE *ceaster* Roman fort (see CHESTER) + *tūn* enclosure, settlement.
Var.: **Kesterton** (chiefly W Midlands).

Chestworth English: habitation name from an unidentified place. The name is now most common in Lancs., but it is a late arrival there and the place in question should probably be sought elsewhere. The second element of the placename is presumably OE *worð* enclosure (see WORTH); the first may be a personal name.

Chétel *see* CHEPTEL

Chetwode English: habitation name from a place in Bucks., so called from the Brit. element *ceto-* wood, with the tautological addition of OE *wudu* (see WOOD) when the old name was no longer understood. Cf. CHEADLE.
Var.: **Chetwood**.

Chetwynd English: habitation name from a place in Shrops., so called from the OE personal name *Ceatta* (see CHATFIELD) + OE *(ge)wind* winding ascent.
Var.: **Chatwin**.

Chevalard *see* CAVALLO

Chevalier French: from OF *chevalier* knight (lit. horseman, rider, LL *caballārius*, a deriv. of *caballus* horse; cf. CAVALLO). In the Middle Ages only men of comparative wealth were able to afford the upkeep of a riding horse. It is likely that in the majority of cases the surname was originally a nickname, or an occupational name for a knight's servant, rather than a status name, for most men of the knightly class belonged to noble families which had more specific surnames derived from their estates.

Vars.: **Chaval(l)ier**; **Lecheval(l)ier**.

Dims.: Fr.: **Chevallereau**, **Chevalleret**.

Chevreuil French: nickname from OF *chevreuil* roe-buck (L *capriōlus*, a deriv. of *caper* goat; cf. CHEEVER), or else a metonymic occupational name for a worker in buckskin.

Vars.: **Chevreul**; **Chevrol(l)ier** (occupational).

Dims.: Fr.: **Chevrolet**. Prov.: **Chabroullet** (Massif Central).

Aug.: Fr.: **Chevrollat**.

Chew English: 1. habitation name from a place in Somerset, so called from a Brit. river name perhaps cogn. with W *cyw* young animal or bird, chicken. 2. habitation name from places in W Yorks. or in the parish of Billington, Lancs., so called from OE *cēo* fish gill, used in the transferred sense of a ravine, in a similar way to ON *gil* (see GILL 2). 3. nickname for a talkative or thievish person, from OE *cēo* chough, a bird closely related to the crow and the jackdaw.

Var.: **Chue**.

Chézelle *see* CASA

Chiarella *see* CLARE

Chicchelli *see* FRANCIS

Chicharro Spanish: nickname for a chirpy individual, from OSp. *chicarro* cricket, cicada (L *cicāda*).

Chichester English: habitation name from the city in Sussex, apparently so called from the OE personal name *Cissa* + OE *ceaster* Roman fort (see CHESTER). *Cissa* is attested as the name of a historical person, but it is of uncertain etymology.

Chick English: 1. metonymic occupational name for someone who bred poultry for the table, from ME *chike* (a shortened form of *chiken*, OE *cīcen* young fowl). In some cases it may have been a nickname from the same word used as a term of endearment. 2. var. of CHEEK.

Var. (of 1): **Chicken**.

Chico Spanish: nickname for a small man, or for the younger of two bearers of the same given name, from Sp. *chico* small, young (of uncertain origin, perhaps from L *ciccum* trifle).

Aug.: **Chicote**.

Chidgley English (Bristol): habitation name from a place called *Chidgley* in W Somerset. The first element of this is probably from an OE personal name of uncertain form and meaning; the second is OE *lēah* wood, clearing.

Chiericetti *see* CLARK

Chiese *see* CHEESEMAN

Chilcott English: habitation name from a place in Somerset, so called from the OE personal name *Cēola* (a short form of various cpd names with a first element *cēol* ship) + OE *cot* cottage, dwelling (see COATES).

Child English: 1. nickname from ME *child*, OE *cild* child, infant, in various possible applications. The word is found in OE as a byname, and in ME as a widely used affectionate term of address. It was also used as a term of status for a young man of noble birth, although the exact meaning is not clear; in the 13th and 14th cents. it was a technical term used of a young noble awaiting elevation to the knighthood. In other cases it may have been applied as a byname to a youth considerably younger than his brothers or to one who was a minor on the death of his father. 2. possibly a topographic name from OE *cielde* spring (water), a rare word apparently derived from *c(e)ald* cold.

Vars.: **Childe**, **Cheeld**, **Chill**.

Patrs. (from 1): **Childs**, **Chil(l)es**.

Childers English: apparently a habitation name from some lost place named *Childerhouse*, from OE *cildra*, gen. pl. of *cild* CHILD + *hūs* house. This may have referred to some form of orphanage perhaps run by a religious order, or perhaps the first element is to be understood in its later sense as a term of status (cf. CHILTON).

Vars.: **Childerhouse**, **Childress**.

Chilton English: habitation name from any of the various places so called, for example in Berks., Bucks., Co. Durham, Hants, Kent, Shrops., Somerset, Suffolk and Wilts. The overwhelming majority are shown by early forms to derive from OE *cild* CHILD + *tūn* enclosure, settlement; cf. CHILDERS. One place of this name in Somerset gets its first element from OE *cealc* chalk, limestone, and one on the Isle of Wight from the personal name *Cēola* (see CHILCOTT).

Chilver English: probably from a ME survival of the OE personal name *Cēolfrið*, composed of the elements *cēol* ship + *frið* peace.

Patr.: **Chilvers**.

Chinery *see* CHÊNE

Chinn English: nickname for someone with a prominent chin or else for someone notably clean-shaven, from OE *cin* chin.

Chiorrini *see* MELCHIOR

Chipman *see* CHAPMAN

Chippendale English (chiefly Lancs.): habitation name from *Chippingdale* in Lancs. near Clitheroe, so called from OE *cīeping* commerce, market (town) (cf. CHAPMAN) + ME *dale* valley (see DALE).

Vars.: **Chippindale**, **Chippindall**.

Chipperfield English: habitation name from a place in SW Herts., near Watford, so called from OE *cēapere* merchant (see CHAPMAN) + *feld* pasture, open country (see FIELD), i.e. probably an open space where markets were held.

Chirac French: habitation name from any of the various places, for example in Charente, Corrèze, and Lozère, so called from the Gallo-Roman personal name *Carius* (a deriv. of the Celt. root *car-* love; cf. CRADDOCK) + the local suffix *-ācum*.

Chisholm Scots: habitation name from *Chisholme* near Hawick in S Scotland, which derives its name from OE *cȳse, cēse* cheese (L *cāseus*; cf. CHEESEMAN) + *holm* piece of dry land in a fen (see HOLME 2) and refers to a waterside meadow good for dairy farming and hence for producing cheeses.

Vars.: **Chisholme**, **Chisolm**.

Chisnall English: habitation name from *Chisnall* Hall in Lancs., in which *Chisnall* is probably derived from an OE adj. **cisen* gravelly, from *cis* gravel + *halh* nook, hollow.

Chiswell English (chiefly Devon): apparently a habitation name from an unidentified minor place. The surname is recorded in the parish of Langford, Devon, in 1244, and again in 1332. There is an area in the parish of Ugborough, Devon, known as Inner and Outer *Chissels*, but this probably derives from the surname rather than vice versa. If it is a habitation name, the placename probably derives either from OE *cis* gravel or from the OE personal name *Cissa* (cf. CHICHESTER) + OE *well(a)* spring, stream (see WELL). The surname also became established in W Leics. in the early 17th cent.

Chittenden English: habitation name from a place in Kent, possibly so called from the gen. case of an OE personal name *Citta* (perhaps a byname derived from *cīð* shoot, sprout) + OE *denn* swine pasture.

Chitty English: 1. nickname from ME *chitte* pup, cub, young of an animal (apparently related to OE *cīð* shoot, sprout; cf. CHITTENDEN). 2. habitation name from a place so called in the parish of Chislet, Kent, or possibly from the manor of *Chiltley* in the parish of Bramshott, Hants, apparently so called from a Brit. hill name **celt* + OE *lēah* wood, clearing.

Vars.: **Chittey(e)**, **Chittie**.

Dim. (of 1): **Chittock** (chiefly Suffolk).

Chiva Catalan: habitation name from *Chiva* de Morella in the province of Castellón. In early records the placename is spelled *Xiva*; it is of uncertain, probably Mozarabic, origin.

Chiverall *see* CHEEVER

Chmielewski Polish: habitation name from any of various places deriving their names from Pol. *chmiel* hops + *-ew* suffix of placenames, with the addition of *-ski* suffix of local surnames (see BARANOWSKI).

Vars.: **Chmielecki**, **Chmieliński**, **Chmielnicki**; **Chmielowiec**; **Chmiel(a)** (probably a metonymic nickname for a drunkard).

Dim.: Czech: **Chmelíček**.

Chodakowski Polish: occupational name for a clog maker, in form a habitation name from Pol. *chodak* clog + *-ów* possessive suffix, with the addition of *-ski*, suffix of surnames (see BARANOWSKI).

Chodkiewicz *see* THÉODORE

Chodosh Jewish (Ashkenazic): nickname for a newcomer to a place (cf. NOVÁK and NEWMAN), from an Ashkenazic pronunciation of Hebr. *chadash* new.

Var.: **Chadash** (Israeli).

Choice English: probably a var. of JOYCE. There is a family tradition among bearers of the name that it means 'chosen', from ME, OF *chois* (of Gmc origin). In the Middle Ages the word was used both for an 'act of choosing' and a 'thing chosen', and as an adj. with the meaning 'chosen', 'select', 'favoured'. It is conceivable that this word could have given rise to a nickname, but in the absence of evidence to support this derivation, the question must remain open: the derivation may be merely the result of folk etymology.

Vars.: **Choyce**, **Choise**, **Choyse**.

Choiseul French: habitation name from a place in Haute-Marne, so called from a L personal name *Causius* + the Gaul. element *ialo* clearing, field.

Chojnacki Polish: topographic name for someone who lived among pine trees, from Pol. *choina* fir tree + *-ak* personal suffix, with the addition of *-ski*, suffix of local surnames (see BARANOWSKI).

Var.: **Chojnowski**.

Cholain *see* KOHL

Cholewiński Polish: occupational name for a bootmaker, in form a habitation name from Pol. *cholewa* upper part of a boot + *-in* possessive suffix, with the addition of *-ski*, suffix of surnames (see BARANOWSKI).

Var.: **Cholewicki**.

Cholmondeley English: habitation name from a place in Ches., so called from the OE personal name *Cēolmund* (composed of the elements *cēol* ship + *mund* protection) + OE *lēah* wood, clearing. The surname is normally pronounced /'tʃʌmlɪ/.

Vars.: **Cholmeley**, **Chumley**, **Chumbly**, **Chambly**.

Cholomin *see* BARTHOLOMEW

Cholwell *see* CALDWELL

Chomel *see* CHAUME

Chomicki *see* THOMAS

Chomont *see* CAUMONT

Chomsky Jewish (E Ashkenazic): habitation name from the town of *Chomsk*, with the addition of the Pol. local suffix *-ski* (see BARANOWSKI). The town was situated in the medieval Grand Duchy of Lithuania, but has successively fallen under the control of Poland and Russia. In America the name is normally pronounced /'tʃɑ:mski:/.

Var.: **Chomski**.

Choneau *see* MICHAEL

Chopin French and English: 1. nickname for a heavy drinker, from OF *chopine*, a (large) liquid measure (from MLG *schōpen* ladle), from which the derived verb *chopiner* has the sense 'tipple', 'drink'. Less plausibly, but more respectably, the surname may have been acquired as a metonymic occupational name for a maker of ladles or vessels used in the casting of metal, which were also called *chopines*. 2. nickname for a pugnacious person, from OF *chopin* violent blow (in form a dim. of *chop* blow, L *colpus*, from Gk *kolaphus*; cf. CAPSTICK).

Vars.: Fr.: **Chopy, Ch(o)upin**. Eng.: **Choppin(g), Choppen**.

Dims.: Fr.: **Chopinel, Chopinet**.

Choque French: **1**. habitation name from *Chocques* in Pasde-Calais, so called from a Picard dial. form of OF *souches* tree stumps (left in a patch of cleared land); see SUCH. **2**. nickname for a clumsy person, from a deriv. of OF *chocqu(i)er* to crash into (of Gmc origin, probably ultimately an imitative formation). **3**. nickname for a tippler, from Norman dial. *choque* toast, act of clinking glasses together, a sense development of the word given in 2.

Vars.: **Chocque, Choc(q)**.

Dims. (of 2 and 3): **Choqu(en)et, Choqueneau**.

Pej. (of 2 and 3): **Choquard**.

Chorley English: habitation name from any of various places, for example in Ches., Herts., Lancs., Shrops., and Staffs., so called from OE *ceorla*, gen. pl. of *ceorl* churl, peasant (cf. CHORLTON) + *lēah* wood, clearing.

Chorlton English: habitation name from any of the various places, in Ches., Lancs., and Staffs., so called from OE *ceorla*, gen. pl. of *ceorl* churl, peasant + *tūn* enclosure, settlement; see CHARLTON. Chorlton cum Hardy in Lancs., however, gets its first element from the OE personal name *Cēolfrið* (a cpd of *cēol* ship + *frið* peace).

Var.: **Cholton**.

Chossec see CHAUSSE

Chouan French: nickname for a raucous person, from OF *chouan* screech-owl (a word of imitative origin, perhaps taken from Gaul., and later altered by folk etymology to the form *chat-huant* howling cat).

Vars.: **Chua(n)t, Cahu**.

Dims.: **Ch(o)uet(te), Cah(o)uet** (later the name of the brown owl, but the terms were of more general meaning in the Middle Ages).

Pejs.: **Ch(o)u(an)ard**.

Chrichton see CREIGHTON

Chrisp see CRISP

Chrispin see CRISPIN

Christian English and French: from the OF given name *Christian* (L *Chrīstiānus* 'follower of *Christ*', L *Chrīstus*, Gk *Khrīstos*, a deriv. of *krīein* to anoint, calqued on Hebr. *mashiach* Messiah). This male given name was introduced into England following the Norman conquest, especially by Bret. settlers. It was also used in the same form as a female name, and in some cases the surname may be metronymic in origin.

Vars.: Eng.: **Christin(e)**. Fr.: **Crestien, Chrétien, Christin(e), Christiné, Christiane, C(h)resti(a)n**.

Dims.: Eng.: **Christie, Christ(e)y** (chiefly Scots and N Irish). Fr.: **Christinet, Crétinon, Crétinot**. Low Ger.: **Crist, Ki(r)st, Korst, Ke(r)st, Ka(r)st, Kirst(e)gen**. Ger. (of Slav. origin): **Krisch(e), Krischke, Kitschold, Kitschelt**. Czech: **Křížek; Křišťál, Krýsl**.

Aug.: Fr.: **Chrétinat**.

Patrs.: Low Ger.: **Kirstens, Kerstens, Ka(r)stens, Carstens; Christensen, Carstensen, Kastensen**. Fris.: **Cassens**. Flem., Norw., Dan.: **Christiansen, Kristiansen, Christensen, Kristensen**. Swed.: **Christiansson, Kristiansson,**

Christensson, Kristensson, Kristersson. Russ.: **Krestyan(in)ov** (largely from the sense 'peasant', 'farmer', 'worker on the land', borne by the word *khrestyanin* since the 14th cent.); **Khristinin** (metr.). Beloruss.: **Khrishtanovich**.

Patrs. (from dims.): Eng.: **Christison** (Scots). Ger.: **Christ(al)ler, Kristeller**. Low Ger.: **Kisting, Ke(r)sting, Kasting; Kürstgens, Corstgens, Körschkes, Köschges, Kerstgens**. Russ.: **Khristin**. Ukr.: **Khristin, Khristich**. Ger. (of Slav. origin): **Kitscher, Kitzer**. Croatian: **Hristić**. Gk: **Christou**.

Christmas English: nickname for someone born on Christmas Day, or who had some other particular association with that time of year, from OE *Crīstesmæsse* mass, festival of Christ.

Var.: **Chrismas**.

Christopher English: from a medieval given name which ostensibly means 'Bearer of Christ' (L *Chrīstopherus*, Gk *Khrīstophoros*, from *Khrīstos* Christ (cf. CHRISTIAN) + *pher-, phor-* carry). This was borne by a rather obscure 3rd-cent. martyred saint. His name was relatively common among early Christians, who desired to bear Christ metaphorically with them in their daily lives, but it was later explained by a wholly legendary story in which he carried the infant Christ across a ford and so became the patron saint of travellers. In this guise he was enormously popular in the Middle Ages, and many inns providing accommodation for travellers were named with this sign; in some instances the surname may have derived originally from residence at or association with an inn.

Vars.: **Stoffer, Stopher** (aphetic forms).

Dims.: Eng.: **Kit(t)**, KIDD; **Kitto(w)** (Cornwall). Fr.: **Christon**. It.: **Cristoforetti, Cristofolini, Toff(ol)etto, Fol(l)etti; Cristofolini, Toffolini, Folini; Cristofanini, Tof(f)anini; Tof(f)anelli**. Czech: **Krištůfek**. Pol.: **Krys(z)ka, Krystek; Krysztowczyk**. Rum.: **Cristea**.

Augs.: It.: **Toffoloni, Toffaloni**.

Patrs.: Eng.: **Christophers(on)**. It.: **De Cristoforo, De Cristofalo** (S Italy). Ger.: **Stoffler, Toffler**. Low Ger.: **Stoffers(en)**. Flem., Du.: **Christoffels, Stoffels**. Dan., Norw.: **Christophersen, Cristoffersen, Kristoffersen**. Swed.: **Kristoffersson**. Russ.: **Khristoforov**. Beloruss.: **Khrishtafovich**. Pol.: **Krysztofowicz; Kr(z)ysztofiak**. Bulg.: **Khristoforov**. Lithuanian: **Krishtopaitis**. Gk: **Christoforou**.

Patrs. (from dims.): Eng.: **Kitts, Kitson**. Rum.: **Cristescu**. Russ.: **Khristyukhin**. Pol.: **Kryszkiewicz; Krysiak**. Gk: **Christofides**.

Chruściel Polish: nickname from Pol. *chruściel* corncrake, a bird with speckled plumage and reddish wings inhabiting fields and meadows. The Pol. word is ultimately derived from Slav. *chrust-* to rustle, and so is cogn. with Russ. *khrushch* may beetle (see KHRUSHCHEV).

Habitation name: **Chruścielewski**.

Chrystal see CRISTAL

Chrzanowski Polish: habitation name from a place named from Pol. *chrzan* horseradish (cogn. with Czech *křen*) + *-ów* possessive suffix, with the addition of *-ski*, suffix of local surnames (see BARANOWSKI).

Russ.: **Khrenov** (patr. in form).

Dim.: Czech: **Křenek**.

Chrząszczyński see KHRUSHCHEV

Chuanard see CHOUAN

Chubb English (chiefly W Country): nickname from the fish, *Leuciscus cephalus*, ME *chubbe* (of unknown origin). The fish is notable for its short, fat shape and sluggish habits. The word is well attested in ME as a description of an indolent, stupid, or physically awkward person, and this is probably the origin of mod. Eng. *chubby*, although the vocab. word has lost any pejorative overtones.

Chuck *see* SUCH

Chudzik Polish: nickname for a thin man, from Pol. *chudy* thin.

Chue *see* CHEW

Chumbly *see* CHOLMONDELEY

Chupin *see* CHOPIN

Church English: topographic surname for someone who lived near a church. The vocab. word comes from OE *cyrice* (LGk *kyrikon*, for earlier *kyriakon* (*dōma*) (house) of the Lord, from *kyrios* lord; cf. KIRILOV).
Vars.: **Churcher, Churchman**. See also KIRK.

Churchill English: habitation name from any of various places, for example in Devon, Oxon., Somerset, and Worcs., so called from OE *cyrice* CHURCH + *hyll* HILL. In some cases (e.g. in Oxon. and Devon) the placenames may originally have contained as their first element the Brit. name *crūc* hill, but if so this was altered early on as the result of folk etymology.

Churchyard English: topographic name for someone who lived by a churchyard, or metonymic occupational name for someone who was employed to look after one, from ME CHURCH + *yard* enclosure (OE *geard*).
Var.: **Churchard**.

Churm English (Yorks.): probably a nickname for a noisy person or a chatterbox, from ME *churme, chirme* hubbub, birdsong (OE *cierm* noise).

Chwedko *see* THÉODORE

Chynoweth *see* CHENOWETH

Cianelli *see* JOHN

Ciardo Italian: from a medieval given name, an aphetic form of RICHARD.
Var.: **Ciardi**.
Dims.: **Ciardelli, Ciard(i)ello, Ciardetti, Ciardini, Ciardulli, Ciardullo, Ciardin** (Venetia). Fr.: **C(h)ardin(eau), Chardy, Chardel, C(h)ardot, C(h)ardon, C(h)ardet, Cardinet**.
Augs.: It.: **Ciardon(e)** (Venetia).

Cibula *see* ZWIEBEL

Ciccetti *see* FRANCIS

Cichle *see* KEIGHLEY

Cichy Polish: nickname for a quiet person, from Pol. *cichy* quiet, calm (cf. TIKHONOV).
Vars.: **Cichoń; Cichosz, Cichocki, Cichecki**.
Dims.: Pol.: **Cichończyk**. Czech: **Ticháček**.
Patr.: Pol.: **Cichowicz**.

Cid Spanish and Portuguese: from a medieval given name, of uncertain origin and meaning. It occurs in L documents of the Middle Ages in the form *Citi*, and is apparently distinct from the honorific title *Cid* (from Arabic *sayyid* lord) borne by Christian overlords with Moslem vassals.

Cieślak Polish: occupational name for a carpenter, from Pol. *cieśla* carpenter (cogn. with Russ. *teslo* adze) + the redundant agent suffix *-ak*.
Vars.: **Cieśla; Ciesielski** (with surname suffix *-ski*; see BARANOWSKI).
Dims.: Pol.: **Cieślik**. Czech: **Tesařik, Tesárek**. Ukr.: **Teslenko**. Beloruss.: **Teslyuk**.
Patr.: Pol.: **Cieślewicz**.

Cifaro S Italian (esp. Campania and Apulia): nickname from the S It. dial. term *cifaro, cifero* devil, demon (an aphetic form of the personal name ascribed to the fallen angel, L *Lūcifer* 'bearer of light', from *lux*, gen. *lūcis*, light + *ferre* to bear, bring). The first syllable was lost because it was understood as the regional form, *lu*, of the def. art.
Vars.: **Cefaro, Cifero**.
Dims.: **Cifariello, Cefariello, Cifarelli**.

Cifuentes Spanish: habitation name from any of various places, for example in the provinces of León and Guadalajara, so called from Sp. *cien* hundred (L *centum*) + *fuentes* springs (L *fontes*; see FONT). The places were so named because of the abundance of natural springs in the area.

Cigler *see* ZIEGLER

Čihák Czech: 1. occupational name for a fowler, Czech *čihăr*, from the verb *čihat* to lie in wait. 2. occupational name for a blacksmith, from the vocab. word *čihák*, which denoted one of the implements used by blacksmiths.

Cimbal *see* ZIMBALIST

Cimerman *see* ZIMMERMANN

Cinelli *see* FRANCIS

Ciobanu Rumanian (partly Jewish): occupational name for a shepherd, from *cioban* shepherd (a borrowing of Turkish *çoban*), with the addition of the def. art. *-u*.
Var.: **Cioban**.

Ciotto *see* FRANCIS

Cipran *see* CEBRIÁN

Circuit English (Beds.): a rare surname, apparently a late respelling, under the influence of folk etymology, of a name representing the local pronunciation of *Southcott* in the parish of Linslade, Bucks. (near the Beds. border).
Vars.: **Sircutt, Sirkett, Surcutt, Surcot, Surcoate, Cercott**.

Cisneros Spanish: habitation name from a place in the province of Palencia, originally named with a deriv. of Sp. *cisne* swan (via OF from L *cycnus*, Gk *kyknos*).

Cissen *see* FRANCIS

Ciszewski Polish: habitation name from a place called *Ciszew* (from Pol. *cisza* silence (cf. CICHY) + *-ew* possessive suffix), with the addition of *-ski*, suffix of local surnames (see BARANOWSKI).

Citroen Dutch and Flemish: metonymic occupational name for a grower or seller of lemons, or perhaps a nickname for a sharp and disagreeable person (cf. CRABBE), from MDu. *citroen* lemon (OF *citron*, from L *citrus* lemon tree).

Patrs.: Jewish: **Citronowicz**, **Cytrynowicz**, **Cytrynowitz**.

City English: of uncertain origin. The earliest form that looks as though it might belong here is William *Citti* of Highclere, Hants, recorded in the 13th cent., but this may well be a form of CHITTY. All present-day non-Jewish bearers of the name seem to belong to a single line, which can be traced back to the early 17th cent. and has always been confined to the London area. It is possible that the original bearer was an immigrant (possibly a Huguenot) who adopted this name on moving to the City of London. The name is also sometimes borne by Jews, in which case its origin is unknown.

Ciurana Catalan: habitation name from a place in the province of Gerona, earlier called *Siverana*. The name is from L *Severiāna* (*villa*) 'estate (see VILLE) of *Severus*'; cf. SÉVERIN.

Claasen see KLAUS

Clachar Scots: occupational name for a stonemason, Gael. *clachair*, an agent deriv. of *clach* stone.

Var.: **Clacher**.

Patr.: **McClacher**.

Clack English: from an OE personal name or byname *Clacc*, or the cogn. ON *Klakkr*. The name is of uncertain origin; it may have been an imitative formation given originally to a chatterer, or it may have described a lumpish person (cf. CLAUGHTON).

Claffey Irish: Anglicized form of Gael. **Mac Fhlaithimh**, patr. from the personal name *Flaitheamh* 'Prince'.

Vars.: **Claffy**; **McClave**.

Clague see CLEGG

Clake see CLEAK

Clamp English: of uncertain origin, probably from the vocab. word denoting an iron band for binding things together (a borrowing from Du., first attested in the 15th cent). This may have been used as a nickname for someone with a 'vice-like' grip, or more plausibly a metonymic occupational name for a smith who specialized in making clamps.

Clancy Irish: Anglicized form of Gael. **Mac Fhlannchaidh**, patr. from the personal name *Flannchadh*, which is derived from *flann* red; cf. FLYNN.

Var.: **Glancy**.

Clapham English: habitation name from any of various places, for example in Beds., Surrey, Sussex, and W Yorks., so called from OE **clop* lump, hillock (cf. CLAPP) + *hām* homestead.

Claplin see McLACHLAN

Clapp English (chiefly Bristol): nickname for a large and ungainly person, ME *cloppe*, *le clop*, from OE **clop* lump, hillock.

Vars.: **Clap**, **Clappe**.

Patrs.: **Clapson** (Sussex); **Clappison** (Yorks).

Clare 1. Irish and English: habitation name from *Clare* in Suffolk, apparently so called from a Brit. river name which may have had the meaning 'bright', 'gentle', or 'warm'. **2.** English: habitation name from *Clare* in Oxon., so called from OE *clǣg* clay + *ōra* slope. **3.** English: from the ME, OF female given name *Cla(i)re* (L *Clāra*, from *clārus* famous), which achieved a moderate popularity, greater on the Continent than in England, through the fame of St Clare of Assisi. See also SINCLAIR. **4.** English: occupational name for a worker in clay, for example someone expert in building in wattle and daub, from a ME deriv. of OE *clǣg* clay, with the agent suffix *-er*.

Vars.: **Claire**, **Clear(e)**, **Clere**.

Aug. (of 3): It.: **Chiaroni**.

Metrs. (from 3): It.: **De Chiara**, **Di Chiara**.

Clarges English: occupational name for the servant of a clergyman, from *clargies*, gen. case of ME *clergie* the clergy, a clergyman (from OF *clergie*, a deriv. of *clerc*, see CLARK; for the change of *-er-* to *-ar-* cf. MARCHANT). In a few cases, the surname may have been acquired by the son of a clergyman in minor orders.

Var.: **Clargis**.

Claridge English: **1.** from the ME, OF female given name *Clarice* (L *Clāritia* 'Fame', 'Brightness', a deriv. of *clārus* famous, bright; cf. CLARE 1). **2.** habitation name from *Clearhedge* Wood in Sussex, which is of obscure etymology; the second element is presumably OE *hecg* hedge, the first is unidentified.

Vars.: **Clarage**. (Of 1 only): **Claris**.

Dim. (of 1): Fr.: **Clarisseau**.

Clark English: occupational name for a scribe or secretary, or for a member of a minor religious order. Originally the word *clerc* denoted a member of a religious order, from OE *cler(e)c* priest, reinforced by OF *clerc* (both from LL *clēricus*, from Gk *klērikos*, a deriv. of *klēros* inheritance, legacy, with reference to the priestly tribe of Levites (see LEVI) 'whose inheritance was the Lord'). For the regular change of *-er-* to *-ar-* see MARCHANT. Clergy in minor orders were permitted to marry and so found families; thus the surname could become established. In the Middle Ages it was virtually only members of religious orders who learned to read and write, so that the term *clerk* came also to be used of any literate man. In many cases the surname may have referred originally to a professional secretary.

Vars.: **Clarke**, **Clerk(e)**.

Dims.: Fr.: **Clergeau**, **Clergeot**, **Clerjot**, **Clergeon**, **Clerget**. It.: **Chiericetti**, **Clericetti**.

Patrs.: Eng.: **Clar(k)son**; **Clarkstone** (Notts.). Fr.: **Auclerc**, **Duclerc**, **Duclert**. Du.: **Clerkx**, **Cler(c)x**. Flem.: **Cler(c)(k)x**.

Equivs. (not cogn.): See at SCRIBE.

Clarkins see CLEARY

Clasby English: apparently a habitation name from an unidentified place, probably in N England and perhaps so called from a Scandinavian form of NICHOLAS (see KLAUS) + Northern ME *by* settlement (ON *býr*).

Vars.: **Clasbey**, **Clasbye**, **Clasbie**, **Clasbery**, **Clasbury**.

Clatworthy English: habitation name from a place in Somerset, so called from OE *clāte* burdock + *worðig* enclosure (see WORTHY 1).

Var.: **Clotworthy**.

Claude French: from a medieval given name (L *Claudius*, a Roman family name derived from *claudus* lame) which was popular as a result of having been borne by a 7th-cent. saint, bishop of Besançon.

Vars.: **Claud**, **Claux**, CLOT.

Dims.: Fr.: **Claudel**, **Claudet**, **Claudin**, **Claudon**, **Claudot**; **Glodeau**; **Clodic** (Brittany). Port.: **Claudino**.

Patrs.: Flem.: **Cloots**, **Clotten(s)**.

Claughton English (chiefly Yorks.): habitation name from a place so called, of which there are two in Lancs. and one in Ches. Ekwall derives the name from ON *klakkr* lump (i.e. lump-shaped hill, but cf. CLACK) + OE *tūn* enclosure, settlement.

Clauzel see CLOSE

Claveau see CRAVO

Clavero Spanish: occupational name for someone who had charge of keys, a chatelain or treasurer or a ceremonial official, from an agent deriv. of OSp. *clave* key (L *clavis*).

Var.: **Llavero**.

Dims.: Prov.: **Clavereau**, **Clavareau**.

Claxton English: habitation name from any of the various places, for example in Co. Durham, Norfolk, and N Yorks., so called from the gen. case of the OE personal name *Clacc* or ON *Klakkr* (see CLACK) + OE *tūn* enclosure, settlement.

Clay English: topographic name for someone who lived in an area of clay soil, or occupational name for a worker in a claypit, from OE *clǣg* clay.

Vars.: **Claye**; **Clayman**; CLARE.

Claydon English: habitation name from any of the various places, for example in Suffolk, Bucks., and Oxon., so called from OE *clǣg* CLAY + *dūn* hill (see DOWN 1).

Var.: **Clayden**.

Clayton English: habitation name from any of the various places, for example in Lancs., Staffs., Sussex, and W Yorks., so called from OE *clǣg* clay + *tūn* enclosure, settlement.

Cleak English: of uncertain origin. The first possible instance is William *Cleike* (Yorks 1176), but this may well be a mistake for *Clerke*. In subsequent records the name is concentrated in Devon, and seems to have been originally a habitation name connected with a piece of land in the parish of Ermington near Plymouth, first recorded in 1278 as *Clekeland(e)*, and still known as *Clickland*; the surnames John *de Clakelond* and Robert *Cleaklond* occur within this parish in 1332 and 1337 respectively. The placename may be from OE *cleaca* stepping stone, boundary stone (of Celt. origin; cf. CLACHAR) + *land* territory.

Vars.: **Cleake**, **Cleek(e)**, **Cleke**, **Cleik(e)**, **Cleeick**, **Clake**, **Click**. See also CLACK.

Clear see CLARE

Cleary Irish: occupational name for a clerk, from Gael. *cléireach* (from LL *clēricus*; cf. CLARK).

Var.: **Clery**.

Patrs.: **McCleary**, **McCleery**, **McC(h)lery**, **McAle(a)ry**, **McAlary**, **McLeary**, **McLeery** (Gael. **Mac Cléirich**).

'Descendant of the clerk': **O'Cle(a)ry** (Gael. **Ó Cléirigh**).

'Descendant of the clerk (dim.)': **O'Clearkane**, **O'Clercan**, **Clerihan**, **Clerkan**, **Clerkin**, **Clarkins** (Gael. **Ó Cléireacháin**, **Ó Cléirchín**).

Cleatherow see CLITHEROE

Cleave see CLIVE

Cleaver English: 1. occupational name for a butcher or someone who split wood into planks by the use of wedges, from OE *clēofan* to split, cut. 2. var. of CLIVE.

Vars.: **Cleever**; **Clover**.

Clee English: 1. habitation name from *Clee* or *Cleobury* in Shrops., which are of uncertain etymology, probably from an ancient Brit. hill-name. Ekwall comments that derivation of this from OE *clǣg* CLAY seems unlikely, since the Clee Hills are noted for their hard rock. 2. topographic name from OE *clawu*, *clēo* claw, cloven hoof, used in the sense of a fork in a river or road.

Cleeick see CLEAK

Cleeve English: habitation name or topographic name, a var. of CLIVE, found chiefly in Gloucs. and Somerset. There are places of this name in Gloucs., Somerset, and Worcs.

Vars.: **Cleeves**; **Cleve** (name of a place in Herefords.).

Cleever see CLEAVER

Cleft see CLIFT

Clegg 1. English (chiefly Lancs. and Yorks.): habitation name from a place in Lancs., so called from ON *kleggi* haystack, originally the name of a nearby hill. 2. Manx: Anglicized form of Gael. **Mac Liaigh** 'son of the physician', from *mac* son + *liaigh* physician (cf. LEACH 1).

Var. (of 2): **Clague**.

Cleghorn Scots: habitation name from either of two minor places of this name in the former county of Lanarks., now part of Strathclyde region.

Cleland 1. Irish: Anglicized form of Gael. *Mac Giolla Fhaoláin*; see WHELAN. 2. habitation name from *Clelland* near Motherwell, probably so called from OE *clǣg* CLAY + *land* land.

Var.: **Clelland**.

Clement 1. English and Dutch: from a ME, OF male given name (L *Clēmens* 'Merciful', gen. *Clēmentis*) which achieved popularity firstly through having been borne by an early saint who was a disciple of St Paul, and later because it was selected as a symbolic name by a number of early popes. There has also been considerable confusion with the originally distinct male given name *Clemence* (in part a female given name, from L *Clēmentia* 'Mercy', an abstract noun derived from the adj.; in part a masc. name from L *Clēmentius*, a later deriv. of *Clēmens*). **2.** Cornish: habitation name from the parish of St *Clement*, near Truro.

Vars.: Eng.: **Clemett**, **Clemitt**.

Dims. (of 1): Eng.: **Clem(m)**; **Clemmey**, **Climie** (largely Scots); **Clem(m)o(w)**, **Climo**, **Clymo**, **Clyma**, **Clymer** (Cornish). Fr.: **Clémentel**, **Clémentet**, **Clemendet**, **Clemendot**, **Clémot**; **Clemenceau**, **Clemencet**, **Clemençon**, **Clemenson**, **Clemanceau**, **Clemançon**. It.: **Clementini**, **Clementucci**. Low Ger.: **Kliemchen**, **Kliemke**. Ger. (of Slav. origin): **Klem(p)ke**, **Klim(p)ke**, **Klampke**, **Klim(m)ek**, **Klima**, **Kli(m)sch**, **Klich(e)**, **Klimschak**. Pol.: **Klimek**; **Klich(e)**. Czech: **Klíma**, **Klimeš**. Beloruss.: **Klimentyonok**, **Klimuk**. Ukr.: **Klimko**, **Klimchuk**, **Klimus**.

Patrs. (from 1): Eng.: **Clements**, **Clemon(t)s**; **Clemetts**; **Clem(m)ens**, **Clem(m)ans**, **Clemence**, **Climance**, **Clemas**, **Climas**; **Cleme(n)tson**, **Cleminson**, **Climenson**, **Clemerson**. It. **De Clemente**, **Di Clemente**. Ger.: **Klemen(t)z**, **Klemz**. Dan.: **Clem(m)ensen**. Russ.: **Klimentov**, **Klimentyev**. Beloruss., Ukr.: **Klimontovich**. Pol.: **Klemensiewicz**. Croatian: **Klemenčić**.

Patrs. (from dims. of 1): Eng.: **Clem(p)son**, **Climpson**. Low Ger.: **Klem(p)s**. Ger. (of Slav. origin): **Klicher**. Russ.: **Klim(k)ov**, **Klim(och)kin**, **Klimushev**, **Klishin**. Beloruss.: **Klimkovich**, **Klimashevich**. Ukr.: **Klim(k)ovich**. Pol.: **Klimowicz**, **Klimkiewicz**; **Klimczak**. Finn.: **Miettinen**.

Habitation names (cogn. with 1): Pol.: **Klimaszewski**, **Klim(k)owski**.

Clench *see* CLINCH

Clendennen *see* GLENDINNING

Clere *see* CLARE

Clergeau *see* CLARK

Clerihew Scots (chiefly Aberdeen): of uncertain origin, not recorded before the 17th cent.

Clermont French: habitation name from any of the various places so called, from OF *clair*, *cler* bright, clear (cf. CLARE 1) + *mont* hill (see MONT), i.e. a hill that could be seen a long way off.

Cléry French: habitation name from any of the various places so called from the Gallo-Roman personal name *Clārius* (a deriv. of *Clārus*; see CLARE 1) + the local suffix *-ācum*.

Cleugh *see* CLOUGH

Cleveland English: regional name from the district around Middlesbrough, so called from OE *clif* cliff (see CLIVE) + *land* land.

Cleverley English: probably a habitation name from *Cleveley* in Lancs., with intrusive -r- under the influence of the vocabulary word *cleverly*. The place gets its name from OE *clif* cliff (see CLIVE) + *lēah* wood, clearing.

Vars.: **Cleverly**, **Cleveley**.

Clewer English (W Midlands): habitation name, probably from either of the two places, in Berks. and Somerset, so called from the OE tribal name *Clifware* dwellers on the hill or slope, from OE *clif* slope (see CLIVE) + *ware* inhabitants.

Click *see* CLEAK

Clifford English: habitation name from any of the various places, for example in Devon, Gloucs., Herefords., and W Yorks., so called from OE *clif* slope (see CLIVE) + *ford* FORD.

Var.: **Clifforth**.

Clift English: topographic name for someone who lived by a crevice in rock, ME *clift* cleft, past part. of *cleave*, *cleeve* to split (OE *cleofian*).

Var.: **Cleft**.

Clifton English: habitation name from any of the numerous places in all parts of England so called, from OE *clif* slope (see CLIVE) + *tūn* enclosure, settlement.

Climance *see* CLEMENT

Clinch English: **1.** habitation name from a place in Wilts., so called from OE **clenc* lump, hill. The same term seems also to have been used of a patch of dry raised ground in fenland surroundings, and the surname may be of topographic origin, from this sense. **2.** occupational name for a maker or fixer of bolts and rivets, from a deriv. of ME *clench(en)* to fix firmly (OE *clencian*).

Vars.: **Clench**. (Of 2 only): **Clink(er)** (N England).

Clindening *see* GLENDINNING

Cline *see* KLEIN

Clingerman *see* KLINGER

Clinton English: habitation name, either from *Glympton* in Oxon., named as 'settlement on the river *Glyme*', or from *Glinton* in Northants, recorded in 1060 as *Clinton* (from an unrecorded OE element akin to MLG *glinde* enclosure, fence + OE *tūn* enclosure, settlement).

Cliquet French: apparently a nickname from OF *cliquet*, the sound of a bell (an imitative formation). This may in effect have been an occupational name for a bellringer or for a wandering pedlar who rang a handbell to advise people of his approach, much like the modern rag-and-bone merchant or ice-cream salesman.

Vars.: **Cliquot**, **Cloquet(te)**.

Clitheroe English: habitation name from a place in Lancs., perhaps from ON *kliðra* song-thrush + *haugr* hill. The first element may alternatively be an OE word, *clӯder* loose stones.

Vars.: **Clitherow**, **Cleatherow**, **Cluderay**.

Clive English: habitation name from a place named from OE *clif* slope, bank, cliff, or topographic name from the same word used independently. The OE word was used not only in the sense of mod. Eng. *cliff* but also of much gentler slopes and frequently also of a riverbank. The surname in the form *Clive* reflects the dat. case of the OE word, originally used after a preposition; the var. in *-s* preserves the OE gen. ending. *Clive* is most common in Ches. and Shrops., and it probably derives principally from the places so called in those two counties.

Vars.: **Clives**, **Clyve**, **Cliff(e)**; **Cleave(s)** (chiefly Devon); CLEEVE.

Clodic *see* CLAUDE

Clohessy Irish: Anglicized form of Gael. **Ó Clochasaigh** 'descendant of *Clochasach*', a personal name apparently derived from *cloch* stone (cf. CLACHAR).

Cloquet see CLIQUET

Close English: 1. topographic name for someone who lived by an enclosure of some sort, such as (in towns) a courtyard set back from the main street or (in country districts) a farmyard, from ME *clos(e)* (OF *clos*, from LL *clausum*, past part. of *claudere* to close, shut). 2. nickname for a reserved or secretive person, from ME *clos(e)* secret.
Vars.: **Cluse, Closs**; CLOWES; **Clowser**.
Dims. (of 1): Fr.: **Clo(u)sel, Clusel, Clo(u)seau, Clo(u)zel, Cl(a)uzel, Clo(u)zeau, Cluzeau(x), Closset, Closson, Clauzet, Clauzin, Ducl(o)uzeau, Descl(o)uzeaux**.

Clot 1. French: var. of CLAUDE. 2. French: var. of *Clos* (see CLOSE). 3. Catalan: topographic name for someone who lived by a pit or hollow, from the dial. term *clot*, used of a depression in the ground (apparently of pre-Roman origin).
Dim. (of 3): **Clotet**.

Clothier English (now mainly Bristol): occupational name for a maker or seller of cloth and clothes, from ME *cloth* (OE *clāð*) + the agent suffix -*(i)er*.
Var.: **Clother**.

Clotworthy see CLATWORTHY

Cloud 1. English: topographic name for someone who lived near an outcrop or hill, from OE *clūd* rock (only later used of the formations in the sky). 2. French: from the Gmc personal name *Hlodald*, composed of the elements *hlōd* fame + *wald* rule, which was borne by a saint and bishop of the 6th cent.
Vars. (of 1): **Cloude**. (Of 2): **Clou(x)** (see also CLOSE).
Dims. (of 2): **Clouet; Closon** (Belgium).

Clough English: topographic name for someone who lived near a precipitous slope, from OE *clōh* ravine.
Vars.: **Cleugh, Cluff; Cloke** (Devon); **Clow, Clew, Clue**; CLOWES, **Clew(e)s** (W Midlands; from the gen. case).

Clout English: metonymic occupational name for a repairer of clothes, shoes, or household utensils, or a nickname for a wearer of much-mended clothes, from ME *clut* patch (OE *clūt*).
Vars.: **Cloutt, Clouter, Cloutman**.

Cloutot see CRAVO

Clover see CLEAVER

Clowes English: 1. var. of CLOUGH (pronounced /klaʊz/). 2. var. of CLOSE (pronounced /kləʊz/).

Cloy see LEWIS

Clucas see LUCAS

Cluderay see CLITHEROE

Clue see CLOUGH

Clune Irish: Anglicized form of Gael. **Mac Glúin**, patr. from the personal name *Glún*. This is either a byname meaning 'Knee', or else a short form of various OIr. cpd

names such as *Glúnfhionn* 'Fair-kneed' or *Glúncoramhn* 'Iron-kneed'.
Vars.: **McClo(o)ne**.

Cluse see CLOSE

Clutterbuck English: of unknown origin, possibly an Anglicized garbling of a Du. name.

Clyde Scots and N Irish: apparently a topographic name for someone who lived on the banks of the river *Clyde* (Gael. *Cluaidh*, probably of pre-Celtic origin), which flows through Glasgow.

Clyma see CLEMENT

Clyne 1. Scots: habitation name from any of various places so called, from Gael. *claon* slope. 2. Jewish (Ashkenazic): Anglicized spelling of KLEIN.

Clynes 1. Scots: var. of CLYNE 1. 2. English: habitation name from *Claines*, just north of Worcester, recorded as *Cl(e)ynes* in the 13th cent. It is by the river Severn, and gets its name from OE *clǣg* CLAY + *nǣss* ness, point of land.

Clynmans see KLEIN

Clyve see CLIVE

Coad English (Devon): probably a metonymic occupational name for a cobbler's assistant, from ME *cōde* cobbler's wax. Alternatively, it may possibly be a topographic name from OCorn. *cuit* wood.
Var.: **Code**.

Coady see CODY

Coakley Irish: Anglicized form of Gael. **Mac Caochlaoich**, patr. from *Caochlaoch*, a personal name composed of the elements *caoch* blind + *laoch* warrior, hero.

Coales see COLE

Coates 1. English: topographic name for someone who lived in a relatively humble dwelling, from the gen. sing. or nom. pl. case of ME *cote, cott* shelter, cottage (OE *cot*). Cf. COTTER 1. 2. English: habitation name from any of the numerous English places named with this word, esp. *Coates* in Cambs. and *Cotes* in Leics. 3. Scots: var. of COUTTS.
Vars.: **Cotes, Coat(t)s, Cottis; Co(a)te** (from the dat. sing.); **Co(a)tman; Dallicoat, Dallicote, Delicate** (with fused ANF preposition and article).

Cobb English: 1. from the ME byname or personal name *Cobbe, Cobba*, or the cogn. ON *Kobbi*, both of which are probably from an element meaning 'lump', used to denote a large man. 2. aphetic form of JACOB.
Vars.: **Cobbe, Cob**.

Cobbold English (chiefly E Anglia): from the ME personal name *Cutebald, Cubald*, OE *Cūðbeald*, composed of the elements *cūð* famous, well-known + *beald* bold, brave.
Vars.: **Cobbald, Cobbett**.

Cobden English: habitation name from either of two places, in Derbys. and Devon, so called from the OE personal name *Cobba* (see COBB 1) + OE *dūn* hill (see DOWN 1).

Cobelli see JACOB

Cobham English: habitation name from a place so called, probably one of those in Kent, Surrey, or Sussex, although the surname is now more common in Lancs. The placenames derive from the OE personal name *Cobba* (see COBB 1) + OE *hām* homestead, except for the one in Surrey, which was originally *Coveham* and so probably derives from the OE personal name *Cofa* + *hām*.

Coblance see KOBLENZ

Coblence see KOBLENZ

Cobley English: habitation name from either of two places in Devon called *Cobley*, from the OE personal name *Cobba* (see COBB 1) + OE *lēah* wood, clearing.

Var.: **Cobleigh**.

Cobo 1. Spanish: popular form of the medieval nickname *Calvo* 'Bald' (L *calvus*; see CHAFF). 2. Spanish: habitation name from any of various minor places. They may have been so called from the same word as in 1, referring to a bare and treeless appearance, or alternatively the placename may be from LL *cova* hollow (of Gmc origin; cf. COVE). 3. Italian: aphetic short form of *Giacobo*; see JACOB.

Vars. (of 1 and 2): **Covo**. (Of 2 only): **Cobos** (the name of places in the provinces of Palencia and Segovia).

Dim.: Sp.: **Covillo**.

Coburn see COCKBURN

Cocci see DOMINIQUE

Coccimano see KUZMIN

Cochrane Scots: habitation name from lands in the parish of Paisley, near Glasgow. The placename is of uncertain origin, perhaps from a Brit. cogn. of W *coch* red (cf. GOUGH 2), although this etymology is not supported by the earliest recorded spelling, *Coueran*.

Vars.: **Cochran**, **Cochren**, **Colqueran**.

Cock English: 1. nickname from the bird, ME *cok*, OE *cocc*, given for a variety of possible reasons. Applied to a young lad who strutted proudly like a cock, it soon became a generic term for a youth and was attached with hypocoristic force to the short forms of many medieval given names (e.g. ALCOCK, *Hancock*, *Hiscock*, *Mycock*). The nickname may also have referred to a natural leader, or an early riser, or a lusty or aggressive individual. The surname may also occasionally derive from the cock used as a house sign. 2. from the ME byname *le Cok*, OE *Cocca*, derived from the word given in 1 above or from the homonymous *cocc* hillock, clump, lump, and so denoting a fat and awkward man. This name is not independently attested, but appears to lie behind a number of placenames and (probably) the medieval given name *Cock*, which was still in use in the late 13th cent.

Dims. (of 1): Eng.: **Cocklin(g)**; **Cock(e)rell**, **Cock(e)rill**, **Cockarill**. Fr.: **Co(c)quet**, **Coc(que)teau**, **Coquot**, **Coquel(et)**, **Coquelin**, **Coclet**, **Coclin**, **Cochet**, **Cochey**, **Cochez**, **Cocheteau**, **Cochin(eau)**, **Cochy**.

Patrs.: Eng.: **Cocks**, Cox; **Coxon**, **Coxen**; **Cocking**. Fr.: **Aucoc**.

Cockayne English: nickname for an idle dreamer, from ME *cokayne* cloud-cuckooland, an imaginary paradise (OF *(pays de) cocaigne*, from MLG *kōkenje*, a dim. of *kōke* cake, since in this land the very houses were supposed to be made of cake).

Cockburn Scots and Northumbrian: habitation name from a place in the former county of Berwicks. (now part of Borders region) so called from OE *cocc* cock (or the byname *Cocca*; see COCK 2) + *burna* stream (see BOURNE). The surname is normally pronounced /'koubʌrn/ (in S England /'kəubɜːn/), apparently to veil the imagined indelicacy of the first syllable.

Var.: **Coburn**.

Cockcroft English (Yorks. and Lancs.): habitation name from an unidentified place named as an enclosure where poultry were raised, from OE *cocc* COCK + *croft* paddock, smallholding (see CROFT).

Var.: **Cockroft**.

Cockell English: from ME, OF *cokille* shell (derived via L from Gk *konkhylion*, a dim. of *konkhē* shellfish). The name could be a metonymic occupational name for a gatherer and seller of shellfish, or it could be a nickname for someone who had been on a pilgrimage to Santiago (cf. KUMSTELLER) and wore a cockle badge in commemoration. The word was also applied in the Middle Ages to a type of woman's head-dress that somewhat resembled the mollusc in form, and so the surname may also have arisen as a metonymic occupational name for a milliner who produced such items.

Vars.: **Cockill**, **Cockle**. Dim.: Fr.: **Coquillon**.

Cocker English: 1. nickname for a bellicose person, from ME *cock* to fight, wrangle (a deriv. of OE *cocc* cock; cf. COCK 1). 2. occupational name for someone who was particularly skilled in building haystacks, from ME *cock* heap of hay (of ON origin, or from OE **cocc* mound, hill; cf. COCK 2).

Cockerham English: habitation name from a place in Lancs., so called from the river *Cocker* (a Brit. name apparently derived from an element **kukro* winding; cf. OIr. *cúcar* crooked, awkward) + OE *hām* homestead. The surname is now most common in this form in the Leeds area; in the var. **Cockram** around Bristol.

Cockman see COOK

Codd 1. English: metonymic occupational name for a maker of purses and bags, from OE *cod* bag. 2. English: metonymic nickname for a man noted for his apparent sexual prowess, from *cod(piece)*, the garment worn in Tudor times prominently over the male genitals. 3. English: metonymic occupational nickname for a fish-monger, from ME *cod*, the fish (of uncertain origin, perhaps a transferred use of 1). 4. Irish: var. of CODY.

Var. (of 1–3): **Codman**.

Dim. (of 1–3): CODLIN.

Code see COAD

Codgbrook English: habitation name from *Cottesbrook* in Northants, so called from the gen. case of the OE personal name **Cott* + OE *brōc* stream (see BROOK).

Var.: **Cotsbrooke**.

Codina Catalan: topographic name for someone who lived on a piece of stony land that could be worked only with difficulty, Cat. *codina* (LL *cotīna*, a deriv. of *cotis* stone).

Codlin English: 1. double dim. of CODD. 2. nickname for a brave man, or ironically for an exceptionally timorous one, from OF *ceur de lion* 'lion heart' (cf. COEUR).
Vars.: **Codling** (Yorks.); **Quodling**, **Quadling** (Norfolk, Suffolk); **Girling**, **Gurling** (Suffolk, Essex, Norfolk).

Codrington English: habitation name from a place in Gloucs., so called from OE *Cūðeringatūn* 'settlement (OE *tūn*) associated with *Cūðhere*', a personal name composed of the elements *cūð* famous, well-known + *here* army.

Codron *see* CALDERON

Cody Irish: 1. Anglicized form of Gael. **Ó Cuidighthigh** 'descendant of *Cuidightheach*', a byname for a helpful person. 2. Anglicized form of Gael. **Mac Óda** 'son of *Óda*', a personal name of uncertain origin. This name was taken by a family in Kilkenny formerly known as *Archdeacon*.
Vars. (of 1): **Coady**; **O'Codihie**, **O'Kuddyhy**, **O'Cuddie**, **Cud(d)ihy**, **Cuddehy**, **Quiddihy**.

Coe English: nickname from the jackdaw, from a S English var. of KAY (for the change of -*ā*- to -*ō*- cf. ROPER). The surname is chiefly found in Essex and Suffolk.
Var.: **Coo**.

Coelli *see* JACOB

Coen *see* COHEN

Coenraets *see* KONRAD

Coeur French: nickname from OF *ceur* heart (L *cor*), given originally to a stout-hearted man, or ironically to a faint-hearted one. In some cases it may have been originally a house name for someone living at the sign of the sacred heart.
Vars.: **Cor**; **Lecour**.
Dim.: **Coeuret**.

Coey *see* COWIE

Coffey Irish: Anglicized form of Gael. **Ó Cobhthaigh** 'descendant of *Cobhthach*', a byname meaning 'Victorious'.
Vars.: **O'Coffey**, **O'Coffie**, **O'Cohey**, **Coffee**, **Cow(h)ey**, **Cowhiy**.

Coffin French and English: metonymic occupational name for a basket maker, from OF *cof(f)in* basket (LL *cophīnus*, from Gk). Mod. Eng. *coffin* represents a specialized development of this word, not attested before the 16th cent. See also KYFFIN.
Vars.: Fr.: **Couffin**, **Co(u)fin**; **Coffinier**. Eng.: **Ca(u)ffin** (Sussex).
Dims.: Fr.: **Co(u)ffinel**, **Coffineau**, **Co(u)ffinet**.

Cogan 1. Irish (of Welsh origin): habitation name from a parish near Cardiff, which may have been named with a W word meaning 'bowl', 'depression'. There is evidence of a family named *de Cogan* in the 12th cent., and by the 13th cent. the name was also associated with Somerset, Devon, Co. Limerick, and Co. Cork. 2. Irish: Anglicized form of Gael. **Mac Cogadháin** 'son of *Cogadhán*', a dim. from a reduced form of the personal name *Cúchogaidh* 'Hound of War'. 3. Jewish (E Ashkenazic): var. of COHEN.
Vars. (of 2): **Coogan**; **Coggan**, **Coggin(s)**; **Gogan**, **Goggin**.

Coggeshall *see* COXALL

Coghill Scots: apparently an Anglicized form of Dan. **Køgel**; cf. KUGEL.

Coghlan *see* COUGHLAN

Cogley *see* QUICKLEY

Cogolo *see* COOK

Cohen 1. Jewish: from Hebr. *kohen* priest. Priests are traditionally regarded as members of a hereditary caste descended from Aaron, brother of Moses. Not all Jews bearing the name *Cohen* belong to the priestly caste: when many Jews were being forced to join the Russian Army for 25 years, a number changed their surnames to *Cohen* because members of the clergy were exempt from service. See also KAPLAN. 2. Irish (Galway): Anglicized form of Gael. *Ó Cadhain*; see COYNE.
Vars.: **Cohan**, **Coen**, **Cohn**. (Of 1 only): **Koh(e)n**, **Cahan**, **Cah(e)n**, **Kah(e)n**, **Cohane**, **Kahan(e)**; **Cohani**, **Cahani**, **Cahany**, **Kahany** (with the Hebr. suffix -*i*); **Cahana**, **Kahana** (from Jewish Aramaic *kahana* the priest); **Cohener**, **Kohener**, **Kohaner**, **Kah(a)ner**; **Cohansky**, **Cahansky**, **Cahansky**, **Kahansky**; **Cogan**, **Kogen**, **Kogan**, **Cagan**, **Kagan** (under Russ. influence, since the Russ. language has no /h/). Hung.: **Kún**.
Patrs. (from 1): **Kohanoff**, **Kahanov**, **Kahanoff**, **Cahanov**, **Cahanoff**, **Kahanow(ich)**, **Kahanowicz**, **Kahanowitz**, **Kahanovitz**, **Kahanovi(t)ch**, **Cahanovitz**, **Cahanovitch**; **Kaganov(ich)**, **Kaganoff**, **Kaganovic**, **Caganovitz**, **Kaganovski**, **Kaganowski** (E Ashkenazic); **Bar-Cohen**, **Barkan**, **Barcan** (with the Jewish Aramaic prefix *bar*- son of).

Cohr *see* KONRAD

Coillard *see* COUILLET

Coimbra Portuguese: habitation name from a place in the province of Beira, first recorded in the form *Colimbria*, from Celt. *Conimbriga*, apparently a cpd of *con* height (cf. CONAN 1) + *briga* hill, fortress (cf. BRYAN).

Coindat *see* QUANT

Coke *see* COOK

Coker English: habitation name from a group of villages in Somerset, so called from a Brit. river name meaning 'crooked'; cf. COCKERHAM.

Colaço Portuguese: nickname for a foundling who was brought up by foster-parents together with their own children, from Port. *colaço* foster brother (LL *collact(ān)eus*, from *con*- with, together + *lac*, gen. *lactis*, milk; the term originally referred to an infant wet-nursed together with a woman's own child).

Colange *see* COULANGE

Colbeck N English: habitation name from any of various minor places, such as *Caldbeck* in Cumb., named with the ON elements *kaldr* cold + *bekkr* stream; cf. CALDWELL and COLBOURNE.
Vars.: **Colebeck**, **Coulbeck**, **Caldbeck**.

Colbourne English: habitation name from a place possibly so named with the OE elements *cōl* cool + *burna* stream (see BOURNE). One such place is *Colburn* near

Catterick in N Yorks., but the surname is now most frequent in Birmingham.

Vars.: **Colbourn**, **Colborn(e)**, **Colburn(e)**.

Colby English: habitation name from places in Norfolk and Cumb., so called from the ON personal name *Koli* (a byname for a swarthy person, from *kol* (char)coal; see COLE 2) + ON *býr* settlement.

Colclough English: habitation name from *Cowclough* in the parish of Whitworth, Lancs., recorded in the 13th cent. as *Colleclogh*, probably from the OE byname *Cola* (see COLE 2) + OE *clōh* ravine (see CLOUGH).

Var.: **Coleclough**.

Colcot *see* CALDICOTT

Coldham English: habitation name from a place in Cambs., so called from OE *c(e)ald* cold + *hām* homestead.

Coldron *see* CALDERON

Cole 1. English: from a ME pet form of NICHOLAS; cf. COLL 1. **2.** English: from a ME personal name derived from the OE byname *Cola* (from *col* (char)coal, presumably denoting someone of swarthy appearance), or the cogn. ON *Koli*. **3.** Scots and Irish: Anglicized form of Gael. **Mac Gille Chomhghaill** (Sc.), **Mac Giolla Chomhghaill** (Ir.) 'son of the servant of (St) *Comhghall*', a personal name, of uncertain origin, borne by an early Ir. saint.

Vars.: **Coull** (Scots). (Of 3 only): **McCole**, **McCool(e)** (see also McDOUGALL); **Coyle**, **Gilhool**.

Patrs. (from 1): **Co(a)les**, **Coules**, **Cowles**; **Coleson**, **Coulson**, **Cowlson**.

Coleman 1. Irish and English: from the OIr. personal name *Colmán*, earlier *Columbán*, a dim. of *Colum(b)* (L *Columba* 'Dove'; see COLOMB). This was the name of an Ir. missionary to Europe, generally known as St *Columban* (*c.*540–615), who founded the monastery of Bobbio in N Italy in 614. With his companion St GALL, he enjoyed a considerable cult throughout central Europe, so that forms of his name were adopted as given names in It. (*Columbano*), Fr. *(Colombain)*, Czech *(Kolman)*, and Hung. *(Kálmán)*. From all of these surnames are derived. In Irish and English, the name of this saint is identical with dims. of the name of the 6th-cent. missionary now generally known as St *Columba* (521–97), who converted the Picts to Christianity, and who was known in Scandinavian languages as *Kalman*. **2.** Irish: Anglicized form of Gael. **Ó Clumháin** 'descendant of *Clumhán*', a personal name of uncertain origin. **3.** English: occupational name for a burner of charcoal or a gatherer or seller of coal, ME *coleman*, from OE *col* (char)coal + *mann* man; cf. COLLIER. **4.** English: occupational name for the servant of a man named COLE. **5.** Jewish (Ashkenazic): Anglicized form of any of the names given at KALMAN.

Vars. (of 1–4): **Colman**, **Coll(e)man**, **Coulman**. (Of 1 only): Scots: **Callum**, **Cullum**.

Patrs. (from 1): Ir.: **McCalman**, **McCalmon(t)** (Gael. **Mac Colmáin**, **Mac Calmáin**).

'Descendant of C. 1': Ir.: **O'Coleman** (Gael. **Ó Colmáin**).

Colenso Cornish: habitation name from a place in the parish of St Hilary, which is of unknown etymology.

Coleridge English: habitation name from two places in Devon so called, from OE *col* (char)coal + *hrycg* ridge.

Colet *see* KOHL

Coletti *see* JACK

Coley English (W Midlands): nickname for a swarthy person, from OE *colig* dark, black (a deriv. of *col* (char)coal; cf. COLE 2).

Vars.: **Colley**, **Collie**.

Colgan *see* QUILL

Coll 1. English: from an aphetic pet form of NICHOLAS. Forms of this name in which the first syllable is lost are found in several European languages. Forms spelled with an initial *K*- are listed at KLAUS. **2.** Irish: var. of COLE 3. **3.** Irish: Anglicized form of the Gael. personal name *Colla*, which was borne by a warrior in Celt. mythology; it is of uncertain etymology. **4.** Catalan: topographic name for someone who lived by a hill or mountain pass, Cat. *coll* (L *collis* hill).

Vars. (of 1–3): **Colle**.

Dims. (of 1): Eng.: **Col(l)in**, COLLING, **Collen**; **Collett**; **Colcock**; **Colkin**. Fr.: **Col(l)et**, **Col(l)in(et)**, **Col(l)inot**, **Coli(g)non**, **Coll(en)ot**, **Coleçon**, **Col(le)son**, **Collechon**; **Collec**, **Colleu(c)** (Brittany). It.: **Colino**, **Colini**, **Colelli**, **Colotti**, **Colozzi**, **Colucci(o)**, **Colaucci**, **Colluc(i)ello**, **Col(a)ussi**, **Colusso**, **Colauzzi**, **Colichio**, **Cullicchi**. Du.: **Collet**, **Colijn**, **Kolijn**. Flem.: **Collin**, **Colson**. (Of 4): Cat.: **Collell**.

Pejs. (of 1): Eng.: **Collard**. Fr.: **Col(l)ard**. It.: **Collazzo**.

Patrs. (from 1): Eng.: **Colls**, **Colson**. It.: **De Cola**, **Di Cola**.

Du.: **Cols**, **Colen**.

Collado Spanish: topographic name for someone who lived by a hill or mountain pass, Sp. *collado* (LL *collātum*, a deriv. of class. L *collis* hill; see COLL 4).

Dim.: Prov.: **Coladon**.

Collan *see* CULLEN

Colleran Irish: Anglicized form of Gael. **Ó Callaráin** 'descendant of *Callarán*', which is probably a dim. of the byname *Callaire* 'Cryer'.

Collier English: occupational name for a burner of charcoal or a gatherer or seller of coal, from ME *cole* (char)coal (see COLE 2 and COLEMAN 3) + the agent suffix *-(i)er*.

Vars.: **Collye(a)r**, **Colyer**, **Colliar(d)**, **Colleer**.

Equiv. (not cogn.): Czech: UHLÍŘ.

Colling English: **1.** from the ON personal name *Kollungr*, a deriv. of *Koli*, or from an OE cogn., *Colling*, a deriv. of *Cola*; see COLE 2. **2.** dim. of COLL, a pet form of NICHOLAS.

Vars.: **Collinge**, **Co(w)ling**.

Patr.: **Collings**.

Collingwood English: habitation name, probably from *Callingwood* in Staffs., although the surname is now more common on Tyneside. The origin of the placename is from a wood whose ownership was disputed (from ME, OF *chalenge* dispute, challenge, L *calumnia* wrong, injury).

Vars.: **Collinwood**, **Collingworth**.

Collins 1. English: patr. from ME *Col(l)in*, a dim. of COLL, itself a pet form of NICHOLAS. 2. Irish: Anglicized form of Gael. *Ó Coileáin* and *Mac Coileáin*; see CULLEN 3.

Vars.: **Collyns**, **Collis**; **Colli(n)son**.

Colmenar Spanish: habitation name from any of the numerous minor places named with this word, a deriv. of Sp. *colmena* beehive (of uncertain origin, perhaps preserving a pre-Roman term derived from the Celt. element *kolmos* straw, a material of which such constructions were commonly made).

Vars.: **Colmenares** (pl.); **Colmenero** (occupational name for a beekeeper).

Dim.: **Colmenarejo**.

Colomb French: 1. metonymic occupational name for a keeper of doves, from OF *colomb* dove (L *columbus*), or a nickname for a person of a mild and gentle disposition. 2. from a given name of the same origin. The name in its Latin forms *Columbus* and *Columba* was popular among early Christians because the dove was considered to be the symbol of the Holy Spirit. See also COLEMAN 1.

Vars.: **Collomb**, **Collomp**, **Col(l)om**, **Col(l)on**; **Colombier**.

Dims.: Fr.: **Co(u)lombet**, **Co(u)lombel**, **Co(u)lombeau**, **Co(u)lombot**; **Colomic** (Brittany). It.: **Colombetti**, **Colombetta**; **Colombin(i)** (in Milan this was the surname regularly used for the foundlings taken into the orphanage of St Catherine there).

Augs.: Fr.: **Co(u)lombat**.

Pej.: It.: **Colombazzi**.

Colqueran see COCHRANE

Colquhoun Scots: habitation name from a place in the former county of Aberdeens. (now part of Grampian region), first recorded in the form *Colqhoun* in 1246. The name appears to derive from Gael. *còil*, *cùil* nook, corner, or *coill(e)* wood + *cumhann* narrow. The regular pronunciation is /kə'hu:n/.

Vars.: **Colhoun** (N Ireland), **Calhoun** (U.S.).

Colreavy see McILWRAITH

Colston English: 1. from a ME given name, *Colstan*, which is probably from ON *Kolsteinn*, composed of the elements *kol* charcoal + *steinn* stone. 2. habitation name from *Colston* (Basset) in Notts., or the nearby *Carcolson*, both of which seem to have originally been named as the settlement (OE *tūn*) of a bearer of the ON name *Kolr*. The first syllable of *Carcolson* was originally the defining prefix *kirk* church. 3. habitation name from *Coulston* in Warwicks., so called from the gen. case of an OE personal name *Cufel* (dim. of *Cufa*) + OE *tūn* enclosure, settlement.

Var.: **Coulston**.

Colt English: 1. metonymic occupational name for someone who looked after asses and horses, from ME, OE *colt* young ass, later also young horse, colt. In N England *colt* was the generic word for working horses and asses. See also COULTHARD. 2. nickname for an obstinate or frisky person, from the same word.

Vars.: **Coult**; **Colter**; **Coltman**.

Coltart see COULTHARD

Colton English: habitation name from any of various places so called. Examples in Norfolk and W Yorks. are

from the OE personal name *Cola* (or the cogn. ON *Koli*; see COLE 2) + OE *tūn* enclosure, settlement. Another in Somerset has as its first element the personal name *Cūla* (of uncertain origin); one in Lancs. has a river name apparently derived from a Brit. word for the hazel; and one in Staffs. may be from OE *colt* COLT.

Colville English and Scots (Norman): habitation name from *Colleville* in Seine-Maritime, so called from the Scandinavian personal name *Koli* (see COLE 2) + OF *ville* settlement, village (see VILLE).

Var.: **Colvill**.

Colwell English: habitation name from places in Northumb. and Devon. The former is so called from OE *col* (char)coal or *cōl* cool + *well(a)* spring, stream (see WELL); the latter has as its first element a Brit. river name, *Coly*, apparently meaning 'narrow'.

Var.: **Colwill**.

Comazzo see JAMES

Combas see COOMBE

Comber see CAMBER

Comerford 1. English: habitation name from *Comberford* in Staffs., so called from the OE personal name *Cumbra* (originally an ethnic name for a British Celt), or from the gen. pl., meaning 'of the British' + OE *ford* FORD. 2. Irish: Anglicized form of Gael. **Mac Cumascaigh** 'son of *Cumascach*', a byname derived from *cumascach* mixer, confuser.

Vars.: **Cummerford**. (Of 2 only): **(Mc)Cumisky**, **(Mc)Cumesky**, **(Mc)Comisky**, **Cumiskey**, **Cumeskey**, **Commiskey**, **Cumish**, **Comisk**.

Comfort English (Kent): 1. nickname or given name from ME *cumfort* (OF *confort* strengthening, succour, from LL *confortāre* to strengthen). 2. habitation name from a lost place, possibly *Comports* near Birling in Kent or *Compworthy* near Oxted in Surrey.

Var.: **Comport**.

Comings see CUMMING

Comley English: nickname for a handsome man, from ME *cumelich* fair, lovely (from OE *(be)cuman* to befit + the adj. suffix *-līc*).

Compagnon French: nickname for a good neighbour or amiable fellow-worker, from the oblique case of OF *compain* companion, fellow (LL *compānio*, gen. *compāniōnis*, mess-mate, from *con-* together, with + *panis* bread).

Vars.: **Compain(g)**, **Compin**, **Cop(a)in**, **Coppin** (from the nom. case).

Dims.: Fr.: **Copinet**, **Copinot**, **Copigneau**. It.: **Compagnini**, **Compagnino**, **Compagnucci**; **Pagnin(i)**, **Pagnotti**, **Pagnussi**, **Pagnut(ti)**.

Augs.: It.: **Compagnoni**, **Compagnone**; **Pagnoni**.

Companys Catalan: from the abstract noun 'company' (cf. COMPAGNON). The name may have referred to one of the members of a nobleman's retinue, or it may derive from a rare medieval given name bestowed on a child in recognition of the companionship he brings to his relatives.

Compton English: habitation name from any of the numerous places throughout England so called from OE *cumb* short, straight valley (see COOMBE) + *tūn* enclosure, settlement.

Var.: **Cumpton**.

Comrie Scots: habitation name from any of various places called *Comrie*, for example in Fife and in the former county of Perths. All are so called from Gael. *comarach*, from *comar* confluence, river-fork, + the local suffix *-ach*.

Comtet *see* COUNT

Conagan *see* CUNNINGHAM

Conan 1. English: from an OBret. personal name, derived from an element meaning 'high', 'mighty', which was introduced into England by followers of William the Conqueror and subsequently into Ireland, where it still has some currency as a given name. 2. Scots: habitation name from a place in the former county of Kincardines. (now part of Grampian region). The placename is of uncertain origin, possibly from early Celt. **Conona* 'hound stream'.

Vars.: **Conen**, **Conant**.

Conaty Irish: Anglicized form of Gael. *Ó Connachtaigh* 'descendant of *Connachtach*', a byname for someone from the province of Connaught.

Dim.: **Conaughton**.

Concannon Irish: Anglicized form of Gael. *Ó Concheanainn* 'descendant of *Cúcheanann*', a personal name composed of the elements *cú* hound, dog + *ceann* head + *fionn* fair, white. Bearers of this surname claim descent from a single 10th-cent. ancestor.

Conceição Portuguese: from a medieval female given name (from LL *conceptio*, gen. *conceptiōnis*, conception, a deriv. of *concipere* to conceive), alluding to the Immaculate Conception of the Virgin Mary.

Conche French: 1. topographic name for someone who lived in or near a hollow or depression in the land, from OF *conche* basin (L *concha* shell, from Gk *konkhē* shellfish; cf. COCKELL), or habitation name from any of the places in France which get their names from this word, as for example *Conques* in Aude and Aveyron. 2. occasionally, perhaps, a metonymic occupational name for a maker or seller of wooden basins or other vessels, which were also named with the word *conche*.

Var.: **Conches**.

Dims.: Fr.: **Conchon**, **Conquet**.

Condamine French: habitation name from a place so called from OF *condumine* condominium, (land held in) joint ownership (LL *condominium*, originally an abstract noun, from *con-* together, with + *dominus* lord, master). Later, by a different interpretation of the compound, the term came to denote land included directly within the feudal lord's own residence and so exempt from taxation.

Vars.: **Condamin**, **Contamin(e)**, **Condemine**, **Condomine**.

Condell Irish: of uncertain, presumably English, origin. It may be a habitation name from *Cundall* in N Yorks, which is of uncertain etymology; or from the group of Dorset villages called *Caundle*, apparently from a Brit. hill-name of uncertain form and meaning.

Condet *see* COUNT

Condom French: habitation name from a place in Aveyron, so called from the Gaul. personal name *Condus* + the Gaul. element *magos* field, plain.

Condon Irish: Anglicized form of Gael. *Condún*, itself a Gaelicized form of the Anglo-Norman habitation name *de Caunteton*. This seems to have been imported from Wales, but probably derives ultimately from *Caunton* in Notts., so called from the OE personal name *Calunōð* (composed of the elements *calu* bald + *nōð* daring) + OE *tūn* enclosure, settlement.

Var.: **Congdon** (Devon).

Conduché *see* DUCHIER

Condy English: topographic name for someone who lived by a water channel, ME, OF *cond(u)it* (LL *conductus*, a deriv. of *conducere* to lead).

Vars.: **Condie** (chiefly Scotland); **Cundy** (chiefly Devon).

Conerding *see* KONRAD

Conesa Catalan: habitation name from a place in the province of Tarragona. The placename is of uncertain origin, and has been explained in terms of various Arabic and pre-Roman elements, as well as more than one Romance source.

Coney English: nickname meaning 'rabbit' or metonymic occupational name for a dealer in rabbits, from ME *cony* (a back-formation from *conies*, from OF *conis*, pl. of *conil*, from L *cuniculus*).

Vars.: **Cony**, **Conie**; **Conning** (from the ONF form *coning*).

Dims.: Prov.: **Conillon**. Sp.: **Conejillo**.

Aug.: It.: **Coniglione**.

Confalonieri *see* GONFALONIERI

Congreve English: habitation name from a place in Staffs., so called from OE *cumb* short valley (see COOMBE) + *grǣfe* grove, brushwood, thicket.

Vars.: **Congr(e)ave**.

Coni *see* JACK

Coninckx *see* KÖNIG

Coningham *see* CUNNINGHAM

Conlan *see* QUINLAN

Conmee *see* MCNAMEE

Conn Irish: short form of any of the names listed under CONNELL, CONNOLLY, CONNOR, and CONROY.

Connell Irish: Anglicized form of Gael. *Ó Conaill* 'descendant of *Conall*', a personal name of uncertain origin, possibly composed of the elements *con* (from *cú* hound) + *gal* valour. The name was popularized by the fame of a 7th-cent. Irish saint, abbot of Inis Caoil.

Vars.: **O'Connell**, **Gunning**.

Conner English: occupational name for an inspector of weights and measures, from ME *connere*, *cunnere* inspector, an agent deriv. of *cun(nen)* to examine, test (OE *cunnian*, from *cunnan* to know).

Connerny *see* MᶜNAIRN

Connolly Irish: Anglicized form of Gael. **Ó Conghalaigh** 'descendant of *Conghalach*', a byname meaning 'Valiant'.

Vars.: **O'Connolly**, **(O')Connally**, **Connelly**, **Conneely**, **Conally**, **O'Conely**, **Conley**.

Connor Irish: Anglicized form of Gael. **Ó Conchobhair** 'descendant of *Conchobhar*', a personal name apparently composed of the elements *cú* hound, dog + *cobhar* desiring. Many present-day bearers of the surname claim descent from a 10th-cent. king of Connaught of this name. In Irish legend, Conchobhar was a king of Ulster who adopted the youthful Cuchulain.

Vars.: **O'Connor**, **Connors**.

Conroy Irish: Anglicized form of Gael. **Ó Conaire** 'descendant of *Conaire*', a byname meaning 'Keeper of the Hound' (an agent deriv. of *cú* hound, dog).

Vars.: **Con(ner)ry**.

Dims.: **O'Conoran**, **O'Coneran**, **Conran**, **Condron**, **Condrin** (Gael. **Ó Conaráin**).

Consell *see* COUNSEL

Considine *see* CONSTANTINE

Constable English: occupational name for the law-enforcement officer of a parish, ME, OF *conestable, cunestable* (LL *comes stabuli* officer (see COUNT) of the stable). The title was also borne by various other officials during the Middle Ages, including the chief officer of the household (and army) of a medieval ruler, and this may in some cases be the source of the surname.

Constance English and French: **1.** from the medieval female given name *Constance* (L *Constantia*, originally a fem. form of *Constantius* (see CONSTANT), but later taken as the abstract noun *constantia* steadfastness). **2.** habitation name from *Coutances* in La Manche, Normandy, which was given its L name of *Constantia* (see above) in honour of the Roman emperor Constantius Chlorus, who was responsible for fortifying the settlement in AD 305–6.

Vars.: Eng.: **Custance**. Fr.: **Coutance**.

Dims. (of 1): Eng.: **Cust**, **Cuss(e)**; **Cussen**, **Cusson** (see also COUSIN and CUTHBERT).

Metr. (from 1): Eng.: **Custerson**.

Metrs. (from 1) (dims.): Eng.: **Cussons**, **Cussens**.

Constant French: from a medieval given name (L *Constans*, gen. *Constantis*, 'Steadfast', 'Faithful', pres. part. of *constāre* to stand fast, be consistent) borne by an 8th-cent. Irish martyr. This surname has also absorbed examples of the name *Constantius*, a deriv. of *Constans*, borne by a 2nd-cent. martyr, bishop of Perugia.

Vars.: **Constans**, **Coutans**, **Contant**, **Coutant**.

Dims.: Prov.: **Constensoux**, **Coutanceau**, **Coutanson**. It.: **Tanzilli**, **Tanzillo**, **Tanzini**, **Tansini**.

Aug.: It.: **Tanzoni**.

Patrs.: It.: **De Costanzo**, **Di Costanzo**.

Constantine **1.** English: from a medieval given name (L *Constantīnus*, a deriv. of *Constans*; see CONSTANT). The name was popular in Continental Europe, and to a lesser

extent in England, as having been borne by the first Christian ruler of the Roman Empire, Constantine the Great (?280–337), in whose honour Byzantium was renamed Constantinople. **2.** Norman habitation name or regional name from *Cotentin (Coutances)* in La Manche; see CONSTANT 2.

Vars.: **Cossentine**, **Consterdine**, **Considine**, COSTAIN.

Dims. (of 1): Eng.: COSTE. Rum.: **Costache**, **Tinu**, **Dinu**. Ger.: **Kost**. Czech: **Kostka**. Pol.: **Kostko**, **Kostiuk**, **Kościuk**, **Kościuszko** (of Beloruss. origin). Ukr.: **Kostenko**, **Kostashchuk**, **Kostyura**. Hung.: **Koszta**, **Kosztka**.

Pej. (from 1 or 2): Fr.: **Costard**.

Patrs. (from 1): Russ., Bulg.: **Konstantinov**. Pol.: **Konstantynowicz**. Croatian: **Konstantinović**. Rum.: **Constantinesco**. Gk: **Constantinou**, **Constantinides**.

Patrs. (from 1) (dim.): Eng.: **Costin(g)s**, **Costons**. Russ.: **Kostin**, **Kostikov**, **Kostyushin**, **Kostyunin**. Beloruss.: **Katusov**. Pol.: **Kostkiewicz**. Croatian: **Kondić**, **Konjević**, **Konjović**; **Kostić**.

Contreras Spanish: habitation name from a place in the province of Burgos. The placename is derived from LL *contrāria* surrounding area, region (from the prep. *contra* opposite, against, hard by).

Converse English: nickname for a Jew converted to Christianity, or more often an occupational name for someone converted to the religious way of life, a lay member of a convent. The name comes from ME, OF *convers* convert (L *conversus*, past part. of *convertere* to turn, change).

Convery Irish: Anglicized form of Gael. **Mac Ainmhire** 'son of *Ainmhire*', a byname meaning 'Fierceness'.

Conway **1.** Welsh: habitation name from *Conwy*, the fortified town on the coast of N Wales, itself named from the river on which it stands. This is of Brit. origin, perhaps from a word meaning 'reedy'. **2.** Scots: habitation name from *Conway* in the parish of Beauly, recorded *c.*1215 as *Coneway* and in 1291 as *Convathe*. It probably gets its name from Gael. *coinmheadh* billet, free quarters, being so named as the district in which the local lord's household troops were billeted. **3.** Irish: Anglicized form of various Gael. names, such as *Mac Conmidhe* (see MᶜNAMEE), **Mac Connmhaigh** ('son of *Connmhach*', a personal name derived from *condmach* head-smashing; also Anglicized as **Conoo**), and **Ó Conbhuide** ('descendant of *Conbhuidhe*', a personal name composed of the elements *cú* hound, dog + *buidhe* yellow).

Var. (of 1): **Conwy**.

Conwell *see* MᶜCONVILLE

Conyer *see* COYNE

Coo *see* COE

Cooch *see* COUCH

Coogan *see* COGAN

Cook **1.** English: occupational name for a cook, a seller of cooked meats, or a keeper of an eating house, from OE *cōc* (L *coquus*). There has been some confusion with COCK. **2.** Jewish (Ashkenazic): in part an Anglicization of the Jewish surnames given below, in part an Anglicization of the Jewish surname **Kuk**, which is of unknown origin; it is some-times Anglicized as **Kook**.

Vars.: **Cooke, Coke**.

Dims.: Pol.: **Kucharczyk, Kucharek**. Ukr.: **Kukharenko**. It.: **Cuocolo, Cocuccio, Cogolo**.

Aug.: It.: **Cogoni**.

Patrs.: Eng: **Cookson, Cuckson, Cux(s)on**; Cox. Low Ger.: **Kocks, Kox**. Beloruss.: **Kukharov**. It.: **Del Coco**.

'Servant of the c.': Eng.: **Cookman, Cockman**.

Equiv. (not cogn.): Russ.: POVAROV.

Cooksey English (chiefly W Midlands): habitation name from a place in Worcs., so called from the gen. case of the OE personal name *Cucu* (perhaps a byname from OE *cwicu* lively) + OE *ēg* island.

Coole Irish: **1.** Anglicized form of Gael. **Mac Cumhaill** 'son of *Cumhall*', a byname meaning 'Champion'. **2.** Anglicized form of Gael. *Mac Dhubhghaill*; see DOUGALL.

Vars.: **Cooil**; **Coolson, Coulson** (see also COLE).

Cooling English: **1.** var. of CULLING. **2.** habitation name from a place in Kent, originally so called from the OE tribal name *Cūlingas* 'people of *Cūl(a)*'; see CULLING. The pronunciation is normally /ˈkʊlɪŋ/, sometimes /ˈkuːlɪŋ/.

Coomans see CHAPMAN

Coombe English: habitation name from any of various places named with OE *cumb* (apparently of Celt. origin) denoting a short, straight valley, or else a topographic name from ME *combe* used independently in the same sense. There are a large number of places in England, mostly spelled *Combe*, named with this word. The vars. in *-e* for the most part derive from the OE dat. case, those in *-(e)s* from the gen.

Vars.: **Co(u)mbe, Coom, Co(o)mb(e)s, Co(o)mber** (see also CAMBER).

Prov.: **Lascombes**. Cat.: **Coma(s)**.

Dims.: Fr.: **Com(b)eau, Combelle(s), Combin, Combet(te), Co(u)met, Combot, Comboul, Coumoul**. Cat.: **Comella(s)**.

Augs.: Fr.: **Combas, Coumas, Coumat**.

Cooney Irish: Anglicized form of Gael. **Ó Cuana** 'descendant of *Cuana*', a personal name derived from *cuanna* elegant, comely.

Vars.: **O'Cooney, Cowney, Cunnea**.

Dims.: **(O')Coonaghan, Counihan, Coonihan, Coonan** (Gael. **Ó Cuanacháin**).

Cooper 1. English: occupational name for a maker and repairer of wooden vessels such as barrels, tubs, buckets, casks, and vats, ME *couper, cowper* (apparently from MLG *kūper*, a deriv. of *kūp* tub, container, which was borrowed independently into Eng. as *coop*). The prevalence of the surname, its cogns., and equivalents bears witness to the fact that this was one of the chief specialist trades in the Middle Ages throughout Europe. **2.** Jewish (Ashkenazic): Anglicized form of *Kupfer* and *Kupper*; see COPPER.

Vars. (of 1): COPPER, COUPAR, **Cupper**; **Kooper**; **Coop(e), Coupe** (Yorks. and Lancs.). (Of 2): **Cooperman**.

Patrs. (from 1): Low Ger.: **Küp(p)ers**. Du., Flem.: **Kui(j)pers, Kuypers, Cuijpers, Cuypers**.

Equivs. (not cogns.): Fr.: CUVIER, TONNELLIER. Ger.: BÖTTCHER, BÜTTNER, KIEFER, SCHÄFFLER. Ger. and Jewish (Ashkenazic):

BODNER, BINDER. Pol. and Jewish (E Ashkenazic): BEDNARZ. Ukr.: BONDAR. Hung.: KÁDÁR.

Coopland see COPELAND

Coopman see COPEMAN

Coornaert see CORNE

Coote English: nickname for a bald or stupid man, from ME *co(o)te* coot (apparently from MLG). The bird was regarded as bald because of the large white patch, an extension of the bill, on its head. It is less easy to say how it acquired the reputation for stupidity.

Var.: **Coot**.

Patrs.: **Coot(e)s**.

Copain see COMPAGNON

Cope English (common in the Midlands and Lancs.): metonymic occupational name for someone who made cloaks or capes, or nickname for someone who wore a distinctive one, from ME *cāpe* (OE *cāp*, reinforced by the cogn. ON *kápa*; both are from LL, see CHAPE). For the change of *-ā-* to *-ō-*, cf. ROPER.

Copeland English and Scots: habitation name from *Copeland* in Cumb. or *Coupland* in Northumb., both so called from ON *kaupland* bought land, a feature worthy of note during the early Middle Ages, when land was rarely sold, but rather held by feudal tenure and handed down from one generation to the next.

Vars.: **Co(u)pland, Coopland, Cowpland**.

Copelli see JACOB

Copeman English: occupational name for a merchant or trader, ME *copman*, from ON *kaupmaðr* (cogn. with OE *cēapman*; see CHAPMAN). *Kaupmaðr* is also found as a personal name in England, and this use may lie behind some cases of the surname.

Vars.: **Copman, Coopman, Coupman**.

Copestake see CAPSTICK

Coplestone English: habitation name from *Copplestone* in the parish of Colebrooke, Devon, so called from the OE element *copel*, of uncertain meaning, possibly 'peaked', + *stān* STONE.

Vars.: **Copleston, Copplestone**.

Copley English (Yorks.): habitation name from any of various places, for example in Co. Durham, Staffs., and Yorks., so called from the OE personal name *Coppa* (apparently a byname for a tall man) or from *copp* hill-top (see COPP) + *lēah* wood, clearing.

Copozzi see CHAPE

Copp English: **1.** topographic name for someone who lived on the top of a hill, from ME *coppe*, OE *copp* summit (a transferred sense of *copp* head, bowl, cogn. with mod. Eng. *cup*, MHG and mod. Ger. *Kopf*, and Pol. *kopa* hill). **2.** nickname for someone with a large or deformed head, from ME *cop(p)* head (the same word as in 1).

Dim. (of 1): Pol.: **Kopka**.

Pejs. (of 2): Eng.: **Copp(e)ard**.

Copper English: **1.** var. of COOPER 1, from ME *copere*, found from the 12th cent. alongside *cupere*. **2.** metonymic occupational name for a worker in copper, OE *coper* (L *(aes) Cyprium* Cyprian bronze).

Cpds (ornamental): Jewish: **Kuperbaum**, **Kuperboim**, **Kiperbaum** ('copper tree'); **Kupferberg**, **Kup(p)erberg** ('copper hill'; *Kupferberg* also exists as a Ger. vocab. word meaning 'copper mine', but this is probably not relevant to any of the Jewish surnames); **Kuperfish** ('copper fish'); **Kup(p)ermintz** ('copper coin'), **Kupferminc** (Pol. spelling); **Kuperschlak** ('copper blow'); **Kupferstein**, **Kupers(h)tein**, **Kupperstein** ('copper stone'); **Kuperstock** ('copper staff'); **Kup(f)erwasser** ('copper water').

Coppersmith 1. English: occupational name for a SMITH who worked in COPPER. **2.** Jewish (Ashkenazic): Anglicization of any of the Jewish surnames listed below.

Coppin *see* COMPAGNON

Copping English: **1.** dim. of JACOB. **2.** topographic name for someone who lived on the top of a hill, from an OE deriv. of *copp* summit (see COPP 1).

Vars. (of 1): **Coppin**, **Coppen**. (Of 2): **Coppinger**.

Coppola S Italian: from the Neapolitan dial. term *coppola*, denoting a type of beret characteristic of the region (cf. CHAPE); either a nickname for a habitual wearer of a beret, or a metonymic occupational name for a maker of such berets.

Var.: **Coppolaro** (occupational name).

Dims.: **Coppolelli**, **Coppoletta**, **Coppoletti**, **Coppolino**.

Aug.: **Coppolone**.

Copsey English (Suffolk): from the ON personal name *Kupsi*. This is of uncertain origin, but is recorded in Domesday Book as *Copsi* and seems to have been used as a fairly frequent given name in the early Middle Ages.

Coquel *see* COCK

Coquillon *see* COCKELL

Cor *see* COEUR

Corain *see* KONRAD

Corbeau *see* CUERVO

Corbeil French: metonymic occupational name for a maker and seller of baskets, from OF *corbeil(le)* basket (LL *corbicula*, a dim. of *corbis* basket). It may also be a habitation name from any of the various places named with this word because of a depression in the ground.

Vars.: **(Le) Corbeiller**, **Corbeillier**.

Corbett English (Norman; esp. common in the W Midlands): nickname meaning 'Little Crow', from ANF *corbet*, a dim. of *corb*; cf. CUERVO.

Vars.: **Corbet**, **Corbitt**.

Corbisier *see* COURVOISIER

Corby 1. English: habitation name from any of various places in N England. Those in Lincs. and Northants are so called from the ON personal name *Kori* (see CORY) + ON *býr* farm, settlement, whereas the one in Cumb. has as

its first element the OIr. personal name *Corc*. **2.** French: dim. of *corb* crow (see CUERVO).

Var. (of 1): **Corbie**.

Corcut *see* CALDICOTT

Corday French: habitation name from any of various places, in Orne, Boucé, and Montrée, so called from the Gallo-Roman personal name *Cordus* ('Young'; cf. CORDERO) + the local suffix *-ācum*.

Corde French: metonymic occupational name for a maker of cord or string, or nickname for a habitual wearer of decorative ties and ribbons, from OF *corde* string (L *c(h)orda*, from Gk *khordē*).

Vars.: **Cordier**, **Cordié**, **Lecordier** (occupational names).

Dims.: Fr.: **Cordet**, **Cordey**, **Cordeix**; **Cordel(le)**, **Cordelet(te)**; CORDONNIER. Eng.: **Cordell**, **Cordall**, **Cordle**.

Cordero Spanish: metonymic occupational name for a shepherd, or nickname meaning 'lamb', from Sp. *cordero* young lamb (L *cordārius*, a deriv. of *cordus* young, new).

Corderoy English: nickname for a proud man, from OF *cuer de roi* king's heart. There is no connection with the name of the fabric, which is not recorded before the 18th cent.

Vars.: **Cord(e)rey**, **Cordurey**, **Corde(a)ry**, **Cordray**.

Córdoba Spanish: habitation name from the city in S Spain, of extremely ancient foundation and uncertain etymology.

Vars.: **Córdova**; **Cordobés**, **Cordovés**.

Cordonnier French: **1.** occupational name for a maker or seller of cord or ribbon, from an agent deriv. of OF *cordon*, a dim. of CORDE. **2.** occupational name for a worker in fine Spanish kid leather, OF *cordoan* (so named from being originally produced at CÓRDOBA).

Vars. (of 1): **Cordon**, **Cordoux**. (Of 2): **Cordouën**, **Cordouant**.

Cordwell English: habitation name from a minor place in the parish of Holmsfield, Derbys. The placename is of uncertain origin; the second element is probably OE *well(a)* spring, stream (see WELL).

Corfield English (W Midlands): habitation name from a place so called by the river *Corve* in Shrops. This gets its name from the river name (which is from OE *corf* cutting) + OE *feld* pasture, open country (see FIELD).

Cork English: metonymic occupational name for a supplier of red or purple dye, ME *cork* (of Celt. origin; cf. CORKERY), or for someone who used it in dying cloth.

Vars.: **Corck**, **Corke**; **Corker**.

Corkery Irish: Anglicized form of Gael. **Ó Corcra** 'descendant of *Corcra*', a personal name derived from *corcair* purple (ultimately cogn. with L *purpur*).

Var.: **Corkerry**.

Dims.: **O'Corcrane**, **O'Corkerane**, **O'Corkran**, **Corcoran**, **Cork(e)ran** (Gael. **Ó Corcráin**); **(O')Corkan**, **Corken**, **Corkin** (Gael. **Ó Corcáin**).

Corless *see* CARLESS

Corlett Manx: Anglicized form of Gael. **Mac Thorliot**, patr. from a personal name of ON origin, composed of the divine name *þórr* + *ljóðr* people.

Corley 1. English: habitation name from a place in Warwicks., recorded in Domesday Book as *Cornelie*, apparently from OE *corna*, a metathesized form of *crona*, gen. pl. of *cron*, *cran* CRANE + *lēah* wood, clearing. 2. Irish: var. of CURLEY.

Corley *see* CURLEY

Cormack Scots: Anglicized form of the Gael. personal name *Cormac*, composed of the elements *corb* raven + *mac* son.

Var.: **Cormick**.

Dim.: **Cormican**.

Patrs.: **McCormack, McCormick** (Gael. **Mac Cormaic**).

Cormier French: topographic name for someone who lived near a sorb or service tree, OF *cormier* (from *corme*, the name of the fruit for which the tree was cultivated, apparently of Gaul. origin).

Dims.: **Cormieau(d), Cormillot, Cormoul**.

Cormode *see* DERMOTT

Cornall English (Lancs.): apparently a habitation name from a lost place in Lancs., perhaps so called from OE *corn* corn, grain or *corn*, a metathesized form of *cron*, *cran* CRANE + *hall* HALL or *halh* nook, recess (see HALE 1).

Corne French: nickname for a cuckold (see HORN 4), or metonymic occupational name for a hornblower or worker in horn, from OF *corne* horn (LL *corna*, originally a contraction of *cornua*, pl. of *cornu*, but later treated as a fem. sing.).

Vars.: **Lacorne; Cornu(t), Cournu, Lecornu, Co(u)rné**.

Dims.: Fr.: **Cornet(te), Cournet, Corney, Cornez; Cornu(d)et, Cornuel, Cornuchet; Cornec, Cornic** (Brittany). Eng.: **Cornet(t)**. Du.: **Cornet**.

Aug.: Fr.: **Cornat**.

Pejs.: Fr.: **Cornard, Cornaud, Cornuau**. Flem.: **Co(o)rnaert**.

Corneille French: 1. from a given name (L *Cornēlius*, an old Roman family name, probably derived from *cornu* horn; cf. CORNE), which was borne by a 3rd-cent. Christian saint and pope. The cathedral of St Cornelius at Aachen was a centre of pilgrimage, and the given name was especially popular in this area in the Middle Ages. 2. nickname for a prattling person, from OF *corneille* crow (LL *cornicula*, a dim. of *cornix* raven).

Vars. (of 1): **Cornély; Cornil, Quernel** (Belgium). (Of 2): **Corn(e)il, Cornille**.

Dims.: (of 1): Beloruss.: **Korneichik**. Ukr.: **Korneichuk**. Pol.: **Korneluk**. Czech: **Kornalík, Kornoušek; Korous, Koreš, Korejs, Kureš**; KORDA. (Of 2): Fr.: **Cornilleau, Cornelleau, Cornillot**.

Patrs. (from 1): Low Ger.: **Cornels, Cornils; Neles, Nellen, Nilles; Nehls(en), Neels**. Du., Flem.: **Cornelisse(n), Nelissen**. Dan.: **Corneliussen**. Russ.: **Kornilov, Kornilyev, Korneev**.

Patrs. (from 1) (dim.): Low Ger.: **Corneljes; Neljes, Nellies, Nilges**. Russ.: **Kornyakov, Kornyshev**.

Cornell 1. English (U.S.): Anglicization of any of the many Continental European surnames derived from the

L given name *Cornelius*; see CORNEILLE 1. 2. Swedish: vernacular form of *Cornelius*. 3. English: var. of CORNWELL. 4. English: var. of CORNHILL.

Corney English: habitation name from places in Cumb. and Herts., so called from OE *corn* corn, grain or *corn*, a metathesized form of *cron*, *cran* CRANE + *ēg* island. It seems possible, from the distribution of early forms, that it may also derive from a lost place in Lancs.

Cornfeld *see* KORN

Cornford English (Sussex, Kent, and Surrey): habitation name from any of several minor place in SE England, named with OE *corn* corn + *ford* FORD. There appears also to have been some confusion with COMFORT.

Cornforth English: habitation name from *Cornforth* in Co. Durham, so called from OE *corn*, a metathesized form of *cron*, *cran* CRANE + *ford* FORD.

Var.: **Cornfoot**.

Cornhill English: 1. habitation name from *Cornhill* in Northumb., so called from OE *corn*, a metathesized form of *cron*, *cran* CRANE + *halh* nook, recess (see HALE 1). 2. English: habitation name from *Cornhill* in London, a medieval grain exchange, so called from OE *corn* corn, grain + *hyll* HILL, or from any other place elsewhere similarly named.

Var.: CORNELL.

Cornier French: 1. occupational name for a hornblower; see CORNE. 2. habitation name for someone who lived on the corner of two streets in a town, from OF *cornier* corner (a deriv. of *corne* horn; see CORNE). 3. topographic name for someone who lived by a dogwood tree, OF *cornier* (L *cornārius*).

Var. (of 3): **Cornoueil**.

Cornish English: regional name for someone from the county of Cornwall, from OE *cornisc* Cornish (from *Corn-* (see CORNWELL 1) + the adj. suffix *-isc*). Not surprisingly, the surname is most common in adjacent Devon, but it is also well established as far afield as Colchester and Preston.

Vars.: **Corn(e)s** (from OF *corneis*).

Cornwell English (now most common in London and Lancs.): 1. regional name from the county of *Cornwall*, so called from the OE tribal name *Cornwealas*. This is from *Kernow*, the native name that the Cornish used to denote themselves (of uncertain etymology, perhaps connected with a Celt. element meaning 'horn', 'headland'), compounded with OE *wealas* strangers, foreigners (see WALLACE), the term used by the Anglo-Saxons for British-speaking people. 2. habitation name from *Cornwell* in Oxon., so called from OE *corn*, a metathesized form of *cron*, *cran* CRANE + *well(a)* spring, stream (see WELL).

Vars. (of 1): **Cornwall; Curnow** (from the native Cornish word); CORNISH.

Coromina Catalan: topographic name for someone who lived on a patch of land not subject to irrigation, Cat. *coromina* (a cogn. of CONDAMINE, although the semantic development is not clear).

Vars.: **Corominas, Coromines, Colomines**.

Corona Spanish and Italian: from Sp., It. *corona* crown (L *corōna* garland, chaplet, diadem), perhaps a house name for someone who lived in a house with this sign or a nickname for someone who had a tonsure in fulfilment of a religious vow.

Vars.: Sp.: **Coronas**; **Coronado**.

Dim.: Jewish **Kroinik**.

Pej.: Fr.: **Couronnaud**.

Cpds (ornamental): Swed.: **Kronberg** ('crown hill'); **Cronholm** ('crown island'); **Kronquist**, **Cronquist** ('crown twig'); **Cronstedt** ('crown homestead'); **Cronström** ('crown river'); **Cronvall**, **Cronwall** ('crown slope'). Jewish: **Kron(en)berg**, **Kronnberg**, **Kronenberger** ('crown hill'); **Kronenblat** ('crown leaf'); **Kronfeld**, **Kron(n)enfeld** ('crown field'); **Krongold** ('crown gold'); **Krongrad** ('crown city'); **Kronkopf**, **Kronkop(p)** ('crown head'); **Kronstein** ('crown stone'); **Kronent(h)al** ('crown valley').

Corot French: topographic name for someone who lived at a corner or angle of land, from a dim. of OF *cor* corner (L *cornu* horn, cf. CORNIER and CORNE).

Corr Irish: Anglicized form of Gael. **Ó Corra** 'descendant of *Corra*', a personal name from *corr* spear, pointed object.

Dims.: **Corrigan**, **O'Corrigane**, **(O')Currigan**, **Corragan**, (Gael. **Ó Corragáin**).

Corral Spanish: topographic name for someone who lived near an enclosure for livestock, Sp. *corral*. This word, which has entered mod. Eng. as a result of contact in the New World, is found in Spain as early as the 11th cent. and is of uncertain etymology, perhaps from a L deriv., **currāle*, of *currus* chariot, as being a run for vehicles. There are numerous places named with this word, in both the sing. and pl. forms, and to a large extent the surname is a habitation name from these.

Var.: **Corrales**.

Corran see CURRAN

Correa Spanish: possibly from Sp. *correa* leather strap, belt, rein, shoelace (L *corrigia* fastening, from *corrigere* to straighten, order, correct). The surname could have arisen as a metonymic occupational name for a maker or seller of any of these articles, or as a nickname for a strong or patient person.

Var.: **Correas**.

Corredor Spanish: occupational name for a messenger, or nickname for a swift runner, from Sp. *corredor* runner (LL *curritor*, for class. L *cursor*, a deriv. of *currere* to run).

Corrie Scots: habitation name from places in Arran, Dumfries, and elsewhere, so called from Gael. *coire* cauldron, applied to a circular hanging valley on a mountain. See also CURRY.

Var.: **Corry**.

Corsan see CARSON

Corselli see BONACCORSO

Corson see CURZON

Corstgens see CHRISTIAN

Cortada Catalan: topographic or occupational name from Cat. *cortada* court, residence, a deriv. of *cort*; see COURT 1.

Dims.: Cat.: **Cortadellas**. Prov.: **Courtadon**.

Cortázar Spanish form of Basque **Kortazar**: topographic name for someone living by an old stable or farmyard, from the Basque elements *korta* stable, cowshed, (farm)yard (a Romance borrowing; see COURT 1) + *za(h)ar, zar* old.

Corte see COURT

Côrte-Real Portuguese: metonymic occupational name for someone who was employed at a royal court, from Port. *côrte* COURT + *real* royal (L *rēgālis*, a deriv. of *rex*, gen. *rēgis*, king).

Corteney see COURTENAY

Cortesini see CURTIS

Cory 1. English: from the ON personal name *Kori*, which is well attested both in Scandinavia and England, but of uncertain meaning. 2. Irish: Anglicized form of Gael. **Ó Comhraidhe** 'descendant of *Comhraidhe*', a personal name of uncertain meaning.

Vars.: **Corey**. (Of 2 only): **O'Corry**, **O'Corrie**, CURRY; WEIR.

Coryton English: habitation name from a place in Devon, so called from a Brit. river name (see CURRY 1) + OE *tūn* enclosure, settlement.

Cosby English: habitation name from a place in Leics., so called perhaps from an OE personal name *Cossa* + ON *býr* farm, settlement.

Coscor see CUSKER

Cosens see COUSIN

Cosgrove 1. English: habitation name from a place in Northants, so called from OE *Cōfesgrāf* 'grove, thicket (OE *grāf*; see GROVE) of **Cōf*', an otherwise unattested personal name. 2. Irish: Anglicized form of Gael. **Ó Coscraigh** 'descendant of *Coscrach*', a byname meaning 'Victorious', 'Triumphant' (from *coscur* victory, triumph).

Vars.: **Cosgrave**. (Of 2 only): **Cosgreave**, **Cosgrive**, **Cosgriff**, **Cosgry**, **O'Cosgra**, **(O')Cosker(r)y**, **Cuskery**.

Dims. (of 2): **Coskeran**, **Cuskern** (Gael. **Ó Coscracháin**).

Cosimelli see KUZMIN

Cossentine see CONSTANTINE

Costain 1. Scots and Irish: Anglicized form of Gael. **Mac Austain** 'son of AUSTIN'. 2. English: var. of CONSTANTINE.

Vars. (of 2): **Costin**, **Coste(a)n**.

Coste 1. French: topographic name for someone who lived on a slope or riverbank, less often on the coast, from OF *coste* (L *costa* rib, side, flank, also used in a transferred topographical sense). There are several places in France named with this word, and the surname may also be a habitation name from any of these. **2.** English: short form of CONSTANTINE.

Vars. (of 1): **Côte**; **Lacoste**; **Delacoste**, **Delacôte**.

Dims. (of 1): Fr.: **Costel(le)**, **Cot(t)el**, **Co(us)teau**, **Cotteaux**, **Co(u)ston**, **Coustet**; **Costiou** (Brittany). Prov.: **Costil(he)**, **Coustille**, **Costy**, **Cot(t)y**. Sp.: **Costilla**.

Aug. (of 1): Fr.: **Coutas**.

Costello Irish: said to be an Anglicized form of Gael. **Mac Oisdealbhaigh** 'son of *Oisdealbhach*', a personal name composed of the elements *os* deer, fawn + *dealbhadh* in the form of, resembling. However, the main family of this name are of Norman origin, and the name may therefore in fact be a deriv. of COSTE.

Vars.: **McCostalaighe**, **McCosdalowe**, **(Mc)Costelloe**, **Costellow**, **Costily**, **Costley**.

Coster **1.** English: metonymic occupational name for a grower or seller of *costards*, a popular variety of large apples, so called from their prominent ribs; cf. COSTE. **2.** Dutch: cogn. of KÜSTER.

Cot **1.** French: aphetic form of a dim. of any of several given names containing the sound /k/ at the beginning of the second syllable, e.g. *Jacquot* (see JACK) or *Nicot* (see NICHOLAS). **2.** Catalan: topographic name for someone who lived by a boundary stone, Cat. *cot* (L *cote* stone), or habitation name from one of the numerous places named with this word.

Var. (of 2): Cat.: **Cots**.

Dims. (of 1): Fr.: **Co(u)tet**, **Cotin(eau)**, **Coutinet**, **Co(u)ton**, **Couthon**, **Coutou(t)**, **Cotot**, **Coutisson**.

Pej. (of 1): Fr.: **Cotard**.

Cote *see* COATES

Coteau *see* COSTE

Cotsbrooke *see* CODGBROOK

Cotte French: metonymic occupational name for a maker of chain mail, from OF *cot(t)e* coat of mail (of Gmc origin). It is unlikely to have been a nickname for a wearer of a coat of mail, since only the richest classes, who already had distinguished family names of their own, could afford to be so well protected in a garment which required many hours of skilled labour to construct. It may perhaps have been used as a nickname for a hard and unfeeling person.

Vars.: **Lacotte**, **Cotté**, **Cottu**.

Dims.: Fr.: **Cottet**, **Cottez**, **Cottey**, **Cottin(eau)**, COTTON, **Cottenet**, **Cott(en)ot**.

Pej.: Fr.: **Cottard**.

Cotter **1.** English: from ME *cotter*, a technical term of status in the feudal system for a serf or bond tenant who held a cottage by service rather than rent, from OE *cot* cottage, hut (see COATES) + *-er* agent suffix. **2.** Irish: Anglicized form of Gael **Mac Oitir** 'son of *Oitir*', a personal name borrowed from ON *Óttarr*, composed of the elements *ótti* fear, dread + *herr* army.

Vars. (of 1): **Cottier**; **Cotman**.

Dims. (of 1): Eng.: **Cotterel(l)**, **Cottrell**, **Cott(e)rill**, **Cotherill** (all chiefly Midlands). Fr.: **Cott(e)rel(l)**, **Cott(e)reau**, **Cottarel**.

Cottle English: **1.** metonymic occupational name for a maker of chain-mail, from an ANF dim. of COTTE. **2.**

metonymic occupational name for a cutler, from OF *co(u)tel*, *co(u)teau* knife (LL *cultellus*, a dim. of *culter* ploughshare).

Vars.: **Cottel(l)**, **Cuttell**, **Cuttill**, **Cuttles**; CUTLER.

Cotton **1.** English: habitation name from any of numerous places throughout England so called from the dat. pl. of OE *cot* cottage, dwelling (see COATES). **2.** French: dim. of COTTE.

Vars. (of 1): **Coton**, **Cottom**, **Cottem**, **Cottam**.

Couaillet *see* CAIL

Couch **1.** Cornish: probably a nickname for a red-haired man, from *cough* red; cf. GOUGH 2. The normal pronunciation of this name is /kuːtʃ/. **2.** English: metonymic occupational name for a maker of beds or bedding, or perhaps a nickname for a lazy man, from ME, OF *couche* bed (a deriv. of OF *coucher* to lay down, L *collocāre* to place).

Vars. (of 1): **Cooch**, **Cough**. (Of 2): **Couche**; **Coucher**, **Coucha**, **Cowcha**; **Couchman**.

Coudert Provençal: topographic name for someone who lived by a grassy patch, Prov. *coudert* (LL *cotericum*, apparently of Gaul. origin). There are various places in SW France named with this word, and the surname may also be a habitation name from any of these.

Vars.: **Couder(c)**.

Coudray *see* COWDREY

Coudwell *see* CALDWELL

Coufal Czech: nickname derived from a dial. form of the verb *couvat* to retreat or go backwards, perhaps applied to a timid or cowardly person.

Couffin *see* COFFIN

Coughlan Irish: Anglicized form of Gael. **Ó Cochláin** 'descendant of *Cochlán*', a byname derived from *cochal* cloak, hood.

Vars.: **O'Coghla(i)ne**, **Coughlin**, **Coghlan**, **Coglin**, **Coughan**.

Couillet French: nickname for a good companion, from OF *couillet*, dim. of *couille* testicle (from L *colea*, a neut. pl. later treated as a fem. sing.).

Vars.: **Couillette**, **Couilleau**, **Couillot**, **Couillon**.

Pejs.: **Co(u)illau(d)**, **Co(u)illard**.

Coulange French: habitation name from any of the various places that derive their names from LL *colōnica (terra)* land cultivated by a 'colonist', a technical term of the feudal system for a peasant labourer who was free in body but bound to the land he worked.

Vars.: **Coulanges**, **Coulonge(s)**, **Col(l)ange**, **Col(l)onge**, **Collongues**; **Coulangeon**.

Coulbeck *see* COLBECK

Coules *see* COLE

Coulet French: **1.** aphetic form of *Nicoulet*, a dim. of NICHOLAS. **2.** topographic name for someone who lived on or near a hill, from a dim. of OF *co(u)l* (L *collis*; see COLL 4). There are various places in Aveyron and SE France named with this word, and the surname may be a habitation name from any of these. **3.** metonymic occupational name for a maker or seller of neckbands, or nickname for a wearer of one, from OF *collet, coulet* neckband, kerchief, a dim. of *co(u)l* neck (LL *collum*).

Coulman *see* COLEMAN

Coulombat *see* COLOMB

Coulson *see* COOLE

Coulston *see* COLSTON

Coult *see* COLT

Coultas English (Yorks.): habitation name or occupational name for someone who lived or worked at a stables, from early mod. Eng. *coulthus*, a cpd of *co(u)lt* COLT + *hus* HOUSE.

Coulter Scots and N Irish: habitation name from places in the former counties of Lanarks. and Aberdeens., so called from Gael. *cùl tir* back land.
Vars.: **Coultar**, **Culter**.

Coulthard N English and Scots: occupational name for someone who looked after asses or working horses, ME *colthart, coltehird*, from OE *colt* ass, young horse (see COLT) + *hierde* herdsman (see HEARD).
Vars.: **Coulthart**, **Colthard**, **Colt(h)art**, **Coltherd**, **Colthert**.

Coulthurst English (Lancs.): apparently a habitation name from an unidentified place so called from OE *colt* ass, young horse (see COLT) + *hyrst* wooded hill (see HURST). *Colthurst* in W Yorks takes its name from a family so called, rather than vice versa.

Coulton English (Lancs.): habitation name from *Coulton* in N Yorks., perhaps so called from OE *colt* ass, young horse (see COLT) + *tūn* enclosure, settlement.

Coumas *see* COOMBE

Counihan *see* COONEY

Counsel English: **1.** nickname for a wise or thoughtful man, from ANF *counseil* consultation, deliberation, also counsel, advice (L *consilium*, from *consulere* to consult). **2.** some of the forms were probably influenced by the similar meaning of ANF *councile* council, assembly (L *concilium* assembly, from the archaic verb *concalere* to call together, summon), and it may also have been an occupational name for a member of a royal council or, more probably, a manorial council.
Vars.: **Co(u)nsell**, **Councel(l)**, **Council**.

Count English: nickname from the Norman title of rank, OF *conte, cunte* (L *comes*, gen. *comitis*, companion, from *com-* together, with + *īre* to go).
Vars.: **Conte**; **Lecount**.
Dims.: Fr.: **Comtet**. Prov.: **Condet**. It.: **Contini** (also Jewish); **Contin(o)**, **Continelli**, **Contuzzi**; **Contiello** (Naples); **Continoli** (Emilia). Port.: **Condinho**.
Patr.: It.: **Del Conte** (Tuscany).
Patr. (from a dim.): It.: **Di Contino**.

Coupar Scots: **1.** habitation name from *Cupar* in Fife, which is probably of Pictish origin, with an unknown meaning. There are several other places similarly named, for example *Cuper* Angus and *Cupar* Maculty (now

Couttie), but these do not seem to have given rise to surnames. **2.** var. of COOPER.
Vars.: **Couper**, **Cowper**.

Coupe *see* COOPER

Coupland *see* COPELAND

Coupman *see* COPEMAN

Courage English and French: nickname from OF *corage, curage* courage, stout-heartedness (a deriv. of *cuer* heart, L *cor*), which was occasionally used in ME as an adj., normally with reference to bodily corpulence. Reaney suggests an alternative derivation from *Cowridge* End in Beds., but it is doubtful what evidence there is to support this.
Dims.: Fr.: **Courageot**, **Courajot**.

Courage *see* KENDRICK

Courbe French: topographic name for someone who lived near a bend in a road or river, from OF *courbe* bend (from the verb *courber* to bend, L *curvāre*). There are a number of minor places throughout France named with this word, and the surname may be a habitation name from one of these. It may also sometimes have been a nickname for a man with a stooping gait.
Dims.: **Courbet**, **Courbin**, **Courbon**, **Courbot**.
Aug.: **Courbat**.
Pej.: **Courbaud**.

Courcelles French: habitation name from the various places that derive their names from LL *corticella* (a dim. of *co(ho)rs*; see COURT 1), probably resulting from the division between heirs of an originally larger estate.
Vars.: **Coursel(le)**, **Courseaux**, **Courcelle**.

Courné *see* CORNE

Couronnaud *see* CORONA

Coursey *see* DECOURCEY

Court **1.** English and French: occupational name or habitation name from OF, ME *court(e), curt* court (L *cohors*, gen. *cohortis*, yard, enclosure). This word was used primarily with reference to the residence of the lord of a manor, and the surname is usually an occupational name for someone employed at a manorial court. **2.** English: nickname from OF, ME *curt* short, small (L *curtus* curtailed, truncated, cut short, broken off).
Vars.: Eng.: **Corte**, **Curt**. (Of 1 only): Eng.: **A'Court** (with ANF preposition); **Courtman**. See also COURTIER. Fr.: **Cour**; **Lacour(t)**, **Laco(u)rte**, **De(la)cour(t)**.
Dims. (of 1): It.: **Cortella**, **Cortello**, **Cortell(ett)i**, **Cortellino**, **Cort(ell)ini**; **Corticelli** (Bologna). Sp.: **Cortina(s)**, **Cortijo**. Cat.: **Cortina(s)**. (Of 2): Cat.: **Curtó**. See also CURTIN and CURZON.
Pej. (of 2): Fr.: **Courtauld**.
Patrs. (from 2): Eng.: **Courts**. Fr.: **Aucourt**. It.: **De Curti(s)**, **Di Curti**. Low Ger.: **Ko(h)rts**. Flem.: **Corten(s)**.

Courtadon *see* CORTADA

Courtenay **1.** English (Norman): habitation name from *Courtenay* in Loiret or Gâtinais, both named from a Gallo-Roman landlord *Curtenus* (a deriv. of L *curtus* short; cf. COURT 2) + the local suffix *-ācum*. **2.** English (Norman): nickname for someone with a snub nose, from OF *c(o)urt*

short (see COURT 2) + *nes* nose (L *nāsus*). **3.** Irish: Anglicized form of Gael. **Ó Curnáin** 'descendant of *Curnán*', an OIr. personal name of uncertain origin.

Vars.: **Courtney, Cort(e)ney, Cortnay**.

Courtier 1. French and English: occupational name for a judge, less often also for a servant employed at the court or residence of a lord, from OF *courtier*, an agent deriv. of *court* (see COURT 1). OF *court* came to be used of a court of law, as local justice was dispensed originally by the lord of the manor. Later he was assisted by advisers, to whom he eventually delegated responsibility entirely for most practical purposes. The surname is unlikely ever to have been acquired by a courtier in the sense of one who frequented a royal court, for those in this position were always of at least knightly class and already held distinctive surnames from their estates. **2.** French: habitation name from places called *Courtier* in Seine-et-Marne and Basses-Alpes, or *Courtié* in Tarn, all of which get their names from LL *co(ho)rtiāre*, a deriv. of *co(ho)rs* court.

Var. (of 1): Eng.: **Curter**.

Courtil French: topographic name for someone who lived by a walled kitchen garden attached to a farm or manor, OF *courtil* walled garden (a deriv. of *court*; see COURT 1). The surname may also have been an occupational name for someone who was employed in a kitchen garden.

Vars.: **Courtille; Courtil(l)ier**.

Dims.: **Courtillet, Courtillon, Courtillol(e)s**.

Courvoisier French: occupational name for a shoemaker, OF *corvisier* (from LL *cordovesārius*, from *Cordove(n)sis*, an adj. deriv. of CÓRDOBA; see CORDONNIER 2).

Vars.: **Corvisier, Corvisy; Crouvoisier, Crouvisier, Crouvezier, Cravoisier; Corbisier, Corbusier, Lecorbusier** (Belgium).

Cousin English and French: **1.** nickname from ME, OF *co(u)sin, cusin* (L *consobrīnus*), which in the Middle Ages, as in Shakespearean English, had the general meaning 'relative', 'kinsman'. The surname would thus have denoted a person related in some way to a prominent figure in the neighbourhood. In some cases it may also have been a nickname for someone who used the term 'cousin' frequently as a familiar term of address. The old slang word *cozen* 'cheat', perhaps derives from the medieval confidence trickster's use of the word *cousin* as a term of address to invoke a spurious familiarity. The patrs. constitute the most frequent forms of this name.

Vars.: Eng.: **Cousen, Cosin; Cussen, Cusson, Cuzen** (see also CONSTANCE and CUTHBERT); **Cushing, Cushion, Cushe(o)n**.

Dims.: Fr.: **Cousinet, Couzinet, Cousiney, Cousinot, Couzineau, Cous(in)ou**.

Patrs.: Eng.: **Cousins, Co(u)sens, Co(u)zens, Cosyns, Cossins, Cossons, Cozins, Cus(s)ins, Cuzons, Cussens, Cussons**.

Cousteau *see* COSTE

Coutance *see* CONSTANCE

Coutanceau *see* CONSTANT

Coutet *see* COT

Couto Portuguese: topographic name for someone who lived by an enclosed pasture, Port. *couto* (LL *cautum*, from the past part. of *cavēre* to make safe, secure).

Dim.: **Coutinho**.

Coutts Scots: habitation name from *Cults* in the former county of Aberdeens. (now part of Grampian region), so called from Gael. *coillte* woods, with the later addition of the Eng. pl. *-s*.

Couturier French: **1.** occupational name for a tailor, from an agent deriv. of OF *cousture* seam (L *consutūra*, from *(con)suere* to sew (together)). **2.** occupational name for a holder of a smallholding, from an agent deriv. of OF *couture* small plot, kitchen garden (LL *cultūra*, in class. L used in the abstract sense 'cultivation', 'agriculture', from *colere* to till, tend).

Vars.: **Couturié, Couturieux, Cou(r)durier, Courdurié; Couture, Coudure**. (Of 1 only): **Cousturier, Cousture**.

Couvert French: topographic name for someone who lived in a shady spot sheltered by trees, from OF *co(u)vert* covered (L *coopertum*, past part. of *cooperire*; cf. COUVREUR). There are villages in Calvados, Manche, Lot, and Haute-Loire that get their name from this word, and the surname may also be a habitation name from any of these.

Couvreur French: occupational name for a roofer, from OF *co(u)vreur*, an agent deriv. of *co(u)vrir* to cover (L *cooperire*, cf. COUVERT). Roofing materials in the Middle Ages might be tiles (cf. TILER), slates (cf. SLATER), or thatch (cf. THATCHER), depending on the regional availability of suitable materials.

Vars.: **Couvreux; Couvrant** (pres. part.).

Cove English: topographic name for someone who lived near a bay or inlet on the coast or an embayment in a river, OE *cofa*. There are places with this name in Devon, Hants, and Suffolk, and the surname may be a habitation name from one of these.

Covelli *see* JACOB

Coveney English: habitation name from a place in Cambs., so called from the gen. case of OE *cofa* (see COVE; the place is in former fenland, where there may have been a bay on a lake or waterway) or of a personal name *Cōfa* (of uncertain origin) + OE *ēg* island. The surname is now established in Ireland as well as in E Anglia.

Coventry English: habitation name from the city in the W Midlands, which is probably so called from the gen. case of the OE personal name *Cōfa* (cf. COVENEY) + OE *trēow* tree.

Coverdale English: habitation name from the place so called in N Yorks, in the valley (ME *dale*) of the river *Cover* (a Brit. name perhaps containing the element which has given W *cau* hollow).

Covillo *see* COBO

Covington 1. Scots: habitation name from *Covinton* in the former county of Lanarks., first recorded in the late 12th cent. in the L form *Villa Colbani*, and twenty years later as *Colbaynistun*. By 1434 it had been collapsed to *Cowantoun*, and at the end of the 15th cent. it first appears in the form *Covingtoun*. It is nevertheless clearly named with the personal name *Colban* (see COLEMAN 1) + OE *tūn* enclosure, settlement; the proprietor in question was a follower of David, Prince of Cumbria, in about 1120. **2.** English: habitation name from a place in Hunts. (now Cambs.), so called from OE *Cōfingtūn* 'Cōfa's settlement'.

Cowan Scots: **1.** common Lowland surname of uncertain origin. None of the explanations put forward is very convincing. The name is not recorded before the middle of the 16th cent. (James *Cowhen*, Berwicks. 1560). **2.** Highland surname of Gael. origin; see EWAN.
Var.: **Cowen**.

Coward English: occupational name for a tender of cattle, ME *cowherde*, OE *cūhyrde*, from *cū* cow + *hierde* herdsman (see HEARD). (The surname has nothing to do with mod. Eng. *coward*, which is from OF *cuard*, app. a pej. from *coue* tail (L *cauda*) with ref. to an animal with its tail between its legs.)
Var.: **Cowherd** (a rare surname, apparently the result of a conscious respelling by a bearer anxious to avoid association with mod. Eng. *coward*).

Cowburn English (Lancs.): habitation name from *Cowburgh*, a minor place in the parish of Kirkham, Lancs. The medieval spellings of the placename indicate uncertainty about whether the final element is OE *burna* stream (see BOURNE) or *burh* fort (see BURKE). The first element is *cū* cow.

Cowcha see COUCH

Cowdell see CALDWELL

Cowden English and Scots: habitation name from any of at least three places so called. One in Northumb. occurs in 1286 as *Colden* and is derived from OE *col* (char)coal + *denu* valley (see DEAN 1); that in E Yorks. occurs in Domesday Book as *Coledun* and is from OE *col* + *dūn* hill (see DOWN 1); while one in Kent occurs in 1160 as *Cudena* and is from OE *cū* cow + *denn* pasture. The last does not appear to have yielded any surnames; the surname is more or less restricted to N England, and is also found in N Ireland, where it may be of Scots origin, from places so called near Dollar and near Dalkieth, Lothian.

Cowdrey English (Norman): habitation name from *Coudrai* in Seine-Maritime or *Coudray* in Eure, or *Cowdray* in Sussex, which seems to have been named after one of these two. All are named from OF *coudraie* hazel copse (a collective of *coudre* hazel tree, LL *colurus*, a metathesized form of class. L *corylus*, from Gk).
Vars.: **Cowdr(a)y**, **Cowd(e)roy**, **Cowdery**, **Coudray**.

Cowdron see CALDERON

Cowell English: habitation name from places in Lancs. and Gloucs. called *Cowhill*, from OE *cū* cow + *hyll* hill.

Cowey see COFFEY

Cowie Scots: habitation name from any of several places of this name, esp. one near Stirling, probably so called from Gael. *colldha*, adj. from *coll* hazel.
Var.: **Coey**.

Cowles see COLE

Cowley 1. English: habitation name from any of the various places so called. One in Gloucs. is named from OE *cū* cow + *lēah* wood, clearing; two in Derbys. get their first element from OE *col* (char)coal; and one near London has it from OE *cofa* recess, bay (see COVE) or the personal name *Cōfa* (cf. COVENEY and COVENTRY). The largest group, however, with examples in Bucks., Devon, Oxon., and Staffs., were apparently named as the wood or clearing of *Cufa*; however, in view of the number of places named with this element, it is possible that it conceals a topographical term as well as a personal name. **2.** Irish and Manx: aphetic form of *Macaulay*; see OLIFF.
Var. (of 2): **Kewley**.

Cowling see COLLING

Cowlishaw see CULSHAW

Cowman see CUMMING

Cowney see COONEY

Cowper see COUPAR

Cowpland see COPELAND

Cox 1. English: patr. from the ME hypocoristic suffix *-coke* (with genitive *-s*), which was attached freely to almost any given name to create a pet form (see COCK). **2.** Flemish: patr. from the occupational term *cok* COOK.

Coxall English: habitation name from *Coggeshall* in Essex, so called from the gen. case of the OE personal name *Cogg* (of uncertain origin) + OE *halh* recess (see HALE 1).
Vars.: **Coggeshall**, **Coxwell**, **Cogswell**.

Coxen see COCK

Coy English: nickname for a quiet and unassuming person, from ME, OF *coi*, *quei* calm, quiet (L *quiētus*).

Coyle Irish: **1.** from the Gael. personal name *Cathmhaol*, composed of the elements *cath* battle + *maol* chief. **2.** Anglicized form of Gael. *Mac Giolla Chomhghaill*; see COLE. **3.** Anglicized form of Gael. *Mac Dhubhghaill*; see COOLE and DOUGALL.

Coyle see COLE

Coyne 1. English: metonymic occupational name for a minter of money, or nickname for a miser, from ME *coin* piece of money (earlier of the die used to stamp money, from L *cuneus* wedge). **2.** Irish: Anglicized form of Gael. **Ó Cúáin** 'descendant of *Cúán*', a byname from a dim. of *cú* hound, dog. **3.** Irish: Anglicized form of Gael. **Ó Cadhain** 'descendant of *Cadhan*', a byname from *cadhan* barnacle goose.
Vars. (of 1): **Conyer** (occupational). (Of 2): **O'Coyne**, **O'Cuayn**, **(O')Quane**, **Quaine**, **Cain**. (Of 3): **O'Coyne**, **(O')Kine**, **Kyne**, CAIN, COHEN; **Barnacle**.
Patr. (from 1): **Conyers**.

Cozens see COUSIN

Cozzi see DOMINIQUE, JACK

Crabbe English and Scots: **1.** nickname for someone with a peculiar gait, from ME *crabbe*, OE *crabba* crab (the crustacean). **2.** topographic name for someone who lived by a crab-apple tree, from ME *crabbe* (apparently of ON origin). It may also have been a nickname for a cantankerous person, a sense which developed primarily from this word, with reference to the sourness of the fruit, but may also have been influenced by the awkward-seeming locomotion of the crustacean.

Vars.: **Crab(b)**. (Of 2 only): **Crabtree**.

Crabet see CHEEVER

Cracknell English: habitation name from either of two places in N Yorks, one called *Crakehall* and the other *Crakehill*, both from ON *kráka* crow (or OE *craca* crake) + OE *halh* recess (see HALE 1). The surname is now more common in E Anglia than in Yorks.

Vars.: **Cracknall**, **Crackel**.

Craddock Welsh: from the OW personal name which gives mod. W *Caradog* 'Amiable' (from the Celt. root *car* love; cf. CAREY). A Brit. bearer of this or a cogn. name is recorded in the L form *Cara(c)tacus* and remembered for his leadership of a revolt against the Roman occupation in the 1st cent. AD.

Vars.: **Cradduck**, **Cradock**, **Cradick**.

Craft see CROFT

Craig Scots: topographic name for someone who lived near a steep or precipitous rock, from Gael. *creag*, a word that has been borrowed in ME *crag(g)*.

Vars.: **Craik** (a place in the former county of Aberdeens., now part of Grampian region); **Carrick** (a district in the former county of Ayrs., now part of Strathclyde region); **Craigie** (from the Gael. locative case); **Cragg(s)** (from ME forms).

Craker see CROAKER

Cramp see CROME

Crampton see CROMPTON

Crandle see RONALD

Crane English: nickname from the bird, OE *cran(uc)*, *cron(uc)*, *corn(uc)* (a term which included the HERON until the introduction of a separate word for the latter in the 14th cent.), probably denoting a tall, thin man with long legs.

Var.: **CRANK**.

Dims.: Ger.: **Kränkel**, **Krenkel**. Low Ger.: **KRANKE**.

Cranfield English: habitation name from a place in Beds., so called from OE *cran(uc)* CRANE + *feld* pasture, open country (see FIELD).

Crank English (chiefly Lancs.): 1. nickname for a cheerful, boisterous, or cocky person, from ME *cranke* lively, lusty, vigorous. 2. var. of CRANE.

Var.: **Cronk**.

Crankshaw English: habitation name from *Cranshaw* in Lancs., so called from OE *cran(uc)* CRANE + *sceaga* grove, thicket (see SHAW).

Vars.: **Cranshaw**, **Cron(k)shaw**, **Crenshaw**.

Cranmer English: habitation name, probably from *Cranmore* in Somerset, so called from OE *cran(uc)* CRANE + *mere* lake, pool (see DELAMARE).

Cranston Scots: habitation name from a place, probably *Cranstoun* Riddel near Dalkeith, so called from the gen. case of the OE byname *Cran* CRANE' + OE *tūn* enclosure, settlement.

Vars.: **Cranstone**, **Cranstoun**.

Crapper see CROPPER

Crasswell see CRESWELL

Crathorne English: habitation name, probably from *Crathorne* in N Yorks., although the surname is now more or less restricted to the W Midlands. The Yorks. place is of uncertain etymology; Ekwall suggests that it may be from OE *craca* crake (cf. CRACKNELL) + *þorn* thorn bush.

Var.: **Craythorne**.

Craven English: regional name from the district of W Yorks. so called, which is probably from a Brit. word, the ancestor of W *craf* garlic. There is probably no connection with ME *cravant* cowardly, feeble, which is of uncertain origin.

Cravo Portuguese: 1. metonymic occupational name for someone who made and sold nails, especially those used in horseshoes, from Port. *cravo* nail (L *clāvus*). 2. topographic name for someone who lived by a spot where pinks grew, from Port. *cravo* pink, carnation (a transferred use of the same word, from the shape of the bud).

Var. (of 1): **Craveiro** (an agent deriv.).

Dims. (of 1): Fr.: **Cloutot**; **Clavel**, **Claveau** (central France).

Cravoisier see COURVOISIER

Craw see CROW

Crawcour see CROAKER

Crawetz see KRAWIEC

Crawford 1. English, Irish, and Scots: habitation name from any of the various places, for example in Dorset and Lancs., England, and Strathclyde, Scotland, so called from OE *crāwa* CROW + *ford* FORD. 2. English: var. of CROWFOOT.

Vars.: **Crauford**, **Crawfurd**, **Craufurd**, **Crawforth**.

Crawley see CROWLEY

Crawshaw English: habitation name from *Crawshaw* Booth in Lancs., so called from OE *crāwa* CROW + *sceaga* grove, thicket (see SHAW).

Vars.: **Crashaw**, **Crawshay**, **Croshaw**, **Crowsher**.

Cray Irish: Anglicized form of Gael. Ó **Craoibhe** 'descendant of *Craobhach*', a byname meaning 'Curly(-headed)' or 'Prolific' (from *craobh* branch, bough).

Vars.: **O'Crevy**, **Creev(e)y**, **Creavagh**; **Creagh**.

Dims.: **O'Crevan**, **Creaven**, **Creavin** (Gael. Ó **Craobháin**).

Creagh see CRAY

Creamer 1. English: occupational name for a seller of dairy products, from an agent deriv. of ME, OF *creme* cream (LL *crāma*, apparently of Gaul. origin). 2. Scots and N Irish: occupational name for a pedlar, a cogn. of KRÄMER. Sir John Skene, in his *De verborum significatione* ('On the Meaning of Words', 1681), explains the term *pedder* as 'ane mechand or *cremer*, quha beris ane pack or *creame* upon his back'. **3.** U.S.: Anglicization of KRÄMER.

Var. (of 2 and 3): **Cramer**.

Creamer *see* KRÄMER

Creaney *see* RAINEY

Crease English: nickname from ME *crease* fine, elegant (OE *crēas*). There is probably no connection with mod. Eng. *crease*, which is first attested in the 16th cent., from earlier *crest* (cf. CRESTE).

Vars.: **Crees(e)**; **Creasey** (chiefly Suffolk).

Crebbin *see* CRIBBIN

Creedon Irish: Anglicized form of Gael. **Ó Críodáin** and **Mac Críodáin** 'descendant' and 'son of *Críodán*', an OIr. personal name of uncertain origin (the ending is dim. in form).

Creegor *see* CROAKER

Creemers *see* KRÄMER

Creggan Irish: Anglicized form of Gael. **Ó Croidheagáin** 'descendant of *Croidheagán*', a personal name from a dim. of *croidhe* heart, used as a term of endearment.

Vars.: **O'Cridigan**, **O'Crigan(e)**, **O'Criane**, **Creddon**, **Creeghan**, **Cre(i)gan**, **Cre(h)an**, **Creane**, **Cree**.

Creighton Scots: habitation name from *Crichton*, 15 miles south-east of Edinburgh, first recorded *c*.1145 in the form *Crechtune*, in 1250 as *Krektun*, and in 1367 as *Creigchton*. The name is probably an early hybrid cpd of Gael. *crioch* border, boundary + ME *tune* farm, settlement (OE *tūn*).

Vars.: **C(h)richton**, **Crichten**, **Crighton**.

Cremin Irish: Anglicized form of Gael. **Ó Croimín** 'descendant of *Croimín*', a byname from a dim. of *crom* bent, crooked; cf. CROME.

Crenel *see* CARNELL

Crennall *see* RONALD

Crenshaw *see* CRANKSHAW

Crépet *see* CRISP

Crepin *see* CRISPIN

Crépy French: habitation name from places in Aisne, Oise, and Pas-de-Calais, all so called from their Gallo-Roman landlord *Crispius* (a deriv. of *Crispus*; see CRISP), with the addition of the local suffix -*acum*.

Crès Provençal: topographic name for someone who lived on a patch of stony ground, from OProv. *cres*, *gres* (of uncertain etymology).

Var.: **Ducrès**.

Dims.: **Cresset**, **Cressin**, **Cressy**, **Cressot**, **Cresseau(x)**, **Cresson**.

Crescent French: from a given name (L *Crescens*, gen. *Crecentis*, 'Growing (sc. in virtue)', pres. part. of *crescere* to grow, increase) borne by an early Christian saint martyred in Galatia under the Roman emperor Trajan.

Vars.: **Cressent**, **Cressan(t)**.

Creste French: topographic name for someone who lived near the crest of a hill, OF *creste* (LL *crista*), or habitation name from any of the numerous places named with this word. It may also in part have been originally a nickname for an arrogant individual, from the same word used with reference to the cock's comb (cf. OF *crester* to strut).

Vars.: **Crète**; **Cresté**, **Crété**, **Cretté** (nicknames).

Dims.: Fr.: **Cretet**, **Créteau(x)**.

Aug.: Fr.: **Crétat**.

Crestian *see* CHRISTIAN

Creswell English: habitation name from any of the various places in England that get their names from OE *cærse* (water)cress + *well(a)* spring, stream (see WELL), as for example in Derbys., Notts., and Staffs.

Vars.: **Cresswell**; **Carswell** (from a place in Berks.); **Caswell** (from places in Dorset, Northants, and Somerset), **Casswell**, **Casewell**; **Craswall** (from a place in Herefords.), **Cras(s)well**, **Caswall**, **Caswill**; **Cressall**, **Cressel**, **Criswell**, **Crissel**; **Kerswell** (from places in Devon and Worcs.), **Kerswill**; **Crassweller**.

Creux French: topographic name for someone who lived by a hollow in the ground, OF *creus(e)* (apparently of Gaul. origin).

Vars.: **Cr(e)use**, **Creuze**; **Lecreux**, **Ducreux**.

Dims.: **Creuzet**, **Cr(e)uset**, **Creusot**, **Creuzot**. Prov.: **Croset**, **Cro(u)zet**, **Crozel**; see also CROSS.

Aug.: Prov.: **Crozat**.

Creveau *see* CRIBLE

Crew English: habitation name from *Crewe* in Ches., so called from OW *criu* weir (mod. W *cryw* weir, ford). This seems to have denoted a wickerwork fence that was stretched across the river Dee to catch fish. The town of *Crewe* near Edinburgh was probably named after this place by settlers from Ches., and may also be a partial source of the surname.

Var.: **Crewe**.

Crewes *see* CRUISE

Crewther *see* CROWTHER

Criado Spanish: nickname for a foster child, from the past part. of Sp. *criar* to raise, bring up (L *creāre* to create, form). In medieval Spain it was a frequent practice for the offspring of a nobleman's vassals to be brought up at his court, and the name may well in some cases have originally been used as a title of honour for one of these.

Cribbin Irish: Anglicized form of Gael. **Mac Roibín**, a patr. from the ANF given name *Robin*, dim. of ROBERT.

Vars.: **Cribbins**, **Crebbin**; **Gribbin**, **Gribben**, **Gribbon** (Ulster).

Crible French: metonymic occupational name for a maker or seller of sieves, from OF *crible* sieve (LL *cribellum*, a dim. of class. L *cribrum*).

Vars.: **Crevel**, **Creveau**, **Cruvel**; **Cribellier**, **Crib(l)ier**, **Crivelier**, **Crevelier**, **Cruvel(h)ier**, **Cruveilh(i)er**.

Crich English: habitation name from the place so called in Derbys., which apparently gets its name from a Brit. element **crūc* hill. The pronunciation is normally /kraitʃ/.

Var.: **Crick** (a place in Northants).

Crichten see CREIGHTON

Crilly see REILLY

Crimond Scots: habitation name from one of the places in Scotland called *Crimond*, probably the one near Peterhead in the former county of Aberdeen., now part of Grampian region. The place is first recorded in 1250 in the form *Creymund*, and is named with the Gael. elements *creachann* bare summit + *monadh* hill.

Crimp English: of uncertain origin, possibly a nickname for a cripple or hunchback, from an unattested blend of ME *cripel* (cf. CRIPWELL) and *crome* (cf. CROME 1). The earliest known bearers are Richard *Crempe*, Richard *Crempa*, and William *Crempa*, all of whom are recorded in S Devon in 1332, and the surname has been almost entirely confined to this locality ever since.

Crindle see RONALD

Cripwell English: nickname for a cripple, from ME *cripel*, *crepel*, *crupel* (OE *crypel*, a deriv. of *crēopan* to creep). The spelling may have been consciously altered to the form of a habitation name to avoid unpleasant associations.

Crisp English: 1. nickname for a man with curly hair, from ME *crisp*, OE *crisp*, *cryps* (L *crispus*), reinforced in ME by an OF word also from L *crispus*. 2. short form of CRISPIN.

Vars.: **Crispe**, **Chrisp**; **Crip(p)s**, **Crippes** (metathesized forms).

Dims. (of 1): Fr.: **Crespet**, **Crespel**, **Crespon**, **Crespoul**, **Crispoul**, **Crépet**, **Crépey**, **Crépon**.

Crispin English and French: 1. from the ME, OF given name *Crispin* (L *Crispīnus*, a family name derived from *crispus* curly-haired; see CRISP). This name was especially popular in France in the early Middle Ages, having been borne by a saint who was martyred at Soissons in AD *c*.285 along with a companion, *Crispiniānus* (whose name is a further deriv. of the same word). 2. dim. of CRISP.

Vars.: Eng.: **Chrispin**, **Crip(p)in**, **Crippen**, **Crepin**. Fr.: **Cre(s)pin**, **Crépin**, **Crespi**, **Crespy**.

Crissel see CRESWELL

Crist see CHRISTIAN

Cristal Scots: from a Sc. pet form of the given name CHRISTOPHER.

Vars.: **C(h)rystal(l)**, **Crystol**, **Kristall**.

Patr.: **McCrystal**.

Cristea see CHRISTOPHER

Critchley see CRUTCHLEY

Crnković see CHERNYAKOV

Croaker English (Norman): habitation name from any of the various places in Normandy, most notably in Calvados, Oise, and Nord, called *Crèvecoeur* 'heartbreak' (from OF *creve(r)* to break, destroy, die (L *crepāre* to rattle) + *ceur* heart (L *cor*)), a reference to the infertility and unproductiveness of the land.

Vars.: **Crawcour**, **Craker**, CROCKER, **Cre(e)gor**.

Croasdale English (Lancs.): habitation name from *Crossdale* in Cumb., so called from the gen. pl. of ON *kross* CROSS + *dalr* valley.

Vars.: **Cros(s)dale**.

Croattini see HORVÁTH

Crocker English (chiefly W Country): 1. var. of CROAKER. 2. occupational name for a potter, from an agent deriv. of ME *crock* pot (OE *croc(ca)*).

Crockett 1. English and Scots (Galloway): nickname for someone who affected a particular hairstyle, from ME *croket* large curl (ONF *croquet*, dim. of *croque* curl, hook, OF *croche*; see CROOK). 2. Scots: Anglicized form of Gael. **Mac Riocaird** 'son of RICHARD'.

Vars.: **Croket**, **Crockatt**.

Crockford English: habitation name from *Crockford* Bridge in the parish of Chertsey, Surrey. The placename is of uncertain origin; the first element may be OE *croc(ca)* pot, used of a hollow in the ground or of a place where potsherds were found, the second is OE *ford* FORD.

Croft English: topographic name for someone who lived by an arable enclosure, normally adjoining a house, OE *croft*. There are several places in England named with this word, and the surname may equally be a habitation name from any of them. *Croft* in Leics. is so called from OE *cræft* craft, skill, also used in the concrete sense of a machine, engine, or mill.

Vars.: **Crofts**, **Craft(s)**, **Cruft(s)**; **Crofter**.

Crofton English: habitation name from any of the various places so called, for example in Cumb., Hants, Kent, Lincs., Wilts., and W Yorks. Most of these are so called from OE *croft* paddock, smallholding (see CROFT) + *tūn* enclosure, settlement, but the one in Kent probably has as its first element OE *cropp* swelling, mound (cf. CROPPER), and that in Lincs. OE *croh* saffron (L *crocus*, from Gk).

Croitoru see KRAWIEC

Cromack see CRUMMOCK

Crombie Scots: habitation name from a place in the former county of Aberdeen. (now part of Grampian region), so called from Gael. *crom(b)* crooked or the Brit. cogn. of this word, ancestor of W *crwm*.

Vars.: **Cromie** (chiefly N Ireland); **Crumbie**, **Crummie**, **Crumm(e)y**, **Crummay**.

Crome English: 1. nickname for a cripple or hunchback, from ME *crome*, OE *crumb* bent, crooked, stooping. 2. metonymic occupational name for a maker, seller, or user of hooks, from ME *crome, cromb* hook, crook (from OE *crumb* bent, reinforced by an OF borrowing from a Gmc cogn.). 3. habitation name from *Croom* in E Yorks., so called from OE *crōhum*, dat. pl. (used originally after a preposition) of *crōh* narrow valley (a cogn. of ON *krá* corner, bend, and related to the words mentioned in 1 and 2 above). 4. habitation name from *Croome* in Worcs., so called from an old Brit. river name ultimately cogn. with the other words mentioned here; cf. W *crwm* crooked, winding.

Vars.: **Croom(e)**. (Of 1 only): **Cromb, Crumb**; **Crump** (chiefly W Midlands), **Cramp**, CRIMP.

Dim. (of 1): Ger.: **Krüm(m)el, Krimmel**. Low Ger.: **Krimpke**.

Patr. (from 1): Flem.: **Crommen**.

Crompton English: habitation name from *Crompton* in Lancs., so called from OE *crumb* bent, crooked (see CROME 1) + *tūn* enclosure, settlement, i.e. a settlement by a bend in a river or road.

Vars.: **Crumpton** (chiefly W Midlands), **Crampton**.

Cromwell English: habitation name from places in Notts. and W Yorks., so called from OE *crumb* bent, crooked (see CROME 1) + *well(a)* spring, stream (see WELL).

Cronholm *see* CORONA

Cronin Irish: Anglicized form of Gael. **Ó Cróinín** 'descendant of *Cróinín*', a byname from a dim. of *crón* swarthy.

Var.: **Crone**.

Cronk *see* CRANK

Cronkshaw *see* CRANKSHAW

Crook English: **1.** from the ON byname *Krókr* 'Crook', 'Bend', originally no doubt bestowed on a cripple or hunchback or a devious schemer, but in early medieval England used as a personal name. **2.** topographic name for someone who lived by a bend in a river or road, or metonymic occupational name for a maker, seller, or user of hooks, from ON *krókr* borrowed into ME as a vocabulary word.

Vars.: **Crooke, Krook**. (Of 1 only): **Croke** (Ireland). (Of 2 only): **Crooker**.

Dims.: Fr.: **Crochet, Crochot, Crochon**.

Pej.: Fr.: **Crochard**.

Patrs. (from 1): Eng.: **Crook(e)s, Crookson**.

Crookshank *see* CRUIKSHANK

Cropper English (chiefly Lancs.): occupational name for a picker of fruit or vegetables or a reaper of corn, from an agent deriv. of ME *crop(en)* to pick, pluck (a deriv. of *crop* produce, OE *cropp* swelling, head of a plant). The word was used also of the polling of cattle and the name may therefore have been given to someone who did this.

Var.: **Crapper**.

Crosby 1. English and Scots: habitation name from any of various places in N England and S Scotland that get their names from ON *kross* CROSS + *býr* farm, settlement. **2.** Irish: var. of CROSS 2 (see below).

Vars.: **Crosbie, Crossby**.

Croset *see* CREUX

Croshaw *see* CRAWSHAW

Cross 1. English: topographic name for someone who lived near a stone cross set up by the roadside or in a marketplace, from ON *kross* (via Gael. from L *crux*, gen. *crucis*), which in ME quickly and comprehensively displaced the OE form *crūc* (see CROUCH). In a few cases the surname may have been given originally to someone who lived by a crossroads, but this sense of the word seems

to have been a comparatively late development. In other cases, the surname (and its European cogns.) may have denoted one who carried the cross in processions of the Christian Church, but in Eng. at least the usual word for this sense was CROZIER. **2.** Irish: Anglicized form of Gael. **Mac an Chrosáin**, a patr. from *crosán* reciter of satirical verse, satirist (originally a cross-bearer in a religious procession; see also CROSBY).

Vars.: **Crosse**. (Of 1 only): **Crossman** (chiefly Somerset). (Of 2 only): **Crossey, Crossin, (Mc)Crossan, McEcrossan, McAncrossane**.

Dims. (of 1): It.: **Crocetti, Crucetti, Crucitti, Crosetto, Crosetti**. Habitation names: Pol.: **Krzyż(an)owski**.

Crossfield English (Yorks.): apparently a habitation name from an unidentified place so called, from ME CROSS + *fe(i)ld(e)* open country, FIELD.

Var.: **Crosfield**.

Crossland English (chiefly W Yorks.): habitation name from a place in the parish of Almondbury, W Yorks., so called from ME CROSS + *land* land.

Vars.: **Cros(se)land**.

Crossley English: habitation name from either of two places in W Yorks. named from ME CROSS + LEE clearing, pasture.

Crossthwaite N English: habitation name from any of several places in NW England that derive their names from ME CROSS + THWAITE clearing.

Vars.: **Crosthwaite, Crosswaite**.

Crosston English: habitation name from *Croston* near Leyland in Lancs., which gets its name from ME CROSS + *tune, tone* enclosure, settlement.

Crothers *see* CARRUTHERS

Crotty Irish: Anglicized form of Gael. **Ó Crotaigh** 'descendant of *Crotach*', a byname for a hunchback.

Crouch English: topographic name for someone who lived by a CROSS, from ME *crouch*, OE *crūc*, a word that was replaced in ME by the ON form *cross*.

Vars.: **Crotch, Crutch**; **Croucher, Crouchman**.

Crouse *see* CRUISE

Crouvezier *see* COURVOISIER

Crovelli *see* CUERVO

Crow 1. English: nickname from the bird, ME *crowe*, OE *crāwa*. **2.** Irish (Munster): Anglicized form of Gael. *Mac Conchradha*; see MCENROE. **3.** Irish: translation of any of various Gael. names derived from *fiach* raven, crow; see FEE.

Vars.: **Crowe** (very common in Ireland); **Craw**.

Crowell English: habitation name from a place in Oxon., so called from OE *crāwa* CROW + *well(a)* spring, stream (see WELL).

Crowfoot English: nickname for someone with splayed feet, or with a foot deformed in some other way.

Crowhurst English: habitation name from places in Surrey and Sussex. The former gets its name from OE *crāwa*

CROW + *hyrst* wooded hill (see HURST); the latter originally had as its first element OE *crōh* narrow valley (see CROME 3).

Var.: **Crowest**.

Crowle English: according to Reaney, this is a habitation name from places in Lincs. and Worcs. The Lincs. place is named from a river (now no longer extant, due to draining) called *Crull* 'winding'; the Worcs. placename is a cpd of OE *croh* saffron or *crōh* bend + *lēah* wood, clearing. However, the surname is more commonly found in Devon and Cornwall than anywhere else. There is no plausible derivation in the Corn. language. The surname is possibly a var. of *Croll* (see KROLL), as Reaney alternatively suggests.

Crowley 1. English: habitation name from any of various places so called from OE *crāwe* CROW + *lēah* wood, clearing. 2. Irish: Anglicized form of Gael. **Ó Cruadhlaoich** 'descendant of *Cruadhlaoch*', a personal name composed of the elements *cruadh* hardy + *laoch* hero.

Vars. (of 1): **Crawley**. (Of 2): **O'Cro(w)l(e)y, Crol(l)y, Crolla**.

Crowther English: occupational name for a player on the *crowd*, ME *crouth, croude*, a type of popular medieval stringed instrument (W *crwth*).

Vars.: **Crowder, Crother, Crewther**.

Patrs.: **Crothers** (see also CARRUTHERS); MCWHIRTER.

Croxford English: habitation name from an unidentified minor place, apparently so called from the gen. case of the ON byname *Krókr* (see CROOK 1) + OE *ford* FORD.

Crozier English and French: occupational name for one who carried a cross or a bishop's crook in ecclesiastical processions, from ME, OF *croisier* (originally an agent deriv. of OF *crois* CROSS, but later associated also with *croce* CROOK).

Vars.: Eng.: **Cros(i)er**. Fr.: **Croisier, Croizier**.

Crucetti *see* CROSS

Cruddace *see* CARRUTHERS

Crudgington English: habitation name from a place in Shrops., earlier *Crugelton*, apparently from the Brit. element *crūc hill (see CRICH) + the explanatory OE *hyll* hill + OE *tūn* enclosure, settlement.

Cruft *see* CROFT

Cruikshank Scots: nickname for a man with a crooked leg or legs, from older Scots *cruik* hook, bend (ME *crook*, ON *krókr*; see CROOK 2) + *shank* leg(-bone) (OE *sceanca*). Black, however, suggests that it is a local name from the river *Cruik* in the former county of Kincardine (now part of Grampian region) + *shank* used in the sense of a 'projecting point of a hill joining it to the plain'.

Vars.: **Cruikshanks; Cruickshank(s), Crookshank(s)**.

Cruise English: 1. nickname from ME *cr(o)us(e)* bold, fierce (apparently from MLG, cogn. with KRAUS). 2. Norman habitation name from a place in France, perhaps *Cruys*-Straëte in Nord, apparently so called from Gaul. *crodiu hard.

Vars.: **Cr(o)use, Crew(e)s, Cruwys**.

Crumb *see* CROME

Crumbie *see* CROMBIE

Crummock English: topographic name for someone who lived near a twisted oak tree, from OE *crumb* crooked, bent (see CROME 1) + *āc* OAK. There is no connection with *Crummock* Water in Cumbria, the name of which is of Brit. origin.

Vars.: **Crummack, Cromack**.

Crumpton *see* CROMPTON

Cruse *see* CREUX

Crutch *see* CROUCH

Crutchley English (W Midlands): apparently a habitation name from an unidentified place so called from OE *crūc* cross (see CROUCH) or Brit. *crūc hill (see CRICH) + OE *lēah* wood, clearing.

Var.: **Critchley**.

Cruveilher *see* CRIBLE

Cryer English: occupational name for a town crier, one whose job was to make public announcements in a loud voice, from ME, OF *criere* (a deriv. of OF *crier* to cry aloud, L *quirītāre*).

Crystal *see* CRISTAL

Ctibor *see* STIBOR

Cubbino *see* JACOB

Cubells *see* CUVIER

Cucci *see* JACK

Cuckson *see* COOK

Cudbird *see* CUTHBERT

Cuddehy *see* CODY

Cudmore English (E Anglia): apparently a habitation name from an unidentified place so called, probably from the OE personal name *Cūða* (a short form of the various cpd names with a first element *cūð* famous, well known) + OE *mōr* marsh, fen (see MOORE).

Var.: **Cutmore**.

Cuerden English: habitation name from a place in Lancs., which according to Ekwall gets its name from Brit. *cerden, W *cerddin* ash tree.

Cuervo Spanish: nickname for a man with strikingly glossy black hair, or for one with a raucous voice, from Sp. *cuervo* raven, rook (L *corvus*).

Dims.: Fr.: **Corbeau, Corbel, Corb(e)let, Corbin**, CORBY. Eng. (Norman): **Corbett**. It.: **Corvini, Corvino, Corbell(in)i, Corbini, Corbucci; Crovelli** (Lombardy).

Cueto Spanish: habitation name from any of various places, for example in the provinces of Biscay, León, Oviedo, and Santander, named with the Sp. topographical term *cueto* crag, hill (of uncertain, probably pre-Roman, origin).

Cuff 1. English: metonymic occupational name for a maker and seller of gloves or nickname for a wearer of particularly fine gloves, from ME *cuffe* glove (of uncertain origin; attested in this sense from the 14th cent., with the modern meaning first in the 16th cent.). 2. Irish: Anglicized form of

Gael. **Mac Dhuibh**, a var. of *Mac Duibh* 'son of the black one'; see DUFF. **3.** Irish: approximate translation of Gael. *Ó Doirnín*; see DORNAN. **4.** Cornish: nickname from Corn. *cuf* dear, kind.

Var.: **Cuffe**.

Cugat Catalan: from the medieval given name *Cugat* (L *Cucuphas*, gen. *Cucuphatis*, apparently of Carthaginian derivation). The name was borne by a 3rd-cent. African saint who was martyred at Barcelona.

Cuijpers *see* COOPER

Cuisine French: metonymic occupational name for someone employed in the kitchens of a great house or monastery, from OF *cuisine* kitchen (LL *coquīna*, from *coquere* to cook; cf. COOK).

Vars.: **Cu(i)sin(ier)**.

Cuker *see* ZUCKER

Culebras Spanish: habitation name from a place in the province of Cuenca, so called from the pl. form of Sp. *culebra* snake (L *colubra*), apparently because snakes were frequently encountered there.

Cullen 1. Scots: habitation name from a place in the former county of Banffs. (now part of Grampian region), so called from Gael. *cùlan*, a dim. of *còil, cùil* nook, recess. **2.** Irish: Anglicized form of Gael. **Ó Cuilinn** 'descendant of *Cuileann*', a byname meaning 'Holly'. **3.** Irish: Anglicized form of Gael. **Ó Coileáin** 'descendant of *Coileán*', a byname meaning 'Puppy', 'Young Dog'. **4.** English: habitation name from the Rhineland city of *Cologne* (OF form of MHG *Köln*, named from L *colōnia* colony). **5.** English: var. of CULLING.

Vars.: **Cullin, Cullon**. (Of 3): **O'Collaine, (O')Collan, Cullane, Culhane**, COLLINS.

Dims. (of 2): **Cullinan(e)**.

Culling English: from a medieval given name, originally an OE patr. from the personal names *Cūl(a)* or *Cēola*. The former may be from a Gmc root *kūl* meaning 'swollen'; the latter is a short form of various cpd names with the first element *cēol* ship.

Vars.: **Cull**; COOLING, CULLEN.

Cullingworth English (Yorks.): habitation name from a place in W Yorks., originally named in OE as the 'enclosure (see WORTH) of the people of *Cūla*' (see COOLING).

Cullum *see* COLEMAN

Cully Irish: Anglicized form of Gael. **Ó Colla** 'descendant of *Colla*', an OIr. personal name of uncertain origin.

Culpepper English: occupational name for a herbalist or spicer, from ME *cull(en)* to pluck, pick (OF *coillir*, from L *colligere* to collect, gather) + *peper* (OE *piper*; see PEPPER).

Vars.: **Cul(l)peper**.

Culreavy *see* MCILWRAITH

Culshaw English (Lancs.): habitation name from *Cowlishaw* near Oldham, Lancs. The placename is recorded as *Cowleshagh* in 1422 and *Colleshawe* in 1558; it

is probably from ME *colly* dark, black (OE *colig*, from *col* (char)coal) + SHAW copse.

Var.: **Cowlishaw**.

Culter *see* COULTER

Culver English: metonymic occupational name for a keeper of doves, or nickname for someone bearing some fancied resemblance to a dove, such as mildness of temper, from OE *culfre* dove (LL *columbula*, a dim. of *columba*; see COLOMB).

Cpd: **Culverhouse** ('dovehouse', topographic).

Culwen *see* CURWEN

Cumberbatch English: habitation name from *Comberbatch* in N Ches., so called from the OE personal name *Cumbra* (originally a byname meaning 'Cumbrian') or the gen. pl. of *Cumbre* 'Britons' + OE *bæce* stream (see BACH 1).

Var.: **Cumberpatch**.

Cumeskey *see* COMERFORD

Cumming English, Scots, and Irish (Norman): from a Bret. personal name derived from the element *cam* bent, crooked (cf. CAMERON and CAMPBELL). This was relatively frequent in Norfolk, Lincs., and Yorks. in the 12th and 13th cents. as a result of Bret. immigration. The Sc. and Ir. families bearing this name and its vars. are apparently all descended ultimately from a companion of William the Conqueror who came from the area of Rouen, where Bret. influence was strong. According to another theory it is a habitation name from *Comines* near Lille, but there is no evidence in favour of this and no early forms with prepositions have been found.

Vars.: **Cuming, Cum(m)ine, Cummin, Commin, Comyn, Commane, Cummane, Cowman**.

Patrs.: Eng.: **Cum(m)in(g)s, Com(m)ings; Cummins, Com(m)ins** (mainly Irish); **Commons**. Gael.: **Mac Coimín**.

'Descendant of C.': Ir.: **O'Co(w)mane, O'Comman, O'Cumyn** (Gael. **Ó Coimín, Ó Cuimín, Ó Comáin**).

Cumpton *see* COMPTON

Cunard English: from the OE personal name *Cyneheard*, composed of the elements *cyne* royal, kingly + *heard* hardy, brave, strong.

Cundy *see* CONDY

Cunha Portuguese: habitation name from any of the numerous places so called. The placename is of uncertain origin; a common early form is *Cuin(h)a*.

Cunliffe English: habitation name from a place in Lancs., near Rishton, recorded in 1246 as *Kunteclive*, from OE *cunte* cunt + *clif* slope (see CLIVE), i.e. 'slope with a slit or crack in it'.

Var.: **Cunnliffe**.

Cunnea *see* COONEY

Cunnell *see* GUNNELL

Cunningham 1. Scots: habitation name from a place near Kilmarnock, first recorded in 1153 in the form *Cunegan*, a Brit. name of uncertain origin. The spelling in -*ham*, first recorded in 1180, represents an assimilation to the Eng.

placename element *-ham*. **2.** Irish: Anglicized form of **Ó Cuinneagáin** 'descendant of *Cuinneagán*', a personal name from a dim. of the OIr. personal name *Conn* 'Leader', 'Chief'.

Vars.: **Cuningham(e), Cunninghame, Coningham, Conyngham**. (Of 2 only): **Conag(h)an, Cunnigan, Cunihan, Cunnahan**; **Kennigan, Kinnegan, Kin(a)ghan, Kinnighan, Kinahan**.

Cunnington English: habitation name from either of two places in Cambs. (one formerly in Hunts.) called *Conington*, from ON *kunung* king, chieftain (probably replacing earlier OE *cyning*) + OE *tūn* enclosure, settlement.

Cupper *see* COOPER

Curd English: metonymic occupational name for a seller of dairy products, from ME *crud(de)*, *curd(de)* curd (cheese) (of uncertain, possibly Celt., origin).

Curland *see* KURLAND

Curless *see* CARLESS

Curley Irish: Anglicized form of Gael. *Mac Toirdhealbhaigh*; see MCTERRELLY.

Vars.: **(Mc)Corley, McCurlye, Kirley, (Mc)Kerley, McKerlie, McKyrrelly; McGorley**.

Curme English: of unknown origin, perhaps a topographic name from early mod. Eng. *corm(e)* service fruit (OF *corme*; cf. CORMIER), attested in the 16th cent.

Vars.: **Cur(ru)m, Curr(o)m**.

Curnow *see* CORNWELL

Curran Irish: Anglicized from of Gael. **Ó Corraidhín** 'descendant of *Corraidhín*', a personal name from a dim. of *corradh* spear; cf. CORR.

Vars.: **Corran, (O')Corrin, O'Corren, O'Corhane, O'Curran(e), O'Currine, O'Carran, Curreen**.

Currigan *see* CORR

Curry 1. English: habitation name from one of the places in Somerset so called from the river *Curry*, on which they stand, the name of which is of unknown origin. **2.** Scots: habitation name from *Currie* in the former county of Midlothian, now part of Lothian region, first attested in this form in 1230. It is apparently from Gael. *curraigh*, dat. of *currach* wet plain, marsh. **3.** Scots: habitation name from *Corrie* in the former county of Dumfries; see CORRIE. **4.** Irish: Anglicized form of Gael. *Ó Comhraidhe*; see CORY 2. **5.** Irish: Anglicized form of Gael. *Ó Corra*; see CORR. **6.** Cornish: habitation name from a place in the parish of Boyton, so called from Corn. *cor* corner + *e(g)y* place.

Vars.: **Currey, Currie**.

Curt *see* COURT

Curter *see* COURTIER

Curtin 1. English: dim. of COURT. **2.** Irish and Scots: Anglicized form of Gael. **Mac Cruitín** 'son of *Cruitín*', a byname for a hunchback.

Vars. (of 2): **McCrutten, McCruttan, (Mc)Curtain, Curtayne**.

Curtis English: **1.** nickname for a refined person, sometimes no doubt given ironically, from OF, ME *curteis*, *co(u)rtois* refined, accomplished (a deriv. of OF *court*, see COURT 1). **2.** nickname for a short person or one who wore

short stockings, from ME *curt* short (see COURT 2) + *hose* leggings (OE *hosa*). Compare SHORTHOUSE. This nickname was borne by William the Conqueror's son Robert, but it is not clear whether it has given rise to any surnames.

Var.: **Curtiss**.

Dim. (of 1): It.: **Cortesini**.

Curwen 1. Scots: habitation name from *Colvend* in the former county of Kirkcudbright, now part of Dumfries and Galloway region. It has been suggested that the placename probably derives from Gael. *cùl a'beinn* at the back of the hill. **2.** Manx: aphetic form of Gael. *Mac Eireamháin*; see IRVING.

Vars. (of 1): **Culwen**. (Of 2): **Curwin, Kermeen**.

Curzon English (Norman): **1.** dim. of COURT. **2.** habitation name from Notre-Dame-de-Courson in Calvados, Normandy, so called from the Gallo-Roman personal name *Curtius* (from *curtus* short; see COURT 2) + the local suffix *-o*, gen. *-ōnis*.

Vars.: **Curson, Corson** (see also CARSON).

Cusack Irish (Norman): habitation name from *Cussac* in Guienne, so called from the Gallo-Roman personal name *Cūcius* or *Cussius* + the local suffix *-ācum*. The surname more or less died out in England, but is quite common in Ireland, where it was taken at the time of the Anglo-Norman invasion and has been Gaelicized as **de Cíosóg**.

Cushen *see* COUSIN

Cusin *see* CUISINE

Cusker Irish: Anglicized form of Gael. **Ó Coscair** 'descendant of *Coscar*', a personal name from *coscur* victory.

Vars.: **O'Coskirr, (O')Cosker, Coscor**.

Cuskern *see* COSGROVE

Cuss *see* CONSTANCE, KISS

Cussen *see* CUTHBERT

Custer *see* KÜSTER

Custódio Portuguese: from a religious byname, chosen to invoke the protection of a guardian angel, Port. *anjo custódio* (LL *angelus custōdius*, from *custos*, gen. *custōdis*, guardian, keeper).

Cusworth English: habitation name from a place in W Yorks., so called from the OE personal name *Cūðsa* (apparently a short form of a name composed of the elements *cūð* famous, well known + *sige* victory) + OE *worð* enclosure (see WORTH).

Var.: **Cushworth**.

Cuthbert English: from the ME given name *Cudbert*, OE *Cuðbeorht*, composed of the elements *cūð* famous, well known + *beorht* bright, famous. The name was borne by a 7th-cent. saint, bishop of Hexham and later of Lindisfarne, and remained popular because of his cult throughout the Middle Ages, especially in N England and the lowlands of Scotland.

Vars.: **Cudbird**, **Cutbirth**.

Dims.: **Cuthbe**, **Cudby**, **Cudd(y)**, **Cutt**; **Cussen**, **Cusson** (see also CONSTANCE and COUSIN).

Patrs.: Eng.: **Cuthbertson**. Sc.: **McCoubr(e)y**, **McCoubrie**, **McCaubrey** (Gael. **Mac Cúthbhréith**).

Patrs. (from dims.): Eng.: **Cutts**, **Cutting**; **Cussens**, **Cussons**.

Cutlack see GULLICK

Cutler 1. English: occupational name for a maker of knives, from an agent deriv. of ME, OF *co(u)tel, co(u)teau* knife (LL *cultellus*, a dim. of *culter* ploughshare; cf. COTTLE). **2.** Jewish (E Ashkenazic): Anglicization of *Kotler* (see KESSEL).

Var. (of 1): **Cuttelar**.

Cutmore see CUDMORE

Cutress see GUTTERIDGE

Cuttell see COTTLE

Cuvier French: occupational name for a maker of barrels and tubs, from an agent deriv. of OF *cuve* vat, tub (LL *cūpa*, of Gmc origin; cf. COOPER).

Dims.: Sp.: **Cubillo**. Cat.: **Cubells**.

Patr.: Flem.: **Cuyvers**.

Cuxon see COOK

Cuypers see COOPER

Cuyvers see CUVIER

Cuzen see COUSIN

Cuzzi see JACK

Cwajgenberg see TWIGG

Cybula see ZWIEBEL

Cygel see ZIEGLER

Cymbalist see ZIMBALIST

Cymerman see ZIMMERMANN

Cytrynowicz see CITROEN

Czajkowski Polish: habitation name from a place named with Pol. *czajka* lapwing (cogn. with Russ. *chaika* seagull) + *-ów* possessive suffix, used in forming placenames, with the addition of the surname suffix *-ski* (cf. BARANOWSKI).

Var.: **Czajka** (probably a nickname).

Czaplicki see CHAPLIN

Czarninski see CHERNYAKOV

Czechowicz see ČECH

Czernas see CHERNYAKOV

Czerwiński Polish: nickname for someone with red hair or a reddish complexion, from Pol. *czerwień* red + *-ski* suffix of surnames (see BARANOWSKI).

Var.: **Czerwieński**.

Dims.: Czech: **Červenka**, **Červinka**.

Czukerman see ZUCKER

Czupryniak Polish: nickname for a man with a thick head of hair, from Pol. *czupryna* head of hair + *-iak* suffix of animate (human) nouns.

Var.: **Czupryński**.

Czyż Polish and Jewish (E Ashkenazic): nickname or, in the case of the Jewish name, ornamental name, from Pol. *czyż(yk)* greenfinch.

Var.: Pol.: **Czyżo**.

Habitation names: Pol.: **Czyżewski**; **Czyżykowski**.

D

Dabbs *see* DOBB

Dąbek *see* DUBNIKOV

Dabney *see* DAUBENEY

D'Aboville *see* ABONVILLE

D'Abramo *see* ABRAHAM

Dąbrowski Polish: habitation name from any of various places called Dąbrowa, from Pol. *dąbrowa* oak grove (from *dąb* oak, pl. *dęby*; see DUBNIKOV), with the addition of -*ski*, suffix of local surnames (see BARANOWSKI).

Da Ca *see* CASA

D'Accardo *see* ACHARD

D'Accorso *see* BONACCORSO

Dach 1. German: habitation name from any of the places, in various parts of Germany, so called from MHG *tāhe*, *dāhe* marsh (OHG *dāha*). **2.** Jewish (Ashkenazic): of uncertain origin, probably from mod. Ger. *Dach* or Yid. *dakh* roof.
Vars. (of 1): **Dacher**, **Dachmann**. (Of 2): **Dachner** ('roofer', occupational name).

Dacheux French: **1.** occupational name for a nailsmith, from a var. spelling of OF *dacheur*, an agent deriv. of *dache* nail (of uncertain origin; cf. DAGG). **2.** habitation name, with fused preposition *de*, from *Acheux* in Somme, so called from LL *apiōsum* patch of smallage or wild celery (a deriv. of *apium* parsley, celery; the word *smallage* was itself originally a cpd of the adj. *small* + ME, OF *ache*).

Dachs 1. German: nickname for someone who resembled a badger in some way, for example in nocturnal habits or in having a streak of white hair among black, from Ger. *Dachs* badger (MHG, OHG *dahs*). **2.** Jewish (Ashkenazic): from Ger. *Dachs* badger, adopted either as an ornamental name or acquired as a nickname, with the same origins as in 1.
Vars.: Jewish: **Taks** (from Yid. *taks* badger), **Tax** (Anglicized spelling).

Dack English: apparently from an OE personal name or byname *Dæcca* (of uncertain origin), which may have survived into the Middle English period as a given name. The surname is found mainly in Norfolk.
Patr.: **Dax**.

Dacre English: habitation name from a place in Cumb. that gets its name from the river on which it stands. This is apparently of Brit. origin, and may originally have meant 'trickling'. The surname is now most common in the Leeds area.

D'Adamo *see* ADAM

Dadd *see* DODD

Daddow *see* DANDO

Dade *see* DAVID

Dadswell English: habitation name from *Dowdeswell* in Gloucs., first recorded in the 8th cent. as *Dogodeswyllan*, from the gen. case of the OE personal name *Dogod* (see DOWDING) + OE *w(i)ell(a)* spring, stream (see WELL).
Var.: **Dowdeswell**.

Daen *see* DANIEL

D'Aeth *see* DEATH

Daffey *see* DAVID

Daft English: nickname for a meek person rather than a stupid one, from ME *daffte* mild, gentle, meek (OE *gedæfte*). The surname survives in the E Midlands in spite of the unfavourable connotations that were acquired by the vocab. word in the 15th cent.

D'Agata *see* AGGIS

Dagg English: metonymic occupational name for a maker or seller of daggers, or nickname for someone who carried one, from OF *dague* dagger (of uncertain origin). ME **Dagger** is a later development of the same word; Fr. **Daguier** is an agent noun derived from it, meaning 'dagger maker'.
Dims.: Eng.: **Daggett**. Fr.: **Dagon(et)**, **Dagonneau**, **Dagot**, **Daguin(ot)**, **Dagu(en)et**, **Dagueneau**.

Dagless *see* DALGLEISH

D'Agnello *see* AGNEW

D'Agnese *see* ANNIS

D'Agnolo *see* ANGEL

Dahlbäck *see* DALE

Dähmel *see* THOMAS

Dahmke *see* ADAM

Dähn *see* DENCH

Daid *see* DAVID

D'Aiello *see* AIELLO

Daile *see* DALE

Dailey *see* DALY

Daimler German: occupational name for a judicial torturer (who applied the thumbscrew), or else a nickname for a cruel person, from an agent deriv. of MHG *diumeln* to torture (a deriv. of *dūme* thumb; see DAUM).
Vars.: **Deimler**, **Däumler**.

Dain English: **1.** nickname for a worthy and honourable citizen, or for a haughty and self-important one, from ME *d(e)igne*, *deyn(e)*, *dain(e)* worthy, fitting (OF *digne*, from L *dignus*). **2.** var. of DEAN. **3.** var. of DENCH.

Vars.: **Daine**, **Dayne**, **Dyne**.

Patrs.: **Daines**, **Daynes**, **Deyns**, **Dines**.

Dainese see DENCH

Daintith English: affectionate nickname or term of address, from ME *deinteth* pleasure, titbit (OF *deintiet*, from L *dignitas*, gen. *dignitātis*, worth, value, a deriv. of *dignus* worthy; cf. DAIN 1). The word was also used as an adj. in the later form *deinte* (OF *deint(i)é*) in the sense 'fine', 'handsome', 'pleasant'. The surname is especially common in Lancs.

Vars.: **Dainteth**, **Dentith**; **Dainty**, **Denty**.

Daintry English: habitation name from *Daventry* in Northants, of which the normal local pronunciation is (or was) /deɪntrɪ/. The place is probably named from the gen. case of an OE personal name or byname *Dafa* (perhaps related to *(ge)dafan* fitting, appropriate) + OE *trēow* tree.

Vars.: **Daintree**, **Daintrey**, **Daventry**.

Dairson see DEAR

D'Ajello see AIELLO

Dakhno see DANIEL

Dakin see DAY

Daladerne see ALADERNE

D'Alayrac see ALAYRAC

D'Albert see ALBERT

Dal Bo see BOEUF

Dalby English: habitation name from any of various places so called from ON *dalr* valley (see DALE) + *býr* farm, settlement. The surname is common in Yorks., and it probably derives mainly from *Dalby* in N Yorks., but similarly named places in Leics. and Lincs. are also possible sources.

Dal Degan see DEAN

Dale English: topographic name for someone who lived in a valley, ME *dale* (OE *dæl*, reinforced in N England by the cogn. ON *dalr*), or habitation name from any of the numerous minor places named with this word.

Vars.: **Daile**, **Dales**; **Deal** (from the Kentish form *del*, and the name of a place in Kent).

Cpds (ornamental): Swed.: **Dahlbäck** ('valley stream'); **Dahlberg** ('valley hill'); **Dahlbom** ('valley tree'); **Dahlborg** ('valley town'); **Dahlgren** ('valley branch'); **Dahlquist** ('valley twig'); **Dahlstedt** ('valley homestead'); **Dahlstrand** ('valley shore'); **Dahlström** ('valley river').

D'Alesco see ALEXIS

D'Alessandro see ALEXANDER

Dal Fabbro see FÈVRE

Dalfin see DAUPHIN

Dal Fiore see FLOWER

Dalgetty Scots: habitation name from a place near Dunfermline, which, according to Watson, derives its name from Gael. *dealg* prickle. There are also lands of the same name in the former county of Aberdeens. (now part of Grampian region) that belonged to a family so called, but it is not clear whether the family took the name from the land or vice versa.

Var.: **Dalgety**.

Dalgleish Scots: habitation name from a place near Selkirk, first recorded in 1383 in the form *Dalglas*, from Gael. *dail* field + *glas* green (cf. GLASS 2), perhaps taken over from Brit. *dollas*, with the same meaning.

Vars.: **Dalgli(e)sh**, **Dalgleas**, **Dagless**, **Daglish**.

Dalhousie Scots: habitation name from a place near Edinburgh, of uncertain etymology. It is recorded *c*.1235 in the form *Dalwussy*, in 1298 as *Dalw(u)lsy*, and in 1461 as *Dalwosie*. It has been suggested that the name originally meant 'field of slander', from Gael. *dail* field + *thuaileas*, gen. of *thuaileas* slander.

Dali see ADELL

D'Alisi see LEWIS

Dalkeith Scots: habitation name from a place near Edinburgh, the etymology of which is probably Brit. *dol* meadow + *cēd* wood.

Dalla Ca see CASA

Dallamore see DELAMARE

Dallas **1.** Scots: habitation name from a place near Forres, probably so called from Brit. *dol* meadow (Gael. *dail*) + *gwas* dwelling. **2.** English: topographic name or name from OE *dæl* valley (see DALE) + *hūs* house, either directly or by way of some placename with this origin, as for example *Dalehouse* in N Yorks.

Var. (of 1): **Dall**.

Dalla Volpe see VOLPE

Dalla Volta see VOLTA

Dallaway English (W Midlands): of uncertain origin. It is possibly a Norman habitation name, with fused preposition *de*, from *Alluyes* in Eure-et-Loire. This placename is recorded in the 6th cent. in the L form *Avallocium*, apparently a deriv. of the Gaul. element *aballo* apple.

Var.: **Dallow**.

Dalle Donne see DAME

Dallicoat see COATES

Dalmas French: from a medieval given name (L *Dalmatius*, originally an ethnic name for someone from *Dalmatia* in modern Yugoslavia; the name may be of Illyrian origin and akin to S Albanian *delme* sheep). The name was borne by a 3rd-cent. bishop of Pavia and a 6th-cent. bishop of Rodez, both of whom were popularly venerated in the Middle Ages.

Vars.: **Damas**; **Dalmais**, **Dalmay**; **Da(l)mace** (learned forms).

Dal Monaco see MONK

D'Aloisio see LEWIS

Dalrymple Scots: habitation name from a place in the former county of Ayrs. (now part of Strathclyde region), said to be so called from Gael. *dail chruim puill* field of the crooked stream.

Dal Savio see SAGE

Dalton English: **1.** habitation name from any of the various places, for example in Cumb., Co. Durham, Lancs., Northumb., and Yorks., so called from OE *dæl* valley (see DALE) + *tūn* enclosure, settlement. **2.** Norman habitation name, with fused preposition *de*, from *Autun* in Seine-et-Loire, whose modern name derives from the L form *Augustodunum*. This is a cpd of the imperial name *Augustus* + the Gaul. element *dūn* hill, fort (cf. DOWN 1).

Vars.: **Daulton**, **Daughton**, **Da(w)ton**. (Of 2 only): **Dautun**, **D'A(l)ton**.

D'Alton see DALTON

Daltry English (Norman): habitation name, with fused preposition *de*, from *Hauterive* in Orne, so called from OF *haute rive* high bank (L *alta rīpa*).

Vars.: **Dawtr(e)y**, **Daughtr(e)y**, **Daughtery**, **Da(u)ltrey**, **Dealtry**, **Doughtery**, **Dowtry**; **Ha(w)try**.

Daly Irish: Anglicized form of Gael. **Ó Dálaigh** 'descendant of *Dálach*', a personal name from *dál* (mod. *dáil*) meeting, assembly.

Vars.: **O'Daly**, **Daley**, **Dail(e)y**, **Dall(e)y**.

Dalziel Scots: habitation name from a place in the Clyde valley, recorded in 1200 in the forms *Dalyell*, *Daliel* and in 1352 as *Daleel*, apparently from Gael. *dail* field + *g(h)eal* white. The *z* in the spelling is not really a /z/ at all; it represents ME ʒ (cf. MENZIES), and the pronunciation, regardless of spelling, was normally /diːˈɛl/ or /darˈɛl/, sometimes /dælˈjɛl/. Black quotes an 'old Galloway rhyme': 'Deil (devil) and Da'yell begins with yae letter; Deil's no gude and Da'yell's nae better'. Nowadays /dælˈziːl/ and /dælˈzɛl/ are also heard.

Vars.: **Dalyell**, **Dalyiel**; **Dalzell** (the latter now being most common in Ireland).

Dam Dutch: topographic name for someone who lived by a dike, esp. one built to keep out the sea, MLG *dam* (the source of the mod. Eng. word *dam*). A homonymous Du. word denotes the game of draughts (from the same source as DAME), but the surname is not likely to be connected with this.

Vars.: **Dam(m)en**; **Van Dam** (partly Jewish), **Van Damme**, **Opdam**, **Damman**, **Dammer**.

Damace see DALMAS

D'Amante see AMANT

Damanti see AMANT

Damaschke see THOMAS

D'Amato see AMEY

D'Ambrogi see AMBROSE

Dame English and French: from OF *dame* lady (L *domina* mistress), originally a nickname for a foppish man or a title of respect for a widow. It may also have been an occupational name for someone in the service of a lady.

Var.: Fr.: **Danne**.

Metrs.: Eng.: **Damson**. It.: **Dalle Donne** (Emilia); **Delle Donne** (Campania).

D'Ameri see AYLMER

Damero see AYLMER

Dametti see ADAM

D'Amici see AMIS

Dammers see DANKMAR

D'Amore see AMOR

Dampier English (Norman): habitation name from any of various places in Normandy named *Dampierre*, in honour of St Peter. The first element, *Dam-* or *Don*, is an OF title of respect (from L *dominus* lord), prefixed particularly to the names of saints.

Var.: **Damper**.

Damyon English: from the medieval given name *Damian* (L *Damiānus*, from a Gk name probably derived from that of the goddess *Damia*, which is probably akin to Gk *damān* to tame, subdue, kill). Damian was the name borne by a famous early Christian saint who was martyred in Cilicia in AD 303 under the emperor Domitian, together with his brother Cosmas. In some accounts the brothers were said to be doctors, and together they were regarded as the patrons of physicians and apothecaries. A later St Damian lived in the 7th–8th cents. and was bishop of Pavia; he may have had some influence on the popularity of the given name in Italy.

Var.: **Damon**.

Dims.: Beloruss.: **Demyanok**, **Demeshko**. Ukr.: **Demyanchuk**, **Demyanets**, **Demchenko**.

Patrs.: Ger.: **Damiani** (Latinized). Flem., Du.: **Damiaens**. Russ.: **Demyanov**. Bulg.: **Damyanov**. Croatian: **Damjanović**.

Patrs. (from dims.): Flem.: **Dams**. Russ.: **Dem(a)kov**, **Demykin**, **Dyom(k)in**, **Dyomyshev**, **Dyomichev**, **Dyomshin**, **Dyominov**, **Dyoshin** (see also DEMIDOV). Ukr.: **Demchinyat**.

Danais see DENCH

D'Anastasio see ANSTICE

Danby English: habitation name from any of several places called *Danby* in N Yorks., originally named in ON as *Danebýr* 'settlement of the Danes', and so cogn. with DENBY.

Dancet see TANZER

Dand see ANDREW

Dandler see TENDLER

Dando English (Norman): habitation name, with fused preposition *de*, from *Aunou* in Orne, Normandy, which gets its name from OF *aunaie* alder grove (see DELANEY).

Var.: **Daddow**.

D'Andrea see ANDREW

Dane see DEAN

Dänecke see DEINHARD

Daněk Czech: **1.** dim. of DANIEL or of any of the Slav. cpd personal names containing the element *dan-* gift, as for example *Danomír*, *Danoslav*, and BOGDANOV. **2.** nickname from the vocab. word *daněk* buck, fallow deer.

Patrs. (from 1): Ger.: **Däniken**. Croatian: **Daničić**.

Danet see JORDAN

D'Angelo *see* ANGEL

Dangerfield English (Norman): habitation name, with fused preposition *de*, from any of the various places in Normandy called *Angerville*, from the ON personal name *Ásgeirr* (from *ás* god + *geirr* spear) + OF *ville* settlement, village. The English surname is now found chiefly in the W Midlands.

Daniel English, French, Portuguese, German, Polish, and Jewish: from the Hebr. male given name *Daniel* 'God is my judge', borne by a major prophet in the Bible. The major factor influencing the popularity of the given name (and hence the frequency of the surname) was undoubtedly the dramatic story in the Book of Daniel, recounting the prophet's steadfast adherence to his religious faith in spite of pressure and persecution from the Mesopotamian kings in whose court he served: Nebuchadnezzar (who went mad) and Belshazzar (at whose feast Daniel interpreted the mysterious message of doom that appeared on the wall, being thrown to the lions for his pains). The name was also borne by a 2nd-cent. Christian martyr and by a 9th-cent. hermit, the legend of whose life was popular among Christians during the Middle Ages; these had a minor additional influence on the adoption of the Christian name. Among Orthodox Christians in E Europe the name was also popular as being that of a 4th-cent. Persian martyr, who was venerated in the Orthodox Church. See also DONALD.

Vars.: Eng.: **Daniell**; **Danniel(l)**, **Danell**, **Dannel**, **Dennell**; **Denial** (with the accent on the first syllable). Fr.: **Deniel**, **Daniau**, **Deniau(d)**. Ger.: **Dan(i)gel**, **Dangl**, **Dannöhl**, **Dan(n)ehl**, **Danneil**. Jewish: **Daniel(l)i**, **Daniely** (with the Hebr. suffix *-i*); **Danielski**, **Danielsky** (E Ashkenazic).

Dims.: Fr.: **Danelet**, **Daniellot**; **Daniélou** (Brittany). It.: **Danelutti**, **Dan(i)elut** (Venetia). Flem.: **Daen**, **Danick**. Beloruss.: **Danilenko**, **Danilchik**. Ukr.: **Dan(il)chenko**, **Danilyuk**, **Danilchik**, **Danilyak**, **Dakhno**. Czech: DAŇEK, **Danihelka**. Hung.: **Dankó**. Jewish (E Ashkenazic): **Danielczyk**.

Patrs.: Eng.: **Daniel(l)s**, **Danels**. It.: **Danielis**. Low Ger.: **Daniels(en)**. Flem., Du.: **Daniels**. Dan.: **Danielsen**. Swed.: **Danielsson**. Ashkenazic: **Daniels**, **Danielso(h)n**. Russ.: **Danilov**, **Danilin**. Beloruss.: **Danilevich**. Ukr.: **Danilovich**. Pol.: **Danilewicz**, **Daniłowicz**. Croatian: **Danilović**. Jewish (E Ashkenazic): **Dani(e)lovitch**. Armenian: **Danielian**.

Patrs. (from dims.): Eng.: **Danson** (chiefly Lancs.; see also ANDREW); **Danks** (chiefly Birmingham). Flem.: **Daens**, **Daenen**. Russ.: **Dankov**, **Danshin**, **Dashkov**, **Dakhov**. Ukr.: **Danovich**, **Dashkovich**. Pol.: **Danielkiewicz**, **Daszkiewicz**. Bulg.: **Danilchev**, **Danev**.

'Son of the wife of D.': Ukr.: **Danilishin**.

Dankmar German: from a Gmc personal name composed of the elements *þank* thought + *mari, meri* famous, renowned.

Dims.: Low Ger.: **T(h)amm**, **Tamme**, **Tan(c)k**, **Tamcke**.

Patr.: Low Ger.: **Dammers**.

Patrs. (from dims.): Low Ger.: **Tammen**, **Tam(m)s**, **Thams(en)**. Fris.: **Tamminga**.

Danne *see* DAME

Dansie English (Norman): habitation name, with fused preposition *de*, from *Anizy* in Calvados, recorded in 1155 in the form *Anisie*. The placename is probably derived from the Gallo-Roman personal name *Anitius* (of uncertain origin) + the local suffix *-ācum*.

Vars.: **Dansey**, **Danc(e)y**, **Dauncey**; **Densey**, **Densie**, **Denzey**; **Dinzey** (W Indies).

Dantas Portuguese: topographic name, with fused preposition *de*, for someone who lived near a group of prehistoric standing stones, from the pl. form of OPort. *anta* dolmen (L *anta* pillar, pilaster).

Dantini *see* DURANT

Danton French: habitation name, with fused preposition *de*, from places in Isère and Haute-Savoie called *Anthon*. The placename is probably from an unrecorded Gaul. personal name rather than from a version of ANTHONY.

D'Antoni *see* ANTHONY

Danvers English (Norman): habitation name, with fused preposition *de*, from *Anvers*, the French form of the name of the Belgian town of Antwerp (Flem. *Antwerpen*, which gets its name from MDu. *an de werfen* at the wharf).

Danzig Jewish (Ashkenazic): local name from the Ger. form of *Gdańsk*, name of the major Baltic port that is now in Poland. The wide distribution and frequency of the name suggests that it may in many cases have been acquired by merchants who had visited the city or who regularly traded with it, as well as those who were actually born there.

Vars.: **Dantzig**, **Danzik**, **Dancyg**; **Danz(i)ger**, **Dancig(i)er**, **Dancyg(i)er**; **Dancigerkron** (an ornamental elaboration; cf. CORONA); **Danz** (from *Dants*, the Yid. name of the city) (Du.); **G(e)danski**, **G(e)dansky** (from the Pol. name of the city). Forms with *-c-* show Pol. influence on the spelling.

Daoust *see* DAVOUT

D'Aquila *see* EAGLE

Darby 1. English: habitation name from *Derby*, the county town of Derbys., and perhaps occasionally from the much smaller town of West *Derby* in Lancs. Both of these get their name from ON *djúr* deer (a cogn. of OE *dēor*; see DEAR 2) + *býr* farm, settlement. The usual spelling of the surname represents the pronunciation of both town and surname. 2. Irish: Anglicized form of Gael. *Ó Duibhdhiormaigh*; see DORMER. 3. Irish: Anglicized form of Gael. *Ó Diarmada*; see DERMOTT.

Vars.: **Darbey**, **Derby**.

Darbyshire English: 1. regional name from the hundred of West Derby in Lancs., which was often referred to in the Middle Ages as *Derbyshire*, from the name of the town + ME *schire* region, administrative district. The surname is still chiefly common in Lancs. 2. regional name from the county of Derbyshire, centred on the city of *Derby* (see DARBY).

Vars.: **Darbishire**, **Derbyshire**.

D'Arco *see* ARCO

Darcy 1. English (Norman): habitation name, with fused preposition *de*, from *Arcy* in La Manche, so called from a Gaul. personal name (which, it has been suggested, may be akin to the Indo-European root *ars*- bear) + the local suffix *-ācum*. 2. Irish: Anglicized form of **Ó Dorchaidhe** 'descendant of the dark one', from *dorcha* dark, gloomy. This has fallen together with the Norman surname, which is certainly attested in Ireland, having been introduced there by Sir William D'Arcy (see below) and Sir John D'Arcy, who was appointed Chief Justiciar of Ireland in the 14th cent.

Vars.: **Darcey**, **D'Arcy**. (Of 2 only): **O'Dor(o)ghie**, **O'Dorchie**, **(O')Dorcey**, **Darky**.

Dard French: from OF *dard* spur (of Gmc origin), and so probably in most cases a metonymic occupational name for a maker or seller of spurs, more rarely perhaps a nickname for a hasty or irritating individual. See also DARDE.

Darde French: from OF *darde* arrow (a byform of DARD; cf. Eng. DART 2), and so probably in most cases a metonymic occupational name for a maker of arrows or a bowman, more rarely perhaps a nickname for a swift runner.

Dims.: **Dardel(et)**, **Dardelin**, **Dardet**. Prov.: **Dardol**. (All of these could also derive from DARD.)

Dare see DEAR

Darell English (Norman): habitation name, with fused preposition *de*, from *Airel* in La Manche, Normandy, so called from LL *areālis*, open space, courtyard (an originally adj. deriv. of *area* threshing floor).

Vars.: **Darrell**; **Dorrell** (chiefly Worcs.).

Dargan Irish: Anglicized form of Gael. **Ó Deargáin** 'descendant of *Deargán*', a byname from a dim. of *dearg* red.

Var.: DORGAN.

Da Riolo see RIEU

Dark English: nickname for someone with dark hair or a dark complexion, from ME *darke*, OE *deorc* dark. The surname is most frequently found in the W Country.

Vars.: **Darke**, **Durk**.

Patr.: **Darkes**.

Darley English: habitation name from either of two places in Derbys., so called from OE *dēor* beast, deer (see DEAR 2) + *lēah* wood, clearing.

Darling English: from ME *derling*, OE *dēorling* darling, beloved one, a deriv. of *dēor* dear, beloved (see DEAR 1). This was quite a common OE byname, which remained current as a given name into the 14th cent. The surname probably derives at least in part from this use, probably in part also from a ME nickname. The surname is common in Scotland and also occurs in Ireland. In these areas it may represent a translation of FARQUHAR.

Vars.: **Dearling**, **Dorling**; **Dyrling** (from the OE byform *dyrling*).

Darlington English: habitation name from a place in Co. Durham, recorded in *c*.1009 as *Dearthingtun*, from OE *Dēornōðingtūn* 'settlement (OE *tūn*) associated with *Dēornōð*', a personal name composed of the elements *dēor* dear + *nōð* daring.

Darlot see ARLOTT

Darmody see DERMOTT

Da Rold see HARROD

Darras French: habitation name, with fused preposition *de*, from various places called *Arras*. The one in Pas-de-Calais gets its name, in much reduced form, from having

once been the seat of the Gaul. tribe of the *Atrebates*; that in Hautes-Pyrénées is named with the Basque elements *harr* stone + *ast* rocky peak; a further example in Ardèche is of impenetrable etymology.

Var.: **Daras**.

D'Arrigo see HENRY

Darroch Scots: 1. habitation name from a place near Falkirk, in the former county of Stirlings., said to be so called from Gael. *darach* oak wood, a deriv. of *dara* oak. 2. from the Gael. personal name *Darach*, a deriv. of *dara* in the sense 'stout-hearted'; cf. ROBUSTI.

Vars.: **Darrach**, **Darragh**, **Darrow**.

Dart English: 1. topographic name for someone living beside the river *Dart* in Devon, which apparently gets its name from a Brit. term meaning 'oak', and is thus a cogn. of DARWIN 2. 2. metonymic occupational name for a maker of arrows, from ME *dart* (OF *darde*; see DARDE).

Darvill English: probably a Norman habitation name, with fused preposition *de*, from *Arville* in Seine-et-Marne, which is so called from the Gmc personal name *Ara* 'Eagle' + OF *ville* settlement, village.

Var.: **Darvell**.

Darwin 1. English: apparently from the OE personal name *Dēorwine*, composed of the elements *dēor* dear + *wine* friend. This name is attested in the 10th cent., but it was apparently not common; nevertheless it may have survived long enough to become a ME given name and so given rise to the surname. 2. English: habitation name from *Darwen* in Lancs., named from the river *Derwent* on which it stands. This seems to be a Brit. name derived from a word meaning 'oak' (cf. W *dâr* oak; see also DARROCH and DART 1). 3. Jewish: of unknown origin.

Var. (of 2): **Darwen**.

Dash English: topographic name for someone who lived near an ash tree, or habitation name from a place named with the OE word *æsc* (see ASH). The ANF preposition *de* of, from, has become fused to the name.

Dashkov see DANIEL

Dashwood English: topographic name for someone living in an ash wood, or habitation name for someone who came from a place called ASHWOOD. The ANF preposition *de* of, from, has become fused to the name.

D'Aton see DALTON

Daub see TAUBER

Daube see TAUBE

Daubeney English (Norman): habitation name, with fused preposition *de*, from any of the various places in N France named with the Gallo-Roman personal name *Albinius* (a deriv. of *albus* white; cf. ALBAN and ALBIN) + the local suffix *-ācum*.

Vars.: **Daubeny**, **Daubney**, **Dabney**, **Dobney**, **D'Aubney**.

Dauchez French: habitation name, with fused preposition *de*, from *Auchel* in Pas-de-Calais. The name is a dim. of that of the nearby *Auchy*, of which it was once a minor dependency. The name *Auchy* itself derives from the

Gallo-Roman personal name *Alcius* (of uncertain origin) + the local suffix *-ācum*.

Daud *see* DAVID

Daudet French: **1.** from OF vernacular pronunciations, such as /dosde/, /dozde/, of the L phrase *Deus dedit* 'God has given', which was occasionally used as a given name in the Middle Ages; cf. DIEUDONNÉ and DONAT. **2.** in Gascony it represents a local form of OProv. *doncel* young knight, squire (LL *dom(i)nicellus*, a dim. of *dominus* master).

Var. (of 1): **Daudé**.

Daugherty *see* DOHERTY

Daughtery *see* DALTRY

Daughton *see* DALTON

Daukes *see* DAW

Daum German and Jewish (Ashkenazic): nickname from Ger. *Daum* thumb (MHG *dūme*, OHG *thūmo*, a cogn. of OE *þūma*). This would have been acquired either by someone with a deformed or missing thumb, or by a very small person (cf. the folk tale of 'Tom Thumb').

Var.: Ger.: **Daumann**.

Daumier Provençal: status name for a farmer who held his land by virtue of contributing a tithe of its produce to the landlord, OProv. *desmier, deumier* (a deriv. of *desme* tithe, L *decima (pars)* tenth).

Dim.: **Daumet**.

Pej.: **Daumard**.

Däumler *see* DAIMLER

Daunay *see* DELANEY

Dauncey *see* DANSIE

Daunderer *see* DONNER

Dauphin French: from a medieval given name (L *Delphīnus*, from *delphis* dolphin). This name was borne by a 4th-cent. saint who was bishop of Bordeaux, and from the early 12th cent. it was in use as a hereditary given name in the family of the counts of Albon, so that it soon came to be used as a title, and led to their territory being known as the *Dauphiné*. When it became part of the Kingdom of France in 1349, the title of *dauphin* thereafter denoted the heir apparent to the throne, and it is possible that in some cases this is the origin of the surname, as a nickname in the sense of 'prince'. The Italian cogns. may derive directly from a nickname for someone supposedly resembling a dolphin in some way.

Vars.: **Delphin, Delphy, Dalfin, Dalphy**.

Dim.: It.: **Dalfinelli**.

Pej.: Fr.: **Dauffard**.

Daval French: topographic name, with fused preposition *de*, for someone who lived downstream from the main settlement, from OF *aval* downstream (L *ad vallem* towards the valley, opposed to *ad montem* (OF *amont*) towards the hill, upstream).

Vars.: **Davau(x), Davault, Daveau**.

Davall *see* DEVILLE

Daveine *see* AVOINE

Davenport 1. English: habitation name from a place in Ches., so called from a Brit. river name (apparently a cogn. of MW *dafnu* to drop, trickle) + OE *port* market town. **2.** Irish: Anglicized form of Gael. **Ó Donndubhartaigh** 'descendant of *Donndubhartach*', a personal name composed of the elements *donn* brown + *dubh* black + *artach* nobleman.

Daventry *see* DAINTRY

Da Vico *see* VICO

David Welsh, Scots, English, French, Portuguese, Czech, and Jewish: from the Hebr. male given name *David* 'Beloved'. The given name has been perennially popular among Jews, in honour of the biblical king of this name, the greatest of the early kings of Israel. His prominence, and the vivid narrative of his life contained in the First Book of Samuel, led to adoption of the given name on a limited scale among Christians throughout Europe in the Middle Ages. The friendship of David and Jonathan (1 Sam. 18: 1–4) was proverbial, adding significance to the name. Its popularity was increased in Britain firstly by virtue of its being the name of the patron saint of Wales (about whom very little is known: he was probably a 6th-cent. monk and bishop) and secondly because it was borne by two kings of Scotland (David I, reigned 1124–53, and David II, 1329–71). Its popularity in Russia is largely due to the fact that this was the church name adopted by St Gleb (d. 1015), one of the two sons of Vladimir, duke of Muscovy, who were martyred for their Christian zeal.

Vars.: Eng.: **Daud, Doud**. Ir.: **Davitt, Devitt, Daid, Dade**; **Taaffe**. Welsh: **Dewi** (an early form); **Dafydd** (a later form); **Daffey, Taffie, Taffee**. Fr.: **Davy**. Jewish: **David(a)i, Davidy** (with the Hebr. ending *-i*); **Davidman, Dawid(man)**.

Dims.: Eng.: DAW, DAY. Sc., Ir.: DAVIE. Fr.: **Davet, Davin(et)**; **Davidou** (Brittany). Prov.: **Davion, Daviot, Davioud**. Beloruss.: **Davydzenko**. Ukr.: **Davydenko**. Czech: **Davídek**.

Patrs.: Eng., Sc.: **Davids, Davidge, Davage**; **Davi(e)s, Davys, Dav(id)son, Davis(s)on**. Ir.: **McDavitt, McDevitt, McCavitt, McKevitt** (Gael. **Mac Daibhéid**); **McDaid, McDade, McCaet**. Sc.: **McDavid**. Rum.: **Davidescu**. Low Ger.: **Davidsen**. Du.: **Davids**. Dan.: **Davidsen**. Swed.: **Davidsson**. Jewish (Ashkenazic): **Davids; Davidso(h)n, Dawidsohn, Davidzon; Davidov(e), Davidof(f), Davidow; Davidowitz, Davidovitz, Davidovits, Davidovic(h), Davidovitch, Davidovics, Davidovicz, Davidowich, Dawidowitz, Dawidowi(ts)ch; Dawidowicz** (Pol. spelling); **Davidovici** (Rumanian spelling); **Davidovsky, Davidowsky, Dawidowsky, Davidofski** (E Ashkenazic; all sometimes Anglicized as *Davis*); **Davidesco, Davidescu** (among Rumanian Jews). Russ.: **Davidov, Davydov; Daudov** (from an Arabic form used in (Muslim) Turkic areas). Beloruss.: **Davidovich**. Pol.: **Dawidowicz**. Croatian: **Davidović, Davið**. Lithuanian: **Dovidaitis, Dovydénas**. Armenian: **Davidian**. Georgian: **Davitashvili**.

Patrs. (from dims.): Russ.: **Davydkov, Davydochkin, Davydychev**. Jewish: **Tewelson, Tevelov** (from Yid. *Teßele*).

Davie 1. Scots and Irish: dim. of DAVID. **2.** English: var. of WAY (see below).

D'Avigdor *see* AVIGDOR

Dávila *see* AVILA

Davin see DEVANE

Da Vinci see VINCENT

Davout French: nickname, originally *d'Avout*, for someone who was born in the month of August (OF *auoust*, from L *(mensis) Augustus*, from the name of the first Roman emperor), or who owed a feudal obligation to help with the harvest in that month.
Vars.: **Daou(s)t**, **Davous(t)**, **Davoud**; **Laoust**.

Daw English: 1. pet form of DAVID. 2. nickname from the (jack)daw, ME *dawe*, a bird noted for its sleek black colour, raucous voice, and thievish nature, any of which characteristics could readily have given rise to a nickname. The word is probably derived from an unattested OE cogn. of OHG *tāha*. 3. Irish: Anglicized form of Gael. Ó Deághaidh, 'descendant of *Deághadh*', a personal name of uncertain etymology. It may be composed of the elements *deagh-* good + *ádh* luck, fate, and some such association seems to lie behind its Anglicization as GOODWIN.
Vars.: (of 1–3): **Dawe**, Dow. (Of 3 only): Ó **Diaghaidh**, **O'Dea(y)**, **O'Daa**, **O'Dawe**, **O'Daye**, **Dea**, DAY, DEE.
Dim. (of 1): **Dawkin**.
Patrs. (from 1): **Daw(e)s**, **Dawson**.
Patrs. (from 1) (dim.): **Dawkins**, **Dawkes**, **Daukes**.

Dawber English (chiefly Lancs.): occupational name for a builder using wattle and daub, from an agent deriv. of the ME verb *daube(n)* to coat with a layer of plaster, from OF *dauber*, L *dēalbāre* to coat with whitewash.

Dawid see DAVID

Dawnay see DELANEY

Dawton see DALTON

Dawtrey see DALTRY

Dax see DACK

Day 1. English: pet form of DAVID. 2. English: from the ME given name *Day(e)* or *Dey(e)*, OE *Dæi*, apparently from OE *dæg* day, perhaps a short form of OE personal names such as *Dægberht* and *Dægmund*. 3. Irish: Anglicized form of Gael. Ó Deághaidh; see DAW.
Vars.: **Daye**, **Dey**; **D'Eye** (apparently no more than an orthographical affectation intended to make the name look French).
Dims. (of 1 and 2): **Daykin** (chiefly E Midlands); **Dakin**.
Patrs. (from 1 and 2): **Deyes**; **Dayson**, **Deason**.
'Servant of D. 1/2': **Dayman**, DIAMOND.

Dayan Jewish: occupational name from Hebrew *dayan* rabbinic judge.
Patrs.: **Ben-Dayan**, **Bar-Dayan**.

Dayczman see DEUTSCH

Dayment see DIAMOND

Dayne see DAIN

D'Azeglio see AIELLO

D'Azzi see ACE

Dea see DAW

Deadman see DEBENHAM

De Agostini see AUSTIN

Deakes see DITCH

Deakin English: occupational name for a deacon, or perhaps more probably for his servant. In ME two forms coalesced: *deakne*, from OE, and *diacne*, from OF. Both are ultimately from LL *diaconus*, from Gk *diakonos* servant.
Vars.: **Deacon**, **Deakan**.
Dims.: It.: **Diagonetti**; **Zaghetto**, **Zaghetti**, **Zaghino**, **Zaghini**, **Zagotto**, **Zagotti** (Venetia). Ukr.: **Dyachenko**.
Patrs.: Eng.: **Deakins**. It.: **Dello Iacono**, **Dello Jacono**. Rum.: **Diaconescu**. Russ.: **Dyakonov**.

Deal see DALE

De Albertis see ALBERT

Dealtry see DALTRY

Deam see DEMPSTER

De Ambrosi see AMBROSE

De Amicis see AMIS

Dean English: 1. topographic name from ME *dene* valley (OE *denu*), or habitation name from a place named with this word. 2. nickname for someone thought to resemble a dean, an ecclesiastical official who was the head of a chapter of canons in a cathedral, or perhaps more probably an occupational name for a servant of a dean. The ME word *deen* is a borrowing of OF *d(e)ien*, from L *decanus* (originally a leader of ten men, from *decem* ten).
Vars.: **Deen**; **Dane** (see also DENCH); DAIN. (Of 1 only): **Deane** (in so far as the final *-e* is a survival of the OE dat. case, and not merely a spelling var.); **Deaner**, **Denner**; DENMAN; **Adeane**, **Atherden**, **A'Deane**.
Dims. (of 2): It.: **Deganut(ti)**.
Patrs. (from 2): Eng.: **Deans** (chiefly Scot.); **Danes**; **Denson**, **Densum**. It.: **Dal Degan**. Flem., Du.: **Dekens**.
'Descendant of the D. 2': Ir.: **O'D(y)eane** (Gael. Ó Déaghain).

De Andreis see ANDREW

De Angelis see ANGEL

De Antoni see ANTHONY

Dear English: 1. from the ME personal name *Dere*, OE *Dēora*, in part a short form of various cpd names with the first element *dēor* dear, in part a byname meaning 'Beloved'. 2. nickname from ME *dere*, OE *dēor* wild animal, or from the adj. of the same form, meaning 'wild', 'fierce'. By the ME period the adj. was falling out of use, and the noun was beginning to be restricted to the sense of mod. Eng. *deer*, so that this may be the sense of the surname in some cases.
Vars.: **D(e)are**, **Deer(e)**; **Dearman**, **Dorman**, **Durman**.
Patrs. (from 1): Eng.: **Dearing**, **De(e)ring**, **Doring**; **Deares**; **Dearson**, **Dairson**. Dan.: **Dyhring**.

Dearden English (Lancs.): habitation name from a place near Edenfield, so called from OE *dēor* beast, deer (see DEAR 2) + *denu* valley (see DEAN 1).
Vars.: **Durden**, **Duerden**.

Dearling see DARLING

Deason see DAY

Deasy Irish: Anglicized form of Gael. **Déiseach**, a nick-name for a member of the vassal community known as the *Déis*, a term of uncertain meaning and origin.

Var.: **Deacy**.

Dêat *see* DIEUDONNÉ

D'Eath *see* DEATH

De Ath *see* DEATH

Death English: **1.** nickname from ME *de(e)th* death, OE *dēað*, which might have been acquired by someone who had played the part of the personified figure of Death in a pageant or play, or else one who was habitually gloomy or sickly. **2.** metonymic occupational name for a gatherer or seller of kindling, from ME *dethe* fuel, tinder (OE *dȳð*). **3.** supposedly a habitation name, with fused preposition *de*, from *Ath* in Belgium. However, modern spellings that divide the name into two elements may be no more than attempts to avoid the unpleasant associations of the vocab. word, and the derivation may in fact be as in 1.

Vars.: **Deeth**, **Dearth**, **D'Eath**, **D'Aeth**, **De Ath**.

Deathridge English (chiefly W Midlands): of uncertain origin. According to Reaney, it is derived from ME *dethewright*, which is an occupational name for one who chopped up wood into tinder, from ME *dethe* tinder (see DEATH 2) + *wryht* maker (see WRIGHT).

Var.: **Detheridge**.

Deavall *see* DEVILLE

Deavin *see* DEVIN

Debank English: Huguenot importation of unknown origin, perhaps a topographic name (with preposition *de*) from F *banc* bench, bank, possibly referring to a terrace on a hillside.

Var.: **Debanc**, **Debanks**.

De Barberi *see* BARBER

De Bassis *see* BASS

De Bastiani *see* SEBASTIAN

Debbage English: habitation name from *Debach* in Suffolk, which derives its name from the OE river name *Dēopa* 'Deep' + OE *bæc* ridge. The surname is largely confined to E Anglia.

Dębecki *see* DUBNIKOV

De Bei *see* BEAU

De Benedetti *see* BENNETT

Debenham English: habitation name from a place in Suffolk, probably so called from the gen. case of the OE river name *Dēopa* (see DEBBAGE) + OE *hām* homestead.

Vars.: **Debnam**, **De(a)dman**.

De Bernardi *see* BERNARD

De Biaggi *see* BLAISE

De Bianchi *see* BLANC

Dębicki *see* DUBNIKOV

De Blase *see* BLAISE

De Boni *see* BON

Debrie French: habitation name, with fused preposition *de*, from *Brie* in Seine-et-Marne, apparently so called from the Gaul. element *briga* hill (cf. BRYAN).

Var.: **Debray**.

Debrie *see* BRIARD

Debrosse *see* BROSSE

De Brouwer *see* BREWER

De Burger *see* BURGER

De Burgh *see* BURKE

Debussy French: habitation name, with fused preposition *de*, from various places called *Bussy*. The placename has two possible origins. On the one hand it may be from a Gallo-Roman personal name *Buccius* (perhaps a deriv. of LL *bucca* mouth, cf. BOCCA) + the local suffix *-ācum*. On the other hand it may also be from LL *buxācum* grove of box trees (see BOX), with perhaps some confusion with *bus*, a regional form of OF *bois* wood (see BUSH).

Debutt *see* THEOBALD

Decamp *see* CHAMP

De Carli *see* CHARLES

De Caro *see* CARO

De Castri *see* CASTRO

Decaux French: habitation name, with fused preposition *de*, from various places called *Caux*. These seem to derive their name from two distinct sources: on the one hand from L *cavus* hollow, and on the other more distantly from a pre-Roman element *kal*, which probably meant 'rock' or 'stone'.

De Cesare *see* CESARE

Decharme *see* CHARME

Déchaux French: nickname for someone in the habit of going barefoot, whether an ascetic or a poor man who could not afford footwear, from OF *deschaux* barefoot (LL *discalceus*, for class. L *discalceātus*, from the privative prefix *dis-* + a deriv. of *calceus* sandal, shoe).

Déchelette *see* ESCHELLE

Dechêne *see* CHÊNE

De Chiara *see* CLARE

Decker **1.** German: occupational name for a thatcher or for a maker of blankets or matting, from an agent deriv. of MHG *decke* covering (from MHG, OHG *decken* to cover), a word which was normally used to refer to roofs, but sometimes also to other sorts of covering; mod. Ger. *Decke* still has the twin senses 'ceiling' and 'blanket'. See also THATCHER. **2.** English: var. of DITCH.

Vars.: (of 1): **Deckert**; **Döcker** (Bavaria); **Deckwer(th)**, **Deckwarth** (see WRIGHT).

Patrs. (from 1): Low Ger.: **Deckers**. Du.: **Dekkers**, **Deckers**.

De Clemente *see* CLEMENT

De Cola *see* COLL

De Costanzo *see* CONSTANT

Decour *see* COURT

Decourcey English (Norman): habitation name, with fused preposition *de*, from any of various places in Normandy called *Courcy*, from the Gallo-Roman personal name *Curtius* (a deriv. of *curtus* short; cf. COURT 2) + the local suffix *-ācum*.
Vars.: **De Courcy**, **(De) Coursey**.

De Cristofalo *see* CHRISTOPHER

De Curti *see* COURT

Dede *see* DERRICK

Dedek *see* DUDEK

Dedman *see* DEBENHAM

De Domenicis *see* DOMINIQUE

De Dona *see* DONAT

Dee 1. Welsh: nickname for a swarthy person, from W *du* dark, black; cf. DUFF. **2.** Irish: var. of DAW 3. **3.** English and Scots: topographic name for someone living on the banks of the river *Dee* in Ches. or one of the same name in Scotland. The origin of both of these is a Brit. word meaning 'sacred'.

Deegan Irish: Anglicized form of Gael. **Ó Duibhginn** 'descendant of *Dubhceann*', a byname from *dubh* black + *ceann* head.
Vars.: **Deegin**, **D(u)igan**, **Deighan**, **Deehan**, **Dig(g)in**; DUFFIN.
Dims.: **O'Duigenain**, **Duignan**, **D(u)ignam**, **Di(e)gnan**, **Dignen** (Gael. **Ó Duibhgeannáin**).

Deeken *see* DERRICK

Deeker *see* DITCH

Deeley English (common in the Birmingham area): of unknown origin, possibly a var. of DALY.

Deem *see* DEMPSTER

Deen *see* DEAN, DENCH

Deeney *see* DENNY

Deer *see* DEAR

Deere *see* DEAR, DWYER

Deery Irish: **1.** Anglicized form of Gael. **Ó Daighre** 'descendant of *Daighre*', a byname meaning 'Fiery'. **2.** var. of DWYER.

Deesen *see* THIESS

Deeth *see* DEATH

Deevey *see* DEVOY

De Facci *see* BONIFACE

De Falco *see* FAULKES

De Fant *see* INFANTE

De Felice *see* FELIX

De Ferrari *see* FARRAR

De Filippi *see* PHILIP

De Florian *see* FLORIANO

De Florio *see* FLEURY

Defond *see* FONT

Defontaine *see* FONTAINE

Deforge *see* FORGE

De Fraine *see* FRAIN

De Franceschi *see* FRANCIS

De Franchi *see* FRANK

de Freitas *see* FREITAS

Deganut *see* DEAN

De Gaspari *see* KASPAR

Degenhard *see* DEINHARD

Degenschein Jewish (Ashkenazic): ornamental name meaning 'sword shine', from Ger. *Degen* sword, rapier + *Schein* shine.
Vars.: **Degenszejn**, **Degenszajn** (E Ashkenazic, Pol. spellings).

De Germano *see* GERMAN

De Giglio *see* LILLY

De Gioia *see* JOY

De Giorgi *see* GEORGE

De Giovanni *see* JOHN

De Giuli *see* JÚLIO

Degli Abati *see* ABBÉ

Degli Antoni *see* ANTHONY

De Gobbi *see* GOBBI

De Grandi *see* GRANT

De Grassi *see* GRASS

De Gregoli *see* GREGORY

De Guglielmo *see* WILLIAM

De Hals *see* HALS

Dehl *see* DERRICK

Dehmel *see* THOMAS

Dehn *see* DEINHARD, DENCH

Deibler *see* TAUBE

Deichman *see* DEUTSCH

Deighan *see* DEEGAN

Deighton English (chiefly Yorks.): habitation name from one of several places in Yorks. so called from OE *dīc* ditch, dyke + *tūn* enclosure, settlement. See also DITTON.
Vars.: **Dighton**, **Dightham**.

Deimler *see* DAIMLER

Deinhard German: from a Gmc personal name composed of the elements *degen* warrior, hero + *hard* hardy, brave, strong.

Vars.: **Degenhard**, **Deinhardt**; **Dönhardt** (Bavaria); **Deinert**, **Dennert**.

Dims.: Ger.: **Dein(lein)**, **Dennerlein**, **Theinel(t)**; **Deindl** (Bavaria); **Thiendl**, **Dienl** (Austria). Low Ger.: **Dehn**, **Denecke**, **Dehn(e)cke**, **Denicke**, **Dänecke**.

Patrs. (from dims.): Low Ger.: **Dehning**, **Dehns**.

Deissmann *see* THIESS

Deitel *see* DERRICK, TEITELBAUM

De Jonghe *see* YOUNG

Deken *see* DERRICK

Dekens *see* DEAN

Dekkers *see* DECKER

Delabrierre *see* BRUYÈRE

Delabrosse *see* BROSSE

De Lacey *see* LACEY

Delachaume *see* CHAUME

Delachaussée *see* CHAUSSÉE

Delachenal *see* CHENAL

Delacoste *see* COSTE

Delacour *see* COURT

Delafield *see* FIELD

Delafon *see* FONT

Delafontaine *see* FONTAINE

Delaforce *see* FORCE

Delaforge *see* FORGE

Delafosse *see* FOSSE

Delafoy *see* FOY

Delagneau *see* AGNEW

Delahunty Irish: Anglicized form of Gael. Ó Dulchaointigh 'descendant of *Dulchaointeach*', a byname composed of the elements *dul* satirist + *caointeach* plaintive.

Vars.: **Ó Dulchonta**; **Delahunt**, **Dolohunty**, **Dulanty**, **Dulinty**.

Delaitre French: topographic name, with fused preposition and article *del*, for someone who lived near a churchyard or cemetery, OF *aitre* (L *atrium* courtyard).

Vars.: **Delaite**, **Delatte**; **Delattre** (see also DELÂTRE).

Delamare English and French: habitation name, with fused preposition *de*, from one of the places in Normandy called *La Mare*, from ONF *la* the + *mare* pool, pond (ON *marr*). In England the surname was later understood as ANF *de la* of the + ME *mere* pool (OE *mere*, a cogn. of the ON word) or *more* moor (OE *mōr*; see MOORE 1).

Vars.: Eng.: **Delamar**, **Delamere**, **Delamore**, **Dallamore**, **Dallimore**, **Dillamore**, **Dol(l)amore**, **Dolle(y)more**, **Dollimore**, **Dollymore**. Fr.: **Delamarre**; **Demare**, **Démare**; **Lamar(r)e**, **Lamard**; **Mare**.

Delamotte *see* MOTTE

Delaney **1.** English (Norman): habitation name, with fused preposition and article *del*, from any of various minor places in Normandy so called from OF *aunaie* alder grove (L *alnētum*, collective of *almus* alder). **2.** Irish: Anglicized form, influenced by the Norman name, of Gael. **Ó Dubhshláine** 'descendant of *Dubhshláine*', a personal name composed of the elements *dubh* black (cf. DUFF) + *slán* challenge, defiance.

Vars.: **Delany**, **Delaun(e)y**, **Deleaney**. (Of 1 only): **Dawney**, **Dawnay**, **Dauney**, **Daunay**; DANDO. (Of 2 only): **O'Dowlaney**, **O'Dulaney**. See also DOLAN.

De Langhe *see* LONG

Delapierre *see* PIERRE

Delaplace *see* PLACE

Delaplanche *see* PLANCHE

De Lapradelle *see* PRÉ

Delarive *see* RIVE

Delarue *see* RUE

Delatouche *see* TOUCHE

Delâtre French: topographic name, with fused preposition and article *del*, for someone who lived by a paved area, or occupational name for someone who tended the hearth in a manor hall, from OF *astre* hearth (LL *astricum*, from Gk *ostrakon* tile).

Vars.: **Dela(i)stre**, **Delestre**; **Delattre** (see also DELAITRE).

De Laurentis *see* LAWRENCE

Delavaivre *see* VAUR

Delavalette *see* VALE

Delavenne *see* AVOINE

Delaville *see* VILLE

Delay *see* DUNLEAVY

Delbalat *see* VALLAT

Del Beccaro *see* BUTCHER

Del Bello *see* BEAU

Delbergue *see* BERGE

Del Bianco *see* BLANC

Del Bono *see* BON

Del Borgo *see* BURKE

Delbouille *see* BOUILLE

Del Bue *see* BOEUF

Delcamp *see* CHAMP

Delcassé *see* CASSE

Del Checolo *see* FRANCIS

Del Coco *see* COOK

Del Conte *see* COUNT

Del Corso *see* BONACCORSO

Del Duca see DUKE

De Lellis see LELLI

De Leo see LYON

De Leonardi see LEONARD

Delépine see ÉPINE

Delétang see ETANG

Del Fabbro see FÈVRE

Del Fante see INFANTE

Del Felice see FELIX

Delgado Spanish and Portuguese: nickname for a thin person, from Sp., Port. *delgado* slender (L *dēlicātus* dainty, exquisite, a deriv. of *dēliciae* delight, joy, from *dēlicere* to lure, seduce). It is also possible that the etymological meaning persisted as a pej. nickname.
Dim.: **Delgadillo**.

Del Giudice see JUDGE

Del Grande see GRANT

Del Greco see GRECO

Del Grosso see GROSS

Delhommeau see ORME

Delhostal see HOSTAL

D'Elia see ELLIS

De Liberto see ALBERT

Delicate see COATES

Delion see LYON

De Lisle see LISLE

Delius see DERRICK

Dell English: topographic name for someone who lived in a small valley, from ME, OE *dell* dell, valley.
Vars.: **Deller**, **Dellar**, DELMAN.

Dell'Abate see ABBÉ

Della Bella see BEAU

Della Casa see CASA

Dell'Agata see AGGIS

Dell'Agnol see ANGEL

Dell'Agostino see AUSTIN

Dell'Amore see AMOR

Dell'Aquila see EAGLE

Dell'Arco see ARCO

Della Vedova see WIDDOW

Della Volpe see VOLPE

Della Volta see VOLTA

Delle Donne see DAME

Delle Grazie see GRACE

Dello Iacono see DEAKIN

Dell'Ongaro see UNGER

Del Lungo see LONG

Del Magro see MAIGRE

Delman 1. English: var. of DELL. **2.** Jewish (Ashkenazic): of unknown origin.
Var. (of 1): **Delleman**.

Delmas see MAS

Del Monaco see MONK

Del Moro see MOORE

De Lorenzis see LAWRENCE

Delorme see ORME

Delort see ORT

Del Paggio see PAGE

Delpech see PUY

Delphin see DAUPHIN

Del Piccolo see PICCINI

Del Prete see PRIEST

Del Principe see PRINCE

Del Ré see RAY

Delrieu see RIEU

Del Rosso see ROUSE

Delroure see ROUVRE

Del Savio see SAGE

Del Sellaio see SELLER

Delsol see SOL

Delsuc see SUC

Del Turco see TURK

De Luca see LUCAS

De Lucia see LUCEY

De Luisi see LEWIS

Del Vecchio see VEAL

Demageard see DOMINIQUE

De Maggio see MAY

De Magistri see MASTER

Demakov see DAMYON

Demann see THOMAS

Demant see DIAMOND

D'Emanuele see EMMANUEL

De Marchi see MARK

Demare see DELAMARE

De Maria see MARIE

De Marini *see* MARIN

De Marney *see* MARNEY

De Martini *see* MARTIN

De Mattei *see* MATTHEW

De Mauro *see* MOORE

Dembinsk *see* DUBNIKOV

Dembitzer Jewish (Ashkenazic): habitation name, Yid. *Dembitser*, for a native or inhabitant of *Dembits*, Yid. name of *Dębica*, a town in SE Poland, which derives its name from Pol. *dęby* oaks, pl. of *dąb* oak (cf. DĄBROWSKI, DUBNIKOV).

Demčák *see* DMITRIEV

De Meis *see* BARTHOLOMEW

De Micheli *see* MICHAEL

Demidov Russian: patr. from the given name *Demid* (earlier *Diomid*, from Gk *Diomēdēs*, composed of the elements *Zeus*, gen. *Dios*, the principle Indo-European god, whose name is akin to the word meaning 'day' + *mēd-* counsel, deliberation). The name was borne by a 3rd-cent. Christian saint martyred in Bithynia under Diocletian.

Dims.: Beloruss.: **Demidyonok**. Ukr.: **Demidas**. See also DAMYON for several forms which may derive from either name.

De Minico *see* DOMINIQUE

Demont *see* MONT

Dempsey Irish: Anglicized form of Gael. **Ó Díomasaigh** and **Mac Díomasaigh** 'descendant' and 'son of *Díomasach*', a byname meaning 'Proud', 'Haughty', from *díomas* pride. The name was occasionally Anglicized as **Proudman** (see PROUD).

Vars.: **Dempsy**; **O'Dempsey**; **McGimpsey**.

Dempster Scots, Manx, and English: occupational name for a judge or arbiter of minor disputes, from OE *dēm(e)stre*, a deriv. of *dēmian* to judge, pronounce judgement. Although this was originally a fem. form of the masc. *dēmere*, by the ME period the suffix *-stre* had lost its fem. force, and the term was used of both sexes (cf. *Baxter* at BAKER, and *Webster* at WEBB). The surname is not common in England, where the term was early replaced by ANF JUDGE, but relatively frequent in Scotland, where until 1747 every laird of a barony could have certain offences within his territory tried by his *dempster*, and on the Isle of Man, where *deemsters* also played an important part in the administration of justice.

Vars.: **De(e)mer**, **Deamer** (from OE *dēmere*, see above); **Deem**, **Deam**, **Dome** (from the OE root word, *dēma, dōma*, which likewise meant arbiter or judge); **De(e)ming** (from OE *dēmung* judgement, act of judging).

Patr.: **Demers**.

Denaghy *see* DONOHUE

Denby English: habitation name from places in Derbys. and W Yorks. This placename has the same origin as DANBY, but the ON first element has been replaced by the cogn. OE *Dene*.

Vars.: **Denb(e)igh**.

Dench English: ethnic name for someone from Denmark, from ME *den(s)ch* Danish (OE *denisc*). The Danes probably originally gained their name from a proto-Gmc cogn. of OE *denu* valley (see DEAN 1), with reference to their inhabitation of a low-lying area. There were many Danes in England in the Middle Ages, not only the long-established settlers in the Danelaw region, but also more recent immigrants.

Vars.: **Dentch**, **Dennish**; **Dence**, **Denns** (N English, Scots); **Danais**, **Dennys**, DENNIS (from ME/OF *danais*); **Dane** (see also DEAN).

Vars.: Fr.: **Danay(s)**, **Danois**, **Daney**, **Dané**. Prov.: **Danès**. It.: **Da(i)nese**, **Da(i)nesi**; **Danise**, **Danisi** (S Italy). Ger.: **Dähn(e)**, **Dehn(e)**. Flem., Du.: **Deen**.

Pej.: Fr.: **Danard**.

Den Dooven *see* TAUBER

Denecke *see* DEINHARD

De Negri *see* NOIR

Deng *see* THON

Dengler German: occupational name for a knife-sharpener, Ger. *Dengler*, from MHG *tengelen* to sharpen instruments (such as large knives, sickles, and scythes), originally by carefully angled hammer blows (from OHG *tangol* hammer).

Vars.: **Teng(e)ler**, **Tengel(mann)**.

Denham English: habitation name from any of various places so called. One in Bucks. (near Uxbridge) and two in Suffolk get the name from OE *denu* valley (see DEAN 1) + *hām* homestead; another in Bucks. (near Quainton) was originally named in OE as *Duningdūn* 'hill (OE *dūn*; see DOWN 1) associated with *Dunna*', a byname meaning 'Brown' (see DUNN 2).

Denholm 1. Scots: habitation name from a place in S Scotland near Hawick, so called from OE *denu* valley (see DEAN 1) + *holm* piece of dry land in a fen (see HOLME 2). 2. English: habitation name from *Denholme* in W Yorks, so called from OE *denum*, dat. pl. of *denu* valley.

Var.: **Denholme**.

Denial *see* DANIEL

De Nicola *see* NICHOLAS

Denley English: apparently a habitation name, perhaps from an unidentified minor place so called from OE *denu* valley + *lēah* wood, clearing.

Var.: **Denly**.

Denman 1. English (chiefly E Midlands): topographic name for someone who lived in a valley; see DEAN 1. 2. Jewish (Ashkenazic): of unknown origin.

Denner *see* DEAN

Dennery French: habitation name, with fused preposition *de*, from either of two places, in Seine-et-Oise and Moselle, called *Ennery*, from the Gmc personal name *Hunheri* (composed of the elements *hūn* bear-cub + *heri, hari* army) + the local suffix *-ācum*.

Denning *see* DINEEN

Dennington English: habitation name from a place in Suffolk, recorded in Domesday Book as *Dingifetuna*, from the OE female personal name *Denegifu* (composed of the elements *Dene* Dane + *gifu* gift) + OE *tūn* enclosure, settlement.

Dennis 1. English: from the medieval given name *Den(n)is* (L *Dionysius*, Gk *Dionysios* (follower) of *Dionysos*', an eastern god introduced to the classical pantheon at a relatively late date and bearing a name of probably Semitic origin). The name was borne by various early saints, including St Denis, the martyred 3rd-cent. bishop of Paris who became the patron of France; the popularity of the name in England from the 12th cent. onwards seems to have been largely due to Fr. influence. The fem. form *Dionysia* (in the vernacular likewise *Den(n)is*) is also found, and some examples of the surname may represent a metronymic form. 2. English: var. of DENCH. 3. Irish: Anglicized var. of DONOHUE.

Vars. (of 1): Eng.: **Den(n)iss**, **Denis(s)**, **Dennes(s)**, **Dinnis**.

Dims. (of 1): Eng.: **Denn(e)**, **Din(n)**, DENNY, **Dennet(t)**, DYE; TENNEY. Fr.: **Deniset**, **Denizet**, **Denisot**, **Denizot**, **Deniseau**, **Denison**; **Niset**, **Nizet**, **Nisot**, **Nizot**; **Donizeau**. It.: **D(i)onisetti**, **D(i)onisetto**. Ger.: **Niess**, **Niesel**, **Nissle**. Low Ger.: **Nies(e)**, **Nys**, **Niesgen**, **Nüss(gen)**; **Nisius** (Latinized). Flem.: **Nys**. Du.: **Nijs**. Czech: **Divíšek**. Pol.: **Dziwisz**. Beloruss.: **D(z)enisenya**. Ukr.: **Denisyuk**.

Pejs.: Fr.: **Denisard**, **Nisard**, **Nizard**.

Patrs.: Eng.: **Den(n)ison**. Dan.: **Dinesen**. Fr.: **Audenis**. It.: **Addionisio**, **Addionizio**. Russ.: **Denisov**, **Denisyev**. Beloruss.: **Denisevich**. Ukr.: **Denisovich**.

Patrs. (from dims.): Eng.: **Dennitts**. Low Ger.: **Dinjes**, **Dinniges**; **Niessen**, **Neissen**, **Nüssen**; **Niesing**, **Neising**. Flem.: **Nyssen(s)**, **Nisen**. Du.: **Nijssen**, **Niessen**, **Niezen**. Russ.: **Denyakin**, **Denyukhin**, **Denyagin**. Beloruss.: **D(z)eniskevich**.

Denniston Scots: habitation name from *Danzielstoun* in the former county of Renfrews. (now part of Strathclyde region), so called from the gen. case of the given name DANIEL + ME *toun*, *tone* settlement (OE *tūn*).

Denny 1. English and Scots: dim. of DENNIS. 2. English: habitation name from a place in Cambs., apparently so called from OE *Dene* Dane + *ēg* island. 3. Scots: habitation name from a town in the former county of Stirlings. 4. Irish: Anglicized form of Gael. **Ó Duibhne** 'descendant of *Duibhne*', a byname meaning 'Ill-tempered', 'Disagreeable'.

Vars.: **Denney**. (Of 3 only): **Deen(e)y**.

de Nógla *see* NANGLE

Den Olden *see* OLD

D'Enrico *see* HENRY

Densey *see* DANSIE

Dent English: 1. habitation name from places in Cumb. and W Yorks., so called from a Brit. hill name cogn. with OIr. *dinn*, *dind* hill. 2. nickname from OF *dent* tooth (L *dens*, gen. *dentis*), bestowed on someone with some deficiency or peculiarity of dentition, or of a gluttonous or avaricious nature.

Dentith *see* DAINTITH

Denton English and Scots: habitation name from any of the numerous places so called. The vast majority, including those in Cambs., Cumb., Dumfries, Co. Durham, Kent, Lancs., Lincs., Norfolk, Northumb., Oxon., Sussex, and W Yorks., get the name from OE *denu* valley (see DEAN 1) + *tūn* enclosure, settlement. An isolated example in Northants appears in Domesday Book as *Dodintone* 'settlement associated with *Dodda*'; see DODD.

Dentz *see* TANZER

Denyer English: nickname for a poor or insignificant man, from the name of a very small medieval coin, ME, OF *denier* (L *dēnārius*, a deriv. of *decem* ten, since the Roman coin was worth ten asses).

Déodat *see* DIEUDONNÉ

De Paoli *see* PAUL

De Pasquale *see* PASCALL

De Pater *see* PATER

De Pero *see* PETER

De Petris *see* PETER

De Pietri *see* PETER

Deplaix *see* PLACE

Deplanche *see* PLANCHE

Depont *see* PONT

De Pretis *see* PRIEST

De Quincey *see* QUINCEY

De Rao *see* ROLLO

Derby *see* DARBY

Derbyshire *see* DARBYSHIRE

De Rege *see* RAY

De Renzis *see* LAWRENCE

Derfler *see* THORPE

Dering *see* DEAR

Dermott Irish: Anglicized form of the Gael. personal name *Difharmait*, composed of the separative prefix *di-* + *farmat* envy, and apparently meaning 'free from envy'. This name was borne in Celtic legend by the lover of Gráinne, and in historical times by Diarmaid Mac Murchadha, the 12th-cent King of Leinster whose appeal to the English for support led directly to the Anglo-Norman invasion of Ireland.

Patrs.: Ir.: **McDermot(t)**, **McDermit**, **McDermid**, **McDerment**. Sc.: **Mac Diarmid**, **McDiarmond**, **McDairmid**, **McDairmond**, **McD(e)armid**, **McDe(a)rmont**, **McDerm(a)id**, **McDermand**. Manx: **Kermode**, **Cormode**.

'Descendant of D.': Ir.: **Dermody**, **Darmody**, DARBY (Gael. **Ó Diarmada**).

Derobert *see* ROBERT

De Rossi *see* ROUSE

Derouet *see* DREW

Derrick English: from the given name *Derrick*, now more commonly spelled *Derek*, earlier *Dederick*. This given name was introduced into England in the 15th cent., from Du. *Diederick, Dirck*; see TERRY. As a surname it is now most common in Somerset.

Dims.: Ger.: **Dieterle**, **Deitel**, **Dietle(in)**, **Diet(h)**, **Dietz(e)**, **Die(t)sch**; **Dietschi** (Switzerland). Low Ger.: **D(i)ede**; **Dietmann**, **Dittman**, **Diehm**; **Dedeke**; **Die(h)l**, **Diehlmann**, **Dihl**, **Dilmann**, **Dehl** (Latinized **Delius**).

Patrs.: Low Ger.: **D(i)ericks**, **Dier(c)ks**, **Dirks**, **Dörks**; **Diedericksen**, **D(i)erksen**, **Dörk(s)en**; **Derering**, **Dierking**. Fris.: **Derksen**. Flem.: **Dier(i)ckx**, **Dierix**, **Dirks**. Du.: **Diedericks**, **Dirks(en)**, **Derks(en)**. Norw., Dan.: **Dideriks**, **Didriksen**.

Patrs. (from dims.): Ger.: **Dietler**, **Detels**. Low Ger.: **Didden(s)**; **Dedeking**, **Dedekind**, **De(e)ken**; **D(i)ehls**, **De(h)lsen**, **Dehling**. Fris.: **Dietjen**, **Dekena**. Flem.: **Diets**, **Didden**.

D'Errico *see* HENRY

Derue *see* RUE

De Ruggero *see* ROGER

Desagnes *see* SAGNE

De Sanctis *see* SAINT

Desbois *see* BOIS

Desborough English: **1.** habitation name from a place in Bucks., so called from OE *dwostle* pennyroyal, an aromatic plant formerly much used in herbal cures + *beorg* hill. **2.** habitation name from a place in Northants, which was originally named in OE as *Dēoresburh* 'fort (OE *burh*; see BURKE) of *Dēor*' (see DEAR 1).

Descamps *see* CHAMP

Descartes French: habitation name, with fused preposition *de*, from places in the parishes of Rochecorbon and Sanzay in Indre-et-Loire called *Les Cartes*.

Deschelle *see* ESCHELLE

Desclouzeaux *see* CLOSE

Desdoights *see* DOUET

Desessard *see* ESSART

Desfontaines *see* FONTAINE

Desforges *see* FORGE

Desfossés *see* FOSSE

Deshorts *see* ORT

De Silvestri *see* SILVESTER

De Simone *see* SIMON

Desmond Irish: Anglicized form of Gael. Ó **Deasmhumhnaigh** 'descendant of the man from S Munster', from *deas* south + *Mumhain* Munster, so called from *Mumhu*, the name (of uncertain origin) of an ancient king of the region. The surname has passed into common use as a given name, not only in Ireland. Cf. ORMOND.

Vars.: **O'Dassuny**, **O'Dasshowne**, **O'Desmonde**, **O'Deason**.

Desnoyers *see* NOYER

Désormeaux *see* ORME

De Souza *see* SOUSA

Despenser *see* SPENCE

Desplanches *see* PLANCHE

Després *see* PRÉ

Desrues *see* RUE

Dessewffy *see* DIDIER

Destaing *see* ETANG

D'Este *see* ESTE

De Stefani *see* STEPHEN

Destombes French: topographic name, with fused preposition and article *des*, for someone who lived by a graveyard, perhaps also an occupational name for a grave digger, from the pl. form of OF *tombe* tomb, grave (LL *tumba* burial mound, from Gk *tymbos*).

Vars.: **Detombes**, **Destombe**.

Destouches *see* TOUCHE

Desvilles *see* VILLE

Desvoivres *see* VAUR

Détang *see* ETANG

Detels *see* DERRICK

Detheridge *see* DEATHRIDGE

Detombes *see* DESTOMBES

De Toni *see* TONEY

de Toulouse *see* TOULOUSE

Dettmers *see* DIETMAR

Deubler *see* TAUBE

Deudat *see* DIEUDONNÉ

Deusing *see* THIESS

Deutsch 1. German: ethnic name given in areas of mixed population to inhabitants speaking a Gmc rather than Slav. language, from Ger. *Deutsch* German (MHG *tiu(t)sch*, OHG *diutisk*, from *diot*, *deot*, people, race, from a Gmc root **þeudō-*). **2.** Jewish (Ashkenazic): regional name for someone who had come from a German-speaking area to another part of Europe.

Vars.: **Deutscher**. (Of 1 only): **Deusch**, **Dutsch**, **Dutz**; **Deutschmann**; **Deutschländer**. (Of 2 only): **Deutschman**; **Deit(s)ch(man)**, **Dayczman** (from Yid. *daytsh*), **Deichman** (see also DITCH); **Taitz**, **Teitz(man)** (from the NE Yid. dial. var. *tayts*).

Dims.: Ger.: **Dutschke**, **Dutzke**.

Devane Irish: **1.** Anglicized form of Gael. Ó **Damháin** 'descendant of *Damhán*', a byname meaning 'Fawn' (a dim. of *damh* ox). **2.** Anglicized form of Ó **Dubháin** 'descendant of *Dubhán*', a byname from a dim. of *dubh* black. There has been considerable confusion with DEVANEY.

Vars. (of 1): Ó **Daimhín**; **Davin(e)**, DEVIN. (Of 2): **O'Doy(a)ne**, **O'Do(w)ane**, **O'Downe**, **(O')Duan(e)**, **Doane**, **Doone**, **Dune**, **Dewan**, **Duffin**; **Kidney** (the result of association with the homonymous *dubhán* kidney).

Devaney Irish: Anglicized form of Gael. Ó **Duibheannaigh** 'descendant of *Duibheannach*', a personal name of uncertain origin; the first element is *dubh* black, the second may be *eanach* marshy place. The surname has become inextricably confused with DEVANE.

Vars.: **Devany, Devenny**.

De Vecchi *see* VEAL

Deventer Dutch: **1.** habitation name from a place in the province of Overijssel, recorded in 772 in the form *Daventre*. According to Bahlow the name is from prehistoric elements meaning 'marshy place'. **2.** occupational name, with fused def. article, for a hawker or pedlar, from an agent deriv. of MDu. *venten* to sell (L *vendere*).

Vars. (of 1): **Van Deventer**. (Of 2): **Venter**.

Dever *see* DWYER

Devereux English (Norman): habitation name, with fused preposition *de*, from *Evreux* in Eure, Normandy; see EVEREST.

Vars.: **Dever(e)aux, Devereu, Deveroux, Deverose**.

De Vettori *see* VICTOR

Devèze French: topographic name for a dweller by an enclosure to which access was forbidden, as for example a park or forest belonging to the lord of the manor, or occupational name for a guardian of such land. The word derives from L *dēfensa*, past part. of *dēfendere* to ward off, prohibit.

Var.: **Ladevèze** (with fused definite article *la*).

De Vico *see* VICO

Deville 1. English: Norman habitation name from *Déville* in Seine-Maritime, probably so called from L *dei villa* 'settlement of (i.e. under the protection of) God'. This name was early interpreted as a prepositional phrase *de ville* or *de val* and applied to dwellers in a town or valley (see VILLE and VALE; and for a similar misapplication cf. DELAMARE). **2.** English: nickname from ME *devyle*, OE *dēofol* devil (L *diabolus*, from Gk *diabolos* slanderer, enemy), referring to a mischievous youth or perhaps to someone who had acted the role of the Devil in a pageant or mystery play. Most of the modern variations in spelling and pronunciation are no more than attempts to disguise the unpleasant connotations of the word (cf., e.g., DEATH for similar processes). **3.** French: var. of VILLE, with fused preposition *de*.

Vars.: **De Ville**. (Of 1 and 2 only): **Devill, Deaville, Deyville, D(e)avall, Devall, Divall, Divell, Davell, Davoll**.

Deville *see* VILLE

Deviller *see* VILLIERS

Devin 1. English and French: nickname, of literal or ironic application, from ME, OF *devin, divin* excellent, perfect (L *dīvīnus* divine, god-like, a deriv. of *dīvus*, byform of *deus* god). **2.** Russian: metronymic from *deva* girl, normally a designation of an illegitimate child. Sometimes it may be a patronymic from a nickname for an effeminate man. **3.** Irish: var. of DEVANE.

Vars. (of 1): **Devine, Devinn, Deavin, Divine**.

Dims. (of 2): Russ.: **Dev(och)kin, Devushkin** (metrs.).

De Vincenzo *see* VINCENT

De Vio *see* VITO

Devissen *see* THIESS

De Vita *see* VITA

Devitt *see* DAVID

Devlin Irish and Scots: Anglicized form of Gael. Ó **Dobh(a)iléin** 'descendant of *Dobhailéan*', a personal name of uncertain origin, probably from a dim. of *dobhail* unlucky, unfortunate.

Vars.: **Ó Doibhlin; O'Devlin**.

De Vogel *see* VOGEL

Devonshire English: regional name for someone from the county of *Devon*. This was originally an ancient Brit. tribal name, OE *Defnas* men of Devon, L *Dumnonii*, perhaps meaning 'worshippers of the god *Dumnōnos*'.

Vars.: **Devonish, Devenish; Devon**.

Devoskin *see* DVORIN

Devoy Irish: Anglicized form of Gael. Ó **Dubhuidhe** 'descendant of *Dubhuidhe*', a personal name probably derived from *dubh* dark, black + *buidhe* sallow.

Vars.: **(O')Deev(e)y, Devey**.

De Vuono *see* BON

Dewan *see* DEVANE

Dewar Scots: **1.** occupational name for a custodian of holy relics (which was normally a hereditary office), from Gael. *deoradh* pilgrim, stranger. **2.** habitation name from a place near Dalkeith, of uncertain etymology. It may derive from the same word as in 1, from having once been the resting place of some relic, or it may be from Gael. *dubh* black, dark (see DUFF) + *ard* height, or from Brit. cogns. of W *du* black, dark + *ar* ploughed land.

Dewey English: of uncertain origin. It may be a Norman habitation name, from *Douai* in Nord, so called from the Gaul. personal name *Dous* (of uncertain meaning) + the local suffix *-ācum*.

Dewhurst English: habitation name from a place in Lancs., apparently so called from the adj. *dewy* + ME *hyrst* wooded hill (see HURST).

Vars.: **Dewhirst, Jewhurst**.

Dewi *see* DAVID

Dexter *see* DYER

Dey *see* DAY

D'Eye *see* DAY

Deyns *see* DAIN

Deyville *see* DEVILLE

Dezsöffi *see* DIDIER

De Zuani *see* JOHN

Dhorme *see* ORME

Dhôtel *see* HOSTAL

D'Hozier *see* DOZIER

Diaconescu *see* DEAKIN

Diago *see* DIEGO

Di Antonio *see* ANTHONY

Diamond 1. English: var. of *Dayman*; see DAY. Forms with the excrescent dental are not found before the 17th cent., and are in part the result of folk etymology. 2. Jewish (Ashkenazic): Anglicized form of various Jewish surnames derived from mod. Ger. *Diamant, Demant*, or Yid. *dime(n)t*, all of which go back to MHG *dīemant* diamond (OF *diamant*, via L from Gk *adamas*, gen. *adamantos*, 'unconquerable', a reference to the hardness of the stone). The name is mostly ornamental, one of the many Ashkenazic surnames based on mineral names, though in some cases (esp. those vars. ending in *-man*) it may have been taken by jewellers. Cf. BRILLANT and JAGLOM.

Vars.: **Diamand, Diamant**. (Of 1 only): **Dayment, D(a)ymond, Dimond, Dimont, Dymont, Dyment**. (Of 2 only): **Diamont, Di(e)mant, Diament, Diment, Demant, Dymant; Dimet(man); Dymetman** (Pol. spelling).

Cpds (of 2): **Diamantstein, Diamandstein, Dimantstein, Diamontstein, Dime(n)tstein, Dyme(n)tsztain, Dymantsztain** ('diamond stone'); **Dimetbarg** ('diamond hill').

Diat *see* DIEUDONNÉ

Di Bartoli *see* BARTHOLOMEW

Di Batista *see* BAPTISTE

Di Baudi *see* BAUD

Dibb English: topographic name for someone living in a hollow, ME *dybbe*. The surname is most common in Yorks., where a number of minor placenames are formed from it.

Var.: **Dibbs**.

Dibbauts *see* THEOBALD

Dibden English: habitation name from a place in Hants, so called from OE *dēop* deep + *denu* valley (see DEAN 1).

Di Bello *see* BEAU

Di Bernardo *see* BERNARD

Di Biagio *see* BLAISE

Di Bono *see* BON

Di Carlo *see* CHARLES

Di Caro *see* CARO

Di Cesare *see* CESARE

Di Chiara *see* CLARE

Dichter 1. German: ostensibly an occupational name for a minstrel or poet, Ger. *Dichter*, from MHG *tichten* to compose, write (L *dictāre* recite, dictate, frequentative of *dīcere* to say). 2. Jewish (Ashkenazic): of uncertain origin. It is probably a nickname from Ger. *Dichter* poet, but could also be an inflected form of Ger. *dicht* thick. In neither case is the reason for the adoption of the word as a surname clear.

Var.: Jewish: **Dychterman** (E Ashkenazic, Pol. spelling).

Dick 1. Scots and English: pet form of RICHARD. Although found in every part of Britain, the form *Dick* is especially common in Scotland. 2. German and Jewish (Ashkenazic): nickname for a stout, thickset man, from Ger. *dick*, Yid. *dik* (MHG *dic(ke)*, OHG *dicki, dichi*). 3. German: topographic name for someone who lived by a thicket or patch of thickly grown undergrowth, from MHG *dicke*, a special use of *dic(ke)* thick (cf. Ger. *Dickicht* thicket).

Vars. (of 1): **Dicke**; DIGG. (Of 2): Jewish: **Dickman(n), Dik(er)man, Dickerman; Dykierman** (Pol. spelling). (Of 2 and 3): **Dicke**. See also DICKER.

Dims. (of 1): Eng.: **Dicken** (chiefly W Midlands), **Dickin, Diggen, Diggon, Dig(g)an; Dickie** (chiefly Scotland and N Ireland), **Dickey** (N Ireland), DIXIE (Scotland).

Patrs. (from 1): Eng.: **Dicks, Dix; Dickson** (chiefly Scotland and N Ireland); **Dixon** (chiefly N England and the Midlands); **Dixson**. (From 2): Eng.: **Thicks**. Flem.: **Dikken**. Du.: **Dikkes**. Patrs. (from 1) (dims.): **Dickin(g)s, Dickens, Dickons, Diggin(g)s, Diggens, Digance; Dicketts; Dickels; Dickinson** (chiefly N England and the Midlands), **Dickison, Dickenson** (chiefly Midlands), **Dicke(r)son, Dickason**.

'Servant of D. 1': **Dickman; Digman** (see also DITCH).

Cpds (of 2): Jewish: **Dikfeld** ('thick field'); **Dickhoff** ('thick farm'); **Dickstein, Diks(h)tein, Diksztejn, Dickenstein** ('thick stone'; *Diksztejn* is a Pol. spelling). All of these compounds are semantically odd, and it is not clear how they were acquired as surnames.

Dicker 1. English: occupational name for a digger of ditches, or topographic name for someone living by a ditch or dyke; see DITCH. 2. English: regional name from an area of E Sussex, near Hellingly, called 'the *Dicker*', from ME *dyker* unit of ten (L *decuria*, from *decem* ten); the reason for the place being so named is not clear. It has been suggested that the reference is to a bundle of iron rods, in which sense *dicras* appears in Domesday Book. Such a bundle could have been the rent for property in this iron-working area. Surname forms such as *atte dicker* occur in the surrounding region in the 13th and 14th cents. 3. German and Jewish (Ashkenazic): inflected form of DICK 2.

Var. (of 3): **Dickert**.

Dicksee *see* DIXIE

Di Clemente *see* CLEMENT

Di Cola *see* COLL

Di Contino *see* COUNT

Di Costanzo *see* CONSTANT

Di Curti *see* COURT

Didden *see* DERRICK

Didier French: from a medieval given name (L *Dēsīderius*, a deriv. of *dēsīderium* desire, longing, given either to a longed-for child, or in expression of the Christian's spiritual longing for God). The name was borne by a 3rd-cent. bishop of Langres and a 6th-cent. bishop of Vienne in the Dauphiné, both of whom were locally venerated as saints.

Var.: **Dizier**.

Dims.: Fr.: **Didion, Did(i)ot, Dideron, Did(e)rot, Didelot, Didelet**.

Patrs.: Hung.: **Dessewffy, Dezsöffi**.

Di Domenico *see* DOMINIQUE

Di Donato *see* DONAT

Diebels *see* THEOBALD

Diede *see* DERRICK

Diegnan *see* DEEGAN

Diego Spanish: from the medieval given name *Diego*, *Diago*, which is of uncertain origin. It was early taken to be an aphetic form of SANTIAGO (cf. Port. *Tiago*), and is commonly taken by English speakers as being a form of JAMES, but this is no more than folk etymology. It is found in the Middle Ages in the L forms *Didacus* and *Didagus*, which Meyer-Lübke derived from Gk *didakhē* doctrine, teaching, but in view of the fact that it is unknown outside the Iberian Peninsula it may possibly have a pre-Roman origin.
Var.: **Diago**.
Patrs.: **Diéguez**, **Díez**; **Díaz**. Port.: **Dias**.

Diemant *see* DIAMOND

Dienl *see* DEINHARD

Dierich *see* DÜRING

Dies *see* THIESS

Diesel S German: from a given name, an aphetic diminutive form of *Mathies*; see MATTHEW.

Diesing *see* THIESS

Diestel *see* DISTEL

Dietmar German: from a Gmc personal name composed of the elements *þeudō*- people, race (OHG *diot*, *deot*) + *meri*, *mari* famous.
Vars.: **Dittmar**, **Dittmer**, **Diemar**, **Diemer**; **Dittmai(e)r**, **Dittmeyr** (the result of folk etymological association with MAYER).
Dims.: Ger.: **Diem**, **Thieme**. Low Ger.: **Dittmann**; TIMM.
Patrs.: Ger.: **Dittmers**. Low Ger.: **Dettmers**.

Dieudonné French: from a medieval given name (OF *Dieudonné* 'God-given', from L *deus* god + *dōnātus* given; cf. DAUDET and DONAT).
Vars.: **Déodat**, **Deudat**, **Dêat**, **Diat**, **Diet**, **Diez**, **Dief** (all from the L form *Deodatus*).

Dieulafoy French: nickname for someone who frequently employed this oath, OF *Dieu* God (L *deus*) + *la foy* (the) faith (L *(illa) fides*).

Di Falco *see* FAULKES

Di Fazio *see* BONIFACE

Di Felice *see* FELIX

Di Filippo *see* PHILIP

Di Fiore *see* FLOWER

Di Folca *see* FOULKES

Di Francesco *see* FRANCIS

Di Franco *see* FRANK

Di Frisco *see* FRANCIS

Di Gaetano *see* GAETANO

Digan *see* DEEGAN

Digan *see* DICK

Digby English: habitation name from *Digby* in Lincs., so called from OE *dīc* dyke (see DITCH) + ON *býr* farm, settlement.

Di Gennaro *see* JANUARY

Digg English: **1.** var. of DICK 1. **2.** nickname from some fancied resemblance to a duck, ME *digge* (of uncertain relation to OE *duce*; cf. DUCKETT).
Vars. (of 2): **Duck**, **Doke**.
Dim.: **Diggle**.
Patrs.: **Digges**. (From 2 only): **Duckes**, **Dooks**.
Patr. (from a dim.): **Diggles**.

Dightham *see* DEIGHTON

Di Giacomettino *see* JAMES

Di Gioia *see* JOY

Di Giorgio *see* GEORGE

Di Giulio *see* JÚLIO

Digman *see* DITCH

Di Gratia *see* GRACE

Di Gregorio *see* GREGORY

Dihl *see* DERRICK

Di Iorio *see* GEORGE

Dike *see* DITCH

Dikerman *see* DICK

Di Lauro *see* LAUR

Di Lazzari *see* LAZAR

Di Leo *see* LYON

Di Leonardi *see* LEONARD

Di Lione *see* LYON

Dillamore *see* DELAMARE

Dilling *see* DOWLING

Dillon **1.** English and French: from the Gmc personal name *Dillo* (of uncertain origin, perhaps a byname from the root *dīl* destroy), introduced into England by the Normans. The surname derives from the OF oblique case of the name, ending in -*n*. **2.** English: habitation name from *Dilwyn* near Hereford, recorded in 1138 as *Dilun*, probably from OE *dīglum*, dat. pl. case (originally used after a preposition) of *dīgol*, *digle* recess, retreat. **3.** Irish (Norman): altered form of *de Leon*; see LYON and also further below. **4.** Irish: Anglicized form of Gael. **Ó Duilleáin** 'descendant of *Duilleán*', a personal name of uncertain origin, probably a var. of *Dallán*, originally a byname meaning 'Blind man'. **5.** Jewish: Anglicized form of **Dilon**, an Ashkenazic surname of uncertain origin, perhaps an altered form of Sefardic *de León*; see LYON.
Var. (of 3): **Dillane**.
Patr. (from 1) (dim.): **Dilks** (chiefly E Midlands).

Dilmann *see* DERRICK

Di Lorenzo *see* LAWRENCE

Di Lucca see Lucas

Di Luisi see Lewis

Dilworth English: habitation name from a place in Lancs. so called from OE *dile*, *dyle* dill (a medicinal herb) + *worð* enclosure (see Worth).

Di Maggio see May

Dimanche see Dominique

Dimant see Diamond

Di Maria see Marie

Di Martino see Martin

Di Mattei see Matthew

Di Mauro see Moore

Dimbleby English: habitation name from *Dembleby* in Lincs., which probably gets its name from an unattested ON antecedent of Northern ME *dimble* ravine with a watercourse in it (cf. mod. Norw. *dembel* pool) + ON *býr* farm, settlement.
Vars.: **Dimblebee**, **Dimbledee**.

Di Meo see Bartholomew

Dimić see Dmitriev

Dimmack see Dymock

Din see Dennis

di Napoli see Napoli

Dineen Irish: Anglicized form of Gael. **Ó Duinnín** 'descendant of *Duinnín*', a byname from a dim. of *donn* brown, dark (see Dunn).
Vars.: **Dinneen**, **Dinan**, **Dunnion**; Dunning, **Denning**; **O'Dunneen**, **O'Dunnion**.

Dines Jewish (Ashkenazic): metr. from the Yid. female given name *Dine* (from the Hebr. name *Dina* Dinah, which appears in Gen. 30: 21) + the Yid. possessive suffix -*s*.
Vars.: **Diness**, **Dinnis**; **Dineso(h)n**, **Dinzon**; **Dinin**, **Dinovitz**, **Dinowitz** (E Ashkenazic).

Dines see Dain

Dingle English: habitation name for someone living in a small wooded dell or hollow, ME *dingle* (of uncertain origin, perhaps akin to *dimble*; cf. Dimbleby). There is a district of Liverpool called *Dingle*.

Dingott Jewish (Ashkenazic): ornamental name composed of Yid. *din(en)* to serve + *got* God, or perhaps of the verb in the imperative, with the sense 'serve God!'

Dinsdale English: habitation name from a settlement on both sides of the river Tees, so partly in Co. Durham and partly in N Yorks. The name is from OE *Dīctūneshalh* 'nook, recess (OE *halh*; see Hale 1) belonging to Deighton'.

Dinswoodie see Dunwoodie

Dinu see Constantine

Dinzey see Dansie

Dion French: habitation name from any of various places called *Dion(s)* and *Dionne*, all apparently derived from a Gaul. element *divon-* (sacred) spring (cf. Dee 3).
Var.: **Dionne**.
Dim.: **Dion(n)et**.

Dionisetti see Dennis

Dios Spanish: nickname from Sp. *Dios* God (L *Deus*). The name seems to have been given either respectfully or mockingly to a notably pious person; in the later Middle Ages it may also have been used as a given name in honour of St John of God (Port. *João de Deus*, 1495–1550).

Di Pasqua see Pask

Di Pierro see Peter

Dipple see Theobald

Dirand see Durant

Dirks see Derrick

Di Roberto see Robert

Di Ruggero see Roger

Di Salvo see Salvi

Disley English: habitation name from a place so called in Ches., the origin of which is uncertain. Early forms were *Distislegh* and *Distelee*. The second element is clearly OE *lēah* wood, clearing; the first is obscure. Ekwall comments that the forms suggest a personal name, but no suitable candidate has been found.

Disney English (Norman): habitation name, with fused preposition *de*, from *Isigny* in Calvados, so called from the Gallo-Roman personal name *Isinius* (a Latinized form of Gaul. *Isina*) + the local suffix -*ācum*.

Disraeli see Israel

Diss English: habitation name from *Diss* in Suffolk, which gets its name from a Norman pronunciation of ME *diche*, OE *dīc* ditch, dyke; see Ditch.

Distel 1. German, Low German, Dutch, and Flemish: topographic name for someone who lived by a patch of ground overgrown with thistles, or perhaps a nickname for a 'prickly' person, from Ger. *Distel* thistle (MHG, MLG, MDu. *distel*; cf. OHG *distil(a)*, OE *ðistel*). 2. Jewish (Ashkenazic): probably in most cases an unflattering name bestowed on Jews by non-Jewish government officials in 18th- and 19th-cent. central Europe.
Vars.: Ger.: **Diestel**, **Distler**, **Di(e)stelmann**. Jewish: **Distelman**; **Distelfeld**.

Ditch English: topographic name for someone who lived by a ditch or dyke, ME *diche*, *dike*, OE *dīc* dyke, earthwork. The medieval dyke was larger and more prominent than the modern ditch, and was usually constructed for purposes of defence rather than drainage. Mod. Eng. *ditch* represents the regular development of the nominative of the OE word; *dyke* may be from OE oblique cases, reinforced by ON *díki*.
Vars.: **Deetch**; **Dike(s)**, **Dyke(s)**, **Deek(e)s**, **Deakes**, **Deex**; Diss; **Ditcher**, **Deetcher**, Dicker, Decker, **Deeker**; **Dickman**, **Digman** (see also Dick).

Ditchburn English: habitation name from a place in Northumb., so called from OE *dīc* DITCH, dyke + *burna* stream (see BOURNE).

Ditchfield English (Lancs.): habitation name from a hamlet near Widnes, so called from OE *dīc* DITCH, dyke + *feld* pasture, open country (see FIELD).

Dittmaier *see* DIETMAR

Dittman *see* DERRICK

Ditton English: **1.** habitation name from any of the numerous places so called, from OE *dīc* DITCH, dyke + *tūn* enclosure, settlement. **2.** from *Ditton* in Shrops., a var. of DODDINGTON.

Var.: DEIGHTON.

Divall *see* DEVILLE

Diver 1. Irish: var. of DWYER. **2.** English, of uncertain origin: possibly from the vocab. word *diver*, an agent deriv. of ME *dive* dip, plunge (OE *dȳfan*), but if so the application is obscure. It may be a nickname for someone compared to a diving bird (cf. DUCKER). **3.** Jewish: of unknown origin.

Patr. (from 2): **Divers**.

Dives French and English (Norman): habitation name from places in Calvados and Oise, both of which get their names from the river *Dive* on which they stand. The name is of Gaul. origin and meant 'sacred' (cf. DEE 3 and DION).

Var.: Fr.: **Dive**.

Diviller *see* VILLIERS

Divine *see* DEVIN

Divíšek *see* DENNIS

Dix *see* DICK

Dixie English: **1.** generally a dim. of DICK 1. **2.** according to Reaney and Dauzat, a nickname for a chorister, from L *dixi* I have spoken, the first word of the 39th Psalm.

Vars.: **Dixey, Dixcee, Dixcey, Dicksee**.

Dizier *see* DIDIER

Djaković *see* JACOB

Djekić *see* JACOB

Djokić *see* JACOB

Djordjević *see* GEORGE

Djurdjević *see* GEORGE

Długoszewski *see* DOLGOV

Dmitriev Russian: patr. from the given name *Dmitri*, from Gk *Dēmḗtrios* (follower) of *Dēmḗtēr*', the goddess of fertility, whose name derives from an obscure element *dē*, sometimes taken as a Doric equivalent of Attic *gē* earth + *mḗtēr* mother. This ostensibly pagan name was in fact borne by several early Christian martyrs, and its popularity in E

Europe is largely due to the fame of a 4th-cent. saint executed under Diocletian.

Vars.: **Dimitriev** (from an earlier unsyncopated form); **Dmitrievski** (a clerical elaboration).

Dims. (patrs.): Russ.: **Mit(k)in, Mitkov, Mityakov, Mityukov, Mityashev, Mityashin, Mityush(k)in, Mitykhin, Mityanin, Mit(r)yaev, Mitasov, Mitusov, Mityagin, Mityurev, Mitrikov, Mitrukov, Mitrosh(k)in, Mitroshinov, Mitrikhin, Michurin** (see also MITROFANOV). Beloruss.: **Mitskevich**. Pol.: **Demkowicz; Mickiewicz** (of Beloruss. origin). Croatian: **Dimić, Mitić**.

Dims. (not patrs.): Beloruss: **Dmiterko, Zmitruk, Zmitrichenko**. Ukr.: **Dmiterko, Dmitruk, Dmitri(ch)enko**. Pol.: **Dmytryk, Demko; Mićka**. Czech: **Demčák, Demčík, Dmíšek**. Hung.: **Deme, Döme**.

Habitation names: Pol.: **Demitrowski, Demkowski**.

Dmytryk *see* DMITRIEV

Doag *see* DOIG

Doane *see* DEVANE

Dobb English: from the medieval given name *Dobbe*, a pet form of ROBERT. The surname is esp. common in N England and the Midlands.

Var.: **Dobbe**.

Dims.: **Dob(b)ie, Dob(b)y, Dobey** (chiefly Scotland); DOBKIN; **Dobbin(g), Dobbyn, Dobing** (chiefly N Ireland); **Dabinett**.

Patrs.: **Dobbs, Dab(b)s; Dobson, Dopson, Dabson**.

Patrs. (from dims.): **Dobbin(g)s; Dob(b)inson, Dobbison, Dobieson**.

Dobbelstein *see* DOPPLER

Dobel 1. English (Norman): nickname from OF *doubel* twin (lit. 'double', from LL *duplus*, class. L *duplex*, from *du(o)* two + *plek-*, a root meaning 'fold'). See also BESSON and JUMEAU. **2.** German: var. of TOBEL.

Vars. (of 1): **Do(u)bell, Do(u)ble, Doubble**. (Of 2): **Dobelmann, Dobler**.

Dobkin 1. English: dim. of DOBB. **2.** Jewish (E Ashkenazic): dim. of DOBRIN.

Döbl *see* TOBIAS

Dobney *see* DAUBENEY

Dobrin Jewish (E Ashkenazic): metr. from the Yid. female given name *Dobre* 'Good'; cf. DOBRYNIN.

Dims.: DOBKIN, **Dopkin** (from the Yid. dim. given name *Dobe*, a pet form of *Dobe*, var. of *Dobre*).

Dobronravov Russian: patr. from the nickname *Dobronravy* 'Pleasant', 'Well-mannered' (a cpd of *dobry* good (cf. DOBRYNIN) + *nrav* manner).

Dobrovolski Russian: compound surname meaning 'good will', composed of the elements *dobry* good (cf. DOBRYNIN) + *volya* will + the (orig. Pol.) suffix of surnames -*ski* (see BARANOWSKI). According to Unbegaun, the Russ. name is a made-up surname of the type assumed by Orthodox priests. Bystroń indicates that the Pol. cogn. is either from villages named *Dobrowole* or *Dobrawola* or from nicknames denoting peasants who had been freed from serfdom. In Czech, on the other hand, Moldanová says that the name was bestowed as a nickname on one who voluntarily accepted serfdom.

Dobrovský Czech: **1.** habitation name from a place called *Dobrovice*, named with the element *dobrý* good. **2.** var. of DOBRÝ.

Dobrý Czech: nickname for a good man, from Czech *dobrý* good.
Var.: DOBROVSKÝ.
Patrs.: Croatian: **Dobrić**. Rum.: **Dobrescu**.

Dobrynin Russian: patr. from the given name *Dobryna*, a short form of the various Slav. personal names with a first element *dobr-* good, kind. Such names, which originated in a pagan culture and not been made respectable by any saint, were frowned upon by the Orthodox Church and not accepted as baptismal names, but nevertheless they were relatively common as unofficial names among the peasantry.
Dim.: Russ.: **Dobryshin** (patr.).

Dobrzyński Polish: habitation name from a place called *Dobrzyń*, named with the element *dobrzy* good.

Dočekal Czech: nickname of uncertain application, from Czech *dočekat* to wait long enough (composed of the perfective prefix *do-* + *čekat* to wait). It may have signified a person who had lived to a great age.
Var.: **Dočkal**.

Docharty *see* DOHERTY

Docker English: habitation name from places in Lancs. and Cumb. so called from ON *dokk* hollow, valley + *erg* shieling or dairy building (of Celt. origin). The name is now found chiefly in the W Midlands.

Döcker *see* DECKER

Dockett *see* DOGGETT

Dockray **1.** English: habitation name from any of several places so called, of which there are four in Cumb. The probable origin is ON *dokk* hollow, valley + *vrá* isolated place; the first element may, however, be OE *docce* dock (the plant). **2.** Irish: Anglicized form of Gael. Ó **Dochraidh** 'descendant of *Dochrach*', a variant of *Dochartach*; see DOHERTY.
Vars.: **Dockeray**, **Dock(e)ry**, **Docwra(y)**.

Dodd **1.** English: from the ME personal name *Dodde*, *Dudde*, OE *Dodda*, *Dudda*, which remained in fairly widespread and frequent use in England until the 14th cent. It seems to have been originally a byname, but the meaning is not clear; it may come from a Gmc root used to describe something round and lumpish—hence a short, plump man. **2.** Irish: var. of DUDDY.
Vars.: **Dod**; **Dadd** (Kent).
Dims. (of 1): Eng.: **Dodell**, **Duddell**, **Duddle**. Fr.: **Dodet**, **Dodin(et)**; **Do(u)in**. It.: **Tozzetti**, **Tozzini**.
Aug. (of 1): It.: **Tozzoni**.
Patrs. (from 1): Eng.: **Dod(d)s**, **Dadds**; **Dodson**, **Dotson**, **Dudson**; **Dodding**.
'Servant of D. 1': Eng.: **Dodman**, **Dudman**.

Doddington English: habitation name from any of the numerous places called *Dod(d)ington*, found in every part of England. The placename generally means 'settlement (OE *tūn*) associated with *Dodda*' (see DODD 1). This

placename has taken the forms *Detton* and *Ditton* in Shrops.
Var.: DITTON.

Dode *see* DUDE

Dodge English (N England): **1.** from the ME given name *Dogge*, a pet form of ROGER. **2.** possibly also a nickname from ME *dogge* dog (OE *docga*, *dogga*).
Vars.: **Doi(d)ge** (SW England).
Dims.: **Dodgin**, **Dodgeo(o)n**.
Patrs.: **Dodgs(h)on**, **Dodgshun**.

Dodsworth English: habitation name from *Dodworth* in W Yorks. (*Dodeswrde* in Domesday Book), which gets its name from the OE personal name *Dodd(a)* (see DODD 1) + OE *worð* enclosure.

Doe English: **1.** nickname for a mild and gentle man, from ME *do* doe (OE *dā*; for the change in the vowel cf. ROPER). **2.** habitation name, with fused preposition *de*, from *Eu* in Seine-Maritime, whose name either represents a dramatic reduction of Latin *Augusta* (city of) Augustus' (cf. DALTON 2), or else derives from the Gmc element *auwa* water-meadow, island.

Doeg *see* DOIG

Doey *see* DUFFY

Dogerty *see* DOHERTY

Doggett English: **1.** nickname, probably with abusive connotations, from a dim. of ME *dogge* dog (OE *docga*). **2.** nickname from ME *dogge* dog + *heved* head (OE *heafod*).
Var.: **Dockett**.

Doherty Irish and Scots: Anglicized form of Gael. Ó **Dochartaigh** 'descendant of *Dochartach*', a byname meaning 'Unlucky' or 'Hurtful'.
Vars.: **O'Doherty**, **(O')Do(u)gherty**, **Dougharty**, **Doghartie**; **Dogerty**, **Daugherty**; **Dockerty**; **Doggart**; **Docherty**, **Docharty** (Scots).

Dohmann *see* THOMAS

Dohnal Czech: nickname from the verb *dohnat* to drive up to or reach a particular point. The application as a surname is uncertain; it may have been given to someone who 'arrived' in a village as opposed to being born there.

Dohnke *see* THON

Doidge *see* DODGE

Doig Scots: Anglicized form of Gael. **Mac Gille Doig** 'son of the servant of *Dog*', an aphetic form of the personal name *Cadog*; see CADDOCK 1.
Vars.: **Doag**, **Doeg**; **Doak** (N Ireland).

Doin *see* DODD

Doke *see* DIGG

Dolamore *see* DELAMARE

Dolan Irish: **1.** Anglicized form of Gael. Ó **Dubhshláin** 'descendant of *Dubhshlán*', a personal name composed of the elements *dubh* dark, black + *slán* challenge, defiance. **2.** Anglicized form of Gael. *Ó Dobhailéin*; see DEVLIN.

Vars. (of 1): **O'Do(w)lane**, **Dowlan**, **Dowlin**, DOWLING. See also DELANEY.

Dolcetta *see* DUCE

Dolé French: nickname for a troubled or anxious person, from OF *dolé*, past part. of *doler*, to rue, regret (L *dolēre* to hurt, *dolet* it is a matter of regret, lit. it hurts).

Var.: **Dollé**.

Dolejš Czech: topographic name for someone living in the lower part of a village, or on the ground floor of a multistorey building divided into apartments, from Czech *dolejší* lower down, downstairs. Compare Hořejš.

Var.: **Dolejší**.

Dim.: **Dolejšek**.

Doley *see* DOYLEY

Doležal Czech: nickname for a lazy or idle person, from the verb *doležat* to have rested up to the present time or long enough (composed of the perfective prefix *do-* + *ležat* to lie down, rest).

Var.: **Doležel**.

Dolgopolov Russ.: according to Unbegaun, this is a nickname for someone who habitually wore long skirts, from Russ. *dolgi* long (see DOLGOV 1) + *pola* skirt. However, the Jewish name *Dolgopolski* means 'long field' rather than 'long skirt'; see POLAŃSKI.

Dolgopolski *see* POLAŃSKI

Dolgov Russian: **1.** patr. from the nickname *Dolgi* 'Long', 'Tall'. **2.** patr. from the nickname *Dolg* 'Debt', 'Duty', acquired perhaps by someone who owed a particular feudal obligation.

Habitation name (from 1): Pol.: **Długoszewski**.

Doliński Polish: topographic name for someone living in a valley, from Pol. *dolina* valley + *-ski* suffix of local surnames (see BARANOWSKI).

Dolittle English: nickname for a lazy man, from ME *do* (OE *dōn*) + *little* (OE *lytel*).

Var.: **Doolittle**.

Dolk Swedish: nickname from Swed *dolk* dagger. This is one of the 'soldiers' names', adopted on military service in the days before surnames came into use in Swedish (i.e. before the 18th cent.), and later retained in civilian life and handed down to descendants as a surname.

Dölker German (chiefly Württemberg): of uncertain origin. It may be a nickname for a stammerer or someone with a speech impediment, from MHG *tolken* to mutter, mumble. Alternatively it may be an occupational name for a translator or interpreter, MHG *tolke*, which is derived from the same verb in the more common sense 'speak'.

Doll English: nickname for a foolish individual, from ME *dolle* dull, foolish (OE *dol*). The byform **dyl(le)* gave rise to ME *dil(le)*, *dul(le)*, mod. Eng. *dull*.

Vars.: **Dol(l)man** (chiefly Midlands).

Dollé *see* DOLÉ

Dolling *see* DOWLING

Dolohunty *see* DELAHUNTY

Dolomieu French: habitation name from a place in the Dauphiné, recorded in the 7th cent. as *Doloimeiacum*, apparently from an otherwise unrecorded Gaul. personal name + the local suffix *-ācum*.

Dolphin *see* DUFFIN

Domagała Polish: nickname for a selfish or demanding person, from Pol. *domagać* demand.

Var.: **Domagalski** (with surname suffix *-ski*; see BARANOWSKI).

Domann *see* THOMAS

Domański Polish: from a deriv. of the OPol. given name *Domarad*, which is composed of the elements *doma* home + *rad* glad, and according to Kupis does not mean 'glad to be at home', but rather 'glad to welcome a guest into one's home'. The (originally local) suffix of surnames *-ski* has been added (see BARANOWSKI).

Dombovsky *see* DUBNIKOV

Döme *see* DMITRIEV

Dome *see* DEMPSTER

Domecq Provençal: topographic name from a Gascon form of OF *demaine* (feudal) estate, land belonging to the lord (LL *dominicum*, a deriv. of *dominus* lord, master; cf. DOMINIQUE).

Var.: **Domec**.

Dömel *see* THOMAS

Dominique French: from a medieval given name (L *Dominicus* of the Lord, from *dominus* lord, master; cf. DOMECQ). It was borne by a Sp. saint (1170–1221) who founded the Dominican order of monks and whose fame gave an added boost to the popularity of the name, already well established because of its symbolic value.

Vars.: **Demange** (Lorraine); **Domange**, **Domenge** (Bordeaux); **Demanche**, **Dimanche** (Paris); **Demo(n)ge** (Burgundy); **Doumic** (Brittany).

Dims.: Fr.: **Domenget**, **Monget**, **Mouget**; **Demangel**, **Mougel**; **Demangeon**, **Mangeon**; **Demangeot**, **Demongeot**; **Demo(u)geot**, **Mangeot**, **Manjot**, **Mongeot**, **Mougeot**; **Demangin**, **Demougin**, **Manjin**, **Mongin**, **Mougin**, **Mangenet**, **Mangeney**, **Ma(n)ginot**, **Mangenot**, **Mo(n)genot**, **Mougenel**. It.: **Dom(en)ichelli**, **Domin(ich)elli**; **Menichelli**, **Menichi(e)llo**, **Minichiello**, **Min(ich)elli**, **Men(e)ghelli**, **Meneghello**, **Minghelli**; **Domin(ich)etti**, **Domeneghetti**, **Domenichetti**; **Men(i)chetti**, **Men(i)chetto**, **Meneghetto**, **Men(e)ghetti**, **Minghetti**; **Domenichini**, **Dominichini**, **Domeneghini**; **Men(i)chini**, **Men(i)chino**, **Men(c)ini**, **Men(e)ghini**, **Meneghino**, **Mengheni**, **Minichini**, **Minichino**, **Minghini**, **Menini**; **Domenicucci**; **Men(i)cucci**, **Men(e)gucci**, **Min(i)cucci**, **Min(i)gucci**, **Menc(i)otti**, **Men(g)otti**, **Mi(n)cotti**, **Min(g)otti**, **Menicocci**, **Minocchi**, **Minicozzi**, **Min(g)ozzi**, **Men(g)ozzi**, **Mengossi**, **Mecocci**, **Mecozzi**, **Mecucci**, **Mecuzzi**, **Mecozzi**; **Cocci**, **Cozzi**, **Gozz(in)i**, **Gozzoli**; **Meneguzzi**, **Meniguzzi**, **Minguzzi**, **Minucci**. Pol.: **Domiczek**. Czech: **Domek**, **Dománek**.

Augs.: Fr.: **Demangeat**. It.: **Domenicone**; **Me(ni)coni**, **Miniconi**, **Menegone**, **Micone**, **Mingone**, **Men(c)oni**, **Men(g)oni**.

Pejs.: Fr.: **Demageard**; **Menjaud**; **Mongeaud**. It.: **Dominicacci**, **Dominigazzo**; **Men(i)cacci**, **Menegazzo**, **Mingazzi**,

Men(eg)azzi, Mecacci; Men(e)gazzi; Mengardo, Mengardi, Mingardo, Mingardi.

Patrs.: It.: **De Domenico, De Domenicis, De Dominici(s), Di Domenico; De Minico; Menis.** Sp.: **Domínguez.** Port.: **Domingues.** Pol.: **Dominiak.**

Habitation name: Pol.: **Miniszewki.**

Domvile *see* DUMVILLE

Don *see* DUNN

Donagh *see* McDONAGH

Donaghey *see* DONOHUE

Donald Scots and Irish: from a Gael. personal name, *Domhnall*, composed of the Celt. elements *dubno-* world + *val-* might, rule.

Vars.: **Donnell, Doull, Doole;** DANIEL.

Patrs.: **Donaldson;** McDONALD, McCONNELL.

'Descendant of D.': **O'Donnell, O'Donill, O'Daniel** (Gael. **Ó Domhnaill**).

'Descendant of D. (dim.)': **(O')Donnellan, (O')Donel(l)an, (O')Donlan, (O')Donlon** (Gael. **Ó Domhnalláin**).

Donat English, French, and German: from a medieval given name (L *Dōnātus*, past part. of *dōnāre*, freq. of *dare* to give). The name was much favoured by early Christians, either because the birth of a child was seen as a gift from God (cf. DAUDET and DIEUDONNÉ), or else because the child was in turn dedicated to God. The name was borne by various early saints, among them a 4th-cent. Italian bishop martyred in *c*.350 under Julian the Apostate, a 6th-cent. hermit of Sisteron, and a 7th-cent. bishop of Besançon, all of whom contributed to the popularity of the given name in the Middle Ages, which was not checked by the heresy of a 4th-cent. Carthaginian bishop who also bore it. Another bearer was a 4th-cent. grammarian and commentator on Virgil, widely respected in the Middle Ages as a figure of great learning.

Vars.: Eng.: **Donnet(t); Donnay; Doney** (Devon and Cornwall). Fr.: **Donnat; Donné, Donnet, Donney.** Ger.: **Donath, Donet.**

Dims.: It.: **Donatelli; Donatiello** (Naples); **Donatini; Donadini** (Venetia).

Augs.: It.: **Donatoni; Donadon(i)** (Venetia).

Patrs.: Ger.: **Donaty** (alteration of *Donáti*, gen. of *Donátus*).

Flem.: **Dons.** It.: **De Donato, Di Donato** (S Italy); **De Dona** (Venetia).

Donegan Irish: Anglicized form of Gael. **Ó Donnagáin** 'descendant of *Donnagán*', a personal name from a dim. of *donn* brown, dark (see DUNN 1).

Vars.: **Dunnigan, Doonican, Dunegain(e),** DUNCAN; **O'Donegan, O'Donegaine, O'Dungan.**

Dönges *see* THON

Dönhardt *see* DEINHARD

Donisetti *see* DENNIS

Donk *see* DUNG

Donker Dutch: nickname for someone with dark hair or a dark complexion, from MDu. *donker, donkel* dark (cf. mod. Ger. *dunkel*).

Patr.: Du.: **Donkers.**

Donleavy *see* DUNLEAVY

Donnelly Irish: Anglicized form of Gael. **Ó Donnghaile** 'descendant of *Donnghal*', a personal name composed of the elements *donn* brown (see DUNN 1) + *gal* valour. It is claimed that most bearers of this surname descend from Donnghal O'Neill, 17th in descent from Niall of the Nine Hostages.

Vars.: **Donneely, O'Donnelly.**

Donner 1. German: nickname for a man with a fierce or blustery temperament, from Ger. *Donner* thunder (MHG *doner*, OHG *thonar*). **2.** Jewish (Ashkenazic): from Ger. *Donner* thunder, one of the many ornamental names derived from vocab. items referring to natural phenomena.

Vars. (of 1): **Donnerer, Donder(er), Daunderer, Dundrer.**

Donohue Irish: Anglicized form of Gael. **Ó Donnchadha** 'descendant of *Donnchadh*', a personal name composed of the elements *donn* brown (see DUNN 1) + *cath* battle.

Vars.: **O'Donohue, O'Donog(h)ue, O'Donohoe, O'Donochowe; O'Donaghie, O'Dunaghy; Donoghue, Dona(g)hue, Donohoe, Donaghoe; Donaghie, Donagh(e)y, Denaghy, Dennehy; Donachie** (Scots); DENNIS.

Donoso Spanish: nickname for a hospitable person, from OSp. *donoso* generous (L *dōnōsus* generous, liberal, a deriv. of *dōnum* gift). The adj. later developed the sense 'witty', 'amusing', and in some cases this may be the meaning of the surname.

Donov *see* DOROFEEV

Donovan Irish: Anglicized form of Gael. **Ó Donndubháin** 'descendant of *Donndubhán*', a personal name composed of the elements *donn* brown (see DUNN 1) + *dubh* black (see DUFF) + the dim. suffix *-án*.

Vars.: **Donavan, Donavin; O'Donovan.**

Doody *see* DUDDY

Doohan *see* DUGGAN

Dooks *see* DIGG

Doolan Irish: Anglicized form of Gael. **Ó Dubhlainn** 'descendant of *Dubhfhlann*', a personal name composed of the elements *dubh* black (see DUFF) + *flann* blood-coloured, red.

Vars.: **O'Doolan, Doolen, Doolin.**

Doole *see* DONALD

Dooley Irish: Anglicized form of Gael. **Ó Dubhlaoich** 'descendant of *Dubhlaoch*', a personal name composed of the elements *dubh* black (see DUFF) + *laoch* champion, hero.

Vars.: **Dooly, O'Dooley, (O')Dowley.**

Doolittle *see* DOLITTLE

Doone *see* DEVANE

Doonican *see* DONEGAN

Döpfler *see* TÖPFER

Dopkin *see* DOBRIN

Doppler German: nickname for a gambler or occupational name for a maker of dice, from an agent deriv. of MHG *dopel(stein)* die (see also TOBEL).

Vars.: **Töppler**; **Doppelstein, Dobbelstein**.

Dopsch *see* TOBIAS

Dopson *see* DOBB

Doran 1. Irish: Anglicized form of Gael. **Ó Deoradháin** 'descendant of *Deoradhán*', a byname representing a dim. of *deoradh* pilgrim, stranger, exile (cf. DEWAR 1). **2.** English: var. of DURANT.

Vars.: **Dorran**. (Of 1 only): **Dorrian, O'D(e)oran**.

Dorant *see* DURANT

Dorcey *see* DARCY

Dore 1. English: habitation name from either of two places, one in Derbys. and the other near Hereford. The former gets its name from OE *dor* door, used of a pass between hills; the latter from a Brit. river name of the same origin as DOVER 1. **2.** Irish: Anglicized form of Gael. **Ó Doghair** 'descendant of *Doghar*', a byname meaning 'Sadness'.

Doré French: nickname from OF *doré* golden (past part. of *dorer* to gild, LL *dēaurāre*, from *aurum* gold), denoting either a goldsmith or someone with bright golden hair.

Sp.: **Dorado**. Port.: **Dourado**.

Dores Portuguese: **1.** nickname for a person oppressed with troubles and anxieties, from the pl. form of Port. *dor* pain, grief (L *dolor*; cf. DOLÉ). **2.** from a medieval female given name, bestowed in allusion to the Marian title *Nossa Senhora das Dores* Our Lady of the Sorrows.

Doret *see* THÉODORE

Dörfle *see* THORPE

Dorgan Irish: **1.** Anglicized form of Gael. **Ó Dorcháin** 'descendant of *Dorchán*', a byname representing a dim. of *dorcha* black, gloomy. **2.** var. of DARGAN.

Dörich *see* DÜRING

Doring *see* DEAR

Dorival French: habitation name, with fused preposition *de*, from any of the places in Charente, Seine-Maritime, and Somme called *Orival*, from L *aurea* golden (i.e. lovely; cf. DORÉ) + *vallis* valley (see VALE). There are also other places throughout France with the same origin but different modern spellings, and these may have contributed to the surname.

Var.: **Dorval**.

Dörken *see* DERRICK

Dörl *see* THOR

Dorling *see* DARLING

Dorme *see* ORME

Dormer 1. English (Norman): nickname for a lazy man or a sleepyhead, from OF *dormeor* sleeper, sluggard (L *dormītor*, from *dormīre* to sleep). **2.** English: apparently a

habitation name in view of the early forms with *de* (see below), but no suitable place of origin has been identified, nor is it clear whether it should be sought in Bucks. or N France. The *de* may be purely honorific. **3.** Irish: Anglicized form of Gael. **Ó Díorma**, a shortened form of **Ó Duibhdhíormaigh** 'descendant of *Duibhdhíormach*', a personal name composed of the elements *dubh* black + *díormach* trooper.

Var. (of 3): **DARBY**.

Dornan Irish: Anglicized form of Gael. **Ó Doirnáin** 'descendant of *Doirnín*', a byname representing a dim. of *dorn* fist.

Vars.: **Durnin** (Gael. **Ó Doirnín**).

Dorofeev Russian: patr. from the male given name *Dorofei* (Gk *Dōrotheos*, composed of the elements *dōron* gift + *theos* God; the same elements in the reverse order make up the name THÉODORE). The name was borne by several early saints, including a 4th-cent. bishop of Tyre much venerated in the Orthodox Church.

Var.: **Dorofanov**.

Dims.: Russ.: **Dorofankin, Dorosh(a)ev, Dor(k)in, Donov**. Beloruss.: **Doroshkevich**. Ukr.: **Dorosh(en)ko; Doroshevich**. Habitation name: Pol.: **Doroszewski**.

Dorrell *see* DARELL

Dorrington English: habitation name from any of several places so called. One in Lincs. and one in Shrops. (near Woore) get the name from OE *Dēoringtūn* 'settlement (OE *tūn*) associated with *Dēor(a)*' (see DEAR 1); another in Shrops. (near Condover) was earlier *Dodintone*, identical with DODDINGTON.

Dorsett English: regional name from the county of *Dorset*, so called from OE *Dorn*, an early name of Dorchester (of Brit. origin, from *durn* fist, probably referring to fist-sized pebbles) + *sǣte* dwellers.

Vars.: **Dorset, Dossett**.

Dorsey English (Norman): habitation name, with fused preposition *de*, from *Orsay* in Seine-et-Orne, recorded in the 13th cent. as *Orceiacum*, from the L personal name *Orcius* + the local suffix *-ācum*.

D'Orsi *see* ORSO

Dossett *see* DORSETT

Dostál Czech: nickname for a reliable, trustworthy person, from Czech *dostát (slovu)* to keep, abide by (one's word).

Dostoevski Russian: habitation name from a village called *Dostoevo*, situated in the Pinsk-Pripet marshes on the border between Poland and the Ukraine.

Dotson *see* DODD

Doubble *see* DOBEL

Doucet *see* DUCE

Doud *see* DAVID

Douet French: **1.** topographic name for someone who lived near a stream or irrigation channel, OF *doit* (L *ductus*, from *ducere* to lead, convey). **2.** dim. of the Gmc personal name *Dodo(n)* (see DODD 1).

Vars. (of 1): **Douit, Douis, Douy; Dudoit, Dudouet, Dudouit, Dudouyt, Dudoy; Desdouets, Desdouits, Desdoights**.

Dim.: **Douetteau**.

Dougall Scots and Irish: from the Gael. personal name *Dubhgall*, composed of the elements *dubh* black (see DUFF) + *gall* stranger (see GALL 1). This was used as a byname for Scandinavians, in particular to distinguish the darker-haired Danes from fair-haired Norwegians.

Vars.: **Dougal, Dougill, Dugall, Dugald; Dowell, Dowall, Doyle**.

Patr.: McDOUGALL.

'Descendant of D.': Ir.: **O'Douill, O'Dowilly, O'Doyle** (Gael. **Ó Dubhghaill**).

Dougan *see* DUGGAN

Dougharty *see* DOHERTY

Doughty English: nickname for a powerful or brave man, esp. a champion jouster, from ME *doughty*, OE *dohtig, dyhtig* valiant, strong.

Vars.: **Douty, Dowty, Dufty**.

Douglas Scots: habitation name from any of the various places so called from their situation on a river named with the Gael. elements *dubh* dark, black (see DUFF) + *glais* stream (a deriv. of *glas* blue; cf. GLASS 2). There are several localities in Scotland and Ireland so named, but the one from which the surname is derived in most if not all cases is 20 miles south of Glasgow, the original stronghold of the Douglas family and their retainers. The traditional pronunciation of the name is /'duːɡləs/, but now /'dʌɡləs/ is more common.

Var.: **Douglass**.

Douillet French: **1.** habitation name from places in Sarthe and Orne, of obscure etymology, perhaps from a personal name. **2.** nickname from OF *douillet* delicate, tender, a dim. of *doux* sweet, soft (see DUCE).

Var. (of 2): **Douillot**.

Pej. (of 2): **Douillard**.

Douin *see* DODD

Doull *see* DONALD

Doumic *see* DOMINIQUE

Dove 1. English: nickname for a mild and gentle person, or metonymic occupational name for a keeper of doves, from ME *dove*, OE *dūfe* dove (or perhaps occasionally from the ON cogn. *dúfa*). The OE word was used as a given name for either sex in the early ME period, and the surname at least in part derives from this use. **2.** Irish: translation of *Mac Calmáin* (see COLEMAN 1). **3.** Scots: var. of DUFF. **4.** Low German: nickname for a deaf man; see TAUBER 3.

Dover 1. English: habitation name from the port in Kent, so called from the river on which it stands, a Brit. name from the word which became W *dwfr* water. **2.** Low German: habitation name from *Doveren* in the Rhineland, of uncertain etymology but perhaps with a Celt. origin and so related ultimately to 1. **3.** Jewish: of unknown origin.

Var. (of 2): Ger.: **Dovermann**.

Dovey *see* DUFFY

Dovidaitis *see* DAVID

Dow 1. English: var. of DAW. **2.** Scots: var. of DUFF.

Var.: **Dowe**.

Patr. (from 1): **Dowson** (see also DUCE).

'Servant of D. 1': **Dowman**.

Dowall *see* DOUGALL

Dowcett *see* DUCE

Dowd *see* DUDDY

Dowdeswell *see* DADSWELL

Dowding English: patr. from an OE personal name, *Dogod* (apparently a deriv. of *dugan* to avail, be of use). The surname is chiefly found in Gloucs. and Somerset.

Var.: **Dowden**.

Dowey *see* DUFFY

Dowlan *see* DOLAN

Dowler English: occupational name for a maker of dowels and similar objects, from an agent deriv. of ME *dowle* dowel (headless peg, bolt) (cf. MLG *dövel*).

Dowley *see* DOOLEY

Dowling 1. English: nickname for a stupid person, ME *dolling*, a deriv. of OE *dol* dull, stupid; see DOLL. **2.** Irish: var. of DOLAN 1.

Vars. (of 1): **Dolling, Dilling**.

Down English: **1.** topographic name from OE *dūn* down, low hill, a common element in placenames. The word is of Celt. origin and was taken into OE from Brit. The surname is chiefly found in SW England. **2.** var. of DUNN.

Vars.: **Downe; Downer; Downman, Dunman**.

Downes *see* DUNN

Downie Irish and Scots: **1.** Anglicized form of Gael. **Ó Dúnadhaigh** 'descendant of *Dúnadhach*', a personal name meaning 'fortress-holder' (from *dún* fortress, fortified hill; see DOWN 1). **2.** var. of MOLONEY. **3.** habitation name from the Scots barony of *Downie* or *Duny* in the parish of Monikie in the former county of Angus (now part of Tayside region), so called from Gael. *dùn* hill (cf. DOWN 1) + the local suffix *-ach*.

Vars.: **Downey, Duny**.

Downton *see* DUNTON

Dowtry *see* DALTRY

Dowty *see* DOUGHTY

Doyle *see* DOUGALL

Doyley English (Norman): habitation name, with fused preposition *de*, from any of several places in Calvados called *Ouilly*, from the Gallo-Roman personal name *Ollius* (of uncertain etymology) + the local suffix *-ācum*.

Vars.: **Dol(l)ey, Dul(e)y; Olley, Ollie** (Norfolk).

Dozier French: topographic name, with fused preposition *de*, for someone who lived near a willow tree or willow grove, from OF *osier* willow (of Gaul. origin).

Vars.: **D'Hozier**; **Lhozier**, **Losier** (with fused definite article); **Osier**.

Dráb Czech: occupational name from Czech *dráb*, which originally meant footsoldier, but also came to denote a servant or retainer, esp. an overseer of workers on an estate.

Dims.: **Drábe(če)k**.

Drabble English: of uncertain origin, perhaps from a dim. of the OE personal name *Drabba*. This too is of uncertain etymology; it may be akin to mod. Eng. *drab* sloven, a word that is first recorded in writing in the 16th cent. but, like many slang terms, may have been in spoken use much earlier.

Drage English: metonymic occupational name for a confectioner, or perhaps a nickname from a term of endearment, from ME *drag(i)e* sweetmeat, sugar-coated spice (OF *dragie*, *dragee*, ultimately from Gk *tragēmata* spices, condiments).

Var.: **Dredge**.

Dragon 1. French and English: nickname or occupational name for someone who carried a standard in battle or else in a pageant or procession, from ME, OF *dragon* snake, monster (L *draco*, gen. *dracōnis*, from Gk *drakōn*, ultimately from *derkesthai* to flash). This word was applied in LL to military standards in the form of a windsock and hence resembling a snake. 2. French: cogn. of DRAKE 1. 3. Jewish: of unknown origin.

Var.: Jewish: **Dragoner**.

Dims.: Fr.: **Draconet**, **Drahonnet**. It.: **Draghetto**, **Draghetti**, **Dragotto**, **Dragotti**.

Drake English: 1. from the OE byname *Draca* 'Snake' or 'Dragon', ME *Drake*, or sometimes from the cogn. ON *Draki*. Both are common bynames and, less frequently, given names. Both the OE and the ON forms are from L *draco* snake, monster (see DRAGON). 2. nickname for someone with some fancied resemblance to a duck, from ME *drake* male duck (from MLG *andrake*; cf. mod. Ger. *Enterich*).

Patr.: Eng.: **Drakes**.

Draksler see DRECHSLER

Drane 1. English: nickname for a lazy man, from ME *drane* drone, male honey bee, long taken as a symbol of idleness (OE *drān*). 2. Irish: Anglicized form of Gael. Ó **Dreain** 'descendant of *Drean*', a byname meaning 'Wren'. 3. Irish: Anglicized form of Gael. Ó *Druacháin*; see DROHAN.

Var.: **Drain**.

Dransfield English: habitation name, perhaps from *Dransfield* Hill in Mirfield, W Yorks., which contains the OE gen. of *drān* drone (see DRANE 1) + *feld* pasture, open country. *Drān* may be a byname in this instance. The surname is mainly found in Yorks.

Draper English: occupational name for a maker and seller of woollen cloth, ANF *draper* (a deriv. of *drap* cloth, possibly of Gaul. origin).

Vars.: **Drapper**, **Drapier**; **Drape**.

Dim.: Fr.: **Draperon**.

Draschner see DRESCHER

Draycott English: habitation name from any of the numerous places in England so called, from OE *dræg* drag, portage, slipway, or sledge (a place where boats were dragged across land or where loads had to be dragged uphill or on sledges across wet ground, from *dragan* to draw, drag) + *cot* cottage (see COATES).

Drayton English: habitation name from any of the very numerous places in England so called from OE *dræg* (see DRAYCOTT) + *tūn* enclosure, settlement.

Dreassi see ANDREW

Drechsler German and Jewish (Ashkenazic): occupational name for a turner, Ger. *Drechsler* (MHG *dreseler* or *dræselære*, OHG *drāslāri*, formed by the addition of a superfluous agent suffix to *drāsil* turner, a primary deriv. of *drāen* to turn, spin). A turner would be responsible for making small objects not just from wood, but also from bone, ivory, and amber, all of which were widely used in the Middle Ages for their decorative value.

Vars.: **Dressler**, **Drexler**. Ger. only: **Drössler** (E Franconia, Thuringia); **Traxler**, **Draxler** (Bavaria, Austria). Jewish only: **Dres(s)ler** (see also THRUSSELL); **Draksler**.

Dredge see DRAGE

Dreier 1. German and Jewish (Ashkenazic): nickname derived from Ger. *drei* three, MHG *drī(e)*, with the addition of the suffix -*er*. This was the name of a medieval coin worth three HELLERS, and it is possible that the Ger. surname may have been derived from this word. More probably, the nickname is derived from some other connection with the number three, too anecdotal to be even guessed at now. 2. Low German: occupational name for a turner of wood or bone, from an agent deriv. of MLG *draeyen* to turn, spin (cf. DRECHSLER).

Vars.: **Dreyer**. (Of 2 only): Low Ger.: **Dreigher**, **Dreger**; **Dreher** (Württemburg).

Dreng see DRING

Drennan Irish: Anglicized form of Gael. Ó **Draighneáin** 'descendant of *Draighneán*', a byname from a dim. of *draighean* blackthorn.

Vars.: **Dr(e)inan**, **Drinnan**, **Drynan**; THORNTON.

Drescher German and Jewish (Ashkenazic): occupational name for a thresher, Ger. *Drescher*, Yid. *dresher*, agent derivs. of MHG *dreschen*, Yid. *dresh(e)n* to thresh (OHG *dreskan*).

Vars.: **Dreschner**. Ger.: **Draschner**; **Trescher**, **Tröscher**, **Trösch(e)**. Jewish: **Dresher**.

Drew 1. English: aphetic var. of ANDREW. 2. English (Norman): from the Gmc personal name *Drogo*, which is of uncertain etymology; it is possibly akin to OSax. *(gi)drog* ghost, phantom, or with a stem meaning 'to bear, carry' (OHG *tragan*). Whatever its origin, the name was borne by one of the sons of Charlemagne, and the name was subsequently popular throughout France in the forms *Dreus, Drues* (oblique case *Dreu, Dr(i)u*), whence it was introduced to England by the Normans. Drogo de Monte Acuto (as his name appears in its Latinized form) was a companion of William the Conqueror and founder of the MONTAGU family, among whom the given name *Drogo* was revived in the 19th cent. **3.** English (Norman): nickname from OF *dru* favourite, lover (originally an adj., apparently from a Gaul. word meaning 'strong', 'vigorous', 'lively', but influenced by the sense of the OHG element *trūt, drūt* dear, beloved). **4.** English (Norman): habitation name from any of various places in France called *Dreux*, from the Gaul. tribal name *Durocasses* (of obscure etymology). **5.** English (Norman): habitation name, with fused preposition *de*, from any of the numerous places in France that get their names from OF *rieux* streams (see RIEU). **6.** Irish: Anglicized form of Gael. **Mac an Druaidh** and **Ó Druaidh** 'son' and 'descendant of the druid'. The word for these ancient Celt. priests is of uncertain origin, possibly akin to Gael. *derb* sure, true or *dara* oak.

Vars.: **Drewe, Dru; Druce, Drewes, Dreux** (the final sibilant representing the Eng. possessive case of 1 or 2, the OF nom. case of 2, or an alternative pronunciation of 4 or 5).

Dims. (of 2): Eng.: **Drewett, Drewitt, Druett, Druitt, Drouet; Drewell.** Fr.: **Drou(h)et, Druot, Drou(h)in, Droin, Drouineau; Derouin, Derouet; Droniou** (Brittany).

Drewery *see* DRURY

Dreyfuss Jewish (W Ashkenazic): habitation name from the town of *Trier* on the Moselle, known in Fr. as *Trèves*; both the Fr. and Ger. names come from L *Augusta Treverorum* 'city of Augustus among the *Treveri*', a Celt. tribal name of uncertain etymology. The form of the surname has been altered by folk etymological association with mod. Ger. *Dreifuss* tripod.

Vars.: **Dre(y)fus, Dreifus(s), Trefus, Treves, Trevis, Trives, Trivis, Trivus, Trivas, Tribus, Trève(s); Trivier.**

Driburg Low German: habitation name from *Driburg* near Höxter in N Rhineland-Westphalia, so called from MLG *tō der Iburg* 'at the Iburg'. This is an old Saxon fortress nearby, which was captured in 775 by Charlemagne; its name is of uncertain origin. The second element is clearly OSax. *burg* fortress (see BURKE), but the first is opaque; according to Bahlow it preserves an ancient name of the settlement.

Driesch Low German: topographic name from the dial. word *drēsch* land used as pasture rather than for the cultivation of crops. There are several minor places of this name in the Rhineland, and the surname may also be a habitation name from any of these.

Var.: **Drieschmann.**

Driesen *see* ANDREW

Driffield English: habitation name from places in Gloucs. and E Yorks., both so called from ME *drit, dirt* mud, manure (ON *drit*) + *feld* pasture, open country (see FIELD).

Var.: **Driffel.**

Driker *see* DRUCKER

Drinan *see* DRENNAN

Dring English: from ON *drengr* young man, but with more than one possible interpretation. It may reflect the personal name (originally a byname) of this form, which had some currency in the most Scandinavian-influenced areas of medieval England. Alternatively it may reflect the ME borrowing of the vocab. word in the sense 'servant', later a technical term of the feudal system of Northumb. for a free tenant who held land by military and agricultural service, sometimes paying rent as well or in commutation.

Var.: **Dreng.**

Drinkwater English: nickname from ME *drink* (OE *drincan*) + *water* (OE *wæter*). In the Middle Ages weak ale was the universal beverage among the poorer classes, and so cheap as to be drunk like water, whereas water itself was only doubtfully potable. The surname was perhaps a joking nickname given to a pauper or miser allegedly unable or unwilling to afford beer, or may have been given in irony to an innkeeper or a noted tippler. The suggestion that some bearers may have been diabetics with voracious unnatural thirsts is interesting but unconvincing. (See also BOILEAU.)

Driscoll Irish: Anglicized form of Gael. **Ó hEidirsceóil** 'descendant of the messenger', from *eidirsceól* go-between, intermediary, news bearer (a cpd of *eidir* between + *sceól* story, news). Most bearers of this surname claim descent from a single 10th-cent. ancestor.

Vars.: **O'Driscoll, O'Driscole, O'Hederscoll, O'Hidirscoll.**

Driver English: occupational name for a driver of horses or oxen attached to a cart or plough, or of loose cattle, from a ME agent deriv. of OE *drīfan* to drive.

Equivs. (not cogn.): Pol.: **WOŹNIAK.**

Drobný Czech: nickname for a small person, from Czech *drobný* small.

Var.: **Drobník, Drobek.**

Drohan Irish: Anglicized form of Gael. **Ó Druacháin** 'descendant of *Druachán*', a byname representing a dim. of *druach* wise man.

Vars.: **Drohane, Droohan, Drohun,** DRANE.

Droin *see* DREW

Dromey *see* DRUMMY

Droop English: nickname from ME *drup* dejected, sad, gloomy (from ON, akin to OE *dropian* to drop).

Drössler *see* DRECHSLER

Droste Low German: occupational name for a steward or head servant, MLG *drotsete* (a cogn. of MHG *truhsæze*, from OHG *truhtsazzo*). The term derives from the elements *truht* body of servants + *sizzen* to sit, in the sense of 'preside'. The term was also used as a title in various different contexts.

Drouilly French: habitation name from a place in Marne, so called from the Gallo-Roman personal name *Drull(i)us* (of uncertain etymology) + the local suffix *-ācum*.

Drovandi *see* ALDOBRANDI

Drożdż Polish: nickname from Pol. *drozd* thrush.
Habitation name: Pol.: **Drozdowski.**

Dru *see* DREW

Drucker Jewish (Ashkenazic): occupational name for a printer, from Ger. *Drucker* or Yid. *druker* printer (agent derivs. of Ger. *drucken*, Yid. *drukn* to print, derived from a Mainz dial. var. of *drücken* to press. Printing was first developed in Mainz in the 15th cent.).

Vars.: **Druck**; **Druker**; **Driker** (S Yid. var. of *Druker*); **Druckier** (Pol. spelling); **Druckmann, Drukman(n)**.

Drummond Scots: habitation name from any of the various places, as for example *Drymen* near Stirling, that get their names from Gael. *dromainn*, a deriv. of *druim* ridge.

Drummy Irish: Anglicized form of Gael. **Ó Droma** 'descendant of *Droma*', a personal name of uncertain origin; it may be from *druim* back (cf. DRUMMOND), and have been given originally to someone with a deformed back.

Vars.: **Dromey, Drumm**.

Drury English (Norman) and French: **1.** nickname from OF *druerie* love, friendship (a deriv. of *dru* lover, friend; see DREW 3). In ME the word also had the concrete meanings 'love affair', 'love token', 'sweetheart'. **2.** from a Gmc personal name composed of the elements *triuwa* truth, trust + *rīc* power.

Vars.: Eng.: **Drew(e)ry, Druery**.

Dryden English: habitation name from an unidentified place, probably in Cumb. or Northumb., where the name is still common, and so called from OE *drȳge* dry + *denu* valley (see DEAN 1).

Drynan *see* DRENNAN

Drysdale Scots: habitation name from *Dryfesdale* near Dumfries, so called from the river *Dryfe* + OE *dæl* valley (see DALE).

Drzewiecki Polish: **1.** habitation name from a village called *Drzewce* (named with Pol. *drzewa* trees) + *-ski* suffix of local surnames (see BARANOWSKI), or topographic name for someone living among trees, from *drzewa* used independently. **2.** nickname for a stiff or upright person, from Pol. *drzewiec* lance + *-ski* general surname suffix (see BARANOWSKI).

D'Souza *see* SOUSA

Duan *see* DEVANE

Dubarry *see* BARRY

Du Bellay *see* BELLAY

Du Bief *see* BÉAL

Dubnikov Russian: patr. from the nickname *Dubnik* 'Oakman' (a deriv. of *dub* oak, cogn. with Czech *dub*, Pol. *dęb*), with ref. to personal strength or to location of residence.

Vars.: **Dubin, Dubov(oi)**.

Dims.: Pol.: **Dąbek**. Czech: **Dubček, Dubík**.

Patrs.: Jewish: **Dembowitz, Dembovitz, Dembovich**.

Collective: Russ.: **Dubrovin**.

Habitation names: Pol.: **Dębowski, Dembowski, Dębicki, Dębecki, Dembiński; Dąbkowski; DĄBROWSKI**. Jewish (E Ashkenazic): **Dombovsky, Dembinsk, Dembinsky, Dembski, Dembowsky**.

Dubois *see* BOIS

Dubonnet *see* BONNET

Du Boulay *see* BOUL

Dubourquet *see* BURKE

Dubreuil *see* BREUIL

Dubuisson *see* BUISSON

Ducamp *see* CHAMP

Ducarme *see* CARNE

Ducasse *see* CASSE

Duce English: nickname from ME *douce, dowce* sweet, pleasant (OF *dolz, dous*, from L *dulcis*). This was also in occasional use as a female given name in the Middle Ages, and some examples may derive from this.

Vars.: **Douce, Dowse; Douch(e)**.

Dims.: Eng.: **Doucet, Dowsett, Dowcett**. Fr.: **Doucet, Doucin(el); Dousset, Doussot, Doussin(et), Doussain(t), Doussinel(le); Douchet, Douchez, Douchin**. It.: **Dolcetti, Dolcetta, Dolcini, Dolcino, Dolciotti**.

Pejs.: Fr.: **Doussard, Douss(in)aud**.

Metrs.: Eng.: **Dowson** (see also Dow). Jewish (Ashkenazic): **Tol(t)zis** (from the Yid. female given name *Toltse*), **Tolces** (Pol. spelling), **Dolcis, Tolciss**.

Duch *see* DUŠEK

Ducharme *see* CHARME

Duchâtelier *see* CHÂTELIER

Duchefdelaville *see* CAPDEVIELLE

Duchemin *see* CHEMIN

Duchêne *see* CHÊNE

Duchet *see* DUKE

Duchier French: occupational name for a tavern-keeper, from an aphetic form of OF *conduchier* (LL *condūcārius*, a deriv. of *condūcere* to conduct, manage).

Vars.: **Ducher, Duché; Conduché**.

Dim.: **Ducheron**.

Duck *see* DIGG

Duckenfield English: habitation name from *Dukinfield* in Manchester, probably so called from OE *dūcena feld* pasture of the ducks; cf. DIGG 2 and FIELD.

Ducker 1. English (E Anglia): nickname from an agent deriv. of ME *douke(n)* to dive, plunge (apparently of native origin and akin to *duck* (the bird); cf. DIGG 2 and DUCKETT 1). **2.** Jewish (Ashkenazic): of unknown origin.

Duckett English: **1.** nickname from a dim. of ME *douke, duk(ke)* duck (OE *duce*; cf. DIGG 2). **2.** nickname from ME *douke, duk(ke)* duck + *heved* head (OE *hēafod*). **3.** nickname from OF *ducquet* owl (a dim. of *duc* guide, leader; see DUKE 1). **4.** from a ME dim. of the OE personal name or byname *Ducca*, of uncertain origin. **5.** from a ME dim. of the given name DUKE.

Vars.: **Ducket, Duckit(t)**.

Duckworth English (chiefly Lancs.): habitation name from *Duckworth* Fold, in the borough of Bury, Lancs., which presumably derives its name from the OE personal name *Ducca* (see DUCKETT 4) + *worð* enclosure (see WORTH).

Duclerc *see* CLARK

Duclouzeau *see* CLOSE

Ducost French: topographic name, with fused preposition and article *du*, from OF *cost* hill (a masc. var. of COSTE, specialized in this sense).
Var.: **Ducos**.

Ducrès *see* CRÈS

Ducreux *see* CREUX

Ducrot French: topographic name, with fused preposition and article *du*, from OF *crot* cave, grotto (a masc. var. of the regional term *crote*, LL *crupta*, from Gk *kryptos* hidden, secret).

Duda Polish, Ukrainian, and Czech: metonymic nickname for a player on the bagpipes, from the Slav. word *duda* bagpipe.
Var.: Czech: **Dudák**.
Dim.: Pol.: **Dudaczyk**.
Patrs.: Russ.: **Dudin**. Beloruss.: **Dudarov**, **Dudorov**. Croatian: **Dudić**. Jewish: **Dudovitz** (E Ashkenazic).
Patrs. (from dims.): Russ.: **Dud(ysh)kin**.

Duddell *see* DODD

Duddy Irish: Anglicized form of Gael. **Ó Dubhda** 'descendant of *Dubhda*', a byname derived from *dubh* dark, black (see DUFF). The surname is very common in Co. Kerry.
Vars.: **Doody**, **(O')Dowd**, DODD.

Dude Low German: from the Gmc personal name *Dudo*, of uncertain etymology. In some cases at least it is apparently a pet form of the compound name *Liudolf* (composed of the elements *leud* people + *wolf* wolf); in the 12th cent. Otto I's son Liudolf was known also as both *Ludo* and *Dudo*. In other cases it may have been originally a byname (cf. DODD 1).
Vars.: **Dü(d)e**, **Dode**.
Patrs.: **Dud(d)en**, **Doden**.

Dudek Polish and Czech: nickname from the vocab. word *dudek* hoopoe. In Pol. the word also means 'simpleton' and this no doubt contributed to the surname, but in Czech no such meaning is attested, and the surname may have originated as a nickname with reference to some other attribute of the bird, such as its repetitive call or its bright plumage.
Vars.: Pol.: **Dudka**. Czech: **Dedek**, **Dydek**.
Patrs.: Pol.: **Dudkiewicz**, **Dutkiewicz**. Jewish (presumably adoptions and alterations of the Pol. surname as ornamental names): **Dudkiewicz**, **Dudkewi(t)z**, **Dudkewich**, **Dudkevich**, **Dudkevi(t)z**.
Habitation name: Pol.: **Dutkowski**.

Duder English: of uncertain origin, perhaps a var. of Welsh *Tudor*; see THÉODORE.

Dudgeon English and Scots: of uncertain origin, but possibly an occupational name for a turner or cutler. The word *dudgeon* (of unknown origin) denoted the wood (probably

boxwood; cf. BOX) used in the handles of knives and daggers in the Middle Ages. Black explains it as a patr. from DODGE, but this seems unlikely.

Dudley English: habitation name from the town in the W Midlands so called from the OE personal name *Dudda* (see DODD 1) + OE *lēah* wood, clearing.

Dudoit *see* DOUET

Düe *see* DUDE

Dueñas Spanish: occupational name for someone who was employed in the quarters of the female members of a noble family, from Sp. *dueñas* ladies (a cogn. of DAME). In a few cases it may have been originally a habitation name, from places in Palencia and Teruel called *(Las) Dueñas*, perhaps of folkloric origin.

Duerden *see* DEARDEN

Dufaure *see* FÈVRE

Dufayard *see* FAGE

Duff Scots and Irish: Anglicized form of Gael. *dubh* dark, black. This word was widely used as a nickname or byname (for a swarthy man or man of dark temperament) and as a personal name. See also DEVANE, DUDDY, DUFFY, and DUGGAN.
Vars.: **Dow**, **Dove**.
Patr.: Sc., Ir.: **McDuff**.

Duffield English: habitation name from places in Derbys. and E Yorks., so called from ON *dúfa* DOVE (perhaps a byname) + OE *feld* pasture, open country (see FIELD).
Vars.: **Duffell**, **Duffill**.

Duffin 1. English: from the ON personal name *Dólgfinnr*, composed of the elements *dólgr* wound, scar + *Finnr* Finn. 2. Irish: var. of DEEGAN and DEVANE 2.
Var. (of 1): **Dolphin** (chiefly W Midlands). See also DAUPHIN.

Duffy 1. Irish: Anglicized form of Gael. **Ó Dubhthaigh** 'descendant of *Dubhthach*', a byname derived from *dubh* black (see DUFF). This name was borne by a 6th-cent. saint who was archbishop of Armagh. 2. Scots and Irish: Anglicized form of Gael. **Mac Dhuibhshíthe** 'son of *Dubhshíth*', a personal name composed of the elements *dubh* black (see DUFF) + *síth* peace.
Vars.: **Duffey**, **Duffie**, **Dowey**, **Dowie**, **Do(v)ey**, **Duthy**, **Duthie**. (Of 1 only): **O'Duff(e)y**, **O'Duffie**, **O'Duhie**, **O'Duhig**, **O'Dowey**. (Of 2 only): **McDuffie**, **McFee**, **McFie**, **McPhee**, **McPhie**, **MacAfee**, **McAffer**, **Maccaffie**, **McCaffer**, **McCov(v)ie**, **McGuffie**, **Machaffie**, **Mehaffy**, **McHaffie**, **McHaffy**.
'Son of the servant of D. 1': **McGildowie**, **McIldowie**, **Dowie**, **Doey**, **Duthy** (Gael. **Mac Giolla Dubhthaigh**).

Duflocq French: of uncertain origin. It probably derives from OF *floc* tuft (L *floccus*). This may be a nickname for someone with a distinctive tuft or quiff of hair, but in view of the fact that it is invariably found with a fused preposition-cum-article *du*, it is more probable that it is a topographic name for someone who lived by a tuft or tump of raised ground.
Vars.: **Duflo(s)**, **Duflot**.

Dufossés *see* FOSSE

Dufresnoy see FRAIN

Dufty see DOUGHTY

Dugage see GAGE

Dugald see DOUGALL

Dugas see GAST

Dugdale English: habitation name from a place so called, probably the hamlet near Uttoxeter, Staffs., now known as *Dagdale*, from the OE personal name or byname *Ducca* (see DUCKETT 4) + OE *dæl* or ON *dalr* valley (see DALE). The surname is now found chiefly in Lancs.

Dugenest see GENEST

Duggan 1. Scots and Irish: Anglicized form of Gael. Ó Dubhagáin 'descendant of *Dubhagán*', a byname representing a double dim. of *dubh* black, dark (see DUFF). 2. Welsh: Anglicized aphetic form of the personal name *Cadwgan, Cadogan* (see CADDOCK 1).
Vars. (of 1): **O'Dooghaine**, **O'Dowgaine**, **O'Duggan**, **O'Doogan**, **(O')Dugan**, **Duggon**, **Duggen**, **Dougan**, **Doohan**.
Patr. (from 2): **Duggins**.

Dugmore English (chiefly W Midlands): of uncertain origin, probably a habitation name from some unidentified place so called from the OE personal name or byname *Ducca* (see DUCKETT 4) + OE *mōr* moor, marsh (see MOORE 1).

D'Ugo see HUGH

Duguid Scots: probably a nickname for a well-intentioned person or do-gooder, from Northern ME *du* do (OE *dōn*) + *gu(i)d* good (OE *gōd*).

Dührig see DÜRING

Duigan see DEEGAN

Duin Dutch: topographic name for someone who lived by a sand dune, MDu. *dūne* (a cogn. of DOWN 1).
Vars.: **Van Duijn**, **Van Duyn**, **Van Duinen**.

Duke English: 1. nickname for someone who gave himself airs and graces, from ME *duk(e)* duke (OF *duc*, from L *dux*, gen. *dūcis*, leader, a deriv. of *dūcere* to lead), or else an occupational name for a servant employed in a ducal household. 2. possibly also from the given name *Duke*, a short form of *Marmaduke*, a given name of Ir. origin, said to be from Ir. *mael Maedoc* 'devotee (*mael*) of *Maedoc*', a given name of uncertain origin, borne by various early Ir. saints, in particular a 6th-cent. abbot of Clonmore and a 7th-cent. bishop of Ferns.
Dims. (of 1): **Duchet**, **Du(c)quet**, **Duchez**, **Duchey**, **Duchon** (all of these may be in part nicknames from the owl, called the 'little guide' in French folklore because of its ability to find its way around in the dark; cf. DUCKETT). It.: **Duchini**.
Patrs.: Eng.: **Dukes**. (From 1 only): Fr.: **Auduc**. It.: **Del Duca** (Naples).

Dulanty see DELAHUNTY

Duley see DOYLEY

Dullea see DUNLEAVY

Dumais see MAS

Dumke see THOMAS

Dummann see THUMB

Dumont see MONT

Dumville English (Norman): habitation name from *Donville* in Calvados, so called from the Gmc personal name *Dono* (of uncertain meaning) or *Dodo* (see DODD 1 and DUDE) + OF *ville* settlement, village (see VILLE).
Vars.: **Dunville**, **Domvil(l)e**; **Dunfield**.

Dunant French: topographic name, with fused preposition-cum-article *du*, from OF *nant* stream (of Gaul. origin).
Var.: **Dunan**.

Dunbar Scots: habitation name from a town on the North Sea coast near Edinburgh, so called from Gael. *dùn* fort + *barr* top, summit (cf. BARR 1).

Duncan Scots and Irish: 1. Anglicized form of Gael. *Duinnchinn*, a byname composed of the elements *donn* dark, brown (see DUNN 1) + *ceann* head. 2. var. of DONEGAN.
Patrs. (from 1): **Duncanson**, **Dunkinson**.

Duncombe English: probably a var. of DUNCAN rather than a habitation name, even though the first element could be OE *dūn* hill (see DOWN 1) and the second OE *cumb* valley (see COOMBE).

Dundas Scots: habitation name from the place so called near Edinburgh, which gets its name from Gael. *dùn* hill (cf. DOWN 1) + *deas* south. The traditional pronunciation is /dən'das/.

Dunderdale English (Lancs. and Yorks.): local name from the district called *Dunnerdale* in Cumb. along the river *Duddon*, which appears in the 12th cent. as *Dudun*, *Dudena*, and *Duthen* (of unexplained origin). The surname is composed of this river name + ME *dale* DALE.

Dundrer see DONNER

Dune see DEVANE

Dunegain see DONEGAN

Dunfield see DUMVILLE

Dunford English: habitation name from *Dunford* Bridge, a hamlet near Penistone, W Yorks., so called from the river *Don* (a Brit. name, possibly meaning 'river') + OE *ford* FORD, or from *Dunford* House in Methley, W Yorks., which is named in OE as *Dunn's ford*' (see DUNN 2).

Dung Low German: topographic name for someone who lived on a piece of raised dry land in marshy surroundings, or habitation name from any of the various places named with the dial. term for such a patch of land, MLG *dung*.
Vars.: **Dungs**, **Düngen**, **Dunk**, **Donk**; **Dunkmann**; **Von der Dunk**.

Dunham English (chiefly Norfolk): habitation name from any of several places so called, of which there is one in Norfolk. Most get the name from OE *dūn* hill (see DOWN 1) + *hām* homestead; one in Ches. originally had as its first element the OE personal name *Dunna* (see

DUNN 2). A place in Lincs. now known as *Dunholme* appears in Domesday Book as *Duneham* and this too may be a partial source of the surname; in this case again the first element is probably from a personal name.

Dunin Russian: **1.** metr. from the female given name *Dunya*, a dim. of *Avdotya* (Gk *Eudokia* 'of good repute', cf. YEVDOKIMOV). The name was borne by a Samaritan penitent who was beheaded under Trajan. **2.** patr. from the nickname *Dyna* (ORuss. *Dunya*) 'Watermelon', given perhaps to a cultivator of this crop or to a person with a large head (cf. ARBUZOV).

Dim.: Russ.: **Dunkin**.

Dunkley English: of uncertain origin, possibly a habitation name from *Dinckley* in Lancs., recorded in 1246 as *Dunkythele* and *Dinkedelay*. The placename is probably named with an old Brit. name, composed of elements meaning 'fort' + 'wood', with the addition of OE *lēah* wood, clearing. The surname is now most common in Northampton.

Dunleavy Irish: Anglicized form of Gael. Ó **Duinnshléibhe** and **Mac Duinnshléibhe** 'descendant' and 'son of *Duinnsliabh*', a personal name composed of the elements *donn* brown + *sliabh* mountain.

Vars.: **O'Dunleavy**, **(O')Donleavy**, **Dunle(e)vy**, **Dunlavy**, **DUN-LOP**; **McAnle(a)vy**, **McAleavy**, **McEnleavy**, **McEnlevie**, **McEnle(i)ve**, **McLeavy**, McLAY, **Killeavy**; **Dunlea**, **Dullea**, **Delea**, **Delee**, **Delay**; **O'Downlay**; **McAlea**, **McConloy**, **McColley**, **McClew**; **Leavy**. See also LIVINGSTONE.

Dunlop 1. Scots: habitation name from a place near Kilmarnock, so called from Gael. *dùn* fort + *lápach* muddy. The traditional pronunciation places the stress on the second syllable, although nowadays it is usually placed on the first. **2.** Irish: Anglicized form of DUNLEAVY. **3.** Irish: Anglicized form of Ó **Lapáin** (**O'Lappin**) 'descendant of *Lapán*', a byname from *lápán* mire, dirt, used figuratively of a poor man.

Var.: **Dunlap** (U.S.).

Dunman *see* DOWN

Dunn 1. Scots and Irish: from Gael. *Donn*, a byname for a person with dark hair or a swarthy complexion, from Gael. *donn* dark, brown. **2.** English: nickname for a man with dark hair or a swarthy complexion, from ME, OE *dunn* dark-coloured. In part it may also derive from an unrecorded ME survival of the OE byname *Dunn(a)* 'Dark'. **3.** Scots: habitation name from *Dun* in the former county of Angus (now part of Tayside region), from Gael. *dùn* fort. Adam *de Dun* was elected to the deanery of Moray in 1255 and William *de Dun*, perhaps a relative, was dean there in 1268.

Vars.: **Dun(ne)**, **Don**, **Donn(e)**, **Down**.

Dims. (of 1): Ir.: DONOVAN, DONEGAN, DINEEN; **Donnan** (chiefly N Ireland). (Of 2): Eng.: **Dunnet(t)**.

Patrs. (from 2): Eng.: **Down(e)s**, **Downing**, DUNNING.

'Descendant of D. 1': Ir.: **O'Dunn(e)** (from Gael. **Ó Duinn**, **Ó Doinn**).

'Son of the servant of D. 1': Ir.: **McIldoon**, **McEldoon**, GUNN (from Gael. **Mac Giolla Dhuinn**).

Dunnicliff *see* TUNNICLIFFE

Dunning 1. English: patr. from DUNN 2. **2.** Scots: habitation name from a place in the former county of Perths., recorded in 1200 as *Dunine* and later as *Dunyn*, from Gael. *dùnan*, a dim. of *dùn* fort. **3.** Irish: var. of DINEEN.

Dunnion *see* DINEEN

Dunoyer *see* NOYER

Dunsford English: habitation name from *Dunsford* in Devon or *Dunsforth* in W Yorks., both so called from the gen. case of the OE byname DUNN + OE *ford* FORD.

Dunstable English: habitation name from a place in Beds., so called from the OE byname *Dunn(a)* (see DUNN 2) + OE *stapol* post, pillar.

Dunstall English: habitation name from places so called in Lincs. and Staffs., which have the same origin as TUNSTALL.

Dunstan English: **1.** from a ME given name *Dunstan*, composed of the OE elements *dunn* dark, brown (see DUNN 2) + *stān* stone. This name was borne by a 10th-cent. archbishop of Canterbury who was later canonized. **2.** habitation name from *Dunstone* in Devon, so called from OE *Dunstānestūn* 'settlement of *Dunstan*' (as in 1). The surname is still chiefly common in Devon, but there are places in other parts of the country with similar names but different etymologies (e.g. *Dunstan* in Northumb., *Dunston* in Lincs., Norfolk, Staffs., and Derbys.), which may possibly have contributed to the surname.

Dunster English: habitation name from a place in Somerset, which derives its name from the gen. case of the OE byname *Dunn(a)* (see DUNN 2) + OE *torr* rocky peak (of Celt. origin).

Dunton English: habitation name from any of various places so called. Most (e.g. those in Essex, Leics., Norfolk, and Warwicks.) get the name from OE *dūn* hill (see DOWN 1) + *tūn* enclosure, settlement. One in Beds. is probably named as *Dunningtūn* 'settlement (OE *tūn*) associated with *Dunna*' (see DUNN 2). One in Bucks probably has as its first element the OE personal name *Dudda* (see DODD).

Var.: **Downton** (there are places spelled thus in Shrops., Herefords., and Wilts.)

Dunwoodie Scots: habitation name from *Dinwoodie* near Dumfries, of uncertain etymology. It is first recorded in 1296 in the form *Dinwithie*, *Dunwythye* (then later 1482 *Donwethy*; 1503 *Dunwedy*; 1578 *Dumwiddie*) and is probably named with Brit. words that are ancestors of W *din* forest + *gwydd* shrubs, bushes.

Vars.: **Din(s)woodie**, **Dinwiddie**.

Duny *see* DOWNIE

Dupaquier *see* PAQUIER

Dupeux *see* PUY

Duplain *see* PLAIN

Dupont *see* PONT

Duportail *see* PORTAIL

Dupré *see* PRÉ

Dupuis see PUITS

Duquemin see CHEMIN

Duquesnay see QUÊNE

Duquet see DUKE

Durant English (Norman) and French: from OF *durant* enduring (pres. part. of *durer* to endure, last, L *dūrāre*, from *dūrus* hard, firm; cf. DURO). This was fairly frequently used in the Middle Ages as a given name in the sense 'Steadfast', and seems also to have been a nickname with the meaning 'obstinate'.
Vars.: Eng.: **Durrant, Dur(r)an(d), Dorant**; DORAN. Fr.: **Durand, Dirand**.
Dims.: Fr.: **Durandeau, Durandet, Durandin, Duranteau, Durantel, Durantet, Durant(h)on, Duranseau**. It.: **D(ur)antini**.
Patrs.: Eng.: **Durrans, Durrance, Dorrins, Dorrance**. Port.: **Durães**.

Durcan Irish: Anglicized form of Gael. **Mac Duarcáin** 'son of *Duarcán*', a byname representing a dim. of *duairc* surly.
Vars.: **Durkan, Durkin**.

Durden see DEARDEN

Dureau French: **1.** nickname from a dim. of OF *dur* hard(y) (see DURO). **2.** patr., originally *(fils) d'hureau*, from the nickname *hureau* scallywag, a dim. of *huré* shock-headed (see HURÉ).
Vars. (of 1): **Durel, Duret**.

Dürer German: **1.** occupational name for a janitor, Ger. *T(h)ürer*, from MHG *tür* door. **2.** In the case of the artist Albrecht Dürer (1471–1528), it has a habitational origin. His grandfather was a Hungarian from *Ajtós* (near Gyula, 46 miles from Nagyvárad, now Oradea in Rumania), so called from Hung. *ajtó* door (cf. DORE 1). The artist's father accordingly adopted the Germanized form *Türer* or *Dürer*, together with a coat of arms showing an open door.

Durham English: habitation name from the city in NE England, so called from OE *dūn* hill (see DOWN 1) + ON *holmr* island (see HOLME 2).
Var.: **Durram**.

Durie Scots: habitation name from a place in Fife, so called from Gael. *dobhar* stream + the local suffix *-ach*.

Düring German: regional name for someone from *Thuringia*. The region is named from its former occupation by the Gmc tribe of the *T(h)uringii*, displaced in the 6th cent. AD. This tribal name has been tentatively connected with the element *tur-* to dare (cf. ON ðora). The surname is especially common in Silesia, Saxony, and Bohemia as a result of the Ger. expansion eastwards during the early Middle Ages.
Vars.: **During, Dühri(n)g, Dürich, Dörich, Dierich**.

Duriz see RIEU

Durk see DARK

Durkheim Jewish (W Ashkenazic): habitation name from *Turkheim* in Alsace, *Dürkheim* on the Isanach in the Palatinate, or *Türkheim* on the Neckar in Württemberg. All of these seem to be named from a Gmc byname *Turinc* 'Thuringian' (see DÜRING) + OHG *heim* homestead.
Vars.: **Durkheimer, Turkheim(er)**.

Durman see DEAR

Durnin see DORNAN

Duro Italian, Spanish, and Portuguese: nickname for a tough or unyielding man, from It., Sp., Port. *duro* hard, tough (L *dūrus*). The word had both the approving sense 'steadfast', 'enduring' (cf. DURANT) and the less favourable sense 'stubborn', 'obstinate', 'cruel'; the nickname may have been bestowed with either motivation.
Var.: It.: **Duri**.
Dims.: It.: **Durin(i)** (Venetia). Fr.: **DUREAU**.

Duroure see ROUVRE

Dürrenmatt Swiss: habitational name from a place so named as the 'barren meadow', from MHG *dürre* barren, infertile (OHG *durri*) + *matte* meadow (a Swabian and Alemannic dial. term, from OHG *matta*; cf. MEAD 1), with the adj. preserving the weak dat. ending originally used after a preposition and def. article.

Dursley English: habitation name from *Dursley* in Gloucs., which is recorded in Domesday Book as *Dersilege*, from the OE personal name *Dēorsige* (composed of the elements *dēor* dear + *sige* victory) + *lēah* wood, clearing.

D'Urso see ORSO

Durtnell English: habitation name from *Dorkinghole*, a lost settlement near Penshurst, Kent. The final element of this placename is *holh* (see HOLE); the first could be a derivative of OE *deorc* DARK.

Duruflé French: apparently a habitation name, with fused preposition and (surprisingly) def. art., i.e. *du* rather than *de*, from places in Côtes-du-Nord and Saint-Doran called *Ruflet*.

Dusap see SAPIN

Duseau see SAULT

Duseigneur see SEIGNEUR

Dušek Czech: from a dim. of the Slav. personal name *Duchoslav*, composed of the elements *duch* spirit + *slav* glory.
Vars.: **Dušák, Duch(ek), Duchoň, Duchaň, Ducháček**.

Dusouchet see SUCH

Dusting see THURSTON

Duteil see TEIL

Dutetre French: topographic name, with fused preposition-cum-article *du*, from OF *tetre* mound, hillock (from LL *termes* (gen. *termitis*) boundary, a re-formation of class. L *termen* (gen. *terminis*) on the pattern of *limes* (gen. *limitis*), a word of similar meaning; the change of sense probably reflects the use of small mounds as clearly identifiable boundaries).
Vars.: **Dutartre, Duteutre**.

Duthie see DUFFY

Duthu *see* TRUC

Dutkiewicz *see* DUDEK

Dutsch *see* DEUTSCH

Dutton English: habitation name from places so called, esp. those in Ches. and Lancs., which get their names from the OE personal name *Dudd(a)* (see DODD 1) + OE *tūn* enclosure, settlement.

Duvallet *see* VALE

Duvaur *see* VAUR

Duverne *see* VER

Duvoisin *see* VOISIN

Duxbury English: habitation name from a place in Lancs., recorded in the early 13th cent. as *D(e)ukesbiri*, from the gen. case of the OE personal name *Deowuc* or *Duc(c)* (both of uncertain etymology; cf. DUCKETT 4) + OE *burh* fort (see BURKE).

Var.: **Duxberry**.

Dvořák Czech: status name for a man who worked at a manor house rather than on the land, from Czech *dvůr* manor, court (cf. Pol. *dwór*). In Moravia the word denoted a freeholder, subject only to the king. This is the fourth most common surname in Czechoslovakia.

Dims.: Czech: **Dvoraček**. Pol.: **Dworczak**, **Dworczyk**.

Habitation names: Czech: **Dvorský** (from places called *Dvůr* or *Dvory*). Pol.: **Dworakowski**; **Dworzyński**.

Dvorin Jewish (E Ashkenazic): metr. from the Yid. female given name *Dvoyre* (from the Hebr. name *Devorah*, lit. 'Bee', whence Eng. *Deborah*) + the Slav. suffix *-in*. The name *Devorah* was borne in the Bible by Rebecca's nurse (Gen. 35: 8) and by a prophetess and judge (Judges 4: 4). The popularity of the Yid. name is due largely to the latter.

Vars.: **Dvoirin** (SE Ashkenazic); **Dvojres** (with Yid. possessive *-s*); **Dvossis** (from *Dvosye*, a by-form of the given name).

Metrs. (from a dim.): **Dvorkin**, **Dworkin**, **Dworkis** (from the dim. given name *Dvorke*); **D(e)voskin**, **Dwoskin** (from the dim. given name *Dvoske*).

Dwire *see* DWYER

Dworakowski *see* DVOŘÁK

Dworkin *see* DVORIN

Dwyer Irish: Anglicized form of Gael. **Ó Du(i)bhuidhir** 'descendant of *Du(i)bhuidhir*', a personal name composed of the elements *dubh* dark, black (cf. DUFF) + *odhar* sallow, tawny.

Vars.: **O'Dwyer**, **O'Du(v)ire**, **Dwire**, **Dwyr**, DIVER, **Dever**, **(O')Deere**, DEERY, DYER.

Dyachenko *see* DEAKIN

Dyason *see* DYE

Dybald *see* THEOBALD

Dychterman *see* DICHTER

Dydek *see* DUDEK

Dye English: from a pet form of the medieval female given name DENNIS. The surname is most common in Norfolk, but found also in Yorks.

Dims.: **Dyet(t)**, **Dyott**.

Metrs.: **Dyson** (chiefly Yorks.); **Dyason**, **Dyerson** (see also DYER); TYSON.

Dyer 1. English: occupational name for a dyer of cloth, ME *dyer* (from OE *dēag* dye; the verb is a back-formation from the agent noun). 2. Irish: var. of DWYER.

Vars.: **Dyster**, **Dexter** (originally these were fem. forms, but from an early period they are used also of men).

Patrs.: **Dyers**; **Dyerson** (see also DYE).

Dyhring *see* DEAR

Dyke *see* DITCH

Dykierman *see* DICK

Dymant *see* DIAMOND

Dyment *see* DIAMOND

Dymock English: habitation name from a place in Gloucs., perhaps so called from a Brit. word akin to W *tymoch* pigsty (a cpd of *ty* house + *moch* pigs), but more probably from *din* fort + *moch* pigs.

Vars.: **Dymick**, **Dymo(c)ke**, **Dim(m)ock**, **Dimmack**, **Dimmick**.

Dymowski Polish: habitation name from a place called *Dymów* (from Pol. *dym* smoke + the possessive suffix *-ów*, often used in forming placenames) + *-ski* suffix of local surnames (see BARANOWSKI), or perhaps a nickname from *dym* used independently, for example with reference to someone whose home was noticeably smoky.

Vars.: **Dymecki**, **Dymkowski**.

Dim. (a nickname, meaning 'Smoky'): **Dymek**.

Dyne *see* DAIN

Dyomichev *see* DAMYON

Dyott *see* DYE

Dyrling *see* DARLING

Dysart Scots: habitation name from any of various places, for example those near Fife and Montrose, so called from Gael. *diseart* hermit's cell, church (from L *dēsertum* desert, waste, solitary spot).

Dyson *see* DYE

Dzenisenya *see* DENNIS

Dzięciełowski Polish: habitation name from a place called *Dzięciłów* (named with Pol. *dzięcioł* woodpecker + *-ów* possessive suffix, often used in forming placenames) + *-ski* suffix of local surnames (see BARANOWSKI).

Dziedzic Polish: status name from Pol. *dziedzic* landowner, squire.

Var.: **Dziedziczak**.

Dzięgielewski Polish: habitation name from a place called *Dzięgielew* (named with Pol. *dzięgiel* angelica, from a Slav. root *dyag-* be strong) + *-ski* suffix of local surnames (see BARANOWSKI).

Dzierżyński Polish: habitation name from a place named with Pol. *dzierżawa* leasehold + *-yń* placename suffix, with the addition of the suffix of local surnames *-ski* (see BARANOWSKI). In some cases this may have been in effect a status name for a leaseholder.

Vars.: **Dzierżawski**, **Dzierżawa**.

Dzikowski Polish: habitation name from a place called *Dzików* (from Pol. *dzik* wild boar + *-ów* possessive suffix, often used in forming placenames) + *-ski* suffix of local surnames (see BARANOWSKI).

Dzugashvili Georgian (partly Jewish): said by Unbegaun to be from an unflattering nickname in the Ossetic language, derived from *dzuka* dross + the patronymic suffix *-shvili*.

E

Eacock *see* EADE

Eade English: **1.** from *Eda*, a ME short form of the female given name *Edith* (OE *Ēadgȳð* 'prosperity battle'). **2.** from a ME short form of ADAM, common esp. in Scotland and N England.

Vars.: **Ead**, **Ede**.

Dims.: **Eacock**; **Eady**, **Eadie** (chiefly Scots); **Eakin** (chiefly Irish; see also HIGGINS).

Patrs./metrs.: **Ead(e)s**, **Edes**, **Ed(e)son**, **Ed(d)ison**; **Eason** (see also McKAY); **E(a)sson**.

Patrs./metrs. (from dims.): **Edkins**, **E(a)kins**.

Eaden *see* EDEN

Eadmeades *see* EDMEAD

Eagan *see* HIGGINS

Eagar *see* EDGAR

Eagle English (mainly E Anglia): **1.** nickname for a lordly, impressive, or sharp-eyed man, from the word denoting the bird, ME *egle*, from OF *aigle* (L *aquila*, replacing OE *earn*; cf. EARLY 1 and EARNSHAW). **2.** habitation name from a place in Lincs., so called from ON *eik* oak + OE *lēah* wood, clearing; cf. OAKLEY. **3.** Norman habitation name from *Laigle* in Orne, Normandy, whose name apparently means 'the eagle', although the reasons for this origin are not clear. The recorded forms may represent the result of the operation of early folk etymology on some unknown original. Matilda *de Aquila* is recorded in 1129 as the widow of Robert Mowbray, Earl of Northumberland.

Var.: **Egle**.

Dims. (of 1): Eng.: **Eaglen**, **Eagling** (Norfolk). It.: **Aquilini**, **Aquilotti**.

Augs. (of 1): It.: **Aquiloni**, **Aquilone**.

Patrs. (from 1): Eng.: **Eagles**. It.: **D(ell)'Aquila**.

Eagles English: **1.** patr. from the nickname EAGLE. **2.** Anglicized form of Fr. **Eglise**, a topographic name for someone who lived near a church (OF *eclise*, from L *ecclēsia*; cf. ECCLES).

Var.: **Eglese**.

Eakin *see* EADE, HIGGINS

Ealey *see* ELY

Eame English: from ME *eme* (maternal) uncle (OE *ēam*), a name presumably given originally to a man who acted as guardian to a niece or a young nephew after the death of the father.

Vars.: **Heam**, **Heme**.

Dims.: Low Ger.: **Öhmke**, **Öhmichen**.

Patrs.: Eng.: **Eames**, **Heams**, **Hemes**. Low Ger.: **Ohms(en)**, **Öhms**. Flem., Du.: **Ooms**, **Oomen**.

Eardley *see* ARDLEY

Earl English: originally, like most of the English names derived from the ranks of nobility, either a nickname or an occupational name for a servant employed in a noble household. The vocab. word is a native one, from OE *eorl* nobleman, and in the Middle Ages was often used as an equivalent of the Norman COUNT.

Vars.: **Earle**, **Hearl(e)**, HARLE, **Hurle**, **Hurll**.

Patrs.: Eng.: **Earles**, **Hurles**.

Early **1.** English: habitation name from any of various places, such as *Earley* in Berks., *Earnley* in W Sussex, and *Arley* in Ches., Lancs., Warwicks., and Worcs., that derive their names from OE *earn* eagle + *lēah* wood, clearing. **2.** English: nickname from OE *eorlīc* manly, noble (a deriv. of *eorl*; see EARL). **3.** Irish: translation of Gael. *Ó Mocháin* (see MOHAN) and other related surnames, as for example *Ó Mochóir*, *O Mochóirghe*, and *Ó Maoil-Mhochóirghe*.

Vars.: **Earley**, **Erleigh**, **Erl(e)y**.

Earner *see* SEEREY

Earnshaw English: habitation name from a place in Lancs., so called from the gen. case of an OE personal name *Earn* 'Eagle' + OE *halh* nook (see HALE).

Earwaker English: from the ME given name *Erewaker*, OE *Eoforwacer*, composed of the elements *eofor* wild boar (cf. EVERARD) + *wacor* watchful, vigilant.

Vars.: **Earwicker**, **Erricker**.

Easman *see* HAYES

Eason *see* EADE, McKAY

East English: topographic name for someone who lived in the eastern part of a town or settlement, or outside it to the east, or regional name for one who had migrated westwards (and hence was regarded as coming from the east; cf. WEST, NORTH, NORRIS, SOUTH, SOUTHAM).

Vars.: **Eastes**, **EASTER**, **EASTMAN**.

Cpds (mostly arbitrary or ornamental coinages, rather than genuine topographic names): Swed.: **Östberg** ('east hill'); **Östlind** ('east lime'); **Östlund** ('east grove'). Jewish (Ashkenazic): **Ostberg** ('east hill'), **Ostfeld** ('east field'), **Ostwald** ('east wood'), **Ostwind** ('east wind').

Easter English: **1.** topographic name for someone living to the east of a main settlement, from ME *easter* eastern (OE *ēasterra*, in form a comparative of *ēast*; see EAST). **2.** habitation name from a group of villages in Essex, so called from OE *eowestre* sheepfold. **3.** nickname for someone who had some connection with the festival of Easter, such as being born or baptized at that time (OE *ēastre*, perhaps from the name of a pagan festival connected with the dawn).

Var. (of 1): **Easterling** (with the Gmc suffix -*ling*).

Dims. (of 1): Ger.: **Österle**, **Österl(e)in**.

Cpds (of cogns. of 1): Swed. (mainly ornamental rather than topographic): **Österberg** ('eastern hill'); **Östergren** ('eastern branch'); **Österholm** ('eastern island'); **Österlund** ('eastern grove'). Jewish (topographic or regional): **Ostersetzer** ('eastern setter'); **Osterweil** ('eastern settlement').

Easterbrook English: topographic name for someone who lived by a brook to the east of a main settlement, from ME *easter* eastern (see EASTER 1) + *brook* stream (see BROOK).

Vars.: **East(a)brook**, **Esterbrook**.

Eastham English: habitation name, now chiefly common in Lancs., from any of various places so called from OE *ēast* EAST + *hām* homestead or *hamm* water-meadow. There are places so named in Ches., Somerset, and Worcs., the first of which seems to have contributed most to the surname.

Eastman English: 1. topographic name, a var. of EAST. 2. from the OE personal name *Ēastmund*, composed of the elements *ēast* grace (or *ēast* east) + *mund* protection. The name survived the Norman Conquest, although it was never very frequent, and is attested in the 13th and 14th cents. in the forms *Estmund* and *Es(t)mond*.

Vars. (of 2): **Eastment**, **Astman**, **Esmond(e)**.

Easton English and Scots: 1. habitation name from any of the numerous places so called. Most are from OE *ēast* EAST + *tūn* enclosure, settlement; examples in Devon and the Isle of Wight get their names from the OE phrase *be ēastan tūne* (place) to the east of the settlement'. Another in Devon gets its first element from the gen. case of the OE personal name *Ælfrīc* (composed of the elements *ælf* elf + *rīc* power) or *Aðelrīc* (composed of the elements *aðel* noble + *rīc* power). One in Essex is from OE *ēg* island + *stān(as)* stone(s). Finally *Easton Neston* in Northants gets its name from OE *Ēadstānestūn* 'settlement of *Ēadstān*', a personal name composed of the elements *ēad* prosperity, riches + *stān* stone.

Eastwood English: habitation name from any of various places so called. Most, such as the one in Essex, get the name from OE *ēast* EAST + *wudu* WOOD, but an example in Notts. originally had as its final element ON *ðveit* meadow (see THWAITE).

Easy English: of uncertain origin, perhaps a nickname for a carefree person, from ME *aisy* at ease, untroubled (OF *aisié*, past part. of *aiser* to put at ease, from *aise* ease, a deriv. of L *adiacens* adjacent, to hand, convenient). The surname is found mainly in Cambs., E Suffolk, and the London area.

Vars.: **Easey**; **Heas(e)y**.

Eaton English: habitation name from any of the numerous places so called from OE *ēa* river or *ēg* island, low-lying land + *tūn* enclosure, settlement.

Var.: **Eyton**.

Eatwell English: habitation name from *Etwall* in Derbys., so called from a short form of some OE cpd name with a first element *Ēad-* prosperity (cf., e.g., EDMOND) + OE *well(a)* spring, stream (see WELL).

Eaves *see* EVE

Eayres *see* AYER

Ebbe *see* EGGEBRECHT

Ebbets *see* HIBBS

Ebblewhite *see* HEBBLETHWAITE

Ebdon English (E Devon and Somerset): habitation name from a hamlet in NE Somerset, near Weston-super-Mare, of uncertain etymology.

Var.: **Ebden**. See also HEBDEN.

Ebe *see* EVERARD

Ebeling *see* EGGEBRECHT

Ebi *see* EVERARD

Ebke *see* EGGEBRECHT

Eble *see* EVERARD

Ebner 1. German: topographic name for someone who lived on a piece of flat ground or a plateau, from MHG *eben(e)* flat, smooth (OHG *eban*), with -*er* suffix of human agents. 2. German: occupational name for an arbiter or judge, MHG *ebenære* (from the same word, in the sense 'fair', 'equitable'). 3. Jewish (Ashkenazic): of uncertain meaning, possibly of the same origin as 1 or 2.

Ebrech *see* EGGEBRECHT

Ebsen *see* EGGEBRECHT

Ebstein *see* EPSTEIN

Eby *see* EVERARD

Eccles Scots and English: habitation name from places near Berwick, Dumfries, Manchester, and elsewhere, all so called from the Brit. word that lies behind W *eglwys* church (from L *ecclesia*, Gk *ekklēsia* gathering, assembly, a deriv. of *ekkalein* to summon, call out). Such places would have been the sites of notable pre-Anglo-Saxon churches or Christian communities.

Var.: **Ecles**.

Eccleston English: habitation name from any of several places so called in Ches. and Lancs., which get their names from an ancient Brit. word meaning 'church' (see ECCLES) + OE *tūn* enclosure, settlement.

Echalié *see* ESCHELLE

Echave Spanish form of Basque **Etxabe**: topographic name for someone who lived on the ground floor of a house, from the Basque elements *etxe* house + *be(e)* bottom, lower part.

Var.: **Echabe**.

Echeandía Spanish form of Basque **Etxeandia**: topographic name for someone who lived in a large house, from the Basque elements *etxe* house + *andi* large + the def. art. -*a*.

Échelle *see* ESCHELLE

Echeverría Spanish form of Basque **Etxeberria**: topographic or habitation name from the Basque elements *etxe* house + *berri* new + the def. art -*a*. This is the origin of the name of a village near Pamplona, now called *Javier*, the birthplace of St Francisco de Jassu XAVIER (1506–52), missionary to East Asia and founding member of the Society of Jesus.

Vars.: **Echeberría**, **Echevarría**, **Echebarría**; **Echéberri**, **Echébarri**, **Echévarri**, **Echávarri**, **Echarri**; **Chávarri**, **Chavarría**.

Echterling see ACHTERMANN

Eck **1.** German and Jewish (Ashkenazic): topographic name for someone living at a corner, Ger. *Eck(e)*, Yid. *ek* (MHG *ecke, egge*, OHG *ecka, egga*). This could have been the corner of two streets in a town or, in the case of the Ger. name, the corner of a field or area of land. **2.** German: short form of any of the various Gmc cpd personal names with a first element *agi(n)*, *agil* edge, point (of a weapon), akin to the word in **1** above); cf., e.g., ECKHARDT, EGGEBRECHT, and EGILOFF. **3.** Swedish: cogn. of OAK.

Vars. (of 1 and 2): **Ecke**, **Egg(e)**. (Of 1 only): Ger.: **Ecker**, **Egger**. Jewish: **E(c)ker**, **Ekler**, **Eckmann**, **E(c)kerman**; **E(c)kerling** (with the Gmc suffix -*ling*); **E(c)khaus**, **Ekhause**, **Ekhaizer**, **Eckheizer**, **Ekhajzer** ('dweller in the corner house'; the last form is a Pol. spelling). (Of 2 only): Ger.: **Ege**, **Egi** (Switzerland). It.: **Aghini**.

Dims. (of 2): **Öckl** (Bavaria); **Eggle** (Swabia); **Eg(g)li** (Switzerland). Low Ger.: **Eckmann**. It.: **Aghini**.

Patrs. (from 2): Ger.: **Eck(e)s**, **Egges**. Low Ger.: **Eggen(s)**, **Egges**, **Egging**. Fris.: **Eggena**. Du.: **Egging**, **Eggink**.

Eckbrett see EGGEBRECHT

Eckersley English (Lancs.): habitation name from a lost place in the parish of Leigh, near Wigan, apparently so called from the gen. case of the OE personal name *Ecgheard* (see ECKHARDT) or *Ecghere* + OE *lēah* wood, clearing.

Eckhardt German: from a Gmc personal name composed of the elements *agi(n)* edge, point + *hard* hardy, brave, strong. The OE cogn. *Ecgheard*, attested in various placenames such as ECKERSLEY and EGERTON, does not seem to have survived the Norman Conquest in sufficient strength to have given rise to a surname.

Vars.: **Eck(e)hard**, **Eckart**, **Eckert**; **Einhart**, **Einert**. Low Ger.: **Eggehart**; **Eggert** (see also EGGEBRECHT); **Ehnert**. Fris.: **Edzart**, **Edzard**. Du.: **Egger**.

Patrs.: Low Ger.: **Eggers**; **Eggerding**, **Eierding** (Westphalia). Du.: **Eggers**.

Eckloff see EGILOFF

Eckstein German and Jewish (Ashkenazic): nickname or ornamental name from Ger. *Eckstein* cornerstone, Yid. *ekshteyn* (from OHG *ecka* corner + *stein* stone), given perhaps to a trusty, reliable person.

Vars.: Jewish: **Ekstein**, **Ekstien**; **Eksztajn** (Pol. spelling).

Ecles see ECCLES

Ecroyd see ACKROYD

Eddington English: **1.** habitation name from a place in Berks., *Eddevetone* in Domesday Book, named from the OE female personal name *Ēadgifu* (composed of the elem-

ents *ēad* prosperity, wealth + *gifu* gift) + OE *tūn* enclosure, settlement. **2.** var. of EDINGTON.

Eddison see EADE

Eddow see BEDDOW

Eddy English (W Country): from the ME given name *Edwy*, OE *Ēadwīg*, composed of the elements *ēad* prosperity, fortune + *wīg* war.

Var.: **Eddie**.

Ede see EADE

Edel **1.** German: from Ger., MHG *edel* noble (OHG *edili*, a deriv. of *adel* nobility). In the Middle Ages this was a term applied to the lowest order of free citizen, ranking below the nobility and knightly class, but above the masses of the servile population. **2.** Jewish (Ashkenazic): from the Yid. female given name *Eydl* 'Noble'. **3.** Jewish (Ashkenazic): ornamental name from mod. Ger. *edel* or Yid. *eydl* noble, splendid, fine. See also ADEL 3.

Vars. (of 1): **Edelmann**, **Ed(e)ler**. (Of 3): **Edelman(n)**, **Eidelman**; **Eidler**, **Aidler**; **E(i)delheit**, **Edelheid** ('nobleness').

Metrs. (from 2): **Eidels**, **Edelso(h)n**, **Eidelson**; **Aides(s)** (from the back-formation *Eyde*, which has also given the surname **Eida**).

Cpds: Jewish (ornamental, from 3): **E(i)delbaum**, **Edelboum** ('noble tree'); **Eidelberg**, **Edelsberg**, **Aidelsberg** ('noble hill'); **Edelsburg** ('noble town'); **Eidelkind** ('noble child'); **E(i)delstein** ('precious stone', 'jewel').

Edelstein see ADEL

Edema see OADE

Eden **1.** English: from the ME given name *Edun*, OE *Ēadhūn*, composed of the elements *ēad* prosperity, wealth + *hūn* bear-cub. **2.** English: habitation name from Castle *Eden* or *Eden* Burn in Co. Durham, both of which derive from a Brit. river name perhaps meaning 'water', recorded by the Greek geographer Ptolemy in the 2nd cent. AD in the form *Ituna*. **3.** Frisian: patr. from the given name *Ede* (see OADE). **4.** Jewish: ornamental name referring to the garden of Eden; cf. LUSTGARTEN.

Vars. (of 1): **Eaden**, **E(a)don**.

Patr. (from 1): **Edens**.

Eder **1.** German: topographic name for someone who lived on a patch of bare, uncultivated land, from Ger. *öd* empty, bare (MHG *(o)ed(e)*, OHG *ōdi*) + -*er* suffix of human nouns. It may also be a habitation name from any of the numerous places named with this element. **2.** Jewish: of uncertain origin, possibly from Hebr. *eder* herd, flock, or (if Ashkenazic) possibly derived as in 1.

Vars. (of 1): **Ederer**, **Öder(er)**.

Edess see BEDDOW

Edgar **1.** English: from the OE personal name *Ēadgār*, composed of the elements *ēad* prosperity, fortune + *gār* spear. The name is found in ME in various forms, e.g. *Edgar*, *Adger*, *Agar*. **2.** Jewish: of unknown origin, possibly an Anglicization of one or more like-sounding Jewish names.

Vars. (of 1): **Eagar**, **Eag(g)er**, **Eg(g)ar**, **Egarr**, **Eg(g)er**, **Edger**, **Adger**; **Agar**, **Ager**; **Adair**; **Odge(a)r**, **Og(i)er** (from the Continental Gmc cogn., introduced into England by the Normans). (Of 2): **Agar**.

Patrs. (from 1): Eng.: **Edgars**, **Eagers**, **Eggars**, **Agars**; **Odgers**.

Edge English: topographic name, esp. in Lancs. and the W Midlands, for someone who lived on or by a hillside or ridge, from OE *ecg* edge (cf. ECK).

Edgeley English: habitation name from places in Ches. and Shrops., so called from OE *edisc* enclosed pasture + *lēah* wood, clearing.

Var.: **Edgley**.

Edgerton *see* EGERTON

Edgeworth English: habitation name from places in Gloucs. and Lancs., so called from OE *ecg* hillside, ridge (see EDGE) + *worð* enclosure (see WORTH).

Var.: **Edgworth**.

Edgington English (W Midlands): apparently a habitation name, of uncertain origin. It may be from a lost place, so called as the 'settlement (OE *tūn*) associated with *Ecgi*', a short form of the various cpd names with the first element *ecg* edge, point (of a weapon). Alternatively, it may be a corruption of *Erdington*, a place in the W Midlands that derives its name from the OE personal name *Ēanrēd* + OE *tūn* enclosure, settlement.

Edington N English and Scots: habitation name from any of various places so called, esp. one in Northumb. originally named in OE as *Idingtūn* 'settlement (OE *tūn*) associated with *Ida*'; see IDE. The place of the same name in Somerset, which may not have contributed to the surname, appears in Domesday Book as *Eduuintone*, from the OE personal name *Ēadwine* (see EDWIN) or *Ēadwynn* (a female personal name composed of the elements *ēad* prosperity, wealth + *wynn* joy) + OE *tūn* enclosure, settlement.

Var.: EDDINGTON.

Edison *see* EADE

Edkins *see* EADE

Edler *see* EDEL

Edlestone 1. English: from the OE personal name *Æðelstān*, composed of the elements *æðel* noble + *stān* stone. 2. Jewish (Ashkenazic): Anglicized form of *Edelstein* (see EDEL).

Vars. (of 1): ALSTON, ASTON.

Edmead English: nickname for a humble or self-effacing person, from ME *edmede* humble, OE *ēadmēde*, a cpd of *ēaðe* easy, gently + *mōd* mind.

Vars. (of 1): **Edmed**, **Edmett**, **Edmott**.

Patrs.: **E(a)dmead(e)s**.

Edmond English and French: from the ME given name *Edmund* (OE *Ēadmund*, composed of the elements *ēad* prosperity, fortune + *mund* protection. In medieval England and France the name was often bestowed in honour of the E Anglian King St Edmund the Martyr (d. 869), who

was killed by pagan Danish invaders, and about whom many legends grew up.

Vars.: Eng.: **Edmund**. Fr.: **Edmont**, **Émon(d)**, **Émont**.

Dims.: Fr.: **Émonet**, **Émonot**; MONET, **Monot**.

Patrs.: Eng.: **Edmon(d)s**, **Edmunds**; **Edmon(d)son**, **Edmundson**, **Edmenson**, **Edminson**. Welsh: **Bedmond** (with the patr. prefix *ap*; sometimes altered to BEAUMONT). Sc.: McKEEMAN.

Edon *see* EDEN

Edrich English: from the ME given name *Edrich, Ederick*, OE *Ēadrīc*, composed of the elements *ēad* prosperity, fortune + *rīc* power.

Vars.: **Edridge**; **Etheridge** (an altered form current since the beginning of the 17th cent., developed from the late 16th-cent. forms *Et(t)riche, Et(t)ridge*).

Edsel *see* ALBERT

Edsen *see* OADE

Edson *see* EADE

Edvardsen *see* EDWARD

Edvinsson *see* EDWIN

Edward English: from the ME given name *Edward*, OE *Ēadward*, composed of the elements *ēad* prosperity, fortune + *w(e)ard* guard. Although apparently of exclusively OE origin, the given name also became popular on the Continent, perhaps as a result of the fame of the two canonized kings of England, Edward the Martyr (962–79) and Edward the Confessor (1004–66). They certainly contributed largely to its great popularity in England.

Var.: **Edwarde**.

Patrs.: Eng.: **Edward(e)s**; **Edwardson**. W: **Bedward**, **Beddard**. Dan., Norw.: **Edvardsen**. Swed.: **Edvardsson**.

Edwin English: from the ME given name *Edwine*, OE *Ēadwine*, composed of the elements *ēad* prosperity, fortune + *wine* friend.

Vars.: **Edwing**, **Edwyn**.

Patr.: Swed.: **Edvinsson**.

Edzard *see* ECKHARDT

Eely *see* ELY

Eerikäinen *see* HERRICK

Effertz *see* EVERARD

Efron Jewish: ornamental name, taken from the biblical placename *Efron*, a mountain mentioned in Josh. 15: 9 and a Benjaminite city mentioned in 2 Chron. 13: 19.

Vars.: **Ephron**, **Evron**; **Efroni**, **Efron(n)y**, **Ephrony**, **Evroni** (with the Hebr. suffix -*i*).

Egan *see* HIGGINS

Egar *see* EDGAR

Egberts *see* EGGEBRECHT

Ege *see* ECK

Egelolf *see* EGILOFF

Eger *see* EDGAR

Egerton English: habitation name from places in Kent and Ches. The former is so called from OE *Egcheardingtūn* 'settlement (OE *tūn*) associated with *Egcheard*' (see ECKHARDT); the second, which is the main source of the surname, is more likely to have been named as the 'settlement of *Egchere*' (in which the second element is OE *here* army).

Vars.: **Eggerton**, **Edgerton**.

Egg *see* ECK

Eggar *see* EDGAR

Eggebrecht German: from a Gmc personal name composed of the elements *agi(l)* edge, point (of a weapon) + *berht* bright, famous. The Eng. cogn. *Egbert* is not found as a surname, in spite of the fame of King Egbert of Wessex.

Vars.: **Ebbrecht**, **Ebrech(t)**, **Ehebrecht**, **Eckebrecht**, **Eckbrett**; **Ehlebracht**, **Eilebrecht**, **E(i)lbracht**, **El(e)brecht**.

Dims.: Fris.: **Ebbe(ke)**, **Ebke(ma)**, **Epp(mann)**.

Patrs.: Ger.: **Eckenbrecher**. Low Ger.: **Ebbers**, **Eppers**; **Elbers**, **Elbertz**, **Elberding** (N Rhineland). Du.: **Egberts**, **Ebbers**.

Patrs. (from dims.): Low Ger.: **Eppen(s)**, **Epping**, **Eppink**.

Fris.: **Ebben**, **Eb(be)sen**, **Ebbing(a)**, **Ebbena**, **Ebeling**.

Eggehart *see* ECKHARDT

Eggerton *see* EGERTON

Eggleston English: habitation name from a place in Co. Durham so called, or from *Egglestone* in N Yorks, both of which are named from the gen. case of the OE personal name *Ecgwulf* (see EGILOFF) + OE *tūn* enclosure, settlement.

Vars.: **Egleston**, **Egglestone**.

Eggleton English: habitation name from a place near Hereford, named in OE as the settlement (OE *tūn*) associated with *Ecgwulf* (see EGILOFF) or *Ecgel* (a derivative of the various cpd names with the first element *ecg*; cf. EDGINGTON).

Egi *see* ECK

Egido Spanish: topographic name for someone who lived by a patch of common land, situated at the edge of a village, OSp. *exido* (L *exitus* exit, way out, a deriv. of *exīre* to go out).

Var.: **Ejido**.

Egiloff German: from a Gmc personal name composed of the elements *agi(l)* edge, point (of a weapon) + *wolf* wolf, cogn. with OE *Ecgwulf*. This was the name of several Lombard kings (ancestors of the Bavarian ducal line of the *Agilolfinger*), who introduced the name to Italy.

Vars.: **Egelolf**, **Egloff**, **Eckloff**, **Egleha(a)f** (Franconia); **Eginolf**, **Egenolf(f)**, **Egenlauf**, **Einolf** (with a first element *agin*, a different extension of the same stem).

Patr.: Swed.: **Elofsson**.

Egle *see* EAGLE

Eglehaaf *see* EGILOFF

Eglese *see* EAGLES

Egleston *see* EGGLESTON

Egli *see* ECK

Eguía Spanish form of Basque **Egia**: topographic name for someone who lived on a mountain ridge, from Basque *egi* ridge, slope + the def. art. *-a*.

Egúsquiza Spanish form of Basque **Eguskiza**: topographic name for someone who lived in a spot that caught the sun, from *eguzki* sun + the suffix of abundance *-tza*.

Ehebrecht *see* EGGEBRECHT

Ehemann *see* EHMANN

Ehlebracht *see* EGGEBRECHT

Ehlend *see* ELEND

Ehler *see* EHLERT

Ehlert Low German: from a medieval given name, composed of the Gmc elements *agil* edge, point (of a weapon) + *hard* brave, hardy, strong or *ward* guard.

Vars.: **Ehler**, **Eiler(t)**.

Dims.: **Ehlermann**, **Eildermann**.

Patrs.: **Ehlers**, **Eilers**; **Ehlerding**, **Eilerding** (Westphalia).

Fris.: **Eil(der)ts**. Dan.: **Ehlers**, **Eiler(t)sen**.

Ehmann **1.** German: nickname for someone under feudal obligations of some particular kind, from MHG *ē* law, contract (OHG *ēwa*) + *mann* man (OHG *man*). **2.** Jewish: (Ashkenazic): nickname from mod. Ger. *Ehemann* husband (the word *Ehe* having progressively become restricted to the marriage contract and then to the state of matrimony itself). At one time in the Austrian Empire, only one son in a Jewish family was officially permitted to marry and start a family of his own: this may have been a surname adopted by such a person.

Var.: **Ehemann**.

Ehmcke *see* AMERY

Ehn Swedish: ornamental name from Swed. *en* juniper. This is one of the many names derived from words denoting natural features, which were used to form Swed. surnames in the 19th cent.

Cpds (ornamental): **E(h)nlund(h)** ('juniper grove'); **E(h)nqvist** ('juniper twig'); **E(h)nström** ('juniper river').

Ehnert *see* ECKHARDT

Ehrlich German and Jewish (Ashkenazic): nickname or ornamental name from Ger. *ehrlich* honourable, honest, or Yid. *erlekh* honest, virtuous (MHG *ērlich* respected, honoured, from OHG *ēra* honour).

Vars.: Jewish: **Erlich(man)**.

Patr.: Jewish: **Erlichson**.

Cpd (ornamental): Jewish: **Erlichgerecht** ('honest and fair').

Ehrmann Jewish (Ashkenazic): ornamental name from mod. Ger. *Ehre* honour + *Mann* man.

Vars.: **Ehre**, **Ehrenmann**.

Cpds (ornamental): **E(h)renberg** ('honour hill'); **Ehrenfeld** ('honour field'); **E(h)renfried** ('honour peace'); **Ehrenfreund** ('honour friend'); **Ehrenhalt** ('honour support'); **Ehrenhaus** ('honour house'); **Ehrenkranz** ('honour garland'); **Ernlib** ('honour love'); **Ehrenpreis** ('honour praise'); **E(h)renreich** ('rich in honour'); **Ehrenstein**, **Ernstein** ('honour stone'), **Ehrent(h)al**, **Erental** ('honour valley'), **Ernwert** ('honourable, respectable'); **Ehrenwort** ('word of honour'); **Ehrenzweig** ('honour twig').

Ehwalt *see* EWALD

Eichel *see* OAK

Eichhorn 1. German: nickname from Ger. *Eichhorn* squirrel (now replaced as a vocab. word by its dim. *Eichhörnchen*). The vocab. word is from OHG *eihhurno*, a cpd of *eih* oak + *urno*, from the ancient Gmc and Indo-European name of the animal, which was later wrongly associated with *hurno* horn. 2. Jewish (Ashkenazic): ornamental name from the vocab. word as in 1.

Eida *see* EDEL

Eidtner *see* AGGIS

Eierding *see* ECKHARDT

Eiffel German and French: regional name for someone from the district bounded by the mid-Rhine, Moselle, and Ardennes known as the *Eifel*. The first record of the placename occurs AD *c*.800 in the L form *in pago Aflense, E(i)flense*. According to Bahlow the term is of pre-Gmc origin.

Vars.: **Eif(f)ler**.

Eigner 1. German: status name originally denoting a smallholder who held his land outright, rather than by rent or feudal obligation. In the Middle Ages this was sufficiently rare to be worthy of remark and was normally a special privilege granted in recognition of some exceptional service. The vocab. word is from MHG *aigen* own (OHG *eigan*), with the addition of the suffix *-er*, denoting human nouns. 2. Jewish (Ashkenazic): from Ger. *Eigner* owner, presumably adopted as an indication of property-owning status.

Var.: **Aigner** (Bavaria).

Eilbracht *see* EGGEBRECHT

Eildermann *see* EHLERT

Einbinder *see* BINDER

Einert *see* ECKHARDT

Einhorn 1. German: nickname from Ger. *Einhorn* unicorn (MHG *einhorn*, OHG *einhurno*, a cpd of *ein* one + *hurno* horn). This may also be a house name, from a house sign depicting the fabulous animal. 2. Jewish (Ashkenazic): ornamental name from Ger. *Einhorn* unicorn.

Var. (of 2): **Ainhorn**.

Einold German: from a medieval given name, composed of the Gmc elements *agin* edge, point (of a weapon) + *wald* rule.

Patr.: Dan.: **Enevoldsen**.

Einolf *see* EGILOFF

Einsiedel German: from MHG *einsidel* solitary settler, hermit, monk (OHG *einsidilio*, a cpd of *ein* one, alone + *sedal* seat, settlement, inspired by L *monachus*; see MONK). The surname may in some cases have referred to an actual hermit, or by extension to a dweller in an isolated situation or an unsociable individual, but more often it is simply a habitation name from places in Bavaria, Austria, and Switzerland called *Einsiedeln*, from having once been the site chosen by hermits (cf. ARMITAGE; and Ger. *München* from MHG *(zu den) münichen* 'at the (place of the) monks').

The famous monastery of this name in Switzerland was founded by a hermit named Meinrad in 830.

Einstein 1. German: habitation name from various places named with a MHG deriv. of *einsteinen* to enclose, surround with stone. In the unsettled social climate of the Middle Ages even relatively minor settlements were commonly surrounded with stone walls as a defence against attack. 2. Jewish (Ashkenazic): adoption of the Ger. name, or else an ornamental name, one of the many ending in *-stein*.

Var. (of 2): **Ainstein**.

Eisen German and Jewish (Ashkenazic): metonymic occupational name for an ironworker or smith, or an ironmonger, from Ger. *Eisen* iron (MHG *īsen*, OHG *īsan*). It may also have been used as a nickname, with reference to the strength and hardness of iron or to its colour, while as a Jewish name it was also adopted as an ornamental name from mod. Ger. *Eisen* iron or the Yid. cogn. *ayzn*.

Vars.: Ger.: **Eis(en)mann, Eiser(mann), Eisler, Eisner**. Jewish: **Aizen, Ajzen, Aizin; Eisenman, Ajsenman, Aizenman, Ajzenman, Aizner, Ajzner** (occupational names).

Cpds (mainly ornamental): Jewish: **Eisenbach** ('iron stream'); **Eisenbaum, Eisenboum, Aizenbaum, Ajzenbaum** ('iron tree'); **Eisenberg(er), Aisenberg, Ajsenberg, Aizenberg, Ajzenberg, Ajzinberg** ('iron hill'); **Eisenfarb** ('iron colour'); **Eisenfeld, Aizenfeld** ('iron field'); **Eisenfish, Ajzenfisz** ('iron fish'); **Eisenhardt, Aizengart** ('iron hard'); **Eisenkeit; Eisenkraft** ('iron chain'); **Eisenkraft** ('iron strength'); **Ajzenkranz** ('iron wreath'); **Eisenpresser** ('iron presser', presumably an occupational name for a blacksmith); **Eisenreich** ('iron rich'); **Eisens(c)her** ('iron scissors or shears'); **Eisenschmidt** ('iron smith', an occupational name); **Eisenschreiber** ('iron writer'; reason for adoption unknown); **Aizenstark** ('strong as iron'); **Eisenstein, Aizenstein, Aizenshtain, Ajzensztein** ('iron stone'); **Eisent(h)al, Aizental, Ajzental** ('iron valley'); **Eisenzweig** ('iron twig').

Eisenbein German: nickname from MHG *īsen* iron (see EISEN) + *bein* leg (OHG *bein*), denoting someone who had an artificial leg made of metal (cf. PETTIFER), or perhaps a metal-worker who manufactured greaves and legarmour.

Eisengrein German: from a Gmc personal name composed of the elements *īsan* iron + *grīm* mask. This is the name born by the wolf in the popular medieval cycle of beast tales, in part in reference to the iron-grey colour of the animal (cf. FARRANT 1), in part a memory of the older association of the wolf with Odin (cf. GRIME). The surname may represent a nickname given in jesting allusion to this. It is found principally in Baden-Württemberg.

Eisenhandler Jewish (Ashkenazic): occupational name for an ironmonger, from Ger. *Eisenhändler* ironmonger, from *Eisen* iron + *Händler* dealer.

Var.: **Eisenhendler**.

Eisenhauer German: occupational name for a worker in iron, from MHG *īsen* iron (see EISEN) + *houwære*, a deriv. of *houwen* to cut, chop, hew (OHG *houwan*).

Vars.: **Haueis(en)**.

Eisenstadt Jewish (Ashkenazic): habitation name from a town formerly in Hungary, now in Austria, known in Yid. as *Ayznshtot* 'Iron City'. See also ASH 2.

Vars.: **Aizens(h)tat, Ajzensta(d)t, Ajzensztad**.

Eisig *see* ISAAC

Eitel German: nickname from MHG *ītel* only, purely, simply (OHG *ītal*, a cogn. of IDLE 3). In the days before surnames had begun to make their mark, bearers of common given names would often have a second given name as a distinguishing feature; someone who did not have such a second given name could be distinguished by this fact in itself, as for example *ītel Hans* (just Hans) as against *Hans Joachim*. The meaning 'vain', 'conceited' is comparatively late and has probably not contributed to the surname.

Vars.: **Eytel**, **Eydel**.

Eithner *see* AGGIS

Ejido *see* EGIDO

Ekberg *see* OAK

Ekdahl *see* OAK

Eke English (E Anglia): habitation name from *Eyke* in Suffolk, named from ON *eik* oak.

Ekedahl *see* OAK

Ekgren *see* OAK

Ekhaizer *see* ECK

Ekholm *see* OAK

Ekins *see* EADE

Ekler *see* ECK

Eklind *see* OAK

Ekroth *see* OAK

Ekstedt *see* OAK

Ekstein *see* ECKSTEIN

Ekvall *see* OAK

Ekwall *see* OAK

Elbaum *see* OHLBAUM

Elbel *see* ALBERT

Elberding *see* EGGEBRECHT

Elborough English: habitation name, probably from a minor place in the parish of Hutton, near Weston-super-Mare in Somerset. It gets its name from the OE personal name *Ella* + OE *bearu* grove.

Vars.: **Elbro(w)**, **Elbra**.

Elcock *see* ELLIS

Elcy *see* ELSEY

Elder English: distinguishing nickname bestowed on the elder (OE *ealdra*, comp. of *eald* OLD) of two bearers of the same given name. At first sight it might be thought to be a topographic name from the tree (OE *ellern*, with later dissimilation), but this origin does not seem to be supported by any evidence from early forms with prepositions.

Eldred *see* ALDRITT

Elebrecht *see* EGGEBRECHT

Elejalde *see* ELIZALDE

Elen *see* ELLEN

Elend German: from MHG *ellende* banished, miserable, luckless (OHG *elilenti*, from *ali* other, foreign + *land* land), apparently used more often as a nickname than as a descriptive term of literal application.

Vars.: **Ellend**, **Ehlend**.

Eles *see* ELLIS

Elesander *see* ALEXANDER

Elfick *see* ELPHICK

Elfin *see* ALPIN

Elford English: habitation name from a place so called from the OE personal name *Ella* (see ELLINGTON) + *ford* FORD, or from OE *alor, elre* alder tree + *ford*. There is a place of this name in Staffs. and another in Northumb., but the surname is now chiefly common in Devon.

Elgar *see* ALGER

Elias *see* ELLIS

Éliet *see* ELLIS

Elin *see* ELLEN

Elington *see* ELLINGTON

Elizalde Basque: topographic name for someone who lived by a church, from *eleiza* church (a Romance borrowing; cf. ECCLES) + the suffix *-alde* by. This also occurs as the name of a village in N Spain, from which the surname may in part be derived.

Var.: **Elejalde** (a common placename).

Elizondo Basque: topographic name for someone who lived near a church, from *eleiza* church (cf. ELIZALDE) + the suffix *-ondo* near, beside. This also occurs as a placename in Navarre, from which the surname may alternatively be derived as a habitation name.

Elkin 1. English: dim. of *Elias*; see ELLIS. **2.** Jewish (E Ashkenazic): metr. from the Yid. female given name *Elke* + the Slav. suffix *-in*.

Patr. (from 1): **Elkins**.

Elkington English: habitation name from a place so called, probably N and S *Elkington* in Lincs., which are named from an OE personal name, possibly *Ēa(n)lāc* + OE *tūn* enclosure, settlement. *Elkington* in Northants did not acquire the name until 1617, before which it was *Eltington* or *Elteton*.

Ellard *see* ALLARD

Ellen English: from the normal medieval vernacular form of the given name *Helen* (Gk *Helenē*, of uncertain origin, perhaps akin to *helanē* torch). This was the name of the mother of Constantine the Great, credited with finding the True Cross; according to legend she was of British origin, and the name was consequently popular in England during the Middle Ages.

Vars.: **Elen**, **El(l)in**, **Elleyne**, **Hel(l)en**, **Hellin**.

Metrs.: **Ellens**, **Ellin(g)s**, **Hellens**.

Ellend *see* ELEND

Eller **1.** German: habitation name from places in the N Rhine and Moselle areas, so called from an old streamname *Elera, Alira*, possibly of Celt. origin. **2.** Low German: topographic name for someone who lived by an alder tree, from MLG *elre, alre* alder (cf. OHG *elira*; the mod. Ger. form *Erle* is from the metathesized *erila*). **3.** Jewish (E Ashkenazic): var. of HELLER, reflecting varieties of Yid. in which there is no /h/. **4.** Italian: Venetian form of the given name HILARY.

Var. (of 1–3): **Ellermann**.

Elleray *see* HILARY

Ellerman *see* ELMAN

Ellif *see* AYLIFF

Ellingham English: habitation name from places in Hants, Northumb., and Norfolk. The first of these is so called from OE *Ēdlingahām* 'homestead (OE *hām*) of the people of *Ēdla*', a personal name derived from a short form of the various cpd names with a first element *ēad* prosperity, fortune; the others may have the same origin or incorporate the personal name *Ella* (see ELLINGTON).

Ellington English: habitation name from places in Cambs., Kent, Northumb., and N Yorks.; most are so called from OE *Ellingtūn* 'settlement (OE *tūn*) associated with *Ella*', a short form of the various cpd names with a first element *ælf* elf, but the one in Kent has its first element from the OE byname *Ealda* OLD.

Var.: **Elington**.

Elliott **1.** English: dim. of ELLIS. **2.** English and Scots: from a ME given name, *Elyat, Elyt*. This represents at least two OE personal names which have fallen together: the male name *Aðelgēat* (composed of the elements *aðel* noble + *Gēat*, a tribal name; see JOCELYN), and the female personal name *Aðelgȳð* (composed of the elements *aðel* noble + *gȳð* battle). The ME name seems also to have absorbed various other given names of OE or Continental Gmc origin, as for example OE *Ælfweald*; see ELLWOOD and see also below. **3.** Scots: Anglicized form of the originally distinct Gael. surname **Elloch, Eloth**, a topographic name from Gael. *eileach* dam, mound, bank.

Vars.: **Elliot, Eliot(t)** (these different spellings have been adopted by different families as a distinguishing feature.)

Ellis English: from the medieval given name *Elis*, the normal vernacular form of *Elijah* (Gk *Elias*, from Hebr. *Eliyahu* 'Jehovah is God'). This name was borne by a biblical prophet, but its popularity among Christians in the Middle Ages was a result of its adoption by various early saints, as for example a 7th-cent. bishop of Syracuse and a 9th-cent. Sp. martyr. In Wales this surname seems to have absorbed forms derived from the W personal name *Elisedd*, a deriv. of *elus* kindly, benevolent.

Vars.: **Elliss, Elis, Ellice, Eles, Elys, Heelis, Hel(l)is, Elias**.

Dims.: Eng.: ELLIOTT; ELKIN; **Elcock, Hellcat, Hillcoat**. Fr.: **Éliet, Éliez, Élion; Al(l)iot; Héliet, Héliot, Hélin**. Ukr.: **Ilyenko, Ilchenko, Ilchuk**.

Patrs.: Eng.: **Ellis(s)on, Elliston**. Welsh: **Bellis(s)**, BLISS. It.: **D'Elia(s)**. Rum.: **Eliesco**. Low Ger.: **Eliassen, Ellissen**. Dan., Norw.: **Eliasen**. Swed.: **Eliasson**. Pol.: **Ilewicz**. Russ.: **Ilyin, Ilmanov** (from an expanded form); **Ilyinski** (a name adopted by

Orthodox priests); **Ilyasov** (from an Arabic form used in the (Muslim) Turkic regions). Armenian: **Helian**. Georgian: **Iashvili**.

Patrs. (from dims.): Eng.: ELSON. Russ.: **Ilyushkin, Ilyukhov, Ilyunin, Ilyasov, Ilyuchyov, Ilyinykh**. Beloruss.: **Yelyashev, Yeliashev**.

'Son of the daughter of E.': Russ.: **Ilyinichnin**.

Elloway *see* ALLOWAY

Ellson *see* ELSON

Ellsworth *see* ELSWORTH

Ellwood English: **1.** habitation name from a place in Gloucs., which is probably named from OE *ellern* elder tree + *wudu* WOOD. **2.** from the OE personal name *Ælfweald*, composed of the elements *ælf* elf + *weald* rule.

Vars.: **Elwood, Allwood**.

Elm English: topographic name for someone who lived near an elm tree or in an elm grove, from ME, OE *elm* elm.

Vars.: **Elm(e)s; Nelm(e)s** (from ME *atten elms*).

Cpds (ornamental): Swed.: **Almberg** ('elm hill'); **Almgren** ('elm branch'); **Almqvist** ('elm twig'); **Almroth** ('elm clearing'); **Almstedt** ('elm homestead'); **Almström** ('elm river').

Elman **1.** Jewish (E Ashkenazic): var. of *Hellmann* (see HELLER), reflecting varieties of Yid. in which there is no /h/. **2.** English: occupational name for a seller of oil, from ME *ele* oil + *man* man; cf. ULMAN 2.

Vars. (of 2): **Elliman, Ellerman**.

Elmar *see* AYLMER

Elmhirst English: habitation name from one of several places in W Yorks. so called from OE *elm* ELM + *hyrst* wooded hill (see HURST).

Var.: **Elmhurst** (the name of places in Somerset and Staffs.).

Elmore English: habitation name from a place in Gloucs., so called from OE *elm* elm + *ofer* ridge.

Elmsley *see* EMSLIE

Elofsson *see* EGILOFF

Elorduy Spanish form of Basque **Elordui**: topographic name for someone who lived by a piece of land overgrown with brambles, from Basque *elor* bramble + the suffix of abundance *-dui*.

Var.: **Elorza** (with a different suffix of the same meaning).

Elorriaga Basque: topographic name for someone who lived by a thorn-bush, from Basque *elorri* hawthorn + the local suffix *-aga*.

Eloy French: from the medieval given name *Eloy* (L *Ēligius*, a deriv. of *ēligere* to choose, elect) made popular by a 6th-cent. saint who came to be venerated as the patron of smiths and horses.

Vars.: **Eloi**, LEY.

Elperin *see* HEILBRONN

Elphey *see* ALVEY

Elphick English: from the ME given name *Elfegh, Alfeg*, OE *Ælfhēah*, composed of the elements *ælf* elf + *hēah* high. The name was sometimes bestowed in honour of St *Alphege* (954–1012), archbishop of Canterbury, who was stoned to death by the Danes, and came to be revered as a martyr.

Vars.: **Elphicke**, **Elfick**, **Elvidge**, **Alphege**.

Elphinston Scots: habitation name from a place in the former county of Midlothian, first recorded in the mid-13th cent. in the form *Elfinstun*; in spite of the superficial approximation to Eng. 'elfin stone', it is likely that the first element is a Gael. personal name altered by folk etymology; cf. ALPIN.

Var.: **Elphinstone**.

Elray *see* HILARY

Elsässer German and Jewish (Ashkenazic): regional name for someone from Alsace (Ger. *Elsass*, Yid. *Elzes*), with the suffix *-er* indicating a native or inhabitant of a place. The name of the region (first attested in L documents in the form *Alisatia*) has traditionally been derived from OHG *ali* other, foreign + *saz* seat, possession, but Bahlow traces the first element back to a river name *Ill* or *Ell*.

Vars.: Jewish: **Elzesser**, **Elzas**.

Elsey English: from the ME given name *El(f)si*, OE *Ælfsige*, composed of the elements *ælf* elf + *sige* victory.

Vars.: **Elsie**, **Elsy**, **Elcy**.

Elshenar *see* ALEXANDER

Elsip *see* ALLSOP

Elson 1. English: habitation name from places in Hants and Shrops. The former is so called from the OE personal name *Æðelswīð* (composed of the elements *æðel* noble + *swīð* strong) + OE *tūn* enclosure, settlement; the latter from the gen. case of the OE personal name *Elli* (see EL-LINGTON) + OE *tūn* settlement or *dūn* hill (see DOWN 1). 2. English: patr. from ELLIS. 3. Jewish (Ashkenazic): patr. from the Yid. male given name *Elye*, from Hebr. *Eliyahu* Elijah (see ELLIS).

Var.: **Ellson**.

Elston English: habitation name from any of various places so called. One in Lancs. gets the name from the OE female personal name *Æðelsige* (composed of the elements *aðel* noble + *sige* victory) + OE *tūn* enclosure, settlement; one in Notts. originally had as its first element the gen. case of the ON byname *Eilífr* 'Everlasting'; one in Wilts. was so named from *Elias* (see ELLIS) Giffard, holder of the manor in the 12th cent.

Elsworth English: habitation name from a place in Cambs., so called from the gen. case of the OE personal name *Elli* (see ELLINGTON) + OE *worð* enclosure (see WORTH).

Var.: **Ellsworth**.

Elton English: habitation name from any of the various places so called. For the most part they derive from the OE personal name *Ella* or *Elli* (see ELLINGTON) + OE *tūn* enclosure, settlement. One in Berks., however, gets its first element from the OE female personal name *Æðelflæd* (composed of the elements *æðel* noble + *flæd* beauty. One in Cambs. has its first element from the personal name *Æðelheah* (composed of the elements *æðel* noble +

hēah high). Finally, the place of this name in Co. Durham probably gets its first element from OE *æl* eel.

Eltringham English: habitation name from a village in Northumb., so called from OE *Ælfheringahām* 'homestead (OE *hām*) of the people of *Ælfhere*'; the *t* was inserted for the sake of euphony after the name had been collapsed in pronunciation. The surname is still largely restricted to the Newcastle area.

Elvey *see* ALVEY

Elvidge *see* ELPHICK

Elvin *see* ALWYN

Elvira Spanish: from the medieval female given name *Elvira*. This is of Gmc origin, probably composed of the elements *gail* happy, content (cf. GALE 1), or perhaps *adel* noble (cf. EDEL), + *wēr* true.

Elwell English: habitation name from a place apparently so called from OE *hæl* omen + *well(a)* spring, stream; the reference is presumably to pagan river worship. This is the origin of a place of this name in Dorset. Two minor places in Devon are probably 'elder-tree spring', from OE *ellern* elder tree + *well(a)*. The surname is now found chiefly in the W Midlands; cf. also HALLIWELL.

Elwes English: from the OF female given name *Eloïse*, introduced into England by the Normans; it is composed of the Gmc elements *heil* hale, sound, healthy + *widi(s)* wide.

Var.: **Elwess**.

Elwin *see* ALWYN

Elwood *see* ELLWOOD

Ely English: habitation name from the cathedral city on an island in the fens N of Cambridge. It is so called from OE *æl* eel + *gē* district.

Vars.: **Eley**, **Eal(e)y**, **Eely**.

Elys *see* ELLIS

Elzas *see* ELSÄSSER

Emanuel *see* EMMANUEL

Emary *see* AMERY

Emberry *see* AMERY

Emblem *see* EMMETT

Embleton English: habitation name from any of various places so called. One in Northumb. is probably from the OE personal name *Æmele* + *dūn* hill; one in Co. Durham was earlier *Elmedene*, from OE *elm* ELM + *denu* valley. Embleton in Cumb. is probably from the personal name *Ēanbald* + OE *tūn* enclosure, settlement.

Emeline *see* EMMETT

Emeric *see* AMERY

Émilien French: from a personal name (L *Aemiliānus*, a deriv. of *Aemilius*, a Roman family name perhaps derived from *aemulus* rival) borne by various early saints, and hence widely used as a given name in the Middle Ages.

Vars.: **Émilian**, **Émilion**; **Mil(l)ien**, **Milian**, **Mil(l)ion** (aphetic forms).

Patr.: Russ: **Yemelyanov**.

Patrs. (from dims.): Russ.: **Yemelyanchikov**, **Yemyashev**.

Emlyn *see* EMMETT

Emmanuel 1. Jewish: from the Hebr. given name *Imanuel* 'God is with us'. **2.** French: from the same name used in the Middle Ages by Christians in honour of a minor 3rd-cent. martyr.

Vars. (of 1): **Emanuel(i)**, **Manuely** (with the Hebr. ending -*i*). (Of 2): Fr.: **Manuel**, **Manueau**, **Manuaud**.

Patrs. (from 1): Jewish: **Emanuelov**; **Manes**, **Manis** (Ashkenazic, from the Yid. male given name *Mane*), **Manin** (E Ashkenazic, with the Slavic possessive suffix -*in*). (From 2): It.: **D'Emanuele**. Swed.: **Emanulsson**. Bulg.: **Manolov**.

Emmel *see* AMERY

Emmett English: from a ME dim. of the female given name *Emma*, introduced into England by the Normans, among whom it was extremely popular. The name is of Gmc origin, originally apparently a hypocoristic form of women's names with a first element *ermin* entire.

Vars.: **Em(m)et**, **Emmott**, **Emmitt**, **Emmatt**, **Hemmett**; **Emeline**, **Emlyn**, **Emblin(g)**, **Emblem**.

Metrs.: Eng.: **Emms**; **Emmison**, **Em(p)son**, **Hemson**.

Émon *see* EDMOND

Emory *see* AMERY

Empereur French: nickname from OF *empereor* emperor (L *imperātor*, originally meaning 'general', 'commander', from the verb *imperāre* to rule, order). The name may have been acquired by someone with an imperious manner, or who had acted the part of an emperor in a pageant, or presided at some festival, or who had won the title by being the champion in a contest.

Var.: **Lempereur** (with fused def. art.).

Fem. forms: Fr.: **Lemprière** (with fused def. art.). It.: **Imperatrice**.

Empson *see* EMMETT

Emslie Scots: habitation name largely confined to the Aberdeen region. It is probably of Eng. origin, from a place called *Elmley*, named with the OE elements *elm* ELM + *lēah* wood, clearing, with an intrusive -*s*-. There are places so called in Kent and Worcs.

Vars.: **Elmslie**, **Elmsl(e)y**.

Emson *see* EMMETT

Encabo Spanish: from OSp. *en* in, at (L *in*) + *cabo* head (see CAP). The precise meaning of the surname is not clear. OSp. *cabo* had various figurative and transferred meanings, the anatomical sense being normally represented by CABEZA, and so the name may have originally denoted a leader or overseer who was placed at the head of a group of workers, or it may be a topographic name for someone who lived at the upper end of a settlement.

Encarnación Spanish: religious byname, or nickname for someone who was born on Christmas Day, celebrated as the feast of the Incarnation of Christ (L *incarnātio*, from *incarnāre* to make flesh, a deriv. of *caro*, gen. *carnis*, flesh).

Encina Spanish: topographic name for someone who lived by a holm oak, Sp. *encina* (OSp. *leçina*, LL *īlicīna*, a deriv. of class. L *īlex*, gen. *īlicis*).

Var.: **Encinas** (the name of various places, for example in the provinces of Salamanca, Valladolid, and Segovia).

Collective: Sp.: **Encinar**.

Ende German: topographic name for someone living at the end of a settlement or street, from MHG *ende* (OHG *enti*).

Vars.: **Endemann**; **Amend(e)**, **Mende**.

Endecott English (Devon): topographic name for someone who lived 'at the end of the cottages', from ME, OE *ende* end + *cot* cottage. One locality so named is *Endicott* in Cadbury, Devon; another is now called *Youngcott*, in Milton Abbot.

Vars.: **Endicott**, **Endacott**.

Enderby English: habitation name from places in Leics. and Lincs., so called from the ON personal name *Eindriði* (composed of the elements *ein* one, sole + *ræði* ruler) + ON *býr* farm, settlement.

Var.: **Endersby**.

Enderl *see* ANDREW

Endlich Jewish (Ashkenazic): from mod. Ger. *endlich* finally, at last; presumably a nickname based on some now irrecoverable incident.

Endricci *see* HENRY

Enevoldsen *see* EINOLD

Enfantin *see* INFANTE

Eng Swedish: ornamental name from Swed. *äng* meadow (ON *eng*), in some cases perhaps chosen as a topographic name by someone who lived beside a meadow. This is one of the many Swedish surnames that were coined in the 19th cent. from vocab. words denoting aspects of the countryside, and which were also used more or less arbitrarily to form compound surnames.

Vars.: **Engh**, **Engman**.

Cpds: **Engberg** ('meadow hill'); **Engblom** ('meadow flower'); **Engborg** ('meadow town'); **Engdahl** ('meadow valley'); **Engholm** ('meadow island'); **Englund** ('meadow grove'); **Engqvist** ('meadow twig'); **Engstrand** ('meadow shore'); **Engström**, **Ångström** ('meadow river'); **Engwall**, **Engvall** ('meadow slope').

Engel 1. German and Dutch: from a short form of various Gmc personal names (cf., e.g., ENGELBERT and ENGELHARD). A number of different elements have fallen together in *Engel*-, mainly *Angel* Angle and *Ingal*, extended form of *Ing*, name of a Gmc god or folk hero. The *Angles* were a Gmc tribe who invaded E and N Britain in the 5th–6th cents. and gave their name to *England* (OE *Englaland*). Cf. ENGLISH. Other elements present in *Engel*- are an extension of *Ang* 'Spike' and, in later names, the Christian *angel* (see below and at ANGEL). **2.** German and Dutch: nickname for a remarkably good or kind person, from Ger. *Engel* angel (MHG *engel*, L *angelus*, from Gk *angelos* messenger). In some cases it may have originated as a house name, from a house bearing the sign of an angel.

See also ANGEL. **3.** Jewish (Ashkenazic): ornamental name from the Ger. vocab. word *Engel* angel (see 2).

Dims. (of 1): Low Ger.: **Engleke, Eng(e)lmann**. Fris.: **Engesma**.

Patrs. (from 1): Ger.: **Engels, Engler, Engling**. Flem.: **Engels, Ingels, Engelen**. Du.: **Engels**. (From 3): Jewish (E Ashkenazic): **Engelowitch**.

Patrs. (from dims. of 1): Low Ger.: **Engelken, Engelking**. (From 3): Jewish: **Engelchin** (altered form of the Ger. dim. vocab. word *Engelchen* 'little angel' under the influence of the Slavic possessive suffix -*in*).

Cpds (of 3): Jewish: **Engel(s)berg** ('angel('s) hill'); **Engel(s)man(n)** ('angel('s) man or husband'); **Engelmayer** ('angel steward'); **Engelrad** ('angel wheel'); **Engelsrath** ('angel's counsel'); **Engelstein** ('angel stone').

Engelbert English, French, and Low German: from a Gmc personal name composed of the elements *engel* (see ENGEL) + *berht* bright, famous. The widespread popularity of the name in France during the Middle Ages was largely a result of the fact that it had been borne by a son-in-law of Charlemagne; in the Rhineland it was more often given in memory of an early medieval martyr of this name, who had been bishop of Cologne (1216–25).

Vars.: Eng.: **Englebert**. Fr.: **Englebert, Englibert, Enjalbert, Enjeubert; Anglebert, Angilbert; Langlebert**. Low Ger.: **Engelbrett**.

Patrs.: Ger.: **Engelbrecher**. Low Ger.: **Engelbertz** (Rhineland).

Engelhard English, German, and Dutch: from a Gmc personal name composed of the elements *engel* (see ENGEL) + *hard* brave, hardy, strong. The personal name was introduced into England by the Normans.

Vars.: Ger.: **Engelhar(d)t**.

Patr.: Low Ger.: **Englerding**.

Englefield English: habitation name from *Englefield* Green in Surrey, so called from the OE personal name *Ingweald* (composed of the elements *Ing*, a divine name (see ING) + *weald* rule) + OE *feld* pasture, open country; or from *Englefield* in Berks., which is named as the 'open land (OE *feld*) of the Angles' (see ENGEL 1).

English 1. English: from OE *Englisc*. The word had originally distinguished Angles (see ENGEL) from Saxons and other Gmc peoples in the Brit. Isles, but by the time surnames were being acquired it no longer had this meaning. Its frequency as an Eng. surname is somewhat surprising. It may have been commonly used in the early Middle Ages as a distinguishing epithet for an Anglo-Saxon in areas where the culture was not predominantly English—for example the Danelaw area, Scotland, and parts of Wales—or as a distinguishing name after 1066 for a non-Norman in the regions of most intensive Norman settlement. However, explicit evidence for these assumptions is lacking, and at the present day the surname is fairly evenly distributed throughout the country. **2.** Irish: see GOLIGHTLY.

Vars. (of 1): **Inglis(h)** (Scotland); **Angliss, Angless, Anglish** (from OF *angleis*); **England**.

Dims. (of 1): Fr.: **Lenglin(ey); Anglichaud**.

Pej. (of 1): Fr.: **Lenglard**.

Engwers *see* INGER

Enion *see* ONION

Enjalbert *see* ENGELBERT

Enlund *see* EHN

Ennion *see* ONION

Enock English: from the medieval given name *Enock* (Gk *Enōkh*, from Hebr. *Chanoch* 'Dedicated'). This was the name borne in the Bible by the eldest son of Cain (Gen. 4: 17) and by the father of Methuselah, who was said to have 'walked with God' (Gen. 5: 22). The surname is relatively common in Wales, but much rarer in England, where it is concentrated on the Warwicks./Oxon. border and probably has a unitary origin.

Var.: **Enoch** (mainly Welsh; a learned form apparently not recorded before the 18th cent.).

Patrs.: Swed.: **Eno(c)ksson, Enochsson**. Jewish (E Ashkenazic): **Hanochov, Hanochow, Hanokhov**.

Enqvist *see* EHN

Enrietto *see* HENRY

Enright Irish: Anglicized form of the Gael. byname *Indreachtach* 'Attacker'.

Ensle *see* ANSELL

Ensor English: habitation name from *Edensor* in Derbys., which derives its name from the gen. case of the OE personal name *Ēadhūn* (see EDEN 1) + OE *ofer* ridge.

Enström *see* EHN

Enterl *see* ANDREW

Entwistle English: habitation name from the village of *Entwisle* in Lancs., so called from OE *henna* (water) hen or *ened* duck + *twisla* tongue of land in a river fork.

Vars.: **Entwisle, Entissle, Entwhistle**.

Eötvös Hungarian: occupational name for a goldsmith, Hung. *ötvös*. The surname retains an older spelling of the word.

Var.: **Ötvös**.

Epelbaum *see* APPLE

Ephron *see* EFRON

Épine French: topographic name for someone who lived by a prominent thorn-bush, OF *espine* (L *spina*), or in an area overgrown with such bushes. Occasionally the name may derive from the same word used in a transferred sense of the crest or ridge of a hill.

Vars.: **Lépine, Delépine**.

Dims.: Fr.: **Espinel, Espinet**. It.: **Spinelli, Spin(i)ello, Spinella, Spinetti, Spinozzi**. Sp.: **Espínola**. Port.: **Espínola, Spínola**.

Aug.: Sp.: **Espinazo**.

Collectives: Fr.: **Espinay, Épinay, Épinoy, Lépinay**. Sp.: **Espinal, Espinar; Espinosa**. Cat.: **Espinós, Espinosa**. Port.: **Espinheira, Espinosa**.

Epp *see* EGGEBRECHT

Epple *see* EVERARD

Epps *see* APPS

Eppstein *see* EPSTEIN

Epstein German and Jewish (Ashkenazic): habitation name, perhaps from *Eppstein* in Bavaria, so called from OHG *ebur* wild boar + *stein* stone.

Vars.: Jewish: **Eppstein**, **Ebstein**; **Epsztejn**, **Epsztajn** (Pol. spellings).

Epsztajn *see* EPSTEIN

Erasmus German: from the personal name (a Latinized form of Gk *erasmos* loved, a deriv. of *erān* to love) borne by a rather obscure early Christian saint who was numbered among the 'fourteen holy helpers' and regarded as the patron of turners and seamen. The fame of the great Humanist scholar Desiderius Erasmus of Rotterdam (?1466–1536) enhanced the popularity of the given name, but not in time to have much effect on the frequency of the surname.

Vars.: **Rasmus** (aphetic), **Asmus**; **Eras**.

Dims.: Ger.: **Rasem**, **Asam**, **Asum**. Low Ger.: **Rassmann**, **Assmann**. Flem., Du.: **Raes**, **Raskin**.

Patrs.: Ger.: **Erasmi** (Latinized); **Asmes(en)**. Low Ger.: **Asmussen**. Dan., Norw.: **Rasmussen**, **Asmussen**.

Erbst *see* HERBST

Erenberg *see* EHRMANN

Erhard German: from a Gmc personal name composed of the elements *ēra* honour (cf. EHRLICH) + *hard* brave, hardy, strong. This Ger. surname has also been adopted by Ashkenazic Jews.

Vars.: **Erhar(d)t**.

Erichs *see* HERRICK

Erlanger German and Jewish (Ashkenazic): habitation name from *Erlangen* in Bavaria, which derives its name from an obscure element *er*, according to Bahlow a prehistoric word for water + the dial. term *wang* water meadow (cf. FEUCHTWANGER and FURTWANGER).

Erleigh *see* EARLY

Erlich *see* EHRLICH

Ermgard German: from a Gmc female personal name composed of the elements *erm(en)* whole, entire + *gard* enclosure, garden.

Vars.: **Irm(in)gard**, **Armgardt**, **Harmgardt**.

Dims.: Fr.: **Mengardon**, **Mengarduque**; **Ermenjon**; **Menjon**, **Mingeon**.

Ermin *see* ARMIN

Ernaud French: hypercorrected form of *Arnaud* (see ARNOLD). Since the pronunciation of *-er-* as *-ar-* in words like *personne* came to be regarded as vulgar, there was a tendency for names containing *-ar-* to receive a 'refined' pronunciation with *-er-*.

Vars.: **Ernau(l)**, **Ernout**.

Erni *see* ARNOLD

Ernlib *see* EHRMANN

Ernmonger *see* IRONMONGER

Ernst 1. German and Dutch: from the Gmc byname *Ernust* 'Seriousness', 'Firmness', or a nickname from

MHG *ern(e)st* seriousness, battle. 2. Jewish (Ashkenazic): nickname from mod. Ger. *ernst* earnest, serious.

Vars. (of 1): **Ernest**. (Of 2): **Ernster** (an inflected form of the Ger. adjective).

Patr.: Ger.: **Ernsting**.

Erpel Low German: 1. nickname from MLG *erpel* drake (apparently from the OSax. byname *Erpo* 'Dark'; cf. the dial. terms *gäret* (see GARRETT) and *gaber* (see GABRIEL) for the goose), or metonymic occupational name for someone responsible for tending ducks. 2. habitation name from a place in the Rhineland called *Erpel*, according to Bahlow a name of pre-Gmc origin.

Errichelli *see* HENRY

Erricker *see* EARWAKER

Errington English: habitation name from a place in Northumb., so called from a Brit. river name apparently akin to W *arian* silvery, bright + OE *tūn* enclosure, settlement.

Erskine Scots: habitation name from a place on the south bank of the Clyde outside Glasgow, first recorded in 1225 in the form *Erskin*. Other early spellings vary (1227 *Yrskin*; 1262 *Ireskin*; 1300 *Harskin, Irschen*). The etymology is not clear: it may be from Celt. elements cogn. with W *ir* green + *esgyn* to ascend.

Erszman *see* HIRSCH

Ertel *see* ORT

Ervin *see* IRVINE

Erwin *see* IRVINE

Esburnham *see* ASHBURNHAM

Escalada Spanish: habitation name from a place in the province of Burgos. The placename is probably a deriv. of *escala* ladder (see ESCHELLE), referring to a terraced slope.

Eschelle French: from OF *eschelle* ladder (L *scāla*, a deriv. of *scandere* to climb). This was probably a topographic name for a dweller by a terraced slope or in a house with an exterior staircase or ladder; perhaps also a metonymic occupational name for a maker or seller of ladders or a nickname for the unique possessor of one in a small village.

Vars.: **Échelle**; **Deschelle**, **Déchelle**; **Leschelle**, **Léchelle**; **Echal(l)ier**, **Echal(l)ié**.

Dims.: Fr.: **Eschalette**, **Eschalotte**; **Déchelette**.

Eschels *see* ASHKETTLE

Escobar Spanish: topographic name for someone who lived in a place overgrown with broom (LL *scopāre*, from *scopa* broom), or habitation name from any of the numerous villages, for example in Murcia, Segovia, and León, named with this word.

Var.: **Escobedo**.

Escoda Catalan: metonymic occupational name for a stone mason, from OCat. *escoda* hammer used in dressing stone (of uncertain origin, perhaps from L *excūdere* to hammer into shape).

Escoffier Provençal: occupational name for a leather-worker or tanner, or for a slaughterman, from an agent deriv. of the OProv. verb *escofia*, used both of dressing leather and of slaughtering animals (from L *exconficere* to finish off).

Vars.: **Escofier**, **Escofié**.

Escorial Spanish: topographic name for someone who lived near a refuse tip or slag heap, OSp. *escorial* (LL *scoriāle*, a deriv. of *scoria* refuse, slag). This was also the name of several villages, including *El Escorial* near Madrid, the site of the royal palace and monastery built by Philip II (1527–98); the surname may be a habitation name from any of these.

Esh *see* ASH

Esherwood *see* ISHERWOOD

Eskenazi *see* ASHKENAZI

Esmond *see* EASTMAN

Espada Spanish, Catalan, and Portuguese: metonymic occupational name for an armourer or a swordsman, from Sp., OCat., Port. *espada* sword (LL *spatha*, from Gk *spathē*, originally denoting a broad, two-edged sword without a point).

Vars.: Sp.: **Espadas**; **Espadero**. Cat.: **Espasa**; **Espadater**, **Espadaté**.

Dims.: It.: **Spadelli**, **Spad(ol)ini**, **Spadotto**, **Spaduzza**, **Spatuzza**, **Spaduzzi**, **Spaducci**.

Augs.: It.: **Spadon(i)**, **Spatoni**.

Pej.: It.: **Spadazzi**.

Espinal *see* ÉPINE

Esposito Italian: surname commonly denoting a foundling, meaning literally 'exposed' (L *expositus*, past part. of *expōnere* to place outside). At the present day this is the commonest surname in Naples.

Vars.: **Espos(u)to**, **Espos(t)i**, **Sposito**.

Esquivel Spanish form of Basque **Aizkibel**: of uncertain origin, possibly a topographic name composed of the Basque elements *aitz* rock, crag + *gibel* rear, back.

Essart French: topographic name for someone who lived in a clearing, OF *essart* (LL *exsartum*, past part. of *exsarire* to weed out, grub up).

Vars.: **Essert** (hypercorrected); **Issart(e)**, **Issert**; **Lessart**, **Lessard**; **Desessarts**, **Desessard**; **Essartier**, **Essertier**.

Dims.: **Essertel**; **Issartel**, **Issarteaux**.

Essex English: regional name for someone from the county of Essex, which is so called from OE *ēast* EAST + *Seaxe* Saxons. The surname is now particularly common in Birmingham.

Esslin *see* ANSELL

Esson *see* EADE

Estagnol *see* ETANG

Este Italian: habitation name from a place in Venetia, originally named in L as *Ateste*. The surname is common in Padua and Venice, and is that of a leading noble family.

Var.: **D'Este**.

Estébanez *see* STEPHEN

Esterbrook *see* EASTERBROOK

Esterházy Hungarian (partly Jewish): from *szerhás* master roofer + *ház* house, the name of the family's original estate in Csallóköz (cf. Old Church Slavonic *strecha* roof).

Estersohn Jewish (Ashkenazic): metr. from the Yid. female given name *Ester* Esther, from Hebr. *Ester*, the name borne in the Bible by a Jewish captive of the Persian King Ahasuerus. According to the biblical story, she became his favourite concubine and managed to save the Jews of Persia from the machinations of the royal counsellor Haman.

Vars.: **Esterson**; **Est(e)rin** (E Ashkenazic).

Dim.: **Esterkin** (E Ashkenazic).

Estival French: **1.** topographic name for a dweller by a patch of summer pasture, OF *estival* (L *aestivāle*, a deriv. of *aestas* summer), or habitation name from one of the several villages named with this word. **2.** metonymic occupational name for a maker of boots and shoes, from OF *estival* (summer) shoe, light boot (of the same origin as 1).

Vars.: **Estivau(x)**.

Dim.: Fr.: **Estivalet**.

Estourneau *see* ÉTOURNEAU

Estreicher *see* OISTRAKH

Etang French: topographic name for someone who lived near a pond or pool, OF *estang* (L *stagnum* standing water, a deriv. of *stāre* to stand).

Vars.: **Esta(i)ng**; **Destan**, **Destaing**, **Détang**, **Delétang**.

Dim.: **Estagnol**.

Etchells English: habitation name from any of various minor places in N England named with the OE term *ēcels* piece of land added to an estate (a deriv. of *ēcan* to increase).

Vars.: **Neachell** (from ME *atten eachel*); **Nechells** (now the name of a district of Birmingham).

Etheridge *see* EDRICH

Etherington *see* HETHERINGTON

Étiennet *see* STEPHEN

Étourneau French: nickname for a sprightly person, or metonymic occupational name for a bird-catcher, from OF *estournel* starling (LL *sturnellus*, a dim. form of class. L *sturnus*).

Vars.: **Étournaud**, **Estourneau**, **Estournel**, **Létourneau**.

Etzel *see* ALBERT

Eugène French: from the personal name (L *Eugenius*, from Gk *Eugenios* 'Well-born', 'Noble') borne by a 3rd-cent. bishop and martyr, who gave the given name some currency during the Middle Ages.

Euler German and Jewish (Ashkenazic): occupational name for a potter, most common in the Rhineland and Hesse, Ger. *Euler (MHG ūl(n)ære*, an agent deriv. of the dial. word *ūl, aul* pot, from L *olla*).

Vars.: Ger.: **Eulner**; **Aul(n)er**.

Eunson *see* EWAN

Euren *see* UREN

Eusébio Portuguese: from the personal name (Gk *Eusebios* 'Revered', from *eu-* good, well + *sebesthai* to honour, respect) borne by a large number of early saints, including a 5th-cent. friend of Jerome popularly credited with the foundation of the monastery of Guadalupe. A 4th-cent. bishop of Samosata in Syria who bore the same name is venerated in the Orthodox Church.
Dims.: Ukr.: **Ovsienko**. Pol.: **Owsik, Owsiejczyk**.
Patrs.: Russ.: **Yevseev, Yevsenov, Ovseev, Avseev**.
Patrs. (from dims.): Russ.: **Yevsikov, Yevsyunin, Yevsyutin**.

Eustace *see* STACE

Eva *see* EVE

Evan 1. Welsh: from the given name *Ifan, Evan* JOHN. 2. Scots: var. of EWAN. 3. Jewish: of unknown origin.
Vars. (of 1): **Heavan, Heaven**.
Patrs. (from 1): Welsh: **Evans, Evens, Evance; Ifans, Ivin(g)s; Avans; Heavans, Heavens**; BEVAN.

Evdakov *see* YEVDOKIMOV

Eve English: from the rare medieval female given name *Eve, Eva* (from Hebr. *Chava*, of uncertain origin, perhaps originally meaning 'Serpent' or akin to *chaya* to live; cf. HYAM). This was, according to the Book of Genesis, the name of the first woman, and in some cases the name may have been acquired by someone (invariably a man) who had played the part in a drama dealing with the Creation. See also KHAVKE.
Var.: **Eva**.
Dims.: **Evett, Evatt, Evitt**.
Metrs.: **E(a)ves; Eve(r)son, Evason, Evison**.
Metrs. (from dims.): **Evetts, Evitts**.

Evelegh English: habitation name from a lost place in Broad Clyst, Devon, so called from OE *ifig* ivy + *lēah* wood, clearing.

Evelyn English: from the ME, OF female given name *Aveline*, a double dim. of the Gmc personal name *Avo*, from the element *avi*, perhaps meaning 'desired, wished for'.
Vars.: **Aveline, Aveling**.
Metr.: Du.: **Eveleens**.

Evens *see* EVAN

Evéquot *see* BISHOP

Everard English: from a Gmc personal name composed of the elements *eber* wild boar + *hard* brave, hardy, strong. The surname was at first found mainly in E Anglia (still one of the principal locations of the var. *Everett*), which was an area of heavy Norman and Breton settlement after the Conquest. This suggests that the personal name may be

of Continental (Norman) origin, but it is also possible that it swallowed up an unattested OE cogn., **Eoforheard*.
Vars.: **Evered, Everid, Everett, Everitt, Everatt**.
Dims.: Ger.: **Ebe, Ebi, Eby, Eble, Eb(er)lein; Eberle, Epple** (Swabia); **Eberl** (Bavaria). Low Ger.: **Ebermann, Evermann, Ewermann**.
Patrs.: Low Ger.: **Ebers, Evers, Ewers; Eber(t)z, Evertz, Effertz** (Rhineland); **Everding**. Flem.: **Everaerts, Evers; Everdey** (Latinized). Du.: **Ever(t)s**.
Patrs. (from dims.): Ger.: **Ebler, Everling**. Low Ger.: **Eveking**.

Everest English (Norman): habitation name from *Evreux* in Eure, Normandy, so called from having apparently been the capital of the *Eburovices*, a Gaul. tribe. This tribal name appears in turn to derive from the river name *Ebura* (now the *Eure*), which may perhaps be akin to a Celt. word for the yew tree (cf. IVE and YORK).
Vars.: **Everist, Everix, Everiss, Evreux**; DEVEREUX.

Everill English: from the OE female personal name *Eoforhild*, composed of the elements *eofor* wild boar + *hild* battle. The surname is chiefly found in the W Midlands.

Everwin *see* IRVINE

Evison *see* EVE

Evreux *see* EVEREST

Evron *see* EFRON

Evstafyev *see* OSTAPOV

Ewald Low German: from a Gmc personal name composed of the elements *ēo* law, custom, right (a rare element in personal names, found mostly in OSax.) + *wald* rule. This name was borne in the 7th cent. by two brothers (distinguished as 'Ewald the White' and 'Ewald the Black') who were missionaries in N Germany. They became the patron saints of Cologne and Westphalia, and so contributed to the popularity of the given name (and hence the eventual frequency of the surname) in these areas.
Vars.: **Ehwalt, Ewold**.
Patrs.: **Ewols(en)**.

Ewan Scots: Anglicized form of the Gael. personal name *Eògann*. This is now generally acknowledged to be a Gael. form of L *Eugenius* (see EUGÈNE), but it was formerly widely believed to be a form of JOHN, and attempts have also been made to derive it from a proto-Celt. name meaning 'born of the yew'.
Vars.: EWEN, **Ewin(g), Hewin, Yewen**, EVAN.
Patrs.: Sc.: **Ewens, Ewin(g)s, Hewins, Youens, Youings; Eunson; McEwan, McEwen, McEwing** (Gael. **Mac Eòghainn**). Ir.: **McKeo(w)n, McCune, McCown, McCone, McGeown, McGuone, Keown**, COWAN.

Ewart English and Scots: 1. from *Ewart*, a Norman form of the given name EDWARD. 2. occupational name for a shepherd, from ME *ewehirde*, from OE *eowu* ewe + *hierde* herdsman (see HEARD). 3. habitation name from a place in Northumb., so called from OE *ēa* river + *worð* enclosure; it is enclosed on three sides by the rivers Glen and Till.
Vars. (of 2): **Yeoward, Yeowart, Youat(t)**, HOWARD.

Ewen 1. Scots: var. of EWAN. **2.** Jewish (Israeli): from Hebr. *even* stone, a translation of the surname *Stein* (see STONE) or any of its compounds.

Ewens see EWAN

Ewer English: occupational name for a transporter or server of water, ME *ewer* (ONF *evier*, OF *aiguier*, from L *aquārius*, a deriv. of *aqua* water). There has been considerable confusion with URE.
Vars.: **Lewer** (with fused ANF def. art.).
Patr.: **Ewers**.

Eweren see UREN

Ewermann see EVERARD

Ewin see EWAN

Ewold see EWALD

Exley English: habitation name from a place in W Yorks., near Halifax, so called from a Brit. *ecclēsia* name meaning 'church' (see ECCLES) + OE *lēah* clearing, wood. The surname is still most common in W Yorks.

Eydel see EITEL

Eyer see AYER

Eyles see ISLES

Eynon see ONION

Eyre see AYER

Eytel see EITEL

Eythner see AGGIS

Eyton see EATON

Ezekiel Jewish: from the Hebr. given name *Yechezkel* 'God will strengthen'.
Vars.: **Yechezkiel**, **Yechesk(i)el**, **Jecheskel**; **Jechezkieli**, **Yecheskely**, **Yecheskiely** (with the Hebr. suffix -*i*); **Heskel**, **Haskel(l)**, **Ha(t)zkel** (Ashkenazic, from the Yid. forms *Kheskl*, *Khatskl*).
Patrs.: (Ashkenazic): **Haskelevic**, **Haskilewitz**, **Hazkelevitch**, **Hazkelevitz**, **Chaskelovic**. (E Ashkenazic): **Yecheskelov**.

Ezquerra Basque: nickname for a left-handed person, from *ezker* left(-handed) + the def. art. -*a*. This term has been taken into the other languages of the Iberian Peninsula (see also IZQUIERDO) in place of the Romance descendants of L *laevus* and *sinister*, since the left side was felt to be ill-omened and the words themselves consequently became taboo.
Var.: **Ezquerro**.

F

Faasen *see* BONIFACE

Fabbretti *see* FÈVRE

Fabian 1. English, French, Polish, Austrian, and Venetian: from a given name (L *Fabiānus*, a deriv. of *Fabius*, a Roman family name perhaps derived from *faba* bean; cf. FAVIER). The given name achieved some popularity in the Middle Ages as having been borne by a 3rd-cent. pope and saint. **2.** Jewish: adoption of the non-Jewish surname under the influence of the Yid. male given name *Fayvish* (see FAIVISH).

Vars.: Fr.: **Fabien**. Pol.: **Fabijan, Fabi(j)ański, Fabicki; Pabi(a)n, Pabiański, Pabich**. Ger.: **Fabigan, Pfabi(g)an, Fabion, Fobian**. It.: **Fabjan; Fabbiano, Fab(b)iani**.

Dims.: Pol.: **Fabi(j)ańczyk, Pabi(j)ańczyk, Pabimak**. Ger.: **Fabel** (also Jewish); **Fabig, Fabisch, Fabianke, Fobianke, Fabianek** (of Slav. origin).

Patrs.: Pol.: **Fabi(j)anowicz; Pabisiak**.

Habitation name: Pol.: **Fabiszewski**.

Fabrikant Jewish (Ashkenazic): occupational name for a factory owner or manufacturer of any type of goods, from Russ. *fabrikant* manufacturer, Ger. *Fabrikant* (from L *fabricans*, gen. *fabricantis*, pres. part. of *fabricāre* to make, a deriv. of *faber*; see FÈVRE).

Vars.: **Fabricant; Fabrykant** (Pol. spelling).

Fabrizio Italian: from the medieval given name *Fabrizio* (L *Fabrīcius*, a Roman family name of unknown, possibly Etruscan, etymology). Already in the Roman period the name was associated by folk etymology with *faber* (see FÈVRE) and L forms of the name were extensively used in the late Middle Ages as equivalents of the various vernacular terms denoting craftsmen.

Vars.: **Fabrizi, Fab(b)rizzi, Fabrici**.

Faccini *see* BONIFACE

Faceto *see* FAGE

Facey *see* VAISEY

Fach *see* WENZEL

Facon *see* FALCON

Fadeev *see* TADIÉ

Fae *see* FAGE

Faers *see* FAIR

Fagan Irish: of uncertain origin. The Gael. form is Ó **Faodhagáin**, but a personal name **Faodhagán* is not known, and it may be a Gaelicized version of a surname of Norman origin.

Fage 1. French: topographic name for someone who lived by a beech tree or beech wood, from OF *fage* beech (LL *fāgea (arbor)*, a deriv. of class. L *fāgus*). **2.** English: nick-

name for a flatterer, from ME *fage* coaxing, flattery, deception (of unknown origin).

Vars. (of 1): **Fages, Laf(f)age; Le Faou** (Brittany).

Dims. (of 1): Fr.: **Faget(te), Lafagette, Fageau, Fajon**. Prov.: **Fayet(te), Lafayette, Fayol(le), Fayot, Fayon, Fayel, Feyel, Feyeux, Fo(u)et, Dufayel, Dufayet**. It.: **Faggin(i), Faggioli, Faggiola, Faggiotto, Fagotti, Fagotto**.

Augs. (of 1): It.: **Faggion(i), Fag(i)one**.

Pejs. (of 1): Fr.: **Fajard**. Prov.: **Fayard, Dufayard**. Sp.: **Fajardo** (Galicia).

Collectives (of 1): It.: **Faet(t)o, Faeti, Faito** (S Italy); **Faedi, Faedo, Faeta, Fae** (N Italy); **Faceto** (Parma).

Fagerberg *see* FAIR

Fagg English (Kent): of uncertain origin, perhaps a var. of FAGE 2 or a nickname from either of two homonymous ME words *fagge*. One apparently denotes a fault in the weave of a piece of cloth, the other is the name of a type of fish; both are attested in OED in only single passages.

Vars.: **Fagge; Vagg**.

Patr.: **Vaggs**.

Fagin *see* FEIGE

Fagot French: metonymic occupational name for a gatherer or seller of firewood, from OF *fagot* bundle of firewood (of uncertain origin, perhaps a distant cogn. of Gk *phakelos* bundle).

Vars.: **Faguet, Fagon**.

Faherty Irish: Anglicized form of Gael. Ó **Fathartaigh** 'descendant of *Fathartach*', a personal name (with a var. *Faghartach*) of unknown meaning.

Fahy Irish: Anglicized form of Gael. Ó **Fathaigh** 'descendant of *Fathach*', a personal name probably derived from *fothadh* base, foundation.

Vars.: **O'Fahy, O'Fa(u)ghy, O'Faye, Fahey, Faughy**, FAY, FOY; GREEN (a result of erroneous association with *faithche* lawn).

Faier *see* FAYERMAN

Faierstein *see* FEUERSTEIN

Faiertag Jewish (Ashkenazic): ornamental name from mod. Ger. *Feiertag* holiday.

Failes English (mainly Cambs.): of uncertain origin, possibly a cogn. of FAILLE 3, from ME *fail(l)e* default, or a var. of FALLAS.

Vars.: **Fails, Fales**.

Faille French: **1.** metonymic occupational name for a maker or seller of a kind of silk material known in OF as *faille* (MHG *pfelle*, from L *palliōlum*, a type of light garment). **2.** metonymic occupational name for a torch-bearer, from OF *faille* torch (LL *facilla*, a dim. of class. L *fax*, gen. *facis*). **3.** nickname for an inept or luckless individual, from

OF *faille* fault, failing, mistake (a deriv. of *faillir* to fail, miss, be wanting, L *fallere* to deceive, disappoint).
Dims.: Fr.: **Faillon**, **Faillot**.

Fainan *see* FINN

Fair English: nickname meaning 'beautiful', from OE *fæger* fair, lovely. The word was also occasionally used as a given name in the Middle Ages, and applied to both men and women.
Vars.: **Faire**, **Fayre**, **Fayer**, **Feyer**, **Phair**, **Phayre**.
Patrs.: **Fair(e)s**, **Fa(i)ers**, **F(a)yers**.
Cpds (ornamental): Swed.: **Fagerberg** ('lovely hill'); **Fagerlund** ('lovely grove'); **Fagerström** ('lovely river').

Fairbairn N English and Scots: probably a nickname from Northern ME *fair* lovely (see FAIR) + *bairn* child (see BARNES 2); cf. FAIRCHILD. Black, however, suggests that it is probably a var. of FREEBORN.
Patrs.: **Fairba(i)rns**.

Fairbank English: habitation name from any of various minor places so called. Most get their names from ME *fair* lovely (see FAIR) + *bank* bank, hill (see BANKS), but in some cases the first elements may derive from OE *fearn* FERN.
Var.: **Fairbanks**.

Fairbrother English: term of relationship, probably meaning 'brother of a FAIR person' or else referring to the better-looking of a pair of brothers. It is quite a common name, and may also in part be derived from *father's brother*, i.e. uncle; cf. EAME.
Vars.: **Far(e)brother**, **Fayerbrother**.

Fairburn 1. English: habitation name from *Fairburn* in Cleveland or *Fairbourne* in Kent, so called from OE *fearn* FERN + *burna* stream (see BOURNE). 2. Scots: habitation name from a place in the former county of Ross and Cromarty, now part of Highland region, originally named with the Gael. elements *far braoin* 'over the wet place', but later altered by folk etymology.
Vars.: **Fairbourn(e)**, **Fairburne**.

Fairchild S English: nickname from ME *fair* lovely (see FAIR) + *child* CHILD; cf. FAIRBAIRN.

Fairclough English (Lancs.): topographical name from ME *fair* lovely (see FAIR) + *cloh* ravine (see CLOUGH), or habitation name from an unidentified place so called.
Vars.: **Faircloth**, **Fairtlough**, **Faircliff(e)**, **Featley**.

Fairfax English: nickname for someone with beautiful long hair, from OE *fæger* lovely + *feax* hair, tresses. This was a common descriptive phrase in ME; the alliterative poem 'Sir Gawain and the Green Knight' refers to 'fair fanning fax' encircling the shoulders of the doughty warrior.

Fairgrieve Scots: of uncertain origin. It may be a combination of the nickname FAIR + the occupational name GRIEVE, but if so both parts may have been altered by folk etymology. Perhaps it is a habitation name, with unexplained variation in the vowel of the second element, from an unidentified place named with the OE elements

fōr pig + *grāf* grove, i.e. a wood where pigs were fed on mast.
Vars.: **Forgrieve**, **Forgrave**.

Fairhead English (Norfolk): nickname from ME *fair* lovely (see FAIR) + *heved* head (OE *hēafod*) or *hood* hood (OE *hōd*).

Fairhurst English (Lancs.): habitation name from a hamlet near Parbold, not far from Wigan, so called from OE *fæger* lovely (see FAIR) + *hyrst* wooded hill (see HURST).
Var.: **Fairest**.

Fairlamb English (said by Reaney to be found in Manchester; also found in Newcastle): ostensibly a nickname from OE *fæger* lovely (see FAIR) + *lamb* LAMB, perhaps from frequent use of this affectionate form of address. More probably, it is a habitation name, altered by folk etymology, from *Farlam* in Cumb., so called from OE *fearn* FERN + the dat. pl. of *lēah* wood, clearing.
Vars.: **Farlam**, **Fairlem**.

Fairley *see* FARLEY

Fairlie Scots: habitation name from a place on the Firth of Clyde, so called from OE *fæger* lovely (see FAIR) + *lēah* wood, clearing.
Vars.: **Fairley** (see also FARLEY); **Fairless** (Northumb.).

Fairman 1. English: occupational name for the servant of a man named FAIR, or a nickname for a handsome man (see FAIR). 2. Jewish (Ashkenazic): presumably an Anglicization of one or more like-sounding Jewish surnames, notably *Feuerman* (see FEUER).
Vars.: **Fierman**, **Fayerman**, **Fireman**. See also FARMAN.

Fairn *see* FERN

Fairnie *see* FERNIE

Fairweather English and Scots: nickname for a person with a sunny temperament; cf. MERRYWEATHER. According to a family tradition, a Scots family of Highland origin assumed this name on migrating southwards, in punning allusion to Job 37: 22, 'Fair weather cometh out of the north'.
Var.: **Fareweather**.

Fairy *see* FEARY

Faist German: nickname for a stout person, from MHG *veiz(e)t* fat, corpulent (OHG *feizit*), a word which was gradually replaced in all dialects of Ger. by the originally Low Ger. FETT or by the unrelated *dick* (cogn. with Eng. *thick*). The vocab. word *feist* survives in mod. Ger. meaning 'corpulent', and this lies behind Jewish cogn.
Vars.: **Feist**, **Feest**, **Fehst**.
Dims.: Ger.: **Faistle** (Swabia); **Faistl** (Bavaria).

Faith English: nickname for a trustworthy person, from ME *fe(i)th* faithfulness, loyalty (OF *feid, feit*, from L *fides*).
Vars.: **Faithful(l)** (from the adj.).

Faito *see* FAGE

Faivish Jewish (Ashkenazic): from the Yid. male given name *Fayvish*, apparently from Gk *Phoebus*, the name of the sun god. This seems to have been used as a trans.

equivalent of Hebr. *Shimshon* (see SAMSON). Alternatively, the Yid. name may derive from LL *Vivus* 'Living', used as a trans. equivalent of Hebr. *Chayim* (see HYAM).

Vars.: **Faibis(h)**, **Faybish**, **Feibish**, **Feibus(c)h**.

Dims.: **Feivel**, **Feiwel**, **Feibel** (from the Yid. dim. given name *Fayvl*).

Patrs. (E Ashkenazic): **Faivisevitz**, **Faivuszevicz**, **Faivuschevitch**, **Fajwshewitz**, **Favshevitz**, **Feibischoff**, **Feibushewitz**.

Patrs. (from dims.): **Faivelson**, **Feivelson**; **Fajwlewicz**, **Fajwlewich**, **Feivlovitz**, **Feiwlowicz**, **Feiwlewicz**, **Feibelovitz** (E Ashkenazic).

Faivre see FÈVRE

Fajard see FAGE

Fajer see FAYERMAN

Fajeraizen Jewish (E Ashkenazic): apparently an ornamental name taken by a blacksmith, from Yid. *fayer* fire + *ayzn* iron.

Fajgenblat see FEIGE

Fajn see FEIN

Fajwlewich see FAIVISH

Fake see FAULKES

Falameev see BARTHOLOMEW

Falchetti see FAULKES

Falcon English: metonymic occupational name for a falconer (see FAULKNER), or nickname for someone thought to resemble a falcon, from ME, OF *faucon, falcun* falcon (L *falco*, gen. *falcōnis*). In a few cases, it may also have been a metonymic occupational name for a man who worked the 16th-cent. piece of artillery named after the bird of prey.

Vars.: **Fa(u)con**. See also FAULKNER.

Dims.: Fr.: **Falcon(n)et**, **Fauconnet**, **Fauconneau**. It.: **Falconetto**.

Augs.: Fr.: **Falcon(n)at**.

Patrs.: Jewish (E Ashkenazic): **Falkoff**, **Falkov(sky)**, **Falkovski**, **Falkowsky**, **Falkowicz**, **Falkowitz**, **Falkovitz**, **Falkovitch**, **Falkievich**.

Cpds.: Jewish (Ashkenazic, ornamental): **Falkenberg** ('falcon hill'); **Falkenflik** (-*flik* is of unknown origin); **Falkenstein** ('falcon stone').

Equiv. (not cogn.): Czech: SOKOL.

Falconar see FAULKNER

Fales see FAILES

Falkingham English (W Yorks.): apparently a habitation name from some place so called from OE *Falcingahām* 'homestead of the people of *Falca*' (a byname meaning 'Falcon'). This may be *Falkenham* in Suffolk, which appears in Domesday Book as *Faltenham*. It is of problematic etymology.

Fall English: topographic name for someone who lived by a clearing or a waterfall, ME *fall* (OE *(ge)feall*, a deriv. of *fealan* to fall).

Vars.: **Falle**, **Faul(l)**, **Fawle**.

Fallas English (Norman): 1. habitation name from *Falaise* in Calvados, birthplace of William the Conqueror. The place is so called from ONF *faleise* cliff (of Gmc origin; cf. FALL). 2. topographic name for someone who lived by a cliff, from the ANF vocab. word.

Vars.: **Fall(i)s**. See also FAILES.

Fallon 1. English: var. of FULLER. 2. Irish: Anglicized form of Gael. Ó *Fallamhain* 'descendant of *Fallamhan*', a byname meaning 'Leader' (from *follamhnas* supremacy).

Vars.: **O'Fallon**, **O'Fallo(w)ne**, **Fal(l)oon**; **Hallon** (Gael. Ó **Fhallamhain**).

Fallow English: topographic name for someone who lived by a patch of fallow land, ME *falwe* (OE *fealh*). The word was used both of land left uncultivated for a time to recover its fertility and of land recently brought into cultivation. 2. nickname for someone with tawny hair, from ME *fallow* yellow, tawny (OE *fealu*, early confused with *fealh* as the colour was understood as being that of exposed soil).

Vars. (of 1): **Fallows** (also borne by Ashkenazic Jews as an Anglicization of one or more like-sounding Jewish surnames); **Fallowes**.

Falvey see FEELY

Fanagan see FINN

Fancello see INFANTE

Fandrich see ANDREW

Fane 1. English: nickname from ME *fein, fayn, fane* glad, well disposed (OE *fægen*). The word seems also to have been occasionally used as a given name in the Middle Ages, and in some instances the surname may derive from this. 2. Welsh: nickname from *fain* slender.

Vars.: **Fayne**, **Va(y)ne**.

Patrs.: **Faynes**, **Va(i)nes**.

Fanier see FENIER

Fann see FENN

Fanner 1. English: occupational name for someone who winnowed corn or performed a similar process on crushed metalliferous rock, from an agent deriv. of ME *fan* fan, winnow (OE *fann*, from L *vannum*). 2. English: topographic name, a var. of FENN. 3. Jewish (Ashkenazic): presumably an Anglicization of one or more like-sounding Jewish surnames.

Vars.: **Vanner**, **Vannar**.

Fanon French: metonymic occupational name for a standard-bearer, from OF *fanon* flag (of Gmc origin, cf. GONFALONIERI). The word was also used by extension for a priest's maniple, and the surname may occasionally have been a nickname from this source.

Fanshaw see FEATHERSTONEHAUGH

Faraday see FEREDAY

Färber German and Jewish (Ashkenazic): occupational name for a dyer, Ger. *Färber*, an agent deriv. of MHG *varwe* colour (OHG *farawa*).

Vars.: **Ferber**. Jewish: **Farber** (in part from Yid. *farber*, in part an Eng. re-spelling of the Ger. word); **Farb(man)**; **Farbiarz**,

Farbiasz (from Pol.): **Farbstein**, **Farbsztein** ('colour stone', an ornamental elaboration).

Patrs.: Low Ger.: **Fervers**, **Ferfers**. Jewish: **Farberso(h)n**; **Ferberov** (E Ashkenazic).

Farbrother *see* FAIRBROTHER

Fareweather *see* FAIRWEATHER

Farey *see* FEARY

Farge *see* FORGE

Fargo Perhaps Welsh, but of unknown origin and not recorded as a surname in Wales.

Faria Portuguese: habitation name from a town in the province of Minho, apparently so called from the personal name *Farus*.

Var.: **Farias**.

Farine **1.** French: metonymic occupational name for a miller or flour-merchant, from OF *farine* wheat flour (L *fārīna*, a deriv. of *fār* coarse grain, spelt). In some cases it may possibly have been originally a nickname for someone with a pale complexion. **2.** Jewish: of unknown origin.

Vars. (of 1): **Far(i)nier** (agent derivs.).

Dims. (of 1): Fr.: **Far(i)nel**, **Far(i)neau**, **Far(i)naux**, **Farinet**, **Farinez**. It.: **Farinelli**, **Farinel(l)a**, **Farinetti**, **Farinola**, **Farinotti**. b

Augs. (of 1): It.: **Farinone**, **Farinon(e)**.

Pejs. (of 1): It.: **Farinacci**, **Farinasso**, **Farinazzo**.

Farkas **1.** Hungarian: nickname from *farkas* wolf. **2.** Jewish (Ashkenazic): Hungarian trans. of the Yid. male given name *Volf* WOLF', or else an ornamental name.

Vars. (of 2): **Farkash** (Eng. spelling); **Farkache** (Fr. spelling).

Farlam *see* FAIRLAMB

Farley **1.** English: habitation name from any of various places, for example in Berks., Derbys., Hants, and Staffs., so called from OE *fearn* FERN + *lēah* wood, clearing. **2.** Irish: Anglicized form of Gael. *Ó Fearghaile*; see FARRELL.

Vars. (of 1): **Farleigh** (the name of places in Hants, Kent, Somerset, Surrey, and Wilts.); **Fairley** (the name of a place in Shrops.; see also FAIRLIE); **Fearnley** (a Yorks. surname).

Farman **1.** English and French: from an ON personal name composed of the elements *fara* to go + *maðr* (acc. *mann*) man. There is also a Continental Gmc personal name *Faraman*, *Fareman* (which Förstemann derives from *fara* family), and this may be the origin of some instances of this surname. **2.** English: occupational name for a pedlar or itinerant merchant, ME *far(e)man* (from an ON vocab. word composed of the same elements as above). **3.** Jewish (Ashkenazic): of unknown origin, presumably a pseudo-Germanization of FORMAN.

Farmer English: occupational name from ME, OF *ferm(i)er* (LL *firmārius*). The term denoted in the first instance a tax-farmer, one who undertook the collection of taxes, revenues, and imposts, paying a fixed (L *firmus*) sum for the proceeds, and only secondarily someone who rented land for the purpose of cultivation; it was not applied to an owner of cultivated land before the 17th cent.

Vars.: **Farmar**, **Fermer**, **Fermor**.

Farmery English: occupational name for a worker at an infirmary, or topographic name for someone who lived by one, from an aphetic form of ME, OF *enfermerie* (LL *infirmāria*, a deriv. of *infirmus* weak, ill). In the Middle Ages an infirmary was generally part of a monastery.

Farn *see* FERN

Farndon English: habitation name from any of the various places, in Ches., Northants, and Notts., so called from OE *fearn* FERN + *dūn* hill (see DOWN 1).

Farnell English: habitation name from any of the many places, such as *Farnell* (Kent, Wilts.), *Farnhill* (W Yorks.), and *Fernhill* (Ches.), named from OE *fearn* FERN + *hyll* HILL. In a few cases it may also derive from Farnell in the former county of Angus, Scotland (now part of Tayside region). Duncan *de Ferneuel* witnessed various documents in Angus in the 13th cent., but the surname is not now common in Scotland.

Vars.: **Farnall**, **Farn(h)ill**, **Fearnall**.

Farnese Italian: habitation name from a minor place near lake Bolsena in central Italy, where the family held land and had established a castle by the 12th cent.

Var.: **Farnes**.

Farnham English: habitation name from any of various places so called. Most, including those in Bucks., Dorset, Essex, Suffolk, Surrey, and W Yorks., get the name from OE *fearn* FERN + *hām* homestead or *hamm* water-meadow. One in Northumb. was originally named *Thirnum*, from the dat. pl. (originally used after a preposition) of OE *pyrne* thornbush, i.e. 'at the thornbushes'.

Farnworth English: habitation name from either of two places in Lancs. so called from OE *fearn* FERN + *worð* enclosure (see WORTH).

Vars.: **Farnsworth**, **Farnorth**.

Faro **1.** Portuguese: habitation name from one of the places named with Port. *faro* beacon (L *pharos*, from Gk; the lighthouse built on the island of *Pharos* at Alexandria was one of the seven wonders of the ancient world), or topographic name for someone who lived near a beacon. Cf. ALFARO and HARO. Some of the places so called may instead derive their names from the Arabic personal name *Harun*. **2.** English: var. of FARRAR.

Farquhar Scots: from the Gael. personal name *Fearchar*, derived from OCelt. elements meaning 'man' + 'dear', 'beloved'.

Vars.: **Farquar**, **Faraquhart**; **Faraker**, **Forker**; **Farragher**, **Far(a)gher** (Ir.).

Patrs.: **Farqu(h)arson**; **McFarqu(h)ar**, **McKer(i)char**, **McKer(i)cher**, **McKerricher**, **McKer(r)acher**, **McCaragher**, **McErchar** (Gael. **Mac Fearchair**).

Farr English and Scots: nickname for a fierce or lusty man, or metonymic occupational name for an oxherd, from ME *farre* bull (OE *fearr*).

Farragut *see* FERRAGUT

Farrant English: **1.** nickname for a person with grey hair or for someone who used to dress in grey, from OF *ferrant* (iron-)grey (a deriv. of *fer* iron, L *ferrum*; cf. FERRO). For the change of -er- to -ar- cf. MARCHANT. **2.** from the medieval given name *Fer(r)ant*, probably in origin an OF form of FERDINAND, but early associated with the colour term.

Vars.: **Ferran(d)**, **Farran(d)**, FARREN.

Dims.: It.: **Ferrantello**, **Ferrantelli**, **Ferrantini**, **Ferrantino**; **Ferrantin** (Venetia).

Patrs.: Eng.: **Farrants**, **Farrance**, **Ferrans**, **Ferens**, **Ference**. Sp.: **Herráez**, **Herráiz**. Port.: **Ferraz**.

Farrar English (in this spelling, most common in Yorks.): occupational name for a smith or worker in iron, from ME, OF *ferreor*, *ferour* (a deriv. of *fer* iron, L *ferrum*; see FERRO). Most forms show the change of *-er-* to *-ar-*, for which see MARCHANT.

Vars.: **Farrier** (Northumb.); FERRIER (Scots and N English); **Ferrer**, **Ferrar**, **Farrer**, **Farra(h)**, **Farrey**, **Farrow**, FARO; **Pharrow**, **Pharaoh** (alteration by folk etymology); **Varah**, **Var(e)y**, **Varrow**, **Vairow**.

Dims.: It.: **Ferrarello**, **Ferraretto**, **Ferrarin(i)**, **Ferrarotti**.

Cat.: **Ferre(i)ró**.

Augs.: It.: **Ferraron(e)**.

Pej.: It.: **Ferraraccio**.

Patrs.: It.: **De Ferrari(s)**.

Farràs Catalan: nickname for a iron-willed or inflexible person, from Cat. *farràs* (made of) iron (LL *ferrāceus*, a deriv. of *ferrum* iron; cf. FERRO).

Var.: **Farreny**.

Farrell Irish: Anglicized form of Gael. **Ó Fearghail** 'descendant of *Fearghal*', a personal name composed of the elements *fear* man + *gal* valour.

Vars.: **O'Farrell**, **O'Ferrall**, **Farrel**, **Ferrell**; **(O')Farrelly**, **O'Ferrally**, FARLEY (Gael. **Ó Fearghaile** or **Ó Fearghailaigh**); **Frawley** (Gael. **Ó Freaghaile**, a metathesized form; see FRIEL).

Farren 1. English: from ME *farhyne*, which is either an occupational name for an oxherd, from OE *fearr* bull (see FARR) + *hīne* servant (see HINE), or a nickname from OE *fæger* handsome (see FAIR) + *hīne* servant. **2.** English: var. of FARRANT. **3.** Irish: Anglicized form of Gael. **Ó Faracháin** 'descendant of *Farachán*', a personal name perhaps derived from *forcha* bolt of thunder, lightning.

Vars.: **Farrin**, **Varran**.

Farrimond English (Lancs.): from a Norman personal name *Faramund*, composed of the Gmc elements *fara* family (see FARMAN 1) + *mund* protection. Alternatively, it may be from an unattested ON personal name *Farmundr*, composed of the elements *fara* to go + *mundr* protection.

Farrington English: habitation name from a place so called, of which there is one in Somerset. The name derives from OE *fearn* FERN + *tūn* enclosure, settlement.

Farris see FERGUS

Farthing English: **1.** nickname denoting someone who paid this amount in rent, or given for some other anecdotal reason, from ME *farden*, *ferthing*, OE *feorðing* quarter of a penny (a deriv. of *fēower* four). **2.** topographic name for someone who lived on a division of land known by this name, from being the fourth part of a larger area. **3.** from the ON personal name *Farþegn*, composed of the elements *fara* to go + *þegn* warrior, hero.

Fasey see VAISEY

Fäsi see JARVIS

Fass German and Jewish (Ashkenazic): metonymic occupational name for a maker or seller of casks and tubs, or nickname for someone as rotund as a barrel. The Ger. name is from MHG, OHG *faz* vat, the Jewish name from mod. Ger. *Fass* or Yid. *fas* cask.

Vars.: **Fäss(l)er**, **Fessler** (agent derivs.).

Fassbinder German and Jewish (Ashkenazic): occupational name for a cooper, Ger. *Fassbinder*, from MHG *faz* cask, tub (see FASS) + *binden* to join, construct (OHG *bindan*). This is the term used for the craft in N Germany; for surnames derived from terms used in other German-speaking regions, see BÖTTCHER, BÜTTNER, and SCHÄFFLER.

Var.: Ger.: **Fassbender**.

Fassbinder see BINDER

Fasset see FAWCETT

Fassini see BONIFACE

Fassnidge English (Bucks): habitation name from a lost place, *Fastendich* near W Wycombe in Bucks., named with the OE elements *fæsten* stronghold + *dīc* ditch.

Var.: **Fastnedge**.

Fastolf English: from the ON personal name *Fastúlfr*, composed of the elements *fast* secure, strong + *úlfr* wolf.

Fath see VOGT

Faucett see FAWCETT

Faucheur French: occupational name for a mower or reaper or for a maker or seller of scythes, from an agent deriv. of OF *fauche* scythe (LL *falca*, for class. L *falx*, gen. *falcis*).

Vars.: **Faucheux**; **Lefaucheur**, **Lefaucheux**; **Fauquer**, **Fauquex**, **Lefauquer**, **Lefauquex** (Normandy, Picardy).

Faucon see FALCON

Faugère see FOUGÈRE

Faughnan Irish: Anglicized form of Gael. **Ó Fachtnáin** 'descendant of *Fachtnán*', a personal name representing a dim. of *Fachtna*, an ancient name of unknown origin.

Faughy see FAHY

Faul see FALL

Faulder see FOLD

Faulkes English: from the Norman given name *Fau(l)ques* (oblique case *Fau(l)que*), originally a Gmc byname meaning 'FALCON'.

Vars.: **Fawlks**, **Fa(w)kes**, **Faux**; **Falkous**, **Falk(h)us**, **Falcus** (Northumb.); **Fa(w)ke**.

Dims.: It.: **Falchetti**, **Falchini**, **Falcucci**.

Patrs.: It.: **De Falco**, **Di Falco**.

Faulkner English and Scots: occupational name for someone who kept falcons for the use of the lord of the manor (a common feudal service), or for someone who operated the siege gun known as a *falcon*.

Vars.: **Falconer**, **Falconar**, **Faulkener**, **Falk(i)ner**, **Faulknor**.

Faurel see FÈVRE

Faust 1. German and Jewish (Ashkenazic): presumably a nickname for a strong or pugnacious person or for someone with a club hand or other deformity of the hand, from Ger. *Faust* fist (MHG, OHG *fūst*). **2.** German: from a personal name (L *Faustus* 'Fortunate', 'Lucky', a deriv. of *favēre* to favour), which was borne by a few relatively insignificant early Christian martyrs. *Fausto* is quite common today as an It. given name, but was not so used until after the Renaissance, hence the absence of It. surnames from this source.

Dims.: Ger.: **Fäustlein**; **Fäustel, Feistel, Feistle** (Swabia).

Patrs. (from 2): Russ.: **Faustov, Favstov, Chaustov**.

Patr. (from 2) (dim.): Russ.: **Faustsev**.

Faustino Portuguese: from a medieval given name (L *Faustīnus*, a deriv. of *Faustus*; see FAUST 2), borne in honour of various early saints, including a 2nd-cent. martyr of Lombardy and a 4th-cent. bishop of Brescia, supposedly his descendant.

Faut see VOGT

Fautley English: of uncertain origin. It is possibly an alteration, influenced by the numerous habitation names in *-ley* (from OE *lēah* wood, clearing), of an unidentified Fr. surname introduced by Huguenot settlers.

Vars.: **Faulty, Faultley**.

Fauvel French: **1.** nickname for someone with a dusky complexion, from a dim. of OF *fauve* tawny (of Gmc origin; cf. FALLOW 2). **2.** nickname for a devious or hypocritical person. The word came to have this sense as a result of being borne by the cunning horse in a popular medieval cycle of beast tales (cf. REYNARD), and was reinforced by associations with OF *favel* story, tale (LL *fabella*, for class. L *fabula*).

Var.: **Fauveau**.

Favard Provençal: nickname from the wild pigeon, OProv. *favart*, a pej. deriv. of *fave* bean (cf. FAVIER). The birds feed greedily on this diet and are responsible for large losses among crops; the nickname presumably denoted similarly gluttonous and destructive individuals.

Var.: **Favart**.

Dims.: **Favardel, Favardon, Favardin**.

Favaretti see FÈVRE

Favier French: occupational name for a grower or seller of beans, OF *favier* (LL *fabārius*, a deriv. of *faba* bean).

Dims.: Fr.: **Fav(e)reau**.

Favshevitz see FAIVISH

Favstov see FAUST

Fawcett English: habitation name from *Fawcett* in Cumb. or *Facit* in Lancs., both so called from OE *fāg, fāh* (brightly) coloured, variegated, flowery + *sīde* slope. *Forcett* in N Yorks. is named from OE *ford* FORD + *(ge)sete* house, settlement, and this may also be a partial source of the surname, which is common esp. in N England.

Vars.: **Fawcitt, Faws(s)ett, Faucett, Fausset(t), Fasset, Fosset, Fossit(t)**.

Fawke see FAULKES

Fawle see FALL

Fay 1. English: nickname for a person believed to have supernatural qualities, from ME, OF *faie* fairy (LL *fāta* fate, destiny, originally neut. pl., but later taken as fem. sing.). **2.** English: nickname for a trustworthy person, from ME, OF *fei* loyalty, trust, a later form of *feit, feid*; cf. FAITH. **3.** English (Norman) and French: habitation name from any of the various places in France named with OF *faie* beech; see FAGE. **4.** Irish: var. of FAHY and FEE.

Vars.: **Faye, Fey**.

Fayard see FAGE

Faybish see FAIVISH

Faydel see FEYDIT

Fayer see FAIR

Fayerbrother see FAIRBROTHER

Fayerman 1. Jewish (Ashkenazic): a deriv. of Yid. *fayer* fire (see FEUER). **2.** English: var. of FAIRMAN.

Vars. (of 1): **Faierman; Fayer, Faier; Fajer(man)** (Pol. spelling).

Fayerman see FAIRMAN

Fayers see FAIR

Fayerstein see FEUERSTEIN

Fayne see FANE

Fazakerley English (Lancs.): habitation name from a minor place in the parish of Walton on the Hill near Liverpool, so called from OE *fæs* border, fringe + *æcer* field, ploughed land + *lēah* wood, clearing.

Vars.: **Fazackerly, Phizackerl(e)y** (pseudo-learned spelling, in imitation of Gk words beginning with *Ph-*).

Fazzini see BONIFACE

Feacey see VAISEY

Feakes see FITCH

Fealey see FEELY

Feamaster see FEMISTER

Feane see FEE

Fear English: **1.** nickname for a sociable person, from ME *fe(a)re* comrade, companion (OE *(ge)fēra*). **2.** nickname for a proud or haughty person, from ME *fere* proud (OF *fier*, L *ferus* wild, savage).

Vars.: **Feare, Phear**.

Patr.: **Fears**.

Fearn see FERN

Fearnall see FARNELL

Fearnley see FARLEY

Fearnside English (Yorks.) and Scots (Aberdeens.): probably a habitation name from one or more unidentified places, apparently so called from OE *fearn* FERN + *sīde* slope, hillside.

Fearon English (Norman): occupational name for a blacksmith or worker in iron, from OF *ferron* blacksmith (L *ferro*, gen. *ferrōnis*, a deriv. of *ferrum* iron; cf. FERRO).

Dims.: Fr.: **Fer(ro)net**, **Fernez**, **Fer(ro)nel**.

Feary English (mostly Lincs.): of uncertain origin, perhaps a habitation name from an unidentified place named with the OE elements *fearr* bull or *fearn* fern + *(ge)hæg* enclosure or *ēg* low-lying land.

Vars.: **Fearey**, **Fery**, **Farey**, **Fairy**.

Feather English: **1.** metonymic occupational name for a trader in feathers and down or a maker of quilts, or possibly also of pens, from ME *fether*, OE *feðer* feather. Feathermongers are recorded from the 13th cent. onwards. **2.** nickname for a very light person or perhaps a person of no account, from the same word as in 1.

Vars.: **Fed(d)er**.

Dim. (of 1): Ger.: **Federle**.

Cpds (ornamental): Jewish: **Federbus(c)h** ('feather bush'); **Federgrün**, **Federgrin** ('feather green', partly Anglicized as **Federgreen**); **Federschneider** ('feather cutter').

Featherstone N English: habitation name from places in Staffs., W Yorks., and Northumb. (but see also FEATHERSTONEHAUGH), which are so called from OE *feðerstān* tetralith, a prehistoric structure consisting of three upright stones capped with a headstone (from OE *fe(o)ðer-* four + *stān* stone).

Vars.: **Fe(a)therston**.

Featherstonehaugh English: habitation name from a place in Northumb. now called FEATHERSTONE, but originally containing the extra element ME *halgh*, OE *halh* nook, recess (see HALE 1). The name is normally pronounced /ˈfænʃɔː/.

Vars.: **Fe(a)therstonhaugh**; **Fanshaw(e)**.

Featley *see* FAIRCLOUGH

Feavearyear *see* FEVEREL

Feavers *see* FÈVRE

Febreau *see* FÈVRE

Febry *see* FEVEREL

Fech *see* WENZEL

Feck *see* FREDERICK

Fedchin *see* THÉODORE

Fedde *see* FREDERICK

Fedder *see* FEATHER

Fedotov Russian: patr. from the given name *Fedot* (Gk *Theodotos* 'God-given', a less common equivalent of *Theodoros* 'God-gift'; see TUDOR). This name was borne by several early Christian saints, among them 4th-cent. bishops of Cyreneia and Laodicea.

Var.: **Fedotyev**.

'Son of the wife of F.': **Fedotikhin**.

Fee Irish: Anglicized form of Gael. **Ó Fiaich** 'descendant of *Fiach*', a byname meaning 'Raven'.

Vars.: FAY, FOY; **O'Fee**, **O'Fay**.

Dims.: **O'Fighane**, **(O')Feehan**, **Fe(g)han**, **Fegan**, **Fe(h)ane** (Gael. **Ó Fiacháin**).

Feehally *see* FITZHENRY

Feek *see* FITCH

Feely Irish: **1.** Anglicized form of Gael. **Ó Fáilbhe** 'descendant of *Fáilbhe*', a byname meaning 'Lively'. **2.** Anglicized form of Gael. **Ó Fithcheallaigh** 'descendant of *Fithcheallach*', a byname meaning 'Chess-player'.

Vars.: **Feeley**, **Feal(e)y**. (Of 1 only): **O'Falv(e)y**, **O'Falvie**, **O'Falie**, **Falvey**. (Of 2 only): **O'Fihily**, **O'Fihillie**, **O'Fielly**, **Fihelly**, **Fe(e)hely**, **Feehily**.

Feemster *see* FEMISTER

Feeney Irish: **1.** Anglicized form of Gael. **Ó Fiannaidhe** 'descendant of *Fiannaidhe*', a byname meaning 'Warrior', 'Champion' (from *fian* army). **2.** Anglicized form of Gael. **Ó Fidhne** 'descendant of *Fidhne*', a personal name apparently derived from *fidh* tree, wood.

Var.: **O'Feeney**.

Feesey *see* VAISEY

Feest *see* FAIST

Feferberg *see* PEPPER

Fegan *see* FEE

Fehan *see* FEE

Fehely *see* FEELY

Fehér Hungarian and Jewish (Ashkenazic): nickname for a fair-skinned or blond-haired person, from Hung. *fehér* white.

Var.: **Fejér**.

Fehst *see* FAIST

Fehster *see* SILVESTER

Fei *see* FEO

Feibel *see* FAIVISH

Feicht German: topographic name for someone who lived by a conspicuous pine tree or in a pine forest, from MHG *viehte* pine (OHG *fiohta*), mod. Ger. *Fichte* spruce. The vowel of the first syllable underwent a variety of changes in different dialects.

Vars.: **Ficht(e)**, **Feucht**, **F(e)icht(n)er**, **Feuchtner**, **Füchter**.

Feidler *see* PFEIDLER

Feierle *see* FEUER

Feige **1.** German: topographic name for someone who lived by a fig tree, or metonymic occupational name for a grower or seller of figs, from Ger. *Feige* fig, MHG *vīge* (OHG *fīga*, from L *fīcus*). **2.** Jewish (Ashkenazic): from the Yid. female given name *Feyge*, a back-formation from *Feygl* (see FEIGEL), as if this contained the dim. suffix -*l*.

Dims. (of 1): Prov.: **Figa(i)rol**. Sp.: **Figueroa** (Galicia). Cat.: **Figuerola**.

Collectives (of 1): Prov.: **Figadère**. Sp.: **Figueredo**. Port.: **Figueiredo**.

Metrs. (from 2): Jewish: **Feiges**, **Feigenson**; **Feigin**, **Fejgin**, **Faigin** (E Ashkenazic); **Fagin** (an Anglicized spelling).

Cpds (of 1, ornamental): Jewish: **Feigenberg**, **Faigenberg** ('fig hill'); **Feigenblat(t)**, **Faigenblat**, **Fajgenblat** ('fig leaf').

Feigel Jewish (Ashkenazic): from the Yid. female given name *Feygl* (from Yid. *foygl* bird (cf. VOGEL and FOWLE), a translation of the Hebr. name *Tsipora* (Eng. *Zipporah*) 'Bird', borne by the wife of Moses).

Metrs.: **Feigelso(h)n**; **Fogelson** (Germanized); **Feig(e)lewitz**, **Feiglin** (E Ashkenazic).

Feigelfuss *see* VOGEL

Feighery Irish: Anglicized form of Gael. **Ó Fiachra** 'descendant of *Fiachra*', a personal name of uncertain origin, probably a deriv. of *fiach* raven (cf. FEE).

Feijoo Spanish (Galicia): metonymic occupational name for a grower or seller of kidney beans, or perhaps a nickname for a small person, from the dial. term *feixó* kidney bean (LL *phaseōlus*).

Feild *see* FIELD

Feimster *see* FEMISTER

Fein 1. German: nickname from MHG *fīn* fine, splendid (a cogn. of FIN). **2.** Jewish (Ashkenazic): ornamental name from mod. Ger. *fein*, Yid. *fayn* fine, excellent.

Vars.: Ger.: **Feine**, **Feiner(t)**, **Feinmann**. Jewish: **Fajn(er)**, **Feiner**, **Feinman**.

Dim.: Ger.: **Feinle**.

Cpds (ornamental): Jewish: **Feinberg** ('fine hill'); **Feinblatt** ('fine leaf'); **Feinbrun** ('fine fountain'); **Feinbus(c)h** ('fine bush'); **Feinburg** ('fine town'); **Feindeitsch** ('fine German'); **Feingang** ('fine gait'); **Feingold**, **Fajngold** ('fine gold'); **Feinholz**, **Fajnhol(t)z** ('fine wood'); **Feinkind** ('fine child'); **Feinkoch** ('fine cook', or from Yid. *faynkukhn* omelette); **Feinmesser** ('fine knife'); **Feinsilber**, **Fajnzylber** ('fine silver'); **Feinstein** ('fine stone'); **Feintuch**, **Fajntuch** ('fine cloth'); **Feinwachs** ('fine wax'); **Feinzak** ('fine sack').

Feinschreiber Jewish (Ashkenazic): occupational name for a scribe who specialized in preparing Torah scrolls, phylacteries, and mezuzot, from mod. Ger. *fein* fine + *Schreiber* writer.

Feio Portuguese: nickname for an ugly person, from Port. *feio* repugnant (L *foedus* foul, shameful).

Feirer *see* FEUER

Feirn *see* FERN

Feist *see* FAIST

Feistel *see* FAUST

Feito Spanish: nickname from the past part. *feito* (L *factus*) of OSp. *fer* to make, do (L *facere*). The word was used of a grown man as opposed to a child, and it is probably in this sense that the surname arose, to designate an adult as opposed to a minor with the same given name.

Feix *see* VITO

Fejér *see* FEHÉR

Fejgin *see* FEIGE

Fekete Hungarian: nickname for a dark-haired or swarthy person, from Hung. *fekete* black.

Feking *see* FREDERICK

Felber 1. German: topographic name for someone who lived by a conspicuous willow tree or a group of such

trees, from MHG *velwe* willow (presumably from an unrecorded OHG cognate of OE *welig*). The vocab. word has now been entirely supplanted by WEIDE 1. Both words ultimately derive from a root meaning 'bent', 'twisted', and refer to the useful suppleness of willow twigs. Some examples may derive from places called *Felben*, from the dat. pl. of the word (originally used after a preposition). **2.** Jewish (Ashkenazic): ornamental name, from the tree.

Vars. (of 2): **Felbert**, **Felberbaum**.

Feldbau *see* FIELD

Feldner 1. German: from MHG *veldener*, a technical term of the feudal system for a vassal or bondsman. The word is a deriv. of OHG *feld* FIELD. **2.** Jewish: ornamental extension of *Feld*; see FIELD.

Var.: **Fellner** (see also FELL 2).

Feldscher Jewish (Ashkenazic): occupational name for an old-time barber-surgeon, who not only cut hair but also pulled teeth, let blood, and applied other remedies. The vocab. word is from Yid. or Russ. *feldsher* (from Ger. *Feldscher* army surgeon, from *Feld* field + *Scher(er)* agent noun from *scheren* to shave, cut). Probably no later than the 20th cent., the occupations of barber and 'barefoot doctor' became separate, but this was probably after the surname had been acquired.

Feliciano Italian, Spanish, and Portuguese: from a medieval given name (L *Fēliciānus*, a deriv. of FELIX). The name was borne by a number of early saints, most notably a 3rd-cent. bishop of Foligno and apostle of Umbria.

Patr.: Pol.: **Felicjaniak**.

Feliński Polish: habitation name from a place called *Felin*.

Var.: **Felińczak**.

Felix 1. English and German: from a medieval given name (L *Fēlix*, gen. *Fēlīcis*, 'Lucky', 'Fortunate'). This was a relatively common Roman family name, apparently first adopted as a nickname by Sulla. It was very popular among early Christians, and was borne by a large number of early saints. **2.** Jewish: presumably an adoption of the non-Jewish surname.

Vars.: Eng.: **Felice**, **Fillis**.

Dims.: It.: **Felicetti**, **Felicini**, **Felicioli**, **Feliciotti**. Fr.: **Félizon**, **F(é)lizot**, **Félissot**, **F(é)lizet**. Pol.: **Felczyk**.

Aug.: It.: **Felicioni**.

Patrs.: It.: **De(l) Felice**, **De Felici**, **Di Felice**. Port.: **Felices**. Pol.: **Feli(k)siak**, **Pelisiak**. Jewish (Ashkenazic): **Felickson**. Habitation name (from a dim.): Pol.: **Felczykowski**.

Felkel *see* VOLK

Fell 1. English (chiefly Northern): topographic name for someone who lived by an area of high ground or by a prominent crag, from Northern ME *fell* high ground, rock, crag (ON *fjall*). **2.** English and Jewish (Ashkenazic): metonymic occupational name for a furrier, from ME, OE *fell* or from Ger. *Fell*, Yid. *fel* (MHG *vel*), all of which words mean 'skin, hide, or pelt'. Yid. *fel* refers to untanned hide, in contrast to *pelts* tanned hide (see PILCHER).

Vars.: Eng.: **Fells**; **Feller**, **Fella**. (Of 2 only): Jewish: **Fel(l)ner**, **Fel(l)man**; **Felhandler** (with mod. Ger. *Händler* dealer or Yid. *hendler*).

Cpds (of 1): Swed.: **Fjellstedt** ('hill homestead'); **Fjellström**, **Fjällström** ('hill stream').

Fellow English: from ME *felagh, felaw*, late OE *feolaga* partner, shareholder (ON *félagi*, from *fé* fee, money + *legja* to lay (down)). In ME the term was used in the general sense of a companion or comrade, and the surname thus probably denoted a (fellow) member of a trade guild (cf. FEAR 1).

Patrs.: **Fellow(e)s** (but see also FIELDHOUSE).

Felmy *see* VOLMER

Felsted English: habitation name from a place in Essex, so called from OE *feld* pasture, open country (see FIELD) + *stede* homestead (see STEAD 1).

Var.: **Felstead**.

Felten *see* VALENTINE

Feltham English: habitation name from places SW of London and in Somerset. The former is so called from OE *feld* pasture, open country + *hām* homestead; the latter from OE *filiðe* hay + *hamm* water meadow.

Felton English: habitation name from any of various places so called. Most of them, including those in Herefords., Shrops., and Somerset (Winford), get the name from OE *feld* pasture, open country (see FIELD) + *tūn* enclosure, settlement. Another place of the same name in Somerset, also known as Whitchurch, has its first element from OE *filiðe* hay. *Felton* Hill in Northumb. gets it from the OE personal name *Fygla* (a deriv. of *fugol* bird; cf. FOWLE). The surname is now found most frequently in the W Midlands of England, though it is also common in the United States.

Femister English and Scots: occupational name for a senior herdsman, from ME *fee* cattle (OE *feoh*) + *master* MASTER.

Vars.: **Fimister**, **Phemister**, **Phimister**, **Whimster**; **Feam(a)ster**, **Feemster**, **Feimster** (U.S.).

Fenaghty Irish: Anglicized form of Gael. **Ó Fionnachta** (often now written **Ó Fiannachta**) 'descendant of *Fionnachta*', a personal name composed of the elements *fionn* fair, white + *sneachta* snow.

Vars.: **Finnerty**, FENTON.

Fenck German: metonymic occupational name for a cultivator of millet or panic grass (MHG *ven(i)ch*, from L *pānicum*), or a topographic name for someone who lived by a patch of land where the crop was grown. There seems also to have been some confusion with MHG *fenich*, a byform of *fēnichel*, mod. Ger. *Fenchel* fennel (see FENNELL).

Var.: **Fenech**.

Fendel *see* INFANTE

Fenegan *see* FINN

Fenemore *see* FINNEMORE

Fenier French: occupational name for a hay merchant, OF *fe(i)nier* (L *f(a)enārius*, from *faenum* hay).

Vars.: **Fenié**, **Fanier**.

Dims.: Fr.: **Feneron**. Prov.: **Fenayrol**, **Fenayroux**.

Fenigson *see* PENNY

Fenlon 1. Irish: Anglicized form of Gael. **Ó Fionnaláin** 'descendant of *Fionnalán*', a personal name from a dim. of *fionn* fair, white (see FINN 1). **2.** English (Huguenot): habitation name from *Fénelon* in the Dordogne, which is of uncertain etymology.

Var. (of 1): **Fenelon**.

Fenn English: topographic name for someone who lived in a low-lying marshy area, from OE *fenn* marsh, bog. The forms with the voiced initial consonant (*V*-) are characteristic of SW dialects of ME. The forms with *Fa-* may represent OE *fænn*, the East Saxon form of *fenn*.

Vars.: **Fann**; **Venn**, **Vann(e)**, **Vance**; **Avann**; **Fenning**, **Fanning**, **Venning** (W Country); **Fenner**, FANNER.

Fris.: **Feenstra**, **Veenstra**; **Venema**. Flem.: **Van de Ven**, **Van den Vinne**, **Venneman**. Du.: **Van den Ven**, **Van (den) Veen**, **Veenman**.

Fennell 1. English: metonymic occupational name for a grower or seller of fennel (OE *finugle, fenol*, from LL *fenuculum*, dim. of *f(a)enum* hay). Fennel was widely used in the Middle Ages as a seasoning. The surname may also have been a topographic name for someone who lived near a patch where the herb was grown, or a nickname for a particularly enthusiastic user of it. **2.** Irish: Anglicized form of Gael. **Ó Fionnghail** 'descendant of *Fionnghal*', a personal name composed of the elements *fionn* fair, white + *gal* valour.

Vars.: **Fennel**. (Of 1 only): **Funnell**, **Fonnell** (forms developed in E Sussex in the 16th and 17th cents.). (Of 2 only): **Fennelly** (Gael. **Ó Fionnghaile** or **Ó Fionnghalaigh**).

Dims. (of 1): It.: **Finoccietti**; **Fenoglietto** (Piedmont).

Fennessy Irish: Anglicized form of Gael. **Ó Fionnghusa** 'descendant of *Fionnghus*', a personal name composed of the elements *fionn* fair, white + *gus* vigour, force.

Fenster German and Jewish (Ashkenazic): metonymic occupational name for a maker of windows, from Ger. *Fenster* window (MHG *venster*, from L *fenestra*). Medieval windows were often just holes in the wall; indeed, the Eng. word *window* derives from ON *vindauga* 'wind eye'. Later they were filled with a frame containing thin layers of translucent horn, and eventually glass, normally only in small pieces leaded together. In the case of the Ger. name, the derivation is in some cases from a habitation name from any of various minor places so called from being in a gap in a range of hills or a clearing in a wood; it may also have been a topographic name for someone who lived in a house remarkable for its windows.

Vars.: Ger.: **Fensterer**, **Fenstermann**. Jewish (Ashkenazic): **Fenstermacher** ('window maker').

Fentiman English: occupational name for a servant or retainer of a family called FENTON.

Var.: **Fenteman**.

Fenton 1. English: habitation name from any of various places, in Lincs., Northumb., Staffs., and S Yorks., so called from OE *fenn* marsh, fen (see FENN) + *tūn* enclosure, settlement. **2.** Irish: Anglicized form of Gael. *Ó Fionnachta*; see FENAGHTY. **3.** Jewish (Ashkenazic): Anglicized form of various like-sounding names, for example *Finkelstein* (see FUNKE).

Var. (of 1): **Venton** (W Country).

Fenwick N English and Scots: habitation name from either of two places in Northumb. or from one in W Yorks., all of which are so called from OE *fenn* marsh, fen (see FENN) + *wīc* dairy farm, outlying village (see WICK). There is also a place in the former county of Ayrs., Scotland (now part of Strathclyde region) which has the same name and origin. This last is the source of at least some early examples of the surname: Nicholaus *Fynwyk* was provost of Ayr in 1313, and Reginald *de Fynwyk* or *Fynvyk* appears as bailie and alderman of the same burgh in 1387 and 1401. The name is usually pronounced /'fenɪk/.

Vars.: **Fennick, Finnick, Vinnick; Fenix, Ph(o)enix; Fenwich** (Scots).

Fenyvesi Hungarian: topographic name for someone who lived in or near a pine forest, Hung. *fenyves* (from *fenyö* pine tree).

Vars.: **Fenyves** (also Jewish (Ashkenazic) ornamental name); **Fenyvessy**.

Fenzl see WENZEL

Feo Italian: from a given name, an aphetic short form of *Maffeo*; see MATTHEW.

Var.: **Fei**.

Dim.: **Feoli**.

Feofilaktov see FILATOV

Féral French: nickname for a man of a cruel disposition or scruffy and uncouth appearance, from OF *féral* wild, bestial (L *ferālis*, from *fera* wild animal).

Ferber see FÄRBER

Ferdinand German and French: from a Spanish (Visigothic) personal name composed of the elements *farð* journey, expedition (or a metathesized form of *frið* peace) + *nanð* daring, brave. The surname is of comparatively recent origin in German-speaking countries and in France, for the given name was not introduced from Spain until the late 15th cent. It was brought to Austria by the Habsburg dynasty, among whom it was a hereditary name, and from Austria it spread to France. The Iberian cogns. given below are of more ancient origin and more frequently found today, since the name was much favoured in the royal house of Castile. It owes its popularity in large measure to King Ferdinand III of Castile and León (1198–1252), who recaptured large areas of Spain from the Moors and was later canonized.

Var.: Fr.: **Fernant**; see also FARRANT.

Patrs.: Sp.: **Hernández, Hernáez, Hernáiz; Fernández, Ferrández; Ferrándiz** (Aragon). Port.: **Fernandes, Fernandez**.

Fereday Irish: Anglicized form of Gael. **Ó Fearadaigh** 'descendant of *Fearadach*', a personal name apparently composed of old Celt. elements meaning 'man' + 'wood'.

Var.: **Faraday**.

Ference see FARRANT

Ferencowicz see FRANCIS

Fergus Scots and Irish: from the Gael. personal name *Fearghus*, composed of the elements *fear* man + *gus* vigour, force. This was the name of an early Irish mythological figure, a valiant warrior, and also of the grandfather of St Columba.

Vars.: **Ferris, Farris** (chiefly N Ireland).

Dim.: **Fergie** (Sc.).

Patrs.: **Fergu(s)son, Fergyson**.

'Descendant of F.': **O'Fearguise, O'Fergus, O'Ferris, O'Farris** (Gael. **Ó Fearghuis**); **O'Farrisa, Farrissy** (Gael. **Ó Fearghusa**).

Fériot see FREDERICK

Fermer see FARMER

Fermin see FIRMIN

Fern 1. English: topographic name for someone who lived in a place where there was an abundance of ferns, from OE *fearn* fern (a collective noun). The forms with voiced initial consonant (*V*-) represent south-western ME developments (cf. FENN). **2.** Jewish: of unknown origin.

Vars. (of 1): **Fearn, Fa(i)rn, Feirn; Fe(a)rne; Ferns, Farnes; Vern(e), Varn(e)s**.

Fernie Scots: habitation name from an estate in Fife, near Cupar, so called from Gael. *fearnach* place of alders, alder wood (from *fearna* alder + the local suffix -*ach*).

Var.: **Fairnie**.

Fernier see FEARON

Ferragut Provençal and Catalan: nickname for a good swordsman, or metonymic occupational name for a master cutler, from OProv., Cat. *ferro* iron (L *ferrum*) + *agut* sharp (L *acūtus*).

Vars.: Prov.: **Farragut, Ferragu(s)**.

Ferrar see FARRAR

Ferrell see FARRELL

Ferrers English (Norman): habitation name from any of various places in Normandy called *Ferrières* 'iron workings' (L *ferrāriae*, a deriv. of *ferrum* iron; cf. FERRO).

Ferriaud see FREDERICK

Ferrier English (chiefly N) and Scots: **1.** var. of FARRAR. **2.** var. of FERRY.

Ferro 1. Italian and Portuguese: metonymic occupational name for someone who worked in iron (L *ferrum*; cf. FARRAR and FEARON), or nickname from the colour or hardness of iron (cf. FARRENT 1 and FARRÀS). **2.** Jewish: of unknown origin.

Vars. (of 1): It.: **Ferri; Fierro** (Campania).

Dims. (of 1): It.: **Ferrett(in)i, Ferrett(in)o, Ferrin(i), Ferrino, Ferrucci, Ferruzzi, Ferrulli, Ferrotti, Ferroli; Ferrillo, Ferrulli** (S Italy).

Augs. (of 1): It.: **Ferron(i), Ferrone**. Fr.: **Ferras**.

Ferry 1. English: metonymic occupational name for a ferryman, or topographic name for someone who lived by a ferry crossing on a river. ME *feri* ferry is from ON *ferja* ferry, ultimately cogn. with the OE verb *ferian* to carry. **2.** Irish: Anglicized form of Gael. **Ó Fearadhaigh**

'descendant of *Fearadhach*', a personal name of uncertain origin, probably an adj. deriv. of *fear* man.

Vars. (of 1): **Ferrey**, **Ferrie**; **Ferriman**, **Ferryman**; FERRIER.

Ferstel *see* FÜRST

Ferster *see* FORSTER

Fertig German and Jewish (Ashkenazic): nickname from Ger. *fertig* ready, prepared (MHG *vertec*, OHG *fertīg*, a deriv. of *vart* journey, expedition, and so meaning originally 'ready for an expedition').

Var.: Ger.: **Förtig** (Bavaria).

Fery *see* FEARY

Fesenko *see* THÉODORE

Fessler *see* FASS

Fester *see* SILVESTER

Fetherston *see* FEATHERSTONE

Fetherstonhaugh *see* FEATHERSTONEHAUGH

Fett Low German: nickname for a fat man, from MLG *vett* fat (cf. OFris. *fett*, *fatt*, OE *fǣt(t)*).

Patr.: Low Ger.: **Fetting**.

Feubre *see* FÈVRE

Feuchère *see* FOUGÈRE

Feucht *see* FEICHT

Feuchtwanger German and Jewish (Ashkenazic): habitation name from *Feuchtwangen* in Franconia, so called from MHG *viuhte* damp (OHG *fūht(i)*) or the dial. term *feuchte* pine, spruce + *wang* meadow, grassland.

Feuer 1. German: metonymic occupational name for a stoker in a smithy or public baths, or nickname for someone with red hair or a fiery temper, from Ger. *Feuer* fire (MHG *viur*, OHG *fuir*). 2. Jewish (Ashkenazic): nickname or ornamental name from mod. Ger. *Feuer* fire. Kaganoff suggests that this is a name often given to or adopted by members of the priestly caste (cf. the Jewish folk belief, found as early as the Talmud, that Kohanim (see COHEN) have a violent temper), but there seems to be no evidence to support this suggestion.

Vars. (of 1): **Feurer**, **Feirer**; **Feuerman(n)**.

Dims. (of 1): **Feuerlein**, **Feierle**.

Feuerbach German: habitation name from a place near Stuttgart, according to Bahlow so called from a prehistoric term for a marsh + OHG *bah* stream (see BACH 1).

Feuerstein 1. German: metonymic occupational name for a seller of flints, or topographic name for someone who lived near an outcrop of flint, from Ger. *Feuerstein* flint (from MHG *viur* fire (see FEUER) + *stein* STONE). 2. Jewish (Ashkenazic): ornamental cpd of the elements FEUER fire + *stein* stone, or ornamental name from the Ger. vocab. word *Feuerstein* flint.

Vars. (of 2): **Faierstein**, **Fayerstein**; **Firestein** (partly Anglicized); **Firestone** (fully Anglicized).

Feverel English: from a ME form of the name of the month of *February* (L *(mensis) februārius*, perhaps a deriv. of *febris* fever, sickness), perhaps originating as a nickname for someone born or found in this bitter month, or for someone who was of a frosty character.

Vars.: **Feave(a)ryear**, **Feveyear**, **Fevyer**; **Febry** (chiefly Bristol).

Fèvre French: occupational name for an iron-worker or smith, OF *fevre* (L *faber* craftsman).

Vars.: **Febvre** (the *-b-* having been introduced by hypercorrection under the influence of the L word); **Feu(b)re** (Brittany); **Fèbre** (Poitou); **Faivre** (Lorraine); **Lefe(b)vre**, **Lefébure**, **Lefeu(v)re**, **Lefeubre**; **Faber(t)** (from the L form often used in medieval documents).

Dims.: Fr.: **Faivret**, **Févret**, **Fevret**; **Febreau**; **Févrichaud**.

Prov.: **Favret**; **Favreau**, **Favrel**, **Faurel**; **Fabron**, **Favr(ich)on**, **Fauron**, **Faurou**; **Fabry**, **Faury**; **Haurillon** (Gascony).

It.: **Fav(a)retti**, **Fab(b)retti**, **Fab(r)etto**, **Fab(b)rini**, **Favruzzi**, **Fab(b)rucci**, **Favaroli**; **Favret(in)**, **Frabet**, **Fav(a)rin**, **Fabbrin** (Venetia); **Frabbetti** (Emilia).

Augs.: It.: **Favarone**, **Fabbroni**, **Frab(b)oni**; **Fav(a)ron** (Venetia).

Patrs.: Prov.: **Dufaure**, **Aufau(v)re**. Eng.: **Fe(a)vers**. It.: **Dal Fabbro**, **Del Fabbro**.

Fewkes *see* FOULKES

Fewster *see* FORSTER

Fewtrell English (W Midlands): of uncertain origin, perhaps from a dim. of the ME occupational term *vewter* keeper of greyhounds (ANF *veutrier*, an agent deriv. of *veutre* greyhound, of Gaul. origin).

Fey *see* FAY

Feydit French: nickname from the past part. of OF *faidir* to banish, outlaw (a deriv. of *faide* feud, vengeance, of Gmc origin).

Var.: **Faydit**.

Dims.: **Feydel**, **Feydeau**, **Faydel**.

Feyel *see* FAGE

Feyer *see* FAIR

Fiala Czech: very common surname, derived from the vocab. word *fial(k)a* violet (the flower). This may have given rise to a surname in various possible ways: as a nickname for a shy, delicate person; as a topographic name for someone who lived where violets grew or, in a town, at a house distinguished with the sign of a bunch of violets; or simply as an ornamental name.

Dims.: **Fialka**; **Fialek** (altered to masc. form).

Fialho Portuguese: nickname for a thin person, from Port. *fialho* fine thread (a deriv. of *fio* thread, L *fīlum*; cf. FILER 2). The nickname is attested in this sense from the 16th cent. and may well have occurred earlier.

Fibonacci Italian: patr. from the nickname *Bonacci*, a pej. of *bono* 'good' (see BON), denoting an excessively pious or a hypocritical person. The first syllable derives from a scribal abbreviation of the L term *filius* son.

Fiche French: topographic name for someone who lived by a stake planted in the ground as a boundary or signpost, from OF *fiche* stake (a deriv. of *ficher* to fix, plant, L *figere*).

Dims.: Fr.: **Fichet**, **Fichot**; **Fiqu(en)et** (Normandy).

Ficht *see* FEICHT

Fick *see* FITCH, FREDERICK

Fidalgo *see* HIDALGO

Fiddes Scots: apparently a habitation name from a place a few miles south of Aberdeen, first recorded in the forms *Futhes* (1240) and *Fothes* (1390), probably from Gael. *fiodhais* wood-place, wood-stance. There is another place of the same name (with similar early forms) in the former county of Kincardine, and this may also have given rise to some examples of the surname.

Fiddian *see* VIVIAN

Fiddy English (Norman): nickname meaning 'son of God', bestowed on an illegitimate child, esp. the illegitimate child of a priest, from ANF *fi(t)z* son (L *filius*) + *Deu* God (L *Deus*).
Vars.: **Fido(e)**.

Fidge *see* FITCH

Fieback German: topographic name for someone who lived by a drovers' road, MHG *vihewec*, from *vehe, vihe, vich* cattle (OHG *feho, fihu*) + *wec* way, path (OHG *weg*). The surname originated chiefly in Saxony, Silesia, and Bohemia.
Vars.: **Fiebeck, Fiebig, Fiebich, Viebig; Fiebiger**.

Fiedler German and Jewish (Ashkenazic): occupational name for a professional player on the fiddle, or nickname for a skilled amateur, from Ger. *Fiedler*, Yid. *fidler* (MHG *videlære*). The instrument (OHG *fidula*) gets its name from LL *vītula*, a deriv. of *vītulāri* to celebrate.

Fiedorowicz *see* THÉODORE

Fieger *see* FÜGER

Field 1. English: topographic name for someone who lived on land which had been cleared of forest, but not brought into cultivation, from OE *feld* pasture, open country (opposed on the one hand to *æcer* cultivated soil, enclosed land (see ACKER) and on the other to *weald* wooded land, uncleared forest; see WALD). 2. Jewish (Ashkenazic): Anglicized and shortened form of any of the Jewish surnames given below.
Vars.: Eng. **Feild; Fields** (from the OE gen. case); **Fielden, Feilden** (from the OE dat. pl. case); **Velden** (S England); **Fielder; Fielding, Feilding; At(t)field; Delafield**.
Flem.: **Van de(r) Velde, Van Velden**. Du.: **Veld, Van den Veldt, Van den Velde(n), Veldman, Veltman**. Jewish: **Feld(er), Feldman(n)**.
Cpds (ornamental unless otherwise stated): Jewish: **Feldbau** ('agriculture', perhaps occupational for a farmer); **Feldbaum** ('field tree'); **Feldberg(er)** ('field hill'); **Feldblum** ('field flower'); **Feldbrin** ('field well', perhaps topographic); **Feldfisher** ('rural fisherman', nickname or occupational name); **Feldharker** ('field smallholder', occupational); **Feldhammer** ('field hammer'); **Feldheim** ('field home'); **Feldhorn** ('field horn'); **Feldhuhn** ('partridge'); **Feldklein** ('field little'); **Feldmark** ('field boundary', perhaps topographic); **Feldmes(s)er** ('field knife' or 'field measurer', occupational name for a surveyor); **Feldmus** ('field-mouse'); **Feldstein** (field stone); **Feldstern** ('field star').

Fieldhouse English (chiefly W Midlands and N England): topographic name for someone who lived in a house (OE *hūs*) in open pasture land (see FIELD). Reaney draws attention to the form *de Felhouse* (Staffs. 1332), and suggests that this may have become *Fellowes* (see FELLOW).

Fiennes English (Norman): habitation name from a place in Pas-de-Calais, recorded in the 11th cent. as *Filnes* and *Finles*. The earliest form of all is *Flidmum* (9th cent.), possibly akin to a Gmc word meaning 'plain' (cf. FILDES). The surname is normally pronounced /faɪnz/.
Vars.: **Fienes, Fynes**.

Fierman *see* FAIRMAN

Fierro *see* FERRO

Fietz *see* VINCENT

Fiévet French: status name for a feudal tenant who held land in return for service, from a dim. of OF *fief* land held in this way (of Gmc origin).
Var.: **Fievez**.

Fife *see* FYFE

Figadère *see* FEIGE

Figdor *see* AVIGDOR

Figgis English: nickname for a trustworthy or reliable person, from a Norman form of OF *ficheis*.
Var.: **Figgess**.

Figiovanni *see* JOHN

Fihelly *see* FEELY

Fijałkowski Polish: habitation name from a place named with OPol. *fijałek, fijałka* violet (mod. Pol. *fiołek*) + *-ów* possessive suffix often used in forming placenames, with the addition of *-ski*, suffix of local surnames (see BARANOWSKI).

Fiksel *see* FOX

Filasov *see* PHILIP

Filatov Russian: patr. from the given name *Filat*, a vernacular form of Gk *Theophylaktos*, composed of the elements *theos* God + *phylakt-* guard, protect. This was the name of a 9th-cent. bishop of Nicomedia, who is venerated in the Orthodox Church.
Vars.: **Feofilaktov, Filakhtov, Filatyev**.

Filby English: habitation name from a place in Norfolk, so called from the ON personal name *Fili* (of uncertain origin) + ON *býr* farm, settlement.
Vars.: **Filbey, Filbee, Philb(e)y**.

Fildes English and Scots (Aberdeen): regional name from a district in Lancs. called The *Fylde*, from OE *(ge)filde* plain.
Var.: **Fyldes**.

Filer English: 1. occupational name for a maker or user of a file (the abrading tool), from an agent deriv. of ME *file* file (OE *fīl*). 2. occupational name for a spinner, from an agent deriv. of ME, OF *fil* thread (L *filum*).

Filkins English: 1. patr. from the medieval given name *Filkin*, a dim. from a short form of PHILIP. 2. habitation name from a place in Oxon. so called, whose name is probably a tribal deriv. of the OE personal name *Filica* (of uncertain origin). Surname forms such as *de Filking(es)* are found in the surrounding area from the 12th and 13th cents.

Fillery English: nickname from ANF *fi(t)z le rei* son of the king. This may have been a nickname bestowed on an illegitimate son of a monarch, but more probably it was either a humorous allusion to a bastard of unknown parentage who claimed an illustrious father or else was bestowed on a man who gave himself airs, acting as if he were of royal blood.

Vars.: **Fillary**, **Fildrey**; FITZROY.

Fillingham English: habitation name from a place in Lincs., so called from OE *Fyglingahām* 'homestead (OE *hām*) of the people of *Fygla*', a personal name from OE *fugol* bird (see FELTON, FOWLE).

Fillmore see PHILLIMORE

Fillon French: nickname for the youngest son in a family, from a dim. of OF *fils* son (L *filius*).

Var.: **Fillion**.

Filosof see PHILOSOPH

Filzer German: occupational name for a maker or seller of felt, MHG, OHG *filz*, with the addition of *-er* suffix denoting agent nouns.

Var.: **Filz**.

Fimichev see YEFIMOV

Fimister see FEMISTER

Fin 1. French: nickname for a clever or elegant man, from OF *fin* fine, delicate, skilled, cunning (originally a noun from L *finis* end, extremity, boundary, later used also as an adj. in the sense 'ultimate', 'excellent'). **2.** Jewish (Ashkenazic): of unknown origin.

Dims.: Fr.: **Finet**, **Finel**, **Finot**.

Finch English: nickname from ME *finch* finch (OE *finc*). In the Middle Ages this bird had a reputation for stupidity. It may perhaps also in part represent a metonymic occupational name for someone who caught finches and sold them as songsters or for the cooking pot. The surname is found in all parts of Britain, but is most common in Lancs. See also FINK.

Fincham English: habitation name from a place in Norfolk, so called from OE *finc* finch + *hām* homestead.

Findlater Scots: habitation name from a place in the former county of Banffs. (now part of Grampian region) so called from Gael. *fionn* white (see FINN) + *leitir* hillside.

Vars.: **Finlater**, **Finlator**.

Findling German and Jewish (Ashkenazic): nickname for a foundling, Ger. *Findling*, MHG *vindelīn* (a deriv. of OHG *findan* to find).

Var.: Ger.: **Findl** (Bavaria).

Finer English: occupational name for a refiner of gold and other metals, from ME *fine(n)* to refine, purify (a deriv. of *fine* fine, pure; see FIN).

Var.: **Finar**.

Finger English, German, and Jewish (Ashkenazic): nickname from ME, MHG, Yid. *finger*, mod. Ger. *Finger* (OE *finger*, OHG *fingar*). The name may originally have denoted a man who had some peculiarity of the fingers, such as possessing supernumerary ones or having lost one or more of them in an accident or fight, or it may have been acquired as the result of some irrecoverable anecdote.

Vars.: Jewish: **Fingerman**; **Fingherman** (Rumanian spelling); **Fingerreich** ('finger rich', possibly a nickname for a person with an extra finger); **Fingeryk** (probably from a Yid. adj. deriv.).

Fingerhut Jewish (Ashkenazic): name bestowed on or taken by a tailor, from mod. Ger. *Fingerhut*, Yid. *fingerhut* thimble (lit. 'finger hat'). The vocab. word also means 'foxglove', but this sense is not relevant to the surname.

Fink German, Jewish (Ashkenazic), and English: nickname (or in the case of the Jewish name, ornamental name) meaning 'Finch', variously from Ger. *Fink* or Yid. *fink* (MHG *vinke*, OHG *finc(h)o*), and Northern ME *fink* (an unpalatalized var. of FINCH).

Vars.: Ger.: **Finker**. Jewish: **Finkman**, **Finkler**. Eng.: **Vin(c)k**.

Dims.: Ger.: **Finkel**, **Finkle** (but see also FUNKE).

Finkelberg see FUNKE

Finlay Scots: from the Gael. personal name *Fionnlagh*, composed of the elements *fionn* white, fair (see FINN) + *laoch* warrior, hero, which seems to have been reinforced by an ON personal name composed of the elements *finn* Finn + *leikr* play.

Vars.: **Findlay**, **Fin(d)ley**, **Fin(d)low**.

Patrs.: **Finlayson**, **Finla(i)son**; MCKINLEY.

Finn 1. Irish: Anglicized form of the Gael. byname *Fionn* 'White'. **2.** English: from the ON personal name *Finnr* Finn, used both as a byname and as a short form of various cpd names with this first element. **3.** Jewish (Ashkenazic): of unknown origin. A connection with Finland seems unlikely.

Vars. (of 1 and 2): **Finne**, **Fynn**, **Phin(n)**.

Patrs. (from 1): Ir.: MCGINN. (From 2): Dan.: **Finsen**.

Patrs. (from 1) (dim.): Ir.: **McKynnan**, **Kinnan** (Gael. **Mac Fhionnáin**).

'Descendant of F. 1': Ir.: **O'Fi(o)nn**, **O'Finne** (Gael. **Ó Finn**).

'Descendant of F. 1 (dim.)': Ir.: **O'Finane**, **O'Fenane**, **O'Fanane**, **Fain(n)an**, **Fin(n)an**, **Fannon**, **Fannin** (Gael. **Ó Fionnáin**); **O'Finegane**, **O'Fenegane**, **Fin(n)igan**, **Fin(n)egan**, **Fenegan**, **Fanagan**, **Finucane** (Gael. **Ó Fionnagáin**).

'Son of the servant of F. 1': Ir.: **McAleenan** (Gael. **Mac Giolla Fhionnain**); MCALINDEN; MCCLINTOCK.

Finnemore English: nickname from OF *fin* fine, splendid (see FIN) + *amour* love (L *amor*).

Vars.: **Fen(n)emore**, **Fenimore**.

Finnerty see FENAGHTY

Finney English: habitation name from one of several places in Ches., so called probably from OE *finig* heap, esp. of wood.

Var.: **Finnie**.

Finnick see FENWICK

Finoccietti see FENNELL

Finster German and Jewish (Ashkenazic): nickname from Ger. *finster* dark, gloomy, or Yid. *fintster* (MHG *vinster*, OHG *finstar, finstrēr*, a byform of *dinstar*). The name may have referred to a person's habitual character or it may have been acquired as a result of some now irrecoverable anecdote.

Var.: Ger.: **Finsterer**.

Dims.: Ger.: **Finsterlin, Finsterle**.

Cpd: Jewish: **Finsterbush** ('dark bush').

Finzel see VINCENT

Fiorella see FLOWER

Fiquenet see FICHE

Firbank English: habitation name from a place in Cumb., so called from ME *firth* woodland (see FIRTH) + *banke* slope (see BANKS).

Var.: **Furbank**.

Fireman 1. Jewish (Ashkenazic): trans. of FAYERMAN and *Feuerman* (see FEUER). 2. English: var. of FAIRMAN.

Fireman see FAIRMAN

Firestein see FEUERSTEIN

Firidolfi see ROLF

Firkin English (W Midlands): metonymic occupational name for a maker of casks and barrels, or nickname for a stout man or a heavy drinker, from ME *fer(de)kyn* small cask (apparently from a MDu. dim. of *vierde* fourth (part); as a measure of capacity a 'firkin' was reckoned as a quarter of a 'barrel').

Patr.: **Firkins**.

Firmin English and French: from the medieval given name *Firmin* (L *Firmīnus*, a deriv. of *firmus* firm, resolute). This name was borne by several early saints, including two bishops of Amiens of the 2nd and 3rd cents.

Vars.: Eng.: **Firman, Furman** (see also FÜHRER). Fr.: **Fermin, Frémin**.

Firrao see ROLLO

Firsht see FÜRST

Firstenberg see FÜRSTENBERG

Firth 1. English and Scots: topographic name from OE *firhð, (ge)fyrhð* woodland or scrub on the edge of a forest. 2. Welsh: topographic name from W *ffrith, ffridd* barren land, mountain pasture (a borrowing of the OE word in 1).

Vars.: **Frith, Frid(d), Fryd, Freeth, Freed(er), Vreede, Frift, Thrift; Fright; Freak(er), Fre(a)ke; Firk(s)**.

Fischbein 1. German: metonymic occupational name for a seller of whalebone, from MHG *(wal)visch* whale + *bein* bone. This elastic bony substance obtained from the upper jaw of whales was much in demand before the development of plastics, and its scarcity made it expensive. 2. Jewish (Ashkenazic): in some cases this name may be occupational, as in 1, but since its high frequency is out of proportion to the small number of Ashkenazic Jews who may have sold whalebone, it is in most cases probably to be interpreted as being composed of Ger. *Fisch* FISH +

Bein bone or leg. If so, it is one of the unflattering surnames imposed by non-Jewish government officials in central Europe when surnames became compulsory, because of its ridiculous connotations.

Vars. (of 2): **Fishb(e)in, Fishbain**.

Fish 1. English: metonymic occupational name for a catcher or seller of fish (cf. FISHER 1) or nickname for someone bearing some supposed resemblance to a fish, from ME *fische, fish*, OE *fisc* fish. 2. Jewish (Ashkenazic): from mod. Ger. *Fisch* or Yid. *fish*, selected either for the same reasons as in 1, or because of its associations with the Hebr. given names *Yona* Jonah and *Efraym* Ephraim. Jonah, in the book of the Bible that bears his name, was swallowed up by a 'great fish'. Ephraim became associated with the fish because he was blessed by his father Jacob (Gen. 48: 16) with the words *veyidgu larov* 'Let them grow into a multitude', the verb *yidgu* containing the root letters of Hebr. *dag* fish.

Vars.: Eng.: **Fishe, Fysh**; FISK. Jewish: **Fisch, Fisz; Fischman(n)**.

Equivs. (not cogn.): It. and other Romance names: PESCE. Pol. and other Slav. names: RYBA.

Dims.: Ger.: **Fisch(e)l, Fischlin**. Jewish: **Fis(c)h(e)l, Fiszel** (from the Yid. male given name *Fishl*, lit. 'Little Fish'); **Fis(c)hlein** (from the Ger. dim. vocab. word).

Patrs. (in form only, lit. 'son of the fish'): Jewish: **Fischsohn, Fishson; Fis(c)hov, Fishof, Fiszow** (E Ashkenazic).

Patrs. (from the Yid. male given name *Fishl*): Jewish: **Fis(c)helson, Fishelzon, Fishlsin; Fishelov; Fischelovitch, Fischelovitz, Fischelewitz, Fish(e)levitz, Fishlovitz, Fiszelewicz**.

Patrs. (from the dim. male given name *Fishke*): Jewish: **Fishkov; Fishkin(d)** (for the excrescent -d, see *Süsskind*); **Fishkinhorn** (apparently an ornamental elaboration of the preceding, with the Ger. element *Horn* horn).

Cpds: Jewish: **Fischauf** ('fish pile'; the second element being mod. Ger. *Hauf* pile); **Fis(c)hbach** ('fish stream'); **Fishbaum** ('fish tree'); **Fish(el)berg** ('fish hill'; -*el*- is dim.: 'little fish hill'); **Fishburger** ('fish citizen'); **Fishfeder** ('fish feather'); **Fis(c)hgrund** ('fish bottom'); **Fischhof(er), Fisherhofer, Fiszhof** ('fish courtyard'; -*er* is a residential suffix); **Fischleiber** ('fish bellies'); **Fishstein** ('fish stone'); **Fisht(h)al** ('fish valley'); **Fischzang** (second element of uncertain origin).

Fisher 1. English: occupational name for a fisherman, ME *fischer*, OE *fiscere*, a deriv. of *fiscian* to catch fish. The name has also been used in Ireland as a loose equivalent of BRADEN. 2. English: topographic name for someone who lived near a fish weir on a river, from ME *fisch* fish (OE *fisc*) + *gere* weir, apparatus (ON *gervi*). 3. Jewish (Ashkenazic): occupational name for a fisherman, mod. Ger. *Fischer*, Yid. *fisher*.

Vars. (of 1): **Fishman**. (Of 3): **Fischer; Fiszer** (Pol. spelling); **Visser** (from Dutch); **Fis(c)hler; Fishner** (partly Anglicized); **Fisherman** (fully Anglicized); **Fis(c)hfanger** ('fish catcher').

Equivs. (not cogn.): Fr. and other Romance names: PÊCHEUR. Pol. and other Slav. names: RYBAK. Hung.: HALÁSZ.

Patrs. (from 1): Eng.: **Fischers**. Low Ger.: **Vissers**. (From 3) Jewish: **Fisherovich** (E Ashkenazic).

Fishwick English (Lancs.): habitation name from a place in Lancs., so called from OE *fisc* FISH + *wīc* outlying farm (see WICK).

Fisk English (E Anglia): metonymic occupational name for a fisherman or fishseller, or nickname for someone supposedly resembling a fish in some way, from ON *fiskr* fish (cogn. with OE *fisc*; see FISH).

Var.: **Fiske**.

Fitch English: although the origins of this surname have been much discussed, no very satisfactory conclusion has been reached. Early forms do not seem to occur with prepositions, so it is not likely to be a habitation name. Reaney rejects the old explanation that it is a nickname derived from early mod. Eng. *fitch* polecat, on the grounds that this word is not found in this form until the 16th cent., whereas the byname or surname *Fitchet* is found as early as the 12th cent. He opts instead for the solution that the name is from OF *fiche* (see FICHE), but with the sense 'iron point', and so a metonymic occupational name for a workman who used an iron-pointed implement.

Vars.: **Fidge**; **Fitcher** (an agent deriv.); **Fick**, **Feak(e)s**, **Feek(s)** (from a Norman form).

Dims.: **Fitchet(t)**, **Fidget**, **Fickett**; **Fitchell**; **Fitchen**, **Ficken**, **Fickin(s)**.

Fitkin *see* VIVIAN

Fitschen *see* FREDERICK

Fitt English (chiefly Norfolk): nickname for a polite and amiable person, from ME *fit* proper, suited (of uncertain origin).

Fitter 1. English: apparently an occupational name for one who prepared things or made them ready. However, the word *fitter* in the sense of a workman appears only in the 19th cent., and the verb to *fit* is not recorded in a relevant sense until the 16th cent. Reaney draws attention to the NE Eng. dial. sense of *fitter* meaning 'coal broker' (although this is not recorded until the 17th cent.). We are either dealing with a very late surname (in which case Reaney's Geoffrey and Hugh *le Fittere* of 1195 and 1231 remain unexplained), or much earlier evidence must be found for the vocab. word. 2. Jewish (Ashkenazic): occupational name for a furrier, from a S Yid. pronunciation of Yid. *futer* fur, furcoat.

Var. (of 2): **Fiter(man)**.

Fittipaldi *see* THEOBALD

Fitton English (chiefly Lancs.): 1. nickname from ME *fitten* lying, deceit (of unknown origin). 2. possibly also a habitation name from *Fitton* Hall in Cambs., which probably gets its name from ON *fit* grassland on the bank of a river + OE *tūn* enclosure, settlement.

FitzAlan *see* ALLEN

Fitzclarence English: this was the surname assumed by George Fitzclarence, Earl of Munster (1794–1842), one of the ten illegitimate children of the Duke of Clarence, later William IV, and Mrs Jordan, one of the leading actresses of the day. He formed his surname by adding the ANF prefix *fitz-* (see FITZGERALD) to his father's title, a revival of one created in 1362 for a son of Edward III, who had married the heiress of CLARE in Suffolk and was given the L title *dux Claresis* or *dux Clareciae*.

FitzGerald Irish (Norman): ANF patr. from the given name *Gerald*; see GARRETT. The name was formed by the addition of the ANF prefix *fi(t)z* son of (L *filius*) to the given name. The Gaelicized form **Mac Gearailt** is common in the Gael.-speaking areas of W Kerry.

Fitzgibbon Irish (Norman): ANF patr. (cf. FITZGERALD) from a dim. of the medieval given name *Gibb*, itself a short form of GILBERT.

Fitzhenry English and Irish (Norman): ANF patr. (cf. FITZGERALD) from the given name HENRY.

Vars.: **Fitzharry**, **Feeharry** (Irish); **Feehally** (Liverpool).

FitzHerbert *see* HERBERT

Fitzhugh English (Norman): ANF patr. (cf. FITZGERALD) from the given name HUGH.

Vars.: **Fitzhugues**; **Fitchew**, **Fit(c)hie**, **Fithye**.

Fitzmaurice Irish (Norman): ANF patr. (cf. FITZGERALD) from the given name *Maurice*; see MORRIS 1.

Fitzner *see* PFÜTZER

Fitzpatrick Irish: occasionally this may be a genuine ANF patr. (cf. FITZGERALD) from the given name PATRICK, but more often it has been adopted as an Anglicized form of Gael. *Mac Giolla Pádraig*; see KILPATRICK.

Fitzpayn *see* PAIN

Fitzrandolph *see* RANDOLPH

Fitzroy English: the surname (from ANF *fi(t)z roy* son of the king; cf. FILLERY) bestowed by Charles II on Henry Fitzroy (1663–90), his illegitimate son by the Duchess of Cleveland. He was created Duke of Grafton in 1675 and was a soldier; he fought under Marlborough and was fatally wounded at the siege of Cork. His descendants include Robert Fitzroy (1805–65), commander of the *Beagle*, the ship in which Darwin made his voyage to S America.

Fitzsimmons Irish (Norman): ANF patr. (cf. FITZGERALD) from the given name SIMON. The name is also found in the Gaelicized form **Mac Síomóin**.

Vars.: **Fitzsimon(s)**, **Fitzsymon(s)**, **Fitzsymonds**.

Fitzsimmons *see* SIMON

Fitzwalter *see* WALTER

Fitzwarin *see* WARING

Fitzwater *see* WATER

Fitzwilliam *see* WILLIAM

Fix *see* VITO

Fjällström *see* FELL

Fjellstedt *see* FELL

Flack 1. English: of unknown origin. The surname is found mostly in Cambs., and so is unlikely to be a var. of FLAGG. It may be akin to the dial. term *flack* to flap about, and so have denoted a scruffily dressed individual. 2. Low German: topographic name apparently derived from a lost word referring to stagnant water.

Vars.: **Flacke**. (Of 2 only): **Flackmann**.

Flagg English: habitation name from places such as *Flagg* in Derbys. and *Flags* in Notts., so called from OE *flage* or ON *flaga* slab, or from ON *flag* turf, sod. The meaning 'standard-bearer' is almost certainly excluded, for the word *flag* in this sense first appears (of unknown provenance) in the 16th cent.

Flaherty Irish: Anglicized form of Gael. Ó **Flaithbheartaigh** 'descendant of *Flaithbheartach*', a byname meaning 'Generous', 'Hospitable' (from *flaith(eamh)* prince, ruler + *beartach* acting, behaving).
Vars.: **O'Fla(g)herty**, **Flagherty**, **Flaverty**, **Flarity**.

Flamank *see* FLEMING

Flamstead English: habitation name from a place in Herts., so called from OE *flēamstede* sanctuary, refuge (a cpd of *flēam* flight + *stede* place, site (see STEAD)).
Vars.: **Flamsteed**, **Flamstede**.

Flanagan Irish: Anglicized form of Gael. Ó **Flannagáin** 'descendant of *Flannagán*', a personal name derived from a dim. of the element *flann* red(dish), ruddy.
Vars.: **Flanaghan**, **Flannagan**, **Flannigan**.

Flanders *see* FLEMING

Flannery Irish: Anglicized form of Gael. Ó **Flannghaile** 'descendant of *Flannghal*', a personal name composed of the elements *flann* red(dish), ruddy + *gal* valour.
Vars.: **O'Flannylla**, **O'Flannelly**, **Flannally**.

Flaschner **1.** German: occupational name for a maker of flasks and bottles, from an agent deriv. of MHG *vlasche* bottle (OHG *flasca*). For the ordinary households of the Middle Ages bottles were made more often from leather than glass, but also sometimes from wood and metal. **2.** Jewish (Ashkenazic): of uncertain origin: possibly as in 1, or possibly an occupational name for a tinsmith, mod. Ger. *Flaschner*.
Vars. (of 1): **Fleschner**; **Pflöschner** (Bavaria); **Flasch(e)**. (Of 2): **Flashner**, **Fleshner**; **Fleschler** ('bottle maker').

Flash **1.** English: topographic name from ME *flasshe* pool, marsh. This is thought to be from ODan *flask* swamp, swampy grassland, shallow water, with -*sh* for -*sk* perhaps due to influence from the synonymous Fr. *flache* (from L *flaccus* soft). **2.** Jewish (Ashkenazic): of uncertain origin, possibly akin to FLASCHNER 2.
Vars.: **Flasher**, **Flashman**.
Dims. (of 1): Fr.: **Flachet**, **Flachot**.
Aug. (of 1): Fr.: **Flachat**.
Pej. (of 1): Fr.: **Flachard**.

Flatt English (chiefly E Anglia): topographic name for someone who lived on a flat, a patch of level or low-lying ground (ON *flat*, *flǫt*).
Var.: **Flatman** (also E Anglian).

Flaubert *see* ROBERT

Flavell English: surname common in the Midlands. *Flavell* was the Normanized form of *Flyford*, Worcs., from OE *ford* with an obscure first element.

Flavien French: from the given name (L *Flāviānus*, a deriv. of *Flāvius*, a Roman family name from *flavus* golden, tawny). This was made popular by two minor saints of the fourth and fifth cents.

Flavin Irish: Anglicized form of Gael. Ó **Flaithimhín** and Ó **Flaitheamháin** 'descendant of *Flaithimhín*' and 'of *Flaitheamhán*'. Both personal names are from dims. of *flaith(eamh)* prince, ruler.

Flax English (E Anglia) and Jewish (Ashkenazic): metonymic occupational name for someone who grew, sold, or treated flax for weaving into linen cloth, from ME *flax* (OE *fleax*) or Ger. *Flachs* (OHG *flahs*).
Vars.: **Flaxman**. Eng.: **Flexman**, **Flexer**. Jewish: **Fla(c)ks**, **Flachs(er)**, **Flaxer**, **Flakser**, **Flaksman**, **Fleksman**.

Fleck German and Jewish (Ashkenazic): from Ger. *Fleck* patch, spot, Yid. *flek* (MHG *vlec(ke)*), of uncertain application. Bahlow suggests various possible reasons for its adoption as a surname, among them the possibility that it is a metonymic occupational name for a user of patches in repairing shoes, clothes, or utensils, or a habitation name from a place named with this word. In some parts of Germany the word denoted a type of round, flat loaf; the surname could perhaps have been a metonymic name acquired by a baker of such loaves. The reasons for the adoption of this word as a Jewish surname are unknown.
Vars.: Ger.: **Fleck(n)er**. Jewish: **Flek**, **Fleckman**.

Fleet English: **1.** habitation name from one of the places so called, in Dorset, Hants, Kent, and Lincs., or from Holt *Fleet* on the river Severn in Worcs., all named with OE *flēot* stream, estuary, creek. It may also be a topographic name from the same word used independently. **2.** nickname for a swift runner, from ME *flete* fleet, rapid (apparently from OE *flēotan* to float, glide rapidly, and so ultimately akin to 1).
Var. (of 1): **Amphlet(t)** (Worcs.; with fused ME preposition *an* on).

Fleetwood English: apparently a habitation name from an unidentified place named with OE *flēot* stream, estuary (see FLEET 1) + *wudu* WOOD. The town of this name in Lancs. got its name in the 19th cent. from its founder, Sir Peter Hesketh Fleetwood, and is not the source of the surname.

Fleksman *see* FLAX

Fleming English: ethnic name for someone from Flanders. In the Middle Ages there was considerable commercial intercourse between England and the Netherlands, particularly in the wool trade, and many Flemish weavers and dyers settled in England. The word reflects an ANF form of OF *flamenc*, from the stem *flam-* + the Gmc suffix -*ing*. The surname is also common in south and east Scotland and in Ireland, where it is sometimes found in the Gaelicized form **Pléimeann**.
Vars.: **Flemming**, **Flemyng**, **Fleeming**, **Fleeman**, **Flamank**, **Flament**, **Flement**, **Le Fleming**; **Flanders**, **Flinders**.
Ger.: **Flaming**, **Flemmi(n)g**, **Flähming**, **Flehmig**, **Flemisch**; **Flander**. Du.: **Vlaming**, **(De) Vlaminck**, **Vleminck**, **(Van) Vlaanderen**. Jewish (Ashkenazic): **Fleming(er)**.
Dim.: Ger.: **Flehmke**.
Pej.: Fr.: **Flamard**.
Patrs.: Eng.: **Flemons**. Flem.: **Vleminckx**. Du.: **Fleminks**.

Fleschler *see* FLASCHNER

Flesher English: occupational name for a butcher. In part it is from ME *flescher*, an agent deriv. of OE *flæsc* flesh, meat; in part a contracted form of ME *fleschewere*, OE *flæschēawere*, in which the second element is an agent noun from *hēawan* to hew, cut (cf. HAUER).

Fletcher English: occupational name for an arrowsmith, ME, OF *flech(i)er* (from OF *fleche* arrow, of Gmc origin; cf. FLOWER 3).

Flett Scots: apparently a habitation name originating in the Orkneys, from a place in the parish of Delting, Shetland, so called from an ON term denoting a strip of arable land or pasture. On the other hand it may be from the ON byname *Fljótr* 'Swift', 'Speedy' (cf. FLEET 2). The surname is now most common around Aberdeen.

Fleurance *see* FLORENCE

Fleurant *see* FLORENT

Fleureau *see* FLOWER

Fleury French and English (Norman): **1.** from the medieval given name *Fleuri* (L *Flōrius*, a deriv. of the Roman family name *Flōrus*, from *flōs*, gen. *flōris*, flower; see FLOWER 1). This name was borne by a 3rd-cent. saint martyred in Nicomedia under Decius. There seems to have been some confusion with a Gmc personal name composed of the elements *hlōd* fame + *rīc* power. **2.** habitation name from any of the various places in N France which get their names from the Gallo-Roman personal name *Florus* (see above, and FLOWER 1) + the local suffix *-ācum*. **3.** nickname from OF *fluri* flowered, variegated (a deriv. of *flur* FLOWER). This could have denoted someone who dressed in an extravagant mixture of colours or perhaps had a blotchy complexion.
Vars.: Fr.: **Flury**. Eng.: **Flury, Flor(e)y**.
Dims. (of 1): Fr.: **Fleuriot**. Prov.: **Flouriot**. It.: **Florino**.
Patrs. (from 1): It.: **De Florio**. Rum.: **Florescu**.

Flewitt English (E Midlands): from the Norman personal name *Flodhard*, composed of the Gmc elements *hlōd* fame + *hard* brave, hardy. The initial *F-* is explained by difficulty experienced by the Normans with the Gmc aspirate (cf. *Flobert* at ROBERT).
Vars.: **Flewett, Flowitt**.

Flinders *see* FLEMING

Flink Jewish (Ashkenazic) and Swedish: nickname from mod. Ger., Yid., Swed. *flink* quick, agile, nimble. As a Swed. name this is one of the group of 'soldiers' names', monosyllabic names adopted (before surnames came into general use in Sweden) by peasants serving in the army, and later transmitted to their descendants. These were the first Swedish surnames.
Vars.: Jewish: **Flinker** (an inflected form, used before a male given name). Swed.: **Flinck**.

Flinn *see* FLYNN

Flint 1. English: topographic name for someone who lived near a notable outcrop of flint (OE *flint*), or nickname for a hard-hearted individual. **2.** Welsh: habitation name from the town of *Flint* in Clwyd, which gave its name to the old

county of Flints. **3.** Jewish: of unknown origin, possibly in some cases a translation of FEUERSTEIN.

Flippen *see* PHILIP

Flizet *see* FELIX

Flobert *see* ROBERT

Flockhart Scots: of uncertain origin, probably a metathesized form of FOLKARD.
Var.: **Flucker**.

Flockton English: habitation name from a place in W Yorks., near Wakefield, so called from the ON personal name *Flóki* (see FLOOK) + OE *tūn* enclosure, settlement.

Flood 1. English: topographic name for someone who lived by a small stream or an intermittent spring (OE *flōd(e)*, from *flōwan* to flow). **2.** Welsh: var. of LLOYD. **3.** Irish: translation of various names correctly or erroneously associated with Gael. *tuile* flood; see TOOLE.
Vars.: **Floud, Fludd, Flude**.
Cpds (of cogns. of 1, ornamental): Swed.: **Flodquist** ('stream twig'); **Flodström** ('stream river').

Flook English: from the ON personal name *Flóki*, originally a byname meaning 'Outspoken', 'Enterprising'.
Var.: **Fluck**.
Patr.: **Flux**.

Florence English and French: **1.** from the medieval given name *Florence*, used by both sexes (L *Flōrentius* (masc.) and *Flōrentia* (fem.), derivs. of *Flōrens*; see FLORENT). Both names were borne by several early Christian martyrs, but in the Middle Ages the masc. name was far more common. **2.** local name for someone from *Florence* in Italy, originally named in L as *Flōrentia*.
Vars.: Fr.: **Florance, Fleurance**.

Florent French: from a medieval given name (L *Flōrens*, gen. *Flōrentis*, pres. part. of *flōrēre* to flourish, bloom, from *flōs*, gen. *flōris*, FLOWER). The name was borne by a number of early saints, amongst them bishops of Cahors in the 4th cent. AD, Orange in the 6th, and Strasbourg in the 7th.
Vars.: **Florant, Fleurent, Fleurant**.

Florentin French (also borne by Sefardic Jews): from a medieval given name (L *Flōrentīnus*, a deriv. of *Flōrens*; see FLORENT). This name was borne by a 6th-cent. saint who was abbot of Arles.

Florescu *see* FLEURY

Flórez Spanish: patr. from the medieval given name *Floro*. This derives in part from the L name *Flōrus* (see FLOWER 1), but has also absorbed the Gmc name *Froila*, a deriv. of the element *fro* lord, master.
Var.: **Flores** (also borne by Sefardic Jews).

Floriano Italian: from a medieval given name (L *Flōriānus*, a further deriv. of *Flōrius*; see FLEURY) borne by a 3rd-cent. saint who was drowned in Noricum during the persecutions of Christians under Diocletian and became the patron of Upper Austria, widely invoked as a protector from the danger of fires.

Vars.: It.: **Florian(i)**, **Floreano**, **Florean(i)**.

Dims.: Pol.: **Florczyk**; **Florek**. Hung.: **Flóris**, **Fóris**.

Patrs.: It.: **De Florian**. Pol.: **Florianowicz**; **Florysiak**. Croatian: **Florjanić**.

Patr. (from a dim.): Pol.: **Florczak**.

Habitation name (from a dim.): Pol.: **Florkowski**.

Flotow German: habitation name from a place on the Weser called *Vlotho* (earlier *Vlotuwe*, from a cogn. of FLOOD) or another in Mecklenburg, near Penzlin, called *Flotow*, which is of Slav. origin.

Var.: **Floto**.

Flower 1. English: nickname from ME *flo(u)r* flower, blossom (OF *flur*, from L *flōs*, gen. *flōris*). This was a conventional term of endearment in medieval romantic poetry, and as early as the thirteenth cent. it is also regularly found as a female given name. The Romance cogns. derive from the L personal names *Flōrus* (borne by a saint active in the Auvergne during the 4th or 5th cents.) and *Flōra* (borne by a 9th-cent. Sp. martyr) as well as formations in the vernacular. 2. English: metonymic occupational name for a miller or flour merchant, or perhaps a nickname for a pasty-faced person, from ME *flo(u)r* flour. This is in origin the same word as in 1, with the transferred sense 'flower, pick of the meal'. Although the two words are now felt to be accidental homophones, they were not distinguished in spelling before the 18th cent. 3. English: occupational name for an arrowsmith, from an agent deriv. of ME *flō* arrow (OE *flā*). For the change of *-ā-* to *-ō-*, cf. ROPER. 4. Welsh: Anglicized form of the W personal name *Llywerch*.

Dims. (of 1): Fr.: **Fleurel(le)**, **Fleureau**, **Fleuret(te)**, **Fleuron**, **Fleurot**. Prov.: **Florel(le)**, **Flouret(te)**. It.: **Fiorell(in)i**, **Fiorell(in)o**, **Fiorella**; **Fiorillo**; **Fioriglio** (S Italy); **Fiorini**, **Fioretti**, **Fioretto**, **Fiorit(t)o**, **Fiorotto**, **Fiorucci**, **Fioruzzi**. Ger.: **Flörl**. Low Ger.: **Flor(ic)ke**.

Augs. (of 1): It.: **Fiorone**, **Fioroni**.

Patrs. (from 1): Eng.: **Flowers**. It.: **Dal Fiore** (Venetia); **Dalla Fior** (Trentino); **Di Fiore** (Sicily); **Floris** (Sardinia). Sp.: FLÓREZ. Low Ger.: **Flöring**. Flem.: **Fleurinck**. Russ.: **Florov**, **Frolov(ski)**, **Florin**. (From 4): Welsh: BLOWER.

Patrs. (from 1) (dim.): Russ.: **Frolkov**, **Frolkin**, **Frolochkin**.

Flowitt *see* FLEWITT

Floyd *see* LLOYD

Fluck *see* FLOOK

Flucker *see* FLOCKHART

Fludd *see* FLOOD

Fluellin *see* LLYWELYN

Flynn Irish: Anglicized form of Gael. Ó Floinn 'descendant of *Flann*', a byname meaning 'Red(dish)', 'Ruddy'.

Vars.: **O'Floin(g)e**, **O'Flynn**, **(O')Flinn**. See also LYNN.

Foakes *see* FOULKES

Foard *see* FORD

Fobian *see* FABIAN

Foch French: habitation name from a place in Ariège, Gascony, of obscure, probably Gaul., etymology.

Var.: **Foix** (representing the original Gascon pronunciation, /fɥa/; now common in Catalonia).

Focken *see* VOLK

Foddy *see* FOODY

Fodor Hungarian and Jewish (Ashkenazic): nickname for a person with curly hair, from Hung. *fodor* curl.

Foet *see* FAGE

Fogarty Irish: Anglicized form of the Gael. personal name *Fógartach*, from *fógartha* banished, outlawed.

Vars.: **Foggarty**, **Fogaty**, **Fogerty**.

Patrs.: **Gogarty**, **Go(g)erty** (Gael. **Mac Fhógartaigh**).

'Descendant of F.': **O'Fogarty**, **O'Fogerty** (Gael. **Ó Fógartaigh**); **O'Hogertie**, **Hogerty**, **Hogart(y)**, HOWARD (Gael. **Ó Fhógartaigh**).

Fogel *see* VOGEL

Fogelson *see* FEIGEL

Fogg English: from ME *fogge* grass left to grow after the hay has been cut, long grass in a water meadow (probably of ON origin), applied either as a topographic name to someone who lived by an area of such grass or as a metonymic occupational name to someone who grazed cattle on it in the winter. The vocab. word is still in use as a dial. term in Craven, Yorks., and in E Lancs. Mod. Eng. *fog* thick mist, first attested in the 16th cent., is perhaps a back-formation from the deriv. *foggy*, which developed the sense 'marshy', 'murky'. It is unlikely to be the source of any surnames.

Foggin English (Northumb.): of uncertain origin, perhaps from a ME given name, a dim. of the various Norman and Scandinavian personal names with the first element *folk* people (see FOULKES).

Var.: **Foggon**.

Foin *see* FOUINE

Foister *see* FORSTER

Foix *see* FOCH

Foizey *see* VAISEY

Fokema *see* VOLK

Fokes *see* FOULKES

Fokin Russian: patr. from the given name *Foka* (Gk *Phōkas*, from *phōkē* seal). This name was borne by several early saints venerated in the Orthodox Church, among them a 2nd-cent. bishop of Sinope (on the Black Sea) who was martyred under Trajan, a 4th-cent. gardener of the same place who was martyred under Diocletian, and a 4th-cent. martyr of Antioch who was suffocated in a bath.

Vars.: **Fokinov**, **Fokanov**.

Folchetti *see* FOULKES

Fold English: topographic name for someone who lived near a pen for animals, or occupational name for someone who worked in one, from ME *fold* pen, enclosure (OE *falod, fald*).

Vars.: **Fould**; **Fo(u)ld(e)s**, **Fowlds**; **Folder**; **Faulds**, **Faulder** (Scots); **Atherfold** ('at the fold').

Földes Hungarian and Jewish (Ashkenazic): occupational name for a farmer, a deriv. of *föld* earth, soil.

Var.: Hung.: **Földesi**.

Foletti *see* CHRISTOPHER

Foley Irish: 1. Anglicized form of Gael. **Ó Foghladha** 'descendant of *Foghlaidh*', a byname meaning 'Pirate', 'Marauder'. 2. Anglicized form of Gael. *Mac Searraigh* (see MCSHARRY), chosen because of its phonetic approximation to Eng. *foal*.

Vars. (of 1): **O'Folowe**, **O'Foley**.

Dim. (of 1): **Folan**.

Folger *see* FULCHER

Foljambe English: nickname for someone with a withered or crippled leg, from OF *fol* foolish, useless (see FOLL) + *jambe* leg (see GAMBE).

Var.: **Fulljames**.

Folk *see* VOLK

Folkard English (Norfolk): from the ME given name *Folc(h)ard*, a Norman name of Gmc origin, composed of the elements *folk* people + *hard* hardy, brave, strong.

Var.: **Folkart**.

Patrs.: Eng.: **Folkerts**. Low Ger.: **Volkerts**, **Folkerts**.

Foll English: nickname for a foolish or eccentric person, from OF *fol* mad, stupid (LL *follis*, originally a noun denoting any of various objects filled with air, but later transferred to vain and empty-headed notions).

Dims.: Eng.: **Follet(t)**, **Follit(t)**.

Follows English (W Midlands): of uncertain origin; perhaps a late var. of FALLOWS or *Fellows* (see FELLOW), which have themselves been considerably confused.

Var.: **Follis**.

Folomeev *see* BARTHOLOMEW

Fölsch *see* VOLK

Fomichkin *see* THOMAS

Fonaryov Russian: patr. from the nickname *Fonar* 'Lamp', 'Lantern' (LGk *phanarion*, a dim. of class. Gk *phanos*, from *phainein* to show, reveal). The reasons for the acquisition of the nickname are not altogether clear; they were probably anecdotal and so are now lost irrecoverably.

Fonin *see* AFANASYEV

Fonnell *see* FENNELL

Fonseca Spanish and Portuguese: topographic name for someone who lived by a spring that dried up during the summer months, from Romance descendants of L *fons* spring, well (see FONT) + *sicca* (fem.) dry.

Font Provençal and Catalan: topographic name for someone living near a spring or well, OProv. *font* (L *fons*, gen. *fontis*).

Vars.: Prov.: **Hont** (Gascony); **Lafon(t)**, **Lafond**; **Defont**, **Defond**; **Delafon(t)**. Cat.: **Fon(t)s**, **Safont**.

Dims.: Prov.: **Fontel(le)**, **Fontin**. Cat.: **Fontelles**.

Fontaine N and central French: topographic name for someone who lived near a spring or well, OF *fontane* (LL *fontāna*, a deriv. of class. L *fons*; see FONT, and cf. MONT and MONTAGNE).

Vars.: **Fonteyne**; **Lafontaine**; **De(la)fontaine**, **Desfontaines**, **Fontanier**, **Fontenier**.

Dims.: Fr.: **Fontanet**, **Fontenet**; **Fontanel**, **Fontenel(le)**, **Fonteneau**. Prov.: **Fontenille**, **Fontenieu**. It.: **Fontanella**, **Fontanelli**; **Fontanino**, **Fontanin(i)**; **Fontanot(ti)**. Sp.: **Fontanillas**. Cat.: **Fontanella(s)**.

Pej.: It.: **Fontanazzi**.

Collectives: Fr.: **Fontenay**, **Fontenoy**. Cat.: **Fontanet**, **Fontanals**.

Fonzone *see* ALFONSO

Foody Irish: Anglicized form of Gael. **Ó Fuada**, 'descendant of *Fuada*', a personal name from *fuad* haste.

Vars.: **O'Foody**, **O'Foodie**, **O'Foedy**; **Foudy**, **Foddy**; SPEED, SWIFT, RUSH.

Fookes *see* FOULKES

Foord *see* FORD

Foorish *see* FOURISH

Foot English (chiefly Devon): nickname for someone with some peculiarity or deformity of the foot, from ME *fot*, OE *fōt*, or in some cases from the cogn. ON byname *Fótr*. Early examples with prepositions, which would support its origin as a topographic name for someone who lived at the foot of a hill, have not been found.

Var.: **Foote** (chiefly Somerset).

Dims.: Eng.: **Footitt** (Notts.). Ger.: **Füssel**; **Füssle** (Swabia); **Füssli** (Switzerland).

Foran Irish: Anglicized form of Gael. **Ó Fuar(th)áin** 'descendant of *Fuar(th)án*', a personal name derived from *fuar* cold.

Var.: **O'Foran**.

Forber *see* FROBISHER

Forbes 1. Scots (now also found in Ireland): habitation name from a place near Aberdeen, so called from Gael. *forba* field, district + the local suffix -*ais*. The placename is pronounced in two syllables, with the stress on the second, and the surname until recently reflected this. Today, however, it is generally a monosyllable. 2. Irish: Anglicized form of Gael. **Mac Fearbhisigh**, patr. from the personal name *Firbhsigh*, composed of Celt. elements meaning 'man' + 'prosperity'. A family of this name in Connacht was famous for its traditional historians.

Forcadell *see* FOURCHE

Force French: topographic name for someone who lived by a fortress or stronghold, OF *force* (LL *fortia*, a deriv. of *fortis* strong; see FORT). There are several places named with this word (for example in Aude, and baronial lands in the Dordogne), and it may also be a habitation name from any of these.

Var.: **Delaforce**.

Forcher German and Jewish (Ashkenazic): topographic name for someone who lived by a conspicuous pine tree or in a coniferous forest, from Ger. *Föhre* pine, MHG *vorhe*.

Vars.: Ger.: **Forchert**, **Forchner**.

Forchheimer Jewish (W Ashkenazic): apparently a habitation name from an unidentified place called *Forchheim* or *Vorchheim*.

Var.: **Vorchheimer**.

Ford 1. English: topographic name for someone who lived near a ford, OE *ford*, or habitation name from one of the many places named with this word. 2. Irish: Anglicized form of various Gael. names, for example *Mac Giolla na Naomh* (see GILDERNEW), *Mac Conshámha* (see KINNEAVY), and *Ó Fuar(th)áin* (see FORAN). 3. Jewish: Anglicization of one or more like-sounding Jewish surnames.

Vars. (of 1): **Foord**, **Foard**, **Forth**; **Forder** (chiefly E Anglia). (Of 1 and 2): **Forde** (very common in Ireland).

Fordham English: habitation name from any of the places in Cambs., Essex, and Norfolk so called, from OE *ford* FORD + *hām* homestead.

Fordyce Scots: habitation name from a place near Banff, so called from Gael. *forba* field (cf. FORBES) + *deas* south.

Forell German: metonymic occupational name for a trout fisher, or nickname for a person bearing some supposed resemblance to a trout, Ger. *Forelle* trout (MHG *forhel*, *forhen*; OHG *forhana*).

Var.: **Forel**.

Forgan 1. Scots: habitation name from a place in Fife, formerly known as *Forgrund*, perhaps from OE *fōr* pig + *grund* ground. 2. Irish: Anglicized form of Gael. *Ó Mhurcháin*; see MORGAN.

Forge English and French: topographic name for someone who lived near a forge or smithy, ME, OF *forge* (from L *fabrīca* workshop, a deriv. of *faber* workman; cf. FÈVRE). The surname is thus in most cases an indirect designation for a SMITH or his assistants and servants.

Vars.: Fr.: **Forgue**, **Farge(s)**; **Laforge**, **Laforgue**; **De(la)forge**, **Desforges**; **Fargier**.

Dims.: Fr.: **Forgette**, **Fargette**; **Fargeon**, **Farjon**, **Forjonnel**.

Aug.: Fr.: **Farjat**.

Forgrave see FAIRGRIEVE

Fóris see FLORIANO

Forker see FARQUHAR

Forlong see FURLONG

Forman 1. English: occupational name for a keeper of swine, ME *foreman*, from OE *fōr* hog, pig + *mann* man. 2. English: status name for a leader or spokesman for a group, from OE *fore* before, in front + *mann* man. The word is attested in this sense from the 15th cent., but is not used specifically of the leader of a gang of workers

before the late 16th cent. 3. Czech and Jewish (Ashkenazic): occupational name for a driver of a horse-drawn vehicle, from Czech *forman* driver (derived, like Pol. and Yid. *furman*, from Ger. *Fuhrmann*; see FÜHRER).

Vars. (of 1 and 2): **Foreman**. (Of 3): Jewish: **Formanski**, **Formansky**, **Furmanski**, **Furmansky**; **Fu(h)rman(n)**.

Dims. (of 3): Czech: **Formánek**. Pol.: **Furmańczyk**, **Furmanek**. Jewish: **Formanek**, **Furmanek**.

Patr. (of 3): Jewish: **Furmanov**.

Formby English: habitation name from the place on Merseyside, so called from ON *forn* old (or perhaps a byname *Forni* with this meaning) + *býr* farm, settlement.

Formentin see FROMENT

Fornarini see FOURNIER

Forrest English: topographic name for someone who lived in or near a royal forest, or occupational name for a keeper or worker in one. ME *forest* was not, as today, a near-synonym of WOOD, but referred specifically to large areas of woodland reserved by law for the purposes of hunting by the king and his nobles; the same applied to the European cogns., both Gmc and Romance. The Eng. word is from OF *forest*, LL *forestis* (*silva*), apparently a deriv. of *foris* outside; the reference was probably originally to woods lying outside a dwelling. On the other hand MHG *for(e)st* has been held to be a deriv. of OHG *foraha* fir (see FORCHER), with the addition of a collective suffix.

Vars.: **Forest**; **For(r)ester**, **Forrestor**, **Forrestier** (see also FORSTER and FOSTER).

Dim.: Fr.: **Forichon**.

Fors Swedish: ornamental name from Swed. *fors* waterfall (ON *fors*), or perhaps in some cases a topographic name adopted by someone who lived by a waterfall. This is one of the many Swedish surnames taken more or less arbitrarily in the 19th cent. from vocab. words referring to natural phenomena, and compounded with other such elements more or less arbitrarily to make compound surnames.

Vars.: **Forss(én)**, **Fors(s)ell**, **Forselius**, **Forslin(g)**, **Forsman**.

Cpds (ornamental): Swed.: **Forsberg** ('waterfall hill'); **Forsgren** ('waterfall branch'); **Forslund** ('waterfall grove'); **Forsström** ('waterfall river').

Forsdick see FOSDYKE

Forshaw English (Lancs.): habitation name from a lost place in the parish of Prescot, Lancs. It is first recorded in 1315 as *Fourocshagh* 'Four Oak Wood' (for the last element see SHAW), and by 1446 had become *Fauroshaw*.

Förstel see FÜRST

Forster 1. English and German: topographic name for someone who lived by a forest, or occupational name for someone employed in one; see FORREST. 2. English (Norman): occupational name for a maker or user of scissors, from OF *forcetier* (a deriv. of *forcettes*, dim. of *forces* clipping shears, L *forfices*). 3. English (Norman): occupational name for a worker in wood, from a metathesized var. of OF *fust(r)ier* (a deriv. of *fustre* block of wood, L *fustis*). 4. Jewish (Ashkenazic): ornamental name from Ger. *Forst* forest.

Vars. (of 1): Ger.: **Förster**, **Ferster**, **Forstner**. (Of 3): **Fewster**, **Foister**, **Foyster**, **Fuster**; see also FOSTER.

Förster *see* FORSTER

Forsyth Scots: from an Anglicized form of the Gael. personal name *Fearsithe*, composed of the elements *fear* man + *sithe* peace. Some early forms with prepositions, as for example William *de Fersith* (Edinburgh 1365), seem to point to an alternative origin as a habitation name, but no placename of suitable form has yet been discovered.

Var.: **Forsythe** (chiefly N Ireland).

Fort English and French: **1.** nickname from OF *fort* strong, brave (L *fortis*). In some cases it may be from the rare L personal name of the same origin borne by an obscure saint whose cult was popular during the Middle Ages in S and SW France. **2.** topographic name for someone who lived near a fortress or stronghold, or occupational name for someone employed in one; cf. FORTIER 1.

Vars.: Eng.: **Forte**. Fr.: **Lefort**.

Dims. (of 1): Fr.: **Fortet**, **Forton**, **Fortin**, **Fo(u)rteau**. Prov.: **Fo(u)rtoul**, **Fortoly**. It.: **Fortino**, **Fortin(i)**, **Fortuzzi**.

Patrs. (from 1): It.: **Fortis**. Sp.: **Ortiz**.

Fortescue English (Norman): nickname for a valiant warrior, from OF *fort* strong, brave (see FORT 1) + *escu* shield (L *scutum*; cf. SQUIRE).

Vars.: **Fortesquieu**, **Foskew**.

Fortgang Jewish (Ashkenazic): presumably from Ger. *Fortgang* continuation; the reason for its adoption or bestowal are unknown (cf. the rarer Ashkenazic surname **Mitgang**).

Fortier French: **1.** occupational name for someone employed at a fortress or castle, from a deriv. of OF *fort* stronghold (from the adj. *fort* strong; see FORT). **2.** occupational name for a worker in wood or metal who made use of a drill, OF *foret* (from *forer* to drill, pierce, L *forāre*).

Var.: **Fourtier**.

Förtig *see* FERTIG

Fortnum English (Norman): nickname for a man with more brawn than brain, from OF *fort* strong (see FORT 1) + *anon*, dim. of *asne* donkey (L *asinus*).

Var.: **Fortnam**.

Fortunato Italian and Portuguese: from a medieval given name (L *Fortūnātus*, a deriv. of *fortūna*; see FORTUNE 1). The L name was fashionable among early Christians, chosen with reference to their joy in the faith. It was borne by a large number of early saints, which further increased its popularity as a given name in the Middle Ages.

Vars.: It.: **Fortunat(i)**.

Fortune **1.** English: nickname for a gambler, from ME, OF *fortune* chance, luck (L *fortūna*); cf. CHANCE and HASARD. In some cases it may derive from the rare medieval given name *Fortune* (L *Fortūnius*). **2.** Scots: habitation name from a place in Lothian, apparently so called from OE *fōr* hog, pig + *tūn* settlement, enclosure; John *de Fortun* was servant to the abbot of Kelso *c.*1200.

Fortwängler *see* FURTWANGER

Forward English: occupational name for a keeper of swine, from OE *fōr* hog, pig (cf. FORMAN 1) + *weard* guardian (see WARD 1).

Var.: **Forwood**.

Foschi *see* FUSCO

Fosdyke English: habitation name from a place in Lincs., so called from the gen. case of the OE byname *Fōt* 'Foot' (or the ON cogn. *Fótr*; see FOOT) + OE *dīc* ditch, dyke (see DITCH).

Vars.: **Forsdyke**, **Forsdike**, **Forsdick**; **Frosdick** (Norfolk).

Foskett English: habitation name from any of various places, such as *Foscott* (Bucks., Oxon.), *Foscote* (Northants, Wilts.), *Foxcott* (Hants), *Foxcote* (Gloucs., Warwicks.), so called from OE *fox* Fox + *cot* shelter, burrow (see COATES).

Foskew *see* FORTESCUE

Fosse English and French: habitation name from some place named with OE *foss* ditch, OF *fosse* (both from L *fossa*, a deriv. of *fodīre* to dig, excavate). In Eng. the term did not survive as a vocab. word into the period when surnames were acquired, and the surname must therefore normally either be an importation from French or refer to any of the various minor places named *Foss(e)*, either from being near the Roman *Fosse* Way, itself named in the OE period from the ditch running alongside it, or from the river *Foss* in Yorks.

Vars.: Eng.: **Foss**; **Vos(s)**. Fr.: **Lafosse**, **Delafosse**.

Dims.: Fr.: **Fosset**, **Fossé**, **Fossez**, **Fossey**, **Dufosset**, **Dufossés**, **Desfossés**. Prov.: **Foussé**.

Augs.: Fr.: **Fossat**. Prov.: **Foussat**.

Fosset *see* FAWCETT

Foster **1.** English: simplified var. of FORSTER, in any of its senses. **2.** English: nickname from ME *foster* foster parent (OE *fōstre*, a deriv. of OE *fōstrian* to nourish, rear, from *fōster* food). **3.** Jewish: of unknown origin, perhaps an Anglicization of one or more like-sounding Jewish surnames, such as FORSTER.

Fothergill English: habitation name from a place in Cumb. or some other place similarly named (e.g. in W Yorks.), from ON *fóðr* fodder, forage + *gil* steep valley, ravine (see GILL 2).

Fotheringham Scots: habitation name from *Fothringham* near Forfar, which seems to have been named after *Fotheringhay* in Northants, which was held in the 12th cent. by the royal family of Scotland as part of the honour of Huntingdon. The Northants place appears in Domesday Book as *Fodringeia*, apparently from OE *fōdring* grazing (a deriv. of *fōdor* fodder) + *ēg* island, low-lying land. In the case of the Scots place, the final element has early been replaced by *-hām* homestead.

Var.: **Fothringham**.

Foucault French: from a Gmc personal name composed of the elements *folk* people + *wald* rule.

Vars.: **Foucau(l)d**, **Foucaut**.

Fouchareau *see* FULCHER

Foudy *see* FOODY

Fouet *see* FAGE

Fougère French: topographic name for someone who lived in a place densely grown with ferns, from OF *foug(i)ere* fern, bracken (from LL *filicāria*, a deriv. of class. L *filix*, gen. *filicis*, fern).

Vars.: **Fouchère**; **Feug(i)ère** (NW France); **Feuchère** (NE France); **Feuquières** (Picardy); **Faug(i)ère** (Puy-de-Dôme).

Dim.: Fr.: **Fougeron**.

Aug.: Fr.: **Fougerat**.

Fouine French: **1.** metonymic occupational name for a maker or user of pitchforks, from OF *foisne* (L *fuscīna* three-pronged fork; cf. FOURCHE). **2.** nickname for a crafty or sly individual, from OF *faïne* weasel, marten (L *fāgīna* (sc. *mustēla* weasel), a deriv. of *fāgus* beech tree (see FAGE), apparently the favourite haunt of the animals).

Vars.: **Fouin**, **Foin(e)**, **Foing**.

Dims.: **Fo(u)ineau**. (Of 1 only): **Foisneau**.

Aug.: **Fouinat**.

Pej.: **Foinard**.

Fould *see* FOLD

Foulerton *see* FULLERTON

Foulkes English: from a Norman given name, a short form of the various Gmc names with the first element *folk* people. See also VOLK.

Vars.: **Folk(e)s**, **Fulk(e)s**; **Fook(e)s**, **Fou(k)x**, **Fo(a)kes**, **Fowkes**; **Fewkes** (chiefly E Midlands); **Volk(e)s**, **Vokes**; **Folk(e)**, **Fulk(e)**, **Fuke**, **Volk(e)**, **Voak** (from the oblique case).

Dims.: Fr.: FOUQUET, **Fouqué**, **Fouchet**; **Fouqueau**. It.: **Folchetti**, **Folc(h)ini**, **Fulcoli**.

Aug.: It.: **Fulconi**.

Patrs.: Eng.: **Folkson**, **Foxon**, **Foxen**. It.: **Di Folca**.

Foulonneau *see* FULLER

Fouquet French: **1.** dim. of FOULKES. **2.** nickname for someone who in some way resembled a squirrel, OF *fouquet* (originally from the given name, but later understood as a dim. of *fou*, *fol* mad; cf. FOLL).

Fourche French: **1.** metonymic occupational name for a maker or user of forked instruments, from OF *fourche* (L *furca* two-pronged fork; cf. FOUINE). **2.** topographic name for someone who lived by a fork in a road or river, from the same word used in this sense.

Var.: **Fourquier** (Normandy).

Dims.: Fr.: **Fourquet**. It.: **Forcella**, **Forcell(in)i**. (Of 2 only): Cat.: **Forcadell**.

Aug.: It.: **Forcone**.

Fourish Irish: Anglicized form of Gael. **Ó Fuarisc(e)** 'descendant of *Fuarisc(e)*', a personal name perhaps derived from *fuar* cold (cf. FORAN).

Vars.: **Foorish**, **Furish**; **Whorisky**, **Horisky**; WATER (by association with *fuaran* well, spring).

Fournel *see* FURNEAUX

Fournier French: occupational name for a baker, OF *fo(u)rnier* (LL *furnārius*, a deriv. of *furnus* oven). As a Fr. surname this is considerably more frequent than BOULANGER, the term which gradually replaced it as a vocab. word during the later Middle Ages.

Vars.: **Fournié**; **Lefournier**, **Lefournié**.

Dims.: Fr.: **Fourneret**. Prov.: **Fourneyron**. It.: **Fornarini**, **Fornarino**, **Fornarotti**.

Patrs.: It.: **Fornaris**, **Forneris**.

Fourrier French: occupational name for a supplier of fodder, from an agent deriv. of OF *fourre* fodder (of Gmc origin).

Vars.: **Fourier**, **Fourié**.

Fourteau *see* FORT

Fourtier *see* FORTIER

Foussat *see* FOSSE

Fowell *see* FOWLE

Fowlds *see* FOLD

Fowle English: nickname for someone who in some way resembled a bird, in part representing a ME continuation of the OE personal name *Fugol* 'Bird', originally a byname.

Vars.: **Fowell**; **Vowell**; **Fuggle**.

Patrs.: **Fowl(e)s**, **Fowells**; **Vowel(l)s**, **Vowles**, **Vouls** (W Country); **Fuggles**.

Fowler English: occupational name for a bird-catcher (a common medieval occupation), ME *fogelere*, *foulere* (OE *fugelere*, a deriv. of *fugol* bird; cf. FOWLE).

Vars.: **Fugler**; **Vowler** (S England).

Equivs. (not cogn.): Czech: PTÁČNÍK, ČIHÁK.

Fox 1. English: nickname from the animal, ME, OE *fox*. It may have denoted a cunning individual or been given to someone with red hair or for some other anecdotal reason; there is no evidence (in the shape of early forms with prepositions) to suggest that it was ever derived from a house sign. This relatively common and readily understood surname seems to have absorbed some early examples of less transparent surnames derived from the Gmc personal names mentioned at FAULKES and FOULKES. **2.** Irish: translation of Gael. *Mac an tSionnaigh* 'Son of the fox'; see SHINNOCK. See also CARNEY. **3.** Jewish (Ashkenazic): Anglicized form of the Jewish cogns. given below, often the result of a desire to avoid association with mod. Eng. *fucks*. **4.** Low German: patr. from the given name *Fock*; see VOLK.

Vars. (of 1–3): **Foxe**. (Of 3): **Foxman**, **Fuchsman**.

Ger.: **Fuchs**. Jewish: **Fuchs(man)**, **Fu(c)ks**, **Fux(sman)**, **Fuksman**; **Fiks(man)** (S Ashkenazic).

Dims. (of 1): Ger.: **Füchsel**. Low Ger.: **Vöske**, **Vössgen**. Jewish: **Fiksel** (from Yid. *fiksl*).

Patrs. (from 1): Low Ger.: **Vossen**, **Vossing**.

Foxall English (W Midlands): habitation name from some minor locality, probably the lost *Foxhale* near Claverley, Shrops., the name of which is derived from OE *fox* Fox + *halh* hollow, recess (see HALE 1). It is less likely that the surname is derived from *Foxhall* in Suffolk (earlier *Foxhole*), which gets its name from OE *fox* + *hol(h)* hollow, depression (see HOLE): the surname is not established in E Anglia.

Foxen *see* FOULKES

Foxley English: habitation name from places in Norfolk, Northants., and Wilts., all of which are so called from OE *fox* Fox + *lēah* wood, clearing.

Foxton English (Yorks.): habitation name from any of the various places so called, of which the most likely source for the surname is the one in N Yorks., which is from OE *fox* Fox + *tūn* enclosure, settlement. The places so called in Co. Durham and Northumb. are from OE *fox* Fox + *denu* valley.

Foxwell English: apparently a habitation name from an unidentified place so called from OE *fox* Fox + *well(a)* spring, stream (see WELL).

Foy 1. French: nickname, from OF *foi* faith (L *fides*), either for a pious person or for someone who frequently used this term in oaths. **2.** French: from the medieval female given name *Foy*, which is from *foi* faith, as above. **3.** Irish: var. of FAHY and FEE.
Vars. (of 1): **Lafoy**, **Delafoy**.

Foyle English and Irish (Norman): topographic name for someone who lived near a pit or man-made hollow, from OF *fouille* pit (a deriv. of *fouillir* to dig up, excavate, LL *fodiculāre*, for class. L *fodīre*; cf. FOSSE). The pit in question could have been a limepit or claypit, or an excavation designed to receive refuse (cf. PITT). There are several minor places in England named with this word, and the surname may also be a habitation name derived from one of these rather than directly from the physical feature.

Foyster *see* FORSTER

Fozard *see* FOZZARD

Fozzard English (chiefly W Yorks.): of unknown origin.
Var.: **Fozard**.

Frabbetti *see* FÈVRE

Frąckiewicz *see* FRANCIS

Fradin *see* FREIDIS

Fragino *see* FRANCIS

Fragneau *see* FRAIN

Fragonard French: nickname, given perhaps to a man with a livid complexion or a birthmark, from OF *frage*, *fraie* strawberry (LL *frāga*, originally a neut. pl. form, but later used as fem. sing.) + the dim. suffix *-on* + the pej. suffix *-ard*.

Fragoso Spanish and Portuguese: topographic name for someone who lived on a patch of rocky ground, from Sp., Port. *fragoso* rocky, uneven (LL *fragōsus*).
Var.: **Fraga** (the name of places in the provinces of Corunna and Huesca).

Frähmke *see* FROMM

Frain English (Norman): topographic name for someone who lived near an ash tree or ash wood, from OF *fraisne*, *fresne* ash (L *fraxinus*).
Vars.: **(De) Fraine**, **Fra(y)ne**, **Frean**, **Freen**, **(De) Freyne**.
Dims.: Fr.: **Fresnel**, **Fresneau**, **Frénel**, **Fréneau**, **Fra(i)gneau**; **Fresnet**, **Fresneix**. Sp.: **Fresnillo**.
Collectives: Eng.: **Franey**, **Fre(e)ney**. Fr.: **Fresnay**, **Fresnoy**, **Frênay**, **Frênais**, **Frênoy**, **Dufresnoy**. Sp.: **Fresneda**.

Frame 1. Scots: of unknown origin. Black notes that 'several persons of this name are recorded in the Commisariot Records of Campsie and of Lanark', and it is now very common in Scotland, esp. around Glasgow. The earliest known instance of the name occurs in 1495. **2.** Jewish: of unknown origin.

Frampton English: habitation name from any of various places so called, of which there are several in Gloucs. and one in Dorset. Most take the name from the river *Frome* (which is apparently from a Brit. word meaning 'fair', 'brisk') + OE *tūn* enclosure, settlement. One near Tewkesbury was originally named in OE as *Frēolingtūn* 'settlement associated with *Frēola*', a short form of any of the various cpd names with the first element *frēo* free. Frampton in Lincs. probably gets its name from the OE byname **Frameca* (a deriv. of *fram* valiant) + OE *tūn*.

Francis 1. English: from a very popular medieval given name (L *Franciscus*, introduced into England in the OF form *François*). This was originally an ethnic name meaning 'Frenchman'; most of the Romance cogns. are ambiguous between derivation from the ethnic name and the given name. The numerous dims., however, almost all belong to the given name, and in Eng. the ethnic name is normally represented by FRENCH. The given name owed much of its popularity during the Middle Ages to the fame of St Francis of Assisi (1181–1226), whose baptismal name was actually *Giovanni* (see JOHN) but who was nicknamed *Francisco* because his father was absent in France at the time of his birth. **2.** Jewish: of uncertain origin, presumably an Anglicization of one or more like-sounding Jewish surnames or an adoption of the non-Jewish surname.
Vars.: Eng.: **Franc(i)es**, **Franses**. Jewish: **Frances**.
Dims.: Sc.: **Francie**, **Francey**. It.: **Francesch(i)elli**, **Ceschelli**, **Schellini**; **Franceschetti**, **Schetti**, **Schettini**; **Franceschini**, **Ceschini**, **Scini**, **Scinelli**, **Schinetti**; **Francescotti**, **Franciotti**, **Cescot(ti)**, **Scotti**, **Scottini**; **Franceschelli**, **Francello**, **Francillo**, **Frangello**; **Franceschino**, **Fragino**; **Francescoccio**, **Francescozzi**, **Francescuccio**, **Francescuzzi**; **Francioli**, **Franzol(in)i**, **Zolini**, **Fransinelli**; **Francino**, **Cino**, **Cinelli**; **Franzini**, **Zini**; **Franzetto**, **Franzitti**, **Zetto**; **Franciotto**, **Ciotto**, **Giotto**, **Giottini**; **Franzotto**, **Zott(ol)i**; **Franzelini**, **Franzonello**, **Franzonetti**; **C(h)ecchi**, **Ch(i)eco**, **C(h)ecchetelli**, **Ceccoli**, **C(h)ec(c)ucci**, **Ceccuzzi**; **Cicco**, **Cicchetto**, **Chicchelli**, **Cichillo**, **Cicchin(ell)i**, **Cicchitello**, **Ciccitti**, **Cicutto**, **Cic(c)olini**, **Ciccolo**, **Cicculi**, **Cicconetti**, **Cic(c)ott(in)i**, **Cicullo**; **Cicci**, **Cic(c)etti**, **Cicciotti**; **Chicco**, **Chicotti**, **Chiechio**, **Sciuscietto**; **Fraschetti**, **Fra(n)scini**; **Fresch(in)i**; **Zecchi**, **Zecchetti**, **Zecchin(i)**, **Zechinelli** (Venetia). Ger.: **Fränzel**, **Frenz(e)l**. Low Ger.: **Franzke**. Du.: **Fransman**. Ger. (of Slav. origin): **Frensch(e)**, **Fronzek**. Czech: **Franěk**, **Froněk**. Pol.: **Frączek**. Beloruss.: **Franchyonok**.
Augs.: It.: **Francesconi**, **Fransecone**; **Francione**, **Franscioni**, **Frascone**, **Frangione**, **Franchioni**, **Fransoni**; **Cescon(i)**.
Patrs.: It.: **De Francesco**, **Di Francesco**, **De Franceschi**, **De Francisci(s)** (Liguria). Low Ger.: **Frantzen**, **Franssen**. Fris.:

Fransema, Frankema. Flem.: **Franssen, Cissen, Ceyssen**. Du.: **Fran(s)sen, Fran(t)zen**. Dan., Norw.: **Frantzen, Frandsen**. Swed.: **Fransson, Franzen**. Pol.: **Franciskiewicz; Ferencowicz** (from the Hung. form of the given name, *Ferenc*). Beloruss.: **Frantsev**. Jewish: **Franzewitch, Fransevich** (E Ashkenazic).

Patrs. (from dims. of 1): It.: **Di Frisco, Del Checolo**. Pol.: **Frankiewicz, Frąc(z)kiewicz; Frą(t)czak, Fron(t)czak; Franiak**.

Habitation name (from a dim.): Pol.: **Frankowski**.

Francombe English (chiefly Bristol): status name from the ANF feudal term *franchomme* free man (see FREE), composed of the elements *franc* free (see FRANK 2) + *homme* man (L *homo*). The spelling has been altered as the result of folk etymological association with the common Eng. placename endings *-combe* and *-ham*.

Vars.: **Frankcombe, Frank(c)om, Francom** (also Bristol); **Frankham**.

Frangipane Italian: nickname from It. *frangere* to break, divide (L *frangere*) + *pane* bread (L *panis*; cf. PAIN 2). A Roman family of this name supposedly acquired it because they distributed bread to the populace during a famine.

Vars.: **Fragapane, Fregapane**.

Frank 1. English: from the Norman given name *Franc*, in origin an ethnic name for a Frank, a member of the Gmc people who inhabited the lands around the river Rhine in Roman times. In the 6th cent., under their leader Clovis I, the Franks established a substantial empire in central Europe, which later developed into the so-called Holy Roman Empire. Their most famous ruler was the Emperor Charlemagne (742–814). Their name is of uncertain ultimate etymology; it may be akin to a Gmc word meaning 'javelin', of which the OE form is *franca*. **2.** English: nickname from ME, OF *franc* liberal, generous (earlier 'free', deriving from the fact that in Frankish Gaul only those of Frankish race enjoyed the status of free men). **3.** German, Flemish/Dutch, Danish/Norwegian, Czech, Hungarian, and Jewish (Ashkenazic): ethnic or regional name for someone from *Franconia* (Ger. *Franken*), a region of SW Germany so called from its early settlement by the Franks.

Vars. (of 1 and 2): Eng.: **Francke**. (Of 3): Ger.: **Franke, Franck(e)**. Flem., Du.: **Franke**. Dan., Norw.: **Franck**. Jewish: **Franken**.

Dims. (of 1 and 2): Fr.: **Franchet, Franquet, Franchineau, Francin(e), Françon, Francillon, Francou(l)**. It.: **Franchelli, Franchetti, Franchitti, Franch(ol)ini, Francucci**. (Of 3): Ger.: **Fränk(e)l, Frenkel, Frankel, Fränkle**. Jewish: **Frank(e)l, Frenk(i)el**.

Augs. (of 1 and 2): It.: **Franconi, Francone**.

Patrs. (from 1): Eng.: **Franks**. It.: **De Franco, Di Franco, De Franchi(s)** (Liguria). (From 3): Ger.: **Franks**. Low Ger.: **Fran(c)ken; Frenking** (N Rhineland). Du.: **Franken**. Jewish: **Frankovits** (E Ashkenazic).

Cpds: Jewish (ornamental unless otherwise stated): **Frankenheim** ('Franconian home', perhaps also a habitation name from a place so called); **Frankenschein** ('Franconian light'); **Frankenstein** ('Franconian rock'); **Frankent(h)al, Frenkental** ('Franconian valley', perhaps also a habitation name from a place so called).

Frankland English: status name for someone who lived on a piece of land held without obligations of rent or service, from ANF *frank* free (see FRANK 2) + ME *land* land; cf. FREELAND.

Franklin English: status name from ME *frankelin* franklin, a technical term of the feudal system, from ANF *franc* free (see FRANK 2) + the Gmc suffix *-ling* (cf. CHAMBERLAIN). The status of the franklin varied somewhat according to time and place in medieval England; in general, he was a free man and a holder of fairly extensive areas of land, a gentleman ranked above the main body of minor freeholders, but below a knight or a member of the nobility. The surname is also borne by Jews, in which case it represents an Anglicization of one or more like-sounding Jewish surnames.

Vars.: **Francklin, Fran(c)klyn, Franklen, Frankling**.

Fraser Scots: of uncertain origin. The earliest recorded forms, of the mid-12th cent., are *de Fresel, de Friselle* and *de Freseliere*. These appear to be Norman, but there is no place in France with a name answering to them. It is possible, therefore, that they represent some Gael. name corrupted beyond recognition by an Anglo-Norman scribe. The Gael. form is **Friseal**, sometimes Anglicized to FRIZZELL. The surname *Fraser* is also borne by Jews, in which case it represents an Anglicization of one or more like-sounding Jewish surnames.

Vars.: **Frazer** (chiefly N Irish); **Frazier** (chiefly U.S.).

Frau 1. German: nickname from Ger. *Frau* lady, MHG *vrouwe* (OHG *frouwa*), given for the most part to an effeminate man. It may also have been an occupational name for a servant employed by a noblewoman or lady. In particular cases there may have been more idiosyncratic origins: for example, at the beginning of the 14th cent. the Minnesinger Heinrich von Meissen was nicknamed *Vrowenlob* 'Lady-praise', because he used the word *vrouwe* as a term of address rather than the more usual *wīp*. **2.** Sardinian: cogn. of FÈVRE.

Fraunhofer German: local name indicating residence and service at a manor (see HOFER) held by a lady (see FRAU), presumably a rich widow. The surname is most common in Bavaria.

Var.: **Frau(e)nhof**.

Frawley *see* FARRELL

Freak *see* FIRTH

Frean *see* FRAIN

Freathy Cornish: of uncertain origin, probably an altered form of *Friday* (see FREITAG). The farm of this name in St Johns parish near Antony in SE Cornwall is probably so called from the surname.

Vars.: **Freethy, Frethey**.

Frebel German: nickname from MHG *vrebel, vrevel* bold, adventurous, daring (OHG *fravalī, frabarī*).

Var.: **Frevel**.

Frech German: nickname from MHG *vrech* eager, bold, brave (OHG *freh* wild, greedy); cf. mod. Ger. *frech* cheeky.

Var.: **Freche**.

Fredberg *see* FRIED

Frederick English: from a Gmc personal name composed of the elements *frid, fred* peace + *rīc* power, introduced into England by the Normans. The name was borne by a canonized 9th-cent. bishop of Utrecht, and was a hereditary name among the Hohenstaufen ruling family; hence its popularity in central Europe.

Dims.: Fr.: **Fériot**, **Ferriot**. It.: **Frizz(ott)i** (Tuscany). Ger.: **Friede**, **Fried(e)l**, **Friedlein**; **Fritz(e)**, **Fritzmann**, **Fritz(e)l**, **Fritzle** (Switzerland); FRIES; **Friesz**, **Freysz**; **Frickel**, **Frickle**. Low Ger.: **Frede(ke)**, **Freke**, **Frick(e)**, **Frickmann**. Fris.: **Fedde(rc)ke**, **Fedde(ma)**, **Feck(e)**, **Fick**, **Vick**. Flem.: FREER, **Frick**. Ger. (of Slav. origin): **Friedsch(e)**, **Frit(z)sch(e)**. Pol.: **Fryś**, **Fryszczyk**.

Augs.: It.: **Federzoni**, **Fedrigon(i)**, **Frizzone**.

Pej.: Fr.: **Ferriaud**.

Patrs.: Eng.: **Fredericks**. Ger.: **Fried(e)richs**; **Friedreicher** (Austria). Low Ger.: **Fred(e)richs**, **Fr(i)ederichs(en)**. Fris.: **Fre(e)r(i)cks**, **Fre(e)rks(en)**, **Frerking**. Flem.: **Frederi(ck)x**, **Fedrix**. Du.: **Fre(de)riks**. Norw., Dan.: **Frederiksen**, **Feddersen**. Swed.: **Fred(e)riksson**, **Freeri(c)ksson**. Pol.: **Frydrychowicz**.

Patrs. (from dims.): Ger.: **Fritzler**, **Fritschler**. Low Ger.: **Frede(r)king**, **Feking**. Fris.: **Feddinga**, **Fecken**, **Fekkena**, **Fitschen**. Pol.: **Fryszkiewicz**.

Habitation name: Pol.: **Frydrychowski**.

Free English (chiefly E Anglia): nickname or term of status from OE *frēo* free (-born), i.e. not a serf.

Vars.: **Freeman**; **Freebody** (see BODY); FRY.

Freeborn English (now most common in N Ireland): term of status for someone who was born a free man (from OE *frēo* FREE + *boren* born), rather than a serf emancipated in later life; cf. FREEDMAN 1.

Vars.: **Freeborne**, **Freebern(e)**, **Freeburn**.

Freedman **1.** English (Yorks.): status name in the feudal system for a serf who had been freed. **2.** Jewish (Ashkenazic): Anglicized form of *Friedmann* (see FRIED).

Freegard English (Wilts.): of uncertain origin, probably imported from Germany in the early 18th cent. It may be an Anglicized form of Ger. **Friedgar**, a rare surname from a Gmc personal name comprised of the elements *frid, fred* peace + *gar* spear.

Var.: **Freeguard**.

Freeland English: status name for someone who lived on a piece of land held without obligations of rent or service, from OE *frēo* FREE + *land* land; cf. FRANKLAND.

Freer **1.** English: nickname for a pious person or for someone employed at a monastery, from ME, OF *frere* friar, monk (L *frāter* brother). **2.** Flemish: cogn. of FREDERICK.

Vars. (of 1): **Fre(e)ar**, **Frere**, **Frier**, **Fryer**, **Friar**.

Patrs. (from 1): Eng.: **Frears(on)**, **Frierson**.

Freestone English (chiefly E Anglia and E Midlands): from the OE personal name *Frēostān*, composed of the elements *frēo* free, noble, generous + *stān* stone.

Fregapane see FRANGIPANE

Freidis Jewish (Ashkenazic): metr. from the Yid. female given name *Freyde* 'Joy'.

Vars.: **Fradis**; **Freidin**, **Fradin** (E Ashkenazic); **Freidlin**; **Fradlin**, **Freidkin**, **Fradkin**, **Fratkin** (from dims.).

Freiling German: status name for a freeman or for a serf who had been freed, from MHG *vrīlinc* freeman or freed man; cf. FREE.

Freins see SÉVERIN

Freitag German and Jewish (Ashkenazic): nickname from Ger. *Freitag* (MHG *vrītac* Friday, OHG *frīatag, frījetag*, a translation of LL *Veneris dies*; Freya was the pagan goddess of love, sometimes considered as equivalent to the Roman Venus. Her name is akin to OE *frīgan* to make love, and ultimately to FRIEND). The Ger. name may have denoted someone born on that day of the week or who performed his feudal service then, but the day was superstitiously considered unlucky throughout the Middle Ages, and it seems more likely that the name was given in allusion to habitual or outstanding bad luck or to a person considered ill-omened; it is found as a byname in this sense in OHG. This is by far the commonest of the surnames drawn from the days of the week, followed by SONNTAG 'Sunday', traditionally a day of good omen. See also MONDAY. Among Jews, it seems to have been one of the group of names denoting days of the week that were distributed at random by government officials.

Var.: **Freytag**.

Freitas Portuguese: topographic name for someone who lived on a patch of stony ground, from Port. (*pedras*) *freitas* broken stones (LL (*petrae*) *fractae*, from the past part. of *frangere* to break, shatter; cf. FRAGOSO).

Var.: **de Freitas**.

Fremantle English (Norman): habitation name from any of the various minor places in France called *Fromentel*, from OF *froid* cold (L *frīgidus*) + *mantel* cloak, coat (LL *mantellum*), or from the place in Hants named in imitation of them. The placename seems to have originated as a sort of nickname for a forest, as providing some sort of inadequate cover for a poor man who could not afford a cloak of his own.

Var.: **Freemantle**.

Frémin see FIRMIN

Frémond French: from a Gmc personal name composed of the elements *frid, fred* peace (or *frija* free, noble, generous) + *mund* protection.

Vars.: **Frémon(t)**.

Dim.: **Frémeau**.

Frênais see FRAIN

French English: ethnic name for someone from France, ME *frensche*. In some cases it may originally have been no more than a nickname for someone who adopted French airs.

Frend see FRIEND

Frenkel see FRANK

Frensch see FRANCIS

Fresco see FRISCH

Frescobaldi Italian: from a Gmc personal name composed of the elements *frisc* fresh, brisk + *bald* bold, daring.

Freshwater English: topographic name for someone who lived by a source of clear drinking water, from ME *fresch* fresh, not salty (OF *freis*, of Gmc origin; cf. FRESCOBALDI)

+ *wæter* water (OE *wæter*). There is a place of this name on the Isle of Wight, which may be a source of the surname.

Fretwell English: habitation name from a minor place in W Yorks., where the surname is commonest, apparently so called from OE *freht* augury + *well(a)* spring, stream (see WELL).

Freud German and Jewish (Ashkenazic): nickname for a person of a cheerful disposition, from Ger. *Freud(e)* joy (MHG *vröude, vreude*).

Vars.: Ger. only: **Freude(mann)**. Jewish only: **Freudman**, **Freudiger** (inflected form of Ger. *freudig* joyous, cheerful, used before a male given name).

Cpds (ornamental): Jewish: **Freudenberger** ('joy hill', with *-er* suffix indicating habitation); **Freudenfels** ('joy cliff'); **Freudenstein** ('joy stone'); **Freudent(h)al** ('joy valley').

Freundl *see* FRIEND

Freville English (Norman): habitation name from *Fréville* in Seine-Maritime, so called from the Gmc personal name or byname *Friso* 'Frisian' + OF *ville* settlement (see VILLE).

Var.: **Freeville**.

Frew Scots: habitation name from the Fords of *Frew*, a fortified site on the river Forth, probably so called from a Brit. element **frwd* current, stream. This place was the lowest crossing-point on the river Forth, and so an important strategic location in the Middle Ages.

Frewin English: from the ME personal name *Frewine*, OE *Frēowine*, composed of the elements *frēo* free, noble, generous (or the rarer *frēa* lord, master) + *wine* friend.

Vars.: **Frewen, Frewing, Frowen, Frowing, Fruen, Fruin**.

Freyse *see* FRIES

Friar *see* FREER

Frías Spanish: habitation name from any of various places, for example in the provinces of Burgos and Teruel, so called from the fem. pl. form of the adj. *frío* cold (L *frīgidus*); a noun such as *aguas* waters or *fuentes* springs has been lost.

Frick *see* FREDERICK

Fricker English: of uncertain origin, perhaps an occupational name for a herald or crier, from the OE agent noun *fricca* with the addition of the ME agent suffix *-er*.

Frid *see* FIRTH

Friebe *see* FRÖBE

Fried 1. German: dim. of FREDERICK. **2.** Jewish (Ashkenazic): from Yid. *frid* peace (cf. mod. Ger. *Friede*), which may sometimes have been chosen as a translation of the Hebr. given name *Shelomo*, whose root letters are the same as those of *shalom* peace (see SALOMON), but which in most cases is simply an ornamental name.

Vars. (of 2): **Frid, Freed; Fried(e)man(n), Fridman(n), Friedler, Friediger, Friedlich, Fridnik** (ornamental elaborations; the last is E Ashkenazic).

Cpds (of 2 or its cogns, ornamental except where otherwise stated): Jewish: **Fri(e)d(en)berg** ('peace hill'); **Friedfertig** ('ready for peace'); **Friedgut** ('peace good'); **Friedhaber** ('one who has peace'); **Friedheim** ('peace home'); **Friedhof** ('peace courtyard', or 'graveyard', in which case it could be a topographic name); FRIEDLAND; **Friedenreich** ('kingdom of peace'); **Fried(en)stein** ('peace stone'); **Friedent(h)al** ('peace valley'); **Fri(e)dwald** ('peace forest'). Swed.: **Fredberg** ('peace hill'); **Fredholm** ('peace island'); **Fredlund** ('peace grove').

Friedland German and Jewish (Ashkenazic): habitation name from any of various places bearing this name, for example in the former German territories of Prussia and Upper Silesia. Bahlow mentions a protected Jewish settlement of this name in Bohemia. As a Jewish name, it is probably in many cases simply an ornamental elaboration of FRIED.

Vars.: Jewish only: **Friedländer, Fri(e)dlander, Fridlender**.

Friel Irish (common in Donegal, and now also in Glasgow): from Gael. **Ó Frighil**, which is probably a metathesized variant of *Ó Fearghail* (see FARRELL).

Frieling *see* FRULING

Friend 1. English: nickname for a companionable person, from ME *frend* friend (OE *frēond*). In the Middle Ages the term was also used to denote a relative or kinsman, and the surname may also have been acquired by someone who belonged to the family of a more important figure in the community. **2.** Jewish: (Ashkenazic): trans. of the Jewish cogns. given below.

Var. (of 1): **Frend**.

Dims.: Ger.: **Freundl** (Bavaria). Low Ger.: **Früngen**.

Patr.: Du.: **Vriens**.

Frier *see* FREER

Fries German, Jewish, and Swedish: **1.** ethnic name for someone from *Frisia* (*Friesland*). The name of this region is ancient and of uncertain etymology; the most plausible speculation derives it from an Indo-European root *prei-* to cut, with reference to the dykes necessary for the cultivation of low-lying land. There is archaeological evidence of the construction of ditches and dams along the southern shores of the North Sea from at least the time of Christ. **2.** occupational name for a builder of dams and dykes. The word was used in this sense in various parts of Germany during the Middle Ages, and is probably a transferred use of the ethnic term, dyke building being a characteristic occupation of Frieslanders. **3.** dim. of *Friedrich* (see FREDERICK).

Vars.: Ger.: **Friese, Freyse**. Swed.: **Fris, Frisell**. Jewish (Ashkenazic): **Friss, Friser, Frizner, Frieslander**.

Dims. (of 1): Low Ger.: **Frieseke**. Jewish: **Friesel**.

Frings *see* SÉVERIN

Frisby English: habitation name from *Frisby* on the Wreake or *Frisby* by Gaulby, or another lost *Frisby* in Leics., all so called from ON *Frísir* Frisians (see FRIES 1) + *býr* farm, settlement.

Frisch 1. German: from a medieval given name, a pet form of FREDERICK. **2.** Jewish (Ashkenazic): nickname from mod. Ger. *frisch*, Yid. *frish* fresh.

Vars. (of 1): **Frische, Frischmann**. (Of 2): **Frish, Fris(c)h(l)er; Fryszer** (Pol. spelling); **Fris(c)hling, Fris(c)hman(n); Fresco, Fresko** (among Sefardic Jews).

Cpds (of 2, ornamental): **Fris(c)hberg** ('fresh hill'); **Frishtag** ('fresh day', or possibly altered by folk etymology from Yid.

frishtik breakfast; all Yid. days of the week end in *-tik*); **Frischwasser** ('fresh water').

Frizzell English (Norman; now most common in N Ireland): **1.** nickname for someone who affected an ornate style of dress, from OF *frisel, fresel* decoration, ribbon, tassel, fringe (a dim. of *frese*, of Gmc origin). **2.** Anglicized form of the Sc. Gael. version, *Friseal*, of the surname FRASER.

Fröbe German: habitation name of Slav. origin, from *vrba* willow, a common element in the placenames of Thuringia, Bohemia, and Silesia.

Vars.: **Fröba, Friebe(n); Fröb(n)er, Frieb(n)er.**

Dims.: Ger.: **Fröbel, Friebel.**

Frobisher English: occupational name for a polisher of metal, in particular someone employed by an armourer to put the finishing touches to his work. The name is a metathesized form of OF *fo(u)rbisseor*, from *fourbir* to burnish, furbish (of Gmc origin).

Vars.: **Furber, Forber.**

Frödden *see* FROUD

Frodsham English (Lancs.): habitation name from a place near Runcorn in Ches., which gets its name from the gen. case of the OE byname *Frōd* (see FROUD) + OE *hām* homestead.

Var.: **Frodson.**

Froggatt English (S Yorks. and Midlands): habitation name from a place in Derbys., near Bakewell, which probably gets its name from OE *frogga* frog (perhaps a byname) + *cot* shelter, cottage (see COATES).

Var.: **Frogget.**

Fröhlich German: nickname for a person with a cheerful temperament, from Ger. *fröhlich* happy, cheerful (a deriv. of *froh* happy, OHG *frō*).

Var.: **Frölich.**

Patr. (from a dim.): Low Ger.: **Fröhlking.**

Fröhmke *see* FROMM

Froikin *see* YEFREMOV

Froissant French: nickname for a strong but clumsy man, from the pres. part. of OF *froisser* to break, shatter (L *frustiāre*, from *frustrum* crumb, scrap).

Pejs.: **Fro(i)ssard, Froissart.**

Frolkin *see* FLOWER

Frome *see* FROOME

Froment French: metonymic occupational name for a corn merchant, from OF *froment* corn, grain (L *frūmentum*).

Dims.: Fr.: **Fromenteau, Fro(u)mentin, Froumenty.** It.: **Formentin(i).**

Augs.: Fr.: **Fromentas.** It.: **Formenton(e).**

Fromkin *see* FRUMIN

Fromm 1. German: nickname for an honourable man, from MHG *vrum, vrom* noble, honourable, trustworthy (from OHG *fruma* use, advantage). **2.** Jewish (Ashkenazic):

nickname for a pious man, from mod. Ger. *fromm* devout, pious (a later sense of the same word as in 1).

Vars.: Ger.: **Fromme(r), Frömmer, Frommann.** Jewish: **From, From(m)er(man); Frum, Frumer(man)** (from Yid. *frum*); **Frymer** (Pol.-based spelling of a S Yid. pronunciation); **Frumak** (from the Yid. pej. term *frumak* hypocrite).

Dims.: Ger.: **Frommel.** Low Ger.: **Frommke, Frö(h)mke, Frä(h)mke.** Jewish: **Fromel.**

Patr.: Low Ger.: **Frömming.**

Fronczak *see* FRANCIS

Froome English: habitation name from any of various places so called from the rivers on which they stand, or simply a topographic name for someone living beside a river with this name, which is apparently cogn. with W *ffraw* fair, fine, brisk; cf. FRAMPTON.

Vars.: **Froom, Frome, Vroome.**

Frosdick *see* FOSDYKE

Frost English, German, and Danish: nickname for someone of an icy and unbending disposition or who had white hair or a white beard, from OE, OHG, ON *frost* frost (a deriv. of the verb 'to freeze').

Froud English: from the OE personal name *Frōd(a)*, originally a byname, or the cogn. ON *Fróði* 'Wise', 'Prudent'.

Vars.: **Fr(o)ude, Frowd(e), Frood.**

Dim.: Fr.: **Frouin.**

Patrs.: Fris., Dan.: **Frödden, Früdden.**

Froumin *see* FRUMIN

Frowen *see* FREWIN

Frude *see* FROUD

Fruen *see* FREWIN

Fruling Jewish (Ashkenazic): from mod. Ger. *Frühling* spring. It may be an ornamental name, or it may be one of the group of names referring to the seasons that were distributed at random by government officials; cf. HERBST, WINTER, and SUMMER. The Ger. vocab. word *Frühling* did not occur before the 15th cent., and has not given rise to any non-Jewish surnames; cf. LENZ 3.

Vars.: **Fruhling; Fri(e)ling** (from Yid. *friling* spring).

Frum *see* FROMM

Frumin Jewish (E Ashkenazic): metr. from the Yid. female given name *Frume* (from *frum* pious; see FROMM 2) + the Slav. suffix *-in*.

Vars.: **Froumin** (Fr. spelling); **Frumson** (Ashkenazic).

Metr. (from the Yid. dim. female pesonal name *Frumke*): **Frumkin, Frumkis, Frumkes; Fromkin** (*-o-* under the influence of mod. Ger. *fromm*).

Früngen *see* FRIEND

Frutos Spanish: **1.** from a medieval given name (L *Fructus* 'Profit', 'Benefit'). The name was borne by an 8th-cent. hermit of Sepúlveda. Together with his brother Valentine and sister Engratia, who were killed by the Moors, he is regarded as the patron of Segovia. **2.** metonymic occupational name for a grower or seller of fruit, Sp. *fruto(s)* (L *fructus*, the same word as in 1, used in this specific sense).

Dims.: Prov.: **Fruchon**, **Fruchou**.

Pej.: Prov.: **Fruchard**.

Cpds (either ornamental or occupational): Jewish: **Frucht(en)baum**, **Fruchtenboim** ('fruit tree'; the latter from Yid. *boym* tree); **Fruchtgarten** ('fruit garden'); **Fruchtlander** ('dweller on fruit land'); **Fruchtnis** ('fruit nut'); **Fruchtzweig** ('fruit twig').

Fry English (chiefly S and SW England): **1.** var. of FREE, from the OE byform *frīg*. **2.** nickname for a small person, from ME *fry* small person, child, offspring (ON *frió* seed).

Var.: **Frye**.

Fryazinov Russian: patr. from the ethnic name *fryazin* Frank, Western European, a borrowing, through Byzantine mediation, of the name of the Franks (see FRANK 1).

Fryd *see* FIRTH

Frydrychowicz *see* FREDERICK

Fryer *see* FREER

Frymer *see* FROMM

Fryszer *see* FRISCH

Fuche *see* FULCHER

Füchsel *see* FOX

Fuchsman *see* FOX

Füchter *see* FEICHT

Fuckart *see* FUGGER

Fudge *see* FULCHER

Fuge *see* FULCHER

Füger German: occupational name for a steward or overseer, Ger. *Füger*, from an agent deriv. of MHG *vüegen* to arrange, dispose (OHG *fuogen*, a deriv. of *fuog* neat, smart).

Vars.: **Fug(e)ner**, **Fiegner**, **Fieger(t)**.

Fugger German: occupational name for a shearer of sheep or of cloth, or a maker and seller of shears, from an agent deriv. of MHG *fucke* shears.

Vars.: **Fucker(t)**, **Fuckart**.

Fuggle *see* FOWLE

Fugler *see* FOWLER

Führer German: occupational name for a carrier or carter, a driver of horse-drawn vehicles, from Ger. *Führer*, MHG *vüerer* (from MHG *vüeren* to lead, transport, OHG *fuoren*, a deriv. of *faran* to travel).

Vars.: Ger.: **Fürer**; **Führ**; **Fuhrmann**.

Fuhrman *see* FORMAN

Fuke *see* FOULKES

Fulcher English (chiefly E Anglia): from a Gmc personal name composed of the elements *folk* people + *hari*, *heri* army, which was introduced into England by the Normans; isolated examples may derive from the cogn.

OE *Folchere* or ON *Folkar*, but these names were far less common.

Vars.: **Fulger**, **Fo(u)lger**; **Fulker**, **Folker**; **Fulsher**, **Foulser**; **Fu(t)cher**, **Fu(d)ger**; **Fullagar**, **Fulleger**.

Dims.: Eng.: **Fudge** (chiefly Somerset); **Fuche**, **Fuge**. Fr.: **Fouchereau**, **Fouchareau**; **Fouquereau**, **Fouqueret**, **Foucreau**, **Foucret**.

Augs.: Fr.: **Fouquerat**, **Foucrat**.

Patrs.: Low Ger.: **Volkers**, **Völkers**; **Volkering**, **Völkering** (Westphalia).

Fulcoli *see* FOULKES

Fulford English: habitation name from places in Devon, Somerset, Staffs., and E Yorks., all so called from OE *fūl* dirty, muddy + *ford* FORD.

Fullbrook English: habitation name from places in Bucks., Oxon., and Warwicks. called *Fulbrook*, from OE *fūl* dirty, muddy + *brōc* stream (see BROOK).

Fuller English: occupational name for a dresser of cloth, OE *fullere* (from L *fullo*, with the addition of the Eng. agent suffix). The ME successor of this word had also been reinforced by OF *fouleor*, *foleur*, of similar origin. The work of the fuller was to scour and thicken the raw cloth by beating and trampling it in water. This surname is found mostly in SE England and E Anglia; see also TUCKER and WALKER.

Vars.: **Voller** (S England); **Fulloon**, FALLON (from OF *f(o)ulun*).

Ger.: **Fuller**. Flem.: **(De) Voller**, **Volder**.

Dim.: Fr.: **Foulonneau**.

Patr.: Eng.: **Vollers**.

Fullerton Scots and N Irish: habitation name from a place so called from OE *fuglere* bird-catcher (see FOWLER) + *tūn* enclosure, settlement. There is a place with this spelling in Hants, but the surname derives chiefly if not exclusively from *Fullerton* near Ayr or *Foulertoun* near Forfar, both in Scotland.

Vars.: **Fullarton**, **Foulerton**.

Fulljames *see* FOLJAMBE

Fullwood English (Midlands): habitation name from places in Notts. and Lancs. called *Fulwood*, from OE *fūl* dirty, muddy + *wudu* WOOD.

Var.: **Fulwood**.

Fulton Scots and N Irish: **1.** contracted form of FULLERTON. **2.** habitation name from a place in the former county of Roxburghs. (now part of Borders region), so called from OE *fugol* bird (see FOWLE) + *tūn* enclosure, settlement.

Funikov *see* AFANASYEV

Funke German: nickname for a small, lively individual, from Ger. *Funke* spark (MHG *vunke*, OHG *funcho*).

Swed.: **Fun(c)k(e)**. Jewish (Ashkenazic, ornamental): **Funk** (from Yid. *funk* spark); **Fink(i)el**, **Finkels**, **Finkelman** (from Yid. *finkl* sparkle).

Cpds (ornamental): Jewish: **Funkenstein** ('spark stone'); **Finkelberg** ('sparkle hill'); **Finkelbrand** ('sparkle torch'); **Finkelkraut** ('sparkle herb'); **Finkelstein**, **Fink(i)elstejn**, **Finkelstejn**, **Finkelsztain** ('sparkle stone').

Funnell *see* FENNELL

Furbank see FIRBANK

Furber see FROBISHER

Furet French: nickname for a vicious person, from OF *furet* ferret, a dim. of *fu(i)r* thief (L *fūr*).
Vars.: **Furon, Fureau**.

Furey Irish: Anglicized form of Gael. **Ó Fiúra**, earlier **Ó Furreidh**. The personal name lying behind these names is of uncertain form and meaning.
Var.: **Fury**.

Furish see FOURISH

Furlong English and Irish: apparently a topographic name from ME *furlong* length of a field (from OE *furh* furrow + *lang* long), the technical term for the block of strips owned by several different persons which formed the unit of cultivation in the medieval open-held system of farming. The surname is now chiefly common in Ireland.
Vars.: **Furlonge(r), Forlong**.

Furman see FIRMIN, FORMAN

Furneaux English (Norman): habitation name from any of the places in N France named from OF *fournel*, a dim. of *four* oven (cf. FOURNIER).
Vars.: **Furnell, Fournel**.

Furness English: local name from the district on the S coast of Cumb. (formerly in Lancs.), earlier *Fuðarnes*, so called from the gen. case (*Fuðar*) of ON *Fuð* 'Rump', the name of the peninsula, formerly of an island opposite the southern part of this district + ON *nes* headland, nose.
Vars.: **Furniss, Furnass**.

Furnival English (Norman): habitation name from *Fournival* in Oise and *Fourneville* in Calvados, both first recorded in the form *Furnivilla*, from a Gallo-Roman personal name *Furnus* (of uncertain origin) or L *furnus* kiln (cf. FOURNIER and FURNEAUX) + OF *ville* settlement (see VILLE). The second element has been later replaced by OF *val* valley (see VALE).
Vars.: **Furnivall, Furnifall**.

Fursdon English: habitation name from any of several minor places in Devon, so called from OE *fyrse* gorse + *dūn* hill (see DOWN).
Var.: **Fursdonne** (a 19th-cent. development).

Furse English (chiefly Devon): topographic name for someone who lived on a piece of land that was thickly grown with gorse, from OE *fyrse* gorse.
Vars.: **Furze(r); Furseman, Furzeman**.

Fürst 1. German: nickname for someone who gave himself princely airs or occupational name for someone who worked in the household of a prince, from Ger. *Fürst* (MHG *füerst* prince, OHG *furisto*, a cogn. of OE *fyrest* first, foremost). **2.** Jewish (Ashkenazic): ornamental name from Ger. *Fürst* prince.
Vars. (of 2): **Furst; Firs(h)t, Firszt** (from Yid. *firsht* duke; *Firszt* is a Pol. spelling); **Firstenfeld** (an ornamental elaboration).
Dims.: Ger.: **Förstel, Ferstel**.

Fürstenberg German and Jewish (Ashkenazic): habitation name from a place in Swabia, so called from the gen. case of OHG *furisto* prince (see FÜRST) + *berg* hill.
Var. (Jewish): **Firstenberg**.

Furtwanger German: habitation name from *Furtwangen* in the Black Forest, so called from OHG *furt* FORD + *wang* water meadow (cf. FEUCHTWANGER).
Vars.: **Furtwängler, Fortwängler**.

Fusco Italian: nickname for someone with dark hair or a swarthy complexion, from It. *fusco* dark (L *fuscus*); in some cases it may be from a medieval given name derived from the Roman family name *Fuscus*, originally of the same meaning.
Vars.: **Fuschi; Fosco, Foschi**.
Dims.: **Fuschini, Fuscolo, Fuscoli, Fuschillo; Foschini, Foscolo, Foscoli**.
Augs.: **Fusconi, Fuscone**.

Füssel see FOOT

Fussell English (Bristol): of uncertain origin, perhaps a Norman metonymic occupational name for a spinner or a maker of spindles, from OF *fusel* spindle (LL *fusellus*, a dim. of class. L *fūsus*).

Fuster see FORSTER

Futcher see FULCHER

Fyall see McFALL

Fyers see FAIR

Fyfe Scots: regional name from the former kingdom of *Fife* in E Scotland, of obscure etymology. Tradition has it that the name is derived from an eponymous *Fib*, one of the seven sons of Cruithne, founding father of the Pictish race.
Vars.: **Fife, Fyffe, Phyffe**.

Fylan see WHELAN

Fyldes see FILDES

Fynes see FIENNES

Fynn see FINN

Fyodorov see THÉODORE

Fysh see FISH

G

Gabaldà see GAVALDÀ

Gabaldón Spanish: habitation name from a place in the province of Cuenca, so called from the Gallo-Roman personal name *Gabalus* (of uncertain meaning) + the Celt. placename element *dūn* hill fort, settlement (see DOWN).

Gabarró Catalan: topographic name for someone who lived on a patch of land overgrown with brambles, from a dim. of OCat. *gavarra* bramble (of pre-Roman origin). Var.: **Gavarró**.

Gabbai Jewish: occupational name, from Hebr. *gabay*, for a trustee or warden of a Jewish public institution, esp. a synagogue, or a manager of the affairs of a Chasidic rabbi. Vars.: **Gabai**, **Gab(b)ay**.

Gaber see HABER

Gäberlein see GABRIEL

Gabert see GEBHARDT

Gabin 1. French: nickname for a man given to mockery and teasing, from a dim. of OF *gab* joke, teasing. The word is of uncertain etymology, but may be akin to ON *gabba* to mock, originally 'open the mouth wide' (cf. JABOUILLE). 2. Jewish (E Ashkenazic): patr. from the Yid. occupational term *gabe* synagogue treasurer (from Hebr. *gabay*; see GABBAI) + the Slav. suffix *-in*.
Vars. (of 1): **Gabet**, **Gabot**. (Of 2): **Gabbin**; **Gabovitch**, **Gabowicz**; **Gabison**, **Gabizon** (Ashkenazic).

Gable N English: of uncertain origin, perhaps a habitation name from one of the minor places named with ON *gaft* gable, applied to a triangular-shaped hill. The mountain called Great *Gable* in Cumb. is named in this way. Var.: **GABLER**.

Gabler 1. German: occupational name for a maker and seller of forks, from an agent deriv. of Ger. *Gabel* fork (MHG *gabel(e)*, OHG *gabala*). The reference is to any of the various pieces of agricultural equipment denoted by this word, for example hay forks, shearlegs, etc. Table forks were not used in Germany for eating before the 16th cent. 2. German: topographic name for someone who lived near a fork in a road or river, from the same Ger. word in this transferred sense. 3. German: habitation name from a place called *Gabel* in Ger., in particular one in Bohemia, which derives its name from the Slav. element *jablo* apple tree (cf. JABŁOŃSKI). 4. English: occupational name for a tax collector or usurer, OF *gabelier*, *gableor* (a deriv. of *gable* tax, revenue, of Gmc origin). 5. English: var. of GABLE. 6. Jewish (Ashkenazic): of unknown origin, perhaps derived as in 1–3 above.
Vars. (of 1–3 and 6): **Gabel**. (Of 1 only): **Gäbler**.

Gabotti see JACOB

Gabriel English, Scots (Aberdeen), French, German, Spanish, Portuguese, and Jewish: from the Hebr. personal name *Gavriel* 'God has given me strength'. This was borne by an archangel in the Bible (Dan. 8: 16 and 9: 21), who in the New Testament announced the impending birth of Jesus to the Virgin Mary (Luke 1: 26–38). It has been a comparatively popular given name in all parts of Europe, among both Christians and Jews, during the Middle Ages and since (cf. MICHAEL and RAPHAEL). In Russia its acceptability was improved by the fact that it was the official name of St Vsevolod (d. 1138).
Vars.: Ger.: **Gaber**. Jewish: **Gavriel**; **Gabrieli**, **Gabriely**, **Gavriel(l)i**, **Gavriel(l)y** (with the Hebr. suffix *-i*); **Gabrielski** (E Ashkenazic).
Dims.: Fr.: **Gabion**. Prov.: **Gab(r)y**, **Graby**. It.: **Gabriel(l)ini**. Ger.: **Gäberlein**; **Gaberl(e)** (S Germany). Ger. (of Slav. origin): **Gabrisch**. Czech: **Kabíček**, **Kabík**. Pol.: **Gabryjańczyk**. Ukr.: **Gavrilyuk**, **Gavril(ch)ik**, **Gavrilechko**, **Gavrilenko**, **Gavrys**. Beloruss.: **Gabrusyonok**, **Gavrilchik**.
Patrs.: Dan., Norw.: **Gabrielsen**. Swed.: **Gabrielsson**. Russ.: **Gavrilov**, **Gavrilin**. Pol.: **Gabriałowicz**, **Gabryłowicz**. Croatian: **Gavrilović**, **Gavrić**. Jewish: **Gabrielov**, **Gabrielow**, **Gabrieloff**, **Gabrilewicz**, **Gabrilovitz**, **Gawryelov**. Armenian: **Gabrielian**, **Kaprilian**.
Patrs. (from dims.): Russ.: **Gavrilichev**; **Gavrikov**, **Gavryutin**; **Gavshikov**, **Gaveshin**, **Gavurin**; **Gashkov**, **Gan(el)in**, **Ganyushkin**, **Ganichev**. Pol.: **Gabarkiewicz**; **Gabrysiewicz**; **Gabrysiak**, **Gawrysiak**, **Gawryszczak**.

Gache 1. Provençal: topographic name for someone who lived by a look-out spot, OProv. *gache* (a deriv. of *gachar* to watch, of Gmc origin), or habitation name from any of the various minor places named with this term. 2. French: metonymic occupational name for a sawyer, from OF *gache* saw (of uncertain origin). 3. French: nickname for a wasteful or destructive person, from OF *gaschier* to spoil, defile (originally 'stain', 'dye', from a cogn. of OHG *wascan* to wash).
Dims.: **Gachet**, **Gachlin**, **Gachenot**, **Gachon**.

Gackl see GEACH

Gädcke see GOTT

Gadd English: occupational name for a driver of cattle or nickname for a persistent and irritating person, from ME *gad* goad, spike, sting (ON *gaddr*). In N England it may in part represent a survival into the ME period of the ON byname *Gaddr*; see GADSBY.

Gaddesden English: habitation name from a place in Herts., recorded in Domesday Book as *Gatesdene*, from the gen. case of the OE byname *Gǣte* 'Goat' + OE *denu* valley (see DEAN 1).
Vars.: **Gad(e)sden**, **Gadsdon**.

Gadea see AGGIS

Gäderts *see* GODDARD

Gadsby English: habitation name from *Gaddesby* in Leics., recorded in Domesday Book as *Gadesbi*, from the gen. case of the ON byname *Gaddr* 'Sting' (see GADD), or from this word used of a spur of land + ON *býr* farm, settlement.
Var.: **Gatsby**.

Gaetano Italian: from a medieval given name, L *Caiētānus*, originally an ethnic name from *Caiēta* in Latium. According to legend the town was named after the elderly nurse of Aeneas, who died on that spot after fleeing with him from the ruins of Troy.
Vars.: **Gaetani**; **Tani**.
Dims.: It.: **Tanini**, **Tanucci**.
Patr.: It.: **Di Gaetano**.

Gaffey *see* CAUGHEY

Gaffican *see* GAVIGAN

Gaffney Irish: Anglicized form of Gael. **Ó Gamhna** 'descendant of *Gamhain*', a byname meaning 'Calf'.
Vars.: **O'Gowney**, **O'Gooney**, **O'Gaeney**.
Dims.: **O'Gownane**, **O'Gownain**, **Goonan(e)** (Gael. **Ó Gamhnáin**).

Gagan *see* GAHAN

Gagarin Russian: patr. from the nickname *Gagara* 'Diving-bird', presumably denoting a strong swimmer.

Gage English and French: **1.** metonymic occupational name for an assayer, an official in charge of checking weights and measures, from ME, OF *ga(u)ge* measure (probably of Gmc origin). **2.** metonymic occupational name for a moneylender or usurer, from ME, OF *gage* pledge, surety against which money was lent (an apparently unrelated word, also of Gmc origin).
Vars.: Eng.: **Gauge**; **Ga(i)ger**. Fr.: **Dugage**.
Dims.: Fr.: **Gaget**, **Gageot**, **Gagelin**; **Gagey** (Burgundy).

Gagern German: habitation name from a place near Rügen on the Baltic coast. The placename is recorded in 1290 as *Gawere*, and is of Slav. origin.

Gagliardini *see* GAILLARD

Gagneux French: occupational name for a farmer or cultivator, from a modified spelling of OF *gagneur*, an agent deriv. of *ga(i)gnier* to till, cultivate (of Gmc origin; cf. WEIDE 2).
Vars.: **Gagnie(u)r**, **Legagneur**, **Legagneux**; **Gaigneux** (Normandy); **Gaignoux** (Ille-et-Vilaine, W France).
Dims.: Fr.: **Gagneron**, **Gagnerot**; **Gagnet**, **Gagnot**, **Gagneau**.
Patr.: Fr.: **Augagneux**.

Gago Spanish and Portuguese: nickname for a man afflicted with a stammer, from Sp., Port. *gago* stammering, stuttering (of imitative origin).

Gahagan *see* GAVIGAN

Gahan Irish: **1.** Anglicized form of Gael. **Mag Eacháin**, patr. from the personal name *Eachán*, a dim. of *each* horse; cf. KEOGH. **2.** Anglicized form of Gael. **Mac Gaoithín**, patr. from the personal name *Gaoithín*, a dim. of *gaoth* wind. This personal name may have been in origin a

short form of *Maolghaoithe*, with the first element *maol* chief, leader.
Vars. (of 1): **Gagan**, **Guihan**, **Gaughan**, **Geghan**, **McGahan**, **Magahan**, **Magann**.

Gahr *see* GEARY

Gai *see* GAY

Gaiger *see* GAGE

Gaigneux *see* GAGNEUX

Gail *see* GALE

Gaillard English (Norman) and French: **1.** from *Gailhard*, a Gmc personal name composed of the elements *gail* gay, joyous (see GALE 1) + *hard* hardy, brave, strong. **2.** nickname for a forceful or boistrous person, from OF *gaile* cheerful (of Gmc origin; cf. GALE 1) + the pej. suffix *-ard*.
Vars.: Eng.: **Gall(i)ard**, **Gaylard**, **Gaylord**.
Dims. (of 1): Fr.: **Gaillardet**, **Gaillardon**; **Gaillourdet**. It.: **Gagliardini**, **Gagliarducci**.
Aug. (of 1): It.: **Gagliardone**.

Gain English (Norman): nickname for a crafty or ingenious person, from an aphetic form of OF *engaine* ingenuity, trickery (L *ingenium* native wit, from *in-* in + *gen-* to be born). The word was also used in a concrete sense of a stratagem or device, particularly a trap.
Vars.: **Ga(i)ne**, **Gaines**; cf. JENNER, and see also INGHAM 2.

Gainsborough English: habitation name from a place in Lincs., so called from the OE personal name *Gegn* (a short form of various cpd names with the first element *gægn* against) + *burh* fortress, town (see BURKE).

Gairdner *see* GARDENER

Gaish *see* WACE

Gaiss *see* GEIST

Gait *see* GATE

Gaitens *see* MCGETTIGAN

Gaites *see* WAITE

Gaitskell *see* GASKELL

Gajda Polish: nickname or metonymic occupational name from Pol. *gajda* bagpipe (from Rumanian *gaidă*, from Turk. *gajda*). In Pol. This word also has the figurative meanings 'fat legs' or 'awkward person'.

Gajer *see* GEIER

Gajownik Polish: occupational or topographic name for a forester or woodman, Pol. *gajownik*, from Pol. *gaj* grove (cogn. with Czech *háj*; see HÁJEK) + *-ów* possessive suffix + *-nik* suffix of human agent nouns.
Var.: **Gajowiak**.
Patr.: Pol.: **Gajewicz**. Croatian: **Gajić**.
Habitation name: Pol.: **Gajewski**.

Galasby *see* GILLESPIE

Gałązka Polish: nickname for a small or physically insignificant person, from Pol. *gałązka* twig.

Galbraith Scots: name for someone descended from a tribe of Britons living in Scotland, from Gael. *gall* stranger (see GALL) + *Bhreathnach* Briton (see BRETT). These were either survivors of the Brit. peoples who had been living in Scotland before the Gael. invasions from Ireland in the 7th cent., or they had perhaps migrated northwards at the time of the Anglo-Saxon invasions. In either case they never became fully integrated with their fellow Celts.

Var.: **Galbreath**.

Galceran Catalan: from the Gmc personal name *Gauzhramn*, composed of the tribal name *Gaut* (see JOCELYN) + *hramn* raven.

Var.: **Galcerà**.

Gałczyński *see* GALL

Galdós Spanish: of Basque origin but of uncertain meaning. The suffix *-os, -oz* occurs in many Basque surnames, particularly in the province of Navarre, and seems generally to have patr. force, but it is not certain whether that is the case here.

Gale English: **1.** nickname for a cheerful or roisterous person, from ME *ga(i)le* jovial, rowdy (from OE *gāl* light, pleasant, merry, reinforced by OF *gail*, of cogn. Gmc origin). **2.** from a Gmc personal name introduced into England by the Normans in the form *Gal(on)*. Two originally distinct names have fallen together in this form: one was a short form of cpd names with the first element *gail* cheerful (cf. GAILLARD), the other was a byname from the element *walh* stranger, foreigner. **3.** metonymic occupational name for a jailer, topographic name for someone who lived near the local jail, or nickname for a jailbird, from ONF *gaiole* jail (LL *caveola*, a dim. of class. L *cavea* CAGE).

Vars.: **Gail**, **Gayle**. (Of 2 only): **Gallon** (chiefly Northumb.). (Of 3 only): **Ga(y)ler**, **Gaylor**, **Jailler**.

Dims. (of 1): Fr.: **Gaillet**, **Gal(l)et**, **Ga(i)llé**, **Ga(i)llot**, **Gaillochet**, **Galichet**, **Galichon**.

Patrs. (from 2): Ger.: **Gailer**, **Geiler(t)**.

Galera Spanish and Catalan: metonymic occupational name for a shipbuilder or a sailor, from Sp., Cat. *galera* galley (L *galea*, from Gk). The word originally denoted a particular type of ship built in Catalonia.

Gálffy *see* GALL

Galhard *see* GAILLARD

Galiana Spanish and Catalan: **1.** from a medieval female given name, a fem. form of GALIANO. **2.** topographic name for someone who lived by the *via Galliana* 'Gaulish path', the pilgrim route from France to the shrine of Santiago de Compostela. The word *galiana* later came to have the weakened sense 'cattle track', but this development is probably too late to lie behind any instances of the surname.

Galiano Spanish: from a medieval given name (LL *Galliānus*, a deriv. of *Gallius*, from *Gallus*; see GALL 2).

Galindo Spanish: from the medieval given name *Galindo*, of predominantly Aragonese origin and distribution, but of unknown etymology.

Patr.: **Galíndez**.

Gałka Polish: nickname from Pol. *gałka* knob, lump, probably denoting someone who was disfigured by a prominent carbuncle.

Patr.: **Gałkiewicz**.

Habitation name: **Gałkowski**.

Galkin Russian: patr. from the nickname *Galka* 'Jackdaw', denoting a thievish or talkative person.

Gall **1.** British: nickname, of Celt. origin, meaning 'foreigner' or 'stranger' (ultimately akin to the Gmc forms mentioned at WALLACE). In the Highlands of Scotland the Gael. term *gall* was applied to people from the English-speaking lowlands and to Scandinavians; in Ireland the same term was applied to settlers who arrived from Wales and England in the wake of the Anglo-Norman invasion. The surname is also found at an early date in Lincs., where it apparently has a Breton origin, having been introduced by Breton followers of the Norman Conquerors. **2.** French and German: from a given name (*Gallus* in L) which was widespread in Europe during the Middle Ages. Its popularity was due to the fame of a 7th-cent. Irish monk, St *Gall* (apparently from the L family name *Gallus*, originally a nickname from *gallus* cock, but later associated with the ethnic term *Gallus* Gaul, probably the same word as in 1). He established a Christian settlement to the S of Lake Constance, which became the monastery later known as St Gall. His given name was taken into Czech as *Havel* and into Pol. as *Gaweł*, the extra syllable being introduced by analogy with L *Paulus*, which yielded Czech *Pavel* and Pol. *Paweł*.

Vars. (of 1): Sc., Ir.: **Gaul(e)**, **Gaw**; GALT, GALLEY. Fr. (Bret.): **Le Gall**, **(Le) Galle**, **(Le) Gallo**.

Dims. (of 1): Fr. (Bret.): **(Le) Gallic**, **Galliou**. (Of 2): Low Ger.: **Gallmann**. Ger. (of Slav. origin): **Gallasch**, **Galuschke**. Czech: **Havlík**, **Havlíček**; **Hálek**, **Halík**; **Kalousek**. Pol.: **Gawlik**.

Patrs. (from 1): Sc., Ir.: **McIngill**, **McAgill**, **McEgill**, **Magill**, **McGill**, GILL (Gael. **Mac an Ghoill**). (From 2): Ger.: **Galler**. Pol.: **Galewicz**. Croatian: **Galić**. Hung.: **Gálffy**, **Gálfi**.

Habitation names (from 2): Pol.: **Galewski**, **Galiński**; **Gawłowski**, **Gawliński**.

Habitation names (from dims. of 2): Pol.: **Gawlikowski**, **Gałczyński**.

Gallagher Irish: Anglicized form of Gael. Ó **Gallchobhair** 'descendant of *Gallchobhar*', a personal name from the elements *gall* strange, foreign + *cabhair* help, support.

Vars.: **Gallacher** (Scot.); **Gallaher**, **Gallogher**, **Galliker**, **Gilliger**; **O'Gallagher**, **O'Galleghure**.

Galland French: nickname for a cheerful or high-spirited person, from the pres. part. of OF *galer* to be in good humour, enjoy oneself (of Gmc origin; see GALE 1 and GAILLARD). The meanings 'gallant', 'attentive to women' are further developments, which may lie behind some examples of the surname.

Vars.: **Galan(d)**, **Gal(l)ant**.

Dims.: Fr.: **Gallandon**, **Galandin**.

Gallatly *see* GOLIGHTLY

Gallear *see* WALLER

Gallego Spanish: regional name for someone from the region of *Galicia* in NW Spain, so called from L *Gallaecia*, a deriv. of the tribal name *Gallaeci, Callaeci*, of unknown origin. The E European region of *Galicia* was Latinized into an identical form when it became part of the Austro-Hungarian Empire in the late 18th cent.; before that it had been the duchy of *Galich* (Pol. *Halicz*).

Var.: **Gallegos**.

Gallen Irish: Anglicized form of Gael. **Ó Galláin** 'descendant of *Gallán*', a personal name from a dim. of *gall* cock.

Gallery *see* MCILWRAITH

Galley 1. English: metonymic occupational name for a seaman, from ME *galy(e)* ship, barge (OF *galie*, of uncertain origin). 2. English: nickname for someone who had been on a pilgrimage to the Holy Land, from a contracted form of the placename *Galilee*. 3. Scots: var. of GALL 1, from the deriv. *gallda* or the collective form *gallaich*.

Vars.: **Gallie**, **Gally**, **Galey**. (Of 2 only): **Galilee**, **Gallally**.

Galliford *see* GULLIVER

Galligai *see* CALLEGARO

Galligan Irish: Anglicized form of Gael. **Ó Gealagáin** 'descendant of *Gealagán*', a personal name from a double dim. of *geal* bright, white.

Gallimard French: of uncertain origin. Dauzat first supposed it to be a nickname from the stem found in mod. Fr. *galimafrée* hotch-potch, confused mass (perhaps from OF *galer* to enjoy oneself (see GALLAND) + *mafrer* to be gluttonous, from MLG *maffelen*) with the addition of a pej. suffix, but in his supplement he derives it from OF *galemart* ink-well, ink-stand.

Var.: **Galimard**.

Gallo Italian and Spanish: 1. nickname from the cock (L *gallus*), given originally to a person with some of the attributes associated with this bird, as for example a fine voice or sexual prowess. 2. from the medieval given name *Gallo*; see GALL 2.

Dims.: It.: **Gallelli**, **Galletti**, **Gallini**, **Gallucci(o)**, **Galluzzi**, **Gallussi**, **Gallozzi**, **Gall(in)otti**.

Augs.: It.: **Galloni**, **Gallone**.

Pejs.: It.: **Gallaccio**.

Gallop English: apparently a nickname for a rash or impetuous person, from mod. Eng. *gallop* run (ME *wallop*, from ONF *walop*, central OF *galop*, probably of imitative origin).

Vars.: **Gallup**, WALLOP.

Galloway Scots: regional name from the area so called in SW Scotland, whose name derives from Gael. *gall* foreigner + *Gaidhel* Gael. From the 8th cent. or before it was a province of Anglian Northumbria. Its Gaelic inhabitants were known as 'the foreign Gaels', who from the 9th cent. onwards tended to be allied with the Norsemen rather than with their fellow Gaels.

Galofre Catalan: from a Gmc personal name composed of the elements *wald* rule or *walh* stranger + *frid, fred* peace.

Dim.: Prov.: **Gaufreteau**.

Patr.: Prov.: **Gaufridy** (Latinized).

Galper *see* HEILBRONN

Galsworthy English: habitation name from a place in Devon, recorded in Domesday Book as *Galeshore*, probably from OE *gagol* sweet gale, bog myrtle + *ōra* slope. The second element has been assimilated to the commoner placename ending *-worthy* (see WORTHY 1). However, some examples may be from places in the parishes of Crowan and Gwennap, Cornwall, called *Goldsworthy*, allegedly from Corn. *gol* field + *erewy* fair, market, i.e. an open space where fairs were held.

Vars.: **Golsworthy**, **Galsery**.

Galt 1. English: nickname from the wild boar, ME *galte, gaute, gault* (ON *goltr*). Wild boars were common in the British Isles from the earliest times, and became extinct only with the clearing of the large tracts of forest which formerly covered the country; hunting them was a favourite pastime in the Middle Ages. 2. Scots: var. of GALL 1.

Vars. (of 1): **Gau(l)t**, **Gaught**, **Gaute**, **Gauld**.

Galtierotti *see* WALTER

Galton English: habitation name from a place in Dorset so called from OE *gafol* tribute + *tūn* enclosure, settlement, denoting an estate held by the payment of rent rather than by feudal gift.

Galván Spanish: from a medieval given name. This is in origin the L name *Galbānus* (a deriv. of the Roman family name *Galba*, of uncertain origin). However, it was used in a number of medieval romances as an equivalent of the Celt. name *Gawain* (see GAVIN), and it is probably this association that was mainly responsible for its popularity in the Middle Ages.

Var.: **Galbán**.

Galve Spanish: from the medieval given name *Galve* (Arabic *Ghālib*), which was borne by several Moorish chieftains in Spanish legends, notably the father-in-law of Almansur, the 10th-cent. vizier of Córdoba. In view of its associations it may also have been used as a nickname; cf. SALADIN.

Patr.: **Gálvez**.

Galvin 1. Irish: Anglicized form of Gael. **Ó Gealbháin** 'descendant of *Gealbhán*', a personal name from the elements *geal* bright + *bán* white. 2. French: nickname for a cheerful drunkard, from OF *galer* to enjoy oneself (see GALLAND), also used in a transitive sense with the meaning 'waste', 'consume' + *vin* wine (L *vīnum*).

Gama Portuguese: apparently a habitation name of Sp. origin, from a place in the province of Santander which is of uncertain etymology, perhaps akin to GAMO (cf. GAMERO 2).

Gamage English (Norman): habitation name from places called *Gamaches* in Eure and Somme, first recorded in the 8th cent. as *Gannapio* and *Gammapium* respectively. The placename is of uncertain etymology; one suggestion is that it was named with the Celt. elements *cam* bent, winding + *apia* water.

Vars.: **Gammage**, **Gammidge**, **Cam(m)idge**.

Gambe French: nickname for a person with some peculiarity of the legs or gait, from the Norman-Picard and

Prov. form of OF *jambe* (LL *gamba*, from Gk *kampē* bend, joint, knee).

Dims.: Fr.: **Gambet**, **Gambin**, **Gambon**; **C(h)ambin**, **C(h)ambet**, **Chambonnet**, **Chambonneau**. It.: **Gambin(o)**, **Gambetta**, **Gambitta**, **Gambella**, **Gambuzza**, **Gambozza**.

Aug.: It.: **Gambone**.

Pejs.: It.: **Gambassi**; **Gambaccini** (dim.).

Gambier French and English (Huguenot): metonymic occupational name for an armourer specializing in the production of leg-pieces, from OF *gambier* greave (a deriv. of *gambe*, *jambe* leg; see GAMBE).

Gamble English: from the ON byname *Gamall* 'Old', which, surprisingly enough, was occasionally used in N England during the Middle Ages as a given name.

Vars.: **Gambell**, **Gammell**, **Gammil**; **Gemmell**, **Gemmill** (Scots).

Dims.: **Gam(b)lin(g)**, **Gamlen**, **Gamlane**.

Patr.: **Gambles**.

Gambourg *see* HAMBURG

Game English: nickname for a merry or sporty person, from ME *gamme* amusement, pastime (OE *gamen*).

Vars.: GAMMON, **Gam(m)an**.

Gamero Spanish: 1. occupational name for a keeper of deer or warden in a park where deer were bred for hunting, from an agent deriv. of GAMO. 2. habitation name from any of various minor places so called, from Sp. *gamero* 'place of deer'.

Gammon English: 1. var. of GAME. 2. from ANF *gambon* ham, a dim. of GAMBE.

Vars.: **Gamon**, **Gammond**.

Gamo Spanish: nickname for a timid person or for a fast runner, from Sp. *gamo* fallow deer (LL *gammus*, of uncertain origin), or perhaps a metonymic occupational name for the warden of a deer park (see GAMERO).

Patr.: **Gámez**.

Gance French: of uncertain origin. It may be a spelling var. of *ganse* ribbon (Prov. *ganso* fastening, buckle, from Gk *kampsos* bent), and so a metonymic occupational name for a maker or seller of ribbons. However, this explanation is rendered doubtful, though not impossible, by the fact that this vocab. word is not attested until the very end of the 16th cent. Alternatively it may be a nickname from a Norman-Picard form of OF *guenche* equivocation, deceit, a deriv. of *guenchir* to move awkwardly, proceed indirectly (of Gmc origin; cf. mod. Ger. *wanken* to hesitate, stumble).

Dims.: **Gancel**, **Ganson**.

Gandelis *see* HANDLER

Gander English: 1. metonymic occupational name for a keeper of geese, or nickname for someone supposedly resembling a gander, from ME *gander*, OE *gand(r)a* gander, male goose. 2. occupational name for a glover; see GAUNT 3.

Gandrich *see* ANDREW

Gandy English (Norman): of uncertain origin. The most plausible suggestion is that it is a nickname for someone who was in the habit of wearing gloves, from OF *ganté*, a deriv. of *gant* glove (see GAUNT 3) or an occupational name

for a glove-maker, OF *gantier*. However, a certain Hugh *de Gandy* was High Sheriff of Devon in 1167; it is possible that his surname is a habitation name from some unidentified place in France or even from Ghent in Flanders (see GAUNT 1).

Vars.: **Gandey**; **Gandee** (apparently a 19th-cent. alteration).

Gane *see* GAIN

Ganelin *see* GABRIEL

Gange English (Norman): of uncertain origin. It may be a habitation name, perhaps from *Ganges* in S France. This is recorded in the 12th cent. as *Agange* and *Aganthicum*, perhaps from a deriv. of L *acanthus* bear's-foot. On the other hand, it may be from the ON personal name *Gangi*, a cogn. of OE *Gegn* (see GAINSBOROUGH).

Gannon Irish: Anglicized form of Gael. **Mag Fhionnán**, patr. from the given name *Fionnán*. This name, from a dim. of *fionn* white, fair, was borne by several early Ir. saints.

Gansel *see* GOOSE

Ganson *see* GAVIN

Gant *see* GAUNT

Ganter 1. German: occupational name for an official in charge of the legal auction of property confiscated in default of a fine; such a sale was known in MHG as a *gant* (from It. *incanto*, a deriv. of LL *inquantāre* to auction, from the phrase *In quantum?* 'To how much (is the price raised)?'). 2. English: occupational name for a glover; see GAUNT 3.

Gapeev *see* AGAPOV

Gapper English (Somerset): 1. nickname for someone whose mouth hung perpetually open, from an agent deriv. of ME *gappen* to gape (ON *gapa*). 2. topographic name for someone who lived by a gap in a chain of hills, from ME *gappe* (ON *gap*, a deriv. of the verb quoted above).

Gara *see* GEARY

Garabedian Armenian: patr. from the given name *Garabed* 'Precursor', the traditional epithet of John the Baptist in the Armenian Church.

Vars.: **Garabetian**, **Karapetian**.

Garand French: nickname for someone who had stood guarantor for the good behaviour or financial responsibility of a member of his family, from the pres. part. of OF *garer* to warrant, guarantee (of Gmc origin, akin to OHG *wār* true).

Var.: **Garant**.

Dims.: **Garandel**, **Garanton**.

Garanin *see* GERASIMOV

Gárate Spanish form of Basque **Garate**: topographic name for someone who lived by a mountain pass, from Basque *gara* heights, summit + *ate* pass.

Garay Spanish form of Basque **Garai**: topographic name for someone who lived by a barn or in an elevated situation, from Basque *garai* barn or the homonymous adj. *garai* high (both of which derive from *gara* heights, summit).

Garber **1.** English: occupational name for someone who bound wheat into sheaves, or who collected wheatsheaves owed in rent, from an agent deriv. of ME, OF *garbe* wheatsheaf (of uncertain origin). **2.** Low German: cogn. of GARBETT or GERBER. **3.** Jewish (Ashkenazic): var. of GERBER.

Var. (of 1): **Garbe**.

Dims. (of 1): Fr.: **Gerberon**; **Gerbet**, **Girbet**, **Gerbeau(x)**, **Girbeau**.

Garbett English (chiefly W Midlands): from *Gerberht*, a Norman personal name composed of the Gmc elements *geri, gari* spear + *berht* bright, famous. Gerbert, archbishop of Rheims, became Pope as Silvester II at the beginning of the 12th cent. There has been some confusion with GARBUTT.

Patrs.: Ger.: **Gerberding**. Low Ger.: **Garberding**, **Garbers**.

Garbo Italian: **1.** apparently a nickname from It. *garbo* graciousness, pleasing manners. **2.** from the name of a street in Florence, the *via del Garbo*, which was populated mainly by workers in *lana del Garbo* wool from the Algarve in Portugal, *Garbo* being the It. name of the Algarve.

Garbutt English (Norman; now chiefly Cleveland and Tyneside): **1.** from *Geribodo*, a Gmc personal name composed of the elements *geri, gari* spear + *bodo* messenger. The name was borne notably by a 7th-cent. saint, bishop of Bayeux; as a result of his fame the name was popular among the Normans and introduced by them into England. **2.** from *Geribald*, a Gmc personal name composed of the elements *geri, gari* spear + *bald* bold, brave. This name owed its popularity largely to a 9th-cent. saint, bishop of Châlons-sur-Seine.

García Spanish: extremely common surname, from a medieval given name of uncertain origin. It is normally found in medieval records in the Latin form *Garsea*, and may well be of pre-Roman origin, perhaps akin to Basque *(h)artz* bear.

Vars.: **Garci**, **Garza**.

Patrs.: Sp., Cat.: **Garcés**.

Gard *see* GUARD

Gardener English: occupational name from ME, ONF *gardin* garden (a dim. of *gard* enclosure, of Gmc origin; cf. GARTH). Reference is normally to a cultivator of edible produce in an orchard or kitchen garden, rather than to a tender of ornamental lawns and flower beds.

Vars.: **Gard(i)ner**, **Gardinor**, GARNER; **Gairdner** (Scots); **Garden**, **Gardyne**; **Jardin(e)**, **Jerde(i)n**, **Jerdan**, **Jerdon** (Scots and Northumb., from the central OF form).

Equivs. (occupational, not cogn.): Czech: ZAHRADNÍK. Pol.: OGRODOWSKI. Hung.: KERTÉSZ.

Gardiennet *see* WARDEN

Garelick *see* GORELIK

Garet French: **1.** metonymic occupational name for a herdsman or topographic name for someone who lived by a covered shelter for animals, OF *garet* shelter, a deriv. of the verb *garer* to guard, protect, shelter (of

Gmc origin). There are villages named with this word in Puy-de-Dôme and Allier, and the surname may also be a habitation name from one of them. **2.** from a dim. of any of various Gmc personal names with the first element *geri, gari* spear or *ward* guard, protect, shelter.

Vars.: **Garel**, **Gareau**, **Gari(o)t**, **Gariou**.

Garfield **1.** English: apparently a habitation name from an unidentified place, probably from a field-name referring to a triangular area (OE *gāra*; see GORE 1) left at the corner of an open field after rectangular furlongs had been laid out. **2.** Jewish: Anglicization of one or more like-sounding Jewish surnames.

Garfinkel *see* GORFINKEL

Garforth English (Yorks.): habitation name from a place in W Yorks., apparently so called from OE *gāra* triangular piece of ground (see GORE 1) + *ford* FORD.

Gargan Irish: Anglicized form of Gael. **Ó Geargáin** and **Mac Geargáin** 'descendant' and 'son of *Geargán*', a personal name from a dim. of *gearg* fierce.

Garland English: **1.** metonymic occupational name for a maker of garlands or chaplets, perhaps also a local name from a house sign. The word is first attested in the 14th cent., from OF, and appears to be of Gmc origin. **2.** habitation name from a minor place, probably *Garland* in Chulmleigh, Devon, named from OE *gāra* triangular piece of land (see GORE 1) + *land* land.

Var.: **Garlant**.

Garlick **1.** English (chiefly Lancs.): metonymic occupational name for a grower or seller of garlic, ME *garlek*, OE *gārlēac* (a cpd of *gār* spear + *lēac* leek, named from the shape of its leaves). It may perhaps also have been a nickname for someone who ate a lot of garlic. **2.** English (chiefly Lancs.): possibly also from a given name, an unrecorded survival into ME of the OE personal name *Gārlāc*, composed of the elements *gār* spear + *lāc* sport, play. **3.** Jewish (E Ashkenazic): Anglicized form of Jewish *Garelik*; see GORELIK.

Vars. (of 1 and 2): **Garlic(ke)**.

Patrs. (from 2): Ger.: **Gerlacher**, **Gerlicher**, **Görlacher**.

Garman *see* GORMAN

Garmendia Basque: topographic name. The first element is unidentified, but the remainder is clearly *mendi* mountain + the def. art. *-a*.

Garner English: **1.** topographic name for someone who lived near a barn or granary, or metonymic occupational name for someone in charge of the stores kept in a granary, from ANF *gerner* granary (OF *gernier*, from LL *grānārium*, a deriv. of *grānum* grain, corn; cf. GRANGER). For the change of *-er-* to *-ar-*, cf. MARCHANT. **2.** var. of WARNER 1, from a central OF form. **3.** contracted var. of GARDENER.

Vars. (of 1): **Garnier**, **Garnar**, **Gerner**.

Dim. (of 1 and 2): GARNETT.

Garnett English: **1.** metonymic occupational name for a grower or seller of pomegranates, from a metathesized form of OF *(pome) grenate* (L *pōmum* fruit, apple + *grānātum* full of seeds, from *grānum* seed, grain). For the change of *-er-* to *-ar-*, cf. MARCHANT. The name of the red-coloured precious stone derives from the same source, comparison being originally made with the rich red of the inside of a pomegranate. **2.** metonymic occupational name for a maker or fitter of hinges, from a dim. of OF *carne* hinge (L *cardo*, gen. *cardinis*). **3.** dim. of GARNER, in either of its first two senses.

Var.: **Garnet**.

Garnham English (Suffolk and N Essex): apparently a habitation name from some unidentified place, so called from the gen. case of the OE personal name *Gāra* (a short form of the various cpd names with the first element *gār* spear) + OE *hām* homestead.

Garnon 1. English: nickname for someone who wore a moustache, from ME, OF *gernon, grenon* moustache. **2.** English and French: dim. of WARNER.

Vars. (of 1): **Garnons, Gernon, Grennan**.

Garnot *see* WARNER

Garrett English (Norman): **1.** from *Gerard*, a personal name introduced to Britain by the Normans, composed of the Gmc elements *geri, gari* spear + *hard* hardy, brave, strong. **2.** from *Gerald*, a personal name introduced to Britain by the Normans, composed of the Gmc elements *geri, gari* spear + *wald* rule.

Vars.: **Garratt, Garrit, Garred, Garrad, Gerrett, Geratt, Gerred, Gerrad, Jarrett, Jarratt, Jarritt, Jar(r)ed, Jarad, Jerratt, Jereatt, Jerred**. (Of 1 only): **Gar(r)ard; Ger(r)ard** (chiefly Lancs.), **Jarrard, Jerrard**. (Of 2 only): **Garrould, Garrod, Gerald, Gerold, Jarro(l)d; Jarrott, Jerrold**.

Dims. (of 1): Fr.: **Gérardet, Girardet, Girardey, Girardez, Gérardin, G(u)irardin, Girardy, Gérardot, Girardot, Gérardeaux, Girardeau**. It.: **Gherardelli, G(h)iriardelli, Gherardini, Girardin(i), Ghelerdini, G(h)ilardini, Gherarducci, Ghelarducci, Girardetti**. Fris.: **Gerritsma**. Du.: **Geerling**. Ger. (of Slav. origin): **Gierek, Gierok, Gi(e)rke, Gierck(e)** (in part shared with GEORGE). Low Ger.: **Geertje**. (Of 2): Fr.: **Giraudeau, Giraudel, Giraudou(x), Giraudot, Giraudy, Géraudel, Géraudy, Girodier, Girodin, Girodon, Giraldon**. It.: **Geraldini, Geroldini**.

Augs. (of 1): It.: **Ghelardoni, Gilardoni, Girardoni, Girardoni**. (Of 2): Fr.: **Giraudat, Girodias**.

Patrs.: Eng.: **Garretts; Garret(t)son, Garrison**; FITZGERALD. (From 1 only): It.: **Gherardesci; Gilardengo, Girardengo**. Ger.: **Gerhartz**. Low Ger.: **Ge(e)rdts, Gehrts, Ge(h)rtz, Gerriets, Gerretz, Geertz, Gerdes, Jertz, Gi(e)raths, Gietz; Gerding; Gerritzen, Gerressen**. Du.: **Geer(i)ts, Gerrets; Gerritse(n), Gerretsen**. Dan.: **Ge(e)rtsen**. (From 2 only): Sp.: **Giráldez**. Port.: **Geraldes**. Ger.: **Gerholz**. Low Ger.: **Garral(t)s, Garrel(t)s, Gerrel(t)s, Gerlts, Gehrels**.

Garric *see* JARRY

Garrido Spanish and Portuguese: nickname from Sp., Port. *garrido* elegant, splendid, ostentatious, in origin apparently the past part. of *garrir* to talk, chatter (L *garrīre*). The word also formerly had the sense 'scandalous', 'wanton', and the surname may sometimes have been given with this meaning.

Garrote Spanish: nickname for a belligerent individual or metonymic occupational name for a crossbowman, from Sp. *garrote* stick, cudgel, also used of a wooden bolt fired from a crossbow and of the weapon itself (of uncertain, possibly Celt., origin).

Gars French: occupational name for a young servant, from OF *gars* boy, lad (apparently of Gmc origin).

Vars.: **Garçon, Garson** (from the oblique case).

Dims.: Fr.: **Garçonnet, Garçonnot, Garsonnin**. Prov.: **Garcin, Garcioux**. It.: **Garzonetti**.

Garside English (Lancs. and Yorks.): habitation name from *Gartside* or *Garside* in Oldham, Lancs., apparently so called from Northern ME *garth* enclosure (ON *garðr*) + *side* hill slope (OE *sīde*).

Var.: **Gartside**.

Garstang English: habitation name from a town in N Lancs., apparently so called from ON *geiri* triangular piece of land (cf. GORE 1) + *stang* pole. Ekwall suggests that the original reference may have been to a boundary mark.

Garston English: habitation name from any of various places so called. Those in Hants and Herts. are named with the OE elements *gærs, græs* grass, grazing + *tūn* enclosure, referring to a paddock. This cpd probably survived into the Middle Ages as a vocab. word. A place of the same name in Lancs. has a different origin, from a metathesized form of OE *grēat* large + *stān* stone.

Garth N English: topographic name for someone who lived near an enclosure, normally a paddock or orchard, from Northern ME *garth* enclosed area, yard (from ON *garðr* enclosure).

Var.: **Gath**.

Garton English: habitation name from a place on the coast near Hull or another on the E Yorks. wolds. They both get their names from ON *garðr* enclosure (see GARTH) + OE *tūn* settlement, place.

Gartzman *see* HERZ

Garvey Irish: Anglicized form of the Gael. personal name *Garbhith*, from *garbh* rough, cruel + a second element of uncertain origin, which has been associated with *bith* fate, (ill) fortune.

Var.: **Garvie** (Scots).

Patr.: Ir.: **MacGarvey** (Gael. **Mac Gairbh(e)ith**).

'Descendant of G.': Ir.: **O'Garvey, O'Garvie** (Gael. **Ó Gairbh(e)ith**).

Garvin Irish: Anglicized form of Gael. **Ó Gairbhín** 'descendant of *Gairbhín*', a personal name derived from *garbh* rough, cruel.

Vars.: **O'Garvin, O'Garven, Garavin, Garvan, Garwin; Girvin, Girvan, Girwin** (N Ireland).

Garwood English: habitation name from an unidentified minor place, probably so called from OE *gāra* triangular piece of land (see GORE 1) + *wudu* WOOD.

Gasbarrini *see* KASPAR

Gascoigne English: regional name for someone from the province of Gascony, OF *Gascogne*. The name of the region derives from that of the Basques, who are found close by and formerly extended into this region as well; they are first named in Roman sources as *Vascōnes*, but the original meaning of the name, derived from a root *eusk-* in the non-Indo-European language that they still speak today, is completely obscure. By the Middle Ages the Basques had been displaced from most of Gascony by speakers of Gascon (a dialect of Occitan, related to French), who were proverbial for their boastfulness.

Vars.: **Gascogne, Gascoyne, Gascon(e), Gasken, Gaskin(g)**.
Cat.: **G(u)asch, Gascó**. Sp.: **Gascón**.
Dims.: Fr.: **G(ou)asquet, Gasquié, Gasquiel, Gascuel**.
Pej.: Fr.: **Gascard**.
Patr.: Eng.: **Gaskens**.

Gash see WACE

Gashkov see GABRIEL

Gąsior Polish: nickname for a stupid person or metonymic occupational name for a keeper of geese, from Pol. *gąsior* gander; cf. GANDER and GOOSE.

Var.: **Gąsiorski** (with surname suffix -*ski*; see BARANOWSKI).
Dim.: **Gąsiorek**.
Patr.: **Gąsiorowicz**.
Patr. (from a dim.): Pol.: **Gąsiorkiewicz**.
Habitation name: **Gąsiorowski**.

Gaskell English (Lancs.): habitation name from *Gatesgill* in Cumb., so called from ON *geit* goat + *skáli* shelter (see SCHOLES).

Vars.: **Gaskill; Gaitskell, Gaitskill**.

Gass 1. German and Jewish (Ashkenazic): topographic name for someone who lived in a narrow lane or alley, Ger. *Gasse*, Yid. *gas* street (MHG *gazze*, OHG *gazza*, a cogn. of ON *gata* road; cf. GATE 1). 2. English: var. of WACE.

Vars. (of 1): Ger.: **Gass(n)er, Gäss(n)er, Gessner**. Jewish: **Gas, Gass(n)er; Gassmann**.

Gast 1. German and Jewish (Ashkenazic): cogn. of GUEST. 2. French: topographic name for someone who lived on a patch of waste land, OF *gast* (of Gmc origin (cf. WÜST), crossed with the ultimately cogn. L *vastum*).

Vars. (of 2): Fr.: **Dugas(t)**.
Cpd (of 1): Jewish: **Gastfreund** ('generous entertainer' or 'welcome guest').

Gastall see WASTELL

Gastl see GUEST

Gaston French: from the OF oblique case of a Gmc personal name, originally probably a byname from *gasti* stranger, guest, host (cf. GUEST). The surname is also found in England and Ireland, where it is probably a Norman importation.

Gate English (chiefly Northern): 1. topographic name for someone who lived by a main road or street, from Northern ME *gate* road, thoroughfare (ON *gata*; cf. GASS 1). 2. topographic name for someone who lived by a gate, from the sing. of GATES. 3. metonymic occupational name for a goatherd, or nickname for a stubborn or particularly smelly person, from ME *gayte* goat, OE *gāt*, or the cogn. ON *geit*. For the Northern ME preservation of -*ā*-, in contrast to the Southern change to -*ō*-, cf. ROPER. 4. metonymic occupa-

tional name for a watchman, from a central OF form of ONF *waite*; see WAITE.

Vars.: **Gait(e), Gaitt**. (Of 1 and 3): **Ga(i)ter, Gayter, Gaytor**. (Of 3 only): **Goate(r), Goatman**.

Gateacre English: habitation name from *Gatacre* in Shrops. or *Gateacre* in Lancs., named with the OE elements *gāt* goat + *acer* cultivated land (see ACKER).

Gatehouse English: habitation name for someone living in the house above the gates of a town or castle, ME *gatehus*.

Gately Irish: Anglicized form of Gael. **Mag Athlaoich**, patr. from the byname *Athlaoch* 'Ex-Warrior', composed of the elements *ath* former + *laoch* warrior, hero.

Gatenby English (Yorks.): habitation name from a place in N Yorks., said to be derived from an OIr. personal name *Gaithan* + ON *býr* farm, settlement.

Gates English: topographic name for someone who lived by the gates of a medieval town. The ME sing. *gate* is from the OE pl., *gatu*, of *geat* gate (see YATE). Since medieval gates were normally arranged in pairs, fastened in the centre, the OE pl. came to function as a sing., and a new ME pl. ending in -*s* was formed. In some cases the name may refer specifically to the Sussex place *Eastergate* (i.e. 'eastern gate'), known also as *Gates* in the 13th and 14th cents., when surnames were being acquired.

Gath see GARTH

Gäthgens see GOTT

Gatsby see GADSBY

Gatterer German: topographic name for someone who lived by the wooden fence surrounding a small community, from Ger. *Gatter* wooden fence (MHG *gater*, from OHG *gataro*) + -*er* suffix denoting human nouns.

Vars.: **Gatter(mann)**.

Gattin see McGETTIGAN

Gatward English: 1. occupational name for a gatekeeper, from OE *gatu* GATES + *weard* guardian (see WARD 1). 2. occupational name for a goatherd, from OE *gāt* goat + *weard* guardian.

Gaubert see JAUBERT

Gauderon see WALTER

Gaufreteau see GALOFRE

Gauge see GAGE

Gaughan see GAHAN

Gaughran Irish: Anglicized form of Gael. **Mag Eachráin**, patr. from the personal name *Eachrán*, of uncertain etymology, perhaps containing the element *each*-horse; cf. GAHAN 1.

Vars.: **McGa(ug)hran, McGawran, McGarran, Mageachrane, Magaher(a)n**.

Gaught see GALT

Gaugin French: of uncertain origin. It may be a dim. form of OF *gauge*, a kind of nut, and so a topographic name for someone who lived by a nut-tree of this type, or a metonymic occupational name for a grower or seller of the nuts.

Vars.: **Gaugain**; **Gauge**; **Gaugier**.

Gaulle, de French: of uncertain origin. It is possibly a Gallicized form of Flem. *De Walle* 'the foreigner, Walloon' (cf. WALLIS). On the other hand, a tradition within the family of the statesman and soldier General Charles de Gaulle connects it with OF *gaule* pole (of Gmc origin). His earliest known ancestor, Richard de Gaulle, was granted land in Normandy in the 13th cent.

Gaumont French: of uncertain origin, probably from a Gmc personal name, *Walmund*, composed of the elements *wala* death in battle + *mund* protection. The second element was assimilated by folk etymology to MONT hill.

Var.: **Gaumond**.

Gaunson see GAVIN

Gaunt English: **1.** local name from the town of *Ghent* in Flanders, from which many wool workers and other skilled craftsmen migrated to England in the early Middle Ages. The surname is found most commonly in W Yorks. around Leeds. The Flem. placename is first recorded in L documents as *Gandi* and *Gandavum*; it is apparently of Celt. origin, but of uncertain meaning. **2.** nickname from ME *gaunt* thin, wasted, haggard (of uncertain, possibly Scandinavian, origin). **3.** metonymic occupational name for a maker and seller of gloves, from OF *gant* glove (of Gmc origin).

Vars. (of 3): **Gant**; **Gaunter**, GANTER, GANDER.

Gauquelin see VAUQUELIN

Gaureschi see WARING

Gäusgen see GOOSE

Gavaldà Catalan: habitation name from *Gavaudan* in S France, which has the same origin as GABALDÓN.

Vars.: **Gavaldó**, **Gabaldà**.

Gavarró see GABARRÓ

Gaveshin see GABRIEL

Gavigan Irish: Anglicized form of Gael. **Mag Eachagáin**, patr. from the personal name *Eachagán*, a double dim. of *each* horse; cf. GAHAN 1.

Vars.: **Gavaghan**, **Gavecan**, **Gaffican**, **Gaffikin**, **Gahagan**, **McGaffigan**.

Gavilán Spanish: nickname for a hawklike person, from Sp. *gavilán* sparrowhawk (of Gmc origin, apparently a deriv. of *gabal* fork (cf. GABLER), referring to the talons of the bird). *Gavilán* was also used in the Middle Ages as a given name, perhaps in part preserving a Gmc byname, and this may also lie behind some examples of the surname.

Gavin English (now also common in Ireland): from a given name popular in the Middle Ages in the ME form *Gawayne* as well as the OF *Gauvin*. The name was introduced from Fr. versions of the Arthurian romances, where this name was borne by one of the knights of the Round Table, the brother of Galahad and Mordred and a nephew of Arthur. It is probably from an OW personal name com-

posed of the elements *gwalch* hawk + *gwyn* white, influenced in part by Bret. forms.

Vars.: **Gaven**, **Gauv(a)in**, **Gawen**; **Gawn(e)** (see also GOUGH); **Wawn(e)**.

Dims.: Fr.: **Gauvreau**, **Gauvrit**, **Gauvry**.

Patrs.: Eng.: **Gawenson**, **Ga(u)nson**.

Gavini see JACOB

Gaw see GALL

Gawen see GAVIN

Gawley see McAULAY

Gawroński Polish: from Pol. *gawron* rook + *-ski* suffix of surnames (see BARANOWSKI), in various possible applications. It may be a nickname for an acquisitive or thievish person, or it may be a habitation name from a place called *Gawrony*.

Gawryelov see GABRIEL

Gawthorpe English (Yorks.): habitation name from any of several places in W Yorks. called *Gawthorpe* or *Gawthrop*, all of which derive their names from ON *gaukr* cuckoo + *þorp* enclosure (see THORPE).

Var.: **Gawthrop**.

Gay **1.** English, French, and Catalan: nickname for a light-hearted or cheerful person; the adj. is of unknown origin, perhaps a borrowing of a Prov. cogn. of JAY. **2.** English (Norman): habitation name from places in Normandy called *Gaye*, from an early proprietor bearing a Gmc personal name cogn. with WADE. **3.** Catalan: from a medieval given name (L *Gaius*, of uncertain, possibly Etruscan, origin; cf. KAY 3). **4.** Irish: see KILDEA.

Vars. (of 1 and 2): Eng.: **Gaye**. (Of 1 only): Fr.: **Gai**, **Leg(u)ay**, **Leguey**.

Dims. (of 1): Fr.: **Gayet**, **Gayon**, **Gayot**.

Pejs. (of 1): Fr.: **Gayard**, **Gayaud**.

Gayer see GEIER

Gaylard see GAILLARD

Gayle see GALE

Gaynor **1.** Irish: Anglicized form of Gael. **Mag Fhionnbhairr** 'son of *Fionnbharr*', a personal name composed of the elements *fionn* fair, white + *barr* top, head. **2.** Welsh: from the female given name *Gaenor* (a form of *Gwenhwyfar*; see JUNIPER 2). **3.** Jewish: of unknown origin.

Vars. (of 1): **McGynnowar**, **Maginnoire**, **Magennure**, **Magenor**.

Gayter see GATE

Gaze see WACE

Gazeley English: habitation name from a place in Suffolk, so called from the gen. case of the OE personal name *Gǣgi* (apparently related to the verb *gǣgan* to turn aside) + OE *lēah* wood, clearing.

Gazzini see AGACE

Gdanski see DANZIG

Geach English (Devon and Cornwall): nickname from ME *geche, ge(c)ke* fool, stupid person (of uncertain origin, but apparently with Gmc cogns.).
Var.: **Geake**.
Dims.: Ger.: **Gackl**, **Gäckle**.
Patrs.: Eng.: **Jeeks**, **Jecks**, **Jex**.

Geai *see* JAY

Geaney Irish: Anglicized form of Gael. **Mag Éanna**, patr. from the personal name *Éanna*, which is of unknown origin.

Gearty *see* GERAGHTY

Geary 1. Irish: Anglicized form of Gael. **Ó Gadhra** 'descendant of *Gadhra*', a personal name derived from *gadhar* hound, mastiff. 2. English: from a Gmc personal name derived from *geri, gari* spear, a short form of the various cpd names with this first element (cf., e.g., GARBETT, GARBUTT, and GARRETT). 3. English: nickname for a wayward or capricious person, from ME *ge(a)ry* fickle, changeable, passionate (a deriv. of *gere* fit of passion, apparently a Scandinavian borrowing).
Vars. (of 1): **O'Geary**, **O'Geiry**, **O'Garey**, **(O')Garry**, **(O')Gara**, **Guiry**, **Gwyre**. (Of 2 and 3): **Gerr(e)y**, **Gerrie** (chiefly Devon). (Of 2 only): **Garey**, **Gar(r)y**; **JARRY**. (Of 3 only): **Gear(e)**, **Geer(e)**; **Ger(r)ish**, **Garrish** (chiefly Somerset).
Dims. (of 2): Fr.: **Gerin**, **Gérin**, **Ger(on)net**, **Gérondeau**; **Géricot**, **Géricault**. Ger.: **Gerle**, **Ge(h)rlein**; **Görl** (Bavaria); **Gerli** (Switzerland). Low Ger.: **Gere(c)ke**, **Gehricke**, **Gehrke**, **Garke**, **Gahr(mann)**, **Ge(h)rmann**, **Giermann**. Fris.: **Jahrmann**, **JARRE**.
Patrs. (from 2): Eng.: **Gearing**, **Geering**. Ger.: **Ge(h)ring**, **Gerung**, **Gö(h)ring** (Bavaria). Low Ger.: **Geers**, **Geeren**, **Gerren(s)**, **Ge(h)rs**, **Ge(h)ring**, **Jhering**, **Ge(h)righ**, **Gehrich**. Fris.: **Jarren**, **Jarr(e)s**, **Jarsen**.
Patrs. (from 2) (dims.): Ger.: **Gerler**, **Gerling**; **Görler**, **Görling** (Bavaria). Low Ger.: **Ger(c)ken(s)**, **Garken**, **Gerking**.

Geaves *see* JEEVES

Geay *see* JAY

Gebb *see* JEFFREY

Gebhardt German: from a Gmc personal name composed of the elements *geb* gift + *hard* brave, hardy, strong. A saint of this name was bishop of Constance around the end of the 10th cent., and his popularity may have had an influence on the continued use of the given name into the Middle Ages.
Vars.: **Gebhard**, **Geber(t)**, **Gebbert**, **Gabert**, **Göbhardt**.
Dims.: Ger.: **Geberl**. Low Ger.: **Gebb(e)**, **Gebecke**, **Ge(e)ve**, **Geffe**, **Gibke**, **Giebecke**.
Patrs.: Ger.: **Geberding**. Low Ger.: **Geb(b)ers**, **Gewers**, **Gevers**, **Geffers**.
Patrs. (from dims.): Low Ger.: **Gebken**, **Gefken**.

Gębski Polish: nickname for a braggart or a foul-mouthed person, or else one with a big mouth in a literal sense, from Pol. *gęba* gob + *-ski* suffix of surnames (see BARANOWSKI).
Vars.: **Gębicki**, **Gembicki**.
Dims.: Czech: **Hubáček**, **Hubálek**.

Gebühr *see* BAUER

Gecht *see* HECHT

Gedanski *see* DANZIG

Geddes Scots: habitation name from a place in the former county of Nairn, which apparently gets its name from a Gael. term for a mountain ridge.
Var.: **Geddis** (chiefly N Ireland).

Geddie Scots: of unknown origin.

Gedge English (E Anglia): nickname from ME *gegge*, a term of abuse or contempt applied to a foolish or loose woman or an awkward or boorish man (of uncertain origin).

Gee English: although this is a common name, especially in N England, it is of very uncertain origin. Forms which certainly belong here are not found before the 16th cent. The existence of the patr. **Geeson** points to a given name, or, less probably, an occupational name or nickname, but this as not been identified.

Geer *see* GEARY

Geerdts *see* GARRETT

Geerooms *see* JEROME

Geest Low German and Dutch: topographic name for someone who lived in an area of barren sandy soil, MLG *gēst*.
Vars.: **GEIST**; **Vergeest**, **Bergeest**, **Borgeest**. Flem., Du.: **Van(der) Geest**, **Van Gheest**, **Geestman**. Fris.: **Geestra**.

Geeve *see* GEBHARDT

Geeves *see* JEEVES

Gefen Jewish (Israeli): ornamental name from Hebr. *gefen* vine, a Hebraicization usually of the various Ashkenazic surnames listed at WEIN.

Geffe *see* GEBHARDT

Geffroy *see* JEFFREY

Geghan *see* GAHAN

Gegner German: topographic name for someone who lived not in the main settlement itself but in the surrounding countryside, from a deriv. of MHG *gegende* (OHG *gegenōti*, a deriv. of *gegin* opposite, against, based on LL *contrāta* region, country, from *contra* opposite, against).

Gehler *see* GELLER

Gehrels *see* GARRETT

Gehrich *see* GEARY

Geier 1. German: nickname from a greedy or rapacious person, from Ger. *Geier* vulture (MHG, OHG *gīr*). Some early examples may be house names, from house signs depicting this bird, and some others may be habitation come from a place near Zwickau called *Geyer*, which is probably ultimately from the same word. 2. Jewish (Ashkenazic): occupational name from Yid. *geyer* pedlar (a deriv. of *geyn* to go) or in some cases perhaps an unflattering name from Ger. *Geier* vulture, as in 1, bestowed by non-Jewish government officials in central Europe at the time when surnames became compulsory.
Vars. (of 1): **Geyer**, **Gayer**. (Of 2): **Gajer** (Pol. spelling), **Geierman**.

Geiger German and Jewish (Ashkenazic): occupational name for a player on the fiddle, from Ger. *Geiger*, an agent deriv. of *Geige* violin, fiddle (MHG *gīge*, Late OHG *gīga*, of uncertain origin).

Geiler *see* GALE

Geindre *see* GENDRE

Geipel *see* GILBERT

Geiss *see* GEIST

Geist 1. German: metonymic occupational name for a goatherd or nickname for a stubborn person, from S Ger. dial. *Geiss* goat (MHG, OHG *geiz*, a cogn. of OE *gāt* and ON *geit*; see GATE). 2. German: house name for someone who lived in a house marked by the sign of the Holy Spirit (normally depicted as a dove), from Ger. *Geist* spirit (MHG, OHG *geist*). Both *Geist* and *Heilgeist* occur as house signs in Frankfurt-am-Main in the mid-14th cent. 2. Low German: var. of GEEST.
Vars. (of 1): **Geiss(er)**, **Gaiss(er)**. (Of 2): **Geister(t)** (Silesia).

Gelatly *see* GOLIGHTLY

Gelbert *see* GILBERT

Geldart English: occupational name for a person responsible for looking after oxen and castrated horses, from ME *geld* sterile, barren (animal) (ON *geldr*) + *herd* herdsman (OE *hierde*; see HEARD).
Vars.: **Geldard**, **Gelder** (Yorks.).

Geldner *see* GOLD

Geldstein *see* HELD

Geles Jewish (Ashkenazic): metr. from the Yid. female given name *Gele* 'Blonde' (cf. GELLER 3).
Vars.: **Gelles(s)**, **Gel(l)is**; **Gelin** (E Ashkenazic).

Gell *see* JULIAN

Gellan *see* GILFILLAN

Geller 1. Low German: habitation name from the N German town of *Geldern* or from the Du. province of *Gelderland*, earlier *Geler* and *Gelre*. Both places get their names from what may be an ancient element descriptive of marshland. 2. German: occupational name for a town crier, Ger. *Geller*, MHG *gellære* (from *gellen* to shout, yell, OHG *gellan*). 3. Jewish (Ashkenazic): nickname for a man with red hair, from the strong form of Yid. *gel* red-headed (MHG *gel* yellow, OHG *gelo*, gen. *gelwes*). There has been considerable confusion with Ger. *Gelb* yellow, since the meaning change from 'yellow' to 'red' took place only in Yiddish and only with reference to people's complexion or hair colouring. 4. Jewish (E Ashkenazic): nickname for a man with light hair or a sallow complexion, a var. of HELLER 3, originating under Russ. influence, since Russ. has no /h/ and alters /h/ in borrowed words to /g/.
Vars.: (of 1): **Gellermann**, **Gelder(mann)**. (Of 2): **Gellert**, **Gehler(t)**. (Of 3): **Gelb(er)**. Jewish only: **Gelb(er)man(n)**, **Gelbert**, GILBERT. (Of 4): **Gel(l)**, **Geler**, **Gel(l)erman**, **Gel(l)man(n)**.
Patr. (from 3): Jewish: **Gelberson**.
Cpds. (of 3; mostly ornamental): Jewish: **Gelband** ('yellow ribbon'); **Gelbart**, **Gelbard**, **Gelbort**, **Gelbord** ('red beard' or 'yellow beard', a nickname); **Gelbaum** ('yellow tree'); **Gelbein** ('yellow leg', a nickname); **Gelberg** ('yellow hill'); **Gilblum** ('yellow flower'); **Gelbrun** ('yellow-brown' or 'yellow fountain'); **Gelfarb** ('yellow colour'); **Gelbfisch** ('yellow fish'); **Gelbgies(s)er**, **Gelbgiser** ('yellow pourer'; apparently occupational, but the occupation in question has not been identified); **Gelbhar** ('red hair' or 'yellow hair', a nickname); **Gelkop(f)** ('red head' or 'yellow head', a nickname); **Gelmond**, **Gelmont** ('yellow moon'); **Gel(b)stein**, **Gel(l)erstein** ('yellow stone'); **Gelbwachs** ('yellow wax').

Gelli *see* AIELLO

Gellibrand *see* GILLIBRAND

Gelling *see* LEWIN

Gelmetti *see* WILLIAM

Gelperin *see* HEILBRONN

Gembicki *see* GĘBSKI

Gemeau *see* JUMEAU

Gemmell *see* GAMBLE

Gemson *see* JAMES

Gencke *see* JOHN

Gendebein *see* JENNEWEIN

Gendelman *see* HANDLER

Gendre French: nickname from OF *gendre* son-in-law (L *gener*), presumably often given with slightly mocking intent to someone who had bettered his lot by marrying the daughter of a rich or influential person.
Vars.: **Legendre**, **G(e)indre**, **Genre**.
Dims.: **Gendreau**, **Gendrot**, **Gendron**, **Gendrin**, **Gendry**.

Genès French: from a medieval given name (L *Genēsius*, from Gk *gnēsios* well-born, legitimate, from the root *gen-* to be born). This was the name of an early Christian martyr under Domitian, and later of a 7th-cent. bishop of Lyons, both of whom helped the name to enjoy a modest popularity. There has, however, been some confusion with GENEST.
Var.: **Geniès**.

Genest French: topographic name for someone who lived by a patch of broom, OF *genest(e)* (LL (*planta*) *genesta*).
Vars.: **Genest(r)e**, **Gine(s)t**, **Gineste**, **Dugene(s)t**. See also GENÈS and GENET.
Dims.: Fr.: **Gene(s)ton**. Prov.: **Genestou(x)**, **Ginestou(x)**.
Augs.: Prov.: **Genestat**, **Ginestat**.
Collectives: Fr.: **Gene(s)tay**.

Genet French: 1. var. of GENEST. 2. aphetic dim. of EUGÈNE. 3. nickname or metonymic occupational name from *genet*, a type of Sp. horse, a jennet. The word *genet* came into OF from Cat. *ginet*, itself a borrowing of Arabic *Zanātah*, the name of a Moorish people renowned for their horsemanship.

Genevois French: local name for someone from the Swiss city of *Geneva*, Fr. *Genève*. The name of the city is of uncertain etymology, but may be akin to L *janua* door, gateway (cf. *Genoa* at JANUARY 2).

Vars.: **Genevoix**, **Genevai**, **Genevay**; **Genève**.

Pej.: Fr.: **Genevard**.

Genn see JANE, JUNIPER

Gennarelli see JANUARY

Genner see JENNER

Genslein see GOOSE

Gentle English: nickname, sometimes perhaps ironic, from ME, OF *gent(il)* well-born, noble, courteous (L *gentilis*, from *gens* family, tribe, itself from the root *gen-* to be born).

Vars.: **Gentile**, **Jentle**; **Gent**, **Jent**; **Gentry**.

Dims.: Fr.: **Gentilleau**, **Gentizon**; **Gentet**, **Gent(h)on**, **Gentot**. It.: **Gentilini**, **Gentillotti**, **Gentillucci**.

Geoffrey see JEFFREY

Geoghegan Irish: Anglicized form of Gael. **Mag Eochagáin**, patr. from the personal name *Eochagán*, probably from a double dim. of *eachadhe* horseman; cf. CAUGHEY.

George English, French, and German: from a Gk personal name, *Geōrgios* (from *geōrgos* farmer, a cpd of *gē* earth, soil + *ergein* to work, till), which was in use in England before the Norman Conquest. Its popularity increased at the time of the Crusades, which brought greater contact with the Orthodox Church, in which there was a thriving cult of an obscure saint of this name, supposedly martyred at Nicomedia in AD 303, although the authenticity of his very existence is doubtful. In 1348 Edward III founded the Order of the Garter under the patronage of St George, and in 1415 his day was made a festival of the highest rank. By the end of the Middle Ages he had acquired an entirely unhistorical legend of dragon-slaying exploits, which caught the popular imagination throughout Europe, and was considered the patron saint of England.

Vars.: Fr.: **Georges**. Ger.: **Georg**, **Jörg**, **Gurg**; **Georgius** (Latinized).

Dims.: Fr.: **Georgel(in)**, **Georgeau**, **George(o)t**, **Georgeon**, **Georger**, **Georgé**. Prov.: **Jorin**, **Joreau**, **Joriot**, **Jorioz**, **Joron**, **Joret**, **Jorez**, **Jorey**. It.: **Giorgetti**, **Giorgini**, **Giorielli**, **Giorietto**; **Iorillo**, **Iorizzo**, **Iorrizzi** (S Italy); **Giorgiutti**, **Giurin(i)**, **Zorzet(ti)**, **Zorzin(i)**, **Zorzutti** (Venetia). Ger.: **Görg(e)l**. Low Ger.: **Görgen**, **Jürgen** (in which a patr. suffix -*en* added to the -*g* of the stem was later confused with the dim. ending -*gen*, -*chen*). Du.: **Jurgen**. Fris.: **Jörn**, **Jürn**, **Jurn**. Flem.: **Gorick** (also found in London); **Horick** (Enghien). Slav. (of Slav. origin): **Jerschke**, **Jerke**, **Jirzik**, **Jirek**, **Jirak**, **Jir(k)a**, **Jorczyk**, **Juhr(k)e**, **Jur(cz)ik**, **Jurick**, **Juschke**, **Juschka**; **Gör(c)ke**, **Göricke**, **Gork(e)**; **Schuricke**, **Schuhrke**; **Tschi(e)rschke**. Czech: **Jiřík**, **Jiříček**, **Jiřička**, **Jiráček**, **Jirásek**, **Jiránek**, **Juránek**, **Jirousek**, **Jir(o)ušek**, **Jiroudek**, **Jiroutek**, **Jiroutka**. Pol.: **Jurek**, **Jurczyk**. Ukr.: **Yurchenko**. Hung.: **Gyurkó**.

Augs.: Fr.: **Jorat** (Switzerland). It.: **Giorgioni**, **Giorgione**; **Zorz(en)oni** (Venetia).

Patrs.: Eng.: **Georgeson** (chiefly Northumb.). It.: **De Giorgi(s)**, **De Giorgio**, **Di Giorgio**, **Di Iorio**; **Giorgeschi**. Rum.: **G(h)eorg(h)escu**. Ger.: **Georges**, **Georgi**, **Gerger**, **Jerger**. Low Ger.: **Görger**, **Jörger**; **Görges**, **Jür(ge)s**, **Juris**, **Jürr(i)es**. Du.: **Jorissen**. Dan., Norw.: **Jørgesen**. Russ.: **Georgiev(ski)** (a

form adopted by members of the Orthodox clergy, from the given-name form *Georgi*, preserved only in ecclesiastical contexts); **Yegorev** (from the ORuss. form of the name, *Yegor(g)i*, a metathesized form of *Georgi*); **Yegorov** (from a less formal version of this form with the final vowel lost); **Yuryev** (from the ORuss. vulgar form *Yur(i)*); **Yur(m)anov** (from extended forms of the popular version). Ukr., Beloruss.: **Yurevich**. Pol.: **Jurewicz**; **Jurczak**. Croatian: **Djor(djev)ić**, **Djurdj(ev)ić**, **Djur(ov)ić**. Bulg.: **Georgiev**. Lithuanian: **Jur(g)aitis**. Gk: **Georg(h)iou**, **Georgeou**, **Georgiades**. Hung.: **Györffy**.

Patrs. (from dims.): Ger.: **Görgler**, **Gergler**. Low Ger.: **Jörgensen**, **Jürgens(en)**. Du.: **Jurgens**. Dan.: **Jörgensen**, **Jurgensen**, **Jurgenson**. Russ.: **Yegorkov**, **Yegorkin**, **Yego(r)shin**, **Yegorchenkov**; **Yurasov**, **Yur(iv)tsev**, **Yurenev**, **Yurikov**, **Yurinov**, **Yuryaev**, **Yuryichev**, **Yur(k)ov**, **Yurlov**, **Yur(y)shev**, **Yur(en)in**, **Yuryatin**, **Yur(och)kin**, **Yurukhin**, **Yurygin**; **Yukhnev**, **Yukh(n)ov**, **Yush(ach)kov**, **Yushmanov**, **Yukh(n)in**, **Yukhtin**, **Yushankin**, **Yush(k)in**. Beloruss.: **Yurkevich**, **Yukhnevich**. Pol.: **Jerzykiewicz**, **Jurkiewicz**. Croatian: **Djurković**, **Djuričić**, **Djurišić**, **Jurišić**. Hung.: **Gyurkovics** (with Slav. ending).

'Son of the wife of G.': Ukr.: **Yurchishin**.

'Son of the daughter of G.': Russ.: **Yegorovnin**.

Habitation names: Pol.: **Jurkowski**, **Jerzykowski**. Czech: **Jirkovský**.

Gepp see JEFFREY

Geraghty Irish: Anglicized form of Gael. **Mag Oireachtaigh** 'son of *Oireachtach*', a byname meaning 'Member of the Assembly'.

Vars.: **McGer(r)aghty**, **McGer(r)ity**, **McGarrity**, **(Mc)Gerety**, **Mageraghty**, **Geraty**, **Gerity**, **Ge(a)rty**, **Jerety**.

Gerald see GARRETT

Geran see WARING

Gerasimov Russian: patr. from the given name *Gerasim* (Gk *Gerasimos*, a deriv. of *geras* honour), which was borne by a 5th-cent. saint, venerated in the Eastern Church, who was chiefly famous for the devotion he is said to have inspired in a lion from whose paw he extracted a thorn.

Vars.: **Garasimov**, **Garaseev**.

Dims.: Russ.: **Gerasov**, **Gerasyutin**, **Gereev**, **Geran(k)in**, **Geranichev**, **Gerakhov**, **Garshin**, **Gar(an)in**, **Garinov** (all patrs.). Ukr.: **Gerasimenko**, **Gerasimchuk**, **Garasimchuk**. Beloruss.: **Gerasimenya**.

Gerbeau see GARBER

Gerber German and Jewish (Ashkenazic): occupational name for a tanner, Ger. *Gerber* (MHG *gerwer*, OHG *(ledar)garawo* leather preparer, a deriv. of *garawen* to prepare, from *gar*, gen. *garawes*, ready, prepared).

Vars.: Ger.: **Gerb**. Jewish: GARBER (from Yid. *garber*).

Dim.: Ger.: **Gerbl** (Bavaria).

Cpds: Ger.: ROTGERBER, WEISSGERBER.

Gerberding see GARBETT

Gercken see GEARY

Gerger see GEORGE

Gergolet see GREGORY

Géricault see GEARY

Gerlacher see GARLICK

German English: **1.** ethnic name from OF *germain* German (L *Germānus*); this sometimes denoted an actual immigrant from Germany, but was also used to refer to a person who had trade or other connections with the country. The L word *Germānus* is of obscure and disputed origin; the most plausible of the etymologies that have been proposed is that the people were originally known as the 'Spear-men', with *geri, gari* spear as the first element. For a similar naming from a characteristic weapon, see FRANK. **2.** from a ME and OF given name, *Germa(i)n*. This was popular in France, where it had been borne by a 5th-cent. saint, bishop of Auxerre, and achieved some currency in medieval England. It derives partly from the tribal name discussed above and partly from the L and OF homonym meaning (full) brother, cousin' (originally an adj. meaning 'of the same stock', from L *germen* bud, shoot). In the Romance languages, esp. It., the popularity of the equivalent given name has been enhanced by association with the meaning 'brother (in God)', and in Sp. the cogn. surname is derived from the vocab. word meaning 'brother' rather than from a given name.

Vars.: **Germann, Germain(e), Germing**; **Jerman, Jermine, Jermyn(n)**; **Jarma(i)n** (W Country).

Dims. (of 2): Fr.: **Germaneau, Germineau, Germinet, Germiny**. It.: **Germanino, Germanini**. Hung.: **Gera**.

Patrs.: Eng.: **Jarmains**. It.: **De Germano** (S Italy).

Germanoff *see* HERMANN

Germly *see* GORMLEY

Gerner *see* GARNER

Gernon *see* GARNON

Geron *see* GIRONA

Gerpott *see* GARBUTT

Gerram *see* JEROME

Gersch *see* HIRSCH

Gershon Jewish: from the Hebr. male given name *Gershon, Gershom*, of uncertain etymology.

Vars.: **Gerson, Gershun, Gershom**; **Gershoni, Gershony, Gershuny** (with the Hebr. ending -*i*).

Patrs.: **G(h)ershensohn** (Ashkenazic); **Gershonov, Gerszonowicz, Gers(c)honowitz, Gershenowitz, Gershanovits** (E Ashkenazic).

Gertz *see* HERZ

Gertzog *see* HERZOG

Gervaiseau *see* JARVIS

Gesche *see* GILBERT

Gesell German: from Ger. *Gesell* companion (MHG *geselle*, OHG *gisell(i)o*, a deriv. of *sal* hall, originally referring to someone who shared living accommodation). In the medieval trade guilds, this word acquired the specialized sense of 'journeyman', i.e. one who had completed his apprenticeship and was working in the workshop of a master craftsman; the surname may well be derived from this spe-

cialized sense, rather than being merely a nickname meaning 'companion' or 'friend'.

Vars.: **Gsell, Gsöll**.

Patr.: Jewish (E Ashkenazic): **Gesellewitz**.

Gessner *see* GASS

Gething *see* GITTING

Getty N Irish: Anglicized form of Gael. **Mag Eitigh**, patr. from the personal name *Eiteach*, which is largely confined to Derry but is of uncertain origin.

Geve *see* GEBHARDT

Geverc *see* GEWIRTZ

Gewers *see* GEBHARDT

Gewirtz Jewish (Ashkenazic): metonymic occupational name for a spicer, from Yid. *gevirts* spice (MHG, OHG *(ge)würz* herb, plant, root; cf. WORT).

Vars.: **Gevirtz(er), Gevirtzman, Gewir(t)zman(n)**; **Gewirzer**; **Gevertz(man)** (from the SE Yid. and a central Yid. form); **Gewirc, Geverc(man)** (Pol. spellings); **Gewu(e)rz, Gewurtz(man)** (from mod. Ger. *Gewürz*).

Geyer *see* GEIER

Ghelardoni *see* GARRETT

Gheorgescu *see* GEORGE

Ghershensohn *see* GERSHON

Ghetti *see* JACK

Ghidelli *see* GUY

Ghiglino *see* WILLIAM

Ghilardini *see* GARRETT

Ghini Italian: from the medieval given name *Ghino*, an aphetic form of *Aghino* (a short form of any of the various Gmc personal names with the first element *agi(n)* edge, point (of a weapon)), *Ughino* (a dim. of *Ugo*, see HUGH), or *Arrighino* (a dim. of *Arrigo*, see HENRY).

Dims.: **Ghinelli, Ghinello, Ghinetti**.

Pej.: **Ghinazzi**.

Ghinsberg *see* GINSBERG

Ghys *see* GILBERT

Giacchello *see* JACK

Giacobazzi *see* JACOB

Giacomasso *see* JAMES

Gianasi *see* JOHN

Gibb Scots and English: from the common medieval pet name *Gib*, a short form of the given name GILBERT.

Var.: **Gipp**.

Dims.: **Giblett, Giblin(g)**, GIBBON.

Patrs.: **Gibbs** (chiefly Midland, W, and SW England, though by no means rare elsewhere); **Gibbes, Gipps, Gypps**; **Gibson** (most common in Scotland, Northumb., and N Ireland); **Gibbeson, Gipson, Gypson**.

Gibbe *see* GILBERT

Gibbon English: **1.** dim. of GIBB. **2.** from the Gmc personal name *Gebwine*, composed of the elements *geba* gift + *wine* friend.

Vars.: **Gibben, Gibbin, Gubbin**.

Patrs. (from 1): **Gibbons, Gibbens, Gibbin(g)s, Gubbins**; FITZGIBBON. Ir.: **McGibbon, McCubbin(e), McCubbing, McKibbin, McKibben, McKibbon** (Gael. **Mac Giobúin**).

Gibke see GEBHARDT

Gibki Polish: nickname for a flexible person (physically or mentally), from Pol. *gibki* supple, pliable.

Gibney Irish: Anglicized form of Gael. **Ó Gibne** 'descendant of *Gibne*', a byname meaning 'Hound'.

Giddings English: habitation name from a group of villages near Huntingdon, called Great, Little, and Steeple *Gidding*, from OE *Gyddingas* 'people of *Gydda*', a personal name of uncertain origin.

Gide French: from the Gmc personal name *Gid(d)o*, of uncertain origin. It may represent a hypocoristic derivative of the various compound personal names containing the element *hild* battle.

Var.: **Gidon** (from the oblique case).

Dim.: **Gidel**.

Giebecke see GEBHARDT

Gielen see GILES

Gieraths see GARRETT

Giermann see GEARY

Gies see GILBERT

Giffard English (Norman) and French: **1.** cogn. of GEBHARDT. **2.** nickname from OF *giffard* chubby-cheeked, bloated (a pej. of *giffel* jaw, cheek, of Gmc origin; cf. mod. Ger. *Kiefer* jaw).

Vars. (of 2): Eng.: **GIFFORD, Jefferd, Jefford**. Fr.: **Giffaut**.

Gifford English: **1.** var. of GIFFARD 2. **2.** habitation name from a place in Suffolk, now *Giffords Hall*. It was originally named in OE as *Gyddingford* 'ford (OE *ford*) associated with *Gydda*'; cf. GIDDINGS.

Giggle see JEKYLL

Giglietti see LILLY

Gigot French: nickname for someone with peculiar legs, from a dim. of OF *gigue* leg, originally a type of small fiddle (of Gmc origin; cf. GEIGER) but applied to the legs because of a supposed similarity of shape.

Vars.: **Gigon, Giguet, Jiguet**.

Gijsbers see GILBERT

Gilardengo see GARRETT

Gilbert **1.** English (Norman), French, and Low German: from *Gislebert*, a Norman personal name composed of the Gmc elements *gīsil* hostage, noble youth + *berht* bright, famous. This given name enjoyed considerable popularity in England during the Middle Ages, partly as a result of the fame of St Gilbert of Sempringham (1085–1189), the founder of the only native English monastic order. This at one time had over twenty houses, but became extinct on the

Dissolution of the Monasteries. **2.** Scots and Irish: Anglicized form of KILBRIDE. **3.** Jewish (Ashkenazic): Anglicization of one or more like-sounding Jewish surnames.

Vars. (of 1): English: **Gilberd, Gilb(e)art, Gil(l)bard, Gilburt, Gilburd, Gilbird, Gelbert; Jelbert, Jelbart** (Devon and Cornwall). Fr.: **Gilibert, Gi(la)bert**. Low Ger.: **Giesebrecht, Gelbert; Schilbert** (Rhineland).

Dims. (of 1): Eng.: GIBB, GIBBON, GILBY. Fr.: **Gi(l)bertin, Gi(l)berton, Gilbon, Gilbain**. Ger.: **Geis(s)el, Geip(p)el, Geipelt**. Low Ger.: **Gies(el), Gieselmann, Gissel, G(i)ese(cke), Gesche, Gibbe**. Flem.: **Ghys**. Dan.: **Giese**.

Patrs. (from 1): Eng: **Gilbertson**. Low Ger.: **Gisbertz, Gilbertz, Gilber(t)s**. Flem.: **Gyselbrechts**. Du.: **Gijsbers**.

Patrs. (from 1) (dim.): Low Ger.: **Ges(ch)en** (Latinized **Gesenius**), **Giesges, Gibbels, Gibbens**. Flem.: **Ghys(el)en**. Du.: **Gijsen, Gijzen**.

Gilblum see GELLER

Gilbride see KILBRIDE

Gilby English: **1.** habitation name from a place in Lincs., so called from the ON personal name *Gilli*, which is abstracted from the various Ir. personal names containing Gael. *giolla* servant (i.e. of a particular saint) + ON *býr* farm, settlement. **2.** dim. of GILBERT.

Var.: **Gilbey**.

Gilchrist Scots: from the Gael. personal name *Gille Crìosd* 'servant of Christ'.

Vars.: **Gilcriest, Gillcrist, Gilgryst**.

Patrs.: **Gilkison, Gilk(e)s; McGilchrist**.

Gildea see KILDEA

Gilder see GOLD

Gildernew Irish: Anglicized form of Gael. **Mac Giolla na Naomh** 'son of *Gilla na Naomh*', a personal name meaning 'servant of the saints'.

Vars.: **McAneave**; FORD.

Gildersleeve English: nickname for an ostentatious dresser, from the ME nickname *gyldenesleve* 'golden sleeve', from OE *gylden* golden (a deriv. of *gold* GOLD) + *slīf, slēf* sleeve.

Var.: **Gildersleve**.

Gilduff Irish: Anglicized form of Gael. **Mac Giolla Dhuibh** 'son of the blackhaired lad'.

Vars.: **McGil(le)duff, McGilleguff, McIlduff, McElduff, (Mc)Kilduff, Killduff; McIlghuie, McAhuie, H(o)uie**.

Giles **1.** English: from a medieval given name of which the original form was L *Ægidius* (from Gk *aigidion* kid, young goat). This was the name of a 7th-cent. Provençal hermit, whose cult popularized the name in a variety of more or less mutilated forms: *Gidi* and *Gidy* in S France, *Gil(l)i* in the area of the Alpes-Maritimes, and *Gil(l)e* elsewhere. This last form was brought over to England by the Normans, but by the 12th cent. it was being confused with the Gmc names *Gisel*, a short form of GILBERT, and *Gilo*, which is from *Gail* (as in GAILLARD). **2.** Irish: Anglicized form of Gael. *Ó Glasáin*; see GLEESAN.

Vars. (of 1): **Gyles, Jiles, Jellis(s)**.

Dims. (of 1): Eng: GILLETT. Fr.: **Gil(l)et, Gill(i)on, Gillot(te), Giloteau, Gilotin, Gilotot, Gillier, Gilliéron, Gillou(in),**

Gil(le)son. It.: **Giletto**, **Gilioli**; **Zilioli**, **Zil(i)otti**, **Zilocchi** (Venetia). Low Ger.: **Gilgmann**, **Ilchmann**, **Ill(ich)mann**. Flem.: **Gil(le)quin**. Czech: **Jílek**.

Aug. (of 1): Fr.: **Giriat**.

Pejs. (of 1): Eng.: **Gillard**, **Jillard**, **Jellard**.

Patrs. (from 1): Eng.: **Gil(l)son** (see also GILL). Ger.: **Gilcher**, **Gilger**, **Gilles**, **Gielen**, **Gieles**, **Gieling**; **Ill(i)es**, **Ilgen**. Flem.: **Gielen**, **Gillen**, **Gillyns**.

Gilfedder see KILFEATHER

Gilfillan Scots: from the Gael. personal name *Gille Fhaoláin* 'servant of (St) *Faolán*'; see WHELAN.

Vars.: **Gilfilland**, **Gillilan(d)**, **Gellan(d)**; **Kilfillan**.

Patrs.: See McCLELLAN.

Gilfoil Irish: Anglicized form of Gael. **Mac Giolla Phóil**, patr. from the personal name *Giolla Phóil* 'servant of (St) PAUL'.

Vars.: **G(u)ilfoyle**, **Kilfoyle**.

Gilham see WILLIAM

Gilhool Irish: Anglicized form of Gael. *Mac Giolla Chomhghaill*; see COLE 3.

Vars.: **Gilhool(e)y**; **McGillecole**, **McGilleghole**, **McGillacoell**.

Gill 1. English: from a short form of the given names GILES, JULIAN, or WILLIAM. In theory the name would have a soft initial when derived from the first two of these, and a hard one when from *William* or from the other possibilities discussed below. However, there has doubtless been much confusion over the centuries, and the modern pronunciation can hardly be taken as a reliable guide to the origin. 2. N English: topographic name for someone who lived by a ravine or deep glen, ME *gil(l)* (ON *gil* gill of a fish, also used in a transferred sense of a ravine). 3. Scots and Irish: Anglicized form of Gael. **Mac Gille** (Sc.), **Mac Giolla** (Ir.), patrs. from an occupational name for a servant or a short form of the various personal names formed by attaching this element to the name of a saint. The ON personal name *Gilli* is probably of this origin (cf. GILBY 1), and may lie behind some examples of the name in N England. 4. Scots and Irish: Anglicized form of Gael. *Mac An Ghoill*; see GALL 1. 5. Dutch: cogn. of GILES. 6. Jewish (Israeli): ornamental name from Hebr. *gil* joy.

Gillanders see ANDREW

Gillespie Scots and Irish: Anglicized form of Gael. **Mac Gille Easbuig** (Sc.), **Mac Giolla Easbuig** (Ir.), patrs. from a byname meaning 'servant of the bishop'.

Vars.: **McGillaspick**; **Gillesp(e)y**, **Gillaspy**, **Gilhespy**, **G(a)lasby**, **Aspig**, **Aspol**, ARCHIBALD.

Gillett English: 1. from a dim. of the given names GILES, JULIAN, or WILLIAM; see GILL 1. 2. topographic name for someone living at the top of a glen or ravine, from Northern ME *gil(l)* glen (see GILL 2) + *heved* head (OE *heafod*).

Vars. (of 1): **Gillet**, **Gill(i)att**, **Giliat**, **Gillyatt**, **Gil(l)iot**, **Gilyot(t)**, **Gillot(t)** (chiefly S Yorks.); **Jillett**, **Jillitt**, **Jellett**; **Gillette** (a fem. form).

Gillian see JULIAN

Gillibrand England (Lancs.): from a Norman personal name *Gillebrand*, composed of the Gmc elements *gīsil* hostage + *brand* sword.

Vars.: **Gillebrand**, **Gellibrand**.

Gillick see GULLICK

Gillies Scots: from the Gael. personal name *Gilla Iosa* 'servant of Jesus'.

Vars.: **Gillis**, LEES.

Patrs.: **Gillison**; **McAleese**, **McAleece**, **McAlish**, **McL(e)ish**, **McLees**, **McLese**, **McLise** (also Ir., from Gael. **Mac Gille Iosa** (Sc.), **Mac Giolla Íosa** (Ir.)).

Gilliger see GALLAGHER

Gilling English: 1. var. of JULIAN. 2. habitation name from places in N Yorks., so called from OE *Gētlingas* or *Gȳðlingas* 'people of *Gētla*' or 'of *Gȳðla*'. The first of these personal names is from a short form of the various cpd names with the tribal name *Gēat* (see JOCELYN) as their first element; the second is from those with a first element *gȳð* battle.

Gillingham English: habitation name from places in Dorset, Norfolk, and Kent, so called from OE *Gȳðlingahām* 'homestead (OE *hām*) of the people of *Gȳðla*'; cf. GILLING 2.

Gillow English: habitation name from a place in Herefords., so called from W *cil* retreat + *llwch* pool.

Gilmartin Irish: Anglicized form of Gael. **Mac Giolla Mhartain**, patr. from the personal name *Giolla Mhartain* 'servant of (St) MARTIN'.

Var.: **Kilmartin**.

Gilmore 1. Scots and Irish: Anglicized form of Gael. **Mac Gille Mhoire** (Sc.), **Mac Giolla Mhuire** (Ir.), patrs. from personal names meaning 'servant of (the Virgin) Mary'. 2. English: habitation name from *Gillamoor* in N Yorks., so called from the nearby town of GILLING + OE *mōr* moor, marsh (see MOORE 1).

Vars. (of 1): **Gillmor(e)**, **Gilmour**, **Gilmer**, **Kilmore**; **McGilmore**, **McGilmour**, **McGilmurry**, **McGillworry**, **McIlmurray**, **McElmurray**; MURRAY.

Gilpin Irish: Anglicized form of Gael. **Mac Giolla Fionn** 'son of the fair-haired lad'; cf. FINN 1.

Gilroy Irish: Anglicized form of Gael. **Mac Giolla Ruaidh** 'son of the red-haired lad'; cf. ROY 1.

Vars.: **McGillaro(w)e**, **McGil(la)roy**, **McKillroe**, **(Mc)Kilroy**, **(Mc)Ilroy**, **McElroy**, **McAlroy**, **McLeroy**.

Gilveil see BELL

Gimel see JUMEAU

Gimelstein see HIMMEL

Gimeno see JIMENO

Gimpel Jewish (Ashkenazic): 1. from the Yid. male given name *Gimpl*, a deriv. of the Ger. given name *Gumprecht* (cogn. of *Gundbert*; see GOMBERT). 2. ornamental name from mod. Ger. *Gimpel* bullfinch, or an unflattering surname from the same word in the sense 'dunce, dupe, simpleton', bestowed by anti-Semitic government officials in 18th- and 19th-cent. central Europe.

Vars.: **Gimpl**; **Gimbel** (W Ashkenazic).

Patrs. (of 1): **Gimp(e)levitch** (E Ashkenazic).

Gimson see JAMES

Gincbarg see GINSBERG

Gindre see GENDRE

Ginest see GENEST

Gingell English (common in Bristol): of unknown origin.

Vars.: **Gingold**, **Gingle**.

Ginn 1. English: metonymic occupational name for a trapper, or nickname for a cunning person, from ME *gin* trick, contrivance, snare (an aphetic form of ME *engin*; see INGHAM 2). **2.** Irish: Anglicized form of Gael. *Mag Fhinn*; see FINN 1.

Var.: **Gynn**.

Ginner see JENNER

Ginsberg Jewish (Ashkenazic): **1.** habitation name from *Gunzberg* in Bavaria, so called from OHG *gen(e)st, gin(e)st* gorse (L *(planta) genesta*; see GENEST) + *berg* hill (see BERG). **2.** habitation name from *Günzburg* in Swabia, which derives its name from the river *Günz* (in early L records *Guntia*, probably of Celt. origin) + OHG *burg* fortress, town. **3.** possibly also a habitation name from *Gintsshprik*, the Yid. name of *Königsberg* ('King's hill') in E Prussia, now Kaliningrad in the Soviet Union.

Vars.: **Ginsberger**, **G(h)inzberg**, **Gunsberg(er)**, **Gunzberg**, **Ghinsberg**, **Gincberg**; **Gincbarg** (with Yid. *barg* hill); **Ginsburg**, **Ginsbo(u)rg**, **Ginzb(o)urg**, **Ghinzburg**; **Ginsburski**, **Ginsborski**, **Ginzburski**, **Ginzbursky**. Ginc- is a Pol. spelling; *Ghin-* is a Rumanian spelling; *-bourg* is a Fr. spelling.

Gioanetti see JOHN

Gioiella see JOY

Giorgeschi see GEORGE

Giottini see FRANCIS

Giovinazzo see JEUNE

Gipp see GIBB

Giráldez see GARRETT

Girbeau see GARBER

Girdwood Scots (SE and central Scotland): habitation name from a place in the parish of Carnwath in the former county of Lanarks. (now part of Strathclyde region). The placename is of uncertain origin, possibly from ME *gerth, girth* band, hoop (ON *gjorð*) + *wode* WOOD.

Giriat see GILES

Girling see CODLIN

Girona Catalan: habitation name from the town of *Gerona* (Cat. *Girona*) in N Spain. The placename is recorded in L sources in the form *Gerunda*, but it is of pre-Roman origin and unknown meaning.

Vars.: **Giró(n)**; **Gironès**.

Girsch see HIRSCH

Girtin see GURTON

Girvan see GARVIN

Gisbertz see GILBERT

Gissing English: habitation name from a place in Norfolk, so called from OE *Gyssingas* 'people of *Gyssa*' or 'of *Gyssi*', an OE or ON personal name representing a short form of the various cpd names with the first element *gīsil* hostage, noble youth (cf., e.g., GILBERT).

Gite see GUTE

Gitter 1. German: topographic name for someone who lived by a gate or barrier, or metonymic occupational name for a janitor, from Ger. *Gitter* grid, grating (MHG *gitter* railing, bar, OHG *getiri*; cf. GATTERER). **2.** German: habitation name from a place near Brunswick, which bears an ancient name of uncertain, probably Celt., origin. **3.** Jewish (S Ashkenazic): cogn. of GOOD.

Var.: **Gitterman**.

Gitting Welsh: **1.** from the W personal name *Gutyn, Guto*, a hypocoristic from of *Gruffydd* (see GRIFFITH). **2.** possibly also a byname from W *cethin* dusky, swarthy.

Var.: **Gething**.

Patrs.: **Gethings**, **Gettens**, **Gettin(g)s**, **Gittens**, **Gittin(g)s**.

Gittoes see GRIFFITH

Giubbini see JOB

Giulianelli see JULIAN

Giulietti see JÚLIO

Giurin see GEORGE

Givenchy French: habitation name from a place in Pas-de-Calais, Picardy, so called from the L personal name *Juventius* + the Gaul. local suffix *-ācum*.

Głąbski Polish: **1.** topographic name for someone living in a low-lying spot or at the bottom of a valley, from Pol. *głąb* depth, bottom. **2.** nickname for a stupid person, from Pol. *głąb* fool (lit., 'cabbage-stalk') + *-ski* suffix of surnames (see BARANOWSKI).

Vars.: **Głąb**; **Głębski**; **Glomski** (U.S. Anglicization).

Habitation names: **Głąbowski**, **Głębowski**; **Głąbicki**, **Głębocki**.

Glad English: **1.** from a short form of the various OE personal names with a first element *glæd* shining, joyful; cf., e.g., GLADWIN. **2.** nickname for a cheerful person, from ME *glad* merry, jolly (from the OE element given above).

Var. (of 2): **Gladman**.

Patrs. (from 1): Eng.: **Glad(d)ing**; **Gladden** (E Anglia).

Gladhill see GLEDHILL

Gladstone 1. Scots: habitation name from a place near Biggar in the former county of Lanarks. (now part of Strathclyde region), apparently so called from the OE *gleoda* kite + *stān* stone. **2.** Jewish (Ashkenazic): Anglicized form of **Glatshteyn**, an ornamental surname composed of the Yid. elements *glat* flat + *shteyn* stone.

Var. (of 1): **Gledstane**.

Gladwin English: from the late OE personal name *Glædwine*, composed of the elements *glæd* shining, joyful + *wine* friend.

Var.: **Gladwyn**.

Glaister Scots: of uncertain origin. The earliest recorded form of the name is *de Glasletter* (1254), which appears to be a habitation name composed of the Gael. elements *glas* green (see GLASS 2) + *leitir* hillside. Later forms such as *de Glacealester* (c.1256), *de Glassester* (1368), and *de Glacestre* (1374) seem to have been influenced by the common Eng. placename element *-cester* (OE *cæster* Roman fort). The forms *Glastre* and *Glastir* appear for the first time in the 15th cent.

Glancy see CLANCY

Glantz Jewish (Ashkenazic): ornamental name from Ger. *Glanz* shine, radiance, Yid. *glants* (MHG, OHG *glanz*, a distant cogn. of GLAD).

Vars.: **Glanz(er)**, **Glantzmann**, **Glanzman**; **Glanzberg** (an ornamental elaboration with Ger. *Berg* hill).

Glanville English (chiefly Devon): **1.** Norman habitation name from a place in Calvados, so called from a Gmc personal name of uncertain form and meaning + OF *ville* settlement (see VILLE). **2.** habitation name from *Glanvill* Farm in Devon, *Clanville* in Somerset and Hants, or *Clanfield* in Hants, or from some other place similarly named, all of which are so called from the OE elements *clæn* clean (i.e. free of brambles and undergrowth) + *feld* pasture, open country (see FIELD).

Vars.: **Glanvill**, **Glan(d)field**.

Glasby see GILLESPIE

Glascott **1.** English: habitation name from *Glascote* in Warwicks., so called from OE *glæs* glass + *cot* hut, shelter; it was probably once a site inhabited by a glass blower. **2.** Welsh: habitation name from *Glascoed* in the former county of Monmouths., so called from W *glas* grey, green + *coed* wood.

Vars.: **Glasscote**, **Glasscock**.

Glasgow **1.** Scots: local name from the city on the Clyde (first recorded in 1116 as *Glasgu*), or from either of two minor places with the same name in the former county of Aberdeens. The etymology of the placename is much disputed; it is most probably from Brit. words that were the ancestors of W *glas* grey, green, blue + *cau* hollows. **2.** Scots and Irish: var. of McCLUSKEY.

Var. (of 1): **Glasscoe**.

Glashen see McGLASHAN

Glass **1.** English: metonymic occupational name for a glazier or glass blower, from OE *glæs* glass (akin to GLAD, referring originally to the bright shine of the material). **2.** Irish and Scots: Anglicized form of any of various Gael. surnames derived from *glas* grey, green, blue; cf., e.g., McGLASHAN. **3.** Jewish (Ashkenazic): ornamental name from mod. Ger. *Glass* glass, or occupational name for a glazier or glass blower.

Vars. (of 1): **Glaze** (W Midlands); **Glassman**; **Glazier**, **Glazyer**, **Glaisher**, **Glaysher**. (Of 3): **Glas**, **Glas(s)er**, **Glasner**, **Glazer**,

Glas(s)man, **Glaserman**; **Glozman** (NE Ashkenazic); **Gluz(er)**, **Gluzman(n)**, **Glusman** (S Ashkenazic); **Gle(j)zer**.
Cpds (of 3, ornamental except where otherwise stated): **Gluzband** ('glass ribbon'); **Glas(s)berg**, **Gluzberg** ('glass hill'); **Glassgold** ('glass gold'); **Glassheib** ('pane of glass', perhaps also occupational); **Gluzschneider** ('glass cutter', occupational).
Equivs. (not cogn.): Eng., Fr.: VERRIER. Pol.: SZKLAR. Jewish (Ashkenazic): STECKLER.

Glatz **1.** German and Jewish (Ashkenazic): nickname for a bald man, from Ger. *Glatze* baldness, MHG *gla(t)z* bald head, bald (a deriv. of MHG, OHG *glat* smooth, shiny, a cogn. of GLAD). **2.** Jewish (Ashkenazic): habitation name from *Glatz*, Ger. name of *Kłodzko* in Lower Silesia.

Vars. (of 2): **Glatzer**.
Dim. (of 1): **Glätzel**.

Glauber see KLUG

Glave see GLEAVE

Glazebrook English: habitation name from a place in Lancs., so called from the *Glaze Brook*, the stream on which it stands (a Brit. name, from a Brit. word that was the ancestor of W *glas* grey, green, blue; cf. GLASS 2) + OE *brōc* stream (see BROOK). The surname is also common in Devon, where it may have an independent origin from a similarly named place, now lost.

Var.: **Glassbrook**.

Glazurin Russian: patr. from the nickname *Glozura*, a deriv. of *glaza* eye, referring to someone with some noticeable peculiarity of the eyes.

Vars.: **Glazyrin**, **Glazov(oi)**, **Glazeev**, **Glazachov**, **Glazatov**, **Glazunov**.

Gleave English (chiefly Lancs.): metonymic occupational name for a maker and seller of swords or nickname for an accomplished swordsman, from ME *gle(y)ve* sword (OF *gleive*, *glaive*, L *gladius*).

Vars.: **Glave**, **Gl(e)aves**.

Głębocki see GŁĄBSKI

Glebov Russian: patr. from the given name *Gleb*, which represents an early borrowing, at the time of the Viking settlement of Kiev, of an ON personal name composed of the elements *gúð* battle, combat + *leifr* love. It is one of the few given names of non-Gk origin officially accepted by the Orthodox church, largely as a result of the enormous popularity of St Gleb (d. AD 1010), who actually bore the Christian baptismal name of DAVID.

Gledhill English: habitation name from a place in W Yorks., so called from OE *gleoda* kite (see GLEED) + *hyll* HILL.

Vars.: **Gledall**, **Gleadell**, **Gleadle**, **Gladhill**.

Gledstane see GLADSTONE

Gleed S English: nickname from ME *glede* kite (OE *gleoda*), probably with reference to the bird's rapacious qualities.

Vars.: **Glede**, **Glide**, **Glyde**.

Gleesan Irish: Anglicized form of Gael. **Ó Glasáin** 'descendant of *Glasán*', a personal name from a dim of *glas* grey, green, blue.
Vars.: **Gleeson, Gleason; (O')Gleasan, O'Glesaine, O'Glassane**; GILES.

Glejzer *see* GLASS

Glen 1. Scots: topographic name for someone who lived in a valley, Gael. *gleann*, or habitation name from a place named with this word, such as *Glen* near Peebles. **2.** English: habitation name from a place in Leics. This bears a Brit. name, probably a cogn. of Gael. *gleann* valley. **3.** Jewish (Ashkenazic): presumably an Anglicization of one or more like-sounding Jewish names.
Vars.: **Glenn.** (Of 1 only): GLYNN.

Glendinning Scots: habitation name from a place in the parish of Westerkirk, Dumfries, recorded in 1384 as *Glendonwyne*. It is apparently so called from Brit. ancestors of the W words *glyn* valley (see GLYNN) + *din* fort + *gwyn* fair, white (see GWYN).
Vars.: **Glenden(n)ing, Clendenning, Clendennen, Clindening.**

Glew English (Yorks.): nickname for a cautious, prudent, or wise man, from ME *glew* wise, prudent (OE *gleaw*).
Var.: **Glue.**

Glick *see* GLÜCK

Glickin Jewish (E Ashkenazic): metr. from the Yid. female given name *Glike* (from Yid. *glik* luck; cf. GLÜCK) + the Slav. suffix -*in*.
Vars.: **Glikin, Glikovsky; Gli(c)kson, Gluekson** (Ashkenazic; the last form is partly Germanized, as if from Ger. *Glück* luck).

Gliddon English (Devon): apparently a habitation name from an unidentified place, possibly *Glidden* in Hants, which is named with the OE elements *glida* kite + *dūn* hill (see DOWN 1); cf. GLEDHILL.

Glide *see* GLEED

Gligoraci *see* GREGORY

Glock German: topographic name for someone who lived by the bell tower of a church, or house name from a house marked by the sign of the bell, from Ger. *Glocke* bell (MHG *glocke, glogge*, OHG *glocka*, apparently ultimately from a Celt. source). It could also be a metonymic occupational name for a sexton, who among other duties was responsible for ringing the church bell; *Glockner* is the usual term for a sexton in some parts of Germany (see also KIRCHNER, MESNER, and OPPERMANN).
Vars.: Ger.: **Glocke; Glock(n)er, Glöckner, Glöckler, Glogger.**
Dims.: Ger.: **Glöckel, Glöckl(e), Glockle, Glöggl** (S Germany and Austria).

Glodeau *see* CLAUDE

Głogowski Polish and Jewish (E Ashkenazic): habitation name from any of various places named with Pol. *głóg* hawthorn + -*ów* possessive suffix, with the addition of the suffix of local surnames -*ski* (see BARANOWSKI). One such place is *Głogów* in W Poland, the Ger. name of which is *Glogau*.

Glohr *see* HILARY

Glomski *see* GŁĄBSKI

Glossop English: habitation name from a place in N Derbys., so called from the gen. case of the OE byname *Glott* (apparently akin to mod. Eng. *gloat*) + OE *hop* valley.

Gloster English: local name from *Gloucester*, the county town of Gloucs. The place originally bore the Brit. name *Glēvum* (apparently from a cogn. of W *gloyw* bright), to which was added the OE element *ceaster* Roman fort (L *castra* legionary camp).

Glover English: occupational name for a maker or seller of gloves, ME *glovere*, agent noun from OE *glōf* glove.

Głowacki Polish: nickname for a clever person or for someone literally with a big head, from Pol. *głowacz* clever person (from *głowa* head) + -*ski* suffix of surnames (see BARANOWSKI).
Var.: **Głowacz.**
Dim.: Czech: **Hlaváček.**
Habitation name: Pol.: **Głowiński.**

Glozman *see* GLASS

Glück 1. German: nickname for a individual considered fortunate, perhaps someone who had had a narrow escape, from Ger. *Glück* luck (MHG *g(e)lücke*, of uncertain origin, not attested before the late 12th cent.). **2.** Jewish (Ashkenazic): ornamental name from mod. Ger. *Glück* luck (Yid. *glik*), or one expressing hope for good luck in the future.
Vars. (of 2): **Glu(e)ck, Gli(c)k; Gluckman(n), Glueckman, Gluecksmann, Glucksman, Gli(c)k(s)man; Glucker, Glik(n)er; Gluecklich, Glicklich** (from the adj. *glücklich* (Ger.), Yid. *gliklekh*, both meaning 'lucky'); **Glucksam, Gliksam** (pseudo-German, with the adj. ending -*sam*).
Cpds (of 2): **Gli(c)ksberg** ('luck hill'); **Glekfeld** ('luck field'); **Glueckselig** ('blissful', expressing hope for a blissful future condition); **Glueckstadt** ('luck city'); **Gluckstein, Gli(c)kstein, Glueckshtin** ('luck stone'); **Glueckstern** ('luck star').

Glue *see* GLEW

Gluekson *see* GLICKIN

Glusman *see* GLASS

Glyde *see* GLEED

Glynn 1. Cornish and Welsh: topographic name for someone who lived in a valley, Corn. *glin*, W *glyn*. **2.** Scots: var. of GLEN 1.
Vars. (of 1): **Glynne, Glyn(e).**

Gnatowski *see* IGNACE

Gnudi *see* BENVENUTI

Goate *see* GATE

Gobbel *see* GODBERT

Gobbi Italian (chiefly Lombardy and Venetia): nickname for a hunchback, from the N Italian regional term *gobbo*.
Var.: **Gobbo.**
Dims.: **Gob(b)etti, Gobbetto, Gobbini.**
Patrs.: **De Gob(b)i(s).**

Gobel French: metonymic occupational name for a maker or seller of goblets and tankards, from OF *gobel* drinking vessel, cup (of Celt. origin; cf. GOBET). The surname is also borne by Ashkenazic Jews, the reason(s) for its adoption being unknown.

Vars.: **Gobeau(x)**, **Goubel**, **Goubeau**; **Goublier**.

Dims.: **Gobelet**, **Gobelot**, **Gobelin**.

Goberman *see* HABER

Gobet French: nickname for a proud or boastful man, from OF *gobet* haughty, vainglorious (apparently from Celt. *gob* mouth, cf. GOBEL).

Var.: **Goubet**.

Göbhardt *see* GEBHARDT

Goble *see* GODBOLD

Goch *see* GOGH

Göcken *see* GOTT

Godbert English: from a medieval given name, *Godebert*, composed of the Gmc elements *gōd* good or *god, got* god + *berht* bright, famous. The name was popularized in England by the Normans, but probably absorbed an OE form *Godbeorht*. An Exeter moneyer named *Godbryt* is recorded in the reign of King Canute (1016–35).

Vars.: **Gobert**; **Godber** (E Midlands).

Dims.: Fr.: **Gobin(ot)**. Ger.: **Gobbel**, **Goppel(t)**, **Göb(b)el**. See also GODBOLD.

Patrs. (from dims.): Ger.: **Göbbels**, **Göbler**.

Godbold English: from a Norman personal name, *Godebald*, composed of the Gmc elements *gōd* good or *god, got* god + *bald* bold, brave.

Vars.: **Godbolt**, **Godball**, **Goble**.

Goddard English (Norman) and French: from *Godhard*, a personal name composed of the Gmc elements *gōd* good or *god, got* god + *hard* hardy, brave, strong. The name was popular in Europe during the Middle Ages as a result of the fame of St Goddard, an 11th-cent. bishop of Hildesheim who founded a hospice on the pass from Switzerland to Italy that bears his name. This surname and the var. *Godard* are also borne by Ashkenazic Jews, presumably as an Anglicization of one or more like-sounding Jewish surnames.

Vars.: Eng.: **Godard**, **Godart**. Fr.: **Go(u)dard**, **Godar(t)**.

Patrs.: Low Ger.: **Göddertz**; **Gäderts** (N Rhineland).

Patrs. (from dims.): Low Ger.: **Gödden**, **Gudden**.

Goddman *see* GOODMAN

Goder *see* GOTT

Godfrey English: from a Norman personal name, *Godefrei*, *Godefroi(s)*, composed of the Gmc elements *god, got* god + *fred, frid* peace. See also JEFFREY.

Vars.: **Godfray**, **Godfree**, **Godfer**, **Gotfrey**.

Dims.: Fr.: **Godfr(a)in**, **Goefrain(t)**.

Patrs.: Low Ger.: **Godeferding**, **Godtfring**; **Goverts**, **Jovers**. Du.: **Govers**. Dan.: **Gotfredsen**.

Godin French and English: from the Gmc personal name *Godino*, a dim. short form of the various cpd names with the first element *god, got* god (cf. e.g. GODBERT, GODBOLD, GODDARD, and GODFREY).

Vars.: Fr.: **Gohin**, **Go(u)in** (see also GWYN). Eng.: **Godden**.

Dims.: Fr.: **Godineau**, **Godinet**; **Gouineau**. Prov.: **Godinou(x)**.

Patr.: Sp.: **Godínez**.

Godley English: habitation name from *Godley* in Ches. or *Goodleigh* in Devon, both of which are so called from the OE byname *Gōda* 'Good' + OE *lēah* wood, clearing.

Vars.: **Godly**; **Goodl(e)y**; **Goodleigh** (a place in Devon).

Godolphin Cornish: habitation name from a place in the parish of Breage, which is of unknown etymology.

Godoy Spanish: habitation name from a place in Galicia. The origin of the placename is uncertain, but a connection has been suggested with the Goth. elements *guðs* god + *wīhs* saint.

Godrich *see* GUTTERIDGE

Godson English: nickname for someone who was the godson (ME *godsune*) of an influential or powerful member of the community, from OE *god* god + *sunu* son. A master would sometimes bestow a special favour on a trusted servant by agreeing to stand godfather to his first child. There has also been some confusion with GOODSON.

Godunov Russian: patr. from the nickname *Godun* (a deriv. of *goditsya* to idle, enjoy oneself), denoting a lazy and self-indulgent person.

Godwin *see* GOODWIN

Goefrain *see* GODFREY

Goemans *see* GOODMAN

Goens *see* GOTT

Goerty *see* FOGARTY

Gofer *see* HOFFMANN

Goff *see* GOUGH

Gofton English (Northumb.): habitation name from a minor place, perhaps *Gofton* in Simonburn, Northumb., earlier *Gofden*, from OE *denu* valley (see DEAN 1), with an uncertain first element.

Gogan *see* COGAN

Gogarty *see* FOGARTY

Gogh Low German: habitation name from any of the various minor places which get their names from an ancient Gmc element *goch, gog* marsh, bog, fen.

Var.: **Goch**.

Gogol Ukrainian and Jewish (E Ashkenazic): nickname or ornamental name from Ukr. *gogol* wild duck, denoting a hunter of the birds or acquired on account of some other association with them.

Goguin French: nickname for a person of easy-going temperament and large appetite, from a dim. of OF *gogue* enjoyment, relaxation, used in some areas also in the more concrete sense 'pudding'; the word is apparently of imitative origin.

Vars.: **Goguy**, **Goguel**.

Dims.: **Goguineau**, **Goguillon**.

Aug.: **Goguelat**.

Gohdens *see* GOTT

Gohin *see* GODIN

Göhring *see* GEARY

Goïc *see* GOUGH

Goichman *see* HOCH

Goicoechea Spanish form of Basque **Goikoetxea**: topographic name for someone who lived in a house situated on a hill or in the upper part of a village, from Basque *goiko* upper (a deriv. of *goi* top; cf. GOYA) + *etxe* house + the def. art. -*a*.

Goin *see* GODIN

Goiri Basque: topographic name for someone who lived near the top of a hill or the upper part of a village, from *goi* top (see GOYA) + the suffix -*iri* near.

Goitia Basque: topographic name for someone who lived on the top floor of a house or at the top of a hill or in the upper part of a village, from *goiti* top part, attic (composed of *goi* top + the local suffix -*ti*) + the def. art. -*a*.

Gołąbek *see* GOLUBEV

Goland *see* HOLLAND

Golby English: apparently a habitation name from an unidentified place, the name of which could be derived from OE *golde* marigold (a deriv. of *gold* GOLD) + ON *býr* farm, settlement. The surname is commonest in the W Midlands, but a placename formed with ON *býr* is not likely to occur in that area; the name is therefore either an alteration of some other name or an importation from further North. It could be a collapsed form of GOLDSBY or a mincing variant of GOODBY.

Gold 1. English and German: metonymic occupational name for someone who worked in gold (OE, OHG *gold*)—a refiner, jeweller, or gilder. **2.** English and German: nickname for someone with bright yellow hair, with reference to the colour of the metal. **3.** English: from an OE personal name *Golda* (or the fem. *Golde*) which persisted into the Middle Ages as a given name. The name was in part a byname from *gold* gold, and in part a short form of the various cpd names with this first element. **4.** Jewish (Ashkenazic): ornamental name from mod. Ger. *Gold*, Yid. *gold* gold. In the U.S. it is often a shortened form of any of the compounds listed below.

Vars. (of 1, 2, and 3): Eng: **Goold**, **Gould**. (Of 1 and 2): Eng.: **Goldman**. (Of 1 only): Eng.: **Gilder**. Ger.: **Göldner**, **Göllner**, **Geldner**, **Gellner**. (Of 2 only): Eng.: **Go(o)lden**, **Goulden**. (Of 4) Jewish: GOLDER, **Goldner**, **Goldman(n)**.

Patrs. (from 3): Eng.: **Golds**, GOLDING.

Cpds (of 4; ornamental unless otherwise stated): Jewish: **Goldbach** ('golden stream'); **Goldband** ('golden ribbon'); **Goldbaum**, **Goldboim** ('golden tree'); **Goldberg**, **Golde(r)nberg** ('golden hill'); **Goldberger** ('person from golden hill'); **Goldblat** ('golden leaf'); **Goldblum** ('golden flower', Anglicized as

Goldbloom); **Goldbren(n)er** ('gold melter', occupational name for a goldsmith); **Goldbruch** ('gold quarry'); **Goldfaber** ('goldsmith', occupational: see FABER); **Goldfaden** ('golden thread'); **Gold(en)farb** ('golden colour'); **Goldfeder** ('golden feather'); **Goldfein**, **Goldfajn** ('fine as gold', Anglicized as **Goldfine**; -*fajn* is a Pol. spelling); **Gold(en)feld** ('golden field'); **Goldfinger** ('golden finger'); **Goldfis(c)h** ('golden fish'); **Goldfis(c)her**; **Goldflam** ('golden flame'); **Goldfleiss** ('golden assiduousness'); **Goldfracht** ('golden freight'); **Goldfri(e)d** ('golden peace'); **Goldfus** ('golden foot', Anglicized as **Goldfoot**); **Goldgart** ('golden garden'); **Goldgewicht** ('golden weight'); **Goldglass** ('golden glass'); **Goldgraber** ('gold digger'); **Goldgrub** ('gold mine'); **Goldhaber** ('possessor of gold' or 'golden oats'); **Goldham(m)er** ('golden hammer'); **Goldhand** ('golden hand'); **Goldhar** ('golden hair', perhaps taken by a blond person); **Goldhecht** ('golden pike'); **Goldhirs(c)h** ('golden deer'); **Goldenhol(t)z** ('golden wood'); **Goldenhorn** ('golden horn'); **Goldkind** ('golden child'); **Goldklang** ('golden sound'); **Goldkorn** ('golden rye'); **Goldkrantz**, **Goldkranc** ('golden wreath', -*kranc* is a Pol. spelling); **Goldlust** ('golden pleasure'); **Goldmacher** ('gold maker', occupational or nickname); **Goldmin(t)z**, **Goldminc** ('gold coin', -*minc* is a Pol. spelling); **Goldmund** ('golden mouth'); **Goldnadel** ('golden needle'); **Goldrat(h)** ('golden counsel'); **Goldreich** ('golden kingdom' or 'rich in gold'); GOLDRING; **Goldrosen** ('golden roses'); **Goldenrot** ('golden red'); **Goldsand** ('golden sand'); **Goldschein** ('golden shine'); **Goldschla(e)ger** ('gold beater', occupational); **Goldsobel** ('golden sable'); **Gold(en)stein** ('gold stone', Anglicized as GOLDSTONE); **Goldstern** ('golden star'); **Goldstoff** ('golden fabric'); **Goldstrom** ('golden stream'); **Goldstuck** ('gold coin'); **Goldenthal** ('golden valley'); **Goldwasser**, **Goldvasser** ('golden water', Anglicized as **Goldwater**); **Goldwein** ('golden wine', Anglicized as GOLDWIN); **Goldwei(t)z** ('golden wheat'); **Goldwerger** (occupational, from Yid. *goldvarger* dealer in items made of gold); **Goldwirth** ('golden host'); **Goldworm** ('golden worm'); **Goldzimmer** ('golden room'); **Goldzweig** ('golden twig'). Of 2 (ornamental): Swed.: **Gullberg** ('gold hill'); **Gullström** ('gold river'); **Gyllenhammar** ('golden hammer'); **Gyllensten** ('golden stone').

Golde Jewish (Ashkenazic): from the Yid. female given name *Golde* 'Gold'.

Var.: **Golda**.

Metrs.: **Goldes**, **Goldis**; **Goldin** (E Ashkenazic).

Golden *see* McGOLDRICK

Golder 1. English: from the OE personal name *Goldhere*, composed of the elements *gold* gold + *here* army. **2.** English: habitation name from a place in Oxon., so called from OE *golde* marigold (a deriv. of *gold* GOLD) + *ōra* slope. **3.** Jewish: var. of GOLD.

Goldfinch English: nickname from the bird, a cpd of OE *gold* GOLD + *finc* FINCH.

Goldie Scots: **1.** dim. of GOLD. **2.** nickname for a wall-eyed person with an unnatural pigmentation of one eye, from ME *gold* GOLD + *ie* eye (OE *eage*).

Vars.: **Gou(l)die**, **Gou(l)dy**. (Of 2 only): **Goldney**.

Golding 1. English: from the late OE personal name *Golding*, formally a patr. from *Golda* 'Gold' (see GOLD 3). **2.** Jewish (Ashkenazic): habitation name from *Golding*, the Yid. name of the town of *Kuldīga* in Latvia.

Goldingay English (W Midlands): apparently a habitation name from an unidentified place. There is a field-name, *Goldenhays*, in Frodsham, Ches., which was *Goulding Hey* in 1684, from ME *golden* golden + *hey* enclosure (see HAY 1). This may once have been a habitation name, and could be the source of the surname.

Goldring 1. English, German, and Jewish (Ashkenazic): from the ME, Ger., or Yid. elements *gold* + *ring*. As an Eng. or Ger. surname it is most probably a nickname for someone who wore a gold ring. As a Jewish surname it is generally an ornamental name. 2. Scots: according to Black, a habitation name from the old 50-shilling lands of Goldring in the bailiary of Kylestewart.

Goldsby English: habitation name from *Goulceby* in Lincs., *Colchesbi* in Domesday Book. Ekwall states that the 'correct' form of the name is *Golkesby*, which would indicate derivation from the gen. case of a personal name *Golk* + ON *býr* farm, settlement. In view of the Domesday Book form, however, Ekwall's other suggestion, that the first element is from the attested ON byname *Kolkr*, seems more plausible.

Goldsmith English: occupational name for a worker in gold, a cpd of OE *gold* GOLD + *smið* SMITH. To a large extent it is an Anglicized form of Ger. or Jewish (Ashkenazic) **Goldschmid(t)**.
Equivs. (not cogn.): Russ. and other Slav. names: ZOLOTARYOV. Jewish: ZOREF. Hung.: EÖTVÖS.

Goldspink English (E Anglia): nickname from the GOLDFINCH. ME *spink* was another name for the finch, probably of imitative origin and largely confined to the N English dialects.

Goldstone English: 1. Anglicized form of Jewish (Ashkenazic) *Goldstein*; see GOLD. 2. from the OE personal name *Goldstān*, composed of the elements *gold* gold + *stān* stone. 3. habitation name from a place in Shrops., so called from the gen. case of the OE personal name *Golda* (see GOLD 3) + OE *stān* stone; or from one in Kent, recorded in the early 13th cent. as *Goldstanestun* 'settlement (OE *tūn*) of *Goldstān*'.
Vars. (of 3): **Goldston**, **Gouldstone**, **Goulston(e)**, **Gols(t)on**, **Guls(t)on**.

Goldthorpe English (Yorks.): habitation name from a place in W Yorks., so called from the OE personal name *Golda* GOLD' + OE *þorp* farm, village.

Goldwin 1. English: from the OE personal name *Goldwine*, composed of the elements *gold* gold + *wine* friend. 2. Jewish (Ashkenazic): Anglicized form of *Goldwein*, a cpd. of GOLD.
Var.: **Goldwyn**.

Golec Polish: nickname from Pol. *golec* (n. deriv. of the adj. *goły* naked) in various possible senses. The basic meaning is 'naked man' or 'hairless man'. It could therefore be a nickname for someone totally destitute, a naked wretch, which is certainly a meaning of the vocab. word. Equally, if not more plausibly, it could be a nickname for a bald or clean-shaven man.
Var.: **Golis**.
Dim.: Czech: **Holeček** (also used as a term of endearment, which may lie behind some cases of this surname).
Habitation names: Pol.: **Goliński**, **Golański**. Czech: **Holíček** (from a placename *Holicky*).

Golightly 1. English: nickname, given perhaps to a messenger, from ME *gō(n)* to go (OE *gān*) + *lihtly* lightly, swiftly (OE *lēoht(līc)*). 2. Scots: altered form of a surname of uncertain origin, possibly an unidentified habitation name. The earliest known bearer is William *Galithli*, who witnessed a charter at the beginning of the 13th cent. Henry *Gellatly*, an illegitimate son of William the Lion, of whom little or nothing is known, was the grandfather of Patric *Galythly*, one of the pretenders to the crown of Scotland in 1291. 3. Irish: Anglicized form of Gael. **Mac an Ghallóglaigh** 'son of the gallowglass', Ir. *gallóglach*. A gallowglass was a mercenary retainer or auxiliary soldier (a cpd of *gall* foreigner (see GALL 1) + *óglach* youth, warrior).
Vars. (of 2): **Gallatly**, **Galletl(e)y**, **Gelatly**, **Gelletly**. (Of 3): **Goligher**, **Goligly**, **Golagley**; INGOLDSBY, ENGLISH.

Gollan see JEKYLL

Golley see GULLY

Golsworthy see GALSWORTHY

Golty see GOULTY

Golubev Russian: patr. from the nickname *Golub* 'Dove' (cogn. with Pol. *gołąb* and ultimately with L *columba*; see COLOMB), denoting a mild-mannered or peace-loving man.
Var.: **Golubinski** (name adopted by members of the Orthodox clergy, with reference to the dove as a symbol of the Holy Spirit).
Dims.: Pol.: **Gołąbik**, **Gołąbek**. Czech: **Holoubek**. Jewish: **Golombek**, **Golombik**.
Habitation names: Pol.: **Gołębiewski**, **Gołębiowski**. Jewish: **Golombursky**, **Golobiwsky**, **Golembiewski**.

Gombert French and Low German: from *Gundbert*, a Gmc personal name composed of the elements *gund* battle, strife + *berht* bright, famous. The name was relatively popular in both France and Germany during the Middle Ages, and was also adopted by Ashkenazic Jews (see also GIMPEL).
Vars.: Fr.: **Gombart**. Low Ger.: **Gumbert**, **Gumpert**, **Gummert**, **Gompert**, **Gommert**.
Patrs.: Low Ger., Du., Flem., and Jewish (Ashkenazic): **Gomper(t)z**, **Gumper(t)z**, **Gompers**.

Gomer English: from ME *Godmer*, a blend of two names, OE *Godmær* and ONF *Godmar*, both composed of the Gmc elements *gōd* good or *god* god + *meri, mari* famous.
Var.: **Gummer**.
Patr.: Eng.: **Gummerson** (Yorks.).

Gomersall English (Yorks.): habitation name from *Gomersal* in W Yorks., so called from the gen. case of an assimilated form of the OE personal name *Gūðmær* (composed of the elements *gūð* battle + *mær* fame) + OE *halh* nook, recess (see HALE 1).

Gomme English: apparently from ME *gome*, OE *guma* man, and so perhaps a nickname or byname, although the exact significance is not clear.
Vars.: **Gomm**, **Goom**; **Gumm(e)**, **Gumb**.
Patrs.: Sp.: **Gómez**. Cat.: **Gomis**. Port.: **Gomes**.

Gonard see HUGH

Goncharov Russian: patr. from the occupational term *gonchar* potter, earlier *gornchar* (a deriv. of *gorn* pot).

Gonfalonieri N Italian: occupational name for a standard-bearer, either in a military context or as the officer of a guild responsible for carrying the banner in religious processions. It was also a title borne by mayors of the Florentine republic, and by other magistrates designated more specifically as *gonfalonieri di giustizia* ('officers of justice'), *gonfalonieri della chiesa* ('officers of the church'), etc. The word is an agent noun derived from It. *gonfalone* standard, from OF *gonfalon* (of Gmc origin, a cpd of the elements *gund* battle + *fan* flag; cf. VAANDRAGER).

Var.: **Confalonieri**.

Gonzalo Spanish: from a Gmc personal name first recorded in the L form *Gundisalvus*. The first element is *gund* battle, strife; the second was perhaps originally *sal* hall, later influenced by L *salvus* safe.

Vars.: **Gonzalvo**, **Gozalo**.

Patrs.: Sp.: **Gonzál(v)ez**, **Gosálvez**. Port.: **Gonçaves**.

Gooch *see* GOUGH

Good English: 1. nickname from ME *gode* good (OE *gōd*). 2. from a medieval given name, a survival of the OE personal name *Gōda*, which was in part a byname and in part a short form of various cpd names with the first element *gōd*.

Vars.: **Goode**, **G(o)ude**, **Gudd**. (Of 1 only): **Legood** (with fused ANF def. art., as often found in medieval records).

Patrs. (from 2): Eng.: **Gooding(e)**, **Goodings**; see also GOODSON.

Goodall English (chiefly Yorks. and Notts.): 1. habitation name from a place in Yorks., either *Goodall* House, a lost place in Leven, E Yorks., or *Gowdall* in W Yorks., named from OE *golde* marigold + OE *halh* nook, recess (see HALE 1). 2. metonymic occupational nickname for a brewer or innkeeper, from ME *gode* GOOD + *ale* ale, malt liquor (OE *ealu*).

Vars. (of 1): **Goodhall**. (Of 2): **Gooda(y)le**.

Gooday English: 1. from the OE personal name *Gōddæg*, composed of the elements *gōd* good, auspicious + *dæg* day. There may also have been some confusion with GOODEY. 2. nickname for someone who made frequent use of the greeting 'good day', cf. GOODEN. 3. forms such as John de Goday (Staffs. 1327) suggest that it may occasionally be a habitation name, perhaps from some minor place named with the OE elements *gōd* good + *(ge)hæg* enclosure (see HAY 1). On the other hand, the *de* in these cases may be purely honorific, indicating gentry status.

Goodbody English: nickname for a good person, from ME *gode* GOOD + *body* person, creature (OE *bodig*).

Vars.: **Goodboddy**, **Goodbaudy**.

Goodby English (W Midlands): nickname for someone who made frequent use of the expression 'God be with you', ME *God b'ye*, not necessarily as a farewell. The first syllable was altered under the influence of parallel expressions such as *good day* and *good even* (see GOODAY 2 and GOODEN), yielding the mod. E vocab. word *goodbye*.

Goodchap English: nickname for a trader who made frequent use of this cry, from ME *gode* GOOD + *ch(e)ap* bargain, barter (cf. CHAPMAN). The mod. Eng. word *cheap* is a reduction of this phrase.

Var.: **Goodcheap**.

Goodchild English (mainly Southern): 1. from a ME given name, a survival of OE *Gōdcild*, composed of the elements *gōd* good + the late OE name-forming element *cild* CHILD. This name may also have been used in the ME period as a nickname for a good person. 2. nickname for someone who was the godchild of an important member of the community; cf. GODSON and its confusion with GOODSON.

Gooden English: nickname from frequent use of the ME salutation (*God ye*) *gooden* 'good evening' (originally *God give you good even*).

Goodenough English: 1. nickname from ME *gode* GOOD + *enoh* enough (OE *genōh*). Reaney suggests that it was bestowed on one who was easily satisfied; it may also have been used with reference to one whose achievements were average, 'good enough' though not outstanding. 2. possibly also a nickname meaning 'good lad' or 'good servant', from ME *gode knave*, from OE *gōd* GOOD + *cnafa* boy, servant.

Vars.: **Goodanew**, **Goodnow**, **Goodner**.

Gooder English: from a ME given name *Godere*, OE *Gōdhere*, composed of the elements *gōd* good + *here* army.

Vars.: **Goodere**, **Gooda**, **Gouda**.

Patr.: **Gooders**.

Gooderick *see* GUTTERIDGE

Goodey English: 1. from a ME female given name *Godeve*, OE *Gōdgifu*, composed of the elements *gōd* good or *god* god + *gifu* gift. This name has perhaps absorbed a less common name with the second element *gūð* battle. 2. nickname for a widow or an independent woman, from ME *goodwife* mistress of a house (from OE *gōd* good + *wīf* woman; cf. GOODMAN 1).

Vars.: **Goodee**, **Good(d)y**, **Goodiff**, **Goodeve**, GOODAY.

Metr.: **Goodison** (Northern).

Goodfellow English: nickname for a congenial companion, from ME *gode* GOOD + *felawe* FELLOW.

Goodfriend English: nickname for a reliable friend or neighbour, from ME *gode* GOOD + *frend* FRIEND.

Goodhew English: 1. nickname for a trusted servant, from ME *gode* GOOD + *hewe* servant (a deriv. of OE *hīwan* retinue, household). 2. from an ON personal name, composed of the elements *guð* battle + *hugi* mind, spirit.

Vars.: **Goodhue**, **Goodhugh**.

Goodlad Scots (common in Orkney and Shetland): nickname for a trusted servant, from ME *gode* GOOD + *ladde* lad, servant (see LADD); cf. GOODHEW 1, GOODENOUGH 2, and GOODSWEN.

Vars.: **Goodlatt**, **Goodlet(t)**.

Goodlake *see* GULLICK

Goodleigh *see* GODLEY

Goodman English: 1. status name from ME *gode* GOOD + *man* man, in part from use as a term for the master of a household; cf. GOODEY 2. In Scotland the term was used of a landowner, however large his estate, who held his land not directly from the crown but from a feudal vassal of the king. 2. from a ME given name *Godeman*, OE *Gōdmann*, composed of the elements *gōd* good or *god* god + *mann* man. 3. from the OE personal name *Gūðmund*, composed of the elements *guð* battle + *mund* protection, or the ON cogn. *Guðmundr*. 4. Jewish (Ashkenazic): Anglicization of any of the Jewish surnames given below.

Vars.: **Goudman**; **God(d)man**.

Patrs. (from 1): Flem., Du.: **Goemans**. (From 3): Swed.: **Gudmundsson**.

Goodrum English (mainly Norfolk): from the ON personal name *Guðormr*, composed of the elements *guð* battle + *ormr* snake, serpent.

Vars.: **Goodram**, **Gooderham**, **Guthrum**.

Goodsir English: 1. nickname for an elderly and venerable gentleman, from ME *goodsire* grandfather, a cpd of *gode* GOOD + *sir(e)*, a form of respect. 2. nickname for one who used the expression 'good sir' to excess as a term of address.

Goodson English (chiefly E Anglia and E Midlands): 1. nickname for a dutiful son, from ME *gode* GOOD + *sune* son. 2. from a ME survival of the OE personal name *Gōdsunu*, composed of the elements *gōd* good + *sunu* son. See also GODSON.

Goodswen English (chiefly Norfolk): nickname for a trusted servant, from ME *gode* GOOD + *sweyn* servant (see SWAN 2).

Goodwill English (Yorks.): nickname for a friendly or amiable person, from ME *gode* GOOD + *will* desire (OE *willa*). The cpd is attested in the sense 'favourable disposition' since before the Norman Conquest.

Goodwin English: from the ME personal name *Godewyn*, OE *Gōdwine*, composed of the elements *gōd* good + *wine* friend.

Vars.: **Godwin**, **Godwyn**.

Goodyear English: from ME *gode* GOOD (OE *gōd*) + *year* year (OE *gear*), of uncertain application as a surname.

Vars.: **Goodyer**, **Goodier**, **Goudier**, **Goodger**, **Gudger**.

Goold *see* GOLD

Goom *see* GOMME

Goonan *see* GAFFNEY

Gooravan *see* McGOVERN

Goose English (now chiefly E Anglia): nickname for a foolish person or metonymic occupational name for a breeder of geese, from OE *gōs* goose. In both Eng. and Low Ger. there has been some confusion with forms of JOYCE.

Var.: **Gooseman**.

Dims.: Ger.: **Gansl**, **Genslein**, **Gänsli**. Low Ger.: **Gäusgen**, **Gösgen**. Jewish: **Ganzel**, **Gans(e)l**, **Genzel**.

Goosen *see* GOSSE

Goosey English: 1. nickname from a place in Berks., so called from OE *gōs* GOOSE + *ēg* island. 2. nickname from OE *gōs* GOOSE + *ēage* eye.

Var.: **Goozee**.

Goppel *see* GODBERT

Gora *see* GÓRSKI

Goracci *see* GREGORY

Görcke *see* GEORGE

Gordeev Russian: patr. from the given name *Gordei*, earlier *Gordi* (from Gk *Gordios*, a name of uncertain and probably non-Gk etymology, borne by the legendary king of Phrygia who tied the 'Gordian knot', which was untied only when Alexander the Great cut it through with his sword). It was also the name of a saint martyred under Diocletian in AD 304 and much venerated in the Orthodox Church.

Dim.: Ukr.: **Hordienko** (Russianized as **Gordienko**).

Gordo Spanish and Jewish (Sefardic): nickname for a fat man, from Sp. *gordo* fat (LL *gurdus*, of uncertain origin). The word is attested as a Sp. byname, though not as a hereditary surname, as early as the 11th cent.

Dim.: **Gordillo**.

Aug.: **Gordón**.

Gordon 1. Scots: habitation name from a place in the former county of Berwicks. (now part of Borders region), apparently so called from Brit. words that were ancestors of W *gor* spacious + *din* fort. 2. English (Norman): habitation name from *Gourdon* in Saône-et-Loire, so called from the Gallo-Roman personal name *Gordus* + the local suffix *-o*, *-ōnis*. 3. Irish: Anglicized form of Gael. **Mag Mhuirneacháin**, patr. from the personal name *Muirneachán*, a dim. of *muirneach* beloved. 4. French: nickname for a fat man, from a dim. of OF *gort, gord* fat (see GORDO). 5. Jewish (E Ashkenazic): probably a habitation name from the Beloruss. city of *Grodno* (Lithuanian *Gardinas*, whence the E Ashkenazic surnames **Gardin(ski)**). It goes back at least to 1657. It was widespread among Jews in Poland by the end of the 17th cent., when two naturalized Polish noblemen, Henry and George Gordon, obtained legislation to prevent its continued adoption by Jews. Various suggestions, more or less fanciful, have been put forward as to its origin. Kaganoff believes it to be an 'Anglicized' form of Russ. *gorodin* townsman (from *gorod* town), but Anglicization was not a factor in E Europe in the 17th cent. There is a family tradition among some bearers that they are descended from a son of the Duke of Gordon who converted to Judaism in the 18th cent., but this would seem to be pure fantasy: the Jewish surname was in existence long before the 18th cent. Others claim descent from earlier Scottish converts, but the Jewish surname existed long before any non-Jew named Gordon converted to Judaism.

Vars. (of 1–4): **G(o)urdon**. (Of 3 only): **McGournaghan**, **McGounasan**. (Of 4 only): **Gordet**, **Gordin**. (Of 5): **Gordin**.

Patrs. (from 5): **Gordonoff**, **Gordonowitz**.

Gore 1. English: habitation name from any of the various places, for example in Kent and Wilts., so called from OE *gāra* triangular piece of land (a deriv. of *gār* spear, with reference to the triangular shape of a spearhead). **2.** French: nickname for a gluttonous and idle individual, from OF *gore* sow (of allegedly imitative origin, reflecting the grunting of the animal).

Vars. (of 1): Eng.: **Gorer**, Gorman. (Of 2): Fr.: **Lagore**.

Dims. (of 2): Fr.: **Go(u)ret**, **Gor(r)on**, **Gorin**, **Go(u)ry**, **Gorel**, **Go(u)reau**, **Gorichon**, **Gori(ll)ot**.

Pej. (of 2): Fr.: **Goraud**.

Goreham English (Norfolk): apparently a habitation name from an unidentified place, so called from OE *gāra* triangular piece of land (see Gore 1) + *hām* homestead.

Var.: **Gorham**.

Gorelik Jewish (Ashkenazic): occupational name for a distiller, Yid. *gorelik* (from a Slav. verb meaning literally 'to burn'; cf. Brenner 1).

Vars.: **Gorelick**, **G(o)ralni(c)k**, **Gorlnik**; **Gareli(c)k** (among Beloruss. Jews; Anglicized Garlick); **Guralni(c)k** (among Ukr. Jews).

Goren Jewish (Ashkenazic): altered form of Horn 5 under Russ. influence, since Russ. has no /h/ and alters /h/ in borrowed words to /g/. In Israel the name has been reinterpreted by folk etymology as being from Hebr. *goren* threshing floor, which is in fact etymologically and semantically unrelated.

Var.: **Gorenn**.

Cpd: **Gorenstein** (alteration, under Russ. influence, of *Hornstein*; see cpds of Horn).

Gorevan see McGovern

Gorey see McCaffrey

Gorfinkel Jewish (Ashkanzic): ornamental name or metonymic nickname meaning 'carbuncle', from Yid. *gorfinkl* or Ger. *Karfunkel* (MHG *carbunkel* jewel, diamond, from LL *carbunculus*, a deriv. of *carbo* glowing coal; cf. Carbonell). The vocab. word denoted both a red precious or semi-precious stone, esp. a garnet or ruby cut into a rounded shape, or a large inflamed area of skin like a large boil.

Vars.: **Gorfunkel**, **Garfinkel**, **Garfunkel**; **Karfunkel** (from Ger. *Karfunkel*); **Karfunkiel** (Pol. spelling), **Gurfinkiel** (S Ashkenazic).

Gorge English and French: topographic name for someone who lived by or in a deep valley, from ME, OF *gorge* gorge, ravine (from OF *gorge* throat, LL *gurga*, from class. L *gurges* whirlpool). There are various places in England and France named with this word, and the surname may be a habitation name from any of these.

Vars.: Eng.: **Gordge**, **Gorch**, **Gorges**.

Dims.: Fr.: **Gorgeau**, **Gorgeon**, **Gorgeot**.

Görhardt see Garrett

Gorick see George

Goring 1. English: habitation name from places in Oxon. and W Sussex, so called from OE *Gāringas* 'people of *Gāra*', a short form of the various cpd names with the first element *gār* spear. For the change of OE *-ā-* to Southern ME *-ō-*, cf. Roper. **2.** Jewish (Ashkenazic): of unknown origin.

Vars.: **Gorin**. (Of 1 only): **Gor(r)inge**.

Göring see Geary

Görlacher see Garlick

Gorman 1. English: from the ME given name *Gormund*, OE *Gārmund*, composed of the elements *gār* spear + *mund* protection. **2.** English: topographic name for someone who lived by or on a triangular patch of land; see Gore 1. **3.** Irish: Anglicized form of Gael. **Mac Gormáin** and **Ó Gormáin** 'son' and 'descendant of *Gormán*', a personal name from a dim. of *gorm* blue. **4.** Jewish (Ashkenazic): of unknown origin.

Vars. (of 1): **Garman**, **Garment**. (Of 3): **MacGorman**, **O'Gorman**.

Gormley Irish: Anglicized form of Gael. **Ó Gormghaile** 'descendant of *Gormghal*', a personal name from *gorm* noble + *gal* valour.

Vars.: **O'Gorm(e)ley**, **O'Gorumley**, **O'Grimley**, **Gormilly**, **Germly**, **Grumley**, Grimley.

Gornall English (Lancs.): apparently a habitation name from a place so called, perhaps *Gornal(wood)* near Birmingham, which probably derives its name from OE *cweorn* mill + *halh* recess, hollow (see Hale 1).

Gorokhov Russian: patr. from the nickname *Gorokh* 'Pea', given perhaps to a market gardener or to a very small man.

Habitation names: Pol.: **Grochowski**, **Grochocki**, **Grochulski**. Czech: **Hráský**, **Hrachovec**. Jewish (E Ashkenazic): **Gorochov(ski)**, **Gorohovski**.

Gorostiaga Basque: topographic name for someone who lived near a holly tree, from *gorosti* holly + the local suffix *-aga*.

Gorostiza Basque: topographic name for someone who lived in an area thickly grown with holly bushes, from *gorosti* holly + the suffix of abundance *-tza*.

Görrissen see Gregory

Gorse 1. French: habitation name from any of various minor places, all of which are probably named from a Celt. word denoting a hawthorn hedge (cf. OIr. *garb* rough). **2.** English: topographic name for someone who lived in an area overgrown with gorse bushes, from OE *gors(t)* gorse (apparently ultimately cogn. with 1).

Vars. (of 1): **Gorsse**, **Gorce**, **Lagorce**. (Of 2): **Gorst**.

Górski Polish and Jewish (E Ashkenazic): topographic name for someone who lived on a hillside or in a mountainous district, from Pol. *góra* mountain, hill + the surname suffix *-ski* (see Baranowski). See also Zagórski.

Vars.: Pol.: **Góral**; **Górny** (from the adj.); **Górak**, **Górczak**, **Górniak**; **Górniok** (Silesian); **Górnicki**, **Górecki**. Jewish: **Gorsky**, **Gurski**, **Gursky**; **Goretzki**, **Guretzky**, **Gora**, **Gura**.

Dims.: Pol.: **Gór(al)czyk**. Czech: **Horáček**, **Horálek**.

Habitation names: Pol.: **Górowski**, **Góralski**.

Gorstidge see Gossage

Gorton English: habitation name from a place in Lancs., so called from OE *gor* dirt + *tūn* enclosure, settlement.

Gorwitz see Horowitz

Gorzkiewicz see Horký

Gosálvez see Gonzalo

Gosch *see* GOTTSCHALK

Gösgen *see* GOOSE

Gosling English: **1.** var., with hard initial, of JOCELYN. **2.** nickname from ME *gosling* young goose (from OE *gōs* + the Gmc suffix *-ling* (cf., e.g., CHAMBERLAIN), partly in imitation of ON *gǽslingr* from *gás*).

Vars. (mainly of 1): **Gossling, Goseling, Gostling, Gos(se)lin, Gosland**.

Gosmin *see* KUZMIN

Gosney English (Yorks.): of uncertain origin, probably a habitation name from some minor place deriving its name from the gen. case of the OE byname *Gōsa* Goose' + OE *ēg* island.

Gossage English: habitation name from the hamlet of *Gorsuch*, Lancs., earlier *Gosefordsich*, from OE *Gōsford* 'goose ford' + *sīc* small stream. *Gorsage Hall* is shown on the 19th-cent. Ordnance Survey map beside the road from Halsall to Scarisbrick.

Vars.: **Gorsuch, Gorstidge, Gostage**.

Gossart **1.** English: occupational name for a keeper of geese, ME *goseherde*, from OE *gōs* GOOSE + *hierde* herdsman, keeper (see HEARD). **2.** French: pej. of GOSSE.

Vars. (of 1): **Gozzard, Gozzett**.

Gosse English (Norman), French, and Low German: from the OF given name *Gosse*, representing the Gmc personal name *Gozzo*, a short form of the various cpd names with the first element *gōd* good or *god, got* god.

Vars.: Eng.: **Goss** (chiefly W Country). Low Ger.: **Gösse**.

Dims.: Eng.: **Gosset(t)**. Fr.: **Gosset, Gossin**.

Patrs.: Flem., Du.: **Goos(s)en(s)**.

Gostellow English: habitation name from *Gorstella* in Ches., so called from OE *gors(t)* GORSE + *hyll* HILL + *hlāw* mound (see LAW 2).

Got Jewish (Ashkenazic): ornamental name from mod. Ger. *Gott* God, Yid. *got*. **2.** French: from a pet form of the personal name *Hugo* (*see* Hugh).

Var.: GOTT.

Cpds.: **Gotajner** ('One God', an expression of monotheistic faith; Pol. spelling); **Gottdenker** ('thinker about God'); **Gott(es)diener, Got(t)esdiner** ('servant of God'); **Gottesdonner** ('God's thunder'); **Gottehrer** ('honourer of God'); **Gottesfeld** ('God's field'); **Gotsforcht** ('fear of God'); **Gottfreund** ('friend of God'); **Gotfri(e)d, Gotfryd, Gottfried** ('God's peace'; see also GODFREY); **Gottesgnade** ('GRACE OF GOD'); **Gottheil, Gotshal** ('God's salvation'); **Got(t)helf, Got(t)hilf** ('God's help'); **Gotkind** ('child of God'; GOTTLIEB; **Gottesmann, Got(t)esman** ('God's man'); **Gottreich** ('kingdom of God'); GOTTSCHALK; **Gott(es)segen** ('God's blessing'); **Gottselig** ('blessed by God').

Got *see* HUGH

Gotfredsen *see* GODFREY

Gothard **1.** English: occupational name for a keeper of goats, ME *gotherde*, from OE *gāt* goat (see GATE 3) + *hierde* herdsman, keeper (see HEARD). **2.** German: cogn. of GODDARD.

Gothmann *see* GOODMAN

Gott **1.** English (Norman) and German: from a personal name, a short form of the various Gmc cpd names with the first element *gōd* good or *god, got* god. **2.** Jewish (Ashkenazic): var. of GOT.

Vars. (of 1): Ger.: **Gotte, Godt, Göth(e)**.

Dims. (of 1): Ger.: **Gott(e)l, Gödel, Götz(e)**. Low Ger.: **Gö(d)tke, Gödeke, Gädtke, Gädcke, Gäde(c)ke**. Fris.: **Jädecke**. Fr.: **Go(u)don, Godot, Godet, Godey**.

Patrs. (from 1): Eng.: **Gotts**. Low Ger.: **Goder, Göder(s), Gohde(n)s, Gödens, Gaden**. Fris.: **Goens**.

Patrs. (from dims. of 1): Ger.: **Göttler**. Low Ger.: **Göttgens, Göttjens, Gäthgens, Göcker, Göcks, Göcken, Göcking**.

Gottlieb **1.** German: from a medieval given name, originally a Gmc personal name composed of the elements *god, got* god + *leoba* love. **2.** Jewish (Ashkenazic): from the Yid. male given name *Gotlib*, derived from the Ger. name given above, or else an ornamental name from Yid. *got* God + *lib* love.

Vars. (of 2): **Gotlieb, Got(t)lib**.

Patrs. (from 2): **Gotlibowicz, Gotlibovski**.

Gottschalk **1.** German: from a medieval given name composed of the MHG elements *got* God (OHG *got*) + *schalk* servant, court jester (OHG *scalc*; cf. MARSHALL and SENESCHAL). **2.** Jewish (Ashkenazic): ornamental name composed of the Ger. elements *Gott* God + *Schalk* servant or jester.

Vars.: **Gottschall, Gottschald; Gutschalk** (also a nickname meaning 'good servant').

Dims.: Ger.: **Göschel**. Low Ger.: **Gosch, Gösch(e)**. Ger. (under Slav. influence): **Gutsch(mann), Gutsch(k)e**.

Patrs. (from dims.): Low Ger.: **Göschen**. Ger. (under Slav. influence): **Gutsch(l)er, Gutschner**.

Gouasquet *see* GASCOIGNE

Goubeau *see* GOBEL

Goubet *see* GOBET

Gouda *see* GOODER

Goudard *see* GODDARD

Goude *see* GOOD

Goudie *see* GOLDIE

Goudier *see* GOODYEAR

Goudman *see* GOODMAN

Goudon *see* GOTT

Gough **1.** English, of Celtic origin: occupational name for a smith, from Gael. *gobha*, Corn./Bret. *goff*. The surname is common in E Anglia, where it is probably of Bret. origin, introduced by followers of William the Conqueror. **2.** Welsh: nickname for a red-haired person, from W *coch* red, showing the mutation of the initial consonant that occurs when the adj. is used attributively with a proper name.

Vars. (of 1): **Goff(e); Gow** (Sc.); **Angove** (Corn.). (Of 2): **Gou(d)ge, Goodge, Gudge; Gutch, Gooch** (mainly E Anglia).

Dims. (of 1): Eng.: **Goffin, Gowen** (both chiefly E Anglia). Bret.: **Goffic, Govic, Go(u)ic**.

Pej. (of 1): Eng.: **Goward** (E Anglia).

Patrs. (from 1): Sc.: **McGow(e)** (Gael. **Mac Gobha**). See also McGOWAN.

Gouin see GODIN

Goujon French: nickname from the gudgeon, OF *gougon* (L *gōbio*, gen. *gōbionis*, a deriv. of *gōbius*, the name of a related fish). The fish is considered easy to catch, and so the nickname may have been used with reference to a greedy or credulous person.
Vars.: **Gougeon**, **Goujou**.

Gould see GOLD

Gouldstone see GOLDSTONE

Goulet French: nickname for a greedy or voracious man, from OF *goulet* gullet, a dim. of *goule* throat (L *gula*). It may also be in part a topographic name for someone who lived by a narrow pass or defile (cf. GORGE).
Var.: **Gouley**.

Goulty English: of unknown origin. No forms have been found before 1544, when Robert *Golty* was married at Debach, Suffolk. The name has always been a rare one, largely confined to Norfolk and Suffolk, and all bearers may well descend from a common ancestor.
Var.: **Golty**.

Gounard see HUGH

Goundry see GRUNDY

Goupil French: nickname for a cunning person, from OF *goupil* fox (LL *vulpiculus*, dim. of class. L *vulpes*, a distant cogn. of WOLF). This was replaced as a vocab. word during the Middle Ages by the modern form *renard*, originally the given name (of Gmc origin; cf. REYNARD) borne by the fox in the popular beast tales.
Vars.: **Goupy**, **Verpy**.
Dims.: **Goupillet**, **Goupillon**, **Guerpillon**.
Pej.: **Verpillat**.

Gourdon see GORDON

Goureau see GORE

Gourlay Scots: of uncertain origin, possibly a habitation name from some place in Normandy. According to Black it is 'probably from some place in England', but elsewhere he mentions a certain Aleyn GURNAY whose seal reads *S(igillum) Alani Gorley*.
Vars.: **Gourley** (chiefly N Ireland), **Gourlie**.

Gous French: nickname from OF *go(u)s* dog, cur (of uncertain origin), widely used as a term of abuse in the Middle Ages. Unlike the majority of surnames derived from offensive nicknames current at that time, this one has survived to the present day. This is no doubt because for some reason the vocab. word fell quickly out of use, so that the name was no longer understood as offensive, and there was no pressure to change it.
Dims.: **Goussin**, **Gousson**, **Gousset**.
Pejs.: **Goussard**, **Goussaud**.

Gouveia Portuguese: habitation name from any of various places so called, in particular a town in the province of Beira Baixa. The placename is first recorded in the L forms *Gaudela* and *Goudela*; it is of obscure origin.

Gouverneur French: occupational name for various sorts of minor administrative officials, from OF *gouverneur* man-

ager, steward (L *gubernātor*, a deriv. of *gubernāri* to steer, control, itself an early borrowing from Gk).

Govan Scots: **1.** occupational name from Gael. *gobhan*, a dim. of *gobha* smith; see GOUGH 1. **2.** habitation name from a place near Glasgow, first recorded *c*.1134 as *Guven*. It is probably from Gael. *gudhbhan*, a dim. of *gudhbh* schoolhouse.

Govenlock see GOWANLOCK

Gover 1. English: of uncertain origin. In part it seems to be a nickname from ME *go(n)* to go (OE *gān*) + *fair* lovely, quiet(ly) (see FAIR), but early examples such as Richard *le Gofiar* (Somerset 1327) point to its origin as an occupational name or perhaps a nickname, from an unknown element. **2.** Jewish: of unknown origin.

Govers see GODFREY

Govic see GOUGH

Govini see JACOB

Gow see GOUGH

Gowanlock Scots: of unknown origin, possibly a habitation name from some minor place that cannot now be identified. The name is first recorded in the Lowlands, (in Edinburgh in 1471, in the form *Gowanlok*), so an Eng. rather than a Gael. etymology should probably be sought.
Vars.: **Gowenlock** (the most common spelling in England); **Govenlock**; **Govinlock** (U.S., Canada).

Gowans see McGOWAN

Gower 1. English (Norman): regional name for someone from the district north of Paris known in OF as *Gohiere*. **2.** English (Norman): habitation name from any of the various places in N France called *Gouy* (from the Gallo-Roman personal name *Gaudius* + the local suffix *-ācum*), with the addition of the ANF suffix *-er*. **3.** English (Norman): from a Norman personal name, *Go(h)ier*, cogn. with the OE name mentioned at GOODER. **4.** Welsh: from the peninsula in S Wales, whose W name is *Gŵyr*. **5.** Jewish: var. of GOVER.
Vars.: **Gowar**, **Guwer**.
Patr. (from 3): Eng.: **Gowers**.

Goya Spanish form of Basque **Goia**, **Goya**: topographic name for someone who lived at the top of a hill or the upper part of a settlement, from Basque *goi* top + the def. art. *-a*.

Gozalo see GONZALO

Gozzard see GOSSART

Gozzi see DOMINIQUE

Graber 1. German: occupational name for a digger of graves or ditches, or an engraver of seals, from an agent deriv. of Ger. *graben* to dig, excavate (OHG *graban*). **2.** Jewish (Ashkenazic): occupational name for a gravedigger, mod. Ger. *Gräber*.
Vars. (of 1): **Grabert**, **Grabner**, **Gräber**, **Grebert**. (Of 2): **Graberman**; **Greber** (from Yid. *greber*).
Dim.: Pol.: **Grabarczyk**.

Grabowski Polish and Jewish (E Ashkenazic): habitation name from any of various places named with Pol. *grab* hornbeam, the wood of which was used for making yokes, with the addition of the surname suffix -ski (see BARANOWSKI). In some cases it may be an occupational name for a yoke-maker.

Vars.: Pol.: **Grab(ski)**. Jewish: **Grabovski**.

Patr.: Pol.: **Grabowicz**.

Graby see GABRIEL

Grace English: 1. nickname from ME, OF grace charm, pleasantness (L grātia). 2. from the female given name Grace, which was popular in the Middle Ages. This seems in the first instance to have been from a Gmc element grīs grey (see GRICE 1), but was soon associated by folk etymology with 1.

Port.: **Graça**.

Dims.: It.: **Grazzini, Grazioli, Graziotti**.

Metrs.: It.: **Di Gratia, Delle Grazie**.

Graczyk Polish: nickname for a gambler or musician (or possibly an actor), Pol. graczyk player, dim. of gracz, agent noun from grać to play, in various senses: to play cards, to play a musical instrument, or to act.

Gradillas Spanish: topographic name for someone who lived at a place where a hillside had been shaped into terraces Sp. gradillas (pl. of gradilla, dim. of grada step, a fem. var. of grado, from L gradus step, a deriv. of gradi to go, proceed).

Grady Irish: Anglicized form of Gael. Ó Gráda 'descendant of Gráda', a byname meaning 'Noble'. The form **Mac Gráda** 'Son of Gráda' (Anglicized **McGrady**) is much rarer.

Vars.: **O'Grady, O'Grada**. See also BRADY.

Graf 1. German: status name from Ger. Graf count, magistrate (MHG grāve, grābe, OHG grāv(i)o), a title denoting various more or less aristocratic dignitaries and officials. In later times it became established as a title of nobility equivalent to the Romance COUNT. The vocab. word also denoted various minor local functionaries in different parts of Germany. In the Grand Duchy of Hesse, for example, it was used for the holder of the comparatively humble office of village headman (cf. MAYER, SCHULTZ, and VOGT). The surname could have originated from any of these senses. 2. Jewish (Ashkenazic): ornamental name selected, like HERZOG and other words denoting titles, because of their aristocratic connotations.

Vars. (of 1): **Grafe** (Rheinland); **Gräfe** (Westphalia); **Grauf** (Swabia); **Grebe** (Hesse). (Of 2): GRAFF, **Grafman**.

Dims. (of 1): Low Ger.: **Greveke**. Czech: **Hrabek**.

Patrs. (of 1): Low Ger.: **Greving, Grewing**. Flem.: **Schrevens**.

Dan.: **Gravesen**.

Patr. (from a dim. of 1): Russ.: **Grafchikov**.

Graff 1. English: metonymic occupational name for a clerk or scribe, from ANF grafe quill, pen (a deriv. of grafer to write, LL grafāre, from Gk graphein). 2. Jewish (Ashkenazic): var. of GRAF.

Grafton English: habitation name from any of the numerous places so called from OE grāf grove + tūn enclosure, settlement.

Graham Scots: habitation name from Grantham in Lincs., recorded in Domesday Book as Graham (as well as Grantham, Grandham, and Granham). See also GRANTHAM.

Vars.: **Grahame, Graeme, Grayham, Greim**.

Grail French: 1. nickname for a thin man, from OF grail lean, slender (L gracilis). 2. nickname for a raucous or thievish person, from OF grail crow, jackdaw (L graculus, perhaps of imitative origin). This word has been retained to the present day in certain regional dialects, but in the standard language it has been replaced by CORNEILLE.

Var.: **Graille**.

Dims.: **Graillet, Grail(l)ot, Graillon, Gralhon, Grol(l)eau, Grollet**.

Graley see GREALEY

Gralnick see GORELIK

Gram Danish: nickname for an irascible person, from Dan. gram angry (ON gramr).

Grame 1. French: nickname for an unfortunate or careworn person, from OF grame trouble, anxiety (of apparently Gmc origin). 2. Provençal: topographic name for someone who lived on a patch of meadowland, from OProv. grame grass, pasture (L gramen).

Var.: **Gramme**.

Gran 1. Swedish: ornamental surname, from Swed. gran Norway spruce, adopted in the 19th cent. This belongs to the large class of ornamental surnames taken from natural features of the landscape. 2. Catalan: cogn. of GRANT 1.

Vars. (of 1): **Grann, Grahn**.

Cpds (of 1): **Granberg** ('spruce hill'); **Granholm** ('spruce island'); **Granlund** ('spruce grove'); **Granlöf** ('spruce leaf'); **Granquist** ('spruce twig'); **Granström** ('spruce river').

Granado Spanish: 1. metonymic occupational name for a grower or seller of pomegranates, from Sp. granado pomegranate (L (pōmum) grānātum; see GARNETT 1). 2. nickname for a (self-)important man, from Sp. granado famous, important, in origin the same word as in 1, but used as an adj. with this sense as a result of confusion with grande (see GRANT 1).

Granda Spanish: habitation name from any of various places in Asturias and Galicia named with the dial. term granda rocky plain, scrub-covered upland with poor soil (of pre-Roman origin). The surname is also borne by Jews, the reasons for its adoption being unknown.

Grandison English and Scots: habitation name from Granson on Lake Neuchâtel. The first known bearer of the surname is Rigaldus de Grancione (fl. 1040). The name was brought to Britain by Otes de Grandison (d. 1328) and his brother, sons of the Lord of Granson. They were among a group of Savoyards who settled in England after Henry III had married a granddaughter of the Count of Savoy.

Granet French: nickname for someone afflicted with pockmarks or similar blemishes, from OF granet, a dim. of grain grain (L grānum).

Vars.: **Granel, Grenot, Grenet(ton)**.

Grange English and French: topographic name for someone who lived by a granary, ME, OF *grange* (L *grānica* granary, barn, from *grānum* grain, corn).

Vars.: Eng.: **Grainge**. Fr.: **Granche**, **Lagrange**.

Granger English and French: occupational name for a farm bailiff, responsible for overseeing the collection of the rent in kind into the barns and storehouses of the lord of the manor. This official had the ANF title *grainger* (OF *grangier*, from LL *grānicārius*, a deriv. of *grānica* granary; see GRANGE).

Vars.: Eng.: **Grainger**. Fr.: **Grangier**, **Grancher**.

Grannell see RONALD

Grant English and (now esp.) Scots: **1**. Norman nickname from ANF *graund*, *graunt* tall, large (OF *grand*, *grant*, from L *grandis*), given either to a person of remarkable size, or else in a relative way to distinguish two bearers of the same given name, often representatives of different generations within the same family. **2**. from a medieval given name, probably a survival into ME of the OE byname *Granta* (see GRANTHAM).

Vars. (of **1**): **Grand** (E Anglia); **Le Grand**.

Dims. (of **1**): Fr.: **Grandel**, **Grandeau**, **Grandet**, **Grandon**, **Grandot**. It.: **Grandin(ett)i**, **Grandotto**.

Augs. (of **1**): It.: **Grandoni**, **Grandone**.

Patrs. (from **1**): It.: **De Grandi**, **(De) Grandis**, **Del Grande**.

Grantham English: habitation name from *Grantham* in Lincs., of uncertain etymology. The final element is OE *hām* homestead; the first may be OE **grand* gravel or perhaps a personal name **Granta*, which probably originated as a byname meaning 'Snarler'. See also GRAHAM.

Granville see GREENFIELD

Grape Low German: metonymic occupational name for a maker of metal or earthenware vessels, from MLG *grope* pot (cf. POTTER, EULER, and TÖPFER).

Vars.: **Gra(a)p**, **Grope**; **Gropius** (Latinized); **Gräper**, **Gröp(p)er**.

Grapes English (E Anglia): of uncertain origin, perhaps a house name from a house bearing the sign of a bunch of grapes. The vocab. word is attested from the 13th cent. (at first in the cpd *wingrape*; cf. WEIN), and comes from OF *grape*, which is probably related to a Gmc element meaning 'hook', perhaps by way of the OF verb *graper* to gather.

Grass 1. English and German: topographic name for someone who lived on a patch of meadowland, from ME *gras* or Ger. *Grass* grass, pasture, grazing (OE *græs*, OHG *gras*). **2**. English: nickname for a stout or corpulent person, from ANF *gras* fat (from L *crassus* (itself used as a family name), with the initial changed under the influence of *grossus*; see GROSS). **3**. Scots: occupational name from Gael. *greusaiche* shoemaker (a deriv. of *gréas* handicraft). A certain John *Grasse* alias *Cordonar* is recorded in Scotland in 1539.

Vars. (of **1**): Ger.: **Gras**; **Grassmann**; **Graser**, **Gräser**. (Of **3**): **Grassick**, **Grassie**, **Gracie**; **Gracey** (N Ireland).

Dims. (of **2**): Fr.: **Grasset**, **Grassot**, **Grassin**, **Grasson**. It.: **Grassell(in)i**, **Grassilli**, **Grasigli**, **Grassetti**, **Grassotti**, **Grassini**.

Patrs. (from **2**): Fr.: **Augras**. It.: **De Grassi**.

Gratien French: from the given name (L *Grātiānus*, a deriv. of *grātus* welcome, pleasing) borne by an early saint who was martyred at Amiens during the reign of the Roman emperor Diocletian.

Gratton English: habitation name from any of various places so called. *Gratton* in Derbys. is from OE *grēat* great + *tūn* enclosure, settlement. *Gratton* in High Bray, Devon, is probably 'great hill', from OE *grēat* + *dūn* (see DOWN). A number of minor places in Devon are from the dial. word *gratton*, *gratten* stubble-field.

Vars.: **Gratten**, **Grattan**.

Grau 1. German: cogn. of GRAY. **2**. French: metonymic occupational name for a maker, seller, or user of agricultural hooks, from OF *grau* hook (apparently of Gmc origin). It may perhaps also be in part a nickname for a hunchback or a devious person; cf. CROOK. **3**. Provençal: topographic name for someone who lived near a canal giving access to the sea, OProv. *grau* (L *gradus* step, from *gradi* to go; cf. GRADILLAS). **4**. Catalan: from a contracted form of the common medieval given name *Guerau*, a popular form of *Gerald*; see GARRETT.

Var. (of **2** and **3**): **Graux**.

Grave 1. English: occupational name from ME *greyve* steward (ON *greifi*, itself from Low Ger. *grēve*; see GRAF). **2**. English: topographic name, a var. of GROVE. **3**. French: topographic name for someone who lived on a patch of gravelly soil, from OF *grave* gravel (of Celt. origin). **4**. Low German: cogn. of GRAF.

Var. (of **3**): Fr.: **Gravier**.

Dims. (of **1**): Eng.: **Graveling** (E Anglia; the suffix *-ling* probably has contemptuous overtones, suggesting petty officialdom). (Of **3**): Fr.: **Gravel(le)**, **Gravelin(e)**, **Graveleau**, **Gravot**.

Patrs. (from **1**): Eng.: **Graves**; **Graves(t)on**, **Grays(t)on**; **Grayshon** (Yorks.).

Graverend French: occupational name for a collector of taxes, OF *graverenc* (of uncertain origin).

Dims.: **Gravereau(x)**, **Graveron**.

Gray 1. English: nickname for someone with grey hair or a grey beard, from OE *græg* grey. In Scotland and Ireland it has been used as a translation of various Gael. surnames derived from *riabhach* brindled, grey; see REAVEY. **2**. English and Scots (Norman): habitation name from *Graye* in Calvados, so called from the Gallo-Roman personal name *Grātus* 'Welcome', 'Pleasing' + the local suffix *-acum*.

Vars. (of **1**): **Grey**; **Legrey** (with the ANF def. art.).

Patr. (from **1**): Flem.: **Schraawen**.

Cpds.: Jewish: **Graubart**, **Graubard**, **Grobard**, **Grubard** ('grey beard', a nickname); **Grauberg** ('grey hill', ornamental); **Grauweis** ('grey-white'); **Grauzalc** ('grey salt', Pol. spelling).

Grčić see GREGORY

Grealey English (Norman): nickname for someone with a pock-marked face, from ONF *greslé* pitted, scarred (from *gresle* hailstone, of Gmc origin).

Vars.: **Grealy**, **Grealish**, **Greelish** (Ireland); **Greel(e)y**, **Gra(y)ley**, **Grelley**; **Gredley**, **Gridley**; GRESLEY.

Dims.: Eng.: **Greslet**. Fr.: **Greslet**, **Greslon**, **Grel(l)on**, **Grelot**.

Greathead English: nickname for someone with a large head, from ME *great* large (OE *grēat*) + *heved* head (OE *hēafod*).

Greatrex English (Midlands): apparently a habitation name from some minor place named as *Great Rakes*, from Northern ME *great* large (OE *grēat*) + *rake* path, track, used in Derbys. in a lead-mining sense 'vertical vein of ore'. In this sense *rake* became the name of several leadmines, including *Greatrake* Mine in Carsington, which could be the source of the surname.

Var.: **Greatorex**.

Greave English: topographic name from OE *græfe* brushwood, thicket, or habitation name from a place named with this word (of which there is one in Lancs.). There has been some confusion with GRAVE and GRIEVE.

Vars.: **Greve**, **Greaves**, **Gre(e)ves**.

Greavison *see* GRIEVE

Grebe *see* GRAF

Greber *see* GRABER

Greco Italian: ethnic name for a Greek, It. *Greco* (L *Graecus*, from *Graecia* Greece). In some cases it may have been merely a nickname for a crafty or guileful person, for these were the qualities traditionally attributed to the Greeks.

Vars.: **Grec(h)i**, **Greg(h)i**, **Grieco**; **Lo Greco** (S Italy). Patr.: It.: **Del Greco**.

Greehy *see* GRIFFIN

Green 1. English: one of the most common and widespread of Eng. surnames, either a nickname for someone who was fond of dressing in this colour (OE *grēne*) or who had played the part of the 'Green Man' in the May Day celebrations, or a topographic name for someone who lived near a village green, ME *grene* (a transferred use of the colour term). 2. Jewish (Ashkenazic): Anglicized form of **Grün** or **Grin**, presumably ornamental names from the mod. Ger. and Yid. words respectively, or short form of any of the cpds listed below. 3. Irish: translation of various Gael. surnames derived from *uaithne* (see HOONEY) and *glas* (see GLASS 2). See also FAHY. 4. Norwegian and Danish: cogn. of GREN.

Vars. (of 1): Eng.: **Gre(e)ne**; **Greening**; **Greenman**, **Greenmon**.

Cpds (ornamental): Jewish: **Grünbaum**, **Gru(e)nbaum**, **Gruenebaum**, **Grunebaum**, **Grinbaum**, **Grinbo(i)m**, ('green tree', partly Anglicized as **Greenbaum**, and **Greenbom**); **Grünberg**, **Gru(e)nberg(er)**, **Grinberg** ('green hill', partly Anglicized as **Greenberg(er)**); **Grünblatt**, **Gruenblat**, **Grunblat(t)**, **Grinblat(t)** ('green leaf', partly Anglicized as **Greenblat(t)**); **Grunfarb** ('green colour'); **Grinfas(s)** ('green barrel'); **Grünfeld**, **Gru(e)nfeld**, **Grinfeld** ('green field', partly Anglicized as **Greenfeld**, **Grinfield**; fully Anglicized as GREENFIELD); **Gringart(en)** ('green garden'); **Grunglas**, **Gringlas(s)** ('green glass', Anglicized as **Greenglass**); **Gruengras**, **Gringras(s)** ('green grass', Anglicized as GREENGRASS); **Grunhaus**, **Grinhaus**, **Greenhoiz** ('green house', Anglicized as GREENHOUSE); **Grünheim**, **Grinheim** ('green home'); **Grünhol(t)z**, **Grinholc** ('green wood', partly Anglicized as **Greenholtz**, fully Anglicized as GREENWOOD; *Grinholc* is a Pol. spelling); **Gru(e)nhut**, **Grinhut** ('green hat'); **Gru(e)nkraut**, **Grinkraut** ('green herb'); **Grinman** ('green man', Anglicized as **Greenman**); **Granseid** ('green silk'); **Grünstein**, **Gru(e)nstein**, **Grinstein** ('green stone', partly Angli-

cized as **Greenstein**, **Greenstien**); **Grintuch** ('green cloth'); **Grün(e)wald**, **Gruen(e)wald**, **Grunwall**, **Grinwald**, **Grinvald** ('green forest', partly Anglicized as **Greenwald**); **Gru(e)nwurzel**, **Grinwurcel** ('green root'; *Grinwurcel* is a Pol. spelling); **Grunzweig** ('green twig', partly Anglicized as **Greenzweig**). Swed.: **Grönberg** ('green hill'); **Grönblad(h)** ('green leaf'); **Gröndahl** ('green valley'); **Grönlund** ('green grove'); **Grönkvist** ('green twig'); **Grönskog** ('green forest'); **Grönstedt** ('green homestead'); **Grönwall**, **Grönvall** ('green pasture').

Greenacre English (E Anglia): topographic name for someone who lived by a patch of luxuriantly fertile land, from OE *grēne* GREEN + *æcer* cultivated land (see ACKER).

Greenaway 1. English: topographic name for someone who lived by a grassy path, from OE *grēne* GREEN + *weg* path (see WAY). 2. Welsh: alteration of the W personal name *Goronwy*, perhaps originally a byname meaning 'Heron'.

Vars.: **Greenway**. (Of 2 only): **Grenow**, **Grono(w)**.

Greener 1. English: habitation name from *Greenhaugh* in Northumb., so called from OE *grēne* GREEN + *halh* nook, recess (see HALE 1). See also GREENHALGH. 2. Jewish (Ashkenazic): Anglicized form of *Griner*; see GREEN.

Greenfield 1. English: habitation name from any of the numerous minor places so called from OE *grēne* GREEN + *feld* pasture, open country (see FIELD). 2. English (Norman): habitation name from any of various places in Normandy called *Grainville*, from the Gmc personal name *Guarin* (see WARING) + OF *ville* settlement (see VILLE). 3. Jewish (Ashkenazic): Anglicized form of *Grünfeld* and its vars.; see cpds at GREEN.

Vars. (of 2): **Grenville**, **Grenfell**, **Granville** (all now chiefly found in Devon).

Greengrass English (E Anglia): apparently a topographic name for someone who lived at a spot where the grass was particularly lush and green, from OE *grēne* GREEN + *græs* GRASS.

Greenhalgh English (Lancs.): habitation name from either of two places in Lancs., both so called from OE *grēne* GREEN + *holh* hollow (see HOLE). See also GREENER.

Vars.: **Greenalf**, **Greenhall**, GREENHOUGH, **Grinaugh**.

Greenham English: habitation name from a place in Berks., so called from OE *grēne* GREEN + *hamm* water meadow or *hām* homestead.

Greenhill 1. English: habitation name from any of the various places in England so called, from OE *grēne* GREEN + *hyll* HILL. 2. Jewish (Ashkenazic): translation of *Grünberg* and its vars.; see cpds at GREEN.

Var. (of 1): **Grinnell**.

Greenhorn Scots: according to Black, a habitation name from an unidentified place, apparently named with the OE elements *grēne* GREEN + *hyrne* corner (see HEARN 2).

Var.: **Greenhorne**.

Greenhough English (Yorks.): 1. habitation name from either of two places, in N and W Yorks., called *Greenhow*, or from *Gerna* in the parish of Downham, Lancs., all of which are named with OE *grēne* GREEN + *hōh* mound (or the cogn. ON *haugr*; see HOE). 2. var. of GREENHALGH.

Var.: **Greenough** (Lancs.).

Greenhouse 1. English: topographic name for someone who lived in a house by a village green, from OE *grēne* GREEN + *hūs* house. The term was not used to denote a glasshouse for the cultivation of 'greens' or sensitive plants until the late 17th cent. **2.** Jewish (Ashkenazic): Anglicized form of *Grünhaus* and its vars.; see cpds at GREEN.

Greenland English: topographic name for someone who lived near a patch of land left open as communal pasturage, from OE *grēne* GREEN + *land* land.

Greenlee see GRINDLEY

Greenslade English: topographic name for someone who lived near a fertile valley, from OE *grēne* GREEN + *slæd* valley, dell.

Greensmith English (chiefly E Midlands and Yorks.): occupational name or nickname for a coppersmith, from ME *grene* GREEN + SMITH, with reference to the characteristic colour of oxidized copper.

Greensmith see SMITH

Greenspan see GRÜNSPAN

Greenwell English (Northumb.): topographic name for someone who lived by a stream among lush pastures, from OE *grēne* GREEN + *well(a)* spring, stream (see WELL), or habitation name from a minor place so named.

Greenwood 1. English: topographic name for someone who lived in a dense forest, from OE *grēne* GREEN + *wudu* WOOD. **2.** Jewish (Ashkenazic): Anglicized form of *Grünholz* and its vars.; see cpds at GREEN.

Greep Cornish: either a nickname from Corn. *cryp* crest, comb, or a habitation name from *Pengreep* in the parish of Gwennap, so called from Corn. *pen* head, top, summit + *gryp*, a mutated form of *cryp* in the sense 'ridge'.

Greer see GRIER

Greet English (now mainly Devon and Cornwall): **1.** topographic name for someone who lived on a patch of gravelly soil or by a gravel pit, from ME *grēt* gravel (OE *grēot*), or an occupational name for a supplier of gravel or a worker in a gravel pit. **2.** nickname for a large person, from ME *grēt* great (OE *grēat*).

Greffuelhe see GRIFFOUL

Gregory English: from a given name that was popular throughout Christendom in the Middle Ages. The name is of Gk origin, *Grēgorios* being a deriv. of *grēgorein* to be awake or watchful, but at an early date the L form *Gregorius* was associated by folk etymology with *grex*, gen. *gregis*, flock, herd, under the influence of the Christian image of the good shepherd. The Gk name was borne in the early Christian cents. by two fathers of the Orthodox Church, St Gregory Nazianzene (*c*.325–90) and St Gregory of Nyssa (*c*.331–95), and later by sixteen popes, starting with Gregory the Great (*c*.540–604). It was also the name of a 3rd-and 4th-cent. apostle of Armenia.

Vars.: **Grigorey**; **Greg(g)or**; **Grigor** (Scots); **GRIER**.

Dims.: Eng.: **Greg(g)**, **Grigg**. Scots: **Greig**, **Grieg**. It.: **Gregoretti**, **Gregoletti**, **Grigoletti**, **Gregorini**, **Gregorutti**, **Gorghetto**; **Gergolet**, **Gregorin**, **Gregolin** (NE Italy); **Gorelli**, **Goretti**, **Gorini**, **Gorioli**, **Gorusso** (N Italy). Flem.: **Gregh**. Ger. (of

Slav. origin): **Gresch(ke)**, **Reschke**, **Greschik**, **Grelka**, **Grelik**, **Grelak**. Czech: **Řehák**; **Řehořek**; **Říhánek**, **Říhošek**. Pol.: **Gr(z)egorek**, **Grzegorzecki**, **Gr(z)egorczyk** (forms with *Gr-* rather than *Grz-* are not typically Polish, although they do occur among Poles); **Grzeszczyk**, **Grzelczyk**; **Grześ**; **Hrycek**, **Hryńczyk**. Ukr.: **Hritzko**, **Hrinchenko**, **Hrishchenko**. Beloruss.: **Hrishanok**. Hung.: **Gerő**.

Augs.: It.: **Grigolon** (NE Italy); **Goroni** (N Italy).

Pejs.: Fr. **Grigaut**. It.: **Gregorace**, **Gregoraci**, **Gligoraci** (Calabria); **Goracci** (N Italy).

Patrs.: Sc.: McGREGOR. It.: **De Gregorio**, **Di Gregorio**, **De Gregoli**, **Grigoriis**. Rum.: **Grigorescu**. Low Ger.: **Greg(g)ersen**; **Gorriessen**, **Görrissen**. Dan., Norw.: **Gregersen**. Russ.: **Grigoryev**, **Grigorov**. Ukr.: **Hrihorovich**. Beloruss.: **Ryhorovich**. Pol.: **Grzegorzewicz**, **Gregorowicz**, **Grygor(ce)wicz**. Croatian: **Gligor(ijev)ić**. Bulg.: **Grigoriev**; **Goranov** (see also GÓRSKI). Georgian: **Grigolashvili**. Armenian: **Grigorian**, **Krikorian**. Gk: **Gregoriou**.

Patrs. (from dims.): Eng.: **Greg(g)s**, **Griggs**, **Gricks**, **Grix**; **Gregson**, **Grigson**. Russ.: **Grigor(ush)kin**, **Grenkov**, **Grinyov**, **Grin(nik)ov**, **Grin(ikh)in**, **Grinishin**, **Grinyakin**, **Grishaev**, **Grish(a)kov**, **Grishan(k)ov**, **Grishelyov**, **Grishenkov**, **Grishinov**, **Grishmanov**, **Grishukov**, **Grish(ak)in**, **Grishagin**, **Grishanin**, **Grishechkin**, **Grishukhin**, **Grishunin**, **Gritsaev**, **Gritskov**, **Gritsunov**, **Grichukhin**, **Grikhanov**. Ukr.: **Hritzkov**. Pol.: **Grzesiak**, **Grzeszczak**; **Grzelak**, **Grzelczak**, **Grzesiewicz**; **Hryckiewicz**, **Hryniewicz**, **Hryniewicki**, **Hryńcewicz**. Croatian: **Grgić**, **Grčić**.

'Son of the wife of G. (dim.)': Russ.: **Grinikhin**. Ukr.: **Hrin(ch)ishin**.

Habitation name: Pol.: **Grzegorzewski**.

Habitation names (from dims.): **Grzelewski**, **Gryglewski**, **Grześkowski**.

Greibel see GRIBOV

Greif 1. German: house name from a house distinguished by the sign of a gryphon, Ger. *Greif* (MHG *grīf(e)*, OHG *grīf(o)*, from L *grȳphus*, Gk *gryps*, of Assyrian origin). **2.** German: nickname for a grasping man, the gryphon in folk etymology having come to be associated with Ger. *greifen* to grasp, snatch (OHG *grīfan*; cf. GRIFFE). **3.** Jewish (Ashkenazic): of uncertain origin, possibly related to 2 above. **4.** N English and Scots: var. of GRIEVE.

Vars. (of 1): Ger.: **Greiff**. (Of 3): **Greifman**, **Greifner**.

Greim see GRAHAM

Greimbl see GRIME

Greither see REUTER

Greitzer Jewish (Ashkenazic): from Yid. *graytser* kreuzer, the old Austro-Hungarian unit of currency. The reason(s) for the adoption of this word as a surname are not known. Cf. *Fenig* (at PENNY) and *Rubel* (at RUBLYOV).

Grémaud see GRIMAUD

Gren Swedish: ornamental surname from Swed. *gren* branch (ON *grein*). In some cases the name may have been chosen with some reference to the notion of the 'branches' making up a family 'tree', but it also falls into the category of words denoting natural features, which were drawn on heavily when Swedish surnames came to be formed wholesale in the 19th cent. The element *gren* was also widely used in forming compounds such as *Lindgren*.

Grenet *see* GRANET

Grennan *see* GARNON

Gresham English: habitation name from a place in Norfolk, so called from OE *græs*, *gærs* grass(land), pasturage + *hām* homestead.

Gresley English: **1.** habitation name from *Gresley* in Derbys. or *Greasley* in Notts., both of which get their name from OE *grēosn* gravel + *lēah* wood, clearing. **2.** nickname from OF *greslé* pock-marked (see GREALEY).
Var.: **Greasley**.

Gretton English: habitation name from places, for example in Gloucs. and Shrops., so called from OE *grēot* gravel + *tūn* enclosure, settlement.
Vars.: **Gritton**, **Gritten**.

Greuze French: nickname for a touchy or hot-tempered individual, from OF *greüse* quarrel, dispute (of unknown origin).
Dim.: **Gruson**.
Pej.: **Greuzard**.

Greville English (Norman): habitation name from *Gréville* in La Manche, so called from a Gmc personal name *Creiz* + OF *ville* settlement (see VILLE).

Grew English: nickname for a tall, scrawny person, from ME, OF *grue* crane (LL *grua*, for class. L *grus*).
Var.: **Grewe**.
Dims.: Eng.: **Grewcock**, **Growcock**, **Gro(o)cock**; **Gro(w)cott**, **Groucutt**. Fr.: **Gruet**, **Gruot**.

Grey *see* GRAY

Grgić *see* GREGORY

Gribbin *see* CRIBBIN

Gribov Russian: patr. from the nickname *Grib* 'Mushroom', given perhaps to a grower or an enthusiastic eater of mushrooms; cf. GRIBOEDOV.
Dims.: Ukr.: **Hribko**. Pol.: **Grzybek**. Ger. (of Slav. origin): **Griebke**, **Greibke**, **Griebsch**, **Greibel**.
Habitation name: Pol.: **Grzybowski**.

Griboyedov Russian: patr. from the nickname *Griboyed*, composed of the elements *grib* mushroom + *yed-* to eat.

Grice English: **1.** nickname for a grey-haired man, from ME *grice*, *gris* grey (OF *gris*, apparently of Gmc origin, and probably a distant cogn. of GRAY 1). **2.** metonymic occupational name for a swineherd or nickname meaning 'pig', from ME *grice*, *grise* pig (ON *gríss*, probably akin to 1).
Vars.: **Grise**, **Griss**, **Le Grice**, **Le Grys**.
Ger.: **Greis(e)**. Low Ger.: **Griese**. Flem.: **De Gryse**. Du.: **De Grijse**.
Dims. (of 1): Eng.: **Grissin**, **Grisson**, **Grissom**. Fr.: **Grisel(in)**, **Griseau**, **Grizeau**, **Gris(e)lain**, **Griset**, **Grisez**, **Grisot**, **Grison(net)**, **Grizon**. It.: **Grisini**.
Aug. (of 1): It.: **Grisoni**.
Pejs. (of 1): Fr.: **Grisard**, **Grizard**.

Grichukhin *see* GREGORY

Gridin Russian: patr. from the medieval given name *Gridya*, in origin a byname meaning 'Guard' (from ON *griði* companion, guard), but used as a dim. of *Gregory* from an early date.
Vars.: **Gridnin**, **Gridnev**, **Gridunov**.

Gridley *see* GREALEY

Griebler *see* GRUBER

Grieco *see* GRECO

Grier Scots: var. of GREGORY.
Var.: **Greer** (chiefly N Ireland).
Patrs.: **Grierson**, **Greerson**.

Griete *see* MARGUERITE

Grieve Scots: occupational name for a steward or manager, ME *greve* (OE (Northumbrian) *græfa*; cf. REEVE and SHERIFF). This word was originally distinct from GRAVE 1, but some confusion has occurred as a result of the close similarity in both form and meaning.
Vars.: **Grief(f)**, **Greef**, GREIF.
Patrs.: **Grieves**, **Grieveson**, **Greavison**, **Gre(e)son**.

Griffe French: nickname for a grasping or vicious person, or perhaps occasionally a more jocular name for a man with an artificial hand, from OF *griffe* claw (of Gmc origin).
Dim.: **Griffon**.
Pejs.: **Griffaut**, **Griffaud**, **Griffard**.

Griffin **1.** Welsh: from a var. of GRIFFITH. **2.** English: nickname for a fierce or dangerous person, from ME *griffin* gryphon; see GREIF. **3.** Irish: Anglicized form of Gael. **Ó Gríobhtha** 'descendant of *Gríobhtha*', a personal name from *gríobh* gryphon (see GREIF).
Vars. (of 3): **O'Grighie**, **O'Greefa**, **(O')Griffy**, **Griffey**, **Greehy**.

Griffith Welsh: from the OW personal name *Gruffydd*, composed of the elements *griff*, of uncertain significance + *udd* chief, lord.
Var.: **GRIFFIN**.
Patrs.: **Griffi(th)s**.
Patrs. (from dims.): **Gittoes**, **Gittus**.

Griffoul Provençal: topographic name for someone who lived by a holly tree, OProv. *griffoul* (L *acrifolium*, from *acer*, gen. *acris*, sharp, pointed + *folium* leaf). See also ACEVEDO.
Vars.: **Agrifoul**, **Aigrefeuille**, **Greffu(e)lhe**, **Grifuel**, **Grifoul**.

Grignon French: **1.** nickname for a proud or contemptuous person, from OF *grignier* to grit the teeth or curl the lips, gestures of fierce contempt. The verb is of Gmc origin and was originally probably an imitative formation suggestive of grunting through clenched teeth; cf. GRANT 2 and GRAHAM. **2.** habitation name from any of the various places, for example in Côte-d'Or and Savoie, so called from the LL personal name *Granius*, *Grinius* + the local suffix *-o*, *-ōnis*.
Pej. (of 1): **Grignard**.

Grill **1.** English: nickname for a fierce or cruel man, from ME *grill(e)* angry, vicious (from OE *gryllan* to rage, gnash the teeth; cf. GRIGNON 1). **2.** German: nickname for a cheerful person, from Ger. *Grille* cricket (MHG *grille* cricket, OHG *grillo*, from LL *grillus*, Gk *gryllos*). The insect is widely supposed to be of a cheerful disposition, no doubt because of its habit of infesting hearths and warm places. The vocab. word is confined largely to S Germany and Austria, and it is in this region that the surname is most frequent. **3.** German: habitation name from a place in Upper Bavaria, perhaps so called from MHG *grille* cricket.

Dims. (of 2): Fr.: **Grillet**, **Grillot**, **Grillon**. Prov.: **Grilhot**. It.: **Grilletti**, **Grilletto**, **Grillini**; **Arillotta**.

Augs. (of 2): It.: **Grilloni**, **Grillone**.

Pej. (of 2): Fr.: **Grillard**.

Patrs. (from 1): Eng.: **Grills**, **Grylls**.

Grimaud French: from *Grimwald*, a Gmc personal name composed of the elements *grīm* mask, helmet + *wald* rule.

Vars.: **Grimault**, **Grimal**, **Grimaux**, **Grémaud**.

Grimble English: from a Norman personal name *Grimbald*, composed of the Gmc elements *grīm* mask, helmet + *bald* bold, brave.

Vars.: **Gribble**, **Gribbell**; **Grumble**, **Grumell**.

Grime English: from the ON personal name *Grímr* (a cogn. of OE *grīma* mask), which remained popular as a given name in the form *Grim* in Anglo-Scandinavian areas well into the 12th cent. It was a byname of Woden with the meaning 'masked person' or 'shape-changer', and may have been bestowed on male children in an attempt to secure the protection of the god. The Continental Gmc cogn. *grīm* was also used as a first element in cpd names (cf. GRIMAUD and GRIMBLE), with the original sense 'mask', 'helmet'. Some examples of the surname may derive from short forms of such names.

Dims.: Ger.: **Greimel**, **Greimbl**.

Patrs.: Eng.: **Grimes**, **Grimson**; **Grimason** (N Ireland).

Grimley 1. English: habitation name from a place in Worcs., probably so called from an OE personal name, *Grīma* (see GRIME) + OE *lēah* wood, clearing. **2.** Irish: var. of GORMLEY.

Grimm German: nickname for a dour and forbidding individual, from OHG *grimm* stern, severe.

Vars.: **Grimme**, GRIMMER.

Grimmer 1. English: from a Norman personal name *Grimier*, composed of the Gmc elements *grim* mask, helmet + *heri*, *hari* army. **2.** German: var. of GRIMM.

Var. (of 2): **Grimmert**.

Grimshaw English: habitation name from one of two places in Lancs., both so called from the ON personal name *Grímr* (see GRIME) or OE *grīma* ghost + OE *sceaga* copse (see SHAW).

Grimston English: habitation name from any of the various places in N and E England so called from the gen. case of the ON personal name *Grímr* (see GRIME) + OE *tūn* enclosure, settlement.

Var.: **Grimstone**.

Grimward English: from a Norman personal name *Grimward*, composed of the Gmc elements *grīm* mask, helmet + *ward* guardian.

Vars.: **Grimwade**, **Grimwood**.

Grinaugh *see* GREENHALGH

Grinbaum *see* GREEN

Grinder English: occupational name for a grinder of corn, i.e. a miller, ME, OE *grindere*, an agent noun from OE *grindan* to grind. Less often it may have referred to someone who ground blades to keep their sharpness or who ground pigments, spices, and medicinal herbs to powder.

Grindley English: habitation name from any of various minor places, for example in Staffs., so called from OE *grēne* GREEN + *lēah* wood, clearing.

Vars.: **Grinley**, **Grinlay**, **Greenl(e)y**, **Greenlee**.

Grindrod English: habitation name from a minor place in the parish of Rochdale, Lancs., so called from OE *grēne* GREEN + *rod* clearing (see RHODES).

Grinnell *see* GREENHILL

Grinshpan *see* GRÜNSPAN

Grinter English: of uncertain origin. It is probably an occupational name for an official in charge of a granary, ANF *grenetier*, but it could also be a var. of GRINDER.

Var.: **Grint**.

Grishka *see* GRUSHIN

Grist English: of uncertain origin. It may be an occupational name for a miller, from the ME abstract noun *grist* grinding (OE *grist*, a deriv. of *grindan*; see GRINDER). The word was not used in the concrete sense of corn to be ground until the 15th cent.

Gritten *see* GRETTON

Grivel French: nickname from the thrush, from a dim. of OF *grive* thrush, itself a fem. of *gri(e)u* Greek (see GRECO), for the birds were thought to spend the winter in Greece. One reason for the giving of the nickname could have been a 'pepper and salt' colouring of the hair, similar to the plumage on the breast of this bird; another was perhaps a propensity to inebriation, since it was a popular belief that the thrush became drunk on the grapes it stole.

Vars.: **Griveau**, **Grivet**, **Grivé**, **Grivot**.

Dim.: **Grivelet**.

Groarke *see* ROURKE

Grob German and Jewish (Ashkenazic): nickname for a boorish individual, from Ger. and Yid. *grob* coarse, crude (MHG *g(e)rop*, OHG *g(e)rob*). As a Jewish name it may sometimes have denoted a fat man, since Yid. *grob* also means 'fat'.

Vars.: Ger.: **Grobe**, **Grobmann**. Jewish: **Grobman**, **Grober(man)**.

Grobard *see* GRAY

Grobelaer Dutch: nickname for a disorderly person, or perhaps an occupational name of some sort, from an agent deriv. of MDu. *grobellen* to turn over, rummage, search.

Vars.: **Grob(b)elaar**; **Grobler**.

Grochocki *see* GOROKHOV

Grocock *see* GREW

Grodzki Polish: from Pol. *gród* castle, fortification (cogn. with Czech *hrad*, Russ. *grad*). Generally, no doubt, this was a topographic name for someone living in or beside a castle or beside the citadel of a fortified town. However, the adj. *grodzki* also occurs in the expression *sąd grodzki* meaning 'castle court', something like a magistrates' court or petty sessions; the surname may therefore also have denoted someone connected with such a court.

Vars.: **Grodziński**, **Grodzicki**.

Dim.: Czech: **Hrádek**.

Grogan Irish: 1. Anglicized form of Gael. **Ó Grúgáin** 'descendant of *Grúgán*', a personal name from a dim. of *grúg* anger, fierceness. 2. Anglicized form of Gael. **Ó Gruagáin** 'descendant of *Gruagán*', a personal name from a dim. of *gruag* hair. The patr. form **Mac Gruagáin** (Anglicized **McGrogan**) is much rarer.

Vars.: **O'Grogaine**, **O'Growgane**, **Groggan**, **Groogan**.

Groleau *see* GRAIL

Grolms *see* JEROME

Gromyko Ukrainian: nickname for a noisy or obstreperous person, from *grom* thunder, crashing, loud noise, perhaps also used with reference to someone who used the word *grom* frequently in an oath.

Vars.: **Gromeko**; **Gromykin** (assimilated to a Russ. patr. form).

Grönberg *see* GREEN

Grono *see* GREENAWAY

Groom English (common in E Anglia): occupational name for a servant or a shepherd, from ME *grōm(e)* boy, servant (of uncertain etymology), which in some places was specialized to mean 'shepherd'.

Var.: **Groome**.

Groombridge English: habitation name from a place in Kent, recorded in 1239 as *Gromenebregge* 'the BRIDGE of the GROOMS'.

Grope *see* GRAPE

Gross German, Jewish (Ashkenazic), and English: nickname for a big man, from Ger. *gross* large, thick, corpulent (MHG, OHG *grōz*, cogn. with OE *grēat* great, large; cf. GREET 2), or, in the case of the Eng. name, from ME, OF *gros* (LL *grossus*, of Gmc origin). The Eng. vocab. word did not develop the sense 'excessively fat' until the 16th cent. The Jewish name has been Hebraicized as **Gadol**, from Hebr. *gadol* large.

Vars. (of 1): Ger.: **Grosse**, **Groos**, **Grosser(t)**, **Grossmann**. Jewish: **Gros**, **Gros(s)man**, **Grossmann**, **Grosser**; GROSZ. (Of 2): Eng.: **Groce**.

Rum.: **Grossu**. Hung.: **Grósz**.

Dims. (of 2): Eng.: **Grosset**. Fr.: **Grosset**, **Grossin**, **Grosson**.

Prov.: **Grousset**, **Groussin**, **Grousson**, **Groussot**. It.: **Grosetti**.

Pejs. (of 2): Fr.: **Grossard**, **Groussaud**.

Patrs. (from 1): Flem., Du.: **Grootaers**, **Grootmans**. (From 2): Fr.: **Augros**. It.: **Del Grosso** (Tuscany).

Cpds: Jewish: **Gros(s)baum**, **Grosboim** ('large tree'); **Gros(s)berg** ('large hill'); **Gros(s)feld** ('large field'); **Grosgluck**, **Grossglick** ('great good fortune'); **Gros(s)gold** ('large gold'); **Grosshaus** ('large house'); **Gros(s)kopf** ('large head', probably

a nickname); **Grossvogel** ('large bird'); **Grosswasser** ('large water').

Grosvenor English (Norman): occupational name for a person who was in charge of the arrangements for hunting on a lord's estate, from ANF *gros* great, chief (see GROSS) + *veneo(u)r* hunter (L *venātor*, from *venāri* to hunt).

Grosz Jewish (E Ashkenazic): 1. nickname, given probably in reference to some now irrecoverable event, from Pol. *grosz*, a coin of small value (MHG *gros(ch)*, med. L *(denārius) grossus* thick coin; cf. GROSS). 2. Hung. spelling of GROSS.

Grout English: metonymic occupational name for a dealer in coarse meal, OE *grūt*, ON *grautr* porridge.

Vars.: **Grut(e)**.

Grove 1. English: topographic name for someone who lived by a grove or thicket, OE *grāf*; for the change of *-ā-* to *-ō-*, cf. ROPER. 2. English (Huguenot): from the French surname **Le Grou(x)** or **Le Greux**, which is of uncertain origin. See below. 3. Low German: cogn. of GROB.

Vars. (of 1): **Groves**, **Grover**; GRAVE.

Grubard *see* GRAY

Grubb English: nickname for a small person, from ME *grub* midget (of uncertain origin).

Var.: **Grubbe**.

Gruber German and Jewish (Ashkenazic): topographic name for someone who lived in a depression or hollow, from Ger. *Grube* pit, hollow (MHG *gruobe* OHG *gruoba*, a deriv. of *graben* to dig; cf. GRABER) + *-er* suffix denoting habitation.

Vars.: **Grüb(n)er**, **Grübler**. Ger. only: **Griebler**; **Grub(e)**, **Grüb**. Jewish only: **Grubner**.

Grudziński Polish: from Pol. *Gridzień* December, a surname bestowed on someone who was born or baptized or who registered a surname in that month.

Gruenbaum *see* GREEN

Gruet *see* GREW

Grulms *see* JEROME

Grumble *see* GRIMBLE

Grumley *see* GORMLEY

Grundy English (chiefly Lancs.): probably a metathesized form of *Gondri*, *Gundric*, an OF personal name introduced to Britain by the Normans. It is composed of the Gmc elements *gund* battle + *rīc* power.

Vars.: **Gundr(e)y**, **Goundry**.

Grünspan Jewish (Ashkenazic): ornamental name from Ger. *Grünspan* verdigris (MHG *gruenspān*, which is a calque of med. L *viride hispanicum* 'Spanish green').

Vars.: **Gru(e)nspan**; **Grynszpan**, **Grinszpan**, **Grins(h)pan** (from Pol. *grynszpan*); **Grins(h)pon**, **Grinspoon** (from Yid. *grinshpon*); **Greenspan**, **Greenspon** (partly Anglicized forms); **Grinspanholz** (an elaboration, with Ger. *Holz* wood).

Grushin Russian: 1. metr. from the female given name *Grusha*, a pet form of *Agrafya*, from L *Agrippina* (a deriv. of *Agrippa*, a family name of obscure, possibly Etruscan, etymology). In W Europe the name is best known as having been borne by the mothers of the Roman emperors Caligula and Nero, neither of whom was a particularly exemplary character, but in the Orthodox Church it is held in high regard as the name of a 3rd-cent. saint martyred under Valerian. **2.** patr. from the nickname *Grusha* 'Pear', given perhaps to a grower or seller of the fruit, or possibly to an individual thought to resemble a pear in some way.

Dims. (of 2): Czech: **Hrušík**. Ger. (of Slav. origin): **Kruschke, Kruschka, Kruschel**. Jewish: **Grus(c)hka, Grushko, Gruszka, Gruszko**; **Grishka**; **Grus(c)hkewitz, Grushkewitch** (patrs. in form).

Habitation name: Pol.: **Gruszczyński**.

Gruson *see* GREUZE

Grut *see* GROUT

Grüter Low German: occupational name for a brewer, from MLG *gruten* to brew, a deriv. of *grut* groats (cf. GROUT), which were sometimes used instead of hops in beer making.

Patrs.: Low Ger.: **Grüters, Gruiters**.

Gruzinov Russian: patr. from the ethnic name *gruzin* Georgian (from the Georgians' own name for themselves, *Gurz*, of somewhat obscure, but presumably Caucasian, etymology).

Var.: **Gruzintsev**.

Gryglewski *see* GREGORY

Grylls *see* GRILL

Grynszpan *see* GRÜNSPAN

Grzegorczyk *see* GREGORY

Grzybek *see* GRIBOV

Grzywacz 1. Polish: nickname from Pol. *grzywacz* ringnecked dove. **2.** Jewish (E Ashkenazic): ornamental name from Pol. *grzywacz* ring-necked dove, one of the many such Ashkenazic names taken from vocab. words denoting birds.

Habitation name: **Grzywaczewski**.

Gsänger S German: habitation name from any of the various minor places called *G(e)seng* or *Gesäng*, from OHG *(gi)seng* clearing (originally one made by burning the vegetation; a deriv. of *(bi)sengan* to burn, singe).

Gscheid S German: topographic name for someone who lived near a boundary, MHG *(ge)scheide* (OHG *(gi)sceida*, a deriv. of *sceidan* to divide, separate), or habitation name from one of the numerous minor places named with this word.

Vars.: **Gscheider, Gschaider**.

Gschwandtner *see* SCHWAND

Gsell *see* GESELL

Guadalupe Spanish: habitation name from a place in the province of Cáceres, so called from Arabic *wad-el-ûbb* 'river of the wolf' or 'river with a curve'. The place is the site of a Hieronymite convent founded in the 14th cent., which possesses a famous image of the Virgin

Mary. A shrine in Mexico has been given the same name, and Our Lady of Guadalupe is regarded as the patron saint of Mexico. Guadalupe has also come to be used as a female given name, but this is almost certainly too late to lie behind any examples of the surname.

Gual Catalan: **1.** topographic name for someone who lived by a ford, Cat. *gual* (LL *vadāle*, a deriv. of class. L *vadum*). The initial consonant has been influenced by Gmc cogns.; cf. WADE. **2.** from a medieval given name of Gmc origin, probably a form of *Waldo*, which is a short form of several cpd names containing the element *wald* rule.

Var. (of 1): **GÜELL**.

Gualter *see* WALTER

Guard English: occupational name from OF *garde* watch, protection (of Gmc origin; cf. WARD 1), also used later in the concrete sense of a watchman.

Var.: **Gard**.

Dims.: Fr.: **Gardet, Gardey, Gardot**. Cat.: **Guardiola**. It.: **Guarducci**.

Guariniello *see* WARING

Gubbin *see* GIBBON

Guber *see* HUBER

Gucci Italian: from a medieval given name, an aphetic form of a dim. of *Ugo* (see HUGH), *Arrigo* (see HENRY), or *Berlinghiero* (see BERINGER).

Vars.: **Guzzi, Guzzo**.

Dims.: **Guccini, Guzz(ol)ini, Guzzetti**.

Guckenheim *see* GUGGENHEIM

Gudd *see* GOOD

Gudden *see* GODDARD

Gudge *see* GOUGH

Gudger *see* GOODYEAR

Gudmundsson *see* GOODMAN

Guedes Portuguese: patr. from the medieval given name *Guede, Gueda*. This is clearly of Gmc origin, but its meaning and derivation are uncertain. It may be akin to GUY.

Güell Catalan: **1.** topographic name for someone who lived by a spring or well, Cat. *güell* (of Gmc origin; cf. WELL). **2.** from a medieval given name of Gmc origin; perhaps from *Gudila*, a deriv. of the element *gūd* battle, or from *Wilia*, a short form of the various cpd names containing the element *will* will, desire. **3.** var. of GUAL.

Guenec *see* GWYN

Guerin *see* WARING

Guerpillon *see* GOUPIL

Guerrazzi *see* WARR

Guest English: nickname for a stranger or newcomer to a community, from ME *g(h)est* guest, visitor (from ON *gestr*, which has absorbed the cogn. OE *giest*).

Dims.: Ger.: **Gastl** (Bavaria); **Gästle** (Swabia).

Guevara Basque: habitation name from a place in the province of Álava. The origin and meaning of the place-name are uncertain; it was recorded in the form *Gebala* by the geographer Ptolemy in the 2nd cent. AD.

Guggenheim Jewish (W Ashkenazic): habitation name from *Gugenheim* in Alsace or *Jugenheim* (earlier *Guggenheim*) near Bensheim. In both cases the second element is from OHG *heim* homestead, while the first is of obscure and disputed etymology.

Vars.: **Gugenheim**, **Guckenheim**; **Guggenheimer**; **Koukenheim** (a Fr. spelling).

Guglielmelli *see* WILLIAM

Guichard French: from a Gmc personal name composed of the elements *wīg* war + *hard* brave, hardy, strong.

Low Ger.: **Wiegard**, **Wieghardt**, **Wieger(t)**, **Wigger(t)**, **Wi(e)chert**, **Wickert**, **Wicher**. Fris.: **Wiart**, **Wiert**.

Dims.: Fr.: **Guichardet**, **Guichardon**, **Guichardot**, **Guichardin**, **Guichon**, **Guichot**, **Guichet(eau)**.

Patrs.: Low Ger.: **Wiegers**, **Wi(e)chers**, **Wiggers**, **Wickerts**; **Wicharz** (N Rhineland). Fris.: **Wiarda**, **Wyerda**, **Wiards**.

Guidelli *see* GUY

Guignard French: 1. nickname for someone with a squint, from OF *guign(ier)* to wink, squint, look askance (of Gmc origin; cf. OE *wincian* to wink) + the pej. suffix -*ard*. 2. from a Gmc personal name composed of the elements *win* friend + *hard* brave, hardy, strong.

Vars. (of 1): **Guignier**, **Guigneux**. (Of 2): **Guin(n)ard**.

Dims.: **Guignardeau**, **Guignet**, **Guignot**, **Guignon**.

Guihan *see* GAHAN

Guijarro Spanish: nickname for a small man or topographic name for someone who lived on stony soil, from Sp. *guijarro* pebble (a pej. deriv. of *guija*, from LL *(petra) aquīlea* sharp stone, from class. L *acūleus* pointed, sharp).

Guilbon *see* WILBERT

Guilfoyle *see* GILFOIL

Guilhermino *see* WILLIAM

Guillain *see* WILL

Guillamon Catalan: from the Gmc personal name *Willimund*, composed of the elements *will* will, desire + *mund* protection.

Guillemin *see* WILLIAM

Guimarães Portuguese: habitation name from any of various places, in particular a town in the province of Minho, so called from L *(villa) Vimaranis* 'estate of *Vimara*', a Gmc personal name probably composed of the elements *wīg* war + *marah* horse.

Guinan Irish: 1. Anglicized form of Gael. **Ó Cuinneáin** 'descendant of *Cuinneán*', a personal name from a dim. of *conn* chief. 2. Anglicized form of Gael. **Ó Cuineáin** 'descendant of *Cuineán*', a personal name from a dim. of *cana* whelp.

Var.: **Guinane**.

Guiness *see* McGUINNESS

Guirardin *see* GARRETT

Guiry *see* GEARY

Guisado Spanish: nickname from OSp. *guisado* (well) prepared, (well) equipped (past part. of the verb *guisar*, LL *wīsāre*, from *wīsa* manner, way, of Gmc origin).

Guise English: regional name for someone from the district of France of this name, which is of unknown etymology.

Guitart Catalan: from the Gmc personal name *Withard*, composed of the element *wit, wid* (see GUY 1) + *hard* hardy, brave, strong.

Guiver English: of uncertain origin; perhaps from an OE personal name composed of the elements *wīg* war and *beorht* famous. However, the earliest known form that seems to belong here is Thomas *Gyva* (Bishops Stortford, Herts., 1489); this is more likely to be from a ME form of the OE female personal name *Gifu*, a short form of any of the various cpd names with a final element *gifu* gift.

Var.: **Guyver**.

Gullberg *see* GOLD

Gullick English: from the ME given name *Gullake*, *Gudloc*, OE *Gūðlāc*, composed of the elements *gūð* battle + *lāc* sport, play, reinforced by the ON cogn. *Gúðleikr*.

Vars.: **Gulick**, **Gillick**; **Goodlake**, **Goodluck**; **Cutlack**, **Cutlock** (Norfolk).

Patr.: Eng.: **Gullickson**.

Gulliver English: nickname for a greedy person, from OF *goulafre* glutton (of uncertain origin).

Vars.: **Gulliford**, **Galliford**, **Galliver**.

Gully English: nickname for a giant or large man, from ME *golias* giant, from the Hebr. personal name *Golyat* Goliath, which occurs in the Bible as the name of the champion of the Philistines, who stood 'six cubits and a span', but was defeated in single combat by the shepherd boy David (I Sam. 17), who killed him with a stone from his sling. The surname is unlikely to be a topographic name for a dweller by a water channel, as the vocab. word *gully* (from OF *goulet* neck of a bottle, a dim. of *goule* throat, L *gula*) is not attested in this sense until the 17th cent.

Vars.: **Golley**, **Gullyes**.

Gulson *see* GOLDSTONE

Gulyaev Russian: patr. from the nickname *Gulyai*, a deriv. of *gulyat* to walk, wander, formerly also 'revel', which is presumably the sense that lies behind the surname.

Gumb *see* GOMME

Gumbel English: from a Norman personal name *Gumbald*, composed of the Gmc elements *gund* battle + *bald* bold, brave.

Dim.: **Gumbley** (W Midlands).

Gumbert *see* GOMBERT

Gummer *see* GOMER

Gunda *see* KONRAD

Gundrey *see* GRUNDY

Gunkel German: metonymic occupational name for a spinner or a maker of spindles, from Ger. *Kunkel* spindle, distaff (MHG *kunkel*, from LL *conicula*, dim. of *cōnus* cone, peg).

Vars.: **Kunkel**, **Künkel**, **Kinkel**; **Künkler**.

Gunn 1. English and Scots: from the ON personal name *Gunnr*, or the fem. form *Gunne*, short forms of the various cpd names with the first element *gunn* battle. **2.** English: metonymic occupational name for someone who operated a siege engine or cannon, perhaps also a nickname for a forceful person, from ME *gunne, gonne* ballista, cannon (originally a humorous application of the female personal name). **3.** Scots: Anglicized form of Gael. **Mac Gille Dhuinn** 'son of the servant of the brown one'; see DUNN 1.

Var. (of 1): **Gun**.

Dims. (of 1): **Gunnet(t)**.

Patrs. (from 1): **Gunns**, **Gunson**.

Gunnell English: from the ON female personal name *Gunnhildr*, ME *Gunnilla, Gunnild*, composed of the elements *gunn* battle + *hild* strife, contention. This was extremely popular in those parts of England that were under Norse influence in the Middle Ages.

Var.: **Cunnell**.

Gunner English: **1.** from the ON female personal name *Gunvǫr*, composed of the elements *gunn* battle + *vǫr* the feminine form of *varr* defender. **2.** occupational name for an operator of heavy artillery; see GUNN 2.

Gunning see CONNELL

Gunsberg see GINSBERG

Gunter English: from the Norman personal name *Gunter* (OF *Gontier*), composed of the Gmc elements *gund* battle + *heri, hari* army.

Var.: **Gunther**.

Dims.: Ger.: **Gunz**, **Gün(t)zel**, **Günzl(ein)**, **Günzelmann**.

Patrs.: Norw., Dan.: **Gundersen**. Swed.: **Gunnarsson**.

Patr. (from a dim.): Ger.: **Günzler**.

Gunton English (E Anglia): habitation name from either of two places, one in Norfolk and the other in Suffolk, so called from the ON personal name *Gunnr* or *Gunne* (see GUNN 1) + OE *tūn* enclosure, settlement.

Guppy English: habitation name from a place in Wootton Fitzpaine, Dorset, so called from the OE personal name *Guppa* (perhaps a short form of a cpd name composed of the elements *gūð* battle + *berht* bright, famous) + *(ge)hæg* enclosure. It is not a nickname from the tropical fish, since this was unknown in medieval England, and was in fact named in the 19th cent. in honour of R. J. L. Guppy, a clergyman in Trinidad who first presented specimens to the British Museum.

Vars.: **Guppey**, **Guppie**.

Gura see GÓRSKI

Guralnick see GORELIK

Gurdon see GORDON

Gurevich see HOROWITZ

Gurfinkiel see GORFINKEL

Gurg see GEORGE

Gurling see CODLIN

Gurnay English (Norman): habitation name from *Gournay*(-en-Brai) in Seine-Maritime, so called from a Gallo-Roman personal name *Gordīnus* + the local suffix *-ācum*.

Var.: **Gurney**.

Gurton English: habitation name from *Girton* in Cambs. and Notts., which get their names from OE *grēot* grit, gravel (or the derived adjective *grēoten*) + *tūn* enclosure, settlement.

Vars.: **Girton**, **Girtin**.

Gusev Russian: patr. from the nickname *Gus* 'Goose', given perhaps to a foolish person, or occupational name for someone who raised geese. The fact that the Eng. and Russ. words sound practically identical is something of a coincidence, for, although the words are ultimately cogn., the rules of Slav. sound changes would lead us to expect a form like *zus* rather than *gus*; there may have been early influence on the Russ. word by Gmc forms. For the Pol. equivalent, see GĄSIOR.

Var.: **Gusakov**.

Dim.: Czech: **Húsek**.

Gusmin see KUZMIN

Gustavsson Swedish: patr. from an ON personal name composed of the tribal name *Gaut* (see JOCELYN) + *staf* staff, cudgel.

Var.: **Gustafsson**.

Gustin see AUSTIN

Gutch see GOUGH

Gute Jewish (Ashkenazic): from the Yid. female given name *Gute* GOOD'.

Var.: **Gite** (from a S Yid. form).

Dim.: **Gittel** (from the Yid. dim. female given name *Gitl*).

Metrs. (from dims.): **Gittelson**; **Gitlin** (E Ashkenazic).

Guthrie 1. Scots: habitation name from a place near Forfar, Tayside, so called from Gael. *gaothair* windy place (a deriv. of *gaoth* wind) + the local suffix *-ach*. **2.** Scots: Anglicized form of Gael. **Mag Uchtre** 'son of *Uchtre*', a personal name of uncertain origin, perhaps akin to *uchtlach* child. **3.** Irish: Anglicized form of Gael. **Ó Flaithimh** 'descendant of *Flaitheamh*', a byname meaning 'Prince'. This Anglicized form seems to be the result of an erroneous association of the Gael. name with *laithigh* mud, and of mud with gutters.

Guthrum see GOODRUM

Gutiérrez Spanish: patr. from the medieval given name *Gutierre*, from a Visigothic personal name of uncertain form and meaning, perhaps a cpd of the elements *gunþi* battle + *hairus* sword.

Gutsch see GOTTSCHALK

Guttenberg German and Jewish (Ashkenazic): habitation name from any of various places, for example in Bavaria, so called from the weak dat. case (originally used after a preposition and article) of OHG *guot* good + *berg* hill. The shortening of the vowel in the first syllable is a feature found in various dialects of German.

Vars.: **Gutenberg**. Jewish only: **Gutenberger**.

Gutteridge English: **1.** from the ME given name *Goderiche*, OE *Gōdrīc*, composed of the elements *gōd* good + *rīc* power. **2.** from the ME given name *Cuterich*, OE *Cūðrīc*, composed of the elements *cūð* famous, well known + *rīc* power.

Vars.: **Gut(t)ridge**. (Of 1 only): **Good(e)ridge**, **Godridge**, **Go(o)drich**, **Good(e)rick**, **Goodwright**. (Of 2 only): **Cutt(e)ridge**, **Cuttriss**, **Cutress**.

Guwer *see* GOWER

Guy 1. English: from a French form of the Gmc personal name *Wido*, of uncertain origin. It may be from the element reflected in OHG *witu*, OE *widu, wudu* wood, or else from that of OHG *wīt*, OE *wīd* wide. Whatever its origins, this name was popular among the Normans in the forms *Wi, Why* as well as in the rest of France in the form *Guy*; both versions are reflected in the Eng. vars. **2.** English: occupational name for a guide, OF *gui* (a deriv. of *gui(d)er* to guide, of Gmc origin). **3.** Jewish: of unknown origin.

Vars.: **G(u)ye**, **Why(e)**, **Wye**; **Guyon**, **Wyon** (from the OF oblique case).

Dims.: Fr.: **Guiet**, **Guyet**, **Guiot**, **Guyot**, **Guyonnet**, **Guyonneau**; **Guit(t)et**, **Guitel**, **Guitonneau**; **Vit(t)et**, **Vuittet**. It.: **Guidelli**, **Guidetti**, **Guidini**, **Guiducci**, **Guiduzzi**, **Guidotti**; **Ghidelli**, **Ghidetti**, **Ghidini**, **Ghidoli**, **Ghi(d)otti**, **Ghiotto** (Lombardy, Emilia). Hung.: **Vida**.

Augs.: It.: **Guidone**, **Guidoni**; **Ghi(d)oni**, **Ghion(e)**.

Patrs.: Eng.: **Guys**, **Guyson**.

Guyardeau *see* WYATT

Guyler English (Nottingham): nickname for a deceitful or treacherous person, from an agent deriv. of ME *guylen* to deceive (a deriv. of *guyle* guile, from OF but of Gmc origin).

Guymer English (Norfolk): from the OF personal name *Guymer*, which was introduced to Britain by the Normans in the form *Wymer*. It is composed of the Gmc elements *wīg* war + *meri, mari* fame. The surname is therefore a doublet of WYMER 1, although this has also absorbed an OE form of the same underlying Gmc name.

Guyton English (Norfolk): habitation name from *Gayton* in Norfolk, probably so called from an OE personal name or stream-name *Gǣga* or *Gǣge* (presumably akin to *gǣgan* to turn aside) + OE *tūn* enclosure, settlement.

Guyver *see* GUIVER

Guzek Polish: nickname for someone with a prominent carbuncle or wart, Pol. *guzek*, a dim. of *guz* knob.

Vars.: **Guziak**; **Guz**.

Patr.: **Guzewicz**.

Habitation name: **Guzowski**.

Guzik Polish: nickname for a small person, from Pol. *guzik* button, originally a dim. of *guz* knob.

Var.: **Guzicki**.

Guzmán Spanish: from a Visigothic personal name, apparently composed of the tribal name *Gaut* (see JOCELYN) + *man* man.

Guzzetti *see* GUCCI

Gwatkins *see* WATT

Gwiazda Polish: nickname meaning 'Star', Pol. *gwiazda*.

Habitation name: **Gwiazdowski**.

Gwinn *see* GWYN

Gwinnett Welsh: regional name from the district in N(W) Wales called *Gwynedd*. The name first occurs in L documents in the form *Venedotia* 'Land of the *Vēnii*', a tribal name of uncertain, though presumably Celt., etymology.

Vars.: **Gwyneth**, **Gwioneth**.

Gwizdka Polish: nickname for someone noted for his cheerful whistling, from a deriv. of Pol. *gwizdać* to whistle.

Var.: **Gwizdała**.

Gwyn Welsh: nickname for a person with fair hair or a noticeably pale complexion, from W *gwyn* light, white, fair. This was also used as a personal name in the Middle Ages, and some early examples may reflect this.

Vars.: **Gwynn(e)**, **Gwinn**; QUINN; WINN.

Dims.: Bret.: **(Le) Guen(n)ec**.

Gwyneth *see* GWINNETT

Gwyre *see* GEARY

Gyatt *see* WYATT

Gye *see* GUY

Gyles *see* GILES

Gyllenhammar *see* GOLD

Gynn *see* GINN, JUNIPER

Györffy *see* GEORGE

Gypps *see* GIBB

Gyselbrechts *see* GILBERT

Gyurkó *see* GEORGE

Gzik Polish: nickname for an irritating person, from Pol. *gzik* gadfly.

H

Haack *see* HAKE

Haagensen *see* HAIN

Haar 1. German and Jewish (Ashkenazic): nickname for someone with a copious or noticeable head of hair, from Ger. *Haar* hair (MHG *hār*). **2.** German: metonymic occupational name for someone who worked with raw flax in the production of linen, from Ger. *Haar* raw flax (a different word from that in 1, from MHG *har*, OHG *haro*). **3.** Low German and Dutch: topographic name for someone who lived on a moor, from MLG *haar* marsh, moor.

Vars. (of 3): Low Ger., Du.: **Van der Haar**, **Verhaar(en)**, **Haaren**, **Ter Haar**.

Dim. (of 1): Ger.: **Härle**.

Haarla Finnish: ornamental name from *haara* branch + the local suffix *-la*; cf. Swed. GREN.

Habbert German: from a Gmc personal name composed of the elements *hadu* battle, strife + *berht* bright, famous.

Vars.: **Happert**, **Habbrecht**.

Dims.: Ger.: **Happel**, HASS. Low Ger.: **Hadeke**. Fris.: **Habbe(ma)**, **Hobbe(ma)**, **Hapke**, **Hatje**. Du.: **Hobbema**. Fr.: **Hablet**, **Hablot**.

Patrs. (from dims.): Fris.: **Hab(be)s**, **Haps**; **Habben**, **Hobben**; **Habbing**, **Hobbing**.

Habenicht German: nickname for a poor man, from Ger. *Habenichts* have-not, a cpd formed from MHG *habe(n)* to have (OHG *habēn*) + *niht* nothing (OHG *niwiht, neowiht*).

Var.: **Habnit**.

Haber German and Jewish (Ashkenazic): metonymic occupational name for a grower of or dealer in oats, from early mod. Ger. *Haber* oats (mod. Ger. *Hafer*; MHG *haber(e)*, OHG *habaro*). As a Jewish surname, it is in many cases ornamental.

Vars.: Ger.: **Hafer**; **Haberer**; **Häberer**; **Habermann**. Jewish: **Haberer**, **Haberman**; **Hober(man)** (from Yid. *hober*); HUBER; **Gaber(man)**, **Goberman** (under Russ. influence; see GOREN); **Aberman** (in regions where Yid. has no /h/).

Dims.: Ger.: **Haberl**, **Häberle(in)**, **Heberl**, **Heberle(in)**.

Cpds.: Jewish: **Haberberg** ('oat hill'); **Haberkorn** ('oat grain', partly Anglicized as **Habercorn**); **Haberfeld** ('oat field', partly Anglicized as **Haberfield**); **Haberstaub**, **Habershtoub** ('oat dust').

Habersham English: metonymic occupational name for a maker of coats of chain mail, from ME, OF *haubergeon* mail jerkin, a dim. of *hauberc* coat of mail, a word of Gmc origin composed of elements meaning 'neck' (see HALS) and 'protection'. After coats of mail became obsolete and the word fell out of use, the name was altered by folk etymology to assume the appearance of a habitation name.

Vars.: **Habershon**, **Haberjam**, **Haversham**, **Havisham**; **Hab(b)eshaw**, **Hab(b)ishaw** (from the OF agent noun *haubergier*).

Hablot *see* ABEL

Habsburg German: habitation name from a castle in Aargau, built in the 11th cent. by Werner, Bishop of Strasburg, and named from the gen. case of MHG *habech* HAWK + *burg* fortress, stronghold.

Var.: **Hapsburg** (an Anglicized form).

Hache 1. French: metonymic occupational name for a maker or user of axes, either for domestic and agricultural purposes or as weapons of war, from OF *hache* axe (of Gmc origin; cf. HACKER). **2.** German: occupational name for a servant, from MHG *hache* lad, boy, servant. **3.** Ger. (of Slav. origin): pet form of HANS.

Vars. (of 1): **Lahache**. (Of 3): **Hach**, **Hachnik**, **Hachnek**.

Dims. (of 1): **Hachet(te)**, **Hachin**, **Hachon**.

Hachner *see* HANS

Hack 1. English: var. of HAKE 1. **2.** Jewish (Ashkenazic): of unknown origin.

Hacker English (chiefly Somerset), German, and Jewish (Ashkenazic): occupational name for a butcher, or less often for a woodcutter, from an agent deriv. of ME *hack(en)*, Ger. *hacken* to chop, cut (OE *haccian*, OHG *hacchōn*). The Jewish surnames in this group may be from Yid. *heker* butcher, *holtsheker* woodcutter (Ger. *Holzhacker*), or *valdheker* lumberjack, or from Ger. *Hacker* woodchopper. Another possibility for Jewish forms spelled with *-e-* is that they are from Yid. *heker* retail or retailer (the exact meaning is unclear); akin to Ger. *Höker* street trader, pedlar (see HAKE).

Vars.: Ger.: **Häcker**, **Hecker** (see also HEDGE); **Hackmann**. Jewish: **Haker**, **He(c)ker**, HACKMANN.

Dims.: Ger.: **Heckerle(in)**.

Hackett 1. English (chiefly W Midlands): dim. of the medieval given name *Hack, Hake*; see HAKE. **2.** Scots: perhaps a habitation name from the lands of *Halkhead* in the former county of Renfrews. (now part of Strathclyde region), apparently so called from ME *hauk, halk* HAWK + *wode, wude* WOOD.

Vars. (of 1): **Haggett**, **Haggitt**, **Acket**. (Of 2): **Halket(t)**.

Patr. (from 1): **Acketts**.

Hacking English: habitation name from a place in Lancs., of uncertain origin. Early forms appear with the definite article, and the name may represent an OE term for a fish weir, a deriv. of *hæcc* hatch or *haca* bolt.

Hackmann 1. German and Jewish (Ashkenazic): var. of HACKER. **2.** Low German: var. of HAKE 2.

Var. (of 1): Jewish: **Hackman**.

Hackwood English: of uncertain origin. It is either an occupational nickname for a woodcutter, from ME *hack(en)* to cut, chop (see HACKER) + *wode* wood, or else a habitation name from some place such as *Hackwood* near Basingstoke, Hants, so called from OE **hacga* hawthorn (see HAW 1) + *wudu* WOOD.

Hacon English: from the ON personal name *Hákon*, originally a byname meaning 'Handy', 'Useful'.
Patrs.: Dan., Norw.: **Håkonsen**. Swed.: **Håkonsson**.

Hadaway *see* HATHAWAY

Hadcock *see* ADAM

Hadden *see* HOWDEN

Haddleton English: habitation name from a lost place near Bingley in W Yorks. called *Hathelton*, later *Halton* (*Hateltun* in Domesday Book). The placename is of uncertain origin; the final element is presumably OE *tūn* enclosure, settlement, but the first element is unidentified.

Haddock English, of uncertain origin. Three possibilities are discussed by Reaney: **1.** metonymic occupational name for a fishmonger or nickname for someone supposedly resembling the fish, from ME *hadduc* haddock (of unknown origin). **2.** from a medieval survival, with added initial *H-*, of an OE personal name *Ædduc*, a dim. of *Æddi*, itself a short form of various cpd names with the first element *ēad* prosperity, fortune. **3.** habitation name from *Haydock* near Liverpool, perhaps so called from W *heiddog* barley farm, a deriv. of *haidd* barley, but more likely from OE *hæþ* HEATH + *hōc* HOOK.

Haddon 1. English: habitation name from any of the various places, in Derbys., Dorset, and Northants, so called from OE *hæð* heathland, heather (see HEATH) + *dūn* hill (see DOWN 1). **2.** Scots: var. of HALDANE 2.

Haddow Scots: habitation name from *Haddo* in the former county of Aberdeens. (now part of Grampian region), so called from ME *half* + Gael. *dabhach*, a land measure equivalent to four ploughgates.

Haddrell *see* HATHERELL

Hadeke *see* HABBERT

Haden English (W Midlands): habitation name from *Haden* Hill near Dudley, which may get its name from OE *hæð* HEATH + *dūn* hill (see DOWN 1).

Hader German and Jewish (Ashkenazic): **1.** nickname for a quarrelsome person, from Ger. *Hader* discord, argument, quarrel (MHG *hader*; cf. the element *hadu* strife, contention, in Gmc personal names). **2.** nickname for a scruffy person or metonymic occupational name for a trader in rags, from Ger. *Hader* tattered clothes, rags (MHG *hader*, OHG *hadara* skins for clothing).
Vars.: Ger.: **Haderer**, **Hadermann**. (Of 2 only): Ger.: **Hodermann**.
Dims.: Ger.: **Häderle**, **Haderlin**.

Hadfield *see* HATFIELD

Hadgkiss *see* HODGE

Hädicke *see* HEYDRICH

Hadley English (chiefly W Midlands): habitation name from a place so called near Telford in Shrops. or another near Droitwich, Worcs., or possibly from any of the places

called *Hadleigh* in Suffolk, Essex, and elsewhere. Most of these get the name from OE *hæð* heathland, heather (see HEATH) + *lēah* wood, clearing. However, the one in Worcs. appears to have as its first element the OE personal name *Hadda* (probably a short form of the various cpd names beginning with *heard* hardy, brave, strong).
Vars.: **Hadleigh** (rare as a surname); **Hadlee**. See also HEADLEY and HEATLEY.

Hadlow English: habitation name from a place in Kent. The second element of this is fairly certainly OE *hlāw* (see LAW 2 and LOW 1); the first may be OE *hāð* heathland, heather (a byform of *hæð*; see HEATH) or perhaps *hēafod* head, chief.

Haensch *see* HANS

Hafer *see* HABER

Hafner German and Jewish (Ashkenazic): occupational name for a potter, from an agent deriv. of Ger. dial. *Hafen* pot, dish (MHG *hafen*, OHG *havan*). This is the normal term for the occupation in S Germany and Austria, and the Ger. surname is confined largely to this area. Other names referring to this occupation may be found at EULER, TÖPFER, and POTTER.
Vars.: **Haffner**, **Hef(f)ner**. Ger. only: **Häfner**.

Haft German and Jewish (Ashkenazic): metonymic occupational name for a maker and seller of various sorts of clamps and fastenings, from Ger. *Haft* clasp (MHG *haft*).
Vars.: **Hafter**. Ger.: **Haftmann**, **Haftenmacher**.
Dim.: Ger.: **Haftel**.

Hagan Irish: Anglicized form of Gael. *Ó hÁgáin* 'descendant of *Ógán*', a personal name from a dim. of *óg* young.
Vars.: **O'Hagan**; **Haggan** (N Ireland).

Hagberg *see* HAIG

Hagen *see* HAIN

Hagerty *see* HEGARTY

Hägg Swedish: ornamental name from *hägg* bird cherry (*Prunus padus*). This is one of the surnames drawn from the vocab. of nature and adopted more or less arbitrarily in the 19th cent.
Cpds.: **Häggberg** ('cherry hill'); **Häggblad** ('cherry leaf'); **Häggblom** ('cherry flower'); **Hägglund** ('cherry grove'); **Häggmark** ('cherry land'); **Häggqvist** ('cherry twig'); **Häggström** ('cherry river').

Haggard English: **1.** nickname from ME, OF *hagard* wild, untamed (of uncertain etymology, perhaps from a Gmc element meaning 'hedge'; cf. HAIG). The word was adopted into ME as a technical term in falconry to denote a hawk that had been captured and trained when already fully grown, rather than being reared in captivity, and the surname could therefore conceivably have developed as an occupational name for a falconer. **2.** said to be an Anglicized form of Dan. ÅGÅRD; see below.
Vars. (of 1): **Haggar(t)**, **Hagard**, **Hagger**.

Haggett *see* HACKETT

Haggis 1. Scots: habitation name from any of the numerous places in the Lowlands so called, apparently from Northern ME *hag* clearing (ON *hǫgg*, akin to HACHE 1 and HACKER) + *hous* house (OE *hūs*). There does not seem to be any direct connection with the vocab. word denoting the typical dish of the region, although this word is itself of uncertain origin. **2.** English (Cambs.): var. of AGGIS.

Vars. (of 1): **Haggish**, **Haggas**.

Hague English: **1.** var. of HAIG. **2.** in a few cases perhaps, a local name from *The Hague* in the Netherlands, Du. *Den Haag*, from *haag* enclosure, a cogn. of ON *hagi*, OE *haga* (see HAIG).

Hahn 1. German: nickname for a proud or lusty person, from Ger. *Hahn* cock (MHG *hane*, OHG *hano*, of which the fem. *henin* is cogn. with OE *henn*, mod. Eng. *hen*). In some cases it may also have been a house name, from a house sign bearing a picture of a cock, or a metonymic occupational name for a chicken farmer. **2.** Jewish (Ashkenazic): ornamental name from Ger. *Hahn* cock, one of the many Ashkenazic surnames based on vocab. words denoting birds or animals. **3.** German: var. of HAIN 4 and 5.

Var. (of 1): **Hahner(t)**.

Hahncke *see* HANS

Haiem *see* HYAM

Haig 1. Scots (Norman): habitation name from any of various places in N France named from ON *hagi* enclosure, a word with cogns. in most Gmc languages (cf. HAY). **2.** English: topographic name for someone who lived by a hedged or fenced enclosure (OE *haga*), or habitation name from a place named with this word (or its ON cogn. *hagi*), esp. three places called *Haigh*, two in W Yorks. and the other near Manchester.

Var.: **Haigh** (chiefly Yorks.).

Dims.: Ger.: **Hägle**, **Hegel(e)**.

Cpds: Swed.: **Hagberg** ('enclosure hill'); **Haglund** ('enclosure grove'); **Hagstedt** ('enclosure homestead'); **Hagstrand** ('enclosure shore'); **Hagström** ('enclosure river').

Haighwood *see* HOGWOOD

Haile *see* HALE

Hailes 1. Scots: habitation name from *Hailes* in Lothian, so called from the ME gen. or pl. form of *hall* HALL. **2.** English: habitation name from *Hailes* in Gloucs., which is an old Brit. river name meaning 'polluted', from a word that is an ancestor of W *halog* dirty. **3.** English: from the gen. or pl. form of OE *halh* nook, recess (see HALE 1).

Vars.: **Hails**. (Of 3 only): **Ha(y)les**; **Hallow(e)s**; **Hallas** (chiefly Yorks.); **Heal(e)s** (Wessex).

Hailey *see* HALEY

Hailwood English: habitation name from *Halewood* in Lancs., so called from OE *halh* nook, recess (see HALE 1) + *wudu* WOOD.

Haime *see* HAMMOND

Hain 1. English: habitation name from any of various places named with ME *heghen*, a weak pl. of *hegh*, from OE *(ge)hæg* enclosure (see HAY 1). *Hayne* is a common minor placename in Devon. **2.** English: from the ME given name *Hain, Heyne*. This is derived from the Gmc personal name *Hagano*, originally a byname meaning 'Hawthorn'. It is found in England before the Conquest,

but was popularized by the Normans. In the Danelaw, it may be derived from ON *Hagni, Hǫgni*, a Scandinavianized version of the same name. **3.** English: nickname for a wretched individual, from ME *hain(e), heyne* wretch, niggard (OE *hēan*). **4.** German: topographic name for someone who lived by a patch of enclosed pastureland, MHG *hagen* (OHG *hagan* hawthorn, hedge). **5.** German: from a Gmc personal name, originally a byname from the same element as in 2 above. **6.** Jewish (Ashkenazic): of unknown origin.

Vars. (of 1–3): **Haine**, **Hayn(e)**. (of 4 and 5): **Hagen**, HAHN. (Of 4): **Haine**, **Hayn**.

Patrs. (from 2): Eng.: HAINES. Dan.: **Haagensen**, **Hågensen**.

Haines 1. English: patr. from the medieval given name HAIN 2. **2.** English: habitation name from *Haynes* in Beds. This name first appears in Domesday Book as *Hagenes* and has been explained in several different ways, none of them very convincing. **3.** Welsh: from the personal name *Einws*, a dim. of *Einion* (of uncertain origin, popularly associated with the vocab. word *einion* anvil).

Vars.: **Hayn(e)s**, **Hanes**, **Heynes**.

Haining *see* HENNING

Hainsworth English (common in W Yorks.): **1.** habitation name from *Hainworth* in W Yorks., so called from an Anglo-Scandinavian form of the Norse personal name *Hagni* or *Hǫgni* (see HAIN 2) + OE *worð* enclosure (see WORTH). **2.** habitation name from AINSWORTH in Lancs., from the OE personal name *Ægen* + *worð* enclosure. Names such as *de Haynesworth* and *de Heynesworth* occur in the surrounding area in the 14th cent.

Hair *see* HARE

Hairon *see* HERON

Haiselden *see* HAZELDEN

Haisell *see* HAZEL

Haiss *see* HIESS

Haitlie *see* HEATLEY

Hajdú Hungarian: from *hajtó* drover. Drovers were armed, and often became highwaymen and mercenaries. *Hajdú* acquired both meanings, but the surname is chiefly associated with the settlement of some 10,000 mercenaries in E Hungary by Prince István Bocskay as a reward for their support. Their towns, dating from 1605, still retain *Hajdú-* as a first element. The word was borrowed into Ger., Pol., and Czech to denote an armed retainer of a nobleman. In Pol. it also denoted a Hung. footsoldier in the Pol. army in the 16th cent. The name is also borne by Hungarian Jews, among whom it is either occupational ('drover') or an adoption of the Hung. name.

Patrs.: Pol.: **Hajdukiewicz**. Croatian: **Hajduković**.

Hájek Czech: **1.** topographic name for someone who lived in or near a thicket or grove, from Czech *hájek* thicket, from *háj* grove, or directly from *háj* grove, the dim. suffix *-ek* being added in forming the surname. **2.** occupational name for a keeper of animals, especially one who looked after horses, from *hejno-* herd, flock.

Vars. (of 2): **Hajný**, **Hejný**, **Hejna**.

Hakala Finnish: ornamental or topographic name from *haka* pasture, paddock + the local suffix *-la*.

Hake 1. English: from the ON byname *Haki*, cogn. with HOOK, and given originally to someone with a hunched figure or a hooked nose. **2.** Low German: occupational name for a pedlar or street trader, from MLG *höken* to carry things about (on one's back). The Eng. word *hawker* derives from a 16th-cent. borrowing of this term.

Vars. (of 1): HACK. (Of 2): **Haack, Hocke; Haker, Haacker, Höck(n)er, Heckner**; HACKMANN.

Patr. (from 1): Eng.: **Hakes**.

Haker see HACKER

Hakkarainen Finnish: patr. from the occupational term *hakkari* woodman, lumberjack (a borrowing of Swed. *hackar*, agent deriv. of *hacka* to chop; cogn. of HACKER).

Häkkinen Finnish: ornamental or topographic name from *häkki* pen, enclosure + the gen. suffix *-nen*.

Håkonsen see HACON

Halary see ALARIC

Hałas Polish: nickname for a noisy person, from Pol. *halas* noise.

Dim.: **Hałaszczyk**.

Halász Hungarian: occupational name for a fisherman, from *hal* fish + *-ász* occupational suffix.

Halbrook see HOLBROOK

Haldane Scots: **1.** from the ON personal name *Halfdanr* or the Late OE Anglicized form of this, *Healfdene*, composed of the elements *healf* half + *Dene* Dane, originally a byname for someone of mixed parentage. **2.** var. of HOWDEN 1.

Vars.: **Halden, Haldin, Hallding, Holdane**.

Halder German: topographic name for someone who lived high on a mountainside, from S Ger. *Halde* slope, hillside (MHG *halde*, OHG *halda*).

Vars.: **Halter, Haldner, Haldermann; Hald, Halt, Häld(e)**.

Hale English: **1.** topographic name for someone who lived in a nook or hollow, from OE *hale*, dat. of *h(e)alh* nook, hollow, recess. In N England the word often has a specialized meaning, denoting a piece of flat alluvial land by the side of a river, originally one deposited in a bend; in the south-east it seems often to have referred to a patch of dry land in a fen. In some cases the surname may be a habitation name from any of the several places in England named with this fossilized inflected form, which would originally have been preceded by a preposition such as *at*. **2.** from a ME given name derived from either of two OE bynames, **Hæle* 'Hero' or **Hægel*, which is probably akin to Gmc *Hagano* 'Hawthorn' (see HAIN 2).

Vars. (of 1): **Haile, Haill; Heal(e), Hele** (chiefly W Country); **Attale** (with fused ME preposition *at*); **Haugh, Hauff** (from the OE nom. case); HAILES (from the gen. sing. or nom. pl.).

Dim. (of 2): **Haylock**.

Hálek see GALL

Haler see HAYLER

Hales see HAILES

Halevy see LEVI

Haley English (chiefly W Yorks.): habitation name from any of various places named with the OE elements *hēg* hay + *lēah* wood, clearing.

Vars.: **Hayley, Hail(e)y, Haly**.

Halford English (chiefly Midlands): habitation name from any of various places so called. Most, for example that in Warwicks., get the name from OE *halh* nook, recess (see HALE 1) + *ford* FORD. One in Shrops. has as its first element ME, OE *hafocere* hawker (see HAWK).

Halfpenny 1. English: nickname from the coin. The first regular issues of round halfpence were made in the reign of Edward I. Before that, there had been sporadic issues, but the term was originally used to denote a silver penny that had been literally (and legally) cut in half to provide smaller change. The nickname may have been bestowed on a man worth very little or on one of small stature. In some instances, the origin may be anecdotal, connected for example with a requirement to pay a rent of a halfpenny. **2.** Irish: Anglicized form of Gael. *Ó hAilpín*; see ALPIN.

Halicz Polish: habitation name from the town of *Halicz*, now in the Soviet Union.

Var.: **Halicki**.

Halket see HACKETT

Hall English, German, Danish/Norwegian, and Swedish: topographic name for someone who lived near a large house, or occupational name for someone employed at a hall or manor (OE *heall*, OHG *halla*, ON *holl*). Some cases may be habitation names from towns named with this word, in particular *Halle* in the south-west corner of East Germany.

Vars.: Eng.: **Halls; Hallman**. Ger.: **Halle(r)** (see also HELLER); **Hal(l)mann**. Swed.: **Hallén, Hallin, Hallman**.

Dims.: Fr.: **Hallet, Hallez**, HALLEY, **Hallé**.

Cpds (mostly ornamental): Swed.: **Hallberg** ('hall hill'); **Hallgren** ('hall branch'); **Hallqvist** ('hall twig'); **Hallström** ('hall river').

Häll Swedish: ornamental or topographic name from Swed. *häll* stone, rock (ON *hallr*).

Cpds (ornamental): **Hällgren** ('stone branch'); **Hällström** ('stone river').

Hallahan Irish: Anglicized form of Gael. Ó hÁilleacháin 'descendant of *Ailleachán*', a personal name from a dim. of *áille* beauty.

Vars.: **O'Halleghane, (O')Hallaghan, Hallihane, Halligan**.

Hallam English (chiefly S Yorks. and E Midlands): regional name from the district in S Yorks. around Sheffield and Ecclesfield so called, or habitation name from the town of this name in Derbys. The Derbys. name is from OE *halum*, dat. pl. of *halh* nook, recess (see HALE 1). The Yorks. district, sometimes called *Hallamshire*, is from *hallum*, dat. pl. of *hall* stone, rock (cf. HÄLL).

Var.: **Hallum**.

Hallard see ALLARD

Hallaway see ALLOWAY

Halley 1. French: dim. from a cogn. of HALL. **2.** N English and Scots: apparently a habitation name from an unidentified place, perhaps named with the OE elements *hall* HALL + *(ge)hæg* enclosure (see HAY 1).

Var.: **Hally**.

Halliday N English and Scots: from OE *hāligdæg* holy day, religious festival. The reasons why this word should have become a surname are not clear; perhaps it was used as a nickname for persons born at Christmas or Easter.

Vars.: **Haliday**, **Hallad(e)y**, **Halleday**, **Hol(l)iday**, **Holyday**, **Holladay**.

Hallin *see* ALLEN

Hallinan Irish: Anglicized form of Gael. **Ó hÁilgheanáin** 'descendant of *Ailgheanán*', a dim. form of a personal name composed of old Celt. elements meaning 'mild person'.

Hallis *see* ALLIS

Hallissey Irish: Anglicized form of Gael. **Ó hÁilgheasa** 'descendant of *Ailgheas*', a personal name meaning 'Desire'.

Halliwell N English (Lancs.) and Scots: habitation name from a place near Manchester, so called from OE *hālig* holy + *well(a)* well, spring, or from any of the numerous other places named with the same elements, such as *Holwell* in Dorset, Leics., Herts., and Oxon., *Halwill* and *Halwell* in Devon, and *Holywell* in Cambs., Cornwall, Clwyd, and Northumb. In medieval times many springs were dedicated to saints, but this usually represented no more than a Christian patina on an earlier pagan and animistic belief. See also HEILBRONN.

Vars.: **Hallawell**, **Hallewell**, **Hallowell**; **Helliwell**; **Holliwell**, **Hollowell**.

Hallon *see* FALLON

Halloran Irish: Anglicized form of Gael. **Ó hAllmhuráin** 'descendant of *Allmhurán*', a personal name from a dim. of *allmhurach* foreigner (from *all* beyond + *muir* sea).

Vars.: **O'Halowrane**, **O'Halloraine**, **O'Halloran**, **O'Hallaran**, **O'Halleran**, **O'Halleron**, **Holloran**.

Hallu French: habitation name from a place in Somme, apparently named with the Gmc elements *hasal* HAZEL + *ōdi* wasteland (see EDER).

Hallworth English: habitation name from either of two places in W Yorks. now called *Holdsworth*, both probably originally from an OE byname *Halda 'Bent' + *worð* enclosure (see WORTH).

Vars.: **Hallsworth**, **Hol(d)sworth**, **Hou(l)dsworth**, **Holesworth**.

Halmshaw *see* HAMPSHIRE

Halonen Finnish: ornamental or anecdotal name from *halko* log, firewood + the gen. suffix -*nen*. If the origin is anecdotal, the circumstances surrounding its adoption as a surname are no longer known.

Halpen *see* ALPIN

Halper *see* ALPERT, HEILBRONN

Hals German and Dutch: from Ger. *Hals*, Du. *hals* neck. Generally this was a nickname for a man with a long neck

or for a conspicuous sufferer from goitre (a common affliction in medieval times, esp. in Alpine regions).

Var.: Du.: **De Hals**.

Cpds: Jewish (Ashkenazic, reasons for adoption unknown): **Halsband** ('neckband'); **Halstuch** ('neckerchief').

Halsall English (Lanc.): habitation name from a place in Lancs. (*Heleshale* in Domesday Book), probably so called from the gen. case of the OE personal name *Hæle* (see HALE 2) + OE *halh* nook, recess (see HALE 1).

Halsey English: probably a habitation name from an unidentified place in the London area, so called from OE *hals* neck of land, channel of water (cf. HALS) + *ēg* island.

Halstead English: habitation name from any of the various places bearing this name, for example in Essex (*Haltesteda* in Domesday Book), Kent, and Leics., all of which are probably so called from OE *(ge)heald* hut, temporary shelter + *stede* site. However, the name is now most frequently found in Lancs., where it is from High *Halstead* in Burnley, which is named as the 'site of a hall', from OE *h(e)all* hall + *stede* place.

Vars.: **Halsted**, **Alstead**.

Halton English: habitation name from any of the many places so called from OE *h(e)alh* nook, hollow (see HALE 1) + *tūn* enclosure, settlement.

Ham 1. English (W Country): topographic name for someone living on low-lying land by a stream; see HAMMER 1. 2. Scots: habitation name from a place in the former county of Caithness (now part of Highland region), so called from ON *hámi* homestead.

Hambly English (W Country): apparently from the ANF given name *Ham(b)lin*, a double dim. of HAMMOND 1.

Vars.: **Hambley**, **Haml(e)y**; **Ham(b)lin**, **Ham(b)lyn**, **Ham(b)ling**, **Hamblen**; **Hamelly** (Cornwall).

Hambro Low German and Danish: habitation name from some minor place apparently named with the Gmc elements *ham* water meadow (see HAMMER 1) + *bru* marsh, bog (see BREUIL).

Hambrook English: habitation name from a place in Gloucs., so called from OE *hān* rock, stone + *brōc* stream.

Hamburg German and Jewish (Ashkenazic): habitation name from the great city at the mouth of the river Elbe, or from some other place so named, from the Gmc elements *ham* water meadow (see HAMMER 1) + *burg* fortress, town (see BURKE).

Vars.: **Hamburger**. Ger.: **Hamborg**, **Hamborch**. Jewish: **Gamb(o)urg** (under Russ. influence; see GOREN).

Hamburgh *see* HANBURY

Hamel 1. German and Jewish (Ashkenazic): habitation name from the city of Hamlin, Ger. *Hameln*, Yid. *Haml*, where the river *Hamel* empties into the Weser. The name of the river probably derives from the Gmc element *ham* water meadow (see HAMMER 1). 2. Dutch: nickname or metonymic occupational name for a shepherd, from MDu. *hamel* wether, castrated ram. 3. French: topographic name for someone who lived and worked at an outlying farm dependent on the main village, OF *hamel* (a dim. from a Gmc element cogn. with OE *hām* homestead).

Vars. (of 1): Ger.: **Hamelmann**. Jewish: HAMMEL.

Dims. (of 3): Fr.: **Hamelin**, **Hamelet**, **Hamelot**.

Hamer 1. English: habitation name from a place in Lancs., so called from OE *hamor* rock, crag. **2.** Flemish, Dutch: metonymic occupational name for a maker of hammers or a user of a hammer, for example in a forge; a cogn. of HAMMER 2. **3.** Jewish (Ashkenazic): var. of HAMMER 2.

Hamill 1. Scots (Norman): habitation name from *Haineville* or *Henneville* in Manche, so called from the Gmc personal name *Hagano* (see HAIN 2) + OF *ville* settlement (see VILLE). **2.** English: nickname for a scarred or maimed person, from ME, OE *hamel* mutilated, crooked.

Vars.: **Hammill**, HAMMEL.

Hamilton Scots and N Irish: habitation name, ultimately not from the town of *Hamilton* near Glasgow (which is derived from the surname), but from what is now a deserted village in the parish of Barkby, Leics. This is so called from OE *hamel* scarred, mutilated, crooked (see HAMILL 2) + *dūn* hill (see DOWN 1). However, some bearers may derive their name from the town founded by the Hamiltons, rather than from being members of the Norman family mentioned below.

Hamlett English (Gloucs.): from a ME given name, a double dim. of HAMMOND 1.

Vars.: **Hamlet**, **Hamblet(t)**.

Hammel 1. English: var. of HAMILL 2. **2.** Ger.: cogn. of HAMEL 2. **3.** Jewish (Ashkenazic): var. of HAMEL 1.

Hammer 1. English and German: topographic name for someone who lived by a patch of flat, low-lying alluvial land beside a stream, OE *hamm*, OHG *ham*. **2.** German and Jewish (Ashkenazic): metonymic occupational name for a maker or user of hammers, for example in a forge, or nickname for a forceful person, from Ger. *Hammer* hammer, Yid. *hamer* (MHG *hamer*, OHG *hamar* stone, hence hammer made of stone).

Vars. (of 1): Eng.: HAM, **Hamm(e)**. (Of 2): Ger.: **Hammermann**. Jewish: HAMER; **Hammerman**.

Dims. (of 2): Ger.: **Hammerl**, **Hämmerle**.

Cpds (of 2): Jewish (Ashkenazic): **Hammerschlag** ('hammer blow'); **Ham(m)erschmidt** ('hammer smith'). Swed. (ornamental): **Hammarbäck** ('hammer stream'); **Hammarberg** ('hammer hill'); **Hammargren** ('hammer branch'); **Hammarlund** ('hammer grove'); **Hammarskjöld** ('hammer shield'); **Hammarstedt** ('hammer homestead'); **Hammarstrand** ('hammer shore'); **Hammarström** ('hammer river').

Hammerstein German and Jewish (Ashkenazic): habitation name from any of various places so called from OHG *hamar* rock, crag (cf. HAMER 1) + *stein* STONE. The Jewish surname is associated in particular with a town formerly in E Prussia (now Czarne in Poland), which once had a large Jewish population.

Var.: Jewish: **Hammerstone** (Anglicized by folk etymology, as if the first element meant 'hammer' rather than 'crag').

Hammerton English: habitation name from any of several places in W Yorks., now *Hamerton* or *Hammerton*, so called from OE *hamor* rock, crag (see HAMER 1) + *tūn* enclosure, settlement.

Hammond English: **1.** from the Norman personal name *Hamo(n)* (from Gmc *Haimo*, a short form of the various cpd names with the first element *haim* home), with excrescent *-d*. **2.** from the ON personal name *Hámundr*, composed of the elements *há* high + *mund* protection. **3.** from the ON personal name *Ámundr*, composed of the elements *á* great-grandfather, ancestor + *mund* protection. This name seems to have been less common than *Hámundr*, and was widely confused with it.

Vars. (of 1): **Ham(m)on**, **Ha(i)me**. (Of 2): **Oman**, **Omond**. Ger.: **Haym**, **Heim**, **Heym**. It.: **Aimo(ni)**.

Dims. (of 1): Eng.: **Hamnet(t)**, HAMLETT, HAMBLY. Fr.: **Hamonet**, **Monet**, **Hamoneau**, **Hémon(n)ot**; **Hamonic**, **Aymonic**, **Mounic** (Brittany). It.: **Aim(on)ino**, **Aimetti**.

Patrs. (from 1): Eng.: **Ham(p)son**; **Ha(i)mes**, **Haymes**. Bret.: **Abhamon**. (From 3): Dan., Norw.: **Amundsen**.

Hampden English: habitation name from a place in Bucks., so called from OE *hamm* water meadow + *denu* valley.

Hampe German: from the MHG personal name *Hampo*, a short form of the cpd name *Hamprecht*, OHG *Hagenberht*, composed of the elements *hagano* hawthorn (cf. HAIN 2) + *berht* bright, famous.

Vars.: **Hempe**, **Hamprecht**, **Hemprecht**, **Hemprich**.

Dims.: **Hamp(e)l**, **Hemp(e)l**.

Hampshire English: **1.** regional name from the S English county, which derives its name from HAMPTON (i.e. the port of Southampton) + OE *scīr* division, district. **2.** regional name from the area of *Hallamshire* in S Yorks., so called from HALLAM + ME *schir* division, administrative region (OE *scīr*). The surname is most common in Yorks., where this second derivation is most likely to be the source.

Vars.: **Hamsher(e)**, **Hamshar**, **Ham(p)shaw**. (Of 2 only): **Halmshaw**.

Hampton English: habitation name from any of the numerous places so called, in all parts of England, including the cities of *Southampton* and *Northampton*. They all share the final OE element *tūn* enclosure, settlement, but the first is variously *hām* homestead, *hamm* water meadow, or *hēan*, weak dat. case, originally used after a preposition and article, of *hēah* high. It is generally impossible to distinguish between these possibilities in individual cases.

Hanauer German and Jewish (Ashkenazic): habitation name from the town of *Hanau* in Hesse, so called from OHG *hano* cock + *ouwa* low-lying land, island.

Var.: Jewish: **Hanau**.

Hanbury English: habitation name from *Hanbury* in Staffs. or Worcs., which get their name from the OE phrase *æt ðǣm hēan byrg* 'at the high fortress'. In some cases it may also be from *Handborough* in Oxon., which is apparently so called from the OE byname *Hagena* 'Hawthorn' (cf. HAIN 2) + OE *beorg* hill.

Vars.: **Handbury**, **Hambury**, **Hamburgh**.

Hance 1. English: patr. from HANN. **2.** English: from a pl. form of HAND 1. **3.** Scots: from a contracted form of ANGUS.

Hancell *see* ANSELL

Hancock English: from a dim. of the ME given name HANN, with the hypocoristic suffix *-cock* (see COCK), which was commonly added to given names. This surname is also borne by Gypsies in Britain.

Var.: **Handcock**.

Patrs.: **Han(d)cocks**, **Hancox**.

Hańczak *see* HANS

Hand 1. English and German: nickname for someone with a deformed hand or who had lost one hand, from ME, OE *hand*, Ger. *Hand* (MHG, OHG *hant*), found in such appellations as *Liebhard mit der Hand* (Augsburg 1383). Cf. FINGER, FOOT, etc. **2.** Irish: Anglicized form of Gael. Ó *Flaithimh*; see GUTHRIE. This Anglicized form is the result of an erroneous association of the Gael. name with *lámh* hand; cf. LAVIN.

Vars. (of 1): Eng.: **Hands** (chiefly W Midlands), HANCE.

Händel *see* HANS

Handford English: habitation name from any of various places, such as *Hanford* in Staffs. and *Handforth* in Ches., so called from OE *hana* cock (cf. HAHN 1), perhaps used as a byname + OE *ford* FORD. See also HANSFORD.

Vars.: **Han(na)ford**, **Han(d)forth**, **Hanfirth**.

Handler German and Jewish (Ashkenazic): occupational name for a merchant or dealer, Ger. *Händler*, an agent deriv. of MHG *handeln* to deal, trade (OHG *hantalōn* to undertake, manage, a deriv. of *hant* HAND).

Vars.: Jewish: **Handeles** (from Pol. *handeles* rag-and-bone man, street buyer of used clothes); **Handel(s)man**; **Gandler**, **Gendler(man)**, **Gandelman**, **Gendel(s)man**, **Gandelis** (under Russ. influence; see GOREN); **Andel(s)man** (in regions where Yid. has no/h/); **Hendel(man)**; **Hendlerski**, **Hendlersky**.

Handley 1. English: habitation name from any of various places, such as *Handley* in Ches., Derbys., and Dorset and *Hanley* in Staffs. and Worcs., so called from the weak dat. case (originally used after a preposition and article) of OE *hēah* high + OE *lēah* wood, clearing. **2.** Irish: Anglicized form of Gael. Ó *hÁinle* 'descendant of *Áinle*', a personal name meaning 'Champion'.

Vars.: **Hanl(e)y**. (Of 2 only): **O'Hanl(e)y**, **O'Hanlee**.

Handrek *see* ANDREW

Handschuh German and Jewish (Ashkenazic): metonymic occupational name for a glover, from Ger. *Handschuh* glove (MHG *hantschuoch*), a cpd of *hant* HAND) + *schuoch* shoe, covering (OHG *scuoh*).

Vars.: **Handschu**. Ger. only: **Hanschuch**, **Hendeschuh**.

Dim.: Ger.: **Handschiegl**.

Handy English: of uncertain origin, perhaps a nickname meaning 'skilful with one's hands', although the vocab. word in this sense is not recorded until the 16th cent. It may alternatively be a var. of HENDY.

Handyside Scots: habitation name from a place in the former county of Berwicks (now part of Borders region), so called from ME *hanging* + *side*, i.e. probably a natural shelf on a hillside, but just possibly a place where executions were carried out.

Var.: **Handasyde**.

Hanes *see* HAINES

Hanham English: habitation name from a place in Gloucs., so called from OE *hānum*, dat. pl. of *hān* rock.

Haning *see* HENNING

Hankin 1. English (chiefly Lancs.): from the ME given name *Hankin*, a dim. of HANN, with the addition of the hypocoristic suffix *-kin*, of Low Ger. origin. **2.** Jewish (E Ashkenazic): metr. from *Khanke* (a pet form of the Yid. female given name *Khane*; see HANNA) + *-in* Slavic possessive suffix.

Var. (of 1): **Hanking**.

Patrs. (from 1): **Hankins(on)**.

Hanks English (Gloucs.): patr. from the ME given name *Hank*, a back formation from HANKIN (with the suffix taken to be *-in*, of OF origin).

Hanlon Irish: Anglicized form of Gael. Ó *hAnluain* 'descendant of *Anluan*', a personal name from the intensive prefix *an-* + *luan* light, radiance, or warrior.

Vars.: **O'Hanlon**, **O'Hanlo(w)ne**, **(O')Handlon**, **Hanlan**.

Hanmer Welsh: habitation name from a place in the former county of Flints. (now part of Clwyd), so called from the Gmc personal name *Hagena* borrowed into OE + *mere* lake, pond.

Hann English: from the medieval given name *Han(n)*, which is usually a short form of *Johan* (see JOHN). In some cases, however, it may be from HENRY and even RANDOLPH (for the replacement of *R-* by *H-* in Gmc names introduced by the Normans, cf. HODGE from ROGER and HOBB from ROBERT).

Dims.: HANKIN, HANCOCK.

Patrs.: HANCE; **Hanson** (chiefly Midlands and N England), **Hansom**.

Hanna 1. English: from the medieval female given name *Hannah* or *Anna* (from Hebr. *Chana* 'He (God) has favoured me (i.e. with a child)'). The name is borne in the Bible by the mother of Samuel (1 Sam. 1: 1–28), and there is a tradition (unsupported by biblical evidence) that it was the name of the mother of the Virgin Mary; this St Anne was a popular figure in the Middle Ages (cf. JOACHIM). **2.** Scots: habitation name from an unidentified place; see below. **3.** Irish: Anglicized form of Gael. Ó *hAnnaigh* 'descendant of *Annach*', a byname meaning 'Iniquity'.

Vars.: **Hannah**. (Of 2 only): **Hannay**.

Dims. (of 1): Jewish (Ashkenazic): **Khan(in)ke**, **Khanele**. (Of 2): **Hann(ig)an**, **(O')Hannon**, **Hanneen** (Gael. Ó *hAnn(ag)áin*).

Metrs. (from 1): Jewish: **Han(e)son**, **Hanis**; **Hanin**, **Chanin** (E Ashkenazic).

Metrs. (from dims. of 1): Jewish: **Hankes**, HANKIN, **Chankin**, **Haninkes**, **Chanlewicz**, **Chaneles** (all E Ashkenazic except the last; the underlying dim. female given names are respectively *Khanke*, *Khaninke*, and *Khanele*).

Hänniger *see* HENRY

Hänninen Finnish: apparently an ornamental name from Finn. *hännys* tail, with the addition of the gen. suffix *-nen*.

Hannington English: habitation name from a place in Wilts., recorded in Domesday Book as *Hanindone*, apparently from the gen. case of the OE byname *Hana* 'Cock' (or the gen. pl., *hanena*, of the vocab. word; cf. HAHN 2) + OE *dūn* hill (see DOWN 1).

Hannover German and Jewish (Ashkenazic): habitation name from the city of *Hannover* in Lower Saxony, whose name is first recorded in the form *Honovere* and is probably composed of a Gmc element *hon*, perhaps meaning 'marsh' and akin to OE *hamm* (see HAMMER 1), + MLG *ōver* bank, shore.

Vars.: Ger.: **Hanover**. Jewish: **Hanower**.

Hanochov see ENOCK

Hanrahan Irish: Anglicized form of Gael. Ó hAnradháin 'descendant of *Anradhán*', a personal name from a dim. of *ánrad(h)* hero, warrior, champion, a title denoting the nobleman next in rank to the king in medieval Ireland. The title was also used to denote court poets of the second rank.

Vars.: **O'Hanrahan**, **O'Harragan**, **O'Horogan**, **O'Hor(i)gan**, **O'Howrane**, **(O')Hourihan**, **(O')Hourigan**, **Hourihan(e)**, **Horrigan**, HORGAN, **Horkan**, HORAN, **Haran**, **Hawrane**.

Hanratty Irish: Anglicized form of Gael. Ó hInreachtaigh 'descendant of the lawyer'; see ENRIGHT.

Hanry see HENRY

Hans German: from a medieval given name, an aphetic form of *Johannes*; see JOHN. The surname is also borne by Ashkenazic Jews, presumably as an adoption of the Ger. surname. Aphetic forms of this name are also found in Slav. languages, and for convenience these are listed here as cogns.

Vars.: **Hanse**; **Honse** (Bavaria). Ger. (of Slav. origin): **Han(n)usch**, **Hanich**, **Han(t)sch**, **Hänisch**, **Haensch**, **Hasch(e)**, HACHE.

Dims.: Ger.: **Hans(e)l**, **Hänsel(in)**, **Hensel**, **Hensolt**; **Ha(h)nel(t)**, **Hand(e)l**, **Händel**, **Hendel**, **Henle**; **Hansi**, **Hänggi**, **Henggi** (Switzerland). Jewish: **Hansel**, **Hendl**. Low Ger.: **Hans(e)mann**, **Han(ne)mann**, **Hahnemann**, **Hens(e)mann**; **Hemmann**; **Hahn(e)(c)ke**, **Hanne(ke)**, **Henne**, **Henne(c)ke**; **Hensgen**. Fris.: **Hannema**. Ger. (of Slav. origin): **Hansli(c)k**, **Hanik**, **Han(n)uschik**, **Han(t)schke**, **Haschke**, **Haschke**. Czech: **Hanousek**; **Hanz(e)l**, **Hanzal**, **Hanzlík**, **Hanzálek**; **Hánek**. Pol.: **Hanke**.

Patrs.: Low Ger.: **Hannessen**, **Han(s)sen**, **Hen(ne)ssen**; **Hansing**, **Hensing**. Flem., Du.: **Hansen**, **Hensen**, **Haesen**. Dan., Norw.: **Han(s)sen**. Swed.: **Hansson**. Pol.: **Hańczak**.

Patrs. (from dims.): Low Ger.: **Hanneken**. Ger. (of Slav. origin): **Henschler**, **Hachner**. Pol.: **Han(usz)kiewicz**.

Hansard English: metonymic occupational name for a cutler, from OF *hansard*, *hansart* cutlass, dagger (of Gmc origin, composed of elements meaning 'hand' (see HAND 1) and 'knife' (see SACHS)).

Hansel see ANSELL, HANS

Hansford English: habitation name from an unidentified place, perhaps *Ansford* in Somerset, which is recorded in Domesday Book as *Almundsford*, from the gen. case of the OE personal name *Ealhmund* (composed of the elements *ealh* temple + *mund* protection) + OE *ford* FORD.

Var.: **Handsford**.

Hanvey Irish: Anglicized form of Gael. Ó hAinbhith 'descendant of *Ainbhtheach*', a byname meaning 'Stormy'.

Hapke see HABBERT

Happs see APPS

Hapsburg see HABSBURG

Haquin see ISAAC

Haran see HANRAHAN

Harbard see HERBERT

Harbaud see HERBAUD

Harber English: metonymic occupational name for a keeper of a lodging house, from late OE *herebeorg* shelter, lodging (from *here* army + *beorg* shelter). For the change of -*er*- to -*ar*- in the first syllable, cf. MARCHANT.

Vars.: **Harbo(u)r**, **Arber**, **Harberer**; **Harbage**, **Herbage**, **Harbidge**, **Harbisher**.

Harborne English (W Midlands): habitation name from a place in Birmingham, so called from OE *horu* dirt + *burna* stream (see BOURNE).

Var.: **Harbron** (Northumb.).

Harbottle English (Northumb.): habitation name from a place in the foothills of the Cheviots, so called from OE *hȳra* hireling (a deriv. of *hȳr* wages, reward) + *bōtl* dwelling. For the development of OE -*y*- in the first syllable to -*e*-, cf. HILL; for the subsequent change of -*er*- to -*ar*-, cf. MARCHANT.

Harcourt 1. English (Norman) and French: habitation name from places in Eure and Calvados, so called from OF *cour(t)* COURT with an obscure first element. 2. English: habitation name from either of two places in Shrops. The one near Cleobury Mortimer gets the name from OE *heafocere* HAWKER + *cot* hut, cottage (see COATES); the one near Wem has as its first element OE *hearpere* HARPER.

Harcus see HERKES

Hard English: 1. from the OE personal name *Heard* or a Norman cogn. *Hard(on)*, both of which are of Gmc origin. This was normally an independent byname meaning 'Hardy', 'Brave', 'Strong', but it also seems to have been a short form of the various cpd names containing this as a first element. 2. nickname for a stern or severe man, from ME *hard* hard, inflexible. 3. topographic name for someone who lived on a patch of particularly hard ground or one that was difficult to farm. This origin is supported by forms with the preposition *de* and article *le*, for example Gilbert *del Hard* (Lincs. 1232); see also HARDAKER.

Var. (of 3): **Harder**.

Dims. (of 1): Eng.: **Harkin**. Ger.: **Härtel**, **Hertel**, **Här(d)tle**, **Hertlein**; **Hörtle** (Bavaria); HERZ; **Hartisch** (E Germany).

Patrs. (from 1): HARDS; HARDING.

Patrs. (from 1) (dims.): Eng.: **Harkins**, **Harkiss**; **Harkess** (Scots).

Hardaker English (Yorks.): topographic name for someone who lived on a patch of poor, stony land, from ME *hard* hard, difficult + *aker* cultivated land (see ACKER), or habitation name from a minor place in Clapham, W Yorks., called *Hardacre*, which has this etymology.

Var.: **Hardacre** (Lancs.).

Hardcastle English (Yorks.): habitation name from a place in Yorks., so named from ME *hard* difficult, inaccessible, impregnable, or perhaps cheerless + *castel* castle, fortress, stronghold (see CASTLE).

Harden English: habitation name from *Harden* in W Yorks., which get its name from OE *hara* HARE + *denu* valley (see DEAN 1). Harden in Staffs., which originally had the same name as *Hawarden* in Clwyd (from OE *hēah* high + *worðign* enclosure) was probably not reduced to its modern form early enough to lie behind any examples of the surname.

Hardenberg German and Dutch: habitation name from any of various places, esp. one near Göttingen, so called from the weak dat. case (originally used after a preposition and article) of MLG *hard* difficult, inaccessible, impregnable + *berg* hill.

Hardiman 1. English: nickname for a brave or foolhardy man, from ME *hardi* HARDY + *man* man. **2.** Irish: Anglicized form of Gael. **Ó hArgadáin** 'descendant of *Argadán*', a personal name from a dim. of *argad* silver.
Var.: **Hardeman**. See also HARDMAN.

Hardin 1. French: cogn. of HARDING. **2.** Jewish: of unknown origin.

Harding English: from the OE personal name *Hearding*, formally a patr. from HARD 1.
Var.: **Arding**.

Hardisty English: habitation name from a place in Yorks., in the parish of Fewston. The placename is recorded in 1379 as *Hardolfsty*, from the OE personal name *Heardwulf* (composed of the elements *heard* hardy, brave, strong + *wulf* wolf) + OE *stīg* path.
Var.: **Hardesty**.

Hardman English (chiefly Lancs.): **1.** occupational name for a herdsman, a var. of *Herdman*; see HEARD. For the change of -er- to -ar-, cf. MARCHANT. **2.** from the OE personal name *Heardmann*, composed of the elements *heard* hardy, brave, strong + *mann* man.

Hardoin see ARDOUIN

Hards English: **1.** patr. from HARD 1. **2.** habitation name from a place in Kent, near Canterbury, called *Hardres* (pronounced /hɑ:dz/), from a ME pl. form of OE **harað* wood (a cogn. of HARDT 1).
Vars.: **Hardes(s)**. (Of 2 only): **Hardres(s)**.

Hardstaff English (Notts.): of uncertain origin, possibly an obscene nickname for a man with a more or less permanent erection, from ME *hard* hard, firm + *staf* wooden pole, rod (OE *stæf*). Alternatively, it may be a habitation name from *Hardstoft* in Derbys., so called from the gen. case of the OE byname *Heorot* HART' + OE *toft* site, plot.

Hardt 1. German: topographic name for someone who lived by a range of wooded hills or by a drovers' road for cattle, both of which are meanings of MHG *hart* (OHG *hard*). **2.** Low German: cogn. of HEARD. **3.** Jewish (Ashkenazic): of unknown origin.
Vars. (of 1): **Har(t)z(er)**, **Harzmann**; **Hort(er)** (S Germany, Austria).

Hardwick English: habitation name from any of various places, for example in Bucks., Cambs., Norfolk, Northants, Worcs., and W Yorks., so called from OE *heorde* herd, flock + *wīc* outlying farm (see WICK).
Vars.: **Hardwicke**, **Herdwick**.

Hardy English and French: nickname for a brave or foolhardy man, from OF, ME *hardi* bold, courageous (of Gmc origin; cf. HARD 1). The surname is also borne by Jews, but the reasons for its adoption are unknown.
Vars.: Eng.: **Hardey**; **Hardie** (Scotland). Fr.: **Hardi**.
Dim.: Fr.: **Hardion**.

Hare 1. English: nickname for a swift runner or a timorous person, from ME *hare* hare (OE *hara*). **2.** Irish: Anglicized form of **Ó hAichir** 'descendant of *Aichear*', a personal name apparently derived from *aichear* fierce, sharp. See also O'HARA.
Vars. (of 2): **Hair** (Scotland), **Haire** (N Ireland); **O'Ha(i)re**, **O'Hagher**, **O'Hahir**, **O'Heare**, **(O')Hehir**.

Harel 1. French: nickname for a boisterous or quarrelsome individual, from OF *harel* tumult, hue and cry (of Gmc origin, apparently an imitative formation). **2.** Jewish (Israeli): ornamental surname from Hebr. *harel*, which is of disputed origin: it is either a cpd of *har* mountain + *el* God or a var. of *ariel*, which is a cpd of *ari* lion + *el* God. Harel is an epithet for the altar in the ancient Jewish temple in Jerusalem and, in mod. Hebrew, for Mount Sinai. Ariel is an epithet for Jerusalem and for the altar in the ancient Jewish temple.
Vars. (of 2): **Harell**, **Har-El**; **Hareli**, **Harely** (with Hebr. suffix -*i*).

Harenc see HERRING

Harford English: habitation name from places in Gloucs. and Devon. The former gets its name from OE *heorot* HART + *ford* FORD, the latter has as its first element OE *here* army.

Hargent see ARGENT

Hargreaves English (Yorks. and Lancs.): habitation name from any of various places, for example in Ches., Northants, and Suffolk, called *Hargr(e)ave*, from OE *hār* grey (see HOARE 1) or *hara* HARE + *grāf* GROVE or *græfe* thicket. An additional source may be a piece of land in the parish of Standen, near Whalley, Lancs., recorded in 1323 as *Hargreves*.
Vars.: **Hargreves**, **Hargreave**, **Hargrave(s)**, **Hargrove(s)**.

Hariot see HENRY

Harju Finnish: ornamental or topographic name from Finn. *harju* ridge, one of the numerous names adopted from the vocab. of the natural landscape in the 19th cent.

Harker English (Northumb.): **1.** habitation name from either of two places in Cumb., or from one in the parish of Halsall, near Ormskirk, Lancs. The places in Cumb. are probably named from ME *hart* male deer (see HART 1) + *kerr* marshland (see CARR). The first element of the one in Lancs. is probably OE *hār* grey (see HOARE 1) or *hara* HARE. **2.** nickname for an eavesdropper or busybody, from an agent deriv. of ME *herkien* to listen (OE **he(o)rcian*).

Harkness Scots: apparently a habitation name from an unidentified place, probably so called from the OE personal name *Hereca* (a deriv. of the various cpd names with the first element *here* army) + OE *næss* headland, cape.

Harland English: habitation name from any of various minor places (including perhaps some now lost) named from OE *hār* grey (see HOARE 1) or *hara* HARE + *land* land, patch of country. The surname is largely concentrated around Middlesbrough.

Var. (U.S.): **Harlan**.

Harle English: **1.** habitation name from a place in Northumb., of whose name the second element is OE *lēah* wood, clearing. The first element may perhaps be an OE personal name *Herela*, a deriv. of the various cpd names with the first element *here* army. **2.** var. of EARL.

Härle see HAAR

Harley English: habitation name from places in Shrops. and W Yorks., so called from OE *hær* rock, heap of stones or *hara* HARE + *lēah* wood, clearing.

Harling English: from a Norman personal name, *Herluin* or *Arluin*, composed of the Gmc elements *erl* warrior + *wine* friend.

Vars.: **Harlin**; **Arling**; **Hurlin(g)**, **Hurlen**; **Urlin(g)**, **Urlwin**.

Harlock see HORLOCK

Harlow English: habitation name from any of various places so called. One in W Yorks. probably gets its name from OE *hær* rock, heap of stones + *hlāw* hill (see LAW 2 and LOW 1); those in Essex and Northumb. have *here* army as the first element, perhaps in the sense 'host', 'assembly'.

Harm see HERMANN

Harmel see HERMELIN

Harmer English: from the ME given name *Heremer*, OE *Heremær*, composed of the elements *here* army + *mær* fame.

Vars.: **Harmar**, **Hermer**.

Harmgardt see ERMGARD

Harmsworth English: habitation name from *Harmondsworth*, to the west of London, so called from the gen. case of the OE personal name *Heremund* (composed of the elements *here* army + *mund* protection) + OE *worð* enclosure (see WORTH).

Harn see HEARN

Harnett see ARNOLD

Harney Irish: Anglicized form of Gael. **Ó hAthairne** 'descendant of *Athairne*', a personal name derived from *aithirne* calf, which was borne by a famous OIr. satirist.

Haro Spanish: habitation name from a place in the province of Logroño, so called from a N Castilian form of Sp. *faro* beacon; cf. FARO and ALFARO.

Harofe see ROFÉ

Har-Paz see PAZ

Harper English and Scots: occupational name for a player on the harp, from an agent deriv. of ME *harp* harp (OE *hearp*). The harper was one of the most important figures of a medieval baronial hall, especially in Scotland and N England, and the office of harper was sometimes hereditary. See also CROWTHER.

Vars.: **Harpour** (with the OF agent suffix *-our*); **Harpur** (chiefly N Ireland); **Harp**.

Harpham English: habitation name from a place in Humberside near Bridlington, so called from OE *hearp* harp (possibly denoting a place where the harp was played, or else from the device called a 'harp', and shaped like one, which was used for purifying sea salt) + *hām* homestead.

Harradine English: habitation name from places in Beds. and Northants called *Harrowden*, from OE *h(e)arg* (pagan) temple (see HARROW) + *dūn* hill (see DOWN 1).

Vars.: **Harraden**, **Harridine**.

Harran see HERON

Harriman English: occupational name for a servant (see MANN) of someone who bore the given name HARRY.

Harrington **1.** English: habitation name from places in Cumb., Lincs., and Northants. The first gets its name from OE *Hæferingtūn* 'settlement (OE *tūn*) associated with *Hæfer*', a byname meaning 'He-goat'; the second may have meant 'settlement on stony ground', from OE *hær* + the suffix *-ing*; the third may contain a word meaning 'heath'. **2.** Irish: Anglicized form of Gael. **Ó hArrachtáin** 'descendant of *Arrachtán*', a personal name from a dim. of *arrachtach* mighty, powerful. See also HERAGHTY.

Vars. (of 1): **Harington**. (Of 2): **O'Haraghtane**, **O'Harrighton**, **O'Herraghton**, **Haroughton**, **Harraughton**.

Harriot see HERRIOT

Harris **1.** English: patr. from the medieval given name HARRY. **2.** Jewish: assumed as an Anglicized form of various like-sounding Jewish names.

Vars.: **Harrison**. (Of 1 only): **Harries** (chiefly Wales).

Harrismith see ARROWSMITH

Harrod English: **1.** from the OE personal name *Hereweald*, its ON cogn. *Haraldr*, or the Continental form *Herold* introduced to Britain by the Normans. These all go back to a Gmc personal name composed of the elements *heri*, *hari* army + *wald* rule, which is attested in Europe from an early date; the Roman historian Tacitus records a certain *Cariovalda*, chief of the Gmc tribe of the Batavi, as early as the 1st cent. AD. **2.** occupational name for a herald, ME *herau(l)d* (OF *herau(l)t*, from a Gmc cpd of the same elements as above, used as a common noun). For the change of *-er-* to *-ar-*, cf. MARCHANT. **3.** var. of HARWOOD. **4.** var. of HERROD 1.

Vars. (of 1 and 2): **Harrold** (W Midlands), **Harroll**; **Har(r)ald**, **Harral(t)**, **Harrel(l)**; **Her(r)ald**, **Her(r)old**, **Herauld**.

Prov.: **Heral**.

Dim. (of 2): Fr.: **Héraudet**.

Patrs. (from 1): Ger.: **Herholz**; **Hörholz** (Bavaria). Swed.: **Haraldsson**. It.: **Da Rold**, **Da Rolt** (misdivided for *D'Arold*).

Harrop English: habitation name from any of several places in W Yorks., or from one in Ches., all of which are so called from OE *hara* HARE + *hop* valley (see HOPE).
Vars.: **Harrap**, **Harrup**.

Harrow 1. English: habitation name from the place in NW London, which derives its name (*Herges* in Domesday Book) from OE *h(e)arg* (pagan) temple. 2. Scots: from various minor places of the same name and etymology.

Harrower Scots and English: occupational name for someone who harrowed cultivated land (perhaps someone who did this as a feudal service on manorial land), from an agent deriv. of ME *harwen* to rake (of Scandinavian origin).
Vars.: **Harrowar**, **Harroway**.

Harry English (chiefly Devon and Cornwall): from the medieval given name *Harry*, which was the usual vernacular form of HENRY, with assimilation of the consonantal cluster and regular change of *-er-* to *-ar-* (cf. MARCHANT).

Harsch 1. German: nickname for a stern or severe man, from Ger. *harsch* harsh, stern (MLG *harsch*, from *harsten* to grow hard, firm; cf. HARD). 2. German: occupational name for a soldier, from MHG *harsch*, *harst* body of troops. 3. Jewish (Ashkenazic): var. of HIRSCH, reflecting a central Yid. pronunciation.
Vars. (of 2): **Harscher**, **Harst(er)**.

Harschbarger *see* HIRSCHBERG

Harshkowitch *see* HIRSCH

Hart 1. English: nickname meaning 'stag', ME *hert*, OE *heorot*, used for someone bearing some fancied resemblance to the animal. The OE word became *hurt* or *hort* in some dialects of ME, esp. western dialects, and these forms are reflected in the vars., but in the standard dialect it became *hert* and later *hart*. 2. Jewish (Ashkenazic): Anglicization of one or more like-sounding Jewish surnames. 3. Irish: Anglicized form of Gael. **Ó hAirt** 'descendant of *Art*', a byname meaning 'Bear', 'Hero' (cf. ARTHUR and CARTON).
Vars. (of 1): **Heart**; **Hurt** (Notts.); **Hort**. (Of 3): **Harte**, **O'-Hart(e)**.
Dims. (of 3): **(O')Hartigan** (Gael. **Ó hArtagáin**).

Hartaud *see* ARTAUD

Hartill English (W Midlands): habitation name, probably from one of the places called *Harthill*, from OE *heorot* HART + *hyll* HILL. There are several places of this name, for example in Ches., Derbys., and W Yorks., but apparently none in the W Midlands. It is possible that the surname represents a truncated deriv. of *Hartlebury* in Worcs. This placename derives from the OE personal name *Heortla* + OE *burh* fort.
Vars.: **Hartle**, **Hartell**.

Hartland English (mainly W Midlands): apparently a habitation name from an unidentified place or region so named from OE *heorot* HART + *land* land. Hartland in Devon was originally *Heorotēg*, from OE *heorot* + *ēg* island; the element *-land* is a later addition. The Devon place is unlikely to be the source of the surname.

Hartley English: habitation name from any of various places so called. Several, in particular those in Hants,

Kent, and Devon, get their names from OE *heorot* HART + *lēah* wood, clearing. One in Northumb. has as its second element OE *hlāw* hill, and one in Cumb. contains *clā* claw, in the sense of a tongue of land between two streams, with an uncertain first element. The surname is widely distributed, but most common in Yorks.
Var.: **Hartly**.

Hartnell English (W Country): of uncertain origin, perhaps a habitation name from an unidentified place, possibly named from the gen. case of the OE byname *Heorta* (from *heor(o)t* HART') + OE *hyll* HILL or *h(e)alh* nook, recess (see HALE 1). If the source is *Hartnoll* in Marwood, Devon, the final element is OE *cnoll* hill (see KNOLL 1).

Hartnett Irish: Anglicized form of Gael. **Ó hAirtnéada** 'descendant of *Airtnéad*', a personal name of uncertain origin. The first syllable is probably from *art* bear, hero; see HART 3.

Hartogs *see* HERZOG

Hartrick *see* ARKWRIGHT

Hartshorn English: habitation name from *Hartshorne* in Derbys., so called from the gen. case of the OE byname *Heorot* HART' + OE *horn* used of a horn-shaped hill (see HORN 3).
Var.: **Hartshorne**.

Hartwell English: habitation name from any of the various places, for example in Bucks., Northants, and Staffs., so called from OE *heorot* HART + *well(a)* spring, stream (see WELL).

Hartwig German: from a Gmc personal name composed of the elements *hard* hardy, brave, strong + *wīg* war.
Vars.: **Härtwig**, **Hertwig**; **Hartig**; **Hattwig**, **Hattwich**.
Patrs.: Ger.: **Hartwiger**. Low Ger.: **Hartwigsen**. Dan.: **Hartvigsen**.

Harty Irish: Anglicized form of Gael. **Ó hA(tha)rtaigh** 'descendant of *Faghartach*', a byname for a noisy person.
Var.: **Hearty**.

Harvánek *see* RAVEN

Harvard English: from the OE personal name *Hereweard*, composed of the elements *here* army + *weard* guard, which was borne by an 11th-cent. thane of Lincs., leader of resistance to the advancing Normans. The ON cogn. *Hervarðr* was also common and, particularly in the Danelaw, it may in part lie behind the surname.
Vars.: **Harward**, **Hereward**.

Harvey 1. English and Scots: from the Bret. personal name *Aeruiu* or *Haerviu*, composed of the elements *haer* battle, carnage + *vy* worthy, which was introduced into England by Bret. followers of William the Conqueror, for the most part in the Gallicized form *Hervé*. The surname is most common in Staffs., Cornwall and S Devon, and E Anglia. For the change of *-er-* to *-ar-*, cf. MARCHANT. 2. Irish: Anglicized form of Gael. **Ó hAirmheadhaigh** 'descendant of *Airmheadhach*', a personal name of uncertain origin. It seems to be a deriv. of *Airmheadh*, the name borne by a mythological physician.

Vars. (of 1): **Harvie** (Scots); **Hervey**; **Herve** (Jersey).

Dims. (of 1): Fr.: **Herv(ou)et**, **Hervochon**.

Patr. (from 1): Bret.: **Abhervé**.

Harwood English and Scots: habitation name from any of various places, for example in the Scottish Borders and in Lancs., Lothian, Northumb., and N Yorks., so called from OE *hār* grey (see HOARE 1) or *hara* HARE + *wudu* WOOD; cf. HARGREAVES and HARLEY.

Vars.: **Harewood** (places in Hants, Herefords., and W Yorks.); HARROD.

Harzbach see HERZ

Hasard English and French: nickname for an inveterate gambler or a brave or foolhardy man prepared to run risks, from ME, OF *hasard* game of chance, later used metaphorically of other uncertain enterprises. The word derives from Arabic *az-zahr*, from *az*, assimilated form of the def. art. *al* + *zahr* die. It appears to have been picked up and brought back to Europe by Provençal crusaders.

Vars.: Eng.: **Haz(z)ard**; **Hassard** (N Ireland); **Hassett** (Ireland); **Assard**. Fr.: **Hazard**, **Hazart**.

Hasch see HANS

Hašek Czech: 1. from a dim. given name, a shortened form of *Haštal* (L *Castulus*, from *castus* pure, chaste) with the dim. suffix -*ek*. 2. altered dim. of the given *Havel* (see GALL 2).

Vars.: **Haš**, **Háša**.

Hasel see HAZEL

Haselden see HAZELDEN

Haselton see HAZELTON

Haselup see HESLOP

Haselwood see HAZELWOOD

Haskel see ASHKETTLE, EZEKIEL

Haskew see ASKEW

Haslam English: topographic name for someone who lived 'by the hazels', or habitation name from *Haslam* in Lancs., in both cases from OE *hæslum*, dat. pl. of *hæsel* HAZEL.

Vars.: **Haslum**, **Haslem**, **Haslen**, **Hesl(eh)am**; **Aslam**, **Aslum**, **Aslen**.

Haslett see HAZLETT

Hasling English: topographic name for someone who lived by a hazel copse, OE **hæsling* (a deriv. of *hæsel* HAZEL; see also HAZLETT).

Vars.: **Haslin**, **Heslin(g)**, **Hessling**.

Haspineall see ASPINALL

Hass 1. German: from a pet form, *Hasso*, of the Gmc personal name *Hadubert* (see HABBERT), or of some other personal name containing *hadu* battle, strife as the first element. 2. German: nickname for a bitter and vicious man, from Ger. *Hass* hatred (MHG, OHG *haz*). 3. Jewish (Ashkenazic): of uncertain origin, perhaps from Ger. *Hass*

hatred, imposed by a non-Jewish government official in central Europe at the time when surnames hbecame obligatory.

Var. (of 1): **Hasse**.

Hassall English: habitation name from a place in Ches., so called from the gen. case of the OE byname *Hætt* 'Hat' (or possibly from the OE vocab. word *hætse* witch) + OE *halh* nook, recess (see HALE 1).

Var.: **Hassell**.

Hasson 1. Scots and N Irish: assimilated form of a patr. from the medieval given name *Hal*, a pet form of HARRY. 2. Jewish (Sefardic): of unknown origin.

Var. (of 2): **Hason**.

Hastings English: 1. habitation name from the place in Sussex, near which the English failed to repel the Norman invasion. It is so called from OE *Hæstingas* 'people of *Hæsta*', a byname from *hæst* violence, fury. 2. patr. from the comparatively rare Norman personal name *Hasten(c)*, *Hastang*. This appears to be of ON origin, composed of the elements *há* high + *steinn* stone.

Vars. (of 2): **Hasting**, **Hastain**.

Hasty English: nickname for a brisk or impetuous person, from ME, OF *hasti* quick (a deriv. of OF *haste* swiftness, of Gmc origin; cf. HASTINGS 1).

Var.: **Hastie** (Scotland).

Haswell English (chiefly Northumb.): habitation name from *Haswell* in Co. Durham (or possibly from one elsewhere), so called from OE *hæsel* HAZEL + *well(a)* spring, stream (see WELL).

Hatch English: topographic name for someone who lived by a gate, OE *hæcce* (normally a gate marking the entrance to a forest or other enclosed piece of land, sometimes a floodgate or sluice-gate), or habitation name from one of the many places named with this word.

Var.: **Hatcher**.

Hatchard see ACHARD

Hatfield English: habitation name from any of the various places, for example in Essex, Herts., Notts., Herefords., Worcs., and E and W Yorks., so called from OE *hǽð* heathland, heather (see HEATH) + *feld* pasture, open country (see FIELD).

Vars.: **Hatfeild**, **Hatful(l)**; **Hadfield** (a place in Derbys.); HEATHFIELD.

Hathaway English: 1. topographic name for someone who lived by a path across a heath, from ME *hath* heath (OE *hǽð*) + *way* way (OE *weg*). 2. from an (apparently rare) OE female personal name, *Heaðuwíg*, composed of the elements *heaðu* strife, contention + *wíg* war, which has Continental cogns. such as Ger. *Hedwig* (OHG *Haduwig*). A St Hedwig lived in the 12th–13th cents.; she was the wife of Henry the Bearded, Duke of Silesia, and founded numerous charitable institutions as well as increasing German influence in Silesia.

Vars.: **Hathway**, **Hadaway**.

Metrs. (from 2) (dims.): Ger.: **Hädscher**. Low Ger.: **Heeschen**.

Hatherell English: probably a habitation name from an unidentified place, possibly so called from OE *hægborn* HAWTHORN + *hyll* HILL.
Vars.: **Hatherill**, **Hatherall**; **Haddrell**, **Had(d)rill**.

Hatherley English (Devon): habitation name from *Hatherleigh* in Devon, or possibly *Hatherley* in Gloucs., both of which get their names from OE *hægborn* HAWTHORN + *lēah* wood, clearing.

Hathorne *see* HAWTHORN

Hatje *see* HABBERT

Hatley English: habitation name from any of a group of places in Beds. and Cambs., so called from OE *hætt* hat (see HATT), probably the name of a hill + OE *lēah* wood, clearing.
Var.: **Hateley**.

Hatry *see* DALTRY

Hatt English: metonymic occupational name for a hatter or nickname for someone noted for the hat or hats that he wore. The bynames *Hætt* and *Hætta* occurred already in the OE period; cf. HASSALL and HATLEY. Some early forms such as Thomas *del Hat* (Oxon. 1279) and Richard *atte Hatte* (Worcs. 1327) indicate that the word was used of a hill shaped like a hat, and in these cases the surname may be topographic in origin.
Var.: **Hatter**.

Hattersley English: habitation name from a place in Ches., of uncertain etymology, perhaps from the gen. case of OE *hēahdēor* deer, stag (a cpd of *hēah* high + *dēor* animal, deer, because the deer was the most prized of the game animals) + OE *lēah* wood, clearing.

Hatton 1. English: habitation name from any of the various places, for example in Ches., Derbys., Lincs., W London, Shrops., Staffs., and Warwicks., so called from OE *hǣð* heathland, heather (see HEATH) + *tūn* enclosure, settlement. 2. French: from the OF oblique case of the Gmc personal name *Hatto*, apparently a short form of the various cpd names with the first element *hadu* strife, contention; cf., e.g., HABBERT and HATHAWAY 2.
Var. (of 2): Fr.: **Haton**.
Dims. (of 2): Fr.: **Hatté**, **Hatin**, **Hatot**.

Hattrick *see* ARKWRIGHT

Hattwich *see* HARTWIG

Hatzkel *see* EZEKIEL

Haueis *see* EISENHAUER

Hauer German and Jewish (Ashkenazic): occupational name for a butcher, a woodcutter, or a stonemason, Ger. *Hauer (Holzhauer, Steinhauer)*, agent derivs. of *hauen* to chop, hack (MHG *houwen*, OHG *houwan*); cf. HACKER.
Var.: **Heuer**.

Hauff *see* HALE

Hauger *see* HUGH

Haughey Irish: Anglicized form of Gael. Ó **hEachaidh** 'descendant of *Eachaidh*', a byname meaning 'Horseman',

from *each* horse (see KEOGH). See also HOWEY and CAUGHEY.

Haughton English: habitation name from any of various places so called. Nearly all, including those in Ches., Co. Durham, Lancs., Northumb., Shrops., and Staffs., get the name from OE *halh* nook, recess (see HALE 1) + *tūn* enclosure, settlement; in the case of one in Notts., however, the first element is OE *hōh* spur of a hill (see HOUGHTON).

Haulbrook *see* HOLBROOK

Häupl *see* HEAD

Hauptmann 1. German: status name for a headman, leader, or captain, Ger. *Hauptmann*, from MHG *houb(e)t*, *houpt* HEAD + *man* man. This word denoted any of various civil and military officials at different times and places. The first element represents the original Gmc word for 'head', but already during the Middle Ages it was being replaced in the literal sense by KOPF, so that today it is retained only in cpds, such as this, where it has the transferred sense 'chief', 'principal'. 2. Jewish (Ashkenazic): probably a name taken by or given to a rabbi, as the head of a Jewish community.
Vars.: Ger.: **Heuptmann**, **Heiptmann**. Jewish: **Hauptman**.

Haurillon *see* FÈVRE

Haurwitz *see* HOROWITZ

Hauschild German: 1. topographic name for someone who lived in a house marked with a shield-shaped sign, from Ger. *Hausschild* house shield, from *Haus* house (MHG, OHG *hūs*) + *Schild* shield (MHG *schilt*, OHG *scilt*). 2. according to Bahlow, who quotes a line from Hans Sachs, it may also be from MHG **Houwschilt*, nickname or byname for a ferocious soldier, from MHG *houw(en)* to chop, hack (see HAUER) + *schilt* shield.
Vars.: **Hauenschild**, **Haufschild**.

Hausser *see* HOUSE

Haüy French: of uncertain origin. It is possible that it is a habitation name from *Havys* in the Ardennes, recorded in the 9th cent. as *Elaviacum*, from the Gaul. personal name *Elavus* + the local suffix *-(i)ācum*. It seems that after the loss of the initial *E-* the *l-* was taken for an elided form of the Fr. def. art. and so also dropped. The present form of the surname can be explained only as the result of a misreading of the written form of the placename.

Havekost Low German: habitation name from any of the various places, principally in Westphalia, so called from MLG *havek* HAWK + *horst* wooded hill (cf. HURST).
Vars.: **Havekoss**, **Havighorst**.

Havelock English: from the ME given name *Havelok*, from ON *Hafleikr*, composed of the elements *haf* sea + *leikr* sport, play. The name was popularized in England in the Middle Ages partly by the ME romance *Havelok the Dane*.

Haversham *see* HABERSHAM

Havet French: metonymic occupational name for someone who used a pickaxe, OF *havet*, a dim. of *hef*, of Gmc origin), or for a manufacturer of pickaxes.
Vars.: **Havot**, **Havon**.

Havken *see* KHAVKE

Havlíček *see* GALL

Havránek *see* RAVEN

Haw English: **1.** topographic name for someone who lived by an enclosure, OE *haga* (a byform of *(ge)hæg*; see HAIG and HAY 1), or habitation name from a place named with this word, such as *Haw* in Gloucs. **2.** from a ME given name, a back-formation from HAWKIN.

Var.: **Hawe**.

Patrs. (from 2): **HAWES**, **Hawson**.

Haward *see* HAYWARD, HOWARD

Hawdon English: habitation name from an unidentified minor place, probably in Northumb., apparently so called from OE *haga* enclosure (see HAW 1) + *dūn* hill (see DOWN 1).

Hawes English: **1.** patr. from HAW 2. **2.** from a Norman female personal name, *Haueis*, from Gmc *Haduwidis*, composed of the elements *hadu* strife, contention + *widi* wide.

Var.: **Hawyes**.

Hawk English (Devon): **1.** metonymic occupational name for a HAWKER or nickname for someone supposedly resembling a hawk in some way, e.g. a fierce or rapacious person or one with a large hooked nose, from ME *hau(l)k*, *haueke* hawk (OE *heafoc*). There was an OE personal name (originally a byname) *H(e)afoc* 'Hawk', which persisted into the early ME period as a given name and may therefore also be a source. **2.** topographic name for someone who lived in an isolated nook, from ME *halke*, one of the forms taken by OE *halh*; see HALE 1.

Var.: **Hawke**.

Dims. (of 1): Eng.: **Hawkett**, **Hawkitt**; **HAWKIN**.

Patr. (from 1): Eng.: **Hawkes** (or a var. of 2).

Hawker English (now found chiefly in the SW Midlands down to Somerset): occupational name for someone who bred and trained hawks, ME *haueker* (an agent deriv. of HAWK). Hawking was a major medieval sport, and the provision and training of hawks for a feudal lord was a not uncommon obligation in lieu of rent. The right of any free man to keep hawks for his own use was conceded in Magna Charta.

Hawkesford English (W Midlands): habitation name from an unidentified place, apparently named with the gen. case of the OE personal name or byname *Heafoc* 'HAWK' + OE *ford* FORD.

Hawkeswood English (W Midlands): habitation name, probably from one of the two places in Shrops. called *Hawkswood*. The one in the parish of Hordley is named with the gen. case of the OE personal name or byname *Heafoc* 'HAWK' + OE *wudu* wood; the one in the parish of Sidbury is earlier *Hokkyswode*, with a first element apparently from the gen. case of an OE personal name *Hocc*.

Hawkin English: from the ME given name *Hawkin*, a dim. of HAWK with the ANF hypocoristic suffix *-in*, or of *Hal*, a pet form of HARRY, with the originally Low Ger. suffix *-kin*.

Vars.: **HAWKING**, **Hawken**.

Patrs.: **Hawkin(g)s**, **Hawkyns**.

Hawking English: **1.** var. of HAWKIN. **2.** var. of HAWKINGE.

Hawkinge English: habitation name from a place in Kent, so called from OE *Hafocing* 'hawk place'; see HAWK 1.

Var.: **Hawking**.

Hawkley English: habitation name from a place, for example one in Hants, so called from OE *heafoc* HAWK + *lēah* wood, clearing.

Hawkshaw English (Yorks.): habitation name from a place in W Yorks., which survives as a field-name, so called from OE *heafoc* HAWK + *sceaga* wood, copse (see SHAW).

Hawksworth English (chiefly Yorks.): habitation name from a place so called in W Yorks., derived from the OE personal name *Hafoc* HAWK' + OE *worð* enclosure (see WORTH). A place similarly named in Notts. may have the same origin, but if so, the early spellings such as *Houkeswurda* must be explained by postulating Scandinavian interference (from the Anglo-Scandinavian form of the personal name, *Hauk*).

Hawley English: habitation name from any of various places so called. One in Kent is, according to Ekwall, named with OE *hālig* holy + *lēah* wood, clearing, and would therefore have once been the site of a sacred grove. One in Hants has as its first element OE *h(e)all* hall, manor (see HALL), or the homonymous *h(e)all* rock, stone (see HÄLL). However, the surname is common mainly in S Yorks. and Notts., and may derive from a lost place called *Hawley* near Sheffield, which is from ON *haugr* mound + OE *lēah* clearing.

Haworth English (Yorks. and Lancs.): **1.** habitation name from *Haworth* in W Yorks., which is so called from OE *haga* enclosure (see HAW 1; here perhaps with the sense 'hedge') + *worð* enclosure (see WORTH). **2.** var. of HOWARTH.

Hawrane *see* HANRAHAN

Hawthorn English: topographic name for someone who lived by a bush or hedge of hawthorn (OE *haguþorn*, *hægþorn*, i.e. thorn used for making hedges and enclosures; cf. HAW 1 and HAY 1), or habitation name from a place named with this word, such as *Hawthorn* in Co. Durham.

Vars.: **Ha(w)thorne** (chiefly N Ireland).

Flem.: **Van Hagendoren**. Du.: **Hagedoorn**.

Hawtin English: **1.** nickname for a proud or disdainful person, from ME, OF *hautain* haughty (a deriv. of *haut* high, lofty, L *altus*). **2.** occupational name for a servant employed in the manor of a feudal lord, from OE *h(e)all* HALL + *þegn* THANE.

Var.: **Hawtayne**.

Hawtry *see* DALTRY

Hay Scots and English: **1.** topographic name for someone who lived by an enclosure, ME *hay(e)*, *heye* (OE *(ge)hæg*, which after the Norman Conquest became confused with

OF *haye* hedge, a word of Gmc origin and ultimately cogn. with the OE word; cf. HEDGE), or habitation name from any of the various places named with this word, including *Les Hays* and *La Haye* in Normandy. The OF and ME word was used in particular to denote an enclosed forest; cf. HAYWOOD. **2.** nickname for a tall man, from ME *hay*, *hey* tall, high (OE *hēah*). **3.** from the medieval given name *Hay*, which represented in part the OE byname *Hēah* 'Tall', in part a short form of the various cpd names with the first element *hēah* high.

Vars.: **Haye**; **Hey(e)** (chiefly Yorks. and Lancs.). (Of 2 only): HIGH.

Dims. (of 1): Fr.: **Hayet**, **Hayot**, **Hayon**. (Of 3): Eng.: **Haylet(t)**; HAYCOCK.

Patr. (from 3): Eng.: HAYES.

Hayat *see* CHAIT

Haycock English (chiefly W Midlands): from a medieval given name, a dim. of HAY 3, formed with the ME hypocoristic suffix *-cock* (see COCK).

Vars.: **Heycock**, **Heacock**.

Patr.: **Hickox**.

Hayday English: nickname for someone having some particular connection with a festival of the Church, from OE *hēah* high + *dæg* day; cf. HALLIDAY.

Hayden 1. English: habitation name from any of various places called *Hayden* or *Haydon*. The three cases of *Haydon* in Northumb. are named from OE *hēg* hay + *denu* valley. Others, for example in Dorset, Herts., Somerset, and Wilts., get the name from OE *hēg* hay (or perhaps *hege* hedge or *(ge)hæg* enclosure) + *dūn* hill. **2.** Irish: Anglicized form of Gael. **Ó hÉideáin** and **Ó hÉidín** 'descendant of *Éideán*' or 'of *Éidín*', personal names from a dim. of *éideadh* clothes, armour.

Vars.: **Haydon**, **Heydon**. (Of 2 only): **O'He(y)den**, **O'Headen**, **O'Headyne**, **O'Hedin**, **(O')Hedian**, **Haydin**.

Haydn *see* HEIDEN

Hayem *see* HYAM

Hayer *see* AYER

Hayes 1. English: habitation name from any of various places, for example in Devon and Dorset, so called from the strong pl. of ME *hay* enclosure (see HAY 1). **2.** English: habitation name from any of various places, for example in Kent, so called from OE *hæs* brushwood. **3.** Irish: Anglicized form of Gael. **Ó hAodha** 'descendant of *Aodh*', a personal name meaning 'Fire' (cf. MCKAY). **4.** English: patr. from HAY 3. **5.** French: pl. cogn. of HAY 3.

Vars.: Eng.: **Hays**; **Hey(e)s** (Lancs.). (Of 3 only): **Atheis**; **Hayesman**, **Heas(e)man**, **Easman**.

Hayfield English (Midlands): habitation name from *Hayfield* in Derbys. or from some other minor place elsewhere having this name. The name is derived from OE *hēg* hay + *feld* pasture, open country (see FIELD).

Hayhoe English: topographic name for someone who lived on a high spur, from OE *hēah* high (see HAY 2) + *hōh* (see HOWE 1), or habitation name from a minor place named with these elements.

Vars.: **Hayhow**, **Heyhoe**, **Heyo**, **H(e)igho**.

Hayhurst English (Lancs.): habitation name from *Hay Hurst* in the parish of Ribchester, Lancs., so called from OE *hæg* enclosure (see HAY 1) or *hēg* hay + *hyrst* wooded hill (see HURST).

Hayler English: **1.** occupational name for a haulier, from an agent deriv. of ME *halien* to haul, transport (OF *haler*, of Gmc origin). **2.** topographic name for someone who lived in a nook or recess; see HALE 1.

Vars.: **Hayller**, **Haylor**, **Haler**.

Hayles *see* HAILES

Hayley *see* HALEY

Hayling 1. English: habitation name from a place in Hants, so called from OE *Hægelingas* 'people of *Hægel*'; see HALE 2. **2.** Welsh: from the OW personal name *Heilyn*, originally a byname meaning 'Cup-bearer'.

Var. (of 2): **Helyn**.

Patrs. (from 2): **Paling**, **Pa(i)lin**, PELLING, **Ballin**, **Bolan** (W *ap Heilyn*).

Haylock *see* HALE

Hayman English (W Country): **1.** topographic name for a man who lived by an enclosure, from HAY 1 + *man*. The term was in many cases in effect a synonym for HAYWARD. **2.** nickname for a tall man; see HAY 2. **3.** occupational name for the servant of someone called HAY 3, with *man* in the sense 'servant'.

Var.: **Heyman**.

Haymes *see* HAMMOND

Hayn *see* HAIN

Haynes *see* HAINES

Hayselden *see* HAZELDEN

Hayter *see* HEIGHT

Hayton English (Northern): habitation name from any of various places, in Cumb., Notts., Shrops., and elsewhere, so called from OE *hēg* hay + *tūn* enclosure, settlement.

Hayward English: occupational name for an official who was responsible for protecting land or enclosed forest from damage by animals, poachers, or vandals, from ME *hay* enclosure (see HAY 1) + *ward* guardian (see WARD).

Vars.: **Heyward**; **Haward** (see also HOWARD).

Haywood English: habitation name from any of various places, for example in Herefords., Notts., Shrops., and Staffs., so called from ME *hay* enclosure (see HAY 1) + *wude* WOOD. It was a common practice in the Middle Ages for areas of woodland to be fenced off as hunting grounds for the nobility. This name may have been confused in some cases with HAYWARD and perhaps also with HOGWOOD.

Hazan *see* CHAZAN

Hazard *see* HASARD

Hazel English: topographic name for someone who lived near a hazel tree or grove, OE *hæsel*.

Vars.: **Hazell, Hasel(l), Haisell; Hessel(s), Heazel(l)** (from the cogn. ON *hesli*); **Haslam** (from the OE dat. pl.); **Has(e)ler, Haselar, Heasler**.

Collectives: Eng.: Hasling, Hazlett.

Cpds (ornamental): Swed.: **Hasselberg, Hesselberg** ('hazel hill'); **Hasselblad, Hesselblad** ('hazel leaf'); **Hasselgren, Hesselgren** ('hazel branch'); **Hasselqvist** ('hazel twig').

Hazelden English: habitation name from any of various places that get their names from OE *hæsel* (or the cogn. ON *hesli*) Hazel + *denu* valley (see Dean 1).

Vars.: **Haizelden, Hayzelden, Haiselden, Hayselden, Hasleden, Haselden, Hes(s)elden, Hesleden, Heseldin, Hazeldon; Ha(y)zeldene, Hazelde(a)ne, Haseldene, Haz(z)eldine, Haz(z)ledine** (Notts.); **Haseldine, Hazeltine, Haseltine, Hes(s)eltine**. See also Hazelton.

Hazelgrave English (W Yorks.): habitation name from a minor place that gets its name from OE *hæsel* (or the cogn. ON *hesli*) Hazel + *grāf* grove or *grǣfe* thicket. *Hazelgrove* in Rishworth and *Hezzlegreave* in Saddleworth, both W Yorks., have this origin.

Hazelton English: habitation name from either of two places so called in Gloucs. At least one and probably both of these derive their name from OE *hæsel* hazel + *denu* valley (see Dean 1). It is possible that there are other minor places elsewhere of this name, in which the second element is OE *tūn* enclosure, settlement. There has been considerable confusion of this name with Hazelden.

Vars.: **Haselton, Heselton, Hastleton**.

Hazelwood English: habitation name from any of various places, for example in Derbys., Suffolk, and W Yorks., so called from OE *hæsel* (or the cogn. ON *hesli*) Hazel + *wudu* Wood.

Vars.: **Haz(z)lewood, Haselwood, Haslewood; Hes(s)elwood, He(a)slewood; Aizlewood**.

Hazkel see Ezekiel

Hazlett English (now chiefly N Ireland): topographic name for someone who lived by a hazel copse, OE **hæslett* (a deriv. of *hæsel* Hazel).

Vars.: **Hazlitt, Haslett, Haslitt, Hezlet(t), Heaslett**.

Heacock see Haycock

Head English (chiefly Kent): **1.** nickname for someone with some peculiarity or disproportion of the head (ME *heved*, OE *heafod*). **2.** topographic name for someone who lived on a hill or at the head of a stream or valley.

Var.: **Heed**.

Dims.: Ger.: **Häup(te)l, Heupl, Heppl**.

Patr. (from 1): Eng.: **Heads** (Northumb.).

Headford English (Bristol): habitation name from an unidentified minor place, apparently so called from OE *hēafod* Head or *hǣð* heathland, heather (see Heath) + *ford* Ford.

Headley English: habitation name from any of various places, for example in Hants, Surrey, Worcs., and W Yorks., so called from OE *hǣð* heathland, heather (see Heath) + *lēah* wood, clearing.

Var.: **Hedley** (places in Co. Durham and Northumb.). See also Hadley and Heatley.

Heafield see Highfield

Heague see McCaig

Heal see Hale

Heald English (Lancs. and Yorks.): topographic name for someone who lived on a hillside, from OE *hylde, hielde* slope.

Vars.: **Held, Hield(s)**.

Heales see Hailes

Healey **1.** English: habitation name from a place near Manchester, so called from OE *hēah* high (see Hay 2) + *lēah* wood, clearing. There are various other places in N England, for example in Northumb. and Yorks., with the same name and etymology, and it is possible that they may also have contributed to the surname. **2.** Irish: Anglicized form of Gael. Ó hÉilidhe 'descendant of the claimant', from *éilidhe* claimant. **3.** Irish: Anglicized form of Gael. Ó hÉalaighthe 'descendant of *Éalathach*', a personal name perhaps from *ealadhach* ingenious.

Vars.: **Healy, Heel(e)y**. (Of 2 and 3): **O'He(a)ly, O'Healie**. (Of 3 only): **O'Healihy**.

Heam see Eame

Heaney Irish: Anglicized form of Gael. Ó hÉanna 'descendant of *Éanna*', a very common personal name of uncertain meaning. It was borne by various early saints, most notably St Éanna of Aran.

Vars.: **(O')Heany, (O')Heney, Heeney**.

Heap English (chiefly Lancs.): habitation name from *Heap* Bridge in Lancs., or topographic name for someone who lived by a hill or heap, from OE *hēap* heap, mound, hill.

Vars.: **Heape, Heaps**.

Heard English (chiefly W Country): occupational name for a tender of animals, normally a cowherd or shepherd, from ME *he(a)rde* (OE *hi(e)rde*, akin to *heord* herd, flock).

Vars.: **Heardman; Herd** (chiefly Scots), **Herdman** (chiefly Northumb.), Hardman, **Hird** (Yorks.), **Hurd** (chiefly Midlands), **Hurdman** (W Midlands); **He(a)rder** (agent derivs. of ME *he(a)rden* to herd, tend animals).

Dim.: Ger.: **Hirtel, Hirtle**.

Hearl see Earl

Hearn **1.** English: var. of Heron 1. **2.** English: topographic name for someone who lived by a bend in a river or in a recess in a hill, both of which are meanings of ME *herne* (OE *hyrne*). It may also be a habitation name from any of the various places, such as *Herne* in Kent and *Hurn* in Dorset, which are named with the OE word. Its exact original sense and its etymology are not clear; it may be a deriv. of *horn* Horn. **3.** English: habitation name from *Herne* in Beds., so called from the dat. pl. (originally used after a preposition) of OE *hær* stone. **4.** Irish: see Ahern.

Vars. (of 2): **Hearne, Hern(e), Hurn(e), Harn; Hernaman, Herniman, Harniman, Horniman, Hurman**.

Hearst see HURST

Heart see HART

Hearty see HARTY

Heaseman see HAYES

Heasey see EASY

Heasler see HAZEL

Heaslett see HAZLETT

Heaslewood see HAZELWOOD

Heaslip see HESLOP

Heath English: topographic name for someone who lived on a heath (ME *hethe*, OE *hǣð*) or habitation name from any of the numerous places, for example in Beds., Derbys., Herefords., Shrops., and W Yorks., named with this word. The same word also denoted heather, the characteristic plant of heathland areas.

Vars.: **Heather**, **Heathman**; HOAD.

Cpds (ornamental): Swed.: **Hed(en)berg** ('heath hill'), **Hedlund** ('heath grove'); **Hedqvist** ('heath twig'); **Hed(en)ström** ('heath river').

Heathcote English: habitation name from any of various places, for example in Derbys. and Warwicks., so called from OE *hǣð* heathland, heather (see HEATH) + *cot* cottage, dwelling (see COATES).

Vars.: **Heathcoat**, **Heathcott**.

Heatherington see HETHERINGTON

Heathfield English: habitation name from any of various places, for example in Somerset and Sussex, so called from OE *hǣð* heathland, heather (see HEATH) + *feld* pasture, open country (see FIELD). Cf. HATFIELD.

Heatley N English and Scots: habitation name from various places so called, of which the most significant is in Ches. near Manchester. However, the surname is now found chiefly in Scotland, N Ireland, and Northumb. The placename is derived from OE *hǣð* HEATH + *lēah* wood, clearing.

Vars.: **Heatlie**, **Haitlie**. See also HEADLEY and HADLEY.

Heaton English (N England): habitation name from any of the numerous places, for example in Lancs., Northumb., and W Yorks., so called from OE *hēah* high + *tūn* enclosure, settlement. Cf. HAMPTON.

Heavan see EVAN

Hebard see HERBERT

Hebblethwaite English (Yorks.): habitation name from *Heblethwaite* in W Yorks., so called from the ME dial. term *hebble* plank bridge (probably of Scand. origin) + Northern ME *thwaite* meadow (see THWAITE).

Vars.: **Hebblewaite**, **Hebblewhite**, **Hepplewhite**, **Ebblewhite**.

Hebborn see HEPBURN

Hebden English (Yorks.): habitation name from a place in W Yorks., so called from OE *hēope* rose-hip + *denu* valley.

Vars.: **Hebdon**; **Hepden**; **Hepton**.

Heberl see HABER

Hébert see HERBERT

Hebich see HAWK

Hecht 1. German: nickname for a rapacious and greedy person, from Ger. *Hecht* pike (MHG *hech(e)t*, OHG *hechit*, *hachit*). It may also have been a metonymic occupational name for a catcher of this unattractive but edible fish. **2.** Jewish (Ashkenazic): ornamental name from Ger. *Hecht* or Yid. *hekht* pike, one of the many Ashkenazic ornamental names taken from vocab. words denoting wildlife.

Vars.: Ger.: **Höcht** (Bavaria). Jewish: **Gecht** (under Russ. influence; see GOREN); **Hechtkopf** ('pike head', presumably one of the unflattering names assigned more or less at random by non-Jewish government officials in 18th- and 19th-cent. central Europe).

Dims.: Ger.: **Hechtl**; **Höchtl** (Bavaria).

Hecker see HACKER

Heckingbottom see HIGGINBOTTOM

Heckner see HAKE

Hector Scots: Anglicized form of the Gael. personal name *Eachdonn*, composed of the elements *each* horse (cf. KEOGH) + *donn* brown (cf. DUNN). The name has been assimilated to that of one of the princes of Troy.

Hedberg see HEATH

Hedderich see HETTERICH

Hedecke see HEYDRICH

Hedegård Danish: habitation name from a placename formed with the elements *hede* HEATH (ON *heiðr*) + *gård* enclosure (ON *garðr*; see GARTH).

Vars.: **Hedegaard**, **Heegård**, **Heegaard**.

Hedge English: topographic name for someone who lived by a hedge, OE *hecg*.

Vars.: **Hedges**; **Hedger**; **Hedgeman**.

Dim.: Fr.: **Hequet**.

Hedgecock see HICK

Hedian see HAYDEN

Hedley see HEADLEY

Heed see HEAD

Heegaard see HEDEGÅRD

Heegan see HIGGINS

Heelan see WHELAN

Heeley see HEALEY

Heelis see ELLIS

Heeney see HEANEY

Heeren see HERR

Heeschen see HATHAWAY

Hefets see HEIFETZ

Heffer English: metonymic occupational name for a cowherd, or perhaps a nickname for a cowlike person, from

ME *heffre, heffour* young cow, heifer (OE *heahf(o)re, heafru*, of obscure derivation).

Var.: **Hefferman**.

Heffernan Irish: Anglicized form of Gael. **Ó hIfearnáin** 'descendant of *Ifearnán*', a personal name from a dim. of *ifreannach* demon (from *ifreann* hell).

Vars.: **O'Hifferane, (O')Hiffer(n)an, Heffernon, Hefferan**.

Heffner *see* HAFNER

Hegan *see* HIGGINS

Hegarty Irish: Anglicized form of Gael. **Ó hÉigceartaigh** 'descendant of *Eigceartach*', a byname meaning 'Unjust'.

Vars.: **O'He(a)gertie, O'Hagirtie, (O')Hagerty, Hegerty, Haggarty, Haggerty, Higerty**.

Hegedüs Hungarian and Jewish (Ashkenazic): occupational name for a player on the fiddle (Hung. *hegedü*, of unknown origin).

Hegel *see* HAIG, HUGH

Heginbotham *see* HIGGINBOTTOM

Hehir *see* HARE

Hehl Low German: 1. from a medieval given name, a short form of various Gmc personal names with the first element *heil* salvation, safety. 2. nickname for a secretive or reclusive person, or topographic name for someone who lived at a remote or concealed spot, from MLG *hēle* secret, concealed.

Var.: **Hehle**.

Dim. (of 1): **Hehlke**.

Patrs. (from 1): Low Ger.: **Hehler**. Dan., Norw.: **Heilsen**.

Hehnke *see* HENRY

Heichman *see* HOCH

Heidecke *see* HEYDRICH

Heidegger German and Swiss: habitation name from *Heidegg* near Zurich or any of the various places in Germany called *Heideck*. All of them get their names from MHG *heide* HEATH + *egge, ecke* corner (see ECK).

Var.: **Heidecker**.

Heiden 1. German: nickname from Ger. *Heiden* heathen (MHG *heiden*, OHG *heidano*, apparently a deriv. of *heida* HEATH, modelled on L *pāgānus*; see PAIN 1). The nickname was sometimes used to refer to a Christian knight who had been on a Crusade to wrest the Holy Land from the Muslims. 2. Jewish (Ashkenazic): of unknown origin. The Ashkenazic surname **Heidenberg** is perhaps an ornamental elaboration.

Var.: **Haydn**.

Heifetz Jewish (Ashkenazic): ornamental name from Hebr. *chefets* delight, pleasure.

Vars.: **Che(i)fetz, Hejfec, Hefetz, Hefets; Haifetz, Chaifetz; Keyfetz**.

Heigho *see* HAYHOE

Height English: topographic name for someone who lived at the top of a hill or on a piece of raised ground, from ME

heyt summit, height (OE *hīehðu*, a deriv. of *hēah* high; cf. HAY 2).

Vars.: **Hight, Hite; Hayter, Haytor**.

Heigl *see* HUGH

Heijne *see* HENRY

Heikkilä Finnish: name borne by a member of a household headed by someone called *Heikki* (a pet form of HENRY). The surname is formed from the given name with the addition of the local suffix -*la*.

Heilbronn Jewish (Ashkenazic): habitation name from a town so called in Württemberg, where there was once a large Jewish community. The town gets its name from OHG *heil(ag)* holy + *brunno* spring, well; cf. HALLIWELL.

Vars.: **Heilbronner; Heilbron, Heilborn, Heilbrun(n), Heilbruner, Heilprun; Heilpern, Halper(n), Halpert, Helper(n), Halp(e)rin, Helprin, Halprin; Galper(n), Galperin, Gelperin** (under Russ. influence; see GOREN); **Alpron, Alper(n)**, ALPERT, **Elper(i)n** (in regions where Yid. has no /h/), **Alperson, Alperin, Alperovi(t)ch, Alperowich, Alperowicz, Alperovitz, Alperovitsh** (patrs.); **Alperstein** (an ornamental elaboration).

Heilsen *see* HEHL

Heim *see* HYAM

Heimbürge German: status name for a village headman, MHG *heimbürge*, a cpd of *heim* homestead, settlement (OHG *heim*) + *bürge* guardian (OHG *burigo*, from the verb *bor(a)gēn* to guard). This was the title regularly used for the office of village headman in Franconia; cf. GRAF, HOFFMANN, MAYER, SCHULTZ, and VOGT.

Vars.: **Heimbürger, Heimburger, Heimberger**.

Heiptmann *see* HAUPTMANN

Heisel *see* HIESS

Heister Low German: topographic name for someone who lived by a conspicuous beech tree, MLG *hēster*.

Var.: **Hester**.

Dim.: Fr.: **Hêtreau**.

Collective: Fr.: **Hétroy**.

Hejfec *see* HEIFETZ

Hejna *see* HÁJEK

Held 1. German, Dutch, and Jewish (Ashkenazic): nickname from Ger. *Held* hero, or Du. or Yid. *held* (MHG, MDu. *held*). As a Jewish name, it is often ornamental. 2. English: var. of HEALD.

Vars. (of 1): Ger.: **Heldt, Heldmann**. Jewish: **Heldman**.

Cpds (of 1; ornamental): Jewish: **Heldenberg** ('hero's hill'); **Heldstein** ('hero stone'), **Geldstein** (the latter under Russ. influence; see GOREN).

Hele *see* HALE

Helen *see* ELLEN

Helian *see* ELLIS

Hell *see* HILL

Heller 1. German: nickname from the small medieval coin known as the *häller* or *heller* because it was first minted (in 1208) at the Swabian town of *(Schwäbisch) Hall*; cf. HALL. 2. Jewish (Ashkenazic): nickname for a person with fair hair or a light complexion, from an inflected form, used before a male given name, of Ger. *hell* light, bright, Yid. *hel* (MHG *hell*). **3.** English: var. of HILL 1.

Vars. (of 2): **Hellerman**, **Heler(man)**, **Hel(l)man**; **Hellerstein** ('bright stone', an ornamental elaboration). See also GELLER and ELLER. (Of 3): **Helle**, **Hellman**.

Hellier English: occupational name for a roofer (tiler or thatcher), from an agent deriv. of ME *hele(n)* to cover (OE *helian*).

Vars.: **Helliar**, **Hel(l)yer**, **Hilliar**, HILLIER, **Hillyar**, **Hil(l)yer**.

Hellings English: of uncertain origin, probably a habitation name. Reaney ascribes it to the village of *Healing* in Lincs. (of the same origin as HAYLING), but since the surname is now found mainly in Devon, it could equally well be a var. of HAYLING or of some other origin entirely.

Helliwell *see* HALLIWELL

Helm 1. English (chiefly Lancs.): topographic name for someone who lived or worked at a rough temporary shelter for animals, ME *helm* (ON *hialmr*, a cogn. of the OE and OHG words in 2 below). **2.** English and German: metonymic occupational name for a maker of helmets, from ME, OE *helm*, Ger. *Helm* (MHG, OHG *helm*). **3.** German: from a medieval given name, a short form of any of the various cpd names containing the element *helm* helmet; cf., e.g., HELMOLD, HELMUND, and WILLIAM.

Vars. (of 1): Eng.: **Helme** (Lancs.), **Helms**.

Dims. (of 3): Ger.: **Helmel**, **Helmle**. Low Ger.: **Helm(e)cke**, **Helmchen**.

Patr. (from 3): Low Ger.: **Helms(en)**.

Patrs. (from 3) (dim.): Low Ger.: **Helmker**.

Helmold German: from a Gmc personal name composed of the elements *helm* helmet + *mund* protection.

Vars.: **Helm(h)olt**.

Patrs.: **Helmhol(t)z**.

Helmsley *see* HEMSLEY

Helmund German: from a Gmc personal name composed of the elements *helm* helmet + *mund* protection.

Vars.: **Hellmund(t)**.

Helper *see* HEILBRONN

Helps English (Southern): of uncertain origin, probably a patr. from an OE personal name *Help*, a short form of a cpd name with the first element *help* help, aid (e.g. *Helprīc*, for which there is placename evidence). Alternatively, it may derive from the cogn. ON female personal name *Hialp*, which is attested.

Helsby English (Lancs.): habitation name from a place in Ches., recorded in Domesday Book as *Helesbe*, which gets its name from ON *hjallr* ledge, used of a ledge on a mountainside + *býr* farm, settlement.

Helyn *see* HAYLING

Hembrey *see* AMERY

Heme *see* EAME

Hémeret *see* HENRY

Hemingway English (W Yorks.): apparently a habitation name from an unidentified minor place in W Yorks., probably in the parish of Halifax, to judge by the distribution of early occurrences of the surname. The placename is from the personal name HEMMING + ME *wey* way, path (OE *weg*).

Var.: **Hemmingway**.

Hemmann *see* HANS

Hemmett *see* EMMETT

Hemming English (chiefly W Midlands), Danish/Norwegian, and Swedish: from the ON personal name *Hemmingr*, originally a patr. from a short form of any of the various cpd personal names with a first element *heim* home.

Patrs.: Eng.: **Hemmings**. Fris.: **Hemminga**. Dan., Norw.: **Hemmingsen**. Swed.: **Hemmingsson**.

Hémonnot *see* HAMMOND

Hempe *see* HAMPE

Hemphill N Irish, originally Scots: habitation name from a place near Galston in the former county of Ayrs. (now part of Strathclyde region), apparently so called from OE *henep* hemp + *hyll* HILL.

Var.: **Hempill**.

Hems English (W Midlands): regional name for someone who lived in the border country between England and Wales, or habitation name from *The Hem*, a village in Shrops., or *Hem* near Montgomery, all from OE *hemm* border (used in a much wider sense than mod. Eng. *hem*).

Hemsley English (chiefly Yorks. and Notts.): habitation name from either of two places in N Yorks. called *Helmsley*. The names are of different etymologies: the one near Rievaulx Abbey is from the OE personal name *Helm* + OE *lēah* wood, clearing, whereas Upper Helmsley, near York, is from the OE personal name *Hemele* + OE *ēg* island, and had the form *Hemelsey* up to at least the 14th cent.

Vars.: **Hemesley**, **Helmsley**.

Hemstock English (Notts.): habitation name from an unidentified minor place; the first element is probably from a personal name of uncertain original form, the second is OE *stoc* place (see STOCK).

Hemsworth English (Yorks.): habitation name from the town in W Yorks., recorded as *Hilmeuuord* and *Hamelesuurde* in Domesday Book. 'This can hardly be anything else than Hymel's *worð*', comments Ekwall, i.e. from the gen. case of the OE personal name *Hymel* (apparently from a short form of names such as *Hūnbeald* 'bear-cub bold' and *Hūnbeorht* 'bear-cub bright') + OE *worð* enclosure (see WORTH).

Hemus English: of uncertain origin, probably a topographic name for someone who lived in a house situated at a border of some sort, from ME *hem(m)* border (see HEMS) + *h(o)us* house (OE *hūs*).

Henchcliff *see* HINCHCLIFFE

Hendel *see* HANS

Hendelman *see* HANDLER

Henderson Scots: patr. from *Hendry*, a chiefly Sc. var. of the given name HENRY; the intrusive *-d-* between *n* and *r* is found also in other languages. Several Scottish bearers of this name have ancestors whose name was *Henryson*.

Hendeschuh *see* HANDSCHUH

Hendra Cornish: habitation name from any of various places so called from Corn. *hendre* winter homestead, the home farm of a people who practised transhumance, from *hen* old + *tre* homestead.

Hendy English (mainly W Country): nickname for a pleasant and affable man, from ME *hende* courteous, kind, gentle (OE *gehende* skilful, handy, a deriv. of *hand* hand). *Hendy* was also sometimes used as a given name in the Middle Ages and some examples of the surname may derive from this rather than from the nickname.

Vars.: **Hendey**, **Henday**.

Patr.: **Hendisson**.

Heneghan Irish: Anglicized form of Gael. Ó **hEidhneacháin** 'descendant of *Eidhneachán*', a personal name of uncertain origin.

Vars.: **Henegan**; BIRD (the result of the association of the Gael. name with *éan* bird).

Heney *see* HEANEY

Hengst German: metonymic occupational name for someone who worked with horses, or nickname for a lustful man, from Ger. *Hengst* stallion (MHG *heng(e)st*, OHG *hengist*). In part it may also have been a house name, from the use of a picture of a horse as a house sign.

Var.: **Hengstmann**.

Hénin French: 1. habitation name from a place in Pas-de-Calais, so called from the Gmc byname *Henno* 'Cock' (see HAHN 1) + the local suffix *-īnum*. 2. metonymic occupational name for a maker or seller of the tall and elaborate head-dresses worn in the Middle Ages by fashionable ladies, known in OF as *hennins*. The word is apparently from MLG *henninck* cock, with reference to the similarity in appearance and function between these garments and the cock's comb.

Var.: **Hennin**.

Henley English: habitation name from any of the various places so called. Most, e.g. those in Oxon., Suffolk, and Warwicks., get the name from the weak dat. case (originally used after a preposition and article) of OE *hēah* high + OE *lēah* wood, clearing. Others, for example one near Ludlow in Shrops., have as their first element OE *henn* hen, wild bird. Others still, for example those in Somerset and Surrey, are ambiguous between the two possibilities.

Var.: **Henly**.

Henn English (chiefly W Midlands): 1. from the ME given name *Henn(e)*, a short form of HENRY. 2. nickname, perhaps for a fussy man, from ME *hen(n)* hen (OE *henn*, related to *hana* cock; cf. HAHN 1).

Dim. (of 1): **Henkin**.

Patr. (from 1): **Henson**.

Hennessy Irish: Anglicized form of Gael. Ó **hAonghusa** 'descendant of ANGUS'.

Vars.: **Hennessey**, **Heness(e)y**, **Hen(n)es(e)y**, **O'Hen(n)es(s)(e)y**, **O'Heanesey**, **Hench(e)y**, **Hinchy**, **Hinsey**.

Henning Scots (most common around Hawick and Dumfries): of uncertain origin. The earliest known occurrence is around 1630.

Vars.: **Ha(i)n(n)ing**.

Hennion *see* ONION

Henry 1. English and French: from a Gmc personal name composed of the elements *haim, heim* home + *rīc* power, introduced into England by the Normans in the form *Henri*. During the Middle Ages this name became enormously popular in England and was borne by eight kings, a record not equalled until the 20th cent. (when EDWARD caught up). Continental forms of the given name were equally popular (Ger. *Heinrich*, Fr. *Henri*, Czech *Jindřich*, etc.). In the period in which the majority of Eng. surnames were formed, a common vernacular form of the name was HARRY; official documents of the period normally used the Latinized form *Henricus*. Eng. *Henry* has absorbed an originally distinct Gmc personal name that had *hagan* hawthorn (cf. HAIN 2) as its first element, and there has also been considerable confusion with AMERY. 2. Irish: Anglicized form of Gael. Ó **hInnéirghe** 'descendant of *Innéirghe*', a byname meaning 'Abandonment', 'Elopement'.

Vars. (of 1): Eng.: **Henrey**; **Hendr(e)y**, **Hendrie** (Scotland); **Hendrick** (Ireland). Fr.: **Henri**, **Hendry**, **Hanry**. (Of 2): **O'Henery**.

Dims. (of 1): Eng.: HERRIOT, HENN, HAWKIN, HAW. Fr.: **Henri(qu)et**, **Henrion**, **Henr(i)ot**, **Hariot**, **Hémeret**; **Riquet** (see also RICHARD); **Mériguet**, **Mérigeau**, **Mérigot**, **Mérigon**; **Mériet**, **Mériel**, **Mériot**. It.: **Enrietto**, **Arrighetti**, **Arrighini**, **Errichelli**, **Errichiello**, **Arrichiello**, **Endrizzi**, **Endricci**, **Arrigucci**. Ger.: **Hein(e)(l)**, **Heyn(e)(l)**, **Heindl(e)**, **Heinle(in)**, **He(i)n(t)ze**, **Heinz(el)**, **Heitz**, **Hin(t)z(e)**. Low Ger.: **Heine(c)ke**, **Heinicke**, **Heinke**, **Hen(c)ke**, **Henkmann**, **Hei(ne)mann**, **Heymann**, **Hehnke**, **Hennemann**. Fris.: **Herrema**, **Harrema**. Flem.: **Heine(man)**. Du.: **Heijne**, **Heyne**, **Henze**, **Heins(ius)**; **Hein**. Ger. (of Slav. origin): **Hein(i)sch**, **Heint(z)sch**, **Heinschke**, **Hinsch(e)**, **Hi(t)schke**, **Hitzschke**, **Hitzke**, **Heinig**, **Hönig**, **Hönack**, **Hönatsch**, **Hön(i)sch**. Czech: **Jind(r)áček**. Finn.: **Heino**. Hung.: **Jendrássik**.

Patrs. (from 1): Eng.: **Hen(e)ries**, HARRIS; **Henryson**, HENDERSON (Scotland); FITZHENRY (Ireland). Sc.: McHENRY. Welsh: PARRY. Sp.: **Enríquez**. Port.: **Henriques**, **Enriques**. It.: **D'Enrico**, **D'Errico**, **D'Arrigo**. Ger.: **Heinritz(e)** (Hesse); **Heinrici** (Latinized). Low Ger.: **Hen(d)richs**, **Hendricks**, **Hinrichs(en)**. Fris.: **Hinners**. Flem.: **Hendricks**, **Hendri(ck)x**, **Hendriksen**. Du.: **Hendriks**, **Hendrix**, **Hendrikse(n)**. Dan., Norw.: **Hen(d)riksen**, **Henrichsen**, **Hinrichsen**. Swed.: **Henriksson**, **Henricsson**.

Patrs. (from 1) (dims.): Scots: HASSON. Ger.: **Heiner(t)**, **Heinzler**, **Hentz(e)ler**, **Hen(t)zer**, **Hin(t)zer**. Low Ger.: **Hein(ek)en**, **Hein(ek)ing**, **Hein(s)sen**, **Henken(s)**, **Henker**, **Hinken(s)**, **Hinksen**, **Henner**. Du.: **Heijnen**, **Heynen**. Flem.: **Heyns**, **Heynen**, **Hens(mans)**. Ger. (of Slav. origin): **Hitscher**; **Henniger**, **Hänniger**. Finn.: **Heinonen**, **Heikkinen**.

Henshaw English: 1. habitation name from a place in Northumb., so called from the gen. case of the OE personal name *Heðīn* (from a short form of the rare cpd names with the first element *hæð* heath) + OE *halh* nook, recess (see

HALE 1). **2.** habitation name from a place in the parish of Prestbury, Ches., and from a lost place in SE Lancs., both so called from ME *hen* hen + *shaw* wood. The name *de Henneshagh* occurs at Rochdale as early as 1325.

Vars.: **Henshall**, **Henshell**, **Hensher**.

Henton English: habitation name from a place so called, probably either *Henton* in Oxon., which is from the OE weak dat. case, originally used after a preposition and article, of *hēah* high (see HAY 2) + OE *tūn* enclosure, settlement, or *Henton* in Somerset, which is from OE *henn* hen (perhaps a byname; cf. HENN 2) + *tūn*. The surname, however, is now chiefly common in Notts.

Henty English (Sussex): according to Reaney this is a habitation name from *Antye* Farm in the parish of Wivelsfield, which gets its name from OE *hēan* (dat. of *hēah* high) + *tēag* enclosure.

Henwood Cornish: habitation name from a place in Linkinhorne parish, so called from OE *henn* hen + *wudu* wood. There is also a place of the same name (but different etymology) in Warwicks., but this does not seem to have given rise to any surnames.

Hepburn N English and Scots: habitation name from a place in Northumb., so called from OE *hēah* high + *byrgen* burial mound, tumulus. Some examples of the surname may derive from *Hebburn* in Co. Durham, which has the same origin, as does *Hebron* in Northumb.

Vars.: **Hebburn**, **Hebborn**, **Hebbourne**.

Hepden *see* HEBDEN

Hepner *see* HÖPFNER

Heppl *see* HEAD

Hepple English (Northumb.): habitation name from a place in Northumb., so called from OE *hēope* rose-hip + *halh* nook, recess (see HALE 1).

Var.: **Heppell**.

Hepplewhite *see* HEBBLETHWAITE

Heptinstall English (Yorks.): habitation name from *Heptonstall* in W Yorks., which derives its name from HEBDEN + OE *stall* cattle-station (or simply 'place'), i.e. 'cattle-stall belonging to Hebden'.

Vars.: **Heptonstall**, **Heppenstall**.

Hepworth English: habitation name from places so called, of which there is one in Suffolk and another in W Yorks., deriving their name from OE *hēope* rose hip + *worð* enclosure (see WORTH). The surname is still largely confined to Yorks., so it seems that the latter place is by far the most likely source of the surname.

Var.: **Hipworth**.

Hequet *see* HEDGE

Heraghty Irish: Anglicized form of Gael. **Ó hOireachtaigh** 'descendant of *Oireachtach*', a byname for a member of an assembly; cf. GERAGHTY.

Herald *see* HARROD

Heras Spanish: habitation name from any of various places, for example in the provinces of Santander and Gua

dalajara, probably so called from the pl. of Sp. *era* threshing floor (L *ārea*). The initial *H-* is silent and in this case inorganic. According to an alternative theory, the placename is derived from L *hedera* ivy.

Herbage *see* HARBER

Herbaud French: from a Gmc personal name composed of the elements *heri, hari* army + *bald* bold, brave.

Vars.: **Herbau(l)t**, **Herbaux**; **Harbaud**, **Harbaut**, **Harbaux**; **Arbaud**.

Herbert English, French, and German: from a Gmc personal name composed of the elements *heri, hari* army + *berht* bright, famous. This OF name, introduced to Britain by the Normans, reinforced the less common OE cogn. *Herebeorht*.

Vars.: Eng.: **Herbit**; **Hebbert**, **Heb(b)ard**; **Harbert**, **Harberd**, **Harbard**, **Harbird**, **Harbord**. Fr.: **Hébert**, **Herbet**, **Harbert**.

Dims.: Eng.: **Hebb**, **Hipkin**; **Hercock**, **Hircock**. Fr.: **Hébertet**, **Hébertot**, **Herbreteau**, **Herb(el)et**, **Herb(el)in**, **Herb(el)ot**, **Harbelot**, **Harbulot**. Low Ger.: **Harr(e)**, **Harck**, **Herck**, **Harich**.

Patrs.: Eng.: **Herbertson**, **Harbertson**, **Harburtson**; **FitzHerbert**. Ger.: **Her(i)bertz**. Low Ger.: **Harbers**, **Harberding**, **Harbring**.

Patrs. (from dims.): Eng.: **Herbi(n)son**; **Harbi(n)son** (chiefly N Ireland); **Hebson**; **Hipkins**, **Hipkiss**. Fris.: **Harbs**.

Herbst German: nickname from MHG *herb(e)st*, which still bore the meaning of its Eng. cogn. *harvest* (of cereals or wine), whereas mod. Ger. *Herbst* has come to mean 'autumn', the time of year when the harvest takes place. The exact application of the nickname is not clear; perhaps it referred to a peasant who had certain obligations to his master at the time of the harvest, or it may have been acquired for some other anecdotal reason which is now lost. **2.** Jewish (Ashkenazic): ornamental name from mod. Ger. *Herbst* autumn, perhaps reflecting the season when the name was first taken or given. In some cases, it seems to have been one of the group of names referring to the seasons that were distributed at random by government officials; cf. FRULING, WINTER, and SUMMER.

Vars.: Jewish: **Herbstman**; **Erbst** (in regions where Yid. has no /h/).

Herd *see* HEARD

Herdwick *see* HARDWICK

Heredero Spanish: nickname for someone who had inherited or was known to be due to inherit property, from Sp. *heredero* heir (LL *hērēditārius*, a deriv. of class. L *hērēs*, gen. *hērēdis*; cf. AYER).

Heredia Spanish: habitation name from any of various places, for example in the province of Álava, so named from the pl. form of LL *hērēdium* hereditary estate (a deriv. of *hērēs*; cf. HEREDERO and AYER), i.e. one that could be passed on to the heirs of its tenant instead of reverting to the overlord.

Hereward *see* HARVARD

Herfahrt German: occupational nickname for a soldier, from MHG *hervart* campaign, military expedition (from OHG *heri* army + *vart* journey).

Vars.: **Her(r)fart**, **Her(r)forth**, **Her(r)furth**, **Her(r)fert**.

Hérisson French: **1.** nickname from OF *hérisson* hedgehog (LL *ēricio*, gen. *ēriciōnis*, for class. L *ēricius*). In the Middle Ages the animal was supposed to have a bad character, and the nickname may have been given in a generalized pej. sense, as well as from more obvious points of comparison, such as an unkempt appearance. **2.** habitation name from places in Allier and Deux-Sèvres, apparently so called from the vocab. word mentioned above; the reference is presumably to some defensive system.
Var. (of 1): **Hérichon**.

Heritage English: status name for someone who held or occupied land inherited from an ancestor, rather than by feudal gift from an overlord, from ME, OF *(h)eritage* inherited property (LL *hēritagium*, from *hērēs* heir; cf. AYER).
Var.: **Heretage**.

Herkes Scots: habitation name from *Harcarse* in the parish of Fogo, Berwicks. The placename is recorded in 1200 as *Harkarres* and in 1328 as *Harcarres*. It is of uncertain origin.
Vars.: **Harkes(s)** (SE Scotland); **Hercus, Harcus** (Orkney).

Herkommer German: habitation name from *Herkheim* in Bavaria. The assimilation to the form of an agent noun from *herkommen* to come forward (i.e. 'new arrival') has been brought about partly by phonetic change and partly by folk etymology.
Vars.: **Herk(he)imer**; **Horkheimer** (also Jewish (W Ashkenazic)).

Herlihy Irish: Anglicized form of Gael. **Ó hIarfhlatha** 'descendant of *Iarfhlaith*', a byname describing a feudal underlord.
Vars.: **O'Herlihy, O'H(i)erlehy, Herley,** HURLEY.

Hermann German: from a Gmc personal name composed of the elements *heri, hari* army + *man* man. This is undoubtedly of very ancient origin, and the 1st-cent. leader of the Cherusci recorded by the L historian Tacitus as *Arminius* has been claimed as the first known bearer, but there are phonetic problems with this interpretation, and his name may rather be a deriv. of the element *Irmen, Ermen*, the name of a god. The surname is also borne by Ashkenazic Jews, probably as an adoption of the Ger. surname.
Vars.: **Herrmann**; **Hörmann** (Bavaria); **Hiermann** (Austria); **Herman** (Jewish).
Dims.: Ger.: **Hermel** (see also HERMELIN), **Hermle, Her(r)l(e), Herlein; Hörl** (Bavaria); **Hierl** (Austria). Low Ger.: **Herm, Harm, Herm(ec)ke, Hermichen.** Ger. (under Slav. influence): HESS, **Hessel, Hetzel, Hetzold, He(t)schold; Hersch(el), Herschmann** (see also HIRSCH); **Men(t)zelmann.** Czech: **Heřmánek.** Fr.: **Armandin.** Eng.: **Harm.** It.: **Armanetti, Armanini, Armanino.**
Patrs.: Jewish (E Ashkenazic): **Hermanoff, Germanoff, Germanov(itz).** Pol.: **Hermanowicz.** Russ.: **Germanov.** Low Ger.: **Hermans, Harmaning.** Du., Flem.: **Hermans(z), Hermanszoon.** Dan., Norw.: **Hermansen.** Swed.: **Hermansson.**
Patrs. (from dims.): Ger.: **Herrler, Her(r)ling; Hörring** (Bavaria). Low Ger.: **Herms(en), Harms(en).** Flem.: **Hermes.** Du.: **Hermsen, Harms(en).** Ger. (of Slav. origin): **Menzler.** Eng.: **Harms.** Finn.: **Manninen.**
Habitation name: Pol.: **Hermanowski.**

Hermelin Jewish (Ashkenazic): ornamental name from Ger. *Hermelin* ermine (MHG *hermelīn*, OHG *harmilī* weasel, a dim. of *harmo*; cf. OE *hearma*).
Vars.: **Harmel** (from Yid. *harml*), **Hermel(e); Harmelin, Harmolin.**

Hermer *see* HARMER

Hermès Provençal: topographic name for someone who lived in a deserted spot or on a patch of waste land, from OProv. *erm* desert, waste (Gk *erēmia*, a deriv. of *erēmos* lonely, solitary) + the local suffix *-ès*. The name has, however, long been associated by folk etymology with that of the Gk god *Hermes*, the etymology of which is unknown.
Var.: **Hermier**.

Hermida Spanish: **1.** cogn. of HERMITE. **2.** habitation name from any of various places, for example in the provinces of Lugo, Orense, and Pontevedra, so called from OSp. *hermida* hermitage, shrine (a later development of the same word as in 1).

Hermitage *see* ARMITAGE

Hermite French: nickname from OF *hermite* hermit (Gk *erēmitēs*; cf. ARMITAGE), which was probably given at least as often to people living in isolated spots (cf. HERMÈS), or not on good terms with their neighbours, as to actual hermits.
Vars.: **Hermitte, Lhermit(t)e.**

Hermoso Spanish: nickname meaning 'fine', 'handsome' (L *formōsus*, from *forma* shape, form, beauty), given either in admiration or in mockery of a dandy.

Hern *see* HEARN

Hernáez *see* FERDINAND

Heron 1. English: nickname for a tall, thin person resembling a heron, ME *heiroun, heyron* (OF *hairon*, of Gmc origin). **2.** Irish: Anglicized form of Gael. **Ó hEaráin** 'descendant of *Earán*', a personal name from a dim. of *earadh* fear, distrust. **3.** Irish: Anglicized form of Gael. **Ó hUidhrín** 'descendant of *Uidhrín*', a personal name probably from a dim. of *odhar* dun-coloured, swarthy. **4.** Irish: Anglicized form of Gael. **Mac Giolla Chiaráin** 'son of the servant of (St) *Ciarán*'; see KIERAN.
Vars. (of 1): **Herro(u)n, Hairon,** HEARN, **Leherne.** (Of 2): **O'Heron, O'Har(a)n, O'Harran(e), Her(r)an, Harran, Harron.** (Of 4): **McIlheron, McElharan.**

Herr 1. German: nickname for someone who gave himself airs and behaved in a lordly manner, from Ger. *Herr* master, lord (MHG *herre*, OHG *herro*). **2.** German: occupational name for someone in the service of the lord of the manor, likewise from Ger. *Herr*, MHG *herre*. **3.** Jewish (Ashkenazic): of unknown origin, possibly originating as in 1 above.
Var.: Ger.: **Herre.**
Dims.: Ger.: **Herrle(i)n.** Low Ger.: **Herrgen.**
Patrs.: Jewish: **Herrenson, Her(r)enzon.** Flem., Du.: **Heeren.**

Herráez *see* FARRANT

Herrema *see* HENRY

Herrgott German: from Ger. *Herrgott* 'Lord God', a cpd of MHG *herre* lord (see HERR) + *got* God. The use of the surname reflects a robust attitude to blasphemy, but the circumstances under which it was acquired are not clear. It may in part be an occupational name for a producer or seller of crucifixes or religious paintings; alternatively, it may be a nickname, either for a frequent user of this expression as an oath, or for arrogant person who behaved 'like God Almighty'.

Vars.: **Hergot**; **Herg(e)t** (Franconia).

Herrick English: from the ON personal name *Eiríkr*, composed of the elements *eir* mercy, peace (a cogn. of OHG *ēra* honour; cf. EHRLICH) + * rík* power. The addition in English of an inorganic *H-* to names beginning with a vowel is a relatively common phenomenon; cf., e.g., HOSKIN and HUCK. It is possible that this name may have swallowed up a less common Gmc personal name with the first element *heri, hari* army. There seems also to have been some confusion with HENRY.

Patrs.: Low Ger.: **Erichs(en)**. Norw., Dan.: **Eriksen**, **Erichsen**. Swed.: **Eriksson**, **Ericsson**. Finn.: **Eerikäinen**.

Herring English: metonymic occupational name for a seller of the fish, ME *hering* (OE *hæring, hēring*). In some cases it may have been a nickname in the sense of a trifle, something of little value, a meaning which is clearly apparent in medieval phrases and proverbial expressions such as 'to like neither herring nor barrel', i.e. not to like something at all.

Vars.: **Hering**; **Harenc** (from the OF word, which is itself of Gmc origin).

Herrington English: habitation name from a place in Co. Durham, so called from OE *Heringtūn* 'settlement (OE *tūn*) associated with *Here*', a short form of the various cpd names with the first element *here* army.

Herriot 1. English and French: dim. (with the suffix -*ot*) of the medieval given name *Herry*, HARRY (a var. of HENRY). **2.** Scots: habitation name from a place, e.g. *Heriot* to the south of Edinburgh, named with ME *heriot*, which denoted a piece of land restored to the feudal lord on the death of its tenant. The ME word is from OE *heregeatu*, a cpd of *here* army + *geatu* equipment, referring originally to military equipment that was restored to the lord on the death of a vassal.

Vars. (of 1): **Harriot**. (Of 2): **Heriot**.

Herrod English (chiefly Notts.): **1.** nickname from the personal name *Herod* (Gk *Hērōdēs*, apparently derived from *hērōs* hero), borne by the king of Judea (d. AD 4) who at the time of the birth of Christ ordered that all male children in Bethlehem should be slaughtered (Matt. 2: 16–18). In medieval mystery plays Herod was portrayed as a blustering tyrant, and the name was therefore given to someone one who had played the part, or who had an overbearing temper. **2.** var. of HARROD (1 or 2).

Var.: **Herod**.

Hersch *see* HIRSCH

Herschberg *see* HIRSCHBERG

Herst *see* HURST

Hertel *see* HARD

Hertwig *see* HARTWIG

Herve *see* HARVEY

Herz 1. German: from a Gmc personal name derived from a short form of the various cpd names with the first element *hard* hardy, brave, strong. **2.** German: nickname for a stout-hearted or kind-hearted individual, from Ger. *Herz* heart (MHG *herze*, OHG *herza*). **3.** Jewish (Ashkenazic): ornamental name from mod. Ger. *Herz* heart, Yid. *harts*. **4.** Jewish (Ashkenazic): from the Yid. male given name *Herts*, which is from MHG *hir(t)z* deer, hart (see HIRSCH).

Vars.: Ger.: **Hertz**. (Of 2 only): Ger.: **Herzen** (also a patr. of 1). (Of 3 and 4): **Herc** (Pol. spelling); **Gertz** (under Russ. influence; see GOREN). (Of 3 only): **Herzer** (from the Yid. pl. *hertser* hearts); **Herzman(n)**, **Hertzmann**; **Gartzman** (under Russ. influence).

Dims. (of 3): **Herzl**, **Her(t)zel**.

Cpds (of 3, mostly ornamental): **Harzbach** ('heart stream'); **Herzbaum** ('heart tree'); **Her(t)z(en)berg**, **Hercenberg**, **Herzberg(er)** ((person from) heart hill'), **Gertzberg** (under Russ. influence); **Hertzburg** ('heart town'); **Herzfeld**, **Harzfeld** ('heart field'); **Hertzheim** ('heart home'); **Harzstark** ('heart-strong'); **Herz(en)stein** ('heart stone'); **Hercwolf** ('heart wolf'); **Herzweig** ('heart twig').

Herzhaft Jewish (Ashkenazic): nickname or ornamental name from the Ger. adj. *herzhaft* bold, courageous.

Var.: **Hertzhaft**.

Herzig Jewish (Ashkenazic): ornamental name from the Ger. adj. *herzig* delightful, charming.

Vars.: **Hertzig**, **Her(t)ziger**.

Herzlich Jewish (Ashkenazic): ornamental name from the Ger. adj. *herzlich* cordial, sincere.

Var.: **Hertzlich**.

Herzog 1. German: from the Ger. title of nobility *Herzog* duke (OHG *herizoho*, from *heri* army + *ziohan* to lead, a calque of the Byzantine title *stratēlatēs* general, commander, from Gk *stratos* army + *elaunein* to lead). The name is unlikely to refer to an actual duke himself; it is normally an occupational name for the servant of a duke or a nickname for one who put on the airs and graces of a duke. **2.** Jewish (Ashkenazic): ornamental name; cf. GRAF and KAISER.

Vars.: Ger.: **Herzig**. Jewish: **Hertzog**, **Hercog**, **Hartzog**; **Gertzog** (under Russ. influence; see GOREN).

Patrs.: Flem., Du.: **Hertogs**. Jewish: **Hartogs**, **Hartogso(h)n** (from the Jewish Dutch male given name *Hartog* 'Duke').

Heschold *see* HERMANN

Heselden *see* HAZELDEN

Heselton *see* HAZELTON

Heselwood *see* HAZELWOOD

Heskel *see* EZEKIEL

Hesketh English (Lancs.): habitation name from places in Lancs. and N Yorks., so called from ON *hestr* horse, stallion (a cogn. of HENGST) + *skeið* racecourse. The ancient Scandinavians were fond of horse-racing and horse-fighting, and introduced both pastimes to England.

Vars.: **Heskett**, **Heskitt**.

Heslam *see* HASLAM

Heslin see HASLING

Heslop English (Northumb.): habitation name from an unidentified place in N England, so called from OE *hæsel* (or the cogn. ON *hesli*) HAZEL + *hop* enclosed valley (see HOPE).

Vars.: **Haslop, Has(e)lup, Heslep, Heslip; H(e)aslip** (N Ireland); **Hislop, Hyslop** (Scotland).

Hesp see APPS

Hess 1. German and Jewish (Ashkenazic): regional name for someone from the state of *Hesse* (Ger. *Hessen*). The placename is first recorded as *Hassia* and probably derives from the *Chatti*, a Gmc tribe mentioned by the Roman historian Tacitus in the 1st cent. AD. 2. Ger. (of Slav. origin): dim. of HERMANN.

Var. (of 1): Ger.: **Hesse**.

Hessel see HAZEL, HERMANN

Hession Irish: Anglicized form of Gael. Ó hOisín 'descendant of *Oisín*', a personal name from a dim. of *os* deer.

Hester see HEISTER

Hetherington English: habitation name from a place in Northumb., probably having the same origin as *Harrington* in Northants. (see HARRINGTON 1).

Vars.: **Heatherington, Etherington**.

Hetman Polish and Jewish (E Ashkenazic): from Pol. *hetman* military leader (from a var. of Ger. HAUPTMANN captain), an occupational name for a military officer or status name for the elected leader of a community, or else a nickname. As a Jewish name, the literal sense 'military leader' never applies.

Hêtreau see HEISTER

Hetschold see HERMANN

Hetterich German: from the Gmc personal name *Hadurīc*, composed of the elements *hadu* battle, strife + *rīc* rule. See also HEYDRICH.

Vars.: **Hed(d)erich**.

Hettmann see HAUPTMANN

Heucheux see HUCHET

Heuer see HAUER

Heugel see HUGH

Heugh N English and Scots: habitation name from any of various places, for example in Co. Durham and Northumb., so called from OE *hōh* spur; see HOUGH, HUFF, HOE.

Heupl see HEAD

Heuptmann see HAUPTMANN

Heurtebise French: perhaps a topographic name for someone living in an exposed situation, buffeted by the north wind, from OF *hurte(r)* to collide, knock against + *bise* north wind (both these elements being of Gmc origin); cf. *Heurtevent* in Calvados. It is also possible that it may have been a humorous nickname for someone with a prominent nose.

Heuse French: metonymic occupational name for a maker or seller of boots and shoes or nickname for someone noted for footwear of an unusual design, from OF *heuse, ho(u)se* boot, shoe (of Gmc origin; cf. HOSIER).

Vars.: **Heuze; Heuzé, Heuzey, Houzé** (nicknames meaning 'shod'; cf. HUSSEY 3).

Dims.: **Houzet, Huzette, Houzel, Houzeaux**.

Pejs.: **H(o)uzard**.

Hevesy Hungarian: 1. habitation name from a place in Hungary called *Heves*. 2. nickname for a man of violent temper, from Hung. *heves* violent, vehement.

Var.: **Hevesi** (partly Jewish (Ashkenazic)).

Hew see HUGH

Heward see HOWARD

Hewin see EWAN

Hewitt English: 1. from the medieval given name *Huet*, a dim. of HUGH. 2. topographic name for someone who lived in an newly made clearing in a wood, ME *hewett* (OE *hīewet*, a deriv. of *hēawan* to chop, cut, hew).

Vars.: **Hewit, Hewet(t), Hewat**. (Of 1 only) **Howet(t), Howat(t); Howitt** (Notts.); **Huet(t), Huitt**.

Patrs. (from 1): **Hewitson, Hewetson; Hewison** (Northumb.); **Howetson, Howatson; Hui(t)son, Huetson**.

Hewlett English (chiefly Worcs.): from the ME given name *Huwelet, Huwelot, Hughelot*, a double dim. of HUGH formed with the dim. suffixes *-el* + *-et* and *-ot*.

Vars.: **Hewlitt, Howlett, Hulett, Hullot**.

Hewson see MCKAY

Hey see HAY

Heycock see HAYCOCK

Heydrich German: from the medieval given name *Heidenreich*, ostensibly composed of the elements *heiden* heathen, infidel (see HEIDEN) + *reich* power, rule, but probably in origin a var. by folk etymology of HETTERICH. The name was extremely popular at the time of the Crusades, the sense 'power over the heathens' being attributed to it.

Vars.: **Heid(en)r(e)ich, Heydenrych, Hädrich**.

Dims.: **Heidel, Hiedle**. Low Ger.: **He(i)decke, Heydicke, Hädicke**.

Heyem see HYAM

Heyer see AYER

Heyes see HAYES

Heyhoe see HAYHOE

Heyman see HAYMAN

Heymann see HENRY

Heynes see HAINES, HYNES

Heyward see HAYWARD

Heywood English (chiefly Lancs.): habitation name from a place near Manchester, so called from OE *hēah* high (see HAY 2) + *wudu* WOOD. There is also a place in Wilts. so called, from OE *(ge)hæg* enclosure + *wudu* (cf. HAYWOOD), although this is probably not the source of the surname.

Heyworth English (Lancs.): habitation name from an unidentified place probably deriving its name from OE *hēah* high (see HAY 2) + *worð* enclosure (see WORTH).

Hezlet *see* HAZLETT

Hibbert English: from the Norman personal name *Hil(de)bert*, composed of the Gmc elements *hild* battle, strife + *berht* bright, famous.

Vars.: **Hibberd**, **Hibbard**, **Hilbert**, **Ilbert**.

Dims.: Ger.: **Hilpl** (Bavaria, Austria). Fris.: **Hibbe**, **Hidde**.

Patrs.: Low Ger.: **Hilbers**, **Ibbers**; **Hilb(e)ring**, **Hilbrink** (Westphalia); **Hilbertz** (Rheinland).

Patrs. (from dims.): Eng.: HIBBS. Low Ger., Dan.: **Ibsen**, **Ipsen**. Fris.: **Hibben**; **Hibbing**, **Ibing**.

Hibbs English (chiefly Devon): 1. patr. from a dim. of HIBBERT. 2. metr. from the medieval female given name *Ibb*, a pet form of *Isabel(le)*; for the initial *H-*, cf. HERRICK. *Isabel* is by origin a var. of *Elizabeth*, a name which owed its popularity in medieval Europe to the fact that it was borne by John the Baptist's mother. The original form of the name was Hebr. *Elisheva* 'my God (is my) oath'; it appears thus in Exod. 6: 23 as the name of Aaron's wife. By NT times the second element had been altered to Hebr. *shabat* rest, Sabbath. The form *Isabella* originated in Spain, the initial syllable being detached because of its resemblance to the def. art. *el*, and the final one being assimilated to the characteristic Sp. fem. ending *-ella*. The name in this form was introduced into France in the 13th cent., being borne by a sister of St Louis who lived as a nun after declining marriage with the Holy Roman Emperor. Thence it was brought to England, where it achieved considerable popularity as an independent given name alongside the root form *Elizabeth*.

Vars.: **Ibbs**, **Ibson**.

Dims.: **Ibbot(t)s**, **Ebbet(t)s**; **Ibbotson**, **Ibbetson**, **Ibbe(r)son**, **Ibbison**.

Hick English: from the medieval given name *Hicke*, a pet form of RICHARD. The substitution of *H-* as the initial resulted from the inability of the English to cope with the velar Norman *R-*; cf. HOBB, HODGE, and also HANN.

Vars.: **Hitch**; **Ick(e)**.

Dims.: **Hickin(g)** (E Midlands), **Hicken** (W Midlands); **Hicklin**, HICKLING; **Higgett**, **Higgitt**, **Higgon**; **Hitchin(g)**, **Hitchen**, **Hitch(e)on** (Lancs., esp. around Burnley); **Hitchcock**, **Hedgecock**, **Hitchcott**, **Hedgecote**, **Hitchcoe**, **Hickock**; **Hiscock**, **Hiscoke**, **Hiscott**, **Hiscutt**, **Hiskett**.

Patrs.: **Hick(e)s** (widely distributed, but most common in the W Country); **Higgs** (chiefly W Midland); **Hitches**; **Ickes**; **Hick(e)son**, **Hixon**; **Higson** (Lancs.); **Hi(t)chisson**.

Patrs. (from dims.): HIGGINS; **Hi(t)chens**, **Hitchin(g)s**, **Hitchcox**, **Hiscocks**, **Hiscox** (chiefly Bristol).

'Servant of H.': **Hickman**, **Hitchman** (chiefly W Midlands); **Higman** (chiefly Devon).

Hickenbotham *see* HIGGINBOTTOM

Hickey Irish: Anglicized form of Gael. *Ó hÍcidhe* 'descendant of *Ícidhe*', a byname meaning 'Doctor', 'Healer'.

Vars.: **O'Hickey**, **O'Hickee**, **Hickie**, **Hicky**.

Hickling English (Notts.): 1. habitation name from a place near Nottingham, so called from the OE tribal name *Hicelingas* 'people of *Hicel(a)*', a personal name or byname of unknown origin. There is also a place of this name and origin in Norfolk, which is another possible source of the surname. 2. dim. of HICK.

Hickmott English (chiefly Yorks. and Lancs.): from the ME given name HICK + ME *maugh, mough* relative (from ON *mágr* or OE *magu*). The exact nature of the relationship is not clear; the ME word meant 'relative by marriage', but was also used occasionally of a female blood relation.

Vars.: **Hitchmough**, **Hitchmouth**.

Hickox *see* HAYCOCK

Hidalgo Spanish: from Sp. *hidalgo* nobleman (attested in this form since the 12th cent.), a contraction of the phrase *hijo de algo* 'son of something'. The expression *hijo de* (L *filius* son + *de* from, of) is used to indicate the abundant possession of a quality, probably influenced by similar Arabic phrases with *ibn; algo* (L *aliquid* something) is used in an elliptical manner to refer to riches or importance. As in the case of other surnames denoting high rank, the name does not normally refer to the nobleman himself, but is usually an occupational name for his servant or a nickname for someone who gave himself airs and graces.

Var.: **Fidalgo** (Aragon).

Hidde *see* HIBBERT

Hiddleston *see* HUDDLESTON

Hide *see* HYDE

Hidler *see* HÜTTLER, HIEDLER

Hie *see* HIGH

Hiedle *see* HEYDRICH

Hiedler S German and Austrian: topographic name for someone who lived by a spring which dried up periodically, from a deriv. of S Ger. dial. *Hi(e)del* intermittent spring.

Vars.: **Hidler** (see also HÜTTLER); **Hiedl**.

Hield *see* HEALD

Hiemer *see* HUBER

Hien *see* HÜHNE

Hierl *see* HERMANN

Hiersemann *see* HIRSEMANN

Hiess S German and Austrian: from a given name, an aphetic short form of *Mathies*; see MATTHEW.

Vars.: **Hies**; **Heiss**, **Haiss**.

Dims.: **Hi(e)sel**, **Heisel**.

Patr. (from a dim.): **Hiesler**.

Hifferan *see* HEFFERNAN

Higerty *see* HEGARTY

Higgett *see* HICK

Higginbottom English: habitation name from a place in Lancs. now known as *Oakenbottom*. The history of the placename is somewhat confused, but it is probably composed of the OE elements *ǣcen* oaken + *botme* broad valley. During the Middle Ages this name became successively *Eakenbottom* and *Ickenbottom*, the second element becoming associated with the dial. word *hicken* or *higgen* mountain ash.

Vars.: **Higginbotham**, **Higginbottam**, **Higenbotham**, **Higenbottam**, **Higinbothom**, **Higgenbottom**, **Heckingbottom**, **Heginbotham**, **Heginbottom**, **Hickinbottom**, **Hickenbotham**.

Higgins 1. English: patr. from the medieval given name *Higgin*, a dim. of HICK. **2.** Irish: Anglicized form of Gael. **Ó hUiginn** 'descendant of *Uiginn*', a byname meaning 'Viking', 'Sea-rover' (from ON *víkingr*). **3.** Irish: Anglicized form of Gael. **Ó hAodhagáin** 'descendant of *Aodhagán*', a personal name representing a double dim. of *Aodh* 'Fire' (cf. McKAY).

Vars.: **Higgens**. (Of 1 only): **Higginson**. (Of 2 and 3): **O'Higgins**. (Of 3 only): **O'Higane**, **O'He(a)gane**, **O'Heaken**, **O'Huggin**, **He(e)gan**, **E(a)gan**; **Eakin** (see also EADE).

High English (chiefly Northumb.): **1.** nickname for a tall man, from ME *hegh, hie* high, tall (OE *hēah*; see also HAY 2). **2.** topographic name for a dweller on a hilltop or high place, from the same word used in a topographical sense. This second use is supported by early forms such as Richard *atte High* (Sussex 1332).

Vars.: **Highe**, **Hie**; **Highman**.

Higham English (Lancs.): habitation name from one of the many places in England so called, of which the most plausible candidate for present-day bearers is that near Burnley. The placename is from OE *hēah* HIGH + *hām* homestead.

Var.: **Hyam**.

Highet Scots: habitation name, probably from *Highgate* in the former county of Ayrs. (now part of Strathclyde region), so called from OE *hēah* HIGH + *geat* GATE.

Vars.: **Hyett**; **Hyatt** (also Jewish, see CHAIT).

Highfield English: habitation name from any of the numerous minor places so called from OE *hēah* HIGH + *feld* pasture, open country (see FIELD).

Var.: **Heafield**.

Highland see HYLAND

Higho see HAYHOE

Hight see HEIGHT

Highton English (Lancs.): habitation name from a place named with the OE elements *hēah* HIGH + *tūn* enclosure, settlement, possibly *Hightown* in SW Lancs. or a similarly named place within the parish of Salford.

Hignett English (Lancs.): from a medieval given name, probably a double dim. of *Higg* (see HICK) formed with the suffixes *-on* + *-et*.

Higonnet see HUGH

Hihn see HÜHNE

Hilary English: **1.** from a medieval male given name (from L *Hilarius*, a deriv. of *hilaris* cheerful, glad, from Gk *hilaros* propitious, joyful). The L name was chosen by many early Christians to express their joy and hope of sal-

vation, and was borne by several saints, including a 4th-cent. bishop of Poitiers noted for his vigorous resistance to the Arian heresy, and a 5th-cent. bishop of Arles. Largely due to veneration of the first of these, the name became popular in France in the forms *Hilari* and *Hilaire*, and was brought to England by the Norman conquerors. **2.** from the much rarer female given name *Eulalie* (from L *Eulalia*, from Gk *eulalos* eloquent, lit. well-speaking, chosen by early Christians as a reference to the gift of tongues), likewise introduced into England by the Normans. A St Eulalia was crucified at Barcelona in the reign of the Emperor Diocletian and became the patron of that city. In England the name underwent dissimilation of the sequence *-l-l-* to *-l-r-* and the unfamiliar initial vowel was also mutilated, so that eventually the name was considered as no more than a feminine form of *Hilary* (of which the initial aspirate was in any case variable).

Vars.: **Hillary**, **Hillery**, **Eller(a)y**, **Elray**.

Dims. (of 1): Eng.: HILL. Fr.: **Hillairet**, **Hilleret**, **Hillairin**, **Hillerin**, **Hillaireau**, **Hillel**, **Hillion**. Ger.: **Lahr**, **Lähr**; **Glohr**, **Klohr**, **Klör**.

Pej. (of 1): Fr.: **Hillard**.

Patrs. (from 1): Sc.: **McKellar**, **MacKeller**, **McEllar**, **McEller** (Gael. **Mac Ealair**). Fr.: **Allilaire**.

Hilbering see HIBBERT

Hildebrand English, French, and German: from a Gmc personal name composed of the elements *hild* battle + *brand* (flaming) sword, introduced into England by the Normans.

Vars.: Eng.: **Hilderbrand**. Fr.: **Hillebrand**. Ger.: **Hille(r)brand**, **Hülle(r)brand**, **Hiltebrandt**, **Hildenbrand**.

Dims.: Eng.: HILL. Ger.: **Hild(t)**, **Hilt**, **Hiltl(e)**; **Hilty** (Switzerland); see also BRAND. Low Ger.: HILL.

Patrs.: Ger.: **Hil(de)brands**. Low Ger.: **Hillebrenner**.

Hildesheim Jewish (WAshkenazic): habitation name from a place near Hanover, recorded in medieval documents in the form *Hildenesheim*. The placename is probably from the gen. case of a personal name derived from a short form of the various Gmc cpd names with a first element *hild* battle, strife + OHG *heim* homestead, but according to Bahlow the first element is a term for a moor or marsh preserved in some modern Fris. dialects.

Vars.: **Hildesheimer**, **Hillesheim**.

Hill 1. English: extremely common and widely distributed topographic name for someone who lived on or by a hill, OE *hyll*. The sound represented by OE *y* developed in various ways in the different dialects of ME: in N England and the E Midlands it became *i*, in SE England *e*, and in the W and central Midlands *u*. Traces of these regional differences may be found in the vars., in spite of the influence of the standard Eng. vocab. word. **2.** English: from the medieval given name *Hill*, a short form of HILARY or of one of the Gmc cpd names with the first element *hild* battle, strife (cf., e.g., HILDEBRAND and HILLIARD). **3.** Low German: dim. of HILDEBRAND. **4.** Jewish (Ashkenazic): Anglicized form of various like-sounding names.

Vars. (of 1): **Hell**, **Hull**; **Hille** (from the OE dat. sing. *hylle*); **Hillam** (from the OE dat. pl. *hyllum*; also the name of a place in

W Yorks.); HILLS; **Hiller**, HELLER; **Hillman**. (Of 3): **Hille**, **Hill(e)mann**, **Hilmann**.

Patrs. (from 3): Low Ger.: **Hillen**, **Hillemans**.

Hillcoat *see* ELLIS

Hilliar *see* HELLIER

Hilliard English: from the Norman female personal name *Hildiarde*, *Hildegard*, composed of the Gmc elements *hild* battle, strife + *gard* fortress, stronghold.

Vars.: **Hilleard**, **Hillyard**, **Hildyard**.

Hillier 1. English: var. of HELLIER. 2. French: cogn. of HILARY.

Hills English: 1. topographic name, a var. of HILL 1. 2. patr. from HILL 2.

Vars.: **Hillis** (N Ireland). (Of 2 only): **Hilson**.

Hilse German: topographic name for someone who lived by a holly tree, MHG *huls* (OHG *hulis*, cogn. with OE *hole(g)n*; cf. HOLME 1).

Dims.: Fr.: **Houssel**, **Housset**, **Houssin**.

Collectives: Fr.: **Houssay(e)**, **Houssais**, **Houssière**.

Hilton English: 1. habitation name from any of various places so called. Most, including those in Cambs. (formerly Hunts.), Cleveland, Derbys., and Shrops., get the name from OE *hyll* HILL + *tūn* enclosure, settlement. Others, including those in Cumb. and Dorset, have early forms in *Hel-* and probably have as their first element OE *hielde* slope (see HEALD) or possibly *helde* tansy. 2. a few early examples such as Ralph *filius Hilton* (Yorks. 1219) point to occasional derivation from a given name, possibly a Norman name **Hildun*, composed of the Gmc elements *hild* battle, strife + *hūn* bear cub.

Var.: **Hylton**.

Hiltunen Finnish: patr. from the given name *Hiltu* (of Gmc origin, probably a deriv. of *hild* battle, strife), with the gen. suffix *-nen*.

Himmel 1. German: habitation name from any of various places named with MHG *himel* heaven, paradise (OHG *himil* heaven, sky), in reference to their pleasant situation and/or the fruitfulness of the soil. 2. Jewish (Ashkenazic): ornamental name from Ger. *Himmel* heaven, selected because of the pleasant associations of the word.

Vars.: Ger.: **Himml**, **Himm(e)ler**, **Himmelmann**. Jewish: **Himel(man)**; **Himlich** ('heavenly').

Cpds (ornamental): Jewish: **Himmelbaum** ('heaven tree'); **Himelberg** ('heaven hill'); **Himmelblau** ('heaven blue'); **Him(m)elbrand** ('sword of heaven'); **Himmelburg** ('heaven town'); **Him(m)elfarb** ('heavenly colour'); **Himmelreich** ('kingdom of heaven'); **Him(m)elschein** ('heavenly light', partly Anglicized as **Himelshine**); **Him(m)elstein** ('heaven stone'), **Himelsztajn** (Pol. spelling), **Gimelstein** (under Russ. influence; see GOREN).

Hinchcliffe English: habitation name from a place in W Yorks., so called from OE *henge-clif* 'steep cliff'.

Vars.: **Hinchcliff**, **Hinchliff(e)**, **Henchcliff(e)**, **Hinchsliff**.

Hinchy *see* HENNESSY

Hinckley English: habitation name from a place in Leics., so called from the OE byname *Hȳnca* (a derivative of *Hūn* 'Bear-cub') + OE *lēah* wood, clearing.

Vars.: **Hinkley**, **Hingley**, **Hinsley**.

Hind English: 1. nickname for a gentle or timid person, from ME, OE *hind* female deer. 2. var. of HINE; for the excrescent dental, cf. DIAMOND.

Vars.: **Hinde**; **Hynd** (Scots). (Of 2): **Hyndman** (N Ireland).

Patrs.: **Hinds**, **Hynds**, HINDES; **Hindson** (Northumb.).

Hindenburg German: habitation name from a place so called from the gen. case of the OHG byname *Hinta* HIND' + OHG *burg* fortress, stronghold.

Hinder 1. German: topographic name for someone who lived at the back of a village or beyond the main settlement, from MHG *hinder* behind, beyond (OHG *hintaro*; mod. Ger. *hinter*); cf. Low Ger. ACHTERMANN. 2. English: probably a nickname from ME *hinder* crafty, treacherous, anxious, fretful (of uncertain origin).

Vars. (of 1): **Hinner**, **Hintner**; **Hinderer**; **Hindermann**.

Hindes 1. English: var. of *Hinds*, patr. from HIND. 2. Jewish (Ashkenazic): metr. from the Yid. female given name *Hinde* HIND'.

Vars. (of 2): **Hindin**, **Hinden** (E Ashkenazic); **Hindels** (from a dim.)

Hindle English: habitation name from a place in the parish of Whalley, Lancs., so called from OE *hind* female deer (see HIND 1) + *hyll* HILL.

Hindley English (Lancs.): habitation name from a place near Manchester, so called from OE *hind* female deer (see HIND 1) + *lēah* wood, clearing.

Var.: **Hindeley**.

Hindmarsh English (Northumb.): habitation name from an unidentified place, probably so called from OE *hind* female deer (see HIND 1) + *mersc* MARSH.

Var.: **Hindmarch**.

Hine English: occupational name for a servant, from ME *hīne* lad, servant (originally a collective term for a body of servants, from OE *hīwan* (pl.) household).

Vars.: **Hyne**, HIND.

Patr.: **Hynes**.

Hiner *see* HYNER

Hines *see* HYNES

Hingle *see* INGLE

Hingston English (Devon): habitation name from a place in Cornwall, apparently so called from the OE byname *Hengest* 'Stallion' (see HENGST) + OE *dūn* hill (see DOWN 1).

Hinken *see* HENRY

Hinks English (W Midlands): apparently a patr. from a medieval given name, perhaps a survival of OE *Hȳnci* or *Hȳnca* (cf. HINCKLEY).

Vars.: **Hin(k)son**.

Hinksey English: habitation name from a place on the Thames just outside Oxford, so called from the gen. case of the OE byname *Hengest* 'Stallion' (see HENGST) + OE *ēg* island, low-lying land.

Hinojosa Spanish: habitation name from any of the numerous places so called, from a deriv. of Sp. *hinoja* fennel (see FENNELL).

Hinton English: habitation name from any of the numerous places so called, which split more or less evenly into two groups with different etymologies. One set (with examples in Berks., Dorset, Gloucs., Hants, Herefords., Somerset, and Wilts.) gets the name from the OE weak dat. *hēan* (originally used after a preposition and article) of *hēah* high + OE *tūn* enclosure, settlement. The other (with examples in Cambs., Dorset, Gloucs., Herefords., Northants, Shrops., Somerset, Suffolk, and Wilts.) gets the first element from OE *hīwan* household, monastery (cf. HINE). The surname is fairly evenly distributed in S and Midland England.

Hipkin *see* HERBERT

Hipólito Spanish and Portuguese: from a medieval given name (Gk *Hippolytos*, composed of the elements *hippos* horse + *luein* to loose). This was the name of a figure in classical mythology who rejected the incestuous love of his stepmother Phaedra, but in the Middle Ages was more closely associated with various minor early Christian saints, especially a bishop of Oporto who was martyred by drowning in the 3rd cent.

Dims.: It.: **Politelli**. Ger.: **Polte**; **Pölt(l)** (S Germany).

Patrs.: Russ.: **Ippolitov**, **Politov**.

Patrs. (from dims.): Ger.: **Poltes**. Russ.: **Polyushkin**, **Polshin**, **Polykhov**, **Polyukhin**, **Polyusov**, **Polunin**, **Polutov**.

Hipworth *see* HEPWORTH

Hircock *see* HERBERT

Hird *see* HEARD

Hiron French and English (Norman): **1.** nickname for a lively person, from OF *hirond*, *arond* swallow; see ARUNDEL. **2.** nickname for a discontented individual, from a dim. of OF *hire* grumble, complaint (of unknown origin).

Vars. (of 1): Fr.: **Ironde**, **Liron(de)**; **Aronde**, **Laronde**.

Patr.: Eng.: **Hirons** (chiefly Birmingham).

Hirsch 1. German: metonymic occupational name for a keeper of deer or nickname for someone who resembled a deer in some way, from Ger. *Hirsch*, MHG *hir(t)z* HART (OHG *hir(u)z*). **2.** Jewish (Ashkenazic): from the Yid. male given name *Hirsh* 'Deer', which is common because of the association of the deer with the Hebr. given name *Naftali*, deriving from the blessing by Jacob of his sons (Gen. 49: 21), in which Naftali is referred to as 'a hind let loose'. **3.** Jewish (Ashkenazic): ornamental name from Ger. *Hirsch* or Yid. *hirsh* deer, one of the many Ashkenazic surnames taken from vocab. words denoting wildlife.

Vars. (of 1): **Hirschmann**, **Hir(t)z**. (of 2 and 3): **Hirsh**; **Hirs(c)hman**; **Hers(c)h(man)**, **Herschman(n)**; **Girs(c)h**,

Gers(c)h, **Gershman** (under Russ. influence; see GOREN); **Erszman** (in regions where Yid. has no /h/).

Dims. (of 1): **Hirschel**, **Hirschle**; **Hirtzel** (Switzerland). (Of 2 and 3): **Hirschel**; **Hers(c)hel** (see also HERMANN); **Hers(c)hko** (among Rumanian Jews).

Patrs. (from 2): **Hirshin**, **Hirschenson**, **Hers(h)enson**, **Hershinson**; **Hershenov**, **Hersc(h)owitz**, **Hersovich**; **Girshov(ich)**, **Girshevich**, **Gershov**, **Gershevich** (under Russ. influence).

Patrs. (from a dim., *Hershke*, of 2): Jewish: **Hershkoff**, **Hers(c)hkowitz**, **Hershkovitz**, **Hers(h)covitz**, **Herscovitch**, **Herscowicz**, **Herscovics**, **Hers(h)kovits**, **Hershkovich**, **Hershkovic**, **Harshkowitch**; **Hershkovici**, **Herscovici** (among Rumanian Jews); **Girshkovich**, **Girshkevich**, **Gershkevich** (under Russ. influence).

Cpds (of 3, ornamental): Jewish: **Hirschenbach** ('deer stream'); **Hirschbein**, **Hers(c)hbein** ('deer leg'); HIRSCHBERG; **Hi(r)schenboim**, **Herschbaum**, **Hershenbaum**, **Herszenbaum** ('deer tree'); **Hershfang** ('deer claw'); **Hirs(c)hfeld**, **Hirsfeld**, **Hers(c)hfeld**, **Girshfeld**, **Gerschfeld** ('deer field', partly Anglicized as **Hirschfield**); **Hershfinger** ('deer finger'); **Hershfinkel** ('deer sparkle'); **Gerschenfus** ('deer's foot'); **Hershenhaus** ('deer house'); **Herszenhaut** ('deerskin'); **Hirsch(h)orn**, **Hers(hen)horn** ('deer horn'); **Hirschkop**, **Hershkopf**, **Hershcopf** ('deer head'); **Hirschkorn**, **Herschkorn** ('deer grain'; in this case the first element could be from Yid. *hirzh* millet, cf. HIRSEMANN); **Hirshprung** ('deer leap'); **Hirsch(en)stein**, **Girshtein**, **Girstejn** ('deer stone'); **Hershenstrauss** ('deer bouquet') **Hirscht(h)al** ('deer valley').

Hirschberg Jewish (Ashkenazic): **1.** habitation name from any of several places in Germany, for example in Thuringia, North Rhine-Westphalia, or what is now *Jelenia Góra* in W Poland, all named with the elements HIRSCH deer + BERG hill. **2.** ornamental name composed of the Ger. vocab. elements *Hirsch* deer + *Berg* hill.

Vars.: **Hirshberg**, **Hers(c)hberg**; **Hirschberger**, **Hars(c)hberger**, **Hars(c)hbarger**.

Hirsemann German: occupational name for a grower of or dealer in millet or panic grass, or topographic name for someone who lived by a patch of land devoted to this crop, from Ger. *Hirse* millet (MHG *hirs(e)*, OHG *hirsi*, *hirso*) + *Mann* man (OHG *man*).

Vars.: **Hiersemann**, **Hirs(ch)er**.

Hirst *see* HURST

Hirtel *see* HEARD

Hirvonen Finnish: patr. from the OFinn. personal name *Hirvo(i)*, from *hirvi* elk.

Hischenboim *see* HIRSCH

Hischke *see* HENRY

Hiscock *see* HICK

Hisel *see* HIESS

Hislop *see* HESLOP

Hitch *see* HICK

Hitchmough *see* HICKMOTT

Hite *see* HEIGHT

Hitler *see* HÜTTLER

Hitscher *see* HENRY

Hixon *see* HICK

Hladík Czech: **1.** nickname for a clean-shaven or bald man, from the Czech adj. *hladký* smooth + the dim. suffix *-ík*. **2.** occupational name for a finisher or polisher of furniture, from a deriv. of the verb *hladit* to polish, burnish, from *hladký*; the word *hladík* is also a technical term in carpentry denoting a kind of rasp or plane.

Var. (of 1): **Hladký**.

Hlava Czech: nickname for someone with some peculiarity of the head, from Czech *hlava* head.

Var.: **Hlavatý** (from the adj. form).

Hlaváček *see* GŁOWACKI

Hloušek Czech: nickname for a deaf man, from Czech *hluchý* deaf + the dim. suffix *-ek*.

Vars.: **Hloužek**, **Hlouch(a)**.

Hnatik *see* IGNACE

Hoad English: topographic name for someone who lived on a heath, from ME *hōth* heath (OE *hāð*, a byform of *hǣð*; see HEATH). This form was restricted in the Middle Ages to SE England, and the surname is still largely confined to Kent and Sussex. In some cases it may be specifically a habitation name from the village of *Hoath* in Kent.

Vars.: **Hoath**, **Ho(a)ther**.

Hoadley English: habitation name from East or West *Hoathley* in Sussex, so called from OE *hāð* HEATH + *lēah* wood, clearing. Cf. HOAD.

Hoare English: **1.** nickname for an old man or someone with prematurely grey hair, from ME *hore*, OE *hār* grey. For the change of OE *-ā-* to ME *-ō-*, cf. ROPER. **2.** topographic name for someone who lived by a slope or shore, OE *ōra*; see ORR 3. For the inorganic *H-*, cf. HERRICK.

Vars.: **Hoar**, **Hore**.

Hoban Irish: Anglicized form of Gael. **Ó hÚbáin** 'descendant of *Úbán*', a personal name of unknown origin.

Hobart *see* HUBERT

Hobb English: from the medieval given name *Hobb(e)*, a pet form of ROBERT. For the altered initial, cf. HICK and HODGE, also HANN. See also DOBB.

Vars.: **Hob**, **Hopp**.

Dims.: **Hobbin**; **Hoblin(g)**, **Hoblyn**; HOPKIN.

Patrs.: **Hobb(e)s**; **Hobbis(s)** (chiefly W Midlands); **Hobson** (most common in W Yorks.); **Hopson**.

Patr. (from a dim.): **Hobbins**.

Hobbe *see* HABBERT

Hobday English (W Midlands): from the given name HOBB + ME *day* servant, i.e. either 'Hobb the servant' or 'servant of Hobb'.

Var.: **Hobdey**.

Hobemann *see* HOFFMANN

Hober *see* HABER

Hobkin *see* HOPKIN

Hobkirk *see* HOPKIRK

Hocek *see* HODEK

Hoch German and Jewish (Ashkenazic): nickname for a tall person, from Ger. *hoch* tall, Yid. *hoykh* (MHG *hōch*, OHG *hōh*, a cogn. of OE *hēah*; see HIGH and HAY).

Vars.: Ger.: **Hoher**, **Ho(c)hmann**, **Höhmann**. Jewish: **Hochman(n)**, **Hocherman**, **Hochner**; **Hojman** (a Spanish spelling); **Goichman** (under Russ. influence; see GOREN); **Heichman** (from NE Yid.).

Patrs.: Flem., Du.: **Hogens**. Jewish: **Hochmanovich** (E Ashkenazic).

Cpds: Jewish: **Hochbaum**, **Hochboim**, **Hochbojm** ('high tree', ornamental, or nickname for a tall person; the last of these is a Pol. spelling); **Hochberg(er)** ((dweller on a) high hill', topographic); **Hochdorf** ('high village', topographic); **Hochfeld(er)** ((dweller in a) high field', topographic); **Hochgeborn** ('high-born', ornamental); **Hochgelernter** ('highly learned', ornamental or a nickname); **Hochgraf** ('high Count', ornamental); **Hochhauser** ('dweller in a high house', topographic); **Hochrad** ('high wheel', ornamental); **Hochschild** ('high shield', ornamental); **Hochsinger** ('high singer', presumably occupational for a cantor); **Hochstadt(er)** ('dweller in a big city', topographic); **Hochstein** ('high rock', ornamental); **Hochstim** ('high voice', a nickname or ornamental var. of *Hochsinger*); **Hochteil** ('high part', topographic); **Hochwald** ('high forest', probably ornamental). Swed. (all ornamental): **Högberg** ('high hill'); **Höglund** ('high grove'); **Högström** ('high river').

Hoche French: nickname for a gambler, from a deriv. of OF *hochier* to shake (of Gmc origin), used especially of playing at dice.

Vars.: **Hochedé**, **Hochedel** ('shake the die').

Dims.: **Hochet**, **Hochon**.

Pej.: **Hochard**.

Höcht *see* HECHT

Hochzeit Jewish (Ashkenazic): presumably a surname taken by someone who was about to get married or who had just been married at the time when the surname was first registered, from Ger. *Hochzeit* wedding (from MHG *hōch(ge)zīt* festival, lit. 'high time').

Hocke *see* HAKE

Hockey English: apparently a habitation name from an unidentified place, probably in S England and named with the OE elements *hocc* mallow + *ēg* island, low-lying land.

Hockley English: habitation name from any of various places, for example in Essex and Warwicks. The former is so called from the OE personal name *Hocca* or the vocab. word *hocc* mallow + *lēah* wood, clearing; the latter from the personal name *Hucca* + *hlāw* hill (see LAW 2 and LOW 1).

Hodd *see* HOOD

Hodder English (chiefly W Country): occupational name for a maker or seller of hoods, from a ME agent deriv. of OE *hōd* HOOD.

Hoddinott Welsh: habitation name from *Hodnet* in Shrops., or any of various places called *Hoddnant* in Wales. The placename is from W *hawdd* pleasant, peaceful + *nant* valley, stream.

Vars.: **Hodinott**; **Hodnett** (now found chiefly in Ireland).

Hodek Czech: from a dim. form of the Czech given name *Hodislav*, composed of the elements *hodi-* be fit, suited + *slav* glory, splendour.

Vars.: **Hodač**, **Hodouš**; **Hoch**, **Hošek**, **Hocek**.

Double dims.: **Hodeček**, **Hodáček**, **Hodoušek**.

Hodermann *see* HADER

Hodes Jewish (Ashkenazic): from the Yid. female given name *Hodes* (Hebr. *Hadasa* 'Myrtle', Eng. *Hadassah*). This was a name of the heroine of the Book of Esther (2: 7), who is more familiarly known in Hebr. and Yid. as *Ester* (from the Babylonian divine name *Ishtar* Astarte).

Vars.: **Hodess**, **Hodas**, **Hodis**, **Hodus**; **Hodys** (a Pol. spelling); **Hudus** (reflecting a S Yid. pronunciation of the name).

Metrs.: **Hodesson**, **Hodison**.

Hodge English: **1**. from the medieval given name *Hodge*, a pet form of ROGER. For the change of initial, cf. HICK and HOBB, also HANN. **2**. nickname from ME *hodge* hog, which occurs as a dial. var. of *hogge*, for example in Ches. placenames; cf. DODGE 2.

Dims.: **Hodgin**, **Hodge(o)n**; **Hodgett**; **Hod(g)kin**, **Hotchkin**, **Hodskin**.

Patrs.: **Hodges**; **Hod(g)son**, **Hodgshon**.

Patrs. (from dims.): **Hodgins**, **Hodgens**, **Hodgetts** (common in the W Midlands); **Hodg(s)kins**, **Hodgki(e)ss**, **Hadgkiss**, **Hotchkins**, **Hotchkis(s)**; **Hodg(e)kinson**, **Hodgkis(s)on**, **Hodgeskinson**, **Hodkinson**.

Hodsdon English: habitation name from *Hoddesdon* in Herts., which gets its name from the OE personal name *Hod* + OE *dūn* hill (see DOWN).

Vars.: **Hodsden**, **Hodgdon**; **Hoddesdon**.

Hoe English: topographic name for someone who lived by a spur of a hill, from the OE dat. case *hō* (originally used after a preposition) of *hōh* (see HUFF, HOUGH). In many cases the surname may be a habitation name from a minor place named with this element, for example one in Norfolk.

Vars.: **Hoo**, **ATTOE**.

Hoes *see* HUFF

Hoetje *see* HUTH

Hoey *see* HOWEY

Hofer S German: topographic name for someone who lived at a particular farmstead, from MHG, OHG *hof* settlement, farm, court + *-er* suffix denoting human nouns.

Vars.: **Hof(f)ert**, **Hofner**, **Höf(n)er**, **Höfler**; **Hoffer** (also Jewish; cf. HOFFMANN 3); **Imhof(f)**.

Hoffmann 1. German: nickname for a farmer who owned his own land as opposed to holding it by rent or feudal obligation, from Ger. *Hof*, MHG *hof* settlement, farm, court (see HOFER) + *mann* man. **2**. E German: occupational name for the manager or steward of an estate, from the same elements as above. The surname, with this sense, was particularly common in Silesia. **3**. Jewish (Ashkenazic): of uncertain origin; Kaganoff suggests that it was selected because of its association with Ger. *hoffen*, Yid. *hofn* to hope, and so expressive of hope for a better future and freedom from persecution. It is also possible that this

is an occupational name, as in 2: many Jews in the Russ. Empire held managerial positions on non-Jewish estates.

Vars. (of 1): **Hofmann** (S Germany); **Hobemann** (Hesse). (Of 3): Jewish: **Hoffman**, **Hofman(n)**; **Gof(f)man** (under Russ. influence; see GOREN); **Hof(f)er**, **Hof(f)ner**, **Gof(f)er** (clearly meaning 'hoper', the latter under Russ. influence); **Of(f)man**, OFFER (in regions where Yid. has no /h/).

Hoffnung Jewish (Ashkenazic): ornamental name from Ger. *Hoffnung* hope, which, like HOFFMANN, may well have been adopted as expressive of hope for a better future.

Vars.: **Hofnung**; **Hofen** (from the verb *hoffen* to hope); **Hof(f)enberg** ('hope hill', an ornamental elaboration); **Hoffmitz** ('hope cap', an ornamental elaboration).

Hoffschläger Low German: occupational name for a shoeing-smith, from an agent deriv. of MLG *huof* hoof (mod. Ger. *Huf*) + *sla(h)en* to strike, hammer (mod. Ger. *schlagen*). High Ger. equivs. for the same occupation are **Hufeisen** 'hoof iron' and **Hufnagel** 'hoof nail'.

Höflich German: nickname for a man of refined behaviour, from Ger. *höflich* polite, well-mannered, refined, MHG *hovelich* (an adj. deriv. of *hof* court (see HOFMEISTER), a calque on OF *courtois* (see CURTIS 1)). See also HÜBSCH.

Hofmeister German: occupational name for the chamberlain in a noble household or an official with similar functions in a religious house, Ger. *Hofmeister*, from MHG *hof* court, household (originally 'settlement' or 'farm'; see HOFER and HOFFMANN) + *meister* MASTER. This name is also borne by Ashkenazic Jews, the reason for its adoption as a Jewish surname being unclear.

Hofrichter German: **1**. occupational name for a judge at a manor court, MHG *hoverichter* (cf. HOFER, HOFFMANN; also RICHTER). **2**. nickname for a hunchback, from the strong form of MHG *hoverecht* hunchbacked (a cogn. of OE *hoferede*).

Var.: **Hoffrichter**.

Hogan Irish: Anglicized form of Gael. *Ó hÓgáin* 'descendant of *Ógán*', a personal name from a dim. of *óg* young. The family claims descent from an uncle of Brian Boru.

Vars.: **O'Hogan(e)**, **O'Hogaine**.

Hogart *see* FOGARTY

Hogarth English (Northumb.) and Scots: probably a var. of HOGGARD, but possibly a habitation name from an unidentified place, the second element of whose name would be Northern ME GARTH enclosure.

Var.: **Hoggarth**.

Hogben English (Kent): nickname for someone with a crippled or deformed hip, from ME *huckbone* hip bone.

Var.: **Hogbin**.

Hogens *see* HOCH

Hogg 1. English (Northumb.) and Scots: metonymic occupational name for a swineherd, from ME *hog* pig (of uncertain origin). It may also occasionally have been a nickname—for a person supposedly resembling a pig in appearance rather than for a dirty person, since in the Middle Ages pigs were not felt to be especially unclean. **2**. Scots and Irish: translation of Gael. *Mac an Bhanbh* 'son of the hog'.

Vars.: **Hogge**; **Hogger**, **Hoggar**.

Hoggard English: occupational name for a keeper of swine, from ME *hog* (see HOGG) + *herd, hard* herdsman (see HEARD).

Var.: **Hoggart**. See also HOGARTH.

Hoghton *see* HUTTON

Hogwood English and Scots (Borders): of uncertain origin, in form evidently a habitation name from a minor place named with ME *hog* (see HOGG) + *wode* WOOD, i.e. 'swine wood'. However, the name apparently alternates from an early date with forms such as *Haigwood*, and if so it may be a N var. of HAYWOOD, or perhaps even 'wood belonging to the HAIG family'.

Vars.: **Haig(h)wood**.

Hohenzollern German: habitation name from a place near Hechingen in Swabia, so called from MHG *hōchen*, weak dat. (originally used after a preposition and article) of *hōch* high (see HOCH) + the ancient placename *Zolorin*, of uncertain etymology.

Hoher *see* HOCH

Hohlbein *see* HOLBEIN

Hoile *see* HOYLE

Hojman *see* HOCH

Holbeche English (Midlands): habitation name from *Holbeach* in Lincs., which derives its name from OE *hol* hollow, sunken + *bæc* back, ridge.

Holbein German: nickname for a bow-legged man, i.e. one with a gap between his knees, from MHG, OHG *hol* hollow + *bein* leg.

Var.: **Hohlbein**.

Holberd *see* HULBERT

Holbrook English: habitation name from any of various places, for example in Derbys., Dorset, and Suffolk, so called from OE *hol* hollow, sunken + *brōc* stream (see BROOK). The name has probably absorbed the Du. **van Hoobroek**, found in London in the early 17th cent., and possibly a similar Low Ger. surname; several American bearers of the name in the 1880 census give their place of birth as Oldenburg or Hanover, Germany.

Vars.: **Holbrooke**, **Houlbrook(e)**, **Holdbrook**, **Holebrook**; **Holbrock**, **Ha(u)lbrook**, **Halbrooks**, **Albrook(s)** (U.S.).

Holcombe English: habitation name from any of various places, for example in Devon, Dorset, Gloucs., Lancs., Oxon., and Somerset, so called from OE *hol* hollow, sunken, deep + *cumb* valley (see COOMBE); cf. HOLDEN.

Vars.: **Holcom(b)**.

Holdane *see* HALDANE

Holdcroft English: habitation name from *Holcroft* in Lancs., so called from OE *holh* hollow, depression + *croft* paddock, smallholding (see CROFT).

Vars.: **Ho(u)lcroft**, **Houldcroft**.

Holden English: habitation name from places in Lancs. and W Yorks., both so called from OE *hol* hollow, sunken, deep + *denu* valley (see DEAN 1); cf. HOLCOMBE.

Vars.: **Houlden**, **Howlden**, **Ho(u)ldin**, **Holding**.

Holder 1. German: topographic name for someone who lived by an elder tree, Ger. *Hol(un)der* (OHG *holuntar, holantar*). 2. Jewish (Ashkenazic): ornamental name from Ger. *Hol(un)der* elder tree. 3. English (chiefly W Midlands): occupational name for a tender of animals, from an agent deriv. of ME *hold(en)* to guard, keep (OE *h(e)aldan*). It is possible that this word was also used in the wider sense of a holder of land within the feudal system.

Vars. (of 1): **Holderer**; **Holdermann**; **Holderbaum**. (Of 3): **Houlder**.

Dims. (of 1): **Hölderl(e)in**, **Hölderle**.

Holderness English: regional name from the coastal district of E Yorks. (Humberside), the origin of which is probably ON *holdr*, a Danelaw rank of feudal nobility immediately below earl + *næs* nose, headland.

Var.: **Holness**.

Holdrup English: of uncertain origin, most probably a habitation name from a place (perhaps in Hants, where the surname seems to have originated) so called from OE *holh* hollow, depression + *prop* village (see THORPE).

Var.: **Holdup**.

Holdsworth *see* HALLWORTH

Hole English (Somerset and Devon): topographic name for someone who lived in or by a depression or low-lying spot, from OE *holh* hole, hollow, depression, akin to the adj. *hol* hollow, sunken, deep.

Vars.: **Houle**, HOYLE; **Hollow**; **Holer**, **Holah**; **HOLMAN**.

Holeček *see* GOLEC

Holford English: habitation name from any of various places, for example in Somerset, so called from OE *hol* hollow, sunken, deep + *ford* FORD.

Vars.: **Houlford**, **Holdford**, **Holdforth**.

Holgado Spanish: from Sp. *holgado* idle (past part. of *holgar* to be idle, enjoy oneself, from LL *follicāre*). It may have been a nickname for an indolent or fun-loving person, or a topographic name for someone who lived on a patch of uncultivated land.

Var.: **Folgado** (Aragon).

Holgate English: habitation name from any of various places, for example in W Yorks., so called from OE *hol* hollow, sunken + ON *gata* road; cf. HOLLOWAY.

Holiday *see* HALLIDAY

Holland 1. English: habitation name from any of the eight villages in various parts of England so called, from OE *hōh* ridge (see HOE) + *land* land. 2. English, German, Jewish (Ashkenazic), Flemish, and Dutch: regional name from *Holland*, a county of the Holy Roman Empire in the Netherlands (for which it has long been used in Eng. as a synonym). The name is generally assumed to be from MLG *hol* hollow, sunken + *land* land, but Bahlow prefers to see in the first syllable an ancient element descriptive of marshland. **3.** Irish: Anglicized form of various Gael. surnames; cf. HOULIHAN, MULHOLLAND, and WHELAN.

Vars. (of 1): **Hollands**, **Howland**, **Hoyland**. (Of 2): **Holla(e)nder**, **Holand(er)**; **Goland**, **Golender** (under Russ. influence; see GOREN).

Hollier English and French: occupational name for a brothel-keeper, ME, OF *hol(l)ier* (a dissimilated var. of *horier*, agent noun from *hore, hure* whore, of Gmc origin). It may also have been used as an abusive nickname.

Vars.: Eng.: **Hollyer**, **Hullyer**; **Hollister** (originally a fem. form; cf. BAXTER).

Pej.: Fr.: **Hollard**.

Hollingsworth English: habitation name from places in Ches. and Lancs. called *Hollingworth*, from OE *hole(g)n* holly (see HOLME 1 and HOLLIS) + *worð* enclosure (see WORTH).

Var.: **Hollingworth**.

Hollington English: habitation name from any of various places, for example in Derbys., Staffs., and Sussex, so called from OE *hole(g)n* holly (see HOLME 1 and HOLLIS) + *tūn* enclosure, settlement.

Hollinshead English: habitation name from an unidentified place in Co. Durham, apparently called *Hollingside* or *Holmside*, from OE *hole(g)n* holly (see HOLME 1 and HOLLIS) + *sīde* side of a hill.

Vars.: **Hollingshead**, **Hollin(g)shed**.

Hollis English: topographic name for someone who lived by a group of holly trees, from ME *holi(n)s*, pl. of *holin, holi(e)* (OE *hole(g)n*; see HOLME 1).

Vars.: **Holliss**, **Holl(i)es**; **Holl(e)y**; **Hollins**, **Holling(s)**, **Hollen(s)** (chiefly Yorks.).

Holliwell *see* HALLIWELL

Holloran *see* HALLORAN

Holloway English: habitation name from any of the numerous minor places so called, from OE *holh* hollow, sunken + *weg* way, path; cf. HOLGATE.

Vars.: **Holl(a)way**, **Holdaway**, **Holoway**.

Hollywood Irish: translation of Gael. **Ó Cuileannáin** 'descendant of *Cuileannán*', a personal name from a dim. of *cuileann* holly tree. See also QUILL.

Holman 1. English, Flemish, and Dutch: topographic name for a dweller in a hollow; see HOLE. **2.** English: topographic name for a dweller by a holly tree or on an island, from ME *holm* (see HOLME) + *man*.

Vars.: Eng.: **Hollman**, **Ho(le)man**. Flem., Du.: **Holleman**.

Holme English and Scots: **1.** topographic name for someone who lived by a holly tree, from ME *holm*, a divergent development of OE *hole(g)n*; the main development was towards mod. Eng. *holly* (see HOLLIS). **2.** topographic name for someone who lived on an island, in particular a piece of slightly raised land lying in a fen or partly sur-

rounded by streams, Northern ME *holm* (ON *holmr*), or habitation name from a place named with this element.

Vars.: **Holmes**, **Hulme(s)**; **Home**, **Hume**; HOMER.

Dan.: **Holm(e)**, **Holmen**. Ger.: **Holm**.

Cpds (of 2; mostly ornamental): Swed.: **Holmberg** ('island hill'); **Holmgren** ('island branch'); **Holmlund** ('island grove'); **Holmqvist** ('island twig'); **Holmstedt** ('island homestead'); **Holmsten** ('island stone'); **Holmstrand** ('island shore'); **Holmström** ('island river').

Holopainen Finnish: patr. from the occupational term *holop* worker, servant.

Holoubek *see* GOLUBEV

Holroyd English: habitation name from any of various minor places in N England so called from OE *hol* hollow, sunken + *rod* clearing (see RHODES).

Vars.: **Holroyde**, **Holdroyd**, **Howroyd**.

Holst Low German, Dutch, and Danish: topographic name for someone who occupied a patch of woodland, from a reduced form of MLG *holtsäte*, a cpd of *holt* wood (see HOLT) + *säte* tenant (from *sitten* to sit). The province of *Holstein*, long disputed between Germany and Denmark, gets its name from the dat. pl. *holsten* of this word (originally used after a preposition); the final syllable has been erroneously altered, on the assumption that it is Low Ger. *sten* stone, which in High Ger. has the form *stein*.

Var.: **Holste**.

Holt English: topographic name for someone who lived in or by a wood or copse, ME, OE *holt*, or habitation name from one of the very many places named with this word. The surname is widely distributed, but rather more common in Lancs. than elsewhere.

Vars.: **Hoult**; **Holter**.

Dims.: Ger.: **Hölzl(e)**. Low Ger.: **Höltje**, **Höltgen**.

Cpds (ornamental unless otherwise stated): Jewish: **Hol(t)zberg**, **Holcberg** ('wood hill'); **Holzblat**, **Holcblat** ('wood leaf'); **Holzdorf** ('wood village'); **Holzhendler** ('wood dealer', occupational); **Holzstein**, **Holcstein** ('wood stone').

Holtham English: habitation name from an unidentified place, presumably named from OE *holt* wood + *hām* homestead. Alternatively, it may be an altered form of HOLTUM.

Holton English: habitation name from any of the numerous places so called. The final syllable represents OE *tūn* enclosure, settlement. The first element has a wide variety of possible origins. In the case of three examples in Lincs. it is OE *hōh* spur of a hill (see HOUGH); for places in Oxon. and Somerset it is OE *halh* nook, recess (see HALE 1); for one in Dorset it may be OE *holh* hollow, depression (see HOLE) or *holt* wood, copse (see HOLT); for a further pair in Suffolk it may be *hola*, gen. pl. of *holh* hollow, but more probably a personal name *Hōla*.

Holtum 1. English (Kent): probably a habitation name from some minor place named with OE *holtum*, dat. pl. of *holt* wood (see HOLT). **2.** Low German: habitation name from any of various places named with the MLG elements *holt* wood + *heim, hēm* homestead.

Var. (of 1): **Holttum**.

Holyoak English: **1.** topographic name, from ME *holy* holy (OE *hālig*) + *oke* (OE *āc* oak), for someone who lived near an oak tree with religious associations. This would have been one which formed a marker on a parish boundary and which was a site for a reading from the Scriptures in the course of the annual ceremony of beating the bounds. **2.** habitation name from the village of *Holy Oakes* in Leics., recorded in Domesday Book as *Haliach*, and no doubt deriving its name as above.

Vars.: **Holyoake**, **Hollyoak(e)**, **Hollyhock**.

Holzapfel German: topographic name for someone who lived by a crab-apple tree or nickname for someone with a sour temperament, from Ger. *Holzapfel* crab-apple (literally 'wood-apple'; cf. HOLT and APPLE).

Homan *see* HOLMAN

Homburg Jewish (Ashkenazic): habitation name from places in Hesse and Saarland, so called from the weak dat. case (originally used after a preposition and article) of OHG *hōh* high (see HOCH) + *burg* town, fortress (see BURKE).

Var.: **Homburger**.

Home *see* HOLME

Homer English (W Midlands): **1.** occupational name for a maker of helmets, from the adopted OF term *he(a)umier* (from *he(a)ume* helmet, of Gmc origin; cf. HELM 2). **2.** var. of HOLME.

Homewood English (Sussex): habitation name from any of various places of this name, in particular one in the parish of Perching recorded as *Homwood* in about 1280; there were others in Chailey and Forest Row. All are probably named from ME *home* homestead, manor (OE *hām*; for the vowel change, cf. ROPER) + *wode* WOOD.

Homfray *see* HUMPHREY

Homm *see* HUMM

Hommeister *see* HOFMEISTER

Hommel *see* HUMMEL

Hommers *see* HUMBERT

Homola Czech: from the vocab. word *homole* cone, in various applications. In some cases it is a habitation name from a place deriving its name from being near a coneshaped hill; in other cases it is a nickname for someone with a pointed or cone-shaped head.

Homolka Czech: nickname for a mild or soft person, from the vocab. word *homolka* (cone-shaped lump of) cream cheese, a dim. of *homole* cone (see HOMOLA).

Hönack *see* HENRY

Hone English: topographic name for someone who lived by a boundary stone or a prominent outcrop of rock, from ME *hōn* stone, rock (OE *hān*, cf. mod. Eng. *hone* whetstone; for the vowel change, cf. ROPER).

Vars.: **Hones**, **Honer**.

Höne German: from the Gmc personal name *Huno*, a short form of the various cpd names with the first element *hūn* (cf., e.g., HUMBOLDT and HUMPHREY). The exact meaning of this element is disputed, but it may be cogn. with ON *húnn* bear cub.

Dims.: Low Ger.: **Hönemann**, **Hönecke**, **Hönk**.
Patr. (from a dim.): Low Ger.: **Hönks**.

Honeen *see* HOONEY

Honegger German: habitation name from any of the various places (including one in Switzerland) that get their names from an uncertain first element + OHG *ecka*, *egga* corner, bend, nook (see ECK).

Var.: **Honecker**.

Honey English (chiefly W Country): metonymic occupational name for a gatherer or seller of honey, OE *hunig*, or nickname from the same word used as a term of endearment, a sense which was common in medieval England.

Vars.: **Hon(n)eyman**.

Cpds (ornamental): Jewish: **Honigbaum** ('honey tree'); **Honig(s)berg** ('honey hill'); **Honigsfeld** ('honey field', Anglicized HONEYFIELD); **Honigstein** ('honey stone'); **Honigwachs** ('honey wax').

Honeyball English: from a given name of uncertain origin, perhaps a Gmc personal name composed of the elements *hūn* bear cub + *bald* bold, brave, or else an altered form of the female given name *Anabel*.

Vars.: **Honniball**, **Hunneyball**, **Hunnibal**, **Honneybell**, **Hunneybell**, **Hunnibell**, **Hunnable**.

Honeycombe English (W Country): **1.** habitation name from *Honeycomb* in Cornwall, so called from OE *hunig* HONEY + *cumb* valley (see COOMBE). **2.** nickname from ME *honeycomb*, used as a term of endearment, for example in Chaucer, in the same way as the simple HONEY.

Honeyfield **1.** English (W Country): topographic name for someone who lived in an area of open land where honey was found or which was regarded as particularly pleasant, from OE *hunig* HONEY + *feld* pasture, open country (see FIELD), or habitation name from an unidentified place named with these elements. **2.** Jewish (Ashkenazic): Anglicized form of *Honigsfeld*; see HONEY.

Honkanen Finnish: ornamental or topographic name from Finn. *honka* pine + the gen. suffix *-nen*.

Honoré French: from a medieval given name (L *Honorātus* 'Honoured'). The name was borne by a 5th-cent. bishop of Arles and a 6th-cent. bishop of Amiens, both of whom became popular minor saints and contributed to the frequency of the name in the Middle Ages.

Honse *see* HANS

Hont *see* FONT

Hoo English (S England and E Anglia): topographic name for someone who lived on a spur of a hill, from the OE dat. case *hō* (originally used after a preposition) of *hōh* (see HOE). In many cases the surname may derive from minor places named with this word, such as *Hoo* in Kent and *Hooe* in Devon and Sussex.

Var.: **Hooe**.

Hood 1. English: metonymic occupational name for a maker of hoods or nickname for someone who wore a distinctive hood, from OE *hōd* hood (a cogn. of HUTH 1 and a distant cogn. of HATT). Some early examples with prepositions seem to be topographic names, referring to a place where there was a natural shelter or overhang, providing protection from the elements. **2.** Irish: Anglicized form of Gael. **Mac hUid** 'son of *Ud*', a personal name of uncertain derivation.

Vars. (of 1): **Hodd(e)**; **Hoods, Hodd(e)s** (local names). (Of 2): **Mahood**.

Hoof *see* HUFF

Hoogland Dutch: topographic name for someone who lived on a piece of raised land, from MDu. *hooch* high (see HOCH) + *land* land.

Hoogstraeten Dutch: topographic name for someone who lived on the principal thoroughfare of a town, from MDu. *hooch* high (see HOCH) + *strāte* STREET; the ending represents the remains of an inflected form following the loss of the preposition and article *van der* 'of the'.

Hook English: from ME *hoke*, OE *hōc* hook, in any of a variety of senses: **1.** metonymic occupational name for someone who made and sold hooks as agricultural implements or employed them in his work. **2.** topographic name for someone who lived by a 'hook' of land, i.e. the bend of a river or the spur of a hill. **3.** nickname (in part a survival of an OE byname) for someone with a hunched back or a hooked nose. A similar ambiguity of interpretation presents itself in the case of CROOK. **4.** Jewish (Ashkenazic): of unknown origin.

Vars.: **Hooke**; **Hooker** (from 1 or 2); **Hook(e)s** (from 2, or patrs. from 3); **Athoke** (from 2).

Hookins *see* HUGH

Hookway English (Devon): habitation name from a place near Crediton, probably so called because the road (OE *weg*) took a detour here around a spur of a hill or bend in a river (see HOOK 2).

Hooley English (N England): habitation name from places called *Hoole* in Ches. and Lancs. The former is so called from the OE dat. case *hole* of *holh* hollow, depression; the latter from ME *hule* hut, shelter (OE *hulu* husk, covering). In both cases the final *-e* is now silent in the placename, but has been retained in the surname, with consequent alteration in the spelling.

Vars.: **Whooley, Hoole**.

Hooney Irish: Anglicized form of Gael. **Ó hUaithnigh** 'descendant of *Uaithneach*', a personal name from *uaithne* green.

Vars.: **O'Honie, O'Howney, Houghney**; GREEN.

Dims.: **O'Hoonin, O'Hownyn, O'Honeen, O'Hunnyn, Ho(u)neen, Huneen, Oonin** (Gael. **Ó hUaithnín**).

Hooper English (widely distributed, but most common in Devon): occupational name for someone who fitted wooden or metal hoops on wooden casks and barrels, an agent deriv. of ME *hoop* hoop, band (a borrowing from MDu.):

Hoose *see* HOUSE

Hoover *see* HUBER

Hopcroft English (E Midlands): habitation name from an unidentified place, probably named with the OE elements *hop* valley among hills (see HOPE) + *croft* paddock, smallholding (see CROFT).

Hope English and Scots: topographic name for someone who lived on a patch of enclosed land or in a small, enclosed valley, ME *hop(e)*, OE *hop*, or habitation name from a place named with this word, of which there are examples in Ches., Devon, Derbys., Herefords., Kent, Lancs., Shrops., Sussex, N Yorks, and Clwyd. The surname is most common in N England and Scotland.

Vars.: **Hopes, Hopping**.

Höpfner German: occupational name for a grower of hops or dealer in hops, or occupational nickname for a brewer, from the use of hops in the manufacture of beer, from Ger. *Hopfen* hops (MHG *hopfe* OHG *hopfo*) + *-er* suffix of agent nouns.

Vars.: **Höpfer, Höptner, Heptner, Hep(p)ner**; **Hopf(n)er** (Bavaria); **Hopf**.

Dim.: Ger. **Höpfli** (Switzerland).

Hopkin English: from a medieval given name, a dim. of HOBB, formed with the addition of the suffix *-kin* (of Low Ger. origin) and subsequent devoicing by assimilation.

Var.: **Hobkin**.

Patrs.: **Hopkins, Hopkinson**; **Hobkins, Hobkinson**.

Hopkirk Scots: habitation name from *Hopekirk* in the parish of Hawick, so called from Northern ME *hop(e)* valley among hills (see HOPE) + *kirk* church (see KIRK).

Var.: **Hobkirk**.

Hopp *see* HOBB

Hopton English: habitation name from any of various places, for example in Derbys., Herefords., Shrops., Staffs., Suffolk, and W Yorks., so called from OE *hop* valley among hills (see HOPE) + *tūn* enclosure, settlement.

Hopwood English: habitation name from a place in Lancs., so called from OE *hop* valley among hills (see HOPE) + *wudu* WOOD.

Horáček *see* GÓRSKI

Horan Irish: **1.** Anglicized form of Gael. **Ó hUghróin** 'descendant of *Ughrón*', a personal name from *ughrach* warlike. **2.** Anglicized form of Gael. **Ó hOdhráin** 'descendant of *Ódhrán*', a personal name (borne, according to legend, by St Patrick's charioteer) from *odhar* dun-coloured (cf. HERON 3). **3.** var. of HANRAHAN.

Hörauf German: from a Gmc personal name, *Heriwulf*, composed of the elements *heri, hari* army + *wulf* wolf. The first syllable embodies a regular development of the vowel in the S German dialects, but the whole name has subsequently been altered by folk etymology to the imperative form of *aufhören* to cease, desist, i.e. as if it meant 'Stop it!'

Horbasch *see* URBAN

Horcajada Spanish: habitation name from places in the provinces of Cuenca and Ávila, so called from a deriv. of HORCAJO.

Horcajo Spanish: habitation name from any of several places so called from Sp. *horcajo* fork (in a road or a river), a deriv. of *horca* fork (the implement; from L *furca*, cf. FOURCHE).

Hordienko *see* GORDEEV

Hore *see* HOARE

Hořejš Czech: topographic name for someone who lived in the upper part of a village or on an upper story of an apartment house, from Czech *hořejš* upper, higher, upstairs. Compare DOLEJŠ.
Var.: **Hořejší**.

Horgan Irish: **1.** var. of HANRAHAN. **2.** var. of MORGAN.

Hörholz *see* HARROD

Horick *see* GEORGE

Horisky *see* FOURISH

Horkan *see* HANRAHAN

Horkheimer *see* HERKOMMER

Horký Czech: nickname for a hot-tempered, choleric, or embittered individual, from Czech *horký* hot, bitter (cogn. with Pol. *gorzki* bitter).
Dims.: Czech: **Horčík, Horčička**.
Patr.: Pol.: **Gorzkiewicz**.
Habitation name: Pol.: **Gorzkowski**.

Hörl *see* HERMANN

Horlacher German: habitation name from *Horlach* in Bavaria or *Horlachen* in Württemberg, both so called from OHG *hor* mud, marsh (cf. HORTON) + *lahha* pool, pond (cf. LAKE); the latter place retains traces of an inflected ending.

Horley English: habitation name from places in Oxon. and Surrey, both so called from OE *horn* tongue of land, spur of a hill (see HORN 3) + *lēah* wood, clearing.

Horlock English: either a more explicit var. of HOARE 1 or else a nickname for someone with just a patch of grey in his hair, from OE *hār* grey + *locc* lock of hair.
Vars.: **Harlock, Horlick**.

Hormaeche Spanish form of Basque **Ormaetxe**: topographic name for someone who lived in a stone house, from Basque *orma* stone wall + *etxe* house.
Vars.: **Hormaechea, Ormaeche(a)**.

Horn English, German, and Danish/Norwegian: from OE, OHG, ON *horn* horn, in a variety of senses: **1.** occupational name for someone who made small articles, such as combs, spoons, and window lights, out of horn. Horn was a commonly used material in the Middle Ages, when glass was for most people prohibitively expensive and plastics had, of course, not been invented. **2.** metonymic occupational name for someone who played the musical instrument, which was made from the actual horn of an animal. This was used not only in recreation and entertainment but also as a signal. **3.** topographic name for someone who lived by a horn-shaped spur of a hill or tongue of land in a bend of a river, or habitation name from any of the places named with this element (for example, one in Surrey on a spur

of a hill and one in Leics. in a bend of a river). **4.** nickname of uncertain application, perhaps referring to some feature of a person's physical appearance, or else used to refer to a cuckolded husband. The notion of the cuckold growing horns is attested from late antiquity and is found in most European languages; the best guess at its origin probably lies in the fact that when a cock was castrated the spurs and comb, outward symbols of its virility, were also removed; the spurs were sometimes grafted to the root of the comb, where they grew into 'horns' of up to several inches in length. This barbarous practice added to the variety of the sport in cock-fighting. **5.** Jewish (Ashkenazic): presumably from Ger. *Horn* horn, adopted as a surname for reasons that are not clear. It may be purely ornamental, or it may refer to the ram's horn (Hebr. *shofar*) blown in the Synagogue during various ceremonies. The latter is probably the reference of the cpd **Hornblas(s)** 'horn blow'.
Vars.: Eng.: **Horne; Horner, Hornor**. Ger.: **Horner, Hörner; Horn(e)mann, Hormann**. (Of 3 only): Eng.: **Athorn(e)**. (Of 5): **Horen, GOREN; Horner; Hornik(er)** ('horn-like').
Dims. (of 4): Ger.: **Hornlein, Hörnle**.
Cpds (mainly ornamental): Swed.: **Hörnfeldt** ('corner field'); **Hörnqvist** ('corner twig'). Jewish: **Hornfeld** ('hornfield'); **Hornreich** ('horn rich'); **Hor(e)nstein** ('horn stone'), **Hornsztajn** (Pol. spelling), **Or(e)nstein, Orensztein** (in regions where Yid. has no /h/); also *Gorenstein* (see at GOREN).

Hornby English (chiefly Lancs., but also found elsewhere): habitation name from any of various places in N England so called. Those in Lancs. and near Bedale in N Yorks. are from the ON personal name *Horni* HORN' + ON *býr* farm, settlement. One in the parish of Great Smeaton, N Yorks., is recorded in Domesday Book as *Horenbodebi* and probably has as its first element an ON personal name composed of the elements *horn* horn + *boði* messenger.

Horncastle English: habitation name from a place in Lincs., so called from OE *horn* tongue of land (see HORN 3) + *ceaster* (Roman) fort (see CHESTER). The town is situated between the rivers Bain and Waring.

Hornet *see* ARNOLD

Horník Czech: occupational name for a miner, Czech *horník* (from *hora* mountain (see GÓRSKI) + *-ník* suffix of agent nouns).
Dim.: **Horníček**.

Horniman *see* HEARN

Hornsby English: habitation name from a place in Cumb., so called from the gen. case of the ON byname *Ormr* 'Serpent' (see ORME 1) + ON *býr* farm, settlement. The form of the name seems to have been influenced by confusion with HORNBY.

Horowitz Jewish (Ashkenazic): habitation name from *Hořovice* in Bohemia, part of Czechoslovakia. The name is a deriv. of the Slav. element *gora* hill (see GÓRSKI).
Vars.: **Horovitz, Horwitz, H(a)urwitz; Gorwitz, Gurvitz, Gur(e)vich, Gurovich** (under Russ. influence; see GOREN); **Urwitz, Urevich** (from S Yid. dialects which have no /h/).

Horrey *see* WOOLDRIDGE

Horridge English: habitation name from *Horwich* in Lancs., so called from OE *hār* grey (see HOARE 1) + *wice* wych elm.

Var.: **Horwich**.

Horrocks English (chiefly Lancs.): habitation name from Great or Little *Horrocks* in Greater Manchester, so called from the pl. form. of the dial. term *hurrock* heaped-up pile of loose stones or rubbish (of uncertain origin).

Horsburgh Scots: habitation name from a place in the parish of Innerleithen in the former county of Peebles (now part of Borders region). The name is first recorded before the Conquest as OE *Horsabrōc* 'brook of the horses'.

Horseford English: habitation name from any of various places, for example in Norfolk, so called (from OE *hors* horse + *ford* FORD) because they lay at fords that could only be crossed on horseback.

Vars.: **Horseforth** (from a place in W Yorks.), **Hosford** (now common in N Ireland).

Horsegood see OSGOOD

Horsey English: habitation name from places in Norfolk, Somerset, and Sussex, so called from OE *hors* horse (perhaps a byname) + *ēg* island, low-lying land.

Horsfall English: habitation name from *Horsefall* in W Yorks., so called from OE *hors* horse (perhaps a byname) + *fall* clearing, place where the trees have been felled (from *fellan* to fell, causative of *feallan* to fall).

Horsfield English: either a var. of HORSFALL, or else a habitation name from an unidentified place named with the elements *hors* horse (perhaps a byname) + *feld* pasture, open country (see FIELD).

Horsler see OSTLER

Horsley English: habitation name from any of various places, for example in Derbys., Gloucs., Northumb., Staffs., and Surrey, so called from OE *hors* horse + *lēah* wood, clearing. The reference is probably to a place where horses were put out to pasture.

Horsman English: occupational name for a stable worker, from OE *hors* horse (cf. Ross 4) + *mann* man. It is unlikely to have been a nickname for a skilled rider, for in the Middle Ages the maintenance and use of a horse was far beyond the means of the mass of common people.

Var.: **Horseman**.

Hort see HARDT, HART

Hörter see HEARD

Horter see HARDT

Hortic see ORT

Hörtle see HARD

Horton English: habitation name from any of the various places so called. The majority, with examples in at least fourteen counties, get the name from OE *horh* mud, slime + *tūn* enclosure, settlement. One in Gloucs. has a different origin, from OE *heorot* HART + *dūn* hill (see DOWN 1).

Horváth Hungarian (partly Jewish): name for a Croat, Hung. *Horváth* (from Slav. *Hrvat*), one of the Slavonic

people who settled in what had been the Roman province of Pannonia in the 7th cent. AD, and who were therefore the southern neighbours of the Magyars when they settled in what is now Hungary in the 10th cent. From 1091 to 1526 Croatia was under Hungarian rule. As a Jewish name, this indicates provenance from Croatia.

Vars.: Hung.: **Horvát**. Jewish: **Horvat**.

Dim.: It.: **Croattini**.

Horwell English (Devon): habitation name from *Horwell* in Colebrook, Devon, which is named with the OE elements *horh* mud, slime + *well(a)* spring, stream (see WELL).

Horwood English: habitation name from places in Bucks. and Devon, the former being so called from OE *horh* mud, slime + *wudu* WOOD. The latter place shows early forms in *Har-* and probably has the same origin as HARWOOD.

Hosbons see HUSBAND, OSBORN

Hose see HUFF

Hoseason Scots. (Shetland): patr. from the given name *Hosea*. This was probably originally *Osie*, a dim. of OSWALD, but was later altered by association with the name of the biblical prophet *Hosea*.

Hosegood see OSGOOD

Hosey see HUSSEY

Hosford see HORSEFORD

Hosier English: occupational name for a maker of leggings, from an agent deriv. of ME *hose* (OE *hosa*). Hose was the regular name for garments worn on the legs until the 18th cent. Cf. HEUSE.

Hoskin English (Devon): from the ME given name *Osekin*, a dim. of the various personal names with an OE first element *ōs* god (cf., e.g., OSBORN, OSGOOD, and OSMOND), or its ON cogn. *ās*. For the inorganic initial *H-*, cf. HERRICK.

Vars.: **Hoskyn**, **Hosken**, **Hosking** (all Devon).

Patrs.: **Hoskin(g)s**, **Hosky(n)s**; **Huskinson**, **Hoskis(s)on**, **Huskisson**.

Hostal French: from OF *hostel*, *hostal*, a house of some size and standing, in which it was possible to accommodate guests in separate rooms (LL *hospitāle*, from *hospes*, gen. *hospitis*, guest; cf. the mod. Fr. *hôtel de ville*). The word was probably used as an occupational name for someone who was employed as a servant in such a grand house, in the later Middle Ages perhaps also a keeper of a hotel as now understood (cf. OSTLER).

Vars.: **Host(e)aux**, **Hôtel**; **O(u)stal**, **O(u)stau**; **Lhostal**, **Loustal**, **Loustau** (with fused def. art.); **Dhôtel** (with fused preposition); **Delho(u)stal**, **Delhoustau** (with fused preposition and def. art.).

Dims.: **Oustalet**, **Oustalot**; **Loustalet**, **Loustalot**.

Hosteller see OSTLER

Hotchen see HUTCHIN

Hotchkin see HODGE

Hôtel see HOSTAL

Hother see HOAD

Hothersall English (Lancs.): habitation name from a place in Lancs., found in ME sources as *Hudereshal* and *Huddeshalh*. Ekwall proposes an etymology from an OE personal name **Huder* + OE *halh* nook, recess (see HALE 1).

Houard French: apparently an occupational name for a humble type of agricultural worker, from OF *houe* hoe (of Gmc origin) + the pej. suffix *-ard*. There has probably also been confusion with HUARD.

Houchen see HUTCHIN

Houdard French: from a Gmc personal name composed of the elements *huld* friendly + *hard* hardy, brave, strong.
Var.: **Houdart**.
Dims.: **Houdin(et)**, **Houdon**, **Houdot**.

Houdek see HUDEC

Houdsworth see HALLWORTH

Houf see HUFF

Hougård Danish: habitation name from a placename composed of the elements *hov* court (cf. HOFER) + *gård* enclosure (cf. GARTH).
Vars.: **Hougaard**, **Hovgård**, **Hovgaard**.

Hough English: habitation name from any of various places, for example in Ches. and Derbys., so called from OE *hōh* spur of a hill (literally 'heel').
Var.: **HUFF**.

Houghney see HOONEY

Houghton English: habitation name from any of the various places so called. The majority, with examples in at least fourteen counties, get the name from OE *hōh* ridge, spur (see HOUGH) + *tūn* enclosure, settlement; cf. HUTTON. *Haughton* in Notts. also has this origin, and may have contributed to the surname. A smaller group of *Houghtons*, with examples in Lancs. and W Yorks., have as their first element OE *halh* nook, recess (see HALE 1). In the case of isolated examples in Devon and E Yorks., the first elements appear to be OE personal names or bynames, of which the forms approximate to **Huhha* and **Hofa* respectively, but the meanings are unknown.

Houghy see HOWEY

Houie see GILDUFF

Houlbrook see HOLBROOK

Houlcroft see HOLDCROFT

Houlden see HOLDEN

Houlder see HOLDER

Houldershaw see OLLERENSHAW

Houle see HOLE

Houlford see HOLFORD

Houlihan Irish: Anglicized form of Gael. **Ó hUalacháin** 'descendant of *Uallachán*', a personal name from a dim. of *úallach* proud, arrogant.

Houliston Scots: habitation name from *Howlison* in the parish of Heriot, Lothian, apparently so called from the

Norman personal name *Hulot* (a dim. of *H(e)ude*, from the Gmc element *hild* battle) + ME *toun* settlement (OE *tūn*).

Hoult see HOLT

Hourigan see HANRAHAN

Hourseau see ORSO

Hourtic see ORT

House English: 1. from OE *hūs*. In the Middle Ages the majority of the population lived in cottages or huts rather than houses, and in most cases this name probably indicates someone who had some connection with the largest and most important building of the settlement, either a religious 'house' or simply the local 'great house'. In some cases it may indicate a 'householder', someone who owned his own dwelling as opposed to being a tenant. 2. a relatively modern respelling of HOWES.
Vars. (of 1): **Hoose**; **Houser**; **Hous(e)man**; **Household(er)**.
Dim.: Low Ger.: **Hüsgen**.
Patrs.: Flem., Du.: **Hui(j)smans**, **Huysmans**.

Housley English: habitation name from *Housley* Hall in Ecclesfield, W Yorks., a cpd of OE *hūs* (see HOUSE 1) with *lēah* wood, clearing.

Houssais see HILSE

Houston Scots: 1. habitation name from a place near Glasgow, so called from the gen. case of the medieval given name HUGH + ME *tune, toun* settlement, village (OE *tūn* enclosure, settlement). The landlord in question is a certain *Hugo* de Paduinan, who held the place *c.*1160. 2. Anglicized form of Gael. *Mac Uistean*; see MCCUTCHEON.
Vars. (of 1): **Houstoun**, **Huston**.

Houton see HUTTON

Houzard see HEUSE

Hovgaard see HOUGÅRD

Hovorka Czech: nickname for a talkative person, Czech *hovorka*, from *hovor* talk, conversation.

Howard 1. English: from the Norman personal name *Huard, Heward*, composed of the Gmc elements *hug* heart, mind, spirit + *hard* hardy, brave, strong. 2. English: from the Anglo-Scandinavian personal name *Hāward*, composed of the ON elements *há* high + *varðr* guardian. 3. English: var. of EWART. 4. Irish: see FOGARTY.
Vars. (of 1): **Heward**, **Hewart**, **Huart**. (Of 2): **Haward**.
Patrs. (from 1): **Hewartson**, **Hewertson**, **Huartson**, **Huertson**.

Howarth English (Lancs.): habitation name from *Howarth* or *Haworth* in the parish of Rochdale, Lancs., apparently so called from OE *hōh* mound (see HOE) + *worð* enclosure (see WORTH). However, if the 13th-cent. form *Halwerdeword* refers to this place, the first element may instead represent a personal name such as OE *Hælweard* or ON *Hallvarðr*.
Vars.: **Howo(u)rth**, HAWORTH.

Howat see HEWITT

Howchin see HUTCHIN

Howcroft English (Yorks. and Lancs.): habitation name from some place named as a smallholding (see CROFT) on the spur of a hill (see HOE), e.g. *Howcroft* in Rimington, W Yorks.

Howden 1. Scots: habitation name from a place so called near Kelso on the Eng. border. Early forms include *Hadden*, *Hauden*, and *Halden*; the placename is probably from OE *halh* nook, recess (see HALE 1) + *denu* valley (see DEAN 1). **2.** English: habitation name from a place in Humberside (formerly E Yorks.), so called from ON *hofuð* head (replacing OE *hēafod*) + OE *denu* valley (see DEAN 1); the first element may have been used in the sense 'principal', 'top', or 'end'.

Vars. (of 1): **Hadden**, HADDON.

Howe English: topographic name for someone who lived by a small hill or a man-made mound or barrow, ME *how* (ON *haugr*), or habitation name from a place named with this word, such as *Howe* in Norfolk and W Yorks. **2.** English: var. of HUGH. **3.** Jewish (Ashkenazic): Anglicized form of one or more like-sounding Jewish surnames.

Vars. (of 1 and 2): **How**; HOWES.

Howell 1. Welsh: from the personal name *Hywel* 'Eminent', popular since the Middle Ages in honour of the great 10th-cent. law-giving Welsh king. **2.** English: habitation name from a place in Lincs., probably so called from the OE personal name *Huna* (a short form of the various cpd names with the first element *hūn* bear cub; cf. HÖNE) + OE *well(a)* spring, stream (see WELL).

Vars.: **How(e)l**.

Patrs. (from 1): **Howel(l)s**, POWELL, BOWELL. See also MCHALE.

Howes English: **1.** topographic name from the pl. of ME *how* barrow (see HOWE 1). **2.** patr. from HUGH.

Vars.: **Howse**, HOUSE.

Howey 1. N English and Scots: from a medieval given name, a dim. of HUGH. **2.** Irish: Anglicized form of Gael. **Ó hEochaidh** 'descendant of *Eochaidh*', a var. of *Eachaidh*; see HAUGHEY.

Vars. (of 1): **Howie**. (Of 2): **Hoey**, **Huey**, **Hoy**; **Houghy**, **O'Hohy**, **O'Huhy**.

Patrs. (from 1): **Howi(e)son**.

Howgate English (Yorks.): habitation name, probably from one of several minor places called *Howgate* in W Yorks., earlier *Holgate* (see HOLGATE). Alternatively, the surname may be from *Huggate* in Humberside, which is named as the 'road by the tumuli' (from ON *haugr* tumulus + *gata* road). This was recorded as *Howgate* in 1406.

Howick English: habitation name from places in Lancs. and Northumb. The former gets its name from OE *hōh* spur of a hill (see HOE) or *hōc* HOOK + *wīc* outlying farm (see WICK); the latter probably originally had as its first element OE *hēah* HIGH, but was later influenced by *hōh*.

Howkins *see* HUGH

Howland *see* HOLLAND

Howlden *see* HOLDEN

Howlett *see* HEWLETT

Howroyd *see* HOLROYD

Hoy *see* HOWEY

Hoyland *see* HOLLAND

Hoyle English (Yorks. and Lancs.): topographic name, a var. of HOLE reflecting a regional pronunciation.

Vars.: **Hoile**; **Hoyles**, **Hoiles**.

Hoyo Spanish: topographic name for someone who lived by a hollow or depression in the ground, Sp. *hoyo* (a byform of *hoya*, from L *fovea* pit).

Var.: **Hoyos** (also a nickname for someone scarred by pockmarks).

Hoz 1. Spanish: topographic name for someone who lived by a narrow pass, Sp. *hoz* (L *fauces* throat, used also in a transferred sense of a defile or gorge). **2.** Spanish: metonymic occupational name for someone who made and sold sickles, or who used them in reaping, from Sp. *hoz* sickle (L *falx*, gen. *falcis*). **3.** Jewish (Ashkenazic): ornamental name from Yid. *hoz* rabbit, one of the many Ashkenazic ornamental surnames taken from words for animals.

Hrabák Czech: nickname for a greedy or miserly person, from a deriv. of the verb *hrabat* to rake in, hoard.

Vars.: **Hrabáč**.

Dims.: **Hrabánek**, **Hrabáček**.

Hrabek *see* GRAF

Hrachovec *see* GOROKHOV

Hradec *see* RADECKÝ

Hrádek *see* GRODZKI

Hrb Czech: nickname for a hunchback, from Czech *hrb* hump.

Vars.: **Hrba**, **Hrbáč**, **Hrbatý**.
Dims.: **Hrbek**, **Hrbáček**.

Hrdlička Czech: nickname meaning 'Turtledove', denoting someone with a mild, peaceable, or affectionate temperament, or metonymic occupational name for a keeper of doves, from Czech *hrdlička* dove.

Hrdý Czech: nickname for a brave, proud, or haughty man, from the Czech adj. *hrdý* (cogn. with Gmc *hard*; see HARD). This is also found as a first element in OCzech personal names such as *Hrděbor*, and this may in some cases account for the origin of the surname.

Var.: **Hrdina**.

Hribko *see* GRIBOV

Hrihorovich *see* GREGORY

Hristić *see* CHRISTIAN

Hron Czech: from an OCzech personal name of uncertain origin; Moldanová suggests that it may be an altered form of *Hroznata*, an OCzech name that is apparently an erroneous translation of *Methodius*, the name of the saint who accompanied St Cyril in bringing Christianity to the Slavs. The error arose because *Methodius* was taken as a deriv. of L *metus* fear and translated with a deriv. of Czech *hrozný* fearful, timid, whereas it is in fact from Gk *methodeia* craft, skill, method.

Vars.: **Hroch**, **Hroz**.

Dims.: **Hroník**, **Hroněk**.

Hrušík *see* GRUSHIN

Hrycek *see* GREGORY

Huard French: **1.** cogn. of HOWARD 1. **2.** nickname for a wise or vigilant person, from OF *huard* owl (a deriv. of *huer* to cry, howl, of imitative origin). There has probably also been some confusion with HOUARD.

Huart *see* HOWARD

Hubáček *see* GĘBSKI

Hubach *see* JACOB

Hubble English (W Midlands): from the Norman personal name *Hubald*, composed of the Gmc elements *hug* heart, mind, spirit + *bald* bold, brave.

Vars.: **Hubball**, **Hubbold**.

Hubený Czech: nickname for a thin man, from Czech *hubený* thin.

Huber 1. German and Dutch: from MHG *huobe* (OHG *huoba*), a measure of land, varying in size at different periods and in different places, but always of considerable extent, appreciably larger than the holding of the average peasant. The surname usually denotes a holder or owner of this amount of land, who would have been a prosperous small farmer and probably one of the leading men of his village. However, it seems also to have been acquired sometimes by men of lower status who merely worked on such a holding in return for a wage, having no land of their own. **2.** Jewish (Ashkenazic): from a S Yid. pronunciation of Yid. *hober* oats; see HABER.

Vars. (of 1): Ger.: **Hüb(n)er**; **Hüf(f)ner** (Franconia); **Hue(b)mer**, **Hiemer** (Bavaria, from *huebmeier*; see MAYER). In the U.S. the surname is often Anglicized as **Hoover**. (Of 2): **Hubner**, **Huberman**; **Guber(man)** (under Russ. influence; see GOREN); **Guberblit** ('oat blossom', an ornamental elaboration).

Patr. (from 1): Du.: **Hubers**.

Hubert English, French, and German: from a Gmc personal name composed of the elements *hug* heart, mind, spirit + *berht* bright, famous. The name was borne by an 8th-cent. bishop of Maastricht who was adopted as the patron of hunters, and helped to increase the popularity of the given name, especially in the Low Countries.

Vars.: Eng.: **Hubbert**, **Hubbart**, **Hubbard**, **Hobart** (this last form being especially common in E Anglia). Ger.: **Hübert**, **Hup(p)recht**.

Dims.: Fr.: **Huberdeau**; **Hubel**, **Hubeau**, **Hub(e)lot**, **Hub(e)lin**, **Hubelet**, **Hubin(et)**, **Huby**. Low Ger.: **Hubbe**, **Hübbe**, **Hup(j)e**, **Hübgen**, **Hüpgen**.

Patrs.: Ger.: **Hubbertz**, **Huppertz**. Low Ger.: **Hüb(b)ers**, **Huppers**. Flem.: **Huybrechts**.

Patrs. (from dims.): Low Ger.: **Hübgens**, **Hüpgens**, **Hübben**, **Hupen**. Flem.: **Huyben(s)**.

Hübsch German: nickname from Ger. *hübsch* polite, refined, agreeable (MHG *hübesch*, *hübisch*, *hövesch*; cf. HÖFLICH). The present-day sense of the vocab. word, 'pretty', 'handsome', 'nice', is a comparatively recent de-

velopment and is unlikely to have affected acquisition of the Ger. surname. However, it underlies all the Jewish cogns. listed below.

Vars.: **Hübscher**, **Hübschmann**.

Dim.: Ger.: **Hübschle**.

Huchet French: metonymic occupational name for a town-crier or herald, from OF *huchet*, a small horn used by such officials to secure the attention of the populace (a word of uncertain, possibly Gmc, origin).

Vars.: **Huchez**; **Huquet** (Normandy, Picardy); **Huchot** (with a different suffix); **Huchier**, **H(e)ucheux**, **Huqueux** (agent nouns).

Pej.: **Huchard**.

Huchon *see* HUGH

Huck English: from the medieval given name *Hucke*, perhaps from the OE personal name *Hucca* (see HUCKNALL) or *Ucca*, which may in some cases be a pet form of OE *Ūhtrǣd*; see UTTRIDGE. (For the inorganic initial *H-*, cf. HERRICK.) Later, however, this name fell completely out of use and the forms became inextricably confused with those of HUGH.

Vars.: **Hucke**, **Hug**.

Dims.: **Huckle**, **Huckel(l)**.

Patrs.: **Huck(e)s**.

'Servant of H.': **Hugman**.

Hucker English (Somerset): occupational name for a pedlar or other tradesman, from an agent deriv. of ME *hukken* to hawk, trade (cf. HAKE 2).

Huckfield English (Somerset): of uncertain origin, perhaps a habitation name from a place named with the OE personal name *Hucca* or *Ucca* (see HUCK) + OE *feld* pasture, open country (see FIELD). Alternatively, it may be a topographic name from some place where an open market was held, from ME *hukken* to hawk, trade (cf. HUCKER) + *fe(i)ld* open space.

Hucknall English (Notts.): habitation name from a place so called in Notts., which was once part of a larger district bearing this name (*Hochenale* in Domesday Book). It is derived from the gen. case of the OE personal name *Hucca* + OE *halh* nook, recess (see HALE 1).

Hudd English: from the popular medieval given name *Hudde*, which is of complex origin. It is usually explained as a pet form of HUGH, but there was a pre-existing OE personal name, *Hūda*, underlying placenames such as *Huddington*, Worcs. This personal name may well still have been in use at the time of the Norman Conquest. If so, it was absorbed by the Norman HUGH and its many dims. Reaney adduces evidence that *Hudde* was also regarded as a pet form of RICHARD.

Var.: **Hutt**.

Dims.: **Huddy** (Devon and Cornwall); **Huddle**.

Patrs.: **Hudson**, **Hutson**.

Huddart *see* WOODARD

Huddleston English: habitation name from a place in W Yorks., so called from the gen. case of the OE personal name **Hūdel* (a deriv. of *Hūda*; see HUDD) + OE *tūn* enclosure, settlement. There is a place of the same name in the parish of Westerkirk in the former county of Dumfries (now part of Dumfries and Galloway region), which seems to have been named from the Yorks. place and may in turn lie behind some examples of the surname in Scotland and N Ireland.

Vars.: **Huddlestone**; **Hiddleston(e)** (Scots).

Hudec Czech: occupational name for a fiddler, Czech *hudec*, from *housti* to play the fiddle.

Dims.: **Hudeček**, **H(o)udek**.

Hudus see HODES

Huebmer see HUBER

Huelin see HUGH

Huertson see HOWARD

Hueson see MCKAY

Huet see HEWITT

Huete Spanish: habitation name from a place in the province of Cuenca. The placename is first recorded in the L form *Opta*, but is of unknown origin.

Huey see HOWEY

Huff English: topographic name for someone who lived by a spur of a hill, OE *hōh* (literally, 'heel').

Vars.: HOUGH, HEUGH, **Hughf(f)**, **Houf(e)**, **Hoof(f)**; **Hoes**, **Hose** (from the pl. *hōs* spurs; *Hose* is also the name of a place in Leics., from which the surname may be derived).

Hüffner see HUBER

Huffton English (Notts.): habitation name from some unidentified place, presumably named with the OE elements *hōh* ridge, spur (see HUFF) + *tūn* enclosure, settlement; it may well be a var. of HOUGHTON or HUTTON.

Hug see HUCK

Hugh English: from the OF personal name *Hu(gh)e*, introduced to Britain by the Normans. This is in origin a short form of any of the various Gmc cpd names with the first element *hug* heart, mind, spirit (cf., e.g., HOWARD 1, HUBBLE, and HUBERT). It was a popular given name among the Normans in England, partly due to the fame of St Hugh of Lincoln (1140–1200), who was born in Burgundy and who established the first Carthusian monastery in England. The popularity of the European cogns. (Fr. *Hugues*, It. *Ugo*, etc.) perhaps owes more to St Hugh of Cluny (1024–1109). In Scotland and Ireland this name has been widely used as an equivalent of Celt. *Aodh* 'Fire' (see MCKAY).

Vars.: **Hugo** (Cornwall; probably a recent reintroduction from France); **Hew(e)**, HOWE.

Dims.: Eng.: **Huget(t)**, HEWITT; **Huggin**, HUTCHIN; **Hug(g)on**; HEWLETT; **Hug(h)lin**, **Huelin**, **Hul(l)in**, **Howlin(g)** (Ireland); **Hewkin**, **Hu(c)kin**; HUDD; HULL; HOWEY. Fr.: **Hugon(n)et**, **Hugu(en)et**, **Huet**, **Higonnet**, **Higounet**, **Igo(u)net**, **Gon(n)et**; **Gounet**; **Hugonneau**, **Gon(n)eau**, **Gon(n)el**, **Gounel**; **Hug(on)ot**, **Huot**, **Gounot**, **Gounod**, **Got**; **Hugonin**, **Hugu(en)in**, **Gon(n)in**, **Gounin**, **Gouny**; **Husson**, **Huchon**, **Husset**; **Huonic** (Brittany). Cat.: **Huguet**. It.: **Ughelli**, **Ughetti**, **Ugoletti**, **Ughini**.

Ug(ol)otti; **Ugolini** (Tuscany). Ger.: **Hügle**, **Hügli(n)**, **Heugel**, **Heugle**, **Heigl**, **Hegel**.

Augs.: It.: **Ugon(i)**.

Pejs.: Eng.: **Huggard**. Fr.: **Gon(n)ard**, **Gounard**.

Patrs.: Eng.: **Hugh(e)s**, **Huws**, **Hew(e)s**, HOWES; **Hughson**, **Hewson**; **Howson** (Yorks.); **Hooson** (Lancs.); FITZHUGH. Welsh: PUGH, BEWES. It.: **D'Ugo**. Ger.: **Hauger**. Flem., Du.: **Huygen(s)**.

Patrs. (from dims.): Eng.: **Hewlin(g)s**, **Howlings**, **Hullins**, **Hulance**; **Hukins**, **Hookins**; **Howkins** (Leicester area); **Huggins**, **Huggens**, **Huggons**.

Hughes see HUGH, MCKAY

Hughf see HUFF

Hühne German: nickname from Ger. *Hüne*, MHG *hiune* giant, monster, bogeyman, from MHG *Hiune* Hun (OHG *Hūni*), a word probably ultimately of Turkic origin.

Vars.: **Hühn**, **Hüne**; **Hihn**, **Hien**.

Huie see GILDUFF

Huijsmans see HOUSE

Huison see HEWITT

Hukin see HUGH

Hulance see HUGH

Hulbert English: from a ME given name *Holbert*, which according to Reaney is probably a survival of an unrecorded OE personal name **Holdbeorht*, composed of the Gmc elements *hold* friendly, gracious + *berht* bright, famous.

Vars.: **Holbert**, **Hulburd**, **Holberd**, **Holbird**.

Hulett see HEWLETT

Hull English: **1.** var. of HILL 1. **2.** pet form of HUGH.

Vars. (of 1): **Hull(e)s**; **Huller**; **Hullah** (Yorks.).

Patrs. (from 2): **Hull(e)s**, **Hulson**.

Hüllebrand see HILDEBRAND

Hullyer see HOLLIER

Hulme see HOLME

Hulse English: habitation name from a place in Ches., recorded in the mid-13th cent. in the forms *Holes*, *Holis*, and *Holys*. This probably represents a ME pl. of OE *holh* hollow, depression (see HOLE).

Hulton English: habitation name from places in Lancs. and Staffs., so called from OE *hyll* HILL + *tūn* enclosure, settlement; cf. HILTON.

Humber English: habitation name from any of the various places so called from their situation on a stream with this name. *Humber* is a common prehistoric river name, of uncertain origin and meaning.

Humberstone English: habitation name from places in Lincs. and Leics. According to Ekwall, the former is so called from the river name HUMBER + OE *stān* stone, while the latter has as its first element the personal name *Hūnbeorht* (see HUMBERT).

Vars.: **Humberston**, **Humblestone**, **Humerstone**, **Hummerston(e)**.

Humbert German and French: from a Gmc personal name composed of the elements *hūn* bear cub + *berht* bright, famous. This was particularly popular in the Netherlands and N Germany during the Middle Ages as a result of the fame of a 7th-cent. St Humbert, who founded the abbey of Marolles in Flanders. A cogn. personal name seems to have existed in OE (see HUMBERSTONE), but did not survive to give rise to a modern surname.

Vars.: Ger.: **Humbrecht**, **Humprecht**, **Humpert**.

Dims.: Fr.: **Humberdot**, **Humb(e)lot**.

Patrs.: Ger.: **Humpertz**. Low Ger.: **Humperding**, **Humperdinck**. Fris.: **Hummers**, **Hommers**.

Humble English (Northumb.): nickname for a meek or lowly person, from ME, OF *(h)umble* (L *humilis* low(ly), mean, base, a deriv. of *humus* ground).

Humboldt German: from a Gmc personal name composed of the elements *hūn* bear cub + *bald* bold, brave. The name was relatively rare, and does not seem to have given rise to cogn. surnames in other European languages.

Var.: **Humbolt**.

Hume *see* HOLME

Humeau *see* ORME

Humm 1. English (Norman): nickname from OF *homme* man (L *homo*), normally representing an ANF translation of MANN. 2. Frisian: short form of HUMBERT and HUMBOLDT.

Vars. (of 1): **Hum**. (Of 2): **Homm**.

Patrs. (from 2): **Hummen**, **Hommen**, **Hommes**.

Hummel 1. German: dim. of HUMBERT and HUMBOLDT. 2. Low Ger.: nickname for a busy or bustling person, from MLG *hommel* bee (of imitative origin, cf. Eng. *humblebee*, now normally altered to the alliterative *bumblebee*). The surname may in some cases have been a metonymic occupational name for a beekeeper.

Vars.: **Hommel**; **Huml**.

Humphrey 1. English: from the OF personal name *Humfrey*, introduced to Britain by the Normans. This is composed of the Gmc elements *hūn* bear cub + *frid, fred* peace. It was borne by a 9th-cent. saint, bishop of Therouanne, who had a certain following in England among Norman settlers. 2. Irish: see OLIFF.

Vars.: **Humph(e)ry**, **Humfrey**, **Homfray**.

Patrs.: Eng.: **Humphr(e)ys**, **Humphries**, **Humphris(s)**, **Humfress**; **Humphers(t)on**. Welsh: **Bo(u)mphrey**, **Bumphries**.

Hund German: metonymic occupational name for a keeper of dogs for hunting or other purposes, or derogatory nickname, from Ger. *Hund* dog (OHG *hunt*).

Var.: **Hundt**.

Dim.: Low Ger.: **Hüngen**.

Patr. (from a dim.): Low Ger.: **Hüngens**.

Huneen *see* HOONEY

Hungar *see* UNGER

Hunnable *see* HONEYBALL

Hunt English: occupational name for a hunter, OE *hunta* (a primary deriv. of *huntian* to hunt). The term was used not only of hunters on horseback of game such as stags and wild boars, which was in the Middle Ages a pursuit restricted to the ranks of the nobility, but also of much humbler bird catchers and poachers seeking food. The word seems also to have been used as an OE personal name (cf. HUNTINGTON and HUNTLEY) and to have survived into the Middle Ages as an occasional given name.

Vars.: **Hunte** (retaining a trace of the OE final vowel); **Hunter** (chiefly Scots; a ME secondary deriv. formed with the addition of the agent suffix *-er*).

Equiv.: Ger.: JÄGER.

Huntington English: habitation name from one of the places that get their names from the gen. pl. *huntena* of OE *hunta* hunter (see HUNT) + *tūn* enclosure, settlement or *dūn* hill (the forms in *-ton* and *-don* having become inextricably confused). In addition, a number of bearers of this name and its vars. can no doubt derive it from the more important town of *Huntingdon* in Cambs. (formerly a county town in its own right), which gets its name from the gen. case of OE *hunta* huntsman, perhaps used as a personal name + *dūn* hill.

Vars.: **Huntingdon**, **Huntinton**.

Huntley 1. English: habitation name from a place in Gloucs., so called from OE *hunta* hunter (perhaps a byname; see HUNT) + *lēah* wood, clearing. 2. Scots: habitation name from a lost place called *Huntlie* in the former county of Berwicks. (now part of Borders region), with the same etymology as in 1. *Huntly* near Aberdeen was named from the Borders place, but does not itself seem to have given rise to any surnames.

Var.: **Huntly**.

Hunwin *see* UNWIN

Huonic *see* HUGH

Hupe *see* HUBERT

Hüpfer German: occupational name for a professional tumbler or acrobat at a fair, or nickname for a restless individual with plenty of energy, from Ger. *Hüpfer* 'hopper', 'jumper', an agent deriv. of *hüpfen* to hop, skip, or jump (OHG *hupfen*, MLG *huppen*, a cogn. of OE *hoppian*, mod. Eng. *hop*).

Vars.: **Hupfer** (S German); **Hupf**; **Hupfauf** ('hop up').

Hupka *see* JACOB

Huquet *see* HUCHET

Hurbank *see* URBAN

Hurd *see* HEARD

Huré French: nickname for someone with an untidy head of shaggy hair, from the past part. of OF *hurer* to bristle, ruffle, stand on end (trans. and intrans.; of uncertain, possibly Gmc, origin).

Vars.: **Hurran**, **Hurren** (from the pres. part.).

Dims.: **Hurel**, **Hureau**, **Hurot**, **Huron**. Eng. (Norman): **Hurrell**.

Pej.: Fr.: **Hurard**.

Hurford English: habitation name from an unidentified place. The second part of the name is clearly OE *ford* FORD; the first is most probably OE *hyrne* corner, bend (see HEARN 2).

Hurle *see* EARL

Hurlen *see* HARLING

Hurley 1. English: habitation name from places in Berks. and Warwicks., so called from OE *hyrne* corner, bend (see HEARN 2) + *lēah* wood, clearing. **2.** Irish: var. of HERLIHY.
Var.: **Hurly**.

Hurman *see* HEARN

Hurrey *see* WOOLDRIDGE

Hurst English: topographic name for someone who lived on a wooded hill, OE *hyrst*, or habitation name from one of the various places named with this word, for example *Hurst* in Berks., Kent, Somerset, and Warwicks., or *Hirst* in Northumb. and W Yorks. For the divergent development of the vowel, cf. HILL 1.
Vars.: **He(a)rst**; **Hirst** (widespread, but most common in W Yorks.).

Hurt *see* HART

Hurtado Spanish: nickname from the past part. of Sp. *hurtar* to rob, conceal (LL *furtāre*, from *furtum* theft, *fur* thief). The reference was probably to an illegitimate offspring, whose existence was concealed, or to a kidnapped child.

Hurwitz *see* HOROWITZ

Husband English: occupational name for a peasant farmer, from ME *husband* tiller of the soil, husbandman. The term (late OE *hūsbonda*, ON *húsbóndi*, a cpd of *hús* HOUSE + *bóndi* BOND) originally described a man who was head of his own household, and this may have been the sense in some of the earliest examples of the surname.
Patrs.: **Husbands**, **Hosbons**.

Húsek *see* GUSEV

Hüsgen *see* HOUSE

Husher *see* USHER

Huskinson *see* HOSKIN

Husset *see* HUGH

Hussey 1. English (Norman): habitation name from *Houssaye* in Seine-Maritime, so called from a collective noun from OF *hous* holly (see HILSE). **2.** English: nickname for a woman who was mistress of her own household, from ME *husewif* (a cpd of OE *hūs* HOUSE + *wīf* woman). No pej. sense is apparent in the word at least until the 17th cent. **3.** English: nickname for someone noted for his boots, from OF *h(e)usé* 'booted' (see HEUSE), either because they were of an unusual design or because he was considered fortunate to have them at all at a time when most of the peasantry had to be content with leggings or sandals. **4.** Irish: Anglicized form of Gael. **Ó hEodhusa** 'descendant of *Eodhus*', a personal name given in bardic families.
Vars.: **Hussy**, **Husey**, **Hosey**; **Hosie** (Scots). (Of 4 only): **O'Hossy**, **O'Hoasy**, **O'Hosey**.

Hustin French: nickname for a quarrelsome person, from OF *hustin* dispute, argument, commotion (of uncertain origin, perhaps from MLG *hutselen* to shake).
Var.: **HUTIN**.

Hustler *see* OSTLER

Huston *see* HOUSTON

Hutchin English and Scots: from the medieval given name *Huchin*, a dim. of HUGH.
Vars.: **Hutcheon** (chiefly Scots); **Hotchen**, **Houchen**, **Howchin**.
Patrs.: **Hutchin(g)s** (chiefly Devon and Somerset); **Hutchison**, **Hutche(r)son** (chiefly Scots); **Hutchin(g)son** (widespread, but most common in N England and N Ireland). See also MCCUTCHEON.

Hüter German: occupational name for a watchman or herdsman, from Ger. *Hüter* protector, agent deriv. of *hüten* to guard, watch over (OHG *huotan*; cf. HUTH 2).

Huth German: **1.** metonymic occupational name for a maker of hats or nickname for a wearer of distinctive hats, from Ger. *Hut(h)* hat (MHG, OHG *huot*; cf. the cogn. HOOD and related HATT; all these words are ultimately akin to OHG *huotan* to protect (see 2 below), since hats were regarded as being primarily for protection rather than ornamentation). **2.** occupational name for a herdsman, MHG *huote* (a primary deriv. of *hüeten* to protect, OHG *huotan*); cf. HÜTER.
Vars.: **Hut(h)er**, **Hüter**, **Huthmann**.
Dims.: Ger.: **Hütel**. (Of 1 only): Low Ger.: **Hoetje**.

Hutin 1. French: nickname for a quarrelsome person, var. of HUSTIN. **2.** Jewish (E Ashkenazic): habitation name from *Hotin*, the Rumanian name of *Khotin* in the Ukraine. Medial *-u-* indicates a S Yid. pronunciation.
Var. (of 2): **Hutiner**.
Dims. (of 1): **Hutinel**, **Hutineau**, **Hut(i)net**.

Hutson *see* HUDD

Hüttler German: agent deriv. of Ger. *Hüttl* little hut, dim. of MHG *hütte* hut (OHG *huttea*). This may have been a topographic name for someone who lived in a small hut, but in Bavaria it was an occupational name for a carpenter (i.e. 'builder of huts').
Vars.: **Hit(t)ler**; **Hidler** (see also HIEDL); **Hütter** (topographic only).

Hutton English and Scots: habitation name from any of the numerous places so called from OE *hōh* ridge, spur + *tūn* enclosure, settlement.
Vars.: **Houton**; **Hoghton** (a place in Lancs.). See also HOUGHTON and HUFFTON.

Huws *see* HUGH

Huxley English: habitation name from a place in Ches., which is probably so called from the gen. case of the OE personal name *Hucc* or from the OE vocab. word *husc, hux* insult, taunt + *lēah* wood, clearing.

Huyben *see* HUBERT

Huygen *see* HUGH

Huysmans *see* HOUSE

Huyton English (Lancs.): habitation name from a place near Liverpool, so called from OE *hȳð* landing place + *tūn* enclosure, settlement.

Huzard *see* HEUSE

Hyam 1. Jewish (Ashkenazic): from the Yid. male given name *Khayim* (from Hebr. *chayim* life). **2.** English: var. of HIGHAM.

Vars. (of 1): **Hyman, Hay(e)m, Hai(e)m, Hayim, Hey(e)m, He(y)im; Chaim.**

Patrs. (from 1): **Hyams, Chaimso(h)n; Haimovich, Khaimovich** (E Ashkenazic).

Hyat *see* CHAIT

Hyatt *see* HIGHET

Hyde English: **1.** topographic name for someone living on (and farming) a place originally named as being a hide of land, OE *hī(gi)d*. This was quite a large amount, varying at different times and places between 60 and 120 acres, and seems from the etymology to have been originally fixed as the amount necessary to support one (extended) family (OE *hīgan, hīwan* household; cf. HIND). **2.** var. of IDE, with inorganic initial *H*-; cf. HERRICK.

Var.: **Hide.**

Hyland 1. English: topographic name for someone who lived on a patch of high ground, from ME *hegh, hie*

HIGH + *land* land (OE *land*); cf. HOOGLAND. **2.** Irish: var. of WHEELAN.

Vars. (of 1): **Highland, Hylands.**

Hylton *see* HILTON

Hynd *see* HIND

Hyne *see* HINE

Hyner English (Suffolk): of uncertain origin, possibly an occupational name for a peasant or agricultural labourer, a var. of HINE, with the addition of the ME agent suffix *-er*.

Var.: **Hiner.**

Hynes 1. Irish: Anglicized form of Gael. **Ó hEidhin** 'descendant of *Eidhin*', a personal name or byname of uncertain origin. It may be a deriv. of *eidhean* ivy, or it may represent an altered form of the placename *Aidhne*. The principal family of this name are descended from Guaire of Aidhne, King of Connacht. From the 7th cent. they provided chiefs of a territory in Galway for over a thousand years. **2.** English: patr. from HINE.

Vars.: **Hines.** (Of 1 only): **O'Heyne, Heynes** (see also HAINES).

Hyslop *see* HESLOP

I

Iacabucci *see* JACOB

Iaccacci *see* JACK

Iacomelli *see* JAMES

Ianelli *see* JOHN

Iashvili *see* ELLIS

Ibáñez *see* JOHN

Ibarra Basque: habitation name from any of several places in the Basque country, so called from *ibar* meadow + the def. art. *-a*.

Ibarruri Basque: habitation name from a place in the province of Biscay, so called from *ibar* meadow + *uri* settlement, village.

Ibbers *see* HIBBERT

Ibberson *see* HIBBS

Iben *see* IVE

Ibing *see* HIBBERT

Ibraimov *see* ABRAHAM

Ibsen *see* HIBBERT

Ibson *see* HIBBS

Icemonger *see* IRONMONGER

Icigson *see* ISAAC

Ick *see* HICK

Ickov *see* ISAAC

Iczkovits *see* ISAAC

Iddon English (Lancs.): from the ON female personal name *Idunn, Iðuna*, probably composed of the elements *iðja* to work, do, perform (cf. IDE) + *unna* to love. The name is often recorded in the L form *Idonea*, as a result of folk etymological association with the fem. form of L *idoneus* suitable.

Dim.: **Innett**.

Metrs.: **Iddins**, **Iddison**; **Ineson** (Yorks.).

Ide English and Low German: from the Gmc personal name *Ida* (from the element *id* to work, do, perform; cf. IDDON), which was used for both men and women. It was popular among the Normans and to some degree was taken up in England. It remained in favour until at least the mid-14th cent., but then died out, to be revived in the 19th cent., perhaps because it sounds like a L or Gk name. (In actual fact, the Gk name *Ida* is that of a mountain, not a woman.) There may also have been an OE male personal name from the same stem, and this could have contributed to the surname. There is a place called *Ide* (pronounced /i:d/) near Exeter in Devon; the etymology

is obscure, perhaps from a river name; it does not seem to have given rise to a surname.

Vars.: Eng.: HYDE. Low Ger.: **Ihde**.

Dim.: Eng.: **Ikin**.

Patrs./Metrs.: Eng.: **I(de)son**, **Izon**. Ger.: **It(t)ensohn**, **Idtensohn**. Low Ger.: **I(h)den**, **Iding**.

Idel *see* IDLE, JUDE

Iding *see* IDE

Idle 1. English: habitation name from a place in W Yorks., perhaps named with a deriv. of OE *īdel* unused ground, patch of waste land. **2.** English: nickname for a lazy person, from ME *idle* idle, indolent (OE *īdel*). **3.** English: var. of ISLES. **4.** Welsh: from the OW personal name *Ithel*; cf. JE-KYLL.

Vars.: **Idel(l)**. (Of 4 only): **Ithell**.

Idtensohn *see* IDE

Ieroushalmi *see* YERUSHALMI

Ifans *see* EVAN

Igel German: nickname from Ger. *Igel* hedgehog (OHG *igil*), given perhaps to a prickly or unapproachable person. There is a place near Trier called *Igel*, but it does not seem to have contributed to the surname. The surname is also borne by Ashkenazic Jews, in which case it is probably one of the unflattering surnames bestowed on Jews by non-Jewish government officials in 18th- and 19th-cent. central Europe.

Cpds (ornamental): Jewish: **Igelberg** ('hedgehog hill'); **Igelfeld** ('hedgehog field').

Ignace French: from a medieval given name (L *Egnatius*, a Roman family name of uncertain, probably Etruscan, etymology). The spelling *Ignatius* appeared in the early Christian era, partly due to folk etymological associations with L *ignis* fire. In this form the name was borne by an early bishop of Antioch who was martyred at Rome under Trajan. As a given name it was not common in the Middle Ages, and the surname is correspondingly infrequent. Its comparative popularity in Catholic countries today is due to the fame of St Ignatius Loyola (Iñigo Yáñez de Oñaz y Loyola, 1491–1556), founder of the Society of Jesus (Jesuits).

Dims.: Ukr.: **Hnatyuk**, **Hnatik**. Beloruss.: **Ihnazenya**, **Ihnatchik**. Czech: **Hnátek**.

Patrs.: Sp.: **Iñiguez**. Russ.: **Ignatov** (also Jewish (E Ashkenazic), an adoption of the Russ. surname); **Ignatyev**. Ukr.: **Hnatovich**. Pol.: **Ignatowicz**, **Nacewicz**; **Ignaczak**. Croatian: **Ignjatović**. Gk: **Ignatides**.

Patrs. (from dims.): Russ.: **Igna(sh)ev**, **Igoshin**, **Igonin**.

Habitation names: Pol.: **Ignatowski**, **Gnatowski**.

Ignoto Italian: nickname for a foundling or bastard, from It. *ignoto* unknown, unacknowledged, i.e. child of an unknown father or unacknowledged by its father (L *ignōtus*, from *in-* not + *(g)nōtus*, past part. of *(g)noscere* to know, acknowledge). The surname is especially common in Sicily.

Var.: **Ignoti**.

Igolkin Russian: patr. from the nickname *Igolka* 'Little Needle' (a dim. of *igla* needle), referring to a tall, thin person or someone with a spiteful tongue.

Igonet *see* HUGH

Igonin *see* IGNACE

Ihde *see* IDE

Ihnatchik *see* IGNACE

Ikin *see* IDE

Ikonnikov Russian: patr. from the occupational term *ikonnik* icon painter (a deriv. of *ikona* ikon, Gk *eikōn* image, from *eikein* to resemble). Icon painting was a common occupation in Orthodox Christian countries, especially Russia, where every church and every devout family possessed images of Christ, the Virgin Mary, and popular saints.

Ilbert *see* HIBBERT

Ilchenko *see* ELLIS

Ilchmann *see* GILES

Iles *see* ISLES

Ilewicz *see* ELLIS

Ilgen *see* GILES

Illes *see* GILES, ISLES

Illingworth English: habitation name from a place in W Yorks. near Halifax, so called from OE *Illingworð* 'enclosure (see WORTH) associated with *Illa*' (a personal name from a short form of the various cpd names with the first element *hild* battle, strife; cf. ILSLEY).

Ilmanov *see* ELLIS

Ilroy *see* GILROY

Ilsley English: habitation name from the villages of E and W *Ilsley* on the Berks. Downs, so called from the gen. case of the OE personal name *Hild* (a short form of any of the various cpd names with the first element *hild* battle, strife) + OE *lēah* wood, clearing.

Ilyasov *see* ELLIS

Imber 1. English: habitation name from places in Surrey and Wilts. The former (also called *Ember*) gets the name from the OE personal name *Imma* (see IMM) + OE *worð* enclosure (see WORTH), the latter from the same personal name + OE *mere* lake, pond (see DELAMARE). **2.** Jewish (Ashkenazic): var. of INGBER, from Yid. *imber* ginger.

Imberman *see* INGBER

Imbery *see* AMERY

Imbrogno Italian: nickname for a muddled or confused person, from a deriv. of It. *imbrogliare* to confuse, embroil (cf. BREUIL).

Imery *see* AMERY

Imhof *see* HOFER

Imm English: from the ME given name *Imma, Emma*, a short form of any of various cpd Gmc personal names with the first element *irmin, ermen* whole, entire (apparently originally the name of a Gmc demigod). The most famous bearer of the name *Imma* in the OE period was the wife of King Canute, who had previously been married to Ethelred. In the early Middle Ages it was often used as a male personal name (cf. IMBER) as well as a female one, but later, under Norman influence, it came to be used almost exclusively for women, being taken as a short form of *Ermingard*.

Metrs.: **Im(m)s**.

Immer German: habitation name from a place in Austria, apparently so called from a river name of obscure origin; there is no connection with Ger. *immer* always.

Var.: **Immermann**.

Imort *see* ORT

Imperatrice *see* EMPEREUR

Impey English: habitation name from any of various minor places named with the OE elements *imp* young tree, sapling + *(ge)hæg* or *haga* enclosure (see HAY 1 and HAIG).

Var.: **Impy**.

Imray *see* AMERY

Ims *see* IMM

Inber *see* INGBER

Ince English: habitation name from places in Lancs. and Ches., so called from a Brit. word corresponding to W *ynys* island, strip of land between two rivers (cf. INNES). **2.** *see* INNOCENTI

Incháustegui *see* INCHAUSTI

Inchausti Spanish form of Basque **Intxausti**: topographic name for someone who lived by a grove of walnut trees, from Basque *intxaur* walnut + *-ti*, suffix of abundance.

Var.: **Incháustegui**.

Inchbald English: from a Gmc personal name composed of the elements *Ingel, Engel* (see ENGEL 1) + *bald* brave, bold, which was introduced into England by the Normans in the form *Inge(l)bald*.

Ineson *see* IDDON

Infante Italian and Spanish: nickname for someone of childish (or childlike) disposition, from It., Sp. *infante* child (L *infans*, gen. *infantis*, from *in-* not + *fāri* to speak). This was also a title borne in medieval Spain by the eldest sons of noblemen before they inherited, and in particular by the son of the king of Castile, and so in Spain the surname may also have originated as a nickname for one of a lordly disposition or as an occupational name for a member of the household of an infante. The Fr. cogn. has the senses 'boy', 'servant', and 'foot soldier'.

Vars.: It.: **Fante**, **Fanti**; **Fant** (Venetia). Sp.: **Infantes**.

Dims.: It.: **Fantino**, **Fantin(ell)i**, **Fantocci**, **Fantozzi**, **Fantucci**, **Fantuzzi**; **Fancello**, **Fanciullo**, **Fanciulli** (Tuscany). In-**fant(ol)ino** (Palermo). Fr.: **Enfantin**, **Fantin**, **Fanton**. Prov.: **Fanty**, **Fantou**. Ger.: **Fendel**.

Augs.: It.: **Fantone**, **Fanton(i)**.

Pejs.: It.: **Fantacci**, **Fantazzi**.

Patrs.: It.: **Del Fante** (N Italy); **De Fant** (Trentino). Eng.: **Fantes**.

Ing English: **1.** from the OE personal name *Ing(a)*, a short form of any of several cpd names with the first element *ing*; cf. INGER 1, INGLE 1, and INGRAM 2. This element is of uncertain origin; it was the name of a minor Norse god associated with fertility, and may be from a Gmc root meaning 'swelling', 'protuberance'. **2.** habitation name from a place in Essex, recorded in Domesday Book as *Inga* and *Ginga*, apparently from an OE tribal name *Gigingas* 'people of *Giga*', a personal name of uncertain etymology, but paralleled on the Continent.

Var.: **Inge**.

Patr. (from 1): **Ings**.

Ingber German and Jewish (Ashkenazic): metonymic occupational name for a spicer, from Ger. *Ingwer* ginger, MHG *ingeber*, *ingewer* (OHG *gingiber(o)*, from OF *gingebre*; the word is ultimately, like the spice, of Oriental origin).

Vars.: Jewish (Ashkenazic): **Ingbar**, **Ingberman**; **Ingberg** (altered under the influence of the many Jewish ornamental surnames ending in *-berg* hill); IMBER, **Inber**, **Imberman**.

Ingels *see* ENGEL

Inger **1.** English (Notts.): from the ON personal name *Ingvarr*, composed of the elements *ing* (see ING 1) + *varr* guard. **2.** Jewish (Ashkenazic): probably from the NE Yid. pronunciation of Yid. *yinger* younger, a name taken by a younger son. **3.** Jewish (Ashkenazic): perhaps also a var. of HUNGER 3.

Vars. (of 1): **Inker** (Somerset). (Of 2 and 3): **Ingerman**.

Patrs. (from 1): Eng.: **Inkerson**. Low Ger.: **Ingwers**, **Engwers**, **Ingwer(t)sen**.

Ingerov *see* UNGER

Ingersoll *see* INKERSALL

Ingham English (chiefly Yorks. and Lancs.): **1.** habitation name from any of several places so called, of which the largest are in Lincs., Norfolk, and Suffolk. The placename is from the OE personal name *Inga* (see ING 1) + OE *hām* homestead. **2.** nickname for a crafty or ingenious person, from OF *engaine*; see GAIN.

Ingle English: **1.** from the ON personal name *Ingialdr*, composed of the elements *ing* (see ING 1) + *gialdr* tribute. This name has become confused with the rarer *Ingólfr*, in which the second element is from *úlfr* wolf. **2.** habitation name from *Ingol* in Lancs., so called from the OE personal name *Inga* (see ING 1) + OE *holh* hollow, depression.

Vars. (of 1): **Ingold**, **Ingall**, **Hingle**.

Patrs. (from 1): **Ingles(on)**.

Ingleby English: habitation name from one of the places, in N Yorks., Derbys., and Lincs., so called from ON *Englabýr* 'settlement (ON *býr*) of the English'.

Inglis *see* ENGLISH

Ingoldsby **1.** English: habitation name from a place in Lincs., so called from the gen. case of the ON personal name *Ingjaldr* (see INGLE 1) + ON *býr* settlement, village. **2.** Irish: see GOLIGHTLY.

Ingram English: **1.** from a Gmc personal name composed of the ethnic name *Engil* (see ENGEL 1) + *hraban* raven, which was introduced into England by the Normans in the form *Eng(u)erran*. **2.** from a Gmc personal name composed of the divine name *Ing* (see ING 1) + *hraban*. This was introduced into England by the Normans, and was reinforced by the ON cogn. *Ingrafn*.

Patr.: **Ingrams**.

Ingres French: of uncertain origin. It may be a nickname from OF *haingre* thin, scrawny (of Gmc origin, probably a cogn. of mod. Eng. *hungry*). The surname is found mostly in SE France.

Iñiguez *see* IGNACE

Inions *see* ONION

Inker *see* INGER

Inkersall English: habitation name from a place in Derbys., recorded in the 13th cent. as *Hinkershil(l)* and *Hinkreshill*. The final element is clearly OE *hyll* HILL; the first may be the ON personal name *Ingvarr* (see INGER) or an OE byname meaning 'Limper' (cf. HINCHCLIFFE and HINCKLEY). Ekwall suggests that it may represent a contracted version of OE *hīgna æcer* monks' field (cf. HINE and ACKER).

Vars.: **Ingersoll**, **Inkersole**, **Ingsole**.

Inman English: occupational name for a keeper of a lodging house, ME *innmann*, from OE *inn* abode, lodging + *mann* man. To this day there remains in English a technical distinction between an inn, where lodgings are available as well as alcoholic beverages, and a tavern, which offers only the latter.

Innes Scots: **1.** habitation name from a barony in the former county of Moray (now part of Grampian region), so called from Gael. *inis* island, esp. in a river, or piece of land between two rivers. **2.** var. of ANGUS.

Vars.: **Inness**, **Innis(s)**, **Inns**.

Innett *see* IDDON

Innocenti Italian: nickname meaning 'innocent' (L *innocens*, from *in-* not + *nocens*, pres. part. of *nocēre* to hurt, harm) and often bestowed on a simpleton, following the Christian notion that simpletons, like children, were incapable of doing evil. The surname is found principally in Tuscany and neighbouring regions and is extremely common in Florence, where it was given as a surname to all foundlings received into the *Spedale degli Innocenti*, an orphanage established in the 15th cent. Occasionally the surname may derive from a given name, borne by a 4th-cent. bishop of Tortona, several popes from the 5th cent. onwards, and a 6th-cent. bishop of Le Mans.

Var.: **Nocenti** (an aphetic form).

Dims.: **Innocentini, Nocentini, Nocentino**. Hung.: **Inc(z)e**.

Inskip English: habitation name from a place in Lancs., the etymology of which is uncertain; the first element has been tentatively connected with W *ynys* island (cf. INCE) and the second with OE *cȳpe* osier basket (for catching fish).

Vars.: **Inskipp, Inskeep**.

Insley English (Midlands): habitation name from an unidentified place, of which the second element is most probably OE *lēah* wood, clearing; the first may be from the gen. case of the OE personal name *Ing* (see ING 1).

Inspektor *see* SPECTOR

Instone English (W Midlands): habitation name from *Innerstone* in Worcs., so called from the gen. case of an OE personal name cogn. with ISNARD + OE *tūn* enclosure, settlement.

Inverarity Scots: habitation name from a place near Forfar, first recorded in 1250 as *Inuerarethin*. The first element is Gael. *inbhir* river-mouth, confluence; the second may be from a Brit. river name originally meaning 'slow'.

Ioannidis *see* JOHN

Ion *see* JOHN

Iordanesco *see* JORDAN

Iorillo *see* GEORGE

Ioselev *see* JOSEPH

Iovinelli *see* JEUNE

Iozefovich *see* JOSEPH

Ippolitov *see* HIPÓLITO

Ipsen *see* HIBBERT

Irby English: habitation name from any of various places, in Lincs., Ches., and N Yorks., so called from ON *Irabýr* 'settlement of the Irish'; cf. IRETON.

Var.: **Ireby** (places in Cumb. and Lancs.).

Iredale English: habitation name from a lost hamlet in Cumb., so called from ON *Íradalr* 'valley (see DALE) of the Irish'. The surname is recorded from the 16th cent.; until recently it was found almost exclusively in the surrounding area.

Var.: **Iredell**.

Ireland English and Scots: ethnic name for someone from *Ireland*, OE *Íraland*, so called from the gen. case of *Íras* Irishmen + *land* land, territory. The stem *Ír-* is taken from the Celt. name for Ireland, *Èriu*, earlier *Everiu*, of uncertain origin. The surname is especially common in Liverpool.

Var.: **Irish**.

Iremonger *see* IRONMONGER

Ireton English: habitation name from either of two places in Derbys. called *Ireton*, or one in N Yorks. called *Irton*, all from the gen. case of OE *Íras* Irishmen (see IRELAND) + OE *tūn* enclosure, settlement. **2.** habitation name from *Irton* in Cumb., so called from the old river name *Irt*, of uncertain origin + OE *tūn* enclosure, settlement.

Var.: **Irton**.

Iriarte *see* URIARTE

Irigoyen Spanish, from Basque: habitation name from a place named as being a village on the top of a hill, from *iri* settlement, village + *goien* highest point, summit.

Irish *see* IRELAND

Irisov Russian: **1.** patr. from the male given name *Iris*, a familiar form of *Irinei* or *Irinarkh*. The former is derived from Gk *Eirēnaios* 'Peaceful', a name borne by a 2nd-cent. bishop of Lyons; the latter comes from Gk *Eirēnarkhos* (composed of the elements *eirēnē* peace + *arkhē* beginning, rule). **2.** surname adopted by Orthodox priests, from *iris* iris (the flower) (Gk *iris* (goddess of) the rainbow). The ending *-ov* was added to give the appearance of a surname of the usual Russ. patr. type.

Irmgard *see* ERMGARD

Ironbuckle *see* ARBUCKLE

Ironde *see* HIRON

Ironmonger English: occupational name for a trader in iron goods, ME *irenmongere*, from OE *īren* iron + *mangere* dealer, trader. Dealers in iron played an important role in the medieval economy, before the advent of cheap mass-production of steel.

Vars.: **Iremonger, Icemonger, Isemonger** (with the first element from the Kentish form *isern*); **Ernmonger, Yernmonger** (with the first element from the cogn. ON *earn, jarn*).

Equiv.: Ukr.: ZALIZNYAK.

Irons English (Norman): habitation name from *Airaines* in Somme, so called from L *harēnas* (acc. case) sands. The form of the name has been altered as a result of folk etymology, associating the name with the metal.

Ironside 1. English: from ME *irenside* (a cpd of OE *īren* iron + *sīde* side), a nickname for an iron-clad warrior. The best-known bearer of this nickname (though not, of course, as a surname) was Edmund Ironside, who was briefly king of England in 1016. **2.** Scots: habitation name from a place in the parish of New Deer in the former county of Aberdeens. This was probably originally named with the OE elements *earn* eagle + *sīde* side (of a hill).

Irrgang German: unflattering nickname for an impatient person or a foolish one, from MHG *irreganc* restless wandering or Ger. *Irrgang* blind alley (a cpd of MHG *irre* mad, aimless (OHG *irri*) + *ganc* going (OHG *gang*)).

Irton *see* IRETON

Irvine 1. Scots: habitation name from *Irvine* in Strathclyde, or from *Irving* in Dumfries and Galloway region. The two names have become confused and are impossible to disentangle. Both are derived from a Celt. river name probably composed of elements cogn. with W *ir, yr* green, fresh + *afon* water. **2.** English: from the ME given name

Irwyn, *Erwyn*, *Everwyn*, OE *Eoforwine*, composed of the elements *eofor* wild boar + *wine* friend. **3.** Irish: Anglicized form of Gael. **Ó hEireamhóin** 'descendant of *Eireamhón*', a personal name of uncertain origin. See also CURWEN and HORAN.

Vars.: **Irvin**, **Ervin(e)**, **Urvine**; **Irving**, **Erving**. (Of 2 only): **Irwin(e)**, **Irwing**, **E(ve)rwin**; **Urwin** (Northumb.). (Of 3 only): **O'Hirwen**.

Irwin *see* IRVINE

Isaac Jewish, French, and English: from the Hebr. male given name *Yitschak*, a deriv. of *tsachak* to laugh. This was the name of the son of Abraham (Gen. 21: 3); the traditional explanation of the name is that Abraham and Sarah laughed with joy at the birth of a son to them in their old age, but a more plausible explanation is that the name originally meant 'may God laugh', i.e. 'smile on him'. Like ABRAHAM, this name has always been immensely popular among Jews and was also widely used in medieval Europe among Christians. Hence it is the surname of many gentile families. In E Europe the given name was popular in both Orthodox (Russ., Ukr., and Bulg.) and Catholic (Pol. and Czech) Churches. The name was borne by a 5th-cent. father of the Armenian Church and by a Sp. saint martyred by the Moorish rulers of Cordoba in AD 851 on account of his polemics against Islam.

Vars.: Jewish: **Isac**, **Isa(a)k**, **Issac**, **Issak**, **Izac**, **Izak**, **Itshak**, **Itz(c)hak**, **Itzhai(e)k**, **I(t)zhayek**, **Izhak**, **Ishak**, **Izsak**, **Jzak**, **Yitshak**, **Yi(t)zhak**, **Yitzhok**, **Eisik**, **Eisig**, **Aizik**, **Aizic**, **Aysik**, **Ajsik** (from *Ayzik*, one of the Yid. forms of the given name); **Is(h)aki**, **Iz(c)haki**, **Izhaky**, **Yitschaky**, **Yitshaki**, **Yitzchaki**, **Yi(t)zhaki**, **Yitzhaky**, **J(i)zhaki**, **Itz(c)haki**, **Itz(c)haky** (with the Hebr. adj. suffix *-i*).

Dims.: Jewish (Ashkenazic): **Itzik**, **Itzig** (from the Yid. dim. *Itsik*). Fr.: **Haquin**. Russ.: **Izachik**. Ukr.: **Izachenko**.

Patrs.: Jewish: **Isaacs**, **Izaks**, **Isaacson**, **Isaaksohn**, **Is(s)acson**, **Isakson**, **I(t)zakson**; **Is(s)akov**, **Is(s)acov**, **Izakov**, **Izacov**, **Isakof(f)**, **Issacof**, **Isacoff**, **Yitzhakov**, **Yitzhakof**, **Itschakov**, **Izhakov**, **Jzhakov**, **Izikov**, **Itzkov**, **Ickov**, **Iskow**, **Isakower**, **Izakowicz**, **Isakowitz**, **I(t)zakovitz**, **Izikovitz**, **Isakovitch**, **Itzkowicz**, **Itzkowitz**, **Itzkovi(t)ch**, **Itzkowitch**, **Itzcovich**, **Itskovitz**, **Itscovitz**, **Ickowicz**, **Ickowics**, **Ickovicz**, **Ickovitz**, **Ickovits**, **Ickovic**, **Iczkovitz**, **Iczkovits**, **Yitzkowitz**, **Yitzkovitz**, **Yitzkovicz**, **Izkovitch**, **Izkovicz**, **Izkovitz**, **Iskowitz**, **Iscowitz** (all E Ashkenazic); **Eisikowitz**, **Eisikowitch**, **Aizikovitch**, **Aizicovitch**, **Aizikowicz**, **Aizikovitz**, **Aiskowitz**, **Eiskovitsh** (E Ashkenazic, based on Yid. *Ayzik*); **I(t)zkovici**, **Ickovici** (Rumanian spellings); **Itzkovsky**, **Izkoveski**; **Itzkin**. Russ.: **Aizikov(ich)**. Bulg.: **Isakov**. Croatian: **Isaković**. Eng.: **Isaacs**, **Isa(a)cson**. Sc., Ir.: **McIsaac**, **McKis(s)ack**. Manx: **Kissack**, **Kissock**. Welsh: **Bissex**. Dan., Norw.: **Isaksen**. Swed.: **Isaksson**, **Isacsson**.

Patrs. (from dims.): Jewish (Ashkenazic): **Itzikson**, **Itzigsohn**, **Izygson**, **Icigson** (based on Yid. *Itsik*). Russ.: **Isachkov**. Pol.: **Iszczak**.

Isambert French: from a Gmc personal name in which the first element probably represents *īsan* iron, but could also be an extended form of *īs* ice; the second element is *berht* bright, famous.

Vars.: **Isembert**, **Isambard**.

Isard *see* IZARD

Isasi Basque: of uncertain origin, partly due to the lack of distinction in Castilian spelling between the Basque sibi-

lants *s* and *ts*. The name appears to come from *isasi* arum lily (a dialect word confined to the Biscay area), but it may also be from *isats* broom (the plant and the implement).

Iscowitz *see* ISAAC

Isembert *see* ISAMBERT

Isemonger *see* IRONMONGER

Iser *see* ISRAEL

Isern Catalan: from a Gmc (probably Visigothic) personal name derived from the element *īsarn* iron.

Ishak *see* ISAAC

Ishchenko *see* JOSEPH

Isherwood English (Lancs.): habitation name from a lost place in the parish of Bolton-le-Moors. The name is first found in Lancs. records in the 13th cent. and is still largely confined to that area.

Vars.: **Esherwood**, **Usherwood**.

Isidore French: from a medieval given name (Gk *Isidōros*, from *Isis*, the name (of uncertain etymology) of an originally Egyptian goddess + *dōron* gift). The name has never been common among non-Jews in W Europe; in E Europe it has been more popular, as it was borne by three saints of the 3rd to 5th cents. much venerated in the Orthodox Church.

Vars.: **Isidor**.

Dims.: Pol.: **Izydorczyk**; **Sidorczyk**. Ukr.: **Sidorenko**. Beloruss.: **Sidorchik**.

Patrs.: Pol.: **Sidorowicz**. Russ.: **Sidorov**, **Sidorin**.

Patrs. (from dims.): Russ.: **Sidorkov**, **Sidorshin**.

'Son of the daughter of I.': Russ.: **Sidorovnin**.

Iskov *see* JOSEPH

Iskow *see* ISAAC

Isles English: topographic or habitation name from ANF *isle*, *idle* island (OF *isel*, L *insula*). As this is a Norman French word, the island in question is more likely to have been in N France than anywhere in Britain.

Vars.: **Iles** (now found mainly in Gloucs.), **Illes**; **Eyles**; IDLE, LISLE.

Islip English: habitation name from places in Northants and Oxon. The former (*Islep* in Domesday Book) is so called from the Brit. river name *Ise*, which originally seems to have meant no more than 'water' + OE *slǣp* slipway, slippery place; the latter (*Ichteslep* in ME, *Gihtslepe* in OE) shares the same second element, but is preceded by a different river name, namely *Ight*, which is probably akin to W *iaith* language, perhaps with the sense 'Chattering'.

Isnard French: from a Gmc personal name composed of the elements *īsan* iron (or ice; cf. ISAMBERT) + *hard* brave, hardy, strong, which acquired some currency in medieval Europe as it was borne by a minor Bavarian saint of the 7th cent. and by a 13th-cent. Italian monk who founded the friary at Pavia.

Ison *see* IDE

Israel Jewish: from the Hebr. male given name *Yisrael* 'Fighter of God', in the Bible a byname bestowed on

Jacob after he had wrestled with the angel at the ford of Jabbok (Gen. 32: 24–8). See also Israeler.

Vars.: **Izrael**; **Yisrael**; **Israelski**; **Is(s)er** (Yid. form); **Srol** (NE Yid. aphetic form); **Srul** (S Yid. aphetic form).

Dim.: **Isserl**.

Patrs.: **Israels(on)**, **Israelov**, **Israelow**, **Israeloff**, **Isrelof(f)**, **Israelovi(t)ch**, **Israelevitch**, **Israelowicz**, **Israelewicz**, **Israelowitz**, **Israelovitz**, **Israelewitz**, **Israelevitz**, **Israelovici** (Rumanian spelling); **Israelashvili** (among Georgian Jews); **Disraeli** (among Italian Jews); **Srolov**, **Sroloff**, **Srulov**, **Srolovitz**, **Srulovich**, **Srulovitz**, **Srulowitz**, **Srulevich**, **Srulewitch**; **Srulovici** (a Rumanian spelling); **Isserso(h)n**, **Iserson**, **Isseroff**, **Iserovich**.

Patrs. (from dims.): **Srulikov**, **Is(s)erles**, **Iserlis**, **Isserlin**.

Israeler Jewish: name adopted with reference to the ancient Kingdom of Israel, destroyed by the Assyrians in 721 BC, or to the concept of Jewish nationhood, or, in modern times, to the state of Israel.

Vars.: **Izraeler**; **Israeli**, **Israely**, **Izraeli**, **Izraely**, **Izreeli**, **Isreeli**, **Yisraeli**, **Yisraely** (with the Hebr. adj suffix -*i*; also derivable from the given name Israel); **Israelit(h)**, **Yisraelit** (with the Hebr. fem. adj. suffix -*it*, but not necessarily fem. in meaning).

Issac see Isaac

Issard see Izard

Issart see Essart

Isser see Israel

Iszczak see Isaac

Itelson see Ittelson

Itensohn see Ide

Ithell see Idle

Itkin see Ittelson

Itschakov see Isaac

Ittelson Jewish (Ashkenazic): metr. from the Yid. female given name *Itl*, a dim. of *Ite*, from the Yid. female given name *Yudes* (from Hebr. *Yehudit* Judith, 'Jewess').

Vars.: **Itelson**; **Itkin** (E Ashkenazic, based on *Itke*, an E yid. dim. of *Ite*).

Ittensohn see Ide

Iturbe Basque: topographic name for someone who lived downstream from a spring, from *iturri* spring + the local suffix -*be*, meaning 'lower down'.

Itzakovitz see Isaac

Ivachyov see John

Ivakhin see John

Ivarsson see Ivor

Ivatt see Ive

Ivchenko see John

Ive English: from the Norman personal name *Ivo*, in origin a short form of any of the various Gmc cpd names with a first element *īv* (ON *ýr*, pl. *ifar*) yew, bow (a weapon generally made from the supple wood of the yew tree). This was a popular name in Normandy and Brittany, and was introduced into England at the time of the Conquest, perhaps reinforcing OE *Ifa*, *Iva*. There was a bishop of Chartres called St Ivo (d. 1115), and a 13th-cent. Bret. saint of this name came to be recognized as the patron of lawyers. St Ives in Cambs. gets its name from a church dedicated to a legendary Persian bishop who is said to have become a hermit there. The more famous *St Ives* in Cornwall is named from a 5th-cent. female Ir. saint more accurately known as *Ia*. Yet another *St Ives*, in Hants, did not originally commemorate a saint at all but is named from a deriv. of OE *īfig* ivy.

Var.: **IVEY**.

Dims.: Eng.: **Ivatt**. Fr.: **Yvelin**, **Ivelain**, **Ivonnet**, **Yvonnet**; **Yvonou**, **Yvenec** (Brittany).

Patrs.: **Ives**; **Iveson**, **Ivison**. Fr.: **Abivon** (Brittany). Ger.: **Iven(s)**, **Iwen**, **Iben(s)**.

Ivers see Ivor

Ivery see Ivory

Ivey English (Devon): 1. var. of Ive. 2. Norman habitation name from *Ivoy* in Cher, so called from OF *ivoie*, a collective from *if* yew tree (of Gmc or Celt. origin).

Vars.: **Ivy**, **Ivie**.

Ivić see John

Ivie see Ivey

Ivings see Evan

Ivison see Ive

Ivković see John

Ivolgin Russian: patr. from the nickname *Ivolga* 'Oriole', given perhaps in admiration for a fine singing voice or with some reference to the striking yellow and black plumage of the bird.

Ivonnet see Ive

Ivor British: from the ON personal name *Ivarr*, of uncertain origin, probably from *īw* yew, bow (see Ive) + *herr* army. The given name was adopted at an early date by the Irish, Scots, and Welsh, much later and more rarely by the English. Many bearers of the modern surname are therefore of Celt. ancestry.

Patrs.: **Ivers(on)**. Sc., Ir.: **MacIvor**, **McIver**, **McEevor**, **McEever**, **McHeever**, **McCure**. Dan., Norw.: **Iversen**. Swed.: **Ivarsson**, **Iwarsson**. Fris.: **Ivers**, **Iwers**; **Ywersen**.

Ivory English (Norman): habitation name from *Ivry*-la-Bataille in Eure, so called from the Gallo-Roman personal name *Eburius* (a deriv. of L *ebur* ivory) + the local suffix -*ācum*.

Var.: **Ivery**.

Ivoshin see John

Ivshin see John

Ivushkin Russian: 1. patr. from the given name *Ivushka*, a dim. of *Ivan*; see John. 2. patr. from the nickname *Ivushka*, a dim. of *iva* willow (which has itself given rise to the surname **Ivin**), perhaps denoting a pliant individual or a topographic name for someone who lived by a willow tree.

Ivy see Ivey

Iwańczyk *see* JOHN

Iwarsson *see* IVOR

Iwen *see* IVE

Iwers *see* IVOR

Izac *see* ISAAC

Izaguirre Spanish form of Basque **Izagirre**, probably a var. of **Aizagirre**, topographic name for someone who lived in a place exposed to the wind, from Basque *aize* wind + *ager, agir* visible, exposed.

Izard 1. English and French: from a Gmc female personal name composed of the elements *īs* ice + *hild* battle, strife, introduced into England by the Normans in the forms *Iseu(l)t, Isolde*. The popularity of the various versions of the legend of Tristan and Isolde led to widespread use of the given name in the Middle Ages. 2. French: from *Ishard*, a Gmc male personal name composed of the elements *īs* ice + *hard* hardy, brave, strong; cf. ISNARD. 3. Provençal: nickname for an agile and sure-footed climber, from OProv. *(bouc) izar* mountain goat (apparently of pre-Roman origin).

Vars. (of 1): Eng.: **Izzard, Izzett, Izat(t), Is(s)ard, Issett, Issit(t), Isso(l)t**.

Izchaki *see* ISAAC

Izdebski Polish: topographic name for someone who lived in a small, isolated dwelling, from Pol. *izdebka* chamber, cell + *-ski* suffix of local surnames (see BARANOWSKI).

Izhak *see* ISAAC

Izikov *see* ISAAC

Izkoveski *see* ISAAC

Izon *see* IDE

Izquierdo Spanish: nickname for a left-handed man, from Sp. *izquierdo* left (a word of pre-Roman origin, akin to Basque *ezker*).

Izrael *see* ISRAEL

Izsak *see* ISAAC

Izydorczyk *see* ISIDORE

Izygson *see* ISAAC

Izzard *see* IZARD

J

Jabłoński Polish: topographic name for someone who lived by an apple tree or apple orchard, or occupational name for a grower or seller of apples, from Pol. *jabłoń* apple tree + *-ski* suffix of local surnames (see BARANOWSKI).

Var.: **Jabłonowski**.

Dims.: **Jabłkowski**; **Jabłonka**.

Patr.: Pol.: **Jabłonowicz**.

Patr. (from a dim.): Pol.: **Jabłkiewicz**.

Jabouille French: nickname for a garrulous person, a deriv. of ONF *jaber* to jabber, chatter (apparently from ON and originally meaning 'to open the mouth wide').

Jacek Polish: from a dim. of the given name *Jacenty* (L *Hyacinthus*, Gk *Hyakinthos*). This was the name of a 3rd-cent. saint who was martyred together with his brother Protus. He enjoyed a certain cult in Portugal as well as in Poland. His name, which is almost certainly of pre-Gk origin, in classical times denoted a flower (not the modern hyacinth, but perhaps the martagon lily), and it was borne by a mythological character from whose blood the flower was supposed to have sprung up.

Patrs.: Pol.: **Jackowicz**, **Jackiewicz**.

Habitation names: Pol.: **Jackowski**, **Jackowiak**; **Jaczewski**.

Jach 1. Polish, Czech, and German (esp. in Slav.-speaking regions): from the given name *Jach*, a dim. of various names beginning with *Ja-*, principally *Jan* (see JOHN), *Jakub* (see JACOB), and, in Pol., *Jacenty* (see JACEK). 2. Jewish (E Ashkenazic): of unknown origin; perhaps an adoption of the non-Jewish surname.

Vars. (of 1): Czech: **Jech**, **Jícha**, **Jač**; **Jaš**, **Ješ**. Ger.: **Jachmann**, **Jochmann**; **Jäch**, **Jach(i)sch**; **Jeche**, **Jecht**, **Jasche**, **Jäsche**; **Jesche**; **Jok(i)sch**, **Jokusch**. (Of 2): **Jachmann**.

Dims. (of 1): Pol.: **Jakowczyk**. Czech: **Jachek**, **Jacháček**; **Jaček**, **Jačka**; **Jašek**, **Jašík**, **Jaška**, **Ješek**. Ger.: **Jaschke**, **Jaschek**, **Jeschke**, **Jeschek**; **Jächel**, **Jächle**; **Jochel**, **Jöchel**; **Jäckl(e)in**, **Jackl**. (Of 2): **Jachel**.

Patrs. (from 1): Pol.: **Jachowicz**. Ger.: **Jachner**, **Jachler**, **Jackner**.

Jachimczak *see* JOACHIM

Jack 1. Scots and English: from the OF given name *Jacques*, the usual Fr. form of L *Jacōbus* JACOB. 2. Scots and English: from a pet form of JOHN, probably a borrowing of the Low Ger. and Du. pet forms *Jankin* and *Jackin*, which are from *Jan* (cf. JANE) + the dim. suffix *-kin*. (The loss of the nasal was a regular development in Low Ger.) In English, the ending came to be associated with the more familiar ANF dim. suffix *-in*, which was then omitted to yield *Jack* as a back-formation. 3. Jewish (Ashkenazic): Anglicization of one or more like-sounding Jewish surnames.

Vars. (of 1 and 2): Eng.: **Jake**, **Jagg**. (Of 1 only): Eng.: **Ja(c)ques** (usually pronounced /'dʒeɪkwɪz/); **Jaquith**.

Dims. (of 1): Eng.: **Jackett** (Cornwall); **Jacot**; **Jacklin(g)** (Notts.); **Je(a)cock**. Fr.: **Ja(c)quot**, **Jacot**, **Jaccoud**, **Jaccoux**, **Jac(qu)otin**, **Jac(qu)oton**, **Jac(qu)otet**, **Jac(qu)o(u)tot**; **Ja(c)quel(et)**, **Ja(c)quelot**, **Ja(c)quel(a)in**, **Ja(c)queau**; **Ja(c)quin(el)**, **Jacqui**, **Ja(c)quinet**, **Ja(c)quinot**, **Ja(c)quenet**, **Ja(c)quenot**, **Ja(c)quenod**, **Quinel**, **Quinet**, **Quinot**, **Quineau(x)**, **Quenel**, **Quenot**, **Queneau(x)**. It.: **Gia(c)chini**, **Iacchino**, **Zacchini**, **Giachinotti**; **Giacchello**, **Iachelli**, **Zachelli**; **Giachetti**, **Iachetti**, **Za(c)chetti**, **Ghetti**; **Iac(ch)ini**, **Iacol(l)o**, **Iacoletti**, **Giacoletti**, **Coletti**, **Iacolucci**; **Iaccello**; **Iacucci**, **Cucci**; **Iacuzzi(o)**, **Cuzzi**; **Giacozzi**, **Iacozzo**, **Cozz(in)i**, **Cozzolini**; **Iacotti**.

Augs. (of 1): It.: **Giac(c)one**, **Giac(c)oni**, **Iacone**, **Zaccone**, **Zacconi**, **Zagone**, **Coni**.

Pejs. (of 1): Fr.: **Ja(c)quard**. It.: **Iaccacci**, **Cacci**.

Patrs. (from 1): Eng.: **Jacks**, **Jaggs**, **Jakes**; **Jackson** (very common in all parts of the British Isles); **Jagson**.

Patrs. (from 1) (dims.): Eng.: **Jacketts**, **J(e)akin(g)s**, **Jacocks**, **Jacox**.

Jackman 1. English: occupational name for the servant of someone who bore the given name JACK. 2. English: Anglicized form of Fr. *Jacquème*; see JAMES. 3. Jewish (Ashkenazic): Anglicization of one or more like-sounding Jewish surnames.

Vars.: Eng.: **Jackaman**, **Jakeman**.

Jacmar *see* JAMES

Jacob English, Jewish, and Portuguese: via L *Jacōbus* from the Hebr. given name *Yaakov*. In the Bible, this is the name of the younger twin brother of Esau (Gen. 25: 26), who took advantage of the latter's hunger and impetuousness to persuade him to part with his birthright 'for a mess of potage'. The name is traditionally interpreted as coming from Hebr. *akev* heel, and Jacob is said to have been born holding on to Esau's heel. In English *Jacob* and *James* are now regarded as quite distinct names, but they are of identical origin (see JAMES), and in most European languages the two names are not distinguished. For convenience, cognates containing *-m-* are listed at JAMES; cognates lacking the *-ob-* syllable are listed at JACK. The principal forms of the given name in other major European languages are French *Jacques* (see JACK); Italian *Giacobo*, *Giacopo*, and *Iacopo* (also *Giacomo*; see JAMES); Spanish *Jaime* (see JAMES) and DIEGO (which is in fact almost certainly of distinct origin but now generally taken as a form of *Jacob*); German *Jakob*; Polish *Jakub*; and Russian *Yakov*. Throughout Eastern Europe, Jewish forms of the name were extremely common, ranging from *Yaakov* through various derivs., including *Yankev* and *Jankl* (see JANKOFF). Aphetic versions of the given name, dropping the initial *Ja-*, were also once common in central Europe and in Italy, hence many of the derivs. listed below.

Vars.: Eng.: **Jacobb(e)**; **Je(a)cop** (Suffolk). Jewish: **Jakov, Yakob, Ya(a)kov**; **Jacobi, Jacoby** (with the Hebr. adj. suffix -*i*); JANKOFF.

Dims.: Eng.: COPPING. It.: **Giacobelli, Giacop(p)ello, Giacovelli, Iacobelli, Iacovelli, Iacoviello, Iaci(v)elli, Sciacovelli, Cobello, Cobelli, Copello, Copelli, Cov(i)ello, Co(v)elli**; **Giacob(b)ini, Giacopini, Iacobini, Iacopini, Iacovino, Iacovini, Coppini, Covino, Cubbino, Cubinelli, Govini, Gavini, Capin(ett)i**; **Giacopetti, Giacovetti, Iacobetto, Iacopetti; Giacobucci, Giacobuzzi, Iacobucci, Iacabucci, Iacopucci, Iacovucci, Iacovuzzi, Cubucci; Giacoppoli, Iacovolo; Iacovozzo, Copozio, Capozzi; Giacobillo, Billo; Covotti, Cabotto, Cavoto, Gabotti, Cavozzi, Gavozzi, Bottin(ell)i, Botticelli; Covolini, Cavolini, Bolino, Bollini, Bolletti**. Ger.: **Köbi**. Low Ger.: **Kob, Ko(o)p, Kopp(e), Koepp(k)e, Köpke, Köbke**. Ger. (of Slav. origin): **Joppich, Jobke, Jopke** (chiefly Silesian); **Huba(ts)ch, Hupka** (Wendish); **Kopisch, Kob(i)sch, Kab(i)sch, K(a)ubisch, Kuba(ts)ch, Kupka, Kupke, Kubek, Kubik, Kuban, Kubin; Kosch(ke), Koschek, Kusch(a), Kusch(k)e, Kuschel, Kuscha(c)k** (see also NICHOLAS). Pol.: **Jakubczyk, Kubik, Kubiczek, Kubyszek; Kupka, Kupczyk**. Czech: **Jakoubek, Koubek, Kubík, Kubáček, Kubíček, Kubička, Kubečka, Kubalek, Kubelka, Kubánek, Kubásek, Kupka; Kopaček**. Hung.: **Jákó, Kubica**. Jewish: **Jekel, Yekel** (from the Yid. dim. *Yekl*); **Jok(e)l, Yokel, Yockelman** (from the Yid. dim. *Yokl*); **Jankel** (see JANKOFF).

Augs.: It.: **Giacoboni, Giacoponi, Iacoboni, Iacovone, Iacavone**.

Pejs.: It.: **Giacobazzi, Giacopazzi, Giacovazzo, Iacobacci, Iacobassi, Iacovazzi, Iacovacci(o)**.

Patrs.: Eng.: **Jacobs(on)**. Low Ger.: **Jakobs(en)**. Flem., Du.: **Jacobs(z), Jacobsen**. Dan., Norw.: **Jacobsen, Jakobsen**. Swed.: **Jacobsson, Jakobsson**. Russ.: **Yakovlev** (from the archaic patr. **Yakovl**, so avoiding -*ovov*); **Yakubov**. Ukr.: **Yakovliv, Yakovich**. Beloruss.: **Yakubovich**. Pol.: **Jakubowicz, Jakucewicz, Kubasiewicz; Jakubiak, Kubiak**. Croatian: **Jakovljević, Jauković; Djaković, Djok(ov)ić, Djek(ov)ić**. Gk: **Iacovides**. Jewish: **Jacobs, Jacobso(h)n, Yakobso(h)n; Jacobskind** ('Jacob's child'); **Yakobov, Yakoboff, Yakubov; Jakubowski, Jakubowsky, Jakubovski, Yakubowski, Yakubovsky; Jacobovitch, Jacobowitz, Jacobowits, Jacobovitz, Jacobovits; Jakubowicz, Jakubowitz, Jakubovitz, Jakubovitch, Jakubovits, Jakubovicz, Jakubovics, Yakobovi(t)ch, Yakobovicz, Yakobovich, Yakobowitz, Yakobowitch, Yakobowitsh, Yakubovitch, Yakubowitch, Yakubowicz, Yakubowitz, Yakubovitz; Yakubovics; Jakovlevitch, Jakovljevic**.

Patrs. (from dims.): Eng.: **Coppins, Coppens**. Low Ger.: **Kob(e)s, Kop(p)s, Köppen, Koppen(s)**. Flem. Du.: **Cops**. Du.: **Coppens, Koppen**. Norw., Dan.: **Jep(pe)sen, Jessen**. Swed.: **Jepsson**. Pol.: **Jakubczak, Kubczak**. Croatian: **Jakšić**. Russ.: **Yashin, Yashaev, Yash(a)nov, Yashunin; Yakhnov, Yakhnin; Yakun(k)in, Yakuntzov, Yakun(n)ikov, Yakunchikov, Yakushev, Yakush(k)in, Yakutin** (these forms are now generally associated with *Yakov*, although in fact they come from an ORuss. given name derived from Scandinavian *Hákon*).

Habitation names: Pol.: **Jakubowski, Jakuszewski**.

Jacquemar *see* JAMES

Jadczak *see* ANTHONY

Jädecke *see* GOTT

Jaén Spanish: local name from a city so called in S Spain. The current form represents an alteration, under the in-

fluence of Arabic, of earlier *Gaén*, from L *Gaiēnum*, a deriv. of the personal name *Gaius* (see GAY 3).

Jaffray *see* JEFFREY

Jäger German: occupational name for a huntsman, Ger. *Jäger*, agent deriv. of *jagen* to hunt (OHG *jagōn*). The surname has also been Latinized as **Venator**.

Vars.: **Jeger**; **Jager** (Austria).

Jagg *see* JACK

Jagger English: occupational name from a word meaning 'pedlar' in the Yorks. dialect, an agent deriv. of ME *jag* pack, load (of unknown origin). All or most present-day bearers of this surname are probably members of a single family, which originally came from Staniland in the parish of Halifax. During the 16th cent. it spread through the Calder valley, and thence to other parts of England.

Patr.: **Jaggers**.

Jagieła *see* JAGIEŁŁO

Jagieło Polish: surname from the princely house of *Jagieło*, who derived it from Władysław *Jagieło* (1348–1434), the Lithuanian founder of the dynasty. The Jagiełos ruled the Kingdom of Poland and the Grand Duchy of Lithuania from 1386 to 1572. The surname in some cases may conceivably indicate genuine descent from a branch of this family, but more often it seems to have been adopted to suggest a connection with, them, or in honour of the dynasty and the glorious period of Polish history that they represent.

Vars.: **Jagieła**; **Jagielski**.

Jaglom Jewish (E Ashkenazic): ornamental name from Hebr. *yahalom* diamond; cf. BRILLANT and DIAMOND. The change from -*h*- to -*g*- is due to Russ. influence.

Var.: **Yaglom**.

Jaher *see* JOHN

Jahier *see* JAYET

Jahrmann *see* GEARY

Jailler *see* GALE

Jaillet French: topographic name for someone who lived on marshy land, from a dim. of OF *jaille* marsh, mud, now a regional term found mainly in W France. It may also perhaps have been a nickname with the sense 'muddy'; in the Jura the word is applied to a cow with dark patches on its side.

Var.: **Jaillon**.

Pej.: **Jaillard**.

Jaimez *see* JAMES

Jain *see* JANE

Jake *see* JACK

Jakeman *see* JACKMAN

Jakimovski *see* JOACHIM

Jakobs *see* JACOB

Jakowczyk *see* JACH

Jambrozek *see* AMBROSE

James English: from a given name that has the same origin as JACOB but that is now felt to be a separate name in its own right. This is largely because in the Authorized Version of the Bible (1611) the form *James* is used in the New Testament as the name of two of Christ's apostles (James the brother of John and James the brother of Andrew), whereas in the Old Testament the brother of Esau is called *Jacob*. The form *James* comes from L *Jacōbus* via LL *Jac(o)mus*, which also gave rise to *Jaime*, the regular form of the name in Sp. (as opposed to the learned *Jacobo*). See also JACK and JACKMAN.

Dims.: Fr.: **Jacquemot**, **Jacquemet**, **Ja(c)quemy**, **Ja(c)queminot**, **Ja(c)queminet**. Prov.: **Jaumet**, **Jam(m)et**, **Jamot**. It.: **Giacomello**, **Giacomelli**, **Giammelli**, **Iacomelli**, **Comello**, **Comelli**, **Comel(l)ini**, **Mello**, **Gia(co)metti**, **Giamitti**, **Iacometti**, **Iamitti**, **Cometto**, **Cometti**; **Giacomini**, **Iacomini**, **Comin(ell)o**, **Comin(ett)i**, **Cominotti**, **Cominoli**; **Giacomucci**, **Gia(co)muzzi**, **Giacomuzzo**, **Giamusso**, **Comucci**, **Comuzzo**, **Comusso**, **Mucci**, **Mucillo**, **Muccino**, **Muzz(in)i**, **Muzzillo**, **Muzzolo**, **Muzzullo**, **Musso**, **Mussett(in)i**, **Muselli**, **Mussilli**, **Mussotti**, MUSSOLINI; **Giacomozzo**, **Camosso**, **Mozz(in)i**, **Mozzetti**; **Comolli**, **Camolli**, **Comoletti**, **Camoletto**; **Comizzoli**, **Mizzi**; **Motto**, **Mottin(ell)i**.

Aug.: It.: **Giacomoni**.

Pejs.: Fr.: **Ja(c)quemar(d)**, **Jacmar(d)**. It.: **Giacomazzo**, **Giacomasso**, **Comazzo**, **Mazzo**.

Patrs.: Eng.: **Jameson**; **Jami(e)son** (chiefly Scot.); **Jemison**, **Jim(p)son**, **Gemson**, **Gimson** (the latter often pronounced with initial /g/). Sc.: **McKeamish**, **McJames** (Gael. **Mac Sheumais**). It.: **Di Giacomo**. Sp.: **Jaimez**.

Patr. (from a dim.): It.: **Di Giacomettino**.

Jaminet see BENJAMIN

Janáček see JOHN

Jane English (chiefly Devon and Cornwall): from the ME given name *Jan*, a var. of JOHN. (As a given name, *Jane* was not specialized as a female form until the 17th cent.)

Vars.: **Jain(e)**, **Jayne**; **Jean**; **Jenn(e)**, **Genn**.

Dims.: **Janet**, **Jennett**; **Jankin**. See also JENKIN.

Patrs.: **Ja(y)nes**, **Jeynes**; **Jean(e)s**, **Jeens**, **Jeneson**; **Jan(ni)s**, **Janson**; **Jenns**, **Jenness**, **Jen(n)ison**.

Jankel see JACOB

Jankoff Jewish (E Ashkenazic): from the male Yid. given name *Yankev*, from Hebr. *Yaakov* (see JACOB).

Vars.: **Yankov**, **Yankow**, **Yankev**, **Yanko**, **Yanku**; **Yankovsky**, **Yankofsky**.

Dim.: **Jankel(l)** (from Yid. *Yankl*).

Patrs.: **Jankovi(t)ch**, **Jankovitz**, **Jankowitz**; **Jankowicz** (Pol. spelling); **Yankowitz**, **Yankovi(t)ch**, **Yankowi(t)ch**, **Yankovitsch**, **Yankovitz**, **Yankovits**.

Patrs. (from dims.): **Jankeloff**, **Yankelevsky**; **Jank(i)elewicz**, **Jankilewicz**, **Jankielowicz**, **Jankelewitz**, **Jankelevitz**, **Jankilevitz**, **Jankelovicz**, **Jankelovits**, **Jankelowitz**, **Jankolowitz**, **Jankolovits**, **Jankulovits**, **Janklowicz**, **Janklewitz**, **Yankelovi(t)ch**, **Yankelevitz**, **Yankelewich**, **Yankelovich**, **Yankelovitz**, **Yankelowitz**, **Yankielewicz**, **Yankilevi(t)ch**.

Janks see JENKS

Jannings see JENNINGS

January English: **1.** nickname or given name for someone born or baptized in January, or having some other particu-

lar connection with that month, which gets its name from L *(mensis) Januārius* (month) of *Janus'*. Janus was the god of gateways and entrances (his name is akin to L *janua* door), and was represented as having two faces, one looking forward at what is to come, the other backward at what is past. In some cases the surname may reflect the L personal name *Januārius*, which was borne by a number of early Christian saints, most famously a 3rd-cent. bishop of Benevento who became the patron of Naples. **2.** local name, altered by folk etymology, from *Genoa* in Liguria. The ME term for a Genoese was *Janaway*, a back-formation from *Janaways*, which was taken as a pl. but is in fact an Eng. spelling of OF *Genoveis*, It. *Genovese* Genoese. Genoa was one of the great seaports of the Mediterranean in medieval times, and merchants and master mariners from there were found in all the coastal and trading towns of Europe. The origin of the name of the city is uncertain. It has been associated with L *janua* door (see above), but is more probably of pre-Roman origin. In the Middle Ages the Genoese were regarded as clever individuals, and it is possible that the surname is sometimes a nickname with this sense.

Var.: (of 2): **Janaways**.

Dims. (of 1): It.: **Gennarelli**, **Gennarino**.

Patr. (from 1): It.: **Di Gennaro**.

Jaquard see JACK

Jaquemar see JAMES

Jara Spanish: habitation name from places in the provinces of Alicante and Cádiz called *La Jara*, from OSp. *jara* wood, thicket (Arabic *šéra*). In some cases the surname may derive directly from the vocab. word, as a topographic name.

Jarad see GARRETT

Jaram see JEROME

Jarcks see TERRY

Jarden see JORDAN

Jardin see GARDENER

Jarmain see GERMAN

Jarmay see JEREMY

Jarosz Polish: from a short form of the given name *Jarosław* (composed of the elements *jaro-* young, robust + *-sław* glory; cogn. with Czech *Jaroslav*), or from some other given name in which *jaro-* forms the first element, or from a dial. form of the given name *Hieronim* JEROME. In some cases it may have originated as a nickname for a vigorous young man, from the adj. *jary*.

Vars.: **Jaros**; **Jarecki**.

Dims.: Pol.: **Jaroszek**, **Jarosik**, **Jaraszek**. Czech: **Jarušek**.

Patrs.: Pol.: **Jarewicz**, **Jaruszewicz**; **Jaroszczak**. Croatian: **Jarić**.

Habitation names: Pol.: **Jaroszewski**, **Jaroszyński**.

Jarre 1. French: metonymic occupational name for a potter, from OF *jarre* earthenware vessel (OProv. *jarra*, from

Arabic *jarrah*, a word brought back by the Crusaders, which has also given Eng. *jar*). **2.** Frisian: cogn. of GEARY 2.

Var. (of 1): **Jarrier**.

Dims. (of 1): **Jarret**, **Jarron**.

Jarren *see* GEARY

Jarry 1. English (Norfolk): var. of GEARY 2. **2.** Provençal: topographic name for someone who lived by an oak tree or oak grove, from OProv. *garric* (masc.) kermes oak or *garrique* (fem.) grove of such oaks.

Vars. (of 1): **Jear(e)y**, **Jary**. (Of 2): **Garric**, **Garrit**; **Jarrige**, **Lajarrige**, **Garrigue**, **Garrique**.

Dims. (of 2): Prov.: **Jarrijon**, **Garrigou**, **Garrioux**.

Järvinen Finnish: ornamental name from Finn. *järvi* lake + the gen. suffix -*nen*, perhaps in some cases chosen as a topographic name by someone who lived by a lake.

Jarvis English: **1.** from the Norman personal name *Gervase*, composed of the Gmc element *geri, gari* spear + a second element of uncertain meaning and original form. (For the change of -*er*- to -*ar*-, cf. MARCHANT.) The name had some currency throughout Europe in the Middle Ages, partly because it was borne by a saint who was martyred under the Roman Emperor Domitian; this saint became one of the patrons of Milan. **2.** habitation name from *Jervaulx* in N Yorks., site of a famous Cistercian monastery, so called from an ANF form of the river name *Ure* (of Brit. origin; it may be cogn. with the Ger. *Isar*, and have some meaning such as 'strongly flowing') + ANF *vaulx* valley (see VALE).

Vars.: **Jervis**. (of 1 only): **Gervis**, **Gervase**; **Jarvie** (Scotland).

Dims. (of 1): Fr.: **Gervaiseau**, **Gervot**. It.: **Gervasini**, **Gervasutti**; **Vasol(in)i**, **Vasolin** (Venetia). Port.: **Gervasinho**. Ger.: **Vaslin**, **Vassle**; **Fäsi(n)** (Switzerland).

Augs. (of 1): It.: **Gervasoni**; **Vason** (Venetia).

Patr. (from 1): Low Ger.: **Gervasing**.

Jarzębowski Polish: habitation name from a place named with Pol. *jarząb* service tree + -*ów* possessive suffix, with the addition of -*ski*, suffix of local surnames (see BARANOWSKI).

Vars.: **Jarzębski**; **Jarząbek**.

Jasche *see* JACH

Jasiak *see* JOHN

Jasiński Polish: probably an elaboration of the given name *Jasiek*, a dim. of *Jan* JOHN, or else a habitation name from some place named with this element.

Var.: **Jasieński**.

Jaspars *see* KASPAR

Jastrow Jewish (Ashkenazic): habitation name from the town of *Jastrowic* in NE Poland (also called *Jastrów*), where there was a large Jewish community.

Var.: **Jastrov**.

Jaszczak *see* JOHN

Jatczak *see* JOHN

Jaubert French: from a Gmc personal name of uncertain origin. The first element is probably the tribal name *Gaut* (see JOCELYN); the second is *berht* bright, famous.

Var.: **Gaubert** (Normandy, Picardy).

Dims.: Prov.: **Joubertin**, **Jouberton**.

Jauković *see* JACOB

Jaumet *see* JAMES

Jaune French: nickname for someone with a sallow skin, from OF *jaune* yellow (L *galbīnus* greenish-yellow, which was itself used as a family name in classical times; cogn. with Ger. *gelb* yellow; cf. GELLER).

Dims.: **Jauneau**, **Jaunet**.

Pejs.: **Jaunard**, **Jaunasse**.

Jáuregui Spanish form of Basque **Jauregi**: topographic name for someone who lived by a manor house, or occupational name for someone who was employed in one, from *jauregi* palace, manor house (a cpd of *jaur* lord + the local suffix -*egi*).

Javier Spanish: from a given name or religious byname bestowed in honour of St Francis *Xavier* (1506–52), Jesuit missionary to the Far East. He was a member of a noble family who took their name from the castle of *Javier* in Navarre, where he was born. The placename is of Basque origin; see ECHEVERRÍA.

Jaworski Polish: topographic name for someone who lived by a maple or sycamore tree, from Pol. *jawor* maple, sycamore + the surname suffix -*ski* (see BARANOWSKI).

Var.: **Jaworowski**.

Jay English and French: nickname from the vocab. word denoting the bird (ME, OF *jay(e)*, *gai*, LL *gaius*, from the personal name *Gaius*; cf. GAY 3), probably referring to an idle chatterer or a showy person, although the jay was also noted for its thieving habits.

Vars.: Fr.: **Geai(x)**, **Geay**, **Legeay**, **Lejay**.

Patrs.: Eng.: **Jay(e)s**.

Jayet French: of uncertain origin, perhaps a metonymic occupational name for a jeweller, from OF *jaiet* jade, which is derived, like It. *geada*, from Sp. *(piedra de) ijada* stone of the flanks (LL *īliata* for class. L *īlia*), so called because it was thought to offer a remedy against kidney stones.

Vars.: **Jayez**, **Jayot**; **Jahier** (agent noun).

Jayne *see* JANE

Jeacock *see* JACK

Jeacop *see* JACOB

Jean *see* JANE

Jeandeau *see* JOHN

Jearey *see* JARRY

Jeavon 1. English: distinguishing name from ANF *jovene* young; see JEUNE. **2.** Welsh: from the given name *Ievan*, an earlier form of EVAN, the W version of JOHN.

Var.: **Jevon**.

Patrs.: **Je(a)vons**.

Jebb *see* JEFFREY

Jech *see* JACH

Jecheskel *see* EZEKIEL

Jechimczyk *see* JOACHIM

Jeckell *see* JEKYLL

Jecks *see* GEACH

Jecock *see* JACK

Jecop *see* JACOB

Jedele *see* ULRICH

Jędrachowicz *see* ANDREW

Jeeks *see* GEACH

Jeens *see* JANE

Jeeves English: metr. from *Geva*, a pet form of the medieval female given name *Genevieve*, introduced into England by the Normans. This is of obscure etymology, but may represent a reworking of a Gaul. name in which the first element meant 'people', the second 'woman'. It was very popular in France, where a 5th-cent. saint bearing it became patroness of Paris.

Vars.: **Jeves, Geaves, Geeves**.

Jefferd *see* GIFFARD

Jeffrey English: from a Norman personal name that appears in ME as *Geffrey* and in OF as *Je(u)froi*. Some authorities regard this as no more than a palatalized form of GODFREY, but early forms such as *Galfridus* and *Gaufridus* point to a first element from Gmc *gala* to sing or *gawi* region, territory. It is possible that several originally distinct names have fallen together in the same form.

Vars.: **Jeff(e)ry, Jeffree, Jeffray, Jeffroy, Jaffrey, Jaffray, Geoffrey, Geoffroy**.

Dims.: Eng.: **Jebb, Jepp(e), Gebb, Gepp, Jeff(e); Jef(f)cock, Jef(f)cott, Jephcott, Jef(f)cote, Jephcote, Jef(f)coat**. Fr.: **Geoffrion, Joufrion, Joffrin; Jaffrennou, Jaffrezic, Jaffrézo** (Brittany).

Patrs.: Eng.: **Jeff(e)ries, Jeff(e)ry(e)s, Jeffer(i)s, Jeffress, Geoffreys; Jefferson**.

Patrs. (from dims.): Eng.: **Jeff(e)s; Jebbs, Jepps; Jebson, Jibson, Jep(pe)son, Gepson, Jephson**.

Jeger *see* JÄGER

Jeggons *see* JEKYLL

Jehaes *see* JOHN

Jehle *see* ULRICH

Jekel *see* JACOB

Jekyll English: of Breton or Cornish origin, from a Celt. personal name, OBret. *Iudicael*, composed of elements meaning 'lord' + 'generous', 'bountiful', which was borne by a 7th-cent. saint, a king of Brittany who abdicated and spent the last part of his life in a monastery. Forms of this name are found in medieval records not only in Devon and Cornwall, where they are of native origin, but also in E Anglia and even Yorks., whither they were imported by Bretons after the Norman Conquest. The vowel of the first syllable is traditionally long, but now often pronounced short.

Vars.: **Jeckell, Jockle, Jiggle, Giggle; Jewell, Juell, Joel(l), Jowle, Joule**.

Dims.: Eng.: **Jiggen, Jickling, Jugg; Jol(l)in, Jowling, Gollin, Jolland, Gollan(d)**.

Patrs.: Eng.: **Jeckells, Jickells, Jickles, Jockelson; Jewels, Joels, Joules, Jo(e)lson**. Welsh: BETHELL.

Patrs. (from dims.): Eng.: **Jiggins, Juggins, Jeggons; Jukes, Jewkes, Jouxson; Jollands, Gollins**.

Jelbart *see* GILBERT

Jelen 1. Czech: nickname from *jelen* stag, perhaps given with reference to the supposed sexual powers of the stag. **2.** Jewish (E Ashkenazic): ornamental name from Czech *jelen* stag, also widely adopted as a translation of HIRSCH.

Vars.: Jewish: **Jel(l)in, Yel(l)en, Yel(l)in, Yel(l)on, Yalin, Yalon, Jelinsky**.

Dims.: Czech: **Jelínek**. Jewish: **Jel(l)inek, Jelinak, Yel(l)inek**. Pol.: **Jelonek, Jelonka**.

Patrs.: Croatian: **Jelenić**. Jewish: **Jelinowicz, Yelinovitz, Yelinsohn**.

Jell *see* JULIAN

Jellard *see* GILES

Jellett *see* GILLETT

Jemison *see* JAMES

Jencke *see* JOHN

Jendrássik *see* HENRY

Jeneson *see* JANE

Jenison *see* JANE

Jenkin English: from the ME given name *Jenkin*, a dim. of JOHN with the addition of the suffix -*kin* (of Low Ger. origin).

Vars.: **Jenken, Jinkin, Junkin**.

Patrs.: **Jenkins, Jinkins; Jenki(n)son, Jenkerson, Junki(n)son**.

Jenks English: patr. from the ME given name *Jenk*, a back-formation from JENKIN with the removal of the supposed ANF dim. suffix -*in*.

Vars.: **Jencks, Jen(c)kes; Janks; Jinks** (W Midlands).

Jenner 1. English (chiefly Kent and Sussex): occupational name for a designer or engineer, from a ME aphetic form of OF *engineor* contriver (a deriv. of *engaigne* cunning, ingenuity, stratagem, device; cf. GAIN and INGHAM 2). Engineers in the Middle Ages were primarily designers and builders of military machines, although in peacetime they might turn their hands to architecture and other more pacific functions. **2.** German: from the given name *Januārius*; see JANUARY 1. The Austrian dial. word for 'January' is *Jänner*, and so it is possible that in Austria this is one of the surnames acquired from words denoting months of the year, for example by converts who had been baptized in that month or people who were born or baptized in that month.

Vars. (of 1): **Jenoure, Genower, Genner, Ginner**.

Jennewein German: from the L personal name *Ingenuīnus* 'True-born', borne by a 7th-cent. saint, bishop of Brixen (now Bressanone) in the S Tyrol.

Vars.: **Gen(n)ewein**, **Gendebein**.

Jennings English: patr. from the ME given name *Janyn*, *Jenyn*, a dim. of JOHN.

Vars.: **Jannings**, **Jennins**, **Jennens**.

Jent see GENTLE

Jentel 1. French: dim. of *Jean* JOHN. 2. Jewish (Ashkenazic): from *Yentl*, a Yid. female given name (ultimately from L *gentilis* well-born, noble; see GENTLE).

Var. (of 2): **Yental**.

Jephcote see JEFFREY

Jeppesen see JACOB

Jerdan see GARDENER

Jereatt see GARRETT

Jeremy English: from the medieval given name of the same form, which enjoyed a modest popularity among Christians as having been borne by the biblical prophet *Jeremiah* (Hebr. *Yirmeyahu* 'may God exalt him'), noted for his lamentations over the faithlessness of Israel.

Vars.: **Jerm(e)y** (Norfolk); **Jarm(e)y**, **Jarmay**.

Patrs.: Russ.: **Yeremeev**, **Yeryomin**. Croatian: **Jerem(ov)ić**. Jewish: **Yermus**, **Yarmus** (from the Yid. form *Yermye*).

Patrs. (from dims.): Russ.: **Yer(sh)in**, **Yerkin**, **Yerk(h)ov**, **Yerasov**, **Yerychov**, **Yeryushev**, **Yeryuchin**. Jewish: **Jermulowicz** (E Ashkenazic, from the Yid. dim. *Yermyele*).

Jerety see GERAGHTY

Jerez Spanish: habitation name from places in the provinces of Badajoz and Cadiz, of unknown etymology. The former, now known in full as Jerez de los Caballeros, was the birthplace of the explorer Vasco Núñez de Balboa (*c*.1475–1519); the latter, Jerez de la Frontera, was an important centre for the manufacture of sherry (named in Eng. from the town) and brandy.

Jerger see GEORGE

Jerman see GERMAN

Jerome English: ostensibly from the medieval given name of the same spelling (OF *Jérôme*, from Gk *Hieronymos*, composed of the elements *hieros* sacred + *onyma* name), which achieved some popularity in France and elsewhere, being given in honour of St Jerome (?347–420), who created the Vulgate, the standard L version of the Bible, working partly from earlier L texts and partly from the original Hebr., Aramaic, and Gk. However, this was a rather rare given name in England in the Middle Ages; the comparative frequency of the surname is explained by the fact that it has also absorbed a Norman personal name, *Gerram*, composed of the Gmc elements *geri*, *gari* spear + *hraban* raven.

Vars.: **Jerrom(e)**, **Jerram**, **Gerram**, **Jerran**, **Jaram**.

Dims.: Ger.: **Grom(me)s**, **Grummes**, **Grolms**, **Grulms**. Czech: **Jarolímek**.

Patrs.: Eng.: **Jer(r)om(e)s**, **Jerrams**, **Jerrans**. Flem.: **Geerooms**; **Rooms**.

Jerozolimski see YERUSHALMI

Jerushalmi see YERUSHALMI

Jervis see JARVIS

Jesche see JACH

Jeschner see JOHN

Jesionowski Polish: habitation name from a place named with Pol. *jesion* ash tree + *-ów* possessive suffix, with the addition of *-ski*, suffix of local surnames (see BARANOWSKI).

Dim.: Pol.: **Jesionek**.

Jespers see KASPAR

Jess see JOSEPH

Jessen see JACOB

Jestice see JUSTICE

Jesus Portuguese: from a medieval given name, taken in honour of Christ. The name *Jesus* is from a Gk form, *Iēsos*, of Hebr. *Yeshua*, a byform of *Yehoshua* (Eng. *Joshua*) 'may Jehovah help him'. In most of Christian Europe this name is felt to be too sacred to bestow on mortal children, but there have been no such inhibitions in Spanish-and Portuguese-speaking areas, where it is extremely popular.

Jetson see JORDAN

Jeulin see JULIAN

Jeune French: from OF *jeuvene* young (L *iuvenis*), used to distinguish the younger of two bearers of the same given name within a community, who might be two brothers, father and son, or no relation at all to each other.

Var.: **Lejeune**.

Dims.: Fr.: **Jeunet**, **Jeuneau**; **Jon(n)et**, **Jonneau**; **Jouvenel**, **Jouvenet**, **Jouvenot**; **Jouvel**, **Jouveau**, **Jouvet**. It.: **Giovinetti**, **Iovinelli**.

Pejs.: Fr.: **Jonnart**. It.: **Giovinazzo**.

Jevain see JOUVIN

Jeves see JEEVES

Jevon see JEAVON

Jew see JULIAN

Jewell see JEKYLL

Jewett see JOWETT

Jewhurst see DEWHURST

Jewry see JURY

Jex see GEACH

Jeynes see JANE

Ježek see YEZHOV

Jeziorski Polish: topographic name for someone who lived by a lake, Pol. *jezioro*.

Vars.: **Jezierski**, **Jeziorny**.

Jhering see GEARY

Jibson see JEFFREY

Jícha see JACH

Jickells see JEKYLL

Jiggen see JEKYLL

Jiguet see GIGOT

Jiles see GILES

Jillett see GILLETT

Jillings see JULIAN

Jimeno Spanish: from a medieval given name of uncertain origin. It has normally been assumed to be a form of SIMON, but this is disputed. The medieval form was *Ximenus*, which Menéndez Pidal derives from L *Siminius*.

Var.: **Gimeno**.

Patrs.: **Jiménez**, **Giménez**; **Ximénez** (archaic spelling).

Jimpson see JAMES

Jindáček see HENRY

Jinkin see JENKIN

Jinks see JENKS

Jira see GEORGE

Jizhaki see ISAAC

Joachim French and German: from the Hebr. male given name *Yoyakim* 'God has granted (a son)', which occurs in the Bible (Neh. 12: 10) and was also borne, according to medieval legend, by the father of the Virgin Mary.

Vars.: Fr.: **Joaquin**. Ger.: **Jochum**, **Joche(i)m**.

Dim.: Pol.: **Jechimczyk**.

Patrs.: Ger.: **Joachimi** (Latinized). Low Ger.: **Joachimsen**, **Jochims(en)**, **Jochens**. Dan.: **Jockumsen**. Russ.: **Akimov**. Pol.: **Jachimowicz**, **Joachimiak**, **Jachimczak**. Jewish: **Joachinsohn**, **Yoachimsohn**; **Jo(a)chimowicz**, **Jochimowich**; **Jakimowski**, **Jakimovski**, **Jakimovsky**, **Yakimov(ski)**, **Yakimovsky** (all apparently from non-Jewish surnames).

Patrs. (from dims.): Russ.: **Akim(a)kin**, **Akimchev**, **Akimchin**, **Akimochkin**, **Akimushkin**, **Akimychev**.

'Son of the wife of J.': Russ.: **Akimikhin**. Ukr.: **Yakimishin**.

Joanaud see JOHN

Joans see JONES

Joass see JOYCE

Job English: **1.** from the personal name (Hebr. *Iyov*) borne by a biblical character, the central figure in the Book of Job, who was tormented by God and yet refused to forswear Him. The name has been variously interpreted as meaning 'Where is the (divine) father?' and 'Persecuted one'. It does not seem to have been used as a given name in the Middle Ages: the surname is probably a nickname for a wretched person or one tormented with boils (which was one of Job's afflictions). **2.** nickname from OF *job, joppe* sorry wretch, fool (perhaps a transferred application of the name of the biblical character). **3.** perhaps also a metonymic occupational name for a cooper, from ME *jubbe, jobbe* vessel containing four gallons (of unknown etymology). This could also have been a metonymic nickname for a heavy drinker or for a tubby person. **4.** metonymic occupational name for a maker or seller (or nickname for a wearer) of the long woollen garment known in ME and OF as a *jube* or *jupe* (cf. mod. Fr. *jupe* skirt). This word ultimately derives from Arabic.

Vars.: **Jobe**, **Jope**, **Jupe**; **Jopp**, **Jubb**, **Jupp**; **Juby**. (Of 3 and 4): **Jobar**, **Jobber**, **Jubber**.

Dims.: Eng.: **Jobin**; **Joblin(g)** **Joplin(g)** (Northumb.). Fr.: **Jobet**, **Jobey**, **Job(el)in**, **Jobineau**, **Jobot**. (Of 4 only): It.: **Giubbini**.

Patrs. (from 1): Eng.: **Jobes**, **Jobson**, **Jopson**.

Patrs. (from 1) (dims.): Eng.: **Jobbins**. Low Ger.: **Jöbken**, **Jöbgen**, **Jöbges**.

Jobert see JAUBERT

Jöbgen see JOB

Jobke see JACOB

Joce see JOYCE

Jocelyn English: from an OF personal name of complex origin, imported into England in the forms *Goscelin*, *Gosselin*, *Joscelin*. The name was known in England before the Conquest, but was spread by the Normans, among whom it was very popular. For the most part it is from the Gmc personal name *Gauzelin*, a dim. from a short form of the various cpd names having as their first element the tribal name *Gaut* (apparently the same as OE *Gēatas*, the Scandinavian people to which Beowulf belonged, and also akin to the name of the *Goths*). However, the name also came to be considered as a dim. of OF *Josse*; see JOYCE.

Vars.: **Jocelyn(e)**, **Josselyn**, **Joselin**, **Joslen**, **Joslin(g)**, **Jos(e)land**, GOSLING.

Jocheim see JOACHIM

Jochel see JACH

Jocić see JOHN

Jockelson see JEKYLL

Jodar Catalan: of uncertain origin, possibly from an Arabic personal name *Ğaudar* or a Gmc personal name composed of the tribal name *Gaut* (see JOCELYN) + *heri, hari* army.

Jöderli see THÉODORE

Jodrellec see CALDERON

Joe see JOSEPH

Joel see JEKYLL, YOEL

Joensen see JOHN

John English: from the Hebr. name *Yochanan* 'Jehovah has favoured (me with a son)' or 'may Jehovah favour (this child)', which was adopted into L (via Gk) as *Johannēs*, and has enjoyed enormous popularity in Europe throughout the Christian era, being given in honour of St John the Baptist, precursor of Christ, and of St John the Evangelist, author of the fourth gospel, as well as others of the nearly one thousand saints of the name. Some of the principal forms of the given name in other European languages are W *Evan, Ioan*; Sc. *Ia(i)n*; Ir. *Séan*; Ger. *Johann, Hans*; Flem., Du. *Jan*; Fr. *Jean*; It. *Giovanni, Gianni, Vanni*; Sp. *Juan*; Port. *João*; Gk *Ioanni*; Czech *Jan*;

Russ. *Ivan*. Polish has surnames both from the W Slav. forms *Jan(usz)* and from the E Slav. form *Iwan*.

There were a number of different forms of the name in ME, including *Jan(e)* (see JANE); *Jen* (see JENKIN); *Jon(e)* (see JONES); and *Han(n)* (see HANN). There were also various ME fem. versions of this name (e.g. *Joan, Jehan*), some of them indistinguishable from the masc. forms. The distinction on grounds of sex between *John* and *Joan* was not firmly established in English until the 17th cent. It was even later that *Jean* and *Jane* were specialized as specifically fem. names in English; bearers of these surnames and their derivs. are more likely to derive them from a male ancestor than a female.

Vars.: **Jon(e)**, **Ion**; JANE. Dims.: Eng.: JENKIN; JOHNCOCK; **Jo(h)nikin**, **Jo(h)nigan** (chiefly Irish); see also JACK. Fr.: **Jean(n)et**, **Joannet**, **Jouan(d)et**, **Jeandet**, **Jantet**, **Jentet**, **Jo(u)an(n)eton**; **J(e)an(n)in**, **Jo(u)an(n)in**, **Jo(u)an(n)y**, **Jan(n)y**, **Jeandin**, **Jentin**, **Jean(n)enet**; **Jean(n)ot**, **Jo(u)an(n)ot**, **Jeandot**, **Jantot**, **Janodet**; **Jean(n)on**, **Jeandon**, **Janton**, **Jenton**; **J(e)an(n)el**, **Jeandel**, **Jantel**, JENTEL, **Jean(n)eau**, **Jou(h)an(d)eau**, **Jeandeau**, **Jenteau**; **Jean(n)equin**, **Jannequin**, **Johanchon**, **Jean(n)esson**, **Jo(u)an(n)isson**, **Janisson**; **Jeandillou**; **Joan(n)ic** (Brittany). It.: **Gi(ov)an(n)elli**, **Giovannilli**, **Gian(i)ello**, **Gianilli**, **Cianelli**, **Ian(n)elli**, **Iannello**, **Ian(n)iello**, **Iannilli**, **Zan(n)elli**, **Zuanelli**, **Zuenelli**, **Van(n)elli**, **Nanelli**; **Gi(ov)an(n)etti**, **Giovanitti**, **Gioanetti**, **Gianeti**, **Gianettini**, **Ian(n)etti**, **Ianniti**, **Ianitti**, **Ianittello**, **Zan(n)etti**, **Zanetto**, **Zoanetti**, **Zanitti**, **Zanettini**, **Zanetello**, **Vannetti**, **Svanetti**, **Nannetti**, **Netti**, **Nitti**; **Gio(v)annini**, **Gian(n)ini**, **Gianinotti**, **Iannini**, **Zan(n)ini**, **Zaninelli**, **Van(n)ini**, **Svanini**, **Nannini**, **Ninn(ol)i**, **Ninotti**; **Gian(n)otti**, **Zan(n)otti**, **Zanotelli**, **Zanutto**, **Zanutti**, **Notti**, **Noto**; **Gian(n)ucci**, **Gianuzzi**, **Ianuccelli**, **Iannuzz(ell)i**, **Ianussi**, **Zanucioli**, **Zanussi**, **Vannucc(in)i**, **Vanucchi**, **Vannozzi**, **Nanuccio**, **Nannuzzi**, **Nozzol(in)i**, **Nucci(tell)i**, **Nuciotti**, **Nuzz(ett)i**, **Nussi**; **Gianolo**, **Gianolini**, **Gianullo**, **Gianulli**, **Zan(n)ol(l)i**, **Zaniolo**, **Zanolini**, **Zanoletti**, **Nol(l)i**; **Zanicchi**, **Zan(n)ichelli**; **Giovanizio**, **Ianizzi**, **Nannizzi**. Sp.: **Juanico**. Ger.: **Jä(h)ne(l)**, **Jä(h)ndel**, **Jahn(d)el**. Low Ger.: **Johnke**, **Jönk(e)**, **Jenne(mann)**. Fris.: **Jansema**. Ger. (of Slav. origin): JACH; **Jä(h)n(c)ke**, **Jä(h)n(i)sch**, **Ja(h)n(i)sch**, **Jä(h)nig**, **Janna(s)ch**, **Jan(n)uschek**, **Janoschek**, **Jen(i)(c)ke**, **Jent(z)sch**, **Gen(i)(c)ke**, **Gent(z)sch**, **Wa(h)n(c)ke**, **Wanka**, **Wan(j)ek**, **Wandtke**; **Nusch(k)e**, **Nuscha**. Pol.: **Janek**, **Janik**, **Janczyk**, **Janasik**, **Janusik**, **Janeczek**, **Jasi(a)k**; JACH; **Jończyk**, **Iwańczyk**, **Waszczyk**. Czech: **Janík**, **Jeník**, **Jančík**, **Janoušek**, **Janeček**, **Janíček**, **Jeníček**, **Janatka**, **Jandl**, **Jand'ourek**, **Janků**; JACH. Ukr.: **Iv(ash)chenko**, **Ivan(en)ko**, **Ivanonko**, **Ivanushka**, **Ivasechko**, **Ivanets**, **Ivakhno**, **Ivanitsa**. Beloruss.: **Yanshonok**, **Yanuk**, **Ivanets**.

Hung.: **Jancsó**, **Jankó**.

Augs.: It.: **Gi(ov)annoni**, **Ian(n)oni**, **Iannone**, **Zan(n)oni**, **Vannoni**, **Nannoni**, **Noni**.

Pejs.: Fr.: **Jeannard**, **Jeannaud**, **J(o)anaud**. It.: **Giovan(n)azzi**, **Giovannacci**, **Giovan(n)ardi**, **Giannazzi**, **Gianazzo**, **Gian(n)assi**, **Gianasi**, **Iannazzi**, **Zuanazzi**, **Zanassi**, **Zanardi**, **Vannacci**, **Nacci**, **Nas(s)i**.

Patrs.: Eng.: **Johns**, JONES; **Johnson**, **Jo(i)nson**, **Joynson**; **Ions** (Northumb.). Sc.: **Ianson**; McLEAN. See also JOHNSTON 2. Ir.: MALONE. Fr.: **A(u)jean**, **Ajam**. It.: **De Giovanni**, **De Zuani**; **Fig(l)iovanni**; **Gianneschi**, **Vaneschi**. Sp.: **Juanes**, **Yáñez**, **Ibáñez**. Rum.: **Ionesco**, **Ionescu**. Low Ger.: **J(oh)an(s)sen**, **Johanning**; **Ja(h)ns**, **Jan(t)z(en)**, **Janning**. Flem.: **Jehaes**, **Jans**, **Jans(s)en(s)**. Du.: **Jans**; **Johansen**, **Janse(n)**, **Janssen(s)**, **Janzen**. Dan.: **Johann(e)sen**, **Johansen**, **Jo(h)nsen**, **J(o)ensen**, **Ja(h)nsen**, **Jantzen**. Swed.: **Johan(ne)sson**, **Jo(h)nsson**, **Jönsson**, **Jansson**. Russ.: **Ivanov**,

Yanov, **Ivanaev**, **Ivantyev**, **Ivanilov**, **Ivanisov**. Pol.: **Januszewicz**, **Janowicz**; **Janiak**, **Janczak**, **Jaszczak**, **Jatczak**, **Iwanowicz**. Croatian: **Jovanović**; **Ivanović**; **Janić**. Bulg.: **Ivanov**. Jewish: **Johannes** (with possessive -s); **Johananov**, **Johananoff**, **Iohananof**. Albanian: **Jonuzi**. Gk.: **Ioannou**, **Io(a)nnidis**. Armenian: **Ionnisian**, **Ohanessian**, **Ogan(es)ian**, **Ovanesian**.

Patrs. (from dims.): Fr.: **Aujouanet**. Low Ger.: **Johäntges**, **Jentge(n)s**. Fris.: **Joontjes**. Flem.: **Nijns**. Ger. (of Slav. origin): **Jä(h)ner**, **Jaher**, **Jeschner**. Pol.: **Janaszkiewicz**, **Jankiewicz**, **Januszkiewicz**, **Jaśkiewicz**, **Iwaszkiewicz**, **Waszkiewicz**. Croatian: **Ivić**, **Iv(an)ković**, **Ivančević**, **Jovašević**, **Jov(ič)ić**, **Jovićević**, **Jovović**, **Jocić**, **Jojić**, **Jončić**, **Janković**, **Jančić**, **Janjić**, **Janošević**, **Janjušević**, **Janićijević**. Russ.: **Ivankov**, **Ivan(n)ikov**, **Ivanch(ik)ov**, **Ivan(ch)enkov**, **Ivantsov**, **Ivan(i)chev**, **Ivanish(ch)ev**, **Ivanyukov**, **Ivanshintsev**, **Ivanusyev**, **Ivan(k)in**, **Ivanchin**, **Ivanikhin**, **Ivan(i)shin**, **Ivanyush(k)in**, **Ivanyutin**, **Ivachyov**, **Ivakhnov**, **Ivashev**, **Ivash(k)ov**, **Ivash(k)in**, **Ivashintsov**, **Ivash(in)nikov**, **Ivashnyov**, **Ivak(h)in**, **Ivashechkin**, **Ivasyushkin**, **Iv(o)shin**, IVUSHKIN; **Yanyshev**, **Yanshin(ov)**, **Yanukhin**, **Yanyushkin**, **Yants(ur)ev**, **Van(k)in**, **Van(k)eev**, **Van(ni)kov**, **Vanshin**, **Vanshenkin**, **Vanshev**, **Vantsov**, **Vanchakov**, **Vanchikov**, **Vanichev**, **Vanichkov**, **Vanichkin**, **Vanyukov**, **Vanya(r)kin**, **Vanyush(k)in**, **Vanyash(k)in**, **Vanyukhin**, **Vanyutin**, **Vanyatin**.

'Son of the wife of J.': Ukr.: **Yankishin**.

'Servant of J.': Eng.: **Janman**, **Jenman**.

Habitation names: Pol.: **Janowski**; **Janaszewski**, **Janiszewski**, **Januszewski**; **Janczewski**, **Iwanicki**, **Iwanowski**. Czech: **Jan(k)ovský**.

Habitation names (from dims.): Pol.: **Jan(i)kowski**, **Waszczykowski**.

Johncock English: dim. of JOHN, with the ME suffix *-cock* (see COCK).

Vars.: **Joncock**, **Jo(h)ncook**.

Johnston 1. Scots: habitation name, deriving in most cases from the place so called in Annandale, in the former county of Dumfries. This is derived from the gen. case of the given name JOHN + ME *tone, toun* settlement (OE *tūn*). There are other places in Scotland so called, including the city of Perth, which used to be known as *St John's Toun*, and some of these may also be sources of the surname. **2.** var. of *Johnson* (see JOHN), with intrusive *-t-*.

Var.: **Johnstone**.

Joice see JOYCE

Joie see JOY

Join see JOUVIN

Joiner English: occupational name for a maker of wooden furniture, ANF *joignour* (OF *joigneor*, from *joinre* to join, connect, L *iungere*).

Var.: **Joyner**.

Patr.: **Joiners**.

Equivs. (not cogn.): Fr.: BOISSIER, CHAPUIS. Ger.: SCHREINER; TISCHLER (also Jewish). Czech: TRUHLÁŘ. Pol. and Jewish (E Ashkenazic): STOLARSKI.

Joinson see JOHN

Jojić see JOHN

Jokel see JACOB

Jokinen Finnish: ornamental name from Finn. *joki* river + the gen. suffix *-nen*, perhaps sometimes chosen as a topographic name by someone who lived by a river.

Jokisch *see* JACH

Joles *see* YOEL

Jolin *see* JEKYLL

Joll *see* JULIAN

Jolly English, Scots, and French: nickname for someone of a cheerful disposition, from ME, OF *joli(f)* merry, happy (apparently of Gmc origin, perhaps ultimately akin to ON *jol* (see YULE), the midwinter festival when everyone celebrated the end of the shortening of the days).

Vars.: Eng.: **Jolley**, **Jollie**, **Jollye**; **Jolliff(e)**, **Juliffe**. Fr.: **Joly**, **Joli(f)**.

Dims.: Fr.: **Joli(v)et**, **Jolivel**, **Joliveau**, **Jolivot**, **Jolliot**, **Jolion**, **Jol(l)et**, **Jol(l)in**.

Jonas 1. English and French: from a medieval given name, which is ultimately from the Hebr. male given name *Yona*, lit. 'Dove'. In the book of the Bible which bears his name, Jonah was appointed by God to preach repentence to the city of Nineveh, but tried to flee instead to Tarshish. On the voyage to Tarshish, a great storm blew up, and Jonah was thrown overboard by his shipmates to appease God's wrath, swallowed by a 'great fish', and delivered by it on the shores of Nineveh. This story exercised a powerful hold on the popular imagination in medieval Europe, and the given name was a relatively common choice. The Hebr. name and its reflexes in other languages (for example Yid. *Yoyne*) have been popular Jewish given names for generations. 2. Jewish (Ashkenazic): Anglicized form of any of the Jewish surnames listed below, or a respelling of *Yonis* or some similar form with Yid. possessive *-s*.

Var.: **Jonah**.

Patrs.: Dan., Norw.: **Jonasen**. Swed.: **Jonasson**. Jewish: **Yonis** (with Yid. possessive *-s*); **Yonovitz** (E Ashkenazic).

Jonchay French: habitation name from any of the various minor places so called from a collective of OF *jonc* rush, reed (L *iuncus*).

Vars.: **Jonchère**, **Joncière**, **Joncherie**.

Jončić *see* JOHN

Joncock *see* JOHNCOCK

Jones 1. English and Welsh: patr. from the ME given name *Jon(e)* JOHN. The surname is especially common in Wales. 2. Jewish: Anglicized form of some like-sounding Jewish surname.

Vars.: Eng.: **Joynes**, **Joans**. See also patrs. of JOHN.

Jonet *see* JEUNE

Jongen *see* YOUNG

Jonkers *see* YOUNGER

Joontjes *see* JOHN

Joosten *see* JOYCE

Jope *see* JOB

Jopke *see* JACOB

Jorat *see* GEORGE

Jorba Catalan: habitation name from a place in the province of Barcelona in N Spain. The placename is of uncertain origin; it is probably pre-Roman.

Jordan 1. English, French, German, and Polish: from the baptismal name of the same spelling, which is taken from the name of the river *Jordan* (Hebr. *Yarden*, from *yarad* to go down, descend, i.e. to the Dead Sea). At the time of the Crusades it was common practice for crusaders and pilgrims to bring back flasks of water from the river, in which John the Baptist had baptized people, including Christ Himself, and to use it in the christening of their own children. Thus *Jordan* became quite a common given name, in commemoration of this. 2. Jewish: ornamental name taken directly from the name of the river.

Vars.: Eng.: **Jord(a)in**, **Jourdan**, **Jo(u)rdon**, **Juden**. Fr.: **Jordain**, **Jourda(i)n**, **Jourde**; **Joudren** (Brittany). Pol.: **Jordański**. Jewish: **Jarden(i)**, **Yarden(i)**, **Jardeny**, **Yardeny** (with the Hebr. suffix *-i*); **Yardinovsky**.

Dims.: Eng.: **Jurd**, **Judd**, JUDE. Fr.: **Jo(u)rdanet**, **Jo(u)rdaney**, **Jourdin(eau)**, **Jourdon**, **Dan(n)et**, **Dan(n)ot**, **Danon**.

Patrs.: Eng.: **Jordens**. Low Ger.: **Jordans**, **Jördens**. Rum.: **Iordanesco**. Bulg.: **Jordanov**.

Patrs. (from dims.): Eng.: **Judson**, **Jutson**, **Jutsum(s)**; **Justum**, **Justham** (metathesized forms); **Jetson**.

Jörg *see* GEORGE

Joscelyn *see* JOCELYN

Jose *see* JOYCE

Joseland *see* JOCELYN

Joselin *see* JOCELYN

Joseph English, French, and Jewish: from the male given name (Hebr. *Yosef* 'may He (God) add (another son)'). In medieval Europe this name was borne frequently, but by no means exclusively, by Jews. In the Book of Genesis, Joseph is the favourite son of Jacob, who is sold into slavery by his brothers but rises to become a leading minister in Egypt (Gen. 37–50); in the New Testament Joseph is the husband of the Virgin Mary.

Vars.: Eng.: **Jessop**, **Jessup**, **Jessep** (representing the usual pronunciation of the name in the Middle Ages). Fr.: **José**. Jewish: **Josef(f)**; **Josephi** (with the Hebr. suffix *-i*).

Dims.: Eng.: **Joe**, **Josey**; **Jess(e)**, **Jessel**, **Jessett**. Ger.: **Jessel**, **Jossel**. Czech: **Joska**, **Jůza**, **Juzek**. Pol.: **Józwik**, **Juszczyk**. Ukr.: **Os(s)ipenko**, **Ishchenko**. Beloruss.: **Asipenko**. Hung.: **Józsa**, **Józsika**, **Szepe**.

Patrs.: Eng.: **Josephs(on)**. Ger.: **Josefs**, **Josefer**; **Josephi**, **Josephy** (Latinized). Dan., Norw.: **Josefsen**, **Josephsen**. Swed.: **Josefsson**. Russ.: **Osipov**; **Yesipov** (N Russia); **Yezafovich**, **Iozefovich** (chiefly Jewish); **Yusupov** (from an Arabic form of the given name, originating among Muslims). Lithuanian: **Jout(ap)aitis**; **Joutapavicius** (Latinized); **Josupeit**, **Josuweit** (Ger. spellings). Pol.: **Józefowicz**; **Józefczak**, **Józefiak**. Croatian: **Josifović**, **Josipović**. Jewish: **Josefso(h)n** (Ashkenazic); **Josephov**, **Josephoff**, **Josefowicz**, **Josefovic**, **Josifovitz**, **Josipovitz**, **Jos(of)ovitz**, **Josowitz**, **Josovich**, **Yosifov**, **Yosevitz** (E Ashkenazic). Armenian: **Ovasapian**.

Patrs. (from dims.): Eng.: **Jesson**. Russ.: **Yeskov**, **Yeskin**, **Yesenev**, **Yesinov**, **Yesichev**, **Yesenin**, **Yesinin**, **Ozintsev**, **Osichev** (see also OSININ). Ukr.: **Iskov**. Pol.: **Juszkiewicz**; **Juszczak**, **Józwiak**, **Józwicki**. Jewish: **Josselso(h)n**, **Joselson**,

Yoselson (Ashkenazic); **Joselovitch, Joselevitch, Joselevitz, Josilevich, Josilowski, Yoseloff, Yos(s)elevitch, Ioselev(ich), Joslow, Joslin, Yoslow(itz), Yosko(witz), Joskowitz, Josskovi(t)z, Joskovitch, Joskowicz** (E Ashkenazic). Lithuanian: **Jozaitis**.

Jou see JOVER

Jouandeau see JOHN

Joubertin see JAUBERT

Joudren see JORDAN

Joufrion see JEFFREY

Jougleux French: occupational name for a jester or entertainer, OF *jougleor* (L *ioculātor*, from *ioculāri* to jest, sport, a deriv. of *iocus* joke, jest).

Joulain see JULIAN

Joule see JEKYLL

Jousset see JOYCE

Joutaitis see JOSEPH

Jouveau see JEUNE

Jouvin French: from the L personal name *Iovīnus*, derived from *Iupiter* (gen. *Iovis*; cf. JULIO), the principal god of pagan Rome. It survived as a given name into the Middle Ages by virtue of having been borne by an obscure early saint whose cult achieved some popularity in W and N France.
Vars.: **Jovin, Jo(u)in, Jev(a)in**.
Dims.: **Jovi(g)net, Jovelin, Jovelet; Join(d)eau, Joinet; Jouon, Jouot, Jouet**.

Jovanović see JOHN

Jovelet see JOUVIN

Jover Catalan: occupational name for a maker of yokes, Cat. *jover* (L *iugārius*, an agent deriv. of *iugum* yoke). This word was apparently also used as an occupational name for an oxherd, hence the relative frequency of the surname.
Vars.: **Jové, Juvé; Jou**.

Jovers see GODFREY

Jowett English (chiefly Yorks.): from the ME given name *Juwet, Jowet* (fem. *Juwette, Jowette*). These originated as dims. (with the ANF suffix *-et(te)*) of *Juwe, Jowe*, vars. of *Jull*, a short form of JULIAN, which were borne by both men and women.
Vars.: **Jowitt, Jewett, Jewitt, Juett**.

Jowle see JEKYLL

Joy English: metonymic nickname for a person of a cheerful disposition, from ME, OF *joie, joye* (LL *gaudia*, for class. L *gaudium*). In some cases it may derive from a given name (normally borne by women) of this origin, which was in sporadic use during the Middle Ages.
Vars.: **Joye, Joie**.
Dims.: Fr.: **Joyet**. It.: **Gioiella, Gioiello**.
Metrs.: Eng.: **Joyes** (see also JOYCE). It.: **De Gioia, Di Gioia**.

Joyce English and Irish: from the Bret. personal name *Iodoc*, a dim. of *iudh* lord, introduced by the Normans in

the form *Josse*. Iodoc was the name of a Bret. prince and saint, the brother of *Iudicael* (see JEKYLL), whose fame helped to spread the name through France and, after the Norman Conquest, England as well. The name was occasionally borne also by women in the Middle Ages, but was predominantly a male name, by contrast with the present usage.
Vars.: **Joi(s)ce, Joss(e), Joass, Joce; Jose** (Devon and Cornwall); GOSSE, CHOICE.
Dims.: Fr.: **Jo(u)sset, Jo(u)sson, Jo(u)ssot, Jo(u)ssin, Joisson; Jos(se)quin** (Belgium); **Jossic** (Brittany). Ger.: **Jostel, Jöstel, Jüstel**.
Patrs.: Ger.: **Josten, Jostes, Jösting**. Flem., Du.: **Joosten**.

Joyner see JOINER

Joynes see JONES

Joynson see JOHN

Jozaitis see JOSEPH

Juanes see JOHN

Jubb see JOB

Judd see JORDAN

Jude 1. English and French: from the vernacular form of the Hebr. male given name *Yehuda* Judah (of unknown meaning), the name of Jacob's eldest son. This was not a popular name among Christians in medieval Europe, because of the associations it had with Judas Iscariot, the disciple who betrayed Christ for thirty pieces of silver. Among Jews, however, the Hebr. name and its reflexes in various Jewish languages (such as Yid. *Yude*) have been popular for generations, hence the many Jewish surnames given below. **2.** French: name for a Jew, OF *jude* (L *Iudaeus*, Gk *Ioudaios*, from Hebr. *Yehudi* member of the tribe of *Judah*, the same word as in 1). **3.** English: pet form of JORDAN.
Var. (of 1): **Judas** (from the learned form of the name).
Dims. (of 1): Jewish: **Yudko, Judelman, Idel(man), Idelchek**.
Patrs. (from 1): Jewish: **Yudayov, Yudin, Judovitch, Judevitch, Judovitz, Judovits, Yudevitz, Yudovitz, Yudowitz, Yudowicz**.
Patrs. (from dims. of 1): Jewish: **Idels, Idelso(h)n; Judelevi(t)ch, Judelevitz, Judelewitz, Yudelevitz, Yudelewitz, Yudelevitz, Idelovitch, Idelovitz, Idelovici; Judkes, Judeikin, Yudeikin, Yudkin, Judkowski, Yudkowski, Judkiewicz, Judkewich, Judkevitz, Judkovicz, Yudkevitz, Yudiovitch**. Fr.: **Judet, Judon, Jud(l)in**. Ger.: **Jüdl**.

Judge 1. English: occupational name for an officer of justice or nickname for a solemn and authoritative person thought to behave like a judge, from ME, OF *juge* (L *iudex*, from *ius* law + *dīcere* to say), which replaced the OE term *dēma* (cf. DEMPSTER). **2.** Irish: trans. of Gael. *breitheamhnach* judge (see BREW).
Dims.: Fr.: **Juget, Jugeau, Jugelet**.
Patrs.: Eng.: **Judges**. It.: **Del Giudice**.

Juell see JEKYLL

Juett see JOWETT

Jugeau see JUDGE

Jugg see JEKYLL

Juhász Hungarian: occupational name for a shepherd, from *juh* sheep + *-ász* occupational suffix.

Juhre see GEORGE

Juillard see JULIAN

Jukes see JEKYLL

Julian English (mainly Devon and Cornwall), French, and German: from a medieval given name (L *Iuliānus*, a deriv. of *Iulius*; see JÚLIO), which had been borne by a number of early saints. In ME the name was borne in the same form by women, whence the mod. girl's name *Gillian*.

Vars.: Eng.: **Julyan**; **Gillian**, **Gillion**, GILLING, **Gellion**. Fr.: **Jullian**, **Jul(l)ien**, **Joul(l)(a)in**, **Jeul(l)in**.

Dims.: Eng.: **Jull**, **Joll(e)**, JOWETT; GILL, GILLETT; **Gell(e)** (E Midlands), **Jell(ey)**, **Jellicoe**; **Jew** (see also JUDE). Fr.: **Juliot**, **Juillot**, **Juillet**. It.: **Giulianelli**, **Giulianini**.

Pejs.: Fr.: **Juliard**, **Juillard**.

Patrs./Metrs.: Eng.: **Julians**, **Jullens**, **Jullings**, **Jillions**, **Jillings**, **Jellings**, **Gillions**, **Gillings**. Russ.: **Ulyanov**, **Ulyan(i)chev**.

Patrs./Metrs. (from dims.): Eng.: **Jules**, **Jolles**; **Jellison**, **Jilson**, **Jew(i)son**, **Jewesson**, **Juson**. Russ.: **Ulyachin**, **Ulyankin**, **Ulyanishchev**, **Ulyash(k)ov**.

Juliffe see JOLLY

Júlio Portuguese: from a medieval given name (L *Julius*, a Roman family name of uncertain etymology, possibly an adj. deriv. of *Iuppiter*, gen. *Iovis*, the supreme god, whose name seems to be akin to words for 'sky', 'light', and 'day'). The name was borne in the Middle Ages in honour of various minor Christian saints, and was nearly as popular as its deriv. JULIAN.

Dims.: It.: **Giulietti**, **Giuliotti**, **Giuliuzzi**; **Zulin**.

Aug.: It.: **Giulioni**.

Patrs.: It.: **De Giuli**, **Di Giulio**. Dan.: **Juliussen**.

Juliussen see JÚLIO

Jumeau French: nickname for a twin, OF *jumeau* (L *gemellus*). There are also various minor places of this name, so called from an anthropomorphic metaphor applied to a pair of rocks or other topographical features, and the surname may possibly be a habitation name from one of these.

Vars.: **Jumel**, **Gemeau(x)**, **Gimel**.

Dim.: Fr.: **Jumelet**.

Jun Czech: nickname for a lively young man, Czech *juný* (ultimately cogn. with Fr. JEUNE and Eng. YOUNG).

Vars.: **Juna**, **Jůn(a)**.

Dim.: **Junek**.

Jung see YOUNG

Juniper English: **1.** topographic name for someone who lived in a place overgrown with juniper bushes (L *jūniperus*, of obscure origin). **2.** from the medieval female given name *Jennifer*, *Junifer*, from W *Gwenhwyfar*, a cpd of *gwen* fair, white + *(g)wyf* smooth, yielding + *fawr* large. This was the name of King Arthur's queen *Guinevere*.

Until the 19th cent. the given name *Jennifer* was characteristically Cornish.

Var. (of 2): **Junifer**.

Dims. (of 2): Corn.: **Genn**, **Gynn**.

Junkers see YOUNGER

Junkin see JENKIN

Jupe see JOB

Jurado Spanish: occupational name for any of various officials who had to take an oath that they would perform their duty properly, from Sp. *jurado* sworn, past part. of *jurar* to swear (L *iurāre*).

Juraitis see GEORGE

Jurd see JORDAN

Jurgen see GEORGE

Jury **1.** English: habitation name from ME, OF *ju(ie)rie* Jewish quarter, most often denoting a non-Jew living in the Jewish quarter of a town, rather than a Jew. Most medieval English cities had their Jewish quarters, at least until King Edward I's attempted expulsion of the Jews from England in 1290. This did not succeed in expelling the Jews, but it did give a licence to persecution and so broke up many of the old Jewish quarters; as a name for a locality this word therefore originated well before the end of the 13th cent.

Var.: **Jewry**.

Juschka see GEORGE

Juson see JULIAN

Just **1.** French, English, Catalan, Polish, Czech, and Danish: from a given name of the same spelling (L *Justus* 'Honourable', 'Upright', a deriv. of *ius* right, law; cf. JUDGE). There were several early saints of this name, among them a 4th-cent. bishop of Lyons and a 6th-cent. bishop of Urgell in Catalonia. **2.** Jewish (NE Ashkenazic): from a Ger. or Pol. spelling of Yid. *yust* well-to-do; cf. MITTELMAN. **3.** German: cogn. of JOYCE.

Vars. (of 1): Fr.: **Juste**, **Jut**, **Jux**. (Of 2): Jewish: **Yust**; **Yuster** (representing a Yid. inflected form); **Yustman**.

Dims. (of 1): Fr.: **Jutel**, **Juteau**, **Jutot**.

Patrs. (from 1): Flem.: **Justens**. Dan.: **Justesen**.

Jüstel see JOYCE

Justham see JORDAN

Justice English: nickname for a fair-minded man, from ME, OF *justice* justice, equity (L *iustitia*, a deriv. of *iustus*; see JUST 1). It may well also have been an occupational name for a judge, for this metonymic use of the word is attested from as early as the 12th cent.

Var.: **Jestice**.

Justin French and English: from a medieval given name (L *Justīnus*, a deriv. of *Justus*; see JUST 1). This name was borne by various early saints, including a 3rd-cent. Parisian martyr and the first archbishop of Tarbes.

Var.: Fr.: **Jutin**.

Dim.: Ukr.: **Ustimenko**.

Patrs.: Russ.: **Ustinov**, **Ustimov**, **Ustyanov**. Ukr.: **Ustimovich**.

Patrs. (from dims.): Russ.: **Ustin(n)ikov**, **Ustyukhin**.

Juszczak *see* JOSEPH

Jut *see* JUST

Jutin *see* JUSTIN

Jutson *see* JORDAN

Juvé *see* JOVER

Jux *see* JUST

Jzak *see* ISAAC

K

Kabanov Russian: patr. from the nickname *Kaban* 'Wild Boar' (a borrowing from a Turkic language).

Kabat Polish: metonymic nickname for someone who habitually wore a jerkin or whose jerkin was particularly noticeable, from Pol. *kabat* jerkin.

Dim.: Czech: **Kabátek**.

Kabeláč Czech: metonymic nickname or occupational name from a deriv. of Czech *kabela* satchel, leather bag, applied to someone who habitually carried such a bag, i.e. a pedlar.

Var.: **Kabelka**.

Kabíček *see* GABRIEL

Kabisch *see* JACOB

Kacev *see* KATZEV

Kachler German: occupational name for a potter, from an agent deriv. of MHG *kachel* pot, earthenware vessel (OHG *chachala*, from LL *caculus*, class. L *cacabus*, coming via Gk from a Semitic source). The surname is common in the Alemannic and Swabian regions, and the vocab. word is still current in Alsace, Switzerland, and the Tyrol. The mod. Ger. sense 'glazed tile' is a fairly recent development, and probably has not contributed to the surname. Cf. EULER, HAFNER, POTTER, and TÖPFER.

Var.: **Kächler**.

Kacperczyk *see* KASPAR

Kaczmarczyk *see* KRETSCHMAR

Kaczor 1. Polish: nickname for someone supposedly resembling a drake, from Pol. *kaczor* drake. 2. Jewish (E Ashkenazic): ornamental name from Pol. *kaczor* drake, one of many taken from vocab. words denoting birds and animals.

Dims.: Pol.: **Kaczorek**. Czech: **Kačírek**.
Habitation name: Pol.: **Kaczorowski**.

Kádár Hungarian and Jewish (Ashkenazic): occupational name for a cooper, Hung. *kádár*.

Kadleček *see* TKACH

Kaesmakers *see* CHEESEMAN

Käfer German: nickname from Ger. *Käfer* bug, beetle (MHG *kever*, OHG *chevar*; cf. Eng. *cockchafer*).

Dims.: **Käferle(in)**.

Kafka 1. Czech: nickname from Czech *kavka* jackdaw (of imitative origin; Pol. *kawka*). 2. Jewish (Ashkenazic): ornamental name from Czech *kavka* jackdaw. According to Kaganov, this was sometimes selected as a Jewish surname because of its phonetic similarity to the Hebr. male given name *Yaakov* (see JACOB), but there does not seem to be any evidence to support this conjecture.

Var.: Czech: **Kavka**.
Habitation names: Pol.: **Kawiński**, **Kawczyński**.

Kagan *see* COHEN

Kagel *see* KOGEL

Kahan *see* COHEN

Kahl German: nickname for a bald man, from Ger. *kahl* bald (cogn. with OE *calu*, used of bare hilltops; see CALLOW 1).

Vars.: **Kahle, Kahler(t)**.

Kahlandt *see* KALAND

Kahoun Czech: of uncertain origin, possibly an ironic nickname for a sluggish or oafish person, from a deriv. of the dial. word *káhat* to move, budge, stir oneself.

Kahr *see* KARMANN

Kahrs *see* MACAIRE

Kain *see* CAIN

Kaindl *see* KONRAD

Kaines *see* KEYNES

Kaiser 1. German: from Ger. *Kaiser* emperor (MHG *keiser*, OHG *keisar*), from the L imperial title *Caesar*, originally itself a family name (see CESARE). This is widely distributed as a Ger. surname, originating partly as a nickname, perhaps for someone who behaved in an imperious manner. It may also have referred to one who had played the part of an emperor in a pageant or play, and it is also recorded as a house name. 2. Jewish (Ashkenazic): ornamental name from Ger. *Kaiser* emperor, adopted like GRAF, HERZOG, etc., because of its aristocratic connotations.

Ger. *Kaiser* was the title borne by Holy Roman Emperors from Otto I (962) to Francis II (who relinquished the title in 1806). Later, it was borne by the ruler of Bismarck's united Germany (1871–1918). The Russ. word *tsar* was formally adopted as a title at his coronation in 1547 by Ivan the Terrible (1530–84), grand duke of Moscow. However, the word was well established in Russia long before this. Ivan's father, Vasily III (1479–1533) and grandfather, Ivan III (1440–1505), both considered themselves successors to the Byzantine Empire, and Ivan III had in fact married the niece of the last Byzantine emperor.

Vars.: Ger.: **Ke(i)ser, Kayser, Keyser**. Jewish (Ashkenazic): **Kaiserman, Keiser(man), Keizer**.
Patrs.: Low Ger.: **Keysers**. Russ.: **Tzaryov**. Croatian: **Cesarić**.
Patr. (from a dim.): Russ.: **Tzarkov**.

Kakosch see KOCHETOV

Kaland German: from MHG *kaland* first day of the month (from L *calendae (dies)* (pl.), a deriv. of the archaic verb *calere* to call, announce; in the early Roman calendar it was on this day each month that the dates of the other, movable, landmarks of the calendar were announced). In medieval Ger. guilds, meetings were normally held on the first day of the month, often accompanied by a good deal of revelry. Some guilds were known as *Kalands-Brüderschaften*. The surname probably denoted a member of such a guild, or someone who took a notable part in organizing the guild's meetings and revels.

Vars.: **Kahlandt**; **Kalander**.

Kälble see CALF

Kalderon see CALDERON

Kaleta Polish: metonymic nickname for someone who habitually wore a leather purse, Pol. *kaleta*.

Kaley see CAYLEY

Kalinin Russian: patr. from the given name *Kalina*, a short form of *Kalinik* (from Gk *Kal(l)inik(i)os*, a cpd of the elements *kalos* fair, lovely or *kallos* beauty, loveliness + *nikē* victory). *Kallinikios* was a 3rd-cent. martyr venerated in the Orthodox Church.

Vars.: **Kal(l)inikov**; **Kalinnikov** (by association with agent nouns in -*nnik* from the common adj. ending -*nny*); **Lin(n)ikov**.

Dims.: Russ. (patrs.): **Kalinkin**, **Kalinkov**, **Kalinychev**, **Kalinichev**, **Kalitsev**; **Linkov**. Ukr.: **Kalenichenko**.

Kalinowski Polish and Jewish (E Ashkenazic): topographic name or ornamental name from Pol. *kalina* snowball ball tree, guelder rose (a species of viburnum), or habitation name from a place called *Kalinów*, which gets its name from these plants.

Vars.: Pol.: **Kaliński**. Jewish: **Kalinski**, **Kalinsky**, **Kalinov(sky)**, **Kalinoff**, **Kalina**.

Dims.: Pol.: **Kalinka**. Ger. (of Slav. origin): **Kalinke**.

Kalisz Polish and Jewish (E Ashkenazic): habitation name from the town of *Kalisz* in W central Poland, which probably derives its name from OPol. *kal* muddy place, slough (see KAŁUŻA).

Var.: **Kaliszewski**.

Dim.: **Kaliszek**.

Kalivoda Czech: 1. nickname for a troublemaker, from Czech *kalit* to stir + *voda* water. 2. habitation name from the town of *Kalivoda* near Nové Strašecí in central Bohemia.

Var.: **Kalvoda**.

Kalker see CHALK

Käll Swedish: ornamental name from Swed. *kjäll* spring, source (ON *kelda*), one of the many words for natural features that were used in the formation of Swed. surnames when these became obligatory during the 18th and 19th cents.

Vars.: **Källén**, **Kjäll(én)**, **Kjell(én)**, **Tjellén**, **Kjellin**, **Kjellman**; **Kjellander**, **Tjellander**.

Cpds: **K(j)ällberg**, **Kjellberg**, **Tjellberg** ('spring hill'); **K(j)ällgren**, **Kjellgren**, **Tjellgren** ('spring branch'); **K(j)ällqvist**, **Kjellqvist** ('spring twig'); **K(j)ällström**, **Kjellström**, **Tjellström** ('spring river').

Kallio Finnish: ornamental name from Finn. *kallio* rock, one of the many words for natural features that were used in the formation of Finn. surnames when these became obligatory during the 18th and 19th cents.

Kalman Jewish (Ashkenazic): from the Yid. male given name *Kalmen*, the everyday form of the Yid. male given name *Kloynemes* (from Hebr. *Kalonimos*, which is from Gk *kalos* fair, lovely, or *kallos* beauty, loveliness (see KALININ) + *onyma* name). The Hebr. given name is first recorded in the Talmud and has been used continuously since then. Among Hungarian Jews, Yid. *Kalmen* became confused in some cases with the Hung. male given name *Kálmán* (see COLEMAN 1).

Vars.: **Kallman**, **Kel(l)man**, **Kol(l)man**; **Klonymus**.

Patrs.: **Kalmanoff**, **Kalmenoff**, **Kalmanowicz**, **Kalmonowski**, **Kalmowitz** (E Ashkenazic); **Kalmans(on)**, **Kalmenson**, **Kalminson** (Ashkenazic).

Kalousek see GALL

Kałuża Polish: topographic name for someone who lived in a muddy or marshy spot, from Pol. *kałuża* puddle, from OPol. *kal* slough.

Vars.: **Kałużka**, **Kałużny**, **Kałużyński**.

Kálvaitis Lithuanian: patr. from the occupational term *kálvis* smith.

Kamelgarn see CAMEL

Kamiński Polish: 1. occupational name for a quarryman or stone-cutter, from Pol. *kamień* stone + -*ski* suffix of surnames. 2. habitation name from any of the several places named with the Pol. word *kamień* stone, e.g. *Kamieniec* in Lower Silesia, with the addition of the local surname suffix -*ski* (see BARANOWSKI).

Vars.: **Kamieński**; **Kamecki**. (Of 1 only): **Kaminiarz**, **Kamieniak**.

Kämpfl see KEMP

Kanaly see McNALLY

Kandeev see KONDRATYEV

Kändler German and Jewish (Ashkenazic): occupational name for a wine steward or cup-bearer, or for a maker of jugs, from Ger. *Kändler*, an agent deriv. of Ger. *Kandel* jug (MHG *kandel*, *kannel*, a dim. of *kanne* can, pot); cf. KANNENGIESSER. The name is most common in Bavaria, Swabia, and E Franconia.

Vars.: **Kendler**; **Kandel** (metonymic).

Kane see CAIN, KEANE

Kania Polish: nickname for a fierce or powerful person, from Pol. *kania* kite, hawk.

Vars.: **Kani(e)cki**, **Kaniera**.

Patr. (from a dim.): **Kankiewicz**.

Habitation name: **Kaniewski**.

Kaňka Czech: derogatory nickname of various possible origins. Czech *kaňka* means 'blot' or 'smudge', but it also means 'runt' or 'stunted gosling'. Alternatively, it may be derived from the verb *kanit*, which means variously 'to tattle or gossip', 'to slobber', or in the reflexive 'to flatter'.

Var.: **Kaňák**.

Kannengiesser German and Jewish (Ashkenazic): occupational name for a maker of metal vessels, from Ger. *Kannengiesser* lit. 'can pourer', i.e. a pewterer, one who poured metal alloy into a mould to make cans, from Ger. *Kanne* can, pot (see CANET) + *giessen* to pour, mould (OHG *giozan*). Ger. *Kannegiesser* is also an old slang word for an alehouse politician, and in some cases the name may be a nickname for such a person.

Vars.: **Kann(e)giesser**; **Kanner**.

Kantor 1. German and Czech: occupational name for a master of music, choirmaster, or village schoolmaster, Ger. *Kantor* (from L *cantor*, a deriv. of *cantāre* to sing; cf. CANT). 2. Jewish (Ashkenazic): occupational name for a cantor (see CHAZAN), from Ger. *Kantor*, as in 1.

Vars.: Jewish: **Kanter(man)**; **Cantor**, **Canter** (Anglicized spellings).

Patrs.: Jewish: **Kanters** (Ashkenazic); **Kantrow**, **Kantorovi(t)ch**, **Kantorowitch**, **Kantorowitsh**, **Kantorowitz**, **Kant(o)rowicz**, **Kant(o)rowitz**, **Cantrowitz**, **Kanterovich**, **Kantarovitch**, **Kantarovitz**, **Kantarowitch**, **Kantarowicz**, **Kantorovsky** (E Ashkenazic).

Kapelushnik *see* CHAPE

Kapf German: topographic name for someone who lived near a prominent hill, from MHG *kapfe* mountain peak, top of a hill (apparently from *kapfen* to look, watch, and so applied to a look-out hill or beacon). This word is still current in the Swabian dialect, and the surname is relatively common in Bavaria, Baden, and Württemberg.

Vars.: **Kapfer(er)**.

Kapitonov Russian: patr. from the given name *Kapiton* (L *Capito*, gen. *Capitōnis*, a Roman family name derived originally from *caput*, gen. *capitis*, head; cf. CABEZA and CAP). This name was borne by a 4th-cent. missionary bishop who preached in the Crimea and S Russia, and by another saint commemorated in the Gk martyrology, of whom nothing more than his name is known.

Kaplan 1. German and Czech: occupational name for a curate, Ger. *Kaplan* (a cogn. of CHAPLIN 1), or nickname for someone resembling a clergyman. 2. Jewish (Ashkenazic): surname used as a translation of COHEN, from Ger. *Kaplan* or Pol. *kapłan* chaplain, curate. Not all Jews bearing this name belong to the priestly caste; at one time in the Russian Empire male Jews other than priests were required to join the Russian army for 25 years, and a number changed their surnames to *Kaplan* in the hope of gaining exemption from military service; cf. COHEN.

Vars.: Jewish: **Kaplanski**, **Kaplinsky**, **Kaplin(ski)**; **Caplan** (an Anglicized spelling); **Kaplanowicz** (patr.).

Kaprilian *see* GABRIEL

Kapuściński Polish: habitation name from a place named from Pol. *kapuścisko* cabbage patch (see KAPUSTA) + *-in* possessive suffix, with the addition of *-ski*, suffix of local surnames (see BARANOWSKI).

Kapusta Polish and Jewish (E Ashkenazic): unflattering nickname, of uncertain application, from Pol. *kapusta* cabbage.

Var.: **Kapuściak**.

Karapetian *see* GARABEDIAN

Karaś Polish and Jewish (Ashkenazic): nickname for someone supposedly resembling a carp, from Pol. *karaś* crucian carp or, in the case of the Jewish name, ornamental name from this word. The word is also found in 16th-cent. Polish with the meaning 'penis', and so the Pol. nickname may be of obscene origin.

Dims.: Pol.: **Karasek**. Czech: **Karásek**.

Patrs.: Pol.: **Karasiewicz**, **Karaszewicz**.

Habitation name: Pol.: **Karasiński**.

Karatygin *see* KOROTYGIN

Karban Czech: metonymic nickname for a gambler, from Czech *karban* gambling.

Karbowiak Polish: occupational name for a overseer, Pol. *karbowy*, from *karbować* to make notches, i.e. to keep records.

Vars.: **Karbownik**, **Karbowski**.

Karch German: metonymic occupational name for a carter, from MHG *karrech* two-wheeled cart (from L *carrūca*, a deriv. of *carrus*; cf. CARRIER).

Vars.: **Karcher**, **Kärcher**, **Kercher**.

Karczewski Polish and Jewish (Ashkenazic): habitation name from a place called *Karczew* (from Pol. *karcz* stump (cf. Czech KRČ) + *-ew* possessive suffix), with the addition of *-ski*, suffix of local surnames (see BARANOWSKI).

Karczmarczyk *see* KRETSCHMAR

Kardos Hungarian and Jewish (Ashkenazic): occupational name for a swordsman, from Hung. *kard* sword, a borrowing from Turkish. The Jewish name is presumably an adoption of the Hung. one.

Karfunkel *see* GORFINKEL

Karg 1. German: nickname from MHG *karc* crafty, cunning (OHG *karag* troubled, preoccupied; mod. Eng. *chary* derives from the cogn. OE *cearig*, a deriv. of *cear* care, worry; cf. CARLESS). 2. Jewish (Ashkenazic): nickname from Yid. *karg* miserly (a different sense development of the same word as in 1), or from mod. Ger. *karg* mean, miserly.

Vars.: **Karger**, Jewish: **Kargman**.

Dim.: Ger.: **Kärgel**.

Karjalainen Finnish: regional name for someone from Karelia, from Finn. *Karjala* Karelia + the locative suffix *-ainen*. Karelia was a region of Finland until 1940, when most of it became part of the Soviet Union.

Kärkkäinen Finnish: patr. from a nickname derived from Finn. *kärkkäs* eager.

Karl *see* CHARLES

Karlin Jewish (E Ashkenazic): habitation name from a place of this name in Belorussia, near Pinsk, in which Jews formed a majority of the population up to the Second

World War. A well-known Chasidic sect originated in Karlin and at one time it attracted so many followers that a (now obsolete) Russian word for 'Chasid' was *Karliner* (of Yid. origin). It is possible that at least some people taking this surname did so because they were members of this sect and not because they were born or lived in Karlin. There is also a Czech town called *Karlin*, but there is no evidence that any of these Ashkenazic surnames derive from it.

Vars.: **Karliner** (with the Yid. suffix *-er* meaning 'native or inhabitant of'); **Karlinski**, **Karlinsky** (with the Slav. adj. suffix *-ski*); **Carlin**, **Carliner** (Anglicized forms).

Karmann German: **1.** occupational name for a maker of baskets and other small containers, from MHG, OHG *kar* vessel + *-man(n)* man. **2.** topographic name for someone who lived by a patch of land at the bottom of a valley used for pasture, from the Tyrolean dial. term *kar* (apparently a specialized use of the word given in 1) + *-mann*.

Vars.: **Kahr**; **Karer**.

Karmeli *see* Carmo

Karpov Russian: **1.** patr. from the given name *Karp* (from Gk *karpos* fruit, used with mystical connotations by early Christians). This was the name of a contemporary of St Paul, of whom nothing is known apart from a passing mention in one of the Epistles, but in the Orthodox Church he is believed to have been a bishop and is revered as a saint. **2.** patr. from the nickname *Karp* 'Carp' (both the Russ. and Eng. words come from OHG *karpfo*, the latter via OF).

Var. (of 1): **Karpeev**.

Ger.: **Karpf**. Low Ger., Flem., Du.: **Karpe**. Jewish (Ashkenazic ornamental names): **Karp(man)**, **Karpf(en)**; **Carp** (an Anglicized spelling). Finn.: **Karppi**, **Karpio**. It.: **Carpio**. Port.: **Carpes**.

Dims. (of 1): Beloruss.: **Karpenya**, **Karpets**. Ukr.: **Karpenko**. Pol.: **Karpik**. Czech: **Karpísek**. Jewish: **Karpel** (in part from the Yid. male given name *Karpl*, a dim. of Yid. *karp* carp).

Patrs. (from 2): Jewish: **Karpoff** (an adoption of the Russ. surname, perhaps under the influence of Yid. *karp* carp). Finn.: **Karpinen**.

Patrs. (from 1) (dims.): Russ.: **Karpushkin**, **Karputkin**, **Karpukhin**, **Karpyshev**, **Karpychev**, **Karpunichev**, **Kartsev**. Jewish: **Karpeles** (from *Karpele*, a dim. of the Yid. given name, + Yid. possessive *-s*).

Habitation name: Pol.: **Karpiński**.

Kärrström *see* Kerr

Karsch *see* Kirsch

Karski Polish: **1.** nickname for a dwarf or for a person of stunted growth, from the Praslovian dial. word *kars* handicapped, stunted (cogn. with Russ. Krivov, Czech *krs* stunted). **2.** nickname for a left-handed person, from Pol. dial. *karśniawy* left-handed (cogn. with Czech *krška* left-hander, from the same element as in 1). Left-handedness was regarded as a deficiency or deformity in many countries of Europe in earlier times.

Var. (of 2): **Karśnicki**.

Dims. (of 1): Czech: **Krsek**. (Of 2): Czech: **Kršek**.

Karslake *see* Carslake

Karssen *see* Christian

Karwacki Polish: **1.** nickname from a deriv. of Pol. dial. *karw* ox. **2.** nickname for someone who habitually wore a waistcoat, from a deriv. of Pol. *karwatka* waistcoat.

Vars. (of 2): **Karwat**, **Karwatek**.

Habitation names (from 1): **Karwowski**, **Karwański**.

Kaschke *see* Lucas

Kashman *see* Cashman

Kaspar German and Polish: from a given name which was especially popular in central Europe up to the 18th cent. Originally a Persian word meaning 'treasurer', it was ascribed by popular tradition in Europe to one of the three Magi. Their supposed remains were brought to Cologne from Constantinople in the 12th cent., and the name gained considerable popularity in Europe after this. See also Balthasar and Melchior.

Vars.: Ger.: **Kasper**, **Kesper**, **Casper**. Pol.: **Kasparski**, **Kasper(ski)**, **Kaszper**; **Sperski** (aphetic form).

Dims.: Pol.: **Kasparek**, **Kasperek**; **Kasprzyk**, **Kacprzyk**, **Kasprzycki**; **Kacperczyk**; **Kaszczyk**. Czech: **Kašpárek**. Fr.: **Gasperin**, **Gasparin**, **Gasparoux**. It.: **Gasperini**, **Gaspar(r)ini**, **Gaspardini**, **Gasbarrini**, **Gasperetti**, **Gaspar(in)etti**, **Gasperotti**, **Gasparotti**, **Gasparelli**, **Gasparoli**; **Sperelli**, **Sperotto** (Venetia); **Parelli**, **Par(r)ini**, **Parrucci** (Tuscany).

Augs.: It.: **Gasperoni**, **Gasparoni**; **Speroni** (Venetia).

Patrs.: Ger.: **Caspary** (also Jewish (Ashkenazic), adoption of the Ger. name). Low Ger.: **Jaspars**, **Jaspers**, **Kespers**, **Caspers**; **Jasparsen**, **Jaspersen**, **Jespersen**. Flem., Du.: **Jaspers**, **Jespers**, **Caspers**. Dan.: **Jespersen**. It.: **De Gasperi**, **De Gaspari**, **Gaspardis**. Pol.: **Kasprowicz**, **Kacprowicz**; **Kasprzak**, **Kacprzak**; **Przykowicz**; **Kasprowiak**. Beloruss.: **Kasperov(ich)**, **Kasparov**.

Patrs. (from dims.): Pol.: **Kasparkiewicz**, **Kasprzykiewicz**.

Habitation name: Pol.: **Kasprowicki**.

Kassidy *see* Cassidy

Kast *see* Christian

Kastner German and Jewish (Ashkenazic): occupational name for a maker of boxes and chests, from Ger. *Kastner*, agent deriv. of *Kasten* chest (MHG *kaste* casket, OHG *kasto*). The Ger. word also denoted a treasurer or other official responsible for financial matters, i.e. one who had control of a money chest, and this may in some cases be the source of the surname.

Vars.: Ger.: **Kästner**, **Kestner**; **Köstner** (Bavaria).

Kaszuba Polish: ethnic name for a Kashubian, Pol. *Kaszuba*, a member of a Slav. people living in N Poland southwest and west of Gdańsk.

Var.: **Kaszubski**.

Kataev Russian: patr. from the nickname *Katai* (from *katat* to roll, turn, spin), denoting a restless individual.

Katan Jewish (Sefardic): nickname from Hebr. *katan* small; cf. Klein.

Vars.: **Kattan**, **Cat(t)an**.

Kate *see* Catlin

Kates *see* Cates

Katona Hungarian and Jewish (Ashkenazic): occupational name for a soldier, Hung. *katona*.

Kats see CATT

Katusov see CONSTANTINE

Katz Jewish (Ashkenazic): acronym from the Hebr. phrase *Kohen TSedek* priest of righteousness. The surname cannot be derived from Hebr. *katsin* rich man, since the Ashkenazic pronunciation of this word always has /o/ in the first syllable.

Vars.: **Katzman(n)**.

Cpd (ornamental): **Katzenstein** (ostensibly Ger. 'cat stone').

Katzenellenbogen Jewish (Ashkenazic): habitation name from *Katzenelnbogen* in the Prussian province of Hesse-Nassau. The place is probably named from the Celt. tribal name *Chattimelibochi*, which is of unknown origin. However, it has been altered by folk etymology as if it meant 'cat's elbow'.

Vars.: **Katz(e)nelson** (sometimes assumed by bearers to be from KATZ, with the addition of *Nelson* (see NEIL) during or after the Napoleonic Wars in honour of the English admiral Lord Nelson, but this is no more than folk etymology).

Katzev Jewish (Ashkenazic): occupational name for a butcher, Yid. *katsev* (from Hebr. *katsav*).

Vars.: **Katsevman**; **Katzeff, Katziff** (-*ff* reflecting a regional Yid. pronunciation); **Katzoff, Kacew** (Pol. spelling), **Kacev, Kaciff**.

Patrs. ('son of the butcher'; E Ashkenazic): **Katzowitz, Katzowitch, Kacowicz**.

Kaubisch see JACOB

Kaucký see KOUTSKÝ

Kaufner see KIEFER

Kauppinen see CHAPMAN

Kavanagh Irish: Anglicized form of the Gael. personal name *Caomhánach* (follower) of (St) *Caomhán*', a personal name from a dim. of *caomh* gentle, tender (cf. KEEFE) which was borne by no less than fifteen early Ir. saints.

Vars.: **Cavana(u)gh**.

Kave see CAVE

Kavka see KAFKA

Kawczyński see KAFKA

Kay English: 1. occupational name for a maker of keys or for someone who held the (often largely ceremonial) office of key-bearer, from OE *cæg* key. 2. topographic name for someone who lived by a wharf or was employed on one, from ME, OF *kay(e)* quay (apparently of Gaul. origin; cf. Bret. *cai* fence). 3. from a ME given name of Celt. origin (OW *Cai*, Corn. *Key*), borne by the boastful foster-brother of King Arthur. This name may be ultimately derived from the old Roman name *Gaius* (see GAY 3). 4. nickname from the jackdaw, Northern ME *kay* (ON *ká*, of imitative origin). See also COE. 5. nickname for a left-handed man, from the Dan. dial. term *kei* left, which was borrowed in the 13th cent. into the dialects of Lancs. and Ches., and survived in this area up to the 19th cent. 6. surname adopted by immigrants to an English-speaking country who originally bore any of various non-English surnames beginning with the letter *K*-.

Vars.: **Kaye, Keay, Key(e)**. See also KEYES. (Of 2 only): **Atkey**.

Kayes see KEYES

Kayley see CAYLEY

Kayne see CAIN

Kazan see CHAZAN

Kazimierski Polish and Jewish (E Ashkenazic): habitation name from a town called *Kazimierz* (from the given name; see KAŹMIERCZAK) + *-ski* suffix of local surnames (see BARANOWSKI). Kazimierz to the NE of Cracow was founded in 1335 by King Casimir the Great (1310–70), and had a substantial Jewish population.

Vars.: Pol.: **Kazimierz, Kaźmierski**. Jewish (E Ashkenazic): **Kazimirski, Kazimi(e)rsky**.

Kaźmierczak Polish: from the Pol. given name *Kazimierz* Casimir (composed of the elements *kazić* to spoil, destroy + *mir* peace, i.e. destroyer of the enemy's peace) + the associative suffix *-czak*, which has patronymic force when used with given names. This name was much used by Pol. royalty, starting with Duke Casimir the Restorer (1015–58), who united the central Polish lands under the Holy Roman Empire. Casimir III, called Casimir the Great (1310–70), presided over a period of great peace and prosperity in Poland. A son of the 15th-cent. Casimir IV, himself called Casimir, became the patron saint of Poland and Lithuania; he spurned his father's ambitions for him to seize the Hungarian throne, and devoted himself instead to a religious life.

Var.: **Kazimierczak**.

Patrs.: Pol.: **Kazimierowicz**. Beloruss.: **Kazimirov**.

Patr. (from a dim.): Pol.: **Kazkiewicz**.

Keable see KEBLE

Keach see KEECH

Keag see MCCAIG

Kealahan see CALLAGHAN

Kealey see KEELEY

Keane 1. Irish: Anglicized form of Gael. Ó **Catháin** 'descendant of *Cathán*', a personal name from a dim. of *cath* battle. 2. English: var. of KEEN.

Vars.: **Kean**. (Of 1 only): **Kane** (see also CAIN), **Cahane**.

Kearney Irish: Anglicized form of Gael. Ó **Ceithearnaigh** 'descendant of *Ceithearnach*', a byname meaning 'Soldier'.

Var.: **O'Kearney**.

Kearns Irish: Anglicized form of Gael. Ó **Céirín** 'descendant of *Céirín*', a personal name from a dim. of *ciar* dark, black (cogn with the Slav. word *cherny*; cf. Russ. CHERNYAKOV).

Kearsley English (Lancs.): habitation name from a place near Manchester, which Ekwall etymologizes as being from OE *cærs, cræs* watercress + *hlāw* hill or *lēah* wood, clearing. There is another place of the same name but different etymology in Northumb., which does not seem to have contributed to the surname.

Keary see CAREY

Keast Cornish: nickname for a fat man, from Corn. **kest* paunch (cf. W *cest* belly, also used as a medieval byname).

Keat *see* KITE

Keating **1.** English: from the OE personal name *Cȳting*, originally a patr. from *Cȳta* KITE'. **2.** Irish: var. of KEATY.

Keatley *see* KEIGHLEY

Keaty Irish: Anglicized form of Gael. **Ó Céatfhadha** 'descendant of *Céatfhaidh*', a byname from *céat(fhadh)ach* reasonable, urbane.

Vars.: **O'Keaty**; KEATING.

Keavane *see* KEEFE

Keay *see* KAY

Keays *see* KEYES

Keble English: nickname given either to a thick, heavy man or to a belligerent individual, from ME *kibble* cudgel (probably of native origin, although no OE forms are attested).

Vars.: **Keeble**, **Keable**, **Kebble**, **Keb(b)ell**, **Kibble**, **Kib(b)el**.

Keddie *see* ADAM

Kedge English: nickname from ME *kedge* brisk, lively, a dial. term confined to E Anglia, and probably of ON origin (cf. mod. Swed. *käck* bold, brisk).

Var.: **Ketch**.

Keeble *see* KEBLE

Keech English: unflattering nickname for a fat, lumpish man, from ME *keech* lump of fat (of unknown origin).

Vars.: **Keetch**, **Kea(t)ch**, **Keitch**.

Keefe Irish: Anglicized form of Gael. **Ó Caoimh** 'descendant of *Caomh*', a byname meaning 'Gentle', 'Kind'.

Vars.: **Keeffe**, **O'Keefe**, **O'Keeve**.

Dims.: **(O')Ke(a)vane**, **Keevane**, **Kevans**, **Cavan**, CAVENDISH (Gael. **Ó Caomháin**).

Keegan Irish: **1.** Anglicized form of Gael. **Mac Aodhagáin**, patr. from the personal name *Aodhagán*, a double dim. of *Aodh* 'Fire'; cf. McKAY. **2.** Anglicized form of Gael. **Mac Thadhgáin**, patr. from the personal name *Tadhgán*, a dim. of the byname *Tadhg* 'Poet'; cf. TIGHE.

Vars. (of 1): **McKeegan**, **McKeagan**, **McKiegan(e)**, **McKeggan**, **McEgan**, **McEgaine**, **McHeagan**. (Of 2): **Kegan**, **Keggin(s)**.

Keeler English (SE England): occupational name for a boatman or boatbuilder, from ME *kele* ship, barge (a borrowing of MDu. *kiel* rather than a direct descendant of OE *cēol*).

Var.: **Keel**.

Keeley **1.** Irish: Anglicized form of Gael. **Ó Caollaidhe** 'descendant of *Caollaidhe*', a personal name derived from *caol* slender, graceful. **2.** English: var. of KEIGHLEY.

Vars. (of 1): **Keely**, **Keal(e)y**; **Queely**, **Queal(l)y**; KIELY.

Keeling English: of uncertain origin, perhaps from a medieval given name, originally an OE patr. from a short form of any of the various cpd personal names with the first element *cēol* keel, ship.

Keemish *see* CAMOYS

Keen **1.** English: nickname from ME *kene* fierce, brave, proud (OE *cēne*). **2.** English: from the ME given name *Kene*, a short form of any of the various OE personal names with the first element *cēne* (see above) or *cyne*-royal (from *cyning* chieftain, king, a deriv. of *cyn(n)* tribe, race, people). **3.** Irish: var. of KEANE.

Var.: **Keene**.

Patr. (from 2): **Kenning**.

Keenlyside N English: habitation name from an unidentified minor place, apparently so called from the OE name *Cēna* (a byname meaning 'Keen', 'Bold' or a short form of various cpd personal names with this first element) + OE *lēah* wood, clearing + *sīde* hillside.

Keep English: occupational name for someone who was employed in the dungeon of a castle, ME *keep* (probably from the verb *keep(en)* to hold, defend, OE *cēpan*).

Keery *see* CAREY

Keeser *see* KESER

Keet *see* KITE

Keetley *see* KEIGHLEY

Keevil English: habitation name from a place in Wilts., recorded in Domesday Book as *Chivele*. It is probably so called either from an OE personal name *Cyfa* (related to *cufa*) or from the gen. pl. of OE *cȳf* tub, vessel + OE *lēah* wood. The second alternative would denote a wood which produced material used for making tubs.

Keeys *see* KEYES

Kegan *see* KEEGAN

Kegg *see* McCAIG

Kegley *see* QUICKLEY

Kehl German: **1.** nickname for someone with some deformity of the throat or neck, perhaps goitre, which was common in the Alpine regions, from Ger. *Kehle* throat (MHG *kel*, OHG *kela*). **2.** topographic name from the same word used in the sense of a narrow gorge or defile, or habitation name from one of the minor places named with this word.

Kehoe *see* KEOGH, KEW

Keig *see* McCAIG

Keighley English: habitation name from a place in W Yorks., recorded in Domesday Book as *Chichelai*, apparently from the OE name *Cyhha* (of uncertain origin) + OE *lēah* wood, clearing.

Vars.: **Keighly**; KEELEY; **K(e)ightley**, **K(e)itley**, **Keatley**, **Keetley**, **Kitlee**; **Cichle** (Wales).

Keight *see* KITE

Keil German: nickname for a large and clumsy individual, from Ger. *Keil* wedge (MHG, OHG *kīl*); this use of the word is reflected in the proverb *auf einem grossen* KLOTZ *gehört ein grosser Keil* ('a great lump needs a great wedge'). Occasionally the surname may have been acquired as an occupational name by someone who made use of wedges, for example in splitting stone, or as a topographic name by someone who lived on a wedge-shaped piece of land. The surname is also borne by Ashkenazic Jews, but the reason(s) for its adoption are unkown.

Cpds (ornamental): Swed.: **Ki(h)lberg** ('wedge hill'); **Ki(h)lgren** ('wedge branch'); **Ki(h)lström** ('wedge river').

Keillips see McKILLOP

Keinrat see KONRAD

Keir see KERR

Keiser see KAISER

Keitch see KEECH

Keith Scots: habitation name from a place so called between Huntly and Elgin. The placename is first recorded in 1187 as *Geth* and in *c*.1220 as *Keth*; it is probably from the Brit. element *cet* wood (cf. W *coed*).

Kelaghan see CALLAGHAN

Kelble see CALF

Kell see KETTLE

Kellaway see CALLOWAY

Kelleher Irish: Anglicized form of Gael. **Ó Céileachair** 'descendant of *Céileachar*', a byname meaning 'Uxorious'.
Var.: **Kelliher**.

Kellett English: habitation name from Nether and Over *Kellet* in N Lancs. near Lancaster, or *Kelleth* in Cumb., all of which derive their names from ON *kelda* spring (see KÄLL) + *hlíð* slope, hillside. The former is the usual source of the surname.
Vars.: **Kellet**, **Kellitt**.

Kellman see KALMAN

Kellner 1. German: occupational name for a person in charge of the wine cellars in a great house or castle, MHG *kelnære* (OHG *kelnari*, agent deriv. of *kellari* cellar, from LL *cellārium*, a deriv. of *cella* small room, storeroom, from *celāre* to hide; cogn. of Eng. SELLER 3). The mod. Ger. sense of *Kellner*, 'waiter', is a comparatively recent development. It has not influenced the Ger. surname, but may lie behind some cases of the Jewish name. 2. Jewish: probably a habitation name from *Keln*, the Yid. name of the city of *Cologne* (Ger. *Köln*).
Vars.: **Kelner**. (Of 1 only): **Keller(t)**, **Kellar(t)**, **Kel(l)ermann**.

Kello English: habitation name from *Kelloe* in Co. Durham, so called from OE *cealf* CALF + *hlāw* hill (see LAW 2 and LOW 1).

Kellogg 1. English: occupational nickname for a pork butcher, from ME *kellen, killen, kullen* to kill, slaughter (OE **cyllan*, a byform of *cwellan*) + *hog* hog, pig (see HOGG). 2. Irish: Anglicized form of Gael. **Ó Ceallaigh**; see KELLY 1. 3. Welsh: of uncertain origin, popularly associated with W *ceiliog* cock.
Var.: **Kellog**.

Kellow Cornish: habitation name from a minor place so called, from Corn. *kellow*, pl. of *kelli* wood, grove (cf. KELLY 3).

Kelly 1. Irish: Anglicized form of Gael. **Ó Ceallaigh** 'descendant of *Ceallach*', originally a byname meaning 'Troublesome', 'Contentious', also said to mean 'Brightheaded'. There were several early Ir. saints who bore this name, and *Kelly* is now the most common of all Ir. surnames. The form **Mac Ceallaigh** 'son of *Ceallach*' (Anglicized **McKelly**, Ulster **Miskelly**) is much rarer. 2. Scots: habitation name from any of various places, such as *Kelly* near Arbroath, named with the Gael. element *coille* wood, grove. 3. English: habitation name from *Kelly* in Devon, named with a Corn. cogn. of 2 (cf. KELLO).
Vars. (of 1): **O'Kelly**, **Kelley**, KELLOGG, **Kelloch**, **Kellock**.

Kelner see KELLNER

Kelsall English: habitation name from a place in Ches., so called from the gen. case of the ME personal name *Kell* (ON *Kell* or *Ketill*) + ME *hale* nook, recess (OE *halh*).
Var.: **Kilshaw**.

Kelsey English: habitation name from a place in Lincs., so called from the gen. case of the OE personal name **Cēnel* (a deriv. of cpd names with the first element *cēne* fierce, brave; cf. KEEN) + OE *ēg* island, low-lying land.

Kelso Scots and N Irish: habitation name from a place so called on the river Tweed, perhaps from OE *cealc* CHALK + *hōh* ridge, spur.

Kember see CAMBER

Kemble 1. English: from the ME given name *Kimbel*, *Chimbel*, OE *Cynebeal(d)*, composed of the elements *cyne-* royal + *beald* bold, brave. 2. English: habitation name from a place in Gloucs., named from a Brit. word related to W *cyfyl* border. 3. Welsh: from a Celt. personal name composed of the elements *cyn* chief + *bel* war. This personal name was borne by an early Brit. chieftain whose name is recorded in a Latinized form as *Cunobelinus*; he provided the inspiration for Shakespeare's *Cymbeline*.

Kemény Hungarian and Jewish (Ashkenazic): nickname for a stern or severe person, from Hung. *kemény* hard.

Kemmelman Jewish (Ashkenazic): 1. occupational name for a maker or seller of combs, from Yid. *keml* comb (a dim. of *kam*) + *man* man. 2. possibly a nickname from Yid. *keml* CAMEL + *man*.
Var.: **Kemelman**.

Kemmis see CAMOYS

Kemp English: occupational name for a champion at jousting or wrestling, ME *kempe* (a weakened sense of OE *cempa* warrior, champion, from *camp* battle, L *campus* plain, field (of battle); cf. CAMPION).
Vars.: **Kempe**.
Dims.: Ger.: **Kämpfl**, **Kempfle**.
Patrs.: Eng.: **Kempson**. Du.: **Kempers**. Finn.: **Kemppainen**.

Kempa Polish: topographic name for someone who lived on a small island or by an isolated clump of trees, from Pol.

kępa islet; the same word is also applied to isolated clumps of trees and to tufts of grass.

Vars.: **Kępa**; **Kempski**; **Kępski**.

Dim.: Pol.: **Kępka**.

Habitation names: Pol.: **Kempiński**; **Kępiński**, **Kępczyński**.

Kempton English: habitation name from *Kempton* in Shrops. or *Kempton* Park near London, recorded in Domesday Book as *Chenpitune* and *Chenetone* respectively. The former is so called from the OE byname *Cempa* 'Warrior' (see KEMP) + OE *tūn* enclosure, settlement; the latter from the OE personal name *Cēna* (see KEENLYSIDE) + *tūn*.

Kendall English: habitation name from *Kendale* in the parish of Driffield, Yorks., or *Kendal* in Cumb. The latter is so called from the Brit. river name KENT + OE *dæl* valley (see DALE); the former is from ON *kelda* spring + ON *dalr* or Late OE *dæl* valley. The surname is very widespread, with a large number of bearers now found as far away as Cornwall.

Vars.: **Kendal, Kendell, Kendle, Kindall, Kindell, Kindle**.

Kendler *see* KÄNDLER

Kendrew *see* ANDREW

Kendrick 1. English: from the ME given name *Cenric*, *Kendrich*, OE *Cynerīc*, composed of the elements *cyne*-royal + *rīc* power. 2. Welsh: from the W personal name *Cyn(w)rig*, *Cynfrig*, possibly composed of the elements *cyn* chief + *(g)wr* man, hero + the suffix of quality -*ig*. 3. Scots: apocopated form of MCKENDRICK; see MCHENRY. 4. Irish: see ENRIGHT.

Vars. (of 1): **Kindrick, Ken(w)rick, Kerrick, Kerrich, Kerridge, Kerrage, Kirrage, Carriage, Courage** (E Anglia); **Kerry** (E Midlands).

Patr. (from 1): **Kerrison**.

Kenerney *see* MCNAIRN

Kenlan *see* QUINLAN

Kennard English: from the ME given name, *Keneward*, OE *Cyneweard*, composed of the elements *cyne*- royal + *heard* hardy, brave, strong or *weard* guard.

Vars. (from the second possibility): **Kenward, Kenwood**.

Kennaway English: from the ME given name *Kenewi*, OE *Cynewīg* or *Cēnwīg*, composed of the elements *cyne*-royal or the rarer *cēne* keen, bold + *wīg* war.

Var.: **Kenway**.

Kenneally Irish: Anglicized form of Gael. Ó *Cionnfhaolaidh* 'descendant of *Cionnfhaoladh*', a personal name derived from *ceann* head + *faol* wolf.

Vars.: **(O')Kennelly, O'Kenneally, (O')Kin(n)eally, Kenne(a)ly**.

Kennedy 1. Irish: Anglicized form of Gael. Ó *Cinnéidigh* 'descendant of *Cinnéidigh*', a personal name derived from *ceann* head + *éidigh* armoured. The name thus meant literally 'helmeted head', but was apparently also a byname for someone with an ugly or deformed head, as in the case of the nephew of Brian Boru, who is claimed as an ancestor by many present-day Kennedys. 2. Jewish: Anglicized form of **Kenedi**, a surname found among Hungarian Jews, which is of unknown origin.

Vars. (of 1): **O'Kennedy, O'Kinedy**.

Kennett English: habitation name from a place in Wilts., so called from the river *Kennet*, on which it stands. This bears an old Brit. name of unknown origin.

Kenngott German: from a Gmc female personal name composed of the elements *kuni* race, people + *gund* battle. This name was popular in the Middle Ages as a result of the fame of St Kunigunde (d. 1039), wife of the Holy Roman Emperor Heinrich II, and also of a Bohemian queen of the same name, the wife of St Wenceslas. In later times the surname has been altered by folk etymology, associating it with Ger. *kennen* to know + *Gott* God.

Vars.: **Könngott, Kunigunde**.

Dims.: **Künne, Kinne**.

Metrs.: **Köngeter, Kingeter**.

Metrs. (from dims.): Ger.: **Kin(t)scher, Küntscher**.

Kennigan *see* CUNNINGHAM

Kenning *see* KEEN

Kenny 1. Scots: Anglicized form of the Gael. personal name *Cionaodha*, of uncertain origin, perhaps composed of the elements *cion* respect, affection + *Aodh*, the name of a pagan god of fire. The personal name thus probably means 'beloved of Aodh', but has also been interpreted as 'ardent love'. 2. Irish: Anglicized form of Gael. Ó *Coinnigh* 'descendant of *Coinneach*', an OIr. personal name borne, for example, by the 6th-cent. monk and saint who gave his name to the town of *Kilkenny* 'Church of Coinneach'.

Vars.: **Kenney, Kinn(e)y, Kinnie**.

Patrs. (from 1): **McKenny, McKinn(e)y, McKinnie, McKe(a)ney, McKenna, McKinna** (Gael. **Mac Cionaodha**).

Patr. (from 1) (dim.): **(Mc)Kennan** (Gael. **Mac Cionaodháin**).

'Descendant of K. 1': **O'Kenn(e)y, O'Kinn(e)y, (O')Kenna, O'Kinna, O'Kenaith** (Gael. Ó **Cionaodha**).

Kent English: regional name from the county of *Kent*, which is of apparently Brit. origin, but uncertain etymology. It may mean 'coastal district', from the Celt. element *canto* (cf. W *cant* rim, border).

Vars.: **Kentish, Kintish**.

Kenton English: habitation name from any of various places so called, which have a number of different etymologies. One near London has the same origin as KEMPTON nearby; one in Northumb. has as its first element OE *cyne*-royal; one in Suffolk may have the same origin as either of the two preceding examples, or it may get its first element from the OE personal name *Cyna*, a short form of the various cpd names with the first element *cyne*- royal; one in Devon is so called from its situation on the river *Kenn*, which bears an old Brit. name of uncertain origin.

Kenworthy English: habitation name from a place in Ches., apparently so called from the OE personal name *Cyna* (see KENTON) or *Cēna* (see KEENLYSIDE) + OE *worðig* enclosure (see WORTHY).

Kenyeres Hungarian: occupational name for a breadseller, from a deriv. of Hung. *kenyér* bread.

Kenyon English (Lancs.): habitation name from a place near Warrington, which is of uncertain etymology. There was formerly an ancient burial mound there and Ekwall has speculated that the name is a shortened form of a Brit. name composed of the elements *crūc* mound (see CRICH) + a personal name cogn. with Welsh *Einion* 'Anvil'.

Keogh Irish: Anglicized form of Gael. **Mac Eochaidh** 'son of *Eochaidh*', a personal name derived from *each* horse.
Vars.: **Keoghoe**, **(Mc)K(e)ough**, **(Mc)Kehoe**, **McKeogh(oe)**, **McKeo**, **McGeogh**, **McEoghoe**.
Dims.: **Keohane**, **Keog(h)an** (Gael. **Mac Eocháin**); see also GAHAN and McGUIGAN. Manx: **Quaggin**, **Weggin**.

Keown see EWAN

Kępa see KEMPA

Kepler see CHAPE

Keppie Scots: habitation name from *Kippo* in Fife, so called from Gael. *ceap, cip* block, tree-stump, hillock + the local suffix *-ach*.
Var.: **Kippie**.

Kerber see KORB

Kerbey see KIRBY

Kercher see KARCH

Kerfoot English (Lancs.): habitation name from an un-identified place, which perhaps derives its name from ME *kerr* wet ground (see KERR) + *fote* foot, bottom of a hill (cf. FOOT).
Vars.: **Kerfod**, **Kerfed**.

Kerk see KIRK

Kerley see CURLEY

Kermeen see CURWEN

Kermode see DERMOTT

Kern German and Jewish (Ashkenazic): from Ger. *Kern* kernel, seed, pip, Yid. *kern* (MHG *kerne*, OHG *kerno*, related to KORN 1). The application as a surname is not clear: it could be a metonymic occupational name for a seller of shelled nuts or for a supplier of seeds, a nickname for a small person, or, in the case of the Jewish name, simply ornamental. See also KERNER.

Kernaghan Irish: Anglicized form of Gael. **Mac Thighearnacháin**, patr. from the personal name *Tighearnachán*, a dim. of *tighearnach* lord, master; cf. TIERNEY.
Var.: **Kernohan**. See also McKIERNAN.

Kernan see McKIERNAN

Kerner 1. German and Jewish (Ashkenazic): occupational var. of KERN, with agent suffix. 2. Low German: occupational name for a carter, from MLG *kerenere*, an agent deriv. of *kar(r)e* cart (cf. CARRIER).
Var. (of 1): Jewish: **Kernerman**.

Kerr Scots and N English: topographic name for someone who lived near a patch of wet ground overgrown with brushwood, Northern ME *kerr* (ON *kjarr*). The pronunciation /ka:(r)/ reflects the ME change of *-er-* to *-ar-* (cf. MARCHANT), seen in the var. spelling CARR. A legend

grew up that the Kerrs were left-handed, from Gael. *cearr* wrong, left-handed.
Vars.: **Ke(i)r**.
Cpd (ornamental): Swed.: **Kärrström** ('marsh river').

Kerrage see KENDRICK

Kerrigan Irish: Anglicized form of Gael. **Ó Ciaragáin** 'descendant of *Ciaragán*', a byname from a double dim. of *ciar* dark, black (cf. KEARNS and CAREY).
Vars.: **Ker(i)gan**, **O'Kerrigane**, **O'Kierrigain**.

Kersch see KIRSCH

Kersey English: habitation name from a place in Suffolk, recorded in Domesday Book as *Careseia*, probably from OE *cærs* watercress + *ēg* island, low-lying land.

Kershaw English: habitation name from *Kirkshaw* in the parish of Rochdale, Lancs., so called from Northern ME *kirk* church (see KIRK) + *shaw* grove (see SHAW). There are two minor places in W Yorks. called *Kershaw*, which may be of the same origin and may also lie behind the surname, but on the other hand they may themselves derive from the surname.
Vars.: **Kersaw**, **Kirshaw**.

Kerslake see CARSLAKE

Kerst see CHRISTIAN

Kerswell see CRESWELL

Kertész Hungarian (partly Jewish): occupational name for a gardener, Hung. *kertész*, from *kert* garden + *-ész* occupational suffix.

Keser 1. German: var. of KAISER. 2. German: cogn. of CHEESEMAN. 3. Low German: status name for someone who held the franchise in respect of a particular electoral procedure, from MLG *ke(e)sen* to chose; cf. KIESER.
Var. (of 3): **Keeser**.

Keser see KAISER

Keserling see KIESSLING

Keshin see McCASHIN

Keslake see CARSLAKE

Kesper see KASPAR

Kessel German: metonymic occupational name for someone who made cooking vessels of various sizes from copper, from Ger. *Kessel* kettle, cauldron (MHG *kezzel*, OHG *kezzil*; cf. KETTLE).
Vars.: **Kessler**; **Kössler** (Bavaria).

Kest see CHRISTIAN

Kestell see CASTLE

Kesterton see CHESTERTON

Kestner see KASTNER

Ketch see KEDGE

Ketchen see KITCHEN

Ketley English: habitation name from a place in Shrops., so called from OE *catta* (wild) cat (see CATT) + *lēah* wood, clearing.

Kett 1. English (Norfolk): var. of KITE. 2. Jewish (Ashkenazic): of unknown origin.

Kettle English: from the ON personal name *Ketill*, a short form of the various cpd names in *-ketill* cauldron (cf. ASHKETTLE and THIRKILL).

Vars.: **Kettel(l)**, **Ketill**, **Kitell**, **Kittle**; **Kell** (Northumb.).

Patrs.: Eng.: **Kettles(s)**, **Kells**; **Kettelson**. Norw., Dan.: **Ketels(en)**, **Kjeldsen**. Swed.: **Kilsson**.

Kettlewell English: habitation name from a place in W Yorks., so called from OE *cetel* KETTLE, deep valley + *well(a)* spring, stream (see WELL).

Ketts see KITE

Kettunen Finnish: patr. from the nickname *Kettu* 'Fox', with the addition of the gen. suffix *-nen*.

Keune see KONRAD

Kevane see KEEFE

Kevern Cornish: habitation name from the parish of *St Keverne* on the Lizard peninsula. The patron of the parish is a rather shadowy figure, whose name is first recorded as *Achobran* in the 10th cent., probably identical with the Irish saint *Accobrán*.

Kew English: 1. occupational name for a cook, ANF *k(i)eu* (L *coquus*; see COOK). 2. Norman habitation name from *Caieu*, a lost town near Boulogne in N France. 3. habitation name from a place in Middlesex, now part of SW London, so called from OE *cǣg* key, projection + *hōh* ridge, slope.

Vars. (of 1): **Le Keux**, **Lequeux**. (Of 2): **Kehoe**, **Keyho(e)** (see also KEOGH).

Kewley see COWLEY

Key see KAY, McKAY

Keyes 1. English: var. of KAY. 2. English (Norman): habitation name from *Guise* in Aisne, Picardy, which is first recorded in the 12th cent. as *Gusia* and is of uncertain etymology. 3. Irish: Anglicized form of Gael. *Mac Aodha*; see McKAY.

Vars.: **Kay(e)s**, **Ke(a)ys**, **Keeys**.

Keyfetz see HEIFETZ

Keyho see KEW

Keynes English (Norman): habitation name from *Cahaignes* in Eure or *Cahaynes* in Calvados, both apparently named from a Celt. element denoting the juniper bush.

Vars.: **Kaines**, **Cain(e)s**.

Keyser see KAISER

Keyte see KITE

Keyworth English: habitation name from a place in Notts., recorded as *Caworde* in Domesday Book, of uncertain etymology. The second element is clearly OE *worð*

enclosure (see WORTH); Ekwall suggests that the first element may be OE *cǣg* key, projection.

Khachaturian Armenian: patr. from the personal name *Khachatur* 'Cross-bearer'.

Khadeev see TADIÉ

Khadkevich see THÉODORE

Khaet see CHAIT

Khaimovich see HYAM

Khanele see HANNA

Khavke Jewish (E Ashkenazic): from *Khavke*, a pet form of the Yid. female given name *Khave* (from Hebr. *Chava* EVE).

Metrs.: **Khavkin**, **Chavkin**, **Havkin**, **Havken**; **Havlin** (based on *Khavele*, a different dim. of *Khave*).

Khazan see CHAZAN

Khilkov see PHILIP

Khimichev see YEFIMOV

Khlebnikov Russian: patr. from the occupational term *khlebnik* baker (from *khleb* bread, a borrowing from a Gmc cogn. of mod. Eng. *loaf*).

Khodasevich see THÉODORE

Khomich see THOMAS

Khrishtafovich see CHRISTOPHER

Khrishtanovich see CHRISTIAN

Khrushchev Russian: patr. from the nickname *Khrushch* 'May Beetle'. This word is ultimately from *khrust-* to rustle, and so is cogn. with Pol. CHRUŚCIEL.

Var.: **Krushchyov**.

Habitation name: Pol.: **Chrząszczyński**.

Khvedko see THÉODORE

Kibbel see KEBLE

Kidd 1. English: nickname for a frisky person or metonymic occupational name for a goatherd, from ME *kid(e)* young goat (of uncertain origin, perhaps from ON *kith*). 2. English: metonymic occupational name for a seller of faggots, from ME *kidde* faggot (of unknown origin). 3. Scots: from a medieval given name, a var. of *Kit* (a pet form of CHRISTOPHER).

Vars.: **Kid(de)**, **Kyd(d)**; **Kidman** (occupational name from 1 or 2).

Patrs. (from 3): **Kydds**, **Kidson**.

Kiddie see ADAM

Kiddle English: topographic name for someone who lived by a fish-weir, ME *kidel* (OF *cuidel*, *quidel*, of Bret. origin).

Var.: **Kiddell**.

Kidney see DEVANE

Kiefer German: 1. occupational name in SW areas of Germany for a cooper, from an agent deriv. of Ger. dial. *Kief(e)*, Ger. *Kufe* barrel (MHG *kuofe*, OHG *kuofa*); a cogn. of Eng. COOPER. 2. topographic name for someone who lived in a pine forest or by an isolated pine tree, from

Ger. *Kiefer* pine. This word, which is first attested in the early 15th cent., results from a combination of the terms *kien* and *forhe*, both meaning 'pine'; *kieboom* is still the normal Flem. and Du. term, and in large parts of Germany the word for the tree is *Föhre*. The surname is also borne by Ashkenazic Jews, among whom it is an ornamental name from the word for tree. **3.** nickname for a glutton or messy eater, from an agent deriv. of MHG *kīfen* to chew (whence mod. Ger. *Kiefer* jaw). **4.** nickname for a combative individual, from MHG *kiffen* to quarrel.

Var. (of 1): **Kiefner**; **Küf(l)er**, **Küf(f)ner**; **Kaufner** (Bavaria); **Kief**.

Kiehne *see* KONRAD

Kiełbasa Polish: metonymic occupational name or nickname from Pol. *kiełbasa* sausage, bestowed either on a seller of sausages or on someone with a fancied resemblance to a sausage.

Var.: **Kiełbasiak**.

Habitation name: **Kiełbasiński**.

Kiely Irish: **1.** Anglicized form of **Ó Cadhla** 'descendant of *Cadhla*', a personal name meaning 'Beautiful'. **2.** var. of KEELEY 1.

Kieran Irish: Anglicized form of the Gael. personal name *Ciarán* (a dim. of *ciar* dark, black), borne by a large number of early Ir. saints.

Patr.: **Kierans**.

Kierevan *see* KIRWAN

Kiernan *see* MCKIERNAN

Kierschner *see* KÜRSCHNER

Kiesel German: nickname, perhaps for someone with a bald head, or topographic name for someone who lived on a patch of gravelly land, from Ger. *Kiesel* pebble, also in a collective sense 'gravel' (MHG *kisel*, OHG *kisil*). There are several minor places named with this word, and the surname may also be a habitation name from any of them. See also KIESSLING 1.

Kieser German: occupational name for an official who tested the weights and measures in use in the public markets and checked foodstuffs on sale for possible adulteration. The MHG word *kieser* derives from *kiesen* to test (OHG *kiosan*, a cogn. of mod. Eng. *choose*; cf. KESER 3).

Kiesewetter German: of uncertain origin. It appears to be either from *kieseln* to hail (from MHG *kisel* pebble, gravel, hailstone; see KIESEL) + *wetter* weather, and so perhaps used for someone of a blustery temperament; or from MHG *kiesen* to test, watch (see KIESER) + *wetter*, and so perhaps denoting an amateur weather prophet. However, as neither of these explanations is particularly convincing, and the surname is found mainly in Saxony and Silesia, it is possible that it represents an alteration through folk etymology of some unidentified Slav. name.

Vars.: **Kisswetter**, **Küssewetter**.

Kiessling German: **1.** topographic name for someone who lived in an area of gravelly soil, from MHG *kiselinc* gravel (a deriv. of OHG *kisil* pebble, gravel (see KIESEL), with the addition of the Gmc suffix *-ing*). There are various minor places named with this word, and the surname may also be

a habitation name from any of these. **2.** patr. from the OHG personal name *Gisilo*, a short form of any of the various cpd names with the first element *gīsil* hostage (cf., e.g., GILBERT).

Vars.: **Kiesling**, **Kies(s)lich**, **K(i)eserling**.

Kigel *see* KUGEL

Kightley *see* KEIGHLEY

Kihlberg *see* KEIL

Kilbane Irish: Anglicized form of Gael. **Mac Giolla Bháin** 'son of the fair-haired lad' (cf. BAIN).

Kilberg *see* KEIL

Kilboy *see* MCEVOY

Kilbride **1.** Irish and Scots: Anglicized form of Gael. **Mac Giolla Brighde** (Ir.) or **Mac Gille Bríghde** (Sc.) 'son of the servant of (St) Brigit'. The name *Brighid* is of uncertain origin, but may mean 'Exalted'; it probably originally denoted a pagan fire goddess, many of whose attributes have become attached to the historical figure of St Brigit of Kildare (452–523), founder of the first Irish convent. **2.** Scots: habitation name from any of the various places with this name, from Gael. *cill Brighde* church (from L *cella* room, cell) of St Brigit.

Vars. (of 1): **McKillbride**, **(Mc)Gil(l)bride**, **McGillvrid(e)**, **MacIlvride**, **MacIlvreed**, **McElvride**, **Micklebride**, **Mackelbreed**; **McBride**, **McBryde**; **Bridson**, **Brydson**, **Brigetson**; BRIDGE, GILBERT.

Kilburn English: habitation name from a place in N Yorks., or one in Derbys., both of which are of uncertain etymology, possibly so called from OE *cylen(e)* kiln (see KILNER) + *burna* stream (see BOURNE). The place of this name in London does not seem to have contributed to the surname.

Kilby English: habitation name from a place in Leics., recorded in Domesday Book as *Cilebi*. It was probably originally named with the OE elements *cild* CHILD + *tūn* enclosure, settlement (cf. CHILTON), the second element being later replaced by the equiv. ON *býr*.

Vars.: **Kilbey**, **Killby**, **Kilbuy**.

Kilcoyne Irish: Anglicized form of Gael. **Mac Giolla Chaoin** 'son of the servant of (St) *Caoin*', a personal name meaning 'Gentle'.

Kildare Irish: Anglicized form of Gael. **Mac Giolla Dhorcha** 'son of the dark-haired lad'.

Vars.: **Kildaire**; **McIlderry**, **McElderry**.

Kildea Irish: Anglicized form of Gael. **Mac Giolla Dhé** 'son of the servant of God', from *Dia* God. The name originated with a monastic family in Donegal in the 11th cent. and has always been more or less confined to NW Ireland.

Vars.: **Gildea**, GRAY.

Kilduff *see* GILDUFF

Kilfeather Irish: Anglicized form of Gael. **Mac Giolla Pheadair** 'son of the servant of (St) PETER'.

Vars.: **Kilfedder**, **Gilfedder**.

Kilfillan *see* GILFILLAN

Kilfoyle *see* GILFOIL

Kilgour Scots: habitation name from a place in Fife, so called from Gael. *coille* wood + *gobhar, gabhar* goat.
Var.: **Kilgore**.

Killeavy *see* DUNLEAVY

Killeen Irish: Anglicized form of the Gael. personal name *Cillín*, a dim. of *Ceallach* (see KELLY 1). The name was borne by various early Ir. saints, including the leader of a 7th-cent. mission to Franconia and Thuringia, hence the popularity of the given name *Kilian* in medieval central Europe, from which several surnames are derived.
Var.: **Killen**.

Killery *see* McILWRAITH

Killick SE English: of unknown origin (apparently not a habitation name, for none of the early forms appear with prepositions).
Var.: **Killik**.

Killigrew Cornish: habitation name from *Killigrew* in St Erme parish, which probably gets its name from Corn. *kelly* grove + *cnow* hazel trees or nuts.

Killingbeck English (Yorks.): habitation name from a place in N Yorks., most probably from an ON personal name *Killing* + ON *bekkr* stream (see BECK).
Var.: **Killingback**.

Killington English: habitation name from a place in Cumb., so called from OE *Cyllingtūn* 'settlement (OE *tūn*) associated with *Cylla*', a personal name of uncertain origin.

Killip *see* McKILLOP

Kilmartin *see* GILMARTIN

Kilminster English (W Midlands): habitation name, probably from *Kidderminster* in Worcs. (recorded as *Kedeleministre* in 1155), which gets its name from the OE personal name *Cydela* (a dim. of *Cydda*) + OE *mynster* monastery church (L *monastērium*).

Kilmore *see* GILMORE

Kilner English: occupational name for a potter or limeburner, from an agent deriv. of OE *cylen(e)* kiln (LL *culīna* kitchen, a deriv. of *coquere* to cook).

Kilpatrick 1. Irish: Anglicized form of Gael. **Mac Giolla Phádraig** 'son of the servant of (St) PATRICK'. **2.** Scots: habitation name from any of various places named in Gael. as *cill Padraig* 'church of (St) PATRICK'.

Kilroy *see* GILROY

Kilshaw *see* KELSALL

Kilsson *see* KETTLE

Kilström *see* KEIL

Kilvert English: apparently from an unattested ON personal name *Ketilfrøðr, Ketilfrith*, Anglicized as *Cytelferð*. This is composed of the elements *ketil* cauldron (cf. KETTLE) + *frøðr, friðr* peace.

Kilvington English: habitation name from one of the places so called: N and S *Kilvington* near Thirsk in N Yorks. or *Kilvington* in Notts. These are either 'settlement (OE *tūn*) associated with *Cynelāf*' or 'settlement associated with *Cynewulf*'. The OE personal names are from *cyne*-royal + *lāf* survivor or *wulf* wolf.

Kimber English: from the OE female personal name *Cyneburh*, composed of the elements *cyne*- royal + *burh* fortress, stronghold. This name was borne by a daughter of the 7th-cent. King Penda of Mercia, who, in spite of her father's staunch opposition to Christianity, was converted and founded an abbey, serving as its head. She was venerated as a saint in the Middle Ages, and children were named after her.
Var.: **Kimbrough**.

Kimberley English (chiefly W Midlands): habitation name from any of various places so called, from different OE personal names + OE *lēah* wood, clearing. *Kimberley* in Warwicks. is first recorded in 1311 in the form *Kynebaldeleye* 'wood of *Cynebald*' (see KEMBLE); *Kimberley* in Notts. is recorded in Domesday Book as *Chinemarelie* 'wood of *Cynemǣr*', a name composed of the elements *cyne*- royal + *mǣr* fame; *Kimberley* in Norfolk is recorded in Domesday Book as *Chineburlai* 'wood of *Cyneburh*' (see KIMBER).
Var.: **Kimberly**.

Kimel *see* KÜMMEL

Kimpton English: habitation name from places in Hants and Herts., so called from the OE personal name *Cyma* (a short from of *Cynemǣr*; see KIMBERLEY) + OE *tūn* enclosure, settlement.

Kinaghan *see* CUNNINGHAM

Kinavan *see* CANAVAN

Kincaid Scots: habitation name from a place near Lennoxtown in Campsie Glen, north of Glasgow, which is first recorded in 1238 as *Kincaith* and in 1250 as *Kincathe*. The former spelling would suggest derivation from Gael. *ceann* head, top + *càithe* pass, whereas the latter would point to *cadha* quagmire as the second element.
Vars.: **Kincade, Kinkead, Kinkaid, Kinkade, Kincaidie**.

Kind German and Jewish (Ashkenazic): nickname for someone resembling a child, Ger. *Kind* (OHG *kind*). In some cases it may also be a shortening of cpd names ending in *-kind*, which is sometimes found as a patr. ending of Jewish surnames, by folk-etymological alteration of the ending *-kin*; see SÜSSKIND.
Var.: Ger.: **Kindt**.
Dims.: Ger.: **Kind(e)l**.

Kindall *see* KENDALL

Kindellan *see* QUINLAN

Kinder English: habitation name from a place in Derbys., the name of which is probably Brit., but of obscure etymology.

Kinderlehrer Jewish (Ashkenazic): occupational name for a teacher in a traditional Jewish elementary school (cf. KNELLER 2). The name is from Ger. *Kinder* children + LEHRER teacher, or the cogn. Yid. *kinder + lerer*.

Var.: **Kinderlerer**.

Kindrick *see* KENDRICK

Kine *see* COYNE

Kineally *see* KENNEALLY

Kinerny *see* McNAIRN

King English: nickname from ME *king*, OE *cyning* king (originally merely a tribal leader, from OE *cyn(n)* tribe, race + the Gmc suffix *-ing*). The word was already used as a byname before the Norman Conquest, and the nickname was common in the Middle Ages, being used to refer to someone who conducted himself in a kingly manner, or to one who had played the part of a king in a pageant, or to one who had won the title in some contest. In rare cases it may actually have referred to someone who had served in the king's household. The surname is also borne by Ashkenazic Jews, among whom it is presumably an Anglicization of KÖNIG or a related form.

Var.: Eng.: **Kinge**.

Dims.: Eng.: **King(g)ett**.

Patrs.: Eng.: **Kings(on)**.

'Servant of K.': Eng.: **Kingman**.

Kingdon English (Devon): habitation name from Higher *Kingdon* in Alverdiscott, Devon, or from *Kendon* in N Bovey, Devon. Both are from OE *cyning* KING + *dūn* hill.

Var.: **Kindon**.

Kingeter *see* KENNGOTT

Kingham English: habitation name from a place in Oxon., so called from OE *Cǣgingahām* 'homestead (OE *hām*) of the people of *Cǣga*', apparently a byname from *cǣg* key, peg.

Kinghorn Scots: habitation name from *Kinghorn* in Fife, *Kyngorn* in 1374, the spelling of which has been affected by folk etymology, but which gets its name from Gael. *ceann* head, height + *gronna* bog.

Var.: **Kinghorne**.

Kingsberg *see* KÖNIGSBERG

Kingsbury English: habitation name from any of several places, for example in NW London, Somerset, and Warwicks. The last mentioned is so called from OE *Cynesburh* 'stronghold (OE *burh*) of *Cyne*', a short form of any of the various cpd names with the first element *cyne-* royal. The others have as the first element OE *cyning* KING, chieftain.

Kingscote English: habitation name from a village near Tetbury, Gloucs., so called from the gen. case of OE *cyning* KING, chieftain + *cot* hut, shelter (see COATES).

Var.: **Kingscott**.

Kingsley English: habitation name from any of the places, in Ches., Hants, and Staffs., so called from from OE *cyningeslēah* 'wood, clearing of the KING, chieftain'.

Kingston English: habitation name from any of the very numerous places in England called *Kingston* or *Kingstone*. Almost all of them, regardless of the distinction in spelling,

were originally named in OE as *cyningestūn* 'settlement of the KING', i.e. royal manor. However, *Kingston* upon Soar in Notts. and *Kingstone* in Somerset are respectively 'royal stone' and 'king's stone', perhaps from some local monument.

Var.: **Kingstone**.

Kington English: habitation name from any of various places in Dorset, Herefords., Warwicks., Wilts., and Worcs. These derive their name either from OE *cyne-* royal or from OE *cyning* KING, chieftain + *tūn* settlement, enclosure, and are thus identical in meaning with KINGSTON, even though the possessive *-s* is missing.

Kingwell English (Devon): habitation name from a place in Somerset, probably so called from OE *cyning* KING, chieftain + *well(a)* spring, stream (see WELL).

Kinig *see* KÖNIG

Kiniry *see* McENERY

Kinkel *see* GUNKEL

Kinloch Scots: habitation name from any of various places that derive their names from Gael. *ceann* head(land) + *loch* loch. The most likely source of the surname is *Kinloch* at the head of Loch Rossie in Fife, where a certain John Kinloch is recorded in charters dating from *c*.1240.

Var.: **Kinlock**.

Kinnaird Scots: habitation name from a place so called on Tayside, which derives its name from Gael. *ceann* head + *aird* height, i.e. 'summit', 'peak'.

Kinnan *see* FINN

Kinnear Scots: habitation name from *Kinneir* in Fife, first recorded at the beginning of the 13th cent. as *Kyner*, apparently from Gael. *ceann* head(land) + *iar* west.

Var.: **Kinneir**.

Kinneavy Irish: Anglicized form of Gael. **Mac Conshnámha** 'son of *Conshnámha*', a personal name composed of the elements *con* dog + *snámh* to swim.

Var.: **McKinnawe**. The name has also been 'translated' FORD, as if from Gael. *Mac an Átha* 'son of the ford'.

Kinneen Irish: Anglicized form of Gael. **Ó Coinín** 'descendant of *Coinín*', a personal name probably from a dim. of *cú*, gen. *con*, hound. As the result of confusion by association with Gael. *coinín* rabbit, the name has also been Anglicized as RABBITT, **Rabitte**, **Rabette**, etc.

Kinney *see* KENNY

Kinsella Irish: Anglicized form of Gael. **Ó Cinnsealaigh** 'descendant of *Cinnsealach*', a byname meaning 'Proud', 'Overbearing'.

Vars.: **O'Kynsillaghe**, **Kinshela**, **Kinsley**.

Kinsey English: from an OE personal name composed of the elements *cyne-* royal + *sige* victory.

Vars.: **Kincey**, **Kynsey**, **Kinzie**.

Kinsman English: from ME *kin(ne)sman* (a cpd of OE *cyn(n)* kin + *man* man), presumably used to refer to someone who was related to an important personage or influential family.

Kintish see KENT

Kintzel see KONRAD

Kiperbaum see COPPER

Kipling English: **1.** habitation name from *Kiplin* in N Yorks., so called from OE *Cyppelingas* 'people of **Cyppel*', an OE personal name of uncertain origin and meaning. **2.** habitation name from *Kipling Cotes* in E Yorks., probably named from OE *Cybbelingcot* 'cottage(s) associated with *Cybbel*', another OE personal name of unknown origin and meaning.

Kippie see KEPPIE

Királyfi see KRÓL

Kirby English: habitation name from any of the numerous places in N England called *Kirby* or *Kirkby*, from ON *kirkja* church (see KIRK) + *býr* settlement.

Vars.: **Kerb(e)y**, **Kirkby**, **Kirkebye**.

Kirchner German: occupational name for a church sexton, from MHG *kirchenære*, a deriv. of *kirche* church (see KIRK). This is the regular term for the occupation in Thuringia; see also KÜSTER, MESNER, and OPPERMANN. The surname is also borne by Ashkenazic Jews, in which use it presumably originally referred to a sexton in a synagogue.

Kirchstein see CHRISTIAN

Kirilov Russian and Bulgarian: patr. from the given name *Kiril* Cyril (Gk *Kyrilos*, from *kyrios* lord; cf. the L equivalent at DOMINIQUE). This was the name borne by a 9th-cent missionary to the Slavs who, together with his companion Methodius, first translated biblical and liturgical texts into Old Slavonic. No Slav. language had previously been written down, and so the two men devised their own system of transcription, based on the Gk alphabet, This remains the basis of the modern Cyrillic scripts. The given name was not in use in the West during the Middle Ages, and surnames derived from it are confined to E Europe.

Vars.: **Kirillov**, **Kiril(l)in**, **Kurilov**, **Kurilin**; **Kiryanov**, **Kuryanov**, **Kirsanov**, **Kursanov**, **Kirisov**, **Kurisov**, **Kirilichev**.

Dims.: Russ.: **Kiril(li)tsev**, **Kirilochkin**, **Kuriltsev**, **Kurilchikov**, **Kurilyov**, **Kurylyov**, **Kurilkin**, **Kurylkin**; **Kirtsov**, **Kireev**, **Kirichev**, **Kirichkov**, **Kiryaev**, **Kiryunchev**, **Kirshov**, **Kir(yak)in**, **Kiryukhin**, **Kiryupin**, **Kiryush(k)in**, **Kiryutin**, **Kirkin**, **Kirsanin**, **Kirshin**; **Kurasov**, **Kurikov**, **Kurinov**, **Kurlov**, **Kurysev**, **Kuryshev**, **Kur(ikh)in**, **Kyryshkin**, **Kurshin** (all patrs.). Ukr.: **Kirilenko**, **Kireiko**, **Kirilyuk**. Beloruss.: **Kireenko**.

Kirk N English and Scots: topographic name for someone who lived near a church or metonymic occupational name for someone who was employed in one, from Northern ME *kirk* church (ON *kirkja*; see further at CHURCH).

Vars.: **Kirke**, **Kerk**, **Kyrke**; **Kir(c)kman**.

Kirkbride N English: habitation name from any of various places so named from having a church (see KIRK) dedicated to St Brigit (cf. KILBRIDE), of which there is one in Cumb. near Carlisle. Cf. KIRKPATRICK.

Var.: **Kirkbright**.

Kirkham N English: habitation name from places in Lancs. and W Yorks., the name of which is a

Scandinavianized form of OE *ciric-hām*, from *cirice* church + *hām* homestead.

Kirkland N English: topographic name for someone who lived on land belonging to the Church, from Northern ME KIRK church + *land* land (OE *land*). There are several villages named with these elements, for example in Cumb., and they may have contributed to the surname. Exceptionally, *Kirkland* in Lancs. has its second element from ON *lund* grove.

Kirkley English: habitation name from a place so called in Northumb., which ostensibly derives its name from ON *kirkja* church (see KIRK) + OE *lēah* wood, clearing. However, it is found as *Crekellawe* in early records; it is therefore derived from Brit. *crūc* hill (see CRICH) + the tautologous OE *hlāw* hill (see LAW 2 and LOW 1).

Kirkpatrick Scots and N Irish: habitation name from any of various places so called from the dedication of their church (see KIRK) to St PATRICK. The order of the elements is the result of Gael. influence.

Kirkup English (Northumb.): apparently a habitation name from an unidentified place, probably named with the Northern ME elements KIRK church + HOPE valley.

Kirkwood Scots: habitation name from any of several places named as being a WOOD belonging to the Church or situated by a church (see KIRK). There are places so called in the former counties of Ayrs., Dumfries, and Lanarks., any of which may have given rise to the surname.

Kirley see CURLEY

Kirner see KÜRNER

Kirrage see KENDRICK

Kirsch **1.** German: topographic name for someone who lived near a cherry orchard or a wild cherry tree, from Ger. *Kirsch(baum)* cherry (tree) (MHG *kirse*, OHG *kirsa*). It may also have been a metonymic occupational name for a gatherer or seller of cherries or a nickname for a man with a ruddy complexion. **2.** Jewish (Ashkenazic): ornamental name, one of the many taken from words for trees and other features of the natural world. The surname is from either the Ger. or the NE or W Yid. form of the word.

Vars. (of 1): Ger.: **Kirsche**. (Of 2): Jewish: **Kirsh** (Anglicized spelling), **Kirs(c)hman**; **Kirsz** (Pol. spelling); **Kersch** (from a S Yid. pronunciation, Anglicized **Kersh**), **Kers(c)hman**; **Karsch** (from a central Yid. pronunciation, Anglicized **Karsh**; also **Karshen**, **Karshon**, from the Yid. pl. *karshn*); **Kirshonovitz**, **Kirsenovitz** (patrs. in form).

Cpds (of 2): Jewish: **Kirs(c)h(en)baum**, **Kirszenbaum**, **Kirsh(en)bom**, **Kirshenboim**, **Kerschenbaum** ('cherry tree'); **Kirs(c)henberg**, **Kirszberg**, **Kirshberg** ('cherry hill'); **Kirschenblatt**, **Kirshenblat(t)**, **Kershenblat** ('cherry leaf'); **Kirschblum**, **Kirs(h)blum** ('cherry flower'); **Kirs(c)henblut** ('cherry blood', from Ger. *Blut* blood, or 'cherry blossom', from Ger. *Blüte* blossom); **Kirshenfeld** ('cherry field'); **Kirschenhaut** ('cherry skin', perhaps a nickname for a man with a ruddy complexion); **Kirschholz**, **Kirsholz**, **Kirszholc** ('cherry wood'); **Kirschensaft** ('cherry juice'); **Kirschstein**, **Kirs(h)tein**, **Kirstain**, **Kerstein**, **Karschenstein** ('cherry stone'; see also CHRISTIAN); **Kirshenzweig**, **Kirszenzweig** ('cherry twig').

Kirschner see KÜRSCHNER

Kirshaw see KERSHAW

Kirton N English: habitation name from any of various places, for example in Lincs., Notts., and Staffs., so called from OE *cirice* church, replaced by ON *kirkja* church (see KIRK), + OE *tūn* enclosure, settlement.

Kirwan Irish: Anglicized form of Gael. **Ó Ciardhubháin** 'descendant of *Ciardhubhán*', a personal name composed of the elements *ciar* dark + *dubh* black + the dim. suffix -*an*.
Vars.: **Kirwen**, **Kirwin**, **Kir(i)van**, **Kier(e)van**; **O'Kirwan**, **O'Kerevan**, **O'Kerrywane**.

Kiselstein see KIESEL

Kiselyov Russian: patr. from the nickname *Kisel*, a type of blancmange containing the juice of various acid fruits such as cranberry. This derives its name from *kisly* sour; the nickname was perhaps used to refer to a person with an acid disposition.
Habitation names: Pol.: **Kisielewski**, **Kiślański**.

Kiss 1. Hungarian (partly Jewish): nickname from *kis* small. At least in the case of the Hung. name, this word was also used in contrast with NAGY as a distinguishing name for the younger of two bearers of the same first name, not necessarily one who was physically smaller. 2. English: metonymic occupational name for a maker of leg armour, normally of leather, from ANF *cuisse* thigh (piece) (L *coxa* thigh).
Vars. (of 1): **Kis**; U.S. **Kish**, **Kisch**. (Of 2): **Cuss(e)** (see also CONSTANCE); **Kisser**, **Kissa**.

Kissack see ISAAC

Kissane Irish: Anglicized form of Gael. **Ó Ciosáin** 'descendant of *Ciosán*', a personal name perhaps derived from a dim. of *ceas* coracle.

Kissinger German and Jewish (W Ashkenazic): habitation name from *Kissingen* in Franconia or *Kissing* in Bavaria, both of which, according to Bahlow, are named with a lost element *kis(s)* denoting a marsh or swamp.

Kissock see ISAAC

Kisswetter see KIESEWETTER

Kist see CHRISTIAN

Kit see CHRISTOPHER

Kitaev see TITO

Kitchen English: metonymic occupational name for a cook or someone who worked in a kitchen, from ME *kychene*, OE *cycen(e)* (L *cucīna*; cf. CUISINE).
Vars.: **Kitchin(g)**, **Ketchen**, **Ketchin**; **Kitchener**; **Kitch(e)man**, **Kitchin(g)man**.

Kite English (chiefly W Midlands): nickname for a fierce or rapacious person, from ME *kete* kite (the bird of prey; OE *cȳta*).
Vars.: **K(e)yte**, **Keight** (W Midlands); KETT; **Keet**, **Keat(e)**.
Patrs.: **Kites**, **Ketts**, **Keat(e)s**; KEATING.

Kiteley English: apparently a habitation name from an unidentified place deriving its name from OE *cȳta* KITE + *lēah* wood, clearing. This may be identical with *Kitley* in Devon.

Kitell see KETTLE

Kitlee see KEIGHLEY

Kitschelt see CHRISTIAN

Kjäll see KÄLL

Kjeldsen see KETTLE

Kjell see KÄLL

Klain see KLEIN

Klampfer see KLEMPNER

Klampke see CLEMENT

Klapper 1. German: nickname for a talkative person or gossip, from an agent deriv. of MHG *klappern* to chatter, rattle (an imitative formation). 2. E German: dial. var. of KLEPPER 1. 3. Jewish (Ashkenazic): of uncertain origin, possibly as in 1 above.
Vars. (of 1): **Klappert**. (Of 2 and 3): **Klapperman**.

Klar 1. German: metr. from the female given name *Klara*, *Clara* (see CLAIRE 1 and SINCLAIR). 2. Jewish (Ashkenazic): ornamental name from mod. Ger. *klar* clear.
Vars. (of 2): **Klahr**, **Klarman(n)**; **Klor** (from Yid. *klor*); **Klurman** (from S. Yid. *klur*).
Cpds (of 2): **Klar(s)feld**, **Klorfeld** ('clear field'); **Klurglus** ('clear glass'); **Klarreich** ('clear rich').

Klaus 1. German: from the medieval given name *Klaus*, still popular in mod. Ger., which originated as an aphetic form of *Niklaus* NICHOLAS. There are, or have been, common aphetic pet forms of NICHOLAS in several European languages, for example Russ. *Kolya*, and many of these have given rise to surnames. Those beginning with *C*- are listed at COLL. 2. Jewish (W Ashkenazic): from Yid. *kloyz* small synagogue or house of study, especially one that is restricted to use by some occupational or social group. The surname was taken by a member of such a group. The vocab. word is related to Ger. *Kloster* monastery; see KLOSTERMANN.
Vars. (of 1): **Klais**, **Kleis**, KLEIST, **Kles(s)**, **Klesse**, **Klus(s)**, **Klöss**, **Klaffs**; **Clausius** (Latinized). (Of 2): **Klausner**, **Kloisner**, **Klousner**.
Dims. (of 1): Ger.: **Kleisel**, **Kleisle**, **Kles(e)l**, **Klessel**, **Klössel**; **Kläwi**, **Klewi** (Switzerland). Low Ger.: **Klassmann**, **Klessmann**, **Klossmann**; **Klag(g)e**, **Klageman**, **Klamman**. Ger. (of Slav. origin): **Kollaschek**, **Klossek**, **Klos(k)a**. Czech: **Kulík**; **Kulíček**, **Kulíšek**.
Patrs. (from 1): Ger.: **Klaiser**, **Kleiser**, **Klös(s)er**, **Kloser**. Low Ger.: **Klaus(s)en**, **Kla(e)sen**, **Claus(s)en**, **Cla(a)sen**, **Classen**, **Klasing**. Fris.: **Klazenenga**. Flem.: **Claesen**, **Claessens**. Du.: **Kla(a)sen**, **Klaassen**, **Claasens**, **Claesens**. Dan.: **Klausen**, **Clausen**. Swed.: **Kla(e)sson**, **Cla(e)sson**. Ger. (of Slav. origin): **Klausewitz**, **Clausewitz**; **Koscher**. Russ.: **Kolyagin**, **Kolin**, **Kolushev**. Croatian: **Kolaković**.
Patrs. (from dims. of 1): Ger.: **Klaves**, **Klebes** (Switzerland). Low Ger.: **Klösges**, **Klag(g)es**. Flem.: **Claeskens**.
Habitation names: Pol.: **Kołakowski**, **Kolczyński**. Czech: **Kolinský**.

Klayman Jewish (E Ashkenazic): possibly an occupational name for a maker of glue, from E Yid. *kley*, Pol. *klej*, or Russ. *klei* glue + *man* man.
Vars.: **Klaiman**, **Klajman**, **Kleiman**.

Klebes *see* KLAUS

Klečák Czech: nickname for a lame man, from a deriv. of OCzech *klecavý* lame (cogn. with Pol. *kulawy*, mod. Czech *kulhavý*).

Var.: **Klečka**.

Dims.: Pol.: **Kulawczyk**, **Kulawik**.

Habitation name: Pol.: **Kulawiński**.

Klee German: apparently from MHG *klē* clover (OHG *klēo*), possibly a topographic name for someone who lived near a field of clover, a nickname of uncertain application, or a metonymic occupational name for someone who grew clover to feed cattle.

Vars.: **Kle(e)man** (see also CLEMENT).

Kleeman *see* CLEMENT

Kleiman *see* KLAYMAN

Klein German, Dutch, and Jewish (Ashkenazic): nickname for a small man, from Ger., Du. *klein* small, Yid. *kleyn* (MHG, MDu. *kleine*, OHG *kleini*, OSax. *klēni*; cogn. with OE *clæne* pure, mod. Eng. *clean*).

Vars.: Ger.: **Kleiner(t)**, **Kleint**; **Klei(n)mann**. Du.: **Kle(i)ne**, **Kl(e)ijn**, **Kl(e)yn**. Jewish: **Kleiner**, **Klein(er)man**; **Klain(er)**, **Klainman**; **Kline(r)**, **Klyne**, **Cline**, **CLYNE** (Anglicized); see also KATAN.

Patrs.: Du.: **Kleynen**, **Kleynermans**. Flem.: **Clynmans**.

Cpds: Jewish (it is hard to tell which are ornamental, which anecdotal, based on some minor incident, and which descriptive or topographic): **Kleinbaum** ('small tree'); **Kleinberg(er)** ((dweller by a) small hill'); **Kleinfeld** ('small field'); **Kleingrub** ('small pit', probably topographic); **Kleinhaus** ('small house', topographic); **Kleinhaut** ('small skin'); **Kleinholz** ('small wood'); **Kleinmintz**, **Kleinmuntz** ('small coin'); **Kleinpeltz** ('small pelt'); **Kleinplatz**, **Kleinplac** ('small place'); **Kleinsinger** ('small singer'); **Kleinstein** ('small stone', ornamental); **Kleinstub** ('small room'); **Kleinstern** ('small star', ornamental); **Kleinzweig** ('small twig', ornamental).

Kleinhändler Jewish (Ashkenazic): occupational name for a retail dealer, i.e. a shopkeeper rather than a merchant, mod. Ger. *Kleinhändler* (lit. 'small trader').

Var.: **Kleinhendler**.

Kleinlerer Jewish (Ashkenazic): occupational name for a teacher of the smallest children in a traditional Jewish elementary school, from Ger. *klein* or Yid. *kleyn* small + Ger. *Lehrer* or Yid. *lerer* teacher.

Kleinschmidt Jewish (Ashkenazic): occupational name for a maker of hand tools, mod. Ger. *Kleinschmidt* (lit. 'small smith').

Kleis *see* KLAUS

Kleist 1. German and Jewish (Ashkenazic): of unknown origin, probably from a habitation name of Slav. etymology. 2. German: var. of KLAUS.

Klemenčić *see* CLEMENT

Klempner N German and Jewish (Ashkenazic): occupational name for a tinker or plumber, an agent deriv. of Ger. *klempern* to clamp, bolt, rivet (of Low Ger. origin, from

klampe clamp, which gradually replaced High Ger. *klampfen*).

Vars.: **Klemperer** (Bavarian). Ger. only: **Klemper(t)**, **Klemptner**; **Klampfer(er)** (Bavaria).

Klepper 1. German: nickname for someone who was under a feudal obligation to provide horses for his lord, from MHG *klepper* horse provided in this way (said to be of imitative origin, from the sound of the hooves). 2. Jewish (Ashkenazic): of uncertain origin, perhaps a var. of KLAPPER 3.

Vars.: (of 1): KLAPPER. (Of 2): **Kleper**.

Klich *see* CLEMENT

Kliegel *see* KLUG

Kliger *see* KLUG

Klijn *see* KLEIN

Klika Czech: apparently from the vocab. word *klika* handle, knob, of uncertain application as a surname. It may be an obscene nickname, with the sense 'penis'.

Var.: **Klik** (altered to masc. gender).

Dim.: **Klička**.

Klincksieck French and German: habitation name from a place in Alsace, of uncertain origin; the first element is probably akin to MHG *klinge* mountain stream (see KLINGE); the second may be akin to MLG *siek* damp, marshy land.

Klinge German: 1. topographic name for someone who lived near a mountain stream, MHG *klinge* (OHG *klinga*, of apparently imitative origin). There are a large number of places named with this word, and the surname may also be a habitation name from any of them. 2. metonymic occupational name for a swordsmith, from MHG *klinge* sword (a later imitative deriv. from the verb *klingen* to ring, clatter).

Vars.: **Kling**, KLINGER, **Klingemann**.

Klinger 1. German: var. of KLINGE. 2. Jewish (Ashkenazic): of unknown origin.

Vars. (of 2): **Klingerman**, **Klingel**, **Kling(man)**; **Clingerman** (an Anglicized spelling). The surnames **Kling(en)stein**, **Klinghof(f)er**, **Klingweil**, and **Klingsberg** may have originated from the combination of this first element with common placename or surname suffixes.

Klöcking *see* KLUG

Klohr *see* HILARY

Kloisner *see* KLAUS

Klonowski Polish: habitation name from a place called *Klonów* (from Pol. *klon* maple tree + *-ów* possessive suffix) + *-ski* suffix of local surnames (see BARANOWSKI).

Var.: **Klonowicz** (patr. in form, perhaps from *klon* used as a nickname; the 16th-cent. Pol. poet Klonowic called himself *Acernus* in Latin).

Klonymus *see* KALMAN

Klopstock German: occupational nickname from MLG *kloppen* to strike, beat (of imitative origin) + *stoc* (tree) stump (see STOCK). The exact meaning of the surname is not clear, since the second element had a variety of technical senses in the crafts of the Middle Ages. One possibility is that it refers to a cutler, who would have made use of a small anvil known by this name in the sharpening of scythes and other instruments which needed their blades honed. The surname is also borne by Ashkenazic Jews, but the reason for its adoption is not certian. It could well be an occupational name for a cutler, which was a not infrequent occupation among Ashkenazic Jews.

Klor *see* KLAR

Kłos Polish: of uncertain origin, perhaps from Pol. *kłos* ear or spike of corn. This could have been a nickname for a small person or else a topographic name for someone living by a cornfield. It is unlikely to be an aphetic form of *Mikołaj* NICHOLAS, for *Kłos* is not recorded as a given name.

Habitation names: **Kłosiński**, **Kłosowski**.

Klostermann German: occupational name for a servant in a monastery or for a lay member of a monastic community, from Ger. *Kloster* monastery (MHG *klōster*, OHG *klōstar*, from LL *clōstrum* monastic cell, from class. L *claustrum* bolt, bar, from *claudere* to close) + *mann* man. The surname may also have denoted someone who farmed land belonging to a monastery and who paid rent in the form of provisions for the monks.

Klotz German and Jewish (Ashkenazic): nickname for a clumsy, awkward man, from Ger. *Klotz* lump, block, or Yid. *klots* (MHG, OHG *klotz*, cogn. with mod. Eng. *clot*, which is similarly used in a transferred sense to denote a stupid person).

Vars.: Ger.: **Klut(h)**. Jewish: **Klots**, **Klotzman(n)**.

Dim.: Ger.: **Klötzel**.

Klouček Czech: nickname for a mischievous, impish person, from Czech *klouček* little boy, imp.

Klöver Low German: occupational name for someone whose job it was to split wood into planks, from MLG *klöven* to cleave, divide (cogn. with OE *clēofan*).

Vars.: **Klöwer**, **Klöber**; **Klüver**, **Klüwer** (also of a court official responsible for placing convicted criminals in the stocks, MLG *kluver*, from *kluven* a slit piece of wood used for this purpose).

Klucznik Polish: occupational or status name for an officer in a manorial or noble household. A *klucznik* was roughly equivalent to a butler; the word is derived from Pol. *klucz* key + *-nik* suffix of agent nouns.

Habitation name: **Kluczyński**.

Klug 1. German: nickname from Eastern MHG *klūc* wise, prudent, or from the Western byform *kluoc*, which had the sense 'noble', 'refined'; both forms probably go back to a single unattested OHG original. 2. Jewish (Ashkenazic): nickname from Ger. *klug* or Yid. *klug* clever, wise.

Vars.: Ger.: **Kluge(r)**; **Glauer(t)**, **Glauber**. Jewish: **Kluger**, **Klugman**; **Kli(e)ger**, **Kli(e)g(er)man** (from a S Yid. pronunication).

Dims.: Ger.: **Klügel**, **Kliegel**.

Patr.: Low Ger.: **Klöcking**.

Klurglus *see* KLAR

Klus *see* KLAUS

Klut *see* KLOTZ

Klüver *see* KLÖVER

Klyn *see* KLEIN

Kmieć Polish: status name for a peasant farmer who had his own land, Pol. *kmieć*.

Var.: **Kmieciak**.

Dim.: Pol.: **Kmiecik**.

Kmoch Czech: from the vocab. word *kmotr* godfather, sponsor (from LL *comater* godmother, from *co-* joint, *co-* + *mater* mother; one of the earliest attested borrowings from Latin in a Slav. language).

Knaggs N English: topographic name for someone who lived by a geographical feature named with the ME word *knagg*, which had various senses, including a stunted dead branch or a jagged crag or outcrop of rock.

Knapp 1. English (chiefly W Country): habitation name from one of the places named with OE *cnæpp* hilltop, of which there are examples in Devon, Hants, and Sussex. It may also be a topographic name from the same word used independently. 2. German: status name for a servant or squire, Ger. *Knappe* (MHG *knappe* boy, lad, OHG *knappo*, a byform of *knabo*, cogn. with OE *cnapa* boy, servant). The surname is also borne by Ashkenazic Jews.

Vars. (of 1): **Knapper**, **Knap(p)man**. (Of 2): Ger.: **Knappe**, **Knab(b)e**.

Dims. (of 2): Ger.: **Knäple**, **Knäble**, **Knable**. Pol.: **Knapik**.

Patrs. (from 2): Ger.: **Knabben**. Flem., Du.: **Kna(e)pen**.

Knapton English (Yorks.): habitation name from one of two places in Yorks., so called from OE *cnapa* boy, servant (perhaps used as a personal name) + *tūn* enclosure, settlement.

Knatchbull English: occupational nickname for a slaughterer and butcher, from ME *knatch(en)*, *knetch(en)* to fell, knock on the head (a byform of *knack(en)*, from Low Ger. or Du.) + *bull* BULL.

Knauer *see* KNORR

Knaus German: 1. nickname for a haughty person, from MHG *knūz* proud, contemptuous (no OHG form is recorded, but the word may nevertheless be akin to OE *cnēatian* to quarrel). 2. topographic name for someone living on a hillock, from *knaus* hillock in the Swabian and Alemannic dialects of German.

Dims.: **Knäusle**, **Kneisel**, **Kneiss(e)l**, **Kneussel**.

Kneale *see* NEIL

Knee *see* NEE

Kneebone English (Devon and Cornwall): of uncertain origin, perhaps in part a nickname for someone with knobbly knees, but probably also in part an alteration by folk etymology of a habitation name from *Carnebone* in the parish of Wendron, Cornwall. The placename is first recorded in 1298 as *Carnebwen*, from Corn. *carn* pile of rocks (cf. CAIRNS) + a second element of uncertain form and meaning.

Knef German: metonymic occupational name for a shoe-maker, from MLG *knīf* (shoemaker's) knife (a cogn. of OE *cnīf*).

Vars.: **Knief**, **Kneif**, **Kneip(p)**, **Kniep(e)**, **Knieper**, **Kneib**.

Kneisel *see* KNAUS

Knell *see* KNILL

Kneller 1. German: nickname for a raucous or disruptive person, from an agent deriv. of MHG *knellen* to make a noise, cause a rumpus. The mod. Ger. slang word *Kneller*, meaning 'poor-quality tobacco', is unlikely to be relevant to the surname. 2. Jewish (Ashkenazic): occupational name for a teacher in a traditional Jewish elementary school, Yid. *kneler*. Cf. KINDERLEHRER. 2. English: var. of KNILL.

Var. (of 2): **Kneler**.

Knepel *see* KNOPF

Knevet *see* KNIGHT

Knežević *see* KNÍE

Knief *see* KNEF

Knight English: status name from ME *knyghte* knight, OE *cniht* boy, youth, serving lad. This word was used as a personal name before the Norman Conquest, and the surname may in part reflect a survival of this. It is also possible that in a few cases it represents a survival of the OE sense into ME, as an occupational name for a domestic servant. In most cases, however, it clearly comes from the more exalted sense that the word achieved in the Middle Ages. In the feudal system introduced by the Normans the word was applied at first to a tenant bound to serve his lord as a mounted soldier. Hence it came to denote a man of some substance, since maintaining horses and armour was an expensive business. As feudal obligations became increasingly converted to monetary payments, the term lost its precise significance and came to denote an honourable estate conferred by the king on men of noble birth who had served him well. Knights in this last sense normally belonged to ancient noble families with distinguished family names of their own, so that the surname is more likely to have been applied to a servant in a knightly house or to someone who had played the part of a knight in a pageant or won the title in some contest of skill.

Vars.: **Knevet(t)**, **Knivit**, **Knivett**, **Knyvett**, **Nevet**, **Nevitt** (reflecting the ANF pronunciation).

Patr.: Eng.: **Knights** (chiefly Norfolk).

Knightley English: habitation name from any of various places, for example in Staffs., so called from OE *cnihtā*, gen. pl. of *cniht* servant, retainer + *lēah* wood, clearing.

Var.: **Knightly**.

Knighton English: habitation name from any of the numerous places named with OE *cnihta*, gen. pl. of *cniht* servant, retainer + *tūn* enclosure, settlement.

Vars.: **Knighten**, **Nighton**.

Knill English: topographic name for someone who lived on a hillock, from OE *cnyll*, a byform of *cnoll* (see KNOLL and KNOWLES).

Vars.: **Knyll**, **Knell**, **Knull**; KNELLER.

Knipe N Irish: habitation name from a place in the former county of Ayrs., Scotland, so called from Gael. *cnap* hill-(ock) (akin to OE *cnæpp*; see KNAPP).

Kníže Czech: nickname meaning 'Prince', Czech *kníže* (ultimately cogn. with Ger. *Knecht* boy, young man, and with Eng. KNIGHT).

Dim.: **Kníěk**.

Patr.: Croatian: **Knežević**.

Knobloch German: metonymic occupational name for a grower and seller of garlic, from a dissimilated form of MHG *klobelouch* (mod. Ger. *Knoblauch*). The word is a cpd. of the elements *klob*- split (cf. KLÖVER) + *louch* leek.

Vars.: **Knoblich**, **Knoflach**; **Knopfloch** (Bavaria).

Knochenhauer Low German: occupational name for a butcher, from MLG *knocke* bone + *houwen* to cut, chop (see HAUER).

Knockton *see* NAUGHTON

Knödel *see* KNOTT

Knoll English: 1. topographic name for someone who lived at the top of a hill, OE *cnoll*, or habitation name from one of the many places named with this word. 2. from an OE byname of the same origin, denoting a short, stout person.

Vars. (of 1): **Knowl(d)er**, **Knowlman**.

Knopf German and Jewish (Ashkenazic): metonymic occupational name for a maker of buttons, normally of horn, from Ger. *Knopf* button (MHG, OHG *knopf*, like other words in *kn*- originally descriptive of a swelling or lump). The Ger. surname may also be a nickname for a small, rotund man or a topographic name for someone who lived by a rounded hillock.

Vars. (all occupational): Ger.: **Knöpfler**; **Knöfler** (Bavaria). Jewish: **Knopfler**; **Knepler** (from Yid. *knepl* button); **Knop(f)macher**, **Knopfelmacher** ('button maker').

Dims.: Ger.: **Knöpfel**, **Knöpfle**, **Knöpfli** (Switzerland); **Knöf(f)el** (Bavaria). Jewish: **Knopl**, **Knep(p)el**. Low Ger.: **Knöpken**.

Knorr 1. German: metonymic nickname for a hunchback or someone with some other bodily protuberance, from MHG *knorre* lump, outgrowth (mod. Ger. *Knorren* knot in a piece of wood). The word is not attested in OHG but is presumably of native origin, belonging in the same group as other nouns beginning with *kn*-. 2. German: topographic name for someone who lived by a small hill or mound, from the same word used in a transferred sense. 3. English: habitation name from *Knarr* Farm and Lake in Cambs., in which the element in question appears to be a cogn. of that in 2.

Vars.: Ger.: **Knorn**, **Knör(r)e**. (Of 2 only): Ger.: **Knauer(t)**, **Knür** (from the byform *knūr*).

Dims. (of 2): Ger.: **Knörndl**; **Knürle**.

Knotek Czech: from Czech *knotek* 'little knot or tangle' (from *knot* knot, tangle + the dim. suffix -*ek*), applied as a nickname either to someone with a tangle of hair or to a dwarf or person of stunted growth.

Knott 1. English: nickname for a lumpish, thickset person, from OE *cnotta* knot, lump, swelling (another member of the large group of Gmc words in *kn*- with related meanings). 2. English: topographic name for someone who lived by a hillock or projecting rock, from ME *knot* hillock (apparently from the same OE source as in 1). **3.** English: from the ON personal name *Knútr*, originally a byname cogn. with 1. This given name became popular in England in the reign of the Danish king Canute (1016–35), and was still in regular use in the 13th cent. **4.** Jewish (Ashkenazic): Anglicization of one or more like-sounding Jewish surnames.

Dims. (of 1 and 2): Ger.: **Knötel**, **Knödel**. Low Ger.: **Knödgen**.

Patrs. (from 3): Eng.: **Knotts(on)**. Dan., Norw.: **Knudsen**.

Swed.: **Knutsson**. Finn.: **Nuutinen**.

Knowles English: **1.** topographic name for someone who lived at the top of a hill, from a gen. or pl. form of ME *knol* (see KNOLL 1). **2.** patr. from the same word used as a byname for a short, stout person (see KNOLL 2).

Vars.: **Knollys**, **Nowles**. (Of 2 only): **Knowlson**; **Knowling**.

Knox Scots, N English, and N Irish: topographic name for someone who lived on a hilltop, from a gen. or pl. form of OE *cnocc* round-topped hill, or habitation name from one of the places called *Knock* in Scotland and N England, in particular one in the former county of Renfrews. The surname is also borne by E Ashkenazic Jews as an Anglicization of one or more like-sounding Jewish surnames.

Vars.: **Knock(er)**.

Dim.: Ger.: **Nöckl**.

Knuckey Cornish: probably a habitation name from *Kenneggy* in the parish of Breage, *Kenegie* in the parish of Gulval, or *Keneggy* in the parish of Kenwyn, all so called from Corn. **keunegy*, pl. of *keunek* reed-bed, marsh.

Knudsen *see* KNOTT

Knull *see* KNILL

Knür *see* KNORR

Knyll *see* KNILL

Knyvett *see* KNIGHT

Kob *see* JACOB

Koblenz Jewish (Ashkenazic) and German: local name from the city of *Koblenz*, situated at the confluence of the Rhine and Mosel. It was founded in 9 BC as a Roman town with the L name of *Confluentes* (*fluvii*) 'confluent rivers', from which the modern name derives. The surname is to a large extent Jewish and has been carried into a number of European languages, where it has been variously spelled.

Vars.: Jewish: **Koblentz**, **Coblen(t)z**; **Koblenc** (a Pol. spelling); **Koblence**, **Coblence**, **Coblance**, **Caublance** (Fr. spellings); **Koblenzer** ('native or inhabitant of Koblenz').

Köbler German: topographic name for someone who lived in a crude or temporary hut, or occupational name for a keeper of animals, an agent deriv. of S Ger. dial. *Kobel* little hut, shelter, or stall (from MHG *kobe* stall, shelter; not attested in OHG, but probably akin to mod. Eng. *cover*).

Vars.: **Kobler** (also borne by Ashkenazic Jews); **Kobel(mann)**.

Kobyłecki Polish: habitation name from a place named from Pol. *kobyła* mare, with addition of the surname suffix *-ski* (see BARANOWSKI).

Vars.: **Kobyłański**, **Kobyliński**.

Kočarek *see* KOCSIS

Koch 1. German: occupational name for a cook, from Ger. *Koch* COOK (MHG *koch*, OHG *choc*, from L *coquus*). **2.** Czech: altered form of any of several obsolete personal names beginning with *Ko-*, for example *Kocián*, *Kojata*, and *Kosmas*. **3.** Jewish (Ashkenazic): of unknown origin.

Vars. (of 1): **Kocher**, **Kochmann**.

Dim. (of 1): **Köchle**.

Kochanek Polish: nickname from Pol. *kochanek* darling, dear (from *kochać* to love), used as a term of address. Prince Karol Stanisław Radziwiłł (1734–90) was generally known as 'Panie Kochanku' (vocative), presumably because he habitually addressed others in this way. In other cases, the word may have been applied as a nickname to a good-looking or amorous man.

Vars.: **Kochaniak**, **Kochański**.

Patr.: **Kochanowicz**.

Habitation name: **Kochanowski**.

Köchel German: habitation name from any of the numerous minor places in Bavaria and the Tyrol that get their names from *Köchel*, a dial. term, of uncertain etymology, said by Bahlow to denote an island of raised land surrounded by marsh.

Vars.: **Köchl(er)**.

Kochetov Russian: patr. from the ORuss. nickname *Kochet* 'Cock', a byform of *kokot*. Both words, which are of imitative origin, from the clucking of farmyard fowls, have been replaced in mod. Russ. by *petukh* (a deriv. of *pet* to sing).

Var.: **Kogutov**.

Dims.: Pol.: **Kokoszko**, **Kokoszka**. Czech: **Kohoutek**, **Kokoška**. Ger. (of Slav. origin): **Kakosch**, **Kakuschke**, **Kokosch(k)a**. Jewish: **Kokotek**, **Kokutak**.

Kociszewski *see* CATT

Kocks *see* COOK

Kocourek *see* CATT

Kocsis Hungarian: occupational name for a coachman, from Hung. *kocsi* coach, which is from the placename *Kocs*, the village where in the 16th cent. coaches were were first made, with the addition of the adjectival ending *-i*. Mod. Eng. *coach* and Fr. *coche* are derived from this Hung. word, as well as Ger. *Kutsche* and Czech *kočí*.

Dim.: Czech: **Kočarek**.

Kodat *see* NIKODÉM

Koefoed *see* KOFOED

Koekemoer Low German and Dutch: habitation name from a place in Westphalia, which probably gets its name from elements meaning 'frog' + 'marsh', 'moor'.

Koenen *see* KONRAD

Koeppe *see* JACOB

Kofoed Danish: uncomplimentary nickname from the elements *ko* cow (ON *kýr*) + *fod* foot (ON *fótr*).

Vars.: **Koefoed**, **Kofod**.

Kofroň Czech: nickname for someone who talked about things that he did not really understand. The word is derived from the placename *Gafron* in Polish Silesia, whose inhabitants had such a reputation.

Var.: **Kofrň**.

Dim.: **Kofránek**.

Kogan *see* COHEN

Kogel 1. Low German: metonymic occupational name for a maker of hoods or nickname for a habitual wearer of a distinctive hood, from MLG *kogel* hood (LL *cuculla*). 2. S German: topographic name from the dial. word *kogel* mountain top. 3. Jewish (Ashkenazic): of unknown origin.

Vars. (of 1): **Kagel(mann)**; **Kogler**, **Kögler**, **Kag(e)ler** (occupational names).

Kogen *see* COHEN

Kogutov *see* KOCHETOV

Kohaner *see* COHEN

Kohl German: metonymic occupational name for a grower or seller of cabbages, from Ger. *Kohl* cabbage (OHG *chōlo*, *kōl(i)*, cogn. with L *caulis* stalk; cf. OF *chol* cabbage).

Var.: Swiss Ger.: **Köhl**.

Dims.: Fr.: **Chol(l)et**, **Chollez**, **Cholley**, **Cholé**, **Choulet**, **Choleau**, **Chol(a)in**, **Cholot**, **Choloux**.

Collective: Cat.: **Colet**.

Köhn *see* KONRAD

Kohoutek *see* KOCHETOV

Kohrts *see* COURT

Koivisto Finnish: ornamental or topographic name meaning 'birch wood', from Finn. *koivo* birch tree + the collective suffix *-isto*.

Kokkonen Finnish: patr. from the OFinn. personal name *Kokko*, a deriv. of the vocab. word *kotka* eagle.

Kokoscha *see* KOCHETOV

Kołacz Polish: metonymic occupational name for a fancy baker, from Pol. *kołacz* a kind of sweet loaf in which the dough has been twisted into an ornamental shape. Loaves of this kind of bread were eaten especially at weddings.

Var.: **Kołacki**.

Kolaković *see* KLAUS

Kolasa Polish: 1. metonymic occupational name for a coachman, from Pol. *kolasa* carriage. 2. perhaps also an aphetic derivative of *Mikołaj* NICHOLAS.

Habitation name: **Kolasiński**.

Kolijn *see* COLL

Kollman *see* KALMAN

Kołodziej Polish: occupational name for a wheelwright, Pol. *kołodziej*, from *koło* wheel.

Var.: **Kołodziejski**.

Dims.: Pol.: **Kołodziejczyk**. Czech: **Kolařík**.

Patr.: Pol.: **Kołodziejczak**.

Komarov Russian: patr. from the nickname *Komar* 'Gnat', 'Mosquito', originally given perhaps to a small and insignificant person or to an irritating one.

Dim.: Czech: **Komárek**.

Komorowski Polish: habitation name for a cottager or tenant, from Pol. *komora* hut, cottage (cf. *komorne* rent), + *-ów* possessive suffix + *-ski* suffix of local surnames (see BARANOWSKI).

Konarski Polish: 1. occupational name for a horse-breeder or for someone who worked with horses, i.e. a groom or ostler, Pol. *koniarz* (from *koń* horse) + the surname suffix *-ski* (see BARANOWSKI). 2. habitation name from the town of *Konary* near Sandomierz, or from some other place similarly named. The placename is likewise derived from *koń* horse or *koniarz* groom.

Dims. (of 1): Czech: **Koňarík**, **Konárek**.

Habitation names: Pol.: **Konarowski**, **Konarzewski**.

Kondić *see* CONSTANTINE

Kondratyev Russian: patr. from the given name *Kondrati*. This is officially derived from Gk *Kodratos* (from L *Quadrātus*; see CARRÉ), which was acceptable as a baptismal name in the eyes of the Orthodox Church because it was the name of several early saints. However, the *-n-* can only be explained by derivation from the Gmc name KONRAD (Pol. *Kondrat*); there has clearly been some confusion between the two names. In the Russ. name, the final *-i* is an example of hypercorrection; it was added after the pattern of Gk names in *-ios*, which lost the vowel in the popular forms but retained it in a learned form.

Var.: **Kondratov**.

Dims.: **Kondrakov**, **Kondrushkin**, **Kondrashov**, **Kondryukhov**, **Kand(r)eev**, **Kondrichev** (all patrs.).

'Son of the wife of K. (dim.)': **Kondrashikhin**.

Kondzyereyonok *see* KUDRAVTSEV

Köngeter *see* KENNGOTT

Konieczny Polish: from the Pol. adj. *konieczny* necessary, although the application is not clear. It may be a status name for someone with 'great expectations', from the expression *dziedzic konieczny* heir apparent.

Vars.: **Skon(i)eczny**, **Skonieczka**, **Skonieczko** (by mis-division).

König 1. German: cogn. of KING. 2. Jewish (Ashkenazic): name chosen as a translation of the Yid. male given names *Meylekh* (from Hebr. *Melech* 'King') and *Elemeylekh* (from Hebr. *Elimelech* 'God is my king'), or an ornamental name, one of several such Ashkenazic surnames based on European titles of nobility or royalty (cf. GRAF, HERZOG, FÜRST, and KAISER).

Var.: Jewish: **Kinig** (from Yid. *kinig*).

Dim.: Jewish: **Kinigel** (alternatively this may be from Yid. *kinigl* rabbit; cf. KROLIKOV).

Patrs.: Flem.: **Conings**, **Conin(ck)x**. Du.: **Konings**. Jewish: **Kinigson**.

Cpds (ornamental elaborations): Jewish: **Kinigstein**; KÖNIGSBERG.

Königsberg 1. Jewish (Ashkenazic) and German: local name from the city of *Königsberg*, former capital of E Prussia, which gets its name from MHG *künigesberc* 'hill of the king', i.e. of King Ottokar II of Bohemia, who founded the city in 1255. It is now in the Soviet Union and called *Kaliningrad*. **2.** Jewish (Ashkenazic): ornamental elaboration of KÖNIG.

Vars.: Jewish: **Konigsberger**; **Kin(i)gsberg**, GINSBERG.

Konopka Polish: nickname meaning 'linnet', perhaps denoting an individual noted for his cheerful singing.

Konovalov Russian: patr. from the occupational term *konoval* horse doctor (a cpd of *kon* horse + *valyat* to throw, i.e. castrate).

Dims.: Beloruss.: **Konoval(ch)ik**, **Konovalyuk**.

Konrad German: from a Gmc personal name composed of the elements *kuoni* daring, brave + *rad* counsel, which has probably fallen together with an originally distinct name in which the first element was *kuni* race, people. The given name was extremely popular during the Middle Ages, being a hereditary name in several ruling families and also widely adopted by the people at large; the expression *Hinz und Kunz* (short forms of HENRY and Konrad) was the Ger. equivalent of 'every Tom, Dick, and Harry'. The surname is also borne by Ashkenazic Jews, presumably as an adoption of the Ger. surname.

Vars.: **Kunrad**, **Ku(h)nert**, **Kundert** (Switzerland); **Kuhnhardt** (with the second element altered to the more common *hard* hardy, brave, strong); **Keinrat** (altered by folk etymology to 'no counsel'); **Kuhnt**, **Kundt**, **Kurt(h)**.

Dims.: Ger.: **Kuhn**, **Kühn(e)**, **Kühn(d)el**; **Kiehne(lt)**, **Kien(d)l**, **Kien(z)le**, **Kienlein** (Austria); **Kienle** (Swabia); **Kaindl**, **Kainz** (Tyrol); **Kunz(e)**, **Künzel(mann)**, **Kin(t)zel**, **Konzel(mann)**, **Kull(mann)**. Low Ger.: **Cohr**; **Keune(ke)**, **Keunemann**, **Keuntje**, **Kö(h)n(e)(ke)**, **Könneke**, **Künneke**, **Kö(h)n(e)mann**. Du.: **Koene**, **Keune**. Ger. (of Slav. origin): **Kuhnke**, **Kunisch**. Czech: **Kuna**, **Kuneš**; **Kunc** (from the Ger. pet form *Kunz*); **Kyncl** (from the Ger. pet form *Künzl*). Ukr.: **Kondratenko**, **Kondratyuk**. Beloruss.: **Kondratenya**, **Kondrachenko**. It.: **Corradetti**, **Corradini**, **Corradino**; **Corain(i)** (Venetia). Hung.: **Gunda**.

Patrs.: Ger.: **Kürten**. Low Ger.: **Konertz**, **Coners**, **Konerding**, **Conerding**, **Conring**, **Ko(h)rding**, **Körting**; **Kordes**, **Cordes**; **Cordsen**, **Corssen**. Flem.: **Coenraets**. Dan.: **Conradsen**. Pol.: **Kondratowicz**. Ukr., Beloruss.: **Kondratovich**. It.: **Corradengo** (Liguria); **Corradeschi** (Tuscany).

Patrs. (from dims.): Ger.: **Künzler**, **Kiezler**. Low Ger.: **Kohnen**, **Köhnen**; **Kohrs**, **Cohrs**, **Kohrsen**, **Köhring**. Du., Flem.: **Koenen**, **Keuning**. Ger. (of Slav. origin): **Kunat(h)**.

Koomans see CHAPMAN

Koop see JACOB

Kooper see COOPER

Kooy Dutch: topographic name for someone who lived by a pen or fold where animals were confined, MDu. *kooy*.

Vars.: **Kooyman**, **Kooi(j)(man)**, **Van (der) Kooi**.

Kop see JACOB

Kopčić see PROKOP

Kopczyński Polish: topographic or habitation name from Pol. *kopczyk* hillock, mound (from *kopa* hill; cogn. with Czech *kopec*), with the addition of *-ski*, suffix of local surnames (see BARANOWSKI).

Vars.: **Kopacki**; **Kopka**.

Kopeć Polish: from OPol. *kopeć* smoke, soot, given perhaps as a nickname to a dirty or swarthy person or to someone who lived in a smoky place, or alternatively perhaps used as an occupational nickname for a chimneysweep.

Dim.: Czech: **Koptik**.

Koper Polish: topographic name from Pol. *koper* dill, fennel, or perhaps an occupational name for a grower or seller of dill or fennel.

Var.: **Koperski**.

Dim.: **Kopernik**.

Habitation name: **Koprowski**.

Kopf **1.** German: metonymic occupational name for a maker or seller of cups or flasks, from MHG *kopf* flask (from LL *cuppa* cask; cf. COOPER). **2.** German: metonymic nickname for someone with some noticeable peculiarity or deformity of the head, from Ger. *Kopf*, the same word as in 1, used in a transferred sense which during the Middle Ages gradually ousted the earlier word *Haupt* (see HEAD). **3.** Jewish (Ashkenazic): from Ger. *Kopf* head, the reasons for its adoption being unclear, but probably as in 2.

Var. (of 3): **Kopman** (from Yid. *kop* head).

Dims. (of 1 and 2): Ger.: **Köpfel**, **Köpfle**, **Köppel**.

Cpds (of 3): **Kopstein** ('head stone', presumably an ornamental elaboration); **Kopfstein** (either an ornamental elaboration or from Ger. *Kopfstein* cobblestone, and so perhaps an anecdotal surname based on some now irrecoverable minor incident).

Kopka see COPP

Kopřiva Czech: from Czech *kopřiva* nettle, presumably either a topographic name or a nickname for a person with a prickly temperament.

Koralyov see KRÓL

Kořán Czech: metonymic occupational name for a herbalist or seller of herbs and spices, from S Czech dial. *kořán* root (cf. Czech *koření* (pl.) spices, Pol. *korzenie*).

Dim.: Czech: **Kořánek**.

Korb **1.** German: metonymic occupational name for a basket-maker, from Ger. *Korb* basket (MHG *korb*, OHG *churp*, from L *corbis*; cf. CORBEIL). **2.** German: metonymic occupational name for a pedlar who carried his goods around in a basket, from the same word as in 1. **3.** Jewish (Ashkenazic): of uncertain origin, probably as in 1 and 2.

Vars.: Ger.: **Körb(l)er**, **Kerb(l)er**, **Kreber**. Jewish: **Korber**; **Korf(f)**, **Korfman(n)**.

Dims.: Ger.: **Körbel**, **Korbel**. Low Ger.: **Korfgen**.

Patrs.: Low Ger.: **Körfers**. (Of 1 only): Flem., Du.: **Korfmakers**.

Korda Czech: from a pet form of the OCzech given name *Kornel* Cornelius (see CORNEILLE 1).

Var.: **Kordač**.

Dim.: **Kordík**.

Kordes see KONRAD

Korecky Czech and Jewish (Ashkenazic): apparently a topographic name for someone living by a watermill, from Czech *koreček* in the dial. sense 'overshot watermill', from Czech *korec* bucket, container.

Var.: **Koreček**.

Korejs *see* CORNEILLE

Körfers *see* KORB

Korhonen Finnish: patr. from the nickname *Korho* 'Deaf'. This is the fourth commonest Finn. surname, so presumably some metaphor is involved in the acquisition of the surname, as deafness is not a noticeably more common affliction in Finland than elsewhere.

Kořínek Czech: nickname for a man with a ruddy, healthy complexion, Czech *kořínek*.

Korland *see* KURLAND

Korn 1. German: metonymic occupational name for a factor or dealer in grain, from Ger. *Korn* grain (MHG, OHG *korn*). 2. Jewish (Ashkenazic): metonymic occupational name as in 1, or ornamental name from Ger. *Korn* grain, Yid. *korn*. 3. Czech: from a short form of the OCzech given name *Kornel* Cornelius (see CORNEILLE 1).

Vars. (of 1): **Körner**, **Kor(ne)mann**.

Dims. (of 1): **Körn(d)le**.

Cpds (of 2; ornamental except where otherwise stated): **Kornberg** ('grain hill'); **Kornblatt**, **Kornblitt** ('grain blossom'); **Kornblau** ('grain blue'); **Kornblum(e)** ('grain flower'); **Kornfein** ('fine as grain'); **Kornfeld** ('grain field', partly Anglicized as **Kornfield**, **Cornfeld**; fully Anglicized as **Cornfield**,); **Korngold** ('grain gold'); **Korngruen** ('grain green'); **Kornhaber** ('grain oats'); **Kornhauser** ((owner of or worker in) a granary', occupational); **Kornhendler** ('grain merchant', occupational); **Kornmehl** ('grain flour', probably occupational for a grain merchant); **Kornreich** ('rich in grain'); **Kornstein** ('grain stone'); **Kornwasser** ('grain water'); **Kornweiss** ('grain white'); **Kornweitz** ('grain wheat'); **Kornzweig** ('grain twig').

Korostelyov Russian: patr. from the nickname *Korostel* 'Landrail' (allegedly of imitative origin).

Var.: **Korostylyov**.

Korotygin Russian: patr. from the nickname *Korotyga* 'Shorty', a deriv. of *korotky* short (ultimately cogn. with L *curtus*; see COURT 2).

Vars.: **Karatygin** (reflecting the actual pronunciation of the unstressed vowels); **Korotkikh** (gen. pl. of the adj.); **Korotky** (apparently nom. sing. of the adj., probably of Ukr. or Beloruss. origin).

Korovnikov Russian: patr. from the occupational term *korovnik* cowherd (a deriv. of *korova* cow).

Korsakov Russian: patr. from the nickname *Korsak* 'Steppe Fox' (a word borrowed from a Turkic language).

Körschkes *see* CHRISTIAN

Körschner *see* KÜRSCHNER

Korst *see* CHRISTIAN

Korts *see* COURT

Kortwright *see* CARTWRIGHT

Kos 1. Czech: nickname from Czech *kos* blackbird. Blackbirds had a reputation for being cunning and devious, even devilish, so the nickname would have been used to refer to a smart or unscrupulous person. The related adj. *kusý*, meaning 'bob-tailed', was likewise applied to the devil. 2. Jewish: of unknown origin. The explanation given in 1 may apply here, or the name may be from Hebr. *kos* (drinking) glass or Yid. *kos* goblet, cup. In the latter case, the surname is probably an anecdotal nickname based on some now irrecoverable minor incident, an assumption supported by the fact that the name is rare. The Ashkenazic surname **Kosman**, on the other hand, is more frequent, and this suggests that it is probably a metonymic occupational name referring to someone who made glasses or cups.

Vars. (of 1): **Kosa**, **Kus**, **Kůs**.

Dim. (of 1): Czech: **Kosík**.

Habitation name: Pol.: **Kosiński**.

Kosch *see* JACOB

Köschges *see* CHRISTIAN

Kościelski Polish: topographic name for someone who lived near a church, from Pol. *kościół* church, with the addition of *-ski*, suffix of local surnames (see BARANOWSKI).

Koskinen Finnish: ornamental name from Finn. *koski* waterfall, rapids + the gen. suffix *-nen*. This was one of the many words for natural features that were used in the formation of Finn. surnames when these became obligatory during the 18th and 19th cents.

Vars.: **Koski**, **Koskela**.

Koslofsky *see* KOZLOV

Kosmala Polish: nickname for a shaggy, unkempt individual, from a deriv. of Pol. *kosmaty* shaggy, hairy.

Var.: **Kosmalski**.

Kosmin *see* KUZMIN

Košnář Czech: occupational name for a basket-maker, from Czech *koš* basket + *-(n)ář* suffix of occupational names.

Vars.: **Koš(n)ar**.

Kosorotov Russian: patr. from the nickname *Kosoroty* 'Wry-mouthed', a deriv. of *kosoi* twisted, awry + *rot* mouth.

Kössler *see* KESSEL

Kost *see* CONSTANTINE

Košťál Czech: apparently from Czech *kost'a* spike, perhaps a nickname for a person of tall and spiky appearance.

Var.: **Košťák**.

Dim.: **Košťálek**.

Kosters *see* KÜSTER

Köstner *see* KASTNER

Kostrzewa Polish: topographic name for someone who lived by a meadow, from Pol. *kostrzewa* meadow grass, fescue, from *kostra* spike (cogn. with Czech *kost'a* spike).

Var.: **Kostrzewski**.

Kosygin Russian: patr. from the nickname *Kosyga* 'Deformed', a deriv. of *kosoi* twisted, crippled, cross-eyed.

Kot'átko *see* CATT

Kotliński Polish: topographic name for someone living in a dale, Pol. *kotlina*, with the addition of *-ski*, suffix of local surnames (see BARANOWSKI).

Var.: **Kotlicki**.

Kotrba Czech: metonymic nickname for someone with a noticeably large or deformed head, or possibly used as a nickname for a headstrong person, from Czech *kotrba* head, skull.

Var.: **Kotrbatý**.

Kotrč Czech: from the vocab. word *kotrč* stick (which had various specialized senses, including 'rudder on a raft'). According to Moldanová, this word was used as a nickname for a small person around Sušice in S Bohemia.

Var.: **Kotrc**.

Koubek *see* JACOB

Koudela Czech: apparently a metonymic occupational name for someone who unravelled old rope to make tow, from *koudel* oakum, tow, or else a nickname for someone with tow-coloured hair. According to Moldanová, however, in Olomouc this is a slang word for a blockhead, and so it may well be a derogatory nickname with this meaning.

Kough *see* KEOGH

Koukenheim *see* GUGGENHEIM

Koutský Czech: topographic name for someone who lived on a corner (from Czech *kout* corner + *-ský* suffix of local surnames), or habitation name from one of the places named with this element. In some cases it also denoted the keeper of a corner shop, and so is an equiv. of Ger. WINCKEL.

Vars.: **Koucký**, **Kautský**, **Kaucký**; **Kout(ný)**; **Koutník**.
Dims.: **Koutek**, **Koutecký**.

Kovac *see* KOWALSKI

Kovanda Czech: nickname meaning 'trueborn', applied to a person of good breeding.

Kowalski Polish and Jewish (E Ashkenazic): occupational name for a blacksmith, Pol. *kowal* (from *kować*, *kuć* to forge, akin to ORuss. *kuzn* forged work; see KUZNETSOV), with the addition of *-ski*, suffix of surnames (see BARANOWSKI).

Vars.: **Kowal**. Jewish only: **Koval(ski)**, **Kovalsky**, **Kowalsky**; **Kovel(man)** (from E Yid. *kovl* smith); **Kovac(s)** (among Hungarian Jews).

Dims.: Pol.: **Kowalczyk**, **Kowalik**. Ukr.: **Kovanko**. Beloruss.: **Kovalyonok**, **Kovalenya**; **Kovalchuk**. Czech: **Kovářík**, **Kováříček**. Ger. (of Slav. origin): **Kowalke**.

Patrs.: Pol.: **Kowalewicz**. Beloruss.: **Kovalevich**. Croatian: **Kovač(ev)ić**, **Ković**. Jewish: **Kowaloff**, **Kowlowitz**.

Habitation names: Pol.: **Kowalewski**, **Kowalczyński**, **Kowaliński**.

Kox *see* COOK

Kozak Polish: 1. name for a *Cossack*, a member of a people descended from a group of runaway serfs who set up a semi-independent military republic in the Ukraine in the 15th and 16th cents. The Cossacks became noted for their military prowess. 2. var. of *Kozieł*; see KOZLOV. 3. Jewish (E Ashkenazic): presumably a nickname for a ruthless person, from Pol. *Kozak* as in 1, unless this is a spelling var. of KOZÁK (see also KOZLOV).

Patr.: Pol.: **Kozakiewicz**.

Kozák Czech: 1. occupational name for a goatherd, Czech *kozák*, or derogatory nickname from the vocab. word *koza* goat (cf. KOZLOV). 2. regional name from the district of *Kozácko* in S Bohemia.

Var. (of 1): **Koza**.

Kozlov Russian and Jewish (E Ashkenazic): patr. in form from the nickname *Kozyol* 'Goat', denoting a stubborn, lecherous, or malodorous man; also perhaps an occupational name for a goatherd. It is not clear how the Jewish surname was acquired.

Vars.: Russ.: **Kozin**. Jewish: **Koziol**; **Kozlovski**, **Kozlow(ski)**, **Koslovsky**, **Koslofsky**; **Kozlovitz**, **Koslovitz**; **Kozloff**, **Koslow**.
Dims.: Czech: **Kozlík**, **Kozelka**.
Habitation name: Pol.: **Kozłowski**.

Kozmin *see* KUZMIN

Kračmarík *see* KRETSCHMAR

Kraft German, Danish, and Jewish (Ashkenazic): metonymic nickname for a strong man, from Ger. *Kraft* or Dan. *kraft* strength (OHG *kraft*). The Ger. and Dan. names possibly also derive from a late survival of the OHG byname *Chrafto* 'Strong' or its ON cogn. *Kraptr*.

Var.: Ger.: **Krafft**.

Kragelić *see* KRÓL

Kraindels Jewish (Ashkenazic): metr. from the Yid. female given name *Kreyndl* (from a dim. of Yid. *kroyn* crown) + Yid. possessive *-s*.

Vars.: From the Yid. female given name *Kreyne* (a back-formation from *Kreyndl*): **Krainin**, **Kreinin**, **Krainovitz** (E Ashkenazic); **Krainis** (Ashkenazic); **Krajnis**, **Krejnis** (Pol. spellings). Germanized forms: **Kro(h)nson**, **Kronzon**.

Krajewski Polish: probably a topographic name for someone who lived on the edge of a parish or other administrative district, from Pol. *kraj* border area + *-ew* possessive suffix + *-ski* suffix of local surnames (see BARANOWSKI).

Krakowiak Polish: local name for someone from the city of Cracow, Pol. *Kraków*.

Var.: **Krakowski** (also Jewish (E Ashkenazic)).

Kraliček *see* KRÓLIK

Krämer German and Jewish (Ashkenazic): occupational name for a shopkeeper, from Ger. *Krämer* (Yid. *kremer*), an agent deriv. of MHG *krām* (OHG *crām*) trading post, tent. The Slav. cogns. listed below are derived from German.

Vars.: Ger.: **Kremer**; **Kromer**, **Krömer**. Jewish: **Kra(e)mer**, **Kramerman**, **Krammer**, **Kremer(man)**. U.S.: **Creamer**.
Dims.: Ukr.: **Kramarenko**, **Kramarchuk**.
Patrs.: Low Ger.: **Kramers**. Flem.: **Cre(e)mers**. Du.: **Kra(e)mers**. Beloruss.: **Kramarov**. Jewish: **Kremers**, **Kremerov**.

Kranewitter *see* KRONEWITTER

Kranke 1. German: nickname from MHG *kranc(k)* thin, slight, weak (the word is not attested in OHG, but appears to be of native origin); towards the end of the surname-forming period the Ger. word *krank* acquired its modern sense 'ill' (replacing MHG *siech* sick) and in some cases the surname may refer to a chronic invalid or a hypochondriac.

The word is akin to mod. Eng. *cringe* (from OE *cringan* to writhe, collapse from wounds). **2.** Low Ger.: dim. of CRANE.

Var. (of 1): **Krankheit** (an abstract noun).

Kränkel *see* CRANE

Kranz 1. German: metonymic occupational name for a maker of chaplets and wreaths or house name for someone who lived at a house distinguished by the sign of a garland, Ger. *Kranz* garland, wreath (MHG *kranz*, OHG *cranz*). **2.** Jewish (Ashkenazic): ornamental name from Ger. *Kranz* or Yid. *krants* wreath, garland.

Vars.: **Krantz**, **Kranzler**. Ger.: **Kränzler**; **Kranzlbinder** (see BINDER). Jewish: **Krantzler**; **Kranc** (a Pol. spelling).

Dims.: Ger.: **Kränz(e)l**, **Kränzle**, **Krenzle**. Low Ger.: **Krantz(c)ke**.

Cpds: Jewish: **Kranzbaum** ('wreath tree'); **Kran(t)zberg**, **Krancberg** ('wreath hill'); **Krancenblum** ('wreath flower'); **Kranzdorf** ('wreath village').

Krapf German: nickname for someone with a hooked nose or a hunched back, from MHG *kräp(f)e* hook (OHG *kräpfo*, akin to mod. Eng. *grapple*, which has come via OF from a Gmc source). The word was also applied to a type of crescent-shaped pastry, and the surname may thus also have been a metonymic occupational name for a baker.

Var.: **Krapp**.

Dims.: Ger. and Jewish (Ashkenazic): **Krapfl**, **Krappel** (reasons for adoption as a Jewish name unclear). Jewish only: **Krep(p)el** (from Yid. *krepl*, a kind of boiled dumpling; reasons for adoption unclear).

Krapotkin *see* KROPOTKIN

Krarup Danish: habitation name from a placename composed of the elements *krage* crow + *rup* settlement (see THORPE).

Krasilnikov Russian: patr. from the occupational term *krasilnik* dyer (from *krasit* to dye, a deriv. of *krasa* brightness, beauty, colour; cf. KRASNIKOV and NEKRASOV).

Var.: **Krasilshchikov**.

Krasnikov Russian: patr. from the nickname *Krasnik* 'Handsome One', from ORuss. *krasny* handsome, a deriv. of *krasa* brightness, beauty, colour; in mod. Russ., since the formation of the surname, the adj. has come to mean 'red', the meaning 'beautiful' being transferred to the byform *krasivy*.

Vars.: **Krasnov**, **Krasnykh**; **Krasavchikov**, **Krasukhin**.

Kraszewski Polish: topographic name for someone who lived in an area where the soil was reddish brown, e.g. containing sandstone, from Pol. *krasz* reddish-brown soil (cogn. with Russ. *krasny* red) + *-ew* possessive suffix + *-ski* suffix of local surnames (see BARANOWSKI).

Kratius *see* PANKRIDGE

Kratochvíl Czech and Jewish (Ashkenazic): nickname for an idle pleasure-seeker, from Czech *kratochvíl* pastime, amusement, entertainment.

Kratschmer *see* KRETSCHMAR

Kratz *see* PANKRIDGE

Kraus German and Jewish (Ashkenazic): nickname for someone with curly hair, from Ger. *kraus* curly(-haired) (MHG *krūs*, not attested in OHG).

Vars.: Ger.: **Krause**, **Krauss**; **Kraushaar**, **Krauskopf**. Jewish: **Krauz(e)**, **Krause(r)**, **Krauzer**, **Krausz(man)**, **Krausman**, **Krauzman**; **Kraushar**, **Krauzhar**.

Dims.: Ger.: **KREISEL**. Czech: **Kroužek**.

Kraut 1. German: metonymic occupational name for a market gardener or herbalist, from Ger. *Kraut* herb, plant (MHG, OHG *krūt*). **2.** Jewish (Ashkenazic): ornamental or occupational-ornamental name from Ger. *Kraut* plant, herb.

Vars.: Ger.: **Krauth**. Jewish (occupational): **Krauter**, **Kreit(n)er**, **Kreitler**, **Kreitman**, **Krautman**.

Dim.: Ger.: **Kräutl**.

Cpds: Jewish (ornamental or occupational-ornamental): **Kraut(en)berg**, **Kreitenberger** ((dweller on a) herb hill'); **Krautblatt** ('herb leaf'); **Krautheim(er)**, **Krauthamer** ('herb homestead(er)', the last reflecting a W Yid. form).

Krawiec Polish and Jewish (E Ashkenazic): occupational name for a tailor, Pol. *krawiec* (derived from OSlav. *kroit* to cut, a distant cogn. of Gk *krinein* to distinguish, judge, and L *cernere* to divide, discern, decide).

Vars.: Pol.: **Krawiecki**. Jewish: **Krav(i)etz**, **Krawetz**, **Kravitz**, **Kravits**, **Krawitz**, **Kravet**, **Kravett(e)**, **Krawet**, **Krawitt**, **Kravetsky**, **Kravetzky**, **Kravitsky**, **Krawi(e)cki**, **Krawiecky**, **Krawatsky**, **Crawetz**; **Croitoru**, **Kroitoru** (among Rumanian Jews).

Dims.: Pol.: **Krawczyk**. Czech: **Krejčík**; **Krajíček**. Jewish: **Kravchuk**, **Krawchuk**, **Kravtshuk**, **Kravchook**, **Krawczuk**; **Krafchik**, **Kravchick**, **Kravtchik**, **Kravc(z)ich**, **Kravzik**, **Krawchick**; **Kravtchinsky**, **Krafchinsky**. Ukr., Beloruss.: **Kravchenko**.

Patrs.: Russ.: **Kravtsov**. Jewish: **Krawzow**.

Habitation name: Pol.: **Krawczyński**.

Krč Czech: nickname for a dwarf or someone of stunted growth, from Czech *krč* stump of a tree, block of wood, stunted tree.

Var.: **Krčál**.

Dim.: **Krček** (also a dim. of *krk* neck).

Krčmarík *see* KRETSCHMAR

Kreber *see* KORB

Kreinin *see* KRAINDELS

Kreisel 1. German: dim. of KRAUS. **2.** German: nickname for a perpetually active and somewhat disorganized person, from Ger. *Kreisel* spinning top (MHG *kriusel*, dim. of *krūs* jug; the vowel of the mod. Ger. word has been influenced by association with *Kreis* circle). **3.** Jewish (Ashkenazic): of uncertain origin, perhaps derived as in 1 and 2 above.

Var.: **Kreisler**.

Kreitenberger *see* KRAUT

Kreith *see* REUTER

Krejčík *see* KRAWIEC

Kremer *see* KRÄMER

Křenek *see* CHRZANOWSKI

Krenkel *see* CRANE

Krenzle see KRANZ

Krepel see KRAPF

Krestyaninov see CHRISTIAN

Kretschmar German: occupational name for an inn-keeper, from MHG *kretscham* inn. The word is of Slav. origin (cf. Czech *krčma* inn, *krčmář* innkeeper; Pol. *ka(r)czma, ka(r)czmarz*).

Vars.: **Kret(z)schmer**, **Kratschmer**; **Kretschmann**, **Kretschmeyer**.

Dims.: Pol.: **Ka(r)czmarek** (*Kaczmarek* is also the name of a place in the Kujawy district near Sandomierz); **Ka(r)czmarczyk**. Czech: **Krčmarík**, **Kračmarík**.

Patr. (from a dim.): Pol.: **Kaczmarkiewicz**.

Kretzing see PANKRIDGE

Krieger 1. German: occupational name for a mercenary soldier, Ger. *Krieger* warrior, soldier (MHG *kriegære*, possibly from LL *(miles) gregārius* common soldier, from *grex* herd, flock, crowd, gen. *gregis*). 2. German and Jewish (Ashkenazic): nickname for a quarrelsome person, Ger. *Krieger*, Yid. *kriger* (from MHG *kriec* quarrelsome, a derivative of *krieg* war, struggle).

Vars. (of 2): Jewish: **Kriger**; **Krigier** (Pol. spelling); **Kri(e)gman**, **Kri(e)gsman**.

Krikorian see GREGORY

Krimmel see CROME

Krisch see CHRISTIAN

Krishtopaitis see CHRISTOPHER

Kristall see CRISTAL

Krivov Russian: patr. from the nickname *Krivoi* 'Defective', 'Deformed', 'Crippled', 'Crooked', or 'One-eyed'.

Var.: **Krivtzov**.

Dims.: Ukr.: **Kriv(ch)enko**. Czech: **Křivánek**.

Habitation name: Pol.: **Krzywański**.

Krochmann see KRÜGER

Krohnson see KRAINDELS

Kroinik see CORONA

Kroitoru see KRAWIEC

Król Polish: nickname from the vocab. word *król* king, presumably given to someone who gave himself regal airs. The vocab. word is derived from the personal name *Karol* CHARLES, for this was the name borne by the Frankish king and Holy Roman Emperor Charlemagne (L *Carolus Magnus*) (?742–814) and by several of his successors.

Var.: **Królak**.

Dims.: Pol.: KRÓLIK. Ukr.: **Korolenko**. Beloruss.: **Korolyonok**. Ger. (of Slav. origin): **Kralik**.

Patrs.: Pol.: **Królewicz**. Beloruss.: **Koralyov**. Russ.: **Korolyov**. Croatian: **Kraljević**, **Kragelić**. Hung.: **Királyfi**.

Królik Pol.: 1. nickname from the vocab. word *królik* rabbit. This is a dim. of KRÓL king, being an attempted calque on a Low Ger. dial. form *kuniklīn*, misanalysed as a dim. of *König*, but in fact from L *cunīculus* (see CONEY). 2. dim. of KRÓL.

Dim.: Czech: **Kraliček**.

Patr.: Russ.: **Krolikov**.

Habitation name: Pol.: **Królikowski**.

Kroll 1. German: nickname for a man with curly hair, from MHG *krol* curly(-haired) (a deriv. of *krol(le)* curl; Eng. *curl* is a cogn., and the whole group is akin to KRAUS). 2. Jewish (E Ashkenazic): possibly as in 1, or alternatively perhaps a var. of Pol. KRÓL.

Kromer see KRÄMER

Kronewitter German (Austria and Tyrol): habitation name from any of several minor places named with the MHG dial. term *kronewitt* juniper bush (a cpd of OHG *krano* crane + *witu* wood).

Vars.: **Kranewitter**, **Kronebitter**, **Kronenbitte**, **Kronenwetter**.

Krook see CROOK

Kropaček Czech: from a dim. of the vocab. word *kropáč* sprinkler, dispenser of holy water. The application as a surname is not clear.

Kropotkin Russian: patr. from a nickname *Krapotka*, denoting an industrious or unsettled person (from *krapotat* to bustle, be busy).

The Moravian cogn. name **Krpata** has the opposite meaning, being from the Moravian dial. word *krpat* to work slowly, dawdle.

Var.: **Krapotkin**.

Krouzek see KRAUS

Krsek see KARSKI

Krtil Czech: nickname from Czech *krt, krtek* mole, perhaps bestowed on an extremely short-sighted person or one thought to look like a mole.

Vars.: **Krt(ek)**.

Krüger 1. German: occupational name for a seller or maker of mugs, jugs, and pitchers, an agent deriv. of Ger. *Krug* jug, pitcher (MHG *kruoc*, OHG *kruog*). Medieval jugs and pitchers were made of leather and metals such as pewter, as well as of earthenware. 2. N German: occupational name for a tavern keeper, Ger. *Krüger*, an agent deriv. of *Krug* inn, tavern (MLG *krūch, krōch*, probably originally a different word from 1, with which it has subsequently fallen together).

Vars. (of 1 and 2): **Kröger**, **Kroger**, **Kruger**; **Krug**, **Kroge** (metonymic); **Krogmann**, **Krochmann**, **Krugmann**.

Dims. (of 1): Ger.: **Krügel**, **Krügle**.

Kruglov Russian: patr. from the nickname *Krugloi* 'Rotund' (from *krug* ring; the Eng. word *ring* is a distant cogn.).

Var.: **Kruglin**.

Kruk 1. Polish: nickname from Pol. *kruk* raven, denoting a person with black hair or perhaps one with a dark and gloomy temperament. 2. Jewish (E Ashkenazic): ornamental name from Pol. *kruk* raven, one of the many such Ashkenazic names taken from words denoting birds.

Habitation names: **Krukowski**; **Kruczkowski**.

Krümel *see* CROME

Krupa Polish and German (of Slav. origin): metonymic occupational name for a dealer in grain, from a Slav. element represented by Pol. *krupa* grain.

Vars.: Pol.: **Krupski**. Ger.: **Kruppa**.

Dims.: Czech: **Krupička**. Ger. (of Slav. origin): **Krupke**.

Habitation name: Pol.: **Krupiński**.

Kruschel *see* GRUSHIN

Kruszyński Polish: of uncertain origin, perhaps either: **1.** topographic name from OPol. *krusza* pear tree or *kruszyna* a kind of buckthorn (*Rhamnus frangula*) + *-ski* suffix of local surnames (see BARANOWSKI). **2.** nickname from the vocab. word *krusza* meaning 'crumb, fragment', and so by extension 'small person'.

Var.: **Kruszyewski**.

Krůta Czech: derogatory nickname for an obstinate, stupid, or headstrong person, from Czech *krůta* turkey.

Vars.: **Kruták**, **Krutský**.

Krylov Russian: patr. from the nickname *Krylo* 'Wing' (from *(po)kryt* to cover), given perhaps to a protective or secretive person; it probably owes its surprising frequency to confusion with derivs. of *Cyril* (see KIRILOV).

Krysiak *see* CHRISTOPHER

Krýsl *see* CHRISTIAN

Krzemiński Polish: habitation name from a place named with Pol. *krzemień* flint, with the addition of *-ski*, suffix of local surnames (see BARANOWSKI).

Vars.: **Krzemień(ski)**, **Krzemionka**, **Krzemieniewski**.

Krzeszewski Polish: habitation name from *Krzeszowice*, near Kraków, or from some other place similarly named. The placename is probably from Pol. *krzesz* the part of a pine which faces north, the wood of which is consequently noticeably more brittle.

Krzywański *see* KRIVOV

Krzyżanowski *see* CROSS

Książek Polish: **1.** nickname meaning 'little priest' or possibly patr. for an illegitimate son of a priest, from Pol. *ksiądz* priest + *-ek* dim. suffix. **2.** nickname meaning 'little prince', from Pol. *książe* prince.

Kubáček *see* JACOB

Kučera Czech: nickname for someone with curly hair, from Czech *kučera* curl. This is the eighth most common Czech surname. Other Czech surnames with the same meaning are *Kudrna* and *Kadeř* (see KUDRYAVTSEV).

Kucharczyk *see* COOK

Kuciński Polish: of uncertain origin, probably a nickname for a dwarf, Pol. dial. *kucin*, with the surname suffix *-ski* (see BARANOWSKI).

Kudravtsev Russian and Jewish (E Ashkenazic): patr. from the nickname *Kudravets* 'Curly', from *kudravy* curly-haired, cogn. with Pol. *kędzior* curl, Czech *kudrna*, *kadeř*.

Dim.: Beloruss.: **Kondzyereyonok**.

Küfer *see* KIEFER

Kugel Jewish (Ashkenazic): unclear whether from Yid. *kugl* (of uncertain etymology) which denotes several different kinds of pudding, or from Ger. *Kugel* 'ball' (MHG *kugel(e)*), which has several derived meanings which might be relevant, or from both.

Vars.: **Kugelman(n)**; **Kugler**; **Kig(h)el** (from S Yid. pronunciations of *kigl*); **Kuglovitz** (in form a patr.).

Kuhl German: topographic name for someone who lived by a hollow or depression, MLG *küle*, or habitation name from one of the numerous minor places in N Germany named with this word. The name has been altered by folketymological association with the High Ger. word *kuhl* cool (MHG *küele*).

Vars.: **Kühl(e)**, **Kühlen**; **Kuhl(e)mann**, **Kulemann**.

Kuhn *see* KONRAD

Kuijpers *see* COOPER

Kujawa Polish: regional name from the district of *Kujawy*, on the left bank of the Vistula between Wrocławek and Bydgoszcz.

Vars.: **Kujawski**, **Kujawiak**.

Kukharenko *see* COOK

Kukla Czech: metonymic nickname from Czech *kukla* hood, probably bestowed on a habitual wearer of a hood.

Dim.: **Kuklík**.

Kukuła Polish: nickname meaning 'Cuckoo', or else a habitation name from a place named with this word.

Var.: **Kukulski**.

Kulawczyk *see* KLEČÁK

Kulemann *see* KUHL

Kulesza Polish: from the Pol. word meaning 'millet gruel', probably a nickname for a weak or insipid person, rather than one who cooked gruel or who sold millet for gruel.

Habitation name: **Kulaszyński**.

Kulíček *see* KLAUS

Kulig Polish: **1.** apparently a nickname from Pol. *kulig* sledge party, cavalcade on sledges, perhaps bestowed on someone who organized or took a prominent part in such a cavalcade. **2.** var. of KULIK.

Patr.: **Kuligowicz**.

Habitation name: **Kuligowski**.

Kulik **1.** Polish: nickname from Pol. *kulik* curlew, or else a habitation name from some place named with this word. **2.** Jewish (E Ashkenazic): meaning and reasons for adoption as a surname not clear.

Vars.: **Kulka**. Pol.: **Kulon**; KULIG.

Patrs.: **Kulikiewicz**. Russ.: **Kulikov** (the Russ. word means 'snipe').

Habitation name: Pol.: **Kulikowski**.

Kull *see* KONRAD

Kümmel German and Jewish (Ashkenazic): metonymic occupational name for a seller of caraway seeds, from Ger. *Kümmel* caraway (MHG *kümmel*, OHG *kumil*, a byform of *kumin*, from L *cumīnum*; the word is ultimately, like the plant itself, of Oriental origin).

Vars.: **Kümmelmann**. Jewish only: **Kimmel**, **Kimel(mann)**, **Kim(m)elman** (from Yid. *kiml*); **Kummel** (Anglicized).

Cpds Jewish (ornamental elaborations): **Kimelfeld** (partly Anglicized as **Kimmelfield**); **Kimelheim**.

Kumsteller German: from a byname for someone who had made the pilgrimage to the alleged tomb of St James the Greater at *Compostela* in Spain, a common penance. The placename is apparently from L *campus* field (see CHAMP) + *stella* star, but this may be no more than folk etymology.

Kún see COHEN

Kuna see KONRAD

Kunigunde see KENNGOTT

Kunkel see GUNKEL

Kupczyk see JACOB

Kuperbaum see COPPER

Küpers see COOPER

Kupka see JACOB

Kuptsov Russian: patr. from the occupational term *kupets*, gen. *kuptsa*, merchant (from *kupit* to buy, a distant cogn. of CHAPMAN).

Kurasov see KIRILOV

Kurek Polish: nickname from Pol. *kurek*, dim. of *kur* cock.

Patrs.: Pol.: **Kurkiewicz**. Russ.: **Kuritsin** ('hen'). Jewish (E Ashkenazic): **Kuritsky**, **Kuritzky** (reasons for adoption as a surname not clear).

Habitation names: Pol.: **Kur(k)owski**; **Kurczewski** (from *kurcze* chicken).

Kureš see CORNEILLE

Kurland Jewish (E Ashkenazic): regional name from Ger., Yid. *Kurland* Courland, which is now part of Latvia. The name of the region comes from the name of the *Kurs*, a Baltic people who, together with the Letts, inhabited this area, + OHG *land* land, territory.

Vars.: **Korland**, **Curland**; **Kurlander**, **Kurlender**, **Korlander** (with -*er* denoting a native or inhabitant); **Kurlandski**, **Kurlansky**, **Korlansky** (adjectival forms); **Kurliandschick**, **Kurliandcik** (dims.).

Kürner German: occupational name for a worker with a hand mill, an agent deriv. of MHG *kürn(e)* hand mill (OHG *quirn*, a cogn. of OE *cweorn* quern). The word and the object were gradually replaced from the 13th cent. by the more efficient apparatus operated by wind, water, or animals, which was named with the loan word *Mühle* (from L *molīna*; see MILL). For a while the vocab. word *Kürn* denoted a granary, before it disappeared completely: some examples of the surname may therefore be equivalents of GRANGER. It may also be a habitation name

from *Kürn* in Bavaria or from some other minor place named with this word.

Var.: **Kirner**.

Kürschner German: occupational name for a furrier, Ger. *Kürschner* (MHG *kürsenære*, from *kürsen* fur garment, OHG *kursinna*, a borrowing from a Slav. language).

Vars.: **Kürssner**, **Ki(e)rschner**, **Körschner**.

Kürstgens see CHRISTIAN

Kurt see KONRAD

Kus see KOS

Kusch see JACOB

Küssewetter see KIESEWETTER

Küster German: occupational name for a sexton or churchwarden, Ger. *Küster* (MHG *kuster*, OHG *kustor*, from LL *custor* guard, warden, from class. L *custos*). The umlaut of the modern form is due to association with other agent nouns in -*er* from OHG -*ari* (L -*ārius*).

Vars.: **Küstermann**, **Kustermann**. U.S.: **Custer**.

Patrs.: Ger.: **Küsters**. Low Ger.: **Kösters**, **Köstering**. Flem., Du.: **Kosters**, **Custers**.

Kutuzov Russian: from a nickname in a Turkic language, *Qutuz* 'Rabid', 'Mad', which has been adapted to the normal pattern of Russ. surnames by the addition of the patr. suffix -*ov*.

Kuusi Finnish: ornamental name from Finn. *kuusi* fir tree, one of the many words for natural features that were used in the formation of Finn. surnames when these became obligatory during the 18th and 19th cents.

Var.: **Kuusinen**.

Kuypers see COOPER

Kužel Czech: apparently from the vocab. word *kužel* head of a distaff. The application as a surname is unclear; it may have been a nickname for an effeminate man.

Var.: **Kužela**.

Dim.: **Kužilek**.

Kuzmin Russian: patr. from the given name *Kuzma* (Gk *Kosmas*, from *kosmos* order, arrangement, (ordered) universe). St Cosmas was martyred together with his brother Damian (see DAMYON) in Cilicia in the early 4th cent. AD, and came to be widely revered in the Eastern Church. The Russ. form of the given name has probably been altered by association with *kuznets* smith (see KUZNETSOV). The surname is also borne by Ashkenazic Jews, as an adoption of the Russian surname.

Vars.: **Kozmin**, **Kosmin**; **Kosminski** (a clerical name); **Kuzminsky** (Jewish).

Dims. (patrs.): Russ.: **Kuz(k)in**, **Kuzyakin**, **Kuzemchikov**, **Kuzichkin**, **Kuzyutin**, **Kuzmishchev**, **Kuzishchin**, **Kuzminov**, **Kuzmichyov**.

Dims. (not patrs.): Ukr.: **Kuzik**. Beloruss.: **Kuzmyanko**. It.: **Cos(i)melli**, **Cos(i)mini**, **Cosmin**, **Gosmin**, **Gusmin** (all predominantly Venetian).

'Son of the wife of K.': Ukr.: **Kuzmishin**.

Kuznetsov Russian: patr. from the occupational term *kuznets* smith (from ORuss. *kuzn* forged work, from *kovat* to forge, ultimately a cogn. of OHG *houwan* to hew; cf. HAUER).

Dim.: Pol.: **Kuźnik**.

Kviat *see* KWIATEK

Kviatkovsky *see* KWIATKOWSKI

Kvist *see* QVIST

Kwapisz Polish: nickname for a busy person or one who was always in a hurry, from a deriv. of Pol. *kwapić* to rush, hasten, hurry.

Patr.: Pol.: **Kwapisiewicz**.

Habitation name: Pol.: **Kwapiński**.

Kwaśniak Polish: nickname for a sour-faced individual, Pol. *kwaśniak*, from *kwaśny* sour, peevish, from *kwas* acid.

Habitation name: **Kwaśniewski**.

Kwiatek **1**. Polish: from the given name *Kwiatek*, dim. of the vocab. word *kwiat* flower. This given name was generally regarded as a vernacular equivalent of *Florián* (L *Floriānus*; see FLORIANO), as was the Czech cogn. *Květoň*. **2**. Polish: var. of KWIECIEŃ. **3**. Jewish (E Ashkenazic): ornamental name from Pol. *kwiat* flower.

Vars.: Jewish: **Kwiat**, **Kviat**; **Kviatek**.

Patr.: Russ.: **Tsvetkov(ski)** (apparently a surname adopted by Orthodox priests).

Kwiatkowski **1**. Polish: habitation name from some place called *Kwiatków* (from Pol. KWIATEK + *-ów* possessive suffix) + *-ski* suffix of local surnames (see BARANOWSKI).

2. Jewish (E Ashkenazic): from the Pol. surname adopted as an ornamental name.

Vars. (of 1): **Kwiatosiński**, **Kwietniewski**. (Of 2): **Kviatkovsky**.

Kwiecień Polish and Jewish (E Ashkenazic): from the Pol. vocab. word *kwiecień* April, adopted by someone who was baptized in that month or, in the case of Jewish bearers, officially took the surname in that month. The cogn. Czech word, *květen*, means 'May'.

Var.: **Kwieciński**.

Kwietniewski *see* KWIATKOWSKI

Kyd *see* KIDD

Kyffin Welsh: habitation name from any of various places named with W *cyffin* boundary, such as the hamlet of *Cyffin* in Powys and the parish of *Gyffin* in Gwynedd.

Vars.: **Caffyn**, COFFIN.

Kyle Scots and N Irish: **1**. regional name from a district in the former county of Ayrs. in SW Scotland. This is so called from the name of the Brit. chieftains who ruled it in the 5th cent., the *Coel Hen*. **2**. habitation name from any of the numerous Scot. places that are so called from Gael. *caol* narrows, strait.

Kyne *see* COYNE

Kynsey *see* KINSEY

Kyrke *see* KIRK

Kyryshkin *see* KIRILOV

Kyte *see* KITE

L

Laakso Finnish: ornamental name from Finn. *laakso* valley, perhaps sometimes chosen as a topographic name by someone who lived in a valley.

Var.: **Laaksonen**.

Labadini *see* ABBÉ

Labarte *see* BARTHE

Labastida *see* BASTIDE

La Bastie *see* BASTIDE

Labelle *see* BEAU

Labern *see* LEYBURN

Labitte French: topographic name, with fused def. art. *la*, for someone who lived by a boulder or roughly carved stone, probably some kind of memorial, OF *bite*. It may also be a habitation name from a minor place so named, and perhaps also an occupational name for a quarryman or a nickname for a lumpish individual.

Labonne *see* BON

Laborier French: occupational name for a worker of any sort, OF *laborier* (from *laborer* to work, toil, L *laborāre*, from *labor* effort); but especially used of someone who worked the land, a farmer.

Var.: **Laborieux**.

Labreneis *see* LAWRENCE

Labretesche *see* BRETÉCHER

Labrosse *see* BROSSE

Labruyère *see* BRUYÈRE

Lacaille *see* CAIL

La Capruccia *see* CHEEVER

Lacassagne *see* CASSAGNE

Lacave *see* CAVE

Lace *see* GLASS

Lacey English and Irish (Norman): habitation name from *Lassy* in Calvados, so called from a Gaul. personal name *Lascius* (of uncertain meaning) + the local suffix -*ācum*. The surname is widespread, but is most common in Notts.

Vars.: **Lacy**, **Lassey**, **De Lac(e)y**; **Leacy** (Ireland, rare).

Lach 1. Polish: name meaning 'Pole', from the Slav. word *Lach* Pole. According to legend, the northern Slav. nations were founded by three brothers called Rus, Lach, and Czech. 2. Polish: topographic name for a dalesman, from OPol. *lach* dalesman, originally the same word as in 1. 3. Czech and German (of Slav. origin): from a given name, a

short form of the name *Ladislav*, *Vlasdislav*, composed of the elements (*v*)*ladi*- government + *slav* glory.

Vars. (of 2): Czech: **Lacha**, **Lachout**, **Laš**.

Dim. (of 2): Czech: **Laček**.

Patr. (from 1): Pol.: **Lachowicz**.

Habitation name (from 1): Pol.: **Lachowski**.

Lachaume *see* CHAUME

Lachaussée *see* CHAUSSÉE

Lachenal *see* CHENAL

Lacher *see* LEICHER

Lachlan Irish: from the Gael. personal name *Lochlann* 'Stranger', originally a byname applied to Viking settlers (from the name used for Scandinavia, a cpd of *loch* lake, fjord + *lann* land). Many Ir. bearers of the name claim descent from Lochlann, a 10th-cent. lord of Corcomroe, Co. Clare.

Vars.: **Lo(u)ghlan**, **Lo(u)ghlin**, **Lo(u)ghlen**, **La(u)ghlan**, **Laughlin**, **Laughland**, **Lafflin(g)**; LOFTUS (Connaught).

Patrs.: **Lackli(n)son**; McLACHLAN.

'Descendant of L.': **O'Lo(u)ghlan**, **O'Lo(u)ghlin**, **O'Lo(u)ghlen**, **O'La(u)ghlan** (Gael. **Ó Lochlainn**).

Lachmann 1. German: topographic name for someone who lived by the boundary of a parish or other administrative unit, from MHG *lāche* boundary stone (OHG *lāh*, of uncertain origin). 2. German: topographic name for someone who lived near a pond or lake, MHG *lache* (OHG *lahha*, mod. Ger. *Lache* puddle; cogn. with OE *laca*, a byform of *lacu*; cf. LAKE). 3. S German: topographic name for someone who lived in or near a small wood or grove, from the Bavarian dial. term *la(i)ch* copse; cf. LEICHER 2. 4. German: occupational name for a physician; see LEACH 1. 5. German (of Slav. origin): cogn. of LACH 1 or 2. 6. Jewish (Ashkenazic): of uncertain origin. It has been suggested that the name was chosen as a translation of the given name ISAAC, which means 'to laugh'; if so the first element here would be mod. Ger. *lachen* or Yid. *lakhn*. Another suggestion is that there may be some connection with E Yid. *lakhman* rag (from Pol. *łachman*). Kaganoff mentions a suggestion that *Lachman* was the way non-Jews in Silesia pronounced the Hebr. given name *Nachman* 'Consolation'. This is questionable, not least because the Yid. form of *Nachman*, the form which people in Silesia would have actually been exposed to, is *Nachmen*, but the spelling var. **Lachmen*, which one would predict if this hypothesis is correct, does not occur. In fact, none of these explanations is really satisfactory, and the origin may be as in 4 above.

Var. (of 6): **Lachman**.

Patr. (from 6): **Lachmanovici** (Rumanian spelling).

Lachs *see* LAX

Lacina Czech: nickname from the Czech vocab. word *lacino* cheaply, apparently bestowed on someone who drove a hard bargain.

Lack see LAKE

Lackenby English: habitation name from a place in N Yorks., of uncertain etymology. The second element is ON *býr* farm, settlement; the first may be the ON personal name *Lakkandi* 'the shouting one' or 'the slow-moving one'.

Lacorne see CORNE

Lacorte see COURT

Lacoste see COSTE

Lacotte see COTTE

Ladbrooke English: habitation name, apparently from *Ladbro(o)ke* in Warwicks., although the surname is now more common in Norfolk than the Midlands. The second element is OE *brōc* BROOK. Early forms with *H-* suggest that the first element may be OE *hlot* lot, choice, decision, and Ekwall suggests that the meaning is therefore 'stream used for divining the future'.

Ladd English: occupational name for a servant, ME *ladde*. The word first appears in the 13th cent. and at first meant 'servant' or 'man of humble birth', the modern meaning of 'young man', 'boy' being a later shift. It is of uncertain origin, perhaps a Scandinavian borrowing, and possibly akin to the verb *lead*.
Patrs.: **Ladds**, **Ladson**.

Lade see LEWIS

Ladefoged Danish: occupational name for an official who was responsible for collecting tithes of produce into the manorial stores, from Dan. *lade* barn (ON *hlaða*; cf. LATHAM) + *foged* overseer (ON *fógutr*, *fóguti*; cf. VOGT).

Ladevèze see DEVÈZE

Ladler English and Scots: probably an occupational name for a maker of ladles, from an agent deriv. of ME *ladel(e)* (OE *hlædel*).
Vars.: **Laidler**; **Ladel(l)**.

Lafage see FAGE

Laffan see LAVIN

Lafferty see LAVERTY

Laffitte French: topographic name, with fused def. art. *la*, for someone who lived near a boundary marker driven firmly into the ground, OF *fitte* (LL *fixta (petra)* fixed stone, from the past part. of *figere* to fix, fasten; cf. FICHE).
Var.: **Laffite**.

Lafflin see LACHLAN

Lafon see FONT

Lafontaine see FONTAINE

Laforge see FORGE

Lafosse see FOSSE

Lafoy see FOY

Lagache see AGACE

Lagan see LOGAN

Lage Portuguese: topographic name for someone who lived by a large flat rock or slab of stone, Port. *lage*, *laja* (of uncertain, possibly Celt., origin).
Var.: **Lages**.

Lager Swedish: ornamental name from Swed. *lager* laurel, bay; one of the many surnames derived from words denoting natural phenomena that were adopted and also used in forming compound surnames in Sweden in the 18th and 19th cents.
Vars.: **Lahger**, **Lagerman**.
Cpds: **Lagerbäch** ('laurel stream'); **Lagerberg** ('laurel hill'); **Lagerborg** ('laurel town'); **Lagercrantz**, **Lagerkran(t)z** ('laurel wreath'); **Lagerdahl** ('laurel valley'); **Lagerfel(d)t** ('laurel field'); **Lagerfors** ('laurel waterfall'); **Lagergre(e)(h)n** ('laurel branch'); **Lagerholm** ('laurel island'); **Lagerlöf** ('laurel leaf'); **Lagerlund** ('laurel grove'); **Lagerquist** ('laurel twig'); **Lagerstedt** ('laurel homestead'); **Lagerstrandt** ('laurel shore'); **Lagerström** ('laurel river'); **Lagerwall**, **Lagervall** ('laurel bank').

Laghlan see LACHLAN

Lagneau see AGNEW

Lagorce see GORSE

Lagore see GORE

Lagrange see GRANGE

Laguna Spanish: topographic name for someone who lived by a pool or pond, Sp. *laguna* (L *lacūna* hollow, hole).
Var.: **Lagunas**.

Lahache see HACHE

Lahger see LAGER

Lahr see HILARY

Lahtinen Finnish: ornamental name from Finn. *lahti* bay, gulf, cove + the gen. suffix *-nen*.
Var.: **Lahti**.

Laicher see LEICHER

Laidlaw Scots: of uncertain origin. According to Black, there is a family tradition that the name comes from LUDLOW in Shrops., England.
Vars.: **Laidler**, **Laidley**. See also LADLER.

Laidler see LADLER

Laikin see LAKIN

Lain see LANE

Laine Finnish: ornamental name from Finn. *laine* wave. This is one of the most common names among those that were derived from words denoting natural features when hereditary surnames were adopted in Finland in the 18th and 19th cents.

Laing see LONG

Laiper see LEAPMAN

Laird Scots and N Irish: probably a status name for a landlord, from Northern ME *laverd*, N dial. var. of *lover(e)d* LORD.

Laister see LISTER

Laithwaite English: habitation name from either of two minor places, one in the parish of Amounderness, Lancs., the other near Prescot in Merseyside (formerly Lancs.). The former gets its name from ON *hlaða* barn (see LATHAM) + *þveit* meadow, piece of land (see THWAITE); in the case of the latter the first element is probably the ON personal name *Leikr*, a short form of the various cpd names containing the element *leikr* sport, play (cf. LAKER 2).

Laitinen Finnish: patr. from the given name *Laiti*, of Gmc origin but uncertain meaning.

Laitner see LEITNER

Laity see LAWTY

Lajarrige see JARRY

Lake English (chiefly W Country): topographic name for someone who lived by a stream, OE *lacu*, or habitation name from a place named with this word, for example in Wilts. and Devon. The mod. Eng. vocab. word *lake* is only distantly related, if at all; it comes via OF from L *lacus*. This meaning, which ousted the native sense, came too late to be found as a placename element, but may lie behind some examples of the surname.

Vars.: **Lack**; **Lakes**; LAKER; **Lakeman**.

Dim.: Fr.: **Lacquet**.

Laker English: **1.** topographic name, a var. of LAKE. **2.** occupational name from Northern ME *leyker* actor, player (an agent deriv. of *leyk(en)* to sport, play, ON *leikja*).

Lakin **1.** Jewish (E Ashkenazic): metr. from *Leyke*, a pet form of the Yid. female given name *Leye* (from the Hebr. female given name *Lea*, literally 'Gazelle' (or 'Weak', from which Eng. *Leah* is derived; see Gen. 29: 16) + the Slav. metr. suffix -*in*. **2.** English: from a medieval given name, a dim. of LAWRENCE; cf. LAW 1 and LARKIN.

Vars.: (of 1): **Laikin**, **Leikin**; **Leyeles** (Ashkenazic, based on *Leye*, a different pet form of *Leye*).

Patr. (from 2): **Lakins**.

Lakser see LAX

Lally see MULLALLY

Lalor see LAWLOR

Lam Danish: **1.** cogn. of LAMB (from ON *lamb*). **2.** nickname for a lame man (from ON *lami*).

Lama Spanish: topographic name for someone who lived on a patch of marshland, Sp. *lama* (LL *lāma*).

Vars.: **Lamas**; **Llama(s)** (Asturias).

Lamadrid see MADRID

Lamard see DELAMARE

Lamarque see MARQUE

Lamartine see MARTIN

Lamb **1.** English: nickname for a meek and inoffensive person or metonymic occupational name for a keeper of lambs, from ME, OE *lamb*. It may also have been a habitation name for someone who lived at a house distinguished by the sign of the paschal lamb, though surnames derived

from house signs are less common in England than in Germany and central Europe. **2.** English: short form of the given name LAMBERT. **3.** Irish: Anglicized form of Gael. *Ó Luain*; see LANE 3.

Var.: **Lambe**.

Dims. (of 1 and 2): Eng.: **Lambie**, **Lamby**, **Lammie**, **Lammey**; **Lam(b)kin**, **Lampkin**; **Lampin**, **Lampen**, **Lammin(g)**. (Of 1 only): Ger.: **Lämmel**, **Lemmel**, **Lammel**, **Lämmle**. Jewish (Ashkenazic): **Lemel** (from the Yid. male given name *Leml*, which is conventionally associated with the Yid. male given name *Osher*, see ASHER).

Patrs. (from 1 and 2): Eng.: **Lam(b)son**, **Lampson**. Flem., Du.: **Lammens**.

Patrs. (from 1 and 2) (dims.): Low Ger.: **Lammeling**. Flem., Du.: **Lammekins**. Jewish: **Lemelson**.

Lambert **1.** English, French, and German: from a Gmc personal name composed of the elements *land* land, territory + *berht* bright, famous. A native OE name *Landbeorht* is attested, and seems to have survived the Norman Conquest, when it was massively reinforced by the Continental form imported by the Normans from France. The name gained yet wider currency in the Middle Ages with the immigration of weavers from Flanders, where St Lambert, bishop of Maastricht *c*.700, was a popular figure. In Italy the name was popular in the Middle Ages as a result of the fame of Lambert I and II, Dukes of Spoleto and Holy Roman Emperors. **2.** English: occupational name for a shepherd, from OE *lamb* (see LAMB 1) + *hierd* (see HEARD).

Vars. (of 1): Eng.: **Lambart(h)**, **Lambard**, **Lampert**, **Lamperd**, **Lampard**, **Lampart**, **Lammert**, **Lambrick**. Ger.: **Lamprecht**, **Lambrecht**, **Lambrich(t)**, **Lammerich**, **Limprecht**, **Limprich(t)**.

Dims. (of 1): Eng.: LAMB. Ger.: **Lamp(e)l**, **Lämpl**, **Lemp(e)l**, **Lemppl**. Low Ger.: **Lamp(e)**, **Lam(p)ke**, **Lamcke**, **Lempke**, **Lem(b)cke**, **Lembke**, **Lemm(e)**. Fr.: **Lamb(l)in**, **Lambinet**, **Lamb(l)ot**, **Lambotin**. It.: **Lambertini** (Emilia); **Lamba** (Naples).

Aug. (of 1): It.: **Lambertoni**.

Pej. (of 1): It.: **Lambertazzi**.

Patrs. (from 1): Eng.: **Lamberts(on)**. Ger.: **Lambrechts**. Low Ger.: **Lamberts**, **Lam(m)ers**, **Lemmers**; **Lambertsen**; **Lambertz**, **Lammertz**, **Lempertz**, **Lemmertz**, **Limpertz** (N Rhineland); **Lammer(d)ing** (Westphalia). Fris.: **Lammenga**. Flem., Du.: **Lambregts**, **Lammer(t)s**, **Lammertse**. It.: **Lambertenghi**, **Lamberteschi**.

Patrs. (from 1) (dims.): Low Ger.: **Lamps**, **Lamping**; **Lamcken**, **Lemmen**. Flem., Du.: **Lampens**, **Lemmen(s)**.

Lambourne English: habitation name from *Lambourne* in Essex or *Lambourn* in Berks., both of which are probably so called from OE *lamb* LAMB + *burna* stream (see BOURNE), i.e. a place where lambs were washed. It is possible, but less likely, that the first element was OE *lām* loam, referring to rich clay soil in the area.

Vars.: **Lambourn**, **Lamborn(e)**, **Lamburn(e)**.

Lambton English: habitation name from a place in Co. Durham, so called from OE *lamb* LAMB + *tūn* enclosure, settlement.

Lamerton English: habitation name from a place in Devon, which derives its name from *Lumburn* Water on which it stands (see LAMBOURNE) + OE *tūn* enclosure, settlement.

Lamont Scots and N Irish: from the medieval given name *Lagman*, which is from ON *Logmaðr*, composed of the elements *log* law (from the verb *legja* to lay down) + *maðr*, gen. *manns*, man.

Vars.: **Lam(m)ond**; **Lawman**, LEMON.

Patrs.: **McLamon(t)**, **McClemment**, **McClements**, **McClymond**, **McClymont** (Gael. **Mac Laomuinn**).

Lamothe *see* MOTTE

Lamouche *see* MOUCHE

Lamoureux *see* AMOUREUX

Lampet English: topographic name for someone who lived near a clay pit or loam pit (ME *lampit*) or occupational name for someone who worked in one. The ME word is from OE *lām* loam, clay + *pytt* pit, hollow (see PITT). The excavation of clay was an important occupation in the Middle Ages as it was widely used in the wattle-and-daub construction of houses, in which wicker hurdles were packed and coated with clay.

Vars.: **Lampitt**, **Lamputt**.

Lancaster English: habitation name from the city in NW England, so called from the river *Lune*, on which it stands, + OE *cæster* Roman fort (L *castra* legionary camp). The river name is probably Brit., perhaps cogn. with Gael. *slán* healthy, salubrious.

Vars.: **Lankester**, **Langcaster**, **Lon(g)caster**, **Lan(g)castle**.

Lance English: from the Gmc personal name *Lanzo*, originally a short form of various cpd names with the first element *land* land, territory (cf., e.g., LAMBERT 1) but later used as an independent name. It was introduced into England by the Normans, among whom it was a popular name with the ruling classes, perhaps partly as a result of association with OF *lance* lance, spear (see LANCIA).

Dims.: Ger.: **Lanzl**, **Lendl**. Low Ger.: **Lendeke**, **Lenk(e)**. It.: **Landini**, **Landino**; **Lanzini**; **Lannino**; **Landucci**, **Landuzzi**.

Augs.: It.: **Landoni**, **Landone**; **Lanzoni**, **Lanzone**.

Lancel *see* ANCEL

Lancia Italian: metonymic occupational name for an armourer or for a soldier who wielded the lance, It. *lancia* (L *lancea*).

Var.: **Lanza**.

Dims.: It.: **Lancini**, **Lanciotti**; **Lanzetta**, **Lanzola**.

Aug.: It.: **Lancioni**.

Lanctin *see* ASHKETTLE

Land English: **1.** topographic name from OE *land*, territory. This had various more specialized senses in the Middle Ages, and was used of the countryside as opposed to a town (as in the ME lyric *My lief is faren in londe*) and of an estate. **2.** topographic name for someone who lived in a forest glade, from ME, OF *la(u)nde* (of apparently Gaul. origin; cf. Bret. *lann* heath), or habitation name from *Launde* in Leics., which is named with this word.

Var. (of 2): **Lawn**.

Cpds (of 1; ornamental): Swed.: **Landberg** ('land hill'); **Land(e)gren** ('land branch'); **Landquist** ('land twig'); **Landström** ('land river').

Landa **1.** Czech: from an aphetic form of the given name *Mikulanda*, a var. of *Mikuláš* (see NICHOLAS). **2.** Jewish (Ashkenazic): presumably a representation of the Yid.

placename *Lande* (see LANDER 2). **3.** Basque: topographic name from the element *landa* field, plot of land. There is a place of this name in the province of Álava, and the surname may in fact be a habitation name from this place.

Var. (of 3): **Landeta** (with the addition of a suffix of abundance).

Lander **1.** German: cogn. of LAND 1, used originally to denote either someone who was a native of the area in which he lived (in contrast to *Neumann*; see NEW) or someone who lived in the countryside as opposed to a town. **2.** Jewish (Ashkenazic): habitation name derived from either of two places called *Landau* in German (from OHG *lant* land, territory + *auwa* damp valley), *Lande* in Yid. The one in the Palatinate was the home of many Jews in the Middle Ages, and when they were expelled in 1545 they moved mostly to Prague, where they adopted the name of the town from which they had come; the other was part of Alsace until the Vienna settlement of 1815 and has given rise to the high frequency of the name in France. **3.** English: var. of LAVENDER.

Vars. (of 1): LANDMANN. (Of 2): **Lande**, LANDA, **Landau(er)**; **Landoj** (Pol. spelling); **Landow(ski)**.

Landmann **1.** German: var. of LANDER 1. **2.** Jewish (Ashkenazic): of uncertain origin, perhaps chosen for its phonetic similarity to Hebr. *lamdan* Talmudic scholar.

Vars. (of 1): Ger.: **Land(e)smann**. (Of 2): **Land(e)sman**, **Lansman**.

Landseer English: topographic name for someone who lived near a border of some kind, ME *landschare*, from OE *land* land, territory + *scearu* boundary.

Lane **1.** English: local name for someone who lived in a lane, ME, OE *lane*, originally a narrow way between fences or hedges, later used of any narrow pathway, including one between houses in a town. **2.** Irish: Anglicized form of Gael. **Ó Laighin** 'descendant of *Laighean*', a byname meaning 'Spear', 'Javelin'. **3.** Irish: Anglicized form of Gael. **Ó Luain** 'descendant of *Luan*', a byname meaning 'Warrior'. **4.** Irish: Anglicized form of Gael. **Ó Liatháin**; see LEHANE. **5.** French: metonymic occupational name for a worker in wool, from OF *la(i)ne* wool (L *lana*). **6.** S French: Gascon cogn. of LAND 2.

Vars. (of 1): **Layne**, **Lain**; **Lanes**; **Loan**, **Lones**. (Of 2): **O'La(y)ne**, **O'Loyne**, **(O')Leyne**, LEAN, LYON. See also LYNE.

Lang *see* LONG

Langan Irish: Anglicized form of Gael. **Ó Longáin** 'descendant of *Longán*', a personal name probably derived from *long* tall, or possibly from the homonymous *long* ship (and so originally a byname for a seafarer).

Vars.: **Langin**, **Longan**, **O'Langan(e)**, **O'Longan(e)**, LONG.

Langdon English: habitation name from any of various places, for example in Devon, Dorset, Essex, Kent, and Warwicks., so called from OE *lang*, *long* LONG + *dūn* hill (see DOWN 1).

Var.: **Longdon** (the name of places in Shrops., Staffs., and Worcs.).

Langenscheidt German: habitation name from any of various minor places in N Germany, so called from the weak dat. case (originally used after a preposition and art.) of MHG *lang* LONG + *scheide* boundary (see SCHEIDT).

Var.: **Langenscheid**.

Langford English: habitation name from any of the numerous places so called from OE *lang, long* LONG + *ford* FORD.

Vars.: **Longford**, **Langsford**.

Langham English: habitation name from any of various places so called. Most, as for example those in Dorset, Norfolk, Leics. (formerly Rutland), and Suffolk, get the name from OE *lang, long* LONG + *hām* homestead, but one in Essex is recorded in Domesday Book as *Laingaham*, from OE *Lāwingahām* 'homestead of the people of *Lāwa*', and one in Lincs. originally had as its second element ME *holm* island (see HOLME 2).

Vars.: **Lanham**; **Longham** (a place in Norfolk, with the same etymology as *Langham* in Essex).

Langlands Scots and N English: habitation name from a property in the former county of Peebles, so called from OE *lang, long* LONG + *land* land, territory.

Langlebert *see* ENGELBERT

Langley English: **1.** habitation name from any of the numerous places named with OE *lang, long* LONG + *lēah* wood, clearing. **2.** from the ON female personal name *Langlif*, composed of the elements *lang* long + *lif* life.

Var.: **Longley** (found chiefly in Notts. and S Yorks.).

Langnese Low German: nickname for someone with a long nose, from MLG *lang* LONG + *nese* nose.

Langridge English: topographic name for someone who lived on or by a long ridge, or habitation name from any of the various places named with the OE elements *lang, long* LONG + *hrycg* ridge, for example in Somerset.

Var.: **Longridge** (places in Lancs. and Staffs.).

Langston English: habitation name from any of various places, for example *Langstone* in Devon and Hants, named with OE *lang, long* LONG, tall + *stān* stone, i.e. a menhir. The surname is now most common in the W Midlands.

Langton English: habitation name from any of numerous places so called from OE *lang, long* LONG + *tūn* enclosure, settlement. Langton in Co. Durham, however, has the same origin as LANGDON.

Vars.: **Longton** (places in Lancs. and Staffs.); **Longtown** (places in Cumb. and Herefords.).

Langtree English: habitation name from places in Devon, Oxon., and Lancs., so called from OE *lang, long* LONG, tall + *trēow* tree.

Lanier French: **1.** occupational name for a worker involved in any of the stages of producing woollen cloth or a seller of the finished material, from an agent deriv. of OF *la(i)ne* wool (L *lana*; cf. LANE 5). **2.** occupational name, with fused def. art., for a pack-driver, from OF *asne* donkey (L *asinus*).

Var. (of 2): **Lasnier**.

Lanigan *see* LENNON

Lansdown English: habitation name from a place in Somerset, *Lantesdune* in early records, probably so called from OE **langet* (see LANT) + *dūn* hill (see DOWN 1).

Lánský Czech: topographic name for someone living near open land or a cleared area of land, from a deriv. of OCzech *lán* open land, cleared area. It may also be a habitation name from any of several places called *Lány*, named with this element.

Lant English (Northumb.): of uncertain origin, perhaps a habitation name from some place named with OE **langet* long strip of ground, long ridge (a deriv. of *lang* LONG).

Lanyon Cornish: habitation name from a place in Madron parish near Penzance, which gets its name from Corn. *lyn* pool + *yeyn* cold.

Laoust *see* DAVOUT

Lapage *see* LAWRENCE

Lapalu *see* PALLU

Lapérière *see* PEAR

Lapid Jewish (Ashkenazic): of uncertain origin, probably from Hebr. *lapid* torch, lightning. The surname may have been adopted as an allusion to any of the numerous Hebr. given names referring to light, such as *Uri* and *Meir*.

Lapidus Jewish (Ashkenazic): of uncertain origin, possibly from the Hebr. given name *Lapidoth*, borne in the Bible by the husband of Deborah (Judg. 4: 4).

Vars.: **Lapiduss**, **Lapidos**, **Lapides**; **Lapidot(h)** (Israeli).

Lapierre *see* PIERRE

Łapiński Polish: of uncertain origin, perhaps a habitation name from some place named with Pol. *łapa* paw, or possibly a nickname from this word, denoting a clumsy person or one with ugly or deformed hands or feet.

Patr.: Russ.: **Lapin**.

Patr. (from a dim.): Russ. and Jewish (Ashkenazic): **Lapkin**.

La Pinta *see* PINTO

Laplace *see* PLACE

Laplanche *see* PLANCHE

Lappalainen Finnish: ethnic name for a Laplander, from Finn. *Lappala* Lapland + the locative suffix *-ainen*. The meaning of the tribal name *Lapp* is unknown; although the Laplanders now speak a language related to Finnish, it is likely that this was adopted at a comparatively late (although still prehistoric) date. They seem to have come originally from central Asia and to have been pushed into their extreme northerly situation by the migrations of the Finns, Goths, and Slavs.

Läpple *see* LEPPER

Lapradelle *see* PRÉ

Lapworth English: habitation name from a place in Warwicks., so called from the OE personal name **Hlappa* + OE *worð* enclosure (see WORTH).

Lara Spanish: habitation name from a place in the province of Burgos.

Laranjeira Portuguese: topographic name for someone who lived by an orange grove, Port. *laranjeira* (a deriv. of *laranja* orange, from Arabic and ultimately from Persian; cf. NARANJO).

Larcher 1. German: from Ger. *Lärche* larch (MHG *larche, lerche*, from LL *larix*, possibly of Celt. origin) + *-er* suffix denoting a human agent or inhabitant. The application is not clear: it may be a topographic name for someone living among larches, an occupational name for a woodman in a larch wood, or a nickname for one tall as a larch. The surname is also borne by Ashkenazic Jews, the reason(s) for its adoption also being unclear. **2.** French: var. of ARCHER, with fused definite article.

Var. (of 1): **Lercher**.

Larder English: metonymic occupational name for a servant in charge of a larder or storeroom for provisions, from ANF *larder* (LL *lardārium*, a deriv. of *lar(i)dum* bacon fat).

Vars.: **Lard(i)ner**.

Large English and French: nickname (literal or ironic) meaning 'generous', from ME, OF *large* generous, free (L *largus* abundant). The Eng. word came to acquire its mod. sense only gradually during the Middle Ages; it is used to mean 'ample in quantity' in the 13th cent., and the sense 'broad' first occurs in the 14th. This use is probably too late for the surname to have originated as a nickname for a fat man.

Vars.: Eng.: **Lardge, Largman**. Fr.: **Lelarge**.
Dims.: Eng.: **Largey**. Fr.: **Largeau(lt), Target(eau), Largeot**.

Largent *see* ARGENT

Larieu *see* RIEU

Larimer *see* LORIMER

Larius *see* HILARY

Larive *see* RIVE

Lark English: **1.** nickname for a merry person or an early riser, from ME *lavero(c)k*, lark (OE *lāwerce*; cogn. with MHG *lerche*). It was perhaps also a metonymic occupational name for someone who netted the birds and sold them for the cooking pot. **2.** from a medieval given name, a byform of LAWRENCE, derived by back-formation from LARKIN.

Vars.: **Larke** (chiefly Norfolk). (Of 1 only): **Laverack, Laverick** (Northumb. and Yorks.).
'Servant of L. 2': Eng.: **Larkman** (E Anglia).

Larkin 1. English: from a medieval given name, a dim. of LAWRENCE, formed with the addition of the ME suffix *-kin* (of Low Ger. origin). **2.** Irish: Anglicized form of Gael. **Ó Lorcáin** 'descendant of *Lorcán*', a personal name from a dim. of *lorc* fierce, cruel.

Vars.: **Larking, Lorkin(g)**.

Larmer *see* ARMER

Larmor *see* ARMOUR

Larnach Scots: regional name (with the suffix *-ach*) for someone from *Lorne* (Gael. *Latharn*), an area in the former county of Argyll, named from an ancient Scottish king bearing the byname *Loarn* 'Fox'.

Var.: **Larnack**.

Larner English: **1.** occupational name for a scholar or schoolmaster, from ME *lern(en)* which meant both 'to learn' and 'to teach' (OE *leornian*). For the change of *-ar-* to *-er-*, cf. MARCHANT. **2.** in the case of a Suffolk family who bore this surname by the 16th cent., ancestors are recorded in the forms *Lawney* (1381) and *de Lauuenay* (1327); this is therefore probably a var. of DELANEY.

Var. (of 1): **LERNER**.

Larochelle *see* ROACH

Laronde *see* HIRON

Larose *see* ROSE

Larrazabal Basque: topographic name for someone who lived by a large expanse of meadowland, from *larre* pasture, meadow + *zabal* broad, wide.

Larrea Basque: topographic name for someone who lived by a patch of meadowland, from *larre* pasture, meadow + the def. art. *-a*. This is also the name of places in the provinces of Álava and Biscay, which may have contributed to the surname.

Var.: **Larrinaga** (with the addition of a local suffix).

Larrett *see* LAWRENCE

Larue *see* RUE

Laš *see* LACH

Lasa Basque: topographic name for someone who lived by a stream, from *lats* stream + the def. art. *-a*.

Lasar *see* LAZAR

Lascelles English (Norman): habitation name from *Lacelle* in Orne, so called from OF *la* the + *celle* hermit's cell (L *cella* small room; cf. SELLER 3).

Var.: **Lessells**.

Lasenby *see* LAZENBY

Lashford *see* LATCHFORD

Łaski Polish: topographic name from Pol. *łas, łaz* clearing in a forest (ultimately cogn. with OE *lēah*).

Var.: **Łasek**.

Laśkiewicz *see* LAZAR

Laskowski Polish and Jewish (E Ashkenazic): habitation name from a place called *Lasków* (Ger. *Laskau*), of which there is one in Lithuania and another in Galicia. They derive their name from Pol. *lasek*, dim. of *las, les* wood.

Vars.: Jewish: **Laskow, Laskov(ski), Laska(u)** (W Ashkenazic); **Lask(i)er, Laskar**.

Lasnier *see* LANIER

Laso Spanish: nickname for a feeble or indolent person, from OSp. *laso* tired, weak(ened) (L *lassus*).

Lasoń Polish: occupational name for a woodman, from Pol. *las, les* wood, forest + *-oń* suffix indicating association or relationship.

Vars.: **Lasota, Lasocki.**

Patr.: **Laśkiewicz.**

Lassalle 1. French: local name or occupational name for someone who lived or worked at a manor house, from OF *sal(e)* hall (mod. Fr. *salle*; see also SALE 1), with fused def. art. *la*. **2.** Jewish: Gallicized spelling of *Lossal*, from *Loslau*, the Ger. name of the town of *Wodisław Śląski* in Silesia.

Var. (of 1): **Lasalle.**

Lassen see LAWRENCE

Lasseter see LEICESTER

Lassey see LACEY

Last 1. English (E Anglia): metonymic occupational name for a cobbler, or perhaps for a maker of cobblers' lasts, from ME *last, lest* the wooden form in the shape of a foot used for making or repairing shoes (OE *lǣste* from *lāst* footprint). **2.** German: metonymic occupational name for a porter, from Ger. *Last* burden, load (MHG *last*). **3.** Jewish (Ashkenazic): of unknown origin, possibly from Ger. *Last* burden, load, in which case the origin is presumably as in 2.

Var. (of 1): **Laster.**

La Stella see STELLA

Lastra Spanish: topographic name for someone who lived by a flat stone slab, probably a boundary marker of some kind, Sp. *lastra* (of uncertain origin; cf. DELÂTRE). There are numerous places in Spain named with this word, and they may also have contributed to the surname.

Var.: **Lastras.**

Łaszczewski Polish: habitation name from a place called *Łaszczew*, which is said by Rospond to have been named in the 16th cent. from a byname *Łaszcz* 'Robber', from Pol. *łaszczyć się* to covet (dial. to rob).

Latch see LEEK

Latches see LEACH

Latchford English: habitation name from any of various places, for example in Ches. and Oxon., so called from OE *lǣcc* stream (cf. LEACH 2) + *ford* FORD.

Vars.: **Lashford, Letchford.**

Lateiner Jewish (Ashkenazic): nickname for a learned man who owned books in Latin (Ger. *Lateiner* Latinist; cf. LATIMER).

Latek Polish: apparently a nickname from Pol. *lato* summer + the dim. suffix *-ek*, perhaps denoting someone of a sunny disposition, or acquired for some anecdotal reason now lost. Cf. SUMMER.

Habitation name: **Latkowski.**

Latham English: habitation name from any of the various places in N England named with the dat. pl. form (used originally after a preposition) of ON *hlaða* barn, as for

example *Latham* in W Yorks., *Lathom* in Lancs., and *Laytham* in E Yorks.

Vars.: **Laytham, Lathom, Lathem; Le(a)tham** (Scotland); **Leathem** (N Ireland); **Leed(h)am, Leedom.**

Latimer English: occupational name for a clerk or keeper of records in Latin, ANF *latinier, latim(m)ier*. Latin was the more or less universal language of official documents in the Middle Ages, displaced only gradually by the vernacular—ANF at first in England, and eventually English.

Vars.: **Lattimer, Latimore, Lat(t)ner, Laturner.**

Latouche see TOUCHE

Latreille see TREILLE

Latter 1. English: occupational name for a worker in wood or nickname for a thin person, from an agent deriv. of ME *latt* thin narrow strip of wood (OE *lætt*). **2.** Jewish: of uncertain origin.

Presumed vars. (of 2): **Latterman, Lattner.**

Latto Scots: according to Black, this is a habitation name from *Laithis* in the former county of Ayr, a minor place of uncertain etymology, which is apparently now lost.

Vars.: **Latta, Lattey, Lawtie, LAWTY.**

Latzarus see LAZAR

Laubreton see BRETT

Lauder Scots and Northumb.: habitation name from *Lauder* in the former county of Berwicks., recorded in 1250 in the form *Lawedir*, in 1298 as *Loweder*, and in 1334 as *Lawadir*; the placename is apparently Brit., perhaps from a cogn. of Bret. *laour* trench, ditch.

Vars.: **Lawder, Lawt(h)er.**

Lauer 1. German: unflattering nickname from MHG *lūre* crafty or cunning person, cheat (apparently originally 'one with narrowed eyes'; the word is akin to mod. Ger. *Lauer* ambush and mod. Eng. *lower*). **2.** German: occupational name for a tanner, MHG *lōwære*, from *lō* (gen. *lōwes*) tannin, which is extracted from the bark of trees (cf. BARKER 1). **3.** German: habitation name from *Lauer* in Franconia, named from the stream on which it stands, in turn perhaps originally named with a Celt. word meaning 'turbulent'. **4.** Jewish (Ashkenazic): of uncertain origin. Any or all of the explanations of the Ger. name are possible.

Var.: **LAUR.**

Lauersen see LAWRENCE

Läufer German: occupational name for a messenger, Ger. *Läufer* runner, an agent deriv. of *laufen* to run (MHG *loufen*, OHG *(h)louf(f)an*).

Laugheran see LOUGHREY

Laughlan see LACHLAN

Laughnan see LOUGHNANE

Laughton English: habitation name from any of the numerous places in England so called. Most of them, as for example those in Leics., Lincs. (near Gainsborough), Sussex, and W Yorks., are named with OE *lēac* leek + *tūn* enclosure. The cpd was also used in the extended sense of a herb garden and later of a kitchen garden. Laughton near Folkingham in Lincs., however, was probably named as *loc-tūn* enclosed farm (see LOCK 2).

Laukkanen Finnish: patr. from a nickname for a brisk and active person, from Finn. *laukka* to gallop, canter.

Laulin *see* NICHOLAS

Laumonier *see* AUMONIER

Launder *see* LAVENDER

Laur 1. French: topographic name for someone who lived by a conspicuous laurel tree, OF *laur* (L *laurus*). 2. French: from a given name of the same etymology, borne by various minor early saints, including a hermit, a martyr, and an abbot. 3. German: var. of LAUER.

Vars. (of 1 and 2): **Laure**. (Of 1 only): **Laurier**.

Dims. (of 1 and 2): Fr.: **Laurel, Laureau, Laurot, Laur(a)in, Lorin**. It.: **Lauriello, Laurini, Laurino**.

Aug. (of 1 and 2): Fr.: **Lauras**.

Collective (of 1): Cat.: **Lloret**.

Patrs. (from 2): It.: **Di Lauro**. Russ.: **Lavrov**.

Lauriol *see* ORIOL

Lautrec French: habitation name from places in Tarn and Haute-Vienne, probably so called from the OProv. def. art. *le* + *autreg* privilege, concession (from *autrejar* to grant, concede, LL *auctōrizāre*), i.e. a community that enjoyed certain special rights.

Lauxmann *see* LUCAS

Lavallette *see* VALE

Lavelle Irish: Anglicized form of Gael. **Ó Maoil Fhábhail** 'descendant of the devotee of (St) *Fábhal*', a personal name meaning 'Movement', 'Travel'.

Vars.: **Lavell; Mulfaul**.

Lavender English: occupational name for a washerman or launderer, ANF *lavend(i)er* (LL *lavandārius*, an agent deriv. of *lavanda* washing, things to be washed, from the gerundive of *lavāre* to wash). The term was applied especially to a worker in the wool industry who washed the raw wool or rinsed the cloth after fulling. There is no evidence for any direct connection with the word for the plant (ME, OF *lavendre*, LL *lavendula*), although the etymology of this word is obscure and it may have been named from the same root, in reference to the use of lavender oil in making soap or of dried heads of lavender in perfuming freshly washed clothes.

Vars.: **Launder**, LANDER.

Lavenier *see* AVOINE

Laver 1. English: occupational name for a washerman, ANF *laver* (an agent deriv. of OF *laver* to wash, L *lavāre*; cf. LAVENDER). 2. S French: nickname for a rich man, from OProv. *aver* possessions, property (from the verb *aver* to have, possess, L *habēre*), with fused def. art. *le*. In SE France the word is used of a flock of sheep (the principal form of property in the area) and the surname

may have been originally an occupational name for a shepherd.

Patrs. (from 1): Eng.: **Lavers** (chiefly Devon and Cornwall), **Lavis(s)** (chiefly W Country).

Laverack *see* LARK

Lavergne *see* VER

Laverty Irish (chiefly N Ireland): Anglicized form of Gael. **Ó Fhlaithbheartaigh** and **Mac Fhlaithbheartaigh** 'descendant' and 'son of *Flaithbheartach*', a personal name composed of the elements *flaith* prince, ruler + *beartach* doer of valiant deeds.

Vars.: **Lafferty; McLaverty**.

Lavery Irish (chiefly N Ireland): anglicized form of Gael. **Ó Labhradha** 'descendant of *Labraidh*', a byname meaning 'Spokesman'.

Var.: **LOWRY**.

Laville *see* VILLE

Lavin Irish: Anglicized form of Gael. **Ó Laimhín**, a reduced form of *Ó Flaithimhín* 'descendant of *Flaithimhín*', a personal name from a dim. of *flaith* prince, ruler.

Vars.: **Laffin, Laffan**; HAND (an erroneous translation, based on the assumption that the Gael. form is *Ó Láimhín*, from a dim. of *lámh* hand, arm).

La Viola *see* VIOLA

Lavoisier French: unflattering nickname for a sly or cunning person, from OF *avoisié* crafty, with fused def. art. and respelling of the ending to coincide with the agent suffix. The word itself is a blend in OF of *voizié* evil, cunning (LL *vitiātus* and *avisé* clever, learned (LL *advisātus*).

Var.: **Levéziel** (Normandy).

La Volpe *see* VOLPE

Lavrenčić *see* LAWRENCE

Lavrov *see* LAUR

Law English and Scots: 1. from a ME pet form of LAWRENCE. 2. topographic name for someone who lived near a hill, Northern ME *law* (from OE *hlāw* hill, burial mound).

Patrs. (from 1): **Law(e)s** (found chiefly in S England), **Lawson**.

Lawder *see* LAUDER

Lawford English: habitation name from a place so called, of which examples are to be found in Essex and Warwicks. These derive their name from the OE personal name *Lealla* (cogn. with the attested OHG *Lallo*, but of unknown meaning) + OE *ford* FORD.

Lawless English: nickname for an unbridled and licentious man, from ME *laghless, lawelas* (a cpd of late OE *lagu* law (from ON) + the native suffix *-l(ē)as* without, lacking). Reaney suggests additionally that this name may have referred to an outlaw (i.e. one from whom the protection of the law had been withdrawn), but this seems unlikely.

Lawley English (chiefly W Midlands): habitation name from a place in Shrops., so called from the OE personal name *Lāfa* (from *lāf* remnant, survivor) + OE *lēah* wood, clearing.

Lawlor Irish: Anglicized form of Gael. **Ó Leathlobhair** 'descendant of *Leathlobar*', a personal name composed of the elements *leath* half (i.e. 'somewhat', 'fairly') and *lobar* leprous, sick. The name seems to have been originally a byname for a man of unhealthy constitution.

Vars.: **(O')Lawler, (O')Lalo(u)r**.

Lawman *see* LAMONT

Lawn *see* LAND

Ławnicki Polish: occupational name for an assessor, Pol. *ławnik* (from *ława* bench), with the addition of the surname suffix -*ski* (see BARANOWSKI).

Var.: **Ławniczak**.

Lawrence English: from the ME and OF given name *Lorens, Laurence* (L *Laurentius* 'man from *Laurentum*', a town in Italy probably named from its laurels or bay trees). The name was borne by a saint who was martyred at Rome in the 3rd cent. AD; he enjoyed a considerable cult throughout Europe, with consequent popularity of the given name (Fr. *Laurent*, It., Sp. *Lorenzo*, Port. *Lourenço*, Ger. *Laurenz*; Czech *Vavřinec*, Pol. *Wawrzyniec* (assimilated to the Pol. vocab. word *wawrzyn* laurel)). The surname is also borne by Jews, among whom it is presumably an Anglicization of one or more like-sounding Ashkenazic surnames.

Vars.: **Lawrance, Laurence, Laurance, Laurens, Lorence, Lowrance**.

Dims.: Eng.: **Lawrie, Laurie; Lawr(e)y** (Devon); LOWRY (N England and Scotland); LAW, LOW, LARKIN, LARK, LAKIN, **Larrie, Larrett**. Fr.: **Laurentin, Laurenty, Laurendin, Laurencin, Laurendeau, Laurenceau, Lorenceau, Laurencet, Laurençot, Lorensot, Laurençon, Laurenson**. It.: **Lorenzetti, Lorenzetto, Lorenzin(i), Lorenzut(ti); Laurito; Renzetti, Renzini; Renzulli, Renzullo; Nencetti, Nencini, Nenciol(in)i**. Sp.: **Laurentino**. Ger. (of Slav. origin): **Lorek, Loricke, Löhrke, Lorck**. Pol.: **Wawrzeńczyk, Wawrzonek, Wawrzyk; Wach**. Czech: **Vavřík, Vavřička, Vavruška**.

Augs.: It.: **Lorenzon(i); Renzoni; Nencioni**.

Patrs.: Eng.: **Lawrenson** (chiefly Lancs.; also adopted as a Jewish surname). Sc.: **Laurenson** (chiefly Orkney and Shetland); MCLAUREN. It.: **(De) Laurentis, De Laurenzis, De Lorenzis, De Lorenzo, Di Lorenzo; De Renzis**. Low Ger.: **Lorentzen, Lohrensen, Lornsen; Lörtzing, Lortzing**. Du.: **Rensen**. Norw., Dan.: **Lorentsen, Loren(t)zen, Lauritsen, Lauritzen, Lauridsen, Lau(e)(r)sen, Laugesen, Larsen, Lassen**. Swed.: **Lorentzson, Larsson**. Pol.: **Wawrzyniak, Wawrzyńczak; Lorentowicz** (from a Ger. form of the given name). Russ.: **Lavrenov, Lavrinov**. Croatian: **Lavrenčić**. Lithuanian: **Laurinaitis**. Latvian: **Labrencis**.

Patrs. (from dims.): Eng.: **Larson**. Pol.: **Wawrzkiewicz, Wachowicz, Wachowiec, Wachowiak; Wasiak, Waszak**. Russ.: **Lavrin, Lavrushin, Lavrukhin, Lavrishchev** (all also from the less common LAUR). Lithuanian: **Loreit, Lorat**.

Habitation name: Pol.: **Wachowski**.

'Servant of L. (dim.)': Eng.: **Lap(p)age** (see PAGE).

Lawtie *see* LATTO

Lawton English: habitation name, common in Lancs. and Yorks., from *Buglawton* or *Church Lawton* in Ches., so called from OE *hlāw* hill, burial mound (see LAW 2) + *tūn* enclosure, settlement.

Lawty 1. English: nickname for a trustworthy person, from ME *lawty* loyalty (OF *léauté*, L *lēgālitas*, a deriv. of *lēgālis*; see LEAL). **2.** Scots: var. of LATTO.

Vars. (of 1): **Laity, Lewt(e)y, L(e)uty**.

Lax 1. German: metonymic occupational name for a salmon fisher or a seller of salmon and other delicacies, from Ger. *Lachs* salmon (MHG, OHG *lahs*, originally meaning 'leaping', 'playful'; cf. LAKER 2). **2.** German: nickname for a lively person, from MHG *lahs* in the sense 'playful', 'leaping'. **3.** Jewish (Ashkenazic): it is unclear to what extent this name is occupational, as in 1, and to what extent it is ornamental, one of the many Ashkenazic surnames taken from words denoting fish, birds, and animals.

Vars. (of 3): **Lachs, Lacks, Lass; Laxer, Lachser, Lakser; Laxman, Lachsman, Laksman**.

Lay *see* LEE

Layborn *see* LEYBURN

Laycock English (chiefly Yorks.): habitation name from *Laycock* in W Yorks. (or possibly from *Lacock* in Wilts.). Both are recorded in Domesday Book as *Lacoc* and seem to be named with OE **lacuc*, a dim. of *lacu* stream (see LAKE).

Var.: **Leacock**.

Layland *see* LEYLAND

Layne *see* LANE

Laytham *see* LATHAM

Layton English: habitation name from any of various places so called, e.g. in Lancs. (near Blackpool) and in N Yorks. The former gets its name from OE *lād* water-course (cf. LOADER 1) + *tūn* enclosure, settlement, the latter from OE *lēac* leek + *tūn* (cf. LAUGHTON, LEYTON, and LEIGHTON).

Lazar Jewish (Ashkenazic), German, and (rarely) English: from the Aramaic male given name *Lazar* (an aphetic form of the Hebr. male given name *Elazar*, composed of the elements *El* God + *azar* help, and meaning 'may God help him' or 'God has helped (i.e., by granting a son)'). In the New Testament, this was the name of the brother of Martha and Mary who was restored to life by Christ (John 11: 1–44). According to an ancient popular tradition, after the death of Christ he came to Provence with his two sisters and became the first bishop of Marseilles. As a Ger. or Eng. name it may in some cases be a nickname for a beggar or especially an outcast leper; this use arises from the biblical parable of Dives and Lazarus (Luke 16: 19–31).

Vars.: Jewish: **Laz(a)rus, Lazerus; Lozerus** (from Yid. *Lozer*). Ger.: **La(t)zarus, Lazer, Lasar, Laser, Leser, Löser**.

Rum.: **Lazăr**. Pol.: **Łazarski**. Hung.: **Lázár**.

Dims.: Jewish: **Lazaruk** (E Ashkenazic). Ukr.: **Lazarchuk**. It.: **Lazzarin(i), Lazzarino, Lazzerini, Lazzarelli, Lazzaretti, Lazzeretti, Lazzarotti, Lazzarotto, Lazzarutti**. Pol.: **Łazarczyk, Łazarek**.

Augs.: It.: **Lazzaroni, Lazzarone, Lazzeroni**.

Patrs.: Jewish: **Lazarson, Lazerson; Lazarin, Lazarow, Lazaroff, Lazarovitch, Lazarowicz, Lazarowics, Lazarowitz, Lazerowitz, Lazarovitz, Lazarofsky** (E Ashkenazic), **Lazarovici** (Rumanian spelling). Russ.: **Lazarev**. Pol.: **Łazarowicz**. Croatian:

Lazarević, Laz(ov)ić. Bulg.: **Lazarov.** It.: **Di Lazzari** (Venetia). Armenian: **Azarian.**

Patr. (from a dim.): Pol.: **Laśkiewicz, Łaszkiewicz.**

Lazenby N English: habitation name from *Lazenby* in N Yorks. or *Lazonby* in Cumb., both so called from ON *leysing* freedman (also used as a byname and personal name) + *býr* farm, settlement.

Var.: **Lasenby.**

Lea *see* LEE

Leach English: **1.** occupational name for a physician, OE *lǣce*. It may also have been a nickname for a demanding or bloodthirsty person, from the bloodsucking creature of the same name, although the metaphor lay originally in calling the animal 'healer' rather than the doctor 'bloodsucker'. **2.** local name for someone who lived by a boggy stream, OE *lǣcc, lǣce* (related to *lacu* stream; see LAKE, LATCHFORD).

Vars. (of 1): **Leche, Lee(t)ch, Leitch.** (Of 2): **Latches, Letcher.**

Leacock *see* LAYCOCK

Leacy *see* LACEY

Leadbetter English: occupational name for a worker in lead, ME *ledbetere*, agent noun from OE *lēad* lead + *bēatan* to beat, strike.

Vars.: **Ledbetter, Leadbeat(t)er, Lidbetter, Leadbitter.**

Leader English: **1.** occupational name for someone who led a horse and cart conveying commodities from one place to another, ME *ledere*, agent noun from OE *lǣdan* to lead. The word may also sometimes have been used to denote a foreman or someone who led sport or dance, but the name certainly did not originate with *leader* in the modern sense 'civil or military commander'; this is a comparatively recent development. **2.** occupational name for a worker in lead, an agent deriv. of OE *lēad* lead; cf. LEADBETTER.

Vars. (of 1): **Leeder** (Norfolk). (Of 2): **Ledder.**

Leaf English: **1.** from the OE personal names *Lēofa* (masc.) and *Lēofe* (fem.) 'Dear', 'Beloved'. These names were in part short forms of various cpd names with this first element (cf., e.g., LEWIN 1 and LEVERIDGE), in part independent affectionate bynames. See also LOVE. **2.** topographic name for someone who lived in a densely foliated area, from ME *lēaf* leaf; a certain Robert Intheleaves is recorded in London in the 14th cent. **3.** as an American surname it is normally a translation of BLATT 'leaf' or an Anglicized form of the Swed. ornamental cpds.

Vars.: **Leafe, Leefe, Lief, Leif, Life, Liff.**

Patrs. (from 1): Eng.: **Leaves, Leavis.**

Cpds (of 2; ornamental): Swed.: **Löfberg, Lövberg** ('leaf hill'); **Löfdahl, Lövdahl** ('leaf valley'); **Löfgren, Lövgren** ('leaf branch'); **Löfquist, Lövquist** ('leaf twig'); **Löfstedt, Lövstedt** ('leaf homestead'); **Löfstrand** ('leaf shore'); **Löfström** ('leaf river').

Leahy Irish: Anglicized form of Gael. *Ó Laochdha* 'descendant of *Laochdh*', a personal name derived from *laoch* hero.

Var.: **Lehigh.**

Leak *see* LEEK

Leal Spanish and Portuguese: nickname for a loyal or trustworthy person, from Sp., Port. *leal* loyal, faithful to

obligations (L *lēgālis*, from *lex*, gen. *lēgis*, law, obligation). Cf. LAWTY 1.

Leaman *see* LEMON

Lean **1.** English (chiefly Devon): nickname for a thin or lean person, from ME *lene* lean, OE *hlǣne*. **2.** Irish and Scots: abbreviated form of McLEAN. **3.** Irish: Anglicized form of Gael. *Ó Laighin*; see LANE 2. **4.** Irish: Anglicized form of Gael. *Ó Liatháin*; see LEHANE.

Var.: **Leane.** (Of 3 and 4): **O'Leane.**

Leapman English: occupational name for a basket-maker, from OE *lēap* basket + *mann* man. The term *lepemakere* denoting a basket-maker occurs in ME.

Vars.: **Leaper, Leeper, Leiper, Laiper** (Scotland); LEPPER.

Lear English: **1.** habitation name from any of various places in N France named with the Gmc element *lār* clearing. **2.** habitation name from *Leire* in Leics., apparently so called from an old Brit. river name, which may be the base of the tribe-name *Ligore* found in LEICESTER.

Learmonth Scots: habitation name from a place in the former county of Berwicks., of uncertain etymology. The second element may be from Gael. *monadh* mountain, moor, but since the place is in the Lowlands, an Eng. (or Scandinavian) etymology should probably rather be sought.

Vars.: **Learmont, Learmond, Leirmonth.**

Learnard *see* LEONARD

Learoyd English (Yorks.): apparently a habitation name from an unidentified place, perhaps named from OE *lēah* wood, pasture + *rod* clearing.

Leary Irish: Anglicized form of *Ó Laoghaire*, 'descendant of *Laoghaire*', a byname originally meaning 'Keeper of Calves', from *loagh* calf. This was the name of a 5th-cent. king of Ireland, after whom the port of *Dún Laoghaire* ('fort, citadel of Laoghaire') is named, and from whom many modern bearers of this name claim descent.

Var.: **O'Leary.**

Leask Scots: habitation name from a place, now called Pitlurg, in the parish of Slains, Aberdeen. The name is first recorded in 1380 in the form *Lask*, but its origin is not known.

Var.: **Leisk.**

Leason *see* LEES

Leatham *see* LATHAM

Leathead *see* LEITHEAD

Leather English (chiefly Lancs. and Yorks.): metonymic occupational name for a leatherworker or seller of leather goods, from ME *lether*, OE *leþer* leather.

Dim.: Ger.: **Lederle.**

Patr.: Eng.: **Leathers.**

Cpds (occupational-ornamental): Jewish: **Lederberg** ('leather hill'); **Lederfajn** ('leather fine', a Pol. spelling); **Ledereich, Lederaich** ('leather rich'); **Lederstein** ('leather stone').

Equiv. (not cogn.): Pol.: SKÓRA.

Leatherbarrow English (Lancs.): habitation name from *Latterbarrow* in Furness, probably so called from ON *látr* lair of a wild animal + OE *bearu* grove, wood.

Leatherland see LITHERLAND

Leathley English: habitation name from a place in W Yorks., which appears to derive its name from OE *hleoða*, dat. pl. of *hlið* slope + *lēah* wood, clearing.

Leaver see LEVER

Leavesley English (Midlands): habitation name from an unidentified place, apparently so called from the gen. case of some OE personal name with the first element *lēof* beloved (cf. LEAF 1) + OE *lēah* wood, clearing.

Leavett see LEVETT

Leavey see LEVY

Leavy see DUNLEAVY, LEVY

Le Bâtard see BASTARD

Lebbel see BEAU

Lebedev Russian and Jewish (E Ashkenazic): patr. from the nickname *Lebed* 'Swan' (a distant cogn. of L *albus* white). The Jewish surnames are ornamental.
Vars.: Russ.: **Lebedinski** (a clergy name). Jewish: **Lebedoff**; **Lebed**, **Lebedinsky**; **Lebedkin** (from a dim.).

Lebègue see BÈGUE

Le Bel see BEAU

Leblanc see BLANC

Leboeuf see BOEUF

Lebon see BON

Lebordais see BOARDER

Leborgne see BORGNE

Lebret see BRETT

Le Canuel see CHENU

Lecapelain see CHAPLIN

Le Carré see CARRÉ

Lecerf see CERF

Lech Polish: from the Pol. given name *Lech*.

Lechat see CATT

Leche see LEACH

Léchelle see ESCHELLE

Lechêne see CHÊNE

Lechevalier see CHEVALIER

Lechner see LEHMANN

Leck see LEEK

Łęcki Polish: topographic name from Pol. dial. *łęk* swamp, waterlogged ground, or from the related *łąka* meadow, with the addition of the surname suffix -*ski* (see BARANOWSKI).

Leckie Scots: habitation name from a place in the parish of Gargunnock, in the former county of Stirlings., so called from a deriv. of Gael. *leac* flagstone (i.e. 'place of flagstones').
Vars.: **Leck(e)y** (N Ireland).

Lecoc see COCK

Lecomber see CAMBER

Le Corbeiller see CORBEIL

Lecorbusier see COURVOISIER

Lecordier see CORDE

Lecornu see CORNE

Lecount see COUNT

Lecour see COEUR

Lecreux see CREUX

Lecue Spanish form of Basque **Lekue**: topographic name for someone who lived at a particular spot outside the main village, from Basque *lek(h)u* place, spot + the local suffix -*ue* (from *(g)une* space, distance). Alternatively it may be a topographic name for someone who lived at a lower spot, in which case it is a var. of **Lekube**, containing the suffix -*be* lower down.

Ledbetter see LEADBETTER

Ledder see LEADER

Leddy Irish: Anglicized form of Gael. **Ó Lideadha** 'descendant of *Lideadh*', a personal name of uncertain origin.
Var.: **Liddy**.

Lederaich see LEATHER

Ledesma Spanish: habitation name from places so called in the provinces of Logroño, Salamanca, and Soria. The placename probably derives from a superlative form of a Celt. adj. meaning 'broad', 'wide' (cf. LEITH).

Ledger English: 1. from a Gmc personal name composed of the elements *liut* people, tribe + *geri, gari* spear, introduced into England in the form *Legier* by Norman settlers. The name was borne by a 7th-cent. bishop of Autun, and although he was martyred for political rather than religious reasons his fame contributed to the popularity of the name in France; in Germany the name was connected with a different saint, an 8th-cent. bishop of Münster. 2. voiced var. of *Letcher* (see LEACH 2), in part a deliberate alteration to avoid unpleasant association with ANF *lecheor* lecher.
Var. (of 1): **Leger**. See also LEGARD and LEGGATT.
Dims. (of 1): Fr.: **Légeret**, **Légerot**, **Légeron**, **Ligereau**, **Ligerot**, **Ligeron**.
Patrs. (from 1): Ger.: **Lüdgering**. Flem.: **Luytgaeren(s)**.

Ledster see LISTER

Lee 1. English: topographic name for someone who lived near a meadow, pasture, or patch of arable land, ME *lee, lea* (from OE *lēa*, dat. case—originally used after a preposition—of *lēah* wood, clearing, a term with cogns. in many European languages; cf. LEICHER 2, LOO, LACHMANN 3, and ŁASKI). 2. English: habitation name from any of the many places names with OE *lēah* wood, clearing, as for example *Lee* in Bucks., Essex, Hants, Kent, and Shrops., and *Lea* in Ches., Derbys., Herefords., Lancs., Lincs., and Wilts. **3.** Irish: Anglicized form of Ó **Laoidhigh** 'descendant of *Laoidheach*', a personal name derived from *laoidh* poem, song (originally a byname for a poet).

Vars. (of 1 and 2): **Lea**, Leigh, Lees; **Lay(e)**, Ley, **Lye** (from the later OE dat. form, preserved in ME as *l(e)ye; Lye* is the name of a place in the W Midlands). (Of 1 only): **L(a)yman, Leyman; At(t)lee, Atley, Atlay, Attle** (with fused preposition); **Atherlee** (with fused preposition and article). (Of 3): **O'Lee, O'Loye, O'L(e)ye, O'Lie**.

Leeb *see* Löwe

Leeburn *see* Leyburn

Leech *see* Leach

Leedam *see* Latham

Leeder *see* Leader

Leeds English: habitation name from the city in W Yorks. The placename is of Brit. origin, appearing in Bede in the form *Loidis* 'People of the *Lāt*', an earlier name of the river Aire, meaning 'the violent one'. *Loidis* was a district name, only later restricted to the town.

Leefe *see* Leaf

Leehan *see* Lehane

Leek English: **1.** topographic name for someone who lived by a stream, from ON *lækr* brook. There are also a number of places named with this word—such as *Leak* in N Yorks., *Leake* in Lincs. and Notts., *Leek* in Staffs., and *Leck* in Lancs.—and the surname may also be from any of these. **2.** metonymic occupational name for a grower or seller of leeks, from OE *lēac*.

Vars.: **Leeke, Leak(e), Leck, Leeks, Leaker.** (Of 1 only): **Latch(es), Letch(er)**, Leach (palatal forms in Southern dialects of ME).

Leeman *see* Lemon

Leeming English: **1.** habitation name from either of two places so called in W Yorks. near Keighley and in N Yorks. near Northallerton. Both are so called from a river name, a deriv. of OE *lēoma* gleam, sparkle. **2.** var. of Lemon (1 and 2).

Leenders *see* Leonard

Leeper *see* Leapman

Lees 1. English: topographic name from ME *lees* fields, arable land, pl. of *lee* (see Lee 1). **2.** English: habitation name from any of the various places named with the nom. pl., *lēas*, of OE *lēah* wood, clearing. Examples of places so named are *Lees* near Ashton-under-Lyne and *Leece* near Barrow-in-Furness. **3.** English: from the medieval female given name *Lece*, a contracted form of *Lettice* (see Lett). **4.** Scots: aphetic form of Gillies.

Vars.: **Leese, Leece.** (Of 4 only): **Leish(man)**.

Metrs. (from 3): **Leeson** (chiefly Northants.); **Leason, Lesson, Lisson**.

Le Faou *see* Fage

Lefaucheur *see* Faucheur

Lefébure *see* Fèvre

Leffeck *see* Levick

Leffel *see* Löffler

Lefkovich *see* Lewkowicz

Le Fleming *see* Fleming

Lefort *see* Fort

Lefournié *see* Fournier

Lefridge *see* Leveridge

Legagneur *see* Gagneux

Le Gall *see* Gall

Legard English (Yorks.): from the Continental Gmc female personal name *Liutgard* (borne by Charlemagne's wife), composed of the elements *liut* people, tribe + *gard* enclosure, which was introduced into England in this form by the Normans. In some cases it may be a var. of Ledger 1, with an excrescent dental. See also Leggatt.

Legay *see* Gay

Legeay *see* Jay

Legendre *see* Gendre

Leger *see* Ledger

Legg English (chiefly W Country): **1.** metonymic nickname for someone with some malformation or peculiarity of the leg(s), or just with particularly long ones, from ME *legg* (ON *leggr*, of obscure further etymology; in the OE period *fōt* (see Foot) denoted both foot and leg). **2.** var. of Leigh.

Var.: **Legge**.

Leggatt English: **1.** occupational name for an ambassador or deputy, from ME, OF *legat* (L *lēgātus*, past part. of *lēgāre* to appoint, ordain, from *lex*, gen. *lēgis*, law, command). The name may have been given to an official elected to represent his village at the manor court. **2.** from a medieval personal name, a var. of Ledger 1 or Legard.

Vars. (mainly of 1): **Legatt, Legat(e), Leggate, Legget(t), Leggitt, Leggott, Legwood**.

Legh *see* Leigh

Legood *see* Good

Le Grand *see* Grant

Legrey *see* Gray

Le Grice *see* Grice

Lehane Irish: Anglicized form of Gael. Ó **Liatháin** 'descendant of *Liathán*', a personal name from a dim. of *liath* grey.

Vars.: **O'Lehane, O'Lyhane, O'Leaghan, L(e)yhane, Leehan(e), Lihane, Lyhan**, Lane, Lean.

Leherne *see* Heron

Lehigh *see* Leahy

Lehmann 1. German: status name for a feudal tenant or vassal, MHG *lēheman, lēnman* (from *lēhen* loan(ed land) + *man* man). The tenant held land on loan for the duration of his life in return for rent or service, but was not free to transfer or divide it. **2.** Jewish (Ashkenazic): of uncertain origin. According to Kaganoff it is normally an occupational name for a banker, pawnbroker, or usurer, from MHG *lēhenen* to lend, and was sometimes adopted as an equivalent of LEVI, apparently because of the coincidence of the first two letters. However, there are phonetic problems with the first of these explanations, while the second seems to be unsupported by any evidence.

Vars. (of 1): **Le(c)hner**, **Lohner**, **Löhner(t)**. (Of 2): **Lehman**.

Lehnertz *see* LEONARD

Lehrer 1. Jewish (Ashkenazic): occupational name for a teacher in a traditional Jewish elementary school, from mod. Ger. *Lehrer*, Yid. *lerer* teacher; cf. KINDERLEHRER, KLEINLERER, and KNELLER 3. **2.** German, and possibly in some cases, Jewish (Ashkenazic): topographic name for someone who lived in a marshy area. There are a number of minor places, mostly in S Germany, named with this element, and the surname may also come from any of them.

Vars. (of 2): **Lehr(mann)**.

Lehtinen Finnish: ornamental name from Finn. *lehti* leaf + the gen. suffix *-nen*. This is one of the many Finn. surnames taken in the 19th cent. from vocab. words denoting features of the natural landscape.

Lehtonen Finnish: ornamental name from Finn. *lehto* grove of trees + the gen. suffix *-nen*. This is one of the many Finn. surnames taken in the 19th cent. from vocab. words denoting features of the natural landscape.

Var.: **Lehto**.

Leib Jewish (Ashkenazic): from the Yid. male given name *Leyb* 'Lion'; cf. LÖWE 2.

Var.: **Leibush** (from Yid. **Leybish**, an extended form of the given name).

Dims.: **Leib(e)l** (from the Yid. dim. male given name *Leybl*).

Patrs.: **Leibso(h)n**; **Leibin**, **Leibov**, **Leibow**, **Leibowicz**, **Leibovi(t)ch**, **Leibowit(s)ch**, **Leibowitz**, **Leibowics**, **Leibovicz**, **Leibovitz**, **Leibovic** (E Ashkenazic), **Leibovici** (Rumanian spelling).

Patr. (from a dim.): **Leiblowicz**.

Leibnitz German: habitation name from one of the various places in Saxony and elsewhere called *Leubnitz* or *Leipnitz* (formerly *Lubenice*). The placename is of Slav. origin and the first element apparently refers to lime trees (cf. LIPPE and LIPSCHUTZ).

Var.: **Leibniz**.

Leibold *see* LEOPOLD

Leicester English: habitation name from the county town of Leics., so called from the OE tribal name *Ligore* (itself adapted from a Brit. river name) + OE *cæster* Roman fort (L *castra* legionary camp). Cf. LEAR 2.

Vars.: **Leycester**; **Lessiter**, **Lissiter**, **Lassiter**, **Lasseter**.

Leicher German: **1.** occupational name for a musician or singer, from an agent deriv. of MHG *leich* music, song (akin to ON *leika* to play, sport; see LAKER 2). **2.** topo-

graphic name for someone who lived in a copse, from the dial. term *la(i)ch* (cf. LACHMANN 3).

Vars.: **Leichner** (also Jewish (Ashkenazic), having a similar origin to 1; presumably an occupational name for a cantor). (Of 2 only): **Laich(n)er**; **Lach(n)er** (see also LAKE).

Leif *see* LEAF

Leigh English: habitation name from any of the numerous places (in at least sixteen counties)—but especially *Leigh* in Lancs.—so called from the nom. case of OE *lēah* wood, clearing (see LEE 1) or from *lēage*, a form of the dat. case of this word.

Vars.: **Legh**, **LEGG**.

Leighton English: habitation name from any of various places so called. Most, as for example those in Beds., Cambs., Ches., Lancs., and Shrops., get the name from OE *lēac* leek + *tūn* settlement; cf. LAUGHTON, LAYTON, and LEYTON.

Leikin *see* LAKIN

Leiner 1. English: cogn. of LANIER. **2.** Jewish (W Ashkenazic): name taken by someone who was good at chanting the Pentateuch at public worship in the synagogue or who regularly did so, from W Yid. *layner* reader (a deriv. of the W Yid. verb *laynen* to read, which comes ultimately from L *legere* to read).

Leinonen Finnish: patr. from the OFinn. personal name *Leino*, originally a byname meaning 'Sad'.

Var.: **Leino**.

Leiper *see* LEAPMAN

Leiprecht *see* LUBRECHT

Leipzig *see* LIPSKI

Leirer German: occupational name for a player on the lyre, from an agent deriv. of Ger. *Leier* lyre (MHG *līre*, OHG *līra*, from L *lȳra*, from Gk).

Var.: **Leyrer**.

Leirmonth *see* LEARMONTH

Leish *see* LEES

Leisk *see* LEASK

Leitão Portuguese: metonymic occupational name for a keeper of pigs, or nickname meaning 'Pig', from Port. *leitão* (suckling) pig (LL *lacto*, gen. *lactōnis*, a deriv. of *lac*, gen. *lactis*, milk; cf. LEITE).

Leitch *see* LEACH

Leite Portuguese: nickname for someone with a notably pale complexion, from Port. *leite* milk (LL *lacte*, for class. L *lac*, gen. *lactis*).

Leitert *see* LEUTHARD

Leith Scots: habitation name from the port near Edinburgh, which takes its name from the river at whose mouth it stands. The river name is from Gael. *Lìte* meaning 'Wet'; compare W *llaith* damp, moist.

Leithead Scots: habitation name from lands in the parish of Kirknewton in the former county of Midlothian. The lands stand at the head of the river known as the Water of LEITH.

Var.: **Leithhead, Leathead**.

Leither *see* LEUTHER

Leitner German and Jewish (Ashkenazic): topographic name for someone who lived on the side of a mountain or slope of a hill, from Ger. *Leite* slope (MHG *līte*, OHG *(h)līta*) + *-(n)er* suffix denoting a native or inhabitant of a place, also an agent noun. The Ger. surname is particularly common in Bavaria and Austria.

Vars.: **Laitner; Leiter** (see also LEADER). Ger. only: **Leuthner**.

Leiva Spanish: habitation name from places in the provinces of Logroño and Murcia. The placename is early recorded in the form *Libia*; it is of uncertain etymology.

Leivers *see* LEVER

Leivick *see* LEVI

Leivik *see* LEVICK

Lejay *see* JAY

Lejeune *see* JEUNE

Le Keux *see* KEW

Leksin *see* LYOKHIN

Leland *see* McCLELLAN

Lelarge *see* LARGE

Lelikov *see* LENIN

Lelli Italian: aphetic form of a dim. from various medieval given names, as for example *Angelo* (see ANGEL) and *Gabriello* (see GABRIEL).

Patrs.: **De Lello, De Lellis**.

Le Lorrain *see* LORRAINE

Lely *see* LILLY

Lemagnan *see* MAGNIEN

Lemaigre *see* MAIGRE

Le Marchand *see* MARCHANT

Lemarignier *see* MARIN

Lemarquis *see* MARQUIS

Lemas *see* MAS

Lembcke *see* LAMBERT

Lemel *see* LAMB

Lemerle *see* MERLE

Lemétais *see* MÉTAYER

Lemon 1. English: from a ME given name *Lefman*, OE *Lēofman*, composed of the elements *lēof* dear, beloved + *mann* man. **2.** English: nickname for a lover or sweetheart, from ME *lem(m)an*, originally a cpd of the same elements as in 1, but used of either sex. There is no connection with the citrus fruit (whose name is of Arabic origin); this could not

be grown in the Eng. climate. **3.** Scots and N Irish: var. of LAMONT.

Vars. (of 1 and 2): **Loveman, Lowman, Luffman, Leaman, Leamon, Le(e)man, Lemmon, Liman, Limon, L(e)aming, Leeming**.

Lemos Portuguese: of uncertain meaning, coming originally from Galicia in W Spain. It is probably from the name recorded in L sources as *Lemavos*, apparently a deriv. of the Celt. element *lemos, limos* elm (cf. LENNOX and LIMA).

Lempereur *see* EMPEREUR

Lenarczyk *see* LEONARD

Lenchenko *see* ALEXANDER

Lendeke *see* LANCE

Leneveu *see* NEVEU

Lenfestey *see* VAISEY

Lenglard *see* ENGLISH

Lengyel Hungarian: ethnic name for a Pole, Hung. *lengyel*, of ORuss. origin.

Lenihan Irish: Anglicized form of Gael. **Ó Leanacháin** 'descendant of *Leanachán*', a personal name of uncertain origin (derivation from *léanach* sorrowful being phonologically impossible).

Vars.: **Lennihan, Lenehan, Len(n)ahan; O'Leneghan, (O')Lenaghan**.

Lenin Russian: one of a group of patrs. from dims. of ALEXANDER. This particular form was chosen as a pseudonym by Vladimir Ilyich Ulanov (1870–1924), with reference to political disturbances among Siberian exiles on the river *Lena*.

Vars.: **Lenkin, Lenshin; Len(k)ov, Lentsov, Lennikov; Lelikov, Lelyakov, Lelyanov, Lelyakin, Lelyashin, Lelyukhin; Lelkin**.

Lenn *see* LYNN

Lennie Scots: habitation name from *Leny* in the parish of Callander in the former county of Perths., so called from Gael. *lèana* bog, marsh + the local suffix *-ach*.

Vars.: **Len(n)y**.

Lennon Irish: **1.** Anglicized form of Gael. **Ó Leannáin** 'descendant of *Leannán*', a byname meaning 'Lover', 'Paramour', 'Concubine'. **2.** Anglicized form of Gael. **Ó Lonáin** 'descendant of *Lonán*', a personal name from a dim. of *lon* blackbird.

Vars.: **(O')Len(n)an(e), (O')Lannan, Lan(n)on, Lannen, Lannin, Linnane, LEONARD. (Of 2 only): O'Lonan(e), O'Lonnan**.

Dims. (of 2): **O'Lonagan, O'Lonegan, O'Lanegane, O'Lannegan, (O')Lanigan, Lannigan** (Gael. **Ó Lonagáin**).

Lennox Scots and N Irish: habitation name from the district near Dumbarton, recorded in 1174 in the form *Leuenaichs*, in the following year as *Levenax*. Apparently it gets its name from Gael. *leamhan* elm + the local suffix *-ach*.

Var.: **Lenox**.

Lenoble *see* NOBLE

Lenoir *see* NOIR

Lenthéric Provençal: from a dim. of a Gmc personal name *Lantier*, composed of the elements *land* land, territory + *hari, heri* army.

Lenton English: habitation name from one of the places so called, in Notts. and Lincs. The former derives its name from the river on which it stands, the *Leen* (an ancient Brit. name) + OE *tūn* settlement, enclosure. The latter, also known as *Lavington*, is probably from the OE personal name *Lēofa* (see LEAF 1) + *tūn*.

Lenz 1. Low German: contracted form of LAWRENCE. **2.** German: cogn. of LANCE. **3.** German: nickname from Ger. *Lenz* spring (MHG *lenze*, OHG *lenzo*, from *lang* LONG, since in this season the days grow longer). The name may have been bestowed on someone who was born in the spring or who owed rent or service at that time of year, or it may have denoted someone who was of a sunny and spring-like disposition. The vocab. word is now somewhat literary or archaic, having been replaced in mod. Ger. by *Frühling*. **4.** Jewish (Ashkenazic): of uncertain origin. It may be one of the class of ornamental names adopted from words denoting the seasons (cf. SUMMER 1, WINTER 2, HERBST, and FRULING), or perhaps an adoption of the Ger. surname.

León Spanish: **1.** cogn. of LYON (1 and 2). **2.** habitation name from the city in NW Spain, so called from L *legio* legion, gen. *legiōnis*, a division of the Roman army. In Roman times the city was the garrison of the 7th legion, known as the *Legio Gemina*.

Leon see LYON

Leonard 1. English: from a Norman personal name composed of the Gmc elements *leo* lion (a late addition to the vocab. of name elements, from L) + *hard*, hardy, brave, strong. A saint of this name, who is supposed to have lived in the 6th cent., but about whom absolutely nothing is known except for a largely fictional life dating from half a millennium later, was popular throughout Europe in the early Middle Ages and was regarded as the patron of peasants and horses. **2.** Irish: var. of LENNON. **3.** Italian: in the U.S., an Anglicization of any of the It. names listed below.

Vars. (of 1): **Len(n)ard**, **Learnard**, **Learned**.

Dims. (of 1): It.: **Leonardelli**, **Leonardini**, **Le(o)narduzzi**; **Lunardelli**. Pol.: **Lenarczyk**. Czech: **Linek**, **Linka**.

Augs. (of 1): It.: **Lenardon(i)**, **Lunardon(i)**, **Linardon**.

Patrs. (from 1): It.: **De Leonardi(s)**, **Di Leonardi**. Low Ger.: **Lennartz**, **Lehnertz**, **Lennerts**, **Linnartz**. Fris.: **Leenderts**. Flem.: **Leenerts**, **Linders**. Du.: **Leenders**. Swed.: **Lennartsson**. Pol.: **Lenartowicz**. Beloruss.: **Lenartovich**.

Leonidov Russian: patr. from the given name *Leonid* (Gk *Leōnidēs*, originally itself a patr. from the byname *Leōn* 'Lion'; cf. LYON 2). The name was borne by various early martyrs of whom little is known, but who are venerated in the Orthodox Church.

Var.: **Levanidov**.

Leontyev Russian: patr. from the given name *Leonti* (Gk *Leōntios*, from *leōn* lion, gen. *leontos*). The name was borne by a number of early Gk martyrs, and also by a 4th-cent. bishop of Caesarea in Cappadocia, all of whom contributed to the popularity of the name in E Europe.

Var.: **Levontyev**.

Leopard see LEPPARD

Leopold German: from a Gmc personal name composed of the elements *liut* people, tribe + *bold* bold, brave. The form of the first element has been affected by the influence of LEONARD. The surname is also borne by Ashkenazic Jews, in which case it is an adoption of the Ger. surname.

Vars.: **Leupold(t)**, **Leipold(t)**, **Leibold**, **Leipelt**, **Luitpold**.

Lepage see PAGE

Lépagneux see PAGNOL

Lepesqueur see PÊCHEUR

Lepeu see PUY

Lépinay see ÉPINE

Le Poideven see POTVIN

Leporini see LEVER

Leppänen Finnish: ornamental name from Finn. *leppä* alder tree + the gen. suffix *-nen*. This is one of the many Finn. surnames taken in the 19th cent. from vocab. words denoting features of the natural landscape.

Leppard English (originating in E Sussex): from ME, OF *lepard* leopard, from LL *leopardus*, a cpd of *leo* lion + *pardus* panther), perhaps a nickname for a stealthy but violent man, or a house name for someone who lived in a house distinguished by the sign of a leopard.

Vars.: **Leopard**, **Lepperd**, **Lippard**.

Lepper 1. German: occupational name from an agent deriv. of MHG *lappe* rag, cloth (OHG *lappa*), apparently denoting a cobbler who repaired footwear with rags rather than leather. Leather shoes in the Middle Ages were a luxury and many people either went barefoot or contented themselves with felt leggings which could easily be repaired with scraps of cloth. **2.** English: var. of LEAPMAN.

Vars. (of 1): **Lepple**, **Läpple**.

Patr. (from 1): **Leppers**.

Lepreux see PREUX

Le Prevost see PREVOST

Leprince see PRINCE

Leproust see PROVOST

Lequeux see KEW

Lerat see RAT

Lercher see LARCHER

Lerner 1. German: occupational name for a pupil or apprentice, Ger. *Lerner*, an agent deriv. of *lernen* to learn (MHG, OHG *lernen*; cf. LARNER). **2.** Jewish (Ashkenazic): from Yid. *lerner* student of the Talmud, an agent deriv. of *lernen* to study (the Talmud). **3.** English: var. of LARNER.

Le Roël see ROACH

Lerondeau see ROUND

Lerouge see RUDGE

Le Rouzic see ROUSE

Lesage see SAGE

Leschelle *see* ESCHELLE

Lešek *see* ALEXANDER

Leser *see* LAZAR

Lesieur *see* SEIGNEUR

Leskinen Finnish: metr. from Finn. *leski* widow.

Leslie Scots: habitation name from a barony in the former county of Aberdeens., which is first recorded *c.*1180 in the form *Lesslyn*. The placename is probably from Gael. *leas celyn* court, garden of hollies. Leslie in Fife is said to be named in imitation of this place; in some cases the surname may come from there.

Vars.: **Lesslie, Lesley.**

Leśniak Polish: occupational name for a woodman or forester, Pol. *leśni(a)k* (from Pol. *les, las* wood, forest + the agent suffixes *-nik, -niak*).

Vars.: **Leśnik, Leśnicki, Lesiak.**

Dim.: Pol.: **Leśniczak.**

Patr.: Pol.: **Leśniewicz.**

Habitation names: Pol.: **Leśniewski, Leśnikowski.**

Lesourd *see* SOURD

Lespagnol *see* PAGNOL

Lessard *see* ESSART

Lessells *see* LASCELLES

Lesseps Provençal: topographic name for someone who lived by a hedge, from OProv. *seps* hedge (L *saepes*), with fused def. art. *le*.

Lessiter *see* LEICESTER

Lesson *see* LEES

Lester *see* LISTER

Lestrange *see* STRANGE

Leszczyński 1. Polish: topographic name for someone who lived by a hazel tree or in a hazel wood, from Pol. *leszczyna* hazel tree + *-ski* suffix of local surnames (see BARANOWSKI). It may also be in part a habitation name from a place named with these elements. 2. Jewish (E Ashkenazic): ornamental name from Pol. *leszczyna* hazel tree + *-ski*, one of the many Ashkenazic ornamental surnames taken from vocab. words denoting features of the natural world.

Letainturier *see* TEINTURIER

Letch *see* LEEK

Letcher *see* LEACH

Letchford *see* LATCHFORD

Letessier *see* TISSIER

Lethaby English: of uncertain origin, probably a habitation name from an unidentified place in N England, of which the second element is ON *býr* farm, settlement; the first has not been satisfactorily identified.

Letham *see* LATHAM

Letherland *see* LITHERLAND

Letort *see* TORT

Letouche *see* TOUCHE

Létourneau *see* ÉTOURNEAU

Lett English: from a medieval female given name, a short form of *Lettice* (L *Laetitia* 'Happiness', 'Gaiety'; see also LEES 2).

Dims.: **Lett(e)y.**

Metrs.: **Letts; Letson, Letsom.**

Leuillet *see* OCHILA

Leupold *see* LEOPOLD

Leuprecht *see* LUBRECHT

Leuthard German: from a Gmc personal name composed of the elements *liut* people, tribe + *hard* hardy, brave, strong.

Vars.: **Leutert, Leitert, Luithardt, Luthard(t).**

Leuther German: from a Gmc personal name composed of the elements *liut* people, tribe + *heri, hari* army.

Vars.: **LUTHER, Leither.**

Dims.: Low Ger.: **Lüthke, Lüt(h)ge, Lüt(t)gen, Lütje(n)** (possibly also from other, rarer Gmc names with *liut* as a first element).

Patrs.: Low Ger.: **Lüd(d)ers, Lüers, Lührs(en), Lü(e)rsen, Lühri(n)g.**

Patrs. (from dims.): Low Ger.: **Lütkens, Lüthgens, Lüttgens, Lütjens.**

Leuthner *see* LEITNER

Leuty *see* LAWTY

Leuvenberg *see* LÖWE

Levalet *see* VALLET

Levallois *see* VALOIS

Levanidov *see* LEONIDOV

Levanneur *see* VANNIER

Levanovich *see* LVOV

Levenherz *see* LÖWE

Levens *see* LEWIN

Lever English: 1. Norman nickname for a fleet-footed or timid person, from OF *levre* hare (L *lepus*, gen. *leporis*). It may also have been a metonymic occupational name for a hunter of hares. 2. topographic name for someone who lived in a place thickly grown with rushes, from OE *lǣfer* rush, reed, iris. Great and Little *Lever* in Lancs. are named with this word (in a collective sense) and the surname may also be derived from them. 3. possibly also from an unrecorded ME survival of an OE personal name, *Lēofhere*, composed of the elements *lēof* dear, beloved + *here* army.

Var.: **Leaver.**

Dims. (of 1): Eng.: LEVERETT. It.: **Leporini, Leporino, Levorin(i), Levrini; Leprotti, Levrotto.**

Aug. (of 1): It.: **Leproni.**

Patrs. (from 3): Eng.: **Lievers; Leivers** (Notts. and Derbys.).

Leverett English: **1.** dim. of LEVER 1. **2.** from the ME given name *Lefred*, OE *Lēofrǣd*, composed of the elements *lēof* dear, beloved + *rǣd* counsel.

Var.: **Leveritt**.

Leveridge English: from the ME given name *Lefric*, OE *Lēofrīc*, composed of the elements *lēof* dear, beloved + *rīc* power.

Vars.: **Leverich**, **Leverick**, **Lefridge**, **Loveridge**, **Loveredge**, **Livery**, **Luffery**.

Leverrier *see* VERRIER

Leverton English: habitation name from any of several places so called. One in Berks. is so called from the OE female personal name *Lēofwaru* (composed of the elements *lēof* dear, beloved + *waru* care) + OE *tūn* enclosure, settlement; one in Lincs. has as its first element OE *lǣfer* rush, reed (see LEVER 2); and N and S *Leverton* in Notts. may contain a river name identical to that in LEAR 2.

Levett English: **1.** Norman nickname from a dim. of ANF *leu* wolf; see LOW 3. **2.** habitation name from any of the various places in Normandy called *Livet*. All are of obscure, presumably Gaul., etymology. **3.** from the ME given name *Lefget*, OE *Lēofgēat*, composed of the elements *lēof* dear, beloved + the tribal name *Gēat* (see JOCELYN). **4.** possibly also from an unrecorded ME survival of the OE female personal name *Lēofgȳð*, composed of the elements *lēof* dear, beloved + *gȳð* battle.

Vars.: **Levet**, **Livett**, **Livitt**, **Leavett**, **Le(a)vitt**.

Levéziel *see* LAVOISIER

Levi Jewish: from the Hebr. male given name *Levi* 'Joining', borne by a son of Jacob and Leah (Gen. 29: 34). Bearers of this given name or surname are Levites, members of the tribe of Levi, who form a hereditary caste who assist the *kohanim* (see COHEN).

Vars.: LEWI, LEVY, **Leve**; **Levit(e)**, **Levitt**, **Lewit(t)**; **Levit(t)an**, **Leviton**; **Lévi**, **Lévy**, **Lévit(t)e**, **Lévitan** (among French-speaking Jews); **Levie(t)** (among Dutch-speaking Jews); **Levinsky**, **Levit(an)sky** (E Ashkenazic); **Halevy**, **Halévi** (with the Hebr. def. art. *ha*).

Dims.: LEVICK, **Leivick** (E Ashkenazic).

Patrs.: **Levis**, LEWIS, **Levites**, **Levitas**; **Levison**, **Levinso(h)n**, **Levinsen**, **Levenson**, **Levenzon** (Ashkenazic); **Leviev**, LEWIN, **Levin(e)**, **Leven(e)**, **Le Vi(g)ne** (a pseudo-Gallicization of *Levin(e)*), **Levinski**, **Levinsky**, **Levinov**, **Levitin** (E Ashkenazic); **Levitov** (either from *Levi(t)* Levite + the Slav. patr. suffix *-in*, or from Hebr. *Levi* Levite + Hebr. *tov* good, i.e. 'good Levite').

Cpds (ornamental elaborations): **Levinberg**, **Levinthal**, **Levinstein** (see also LÖWE).

Levick **1.** English: nickname from ANF *l'eveske* 'the BISHOP'. **2.** English: from the ME given name *Lefeke*, OE *Lēofeca*, a deriv. of *Lēofa* (see LEAF 1). **3.** Jewish (E Ashkenazic): from Yid. *Leyvik*, a dim. of the male given name *Leyvi*; see LEVI.

Vars. (of 1 and 2): **Livick**, **Livock**, **Leffeck**. (Of 1 only): **Veck**, **Vick** (by wrong division). (Of 3): **Leivik**, **Levak**.

Patrs. (from 2): **Lucking** (from OE *Lēofecing*). (From 3): **Levikson**, **Levakov**.

Levillain *see* VILLAIN

Levingston *see* LIVINGSTONE

Levkovits *see* LEWKOWICZ

Levontyev *see* LEONTYEV

Levy **1.** Jewish: var. of LEVI. **2.** English: from the ME given name *Lefwi*, OE *Lēofwīg*, composed of the elements *lēof* dear, beloved + *wīg* war. **3.** French: habitation name from *Lévy*(-Saint-Nom) in Seine-et-Oise, so called from the Gallo-Roman personal name *Laevius* (from L *laevus* left) + the local suffix *-ācum*. Members of a noble family originally from this place followed Simon de Montfort on the Albigensian crusade, and were granted an estate at Mirepoix in Arriège.

Vars. (of 1 and 2): **Leavy**, **Le(a)vey**. (Of 3): **Lévis**.

Lewandowski Polish: habitation name from an estate called *Lewandów* (probably named from the Pol. personal name *Lewanda*, or Beloruss. *Levon*, forms of *Leo* (see LYON 2) + *-ów* possessive suffix), with the addition of *-ski*, suffix of local surnames (see BARANOWSKI). A possible alternative derivation for the placename is from a var. of *lawenda* lavender.

Lewellin *see* LLYWELYN

Lewer *see* EWER

Lewin **1.** English: from the ME given name *Lefwine*, OE *Lēofwine*, composed of the elements *lēof* dear, beloved + *wine* friend. This was the name borne by an Eng. missionary who became the patron of Ghent, and the given name was consequently popular in the Low Countries during the Middle Ages. **2.** Jewish (E Ashkenazic): patr. from LEVI. **3.** Manx: Anglicized form of Gael. **Mac Giolla Guillin** 'son of the servant of WILLIAM'.

Vars. (of 1): **Lowin**, **Lowen**. (Of 3): **Gelling**.

Patrs. (from 1): Eng.: **Lewins**, **Lewens**, **Livens**. Low Ger.: **Lewens**, **Levens**.

Lewis **1.** English: from *Lowis*, *Lodowicus*, a Norman personal name composed of the Gmc elements *hlod* fame + *wīg* war. This was the name of the founder of the Frankish dynasty, recorded in L chronicles as *Ludovicus* and *Chlodovechus* (the latter form becoming OF *Clovis*, *Clouis*, *Louis*, the former developing into Ger. *Ludwig*). The name was popular throughout France in the Middle Ages and was introduced into England by the Normans. On the continent it was a hereditary name borne by many Fr. kings and by the Bavarian WITTELSBACHS. **2.** Welsh: Anglicized form of LLYWELYN. **3.** Scots: local name from the Hebridean island of *Lewis*. This seems to have been named with ON *hlóðr* silent, melancholy or *ljoð* song + *hús* house, but these rather fanciful forms may well represent the workings of folk etymology on some more ancient name. **4.** Scots and Irish: Anglicized form of Gael. **Mac Lughaidh** 'son of *Lugaidh*'. This is one of the most common OIr. personal names. It is derived from *Lugh* 'Brightness', which was the name of a Celtic god. In Scotland the name was taken as a Gaelicized form of *Lewie*, a pet form of the given name *Lewis* (as in 1). **5.** Jewish (Ashkenazic): patr. from LEVI or Anglicization of some like-sounding Jewish surname.

Vars. (of 1): **Louis**, **Lowis**. (Of 4): **(Mc)Cloy**.

Dims. (of 1): Fr.: **Louiset**, **Louisot**, **Luizet**, **Louichon**. It.: **Lodovichetti**, **Luiselli**, **Luisetti**. Ger.: **Lude**, **Lutz(mann)**, **Litzmann**, **Lutsch**; **Lotze** (Hesse); **Ludl** (Bavaria); **Lösel**. Low

Ger.: **Lode(mann)**, **Lade(mann)**, **Lohde**, **Löhde**, **Lödeke**; **Lo(o)s**, **Lose(mann)**, **Lossman**, **Loseke**.

Pej. (of 1): Fr.: **Luizard**.

Patrs. (from 1): Fr.: **Ludovici** (Latinized). It.: **D'Aloisio**, **D'Aluisio**, **D'Alisi**, **De Luisi**, **Di Luisi**. Fris.: **Luickinga**. Flem.: **Luyckx**, **Louckx**, **Loix**. Du.: **Lodewijks**. Dan.: **Ludvigsen**. Pol.: **Lud(wi)kiewicz**; **Ludwiczak**, **Ludwisiak**.

Patr. (from 1) (dim.): Low Ger.: **Löding**.

Lewit *see* LEVI

Lewkowicz 1. Polish: patr. from a dim. of the given name *Lew* 'Lion' (see Lvov and LYON 2). **2.** Polish: perhaps also a patr. from the nickname *Lewek* 'Left-handed', a dim. of LEWY 1. **3.** Jewish (E Ashkenazic): patr. of uncertain origin, possibly as in 1 and 2.

Vars. (of 1): **Lwowicz** (not dim.). (Of 1 and 2): **Lewicki**, **Lewiński**. (Of 3): **Lewkowitz**, **Levkowitz**, **Lewkovitz**, **Levkovitz**, **Levkovits**, **Lefkovitz**, **Lefkowicz**, **Lefkowits**, **Lefkovits**, **Lefkovich**.

Lewtey *see* LAWTY

Lewy 1. Polish: nickname for a left-handed person, from Pol. *lewy* left. **2.** Jewish (Ashkenazic): probably in most cases a var. of LEVI, but possibly also derived as in 1.

Vars. (of 1): **Lewiak**. (Of 2): **Lewi**.

Patr. (from 1): Pol.: LEWKOWICZ.

Lexa *see* ALEXANDER

Ley 1. English: var. of LEE 1 and 2. **2.** French and German: var. and cogn. of ELOY.

Leybish *see* LEIB

Leyburn English: habitation name from *Leyburn* in N Yorks. or *Leybourne* in Kent. The former is so called from the OE personal name **Lylla* (a byform of the attested *Lulla*) + OE *burna* stream (see BOURNE). The latter probably has as its first element OE *hlīg*, a byform of *hlēow* shelter.

Vars.: **Leyborne**, **Laybo(u)rn**, **Leeburn**, **Lyburn**, **Labern**.

Leycester *see* LEICESTER

Leyden Irish: Anglicized form of Gael. **Ó Loideáin** 'descendant of *Loideán*', a personal name of uncertain origin.

Vars.: **L(e)ydon**.

Leyeles *see* LAKIN

Leyes *see* ELLIS

Leyhane *see* LEHANE

Leyland English (Lancs.): topographic name or habitation name from ME *layland*, OE *lǣgeland* land left lying uncultivated. This is the name of a place in Lancs., and the present-day distribution of the surname suggests that this place is the source for most bearers. Others may, however, get their name from the same word used in other parts of the country.

Var.: **Layland**.

Leyman *see* LEE

Leyne *see* LANE

Leyrer *see* LEIRER

Leyten *see* ALLIS

Leyton English: **1.** habitation name from *Leyton* in Essex, so called from the Brit. river name *Lea* (of uncertain etymology, perhaps from the Celt. element *lug*- light) + OE *tūn* enclosure, settlement. **2.** var. of LAYTON or LEIGHTON.

Lhermite *see* HERMITE

Lhostal *see* HOSTAL

Lhoták Czech: topographic name from the vocab. word *lhota* village or habitation name from any of the many small places named with this word.

Vars.: **Lhota**, **Lhotský**.

Lhozier *see* DOZIER

Libby English (Devon): from a medieval female given name, a pet form of *Elizabeth*; see HIBBS 2.

Liber *see* LIEB

Libertini *see* ALBERT

Libes Jewish (Ashkenazic): metr. from the Yid. female given name *Libe*, from *lib* dear, beloved (cf. LIEB).

Vars.: **Li(e)bis**; **Libin**, **Libov(itz)**, **Libovits**, **Libowicz** (E Ashkenazic), **Libovici** (Rumanian spelling).

Metr. (E Ashkenazic, from a dim., Yid. *Libke*): **Libkowicz**.

Libschitz *see* LIPSCHUTZ

Libsky *see* LIPSKI

Li Cari *see* CARO

Licastri *see* CASTRO

Licciardello *see* RICHARD

Licence *see* LISON

Lichfield English: **1.** habitation name from the city in Staffs. The first element preserves a Brit. name recorded as *Letocetum* during the Romano-British period. This means 'grey wood', from words which are the ancestors of W *llwŷd* grey and *coed* wood. By the OE period this had been reduced to *Licced*, and the element *feld* pasture, open country (see FIELD) was added to describe a patch of cleared land within the ancient wood. **2.** habitation name from *Litchfield* in Hants, recorded in Domesday Book as *Liveselle*. This is probably from OE *hlif* shelter + *scylf* shelf, ledge. The subsequent transformation of the placename may be the result of folk etymological association with OE *hliδ*, *hlid* slope + *feld* open country.

Var.: **Litchfield**.

Licht 1. German: metonymic occupational name for a chandler, from Ger. *Licht* light, MHG *lieht* candle (MHG *lieht*, OHG *lioht*). **2.** Jewish (Ashkenazic): occupational name as in 1, or else an ornamental name, perhaps chosen in some cases in allusion to one of the various male Hebr. given names referring to light, such as *Uri* and *Meir*. **3.** Low German: cogn. of LIGHT 2.

Vars. (of 1 and 2): **Licht(n)er**, **Lichtmann** (occupational). (Of 2): **Likht**; **Lichtig(er)**, **Likhtiger**, **Likhtikman** (from Yid. *likhtik* bright (i.e. 'full of light')); **Licht(er)man**, **Lichtermann** (occupational).

Cpds (of 2; all ornamental): **Lichtbach** ('light stream'); **Lichtenbaum** ('light tree'); **Lichtenberg** ('light hill'); **Lichtblau** ('light blue'); **Lichtbrun** ('light brown'); **Lichtenfeld** ('light field'); **Lichtenholz** ('light wood'); **Lichtschein**, **Lichtszain** ('light shine'), **Lichtszajn** (Pol. spelling); **Licht(en)stein**, **Lichtensztein** ('light stone'; see also LIECHTENSTEIN); **Lichtenthal** ('light valley').

Lichtzer German: occupational name for a chandler or candle-maker, Ger. *Lichtzieher*, from MHG *lieht* candle (see LICHT 1) + *zieher*, an agent deriv. of *ziehen* to draw, dip. Candles were made by repeatedly dipping the wicks into tubs of molten wax.

Lidbetter *see* LEADBETTER

Liddell N English and Scots: habitation name from any of various places in Cumb. and the Scots Borders called *Liddel*, from the OE river name *Hlȳde* 'Loud' + OE *dæl* valley (see DALE).

Vars.: **Liddel, Lidell, Liddle, Liddall, Lydall**.

Liddiard English: habitation name from *Lydiard* in Wilts. or *Lydeard* in Somerset, both of which apparently preserve a Brit. name composed of W *garth* hill with an obscure first element.

Liddiatt English and Scots: topographic name from ME *lidyate* gate in a fence between ploughed land and meadow (OE *hlid-geat* swing-gate), or habitation name from one of the places named with this word, as for example *Lidgate* in Suffolk or *Lydiate* in Lancs.

Vars.: **Lidgate, Lydiate, Liggat(t); Liggett** (N Ireland); **Lidgett**.

Liddicoat English (Devon and Cornwall): habitation name from any of various places in E Cornwall now known as *Lidcott, Lydcott, Ludcott*, and *Lidcutt*. All get their names from OCorn. *luit* grey + *cuit* wood; cf. LICHFIELD 1.

Liddy *see* LEDDY

Lidster *see* LISTER

Lidstone English: habitation name from a place in Devon, so called from the gen. case of the OE personal name *Lēofede* (a deriv. of *Lēofa*; see LEAF 1) + OE *tūn* enclosure, settlement.

Lieb 1. German and Jewish (Ashkenazic): nickname for a pleasant or agreeable person, from Ger. *lieb* or Yid. *lib* dear, beloved (MHG *lieb*, a cogn. of OE *lēof*; see LEAF 1). 2. German: from a medieval given name, a short form of the various cpd Gmc personal names with the first element *lieb*. 3. German (of Slav. origin): from a short form of the various cpd Slav. personal names with a first element *lubo-* love (ultimately cogn. with 1).

Vars. (of 1): **Liebe(r), Lieb(er)mann**. Jewish only: **Lieb(er)man; Liber, Liberman(n), Libman, Li(e)blich** ('lovely'); **Li(e)bling** ('darling'); **Lib(e)st** ('dearest').

Dims. (of 1): **Li(e)blein**. (Of 2): **Li(e)bi(n)g, Lieb(i)sch**.

Cpds (of 1): Jewish: **Liebfreund, Liberfreund** ('dear friend'); **Li(e)bermens(c)h, Liebermensz** ('dear person'); **Li(e)bso(h)n, Li(e)berso(h)n** ('dear son'); **Libertal** ('dear valley').

Liebis *see* LIBES

Liebschutz *see* LIPSCHUTZ

Liechtenstein 1. Austrian: habitation name from a castle near Vienna. The noble family of this name trace their descent from Hugo of Liechtenstein, who lived in the early 12th cent. The tiny European principality of this name was created in 1719 when the Austrian family holding the barony of Schellenberg acquired the county of Vaduz, which is now the capital of the principality. 2. Jewish (Ashkenazic): ornamental cpd of LICHT light + STEIN stone.

Lief *see* LEAF

Liepe *see* LIPPE

Liepmann *see* LIPMAN

Lievers *see* LEVER

Lifchic *see* LIPSCHUTZ

Life *see* LEAF

Ligereau *see* LEDGER

Liggat *see* LIDDIATT

Light English: 1. nickname for a happy, cheerful person, from ME *lyght*, OE *lēoht* light (not dark), bright, cheerful. 2. nickname for someone who was busy and active, from ME *lyght*, OE *līoht* light (not heavy), nimble, quick. The two words *lēoht* and *līoht* were originally distinct, but they were confused in Eng. from an early period. 3. nickname for a small person, from ME *lite*, OE *lȳt* LITTLE, influenced by *lyght* as in 1 and 2.

Vars.: **Lyte; Lightman, Lyteman, Lit(t)man, Lut(t)man**.

Dims. (of 2): Ger.: **Leichtl(e)**.

Lightbody Scots and N English: 1. nickname for a cheerful person or a busy and active one; cf. LIGHT (1 and 2) + BODY. 2. nickname for a small person, from ME *lite* little (see LIGHT 3) + BODY.

Lightfoot English (chiefly N England, esp. Liverpool): nickname for a fast runner, from ME *lyght* light, nimble, quick (OE *līoht*; cf. LIGHT 2) + *fote* foot (OE *fōt*; cf. FOOT).

Lightowler English (Yorks. and Lancs.): habitation name from the village of *Lightollers* in Lancs., so called from OE *lēoht, līht* light, bright (cf. LIGHT 1) + *aloras* alders (cf. OLLERENSHAW).

Vars.: **Lightowlers, Lightoller(s)**.

Ligier *see* LEDGER

Lihane *see* LEHANE

Likht *see* LICHT

Likoff *see* LUKOV

Lilburn English, Scots, and N Irish: habitation name from a village in Northumb., so called from the OE personal name *Lilla* (of uncertain origin, perhaps a nursery word; cf. LILLO) + OE *burna* stream (see BOURNE).

Lillicrop English (chiefly Devon): nickname for someone with very fair hair, from OE *lilie* lily (see LILLY 2) + *cropp* top, head (see CROPPER).

Var.: **Lillicrap**.

Lillo Spanish: from a medieval given name recorded in the L forms *Lilus* and *Lilius*. It is of uncertain, probably Gmc (cf. LILBURN), origin and unknown meaning.

Lilly English: 1. from a dim. of the female given name *Elizabeth* (see HIBBS 2). 2. nickname for someone with very fair hair or skin, from ME, OE *lilie* lily (L *līlium*).

The It. cogn. *Giglio* was used as a given name in the Middle Ages. In Eng. and other langs. there has also been some confusion with forms of GILES. **3.** habitation name from *Lilley* in Herts. or in Berks. The Herts. place is named from OE *līn* flax + *lēah* wood, clearing (see LINDLEY 1). The Berks name is OE *Lillinglēah* 'wood associated with *Lilla*'.

Vars.: **Lil(l)ey, Lil(l)ie, Lely; Lill(e)yman, Lilliman.**

Dims. (of 2): It.: **Giglietti, Giglietto, Gigliucci, Giglioli, Gigliotti; Zigliotto, Zigliotti.**

Aug. (of 2): It.: **Giglioni.**

Pej. (of 2): It.: **Zeggiato.**

Patrs. (from 2): Eng.: **Lillis** (now found chiefly in Ireland). It.: **De Giglio.**

Cpds (of 2; ornamental): Swed.: **Lilje(n)berg** ('lily hill'); **Liljeblad(h)** ('lily leaf'); **Lilje(n)dahl** ('lily valley'); **Liljegren** ('lily branch'); **Liljeqvist** ('lily twig'); **Liljero(o)s** ('lily rose'); **Liljestrand** ('lily shore'); **Lilje(n)ström** ('lily river'). Jewish: **Lilienberg** ('lily hill'); **Lilienblum** ('lily flower'); **Lilienfeld** ('lily field'); **Lilienstein** ('lily stone'); **Lilient(h)al** ('lily valley').

Lillywhite English: nickname for someone with very fair hair or complexion, who was 'as white as a lily'.

Var.: **Lilywhite.**

Lima Portuguese: apparently a topographic name for someone living on the banks of the river of this name (of pre-Roman origin, probably akin to a Celt. element meaning 'elm'; cf. LEMOS and LENNOX).

Liman *see* LEMON

Limb *see* LUMB

Limbert *see* LOMBARD

Limpertz *see* LAMBERT

Linacre English: topographic name for someone who lived near a field where flax was grown for the manufacture of linen cloth, from OE *līn* flax + *æcer* (cultivated) field (see ACKER). In part the surname may derive directly from *Linacre* in Lancs. or Cambs., both of which get their names from this source.

Vars.: **Linaker, Lineker, Liniker, Linnecar, Lin(n)egar.**

Linardon *see* LEONARD

Linares Spanish: habitation name from any of various places so called, from the pl. form of Sp. *linar* flax field (L *līnāre*, a deriv. of *līnum* flax).

Lince *see* LYNCH

Lincoln English: habitation name from the city of *Lincoln*, so called from an original Brit. name *Lindo-* lake (cf. W *llyn*) + L *colōnia* settlement, colony. The town was an important administrative centre during the Roman occupation of Britain and in the Middle Ages it was a centre for the manufacture of cloth, including the famous 'Lincoln green'.

Var.: **Linkin.**

Linde German: topographic name for someone who lived by a conspicuous lime tree, Ger. *Linde* (MHG *linde*, OHG *linta*). There are several places, especially in N Germany, named with this word, and the name may also be a habitation name from any of these. The word was also used in a

number of OHG women's given names, with the meaning 'Shield' or 'Spear' (shields and spears being made from the hard wood of the lime); it is possible that the surname in some cases is a deriv. of a short form of one of these. As a Jewish (Ashkenazic) name, it is ornamental, adopted from the vocab. word for the tree.

Vars.: **Linden, Lind(n)er, Linde(r)rmann.** Ger. only: **Lingner.** Jewish only: **Lind, Lindeman, Lind(en)man** (possibly also topographic for a man who lived by a conspicuous lime tree).

Dim.: Ger.: **Lindl.**

Cpds (ornamental): Jewish: **Lindenbaum** (also Ger.), **Lindenboim** ('lime tree'); **Lindenberg** ('lime hill'); **Lindenblat(t)** ('lime leaf'); **Lindenbluth** ('lime blossom'); **Lindenfeld** ('lime field'); **Lindenstrauss** ('lime bouquet'); **Lindwasser** ('lime water'). Swed.: **Lindbäck** ('lime stream'); **Lind(e)berg** ('lime hill'); **Lindberg(h)** ('lime hill'); **Lindblad(h)** ('lime leaf'); **Lindblom** ('lime flower'); **Linbo(h)m** ('lime tree'); **Lind(e)borg** ('lime town'); **Lind(e)gren** ('lime branch'); **Lindholm** ('lime island'); **Lindelöf** ('lime leaf'); **Lindmark** ('lime land'); **Lindqvist** ('lime twig'); **Lindro(o)s** ('lime rose'); **Lind(e)rot(h)** ('lime root'); **Lindsjö** ('lime sea'); **Lindskog** ('lime copse'); **Lindstedt** ('lime homestead'); **Lindstrand** ('lime shore'); **Lindström** ('lime river'); **Lind(e)wall, Lind(e)vall** ('lime bank').

Lindegård Danish: topographic or habitation name composed of the elements *lind* lime tree + *gård* enclosure.

Var.: **Lindegaard.**

Linden *see* MCALINDEN

Lindhardt Danish: from an ON personal name composed of the elements *lind* lime, shield, spear + *harðr* hardy, brave, strong.

Lindley English: **1.** habitation name from either of two places in W Yorks. called *Lindley*, or from *Linley* in Shrops. and Wilts., all so called from OE *līn* flax + *lēah* wood, clearing, with epenthetic *-d-*; cf. LILLY 3. **2.** habitation name from the other *Lindley* in W Yorks. (near Otley), so called from OE *lind* lime tree (see LINDE and LINE 1) + *lēah* wood, clearing. Lindley in Leics. probably also has this origin, and is a further possible source of the surname.

Vars.: **Lin(g)ley.**

Lindop English (Yorks.): habitation name from an unidentified place, presumably named with the OE elements *lind* lime tree (see LINDE and LINE 1) + *hop* enclosed valley (see HOPE).

Lindsay **1.** English and Scots: habitation name from *Lindsey* in Lincs. This is first found in the form *Lindissi*, apparently a deriv. of the Brit. name of LINCOLN. To this has later been added the OE element *ēg* island, since the place was virtually cut off by the surrounding fenland. **2.** English: habitation name from *Lindsey* in Suffolk, named in OE as *Lelleseg* 'island of *Lelli*', a personal name representing a byform of *Lealla*, cogn. with the attested OHG *Lallo*. **3.** Irish: Anglicized form of various Gael. surnames, as for example *O Loingsigh* (see LYNCH 1), *Mac Giolla Fhionntóg* (see FINN), and *Ó Floinn* (see FLYNN).

Vars.: **Linsey, Lincey.**

Lindsell English: habitation name from a place in Essex, so called from OE *lind* lime tree (see LINDE and LINE 1) + *(ge)sell* shelter, hut.

Line English: **1.** topographic name for someone who lived by a lime tree, ME *lind, line* (OE *lind*, cf. LINDE; mod. Eng. *lime* is an ill-explained alteration of the second form). **2.** from the medieval female given name *Line*, an aphetic form of *Cateline* (see CATLIN) and of various other names, such as *Emmeline* and *Adeline*, containing the ANF dim. suffix *-line* (originally a double dim., composed of the elements *-el* and *-in*).

Vars.: LYNE. (Of 1 only): **Lind(er)**, **Lynde**, **Lynds**.

Metrs. (from 2): **Lines**, **Lynes**.

Lineham *see* LYNEHAM

Linforth English: habitation name from Great and Little *Linford* in Bucks. or *Lynford* in Norfolk. The former may have OE *hlyn* maple as its first element; the latter is more likely to contain *līn* flax. The second element in each case is OE *ford* FORD.

Vars.: **Linford**, **Linfoot**.

Ling English (E Anglia): habitation name from *Lyng* in Norfolk, which Ekwall suggests may be derived from OE *hlinc* hillside.

Lingen English: habitation name from a place in Herefords., so called from an old Brit. stream-name, perhaps composed of words which became W *llyn* water + *cain* clear, beautiful. The spelling *Lingham* in Domesday Book reflects scribal assimilation to the common placename element *-ham* homestead.

Lingwood English (E Anglia): habitation name from a place in Norfolk, so called from OE *hlinc* hillside + *wudu* WOOD.

Linikov *see* KALININ

Link 1. German and Jewish (Ashkenazic): nickname for a left-handed person, from Ger. *Linke* left hand (MHG *linc* left, OHG *lenka* left hand). In Europe left-handers have long been regarded with suspicion as clumsy, awkward, deviant, and even untrustworthy. **2.** English: topographic name, var. of LYNCH 2.

Vars. (of 1): Ger.: **Linke**, **Linkhand**. Jewish: **Linker**.

Linkin *see* LINCOLN

Linklater Scots: habitation name from either of the places of this name in the Orkneys, so called from ON *lyng* heather + *klettr* rock.

Var.: **Linkletter**.

Linn *see* LYNN

Linnane *see* LENNON

Lino Portuguese: from a medieval given name (L *Linus*, from Gk, but of unknown ultimate origin and meaning). According to classical legend this was the name of a celebrated singer and poet, the son of Apollo and the teacher of Orpheus and Hercules. Later it was borne by a 1st-cent. saint, the immediate successor of St Peter as Pope.

Linton English and Scots: habitation name from any of the numerous places so called, found in every part of England and in the Scottish Borders. The second element is in all cases OE *tūn* enclosure, settlement. The first in the case of *Linton* in Northumb. is a Brit. river name, *Lyne* (related to

W *lliant* stream). The other places of this name normally have as their first elements OE *lind* lime tree or *līn* flax, but occasionally perhaps *hlynn* torrent or *hlinc* hillside. On the basis of geographical situation the meaning 'torrent' would be appropriate to *Linton* near Skipton in W Yorks.

Lion *see* LYON

Lipgens *see* PHILIP

Lipin Jewish (E Ashkenazic): patr. from the Yid. male given name *Lipe* (a short form of LIPMAN) + the Slav. suffix *-in*.

Vars.: **Lipovitch**, **Lipovitz**, **Lipowicz**; **Lipso(h)n** (also W Ashkenazic).

Dims.: **Lipkin**, **Lipkes** (see also LIEBSOHN); **Lipka** (see also LIPPE).

Lipman Jewish (Ashkenazic): from the Yid. male given name *Lipman*, composed of the Yid. words *lib* dear, beloved + *man* man. (In some cases the surname may have been formed directly from these elements.)

Vars.: **Li(e)pmann**.

Patr.: **Lipmanovicz** (E Ashkenazic).

Lipp 1. English: metonymic nickname for someone with large lips or with some deformity of the lips, from ME *lippe* (OE *lippa*). **2.** English: perhaps from a ME given name, *Leppe* or **Lippe*, apparently from OE *Lēofa* (see LEAF 1). **3.** German: var. of LIPPE 1 and 2.

Patr. (from 2): **Lipson**.

Lippard *see* LEPPARD

Lippe German: **1.** aphetic pet form of PHILIP. **2.** from a pet form of any of the various Gmc personal names in which the first element is *liut* people, tribe is combined with a second element beginning with *b-*, such as *-berht* famous, *-bald* bold, or *-brand* sword, causing assimilation of the cluster *-tb-* to *-pp-*. **3.** habitation name from the duchy of *Lippe*, which became an independent state in the 12th cent. under Bernard, Lord of Lippe. This title was taken from the name of a castle held by the family, which probably has the same origin as in 5 below. **4.** topographic name for someone living on the banks of the river *Lippe* in Westphalia, which is of uncertain etymology. It is extremely ancient, being recorded by the Roman historian Tacitus in the form *Lupia*. **5.** topographic name (of Slav. origin) for someone who lived among lime trees, from *lipa* lime (cf. LIPSKI).

Dims. (of 1): Ger.: **Lippl**. Low Ger.: **Lipgen**. (Of 5): Ger. (of Slav. origin): **Lip(p)ke**, **Lipka**, **Lippek**. Jewish: **Lipka** (see also LIPIN).

Patrs. (from 1): Low Ger.: **Lip(p)s**; **Lipsius** (Latinized). Flem., Du.: **Lips**, **Lippen(s)**.

Habitation name (from 5): **Liepe** (the name of several places in Brandenburg and Pomerania).

Lippiatt English: habitation name from *Lipiate* in Somerset or *Lypiatt* in Gloucs., both so called from OE *hlīepgeat* 'leap-gate', a gate which was low enough to be jumped by horses and deer but presented an obstacle to sheep and cattle.

Vars.: **Lippiet**, **Lipyeat**.

Lipschutz Jewish (Ashkenazic): habitation name from *Leobschütz* in Upper Silesia or *Liebeschitz* in Bohemia.

The placenames are of Slav. origin, and are probably derived from *lipa* lime (see LIPPE 5).

Vars.: **Lipschütz, Liebschutz, Libschitz, Lipschitz, Lifs(c)hutz, Lifs(c)hitz, Lifshits, Lifchitz, Lifshytz, Lifs(c)hiz, Lifshic, Lifchic, Livschutz, Livs(c)hitz, Livshits, Liwshitz; Lifszec, Lifszic, Lifszyc** (Pol. spellings); **Lüpschütz, Lufschutz** (hypercorrected).

Lipski 1. German and Jewish (E Ashkenazic): habitation name from *Lipsk*, the former name of *Leipzig* in E Germany. The placename derives from the Slav. element *lipa* lime (see LIPPE 5). 2. Polish: habitation name from any of the many places named from Pol. *lipa* lime, for example *Lipno* in N central Poland.

Vars. (of 1): Jewish: **Lipsky, Libsky; Lipsker** ('native or inhabitant of Lipsk'), **Lipskier** (Pol. spelling); **Leipzig(er)** (Ger. forms). (Of 2): **Lipiński, Lipowski**.

Liptrot English: of uncertain origin; according to Harrison it is from a Gmc personal name composed of the elements *liob* dear + *trūt* beloved. The surname is now quite common in Lancs., but seems to be a comparatively recent importation into the county.

Var.: **Liptrott**.

Liron *see* HIRON

Lis Polish and Jewish (E Ashkenazic): nickname for a cunning person or, in the case of the Jewish name, ornamental name, from Pol. *lis* fox.

Vars.: Pol. **Lisiak; Lisiecki**. Jewish: **Liss, Lys(s), Lis(s)man, Lissak**.

Dims.: Pol.: **Lisek, Lisik**. Ukr.: LYSENKO.

Habitation names: Pol.: **Lisowski, Liszewski**.

Lisboa Portuguese: habitation name from *Lisbon* (Port. *Lisboa*), the principal city of Portugal. The name is first recorded in the L form *Olisipo* and is of uncertain, possibly Carthaginian, origin.

Lisciardelli *see* ALEXANDER

Lisle English (Norman): 1. topographic name for someone who lived on an island, OF, ME *isle* (L *insula*), with fused def. art. *l'*. 2. habitation name for someone from the Fr. town of *Lille*, which derives its name from OF *isle* (the same word as in 1).

Vars.: **De Lisle, (De) Lyle**; ISLES.

Lison English and French: habitation name from a place in Calvados, Normandy, of obscure etymology.

Vars.: Eng.: **Lysons, Licence**. Fr.: **Liçon**.

Lissiter *see* LEICESTER

Lisson *see* LEES

List German and Dutch: nickname for a cunning or wily individual, from Ger. *List*, Du. *list* guile, ingenuity, stratagem, device (OHG, MLG *list*).

Var.: Ger.: **Listmann**.

Dim.: Ger.: **Listl**.

Lister 1. English: occupational name for a dyer, ME *litster*, an agent deriv. (originally fem.; cf. *Baxter* at BAKER, *Webster* at WEBB) of *lit(t)e(n)* to dye (ON *lita*). The term was used principally in E Anglia and N and E England, and to this day the surname is found principally

in these regions, especially in Yorks. 2. Scots: Anglicized form of Gael. **Mac an Fleisdeir** 'son of the arrow-maker'; cf. FLETCHER. The family of this name originated in Drimfearn in the 10th cent.; they served as hereditary arrow-makers to the clan McGregor in Glenorchy. The surname has also been associated with the Gael. vocab. word *leastar* cup, boat, receptacle (used in a figurative sense of people as recipients of divine grace), but this is not the etymology. 3. Jewish (Ashkenazic): of uncertain origin.

Vars.: **Lyster, Lester, Lestor**. (Of 1 only): **Litster, Lidster, Ledster**. (Of 2 only): **McInlester, McLeister, Laister**.

Liston 1. English: habitation name from a place in Essex, so called from the OE personal name **Lissa* (probably a pet form of *Lēofsige*; see LIVESEY 2) + OE *tūn* enclosure, settlement. 2. Scots: habitation name from places in the former counties of W Lothian and Midlothian, which probably have the same origin as in 1.

Liszt Hungarian: 1. metonymic occupational name for baker or miller, from *liszt* flour, perhaps also a nickname for a white-haired person or someone with a very pale complexion. 2. Hungarian spelling of LIST.

Litchfield *see* LICHFIELD

Litherland English: habitation name from the district so called near Liverpool, consisting of *Uplitherland* and *Downlitherland*. The placename is derived from ON *hliðar*, gen. of *hlið* slope + *land* land.

Vars.: **Le(a)therland**.

Lithgow Scots: habitation name from *Linlithgow*, between Edinburgh and Falkirk, which was probably named with Brit. words related to W *llyn* lake, pool + *llaith* damp + *cau* hollow. In the 13th and 14th cents. the name appears both with and without the first syllable. It has been assumed that *Lithgow* was the name of the settlement and *Linlithgow* that of the lake. *Lithgow* was associated by folk etymology with Gael. *liath* grey + *cu* dog, and such a figure appears on the medieval borough seal.

Vars.: **Lithgoe; Lythgoe** (now commonly found in Lancs.).

Litman *see* LIGHT

Litster *see* LISTER

Little 1. English: nickname for a small man or distinguishing epithet for the younger of two bearers of the same given name, from ME *littel* (OE *lȳtel*, originally a dim. of *lȳt*; cf. LIGHT 3). 2. Irish: translation of BIGG.

Vars.: **Littell; Lyt(t)le** (chiefly N Ireland); **Littler**.

Littleboy English (E Anglia): occupational nickname from ME *littel* small + *boy* lad, servant; cf. LITTLEPAGE.

Littlefair English: nickname from ME *littel* small + *fere* companion (see FEAR 1).

Littleford English (chiefly W Midlands): habitation name from some minor place named with OE *lȳtel* small + *ford* FORD.

Littlehales English (chiefly W Midlands): habitation name from *Little Hales* near Newport, Shrops., which is named with OE *lȳtel* small + *halh* nook, recess (see HALE 1).

Littlejohn Scots and English: distinguishing epithet for the smallest of two or more bearers of the extremely common given name JOHN; cf. MEIKLEJOHN. In some cases the nickname may alternatively have been bestowed on a large man, irrespective of his actual given name, in allusion to the character in the Robin Hood legend, whose nickname was of ironic application.

Var.: **Litteljohn**.

Patr.: **Littlejohns**.

Littlepage English: occupational nickname from ME *littel* small + PAGE servant, groom.

Littleproud English: unflattering nickname for a person considered to be of slight worth, from ME *littel* small + ME, OF *prod* valiant, gallant (from L *prōdesse* to be of value, use; cf. PROUD).

Littleton English: habitation name from any of various places, mostly in SW England, but also in Gloucs. and Worcs., so called from OE *lȳtel* small + *tūn* enclosure, settlement.

Var.: **Lyttleton**, **Lyttelton**.

Littlewood English (chiefly Yorks.): habitation name from any of several minor places in W Yorks., *Littlewood* in Wooldale being a well-recorded instance. They are named with OE *lȳtel* small + *wudu* WOOD.

Littleworth English: habitation name from any of various places, for example in Berks., Bucks., and Warwicks., so called from OE *lȳtel* small + *worð* enclosure (see WORTH).

Littley English: **1.** nickname for someone with disconcertingly small eyes, from ME *littel* small + *ey* eye (OE *ēage*). **2.** habitation name from a minor place named with OE *lȳtel* small + *(ge)hæg* enclosure (see HAY 1). There is a lost *Littley* in Kirby Malzeard, W Yorks., which could be the source of the surname.

Litton English: habitation name from any of the places so called, as for example in Derbys., Dorset, Somerset, and W Yorks. In most cases the names are from OE *hlȳde* torrent (from *hlūd* loud, roaring) + *tūn* enclosure, settlement, but some examples may originally have had as their first element *hlid(-geat)* gate (cf. LIDDIATT).

Vars.: **Litten**, **Lytton**.

Littwak Jewish (E Ashkenazic): regional name from Yid. *Lite* 'Lithuania' (Pol. *Litwa*; see LITWIN 2). In Ashkenazic culture, the region referred to as *Lite* encompassed not only Lithuania but also Latvia, Estonia, Belorussia, parts of the N Ukraine, and parts of NE Poland.

Vars.: **Litwa(c)k**, **Litva(c)k**, LITWIN; **Lut(t)wak**, **Lutwick**, **Lutvak** (hypercorrected forms in S Yid. regions); **Littau**, **Lit(t)auer**, **Litewski**, **Litowski**, **Litovsky**; **Litai** (Israeli).

Litwin **1.** English: probably from an OE personal name, *Lēohtwine, composed of the elements *lēoht* light, bright + *wine* friend. The name is not attested in pre-Conquest documents, but a certain *Lihtuuinus* is recorded in Domesday Book. **2.** Polish: ethnic name for someone from Lithuania, Pol. *Litwa* (of uncertain etymology, per-

haps ultimately from a Baltic word meaning 'coast'). **3.** Jewish (E Ashkenazic): var. of LITTWAK.

Vars. (of 3): **Littwin**, **Litvin**; **Lutwin** (hypercorrected, from S Yid. regions).

Dims. (of 2): Ukr.: **Litvinenko**. Beloruss.: **Litvinyonok**. (Of 3): Jewish: **Litvintchouk**.

Patrs. (from 2): Pol.: **Litwinowicz**. Russ.: **Litvinov**. (From 3): Jewish: **Litvinov**, **Litvinoff**.

Lityński Polish: of uncertain origin, perhaps a nickname derived from Pol. *lit* goodwill gift, small bribe.

Litzmann see LEWIS

Livens see LEWIN

Livermore English: probably a habitation name from *Livermere* in Suffolk. This is first found in the form *Leuuremer* (*c*.1050), which suggests derivation from OE *læfer* rush, reed (see LEVER 2) + *mere* lake. However, later forms consistently show *i* in the first syllable, suggesting OE *lifer* liver, referring either to the shape of the pond or to the coagulation of the water.

Liversidge English (Yorks.): habitation name from *Liversedge* in W Yorks., named in OE as *Lēofheresecg* 'ridge, bank of *Lēofhere*' (see LEVER 3).

Var.: **Liversedge**.

Livery see LEVERIDGE

Livesey English (chiefly Lancs.): **1.** habitation name from a place in Lancs., so called from ON *hlíf* protection, shelter (or an unrecorded OE cogn.) + OE *ēg* island. **2.** possibly in a few cases from an OE personal name composed of the elements *lēof* dear, beloved + *sige* victory.

Vars.: **Livesay**, **Livsey**; **Livesley** (influenced by the many placenames and surnames ending in *-ley*).

Livett see LEVETT

Livick see LEVICK

Livieri see OLIVER

Livingstone **1.** Scots: habitation name from a place in Lothian, originally named in ME as *Levingston*, from an owner called *Levin* (see LEWIN 1), who appears in charters of David I in the early 12th cent. **2.** Irish: Anglicized form of Gael. *Ó Duinnshléibhe* and *Mac Duinnshléibhe*; see DUNLEAVY. **3.** American: Anglicized form of the Jewish surname *Löwenstein* (see LÖWE 2).

Vars.: **Livingston**, **Levingston(e)**.

Livschitz see LIPSCHUTZ

Liwshitz see LIPSCHUTZ

Ljung Swedish: ornamental name from Swed. *ljung* heather (ON *lyng*; see LING). This is one of the many Swed. surnames taken in the 19th cent. from vocab. words denoting features of the natural landscape, and used extensively in forming cpd surnames. In the U.S. it has often been Anglicized to YOUNG.

Var.: **Ljungman**.

Cpds: Swed.: **Ljungberg** ('heather hill'); **Ljungdahl** ('heather valley'); **Ljungren** ('heather branch'); **Ljungholm** ('heather island'); **Ljunglöf** ('heather leaf'); **Ljunqvist** ('heather twig'); **Ljungstedt** ('heather homestead'); **Ljungström** ('heather river').

Lladó *see* LLEDÓ

Llama *see* LAMA

Llavero *see* CLAVERO

Lledó Catalan: topographic name for someone who lived near a nettle tree, from Cat. *lledó* nettle fruit (LL *lōto*, gen. *lōtōnis*, for class. L *lōtus*, from Gk). There is a place named with this word in the province of Teruel, which may also be a partial source of the surname.
Var.: **Lladó** (a place in the province of Gerona).

Llewelin *see* LLYWELYN

Llopis *see* LOPE

Lloret *see* LAUR

Lloyd Welsh: nickname for a person with grey hair or who habitually dressed in grey, from W *llwyd* grey.
Vars.: **Loyd**; **Floyd(e)**, **Floyed**, FLOOD.
Patrs.: **Bloyd**, BLOOD, **Blud**.

Llywelyn Welsh: from an OW personal name, apparently derived from the element *llyw* leader, although the exact formation is unclear.
Vars.: **Llywellin**, **Llewel(l)yn**, **Llewel(l)in**, **Llewhellin**, **Lewellin**, **Fluellin**; LEWIS.

Lo *see* LOO

Loach English (Midlands): nickname from ME *loch(e)* loach, a type of small fresh-water fish formerly prized as a delicacy (OF *loche*, of uncertain origin).

Loachead *see* LOCHHEAD

Loader English: 1. topographic name for someone who lived by a road or a watercourse, OE *lād* (from the verb *lǣdan* to lead, go). In placenames this OE word generally denotes a man-made drainage channel. For the change in the vowel, cf. ROPER. 2. occupational name for a carter, from ME *lode(n)* to carry, transport (deriving phonetically from the word given above, but influenced in its meaning by ME *lade(n)*, from OE *hladan* to load).
Vars.: **Loder**, **Load(s)man**. (Of 1 only): **Load(e)s** (chiefly E Anglia).

Loan *see* LANE

Loaring *see* LORRAINE

Lobato *see* LOW

Lobb English: habitation name from a place in Devon, recorded in Domesday Book as *Loba*, apparently a topographical term of uncertain meaning, perhaps 'lump', 'hill'; the village is situated at the bottom of a hill. There is also a place of the same name in Oxon. (recorded in 1208 as *Lobbe*), but the historical and contemporary distribution of the surname makes it unlikely that it ever derives from this place, or from the ME, OE word *lobbe* spider.
Vars.: **Lob(be)**.

Lobel 1. French: nickname for a deceitful individual or for a flatterer, from a dim. of OF *lobe* flattery (of Gmc origin; cf. OHG *lob* praise). 2. Jewish (Ashkenazic): pseudo-Ger-

manized form of the Yid. male given name *Leybl*, a dim. of *Leyb* (see LEIB).
Vars. (of 1): **Lobeau**. (Of 2): **Löbel**.

Lo Casto *see* CASTRO

Lochhead Scots: local name for someone who lived at the head of a loch; cf. KINLOCH.
Vars.: **Lochead**, **Loachead**, **Lockhead**.

Lochrane *see* LOUGHREY

Lock 1. English: metonymic occupational name for a locksmith, from ME, OE *loc* lock, fastening. 2. English: topographic name for someone who lived near an enclosure, a place that could be locked, ME *loke*, OE *loca* (a deriv. of *loc* as in 1). ME *loke* was also used esp. of a barrier on a river, which could be opened and closed at will, and by extension of a bridge. The surname may thus also have been a metonymic occupational name for a lock-keeper. 3. English and German: nickname for a person with fine hair, from OE, OHG *loc* lock (of hair), curl (probably also ultimately identical with *loc* as in 1). 4. N English and Scots: see LUCAS.
Var.: **Locke**. (Of 1 only): Eng.: **Lock(i)er**, **Lockye(a)r** (agent derivs.).
Dim. (of 3): Ger.: **Löckle** (Swabia).

Locket *see* LUCAS

Lockhart Scots: of uncertain origin, probably from a Gmc personal name composed of the elements *loc* lock, bolt (see LOCK 1) + *hard* hardy, brave, strong.
Var.: **Lockart**.

Lockley English (W Midlands): habitation name from some minor place, probably *Lockleywood* in Hinstock, Shrops., that gets its name from OE *loca* enclosure (see LOCK 2) + *lēah* wood, clearing.

Lockwood English: habitation name from a place in W Yorks., probably so called from OE *loca* enclosure (see LOCK 2) + *wudu* WOOD. It seems likely that all present-day bearers of the name descend from a single family which originated in this place. There is another place of the same name in Yorks. (Cleveland), first recorded in 1273 as *Locwyt*, from ON *lok* fern + *viðr* wood, brake, but it is not clear whether it has given rise to a surname.

Lode *see* LEWIS

Loder *see* LOADER

Lodge English: local name for someone who lived in a small cottage or temporary dwelling, ME *logge* (OF *loge*, of Gmc origin). The term was used in particular of a cabin erected by masons working on the site of a particular construction project, such as a church or cathedral, and so it was probably in many cases equivalent to an occupational name for a mason.
Dims.: Fr.: **Logé**, **Logez**.
Aug.: Fr.: **Logeat**.

Loe *see* LOO

Loeffler *see* LÖFFLER

Löfberg *see* LEAF

Löffler German and Jewish (Ashkenazic): occupational name for a maker or seller of spoons, which in the Middle Ages were normally carved from wood, or more rarely from bone or horn. The word is an agent deriv. of Ger. *Löffel* (MHG *leffel*, OHG *leffil*).

Vars.: Ger.: **Leffler**; **Löffel**, **Leffel**. Jewish: **Loeffler**, **Lefler** (occupational); **Leffel** (meaning 'spoon'; reason(s) for adoption uncertain).

Loftus 1. English (Yorks.): habitation name from *Loftus* in N Yorks., *Lofthouse* in W Yorks., or *Loftsome* in E Yorks. All get their names from ON *lopt* loft, upper storey + *hús* house, the last deriving from the dat. pl. form. Houses built with an upper story (which was normally used for the storage of produce during the winter) were a considerable rarity among the ordinary people of the Middle Ages. **2.** Irish: Anglicized form of *Ó Lachtnáin* (see LACHLAN) or *Ó Lochlainn* (see LOUGHNANE).

Vars. (of 1): **Loft(i)s**, **Lofthouse**.

Logan 1. Scots and N Irish: habitation name from any of the places so called, principally that near Auchinleck. They all get their names from Gael. *lagan*, a dim. of *lag* hollow. **2.** Irish: Anglicized form of Gael. *Ó Leocháin* 'descendant of *Leochán*', a personal name of uncertain origin, perhaps a dim. of the OIr. name *Leo*, or akin to *leochail* delicate, fragile.

Vars.: (of 2): **O'Logan**, **O'Loughane**, **O'Lochan**, **O'Lagan(e)**, **Lo(u)ghan**, **Lagan**, **Lohan**.

Logé see LODGE

Loghlan see LACHLAN

Logie Scots: habitation name from any of the various places so called, from Gael. *lag* hollow + the local suffix -*ach*.

Var.: **Loggie**.

Lo Greco see GRECO

Logue see MOLLOY

Loh see LOO

Lohan see LOGAN

Lohde see LEWIS

Lohner see LEHMANN

Lohrensen see LAWRENCE

Loiselet see UCCELLO

Loix see LEWIS

Loker see LUKER

Lo Mancuso see MANCO

Lomax English: habitation name from a lost place near Bury in Lancs., recorded in the Middle Ages as *Lumhalghs*, and apparently named with the OE elements *lumm* pool (see LUMB) + *halh* nook, recess (see HALE 1).

Vars.: **Lo(o)mas**, **Loomis**, **Lummis**, **Lummus**.

Lombard English (also Scots and Irish) and French: **1.** ethnic name for someone from *Lombardy* in Italy. The region is named from the Gmc tribe which overran the area in the 6th cent. AD; its name is attested only in the Latin-ized form *Langobardi*, but is clearly composed of Gmc elements meaning 'long-beards' (cf. LONG and BEARD). **2.** occupational name for a banker or money-lender. Many of the early It. immigrants to England were involved in such dealings, and the name came to be used from the 14th cent. onward as a generic term for a financier.

Vars.: Eng.: **Lumbard**, **Lumbert**, **Limbert**. Fr.: **Lombart**.

Dims.: Fr.: **Lombardet**, **Lombardot**. Prov.: **Lombardy**. It.: **Lombardelli** (Lombardy); **Lombarini**, **Lombarino** (Tuscany).

Lombe see LUMB

Lomonosov Russian: patr. from the nickname *Lomonos* 'Broken Nose' (from *lomit* to break + *nos* nose). The name was presumably originally given to a man whose nose had been broken and had set crooked, but there may possibly be some connection with the plant 'virgin's bower', a kind of clematis, which is called *lomonos* for obscure reasons, probably the result of some lost anecdote.

Loncaster see LANCASTER

London 1. English: habitation name for someone who came from *London* or nickname for someone who had made a trip to London or had some other connection with the city. The placename is of Brit. origin and obscure etymology; it is recorded by the Roman historian Tacitus in the Latinized form *Londinium*, and may be connected with the Celt. element *lond* wild, bold, perhaps as a tribal name. **2.** Jewish (Ashkenazic): of uncertain origin. It is hardly likely to be of the same origin as 1, since Ashkenazic migration has always been largely from the Continent to Great Britain rather than in the reverse direction. The name may have been chosen to reflect Ashkenazic Hebr. *lamdon*, Yid. *lamdn* Talmudic scholar.

Vars. (of 1): **Lundon**, **Lonnon**, **Lunnon**. (Of 2): **Londin(ski)**, **Londner**.

Lones see LANE

Loney see LOONEY

Long 1. English: nickname for a tall person, from OE *lang*, *long* long, tall (cogn. with L *longus*, from which derive the Romance forms quoted below). **2.** Irish: Anglicized form of Gael. *Ó Longáin*; see LANGAN.

Vars. (of 1): **Lang**; **Laing** (Scots); **Longman**, **Langman**.

Dims. (of 1): Fr.: **Longeau(x)**, **Longet**, **Longin**, **Lonjon**; **Longuet(eau)**. It.: **Longhin(i)** (Venetia), **Lunghini**, **Longhetti**, **Lunghetti**.

Augs. (of 1): Fr.: **Lonjas**. It.: **Longon(i)** (Lombardy).

Pejs. (of 1): Fr.: **Longeard**, **Longaud**. It.: **Longato** (Venetia).

Patrs. (from 1): Flem.: **Langmans**. It.: **Del Lungo** (Tuscany); **Del Luongo** (Naples).

Cpds (from cogns. of 1, ornamental unless otherwise stated): Jewish (Ashkenazic): **Langbaum** ('tall tree'); **Langbart**, **Langbord**, **Langburt** ('long beard', a nickname); **Langberg** ('long hill'); **Langfuss** ('long foot', a nickname); **Langholz** ('long wood'); **Langleben** ('long life', a 'hopeful' name); **Langent(h)al** ('long valley').

Longan see LANGAN

Longbottom English (W Yorks.): topographic name for someone who lived in a long valley, from ME *long* + *bodme* (see BOTTOM). *Longbottom* in Luddenden Foot, W Yorks., may be the origin.

Var.: **Longbotham**.

Longden English: habitation name from any of various places, for example *Longden*, the ME form that underlies *Longdendale* in Ches. and Derbys. This is a cpd of OE *lang*, *long* LONG + *denu* valley (see DEAN 1). A place called *Longden* in Shrops., however, has the same origin as LANGDON, so there has clearly been some confusion between the two forms.

Longdon see LANGDON

Longfellow English: nickname for a tall person who was a good companion; see LONG 1 and FELLOW.

Longfield English: topographic name for someone who lived by an extensive piece of open country or pastureland; see LONG and FIELD. There is a place so named in Kent, and there are several in W Yorks., where the surname is common. Two places now called *Longville* in Shrops. also have this origin.

Longford see LANGFORD

Longham see LANGHAM

Longhurst English: habitation name from any of various places, such as *Longhirst* in Northumb., named with the OE elements *lang*, *long* LONG + *hyrst* wooded hill (see HURST).

Longley see LANGLEY

Longmire English: habitation name from a minor place in the parish of Windermere, Cumb., so called from ME *long* LONG + *myre*, *myer* marsh, bog (ON *mýrr*).

Var.: **Longmires**.

Longmore English: topographic name for someone who lived in an extensive area of marsh or fen; see LONG and MOORE 1. The surname is now found chiefly in the W Midlands.

Var.: **Longmuir** (Scots).

Longridge see LANGRIDGE

Longsdon English: habitation name from *Longsdon* in Staffs. or *Longstone* in Derbys. Both seem to derive from the gen. case of a OE hill name *Long* 'Long' + OE *dūn* hill (see DOWN 1).

Longstaff English: apparently an occupational name for a tipstaff or beadle who carried a long staff as a badge of office; perhaps also a nickname for a very tall, thin man, or even an obscene nickname for a man with a long sexual organ. The surname is found chiefly in NE England.

Var.: **Langstaff**.

Longton see LANGTON

Longworth English: habitation name from any of various places, for example in Berks. and Lancs., so called from OE *lang*, *long* LONG + *worð* enclosure (see WORTH).

Lonjas see LONG

Lönn Swedish: ornamental name from Swed. *lönn* maple tree, one of the many Swed. surnames taken in the 19th cent. from vocab. words denoting features of the natural landscape.

Cpds: **Lönn(e)berg** ('maple hill'); **Lönn(e)gren** ('maple branch'); **Lönnqvist** ('maple twig').

Lonsdale English: habitation name from places in Lancs. and S Cumb., named in OE as *Lunesdæl* 'valley (see DALE) of the river *Lune*'. This ancient Brit. river name is the same as in the first element in LANCASTER, through which city the river runs.

Var.: **Londsdale**.

Loo Low German, Flemish, and Dutch: topographic name for someone who lived in a grove or clearing, MLG, MDu. *lō* (a cogn. of MHG *lōch*, OHG *lōh* (cf. LACHMANN 3 and LEICHER 2) and OE *lēah* (see LEE 1)). The word is a common element in placenames, as for example *Waterloo*, the town in Brabant where Napoleon was finally defeated in 1815.

Vars.: **Lo(e)**, **Loh**, **Zumloh**, **Van (de) Loo**, **Van Loon**, **Looman(n)**.

Loobey Irish: Anglicized form of Gael. Ó *Lúbaigh* 'descendant of *Lúbach*', a byname originally applied to a cunning person.

Look see LUCAS

Looker see LUKER

Loom see LUMB

Loomas see LOMAX

Looney Irish: Anglicized form of Gael. Ó *Luanaigh* 'descendant of *Luanach*', a personal name derived from *luan* warrior (cf. LANE 3 and LAMB 3).

Vars.: **O'Looney**; **Lowney**; **Loney**, **Luney**, **Lunny** (N Ireland); **Lonie** (Scotland).

Loos see LEWIS

Lo Papa see PAPA

Lope Spanish: from a medieval given name. This may be from L *Lupus* 'Wolf', but the manner of derivation is not clear; the Sp. vocab. word has become *lobo* (see LOW 3).

Patrs.: Sp.: **López** (one of the commonest of all Spanish surnames). Cat.: **Llopis**. Port.: **Lopes**.

Lo Pinto see PINTO

Loran see LOUGHREY

Lorat see LAWRENCE

Lorca Spanish: habitation name from places in the provinces of Murcia and Navarre.

Lord 1. English: nickname for someone who behaved in a lordly manner, or had earned the title in some contest of skill, or had played the part of the 'Lord of Misrule' in the Yuletide festivities. It may also sometimes have been an occupational name for a servant in the household of the lord of the manor, or possibly a status name for a landlord or the lord of the manor himself. The word derives from OE *hlāford*, earlier *hlāf-weard*, lit. 'loaf-keeper', since the lord or chief of a clan was responsible for providing food for his dependants. **2.** Irish: translation of Gael. *Ó Tighearnaigh* (see Tierney) and *Mac Thighearnáin* (see McKiernan).

Lordan Irish: Anglicized form of Gael. **Ó Lórdáin** 'descendant of *Lórdán*', a personal name of unknown origin. The surname is particularly common in W Cork.

Lo Ré *see* Ray

Loria *see* Luria

Lo Riccio *see* Ricci

Lorie *see* Lowry

Lorieu *see* Oriol

Lorimer English and Scots: occupational name for a maker and seller of spurs, bits, and other small metal attachments to harness and tackle, from ANF *lorenier*, *loremier* (an agent deriv. of OF *lorain* tackle, harness, LL *lōrānum*, from class. L *lōrum* harness, strap).

Vars.: **Lorrimer**, **Larimer**.

Lorin *see* Laur

Lorkin *see* Larkin

Lorraine French and English: regional name from *Lorraine* in NE France, so called from the Gmc tribal name *Lotharingi* 'people of *Lothar*' (a personal name composed of the elements *hlod* famous, renowned + *hari*, *heri* army); cf. the mod. Ger. name of the region, *Lothringen*.

Vars.: Fr.: **(Le) Lorrain**. Eng.: **Loraine**; **Lor(r)ain**, **Lo(a)ring**. Ger. and Jewish (W Ashkenazic): **Lotring**, **Lot(h)ringer**.

Lorton English: habitation name from a place in Cumb. The second element of this is clearly OE *tūn* enclosure, settlement; according to Ekwall, the first may be a ON name *Hlóra* 'Roarer' (akin to OE *hlōwan* to low, roar), applied to the beck on which Lorton stands.

Łoś Polish: nickname for a large, ungainly person, from Pol. *łoś* elk.

Var.: **Łosiak**.

Los *see* Lewis

Losa Spanish: topographic name for someone who lived by a flat stone slab, perhaps a boundary marker of some kind, Sp. *losa* (of pre-Roman origin, probably Celt.; cf. Gael. *leac*, W *llech*).

Losada Spanish: topographic name for someone who lived by an area paved with flagstones, Sp. *losada* (from *losar* to pave, a deriv. of Losa).

Löser *see* Lazar

Loseto *see* Zito

Losier *see* Dozier

Lothian Scots: regional name from the region in SE central Scotland. This is very ancient and is of unknown origin.

Vars.: **Lowthian**, **Louthean**, Lowden.

Lothringer *see* Lorraine

Lott English: from a medieval given name introduced by the Normans, of uncertain origin. It may be the Hebr. personal name *Lot* 'Covering', which was relatively popular in N France, or an aphetic form of various names formed with the dim. suffix *-lot* (originally a combination of *-el* + *-ot*).

Var.: **Lotte**.

Patr.: **Lots**.

Lotze *see* Lewis

Loubat *see* Low

Louckx *see* Lewis

Loud English: **1.** nickname for a noisy person, from ME *lude* loud (OE *hlūd*), perhaps in part preserving the OE byname *Hlūda* that Ekwall postulates to explain the placenames *Loudham* (Suffolk) and *Lowdham* (Notts.). **2.** topographic name for someone who lived by a roaring stream, OE **hlȳde*, or habitation name from any of the places named from this word, e.g. *Lyde* in Hereford and Somerset. **3.** habitation name from *Louth* in Lincs., so called from its position on the river *Lud* (OE *Hlūde* 'Loud').

Var.: **Lowde**.

Louden *see* Lowden

Loughan *see* Logan

Loughlan *see* Lachlan

Loughnane Irish: Anglicized form of Gael. **Ó Lachtnáin** 'descendant of *Lachtnán*', a personal name from *lachtna* grey.

Vars.: **O'Lo(u)ghnane**, **O'Loughnan**, **O'Laghnane**, **Lough(nan)**, **Laughnan**.

Loughrey Irish: Anglicized form of Gael. **Ó Luachra** 'descendant of *Luachra*', a personal name derived from *luachair* rushes, sedges.

Vars.: **Loughry**, **Lockery**, **O'Lucry**, **O'Logher**; Rush.

Dims.: **O'Lucherin**, **O'Loghrane**, **O'Loughran**, **Lough(e)ran**, **Loughren**, **Laugheran**, **Lochrane**, **Loughrane**, **(O')Loran** (Gael. **Ó Luchaireáin**).

Loukes *see* Lucas

Louria *see* Luria

Lourie *see* Lowry

Louro Portuguese: nickname for someone with hair of a blonde or light chestnut colour, Port. *louro* (of uncertain etymology; in form it appears to be from L *laurus* laurel (see Laur 1), but the semantic development is not clear).

Loustal *see* Hostal

Louthean *see* Lothian

Louveton *see* Lovatt

Lo Vasco *see* Vasco

Lovatt **1.** English (chiefly Staffs.): nickname from ANF *lo(u)vet* wolfcub, young wolf (see Low 3). **2.** Scots: habitation name from *Lovat* near Beauly, in the former county of Inverness, which is from Gael. *lobh* rot, putrefy + *-ait* place.

Vars.: **Lovat**, **Lovett**, **Lovitt**.

Dims. (of 1): Fr.: **Louveton**, **Lovetot**.

Lövberg *see* LEAF

Love 1. English: from a ME given name, from the OE female personal name *Lufu* 'Love', or the masc. equivalent *Lufa*. Cf. LEAF 1. 2. English and Scots: nickname from ANF *louve* female wolf (a fem. form of *lou*; cf. LOW 3). This nickname was fairly commonly used for men, in an approving sense. It may have been bestowed on a staunch soldier, with reference to the ferocity with which the she-wolf defends her young. No doubt it was reinforced by crossing with post-Conquest survivals of the masc. version of 1. 3. Irish: erroneous translation of MCKINNON.

Var.: **Luff**.

Dims. (of 1): Eng.: **Lovekin**, **Lufkin**.

Loveday English: 1. from the ME female given name *Loveday*, OE *Lēofdæg*, composed of the elements *lēof* dear, beloved + *dæg* day. 2. nickname for someone who had some particular association with a 'loveday'. According to medieval custom this was a day set aside for the reconciliation of enemies and amicable settlement of disputes.

Lovegrove English: apparently a habitation name from an unidentified place named with the OE personal name *Lufa* (see LOVE 1) + OE *grāf* grove, thicket.

Lovelace English: 1. nickname for a philanderer, from ME *lufelesse* loveless, without love (OE *lufu-lēas*), probably in the sense 'fancy free'. 2. some early examples, such as Richard *Lovelas* (Kent 1344), may have as their second element ME *las(se)* girl, maiden (of disputed etymology); cf. TIPLADY.

Vars.: **Loveless**, **Lowles(s)**.

Lovell English: dim. of LOW 3, i.e. a nickname from ANF *lou* wolf (L *lupus*) + the dim. suffix *-el*.

Vars.: **Lovel**, **Lowell**.

Lovelock English: nickname for a dandy, from ME *love-lock*, a lock of hair, sometimes an artificial one, curling over the forehead or ears in a variety of fashionable styles.

Var.: **Loveluck**.

Lovely English: nickname for an amiable person, also perhaps sometimes given in an ironical sense, from ME *luvelich* (OE *luf(e)līc*). During the main period of surname formation the word was used in an active sense, 'loving', 'kind', 'affectionate', as well as the passive 'lovable', 'worthy of love'. The meaning 'attractive', 'beautiful' is not clearly attested before the 14th cent., and remained rare throughout the Middle Ages.

Loveman *see* LEMON

Loven *see* LOWN

Lovenzon *see* LÖWE

Lo Verde *see* VERDE

Loveredge *see* LEVERIDGE

Lovick English (Norfolk): from the ME given name *Loveke*, OE *Lufeca*, a deriv. of *Lufa* (see LOVE 1).

Lovini *see* LOW

Low 1. English: topographic name for someone who lived near a hill, from OE *hlāw* (see LAW 2; for the change of -*ā*- to -*ō*- in the Midland and Southern dialects of ME, cf. ROPER). 2. English: nickname for a short man, from ME *lāh* (ON *lágr*; the word was adopted first into the Northern dialects of ME, where Scand. influence was strong, and then spread south, with regular alteration of the vowel quality). 3. English (Norman): nickname for a crafty or dangerous person, from ANF *lou*, *leu* wolf (L *lupus*). Wolves were relatively common in Britain at the time when most surnames were formed, as there still existed large tracts of uncleared forest. 4. Scots: from a pet form of LAWRENCE; cf. LOWRY 1. 5. Jewish (Ashkenazic): Anglicized form of LÖWE 2.

Var.: **Lowe**.

Dims. (of 3): Eng.: LOVATT, LEVETT, LOVELL. Fr.: **Loupot**. Prov.: **Louvion**, **Louviot**; **Louvihoux** (Gascony). It.: **Lupi(ci)ni**, **Lup(p)ino**, **Lovini**, **Luvini**; **Lovotti**, **Luvotti**, **Lu(v)otto**; **Lup(p)oli**. Sp., Port.: **Lobato**.

Augs. (of 3): Prov.: **Loubat**. It.: **Lupone**.

Patrs. (from 3) It.: **Lup(p)is**. Rum.: **Lupesco**, **Lupescu** (in part Jewish, translating WOLF). (From 4): Sc.: **Lowson**.

Lowde *see* LOUD

Lowden English (chiefly Northumb.) and Scots: 1. var. of LOTHIAN. 2. habitation name from *Loudoun* near Cunningham in the former county of Ayrs., probably so called from Northern ME *low* flame, beacon (ON *loge*) + *doun* hill (see DOWN 1).

Vars.: **Lowdon**, **Louden**, **Loudon**.

Löwe 1. German: nickname for a brave or regal person, from Ger. *Löwe* lion (MHG *lēwe*, *louwe*, OHG *lēwo*, *louwo*; the word is probably borrowed from L (cf. LYON 1), although the phonetic development is not clear). In some cases the surname may have been originally a house name, from a house distinguished by the sign of a lion. 2. Jewish (Ashkenazic): from Ger. *Löwe* lion, translating the Yid. male given name *Leyb* (see LEIB), or, at least in some cases, chosen because of the association of the animal with the tribe of Judah; in the blessing of Jacob (Gen. 49: 9) Judah is likened to a lion's whelp. There has also been considerable confusion with LEVI, especially among the cpds.

Vars. (of 1): **Löw**; **Leeb** (S Germany); **Löb(e)** (Alsace).

Patrs. (of 2): **Lowensohn**, **Lovenzon**.

Cpds (of 2; purely ornamental or, in some cases, ornamental elaborations associated with the given name *Leyb*): **Löwenberg** ('lion hill'; **Leuvenberg** among Dutch Jews); **Lowenhar** ('lion hair', i.e. 'mane'); **Levenherz** ('lion heart'); **Lowenstark** ('strong as a lion'); **Löwenstein**, **Levenstein** ('lion stone', Anglicized LIVINGSTONE); **Löwenthal**, **Leventhal** ('lion valley').

Lowen *see* LEWIN

Lowis *see* LEWIS

Lowles *see* LOVELACE

Lowman *see* LEMON

Lown English: 1. from the ME given name *Lovin*, OE *Lēofhūn*, composed of the elements *lēof* dear, beloved +

hūn bear cub. **2.** habitation name from the city of *Louvain* in Belgium (Flem. *Leuven*).

Var.: **Loven**.

Patrs. (from 1): **Lown(e)s**, **Lowndes**; **Loynes** (Norfolk).

Lowney *see* LOONEY

Lowrance *see* LAWRENCE

Lowry **1.** N English and Scots: dim. of LAWRENCE. **2.** Irish: Anglicized form of Gael. *Ó Labhradha*; see LAVERY.

Vars.: **Lowery**, **Lowrey**, **Low(e)rie**, **Lor(r)ie**, **Lo(u)ry**, **Lourie**. (Of 2 only): **O'Lowry**, **O'Lawry**.

Patrs. (from 1): **Lowries**, **Lowri(e)son**, **Lorrison**.

'Servant of L. 1': **Lorriman**.

Lowther English: habitation name from a place in Cumb., so called from the river on which it stands. The name is of obscure etymology, perhaps of Brit. origin and equivalent to LAUDER, or from ON *lauðr* froth, foam + *á* river.

Lowthian *see* LOTHIAN

Lowton English: habitation name from a place in Lancs., so called from OE *hlāw* hill + *tūn* settlement, enclosure; cf. LAWTON.

Loyd *see* LLOYD

Loynes *see* LOWN

Loyola Spanish form of Basque **Loiola**: habitation name from a place in the province of Guipúzcoa, so called from Basque *loi* mud + the local suffix *-ola*.

Lozano Spanish: nickname for an elegant or haughty person, from OSp. *loçano* splendid, later 'good-looking' (LL *lautiānus*, from class. L *lautus, lavātus*, originally the past part. of *lavāre* to wash).

Lozerus *see* LAZAR

Lozito *see* ZITO

Luášek *see* LUCAS

Lübbe Low German: short form of the given names LEOPOLD and LUBRECHT.

Var.: **Luppe**.

Dim.: **Lübke**.

Patrs.: **Lübben**, **Lübbing**.

Patrs. (from dims.): **Lübken**, **Lübking**.

Lubbock English: habitation name from the port of *Lübeck* in NW Germany, or nickname for a merchant who had professional connections with the place. Lübeck was a major commercial centre of the Hanseatic League in the Middle Ages. Its name derives from Wendish *Liubice* 'lovely' (cf. LIEB 3).

Lubrecht German: from a Gmc personal name composed of the elements *liut* people, tribe + *berht* bright, famous.

Vars.: **Lubrich(t)**, **Leiprecht**, **Leuprecht**.

Patrs.: Low Ger.: **Lübbers**, **Lüppertz**, **Lüber(d)ing**.

Lucas English, French, Spanish, Portuguese, and Flemish/Dutch: from the given name *Lucas*, a L form of Gk *Loucas* 'man from *Lucania*'. Lucania was a region of S Italy that was perhaps originally named in an Italic dialect

with a word meaning 'bright', 'shining' (cf. LÚCIO). The name owed its popularity in the Middle Ages to St Luke the Evangelist.

Vars.: Eng.: **Luke**, **Luck** (the medieval vernacular forms); **Look**, **Lock** (N England and Scotland); **Lugg** (Devon). Fr.: **Luc**. Flem., Du.: **Lukas**.

Dims.: Eng.: **Luckett**; **Locket(t)**, **Lockitt** (N England); **Lockie**, **Lockey** (Scotland). Fr.: **Lucazeau**; **Luquet**, **Lucot**.

Prov.: **Lugol**. It.: **Luc(c)helli**, **Luc(c)hetti**, **Luc(c)hini**, **Lucotti**. Low Ger.: **Lauxmann**. Ger. (of Slav. origin): **Lukaschek**, **Kaschke**. Czech: **Luášek**; **Kašek**, **Kašík**. Pol.: **Łukasik**, **Łulka**. Ukr.: **Lukashenko**. Beloruss.: **Lukashenya**.

Aug.: It.: **Luconi**. Czech: **Kašák**.

Pej.: Fr.: **Lucaud**.

Patrs.: Eng.: **Luckes**, **Looks**, **Loukes**. Sc.: **McLucas**, **McLuga(i)sh**, **McLugish** (Gael. **Mac Lucais**). Manx: **Clucas**. It.: **De Luca**, **Di Lucca**. Low Ger.: **Lukasen**, **Luxen**. Du.: **Lucassen**. Russ.: **Lukin(ov)**. Ukr.: **Lukashevich**. Pol.: **Łukaszewicz**, **Łukasiewicz**, **Łukowicz**. Croatian: **Luk(ov)ić**. **Lukač**. Bulg.: **Lukanov**.

Patrs. (from dims.): Sc.: **McLu(c)kie**, **McLucky**. Russ.: **Lukashev**, **Lukonin**, **Lukichyov**, **Lukinykh**. Pol.: **Łukaszkiewicz**, **Łuczkiewicz**. Croatian: **Lučić**.

'Servant of L.': Eng.: **Lukeman**, **Luckman**.

Habitation names: Pol.: **Łukaszewski**, **Łukowski**.

Lucca Italian: **1.** cogn. of LUCAS. **2.** habitation name from the Tuscan city of *Lucca*, or from a smaller place of the same name in Sicily. Both appear to have been originally named with a Celt. element meaning 'marshy'.

Vars. (of 2): **Lucches(in)i** (Tuscany); **Lucchese** (Sicily).

Lucena Spanish: habitation name from any of various places, especially in Andalusia, so called from LL *Lūciēna (villa)* 'estate of *Lūcius*' (see LÚCIO).

Lucey **1.** English and Irish (Norman), and French: habitation name from any of various places in Normandy and N France originally named with the L personal name *Lūcius* (see LÚCIO) + the local suffix *-ācum*. **2.** English: from the medieval female given name *Lucie* (L *Lūcia*, a fem. form of *Lūcius*). The name was borne by a young Sicilian maiden and an aged Roman widow, both martyred under Diocletian and venerated as saints. **3.** Irish: Anglicized form of Gael. **Ó Luasaigh**, an altered form of *Mac Cluasaigh* 'son of *Cluasach*', a byname originally denoting someone with large ears (from *cluas* ear).

Vars.: **Lucy**. (Of 2 only): Eng.: **Luce** (the normal medieval vernacular form); **Lucia** (Latinized).

Dims. (of 2): Fr.: **Lucet(te)**.

Metr. (from 2): It.: **De Lucia**.

Lucien French: from a given name (L *Luciānus*, a deriv. of *Lucius*; see LÚCIO), borne by a number of minor early Christian martyrs.

Patrs.: Russ.: **Lukianov**. Ukr.: **Lukianovich**.

Lúcio Portuguese: from a medieval given name (L *Lūcius*, an ancient Roman personal name probably derived from *lux* light, gen. *lūcis*). The name was borne by a large number of early Christian saints, and was accordingly moderately popular in the Middle Ages.

Luckhurst English: of uncertain origin. It is found principally in Kent and may be a habitation name from a place in the parish of Mayfield, Sussex, recorded in 1553 as

Lukkars Croche. The first part of this seems to be from a family name recorded in 1296 as *Luggere*; the second is ME *croche* cross. The etymology of *Lukkar* or *Luggere* is unknown. If this is really the source of the surname, it has been altered fairly radically by folk etymology, to assimilate to the common placename element HURST.

Var.: **Lukehurst**.

Lucking *see* LEVICK

Luckoff *see* LUKOV

Lucraft English: habitation name from *Luckcroft* in Ashwater, Devon, named with OE *loca* enclosure (see LOCK 2) + *croft* paddock (see CROFT).

Var.: **Luckraft**.

Lüdders *see* LEUTHER

Lude *see* LEWIS

Lüdgering *see* LEDGER

Ludlow English: habitation name from a place in Shrops., so called from the OE river name *Hlūde* (from *hlūd* loud, roaring) + *hlāw* hill (see LAW 2 and LOW 1). See also LAIDLAW.

Lueger *see* LUGER

Lüers *see* LEUTHER

Luff *see* LOVE

Luffery *see* LEVERIDGE

Luffman *see* LEMON

Lufschutz *see* LIPSCHUTZ

Luger 1. German: habitation name from any of the minor places in Germany named from MHG *luoc* hiding place, ambush (from OHG *luogen* to watch, (lie in) wait; cf. OE *lōcian* to look). *Lueg* is a common placename in the Tyrol, and the surname is particularly frequent in Bavaria and Austria. 2. Jewish (Ashkenazic): of uncertain origin, perhaps a derogatory name from mod. Ger. *Lüger* liar, imposed by anti-Semitic government officials in 18th- and 19th-cent. central Europe.

Vars. (of 1): **Lugert**; **Lueger**.

Lugg *see* LUCAS

Lugo Spanish: habitation name from a city in Galicia. This was a Roman settlement under the name of *Lucus Augusti* 'grove, wood of Augustus', but that may have been no more than an adaptation of an earlier name derived from that of the Celt. god *Lugos*.

Lührig *see* LEUTHER

Luickinga *see* LEWIS

Luithardt *see* LEUTHARD

Luitpold *see* LEOPOLD

Lukač *see* LUCAS

Lukehurst *see* LUCKHURST

Luker English: 1. habitation name from *Lucker* in Northumb., so called from ON *ló* sandpiper + *kiarr* marsh, wetland (see KERR). 2. occupational name for someone who had to watch or look after something, as for example a watchman or a keeper of animals, from ME *luk(en)* to look (OE *lōcian*).

Vars.: **Lo(o)ker**.

Lukianov *see* LUCIEN

Lukov 1. Jewish (Ashkenazic): habitation name from *Lüchow* in Lower Saxony. 2. Russian: patr. from the nickname *Luk* 'Onion' (an early borrowing from a Gmc cogn. of mod. Eng. *leek*), perhaps given originally to a market gardener. 3. Russian: patr. from the nickname *Luk* 'Bow', bestowed on a skilled archer or perhaps on someone with a deformed spine.

Vars. (of 1): **Lukof(f)**, **Luckoff**; **Likoff** (from a S Yid. form of the name); **Lukovsky**, **Lukowsky**.

Łulka *see* LUCAS

Lumb English: habitation name from places so called in Lancs. and W Yorks., both apparently originally named with OE **lum(m)* pool. The word is not independently attested, but appears also in LOMAX and LUMLEY, and may be reflected in the dial. term *lum* denoting a well for collecting water in a mine. The vars. preserving traces of inflected forms suggest that the surname derives also in part directly from this term used as a vocab. word in the Middle Ages.

Vars.: **Lum**, **Loom**, **Limb**; **Lo(o)mbe**, **Loomes**.

Lumbard *see* LOMBARD

Lumbreras Spanish: metonymic occupational name for a maker of lamps, from the pl. of Sp. *lumbrera* lamp (OSp. *lumnera*, from L *lūmināria*, a deriv. (originally neut. pl. but later taken as fem. sing.) of *lūmen*, gen. *lūminis*, light).

Lumby English (Yorks.): habitation name from a place between Leeds and Selby (now in Humberside), so called from ON *lundr* grove, wood (see LUND) + *býr* farm, settlement.

Lumley N English: habitation name from a place in Co. Durham, so called from OE **lum(m)* pool (see LUMB) + *lēah* wood, clearing.

Var.: **Lumbley**.

Lummis *see* LOMAX

Lumsden Scots: habitation name from a place in the parish of Coldingham, Berwicks. The first element of the placename is of uncertain origin, apparently the gen. case of a personal name; the second is probably OE *denu* valley (see DEAN 1).

Var.: **Lumsdaine**.

Luna Spanish (Aragon) and Jewish (Sefardic): As a Spanish name, a topographic name for someone who lived by an open courtyard, from the Aragonese dial. term *luna* (L *lūmina*, pl. of *lūmen* light); in part it may be a habitation name from a place so called in the province of Saragossa in Aragon. As a Jewish name, its origin is not clear.

Luňák Czech: nickname meaning 'Hawk'.

Lunardelli *see* LEONARD

Lund English, Swedish, and Danish/Norwegian: topographic name for someone who lived in a grove, ON *lundr*; the word was adopted into the Northern dials. of ME and also into ONF. There are a number of places in England named with this word, as for example *Lund* in Lancs. and E and W Yorks., *Lunt* in Lancs., and *Lound* in Lincs., Notts., and Suffolk, and the surname may also derive from any of these. When surnames became obligatory in Sweden in the 19th cent., this was one of the most popular among the many terms denoting features of the natural landscape which were adopted as surnames, usually compounded with some other such term.

Vars.: Eng.: **Lunt** (chiefly Liverpool), **Lunn**. Swed.: **Lundh**, **Lundell**, **Lundén**, **Lundin**, **Lundman**.

Cpds (ornamental): Swed.: **Lundbäck** ('grove stream'); **Lundberg**, **Lundebergh** ('grove hill'); **Lundblad(h)** ('grove leaf'); **Lundbo(h)m** ('grove tree'); **Lundborg** ('grove town'); **Lundahl** ('grove valley'); **Lund(e)gren** ('grove branch'); **Lundholm** ('grove island'); **Lundkvist**, **Lund(e)qvist** ('grove twig'); **Lundmark** ('grove land'); **Lundstedt** ('grove homestead'); **Lundström** ('grove river'); **Lundwall**, **Lundvall** ('grove bank').

Lundon *see* LONDON

Lundy 1. Scots and N Irish: habitation name from any of several places called *Lundie*, for example one near Doune in the former county of Perths. These derive their names from Gael. **lunnd* marsh. 2. Irish: variant of MCALINDEN

Var.: **Lundie**.

Luney *see* LOONEY

Lunghetti *see* LONG

Luotto *see* LOW

Lupesco *see* LOW

Luppe *see* LÜBBE

Lüppertz *see* LUBRECHT

Lüpschütz *see* LIPSCHUTZ

Lupton English: habitation name from a place in the former county of Westmorland, now part of Cumb. The placename is recorded in Domesday Book as *Lupetun*, and probably derives from an OE personal name **Hluppa* (of uncertain origin) + OE *tūn* enclosure, settlement.

Luquet *see* LUCAS

Luria Jewish (Sefardic and Ashkenazic): of uncertain origin, possibly a habitation name from *Luria* in the province of Treviso, Italy, or *Loria* near Bassano, Italy.

Vars.: **Luriah**, **Lurie**, **Lurya**, **Lurye**, **Loria**, **Lorie**; **Lurja**, **Lurje** (Pol. spellings); **Louria**, **Lourié** (Fr. spellings).

Lürsen *see* LEUTHER

Luscombe English (Devon): habitation name from any of the five villages of this name in Devon, all probably so called from OE *hlōse* pigsty + *cumb* valley (see COOMBE).

Lusher *see* USHER

Lussato *see* LUZZATTO

Lustgarten Jewish (Ashkenazic): from mod. Ger. *Lustgarten* pleasure garden (a cpd of *Lust* enjoyment,

pleasure (cf. LUSTIG) + *Garten* garden), presumably a reference to the Garden of Eden.

Lustig German and Jewish (Ashkenazic): nickname for a person of a cheerful disposition, from Ger. *lustig* merry, carefree (MHG *lustig*, a deriv. of *lust* enjoyment, pleasure).

Vars.: Ger.: **Lust**, **Lüstel**. Jewish: **Lustik**, **Lustig(i)er**, **Lust(ig)man**.

Lütge *see* LEUTHER

Luthard *see* LEUTHARD

Luther 1. German: var. of LEUTHER. 2. English: occupational name for a player on the lute, ME, OF *luthier* (from OF *lut*, via OProv. from Arabic *al* 'ūd 'the wood').

Vars. (of 2): Eng.: **Lut(t)er**.

Lutman *see* LIGHT

Luton English: habitation name from the town in Beds. (which derives its name from the river *Lea* + OE *tūn* enclosure, settlement) or, more plausibly in view of the pattern of distribution, from *Luton* in Devon (near Teignmouth), so called from the OE female personal name *Lēofgifu* (composed of the elements *lēof* dear, beloved + *gifu* gift) + *tūn*. A further possible source of the name is *Luton* in Kent, named as the 'settlement (OE *tūn*) associated with *Lēofa*'.

Lutsch *see* LEWIS

Lutt English: from a medieval given name which probably preserves an OE byname **Lutt(a)*, derived from *lȳt* small (see LIGHT 3).

Dim.: **Lutkin** (E Anglia).

Lutton English (now found mainly in N Ireland): habitation name from any of the various places so called—in Northants, Devon, Lincs., and elsewhere. The one in Northants is OE *Ludingtūn* 'settlement associated with *Luda*', a personal name of uncertain origin; that in Cornwood, Devon, is OE *Ludantūn* 'Luda's settlement'; that in Lincs is 'pool settlement', from OE *luh* pool (a borrowing from W *llwch*) + *tūn*. *Lutton* in Yorks. is 'settlement on the river *Hlūde*' (see LOUD).

Luttrell English (Norman): nickname from the otter or metonymic occupational name for a hunter of otters (for their pelts), from a dim. form of OF *loutre* otter (L *lutra*).

Luttwak *see* LITTWAK

Lutwin *see* LITWIN

Lutwyche English (W Midlands): habitation name from a place in Shrops., the second element of which is OE *wīc* outlying village (see WICK). According to Ekwall, the first element is from an OE word **lōt*, 'no doubt identical with Du. *loete*, LG *lōte*, a shovel used to remove mud from ditches and canals'.

Luty *see* LAWTY

Luvini *see* LOW

Luxen *see* LUCAS

Luxford English: habitation name from an unidentified place, no doubt named as the FORD belonging to a bearer of the given name or surname *Luke, Luck* (see LUCAS).

Luxmoore English (Devon): habitation name from an un-identified place, probably in Devon, recorded in medieval documents as *Lukesmore*, and apparently derived from the gen. case of the given name *Luke, Luck* (see LUCAS) + ME *more* marsh, fen (see MOORE 1).

Var.: **Luxmore**.

Luxton English: habitation name from a minor place, probably one of two in Devon, so called from the gen. case of the ME given name *Luke, Luck* (see LUCAS) + ME *tune, tone* settlement (OE *tūn*).

Luyckx *see* LEWIS

Luytgaeren *see* LEDGER

Luz 1. Portuguese: religious byname from a title of the Virgin Mary, *Maria da Luz* 'Mary of Light' (from L *lux*, gen. *lūcis*). **2.** Jewish (Israeli): ornamental name from Hebr. *luz* almond, usually if not always a Hebraicization of MANDEL 3.

Luzak Polish: nickname meaning 'Loose Horse', i.e. one not harnessed but led behind the waggon as a spare. It may have been bestowed on someone who was not felt to be doing his fair share of a job of work.

Luzzatto Italian and Jewish (Sefardic): regional name for someone from *Lusatia* (Ger. *Lausitz*), the region between the Elbe in Germany and the Oder in W Poland.

Vars.: **Luzzato, Luzzat(t)i, Lussato**.

Lvov Russian: patr. from the name *Lev* (gen. *Lva*) 'Lion' (an early borrowing from Gmc; cf. LÖWE). This word may occasionally have been used as a nickname for a fierce or brave fighter, but normally it was taken as a vernacular equivalent of the given name *Leon* (see LYON 2).

Dims.: Russ.: **Levkov, Lyov(ysh)kin, Levshukov, Levykin, Levashov, Lyovshin, Levoshin, Levishchev**. Ukr.: **Levchenko** (not patr.). Beloruss.: **Levashenya** (not patr.); **Levanovich** (patr.).

Lvovski *see* LWÓWSKI

Lwowicz *see* LEWKOWICZ

Lwówski Polish and Jewish (E Ashkenazic): habitation name from *Lwów*, the Polish name of the city known in Russ. as *Lvov*, in Ukr. as *Lviv*, and in Ger. as *Lemberg*. It is now in the Ukraine and so part of the Soviet Union, but was for long a major centre of Polish culture.

Vars.: Jewish: **Lwowsky, Lvovski, Lvovsky**.

Lyakin *see* LYOKHIN

Lyal Scots: probably from an ON personal name *Liulfr*, composed of an uncertain first element + *úlfr* wolf, although Reaney gives this as a dim. of *Lyon* or *Lionel*.

Vars.: **Lyall, Lyel(l)**.

Lyburn *see* LEYBURN

Lydall *see* LIDDELL

Lydiate *see* LIDDIATT

Lydon *see* LEYDEN

Lye *see* LEE

Lyel *see* LYAL

Lyhan *see* LEHANE

Lyle *see* LISLE

Lyman *see* LEE

Lynch 1. Irish: Anglicized form of **Ó Loingsigh** 'descend-ant of *Loingseach*', a personal name (originally a byname) meaning 'Mariner' (from *long* ship; cf. LANGAN). **2.** Irish (Anglo-Norman): Anglicized form of Gael. **Linseach**, it-self a Gaelicized form of ANF *de Lench*, the version found in old records. This would appear to be a local name, but its origin is unknown. One family of bearers of this name were of Norman origin, but became one of the most im-portant tribes of Galway. **3.** English: topographic name for someone who lived on a slope or hillside, OE *hlinc*, or per-haps a habitation name from *Lynch* in Somerset or *Linch* in Sussex, both of which are named with this word.

Vars.: (of 1): **(O')Lynchy, O'Lynche, O'Lensie, Linch(e)y**, LIND-SAY. (Of 2): **Linch, Lince, LINK, Linck**.

Dims. (of 1): **O'Lyneseghane, Lynchaha(u)n, Lynchehan** (Gael. **Ó Loingseacháin**).

Lynde *see* LINE

Lyndon English (Midlands): habitation name from a place in Leics. (formerly Rutland), so called from OE *lind* lime tree (cf. LINDE and LINE 1) + *dūn* hill (see DOWN 1).

Lyne 1. English: var. of LINE. **2.** Irish: var. of LANE. **3.** Scots: habitation name from a place in the former county of Peebles., so called from Gael. *linne* pool, stream.

Var. (of 3): **LYNN**.

Lyneham 1. English: habitation name from places in Devon, Oxon., and Wilts., all so called from OE *līn* flax + *hām* homestead or *hamm* water meadow. **2.** Irish: Angli-cized form of Gael. **Ó Laidhghneáin** 'descendant of *Laidhghneán*', a personal name that occurs in OIr. geneal-ogies. It is of uncertain origin, perhaps a dim. of *ladhgh* snow and meaning 'Snowflake'.

Vars.: **Lineham, Lyn(h)am**. (Of 2 only): **Linehan**.

Lynn 1. Scots: var. of LYNE 3. **2.** Irish: Anglicized form of Gael. *Mac Fhloinn* and *Ó Fhloinn*; see FLYNN. **3.** English: habitation name from any of the various places so called in Norfolk, in particular King's *Lynn*, an important centre of the medieval wool trade. The placename is probably from a Brit. word, an ancestor of W *llyn* lake. **4.** Jewish: Angli-cization of the Ashkenazic surname **Lin(n)**, which is of unknown origin.

Vars.: **Lynne, Linn, Lenn**.

Lyokhin Russian: one of a group of patrs. from dims. of the given name *Aleksei* (see ALEXIS).

Vars.: **Lyoshin; Lyalin, Lyal(ya)kin, Lyalikov, Lyakin, Lya(ki)shev, Lyashutin; Leksin**.

Lyon 1. English and French: nickname for a fierce or brave warrior, from OF, ME *lion* (L *leo*, gen. *leōnis*). **2.** English and French: from the name *Leo(n)* (from L *leo* lion, or the cogn. Gk *leōn*), borne by numerous early martyrs and thir-teen popes. On the Continent the given name was relatively popular because of the numerous saints who bore it, and also because the lion was the symbol of the evangelist St Mark. In England, however, it was rare throughout the Middle Ages. **3.** English and French: habitation name from the town of *Lyon* in central France (sometimes known in mod. Eng. as *Lyons*), or from the smaller *Lyons*(-la-Forêt) in Eure, Normandy. The name of the former place is recorded in the 1st cent. BC as *Lugdunum*, apparently from Gaul. elements meaning 'raven', 'crow' + 'hill', 'fort'. **4.** Irish: Anglicized form of Gael. *Ó Laighin*; see LANE 2.

Vars. (of 1–3): Eng.: **Lion**, **Leon**. Fr.: **Lion**, **Léon**. (Of 3 only): Eng.: **Lyons**. Fr.: **Lions**, **Lyonnais**.

Dims. (of 1 and 2): Fr.: **Lyonnel**, **Lion(n)el**; **Lyonnet**, **Lion(n)et**. It.: **Leonelli**, **Leonello**, **Lionelli**, **Lionello**; **Leonetti**, **Leonetto**, **Leonotti**.

Patrs. (from 1 and 2): Fr.: **Delion**. It.: **De Leone**, **Di Lione**; **De Leonibus** (Latinized); **De Leo**, **Di Leo**; **Leoneschi**.

Lyosik *see* ALEXIS

Lyovkin *see* LVOV

Lys *see* LIS

Lysaght Irish: Anglicized form of Gael. **Mac Giolla Iasachta** 'son of the servant of the foreigner', from *iasachta* strange, foreign.

Vars.: **Lysa(ch)t**; **McLysaght**; **McGillesachta**, **McGillisachia**, **McGillysachtie**.

Lysenko Ukrainian: **1.** nickname from a dim. of *lys* fox (cf. LIS). **2.** nickname from a dim. of the adj. *lysy* bald (cf. ŁYSIAK).

Łysiak Polish: nickname for a man with a bald pate, from Pol. *lysy* bald + *-iak* noun suffix.

Dims.: Pol.: **Łysek**. Beloruss.: **Lysyononok**. Ukr.: LYSENKO.

Lysons *see* LISON

Lyster *see* LISTER

Lyte *see* LIGHT

Lythe English: **1.** topographic name for someone who lived on a hillside, from OE *hlið*, ON *hlíð* slope. **2.** nickname for a mild or gentle person, from ME *lithe* mild (OE *līðe*).

Lythgoe *see* LITHGOW

Lytle *see* LITTLE

Lyttelton *see* LITTLETON

Lytton *see* LITTON

Lyubimov Russian: patr. from the nickname *Lyubimy* 'Dear', 'Beloved' (from the root *lyub-* love; cf. LIEB 3).

M

Maas Low German and Dutch: **1.** aphetic form of THOMAS. **2.** topographic name for someone living on the banks of the river *Maas*, which flows through Belgium and Holland. It was originally named as the *Mosa*, a name of apparently Celto-Ligurian origin and uncertain meaning.

Vars. (of 1): MAS, **Ma(a)ss**. (Of 2): **Vermaas**.

Dims. (of 1): Low Ger.: **Massmann**, **Maascke**. Ger. (of Slav. origin): **Mas(ch)ek**, **Mas(ch)ke**. Fr.: **Masset**, **Massin(ot)**, MASSON, **Mass(ic)ot**, **Massiquot**, **Massoud**. It.: **Mas(s)ini**, **Masin(o)**, **Masolini**, **Maselli**, **Mas(i)ello**, **Mas(s)etti**, **Masetto**, **Masotti**, **Masutti**, **Masutto**, **Masuzzo**, **Masucci(o)**, **Masolo**, **Masullo**, **Massuli**.

Patrs. (from 1): Low Ger.: **Maasen**, **Massen(s)**. Flem.: **Maesen**. It.: **Masellis**. Lithuanian: **Masionis**.

Mabb English: from the medieval female given name *Mab(be)*, a short form of ME, OF *Amabel* (from L *amābilis* loveable). This has survived into the 20th cent. in the aphetic form *Mabel*.

Var.: **Mapp**.

Dims.: **Mabbot**, **Mabbett**, **Mabbutt**.

Metrs.: **Mabbs**, **Mabson**; **Mobbs** (Norfolk).

Mabon 1. Scots: from the medieval given name *Maban*, *Mabon*, which according to Black is cogn. with W *Mabon*, and represents Brit. *Maponos* 'Great Son'. On the other hand the given name could possibly be a dim. of ME *Mab(be)* (see MABB). **2.** Jewish: a name borne by French Jews, of unknown origin.

Vars. (of 1): **Maben**, **Maybin**.

Mac- For Scots and Irish names beginning thus, see Mc-.

Mac Adaidh see ADAM

MacAfee see DUFFY

Mac Aileáin see ALLEN

Mac Ailpín see ALPIN

Mac Aindrín see ANDREW

Macaire French: from the OF given name *Macaire*, Gk *Makarios* (from *makar* fortunate, blessed) borne by two obscure 4th-cent. Egyptian saints.

Var.: **Maquaire**.

Patrs.: Ger.: **Kahrs**. Pol.: **Makarewicz**. Russ.: **Makarov**, **Makaryev**. Georgian: **Makaradze**. Armenian: **Markarian**.

Patrs. (from dims.): Russ.: **Makarochkin**, **Makarytsev**. Ukr.: **Makarishin**.

'Son of the wife of M.': Russ.: **Makarikhin**.

Mac Alastair see ALEXANDER

Macalpin see ALPIN

Macaluso Italian: status name for a freed serf, from the Sicilian dial. term *macalusciu*, *macaluggiu* freedman (Arabic *maḥlūǧ*, a deriv. of *ḥalaǧa* to free, liberate).

Mac Ambróis see AMBROSE

Mac an Aba see ABBOTT

Mac an Baird see BARD

Mac an Bhreatnaich see BRETT

Mac an Easpuig see BISHOP

Mac an Ghobhann see McGOWAN

Mac an Ghoill see GALL

Mac an Stocaire see STOKER

Mac Artáin see McCARTNEY

Mac Artair see ARTHUR

Mac Ascaidh see ASHKETTLE

Mac Asgaill see ASHKETTLE

Mac Beathain see BEAN

Mac Bheathain see BEAN

Mac Bhiocair see VICKAR

Mac Biorna see BURNEY

Mac Briain see BRYAN

Maccaffie see DUFFY

Mac Calmáin see COLEMAN

Mac Carlais see CHARLES

MacCaslane see McAUSLAN

Mac Cearbhaill see CARROLL

Mac Chonnigh see McKENZIE

Mac Cionaodha see KENNY

Mac Cléirich see CLEARY

Mac Coimín see CUMMING

Mac Colmáin see COLEMAN

Mac Cormaic see CORMACK

Mac Cúthbhréith see CUTHBERT

Mac Daibhéid see DAVID

Mac Diarmid see DERMOTT

Macé see MASSEY

Mace English: from a medieval given name. This was probably originally of Gmc derivation, representing OE *Mæssa* (cf. MASSINGHAM) or the cogn. OHG *Mas(s)o*, but during the Middle Ages it came to be taken as a pet form of MATTHEW.

Var.: **Masse**.

Mac Ealair *see* HILARY

Macedo *see* MANZANO

Macek *see* MATTHEW

Mac Eocháin *see* KEOGH

Mac Eòghainn *see* EWAN

Mac Fearchair *see* FARQUHAR

Mac Fhionnáin *see* FINN

Mac Fhógartaigh *see* FOGARTY

Mac Gairbheith *see* GARVEY

MacGarvey *see* GARVEY

Mac Gille Andrais *see* ANDREW

Mac Gille Iosa *see* GILLIES

Mac Giobúin *see* GIBBON

Mac Giolla Dhuinn *see* DUNN

Mac Giolla Dubhthaigh *see* DUFFY

Mac Giolla Fhionnain *see* FINN

Mac Giolla Íosa *see* GILLIES

Mac Gobha *see* GOUGH

Mac Gofraidh *see* McCAFFREY

MacGorman *see* GORMAN

Mach **1.** Czech, Polish, and German (of Slav. origin): from the given name *Mach*, a pet form of Czech *Matěj*, Pol. *Maciej*, etc. (see MATTHEW). The Czech name is also a pet form of other names beginning with *Ma-*, e.g. *Marek* (see MARK) and MARTIN. **2.** Jewish (Ashkenazic): of unknown origin.
Vars. (of 1): Czech: **Mácha**, **Máchač**, **Máchal(a)**, **Macháň**, **Machoň**. Pol.: **Machała**, **Machnicki**, **Machocki**. Ger.: **Mache**, **Macha**.
Dims.: Czech: **Macháček**, **Machálek**, **Machek**, **Machotka**.

Machado Spanish and Portuguese: metonymic occupational name for a maker, seller, or user of a hatchet, Sp., Port. *machado* (a deriv. of MACHO 2). In part it may also be a habitation name from a place in the province of Lugo, Spain, but alternatively the placename may be derived from the surname rather than the other way about.

Machaffie *see* DUFFY

Machan *see* MAUGHAN

Macherzyński Polish: offensive nickname for a man of weak character, from Pol. dial. *macherzyna* bladder, scrotum.

Machiavelli Italian: nickname for a notorious philanderer, from It. *malo* bad (see MALO) + *chiavello* nail, spike (LL *clavellus*, a dim. of class. L *clavus*), also used of the penis. The surname is first recorded in Genoa in 1148 in the Latinized form *Malclavellus* and is found at Savona in the 14th cent. as *Malusclavus*. Today the surname is principally confined to Liguria, Emilia, and Tuscany.
Vars.: **Macchiavelli**, **Ma(c)chiavello**.

Machin English: occupational name for a stonemason, ANF *machun* (a Norman var. of OF *masson*; see MASON).
Vars.: **Machon**, **Machen(t)**, **Meachin**, **Meachen**, **Meachem**, **Meacham**, **Meecham**.

Macho Spanish: **1.** nickname for a virile, bold man, from Sp. *macho* male (L *masculus*; cf. MALE). **2.** nickname for a forceful person or metonymic occupational name for a smith, from Sp. *macho* sledgehammer (probably from LL *marculus* hammer (cf. MARTEL), crossed with Sp. MAZA).

Maciak *see* MATTHEW

MacIlvreed *see* KILBRIDE

MacIvor *see* IVOR

Mack **1.** Scots (Berwicks.): from the ON personal name *Makkr*, a form of MAGNUS. **2.** Chiefly U.S.: simplified form of any of the various Scots and Irish names beginning *Mc-*.
Var. (of 1): **Maccus**.

Mackelbreed *see* KILBRIDE

Mäckelburg *see* MECKLENBURG

MacKeller *see* HILARY

Mackereth *see* McCRAE

Mackintosh *see* McINTOSH

Mackover *see* MAKOWSKI

Mackworth English: habitation name from a place in Derbys., so called from the OE personal name *Macca* (of uncertain origin) + OE *worð* enclosure (see WORTH).

Mac Laomuinn *see* LAMONT

Maclehose Scots: Anglicized form of Gael. **Mac Gille Thamais** 'son of the servant of (St) THOMAS'.

Mac Lucais *see* LUCAS

Mac Marcuis *see* MARK

Mac Mathghamhana *see* McMAHON

Mac Muircheartaigh *see* MORIARTY

MacMuiris *see* MORRIS

Mac na Ceardadh *see* CAIRD

Mac Neacail *see* NICHOLAS

Macourek *see* MATTHEW

Mac Phádraig *see* PATRICK

Mac Phaid *see* PATE

Macquarie *see* McQUARRY

Mac Raghailligh *see* REILLY

Mac Raighne *see* RAINEY

Mac Raonuill *see* RONALD

Mac Réamoinn *see* RAYMOND

Mac Riabhaich *see* REAVEY

Mac Ruaidhrí *see* RORY

Mac Ruiarc *see* ROURKE

Mac Sheumais *see* JAMES

Mac Shimidh *see* SIMON

Mac Shuibhne *see* SWEENEY

Mac Síthigh *see* SHEEHY

Mac Thámhais *see* McTAVISH

Mac Thomaidh *see* McCOMB

Mac Uaitéir *see* WALTER

Mączyński Polish: habitation name from a place named with Pol. *mąka* flour + *-yn* possessive suffix, with the addition of the suffix of local surnames *-ski* (see BARANOWSKI). In effect, it is probably an occupational name for a flour-dealer.

Madariaga Basque: topographic name for someone who lived by a wild pear tree, from Basque *madari* + the local suffix *-aga*.

Maddei *see* AMADEI

Madden Irish: Anglicized form of Gael. Ó Madaidhín 'descendant of *Madaidhín*', a personal name from a dim. of *madadh* hound, mastiff.
Vars.: **Madine**; **O'Madden**, **O'Maddane**; **O'Madagane**, **O'Madigane**, **Mad(d)igan** (Gael. Ó Madagáin).

Maddens *see* MAUDLING

Madder English: **1.** metonymic occupational name for a dyer or seller of dye, from ME *mad(d)er* madder (OE *mædere*), a dark red dye obtained from plant roots. **2.** nickname for a person with a ruddy complexion, from the same word used in a transferred sense.
Vars.: **Mader** (also Jewish, of unknown origin); MATHER. (Of 2 only): **Maddern** (an adj. deriv.).

Maddison English: metr. from the medieval female given name *Madde*, a form of *Maud* (see MOULT 1) or of *Magdalen* (see MAUDLING).
Var.: **Madison**.

Madeira Portuguese: **1.** metonymic occupational name for a carpenter, from Port. *madeira* wood, timber (LL *māteria*, from class. L *māteries* material, substance). **2.** nickname for a stupid person, from the same word in a transferred sense, i.e. 'blockhead'. **3.** (rarely) local name from the island of *Madeira*, which was named with Port. *madeira* timber because of the timber that grew there. The island was colonized in the 15th cent. under the patronage of Prince Henry the Navigator.

Madeley English: habitation name from any of various places (one in Shrops. and two in Staffs.), so called from the OE byname **Māda* (probably a deriv. of *mād* foolish) + OE *lēah* wood, clearing.

Madge *see* MARGUERITE

Madoc Welsh: from the OW personal name *Matoc* (possibly a dim. of *mad* fortunate, good), which survives in the mod. W given name *Madog*.
Vars.: **Maddock**, **Maddick**, **Mattock**, **Mattick**, **Mattuck**, **Mattack**.
Patrs.: Welsh: **Mad(d)ocks**, **Maddox**, **Maddicks**, **Mattocks**, **Mattacks**.

Madrid Spanish: habitation name from what is now the principal city of the Spanish peninsula. Throughout the Middle Ages it was of only modest size and importance, and did not become the capital of Spain until 1561. Its name is of uncertain origin, most probably a deriv. of LL *mātrix*, gen. *mātricis*, riverbed, much changed by Arabic mediation; cf. MADRIGAL. There are other, smaller places of the same name in the provinces of Burgos and Santander, and these may also be partial sources of the surname.
Var.: **Lamadrid**.

Madrigal Spanish: habitation name from any of various places, for example in the provinces of Avila, Burgos, Cáceres, and Guadalajara, apparently so called from LL *mātricāle*, a adj. deriv. of *mātrix* womb, riverbed; cf. MADRID.

Madsen *see* MATTHEW

Madureira Portuguese: habitation name from any of various places so called from LL *mātūrāria* place for ripening fruit and vegetables (a deriv. of *mātūrus* ripe).

Maesen *see* MAAS

Maestacci *see* MASTER

Maeterlinck Belgian: occupational name for an official responsible for dispensing corn from a central warehouse, from MDu. *meten* to measure out + the Gmc suffix *-ling* (cf. CHAMBERLAIN).

Maffetti *see* MATTHEW

Magahan *see* GAHAN

Magaheran *see* GAUGHRAN

Magalhaēs Portuguese: habitation name from any of various minor places. The placename is of uncertain origin; the first element may be akin to Celt. *magal* large.

Magann *see* McGANN

Magauran *see* McGOVERN

Magaw *see* MEGAW

Magdelon *see* MAUDLING

Magee *see* McKAY

Magennis *see* McGUINNESS

Magennure *see* GAYNOR

Magenza *see* MAINZ

Mager *see* MAJOR

Mageraghty *see* GERAGHTY

Magermans *see* MAIGRE

Magg English (chiefly Somerset and Wilts.): from the medieval female given name *Mag(ge)*, a pet form of *Margaret* (see MARGUERITE).

Vars.: **Mogg**; **Mudge** (Devon).

Metrs.: **Maggs**, **Magson**, **Megson**; **Mox(s)on**, **Mox(s)om**, **Moxham**.

Maggi *see* MARGUERITE

Maggini *see* MAY

Magid Jewish (Ashkenazic): occupational name for a preacher, Hebr. *magid*, Yid. *maged*.

Vars.: **Maged** (from Yid. *maged*); **Magit** (reflecting a regional Yid. pronunciation).

Patrs.: **Magidson**; **Magidov(itz)** (E Ashkenazic).

Magill *see* GALL

Maginn *see* MCGINN

Maginot *see* DOMINIQUE

Magistrelli *see* MASTER

Magnien French: occupational name for an itinerant tinker or locksmith, OF *ma(i)gna(i)n* (lit. 'worker', from a LL deriv. of *machina* work, trade, earlier 'contrivance', 'device').

Vars.: **Meignien**, **M(e)ignan**, **Mégni(e)n**; **Lema(i)gnan**, **Lemaign(i)en**.

Dims.: It.: **Magnanelli**, **Magnanini**.

Magnol French: habitation name from places in Loire, Lot, and Puy-de-Dôme, all so called from a dim. of OProv. *magnan* silkworm (lit. 'worker'; cf. MAGNIEN). The farming of silk worms was an important occupation in S France during the Middle Ages.

Magnus 1. English, Swedish, Danish/Norwegian, and German: from the Scandinavian personal name *Magnús*. This was borne by Magnus the Good (d. 1047), king of Norway, who was named after the Emperor Charlemagne, L *Carolus Magnus* CHARLES the Great'. The name spread from Norway to the east Scandinavian royal houses, and became popular all over Scandinavia and thence in the English Danelaw. **2.** Jewish: of unknown origin. It may be related to the Jewish surname **Magnes**, which is likewise of unknown origin.

Dims.: Fr.: **Maignet**, **Maignon**. It.: **Magnetti**, **Magnozzi**.

Augs.: It.: **Magnoni**, **Magnone**.

Patrs.: Eng.: **Magnu(s)son**; MANSON. Sc., Ir.: MCMANUS.

Swed.: **Magnusson**; **Månsson** (Anglicized in the U.S. as **Monson**). Dan.: **Magnussen**.

Magorlick *see* MCGOLDRICK

Magragh *see* MCCRAE

Magrannell *see* RONALD

Magreavy *see* REAVEY

Magriñá Catalan: from the medieval given name *Magrinyá* (L *Macrīniānus*, a deriv. of the Roman family name *Macrīnus*, from *macer* lean; cf. MAIGRE).

Magueen *see* SWEENEY

Maguier *see* MCGUIRE

Magyar Hungarian: name meaning 'Hungarian'. The Magyar people seem to have come originally from the Urals, but between the 5th and 9th cents. they lived in the north Caucasus and were closely associated with the Turkic peoples ther. They were forced to migrate westward as a result of Bulgarian expansionism and settled in their present territory at the end of the 9th cent.

Maher Irish: Anglicized form of Gael. **Ó Meachair** 'descendant of *Meachar*', a byname meaning 'Hospitable'.

Vars.: **O'Meagher**, **Meacher**.

Mahew *see* MAYHEW

Mahler 1. German: occupational name for a painter, esp. a painter of stained glass, from an agent deriv. of Ger. *malen* to paint (MHG *mālen*, OHG *mālōn* to mark, from *māl* point, mark). **2.** Jewish (Ashkenazic): presumably an adoption of the Ger. surname or an occupational name for an artist or a housepainter. Kaganoff suggests that the name was occasionally used as an equivalent of LEVI, but there seems to be no evidence to support this hypothesis.

Vars.: Ger.: **Mähler**; **Mehler** (Rhineland, Hesse); **Möhler** (Bavaria).

Mahlke *see* MALÝ

Mahon Irish: **1.** Anglicized form of the Gael. personal name or byname *Mathghamhain* 'Bear'. **2.** Anglicized form of Gael. **Ó Mocháin**; see MOHAN.

Patr. (from 1): MCMAHON.

'Descendant of M. 1': **(O')Mahon(e)y** (Gael. **Ó Mathghamhna**).

Mahood *see* HOOD

Mahorry *see* MCAREE

Mahoudeau *see* MOULT

Mai *see* MAY

Maia Portuguese: habitation name from any of several places so called. The most important is first recorded in the form *Amaia*, and is probably of pre-Roman origin. Others may get their names from Port. *maia* flowering broom (from *maio* month of MAY).

Maiden English: nickname for a man of effeminate appearance, from ME *maiden*, the usual word for a young girl (OE *mægden*).

Maidment English: occupational name for a servant employed by a (young) woman or at a convent, from ME *maid(en)* + *man*. For the excrescent *-t*, cf. DIAMOND.

Vars.: **Maitment**; **Maidman** (also borne by at least one Ashkenazic Jewish family in the U.S., in which case the origin is unknown).

Maier *see* MAYER

Maignet *see* MAGNUS

Maigre French: nickname for a thin person, from OF *maigre* thin, slender (L *macer* delicate).

Var.: **Lemaigre**.

Dims.: Fr.: **Maigret**, **Meigret**, **Mégret**, **Maigrot**. Prov.: **Magret**, **Magrin**, **Magron**, **Magrou**. It.: **Magretti**, **Magrin(i)**, **Magrino**, **Magherini**, **Magrotti**. Ger.: **Mägerl(ein)**, **Megerle**.

Augs.: It.: **Magroni**, **Magrone**.

Patrs.: Eng.: **Meagers**. It.: **Magris** (Venetia); **Del Magro**. Flem., Du.: **Magermans**.

Maigrot *see* MAIGRE

Maile *see* MAUL

Mailer 1. English: occupational name for an enameller, from an aphetic form of ME *ameillur*, ANF *esmailour* (an agent deriv. of *esmail* enamel, a word of Gmc origin akin to mod. Eng. *(s)melt*). **2.** English: occupational name for a maker of chain mail, from ME, OF *maille* mail, mesh (L *macula* mesh, spot, stain). **3.** Scots: habitation name from a place in the former county of Perths., perhaps so called from the Gael. elements *maol* bare + *ard* height. It is recorded as *Malere* in 1296 and *Maller* in 1380. The surname is most common around Stirling. **4.** Welsh: from the OW personal name *Meilyr*, derived from an original Celt. form **Maglorīx*, composed of the elements *maglos* chief + *rīx* ruler. **5.** Welsh: habitation name from *Maelor* in Clwyd, so called from the W personal name *Mael* + W *or* land, territory. **6.** Jewish (Ashkenazic): of uncertain origin, possibly an occupational name for a charcoal burner, from mod. Ger. *Meiler* charcoal kiln.

Vars. (of 1–5): **Mailler, Maylor, Meyler.**

Main *see* MAYNE

Mainerd *see* MAYNARD

Maingaut French: from a Gmc personal name, *Magengaut*, composed of the elements *magin* strength (cogn. with Eng. *main*) + the tribal name *Gaut*. For spellings without *-i-*, the first element may be *man* man.

Vars.: **Mangaut, Ma(i)ngaud.**

Mainland Scots: local name found almost exclusively on the Shetland islands, especially in the parish of Dunrossness, and also in parts of the Orkneys. It is a local name from the principal island of the Shetlands, which is so called. The principal island of the Orkneys is also called *Mainland*, but it is probably not the source of the surname.

Mains Scots and N English: topographic name for a dweller at the chief farm (or home farm) on an estate, Sc. *mains*, or habitation name from any of the various minor places named with this word (originally an aphetic form of *domain*, later associated with the adj. *main* principal).

Mainwaring English (Norman): habitation name from a lost place, of uncertain location, named in ANF as *mesnil Warin* 'domain of *Warin*' (see WARING). The surname has gone through a large number of var. spellings; it is normally pronounced /'mænərɪŋ/.

Vars.: **Manwaring, Mannering.** See also MANDRY.

Mainz Jewish: habitation name from the city of *Mainz* in W Germany, which is so called from the river *Main*, on which it stands. The river name is ancient and has many cogns. throughout Europe, but its meaning is obscure.

Vars.: **Mainzer, Meinzer; Magenza** (from a form closer to the L name of the city, *Maguntia*).

Maiorov Russian: **1.** patr., of relatively recent origin, from the army rank *maior* major (borrowed in the 16th cent. from Ger.). **2.** surname adopted by members of the Orthodox clergy, from the learned nickname *maior* older, senior, with the addition of the normal patr. suffix *-ov*.

Mair 1. Scots: occupational name for an officer of the courts whose functions resembled those of an Eng. beadle and who was known as a *mair* (cf. MAYER 1). **2.** Jewish: var. of MAYER 3.

Patr. (from 1): **Mairs** (chiefly N Ireland).

Maisme *see* MAXIME

Maistrelli *see* MASTER

Maites Jewish (Ashkenazic): metr. from the Yid. female given name *Meyte* (from MHG *maget* maiden; cf. MAKIN 2) + the Yid. possessive suffix *-s*.

Vars.: **Mat(t)es, Matus, Matis** (see also MATTHEW); **Meites, Meitus; Maitin, Meitin** (E Ashkenazic).

Metrs. from a dim. (*Meytl*): **Mait(e)les, Ma(j)teles, Mat(a)lis, Meitlis, Maitlis; Majtlis** (Pol. spelling, reflecting the central Yid. pronunciation of the given name); **Matelson; Matlow, Matalovitch, Mat(a)lovsky, Matlovski.**

Maitland Scots and English (Norman): of uncertain origin, possibly a nickname for an ungracious individual, from ANF *maltalent, mautalent* bad temper (LL *malum* bad + *talentum* inclination, disposition). However, there is a place called *Mautalant* in Pontorson, France, so named from its unproductive soil, and this may well be a partial source of the surname. The present spelling is the result of a contracted pronunciation and folk etymological identification with the common topographic element *land*.

Maizel *see* MAUS

Majblat *see* MAY

Majchrowicz *see* MELCHIOR

Majerczyk *see* MAYER

Majewski Polish and Jewish (Ashkenazic): surname adopted with reference to the month of MAY, Pol. *maj*, with the addition of the common surname ending *-ewski*. Surnames derived from months were often taken, for example, by converted Jews to mark the month in which they were converted to Christianity or baptized. In other cases, it simply marks the month in which a surname was registered.

Var.: **Majkowski.**

Major 1. English: from the Norman personal name *Malg(i)er, Maug(i)er*, composed of the Gmc elements *madal* council + *gari, geri* spear. **2.** Jewish (E Ashkenazic): var. of MAYER 3.

Vars. (of 1): **Ma(u)ger.**

Majoral *see* MAYORAL

Majstorović *see* MASTER

Majteles *see* MAITES

Makaradze *see* MACAIRE

Makepeace English: nickname for a person known for his skill at patching up quarrels, from ME *mak(en)* to make (OE *macian*) + *pais* peace (see PACE).

Var.: **Makepiece.**

Mäki Finnish: ornamental name from Finn. *mäki* hill, perhaps sometimes chosen as a topographic name by someone who lived on or near a hill.

Vars.: **Mäkelä** (with collective suffix), **Mäkinen** (with gen. suffix).

Makin N English (Lancs. and Yorks.): **1.** dim. of MAY, which is itself a pet form of MATTHEW. **2.** nickname for an effeminate man, from ME *maid(en)* girl, young woman (see MAIDEN) + the dim. suffix *-kin*. It is possible, but unlikely, that it may also have been of more literal application as an occupational name for a female servant.

Vars.: **Maykin**; **Meakin** (chiefly Notts.), **Meaken**; **Making**.

Patrs. (from 1): **Makins**, **Maykin(g)s**, **Meakin(g)s**, **Meekin(g)s**; **Makinson** (Lancs.).

Makonin *see* MAXIME

Makowski Polish and Jewish (E Ashkenazic): habitation name from the town of *Maków* (Yid. *Makeve*), so called from Pol. *mak* poppy (a word probably ultimately cogn. with, rather than borrowed from, Gk *mēkon*), + *-ów* possessive suffix used in forming placenames.

Vars.: Pol.: **Makówka**. Jewish: **Ma(c)kover**, **Makower** (clearly habitation names); **Makov**, **Makovski**, **Makowsky**, **Makovsky** (probably ornamental names from Pol. *mak* poppy).

Maksakov *see* MAXIME

Malaghan *see* MILLIGAN

Malave Jewish (E Ashkenazic): habitation name from *M(e)lave*, Yid. name of the town of *Mława* in Poland.

Vars.: **Mlawer**, **Melaver**; **Malavski**, **Malavsky**, **Malawsky**.

Malcharek *see* MELCHIOR

Malcolm Scots: from the Gael. personal name *Mael-Colum* 'devotee of (St) *Columba*' (see COLOMB).

Var.: **Malcom**.

Patrs.: **Malco(l)mson** (chiefly N Ireland).

Mald *see* MOULT

Maldonado Spanish: nickname for an ugly or stupid person, from Sp. *mal donado* ill-favoured. The phrase is a cpd of *mal* badly (L *male*, a deriv. of *malus*; see MALO) + *donado* given, endowed (L *donātus*, past part. of *donāre*; cf. DONAT).

Male English: nickname for a particularly virile man, from ME *male* masculine (OF *masle, madle*, L *masculus*).

Vars.: **Mayle**, **Mayell**, **Mayall**.

Dims.: Prov.: **Masclet**. It.: **Maschietto**, **Mascolino**.

Malebranche French: nickname from OF *mal(e)* bad (see MALO) + *branche* branch. The original significance of the name is not easy to determine; there may have been some jocular reference to an illegitimate branch of a noble family.

Malet **1.** English: from the medieval female given name *Malet*, a dim. of *Mal(le)*, pet form of *Mary* (see MARIE), and so a var. of MALIN 1 with a different dim. suffix. **2.** English: var. of MALLARD 1. **3.** English: nickname for an unfortunate person, from OF *maleit* accursed (L *maledictus*, the opposite of *benedictus*; cf. BENNETT). **4.** English and French: nickname for a fearsome warrior or metonymic occupational name for a smith, from OF

ma(i)let, dim. of *ma(i)l* hammer (see MALLE 1). **5.** French: from a dim. of the given name *Malo*, which was relatively popular in Brittany in the Middle Ages, having been borne by a 6th-cent. Welsh missionary to the area. His name is also recorded in the Latinized form *Maclovius*, and perhaps has some connection with Celt. *megalos* chief, leader.

Vars.: Eng.: **Mallet(t)**. Fr.: **Mallet**, **Mallez**.

Dim. (of 3): Fr.: **Malouet**.

Malfi *see* AMALFI

Malherbe French: topographic name for someone who lived on a patch of ground overgrown with weeds, from OF *mal(e)* bad (see MALO) + *herbe* plant (L *herba* grass).

Vars.: **Malherb**, **Malerbe**; **Malesherbes** (a place in Loiret).

Pej.: Fr.: **Malherbaud**.

Malin **1.** English: from the medieval female given name *Malin*, a dim. of *Mal(le)*, pet form of *Mary* (see MARIE). **2.** Jewish (E Ashkenazic): metr. from the Yid. female given name *Male* (a back-formation from *Malke* (see MALKIN), as if it contained the Slav. dim. suffix *-ke*) + the Slav. metr. suffix *-in*. In a few cases it may originate as in 3 below. **3.** Russian: patr. from the nickname *Mala* 'Small One'; see MALÝ.

Vars. (of 1): **Mallin**; **Mallen** (see also MELLON). (Of 2): **Malis**.

Metrs. (from 1): Eng.: **Malli(n)son**, **Malleson**.

Malinowski Polish and Jewish (E Ashkenazic): habitation name from a place named with Pol. *malina* raspberry, possibly in effect an occupational name for a grower of the fruit. As a Jewish name, it may well be ornamental, one of the many Ashkenazic surnames taken from vocab. words for fruit and plants.

Vars.: Pol.: **Maliński** (also from a nickname). Jewish: **Malina**; **Maliniak**; **Malin(ov)sky**, **Malinovski**, **Malinowsky**.

Patrs. (from a nickname): Russ., Bulg.: **Malinov**. Jewish: **Malinov(itz)**, **Malinowitz**.

Malise *see* MELLIS

Małkiewicz *see* MALÝ

Malkin **1.** English: from a medieval female given name, a dim. of *Mal(le)* (see MALIN), with the hypocoristic suffix *-kin*. **2.** Jewish (E Ashkenazic): metr. from the Yid. female given name *Malke* (from Hebr. *Malka* 'Queen') + the Slav. metr. suffix *-in*.

Vars. (of 1): **Maulkin**. (Of 2): **Malkes**; **Malkind** (influenced by Yid. *kind* child; see SÜSSKIND); **Malkinson** (with a Gmc suffix added to the Slav. one).

Metr. (from 1): Eng.: **Malkinson**.

Mallard English: **1.** from the OF personal name *Malhard*, composed of the Gmc elements *madal* council + *hard* hardy, brave, strong. This was introduced to Britain by the Normans. **2.** nickname for someone supposedly resembling a drake or male wild duck, ME, OF *malard* (originally a pej. from OF *ma(s)le* MALE).

Vars. (of 1): **Maylard**, **Maylett**, MALET.

Mallarmé French: nickname for a poorly accoutred warrior, perhaps one who could barely afford the knight's service he had inherited, from OF *mal* badly (L *male*) + *armé* armed (L *armātus*, from *arma* arms).

Vars.: **Malarmé**, **Mal(l)armey**.

Malle French: **1.** metonymic occupational name for a smith, or nickname for a fierce fighter, from OF *ma(i)l* hammer (L *malleus*). **2.** metonymic occupational name for a maker of bags or nickname for someone who habitually carried one, from OF *male* bag (of Gmc origin).

Mallen *see* MELLON

Mallory English (Norman): nickname for an unfortunate person, from OF *malheure* unhappy, unlucky. The etymology from *maloret* ill-omened (L *male* badly + *augurātus*) is less likely for the surname that has actually survived, although it does lie behind other medieval Norman surnames, now defunct.

Vars.: **Malory**, **Mal(l)ary**, **Mallery**, **Mallerie**, **Mallorie**.

Malloy *see* MOLLOY

Mally Irish: Anglicized form of Gael. **Ó Máille** 'descendant of the nobleman', from *mál* prince, champion, poet.

Vars.: **Malley**, **Meall(e)y**, **Melly**, **Melia**; **O'Mall(e)y**, **O'Mallie**, **O'Mailie**, **O'Maely**, **O'Meal(l)y**.

Malm Swedish: arbitrary or ornamental name, from Swed. *malm* ore (ON *málmr*), adopted in some cases by people having something to do with the copper-mining industry.

Cpds: **Malmberg** ('ore hill'); **Malmborg** ('ore town'); **Malmgren** ('ore branch'); **Malmqvist** ('ore twig'); **Malmsten** ('ore stone'); **Malmström** ('ore river').

Malo Spanish: nickname for an unpleasant individual, from Sp. *malo* bad, evil (L *malus*).

Malone Irish: Anglicized form of Gael. **Ó Maoil Eoin** 'descendant of the devotee of (St) JOHN'.

Var.: **Mallon**.

Maloney *see* MOLONEY

Malpas English (Norman) and French: habitation name from any of various places named, because of the difficulty of the terrain, from OF *mal pas* bad passage (L *malus passus*). Places in Ches., Cornwall, Gwent, and elsewhere were given this name by Norman settlers. A place in Rousillon which was so called in the 12th cent. was subsequently renamed *Bonpas* for the sake of a better omen.

Vars.: Eng.: **Malpass**, **Malpuss**, **Melpuss**, **Morpuss**. Fr.: **Maupas(sant)**.

Malpighi Italian: nickname for an idle chatterer or malicious gossip, from It. *mala* (fem.) bad, evil (see MALO) + *piga*, a dial. term for the magpie (L *pica*; cf. PYE 1).

Malt *see* MOULT

Maltby English: habitation name from *Maltby* in Cleveland, Lincs., and N and W Yorks., or *Mautby* in Norfolk, all so called from the ON byname *Malti* 'Sharp', 'Bitter' + ON *býr* farm, settlement.

Vars.: **Mau(l)tby**.

Malter English: **1.** occupational name for a brewer who used malt, from an agent deriv. of ME *malt* malt, germinated barley (OE *mealt*). **2.** topographic name for someone who lived on a patch of unprofitable land, from OF *male terre* bad land (L *mala terra*).

Vars. (of 1): **Maltster** (originally a fem. form); **Maltman** (Sc.).

Malthus English: topographic name for someone who lived at a malt-house, ME *malthuse* (from OE *mealt* + *hūs*), and so in effect an occupational name for a brewer. The malt-house was the building in which the cereal was dried in an oven after it had been soaked in water to make it germinate.

Vars.: **Malthouse**, **Maltus**, **Maltas**.

Maltravers English (Norman): apparently a local surname from an unidentified place, presumably named from OF *mal travers* bad crossing (LL *malum traversum*), perhaps at the site of a difficult ford. Cf. MALPAS.

Vars.: **Mat(t)ravers**, **Matraves**.

Malý Czech: from the Czech adj. *malý* small. This was both a nickname for a physically small man and a pet name for a child, which was sometimes retained in adult life. The cogn. noun *malec*, in Pol. as well as Czech, has the additional sense 'young man', which probably also underlies some surnames.

Vars.: **Malec**, **Maleč**, **Malecký**, **Malák**, **Malát**.

Dims.: Czech: **Málek**, **Malík**, **Maleček**. Pol.: **Malczyk**, **Małek**, **Małecki**. Ukr.: **Malko**. Ger. (of Slav. origin): **Ma(h)lke**, **Malek**, **Malicke**.

Patrs.: Russ. and Jewish: **Malov**, MALIN. Pol.: **Malisiewicz**.

Patrs. (from dims.): Russ.: **Maltsev**, **Maltsov**, **Maleev**, **Male(n)in**, **Maleinov**, **Malnev**, **Malenkov**, **Mal(i)kov**, MALIN, **Malyagin**, **Malyav(k)in**, **Malyugin**, **Malyukin**, **Malyukov**, **Malyut(k)in**, **Malyk(h)in**, **Malygin**, **Malyshev**, **Malyshkin**, **Malushin**. Pol.: **Małkiewicz**. Croatian: **Maletić**.

Habitation names: Pol.: **Malewski**, **Maliszewski**.

Habitation names (from dims.): Pol.: **Małkowski**, **Malczewski**.

Manahan *see* MONAGHAN

Manally *see* McNALLY

Mañas Spanish: nickname for a devious character or alternatively for an astute or skilful person, from the pl. form of Sp. *maña* trick, strategem (LL *mania*, a deriv. of *manus* hand).

Mancebo Spanish: occupational or status name for a serf or servant, OSp. *mancebo* (LL *mancipus*, from class. L *mancipium* slave).

Manchester English: habitation name from the city in NW England, formerly part of Lancs. This is so called from *Mamucio* (an ancient Brit. name containing the element *mammā* breast, and meaning 'breast-shaped hill') + OE *ceaster* (Roman) fort (L *castra* legionary camp).

Manco Italian: nickname for a left-handed person, from the It. adj. *manco*. The name is found in this form largely in S Italy.

Vars.: **Mango**; **Manka** (Sardinia); **(Lo) Mancuso**, **Mancusi**, **Manguso**, **Mangusi**, **Moncuso** (Calabria, Sicily); **Mancosu** (Sardinia).

Dims.: **Mancin(ell)i**, **Mancinetti** (Tuscany, NW Italy); **Mancin** (Venetia).

Aug.: **Manconi**.

Mandel **1.** German and Jewish (Ashkenazic): from Ger. *Mandel* almond or its Yid. cogn. *mandl* (MHG *mandel*, OHG *mandala*, from LL *amandula*, from Gk *amygdale*, probably of Semitic origin). This could have been a topographic name for someone who lived by an almond tree or a metonymic occupational name for a seller of almonds. In the case of the Jewish name, it is one of the many ornamental surnames referring to different types of trees and their fruit. **2.** S German and Austrian: dim. of the medieval given name MANN.

Vars. (of 1): Jewish: **Mandell** (U.S.); **Mandelman** (occupational).

Cpds (of 1; ornamental): Jewish: **Mandelbaum, Mandelboim** ('almond tree', Anglicized **Mandlebaum**); **Mandelberg** ('almond hill'); **Mandelblatt** ('almond leaf'); **Mandelblitt** ('almond blossom'); **Mandelmilch** ('almond milk'); **Mandelstam(m)** ('almond trunk'); **Mandeltort** ('almond cake'); **Mandelzweig** ('almond twig').

Mander English: of uncertain origin. It may be a nickname for a beggar, from an agent deriv. of *maund* beg (probably from OF *mendier*, LL *mendicare*); this word is not attested before the 16th cent., but may well have been in use earlier. Alternatively it may be an occupational name for a maker of baskets, from an agent deriv. of ME *maund* basket (OF *mande*, of Gmc origin); or perhaps for someone in some position of authority, from an aphetic form of ME *coma(u)nder* (from *coma(u)nden* to command, ANF *comaunder*, OF *comander*, LL *commandāre*).

Vars.: **Maund(er)**.

Patrs.: **Ma(u)nders, Manderson**.

Mandeville English (Norman): habitation name from any of various places in France called *Mann(e)ville* (from the Gmc personal name *Manno* (see MANN 2) + OF *ville* settlement) or *Magneville* (from OF *magne* great + *ville* settlement).

Vars.: **Manville, Manvell, Manwell**.

Mandry English or Welsh: apparently a var. of MAINWARING. The latter name is pronounced /'mændrɪ/ in the Ammanford district of Wales, but not so spelled there. This spelling is, however, found in Neath. The earliest known record of the name is the marriage of Sarah *Mandrey* in the city of London in 1688.

Mané Catalan: from a Gmc personal name composed of the elements *magin* strength + *heri, hari* army.

Var.: **Mañés**.

Manes *see* EMMANUEL

Manfelloto *see* MEIFFERT

Mangan Irish: Anglicized form of Gael. **Ó Mongáin** 'descendant of *Mongán*', originally a byname for someone with a luxurious growth of hair (from *mong* hair, mane).

Mangaud *see* MAINGAUT

Mangenet *see* DOMINIQUE

Manger *see* MENGER

Mangia Italian: nickname for a glutton, a deriv. of It. *mangiare* to eat (L *manducāre* to chew).

Dims.: It.: **Mangini** (Tuscany, Liguria); **Mangiullo, Mangiulli**. Fr.: **Mangot, Manguet, Manguin**.

Aug.: It.: **Mangione**.

Mango *see* MANCO

Mangold 1. English: of uncertain origin. Reaney gives it as a var. of **Mangnall**, which he derives from OF *mangonelle*, a war engine for throwing stones. It may alternatively be identical in origin with the German name in 2 below, but there is no evidence of its introduction to Britain as a given name by the Normans, which is normally the case for English surnames derived from Continental Gmc personal names. **2.** German: from a Gmc personal name *Managold*, composed of the elements *manag* much (cogn. with mod. Eng. *many*) + *wald* rule.

Patrs. (from 2): Low Ger.: **Mangels(en), Mangholz**.

Manikhin *see* MARIE

Manin *see* EMMANUEL

Manjón Spanish: of uncertain origin, perhaps from a LL personal name *Mancio*, gen. *Manciōnis*, a deriv. of *Mancius*.

Manley English: **1.** habitation name from places in Devon and Ches., so called from OE *(ge)mǣne* common, shared + *lēah* wood, clearing. The surname is still chiefly found in the regions around these villages. **2.** nickname from ME *mannly* manly, virile, brave (OE *mannlīc*, originally 'man-like').

Vars.: **Manly, Manleigh**.

Mann 1. English and German: nickname for a fierce or strong man, or for a man contrasted with a boy for some reason, from ME, MHG *man*, mod. Ger. *Mann* (OE *mann*, OHG *man*). In some cases it may have arisen as an occupational name for a servant, from the medieval use of the term to describe a person of inferior social status. **2.** English and German: from a Gmc personal name, found in OE as *Manna*. This originated either as a byname or else as a short form of any of the various cpd names containing this element, such as HERMANN. **3.** Jewish (Ashkenazic): of uncertain origin. Possibly it is from Hebr. and Yid. *man* manna, and is thus expressive of faith in God. Another possibility is that it comes from the Yid. male given name *Man* (cogn. with the Gmc name mentioned in 2), which is sometimes taken as a short form of the Hebr. given name *Menakhem*. See also MENDEL.

Vars. (of 1): Eng.: **Man**. (Of 3): (E Ashkenazic): **Mannsky, Manski; Monsky** (reflecting the pronunciation of Yid. *man* found in Podolia, Moldavia, and Bessarabia).

Dims. (of 2): Ger.: MANDEL, **Männel, Männle**. Fr.: **Manet(eau), Manin**. It.: **Mannelli, Mannello, Man(n)ini, Man(n)ino, Man(n)etti, Mannucci, Mannuzzi**.

Augs. (of 2): It.: **Mannoni, Mannone**.

Patrs. (from 1 and 2): Eng.: **Manning**, MANSON. Ger.: **Mann(e)s**. (From 2): Low Ger.: **Manssen**. It.: **Manneschi**. (From 3): Jewish: **Manzon, Manis, Manin**.

Mannell *see* MEYNELL

Mannering *see* MAINWARING

Manners English (Norman): habitation name from *Mesnières* in Seine-Maritime, recorded in the 13th cent. as *Maneria*, a deriv. of L *manēre* to remain, abide, reside. See also MENZIES.

Mannheim Jewish (Ashkenazic): habitation name from the city in SW Germany (formerly the residence of the electors Palatine), so called from the Gmc personal name

Manno (see MANN 2) + OHG *heim* homestead. It seems that all bearers of the surname are Jews who have acquired it relatively recently. Mannheim was not fortified or chartered until the beginning of the 17th cent., until which time it was just a small fishing village.

Vars.: **Manheim, Man(n)heimer**.

Mannin Irish: Anglicized form of Gael. **Ó Mainnín** 'descendant of *Mainnín*', probably an assimilated form of *Mainchín*, a dim. of *manch* monk.

Vars.: **Mannion, Manning**.

Manninen *see* HERMANN

Mannington *see* MERITON

Mannish *see* McNEICE

Manntschke *see* SIMON

Manrique Spanish: from the medieval given name *Manrique*, composed of the Gmc elements *mann* man + *rīc* power.

Mansell English (chiefly W Midlands): **1.** Norman habitation or regional name from OF *mansel* inhabitant of Le Mans or the surrounding area of *Maine*. The town was originally named in L *(ad) Ceromannos*, from the name of the Gaul. tribe living there, the *Ceromanni* (of unknown etymology). The name was reduced to *Celmans* and then became *Le Mans* as a result of the mistaken identification of the first syllable with the OF demonstrative adj. **2.** status name for a particular type of feudal tenant, ANF *mansel*, who occupied a *manse* (LL *mansa* dwelling), a measure of land sufficient to support one family; cf. HYDE, HUBER. **3.** some early examples, such as Thomas *filius Manselli* (Northumb. 1256), point to derivation from a personal name, perhaps the Gmc deriv. of MANN 2 Latinized as *Manzellinus*.

Vars.: **Mansel, Mancell, Maunsell**.

Manser English: **1.** from the male given name *Manasseh* (Hebr. *Menashe* 'One who causes to forget'), borne occasionally in the Middle Ages by Christians as well as by Jews. Hebr. *Menashe* and its reflexes in other Jewish languages have always been popular among Jews. **2.** occupational name for someone who made handles for agricultural and domestic implements, from an agent deriv. of ANF *mance* handle (OF *manche*, LL *manicus*, a deriv. of *manus* hand).

Var.: **Mancer**.

Dim. (of 1): Jewish (E Ashkenazic): **Menashko** (among Rumanian Jews).

Patrs. (from 1): Jewish: **Menashes**; **Menasherov**; **Manaschewitz, Manesewic**.

Mansfield English: habitation name from a place in Notts. The early forms, from Domesday Book to the early 13th cent., show the first element uniformly as *Mam-*, and it is therefore likely that this was a Brit. hill-name meaning 'Breast' (cf. MANCHESTER), with the later addition of OE *feld* pasture, open country (see FIELD) as the second element. The surname is now widespread throughout Midland and S England and is also common in Ireland.

Mansilla Spanish: habitation name from any of various places, for example in the provinces of Burgos, León, Logroño, and Segovia, so called from Sp. *mansilla*, a dim. of LL *mansa* dwelling (class. L *mansio*, a deriv. of *manēre* to remain, abide).

Manso Spanish and Portuguese: nickname for a mild and inoffensive person, from Sp., Port. *manso* tame, docile (LL *mansus*, class. L *mansuētus*, past part. of *mansuescere* to tame, lit. 'accustom to the hand').

Manson 1. Scots: patr. from the given name MAGNUS. **2.** English: patr. from the ME nickname or byname MANN.

Månsson *see* MAGNUS

Mantegna Italian: from an aphetic form of the medieval given name *Diotimantegna* 'God preserve you'.

Mantell 1. English: metonymic occupational name for a maker of overgarments, or nickname for someone who wore a cloak of a particularly conspicuous design, from ANF *mantel* cloak, coat (LL *mantellus*, probably of Celt. origin; cf. W *mantell* cloak). **2.** Jewish (Ashkenazic): probably from Ger. *Mantel* or Yid. *mantl* coat, which are related to 1 above.

Vars.: **Mantel**. (Of 1 only): **Mantle**.

Dims.: Fr.: **Mantelet, Mantelin**. Jewish: **Mantelik**.

Manthorpe English: habitation name from either of two places in Lincs., so called from the ON personal name *Manni* (a deriv. of *maðr*, gen. *mannes*, man; cf. MANN) + ON *þorp* settlement (see THORPE).

Manton English: habitation name from any of the various places so called, for example in Leics., Lincs., Notts., and Wilts. For the most part the first element is either OE *(ge)mǣne* common, shared (cf. MANLEY), or the OE byname *Mann(a)* (see MANN). However, in the case of *Manton* in Lincs., the early forms show clearly that it was OE *m(e)alm* sand, chalk, with reference to the poor soil of the region. The second element is in each case OE *tūn* enclosure, settlement.

Manzano Spanish: topographic name for someone who lived by an apple tree or orchard, from Sp. *manzano* apple tree (OSp. *maçano*, from *maçana* apple, LL *(māla) Mattiāna* (originally neut. pl., then fem. sing.), a type of apple named in honour of the 1st cent. BC horticultural writer Gaius *Matius*).

Collectives: Sp.: **Manzanares**. Port.: **Macedo**.

Manzo Italian: nickname for someone supposedly resembling an ox, It. *manzo* (from LL *mansus* tame (see MANSO), specialized in the sense of an ox tamed to the plough), or metonymic occupational name for someone who worked with oxen.

Vars.: **Manzi, Mansi**.

Dim.: **Manzitto**.

Aug.: **Manzoni**.

Maple English: topographic name for someone who lived by a maple tree, ME *mapel*, OE *mapul*.

Var.: **Maples**.

Mapp *see* MABB

Maquaire see MACAIRE

Maqueda Spanish: habitation name from a place in the province of Toledo, so called from the Arabic name of a fortress established there, derived from Ar. *makāda* firm, fixed.

Maranc see POMERANTZ

Marañón Spanish: habitation name from a place in the province of Navarre, apparently so called from a deriv. of Sp. *maraña* thicket, dense foliage (of uncertain, probably pre-Roman, origin).

Marcelino Portuguese: from a personal name (L *Marcellīnus*, a deriv. of *Marcellus*; see MARCELO) borne by several early saints, including the friend of St Augustine to whom *De Civitate Dei* was dedicated.

Marcelo Portuguese: from a personal name (L *Marcellus*, a dim. of *Marcus*; see MARK 1). This was borne by a large number of minor early saints, and consequently became popular as a given name during the Middle Ages.
Vars.: Fr.: **Marcel, Marceau**.
Dims.: Fr.: **Marcel(l)et, Marcel(l)eau, Marcelot, Marcelon**.

Marcereau see MERCER

March 1. English: topographic name for someone who lived on the border between two territories, esp. in the Marches between England and Wales or England and Scotland, from ANF *marche* boundary (of Gmc origin; cf. MARK 2 and MARQUE 1). In some cases, the surname may be a habitation name from *March* in Cambs., which was probably named from the locative case of OE *mearc* boundary. 2. English: from a nickname or given name for someone who was born or baptized in the month of March (ME, OF *march(e)*, L *Martius (mensis)*, from the name of the god *Mars*) or who had some other special connection with the month, such as owing a feudal obligation then. 3. Catalan: cogn. of MARK 1.

Marchant English, French, and Jewish: occupational name for a buyer and seller of goods, from OF, ME *march(e)ant* (LL *mercātans*, pres. part. of *mercātāre*, from *mercātus*, past part. of class. L *mercāri* to trade, from *merx*, gen. *mercis*, commerce, exchange, merchandise). In the Middle Ages the term was used mainly of a wholesale dealer. The surname shows the regular ME, OF change of *-er-* to *-ar-*, although in the Eng. vocab. word the original vowel was later restored under learned (etymological) influence.
Vars.: Eng.: **Marchent, (Le) Marchand, Le Marchant; (Le) Marquand** (from a Norman form); **Merchant**. Fr.: **Marcant, Marc(h)and; Marquant, Marquand**. Jewish: **Marchand**.
Dims.: Fr.: **Marchandel, Marcantel, Marchandon, Mercanton**. It.: **Marcantelli, Mercantini**.
Aug.: It.: **Mercantone**.
Patr.: Fr.: **Aumarchand**.
Equivs.: Ger.: HANDLER. Czech: SOUKUP. Pol.: TARGOWNIK. Russ.: KUPTSOV. Rum.: NEGUS.

Marchewa Polish: nickname from Pol. *marchew* carrot (Czech *mrkev*), given no doubt to a person with carrot-coloured hair.
Var.: **Marchwicki**.
Dims.: Pol.: **Marchewka**. Czech: **Mrkvička**.
Patr.: Croatian: **Mrkić**.

Marden English: habitation name from any of various places so called, which have a number of different origins. One in Wilts. is so called from OE *mearc* boundary + *denu* valley; one in Sussex from OE *(ge)mǣre* boundary + *dūn* hill; one in Kent from OE *m(i)ere* mares + *denn* pasture; and one in Herefords. from Brit. *magno-* plain + OE *worðign* enclosure.
Var.: **Mardon**.

Mare see DELAMARE

Marek Czech: 1. from the personal name *Marek*, the Czech equivalent of MARK. *Marek* is also the usual Pol. form of the given name, but it does not seem to be used as a Pol. surname. 2. from a dim. of MARTIN or *Mauritius* (see MORRIS).
Vars.: **Mareš, Mára**.
Dims.: **Mareček, Maršík, Mařík**.

Marfleet English (Yorks. and Lincs.): habitation name from a village in Humberside, near Hull, which is so called from OE *mere* lake, pond + *flēot* stream.
Var.: **Marflit** (Yorks.).

Marguerite French: from the LL female personal name *Margarita* 'Pearl' (the vocab. word was borrowed into Greek and Latin from a Semitic source, and is probably of Persian origin). This was borne by several early Christian saints, and became a popular female given name throughout Europe. The usual ME form was *Margerie*.
Vars.: Fr.: **Margueritte, Margeride, Margaride, Margalide, Margerit, Marg(u)erie, Marguery, Margry; Magritte** (Belgium).
Dims.: Fr.: **Margeridon; Marg(u)erin, Marg(u)eron; Margot(eau), Margotin, Marguet, Marguin**. Eng.: **Madge**, MAGG; **Madgett, Meggett, Meggitt, Meggat**. Ger.: **Maggi** (Switzerland). Flem., Du.: **Griete**.
Metrs.: Eng.: **Marger(r)ison, Marger(e)son, Margetson, Margesson, Margi(t)son, Marginson; Marget(t)s**.

Marie French: from the extremely popular medieval female given name, L *Maria*. This was the name of the mother of Christ in the New Testament, as well as several other New Testament figures. It derives from Aramaic *Maryam* (Hebr. *Miryam*), but the vernacular forms have been influenced by the Roman family name *Marius* (of uncertain origin). The Hebr. name is likewise of uncertain etymology, but perhaps means 'Wished-for Child', from an Egyptian root *mrj* with the addition of the Hebr. fem. dim. suffix *-am*. St Jerome understood it as a cpd of *mar* drop + *yam* sea, which he rendered as L *stilla maris*, later altered to *stella maris* star of the sea, whence the liturgical phrase. A Latin masc. adj. form, *Mariānus*, was applied by Christians to devotees of the Virgin Mary, and lies behind several of the surnames listed here.
Dims.: Fr.: **Mariel(le), Mariet(te), Mariéton, Marion(eau), Mariot(te), Mariolle**. Eng.: **Mar(r)ion, Maryon, Mar(r)ian, Maryan**; MARRIOTT; **Merrikin**. Pol.: **Marusik**. Czech: **Maroušek, Marušák, Maruška, Maryška**. Ukr.: **Marishenko, Marusyak**,

Marushak, **Marunchak**. Jewish (E Ashkenazic): **Mariamchik** (consists of a central Yid. pronunciation of the Yid. female given name *Miryem* Miriam + the E Yid. dim. ending *-tshik*).

Pejs.: Fr.: **Mariaud**, **Mariault**.

Metrs.: Eng.: **Marrison** (chiefly Norfolk). Flem.: **Marien**. It.: **De Maria**, **Di Maria**. Russ.: **Mar(y)in**. Croatian: **Mar(ič)ić**, **Marjanović**.

Metrs. (from dims.): Eng.: **Marians**. Russ.: **Mariyushkin**, **Marikhin**, **Maryakhin**, **Maryashkin**, **Maryushkin**, **Maryasin**, **Mash(k)in**, **Mashikhin**, **Mashenkin**, **Mashutkin**, **Man(ikh)in**, **Manyurin**. Ukr.: **Marusin**. Croatian: **Marušić**.

Habitation name: Pol.: **Maruszewski**.

Marimon Catalan: of uncertain origin. It has been explained as a habitation name from *Miremont* in Garonne, France, so called from OProv. *mirar* to look, watch + *mont* hill (i.e. 'look-out hill'), and as from a medieval given name composed of the Gmc elements *ber(i)* bear + *mund* protection, but neither of these etymologies is very convincing.

Marin **1.** French: from a personal name (L *Marīnus*, a Roman family name derived from *Marius*; cf. MARIE). This was borne by several minor early saints. **2.** French: occupational name for a sailor, OF *marin* (LL *marīnus*, a deriv. of *mare* sea). **3.** Jewish (Ashkenazic): of unknown origin.

Vars. (of 2): **Marinier**, **Lemari(g)nier**. (Of 3): **Marinberg** (evidently an ornamental elaboration).

Dims. (of 1): It.: **Marin(i)ello**, **Marinelli**, **Marinetto**, **Marinetti**, **Marinucci**, **Marinuzzi**, **Marinolli**, **Marinotti**, **Marinotto**. (Of 3): **Marinczik** (E Ashkenazic).

Aug. (of 1): It.: **Marinoni**.

Pejs. (of 1): It.: **Marinacci(o)**, **Marinazzo**, **Marinato**.

Patrs. (from 1): It.: **De Marini(s)**. Rum.: **Marinescu**. Croatian: **Marin(ov)ić**. Bulg.: **Marinov**. Pol.: **Marynowicz**. (Of 3): **Marinoff**, **Marinow** (E Ashkenazic); **Marinescu** (among Rumanian Jews).

Patr. (from a dim. of 1): Croatian: **Marinković**.

Habitation name: Pol.: **Marynowski**.

Marivaux French: habitation name from places called *Marivaux* in Aisne, Oise, and Seine-et-Oise, or *Marival* in Aisne and Haute-Savoie. The second element is presumably OF *val* valley (see VALE); the first is of uncertain origin.

Var.: **Marival**.

Marjoram English (Norfolk): apparently from the name of the herb, ME *majorane*, *mageram* (via OF from med. L *majorana*, of obscure derivation).

Marjoribanks Scots: according to Black, this name was adopted by a family previously known as JOHNSTON, when, in the early 16th cent., they acquired the lands of *Ratho-Marjoribankis* in Renfrew. This estate was so called from having been bestowed on Robert the Bruce's daughter *Marjorie* (see MARGUERITE) on her marriage in 1316 to Walter the High Steward. The pronunciation is normally /'mɑːtʃbæŋks/.

Var.: **Marchbanks**.

Mark **1.** English: from L *Marcus*, the personal name of St Mark the Evangelist, author of the second Gospel. The name was borne also by a number of other early Christian saints. *Marcus* was an old Roman name, of uncertain (possibly non-Italic) etymology; it may have some connection with the name of the war god *Mars* (cf. MARTIN). The given name was not as popular in England in the Middle Ages as it was on the Continent, especially in Italy, where the evangelist became the patron of Venice and the Venetian Republic, and was allegedly buried at Aquileia. **2.** English: topographic name for someone who lived on a boundary between two districts (OE *mearc*), or habitation name from any of the various places named with this word, such as *Mark* in Somerset. See also MARCH 1 and MARQUE 1. **3.** Jewish (Ashkenazic): in many cases an Anglicization of any of several like-sounding Jewish surnames. However, since *Mark* has also been an Ashkenazic surname in E Europe, where English influence is out of the question, there must be at least one other explanation too.

Vars. (of 2): **Marke**, MARKS.

Dims. (of 1): Fr.: **Marquet**, **Marquot**. It.: **Marchel(li)**, **Marchello**, **Marchet(ti)**, **Marchetto**, **Marchitto**, **Marchitelli**, **Marchitiello**, **Marchetiello**, **Marchin(i)**, **Marcolin(i)**, **Marchiol(i)**, **Marcocci(o)**, **Marcozzi**, **Marcucci(o)**, **Marcuzzi**, **Marcuzzo**. Ger.: **Mark(e)l**, **Merkel**, **Merkle**, **Märkli(n)**. Pol.: **Marczyk**. Ukr.: **Marchenko**.

Augs. (of 1): It.: **Marcon(i)**, **Marcone**.

Patrs. (from 1): Eng.: MARKS, **Markson**. Sc.: **McMarquis** (Gael. **Mac Marcuis**). It.: **De Marchi(s)**. Sp.: **Márquez**. Port.: **Marques**. Low Ger.: **Marcussen**, **Marx(s)en**. Flem., Du.: **Merckx**. Dan., Norw.: **Markussen**, **Marcussen**. Russ.: **Mark(os)ov**. Ukr.: **Markovich**. Pol.: **Markowicz**, **Markiewicz**, **Marczak**. Croatian: **Marković**. Bulg.: **Markov**. Jewish: **Markson**; **Marcov**, **Marcoff**, **Markovitch**, **Marcovi(t)ch**, **Markovic(h)**, **Marcovic**, **Marcovicz**, **Marcovits**, **Markovitz**, **Marcovits**, **Markovits**, **Marcowi(t)ch**, **Marcowic(z)**, **Marcowitz**, **Markowitz**, **Markewitz**, **Markovski**, **Markovsky**, **Markowsky** (E Ashkenazic); **Marcovici**, **Markovici** (among Rumanian Jews). Armenian: **Margossian**. Lithuanian: **Morkúnas**.

Patrs. (from 1) (dims.): Russ.: **Markush(k)in**, **Markushev**, **Mar(k)tsev**, **Markisov**, **Markichev**.

Habitation names: Pol.: **Markowski**, **Marczewski**, **Marczyński**.

Markarian *see* MACAIRE

Marker **1.** English: topographic name for someone who lived by a boundary; see MARK 2. It is notable that early examples of the surname tend to occur near borders, for example on the Kent/Sussex boundary. In the U.S.A., the name is also an Anglicization of the Ger. cogns. listed below. **2.** English: possibly also an occupational name from an agent deriv. of ME *mark(en)* to put a mark on (OE *mearcian*), although it is not clear what the exact nature of the work of such a 'marker' would be. **3.** English: relatively late development of MERCER. There is one family in Clitheroe, Lancs., who spelled their name *Mercer* or *Marcer* (cf. MARCHANT) in the 16th cent., but *Marker* in the 17th. **4.** Jewish (Ashkenazic): of unknown origin. Compare MARK 3.

Var. (of 4): **Merker**.

Markey Irish: Anglicized form of Gael. **Ó Marcaigh** 'descendant of *Marcach*', a byname meaning 'Knight', 'Horseman'.

Dims.: Ir.: **O'Markaghaine**, **O'Marcahan**, **Marca(ha)n**, MARKHAM (Gael. **Ó Marcacháin**).

Markham **1.** English: habitation name from a place in Notts., so called from OE *mearc* boundary (see MARK 2) + *hām* homestead. **2.** Irish: Anglicized form of Gael. *Ó Marcacháin*; see MARKEY.

Markland English (Lancs.): habitation name from a place in the parish of Wigan, so called from OE *mearc* boundary (see MARK 2) + *lanu* lane.

Var.: **Martland**. See also MARLAND and MARSLAND.

Marklew English (W Midlands): probably a habitation name from an unidentified place, perhaps named with OE *mearc* boundary (see MARK 2) + *hlǣw* hill (a byform of *hlāw*; cf. LAW 2 and LOW 1). Alternatively, the second element could conceivably be a river name (there is a river *Lliw* in Wales, and a *Lew* in Devon, the names of which are derived from a Celt. element meaning 'bright', 'shining').

Var.: **Martlew**.

Marks 1. English: patr. from MARK 1. **2.** English: topographic name, var. of MARK 2. **3.** German: contracted form of *Markus*, the Ger. version of MARK 1. **4.** Jewish (W Ashkenazic): adoption of the Ger. surname, chosen under the influence of various like-sounding Jewish given names.

Vars. (of 3 and 4): **Marx**.

Markwardt German (common esp. in N Germany): occupational name for a frontier guard, Ger. *Markwart*, from *Mark* frontier, boundary (see MARK 2) + *Wart* guard (MHG, OHG *wart*, cogn. with OE *weard*; see WARD). In MHG folk stories *Markwart* occurs as a nickname for a jay; it is possible that this use influenced the acquisition of the surname to some extent.

Vars.: **Markward**, **Marquardt**.

Patr.: Dan.: **Marquardsen**.

Marland English (S Lancs.): habitation name from a minor place in the parish of Rochdale, so called from OE *mere* lake, pool + *land* land. There may also have been some confusion with MARKLAND.

Marler English: topographic name for someone who lived on a patch of clay soil, ME *marl* (OF *marle*, LL *margila*, from earlier *marga* (prob. of Gaul. origin), with the ending added under the influence of the synonymous *argilla*).

Var.: **Marlor**.

Marley English: habitation name from any of the various places so called, for example in Devon, Kent, and W Yorks. According to Ekwall, the first element of these placenames is respectively OE *(ge)mǣre* boundary, *myrig* pleasant, and *mearð* (pine) marten. The second element in each case is OE *lēah* wood, clearing.

Vars.: **Marlee**, MARLOW.

Marlow English: **1.** habitation name from the town in Bucks., on the Thames, so called from OE *mere* lake, pool + *lāfe* remnants, leavings, i.e. a boggy area remaining after a lake had been drained. **2.** var. of MARLEY.

Var.: **Marlowe**.

Marney English (Norman): habitation name from *Marigni* in La Manche, so called from the Gallo-Roman personal name *Marīnius* + the local suffix *-ācum*.

Vars.: **Marnie**, **De Marney**.

Maroto Spanish: probably a nickname for a lascivious person, from OSp. *marueco* ram (of pre-Roman origin).

Marouzeau Provençal: habitation name from a farm named with the OProv. elements *mas* farm(stead) (see

MAS) + *rouzeau*, a nickname for a red-haired proprietor (cf. RUSSELL).

Vars.: **Marozeau**, **Marouzé**.

Maroz see MRÓZ

Marple English: habitation name from a place in Ches., so called from OE *(ge)mǣre* boundary + *pōl* pool or *pyll* steam.

Var.: **Marples** (now found chiefly in S Yorks.).

Marpurch see MORPURGO

Marque French: **1.** topographic name for someone who lived near a boundary, OF *marque* (of Gmc origin; cf. MARK 2 and MARCH 1). **2.** metonymic nickname for someone with a noticeable birthmark, or who had suffered the disfigurement of branding (a relatively common medieval punishment; cf. BRENNAN 2), from OF *marque* mark (a transferred sense of 1). **3.** metonymic occupational name for a coiner, or nickname with a lost anecdotal origin, from OF *marc*, a coin of high value. The vocab. word is of uncertain etymology, but may be of the same origin as above, from the design marked on it.

Var. (of 1 and 2): **Lamarque**.

Marquis 1. French (Norman) and English: nickname for someone who behaved like a marquess or occupational name for a servant in the household of a marquess, from ONF *marquis*. The title originally referred to the governor of a border territory (cf. MARQUE 1). Marquesses did not form part of the original Fr. feudal structure of nobility; the title was first adopted by the Counts of Toulouse because of their possessions in the border region beyond the Rhône. **2.** Scots: var. of *McMarquis* (Gael. *Mac Marcuis*), a patr. from MARK 1.

Vars. (of 1): Fr.: **Lemarquis**; **Marchis**.

Dims. (of 1): Fr.: **Marquiset**. It.: **Marchisello**, **Marchiselli**, **Marchisini** (Emilia); **Marchesin** (Venetia); **Marchesotti**.

Aug. (of 1): It.: **Marchesoni**.

Marr 1. English: habitation name from *Marr* in W Yorks., which is of uncertain etymology. It may have been named with ON *marr*, a rare word used normally of the sea, but perhaps also of a marsh or fen, as reflected in modern dial. forms. **2.** Scots: habitation name from *Mar* in the former county of Aberdeens., the etymology of which is equally uncertain, and possibly identical with that of 1.

Vars.: **Marre**, **Marrs**.

Marrel see MORRELL

Marrington see MERITON

Marriott English: from the medieval female given name *Mariot*, a dim. of *Mary* (see MARIE).

Vars.: MARRYAT, MERRIOT.

Marron Irish: Anglicized form of Gael. **Ó Mearáin** 'descendant of *Mearán*', a personal name from a dim. of *mear* lively.

Marryat English: **1.** from a ME given name, *Meryet*, OE *Mǣrgēat*, composed of the element *mǣr* boundary + the tribal name *Gēat* (see JOCELYN). **2.** var. of MARRIOTT.

Var.: **Maryatt**. See also MERRIOT.

Marsden English: habitation name from places in Lancs. and W Yorks., so called from OE *mearc* boundary (see MARK 2) + *denu* valley (see DEAN 1), i.e. a valley forming a natural boundary.

Marsh English: topographic name for someone who lived by or in a marsh or fen, OE *mersc* (for the change of *-er-* to *-ar-*, cf. MARCHANT).

Vars.: **Mersh**; **Mars**, **Mash**; **Ma(r)shman**.

Dim.: It.: **Marescotti**.

Marshall English and Scots: occupational name from ME, OF *maresc(h)al* marshal. The term is of Gmc origin (cf. OHG *marah* horse, mare + *scalc* servant), and was originally applied to a man who looked after horses. By the heyday of surname formation it referred on the one hand to one of the most important servants in every great household (in the royal household a high official of state), and on the other to a humble shoeing smith or farrier. A similar wide range of meanings is found in other languages: for example, in Polish a *marszałek* can be anything from a field marshal or the chairman of the Polish parliament to the senior servant in a household. The surname is also borne by Jews, presumably as an Anglicization of one or more like-sounding Jewish surnames.

Vars.: **Marschall**; **Ma(r)skell**, **Maskall**, **Mascall**, **Maskill** (from ANF forms).

Dims.: Fr.: **Marchaudon**; **Mesclou** (Brittany). Ger. (of Slav. origin): **Marschallek**, **Marschollek**. Pol.: **Marszałek**. Czech: **Maršálek**.

Marsham English: habitation name from a place in Norfolk, so called from OE *mersc* MARSH + *hām* homestead.

Marsland English (chiefly S Lancs.): habitation name, probably from some place named as being a boggy place, from OE *mersc* MARSH + *land* land. Alternatively, it may be a var. of MARKLAND.

Marston English: habitation name from any of the numerous places so called, of which there are examples in at least sixteen counties. All get their names from OE *mersc* MARSH + *tūn* enclosure, settlement.

Var.: **Marson**.

Martel English and French: **1.** from a medieval given name, a dim. of MARTIN or of MARTHE. **2.** metonymic occupational name for a smith or nickname for a forceful person, from OF *martel* hammer (LL *martellus*, a var. of *martulus*, *marculus*; cf. MACHO). Charles Martel, the grandfather of Charlemagne, gained his byname from the force with which he struck down his enemies in battle.

Vars.: Eng.: **Martell**. Fr.: **Marteau**; **Martel(l)ier** (occupational).

Dims.: Fr.: **Martelet**, **Marteret**. It.: **Martellini**, **Martellino**, **Martelotti**, **Martelotto**.

Marthe French and German: from the female name which appears in the Gk New Testament as *Martha* (Aramaic *Marta* 'Lady'), borne by the sister of Lazarus and Mary (of Bethany).

Vars.: Ger.: **Morthe**, **Merta**.

Dims.: Fr.: **Mart(h)on**, **Martot**, MARTEL, **Marthelot**.

Martial French: from a personal name (L *Martiālis*, originally a family name, apparently derived from that of the war god *Mars*; cf. MARTIN). This was borne by a minor 3rd-cent. saint, the first bishop of Limoges.

Vars.: **Marsal**, **Marseau**, **Marsau(l)t**, **Marsaud**.

Dim.: Fr.: **Marsallon**.

Martin English, Scots, Irish, French, German, Czech, Flemish/Dutch, and Danish/Norwegian: from a personal name (L *Martīnus*, a deriv. of *Mars*, gen. *Martis*, the Roman god of fertility and war, whose name may derive ultimately from a root *mar* gleam). This was borne by a famous 4th-cent. saint, Martin of Tours, and consequently became extremely popular throughout Europe in the Middle Ages. It is one of the few saints' names other than the names of OE saints found in England before the Conquest.

Vars.: Eng.: **Marten**, **Martyn**. Fr.: **Martine**, **Lamartine** (fem. forms). Flem., Du.: **Martijn**, **Martyn**, **Marten**.

Dims.: Fr.: **Martineau** (also common in Birmingham); **Martinet**, **Martinon**, **Martinot**; **Tinot** (an aphetic form). It.: **Martinello**, **Martinelli**, **Martinetto**, **Martinetti**, **Martinol(l)i**, **Martinotti**, **Martinuzzi**. Ger.: **Märtl**, **Mertel**; **Mörtel** (Bavaria); **Marti**, **Marty** (Switzerland). Low Ger.: **Mertgen**; **Tienke** (see also AUSTIN). Flem., Du.: **Meert**. Ger. (of Slav. origin): **Martsch(ke)**, **Martschik**, **Mertsching**. Ukr.: **Martinyuk**, **Martinets**. Pol.: **Martynka**, **Marciek**. Czech: **Martínek**; MAREK.

Augs.: Fr.: **Martinat**. It.: **Marti(g)noni**, **Martignon**. Czech: **Martinec**. Pol.: **Marciniec**.

Patrs.: Eng.: **Martins**, **Martyns**, **Martens**; **Martinson**. Sc.: **McMartin**. It.: **De Martino**, **Di Martino**, **De Martini**, **(De) Martinis**. Sp.: **Martínez**. Port.: **Martins**. Ger.: **Martini** (Latinized). Low Ger.: **Martens(en)**, **Me(h)rtens**; **Marti(e)n(s)sen** (N Rhineland). Flem., Du.: **Martens**, **Me(e)rtens**. Dan., Norw.: **Martin(us)sen**, **Mortensen**. Swed.: **Martinsson**, **Mårtensson**. Croatian: **Mart(inov)ić**. Pol.: **Marciniak**; **Marcinowicz**, **Martynowicz**. Ukr.: **Martinovich**. Russ.: **Martynov**. Lithuanian: **Martinaitis**. Hung.: **Mártonfi**, **Mártonf(f)y**.

Patrs. (from dims.): Low Ger.: **Mertz**; **Tienken**. Russ.: **Martyshkin**, **Mart(y)ushev**, **Martusov**, **Martygin**, **Martyntsev**, **Martyanychev**. Beloruss.: **Martsinkevich**. Pol.: **Marcinkiewicz**. Lithuanian: **Marcinkus**. Finn.: **Martikainen**.

'Son of the wife of M.': Russ.: **Martynikhin**.

Habitation names: Pol.: **Marcinkowski**, **Marciszewski**. Czech: **Martinovský**.

Martindale English: habitation name from a place in Cumb., first recorded in 1220 in its present form. There is a chapel of St Martin here, and the valley (see DALE) may be named from this. Alternatively, there may have been a landowner here called *Martin*, and the church dedication may be due to popular association of his name with that of the saint.

Martorell Catalan: from a medieval given name of this form and uncertain origin, probably from LL *Martyrellus*, a dim. of *martyr* martyr (originally 'witness (to the faith)', from Gk *martyrein* to bear witness). There are also places in the provinces of Barcelona and Valencia so called from early proprietors, and in some cases the surname may be a habitation name from one of them.

Marvel English: **1.** nickname for a person considered prodigious in some way, from ME, OF *merveille* miracle (L *mīrābilia*, originally neut. pl. of the adj. *mīrābilis* admirable, amazing). The nickname was no doubt sometimes given with mocking intent. **2.** Norman habitation name, from places called *Merville*. The one in Nord is named from OF *mendre* smaller, lesser (L *minor*) + *ville* settlement; that in Calvados seems to have as its first element a Gmc personal name, probably a short form of a cpd name with the first element *mari, meri* famous.

Var.: **Marvell**.

Marwick Scots: habitation name from a place in the Orkneys, so called from ON *marr* sea, lake, marsh (see MARR) + *vík* bay. The surname is also borne in the U.S. by Jews, as an Anglicized form of one or more Ashkenazic surnames.

Marwood English: 1. habitation name from a place so called, probably the one in Co. Durham, which Ekwall derives from OE *māra* greater, larger (cf. mod. Eng. *more*) + *wudu* WOOD. 2. Norman nickname for a person believed to have the power of casting the 'evil eye', from ONF *malreward*, a cpd of *mal* evil, bad + *reward* (OF *regard*) look.

Mas 1. Low German and Dutch: aphetic form of THOMAS. 2. Provençal and Catalan: topographic name for someone who lived in an isolated dwelling in the country, rather than in a village, from OProv., Cat. *mas* farm(stead) (LL *mansum, mansus*).

Vars.: (of 1): **Masius** (Latinized). (Of 2): Prov.: **Lemas**; **Duma(i)s**, **Duma(i)t**, **Dumès**, **Dumé(e)**, **Dumeix**, **Dume(t)z**, **Dumay**, **Delmas**; **Aumas**. Cat.: **Delmàs**.

Dims. (of 2): Prov.: **Maset**, **Masot**, **Mazet**, **Dumazet**, **Mazel**, **Mazeau**, **Dumazel**, **Dumazeau**, **Mazin**, **Mazot**. Cat.: **Mas(s)ó** (see also MASON).

Máša Czech: from the given name *Máša*, a pet form of any given name beginning with *Ma-*, in particular *Matěj* (see MATTHEW), MARTIN, and *Mauritius* (see MORRIS). It may also be an aphetic form of *Tomáš* (see THOMAS).

Vars.: **Mašát**, **Mašata**, **Mašín**.

Dims.: **Mašek**, **Maška**.

Mascall see MARSHALL

Maschek see MAAS

Maschietto see MALE

Masdeu Catalan: habitation name from a farm named with the elements *mas* farm(stead) (see MAS) + *Deu* God (L *deus*); several places were so called in the Middle Ages as a pious invocation of God's blessing on the holding.

Masefield English: apparently a habitation name from an unidentified place, perhaps in the W Midlands, and possibly named with the OE personal name *Mæssa* or the medieval given name MACE + OE *feld*, ME *feild* pasture, open country (see FIELD).

Mash see MARSH

Mashenkin see MARIE

Masheter English: of problematic origin. Reaney's evidence suggests that it derives from the Tudor surname *Masherudder* (York 1517). This would be an occupational nickname for a worker in a brewery, from ME *mash* malt mixed with hot water to form wort (OE *māsc*) + *rudder* (OE *roþer*), i.e. a rudder-shaped implement used to stir the fermenting mass.

Vars.: **Mashiter**, **Mashe(d)der**, **Masseter**, **Messiter**.

Mašić see MATTHEW

Maslin English: 1. from the medieval given name *Masselin*. This originated as an OF dim. of Gmc names with the first element *mathal* speech, counsel. However, it was later used as a dim. of MATTHEW (see MACE). A fem. form, *Mazelina*, was probably originally a dim. of *Matilda*. 2. possibly also a metonymic occupational name. Reaney suggests that this referred to a maker and seller of wooden bowls, from ME, OF *maselin* bowl or goblet of maple wood (a dim. of OF *masere* maple wood, of Gmc origin). It is also possible that in some cases it derives from one of the homonymous dial. terms *maslin*, one of which means 'brass' (OE *mæslen, mæstling*; cf. MESSINGER 2), the other 'mixed grain' (OF *mesteillon*, LL *mixtilio*, a deriv. of *mixtus* mixed).

Vars.: **Maslen**, **Masling**.

Maslov Russian and Jewish (E Ashkenazic): patr. from the Russ. vocab. word *maslo* butter, presumably used as an occupational name for a dairyman, or acquired for some anecdotal reason now lost.

Vars.: Jewish: **Maslow**, **Maslovitz**; **Maslo** (not a patr.); **Maslovaty** (an adj. deriv.).

Mason English and Scots: occupational name for a stonemason, ME, OF *mas(s)on* (apparently of Gmc origin, perhaps akin to OE *macian* to make or *mattuc* mattock). See also MASSON and MACHIN.

Patr.: Fr.: **Aumasson**.

Massalovo see MAZZA

Massarelli see MAZIER

Masse see MACE

Massey English (Norman) and French: habitation name from any of various places in N France which get their names from the Gallo-Roman personal name *Maccius* + the local suffix *-ācum*.

Vars.: Eng.: **Massy**, **Mac(e)y**. Fr.: **Macey**, **Macé**, **Massé**.

Massingberd English: nickname for someone with a tawny beard, from ME *massing* brass (probably of Scandinavian origin; cf. MESSINGER 2) + BEARD.

Var.: **Massingbird**.

Massingham English: habitation name from a place in Norfolk, so called from OE *Mǣssinghām* 'homestead (OE *hām*) associated with **Mǣssa*'.

Masson 1. Scots: var. of MASON. 2. French: cogn. of MASON. 3. French: aphetic form of *Thomasson*, dim. of THOMAS (cf. MAAS 1).

Dims. (of 3): Fr.: **Massoneau**, **Massonet**, **Massenet**.

Mastalerz Polish: occupational name for a stableman or groom, Pol. *masztalerz*.

Master English and Scots: nickname for someone who behaved in a masterful manner, or occupational name for someone who was master of his craft, from ME *maister* (OF *maistre*, L *magister*). In early instances this surname was often borne by people who were franklins or other substantial freeholders, presumably because they had labourers under them to work their lands, and unlike smaller free tenants did not just till their property themselves. In Scotland the eldest sons of barons had this title, and the name may also have been acquired as an occupational nickname by a servant who worked in the household of the eldest son of a baron.

Var.: **Meystre**.

Dims.: Fr.: **Mai(s)tret**, **Maitrot**. Prov.: **Mestrel**, **Métreau**. It.: **Maestrello**, **Maestrelli**, **Ma(i)strelli**, **Maistrello**, **Magistrelli**, **Magistretti**, **Maestrini**, **Mastrillo**, **Mastrilli**, **Mastruzzo**, **Masciullo**.

Aug.: It.: **Maestrone**.

Pej.: It.: **Maestacci**.

Patrs.: Eng.: **Masters**; **Masterson**. Sc.: MCMASTER. Fr.: **Aumaître**. It.: **De Magistri**, **(De) Magistris**. Low Ger.: **Meistering**. Flem., Du.: **Smeesters**, **Smeysters**. Russ.: **Mashtakov** (from the vocab. word borrowed via Pol. from Ger.). Croatian: **Majstorović**.

'Servant of the master': Eng.: **Masterman**.

Masterton Scots: habitation name from a place in Fife, so called from the Older Sc. title *maister* (see MASTER) + ME *tune* village, settlement. The lands were once held by a tenant referred to in the Latinized form *Magister Ailricus*, and their name may derive from him.

Mata Spanish, Catalan, and Portuguese: topographic name for someone who lived by a plantation of trees, OSp. *mata* (of uncertain origin).

Vars.: Sp.: **Matas**. Port.: **Matos**. Both these forms are also found as Jewish surnames, but the reasons for their adoption are unclear.

Dim.: Sp.: **Matilla**.

Matalis *see* MAITES

Matchett N Irish: of uncertain origin, possibly a dim. of MATTHEW. The surname **Matches** is found in the Orkney and Shetland islands, and was formerly used as a given name there; it has been supposed to derive from a Scandinavian form of MATTHEW.

Mateer *see* MCINTYRE

Matesanz Spanish: apparently from a combination of the given names *Mate* (see MATTHEW) + *Sanz* (see SANCHO); cf. ROBESPIERRE.

Mather English: **1.** occupational name for a mower or reaper of grass or hay, OE *mǣðere* (cf. MEAD 1 and MOWER). Hay was formerly of great importance, not only as feed for animals in winter but also for bedding. **2.** in S Lancs., where it has long been a common surname, it is probably a relatively late development of MADDER.

Var.: **Mathur**.

Dim. (of 1): Ger.: **Mederle**.

Patr.: Eng.: **Mathers**.

Matravers *see* MALTRAVERS

Mattack *see* MADOC

Matthew English and Scots: from the ME given name *Mathew*, of biblical origin, ultimately from the Hebr. male given name *Matityahu* 'Gift of God', recorded in the Gk New Testament in the form *Matth(a)ias*. This was taken into L as both *Matthias* and *Matthaeus*, the former being used for the apostle and the latter for the evangelist. However, the distinction was not consistently made,

and in most languages the two forms have completely fallen together again (vernacular forms of the given name, e.g. OF *Matheu*, Sp. *Mateo*, It. *Matteo*, etc., normally being derived from *Matthaeus*).

Vars.: **Mathew**; **Ma(t)thias** (a learned form, found chiefly in Wales); MAYHEW.

Dims.: Eng.: **Matt(in)**, **Matten**, **Mat(t)on**, **Matkin**; see also MACE and MESLIN. Fr.: **Mathivet**, **Mathivon**, **Mathevet**, **Mathevon**; **Mathe(lin)**, **Mathely**, **Mathelon**, **Math(i)ot**, **Mathon(net)**, **Matteau**; **Mat(h)ou** (Brittany). It.: **Mattiello**, **Mattielli**, **Matteini**, **Matt(e)ucci**, **Matteuzzi**, **Mattiuzzi**, **Matt(i)ussi**, **Matteoli**, **Mattioli**, **Matteotti**; **Maffetti**, **Maffini**, **Maf(f)ucci**, **Maffiol(ett)i**, **Maffezzoli**, **Maffiotti**, **Maffulli**; **Mazzilli**, **Mazziotti**, **Mazzullo**. Ger.: **Matthäi** (Switzerland); **Matz(e)l**, **Metzel** (Bohemia, Bavaria); see also HIESS and DIESEL. Ger. (of Slav. origin): **Matz(ke)**, **Matschke**, **Mätschke**, **Metschke**, **Metzke**, **Metzi(n)g**, **Matschek**, **Matschuk**, **Matschoss**, **Mattschas**, **Mattke**, **Mattek**. Czech: **Matěj(í)ček**, **Matějka**, **Matiásek**, **Matoušek**, **Matuška**; **Macek**, **Macourek**. Pol.: **Matuszyk**, **Matysik**, **Mateuszczyk**, **Matyjasik**; **Macieiczyk**, **Maciaszek**, **Maciaszczyk**. Ukr.: **Matveiko**, **Matyushenko**. Beloruss.: **Matyushonok**, **Mateiko**. Jewish (E Ashkenazic): **Matuschek**.

Augs.: Fr.: **Mathivat**. It.: **Matteoni**, **Mattioni**; **Maffioni**, **Maff(i)one**.

Pejs.: It.: **Matteacci**, **Mattiacci**, **Mattiazzi**, **Mattiazzo**, **Mattiassi**, **Mattiato**.

Patrs.: Eng.: **Ma(t)thew(e)s**; **Ma(t)thewson**. It.: **De Mattia**, **De Mattei**, **Di Mattei**, **Di Matteo**, **(De) Matteis**. Rum.: **Mateescu**. Ger.: **Mattäser** (Bavaria). Low Ger.: **Matthiessen**, **Matthe(e)(s)sen**. Dan., Norw.: **Mathia(s)sen**, **Mathi(s)sen**, **Matthie(s)sen**. Swed.: **Matt(h)isson**. Croatian: **Mat(ej)ić**, **Matij(aš)ević**, **Matović**. Pol.: **Mackiewicz**; **Matusiak**, **Matuszak**, **Matysiak**, **Maciejak**, **Maciak**. Beloruss.: **Mateev**. Russ.: **Matveyev**, **Matveichev**. Jewish: **Matusson** (Ashkenazic); **Mat(t)usov**, **Matussov**, **Matussow**, **Matusovsky**, **Matis(s)off**, **Mattosof**, **Mattusevich**, **Matussevich**, **Matushevitz**, **Matuszak** (E Ashkenazic). Lithuanian: **Matelyunas**, **Maciunas**, **Matelaitis**. Armenian: **Matevosian**, **Matessian**. Georgian: **Matiashvili**.

Patrs.: (from dims.): Eng.: **Mathi(e)s**, **Ma(t)thys**; **Matti(n)son**, **Mattingson**, **Matterson**; **Matt(e)s**, **Ma(t)thes**; **Matson**. Sc.: **Ma(t)thi(e)son**, **Matheson**. Low Ger.: **Matzen**. Dan., Norw.: **Madsen**. Swed.: **Mattsson**. Russ.: **Matantsev**, **Matasov**, **Matusov**, **Matyatin**, **Matyugin**, **Matyukov**, **Matyushkin**, **Matashkin**, **Matyashev**, **Matoshin**, **Matokhin**, **Matanin**, **Matonin**. Ukr.: **Matskiv**, **Matushevich**. Beloruss.: **Matevushev**, **Matusevich**, **Matskevich**. Pol.: **Matuszkiewicz**; **Matczak**. Lithuanian: **Matz(k)aitis**, **Matz(k)eitis**. Croatian: **Matković**, **Mašić**.

'Servant of M.': Eng.: **Mat(t)hewman**.

'Relative of M.': Eng.: **Mattimoe** (cf. MAW 2).

Habitation names: Pol.: **Matuszewski**, **Matuszyński**, **Maciejewski**. Czech: **Matějovský**.

Mattila Finnish: name borne by a member of a household headed by someone called *Matti* MATTHEW, from the Finn. given name + the local suffix *-la*.

Mattingley English: habitation name from a place in Hants, originally named in OE as *Mattinglēah* 'wood, clearing associated with *Matta*'.

Var.: **Mattingly**.

Mattlin *see* MEAD

Maturin French: from a personal name, L *Mātūrīnus* (a deriv. of *Mātūrus* 'Timely'), borne by a 3rd-cent. saint who was responsible for spreading the gospel in the district of Sens.

Vars.: **Mathurin**.

Dims.: **Mathorel**, **Mathoré**, **Mathorez**; **Matheron**.

Augs.: **Mat(h)erat**.

Maud *see* MOULT

Maudling English: from the ME vernacular form, *Maudeleyn*, of the Gk female given name *Magdalēnē*. This is a byname, meaning 'woman from *Magdala*' (a village on the Sea of Galilee, deriving its name from Hebr. *migdal* tower, itself from the adj. *gadol* large), which was given in the New Testament to the woman cured of evil spirits by Jesus (Luke 8: 2), who later became a faithful follower. The popularity of the given name increased with the supposed discovery of her relics in the 13th cent.

Dims.: Fr.: **Ma(g)delon**, **Madon**, **Madot**, **Madoz**.

Metr.: Ger.: **Madlener**.

Metrs. (from dims.): Eng.: MADDISON. Flem.: **Maddens**.

Maudslay *see* MAWDESLEY

Maufe English: **1.** nickname for an untrustworthy person, from the ANF elements *mal, mau* bad + *fei, foi* faith. **2.** variant of MAW 2.

Mauger *see* MAJOR

Maughan 1. Scots: habitation name from *Machan* (now also called *Dalserf*) in the former county of Lanarks., named with a dim. form of Gael. *machair* (river) plain. **2.** Irish: Anglicized form of Gael. *Ó Mocháin*; see MOHAN. **3.** Welsh: habitation name from either of two places in the former county of Monmouths., one of which is called *(St) Maughan* (an Anglicized form of W *Llanfocha* 'Church of St *Mochan*'), and the other *Machen* 'Place of *Cain*'.

Vars.: **Maugham**, **Ma(u)chan**.

Maul German: nickname for someone with a deformed mouth, or for someone who made excessive use of the mouth in eating, drinking, or talking, from Ger. *Maul* mouth, gob (MHG *mūl(e)*, OHG *mūla*). It is also possible that in some cases the surname may derive from MHG *mūl* mule (mod. Ger. *Maultier, Maulesel*) or even MHG *mūl(ber)* mulberry (mod. Ger. *Maulbeere*).

Vars.: **Mäule**, **Maile**.

Dim.: Low Ger.: **Muhlke**.

Mauleverer English (Norman): nickname from OF *mal leverier* bad harrier (L *malus leporārius*). The name is apparently of anecdotal origin, and the reasons for its adoption as a surname are not clear. It is also the name of a place in Seine-Maritime, but this is probably so called from the family name of a Norman family who held it, rather than vice versa.

Maulkin *see* MALKIN

Maultby *see* MALTBY

Maund *see* MANDER

Maunsell *see* MANSELL

Maupas *see* MALPAS

Mauran *see* MORANT

Mauras *see* MOORE

Maurer 1. German: occupational name for a builder of defensive walls or the walls of substantial buildings from stone or brick, from an agent deriv. of Ger. *Mauer* wall (MHG *mūre*, OHG *mūra*, from L *mūrus*; cf. MURAT). In the Middle Ages the majority of dwellings were built of wood (or lath and plaster); a *Maurer* would have been employed mainly in building defensive walls, castles, churches, and other public buildings. **2.** Jewish (Ashkenazic): occupational name for a mason or bricklayer, mod. Ger. *Maurer*.

Vars.: **Meurer**, **Mauer(mann)**.

Mauriac Provençal: habitation name from any of various places, for example in Cantal and Gironde, so called from the L personal name *Maurus* (see MOORE 3) + the local suffix *-ācum*.

Maurice *see* MORRIS

Maus 1. German: nickname for someone supposedly resembling a mouse, in appearance or timidity, or else a metonymic occupational name for a catcher of mice and rats, from Ger. *Maus* mouse (MHG, OHG *mūs*). **2.** Jewish (Ashkenazic): from Ger. *Maus* mouse, one of the most common of the unflattering surnames imposed on Jews by non-Jewish government officials in 18th- and 19th-cent. central Europe.

Vars.: Ger.: **Mauser**, **Meuser**; **Muser** (Switzerland). Jewish: **Meislish** ('mousy').

Dims.: Ger.: **Mäusel**, **Meusel**, **Meisel**, **Meissl**. Pol.: **Myszka** (from Pol. *myszka* mouse). Jewish: **Meisel(man)**, **Maizel**; **Meisel(e)s**, **Majzels** (patrs. in form; *Majzels* is a Pol. spelling).

Habitation names: Pol.: **Myszk(or)owski**.

Mavrić *see* MOORE

Maw English: **1.** from the OE personal name *Mawa*, perhaps originally a byname from OE *mǣw* (sea-)mew, or alternatively akin to OE *māwan* to mow. **2.** nickname for someone who was related to an important local personality, from ME *maugh, maw* relative, esp. by marriage (from OE *māge* female relative). This element is also found in compound names such as WATMOUGH. **3.** topographic name, apparently from OE **māwe* meadow. Some early forms, such as Sibilla *de la Mawe* (Suffolk 1275), clearly indicate a topographic origin, by the preposition and article.

Vars.: **Mawe**, **Mowe**, **Mew(e)**. (Of 2 only): **Mough**, MAUFE, **Muff**. Patrs. (from 1): Eng.: **Mawson**, **Mawsom** (see also MOULT).

Mawdesley English: habitation name from a place in Lancs., recorded in 1219 as *Madesle* and in 1269 as *Moudesley*, i.e. probably 'clearing of *Maud*' (see MOULT 1).

Vars.: **Mawdsley**, **Maudsley**, **Maudslay**.

Mawhinney *see* McKENZIE

Mawsom *see* MOULT

Max German: from a short form of the given name *Maximilian* (L *Maximilliānus*, a deriv. of *Maximillus*, dim. of *Maximus* 'Greatest'), borne by a 3rd-cent. saint venerated particularly in the region of Passau, where he founded a church. This given name was comparatively rare at the most productive period of surname formation; it gained popularity from the Holy Roman Emperor Maximilian I

(b. 1459), who was named by his father, Frederick III of Austria, in honour of the Roman heroes Q. Fabius Maximus and Scipio Aemilianus, as if with a combination of their names. The name is also borne by Ashkenazic Jews, presumably as an adoption of the Ger. surname.

Maxey English: habitation name from a place in Northants, so called from the gen. case of the N English personal name MACK + OE ēg island, low-lying land.

Maxime French: from the personal name (L *Maximus* 'Greatest', superlative of *magnus* great; cf. MAGNUS), borne by a number of minor early Christian saints. The Jewish names mentioned below are adoptions of the non-Jewish surnames.

Vars.: **Maxim** (also Jewish); **Maisme**, **Mesme** (vernacular forms); **Maismon**, **Mesmon** (from the oblique case).

Dims.: Ukr.: **Maksimonko**. Beloruss.: **Maksimyonok**, **Maksimuk**.

Patrs.: Russ.: **Maksimov** (also Jewish). Ukr.: **Maksimovich**. Pol.: **Maksymowicz**. Croatian: **Maks(imov)ić**.

Patrs. (from dims.): Russ.: **Maksimychev**, **Maksakov**, **Maksyatkin**, **Maksyutin**, **Makonin**. Ukr.: **Maksimat**.

Maxwell 1. Scots: habitation name from a place near Melrose in the former county of Roxburgh. The placename is first recorded in 1144 in the form *Mackeswell* 'spring, stream (see WELL) of MACK'. 2. Jewish: arbitrary adoption of the Scots name, or Anglicization of one or more like-sounding Jewish surnames.

May 1. English: pet form of MATTHEW; cf. MAYHEW. 2. English, French, and German: from a nickname or given name from the month of May (ME, OF *mai*, MHG *meie*, from L *Maius (mensis)*, from *Maia*, a rather obscure goddess of fertility, whose name is derived from the same root as *maius* larger and *maiestas* greatness). This may have been bestowed on someone born or baptized in the month of May, or it may have been used to refer to someone of a particularly sunny disposition, or who had some anecdotal connection with the month of May, such as owing a feudal obligation then. 3. English: nickname from ME *may* young man or woman (of uncertain origin, probably originally meaning kinsman or kinswoman). 4. Jewish (Ashkenazic): ornamental name from Yid. *may* lilac.

Vars.: Eng.: **Maye**, **Mey(e)**. (Of 2 only): Ger.: **Mai**, **Mei**, **Mey**.

Dims.: (of 1): Eng.: MAKIN; **Maycock**, **Meacock**. (Of 2): It.: **Maggini**, **Maggiol(in)i**.

Patrs.: (from 1): Eng.: **May(e)s**, **Mayze**, **Meyz**, **Mease**. (From 2): It.: **De Maggio**, **Di Maggio**. Pol.: **Majewicz**.

Cpds (of 4): **Meibaum** (from Ger. *Maibaum* 'maypole' or Yid. *mayboym* 'lilac tree'); **Mayberg(er)**, **Meiberg** ((dweller on the) lilac hill'); **Majblat** ('lilac leaf'; Pol. spelling); **Mayblum**, **Meiblum** ('lilac flower', or based on Ger. *Maiblüme* 'lily of the valley'); **Meit(h)al** ('lilac valley', in Israel often taken as being from Hebr. *mey-tal* dew water).

Mayall *see* MALE

Maybin *see* MABON

Maybury English (W Midlands): habitation name, almost certainly not from the place near Woking in Surrey, which is not recorded until 1885 and may well be named from the surname. The origin is probably some unidentified place somewhere farther north.

Mayer 1. English: status name or occupational name for a mayor, ME, OF *mair(e)* (from L *māior* greater, superior; cf. MAYOR). In France the title denoted various minor local officials, and the same is true of Scotland (see MAIR 1). In England, however, the term was normally restricted to the chief officer of a borough, and the surname may have been given not only to a citizen of some standing who had held this office, but also as a nickname to a pompous or officious person. 2. German: occupational name, originally for a village headman or similar official, from MHG *meier* (OHG *meior*, of the same origin as above). The Ger. term also acquired the sense 'steward', 'bailiff', and later came to be used also to denote a (tenant) farmer. 3. Jewish (Ashkenazic): from the Yid. male given name *Meyer* (from Hebr. *Meir* 'Enlightener', a deriv. of Hebr. *or* light).

Vars. (of 1): MAYOR. (Of 2): Ger.: **Maier**, **Meyer**, **Meier**. Pol., Czech: **Majer**. (Of 3): Jewish: **Maier**, **Meyer**, **Meier**, **Majer**, MAJOR, **Meyr**; MAIR, **Meir** (not exclusively Ashkenazic); **Meiri**, **Meiry** (Israeli, with the Hebr. suffix -*i*).

Dims. (of 1): Fr.: **Mairel**, **Maireau**, **Mairot**, **Méret**, **Mérey**, **Mérot**. (Of 2): Ger.: **Mayerl**, **Maierl** (Bavaria, Austria). Pol.: **Majerczyk**. (Of 3): Jewish: **Majerczyk**, **Majorczyk**, **Majorchick**, **Mayorczyk**, **Mayorchik**, **Meirtchak** (E Ashkenazic).

Patrs. (from 1): Eng.: **Mayers**, **M(e)yers**, **Miers**. (From 2): Ger.: **Mayers**. Low Ger.: **Meggers**; **Meyering**, **Meyerinck**. Flem., Du.: **Meyers**, **Smeyers**; **Meyerink**. (From 3): Jewish: **Meyers**; **Mayerso(h)n**, **Maierson**, **Meyerso(h)n**, **Mejerson**, **Mairson**, **Meirso(h)n**, **Me(e)rson**; **Mayerovitch**, **Maieroff**, **Meyerovitch**, **Meyerovitz**, **Meyerowitz**, **Majerowitz**, **Majerowits**, **Majerowicz**, **Mayorovits**, **Mairoff**, **Mairov(itch)**, **Mairovitz**, **Mairowitz**, **Mairowicz**, **Meirovic**, **Meirovi(t)ch**, **Meirowitch**, **Meirovitz**, **Meirowi(t)z**, **Meirowicz**, **Meerov**, **Meerovi(t)ch**, **Meerovitz**, **Meerowitz** (E Ashkenazic); **Meirovici** (among Rumanian Jews); **Meirshvili** (among Georgian Jews); **Meirov**, **Meirow** (not exclusively Ashkenazic).

Mayfield English: habitation name from places in Staffs. and Sussex. The former is so called from OE *mæddre* MADDER + *feld* pasture, open country (see FIELD); the latter has its first element from OE *mægðe* mayweed. The surname itself is common in Notts., and it may be that an additional place of origin is to be sought in this area.

Mayhew English: from the Norman given name *Mahieu*, a var. of *Mathieu*; see MATTHEW.

Vars.: **Mahew**, **Mehew**, **Mayo(w)**.

Maykin *see* MAKIN

Maylard *see* MALLARD

Maylor *see* MAILER

Maynall *see* MEYNELL

Maynard English (Norman) and French: from the Continental Gmc personal name *Mainard*, composed of the elements *magin* strength + *hard* hardy, brave, strong.

Vars.: Eng.: **Mainerd**. Fr.: **Meynard**, **Ménard**; **Mesnard** (hypercorrected).

Patrs.: Low Ger.: **Mein(d)ers**, **Mein(ert)z**, **Men(t)z**, **Menzen**. Fris.: **Minners**; **Meents**; **Meendsen**, **Meenzen**; **Minten**.

Mayne English (Norman): 1. from the Continental Gmc personal name *Maino*, *Meino*, a short form of the various cpd names with a first element *magin* strength, might (cf., e.g., MAYNARD and MEIFFERT). **2.** regional name for someone from the Fr. province of *Maine*; cf. MANSELL 1. **3.** nickname for a large man, from ANF *magne, maine* great, tall (L *magnus*). **4.** nickname for someone with a deformed or missing hand, from OF *main* hand (L *manus*).

Var.: **Main**.

Dims. (of 1): Ger.: **Meinel, Mein(d)l**. Low Ger.: **Mein(e)(c)ke, Menne(c)ke, Me(h)nke, Menk**. Fris.: **Min(c)k(e), Minkema**. It.: **Mainello, Mainelli, Mainetto, Mainetti, Mainoli**.

Patrs. (from 1): Low Ger.: **Meyns, Me(i)ns; Me(i)nsen; Meynen; Meinen; Menning**. Fris.: **Meenen; Minning, Meenenga; Mennenga**. It.: **Mainis**.

Patrs. (from 1) (dims.): Low Ger.: **Mein(e)ken, Mencken; Meineking, Menneking**. Fris.: **Meenken, Meemken**.

Mayne *see* McMANUS

Mayol Catalan: topographic name for someone who lived by a plantation of young vines or metonymic occupational name for someone employed to watch over such a plantation, from Cat. *mayol, mallol* young vine, vine shoot (LL *malleolus*).

Mayor **1.** English (Lancs.): var. of MAYER 1. **2.** Spanish: nickname of the elder of two bearers of the same given name, from Sp. *mayor* elder (L *māior (nātū)*, lit. 'greater by birth'). The term was also occasionally used as a female given name in Spain in the Middle Ages, and this may be a partial source of the surname. **3.** Jewish: of uncertain origin, possibly a var. of MAYER 3.

Mayoral Spanish and Catalan: occupational name for the foreman of a gang of agricultural workers or the leader of a group of herdsmen, Sp., Cat. *mayoral* (LL *māiorālis*, originally an adj. deriv. of *māior*; cf. MAYER and MAYOR).

Var.: Cat.: **Majoral**.

Mayordomo Spanish: occupational name for a steward or butler in a great house, Sp. *mayordomo* (LL *māior domūs* head of the household). Sometimes the same term was used in an extended sense of the headman or mayor of a settlement; cf. MAYER 1.

Maza Spanish: metonymic occupational name for someone who had a mace as a symbol of office or who carried one in ceremonial possessions, from Sp. *maza* mace (LL *mattea*, probably of Gmc origin; cf. OE *mattuc* mattock). In some cases it may have been used as an occupational nickname for a soldier who used a mace in its original function as a weapon.

Mazeau *see* MAS

Mazier Provençal: topographic or status name for the holder of an isolated farmstead, from an agent deriv. of *mas* isolated farm; cf. MAS. The It. cogns. were used as technical terms of feudalism for a tenant farmer; in S Italy the term *Massaro* was also used of a steward managing lands on behalf of an absentee landlord.

Vars.: **Mazié; Mazerand, Mazerant**.

Dims.: Fr.: **Mazereau, Mazeret, Mazerin**. It.: **Massarelli; Massarin(i)** (Venetia); **Massarino** (Liguria); **Massarol(l)i, Massariolo; Massarotti, Massarotto; Massarut(ti), Massarutto** (Venetia).

Aug.: Fr.: **Mazeyrat**.

Mazo Spanish: nickname for a forceful person or metonymic occupational name for someone who made use of a mallet, Sp. *mazo* (a byform of MAZA; cf. MACHO 2). The surname is also borne by Jews, the reason(s) for its adoption being unclear.

Mazur Polish and Jewish (E Ashkenazic): regional name for someone from one of two provinces of Poland: Masovia (Pol. *Mazowsze*) or Masuria (Pol. *Mazury*) in NE Poland, famous for its lakes. Masuria is so called because it was colonized by settlers from Masovia, replacing the Baltic inhabitants. The primary meaning of *Mazur* in Polish is someone from Masovia.

Vars.: Pol.: **Mazurowski**. Jewish: **Mazer; Mazurski, Mazursky**.

Dim.: Pol.: **Mazurek**.

Patr.: Pol.: **Mazurkiewicz**.

Mazza Italian: nickname for a destructive individual, a deriv. of It. *mazzare* to kill, destroy (L *mactāre*).

Dims.: **Mazzetto, Mazzetti, Mazzino, Mazzini, Mazzola, Mazz(u)oli, Mazzoletti, Mazzotta, Mazzotti**.

Augs.: **Mazzone, Mazzoni**.

The numerous cpds, such as **Mazzabue** ('kill bull'), **Mazzacane** ('kill dog'), **Mazzacurati** ('kill curate'), **Mazzagalli** ('kill cock'), **Mazzagreco** ('kill Greek'), **Massalovo** ('kill wolf'), **Mazzanobile** ('kill noble'), **Mazzalorso** ('kill bear'), **Mazzapica** ('kill magpie'), and **Mazzavillani** ('kill churl'), are all elaborations, in some cases no doubt humorous and suggested by some now-forgotten incident.

Mazzilli *see* MATTHEW

Mazzo *see* JAMES

McAbrahams *see* BRAIN

McAckolly *see* QUILLY

McAdam *see* ADAM

McAffer *see* DUFFY

McAgill *see* GALL

McAgown *see* McGOWAN

McAhuie *see* GILDUFF

McAig *see* McCAIG

McAimon *see* McKEEMAN

McAirter *see* ARTHUR

McAlary *see* CLEARY

McAlaster *see* ALEXANDER

McAlea *see* DUNLEAVY

McAlear *see* McCLURE

McAleece *see* GILLIES

McAleenan *see* FINN

McAlinden Irish: Anglicized form of Gael. **Mac Giolla Fhiontáin** 'son of the servant of (St) *Fiontán*'. This name, a deriv. of *fionn* white, was borne by various early saints, including 6th-cent. disciples of St Columba and St Comgall.

Vars.: **Linden; Lindie, Lundy**.

McAline *see* ALLEN

McAlivery Irish: Anglicized form of Gael. **Mac Giolla Gheimhridh** 'son of the servant of *Geimhreadh*', a byname meaning 'Winter'.

McAll *see* McCall

McAllay *see* McAulay

McAllum *see* McCollum

McAloon *see* McLean

McAlroy *see* Gilroy

McAnally *see* McNally

McAnaspie *see* Bishop

McAnchelly *see* Quilly

McAncrossane *see* Cross

McAndrew *see* Andrew

McAne *see* McKane

McAneave *see* Gildernew

McAnern *see* McNairn

McAnleavy *see* Dunleavy

McAnn *see* McCann

McAnulty *see* McNulty

McAra Scots: patr. from the Gael. occupational term *ara* driver, charioteer. The surname is esp. common in the Perth area.

Vars.: **McCar(r)a**, McAree.

McArdle Irish: Anglicized form of Gael. **Mac Ardghail**, patr. from the personal name *Ardghal*, composed of the elements *ard* height + *gal* valour.

Vars.: **McArdell**, **McCardle**.

McAreavey *see* McIlwraith

McAree **1.** Irish: Anglicized form of Gael. **Mac Fhearadhaigh**, patr. from the byname *Fhearadhach* 'Manly', 'Brave' (from *fear* man). **2.** Scots: var. of McAra.

Vars. (of 1): **McHarry**, **Mahorry**; **McKarr(y)e**, **McKerry**, **McKeary**; **McCarrie**, **McGarry**, **Megarry**; **McFaree**, **McFarry**, **McFerry**; **McVarry**, **McVerry**. The name has also been erroneously translated King, as if from *Mac an Rígh* 'son of the king'.

McArtair *see* Arthur

McArtan *see* McCartney

McArthy *see* McCarthy

McAsgill *see* Ashkettle

McAsinagh *see* Tinney

McAslan *see* McAuslan

McAteer *see* McIntyre

McAulay Scots: **1.** Anglicized form of Gael. **Mac Amhalghaidh**, patr. from the old Gael. personal name *Amhalghadh*. **2.** Anglicized form of Gael. **Mac Amhlaoibh** or **Mac Amhlaidh**, patrs. from Gael. forms of the ON personal name *Áleifr, Óláfr* Olaf (cf.

Oliff). These names originated in the Hebrides, where Scandinavian influence was particularly strong.

Vars.: **McAull(a)y**, **McAuley**, **McAllay**, **McAlley**; **McCaulay**, **McCauley**, **McCally**; **Cawley**, **Gawley**.

McAuslan Irish and Scots: Anglicized form of Gael. **Mac Ausaláin**, patr. from a Gael. form of the given name Absolom.

Vars.: **McAuslane**, **McAusland**, **McAuselan**, **McA(u)slin**, **McAslan(d)**; **McCa(u)slan(d)**, **MacCaslane**, **McCasline**.

McAvinchy Irish: Anglicized form of Gael. **Mac Dhuibhinse**, patr. from the personal name *Duibhinse*, composed of the elements *dubh* black + *inis* island; see also Vincent.

McAvish *see* McTavish

McAvoy *see* McEvoy

McAward *see* Bard

McAy *see* McKay

McBain *see* Bean

McBean *see* Bean

McBeth Scots: from the Gael. personal name *Mac Beatha* 'Son of Life', i.e. 'man of religion'.

Vars.: **McBeath**, **McBeith**; **McBay**, **McBey**; **McVay**, **McVey**, **McVeagh**, **McVeigh**, **McVie** (Gael. **Mac Bheatha**).

McBirney *see* Burney

McBlain *see* Blain

McBratney *see* Brett

McBrayne *see* Brain

McBreive *see* Brew

McBride *see* Kilbride

McBrien *see* Bryan

McBrohoon *see* Brain

McBurney *see* Burney

McCabe Scots and Irish: Anglicized form of Gael. **Mac Cába**, patr. from the byname *Cába* 'Cape' (presumably denoting a wearer of a distinctive cape).

McCaddie *see* Adam

McCaet *see* David

McCaffer *see* Duffy

McCafferty Irish: Anglicized form of Gael. **Mac Eachmharcaigh**, patr. from the personal name *Eachmharcach*, composed of the elements *each* horse (see Keogh) + *marcach* rider, knight (see Markey).

Vars.: **McCafferchie**, **McCafferkie**, **McCafferky**, **McCaffarky**, **McCagherty**, **McCaugherty**, **McCaverty**, **McCaharty**, **McCaherty**, **McCaffert**; **Cafferty**, **Cafferky**.

McCaffrey Scots and Irish: Anglicized form of Gael. **Mac Gafraidh**, patr. from a Gael. form of an ON personal name composed of the elements *guð* god + *fróðr* wise.

Vars.: **McCaffery**, **McCaffray**, **McCaffrae**; **McGorrie**, **Gorry**, **Gorey** (Gael. **Mac Gofraidh**).

McCahey see CAUGHEY

McCaig Irish and Scots (Ayr, Galloway): Anglicized form of Gael. **Mac Thaidhg**, patr. from the byname *Tadhg* 'Poet', 'Philosopher'; see also TIGHE and MONTAGU.

Vars.: **McKaig, McKa(i)g(u)e, McKeige, (Mc)Keag(ue), McHaig, McHeigh, Heague, McAig; Keig, Kegg** (Manx).

McCairtair see ARTHUR

McCale see MCKAIL

McCall 1. Irish: Anglicized form of Gael. **Mac Cathmhaoil**, patr. from the personal name *Cathmhaol*, composed of the elements *cath* battle + *maol* chief. 2. Scots: var. of MCKAIL.

Vars.: **McCaul(l), McKall, McGALL, McAll.**

McCallan see CALLAN

McCallerie see MCILWRAITH

McCallister see ALEXANDER

McCallum see MCCOLLUM

McCally see MCAULAY

McCalman see COLEMAN

McCambridge see AMBROSE

McCandless Irish: Anglicized form of Gael. **Mac Cuind(i)lis**, patr. from the personal name *Cuindleas*, of uncertain derivation.

Vars.: **McCandlish, C(h)andlish.**

McCann Irish: Anglicized form of Gael. **Mac Cana**, patr. from the byname *Cana* 'Wolf Cub'. There has been considerable confusion with MCGANN.

Vars.: **McCanna, (Mc)Canny; McAnn(a).**

McCanon see CANNON

McCara see MCARA

McCaragher see FARQUHAR

McCardle see MCARDLE

McCarlish see CHARLES

McCarney Irish: Anglicized form of Gael. **Mac Cearnaigh**, patr. from the byname *Cearnach* 'Victorious'. See also CARNEY.

McCarnon see MCKIERNAN

McCarrick Irish: Anglicized form of Gael. **Mac Concharraige**, patr. from the personal name *Cúcharraige*, composed of the elements *cú* hound, dog + *carraig* rock.

Vars.: **McCarrach, Carrigy.**

McCarrie see MCAREE

McCarroll see CARROLL

McCarron Irish: Anglicized form of Gael. **Mac Carrghamhna**, patr. from the personal name *Corrghamhain*, composed of the elements *corr* pointed, sharp + *gamhain* calf.

McCarthy Irish: Anglicized form of Gael. **Mac Cárthaigh**, patr. from the byname *Cárthach* 'Loving' (cf. CRADDOCK).

Vars.: **McCarty, McCartie; McCarhie, McCarha; McArthy.**

McCartney Scots and Irish: Anglicized form of Gael. **Mac Artaine** (Sc.), **Mac Artnaigh** (Ir.), patr. from a dim. of the byname *Art* 'Bear', 'Hero' (cf. ARTHUR).

Vars.: **McArtney.** Ir. only: **McCartan, McCarten, McCartin, McArtan, Carton** (Gael. **Mac Artáin**).

McCashin Irish: Anglicized form of Gael. **Mac Caisín**, patr. from the byname *Caisín*, from a dim. of *cas* curly (-headed); cf. CASSIDY.

Vars.: **(Mc)Cassin, Cashi(o)n, Cashe(e)n, McKasshine, Keshin.**

McCaskell see ASHKETTLE

McCaslan see MCAUSLAN

McCateer see MCINTYRE

McCaubrey see CUTHBERT

McCaulay see MCAULAY

McCause see MCTAVISH

McCauslan see MCAUSLAN

McCaverty see MCCAFFERTY

McCaw see MEGAW

McCay see MCKAY

McChlery see CLEARY

McChruiter see MCWHIRTER

McClacher see CLACHAR

McClaron see MCLAREN

McClatchie Irish and Scots (Ayr, Galloway): Anglicized form of Gael. **Mac Gille Eidich** 'son of the servant of (St) *Eidich*', a personal name of uncertain origin.

Vars.: **McClatch(e)y, McLatchie, McLatchy, McLetchie.**

McClave see CLAFFEY

McClay see MCLAY

McClean see MCLEAN

McCleary see CLEARY

McClellan Scots and Irish: Anglicized form of Gael. **Mac Gille Fhaolain** (Sc.) and **Mac Giolla Fhaoláin** (Ir.) 'son of the servant of (St) *Faolán*'; see GILFILLAN and WHELAN.

Vars.: **McClelland, McLellan, McLel(l)and, McGillallen; CLELAND, Leland.**

McClements see LAMONT

McClenaghan Scots: Anglicized form of Gael. **Mac Gille Onchon** 'son of the servant of (St) *Onchú*', an OIr. personal name perhaps meaning 'Mighty Hound'. St Onchú was a 6th-cent. Irish pilgrim and collector of holy relics.

Vars.: **McClanaghan, McClan(n)achan, McLanaghan, McLanachan.**

McClennan Scots: Anglicized form of Gael. **Mac Gille Fhinneain** 'son of the servant of (St) *Fionnán*', a personal name representing a dim. of *fionn* white. There were several early Irish saints of this name, most notably a 7th-cent. bishop who governed the Church established in Northumb. and evangelized parts of S England.
Var.: **McLennan**.

McClew *see* DUNLEAVY

McClintock Scots and Irish: Anglicized form of Gael. **Mac Gille Fhionndaig** (Sc.), **Mac Giolla Fhiontóg** (Ir.) 'son of the servant of (St) *Finndag*', a personal name representing a dim. of *fionn* white.

McClone *see* CLUNE

McCloud *see* MCLEOD

McCloy *see* LEWIS

McClune *see* MCLEAN

McClung Scots: Anglicized form of Gael. **Mac Luinge**, patr. from a personal name which is probably derived from *long* ship or the homonymous *long* tall.
Vars.: **McCluny**, **McLung**.

McClure Scots: **1.** Anglicized form of Gael. **Mac Gille Uidhir** 'son of the servant of (St) *Odhar*', whose name means 'Sallow'. Cf. HORAN and McGUIRE. **2.** Anglicized form of Gael. **Mac Gille Dheòradha** 'son of the servant of the pilgrim'; cf. DEWAR.
Vars. (of 1): **McCloor**, **McLure**, **McLeur**, **McAlear**, **McAleer**.

McClurg Scots: Anglicized form of Gael. **Mac Luirg**, patr. from the personal name *Lorg*, of uncertain origin.
Var.: **McLurg**.

McCluskey Irish: Anglicized form of Gael. **Mac Bhloscaidhe**, patr. from the personal name *Bloscadh*, which is probably a deriv. of *blosc* loud noise.
Vars.: **McClusky**, **McClosk(e)y**, **McCluskie**; **McLusky**, **McLuskie**; GLASGOW.

McClymond *see* LAMONT

McCole *see* COLE, McDOUGALL

McColl *see* QUILL

McColley *see* DUNLEAVY

McCollum Scots: Anglicized form of Gael. **Mac Coluim**, patr. from a Gael. form of the given name *Columba*; see COLOMB.
Vars.: **McCollam**, **McCallum**, **McAllum**.

McComb Scots: Anglicized form of Gael. **Mac Thóm**, patr. from a Gael. pet form of the given name THOMAS.
Var.: **McCombe**.
Dims.: **McC(h)ombich**, **McCom(b)ie**, **McOmie** (Gael. **Mac Thomaidh**).

McComish *see* McOMISH

McComisky *see* COMERFORD

McConachie *see* McDONAGH

McConamy *see* McNAMEE

McCone *see* EWAN

McConnell **1.** Scots: Anglicized form of Gael. *Mac Dhomhnuill*, patr. from the personal name *Domhnall*; see DONALD and McDONALD. **2.** Irish: Anglicized form of Gael. **Mac Conaill**, patr. from the personal name *Conall* (see CONNELL).
Vars.: **McConnel**, **McConnal** (Of 1 only): **(Mc)Whannell**.

McConville Irish: Anglicized form of Gael. **Mac Conmhaoil**, patr. from the personal name *Conmhaol*, apparently composed of the elements *cú* hound + *maol* bald.
Vars.: **(Mc)Conwell**.

McCorc *see* McGURK

McCord Irish: Anglicized form of Gael. **Mac Cuairt** and **MacCuarta**, patrs. from a personal name of uncertain origin.
Vars.: **McCoard**, **McCourt**.

McCorkell *see* THIRKILL

McCorley *see* CURLEY

McCormack *see* CORMACK

McCorry Irish: Anglicized form of Gael. **Mac Gothraidh**, patr. from a Gael. form of the given name GODFREY.

McCosdalowe *see* COSTELLO

McCosh Scots: Anglicized form of Gael. **Mac Coise**, patr. from the byname *Cos* 'Footsoldier', 'Messenger'.

McCosker *see* McCUSKER

McCoubrey *see* CUTHBERT

McCoulie *see* McCULLOCH

McCovie *see* DUFFY

McCoy *see* McKAY

McCracken N Irish and Scots (Galloway): of uncertain origin, possibly from Gael. **Mac Neachtain** (see McNAUGHTON), with the interchange of *n* and *r* characteristic of Ulster.
Vars.: **McCraken**, **McCrackan**; **McGrattan**.

McCrae Scots and Irish: Anglicized form of Gael. **Mag Raith**, patr. from the byname *Rath* 'Grace', 'Prosperity'.
Vars.: **McCray(e)**, **McCrea**, **McCree**, **McCrie**, **McCraw**, **McCr(e)agh**, **McCreath**, **McCraith**, **McCreith**, **McCreight**; **McGra(w)**, **McGragh**, McGRATH; **McRay**, **McRea**, **McRee**, **McRie**, **McRaw**, **McRaith**, **McReath**; **McWray**; **Magraw**, **Magragh**, **Magrath**, **Megraw**, **Megrath**, **Mackereth**. See also REITH.

McCrandle *see* RONALD

McCrank *see* RAINEY

McCranor *see* TRAINOR

McCready Irish: Anglicized form of Gael. **Mac Riada**, patr. from the byname *Riada* 'Trained', 'Expert'.
Vars.: **McCre(a)d(d)ie**, **McReady**, **McRe(a)die**.

McCreavy *see* REAVEY

McCreery Scots: Anglicized form of Gael. **Mac Ruidhrí**, patr. from the personal name *Ru(a)idhrí*; see RORY.
Vars.: **McCre(a)ry**, **McCririe**.

McCreesh *see* McNEICE

McCrimmon Scots: Anglicized form of Gael. **Mac Ruimein**, patr. from a Gael. form of the ON personal name *Hróðmundr*, composed of the elements *hród* fame + *mundr* protection.

McCrory *see* RORY

McCrossan *see* CROSS

McCrudden Irish: Anglicized form of Gael. **Mac Rodáin**, patr. from the personal name *Rodán*, a deriv. of *rod* spirited; cf. RODEN.

McCrumm Scots: Anglicized form of Gael. **Mac Chruim**, patr. from the byname *Crum* 'Bent', 'Twisted'.

McCruttan *see* CURTIN

McCrystal *see* CRISTAL

McCubbin *see* GIBBON

McCue *see* McKAY

McCulloch Irish and Scots (Glasgow): Anglicized form of a Gael. patr. from a personal name apparently derived from *cullach* wild boar—some families in N Sligo have indeed translated the name as **Boar**. It is, however, possible that it was originally *Cú-Uladh* 'Hound of Ulster' and has undergone alteration as a result of folk etymology.
Vars.: **McCullach**, **McCullagh**, **McCullough**; **McCully**, **McCullie**, **McCoulie**.

McCumesky *see* COMERFORD

McCune *see* EWAN

McCure *see* IVOR

McCurlye *see* CURLEY

McCurrey *see* McMURRAY

McCurtain *see* CURTIN

McCusker Irish: Anglicized form of Gael. **Mac Oscair**, patr. from a Gael. form of the ON personal name *Ásgeirr*, composed of the elements *ans* god + *geirr* spear.
Var.: **McCosker**.

McCutcheon Scots: Anglicized form of Gael. **Mac Uisdein**, patr. from the personal name *Uisdean*, a Gaelicized form of OF *Huchon* (see HUTCHIN).
Vars.: **McCutchen**, **McHutche(o)n**, **McHutchin**, **McQuistan**, **McQuisten**, **McQuistin**, **McQuiston**, **McQueston**, **McQuaston**, **McWhiston**, HOUSTON.

McDade *see* DAVID

McDairmid *see* DERMOTT

McDearmid *see* DERMOTT

McDearmid *see* DERMOTT

McDevitt *see* DAVID

McDiarmond *see* DERMOTT

McDonagh Scots and Irish: Anglicized form of Gael. **Mac Donnchaidh** (Sc.) and **Mac Donnchadha** (Ir.), patrs. from the given name *Donnchadh*; see DONOHUE.
Vars.: **McDonnagh**, **McDonaugh**, **McDon(n)ach**, **McDono(u)gh**, **McDona**; **McDonoghue**, **McDonnoghie**, **McDonaghy**, **McDon(a)chie**, **McDonachy**, **McDunphy**; **McConaghy**, **McCon(n)achie**, **McCon(n)echie**, **McCon(n)ochie**, **McConoughey**, **McConachy**, **McCon(e)chy**, **McConkey**, **McKonochie**, **McOnachie**, **McOnechy**, **McOnochie**; **Dono(u)gh**, **Don(n)agh**.

McDonald Scots: Anglicized form of Gael. **Mac Dhomhnuill**, patr. from the personal name *Domhnall*; see DONALD.
Vars.: **McDon(n)ell**, **McDona(i)ll**, **McDaniel**; McCONNELL.

McDougall Scots: Anglicized form of Gael. **Mac Dhubhghaill**, patr. from the given name *Dubhghall*; see DOUGALL.
Vars.: **McDougal**, **McDugal(d)**, **McDoual(l)**, **McDowall**, **McDo(w)ell**, **McDuall**, **McDool**; **McCool(e)**, **McCole** (see also COLE 3); COOLE.

McDowney *see* MOLONEY

McDuff *see* DUFF

McDugal *see* McDOUGALL

McDunphy *see* McDONAGH

McEa *see* McKAY

McEabuoy *see* McEVOY

McEan *see* McKANE

McEbrehowne *see* BRAIN

McEcrossan *see* CROSS

McEdmond *see* McKEEMAN

McEever *see* IVOR

McEgaine *see* KEEGAN

McEgill *see* GALL

McEgown *see* McGOWAN

McElane *see* ALLEN

McElderry *see* KILDARE

McEldoon *see* DUNN

McEldowney *see* MOLONEY

McElduff *see* GILDUFF

McElharan *see* HERON

McElhinney Irish: Anglicized form of Gael. **Mac Giolla Choinnigh** 'son of the servant of (St) *Coinneach*' (see KENNY 2).

McElhuddy *see* McGILLICUDDY

McElistrim *see* ALEXANDER

McEllar *see* HILARY

McElmurray *see* GILMORE

McElreath *see* McILWRAITH

McElroy *see* GILROY

McElvride *see* KILBRIDE

McElwain *see* MCILWAINE

McEnally *see* MCNALLY

McEnarhin *see* MCNAIRN

McEnery Irish: Anglicized form of Gael. **Mac Innéirghe**, patr. from the personal name *Innéirghe*, apparently a deriv. of the verb *éirghe* to arise, ascend.

Vars.: **McEnerie**, **McEn(i)ry**; **McIneirie**; **McKen(n)ery**, **McKeneyry**; **McKeniry**; **McNeiry**; **Kiniry**.

McEnkelly *see* QUILLY

McEnleavy *see* DUNLEAVY

McEnnesse *see* MCGUINNESS

McEnroe Irish: Anglicized form of Gael. **Mac Conchradha**, patr. from the personal name *Conchradh*, composed of *cú* hound + a second element of uncertain meaning.

Vars.: **McEnchrow**, CROW.

McEntaggart *see* TAGGART

McEntee Irish: Anglicized form of Gael. **Mac an tSaoi** 'son of the scholar, wise man'.

McEnteer *see* MCINTYRE

McEoghoe *see* KEOGH

McErchar *see* FARQUHAR

McErlean Scots: Anglicized form of Gael. **Mac an Fhirléighinn** 'son of the lector'; this was the title held by the head of a monastic school.

Vars.: **McErlain**, **McNerlan**, **McNerlin**.

McEtterick *see* MCKETTRICK

McEvoy Irish: Anglicized form of Gael. **Mac Giolla Bhuidhe** 'son of the yellow-haired lad'.

Vars.: **McAvoy**, **McEabuoy**, **McElwee**, MCKELVEY, **Kilboy**.

McEvrehune *see* BRAIN

McEwan *see* EWAN

McFadden Scots and Irish: Anglicized form of Gael. **Mac Phaid(e)in** (Sc.) and **Mac Pháidín** (Ir.), patrs. from Gael. dim. forms of the given name PATRICK.

Vars.: **McFadin**, **McPha(i)den**, **McFayden**, **McFeyden**, **McFadye(a)n**, **McFadz(e)an**, **McFadion**, **McFadyon**, **McFadzeon**, **McFadzein**, **McFadwyn**.

McFade *see* PATE

McFall Scots and Irish: Anglicized form of Gael. **Mac Phàil** (Sc.) and **Mac Phóil** (Ir.), patrs. from Gael. forms of the given name PAUL.

Vars.: **McFaul**, **McFail**, **McVail**, **McPhail**, **McPhial**, **McPhiel**, **(Mc)Fyall**; QUAIL.

McFaree *see* MCAREE

McFarlane Scots and Irish: Anglicized form of Gael. **Mac Pharthalàin**, patr. from *Parthalán*, a personal name from L *Bartholomaeus* (see BARTHOLOMEW).

Vars.: **McFarlan(d)**, **McFarlin**, **McPharlain**, **McPharland**, **McPar(t)lan(d)**, **McParlane**, **McParlin**.

McFarquar *see* FARQUHAR

McFeat *see* PATE

McFee *see* DUFFY

McFerran Irish: Anglicized form of Gael. **Mac Fearáin**, patr. from the personal name *Fearán*, a dim. of *fear* man.

McFerry *see* MCAREE

McFetridge Scots: Anglicized form of Gael. **Mac Pheadruis**, patr. from a Gael. form of the given name PETER.

Vars.: **McPhetrish**, **McFedri(e)s**.

McFie *see* DUFFY

McFun *see* MCMUNN

McGaffey *see* CAUGHEY

McGaffigan *see* GAVIGAN

McGahan *see* GAHAN

McGahran *see* GAUGHRAN

McGale *see* MCKAIL

McGall Scots: **1.** var. of MCCALL. **2.** Anglicized form of Gael. **Mac Goill**, patr. from the byname *Gall* 'Stranger'; cf. GALL 1.

McGann Irish: Anglicized form of Gael. **Mag Annaidh**, patr. from the personal name *Annadh*, the meaning of which is unknown. There has been considerable confusion with MCCANN.

Var.: **Magann** (see also GAHAN).

McGarrigle Irish: Anglicized form of Gael. **Mag Fhearhgail**, patr. from the personal name *Fearghal*, composed of the elements *fear* man + *gal* valour.

McGarrity *see* GERAGHTY

McGarry *see* MCAREE

McGaw *see* MEGAW

McGee *see* MCKAY

McGeogh *see* KEOGH

McGeorge Scots: not a patr. from the given name GEORGE, but an Anglicized form of Gael. **Mac an Deoir** 'son of the pilgrim, relic keeper'; cf. DEWAR.

Vars.: **McJerrow**, **McJarrow**; **McIndeor**, **McIndewer**, **McKinde(wa)r**.

McGeown *see* EWAN

McGeraghty *see* GERAGHTY

McGettigan Irish: Anglicized form of Gael. **Mag Eiteagáin**, patr. from the personal name *Eiteagán*, a dim. of *eite* wing (perhaps originally a byname for a swift runner).

Vars.: **Gattin(s)**, **Gaitens**.

McGhee *see* MCKAY

McGibbon *see* GIBBON

McGilbride *see* KILBRIDE

McGilchrist see GILCHRIST

McGildowie see DUFFY

McGildowney see MOLONEY

McGilduff see GILDUFF

McGill see GALL

McGillacoell see GILHOOL

McGillallen see McCLELLAN

McGillaroe see GILROY

McGillaspick see GILLESPIE

McGillereogh see McILWRAITH

McGillesachta see LYSAGHT

McGillicuddy Irish: Anglicized form of Gael. **Mac Giolla Chuda** 'son of the servant of (St) *Chuda*'. This was the name of a 7th-cent. abbot-bishop of Rathin in Westmeath.
Vars.: **McGillacuddy**, **McElhuddy**.

McGilligan 1. Scots: Anglicized form of Gael. **Mac Gille Fhaolagain** 'son of the servant of (St) *Faolagan*', a personal name representing a double dim. of *faol* wolf (cf. WHELAN and McCLELLAN). 2. Irish: Anglicized form of Gael. **Mac Giollagáin**, patr. from the personal name *Giollagán* (a dim. of *giolla* servant).
Vars.: **McGilligin**, **McKilligan**, **McKilligin**, **McKillican(e)**.

McGillivray Scots and Irish: Anglicized form of Gael. **Mac Gille Bhrath** (Sc.) and **Mac Giolla Bhraith** (Ir.), patrs. from a given name meaning 'Servant of Judgment'.
Vars.: **McGillvray**, **McGilvra(y)**, **McGillavery**, **McGillivry**, **McGillivrie**, **McGil(l)vary**, **McGilvery**.

McGillworry see GILMORE

McGilp see McKILLOP

McGilvane see McILWAINE

McGilveil see BELL

McGilvernock see WARNOCK

McGimpsey see DEMPSEY

McGinley Irish: Anglicized form of Gael. **Mag Fhionnghaile**, patr. from the personal name *Fionnghal*, composed of the elements *fionn* fair + *gal* valour. According to Black it has no connection with McKINLEY.

McGinn Irish: Anglicized form of Gael. **Mag Fhionn**, patr. from the personal name *Fionn*; see FINN.
Vars.: **McGin(g)**, **McGenn**, **McKinn**, **McKing**, **Maginn**, **Meggin**.

McGinnis see McGUINNESS

McGinty Irish: Anglicized form of Gael. **Mag Fhionnachtaigh**, patr. from the personal name *Fionnshneachtaigh*, composed of the elements *fionn* white + *sneachtach* snow.

McGirr Scots and N Irish: Anglicized form of Gael. **Mac an Gheairr** 'son of the short man', sometimes translated into English as SHORT.

McGivern see McGOVERN

McGlashan Scots: Anglicized form of Gael. **Mac Glasain**, patr. from the personal name *Glasan*, originally a byname from a dim. of *glas* grey, green, blue (see GLASS 2).
Vars.: **McGlashen**, **McGlasson**; **Glashen**.

McGloin see McLEAN

McGloughlin see McLACHLAN

McGoldrick Irish: Anglicized form of Gael. **Mag Ualghairg**, patr. from the personal name *Ualgharg*, apparently composed of old Celt. elements meaning 'proud' + 'fierce'.
Vars.: **McGolrick**, **Magorlick**, **McWalrick**, **Golden**.

McGonigle Irish: Anglicized form of Gael. **Mac Congail**, patr. from the personal name *Congal*, composed of old Celt. elements meaning 'high' and 'valour'.
Var.: **McGonagle**.

McGorley see CURLEY

McGorrie see McCAFFREY

McGounasan see GORDON

McGovern Irish: Anglicized form of Gael. **Mag Shamhr(adh)áin**, patr. from the personal name *Samhradháin*, a dim. of *samhradh* summer.
Vars.: **McGaveran**, **McGovran**, **McGivern**, **McGowran**, **McGouran**, **Magover(a)n**, **Magawran**, **Magaur(a)n**, **Magurn**, **Gooravan**, **Gorevan**, **Gorevin**.

McGow see GOUGH

McGowan 1. Scots and Irish: Anglicized form of Gael. **Mac Gobhann** (Sc.) and **Mac Gabhann** (Ir.), patrs. from occupational bynames meaning 'Smith'. 2. Scots: Anglicized form of Gael. **Mac Owein**, patr. from the given name *Owen* or EWAN. One family of this name is probably descended from a king of the Strathclyde Britons (killed 1018), recorded by Simeon of Durham in the L form *Eugeni*.
Vars. (of 1): **McGowing**, **McGow(e)n**, **McGoun(e)**, **Magowan**. Sc. only: **McAgown**, **McEgown**, **McIgo(i)ne** (Gael. **Mac an Ghobhann**); **Gowans**.

McGra see McCRAE

McGrain see RAINEY

McGrandell see RONALD

McGrath Irish: the normal Ir. form corresponding to Sc. McCRAE.

McGrattan see McCRACKEN

McGreal see NEIL

McGreave see REAVEY

McGregor Scots: Anglicized form of Gael. **Mac Griogair**, patr. from a Gael. form of the given name GREGORY.
Vars.: **McGr(e)igor**.

McGrory see RORY

McGuffie see DUFFY

McGuggy see CAUGHEY

McGuigan Irish: Anglicized form of **Mac Guagáin**, an altered version of *Mag Eochagáin*; see GEOGHEGAN.
Vars.: **McG(o)ugan, McGucki(a)n; McWiggan**.

McGuinness Irish: Anglicized form of Gael. **Mag Aonghuis**, patr. from the given name *Aonghus*; see ANGUS.
Vars.: **McGinnis, McEnnesse, McEnnis, McInnes, McInch, McKinch, McHinch; Maguin(n)ess, Maginness, Maginnis, Magennis, Meginniss; Guin(n)ess**.

McGuire Irish: Anglicized form of Gael. **Mag Uidhir** 'son of *Odhar*', a byname meaning 'Sallow'. According to legend, St Odhar was St Patrick's charioteer. See also McCLURE and HORAN.
Vars.: **McGwir(e), McGui(v)er, Maguire, Maguier**.

McGuone see EWAN

McGurk 1. Scots: Anglicized form of Gael. **Mag Coirc**, patr. from the personal name *Corc* 'Heart'. 2. Irish: Anglicized form of Gael. **Mag Oirc**, patr. from the personal name *Orc*, of uncertain origin, perhaps from *orc* pig.
Vars.: **McGuirk, McCorc**.

McGynnowar see GAYNOR

McHaffie see DUFFY

McHaig see McCAIG

McHale Irish: 1. Anglicized form of Gael. **Mac Céile**, patr. from the byname *Céile* 'Companion'. 2. from **Mac Haol**, a Gaelicized form of HOWELL that was adopted by a Welsh family of this name who settled in Co. Mayo.

McHarnon see McKIERNAN

McHarry see McAREE

McHeagan see KEEGAN

McHeever see IVOR

McHeigh see McCAIG

McHenry Scots and Irish: Anglicized form of Gael. **Mac Eanruig** (Sc.) and **Mac Éinrí, Mac Eanraic** (Ir.), patrs. from Gael. forms of the given name HENRY.
Vars.: **McHendry, McHendrie; McHendrick, McKendrick**.

McHinch see McGUINNESS

McHugh see McKAY

McHutchen see McCUTCHEON

McIan see McKANE

McIgoine see McGOWAN

McIlderry see KILDARE

McIldoon see DUNN

McIldowie see DUFFY

McIldowney see MOLONEY

McIlduff see GILDUFF

McIlheron see HERON

McIliams see McWILLIAM

McIllrick see McILWRAITH

McIlmurray see GILMORE

McIlroy see GILROY

McIlvernock see WARNOCK

McIlwaine Scots: Anglicized form of Gael. **Mac Gille Bheathain** 'son of the servant of (St) *Beathan*', a personal name representing a dim. of *beathe* life.
Vars.: **McIlvain(e), McIlvane, McIlvean, McIlveen, McIlvenna, McIlvenny; McElwain; McKilvain; McGilvane**. The name is sometimes further Anglicized as MELVIN.

McIlwraith Scots and Irish: Anglicized form of Gael. **Mac Gille Riabhaich** (Sc.) and **Mac Giolla Riabhaigh** (Ir.) 'son of the brindled lad'; cf. REAVEY.
Vars.: **McIl(w)rath, McIl(a)raith, McIlarith, McIl(le)riach, McIlreach, McIlurick, McIllrick, McGillreich** (Sc.); **McIlravy, McIlrea; McEl(w)reath, McElreavy, McAre(a)vey, McGillereogh, McGilrae, Gallery, McCalreogh, McCalreaghe, McCallerie, Colreavy, Culreavy, Callery, Killery** (Ir.).

McInally see McNALLY

McInch see McGUINNESS

McInchelly see QUILLY

McIndeor see McGEORGE

McIneirie see McENERY

McInerney see McNAIRN

McIngill see GALL

McInlester see LISTER

McInstocker see STOKER

McIntaggart see TAGGART

McIntosh Scots: Anglicized form of Gael. **Mac an Toisich** 'son of the chief, leader, thane'.
Vars.: **McKintosh, Mackintosh; Tosh, Tos(c)hach, Tosha(c)k**.

McIntyre Scots: Anglicized form of Gael. **Mac an tSaoir** 'son of the carpenter or mason'.
Vars.: **McInteer; McEntire, McEnteer; McAteer; McCateer; McTear, McTier; Matier, Mateer; Tear(e), Tier, Tyr(i)e**.

McIsaac see ISAAC

McIver see IVOR

McJames see JAMES

McJarrow see McGEORGE

McJerrow see McGEORGE

McKage see McCAIG

McKaghone see McMAHON

McKail 1. Scots: Anglicized form of Gael. **Mac Cathail**, patr. from the personal name *Cathal*; see CAHILL. 2. Irish: Anglicized form of Gael. *Mac Céile*; see McHALE.
Vars.: **McKale, McCale, McGale**.

McKale see McKAIL

McKall see McCALL

McKane Scots: Anglicized form of Gael. **Mac Iain**, patr. from a Gael. form of the given name JOHN.
Vars.: **McKain, McKean(d), McAne, McEan, McIan**.

McKarre *see* McAREE

McKarrill *see* CARROLL

McKaskil *see* ASHKETTLE

McKasshine *see* McCASHIN

McKay Scots and Irish: Anglicized form of Gael. **Mac Aodha**, patr. from the personal name *Aodh* 'Fire', originally the name of a pagan god.
Vars.: **McKoy, McKey, McKee, McKie; McCay, McCoy; McG(h)ee, McGhie; McHugh, McCue; McEa, McAy; Mag(g)ee; Quay(e), Key** (Manx); KEYES; **Hughes, Hueson, Hewson,** (see also HUGH); **Eason** (see also EADE); **Ayson**.

McKeag *see* McCAIG

McKeagan *see* KEEGAN

McKeamish *see* JAMES

McKean *see* McKANE

McKeaney *see* KENNY

McKeary *see* McAREE

McKechnie Scots: Anglicized form of Gael. **Mac Eacharna**, patr. from the personal name *Eacharn*, a deriv. of *each* horse.

McKeeman Scots: Anglicized form of Gael. **Mac Eamoinn**, patr. from a Gael. form of the given name ED-MOND.
Vars.: **McEdmond, McAimon**.

McKehoe *see* KEOGH

McKeith *see* SHEEHY

McKellan *see* ALLEN

McKellar *see* HILARY

McKelvey 1. Scots: Anglicized form of Gael. **Mac Shealbhaigh**, patr. from the personal name *Sealbhach*, of uncertain origin. 2. Irish: Anglicized form of Gael. *Mac Giolla Bhuidhe*; see McEVOY.
Vars.: **McKelvy, McKelvie, McKilvie**.

McKendrick *see* McHENRY

McKenery *see* McENERY

McKenzie Scots: Anglicized form of Gael. **Mac Coinnich**, patr. from the byname *Coinneach* 'Comely' (a deriv. of *cann* fair, bright). The name was formerly pronounced /məˈkenjiː/; cf. MENZIES.
Vars.: **McQuenzie; McWhinnie, McW(h)inney, McWeeney, Mawhinney, Mewhinney** (Gael. **Mac Chonnigh**).

McKeon *see* EWAN

McKeracher *see* FARQUHAR

McKerley *see* CURLEY

McKettrick Scots: Anglicized form of Gael. **Mac Shitrig**, patr. from a Gael. form of the ON personal

name *Sigtryggr*, composed of the elements *sigr* victory + *tryggr* true.
Vars.: **McKetterick, McKitt(e)rick, McEtterick**.

McKevitt *see* DAVID

McKey *see* McKAY

McKibben *see* GIBBON

McKie *see* McKAY

McKiegan *see* KEEGAN

McKiernan Irish: Anglicized form of Gael. **Mac Thighearnáin**, patr. from a dim. of the byname *Tighearna* 'Lord', 'Master'; cf. TIERNEY.
Vars.: **K(i)ernan, Kernon, McKernan(e), McCarnon, McHarnon,** LORD.

McKilduff *see* GILDUFF

McKillbride *see* KILBRIDE

McKilliam *see* McWILLIAM

McKillican *see* McGILLIGAN

McKillop Scots: Anglicized form of Gael. **Mac Fhilib**, patr. from a Gael. form of the given name PHILIP.
Vars.: **McGilp, Killip, Keillips**.

McKillroe *see* GILROY

McKilvain *see* McILWAINE

McKimm Scots: Anglicized form of Gael. **Mac Shim**, patr. from a Gael. pet form of the given name SIMON.
Var.: **McKim**.

McKimmie *see* SIMON

McKinch *see* McGUINNESS

McKinder *see* McGEORGE

McKing *see* McGINN

McKinley Scots: Anglicized form of Gael. **Mac Fhionnlaoich**, patr. from the personal name *Fionnlaoch*; see FINLAY.
Vars.: **McKin(d)lay**.

McKinna *see* KENNY

McKinnawe *see* KINNEAVY

McKinnerkin *see* McNAIRN

McKinnon Scots and Irish: Anglicized form of Gael. **Mac Fhionghuin**, patr. from an old Gael. personal name meaning 'Fair Born' or 'Beloved Son'. The surname has also been erroneously translated LOVE, as if from Gael. *Mac Ionmhuinn*.

McKinstry N Irish: Anglicized form of Gael. **Mac an Aistrigh**, a simplified version of *Mac an Aistrighthigh* 'son of the traveller'. The name is now largely confined to Ulster, but seems to have originated in Galloway.

McKintosh *see* McINTOSH

McKisack *see* ISAAC

McKitterick *see* McKETTRICK

McKnight *see* McNaughton

McKnockatir *see* McNucator

McKnulty *see* McNulty

McKonochie *see* McDonagh

McKough *see* Keogh

McKoy *see* McKay

McKrevie *see* Reavey

McKynnan *see* Finn

McKyrrelly *see* Curley

McLachlan Scots: Anglicized form of Gael. **Mac Lachlainn**, patr. from the personal name *Lachlann*; see LACHLAN.
Vars.: **McLachlane**, **McLauchlan(e)**, **McLauchlin**, **McLaughlan(e)**; **McLaughlin**, **McLochlin**, **McLo(u)ghlin**, **McGloughlin** (Ir.); **Claplin** (Manx).

McLain *see* McLean

McLamon *see* Lamont

McLanachan *see* McClenaghan

McLaren Scots: Anglicized form of Gael. **Mac Labhruinn**, patr. from a Gael. form of the given name LAWRENCE.
Vars.: **McLaran**, **McLauren**, **McLaurin**, **McLawring**, **McClaron**.

McLarnon N Irish: Anglicized form of Gael. **Mac Giolla Earnáin** 'son of the servant of (St) *Ernán*'. The name was borne by several early Irish saints, most notably a nephew of St Columba.
Var.: **McLernon**.

McLatchie *see* McClatchie

McLaverty *see* Laverty

McLay Scots: of uncertain origin, probably an Anglicized and drastically reduced form of Gael. **Mac Dhuinnshléibhe**, patr. from the personal name *Duinnshléibhe*; see DUNLEAVY. On the other hand it is possible that the *McLeays* of Sutherland are descended from Ferchard *Leche* (see LEACH), recorded in 1386, and in this case the name would be from Gael. *Mac an Léigh* 'son of the physician'.
Vars.: **McLae**, **McLea(y)**, **McClay**.

McLea *see* McLay

McLean Scots and Irish: Anglicized form of Gael. **Mac Gille Eáin** (Sc.) and **Mac Giolla Eóin** (Ir.) 'son of the servant of (St) JOHN'.
Vars.: **McLane**, **McLain(e)**, **McLune**, **McLoon(e)**; **McClean(e)**, **McClune**, **McGlone**, **McGloin**, **McAloon**.

McLeary *see* Cleary

McLeavy *see* Dunleavy

McLees *see* Gillies

McLeister *see* Lister

McLeland *see* McClellan

McLennan *see* McClennan

McLeod Scots: Anglicized form of Gael. **Mac Leòid**, patr. from a Gael. form of the ON byname *Ljótr* 'Ugly'.
Var.: **McCloud**.

McLernon *see* McLarnon

McLeroy *see* Gilroy

McLetchie *see* McClatchie

McLeur *see* McClure

McLise *see* Gillies

McLochlin *see* McLachlan

McLoon *see* McLean

McLucas *see* Lucas

McLune *see* McLean

McLung *see* McClung

McLure *see* McClure

McLuskie *see* McCluskey

McLysaght *see* Lysaght

McMahon Irish: Anglicized form of Gael. **Mac Mathghamhna**, patr. from the byname *Mathghamhain*; see MAHON.
Vars.: **McMachon**, **McMa(c)han**, **McMaghon(e)**, **McMa(g)hen**, **McKaghone**, **McMann**; **McMahouna**, **McMaghowney** (Gael. **Mac Mathghamhana**).

McManamon *see* McMenemy

McManus Irish: Anglicized form of Gael. **Mac Maghnuis**, patr. from a Gael. form of the given name MAGNUS.
Vars.: **McMannas**, **McMannes**, **Mayne(s)**.

McMarquis *see* Mark

McMartin *see* Martin

McMaster Scots: Anglicized form of Gael. **Mac Maighstir**, patr. from the Gael. title *maighstir* MASTER.
Var.: **McMasters**.

McMearty *see* Moriarty

McMeekin Irish and Scots (Galloway): Anglicized form of Gael. **Mac Miadhacháin**, patr. from the personal name *Miadhachán*, a dim. of *miadhach* honourable.
Vars.: **McMeeking**, **McMikin**, **McMicking**, **McMeekan**, **McMei(c)kan**, **McMi(c)kan**, **McMeckan**, **McMeeken**, **McMi(c)ken**, **McMeechan**, **McMeecham**, **McMichan**, **McMychen**.

McMenemy Irish: Anglicized form of Gael. **Mac Meanm(n)a**, patr. from a personal name meaning 'Mind', 'Courage', 'Spirit'.
Vars.: **McMenamy**, **McMenamie**.
Dims.: **McMenamin**, **McManamon**.

McMenigall *see* McMonagle

McMichael Scots: Anglicized form of Gael. **Mac Micheil**, patr. from a Gael. form of the given name MICHAEL.
Vars.: **McMicheal**, **McMichail**.

McMichan *see* MᶜMEEKIN

McMichie *see* MICHIE

McMillan Scots: Anglicized form of Gael. **Mac Maoláin**, patr. from the byname *Maolán*, a dim. of *maol* bald, tonsured. The name normally referred to a wearer of the tonsure, and, in a transferred sense, to a devotee of a particular saint. See also MULLEN.

Vars.: **McMillen; McMullan, McMullen, McMullin, McMullon; McMowlane, McMoylan.**

McMiritee *see* MORIARTY

McMonagle Irish: Anglicized form of Gael. **Mac Maonghail**, patr. from the personal name *Maonghal*, composed of the elements *maoin* wealth + *gal* valour.

Vars.: **McMunagle, McMenigall.**

McMordie Scots: Anglicized form of Gael. *Mac Muircheartaigh*, patr. from the personal name *Muircheartach*; see MORIARTY.

Vars.: **McMurdo, McMurtough, McMurthoe, McMurty.**

McMoriertagh *see* MORIARTY

McMorland Scots: Anglicized form of Gael. **Mac Murghalain**, patr. from the personal name *Murghalan*, composed of the elements *muir* sea + *gal* valour + the dim. suffix -*an*.

Var.: **McMoreland.**

McMorris *see* MORRIS

McMorrough Irish: Anglicized form of Gael **Mac Murchadha**, patr. from the personal name *Murchadha*, composed of the elements *muir* sea + *cadh* warrior. See also MURPHY.

Vars.: **McMorrow, McMoroghoe, McMurroghowe, (Mc)Murchie, McMurphew; Morrowson, Murchison.**

McMowlane *see* MᶜMILLAN

McMreaty *see* MORIARTY

McMullan *see* MᶜMILLAN

McMunagle *see* MᶜMONAGLE

McMunn Scots: Anglicized form of Gael. **Mac Gille Mhunna** 'son of the servant of (St) *Munnu*'. This name, which is also found in the form *Mundu*, from earlier *Mo-Fhindu*, is a hypocoristic form of *Fionntan* with the affective prefix *mo*- my.

Vars.: **McPhun, McFun(n).**

McMurchie *see* MᶜMORROUGH

McMurdo *see* MᶜMORDIE

McMurihertie *see* MORIARTY

McMurphew *see* MᶜMORROUGH

McMurray Irish: Anglicized form of Gael. *Mac Muireadhaigh*, patr. from the given name *Muireadhach*; see MURDOCH.

Vars.: **McCurrey, McCurrie.**

McMurthoe *see* MᶜMORDIE

McMychen *see* MᶜMEEKIN

McNab *see* ABBOTT

McNair 1. Scots: Anglicized form of Gael. **Mac Iain Uidhir** 'son of sallow JOHN'. This form seems to have originated in Ross. 2. Scots: Anglicized form of Gael. **Mac an Oighre** 'son of the heir'. This form seems to have originated in Perthshire. 3. Irish: Anglicized form of Gael. **Mac an Mhaoir** 'son of the steward, keeper'. The principal Irish family of this name held the hereditary post of Keeper of the Book of Armagh at *Ballymoyer* (Gael. *Baile an Mhaoir* 'town of the keeper').

Vars.: **McNeir, McNuir, McNayer, McNuyer, Menair,** WEIR.

McNairn Irish: Anglicized form of Gael. **Mac an Airchinn(igh)** 'son of the *erenagh*', a steward of church lands.

Vars.: **McNern, McNarin, McNaryn, (Mc)Ner(hen)ny, (Mc)Nirney; McInerney; McAnern(y); McEnerny, McEnarhin, McEnerin; McKinnerkin; McKinnertin; Minnerk; Kenerney, Kinerny, Connerny.**

McNakard *see* CAIRD

McNally Irish: Anglicized form of Gael. **Mac an Fhailghigh** 'son of the poor man'.

Vars.: **McAn(n)ally, McAnnulla; McInally; McEnally; Manally, Menally; Canally, Kanaly; Nally; McNarry.**

McNamara Irish: Anglicized form of Gael. **Mac Conmara**, patr. from a personal name composed of the elements *cú* hound + *muir* sea.

Vars.: **McNamarra, McNamarrow.**

McNamee Irish: Anglicized form of Gael. **Mac Conmidhe, Mac Conmeadha**, patr. from a personal name meaning 'Hound of Meath'.

Vars.: **McConmea, McConmay, McConvea, (Mc)Convey, (Mc)Convoy; McConomy, McConamy, Conmey, Conmee,** CONWAY; MEE, **Meath** (see also comment at MEAD).

McNaughton Scots: Anglicized form of Gael. **Mac Neachdainn**, patr. from the personal name *Neachdàn*, an old Celt. name of uncertain origin.

Vars.: **McNaughtan, McNaughten, McNauchton, McNauchtan, McNauton, McNachtan, McNaghten; McNaught, McNeight; McKnight, McNutt** (Ulster); **McNitt** (U.S.). See also MᶜCRACKEN and NAUGHTON.

McNay *see* MᶜNEE

McNeal *see* NEIL

McNecaird *see* CAIRD

McNee Scots: Anglicized form of Gael. **Mac Niadh**, patr. from the byname *Nia* 'Champion'.

Vars.: **McNea, McNia, McNey, McNeigh, McNay.**

McNeice Irish: Anglicized form of Gael. **Mac Naois**, a shortened form of *Mac Aonghuis* 'son of ANGUS'.

Vars.: **McNeese, McNess, McNisse, McN(e)ish, Mannish, Mannix, Minnish, Minch; McCreesh** (Ulster); **Neis(s)on, Neeson.**

McNeilly Scots (Galloway) and N Irish: Anglicized form of Gael. **Mac an Fhilidh** 'son of the poet'.

Vars.: **McN(e)illie, McNeely, McNelly, Meneely; Neilly, Neely** (N Ireland).

McNeiry *see* MᶜENERY

McNelis Scots: Anglicized form of Gael. **Mac Niallghuis**, patr. from the personal name *Niallghus*, composed of the elements *niall* champion + *gus* choice.
Vars.: **(Mc)Neelis**.

McNerlan *see* McERLEAN

McNern *see* McNAIRN

McNevin *see* NEVIN

McNichol *see* NICHOLAS

McNidder Scots: Anglicized form of Gael. **Mac an Fhigheadair** 'son of the weaver'.
Var.: **McNider**.

McNiel *see* NEIL

McNillie *see* McNEILLY

McNirney *see* McNAIM

McNish *see* McNEICE

McNitt *see* McNAUGHTON

McNiven *see* NEVIN

McNokerd *see* CAIRD

McNucator Scots: Anglicized form of Gael. **Mac an Fhucadair** 'son of the fuller'.
Vars.: **Nucator, McKnockatir**.

McNuir *see* McNAIR

McNulty Irish: Anglicized form of Gael. **Mac an Ultaigh** 'son of the Ulsterman'.
Vars.: **McAnulty, McKnulty, Nulty**.

McNutt *see* McNAUGHTON

McOmie *see* McCOMB

McOmish Scots: Anglicized form of Gael. **Mac Thómais**, patr. from a Gael. form of the given name THOMAS.
Var.: **McComish**.

McOnachie *see* McDONAGH

McPake *see* McPEAKE

McParlan *see* McFARLANE

McPeake Irish: Anglicized form of Gael. **Mac Péice**, patr. from the personal name *Péic*, of uncertain origin.
Var.: **McPake**.

McPerson *see* McPHERSON

McPhade *see* PATE

McPhaden *see* McFADDEN

McPhail *see* McFALL

McPharlain *see* McFARLANE

McPhedric *see* PATRICK

McPhee *see* DUFFY

McPherson Scots: Anglicized form of Gael. **Mac an Phearsain** 'son of the parson' (see PARSONS).
Var.: **McPerson**.

McPhetrish *see* McFETRIDGE

McPhilip *see* PHILIP

McPhun *see* McMUNN

McQuaid Irish: Anglicized form of Gael. **Mac Uaid**, patr. from a Gael. form of the given name *Wat* (see WALTER).
Vars.: **McQuade, McQuoid, Qua(i)d**.

McQuarry Scots: Anglicized form of Gael. **Mac Guaire**, patr. from an old Gael. personal name meaning 'Proud', 'Noble'.
Vars.: **McQuarrey, McQuar(r)ie, Macquarie, McWharrie**. See also QUARRY.

McQuaston *see* McCUTCHEON

McQueen Scots: Anglicized form of Gael. *Mac Shuibhne*, patr. from the personal name *Suibhne*; see SWEENEY. This name was also used as a Gael. form of the ON byname *Sveinn* (see SWAIN).

McQueenie *see* SWEENEY

McQuenzie *see* McKENZIE

McQuillan Irish: Anglicized form of Gael. **Mac Uighilín**, patr. from a Gael. form of OF *Huguelin*, a double dim. of the given name HUGH.

McQuilliam *see* McWILLIAM

McQuilly *see* QUILLY

McRaith *see* McCRAE

McRanald *see* RONALD

McRea *see* McCRAE

McReadie *see* McCREADY

McReavy *see* REAVEY

McReilly *see* REILLY

McRie *see* McCRAE

McRitchie *see* RICH

McRobb *see* ROBERT

McRobbie *see* ROBY

McRobin *see* ROBIN

McRoory *see* RORY

McRury *see* RORY

McSeveny *see* SWEENEY

McShane *see* SHANE

McShanley *see* SHANLEY

McSharry Irish: Anglicized form of Gael. **Mac Searraigh**, patr. from the byname *Searrach* 'Foal', and sometimes further Anglicized as FOLEY.
Var.: **McSherry**.

McShee *see* SHEEHY

McSorley *see* SORLEY

McSparran *see* SPORRAN

McStoker *see* STOKER

McSween *see* SWEENEY

McTaggart *see* TAGGART

McTague *see* MONTAGU

McTavish Scots: Anglicized form of Gael. **Mac Támhais**, patr. from a Gael. form of the given name THOMAS.

Vars.: **McCavish**, **McAvish**, **McCaw(i)s**, **McCause** (Gael. **Mac Thámhais**). See also McOMISH.

McTeague *see* MONTAGU

McTear *see* McINTYRE

McTerrelly Irish: Anglicized form of Gael. **Mac Toirdhealbhaigh**, patr. from the personal name *Toirdhealbhach*, composed of the elements *Tor* Thor + *dealbhach* like, in the shape of.

Vars.: **McTorrilogh**, **McTurlogh**, **McTirlay**, **Torley**, **Turley**; **McTerrens**, **Terrance**, TERRY. See also CURLEY.

McTier *see* McINTYRE

McTigue *see* MONTAGU

McTimney *see* TIMONY

McTirlay *see* McTERRELLY

McTorrilogh *see* McTERRELLY

McTurk Scots: Anglicized form of Gael. **Mac Tuirc**, patr. from the byname *Torc* 'Boar'.

McTurlogh *see* McTERRELLY

McUre *see* URE

McVail *see* McFALL

McVain *see* BEAN

McVarish *see* MORRIS

McVarnock *see* WARNOCK

McVarry *see* McAREE

McVay *see* McBETH

McVeagh *see* McBETH

McVerry *see* McAREE

McVicar *see* VICKAR

McVie *see* McBETH

McVitie Scots (Ayr, Galloway): of uncertain origin, possibly an Anglicized form of Gael. **Mac an Bhiadhtaigh** 'son of the victualler'.

Vars.: **McVittie**, **McVitty**.

McVittie *see* McVITIE

McVrehoune *see* BRAIN

McWalrick *see* McGOLDRICK

McWalter *see* WALTER

McWard *see* BARD

McWeeney *see* McKENZIE

McWhan *see* SWEENEY

McWhannell *see* McCONNELL

McWharrie *see* McQUARRY

McWhinney *see* McKENZIE

McWhirter Scots: Anglicized form of Gael. **Mac Chruiteir**, patr. from the occupational byname *Cruiteir* 'Harpist', 'Fiddler'; cf. CROWTHER.

Var.: **McChruiter**.

McWhiston *see* McCUTCHEON

McWiggan *see* McGUIGAN

McWilliam Scots: Anglicized form of Gael. **Mac Uilleim**, patr. from a Gael. form of the given name WILLIAM.

Vars.: **McWilliams**, **McQuilliam(s)**, **Quilliam**, **McKilliam(s)**, **McIliams**.

McWinney *see* McKENZIE

McWray *see* McCRAE

Meacham *see* MACHIN

Meacher *see* MAHER

Meacock *see* MAY

Mead English: **1.** topographic name for someone who lived near a patch of grassland used as pasture, from ME *mede*, OE *mæd* meadow. **2.** metonymic occupational name for a brewer or seller of mead (OE *meodu*), a type of alcoholic beverage made by fermenting honey.

Vars.: **Meade** (chiefly Ir.; see below). (Of 1 only): **Meads**, **Medd**, **Medding(s)**, MEADOW; **Medland** (W Country).

Dim. (of 1): Ger.: **Mattlin**.

Meadow English: topographic name for someone who lived by a meadow (cf. MEAD 1). The form *meadow* derives from the dative case, *mædwe*, of OE *mæd*.

Vars.: **Meadows**, **Medewe(s)**.

Meaken *see* MAKIN

Mealing English: common surname in the Bristol area, of unknown origin. It may be a var. of MELLING.

Mealley *see* MALLY

Meaney Irish: Anglicized form of Gael. **Ó Maonaigh** 'descendant of *Maonach*', a personal name derived from *maoineach* rich.

Vars.: **Meany**, **Meeny**, **O'Mo(o)ney**, **O'Moyney**, **O'Moeney**, **Mooney**, MONEY.

Mear English: **1.** topographic name for someone who lived by a pond, OE *mere*; cf. DELAMARE and MEER 1. **2.** topographic name for someone who lived near a boundary, OE *(ge)mære*.

Vars.: **Mear(e)s**, **Meers**.

Meara *see* O'MARA

Mearns Scots: **1.** habitation name from a place in the former county of Renfrews., so called from Gael. *maiorne* office or province of a MAIR. **2.** local name for a region more or less coinciding with the former county of

Kincardine, called *The Mearns* (apparently of the same origin as in 1).

Meath *see* McNamee

Meatyard English: of uncertain origin, perhaps from a minor place named with the OE elements *mǣd* meadow (see Mead 1) + *geard* enclosure. The name is documented in Dorset from the early 13th cent., and seems to have originated around the river Stour, south-west of Shaftesbury.

Vars.: **Met(e)yard**.

Meazzi *see* Bartholomew

Mecacci *see* Dominique

Mechel *see* Moult

Mechsner *see* Meisner

Mecklenburg German and Jewish (Ashkenazic): regional name for someone from the province of this name in N Germany, or habitation name from its capital, so called from MLG *mekele* big, great (cf. Meikle) + *borch* fortress, city (cf. Burke). The adj. retains the weak dat. ending used after the lost prepositional phrase *to der* 'at the'.

Vars.: Ger.: **Mäckelburg, Meckelburg, Mechlenburg**.

Medcalf *see* Metcalf

Medd *see* Mead

Medeiros Portuguese: habitation name from any of various places named with Port. *medeiro* place where shocks of maize are gathered (a deriv. of *meda* shock, stack, L *mēta* (pyramid-shaped) post).

Mederle *see* Mather

Medewe *see* Meadow

Medhurst *see* Midhurst

Mediavilla Spanish: topographic name for someone who lived in the centre of a settlement, from Sp. *media* (fem.) middle (L *media*) + *villa* village, settlement (see Ville).

Medici Italian: occupational name for a physician, It. *medico* (L *medicus*, from *medēre* to cure, heal).

Medina Spanish and Catalan: habitation name from any of the several places, as for example *Medina*-Sidonia in Cádiz and *Medina* del Campo in Valladolid, so called from Arabic *medina* city. The surname is also borne by Sefardic Jews, the reason(s) for its adoption being unclear.

Medler English (Norfolk): habitation name from *Madehurst* in Sussex, which gets its name from OE *mǣd* meadow (see Mead 1) + *hyrst* wooded hill (see Hurst). This placename appears in 12th-cent. records in the Normanized form *Medl(i)ers*. The surname is found in Norfolk as early as the 13th cent. in the form *de Medlers*; the landowning family who bore it were in vassalage to the Earl of Surrey, who had large estates in both Sussex and Norfolk.

Medley English: 1. habitation name, either a var. of Madeley, or from *Medley* on the Thames in Oxon., so called from OE *middel* middle + *ēg* island. 2. nickname for an aggressive person, from ME, OF *medlee* combat, conflict (LL *misculāta*).

Mednik Jewish (E Ashkenazic): 1. occupational name for a copper-worker, from Pol. *med* copper + *-nik* suffix of occupational names. 2. occupational name for a brewer or seller of mead, a cogn. of Eng. Mead 2.

Vars.: **Mednikor, Mednicki, Mednitzky, Mednitzki**.

Mędrzak Polish: nickname for a wise man, from Pol. *mędrzy* wise, clever, cogn. with Czech *moudrý* wise; cf. Pol. *mędrzec* wise man, philosopher.

Var.: **Mędrzycki** (also Jewish (E Ashkenazic)).

Medvedev Russian: patr. from the nickname *Medved* 'Bear' (lit. 'Honey-eater'), referring to a large, strong, or clumsy person.

Dim.: Ukr.: **Medvedko**.

Mee Irish: 1. Anglicized form of Gael. *Mac Conmidhe*; see McNamee. 2. Anglicized form of Gael. *Ó Miadhaigh* 'descendant of *Miadhach*', a byname meaning 'Honourable'.

Dim. (from 2): Meehan.

Patr.: **Meeson**.

Meecham *see* Machin

Meehan Irish: 1. Anglicized form of Gael. *Ó Miadhacháin*, from a dim. of the personal name *Miadhach*; see Mee 2. 2. Anglicized form of Gael. *Ó Maotháin* 'descendant of *Maothán*', a personal name representing a dim. of *maoth* moist, soft, tearful.

Vars.: **O'Meehan, Meegan, Meechan**.

Meek English and Scots: nickname for a self-effacing person or a gentle and compassionate one, from ME *meek* humble, submissive, merciful (ON *mjúkr*).

Var.: **Meeke**.

Patr.: **Meeks**.

Meekings *see* Makin

Meemken *see* Mayne

Meendsen *see* Maynard

Meeny *see* Meaney

Meer 1. Flemish, Dutch: topographic name for someone who lived by a pool or pond, MDu. *mere*; cf. Mear 1. 2. Jewish: of uncertain origin, possibly a var. of Mayer 3.

Vars. (of 1): **Van der Meer, Vermeer(en), Termeer, Meerman**.

Meerov *see* Mayer

Meers *see* Mear

Meersand Jewish (Ashkenazic): ornamental name composed of the Ger. elements *Meer* sea + *Sand* sand, chosen in reference to Gen. 32: 13, where Jacob is promised that his descendants shall be as numerous as the grains of sand on the shore.

Var.: **Mersand** (an Anglicized form).

Meert *see* Martin

Meesen *see* Bartholomew

Mefet *see* Moffatt

Megahey *see* CAUGHEY

Megalini *see* MICHAEL

Megarry *see* McAREE

Megaw Scots and Irish: Anglicized form of Gael. **Mag Ádhaimh**, patr. from a Gael. form of the given name ADAM.
Vars.: **Magaw, McGaw, McCaw**.

Megerle *see* MAIGRE

Meggat *see* MARGUERITE

Meggers *see* MAYER

Meggin *see* McGINN

Megía *see* MEJÍA

Meginniss *see* McGUINNESS

Mégnien *see* MAGNIEN

Megnot *see* MIGNOT

Megrath *see* McCRAE

Megson *see* MAGG

Mehaffy *see* DUFFY

Mehew *see* MAYHEW

Mehl *see* MELBER

Mehler *see* MAHLER

Mehnke *see* MAYNE

Mehrtens *see* MARTIN

Mei *see* MAY

Meier *see* MAYER

Meiffert German: from the Gmc personal name *Mag(in)frid*, composed of the elements *mag(in)* strength, might + *frid* peace.
Vars.: **Meifert; Meyf(f)arth, Maifahrt**.
Dims.: It.: **Manfredini, Manfrin(i), Manfriello, Manfrellotti, Manferlotti, Manfellotti, Manfelloto, Manfrotto**.
Augs.: It.: **Manfr(ed)oni**.
Patrs.: Low Ger.: **Meiferts, Meivers**.

Meignan *see* MAGNIEN

Meigret *see* MAIGRE

Meikle Scots: nickname for a big man, from Older Sc. *meikle, mekill* great, large (ON *mikel*, a cogn. of OE *micel* large).
Vars.: **Mickle; Muckle** (Northumb.).

Meiklejohn Scots: distinguishing name for the largest or eldest (see MEIKLE) of two or more bearers of the given name JOHN.
Vars.: **Micklejohn, Mucklejohn**.

Meillet *see* MILLET

Meincke *see* MAYNE

Meinders *see* MAYNARD

Meinzer *see* MAINZ

Meireles Portuguese: habitation name from any of several minor places so called. The placename is of unknown origin; an earlier form is *Maioreles*.

Meis *see* BARTHOLOMEW

Meisel *see* MAUS

Meisner German and Jewish (Ashkenazic): habitation name from the E German town of *Meissen*, earlier *Michsen*, apparently so called from a Slav. element *misna* marsh. The town was famous in the Middle Ages for the fine linen cloth produced there, and the Ger. surname may also be an occupational name for a manufacturer or seller of such wares.
Vars.: Ger.: **Meissner, Me(i)chsner, Me(i)xner**.

Meistering *see* MASTER

Meites *see* MAITES

Mejerson *see* MAYER

Mejía Spanish: religious byname, from a vernacular form of L, Gk *Messias* Messiah.
Vars.: **Mejías, Megía(s)**.

Mék *see* MIČKA

Melane *see* MULLEN

Melaver *see* MALAVE

Melber German: occupational name for a miller or flour merchant, from an agent deriv. of MHG *mel* (gen. *melwes*) flour (OHG *melo*, gen. *melawes*).
Vars.: **Melbert; Möhlber(t)** (Bavaria); **Mehl(mann)**.

Melbourne English: habitation name from any of various places. Melbourne in E Yorks. is recorded in Domesday Book as *Middelburne*, from OE *middel* middle + *burna* stream (see BOURNE); the first element was later replaced by the cogn. ON *meðal*. Melbourne in Derbys. has as its first element OE *mylen* MILL, and *Melbourn* in Cambs. probably OE *melde* milds, a type of plant.

Melchior German and Danish: from the male given name *Melchior* (apparently ultimately derived from Hebr. *melech* king + *or* light, splendour), which was ascribed by popular Christian tradition to one of the Magi. The surname is also borne by Ashkenazic Jews, in which case it represents an adoption of the Ger. surname.
Vars.: Ger.: **Melcher(t)**.
Dims.: It.: **Chiorrini** (Venetia). Ger. (of Slav. origin): **Malcharek**. Czech: **Melíšek**.
Patrs.: Dan.: **Melchiorsen**. Low Ger., Flem., Du.: **Melchers**. Pol.: **Majchrowicz, Majchrzak**.
Habitation name: Pol.: **Majchrowski**.

Meldon *see* MULDOON

Meldrum Scots: habitation name from a place in the former county of Aberdeens., first recorded in 1291 as *Melgedrom*, from the OGael. elements *mal(a)g* noble + *druim* ridge.

Mélendez *see* MENÉNDEZ

Melero Spanish: occupational name for a collector or seller of honey, Sp. *melero* (LL *mellārius*, an agent deriv. of *mel*, gen. *mellis*, honey).

Melgar Spanish: topographic name for someone who lived by a field of lucerne, Sp. *melgar* (a collective deriv. of *mielga* lucerne, LL *mēlica*, for class. L *Mēdica (herba)* plant from Media). There are several places in Spain named with this word; the surname may be a habitation name from any one of them.

Melhuish English: habitation name from a place in Devon, so called from OE *mǣl(e)* brightly coloured, flowery + *hīwisc* hide of land.
Vars.: **Mell(hu)ish**.

Melia *see* MALLY

Melican *see* MILLIGAN

Melior *see* MILLIER

Mellado Spanish: nickname for a gap-toothed person, from the Sp. adj. *mellado* (past. part. of *mellar* to chip, of uncertain, probably pre-Roman, origin).

Mellanby English: habitation name from places in Cumb. and N Yorks. called *Melmerby*. These get their names from the ON personal name *Melmor* (from Ir. *Mael-Muire* 'Devotee of (the Virgin) Mary') + ON *býr* farm, settlement, or, in the case of *Melmerby* near Ripon, from ON *malmr* sandy field + *býr*.

Mellard *see* MILLWARD

Meller *see* MILLER

Melling English (Lancs.): habitation name from places near Lancaster and near Liverpool. Both are probably so called from the OE tribal name *Me(a)llingas* 'people of *Mealla*'.

Mellis 1. English: habitation name from a place in Suffolk, so called from OE *mylenas*, plur. of *mylen* MILL. **2.** Scots and Irish: from the Gael. personal name *Maol Íosa* 'Devotee of Jesus'.
Vars.: **Melliss, Melles, Melis**. (Of 2 only): **Malise; Mellows** (see also MELLOR).

Mello *see* JAMES

Mellon Irish: Anglicized form of Gael. **Ó Mealláin** 'descendant of *Meallán*', a personal name representing a dim. of *meall* pleasant.
Vars.: **Mellan; Mallen** (see also MALIN).

Mellor English: habitation name from places in Lancs., W Yorks., and Derbys., earlier recorded as *Melver*, and named from ancient Brit. words that are ancestors of W *moel* bare + *bre* hill.
Vars.: **Mellors; Mellows** (see also MELLIS).

Melnikov Russian and Jewish (E Ashkenazic): patr. from the occupational term *melnik* miller (from *melit* to grind).
Vars.: Jewish: **Melni(c)k**.

Melpuss *see* MALPAS

Melrose Scots: habitation name from a place near Galashiels in the Scots Borders, so called from ancient Brit. words that were ancestors of W *moel* bare, barren +

rhos moor, heath. The Bret. and Ir. cogns. of the second element mean 'hillock', 'promontory', and this may also have been the sense here.

Melton N English: habitation name from any of various places, for example in Leics., Lincs., Norfolk, and E and W Yorks., all of which have the same origin as MIDDLETON, with OE *middel* replaced by ON *meðal* under Scandinavian influence.

Melville 1. Scots (Norman): habitation name from one of the various places in Normandy called *Malleville*, from L *mala* (fem.) bad (see MALO) + *ville* settlement (see VILLE). **2.** Irish: Anglicized form of Gael. **Ó Maoil Mhichíl** 'son of the devotee of (St) MICHAEL'.
Vars.: **Melvil**. (Of 1 only): **Melvin**. (Of 2 only): **O'Mulmichell, O'Mulveill, (O')Mulvihil(l)**.

Melvin 1. Scots: var. of MELVILLE 1. **2.** Scots: Anglicized form of Gael. *Mac Gille Bheathain*; see MCILWAINE. **3.** Irish: Anglicized form of Gael. **Ó Maoil Mhín** 'descendant of the devotee of (St) *Mín*', a personal name derived from *mín* soft, gentle.
Vars. (of 3): **O'Mullwine, Mul(l)veen, Mulvin, Molvin**.

Memoli *see* WILLIAM

Memory *see* MOWBRAY

Mena Spanish: habitation name from a place in the province of Burgos, so called from OSp. *mena* battlement (L *minae* (pl.)). The name may also have been used in a transferred sense for anyone who lived on a pinnacle or high spot. It is also borne by Jews, but the reasons for its adoption are not clear.

Menair *see* MCNAIR

Menally *see* MCNALLY

Menasherov *see* MANSER

Menazzi *see* DOMINIQUE

Menchaca Basque: habitation name from a minor place, so called from a personal name (of uncertain form and meaning) + the local suffix *-aca*.

Mencken *see* MAYNE

Mende *see* ENDE

Mendel Jewish (Ashkenazic): from the Yid. given name *Mendl*, a dim. of *Man* (see MANN 3).
Patrs.: **Mendel(s)so(h)n, Mendelzon; Mendelovi(t)ch, Mendelovic, Mendelovicz, Mendelowicz, Mendelovics, Mendelowisz, Mendelovitz, Mendelowitz, Mendelovits, Mendlovic, Mendelevitch, Mend(e)levitz, Mend(e)lewicz, Mendelevsky, Mendlevich** (E Ashkenazic), **Mendelovici** (among Rumanian Jews).

Mendham English: habitation name from a place in Suffolk, so called from the OE personal name *Mynda* (a byform of *Munda*, a short form of the various cpd names containing the element *mund* protection) + OE *hām* homestead.

Mendieta Basque: habitation name from places in the provinces of Álava and Biscay, so called from *mendi* mountain + the suffix of plurality *-eta*.

Mendizabal Basque: habitation name from a placename composed of the elements *mendi* mountain + *zabal* wide, broad.

Mendoza Spanish (of Basque origin): habitation name from a place in the province of Alava, so called from Basque *mendi* mountain + *otz* cold + the def. art. *-a*.

Meneely *see* McNeilly

Menel *see* Meynell

Menéndez Spanish: patr. from the medieval given name *Menendo*, from the Visigothic personal name *Hermenegild*, composed of the elements *ermen, irmen* whole, entire + *gild* tribute. The personal name was borne by a 6th-cent. member of the Visigothic royal house, who was converted from Arianism to the Catholic faith and became an enormously popular saint, as a result of which the given name was very common in Spain in the Middle Ages.

Vars.: **Mélendez**, **Méndez**.

Meneses Spanish and Portuguese: habitation name from any of several places, notably in the province of Palencia, Spain, originally established by settlers from Mena.

Mengardon *see* Ermgard

Menger German: occupational name for a retail trader in unspecified goods, MHG *mengære, mangære* (from LL *mangō* salesman, with the addition of the Gmc agent suffix).

Vars.: **Manger**; **Menge(l)**, **Meng(e)le(r)**.
Patr.: Low Ger.: **Mangers**.

Menshikov Russian: patr. from the distinguishing nickname *Menshik* (from *menshoi* smaller, younger), often used to distinguish between two bearers of the same given name. Compare Bolshakov.

Vars.: **Mensh(chik)ov**.

Menteith *see* Monteith

Mentz *see* Maynard

Mentzelmann *see* Hermann

Menuhin Jewish (E Ashkenazic): metr. from the Yid. female given name *Menukhe* (from Hebrew *menucha* tranquillity, stillness) + the Slav. suffix *-in*.

Vars.: **M(e)nuchin**, **M(e)nukhin**.
Dims.: **Mnus(h)kin**.

Menzies Scots (Norman): var. of Manners, in which the *z* originally represented ME ȝ, a sound similar to mod. Eng. *y* /j/. The surname is still pronounced /ˈmɪŋɡɪz/ in Scotland. It has also been Gaelicized **Mèinn**, from which come the Eng. forms **Mein** and **Mien**. The patr. forms **McMenzies**, **McMon(n)ies**, **McMin(n)**, and **McMyn** represent adapations of the name to the predominant pattern of Highland surnames.

Mercadier Provençal: occupational name for a tradesman, OProv. *mercadier* (LL *mercātārius*, a agent deriv. of *mercātus* trade; cf. Mercado 1).

Vars.: **Merchadier**, **Mercadié**.

Mercado 1. Spanish: topographic name for someone who lived by a market place, Sp. *mercado* (L *mercātus* trade, commerce, from *mercāri* to trade, deal, aderiv. of *merx* merchandise; cf. Mercadier and Marchant). There are a number of minor places in Spain named with this word, and the surname may also be a habitation name from any of these. 2. Jewish (Sefardic): either of the same origin as 1, or else possibly from the Sefardic male given name *Merkado* 'Bought' (from the past part. of Judezmo *merkar* to buy). This was a name given to or assumed by someone who had escaped some great danger or recovered from a life-threatening illness; he was 'bought' or taken under the protection of a relative or friend, and had his name changed to *Merkado* in order to confuse the Angel of Death, who, it was believed, would make further attempts to take the life of which he had been baulked (cf. *Alt* at Old).

Var. (of 2): **Merkado**.

Mercanton *see* Marchant

Mercer English: occupational name for a trader, from OF *mercier* (LL *mercārius*, an agent deriv. of *merx*, gen. *mercis*, merchandise; cf. Marchant, Mercado). The term was applied in ME particularly to one who dealt in textile fabrics, especially the more costly and luxurious fabrics such as silks, satin, and velvet.

Vars.: **Mercier**; **Merchier** (from the Norman form); Marker.
Dims.: Fr.: **Merceron**, **Marceron**, **Mercereau**, **Marcereau**, **Marcireau**, **Mercerot**.

Merckx *see* Mark

Meredith Welsh: from the personal name *Meredydd* or, more commonly, *Maredudd*. The OW form is *Morgetiud*, of which the first element may mean 'pomp, splendour' and the second is *udd* lord. See also Beddow.

Vars.: **Merredy**, **Merriday**, **Merridew**.

Mergin *see* Bergin

Mériel *see* Henry

Mérimée French: of uncertain origin. Tradition in the family of the novelist Prosper Mérimée (1803–70) derived the name from an Eng. nickname *Merrymaid*, but this is probably merely fanciful.

Merino Spanish: occupational or status name from Sp. *merino*, the title of a royal or seigneurial functionary who had wide legal and military jurisdiction over a district. The word is from LL *māiorīnus*, a deriv. of *māior* (cf. Mayer and Mayoral).

Meriton English: habitation name of uncertain origin, probably from places in Shrops. and Co. Durham called *Merrington*. Merrington in Shrops. is from OE *myrge* pleasant (see Merry) + *dūn* hill (see Down 1). *Kirk Merrington* in Co. Durham is from *Mǣringtūn*, 'settlement (OE *tūn*) associated with *Mǣra*', a personal name meaning 'Famous'.

Vars.: **Merrington**, **Mirrington**, **Marrington**, **Morrington**; **Mannington**.

Merker *see* Marker

Merle French: nickname from OF *merle* blackbird (L *merula*). This bird seems in the Middle Ages to have been regarded at times as a foolish creature like the magpie, and at other times as a cunning rogue like the jackdaw. In Italy today it is generally thought of as shrewd, but in

Milan it is a byword for simplicity, and in Sicily it is noted for its timorousness. The surname could have been acquired in any of these senses. It may also in part have been a metonymic occupational name for a catcher of blackbirds for the cooking pot.

Vars.: **Lemerle**, **Lemesle** (nicknames, with fused def. art. *le*); **Merlier** (occupational).

Dims.: Fr.: **Merlet**, **Merlot**, **Merloz**, **Merleau**. It.: **Merletti**, **Merletto**, **Merlini**, **Merlino**, **Merlotti**.

Augs.: Fr.: **Merlat**. It.: **Merloni**.

Pejs.: Fr.: **Merlaud**, **Merlault**.

Patr.: Fr.: **Aumerle** (found chiefly in the *département* of Indre).

Merlin 1. French: from the W personal name *Myrddin*, obtained by back-formation from the placename *Caerfyrddin* (i.e. *Carmarthen*), wrongly analysed as a cpd of W *caer* fort + a personal name *Myrddin*. In fact it represents the Romano-Celtic placename *Moridunum* 'Sea Fort'. *Merlinus* was a Latinized form of *Myrddin* devised by Geoffrey of Monmouth and popularized in the Arthurian romances. **2.** Jewish: of unknown origin.

Merrick 1. English: from an OF personal name introduced to Britain by the Normans, composed of the Gmc elements *meri, mari* fame + *rīc* power. **2.** Scots: habitation name from a place near Minigaff in Dumfries and Galloway, so called from Gael. *meurach* branch or fork of a road or river. **3.** Welsh: from the W given name *Meuric*, a form of *Maurice* (see MORRIS).

Var. (of 3): **Meyrick**.

Merrifield English: habitation name from any of various places, such as *Merryfield* in Devon and Cornwall or *Mirfield* in W Yorks., all named with the OE elements *myrige* pleasant (see MERRY) + *feld* pasture, open country (see FIELD).

Var.: **Mirfield**.

Merrill English: **1.** from the female personal name *Muriel*, composed of the Celt. elements *muir* sea + *gael* bright. The given name was particularly common during the Middle Ages in E Anglia, where it was introduced by Bret. settlers accompanying and following William the Conqueror; it was also frequent in N England, where it was brought by Norsemen from Ireland, and in W England, due to Welsh influence. **2.** habitation name from any of various minor places named with the OE elements *myrige* pleasant (see MERRY) + *hyll* HILL.

Vars.: **Merril**, **Merrel**, **Merrall**, **Murril**, **Murrell**.

Metrs. (from 1): **Merrills**, **Merrells**, **Merralls**, **Murrells**, **Mirralls**.

Merriot English: **1.** habitation name from a place in Somerset, so called from OE *(ge)mǣre* boundary or *miere* mare + *geat* gate. **2.** var. of MARRIOTT or MARRYAT, as a result of hypercorrection.

Vars.: **Merrett** (W Country); **Merryett**, **Mer(r)it(t)**.

Merry English: nickname for someone of blithe or cheerful disposition, from ME *merry* lively, happy (OE *myr(i)ge* pleasant, agreeable).

Vars.: **Merriman**, **Merriment**.

Merryweather English: nickname for someone of a sunny disposition, from ME MERRY + *wether* weather (OE *weder*).

Vars.: **Merrywether**, **Merriweather**, **Mereweather**.

Mersand *see* MEERSAND

Mersh *see* MARSH

Merson *see* MAYER

Merta *see* MARTHE

Mertel *see* MARTIN

Merton English: habitation name from *Merton* in S London, Devon, Norfolk, and Oxon.; *Marton* in Ches., Cleveland, Humberside, Lincs., Shrops., N Yorks., and Warwicks.; or *Martin* in Hants and Lincs. All of them derive their names from OE *mere* lake, pool (see MEAR) + *tūn* enclosure, settlement.

Merwe, van der Dutch: local name from the river *Merwede* in the province of S Holland.

Mesa Spanish: topographic name for someone who lived on a plateau, OSp. *mesa* (L *mensa* table), or habitation name from any of the several places named with this term, for example in the provinces of Cadiz, Jaén, and Toledo.

Mesclou *see* MARSHALL

Mesme *see* MAXIME

Mesnard *see* MAYNARD

Mesner German: occupational name for a sexton, churchwarden, or verger, S Ger. and Austrian dial. *Mesner* (MHG *mesnære*, OHG *mesinâri*, from LL *ma(n)siōnārius*, a deriv. of *mansio*, gen. *mansiōnis*, house (of God), church).

Vars.: **Messner** (a result of association with *Messe* mass; this form is also borne by Ashkenazic Jews, as a translation of Yid. or Hebr. terms for the sexton of a synagogue); **Mes(s)mer** (Swabia, Switzerland; by analogy with surnames in *-mer* from place names in *-heim* homestead); **Mössner**, **Mössmer** (Bavaria).

Mesquita Portuguese: habitation name from any of various places named during the Moorish occupation with the Port. term *mesquita* mosque (Arabic *másǧid*, from *sáǧad* to prostrate oneself).

Messeguer Catalan: occupational name for a harvester or someone who kept watch over harvested crops, OCat. *messeguer* (LL *messicārius*, agent deriv. of *messis* harvest; cf. MESSER 3).

Messenger English: occupational name, from ME, OF *messag(i)er* carrier of messages (an agent deriv. of *message*, LL *missāticum*, from *missus* sent). For the inserted nasal, cf. PASSENGER.

Vars.: MESSINGER, **Message**.

Messer 1. German and Jewish (Ashkenazic): metonymic occupational name for a cutler, from Ger. *Messer* knife or its Yid. cogn. *meser* (MHG *mezzer*, a back-formation from *mezzeres* (taken as a gen. case), OHG *mezzirahs*, *mezzisahs*, a cpd of *maz* food, meat + *sahs* knife, sword, cogn. with OE *meteseax*). **2.** German: occupational name for an official in charge of measuring the dues paid in kind by tenants, an agent deriv. of MHG *mezzen* to measure (OHG *mezzan*, from *mez* measure, portion). See also MAETERLINCK. **3.** Scots: occupational name for someone who kept watch over harvested crops, Older Sc. *mess(i)er*, from OF *messier* harvest master (LL *messicārius*; cf. MESSEGUER).

Vars. (of 1): Ger.: **Messerer**; **Messerschmidt**, **Messerschmitt** ('knife smith'; cf. NAYSMITH). Jewish: **Meser**, **Mes(s)erman**. See also METZ.

Dim. (of 1): Ger.: **Messerle**.

Messina Italian: habitation name from the ancient Sicilian city of this name. It was named *Messana* in the 5th cent. BC when it was captured by Anaxilaos of Rhegium; previously it had been known as *Zancle*.

Vars.: **Messana**; **Messinese**; **Messineo**, **Messaneo** (S Calabria).

Dims.: **Messinetti**, **Messanelli**.

Messinger 1. English: var. of MESSENGER. **2.** German and Jewish (Ashkenazic): occupational name for a worker in brass, from an agent deriv. of Ger. *Messing* brass (MHG *messinc*, from Gk *Mossynoikos (khalkos)* Mossynoecan bronze, named after the people of NE Asia Minor who first produced the alloy).

Var. (of 2): **Messing**.

Messiter *see* MASHETER

Mestadié *see* MÉTAYER

Meste *see* METZ

Mestivier *see* MÉTIVIER

Mestrel *see* MASTER

Métayer French: status name for a tenant farmer who held land on condition of sharing its produce equally with the landlord, OF *meitier* (an agent deriv. of *meitié* half, LL *mediētas*, from *medius* middle).

Vars.: **Métayé**, **Métoyer**, **Métadier**; **Mestayé**, **Mestadier**, **Mestadié** (hypercorrected forms); **Métais**, **Lemétais**.

Metcalf English (Yorks.): of uncertain origin, probably from ME **metecalf* 'meat calf', i.e. a calf being fattened up to be slaughtered for meat at the end of the summer (from OE *mete* food, meat + *c(e)alf* calf). It is thus either an occupational name for a herdsman or slaughterer, or a nickname for a sleek and plump individual, from the same word in a transferred sense. The variants in *med-* appear early, and suggest that the first element was associated by folk etymology with ME *mead* meadow, pasture.

Vars.: **Metcalfe**, **Medcalf(e)**, **Mitcalfe**.

Meteyard *see* MEATYARD

Methven Scots: habitation name from a place near Perth, recorded in 1150 in the form *Matefen*, at the end of the same cent. as *Mafen*, and at the beginning of the 13th cent. as *Methfen*. The placename is probably derived from Brit. cogns. of W *medd* mead + *maen* (mutated to *faen*) stone, but its significance is not clear.

Var.: **Methuen**.

Métivier French: occupational name for a harvester, or rather a feudal tenant who owed a particular duty of service at the time of the harvest, from an agent deriv. of OF *métive* harvest (L *messis aestiva* summer harvest).

Var.: **Mestivier**.

Métreau *see* MASTER

Metschke *see* MATTHEW

Mett *see* MOULT

Metternich German: habitation name from either of two places in the Rhineland. The Austrian statesman and diplomatist Prince Klemens von Metternich (1773–1859) was born in Coblenz into a Rhenish noble family. One ancestor had been elector and archbishop of Trier, and his father was hereditary chamberlain to the archbishop of Mainz and Austrian ambassador to various Rhenish courts.

Metz 1. Jewish (Ashkenazic): habitation name from *Metz* in Lorraine. **2.** Low German: occupational name for a cutler, from a regional var. of MESSER 1.

Vars. (of 1): **Metzer**. (Of 2): **Meste**; **Mestemacher**; **Mestwerdt**, **Mestwarb** (see WRIGHT).

Metzger German and Jewish (Ashkenazic): occupational name for a butcher, Ger. *Metzger* (MHG *metziger, metzjer*, an agent deriv. of *metzjen* to slaughter, itself a back-formation from the agent noun *metzeller*, from L *macellārius* slaughterer).

Vars.: **Mezger**. Ger. only: **Mezler**.

Meugnot *see* MIGNOT

Meulders *see* MILLER

Meurer *see* MAURER

Meusel *see* MAUS

Meuwissen *see* BARTHOLOMEW

Mew *see* MAW

Mewhinney *see* MCKENZIE

Mexner *see* MEISNER

Mey *see* MAY

Meyer *see* MAYER

Meyfarth *see* MEIFFERT

Meyler *see* MAILER

Meynard *see* MAYNARD

Meynell English: **1.** topographic name for someone who lived not in the main village, but in an isolated dwelling in the country, ME *meinil, mesnil*, OF *mesnil* (LL *mansiōnillum*, a dim. of *mansio* house, dwelling). There are several minor places in France named with this word and the surname may also be a habitation name from any of these. In England the vocab. word was used in particular to denote a fortified manor occupied by a landlord; the surname may also have been an occupational name for someone who was employed at such a manor. **2.** from a Norman female personal name composed of the Gmc elements *magin* strength, might + *hild* battle.

Vars.: **Maynell**, **Maynall**, **Mennell**, **Menel**; **Mannell** (Devon).

Meynen *see* MAYNE

Meyrick *see* MERRICK

Meystre *see* MASTER

Mezger *see* METZGER

Miall *see* MYHILL

Miatt *see* MYATT

Miazzi *see* BARTHOLOMEW

Michael 1. English: from the ME given name *Michael* (learned form; cf. MITCHELL). This is ultimately from Hebr. *Micha-el* 'Who is like God?', a name borne by various minor biblical characters as well as by an archangel, the protector of Israel (Dan. 10: 13, 12: 1; Rev. 12: 7). In Christian tradition, Michael was regarded as the warrior archangel, conqueror of Satan, and the given name was correspondingly popular throughout Europe, especially in knightly and military families. See also MYHILL. 2. Jewish: from a Jewish given name such as Hebr. *Michael* or Yid. *Mikhl*. The Hebr. adjectival forms **Michaeli** and **Michaely** are also in use as Jewish surnames.

Dims.: Eng.: MYATT. Sc.: MICHIE. Fr.: **Mich(el)et, Miquelet, Miché, Michey, Michez, Miguet; Mich(el)in, Michenet, Michenot; Mich(el)ot, Migot; Mich(el)on, Chon(n)eau(x), Chonet, Chonez, Chonillon, Mic(h)ou(d), Micoux, Michal(l)on, Miquelon.** It.: **Mich(i)eletti, Mich(i)eletto, Micaletti, Micaletto, Migaleddu; Michelini, Michelino, Mich(i)elin, Micalini, Migalini, Megalini; Michelutti, Micheluz(zi), Michelucci, Michelotti, Michelotto, Michelozzi, Michelozzo, Micalizzi, Micalizio, Migalizzi, Megalizzi; Michi, Mico, Michetti, Micoli.** Ger. (of Slav. origin): **Mikisch; Mich(a)lik, Michling, Michalke, Michelk, Michnik; Misch(e), Mischke, Mischok, Mischak, Mischan(ek), Mischnik.** Czech: **Michálek,** MIČKA. Pol.: **Michalczyk, Michalik.** Ukr.: **Mikhalchenko, Mishchenko, Mishurenko.** Beloruss.: **Mikhalenya.** Hung.: **Mikó.**

Augs.: It.: **Micheloni, Michelone, Mic(i)elon, C(h)elon(i).** Czech: **Michalec.**

Pejs.: Fr.: **Michelaud, Michallaud, Michaut, Michaux; Miquelard, Michard.** It.: **Michelacci, Michelazzi, Mich(i)elazzo, Michelassi, Michelato; Chelazzi.**

Patrs.: Eng.: **Michaels, Miggles; Michaelson.** Sc.: McMICHAEL. It.: **Michaelis, De Micheli(s).** Port.: **Migueis.** Rum.: **Mihăilescu, Mihaileanu, Mihaileano.** Ger.: **Michel(i)s, Michler.** Low Ger.: **Miche(e)lsen.** Flem., Du.: **Mich(i)els.** Dan., Norw.: **Mich(a)elsen, Mikkelsen.** Swed.: **Mickelsson.** Russ.: **Mikhailov, Mikhailin, Mikhantyev, Mikhailychev, Mikhailichev.** Ukr.: **Mikailiv.** Beloruss.: **Mikalaevich.** Pol.: **Michałowicz, Michalewicz, Mich(n)iewicz; Michalak.** Croatian: **Mihajlović, Mihailović.** Bulg.: **Mikhailov.** Jewish: **Michael(i)s, Michaelson; Michaelov(itch); Michaelovici** (Rumanian spelling), **Michaelowici; Michels, Michils, Michlis, Michelson** (Ashkenazic, from Yid. *Mikhl*); **Michlin, Michelevitz** (E Ashkenazic). Gk: **Michaelides.** Armenian: **Mikaelian.** Georgian: **Mikladze.**

Patrs. (from dims.): Russ.: **Mikhalkov,** MISHKIN, **Mishukov, Mishutushkin, Mishechkin, Mishenkin, Mishatkin, Mishenev, Mishunov, Mikhnov, Mikhnev, Mishanin, Mishenin, Mishutin, Mishurov, Mishurin, Mishulin.** Ukr.: **Mitsnovich, Mikhalchat.** Beloruss.: **Mikhnevich.** Croatian: **Mijalković, Mij(at)ović, Mijušković; Mikić, Mihić, Mić(ov)ić, Mićanović.** Pol.: **Michałkiewicz; Miśkiewicz, Miszkiewicz; Miszczak; Misiak.** Ger. (of Slav. origin): **Misch(n)er.** Finn.: **Mikkonen.** Lithuanian: **Mishkunas.** Armenian: **Mikoyan.**

Habitation names: Pol.: **Michalewski, Michałowsky.** Jewish: **Michaelowsky.**

Michell *see* MITCHELL

Michelmore *see* MITCHELMORE

Michie Scots (Aberdeen): from the old Sc. given name *Michie*, a dim. of MICHAEL.
Patrs.: **McMichie, Mich(i)eson, Mitchi(e)son.**

Michurin *see* DMITRIEV

Mička Czech: from a given name, a pet form of *Mikuláš* (see NICHOLAS) or of *Michal* (see MICHAEL).
Vars.: **Micka, Mék, Mičan.**

Mickeleit *see* NICHOLAS

Mickle *see* MEIKLE

Micklebride *see* KILBRIDE

Micklejohn *see* MEIKLEJOHN

Micklethwaite English (Yorks.); habitation name from one of several places in W Yorks. named with the ON elements *mekil* great, big (see MEIKLE) + *þveit* meadow (see THWAITE).

Micklewright English (now chiefly W Midlands): distinguishing nickname from Northern ME *mekill* great, big (see MEIKLE) + *wriht* WRIGHT.

Micone *see* DOMINIQUE

Middleditch English: habitation name from a minor place named with the OE elements *midel* middle + *dic* ditch, dyke (see DITCH). This survives as a Cheshire field-name, which may be the source of the surname.

Middlehurst English (Lancs.): probably a habitation name from *Middleforth* in Lancs.; the two placename elements *-hurst* and *-forth* are sometimes confused in surnames in N England.

Middlemass Scots: regional name from a district near Kelso in the Borders region, so called from Northern ME *midelmast* middlemost.
Vars.: **Middlemas, Middlemiss, Middlemist, Middlemost.**

Middler Scots: habitation name from *Midlar* near Aberdeen, which is of unknown derivation. The placename is apparently first recorded in 1513, as *Maidlare*.

Middleton English and Scots: habitation name from any of the places so called. In over thirty instances from many different areas, the name is from OE *midel* middle + *tūn* enclosure, settlement. However, *Middleton* on the Hill near Leominster in Herefords. appears in Domesday Book as *Miceltune*, the first element clearly being OE *micel* large, great (cf. MEIKLE). *Middleton* Baggot and *Middleton* Priors in Shrops. have early spellings that suggest *gemȳðhyll* (from *gemȳð* confluence + *hyll* hill) + *tūn* as its origin.
Var.: **Myddleton.**

Midgley English: habitation name from any of several places in W Yorks., or minor places in Ches., so called from OE *micg(e)* midge + *lēah* wood, clearing.

Midhurst English: habitation name from a place in Sussex, so called from OE *mid* amongst + the pl. of *hyrst* wooded hill (see HURST).
Var.: **Medhurst.**

Mielczarek Polish: **1.** occupational name for a maltster, dim. of *mielczarz*, dial. var. of Pol. *mielcarz*. **2.** nickname for a dusty person, in particular a miller, from Pol. *miałki* dusty (from *miał* dust, akin to *mielenie* grinding, and ultimately to Eng. MILL).

Vars.: **Milczarek**, **Mi(e)lczarski**.

Miell *see* MYHILL

Mierosławski Polish: from a Slav. personal name composed of the elements *mer* great, famous (ultimately cogn. with the Gmc element *meri, mari* famous, but early confused with Slav. *mir* peace) + *slav* fame, glory, with the addition of the surname suffix *-ski* (see BARANOWSKI).

Miers *see* MAYER

Mierzejewski Polish: habitation name from a place called *Mirzejewo* (from Pol. *mierzeja* spit, sandbar + *-ew* possessive suffix) with the addition of *-ski*, suffix of local surnames (see BARANOWSKI).

Miettinen *see* CLEMENT

Migaleddu *see* MICHAEL

Mighell *see* MYHILL

Mignan *see* MAGNIEN

Mignot French: nickname for an amiable or good-looking person, from OF *mignot* pretty, nice (of uncertain origin).

Vars.: **Me(u)gnot**, **Migne**, **Mignon**.

Dims.: **Mignoton**, **Mignonneau**.

Mihaileano *see* MICHAEL

Mijalković *see* MICHAEL

Mika *see* NICHOLAS

Mikaelian *see* MICHAEL

Mikeshin *see* NIKITIN

Mikkola Finnish: name borne by a member of a household headed by someone called *Mikko*, Finn. pet form of MICHAEL. The surname is formed from the pet name + the local suffix *-la*.

Míl Czech: **1.** affectionate nickname for an attractive person, from Czech *milý* dear, beloved. **2.** from a short form of any of the Slav. cpd names containing the element *mil* mercy (cf. MILES 1), as for example *Miloslav* and *Bohumil*.

Var. (of 1): **Milec**.

Dim. (of 1): Czech: **Miláček** (also a vocab. word meaning 'darling', which in some cases may be the source of the surname).

Patrs. (from cogns. of 2): Croatian: **Mil(ošev)ić**, **Milo(je)vić**, **Miljević**, **Milačić**, **Milćević**; **Milosavljević**, **Milisavljević**.

Patrs. (from dims. cogn. with 2): Croatian: **Milekić**, **Milojković**, **Miljković**.

Milà Catalan: nickname for a rapacious person, from Cat. *milà* kite (LL *mīlvānus*, a deriv. of class. L *mīlvus*).

Milano Italian (partly Jewish): habitation name for someone who came from Milan, It. *Milano* (from L *Mediolān(i)um*, composed of apparently Celt. elements meaning 'middle' + 'plain').

Vars.: It.: **Milan(i)**, **Milanese**, **Milanesi**.

Milborne English: habitation name from places in Dorset and Somerset, so called from OE *mylen* MILL + *burna* stream (see BOURNE). See also MELBOURNE, MILBOURNE, and MILBURN.

Milbourne English: habitation name from places in Northumb. and Wilts., so called from OE *mylen* MILL + *burna* stream (see BOURNE). See also MELBOURNE, MILBORNE, and MILBURN.

Milburn English (Northumb. and Cumb.): habitation name from a place in Cumb., so called from OE *mylen* MILL + *burna* stream (see BOURNE). See also MILBO(U)RNE and MELBOURNE.

Milczarek *see* MIELCZAREK

Mildmay English: nickname for an innocuous individual, from ME *mild(e)* tame, gentle (OE *milde*) + *may* maiden (see MAY 3).

Miles **1.** English (Norman): via OF from the Gmc personal name *Milo*, of uncertain etymology, but perhaps ultimately akin to the Slav. element *mil-* mercy (cf. MÍL 2). The name was introduced into England by the Normans in the form *Miles* (oblique case *Milon*). In Eng. documents of the Middle Ages the name normally appears in the Latinized form *Milo* (gen. *Milōnis*), but the normal ME form was *Mile*, so the final *-s* must usually represent the possessive ending, i.e. 'son or servant of Mile'. **2.** English: patr. from an OF contracted form of MICHAEL (cf. MYHILL). **3.** English: occupational name for a servant or retainer, from L *miles* soldier, sometimes used as a technical term in this sense in medieval documents. **4.** Jewish: of unknown origin.

Var. (of 1–3): **Myles**.

Dims. (of 1): Fr.: **MILLET**, **Mil(l)ot**.

Patrs. (from 1): Eng.: **Mil(e)son**, **Milsom**.

Milford English: habitation name from any of numerous places, for example in Derbys., Devon, Hants, Norfolk, Staffs., and Surrey, so called from OE *mylen* MILL + *ford* FORD.

Milgrim Jewish (Ashkenazic): ornamental name from Yid. *milgrim, milgroym* pomegranate (ultimately from LL *mille granāta* thousand seeds).

Vars.: **Milgro(u)m**, **Milgroom**, **Milgr(a)um**, **Mil(li)gram**.

Milhaud French (partly Jewish): habitation name from *Millau* in Aveyron, so called from the L personal name *Aemilius* (see ÉMILIEN) + the local suffix *-ācum*.

Vars.: Fr.: **Mil(l)au**, **Milhavés**, **Millavois**.

Milian *see* ÉMILIEN

Mill English and Scots: topographic name for someone who lived near a mill, ME *mille, milne*, OE *mylen(e)* (from L *molīna*, a deriv. of *molere* to grind). It was usually in effect an occupational name for a worker at a mill and indeed for the miller himself (cf. MILLER and MILLWARD). The mill, whether powered by water, wind, or (occasionally) animals, was an important centre in every medieval settlement; it was normally operated by an agent of the local landowner, and individual peasants were compelled to come to him to have their corn ground into flour, a proportion of the ground corn being kept by the miller by way of payment.

Vars.: **Mille**, **Miln(e)**; **Mills** (the commonest form of this name), **Milles**, **Millis**, **Miln(e)s**, **Mil(l)man**; MULLEN.

Dims.: Fr.: **Moulinet**, **Moulinot**, **Moulineau**. It.: **Molinelli**, **Molinetti**. See also MOLYNEUX.

Pej.: It.: **Mullinacci**.

Cpds: Jewish: **Muehlbauer**, **Milbauer** ('mill builder', occupational name roughly equivalent to Eng. WRIGHT); **Milberg** ('mill hill', probably local); **Milfirer** ('mill director', occupational); **Muehlrad**, **Mil(e)rad** ('mill wheel', ornamental-occupational); MILLSTEIN.

Millen see MULLEN

Miller English: occupational name for a miller. The word represents the Northern ME term, an agent deriv. of *mille*, *milne* MILL, reinforced by the cogn. ON *mylnari*; in S, W, and Midland England the equivalent MILLWARD was used.

Vars.: **Millar** (Scot.); **Milner** (commonest in Yorks., retaining the -n- of the ME and OE word); **Meller**.

Dims.: Fr.: **Mugn(er)ot**, **Mugniot**. It.: **Molinaroli**, **Molinarolo**, **Munaretti**, **Munaretto**, **Munarin(i)**, **Munerotto**, **Mugnaini**. Pol.: **Młynarczyk**. Czech: **Mlnařík**, **Minařík**; **Mlejnek**.

Aug.: It.: **Muneron** (Venetia).

Patrs.: Eng.: **Mellers** (see also MELLOR). Fr.: **Aumeunier**. Low Ger.: **Möllering**. Flem., Du.: **M(e)ulders**, **Smulders**, **Smolders**, **Molenaers**.

Equivs. (not cogns.): Fr.: CASSEGRAIN, FARINE. Hung.: LISZT.

Millet 1. French and English: metonymic occupational name for a grower or seller of millet or panic grass, from a dim. form of OF *mil* (L *milium*). In some cases it may have been a nickname for someone suffering from a skin disease, with blisters resembling grains of millet (cf. mod. Eng. *miliary* fever). **2.** French: dim. of MILES 1. **3.** Catalan: topographic name for someone who lived by a field of millet, Cat. *millet* (L *miliētum*, a deriv. of *milium*).

Vars. (of 1): Eng.: **Millett**. Fr.: **Meillet**.

Millichamp English: habitation name from *Millichope* in Shrops., recorded in Domesday Book as *Melicope*, composed of the OE elements *mylen* MILL + *hlinc* hill (see LYNCH 3) + *hop* enclosed valley (see HOPE). It probably referred to location at the foot of a hill with a windmill on it.

Vars.: **Millichap**, **Millichop(e)**, **Millichip**, **Millership**.

Millier English (Somerset): of uncertain origin, probably a habitation name from an unidentified place named with the OE elements *mylen* MILL + *gear* weir.

Vars.: **Milliar**, **Milyear**, **Melliar**, **Mel(l)ior**.

Milligan Irish: Anglicized form of Gael. **Ó Maolagáin** 'descendant of *Maolagán*', a personal name from a double dim. of *maol* bald, tonsured; cf. MULLEN and McMILLAN.

Vars.: **Milligen**, **Millican**, **Milliken**, **Millikin**, **O'Milligane**, **Mulligan**, **Mul(la)gan**, **Mullikin**, **O'Mullegan**, **O'Mul(le)ghan**, **Melican**, **O'Mellegan**; **Molohan**, **O'Mol(l)eghan**, **O'Mollegane**, **O'Moylegane**; **Malaghan**.

Millington English: habitation name from places in Ches. and E Yorks., so called from OE *mylen* MILL + *tūn* enclosure, settlement. See also MILTON.

Millstein Jewish (Ashkenazic): occupational-ornamental name for a miller, from Yid. *milshteyn* millstone.

Vars.: **Mils(h)tein**; **Milsztejn** (Pol. spelling).

Millward English (chiefly W Midlands): occupational name for someone in charge of a mill, from OE *mylen* MILL + *weard* guardian. In S(W) England and the W Midlands this was the normal medieval term for a miller.

Vars.: **Milward**; **Millard** (chiefly Gloucs. and Worcs.); **Millwood**, **Mellard**.

Milton English: habitation name from any of the numerous places so called. The majority, with examples in at least fourteen counties, get the name from OE *middel* middle + *tūn* enclosure, settlement (cf. MIDDLETON); a smaller group, with examples in Cumb., Kent, Northants, Northumb., Notts., and Staffs., have as their first element OE *mylen* mill (cf. MILLINGTON). The surname is most common in Beds.

Milz German: **1.** metonymic nickname for a cantankerous, splenetic individual, from Ger. *Milz* spleen (MHG *milz(e)*, OHG *milza*). According to medieval theory of humours, an excess of bile from the spleen was responsible for ill temper. **2.** habitation name from a place so called in Thuringia.

Var.: **Miltz**.

Minařík see MILLER

Minch see McNEICE

Minck see MAYNE

Mincotti see DOMINIQUE

Mindel Jewish (Ashkenazic): from the Yid. female given name *Mindl*, a dim. of *Mine* (see MINN).

Metr.: **Mindlin** (E Ashkenazic).

Miner English: occupational name for someone who built mines, either for the excavation of coal and other minerals, or as a technique in the medieval art of siege warfare. The word represents an agent deriv. of ME, OF *mine* mine (apparently of Gaul. origin, cogn. with Gael. *mein* ore, mine).

Var.: **Minor**.

Patrs.: **Miners** (chiefly Cornwall, where there were extensive tin mines), **Minors**.

Equiv. (not cogn.): Czech: HORNÍK.

Mingay English (now chiefly Norfolk): from a Bret. personal name composed of the elements *men* stone + *ki* dog, which was introduced into England by settlers from N France accompanying William the Conqueror and following in his wake.

Var.: **Mingey**.

Mingeon see ERMGARD

Minihan see MONAGHAN

Minn English: from the medieval female given name *Minne*. This seems to have been in origin a Gmc personal name from OHG *minna* love, but in the late Middle Ages it was also used as a short form of *Willemina*, a fem. version of WILLIAM.

Var.: **Mynn**.

Dims.: **Minnett**, **Minnitt**.

Metrs.: **Minns** (chiefly Norfolk). Jewish (Ashkenazic): **Mines(s)** (consisting of the Yid. female given name *Mine* (see MINDEL) + the Yid. possessive suffix *-s*).

Minnerk *see* McNAIRN

Minners *see* MAYNARD

Minogue Irish: Anglicized form of Gael. **Ó Muineog** 'descendant of *Muineog*', a personal name representing a dim. of *manach* monk.

Var.: **Minnock**.

Minshull English: habitation name from a pair of villages in Ches., on either side of the river Weaver, recorded in Domesday Book as *Maneshale*, from the gen. case of the OE personal name *Mann* + OE *scylf* shelf, ledge.

Minter English: occupational name for a moneyer, OE *myntere* (cogn. with Ger. *Münzer*, Yid. *mintser*, whence the derivs. listed below), an agent deriv. of *mynet* coin, from LL *monēta* money, originally an epithet meaning 'Counsellor' (from *monēre* to advise) of Juno, at whose temple in Rome the coins were struck. The Eng. term was used at an early date to denote a workman who stamped the coins; later it came to denote the supervisors of the mint, who were wealthy and socially elevated members of the merchant class, and who were made responsible for the quality of the coinage by having their names placed on the coins.

Var.: **Mintor**.

Dims.: Fr.: **Monnereau**, **Monneret**, **Monnerot**.

Minto Scots: habitation name from a place near Denholm in the Borders, so called from the Brit. word that became W *mynydd* hill, with the later addition of ME *ho(e)* ridge, hill (OE *hōh*, see HOE) after the original meaning of the first element had been forgotten.

Minton English: habitation name from a place in Shrops., so called from W *mynydd* hill + OE *tūn* enclosure, settlement.

Miot *see* MYATT

Miquelard *see* MICHAEL

Miralles Catalan: habitation name from any of the various minor places in NE Spain named with Cat. *miralla* watchtower, look-out post (cf. MIRANDA).

Miranda Spanish, Catalan, Portuguese, Jewish (Sefardic), and Italian: habitation name from any of various places so called. The origin of this frequent placename is uncertain. It seems to be from the neut. pl. of L *mīrandus* wondrous, lovely (gerundive of *mīrāri* to wonder at, respect), but it is also possible that it was used in the sense of a watch-tower or look-out post; cf. MIRALLES.

Var.: It.: **Amiranda**.

Mirfield *see* MERRIFIELD

Mirón Spanish: from a medieval given name of Gmc origin. The name is found in the L form *Miro*, gen. *Mirōnis*,

and may represent a short form of the various Gmc cpd names with the first element *meri, mari* famous.

Dim.: Cat.: **Miret**.

Mironov Russian: patr. from the given name *Miron* (Gk *Myron*), borne by a 3rd-cent. saint who was martyred at Cyzicus on the Sea of Marmora, and subsequently venerated in the Orthodox Church.

Dims.: Russ.: **Mironichev**, **Miroshkin** (patrs.).

Mirralls *see* MERRILL

Mirrington *see* MERITON

Mirski Polish and Jewish (E Ashkenazic): nickname for a peaceable individual, from Pol. *mir* peace, respect for others + the general surname suffix *-ski* (see BARANOWSKI). It may also be a habitation name for a native or inhabitant of *Mir*, a town in Belorussia.

Var.: **Mirecki**.

Habitation name: **Mirowski**.

Misch *see* MICHAEL

Mišek *see* NICHOLAS

Mishkin 1. Russian: patr. from the given name *Mishka*, a pet form of *Mikhail* MICHAEL. 2. Jewish (E Ashkenazic): patr. from *Mishke*, a pet form of the Yid. given names *Mikhl* MICHAEL and *Moyshe* MOSES.

Var. (of 2): MISKIN.

Miskin 1. English: nickname for a young man, from ANF, OF *meschin* (via It. *meschino* wretched, small, from Arabic *miskīn* poor). The word seems to have been used to distinguish a younger from an older bearer of the same given name, but it also had a somewhat derogatory connotation. 2. Jewish (E Ashkenazic): var. of MISHKIN.

Misrachi *see* MIZRACHI

Mitasov *see* DMITRIEV

Mitcalfe *see* METCALF

Mitchell English, Scots, and Irish: from the ME, OF given name *Michel*, the regular vernacular form of MICHAEL.

Vars.: **Mitchel**, **Michell** (Devon and Cornwall).

Patrs.: Eng.: **Mi(t)chelson**.

Mitchelmore Scots and Irish: distinguishing name for the largest or eldest of several bearers of the given name *Michel* (see MITCHELL), with the addition of the Gael. adj. *mór* big (see MOORE 5).

Var.: **Michelmore**.

Mitchieson *see* MICHIE

Mitford English: habitation name from a place in Northumb., so called from OE *(ge)mӯðe* confluence + *ford* FORD.

Mitić *see* DMITRIEV

Mitrofanov Russian: patr. from the given name *Mitrofan* (Gk *Mētrophanēs*, from *mētēr* mother (sc. of God) + *phainein* to reveal, display). This name was borne by a 4th-cent. bishop of Byzantium, who became a popular saint in the Orthodox Church, although little is known about his life.

Var.: **Mitrofanyev**.

Mitsnovich *see* MICHAEL

Mittelman Jewish (Ashkenazic): nickname for a wealthy man, from Yid. *mitlman* man of means, from Yid. *mitl* means, resources (Ger. *Mittel*) + *man* man.

Vars.: **Mitelman**, **Mit(t)elmann**; **Mittleman** (Anglicized).

Mitter German: topographic name for someone who lived on a farm that was in the middle between two others, esp. if the others were both inhabited by men with the same personal name (e.g. *Mitter Hans*), from the strong form of MHG *mitte* mid, middle (OHG *mitti*).

Var.: **Mitterer**.

Cpds: **Mitterhofer** ('middle farmer'); **Mittermeier** ('middle steward'); **Mittermüller** ('middle miller'); **Mitterreiter**, **Mitterreuter** ('dweller in the middle clearing').

Mittmann German: (Silesian) status name for a tenant farmer who payed rent, from a dial. pronunciation with short vowel of MHG *miete* rent (OHG *mieta*) + *mann*.

Var.: **Mitter(er)**.

Mitton English: habitation name from places in Lancs., Worcs., and W Yorks., so called from OE *(ge)mȳðe* confluence, place where two streams meet (a deriv. of *mūð* mouth) + *tūn* enclosure, settlement. See also MYTON.

Mixa *see* NICHOLAS

Mizen English: habitation name from *Misson* in Notts., apparently so called from a lost Gmc element denoting a marshy place, akin to MOSS 1 and reflected also in the Belgian placename *Muizen* and the Du. *Mijsen*.

Vars.: **Mizzen**, **Mizon**.

Mizerski Polish: nickname for a wretchedly poor person, from Pol. *mizerny* poor, wretched, impoverished.

Mizon *see* MIZEN

Mizrachi Jewish: from Hebr. *mizrachi* eastern, man from the East.

Vars.: **Mizrahi**, **Mizrahy**, **Misra(c)hi**.

Mizzi *see* JAMES

Mlawer *see* MALAVE

Mlejnek *see* MILLER

Mlnařík *see* MILLER

Mnuchin *see* MENUHIN

Mo Swedish: topographic name for someone who lived on a sand-dune or heathland, Swed. *mo*, or arbitrarily adopted ornamental surname from this word.

Vars.: **Moe**, **Mo(h)lén**, **Mo(h)lin**.

Cpds: **Moberg** ('dune hill'); **Mogren** ('dune branch', ornamental).

Moan *see* MOHAN

Moat Scots and N English: habitation name from either of two places in the former county of Dumfries, so called from ME *mote* moat, ditch (originally referring to the whole system of fortifications; see MOTTE). In some

cases it may have referred originally to residence in or near some other moated dwelling.

Mobbs *see* MABB

Moberg *see* MO

Moberly English: habitation name from *Mobberley* in Ches., so called from OE *(ge)mōt* meeting, assembly + *burh* enclosure, fortification + *lēah* wood, clearing, i.e. a clearing where there was a fortified site at which assemblies were held.

Var.: **Mobley**.

Mockridge *see* MUGGERIDGE

Moczkowski Polish: habitation name from a place named with Pol. *moczary* marsh + *-(e)k* dim. suffix + *-ów* possessive suffix, with the addition of *-ski*, suffix of local surnames (see BARANOWSKI).

Modigliano Italian: probably a habitation name from *Modigliana* in Tuscany. The surname is now most common around Livorno and is to a large extent borne by Jews.

Var.: **Modigliani**.

Modrzejewski Polish: topographic name for someone living in a larch wood, from Pol. *modrzew* larch, or habitation name from a place named with this element.

Var.: **Modrzewski**.

Moe *see* MO

Moen *see* MOHAN

Moens *see* SIMON

Moët French: nickname of uncertain origin, apparently a dim. of either OF *moe* lip, mouth (of Gmc origin; cf. Du. *mouwe* grimace) or the homonymous OF *moe* seagull (also of Gmc origin; cf. MAW 1).

Vars.: **Mouet**, **Mouez**.

Moffatt Scots and N Irish: habitation name from a place in the former county of Dumfries, so called from Gael. *magh* plain, field + *fada* long.

Vars.: **Moffett** (chiefly N Ireland); **Moffitt**, **Muffatt**, **Muffett**, **Meffat**, **Mefet**.

Mogenot *see* DOMINIQUE

Mogg *see* MAGG

Moggridge *see* MUGGERIDGE

Moghan *see* MOHAN

Mogren *see* MO

Mohan Irish: Anglicized form of Gael. **Ó Mocháin** 'descendant of *Mochán*', a personal name from a dim. of *moch* early, timely. It has been occasionally translated into English as EARLY.

Vars.: **O'Mochaine**, **(O')Mo(u)ghan(e)**, **O'Moon**, **Moohan**, **Mo(w)en**, **Moan**, MOON, MAUGHAN, VAUGHAN.

Mohlén *see* MO

Möhler *see* MAHLER

Möhring *see* MOORE

Moinard *see* MONK

Moir *see* MOORE

Moise *see* MOSES

Moita Portuguese: topographic name for someone who lived at a spot covered with dense undergrowth, Port. *moita* (of uncertain origin, apparently akin to MATA).

Mojsilović *see* MOSES

Molchanov Russian and Jewish (E Ashkenazic): patr. from the Russ. nickname *Molchan* (from *molchat* to be silent), denoting a taciturn individual. As a Jewish name it may be based on some now irrecoverable minor incident.

Vars.: Jewish: **Molchan(ov)sky**.

Mold *see* MOULT

Mole English: **1.** nickname for someone supposedly resembling the burrowing mammal, ME *mol(le)* (from Du. or Low Ger. *mol*), for example in having poor eyesight. **2.** nickname for someone with a prominent mole or blemish on the face, from ME *mōl* (OE *māl*).

Molén *see* MO

Molenaers *see* MILLER

Molero *see* MUELA

Molesworth English: habitation name from a place in Cambs., so called from OE *Mūlesworð* 'enclosure (see WORTH) of *Mūl*', a byname meaning 'Mule'. It may also come in part from *Mouldsworth* in Ches., so called from OE *molda* crown of the head, top of a hill + *worð* enclosure.

Mølgård Danish: habitation name from a placename composed of the elements *møl* MILL + *gård* enclosure (see GARTH).

Var.: **Mølgaard**.

Molinelli *see* MILL

Molins *see* MULLEN

Moll 1. English (Norfolk): from the medieval female given name *Moll(e)*, a pet form of *Mary* (see MARIE). **2.** S German: nickname from a Swabian and Alemannic dial. term for a stout person. **3.** Catalan: nickname for a weak or ineffective person, from Cat. *moll* soft, weak (L *mollis*).

Molloy Irish: **1.** Anglicized form of Gael. Ó **Maolmhuaidh** 'descendant of *Maolmhuadh*', a personal name composed of the elements *maol* chieftain + *muadh* proud. **2.** Anglicized form of Gael. Ó **Maol Aodha** 'descendant of the devotee of (St) *Aodh*'; see McKAY. **3.** Anglicized form of Gael. Ó **Maol Mhaodhóg** 'descendant of the devotee of (St) *Maodhóg*'; see MADOC.

Vars.: **Mulloy**, **Malloy**. (Of 3 only): **Logue** (chiefly N Ireland).

Molohan *see* MILLIGAN

Moloney Irish: **1.** Anglicized form of Gael. Ó **Maol Dhomhnaigh** 'descendant of the devotee of the Church'. **2.** Anglicized form of Gael. **Mac Giolla Dhomhnaigh** 'son

of the servant of the Church'. Both names were occasionally used for the illegitimate children of priests.

Vars.: **Molony**, **Maloney**, DOWNIE. (Of 1 only): **Mullo(w)ney**, **Mul(l)downey**. (Of 2 only): **McGildowney**, **McIldowney**, **McEldowney**, **McDowney**.

Molotov Russian: patr. from the nickname *Molot* 'Hammer' (from *molot* to grind), referring to a fierce fighter (cf. MALET 4 and MARTEL 2) or to someone who used such an implement in his work.

Dim.: Russ.: **Molotkov**.

Moltke Low German: metonymic occupational name for a maltster, from a dim. of MLG *molt, mout* malt.

Molvin *see* MELVIN

Molyneux English and Irish (Norman): habitation name from *Moulineaux* in Seine-Maritime, so called from the pl. form of OF *moulineau*, a dim. of *moulin* MILL.

Vars.: **Molineaux**.

Mombrun French and English (Norman): habitation name from places in Aude, Haute-Garonne, Lot, and Lozère called *Montbrun*, from OF *mont* hill (see MONT) + *brun* BROWN.

Vars.: Eng.: **Monbrun**, **Monbrum**, **Mombrum**.

Momery *see* MOWBRAY

Momigliano Jewish: Italianized form of a habitation name from *Montmélian* in Savoy, so called from OF *mont* hill (see MONT) + the Gaul. name *Mediolanum* (see MILANO). This is now no more than a village, but during the Middle Ages it was the capital of a county with a considerable Jewish population. In Italy the name is most common in Piedmont and Lombardy.

Mommsen Low German: patr. from the medieval given name *Mumm(o)*. This is probably a short form of a Gmc personal name composed of *mund* protection + a second element beginning with *m-*, such as *man* man or *muot* courage.

Vars.: **Mummsen**; **Mommen**, **Mummen**.

Monaboe *see* ABBOTT

Monaghan Irish: Anglicized form of Gael. Ó **Manacháin** 'descendant of *Manachán*', a personal name representing a dim. of *manach* MONK.

Vars.: **O'Monaghan**, **(O')Monahan**, **O'Managhane**, **(O')Manahan**, **Minihan(e)**.

Monash Jewish (Ashkenazic): from *Monish*, a pet form of the Yid. male given name *Menakhem*, which is from the Hebr. male given name *Menachem*, lit. 'Consoler'.

Patr.: **Monosson**.

Monasterio Spanish: topographic name for someone who lived near a monastery (LL *monastērium*, from Gk *monastērion*, a deriv. of *monos* alone; cf. MONK 1), or occupational name for someone employed in one.

Monbrum *see* MOMBRUN

Moncey *see* MOUNSEY

Monclús Catalan: habitation name from any of the places situated on the mountain ridge of *Montclús* in N Spain. The placename is from LL *mons clausus* (en)closed hill, apparently referring to the fact that the high ground is shut in by rivers on either side.

Moncrieff Scots: habitation name from *Moncreiff* near Perth, so called from Gael. *monadh* hill + *craoibhe*, gen. of *craobh* tree.

Vars.: **Moncreiff(e)**.

Moncur Scots: evidently a habitation name, possibly of Norman origin. The first known bearer of the name is Michael *de Muncur*, who witnessed a charter in the first half of the 13th cent.

Moncuso *see* MANCO

Mondadori Italian: occupational name for a selector of the fleeces to be used in producing wool, from a Venetian dial. form of OIt. *emendatore* corrector (LL *emendātor*, from *emendāre*, a deriv. of *menda* fault).

Monday 1. English: from the ON personal name *Mundi*, a short form of the various cpd names containing the element *mundr* protection. 2. English: nickname for someone who had some particular association with this day of the week (OE *mōnandæg* day of the moon), normally because he owed feudal service then. It was considered lucky to be born on a Monday (and unlucky on a Friday; cf. FREITAG). 3. Irish: Anglicization of *Mac Giolla Eoin* 'son of the servant of Eoin', by confusion of the last part of the name with Irish *Luain* Monday.

Vars.: **Mondy**; **Mund(a)y**.

Monelli *see* SIMON

Monet French: from an aphetic form of a dim. of either of two given names, *Hamon* (see HAMMOND 1) and *Émon* (see EDMOND).

Var.: **Monnet**.

Monet *see* HAMMOND

Money 1. English: nickname for a rich man or metonymic occupational name for a moneyer, from ME *money(e)* money (OF *moneie*, L *monēta*; cf. MINTER). 2. Irish: Anglicized form of Gael. *Ó Maonaigh*; see MEANEY.

Moneypenny English and Scots: probably a nickname for a rich man or a miser, from ME *many* many (OE *manig*, *monig*) + *peny* PENNY (OE *penig*).

Var.: **Monypenny**.

Mongeaud *see* DOMINIQUE

Moniz *see* MUÑO

Monk 1. English: nickname for someone of monkish habits or appearance, or occupational name for a servant employed at a monastery, from ME *munk*, *monk* monk (OE *munuc*, *munec*, from LL *monachus* Gk *monakhos* solitary, a deriv. of *monos* alone). 2. Irish: translation of MINOGUE and MONAGHAN. 3. Jewish (Ashkenazic): of unknown ori-

gin. The Jewish surnames **Munk(e)** may or may not be related.

Vars.: Eng.: **Monck, Mun(c)k, Monnick**.

Dims.: Fr.: **Moinet, Moinot, Moynet, Moynot, Moiné, Moinel, Moineau**. It.: **Monac(h)ello, Monacelli, Monachino**.

Aug.: Fr.: **Moinat**.

Pejs.: Fr.: **Moinard, Moinaud, Moynard, Moinault**.

Patrs.: Eng.: **Monks, Munks**. Fr.: **Aumoine**. It.: **Del Monaco, Dal Monaco**.

'Servant of the m.': Eng.: **Monkman, Munkman**.

Monkhouse English: topographic name for someone who lived in a house near or owned by a monastery, or occupational name for someone who worked in a house where monks lived, i.e. a monastery.

Monnereau *see* MINTER

Monot *see* EDMOND

Monreal Catalan: habitation name from *Montréal* in Aude, France, so called from L *mons rēgālis* royal hill, or from a similarly named place in the province of Tarragona in Spain.

Monro *see* MUNRO

Monsky *see* MANN

Monson *see* MAGNUS

Mont French: topographic name for someone who lived on or near a hill, OF *mont* (L *mons*, gen. *montis*).

Vars.: **Demont, Dumont**.

Dims.: Fr.: **Montel, Monteau(x), Montet, Montillon**. It.: **Mont(ic)elli, Montello, Montin(i)**. Sp.: **Montejo, Montilla**.

Aug.: Fr.: **Montat**.

Montagne French: topographic name for someone who lived on or near a hill, from OF *montaine* hill, (small) mountain (LL *montānea*, originally neut. pl. of an adj. deriv. of *mons*; cf. MONT).

Vars.: **Montaigne**; **Monta(g)nier, Montagnié**.

Dims.: Fr.: **Montagnon**. It.: **Montagnino, Montagnini, Montanelli**.

Aug.: It.: **Montagnoni**.

Montagu 1. English (Norman) and French: habitation name from a place in La Manche, so called from OF *mont* hill (see MONT) + *agu* pointed (L *acūtus*, from *acus* needle, point). 2. Irish: Anglicized form of Gael. **Mac Taidhg**, patr. from the byname *Tadhg* 'Poet', 'Philosopher'; see TIGHE, and also McCAIG.

Vars.: (of 1): Eng.: **Montague, Montacute**. Fr.: **Montaigu, Montagut** (also from other places). (Of 2): **McT(e)ague, McT(e)igue**.

Montalvo Spanish: habitation name from places in the provinces of Cuenca and Logroño called *Montalbo*, from Sp. *monte* hill (see MONT) + *albo* white (L *albus*).

Montaner Catalan: occupational name for a warden in charge of game forests on a wooded upland, Cat. *muntaner* (LL *montānārius*, a deriv. of *montānea*; cf. MONTAGNE).

Vars.: **Montané, Muntané**.

Montefiore Italian (largely Jewish): either an ornamental name or a habitation name from an unidentified place, from It. *monte* hill (see MONT) + *fiore* flower (L *flōs*, gen. *flōris*).

Monteith Scots: habitation name from a place in the former county of Perths., so called from Gael. *mon* hill pasture + *Teith*, a river name of obscure origin.

Vars.: **Menteith**, **Monteath**.

Montenegro Spanish: habitation name from a place in the province of Soria, so called from Sp. *monte* hill (see MONT) + *negro* black (L *niger*).

Montero Spanish: occupational name for a beater or other assistant at a hunt, from an agent deriv. of Sp. *monte*, which as well as meaning 'hill' (see MONT) was also used in the transferred sense of a game forest on wooded upland (cf. MONTANER). The occupational term was itself also used as a title for various palace functionaries, and some cases of the surname may derive from this.

Montessori Italian: habitation name from a place in Tuscany, so called from It. *monte* hill (see MONT) + *tessoro* TREASURE.

Monteverde Italian: habitation name from any of various places so called, from It. *monte* hill (see MONT) + *verde* green (L *viridis*).

Var.: **Monteverdi**.

Montfort French and English (Norman): habitation name from any of the numerous places so called, from OF *mont* hill (see MONT) + *fort* strong, impregnable (L *fortis*). A Norman bearer of this name, from *Montfort*-sur-Risle in Eure, near Brionne, accompanied William the Conqueror in his invasion of England.

Vars.: Eng.: **Mountfort**, **Montford**, MOUNTFORD.

Montgolfier French: habitation name from a place in Arèche, so called from OF *mont* hill (see MONT) + a Gmc personal name composed of the elements *wulf* wolf + *heri, hari* army.

Montgomery English, Scots, and N Irish (Norman): habitation name from a place in Calvados, so called from OF *mont* hill (see MONT) + a Gmc personal name composed of the elements *guma* man + *rīc* power.

Vars.: **Montgomerie**, **Montgomry**.

Montilla Spanish: habitation name from a place in the province of Córdoba, so called from L *Montella*, pl. form of *montellum*, a dim. of *mons* hill (see MONT).

Montmorency French: habitation name from a place in Seine-et-Oise, so called from OF *mont* hill (see MONT) + the Gallo-Roman personal name *Maurentius*, apparently a cross between *Maurus* (see MOORE 3) and *Laurentius* (see LAWRENCE).

Montoliu Catalan: habitation name from either of two places in the province of Lérida, both so called from L *mons olivi* hill of the olive tree (cf. MONT and OLIVA).

Var.: **Montolio**.

Montoro Spanish: habitation name from a place in the province of Córdoba, of uncertain etymology. It was probably originally named with a LL deriv., **montorium*, of L *mons* hill (see MONT), but the name may possibly be from L *mons aureus* golden hill.

Montserrat Catalan: local name from a hill in the province of Barcelona, so called from Cat. *mont* hill (see MONT) + *serrat* jagged (L *serrātus*, a deriv. of *serra* saw). The frequency of the surname is probably to be explained as a result of its adoption as a religious byname, since the monastery of Montserrat was famous for its shrine of the Black Madonna, regarded as the patroness of Catalonia.

Monzón Spanish: habitation name from a place in the province of Huesca, Aragon, which is of uncertain etymology. Medieval forms include *Mon(t)ssone* and *Montisoni*, and it appears to be a deriv. or cpd of *monte* hill (see MONT).

Moody English: nickname for a courageous, arrogant, or foolhardy person, or one quickly moved to anger, from ME *modie* impetuous, haughty, angry (OE *mōdig* brave, proud, from *mōd* spirit, mind, courage).

Vars.: **Moodey**; **Moodie** (Scots); **Muddiman**, **Muddeman**.

Moohan see MOHAN

Moon 1. English (Norman): habitation name from *Moyon* in La Manche, so called from the Gallo-Roman personal name *Modius* (from L *modus* measure) + the local suffix -*o* (gen. -*ōnis*). 2. English: nickname from ANF *moun* MONK. 3. Cornish: nickname for a slender person, from Corn. *mon* thin. 4. Irish: Anglicized form of Gael. *Ó Mocháin*; see MOHAN.

Vars.: **Moone**. (Of 2 only): **Munn**.

Patrs. (from 2): **Munns**, **Munson**.

Mooney see MEANEY

Moor see MOORE, MORRIS

Moorby English: habitation name from a place so called, probably the one in Lincs., which gets its name from ON *mór* marsh, fen (a cogn. of OE *mōr*; see MOORE 1) + *býr* farm, settlement.

Moorcroft English (chiefly Lancs.): habitation name from one of several places in W Yorks., or from a lost place near Ormskirk in Lancs. called *Morcroft*. All derive their names from OE *mōr* marsh, fen (see MOORE 1) + *croft* paddock, smallholding (see CROFT).

Var.: **Moorcraft**.

Moore 1. English: topographic name for someone who lived on a moor or in a fen, both of which were denoted by ME *more* (OE *mōr*), or habitation name from any of the various places named with this word, as for example *Moore* in Ches. or *More* in Shrops. 2. English: nickname for a man of swarthy complexion, from OF *more* Moor, Negro (L *Maurus*, ultimately from Phoenician *mauharim* Eastern). 3. English: from a personal name of the same origin as in 2 above, which was borne by several early saints. The given name was introduced into England by the Normans, but was never as popular in England as on the Continent. 4. Irish: Anglicized form of Gael. *Ó Mórdha* 'descendant of *Mórdha*', a byname meaning 'Great', 'Proud', or 'Stately'. 5. Scots and Welsh: nickname for a large man, from Gael. *mór*, W *mawr* big, great.

Vars.: **Moor**. (Of 1 only): **Mo(o)res**, **Moors** (rarely perhaps also patrs. from the given name); **Atmore**, **Amoore**; **Moorman**,

Mor(e)man. See also MUIR. (Of 4 only): **O'Moore**, **O'Mora**, **(O')Morey**. (Of 5 only): Sc.: **Moir** (Aberdeen), **More**.

Dims. (of 2 and 3): Eng.: MORRELL; **Mor(r)in**, **Morren**, **Mo(o)ring**; **Moorcock** (perhaps also a nickname from the bird). Fr.: **Maurin**, **Mo(u)rin**, **Mor(i)net**, **Morineau**; **Mauret**, **Mouret**, **Mo(u)ré**; **Mo(u)rot**; **Mauron**, **Moron**, **Maurou(x)**. It.: **Maurino**, **Maurin(i)**, **Morin(i)**, **Morino**; **Moret(ti)**, **Moretto**, **Moriotto**, **Moriotti**, **Morozzi**, **Morucci**, **Moruzzi**, **Morucchio**. Ger.: **Mörle**. Low Ger.: **Mö(h)rke**, **Möri(c)ke**.

Augs. (of 2 and 3): Fr.: **Mauras**. It.: **Moroni**.

Pejs. (of 2 and 3): It.: **Morazzi**, **Moras(si)**, **Morasso**.

Patrs. (from 2 and 3): It.: **De Mauro**, **Di Mauro**, **Del Moro**. Low Ger.: **Mö(h)ring**. Flem.: **Moors**. Russ.: **Mavrov**. Croatian: **Mavrić**.

Patr. (from 2 and 3) (dim.): Russ.: **Mavrishchev**.

Moorfield English (Lancs.): probably an altered version of the Norman baronial name *de Morville*, borne by a family who held land in Yorks. and N Lancs. in the 12th and 13th cents.

Moorhead *see* MUIRHEAD

Moorhouse English (chiefly Yorks.): habitation name from any of various places, for example in W Yorks., named with the OE elements *mōr* marsh, fen (see MOORE 1) + *hūs* HOUSE.

Vars.: **Morehouse**, **Morres**, MORRIS.

Moorley *see* MORLEY

Mór *see* MORRIS

Mora Spanish and Portuguese: topographic name for someone who lived by a mulberry or blackberry bush, from Sp. *mora* mulberry, blackberry (LL *mōra*, originally the pl. of class. L *mōrum*). There are numerous places named with this word, and the surname may also be a habitation name from any of these. It is also possible that it was used as a nickname, with reference to the dark colour of the berries.

Vars.: Sp.: **Moral(es)**. Port.: **Moreira**.

Dims.: Sp.: **Morilla(s)**.

Collectives: Sp.: **Moraleda**. Port.: **Morais**.

Moran 1. English: var. of MORANT; the accent is normally on the second syllable. **2.** Irish: Anglicized form of Gael. **Ó Móráin** 'descendant of *Morán*', a personal name meaning 'Great', 'Large' (cf. MOORE 5); the accent is normally on the first syllable.

Vars. (of 2): Ir.: **O'Moraine**, **O'Moran(e)**.

Morant English and French: from an OF personal name of uncertain etymology. It appears to be a byname meaning 'Steadfast', 'Enduring', from the pres. part. of OF *(de)morer* to remain, stay (cf. DURANT), but this may be no more than the reworking under the influence of folk etymology of some unrecognized Gmc original.

Vars.: Eng.: **Moran**. Fr.: **Morand**, **Mauran(d)**.

Dims.: Fr.: **Morandeau**, **Maurandi**. It.: **Morandin(i)**, **Moranduzzo**.

Aug.: Fr.: **Morandat**.

Moras *see* MOORE

Morata Spanish: habitation name from any of various places so called, for example in the provinces of Jaén, Madrid, Murcia, and Saragossa. The placename is probably

from LL *morāta* dwelling, residence (from *morāre* to remain, stay; cf. MORANT).

Dim.: **Moratilla** (the name of two places in the province of Guadalajara).

Moravec Czech: regional name for someone from Moravia (Czech *Morava*, named from the river of the same name), a district of N central Czechoslovakia, which from the 11th cent. onwards was a crownland of the kingdom of Bohemia. Protestantism has flourished in Moravia since the 16th cent.

Var.: **Morava**.

Dim.: **Moravčík**.

Morcillo Spanish: nickname for someone with dark skin or hair, from Sp. *morcillo* dark, black (LL *mauricellus*, a dim. of class. L *Maurus* Moor; cf. MOORE 2).

Morcombe English: habitation name, probably from *Morecombelake* in Dorset (recorded as *Mortecumbe* in 1240). The second element of this is OE *cumb* short valley (see COOMBE); the first is probably an OE personal name, **Morta* (see MORT). For the third element, see LAKE. The surname is certainly not from *Morecambe* in Lancs., which is named with an 18th-cent. coinage, based on identification of *Morecambe Bay* with Ptolemy's *Morikambē*.

Var.: **Morcom**.

Mordaunt English (Norman): nickname for a person with a sharp tongue, from ANF *mordaunt* biting, spiteful (pres. part. of OF *mordre* to bite, L *mordere*).

Morehead *see* MUIRHEAD

Morehouse *see* MOORHOUSE

Moreland Scots and N English: habitation name from any of various places, notably in the Borders region and in the former county of Kinross, named with OE *mōr* marsh, fen, moor (see MOORE 1) + *land* land.

Var.: **Morland**.

Moreno 1. Spanish and Portuguese: nickname for someone with dark hair and a swarthy complexion, from Sp., Port. *moreno* dark-haired (of uncertain origin, probably from LL *maurīnus*, a deriv. of class. L *Maurus* Moor; cf. MOORE 2 and MORCILLO). **2.** Jewish (Sefardic): probably of the same origin as the Spanish and Portuguese names. It has been suggested that this was a name for a rabbi, from the Hebr. honorific title *morenu* 'our master', but this is unlikely since this Hebr. word would normally give a name ending in *-u*, not *-o*. However, the Hebr. word is probably the source of the Ashkenazic surnames **Moreinu** and **Moreinis** (the latter having Yid. possessive *-s*).

Var. (of 1): Sp.: **Morena** (a fem. form).

Moresby English: habitation name from a place in Cumb., so called from the OF given name *Maurice* (see MORRIS 1) + the Northern ME local element *by* farm, settlement (ON *býr*).

Morgado Portuguese: distinguishing name for the eldest son of a family, from Port. *morgado* first-born, heir (LL *māioricātus*, a deriv. of *māior*; cf. MAYOR).

Morgan Welsh, Scots, and Irish: from an old Celt. personal name (of which *Morien* is the more usual development in Welsh), apparently composed of elements meaning 'sea' + 'bright' (although 'Great Defender' is also a possible interpretation).

'Descendant of M.': Ir.: **(O')Murchan**, **O'Morghane**, **O'Moraghan**, **Morchan**, **Morkan**, **Morkin**, **Murkin** (Gael. **Ó Murcháin**); FORGAN, HORGAN, ORGAN (Gael. **Ó Mhurcháin**).

Morgenrot Jewish (Ashkenazic): from mod. Ger. *Morgenrot* dawn, sunrise (lit. 'morning red'), one of a group of Jewish ornamental names taken from words referring to natural phenomena; cf. MORGENSTERN and ABENDROTH.

Var.: **Morgenroth**.

Morgenstern Jewish (Ashkenazic): from mod. Ger. *Morgenstern* morning star, Yid. *morgn-shtern*, one of the class of Jewish ornamental names taken from natural phenomena.

Moriarty Irish: Anglicized form of the Gael. personal name *Muircheartach*, composed of the elements *muir* sea + *ceardach* skilled, i.e. skilled navigator.

Patrs.: **McMoriertagh**, **McMurihertie**, **McMiritee**, **McMreaty**, **McMe(a)rty** (Gael. **Mac Muircheartaigh**). See also McMORDIE.

'Descendant of M.': **O'Morierty** (Gael. **Ó Muircheartaigh**).

Mörk Swedish: nickname for someone with dark hair or a swarthy complexion, uncharacteristic of Scandinavian people, from Swed. *mörk* dark (ON *myrkr*, whence also ME *murk(y)*).

Morkúnas *see* MARK

Morley English: habitation name from any of the various places called *Morley* (e.g. in Ches., Derbys., Co. Durham, Norfolk, and W Yorks.), or *Moreleigh* in Devon, all of which are so called from OE *mōr* marsh, fen (see MOORE 1) + *lēah* wood, clearing.

Vars.: **Moorley**, **Morely**; **Moralee** (Northumb.).

Morling English: of uncertain origin, most likely a double dim. (with the ANF suffixes *-el* and *-in*) of the medieval given name *More*; see MOORE 3 and MORRELL.

Var.: **Morlin**.

Morón Spanish: habitation name from places in the provinces of Seville and Soria. The former, and possibly the latter also, is probably named from Arabic *maurûr* 'hidden', from the past. part. of *wárrà* to hide, bury.

Moroney Irish: Anglicized form of Gael. **Ó Maol Ruanaidh** 'descendant of the devotee of (St) *Ruanaidh*'; see ROONEY.

Vars.: **Morooney**, **Murroney**, **Mulro(o)ney**, **O'Moronie**.

Morpeth English (Northumb.): habitation name from the town of this name, so called from OE *morð* murder + *pæð* path. The reasons for this grisly appellation have long ago been lost.

Var.: **Morpat** (Sc.).

Morphy *see* MURPHY

Morpurgo Jewish: habitation name borne by Jews in Italy, either from the city of *Maribor* in Slovenia (known in It. as *Marburgo*, in Ger. as *Markburg*) or from *Marburg* in Germany.

Vars.: **Marpurg**, **Marpurch**.

Morpuss *see* MALPAS

Morrell English: from the medieval given name *Morel*, a dim. of *More* (see MOORE 3) with the hypocoristic suffix *-el*.

Vars.: **Morel(l)**, **Morrel**, **Mor(r)ill**, **Morrall**, **Murrill**, **Marrel**.

Dims.: Eng.: **MORLIN**. Fr.: **Morellet**, **Mor(e)let**, **Morel(l)on**, **Mor(e)lot**, **Mourlot**.

Morrington *see* MERITON

Morris 1. English, Welsh, Scots, and Irish: from an OF personal name introduced to Britain by the Normans, *Maurice* (L *Mauritius*, a deriv. of *Maurus*; cf. MOORE 3). This was borne by several minor early Christian saints, including a 3rd-cent. Swiss martyr. **2.** Jewish: Anglicization of any of various like-sounding Jewish surnames.

Vars. (of 1): **Morriss**, **Morrish**; **Morrice** (Sc., chiefly Aberdeen), **Maurice**; **Morse**, **Morce**, **Morss**. (Of 2): **Morse**.

Dims.: Fr.: **Mauricet**, **Maurisset**, **Moricet**, **Morisset**, **Morizet**, **Maurisseau**, **Maurisson**, **Morisson**, **Maurizot**, **Morizot**. Czech: **Mourek**. Hung.: **Moor**, **Mór(a)**.

Aug.: Fr.: **Maurissat**.

Patrs.: Eng.: **Mor(r)ison** (also Sc.). Sc.: **McMorris** (Gael. **MacMuiris**); **McVarish** (Gael. **Mac Mhuiris**). Ir.: **McMorris**, FITZMAURICE. Ger.: **Moritzer**. Low Ger.: **Moritzen**. Flem., Du.: **Morissen**. Dan., Norw.: **Mouritsen**, **Mouritzen**, **Mauritzen**.

Morrissey Irish: Anglicized form of **Ó Muirgheas** 'descendant of *Muirgheasa*', a personal name apparently derived from the elements *muir* sea + *geas* taboo, prohibition.

Vars.: **O'Morrissey**, **O'Murrissa**, **O'Morisa**, **Mor(r)issy**, **Morrisey**.

Dims.: **O'Murghesan**, **O'Morrisane** (Gael. **Ó Muirgheasáin**).

Morrow Irish and Scots: Anglicized form of the Gael. personal name *Murchadh*, composed of the elements *muir* sea + *cadh* warrior; cf. McMORROUGH and MURPHY.

Vars.: **Morrough**, **Murrow**, **Murrough**.

Morrowson *see* McMORROUGH

Mort 1. English (Lancs.): of uncertain origin. The most plausible suggestion is that it is a Norman nickname from OF *mort* dead (L *mortuus*), presumably referring to a person of deathly pallor or unnaturally still countenance. However, it could also be the result of survival into the ME period of an OE personal name, **Morta*, postulated by Ekwall to explain various placenames (cf. MORCOMBE and MORTLOCK). **2.** French: either a nickname from OF *mort* dead (see above), or alteration, by folk etymology, of the given name *Mor(e)* (see MOORE 3).

Mortagh *see* MURDOCH

Mortensen *see* MARTIN

Morthe *see* MARTHE

Mortiboys English (W Midlands): apparently a Norman habitation name from an unidentified place named with OF *mort* dead (see MORT) + *bois* wood (see BOIS).

Mortimer English (Norman): habitation name from *Mortemer* in Seine-Maritime, so called from OF *mort(e)* dead (see MORT) + *mer* sea (L *mare*). The placename probably referred to a stagnant pond or partly drained swamp;

there may also have been an allusion to the biblical Dead
Sea seen by crusaders.

Vars.: **Mortimor(e)**, **Murtimer**.

Mortlock English: probably a habitation name from
Mortlake in Surrey, recorded in Domesday Book as
Mortelaga and *Mortelage*, apparently from the OE byname
*Morta (see MORT 1) + OE *lag* marshy meadow or *lacu*
stream (see LAKE).

Morton 1. English and Scots: habitation name from any of
the many places called *Mor(e)ton*, from OE *mōr* marsh, fen,
moor (see MOORE 1) + *tūn* enclosure, settlement. **2.** Swedish: cogn. of MARTIN. **3.** Jewish (Ashkenazic): presumably
an Anglicization of one or more like-sounding Jewish surnames.

Var. (of 1): Eng.: **Moreton**. See also MURTON.

Mosby English (Yorks.): habitation name, probably from
Mosbrough in S Yorks. (*Moresburh* in Domesday Book),
which gets its name from OE *mořes*, gen. sing. of *mōr*
marsh, fen, moor (see MOORE 1) + *burh* fortress (see BURY).

Moscardi *see* MOUCHE

Moseley English (chiefly W Midlands): habitation name
from one of several places called *Mos(e)ley* in central, W,
and NW England. The obvious derivation is from OE *mos*
peat bog (see MOSS 1) + *lēah* wood, clearing, but the one in
S Birmingham (*Museleie* in Domesday Book) had as its first
element OE *mūs* mouse, while one in Staffs. (*Molesleie* in
Domesday Book) had the gen. case of the OE byname *Moll*.

Vars.: **Mousley** (Birmingham); **Mosley** (chiefly S Yorks. and
Lancs.).

Moses Jewish, English, and French: from the name of the
Israelite leader *Moses* in the Book of Exodus, who led the
Israelites out of Egypt. The Hebr. form of the name,
Moshe, is probably of Egyptian origin, a short form of
any of the various theophoric personal names, such as
Rameses and *Tutmosis*, meaning 'conceived by (a certain
god)'. However, very early in its history it acquired a
folk etymology, being taken as a deriv. of the Hebr. root
mšh to draw (something from the water), a reference to the
story of the infant Moses being discovered among the
bullrushes by Pharaoh's daughter. See also MOSS 2.

Vars.: Jewish: **Mozes**, **Moshe**. Eng.: **Moyses**; **Moyse**, **Moise**,
Moyce; **Moyes** (Sc.). Fr.: **Moyse**, **Moïse**.

Dims.: It.: **Moselli**, **Mosello**, **Mosetti**. Czech: **Mojžíšek**. Ukr.:
Mosienko.

Patrs.: Jewish: **Mos(s)esohn**, **Mosezon**, **Moshes** (Ashkenazic);
Moise(i)ev, **Moisseef**, **Mosaiov**, **Mosayov**, **Mosheyov**,
Mosheyoff, **Moshaiov**, **Moshaiow**, **Moshayov**, **Moshayof**,
Moshevitch, **Moshevitz**, **Moschowitsch** (E Ashkenazic);
Moisescu (among Rumanian Jews); **Mosheshvili**, **Mosheshvily**
(among Georgian Jews); **Musayov**, **Musaiov**, **Mussaioff**,
Moussaieff (via Russ. from the Arabic form). Russ.: **Mo(i)seev**,
Mos(e)ichev; **Musin**, **Musaev**, **Muzaev** (from the Arabic form
Mūsā used in the Turkic languages). Croatian: **Mojsilović**. Arme-
nian: **Movesian**.

Patrs. (from dims.): Jewish: **Moskovi(t)ch**, **Moscovitch**,
Moskowi(t)ch, **Moskovic**, **Moskowicz**, **Moscowicz**, **Moskovicz**,
Moscovicz, **Moskowics**, **Moskovics**, **Moskowitz**, **Moscowitz**,
Moskovitz, **Moscovi(t)z**, **Moskowits**, **Moskovits**,
Moshkovi(t)ch, **Moshcovitch**, **Moshkowich**, **Moszkowicz**
(Pol. spelling), **Moszkovicz**, **Moshkowitz**, **Moshkovi(t)z**,

Moshcovitz (E Ashkenazic); **Moskovici**, **Moscovici** (among Rumanian Jews). Russ.: **Mosyagin**. Pol.: **Moszkowicz**.

Moskowski Jewish (E Ashkenazic): ostensibly a habitation name from the city of *Moscow* or regional name from
Muscovy (both named in Russ. as *Moskva*). However, the
reference is probably merely to someone who had been on a
trip to Moscow, as there were very few Jews living in Moscow or the surrounding region in the early 19th cent., when
most Jews in the Russian Empire adopted family names.
Alternatively, the name may in fact be an alteration of
Moskovich (see patrs. at MOSES), under the influence of
the placename. The city takes its name from that of the
river on which it stands, which seems, like so many old
river names, to have originally meant no more than
'damp', 'wet'.

Var.: **Moskowsky**.

Moss 1. English: topographic name for someone who lived
by a peat bog (ME, OE *mos*), or habitation name from a
place named with this word. It was not until later that the
vocab. word came to denote the class of plants characteristic of a peat-bog habitat, under the influence of the ON
cogn. *mosi*. **2.** English: from the normal medieval vernacular form of the given name MOSES. **3.** Jewish (Ashkenazic):
of uncertain origin. It may be an Anglicization of MOSES or
some other like-sounding Jewish name.

Vars. (of 1): **Mosse**, **Mossman**.

Dim. (of 1): Ger.: **Mösl**.

Cpd (of 1; arbitrary or ornamental): Swed.: **Mossberg** ('bog hill').

Mössmer *see* MESNER

Most 1. German: metonymic occupational name for a producer or seller of must, i.e. unfermented grape juice, Ger.
Most (MHG, OHG *most*, from L *mustum (vīnum)* young,
i.e. fresh, wine). The same term was also used of perry and
cider, since these do not keep well and have to be drunk
quickly while still fresh. **2.** Flemish and Dutch: cogn. of
MOSS 1. **3.** Jewish (E Ashkenazic): from Pol. and Russ.
most bridge

Vars. (of 1): **Mös(s)t**; **Mostert**, **Mustert**. (Of 2): Flem., Du.:
Mostinck, **Van der Most**.

Motel 1. Jewish (Ashkenazic): from Yid. *Motl*, a pet form
of the Yid. male given name *Mortkhe*, from Hebr.
Mordechay Mordecai (of Akkadian origin), name of the
hero of the Book of Esther in the Bible, who with the
help of his cousin Esther saved the Jews of Persia from
destruction. Cf. ESTERSOHN. **2.** French: dim. of MOTTE.

Patr. (from 1): **Motelsohn**.

Mothersole English: **1.** habitation name from
Moddershall in Staffs., so called from OE *Mōdrēdeshalh*
'recess (see HALE 1) of *Mōdrēd*', a personal name composed
of the elements *mōd* heart, spirit, courage + *rēd* counsel,
wisdom. **2.** perhaps also a nickname for a person who was
in the habit of swearing with the oath 'on my *mother's soul*',
but this is probably no more than folk etymology.

Var.: **Mothersill**.

Motion Scots: of unknown origin, perhaps a nickname for
a restless person, from ME, OF *motion* movement (LL
mōtio, gen. *mōtiōnis*, a deriv. of *mōvēre* to move). However,
there are difficulties with this suggestion, principally the

fact that *motion* was a learned word, and is not attested before the 15th cent.

Motte French and English: topographic name for someone who lived by a fortified stronghold, OF, ME *motte* (of apparently Gaul. origin, referring originally to a hillock or mound; see also MOAT). The surname may also be a habitation name from any of the places in France named with this word.
Vars.: Fr.: **Mot(h)e**; **Lamotte**, **Lamothe**, **Delamotte**; **Mot(t)ier**. Eng.: **Mote**, **Mott**.
Dims.: Fr.: MOTEL, **Mot(t)et**, **Motton**.

Mottershead English: habitation name from a lost place in the parish of Mottram, Ches., recorded in the 13th cent. as *Mottresheved*, from the gen. case of the OE byname *Mōtere* 'Speaker' + ME *heved* head(land), hill.
Var.: **Mottishead**.

Mottinelli *see* JAMES

Motton *see* MUTTON

Mottram English: habitation name from either of two places in Ches. It is possible that the name originally denoted a building where village assemblies were held, from OE *(ge)mōt* meeting + *ærn* house, hall. Other possibilities are that the name derives from OE *(ge)mōt-rūm* 'meeting space', or *(ge)mōt-treum* 'assembly trees'.

Mouat *see* MOWAT

Moubray *see* MOWBRAY

Mouche French: nickname from the housefly, OF *mouche* (L *musca*), denoting a small, light person, an insignificant one, or an irritating one.
Vars.: **Mouque**; **Lamouche**, **Lamouque**.
Dims.: Fr.: **Mouchot(te)**, **Mouchel(et)**, **Mouchet**, **Mouchez**, **Mouquet**. It.: **Moschella**, **Moschelli**, **Moschetta**, **Moschetti**, **Moschetto**, **Moschin(i)**, **Moschino**, **Moschitta**, **Moscolini**, MUSSOLINI.
Augs.: It.: **Moscone**, **Moscon(i)**. Cat.: **Moscardó**.
Pejs.: It.: **Moscardo**, **Moscardi**.

Mouet *see* MOT

Mougel *see* DOMINIQUE

Mough *see* MAW

Moughan *see* MOHAN

Moule *see* MULE

Moulineau *see* MILL

Moult English: **1.** from the ME female given name, *Ma(ha)lt*, *Mau(l)d*, a var. of the Norman name *Mathilde*, *Matilda*, composed of the Gmc elements *maht* might, strength + *hild* battle. The learned form *Matilda* was much less common than the vernacular *Mahalt*, *Maud* and the aphetic pet form TILL. The name was borne in England by the daughter of Henry I, who disputed the throne of England with her cousin Stephen for a number of years (1137–48). In Germany the popularity of the name in the Middle Ages was augmented by its being borne by a 10th-cent. saint, wife of Henry the Fowler and mother of Otto the Great. **2.** nickname for a bald man, or someone

who suffered from some deformity of the skull, from ME *mould* top of the head (OE *molda*).
Vars. (of 1): **Mo(u)ld**, **Moule**, **Moull**, **Ma(u)lt**, **Mald**, **Maud(e)**, MUDD, MOWAT.
Dims. (of 1): Fr.: **Mahoudeau**. Ger.: **Metze**; **Mechel** (Hesse). Low Ger.: **Mett(e)**, **Mettke**.
Metrs. (from 1): Eng.: **Moulds**, **Moulding**; **Maudson**, **Malson**, **Mo(u)lson**; **Mawson**, **Mawsom** (see also MAW).
Metrs. (from 1) (dims.): Ger.: **Metzen**. Low Ger.: **Vermette**.

Moulton English: habitation name from any of the various places with this name, as for example in Ches., Lincs., Norfolk, Northants, Suffolk, and N Yorks. For the most part these are named with the OE byname *Mūla* 'Mule' + OE *tūn* enclosure, settlement, but in some cases they may have been originally farms where mules were reared or kept. for the place in Norfolk the first element was probably a personal name *Mōda*, a short form of the various cpd names with a first element *mōd* spirit, mind, courage (cf. MOODY).

Mounic *see* HAMMOND

Mounsey English (Norman): habitation name from *Monceaux* in Calvados and Orne, or *Monchaux* in Nord and Seine-Maritime. All get their name from the pl. form of OF *moncel* hillock (LL *monticellum*, a dim. of *mons*; cf. MONT).
Vars.: **Mo(u)ncey**, **Munsey**, **Munchay**; **Mounsie**, **Muncie** (Sc.).

Mountbatten English: translation of the Ger. habitation name **Battenberg**, from a place on the river Eder. The placename consists of the element *bat*, of uncertain meaning, perhaps describing a water-meadow (cf. BATE 3) + OHG *berg* hill.

Mountford English (chiefly W Midlands): **1.** Anglicized form of the Norman name MONTFORT. **2.** possibly also a habitation name from *Mundford* in Norfolk, so called from the OE personal name *Munda* (from *mund* protection) + *ford* FORD.
Vars.: **Mun(d)ford**, **Mumford**.

Mountfort *see* MONTFORT

Mountney English (Norman): habitation name from any of numerous places called *Montigni*, from the Gallo-Roman personal name *Montinius* + the local suffix *-ācum*.

Mouré *see* MOORE

Mourek *see* MORRIS

Mourlot *see* MORRELL

Mousley *see* MOSELEY

Moussaieff *see* MOSES

Moutenet *see* MUTTON

Moutinho Portuguese: of uncertain origin, possibly a habitation name from a place called *Moitinha*, a dim. of MOITA.

Movesian *see* MOSES

Mowat Scots and N English: **1.** from a medieval female given name, *Mohaut*, var. of *Mau(l)d*; see MOULT 1. **2.** occupational name for an official in charge of communal pasture land, ME *moward*, *maward*, from OE *māwe* meadow (see MAW 3) + *weard* guardian (see WARD 1). **3.** habitation name from any of various places in N France called *Mon(t)haut*, from OF *mont* hill (see MONT) + *haut* high (L *altus*).

Vars.: **Mowatt**, **Mouat(t)**.

Mowbray English (Norman): habitation name from *Montbrai* in La Manche, so called from OF *mont* hill (see MONT) + *brai* mud, slime (of Gaul. origin).

Vars.: **Mowbury**, **Moubray**, **Mumbray**, **Momery**, **Mummery**, **Memory**, **Mulb(e)ry**, **Mulberry**.

Mowe see MAW

Mowen see MOHAN

Mower English (chiefly Norfolk): occupational name for someone responsible for mowing pasture lands to provide hay, from an agent deriv. of ME *mow(en)* to mow (OE *māwen*; cf. MAW 1 and MATHER 1).

Mowl see MULE

Moxham see MAGG

Moyano Spanish: from a medieval given name, LL *Modiānus*, a deriv. of *Modius* (from L *modus* measure).

Moyce see MOSES

Moylan see MULLEN

Moyle Cornish: nickname for a bald man, from Corn. *moyl* bald.

Moynard see MONK

Moynihan Irish: Anglicized form of Gael. Ó **Muimhneacháin** 'descendant of *Muimhneachán*', a dim. of the byname *Muimhneach* 'Munsterman'.

Var.: **Moynan**.

Mozart German: of uncertain origin, probably from a Gmc personal name composed of the elements *mōd* spirit, mind, courage + *hard* hardy, brave, strong.

Var.: **Mozet**.

Mozes see MOSES

Mozet see MOZART

Mozo Spanish: nickname or occupational name from Sp. *mozo* boy, lad, servant (of uncertain origin, perhaps from L *mustus* young, fresh (cf. MOST 1) or from a pre-Roman element *muts-* pruned, shorn, referring to the custom among youths and lowly individuals of wearing their hair short (cf. PSCHORR and TOUS)).

Mozzetti see JAMES

Mráček Czech: nickname for a person of a gloomy disposition, from Czech *mráček* small dark cloud, dim. of *mrak* cloud, also used in the sense 'gloom'.

Habitation name: Pol.: **Mroczkowski**.

Mrázek see MRÓZ

Mrkić see MARCHEWA

Mroczkowski see MRÁČEK

Mrówka Polish: nickname from Pol. *mrówka* ant, applied to a person of small stature, or perhaps to a busily active one.

Habitation name: **Mrowiński**, **Mrówczyński**.

Mróz Polish: **1.** from an aphetic form of the Pol. given name *Ambroży* AMBROSE. **2.** nickname for a white-haired man or alternatively for one of an icy and unsociable disposition, from Pol. *mróz* hoarfrost.

Dims. (of 1 and 2): Pol.: **Mrozek**. (Of 2 only): Czech: **Mrázek**.

Patr. (from 1): Pol.: **Mrozowicz**.

Habitation names (from 1 or 2): Pol.: **Mrozowski**, **Mroziński**. (From 1 only): Pol.: **Mrożewski**.

Mucci see JAMES

Much see MUTCH

Muckle see MEIKLE

Mucklejohn see MEIKLEJOHN

Mucklow English (W Midlands): habitation name from *Mucklows* Hill, to the W of Birmingham, or *Muckley* Corner near Lichfield, Staffs. Both names are from OE *micel* large + *hlāw* hill, here perhaps tumulus.

Mudd English: **1.** from a medieval female given name, var. of *Maud*; see MOULT 1. **2.** from the OE personal name *Mōd(a)*, a short form of the various cpd names containing the element *mōd* spirit, mind, courage (cf. MOODY). **3.** topographic name for someone who lived in a particularly muddy area, from ME *mud* (MLG *mudde*), perhaps also a metonymic occupational name for a dauber (one who constructed buildings of wattle and daub).

Muddeman see MOODY

Mudge see MAGG

Muehlbauer see MILL

Muela Spanish: **1.** metonymic occupational name for someone who made or sold mill wheels, from Sp. *muela* mill wheel (L *mola*). **2.** topographic name for someone who lived on a hill with a flat top, from the same word used in a topographic sense. There are numerous places called *La Muela*, and the surname may be a habitation name from any of these.

Vars.: **Muelas**. (Of 1 only): **Molero**.

Muff see MAW

Muffatt see MOFFATT

Muggeridge English: habitation name from *Mogridge* in Devon. The second element of this placename is clearly OE *hrycg* ridge, spur; the first is probably from an OE personal name *Mogga*.

Vars.: **Mug(g)ridge**, **Mog(g)ridge**, **Mockridge**.

Mugnaini see MILLER

Muhlke see MAUL

Muir Scots and N English: topographic name for someone who lived on a moor, from a Northern dial. var. of ME *more* (see MOORE 1).

Var.: **Mure**.

Muirhead Scots: habitation name from any of the places in S Scotland so called, from Northern ME *muir* moor (see MUIR) + *heid* head, end.

Vars.: **Moorhead** (N Ireland), **Morehead**.

Mukhin Russian: patr. from the nickname *Mukha* 'Fly', denoting a small and irritating person, or someone considered of no importance.

Habitation names: Pol.: **Muszyński**. Jewish (E Ashkenazic): **Muszinsky** (reason(s) for acquisition not clear).

Mulberry see MOWBRAY

Mulcahy Irish: Anglicized form of Gael. Ó Maolchathaigh 'descendant of the devotee of (St) *Cathach*', a byname meaning 'Warlike'.

Vars.: **Cahy**, CAUGHEY.

Mulcaster see MUNCASTER

Mulcreevy Irish: Anglicized form of Gael. Ó Maolchraoibhe 'descendant of the devotee of (St) *Craobh*'.

Vars.: **O'Mulcreevy**; **Mulgrew**, **Mulgrue**, **Mulgroo**.

Muldoon Irish: Anglicized form of Gael. Ó Maoldúin 'descendant of *Maoldúin*', a personal name composed of the elements *maol* chief + *dún* fortress.

Vars.: **O'Muldoon**, **Muldon**, **Meldon**.

Muldowney see MOLONEY

Mule English: 1. from a medieval given name, perhaps OE *Mūl* (from OE *mūl* mule, halfbreed). This was the name of a brother of Ceadwalla, King of Wessex (d. 675), and is also found as a placename element. However, it may not have survived to the Conquest, and Domesday Book *Mule*, *Mulo* may instead represent ON *Mūli*, which is probably from ON *mūli* muzzle, snout. 2. nickname for a stubborn person or metonymic occupational name for a driver of pack-animals, from ME *mule* mule (OE *mūl*, from L *mūla*, reinforced by OF *mule*, from the same source). 3. from the medieval female given name *Mulle*, var. of *Molle*, a pet form of *Mary* (see MARIE).

Vars.: **Moule**, **Mowl(e)**.

Dims.: (of 2): Eng.: **Mullet(t)**. Fr.: **Mul(l)et**, **Mulin**.

Pej. (of 2): Fr.: **Mulard**.

Metr. (from 3): Eng.: **Mowles**.

Mulfaul see LAVELLE

Mulgan see MILLIGAN

Mulhall Irish: Anglicized form of Gael. Ó Maolchathail 'descendant of the devotee of (St) *Cathal*' (see CAHILL).

Mulhern Irish: Anglicized form of Gael. Ó Maoilchiaráin 'descendant of the devotee of (St) *Ciarán*' (a byname from a dim. of *ciar* black).

Vars.: **Mulkerrin**, **Mulkern(s)**.

Mulholland Irish: Anglicized form of Gael. Ó Maolchalann 'descendant of the devotee of (St) *Calann*' (see CALLAN).

Mullally Irish: Anglicized form of Gael. Ó Maolalaidh 'descendant of *Maolaladh*', a personal name composed of the elements *maol* chieftain + *aladh* speckled, piebald.

Vars.: **O'Mullally**, **Mullal(e)y**, **Lally**.

Mullarkey Irish: Anglicized form of Gael. Ó Maoilearca 'descendant of the devotee of (St) *Earc*'.

Mullen 1. Irish: Anglicized form of Gael. Ó Maoláin 'descendant of *Maolán*', a byname meaning 'Tonsured One', 'Devotee' (from *maol* bald; cf. MILLIGAN and MCMILLAN). 2. English: topographic name for someone who lived by a MILL, or occupational name for a MILLER, from ANF *mo(u)lin, mulin* mill.

Vars.: **Mullens**, **Mullin(s)**, **Mullings**, **Millen(s)**. (Of 1 only): **Mullan(e)**, **Mulhane**, **Mullon**, **Millen**, **Milling**, **Mollan**, **Moylan**, **Melane**, **(O')Moylane**, **O'Mullan(e)**, **O'Mollane**, **O'Melane**. (Of 2 only): **Molins**; **Mullin(g)er**, **Mullin(d)ar** (agent derivs.).

Mullinacci see MILL

Mullis English (W Midlands): topographic name for someone who lived by a mill(house), from ME *mulle* mill (W dial. form of OE *mylen*) + *hus* house, or occupational name for someone who worked in one.

Mulloy see MOLLOY

Mullveen see MELVIN

Mulqueen Irish: Anglicized form of Gael. Ó Maolchaoine 'descendant of the devotee of (St) *Caoine*' (see CAIN).

Mulroney see MORONEY

Mulroy Irish: Anglicized form of Gael. Ó Maolruaidh 'descendant of *Maolruadh*', a personal name composed of the elements *maol* chief + *ruadh* red.

Mulryan Irish: Anglicized form of Gael. Ó Maoilríaghain 'descendant of the devotee of (St) *Ríaghan*' (see RYAN).

Vars.: **Mulryne**, **Mulrine**, **Mulran**; **O'Mulr(o)yan**, **O'Mulrigan**, **O'Mulrean**.

Mulvaney Irish: Anglicized form of Gael. Ó Maoilmheana 'descendant of the devotee of (St) *Meana*' (a personal name apparently from *mion* mite, small thing).

Vars.: **Mulvenna**, **Mulvany**.

Mulvey Irish: Anglicized form of Gael. Ó Maoilmhiadhaigh 'descendant of the devotee of (St) *Miadhach*' (a byname meaning 'Honourable').

Mulvihil see MELVILLE

Mumbray see MOWBRAY

Mumby English: habitation name from a place in Lincs., so called from the ON personal name *Mundi* (see MONDAY 1) + ON *býr* farm, settlement.

Mumford see MOUNTFORD

Mummen see MOMMSEN

Munaretti see MILLER

Muncaster English: habitation name from a place in Cumb., known in the Middle Ages as *Mulcaster*, from the OE byname *Mūla* 'Mule', or possibly the ON personal name *Múli* (from *múli* muzzle, snout; see MULE 1) + OE *ceaster* (Roman) fort (L *castra* legionary camp).

Var.: **Mulcaster**.

Munchay see MOUNSEY

Munck see MONK

Munday see MONDAY

Munden English: habitation name from a place in Herts., so called from the OE personal name *Munda* (a short form of any of the various cpd names containing the element *mund* protection) + OE *denu* valley (see DEAN 1).

Mundford see MOUNTFORD

Municio Spanish: of uncertain origin, probably from an old given name, which appears in medieval sources in the L forms *Munitius* and *Munnitus* and is probably related to MUÑO.

Muñiz see MUÑO

Munn see MOON

Munnelly Irish: Anglicized form of Gael. **Ó Maonghaile** 'descendant of *Maonghal*', a personal name composed of the elements *maon* riches + *gal* valour.

Muño Spanish: from an old given name that appears in medieval sources in the L forms *Munnius* and *Monnius*. It is of uncertain origin, perhaps from a Gmc short form of the various cpd personal names with the first element *mund* protection.

Patrs.: **Muñiz**, **Muñoz**. Port.: **Moniz**.

Munro Scots: local name for someone who had migrated from the mouth of the river *Roe* in Derry, N Ireland; the surname is derived from *mun*, mutated form of Gael. *bun* root, river-mouth + *Rotha*, the Gael. name of the river.

Vars.: **Munroe**, **Munrow**, **Monro(e)**.

Muntané see MONTANER

Murat Provençal: habitation name from any of various places so called, from OProv. *murat* fortified (L *mūrātus*, a deriv. of *mūrus* wall; cf. MURO).

Dim.: **Muratet**.

Murchan see MORGAN

Murchie see MCMORROUGH

Murcia Spanish: habitation name from the town, or regional name from the province of this name in SE Spain, apparently so called from L *(aqua) murcida* stagnant water. Alternatively, it may derive from L *Murcia, Murtia*, the name of an obscure Roman or Italic goddess, later used as an epithet of Venus, as if from *myrta, murta* myrtle.

Var.: **Murciano** (also borne by Sefardic Jews).

Murdoch Scots: Anglicized form of the Gael. personal name *Muire(adh)ach*, a deriv. of *muir* sea.

Vars.: **Murdock** (N Ireland); **Murdough**, **Murdow**, **Murdy**, **Mortagh**, **Murt(h)a**. See also MCMURRAY.

Mure see MUIR

Murgatroyd English (W Yorks., chiefly Halifax and Bradford): habitation name from a lost place near Halifax, apparently so called from the medieval female given name *Marg(ar)et* (see MARGUERITE) + Northern ME *royd* clearing (OE *rod*).

Murnane Irish: Anglicized form of Gael. **Ó Murnáin**, a contracted form of *O Manannáin* 'descendant of *Manannán*', a name borne in Celt. mythology by a sea-god.

Muro Spanish: topographic name for someone who lived near a fortification (Sp. *muro*, from L *mūrus* wall), or habitation name from any of the numerous places named with this element (cf. MURAT).

Dims.: Sp.: **Muriel**, **Murillo**.

Murphy Irish: Anglicized form of Gael. **Ó Murchadha** 'descendant of *Murchadh*', a personal name composed of the elements *muir* sea + *cadh* warrior.

Vars.: **O'Murphy**, **(O')Morphy**, **O'Morchoe**. See also MORROW and MCMORROUGH.

Murray 1. Scots: regional name from *Moray* in NE Scotland, apparently so called from old Celt. elements meaning 'sea' + 'settlement'. **2.** Irish: Anglicized form of Gael. *Mac Muire(adh)aigh*; see MCMURRAY. **3.** Irish: Anglicized form of Gael. *Mac Giolla Mhuire*; see GILMORE. **4.** English: var. of MERRY; for the varied treatment of OE *-y-*, cf. HILL 1.

Vars.: **Murr(e)y**, **Murrie**.

Murrell see MERRILL

Murrill see MORRELL

Murroney see MORONEY

Murrough see MORROW

Murtimer see MORTIMER

Murton N English: habitation name from any of various places, in Cumb., Co. Durham, N Yorks., and elsewhere, all so called from OE *mōr* marsh, fen, moor (see MOORE 1) + *tūn* enclosure, settlement; cf. MORTON.

Musaev see MOSES

Muselli see JAMES

Muser see MAUS

Musgrave English: habitation name from a pair of villages in Cumb., so called from OE *mūs* mouse (perhaps a byname) + *grāf* GROVE. The Norman surname *de Mucegros*, established in Herefords. and elsewhere in the 12th and 13th cents., is probably unrelated and has died out.

Var.: **Musgrove**.

Musiał Polish: a fairly common surname, as is its Czech cogn.; both are of uncertain origin. It appears to be a nickname from the masc. sing. past tense of *musieć* must. If this is right, it means something like 'he had to', 'he was forced to', but the circumstances in which this vocab. word gave rise to a surname are not known.

Dims.: Pol.: **Musiałek**. Czech: **Musílek**.

Patr.: Pol.: **Musiałowicz**.

Habitation name: Pol.: **Musiałowski**.

Musset French: habitation name from any of various minor places named with a dim. form of OF *musse* hiding-place, ambush (from *musser, mucier* to hide, of Gaul. origin).
Vars.: MUSSON, **Mussot**.
Dim.: **Mussillon**.

Mussolini Italian: **1.** metonymic occupational name for a seller of muslin, It. *mussolina* (Arabic *mauçilīy*, from the name of *Mosul* in Iraq, where it was first manufactured). **2.** nickname from a double dim. of *mussa* fly; cf. MOUCHE. **3.** from a double dim. of an aphetic form of the given name *Iacomus*; see JAMES.

Musson 1. English (chiefly Notts.): of uncertain origin, ostensibly a patr. **2.** French: var. of MUSSET.

Mustard English: metonymic occupational name for a dealer in spices, or nickname for someone with a hot temper or a vicious tongue, from ME, OF *mo(u)starde* mustard (a deriv. of *mo(u)st* unfermented wine (see MOST 1), in which the mustard seeds were originally prepared).
Var.: **Mustart**.

Mustert *see* MOST

Mustoe English: topographic name for someone who lived near a piece of open ground used as a meeting-place, from ME *motestow*, from OE *(ge)mōt* meeting, assembly (a deriv. of *mētan* to meet) + *stōw* place, site (see STOW).
Vars.: **Musto(w)**.

Mustonen Finnish: patr. from the nickname *Musto* 'Black', denoting someone with dark hair or a dark complexion, or who habitually dressed in black.

Muszinsky *see* MUKHIN

Mutch Scots: nickname for a large (tall or fat) person, from ME *muche* great, a shortened form (probably a back-formation, as if from a dim. with the ANF suffix -*el*) of *muchel*, OE *mycel* (cf. MEIKLE).
Var.: **Much**.

Mutterperl *see* PEARL

Mutton English (chiefly Devon): nickname for a gentle but unimaginative person, one thought to resemble a sheep, or metonymic occupational name for a shepherd, from ANF

m(o)uto(u)n sheep (OF *mouton*, probably of Gaul. origin; cf. Bret. *maout* sheep).
Var.: **Motton**.
Dims.: Fr.: **Moutonneau, Moutonnet, Mout(h)enet, Mouthenot**.

Muzaev *see* MOSES

Mužík Czech: affectionate nickname for a man of short stature, from a vocab. word derived from *muž* man.

Muzzi *see* JAMES

Myall *see* MYHILL

Myasnikov Russian: patr. from the occupational term *myasnik* butcher (from *myaso* meat).

Myatt English (chiefly W Midlands): from the ME given name *Myat*, formed from a truncated version of *Mihel* (see MYHILL) + the dim. suffix -*at* (from OF -*et*, crossed with the originally pej. OF -*ard*).
Vars.: **Miatt, Myott, Miot**.

Myddleton *see* MIDDLETON

Myers *see* MAYER

Myerscough English (Lancs.): habitation name from a place in Lancs., so called from ON *mýrr* marsh, mire + *skógr* copse (cf. SHAW).

Myhill English (Norfolk): from the ME, ANF given name *Mihel*, a vernacular form of MICHAEL.
Vars.: **Mighell, Mighill; Miell, Miall, Myall**.
Dim.: Fr.: **Miellet**.

Mykyta *see* NIKITIN

Myles *see* MILES

Mynn *see* MINN

Myott *see* MYATT

Myslivec Czech: occupational name for a hunter or game-keeper, from a vocab. word ultimately derived from *mysl* mind.
Dim.: **Mysliveček**.

Myszka *see* MAUS

Myton English: habitation name from *Myton* in Warwicks. or *Mytton* in Shrops., both so called from OE *(ge)mȳðe* confluence, place where two streams meet + *tūn* enclosure, settlement. See also MITTON.
Var.: **Mytton**.

N

Nabais Portuguese: metonymic occupational name for a turnip farmer or topographic name for someone who lived by turnip fields, from the pl. form of Port. *nabal* turnip field (LL *nāpāle*, a deriv. of *nāpus* turnip; cf. NEAPE).

Nabarro see NAVARRO

Nabokov Russian: apparently a patr. from a nickname *Nabok*, derived from the phrase *na bok* (with the accent on the preposition) on(to) one's side; the application of the nickname is not clear. Compare BOCZEK.

Nacci see JOHN

Nacewicz see IGNACE

Nachimovski see NAHUM

Nachmann Jewish: from the Hebr. male given name *Nachman*, which is probably a var. of the biblical male given name *Nachum* 'Consoled' (see NAHUM).

Vars.: **Na(c)hman**; **Na(c)hmani**, **Na(c)hmany** (with the Hebr. suffix -*i*).

Patrs.: **Nachmanson** (Ashkenazic); **Nachmanovitz**, **Nachmanowitz**, **Nachminovitch** (E Ashkenazic, the latter reflecting Yid. *Nakhmen*); **Nachmanovici**, **Nachminovici** (Rumanian spellings).

Nader see NÄHER

Nadin see NOEL

Nadler English, German, and Jewish (Ashkenazic): occupational name for a maker of needles, or in some cases perhaps for a tailor, from an agent deriv. of ME *nadle* needle, Ger. *Nadel* (OE *nǣdle*; MHG *nādel(e)*, OHG *nād(a)la*; cf. NÄHER). Needles in the Middle Ages were comparatively coarse articles made from bone.

Vars.: Eng.: **Needler**; **Ne(e)lder**, **Nayldor**; **Neilder** (mainly Cornwall and Devon); **Needle**. Ger.: **Nold(n)er**, **Nöldner**, **Nöllner**, **Nadel**. Jewish: **Nadel(man)**; **Nodelman** (from Yid. *nodl* needle); **Nudel(man)**, **Nudler** (from a S Yid. pronunciation of *nodl*).

Cpds: Jewish: **Nadelstecher** ('needle sticker', probably a derogatory nickname for a tailor); **Nadelstern** ('needle star', occupational-ornamental); **Nadelstock** ('needle staff', occupational-ornamental).

Nádvorník Czech: occupational name for a chamberlain, head servant, or overseer, from Czech *na* on, over + *dvůr* household, court (see DVOŘÁK) + -*ník* suffix of agent nouns. The vocab. word is more or less equivalent to Ger. HOFMEISTER.

Naesmith see NAYSMITH

Naftali Jewish: from the Hebr. male given name *Naftali* 'I have struggled', borne by one of the twelve sons of Jacob. On his death bed Jacob blessed him with the words 'Naphtali is a hind let loose: he giveth goodly words' (Gen. 49: 21), and it is possible that in at least some cases surnames

meaning 'deer' have been chosen by Jews in allusion to this; see, e.g., CERF 2 and HIRSCH 2.

Vars.: **Naftaly**, **Nafthalie**.

Patrs.: **Naftalis(on)** (Ashkenazic); **Naftalin**, **Naftalovici** (E Ashkenazic; the latter is a Rumanian spelling); **Naftolin** (reflecting the NE Yid. pronunciation of the given name); **Naftulis**, **Naftulin** (reflecting a S Yid. pronunciation of the given name).

Nafz German: nickname for a sleepyhead, from a deriv. of MHG *nafzen* to take a nap (OHG *(h)naffezan*).

Vars.: **Nafz(g)er**, **Nefzger**.

Nagar Jewish (Ashkenazic): occupational name for a carpenter, Hebr. *nagar*.

Vars.: **Naggar**; **Nager** (if this name is indeed related to *Nagar*, it shows alteration of the final vowel under Yid. influence; if not, it is from *Näger* (see NÄHER); **Nagari** (with the Hebr. suffix -*i*).

Patr. (E Ashkenazic): **Nagarin** (with the Slav. suffix -*in*).

Nagelberg see NAYLOR

Näger see NÄHER

Naghten see NAUGHTON

Nagle see NANGLE

Nagy Hungarian and Jewish (Ashkenazic): nickname for a large man, from Hung. *nagy* big. As a Hung. name it is contrasted with KISS and used to describe the older of two bearers of the same given name.

Näher German: occupational name for a tailor, from an agent deriv. of Ger. *nähen* to sew (MHG *najen*, OHG *nājan*; cf. NADLER).

Vars.: **Näger**, **Neher**, **Neger**, **Nei(g)er**; **Nader**, **Näder**; **Nather**, **Nät(h)er**, **Nether**.

Nahman see NACHMANN

Nahum Jewish: from the Hebr. male given name *Nachum* 'Consoled', borne by a minor prophet, the author of the Book of the Bible that bears his name. The Russ. form of the name, *Naum*, is widespread even among non-Jews, because of folk-etymological association with Russ. *naumnik* genius, from the root *um* mind.

Vars.: **Naum** (from the Russ. given name); **Nahumi** (with the Hebr. ending -*i*).

Dims.: Ukr.: **Naumenko**. Beloruss.: **Navumenko**, **Naumchik**, **Navumchik**.

Patrs.: Jewish: **Nahumson**, **Na(c)himson**, **Nachimzon** (Ashkenazic); **Nakhumovich**, **Na(c)humovsky**, **Nachimovski** (E Ashkenazic); **Nochimowski** (NE Ashkenazic, from Yid. *Nokhem*, a reflex of the Hebr. given name); **Nukhimovich**, **Nuhimovsky** (S Ashkenazic, from a S Yid. pronunciation of the Yid. given name). Russ.: **Naumov**. Beloruss.: **Navumov**. Croatian: **Naumović**.

Patrs. (from dims.): Russ.: **Naumshin**, **Naumychev**.

Nairn Scots: habitation name from the town of this name, east of Inverness, so called from the river at whose mouth it stands. The river name is of ancient and disputed origin.

Var.: **Nairne**.

Naisbet see NISBIT

Naish see NASH

Naismith see NAYSMITH

Nakhumovich see NAHUM

Nalder English: topographical name for someone who lived by an alder, a var. of ALDER 2 by misdivision from ME *atten al(d)re* at the alder; cf. NASH and NOAKE.

Derivs.: **Naldrett**, **Neldrett** (from *atten al(d)rett* by the alder grove).

Naldini see NAUD

Nally see McNALLY

Nanard see NEAME

Nancarrow Cornish: habitation name from places in the parishes of St Allen and St Michael Penkivel, so called from Corn. *nans* valley + *carow* deer, stag or *garow* rough.

Nanelli see JOHN

Nangle English and Irish (Norman): var. of ANGLE, from a misdivision of ME *atten angle*.

Vars.: **N(e)agle** (reflecting the OF pronunciation with a nasalized vowel); **de Nógla** (a Gaelicized form).

Nankervis Cornish: habitation name from a place in St Enoder parish, so called from Corn. *nans* valley + an uncertain second element, possibly **cerwys*, an unattested pl. of *carow* stag. Compare NANCARROW.

Nankivell Cornish: habitation name from a place in the parish of St Mawgan in Pydar, so called from Corn. *nans* valley + a personal name *Cuvel*.

Nanne Low German and Danish: from a Fris. personal name, in origin probably a nursery term, but in the Middle Ages also taken as a short form of various Gmc cpd names containing the element *nand* daring, brave (cf., e.g., FERDINAND).

Dims.: **Nanneke**, **Nenneke**.

Patrs.: **Nannen**, **Nansen**, **Nanning(a)**.

Napier Scots, English, and French: occupational name for a seller of table linen or for a 'naperer', the servant in charge of the linen in use in a manor house. The name represents ME, OF *nap(p)ier*, an agent deriv. of OF *nappe* table cloth (L *mappa*, of apparently Punic origin).

Vars.: Eng.: **Nap(p)er**.

Napleton see APPLETON

Napoleoni Italian: from the Corsican given name *Napoleone*, of uncertain origin. It has been suggested that it is from the Gmc personal name *Nibelung* 'son of Mist, Fog' (see NIEBLICH), but in folk etymology it has been associated with the city of *Naples* (see NAPOLI) + It. *leone* lion.

Vars.: **Napolioni**; **Nebuloni**, **Nebulone** (Lombardy); **Nuvoloni**, **Nuvolone** (Lombardy, Liguria).

Napoli Italian: habitation name from the Campanian city of *Naples* (It. *Napoli*, L *Neapolis*, from Gk *nea* new + *polis* city; it was an ancient Gk colony taken over by the Romans in the 4th cent. BC).

Vars.: **di Napoli**; **Napoletano**, **Napolitano**.

Nápravník Czech: status name for a feudal tenant, who held land as of right in return for various duties to his lord, from Czech *na* on, over + *právo* right, entitlement + *-ník* suffix of agent nouns.

Naquet French: occupational name for a young lad or serving man, OF *naquet* (apparently a dim. of *naque* mucus, snot, a word of uncertain origin).

Var.: **Naquin**.

Pej.: **Naquard**.

Naranjo Spanish: metonymic occupational name for a grower of oranges or topographic name for someone who lived by an orange grove, from Sp. *naranjo* orange tree (from *naranja* orange, Arabic *nārángya*, probably derived via Sanskrit and Persian from a Dravidian language). The word *orange* reached Eng. from Sp. via OF and OProv., in which languages the initial *n-* had already been sporadically lost.

Dims.: It.: **Aranzello**, **Ranzetti**.

Narciso Portuguese: from a medieval given name (L *Narcissus*, from Gk *Narkissos*, the name of a flower). This name was borne, according to classical myth, by a vain youth who was so transfixed by his own beauty that he ignored the blandishments of the nymph Echo and stared at his own reflection in water until he faded away and turned into the pale but lovely flower that bears his name. It was also borne by several early Christian saints, in particular by a bishop who was said to have been put to death, together with his deacon Felix, in Catalonia AD *c.*307. The given name owes its popularity to this saint rather than to the mythological youth.

Nardi 1. Italian: from an aphetic form of any of the various medieval It. given names (of Gmc origin) ending in the syllable *-nard(o)*; cf., e.g., BERNARD, LEONARD, and REYNARD. 2. Jewish (Israeli): ornamental name from Hebr. *nerd* nard, an aromatic plant.

Var. (of 1): **Nardo**.

Dims. (of 1): **Nardelli**, **Nard(i)ello**, **Nardin(i)**, **Nardulli**, **Narducci**, **Narduzzi**. Fr.: **Nardet**, **Nardeau**, **Nardin**, **Nardon(neau)**, **Nardou(x)**.

Augs. (of 1): It.: **Nardon(i)**, **Nardone**.

Nardoni see BERNARD

Narracott see NORTHCOTT

Nascimento Portuguese: religious byname from Port. *nascimento* birth, nativity (LL *nascimentum*, from *nasci* to be born). This was one of the epithets of the Virgin (*Maria do Nascimento*), and was also used as a given name for children born at Christmas.

Nash 1. S English: topographic name for someone who lived by an ash tree, a var. of ASH by misdivision of ME *atten ash* 'at the ash'; cf. NALDER and NOAKE. 2. Jewish: of unknown origin, possibly an Anglicized form of one or more like-sounding Jewish surnames.

Var. (of 1): **Naish** (chiefly Wilts. and Somerset).

Nasi *see* JOHN

Naslednikov Russian: patr. from the nickname *Naslednik* 'Heir' (a deriv. of *(na)sledit* to follow (on)), given perhaps to a man who had inherited a great deal of money, or perhaps merely to someone with great expectations.

Nasmith *see* NAYSMITH

Nassau German: habitation name from the small town of *Nassau*, formerly the seat of an independent duchy. The name comes from OHG *nazz* damp, wet + *ouwa* water meadow.

Nast German: topographic name for someone who lived in a thickly wooded area, or metonymic occupational name for a woodcutter, from MHG *nast* branch, a regional var. of *ast*, resulting from the misdivision of forms such as *ein ast* 'a branch'.

Var.: **Ast** (also Jewish, of unknown origin, perhaps to be explained in the same way as the Ger. name).

Dim.: **Nestle** (Switzerland), Gallicized as **Nestlé**.

Nastić *see* ANSTICE

Nathan Jewish and English (Notts.): from the Hebr. male given name *Natan* 'Given' (i.e. by God; cf. *Jonathan* and *Nathaniel*), borne by a minor biblical prophet (2 Sam. 7: 2). The given name was a comparatively rare one among non-Jews in the Middle Ages (although always common among Jews); as a modern surname it is most frequently Jewish.

Vars.: Jewish: **Natan**; **Nusan**, **Nusen** (based on S Yid. pronunciations). Eng.: **Natan**; **Nation** (W Midlands; altered by folk etymology).

Dims.: Jewish: **Nuta** (based on a S Yid. pronunciation).

Patrs.: Jewish: **Nat(h)ans**, **Nat(h)anso(h)n**, **Nat(h)anzon**, **Natenzon**, **Nathansen**, **Nusinzon** (Ashkenazic); **Nus(s)inov**, **Nusynowicz**, **Nusynowitz**, **Nusinowitz**, **Nus(s)inovitz**, **Nusynowicz** (E Ashkenazic, from S Yid. pronunciations); **Natanov** (not exclusively Ashkenazic).

Patrs. (from dims.): Jewish: **Notes**, **Notowitz**, **Nutin**; **Notkin**, **Notkovich**, **Nutkevitch**, **Nutk(i)ewicz**, **Nutkewitz**, **Nutkevitz**; **Noszkes**, **Noskes**, **Noskovitz**, **Noskowitz**.

Näthbom *see* NUTT

Nather *see* NÄHER

Natten *see* NAUGHTON

Nauber *see* NEUBAUER

Naud 1. French: from an aphetic form of various medieval given names derived from Gmc personal names ending in the element *wald* rule; cf., e.g., ARNOLD and REYNOLD. **2.** Provençal: cogn. of the given name NOEL. **3.** Provençal:

metonymic occupational name for a sailor or boat-builder, from OProv. *nau* boat, ship (L *navis*).

Vars. (of 1): **Naude**, **Nault**.

Dims. (of 1): Fr.: **Naudet**, **Naudin**, **Naudot**, **Naudon**. Low Ger.: **Nöl(de)ke**. It.: **Naldini**, **Nallini**.

Aug. (of 1): It.: **Naldone**.

Patrs. (from 1): Low Ger.: **Nolten**, **Nolting**, **Nölting**.

Patrs. (from 1) (dim.): Low Ger.: **Nölker**, **Nölken**.

Naughton 1. Irish: Anglicized form of the Gael. personal name *Neachtan*. This was the name of the god of water and the sea in Irish mythology. It has been suggested that the name is derived from L *Neptūnus* Neptune, the Roman sea-god. **2.** English: habitation name from a place in Suffolk, so called from OE *nafola* navel, depression + *tūn* enclosure, settlement.

Vars. (of 1): **Naughtan**, **Na(u)ghten**, **Nochtin**, **Nocton**, **Knockton**, **Natten**, **Natton**, NORTON.

'Descendant of N. 1': **O'Naughton**, **O'Naghtan**, **O'N(e)aghten** (Gael. **Ó Neachtain**).

Naugolnikov Russian: patr. from *Naugolnik*, denoting someone who lived at a corner, from *na* on, at + *ugol* corner + *-nik* suffix of agent nouns.

Naum *see* NAHUM

Nava Spanish: habitation name for someone who lived on a flat, treeless area of upland, Sp. *nava* (a word of pre-Roman origin). There are numerous places named with this element, any of which may also have given rise to the surname. The name is also borne by Sefardic Jews, the reason(s) for its adoption being unknown.

Var. (Sp. only): **Navas**.

Navarrete Spanish: habitation name from places in the provinces of Logroño and Álava, so called from the Basque elements *Nafar* Navarrese (see NAVARRO) + *ate* pass, defile.

Navarro Spanish and Jewish (Sefardic): regional name for someone from Navarre (Sp. *Navarra*), now divided between Spain and France, but in the Middle Ages an independent Basque kingdom. Its name may have some connection with Sp. *nava* treeless plateau (see NAVA).

Vars.: **Nabarro**. Jewish only: **Navaro**.

Navàs Catalan: habitation name from a place in the province of Barcelona, so called from the pre-Roman element NAVA + the suffix *-às*, which is of Celt. origin and uncertain significance.

Navière *see* NEAPE

Navin *see* NEVIN

Navrátil Czech: nickname from the masc. sing. past tense of the verb *navrátit* to return, perhaps originally used to refer to someone who had returned to his native community after a prolonged absence. The Czech surname does not have the meaning 'Convert' borne by the Pol. cogn. NAWROCKI.

Navumchik *see* NAHUM

Nawrocki Polish: name adopted by a religious convert, in particular a Jew who had converted to Christianity, from Pol. *nawróc* to turn.

Var.: **Nawrot**.

Nay *see* NYE

Naybour *see* NEIGHBOUR

Nayldor *see* NADLER

Naylor English: occupational name for a maker of nails, from an agent deriv. of ME *nayl* nail (OE *nægel*).

Vars.: **Nayler**, **Naylar**.

Patrs.: Flem., Du.: **Nagelma(e)kers**.

Cpds (ornamental elaborations of *Nagel*): Jewish (Ashkenazic): **Nagelberg** ('nail hill'); **Nagelstein** ('nail stone').

Naysmith Scots and English: occupational name for a maker of knives or of nails, from OE *cnīf* knife or *nægel* nail + *smið* SMITH.

Vars.: **Naismith**, **Na(e)smith**, **Nasmyth**.

Nazaire French: from the given name *Nazaire*, which was relatively common in the Middle Ages in France as a result of the popularity of a 5th-cent. saint so called, abbot of Lérins. The given name represents a vernacular form of L *Nazareus* or Gk *Nazarios*, a deriv. of *Nazareth* (Hebr. *Natserat*, perhaps from a root meaning 'to guard, protect'), applied to early Christians as followers of Jesus of Nazareth and accepted by them as an honourable personal name.

Patrs.: Russ.: **Nazarov**, **Nazaryev(ykh)**. Armenian: **Nazarian**.

Patrs. (from dims.): Ger.: **Zarges**, **Zerges**, **Zerr(i)es**. Russ.: **Nazartsev**.

Neachell *see* ETCHELLS

Neagle *see* NANGLE

Neal English: var. of NEIL. This is the usual spelling of the surname in S and central England, derived from ME forms of the given name such as *Neel*.

Vars.: **Neale**, **Neall**.

Patr.: **NELSON**.

Nealon *see* NEIL

Neame English: **1.** var. of ME *eame* uncle (see EAME), arising from misdivision of the common term of address *mine eame* 'my uncle'. **2.** nickname for a very short man, from OF *nain* dwarf (L *nānus*). In ME, Fr. nasalized vowels with *n* or *m* were regularly confused.

Dims. (of 2): Fr.: **Nanet**, **Naneix**, **Naneau**, **Nanin**, **Nanot**.

Pej. (of 2): Fr.: **Nanard**.

Neape English: metonymic occupational name for a grower or seller of turnips and other root vegetables (perhaps also a nickname), from ME *neep* turnip (OE *næp*, from L *nāpus*; cf. NABAIS).

Var.: **Neep**.

Collective: Fr.: **Navière**.

Neary Irish: Anglicized form of Gael. **Ó Náraigh** 'descendant of *Nárach*', a byname meaning 'Modest'.

Neat English: metonymic occupational name for a herdsman in charge of cattle or nickname for someone thought to resemble an ox or a cow, from ME *neat* ox, cow (OE *nēat*).

The mod. Eng. adj. *neat* (via Fr. from L *nitidus* clean, shining) does not occur before the 16th cent., after the main period of surname formation.

Var.: **Neate**.

Neave *see* NEVE

Nébodon *see* NEVEU

Nebulone *see* NAPOLEONI

Nechells *see* ETCHELLS

Nedergård Danish: habitation name from a placename composed of the elements *neder* lower + *gård* enclosure; cf. OVERGÅRD.

Vars.: **Nedergaard**; **Neegård**, **Neegaard**.

Nedham *see* NEEDHAM

Nee Irish: Anglicized form of Gael. **Ó Niadh** 'descendant of *Nia(dh)*', a byname meaning 'Warrior'.

Vars.: **O'Nee**, **O'Nea**, **O'Ney**, **(O')Knee**. See also NEVILLE.

Need English: probably a nickname for an impoverished person, from ME *nede* poverty, hardship (OE *nēd*).

Needham English: habitation name from places in Derbys., Norfolk, and Suffolk, so called from OE *nēd* need, hardship + *hām* homestead, i.e. a place that provided a poor living.

Var.: **Nedham**.

Needle *see* NADLER

Neefken *see* NEVE

Neegaard *see* NEDERGÅRD

Neel *see* NEIL

Neelis *see* MCNELIS

Neels *see* CORNEILLE

Neely *see* MCNEILLY

Neenan *see* NOONAN

Neep *see* NEAPE

Neesen *see* ANNIS

Neeson *see* MCNEICE

Nefgen *see* NEVE

Nefimanov *see* YEFIMOV

Neger *see* NÄHER

Negrato *see* NOIR

Negus **1.** English: of uncertain origin. It is conceivably a topographic name for someone who lived in a house that was near but not in a main settlement, from OE *nēah* near + *hūs* house. Other writers claim a Corn. origin for it, but this does not seem plausible. **2.** Rumanian: occupational name for a merchant (LL *negōtiātor*, from *negōtiāri* to trade, deal, a deriv. of *negōtium* business, affair).

Var. (of 2): **Negustor**.

Neher *see* NÄHER

Nehls *see* CORNEILLE

Neier *see* NÄHER

Neighbour English: from ME *nechebure* (a cpd of OE *nēah* near + *gebūr* dweller; cf. BAUER). This may have been used as a nickname for someone who was a 'good neighbour', or more probably it derives from the common use of the word as a term of address.
Var.: **Naybour**.

Neil Irish, Scots, and English: from a given name of Ir. origin, Gael. *Niall* (gen. *Néill*), thought to mean 'Champion'. This was adopted by Norsemen in the form *Njáll*, and was brought to England both directly from Ireland by Scandinavian settlers and indirectly by the Normans. Among the latter it had taken the form *Ni(h)el*, which was altered by folk etymology to the L form *Nigellus* (see NIGEL).
Vars.: **Neill** (chiefly N Irish; also Scots); **Neild**; NEAL; **Neel(e)**; **Neeld**; NELL; **Niall, Niell, Niel(d), Nihell, Nihill**.
Patrs.: Eng.: **Neels, Niles**; **Neilson** (Sc.); **Ni(e)lson**. Sc., Ir.: **McNeil(l), McNeille, McNeal(l), McNeale, McNeel, McNiel; McGreal** (Ulster). Manx: **Kneale**. Dan., Norw.: **N(i)elsen**. Swed.: **Ni(e)lsson**.
'Descendant of N.': Ir.: **O'Neil(l), O'Neal** (Gael. **Ó Néill**).
'Descendant of N. (dim.)': Ir.: **(O')Neilane, (O')Nillane, (O')Ne(y)lane, Ne(i)lan, Nilan, Nilon, Nealon, Neylon, Neylan(d), N(e)iland, Neelan(d), Neelands** (Gael. **Ó Nialláin**).

Neil *see* NEIL

Neilder *see* NADLER

Neilly *see* McNEILLY

Neising *see* DENNIS

Neison *see* McNEICE

Nejedlý Czech: nickname for an unpleasant or unsavoury individual, from the adj. *nejedlý* unappetizing, inedible, from *ne* not + *jedlý* edible.

Nekludov Russian: patr. from the nickname *Neklud* 'Disorder', 'Disarray', referring to an untidy or clumsy person. Uncomplimentary nicknames such as this might also be given by fond parents to their children as familiar names, in the hope that they would discourage evil spirits from paying too much attention (cf. NEKRASOV).
Var.: **Nekhlyudov**.

Nekolný Czech: nickname for a stubborn person, from Czech *ne* not + the rare or obsolete adj. *kolný* unstable (mod. Czech *kolísavý*).
Vars.: **Nekola, Nekula**.

Nekrasov Russian: patr. from the nickname *Nekras* 'Ugly' (from the negative particle *ne-* + *kras* beauty, colour, brightness). This seems often to have been given as an apotropaic familiar name, expressing the parents' wish that a child should grow up handsome (cf. NEKLUDOV). The surname is also borne among E Ashkenazic Jews, among whom it presumably represents an adoption of the Russ. surname.

Nelan *see* NEIL

Nelder *see* NADLER

Neles *see* CORNEILLE

Nell English: from the ME given name *Nel(le)*, a var. of NEIL.
Patr.: Eng.: NELSON.

Nelmes *see* ELM

Nelson English: patr. from NELL or NEAL, both of which go back to the same original Ir. personal name, *Niall* (see NEIL).

Nemchinov Russian: patr. from the name *Nemchin* German. In OSlav. this word was evidently used to denote any foreigner, being derived from *nemoi* dumb, referring to an inability to speak intelligibly. The Gk word *barbaros* had a similar meaning (cf. BARBARY).
Var.: **Nemtsev**.
Dims.: Ukr.: **Nimchenko**. Pol.: **Niemczyk**. Czech: **Němeček**. Ger. (of Slav. origin): **Niemtschke**. Jewish: **Niemczyk, Niemtchik, Niemchenok**.

Nemes Hungarian: status name or nickname from the adj. *nemes* possessing noble rights and privileges.

Nemmock *see* NIMMO

Nencetti *see* LAWRENCE

Nenneke *see* NANNE

Nepveu *see* NEVEU

Neretti *see* NOIR

Nerhenny *see* McNAIRN

Neruda Czech: nickname for a difficult or unsociable individual, from the adj. *neródný* inflexible, surly.
Var.: **Nerud**.

Nesbit *see* NISBIT

Nesen *see* ANNIS

Ness English and Scots: topographic name for someone who lived on a headland or promontory, Northern ME *ness* (ON *nes*), or habitation name from any of the places named with this term, for example *Ness* in Ches. and N Yorks. The name is now most common in Scotland. It coincides in form with the Gael. personal name *Ness*, but there is no evidence to suggest that the two are connected.

Nesterov Russian: patr. from the given name *Nester* (Gk *Nestōr*, the name of an old and wise hero in Homer's *Iliad*). The name is of uncertain etymology, perhaps from Gk *neisthai* to return (safely). It was borne by a 3rd-cent. Pamphilian bishop who became a popular saint in the Orthodox Church.
Var.: **Nesterin**.
Dims.: Croatian: **Nešković, Neš(ov)ić**.

Nestle *see* NAST

Nether *see* NÄHER

Nethercott English: topographic name for someone who lived in a cottage at the lower end of a settlement (from ME *nether(e)* lower (OE *neoðera*) + *cot* cottage (see COATES)), or habitation name from *Nethercote* in Oxon. or *Nethercot* in Northants, both of which are named with these elements.

Netherton English: habitation name from a place named with the OE elements *neoðera* lower + *tūn* enclosure, settlement. This could be the one in Worcs. or the one in Northants, but is more likely to be from one of the eight places so called in Devon, where the surname is most common.

Netherwood English: habitation name from some place named as the 'lower wood', from OE *neoðera* lower + *wudu* Wood.

Netti *see* John

Nettlefold English: habitation name from a minor place, probably the lost settlement of *Nettlefold* in Dorking, Surrey. This is named from OE *netele* nettle + *fal(o)d* enclosure (see Fold) or *feld* pasture, open country (see Field).

Var.: **Nettlefield**.

Nettleton English (Yorks.): habitation name from a place so called, probably the one in Lincs., although there is also one in Wilts. The name is derived from OE *netele* nettle + *tūn* enclosure, settlement.

Neubauer 1. German: nickname for an agricultural worker who was new to an area, from MHG *niuwe* new + *gebūre* peasant (see Bauer). 2. Jewish (Ashkenazic): apparently an adoption of the Ger. surname (Jews were not usually agricultural workers at the time when surnames were acquired). Alternatively, the name may have been taken by someone who had just built a new house (from mod. Ger. *neu* new + *bauen* to build), or it may have been intended to express hope for the rebuilding of the Temple in Jerusalem (from mod. Ger. *Neubau* new building, reconstruction).

Vars.: Ger.: **Neuber(t)**, **Neuper(t)**, **Nauber**.

Neužil Czech: descriptive nickname for a miser, from Czech *ne* not + *užilý* generous.

Nevado Spanish: nickname for someone with snow-white hair, from Sp. *nevado*, past part. of *nevar* to snow (LL *nivāre*, from *nix* snow, gen. *nivis*; cf. Nieves).

Nevalainen Finnish: ornamental name from Finn. *neva* marsh + the locative/patr. suffix *-lainen*.

Neve English (Norfolk): from ME *neve* nephew (OE *nefa*), presumably denoting the nephew of some great personage, or perhaps an orphan who was brought up in in the guardianship of his uncle (cf. Eame).

Vars.: **Neave**, **Neeve**.

Dims.: Low Ger.: **Neefken**, **Nefgen**.

Patrs.: Eng.: **Neaves**, **Neeves**. Low Ger.: **Neeven**. Flem.: **Neefs**, **Neven**.

Nevet *see* Knight

Neveu French: from OF *neveu* nephew (L *nepos*, gen. *nepōtis*); for the application(s) as a surname, cf. Neve.

Vars.: **Neveux**, **Nepveu**; **Leneveu**.

Dim.: Prov.: **Nébodon**.

Neville 1. English and Irish (Norman): habitation name from *Neuville* in Calvados or *Néville* in Seine-Maritime, both so called from OF *neu(f)* new (L *novus*) + *ville* settlement (see Ville). 2. Irish: a further Anglicization of Gael. *Ó Niadh* (see Nee) and of Nevin.

Vars.: **Nevile**, **Nevill**; **Newell**, **Newill**.

Nevin 1. Scots and Irish: Anglicized form of Gael. **Mac Naoimhín**, patr. from a personal name representing a dim. of *naomh* saint. 2. Irish: Anglicized form of Gael. **Mac Cnáimhín** and **Ó Cnáimhín** 'son' and 'descendant of *Cnámh*', a byname meaning 'Bone', apparently used to refer to a thin man.

Vars.: **Neven**, **Navin**; **Niven** (Sc.); Neville. (Of 1 only): **McNevin**, **McNiven**; **Nevins**, **Nevi(n)son** (chiefly Sc.). (Of 2 only): **O'Knavin**.

New English: 1. nickname for a newcomer to an area, from ME *newe* new (OE *nēowe*, *nīwe*). 2. topographic name for someone who lived by a yew tree, from a misdivision of the ME phrase *atten ew* at the yew (OE *æt ðæm ēowe*).

Patrs. (from 1): Eng.: **Newson** (Norfolk); **Newing**.

Cpds (of 1; mostly ornamental): Swed.: **Nyberg** ('new hill'); **Nyblom** ('new flower'); **Nygren** ('new branch'); **Nyholm** ('new island'); **Nylander** ('dweller on new land'); **Nylund** ('new grove'); **Nyqvist** ('new twig'); **Nystedt** ('new homestead'); **Nyström** ('new river').

Newall English: topographic name for someone who lived at a 'new hall' (cf. New 1 and Hall), occupational name for someone who worked in one, or habitation name from a place named with these elements.

Newberry English: habitation name from any of the many places named with the OE elements *nēowe* New + *burh* fortress, town (see Berry 1 and Bury).

Vars.: **Newbery**, **Newbury**, **Newb(o)rough**, **Newburgh**.

Newbold English: nickname for someone who lived in a newly constructed dwelling, from OE *nēowe* New + *bold* building (see Bold 2). There are several places (in Ches., Derbys., Lancs., Leics., Northants, Notts., Warwicks., and Worcs.) named with these elements, and the surname may also be derived from any or all of them.

Vars.: **Newbould**, **Newbo(u)lt**; **Newbald** (places in E Yorks.).

Newby English: habitation name from any of the various places in N England named with the ME elements *newe* New + *by* farm, settlement (of ON origin); cf. Newton.

Newcombe English: nickname for a new arrival in a place, from ME *newe* New + *come* comer (OE *cuma*, *cumen*, past part. of *cuman* to come). The intrusive -*b*- is the result of the influence of placenames ending in -*combe* (see Coombe).

Vars.: **Newcome(n)**.

Newell *see* Neville

Newey English (W Midlands): topographic name for someone who lived at a 'new enclosure', from OE *nēowe* New + *haga* enclosure (see Haig 2), or habitation name from some minor place named with these elements. *Newhay* and *Newhey* occur several times as placenames in Ches.

Var.: **Neway**.

Newham English: habitation name from any of the various places, for example in Northumb. and N Yorks., so called from OE *nēowe* New + *hām* homestead.

Vars.: **Newnham**, **Nuneham** (with the adj. retaining the weak dat. -*an* inflection, originally used after a preposition and article).

Newhouse English: topographic name for someone who lived in a 'new house' (cf. NEW and HOUSE), or habitation name from some minor place named with these elements. See also NEWSOME.

Newland English: topographic name for someone who lived by a patch of land recently brought into cultivation, or recently added to the village, or habitation name from any of a number of settlements called *Newland* for this reason; cf. NEW and LAND 1.

Var.: **Newlands** (as a Scots name this derives from either of two places so called, a barony in Kincardine and a parish in Peebles).

Newman English: nickname for a newcomer to a place, from ME *newe* NEW + *man* man. This form has also been used as an Anglicization of many of the cogns. listed below and of non-cogn. equivalents such as CHODOSH, or more distantly related cogns. such as the group listed at NOVÁK.

Newport English: habitation name from any of several towns so called, from OE *nēowe* NEW + *port* market town (see PORT 2). The name is common in Bristol, where it probably derives from Newport in Gwent, just across the Bristol Channel.

Newsome English (chiefly Yorks.): habitation name from a place named with the OE phrase *(æt δǣm) nēowan hūsum* (at the) new houses. This and some of the vars. listed below are common as placenames in N England.

Vars.: **Newsom**, **Newsam**, **Newsum**; **Newson** (see also NEW); **Newsham** (chiefly Lancs.); **Newsholme** (places in Humberside and Lancs.).

Newstead 1. English: habitation name from any of the various places in Lincs., Notts. (*Newstead* Abbey), and elsewhere, so called from OE *nēowe* NEW + *stede* place (see STEAD 1). 2. Jewish (Ashkenazic): Anglicized form of **Neustadt**, which is equivalent in meaning to NEWTON.

Newton English: habitation name from any of the many places so called, from OE *nēowe* NEW + *tūn* enclosure, settlement. According to Ekwall, this is the commonest Eng. placename. For this reason, the surname has a highly fragmented origin.

Ney *see* NYE

Neylan *see* NEIL

Neyrat *see* NOIR

Niall *see* NEIL

Niblett English: of unknown origin, possibly a nickname from a double dim. of ME *nibbe*, dial. form of *neb* beak, referring to someone with a prominent or beaklike nose.

Nice English: nickname from ME, OF *nice* foolish, simple (L *nescius* ignorant). In the 14th cent. the Eng. word also acquired the sense 'wanton' and in the 15th cent. 'coy', 'shy', both of which meanings may be reflected in the surname. The sense 'fastidious', 'precise', 'minute' developed only in the 16th cent., probably too late to have given rise to any surnames, and the present-day sense of general approbation is not clearly attested until the late 19th cent.

Nicholas English and Welsh: from the given name (Gk *Nikolaos*, from *nikān* to conquer + *laos* people). Forms with *-ch-* are the result of hypercorrection (cf. ANTHONY).

The name was popular among Christians throughout Europe in the Middle Ages, largely as a result of the fame of a 4th-cent. Lycian bishop, about whom a large number of legends grew up, and who was venerated in the Orthodox Church as well as the Catholic. E European forms of this name are spelled with initial *M-*: Czech *Mikuláš*, Pol. *Mikołaj*. Aphetic short forms (without the first syllable) were also common in most European languages; surnames derived from these are listed at COLL 1 and KLAUS. The normal ME vernacular form was *Nicol*, and this was also sometimes borne by women as well as the feminine forms *Nicole* and *Nicola*.

Vars.: **Nic(o)las** (Wales), **Nickless** (W Midlands); **Nichol(l)**, **Nicoll**, **Nic(k)ol**, **Nickal**, **Nickel(l)**, **Nickle**.

Dims.: Eng.: **Nicklin** (W Midlands, esp. Staffs.). Fr.: **Nicol(l)et**, **Niclot**, **Nicollic** (Brittany). Prov.: **Nicolou**, **Nicloux**. It.: **Nic(c)olini**, **Nicoletti**, **Nicorini**, **Nicorelli**, **Nic(c)olucci**, **Nicolussi**. Ger.: **Nick**, **Nick(e)l**, **Nigg**, **Niggl(i)**; **Läule**, **Laulin** (Switzerland); **Nick(l)isch**, **Nick(u)sch**, **Nitsch(k)e**, **Ni(e)tzsche**, **Nitzschke**, **Nitschold**, **Nietzschold**, **Niezold**, **Ni(e)tschmann**, **Nitzschmann** (of Slav. origin). Czech: **Mikulášek**, **Mikulík**, **Mikulka**; **Míka**, **Mika**, **Mikeš**, **Miksa**, **Mixa**; **Mikolášek**, **Míšek**, **Miška**, MIČKA. Pol.: **Mikołajczyk**

Patrs.: Eng.: **Nichol(l)s**, **Nickol(l)s**, **Nicolls**, **Niccols**, **Nicholes**, **Nickoles**, **Nicholds**, **Nickolds**, **Nickalls**, **Nickel(l)s**; **Nic(h)olson**, **Nickleson**. Scot.: **McNicholas**; **McNic(h)ol(l)**, **McNickle** (Gael. **Mac Neacail**). It.: **De Nicola**. Rum.: **Nicolescu**, **Niculescu**. Low Ger.: **Nicolassen**, **Nicklassen**, **Nickelsen**; **Nicolaï** (Latinized); **Nicolaisen** (hypercorrected). Dan., Norw.: **Niclasen**; **Nicolaisen**, **Nicolajsen**, **Nikolajsen**. Swed.: **Niklasson**. Russ.: **Nikolaev(ski)**, **Nicolin**, **Nikulin**, **Mikulin**. Ukr.: **Mikulich**. Pol.: **Mikołajewicz**. Croatian: **Nikolajević**, **Nik(ol)ić**. Bulg.: **Nikolaev**, **Nikolov**. Lithuanian: **Nicoleit**, **Nickeleit**, **Mickeleit**; **Mikolyunas**. Latvian: **Nicolovius**. Gk: **Nicolaou**, **Nicolaides**. Armenian: **Nicogossian**. Georgian: **Nikolaishvili**, **Nikoleish(i)vili**; **Nikolodze**.

Patrs. (from dims.): Eng.: **Nicholetts**; **Nix** (Notts.), **Nick(e)s**; NIXON; **Nickinson**, **Nickisson**; **Nickerson** (Norfolk). Ger.: **Nicks**, **Nix**. Ger. (of Slav. origin): **Nitsch(k)er**. Russ.: **Nikolyukin**, **Nikashin**. Croatian: **Nik(š)ić**, **Nikčević**.

'Servant of N. (dim.)': Eng.: **Nickman**.

Habitation names: Czech: **Mikšovský**, **Miškovský**. Jewish (E Ashkenazic): **Nikolajewski**, **Nikolajewsky**, **Nikolayevski** (either adoptions of non-Jewish surnames, or else from Yid. *Nikelayevsker soldat*, a nickname given to Jews who, during the reign of Tsar Nicholas I, had been required to serve for 25 years in the Russ. army; cf. COHEN, KAPLAN).

Nickson *see* NIXON

Nie *see* NYE

Nieblich German: from a medieval given name, representing the Gmc clan name *Nibelung* 'son, descendant of Mist (or Fog)' (cf. mod. Ger. *Nebel* mist, fog). In Gmc mythology the Nibelungs were the doomed possessors of an immense hoard of treasure.

Vars.: **Niebli(n)g**.

Nieder German and Jewish (Ashkenazic): topographic name for someone who lived at the lower end of a settlement, from Ger. *nieder* lower (MHG *nider*, OHG *nidar*). In some cases it may have referred to someone who lived on the lower floor of a house of two or more storeys.

Vars.: Ger.: **Niederer** (comp.); **Niederst** (sup.); **Niedermann**. Jewish: **Niederman**.

Niedzielski Polish: nickname from Pol. *niedziela* Sunday, denoting someone baptized or born on a Sunday, or acquired for some anecdotal reason.

Niel *see* NEIL

Niemchenok *see* NEMCHINOV

Nieminen Finnish: ornamental name from Finn. *niemi* peninsula, headland + the gen. suffix *-nen*. It may in some cases have been chosen as a topographic name, but as this is the second commonest Finnish surname, many adoptions were probably arbitrary.

Vars.: **Niemi(lä)**.

Nierenberg Jewish (Ashkenazic): habitation name from the city of Nuremberg in N Bavaria, Yid. *Nirnberg*, Ger. *Nürnberg*.

Vars.: **Nir(e)nberg**; **Nur(e)nberg**, **Nürnberg**.

Nies *see* DENNIS

Niesen *see* ANNIS

Nieswand Low German: apparently a habitation name from some minor place, now altered out of all recognition by folk etymological association with *Nies*, a Low Ger. aphetic form of the given name DENNIS + MLG *wand* wall.

Vars.: **Nieswandt**, **Niesewand(t)**.

Nieto Spanish: nickname for someone descended from a prominent elder in a community, or one whose memory was respected, from Sp. *nieto* grandson (LL *neptus*, for class. L *nepos*, gen. *nep(ō)tis*, grandson, nephew; cf. NEVEU).

Nietschmann *see* NICHOLAS

Nieves Spanish: religious byname, from the title *María de las Nieves* 'Mary of the Snows', given particularly to children born on 5 August, on which date the Virgin allegedly once caused it to snow in Rome. It is possible that the surname also derives from a nickname with the same meaning as NEVADO.

Niewiadomski Polish: nickname from Pol. *niewiadomy* unknown, referring to a stranger of unknown origin (i.e. a newcomer to a district), or to a foundling, whose parentage was unknown.

Niewiarowski Polish: nickname for an atheist or unbeliever, from Pol. *nie* not, no + *wiara* faith, religion, with the addition of the surname suffix *-ski* (see BARANOWSKI).

Nigel Scots and English: from the Latinized personal name *Nigellus*, which was popular among the Normans. It is in actual fact a form of NEIL, but was taken by folk etymology to be a dim. of L *niger* black, dark.

Nigg *see* NICHOLAS

Nightingale English: nickname for someone with a good voice, from ME *nichti(n)gale* (OE *nihtegal*, from *niht* night + *galan* to sing; cogn. with Ger. *Nachtigall*).

Var.: **Nightingall**.

Nighton *see* KNIGHTON

Nigrelli *see* NOIR

Nihell *see* NEIL

Nijns *see* JOHN

Nijs *see* DENNIS

Nikashin *see* NICHOLAS

Nikiforov Russian: patr. from the given name *Nikifor* (Gk *Nikēphoros*, from *nikē* victory + *phorein* to carry, bear). Although of pagan origin, the name was popular among early Christians in allusion to Christ's victory over Death, and was borne in particular by a (possibly fictional) 3rd-cent. martyr of Antioch, as well as various other early saints who helped to make the name a popular one in E Europe.

Nikitin Russian and Ukrainian: patr. from the given name *Nikita* (Gk *Nikētas*, a deriv. of *nikān* to conquer). The name was popular among early Christians for the same reasons as *Nikēphoros* (see NIKIFOROV) and was borne by several saints, including a 4th-cent. converted Ostrogoth and a 5th-cent. missionary to Dacia. Both are more honoured in the Orthodox Church than the Roman Catholic, and the given name is accordingly largely confined to E Europe.

Vars.: Russ.: **Nikitaev**, **Mikitin**. Ukr.: **Mykyta** (not patr.).
Dims.: Russ.: **Nikitnikov**, **Nikishov**, **Mikeshin** (patrs.). Ukr.: **Nikitenko**, **Nikityuk**, **Mikitenko**, **Mikitka**.

Nikodém Czech: from the given name *Nikodém* (Gk *Nikodēmos*, from *nikē* victory + *dēmos* people). The name was adopted in E Europe in honour of the Nicodemus mentioned in the New Testament, a member of the Sanhedrin who helped to bury Christ after he was taken down from the cross.

Vars.: **Nykodým**; **Kodým**, **Kodeš**, **Kodat** (aphetic).

Nilan *see* NEIL

Nilges *see* CORNEILLE

Nimchenko *see* NEMCHINOV

Nimmo Scots: of unknown origin. The earliest forms that belong here are probably *Newmoch* (1459), *Nemoch* (1490), and *Nemok* (1587). Forms with *-i-* are not found before the 17th cent.

Vars.: **Nemo**, **Nemmock**.

Ninni *see* JOHN

Niño Spanish: nickname from Sp. *niño* child, boy (of uncertain origin; apparent cogns. are found in various dialects of Catalonia, Provence, and S Italy). This was often given to a first-born son as a familiar name, and in some cases persisted to adulthood.

Nirenberg *see* NIERENBERG

Nirney *see* McNAIRN

Nisard *see* DENNIS

Nisbaum *see* NUTT

Nisbit Scots and N English: habitation name from any of several places in the Border region called *Nisbit* or *Nesbit(t)*, from Northern ME *nese* nose (from ON) + *bit* mouthful, piece of ground (OE *bita*) or *bit* bend (OE *byht*). The placenames refer either to a piece of raised land sticking up like a nose, or to a bend in a river shaped like a nose.

Vars.: **Nisbet**; **Nesbit(t)** (esp. N Ireland); **Naisbit(t)**, **Naisbet**.

Nish *see* ANGUS

Nissen 1. Jewish (Ashkenazic): from the Yid. male given name *Nisn*, (from Hebr. *nisan*, the name of a Jewish month), presumably at first given to boys born in that month; cf. ODER 2. **2.** German and Danish: patr. from the Scandinavian given name *Niss*, a greatly contracted form of NICHOLAS. This surname is still largely confined to its original home in Schleswig.

Vars. (of 1, not exclusively Ashkenazic): **Nis(s)an**; **Nissani**, **Nissany** (with the Hebr. ending *-i*).

Dims. (of 1): **Nis(s)el** (also perhaps from Yid. *nisl*, a dim. of *nus* nut, and so one of the many ornamental surnames derived from plant names).

Patrs. (from 1): **Nissenso(h)n**, **Nisenzon**, **Nis(s)anov**.

Patrs. (from 1) (dims.): **Niselovitz**, **Niselevich**; **Nusilevitz** (hypercorrected).

Nitsche *see* NICHOLAS

Nitti *see* JOHN

Niven *see* NEVIN

Nix *see* NICHOLAS

Nixon N English, Scots, and N Irish: patr. from the ME given name *Nik(ke)*, a short form of NICHOLAS.

Vars.: **Nickson** (Lancs.), **Nixson**.

Nizard *see* DENNIS

Noade English: topographic name resulting from misdivision of ME *atten oade* at the heap (OE *æt ðǣm āde*, from *ād* heap, (funeral) pyre; for the change of *-ā-* to *-ō-*, cf. ROPER). The meaning of OE *ād* is complex: it may refer to an ancient burial mound, a grassed-over refuse heap, a natural mound, or a high spot used as the site for a beacon.

Vars.: **Noad**, **No(a)des**.

Noake English (chiefly W Midlands): topographic name for someone who lived by an oak tree, from a misdivision of ME *atten oke* at the oak. The form *atten* (from OE *æt ðǣm*) was used more or less indiscriminately in ME as distinctions of grammatical gender ceased to be felt. Strictly, it was used only with masc. nouns, the fem. equivalent being *atter* (OE *æt ðǣre*). Other names resulting from similar misdivision include NALDER and NASH.

Vars.: **Noak**, **Noke**, **Nock**, **Noak(e)s**, **Nokes**.

Nobb English (Norfolk): from a medieval given name, a pet form of ROBERT.

Patrs.: **Nobbs** (Norfolk), **Nop(p)s**, **Nobes**.

Patr. (from a dim.): **Nopkins**.

Nobelius Swedish: Latinized form of a habitation name from a place called *Nöbbelöv*. This is one of the rare genuine habitation names in Swedish, as distinct from ornamental coinages, which sometimes look like topographic names.

Var.: **Nobel**.

Noble 1. English, Scots, and French: nickname from ME, OF *noble* high-born, distinguished, illustrious (L *nobilis*), referring to someone of lofty birth or character, or ironically to someone of exceedingly humble birth and station. **2.** Jewish (Ashkenazic): in at least one family, an Anglicized form of **Knöbel**, a surname derived from an archaic Ger. word for a servant. This was a famous rabbinical family which came from Wiener Neustadt to Sanok in Galicia in the 17th cent.; several members subsequently emigrated to the U.S. **3.** Jewish (Ashkenazic): probably also an Anglicized form of the Ashkenazic surname *Knobel* 'garlic' (see KNOBLOCH).

Var. (of 1): Fr.: **Lenoble**.

Patrs. (from 1): Eng.: **Nobles**. Flem., Du.: **Nobels**.

Noblett English (Lancs.): **1.** dim. of NOBLE 1. **2.** double dim. of NOBB.

Var.: **Noblet**.

Nocenti *see* INNOCENTI

Nochimowski *see* NAHUM

Nochtin *see* NAUGHTON

Nock *see* NOAKE

Nöckl *see* KNOX

Nodelman *see* NADLER

Nodes *see* NOADE

Noe *see* NOY

Noel English and French: nickname for someone who had some particular connection with the Christmas season, such as owing the particular feudal duty of providing a yule-log to the lord of the manor, or having given a memorable performance as the Lord of Misrule; see also YULE. The name is from ME, OF *no(u)el* Christmas (L *natālis (dies)* birthday, from *nasci* to be born). It was also used as a given name for someone born during the Christmas period; cf. NASCIMENTO.

Vars.: Eng.: **Nowell**, **Nowill**. Fr.: **Nouau**, **Nou(h)aud**.

Dims.: Fr.: **Noellet**. Prov.: **Nadin**, **Nadot**.

Nogin Russian: patr. from the nickname *Noga* 'Foot', 'Leg', acquired presumably on account of some lameness or deformity.

Noice *see* NOY

Noir French: nickname for someone with notably dark hair or complexion, from OF *noir* black (L *niger*).

Var.: **Lenoir**.

Dims.: Fr.: **Noiret**, **Noyret**, **Noirez**, **Néret**, **Noiré**, **Néré**, **Noireau(x)**, **Noirot**, **Néreau**, **Nérot**, **Noiron**, **Néron**, **Noirtin**, **Nerisson**. Prov.: **Negrel**, **Negron**; **Neyret**, **Neyron**, **Neyroud**. It.: **Negrelli**, **Negrello**, **Ne(g)rini**, **Negrin(o)**, **Negrotto**, **Neretti**, **Nerucci**, **Nerozzi**, **Nigrelli**, **Nigr(i)ello**.

Augs.: Fr.: **Nérat**. Prov.: **Neyrat**. It.: **Ne(g)roni**, **Ne(g)rone**.

Pejs.: Fr.: **Noiraud**, **Néraud**, **Noireau(l)t**. Prov.: **Neyraud**. It.: **Negrato**.

Patrs.: It.: **De Negri(s)**, **Nigris**. Rum.: **Negresco**.

Noke *see* NOAKE

Nolan Irish: Anglicized form of Gael. **Ó Nualláin** 'descendant of *Nuallán*', a personal name representing a dim. of *nuall* famous, noble.

Vars.: **O'No(u)lane, (O')Noland, (O')Nowlan**.

Nöldeke *see* NAUD

Nolder *see* NADLER

Noli *see* JOHN

Nolin *see* BERNARD

Noni *see* JOHN

Noon 1. English: nickname for a bright and cheerful person, from ME *none* noon (the time of brightest sunshine). The word is derived from L *nōna (hora)*, originally denoting the ninth hour, i.e. about three o'clock. The change in meaning of the vocab. word, from mid-afternoon to midday, probably occurred as a result of monastic meal times being brought forward. **2.** Irish: var. of NOONE.

Noonan Irish: Anglicized form of Gael. **Ó hIonmhaineáin** 'descendant of *Ionmhaineán*', a personal name derived from *Ionmhain* beloved.

Vars.: **Nunan, Neenan**.

Noone Irish: Anglicized form of Gael. *Ó Nuadháin* 'descendant of *Nuadhán*', a personal name derived from *Nuadha*, the name of several ancient Celt. gods.

Vars.: **O'Now(a)n, O'Nown**, NOON.

Nopkins *see* NOBB

Norbury English: habitation name from any of various places, for example in Ches., Derbys., Shrops., Staffs., and Surrey, so called from OE *norð* NORTH + *burh* fortress, town (see BURY).

Norchard *see* ORCHARD

Norcross English (Lancs.): habitation name from a minor place near Blackpool, so called from OE *norð* NORTH + *cros* CROSS.

Norfolk English: regional name from the county of *Norfolk* in E Anglia, so called from an OE tribal name composed of the elements *norð* NORTH + *folc* people (in contrast to the *sūðfolc* of Suffolk).

Norgård Danish: habitation name from a placename composed of the elements *nord* NORTH + *gård* enclosure.

Vars.: **Norgaard; Norregård, Norregaard**.

Norgrove English (W Country): habitation name from an unidentified place, presumably named with the OE elements *norð* NORTH + *grāf* GROVE.

Noriega Spanish: habitation name for a place in the province of Oviedo, whose name is perhaps akin to Sp. *noria* water-wheel (from Arabic *nā'ūra*, a deriv. of *nā''ar* to creak).

Norman 1. English: name applied either to a Scandinavian settler or to someone from Normandy in N France. The Scandinavian adventurers of the Dark Ages called themselves *norðmenn* (nom. sing. *norðmaðr*) 'men from the North'. When they settled in England and N France the term was adopted by the local population as *Norþmann* and *Norman(t)* respectively. The pre-Conquest Scandinavian settlers in England were fairly readily absorbed, and

Nor(þ)mann came to be used as a byname and later as a personal name, even among the Saxon inhabitants. It would have been the more easily assimilated because *norð* and *mann* were both Gmc name-forming elements in their own right, so in fact the compound name could have been formed without any specific reference to Scandinavians. The word gained a new use when England was settled by invaders from Normandy, of Scandinavian origin but by now largely integrated with the native population and speaking a Romance language, retaining only their original Gmc name. **2.** Jewish (Ashkenazic): of uncertain origin. In at least one case it is an Anglicized form of **Novominsky**, the name of a family from Uman in the Ukraine. On coming to the United States around 1900, a member of this family changed his name to *Norman*, after which some relatives in Russia adopted this name instead of *Novominsky*. **3.** Swedish: cogn. of NORTH.

Var. (of 1): **Normand**.

Noronha Portuguese: of uncertain origin. In the Middle Ages the name appears as *Loronha*; it is probably related to the Galician placename *Loroño*.

Norrington English: **1.** topographic name for someone living to the north of a main settlement, OE *norð in tūne*. According to Reaney, possible sources include *Norrington* near Alvediston, Wilts., *Norrington* End Farm in Redbourn, Herts., and *Northingtown* Farm in Grimley, Worcs., but there were no doubt others, now lost. The form of the name has been influenced by the common placename ending *-ington*. **2.** habitation name from the city of *Northampton*, originally named with the elements NORTH + HAMPTON.

Var.: **Nor(th)ington**, NORTON.

Norris English and Scots: **1.** regional name for someone who had migrated from the North (i.e. further north in England, or from Scotland or Scandinavia), from OF *nor(r)eis* northerner. **2.** topographic name for someone who lived in a house on the north side of a settlement or estate, from OE *norð* north + *hūs* house. **3.** occupational name for a wet nurse or foster mother, from OF *nurice* (L *nutrix*, gen. *nutricis*).

Vars.: **Noriss, Norrish; Nor(r)ie** (Scots). (Of 1 only): **Norreys**. (Of 3 only): **Nurrish, N(o)urse**.

North 1. English: topographic name, from OE *norð* north, for someone who lived in the northern part of a village or to the north of a main settlement (cf. NORRINGTON 1), or regional name for someone who had migrated from the north (cf. NORRIS 1). **2.** Irish: regional name for someone from Ulster, the northern area of Ireland, in part as an Anglicized form of Gael. *Mac an Ultaigh* (see McNULTY).

Vars.: Eng.: **Northe(r)n**.

Cpds (mostly arbitrary combinations rather than genuine habitation names): Swed.: **Nor(d)berg** ('north hill'); **Norrby** ('north settlement'); **Nordahl** ('north valley'); **Nor(d)gren** ('north branch'); **Nordlund** ('north grove'); **Nordlöf** ('north leaf'); **Nordmark** ('north land'); **Nordqvist** ('north twig'); **Nor(d)ström** ('north river'); **Nordwall, Nordvall** ('north bank').

Northall English (W Midlands): habitation name from an unidentified place named with the OE elements *norð* NORTH + *h(e)all* HALL or *h(e)alh* nook, recess (see HALE 1).

Northcott English: habitation name from any of various minor places so called from OE *norð* NORTH + *cot* cottage, shelter (see COATES).

Vars.: **Norcott, Norcutt, Norkutt, Norkett; Northcote; Narracott.**

Northey English (Devon): habitation name, probably from *Northay* in Hawkchurch, Devon, named with the OE elements *norð* NORTH + *(ge)hæg* enclosure (see HAY 1).

Northfield English: habitation name from any of various places, for example in S Birmingham, so called from OE *norð* NORTH + *feld* open country, pasture (see FIELD).

Northmore English (Devon and Cornwall): topographic name for someone who lived on the northern part of a moor (presumably of Bodmin Moor, Dartmoor, or Exmoor), from ME *north* NORTH + *more* moor (see MOORE 1).

Norton English: **1.** habitation name from any of the many places so called, from OE *norð* NORTH + *tūn* enclosure, settlement. **2.** var. of NORRINGTON. **3.** var. of NAUGHTON 1.

Norwood English: habitation name from any of the many places so called, from OE *norð* NORTH + *wudu* WOOD.

Var.: **Northwood.**

Nosek Czech: nickname for someone with a noticeable nose, from Czech *nos* nose + the dim. suffix *-ek*. Since the suffix is diminutive, the nose in question could have been either remarkably large or remarkably small.

Var.: **Nosák** ('big nose').

Noskes see NATHAN

Notbohm see NUTT

Notes see NATHAN

Nothard see NUTTER

Notley English: habitation name from places, for example in Bucks. and Essex, so called from OE *hnutu* nut + *lēah* wood, clearing.

Notman **1.** Scots: probably an occupational name for a dealer in nuts, from ME *not(e), nut* (see NUTT) + *man* (OE *mann*), although Black expresses reservations about this derivation. Maybe it is a var. of NOTT. **2.** Jewish (Ashkenazic): probably a nickname for a poor man, from mod. Ger. *Not* need, want + *Mann* man.

Vars. (of 2): Jewish: **Nottman, Nothmann.**

Noto see JOHN

Nott English: nickname for a bald man or one who kept his hair extremely close-cropped, from ME *not* bald (OE *hnot*). The word was also used of pollarded cattle and trees, and the surname may perhaps in part be a metonymic occupational name for a herdsman or a topographic name for someone who lived by a stunted tree. See also KNOTT.

Patrs.: **Notting, Notts.**

Nottage English: nickname from ME *notehache* nuthatch (apparently from OE *hnutu* nut + *haccian* to break, crack).

Var.: **Nottidge.**

Notton English (Wilts.): habitation name from places in Wilts. and Dorset, so called from OE *nēat* cattle (see NEAT) + *tūn* enclosure, settlement.

Nouau see NOEL

Nourse see NORRIS

Nouveau see NUEVO

Novais Portuguese: habitation name from any of various minor places so called, from L *Novāles*, pl. of *novālis* clearing, land recently cleared and brought into cultivation (an adj. deriv. of *novus* new; cf. NUEVO).

Novák Czech: nickname from Czech *nový* new, generally referring to a newcomer to a place (cf. NEWMAN). However, the name also denoted a shoemaker who made new shoes (as distinct from a cobbler who repaired old ones). This is the most common Czech surname, and the var. *Novotný* is the third most common. The Pol. cogn. *Nowak* is also extremely common.

Vars.: **Novotný, Nový.**

Dims.: Czech: **Nováček.** Pol.: **Nowaczyk.** Ukr.: **Novichenko.**

Patrs.: Russ.: **Novikov.** Croatian: **Novaković, Nov(i)čić.** Jewish (E Ashkenazic): **Novikov, Novikoff, Novakovsky.**

Habitation names: Pol.: **Nowakowski, Nowiński.**

Novel see NUEVO

Nowaczyk see NOVÁK

Nowell see NOEL

Nowers see OVER

Nowlan see NOLAN

Nowles see KNOWLES

Noy **1.** English: from ME *Noye*, vernacular form of the Hebr. male given name *Noach* Noah, which is said to mean 'Long-lived'. According to the Book of Genesis, Noah, having been forewarned by God, built an ark into which he took his family and representatives of every species of animal, and so was saved from the flood that God sent to destroy the world because of human wickedness. The given name was not common among non-Jews in the Middle Ages, but the biblical story was an extremely popular subject for miracle plays. In most cases, therefore, the surname probably derives from a nickname referring to someone who had played the part of Noah in a miracle play or pageant, rather than from a given name. **2.** Jewish (Israeli): ornamental name from Hebr. *noy* decoration, adornment, in part adopted as a Hebraicized form of various Ashkenazic surnames containing the unrelated Ger. element *neu*, e.g. *Neumann* (see NEWMAN).

Var. (of 1): **Noe.**

Patrs. (from 1): Eng.: **Noyes, Noyce, Noise, Noice.**

Noyer French: topographic name for someone who lived near a (wal)nut tree, OF *noyer* (LL *nucārius*, from *nux*, gen. *nucis*, nut).

Vars.: **Dunoyer, Desnoyers.**

Noyret see NOIR

Nozzoli see JOHN

Nucator see McNUCATOR

Nuccii see JOHN

Nudd English: common Norfolk surname, of unknown origin. The suggestion that it is a var. of HUDD with the initial altered under the influence of pairs such as HOBB and NOBB is not very plausible. There are phonological difficulties in accepting it as a var. of NUTT.

Nudel *see* NADLER

Nuevo Spanish: nickname for a newcomer to an area, from Sp. *nuevo* new (L *novus*). The word was also occasionally used in the Middle Ages as a given name, particularly for a child born after the death of a sibling, and this may also be a source of the surname.

Var.: **Novo**.

Dims.: Sp.: **Novillo**. Fr.: **Nouvel, Nouveau, Nouvet**. It.: **Nov(i)ello, Novel(li)**.

Nugent English and Irish (Norman): habitation name from any of several places in N France, such as *Nogent-sur-Oise*, named with L *Novientum*, apparently an altered form of a Gaul. name meaning 'new settlement'.

Nuhimovsky *see* NAHUM

Nukhimovich *see* NAHUM

Nulty *see* McNULTY

Nunan *see* NOONAN

Nuneham *see* NEWHAM

Nunn English: nickname for a pious and demure man, or occupational name for someone who worked at a convent, from ME *nunn* nun (OE *nunne*, from L *nonna*, originally a respectful term of address for an elderly woman. The L word probably originated as a nursery term).

Patr.: **Nunns**.

Nuño Spanish: from a medieval given name, which is first attested in the L forms *Nunnius* and *Nonnius* and is of uncertain origin. There may be some connection with MUÑO.

Patrs.: Sp.: **Núñez**. Port.: **Nunes** (also borne by Sefardic Jews, in which case it is an adoption of the non-Jewish name).

Nurenberg *see* NIERENBERG

Nuriev Russian: patr. from the Islamic given name *Nuri*, which means 'Light' in Arabic and was originally an epithet of Allah.

Vars.: **Nure(y)ev**.

Nurmi Finnish: ornamental name from Finn. *nurmi* lawn, pasture; one of the many Finn. surnames formed in the 19th cent. from vocab. words denoting natural features.

Var.: **Nurminen**.

Nurrish *see* NORRIS

Nusan *see* NATHAN

Nusbaum *see* NUTT

Nuscha *see* JOHN

Nusilevitz *see* NISSEN

Nüss *see* DENNIS

Nuta *see* NATHAN

Nuti *see* BENVENUTI

Nutt English: from ME *not(e)*, *nut* nut (OE *hnutu*); either a metonymic occupational name for a gatherer and seller of nuts, or nickname for a man supposedly resembling a nut (e.g. in having a rounded head and dark complexion).

Patr.: Eng.: **Nutting**.

Cpds (meaning 'nut tree'): Ger.: **Nussbaum, Nussba(u)mer**. Low Ger.: **Not(te)bohm, Näthbom**. Flem., Du.: **Noteboom**. Jewish (Ashkenazic): **Nus(s)(en)baum, Nus(s)boim, Nis(s)(en)baum, Nis(en)boim, Nissnbaum, Nis(se)lbaum** (all ornamental).

Nuttall English: habitation name from some place named with the OE elements *hnutu* nut (see NUTT) + *h(e)alh* nook, recess (see HALE 1). In some cases this may be *Nuthall* in Notts., but the surname is common mainly in Lancs., and a Lancs. origin is therefore more likely. *Nuttall* in Bury, Lancs., was earlier *Notehogh*, from OE *hnutu* + *hōh* hill-spur (see HOE).

Var.: **Nuthall**.

Nutter English: 1. occupational name for a keeper of oxen, from an agent deriv. of ME *nowt* beast, ox (from ON *naut*, a cogn. of OE *nēat*; cf. NEAT). 2. occupational name for a scribe or clerk, from ME *notere* (OE *nōtere*, from L *notārius*, an agent deriv. of *nota* mark, sign).

Var. (of 1): **Nothard** (see HEARD).

Nuutinen *see* KNOTT

Nuvolone *see* NAPOLEONI

Nuzzetti *see* JOHN

Nyberg *see* NEW

Nye English: topographic name arising from a misdivision of ME *atten (e)ye* which means both 'at the river' and 'at the island', from OE *ēa* river and *ēg* island respectively. Both these words were actually fem. in OE, and so should have been preceded only by ME *atter* (see RYE), but distinctions of gender ceased to be carefully maintained in the ME period. Cf. NALDER, NASH, and NOAKE.

Vars.: **Nie, Ney, Nay**.

Nyegaard *see* NYGÅRD

Nygaard *see* NYGRÅD

Nygård Danish: habitation name from a placename composed of the elements *ny* NEW + *gård* enclosure.

Vars.: **Nygaard; Nyegård, Nyegaard**.

Nygren *see* NEW

Nyhan Irish: Anglicized form of Gael. **Ó Niatháin** 'descendant of *Niathán*', a diminutive of *Niath* 'Warrior' (a later spelling of *Nia(dh)*; cf. NEE).

Nyholm *see* NEW

Nykodým *see* NIKODÉM

Nylander *see* NEW

Nyqvist *see* NEW

Nys *see* DENNIS

Nystedt *see* NEW

O

Oade English: **1.** from a ME given name *Ode*, in which personal names of several different origins have coalesced: principally OE *Od(d)a*, ON *Od(d)a* and Continental Gmc *Odo*, *Otto*. The first two are short forms from names with the first element OE *ord*, ON *odd* point of a weapon. The Continental Gmc names are from a short form of cpd names with the first element *od-* prosperity, riches (cogn. with OE *ēad-*; cf. EADE). The situation is further confused by the fact that all of these names were Latinized as *Odo*. *Odo* was the name of the half-brother of the Conqueror, archbishop of Bayeux, who accompanied the Norman expedition to England and was rewarded with 439 confiscated manors. The German name *Odo* or *Otto* was a hereditary name in the Saxon ruling house, as well as being borne by Otto von Wittelsbach, who founded the Bavarian ruling dynasty in the 11th cent., and the 12th-cent. Otto of Bamburg, apostle of Pomerania. **2.** topographic name for someone who lived near a mound or heap; see NOADE.

Vars. (of 1): **Odd(e)**, **Ott**; **Otton**, **Otten**, **Oaten** (from the OF oblique case).

Dims. (of 1): Eng.: **Oddie**, **Odd(e)y**, **Odlin(g)**. Fr.: **Od(el)in**, **Ody**, **Oudin(eau)**, **O(u)dinet**, **O(u)dinot**, **O(u)det**, **Oudot**. It.: **Odello**, **Odetti**, **Oddino**, **Od(d)(ic)ini**, **Odicino**, **Oddenino**, **Ottonello**, **Ottonelli**, **Otanelli**, **Otino**, **Ottin(i)**, **Ottoli**, **Ottolino**, **Ottolin(i)**. Ger.: **Ottel**, **Öttel**, **Öttle**. Low Ger.: **Otke**, **Ötke**, **Odeke**, **Ocke**, **Ödgen**, **Odemann**. Fris.: **Edema**.

Pejs. (of 1): It.: **Odazzi**, **Odazio**, **Odasso**, **Odasi**.

Patrs. (from 1): Eng.: **Oades**, **Oat(e)s**, **Otis**. Low Ger.: **Otten(s)**, **Oden(s)**, **Ottsen**, **O(u)tzen**. Fris.: **EDEN**, **Edens**, **Edsen**; **Odinga**. Flem., Du.: **Otten(s)**. Dan., Norw.: **Ottesen**, **Ottosen**, **Otzen**. Swed.: **Ottosson**.

Patrs. (from dims. of 1): Ger.: **Ottler**. Low Ger.: **Oetken**, **Oetjen**, **Ötker**, **Öcker**, **Ockens**.

Oag see OGG

Oak English: topographic name for someone who lived near an oak tree or in an oak wood, from ME *oke* oak (OE *āc*; for the Southern ME change of *-ā-* to *-ō-*, cf. ROPER), also used in the sing. in a collective sense. In some cases the surname may be a habitation name from minor places named with this word, such as *Oake* in Somerset. It is possible that it was sometimes also used as a nickname for someone 'as strong as oak'.

Vars.: **O(a)ke**, **Oak(e)s**, **Oaker**; **Attoc(k)**, **At(t)ack**; **Aikman** (Scots). See also NOAKE and ROCK 2.

Dims.: Ger.: **Eichele**, **Aichele**. Jewish: **Eichel**, **Aihel(baum)**.

Cpds (ornamental): Swed.: **Ekberg(h)** ('oak hill'); **Ekblad(h)** ('oak leaf'); **Ekblom** ('oak flower'); **Ek(e)dahl** ('oak valley'); **Ek(e)gren**, **Ekengren** ('oak branch'); **Ekholm** ('oak island'); **Eklind** ('oak lime'); **Ek(e)löf**, **Ek(e)löv** ('oak leaf'); **Ek(e)lund(h)** ('oak grove'); **Ekroth** ('oak clearing'); **Ekstedt** ('oak homestead'); **Ekstrand** ('oak shore'); **Ekström** ('oak river'); **Ekwall**, **Ekvall** ('oak bank'). Jewish: **Eichelberg** ('oak hill'); **Eichenblat**, **Aichenblat(t)** ('oak leaf'); **Eichengruen** ('oak green'); **Eich(en)holz**, **Eichengolz**, **Aichenhol(t)z** ('oak wood'; *-golz*

under Russ. influence, since Russ. has no /h/ and changes /h/ in borrowed words to /g/); **Eichenstein** ('oak stone'); **Eich(en)wald**, **Aichenwald** ('oak forest').

Oakden see OGDEN

Oakland English: topographic name for someone who lived on a patch of land marked by its oak tree or trees, from ME *oke* OAK + *land*.

Oakley English: habitation name from any of the numerous places in S and central England named with the OE elements *āc* OAK + *lēah* wood, clearing.

Vars.: **Oakeley**, **Okel(e)y**, **OGLEY**. See also EAGLE 2.

Oastler see OSTLER

Oaten see OADE

Oatley English: **1.** habitation name from *Oteley* in Ellesmere, Shrops., named with the OE elements *āte* oats + *lēah* wood, clearing. **2.** var. of OAKLEY.

O'Balivan see BALFE

O'Banane see BANNAN

Ó Beagáin see BEGG

O'Beirne see BYRNE

Ober German: topographic name for someone who lived at the upper end of a village, from Ger. *ober-* upper (MHG *ober*, *obar* above, OHG *ubar*). In some cases, it may have denoted someone who lived on an upper floor of a building with two or more storeys. Cf. NIEDER.

Vars.: **Oberer** (comparative); **Oberst** (superlative); **Zobrist** (Switzerland); **Obermann** (U.S. **Oberman**).

Oberg see ÅBERG

Öberg see ÖMAN

Oberholz German: topographic name for someone who lived in a place known as the 'upper wood', or on the far side of a wood from the main settlement, from Ger. *ober-* upper or MHG *ober* above, beyond (see OBER) + *Holz* wood (see HOLT).

Var.: **Oberholtz**.

Oberlin see ALBERT

Obin see ALBIN

Oblomov Russian: patr. from the nickname *Oblom* (from *oblomat* to shatter, smash), presumably referring to a strong or clumsy person.

O'Boghan see BOWEN

Obolensky Russian: habitation name adopted by a princely family from their estates at *Obolensk*.

O'Boughelly see BUCKLEY

O'Boyle *see* BOYLE

O'Brackan *see* BRACKEN

O'Bradane *see* BRADEN

O'Braddigan *see* BRADY

O'Branagan *see* BRANNIGAN

Obray *see* AUBREY

O'Brean *see* BREEN

O'Breassell *see* BRAZIL

O'Brenane *see* BRENNAN

O'Brian *see* BRYAN

O'Broghan *see* BANKS

O'Brognan *see* BROGAN

O'Brollaghan *see* BROLLY

Ó Bruic *see* BROCK

O'Buhilly *see* BUCKLEY

O'Bynnan *see* BANNAN

O'Byrne *see* BYRNE

O'Caherny *see* CARNEY

O'Cahill *see* CAHILL

O'Cahsedy *see* CASSIDY

O'Callaghan *see* CALLAGHAN

Ocaña Spanish: habitation name from places in the provinces of Almería and Toledo. The placename is probably of pre-Roman origin, and may be akin to the North(-Eastern) Italian placenames *Oc(c)a* and *Occagno*, which have been claimed to be of Ligurian derivation.

O'Canavan *see* CANAVAN

O'Cannan *see* CANNON

Ó Caomháin *see* KEEFE

O'Carran *see* CURRAN

O'Carroll *see* CARROLL

O'Casey *see* CASEY

Occhillo *see* OCHILA

Ó Cearbhaill *see* CARROLL

Ochila Rumanian: nickname for a one-eyed man or for someone with some other defect of the eyes, such as squinting. The name is a deriv. of the word *ochi* eye (L *oc(u)lus*), and is applied also to a one-eyed monster in Rumanian folk-tales.

Dims.: Fr.: **Oeuillet**, **Leuillet**, **Leuillot**. It.: **Ochiello**, **Occhillo**, **Occhini**, **Occhino**, **Ochiuzzi**; **Occhiuto**, **Occhiuti** (Calabria).

Aug.: It.: **Occhioni**.

Ochoa Spanish form of Basque **Otxoa**: from a personal name, probably originally a byname from Basque *otso* wolf + the def. art. *-a*.

Ó Cionaodha *see* KENNY

Ocke *see* OADE

Ockenden English: habitation name from *Ockendon* in Essex, which appears in Domesday Book as *Wochenduna*, apparently from the gen. case of an OE personal name *Wocca* + OE *dūn* hill (see DOWN 1).

Ocker German: topographic name for someone living on the banks of the river *Ocker* in the Harz mountains, which perhaps derives its name from a Celt. word for the salmon, cogn. with Corn. *ehoc*.

Var.: **Ockermann**.

Öckl *see* ECK

O'Clearkane *see* CLEARY

O'Codihie *see* CODY

O'Coffey *see* COFFEY

O'Coghlaine *see* COUGHLAN

O'Cogley *see* QUICKLEY

O'Coleman *see* COLEMAN

O'Collaine *see* CULLEN

O'Comane *see* CUMMING

O'Conely *see* CONNOLLY

O'Coneran *see* CONROY

O'Conlan *see* QUINLAN

O'Connell *see* CONNELL

O'Connor *see* CONNOR

O'Coonaghan *see* COONEY

O'Corcrane *see* CORKERY

O'Corhane *see* CURRAN

O'Corrie *see* CORY

O'Corrigan *see* CORR

O'Cosgra *see* COSGROVE

O'Cosker *see* CUSKER

O'Coyne *see* COYNE

O'Crevan *see* CRAY

O'Criane *see* CREGGAN

O'Croley *see* CROWLEY

Ó Cuanacháin *see* COONEY

O'Cuayn *see* COYNE

O'Cuddie *see* CODY

O'Cuill *see* QUILL

O'Cuirk *see* QUIRKE

O'Cumyn *see* CUMMING

O'Curran *see* CURRAN

O'Currigan *see* CORR

O'Cwigley *see* QUICKLEY

O'Daa *see* DAW

Ó Daimhín *see* DEVANE

O'Daly *see* DALY

Odam English: nickname for someone who had done well for himself by marrying the daughter of a prominent figure in the local community, from ME *odam* son-in-law (OE *āðum*).
Vars.: **Odham** (altered by folk etymology as if derived from a placename in *-ham*); **Odom**.
Patrs.: **Od(h)ams**.

O'Daniel *see* DONALD

Odasi *see* OADE

O'Dasshowne *see* DESMOND

Odd *see* OADE

O'Dea *see* DAW

O'Deane *see* DEAN

O'Deason *see* DESMOND

O'Deere *see* DWYER

O'Deevey *see* DEVOY

Odeke *see* OADE

Odell English: habitation name from a place in Beds., also called *Woodhill*, from OE *wād* woad (a plant collected for the blue dye that could be obtained from its leaves) + *hyll* HILL.
Vars.: **O'Dell** (altered by folk etymology as if of Ir. origin); WADDELL.

O'Dempsey *see* DEMPSEY

O'Deoran *see* DORAN

Oder 1. German: topographic name for someone living on the banks of the central European river of this name. It rises in Poland, and its lower course forms the present-day border between Poland and E Germany. Its name is ancient, and is probably from a pre-Slav. element perhaps cogn. with Gk *hydōr* water, Gael. *odhar* dun, sallow, mod. Eng. *otter*. **2.** Jewish (Ashkenazic): possibly as in 1, or from a W or NE Yid. pronunciation of Yid. *adar*, the name of a month of the Jewish calendar. This is considered a happy time of year mainly because the festival of Purim is celebrated during this month and because Jewish tradition has it that Moses was born in this month.
Vars. (of 2): **Adar(i)**, **Adary** (with the Hebr. suffix *-i*, from the name of the month); **Oderberg** (presumably an ornamental elaboration).

Öder *see* EDER

O'Devlin *see* DEVLIN

Odgear *see* EDGAR

Ödgen *see* OADE

Odham *see* ODAM

Ó Diaghaidh *see* DAW

Ó Diarmada *see* DERMOTT

Odicini *see* OADE

Odlin *see* OADE

O'Doane *see* DEVANE

O'Dogherty *see* DOHERTY

Ó Doibhlin *see* DEVLIN

Ó Doinn *see* DUNN

Ó Doirnín *see* DORNAN

O'Dolane *see* DOLAN

Odom *see* ODAM

Ó Domhnaill *see* DONALD

O'Donaghie *see* DONOHUE

O'Donegaine *see* DONEGAN

O'Donelan *see* DONALD

O'Donleavy *see* DUNLEAVY

O'Donnelly *see* DONNELLY

O'Donovan *see* DONOVAN

O'Doogan *see* DUGGAN

O'Doolan *see* DOOLAN

O'Dooley *see* DOOLEY

O'Doran *see* DORAN

O'Dorcey *see* DARCY

O'Dougherty *see* DOHERTY

O'Douill *see* DOUGALL

O'Dowane *see* DEVANE

O'Dowd *see* DUDDY

O'Dowey *see* DUFFY

O'Dowlaney *see* DELANEY

O'Driscole *see* DRISCOLL

O'Duan *see* DEVANE

Ó Dubhghaill *see* DOUGALL

O'Duffey *see* DUFFY

O'Dugan *see* DUGGAN

Ó Duibhgeannáin *see* DEEGAN

O'Duire *see* DWYER

O'Dulaney *see* DELANEY

Ó Dulchonta *see* DELAHUNTY

O'Dunaghy *see* DONOHUE

O'Dungan *see* DONEGAN

O'Dunleavy *see* DUNLEAVY

O'Dunn *see* DUNN

O'Dunneen *see* DINEEN

O'Dwyer *see* DWYER

Ody see OADE

O'Dyeane see DEAN

Oetjen see OADE

Oeuillet see OCHILA

O'Faghy see FAHY

O'Falie see FEELY

O'Fallon see FALLON

O'Fanane see FINN

O'Farrell see FARRELL

O'Farris see FERGUS

O'Fay see FEE

O'Fearguise see FERGUS

O'Fee see FEE

O'Feeney see FEENEY

Ofen see OFFEN

O'Fenane see FINN

O'Feolane see WHELAN

O'Fergus see FERGUS

O'Ferrall see FARRELL

Offen 1. German: nickname for someone with a straight-forward or open nature, from Ger. *offen* open (OHG *offan*). 2. German: metonymic occupational name for a baker, or for someone who had charge of the communal village oven and was empowered to exact payment in kind for its use, from Ger. *Ofen* oven (MHG *oven*, OHG *ovan*). 3. German: habitation name from Buda, part of Budapest in Hungary, which was known in MHG as *Ofen*. 4. Jewish (Ashkenazic): of unclear origin. Any one of the foregoing explanations is possible, but none is certain. In the case of 1, the relevant vocab. words are Ger. *offen* and Yid. *ofn*; in the case of 2, Ger. *Ofen*; and in the case of 3, mod. Ger. *Ofen*.

Vars.: **Ofen**. (Of 2 only): **Of(f)ener**. (Of 4): **Offner**.

Offer 1. English (Norman): occupational name for a goldsmith, from ANF *orfrer*, OF *orfevre* (L *aurifaber*, from *aurum* gold + *faber* maker; cf. FÈVRE). 2. Jewish: of unknown origin; possibly a var. of *Hoffer* (see HOFFMANN 3), reflecting varieties of Yiddish with no /h/. Derivation from the Hebr. male given name *Ofer* is impossible since that is a 20th-cent. coinage.

Var. (of 1): **Orfeur**.

Offermann see OPPERMANN

Officer English: 1. occupational name for the holder of any office, from ANF *officer* (an agent deriv. of OF *office* duty, service, L *officium* service, task). 2. occupational name for a sewer of gold embroidery, from ANF *orfroiser* (an agent deriv. of OF *orfrois*, LL *auriphyrigium* Phrygian gold—the Phrygians being famed in antiquity for their gold embroidery).

Var. (of 1): **Office**.

Offield see OLDFIELD

Offman see HOFFMANN

Offord English: habitation name from a place in Cambs., so called from OE *uppe* up(stream) + *ford* FORD.

Ó Fhallamhain see FALLON

Ó Fhógartaigh see FOGARTY

Ofield see OLDFIELD

O'Fielly see FEELY

O'Fighane see FEE

O'Finane see FINN

Ó Fionnghaile see FENNELL

O'Flagherty see FLAHERTY

O'Flannelly see FLANNERY

O'Flinn see FLYNN

Ofman see HOFFMANN

O'Foedy see FOODY

O'Fogarty see FOGARTY

O'Folane see WHELAN

O'Foley see FOLEY

O'Folowe see FOLEY

O'Foran see FORAN

Ó Freaghaile see FARRELL

O'Fylan see WHELAN

O'Gaeney see GAFFNEY

Ó Gairbheith see GARVEY

O'Gallagher see GALLAGHER

Oganesian see JOHN

O'Gara see GEARY

O'Garven see GARVIN

O'Garvey see GARVEY

Ogborne English: habitation name from a pair of villages in Wilts. called *Ogbourne*, from the OE personal name *Oc(c)a* + OE *burna* stream (see BOURNE).

Ogden English: habitation name from some minor place, probably the one in W Yorks., so called from OE *āc* OAK + *denu* valley (see DEAN 1).

Var.: **Oakden**.

O'Geary see GEARY

Oger see EDGAR

Ogg Scots: Anglicized form of a nickname from the Gael. adj. *óg* young, used to distinguish the junior of two bearers of the same given name.

Var.: **Oag**.

Ogier see EDGAR

Ogill see OGLE

Ogilvie Scots: habitation name from a place near Glamis in the former county of Angus, which is first recorded *c*.1205 in the form *Ogilvin*. It probably gets its name from Brit. (pre-Gael.) cogns. of OW *ugl* high + *ma* plain, place (mutated to *fa*) or *ban* hill (mutated to *fan*).
Vars.: **Ogilvy**, **Ogilwy**; **Ogilby** (N Ireland).

O'Glassane *see* GLEESAN

Ogle Scots and N Irish: habitation name from a place in Northumb., so called from the OE personal name *Ocga* + OE *hyll* HILL.
Var.: **Ogill**.

Oglethorpe English: habitation name from a place in W Yorks., so called from the ON personal name *Oddketill* (composed of the elements *odd* point of a weapon + *ketill* cauldron) + ON *þorp* village, settlement.

Ogley English: **1.** var. of OAKLEY. **2.** habitation name from a place in Staffs., so called from the OE personal name *Ocga* + OE *lēah* wood, clearing.

O'Gooney *see* GAFFNEY

O'Gorman *see* GORMAN

O'Gormeley *see* GORMLEY

Ograbek Polish: nickname, of uncertain application, from Pol. *ograbek*, sing. of *ograbki* remnants, gleanings. This could be a nickname for an insignificant or unwanted person, or perhaps a metonymic occupational name for a gleaner.

O'Grada *see* GRADY

O'Greefa *see* GRIFFIN

Ögren *see* ÖMAN

O'Grimley *see* GORMLEY

Ogrodowski Polish: occupational name (in form a habitation name) for a market gardener or owner of an orchard or smallholding, Pol. *ogród*.
Var.: **Ogrodzki**.
Dim. **Ogrodowczyk**.
Patr.: **Ogrodowicz** (also Jewish (E Ashkenazic)).

O'Grogaine *see* GROGAN

O'Guindelane *see* QUINLAN

Ogurtsov Russian: patr. from the nickname *Oguréts* 'Cucumber' (an early borrowing from Gk), given perhaps originally to a grower or seller of these vegetables.

O'Hagan *see* HAGAN

O'Hagerty *see* HEGARTY

O'Hagher *see* HARE

O'Hallaghan *see* HALLAHAN

O'Hallaran *see* HALLORAN

O'Hallyn *see* ALLEN

O'Halpen *see* ALPIN

O'Handlon *see* HANLON

Ohanessian *see* JOHN

O'Hanlee *see* HANDLEY

O'Hannon *see* HANNA

O'Hanrahan *see* HANRAHAN

O'Hara Irish: Anglicized form of Gael. **Ó hEaghra** 'descendant of *Eaghra*', a personal name of uncertain derivation; cf. HARE.
Var.: **O'Hora**.

O'Haraghtane *see* HARRINGTON

O'Haran *see* HERON

O'Hart *see* HART

O'Headen *see* HAYDEN

O'Heagane *see* HIGGINS

O'Heagertie *see* HEGARTY

O'Healie *see* HEALEY

O'Heanesey *see* HENNESSY

O'Heany *see* HEANEY

O'Heare *see* HARE

O'Hederscoll *see* DRISCOLL

O'Henery *see* HENRY

O'Herlehy *see* HERLIHY

O'Heron *see* HERON

O'Herraghton *see* HARRINGTON

O'Heyne *see* HYNES

Öhgren *see* ÖMAN

O'Hickee *see* HICKEY

O'Hidirscoll *see* DRISCOLL

O'Hierlehy *see* HERLIHY

O'Hifferan *see* HEFFERNAN

O'Higane *see* HIGGINS

O'Hirwen *see* IRVINE

Ohlbaum Jewish (Ashkenazic): ornamental name, from Ger. *Ölbaum* olive tree (lit. 'oil tree').
Vars.: **Elbaum** (mixed Yid.-Ger. form); **Elbum**, **Elbo(i)m**, **Elboym** (from Yid. *eylboym* olive tree).

Ohlenschlager German: occupational name for an extractor of linseed oil. Oil was extracted from linseed by striking the grains with a heavy wooden hammer. The name is thus derived from MHG *oli(e)* oil + *sla(h)en* to strike, smite.
Vars.: **Öhl(en)schlager**, **Öhl(en)schläger**, **Ohligschlager**, **Ohligschläger**, **Öhlschlegel**.

Öhlerking *see* ULRICH

Ohlsen *see* OLIFF

Öhman *see* ÖMAN

Öhmichen *see* EAME

O'Hoasy *see* HUSSEY

O'Hogaine *see* HOGAN

O'Hogertie *see* FOGARTY

O'Hohy *see* HOWEY

O'Honeen *see* HOONEY

O'Hora *see* O'HARA

O'Horgan *see* HANRAHAN

Ohrbach *see* AUERBACH

O'Huggin *see* HIGGINS

O'Huhy *see* HOWEY

O'Hunnyn *see* HOONEY

Oistrakh Jewish (Ashkenazic): regional name for someone from Austria, from an older pronunciation of Yid. *Estraykh* (Ger. *Österreich*, from OHG *ōstar* eastern + *rīhhi* kingdom).

Vars.: **Ostreich(er)** (Ger.-based syncopated forms); **Estreicher** (Ger.-based romanization of Yid. *estraykher* Austrian); **Österreicher** (from Ger.); **Osterreicher** (from the prec., with omission of umlaut).

Ojala Finnish: topographic name, from Finn. *oja* ditch + the local suffix *-la*.

Ojeda Spanish: topographic name for someone living on the banks of the river *Ojeda* in the province of Soria, which is probably so called from L *folia* leaves (cf. RIOJA) + the collective suffix *-ēta*.

Oke *see* OAK

O'Kearney *see* KEARNEY

O'Keaty *see* KEATY

O'Keavane *see* KEEFE

O'Kegley *see* QUICKLEY

O'Kelaghan *see* CALLAGHAN

Okeley *see* OAKLEY

O'Kelly *see* KELLY

O'Kenaith *see* KENNY

O'Kennavain *see* CANAVAN

O'Kenneally *see* KENNEALLY

O'Kennedy *see* KENNEDY

O'Kennellan *see* QUINLAN

Okeover English: habitation name from a place in Staffs., so called from OE *āc* OAK + *ofer* bank, slope (see OVER).

O'Kerevan *see* KIRWAN

O'Kerrigane *see* KERRIGAN

O'Kierrigain *see* KERRIGAN

O'Kine *see* COYNE

O'Kineally *see* KENNEALLY

O'Kinedy *see* KENNEDY

O'Kinna *see* KENNY

O'Kirwan *see* KIRWAN

O'Knavin *see* NEVIN

O'Knee *see* NEE

Oksanen Finnish: ornamental or arbitarily chosen name, from Finn. *oksa* branch + the gen. suffix *-nen*.

O'Kuddyhy *see* CODY

O'Kynsillaghe *see* KINSELLA

O'Lagan *see* LOGAN

O'Laghlan *see* LACHLAN

O'Laghnane *see* LOUGHNANE

Olalla Spanish: habitation name from a place in the province of Teruel, first recorded in the form *Olalia*, and probably named from the dedication of its church to St *Eulalia* (see HILARY 2).

O'Lalor *see* LAWLOR

O'Lane *see* LANE

O'Lanegane *see* LENNON

O'Langan *see* LANGAN

Olausson *see* OLIFF

O'Lawry *see* LOWRY

Olbrechts *see* ALBERT

Olcha *see* OLSZEWSKI

Olczak *see* ALEXIS

Old English: from ME *old* (OE *eald*), not necessarily implying old age, but rather used to distinguish an older from a younger bearer of the same given name. See also ELDER.

Vars.: **Ould**; **Auld**, **Ault**, **Aude** (Sc.); **Ol(d)man**.

Patrs.: Eng.: **O(u)lds**. Low Ger.: **Alden**, **Old(s)en**. Flem., Du.: **Den Olden**, **Den Ouden**. Jewish (from the Yid. male given name *Alter*): **Alters(on)** (Ashkenazic); **Alterovitch**, **Alterowitz**, **Alterovitz** (E Ashkenazic); **Alterovici**, **Alterescu** (among Rumanian Jews).

Metrs.: Jewish: **Altes**, **Altovsky** (from the Yid. female given name *Alte*, fem. equivalent of *Alter*; see above).

Cpds: Jewish: **Altbach** ('old stream'); **Altbauer** (meaning unclear); **Altbaum** ('old tree'); **Altberg** ('old hill'); **Althaus** ('old house'); **Altheim** ('old home'); **Althoff** ('old court'); **Altholz** ('old wood'); **Altsta(e)dter** ('dweller in the old town'); **Altstein** ('old stone'); **Alterthum** ('antiquity').

Oldcastle English: habitation name from a place in Ches., so called from OE *eald* OLD + *castel* fortified settlement (see CASTLE).

Olden *see* ALDEN

Oldenburg Low German: habitation name from a place so called, from the weak dat. case (originally used after a preposition and article) of MLG *ald, old* OLD + MLG *burg* fortress, town (see BURKE).

Oldershaw *see* OLLERENSHAW

Oldfield English: habitation name from any of various minor places so called, from OE *eald* OLD + *feld* pasture, open country (see FIELD). The surname is widespread, but most common in W Yorks.

Vars.: **O(f)field**, **Allfield**.

Oldham English: habitation name from the place in Lancs., so called from ME *ald, old* OLD + *holm* island, dry land in a fen, promontory (see HOLME 2).

Oldroyd English (Yorks.): habitation name from any of various minor places in N England so called from ME *ald, old* OLD + *royd* clearing (OE *rod*).

O'Leaghan *see* LEHANE

O'Leane *see* LEAN

O'Leary *see* LEARY

Olechnowicz *see* ALEXIS

O'Lee *see* LEE

O'Lenaghan *see* LENIHAN

O'Lenan *see* LENNON

Olenchenko *see* ALEXANDER

O'Lensie *see* LYNCH

Olerenshaw *see* OLLERENSHAW

Olesen *see* OLIFF

O'Leyne *see* LANE

O'Lie *see* LEE

Olier *see* OYLER

Oliff English: from the ON personal name *Óleifr* Olaf (earlier *Anleifr*), composed of the elements *ans* god + *leifr* relic (from *leifa* to leave). The name was a common Scandinavian one, and became popular also in N Scotland and Ireland, which received Scandinavian colonists at an early date. The name continued to be popular in the Middle Ages, in part as a result of the fame of St Olaf, King of Norway, who brought Christianity to his country *c*.1015.

Vars.: **Ol(l)iffe**, **Olliff**.

Patrs.: Dan., Norw.: **Olufsen**, **Ovesen**, **Olesen**, **Ohlsen**; **Olsen** (also common in Newcastle). Swed.: **Olavsson**, **Olofsson**, **Olausson**, **O(h)lsson**. See also MCAULAY.

Olimpiev Russian: patr. from the given name *Olimpi* (Gk *Olympios*, a deriv. of *Olympos*, the traditional home of the gods), borne by a 4th-cent. saint, bishop of Aenos in Rumelia.

Vars.: **Alimpiev**, **Alimov**.

Oliphant English, Scots, French, and German: from ME, OF, MHG *olifant* elephant (LL *olifantus*, for class. L *elephantus*, Gk *elephas*, gen. *elephantis*; the modern words have been re-formed from the class. L). The circumstances in which this word was applied as a surname are not clear. It may have been a nickname for a large, clumsy individual, or a metonymic occupational name for a worker in ivory, or a house name from a house distinguished with the sign of an elephant.

Vars.: **Olifant**, **Olivant**.

Oliva Italian, Spanish, Catalan, and Jewish (Sefardic): topographic name for someone who lived by an olive grove, or metonymic occupational name for a gatherer or seller of olives or an extractor or seller of olive oil, perhaps sometimes also a nickname for someone with a sallow complexion. The vocab. word in all these languages comes from L *olīva* olive; the forms from the LL deriv. *olīvārius* olive tree have been confused with the personal name OLIVER.

Vars.: It.: **Olivi**, **Olivo**; **Uliva** (Venetia); **Ulivi** (Tuscany); **Olivari**. Sp.: **Olivas**; **Olivera**. Cat.: **Olivera**.

Dims.: It.: **Olivella**, **Olivelli**, **Olivello**, **Ulivelli**, **Olivetta**, **Olivetti**, **Olivotti**. Prov.: **Olivet**. Cat.: **Olivella**.

Pejs.: It.: **Olivazzi**, **Olivato**.

Collectives: It.: **Oliveto**, **Oliveti**. Sp.: **Olivar(es)**. Cat.: **Olivar**.

Oliver English, Scots, French, Catalan, and German: from the OF given name *Olivier*, which was brought to England by the Normans from France. It was popular throughout Europe in the Middle Ages as having been borne by one of Charlemagne's paladins, the faithful friend of Roland, about whose exploits there were many popular romances. The name ostensibly means 'olive tree' (see OLIVA), but this is almost certainly the result of folk etymology working on a personal name of Gmc origin, perhaps one cogn. with ÁLVARO. The surname is also borne by Jews, apparently as an adoption of the non-Jewish surname.

Vars.: Eng.: **Olver** (Devon). Fr.: **Ol(l)ivier**. Cat.: **Olivé**.

Dims.: Fr.: **Olivreau**. It.: **Vierin(i)**, **Vierucci**.

Olkowicz *see* ALEXIS

Oller Catalan: occupational name for a potter, Cat. *oller* (LL *ollārius*, from *olla* pot; cf. EULER).

Var.: **Ollé**.

Ollerenshaw English: habitation name from a place in Derbys., so called from OE *ælren* aldern, of alders (an adj. deriv. of *alor*; see ALDER 2) + *sceaga* wood, copse (see SHAW).

Vars.: **Olerenshaw**, **Olorenshaw**, **Ollarenshaw**; **Ollerearnshaw** (by confusion with EARNSHAW); **Oldershaw**, **Houldershaw**.

Öllerking *see* ULRICH

Ollerton English (Lancs.): habitation name from places so called in Ches., Notts., and Shrops. The first two are named from OE *alor* ALDER + *tūn* enclosure, settlement. *Ollerton* in Shrops., which is earlier found as *Alvereton*, is from an OE personal name, perhaps *Ælfhere* + OE *tūn* enclosure, settlement.

Olley *see* DOYLEY

Ollier *see* OYLER

Olliff *see* OLIFF

Ollivier *see* OLIVER

Olman *see* OLD

Olmo Italian and Spanish: topographic name for someone who lived by a conspicuous elm tree (L *ulmus*).

Vars.: It.: **Olmi**. Sp.: **Olmos**.

Collectives: Sp.: **Olmedo**, **Olmeda**.

Olney English: habitation name from places so called in Bucks. and Northants. The former gets its name from OE

Ollanēg 'island (OE *ēg*) of *Olla*'; the latter from OE *āna* one, single, solitary + *lēah* wood, clearing, with later metathesis of *-nl-* to *-ln-*.

O'Lochan *see* LOGAN

Olofsson *see* OLIFF

O'Logher *see* LOUGHREY

O'Loghlan *see* LACHLAN

O'Loghnane *see* LOUGHNANE

Ó Loingseacháin *see* LYNCH

O'Lonagan *see* LENNON

O'Longan *see* LANGAN

O'Looney *see* LOONEY

Olorenshaw *see* OLLERENSHAW

O'Lowry *see* LOWRY

O'Loye *see* LEE

O'Loyne *see* LANE

Olsen *see* OLIFF

Olszewski **1.** Polish: habitation name from one of the places named with Pol. *olcha, olsza* alder + *-ew* possessive suffix, with the addition of *-ski*, suffix of local surnames (see BARANOWSKI). It may perhaps also be a topographic name for someone living by an alder. **2.** Jewish (E Ashkenazic): ornamental name from Pol. *olcha, olsza* alder.

Vars.: Pol.: **Olszak** (topographic only); **Olszacki, Olszycki, Olszański, Olszyński.** Jewish: **Olshevski, Olshevsky, Olchovski, Volchonsky; Olcha, Olchik.**

Oltukhov *see* YEVTIKHIEV

O'Lucherin *see* LOUGHREY

Olufsen *see* OLIFF

Olver *see* OLIVER

O'Lye *see* LEE

O'Lyhane *see* LEHANE

O'Lynche *see* LYNCH

Olyonov *see* ALEXANDER

Olyoshin *see* ALEXIS

O'Madagane *see* MADDEN

O'Maely *see* MALLY

O'Mahoney *see* MAHON

Öman Swedish: ornamental name from Swed. *ö* island (ON *ey*) + *man* man (ON *maðr*), sometimes adopted as a topographic name by someone who lived on an island.

Var.: **Öhman.**

Cpds (ornamental): **Öberg** ('island hill'); **Ö(h)gren** ('island branch'); **Öqvist** ('island twig'); **Öström** ('island river').

O'Managhane *see* MONAGHAN

O'Mara Irish: Anglicized form of Gael. **Ó Meadhra** 'descendant of *Meadhra*', a personal name derived from *meadhar* mirth, joy.

Vars.: **(O')Meara.**

O'Marcahan *see* MARKEY

O'Meagher *see* MAHER

O'Meally *see* MALLY

O'Meara *see* O'MARA

O'Meehan *see* MEEHAN

O'Melane *see* MULLEN

O'Mellegan *see* MILLIGAN

Ó Mhurcháin *see* MORGAN

O'Milligane *see* MILLIGAN

O'Mochaine *see* MOHAN

O'Moeney *see* MEANEY

O'Moleghan *see* MILLIGAN

O'Mollane *see* MULLEN

O'Monaghan *see* MONAGHAN

Omont *see* OSMOND

O'Moore *see* MOORE

O'Moraghan *see* MORGAN

O'Moraine *see* MORAN

O'Morchoe *see* MURPHY

O'Morierty *see* MORIARTY

O'Morisa *see* MORRISSEY

O'Moronie *see* MORONEY

Ó Muircheartaigh *see* MORIARTY

Ó Muirgheasáin *see* MORRISSEY

O'Mulcreevy *see* MULCREEVY

O'Muldoon *see* MULDOON

O'Mulghan *see* MILLIGAN

O'Mullally *see* MULLALLY

O'Mullan *see* MULLEN

O'Mullwine *see* MELVIN

O'Mulmichell *see* MELVILLE

O'Mulrean *see* MULRYAN

O'Multilly *see* TULLY

O'Murchan *see* MORGAN

O'Murphy *see* MURPHY

O'Naghtan *see* NAUGHTON

Onciulesco *see* UNCLE

Ondráček *see* ANDREW

O'Nea *see* NEE

O'Neaghten see NAUGHTON

O'Neal see NEIL

Ongarelli see UNGER

O'Nillane see NEIL

Onion 1. Welsh: from the W personal name *Einion*. This is probably from the L personal name *Anniānus*, but no doubt enjoyed its wide popularity as a result of folk etymological associations with W *einion* anvil and *uniawn* upright, just. **2.** English: metonymic occupational name for a grower or seller of onions, from ME *oyn(y)on, unyon* (OF *oignon*, from L *unio*, gen. *uniōnis*, a deriv. of *unus* one, since the plant produces only a single unit, as contrasted with garlic with its many cloves).

Vars.: **Onyon**. (Of 1 only): **Anyon, Anyan, Annion, Eynon, En(n)ion, Hennion**.

Patrs. (from 1): **Onions, Onians, Inions**; **Beynon** (with the Welsh prefix *ap, ab*).

Patr. (from 1) (dim.): BAINES.

O'Noland see NOLAN

O'Nowan see NOONE

Onslow English: habitation name from a place in Shrops., which appears in Domesday Book in the form *Andeslave*, and is probably named as the 'hill or burial-mound (OE *hlāw*; see LAW 2 and LOW 1) of *Andhere*', an otherwise unattested personal name composed of the elements *and* spirit, soul + *here* army.

Onyon see ONION

Oomen see EAME

Oonin see HOONEY

Opatovsky see APT

Opdam see DAM

Opel see ALBERT

Openhaime see OPPENHEIM

Openshaw English (Lancs.): habitation name from a place in Greater Manchester, so called from OE *open* open, i.e. not surrounded by a hedge + *sceaga* copse (cf. SHAW).

Opfermann see OPPERMANN

O'Phelane see WHELAN

Opie Cornish: from the medieval given name *Oppy, Obby*, a dim. of various names such as OSBORN, *Osbert*, and *Osbald*.

Oppenheim Jewish (W Ashkenazic): habitation name from a place in Hesse, on the Rhine between Mainz and Worms, so called from an obscure first element (Bahlow favours a prehistoric element referring to a marsh or fen) + OHG *heim* homestead.

Vars.: **Oppenhaim, Openhaime, Openheim**; **Openhajm** (Pol. spelling); **Op(p)enheimer** ('native or inhabitant of Oppenheim').

Oppermann Low German: occupational name for a churchwarden or sexton, with particular reference to his task of taking the collection, from MLG *opper(gilt)* dona-

tion (from *oppern* to donate, sacrifice, LL *operāri*) + *mann* man.

Vars.: **Opfermann**; **Offermann** (also Jewish, presumably an occupational name for the sexton of a synagogue).

Patr.: Low Ger.: **Offermanns**.

O'Prey Irish: Anglicized form of Gael. **Ó Préith**, from a personal name that is probably of Pictish origin.

Vars.: **Prey, Pray**.

O'Quane see COYNE

O'Quigley see QUICKLEY

O'Quill see QUILL

O'Quin see QUINN

O'Quinelane see QUINLAN

O'Quirk see QUIRKE

Öqvist see ÖMAN

O'Raghtagan see RATTIGAN

O'Rahilly see REILLY

Ó Ráighne see RAINEY

Oram see ORME

Orange English: of uncertain origin, discussed by Reaney. A certain William *de Orenge* mentioned in Domesday Book probably derives his name from *Orange* in the *département* of Mayenne. Later medieval examples probably come from a female given name, *Orenge*, of obscure derivation.

Orbach see AUERBACH

Orchard English: topographic name for someone who lived by an orchard, or metonymic occupational name for a fruit grower, from ME *orchard* (OE *ortgeard, orceard*, a cpd of *wort, wyrt* plant (later associated with L *hortus* garden; see ORT 1) + *geard* yard, enclosure).

Var.: **Norchard** (by misdivision of ME *atten orchard* 'at the orchard').

Ord 1. English (Northumb.): habitation name from a place in Northumb., so called from OE *ord* point; cf. ORT 3. **2.** English: from a Gmc personal name; see ORT 2. **3.** Scots: habitation name from various minor places named with Gael. *ord* hammer, used as a topographical term for a rounded hill.

Var.: **Orde**.

Ordelt see ORT

Ordóñez Spanish: patr. from the medieval given name *Ordoño*, of uncertain origin and meaning.

O'Reagan see REGAN

O'Really see REILLY

O'Reaney see RAINEY

O'Reddie see READY

O'Ree see REAVEY

O'Reedan see RIORDAN

Orellana Spanish: habitation name from either of two places in the province of Badajoz, probably so called from L *Aurēliāna (villa)* 'estate of *Aurēlius*', a Roman family name.

Orenstein *see* HORN

Orfeur *see* OFFER

Orff German: **1.** habitation name from a place in Hesse, near Kassel, now known as *Urff*, but recorded in 1184 as *Orpha*. Its etymology is obscure. **2.** contracted form of a Gmc personal name composed of the elements *ort* point (of a spear, sword) + *wulf* wolf. **3.** metonymic occupational name for a fisherman or fish-seller, or nickname for a person thought to resemble a fish, from *orf*, a dial. word for a type of fish of the carp family.

Orford English: habitation name from any of various places so called. One in Suffolk gets its name from OE *ōra* shore (see ORR 3) + *ford* FORD, whereas that in Lancs. is from ME *overe* upper (OE *uferra*; cf. OBER) + *ford*. A third example, in Lincs., is recorded as *Erforde* in Domesday Book, but later forms have *I-*, suggesting a derivation from OE *Iraford* 'ford of the Irish'.

Organ **1.** English: metonymic occupational name for a player of a musical instrument (not necessarily what is now known as an organ), from ME *organ* (OF *organe*, LL *organum* device, (musical) instrument, Gk *organon* tool, from *ergein* to work, do). **2.** English: from a rare medieval given name, attested only in the Latinized forms *Organus* (masc.) and *Organa* (fem.). Its etymology is obscure; it may represent a reworking of a Celt. name. **3.** Welsh: see MORGAN.

Var. (of 1): **Organer**.

O'Ria *see* REAVEY

O'Riegaine *see* REGAN

O'Riellie *see* REILLY

Orieux *see* ORIOL

O'Rinne *see* WREN

Oriol Provençal and Catalan: nickname for a man with bright yellow hair, from OProv., Cat. *oriol* oriole, a yellow bird (LL *aureolus*, a dim. of *aureus* golden, from *aurum* gold).

Vars.: Prov.: **Oriou, Orieux, Oriot**; **Auriol, Auriou**; **Loriol, Lauriol, Lorieu(x), Loriot**.

O'Riordan *see* RIORDAN

Orive Spanish form of Basque **Oribe**: topographic name for someone living in the lower part of a village, from *uri, iri* settlement (see URIA) + *be(h)e* lower part; cf. URIBE.

Orlandelli *see* ROWLAND

Orlov **1.** Russian: patr. from the nickname *Oryol* 'Eagle' (cogn. with Pol. *orzel*, Czech *orel*). This word is a distant cogn. of Gk *ornis* bird, but was specialized in the Slav. languages to denote the king of the birds. **2.** Jewish (E Ashkenazic): patr. from the Russ. vocab. word *oryol* eagle, one of the many Ashkenazic ornamental surnames derived from words denoting birds.

Vars.: Russ.: **Orlovski** (surname adopted by Orthodox clergy, in reference to the eagle as a symbol of St John the Evangelist). Jew-

ish: **Orlovitch, Orlovitz, Orlowitz**; **Orlovsky, Orlowsky, Orlowski**.

Dims.: Pol.: **Orlik, Orlicki**. Czech: **Orlický, Vorlický**; **Vorlíček**.

Habitation names: Pol. **Orłowski, Orlikowski, Orliński**.

Ormaeche *see* HORMAECHE

Orme **1.** N English: from the ON personal name *Ormr*, originally a byname meaning 'Snake', 'Serpent', 'Dragon' (cogn. with OE *wyrm* worm, which originally had the same range of meanings). **2.** French: topographic name for someone who lived near a conspicuous elm tree, from OF *orme* (L *ulmus*; see OLMO).

Vars. (of 1): Eng.: **Oram, Or(r)um**. (Of 2): Fr.: **D(h)orme, Delorme**.

Dims. (of 1): Ger.: **Würmle, Würmlin**. Low Ger.: **Wörm(b)ke**. (Of 2): Fr.: **Ormeau, Delormeau, Delhommeau(x), Désormeaux**; **Humeau** (E France); **Ormesson**.

Patrs. (from 1): Eng.: **Ormes**. Ger.: **Würmeling**.

Collective (of 2): Fr.: **Dormeuil**.

Ormerod English (Lancs.): habitation name from a place in Lancs., so called from the ON personal name *Ormr* (see ORME 1) or *Ormarr* (composed of the elements *orm* serpent + *herr* army) + OE *rod* clearing.

Var.: **Ormrod**.

Ormiston Scots: habitation name from places in the former counties of Roxburgh and E Lothian, so called from the gen. case of the ON personal name *Ormr* (see ORME 1) + OE *tūn* enclosure, settlement.

Var.: **Ormston** (Northumb.).

Ormond Irish (common in the Cork and Waterford areas): Anglicized form of Gael. **Ó Ruaidh** 'descendant of *Ruadh*', a byname meaning 'Red', altered by folk etymology to resemble a regional name from the ancient region of of E Munster known as *Ormond* (Gael. *Ur Mhumhain*).

Vars.: **Ormonde, Orman**.

Ormsby English: habitation name from *Ormsby* in Lincs. and N Yorks., or *Ormesby* in Norfolk, all so called from the gen. case of the ON personal name *Ormr* (see ORME 1) + ON *býr* farm, settlement.

Ormshaw English (Lancs.): habitation name from an unidentified place, apparently named with the personal name ORME and the local element SHAW.

Var.: **Ormesher**.

Ornstein *see* HORN

O'Roan *see* RUANE

O'Rodane *see* RODEN

O'Roddy *see* READY

O'Ronane *see* RONAN

O'Roney *see* ROONEY

O'Rorke *see* ROURKE

Orozco Basque: habitation name from a place in the province of Biscay, of unclear etymology; the first element may derive from Basque *oru* plot of land.

Orpin English: metonymic occupational name for a herbalist, from ME, OF *orpin(e)* yellow stonecrop (from LL *auripigmentum* yellow arsenic, lit. 'golden pigment'), a plant widely esteemed for its reputed capacity to heal wounds.

Var.: **Orpen**.

Orr 1. N English, Scots, and N Irish: from the ON byname *Orri* 'Black-cock'. **2.** Scots: nickname for someone with a sallow complexion, from Gael. *odhar* pale, dun. **3.** English: topographic name for someone who lived on a shore or on the edge of a hill, from OE *ōra* edge, or habitation name from a place named with this word, as for example *Ore* in Sussex or *Oare* in Berks., Kent, and Wilts. **4.** Jewish (Israeli): ornamental name from Hebr. *or* light.

Orrey *see* WOOLDRIDGE

Orrick English (Northumb.): from a ME survival of the OE personal name *Ordrīc*, composed of the elements *ord* point (of a sword, spear) + *rīc* power.

Var.: **Orridge** (Notts.).

Orrum *see* ORME

Ors *see* ORT

Orso Italian: nickname for someone thought to resemble a bear (e.g. a large, lumbering person), or local name for someone who lived in a house distinguished with the sign of a bear, from It. *orso* bear (L *ursus*).

Vars.: **Orsi**; **Urso**, **Ursi** (S Italy).

Dims.: It.: **Orselli**, **Orsello**, **Orsetti**, **Ors(ol)ini**, **Orsolino**, **Orsolillo**, **Orsucci**, **Ursillo**, **Ursino**, **Ursini**. Fr.: **Oursel(in)**, **Orsel**, **Orseau**, **Hourseau**, **Orset**.

Augs.: It.: **Orsoni**, **Orsone**.

Patrs.: It.: **D'Orso**, **D'Orsi**, **D'Urso**.

Országh Hungarian: topographic name from Hung. *ország* land, territory.

Ort 1. Provençal: metonymic occupational name for a gardener or topographic name for someone who lived near an enclosed garden, OProv. *ort* (L *hortus*). **2.** German: from a Gmc personal name *Ort*, a short form of the various cpd names with the first element *ord* point (of a sword, spear). **3.** German: topographic name for someone who lived at the top of a hill or the end of a settlement, from OHG *ort* (see 2 above), in the transferred sense 'tip', 'extremity'. In mod. Ger. the word has come to mean 'point', 'spot', 'place'.

Vars. (of 1): **Delort**, **Or(t)s**, **Des(h)orts**. (Of 3): **Ortner**, **Ortler**; **Amort**, **Imort**.

Dims. (of 1): Prov.: **Ortet**, **Orteau(x)**; **Ourtic**, **Ho(u)rtic**. Cat.: **Ortells**, **Orteu**. (Of 2): Ger.: **Örtel(t)**, **Ert(e)l**, **Ertelt**, **Ordelt**, **Artelt**.

Ortega Spanish and Catalan: habitation name from any of various places, for example in the provinces of Burgos, La Coruña, and Jaén, of uncertain etymology. It may represent an altered form of Sp. *ortiga* nettle (L *urtīca*), or be from L *hortus* garden, orchard (cf. ORT 1) + the local suffix *-eca*.

Ortiz *see* FORT

Orton English and Scots: habitation name from any of various places so called. All those in England share a second element from OE *tūn* enclosure, settlement, but the first element in each case is more difficult to determine. Examples in Cambs. and Warwicks. are on the banks of rivers, so that there it is probably OE *ōfer* riverbank; in other cases it is impossible to decide between *ofer* ridge and *ufera* upper. Orton in Cumb., exceptionally, probably has as its first element the ON byname *Orri* 'Black-cock' (see ORR 1), and Orton near Fochabers, Scotland, probably gets its name from Gael. *oir*, loc. case of *or* border, edge + *dùin*, gen. case of *dùn* fort.

Ortuño Spanish: from a medieval given name (L *Fortūnius*, a deriv. of *fortūna* chance, (good) fortune).

Ó Ruairc *see* ROURKE

O'Ruane *see* RUANE

O'Ruddane *see* RODEN

O'Ruddy *see* READY

Orum *see* ORME

Orwell 1. English: habitation name from a place in Cambs., so called from the OE topographical term *ord* tip, top, extremity (cf. ORT 3) + *well(a)* spring, stream (see WELL). **2.** Scots: habitation name from a place in the former county of Kinross, first recorded in 1330 in the form *Urwell*, probably from Gael. *ùr* new + *baile* (in combination *bhail*) village.

O'Ryan *see* RYAN

Orzechowski Polish: **1.** habitation name from a place named with Pol. *orzech* nut, hazel-nut, + *-ów* possessive suffix, with the addition of the suffix of local surnames *-ski* (see BARANOWSKI). In some cases it may also be a topographic name for someone who lived by a nut-tree. **2.** nickname from Pol. *orzechowy* hazel (adj.), applied to the colour of the hair.

Ös *see* OSWALD

O'Sawra *see* SUMMER

Osborn English: from the ON personal name *Ásbjorn*, composed of the elements *ás* god + *björn* bear. This was established in England before the Conquest, in the late OE form *Ōsbern*, and was later reinforced by the Norman *Osbern*.

Vars.: **Osborne**, **Osbourn(e)**, **Osburn**, **Osbon**, **Osband**, **Usborne**, **Hosburn**.

Patr.: Eng.: **Hosbons**.

O'Scandall *see* SCANNELL

Ösch *see* OSWALD

O'Scollee *see* SCULLY

Oscroft English: apparently a habitation name from an unidentified place, the second element of which appears to be OE *croft* paddock, smallholding (see CROFT). The first element may be a short form of an OE personal name containing the element *ōs* god (e.g. *Oswine*; see OSWIN) or its ON cogn. *ás* (see, e.g., OSBORN).

Ó Seanacháin *see* SHANE

Oseletti *see* UCCELLO

O'Serie *see* SEEREY

Oserovitch *see* OSHER

O'Sesnane see SEXTON

Osgood English: from the ON personal name *Ásgautr*, composed of the element *ás* god + the tribal name *Gaut* (see JOCELYN). This was established in England before the Conquest, in the late OE forms *Ōsgot* or *Ōsgod*, and was later reinforced by the Norman *Ansgot*.

Vars.: **Angood**, **Angold**; **Hosgood**, **Ho(r)segood**.

O'Shanahan see SHANE

O'Shanesy see SHAUGHNESSY

O'Shanley see SHANLEY

O'Shea see SHEA

O'Sheahan see SHEEHAN

O'Sheal see SHIELD

Osher Jewish (Ashkenazic): from the Yid. male given name *Osher* (Hebr. ASHER 'Blessed').

Vars.: **Osheri** (from Hebr. *osher* happiness + the Hebr. ending *-i*); USHER.

Dim.: **Osherenko** (SE Ashkenazic).

Patrs. (E Ashkenazic): **Osh(e)rov**, **Osheroff**, **Oserow**, **Os(h)erovitch**, **Os(h)erovitz**, **Oshrovitz**, **Osherowitz**, **Osherowicz**, **Osherowich**, **Osherovsky**; **Oszerowski** (Pol. spelling).

O'Sheridane see SHERIDAN

O'Shesnan see SEXTON

O'Shirie see SEEREY

Oshrov see OSHER

O'Shydie see SHEEDY

Osichev see JOSEPH

Osiecki Polish: topographic name for someone living by a water meadow, Pol. *osiek*.

O'Siegall see SHIELD

Osier see DOZIER

Osinin Russian: **1.** patr. from the given name *Osinya*, a pet form of *Osip*; see JOSEPH. **2.** patr. from the nickname *Osina* 'Aspen', used to refer to a very timid person, or to someone who suffered from a nervous tremor.

O'Slattery see SLATTERY

Osler see OSTLER

O'Slowey see SLOWEY

Osmond English and French: from the ON personal name *Ásmundr*, composed of the elements *ás* god + *mund* protection. This was established in England before the Conquest, coalescing with the independent OE form *Ōsmund*, and was later reinforced by the Norman *Osmund*.

Vars.: Eng.: **Osmund**, **Osmon**, **Osman(t)**, **Osment**, **Osmint**. Fr.: **O(s)mont**.

Osorio Spanish: from a medieval given name, of uncertain origin. It is probably a metathesized form of L *Orosius* (Gk *Orosios*, a deriv. of *oros* mountain), the name borne by a 4th-cent. Iberian theologian and historian, who was famous in Spain throughout the Middle Ages.

O'Spallane see SPILLANE

Ossipenko see JOSEPH

Ossowski Polish: common surname of uncertain origin. In form it is a habitation name; it may perhaps be from a place named from a personal nickname derived from Pol. *osowiały* miserable, depressed.

Ostal see HOSTAL

Ostapov Russian: patr. from the given name *Ostap* (Gk *Eustathios*, from *eu* good, well + *stat-* to stand). This rare name was early confused with *Eustakhios* Eustace (see STACE). The forms have been further affected by confusion with *Osip* JOSEPH and other given names.

Vars.: **Astapov**, **Ostafyev**, **Astafyev**, **Evstafyev**, **Astfimov**, **Ostanov**.

Dims.: Russ.: **Ostankin**, **Ostashkin**, **Ostashkov**, **Astashkin**, **Astashov**, **Astashev**, **Astachov**, **Tafintsev** (all patrs.). Ukr.: **Ostashko**, **Ostapets**. Beloruss.: **Ostepenya**, **Astapenya**, **Astapchyonok**, **Astapchuk**.

'Son of the wife of O.': Ukr.: **Ostapishin**.

Ostberg see EAST

Österberg see EASTER

Østergård Danish: habitation name from a placename composed of the elements *øster* eastern + *gård* enclosure.

Var.: **Østergaard**.

Osterreicher see OISTRAKH

Ostler English: occupational name for an innkeeper, from ME *(h)osteler* (OF *(h)ostelier*, an agent deriv. of HOSTAL). This term was at first applied to the secular officer in a monastery who was responsible for the lodging of visitors, but it was later extended to keepers of commercial hostelries, and this is probably the usual sense of the surname. The more restricted mod. Eng. sense, 'groom', is also a possible source.

Vars.: **Oastler**, **Osler**; **Host(el)ler**, **Hustler**, **Horsler**.

Öström see ÖMAN

Ostrowski Polish: habitation name from any of the many places in different parts of Poland named with Pol. *ostrów*, which denotes both an island in a river and a water meadow bounded by ditches. In some cases it may be a topographical name for someone who lived on a river island or in a water meadow.

Ostrý see VOSTRÝ

O'Sullivan see SULLIVAN

Osuna Spanish: habitation name from a place in the province of Seville, so called from Arabic *Oxuna*, perhaps from LL *Ursīna (villa)* 'estate of *Ursus*', a byname meaning 'Bear'.

Oswald N English and Scots: from an OE personal name composed of the elements *ōs* god (Continental Gmc *ans*) + *weald* power. In the ME period, this fell together with the less common ON cogn. *Asvaldr*. The name was introduced to Germany from England, as a result of the fame of St Oswald, a 7th-cent. king of Northumb., whose deeds were reported by Celtic missionaries to S Germany. The name

was also borne by a 10th-cent. Eng. saint of Dan. parentage, who was important as a monastic reformer.
Dims.: Ger.: **Ös(ch)**, **Öschlin**.

Oswell English: of uncertain origin, possibly a habitation name, of which the second element appears to be OE *well(a)* spring, stream (see WELL). The first element may be a short form of an OE personal name containing the element *ōs* god (e.g. *Oswine*; see OSWIN) or its ON cogn. *ás* (see, e.g., OSBORN).

O'Swerte *see* SEWARD

Oswin English: from a ME survival of the OE personal name *Ōswine*, composed of the elements *ōs* god + *wine* friend.

Oszerowski *see* OSHER

Ó Tadhgán *see* TIGHE

Otanelli *see* OADE

Otava *see* VOTAVA

O'Tearney *see* TIERNEY

Otero Spanish: habitation name from any of the numerous places in N and NW Spain so called, from Sp. *otero* height, hill (LL *altārium*, a deriv. of *altus* high).

O'Tiernan *see* TIERNEY

Otino *see* OADE

Otke *see* OADE

O'Toole *see* TOOLE

O'Toomey *see* TWOMEY

O'Towie *see* TUOHY

O'Trasey *see* TREACY

O'Trehy *see* TROY

O'Trevir *see* TREVOR

Ott *see* OADE

Otter English: **1.** metonymic occupational name for an otter hunter, or nickname for someone supposedly resembling an otter, from ME *oter* (OE *otor*). **2.** from the late OE personal name *Ohthere*, a borrowing of ON *Óttar*, composed of the elements *ótti* fear, dread + *herr* army.

Ottolenghi Italian (Jewish): Italianized form of a habitation name from *Öttlingen* in Bavaria. Jews were repeatedly expelled from this town in the 15th and 16th cents. and many of them settled in N Italy, particularly in Piedmont and Lombardy.

Ottoway English: from either of two Norman personal names: *Otoïs*, composed of the Gmc elements *od* prosperity, riches + *widis* (from *wid* wide or *witu* wood), or *Otewi*, in which the second element is *wīg* war.
Vars.: **Ottaway**, **Otterway**, **Ot(t)way**.
Dims.: **Otte(r)well**, **Ottewill**, **Ottiwell** (from OF *Otuel*).

O'Tuale *see* TOOLE

Ötvös *see* EÖTVÖS

Otway *see* OTTOWAY

O'Twohill *see* TOOLE

O'Twohy *see* TUOHY

O'Twomey *see* TWOMEY

Otzen *see* OADE

Oudet *see* OADE

Ough English: a fairly common surname in Cornwall, of unknown origin. It is not from the Corn. language.

Oughtright *see* UTTRIDGE

Ould *see* OLD

Ourry *see* WOOLDRIDGE

Oursel *see* ORSO

Ourtic *see* ORT

Ousley S English: apparently a habitation name from an unidentified place, perhaps a cpd of the river name *Ouse* (OE *Usa*, of ancient Brit. origin, from *ud-* water) + OE *lēah* wood, clearing.
Vars.: **Ouseley**, **Owsley**.

Oustal *see* HOSTAL

Outin *see* AUSTIN

Outridge *see* UTTRIDGE

Outzen *see* OADE

Ovanesian *see* JOHN

Óváry Hungarian: topographic name for someone who lived by an old castle, composed of the elements *ó* old + *vár* castle, or habitation name from a place so named.
Var.: **Óvári**.

Ovasapian *see* JOSEPH

Ovdkimov *see* YEVDOKIMOV

Ovejero Spanish: occupational name for a shepherd, Sp. *ovejero* (LL *oviculārius*, agent. deriv. of *ovicula* sheep, a dim. of class. L *ovis*).

Ovenden English: habitation name from a place in W Yorks., so called from the gen. case of the OE personal name *Ofa* + OE *denu* valley (see DEAN 1). In some cases the surname may also derive from *Ovingdean* in Sussex, named as the 'valley of the people of *Ufa*'.

Over English: topographic name for someone who lived on the bank of a river or on a slope (from OE *ōfer* seashore, riverbank, or from the originally distinct word *ofer* slope, bank, ridge). The two terms, being of similar meaning as well as similar form, fell together in the ME period. The surname may also be a habitation name from places named with one or other of these words, which can only be distinguished with reference to their situation. *Over* in Cambs. is on a riverbank, whereas examples in Ches. and Derbys. are not; *Over* in Gloucs. is on the bank of the Severn, but also at the foot of a hill.
Vars.: **Ower(s)**, **Nowers**.

Overall English: topographic name composed of the ME elements *overe*, *uvere* upper (OE *ufera*) + *hall* HALL.
Vars.: **Overal**, **Overell**, **Overill**.

Overend English (Yorks.): topographic name for someone who lived at the 'upper end' of a settlement, from ME *overe, uvere* upper (OE *ufera*) + *end* end (OE *ende*).

Overgård Danish: habitation name from a placename composed of the elements *over* upper + *gård* enclosure; cf. NEDERGÅRD.

Var.: **Overgaard**.

Overton English: habitation name from any of the numerous places so called. Most get the name from OE *ufere* upper + *tūn* enclosure, settlement; others have the first element from OE *ōfer* riverbank or *ofer* slope (see OVER).

Overy English: habitation name from a place named with the OE phrase *ofer īe* over, across the river, for example *Overy* in Oxon.

Ovesen *see* OLIFF

Oviedo Spanish: habitation name from the city in N Spain, found in early records in the L form *Ovetum*. It is of unknown origin.

Ovseev *see* EUSÉBIO

Ovtukhov *see* YEVTIKHIEV

Owczarz Polish: occupational name for a shepherd, Pol. *owczarz*.

Dims.: **Owczarek**, **Owczarczyk**.

Owen Welsh: from the W personal name *Owain*, in origin probably a borrowing of L *Eugenius* (see EUGÈNE).

Patr.: **Bowen** (*ap Owain*).

Ower *see* OVER

O'Whalen *see* WHELAN

Owsiejczyk *see* EUSÉBIO

Owsley *see* OUSLEY

Oxenham English (W Country): habitation name from *Oxenham* in S Tawton, Devon, named with OE *oxan*, gen. pl. of *oxa* ox + *hamm* water meadow.

Oxley English: habitation name from any of various places, for example *Oxley* in Staffs. and *Ox Lee* near Hepworth (W Yorks.), so called from OE *oxa* ox + *lēah* wood, clearing.

Var.: **Oxlee**.

Oxnard English: occupational name for a keeper of oxen, from OE *oxan* oxen + *hierde* herdsman (see HEARD).

Oyler English: occupational name for an extractor or seller of oil, from a metathesized form of ANF *olier* (from *oile* oil, L *oleum* (olive) oil; cf. OLIVA). In N England linseed oil obtained from locally grown flax was more common than olive oil.

Var.: **Olier**.

Ozintsev *see* JOSEPH

P

Paapke *see* POPE

Pabelik *see* PAUL

Pabian *see* FABIAN

Pacák Czech: **1.** nickname for a bungler, from a deriv. of the OCzech verb *pacat* to bungle, botch. **2.** habitation name from a place called *Pacov*.

Var. (of 2): **Pacovský**.

Pacandet *see* PAIN

Pace English: nickname for a mild-mannered and even-tempered man, from ME *pace, pece* peace, concord, amity (ANF *pace*, from L *pax*, gen. *pācis*). There has been considerable confusion with *Pash* (see PASK).

The It. cogn. *Pace* /'pɑtʃɛ/ was used as a given name in the Middle Ages, and the many It. derivs. are mostly from this. The Sp. and Port. cogns. were often assumed, as approximate translations of the Hebr. given name *Shelomo* (see SALOMON), by Jews converted to Christianity; in other cases they derive from a title of the Virgin, *María de la Paz* (Sp.), *Maria da Paz* (Port.).

Vars.: **Paice**, PAYS, **Payze**, **Peace**.

Dims.: Fr.: **Pachot**. Prov.: **Pa(s)choud**. It.: **Pacelli**, **Paciello**, **Pacilli**, **Paselli**, **Pasello**, **Pacetti**, **Pasetti**, **Pasetto**, **Pacitti**, **Pacin(ott)i**, **Pacino**, **Pasin(i)**, **Pasino**, **Pasinetti**, **Pasol(in)i**, **Pasolli**, **Paciotti**, **Pasotti**, **Pasotto**, **Pasutti**, **Pasutto**, **Paciullo**.

Pačes Czech: **1.** nickname for someone with an unruly mop of hair, from Czech *pačesy* mop or shock of hair. **2.** from an OCzech personal name, *Pačeslav*, composed of the elements *pač* stronger (comparative of *paký* strong) + *slav* glory.

Vars. (of 2): **Pač**, **Páč**.

Pacey English (Norman): habitation name from *Pacy-sur-Eure*, which has the same origin as PASSY.

Var.: **Pacy**.

Pach *see* BACH

Pache *see* PAUL

Pacheco Spanish and Portuguese: of uncertain origin. It is possibly from a dim. of the given name *Francisco* (see FRANCIS); the form *Pachico* is in use in the Basque country, and *Pachón* and *Pachu* are found elsewhere in Spain. Alternatively, it may be related to a root *pag-, pak-* found in various Romance languages signifying heaviness or fatness, and so be a nickname for a large, fat man.

Pacholski Polish: occupational name for a manservant, from Pol. *pachoł(ek)* servant + *-ski* suffix of surnames (see BARANOWSKI).

Dims.: Pol.: **Pacholczyk**. Ger. (of Slav. origin): **Pacholek**, **Pacholke**.

Pächt *see* PETER

Pacifico **1.** Italian: from the medieval given name *Pacifico* 'Peaceful', 'Peace-loving' (L *Pacificus*, from *pax* (gen. *pācis*) peace + *facere* to make, create). **2.** Italian (Jewish): surname adopted as an approximate translation of the Hebr. given name *Shelomo* (see SALOMON).

Var.: **Pacifici**.

Pack English (Kentish): from a medieval given name, *Pack*, possibly a survival of the OE personal name **Pacca* (see PACKHAM), although this is found only as a placename element and appears to have died out fairly early on in the OE period. The ME given name is perhaps more likely to be an altered form of PASK.

Vars.: **Packe**, **Paik**; **Patch** (chiefly Bristol).

Packard English: **1.** pej. name for a pedlar, from ME *pa(c)k* pack, bundle (see PACKER 2 and PACKMAN 1) + the ANF pej. suffix *-ard*. **2.** pej. deriv. of the ME given name PACK. **3.** from the Norman personal name *Pachard*, *Baghard*, composed of the Gmc elements *pac, bag* fight (see BACON 2) + *hard* hardy, brave, strong.

Packer **1.** English: occupational name for a wool-packer, an agent deriv. of ME *pack(en)* to pack (from *pa(c)k* package, from MLG *pak*, of unknown origin). **2.** German and Jewish (Ashkenazic): occupational name for a wholesale trader, one who sold goods in large packages rather than broken down into smaller quantities. The term is an agent deriv. of Ger. *Pack* package (of the same MLG origin as the Eng. word).

Packham English: habitation name from *Pagham* in Sussex or *Pakenham* in Suffolk, apparently named as the homesteads (OE *hām*) of bearers of the OE personal names **Pæcga* and **Pac(c)a* respectively. **Pæcga* is an unattested byform of the attested *Pæga*. **Pac(c)a*, though apparently present in a number of placenames, including PACKWOOD, is unattested in its own right and remains unexplained.

Vars.: **Padgham** (from the place in Sussex); **Pakenham** (from the place in Suffolk).

Packman **1.** English and Jewish (Ashkenazic): occupational name for a pedlar or hawker, one who carried his pack of goods for sale with him. **2.** English: occupational name for the servant of someone called PACK.

Var. (of 1): Jewish: **Pakentreger** (from Yid. *pakn-treger* pack-carrier).

Packwood English: habitation name from a place in Warwicks., so called from the OE personal name **Pac(c)a* (see PACKHAM) + *wudu* WOOD.

Pacock *see* PEACOCK

Pacquet *see* PAQUET

Pacześ *see* PAKUŁA

Padan *see* PATRICK

Paddock English: **1.** topographic name for a dweller in a paddock or enclosed meadow, from ME *parrock* (OE *pearruc*; cf. PARR 1 and PARK 1). The change of -*rr*- to -*dd*- did not occur before the 17th cent., and is not readily explained. **2.** nickname for someone considered to resemble a toad or frog, from ME *paddock*, dim. of *pad* (from ON *padda*, apparently from the root *pa(d)* marsh, bog).

Paddon N English: **1.** habitation name from some minor place so called, perhaps from OE *pæð* path + *dūn* hill (see DOWN 1). **2.** dim. of PATRICK; cf. PATE.

Paderewski E Polish or Ukrainian: habitation name from a place called *Paderew*. The location of this is uncertain, as is the etymology, though this is most likely the same as that of *Padarzewo* in Środa region, i.e. probably from an OPol. personal name *Podarz*.

Var.: W Pol.: **Padarzewski**.

Padfield N English: habitation name from a place in Derbys. (or some other minor place with the same name), so called from the OE personal name *Pad(d)a* (attested, but of disputed origin) + OE *feld* pasture, open country (see FIELD).

Padgett *see* PAGE

Padgham *see* PACKHAM

Padilla Spanish: habitation name from any of the various minor places, for example in the provinces of Burgos, Guadalajara, and Valladolid, so called from Sp. *padilla* frying-pan, breadpan (L *patella*, a dim. of *patina* shallow dish), a word which was commonly used in the topographical sense of a gentle depression.

Padmore English: **1.** habitation name from a place, for example in the parish of Onibury, Shrops., so called from late OE *padde* toad (cf. PADDOCK 2) + OE *mōr* marsh (see MOORE 1). **2.** var. of PATMORE.

Padovano Italian (partly Jewish): habitation name from the city of Padua, It. *Padova* (L *Patavium*, of obscure etymology).

Vars.: It.: **Padovan(i)**, **Padoan(i)**, **Paduan(i)**, **Paduano**, **Pavna(i)**. Jewish: **Padova**; **Padover**, **Padawer** (Ashkenazic).

Dims.: It.: **Pavanelli**, **Pavanello**, **Pavanetti**, **Pavanetto**, **Pavanini**.

Padrós *see* PEDROSA

Páez *see* PELAYO

Paffen *see* POPE

Pagan N English and Scots: of uncertain origin, probably from a more formal version of the medieval given name *Payne* (see PAIN 1). The name does not occur in this form before the 16th cent., and so probably represents a learned respelling. In America it has often been used as an Anglicization of the Italian surname *Pagano*, itself a cogn. of PAIN 1.

Vars.: **Pagen**, **Pagin**, **Pagon**.

Paganelli *see* PAIN

Page English and French: occupational name for a young servant, ME, OF *page* (from It. *paggio*, apparently ultim-

ately from Gk *paidion*, dim. of *pais* boy, child). The surname is also common in Ireland, where it has been Gaelicized **Mac Giolla** (see GILL 3).

Vars.: Eng.: **Paige**. Fr.: **Lepage**.

Dims.: Eng.: **Paget(t)**, **Padgett**. Fr.: **Pag(en)et**, **Page(n)ot**, **Pajot**, **Pageon**.

Pejs.: Fr.: **Pageard**, **Pageaud**.

Patr.: It.: **Del Paggio**.

Pagels *see* PAUL

Paggiarin *see* PAILLIER

Pagliacci *see* PAILLE

Pagnin *see* COMPAGNON

Pagnol French: ethnic name from an aphetic form of OF *espaignol* Spaniard (L *Hispāniōlus*, from *Hispānia* Spain, a name probably ultimately of Phoenician origin). The It. cogns. were often nicknames referring to people of extreme haughtiness or elegance, which were believed to be characteristics of Spaniards; the painter Giuseppe Maria Crespi (1665–1737) was nicknamed *lo Spagnuolo* because of his foppish dress.

Vars.: **Pagnoul**, **Pagnoux**; **Lespagnol**, **Lespagnoud**, **Lépagnol**, **Lépagneux**.

Dims.: Fr.: **Pagnon**, **Pagnot**. It.: **Spagnoleto**, **Spagnoletti**.

Pej.: Fr.: **Pagnard**.

Pagram *see* PILGRIM

Pahl *see* PAUL

Pahlke *see* PEEL

Pahnke *see* PANK

Paice *see* PACE

Paige *see* PAGE

Paik *see* PACK

Pailin *see* HAYLING

Paille French: metonymic occupational name for someone who gathered straw or used it to make hats or mattresses, from OF *paille* straw (L *palea*). It may also have been a nickname for someone with straw-coloured hair.

Dims.: Eng.: PALLETT. It.: **Pa(gl)ietta**, **Paiola**, **Paiotta**, **Paglicci**, **Pagliocca**, **Pagliucca**.

Aug.: It.: **Paglione**.

Pejs.: Fr.: **Paillard** (denoting a man who slept on a bed of straw, being too poor to afford anything better; later applied as a general term of abuse for a vagabond or ragamuffin). It.: **Pagliazzi**, **Pagliacci**.

Paillier French: **1.** occupational name for someone who gathered or used straw, from an agent deriv. of PAILLE (LL *paleārius*). **2.** topographic name for someone who lived near a straw-loft or barn (LL *paleārium*).

Var.: **Pailler**.

Dims.: Fr.: **Pailleret**. It.: **Pagliarolo**, **Pagliaroli**, **Pagliarulo**; **Paggiarin** (Venetia).

Pain 1. English: from a ME given name *Pain(e)*, *Payn(e)* (OF *Paien*, from L *Pāgānus*). The L name is a deriv. of *pāgus* outlying village, and meant at first a rustic, then a civilian as opposed to a soldier, and finally a heathen (one not enrolled in the army of Christ). In spite of its unchristian associations this was a popular name in the early Middle Ages. Some of the Romance cogns. may have originated as topographic names in the original sense 'country-dweller'. **2.** French: metonymic occupational name for a baker of bread or for a pantryman (see PANTHER), from OF *pain* bread (L *pānis*).

Vars. (of 1): Eng.: **Pa(i)ne**, **Payn(e)**, **Payen**, **Payan**; PAGAN. (Of 2): Fr.: **Pan(n)ier**, **Pagnier**, **Pagniez**.

Dims. (of 1): Eng.: **Paynell**. Fr.: **Pacandet**. It.: **Paganino**, **Paganin(i)**, **Paganelli**, **Paganetto**, **Paganetti**, **Paganucci**, **Paganuzzi**, **Paganotto**. (Of 2): It.: **Panelli**, **Panello**, **Panetti**, **Pagnotto**, **Panozzo**.

Augs. (of 1): It.: **Paganoni**. (Of 2): It.: **Pagnone**.

Patrs. (from 1): Eng.: **Pa(i)nes**, **Paynes**; **Fitzpayn**.

Painter English: occupational name for a painter (normally of stained glass), from ME, OF *peinto(u)r*, oblique case of *peintre* (LL *pinctor*, for class. L *pictor*, from *pingere* to paint).

Var.: **Paynter**.

Dim.: It.: **Pintoricchio**.

Painty see PENTY

Pairpoint see PIERREPONT

Pais see PELAYO

Paisant see PAYS

Paish see PASK

Paisley Scots: habitation name from a place in Strathclyde, now a suburb of Glasgow. It is first recorded in 1157 as *Passeleth*, then in 1158 as *Paisleth* and in 1163 as *Passelet*, *Passelay*; it may be derived from LL *basilica* church.

Paiva Portuguese: topographic name for someone living by the river *Paiva* in N Portugal. The river name is recorded in the Middle Ages as *Pavia*, identical in form with the It. town *Pavia* (see PAVEY 2).

Paixão Portuguese: religious byname from Port. *paixão* passion (L *passio*, gen. *passiōnis*, a deriv. of *pati* to suffer), borne in commemoration of Christ's passion, in particular by someone born on Good Friday.

Pajor Polish: nickname for a quarrelsome person, derived from a dial. form of Pol. *pojować* to shout, quarrel.

Pajot see PAGE

Pakenham see PACKHAM

Pakentreger see PACKMAN

Pakes see PASK

Pakuła Polish: nickname for someone with tow-coloured hair, or perhaps an occupational name for someone who worked with linen or hemp, from Pol. *pakuły* tow (also called *pacześ*).

Vars.: **Pakulski**; **Pacześ**, **Paczesny**.

Palacín Spanish: occupational name for someone who was employed at a royal or noble court (cf. COURTIER 1 and HOFFMANN), or nickname for a courteous individual (cf. CURTIS 1 and HÖFLICH). The name is from OSp. *palacin*

'of the palace', the result of a cross between *palatino* and *palaciano* (respectively from L *palatīnus* and LL *palatiānus*, both derivs. of *palātium*; see PALACIO).

Palacio Spanish: topographic name for someone who lived near a royal or noble mansion, or occupational name for someone who was employed in one, from Sp. *palacio* palace, manor, great house (L *palātium*, a vocab. word derived from the *Palātium* or *mons Palātīnus* in Rome (of uncertain etymology), site of the emperor Augustus' golden house).

Vars.: **Palacios**; **Pazos** (Galicia; also from any of the numerous places so called in that region, for example in the provinces of Corunna, Orense, and Pontevedra).

Dims.: Cat.: **Palou**. It.: **Palazzetti**, **Palazzini**, **Palazzolo**, **Palazzoli**, **Palazzotto**.

Pałasz Polish: nickname from Pol. *pałasz* sabre, applied to a fierce or combative individual, or to a soldier.

Palczewski Polish: habitation name from a place called *Palczewo*, named with the element *palec* finger, toe (cf. PALUCH).

Pálek see PAUL

Palencia Spanish: habitation name or regional name from the city or region of this name in N Spain, a seat of the Castilian kings during the 12th and 13th cents. It is first recorded in the L forms *Pal(l)antia* and *Pelentia*, and is of uncertain origin.

Paler see PAYLER

Palermi Italian: habitation name from the Sicilian town of *Palermo*, an ancient Phoenician foundation of uncertain etymology.

Var. (also in part Jewish): **Palermo**.

Palethorpe English (Notts.): apparently a habitation name from an unidentified place, the second element of which is ON *þorp* settlement (see THORPE). The first may be the personal name *Pal(l)a*, which Ekwall postulates as an etymon for PALGRAVE in Suffolk.

Paley **1.** English: of uncertain origin, probably a habitation name from an unidentified place in Yorks. **2.** Jewish (Ashkenazic): of unknown origin.

Palfrey English: metonymic occupational name for a man responsible for the maintenance and provision of saddle-horses, from ME *palfrey* saddle-horse (OF *palefrei*, from LL *paraverēdus*, a cpd of Gk *para* beside + Gaul. *verēd* (light) horse; the L term has also given mod. Ger. *Pferd* horse).

Vars.: **Palfery**, **Parf(f)rey**; **Palfre(y)man**, **Palfreeman**, **Palphreyman**, **Palframan**, **Parfrement**.

Palgrave English (E Anglia): habitation name from places so called in Norfolk and Suffolk, both of rather doubtful, but clearly distinct, etymology. *Palgrave* in Suffolk appears in Domesday Book as *Palegraua* and is most likely so called from the gen. pl. of OE *pāl* pole + *grāf* grove, though Ekwall also suggests that a personal name, *Pal(l)a*, may underlie the first element. Great and Little *Palgrave* in Norfolk consistently lack the -*l*- in early forms (Domesday Book *Pag(g)raua*), and the first element may be from a per-

sonal name of the problematical group discussed at
PACKHAM.

Palin *see* HAYLING

Pałka Polish: from Pol. *pałka* truncheon, club, used as a
nickname applied either to a thin, stiff person, or to one
renowned for his use of the truncheon.
Habitation name: **Pałczynski**.

Pallejà Catalan: habitation name from a place in the province of Barcelona, so called from LL *Palladiānus (fundus)*
estate of *Palladius*, a personal name derived from Gk *Pallas*, gen. *Pallados*, an epithet of the goddess Athene (of
unknown origin, probably originally the name of a distinct
but obscure goddess).

Pallet *see* PEEL

Pallett English: metonymic occupational name for a
maker of straw mattresses or nickname for someone who
slept on one (i.e. someone who could not afford a better
bed), from ME, OF *pa(i)llet* heap of straw, straw mattress,
a dim. of PAILLE straw.

Palliser English: occupational name for a maker of paling
and fences, from an agent deriv. of OF *pal(e)is* palisade
(from LL *pālicium*, a deriv. of *pālus* stake, pole).
Vars.: **Pal(l)ister**, **Palser**; **Pallis**.

Pallu French: topographic name for someone who lived
near a marsh or fen, OF *palu* (L *palūs*), or habitation name
from any of the numerous minor places named with this
word.
Vars.: **Palu(t)**, **Palud**; **Lapalu(e)**, **Lapalud**, **Lapalus**.
Dim.: **Paluel**.
Aug.: **Paluat**.

Palmer English: nickname for someone who had been on a
pilgrimage to the Holy Land, ME, OF *palmer, paumer*
(from *palme, paume* palm tree, L *palma*). Such pilgrims
generally brought back a palm branch as proof that they
had actually made the journey, but there was a vigorous
trade in false souvenirs, and the term also came to be applied to a cleric who sold indulgences. Some of the European cogns. may also be topographic names referring to
dwellers near a palm tree or grove.
Vars.: **Palmar**, **Paumier**, **Palmes**.
Dims.: It.: **Palmerin(i)**, **Palm(er)ucci**.
Cpds (ornamental): Swed.: **Palmberg** ('palm hill'); **Palmgren**
('palm branch'). Jewish (Ashkenazic): **Palmenbaum** ('palm
tree'); **Palmholz** ('palm wood').

Palomar Spanish: habitation name from any of the numerous places so called, from Sp. *palomar* pigeon loft,
dovecot (LL *palumbāre*, a deriv. of *palumbus* pigeon; see
PALOMO).
Var.: **Palomares**.

Palomo Spanish: nickname for a mild and inoffensive individual, or metonymic occupational name for a keeper of
pigeons, from Sp. *palomo* pigeon (LL *palumbus*, class. L
palumbēs). The It. cogn. also has dial. meanings 'butterfly'
and 'dogfish', and it is possible that in some cases the nickname has one of these senses.
Var.: **Palomero** (occupational).
Dims.: Sp.: **Palomino**. It.: **Palombella**, **Palombino**, **Palombini**.

Pålsson *see* PAUL

Paluch Polish: nickname from Pol. *paluch* thumb (augmentative of *palec* finger). This was used to denote a
small person or a dwarf, although it may also have been
applied to someone with a deformed or missing thumb.
Patr. (from a dim.): Pol.: **Paluszkiewicz**.
Habitation name: Pol.: **Paluszewski**.

Pamies Catalan: habitation name from *Pamiers* in Ariège,
S France, so called from med. L *castrum Appamiae*, a name
given to it in the 12th cent. by its lord, Roger II of Foix, in
memory of the town of *Apamea* in Syria, where he had
fought in the 1st Crusade.
Vars.: **Pàmies**, **Pamias**.

Pammenter *see* PARMENTER

Panadés Catalan: of uncertain origin, probably a habitation name from *Penedès*, a region in the province of Tarragona. The placename probably derives from LL
pinnētense, a deriv. of *pinnētum*, itself a collective of L
pinna rock, crag (see PEÑA).

Panasik *see* AFANASYEV

Pane *see* PAIN

Panek Polish: nickname from a dim. of Pol. *pan* master,
used either affectionately, in the sense 'little master', or
contemptuously, in the sense 'lordling'.
Var.: **Panas** (not dim.).
Patrs.: Pol.: **Pankiewicz**; **Panasewicz** (not dim.). Russ.: **Panov**.
Habitation name: Pol.: **Pankowski**.

Paniagua Spanish: ostensibly a nickname from Sp. *pan y
agua* bread and water (L *panis et aqua*), maybe denoting a
poor man unable to afford a better diet, or else a miser. It
seems more likely, however, that the name is an alteration
by folk etymology of the OSp. occupational term
apaniguado servant, retainer (from the past part. of
apaniguar to provide bread for, LL *appānificāre*, a deriv.
of *pānis* bread; cf. PAIN 2).

Panizo Spanish: metonymic occupational name for a
grower or seller of millet, panic grass, or topographic
name for someone who lived by a field devoted to the
crop, Sp. *panizo* (LL *panīcium*, class. L *panīcum*).

Pank 1. English: from a short form of the medieval given
name *Pancras*; see PANKRIDGE. 2. German (of Slav. origin):
cogn. of PANEK.
Vars. (of 2): **Pa(h)nke**.

Pankhurst English: the conventional explanation of this
name, put forward by Reaney and others, is that it is a var.
of PENTECOST, with late assimilation to the local ending
-*hurst* (see HURST). However, McKinley has gathered evidence that suggests that it is a habitation name, probably
from *Pinkhurst* in Sussex or Surrey. The Sussex place
called *Pankhurst* is said to be derived from the surname
Pentecost, and the hypothesis that it is derived from a surname rather than vice versa is supported by the absence of
early forms.

Pankridge English: from the medieval given name
Pancras, the vernacular form of L *Pancratius* (Gk
Pankratios, from *pankratēs* all-in wrestler, from *pan* all,

every + *kratein* to conquer, subdue, re-analysed by early Christians as meaning 'Almighty' and thus a suitable epithet of Christ). The name was fairly popular in England during the Middle Ages, for in the 7th cent. the relics of an early martyr of this name had been sent to England by the Pope.

Var.: **Panckridge**.

Dims.: Eng.: PANK. Ger.: **Kratz** (Latinized as **Kratius**), **Krätzel**. Low Ger.: **Kratzke**, **Kratzmann**.

Patrs.: Ger.: **Pankrazer**. Russ.: **Pankratov**, **Pankratyev**.

Patrs. (from dims.): Ger.: **Kretzing**, **Kratzig**. Russ.: **Pankrushin**, **Pankeev**.

'Son of the wife of P.': Russ.: **Panchishin**.

Pannaman *see* PENNY

Pantaleone Italian: from a given name (Gk *Panteleiōn*, from *pas*, gen. *pantos*, all, every + *eleiōn*, pres. part. of *eleein* to forgive, pardon, have mercy). This name was borne by a saint martyred under Diocletian, perhaps at Nicomedia, and regarded as a patron of physicians, having allegedly been one himself. He was honoured in the East as early as the 5th cent., but his cult did not reach the West until the 11th cent., when he was adopted as the patron of Venice. In the 14th cent. the name was used for a character in the Harlequinade, a foolish old Venetian, and in some later cases the surname may have arisen as a nickname referring to this character. It was from his typical costume that the term *pantaloon(s)* came to be used of a type of loose-fitting breeches, whence the mod. Eng. short form *pants*.

Vars.: **Pantaleo**, **Pantalone**, **Pantaloni**, **Pantele(on)i**.

Dims.: Ger.: **Pant(e)l**, **Pantele**, **Bantele**, **Bentele**, **Bentlin**; **Bantli** (Switzerland). Low Ger.: **Pantelmann**. Albanian: **Panshi**, **Pançi**.

Patrs.: Croatian: **Pantelić**, **Pant(ov)ić**. Bulg.: **Pantleev**.

Patr. (from a dim.): Bulg.: **Pantchev**.

Panther English: 1. occupational name for a servant in charge of the supply of bread and other provisions in a monastery or large household, from ME *panter* (OF *panetier*, from LL *pānitārius*, an expansion of *pānārius*, from *pānis* bread; see PAIN 2). 2. perhaps also a house name from a house bearing the sign of a panther (OF *panthère*, via L from Gk *panthēr*, which was taken in the ancient world to be a cpd of Gk *pan* all, every + *thēr* beast, but more probably represents an independent IE word; cf. Skt *pundarika* tiger).

Panton English: habitation name from a place in Lincs., for which Ekwall suggests derivation from an unattested OE word **pamp* hill, ridge + OE *tūn* enclosure, settlement.

Panzer 1. German: metonymic occupational name for an armourer, from MHG *panzi(e)r* coat of mail (from OF *pancier* stomach, armour for the stomach, body armour, LL *panticiārium*, from L *pantices* bowels; cf. PAUNCEFOOT). 2. Jewish (Ashkenazic): of unknown origin.

Vars. (of 1): **Panzner**; **Ban(t)zer** (S Germany).

Paolacci *see* PAUL

Papa Italian: nickname from It. *papa* father, priest, pope. In S Italy it is generally a nickname for someone thought to resemble a priest, or in some cases for the illigitimate child of a priest, but in the North it is more often a nickname meaning POPE, denoting a vain or pompous man.

Var.: It.: **Lo Papa**.

Dim.: It.: **Papotto**.

Pejs.: S It.: **Papaccio**, **Papazzo**.

Papatov *see* POPOV

Papen *see* POPE

Papigay *see* POBGEE

Papillon French and English: nickname for a dainty or inconstant person, from OF *papillon* butterfly (L *papilio*, gen. *papiliōnis*).

Vars.: Fr.: **Parp(a)illon**.

Pejs.: Fr.: **Papillard**, **Papillaud**.

Papot French: nickname from OF *paper* to munch, eat (LL *pappāre*, in origin a nursery word). The sense of the nickname is not entirely clear, but it may have been given originally to a glutton. The form **Papin** also had the meaning 'pap' or 'pulp', and may have denoted a toothless old man incapable of taking more solid nourishment; **Papon** also meant 'grandfather', 'old man', perhaps for the same reason, or as an independent nursery formation from *papa* father.

Dims.: Fr.: **Papineau**, **Papinot**, **Papponeau**, **Paponnot**.

Aug.: It.: **Pappone**.

Paprocki Polish: topographic name for someone who lived in a place where ferns grew in abundance, from Pol. *paproć* fern + *-ski* suffix of (originally) local surnames (see BARANOWSKI).

Papworth English: habitation name from a place in Cambs., so called from an OE personal name *Papa* + OE *worð* enclosure (see WORTH).

Paquet French: 1. dim. of the Fr. given name *Pascal* (see PASCALL). 2. metonymic occupational name for a gatherer or seller of firewood or kindling, from OF *pacquet* bundle (of faggots), dim. of *paque* parcel (from MDu.; cf. PACKER).

Vars.: **Paquette** (fem.); **Pacquet**, **Paquot**, **Paquin**.

Dims.: **Paqueteau**, **Paquetot**, **Pacteau**, **Pactot**.

Paquier French: topographic name for someone who lived near a piece of land used for (communal) grazing, OF *pasquier* (LL *pascuārium*, from *pascere* to graze), or habitation name from a place named with this word.

Vars.: **Pasquier**, **Pasquié**; **Pasquer** (Brittany); **Dupa(s)quier**.

Dims.: **Paquereau**. Prov.: **Pascarel**.

Paradowski Polish: nickname for a swaggerer, from Pol. *paradować* to swagger (from *parada* parade, display) + *-ski* suffix of surnames (see BARANOWSKI).

Paragreen *see* PILGRIM

Páramo Spanish: topographic name for someone who lived on a patch of waste land or a bare plateau, Sp. *páramo* (found in the LL of the peninsula as *paramus*, but of uncertain origin). The surname may also be a habitation name from one of the places, for example in the provinces of Lugo and Oviedo, named with this element.

Parant 1. French: occupational name for someone involved in the finishing stages of some manufacturing process, from OF *parant*, pres. part. of *parer* to prepare, make ready (L *parāre*; cf. PARMENTER). **2.** English and French: var. of PARENT.

Vars. (of 1): **Paran** (also Jewish, of unknown origin; cf. PARENT); **Paraire**.

Dim.: **Paranteau**.

Pardal 1. Portuguese: nickname for someone supposedly resembling a sparrow, presumably a small or chirpy person or one of tawny colouring, from Port. *pardal* sparrow, a deriv. of the adj. *pardo* (see PARDO), referring to the colour of the bird. **2.** Jewish: of unknown origin.

Pardelli *see* BARD

Pardo 1. Spanish and Portuguese: nickname for someone with tawny hair, from *pardo* dusky, brown, dark grey (from L *pardus* leopard; in LL this word was joined with the more familiar term *leo* lion to yield the word *leopardus* (see LEPPARD) and the second element, *-pardus*, was taken to be a distinguishing adj. referring to the dark spots and so acquired the status of an independent vocab. element). **2.** Jewish: of unknown origin.

Pardoe English: nickname from a favourite oath, OF *par Dieu* by God (LL *de parte Dei* for God's sake), which was adopted into ME in a variety of more or less mangled forms.

Vars.: **Pardew**, **Pard(e)y**, **Perdue**. See also PURDY.

Paredes Spanish and Portuguese: topographic name for someone who lived in a lean-to built up against the wall of a larger building, from *pared* (house) wall (L *paries*, gen. *parietis*). Servants often lived in buildings of this sort outside manor houses, and masons constructed huts of this kind on the site of their labours, making temporary use of the walls of the new building. There are also a large number of places named with this word, and the surname may also be a habitation name from any of these.

Parejo Spanish: nickname for a companion or partner in an enterprise, Sp. *parejo* (LL *pāriculus*, a dim. of class. L *pār* equal, like; cf. PEAR 2). The fem. form **Pareja** meant 'wife', and may have denoted a woman who managed the affairs of a household in the absence of her husband.

Parell *see* PETER

Parellada Catalan: habitation name from any of various minor places so called, from the name of a measure of land, originally the amount that could be ploughed in a day by a pair of oxen (a deriv. of *parell* pair, from LL *pāriculus*; cf. PAREJO).

Parelli *see* KASPAR

Parent English and French: **1.** nickname from ME, OF *parent* parent, relative (L *parens*, gen. *parentis*, pres. part. of *parere* to give birth, be a parent), referring to someone who was related to an important member of the community. **2.** nickname for someone of striking or imposing appearance, from ME, OF *parent* notable, impressive (L *pārens*, gen. *pārentis*, pres. part. of *pārēre* to appear, seem).

Vars.: Eng.: **Parrent**, **Parrant**, PARANT.

Dims.: Fr.: **Parentin**, **Parenteau**.

Pej.: Fr.: **Parentaud**.

Parffrey *see* PALFREY

Parfitt English: nickname, probably originally denoting an apprentice who had completed his period of training, from ME *parfīt* fully trained, well versed (OF *parfit(e)* complete(d), from L *perfectus*, past part. of *perficere* to finish, accomplish). For the change of *-er-* to *-ar-*, cf. MARCHANT. The mod. Eng. vocab. word *perfect* is a learned recoinage from L.

Vars.: **Parf(a)it**, **Parfect**, **Perfitt**, **Perfett**, **Perfect**.

Pargetter English: occupational name for a (decorative) plasterer, an agent deriv. of OF *pargeter*, *parjeter* to plaster, daub (from *par* (all) over, L *per* + *jeter* to throw, cast, L *iactāre*). Pargetting is a style of house decoration particularly common in E Anglia.

Vars.: **Pargeter**, **Pargiter**.

Parham English: habitation name from places in Suffolk and Sussex, so called from OE *pere* PEAR + *hām* homestead. For the change of *-er-* to *-ar-*, cf. MARCHANT.

Var.: **Parram**. See also PARNHAM, PERHAM.

Parin *see* PEAR

París *see* APARICIO

Parish English: **1.** local name for someone from the French capital, *Paris*, the name of which is derived from that of a Gaul. tribe, recorded in L sources as the *Parisii*; the original meaning of the tribal name cannot even be guessed at. **2.** from the rare medieval given name *Paris*, probably in origin an OF form of PATRICK, but associated with the name of the Trojan prince *Paris*, which has been speculatively traced to an original Illyrian form *Voltuparis* or *Assoparis* 'Hawk'.

This, the most common form of the name in Eng., is the result of confusion between *-s* and *-sh* (cf. NORRIS) reinforced by folk etymological association with the mod. Eng. vocab. word *parish* (ME *parosse*, *paroche*, *parissche*, from OF *paroisse*, Gk *paroikia*). In the 17th and 18th cents. the surname was occasionally bestowed on foundlings brought up at the expense of the parish.

Vars.: **Parrish**, **Par(r)is**.

Dims. (of 1): Fr.: **Parisel**, **Parizel**, **Pariset**, **Parizet**, **Parisot**, **Parizot**, **Parigot**. It.: **Parisini**, **Parigini**, **Parisotti**.

Pejs. (of 1): It.: **Parisato**, **Parisatti**.

Pařizek Czech: habitation name from a place so called near Sobotka, which derives its name from Czech *pařez* tree stump.

Park English: **1.** metonymic occupational name for someone employed in a park (ME, OF *parc*, of Gmc origin; cf. PADDOCK 1), or topographic name for someone who lived in or near a park. In the Middle Ages a park was a large enclosed area where the landowner could hunt game; cf.

FORREST. **2.** dim. of PETER, a back-formation from PAR-KIN.

Vars.: **Parke**. (Of 1 only): **Parrock**, **Parruck**, **Parrack** (from cogn. vocab. words).

Dims. (of 1): Fr.: **Parquet**, **Parquin**.

Patrs. (from 2): Eng.: **Park(e)s**, **Perks**.

'Servant of P. 2': Eng.: **Parkman**.

Parker 1. English: occupational name for a gamekeeper employed in a medieval park, from a ME agent deriv. of PARK 1. **2.** Jewish: presumably an Anglicization of one or more like-sounding Jewish names.

Parkhill Scots and N Irish: habitation name from a place in the barony of Tarbolton in the former county of Ayrs., presumably a cpd of PARK 1 + HILL.

Parkhouse English: topographic name for someone who lived in a warden's lodge in a park; see PARK 1 and HOUSE.

Parkin English: from the ME given name *Perkin, Parkin*, a dim. of PETER with the hypocoristic suffix -*kin*; for the change of -*er*- to -*ar*-, cf. MARCHANT.

Vars.: **Parkyn**; **Perkin**, **Perken**.

Patrs.: **Parkins** (also Jewish, presumably an Anglicization of one or more like-sounding Jewish names); **Perkins**, **Purkins**; **Parkinson**.

Parley English and Scots: habitation name from any of various places, for example E and W *Parley* on the Hants-Dorset borders, north of Bournemouth, so called from OE *pere* PEAR + *lēah* wood, clearing.

Vars.: **Parly**, **Parlie**.

Parmenter English: occupational name for a maker of facings and trimmings, ME, OF *par(e)mentier* (from *parement* fitting, finishing, LL *parāmentum*, a deriv. of *parāre* to prepare, adorn; cf. PARANT 1).

Vars.: **Parmi(n)ter**, **Parmeter**, **Pammenter**.

Dims.: Fr.: **Parmentel(ot)**. Jewish (E Ashkenazic): **Pas(s)manik**.

Parnell English: from the medieval female given name *Parnell*, a vernacular form of L *Petrōnilla*. This is a dim. of *Petrōnia*, fem. of *Petrōnius*, a Roman family name of uncertain, probably Etruscan, etymology. It was borne by an early Roman martyr about whom very little of historical value is known; a 6th-cent. biography makes her a daughter of St PETER, no doubt as a result of folk etymological association of their names.

Vars.: **Parnall**, **Parnwell**; **Purnell** (Gloucs. and Somerset); **Pennell**, **Pennall**.

Dim.: Eng.: PENN.

Parnes Jewish (Ashkenazic): occupational name for the president of a Jewish community, Yid. *parnes* (from Hebr. *parnas*).

Var.: **Parness** (often stressed on the final syllable, under the influence of Eng. words such as *duress* and *caress*); **Parnas(s)** (from the Hebr. form), **Parnasz** (Hung. spelling).

Parnham English: habitation name from a place in Dorset, so called from OE *peren*, adj. from *pere* PEAR + *hām* homestead.

Paron *see* PATRONE

Parpaillon *see* PAPILLON

Parr 1. English: habitation name from a place in Lancs., so called from OE **pearr* enclosure (a dim. of which is reflected in PADDOCK 1 and PARK 1). **2.** Low German: from MLG *parre* parish, district, perhaps a nickname for a foundling. According to Ekwall, this word is cogn. with the one in 1 above, and has no connection with mod. Eng. *parish* (see PARISH).

Parra Spanish and Catalan: topographic name for someone who lived by an enclosure with some form of trellis or interwoven fencing, OSp., OCat. *parra* (mod. Sp., Cat. *parra* trellis, arbour, vine; the word is of uncertain, possibly Gmc, origin; cf. PARR 1). There are also numerous places named with this word, from which the surname may also derive as a habitation name.

Var.: Sp.: **Parras**.

Dim.: Sp.: **Parrilla** (in part from places so named in the provinces of Cadiz, Córdoba, Málaga, and Valladolid).

Parramon Catalan: from a contracted form of the given names *Pere* (see PETER) + *Ramon* (see RAYMOND).

Parren *see* PERRIN

Parrott English: **1.** from a ME given name which took various forms—*Perot, Parot, Paret*, etc., all dims. of PETER. The talking bird seems to get its name from this (cf. the *robin* from a dim. of ROBERT; also the *jackdaw* and *magpie*), but it was not so called until the 16th cent., rather too late to have given rise to a surname. (For names derived from the earlier term for a parrot, see POBGEE). **2.** habitation name from N and S *Perrott* in Somerset, which take their name from the river *Parret* on which they stand. This is of unknown origin.

Vars. (of 1): Eng.: **Parrot**, **Parret(t)**, **Parratt**; **Perot(t)**, **Peret(t)** (chiefly Somerset); **Perrat**.

Dims. (of 1): Fr.: **Perrotin**, **Perroton**, **Perroteau**. It.: **Pedrotini**, **Rotellini**; **Petrettini**; **Pierettini**.

Parry 1. Welsh: patr., with a reduced form of the W element *ap*, from the given name HARRY. **2.** French: cogn. of PARISH 1.

Vars. (of 1): BARRY; **Pend(r)y**, **Bend(r)y** (from W *ap* HENDRY).

Parslow English (Norman): nickname from an OF phrase composed of the elements *passe(r)* to pass, cross (LL *passāre*, from *passus* step, pace) + *l'ewe* the water (L *(illa) aqua*). The nickname probably at first denoted a merchant who was in the habit of travelling overseas, or else someone who had been on a pilgrimage or crusade; but it may also have been used as a topographic name for someone who lived on the opposite side of a watercourse from the main settlement (cf. PASSMORE).

Vars.: **Parsloe**, **Paslow**, **Pa(r)sley**, PASHLEY.

Parsonage English: topographic name for someone who lived at or by a parson's house, from ME, OF *personage* benefice, living, hence the house and estate held by a parson.

Parsons English: **1.** occupational name for the servant of a parish priest or parson, or patr. denoting the child of a parson, from the possessive case of ME *persone, parsoun* (OF *persone*, from L *persōna* person, character). The reasons for the semantic shift from 'person' to 'priest' are not certain; the most plausible explanation is that the local priest was regarded as the representative person of the parish. For the change of -er- to -ar-, cf. MARCHANT. See also McPHERSON. **2.** Many early examples are found with prepositions (e.g. Ralph *del Persones* 1323); these are habitation names, with the omission of *house*, in effect occupational names for servants employed at the PARSONAGE.

Partanen Finnish: patr. from the nickname *Parta* 'Beard'.

Partington English (Lancs.): habitation name from a place in Greater Manchester, so called from OE *Peartingtūn* 'settlement (OE *tūn*) associated with **Pearta*', a personal name not independently recorded.

Parton English (chiefly W Midlands): habitation name from any of various places so called, which mostly get the name from OE *peretūn* pear orchard (a cpd of *pere* pear + *tūn* enclosure; cf. APPLETON), with later change of -er- to -ar- (cf. MARCHANT). There are examples in Gloucs., two in Cumb., and one in Scotland; the last gets its name from Gael. *portan*, a dim. of *port* harbour (see PORT). The distribution of the surname makes it probable that in most cases it is from the place in Gloucs.

Partridge 1. English: from ME *pertriche* partridge (OF *perdrix*, from L *perdix*, gen. *perdicis*), either a metonymic occupational name for a hunter of the bird, or a nickname from some fancied resemblance, or a house name for someone living in a house distinguished by the sign of a partridge. For the change of -er- to -ar-, cf. MARCHANT. **2.** Irish and English: var. of PATRICK.

Vars.: **Partriche**, **Partrick**.

Dims. (of 1): Fr.: **Perdrizet**, **Perdrizot**, **Perdrig(e)on**, **Perdriget**.

Parviainen Finnish: habitation name for someone who lived in an upper storey or in a house with an upper storey, from Finn. *parvi* garret, attic, with the addition of the locative suffix -*ainen*.

Pascall English: from the medieval given name *Pascal* (L *Paschālis*, from *pascha* Easter, via Gk and Aramaic from Hebr. *pesach* Passover; cf. PEISACH). The name was introduced into England from France; it was popular throughout Catholic Europe, mainly in honour of the festival of Christ's crucifixion and resurrection, but also in honour of a 9th-cent. pope and saint who had borne the name.

Vars.: **Paskell**, **Pasquill**.

Dims.: Eng.: **Pass(e)**. Fr.: **Pascalin**, **Pasquelin**, **Pascot**, **Pasquet**, **Pasquez**; PAQUET. It.: **Pasqualini**, **Pasqualino**, **Pascalino**, **Pasqualetto**, **Pasqualetti**, **Pascaletto**, **Pasqualotto**, **Quarello**.

Pej.: Fr.: **Pasquard**.

Patrs.: It.: **De Pasquale**, **(De) Pasqualis**, **Pascalis**. Rum.: **Pasculesco**.

Pascarel see PAQUIER

Paschek see PAUL

Paschoud see PACE

Pascoe English (Cornwall): from the medieval given name PASK, with -*oe*, -*ow* as a hypocoristic suffix.

Var.: **Pascow**.

Pashley English: **1.** habitation name from a place in the parish of Ticehurst, Sussex, so called from an OE personal name **Pæcca* (related to **Pacca*; see PACKHAM) + OE *lēah* wood, clearing. A district of Eastbourne bearing this name derives it from the surname; a family so called had moved there from Ticehurst by the later part of the 13th cent. **2.** possibly also a var. of PARSLOW. The surname is now chiefly common in S Yorks, which would anyway raise a question mark over its derivation from a Sussex placename.

Pask English: nickname for someone who was born at Easter, or had some other particular connection with that time of year, such as owing a feudal obligation then, from ME *paske* Easter (OF *pasque*, L *pascua*, earlier *pascha* (cf. PASCALL); the altered form seems to be the result of association with L *pascuum* pasture (cf. PASTOR)). *Pask*, *Pash*, and *Pack* were sometimes used as vernacular given names in medieval England, equivalent to PASCALL.

Vars.: **Paske**, **Pasque**; **Pash(e)**, **Paish** (from the byform *pasche*, L *pascha*).

Dims.: Eng.: **Paskin** (W Midlands); **Patchett**, **Patchin(g)**. It.: **Pasquelli**, **Pasquetti**, **Paschetti**, **Paschetto**, **Pasquino**, **Paschini**, **Pasquin(ell)i**, **Pascucci**, **Pascuzzi**, **Pascuzzo**, **Pasquinucci**, **Pasquinuzzi**, **Pascutti**, **Pascutto**, **Pasquotti**, **Pascotti**, **Pascullo**, **Pascol(ett)i**, **Pascolo**, **Pascolini**, **Pascolutti**.

Pejs.: It.: **Pasquazzo**, **Pasquato**, **Pasquati**.

Patrs.: Eng.: **Pakes**. It.: **Di Pasqua**.

'Servant of P.': Eng.: **PACKMAN**, **Paxmann**.

Pasley see PARSLOW

Pasmanik see PARMENTER

Passenger English: nickname for a traveller (until the 19th cent., the vocab. word *passenger* denoted one who travelled on foot as well as one carried on horseback or in a carriage), from ME, OF *passager* (a deriv. of *passage* journey, LL *passāticum*, from *passāre* to proceed, go, cross; cf. PARSLOW and PASSMORE). For the intrusive -n-, cf. MESSENGER. The name was applied to an itinerant merchant or workman who did not stop long in any community, but was always just passing through.

Passifull see PERCIVAL

Passler see PETER

Passmanik see PARMENTER

Passmore English (chiefly Devon and Somerset): **1.** nickname from ME *pass(en)* to pass, go across (LL *passāre*; cf. PASSENGER) + *more* marsh, fen (see MOORE 1), bestowed no doubt on someone who lived on the far side of a tract of moorland near the main settlement, or on someone who was familiar with the safe routes across a moor. **2.** several early forms have -*e*- in place of -*o*- in the second syllable, and may have a different origin. They could represent an ANF nickname *Passemer*, from *passe(r)* to cross (as above) + *mer* sea, ocean (L *mare*), similar in significance to PARSLOW, or the second element could be from OE *mere* lake, marsh.

Var.: **Pasmore**.

Passy French: habitation name from any of the numerous places so called from the Gallo-Roman personal name *Paccius* + the local suffix -*ācum*.

Pasterfield see BASKERVILLE

Pasternak Polish, Ukrainian, Russian, and Jewish (E Ashkenazic): from Pol., Ukr., Russ., and E Yid. *pasternak* parsnip (MHG *pastinake*, from L *pastināca*), apparently a nickname or arbitrarily adopted surname taken from the plant. In the case of the Jewish name, this is one of the many ornamental names based on words denoting plants.

Vars.: **Pasternack**, **Pastinack**.

Paston English: habitation name from any of several places so called. Examples in Norfolk and Northants apparently get the name from OE *pæsc(e)* puddle, pool + *tūn* enclosure, settlement; one in Northumb. is OE *Pallocestūn* 'settlement of *Palloc*', an otherwise unattested personal name.

Pastor 1. English, French, Spanish, and Catalan: occupational name for a shepherd (ANF *pastre* (oblique case *pastour*), Sp., Cat. *pastor*, from L *pastor*, an agent deriv. of *pascere* to graze (trans.)). The religious sense of a spiritual leader was rare in the Middle Ages, and insofar as it occurs at all seems always to be a conscious metaphor; it is unlikely, therefore, that this sense lies behind any examples of the surname. 2. German and Dutch: Latinized form of various vernacular terms meaning 'shepherd' (cf., e.g., SCHÄFER), adopted in the 16th and 17th cents. 3. Jewish: of uncertain origin.

Vars. (of 1): Fr.: **Pastour**, **Pasteur**, **Pastre**. (Of 3): Jewish: **Paste(u)r**.

Dims. (of 1): Fr.: **Pa(s)tourel**, **Pa(s)toureau**. It.: **Pastorino**, **Pastorini**, **Past(o)rello**, **Pastorelli**.

Pastukhov Russian: patr. from the occupational term *pastukh* shepherd (from *pasti* to graze (trans.), ultimately a cogn. of L *pascere*; cf. PASTOR).

Patch *see* PACK

Patchett *see* PASK

Pate English and Scots: 1. from the given name *Pat(t)*, *Pate*, a short form of PATRICK. 2. nickname for a man with a bald head, from ME *pate* head, skull (of unknown origin).

Var. (of 1): **Patt**.

Dims. (of 1): **Patey**; **Pat(t)on**, PADDON, PATTEN.

Patrs. (from 1): **Pates**; **McPhaid**, **McPhade**, **McFade**, **McPhate**, **McFait**, **McFeat(e)** (Gael. **Mac Phaid**).

Patrs. (from dims of 1): **Pattinson**, **Pat(t)ison**, **Pattyson**, **Patte(r)son**, **Paterson**. See also McFADDEN.

'Servant of P. 1': **Pateman**, **Pat(t)man**.

Pater Dutch: nickname for a solemn or pompous man, from MDu *pater* father superior (in a religious order; from L *pater* father).

Var.: **De Pater**.

Patera Czech: from a blend of the two common given names *Pavel* (see PAUL) and *Petera* (see PETER). The formation was also influenced by the L word *pater* father.

Paternoster English, French, and German: metonymic occupational name for a maker of rosaries, from L *pater noster* Our Father, the opening words of the Lord's Prayer, which is represented by large beads punctuating the rosary. The surname may also have been originally a nickname for an excessively pious individual or for someone who was under a feudal obligation to say paternosters for his master as part of the service by which he held land.

Vars.: Fr.: **Patenôtre**, **Peternot(te)**, **Paternault**. Ger.: **Ternoster** (an aphetic form).

Patience 1. English: nickname from ME, OF *patience* (L *patientia*, from *patiens*, gen. *patientis*, patient, pres. part. of *pati* to endure), given perhaps to a notably long-suffering individual or to someone who had represented this abstract virtue in a morality play. 2. Jewish (Ashkenazic): this surname has been used in the U.S. as a translation of GEDULD.

Var.: **Patient**.

Patmore English: habitation name from a place in Herts. which appears in Domesday Book as *Patemere*, from an OE personal name *P(e)atta* (perhaps an assimilated form of *Pearta*; see PARTINGTON) + OE *mere* lake, pool.

Var.: PADMORE.

Patočka Czech: nickname for a beer drinker or metonymic occupational name for a brewer, from a dim. of Czech *patoky* thin beer, porter.

Var.: **Patoka**.

Patora Polish: 1. nickname from Pol. dial. *patorny* bad, evil. 2. nickname from Pol. dial. *patoroczny* clumsy, inept.

Var.: **Patura**.

Patoureau *see* PASTOR

Patrick English: from a given name (L *Patricius* son of a noble father, member of the patrician class, the Roman hereditary aristocracy). This was the name of a 5th-cent. Romano-Briton who became the apostle of Ireland, and it was largely as a result of his fame that the given name was so popular in the Middle Ages.

Vars.: **Pattrick**, PARTRIDGE.

Dims.: Eng., Sc.: PETRIE; **Padan**, **Padyn**, **Pedan**, **Peden**. Fr.: **Patricot**, **Patrigeon**.

Patrs.: Sc.: **McPhedric** (Gael. **Mac Phádraig**). Ir.: FITZPATRICK; see also KILPATRICK. Russ.: **Patrikeev**.

Patrs. (from dims.): Sc., Ir.: McFADDEN. Russ.: **Patrushev**, **Patrikeivin**.

Patrone Italian: nickname from It. *patrone* master (L *patrōnus*, a deriv. of *pater* father). The term had various senses in the Middle Ages; it was applied, for example, to the master of a ship, and also to the former owner of a freed serf, who still enjoyed certain rights over him.

Vars.: **Patroni**, **Patrono**; **Paroni**, **Pa(t)ron** (Venetia); **Patruno** (Apulia).

Patt *see* PATE

Patte French: nickname, applied presumably to a man with large and clumsy hands or feet, from OF *pat(t)e* paw (of apparently Gaul. origin).

Vars.: **Pat(h)é**, **Patey**, **Patez**, **Patu** ('with paws').

Dims.: **Paton**, **Patou(x)**, **Patout**.

Augs.: Fr.: **Patat**. Sp.: **Patón**.

Pejs.: Fr.: **Pataud**, **Patard**, **Patart**.

Patten English: 1. dim. of PATE 1. 2. metonymic occupational name for a maker or seller of clogs, or nickname for a wearer of them, from ME *paten* clog (OF *patin*, of uncertain origin, but perhaps akin to PATTE).

Var.: **Pattin**.

Dims. (of 2): Fr.: **Patinet, Patineau**.

Pattenden English: habitation name from a place in Kent, named in OE as the 'swine pasture (OE *denn*) associated with *Peatta*' (cf. PATMORE).

Patullo Scots: habitation name from either of two places, in the former counties of Fife and Perths., called *Pittilloch*, from the Pictish element *peit* portion (of land) + Gael. *tulach* hill.

Vars.: **Pattullo, Pat(t)illo**.

Patvine *see* POTVIN

Patzelt *see* PETER

Pauer *see* BAUER

Pauker German and Jewish (Ashkenazic): occupational name for a drummer, Ger. *Pauker* (MHG *pūkære*, agent deriv. of *pūke* drum (mod. Ger. *Pauke*), of uncertain, possibly imitative, origin).

Vars.: Ger.: **Peuker**; **Peuchert** (Silesia); **Peickert** (Silesia, Saxony); **Baiker(t)**. Jewish (Ashkenazic): **Paucker**.

Paukov Russian: patr. from the nickname *Pauk* 'Spider'.

Paul English, French, German, and Flemish/Dutch: from the given name (L *Paulus* 'Small'), which has always been popular in Christendom. It was the name adopted by the Pharisee Saul of Tarsus after his conversion to Christianity on the road to Damascus (AD *c*.34). He was a most energetic missionary to the gentiles in the Roman Empire, and perhaps played a more significant role than any other of Christ's followers in establishing Christianity as a major world religion. The name was borne also by numerous other early saints. The surname is also occasionally borne by Jews; the reasons for this are not clear.

Vars.: Eng.: **Paull** (chiefly Devon and Cornwall); **Paule, Pawle**, POOL, POWELL. Fr.: **Pol**. Ger.: **Pahl, Pohl**; **Paulus** (Latinized). Flem., Du.: **Pau(w)el**.

Dims.: Eng.: **Paul(l)ey, Pauly**, PAWLEY; **Powley** (E Anglia); **Paulin(g), Paulling, Pawlyn, Pawling, Powling**; PAWLETT. Fr.: **Pauleau, Paulet, Paulin, Pauly, Polin, Paulot, Paulon, Paulou**. It.: **Pa(v)olini, P(a)olino, Polini, Paolinelli, P(a)oletti, Paoletto, Pauletti, Pauletto, Polet(to), P(a)olotti, P(a)olotto, Paolozzi, Paolillo, Paulillo, Pavolillo, P(a)olucci, Paulucci, Pauluzzi, Poluzzi, Paolicchi**. Port.: **Paulino**. Low Ger.: **Paulmann**. Ger. (of Slav. origin): **Paulack, Paulig, Paulich, Pawelke, Pawellek, Pawlick, Pabelik, Paulitschke, Paulisch, Pallas(ch), Pallaske, Palleske, Paulusch, Palluschek, Pavlitschek; Paschek, Paschke, Pache**. Czech: **Pavelka; Pavlí(če)k, Pavlášek; Pávek, Pálek, Pašek**. Pol.: **Pawełek, Pawełczyk, Pawlaczyk, Pawlik, Paszek, Pasek**. Ukr.: **Pavlik, Pavluk, Pavlenko**.

Augs.: Fr.: **Paulat**. It.: **P(a)olon(i), Paolone**. Pol.: **Pawelec**.

Pejs.: Eng.: POLLARD. It.: **P(a)olacci, Paulazzi, P(a)olazzi**.

Patrs.: Eng.: **Paulson, Po(u)lson, Poulsom, Poulsum**. Sc.: McFALL. Manx: QUAIL. Fr.: **Aupol**. It.: **De Paoli(s)**. Ger.: **Pauler, Pahler; Pauli, Pauly** (Latinized). Low Ger.: **Pauls(en), Pawels, Pagels(en); Pöhls(en), Pöhling**. Fris.: **Pau(g)els, Paulsen**. Flem., Du.: **Pau(we)ls**. Dan., Norw.: **Paulsen, Pallesen, Poulsen, Povlsen**. Swed.: **Paulsson, På(h)lsson; Pauli** (Latinized). Russ.: **Pavlov, Pavelyev**. Pol.: **Pawłowicz**. Lithuanian: **Paulat(h), Pauleit; Poweleit, Pauluweit** (Ger. spell-

ings). Croatian: **Pavlov(ić), Pav(e)lić, Pavić, Paljić**. Hung.: **Pálf(f)i, Pálf(f)y**. Armenian: **Pogosian, Bogosian**.

Patrs. (from dims.): Eng.: **Pollins**. Russ.: **Pavlen(k)ov, Pavlikov, Pavlishchev, Pavlishintsev, Pavyuchikov, Pavlyuk(h)ov, Pavyushkov, Pavlitsev, Pavlikhin, Pavlukhin, Pavlush(k)in, Pavlygin; Pavshukov, Pavkin, Pavshin; Pashaev, Pashenkov, Pashintsev, Pashinov, Pashkeev, Pashkov, Pashnev, Pashanin, Pashetkin, Pashikhin, Pash(in)(k)in, Pashunin, Pashutin**. Pol.: **Pawełkiewicz, Pawlikiewicz; Paszkiewicz; Pawełczak, Paszak**. Croatian: **Pavličić, Pavičević, Pavković**.

'Son of the wife of P. (dim.)': Russ.: **Pavlikhin, Pashikhin**.

Habitation names: Pol.: **Pawłowski, Pawliński, Pawlikowski; Paszkowski, Pasikowski**. Czech: **Pavlovský**.

Paulet *see* PAWLETT

Pauncefoot English (Norman): nickname for a man with a large belly, from ANF *paunc(h)e* stomach, gut (OF *paunce*, from L *pantices* bowels, intestines) + *vout, vaut* vaulted, arched, rounded (L *volūtus*, past part. of *volvere* to turn).

Vars.: **Pauncefote, Pauncefort; Ponsford** (perhaps also from a place in Devon).

Paustian *see* SEBASTIAN

Paustovski Belorussian: habitation name from any of several minor settlements called *Paustovo*, from the dedication of the local church to St *Faustus* (see FAUST 2).

Pavanelli *see* PADOVANO

Paveley *see* PAWLEY

Pavelić *see* PAUL

Pavey English: 1. from the medieval female given name *Pavia*, which is of uncertain origin. 2. habitation name from the It. town of *Pavia* in Lombardy, N Italy.

Vars.: **Pavy, Pavie**.

Dims. (of 1): Eng.: **Pavett, Pavitt**.

Pavier English: occupational name for a layer of paving, from ME, OF *pavier* (an agent deriv. of OF *paver* to pave, L *pavīre* to beat, ram down; the difference in declension suggests that the OF verb may be a back-formation from *pavement* laid floor, L *pavīmentum*).

Vars.: **Pav(y)er, Pavio(u)r**.

Paw English: 1. nickname from ME *pawe*, OE *pāwa* PEACOCK. 2. var. of PAUL.

Var.: **Pawe**.

Patr. (from 2): **Pawson** (Yorks).

Pawełczak *see* PAUL

Pawlett English: 1. dim. of PAUL. 2. habitation name from a place in Somerset, apparently so called from OE *pāl* pole + *flēot* stream, i.e. a stretch of water with mooring posts or with piles to support the banks.

Vars.: **Paulet**.

Pawley English: 1. Norman habitation name from *Pavilly* in Seine-Maritime, which is so called from the Gallo-Roman personal name *Pavilius* + the local suffix *-ācum*. 2. dim. of PAUL.

Vars. (of 1): **Pav(e)l(e)y**.

Paxmann *see* PASK

Paxton English and Scots: habitation name from places in Cambs. and the former county of Berwicks., so called from OE *Pæccestūn* 'settlement of *Pæcc*', a personal name related to the **Pacca* discussed at PACKWOOD.

Pay S English: **1.** var. of *Pea, Pee* (see PEACOCK). **2.** from an early medieval given name, apparently masc. but of uncertain origin, perhaps derived from 1 (cf. PAW).

Var.: **Pey**.

'Servant of P.': **Payman**, **Peyman**.

Payan see PAIN

Payeur French: occupational name for an official responsible for settling accounts, from OF *payeur* (LL *pācātor*, from *pācāre* to appease, requite, a deriv. of *pax*, gen. *pācis*, peace, concord).

Var.: **Payer**.

Dims.: **Payet**, **Payot**, **Payon**.

Payler English: occupational name for a maker of pots and pans, from an agent deriv. of ME *pail(e)* (OF *paelle* frying pan, cooking pan; cf. PADILLA).

Vars.: **Paler**, **Paylor**.

Paynter see PAINTER

Pays 1. French: occupational name for a peasant farmer or agricultural labourer, OF *pays* peasant (LL *pāgēnsis*, a deriv. of *pāgus* village, country district; cf. PAIN 1). **2.** English: var. of PACE.

Vars. (of 1): **Paysan(t)**, **Paisant**.

Payton English: habitation name from *Peyton* in Sussex (so called from the OE personal name *Pǣga* + OE *tūn* enclosure, settlement) or from some other place similarly named. The surname is common in the W Midlands. *Peyton* in Essex has probably not contributed; it is recorded in Domesday Book as *Pachenhou* 'ridge, spur (see HOE) of *Pac(c)a*', and even in the 16th cent. it was still *Pakenho* or *Patenhall*.

Payze see PACE

Paz 1. Spanish and Portuguese: cogn. of PACE. **2.** Jewish (Israeli): ornamental name from Hebr. *paz* pure gold.

Cpd (of 2): **Har-Paz** (translation of GOLDBERG, with Hebr. *har* mountain).

Pazdera Czech: **1.** occupational name for a flax-dresser, from Czech *pazdero* flax. **2.** nickname for an untidy person or a person of ill repute, from metaphorical uses of the preceding word.

Var.: **Pazdernik**.

Pazos see PALACIO

Peabody English: probably a nickname for a showy dresser, from ME *pē* PEACOCK + *body* BODY, person.

Peace see PACE

Peachey English: nickname for a reprobate, probably given more often in jest than as a mark of censure, from OF *pech(i)e* sin (L *peccātum*, past part. of *peccāre* to sin, err).

Vars.: **Pe(t)chey**; **Peach(e)**, **Peech**, **Petch(e)**.

Peacock English: nickname for a vain, strutting person or for a dandy, from ME *pē*, *pā*, *pō* peacock (OE *pēa*, *pāwa*, ON *pá*; cogn. with or taken from L *pāvo*, gen. *pāvōnis*), with the later disambiguating addition of *cok* male bird (see COCK). In some cases it may be a house name from a house distinguished by the sign of a peacock.

Vars.: **Peacocke**, **Peecock**, **Pacock**, **Pocock(e)**; PAW, PAY, POWE; **Poe** (from ON *pá*); **Pea**, **Pee**.

Peaddie see PETER

Peagram see PILGRIM

Peak English: topographic name for someone living by a pointed hill, or regional name from the *Peak* District (OE *Pēaclond*) in Derbys., from OE *pēac* peak, pointed hill (found only in placenames). This word is not directly related to OE *pīc* point (ed hill), which yielded PIKE; there is, however, evidence of confusion between the two surnames.

Vars.: **Peake(r)**, **Peakman**; **Peek** (Norfolk); PECK.

Peale see PEEL

Peaple see PEPYS

Pear English: **1.** metonymic occupational name for a grower or seller of pears, or topographic name for someone who lived by a pear tree or pear orchard, from ME *pe(e)re* pear (OE *pere*, *peru*, from L *pirum*). **2.** nickname from ME *pere* peer, companion (OF *pe(e)r*, from L *pār* equal).

Vars. (mostly of 1): **Pee(a)r**, **Pere**; **Pearman**, **Pearmund**; **Peartree**. See also PERRY.

Dims. (of 1): Fr.: **Poirot**. It.: **Peretto** (see also PARROTT), **Piretto**, **Predda**, **Prodda**, **Piroddi** (Sardinia). Sp.: **Perella**. Cat.: **Perellas**. (Of 2): Prov.: **Pari(o)n**, **Pariot**.

Collectives (of 1): Prov.: **Lapérière**. Sp.: **Pereda**.

Pearce English: from the ME given name *Piers*, the regular vernacular form of PETER. Since the given name ends in *-s*, surnames that originated as patrs. in *-s* are indistinguishable from those derived directly from the base form.

Vars.: **Pears(e)** (chiefly Cornwall); **Pierce**, **Piers(e)** (chiefly Ireland); **Peers**, **Perce**, **Pers(s)e**, **Perris**.

Patrs.: **Pearson**, **Pierson**.

Pearcey see PERCY

Pearl 1. English: metonymic occupational name for a trader in pearls, which in the Middle Ages were fashionable among the rich for the ornamentation of clothes, from ME, OF *perle* (LL *perla*, perhaps from *perna* mussel (originally 'ham'; the sense transfer was no doubt due to a supposed similarity in shape)). **2.** Jewish (Ashkenazic): ornamental name, or Anglicized form of the Yid. female given name *Perl* 'Pearl', a translation of Hebr. *Margalit* (see MARGUERITE).

Vars.: Jewish: **Per(e)l**, **Perle**; **Per(e)lman(n)** (Anglicized **Pearlman**); **Perelsman**, **Perlesman** ('husband of *Perl*').

Metrs. (from the given name): Jewish: **Perles**, **Perlis**, **Perlus**, **Perelson**; **Perlov**, **Perlow(ski)**, **Perlin(ski)** (Anglicized **Pearlin**).

Cpds (ornamental): Jewish: **Perlberg(er)** ('pearl hill'); **Perlgut** ('pearl good(s)'); **Per(e)lmut(t)er**, **Mutterperl** ('mother of pearl'); **Perlrot(h)** ('pearl red'); **Perlschein** ('pearl shine'); **Per(e)lstein** ('pearl stone', partly Anglicized as **Pearlstine**); **Perlszweig** ('pearl twig').

Pearpoint see PIERREPONT

Peart N English and Scots: of uncertain origin, perhaps a habitation name from *Pert* on the North Esk near Montrose, so called from a Pictish or Celtic term for a wood or copse.

Pease English: metonymic occupational name for a grower or seller of peas, or nickname for a small and insignificant man, from ME *pese*, originally a collective singular (OE *peose, pise*, from L *pisa*), from which the mod. E vocab. word *pea* is derived by folk etymology, the singular having been taken as a plural.

Peasey *see* PUSEY

Pebjoy *see* POBGEE

Pech *see* PETER, PUY

Péchels Provençal: habitation name from an unidentified place named with the pl. form of a dim. of OProv. *pech* hill, plateau (see PUY).

Pecher 1. German and Jewish (Ashkenazic): occupational name for a boiler of pitch, from an agent deriv. of Ger. *Pech*, Yid. *pekh* pitch (MHG *pech*, OHG *peh*, from L *pix* pitch; cf. PÈGUE). 2. German: metonymic occupational name for a turner of wooden vessels, from MHG *becher* beaker, goblet, pitcher, jug (cf. BECHER 1). For the alternation of /p/ and /b/, cf. BIRNBAUM and its vars. 3. German: nickname for an unlucky fellow, from Ger. *Pech* bad luck (a transferred sense of the same word as in 1) + *-er* suffix of agent nouns.

Vars. (of 1): Jewish: **Pechner**; **Pechwasser** ('pitch water').

Pêcheur French: occupational name for a fisherman, from an agent deriv. of OF *pesche* fish (see PESCE).

Vars.: **Pêcheux, Pescheur, Pescheux; Pe(c)queur, Pe(c)queux** (Normandy, Picardy); **Pesque(u)r, Pesqueux, Lepesqueur** (Brittany).

Pechey *see* PEACHEY

Pechon *see* PETTIT

Pechstein *see* BECHSTEIN

Peck English: 1. metonymic occupational name for someone who dealt in weights and measures, for example a corn factor, from ME *pekke* peck (an old measure of dry goods equivalent to eight quarts or a quarter of a bushel). 2. topographic name, a var. of PEAK.

Peckham English: habitation name from one of the places so called, in Kent and S London, possibly from OE *pēac* hill (see PEAK) + *hām* homestead.

Pecora Italian: metonymic occupational name for a keeper of flocks of sheep and goats, from It. *pecora* flock (from L *pecus*, gen. *pecoris*).

Vars.: **Pecori, Peguri; Pecoraro, Pecora(r)i, Pegoraro, Pegorari, Pegorer**.

Dims.: **Pecorella, Pecorelli, Pegoretti, Pecorini, Pegorin(i)**.

Pedan *see* PATRICK

Peddie *see* PETER

Peder *see* BADER

Pedler English: 1. occupational name for a pedlar, from ME *pedler, pedlar*, apparently a dissimilated var. of *pedder*,

peddar, from *pedde* pannier, basket (of uncertain origin), in which goods were carried from place to place. 2. nickname for a fleet runner, from OF *pie de lievre* hare's foot (LL *pēs de lepore*); cf. PEDLEY.

Vars.: **Pedlar, Pegler, Pidler**. (Of 1 only): **Pedder, Peddar**.

Equivs. (not cogn.): Fr.: TROSSIER. Ger.: TRAGER, KORB. Du.: DEVENTER. Jewish: GEIER. Pol.: BEDWINEK. Czech: KABELÁČ. Russ.: PESHKOV.

Pedley English (Norman): nickname for a stealthy person, from OF *pie de leu* wolf's foot (LL *pēs de lupo*); cf. PEDLER 2.

Var.: **Pedlow, Pellew, PELLOW**.

Pedoux *see* POU

Pedraza *see* PIERRE

Pedrick *see* PETHICK

Pedrinelli *see* PERRIN

Pedró Catalan: habitation name from any of several minor places so called from Cat. *pedró* large stone, pedestal (LL *petro*, gen. *petrōnis*, a deriv. of *petra* stone; cf. PIERRE 2).

Pedrosa Spanish, Catalan, and Portuguese: habitation name from any of various places, for example in the provinces of Burgos, Lugo, and Orense, so called from LL *Petrōsa* 'Place of Stones' (neut. pl. or fem. sing. of *petrōsus*, an adj. deriv. of *petra* stone; cf. PIERRE 2).

Vars.: Cat.: **Padrós**. Port.: **Pedroso**.

Pedrotini *see* PARROTT

Pędziwiatr Polish: nickname for a restless person given to impractical and fanciful schemes, from Pol. *pędzić* to chase + *wiatr* the wind.

Pee *see* PEACOCK, PETER

Peear *see* PEAR

Peebles Scots: habitation name from the town on the river Tweed in SE Scotland, or from a smaller place of the same name in the parish of St Vigeans, Angus. Both places probably get the name from a Brit. element that became W *pebyll* tent, pavilion, to which the Eng. pl. *-s* has been added.

Peech *see* PEACHEY

Peek *see* PEAK

Peel English: nickname for a tall thin man, from ANF *pel* stake, pole (OF *piel*, from L *pālus*). It may also have been a topographic name for someone who lived by a stake fence or in a property defended by one, or a metonymic occupational name for a builder of such fences (cf. PALLISER).

Vars.: **Peele, Peale, Piele, Peile**.

Dims.: Fr.: **Pieuchot**. Prov.: **Pallet, Pallez**. Low Ger.: **Pahlke**.

Peer *see* PEAR

Peers *see* PEARCE

Peever *see* PEPPER

Peffer *see* PEPPER

Pegg English: metonymic occupational name for a maker or seller of wooden pegs, from ME *pegge* (from MDu., of uncertain origin), perhaps also a nickname for a person with a wooden leg.

Peggram *see* PILGRIM

Pegler *see* PEDLER

Pegorari *see* PECORA

Pègue Provençal: metonymic occupational name for a boiler of pitch (cf. PECHER 1) or nickname for someone with very dark, 'pitch-black' hair, from OProv. *pegue* pitch (L *pix*, gen. *picis*).

Dims.: **Pegeon**, **Pe(u)geot**, **Peguet**.

Pej.: **Pegeaud**.

Pehrsson *see* PETER

Pei *see* PETER

Peickert *see* PAUKER

Peile *see* PEEL

Peinado Spanish: nickname for a well-groomed person or for someone with naturally smooth rather than curly hair, from Sp. *peinado*, past. part. of *peinar* to comb (LL *pectināre*, a deriv. of *pecten* comb, gen. *pectinis*, itself a deriv. of class. L *pectere* to comb).

Peipers *see* PIPER

Peircey *see* PERCY

Peirier *see* PERRIER

Peisach Jewish (Ashkenazic): from the Yid. male given name *Peysekh* (from Hebr. *pesach* Passover).

Vars.: **Pes(s)a(c)h**.

Patrs.: **Pesahson**; **Peisachovitz**, **Peisachowitch**, **Pesachov**, **Pesakhowich**, **Pessahov(itz)**, **Pesa(c)hovitz** (E Ashkenazic).

Peiser **1.** English: var. of PEYZER. **2.** Jewish (Ashkenazic): of unknown origin.

Peisson *see* PESCE

Pękala Polish: nickname from the Pol. dial. term *pękal* short, fat man.

Var.: **Pękalski**.

Pekárek *see* PIEKARSKI

Pěkný Czech: nickname for a man who was either fairhaired or handsome, Czech *pěkný*.

Peláez *see* PELAYO

Pelayo Spanish: from a medieval given name, from Gk *Pelagios* (a deriv. of *pelagos* (open) sea). The name was borne by a 10th-cent. Christian martyr, a young boy tortured and killed by the Moors of Córdoba for refusing to renounce his faith. His fame led to the given name being very popular in Spain in the Middle Ages; it was borne also by the semi-legendary first king of the Reconquest. The name was also borne by various other early martyrs, but in other European countries it has not been popular because of its association with the British heretic *Pelagius*.

Patrs.: Sp.: **Peláez**, **Páez**, **Báez**. Port.: **Pais**.

Pełczyński Polish: habitation name, probably from *Pełczyn*, a placename derived from PEŁKA army, or

Pełczyce in NW Poland, the Ger. name of which is BERNSTEIN.

Pelerin *see* PILGRIM

Pelham English: habitation name from a place in Herts., so called from the OE personal name *Pēotla* (a deriv. of *Pēot*, perhaps a short form of the various cpd personal names with the first element *Peoht* Pict) + OE *hām* homestead.

Pelikán Czech: house name from a house marked with the sign of a pelican (Czech *pelikán*). The pelican was regarded as a symbol of Christian piety: the female pelican was supposed, in medieval religious folklore, to feed her young with her own blood by plucking the feathers from her breast.

Pelisiak *see* FELIX

Pelisse French: metonymic occupational name for a maker of fur garments or nickname for a wearer, from OF *pellice* fur cloak (LL *pellīcia* from *pellis* skin, fur; cf. PELLETIER).

Vars.: **Pel(l)isier**, **Pélissier**, **Pélissié**, **Pelicier**, **Pélicier**; **Plissonier**.

Dims.: Fr.: **Pellisson**, **P(é)lisson**, **Plissoneau**, **Plichon**, **Plichet**. It.: **Pellicciotta**.

Augs.: It.: **Pelliccioni**, **Pel(l)izzon(i)**, **Pellissoni**, **Pellissone**.

Pełka Polish: apparently from a short form of a given name containing the element *pełka* army. This is found in several Slav. compound names such as *Świętopełk* ('holy' + 'army'). Alternatively, this name may simply be a dial. var. of PAŁKA.

Pell English: **1.** from the ME given name *Pell*, a pet form of PETER. **2.** metonymic occupational name for a dealer in furs, from ME, OF *pel* skin (cf. PELLETIER and PILCHER). **3.** topographic name, a var. of PILL 1.

Dim. (of 1): **Pelly**.

Pellé French: nickname for a bald man, from OF *pelé* (past part. of *peler* to peel, strip (esp. of hair), L *(de)pilāre*, from *pilus* hair; the spelling has been influenced by L *pellis* skin, hide).

Var.: **Pelé**.

Pej.: Fr.: **Pelard**.

Peller *see* PILL

Pelletier French: occupational name for a furrier, from OF *pelletier* (a deriv. of *pellet*, dim. of *pel* skin, hide, from L *pellis*).

Var.: **Peltier**.

Pellew *see* PEDLEY

Pelling English: **1.** habitation name from *Peelings*, a minor place in Sussex, recorded in Domesday Book as *Pellinges*, apparently from the OE tribal name *Pydelingas* 'people of *Pydel*', a personal name which may be derived from the root *pud-* to swell, be fat. **2.** See HAYLING.

Pellow **1.** Cornish: deriv. of PELL 1; for the ending, cf. PASCOE. **2.** English: var. of PEDLEY.

Peltonen Finnish: ornamental or topographic name from *pelto* field + the gen. suffix *-nen*.

Var.: **Peltola** (with a local suffix).

Pemberton English: habitation name from a place in Greater Manchester, so called from the Brit. element *penn* hill, head + OE *bere* barley + *tūn* enclosure, settlement (see BARTON).

Peña Spanish: topographic name for someone who lived near a large jutting rock or crag, Sp. *peña* (probably from L *penna*, *pinna* pinnacle, battlement, originally 'feather', or else of Celt. origin (cf. PENDLEBURY)). The surname is no doubt also a habitation name from any of the numerous minor places named with this term.

Vars.: **Peñas**; **Pina** (a place in the province of Saragossa).

Dims.: Sp.: **Pinilla** (see also PINE). It.: **Pennella**, **Pennelli**, **Penniello**, **Pennetta**, **Pennetti**, **Pennino**, **Pennini**.

Augs.: It.: **Pennone**, **Pennoni**.

Pejs.: It.: **Pennacci**, **Pennazzi**.

Pendegast see PRENDERGAST

Pender see PINDER

Pendlebury English (Lancs.): habitation name from a place in Greater Manchester so called from the hill name *Pendle* (composed of the Brit. element *penn* hill, head + a tautologous OE *hyll*) + OE *burh* fort, town (see BURY).

Pendleton English: habitation name from a place near PENDLEBURY, or another in Lancs., both of which are so called from the hill name *Pendle* + OE *tūn* enclosure, settlement.

Var.: **Pendelton**.

Pendreigh Scots: habitation name from any of various places apparently named with the Brit. phrase *pet an drych* croft of the view.

Vars.: **Pendrigh**, **Pendrich**; **Pittendr(e)igh**, **Pettendrich**.

Pendry see PARRY

Penev see STEPHEN

Penfold English (mainly Kentish): metonymic occupational name for someone in charge of a pound where stray animals were kept, from ME *punfold*, OE *pundfald* (cf. POUND and FOLD), or topographic name for someone who lived by such a pound.

Var.: **Pinfold**.

Pengelly Cornish: habitation name from any of the places (in thirteen parishes) so called from Corn. *pen* head, top, end + *kelly* (mutated *gelly*) copse, grove.

Vars.: **Pengelley**, **Pengill(e)y**.

Penhaligon Cornish: habitation name from a place in the parish of Bodmin, so called from Corn. *pen* head, top, end + *helygen* willow treee.

Penman Scots: habitation name from a lost place in the Border region, apparently derived from the Brit. elements *penn* hill, head + *maen* stone.

Penn English: **1**. metonymic occupational name for a shepherd or an impounder, from ME, OE *penn* (sheep) pen. **2**. habitation name from various places, e.g. *Penn* in Bucks. and Staffs., named with the Brit. element *pen* hill, which was apparently adopted into OE. **3**. pet form of PARNELL.

Var.: (of 1): **Penner**. See also PINDER.

Patrs. (from 3): **Pen(n)son**.

Penna **1**. Cornish: of uncertain origin. The form *Pennow* is recorded in 1524, and this name is probably derived from it. This seems to be Corn. *pennow* heads, pl. of *penn* head, but it may be Corn. *penn* + the ME dim. suffix *-oe* (see PASCOE). **2**. Italian: topographic name from a cogn. of Sp. PEÑA.

Pennacci see PEÑA

Pennall see PARNELL

Pennetier see PANTHER

Pennington English: habitation name from places in Lancs., Cumb., and Hants. The latter two are so called from OE *pening* PENNY (used as a byname or from a tribute due on the land) + *tūn* enclosure, settlement. The place of this name in the parish of Leigh in Lancs. is recorded in the 13th cent. as *Pinington* and *Pynington*, and may be from OE *Pinningtūn* 'settlement associated with *Pinna*'; the var. **Pinnington** derives specifically from this place.

Penny English: nickname from the coin (OE *peni(n)g*, cogn. with OHG *pfenning*, ON *penningr*). This was the common Gmc unit of value when money was still an unusual phenomenon, and by no means denoted a coin of little value, as it does today. It was the only unit of coinage in England until the early 14th cent., when the groat and the gold noble were introduced. It was a silver coin of considerable value, and the nickname may therefore have denoted a person of some substance. There is some evidence that the word for the coin was used in OE times as a byname (cf. PENNINGTON).

Vars.: **Penney**, **Pennie**, **Penning**.

Patrs.: Eng.: **Pennings**. Jewish: **Fenigson**.

'Servant of P.': **Pennyman**, **Penniman**, **Pannaman**.

Pennycuick Scots: habitation name from *Penycuik* near Edinburgh, recorded in 1250 as *Penicok* and in 1296 as *Penycoke*, apparently from Brit. cogns. of W *pen* hill and *cog* cuckoo.

Vars.: **Penneycuik**, **Pennecuik**, **Pennycook**, **Pennycock**.

Penrose Cornish and Welsh: habitation name from any of the places so called, in ten parishes of Cornwall, several times in Wales, and in Herefords. near the Welsh border. All are so called from the Celt. elements *pen* head, top, end + *ros* heath, moor.

Penswick English: habitation name from *Painswick* in Gloucs., so called from the possessive case of the ME given name PAIN + ME *wick* outlying settlement (see WICK). The place is recorded in Domesday Book simply as *Wiche*, but was later held by Pain FitzJohn (d. 1137), from whose name the first element of the placename is derived. The surname is now most common in Lancs., where it was introduced apparently as late as the 19th cent. and ramified exceptionally rapidly.

Pentecost English: nickname for someone who was born at Whitsuntide or had some particular connection with that time of year, such as owing a feudal obligation then. The name is from ME, OF *pentecost* (Gk *pentēcostē (hēmera)* fiftieth (day) (after Easter)).

Vars.: **Pentercost, Penticost, Pentycross, Perrycost**. See also PANKHURST.

Pentland Scots: habitation name from a place in the former county of Midlothian, of uncertain etymology, perhaps from ME *pent* (i.e. enclosed) *land*.

Pentreath Cornish: habitation name from a place in the parish of Breage, so called from Corn. *pen* head, top, end + *treth* beach, shore.

Penty W English: of uncertain origin, perhaps a back-formation from ME *pentis, pent(h)us* penthouse, and so a topographic name for someone who lived in one. This form of the vocab. word is found in W *penty* penthouse.

Vars.: **Pentey, Painty**.

Penwarne Cornish: habitation name from places in the parishes of Mawnan, Cuby, and Mevagissey, all so called from Corn. *pen* head, top, end + *gwern*, which means both 'marsh' and 'alder trees'.

Var.: **Penwarden** (a place in the parish of South Hill).

Penzer see PEYZER

Peopall see PEPYS

Pépineau see PEPYS

Peplow English: habitation name from a place in Shrops., recorded in Domesday Book as *Papelau*. This may be from OE *pyppel* pebble + *hlāw* hill (see LAW 2 and LOW 1).

Var.: **Peploe** (chiefly Scots.).

Pepper 1. English: metonymic occupational name for a spicer, from ME *peper, piper* pepper (OE *piper, pipor*, from L *piper*). The surname may also be a nickname for a small man or one with a fiery temper, or anecdotal for someone who paid a peppercorn rent. **2.** Jewish (Ashkenazic): Anglicized form of **Pfef(f)er**, derived from Ger. *Pfeffer* pepper, or **Fef(f)er**, from Yid. *fefer*. These are ornamental names, belonging to the large class of Ashkenazic names taken from words denoting plants. It is also possible that it may represent a punning translation of Hebr. *pilpul*, lit. 'pepper', fig. 'Talmudic debate', with reference to someone who was a sharp reasoner.

Vars.: Eng.: **Peppar; Peever, Peffer(s)** (from ANF *pivre*). Jewish: **Peper; Peperman, Fef(f)erman; Peperni(c)k** (E Ashkenazic, an agent deriv.).

Dims.: Eng.: **Peperel, Pepp(e)rell, Pepperall, Peperwell; Peverel(l), Peverill, Peverall**. Fr.: **Peuvret, Prevel**. Ger.: **Pfefferle(in)**.

Cpds (not clear whether merely ornamental, or ornamental extensions of 'pepper' with reference to a sharp reasoner): Jewish: **Pfefferbaum** ('pepper tree'); **Feferberg** ('pepper hill'); **Pfefferbluth** ('pepper blossom'); **Feferkichen** ('pepper cake'); **Pfefferkranz** ('pepper wreath').

Pepys English: from the OF personal name *Pepis*, oblique case *Pepin*, introduced to Britain by the Normans. It is of uncertain origin, perhaps originally a byname meaning 'Terrible', 'Awe-inspiring', from a root *bib-* to tremble. It was borne by several Frankish kings, most notably Pepin le Bref, father of Charlemagne, and remained popular throughout the early Middle Ages. The pronunciation is normally /pi:ps/.

Vars.: **Pep(p)in, Pippin, Pipon**.

Dims.: Eng.: **Pepall, Peaple, People, Peopall; Peppett, Peppiatt, Peppiett**. Fr.: **Pépineau(x), Pépinot**.

Patr. (from a dim.): Eng.: **Peoples**.

Pequeur see PÊCHEUR

Peracco see PETER

Peralta Spanish, Catalan, and Portuguese: habitation name from any of various places, for example in the provinces of Huesca and Navarre, so called from L *petra alta* high rock.

Pérard see PIERRE

Perce see PEARCE

Percival English: from the personal name *Perceval*, first found as the name of the hero of an epic poem by the 12th-cent. Fr. poet Crestien de Troyes, describing the quest for the holy grail. The origin of the name is uncertain; it may be associated with the Gaul. personal name *Pritorīx* or it may be an alteration of the Celt. name *Peredur* (perhaps from OW *peri* spears + *dur* hard, steel). It seems to have been altered as the result of folk etymological association with OF *perce(r)* to pierce, breach (LL *pertūsiāre*, reformed from *pertūsus*, past part. of class. L *pertundere*) + *val* valley (see VALE); cf. PERCY 2. The same hero was celebrated by the German epic poet Wolfram von Eschenbach under the name *Parzifal*, and with the spread of Arthurian romance the name became popular throughout W Europe.

Vars.: **Perceval, Percifull, Passifull, Purcifer**.

Percy English (Norman): habitation name from any of various places in N France, so called from the Gallo-Roman personal name *Persius* + the local suffix *-ācum*. The suggestion has also been made that it is a nickname from OF *perce(r)* to pierce, breach (cf. PERCIVAL) + *haie* hedge, enclosure (cf. HAY 1), referring either to a soldier remembered for his breach of a fortification, or in jest to a poacher who was in the habit of breaking into a private park.

Vars.: **Percey, Persay, Pearc(e)y, Pears(e)y, Pierc(e)y, Peircey; Pursey** (Somerset).

Perdrigeon see PARTRIDGE

Perdue see PARDOE

Pere see PEAR

Peregrín see PILGRIM

Perek Polish: of uncertain origin, probably a nickname or metonymic occupational name from a dim. of the Poznań dial. word *perka, pyrka* potato.

Var.: **Perka**.

Habitation name: **Perkowski**.

Perel see PEARL

Perelló Catalan: topographic name for someone who lived by a wild pear tree, from Cat. *perelló* wild pear (a double dim. of *pera* PEAR). There are places named with this word in the provinces of Tarragona and Valencia, and the surname may in part derive from them.

Perepyolkin Russian: patr. from a dim. of the nickname *Perepel* 'Quail', denoting presumably either a hunter of quails or an individual thought to be as timid as a quail.

Perevodchikov Russian: patr. from the occupational term *perevodchik* interpreter, translator (from *perevodit* to translate, from *pere-* across + *vodit* to lead, a calque of Fr. *traduire*, from L *tra(ns)ducere*).

Perfect *see* PARFITT

Perham English: habitation name from any of various places (for example those in Suffolk and Sussex now called PARHAM as the result of a regular ME development) originally named with the OE elements *peru* PEAR + *hām* homestead.

Vars.: **Perram**.

Perken *see* PARKIN

Perks *see* PARK

Permann *see* BERMANN

Permenter German: occupational name for a preparer or seller of parchment, an agent deriv. of Ger. *Pergament* parchment (so called from the ancient city of *Pergamon* in Asia Minor, where the technique of producing the material originated). Parchment was in general use well into the 15th cent.

Vars.: **Pergament**; **Berm(it)ter**.

Peron *see* PIERRE

Perot *see* PARROTT

Perov Russian: patr. from the nickname *Pero* 'Feather', 'Pen', denoting either a small, light person, or a clerk, on account of his use of a quill pen.

Perrier French: occupational name for a quarryman, OF *perrier*, an agent deriv. of *pierre* stone, rock (see PIERRE 2).

Vars.: **Pierrier**; **Peirier**.

Perrin English and French: from the ME, OF given name *Perrin*, a dim. of PETER.

Vars.: Eng.: **Perring** (chiefly Devon), **Perryn**, **Perren**, **Parren**. Fr.: **Perrain**, **Perrein**, **Prin**.

Dims.: Fr.: **Perrinet**, **P(é)rinet**; **Perrineau**, **Périnel**; **Perren(n)et**, **Pernet**, **Pernin**, **Pernot**, **Pernod**, **Pernollet**. It.: **Pe(d)rinelli**, **Perinello**, **Rinelli**, **P(e)rinetti**, **Rinetti**, **Rinucc(in)i**.

Patr.: Eng.: **Perrins** (chiefly W Midlands).

Perrowne English: Huguenot name, from the F given name *Perron*, a S French dim. of PIERRE.

Vars.: **Perron**, **Perowne**.

Perry 1. English: topographic name for someone who lived near a pear tree, ME *per(r)ie* (OE *pyrige*, a deriv. of *pere* pear). **2.** Welsh: patr., with the W prefix *ap-*, from the medieval given name *Herry*, an assimilated form of

HENRY. **3.** Jewish (Israeli): ornamental name from Hebr. *peri* fruit, reward.

Vars. (of 1): **Pery**, **Perrie**; **Pir(r)ie** (Scots); **Pur(r)y**; **Per(r)yman**, **Per(r)iman**, **Perriment**. (Of 3): **Pery**, **Per(r)i**.

Perrycost *see* PENTECOST

Pershing *see* PFIRSICH

Pertek Polish: nickname from the Pol. dial. term *pertek*, referring to a small, sprightly man.

Patr.: **Pertkiewicz**.

Perthold *see* BERTHOLD

Pertini *see* BERT

Pertwee English (Norman): habitation name from any of the various places in N France called *Pert(h)uis*, *Pertuy*, or *Pertus*, from OF *pertuis* ravine, gorge, cave (LL *pertūsium*, from *pertūsus*, past part. of *pertundere* to pierce, breach; cf. PERCIVAL and PERCY 2). The Fr. cogns. can also be topographic names for someone living by a ravine.

Var.: **Pertuce**.

Dims.: Fr.: **Pertuiset**, **Pertuisot**.

Pesach *see* PEISACH

Pesce Italian: metonymic occupational name for a fisherman or fishmonger (cf. PÊCHEUR) or nickname for someone supposedly resembling a fish, It. *pesce* (L *piscis*).

Vars.: **Peschi(o)**.

Dims.: It.: **Pescetto**, **Pesc(iol)ini**. Fr.: **Poisson(net)**, **Poissenot**, **Poyssenot**. Prov.: **Peisson**, **Peysson(eau)**. Port.: **Peixoto**, **Peixinho**. Jewish (Sefardic): **Peixotto** (reason for adoption unknown).

Aug.: It.: **Peschione**.

Peschel *see* PETER

Pescheur *see* PÊCHEUR

Peshin Jewish (E Ashkenazic): metr. from the Yid. female given name *Peshe*, *Pesye*, which is of uncertain origin; it may be an altered form of *Bashe*, *Basye*, from Hebr. *Batya* 'daughter of God'; cf. BASKIN.

Var.: **Peshes**.

Dims.: **Pessel**; **Pesselov**, **Pes(h)kin** (metrs.).

Peshkov Russian: patr. from the nickname *Peshki* 'Pedestrian', 'Foot-traveller', denoting someone who travelled about but was too poor to be able to afford the humblest form of transport, for example a pedlar.

Peso Spanish: nickname for a heavy person or metonymic occupational name for someone responsible for testing weights and measures, from Sp. *peso* weight (LL *pensum*, from the past part. of *pendere* to weigh; cf. PEYZER).

Pessoa Portuguese: nickname from Port. *pessoa* person, human being (L *persōna*; cf. PARSONS). The original application of the nickname is not clear; it may have had contemptuous overtones, or it may have denoted an important personage.

Pest *see* SEBASTIAN

Pestalozzi Italian: nickname for a butcher, from It. *pesta(re)* to pound, crush (LL *pistāre*, a reformation from *pistus*, past part. of class. L *pinsere*) + the dial. term *lozzo* bone.

Pestana Portuguese: nickname for someone who had long eyelashes or bushy eyebrows, from Port. *pestana* eyelash, also used in the Middle Ages of the eyebrow; the word is of unknown origin, probably from a pre-Roman term.

Pestelard *see* PISTOL

Pesterfield *see* BASKERVILLE

Pétain *see* PETTER

Petch *see* PEACHEY

Pételat *see* PISTOL

Peter English, German, and Flemish/Dutch: from the given name (Gk *Petros*, from *petros* rock, stone, a byform of *petra*; cf. PERRIER and PIERRE 2): The name was extremely popular throughout Christian Europe in the Middle Ages, as it had been bestowed by Christ as a byname on the apostle Simon bar Jonah, the brother of Andrew. The name, chosen by Christ for its symbolic significance, is a translation of Aramaic *kefa* rock (John 1: 42, Matt. 16: 18); St Peter is regarded as the founding father of the Christian Church in view of Christ's comment, 'Thou art Peter and upon this rock I will build my Church'. In Christian Germany in the early Middle Ages this was the most frequent given name of non-Gmc origin, being overtaken in the 14th cent. by JOHN and NICHOLAS. In England the vernacular form *Piers* (from OF *Piers*, oblique case *Pierre*) was usual at the time when surnames were being assumed; see PEARCE. The usual form of the given name in mod. Fr. is *Pierre*; in It. *Pietro*; in Sp. and Port. *Pedro*; in Russ. *Pyotr*; in Pol. *Piotr*; and in Czech *Petr*. The surname is also occasionally borne by Jews, in which case it represents an adoption of a non-Jewish surname.

Vars.: Eng.: **Petre**; **Pether** (Cornwall). Flem., Du.: **Peeter**, **Pieter**, **Peer**.

Dims.: Eng.: **Peet**, **Peat**, PELL; **Peattie**, **Pe(a)ddie** (N England and Scotland); **Perell**, **Parell**; PERROWNE; PERRIN; PARROTT; PARKIN; PETHICK (Cornwall); PETRIE (Scotland). It.: **Pe(t)relli**, **Pitrelli**, **Perrelli**, **Pe(t)r(i)ello**, **Pe(t)rilli**, **Pe(t)rillo**, **Pitrillo**, **Pirello**, **Pirelli**, **Perrillo**, **Pedr(i)elli**, **Perillio**, **Petrelluzzi**, **Petrozz(in)i**, **Pedrozzi**, **P(i)erozzi**, **Pirozzi**, **Pirozzolo**, **P(e)rozzo**, **Prozillo**, **Perocci**; **Petrucco**, **P(i)etrucci**, **Pedrucci**, **P(i)erucci**, **Prucci**, **Pieruccio**, **Perrucci(o)**, **Petruccelli**, **Petrucc(h)ini**, **Petruzzi**, **P(i)eruzzi**, **Pe(t)ruzzo**, **Petruzzio**, **Petruzzelli**, **Petruzziello**, **Perut(ti)**, **Perutto**, **Petruzziello**, **Petrussi**, **Prusso**; **Petrizz(ell)i**, **Periz(zi)**, **Pedrizzoli**, **Petroccello**, **Petroselli**, **Petriccelli**, **Petroccini**, **Petriccini**, **Petricciolo**, **Petrocchi**, **Pedrocco**, **Pedrocchi**, **Pirocchi**; **Petrol(in)i**, **Petrol(in)o**, **Pedrol(in)i**, **Pe(t)rolo**, **Pedrioli**, **Pe(i)roli**, **Pirioli**, **Pirolini**, **Pittoli**, **Petrolli**, **Pedrollo**, **Pe(t)rullo**, **Perrulo**, **Perulli**, **Perruli**; see also PARROTT and PERRIN. Ger.: **Pischel** (Silesia); **Pöschel** (Bavaria). Low Ger.: **Pe(e)termann**. Fris.: **Pie(te)rsma**. Flem., Du.: **Pie(t)**, **Pee**. Ger. (of Slav. origin): **Pet(e)rick**, **Petrusch**, **Pietruschka**, **Pet(r)asch**, **P(i)etsch**, **Pietz(ke)**, **Petz(old)**, **Petzolt**, **Pötzold**, **Patzelt**, **Pes(s)olt**, **Pessold**, **Piesold**, **Pessel**, **Posselt**, **Poss(e)**, **Possa**, **Possek**, **Pe(t)schel(t)**, **Peschke**, **Peschka**, **Peschmann**; **Pech(t)**, **Pecht**, **Pächt**, **Pechan**, **Pech(h)old**; **Piche**, **Pioch**, **Piech(a)**, **Piechnik**, **Pichan**, **Pichmann**; **Perschke**, **Pers(i)cke**, **Persich**, **Persian**. Czech: **Petráček**, **Petrášek**, **Petrásek**, **Petránek**; **Petřík**, **Petříček**, **Petřína**; **Pešek**, **Pešík**, **Pech(a)**; **Pecháček**.

Pol.: **Pietrzyk**, **Pietrzycki**, **Pietrasik**, **Pietraszek**, **Pietruszka**, **Pietranek**. Ukr.: **Petrus**, **Petrik**, **Petrenko**, **Petrushanko**, **Petlyura**. Beloruss.: **Petruk**. Jewish (E Ashkenazic, adoptions of non-Jewish surnames): **P(i)etruszka**, **Petrus(h)ka**. Hung.: **Pet(t)kó**, **Petö**, **Petri**.

Augs.: It.: **P(i)etroni**, **Troni**, **Pedron(i)**, **Spedroni**, **P(i)eroni**, **Peron(e)**, **Perroni**, **Perrone**, **Pirrone**, **Peirone**, **Pitone**.

Pejs.: It.: **Petrazzi**, **Trazzi**, **Pedrazzi**, **P(i)erazzi**, **Pirazzi**, **Perazzo**, **Petracc(h)i**, **Spedracci**, **Pieracci**, **Raccio**, **Pe(t)racco**, **Pe(t)rasso**, **Pitrasso**, **Perassi**.

Patrs.: Eng.: **Peters(on)**; **Pethers**, **Pithers** (Cornwall). Sc.: McFETRIDGE. It.: **De Pietri**, **De Pietro**, **Di Pietro**, **Di Pierro**, **De Pero**, **(De) Petris**, **Perris**. Sp.: **Pérez**. Cat.: **Peris**, **Piris**. Port.: **Peres**, **Pires**. Rum.: **Petrescu**. Ger.: **Petri**, **Petry** (Latinized). Low Ger.: **Pet(t)ers**, **Pieters**, **Peers**. Fris.: **Pietringa**. Flem., Du.: **Pe(e)ters**, **Pieters**; **P(i)eterse(n)**; **Petri**. Norw., Dan.: **Petersen**, **Pedersen**. Swed.: **Pet(t)ersson**, **Pe(h)rsson**. Pol.: **Pietrowicz**, **Piotrowicz**; **Pietrzak**, **Pietrasiak**, **Pietrusiak**. Russ.: **Petrov(ykh)**. Croatian: **Petr(ov)ić**; **Per(ov)ić**, **Pešić**. Bulg.: **Petrov**. Jewish (E Ashkenazic, adoptions of non-Jewish surnames): **Petrov**, **Petroff**. Lithuanian: **Petráitis**, **Petrulis**, **Petronis**, **Petráuskas**. Gk: **Petrou(lis)**. Armenian: **Petrosian**, **Bedrosian**. Hung.: **Péterf(f)y**, **Petöfi**.

Patrs. (from dims.): Flem., Du.: **Pien(s)**, **Pergens**. Ger. (of Slav. origin): **Pietzker**, **Pietzner**, **Pessler**, **Pässler**, **Passler**. Russ.: **Petra(ch)kov**, **Petrash(k)ov**, **Petrishchev**, **Petryashov**, **Petrun(k)in**, **Pet(r)aev**, **Pet(ru)ichev**, **Petin(ov)**, **Petugin**, **Petyakov**, **Petyan(k)in**. Pol.: **Pietruszewicz**, **Pietrusikiewicz**, **Pietrkiewicz**. Ukr.: **Petrus(k)evich**, **Petrichat**. Beloruss.: **Petrush(k)evich**, **Petrashkevich**. Croatian: **Petković**; **Perišić**. Bulg.: **Petkov**.

Habitation names: Pol.: **Piotrowski**, **Pietrowski**, **Pietruszewski**; **Pietrzykowski**; **Petrykowski**. Jewish (E Ashkenazic): **Piotrkowski**, **Piotrkowsky**, **Piotrkovski**, **Piotrkovsky**.

Peternot *see* PATERNOSTER

Pethick Cornish: from the Corn. given name *Petroc* or *Pedrek*, a dim. of PETER. St Petroc is a local saint, of whom very little of historical value is known, but who is commemorated in several placenames, including *Padstow* (earlier *Sancte Petroces stow*).

Vars.: **Petherick**, **Pedrick**.

Pethybridge English (Cornwall and Devon): habitation name from a place near Lustleigh in S Devon, so called from the OE personal name *Pyd(d)a* or *Pidda* (cf. PIDDINGTON) + ME *brigge* BRIDGE.

Petipa French: 1. nickname for a man with a mincing gait, from OF *petit* small (see PETTIT) + *pas* step, stride (L *passus*). 2. habitation name from any of the various minor places named with the OF elements *petit* small, narrow + *pas* passage (L *passus*, originally the same word as in 1 above).

Petrettini *see* PARROTT

Petrie Scots: 1. dim. of PETER. 2. dim. of PATRICK.

Pett *see* PITT

Pettendrich *see* PENDREIGH

Petter 1. English (Norman): nickname for a flatulent person, from an agent deriv. of OF *peter* to fart (from *pet* a fart,

L *peditum*, past part. of *pedere* to fart). **2.** Low German: var. of PETER.

Vars. (of 1): **Pet(t)our**.

Dims. (of 1): Fr.: **Pét(a)in**, **Péton**, **Pétot**.

Aug. (of 1): Fr.: **Pétat**.

Pejs. (of 1): Fr.: **Pétard**, **Pethard**, **Pétaud**.

Pettifer English (Norman): nickname from OF *pie de fer* iron foot (LL *pēs de ferro*), given perhaps to someone with an artificial foot or leg, or to a tireless walker.

Vars.: **Pettyfer**, **Pettipher**, **Pettefer**, **Pettiver**, **Pettyfor**, **Pettafor**, **Pettiford**, **Pettifar**, **Pettefar**, **Puddifer**; **Pot(t)iphar** (altered by folk etymology to conform to the name of Pharaoh's captain of the guard in Gen. 39).

Pettigrew Scots (Norman): apparently a nickname for a small man, from OF *petit* little, small (see PETTIT) + *cru* growth (past part. of *creistre* to grow, increase, L *crescere*). Another explanation is that it is a nickname for a man with long thin legs, from OF *pie de grue* crane's foot (LL *pēs de gruā*).

Vars.: **Petticrew**, **Petticrow**, **Pettigree**, **Pet(t)egree**.

Pettingell English: ethnic name for someone from Portugal. The name derives from LL *Portucale*, originally referring only to the area around the trading base of Oporto (*Portus Cales*, from L *portus* port, harbour (see PORT 2) + *Cales*, the ancient name of the town). In some cases the surname may be no more than a nickname for someone who had business connections with Portugal.

Vars.: **Pettingall**, **Pettingale**, **Pettingill**, **Pettengell**, **Pettengill**, **Puttergill**, **Portingale**, **Portugal**.

Pettit English: nickname for a small person, or for the younger of two bearers of the same given name, from ANF *petit* small (a word of obscure and isolated origin, probably a nursery word).

Vars.: **Petit**, **Petyt**, **Pettitt**, **Pettet**, **Pittet**, **Petty**, **Pettie**.

Dims.: Fr.: **Petiteau**, **Peti(t)et**, **Peti(t)on**, **Peti(t)ot**, **Petetot**, **Petetin**, **Pit(t)iot**; **Péchin**, **Péchon**, **Pechon**, **Péchou(x)**, **Péchot**, **Pechot**.

Patr.: Fr.: **Aupetit**.

Petukhov Russian: patr. from the nickname *Petukh* 'Cock' (from *pet* to sing), denoting a lusty or self-important person.

Peu see PUY

Peuchert see PAUKER

Peugeot see PÈGUE

Peutherer Scots and English: occupational name for a pewterer, someone who made articles of pewter (an alloy of tin and lead), from ME *peutrer* (OF *peautrier*, an agent deriv. of *peau(l)tre* pewter, the further etymology of which is unknown).

Vars.: **Pewterer**, **Powter**, **Pouter**.

Peuvret see PEPPER

Peverall see PEPPER

Pevzner Jewish (Ashkenazic): of uncertain origin, possibly from Yid. *Poyzner*, a habitation name from the city

of *Poznań* (Ger. *Posen*, Yid. *Poyzn*) in Poland. See POZNAŃSKI.

Var.: **Pevsner**.

Pew see PUGH

Pewsey English: habitation name from a place so called in Wilts., recorded in Domesday Book as *Pevesie*, apparently from the gen. case of an OE personal name **Pefe*, not independently attested + OE *ēg* island.

Var.: **PUSEY**.

Pewterer see PEUTHERER

Pey see PAY, PUY

Peyraud see PIERRE

Peysson see PESCE

Peyzer English: occupational name for an official in charge of weights and measures, especially one whose duty it was to weigh rent or tribute received, from ANF *peiser*, *poiser* weigher (LL *pensārius*, a deriv. of *pensāre* to weigh, for class. L *pendere*, past part. *pensus*).

Vars.: **P(e)iser**, **Peizer**, **Pyser**, **Pyzer**, **Po(y)ser**, **Poyzer**; **Penzer** (with -*n*- reflecting a trace of the L word).

Pezey see PUSEY

Pezout see POU

Pezron see PIERRE

Pfabian see FABIAN

Pfäffle see POPE

Pfaitler see PFEIDLER

Pfeffel see POPE

Pfefferbaum see PEPPER

Pfeidler S German and Austrian: occupational name for a maker of goatskin garments, S Ger. dial. *Pfeidler* (mod. sense 'shirtmaker'), an agent deriv. of a dim. of MHG *pfeit* goatskin cloak (OHG *pfeit*, from Gk *baitē*).

Vars.: **Pfeitler**, **Pfaitler**, **Feidler**.

Pfeil German: metonymic occupational name for an arrowsmith, or perhaps a nickname for a tall thin man, from Ger. *Pfeil* arrow (MHG, OHG *pfīl*, from L *pīlum* spike, javelin; cf. PILE 1).

Vars.: **Pfeiler**; **Pfeilschmidt** (see SMITH).

Dims.: Low Ger.: **Pielk(e)**.

Pfersching see PFIRSICH

Pfirsich German: metonymic occupational name for a grower or seller of peaches, from Ger. *Pfirsich* peach (MHG *pfersich*, from LL *persica*, for class. L *persicum (malum)* Persian apple).

Vars.: **Pfersich**, **Pfirsching**, **Pfersching**, **Pförsching**; **Pershing** (U.S.).

Pfister S German: occupational name for a baker, southern MHG *pfister* (from L *pistor* baker, miller, from *pinsere*, past part. *pistus*, to grind, mill).

Var.: **Pfisterer** (with the addition of the Ger. agent suffix).

Dims.: It.: **Pistorello**, **Pistorino**, **Pistorini**.

Pfitzer *see* PFÜTZER

Pflimlin *see* PLUM

Pflöschner *see* FLASCHNER

Pförsching *see* PFIRSICH

Pföstl *see* POST

Pfützer German: topographic name for someone who lived by a well or a pond, MHG *pfütze* (mod. Ger. *Pfütze* puddle; from L *puteus* well; cf. PUITS).

Vars.: **Pfützner**; **Pfitz(n)er** (Austria); **Fitzner** (Silesia); **Pfützmann, Pfitzmann**.

Phair *see* FAIR

Phaisey *see* VAISEY

Phalip *see* PHILIP

Pharaoh *see* FARRAR

Phear *see* FEAR

Pheasey *see* VAISEY

Phelan *see* WHELAN

Phelip *see* PHILIP

Phemister *see* FEMISTER

Phenix *see* FENWICK

Phethean *see* VIVIAN

Philan *see* WHELAN

Philbert French: from *Filibert*, a Gmc personal name composed of the elements *filu* very + *berht* bright, famous, which was borne by a 7th-cent. saint, abbot of Jumièges. The spelling has been influenced by the various given names of Gk origin containing the element *phil-* love; cf. e.g. PHILIP.

Var.: **Philibert**.

Philbey *see* FILBY

Philip English, French, Dutch/Flemish, and Danish/ Norwegian: from the Gk name *Philippos* (from *philein* to love + *hippos* horse), borne by one of the apostles, as well as by various other early saints. Unusually for a common Christian name, it seems to owe its popularity more to the medieval romances about Alexander the Great, whose father was Philip of Macedon, than to any saint. The surname is also occasionally borne by Jews, in which case it represents an adoption of a non-Jewish surname or an Anglicization of some like-sounding Jewish surname.

Vars.: Eng.: **Philipp, Phillip, Phil(l)p, Phelp, Phalp**. Fr.: **Philippe, Phélip, Félip, Phélit, Phelip, Phalip**. Flem., Du.: **Filip**. Jewish: **Philipp, Phillip, Filip**.

Dims.: Eng.: PHILPOTT, **Philott**; **Phippin, Phippen**; **Philcock, Philcott**. Fr.: **Philip(p)eau(x), Phélipeau, Philip(p)et, Philip(p)on, Phlipon**. It.: **Filippini, Lippini, Filippelli, Filippello,**

Lippiello, Filippetti, Filippucci, Filipputti, Filippozzi. Czech: **Filípek**. Pol.: **Filipek**. Ukr.: **Pilipyak, Pilipets, Pikhno**.

Augs.: It.: **Filippone, Filipponi**.

Pejs.: Fr.: **Philip(p)ault, Philip(p)art, Philip(p)ard**. It.: **Filippazzo**.

Patrs.: Eng.: **Phil(l)ip(p)s, Phillis**; **Phil(l)ps**; **Phel(i)ps** (S and SW England); **Phip(p)s**; **Philip(p)son, Phillipson**; **Phipson**. Sc.: **McPhilip, McPhillips**, MCKILLOP. It.: **De Filippo, De Filippi(s), Di Filippo**. Ger.: **Philippi** (Latinized). Low Ger.: **Philipps(en), Ph(i)lips, Flips(en)**. Flem., Du.: **Philips, Flippen**. Dan., Norw.: **Philipsen**. Swed.: **Philipsson**. Jewish (Ashkenazic): **Phil(l)ips, Philip(p)sohn, Filipson**. Russ.: **Filippov, Filip(p)yev**. Pol.: **Filipowicz; Filipczak, Filipiak**. Croatian: **Filip(ov)ić, Pilipović**. Bulg.: **Filipov**. Gk.: **Philippou**.

Patrs. (from dims.): Eng.: **Fills, Philson, Filson**; **Phillins**, FILKINS, **Phil(l)cox**. Low Ger.: **Lipgens**. Russ.: **Filipchikov, Filipychev, Fil(k)ov, Fil(ya)ev, Fil(k)in, Filyakov, Filyukov, Filchakov, Filinkov, Filyushkin, Filyashin, Filchagin, Filisov, Filasov, Filochov, Filintsev, Filshin, Khilkov**. Croatian: **Piletić**.

Habitation name: Pol.: **Filipczyński**.

Phillimore English: from a Norman personal name, *Filimor*, composed of the Gmc elements *filu* very + *meri, mari* famous. The spelling has been altered under the influence of PHILIP.

Vars.: **Fil(l)more**.

Philosoph Jewish (Ashkenazic): Germanized form of a Yid. nickname from *filesof, pilesof* philosopher, also used ironically to mean 'ignoramus'.

Vars.: **Philossoph, Philozof, Filosof(f), Filozof, Pilos(s)of**.

Philpott English (mainly Kentish): from the ME given name *Phil(i)pot*, a dim. of PHILIP with the hypocoristic suffix *-ot*.

Vars.: **Phillpott, Phil(l)pot, Phillippot**, POTT.

Patrs.: Eng.: **Phil(l)pots, Philpotts**.

Phimister *see* FEMISTER

Phin *see* FINN

Phizackerley *see* FAZAKERLEY

Phlipon *see* PHILIP

Phoenix *see* FENWICK

Phyffe *see* FYFE

Phythian *see* VIVIAN

Piaget French: metonymic occupational name for the keeper of a toll booth. The surname is found principally around Lyon, and represents a local pronunciation of OF *péaget*, a dim. of *péage* toll (booth) (from LL *pediaticum* right to cross, set foot on, from *pēs*, gen. *pedis*, foot).

Pianella *see* PLAIN

Piasecki Polish: topographic name for someone who lived in a sandy place, from Pol. *pias(ek)* sand, or habitation name from a place named with this element.

Vars.: **Piaskowski**; **Piasny**; **Piaseczny** (probably a habitation name from *Piaseczno*, just S of Warsaw); **Piaskowiak** (also an occupational name for a dealer in sand).

Piątkowski Polish: from the Pol. given name *Piątek* 'Friday', with the addition of the common surname ending *-owski*. Illegitimate children were often given the name of the day of the week on which they were baptized; even more frequently, converted Jews took as a surname the name of the day on which they were baptized.

Var.: **Piątek**.

Patr.: Pol.: **Piątkiewicz**.

Piazzini see PLACE

Picard see PIKE

Picazo Spanish: nickname from Sp. *picazo* magpie, given perhaps to a talkative or thievish person, or to someone who had a streak of white among black hair. The word seems to derive from L *pīca* (see PYE 1), but the suffix is obscure.

Piccini Italian: nickname for a small person, from It. *piccino* small (of uncertain etymology, perhaps related to the group of words discussed at PIKE).

Vars.: **Piccin**, **Pizzin(i)** (Venetia); **Piccinni**, **Piccinno** (Tuscany); **Picc(i)oli**, **Picc(i)olo**, **Pizz(i)oli**, **Pizz(i)olo**, **Picci(o)tto**, **Picciocchi**, **Picciulli**, **Picciullo**, **Picciuzzo**.

Dims.: It.: **Piccinelli**, **Pizzinelli**, **Piccinin(i)**, **Piccinino**, **Pizzinini**; **Piccolin(i)**, **Piccolino**, **Picolotto**.

Patr.: It.: **Del Piccolo**.

Piccolomo Italian: nickname for a small man, from It. *piccolo* small (see PICCINI) + *uomo* man (L *homo*, gen. *hominis*).

Var.: **Piccolomini**.

Pichan see PETER

Pichl see BÜHLER

Pick 1. English: metonymic occupational name for someone who made or used a pick or pickaxe as an agricultural or excavating tool, from ME *pi(c)k*. This is probably from OE *pīc* (see PIKE 3), although the shortening of the vowel is something of a mystery. See also PEAK. **2.** Jewish (E Ashkenazic): of unknown origin.

Dims. (of 1): **Pickin**, **Picken**.

Pickard English: **1.** regional name for someone from Picardy (Fr. *Picardie*) in N France, a region adjoining Normandy, from which many of William the Conqueror's companions and followers came. **2.** some early examples, such as Paganus *filius Pichardi* (Hants 1160), seem to point to derivation from a Gmc personal name, probably composed of the elements *bic* sharp point, pointed weapon + *hard* hardy, brave, strong.

Var. (of 2): PITCHER.

Dims.: It.: **Pic(c)ardino**.

Pickerden English: of uncertain origin. From its form it would appear to be a habitation name, but no suitable placename is known. The first known bearer is a certain William Pickerden of Hastings, Sussex, recorded in 1591, and if the William *Picardin* whose will was proved at Hastings in 1593 is the same person, it may be a dim. of PICKARD. The surname has been strongly concentrated in E Sussex from its first occurrence to the present day, and it seems likely that all bearers belong to a single family.

Pickerell English: nickname for a sharp and aggressive person, from ME *pykerell* young pike (from ME *pyke* pike (the fish) + *-ell* dim. suffix).

Vars.: **Pick(e)rill**, **Pickrell**.

Pickering English: habitation name from a town in N Yorks., so called from an OE tribal name *Piceringas*. Ekwall suggests that this is earlier *Pīcōringas* 'people on the ridge (see ORR 3) of the pointed hill (see PIKE 1)'.

Var.: **Pickerin**.

Pickersgill English (Yorks.): habitation name from a place in W Yorks., apparently originally named as 'Robber's Ravine', from ME *pyker* thief + *gill* gully (see GILL 2).

Var.: **Pickersgil**.

Pickett see PIGGOTT

Pickford English: habitation name, perhaps from *Pickforde* 'pig ford' in Ticehurst, Sussex. The surname is now most common in the Manchester region, but it does not seem to have reached there before the 17th cent.

Pickholz Jewish (Ashkenazic): ornamental name from Yid. *pikholts* woodpecker (from Ger. *picken* to peck + *Holz* wood), one of the large group of Ashkenazic surnames taken from words denoting birds and animals.

Var.: **Pikholz**.

Pickles English (Yorks.): topographic name for someone who lived by a small field or paddock, ME *pigh(t)el* (of obscure origin).

Vars.: **Pickless**, **Pighills**.

Pickup English: habitation name from a place in Lancs., so called from OE *pīc* point (see PIKE 1) + *copp* top, i.e. a hill with a sharp peak.

Picton English: habitation name from any of various places, for example in Ches. and N Yorks., so called from OE *pīc* point, peak (or the derived byname *Pīca*; see PIKE 1 and 6) + *tūn* enclosure, settlement.

Var.: **Pickton**.

Pidal Spanish: topographic name for someone who lived by a plant nursery or metonymic occupational name for a nurseryman, from OSp. *pibdal* nursery (LL *pīpītāle*, a deriv. of *pīpīta* seed, class. L *pītuīta* gum exuded from trees).

Piddington English: habitation name from places so called in Northants and Oxon., both from OE *Pydingtūn* 'settlement (OE *tūn*) associated with *Pyda*'.

Pidgeon English: **1.** metonymic occupational name for a hunter of wood pigeons, or nickname for a foolish or gullible person, since the birds were easily taken. ME *pigeon* (from OF *pijon* young bird, LL *pipio*, gen. *pipiōnis*, an imitative formation) was also used to denote a young DOVE. **2.** from *Pet(y)jon*, a nickname from ME *pety* small (see PETTIT) + the given name JOHN. Cf. LITTLEJOHN.

Vars. (of 1): **Pid(e)on**, **Pidgen**, **Piggin**.

Pidler see PEDLER

Pie see PETER

Piechota Polish: **1.** nickname for someone who travelled about on foot, from Pol. *na piechotę* on foot (the vocab. word is not found in the nominative). Cf. Russ. PESHKOV. **2.** from a pet form of *Piotr* PETER.

Var.: **Piechocki**.

Patr. (from 2): **Piechowiak**.

Piedade Portuguese: religious byname from Port. *piedade* compassion, pity (L *pietas*, gen. *pietātis*), an attribute of the Virgin Mary, *Maria da Piedade*.

Piegrome *see* PILGRIM

Piekarski Polish: occupational name for a baker, from Pol. *piekarz* baker + *-ski* suffix of surnames (see BARANOWSKI).

Var.: **Piekarz**.

Dim.: Czech: **Pekárek**.

Piele *see* PEEL

Pielk *see* PFEIL

Pieńkowski Polish: topographic name for someone who lived where hemp was grown, from Pol. *pieńka* hemp + *-ów* possessive suffix, + *-ski* suffix of local surnames (see BARANOWSKI).

Piepers *see* PIPER

Piera Catalan: habitation name from a place in the province of Barcelona, so called from an aphetic form of OCat. *apiera* beehive (L *apiāria*, a deriv. of *apis* bee). In some cases it may also derive from the vocab. word and be a metonymic occupational name for a beekeeper.

Var.: **Pié**.

Pierce *see* PEARCE

Piercey *see* PERCY

Pierettini *see* PARROTT

Pierre French: **1.** from the Fr. given name *Pierre*, a cogn. of PETER. **2.** topographic name for someone who lived on a patch of stony soil or by a large outcrop of rock, from OF *pierre* stone, rock (L *petra*, from Gk). It may also be a metonymic occupational name for a quarryman or stone-carver; cf. PERRIER.

Vars. (of 2): **Lapierre**, **Delapierre**.

Dims. (of 1): Fr.: **Pérel**, **Péreau**, **Perreau**, **P(i)erron**, **Perronet**, **P(ey)ron(et)**, **Péronel**, **Perronel**, **Péroneau**, **Perron(n)eau**, **Peyroneau**, **Perron(n)in**, **Peyronin**, **Pe(y)rony**, **Perronot**, **Perruc**, **Peyruc** (Brittany). Prov.: **Pe(d)ron**, **Pezron**, **Pierrou**, **Perroux**. See also PARROTT and PERRIN.

Augs. (of 1): Fr.: **P(i)errat**, **Piérat**.

Pejs. (of 1): Fr.: **P(i)errard**, **P(i)érard**; **Perrau(l)t**, **Perriault**, **Pérau(l)t**, **Peyraud**.

Collectives (of 2): Sp.: **Pedraza** (places in the provinces of Lugo and Segovia), **Pedrera** (a place in the province of Sevilla), **Pedreira** (Galicia). Port.: **Pedreira**.

Pierrepont French and English (Norman): habitation name from any of various places, for example in Aisne and Calvados, so called from OF PIERRE stone + PONT bridge.

Vars.: Eng.: **Pierrepoint**, **Pierpon(t)**, **Pearpoint**, **Pairpoint**.

Pierrier *see* PERRIER

Pierzchała Polish: nickname for a harum-scarum or hothead, from a deriv. of the verb *pierzchać*, which in OPol. meant 'to be angry' (it has since acquired the meaning 'to run away').

Var.: **Pierzchalski**.

Pigault *see* PIKE

Pigg English (Northumb.): metonymic occupational name for a swineherd or nickname for someone supposedly resembling a pig or young hog, ME *pigge* (of uncertain origin; although an OE form is not attested, there is oblique evidence for it in the word *picbrēd* pigfood, i.e. acorns).

Piggin *see* PIDGEON

Piggott English: from the ME, OF given name *Picot*, *Pigot*, a dim. of *Pic* (see PIKE 6). In ME, the form *Piket* (OF *Picquet*) was also common.

Vars.: **Pigott**, **Pig(g)ot**, **Pygott**, **Picot**; **Pi(c)kett**, **Pykett** (Notts.).

Dim.: Fr.: **Piqueton**.

Piggrem *see* PILGRIM

Pighills *see* PICKLES

Pigler *see* BÜHLER

Pike English: **1.** topographic name for someone who lived near a hill with a sharp point, from OE *pīc*, which was a relatively common placename element (cf. PICKERING and PICKUP). **2.** metonymic occupational name for a pike fisherman or nickname for a predatory individual, from ME *pike* (OE **pīc*, the fish being named from its pointed jaw). **3.** metonymic occupational name for a user of a pointed tool for breaking up the earth, ME *pike* (cf. PICK). **4.** metonymic occupational name for a medieval foot-soldier who used a pike, a weapon consisting of a sharp pointed metal end on a long pole, ME *pic* (OF *pique*, of Gmc origin). **5.** nickname for a tall, thin person, from a transferred sense of one of the above. **6.** from a Gmc personal name (derived from the root 'sharp', 'pointed' underlying all of the above), found in ME and OF as *Pic*. **7.** nickname from OF *pic* woodpecker (from L *pīcus*, perhaps named from its pointed beak and so ultimately cogn. with the other words of this group; see also PYE, SPEIGHT, and PICKHOLZ).

Var.: **Pyke**. See also PICK and PEAK.

Dims.: Fr.: **Picon**, **Pichon**, **Pichonneau**. (Of 2 only): Eng.: PICKERELL. (Of 6 only): Eng.: PIGGOTT.

Augs. (of 6): It.: **Picchioni**, **Pigoni**.

Pejs.: Fr.: **Pic(h)ard** (see also PICKARD); **Pic(h)aud**, **Pic(h)ault**, **Pigault**.

Pikett *see* PIGGOTT

Pikhno *see* PHILIP

Pikholz *see* PICKHOLZ

Pilcher English (Kentish): occupational name for a maker or seller of *pilches*, or nickname for a habitual wearer of one of these. A *pilch* was a kind of coarse leather garment with the hair or fur still on it (OE *pylece*, from LL *pellīcia*, a deriv. of *pellis* skin, hide, from which Ger. *Pelz* hide (OHG *pelliz*) is also derived). Cf. FELL. In early 17th-cent. English, *pilcher* was a popular term of abuse, being confused or punningly associated with the unrelated verb *pilch* to steal and with the unrelated noun *pilchard* a kind of fish.

Vars.: **Pilger**; **Pilch**.

Pile 1. English: topographic name for someone who lived near a stake or post serving as a landmark, ME *pile* (OE *pil*, from L *pilum* spike, javelin; cf. PFEIL). **2.** French: topographic name for someone who lived in a depression or hollow, from OF *pile* trough, mortar (L *pila* mortar; both *pilum* and *pila* are derivs. of *pinsere* to grind, crush (cf. PFISTER and PISTOL)). The surname may perhaps also have been a metonymic occupational name for someone who made or used such vessels.

Var. (of 1): **Pyle**.

Dims. (of 2): **Pil(l)et**, **Pil(l)ot**, **Pil(l)on**.

Pilgrim English: nickname for a person who had been on a pilgrimage to the Holy Land (cf. PALMER) or to some seat of devotion in Europe such as Santiago de Compostella or Rome (cf., e.g., KUMSTELLER and ROMAN), or to one nearer home, for example the tomb of St Thomas à Becket at Canterbury. Such pilgrimages were often imposed as penances, graver sins requiring more arduous journeys. The word *pilgrim* is from ME *pilegrim*, *pelgrim*, OF *pelegrin* (L *peregrinus* traveller, a deriv. of *peregre* abroad, from L *per agros* lit. 'through the fields', from *ager* field). Pilgrim was also occasionally used as a given name, and the surname may in some cases be derived from this use.

Vars.: **Pilgram**, **Peagrim**, **Piggrem**, **Pigram**, **P(e)agram**, **Peg(g)ram**, **Pegrum**, **Pi(e)grome**; **Pelerin**; **Peregrine**, **Paragreen**.

Dims.: It.: **Pellegrinelli**, **Pellegrinetti**, **Pellegrinotti**.

Pilipets *see* PHILIP

Pilkington English: habitation name from a place in the parish of Prestwich, Lancs., so called from OE *Pilecingtūn* 'settlement (OE *tūn*) associated with *Pileca*'.

Pill English (Devon and Cornwall): **1.** topographic name for someone who lived by a stream or creek, OE *pyll*. **2.** nickname for a small, round person, from ME, OF *pil(l)e* ball (LL *pilula*, a dim. of class. L *pila*).

Vars. (of 1): PELL; **Piller**, **Peller**, **Puller**; **Pillman**, **Pel(l)man**, **Pul(l)man**; **Pilling**.

Pillay English: habitation name from either of two places now called *Pilley*. One in S Yorks. is recorded as *Pillei* in Domesday Book and as *Pillay* in the late 12th cent. It is probably from OE *pil* pile, post (see PILE 1) + *lēah* wood, clearing, i.e. a wood where timber for piles could be obtained. One in Hants appears in Domesday Book as *Piste(s)lei*, but has later spellings resembling those for *Pilley* in Yorks., and may have the same etymology.

Var.: **Pilley**.

Piller *see* BÜHLER

Pilosof *see* PHILOSOPH

Pilshchikov Russian: patr. from the occupational term *pilshchik* sawyer (from *pilit* to saw).

Dims.: Pol.: **Pilarczyk**, **Pilarek**.

Pilz German and Jewish (Ashkenazic): metonymic occupational name for a gatherer or grower of mushrooms,

from Ger. *Pilz* mushroom (MHG *bül(e)z*, OHG *buliz*, from L *bōlētus*).

Vars.: **Piltz**. Ger. only: **Bilz**. Jewish only: **Pilzer**.

Pimenta Portuguese: metonymic occupational name for a grower of peppers, from Port. *pimenta* red pepper (LL *pigmenta*, from class. L *pigmentum* paint, pigment, a deriv. of *pingere* to paint; cf. PAINTER and PINTO). The fruit was so called because of its bright colour. The surname may also have arisen as a nickname for someone with a red face or a quick temper or wit.

Dim.: **Pimentel** (also Jewish (N Sefardic), reason for adoption unknown). The Jewish name has also been altered to **Pimenthal** by association with the many ornamental Ashkenazic names ending in *-t(h)al* valley.

Pimm English: from the medieval female given name *Pymme*, *Pimme*, vernacular short forms of *Euphemia*, a Gk name composed of the elements *eu* well + *phēnai* to speak, i.e. to avoid words of ill omen. The name was adopted by early Christians in the sense 'praise of God' or 'good repute', and was borne by a 4th-cent. virgin martyr burnt at the stake in Chalcedon. It was popular in England in the Middle Ages, official documents usually recording only the learned form.

Vars.: **Pim**, **Pym(m)**.

Dims.: **Pim(b)let(t)** (chiefly Lancs.); **Pim(b)lott**.

Pinard French: nickname from OF *pinard*, a small medieval coin, so called because it bore the device of a pine cone (see PINE). The name may have denoted someone who paid a rent of this amount; the term seems also to have been used as a derogatory term for a rich man or miser.

Var.: **Pinart**.

Dims.: **Pinardel**, **Pinardeau**, **Pinardon**.

Pinch English: nickname for a chirpy person, from ME *pinch*, *pink* (chaf)finch (OE *pinc(a)*; cf. FINCH and FINK).

Var.: **Pin(c)k**.

Dim.: Eng.: **Pinkett**.

Patr.: Eng.: **Pinks**.

Pinchas Jewish: from the Hebr. male given name *Pinechas* (of Egyptian origin).

Vars.: **Pinhas**; **Pinches** (from the Yid. form *Pinkhes*); **Pinchasi**, **Pinhas(s)i**, **Pinhasy** (with the Hebr. ending *-i*). See also FINCH.

Dim.: **Pinko** (from Yid. *Pinke*).

Patrs.: **Pin(c)hasov**, **Pinchasow**, **Pinhassof**, **Pinhasovi(t)ch**, **Pinhassovitch**, **Pinhassovitz** (E Ashkenazic).

Patrs. (from dims.): (Ashkenazic): **Pin(n)es**, **Pinus**, **Pinas**, PINSON (from Yid. *Pinye*); **Pineles** (from Yid. *Pinyele*). (E Ashkenazic, from E Yid. *Pinke*): **Pinkus**, **Pincus**, **Pinkas**, **Pincas**, **Pinkason**, **Pincov**, **Pincovich**, **Pinkowitz**, **Pincowitz**, **Pink(as)ovitz**, **Pincowski**; **Pincovici** (among Rumanian Jews); **Pinkoffs**, **Pincoffs** (with double suffix: Slav. *-ov* + Yid. *-s*).

Pinchbeck English: habitation name from a place in Lincs., apparently so called from OE *pinc(a)* (chaf)finch (see PINCH) + *bæc* back, ridge.

Var.: **Pinchback**.

Pincher English: nickname from ME *pinch(en)* to pinch, grip (from a Norman version of OF *pincier*, from LL *punctiāre* to prick, pierce, punch (freq. of *pungere*, past part. *punctus*), with the vowel altered by crossing with words of the PIKE group). The verb also had the transferred senses 'carp', 'cavil', and 'dispense meanly', and this may well be the origin of the surname.

Pejs.: Fr.: **Pinsard**; **Pinchard**, **Pinchart**, **Pinchaut** (Normandy).

Pinder English: occupational name for an official who was responsible for rounding up stray animals and placing them in a pound, from an agent deriv. of ME *pind(en)* to shut up, enclose (OE *pyndan*).

Vars.: **Pindar**, **Pindor**, **Pender**.

Pine English: topographic name for someone who lived by a conspicuous pine tree or in a pine forest, from ME *pine* (OE *pīn*, from L *pīnus*, reinforced by OF *pin* from the same source). It may also be a habitation name from various places named with this word, such as *Le Pin* in Calvados; in other cases it may originally have been a nickname for a tall, thin man, supposedly resembling a pine tree.

Var.: **Pyne**.

Dims.: Eng.: **Pinnell**, **Pinel**. Fr.: **Pineau(x)**, **Pinet**, **Pinot(eau)**, **Pinon**. Prov.: **Pinets**. It.: **Pinelli**, **Pinello**, **Pinetti**, **Pinotti** (all in part also from aphetic dim. forms of given names such as JACOB, JOSEPH, and PHILIP). Sp.: **Pinilla** (see also PEÑA). Cat.: **Piñol**.

Aug.: Fr.: **Pinat**.

Collectives: Fr.: **Pinoy**. Prov.: **Pinède**. Sp.: **Pinedo**, **Pineda**, **Pinar**. Cat.: **Pineda**. Port.: **Pinhal**.

Pinfold see PENFOLD

Pinilla see PEÑA

Pinkerton Scots and N Irish: habitation name from a place near Dunbar in the former county of E Lothian. The placename is probably of Eng. origin, with a final element from OE *tūn* enclosure, settlement, but the first part is obscure.

Pinkney English (Norman): habitation name from *Picquigny* in Somme, so called from a Gmc personal name *Pincino* (of obscure derivation) + the local suffix *-(i)ācum*.

Var.: **Pinckney**.

Pinner English: **1.** occupational name for a maker of pins or pegs, from an agent deriv. of ME *pin* (OE *pinn*, apparently from L *pinna*; cf. PEÑA). **2.** occupational name for a maker or user of combs, ANF *peigner* (from *peigne* comb, L *pecten*; cf. PEINADO). **3.** habitation name from *Pinner*, now part of NW London, which derives its name from OE *pinn* pin, peg + *ōra* slope, ridge. The first element probably denoted a topographical projection, although it is also possible that it represents a byname.

Pinson 1. English and French: nickname from OF *pinson* finch (LL *pincio*, gen. *pinciōnis*, apparently of Gmc origin; cf. PINCH), perhaps applied to a bright and cheerful person. **2.** English and French: metonymic occupational name for someone who made use of pincers or forceps in his work, from OF *pinson* pincers (a deriv. of *pincier* to pinch; cf. PINCHER). **3.** Jewish (Ashkenazic): patr. from *Pine*, a pet form of the Yid male given name *Pinkhes* (see PINCHAS).

Vars. (of 1 and 2): Eng.: **Pinshon**, **Pinch(e)on**, **Pinching(g)**, **Pinchen** (Norman forms); **Pinsent**. Fr.: **Pinçon**; **Pinchon** (Normandy, Picardy).

Pinto Spanish, Portuguese, Italian, and Jewish (Sefardic): nickname for a person with a blotchy complexion or pep-

per-and-salt hair, from *pinto* mottled (LL *pinctus*, for class. L *pictus*, past part. of *pingere* to paint).

Vars.: Sp.: **Pintado**. Port.: **Pinta** (partly Jewish, Anglicized **Pinter**). It.: **Pintus**, **Lo Pinto**, **La Pinta** (Sicily).

Pintoricchio see PAINTER

Pioch see PETER, PUY

Piper English: occupational name for a player on the pipes, ME *pipere*, OE *pīpere* (an agent deriv. of *pīpe* pipe (cogn. with Ger. *Pfeife* whistle, pipe, OHG *pfīfa*), from LL *pīpa*, from *pīpāre* to pipe, squeak, of imitative origin; cf. PIDGEON).

Vars.: **Pyper**; **Pipe(s)**.

Patrs.: Low Ger.: **Pi(e)pers**, **Peipers**.

Pipon see PEPYS

Piqueton see PIGGOTT

Pirazzi see PETER

Piretto see PEAR

Pirie see PERRY

Pirkis see PURCHASE

Pirkl see BIRCH

Pirpamer see BIRNBAUM

Pisani Italian: habitation name from the city of *Pisa* in Tuscany. This was probably founded by Greek colonists, but before coming under Roman control it was in the hands of the Etruscans, who seem to have given it its name. At any rate, the placename is of obscure meaning.

Vars.: **Pisano**; **Pisanu** (Sardinia); **Pisa**.

Dims.: **Pisanelli**, **Pisan(i)ello**.

Pisarski Polish: occupational name for a clerk or scribe, Pol. *pisarz* (from *pisać* to write), with the addition of the surname suffix *-ski* (see BARANOWSKI). Cf. SCHREIBER and SOFER for names with similar meanings.

Vars.: **Pisarz**, **Pisera**.

Dims.: Pol.: **Pisarek**, **Pisarczyk**. Czech: **Písařík**. Ukr.: **Pis(s)arenko**.

Patrs.: Russ.: **Pisarev**. Jewish (E Ashkenazic): **Pisareff**.

Patr. (from a dim.): Pol.: **Pisarkiewicz**.

Pischel see PETER

Piscopello see BISHOP

Piser see PEYZER

Piskač Czech: metonymic occupational name or nickname for someone who played a fife or penny whistle, from Czech *piskač* (also *pištec*) whistle.

Var.: **Pištěk**.

Dim.: **Piskáček**.

Pistol English: metonymic occupational name for an apothecary or grocer, from ME, OF *pistel*, *pestel* pestle

(L *pistillum*, later *pestillum*, from *pinsere*, past part. *pistus*, to crush, grind).

Var.: **Pestell**.

Dims.: Fr.: **Pétrel**, **Pétron**; **Pestureau**.

Augs.: Fr.: **Pétel(l)at**, **Pételaz**, **Pettelat**.

Pej.: Fr.: **Pestelard**.

Pistorello *see* PFISTER

Pitarch Catalan: of uncertain origin, apparently from the Fr. surname *Pitard*; see PYTHON.

Pitard *see* PYTHON

Pitcher English (chiefly E Anglia): **1.** occupational name for a caulker, one who sealed the seams of a ship with pitch, from an agent deriv. of ME *pich* (OE *pic*; cf. PECHER 1 and PÈGUE). **2.** var. of PICKARD 2.

Patr.: **Pitchers**.

Pitchford English: habitation name from a place near Shrewsbury, where there was a bituminous well; the name is derived from OE *pic* pitch (see PITCHER) + *ford* FORD.

Var.: **Pitchforth**.

Pite English: of uncertain origin, probably a var. of PITT.

Pithers *see* PETER

Pitiot *see* PETTIT

Pitkänen Finnish: patr. from the nickname *Pitkä* 'Tall'.

Pitt English: topographic name for someone who lived by a pit or hollow, OE *pytt*, or habitation name from a place named with this word, e.g. *Pitt* in Hants or *Pett* in E Sussex. For the variation in the vowel, cf. HILL 1.

Vars.: **Pitts**, **Pett(s)**; **Putt(s)** (Devon and Cornwall); **Pit(t)man**, **Pettman**, **Putman**; **Pitter**, **Putter**.

Pittaway English (W Midlands): of uncertain origin, probably a habitation name from an unidentified place named with the OE elements *pytt* pit, hollow (see PITT) + *weg* path (see WAY).

Pittendreigh *see* PENDREIGH

Pittner *see* BÜTTNER

Piwoński Polish: ostensibly an ornamental nickname from *piwonia* peony, this is probably a 'polite' alteration of **Piwocha** 'beer drinker'.

Piwowarski Polish: occupational name for a brewer, Pol. *piwowar* (from *piwo* beer + *warić* to brew), with the addition of the surname suffix -*ski* (cf. BARANOWSKI).

Pizarro Spanish: topographic name for someone who lived near a slate quarry or occupational name for someone who worked in one; perhaps also a topographic name for someone who lived in a house with a roof of slate, or a nickname from the colour. The name is from Sp. *pizarra* slate, of uncertain etymology. It seems to be taken from Basque, and may have been originally *lapitz-arri*, a cpd of the borrowed L *lapideus* (an adj. deriv. of *lapis* stone) + the native *arri* stone, with the initial syllable being lost by folk etymology, it being taken as the fem. form of the Sp. definite article.

Pizey *see* PUSEY

Pizzin *see* PICCINI

Plab *see* BLAU

Place English and French: **1.** topographic name for someone who lived in the main market square of a town or village, ME, OF *place* (LL *platea (via)* broad street, from Gk *platys*, fem. *plateia*, broad, wide). **2.** metonymic occupational name for a fishmonger, or perhaps a nickname for a thin person, from ME, OF *plaise* plaice, flat fish (LL *platessa*, apparently akin to 1). **3.** topographic name for someone who lived near a quick-set fence, ME, OF *pleis* (L *plexum*, past part. of *plectere* to plait, weave, intertwine).

Vars.: Eng.: **Plaice**. (Of 1 only): Fr.: **Plasse**, **Laplace**, **Delaplace**. (Of 3 only): Eng.: **Pl(e)ass**, **Pleace**, **Pleece**.

Dims. (of 1): It.: **Piazzini**, **Piazzol(l)a**, **Piazzoli**.

Plaček Czech: nickname for a discontented, miserable person, from Czech *plaček* moaner, weeper, from *pláč* to cry, bewail one's lot.

Plachý Czech: nickname for a shy, timid person, from Czech *plachý* shy.

Var.: **Plachký**.

Plackett English (Notts.): probably a nickname from early mod. Eng. *placket* (from OF, a deriv. of *plaquier* to lay flat). The word denoted an extra piece of material in a garment or a slit in the top of a skirt, also the female sex organs, and hence a woman considered as an object of sexual desire. The word is not attested in OED until Shakespeare, for whom it clearly had bawdy connotations, but it was probably in colloquial use earlier. The surname is presumably of obscene origin, perhaps a nickname for a person noted for sexual activity.

Plain French: topographic name for someone who lived on a plain or plateau, OF *plan* (L *plānum*, from the adj. *plānus* flat, level).

Vars.: **Plan**, **Plaine**; **Duplain**, **Duplan(t)**.

Dims.: Fr.: **Planet**, **Planeix**, **Planel(le)**, **Planeau**. It.: **Pianella**, **Pianelli**, **Pianetti**. Cat.: **Planella**, **Planells**.

Augs.: It.: **Pianon(e)**.

Planche French: from OF *planche* plank (LL *planca*, akin to L *plancus* flat-footed, which was a Roman family name, and Gk *plax*, gen. *plankos*, flat surface, *platys* broad, flat; cf. PLACE 1). It is not clear how this word was applied as a surname: it may be a topographic name for someone who lived near a plank-bridge over a stream, a metonymic occupational name for a carpenter, or a nickname for a thin person, i.e. one seen as being as flat as a board.

Vars.: **Planque**; **Laplanche**, **Laplanque**; **Desplanches**, **De(la)planque**.

Dims.: Fr.: **Planchet(te)**, **Planquette**, **Planchon**, **Plançon**, **Plancon**. Ger.: **Plankl**.

Pej.: Fr.: **Planchard**.

Plant English: **1.** metonymic occupational name for a gardener, from ME *plant* young tree, herb (OE *plante*, from L *planta* cutting, shoot, reinforced by OF *plante* from the same source). **2.** perhaps also a nickname for a tender or delicate individual, from the same word in a transferred sense.

Var.: **Plante**.

Plas, van den Dutch: topographic name for someone who lived by a dip in a road, which filled up with water in the winter months, from MDu. *plas* puddle, pool, plash.

Plaschke *see* BLAISE

Plaster English: 1. metonymic occupational name for a plasterer, from ME *plaster* (OF *plastre*, from L *(em)plastrum*, Gk *emplastron*, a deriv. of *emplassein* to shape, form). 2. habitation name from any of various places called *Plaistow* (in E London, Derbys., Sussex, and elsewhere), from OE *plegestōw* playground (cf. PLAYER and STOW).

Vars. (of 2): **Pla(i)stow**.

Platonov Russian: patr. from the given name *Platon*. The Gk byname *Platōn* 'Flat(-footed)' (from *platys* broad, flat; cf. PLACE 1 and PLATT) was borne not only by the ancient philosopher known in Eng. as *Plato*, but also by a 4th-cent. Christian martyr venerated in the Orthodox Church, and for this reason the given name became fairly common in Russia.

Dims.: **Platon(n)ikov**, **Platoshkin**, **Platygin** (all patrs.).

'Son of the wife of P.': **Platonikhin**.

Platt 1. English: nickname for a thin man, from OF *plat* flat (LL *plat(t)us*, from Gk *platys* broad, flat; cf. PLACE 1). It may also be a topographic name for someone who lived on a piece of flat land or by a plank-bridge; *Platt* Bridge in Lancs. is named from this dial. sense of the ME word, and may well be the main source of the surname, which is still found principally in the surrounding area. 2. Jewish (Ashkenazic): of unknown origin.

Var. (of 1): **Platts**.

Dims. (of 1): Eng.: **Platten** (Norfolk). Fr.: **Platel**, **Plateau**.

Pejs. (of 1): Fr.: **Plat(t)ard**.

Player English: occupational name for an actor or musician or nickname for a successful competitor in contests of athletic or sporting prowess, from an agent deriv. of ME *pleyen* to play (OE *plægian*, *plegan*).

Playfair Scots: 1. var. of PLAYFORD. 2. nickname for an enthusiastic participant in athletic activities, from ME *pley* sport, play (cf. PLAYER) + *fere* companion (see FEAR 1).

Var.: **Playfer**.

Playford English: habitation name from a place in Suffolk, so called from OE *plæga*, *plega* sport, play + *ford* FORD. The reason for the name is not clear; the place may have been the site of sporting contests, or it may have been so named from animals playing there.

Var.: PLAYFAIR.

Pleace *see* PLACE

Pleaden *see* BLEVIN

Pleasance English: 1. from the medieval female given name *Plaisance* 'Pleasantness', regarded as a specifically fem. form of the much rarer *Plaisant* (pres. part. of OF *plaire*, from L *placere* to please), of common gender (cf. CONSTANT and CONSTANCE). 2. habitation name from

the N Italian city of *Piacenza*, so called from L *Placentia* (neut. pl. of the pres. part. of *placere*).

Var.: **Pleasaunce**.

Plechatý Czech: nickname for a bald-headed man, from Czech *plechatý*, *plešatý* bald.

Var.: **Plecháč**.

Plecitý Czech: nickname for someone with broad shoulders, from Czech *plecitý* broad-shouldered.

Plemyannikov Russian: patr. from the nickname *Plemyannik* 'Nephew', 'Kinsman', denoting someone who was related to some prominent member of the community or who had inherited wealth from a relative.

Plenderleith Scots: habitation name from a place in the former county of Roxburgh, the name of which is of uncertain derivation. It may be from Brit. *pren* timber + *dre* farm, plus an uncertain final element, possibly a river name meaning 'Broad' (see LEITH).

Var.: **Plenderleath**.

Plenty English: nickname from ME *plente(th)* plenty, abundance (OF *plentet*, from LL *plēnitas*, gen. *plēnitātis*, a deriv. of *plēnus* full), given perhaps to a wealthy man or else to a heavy drinker or eater. The word was also used as an adj. in the Middle Ages; cf. DAINTITH.

Plessing *see* BLAISE

Pleuman *see* PLOWMAN

Plewright *see* PLOWRIGHT

Plichet *see* PELISSE

Plimmer *see* PLUMMER

Ploch *see* VLACH

Płóciennik *see* PŁUCIENNIK

Plomer *see* PLUMMER

Plomley *see* PLUMLEY

Płoński Polish: habitation name from the town of *Płońsk*, NW of Warsaw.

Płoszaj Polish: occupational name for someone whose job was to frighten birds away from crops, from a deriv. of Pol. *płoszyć* to frighten.

Vars.: **Płoszajski**; **Płoszyński** (formally a habitation name).

Plotka Jewish (E Ashkenazic): from Pol. *płotka*, dim. of *płoć* roach, one of the many ornamental names based on fish names.

Vars.: **Plotke**; **Plotkin** (formally a patr.).

Plotnik Jewish (E Ashkenazic): occupational name from Russ. *plotnik* carpenter (originally a maker of wattles and wooden fences, from *plot* plaited, woven object).

Vars.: **Plotnick**; **Plotnicki**, **Plotni(t)zki**, **Plotni(t)zky**, **Plot(t)**.

Patrs.: **Plotnikov**, **Plotnicov**.

Plouvier French: 1. topographic name for someone who lived near a gutter or drainage channel, OF *plo(u)vier* (LL *pluviārium*, from *pluvia* rain). 2. nickname from the plover or rainbird, OF *plo(u)vier* (LL *pluviārius*).

Var.: **Plovier**.

Plovier *see* PLOUVIER

Plowden English: habitation name from a place in Shrops., so called from OE *plæga, plega* play, sport + *denu* valley (see DEAN 1); cf. PLAYFORD. The vowel of the first syllable is not easy to explain, but it occurs as early as 1286, a single generation after the unambiguous *Plaueden, Pleweden* of 1252.

Plowman English: occupational name, from OE *plōh* plough + *mann* man; it was probably given more often to a PLOWRIGHT than to a ploughman in the modern sense, since ploughing was shared at the appropriate season by virtually all male members of the agricultural community.

Vars.: **Pleuman**; **Plows**, **Plews**.

Plowright English: occupational name for a maker of ploughs, from OE *plōh* plough + *wyrhta* WRIGHT.

Var.: **Plewright**.

Equivs.: Low Ger.: **Plomaker**, **Plögemaker**; **Pluymaker**, **Plümaker** (Rhineland).

Płuciennik Polish: occupational name for a linen-draper, Pol. *płóciennik*, from *płótno* linen + *-nik* suffix of agent nouns.

Var.: **Płóciennik**.

Plum English: topographic name for someone who lived by a plum tree, from OE *plūme* plum (L *prūna*, originally a neut. pl., but later taken as fem. sing.).

Vars.: **Plumb**, **Plum(b)e**; **Plum(p)tre(e)**.

Dims.: Ger.: **Pflimlin** (Switzerland). Low Ger.: **Plum(e)ke**, **Plümecke**. Fr.: **Prunel**, **Pruneau**, **Prunet**.

Plumley English: habitation name from any of various places so called, the chief of which is in Ches. near Knutsford. The name is derived from OE *plūme* PLUM + *lēah* wood, clearing.

Vars.: **Plomley**, **Plumbley**.

Plummer English: 1. topographic name for someone who lived near a plum tree; see PLUM. 2. occupational name for a dealer in feathers, from an agent deriv. of ME, OE *plume* feather (L *plūma*). 3. occupational name for a worker in lead, especially a maker of lead pipes and conduits, a plumber (ANF *plom(m)er, plum(m)er*, from *plom(b)*, *plum(b)* lead, L *plumbum*).

Vars.: **Plumer**; **Plomer** (pronounced /'pluːmə(r)/); **Plimmer** (W Midlands).

Plumstead English: habitation name from any of various places, for example in Norfolk, so called from OE *plūme* PLUM + *stede* site (see STEAD).

Plunkett English and Irish (Norman): 1. habitation name from a metathesized form of *Plouquenet* in Ille-et-Villaine, Brittany, so called from Bret. *plou* parish (from L *plebs* people) + *Guenec*, the personal name (a dim. of *guen* white) of a somewhat obscure saint. 2. An alternative explanation is that this is a metonymic occupational name for a maker or seller of blankets, from ME *blaunket* (ANF *blancquet*, a dim. of *blanc* white), but replacement of /b/ by /p/ is not usual in English.

Vars.: **Plunket**, **Plumkett**, **Plucknett**; **Pluincéid** (a Gaelicized form).

Pluntsch *see* BLUNTSCHLI

Pluta Polish: nickname from the Pol. dial. term *pluta* bad weather, rain, sleet, or puddle, perhaps denoting someone of a gloomy temperament.

Habitation name: **Pluciński**.

Plutheroe *see* PROTHEROE

Pluymaker *see* PLOWRIGHT

Plzák Czech: habitation name for someone from the city of Pilsen in Czechoslovakia, Czech *Plzeň*.

Pobgee English: nickname from ME *popinjay, papejai* parrot (OF *papageai*, from Arab. *bab(b)aghā*, perhaps of imitative origin; the ending was altered by folk etymological association with JAY). The nickname was probably acquired by a talkative person or by someone who habitually dressed in bright colours, but occasionally it may have denoted one who was connected with or who excelled at the medieval sport of tilting or shooting at a wooden parrot on a pole.

Vars.: **Pebjoy**, **Pobjoy**, **Pop(e)joy**, **Papigay**.

Patr.: Russ.: **Popugaev**.

Poch Catalan: nickname for a small man, from Cat. *poch* little, small (L *paucus*).

Pochet *see* POKE

Pockney English (Sussex): habitation name, probably from *Puckney* Gill in the parish of Charlwood, Surrey, which is so called from the gen. pl. of OE *pūca* goblin + OE *ēg* island. The surname is first found in Sussex in 1332 as *atte Pukenegh*, and occurs also in Surrey at about the same date. From the 14th to the 17th cent. it was largely confined to a small area of central Sussex around W Grinstead.

Vars.: **Pokney**, **Pocknee**.

Pocock *see* PEACOCK

Podczaski Polish: occupational name from Pol. *podczaszy* butler, wine steward, one who served drinks and organized weddings.

Podevin *see* POTVIN

Podgórski Polish: topographic name for someone who lived at the foot of a hill, from the elements *pod* under + *góra* hill, mountain + *-ski*, suffix of local surnames (see BARANOWSKI).

Podkidyshev Russian: patr. from the nickname *Podkidysh* 'Foundling' (from *podkidyvat* to abandon a baby, a cpd of *pod* under, secretly + *kidat* to throw).

Podlesiak Polish: topographic name for someone who lived near a wood, from Pol. *pod* near + *les* wood + *-(i)ak* suffix denoting human nouns. The two vars. listed below are probably regional names from the district of *Podlasie* in Poland, which gets its name from these elements.

Vars.: **Podlasiak**, **Podlaski** (regional names).

Podmore English: habitation name from *Podmore* in Staffs. or *Podimore* in Somerset, both of which are of uncertain origin, possibly from a rare ME word *pod, pad* frog (cf. PADDOCK 2) + *more* fen, marsh (see MOORE 1).

Podolski Polish and Jewish (E Ashkenazic): regional name for someone from Podolia in the Ukraine (Pol. *Podole*, Yid. *podolye*), a region which had a large Jewish population from the Middle Ages up to the Second World War. It is also possible that in some cases the Jewish names listed here derive from *Podol*, the only district of Kiev in which Jews were permitted to live in the 1880s. However, since all Ashkenazic Jews in the Russian Empire had surnames by that decade, it would have to be shown that Jews were living in Podol earlier (at least by 1844) if this explanation is to be established as correct.

Vars.: Jewish: **Podolsky**; **Podoly**, **Podell**, **Podol(i)er** (from Yid. *podolyer* native or inhabitant of Podolia); **Podolov**, **Podoloff**.

Podroužek Czech: from a dim. form of Czech *podruh*, a status term denoting a tenant on an estate who held his land in return for labour rather than for a cash rent.

Poe *see* PEACOCK

Poeuf *see* PUY

Poggetti *see* PUY

Poggs English: metr. from the ME female given name *Pogg(e)*, var. of *Mogg(e)*, a dim. of *Margaret* (cf. mod. Eng. *Peggy*).

Vars.: **Pogson**, **Poxon**.

Pogoński Polish: nickname for a Lithuanian, from Pol. *pogoń* the Lithuanian coat of arms.

Patr.: **Pogonowicz**.

Pogorzelski Polish: nickname for someone who had lost his home and his property in a fire, from a deriv. of *pogorzeć* to burn down. It may also be a habitation name from the town of *Pogorzela* in W Poland, which gets its name from this word.

Pogosian *see* PAUL

Pohl *see* PAUL

Pohořelý *see* POGORZELSKI

Poidevin *see* POTVIN

Poillon *see* POU

Poincaré French: nickname for a fierce fighter, from OF *poing carré* square fist (L *pugnus quadrātus*). The surname is found mainly in the Meuse and Champagne regions.

Poinçon French: metonymic occupational name for a maker or user of any pointed instrument, OF *poinson* (LL *punctio*, gen. *punctiōnis*, from *pungere* to pierce, punch; cf. PINSON 2).

Vars.: **Poinson**, **Poinçot**, **Poinsot**; **Poinset** (Anglicized **Poinsett**, see below).

Dims.: Fr.: **Poincelin**, **Poincelot**, **Poincelet**; **Poinsignon**, **Poincignon**.

Pointer English (E Anglia): occupational name from ME *pointer* point maker, an agent deriv. of *point*, a kind of lace used to fasten together the doublet and hose (OF *pointe* point, sharp end, LL *puncta*, from *pungere* to pierce).

Var.: **Poynter**.

Pointon English: habitation name from a place in Lincs., so called from OE *Pohhingtūn* 'settlement (OE *tūn*) associated with *Pohha*', a byname apparently meaning 'Bag' (cf. POKE).

Var.: **Poynton**.

Points English (Norman): **1.** from the medieval given name *Ponc(h)e*, *Pons*, ultimately from *Pontius*, a Roman family name of uncertain origin, perhaps an ethnic name for someone from *Pontus* (named from Gk *pontos* ocean) in Asia Minor, or an Italic cogn. of L *Quintus* 'Fifth(-born)'. The name was borne by two 3rd-cent. saints, a Carthaginian deacon and a martyr of Nice, but was not widely popular in the Middle Ages because of the inhibiting influence of the even more famous Pontius Pilate. In some cases, though, the surname may have been originally used for someone who had played the part of this character in a religious play. **2.** habitation name from *Ponts* in La Manche and Seine-Maritime, Normandy; see PONT.

Vars.: **Poyntz**. (Of 1 only): **Punch**.

Dims. (of 1): Eng.: **Pointel**. Fr.: **Ponci(n)**, **Poncy**, **Poncet**, **Punchet**, **Punchon**. It.: **Ponzetti**, **Punzetti**, **Punzetto**.

Augs. (of 1): It.: **Ponzoni**, **Ponzone**, **Punzone**.

Pejs. (of 1): Eng.: **Ponsard**. Fr.: **Punchard**.

Patr. (from 1): Eng.: **Ponson**.

Poireau French: metonymic occupational name for a grower or seller of leeks, from OF *poireau* leek (LL *porrellum*, a dim. of class. L *porrum*; the first syllable seems to have been altered by the influence of *poire* PEAR).

Vars.: **Poirel**, **Poiraux**, **Po(u)reau**, **Pouriau**, **Pouriel**, **Pourrel**.

Poirot *see* PEAR

Poissenot *see* PESCE

Poke English: metonymic occupational name for a maker of bags and purses, or nickname for someone who was in the habit of carrying a distinctive bag or purse, from ME *poke* purse, bag (ANF *poque*, of Gmc origin, cogn. with OE *pohha*).

Vars.: **Pouch(er)**, **Pougher**.

Dims.: Eng.: **Pocket(t)**. Fr.: **Pocquet**, **Po(u)chet**, **Po(u)chon**, **Pochot**.

Pokney *see* POCKNEY

Pokorný Czech: nickname for a humble or self-effacing person, from Czech *pokorný* lowly, humble, meek.

Pokrovski Russian: surname adopted by members of the Orthodox clergy, formed from *pokrov* feast of the Intercession of the Holy Virgin (lit. 'covering', 'protection', from *pokryt* to cover over). This feast, celebrated on 1 October, commemorates the salvation of Constantinople from the Saracens in the mid-10th cent., allegedly as the result of an apparition of the Holy Virgin.

Pol 1. Dutch: topographic name for someone who lived by a grassy mound, from MDu. *pol* tussock. **2.** Catalan: cogn. of PAUL. **3.** French: var. of PAUL.

Vars. (of 1): **Poll**, **Pols**, **Van den Pol(l)**; **Polman** (also Jewish).

Polak Polish and Jewish (Ashkenazic): ethnic name for a Pole or regional name for someone from Poland. In the case of the Ashkenazic name and its vars., the reference is to a Jew from Poland or other Slav.-speaking region. The name of the country (Pol. *Polska*) derives from a Slav. element *pole* field, open country, cleared land (cf. POLAŃSKI); to this has been added *-ak*, suffix denoting a human subject.

Vars.: Pol.: **Pol**, **Polka**; **Pol(a)kowski**. Jewish: **Polack**, **Pollack**, **Polliak**, POLLOCK; **Bollack**, **Bol(l)ag** (W Ashkenazic); **Polski**, **Polsky**; **Pol(a)kowski**; POOL.

Dims.: Pol.: **Polaczek**. Czech: **Poláček**, **Polášek**. Jewish: **Pola(t)chek**, **Polatshek**, **Pol(l)atsek**, **Polacek**.

Patrs.: Jewish: **Polyakov**, **Poliakov(e)**, **Poliakow**; **Polakevitch**, **Polakiewicz**. Russ.: **Polyakov**.

Polański Polish: **1.** ethnic name (with the surname suffix *-ski*: see BARANOWSKI) for a Pole, or more specifically for a descendant of the *Polanie*, one of the original Polish tribes. **2.** topographic name for someone who lived in a clearing, from *polana* glade, clearing (a deriv. of *pole* field).

Vars.: **Polanowski**, **Poliński**; **Polczynski**; **Polawski**.

Cpd (of 2): Jewish: **Dolgopolski** ('long field').

Polglase Cornish: habitation name from any of several places whose name is composed of the Corn. elements *pol* pool, pond + *glās* blue, green, grey.

Politelli *see* HIPÓLITO

Polívka Czech: apparently a nickname from Czech *polevka* soup, broth, stock, perhaps denoting a cook or seller of broth.

Polk 1. German (of Slav. origin): from a dim. of a short form of a Slav. personal name composed of the elements *bole* great, large + *slav* glory. This name was a favourite during the Middle Ages among the Silesian ruling class and was widely imitated by their subjects. **2.** German: ethnic name for a Pole; see POLAK. **3.** U.S.: contracted form of POLLOCK.

Vars. (of 1): **Polke**, **Polka**, **Pulke**.

Polkinghorne Cornish: habitation name from a place in the parish of Gwinear, recorded in 1316 as *Polkenhoern*, from Corn. *pol* pool, pond + the OCorn. personal name *Kenhoern* (literally 'Hound-Iron').

Pollard English: **1.** nickname for a person with a large or unusually shaped head, from ME *poll* head (MLG *polle* (top of the) head) + the pej. suffix *-ard*. The term *pollard* denoting an animal that has had its horns lopped is not recorded before the 16th cent., and of a tree similarly truncated not until the 17th cent., so both these senses are almost certainly too late to have contributed to the surname. **2.** pej. of PAUL.

Pollini *see* POULE

Pollock 1. Scots: habitation name from a place in Strathclyde, apparently so called from a dim. of a Brit. cogn. of Gael. *poll* pool, pit. **2.** Jewish (Ashkenazic) and German: ethnic name for someone from Poland. In the case of the Ashkenazic name, the reference is to a Jew from Poland or from some other Slav.-speaking region; cf. POLAK.

Var.: **Pollok**.

Polly English (Norman): nickname for a courteous or amiable person (perhaps also sometimes given ironically to a

boor), from OF *poli* agreeable, polite (lit. 'polished', past part. of OF *polir*, L *polīre*).

Var.: **Polley**.

Dims.: Fr.: **Pol(l)iet**, **Pol(l)iot**.

Pej.: Fr.: **Poliard**.

Polman *see* POOL

Polster German: metonymic occupational name for a maker or seller of cushions, or nickname for a plump man, from Ger. *Polster*, *Bolster* cushion, pillow, bolster (OHG *polstar*).

Var.: **Bolster**.

Dim.: **Pölsterl**.

Polyblank English (Norman): apparently a nickname for someone with fair hair, from OF *poil* hair (L *pilus*) + BLANC white. However, the name consistently shows an extra syllable in the middle (represented normally as *y*, sometimes as *i* or *e*, in isolated cases as *o*, *a*, *ay*, *ey* and *er*), which is not easy to explain.

Vars.: **Pulleyblank**, **Pulliblank**.

Pomerantz 1. German: metonymic occupational name for an importer or seller of bitter (Seville) oranges, Ger. *Pomeranze* (MHG *pomeranz*, med. L *pōmarancia*, composed of **arancia*, the name imported with the fruit (cf. NARANJO), with the explanatory L *pōmum* apple, fruit (cf. POMEROY)). **2.** Jewish (Ashkenazic): from Yid. *pomerants* orange, one of the many ornamental names taken from plants.

Vars.: **Pomeranz**. (Of 2 only): **Pomerants**, **Pomeranc(e)**, **Pomrince**, **Pomrinse**; **Marantz**, **Maranc**, **Marans** (from the aphetic Yid. form *marants*).

Dims.: Jewish: **Pomeranzik**, **Pomaranzik**, **Pomeranchik**.

Cpds (ornamental): Jewish: **Marantenboim** ('orange tree'; the spelling is Rumanian); **Pomeranzblum**, **Pomerancblum** ('orange flower').

Pomeroy English (Norman; found mainly in Devon): habitation name from any of the various places in NE France named with OF *pommeroie*, *pommeraie* apple orchard (collective of *pomme* apple, L *pōmum*).

Vars.: **Pomery**, **Pomroy**, **Pummery**.

Pomfret English: habitation name from *Pontefract* in W Yorks., so called from OF *pont freit* broken bridge (from L *pons* (gen. *pontis*) bridge + *fractus*, past part. of *frangere* to break). The name is recorded in the medieval period in L (*Pontefracto* 1090) and in Fr. (*Puntfreit* 1226). The modern placename spelling derives from the L form, while the local pronunciation is from the Fr.

Vars.: **Pomfrett**, **Pumfrett**, **Pomphrett**, **Pontefract**.

Pomorski Polish: regional name from *Pomerania* in NW Poland (Pol. *Pomorze*, Ger. *Pommern*, from Pol. *po-* up to, beside + *morze* the sea).

Dim.: Ger.: **Pommerenke**.

Pomphrey Welsh: patr., with a reduced form of the W element *ap*, from the given name HUMPHREY.

Vars.: **Pomfrey**, **Pomphray**, **Pumphrey(s)**, **Pumphery**, **Pumfray**.

Poncet *see* POINTS

Pond English: topographic name for someone who lived beside a pond or lake, from ME *pond* enclosed expanse of water, especially a man-made one (an altered form of POUND).

Var.: **Ponder**.

Ponomaryov Russian: patr. from the occupational term *ponomar* sexton, churchwarden (from Late Gk *paramonarios*, a deriv. of *paramonē* service, support, from *paramenein* to remain beside, support; the Gk prefix has been replaced by a Slav. one of similar meaning, and the nasals have undergone metathesis).

Dim.: Ukr.: **Ponomarenko** (not patr.).

Ponsford *see* PAUNCEFOOT

Ponsonby English: habitation name from a place in Cumb., so called from the ME nickname, *Puncun*, of a 12th-cent. owner (see POINÇON) + northern ME *by* settlement (ON *býr*).

Pont English, French, and Catalan: topographic name for someone who lived near a bridge, ANF, OF, Cat. *pont* (L *pons*, gen. *pontis*).

Vars.: Fr.: **Depont**, **Dupont**.

Dims.: Eng.: **Pontin(g)**. Fr.: **Pontet**, **Pontel**, **Pontin**, **Pont(ill)on**. It.: **Pontello**, **Pontel(li)**, **Pontillo**, **Pontini**; **Ponticiello**, **Ponticeli** (Naples).

Augs.: It.: **Ponton(i)**.

Pontefract *see* POMFRET

Pook English: nickname from ME *pook, puck* goblin, evil spirit (OE *pūca*; cf. POCKNEY).

Vars.: **Pouck**, **Pooke**.

Pool 1. English: topographic name for someone who lived near a pool or pond, OE *pōl*. 2. English: var. of PAUL. 3. Dutch (largely Jewish): ethnic name for someone from Poland. In the case of the Jewish name, the reference is to a Jew from Poland or from some other Slav.-speaking region; cf. POLAK.

Vars. (of 1): Eng.: **Poole**, **Po(o)lman**.

Pooley English: 1. habitation name from a place so called in Warwicks. No forms of the name are recorded before the 13th cent., when *Povele, Poueleye, Powelee, Pouelee*, and *Poleye* are all found. The second element is OE *lēah* wood, clearing; the first is a word *pofel*, found occasionally in placenames, the meaning of which has not been established. 2. habitation name from *Pooley* Bridge in Cumb., so called from OE *pōl* POOL + ON *haugr* hill, mound.

Poolton *see* POULTON

Poor *see* POWER

Pope English: nickname from the ecclesiastical title for the head of the Roman Catholic Church, ME *pope* (OE *pāpa*, from LL *pāpa* bishop, pope, from Gk *pappas* father, in origin a nursery word; for the change of -*ā*- to -*ō*- cf. ROPER). In the early Christian Church, the L term was at first used as a title of respect for male clergy of every rank, but in the Western Church it gradually came to be restricted to bishops, and then only to the bishop of Rome; in the Eastern Church it continued to be used of all priests (see POPOV). The nickname would have been used for a

vain or pompous man, or for someone who had played the part of the pope in a pageant or play.

Dims.: Ger.: **Pfäffle**, **Pfeffel(in)**. Low Ger.: **Pa(a)pke**, **Päpke**.

Patrs.: Ger.: **Papen**, **Paffen**. Croatian: **Papić**.

Habitation name: Pol.: **Papiewski**.

Popejoy *see* POBGEE

Popham English: habitation name from a place in Hants, so called from an unexplained first element *pop* + OE *hām* homestead.

Popkiss English: of uncertain origin, ostensibly an assimilated form of *Popkins*, from W *ap Hopkin* 'son of *Hopkin*' (see HOBB). It is a rare surname, which has not been traced before the 18th cent. and has always been strongly localized in the Dover area. It is probable that all bearers descend from a certain Peter *Popkes*, who was married at Dover in 1748; it has not been possible to discover anything of his origins.

Var.: **Popkess**.

Popławski Polish: topographic name for someone who lived by a water-meadow, from Pol. *popław* water-meadow + -*ski* suffix of local surnames (see BARANOWSKI).

Popov 1. Russian, Bulgarian, and Croatian: patr. from the occupational term *pop* priest (from Gk *pappas*; see POPE). The name may occasionally derive from a nickname, but celibacy was not enjoined on priests of the Orthodox Church and so the name normally means literally 'son of the priest'. 2. Jewish: of unknown origin, probably an adoption of the Russ. surname.

Vars.: Bulg.: **Papatov**. Croatian: **Pop(ov)ić**.

Dim.: Ukr.: **Popenko**.

Popp 1. German: from a Gmc personal name *Poppo, Boppo*, of uncertain origin and meaning, perhaps originally a nursery word. It was a hereditary given name among the counts of Henneberg and Babenberg in E Frisia between the 9th and 14th cents. 2. Jewish (Ashkenazic): habitation name from either of the cities called *Frankfurt*, on the Main and on the Oder. These are both named from OHG *Frankena furt* FORD of the FRANKS'. In Jewish writings the placename was commonly abbreviated to *Ff* and read as /pop/, since in unpointed Hebr. and Yid. the same letter can be read as /f/ or as /p/.

Vars. (of 1): **Poppe**, **Bopp**, **Bopf**. (Of 2): **Popper**.

Dims. (of 1): Ger.: **Pöpp(e)l**, **Böppel**, **Böpple**. Fris.: **Popkema**. Czech: **Popel(ka)** (the Czech word *Popelka* is the equivalent of Cinderella, being associated with the vocab. word *popel* ashes).

Patrs. (from 1): Ger.: **Popper**. Low Ger.: **Poppen**. Fris.: **Poppinga**.

Patrs. (from 1) (dim.): Low Ger.: **Popken**.

Poppleton English (W Yorks.): habitation name from a place in W Yorks., so called from OE *popel* pebble + *tūn* enclosure, settlement.

Popplewell English (W Yorks.): habitation name from any of several places in W Yorks., for example in the parish of Cleckheaton. The second element is OE *well(a)* spring, stream (see WELL); the first may be *popel* pebble, or a word meaning 'bubbling spring'.

Porcellazzi *see* PURCELL

Porcher English and French: occupational name for a swineherd, ME, OF *porch(i)er* (LL *porcārius*, an agent deriv. of *porcus* pig; cf. PURCELL).
Vars.: Fr.: **Pourcher, Po(u)rquier, Porché, Pourquié, Porchez**.
Dims.: Fr.: **Porcheron**. Prov.: **Pourcheiroux**.

Poreau *see* POIREAU

Porkiss *see* PURCHASE

Porras Spanish and Catalan: nickname for a thickset or belligerent person, from the pl. form of Sp., Cat. *porra* cudgel, club (probably from L *porrum* leek (see POIREAU), because of similarity in shape).

Port 1. English: topographic name for someone who lived near the gates of a town (and in many cases was in charge of them; thus in part a metonymic occupational name equivalent to PORTER 1), from ME *port* gateway, entrance (OF *porte*, from L *porta* door, entrance). 2. English: topographic name for someone who lived near a harbour or in a market town, from the homonymous ME *port* (OE *port* harbour, market town, from L *portus* harbour, haven, reinforced in ME by OF *port*, from the same source). 3. Jewish: of unknown origin.
Vars. (of 1 and 2): **Porte; Portman**.
Dims. (of 1): Sp.: **Portela, Portilla**. Cat.: **Portella**. Port.: **Portela**. (Of 2): Sp.: **Portillo**. Cat.: **Portell**. It.: **Portelli**.

Portail French: topographic name for someone who lived near the gates of a town, or metonymic occupational name for a gatekeeper, from OF *portal* gateway (LL *portāle*, a deriv. of *porta* door, entrance); cf. PORT 1 and PORTER 1.
Var.: **Duportail** (with fused preposition and def. art.).

Portch English: topographic name for someone who lived in a building with a covered entrance, or nickname for a beggar who was in the habit of stationing himself in the porch of a church, from ME *porch* (OF *porche*, LL *porticus*, a deriv. of *porta* door, entrance; cf. PORT 1 and PORTER 1).

Porteous Scots: of uncertain origin, perhaps a topographic name for someone who lived in the lodge at the entrance to a manor house, from ME *port* gateway, entrance (see PORT 1) + *hous* HOUSE.

Porter English: 1. occupational name for the gatekeeper of a town or the door-keeper of a large house, ME *porter* (OF *portier*, LL *portārius*, an agent deriv. of *porta* door, entrance; cf. PORT 1). 2. occupational name for a man who carried loads for a living, esp. one who used his own muscle power rather than a beast of burden or a wheeled vehicle (see CARTER). This sense is from OF *porteo(u)r* (LL *portātor*, from *portāre* to carry, convey).
Dims. (of 1): Fr.: **Portereau, Port(e)ret, Porterot, Port(e)ron**.
Aug. (of 1): Fr.: **Porterat**.
Equivs. (of 1): Prov.: BADIER. Ger.: DÜRER, GITTER.

Portingale *see* PETTINGELL

Portnov Russian and Jewish (Ashkenazic): patr. from the occupational term *portnoi* tailor (an adj. deriv. of *port* uncut cloth).
Vars.: Russ.: **Portnyakov, Portnyagin**. Jewish: **Portnoi, Portnoy, Portnoj** (not patrs.)

Portwin *see* POTVIN

Poruchikov Russian: patr. from the occupational term *poruchik* lieutenant, deputy, steward (from *poruchit* to hand over, entrust, from *ruka* hand).

Posada Spanish: metonymic occupational name for an innkeeper or for someone who worked at an inn, from Sp. *posada* inn (a deriv. of *posar* to rest, stay, LL *pausāre*, from Gk).

Poser *see* PEYZER

Posner *see* POZNAŃSKI

Pospíšil Czech: nickname for a busy or active individual, from Czech *pospíšit* to be in a hurry.

Poss *see* PETER

Post 1. Low German: topographic name for someone who lived near a post or pole (MLG *post*, from L *postis*), presumably one of some significance, e.g. serving as a landmark or boundary. 2. Jewish: of unknown origin.
Dim. (of 1): Ger.: **Pföstl**.

Poste French: apparently a topographic name from OF *poste* post, pole (L *postis*; see POST). However, the word in Fr. was used also of the pillory, and so the surname may in part be a metonymic occupational name for the official in charge of overseeing the punishment, or a nickname for someone who had frequently suffered it.
Dims.: **Po(s)tel, Po(s)teau, Pouteau**.

Postgate English (Yorks.): habitation name from a place in N Yorks., so called from northern ME *post(e)* post, pole (from OF; see POSTE) + *gate* road (ON *gata*), i.e. a road marked by posts.
Vars.: **Posgate, Poskett, Poskitt**.

Postigo Spanish: topographic name for someone who lived by a minor opening in the walls of a city, as opposed to the main gateway, from Sp. *postigo* postern gate (LL *postīcum*, a deriv. of *post* behind).

Postle English: nickname from an aphetic form of ME *apostel* apostle (OE *apostol*, via L from Gk *apostolos* messenger, delegate, from *apostellein* to dispatch). The nickname may have been used for someone who had played the part of one of the twelve apostles in a play or pageant, or for a particularly zealous Christian. The word seems also to have been occasionally used as a personal name; cf. POSTLETHWAITE.
Vars.: **Post(h)ill, Possell**.

Postlethwaite English: habitation name from a minor place in the parish of Millom, Cumb. The name is not recorded until the 13th cent. The first element is probably from ME *apostel* apostle, used as a nickname or personal name (see POSTLE). Alternatively, it may represent a survival of an OE personal name, *Possel*. The second element is northern ME *thwaite* clearing (ON *þveit*; see THWAITE).
Vars.: **Posselwhite, Posnett(e)**.

Poteau *see* POSTE

Potiphar *see* PETTIFER

Potocki Polish and Jewish (E Ashkenazic): topographic name for someone who lived by a brook or stream, from Pol., Czech *potok* stream.

Var.: Jewish: **Potok**.

Pott English: **1.** from a medieval given name, an aphetic form of PHILPOTT. **2.** topographic name for someone who lived by a depression in the ground, from ME *pot* (cf. POTTER) used in this transferred sense, or habitation name from one of the minor places deriving their name from this element.

Dims. (of 1): **Potkin**; **Pottle**, **Potell**.

Patr. (from 1): **Potts**.

Patr. (from 1) (dim.): **Potkins**.

'Servant of P. 1': **Pot(is)man**.

Potter English: occupational name for a maker of drinking and storage vessels, from an agent deriv. of ME *pot* (OE *pott*, from LL *pottus* (perhaps an altered form of *pōtus* drink, draught), reinforced by OF *pot* from the same source). In the Middle Ages the term covered workers in metal as well as earthenware and clay.

Dim.: Fr.: **Poterot**.

Equivs. (not cogns.): Sp.: CANTARERO. It.: VASARI. Ger. and Jewish (Ashkenazic): HAFNER, KACHLER, TÖPFER, EULER. Russ.: GONCHAROV. Pol.: ZDUNIAK.

Potterall *see* PUTTERILL

Pottinger English: occupational name for a maker or seller of potage, a thick soup or stew. The name represents ME, OF *potagier* (an agent n. from *potage*, a deriv. of *pot*; see POTTER). For the intrusive -*n*-, cf. MESSENGER and PASSENGER.

Var.: **Pottage**.

Pottock *see* PUTTOCK

Potton English: habitation name from a place in Beds., so called from OE *pott* pot + *tūn* enclosure, settlement. The significance of the first element is not clear; this may have been a place where pots were made, or the word may have been used in a topographical sense of a hollow depression.

Potvin English: regional name from OF *Poitevin*, denoting someone from *Poitou* in W France, so called from L *Pictāvum*, the region of the *Pictāvi* or *Pictōnes*. The name of this Gaul. tribe was probably cogn. with, if not identical to, that of the Brit. *Picts*, but the meaning is unknown.

Vars.: **(Le) Poidevin**, **Le Poideven**, **Pod(e)vin**, **Patvine**, **Potwin**, **Portwin(e)**, **Putwaine**, **Puddifin**, **Puddifant**, **Puttifent**.

Potyomkin Russian: patr. from the nickname *Potyomki* 'Darkness', 'Nightfall' (from *tyomni* dark), which was probably originally given for some anecdotal reason.

Pötzold *see* PETER

Pou **1.** French: nickname from OF *poiul* louse, flea (LL *pediculus, peduculus*, a dim. of class. L *pedis*), denoting a small or despised person, or someone who was infested with lice or fleas. **2.** Catalan: cogn. of PUITS.

Vars. (of 1): **P(ed)oux**, **Pezout**; **Pouilleux**. (Of 2): **Pous**.

Dims. (of 1): **Pouillet**, **Pouillot**, **Poillon**.

Pejs. (of 1): **Pouillard**, **Pouillaud**.

Pouch *see* POKE

Poueigh *see* PUY

Poule French: metonymic occupational name for a breeder of chickens or nickname for a timorous person, from OF *poule* chicken (LL *pulla (avis)* young bird; cf. PULLEN).

Vars.: **Poul(le)**.

Dims.: Fr.: **Poulin**, **Poul(l)et**, **Poul(l)ot**, **Poul(e)teau**. It.: **Pollini**; **Puddinu** (Sardinia).

Augs.: Fr.: **Poulat**, **Poulas**. It.: **Polloni**.

Pejs.: Fr.: **Poulard**, **Poulastre**.

Poulsen *see* PAUL

Poulton English: habitation name from any of the various places, for example in Ches., Gloucs., Kent, and Lancs., so called from OE *pōl* POOL + *tūn* enclosure, settlement.

Var.: **Poolton**.

Pound English: topographic name for someone who lived near an enclosure in which animals were kept, ME *p(o)und* (of uncertain, presumably native, origin; cf. PENFOLD), or metonymic occupational name for an official responsible for rounding up stray animals and placing them in a pound.

Vars.: **Pounds**, **Pund**; **Pounder**, **Poynder**.

Pountney English: habitation name from a place in Leics. now known as *Poultney*, but recorded in Domesday Book as *Pontenei*. The Domesday form shows the common Norman French substitution of -*n*- for OE -*l*-. The placename derives from the gen. case of the OE personal name *Pulta* + OE *ēg* island.

Vars.: **Poul(t)ney**, **Pulteney**.

Pourcheiroux *see* PORCHER

Poureau *see* POIREAU

Poussin French: nickname from OF *poussin* chick (LL *pullicīnus*, a deriv. of *pullus*; cf. POULE and PULLEN), apparently denoting a small man.

Var.: **Pouchin**.

Dims.: **Pous(s)ineau**, **Pouzinot**, **Poussinet**.

Pouteau *see* POSTE

Pouter *see* PEUTHERER

Poutrel *see* PUTTERILL

Pouvereau *see* POWER

Pouzet *see* PUITS

Povarov Russian: patr. from the occupational term *povar* cook (from *povarit* to cook, boil).

Poveda Spanish: topographic name for someone who lived near a grove of poplars, OSp. *poveda*, a collective of *povo, pobo* (white) poplar (LL *pōpus*, a back-formation from class. L *populus*, taken as a dim.). There are also several places named with this word, and they may have contributed to the surname.

Poverelli *see* POWER

Povey English: of uncertain origin; according to Smith it is a nickname deriving from a dial. term for the owl. The name is most common in London and Birmingham, with a smaller concentration in Bristol.

Povlsen *see* PAUL

Powderill *see* PUTTERILL

Powe English: **1.** nickname from ME *pō* PEACOCK. **2.** Welsh: patr., with a reduced form of the W element *ap*, from the given name HOWE, a var. of HUGH.

Var.: **Pow** (chiefly Scots.).

Poweleit *see* PAUL

Powell 1. Welsh: patr., with a reduced form of the W element *ap*, from the given name *Hywel* (see HOWELL). **2.** English: var. of PAUL.

Vars. (of 1): **Powles**; BOWELL.

Power 1. English and Irish (Norman): habitation name from OF *Pohier* native of *Pois*, a town in Picardy, apparently so called from OF *pois* fish (cf. PESCE) because of its well-stocked rivers. **2.** English: nickname for a poor man, or ironically for a miser, from ME, OF *povre, poure* poor (L *pauper*).

Vars.: **Powers**; **Poor(e)**.

Dims. (of 2): Fr.: **Pouv(e)reau**. It.: **Poverelli**.

Pownall English: habitation name from a place in Ches., first recorded in the 12th cent. as *Pohenhale*, from the gen. case of the OE personal name *Pohha* + OE *halh* nook, recess (see HALE 1).

Var.: **Powney**.

Powter *see* PEUTHERER

Poxon *see* POGGS

Poy *see* PUY

Poynder *see* POUND

Poyner 1. English (Norman): nickname for someone who was handy with his fists, from OF *poigneor* fighter (L *pugnātor*, from *pugnāre* to fight, a deriv. of *pugnus* fist). **2.** Welsh: Anglicized form of the patr. phrase *ab Ynyr* son (W *ab, ap*) of *Ynyr* (a personal name, apparently from L *Honorius*; cf. HONORÉ).

Vars. (of 1): **Poynor**, **Punyer**. (Of 2): **Bonner**, **Bunner**.

Poynter *see* POINTER

Poynton *see* POINTON

Poyntz *see* POINTS

Poyser *see* PEYZER

Poyssenot *see* PESCE

Pozetti *see* PUITS

Poznański Polish and Jewish (Ashkenazic): habitation name from the city of *Poznań* (Ger. *Posen*) in W central Poland, + *-ski* suffix of local surnames (see BARANOWSKI). The name of the city is said to be derived from the verb *poznać się* to get to know someone, and is associated with the story of the meeting of the Polish king Bolesław Chrobry and the German emperor Otto III at the funeral of St Wojciech in the 11th cent.

Vars.: Jewish: **Posner**; PEVZNER.

Pozzoli *see* PUY

Prack *see* BRACK

Pradeau *see* PRÉ

Praetorius German: Latinized form of various surnames meaning 'leader' or 'headman', e.g. MAYER and SCHULTZ; it is a deriv. of L *praetor*, the title of various officials in republican and imperial Rome (probably a contracted form of *praeitor*, from *praeire* to go before).

Var.: **Pretorius**.

Prager Jewish (Ashkenazic) and German: habitation name from the city of Prague (Ger. *Prag*, Czech *Praha*), the capital of Czechoslovakia. The name may also have been applied to or taken by someone who came from elsewhere in Bohemia, the name of the nearest large town being preferred to a more precise local designation. It is possible that in some cases the name may derive from *Praga* on the Vistula opposite Warsaw, known in Yid. as *Prage*.

Vars.: Jewish: **Pragerman**; **Proger** (from the Yid. name of the Bohemian city, *Prog*); **Van Praag(h)** (among Jews in Holland).

Prais *see* PREUSS

Prakepyonok *see* PROKOP

Prandin *see* BRAND

Prášek Czech: occupational nickname for a miller's apprentice, from Czech *prášek* dust, flour (a dim. of *prach* powder, cogn. with Pol. *proch*; cf. PROCHOWNIK).

Prata 1. Italian: cogn. of PRÉ. **2.** Portuguese: metonymic occupational name for a worker in silver, Port. *prata* (LL *plata* sheet metal, apparently from *plat(t)us* flat, from Gk; cf. PLATT).

Var. (of 2): **Pratas**.

Pratt English: nickname for a clever trickster, from OE *prætt* trick, which is found in use as a byname in the 11th cent. ME *pratt(e)* is not recorded as a vocab. word until the 15th cent.

Dims.: **Pratten**, **Pratlett**.

Praundl *see* BROWN

Pray *see* O'PREY

Prazeres Portuguese: religious byname, from Port. *prazeres* joys (from L *placēre* to please, delight); the reference is to the Seven Joys of the Blessed Virgin (cf. DORES for the complement).

Prchal Czech: nickname for a fugitive or deserter, Czech *prchal*, from *prchat* to run away.

Dim.: **Prchlík**.

Pré French: topographic name for someone who lived near a meadow, OF *pred* (L *prātum*; the fem. forms are from LL *prāta*, originally the pl. of this word), or habitation name from any of the numerous minor places named with this word.

Vars.: **Prée**, **Prey**, **Prez**; **Laprée**, **Lapraye**; **Dupré**, **Després**, **Desprez**.

Dims.: Fr.: **Préau(x)**, **Pr(é)el**. Prov.: **Pradeau(x)**, **Pradel(le)**, **(De) Lapradelle**, **Pradine**, **Prad(ill)on**, **Pradoux**. It.: **Pratelli**, **Pratella**, **Pradel(la)**, **Pradetto**, **Pratolini**, **Pradolin**. Sp.: **Pradillo**.

Prebble English (chiefly Kent): of uncertain origin. It may be a habitation name from a Norman place named with the elements PRÉ + VILLE, but this theory has not been supported by evidence in the shape of early forms.

Vars.: **Preble**, **Pribul**.

Precious English (mainly Yorks. and Norfolk): nickname for a valued member of the community (perhaps sometimes used ironically), from ME, OF *precios* (LL *pretiōsus*, a deriv. of *pretium* price, prize). It may also derive from a medieval female given name, originally an affectionate nickname.

Var.: **Pretious**.

Predda see PEAR

Preece see PRICE

Preedy Welsh: **1.** occupational name for a bard, W *prydudd*. **2.** from the personal name *Predyr*, *Peredur*, which was borne, in Arthurian legend, by one of the knights of the Round Table; see also PERCIVAL.

Var.: **Pridd(e)y**, **Preddy**.

Preis see PREUSS

Preist see PRIEST

Premack see PRIMAK

Prendergast English: of uncertain origin; said by its bearers to be the name of Flemish settlers in Normandy, who took their name from a lost place, *Brontegeest* (*Prentagast*) in Flanders near Ghent.

Vars.: **Pendergast**, **P(r)endegast**, **P(r)end(er)grast**, **Prendergrass**, **Prendeguest**, **Prendergat**.

Prentice 1. English and (esp.) Scots: nickname from an aphetic form of ME, OF *aprentis* apprentice (from OF *aprendre* to learn, understand, L *appre(he)ndere* to understand, grasp). **2.** Irish: Anglicized form of *Ó Pronntaigh*; see PRUNTY.

Vars. (of 1): **Prentis(s)**.

Prescott English: habitation name from any of the places so called, in SW Lancs. (now Merseyside), Gloucs., Oxon., and Shrops. (two), all of which are named from OE *prēost* PRIEST + *cot* cottage, dwelling (see COATES). The surname is most common in N England, and so it seems likely that the first of these places is the most frequent source.

Vars.: **Prescot**, **Priscott**, **Preskett**, **Prescod**.

Presland English: topographic name for someone who farmed land held by the Church, from OE *prēost* PRIEST + *land* land.

Vars.: **Pressland**, **Priestland**.

Presley see PRIESTLEY

Preston N English: habitation name from any of the extremely numerous places (most notably one in Lancs.) so called from OE *prēost* PRIEST + *tūn* enclosure, settlement; the meaning may have been either 'village with a priest' or 'village held by the Church'.

Prestwich English: habitation name from places in Lancs. (now Greater Manchester) and Northumb., so called from OE *prēost* PRIEST + *wīc* outlying settlement (see WICK). Cf. PRESTON.

Var.: **Prestige**.

Pretheroe see PROTHEROE

Pretorius see PRAETORIUS

Pretty English (chiefly E Anglia): nickname for a fine or handsome fellow, from ME *prety*, *prity* fine, pleasing, excellent (OE *prættig* clever, artful, wily, from *prætt* trick; see PRATT).

Vars.: **Pritty**; **Pret(t)yman** (E Anglia).

Preuss German and Jewish (Ashkenazic): regional name for someone from Prussia (Ger. *Preussen*), a former state of N Germany, so called from the tribal name of the *Prūsen*, a Baltic tribe displaced by the Germans during the 13th cent. Their name is of unknown origin, although it has been suggested that it may be connected with that of the Frisians (see FRIES).

Vars.: Ger.: **Preussner**, **Preussler**; **Preiss(ner)**, **Preissler** (S Germany); **Prutz** (E Germany). Jewish: **Preiss(s)**, **Prais(s)**, **Preiser**, **Preissler**, **Preissman** (from Yid. *Prays* Prussia, or from a S Ger. pronunciation of *Preuss*); PRICE (Anglicized).

Patr.: Jewish: **Preiserowicz** (E Ashkenazic).

Habitation names: Pol.: **Prusz(cz)yński**.

Preux French: nickname for a much admired man, perhaps also sometimes given in a spirit of irony, from OF *proz* good, excellent (LL *prodis*, a back-formation from the impersonal verb *prodesse* to be (to the) good; the verb is in fact a cpd of *pro-* for, advantageous + *esse* to be, with epenthetic *-d-*, but was reinterpreted as a contraction of *prode esse*, from which the masc. form of the adj. was derived).

Vars.: **Lepreux**, **Prou(x)**, **Leproux**.

Prevedel see PRIEST

Prevel see PEPPER

Prevost French: occupational name for any of various officials in a position of responsibility, from OF *prevost* (L *praepositus*, past part. of *praeponere* to place in charge).

Vars.: **Prévost**, **Prévôt**, **Le Prevost**.

Dims.: **Prévostel**, **Prévo(s)teau**, **Prévotet**.

Prew see PROWSE

Prey see O'PREY

Pribul see PREBBLE

Price 1. Welsh: one of the commonest of W surnames, a patr., with a reduced form of the W element *ap*, from the given name RHYS. **2.** English: the name is also found very early in parts of England far removed from Welsh influence (e.g. Richard *Prys*, Essex 1320), and in such cases presumably derives from ME, OF *pris* price, prize (L *pretium*; cf. PRECIOUS). **3.** Jewish (Ashkenazic): Anglicized form of any of the Jewish surnames listed at PREUSS.

Vars.: **Pryce**. (Of 1 only): **Preece**.

Prickett see PRYKE

Priddey see PREEDY

Prideaux Cornish: habitation name from a place in the parish of Luxulyan, which is first recorded in the 12th and 13th cents. in the form *Pridias*, perhaps from Corn. *prȳ* clay + an unknown word. Later forms of the placename, and hence the surname, show the results of folk etymological assimilation to Fr. *près d'eaux* 'near waters' or *pré d'eaux* 'meadow of waters'.

Var.: **Priday**.

Pridham English (Norman): nickname from OF *prud'-homme* wise, sensible man, a cliché term of approbation from the chivalric romances. It is a cpd of OF *proz, prod* good (cf. PREUX), with the vowel influenced by crossing with *prudent* wise (L *prūdens*, gen. *prūdentis*, from *providēre* to foresee) + *homme* man (L *homo*, gen. *hominis*).

Vars.: **Prodham**, **Prudham**, **Prudhomme**; **Purdham**, **Purdom**, **Purdon** (metathesized forms).

Dim.: Fr.: **Prudhommeau**.

Prier *see* PRIOR

Priest English: nickname from ME *pr(i)est* minister of the Church (OE *prēost*, from L *presbyter*, Gk *presbyteros* elder, counsellor, cpd of *presbys* old man). It may also have been an occupational name for someone in the service of a priest, and occasionally it may have been used to denote someone suspected of being the son of a priest.

Vars.: **Preist**, **Prest(t)**, **Press**, **Prust**; **Prester**, **Presser** (from OF forms).

Dims.: It.: **Privitelli**; **Prevedel(lo)** (Venetia); **Prestino**.

Patrs.: It.: **Del Prete**, **De Pretis**.

'Servant of the p.': Eng.: **Priestman**; **Pres(s)man** (also Jewish, of unknown origin).

Priestley English: habitation name from any of the various minor places so called, especially the one in N Yorks. These are named from OE *prēost* PRIEST + *lēah* wood, clearing, i.e. a wood or clearing belonging to the Church.

Vars.: **Priestly**, **Pressl(e)y**, **Presley**, **Presslee**, **Presslie**, **Prisley**.

Prieto Spanish: nickname for a dark-haired or dark-skinned man, from OSp. *prieto* dark, black (from the verb *apretar* to squeeze, compress, a metathesized form of *apetrar*, LL *appectorāre* to hold close to the chest (from *pectus*, gen. *pectoris*, chest)). The use as a colour term seems to have derived originally from its application to rain-clouds and fog.

Primak Jewish (E Ashkenazic): from Slavic *primak* adopted member of a family. The exact application of the name is unclear. It could have been taken by or given to an adopted child or by a married student of Jewish law, supported, following Jewish tradition, by his father-in-law so that he would be free to devote all his time to his studies.

Vars.: **Primack**, **Prema(c)k**.

Prime English: from a ME personal name or nickname. The personal name existed in OE, and is probably derived from OE *prim* early morning (from L *prīmus* first, used as the name of one of the canonical hours). A possible source of the word as an ME nickname is ME, OF *prim(e)* fine, excellent (L *prīmus* first, best).

Vars.: **Prin(n)**, **Pring**, **Prinne**, **Prynn(e)**.

Primrose Scots: habitation name from a place in the parish of Dunfermline, so called from Brit. equivalents of W *pren* tree + *rhos* moor, later altered by folk etymological association with the name of the flower (LL *prima rosa* first(-flowering) rose).

Var.: **Primerose**.

Primrose

Prin *see* PERRIN

Prince 1. English and French: nickname from ME, OF *prince* (L *princeps*, gen. *principis*, from *prīmus* first + *capere* to take), presumably denoting someone who behaved in a regal manner or who had won the title in some contest of skill. 2. Jewish (Ashkenazic): Anglicized form of the ornamental name *Prinz* (see below; compare GRAF, BARON, HERZOG, KAISER, etc.).

Vars.: Eng.: **Prins**. Fr.: **Leprince**.

Patr.: It.: **Del Principe**. Flem., Du.: **Prinsen**, **Prinzen**.

Pringle Scots and English (Northumb.): habitation name from a place near Stow in the former county of Roxburghs., formerly called *Hop(p)ringle*, from ME *hop* enclosed valley (see HOPE) + a name of ON origin composed of the byname *Prjónn* 'Pin', 'Peg' + *gil* narrow valley, ravine (see GILL 2).

Prior English: nickname or occupational name from ME *prior* prior, a monastic official immediately subordinate to an abbot (OE *prior*, from L *prior* superior, reinforced by OF *pri(o)ur* from the same source). The surname probably most often originated as an occupational name for a servant of a prior.

Vars.: **Prier**, **Pryer**, **Pryor**.

Priscott *see* PRESCOTT

Prisley *see* PRIESTLEY

Pritchard Welsh: patr., with a reduced form of the W element *ap*, from the given name RICHARD.

Var.: **Prichard**.

Pritchatt *see* PRYKE

Pritty *see* PRETTY

Privat French: from the given name (L *Prīvātus* 'Secluded', 'Withdrawn', from the past part. of *prīvāre* to deprive) borne by a 3rd-cent. saint and martyr, bishop of Mende, as well as various other early saints.

Vars.: **Privé**, **Privey**, **Privez**.

Privett English: habitation name from a place in Hants, which seems to get its name from an OE word *pryfet* privet copse. This element is thought to occur in other placenames, including *Privett* Farm in Standlynch, Wilts., which may also be a partial source of the surname, but the vocab. word for the shrub is not recorded before the 16th cent.

Privitelli *see* PRIEST

Probert Welsh: patr., with a reduced form of the W element *ap*, from the given name ROBERT.

Probin *see* ROBIN

Procházka Czech: occupational name for an itinerant tradesman, especially a travelling butcher, literally a 'walker', from a deriv. of Czech *procházet* to walk, stroll, saunter. It could also be a nickname for an idle person, from the same word in the sense of one who sauntered idly from place to place. This is one of the most common Czech surnames.

Prochownik Polish and Jewish (E Ashkenazic): occupational name for a manufacturer of or trader in any type of powder, especially gunpowder, from an agent deriv. of *proch* powder.

Var.: Pol.: **Prochowski**.

Proctor English (most common in the north): occupational name for a steward, ME *prok(e)tour* (contracted from OF *procurateour*, L *prōcūrātor* agent, from *prōcūrāre* to manage, a cpd of *prō* for, on behalf of + *cūrāre* to deal with). The term was used most commonly of an attorney in a spiritual court, but also of other officials such as collectors of taxes and agents licensed to collect alms on behalf of lepers and enclosed orders of monks.

Vars.: **Procktor**, **Proc(k)ter**.

Prodda see PEAR

Prodham see PRIDHAM

Profumo Italian (Liguria): metonymic occupational name for a maker or seller of scents and aromatic oils, from It. *profumo* perfume (from *perfumare* to perfume, L *perfūmāre* to smoke through, with change of prefix). The name may also have been a nickname for someone who made liberal use of perfume, or ironically for someone who was exceptionally evil-smelling even by medieval standards. It was also used as an affectionate familiar name, since perfume was very precious in the Middle Ages.

Proger see PRAGER

Proietto Italian: nickname given to a foundling, from It. *proietto* rejected, abandoned (L *prōiectus*, past part. of *prōicere* to cast forth). The surname is found mainly in Rome, and is still relatively frequent, in spite of its transparently unfavourable meaning. Cf. ESPOSITO.

Var.: **Proietti**.

Prokhorov Russian: patr. from the given name *Prokhor* (Gk *Prokhoros*, from *pro* before, in front + *khorein* to dance, sing). This is the name supposedly borne by a 1st-cent. saint ordained by the apostles, who is said to have subsequently become bishop of Nicomedia and been martyred at Antioch.

Dims.: Russ.: See at PROKOP. Beloruss.: **Prokhorchik** (not patr.).

'Son of the wife of P.': Russ.: **Prokhorikhin**.

Prokop Czech, Polish, Ukrainian, and Belorussian: from the given name *Prokop* (Gk *Prokopios*, from *pro* before, in front + *kopē* cut; i.e. 'Pioneer'). This was the name of the first victim of Diocletian's persecutions in Palestine in AD 303. He was greatly venerated in the Orthodox Church, whence the popularity of the Russ. given name *Prokofi* (a hypercorrected version of the Gk name, since Russian *p* was often used for Gk *ph*; cf. STEPHEN). The popularity of the name in central Europe is largely due to a later St *Prokop*, the patron saint of Bohemia, who founded the Sazaba abbey in Prague in the 11th cent.

Dims.: Czech: **Prokůpek**; **Průcha**, **Průša**; **Prokoš**, **Prokeš**, **Prošek**. Pol.: **Prokopczyk**. Beloruss.: **Prokopchik**,

Prakepyonok. Ger. (of Slav. origin): **Prok(i)sch**, **Prox**; **Broksch**, **Bruck(i)sch**, **Brox**.
Aug.: Czech: **Prokopec**.
Patrs.: Ukr., Beloruss.: **Prokopovich**. Russ.: **Prokofyev**. Bulg.: **Prokofiev**.
Patrs. (from dims.): Russ.: **Prokoshkin**, **Prokoshev**, **Prokonov**, **Prokunin**, **Prokhnov**; **Pron(yak)ov**, **Pron(k)in**, **Pronichkin**, **Pronyaev**, **Pronchishchev**, **Pronichev**, **Proshchin** (shared with PROKHOROV). Croatian: **Prokić**, **Kopčić**.

Pron see PIERRE

Pronk Dutch: nickname for an ostentatious dresser, from MDu. *prunk, pronk* finery, show, display.

Pronty see PRUNTY

Proom English: of uncertain origin, perhaps an importation, via the Low Countries, of a habitation name derived from *Prüm* near Trier in Germany.

Var.: **Proome** (a 20th-cent. alteration).

Proschek see AMBROSE

Prosser Welsh: patr., with a reduced form of the W element *ap*, from the given name *Rhosier*, the W form of ROGER.

Protais French: from the OF given name *Protais* (from Gk *Protāsios*, a deriv. of *Protās*, a short form of various cpd personal names with the first element *prōtos* first). This was the name of a 1st-cent. saint martyred together with his brother Gervasius (see JARVIS 1), as well as of a 4th-cent. bishop of Milan and a 6th-cent. bishop of Avence.

Vars.: **Prothais**, **Protas**, **Protat**.
Dims.: **Proteau(x)**, **Protet**, **Prothin**, **Prothon**.

Protheroe Welsh: patr., with a reduced form of the W element *ap*, from the given name *Rhydderch* (see RODERICK 2).

Vars.: **Prothero**, **Protherough**, **Pretheroe**; **Prydderch**, **Prytherch**, **Prytherick**; **Plutheroe**.

Protopopov Russian: patr. from the occupational term *protopop* arch-priest (Late Gk *prōtopappas*, from *prōtos* first + *pappas* priest; cf. POPE and POPOV).

Prou see PREUX

Proud English (chiefly Northumb.): nickname for a vain or haughty man, from ME *prod, prud* proud (late OE *prūd*, from the oblique form of OF *proz*; see PREUX and PRIDHAM).

Vars.: **Proude**; **Prout** (Cornwall).

Proudfoot Scots and English: nickname for someone with a haughty gait, from ME *prod, prud* PROUD + *fote* FOOT.

Provan Scots: habitation name from a place near Glasgow, so called from ME *provend, prebend* land providing revenue for a holder of religious office (OF *probende, prebende*, LL *praebenda* supplies, things to be supplied, from the neut. pl. form of the gerundive of *praebēre* to provide, furnish; for the alteration in the prefix, cf. PROVOST). The place was formerly held by the prebendary of Barlanark, one of the canons of Glasgow cathedral.

Vars.: **Provand**, **Proven**.

Provazník Czech: occupational name for a rope-maker, from Czech *provaz* rope + *-ník* suffix of agent nouns.

Province English: regional name for someone from *Provence* in S France, which is so called from L *prōvincia* province, sphere of office, because it was the first Roman province to be established outside Italy.
Var.: **Provins**.

Provost English: occupational name for the head of a religious chapter or educational establishment, or, since such officials were usually clergy and celibate, a nickname for a self-important person who behaved like a headmaster. The ME word *provost* (OE *profost*, reinforced by OF *provost*) is from L *prōpositus*, a byform of *praepositus* (see PREVOST).
Vars.: **Provest**, **Provis**, **Proust**.

Prowse English: nickname for a redoubtable warrior, from ME *prou(s)* brave, valiant (OE *proux*, *preux*; see PREUX).
Vars.: **Prouse**, **Prewse**, **Pruce**; **Prow**, **Prew**, **Prue**.
Dims.: **Prewett**, **Pruett**, **Pruitt**.

Prozillo see PETER

Prucci see PETER

Pruce see PROWSE

Průcha see PROKOP

Prudham see PRIDHAM

Prudhoe English: habitation name from a place in Northumb., so called from the late OE byname *Prūda* (from *prūd* PROUD) + OE *hōh* ridge (see HOE).

Pruen English: of uncertain origin, probably Dutch or Flemish.
Vars.: **Pruin**, **Pruyn**.

Pruneau see PLUM

Prunner see BOURNE

Prunty Irish: Anglicized form of Gael. **Ó Proinntigh** 'descendant of *Proinnteach*', a personal name meaning 'Bestower' (originally a byname denoting a generous person).
Vars.: **Pronty**, **Brunty**, **Brontë**, PRENTICE.

Prust see PRIEST

Pruszczyński see PREUSS

Pryce see PRICE

Prydderch see PROTHEROE

Pryde English and Scots: nickname from ME *pryde*, *pride* (late OE *prȳde*, a deriv. of *prūd* PROUD), denoting an arrogant man, or referring to someone who had played the part of this personified vice in a pageant of the Seven Deadly Sins. **2.** Welsh: nickname from *prid* precious, dear.

Pryer see PRIOR

Pryke English: metonymic occupational name for a maker or user of any of various pointed instruments, or nickname for a tall, thin man, from ME *prik(e)*, *prich* point, prick (OE *pric(a)*).
Dims.: **Prickett**, **Pritchet(t)**, **Pritchatt**.

Prynn see PRIME

Przybysz Polish: nickname for someone who had recently arrived in a district, from Pol. *przybysz* newcomer. Cf. NEWMAN, NOVÁK.
Vars.: **Przbył(a)**, **Przybyłak**; **Przybylski** (a common Pol. name, said by Bystroń to have been frequently given to foundlings).
Dim.: Pol.: **Przybyłek**.
Habitation names: Pol.: **Przybyłowski**, **Przybyszewski**.

Przygoda Polish: apparently a nickname from Pol. *przygoda* adventure, although the application is not clear. It probably refers to some now forgotten incident, but may have been used for an adventurous individual.
Vars.: **Przygodzki**, **Przygocki**.

Przykowicz see KASPAR

Pschorr S German: nickname for a person with close-cropped hair, from MHG *beschorner* shorn, strong form of the past part. of *(be)schern* to shear. In the Middle Ages this would have indicated lowly status, for only free men had the right to wear their hair long; cf. TOUS.
Vars.: **Pschorn**, **Beschor(e)n**, **Beschorner**.

Ptáčník Czech: occupational name for a fowler, from Czech *pták* bird + *-ník* suffix of agent nouns.

Pták Czech: nickname for a small, light person, from Czech *pták* bird.
Dim.: Czech: **Ptáček**.

Ptaszyński Polish: habitation name from a place named *Ptaszyn*, from Pol. *ptak* bird, or alternatively from a place where someone nicknamed *Ptaszek* 'Little Bird' lived. The nickname has the additional sense 'Cunning Rogue'.
Var.: **Ptasiński**.

Puccini Italian: aphetic form of a double dim. of any of various given names with the final consonant *p*, as for example *Filippo* (see PHILIP), *Giuseppe* (see JOSEPH), and *Iacopo* (see JACOB).

Puch see PUY

Puchner see BUCH

Puddephat English: nickname for someone compared in shape to a round barrel, from ME PUDDY round-bellied + *fat* vat.
Vars.: **Pudephat**, **Puddefoot**, **Pud(d)ifoot**, **Puttifoot**.

Puddifant see POTVIN

Puddifer see PETTIFER

Puddinu see POULE

Puddy English: nickname for a rotund person, from ME *puddy* round-bellied (of uncertain immediate origin, but evidently akin to the Gmc element *pud-* to swell, bulge).

Pudge see PUGH

Puebla Spanish: habitation name from any of the many places in Spain so called, from OSp. *puebla* village, settlement (a deriv. of *poblar* to settle, populate, LL *populāre*, from *populus* people). The term was applied to a variety of deliberate settlements and resettlements, including those established in border areas or set up by foreigners or Jews.

Puech *see* PUY

Puey Catalan: nickname for a young person, or the younger of two bearers of the same given name, from Cat. *puey* boy (LL *puellus*, a dim. of class. L *puer*).

Pugachyov Russian: patr. from the nickname *Pugach* 'Owl' (of imitative origin, or from *pugat* to frighten, alarm).

Puget *see* PUY

Pugh Welsh: patr., with a reduced form of the W element *ap*, from the given name HUGH.
Vars.: **Pughe**, **Pudge**, **Pew**, POWE, PYE.

Pugmire English: habitation name from a lost place in Yardley, E Birmingham, recorded in 1645 as *Puggmyre* Farm. This derives from the name of its 13th-cent. landlord, Robert *Pugg*, whose surname is of unknown etymology + ME *myre* mire, bog.

Puig *see* PUY

Puits French: topographic name for someone who lived by a well, OF *puts* (L *puteus* well, pit).
Vars.: **Puis**, **Dupui(t)s**.
Dims.: Prov.: **Pouzet**, **Pouzin**, **Pouzol**. It.: **Pozetti**, **Pozetto** (also nicknames for a pock-marked man); **Pozzoli**, **Pozzolo** (see also PUY); **Puzzolo**, **Puzzulu** (Sardinia). Sp.: **Pozuelo**.

Pujadas Catalan: topographic name for someone who lived on a piece of rising ground, Cat. *pujada* (a deriv. of *puig*; see PUY).

Pujol *see* PUY

Pulford English: habitation name from a place in Ches., so called from OE *pōl* POOL + *ford* FORD.

Pulham English: habitation name from places in Dorset and Norfolk, so called from OE *pōl* POOL + *hām* homestead.

Pulke *see* POLK

Pullen English: metonymic occupational name for a horse-breeder or nickname for a frisky person, from OF *poulain* colt (LL *pullāmen*, a deriv. of *pullus* young animal; cf. POULE).
Vars.: **Pullein(e)**, **Pulleyn**, **Pullin**, **Pullan**.

Puller *see* PILL

Pulleyblank *see* POLYBLANK

Pulteney *see* POUNTNEY

Pulver German and Jewish (Ashkenazic): metonymic occupational name for an apothecary who dispensed various types of medicinal powder, from Ger. *Pulver* powder (LL *pulver*, for class. L *pulvis*, gen. *pulveris*). From the 15th cent. it may also have been used of a manufacturer of gunpowder.
Var.: **Pulvermacher**.

Pulvertaft Irish: of uncertain origin, possibly a var. of the extinct Lincs. surname *Pulvertoft*, which may have been a habitation name from some lost place. *Pulver* is probably an old stream name, preserved also in *Pulverbatch*, Shrops., derived from ON *puldra* to gush; *-toft* is a common N English placename element, from ON *topt* homestead, although in the earliest known instance of the surname the second element seems to be CROFT.

Pumfray *see* POMPHREY

Pumfrett *see* POMFRET

Pummell English: of uncertain origin. It appears to derive from ME, OF *pomel* bump, hillock (LL *pōmellum*, dim. of *pōmum* apple, fruit), perhaps as a topographic name.

Pummery *see* POMEROY

Punainen Finnish: patr. from the nickname *Puna* 'Red', denoting a man with red hair.
Var.: **Punanen**.

Punch *see* POINTS

Pund *see* POUND

Punton Scots and N English: of uncertain origin, probably a habitation name from *Ponton* or PANTON in Lincs., both of which have the same etymology.

Punyer *see* POYNER

Purcell English: metonymic occupational name for a swineherd or nickname, perhaps affectionate in tone, from OF *pourcel* piglet (L *porcellus*, a dim. of *porcus*; cf. PORCHER).
Dims.: It.: **Porcellino**, **Porcellini**, **Porcellotto**, **Porcelletti**.
Pej.: It.: **Porcellazzi**.

Purchase English: metonymic occupational name for an official responsible for obtaining the supplies required by a monastery or manor house, from ANF *purchacer* to acquire, buy (OF *pourchacier*, from *chacier* to chase, catch (L *captāre*; cf. CATCHPOLE) with the addition of the intensive prefix *p(o)ur*, L *prō*).
Vars.: **Purchas**, **Purches(e)**; **Purkis(s)**, **Purkess**, **Pirkis(s)**, **Porkiss**.

Purcifer *see* PERCIVAL

Purdham *see* PRIDHAM

Purdy English: nickname for someone who made frequent use of the ANF oath *pur die*, from OF *p(o)ur Dieu* by God (L *prō Deo*).
Vars.: **Purdey**, **Purdye**, **Purday**, **Purdu(e)**; **Purdie** (Scots).

Purkins *see* PARKIN

Purnell *see* PARNELL

Purry *see* PERRY

Purser 1. English: occupational name for someone who made or sold purses and bags, or for an official in charge of expenditure, from an agent deriv. of ME *purse* (OE *purse*, from LL *bursa*). **2.** Scots: translation of Gael. *Mac Sparáin*; see SPORRAN.
Var.: **Purse**.

Pursey *see* PERCY

Purton English: habitation name from any of the places so called, in Gloucs., Staffs., and Wilts., from OE *pirige* pear tree (see PERRY 1) + *tūn* enclosure, settlement; cf. PARTON.

Purves Scots and N English: probably a metonymic occupational name for an official responsible for obtaining the supplies required by a monastery or manor house, from ME *purveys* provisions, supplies (from *purvey(en)*, OF *porveoir* to provide, supply, L *prōvidēre* to foresee, anticipate). According to Black it is a topographic name from ME, OF *parvis* church portico (from an altered form of L *paradīsus* Paradise), but the consistent *u* or *o* of the first syllable in early forms is hard to reconcile with this explanation.

Vars.: **Purvis** (Northumb.); **Purvess**; **Purvey**.

Pusey 1. English: habitation name from *Pusey* in Berks., so called from OE *peose, piosu* pea(s) (see PEASE) + *ēg* island, low-lying land. **2.** French: habitation name from *Pusey* in Haute-Saône, so called from a Gallo-Roman personal name *Pusius* + the local suffix *-ācum*.

Vars. (of 1): **Peasey**, **Pezey**, **Piz(z)ey**, **Pizzie**; PEWSEY. (Of 2): **Puss(e)y**.

Pushkar Jewish (E Ashkenazic): occupational name for a gunsmith or cannon maker; cf. PUSHKIN.

Dims.: Ukr.: **Pushkarenko**. Beloruss.: **Pushkarchuk**.

Patrs.: Russ.: **Pushkarev**. Beloruss.: **Pushkarevich**.

Pushkin Russian: patr. from the nickname *Pushka* 'Cannon' (originally 'container', 'magazine', from OHG *buhsa* box, L *buxis*; see BOX), denoting a bombastic person or used as an occupational name for a gunner or gunsmith.

Pustelnik Polish: nickname for a solitary individual, from Pol. *pustelnik* hermit.

Putman *see* PITT

Putnam English: habitation name from either of the places, in Herts. and Surrey, called *Puttenham*, from the gen. case of the OE byname *Putta* 'Kite' + OE *hām* homestead.

Var.: **Puttenham**.

Puttergill *see* PETTINGELL

Putterill English: metonymic occupational name for someone responsible for keeping horses, or nickname for a frisky and high-spirited person, from OF *poutrel* colt (LL *pultrellus*, from *pullus* young animal; cf. PULLEN).

Vars.: **Puttrell**, **Poutrel**, **Potterall**, **Pott(e)rill**, **Powdrell**, **Powd(e)rill**; **Purtill**.

Puttfarken Low German: nickname for a dirty or slovenly person, from MLG *put(t)* puddle (see PFÜTZER) + *farken* piglet (dim. of a cogn. of OE *fearh*).

Var.: **Putfarken**.

Puttifent *see* POTVIN

Puttock English: nickname for a rapacious or greedy person, from ME *puttock* kite (a dim. of OE *putta*; cf. PUTNAM).

Vars.: **Puttick**, **Puttack**, **Puttuck**, **Pottock**.

Puxbaum *see* BUCHS

Puy Provençal and Catalan: topographic name for someone who lived at a high place, or habitation name from any of the numerous places in S France and NE Spain named with OProv., Cat. *puy* hill(ock) (L *podium* platform, from Gk *podion*, a dim. of *pous*, gen. *podis*, foot).

Vars.: Prov.: **Peu(x)**, **Pey**, **Pou(e)y**, **Poy**, **Pu(e)ch**, **Pe(u)ch**, **Pioch**, **Poueigh**, **Poeuf**; **Lepeu(t)**; **Dupeux**, **Dupouy**, **Delpu(e)ch**, **Delpech**. Cat.: **Puig**.

Dims.: Prov.: **Puechon**, **Puget**, **Pugin**; see also PÉCHELS. Cat.: **Puyol**, **Pujol**. It.: **Poggetti**, **Poggini**, **Poggiol(in)i**; **Pozzol(in)i**, **Pozzolo** (from places in Tuscany and Liguria; see also PUITS).

Puzzolo *see* PUITS

Pye 1. English (especially common in Lancs. and E Anglia): nickname (for a talkative or thievish person) from the magpie, ME, OF *pie, pye* (L *pīca*). The mod. Eng. name of the bird, not found before the 17th cent., is from the earlier dial. term *maggot-pie*, formed by the addition of a dim. of the female given name *Margaret*. **2.** English: metonymic occupational name for a baker or seller of pies, from ME *pie* (of unknown origin, possibly from the bird). **3.** Welsh: patr., with a reduced form of the W element *ap*, from the given name HUGH.

Pygott *see* PIGGOTT

Pyke *see* PIKE

Pykett *see* PIGGOTT

Pyle *see* PILE

Pym *see* PIMM

Pyne *see* PINE

Pyper *see* PIPER

Pyser *see* PEYZER

Pytel Polish: metonymic occupational name for a bolter of flour, from Pol. *pytel* bolting cloth, sieve.

Python French: nickname for an unfortunate individual, from a dim. of OF *pite* pitable, from *pité* pity, mercy, LL *pietās*.

Vars.: **Pit(h)on**, **Pitou**; **Pitet**, **Pitel**.

Pejs.: **Pitard**, **Pitault**.

Q

Quad *see* McQuaid

Quadling *see* Codlin

Quaggin *see* Keogh

Quail 1. English: nickname from the bird, ME, OF *quaille* (LL *quacula*, probably of imitative origin), no doubt denoting a timorous, lecherous, or fat person, all of which qualities were ascribed to the bird. **2.** Irish: var. of Quill 1. **3.** Irish and Manx: Anglicized form of Gael. *Mac Phóil*; see McFall. **4.** Jewish: in one family this is an Anglicized form of the Ashkenazic ornamental surname **Kvalvaser** (Yid.: 'spring water').

Vars.: **Quaile**, **Qua(y)le**.

Dims. (of 1): It.: **Quaglino**, **Quagliotto**, **Quaglietta**.

Quaine *see* Coyne

Qualtrough Manx: from an aphetic form of Gael. **Mac Ualtair**, patr. from the given name Walter, with the addition of the adj. suffix *-agh*, in a collective or patronymic sense.

Vars.: **Qualterough**; **Qualter(s)**.

Quant English: nickname for a person admired for his good sense or skill, or regarded as cunning or crafty, or noted for elegance and fine dress, from ME, OF *cointe*, *quointe* (L *cognitus* known (past part. of *cognōscere* to discover), later used also in the active sense 'knowing', 'clever', 'cunning'). The OF word developed the sense 'skilfully made', 'attractive', and this meaning was also taken into ME, eventually developing into 'unusual' (mod. Eng. *quaint*).

Dim.: Eng.: Quantrill.

Augs.: Fr.: **Cointat**, **Coindat**.

Quantrill English (E Anglia): nickname for a dandy or an elegant person, from ME, OF *cointerel*, a deriv. of *coint* skilled, attractive (see Quant).

Vars.: **Quantrell**, **Quintrell**.

Quard *see* Bard

Quarello *see* Pascall

Quaresma Portuguese: religious byname for someone born during Lent, Port. *quaresma* (LL *quadrāgēsima*, from *quadrāgēsimus*, a deriv. of *quadrāginta* forty, referring to the forty days of Lent, commemorating Christ's forty days in the wilderness).

Quark 1. German: metonymic occupational name for a maker and seller of curd cheese, Ger. *Quark* (MHG *quark*, from Slav. *tvarog*, borrowed first into E Ger. dialects and then spreading throughout the German-speaking lands during the Middle Ages). **2.** Manx: aphetic form of Gael. **Mac Mhairc**, patr. from the given name Mark.

Vars. (of 1): **Quarch**, **Quarg**.

Quarles English: habitation name from a place in Norfolk, recorded in Domesday Book as *Huerueles*, from OE *hwerflas*, pl. of *hwerfel* circle. The name perhaps originally referred to a prehistoric stone circle, although no trace of any such feature remains today.

Quarmby *see* Wharmby

Quarrell English: **1.** metonymic occupational name for a maker of crossbow bolts or nickname for a short, stout man, from ME, OF *quar(r)el* bolt for a crossbow (LL *quadrellum*, a dim. of *quadrum* square). Cf. Bolt 2. **2.** nickname for a troublemaker, from ME, OF *querel* complaint, accusation (LL *querella*, for class. L *querūla*, a deriv. of *queri* to complain). For the change of *-er-* to *-ar-*, cf. Marchant.

Dim. (of 1): Fr.: **Carrelet**.

Quarrier *see* Carrier

Quarry 1. English (Norman): nickname for a thickset or portly man, from ONF *quaré* square-shaped (L *quadrātus*, from *quadrum* square); cf. Carré. **2.** English: topographic name for someone who lived near a stone quarry, or metonymic occupational name for someone who worked in one, from ME *quarey*, *quarer(e)* (ONF *quarrere*, a deriv. of *quaré* in the specialized sense 'dressed stone'). **3.** Manx: aphetic form of Gael. *Mac Guaire*; see McQuarry.

Var.: **Quarrie**.

Quartermain English (Norman): nickname meaning 'four hands', perhaps denoting a person who was in the habit of wearing heavy gloves, esp. of mail, or one who worked so fast or was so dextrous that he seemed to have four hands, from OF *quatre* four (L *quattuor*) + *main* hand (L *manus*).

Vars.: **Quartermaine**, **Quarterman**, **Quatermain(e)**.

Quay *see* McKay

Queally *see* Keeley

Queille French: habitation name from any of the places called *La Queille*, of which there is one in Calvados and another in Corrèze, or one called *Laqueille* in Puy-de-Dôme. All were originally named *l'accueil*, from OF *accueil* welcome (from *accueillir* to welcome, LL *accolligere* to gather (together) to oneself) with fused def. art. and consequent misdivision.

Var.: **Queuille**.

Quemin *see* Chemin

Quêne French: **1.** nickname from Norman forms of OF *chiene* bitch (fem. of *chien* dog, L *canis*). **2.** topographic name for someone who lived by an oak tree, from a Nor-

509

man or Picard form of CHÊNE. **3.** aphetic var. of the given name *Jacqème*; see JAMES.

Vars. (of 2): **Quesne, Duquesne**.

Dims. (of 2): **Quesnet, Quénet, Quesnel, Quénel, Quesneau, Quéneau, Quesnot**.

Collectives (of 2): **Quesnay, Quesney, Quesnoy; Duquesnay, Duquesnoy**.

Queneau *see* JACK

Quennell English: from the ME female given name *Quenilla, Quenilde*, from OE *Cwēnhild*, composed of the elements *cwēn* woman + *hild* battle.

Vars.: **Quenell, Quinell**.

Quenu *see* CHENU

Quer Catalan: habitation name from any of various places named with the OCat. element *quer* rock (of pre-Roman origin and apparently akin to Basque *arri*).

Dims.: **Querol, Queró**.

Queralt Catalan: habitation name from any of various places so called from OCat. *quer* rock (see QUER) + *alt* high (L *altus*).

Quernel *see* CORNEILLE

Quesada Spanish: habitation name from a place in the province of Jaén, of uncertain etymology. There may be some connection with OSp. *requexada* corner, tight spot, apparently a deriv. of *quexar* to afflict, oppress (L *quassāre* to shake, break, frequentative of *quatere* to shake).

Quesnay *see* QUÊNE

Quested English: of uncertain origin, probably a habitation name from the lost village of *Questers* (earlier *Quernstede*) in the parish of Sampford, Essex, so called from OE *cweorn* quern, hand-mill + *stede* site (see STEAD).

Quick 1. English: nickname for a lively or agile person, from ME *quik*, OE *cwic* alive, lively. **2.** English: topographic name for someone who lived by one of the various types of vegetation named from this word: couch grass, which grows rapidly and is difficult to eradicate (OE *cwice*); the aspen, whose leaves tremble as if they are alive (OE *cwictrēow*); or the poplar, which is widely used to make quickset fences (OE *cwicbēam*). **3.** English: topographic name for someone who lived at an outlying dairy farm, from OE *cū* cow + *wīc* outlying settlement (see WICK). **4.** Cornish: topographic name for someone who lived in a wood, Corn. *gwyk*, or habitation name from a minor place named with this word, as for example *Gweek* in the parish of Constantine.

Vars.: Eng.: **Quicke**. (Of 1 only): QUICKLEY.

Quickley 1. English: var. of QUICK 1, from ME *quiklich*, OE *cwiclīc* lively. **2.** Irish: Anglicized form of Gael. **Ó Coigligh** 'descendant of *Coigleach*', a byname apparently representing a simplified form of *coigeallach* untidy person.

Vars. (of 2): **(O')Quigl(e)y, O'Cwigley, (O')Cogley, O'Coigley, (O')Kegley**.

Quiddihy *see* CODY

Quijada Spanish: nickname for a person with a prominent jaw, Sp. *quijada* (a deriv. of OSp. *quexa*, from LL *capsea*, itself a deriv. of *capsa* box (cf. CASE 1)).

Quilici Italian: from the given name *Quilico*, an altered form of *Quirico*, borne by a (probably fictitious) 4th-cent. infant saint, said to have been martyred at Tarsus with his mother Julitta, who was honoured in the Middle Ages as a patron of children. The name is of uncertain origin. It seems to result from the crossing of two other names, both borne by several early saints: L *Quirīnus*, originally a title borne by Romulus, founding father of Rome, which is derived from the Sabine city of *Cures*, and Gk *Kyriakos*, a deriv. of *kyrios* lord, master.

Vars.: **Quilico, Quirico**.

Dim.: **Quilichini**.

Aug.: **Quiriconi**.

Patrs.: Sp.: **Quílez**. Cat.: **Quiles, Quilis**.

Quill 1. Irish: Anglicized form of Gael. **Ó Cuill** 'descendant of *Coll*', a personal name from *coll* hazel tree. **2.** Scots: Anglicized form of Gael. **Mac Cuill** 'son of *Coll*', the same name as in 1.

Vars. (of 1): QUAIL, **O'Quill, O'Cuill**. (Of 2): **McColl**.

Dims. (of 1): **Quill(ig)an, Col(l)gan**.

Quilliam *see* McWILLIAM

Quilly Irish: **1.** Anglicized form of Gael. **Mac Conchoille** 'son of *Cú Choille*', a personal name from *cú* dog + *coille*, gen. of *coill* wood, forest. **2.** Anglicized form of Gael. **Mac an Choiligh** 'son of the cock', from *coileach* cock.

Vars.: **McQuilly**. (Of 2 only): **McAnchelly, McInchelly, McEnkelly, McAckolly**.

Quilter English: occupational name for a maker of quilts and mattresses, and also of the quilted garments worn in battle by those who could not afford armour made of metal, from an agent deriv. of ME, OF *cuilte, coilte* quilt, mattress (L *culcita* mattress).

Quincey English (Norman): habitation name from any of several places in France deriving their names from the Gallo-Roman personal name *Quintus* 'Fifth(-born)' + the local suffix *-ācum*. The earliest bearers of the name in England were from *Cuinchy* in Pas-de-Calais, but other stocks may be from *Quincy*-sous-Sénard in Seine-et-Oise or *Quincy*- Voisins in Seine-et-Marne.

Vars.: **De Quincey, Quincy, Quinsey, Quinsee**.

Quineau *see* JACK

Quinell *see* QUENNELL

Quinlan Irish: **1.** Anglicized form of Gael. **Ó Caoindealbháin** 'descendant of *Caoindealbhán*' a personal name composed of the elements *caoin* comely, fair + *dealbh* form + the dim. suffix *-án*. **2.** Anglicized form of **Ó Conailláin** 'descendant of *Conaillán*' a personal name representing a dim. of *Conall*; see CONNELL.

Vars.: **O'Connellaine, Connellan, (O')Conlan, Conlon, Conlin**. (Of 1 only): **O'Quinelane, O'Guindelane, O'Kenolan, (O')Kennellan, Quinlivan, Quinlevan, Kin(del)lan, Kenlan**.

Quinn Irish: Anglicized form of Gael. **Ó Cuinn** 'descendant of *Conn*', a byname meaning 'Leader', 'Chief'.

Vars.: **(O')Quin(e), O'Quyn**.

Quiñones Spanish: topographic name for someone who lived on a piece of land that was shared out among a group of co-tenants for sowing, Sp. *quiñón* (L *quīnio*, gen. *quīniōnis*, group of five, a deriv. of *quinque* five).

Quintana Spanish and Catalan: topographic name for someone who lived on a piece of land subject to rent of one-fifth of its produce, from Sp., Cat. *quintana* a fifth (LL *quintāna*, a deriv. of *quintus* fifth). There are numerous places named with this word, and the surname may also be a habitation name from any of these.

Dim.: Sp.: **Quintanilla**.

Quinton English: **1.** habitation name from any of the places, for example in Gloucs., Northants, and Birmingham, so called from OE *cwēn* queen + *tūn* enclosure, settlement (cf. KINGSTON). **2.** from the OF given name *Quentin*, *Quintin* (L *Quintīnus*, a deriv. of *Quintus* 'Fifth(-born)'; cf. QUINCEY), which was introduced into England by the Normans, but never became widely popular. **3.** Norman habitation name from any of the places in N France named from St Quentin of Amiens, a 3rd-cent. Roman missionary to Gaul, as for example *Saint-Quentin* in La Manche or *Saint-Quentin*-en-Tourmont in Somme, the site of his martyrdom.

Quintrell *see* QUANTRILL

Quirke Manx and Irish: Anglicized form of Gael. **Ó Cuirc** 'descendant of *Corc*', a personal name from *corc* heart, or *curc* tuft of hair. It is sometimes translated **Oates**, as if from *coirce* oats.

Vars.: **Quirk**; **O'Quirk(e)**, **O'Cuirk**.

Quiroga Spanish: habitation name from places (of unknown etymology) in the provinces of Lugo and Orense.

Quirós Spanish: habitation name from any of various places in W Spain, most notably one in the province of Oviedo. The placename is of unknown origin; there may be some connection with the Galician dial. term *queiroa*, which denotes a kind of heather.

Quist *see* QVIST

Quodling *see* CODLIN

Qvist Swedish: ornamental surname, from Swed. *quist* twig (ON *kvistr*). When surnames were adopted on a large scale in the 19th cent. in Sweden, *qvist* was one of the elements that were widely used in combination with other words denoting natural features to form surnames such as *Lindqvist* and *Blomqvist*.

Vars.: **Quist**, **Kvist**.

R

Rabadán Spanish: occupational name for a shepherd boy, Sp. *rabadán* (Arabic *rabb ad-da'n* 'the one with the sheep').

Rabaud French: from the OF personal name *Radbaud*, *Rabbaud*, composed of the Gmc elements *rād* counsel, advice + *bald* bold, brave.
Var.: **Rabault**.
Dims.: Low Ger.: **Rabbe(ke)** (see also RABBITT).
Patr.: Ger.: **Rappolder** (Austria).

Rabb see ROBERT

Rabbitt 1. English: dim. of *Rabb*, a pet form of ROBERT. 2. English: from the Norman personal name *Radbode*, *Rabbode*, composed of the Gmc elements *rād* counsel, advice + *bodo* message, tidings, introduced by the Normans. 3. Irish: erroneous translation of Gael. *Ó Coinín*; see KINNEEN.
Vars.: (of 1): **Rabet**. (Of 3): **Rabbitte**.
Dims.: (of 2): Low Ger.: **Rabbe(ke)** (see also RABAUD).
Patrs. (from 1 and 2): Eng.: **Rabbit(t)s**, **Rabet(t)s**, **Rabbatts**.

Rabeau see RAVEL

Rabey see ROBY

Rabin Jewish (E Ashkenazic): status name from Pol. *rabin* rabbi (ultimately from Hebr. *rav*).
Vars.: **Rabinski**, **Rabinsky**; **Ravin(sky)**, **Ravinzki** (from Russ. *ravin*); **Rabiner** (from Ger. *Rabbiner*; also W Ashkenazic); **Raff** (W Ashkenazic; from Low Ger.); **Rab(b)ino** (among It. Jews, from the It. word for 'rabbi'); **Rabenu** (a Hebr. phrase meaning 'our rabbi'); ROBIN.
Patrs.: **Rabin(er)son**, **Rabinsohn**, **Robinso(h)n**, **Robinzon** (Ashkenazic); **Rabinow**, **Rabinov**, **Robinov**, **Robinow**, **Rabinowicz**, **Ravinovicz**, **Rabinowit(s)ch**, **Rabinovi(t)ch**, **Rabinovitsh**, **Rabinowitz**, **Rabinovitz**, **Rabinovits**, **Rabinovics**, **Robinovich**, **Robinovitz** (E Ashkenazic), **Rabinovici** (among Rumanian Jews).

Rabl see RAVEN

Rabone see RATHBONE

Racamier see RÉCAMIER

Raccio see PETER

Rachet French: nickname for a bald man, from a dim. of North-Eastern OF *rache* bald (of uncertain origin, perhaps from L *rāsus* clean-shaven, past part. of *rādere* to scrape; cf. RAYER 2). The surname is found largely in the Burgundy and Champagne regions.
Var.: **Rachez**.

Rachlin see ROCHLIN

Racine French: metonymic occupational name for a grower or seller of root vegetables, or nickname for a ten-acious and stubborn person, from OF *racine* root (LL *rādīcīna*, a deriv. of class. L *rādix*, gen. *rādīcis*).
Vars.: **Rachine** (Normandy); **Rassinier**, **Racineux**, **Rassineux** (agent derivs.).
Dims.: **Racinet**; **Rachinel** (Normandy).

Rackcliff see RATCLIFFE

Rackel see RAT

Rackham English: habitation name from a place in Sussex, so called from OE *hrēac* mound, (hay)rick (probably the name of a nearby hill) + *hām* homestead.

Rackley English: apparently a habitation name from an unidentified place, which would derive its name from OE *hrēac* mound (cf. RACKHAM) or *hraca* throat, gulley + *lēah* wood, clearing.

Ractigan see RATTIGAN

Rácz Hungarian: from Hung. *rác* Serbian, derived from the Serbian placename *Ras*, the capital of medieval Serbia.

Raczek see RAK

Raczyński Polish: habitation name from a village called *Raczyn* or *Raczyno*.

Radbone see RATHBONE

Radcliff see RATCLIFFE

Raddie see READY

Radecke see RAT

Radecki Polish: from a dim., *Radek*, of any of various Slav. personal names containing a first element *rad* glad. In Pol., the most common such names are *Radosław* (Czech *Radoslav*), in which the second element means 'glory' and *Radomierz* (Czech *Radomír*), in which the second element means 'great, famous'.
Vars.: **Radek**, **Radke**.
Patrs.: Pol.: **Radkiewicz**. Croatian: **Radić**, **Radović**, **Radojević**, **Radoj(i)čić**; **Radojković**; **Radošević**, **Radišić**; **Radunović**, **Radjenović**, **Radonjić**, **Radenković**, **Radaković**, **Radulović**; **Radovanović**; **Rad(o)manović**. Bulg.: **Raikov**. Rum.: **Rădulescu**, **Rad(u)lesco**. Hung.: **Radics**.

Radecký Czech: habitation name from any of several places in Bohemia, for example *Hradec (Králové)* (Ger. *Königgrätz*) or *Radeč*.
Vars.: **Hradecký**, **Hradec**.

Rademaker Low German and Dutch: occupational name for a wheelwright, from MLG, MDu. *rat* wheel + *makære* maker. The term was also used by extension for a builder of

512

carts, and so is an equivalent of N Ger. STELLMACHER and S Ger. WAGNER.

Vars.: Low Ger.: **Rademacher**, **Ra(h)maker**, **Ramacker**, **Ramecker**; **Re(de)ker**.

Patrs.: Low Ger.: **Ra(h)makers**, **Ramachers**, **Rameckers**, **Rademächers**. Flem.: **Raemakers**.

Radford English: habitation name from any of the various places so called, for example in Devon, Notts., Oxon., Warwicks., and Worcs. Most are named from OE *rēad* red (see READ 1) + *ford* FORD, but it is possible that in some cases the first element may be a deriv. of OE *rīdan* to ride, with the meaning 'ford that can be crossed on horseback'.

Vars.: **Radforth**, **Radfirth**, **Ratford**; **Red(di)ford**, **Retford**.

Radigue Provençal: of uncertain origin. It is largely confined to Gascony and is perhaps a deriv. of OProv. *razigar* to tear out, uproot (L *ērādīcāre*, from *rādix*, gen. *rādīcis*, root; cf. RACINE); if so, it is presumably a topographic name for someone who lived on a patch of cleared land.

Dims.: **Radiguet**, **Radigon**.

Radley English: habitation name from a place so called from OE *rēad* red (see READ 1) + *lēah* wood, clearing; cf. REDSHAW and REDWOOD. There are places of this name in Berks. and Devon.

Var.: **Radleigh**. See also RALEIGH.

Radmore English (Devon): habitation name from an unidentified place, apparently originally named with the OE elements *rēad* red (see READ 1) + *mōr* moor (see MOORE 1).

Radnedge English: habitation name, probably from *Radnage* in Bucks., which gets its name from OE *(æt þǣm) rēadan æc* (at the) red oak'.

Radomski Polish: habitation name from the city of *Radom* in central Poland, S of Warsaw. The placename is derived from the OSlav. personal name *Radomir*.

Radziejewski Polish: habitation name from the town of *Radziejów* in N central Poland, so called from an OPol. personal name *Radziej* (derived from the suffix *rad(z)-* together) + *-ów*, *-ew* possessive suffix, with the addition of the surname suffix *-ski* (see BARANOWSKI).

Vars.: **Radzikowski**, **Radziński**.

Dims. (of the personal name): **Radzik**, **Radzicki**.

Radziwiłł Polish: from Lithuanian *radvila* foundling. In spite of its humble origin, this surname has enjoyed considerable prestige as the name of one of the leading noble families of Poland.

Vars.: **Radziwilski**, **Radziwił(ł)owski** (from placenames derived from this surname); **Radziwill** (U.S.).

Raeburn Scots: habitation name from a place in the Scottish Borders, so called from Northern ME *ray* roebuck (see RAY 2) + *burn* stream (see BOURNE).

Raemakers see RADEMAKER

Raes see ERASMUS

Rafaeli see RAPHAEL

Rafanel see RAVANO

Rafe see RALPH

Raff see RABIN

Rafferty Irish (esp. Ulster): Anglicized form of Gael. Ó Rabhartaigh or Ó Robhartaigh 'descendant of *Robhartach*', a personal name apparently meaning 'Wielder of Prosperity'.

Ragazzo Italian: occupational name for a servant, from It. *ragazzo* boy, lad, servant.

Vars.: **Ragazzi**, **Regazzi**, **Regazzo**.

Dims.: **Ragazzini**, **Regazzini**.

Augs.: **Ragazzoni**, **Ragazzone**, **Regazzoni**.

Raggett English: nickname for a person of unkempt appearance, from ME *ragged* shaggy, rough (from ON *roggvaðr* tufted); the noun *rag* is a back-formation from this. The surname is localized in the Odiham area of Hants. in the 17th cent.

Ragnarsson see RAYNER

Ragoneau see RAINE

Rahier see RAYER

Rahlke see ROLLO

Rahmaker see RADEMAKER

Rahn German: 1. nickname for a person with dark hair or a swarthy complexion, from MHG, OHG *rān*, *rām* soot, dirt. 2. nicknickname for a thin person, from MHG *rān* slender (of uncertain origin). 3. from a short form of any of various Slav. personal names, such as *Ranoslav* and *Ranomir*, with the first element *rano* early.

Dims. (of 3): **Rahncke**, **Ran(t)ke**, **Ranek**, **Rahnsch**, **Ranisch**, **Ranusch**, **Ränisch**.

Raiber see RÄUBER

Raikes English: topographic name for someone who lived by a narrow pass or cleft in a hillside, from OE *hraca* throat, also commonly used with this transferred sense.

Vars.: **Rake(s)**.

Raikov see RADECKI

Raiment see RAYMOND

Rainalder see REYNOLD

Rainard see REYNARD

Rainbird English: from an OF personal name, *Rainbert*, composed of the Gmc elements *ragin* counsel + *berht* bright, famous. This was introduced to Britain by the Normans. The form of the name has been affected by folk etymological association with *rainbird*, a vernacular name of the plover (cf. PLOUVIER 2).

Vars.: **Raynbird**, **Rambert**, **Ram(b)art**.

Rainbow 1. English: from an OF personal name, *Rainbaut*, composed of the Gmc elements *ragin* counsel + *bald* bold, brave. This was introduced to Britain by the Normans. The form of the name has been affected by folk etymological association with the natural phenomenon. 2. Jewish (Ashkenazic): Anglicized form of

Regenbogen (mod. Ger. 'rainbow'), one of the group of ornamental names based on natural phenomena.

Vars. (of 1): **Rambaut, Rimbault, Renbold, Ramble, Rammell, Raybould**.

Raine 1. English and French: from a short form of any of the various Gmc personal names with the first element *ragin* counsel (see, e.g., RAYMOND, REYNOLD). **2.** English: from the medieval female given name *Reine* (from OF *reine* queen, L *rēgīna*). **3.** Jewish (Ashkenazic): from the Yid. female given name *Rayne*, cognate with 2 and used as a translation of Hebr. *Malka* 'Queen'. **4.** English and French: nickname from OF *raine* frog (L *rāna*). **5.** Scots: habitation name from *Raine* in the former county of Aberdeens., so called from Gael. *rath chàin* ford of the tax or tribute.

Vars.: Eng.: **Rayne, Rain**. (Of 1 only): Fr.: **Renne; Rainon, Renon** (from the oblique case).

Dims. (of 1): Eng.: **Raincock**. Fr.: **Raineau, Ragoneau(x), Rag(on)ot, Ragueneau, Ragu(en)et, Raguin**. Ger.: **Reinel, Reinle, Rein(d)l; Rein(t)sch, Re(i)nisch, Rentsch(ke); Rön(t)sch, Rönisch**. Low Ger.: **Reinmann, Rai(n)mann; Reine(c)ke, Reinick(e), Reinege, Reinke, Renneke**. It.: **Ranucci, Ranuzzi**.

Patrs. (from 1): Eng.: **Raines**. Low Ger.: **Reins, Reinen, Rehnen, Reenen, Rennen**.

Metrs. (from 3): Jewish: **Rainin** (E Ashkenazic); **Raines, Ra(i)nis, Reines, Reinis, Reinuss, Renus**.

Patrs. (from 1) (dims.): Low Ger.: **Reine(c)ken, Reinicken, Reinken(s), Rennsen, Reining, Rennings, Rein(e)king**. Fris.: **Reininga, Reinkena**.

Rainer *see* RAYNER

Rainey Scots and Irish: from a dim. of a short form of any of the various Gmc personal names with a first element *rand* (shield) rim (cf. RAND 1) or *ragin* counsel. The given name was most frequently used as a form of RANDOLF and REYNOLD.

Vars.: **Rainy, Rain(n)ie, Raney, Rannie, Rean(n)e)y, Renn(e)y, Rennie**.

Patrs.: **Renison; Creaney** (Gael. **Mac Raighne**); **McCrank, McGrane, McGrain** (Gael. **Mac Raing**).

'Descendant of R.': **O'Reaney** (Gael. **Ó Ráighne, Ó Raighne**).

Rainford English: habitation name from a place in Lancs., so called from *Regna, a short form, not independently attested, of OE cpd personal names with the first element *regen* counsel + OE *ford* FORD.

Var.: **Rainsford**.

Rainger *see* RANGER, RINGER

Raison English and French: nickname for an intelligent person, from ME, OF *raison* reasoning, intellectual faculty (L *ratio*, gen. *ratiōnis*, a deriv. of *rēri* to think).

Vars.: Eng.: **Reason**. Fr.: **Raisonnier**.

Raistrick English: habitation name from *Rastrick* in W Yorks., the origin of which is obscure; it may mean 'resting-place ridge'.

Var.: **Rastrick**.

Rajala Finnish: topographic name for someone living near a border, from Finn. *raja* boundary, border + the local suffix *-la*.

Rajchbart *see* RICH

Rajnerman *see* RAYNER

Rajski Polish and Jewish (Ashkenazic): **1.** topographic name for someone living in a marshy or muddy spot, from OPol. *raj(a)* marsh, mud + *-ski* suffix of surnames (see BARANOWSKI). **2.** nickname for someone who lived in a pleasant spot or in happy circumstances, from Pol. *raj* paradise + *-ski*. As a Jewish name, this may well be ornamental in origin.

Var.: **Raj**.

Habitation names: **Rajewski**. Pol. only: **Rajkowski** (from a dim.).

Rak Polish, Czech, and Jewish (E Ashkenazic): apparently from the Slav. vocab. word *rak* crab, crayfish. The reasons for its acquisition as a surname are not clear. It may be a nickname, and in areas where crabs were familiar may have been applied to someone who did not walk straight or to one who was not entirely 'straight' in his dealings. In some cases it represents a translation of Ger. *Krebs* (see CRABBE), and as an Ashkenazic name may have been one of the unflattering surnames bestowed on Jews by non-Jewish government officials in 18th- and 19th-cent. Eastern Europe.

Dim.: Pol.: **Raczek**.

Habitation names: Pol. and Jewish: **Rakowski** (from any of several places called *Raków*, including one S of Warsaw and another in Belorussia, which was a frontier town between Poland and the Soviet Union 1921–39). Pol. only: **Rakowiecki** (from *Rakowiec*, S of Warsaw).

Habitation name (from the dim. *raczek*): Pol. and Jewish: **Raczkowski**.

Rake *see* RAIKES

Rakhmaninov Russian: patr. from the ORuss. ethnic name *rakhmanin* Indian (ultimately from Skt *brāhmana* Brahmin), used as a nickname for someone of swarthy appearance.

Rákos Czech: **1.** topographic name for someone who lived by a reedbed or patch of bulrushes, Czech *rákos*. **2.** metonymic occupational name for a basketmaker, from the same word in the sense of cane or wickerwork.

Vars.: **Rokos**. (Of 2 only): **Rákosník**.

Rakušan Czech: ethnic name for an Austrian, from a deriv. of Czech *Rakousko* Austria.

Raleigh English: habitation name from *Raleigh* in Devon, recorded in Domesday Book as *Radeleia*, from OE *rēad* red (see READ 1) + *lēah* wood, clearing; cf. RADLEY. The placename is pronounced /'rɔːlɪ/, and this is also the traditional pronunciation of the surname (James I punned the name of Sir Walter with *rarely*); nowadays the pronunciations /'rɑːlɪ/ and /'rælɪ/ are also found.

Vars.: **Ralegh, RAYLEIGH; Ra(w)ley, Rall(e)y**.

Rallin *see* RAWLING

Ralph English: from an ON personal name composed of the Gmc elements *rad* counsel, advice + *wolf* wolf. This was first introduced into England by Scandinavian settlers in the ON form *Ráðúlfr*, and was reinforced after the Conquest by the Norman form *Ra(d)ulf*.

Vars.: **Ralf(e)**; **Rafe**, **Raff**; Raw, **Rawle**, **Rawll**.

Dims.: Eng.: Rawling. Fr.: **Raulet**; **Raulic** (Brittany).

Patrs.: Eng.: **Ralphs**, **Ralfs**; **Raves**; **Ra(w)les**, **Ralls**; **Ralphson**. Low Ger.: **Ralf(e)s**, **Ralwes**.

Ram 1. English: nickname for a forceful or lusty individual, from ME, OE *ram(m)* male sheep (in part perhaps representing a continued use of an OE byname). It may also occasionally have been a metonymic occupational name for a shepherd, or a house name for someone who lived 'at the sign of the ram'. **2.** French: topographic name for someone who lived in a thickly wooded area, from OF *ra(i)m* branch (L *rāmus*). It seems likely that it was also used as a nickname for someone who had some particular connection with Palm Sunday, for which the Fr. term is *(dimanche des) rameaux*, and there may in some cases have been some reference to the 'branches' of a family tree. **3.** Swedish: topographic name for someone who lived near a border or boundary, Swed. *ram*. **4.** Jewish (Israeli): ornamental name from Hebr. *ram* lofty.

Vars. (of 1 and 4): **Ramm**. (Of 2): **Rame(s)**.

Dims. (of 1): Eng.: **Ramplin(g)**. (Of 2): Fr.: **Ramel(et)**, **Rameau(x)**, **Ram(e)lot**, **Ramet**, **Ramey**. Port.: **Ramalhete**.

Pej. (of 2): Fr.: **Ramard** (the sense is probably as in Ramage).

Collective (of 2): Port.: **Ramalho**.

Cpds (of 3, topographic or ornamental): Swed.: **Ramberg** ('border hill'); **Ramstedt** ('border homestead'); **Ramström** ('border river').

Ramachers *see* Rademaker

Ramage Scots: nickname for a savage or unpredictable individual, from ME, OF *ramage* wild (of a bird of prey) (LL *rāmaticus*, from *rāmus* branch; cf. Savage).

Ramart *see* Rainbird

Rambaut *see* Rainbow

Ramírez *see* Reinmar

Ramond *see* Raymond

Ramsbottom N English: habitation name from a place in Lancs., so called from OE *hramsa* wild garlic + *boðm* valley (see Bottom).

Var.: **Ramsbotham**.

Ramsdale N English: habitation name from a place in N Yorks., so called from OE *hramsa* wild garlic (or possibly the gen. case of the byname *Ram(m)* Ram') + *dæl* valley (see Dale).

Ramsden N English: habitation name from any of various places so called from OE *hramsa* wild garlic (or possibly the gen. case of the OE byname *Ram(m)* Ram') + *denu* valley (see Dean 1). There are villages so named in Essex, Kent, Oxon., and Warwicks., but the surname is most common in Yorks., where there are several minor places so called, *Ramsden* in the parish of Kirkburton being a well-recorded instance.

Ramsey Scots: **1.** habitation name from places in Hunts. (now part of Cambs.) and Essex, so called from OE *hramsa* wild garlic + *ēg* island, low-lying land. **2.** habitation name

from a place in the parish of Whithorn, in the former county of Wigtown, so called from the gen. case of the OE byname *Ram(m)* Ram' + *ēg*.

Var.: **Ramsay**.

Ramshaw English: habitation name from a place in Co. Durham, probably so called from OE *hramsa* wild garlic + *sceaga* wood, copse (cf. Shaw).

Ramskill English (Yorks.): habitation name from *Ramsgill* in W Yorks., so called from OE *hramsa* wild garlic (or possibly the gen. case of the OE byname *Ram(m)* 'Ram' or the ON byname *Hrafn* 'Raven') + ON *gil* ravine (see Gill 2).

Ranald *see* Ronald

Ranalder *see* Reynold

Rand English: **1.** from the ME given name *Rand(e)*, a short form of any of the various Gmc cpd personal names with the first element *rand* (shield) rim, as for example Randolph. **2.** topographic name for someone who lived on the margin of a settlement or on the bank of a river (from OE *rand* rim, used in a topographical sense), or habitation name from a place named with this word, as for example *Rand* in Lincs. and *Rand* Grange in N Yorks.

Vars.: **Rant**. (Of 1): **Randon** (from the OF oblique case).

Dims. (of 1): Eng.: Randall, Rankin; **Randy**, Rainey.

Patrs. (from 1): Eng.: **Rands**, **Rance**; **Ranson**, **Ransom(e)** (chiefly E Anglia).

Randall English: from the ME given name *Randel*, a dim. of Rand with the ANF hypocoristic suffix *-el*.

Vars.: **Randell**, **Randle**; **Rendall**, **Rendell**, **Rendle**.

Patrs.: **Randles**; **Randlesome**, **Randerson**.

Randolph English: from a Gmc personal name composed of the elements *rand* rim (of a shield), shield + *wolf* wolf. This was first introduced into England by Scandinavian settlers in the ON form *Rannúlfr*, and was reinforced after the Conquest by the Norman form *Randolf*.

Patr.: Eng.: **Fitzrandolph**.

Ranek *see* Rahn

Raney *see* Rainey

Ranger English: occupational name for a gamekeeper or warden, ME *ranger*, an agent deriv. of *range(n)* to arrange, dispose (OF *ranger*, from *rang* rank, of Gmc origin).

Var.: **Rainger**.

Ranis *see* Raine

Rank English: **1.** nickname for a powerfully built man or someone of violent emotions, from the ME adj. *rank* (OE *ranc* proud, rebellious). **2.** from a medieval given name, a back-formation from the dim. Rankin.

Rankin Scots and N English: from the medieval given name *Rankin*, a dim. of Rand 1, with the hypocoristic suffix *-kin* (of Low Ger. or Du. origin).

Vars.: **Rankine**, **Ranking**, **Ranken**.

Ranner *see* Rayner

Ranshaw *see* Renshaw

Ransley *see* Rawnsley

Ranta Finnish: ornamental name, perhaps chosen for topographic reasons by someone who lived near the coast, from Finn. *ranta* shore.

Vars.: **Rantala**, **Rantanen**.

Ranzetti *see* NARANJO

Rapa Italian: **1.** metonymic occupational name for a grower or seller of turnips, from It. *rapa* turnip (LL *rāpa* (fem.), originally the pl. form of class. L *rāpum* (neut.)). **2.** derogatory nickname for a stupid person, from the same word in a transferred sense.

Vars.: **Rapi**; **Rava**, **Ravi** (N Italy).

Dims.: It.: **Rapetti**, **Rapetto**, **Rapini**, **Rapino**, **Rapucci**, **Rappuzzi**; **Ravetta**, **Ravetti**, **Ravina**, **Ravella**, **Ravelli**.

Raphael Jewish, English, and French: from the Hebr. male given name *Refael*, composed of the elements *rafa* to heal + *el* God. This name was borne by one of the archangels, but for some reason it was less popular among Christians in the Middle Ages than the other names of archangels, MICHAEL and GABRIEL, except perhaps in Italy. Such currency as it did enjoy was largely the result of the part played by the angel in the Apocryphal tale of Tobias.

Vars.: Jewish: **Rafael**, **Rephael**, **Refael**; **Raphaeli**, **Rephaeli**, **Rafaeli**, **Refaeli**, **Raphael(l)y**, **Rafaely**, **Refaely** (Israeli, with the Hebr. ending *-i*). Fr.: **Raphel**. Eng.: **Raffel**, **Raffle**, **Raffield**.

Patrs.: Jewish (E Ashkenazic): **Raphaelov**, **Raphaelof(f)**, **Rafaelof(f)**, **Rafaelovich**, **Rafaelovitz**, **Refaelov(e)**, **Refalovicz**, **Refalovitch**; **Rafaelovici** (a Rumanian spelling). Croatian: **Rafajlović**. Eng.: **Raffles**.

Raphanel *see* RAVANO

Rapkins *see* ROBERT

Raposo Portuguese: nickname for a cunning person, or else for someone with reddish brown hair, from Port. *raposo* fox, a deriv. of *rabo* tail, with reference to the spectacular brush of the animal. The origin of *rabo* is not clear, but it has been suggested that it is from L *rāpum* turnip (cf. RAPA), because of the resemblance between the shaggy tap root of the turnip and the tail of an animal.

Rapp **1.** Swedish: 'soldier's name', one of the monosyllabic names adopted by soldiers in the 17th cent., before surnames became general in Sweden, from Swed. *rapp* quick, prompt. **2.** German and Jewish (Ashkenazic): cogn. of RAVEN.

Rappaport Jewish (Ashkenazic): of uncertain origin. Most people bearing this name are descended from Avrom-Menakhem Ben-Yankev Hakoyen Rapa, who lived in Porto, Italy, at the beginning of the 16th cent. In his case *Rapa* was an ornamental name, from Ger. *Rappe* RAVEN. According to one explanation his descendants added the name of their city, Porto, in order to distinguish themselves from unrelated Jews surnamed *Rapa*; according to another, there was a marriage between the *Rapa* and *Porto* families, and the issue of this union took the cpd name. In any case, because this was a distinguished family, some unrelated Jews adopted may have the surname for the sake of its prestige.

Vars.: **Rapaport**, **Rap(p)oport**.

Rappl *see* RAVEN

Rappolder *see* RABAUD

Rasch **1.** German: nickname for a nimble person, from Ger. *rasch* quick (OHG *rasc*; cf. ON *rǫskr* bold). **2.** German (of Slav. origin): dim. from a short form of any of various Slav. personal names with the first element *rad* glad (see RADECKI) or *rano* early (see RAHN 3).

Dims. (of 2): Ger.: **Raschke**, **Raschka**, **Ratzke**, **Ratzka**, **Raschek**, **Ratzek**, **Rassek**. Czech: **Rašek**, **Raška**.

Rasem *see* ERASMUS

Rash **1.** English: var. of ASH; the name has arisen as the result of the misdivision of ME *atter ashe* 'at the ash tree' (OE *æt þēre æsce*). **2.** Jewish: of unknown origin.

Raskin *see* ERASMUS

Rasp German: probably a nickname for a miser, from MHG *raspen* to scrape together (OHG *raspōn*).

Rasputin Russian: patr. from a nickname composed of the elements *raz* apart, away + *put* journey, which is capable of various interpretations. On the one hand *rasputye* is a road-fork or parting of the ways, and it seems likely that the most famous bearer of the name, the monk Grigori Yefimovich Rasputin (1872–1916), himself derived the name from this, since his birthplace is said to have been situated on a road fork. His enemies, however, took it to be from *rasputny* deviant, debauched, and it is likely that he himself enjoyed the ambiguity, since he was a member of the Khlysty sect, who believed that sinning was a prerequisite of salvation.

Rassineux *see* RACINE

Rastel *see* RATEAU

Rastrick *see* RAISTRICK

Rat **1.** French: nickname for a sly and agile individual, from OF *rat* rat (apparently of Gmc origin). **2.** German and Jewish (Ashkenazic): nickname for a wise person, from Ger. *Rat* counsel, advice (MHG, OHG *rāt*). **3.** German: from a short form of any of the various Gmc cpd personal names with the first element *rāt* counsel, advice.

Vars. (of 1): **Lerat**. (Of 2): Jewish: **Rath**. (Of 2 and 3): Ger.: **Rath(e)**.

Dims. (of 1): Fr.: **Ratet**, RATEAU, **Rat(ill)on**, **Ratin(eau)**, **Raty**. (Of 3): Ger.: **Rack(e)l**. Low Ger.: **Rademann**, **Rade(c)ke**, **Redeke**, **Rathke**, **Rathgen**, **Rathje(n)**. Fr.: **Radet**, **Radot**.

Cpds (of 2): Jewish: **Rathaus(e)** (topographic name for someone who lived by a town hall; Anglicized as **Rathouse**).

Ratajski Polish: occupational name for a ploughman, from Pol. *rataj* ploughman + *-ski* suffix of surnames (see BARANOWSKI).

Dim.: Pol.: **Ratajczyk**.

Ratchford *see* ROCHFORD

Ratcliffe English (chiefly Lancs.): habitation name from any of the places, in various parts of England, called *Ratcliff(e)*, *Radcliffe*, *Redcliff*, or *Radclive*, all of which derive their names from OE *rēad* red (see READ 1) + *clif* cliff, slope, riverbank (see CLIVE).

Vars.: **Rat(t)cliff**, **Radcliff(e)**, **Radclyffe**, **Ratliff(e)**, **Rack(c)liff(e)**; **Red(i)cliffe**, **Redclift**, **Reddecliff**.

Rateau French: **1.** metonymic occupational name for someone who made or used rakes, or nickname for a tall, thin man, from OF *rastel* rake (LL *rastellum*, a dim. of class. L *rastrum*). **2.** dim. of RAT 1.

Vars.: **Ra(s)tel**, **Ratheau**, **Rateaux**, **Rateaud**.

Ratford *see* RADFORD

Rathbone English: apparently a habitation name from *Radbourn* in Warwicks. or *Radbourne* in Derbys., both of which seem to get their names from OE *hrēod* reeds (a collective sing.) + *burna* stream (see BOURNE).

Vars.: **Ra(d)bone**; **Rathbourn**, **Rathborne**.

Ratner Jewish (Ashkenazic): habitation name from *Ratno* in the Ukraine or *Rathenau* near Brandenburg.

Vars.: **Rattner**; **Rathenau** (from the Ger. placename).

Rattigan Irish: Anglicized form of **Ó Reachtagáin** 'descendant of *Reachtagán*', a personal name from a dim. of *reachtaire* steward, administrator.

Vars.: **O'Raghtagan**, **Roghtigan**, **Ra(c)tigan**, **Ratican**, **Rhatigan**, **Rhategan**.

Rattray Scots: habitation name from a feudal barony in the former county of Perths., apparently so called from Brit. cogns. of Gael. *rath* fortress + W *tref* settlement.

Ratzek *see* RASCH

Räuber German: derogatory nickname (hardly an actual occupational name) from Ger. *Räuber* robber, bandit, highwayman (MHG *roubære*, OHG *roubari*, from *roub, roup* booty, spoils; cf. ROPERO).

Vars.: **Rauber**; **Raiber** (Austria; also born by Ashkenazic Jews).

Dim.: Ger.: **Raible** (Swabia).

Raucci *see* ROLLO

Rauch German and Jewish (Ashkenazic): nickname for a shaggy or unkempt person, from Ger. *rauch* rough, hairy (MHG, OHG *rū(h)*).

Vars.: Ger.: **Rau(h)**. Jewish: **Rau**.

Raulet *see* RALPH

Raulin *see* RAWLING

Raun *see* RUANE

Rautainen Finnish: patr. from the Finn. adj. *rautainen* 'made of iron', used as an ornamental name, as a nickname referring to the strength or colour of the metal, or as an occupational name for a blacksmith.

Rautenbach German: habitation name from a place in Saxony, so called from MLG *rūte* rue (L *rūta*) + *bach* stream (see BACH).

Rauter *see* REUTER

Rava *see* RAPA

Ravaillac French: habitation name from a lost place in SW France, so called from the Gallo-Roman personal name *Ravilius* + the local suffix *-ācum*.

Ravano Italian: metonymic occupational name for a grower or seller of horse-radish, It. *ravano* (L *raphanus*, from a Gk word akin to the roots of RAPA and REPIN).

Vars.: **Rava(g)ni**.

Dims.: **Ravanelli**, **Ravanello**. Fr.: **Ravenel**, **Raveneau**, **Raffenel**, **Raffeneau**, **Rappeneau**, **Raphanel**, **Rafanel**.

Ravel 1. French: metonymic occupational name or nickname from OF *ravel*, a dim. of *rabe, rave* turnip (see RAPA). In part it may also be a habitation name from a place named with this word, as for example *Ravel* in Puyde-Dôme. **2.** Provençal: habitation name from a place in Drôme, so called from OProv. *revel* rebel (L *rebellis*, from *re-* again, back + *bellum* war).

Vars. (of 1): **Raveau**; **Rabel**, **Rabeau**. (Of 2): **Revel**.

Raven English: nickname for a thievish or dark-haired person, from ME *raven* (OE *hræfn*). In some cases it may be from a personal name derived from this element, a survival into ME of the ON byname *Hrafn* or of an unattested OE cogn. name (*Hræfn*), which is probably present in placenames such as RAVENSCROFT and RAWNSLEY. In central European languages, the cogns. are also found in use as nicknames. In England, a few early forms such as William *atte Raven* (London 1344) suggest that it may also in part be derived from a house sign.

Var.: **Revan**.

Dims.: Ger.: **Rabl**, **Rappl**, **Räppli**. Czech: **Havránek**, **Harvánek**.

Patrs.: Eng.: **Ravening**; **Ravens**, **Revans**, **Revens**.

Ravenscroft English: habitation name from a place in Ches., so called from the gen. case of the OE byname *Hræfn* RAVEN' + OE *croft* paddock, smallholding (see CROFT).

Ravenshaw *see* RENSHAW

Raventós Catalan: of uncertain origin, perhaps an altered form of the rarer surname **Revoltós**, a nickname from Cat. *revoltós* rebellious, difficult (a deriv. of *revolt* revolt, rebellion; cf. REVUELTA). The alteration of the surname may have come about partly to avoid the unfavourable connotations, partly as a result of connection with VENTÓSA.

Raves *see* RALPH

Ravin *see* RABIN

Raw English: **1.** from a medieval given name, a var. of RALPH. **2.** topographic name, a northern var. of ROWE 1.

Var.: **Rawe**.

Patrs. (from 1): **Raw(e)s**, **Rawse**; **Rawson** (chiefly S Yorks.).

Rawcliffe English: habitation name from places in Lancs. and N and W Yorks., so called from ON *rauðr* red (probably replacing the cogn. OE *rēad*; cf. RATCLIFFE) + OE *clif* cliff, slope, riverbank (see CLIVE).

Vars.: **Rawcliff**, **Rawcliffe**.

Rawle *see* RALPH

Rawley *see* RALEIGH

Rawling English: from the ME given name *Rawlin*, OF *Raulin*, a double dim. of RAW 1, with the ANF suffixes *-el* and *-in*.

Vars.: **Rawlin**, **Raulin**, **Rallin(g)**.

Patrs.: Eng.: **Rawling(g)s**, **Rawlyns**, **Rawlence**, **Raulins**, **Rallin(g)s**; **Rawlin(g)son**, **Rawlison**, **Rallison**.

Rawnsley English: habitation name from a place in W Yorks., apparently so called from the gen. case of the OE byname *Hræfn* RAVEN' + OE *hlāw* hill (see LAW 2).

Var.: **Ransley**.

Rawsthorne English: habitation name from *Rostherne* in Ches., so called from the gen. case of the ON byname *Rauðr* 'Red' + ON or OE *þorn* thorn bush.

Vars.: **Rawsthorn**, **Rawstorn(e)**, **Rawstron**, **Rosthorne**, **Rostron**, **Rostern(e)**.

Ray 1. English (Norman): nickname from OF *rey*, *roy* king (from L *rex*, gen. *regis*), denoting someone who behaved in a regal fashion or who had earned the title in some contest of skill or by presiding over festivities. **2.** English: nickname for a timid person, from ME *ray* female roe deer (OE *rǣge*) or northern ME *ray* roebuck (OE *rā*; for the vowel development, cf. ROPER). **3.** English: topographic name, a var. of RYE (1 and 2). **4.** English: habitation name, a var. of WRAY. **5.** Jewish (Ashkenazic): of unknown origin.

Vars. (of 1–4): **Raye**, **Rey**. (Of 1 only): **Roy**. (Of 2 only): **Roe(buck)**.

Patrs. (from 1): Eng.: FITZROY. It.: **Del Ré**, **De Rege**, **(De) Regis**, **(De) Regibus**.

Raybould *see* RAINBOW

Rayer 1. English: from the Norman personal name *Raher*, composed of the Gmc elements *rad* counsel, advice + *heri*, *hari* army. **2.** French: occupational name for a barber, OF *raier* (from *rère* to shave, L *rādere*).

Vars. (of 2): **Rayeur**, **Rahier**.

Rayleigh English: **1.** habitation name from a place in SE Essex, so called from OE *rǣge* female roe deer (see RAY 2) + *lēah* wood, clearing. **2.** var. of RALEIGH.

Rayman *see* RYE

Raymond English and French: from the Norman personal name *Raimund*, composed of the Gmc elements *ragin* counsel + *mund* protection.

Vars.: Eng.: **Raymont**, **Rayment**, **Raiment**. Fr.: **Raimond**, **Reymond**, **Rémon(d)**, **Rémont**, **Ramon(d)**.

Dims.: Fr.: **Remondeau**, **Remondon**. Prov.: **Ramondou**, **Ramon(d)enc**, **Raymonenc(q)**, **Ramonic**. It.: **Raimo**; **Ramondelli**, **Ramondini**, **Ramondino**, **Rimondini**. Ger.: **Reim**.

Patrs.: Ir.: **Redmond(s)** (Gael. **Mac Réamoinn**).

Raynard *see* REYNARD

Raynaud *see* REYNOLD

Raynbird *see* RAINBIRD

Rayne *see* RAINE

Rayner 1. English: from the Norman personal name *Rainer*, composed of the Gmc elements *ragin* counsel + *hari*, *heri* army. **2.** Jewish (Ashkenazic): apparently an ornamental name from mod. Ger. *rein* or Yid. *reyn* pure.

Vars. (of 1): **Raynor**, **Rainer**, **Reyner**, **Reiner**, **Ranner**, RENNER. (Of 2): **Reiner**, **Rainer**; **Rajnerman** (Pol. spelling).

Patrs. (from 1): Ger., Flem., Du.: **Reiners**. Swed.: **Ragnarsson**.

Raynouard *see* RENOUARD

Razgovorov Russian: patr. from the nickname *Razgovor* 'Conversation', denoting a gossip or chatterbox.

Rea *see* RYE

Reacher *see* RICHER

Read English: **1.** nickname for a person with red hair or a ruddy complexion, from ME *re(a)d*, OE *rēad* red (the shortening of the vowel in the mod. Eng. vocab. word is not well explained, though it is parallelled in *bread*, *dead*, and *lead*, where the spelling is more conservative). **2.** topographic name for someone who lived in a clearing in woodland, OE *rīed*, *rȳd*; cf. RHODES and REUTER 1. **3.** habitation name from various places: *Read* in Lancs., the name of which is a contracted form of OE *rǣgheafod*, from *rǣge* female roe deer + *hēafod* head(land); *Rede* in Suffolk, so called from OE *hrēod* reeds; or *Reed* in Herts., so called from OE *rȳht* brushwood.

Vars. (of 1): **Reade**, **Reed**, **Red(d)**; **Reid** (Scots); **Re(a)dman** (see also READER). (Of 2): **Ride**, **Ryde**; RIDER; **Attride**, **Attryde**.

Reader English: occupational name for someone who thatched cottages with reeds, from an agent deriv. of ME *rēd(en)* to cover with reeds (from OE *hrēod* reed).

Vars.: **Re(e)der**; **Reedman**, **Readman** (see also READ).

Patrs.: **Readers**, **Reeders**.

Readhead *see* REDHEAD

Reading English: **1.** habitation name from the county town of Berks., which gets its name from OE *Rēadingas* 'people of *Rēad(a)*', a byname meaning 'Red' (see READ 1). **2.** topographic name for someone who lived in a clearing, from OE *ryding*, a deriv. of *rīed*, *rȳd* (see READ 2).

Vars.: **Red(d)ing**. (Of 2 only): **Rid(d)ing**, **Ryding(s)** (Lancs.).

Readwin *see* REDWIN

Ready 1. English: nickname for a provident man, from ME *readi* prepared, prompt (OE *(ge)rǣde*, of uncertain origin, perhaps a deriv. of *rǣd* counsel, advice). **2.** Scots: habitation name from *Reedie* in the former county of Angus, whose name is of uncertain origin. **3.** Irish: Anglicized form of Gael. **Ó Rodaigh** 'descendant of *Rodach*', a personal name probably derived from *rod* spirited, furious (cf. RODEN 1).

Vars.: **Readey**, **Re(a)ddie**, **Re(a)ddy**, **Raddie**. (Of 2 only): **Reedie**, **Reiddie**, **Reidy**. (Of 3 only): **(O')Roddy**, **(O')Ruddy**, **O'Reddie**.

Dims. (of 3): **O'Rodeghan**, **Rodaughan**, **Rudihan**, **Rudican**, **Redehan**, **Redahan** (Gael. **Ó Rodacháin**).

Reagan *see* REGAN

Real Spanish: **1.** habitation name from any of the numerous places so called, from Sp. *real* encampment, rural property (Arabic *rah(á)l* farmhouse, cabin). **2.** nickname for someone who behaved in a regal manner or occupational name for someone in the service of the king, from Sp. *real* royal (L *regālis*, from *rex*, gen. *regis*, king; cf. RAY 1).

Realff *see* RELPH

Really *see* REILLY

Reaney *see* RAINEY

Rearden *see* RIORDAN

Rease *see* RHYS

Reason *see* RAISON

Réaumur French: habitation name from a place in Vendée, so called from OF *réal* royal (see REAL 2) + *mur* fortress, redoubt (L *mūrus* wall, fortification).

Reavell see REVELL

Reaves see REEVES

Reavey Irish: Anglicized form of Gael. *Riabhach*, a byname meaning 'Brindled', 'Grizzled'.

Patrs.: **McReavy**, **McCreavy**, **McCreevy**, **McCreve(y)**, **McKrevie**, **McGreavy**, **McGreevy**, **McGrievy**, **McGrevye**, **McGreave**, **Magreavy**, **Magreevy** (Gael. *Mac Riabhaich*).

'Descendant of R.': **O'Revoay**, **O'Reogh**, **O'Ria**, **O'Ree** (Gael. *Ó Riabhaigh*).

Rebelo Portuguese: habitation name from the medieval town of *Rabelo*, perhaps so called from a deriv. of Port. *rabo* tail (cf. RAPOSO), i.e. a projecting strip of land.

Rebert see ROBERT

Rebhun 1. German: metonymic occupational name for a hunter of partridges or nickname for someone supposedly resembling a partridge in some way, from Ger. *Rebhuhn* male partridge (MHG *rephuon*, OHG *reb(a)huon*). **2.** Jewish (Ashkenazic): ornamental name from the word denoting the bird, Ger. *Rebhuhn*, one of the many Ashkenazic surnames derived from words for birds and animals.

Var.: **Rebhahn** (from Ger. *Rebhahn* female partridge).

Rebmann German: occupational name for a vine-dresser, from Ger. *Rebe* vine, young shoot (MHG *rebe* planting, esp. of a vine, OHG *reba*) + *Mann* man.

Rebollo Spanish: habitation name from any of various places, for example in the provinces of Segovia and Soria, so called from Sp. *rebollo* shoot (LL *repullus*, from class. L *pullus* young animal; cf. POULE and PULLEN). It is possible that in some cases it may have been a nickname in the sense 'offspring', 'son'.

Rebours French: nickname for someone with bushy and unkempt hair, from OF *rebours* shaggy (LL *reburrus*, probably from *burrus* coarse cloth (see BOURE); later *rebursus*, by hypercorrection and crossing with *reversus*, past part. of *revertere* to turn back).

Vars.: **Rebour**, **Rebous**, **Rebout**.

Dims.: **Rebourseau(x)**, **Rebourset**, **Reboussin**.

Récamier French: occupational name for an embroiderer, from an agent deriv. of OF *recamer* to embroider.

Var.: **Racamier**.

Recasens Catalan: from a Visigothic personal name composed of the elements *rīc* power + *sinð s* way, path. In view of its frequency it is probably in part also a habitation name from either of the two places in the province of Gerona called *Requesens*, from an early proprietor.

Recio Spanish: nickname for a strong or tough man, from the Sp. adj. *recio* (apparently related to L *rigidus* stiff, hard, but the phonetic development is not clear).

Reckitt see RICH

Record see RICKWOOD

Red see READ

Redahan see READY

Redcliffe see RATCLIFFE

Reddan see RODEN

Reddick Scots and N Irish: habitation name from *Rerrick* or *Rerwick* in the former county of Kirkcudbright, probably so called from OE *reafere* robber, reiver + *wīc* outlying settlement (see WICK). It is also possible that the first element was ON *rauðr* red, partially replaced by the native equivalent, which would better explain the pronunciation preserved in the surname.

Var.: **Riddick**.

Reddiford see RADFORD

Redding see READING

Reddington English: probably a var. of READING 1, from the placename + the ME suffix -*tune* (OE *tūn* settlement). However, the surname is quite common in Lancs. and Yorks., and so perhaps a northern place named as the 'settlement associated with *Rēad(a)*' is to be sought.

Reddish English: habitation name from *Reddish* in Lancs. or *Redditch* in Worcs., which are respectively 'reed ditch' (OE *hrēod* + *dīc*) and 'red ditch' (cf. READ 1). The surname is now common in Notts.

Redeke see RAT

Redeker see RADEMAKER

Reder see READER

Redfern English: habitation name from *Redfern* near Rochdale, Greater Manchester, so called from OE *rēad* red + *fearn* fern, bracken.

Var.: **Redfearn**.

Redgate English (Notts.): habitation name from an unidentified place probably deriving its name from OE *rēad* red + ON *gata* road; cf. REDPATH. There is a *Redgate* Wood in Kirklington, Notts., but this placename may be of comaparatively recent origin.

Redgewell see RIDGEWELL

Redgrave English (E Anglia): habitation name from a place in Suffolk, so called from OE *hrēod* reed + *græf* excavation, ditch or OE *rēad* red + *grāfa* grove.

Redhead English and Scots: nickname for someone with red hair, from ME *re(a)d* red (see READ 1) + *heved* head (OE *hēafod*). In some cases it is possibly also a topographic name with the sense 'red headland'.

Var.: **Readhead**.

Redman see ROTH

Redmayne English: habitation name from *Redmain* in Cumb., near Cockermouth, the derivation of which is uncertain. Ekwall suggests that it may be from ME *re(a)d* red + the N Eng. dial. term *man* cairn (of Celt. origin). Another suggestion is W *rhyd* ford + *main* stone.

Redmond see RAYMOND

Redondet see ROUND

Redouté French: nickname for a formidable individual, from the past part. of OF *redouter* to fear (LL *redubitāre*, from the intensive prefix *re-* + *dubitāre* to hesitate, waver).

Redpath Scots: habitation name from a place in the former county of Berwicks., probably so called from OE *rēad* red + *pæð* path; cf. REDGATE.

Var.: **Ridpath**.

Redshaw N English: habitation name, perhaps from *Radshaw* Gill in Fewston, W Yorks., named with the OE elements *rēad* red + *sceaga* copse; cf. RADLEY and REDWOOD.

Redsmith *see* SMITH

Redwin English: from an OE personal name composed of the elements *rǣd* counsel, advice + *wine* friend.

Var.: **Readwin**.

Redwood S English: apparently a habitation name from some minor place so called, probably from OE *rēad* red + *wudu* WOOD; cf. RADLEY and REDSHAW. The reference is probably to birch trees as they appear in the spring.

Reece *see* RHYS

Reed *see* READ

Reeder *see* READER

Reedie *see* READY

Reekie Scots: of uncertain origin, possibly a habitation name from *Reikie* in the former county of Aberdeens., or an altered spelling of *Rikie*, a dim. of RICHARD. It is also possible that it originated as a nickname meaning 'Smoky', from the Sc. dial. term *reek* smoke.

Reely *see* REILLY

Reeman *see* RYE

Reendels *see* REYNOLD

Reenen *see* RAINE

Reents *see* REYNARD

Reeve English (most common in E Anglia): occupational name for a steward or bailiff, the precise character of whose duties varied from place to place and at different periods. The vocab. word is from ME *reeve* (OE *(ge)rēfa*, the etymology of which is disputed; there is apparently no connection with Ger. GRAF). See also GRIEVE, GRAVE 1, and SHERIFF.

Reeves English: 1. patr. from REEVE. 2. topographic name for someone who lived on the margin of a wood, from a misdivision of the ME phrase *atter eaves* at the edge (OE *æt þære efese*).

Vars.: **Reaves**, **Revis**.

Refael *see* RAPHAEL

Refoy English: of uncertain origin; the first known bearer in England is Francis Refoy, who was living at Slindon, Sussex, in 1740. The family are Catholics, and may well have immigrated from Continental Europe.

Regan Irish: Anglicized form of Gael. **Ó Ríagáin** 'descendant of *Riagán*', a personal name of uncertain origin,

perhaps akin to *ríodhgach* impulsive, furious. Bearers of the surname sometimes claim descent from a nephew of Brian Boru called Riagán. See also RYAN.

Vars.: **(O')Reagan**, **O'Regan(e)**, **O'Riegaine**.

Regazzi *see* RAGAZZO

Reger 1. German: nickname from MHG *re(i)ger* heron (OHG *(h)reigaro*), no doubt bestowed on a tall, thin person with long spindly legs. 2. German: nickname for a passionate person, from an agent deriv. of MHG *regen* to be excited, moved. 3. Jewish (Ashkenazic): nickname from mod. Ger. *rege* industrious, quick, nimble.

Var. (of 3): **Regerman**.

Regibus *see* RAY

Regidor Spanish: occupational name for an alderman or similar official, Sp. *regidor* (from *regir* to rule, govern; cf. RÉGIS 1).

Régis French: 1. occupational name for a local dignitary, a deriv. of OF *régir* to rule, manage (L *regere*; cf. REGIDOR). 2. from L *rēgis*, gen. case of *rex* king (see RAY 1); perhaps an occupational name for someone employed in the royal household, or a patr. from a nickname.

Vars. (of 1): **Régissier**, **Regisser**.

Regnard *see* REYNARD

Rego Portuguese: topographic name for someone who lived by a ditch or channel used for irrigation or drainage, Port. *rego* (of pre-Roman origin).

Řehák Czech: ostensibly a nickname meaning 'Redstart', a kind of field warbler. However, in many cases this may well be a pet form of the given name *Řehoř*, the Czech form of GREGORY.

Dim.: **Řeháček**.

Rehnen *see* RAINE

Řehořek *see* GREGORY

Reibisch *see* RYBA

Reichartz *see* RICHARD

Reichbach *see* RICH

Reichenbach German and Jewish (Ashkenazic): habitation name from any of various minor places, particularly in Baden-Württemberg, so called from OHG *rīhhi* rich, powerful (i.e. strongly-flowing; cf. RICH 1) + *bah* stream (see BACH); the adj. retains the weak dat. ending originally used after a preposition and def. art.

Reicholz *see* RICKWOOD

Reid *see* READ

Reiddie *see* READY

Reielts *see* REYNOLD

Reignard *see* REYNARD

Reilly Irish: Anglicized form of the Gael. personal name *Raghailleach*, OIr. *Roghallach*, of unknown origin.

Vars.: **Reily, Rielly, Real(l)y, Reely**; RILEY.

Patrs.: **McReilly, Crilly** (Gael. **Mac Raghailligh**).

'Descendant of R.': **O'Reil(l)y, O'Rielly, O'Riellie, O'Rahilly, O'Real(l)y, O'Reallye, O'Reely, O'Reyley** (Gael. **Ó Raghailligh**).

Reim *see* RAYMOND

Reindl *see* RAINE

Reiner *see* RAYNER

Reinmar German: from a Gmc personal name composed of the elements *ragin* counsel + *meri, mari* fame.

Patrs.: Low Ger.: **Re(i)mers**. Flem., Du.: **Reijmers, Reymers, Remmers**. Sp.: **Ramírez**.

Reis 1. German: topographic name for someone who lived in an overgrown area, from MHG, OHG *rīs* undergrowth, brushwood (mod. Ger. *Reis*). **2.** Jewish (Ashkenazic): of unclear origin: possibly an ornamental name from Ger. *Reis* twig, branch (the same word as in 1 in a transferred sense). Cf. ZWEIG. It may also be a metonymic occupational name for a dealer in rice, from mod. Ger. *Reis* rice. **3.** Portuguese: nickname meaning 'King'; see RAY.

Vars. (of 2): **Reiss, Reisman(n)**.

Reisen Jewish (Ashkenazic): **1.** possibly an ornamental name from NE Yid. *reyzn* roses (Standard Yid. *royzn*); see ROSE 3. **2.** possibly also a habitation name from *Reisen*, which is the Ger. name of *Rydzyna* in the province of Poznań, Poland.

Var. (of 2): **Reisner**.

Reisenberg *see* ROSE

Reitbard *see* ROTH

Reitberg *see* ROTHENBERG

Reiten *see* REUTER

Reith 1. Scots: of uncertain origin, possibly a var. of *McCreath* (see MCCRAE), with the loss of the patr. prefix. **2.** German: var. of REUTER 1.

Reker *see* RADEMAKER

Relandeau *see* ROWLAND

Relin *see* ROLLO

Relph English: from the OF personal name *Riulf*, composed of the Gmc elements *rīc* power + *wulf* wolf. This was introduced to Britain by the Normans.

Vars.: **Relf(e), Realff**.

Remers *see* REINMAR

Remington *see* RIMMINGTON

Remondeau *see* RAYMOND

Remy French: from a medieval given name, which represents a falling together of two distinct L names: **1.** *Rēmigius* (a deriv. of *rēmex*, gen. *rēmigis*, rower, oarsman, from *rēmus* oar + *agere* to wield); this was borne by a 6th-cent. bishop of Rheims who brought Christianity to the W Franks and who baptized Clovis. **2.** *Remedius* (from *remedium* cure,

remedy, a deriv. of *(re)medēri* to treat, heal), which was borne by various minor saints of the 8th to 10th cents.

Var.: **Remi** (also Jewish, of unknown origin).

Dims.: Fr.: **Remi(ll)on, Remiot**. (Of 1 only): Fr.: **Remigeau, Remigeon**. (Of 2 only): It.: **Rimediotti**.

Patr.: Flem.: **Remiens**.

Renad *see* REYNARD

Renaldini *see* REYNOLD

Renbold *see* RAINBOW

Rendall *see* RANDALL

Render N English: of uncertain origin, perhaps an occupational name for a woodcutter or a butcher, from an agent deriv. of ME *rend(en)* to divide, split (OE *rendan*).

René French: from a given name (L *Renātus* 'Reborn') borne by a 4th-cent. saint, and popular in France throughout the Middle Ages because of its transparent reference to Christian spiritual rebirth.

Var.: **Resnais** (a hypercorrected form).

Renisch *see* RAINE

Renison *see* RAINEY

Renner English and German: **1.** occupational name for a messenger, normally a mounted and armed military servant, from an agent deriv. of ME, MHG *rennen* to run. **2.** var. of RAYNER 1.

Renouard French: from *Reginward*, a Gmc personal name composed of the elements *ragin* counsel + *ward* guard.

Vars.: **Reynouard, Raynouard**.

Rensburg, van Dutch: habitation name from *Rendsburg* in the province of Holstein.

Rensen *see* LAWRENCE

Renshaw English: habitation name from *Renishaw* in Derbys., so called from the ME given name REYNOLD + *shawe* copse (see SHAW). The name is still chiefly common in Derbys., S Yorks., and Lancs.

Vars.: **Ra(ve)nshaw, Ravenshear; Renshall, Renshell**.

Renton Scots: habitation name from a place in the former county of Berwicks., 'settlement (OE *tūn*) associated with *Regna*' (a short form of the various cpd personal names with the first element *regen* govern).

Rentoul *see* RINTOUL

Renwick English and Scots (pronounced /'rɛnɪk/): habitation name from a place in Cumb., so called from the OE byname *Hræfn* RAVEN' + *wīc* outlying settlement (see WICK).

Rephael *see* RAPHAEL

Repin Russian: patr. from the nickname *Repa* 'Turnip' (cogn. with Pol. *rzepa* and Czech *řepa*, and ultimately with It. RAPA), denoting a grower or seller of the vegetable or an impassive or slow-witted individual. The Pol. cogn.

is also a nickname for a sturdy, vigorous person (cf. the expression *zdrowy jak rzepka* 'healthy as a turnip').

Dims.: Pol.: **Rzepka**. Czech: **Řepka**.

Habitation names: Pol.: **Rzepkowski**, **Rzepczyński**.

Repton English: habitation name from a place in Derbys., so called from OE *Hrypa*, gen. pl. of the tribal name *Hreope* (cf. RIPPON) + *dūn* hill (see DOWN 1).

Requena Spanish: habitation name from places in the provinces of Palencia and Valencia, apparently so called from a short form of any of the various Visigothic cpd personal names with the first element *rīc* power, with the addition of the local suffix -*ena*.

Reschke see GREGORY

Resende Portuguese: habitation name from any of various places, for example in the province of Beira, so called from the gen. case of a Visigothic personal name composed of the elements *rēðs* counsel, advice + *sinðs* way, path.

Resnais see RENÉ

Restif see RÉTIF

Restorick Cornish: habitation name from a farm called *Restowrack* in the parish of St Dennis, named from Corn. *ros* hill-spur + *dowrek* watery.

Retallack Cornish: habitation name from any of four places in Cornwall. Two of them are from Corn. *res* ford + *helyk* willow trees; the other two are either from *res* + *halek* muddy, marshy, or from *res* + *talek* steep-browed (which also occurs as a personal name).

Var.: **Retallick**.

Retchford see ROCHFORD

Retford see RADFORD

Rethel see ROTH

Rétif French: nickname for an obstinate or awkward individual, from OF *restif* unmoving, stubborn (LL *restīvus*, from *restāre* to remain still).

Vars.: **Restif**, **Réty**; **Retief** (S Africa).

Retter 1. English: occupational name for someone who prepared flax to be made into linen, from an agent deriv. of ME *rett(en)* to soak flax stems in water (in order to rot the soft parts and release the linen fibres). 2. English: occupational name for a maker of fishing nets, OF *retier* (L *rētiārius* (earlier, a gladiator who fought with a net), a deriv. of *rēta* net). 3. Jewish (Ashkenazic): probably from Ger. *Retter* rescuer, saviour (an agent deriv. of *retten* to save). The reasons for its adoption as a surname are unknown: it is probably anecdotal, based on some now irrecoverable incident.

Rettig 1. German: metonymic occupational name for a grower or seller of radishes, from Ger. *Rettich* radish (MHG *rætich*, OHG *rātih*, from L *rādix*, gen. *rādīcis*, root; cf. RACINE). 2. Jewish (Ashkenazic): occupational or ornamental name from the Ger. word for the plant.

Vars. (of 1): **Rettich**. (Of 2): **Retig**.

Reubel see ROBERT

Reuben Jewish: from the Hebr. given name *Reuven* (interpreted in Gen. 29: 32 as *reu* behold + *ben* son). This biblical name may well have influenced the selection of Ashkenazic surnames that are ostensibly derived from mod. Ger. *Rubin* ruby, Yid., Pol., Russ., Ukr. *rubin* (from LL *rubīnus (lapis)*, a deriv. of *rubeus* red; cf. RUDGE 3); see the cpds listed below.

Vars.: **Ruben**, **Rubin(sky)**, **Reuven**.

Dims.: Jewish: **Rubel**, **Ruvel** (from a NE Yid. form); **Rivel**, **Rival** (from a S Yid. form); **Rubenchik**, **Rubenczyk**, **Rubenczik**, **Rubinchik**, **Rubi(ne)k**, **Rubanenko** (E Ashkenazic).

Patrs.: Jewish: **R(e)ub(b)ens** (see also ROBERT), **Rubinsohn** (Ashkenazic); **Rivenzon** (S Ashkenazic); **Rub(e)nov**, **Rubinov**, **Rubinow**, **Rubenovic**, **Rubinowicz**, **Rubinowitz**, **Rubinowi(t)ch**, **Rubinowitsch**, **Rubinovi(t)sch**, **Rubinivitz** (E Ashkenazic); **Rubinovici** (among Rumanian Jews).

Patrs. (from dims.): Jewish: **Riveles**, **Rivilis**, **Rivlin** (S Ashkenazic; see also RIFKIN).

Cpds (ornamental): Jewish: **Rubinfeld**, **Rubenfeld** ('ruby field'); **Rubinfajn** ('ruby fine'); **Rubinlicht** ('ruby light'); **Rubinsaft** ('ruby juice'); **Rubins(h)tein**, **Rubinsztein** ('ruby stone').

Reuss German: ethnic name for someone from Russia, from Ger. *Reusse*, MHG *riusse* Russian (cf. RUSAKOV 1). In some cases, as shown by the example below, it was merely a nickname for someone who had some connection with an E Slav. region.

Reuter 1. German: topographic name for someone who lived in a clearing or occupational name for a clearer of woodland, from an agent deriv. of MHG *(ge)riute* clearing (OHG *riuti*; cf. READ 2 and RHODES). 2. German: derogatory nickname (hardly an actual occupational name) from MHG *riutære* footpad, highwayman (MDu. *ruiter, rütær*, from LL *ruptuārius*, a deriv. of *rupta (via)* road, lit. 'broken way'). 3. Jewish (Ashkenazic): of uncertain origin, possibly as in 1 or 2, possibly an adoption of the German surname.

Vars. (of 1): **Reuther**; **Reit(h)er**, REITH, **Reithmann**, **Reiten**, **Rauter**, **Rauth(mann)**; **Greut(er)**, **Greither**, **Kreith(er)**, **Kreuter**. (Of 3): **Reiten**, **Rauth(mann)**, **Rautman**, **Kreuter**.

Patrs. (from 2): Low Ger.: **Reuters**, **Rüters**.

Revan see RAVEN

Revel see RAVEL

Revell English: nickname for a boisterous person, from ME, OF *revel* festivity, tumult, riot (from OF *reveler* to revel, LL *rebellāre* to rebel, riot; cf. RAVEL 2).

Vars.: **Revel(s)**, **Revill(e)**, **Reavell**.

Revett see RIVETT

Revilla Spanish: habitation name from any of the numerous places so called, from OSp. *revilla* dependent settlement (a deriv. of *villa*; see VILLE).

Revis see REEVES

Revuelta Spanish: nickname for a quarrelsome or argumentative person, from Sp. *revuelta* squabble (LL *revolta* revolt, rebellion, from the past part. of *revolvere* to turn round; cf. RAVENTÓS).

Rew see ROWE

Rewan see RUANE

Rey see RAY

Reymers see REINMAR

Reymond see RAYMOND

Reynard English and French: from a Gmc personal name composed of the elements *ragin* counsel + *hard* hardy, brave, strong, which was introduced into England by the Normans in the form *Re(i)nard*. This was the name borne by the cunning fox in the popular medieval cycle of beast-tales, with the result that from the 13th cent. it began to replace the previous OF word for the animal (see GOUPIL). Some Fr. examples may be nicknames for crafty individuals, referring to the fox's reputation for cunning.

Vars.: Eng.: **Renhard, Rennard, Renyard**. Fr.: **Reinard, Raynard, Rainard, Rena(r)d, Re(i)gnard**.

Dims.: Fr.: **Renardet, Renardin, Renardeau, Renardot**. Ger.: **Reindel, Renardin**. Fris.: **Reintsema**.

Patrs.: Ger.: **Reinartz**. Low Ger.: **Reinerts; Reinerding, Renting**. Fris.: **Reints, Reents**.

Patr. (from a dim.): Low Ger.: **Reintjes**.

Reyner see RAYNER

Reynold English: from a Gmc personal name composed of the elements *ragin* counsel + *wald* rule, which was first introduced to England by Scandinavian settlers in the ON form *Rögnvaldr* (see RONALD), and greatly reinforced after the Conquest by the Norman forms *Reinald, Reynaud*. The surname is occasionally also borne by Jews, in which case it presumably represents an Anglicization of one or more like-sounding Jewish surnames.

Vars.: **Reynell, Rennell, Rennoll, Rennold; Renaud, Renaut**.

Dims.: Fr.: **Renaudel, Renaudeau, Renaudet, Renaudin, Renaudot, Renaudon; Renauleau, Renolleau**. It.: **Rinaldelli, Rinaldin(i), Rinaldini, R(a)inalducci, Rinalduzzi**.

Patrs.: Eng.: **Reynolds, Reynalds, Rennolds, Renals, Rennels; Reynoldson**. It.: **R(a)inaldis; Rinaldeschi** (Tuscany). Ger.: **Ra(i)nalder, Rainalter; Reinhol(t)z; Rainals** (Austria). Low Ger.: **Rei(n)elts**. Fris.: **Reendels**.

Reynouard see RENOUARD

Řezáč Czech: occupational name for a woodcutter, an agent noun from the verb *řezat* to cut, trim, lop, and so a byform of *Řezník* butcher (see RZEŹNIK).

Rhategan see RATTIGAN

Rhein German: topographic name for someone who lived by the river *Rhine*, which is first recorded in the Roman period in the form *Rhenus*; it may be derived from a Celt. element meaning 'to flow'.

Rhind see RIND

Rhodes English (chiefly Yorks.): topographic name for someone who lived in a clearing in woodland, OE *rod*. This most common form of the name has been influenced in spelling by the Gk island of *Rhodes* (Gk *Rhodos*, perhaps ultimately akin to ROSE 1). There does not seem to be any connection with mod. Eng. *road* (OE *rād* 'riding'), which was not used of a thoroughfare on land until the 16th cent.

Vars.: **Rhoades, Road(s); Royds; Rodd**.

Rhynd see RIND

Rhys Welsh: from one of the most common of OW personal names, *Rīs* 'Fiery Warrior'. This was the name of the last ruler of an independent kingdom of Wales, Rhys ap Tewder, who died in 1093 unsuccessfully opposing the Norman advance.

Vars.: **Rees(e), Reece, Rease, Rice**.

Patr.: PRICE.

Rian see RYAN

Riba see RYBA

Riback see RYBAK

Ribalta Catalan: topographic name for someone who lived by a high riverbank, from Cat. *riba* bank (see RIVE) + *alta* (fem.) high (L *alta*). There are various minor places in E Spain named with these elements, and the surname may also derive from any of them.

Ribaud French: nickname for a notorious reprobate, from a pej. deriv. of OF *riber* to live licentiously (of Gmc origin). The term was also used to denote a member of the lowest class of servants, who had to carry out the most unpleasant and dangerous tasks, so that it may in part also have been originally an occupational name.

Vars.: **Ribau(l)t, Riboud, Ribout; Ribard**.

Dims.: Fr.: **Ribot(on), Ribon, Ribet**.

Ribbe see RIPPERT

Ribbentrop German: habitation name from a place in Lippe, recorded in 1564 in the form *Ribbrachtingdorp*, i.e. 'village (see THORPE) of the people of *Ribbracht*', a Gmc personal name composed of the elements *rīc* power + *berht* bright, famous; cf. RIPPERT.

Ribereau see RIVERS

Ribó Catalan: 1. nickname, a var. of *Ribot*; see RIBAUD. 2. topographic name, a dim. of *Riba*; see RIVE.

Ribra see RUBBRA

Ricci Italian: nickname for a person with curly hair, from It. *ricco* curly.

Vars.: **(Lo) Riccio, Rizzi, (Lo) Rizzo; Risso** (Liguria).

Dims.: **Riccelli, Rizzelli, Rizz(i)ello, Rizzillo, Riccetti, Rizzetti, Rizzetto; Riccini** (partly Jewish), **Rizzini, Riciol(in)i, Ricciolino, Rizz(i)oli, Rizzolo, Rissolo, Ricciulli, Ricciotti, Rizzotti, Rizzotto**.

Augs.: **Riccioni, Rizzon(i), Rizzone, Rissone**.

Rice see RHYS

Rich English: 1. nickname for a wealthy man (or perhaps in some case an ironic nickname for a pauper), from ME, OF *riche* rich, wealthy (of Gmc origin, akin to Gmc *rīc* power). 2. from a medieval given name, a short form of RICHARD, or less commonly of some other cpd name with this first element (cf., e.g., RICHER). 3. habitation name from the lost village of *Riche* in Leics., apparently so called from an OE element **rīc* stream or, here, drainage channel. Some early forms of the surname, such as Ricardus *de la riche* (Hants 1200) and Alexander *atte Riche* (Sussex 1296) probably derive from minor places named with this element in southern counties, as for example Glynde *Reach* in Sussex.

Vars.: **Riche, Ritch; Richman** (see also RICHMOND). (Of 2 only): **Rick**.

Dims. (of 1): Fr.: **Richet(on), Richez, Richon, Richou**. It.: **Ricchini, Ricchino**. Ger.: **Reichel, Reichlin**. (Of 2): Eng.:

Ritchie (chiefly Scots); **Ricket(t)**, **Reckitt**. Ger.: **Reichel(t)**, **Reickl**, **Rietsche(l)**. Fris.: **Ritzke**.

Augs. (of 1): It.: **Riccone**. Sp.: **Ricote**.

Patrs. (from 2): Eng.: **Riches**; **Ricks(on)**, RIX, **Rixon**. Ger.: **Ritzer**, **Ritzen**, **Ritscher**, **Ritschen**. Low Ger.: **Ricks**, **Rix(en)**, **Ricken(s)**. Fris.: **Rickena**, **Rykena**.

Patrs. (from 2) (dims.): Eng.: **Richies**; **Ricketts** (chiefly W Midlands). Sc.: **McRitchie**. Ger.: **Reichler**.

Cpds (from cogns. of 1; ornamental unless otherwise stated): Jewish (Ashkenazic): **Reichbach** ('rich stream', may also be topographic; see also REICHENBACH); **Reichbart**, **Reichbard**, **Rajchbart** ('rich beard', nickname; *Rajchbart* is a Pol. spelling); **Reichenbaum** ('rich tree'); **Reich(en)berg** ('rich hill'); **Reichfeld** ('rich field'); **Reichgold** ('rich gold'); **Reichgott** ('rich God'); **Reichkind** ('rich child'); **Reichnadel**, **Reichnudel** ('rich needle', perhaps ornamental-occupational for a tailor); **Reich(en)stein** ('rich stone'); **Reichent(h)al** ('rich valley'); **Reichtaler** ('rich dollar' or 'dweller in a rich valley').

Richard English, French, German, and Flemish/Dutch: from a Gmc personal name composed of the elements *rīc* power + *hard* hardy, brave, strong. This is found in OE, but was popularized in England by the Normans. See also DICK and HICK. There was considerable confusion with the rarer RICHER (for a similar situation, cf. SIMON).

Vars.: Eng.: **Ritchard**, **Ricard(e)**, **Riccard**; **Rickard** (Devon and Cornwall); **Rickerd**, **Rickert**. Fr.: **Ricard**, **Rig(u)ard**.

Ger.: **Reich(h)ardt**, **Reichert**, **Richardt**. Flem.: **Rickaert**, **Rykert**.

Dims.: Fr.: **Richardeau**, **Rigardeau**, **Ric(h)ardet**, **Ric(h)ardin**, **Ric(h)ardon**, **Ric(h)ardot**, **Ricardou**. It.: **Ricc(i)ardelli**, **Ricciardello**, **Riccardini**; **Ricciardiello** (Naples); **Rizzardini**; **Licciard(i)ello**.

Patrs.: Eng.: **Richard(e)s**, **Ric(k)ards**, **Rickardes**; **Richardson**; **Ritson** (Northumb. and Yorks). Welsh: PRITCHARD. Ger.: **R(e)ichar(t)z**, **Reicherz**. Low Ger.: **Rickertsen**. Fris.: **Richten**, **Rigts**. Swed.: **Rickardsson**, **Richardsson**.

Richer English (chiefly Essex): from a Gmc personal name composed of the elements *rīc* power + *heri*, *hari* army, introduced into England by the Normans in the form *Richier*, but largely absorbed by the much more common RICHARD.

Vars.: **Reacher**, **Ricker**.

Patr.: Eng.: **Rickers**.

Richmond English: habitation name from any of the numerous places so called, in N France as well as in England. These are named with the OF elements *riche* rich, splendid (see RICH 1) + *mont* hill (see MONT). Richmond in N Yorks. was named after a *Richmont* in France immediately after the Norman Conquest, and in many if not most cases the Eng. surname can be derived from this place. Richmond in SW London received this name only in the reign of Henry VII, in honour of the king, who had been Earl of Richmond until he came to the throne. Previously the place was known as *Sheen*; it is unlikely to be the source of the surname of anyone called *Richmond*.

Vars.: **Richmont**; **Richman** (see also RICH).

Richter 1. German: occupational or status name for an arbiter or judge, Ger. *Richter* (MHG *rihtære*, from *rihten* to make right). The term was mostly used in the Middle Ages to denote a part-time settler of disputes rather than a full-time legal official. Such communal conciliators held a position of considerable esteem in rural communities; in E Germany the term came to denote a village headman, which was often a hereditary office. It is in this region that the surname is most frequent. **2.** Jewish (Ashkenazic): translation of DAYAN.

Dim. (of 1): Czech: **Rychtářík**.

Patrs. (from 1): Low Ger.: **Richters** (N Rhineland); **Richtering** (Westphalia).

Rickwood English: **1.** from *Richold*, a Norman personal name composed of the Gmc elements *rīc* power + *wald* rule. Reaney also cites *Ricolda* as a fem. name, from Gmc *rīc* power + *hild* battle. **2.** from *Richward*, a Norman personal name composed of the Gmc elements *rīc* power + *ward* guard. Both names were introduced into England by the Normans, but neither became particularly popular, and they were confused early.

Vars. (of 1): **Richold**. (Of 2): **Rickward**, **Rickword**, **Record**.

Dims. (of 1): Fr.: **Rigaudet**, **Rigaudin**.

Patrs. (from 1): Ger.: **Reicholz**. Low Ger.: **Rickolts**, **Rickelts**. (From 2): Eng.: **Records**.

Riddell Scots and N English: **1.** regional name from *Ryedale* in N Yorks., the valley (see DALE) of the river *Rye* (which bears a Brit. name). **2.** from a Norman personal name, *Ridel*. Reaney explains this as a nickname from OF *ridel* small hill (a dim. of *ride* fold, of Gmc origin), but a more probable source is a Gmc personal name derived from the element *rīd* ride.

Vars.: **Riddel**, **Riddle**, **Riddall**, **Rid(e)al**.

Ridding see READING

Ride see READ

Rider English: **1.** occupational name for a mounted warrior or messenger, late OE *rīdere* (from *rīdan* to ride), a term quickly displaced after the Conquest by the new sense of KNIGHT. As an Ir. surname it is a translation of a Gael. name; see MARKEY. **2.** topographic name for someone who lived in an clearing in woodland; cf. READ 2.

Var.: **Ryder**.

Patrs. (from 1): Low Ger.: **Ridders**, **Ritters**, **Riddering**.

Ridge 1. English: topographic name for someone who lived on or by a ridge, ME *rigge*, OE *hrycg*. **2.** Irish: translated form of Gael. **Mac Con Iomaire** 'son of *Cú Iomaire*', a byname meaning 'Hound (i.e. watchdog) of the Ridge (i.e. border)'. This surname is common in Galway.

Vars. (of 1): **Rigg(e)**, **Riggs** (northern, from an ON cogn.; cf. RIGBY); RUDGE, **Ruggs**, **Rugman**; **Atteridge**.

Ridgewell English: habitation name from *Ridgewell* in Essex, so called from OE *hrēod* reed + *well(a)* spring, stream (see WELL).

Vars.: **Ridgwell**, **Redg(e)well**.

Ridgway English (chiefly Lancs.): topographic name for someone who lived on an ancient way along a ridge, from OE *hrycg* RIDGE + *weg* path, road (see WAY), or habitation name from some minor place of this name.

Var.: **Ridgeway**.

Ridler English: occupational name for a sifter of flour and meal, from an agent deriv. of ME *rid(e)len* to sift (from OE *hriddel* sieve).

Ridley English: habitation name from any of various places in England so called, esp. the one in Northumb., which, like that in Ches., is clearly derived from OE *geryd* channel + *lēah* wood, clearing. Those in Essex and Kent appear in Domesday Book as *Retleia* and *Redlege* respectively, and get their names from OE *hrēod* reed + *lēah*.

Ridout English: of uncertain origin. It might seem to be an occupational nickname for a rider, from ME *rid(en)* to ride + *out* out, forth, but this is probably no more than folk etymology.

Vars.: **Rideout**, **Ridoutt**.

Ridpath *see* REDPATH

Ridsdale English (Yorks.): habitation name from *Ridsdale* or *Redesdale* in Northumb., so called from its position in the valley (see DALE) of the river *Rede*, whose name is derived from OE *rēad* red.

Riebisch *see* RYBA

Riedel *see* RODE

Riefenstahl Low German: occupational nickname for a polisher of weapons and armour, from the MLG phrase *wrīve den stāl* polish the steel, from *wrīven* to rub, polish + *den* (acc.) def. art. + *stāl* STEEL.

Var.: **Riefstahl**.

Rieflin *see* ROLF

Rielly *see* REILLY

Riemer German and Jewish (Ashkenazic): occupational name for a maker of leather reins and similar articles, Ger. *Riemer* and Yid. *rimer* belt-maker (MHG *riemœre*, an agent deriv. of *rieme(n)* strap, belt, thong, OHG *riomo*).

Vars.: Ger.: **Rieme**, **Rie(h)m** (metonymic); **Riem(en)schneider** (see SCHNEIDER). Jewish: RIMER; **Rymer** (E Ashkenazic, a Pol. spelling); **Rimerman**.

Riepe *see* RIPPERT

Riepel *see* ROBERT

Riera Catalan: topographic name for someone who lived by a flood-stream, Cat. *riera* (LL *rīvāria*, a deriv. of *rīvus* stream; cf. RIEU). There are various places in N Spain named with this word, for example in the province of Tarragona, and the surname may also be a habitation name from any of these.

Riesco Spanish: topographic name for someone who lived near an outcrop of rock or nickname for a hard-hearted individual, from OSp. *riesco* steep crag (of uncertain origin, perhaps akin to L *resecāre* to cut; cf. RIESGO).

Var.: **Risco**.

Riese Jewish (Ashkenazic): nickname for an exceptionally tall or bulky person, from mod. Ger. *Riese* giant. In some cases the name may have been used to refer ironically to a particularly short man.

Vars.: **Ries**, **Riz** (from Yid. *riz* giant). The name has sometimes been Anglicized as REESE (see also RHYS).

Riesgo Spanish: nickname for an awkward or quarrelsome person, from OSp. *riesgo* discord (perhaps akin to L *resecāre* to cut, divide; cf. RIESCO).

Rietsche *see* RICH

Rietveld Dutch: topographic name for someone living by a reedbed, from Du. *riet* reed (OSax. *hriod*) + *veld* uncultivated land (see FIELD).

Rieu Provençal: topographic name for someone who lived near a stream, OProv. *rieu* (L *rīvus*), or habitation name from any of the numerous places named with this word.

Vars.: **Rieux**, **Rieuf**; **Rio(u)**; **Larieu**, **Sarieu**; **Delrieu**, **Durrieu**; **Duriz**, **Duruz**, **Dury** (Switzerland).

Dims.: Prov.: **Riol(s)**, **Rivol(l)et**. It.: **Rivolo**, **Da Riolo**; **Rivelli**; **Riet(t)i**, **Riozzi**.

Rifkin Jewish (E Ashkenazic): metr. from the Yid. female given name *Rifke* (from the Hebr. name *Rivka* Rebecca, meaning 'Heifer'), with the addition of the Slav. metr. suffix *-in*.

Vars.: **Rifkind**, **Rivkin(d)**, **Ryvkin(d)** (for the excrescent *-d*, see SÜSSKIND); **Rivkovich**, **Rivkes**; **Rives** (from the female given name *Rive*, a back-formation from *Rivke*, taken as a supposed dim.); **Riveles**, **Rivelis**, **Rivlin** (from *Rivele*, a pet from of *Rive*; see also REUBEN).

Rigard *see* RICHARD

Rigaudet *see* RICKWOOD

Rigby English (chiefly Lancs.): habitation name from *Rigby* in Lancs, named with ON *hryggr* ridge + *býr* farm, settlement.

Rigg *see* RIDGE

Rigglesford *see* WRIGGLESWORTH

Rigley *see* WRIGLEY

Řihánek *see* GREGORY

Rikin Jewish (E Ashkenazic): metr. from the Yid. female given name *Rike* (of uncertain origin) + the Slav. metr. suffix *-in*.

Vars.: **Rykowicz**; **Riklin**, **Riklis** (from the dim. *Rikl*).

Riley 1. Irish: var. of REILLY. 2. English: habitation name from *Ryley* in Lancs., so called from OE *ryge* RYE + *lēah* wood, clearing. There is a *Riley* with the same meaning in Devon, but it does not seem to have contributed to the surname, which is more common in N England.

Var. (of 2): **Ryley**.

Rimbault *see* RAINBOW

Rimediotti *see* REMY

Rimer 1. English (Lancs.): occupational name for a poet, minstrel, or balladeer, from an agent deriv. of ME *rime(n)* to compose or recite verses (OF *rimer*, from *rime* metre, L *rhythmus*). 2. Jewish (Ashkenazic): var. of RIEMER.

Var. (of 1): Eng.: **Rimmer**.

Rimerman *see* RIEMER

Rimmington English: habitation name from *Rimington* in Yorks., so called from the old name of the stream on which it stands (OE *Riming* 'Boundary Stream') + OE *tūn* enclosure, settlement.

Var.: **Remington**.

Rimon Jewish (Israeli): ornamental name from Hebr. *rimon* pomegranate, in part a Hebraicization of MILGRIM and *Granat* (see GARNETT 1).

Var.: **Rimmon**.

Rimondini *see* RAYMOND

Rimpler *see* RUMBOLD

Rinaldelli *see* REYNOLD

Rincón Spanish: topographic name for someone who lived by a corner, Sp. *rincón* (OSp. *re(n)cón*, from Arabic *ruk(ú)n*).

Rind 1. Scots: habitation name from a small place in the former county of Perths. called *Rhynd*, from Gael. *roinn* point of land. 2. Jewish (Ashkenazic): of uncertain origin, possibly from Ger. *Rind*, Yid. *rind* head of cattle, or a shortening of the ornamental Ashkenazic surname **Baumrind** (from Ger. *Baumrinde* tree-bark).

Vars. (of 1): **Rhind**, **Rhynd**.

Rinelli *see* PERRIN

Ring English, German, Danish/Norwegian, and Swedish: metonymic occupational name for a maker of rings (from OE, OHG *hring*, ON *hringr*), either to be worn as jewellery or as component parts of chain-mail, harnesses, and other objects. In part it may also have arisen as a nickname for a wearer of a ring. Latterly, in Scandinavia it was adopted as an ornamental name.

Vars.: Eng.: **Rings**. Ger.: **Rin(c)k(e)**.

Dims.: Ger.: **Ringel**, **Ringle**.

Ringer English: 1. from the OF personal name *Reinger*, *Rainger*, composed of the Gmc elements *ragin* counsel + *geri, gari* spear. This was introduced to Britain by the Normans. 2. occupational name for a maker of rings (see RING) or for a bell-ringer (from ME *ring(en)* (trans.), OE *hringan* (intrans.)).

Var. (of 1): **Rainger**.

Ringrose English: of uncertain origin. It is first attested in Norwich in 1259 as *Ringerose*, and later forms show no significant variation. Unless it had already been drastically altered by folk etymology at that early date, it is probably from ME RING + ROSE, but if so the original meaning is far from clear.

Rinne *see* WREN

Rintoul Scots: habitation name from a minor place now lost, which was in Fife near Kinross. The etymology of the placename is obscure.

Var.: **Rentoul**.

Rioja Spanish: regional name for someone from the region of *Rioja* in N Castile, which is centered on Logroño. The region is named from the river *Oja*, which flows through it; the Sp. word *río* river has become fused with the river name. This is first recorded in the form *Ol(i)a*, and may possibly be derived from L *folia* leaves (cf. OJEDA).

Riordan Irish: Anglicized form of Gael. **Ó Ríoghbhárdáin** 'descendant of *Ríoghbhárdán*', a byname composed of *ríogh-* royal + a dim. of *bárd* bard, poet.

Vars.: **O'Riordan**, **O'Riourdane**, **O'Riverdan**, **O'Reedan**, **Reardon**, **Rearden**.

Ripley English: habitation name from any of various places, esp. one in W Yorks., so called from OE *ripel* strip of land + *lēah* wood, clearing.

Ripoll Catalan: habitation name from a place in N Spain, the site of a famous medieval monastery, originally named with the L elements *rīvus* stream (see RIEU) + *pullus* dark grey.

Var.: **Ripollès**.

Rippe 1. French: nickname for a sufferer from scabies, OF *ripe* (from *riper* to itch, scratch, tear, of Gmc origin). 2. Low Ger.: dim. of the given name RIPPERT.

Dims. (of 1): Fr.: **Ripot(eau)**, **Ripon**, **Ripoche**.

Ripper English: occupational name for someone who made or sold baskets, or else carried wares about in a basket, from an agent deriv. of ME *(h)rip* basket (ON *hrip*).

Rippert French and Low German: from a Gmc personal name composed of the elements *rīc* power + *berht* bright, famous.

Vars.: Fr.: **Ripert**, **Ribert**. Low Ger.: **Ribbert**.

Dims.: Low Ger.: RIPPE, **Ribbe**, **Rip(p)ke**. Fris.: **Riepe**.

Patrs. (from dims.): Low Ger.: **Rippen(s)**, **Ripping**. Fris.: **Riepen(a)**.

Rippon English: habitation name from *Ripon* in N Yorks., so called from OE *Hrypum*, dat. pl. (originally used after a preposition) of a tribal name of obscure etymology; cf. REPTON.

Riquet *see* HENRY

Risby English: habitation name from any of various places, for example in Lincs., Suffolk, and E Yorks., so called from ON *hrís* brushwood (cf. REIS 1 and RISLEY) + *býr* farm, settlement.

Rischer *see* RUSH

Risco *see* RIESCO

Riseborough English (Norfolk): habitation name, of uncertain origin. It could be from Princes *Risborough* in Bucks. (from OE *hrīsen*, an adj. deriv. of *hrís* brushwood + *beorgas* hills).

Var.: **Risebrow**.

Risk *see* RUSK

Risley English: habitation name from *Risley* in Derbys. and Lancs., or *Riseley* in Beds. and Berks., all so called from OE *hrīs* brushwood + *lēah* wood, clearing.

Risso *see* RICCI

Rita Portuguese: from a female given name, an aphetic form of *Margharita* Margaret (see MARGUERITE), chosen in particular in honour of a 15th-cent. It. saint who bore the name in this form.

Ritch *see* RICH

Ritchard see RICHARD

Ritters see RIDER

Rival see REUBEN

Rive French: topographic name for someone who lived on the bank of a river or the shore of a lake, OF *rive* (L *rīpa*).
Vars.: **Rives**; **Larive**, **Delarive**.
Dims.: Fr.: **Rivet**, **Riveau**, **Rivelon**. It.: **Rivetti**. Cat.: RIBÓ.

Riveles see RIFKIN

Rivelli see RIEU

Rivero Spanish: topographic name for someone who lived on a patch of raised land beside a river, Sp. *ribero* (LL *rīpārium*, a deriv. of *rīpa*; see RIVE).

Rivers English (Norman): habitation name from any of various places in N France called *Rivières*, from the pl. form of OF *rivière* river (originally meaning 'riverbank', from L *rīpāria*, a deriv. of *rīpa* bank; cf. RIVE and RIVERO). The absence of Eng. forms without the final -*s* makes it unlikely that it is ever from the borrowed ME vocab. word *river*, but the French and other Romance cogns. do normally have this sense.
Dims.: Prov.: **Ribereau**, **Riberole**, **Ribe(y)rolles**.
Aug.: Prov.: **Ribeyras**.

Rivett English (E Anglia): metonymic occupational name for a metalworker, from ME, OF *rivet* small nail or bolt (from OF *river* to fix, secure, of unknown origin).
Var.: **Revett**.

Rix English (E Anglia): 1. patr. from the given name *Rick*, a var. of RICH 2. 2. topographic name for someone who lived on a piece of land thickly grown with rushes, from OE (W Saxon) *rixe* rush (coll. sing.), a metathesized form of *rysc*; cf. RUSH 1. 3. Low German: see RICH

Riz see RIESE

Rizzardini see RICHARD

Rizzelli see RICCI

Roach English: topographic name for someone who lived by a rocky crag or outcrop, from ME, OF *roche* (later replaced in England by *rock*, from the Norman byform *rocque*; cogns. are found in other Romance languages, but the origin is unknown). Some early examples of the surname derive from various places in Normandy, as for example *Les Roches* in Seine-Maritime, named with this word.
Var.: **Roche** (Irish).
Dims.: Eng.: **Rochelle**, **Rotchell**, **Rockell**, **Rockall**. Fr.: **Rochel(le)**, **Larochelle**, **Rochet(te)**, **Larochette**, **Rochon**; **Rohel**, **(Le) Roël** (Brittany). Prov.: **Ro(c)quet(te)**; **Rouchet**, **Rouché**, **Rouchès**, **Rouchon**, **Rouchoux**, **Rouchousse**.

Road see RHODES

Roadknight English: occupational name for a mounted retainer, ME *rōdknicht* (OE *rādcniht*, from *rād*, an abstract deriv. of *rīdan* to ride + *cniht* servant (see KNIGHT)).
Var.: **Rodknight**.

Roaf see ROLF

Roake see ROCK

Roan see RUANE

Robalo Portuguese: metonymic occupational name for a fisherman, or nickname, from Port. *robalo* snook (*Centropomus undecimalis*, a marine fish). The word is of uncertain origin, perhaps a metathesized form of **lobarro*, a deriv. of *lobo* wolf (cf. Low 3).

Robatham see ROWBOTTOM

Robert English, French, Catalan, Low German, and Dutch: from a Gmc personal name composed of the elements *hrōd* renown + *berht* bright, famous. This is found occasionally in England before the Conquest, but in the main it was introduced into England by the Normans and quickly became popular among all classes of society. See also DOBB, HOBB, and NOBB. The surname is also occasionally borne by Jews, as an Anglicization of one or more like-sounding Jewish surnames.
Vars.: Eng.: **Robart**. Fr.: **Robart**, **Robard**, **Rebert**; ROPER, **Ro(s)pars**, **Ropartz** (Brittany); **Flobert**, **Flaubert** (from a byform with the first element *hlōd*; cf. LEWIS). Low Ger.: **Robbert**, **Rub(b)ert**, **Ropert**, **Rup(p)ert**.
Dims.: Eng.: **Robb**, **Rabb**; ROBIN; **Roby** (Scotland); RABBITT, **Roblett**, **Roblin**, **Rablin**, **Rablan**. Fr.: **Robertet**, **Robardet**, **Robardey**, **Robertot**; **Robet**, **Robé**, **Robey**, **Robez**, **Robel(in)**, **Roblin**, **Rob(e)let**, **Rob(e)lot**, **Rob(i)ot**, **Robion**, **Robiou**, **Robeçon**, **Robichon**, **Rebichon**, **Robuchon**, **Robic** (Brittany). It.: **Robertelli**, **Rubertelli**, **Rubartelli**, **Robertucci**. Ger.: **Ropp**, **Robbel**, **Rupp(el)**, **Rüpel**, **Rüppele** (Swabia); **Rüppeli(n)** (Switzerland); **Riep(e)l** (Bavaria); **Reubel**, **Reuble** (see also REUBEN). Low Ger.: **Robbe**, **Röpe**, **Röb(be)ke**, **Röp(c)ke**, **Rübke**, **Rüpke**.
Pejs.: It.: **Robertacci**, **Robertazzi**.
Patrs.: Eng.: **Roberts** (also Jewish), **Robers**, **Robarts**, **Robberds**; **Rober(t)son** (especially common in Scotland). Sc.: **McRobert(s)**. Welsh: PROBERT. Fr.: **Derobert**. It.: **De Roberto**, **Di Roberto**, **(De) Robertis**, **Rubertis**. Ger.: **Ruprechter**; **Ruperti** (Latinized). Low Ger.: **Roberts(en)**, **Robberts**, **Rubberts**; **Robertz**, **Ruppertz** (N Rhineland). Swed.: **Robertsson**.
Patrs. (from dims.): Eng.: **Robbs**; **Rob(e)son** (Northumb.); **Rabson**; **Rapson** (Cornwall); **Ropkins**, **Rapkins**. Sc.: **McRobb**. Low Ger.: **Robben**, **Röbken**, **Röbker**, **Röpkes**, **Röpking**. Flem., Du.: **Rops**, **Rub(b)ens**.

Robertshaw English (W Yorks.): habitation name from a lost place in Heptonstall, W Yorks., taking its name from an owner ROBERT + ME *shawe* copse (OE *sceaga*).
Var.: **Robshaw**.

Robespierre French: from a combination of the given names ROBERT and PIERRE. The spelling with -*s*- is the result of hypercorrection of the form *Robépierre*, from earlier *Rober(t)pierre*.

Robin 1. English and French: from the medieval given name *Robin*, a dim. of ROBERT, from the short form *Rob* + the hypocoristic suffix -*in*. 2. Jewish (Ashkenazic): possibly a var. of RABIN.
Vars. (of 1): Eng.: **Robbin**, **Robyn**.
Dims. (of 1): Fr.: **Robinet**, **Robinot**, **Robineau**. Prov.: **Roubineau**, **Roubinet**.
Patrs. (from 1): Eng.: **Rob(b)ins**, **Rob(b)ens**, **Robyns**; **Robi(n)son**. Sc.: **McRobin**. Welsh: **Probin**, **Brobin**, **Broben**.

Robinov see RABIN

Robledo *see* ROUVRE

Robottom *see* ROWBOTTOM

Robusti Italian: nickname for a strong and hardy person, from the It. adj. *robusto* (L *rōbustus*, from *rōbur* (heart of) oak; cf. ROUVRE).

Roby English and Scots: **1.** dim. of ROBERT. **2.** habitation name from *Roby* in Lancs. (now Merseyside), so called from ON *rá* pole, boundary mark + *býr* farm, settlement.
Vars. (of 1): **Rob(b)ie**. (Of 2): **Rab(e)y**, **Rabie** (also from *Raby* in Ches. and Co. Durham, with the same etymology).
Patr. (from 1): Sc.: **McRobbie**.

Roch 1. French: from a Gmc personal name of uncertain origin. It may have been originally a byname meaning 'Crow' (cf. OHG *hruoh*, OE *hrōc*, an imitative formation), but Dauzat derives it from a root *hroc* rest. The name was reasonably common in the Middle Ages and was often given in honour of a 14th-cent. saint of Montpellier remembered for his miraculous healings during an outbreak of the plague. **2.** Jewish: of unknown origin.
Var. (of 1): **Roz** (see also ROSE).
Dims. (of 1): It.: **Rocchelli**, **Rocchetti**, **Rocchini**, **Rocuzzo**.
Augs. (of 1): It.: **Roccon(i)**.
Patrs. (from 1): Low Ger.: **Rochs**, **Rochussen**.

Roche *see* ROACH

Rochester English: habitation name from the town in Kent, recorded by Bede (*c.*730) under the names of both *Dorubrevi* and *Hrofæcæstre*. The former represents the original Brit. name, composed of the elements *duro-* fortress and *brīvā* bridge. The second represents a contracted form of this (possibly affected by folk etymological connection with OE *hrōf* roof) combined with an explanatory OE *cæster* Roman fort (from L *castra* military camp). There is a much smaller place in Northumb. also called *Rochester*, which seems to have been named in imitation of the more important one, but which is a more than occasional source of the surname. In a few cases there may also have been confusion with *Wroxeter* in Shrops., recorded in Domesday Book as *Rochecestre*.
Vars.: **Rogister**, **Rossiter**.

Rochford English: habitation name from either of two places so called, in Essex and Worcs. In both cases the name probably derives from the gen. case of OE *ræcc* hunting dog (perhaps a byname) + OE *ford* FORD, but its development has been influenced by the common Fr. placename composed of the elements *roche* rock (see ROACH) + *fort* strong (L *fortis*).
Vars.: **Ratchford**, **Retchford**.

Rochlin Jewish (NE Ashkenazic): metr. from the Yid. female given name *Rokhl* (from the Hebr. female name *Rachel* 'Ewe') + the Slav. metr. suffix *-in*.
Var.: **Rachlin** (a Hebraicized form found in Israel).

Rock English: **1.** topographic name for someone who lived near a notable crag or outcrop, from ME *rocc* rock (see ROACH), or habitation name from a place named with this word, as for example *Rock* in Northumb. **2.** topographic name for someone who lived near a large oak

tree (see OAK), from a misdivision of ME *atter oke* at the oak. *Rock* in Worcs. gets its name in this way, and the surname may in some cases be a habitation name from this source. **3.** metonymic occupational name for a spinner of wool or a maker of distaffs, from ME *rok* distaff (from ON *rokkr* or MDu. *rocke* or an unattested OE cogn.).
Vars.: **Rocke**; **Rocks**. (Of 2 only): **Ro(a)ke**. (Of 3 only): **Rocker**, **Rooker**, **Rucker**.

Rockefeller German: habitation name from the village of *Rockenfeld* near Neuwied in the Rhineland (so called from MHG *rocke* RYE (OHG *rocko*) + *feld* open country; see FIELD) + *-er* suffix denoting a native or inhabitant.

Rockley English (Notts.): habitation name from a place near Retford, so called from OE *hrōc* rook (perhaps a byname) + *lēah* wood, clearing. There is also a place so called in Wilts., which is a possible alternative source of the surname.

Rockwell English: habitation name from places in Bucks. and Somerset. The former was earlier *Rockholt*, and is so called from OE *hrōc* rook (perhaps a byname) + *holt* wood. The second element of the Somerset place is probably (and more predictably) OE *well(a)* spring, stream (see WELL).

Rocquette *see* ROACH

Rodaughan *see* READY

Rodd *see* RHODES

Roddam English: habitation name from *Roddam* Hall near Alnwick in Northumb., which is named from the dat. pl., *rodum* (originally used after a preposition) of OE *rod* clearing (see RHODES).
Var.: **RODEN**.

Roddy *see* READY

Rode 1. French: from a short form of any of the various Gmc personal names with the first element *hrod* renown (cf. ROTH 3). **2.** French: topographic name for someone who lived in a clearing in woodland, OF *rode* (of Gmc origin; cf. RHODES). **3.** Low German: cogn. of RHODES. **4.** Danish and Norwegian: cogn. of ROTH 1 and 2. **5.** Provençal: metonymic occupational name for a wheelwright or topographic name for someone who lived by a waterwheel, from OProv. *rode* wheel (L *rota*).
Vars. (of 1): **Rodon** (from the oblique case). (Of 3 and 4): **Rohde**. (Of 5): **Ro(u)dier**, **Ro(u)dié**.
Dims. (of 1): Fr.: **Rodin**, **Rodot**, **Rodilon**. Ger.: **Rüdel**, **Riedel**. (Of 5): Prov.: **Rodel**, **Ro(u)det**, **Roudeix**.
Patrs. (from 1): Low Ger.: **Röd(d)ing**. Flem., Du.: **Rutten**.

Roden 1. Irish: Anglicized form of Gael. Ó Rodáin 'descendant of *Rodán*', a personal name derived from *rod* hearty, lively, furious, spirited; cf. READY 3. **2.** English: var. of RODDAM.
Vars.: **Rodden**, **Rod(d)an**. (Of 1 only): **O'Rodane**, **O'Ruddane**, **(O')Rudden**, **Ruddon**, **Reddan**, **Reddin**.

Ródenas Spanish: habitation name from a place in the province of Teruel, so called from a fem. pl. form of the adj. *rodeno*, a Mozarabic dial. form of OSp. *roano* reddish (see RUANO); the noun *tierras* land is probably to be understood.

Rodera Spanish: topographic name for someone who lived by a cart track, Sp. *rodera* (LL *rotāria*, a deriv. of *rota* wheeel; cf. RODE 5).

Var.: **Roderas** (more frequent).

Roderick 1. English: from the Gmc personal name *Hrōdrīc*, composed of the elements *hrōd* renown + *rīc* power, introduced into England by the Normans in the form *Rodric*, but not frequent during the Middle Ages. 2. Welsh: Anglicized form of the personal name *Rhydderch*, originally a byname meaning either 'Reddish-brown' or else 'Very Famous'.

Patrs. (from 1): Sp.: **Rodríguez**, **Ruiz**. Port.: **Rodrigues**. Jewish (Sefardic): **Rodriques**, **Rodriguez** (adoptions of the Sp. and Port. names). (From 2): Welsh: PROTHEROE.

Rodés Catalan: habitation name from a place in the province of Lérida. This probably has the same origin as *Rodez* in the *département* of Aveyron, France, which is first recorded in the 6th cent. in the L form *Rutensis*, apparently from the Gaul. tribal name *Ruteni*, of unknown origin.

Rodge see ROGER

Rodknight see ROADKNIGHT

Rodney English: habitation name from a minor place in Somerset, an area of land in the marshes near Markham. This is first recorded in the form *Rodenye*; it derives from the gen. case of the OE personal name *Hroda* (a short form of the various cpd names with the first element *hrōð* renown; cf. RODE 1) + OE *ēg* island, dry land in a fen.

Rodway English: habitation name from a place in Somerset, so called from OE *rād* riding (a deriv. of *rīdan* to ride) + *weg* way, path, i.e. a path suitable for passage on horseback as well as on foot.

Var.: **Rodaway**.

Rodwell English (chiefly E Anglia): apparently a habitation name from an unidentified place (probably not the district of Weymouth in Dorset), perhaps so called from the OE personal name *Hroda* (see RODNEY) + OE *well(a)* spring, stream.

Roe see RAY

Roebotham see ROWBOTTOM

Roël see ROACH

Roelands see ROWLAND

Roelofs see ROLF

Rofé Jewish: occupational name from Heb. *rofe* physician (a deriv. of *rafa* to heal; cf. RAPHAEL).

Vars.: **Rofe(h)**, **Rophe**, **Roff(e)** (see also ROLF); **Harofé**, **Harofe** (with the Hebr. def. article).

Rofe see ROLF

Roffey English: habitation name from a place in Sussex, near Horsham, so called from OE *rūh* rough (cf. RAUCH) + *(ge)hǣg* enclosure (see HAY 1).

Rogacki Polish: topographic name for someone who lived on a 'horn' of land, i.e. an outlying, projecting edge of a settlement or administrative division, from Pol. *róg* horn, projection, with the surname suffix *-ski* (see BARANOWSKI).

Vars.: (also Jewish (E Ashkenazic)): **Rogowski**, **Rogaczewski**.

Rogalski 1. Polish: from the Pol. dial. term *rogala* ox (a deriv. of *róg* horn), with the surname suffix *-ski* (see BARANOWSKI). This was perhaps applied as a nickname for a large, strong man, or taken from a house sign showing an ox or a pair of horns. 2. Jewish (Ashkenazic): the reasons for its adoption as a Jewish surname are unclear; it may be an ornamental name.

Vars.: **Rogulski**, **Rogala**; **Rogaliński** (possibly also a habitation name from the town of *Rogalin* in Great Poland).

Patr.: Pol.: **Rogalewicz**.

Roger 1. English, French, Catalan, and Low German: from a Gmc personal name composed of the elements *hrōd* renown + *geri, gari* spear, which was introduced into England by the Normans in the form *Rog(i)er*. The cogn. ON *Hróðgeirr* was a reinforcing influence in Normandy. See also DODGE and HODGE. 2. Irish: Anglicized form of *Mac Ruaidhrí*; see RORY.

Vars. (of 1): Eng.: **Rodgier**, **Rogger**; **Rodger** (Scotland); **Rosser** (Wales). Fr.: **Rogier**, **Rogez**. Low Ger.: **Rogger**, **Röttger**, **Röttcher**, **Rödi(n)ger**.

Dims. (of 1): Eng.: **Rodge(tt)**, RUDGE. Fr.: **Rogeron**, **Rogerot**, **Roget**, **Rogeon**. Flem., Du.: **Rogge**.

Aug. (of 1): It.: **Roggerone**.

Patrs. (from 1): Eng.: **Rogers(on)**; **Rodgers(on)** (Scotland, N Ireland). Welsh: PROSSER. It.: **De Rugg(i)ero**, **Di Rugg(i)ero**. Low Ger.: **Ruttgers**, **Röttgers**. Flem., Du.: **Rutgers**, **Roggers**.

'Servant of R. 1 (dim.)': Eng.: **Rodgeman**, **Roggeman**.

Roghtigan see RATTIGAN

Rogister see ROCHESTER

Rogov Jewish (E Ashkenazic): habitation name from *Raguva* near Kaunas in Lithuania, formerly known by the Russ. name *Rogovo*.

Vars.: **Rogoff**, **Rogow**; **Rogowski**, **Rogowsky**, **Rogovsky**; **Rogover** (from Yid *Rogever* native or inhabitant of *Rogeve*, the Yid. name of the town).

Rogoziński Polish and Jewish (E Ashkenazic): habitation name from some place named with Pol. *rogoża* bulrush, for example *Rogoźnica, Rogoźnik, Rogoźno*, or *Rogoźno*.

Rohan 1. French: habitation name from a place in Morbihan, in Brittany. There is also another place of the same name in Deux-Sèvres, which may have contributed to the surname. 2. Irish: var. of RUANE.

Rohde see RODE

Rohel see ROACH

Rohfsen see ROLF

Rohling see ROLLO

Rohr 1. German: topographic name for someone who lived in an area thickly grown with reeds, from Ger. *Rohr* reed, MHG *rōr* (a collective sing.), or habitation name from one of the several places named with this word. **2.** Jewish: of uncertain origin, possibly as in 1.

Vars. (of 1): **Röhr**, **Rohrer**, **Rohrmann**.

Dims. (of 1): Ger.: **Röhrle**. Low Ger.: **Röhreke**.

Collectives (of 1): Ger.: **Röhrich(t)**, **Rörig**.

Rois see ROSE

Roisman see ROSEMAN

Roit see ROTH

Rojas Spanish: from the fem. pl. form of *rojo* red (see ROUSE). It is probably a topographic name, with some noun to be understood such as *tierras* land (cf. RÓDENAS) or *aguas* water.

Rojek Polish and Jewish (E Ashkenazic): apparently a nickname from Pol. dial. *rojek*, a kind of small ox from the mountain regions of S Poland (a deriv. of *róg* horn; see ROGALSKI). As a Jewish name, it is probably purely ornamental.

Habitation name: **Rojewski**.

Rojter see ROTH

Roke see ROCK

Rokos see RÁKOS

Rolance see ROWLAND

Rolf English: from the ME given name *Rolf*, composed of the Gmc elements *hrōd* renown + *wulf* wolf. This name was especially popular among Nordic peoples in the contracted form *Hrólfr*, and seems to have reached England by two separate channels; partly through its use among pre-Conquest Scandinavian settlers, partly through its popularity among the Normans, who, however, generally used the form *Rou(l)* (see ROLLO).

Vars.: **Ro(a)lfe**, **Rolph**, **Rulf**; **Roff(e)**, **Ruff**, **Roaf**, **Rofe**, **Roof(e)**, **Rouf(f)**, **Rove**.

Dims.: Eng.: **Ruffell**, **Ruffle** (Essex). It.: **Rolfini**. Ger.: **Rüffli**, **Rieflin** (Switzerland).

Patrs.: It.: **Firidolfi**. Ger.: **Rudolfer**. Low Ger.: **Ro(h)lfs**, **Rohfsen**, **Rohlfing**. Flem., Du.: **Roelofs(en)**, **Roelvink**.

Patr. (from a dim.): Eng.: **Ruffles**.

Rollo English: from a Latinized form, common in early medieval documents, of *Rou(l)*, the usual Norman form of ROLF.

Vars.: **Roll(e)**, RULE, ROWE.

Dims.: Eng.: **Rollet(t)**, **Rollit(t)**, **Rowlett**, **Rowlatt**; **Rol(l)in(g)**, **Rowling**. Fr.: **Ro(u)l(l)et**, **Rol(l)in**, **Relin**, **Roul(l)y**, **Rollot**, **Roulot**. It.: **Raucci(o)**. Low Ger.: **Rollman**, **Rullmann**, **Rühlemann**, **Rahlmann**; **Rö(h)lke**, **Rühlicke**, **Rülke**, **Rahlke**.

Patrs.: Eng.: **Rolls**, **Rol(l)es**, **Rowles**; **Rowlson**, **Roulson**. It.: **Firrao**, **De Rao**. Low Ger.: **Rohls(en)**, **Rahls**; **Röhli(n)g**, **Rohling**.

Patrs. (from dims.): Eng.: **Rollin(g)s(on)**, **Rollison**, **Roli(n)son**, **Rollerson**, **Rollason**, **Rowlings(on)**, **Rowli(n)son**, **Rowlerson**.

Rolo Portuguese: **1.** nickname for a person with curly hair, from Port. *rolo* roll, coil, curl (LL *rotulus*, a dim. of *rota* wheel; cf. RODE 3). **2.** nickname for a troublesome or ob-

streperous person, from the same word used in the sense 'rumpus', 'uproar'.

Rolston English: habitation name from any of various places, such as *Rowlston* on the coast in Humberside, *Rolleston* in Leics., Notts., and Staffs., or *Rowlstone* in Herefords., near the Welsh border. Most of these are so called from the gen. case of the ON personal name *Hrólfr* (see ROLF) or of the OE cogn. name *Hrōðwulf* + OE *tūn* enclosure, settlement. In the case of the Notts. place, however, the first element is from the gen. case of the ON personal name *Hróald* (see ROWETT).

Vars.: **Rolleston**, **Rolstone**, **Roulston**, **Row(le)ston(e)**.

Romagosa Catalan: habitation name from any of several places in N Spain, so called from *romagosa*, fem. of Cat. *romagós*, *romegós* thistly, prickly (LL *rumicōsus*, from *rumex*, gen. *rumicis*, sorrel); a noun such as 'land' is presumably to be understood.

Roman 1. English, French, Catalan, Rumanian, Polish, Ukrainian, and Belorussian: from the L personal name *Rōmānus* (originally an ethnic byname from *Rōma* Rome, of obscure, probably pre-Italic, origin), borne by several early saints, including a 7th-cent. bishop of Rouen. It was also the baptismal name of St Boris (see BORISOV). The name was popular in N France in the early Middle Ages and was introduced into England by the Normans, but did not become common. **2.** English, French, and Catalan: regional or ethnic name for someone from Rome or from Italy in general, or nickname for someone who had some connection with Rome, as for example having been there on a pilgrimage (cf. ROMERO).

Vars. (of 1 and 2): Eng.: **Romain(e)**, **Romayn(e)**. Fr.: **Romain**, **Romand**. Cat.: **Romà**. (Of 1 only): Pol.: **Romański**. (Of 2 only): Eng.: **Rome**, **Room(e)**. Fr.: **Rom(m)e**.

Dims. (of 1 and 2): Fr.: **Romanet**. It.: **Romanelli**, **Roman(i)ello**, **Romanetti**, **Romanino**, **Romanin(i)**, **Romanucci**. (Of 1 only): Ukr.: **Romaniuk**, **Romanchuk**, **Romanets**. Beloruss.: **Romanenya**.

Pej. (of 1 and 2): It.: **Romanazzi**.

Patrs. (from 1 and 2): Eng.: **Romans**. (From 1 only): Russ.: **Romanov**, **Rominov**; **Romanoff** (U.S.). Ukr., Beloruss.: **Romanovich**. Pol.: **Romanowicz**.

Patrs. (from 1) (dims.): Russ.: **Romanychev**, **Romin**, **Romashov**. Ukr.: **Romanitsa**, **Romanchat**.

'Son of the wife of R. 1': Russ.: **Romanikhin**.

Habitation name: Pol.: **Romanowski**.

Rombouts see RUMBOLD

Rombulow see RUMBELOW

Romero Italian and Spanish: **1.** regional or ethnic name for a Roman or more generally for an Italian (cf. ROMAN 2), from L *Rōmaeus*, Gk *Rōmaios*, with the ending influenced by the common L agent suffix *-ārius*. **2.** nickname for a pilgrim. The vocab. word came to have this sense because it was originally applied to travellers from the Western (Roman) Empire who had to pass through the Eastern (Byzantine) Empire on their way to the Holy Land. Later it was also used of pilgrims to Rome and to Santiago de Compostela.

Vars.: It.: **Romerio**, **Romeo**, **Romei**.

Romilly 1. English (Norman) and French: habitation name from any of various places in N France, as for example *Romilly* in Eure or *Remilly* in La Manche, so called from the Gallo-Roman personal name *Rōmilius* (a deriv. of *Rōmulus*, the founding father of Rome) + the local suffix *-ācum*. **2.** habitation name from *Romiley* in Greater Manchester, so called from OE *rūm(ig)* spacious, roomy + *lēah* wood, clearing.

Rommel Low German, Flemish, and Dutch: nickname for an obstreperous person, from MLG, MDu. *rummeln, rumpeln* to make a noise, create a disturbance (of imitative origin).

Vars.: **Römmele, Römmler; Rummel, Rümmele, Rümmler**.

Romney English: habitation name from a place in Kent, so called from an obscure first element *Rumen* + OE *ēa* river (see RYE).

Var.: **Rumney**.

Romo Spanish: nickname for someone with a snub nose, from Sp. *romo* blunt, foreshortened (of uncertain etymology, perhaps from L *rhombus*, itself a borrowing from Gk, with reference to the two obtuse angles of this figure).

Romsay see RUMSEY

Ronald Scots: Anglicized form of the Gael. personal name *Raonull*, which is a borrowing from ON *Rögnvaldr* (see REYNOLD).

Var.: **Ranald**.

Patrs.: **Ronaldson, Ranaldson; McRanald, McRannal, Magrannell, Grannell, (Mc)Crandle, (Mc)Crindle, McCrindell, McGrandell, (Mc)Crangle, (Mc)Cringle, Crennall** (Gael. **Mac Raonuill**).

Ronan Irish: Anglicized form of Gael. **Ó Rónáin** 'descendant of *Rónán*', a personal name apparently representing a dim. of *rón* seal.

Vars.: **(O')Rona(y)ne**.

Roncero Spanish: nickname for a deceitful person or a flatterer, from the OSp. adj. *roncero* (a deriv. of *ronce* deception, flattery, from Arabic *ramz, rumz* allusion, figurative expression (as opposed to plain speech)).

Roncin French: metonymic occupational name for someone in charge of horses used as pack-animals or for pulling carts rather than for riding, from OF *roncin* workhorse (of obscure etymology). The word also developed the meaning 'drudge', and so may also have been a nickname for a hard-pressed servant.

Var.: **Ronsin**.

Pej.: Fr.: **Ronsard**.

Rondeau see ROUND

Roney see ROONEY

Rongier French: nickname from an agent deriv. of OF *ronger* to gnaw (from L *rumigāre* to ruminate, with the vowel influenced by crossing with *rōdere* to gnaw). The significance of the name is not entirely clear. It may have been bestowed on a usurer or a grumbler or for some more anecdotal reason.

Dims.: **Rongeron, Ronget**.

Rönisch see RAINE

Rönnberg see ROWNTREE

Rønne Danish: topographic name for someone who lived in a very humble dwelling, from Dan. *rønne* hovel.

Var.: **Rønn**.

Ronson see ROWLAND

Roobottam see ROWBOTTOM

Roof see ROLF

Rook English: **1.** nickname from the bird (OE *hrōc*), given to a person with very dark hair, or for some other reason. **2.** some early examples, such as Robert *of ye Rook* (London 1318) and Henry *del Rook* (Staffs. 1332), point clearly to a local name of some kind. The first of these could be from a house sign, the second may well be a var. of ROCK 1.

Vars.: **Rooke, Ruck**.

Patrs. (from 1): **Rook(e)s**.

Rooker see ROCK

Rookledge see ROUTLEDGE

Room see ROMAN

Rooms see JEROME

Roon see RUANE

Rooney Irish: Anglicized form of Gael. **Ó Ruanaidh** 'descendant of *Ruanaidh*', a byname meaning 'Champion'.

Vars.: **O'Rownoe, (O')Roney, ROWNEY**.

Roop see ROPER

Roos see ROSS

Roosevelt Dutch: topographic name for someone living by an area of uncultivated land overgrown with roses, from Du. *roose* ROSE + *velt* open country (cf. FIELD).

Root 1. English: nickname for a cheerful person, from ME *rote* glad (OE *rōt*). **2.** English: metonymic occupational name for a player on the rote, an early medieval stringed instrument (ME, OF *rote*, of uncertain origin but apparently ultimately akin to W *crwth*; cf. CROWTHER). **3.** Dutch: topographic name for someone who lived by a retting place (Du. *root*, a deriv. of *ro(o)ten* to ret, akin to mod. Eng. *rot*), where flax was soaked in tubs of water until the stems rotted to release the linen fibres.

Vars. (of 1 and 2): Eng.: **Roote, Rutt**. (Of 2 only): Eng.: RUTTER. (Of 3 only): Du.: **Rooth**.

Patrs. (from 1): **Root(e)s**.

Rootham English: habitation name from *Wrotham* in Kent, so called from the OE byname **Wrōta* (from *wrōt* snout) + OE *hām* homestead. The spelling of the surname reflects the present pronunciation of the placename.

Ropars see ROBERT

Roper 1. English: occupational name for a maker or seller of rope. The word is an agent deriv. of OE *rāp*; in the SE Midland dialect of Eng., which became standard, OE *-ā-* /ɑ:/ became ME *-ō-* /o:/ and eventually mod. Eng. /əʊ/, whereas in the N Eng. dialects it was preserved, becoming mod. Eng. /eɪ/, so that the var. **Raper** is still common in

Yorks., in spite of its obvious undesirable modern connotations. **2.** French (Brittany): var. of ROBERT.

Vars. (of 1): **Rooper**; **Rope(s)**, **Roop(e)**.

Equivs. (not cogn.): Ger.: SEILER. Czech: PROVAZNÍK.

Ropero Spanish: occupational name for a seller of clothes or for someone who was in charge of the working clothing held in common by a group of workers, from an agent deriv. of Sp. *ropa* clothes (of Gmc origin; the meaning was originally 'spoils', 'plunder'; cf. RÄUBER).

Rophe *see* ROFÉ

Roquet *see* ROACH

Rörig *see* ROHR

Rorke *see* ROURKE

Rory Scots and Irish: Anglicized form of the Gael. personal name *Ruaidhrí*, originally composed of Celt. elements meaning 'red' (also 'powerful', 'mighty') and 'rule'.

Vars.: **Rorie**; ROGER.

Patrs.: **Rorison**; **McRo(o)ry**, **McRury**, **McCrory**, **McGrory**, MCCREERY (Gael. **Mac Ruaidhrí**).

Rosa 1. Italian and Catalan: cogn. of ROSE 1. **2.** Polish and Czech: apparently from Pol., Czech *rosa* dew, perhaps applied as a nickname. However, in the Mazovian dial. of Polish *rosa* also means a cornflower, and the Pol. name may therefore be of topographic origin, while the Czech word also has other meanings, including waste from a mill or the outflow of a millstream. Moldanová suggests also that it may also be a short form of the given name *Rostislav*.

Vars.: Pol.: **Rosiak**, **Roszak**, **Rosicki**. Czech: **Rosák**.

Dims.: Pol.: **Roszczyk**. Czech: **Rosík**.

Habitation names: Pol.: **Roszkowski**; **Rosiński**.

Rosado Spanish and Portuguese: nickname for someone with a notably 'pink and white' complexion, from Sp., Port. *rosado* pink (LL *rosātus*, a deriv. of *rosa* ROSE).

Rosal Spanish: topographic name for someone who lived by a rose bush, Sp. *rosal* (LL *rosāle*, a deriv. of *rosa* ROSE). There are numerous places named with this word, for example in the provinces of Granada, Huelva, Orense, and Pontevedra, and the surname may also derive from any of these.

Var.: **Rosales**.

Rosário Portuguese: religious byname from *rosário* rosary, given in particular to someone who was born on the festival of Our Lady of the Rosary, celebrated on the 1st Sunday in October. The word derives from LL *rosārium* rose garden (a deriv. of *rosa* ROSE), and was transferred to a set of devotions dedicated to the Virgin Mary as the result of the medieval symbolism which constantly compared her to a rose.

Roscoe English: habitation name from a place in Lancs., so called from ON *rá* roebuck (see RAY 2) + *scógr* copse (see SHAW).

Rose 1. English, French, and German: from the name of the flower, ME, OF *rose*, Ger. *Rose*, MHG *rose* (L *rosa*), in various applications. In part it is a topographic name for someone who lived at a place where wild roses grew. In a town, it can also be a house name from a house bearing the sign of the rose. It is also found, especially in Europe, as a nickname for a man with 'rosy' complexion. Latterly, in Scandinavia the cogns. were adopted as ornamental names. **2.** English: from the medieval female given name *Rose*, *Royse*, popularly associated with the flower, but in fact originally from a Gmc personal name. This is recorded in Domesday Book in the form *Rothais*, and is apparently composed of the elements *hrōd* renown + *haid(is)* kind, sort. **3.** Jewish (Ashkenazic): ornamental surname from the word for the flower (Ger. *Rose*, Yid. *royz*), or metronymic from the Yid. female given name *Royze*, derived from the word for the flower.

Vars. (of 1): Fr.: **Roze**, **Larose**, **Laroze**; **Roz** (Brittany; see also ROCH). (Of 2): Eng.: **Royse**, **Royce**. (Of 3): Jewish: **Rois(en)**, **Roiz**, **Roiz(i)n**, REISEN; ROSEMAN.

Dims. (of 1): Fr.: **Roset**, **Ro(u)zet**, **Rosin**; **Rozec** (Brittany). It.: **Rosell(in)i**, **Rosiello**, **Rosett(in)i**, **Rosina**, **Rosin(i)**, **Rosita**. Ger.: **Rösel**, **Rösle(n)**. Low Ger.: **Rösgen**. Czech: **Růžek**.

Augs. (of 1): It.: **Rosone**, **Roson(i)**.

Cpds (ornamental): Swed.: **Ros(en)berg** ('rose hill'); **Rosenblad(h)** ('rose leaf'); **Rosencran(t)z** ('rose wreath, rosary'); **Rosendahl** ('rose valley'); **Rosengren** ('rose branch'); **Ros(en)qvist** ('rose twig'). Jewish: **Rosenbaum**, **Rosenboim**, **Rosenbojm**, **Roizenbaum** ('rose tree'); **Rosenberg(er)**, **Rosenbarg**, **Reisenberg** ((inhabitant of) rose hill); **Rosenblatt**, **Rosenblat(h)** ('rose leaf'); **Rosenblum** (U.S. **Rosenbloom**; 'rose flower'); **Rosenbus(c)h** ('rose bush'); **Rosendorf** ('rose village'); **Rosenfarb** ('rose colour'); **Rosenfeld(er)** ((inhabitant of) rose field', partly or completely Anglicized as **Rose(n)field**); **Rosenfrucht** ('rose fruit'); **Rosengart(en)** ('rose garden'); **Rosenhaupt** ('rose head'); **Rosenhaus** ('rose house'); **Rosenkran(t)z**, **Rosenkranc(e)** ('rose wreath'); **Rosensaft** ('rose juice'); **Rosenschein** (U.S. **Rosenshine**; 'rose shine'); **Rosens(h)tein**, **Reisenstein** ('rose stone'); **Rosenstengel** ('rose stem'); **Rosenstiel** ('rose stalk'); **Rosens(h)to(c)k** ('rose bush'); **Rosenshtrom** ('rose river'); **Rosent(h)al**, **Rosent(h)ol(er)** ((inhabitant of) rose valley'); **Rosenwald** ('rose wood'); **Rosenwasser**, **Rosenvasser** ('rose water'); **Rosenzweig**, **Rosenzveig**, **Rosencwaig** ('rose twig').

Roselló Catalan: habitation name from a place in the province of Lérida or a region in S France (*Rousillon*). Both places first appear in the L form *Ruscino*, gen. *Ruscinōnis*. They are of pre-Roman origin and obscure meaning.

Var.: **Rosselló**.

Roseman 1. English: from the medieval female given name *Rosemunde*, apparently originally a Gmc cpd of the elements *hros* horse + *mund* protection, but early associated in the popular mind with the L phrase *rosa munda* pure rose, an epithet of the Virgin Mary. **2.** Jewish (Ashkenazic): ornamental name or name adopted by the husband of a woman bearing the Yid. given name *Royze* (see ROSE 3).

Vars. (of 1): **Rosoman**; **Rosamond** (also Fr., and in London and elsewhere partly of Huguenot origin). (Of 2): **Rosemann**, **Roisman**, **Roizman**, **Royzman**; **Rosenman(n)** (the latter is probably only ornamental).

Roses Catalan: habitation name from a place in the province of Gerona, of uncertain etymology (it has been guessed to have some connection with the name of the Gk island of *Rhodes*, which is perhaps distantly related to ROSE 1).

Var.: **Rosas**.

Roseveare Cornish: habitation name from either of two places so called. The one in St Austell is so called from Corn. *ros* moor + *mur* great, large; the other, in St Mawgan in Meneage, is from *res* ford + *mur*. In both cases, the initial *m-* of the adj. is mutated to *v-*.

Vars.: **Rosevear**, **Roseveer**, **Roseveor**.

Rosewall Cornish: habitation name from a place in the parish of Towednack, recorded in 1327 in the form *Ryswal*, from Corn. *res* ford + possibly *(g)wall* rampart.

Var.: **Rosewell**.

Roskilly Cornish: habitation name from a place in the parish of St Keverne, so called from Corn. *ros* moor + *kelly* grove.

Var.: **Roskelly**.

Rospars see ROBERT

Ross 1. English and Scots (Norman): habitation name from *Rots* near Caen in Normandy, probably named with the Gmc element *rod* clearing; cf. RHODES. This was the original home of a family *de Ros*, who were established in Kent in 1130. **2.** English and Scots: habitation name from any of various places called *Ross* or *Roos(e)*, deriving the name from W *rhós* upland or moorland, or from a Brit. ancestor of this word, which also had the sense 'promontory'. This is the sense of the cogn. Gael. word *ros*. Known sources of the surname include *Roos* in E Yorks (now Humberside) and the region of N Scotland known as *Ross*, part of the former county of Ross and Cromarty. Other possible sources are *Ross*-on-Wye in Herefords., *Ross* in Northumb. (which is on a promontory), and *Roose* in Lancs. **3.** English and German: from the Gmc personal name *Rozzo*, a short form of the various cpd names with the first element *hrod* renown, introduced into England by the Normans in the form *Roce*. **4.** German: metonymic occupational name for a breeder or keeper of horses, from S Ger. *Ross* horse (MHG *ros*, OHG *hros*), perhaps also a nickname for someone thought to resemble a horse or a house name for someone who lived at a house distinguished by the sign of a horse. **5.** Jewish (Ashkenazic): in some cases, of the same origin as in 4, in others an Anglicization of any of the Jewish surnames listed at ROSE.

Vars. (of 2): **Roos(e)**.

Rossall English: habitation name from *Rossall* in Lancs. and Shrops, so called from OE *hros, hors* horse + *halh* nook, recess (see HALE 1).

Rosseels see RUSSELL

Rosser see ROGER

Rosset see ROUSE

Rossignol French: nickname for a person with a good singing voice, or ironically for a raucous person, from OF *rossignol* nightingale (OProv. *rossinhol*, from LL *lusciniólus*, class. L *lusciniôla*, dim. of *luscinia*).

Vars.: **Roussignol**, **Rossignon**, **Rossigneux**.

Rossington English: habitation name from a place in W Yorks., apparently named in OE as *Rosingtún* 'enclosure, settlement associated with a moor' (the first element being akin to W *rhós* moor, heath).

Rossiter see ROCHESTER

Rostaing French: from a Gmc personal name composed of the elements *hrod* renown + *stán* stone.

Vars.: **Roustaing**, **Ro(u)stang**, **Rostand**, **Roustan**.

Rostern see RAWSTHORNE

Rostropovich Belorussian: patr. from the nickname *Rastrop* 'Shock-headed person'; the vowel of the first syllable has been hypercorrected under Russ. influence, since in that language unaccented *o* is pronounced as *a*.

Rotchell see ROACH

Rotellini see PARROTT

Rotgerber German and Jewish (Ashkenazic): occupational name for someone who dressed leather with tannin (cf. BARKER 1 and TANNER 1), as opposed to using alum salts (cf. WEISSGERBER and WHITTIER). The word is a cpd of Ger. *rot* red (see ROTH 1) + GERBER.

Roth 1. German and Jewish (Ashkenazic): nickname for a person with red hair, from Ger. *rot* red (MHG, OHG *rôt*; a cogn. of READ 1). As a Jewish surname it is also at least partly ornamental: its frequency as a Jewish surname is disproportionate to the number of Jews who one may reasonably assume were red-headed during the period of surname adoption. **2.** German and English: topographic name for someone who lived in a clearing; see RHODES. **3.** German: from a short form of any of the various Gmc personal names with the first element *hrod* renown; cf. RODE 1 and ROSS 3.

Vars. (of 1): Ger.: **Rothe**, **Rother(t)**. Jewish: **Rot(er)**; **Roit(er)**, **Royter** (from Yid. *royt*), **Rojter** (Pol. spelling); **Rot(h)man(n)**, **Rottmann**, **Rot(t)erman**, **Roitman**; **Reitman** (from the NE Yid. pronunciation of Yid. *royt* red); **Redman** (Anglicized); **Rothmensch**, **Rotmensh**, **Rotmench**; **Rotmensz** (Pol. spelling). See also ROTHMANN.

Dims. (of 1): Ger.: **Röthel**, **Rethel**, **Röthlein**. Low Ger.: **Rötchen**.

Cpds (of cogns. of 1, ornamental except where otherwise stated): Jewish: **Rotapel** ('red apple'); **Rot(er)band** ('red ribbon'); **Rotbart(h)**, **Rotbard**, **Reitbard**, **Reitbord** ('red beard', nickname); **Rotbaum** ('red tree'); **Rotblat**, **Reitblatt** ('red leaf'); **Ro(i)tblit** ('red blossom'); **Rotblum** ('red flower'); **Rotfarb** ('red colour'); **Rot(h)feld**, **Rottfeld** ('red field'); **Rotgold** ('red gold'); **Rotholz**, **Rotgolz** ('red wood'); **Rotkirch** ('red church', probably topographic); **Rot(h)kopf**, **Roitkof** ('red head', nickname); **Rotleder** ('red leather', perhaps ornamental-occupational); **Rotermund** ('red mouth', perhaps nickname or anecdotal); **Rotrubin** ('red ruby'); **Rot(h)stein**, **Rotshtein**, **Rotsztejn** ('red stone'); **Rotwald** ('red forest').

Rothenberg Jewish (Ashkenazic): habitation name from a place so called in W Bavaria, or possibly from some other place similarly named, e.g. one in Upper Lusatia in East Germany. The placename is from OHG *rôt* red (with the weak dat. ending *-en*, originally used after a preposition and def. art.) + *Berg* hill.

Vars. (also merely ornamental, composed of the elements *rot* red + *berg* hill): **Rot(t)enberg**, **Rut(t)enberg**; **Routenberg** (Fr. spelling); **Rothenberger**; **Rothberg**, **Rutberg**; **Reitberg(er)** (from the NE Yid. pronunciation of Yid. *royt* red).

Rotherforth see RUTHERFORD

Rotherham English: habitation name from the town in S Yorks., so called from the ancient Brit. river name *Rother* (of obscure meaning) + OE *hām* homestead.

Var.: **Rotheram**.

Rothmann German: **1.** var. of ROTH, in any of its senses. **2.** (in Saxony and Silesia) occupational name for a counsellor or nickname for a man respected for his opinions and advice, from a dial. var. of Ger. *Rat* counsel (MHG *rāt*) + *Mann* man.

Rothschild Jewish (Ashkenazic): house name from a house distinguished with a red sign (see ROTH 1 and SCHILD 2). The famous banking family of this name took it from a house so marked in the Jewish quarter of Frankfurtam-Main, but the name has also been adopted by many Ashkenazic Jews unrelated to the family. In Britain the surname is normally given the spelling pronunciation /'rɒθstʃaɪld/; the original pronunciation is /'roːtʃɪlt/.

Vars.: **Rotschild**; **Rothchild** (U.S.).

Rothwell English: habitation name from any of the places, in Lincs., Northants, N Yorks., and elsewhere, so called from OE *roð(u)* clearing (a byform of *rod*; cf. RHODES) + *well(a)* spring, stream (see WELL).

Var.: **ROWELL** (representing the local pronunciation of the place in Northants).

Röttcher *see* ROGER

Rouane *see* RUANE

Roubíček Czech and Jewish (Ashkenazic): nickname for a cringing person, from a dim. of the vocab. word *roub* graft, binding (cf. the expression *svázat do roubu* to bind someone's arms and legs), akin to the verb *roubat* to cut.

Roubineau *see* ROBIN

Roubottom *see* ROWBOTTOM

Rouček Czech (Moravian): nickname for someone with a deformed or missing hand, from the vocab. word *roučka* handle.

Rouché *see* ROACH

Roudeix *see* RODE

Rouf *see* ROLF

Rougeau *see* RUDGE

Roughley *see* ROWLEY

Roulet *see* ROLLO

Roulston *see* ROLSTON

Round English (chiefly W Midlands): nickname for a plump person, from ME, OF *rond', rund* fat, round (L *rotundus*, a deriv. of *rotāre* turn, from *rota* wheel; cf. RODE 3).

Dims.: Eng.: **Roundell**, RUNDLE. Fr.: **Rondel, Lerondel, Rondeau, Lerondeau, Rond(el)et, Rondot, Rondou**. Prov.: **Redondet, Redon(n)et, Redondin**.

Patrs.: Eng.: **Rounds, Rounce**.

Roundtree *see* ROWNTREE

Rourke Irish: Anglicized form of the Gael. personal name *Ruarc*, perhaps from *ruarc* heavy shower of rain.

Var.: **Rorke**.

Patrs.: **Groarke** (Gael. **Mac Ruiarc**).

'Descendant of R.': **O'Ro(u)rke, O'Ro(w)warke** (Gael. **Ó Ruairc**).

Rouse English: nickname for a person with red hair, from ME, OF *rous* red(-haired) (L *russ(e)us*). For Slav. cogns., see RUDAKOV.

Vars.: **Rous, Rowse, Russ**.

Dims.: Eng.: RUSSELL (which also see for further Eng., Fr., and It. dims.). Fr.: **Ro(u)sset, Rossey, Roussin(eau), Roussy, Rosson, Roussot; (Le) Rouzic, Rousic** (Brittany). It.: **Rossett(in)i, Rossett(o), Rossitti, Rossitto, Russetti, Rossin(i), Rossino, Russino, Rossotti, Rossotto, Russotti, Russotto**.

Augs.: It.: **Rosson(i), Rossone**.

Patrs.: Fr.: **Auroux**. It.: **De Rossi** (partly Jewish; reasons for adoption unclear); **Del Rosso, De Russi**.

Rousel *see* RUSSELL

Roussignol *see* ROSSIGNOL

Roustaing *see* ROSTAING

Rout English (now chiefly E Anglia): probably a topographic name for someone who lived by a patch of rough ground, from a hypothetical OE word **rū(we)t* or *rūhet*, derivs. of *rūh* rough, overgrown; cf. RAUCH. There are places called *Ruffet(t)* in Surrey and Sussex which are thought to have this origin.

Routenberg *see* ROTHENBERG

Routledge English and Scots: of uncertain origin. If it is a habitation name, the location and etymology of the place from which it derives are obscure. The name is found mainly on the English/Scottish borders. The place in Cumb. now called *Routledge* Burn seems to have received its name in the 16th cent. from a member of the family rather than vice versa.

Vars.: **Rutledge, Rudledge, Rookledge, Rucklidge**.

Rouvre Provençal: topographic name for someone who lived by a notable oak tree or in an oak forest, from OProv. *rouvre* oak (L *robur*; cf. ROBUSTI).

Vars.: **Roure, Durou(v)re, Delroure**.

Dims.: Fr.: **Rouvreau, Rouvet, Rouveix**.

Collectives: Fr.: **Rouvroy, Rouvray, Rouvrais, Rouvière, Rouveyre**. Sp.: **Robledo, Robredo**. Cat.: **Rovira**.

Rouzet *see* ROSE

Rove *see* ROLF

Rover English: **1.** occupational name for someone who constructed or repaired roofs, from an agent deriv. of ME *roof* (OE *hrōf*). In the Middle Ages roofs might be thatched with reeds or straw, or covered with tiles, slates, or wooden shingles. **2.** nickname for an unscrupulous individual, from ME *rover* pirate, robber (from MLG *rōver*; cf. RÄUBER). The verb *rove* to wander is probably a back-formation from this, and is not attested before the 16th cent., so it is unlikely to lie behind any examples of the surname.

Var. (of 1): **Ruffer**.

Rovira *see* ROUVRE

Rowan *see* RUANE

Rowberry *see* RUBBRA

Rowbottom English: topographic name for someone living in an overgrown valley, from OE *rūh* rough, overgrown (cf. RAUCH) + *boðm* valley (see BOTTOM). The surname is now most common in Lancs., but does not seem to be found there before 1500. The surname may be a habitation name from an unidentified place so called.

Vars.: **Robottom**, **R(o)ubottom**, **Rowbottam**, **Roobottam**, **Rowbotham**, **Roebotham**, **Robatham**, **Robathan**.

Rowden English: habitation name from a place near Hereford, so called from OE *rūh* rough, overgrown (cf. RAUCH) + *dūn* hill (see DOWN 1).

Rowe English: **1.** topographic name for someone who lived by a hedgerow or in a row of houses built next to one another, from ME *row* (Northern ME *raw*, from OE *rāw*). **2.** from the medieval given name *Row*, a var. of *Rou(l)* (see ROLLO) or a short form of ROWLAND.

Vars.: **Row**. (Of 1 only): RAW; **Rew**, RUE (from the OE byform *rǣw*).

Dims. (of 2): ROWELL, ROWETT.

Patrs. (from 2): **Rowes**, **Rowson**.

Rowell English: **1.** habitation name, a var. of ROTHWELL. **2.** habitation name from a place in Devon, so called from OE *rūh* rough, overgrown (cf. RAUCH) + *hyll* HILL. **3.** from a medieval given name, a dim. of ROWE 2.

Rowett English: from a medieval given name composed of the Gmc elements *hrōd* renown + *wald* rule, which was introduced into England by Scandinavian settlers in the form *Hróaldr*, and again later by the Normans in the form *Ro(h)ald*. This name has absorbed a much rarer one with the second element *hard* hardy, brave, strong, which was introduced into England by the Normans in the form *Ro(h)ard*. It has also sometimes been used a dim. of ROWE 2, itself both a var. of ROLLO and a short form of ROWLAND.

Vars.: **Rowet**, **Rowat(t)**.

Rowland English: **1.** from *Rol(l)ant*, a Norman personal name composed of the Gmc elements *hrōd* renown + *land* land, territory. This was popular throughout Europe in the Middle Ages as a result of the fame of Charlemagne's warrior of this name, who was killed at Roncesvalles in AD 778. **2.** habitation name from places in Derbys. and Sussex, so called from ON *rá* roebuck (see RAY 2) + *lundr* wood, grove (see LUND).

Vars.: **Rol(l)and**.

Dims. (of 1): Fr.: **Rolandeau**, **Relandeau**. It.: **Rolandino**; **Orlandini**, **Orlandelli**, **Orlanducci**.

Aug.: It.: **Orlandoni**.

Patrs.: Eng.: **Rowlands**, **Rolance**, **Rollons**; **Rowlandson**, **Ro(w)nson**. Flem., Du.: **Roeland(t)s**.

Rowlatt *see* ROLLO

Rowleston *see* ROLSTON

Rowley English: habitation name from any of the various places, in Devon, Co. Durham, Staffs., and Yorks., so

called from OE *rūh* rough, overgrown (cf. RAUCH) + *lēah* wood, clearing.

Var.: **Roughley** (Lancs.).

Rowney **1.** English: habitation name from a place in Herts. so called from OE *rūh* rough, overgrown (with the remains of the weak dat. ending *-en*, originally used after a preposition and def. art.) + *(ge)hæg* enclosure (see HAY 1), or from various other minor places of the same origin. **2.** Irish: Anglicized form of Gael. *Ó Ruanaidh*; see ROONEY.

Rowntree English: topographic name for someone who lived by a rowan or mountain ash, from ME *rown* (ON *rogn*) + *tree* (OE *trēow*).

Vars.: **Roun(d)tree**; **Rowen**.

Cpds (ornamental): Swed.: **Rönnberg(h)** ('rowan hill'); **Rönnqvist** ('rowan twig').

Rowse *see* ROUSE

Rowsell *see* RUSSELL

Roxburgh Scots: habitation name from a place near Kelso, so called from the gen. case of the OE byname *Hrōc* ROOK' + OE *burh* fort, manor (see BURY).

Roy **1.** Scots: nickname for a person with red hair, from Gael. *ruadh* red (ultimately cogn. with READ 1, ROTH 1, RUDAKOV, and RUDD). **2.** English (Norman): var. of RAY 1. **3.** French: cogn. of RAY 1.

Royan *see* RUANE

Royce *see* ROSE

Roycraft *see* RYCROFT

Royds *see* RHODES

Royle English (chiefly Lancs.): habitation name from a place in Lancs., so called from OE *rā* roe deer (see RAY 2) + *hyll* HILL.

Vars.: **Royal(l)**; **Ryal(l)**, **Ryle**, **Ryhill** (also in part from places such as *Ryal* and *Ryle* in Northumb. and *Ryhill* in Humberside and W Yorks., so called from OE *ryge* RYE + *hyll*).

Royston English: **1.** habitation name from a place in Herts., recorded in 1262 as *Croyroys*, from OF *croiz* cross (L *crux*, gen. *crucis*) + the female given name *Royse* (see ROSE 2). Ekwall mentions forms from only twenty years later in which the placename first more or less assumes its modern form. It is not clear, however, whether this is to be interpreted as 'Royse's stone' (with the second element ME *stōn*, from OE *stān*) or 'settlement at (Croiz) Royse' (with the second element ME *toun*, from OE *tūn*). **2.** habitation name from a place in W Yorks., so called from the gen. case of the OE byname *Hrōr* 'Vigorous' (or its ON cogn. *Róarr*) + OE *tūn* enclosure, settlement. **3.** Jewish (Ashkenazic): presumably an Anglicization of one or more like-sounding Jewish surnames.

Royter *see* ROTH

Royzman *see* ROSEMAN

Roz *see* ROCH, ROSE

Rozas Spanish: habitation name from any of various places so called, from the pl. form of Sp. *roza* cleared land ready for ploughing (from *rozar* to clear, plough, LL *ruptiāre*, from the past part. *ruptus* of class. L *rumpere* to break).

Rozdestvenski Russian: surname adopted by members of the Orthodox clergy in honour of the feast of Christmas, Russ. *rozdestvo* (from *roditsya* to be born).

Var.: **Rozestvenski**.

Rozwadowski Polish: habitation name from the town of *Rozwadów* in SE Poland.

Ruane Irish: Anglicized form of Gael. **Ó Ruadháin** 'descendant of *Ruadhán*', a personal name from a dim. of *ruadh* red (cf. ROY 1).

Vars.: **O'Ruane**, **O'Rowane**, **(O')Roan**, **Ro(u)ane**, **Rowan**, **ROHAN**, **Rewan**, **Royan**, **Raun**, **Roon**.

Ruano Spanish: **1.** occupational name for a common soldier, OSp. *ruano* (apparently a deriv. of *ru(g)a* street (see RUE 1), perhaps because such soldiers were recruited in the street). **2.** nickname for someone with reddish hair, from Sp. *roano*, *ruano* reddish, roan (apparently from a Goth. cogn. of READ 1 and ROTH 1).

Rubartelli *see* ROBERT

Rubbens *see* REUBEN

Rubbra English: habitation name from any of various places, such as *Roborough* in Devon, *Rowberrow* and *Ruborough* Hill in Somerset, *Rubery* near Birmingham, and *Rowborough* in the Isle of Wight, named from OE *rūh* rough, overgrown + *beorg* hill.

Vars.: **Ribra**, **Ruber(r)y**, **Rowb(er)ry**, **Rowbury**.

Rübel German: metonymic occupational name for a cultivator of rape, grown for use as a fodder crop and for the oil obtained from its seeds. The name represents a dim. form of MHG *ruobe* (L *rāpum*; cf. RAPA and RAVEL). It is possible that the surname may in some cases derive from a nickname given with reference to the bright yellow flowers or unpleasant smell of the plant.

Rublyov Russian: patr. from the nickname *Rubl* 'Rouble', a unit of currency, denoting someone who payed a rent or tax of this amount, or acquired for some more anecdotal reason. The etymology of the word is uncertain: it may be a deriv. of *rubit* to chop, hack, and so may mean 'portion', 'fraction', but others have connected it with the Indian *rupee*, from Skt *rūpya* wrought silver.

Rubottom *see* ROWBOTTOM

Ruciński *see* RUTECKI

Ruck *see* ROOK

Rucker *see* ROCK

Rucklidge *see* ROUTLEDGE

Rudakov Russian: patr. from the nickname *Rudak* 'Redhaired man' (from *rudy* red(-haired), akin to *ruda* ore; cf. READ 1, ROTH 1, and RUDD 1).

Dims.: Ukr.: **Rudeiko**, **Rudenko**. Beloruss.: **Rudzko**, **Rudyonok**; **Rudzevich** (patr.).

Habitation names: Pol.: **Rudnicki**; **Rudziński** (from the town of *Rudnik* in SE Poland, or from some other place similarly named with the Slav. word *rudy* red).

Rudd 1. English: nickname for a person with red hair or a ruddy complexion, from ME *rudde*, OE *rud(ig)* red, ruddy. **2.** Jewish (Ashkenazic): Anglicized, shortened form of various surnames beginning with the syllable *Rud-*.

Vars. (of 1): **Ruddy**, **Rudman**.

Dims. (of 1): **Rudkin**, **Rudling**.

Rudden *see* RODEN

Ruddiforth *see* RUTHERFORD

Ruddock English: nickname from the robin, ME *ruddock* (OE *ruddoc*, *rudduc*, a dim. of *rud(ig)* red; cf. RUDD 1).

Var.: **Ruddick** (Northumb.).

Ruddy *see* READY

Rüdel *see* RODE

Rudge English (W Midlands): **1.** topographic name from West Midland ME *rugge*, a var. of *rigge* RIDGE, or habitation name from the village of *Rudge* in Shrops., which is named with this element. **2.** from a medieval given name, a dim. of ROGER. **3.** nickname for a person with red hair or a ruddy complexion, from OF *r(o)uge* red (L *rubeus*).

Var. (of 3): **Lerouge**.

Dims. (of 3): Fr.: **Rouget(et)**, **Rougeau(x)**, **Rougeot**, **Roujon**, **Roujou**.

Patr. (from 2) (dim.): Eng.: **Ruggles**.

Rudledge *see* ROUTLEDGE

Rudolfer *see* ROLF

Rue 1. French: topographic name for someone who lived on a track or pathway, OF *rue* (L *rūga* crease, fold). **2.** English: var. of *Rew*; see ROWE 1.

Vars. (of 1): Fr.: **Larue**, **De(la)rue**, **Delrue**, **Desrues**.

Ruff *see* ROLF

Ruffer *see* ROVER

Ruffin French: from a personal name (L *Rūfīnus*, a deriv. of *Rūfus*; see RUFFO 1), borne and popularized by various minor early saints, including a 3rd-cent. martyr of Soissons and a 4th-cent. Church Father.

Var.: **Rufin**.

Dim.: It.: **Ruffinelli**.

Aug.: It.: **Ruffinoni**.

Ruffo S Italian: **1.** from a personal name (L *Rūfus*, originally a nickname for someone with red hair, from a byform of *rubeus* (see RUDGE 3), taken from another Italic dialect). This name was borne by various minor early saints, and occasionally used as a given name in the Middle Ages. **2.** from a personal name of Gmc origin but uncertain form and meaning. The Calabrian noble family of this name are said to have come to S Italy with the Normans.

Var.: **Ruffi**.

Dims.: It.: **Ruf(f)olo**, **Ruffoli**.

Ruggles *see* RUDGE

Ruggs *see* RIDGE

Rühlemann *see* ROLLO

Ruisdael *see* RUYSDAEL

Ruiz *see* RODERICK

Rule 1. English: from a medieval given name, a var. of *Rou(l)*; see ROLLO. 2. Scots: habitation name from a place in the former county of Roxburghs., so called from the stream on which it stands. This name is of uncertain origin, possibly cogn. with W *rhull* hasty, rash.

Rulf *see* ROLF

Rullmann *see* ROLLO

Rumbelow English: habitation name from any of two or three minor localities originally named with OE *þreom* (dat. of *þrēo* three) + *hlāwum* (dat. pl. of *hlāw* hill, tumulus (see LAW 2)), i.e. 'at the three tumuli'. The word *rumbelow* is attested from the 14th cent. as a meaningless combination of syllables sung by sailors to keep time while rowing, and the surname used to be thought to be a generic name for a sailor, but Reaney has produced convincing evidence in favour of the local-name hypothesis; a certain Richard *Thrimelowe* (1334) lived in Aston (Birmingham), where there is a locality called *the Rumbelow*.

Vars.: **Rumbellow**, **Rombulow**.

Rumbold English: from the Norman personal name *Rumbald*, composed of the Gmc elements *rūm* wide, spacious (or, more plausibly, a byform of *hrūm* renown) + *bold* bold, brave.

Vars.: **Rumbolt**, **Rumbol(l)**, **Rumball**, **Rumbell**, **Rumble**, **Rumpole**.

Patrs.: Eng.: **Rumbles**. Ger.: **Rumpler**, **Rümpler**, **Rimpler**.

Flem.: **Rombouts**; **Boudts**.

Rummel *see* ROMMEL

Rumney *see* ROMNEY

Rump English: nickname for a person with a large behind, from OE *rumpe* buttocks. Despite the faintly obscene or derogatory connotations of the vocab. word, the surname survives in Norfolk.

Rumsey English: habitation name from *Romsey* in Hants, so called from the gen. case of the OE personal name *Rūm* (a short form of cpd names with the first element *rūm*) + OE *ēg* island, dry land in a fen.

Vars.: **Romsey**, **Romsay**, **Rumsay**.

Runacres English: topographic name for someone who lived by a field where rye was grown, from OE *rygen*, an adj. deriv. of *ryge* RYE + *æcer* cultivated land (see ACKER). *Renacres* near Liverpool (*Runacres* in 1284) is a possible source.

Vars.: **Runnacles**, **Runicles**, **Runagle**, **Runnagall**.

Rundle English (Devon and Cornwall): 1. nickname, a dim. of ROUND. 2. habitation name from *Rundale* in the parish of Shoreham, Kent, so called from OE *rūm(ig)* roomy, spacious + *dæl* valley.

Vars.: **Rundell**, **Rundall**.

Runge German: from MHG *runge* staff, stick (OHG *runga*). The precise sense of the surname is not clear, but the vocab. word was used in particular of the handle by which a horse-drawn waggon was led by someone walking beside it; thus it is possibly a metonymic occupational name for a carter.

Ruotsalainen Finnish: name for a Swedish-speaker or someone from Sweden, from Finn. *ruotsalainen* Swede, from *Ruotsala* Sweden + *-ainen* locative suffix.

Rupert *see* ROBERT

Rusakov Russian: 1. patr. from the name *Rusak* (Great) Russian. The name derives ultimately from a Scandinavian term meaning 'rower', 'oarsman', the Russian state having been first established in the 9th cent. by Varangian (i.e. Norse) settlers who rowed up the rivers from the Baltic. 2. patr. from the nickname *Rusak*, a deriv. of *rusi* light brown (akin to the vocab. words that lie behind RUDAKOV and RYZHAKOV).

Var. (of 1): **Rusinov**.

Dims. (of 1): Pol.: **Rusek**, **Ruszczyk**, **Rusin**. Czech: **Rusek**.

Patrs. (from dims. of 1): Pol.: **Ruszkiewicz**, **Rusinkiewicz**.

Habitation names (from dims. of 1): Pol.: **Ruszkowski**, **Ruszczyński**.

Rush 1. English: topographic name for someone who lived near a clump of rushes, from ME *rush* (a collective sing., OE *rysc*). 2. Irish: Anglicized form of Gael. **Ó Ruis** 'descendant of *Ros*', a personal name perhaps from *ros* wood. In S and SW Ulster it has also been used as a translation of *Ó Fuada* (see FOODY), and in Connaught for *Ó Luachra* (see LOUGHREY).

Vars. (of 1): **Rusher**, **Rischer**.

Rushforth English (W Yorks.): habitation name from an unidentified place, possibly *Rushford* in Devon, Norfolk, or Warwicks. However, in view of the distribution of the surname, a more likely source is *Ryshworth* in Bingley, W Yorks., which was earlier called *Rushford* (from OE *rysc* rushes + *ford* FORD).

Var.: **Rushfirth**.

Rushmer English (E Anglia): habitation name from *Rushmere* in Suffolk, near Lowestoft, so called from OE *rysc* rushes + *mere* pond, lake.

Var.: **Rushmere**.

Rushton English: habitation name from any of the various places, for example in Ches., Northants, and Staffs., so called from OE *rysc* rushes + *tūn* enclosure, settlement.

Rushworth English (W Yorks.): habitation name from *Rishworth* in W Yorks., so called from OE *rysc* rushes + *worð* enclosure (see WORTH).

Rusk Scots: of uncertain origin, probably a topographic name from the Gael. element *riasg* marsh, bog.

Var.: **Risk**.

Ruskin 1. English: probably a dim. of the medieval given name ROSE 2. 2. Scots: occupational name for a tanner, from Gael. *rusg(aire)an*, dim. form of *rusgaire* peeler (of bark).

Russ *see* ROUSE

Russell English, Scots, and Irish: from *Rousel*, a common ANF nickname for someone with red hair, representing a dim. of ROUSE with the hypocoristic suffix *-el*.

Vars.: **Russel**, **Rous(s)el(l)**, **Rowsell**, **Russill**.

Dims.: Fr.: **Rouselet**, **Rousselin**, **Rousselot**. It.: **Rossellini**.

Patrs.: Fr.: **Aurousseau**. Flem.: **Rosseels**.

Rust English (chiefly E Anglia) and Scots: nickname for someone with red hair or a ruddy complexion, from OE *rūst* rust (from a Gmc root meaning 'red'; cf. READ 1 and ROTH 1).

Ruston English: habitation name from any of the various places so called, for example in Norfolk, N Yorks., and Humberside. The two villages of this name in Norfolk are recorded in Domesday Book as *Ristuna*, and are from OE *hrīs* brushwood + *tūn* enclosure, settlement; *Ruston* Parva in Humberside appears in Domesday Book as *Roreston*, from the gen. case of the ON byname *Hrór* 'Vigorous' + OE *tūn; Ruston* in N Yorks. is *Rostune* in Domesday Book, apparently from OE *hrōst* roost, roof + *tūn*, referring to a building with an unusual roof.

Rutberg *see* ROTHENBERG

Rutecki Polish: topographic name for someone who lived by a patch of rue, Pol. *ruta* (L *rūta*).

Vars.: **Ruta**.

Habitation name: **Ruciński**.

Rüters *see* REUTER

Rutgers *see* ROGER

Ruth English: nickname for a charitable person, or for a wretched one, from ME *reuthe* pity (a deriv. of *rewen* to pity, OE *hrēowan*). The given name *Ruth* was little used in the Middle Ages among non-Jews, and is unlikely to have had any influence on the surname.

Rutherford Scots: habitation name from a place in the Scottish Borders near Roxburgh, so called from OE *hryðer* cattle + *ford* FORD. There is another place of the same name and etymology in N Yorks., but this does not seem to have contributed to the surname, which is principally found in the Borders and Lowlands of Scotland.

Vars.: **Rutherfoord**, **Rutherfurd**, **Rutterford**, **Rotherforth**, **Ruddiforth**, **Rudeforth**.

Ruthven Scots: habitation name, traditionally pronounced /ˈriːvən/, from various places in Scotland, esp. one near Coldstream in the Borders region, and one near Perth. There are two possible etymologies: from ON *rauðr* red + *fen* fen, marsh, or from Gael. *ruadh* red + *abhuinn* river.

Rutkowski Polish: habitation name from a village called *Rutki*, which according to Rospond is derived from the personal name *Rudek*. This is either a byname meaning 'Red-haired' (see RUDAKOV), or a short form of a cpd personal name with *rudy* red as its first element.

Patr. (from *Rudek*): **Rutkiewicz**.

Rutland English: regional name from the former English county of this name, so called from the OE byname *Rōta* (from *rōt* cheerful, glad; see ROOT 1) + *land* land, territory.

Rutledge *see* ROUTLEDGE

Rutt *see* ROOT

Rutten *see* RODE

Rutter English: 1. occupational name for a player on the rote; see ROOT 2. 2. nickname for an unscrupulous person, from OF *ro(u)tier* robber, highwayman, footpad (see REUTER 2).

Ruvel *see* REUBEN

Ruysdael Dutch: habitation name from a minor place, so called from MDu. *ruis* rush + *dal* valley.

Var.: **Ruisdael**.

Růžek *see* ROSE

Ryal *see* ROYLE

Ryan Irish (one of the commonest surnames in Ireland): 1. simplified form of MULRYAN. The surname from this source is particularly common in Tipperary. 2. Anglicized form of Gael. **Ó Riain** 'descendant of *Rian* or *Riaghan*', a personal name of uncertain origin. There has been considerable confusion with REGAN.

Vars.: **O'Ryan**, **Rian**.

Ryba Polish, Czech, and Jewish (E Ashkenazic): metonymic occupational name, nickname, or ornamental name from the Slav. term *ryba* fish. As an occupational name it may have denoted a fisherman (cf. RYBAK) or a seller of fish. As a nickname it may have been bestowed on account of some fancied physical resemblance to a fish.

Vars.: Pol.: **Rybicki**. Czech: **Rybín**, **Rybka**. Jewish: **Riba**, **Ryb(icki)**.

Dims.: Ger. (of Slav. origin): **Reibke**, **Riebisch**, **Reibisch**.

Patrs.: Pol.: **Rybowicz**. Russ.: **Rybin**.

Patr. (from a dim.): Russ.: **Ryb(ush)kin**.

Habitation names: Pol.: **Rybiński**, **Rybczyński**.

Rybak Polish, Ukrainian, and Jewish (E Ashkenazic): occupational name for a fisherman, an agent deriv. of RYBA fish.

Vars.: Pol.: **Rybarz**. Jewish: **Riba(c)k**.

Dims.: Pol.: **Rybarczyk**, **Rybiałek**. Ukr.: **Rybal(chen)ko**.

Patrs.: Pol.: **Ryba(r)kiewicz**. Ukr.: **Rybalka**. Jewish: **Rybalow**. Russ.: **Rybakov**, **Ryba(l)kin**.

Rybniček Czech: topographic name for someone who lived by a fishpond, from a dim. of Czech *rybnik* fishpond.

Rychtářík *see* RICHTER

Rycroft English: topographic name for someone who lived by a smallholding (see CROFT) where RYE was grown.

Vars.: **Rycraft**; **Roycroft**, **Roycraft** (chiefly Irish).

Ryde *see* READ

Ryder *see* RIDER

Ryding *see* READING

Rye English: 1. topographic name for someone who lived on an island or patch of firm ground surrounded by fens, from a misdivision of the ME phrase *atter ye* at the island (OE *æt þære īge*, from *ēg* island). 2. topographic name for someone who lived near a river or stream, from a misdivision of the ME phrase *atter eye* at the river (OE *æt þære eā* at the river, from *ēa* river). 3. topographic name for someone living at a place where rye (OE *ryge*) was grown, or perhaps a metonymic occupational name for someone who grew it.

Vars. (of 1 and 2): RAY, **Rea(y)**; **R(a)yman**, RAIMAN, **Reaman**, **Reeman**. See also NYE.

Ryhill *see* ROYLE

Ryhorovich *see* GREGORY

Rykena *see* RICH

Rykert *see* RICHARD

Rykowicz *see* RIKIN

Ryland English: topographic name for someone who lived near a piece of land where rye was grown, from OE *ryge* RYE + *land* land.

Vars.: **Rylands**, **Rylance**.

Ryle *see* ROYLE

Ryley *see* RILEY

Ryman *see* RYE

Rymer *see* RIEMER

Rynn *see* WREN

Ryšánek *see* RYZHAKOV

Rysev Russian: patr. from the nickname *Rys* 'Lynx', given perhaps to a sly person. The lynx was native to the forests of E Europe until the 19th cent., and in Russ. was originally named from its colour; cf. RYZHAKOV.

Var.: **Rysin**.

Ryvkin *see* RIFKIN

Ryzhakov Russian: patr. from the nickname *Ryzhak* 'Red-haired man' (from *ryzhi* red, lit. rust-coloured; the name is akin to the roots mentioned at RUSAKOV 2 and RUDAKOV, and is ultimately cogn. with L *russ(e)us* (see ROUSE)).

Vars.: **Ryzh(i)kov**, **Ryzhochin**, **Ryzhov**, **Ryzhago**.

Dim.: Czech: **Ryšánek**.

Rzepczyński *see* REPIN

Rzetelski Polish: nickname for a man noted for his honesty and fair dealing, from Pol. *rzetelny* honest, fair + the surname suffix -*ski* (see BARANOWSKI), or else from the same word in the sense 'likeable' or 'handsome'.

Rzeźnik Polish: occupational name for a butcher, Pol. *rzeźnik*, from a deriv. of Pol. *rzeźać* to slaughter (cf. Czech *řezat* to cut and the surname ŘEZÁČ).

Var.: **Rzeźnicki**.

S

Saarinen Finnish: ornamental name from Finn. *saari* island + the gen. suffix *-nen*, chosen in some cases as a topographic name by someone who lived on or by an island.
Var.: **Saari**.

Saavedra Spanish (Galicia): habitation name composed of the dial. words *saa* hall (see SALE 1) + *vedra* (fem.) old (L *vetus*, gen. *veteris*).

Sabbato Italian: from a nickname or given name bestowed on someone born on a Saturday, which was considered a good omen, from It. *sabbato* Saturday (LL *sabbatum*, Gk *sabbaton*, from Hebr. *shabaton*, a deriv. of *shabat* rest).
Var.: **Sabato**.
Dims.: It.: **Sab(b)atini**, **Sab(b)atino**, **Sab(b)atelli**, **Sabatello**, **Sab(b)atiello**, **Sab(b)atucci**; **Zabatino** (Sicily); **Sab(b)adin(i)** (N Italy).

Sabberton English (E Anglia): probably a habitation name from any of the various places, in Derbys., Gloucs., Lincs., and Sussex, called *Sapperton*, from OE *Sāperatūn* 'settlement (OE *tūn*) of the soap-makers' (cf. SOPER). The place in Sussex is frequently found in forms such as *Saberton* and *Sabirton* as late as the 16th cent. The place in Lincs. is the most likely source of the E Anglian surname, as there was a good deal of migration from that region in connection with the medieval wool-trade.

Sabháiste *see* SAVAGE

Sabin 1. English and French: from the OF masc. given name *Sabin* or the fem. *Sabine* (L *Sabīnus*, *Sabīna*, member of the Sabine tribe, an ancient Italic people of central Italy whose name is of uncertain origin). The masc. name was borne by at least ten early saints, but the fem. form was more common in England in the Middle Ages. 2. Jewish (Ashkenazic): of unknown origin.
Vars. (of 1): Eng.: **Sab(b)en**, **Saban**; **Sabine**. Fr.: **Savin**, **Sevi(n)**; **Sabine**, **Savine**, **Sevène** (fem. forms); **Sabina** (fem., Brittany). (Of 2): **Sabine** (an Anglicized form).
Dims.: Eng.: **Sablin(e)**. Fr.: **Savineau**, **Savignon**, **Sevenet**.
Patrs.: Flem., Du.: **Sevens**. Russ.: **Savinov**, **Savinykh**. Bulg.: **Savov**.

Sabouret *see* SAVOUREUX

Sabrier Provençal: occupational name for a preparer or seller of spiced foods, from an agent deriv. of OProv. *sabre* flavour (L *sapor*; cf. SAVOUREUX). The denotation of this word was extended to sauces, bacon, and other highly flavoured foodstuffs, which were extremely common in the Middle Ages, since the spices functioned as preservatives as well as flavourings.
Var.: **Sabrié**.

Saburov Russian: patr. from the Turkic given name *Sabur*, from Arabic *Sābūr* 'the Patient one', an epithet of Allah.

Sacerdote Italian (Jewish): name assumed by a member of the priestly caste (see COHEN), from It. *sacerdote* priest (L *sacerdōs*, gen. *sacerdōtis*).

Šach *see* SALOMON

Sachariasch *see* ZACHARY

Sacher Jewish (Ashkenazic): of uncertain origin, possibly from: 1. the Yid. male given name *Skharye*, from the Hebr. name *Zecharya*; see ZACHARY. 2. the Yid. male given name *Sokher*, from the Hebr. name *Yissachar* (Eng. *Issachar*) 'Hired'. 3. the Yid. occupational term *soykher* merchant (from Hebr. *socher*). However, none of these three explanations is really convincing, for phonological reasons.
Var.: **Sachar**.
Patrs.: **Sachers**; **Sacharov**, **Sacharow** (E Ashkenazic).

Sachs 1. German: regional name from Saxony, Ger. *Sachsen*. The region is called after the Gmc tribe which settled there in Roman times; they in turn seem to have been named from a kind of knife or dagger that they used (see MESSER 1). 2. Jewish (Ashkenazic): of uncertain origin, possibly as in 1 above, or else adopted in memory of persecuted forebears, an acronym of the Hebr. phrase *Zera Kodesh SHemo* 'his name is of the seed of holiness'.
Vars. (of 1): **Sachse**. (Of 2): **Zaks**, **Sa(c)ks**, **Sax**.
Dims. (of 1): Fr.: **Sachsé**, **Saisset**. It.: **Sassoli**.

Sack 1. English: metonymic occupational name for a maker of sacks or bags, from OE *sacc* (LL *saccus*, Gk *sakkos*, probably ultimately of Semitic origin). 2. Jewish (Ashkenazic): of uncertain origin, possibly an acronym of the Hebr. phrase *Zera Keshodim* 'Seed of the Holy'.
Vars. (of 1): **Sa(t)ch**; **Sa(c)ker**, **Sackur**, SECKER. (Of 2): **Sackheim**, **Zakheim**, **Zakheym** (ornamental extensions).
Dims. (of 1): Eng.: **Sackett**; **Satchel(l)**. Fr.: **Sachet**, **Sachot**. Prov.: **Saquet(oux)**. It.: **Sacchet(ti)**, **Sacchetto**, **Sacchini**, **Saccucci**.
Augs. (of 1): It.: **Saccon(i)**, **Saccone**.

Sackville English (Norman): habitation name from *Saqueneville* in Eure, so called from the Gmc personal name *Sachano* (apparently a deriv. of the element *sakō* quarrel, dispute) + OF *ville* settlement (see VILLE).
Var.: **Sackwild**.

Sacramento Portuguese: religious byname from Port. *sacramento* sacrament (L *sacrāmentum* oath, a transparent deriv. of *sacer* sacred, re-analysed in Christian terminology).

Sadd English (E Anglia): nickname for a serious or solemn person, from ME *sad* serious, grave (OE *sæd* weary, tired).

The mod. Eng. sense 'unhappy' did not develop until the 15th cent.

Saddington English: habitation name from a place in Leics., recorded in Domesday Book in the forms *Sadintone* and *Setintone*. The first element may be a reduced form of an OE personal name; Ekwall suggests *Sǣgēat* (from *sǣ* sea + the tribal name *Gēat*), in which case the etymology is 'settlement (OE *tūn*) associated with *Sǣgēat*'.

Sade French: 1. habitation name from the village of *Saddes* in Avène. 2. nickname for a pleasant or amiable person, from OF *sade* agreeable (originally of taste, from L *sapidus*; cf. SAVOUREUX).

Sadler English and Low German: occupational name for a maker of saddles, from an agent deriv. of ME, MLG *sadel* (OE *sadol*, OSax. *zadel*).
Vars.: Eng.: **Saddler**; **Sadlier** (chiefly common in Ireland). Low Ger.: **Sedler**; **Sadelmacher**.

Sadowski Polish, German (of Slav. origin), and Jewish (E Ashkenazic): habitation name from any of several places named with Pol. *sad* orchard + the possessive suffix *-óv*, such as *Sadowa* in NE Poland, with the addition of the suffix of local surnames *-ski* (see BARANOWSKI).
Vars.: Jewish: **Sadowsky**, **Sadovski**, **Sadovsky**; **Sadovnik**, **Sadownik** (occupational names).

Sáenz see SANCHO

Saer see SAYER

Šafařík see SCHAFFER

Saffer English (Norman): nickname for a greedy person, from OF *saffre* glutton (of unknown etymology).

Safont see FONT

Safran 1. German: metonymic occupational name for a spicer or nickname for someone with blond hair, from Ger. *Safran* saffron, a spice which is bright yellow or orange in colour (MHG *saffrān*, from OF *safran*, Arabic *za'farān*). 2. Jewish (Ashkenazic): occupational name as in 1, or ornamental name (one of the many taken from words denoting plants).
Vars.: **Saffran**. Jewish only: **Shafran(ski)**, **S(h)afranovitch**, **Zaf(f)ren**.
Dim.: Czech: **Šafránek**.

Sagal see SEGAL

Sagan Polish: metonymic occupational name for a maker of pots and pans, from Pol. *sagan* kettle, or nickname from the same word in a less clear application.
Var.: **Sagański** (with *-ski* suffix of surnames; see BARANOWSKI).
Habitation name: **Saganowski**.

Sagar see SEAGAR

Sagarra see SEGARRA

Sage English and French: nickname for a wise man, from ME, OF *sage* learned, sensible (LL *sapius*, from *sapere* to taste, discern, discriminate).
Var.: Fr. **Lesage**.
Dims.: Fr.: **Sagel**, **Saget**, **Sageon**, **Sageot**. Prov.: **Saivet**. It.: **Saviotti**, **Savioli**, **Saviozzi**.
Patrs.: It.: **Del Savio**; **Dal Savio** (Venetia, where *savio* was a title of office for the city councillors during the Middle Ages).

Sägebrecht see SIEBERT

Sagne Provençal: topographic name for someone who lived by a patch of marshy land, from OProv. *sagne* fen, bog (from *sagnier* to bleed, L *sanguināre*, a deriv. of *sanguis*, gen. *sanguinis*, blood).
Vars.: **Saigne**, **Sagnes**, **Desagnes**; **Sa(n)gnier**, **Saignier**, **Sannier**, **Sannié**.

Sahlberg see SALE

Sahuc see SUREAU

Saiger see SEAGAR

Saigne see SAGNE

Sailer see SAYLOR

Sainclair see SINCLAIR

Sainer see SENIOR

Sainsbury English: habitation name from *Saintbury* in Gloucs., recorded in the 12th cent. as *Seynesbury*. The placename is probably from the gen. case of the OE male personal name *Sǣwine* (composed of the elements *sǣ* sea + *wine* friend) + OE *burh* fort, town (see BURY).
Vars.: **Saintsbury**, **Sainsberry**, **Sinisbury**.

Sainson see SAMSON

Saint English and French: nickname for a notably pious individual, from ME, OF *saint*, *seint* (L *sanctus* blameless, holy). The vocab. word was occasionally used in the Middle Ages as a given name, esp. on the Continent, and this may have given rise to some instances of the surname.
Vars.: Eng.: **Sa(u)nt**. Fr.: **Sant**, **Sa(i)ns**.
Dims.: Fr.: **Sainteau**, **Saintin**, **Saint(ign)on**, **Santot**; **Sansuc** (Brittany). It.: **Santel(li)**, **Santello**, **Santilli**, **Santillo**, **Santulli**, **Santullo**, **Santin(i)**, **Santino**, **Santucci**, **Santuzzo**.
Augs.: It.: **Santon(i)**.
Patrs.: It.: **De Santi** (Venetia); **De San(c)tis** (S Italy). Swed.: **Santesson**.

Saint-Supéry see SAINT-EXUPÉRY

Sainte-Beuve French: habitation name from a place in Seine-Maritime, Normandy, so called from the dedication of its church to a 7th-cent. saint, abbess of Rheims, who bore the Gmc personal name *Bova*, which is of uncertain etymology.

Saint-Exupéry French: habitation name from either of the places, in Corrèze and Gironde, so called from the dedication of their churches to a 5th-cent. archbishop of Toulouse, St *Exsuperius* (a deriv. of LL *exsuper* (far) above).
Var.: **Saint-Supéry**.

Saint-Georges French: habitation name from any of the numerous places so called from the dedication of their churches to St GEORGE.

Sainthill English: habitation name from a hamlet in Devon, recorded in the 13th cent. as *Sengethill*, from OE *senget* place cleared by burning (from *sencgan* to burn) + *hyll* HILL. Later forms of the name include *Se(i)nthill*, *Sainthyll*, and *St Hill*.

Saint-Jean French: habitation name from any of the extremely numerous places so called from the dedication of their churches to a St JOHN.

Saint-Just French: habitation name from any of the numerous places so called from the dedication of their churches to a 4th-cent. bishop of Lyons, St *Justus* (see JUST).

Saint-Laurent French: habitation name from any of the numerous places so called from the dedication of their churches to St LAWRENCE.

Saint-Saëns French: habitation name from a place near Rouen in Seine-Maritime, Normandy, so called from the abbey founded there under a 7th-cent. Irishman, St *Sidōnius*, whose name is of obscure origin. It is probably in origin a L ethnic name from the Phoenician city of *Sidon*, but was widely associated with Gk *sindon* winding sheet, shroud (cf. SENDALL).

Sáinz *see* SANCHO

Saisset *see* SACHS

Saivet *see* SAGE

Saker *see* SACK

Sakharov *see* ZACHARY

Sakhnov *see* SASHIN

Saks *see* SACHS

Saladin French: nickname for a blustering or tyrannical individual, from the Arabic title, *Salāh-ad-Dīn* 'Justice of the Faith', of the great Moslem leader Yusuf ibn-Ayyub, who opposed, for the most part successfully, the Crusades undertaken by Richard I of England and Philip II of France, and became in popular French imagination a monster as great as Herod.

Salamanca Spanish: habitation name from the city of *Salamanca* in W Spain, which is of pre-Roman foundation and obscure etymology. During the Middle Ages it was one of the leading cultural centres of Europe, and the surname may in some cases have been a respectful nickname for someone who had visited the city.

Salazar Spanish and Portuguese: habitation name, ultimately of Basque origin, from Romance *sala* hall (see SALE 1) + Basque *zahar* old; cf. SAAVEDRA. In some cases the surname may derive from a place so called in the province of Burgos.

Salcedo *see* SAUCE

Šalda *see* SALOMON

Sale English: 1. occupational name for someone employed at a manor house, ME *sale* (from OE *sæl* hall, reinforced by OF *salle*, also of Gmc origin). 2. topographic name for someone who lived by a sallow tree, ME *sale* (OE *salh*; cf. SAUCE), or habitation name from a place named with this word, for example *Sale* in Greater Manchester.

Vars.: SALES, SEAL, **Sall(es)**.

Dims. (of 1): Fr.: **Sal(l)et**, **Sallez**. Prov.: **Salon**, **Salou**, **Salot**.

Cpds (of 1, ornamental): Swed.: **Sahlberg** ('hall hill'); **Sahlström** ('hall river').

Salé French: 1. nickname for an amusing or witty person, from the OF adj. *salé*, lit. salted, salty (LL *salātus*, from *sal* salt). 2. topographic name for someone who lived in a salt marsh, from the same word used in a literal sense.

Var.: **Sallé**.

Šálek *see* SALOMON

Sales 1. English and Catalan: topographic name; see SALE 2. 2. Portuguese: habitation name from a place that is probably so called from a Gmc personal name of uncertain form and derivation. 3. Portuguese: religious byname adopted since the 17th cent. in honour of St Francis of *Sales* (1567–1622), who was born at the Château de *Sales* in Savoy.

Salguero Spanish: 1. topographic name for someone who lived by a weeping willow, Sp. *salguero* (LL *salicārius*, a deriv. of class. L *salix*, gen. *salicis*, willow; see SAUCE). 2. it is also possible that the name is sometimes derived from a homonymous archaic term denoting a spot where salt was given to cattle (LL *salicārium*, a deriv. of *salicāre* to give salt to, from *sal* salt; cf. SALÉ).

Salido Spanish: nickname for an exile, OSp. *salido*, past part. of *salir* to go out (L *salīre* to leap; cf. SAUTOUR and SAYLOR). The name may also have been acquired by someone who had spent a period abroad.

Salinas Spanish: topographic name for someone who lived near a salt works, Sp. *salinas* (L *salīnae*, a deriv. of *sal* salt; cf. SALÉ), or occupational name for someone who worked at one.

Var.: **Salinero** (an agent deriv.).

Salinger 1. English (Norman): habitation name from *Saint-Léger* in La Manche or *Saint-Léger*-aux-Bois in Seine-Maritime, both so called from the dedication of their churches to St Leger (see LEDGER), the martyred 7th-cent. bishop of Autun. 2. Jewish (Ashkenazic): of uncertain origin, possibly an altered form of a habitation name from *Solingen* in N Germany. The expected deriv. of *Solingen* is *Solinger*, but this apparently does not occur as a surname.

Vars. (of 1): **Salingar**, **Sallagar**, **Seli(n)ger**, **Sellinger**. (Of 2): **Salingar**, **Selinger**.

Salisbury English: 1. habitation name from the city in Wilts., the Roman name of which was *Sorviodūnum* (of Brit. origin). In the OE period the second element (from Celt. *dūn* fortress) was dropped and *Sorvio-* (of unsolved meaning) became *Searo-* in OE as the result of folk etymological association with OE *searu* armour; to this an explanatory *burh* fortress, manor, town (see BURY) was added. The town is recorded in Domesday Book as *Sarisberie*; the change of -*r*- to -*l*- is a later result of dissimilation. 2. habitation name from *Salesbury* in Lancs., so called from OE *salh* willow (see SALE 2) + *burh* fortress, manor.

Vars.: **Salisberry, Salesbury, Sal(u)sbury**.

Salivonok *see* SELWYN

Salked N English: habitation name from *Salkeld* in Cumb., so called from OE *salh* willow (see SALE 2) + *hylte* wood.

Sallaway *see* SELWAY

Salminen Finnish: ornamental name from Finn. *salmi* strait + the gen. suffix *-nen*, perhaps chosen in some cases as a topographic name by someone who lived by a strait.

Var.: **Salmi**.

Salmon 1. English and French: from the ME, OF given name *Salmon, Saumon*, a contracted form of SALOMON. 2. Jewish (Ashkenazic): from the Yid. male given name *Zalmen*, derived via a German form from Hebr. *Shelomo*; see SALOMON. 3. Irish: translated form of Gael. *Ó Bradáin*; see BRADEN.

Vars. (of 1): Eng.: **Salmond, Salman, Salmen**. Fr.: **Salman, Solmon**. (Of 2): Jewish: **Salman, Zalmon, Zalman, Zalmen**.
Patrs. (from 1): Eng.: **Salmons, Sammon(d)s**. Swed.: **Salmonsson**. (From 2): Jewish: **Salmanso(h)n, Salmenson, Zalmanson; Salmonov, Salmanov, Zalmonovich, Zalmanov, Zalmanoff, Zalmanovi(t)ch, Zalmanovicz, Zalmanovics, Zalmanowitz, Zalmanovitz, Zalmenov(itz)** (E Ashkenazic); **Zalmanovici** (a Rumanian spelling).

Salomon Jewish, English, French, Venetian, German, Danish/Norwegian, Polish, and Hungarian: ultimately from the Hebr. male given name *Shelomo* (a deriv. of *shalom* peace; cf. SHOLEM), which was fairly widespread in the Middle Ages among Christians and has for generations been a popular Jewish name. Among Christians it was also used as a nickname for a man who was considered wise, and for someone who had played the part of King Solomon in a miracle play.

Vars.: Jewish: **Salamon, Salaman, SALMON; Suliman** (from the Arabic form of the given name). Eng.: **Salamon, Salaman, SALMON**. Fr.: **Salamon, Solomon, SALMON; Salaün** (Brittany). It.: **Salomone, Salomon(i), Salamone, Salamon(i); Salamo** (Calabria). Ger.: **Saleman**. Pol.: **Salamon**. Czech: **Šalamoun**. Hung.: **Salamon**.
Dims.: Jewish: **Salomonczyk; Slomka** (from Yid. *s(h)loyme*). Czech: **Šach, Šalda, Šálek**.
Patrs.: Jewish: **Salomonson; Salomonof, Salomonivitch, Salom(on)owicz, Salomonovitz, Salomonowitz, Salam(on)ovitz, Salamonovits, Salomanof(f), Sulimani** (with the Arabic suffix *-i*); **Sulimanian** (among Iranian Jews); **Shlomov, Shlomof; Shlomowitz, S(h)lomovitz, Szlomowicz, Schlomovitz, S(h)lomovits, Shlomovics, Schlomovich, Shlomovi(t)ch, Schlomowich; S(h)lomovici** (a Rumanian spelling); **Shlemovich, Sleymovich** (from NE Yid. forms); **Salomons, Salamans**. Flem., Du.: **Salomons**. Norw., Dan.: **Salomonsen**. Swed.: **Salomonsson**.
Patrs. (from dims.): Jewish (E Ashkenazic): **Shlomkowitz, Shlomkovitz, Schlomkowich**.

Salonen Finnish: ornamental name from Finn. *salo* forested wilderness + the gen. suffix *-nen*, perhaps chosen in

some cases as a topographic name by someone who lived by such a place.

Var.: **Salo**.

Sälström *see* SEALEY

Salt English: metonymic occupational name, a var. of SALTER 1, or habitation name from a place in Staffs., so called from a salt pit there.

Vars.: SAULT, **Saltman**.
Cpds (ornamental elaborations): Jewish (Ashkenazic): **Salzberg, Zalt(z)berg, Zalcberg, Zalsberg** ('salt hill'); **Salzstein, Zalcstein** ('salt stone'); **Zalcwasser** ('salt water').

Salter English: 1. occupational name for an extractor and seller of salt (OE *s(e)alt*), a precious commodity in medieval times. 2. metonymic occupational name for a player on the psaltery, ME, OF *saltere* (L *psaltērium*, Gk *psaltērion*, from *psallein* to sound), a kind of stringed instrument.

Var.: SAUTER.
Dim.: Pol.: **Solarek** (also means 'salt-barrel').
Habitation names: Pol.: **Solecki** (from any of a number of places called *Solec*); **Soliński**.

Salthouse English (Lancs.): occupational name for a worker at a salt-works, topographic name for someone who lived by a salt-works, or habitation name from one of the minor places named from a salt-works. There are examples in Lytham St Annes and in Furness, among other places.

Var.: **Salters** (chiefly N Ireland).

Saltilo *see* SAULT

Saltykov Russian: patr. from the Turkic byname *Satyq, Satuq* 'Sold', presumably borne originally by a serf or someone who had been sold into slavery.

Salvador Spanish, Catalan, and Portuguese: from a popular medieval and modern given name (L *Salvātor* 'Saviour', a deriv. of *salvāre* to save; cf. SAUVÉ), borne in honour of Christ. The given name is also popular in Italy, esp. in the south, partly as a result of Sp. influence.

Dims.: It.: **Salvatorello, Salvatorelli**.

Salvage *see* SAVAGE

Salvi French and Italian: from a personal name (L *Salvius*, a deriv. of *salvus* safe; cf. SAUVÉ) borne by various early saints, among them a 6th-cent. bishop of Albi and a 7th-cent. bishop of Amiens.

Vars.: Fr.: **Salvy, Sauvy**. It.: **Salv(i)o**.
Dims.: It.: **Salvetti, Salvin(ell)i, Salvinello, Salvioli, Salvucci**.
Augs.: It.: **Salvioni, Salvione**.
Patr.: It.: **Di Salvo**.

Šamal Czech: nickname for someone with some peculiarity of the gait, from a deriv. of Czech *šámat* to shuffle or limp.

Sambell *see* SEMPLE

Sambrook English: habitation name from a place in Shrops., so called from OE *sand* SAND + *brōc* stream (see BROOK).

Samet 1. German and Jewish (Ashkenazic): metonymic occupational name for a maker or seller of velvet, Ger.

Samt, Yid. *samet* (MHG *samet*, ultimately from Gk *hexamiton*, a cpd of *hex* six + *mitos* thread). **2.** Jewish: acronymic name from the Hebr. letters SMT, representing the phrase *SiMan Tov* 'lucky sign', 'good omen' or *Sor Mera vaase Tov* 'turn from evil and do good', which was inscribed on the lecterns of the reader's desk in Ashkenazic synagogues in E Europe.

Vars. (of 1): Ger.: **Sameth, Samm(e)t, Sambeth**. Jewish (E Ashkenazic): **Sametnik** (an agent deriv.).

Samman *see* SAND

Sampaio Portuguese: habitation name from a place named from the dedication of its church to St *Pelagius*; see PELAYO.

Samper English (Norman): habitation name from any of the various places in N France called *Saint-Pierre*, from the dedication of their churches to St PETER.

Vars.: **Samber, Semper, Sember, Simper, Symber**.

Sampford *see* SANDFORD

Samson English, French, German, Jewish, and Flemish/Dutch: from the biblical name *Samson* (Hebr. *Shimshon*, a dim. of *shemesh* sun). Among Christians it may sometimes have been chosen as a given name or nickname in direct reference to the great strength of the biblical character, but a more common association was with the 6th-cent. Welsh bishop *Samson*, who travelled to Brittany, where he died and was greatly venerated. His name, which may be an altered form of a Celt. original, was popularized in England by Bret. followers of William the Conqueror, and to some extent independently from Wales.

Vars.: Eng.: **Sampson, Samsin; Sansom(e), Sansum, Sansam** (chiefly Somerset). Fr.: **Sa(i)nson**. Ger.: SIMSON. Jewish: **Shimshon, Shimsoni, Shimsony** (with the Hebr. suffix -*i*).

Dims.: Eng.: **Sam(me), Sanne, Sankin**. Fr.: **Sansot, Sansonnet**. It.: **Sansonetti**.

Patrs.: Jewish (E Ashkenazic): **Samsonov(ich), Samsonovitz; Szimszewicz, Shimshovits** (from Yid. *Shimshn*).

Samuel English, French, German, and Jewish: from the biblical male given name *Samuel* (Hebr. *Shemuel* 'Name of God').

Vars.: Eng.: **Samwell**. Ger.: **Samel**. Jewish: **Schmuel, Szmu(e)l; Shmil** (a S Yid. form); **S(c)hmueli, S(c)hmuely** (with the Hebr. suffix -*i*); **Shmouel, Schmoueli** (semi-Gallicized spellings).

Dims.: Pol.: **Samulczyk, Smulczyk**. Czech: **Samek**. Ukr.: **Samus**. Beloruss.: **Samuilyonok**. Hung.: **Samu**.

Patrs.: Eng.: **Samuels(on)**. Dan., Norw.: **Samuelsen**. Swed.: **Samuelsson**. Jewish: **Sam(u)elsohn; S(h)mulevich, Szmulewicz, Szmulewitz, Shmuilov(ich)** (NE Ashkenazic); **Shmilovitch, Shmilovitz** (S Ashkenazic). Russ.: **Samylov, Samoilov, Samylin**. Pol.: **Smuliewicz; Samulak**. Lithuanian: **Samelionis**. Armenian: **Smulian**.

Patrs. (from dims.): Eng.: **Sam(m)s**. Jewish: **Schmelkes, Schmelkin** (E Ashkenazic). Russ.: **Samoshkin, Samyshkin, Samokhin, Samukhin, Samonin, Samunin, Samus(y)ev, Samugin, Simulev**. Beloruss.: **Samusev**.

Samways English: nickname for a stupid person, from ME *samwis* dull, foolish (OE *sāmwīs*, from *sām* half + *wīs* wise).

Sanahuja Catalan: habitation name from *Sanaüja* in the province of Lérida. The placename is certainly not of Ro-

mance origin and more than one Basque etymology has been proposed.

Sancho Spanish and Portuguese: from an extremely common medieval given name (L *Sanc(t)ius*, seemingly a deriv. of *sanctus* (see SAINT), but in fact probably an approximation to an earlier pre-Roman personal name (cf. DIEGO)). The given name was borne by a 9th-cent. martyr of Cordova.

Var.: **Sanz**.

Patrs.: Sp.: **Sánchez, Sáe(n)z, Sái(n)z; Sánchiz** (Aragon). Cat.: **Sanchís, Sanchis, Sanchiz**. Port.: **Sanches**.

Sanctuary *see* SENTRY

Sand 1. English, Scots, German, Danish/Norwegian, and Swedish: topographic name for someone who lived on patch of sandy soil, from ME, Ger., Dan., Swed. *sand* (OE *sand*, OHG *sant*, ON *sandr*). **2.** English, Scots, and Danish/Norwegian: short form of ALEXANDER (cf. SANDER). **3.** Jewish (Ashkenazic): ornamental name, perhaps adopted in reference to God's promise to the Jewish people that they would be as many as the grains of sand upon the shore of the sea; cf. MEERSAND.

Vars. (of 1): Eng.: **Sand(e)s, Sandys** (also patrs. from 2). Ger.: **Sande, Sandt; Sand(e)mann, San(n)mann, Samman; Sandner**. Swed.: **Sandh, Sandin, Sandén, Sandman**, SANDELL. (Of 3): Jewish: **Zand**.

Cpds (of 1, ornamental elaborations): Swed.: **Sandberg** ('sand hill'); **Sandgren** ('sand branch'); **Sandlund** ('sand grove'); **Sandmark** ('sand territory'); **Sandquist** ('sand twig'); **Sandström** ('sand river'). (Of 3): Jewish: **Sandberg, Zandberg** ('sand hill'); **Sandgarten** ('sand garden'); **Sandhaus** ('sand house'; Anglicized **Sandhouse**); **Sandstein, Zandsztajn** ('sand stone'; the latter is a Pol. spelling).

Sandak Jewish: from Hebr. *sandak* godfather (Gk *syndikos* defendant's advocate, from *syn* with + *dikē* judgement), a role normally undertaken by some particularly respected member of the family or of the Jewish community.

Vars.: **Sandek, Sandik** (from Yid. *sandek*).

Sandbach English: habitation name from a place in Ches., so called from OE *sand* SAND + *bæce* stream (see BACH).

Sandell 1. English: topographic name for someone who lived by a sand-hill or sandy slope, from OE *sand* SAND + *hyll* HILL or *hylde* slope. **2.** Swedish: ornamental name, from Swed. *sand* SAND + the element -*el(l)* abstracted arbitrarily from other surnames such as *Nobel*.

Vars. (of 2): **Sandel(in), Sandelius**.

Sander English, Scots, and German: from the medieval given name *Sander*, an aphetic form of ALEXANDER.

Var.: Sc.: **Saunder**.

Dims.: Eng.: **Sandercock** (Devon); **Sandow** (Cornwall). Fr.: **Sandrin**. Prov.: **Sandeyron**. It.: **Sandrelli, Sandrin(i), Sandrolini, Sandrucci**.

Augs.: It.: **Sandron(i)**.

Patrs.: Eng., Sc.: **Sa(u)nders, Sandars; Sa(u)nderson, Sandeson, Sandi(e)son**. Low Ger.: **Sanders(en), Sandering**. Jewish: **Senders, Senderov(ski), Senderowsky, Senderoff, Senderovitch, Send(e)rovitz, Send(e)rowitz, Send(e)rowicz,**

Senderovicz, **Senderovits** (E Ashkenazic). Croatian: **Sand(ov)ić**.

'Servant of S.': Eng.: **Sande(r)man**.

Sandford English: habitation name from any of the various places, for example in Berks., Devon, Dorset, Oxon., and Shrops., so called from OE *sand* SAND + *ford* FORD.

Vars.: **Sanford**; **Sampford** (places in Devon, Essex, and Somerset); **Sandiford** (a lost place, probably in Yorks.), **Sandeford**, **Sandifer**, **Sandever**, **Sandyfirth**.

Sandham N English: apparently a habitation name, perhaps from an unidentified place named with the OE elements *sand* SAND + *hām* homestead. Alternatively, it may be from any of the several places in Yorks. called *Sandholme*, named from ON *sandr* sand + *holmr* island.

Sandilands Scots: habitation name from a district in Clydesdale, so called from the sandy soil.

Sandler 1. English (Norman): habitation name from *Saint-Hilaire*-du-Harcouët in La Manche, which gets its name from the dedication of its church to St HILARY, or alternatively from either of the places, in La Manche and Somme, called *Saint-Lô*. Both of the latter are named from a 6th-cent. St *Lauto*, bishop of Coutances; his name is of variable form in the sources and uncertain etymology. 2. Jewish (Ashkenazic): occupational name for a shoemaker or cobbler, Yid. *sandler* (from Hebr. *sandelar*, from LL *sandalārius*, an agent deriv. of *sandalium* shoe, a word that is apparently ultimately of Persian origin).

Vars. (of 1): **Santler**, **Sendler**. (Of 2): **Sandlerman**; **Sandlar** (from the Hebr. word).

Sandoval Spanish: habitation name from a place in the province of Burgos, earlier called *Sannoval*, from L *saltus* grove, wood (see SAULT) + *novālis* newly cleared land (see NOVAIS).

Sandy English: 1. habitation name from a place in Beds., so called from OE *sand* SAND + *ēg* island, dry land in a fen. 2. from the ON personal name *Sand(i)*, a short form of the various cpd names with a first element that is either *sand* truth or *sandr* sand.

Sanftleben *see* SENF

Sanger 1. English: occupational name for a singer or chorister, or nickname for a person who was always singing, from OE *sangere, songere* singer (a deriv. of *singan* to sing); the var. **Singer** represents a ME recoinage from the verb *sing(en)*. 2. Jewish (Ashkenazic): occupational name for a cantor, from Ger. *Sänger* singer. See also KAZAN.

Vars.: Eng.: **Songer**; **Sangster** (Scots; in form, early ME *-ster* is a fem. agent suffix, contrasted with the masc. *-er*, but by the period of surname formation, the distinction was pretty well lost). Jewish: **Zing(h)er** (from Yid. *zinger*); **Singman**.

Dim.: Jewish (E Ashkenazic): **Zingerenko** (with the Ukr. dim. suffix *-enko*).

Patrs.: Eng.: **Singers**. Flem., Du.: **Sangers**, **Sengers**, **Zangers**. Jewish (E Ashkenazic): **Zingerevich**, **Zingerevitz**.

San José Spanish: habitation name from any of various places, for example in the provinces of Almería, Cadiz, and Seville, so called from the dedication of their churches to St JOSEPH.

Sanichkin *see* SASHIN

Sankey 1. English: habitation name from a place in Lancs., apparently so called from a Brit. river name, perhaps meaning 'Sacred', 'Holy'. 2. Irish: Anglicized form of Gael. **Mac Seanchaidhe** 'son of the chronicler'. The name is nevertheless not common in Ireland.

Var.: **Sanky**.

San Martín Spanish: habitation name from any of the numerous places so called from the dedication of their churches to St MARTIN.

San Miguel Spanish: habitation name from any of the numerous places so called from the dedication of their churches to St MICHAEL.

San Román Spanish: habitation name from any of the numerous places so called from the dedication of their churches to St ROMAN.

San Segundo Spanish: habitation name from some minor place so called from the dedication of its church to St *Secundus* (see SEGOND).

Sankin *see* SAMSON

Sannié *see* SAGNE

Sans *see* SAINT

Santa María Spanish: habitation name from any of the extremely numerous places so called from the dedication of their churches to the Blessed Virgin Mary, or to some other St Mary (cf. MARIE).

Santana Spanish, Catalan, and Portuguese: habitation name from any of the numerous places so called from the dedication of their churches to St *Anne* (see HANNA).

Santiago Spanish and Portuguese: habitation name from any of the numerous places so called from the dedication of their churches to St JAMES. The apostle St James the Greater is the patron of Spain, following a 9th-cent. legend that he visited and evangelized the country after the death of Christ, rather than meeting a speedy end under Herod Agrippa. The scene of his alleged burial at Compostela was a place of pilgrimage from all over Europe throughout the Middle Ages.

Var.: Port.: **Tiago** (an aphetic form, the result of misdivision).

Santoro Italian: from a nickname or given name for someone who was born on All Saints' Day, It. *santoro* (LL *sanctorum (omnium dies festus)*).

Vars.: **Santori(o)** (Naples); **Santorum** (Trentino).

Dims.: **Santorelli**, **Santoriello**, **Santorini**.

Sanvoisin French: nickname for someone who lived in a remote situation, from OF *sans* without (L *sine*, apparently crossed with *absens*, pres. part. of *abesse* to be absent, lacking) + *visin* neighbour (see VOISIN).

Saoul *see* SOUL

Sapeyre *see* PIERRE

Sapin French: topographic name for someone who lived near a fir tree, or in a coniferous forest, from OF *sapin* fir (LL *sapīnus*). The OF byform *sap* may be a backformation from a supposed dim., but it may also represent the survival of an earlier form of the word, of Gaul. origin, to which was added the L adj. ending -*īnus*, perhaps as a result of association with *pīnus* PINE.

Vars.: **Sapy**; **Dusapin**; **Dusap(t)**.

Sapiński Polish: nickname for someone who wheezed a lot, from OPol. *sapać* to wheeze, hiss, or habitation name from a place named with this element in the sense 'quagmire'.

Var.: **Sapieha** (traditionally derived from Gk *sophia* wisdom, but this is no more than folk etymology).

Sapir Jewish (Ashkenazic): **1.** ornamental name from Hebr. *sapir* sapphire. **2.** said to be a habitation name from the Ger. town of *Speyer* (Eng. *Spires*), which had a large Jewish population in the Middle Ages; cf. SHAPIRO, SPIER, and SPIRE. However, there are phonological problems with this explanation.

Vars. (of 1): **Saphir(e)**; **Saphyr** (influenced by the spelling of Eng. *zephyr*); **Saperstein**.

Sapozhnikov Russian and Jewish (E Ashkenazic): patr. from Russ. *sapozhnik*, occupational name for a cobbler, an agent noun from *sapog* boot.

Vars.: Jewish: **Saposhnikov**, **Sapochnikov**, **Sapoznikov**, **Sapoznikow**, **Sapojnikov**, **Sapojnikoff** (patrs.); **Saposhnik**, **Sapoznik**.

Sapsford English: habitation name from *Sawbridgeworth* in Herts., which is recorded in 1568 as *Sapsforde*. The first element represents the gen. case of the OE personal name *Sǣbeorht*, composed of the elements *sǣ* sea + *beorht* bright, famous; the second is from OE *worð* enclosure (see WORTH), but has been confused with *ford* FORD.

Saquet *see* SACK

Saraiva Portuguese: of uncertain origin, possibly a habitation name from *Sarabia* in Galicia.

Sarch *see* SURRIDGE

Sardinha Portuguese: metonymic occupational name for a fisher of sardines (or perhaps a nickname), from Port. *sardinha* sardine (L *sardīna*, from Gk; the further etymology of the vocab. word is unclear, but it may be connected with the name of the island of *Sardinia*; cf. SARDOU).

Sardou Provençal: ethnic name for someone from Sardinia, a dim. of OProv. *sarde* Sardinian. The name of the island is of uncertain origin; cf. SARDINHA.

Vars.: **Sardet**, **Sardin**.

Sare *see* SAYER

Saretti *see* BALTHASAR

Sarfatti Jewish: ethnic name adopted in Italy by migrants from France and Spain, from Hebr. *Tsarefati*, a deriv. of *Tsarefat*, originally designating a Phoenician city on the eastern shore of the Mediterranean mentioned in the Book of Obadiah (rendered in the Vulgate as *Sarepta*). Under the influence of Gk *Hesperides* 'Western Islands', Jews associated the name *Tsarefat* first with France, then with France and the Iberian Peninsula (beginning in the 10th cent.), and finally with the whole of Western Europe

(from about the 14th cent.). In today's Hebr. the meaning of the word is 'France'.

Vars.: **Sarfati**, **Sarfat(t)y**, **Zarfat(t)i**, **Zarfaty**, **Serfati**, **Serfaty**.

Sargant *see* SERGEANT

Sarieu *see* RIEU

Sarkin *see* SORIN

Sarkisian *see* SERGIO

Sarmiento Spanish: apparently a nickname for a tall, thin person, from Sp. *sarmiento* vine shoot (L *sarmentum* shoot, from *sarpere* to trim, prune).

Sarpot *see* SERPE

Sarrail Provençal: metonymic occupational name for a locksmith, from OProv. *sarrail* lock (LL *serrālium*, a deriv. of *serra* bolt, bar). For the change of -*er*- to -*ar*-, cf. MARCHANT.

Vars.: **Sarraille**, **Sarralh**; **Sarraillier**, **Sarraillié**, **Sarralhier**, **Sarralhié**.

Sarran *see* SERRE

Sarson English: **1.** nickname for someone of swarthy appearance, or for an unruly person, or perhaps for someone who had taken part in a Crusade, from ME, OF *sarrazin* Saracen (via L and Gk from a Semitic term, perhaps akin to Arab. *sharq* sunrise, east, from *shāraqa* to rise). **2.** patr. from the medieval male given name *Sa(h)er*; see SAYER. **3.** metr. from the Hebr. female given name *Sara* 'Princess', borne by the wife of Abraham. This given name was not common in the Middle Ages except among Jews; cf. SORIN.

Dim. (of 1): It.: **Sarcinelli**.

Patr. (from 1): Eng.: **Sarsons**.

Sartre French: occupational name for a tailor, OF *sartre* (oblique case *sartor*, from L *sartor*, a deriv. of *sarcīre* (past part. *sartus*) to mend, patch).

Vars.: **Sa(s)tre**, **Sarthre**; **Sartor**.

Dims.: Fr.: **Sart(h)on**, **Sart(h)ou**. It.: **Sartorelli**, **Sartoret(to)**, **Sartini**, **Sartucci**.

Aug.: It.: **Sartoni**.

Sarvis *see* SERVIS

Šašek Czech: nickname meaning 'fool' or 'buffoon'.

Sashin Russian: patr. from the given name *Sasha*, one of a group of aphetic pet forms and dims. of ALEXANDER.

Vars.: **San(yut)in**, **Sa(kh)nov**.

Dims.: **Sashkin**, **Sash(en)kov**, **San(ich)kin**, **Sankov**.

Sason Jewish (non-Ashkenazic): from the Hebr. male given name *Sason* 'Joy', or ornamental name from the vocabulary word.

Vars.: **Sasson**; **Sassoon** (an Anglicized spelling); **Sassoun** (a Gallicized spelling); **Sassoni** (with the Hebr. adj. suffix -*i*).

Patrs.: **Ben-Sasson**; **Sassonov**.

Sassoli *see* SACHS

Sastre *see* SARTRE

Satch *see* SACK

Satre *see* SARTRE

Satterthwaite English: habitation name from a place in the Lake District, so called from OE *sætr* shieling + ON *þveit* pasture (see THWAITE).

Vars.: **Satterfitt**, **Setterfield**.

Saturnin French: from a given name (L *Saturnīnus*, a Roman family name, from *Saturnus*, the god of agriculture and vegetation, whose name is a deriv. of the root *sat*-plant, sow). This was borne by a large number of early saints, including the 3rd-cent. first bishop of Toulouse.

Vars.: **Sernin**, **Sornin**, **Cernin**, **Cerny**.

Satz Jewish (Ashkenazic): acronym from the Hebr. phrase *Zera TSadikim* 'seed of the righteous', assumed in a spirit of pious respect for one's ancestors. See also SCHATZ.

Vars.: **Zatz**; **Zac** (a Polish spelling).

Sauber German and Jewish (Ashkenazic): nickname for a tidy or well-groomed person, from Ger. *sauber* clean (MHG *sūber* smart, neat).

Vars.: Ger.: **Saubert**; **Säuberlich**, **Seuberlich**, **Seiberlich**. Jewish: **Sauberman**; **Soiberman**, **Zoiberman** (from Yid. *zoyber*).

Saüc *see* SUREAU

Sauce French: topographic name for someone who lived by a willow tree, OF *saus* (L *salix*, gen. *salicis*; cf. SALE).

Vars.: **Sausse**, **Sauze**.

Dims.: Fr.: **Saucet**, **Saucey**, **Sausset**, **Sauzet**. It.: **Sal(ic)etti**, **Sal(ic)ini**, **Salizzoli**.

Collectives: Fr.: **Saussure**; **Saulxures** (Lorraine). It.: **Saliceti**. Sp.: **Salcedo** (places in the provinces of Álava, Lugo, and Oviedo).

Sauer German and Jewish (Ashkenazic): nickname for a cross or cantankerous person, from Ger. *sauer* sour (MHG *sūr*, cogn. with Eng. *sour*, OE *sūr*).

Vars.: Ger.: **Sauermann**. Jewish: **Sauerman(n)**; **Zoyer** (from Yid. *zoyer*).

Dims.: Ger.: **Säuerle**, **Seyerlin**.

Cpds: Jewish (reason for adoption unknown, perhaps bestowed by non-Jewish government officials): **Sauerbrunn** ('sour well'); **Sauerquell** ('sour spring'); **Sauerstrom** ('sour river'); **Sauerteig** ('sour dough').

Saul English, French, German, and Italian: from the given name *Saul* (Hebr. *Shaul* 'Asked-for (child)'), the name of the king of Israel whose story is recounted in the first book of Samuel. In spite of his success in uniting Israel and his military prowess, Saul had a troubled reign, not least because of his long conflict with the young David, who eventually succeeded him. Perhaps for this reason, the given name was not particularly common in medieval times; hence the surname too is comparatively rare. A further disincentive to its popularity as a Christian name was the fact that it was the original name of St Paul, borne by him while he was persecuting Christians, and rejected by him after his conversion to Christianity. It may in part have arisen as a nickname for someone who had played the part of the biblical king in a religious play.

Vars.: Eng.: **Saull**, **Sawle**. It.: **Saul(l)e**, **Saul(l)i**, **Saullo**.

Dims.: It.: **Saulino**. Jewish: **Shaulick** (E Ashkenazic).

Patrs.: Jewish: **Shaulson** (Ashkenazic); **Shaulov**, **Shauloff** (E Ashkenazic).

Sault 1. English: var. of SALT. 2. French: topographic name for someone who lived near a grove or small wood, OF *saut* (L *saltus*).

Vars. (of 2): Fr.: **Dussau(l)t**, **Dussaud**; **Duss(e)aux**, **Duseau(x)**. Dims. (of 2): It.: **Saltilo**. Sp.: **Sotelo**, **Sotillo(s)**.

Saunder *see* SANDER

Saunt *see* SAINT

Saurat *see* SOAR

Sauter 1. German: occupational name for a shoemaker or cobbler (rarely a tailor), from MHG *sūter*, *siuter*, *sūtære* (from L *sūtor*, an agent deriv. of *suere* to sew). See also SCHUSTER. 2. English: var. of SALTER.

Vars. (of 1): **Seut(t)er**; **Seiter** (Swabia); **Sutter(er)** (Switzerland); **Saut(t)**. (Of 2): **Saulter**, **Sautter**.

Dims. (of 1): Ger.: **Seuterle**, **Seuterlin**, **Seit(t)erle**, **Sütterle**, **Sütterlin**.

Sautour French: occupational name for a tumbler or acrobat, OF *sauteour* (L *saltor*, an agent deriv. of *salīre*, past part. *saltus*, to spring, leap; cf. SAYLOR).

Dims.: **Saut(e)reau**, **Sauterel**, **Sauteron**.

Sauvage *see* SAVAGE

Sauvan *see* SELWYN

Sauvé French: nickname for someone who had had a narrow escape, or from a given name with a religious significance referring to Christian salvation, from OF *sauvé* saved (past part. of *sauver* to save, L *salvāre*).

Sauvy *see* SALVI

Savage English: nickname for a wild or uncouth person, from ME, OF *salvage, sauvage* untamed (LL *salvaticus*, a deriv. of L *silva* wood, influenced by L *salvus* whole, i.e. natural).

Vars.: **Sauvage**, **Salvage**, **Sa(l)vidge**, **Savege**. The surname is also relatively common in Ireland, where it has been Gaelicized **Sabhaois** and **Sabháiste**.

Dims.: Fr.: **Sauvageon**, **Sauvageau**, **Sauvageot**. It.: **Selvaggini**.

Savasteev *see* SEBASTIAN

Savatier French: occupational name for a shoemaker or cobbler, OF *savatier* (an agent deriv. of *savate* slipper, shoe, a borrowing from Arabic or some oriental language). The term also acquired the pej. sense 'botcher' and in some cases the surname may perhaps have arisen as an abusive nickname with this meaning.

Var.: **Savetier**.

Savelyev Russian: patr. from the given name *Saveli* (L *Sabellius*). Sabellius (*fl.* 215) was an early Christian theologian who was excommunicated by Pope Calixtus I, but whose ideas enjoyed a considerable cult in the East. The name *Sabellius* is an ethnic term, of uncertain origin, denoting a member of a minor Italic tribe that was subdued by the Romans in ancient times; cf. SABIN.

Var.: **Savyolov**.

Dims.: Russ.: **Savlichev** (patr.). It.: **Savellini**.

Savić *see* SAWICKI

547

Savignac French: habitation name from any of the various places, mostly in SW France, so called from the Gallo-Roman personal name *Sabinius* (a deriv. of *Sabinus*; see SABIN) + the local suffix *-ācum*.

Vars.: **Savignat**, **Savigny**.

Savignon *see* SABIN

Saville English (Norman): habitation name from a place in N France, of which the identity is not clear. It is probably *Sainville* in Eure-et-Loire, so called from OF *saisne* Saxon (see SACHS 1) + *ville* settlement (see VILLE).

Vars.: **Savil(l)**, **Savile**, **Save(a)ll**, **Seville**.

Savioli *see* SAGE

Savoie French: regional name from Savoy, Fr. *Savoie*, which was consolidated in the 11th cent. by Count Humbert the White-handed, feudal lord of the kingdom of Arles. His descendants formed the great European noble house of Savoy, with large holdings in France, Switzerland, and Italy. Piedmont was closely connected with Savoy as early as the 11th cent., since Humbert acquired a number of possessions there through marriage.

Vars.: **Savoye**, **Savois**; **Savoyer**, **Savoyen**, **Savoyant**.

Savory English: from a Gmc personal name composed of the elements *saba*, of uncertain meaning + *rīc* power, which was introduced into England by the Normans in the form *Savaric*.

Vars.: **Savoury**, **Savary**, **Savery**, **Severy**.

Savoureux French: nickname for a pleasant or amiable person, from OF *savoureux* tasty, agreeable (LL *saporōsus*, from *sapor* flavour, taste).

Vars.: **Savreux**; **Savouré**.
Dims.: Fr.: **Savouret**, **Savourez**. Prov.: **Sabouret**, **Saboureau**, **Sabourin**.
Aug.: Fr.: **Savourat**.

Sawell *see* SEWELL

Sawicki Polish: from the given name *Sawa* (from Gk *Sabbas*, the name of a saint who died in 532), with the addition of *-ski*, suffix of surnames (see BARANOWSKI).

Dim.: Pol.: **Sawczyk**.
Patrs.: Pol.: **Sawicz**. Croatian: **Savić**, **Savićević**.
Patr. (from a dim.): Croatian: **Savković**.

Sawle *see* SAUL

Sawyer English: occupational name for someone who earned his living from sawing wood, ME *saghier*, an agent deriv. of *sagh(en)* to saw (from OE *sagu* a saw); for the inserted glide, cf. BOWYER. The ME word absorbed the ANF term for a sawyer, *syour* (see SEWER 3).

Var.: **Sawer**; see also SAYER.
Patr.: Eng.: **Sawyers**.
Equivs. (not cogn.): Fr.: GACHE. Pol.: TRACZ. Russ.: PILSHCHIKOV.

Sax *see* SACHS

Saxby English: 1. habitation name from places in Leics. and Lincs., so called from the ON byname *Saksi* 'Saxon' (or the gen. of the OE folk-name *Seaxe*, ON *Saksar*; cf. SACHS 1) + ON *býr* farm, settlement. 2. from ME *sakespey*,

OF *sacquespee*, a nickname for someone quick to take offence and draw his sword, from OF *sacque(r)* to draw, extract (from *sac* SACK) + *espee* sword (L *spatha*; cf. ESPADA).

Saxon English (Lancs.): 1. var. of SAXTON. 2. from the medieval given name *Saxon*, originally an ethnic byname for someone from Saxony; cf. SACHS 1.

Saxton English: 1. habitation name from places in Cambs. and W Yorks., both so called from OE *Seaxe* Saxons (cf. SACHS 1) + *tūn* enclosure, settlement. 2. occupational name, a var. of SEXTON 1.

Say English: 1. Norman habitation name from *Sai* in Orne or *Say* in Indre, perhaps so called from a Gaul. personal name *Saius* + the local suffix *-ācum*. 2. metonymic occupational name for a maker or seller of *say*, a kind of finely textured cloth (from OF *saie*, L *saga*, pl. of *sagum* military cloak). The surname may also have denoted a habitual wearer of clothes made of this material.

Var.: **Saye**.

Saycell *see* CECIL

Sayer 1. English: from the ME personal name *Saher* or *Seir*. This is probably a Norman introduction of the Continental Gmc personal name *Sigiheri*, composed of the elements *sigi* victory + *heri* army. However, it could also represent a ME survival of an unrecorded OE name, **Sǣhere*, composed of the elements *sǣ* sea + *here* army. 2. English: occupational name for a woodcutter, from ME *saghier* (see SAWYER) or OF *seieor* (see SEWER 3). 3. English: occupational name for a professional reciter, from an agent deriv. of ME *say(en)*, *sey(en)* to say (OE *secgan*). 4. English: occupational name for an assayer of metals or a taster of food, from an aphetic form of ME *assayer* (an agent deriv. of *assay* trial, test, OF *essay*, from LL *exagium*, a deriv. of *exagmināre* to weigh). 5. English: occupational name for a maker or seller of the type of cloth known in ME as *say*; cf. SAY 2. 6. Welsh: occupational name from W *saer* wright, artificer, carpenter (cf. MCINTYRE).

Vars.: **Sa(y)re**, **Saer**, **Se(e)ar**.
Patrs.: Eng.: **Sayers**, **Seyers**; **Sear(e)s**, **Seers**; **Searson**, SARSON. (From 1 only): Low Ger.: **Siegers**, **Se(e)gers**. Dan., Norw.: **Sejersen**.

Saylor English: occupational name for a dancer or acrobat, OF *sailleor* (L *salītor*, from *salīre* to jump, leap; cf. SAUTOUR).

Vars.: **Sailer**, SEILER.

Sayman *see* SEAMAN

Saywell *see* SEWELL

Scaife N English: nickname for an awkward or difficult man, a tyke, or else one who was physically misshapen, from Northern ME *skafe* misshapen, crooked; awkward, difficult (ON *skeifr*).

Vars.: **Skaife**, **Scafe**.

Scale *see* SCHOLES

Scallan *see* SCULLY

Scammell English: of uncertain origin, perhaps from a ME given name **Skammel*, dim. of an ON byname from *skammr* short.

Scannell Irish: Anglicized form of Gael. **Ó Scannail** 'descendant of *Scannal*', a byname meaning 'Contention'.

Vars.: **O'Scandall**, **O'Scannill**, **O'Scannell**.

Dims.: **O'Scanlaine**, **(O')Scanlan**, **(O')Scan(d)lon** (Gael. **Ó Scannláin**).

Scantlebury English (W Country): of unknown origin, perhaps a habitation name from *Kentisbury* or *Kentisbeare* in Devon, with excrescent initial *S*-. Both these places derive their first element from the OE personal name *Cæntel*; the second is in the one case *burh* fort (see BURY) and in the other *bearu* grove (see BEER).

Scarborough English: habitation name from the town on the coast of N Yorks., so called from the ON byname *Skarði* (see SCARTH 2) + ON *borg* fortress, town.

Scarfe English: nickname for someone bearing some supposed resemblance to a cormorant, Northern ME *scarfe* (ON *skarfr*), or else a survival into ME of the ON byname *Scarfi*, from the same source.

Vars.: **Scarf(f)**, **Scarffe**.

Scargill English: habitation name from a place in N Yorks., so called from the ON bird name *skraki*, a diving duck + ON *gil* valley, ravine (see GILL 2).

Scarisbrick English: habitation name from a place near Liverpool, so called from the gen. case of the ON personal name *Skar* + ON *brekka* slope, hill.

Vars.: **Sizebrick**, **Siosbrick**.

Scarlett English: metonymic occupational name for a dyer or for a seller of rich, bright fabrics, from OF *escarlate* scarlet cloth (LL *scarlāta, scarlētum*, of uncertain, probably Semitic, origin).

Var.: **Scarlet**.

Scarso Italian: nickname for a poor man or for a miser, from It. *scarso* scarce, scant (LL *excarpsus*, for class. L *excarptus*, past part. of *excarpere* to excerpt, pick out).

Var.: **Scarsi**.

Dims.: **Scarsello**, **Scarselli**, **Scarsini**.

Scarth N English and Scots (esp. Orkneys): **1.** habitation name from any of the various places named with the ON topographical term *skarð* gap, notch. **2.** from the ON byname *Skarði* 'Hare-lipped', a deriv. of the element given above.

Scatchard English: of uncertain origin, perhaps a derisory nickname for a long-legged man, from ANF *(e)scache* stilt + the pej. suffix *-ard*.

Scattergood English: nickname for a man who was careless and free with money, perhaps a philanthropist who gave his goods to the poor, from ME *skater(en)* to squander, dissipate (apparently a byform, under Scandinavian influence, of *shatter*) + *gode* property, goods, wealth.

Šćepanović see STEPHEN

Schachter see SCHECHTER

Schade see SHADE

Schadow German: habitation name from a place in the Spreewald, whose name is of Slav. origin.

Schäfer **1.** German: occupational name for a shepherd, Ger. *Schäfer*, an agent deriv. of *Schaf* sheep (MHG *schāf*, OHG *scāf*). **2.** Jewish (Ashkenazic): because of the small number of Jewish shepherds at the time when most Ashkenazic Jews adopted surnames (in the late 18th and early 19th cents.), it is unlikely that this common Jewish surname can be given a literal interpretation. Perhaps it was adopted as a reference to God ('The Lord is my Shepherd'; Ps. 23: 1), or perhaps in allusion to King David, who was a shepherd in his boyhood.

Vars.: Jewish: **Schaf(f)er**, **S(c)hef(f)er**; **Szefer** (a Pol. spelling); Sheferman.

Patrs.: Low Ger.: **Schäpers**, **Sche(e)pers**, **Schiepers**. Flem., Du.: **Schepers**.

Schaffer **1.** German: occupational name for a steward or baliff, from an agent deriv. of Ger. *schaffen* to manage, run (OHG *scaffan, scaffōn*). **2.** Jewish (Ashkenazic): var. of SCHÄFER.

Vars. (of 1): **Schaffner**, **Scheffner**, **Schäffer**, **Schöfer**.

Dims. (of 1): Ger.: **Schafferlin**. Czech: **Šafařik**.

Patr. (from 1): Low Ger.: **Scheffers**.

Schäffler German (Bavaria): occupational name for a cooper, an agent deriv. of *Schäffl*, dim. of the S Ger. dial. term *Schaff* tub, butt.

Vars.: **Scheffler**, **Schöffler**; **Scheff(e)l**, **Schöffel**.

Schakespear see SHAKESPEARE

Schalk German: occupational name for a servant or, more specifically, a jester, MHG *schalk* (OHG *scalc*); cf. also GOTTSCHALK, MARSHALL, SENESHAL. Later the word came to be used as a term of reproach, 'knave', and some cases of the surname may reflect this use.

Var.: **Schalch**.

Dims.: **Schalkl**, **Schälkle**.

Schäpe see STEPHEN

Schapiro see SHAPIRO

Scharfherz see SHARP

Scharnhorst German: habitation name from any of various ous places, for example near Dortmund in Westphalia and also near Verden and to the north of Celle, apparently so called from the Gmc elements *skarn* damp, dirty + *horst* wood(ed hill) (cf. HURST).

Scharnke see CHERNYAKOV

Scharrer German: **1.** occupational name for a carder of wool, from an agent deriv. of Ger. *scharren* to scrape, scratch (akin to OHG *scerran*). **2.** habitation name from any of the various places, such as *Scharr* in Switzerland and the Upper Palatinate or *Scharre* in Saxony, named from OHG *scara* wooded area, with the suffix *-er* denoting an inhabitant of a place.

Schatz **1.** German: metonymic occupational name for a treasurer, from Ger. *Schatz* treasure (MHG *scha(t)z*, OHG *skaz*). It may also have been a nickname for a rich man (or ironically for a miser), or else for a well-liked person or a ladies' favourite, from the use of the vocab. word as a term of endearment. **2.** Jewish (Ashkenazic): acronymic name from the Hebr. phrase *SHeliach-TSibur* 'emissary of the congregation', an epithet of the cantor.

Vars. (of 1): **Schatz(l)er**, **Schätz(l)er**; **Schatzmann**. (Of 2): **Shatz**, **Szatz**; **Shatski**, **Shatsky** (E Ashkenazic adjectival forms); **Shatzov**, **Shatzkin** (patrs., the latter based on a dim. form).

Dims. (of 1): Ger.: **Schatzl**, **Schätzl**.

Cpd (of 1, ornamental): Jewish (Ashkenazic): **S(c)hatzberg** ('treasure hill').

Schauchet *see* SHOIKHET

Schauer 1. German: occupational name for an official inspector, for example the official overseer of a market, MHG *schouwer*, agent deriv. of *schouwen* to look, inspect (OHG *scouwōn*). 2. Jewish (W Ashkenazic): ornamental name from a W Yid. pronunciation of Hebr. *shor* ox, perhaps taken by bearers of the given name JOSEPH because the biblical character of this name is compared to an ox in Deut. 33: 17: 'His glory is like the firstling of his bullock'. See also BICK 2.

Vars. (of 1): **Schauert**, **Schauber**. (Of 2): **S(c)hor(r)**, **Schorman(n)**; **Szor** (a Pol. spelling); **S(c)hory**, **Shori** (with the Hebr. suffix -*i*); SHORE.

Schechter Jewish (Ashkenazic): occupational name for a ritual slaughterer, Ger. *Schächter* (agent deriv. of *schächten*, from the Yid. verb *shekhtn*, whose stem is from Hebr. *shachat* to slaughter). See also SHOIKHET.

Vars.: **Schächter**, **Scha(e)chter**, **Schacter**, **Shechter**, **Schecter**, **Szechter**, **Schechner**, **S(c)hecht(er)man**.

Schecker German: occupational name for an armourer, an agent. deriv. of MHG *schecke* quilted jacket, coat of mail.

Vars.: **Scheck(e)**, **Schegg**, **Schöck**; **Scheckenmacher**, **Scheggenmacher**.

Scheidt German: topographic name for someone who lived near a boundary or watershed, MHG *scheide* (OHG *sceida*, from *sceidan* to part, divide), or habitation name from any of the numerous places named with this word.

Vars.: **Scheit**, **Schaid(t)**; **Scheid(l)er**.

Scheinis Jewish (Ashkenazic): metr. from the Yid. female given name *Sheyne* (from Yid. *sheyn* beautiful, which is from MHG *schoene*; cf. SCHÖN) + the Yid. possessive suffix -*s*.

Vars.: **Sheinis**, **S(c)heines**; **Sheinenson**, **Scheineson**; **Szenes**, **S(c)heinin** (E Ashkenazic).

Dims.: **Sche(i)ndel** (from Yid. *Sheyndel*); **Scheinkin** (metr., from Yid. *Sheynke*).

Schell German: nickname for a wild or obstreperous person, from MHG *schel* noisy, loud.

Vars.: **Schelle(r)**, **Schöll(er)**; **Schellig**, **Schölig**.

Schellini *see* FRANCIS

Schemmel German: metonymic nickname for a cripple, from MHG *schemel* crutch (also meaning 'bench' or 'stool', OHG *scamil*, from L *scamillus* raised platform).

Var.: **Schemel**.

Schenke German: occupational name for a cup-bearer or server of wine, MHG *schenke* (OHG *scenko*, from *scenken*

to pour out, serve). The vocab. word was also used as an occupational name for a tavern keeper (hence the sense of the mod. Ger. word, 'inn', tavern'). In another development, the word came to be used as an honorary title for a high court official (cf. BUTLER); the surname may additionally derive from either of these senses.

Vars.: **Schenk**, **Schenck(e)**; **Schenker** ('tavern keeper').

Schepe *see* STEPHEN

Scherschewski *see* SIEROTA

Scherzer 1. German: occupational name for a jester or nickname for a facetious person, an agent deriv. of Ger. *Scherz* joke (MHG *scherz* amusement, game). 2. Jewish (E Ashkenazic): possibly a habitation name from *Scierza* in Galicia, Poland, or an occupational name akin to 1, referring to an entertainer at Jewish weddings.

Vars.: **Schertzer**; **Scher(t)z** (metonymic).

Scheuer 1. German: topographic name for someone who lived near a tithe-barn, or metonymic occupational name for an official responsible for receiving the tithes of agricultural produce rendered, from MHG *schiur(e)*, *schiuwer* barn, granary (OHG *scūra*, *sciura*). 2. Jewish (Ashkenazic): of uncertain origin, perhaps taken by someone who lived near or owned a barn.

Vars.: (Of 1): **Scheurer**, **Scheuermann**. (Of 2): **Scheuerman(n)**; **Scheier**, **Schaier** (presumably from Yid. *shayer* barn).

Vars.: Low Ger.: **Verschuer**, **Terschüren**; **Scheu(ne)mann**, **Schü(ne)mann**. Flem.: **Van der Schueren**; **Schuerman**. Du.: **Verschoor**, **Verschuren**, **Schuurman**.

Schiaparelli Italian: occupational name for a woodcutter, from a dim. of the Ligurian dial. term *sciaparo* (an agent deriv. of *sciapà* to split, cleave).

Schick 1. German: nickname for a pleasant and well-behaved person, from Ger. *schick* polished, courteous, proper, fitting (from Ger., MHG *schicken* to be fitting or appropriate; the Fr. adj. *chic* is from the Ger.). 2. Jewish (Ashkenazic): of uncertain origin, either of similar derivation to 1 above, or perhaps an acronym of the Hebr. phrase *SHem yisrael Kodesh* 'the name of Israel is holy'.

Vars. (of 1): **Schicke**, **Schicker(t)**. (Of 2): **Shi(c)k**.

Dims. (of 1): **Schick(e)l**, **Schickele**.

Schief German: nickname for someone suffering from some deformity, from Ger., MLG *schief* crooked.

Vars.: **Scheef(e)**, **Scheff**, **Scheve**, **Scheewe**.

Schiementz *see* SIMON

Schieve *see* SHERIFF

Schilbert *see* GILBERT

Schild 1. German: metonymic occupational name for a maker or painter of shields, from Ger. *Schild* shield (MHG *schilt*, OHG *scilt*). 2. Jewish (Ashkenazic): of uncertain origin, probably a house name for someone who lived in a house marked with a sign, from Ger. *Schild*, Yid. *shild* sign; cf. ROTHSCHILD and SCHWARZSCHILD.

Vars.: **Schildt**, **Schilder**, **Schilter**. (Of 2 only): **Schildhaus**. Dim.: Low Ger.: **Schilgen**.

Schiller 1. German: nickname for a person with a squint, from an agent deriv. of MHG *schilhen* to squint (from *schelh* squinting, OHG *scelah*). **2.** Jewish (S Ashkenazic): see SCHULER 2.

Vars. (of 1): **Schilcher**. (Of 2): **Shil(l)er**.

Schilling German: nickname from the coin, Ger. *Schilling* (MHG *schilling*, OHG *scilling*, a deriv. of *scilt* shield). The surname may have referred originally to a rent or fee owed, or have some other anecdotal origin, now irrecoverable.

Vars.: **Schelling**. (Under Slav. influence): **Schilla(c)k**, **Schellack**, **Schellach**, **Schillok**, **Schilloga**.

Patr.: Flem.: **Schellinckx**.

Schimmel 1. German and Dutch: nickname for a man with grey or white hair, from MHG, MDu. *schimel*, a term used to denote both mildew and a white horse. OHG forms are not found, and the semantic development is not entirely clear. **2.** Jewish (Ashkenazic): of uncertain origin, probably an unflattering nickname, meaning 'mildew', imposed by a non-Jewish government official.

Schimpf 1. German: nickname for a humorous or playful person, from MHG *schimpf* sport, play, amusement (OHG *scimpf*). **2.** Jewish (Ashkenazic): of uncertain origin, probably an unflattering nickname from mod. Ger. *Schimpf* insult, complaint, imposed by a non-Jewish government official.

Vars.: Ger.: **Schimpp**, **Schempf**, **Schempp**; **Schimpfer**.

Dim.: Ger.: **Schimpfle**.

Schinasi *see* ASHKENAZI

Schlecht German: **1.** nickname for a straightforward person, from MHG, OHG *sleht* direct, natural (which later came to mean 'defective', 'bad'; a cogn. of SLIGHT 1). **2.** habitation name from any of various minor places, named from OHG *sleht* in the sense 'flat'. There are places so named for example in Mecklenburg and the Upper Palatinate.

Vars.: **Schlicht(e)**, **Schlichter**, **Schlichtmann**.

Patrs. (from 1): Low Ger.: **Schlichting**. Flem., Du.: **Slechten**.

Schlegel German: metonymic occupational name for a smith, or nickname for a forceful person, from MHG *slegel* sledgehammer (OHG *slegil*, a deriv. of *slahan* to strike).

Vars.: **Schlegl**, **Schlögl**.

Schleicher German and Jewish (Ashkenazic): nickname for a furtive or stealthy person, from an agent deriv. of Ger. *schleichen* to creep silently (MHG *slichen*, OHG *slihhan*).

Vars.: Ger.: **Schleich**. Jewish: **Shleicher**.

Schleier German: metonymic occupational name for a maker or seller of veils, from Ger. *Schleier* veil or headscarf (MHG *sleier*, *sloier*, of uncertain origin).

Vars.: **Schleyer**, **Schlayer**; **Schleirmacher**.

Schleifer 1. German: occupational name for a polisher of swords and armour (cf. FROBISHER), or a grinder of knives or diamonds, from an agent deriv. of Ger. *schleifen* to grind, polish (MHG *slifen*, OHG *slifan*). **2.** German and Jewish (Ashkenazic): habitation name for someone who came from *Schleife* in Silesia.

Vars. (of 1): Ger.: **Schleif**. Jewish: **Schleifman**.

Schlein Jewish (Ashkenazic): ornamental or occupational-ornamental name from Yid. *shlayn* tench (Ger.

Schlei(e), MHG *slī(g)e*, *slīhe*, OHG *slīo*). This is one of the many Ashkenazic ornamental names taken from words denoting fishes.

Schlessinger German: regional name for someone from Silesia (Ger. *Schlesien*, *Schlesing*, Pol. *Śląsk*), so called from the *Silingae*, a Gmc tribe which occupied the region before being expelled by Slavs in the 4th cent. AD. The region is now part of Poland, but was formerly under German administration. Other places named with the same element include *Schleusingen* in Saxony, *Schlenzig* in Pomerania, and *Schlenz* in Silesia itself, and it is possible that in some instances the surname derives from one of these.

Vars.: **Sles(s)inger**, **Slazenger** (Anglicized forms); **Schlensok**, **Schlensog** (of Slav. origin).

Schlick 1. German: nickname for a glutton, a deriv. of MHG *slicken* to gulp, swallow (OHG **sluckōn*). **2.** Low German: topographic name for someone who lived in a marshy area, from MLG *slik* slime, bog. **3.** Jewish (Ashkenazic): of uncertain origin, probably an unflattering name from mod. Ger. *Schlick* slime, mud, imposed by a non-Jewish government official.

Vars. (of 1): **Schluck(er)**. (Of 2): **Schlicke**, **Schlickmann**, **Schlich**.

Schliemann 1. Low German: occupational name for a seller of freshwater fish, from MLG *slie* tench + *mann* man. **2.** German: topographic name for someone who lived near a sloe tree, or occupational name for someone who sold sloes, from MHG *slēhe* sloe (OHG *slēha*, *slēwa*) + *mann* man.

Vars. (of 1): **Schlie**. (Of 2): **Schlee(mann)**.

Schliesser 1. German: occupational name for a jailer, Ger. *Schliesser*, or for a chatelain or steward in charge of the keys to the pantry and storerooms, MHG *sliezer*, agent deriv. of *sliezen* to shut, lock (OHG *sliozan*). **2.** Jewish (Ashkenazic): of uncertain origin, perhaps an adoption of the relatively common German surname.

Var.: Ger.: **Schleusser**.

Schlomkowich *see* SALOMON

Schloss 1. German: metonymic occupational name for a locksmith, from Ger. *Schloss* lock (MHG, OHG *sloz*, a deriv. of *sliozen* to shut, lock; cf. SCHLIESSER). **2.** German: topographic name for someone who lived in or near a castle, or who or was employed at a castle, Ger. *Schloss* castle (originally the same word as in 1). **3.** Jewish (Ashkenazic): of uncertain origin, either an occupational cogn. of 1 or an ornamental name related to 2.

Vars. (of 1 and 2): **Schlösser**, **Schlossmann**. (Of 1 only): **Schlossmacher**, **Schlosshauer**.

Schlossberg Jewish (Ashkenazic): habitation name from any of various places in Germany so called, because they were the sites of castles (see SCHLOSS 2) on hills (see BERG).

Var.: **Szlosberg** (a Pol. spelling).

Schlunk German: topographic name for someone who lived in a narrow valley or ravine, MHG dial. *slunk* (cogn. with mod. Ger. *Schlund* throat, chasm), or perhaps a nickname from this word.

Schmädicke *see* SMITH

Schmalz 1. German: metonymic occupational name for a chandler, from Ger. *Schmalz* tallow, grease, fat (MHG, OHG *smalz*), or perhaps a nickname for a fat or unctuous man. 2. Jewish (Ashkenazic): of uncertain origin, perhaps a nickname from Ger. *Schmalz* or Yid. *shmalts* animal fat.

Vars.: Ger.: **Schmaltz**; **Schmolz** (Bavaria). Jewish: **Schmalzer** (apparently an occupational name for someone who dealt in animal fat).

Dims.: Ger.: **Schmalzl**, **Schmälzle**; **Schmolzl** (Bavaria).

Schmelkes *see* SAMUEL

Schmuck German: metonymic nickname for someone who wore a prominent jewel or ornament, from Ger. *Schmuck* jewel, ornament (MHG *smuc* jewel, finery).

Schnabel German and Jewish (Ashkenazic): nickname for a gossip or a glutton, or for someone with a long nose, from Ger. *Schnabel* beak, mouth (MHG *snabel*, OHG *snabul*).

Schneck German and Jewish (Ashkenazic): nickname for a slow or indolent worker, from Ger. *Schneck(e)*, Yid. *shnek* snail (MHG *snecke*, OHG *snecko*). The same Ger. vocab. word was also used to denote slugs and leeches, and the surname may in some cases refer to one of these creatures, e.g. as a nickname for a 'slimy' or clinging person, or in the case of the Jewish name, simply an unflattering name imposed by a non-Jewish government official.

Vars.: Ger.: **Schnicke**; **Schnegg(e)**, **Schnigge**, **Schnegel** (chiefly S German and Austrian).

Schneeberg *see* SNOW

Schneider German and Jewish (Ashkenazic): occupational name for a tailor, Ger. *Schneider*, Yid. *shnayder* (MHG *snīdære*, an agent deriv. of *snīden* to cut, OHG *snīdan*). The vocab. word is probably a loan translation of OF *tailleur* (see TAYLOR), replacing the earlier *nātære*, from *nāten* to sew.

Vars.: Ger.: **Schneidermann**. Jewish: **Snider**, **Snyder** (Anglicized forms); **Schneid(er)man**; **Sznajderman** (a Pol. spelling).

Patrs.: Jewish: **Shneiderov** (E Ashkenazic). Low Ger.: **Schneiders**, **Schnie(de)rs**. Flem.: **Sn(e)yders**, **Snieders**. Du.: **Snijders**. Eng.: **Sniders**, **Snyders**.

Schneir Jewish (Ashkenazic): from the Yid. male given name *Shneyer* (ultimately from L SENIOR 'Elder').

Vars.: **Schneu(e)r**, **Shneur**, **Shneor**; **Sznejor** (a Pol. spelling).

Patrs.: **Schneerso(h)n**, **Schneurso(h)n**, **Shneerson**; **Schneirovitz** (E Ashkenazic).

Schnitzer German and Jewish (Ashkenazic): occupational name for a woodworker, from an agent deriv. of Ger. *schnitzen* to cut, carve (MHG *snitzen*).

Vars.: Ger.: **Schnitz(ler)**; **Schnetz**, **Schnetz(l)er**. Jewish: **Schnitzler**.

Schnur German and Jewish (Ashkenazic): metonymic occupational name for a maker of cords and rope, from Ger. *Schnur*, Yid. *shnur* cord, rope (MHG *snuor*).

Vars.: Ger.: **Schnürer**; **Schnierer** (Bavaria). Jewish: **Shnur**, **Schnurman**, **Schnurmacher**; **Schnirr**, **Schnirman**, **Schnirer** (from a S Yid. pronunciation).

Dims.: Ger.: **Schnürle**; **Schnierl** (Bavaria). Low Ger.: **Schnürchen**.

Schnurrer German: of uncertain origin, possibly: 1. occupational name for a jester or nickname for a merry prankster, from MHG *snurræere* jester. 2. occupational name for a busker, one who begged by playing the *Schnurrpfeife*, an instrument similar to a penny whistle. 3. nickname for someone with something odd about his mouth, from Ger. *Schnurre* mouth (MLG *snurre*). 4. occupational name for a night-watchman, an agent deriv. of Ger. *Schnurre* rattle; night-watchmen carried rattles.

Vars.: **Schnurr(e)**; **Schnorr(er)**.

Schofield English (mainly Northern): habitation name from any of various minor places, in Lancs. and elsewhere, named from ME *sc(h)ole* hut (see SCHOLES) + *feld* pasture, open country (see FIELD).

Vars.: **Sc(h)ol(e)field**, **Scoefield**, **Sco(f)field**.

Scholar English: Reaney makes this a local name from ON *skáli* hut (see SCHOLES) + *erg* shieling. However, it seems equally probable that it is a nickname for a person who could read and write, in the days when education was the exception rather than the rule; cf. SCHULER, SCULLY.

Vars.: Eng.: **Scholer**, **Scollard**; **Scoular** (Scots).

Scholes N English: topographic name for someone who lived in a rough hut or shed, Northern ME *scale*, later also *sc(h)ole* (from ON *skáli*), or habitation name from one of the various places named with this word, as for example *Scholes* in W Yorks. or *Scales* in Lancs. and Cumb.

Vars.: **Schoales**, **Scoles**, **Scale(s)**; **Scoyles** (Norfolk).

Scholey N English: topographic name for someone who lived in a wood or clearing with a hut in it, from ON *skáli* hut (see SCHOLES) + OE *lēah* wood, clearing. This cpd occurs several times as a minor placename in W Yorks.

Scholl 1. German: nickname for a lumpish person, from Ger. *Scholle* clod of earth (OHG *scolla, scollo*). 2. Jewish (Ashkenazic): cogn. of 1, or acronymic surname from the Hebr. phrase *SHevach Leel* 'praise to God'.

Var. (of 2): **Shol**.

Schön German: nickname for a handsome or pleasant man, from Ger. *schön* fine, beautiful; bright; refined, friendly, nice (MHG *schœne*, OHG *skōni*). 2. Jewish (Ashkenazic): ornamental name from the same vocab. word as in 1, in any of its senses.

Vars.: Ger.: **Schöne**, **Schöner(t)**, **Schonert**, **Schön(e)mann**; **Schönherr**. Jewish: **S(c)ho(e)n**; **S(c)hein(er)**, **Scheyn**, **Shain**, **Szejn**, **Szajn(er)**; (from Yid. *sheyn*; *Szajn* is a Pol. spelling); **Scheinman(n)**, **S(c)heinerman**, **Sheinman**, **Schainman**; **Schen(man)**.

Dims.: Ger.: **Schönle(in)**, **Schinle**. Low Ger.: **Schöneke**.

Patr.: Low Ger.: **Schöning**.

Cpds (ornamental): Jewish: **Scho(e)nbach**, **S(c)heinbach**, **Shainbach** ('lovely stream'); **Scho(e)nbaum**, **S(c)heinbaum**, **Sheynbaum**, **Shainbaum**, **Szejnbojm** ('lovely tree'); **Sheinbein**, **Schenbein** ('lovely bone'); **Schönberg**, **S(c)ho(e)nberg(er)**, **S(c)heinberg(er)**, **Shainberg**, **Sheinerberg**, **Szejnberg**, **Schenberg** ('lovely hill'); **Scheinblatt** ('lovely leaf'); **Schonblum** ('lovely flower'); **Sho(e)nbrot**, **Szenbrot** ('lovely bread'); **Scheinbrun** ('lovely well'); **S(c)hondorf** ('lovely village'); **S(c)heinfein** ('lovely and fine'); **Scho(e)nfeld**, **Shoenfeld**, **Sche(i)nfeld**, **Sheinfeld**, **Shainfeld**, **Sze(i)nfeld**, **Szainfeld** ('lovely field'); **Scheinfuchs** ('lovely fox'); **S(c)heingarten** ('lovely garden'); **Scho(e)ngut**, **Shongut**, **Scheingut** ('lovely and good'); **Sheinhaus** ('lovely house'); **Schoenherz**, **Scheinherz** ('lovely heart'); **Scho(e)nholz, S(c)heinholz** ('lovely wood'); **Schoenhorn, S(c)heinhorn** ('lovely horn'); **Shainkind, Sheinkinder** ('lovely child(ren)'); **Schonkopf** ('lovely head'); **Schoenlicht** ('lovely light'); **Schoenrock, Scheinrok, Szeinrok** ('lovely coat'); **S(c)honshein** ('lovely shine'); **Schonstadt** ('lovely city'); **Shonstein** ('lovely stone'); **Schonthal, Sheintal, Schenthal** ('lovely valley'); **S(c)heintuch** ('lovely cloth'); **Schoenwald, Scheinwald** ('lovely forest').

Schöngauer German: regional name from *Schöngau* in Upper Bavaria, so called from OHG *skōni* lovely (see SCHÖN) + *gewi* region, area.

Schöttle *see* SCOTT

Schpitz *see* SPITZ

Schraawen *see* GRAY

Schramm German and Jewish (Ashkenazic): metonymic nickname for a person with a prominent scar, from Ger. *Schramme*, Yid. *shram* scar (MHG *schram(me)*).

Vars.: Ger.: **Schramme; Schrimp(f), Schrempf, Schrempp**.

Dims.: Ger.: **Schrammel, Schremmel**. Low Ger.: **Schramke**. Czech: **Šrámek**.

Schreiber 1. German: occupational name for a clerk, from an agent deriv. of Ger. *schreiben* to write (MHG *schrīben*, OHG *scrīban*, from L *scrībere*; see also SCRIBE and SCRIVEN). **2.** Jewish (Ashkenazic): from Ger. *Schreiber*, Yid. *shrayber* writer, adopted as a translation of Hebr. SOFER scribe (cf. *Pisareff* at PISARSKI).

Vars.: Ger.: **Schreber** (Saxony). Jewish: **Szreiber, Schreibman(n)**.

Patr.: Low Ger.: **Schrievers**.

Schreier 1. German: occupational name for a town crier, or nickname for a noisy individual, from an agent deriv. of Ger. *schreien* to shout, cry (MHG *schrī(e)n*, OHG *scrīan*). **2.** Jewish (Ashkenazic): from Ger. *Schreier*, Yid. *shrayer* shouter, either a nickname for a noisy person, or, possibly, an occupational name for a person whose duty it was to summon Jews to public worship.

Vars.: Ger.: **Schreiert, Schrei**. Jewish: **Shreier, Szrayer**.

Schreiner German: occupational name for a joiner, Ger. *Schreiner* (MHG *schrīnære*, an agent deriv. of *schrīn* chest, box, OHG *skrīni*, from L *scrīnium* bookcase). The vocab. word and the surname are found mainly in W parts of Germany; the term in N, E, and S German-speaking regions was TISCHLER.

Var.: **Schreinert**.

Schrevens *see* GRAF

Schröder N German: occupational name for a tailor, from an agent deriv. of MLG *schröten, schräten* to cut. The same term was also occasionally used to denote a shoemaker, whose work included cutting leather, and, for reasons that are not clear, also a drayman, one who delivered beer and wine in bulk to customers. The surname may have been acquired in any of these senses.

Vars.: **Schröter, Schrader**.

Patrs.: Low Ger., Flem., Du.: **Schreu(de)rs, Schrörs**.

Schübel German: apparently from MHG *schubel, schübel* bunch, clump, tuft; of uncertain application. It may have

been a topographic name for someone who lived near a hillock or a clump of trees. In Bavaria it seems also to have been a nickname for a plump little fellow, from the same vocab. word used in a transferred sense.

Var.: **Schübler**.

Schubert German and Jewish (Ashkenazic): occupational name for a shoemaker or cobbler, from MHG *schuouch* shoe (see SCHUH) + *würhte* maker (see WRIGHT). The sound /b/ was often substituted for /v/ in southern and south-eastern dialects of German.

Vars.: **Schubart, Schubort, Schuwart, Schuchert, Schuckert, Schuh(h)ardt**.

Schuh German: metonymic occupational name for a maker or repairer of shoes, from Ger. *Schuh* shoe (MHG *schuoch*, OHG *scuoh*); see also SCHUBERT and SCHUSTER.

Vars.: **Schuch, Schuck, Schug; Schu(h)mann, Schuckmann; Schu(h)macher** (Anglicized **S(c)hoemaker**).

Dims.: Ger.: **Schü(h)le, Schühlein, Schü(c)hel, Schügl, Schiegel, Schigl, Schiele** (Swabia); **Schieli** (Switzerland).

Schuhrke *see* GEORGE

Schuler 1. German: occupational name for a scholar or a student training to be a priest, from an agent deriv. of Ger. *Schule* school (MHG *schuol(e)*, OHG *scuola*, from L *schola* sect, Gk *skholē* leisure, pastime). **2.** Jewish (Ashkenazic): occupational name for a Talmudic scholar or the sexton of a synagogue, from an agent deriv. of Yid. *shul* synagogue (likewise ultimately from L *schola*).

Vars. (of 1): **Schuller** (Latinized **Schullerus**), **Schül(l)er**. (Of 2): **Schuller**, SCHILLER, **Schulman, Szulman, Shi(e)lman; S(z)koler, Szkolerman; S(c)hkolnik, Szkolnik, Skolni(c)k, Scolnik, Scolnic, Skulnik, Skoolnik, Schoolnik** (E Ashkenazic); **Schulsinger, Szulsinger** (names adopted by cantors; cf. *Singer* at SANGER).

Patrs. (from 2): Jewish: **Skolnikov**.

Schulmeister Jewish (Ashkenazic): occupational name for a teacher in a Jewish school, from mod. Ger. *Schulmeister* schoolmaster.

Schultz 1. German: status name for a village headman, from a contracted form of MHG *schultheize* (OHG *sculdheizo*). The term originally denoted a man responsible for collecting dues and paying them to the lord of the manor; it is a cpd of *sculd(a)* debt, due + a deriv. of *heiz(z)an* to command. **2.** Jewish (Ashkenazic): reason for adoption uncertain, perhaps taken by or given to a rabbi, seen as the head of a Jewish community (cf. HAUPTMANN and *Oberman* at OBER).

Vars. (of 1): **Schulz, Schul(t)ze, Schulthe(i)ss; Scholz, Scholtis** (Saxony, Silesia). (Of 2): **Schulz**.

Dims. (of 1): Ger.: **Schölzel, Schelzel**. Pol.: **Sołtysik**.

Patrs. (from 1): Low Ger.: **Schulten, Schülting**. Flem.: **Schouteden, Scholts**. Du.: **Scholten(s), Schouten**.

Habitation name: Pol.: **Szulczewski**.

Schüssel 1. German: metonymic occupational name for a turner, from MHG *schüssel(e)* small wooden bowl (OHG *skussila*). **2.** Jewish (Ashkenazic): from mod. Ger. *Schüssel* dish. The reason for its assumption is not known, but the fact that it is not a common surname suggests that it may be an anecdotal name derived from some now irrecoverable minor incident.

Var.: Ger.: **Schüssler**.

Schuster German and Jewish (Ashkenazic): occupational name for a maker or repairer of shoes, from Ger. *Schuster*, Yid. *shuster* (MHG *schuochsūtære*, a cpd of *schuoch* shoe (see SCHUH) + *sūtære* sewer (see SAUTER)).

Vars.: Jewish: **Shuster**, **S(c)husterman**.

Dims.: Ger.: **Schüst(er)l**, **Schiesterl**, **Schiest(e)l**.

Schutz 1. German: occupational name for a watchman or guard, from a deriv. of MHG *schützen* to guard, protect; the word originally denoted either the warden of a park or piece of common land or a night-watchman in a town. 2. Jewish (Ashkenazic): of uncertain origin, possibly an adoption of the relatively common Ger. surname.

Vars.: Jewish: **Schutzer**, **Schutzman**.

Schützbier German: nickname for a belligerent person, from MHG *schüt(t)en* to brandish, flourish, shake (OHG *skutten*) + *sper* SPEAR (cf. SHAKESPEARE). A knight named Diderich *Schuzcesper* is recorded in 1316 in Hessen, and a Low Ger. Reimbert *Scudesper* in 1174. In more recent times the surname has been altered by folk etymological association with mod. Ger. *schützen* to protect (see SCHUTZ) and *Bier* beer.

Schütze German: occupational name for a bowman, Ger. *Schütze* (MHG *schütze*, OHG *scuzz(i)o*, from *skiozan* to shoot).

Var.: **Schütz**.

Schwab German and Jewish (Ashkenazic): regional name for someone from Swabia, Ger. *Schwaben*, so called from a Gmc tribe recorded from the 1st cent. BC in the L form *Suebi* or *Suevi*, of uncertain origin. This region in S Germany was an independent duchy from the 10th cent. until 1313, when the territory was broken up.

Vars.: Ger.: **Schwob**. Jewish: **Schwabe**.

Dims.: Ger.: **Schwäble**; **Schwabel** (also Jewish, of uncertain origin).

Schwälble *see* SWALLOW

Schwand German: topographic name for someone who lived in a glade or clearing, MHG *swand* (from *swinden* to thin out, disappear, OHG *swintan*).

Vars.: **Schwandt**, **Schwende(mann)**; **Schwand(n)er**, **Gschwandtner**, **Schwend(n)er**, **Schwendler**.

Schwaneke *see* SWAN

Schwarz German and Jewish (Ashkenazic): nickname for someone with black hair or a dark complexion, from Ger. *schwarz*, Yid. *shvarts* dark, black (MHG, OHG *swarz*, a cogn. of OE *swart* dark, swarthy).

Vars.: **Schwartz**, **Schwar(t)ze(r)**, **Schwar(t)zmann**.

Dim.: Ger.: **Schwärzel**.

Patrs.: Low Ger.: **Schwarten**, **Schwarting**. Flem.: **Swerts**. Du.: **Zwarts**.

Patr. (from a dim.): Du.: **Zwartjes**.

Schwarzkopf German and Jewish (Ashkenazic): nickname for someone with dark hair, from Ger. *schwarz* black, dark (see SCHWARZ) + *kopf* head (see KOPF).

Var.: **Schwartzkopf**.

Schwarzschild Jewish (Ashkenazic): from Ger. SCHWARZ black + SCHILD sign; in at least some cases this was a house name for someone who lived in a house marked by a black sign. Cf. ROTHSCHILD.

Schwebel 1. German: apparently a dim. of SCHWAB. 2. Jewish (Ashkenazic): of uncertain origin, possibly from Yid. *shvebl* sulphur, in which case the reason for its assumption is unknown.

Schweder German: ethnic name for a Swede (cf. SVEDIN).

Var.: **Schwed**.

Habitation name: Pol.: **Szwedziński**.

Schweiger German and Jewish (Ashkenazic): nickname for a somewhat taciturn or 'deep' person, from an agent deriv. of Ger. *schweigen*, Yid. *shvaygn* to be silent.

Schweitzer German and Jewish (Ashkenazic): ethnic name for a Swiss, Ger. *Schweizer*, from Ger. *Schweiz* + the suffix *-er* denoting a native or inhabitant of a place. As a Jewish name, it denotes a Jew from Switzerland. The Polish cogn. vocab. word acquired the additional senses of a commissionaire and a verger in a church.

Vars.: **Schweizer**. Jewish only: **Szweitzer**.

Schwemmer German: 1. occupational name for someone who floated logs downstream from the forests where they were felled, from an agent deriv. of MHG *swemmen*, causative of *swimmen* to float, swim. 2. topographic name for someone who lived by a deep ford where horses could be made to swim across, MHG *swem(me)*, from the same word as in 1.

Schwennen *see* SWAIN

Schwepe Low German: metonymic occupational name for a roof-builder, from MLG *swepe* rafter.

Vars.: **Schweppe** (also Jewish); **Schwepenhauer**.

Schwertl *see* SWORD

Schwimmer German and Jewish (Ashkenazic): nickname for a good swimmer, from an agent deriv. of Ger. *schwimmen*, Yid. *shvimen* to swim.

Var.: Jewish: **Schwimer**.

Schwippe German: metonymic occupational name for a driver or nickname for a brutal man, from early mod. Ger. *schwuppe* whip (of Gmc origin, probably akin to mod. Eng. *sweep* and *swoop*), now replaced as a vocab. word by the Slav. borrowing *Peitsche*.

Vars.: **Schwibbe**, **Schwöpe**.

Dims.: **Schwippl**. Low Ger.: **Schwippke**.

Sciacovelli *see* JACOB

Scimonelli *see* SIMON

Scinelli *see* FRANCIS

Sclater *see* SLATER

Scobie Scots: habitation name from a lost place in the former county of Perths., so called from Gael. *sgolbach* thorny place.

Scoefield see SCHOFIELD

Scoles see SCHOLES

Scollard see SCHOLAR

Scolnic see SCHULER

Scopes English: of uncertain origin, perhaps a topographic name from ME *scōpe* scoop, ladle, shovel (of Low Ger. origin), used in the transferred sense of a hollow in the ground. However, this does not occur as a placename element. According to Barber it is a patr. from OE *scōp* poet, minstrel, a word last attested at the beginning of the 13th cent. before its revival as a conscious archaism in the 19th cent.

Scorer N English: **1.** occupational name for someone who kept accounts, from an agent deriv. of ME *score(n)* to record (ON *skora*). **2.** occupational name for a scout or a spy, ME *scorer* (OF *escoreor*, an agent deriv. of *escorir* to reconnoitre, L *excurrere* to run out, make a sally).

Vars.: **Scorrer**, **Scorah**.

Scorthals see SHORTALL

Scorza Italian: occupational name for a tanner or nickname for a vicious man, from a deriv. of It. *scorzare* to skin, flay (L *excoriāre*, from *corium* skin, hide).

Var.: **Scorcia**.

Dims.: **Scorzelli**, **Scorziello**, **Scorzetti**.

Augs.: **Scorzon(e)**, **Scorsone**.

Scothern English: habitation name from a place in Lincs., recorded in Domesday Book as *Scotstorne*, from the gen. case of the OE byname *Scott* 'Irishman' (see SCOTT) + OE *þorn* thornbush (see THORN 1).

Scotland **1.** English: ethnic name for someone from Scotland (cf. SCOTT). **2.** English: from the rare Norman personal name *Escotland*, composed of the ethnic name *Scot* + *land* territory. **3.** Scots: habitation name from *Scotland(well)* near Loch Leven in Kinross.

Scott English and Scots: ethnic name for someone from Scotland or, more commonly, for a Gaelic-speaker within Scotland. The Gaelic-speaking peoples in Scotland came originally from Ireland, and it is possible that their name is connected with OW *ysgthru* to cut, carve, referring to their habit of tatooing themselves with iron points.

Dim.: Ger.: **Schöttle**.

Patrs.: Eng.: **Scotts**, **Scotson**.

Scotti see FRANCIS

Scougall Scots: habitation name from *Scoughall* on the coast near North Berwick, so called from ON *skógr* wood (cf. SHAW) + OE *halh* nook, recess (see HALE 1).

Scrase English: of unknown origin. It is an established surname in E Sussex as early as the 13th cent., and is still relatively common in the W Country, but none of the early forms give any clue as to its meaning.

Screech English (Devon and Cornwall): of uncertain origin, perhaps a nickname for a person with a strident voice, from early mod. Eng. *screche* screech, or just possibly a habitation name from *Screek* Wood in the parish of St Martin by Looe. This place was earlier known as *Loscruk*, from Corn. *lost* tail + *cruc* barrow (the first element referring to the long, thin shape of the feature).

Scribe French: occupational name for a clerk or copyist, OF *scribe* (L *scrība*, a deriv. of *scrībere* to write; cf. SCHREIBER and SCRIVEN).

Var.: **Scrive**.

Dim.: Fr.: **Scribot**.

Equivs. (not cogn.): Jewish (Ashkenazic): PISARSKI, SOFER. Russ. PEROV.

Scrimgeour Scots and English: occupational name for a fencer or fencing-master, from OF *eskermisseo(u)r* fencer (from *eskermir* to fence, skirmish, fight hand-to-hand, of Gmc origin; cf. OHG *skirmen* to defend). Fencing-masters always found plentiful employment in medieval England, although they were officially banned from the City of London because of their dangerous influence.

Vars.: **Scrimgeoure**, **Scrymgeo(u)r**, **Scrimger**, **Scrimi(n)ger**, **Skrimshire**, **Scrimshaw**; **Skirmer**, **Skermer**, **Scurmer** (the last three being derivs. of ME *skirme(n)* to fight).

Scriven English: occupational name for a clerk or copyist, from OF *escrivein*, *escrivain* writer, scribe (LL *scrībānus*, for class. L *scrība*; cf. SCRIBE).

Vars.: **Scrivener**, **Scrivenor** (with the addition of the ME agent suffix); **Scribner**.

Patrs.: Eng.: **Scrivens**, **Scrivin(g)s**.

Scrope English: of uncertain origin, said to be from an ON byname meaning 'Crab'.

Scruton English: habitation name from a place in N Yorks., so called from the ON byname *Skurfa* 'Scurf' + OE *tūn* enclosure, settlement.

Var.: **Scrutton**.

Scrymgeor see SCRIMGEOUR

Scuce see SKUSE

Scudamore English (West Country): of uncertain origin, perhaps a habitation name from an unidentified place so called from OE *scīte* shit, dung + *mōr* moor, fen.

Vars.: **Skidmore**, **Skitmore**.

Scull English: nickname for a bald-headed man or someone of cadaverous appearance, from ME *sc(h)olle*, *sc(h)ulle* skull (probably of Scandinavian origin).

Scully Irish: Anglicized form of Gael. Ó Scolaidhe 'descendant of the scholar', from *scolaidhe* scholar.

Vars.: **O'Scully**, **O'Scollee**, **Skelly**, **Skally**, **Scally**.

Dims.: **Scull(i)on**, **Scallan**, **Scalon** (Gael. Ó Scoláin).

Scurmer see SCRIMGEOUR

Scurrell see SQUIRREL

Scutt English: **1.** occupational name for a scout or spy, ME *scut* (OF *escoute*, from *escouter* to listen, L *auscultāre*).

2. nickname for a swift runner, from ME *scut* hare (of uncertain origin).

Vars. (of 1): **Scudder** (with the addition of the ME agent suffix). (Of 2): **Skitt**.

Seabra Portuguese: apparently a habitation name from *Senabria* in Spain, which was perhaps originally named with the Celt. elements *sena* old + *briga* height, hill.

Seabrook English: habitation name from a place in Bucks., so called from the OE river name *Sǣge*, apparently meaning 'Trickling', 'Slow-moving' + OE *brōc* stream (see BROOK).

Seach *see* SYKES

Seacombe English: habitation name from a place in Ches., named with the OE elements *sǣ* sea + *cumb* valley (see COOMBE).

Seagar English: from the ME given name *Segar*, OE *Sǣgar*, composed of the elements *sǣ* sea + *gār* spear.

Vars.: **Seager**, **Seegar**, **Se(e)ger**; **Sagar**, **Sa(i)ger**; **Segger**.

Patrs.: **Seagars**, **Seagers**, **Saggers**.

Seagrave English: habitation name from a place in Leics., recorded in Domesday Book as *Satgrave* and *Setgraue*, probably from OE *(ge)set* fold, pen or *sēað* pit, pool + *grāf* grove or *grǣf* ditch.

Vars.: **Segrave**, **Seagrove**, **Seagrief**.

Seal English: **1.** topographic name; var. of SALE. **2.** metonymic occupational name for a maker of seals or signet rings, from ME, OF *seel* seal (L *sigillum*, a dim. of *signum* sign). **3.** metonymic occupational name for a maker of saddles, from OF *seele* saddle (see SELLER 2). **4.** nickname for a plump or ungainly person, from the aquatic mammal, ME *sele* (OE *seolh*).

Vars.: **Seale**, **Seel**, **Zeal(e)**. (Of 2 and 3): **Sealer**.

Patrs. (from 4): Eng.: **Seal(e)s**, **Seels**.

'Servant of S. 4': Eng.: SELMAN.

Sealey English: nickname for a person with a cheerful disposition, from ME *seely* happy, fortunate (OE *sǣlig*, from *sǣl* happiness, good fortune), which was also occasionally used as a female given name during the Middle Ages. The sense 'pitiable', which developed into mod. Eng. *silly*, is not attested before the 15th cent.

Vars.: SELLEY; **Seal(l)y**, **Seel(e)y**, **Seelly**, **Sill(e)y**, **Sellick**; **Ceel(e)y**, **Ceiley**, **Cely**, **Zeal(l)ey**, **Zelley**; SELMAN.

Cpd (ornamental): Swed.: **Sälström** ('lovely river').

Seaman English (Norfolk): **1.** from *Sǣmann*, an OE personal name composed of the elements *sǣ* sea + *mann* man. **2.** occupational name for a sailor.

Vars.: **Se(e)man**, **Seyman**, **Sayman**, **Seamenn**.

Patrs.: **Se(m)mens** (Devon and Cornwall), **Semmence**; **Seamons**.

Seanor *see* SENIOR

Sear *see* SAYER

Search *see* SURRIDGE

Seargeant *see* SERGEANT

Searle English: from the Norman personal name *Serlo*, Gmc *Sarilo*, *Serilo*. This was probably originally a byname

cogn. with ON *Sorli*, and akin to OE *searu* armour, meaning perhaps 'Defender', 'Protector'.

Vars.: **Searl**, **Serle**, **Serrell**.

Patrs.: **Searl(e)s**.

Seartáin *see* SHORTALL

Seath *see* SHEEHY

Seaton English and Scots: habitation name from any of the various places so called. The majority, for example those in Cumb., Devon, Co. Durham, Northumb., and E and N Yorks., are named with OE *sǣ* sea, lake + *tūn* enclosure, settlement. One in Leics. (formerly Rutland), however, seems to have as its first element a stream name *Sǣge* (see SEABROOK) or a personal name *Sǣga*, a short form of a cpd name such as SEAGAR. One in Kent is named with OE *seten* plantation, cultivated land (from *settan* to set, plant). The Scottish place of this name, near Longniddry, is so named because it was held from the 12th cent. by a Norman family *de Sey*, from *Say* in Indre (see SAY 1).

Var.: **Seton**.

Sebastian German: from the given name *Sebastian* (L *Sebastiānus*, originally an ethnic name meaning 'man from *Sebastia*', a city in Pontus named from Gk *sebastos* revered). The name was borne by a 3rd-cent. martyr who became the patron saint of Nuremberg, hence (in part) its popularity in Germany. The surname is also sometimes born by Jews, presumably as an adoption of the Ger. surname.

Vars.: **Sebass**, **Ba(u)stian**, **Paustian**.

Dims.: Ger.: **Bast**, **Bästl(e)**, BEST, **Pest(lin)**. Low Ger.: **Bastke**, **Bes(t)gen**. It.: **Sebastianelli**, **Sebastianini**, **Sebastianutto**, **Sebastianutti**, **Bastianel(li)**, **Bastiaelli**, **Bastia(n)ello**, **Bastianetto**, **Bastianini**, **Bastianutti**, **Bastianutto**. Czech: **Šebek**. Hung.: **Sebök**.
Augs.: Fr.: **Bastiat**. It.: **Bastianon**.
Patrs.: Flem.: **Basteyns**. Du.: **Bastiaanse(n)**. It.: **De Bastiani**. Russ.: **Savasteev**.
Patrs. (from dims.): Low Ger.: **Basten**, **Basting**, **Bestges**. Russ.: **Savoskin**, **Savonichev**.

Sébilleau *see* SIBLEY

Sebrecht *see* SIEBERT

Seccombe English (Devon): habitation name from either of two places in Devon, both so called from the OE personal name *Secca* + OE *cumb* valley (see COOMBE).

Var.: **Secombe**.

Secker 1. English: var. of *Sacker*; see SACK. **2.** Low German: topographic name for someone who lived in an area of wetland, MLG *seck*. **3.** Jewish (Ashkenazic): of unknown origin, possibly as in 1.

Seckerson *see* SEXTON

Seco Spanish: nickname for a thin and apparently bloodless person, from Sp. *seco* dry (L *siccus*).

Dims.: Fr.: **Sechet**, **Séchet**.

Second *see* SEGOND

Sęczkowski *see* SUK

Seddon English: of uncertain origin, perhaps a habitation name from an unidentified place, the last element of which could well be OE *dūn* hill. Without early forms, it is impossible even to speculate what the first element might be. The surname is extremely common in Lancs., esp. in the Manchester area, where it was first recorded in the 14th cent.

Sedge English: topographic name for someone who lived in a place overgrown with sedge and reeds, or metonymic occupational name for someone who made use of these materials in thatching, from OE *secg* sedge.
Vars.: **Sedger**, **Sedgeman**.

Sedgley English (W Midlands): habitation name from a place near Dudley, so called from the OE byname *Secg* 'Warrior' + OE *lēah* wood, clearing.

Sedgwick English: habitation name from *Sedgwick* in Cumb., so called from the ME personal name *Sigg(e)* (from ON *Siggi* or OE *Sicg*, short forms of the various cpd names with the first element 'victory') + OE *wīc* outlying settlement, dairy farm (see WICK); or from *Sedgewick* in Sussex, so called from OE *secg* SEDGE + *wīc*.
Vars.: **Sedgewick(e)**, **Sedwick**, **Sidg(e)wick**.

Sedlák Czech: occupational or status name for a peasant or farmer, Czech *sedlák*, the equivalent of Ger. BAUER. A *sedlák* was a comparatively rich farmer, with more land than a *zahradník* (smallholder) or a *chaloupník* (cotter).
Dim.: Czech: **Sedláček**.

Sedler see SADLER

Sedman see SEED

Sedov Russian: patr. from the nickname *Sedoi* 'Grey (-haired)'.

Sędzicki Polish: 1. occupational name from Pol. *sędzia* judge, or nickname for a wise person. 2. nickname from *sędziwy* grey-haired. There is no direct cogn. relationship between this Pol. word and Russ. *sedoi* (see SEDOV), although they both mean 'grey-haired'. The connection between *sędziwy* and *sędzia* is also unclear, although presumably it has something to do with the association between judges and grey hair. The Pol. cogn. of *sedoi* is *szady*, which also means 'grey-haired'.
Vars.: **Sędicki**, **Sędziński**.
Patr.: **Sędkiewicz**.
Habitation name: **Sędkowski**.

See English: topographic name for someone who lived by the sea-shore or beside a lake, from ME *see* sea, lake (OE *sǣ*).
Cpds (mostly ornamental): Swed.: **Sjöberg** ('sea hill'); **Sjöborg** ('sea town'); **Sjöblom** ('sea flower'); **Sjögren** ('sea branch'); **Sjöholm** ('sea island'); **Sjölund** ('sea grove'); **Sjöqvist** ('sea twig'); **Sjöstedt** ('sea homestead'); **Sjöstrand** ('sea shore'); **Sjöström** ('sea river').

Seear see SAYER

Seed English (chiefly Lancs.): metonymic occupational name for a gardener or husbandman, or nickname for a small person, from ME *sede* seed (OE *sǣd*).
Vars.: **Se(e)dman**, **Seeds**.

Seef see SIEFF

Seefried see SIEGFRIED

Seegar see SEAGAR

Seel see SEAL

Seeley see SEALEY

Seelig see SELIG

Seeman see SEAMAN

Seemund see SIEGMUND

Seener see SENIOR

Seerey Irish: Anglicized form of Gael. **Ó Saoraidhe** 'descendant of *Saoraidhe*', a personal name derived from *saordha* noble.
Vars.: **Seery**; **O'Seyry**, **O'Serie**; **O'Shirie**, **O'Shyry**, **O'Shrue**; **Earner** (a translated form, the result of erroneous association with *saothraidhe* worker, earner).

Seffers see SIEGFRIED

Sefton English: habitation name from a place in Lancs., so called from ON *sef* rush + OE *tūn* enclosure, settlement.
Var.: **Sephton**.

Segal 1. Jewish (Ashkenazic): acronym of the Hebr. phrase *SeGan Levia* 'second-rank Levite'. 2. French: metonymic occupational name for a grower or seller of rye, OF *segal* (L *secale*).
Vars. (of 1): **Sagal**, **Se(i)gel**, **SIEGEL**, **Chagal(l)**; **Segelstein** (an ornamental elaboration). (Of 2): **Ségal**, **Segall**, **Sigal**.
Dim. (of 1): **Segalczyk**.
Patrs. (from 1): **Segals(on)**; **Segalescu** (Rumanian); **Segalov**, **Segalovi(t)ch**, **Segalowitz**, **Segalowitsch**, **Sagalov(ich)**, **Shagalov** (E Ashkenazic).

Segarra Catalan: habitation name from a place of uncertain etymology (possibly derived from Basque *sagar* apple tree + the def. art. *-a*, although the alteration of the first vowel cannot be readily explained).
Var.: **Sagarra**.

Segbers see SIEBERT

Segemund see SIEGMUND

Seger see SEAGAR

Segers see SAYER

Seggeling see SIEGEL

Segond French: from the medieval given name *Segond* (L *Secundus* 'Second(-born)' or 'Favourable', a deriv. of *sequi* to follow), borne in honour of various minor early saints.
Var.: **Second**.
Dims.: **Segondin**, **Segondy**.
Aug.: **Secondat**.

Segovia Spanish: habitation name from the town in central Spain of this name, which is of uncertain origin (possibly containing the Celt. element *sego* victory).
Var.: **Segoviano**.

Segrave see SEAGRAVE

Seguí Catalan: from a Gmc personal name composed of the elements *sigi* victory + *wine* friend.

Dims.: Prov.: **Séguineau, Séguinot, Séguiniol.**

Ségur Provençal: habitation name from any of various minor places so called from OProv. *ségur* safe, well-defended (L *sēcūrus* carefree, from *sē-* without + *cūra* care, anxiety).

Var.: **Ségura.**

Dims.: Prov.: **Séguret, Siguret.**

Seiberlich *see* SAUBER

Seibers *see* SIEBERT

Seide German: metonymic occupational name for a manufacturer or seller of silk, Ger. *Seide* (MHG *sīde*, from LL *sēta*, originally denoting animal hair).

Vars.: **Seidemann, Seidler.**

Cpds (ornamental): Jewish (Ashkenazic): **Seidenband** ('silk ribbon'); **Seidenbaum** ('silk tree'); **Seidenberg** ('silk hill'); **Seidenfeld** ('silk field'); **Seidenschnir, Zajdensznir** ('silk rope', the latter a Pol. spelling); **Seidenwurm, Zajdenvorm** ('silk worm', the latter a partly Pol. spelling).

Seifart *see* SIEGFRIED

Seigel *see* SEGAL

Seigneur French: derisive nickname for a peasant who gave himself airs and graces, or occupational name for someone in the service of a great lord, from OF *segneur* lord (L *senior* elder). The It. cogns. came to be used also as titles of respect for professional men such as notaries.

Vars.: **Sieur, Lesieur, Lesieux; Sire, Lesire.**

Dims.: Fr.: **Seigneuret, Seigno(u)ret; Siret, Siron, Sirot(eau).** It.: **Signorini, Signorino, Signorelli, Signor(i)ello, Signoretti.**

Aug.: It.: **Signoroni.**

Pej.: It.: **Signoraccio.**

Patr.: Fr: **Duseigneur.**

Seignior *see* SENIOR

Seiler 1. German: occupational name for a rope-maker, from an agent deriv. of Ger. *Seil* rope (MHG, OHG *seil*). 2. Jewish (Ashkenazic): of unknown origin, possibly an occupational name as in 1 above, or possibly a surname adopted as an (imperfect) anagram of the Hebr. given name *Yisrael* (see ISRAEL). The latter explanation is the less convincing one. 3. English: var of SAYLOR.

Vars. (of 3): **Seyler, Seiller.**

Seis *see* SEUSS

Seisill *see* CECIL

Seiter *see* SAUTER

Seixas Portuguese and Jewish (Sefardic): topographic name for someone who lived on a patch of stony ground, from Port. *seixas* rocks, pl. of *seixa* (L *saxa*, originally itself the pl. of the neut. noun *saxum*, but later taken as a fem. sing.).

Sejersen *see* SAYER

Séjournant French: nickname for a newcomer or temporary visitor to a community, from the pres. part. of OF *séjourner* to sojourn, stay (LL *subdiurnāre* to spend the day, from *diēs* day).

Vars.: **Séjourné, Séjournet.**

Sękowski *see* SUK

Selby English: habitation name from a place in W Yorks., so called from ON *selja* willow (cf. SALE 2) + *býr* farm, settlement. The surname is now very common in Notts.

Vars.: **Selbey, Selbie.**

Seld S German: topographic name for an inhabitant of a croft (a hut with a small kitchen-garden, but no agricultural land attached), MHG *selde*.

Vars.: **Seldt(e): Seldner, Sellner, Söldner, Söllner; Seldmann, Seltmann.**

Selden English: habitation name from *Selden* Farm in the parish of Patching, Sussex, probably so called from OE *s(e)alh* willow (see SALE 2) + *denu* valley (see DEAN 1).

Vars.: **Seldon, Seldom.**

Seldes *see* ZELDES

Self English (E Anglia): from the ME given name *Saulf*, OE *Sǣwulf*, composed of the elements *sǣ* sea + *wulf* wolf.

Var.: **Selfe.**

Selfridge English: of uncertain origin, perhaps a habitation name from an unidentified minor place, which might be so called from OE *scelf* shelf + *hrycg* ridge.

Selig 1. German: cogn. of SEALEY. 2. Jewish (Ashkenazic): from the Yid. male given name *Zelik* 'Fortunate', 'Blessed' or from the mod. Ger. vocabulary word *selig* of the same meaning (cf. SEALEY).

Vars. (of 1): **Seelig, Se(e)liger, Seligmann.** (Of 2): **Sellig, Zelig, Seligman(n), Zeligman(n), Zelik.**

Patrs. (from the given name): Jewish: **Seligso(h)n, Zeligson, Selikson; Zelikov, Zelikovi(t)ch, Zelikowicz, Zelikovitz; Zelicovici** (a Rumanian spelling); **Zeligowski, Zelikowsky, Zelicovski, Zelichovsky, Zelichowski, Zelikin, Zelicki, Zelitzki** (E Ashkenazic).

Seliger *see* SALINGER

Seliverstov *see* SILVESTER

Selkirk Scots: habitation name from the town of *Selkirk* in the Borders region of Scotland, so called from ME *sale, sele* hall, manor (see SALE 1) + *kirk* church (see KIRK).

Var.: **Selcraig** (an altered form of the placename current in the 16th–18th cents.).

Sell 1. English: topographic name for someone who lived in a rough hut of the type normally occupied by animals, ME *selle*, OE *(ge)sell*. In many cases the name may have been in effect an occupational name for a herdsman. 2. U.S.: Anglicized form of SZÉLL.

Vars. (of 1): **Selle, Sells, Zell(e); SELLER.**

Seller English and Scots: 1. topographic name, a var. of SELL 1. 2. occupational name for a saddler, ANF *seller* (OF *sellier*, L *sellārius*, a deriv. of *sella* seat, saddle, from *sedēre* to sit). 3. metonymic occupational name for someone employed in the cellars of a great house or monastery, from ANF *celler* cellar (OF *cellier*, LL *cellārium*, a deriv. of *cella* small room, store-room, from *celāre* to hide), or a reduction of the ME agent deriv. *cellerer*. 4. occupational name for a tradesman or merchant, from an agent deriv. of ME *sell(en)* to sell (OE *sellan* to hand over, deliver).

Vars.: **Sellar**, **Sellier**, **Cellier**.

Dims. (of 2): Fr.: **Selleret**. It.: **Sellaroli**.

Patrs.: Eng.: **Sellers**, **Sellars**, **Sellors**. (From 2 only): It.: **Del Sellaio**.

Selley English: **1.** (chiefly Devon) var. of SEALEY. **2.** habitation name from *Selly* Oak in Birmingham, which is a var. of SHELLEY by origin.

Var.: **Selly**.

Sellick *see* SEALEY

Selman English: **1.** nickname for a happy or fortunate man; see SEALEY. **2.** occupational name for a servant employed by a bearer of the name SEALEY or SEAL 4.

Vars.: **Sellman**, **Sil(l)man**.

Selmini *see* ANSELL

Selous English: of uncertain origin, perhaps a habitation name from an unidentified place named with the OE elements *s(e)alh* willow (see SALE 2) + *hūs* house.

Selvaggini *see* SAVAGE

Selway English: from a ME given name, *Salewi*, probably from an unattested OE personal name, **Sǣlwīg*, composed of the elements *sǣl* good fortune (cf. SEALEY) + *wīg* war.

Vars.: **Sal(la)way**, **Salloway**, **Salwey**.

Selwood English: habitation name from a place in Somerset, so called from OE *s(e)alh* willow (see SALE 2) + *wudu* WOOD.

Var.: **Sellwood**.

Selwyn English: **1.** from the ME, OF given name *Seluein* (L *Silvānus*, a deriv. of *silva* wood; cf. SILVA), bestowed in honour of various minor early Christian saints. **2.** from a ME given name, *Selewyne*, from the OE personal name *Selewine*, composed of the elements *sele* hall + *wine* friend.

Vars.: **Selwyne**, **Selwin(e)**. (Of 1 only): **Sa(l)vin**, **Sauva(i)n**, **Sauven**, **Sylvaine**.

Dims. (of 1): Eng.: **SILL**. Fr.: **Sauvignon**, **Sauvanet**, **Sauvanon**. It.: **Salva(g)nini**. Beloruss.: **Selivonok**, **Salivonok**.

Aug. (of 1): It.: **Salvagnoni**.

Patrs. (from 1): It.: **Salvagneschi**. Russ.: **Selivanov**, **Selifanov**, **Selifonov**.

Semakin *see* SIMON

Seman *see* SEAMAN

Sember *see* SAMPER

Semkin *see* SIMKIN

Semmel German and Jewish (Ashkenazic): metonymic occupational name for a baker of white rolls (Ger. *Semmel*, Yid. *zeml*), from fine wheat-flour, MHG *semel(e)*, *simel* (OHG *semala*, *simila*, from L; ultimately, via Gk, from Arabic). Such rolls were in contrast to the coarse ryebread that was and is the norm in many households. The Ger. surname may also be an occupational name for a dealer in fine wheat-flour.

Vars.: Ger.: **Semel**, **Simmel**; **Sem(m)ler**, **Simmler**, **Semmelmann**; **Semmelweis** (with MHG *weize* wheat). Jewish:

Semel, **Simel**, **Zemel**; **Semler**, **Simler**, **Zemler**, **Zimler**; **Zemelman**.

Dims.: It.: **Semolini**. Fr.: **Sim(o)ulin**.

Sempf *see* SENF

Semple **1.** Scots, N Irish, and English (Norman): habitation name from any of various places in Normandy called *Saint-Paul* or *Saint-Pol*, from the dedication of their churches to St PAUL. **2.** nickname from ME, OF *simple* simple, straightforward, humble (L *simplus*).

Vars. (of 1): **Sempill**, **Sample**, **Sambell**, **Simble**, **Simpole**.

Dims. (of 2): Fr.: **Simplot**. It.: **Semplicini**.

Semrád Czech: from a Czech personal name, *Sěmirad*, composed of the elements *sěmi* person + *rad* nimble, swift.

Vars.: **Semerád**, **Semirád**.

Sena Portuguese: apparently a religious byname adopted in honour of St Catherine of *Siena* (Port. *Sena*). This saint was born in 1347 at Siena in Tuscany, the daughter of a wool-dyer with the surname Benincasa, and combined her work among the poor of the town with an influential role in ecclesiastical politics.

Sénac French: habitation name from a place in Hautes-Pyrénées, so called from the Gaul. personal name *Senos* (from the root *sen-* old) + the local suffix *-ācum*.

Senchenko *see* SIMON

Sendall English: probably a metonymic occupational name for a merchant dealing in fine silk, ME, OF *sendal* (apparently ultimately from Gk *sindōn* fine linen cloth, winding sheet, shroud). The meaning 'winding sheet, shroud' also attached to the ME word, and so it is possible that in some cases the surname originated as an occupational name for an undertaker.

Senderoff *see* SANDER

Sendler *see* SANDLER

Sendra Catalan: **1.** from a Gmc (Visigothic) personal name composed of the elements *sinðs* path + *rēðs* counsel, attested in placenames such as *Vilasendra*. **2.** nickname for someone with grey hair or an unhealthy complexion, from Cat. *cenda* cinders, ash (L *cinis*, gen. *cineris*).

Seneschal English: nickname for an officious man or occupational name for a seneschal, an official in a large household who was responsible for overseeing day-to-day domestic arrangements, ME, OF *seneschal* (of Gmc origin, composed of the elements *sini* old (ultimately cogn. with the root of SEIGNEUR) + *scalc* servant (see SCHALK)). The seneschal of a royal or ducal household in the Middle Ages was a very powerful man indeed, often having control over the administration of justice, among other things.

Vars.: **Seneschall**, **Senchell**, **Sene(s)cal**, **Senskell**, **Sensicall**, **Sensicle**.

Senet *see* SINNOTT

Senf German: **1.** metonymic occupational name for a dealer in mustard or nickname for someone with a fiery temper, from Ger. *Senf(t)* mustard (MHG *sen(e)f*, OHG *senef*, from L *sinapi*, a borrowing from Gk and probably ultimately from an oriental language). **2.** nickname for a helpful or friendly person, from MHG *senfte* soft, accommodating (OHG *semfti*), mod. Ger. *sanft*.

Vars.: **Sempf**, **Senff**, **Senft**. (Of 2): **Senftleber** ('easy liver'); **Senftleben**, **Sanftleben** ('easy life').

Sengers *see* SANGER

Senior 1. English: nickname for a peasant who gave himself airs and graces, from ANF *segneur* lord (see SEIGNEUR). **2.** English: distinguishing nickname for the elder of two bearers of the same given name (e.g. father and son or two brothers), from L *senior* elder. **3.** Jewish (Ashkenazic): reason for adoption unknown.

Vars.: Eng. (mainly of 1): **Seignior**, **Senier**, **Senyard**, **Sinyard**, **Sinyer**, **Seyner**, **Seynor**, **Sainer**, **Seanor**, **Seener**, **Seeney**.

Sentís Catalan: habitation name from a place whose name is of uncertain origin. It may derive from the dedication of the local church to St *Thyrsus*, a 3rd-cent. martyr of Apollonia in Phrygia, who was honoured with a full office in the Mozarabic liturgy. Alternatively, it may be from L *senticētum* thorn brake (a collective of *sentis* thorn bush, briar).

Sentry English: topographic name for someone who lived near a shrine, ME, OF *seintuarie* (LL *sanctuārium*, a deriv. of *sanctus* holy; cf. SAINT), or a nickname for someone who had had occasion to take sanctuary in a church or monastery, where he would have been afforded immunity from arrest or injury. The mod. Eng. occupational term *sentry* 'guardsman' is not attested before the 17th cent., and so is unlikely to be the source of the surname.

Vars.: **Santry**, **Sanctuary**.

Sephton *see* SEFTON

Seppälä Finnish: topographic name for someone who lived in the house of a smith, from *seppä* (black)smith + the local suffix *-la*.

Seppänen Finnish: patr. from the occupational term *seppä* (black)smith.

Seppings English (E Anglia): nickname meaning 'sevenpence' (recorded in the form *Sevenpen(n)ys* in 1524), bestowed on someone who paid a rent of this amount or for some now irrecoverable anecdotal reason.

Var.: **Sippings**.

Sepúlveda Spanish: habitation name from any of various places so called, for example in the provinces of Salamanca and Segovia. The name is probably a deriv. of Sp. *sepultar* to bury (LL *sepultāre*, for class. L *sepelīre*, past part. *sepultus*), but the ending has not been satisfactorily explained.

Sequeira Portuguese: topographic name for someone who lived by a patch of dry, infertile land or a piece of land used for drying crops or bleaching clothes in the sun. The term derives from LL *siccāria*, a deriv. of *siccus* dry (see SECO), and has named various places, which may also be sources of the surname.

Serafim Portuguese: from a medieval given name, L *Seraphīnus*, from Hebr. *serafim*. This term was applied to the six-winged creatures described in Isaiah 6, and regarded in the Middle Ages as a class of angels; it is the pl. form of Hebr. *saraf*, probably a deriv. of *saraf* to burn. In part the Port. surname may represent a religious byname adopted in honour of the Capuchin monk St Seraphinus (1540–1604, formally canonized in 1767).

Patr.: Pol.: **Serafinowicz**.

Serbinov Russian: patr. from the name *serbin* Serb. The Serbs originally came from what is now Galicia in Poland, and migrated to the Balkan peninsula in the 6th and 7th cents. AD.

Dims.: Czech: **Srbek**, **Srbík**.

Serck *see* SURRIDGE

Seretti *see* BALTHASAR

Serfati *see* SARFATTI

Sergeant English and French: occupational name for a servant, ME, OF *sergent* (L *serviens*, gen. *servientis*, pres. part. of *servīre* to serve). The surname probably originated for the most part in this general sense, but the word also developed various specialized meanings (being used for example as a technical term for a tenant by military service below the rank of a knight, and as the name for any of certain administrative and legal officials in different localities). For the change of *-er-* to *-ar-*, see MARCHANT.

Vars.: Eng.: **Sergeaunt**, **Sergean**, **Sergant**, **Sergent**, **Serje(a)nt**, **Seargeant**, **Searjeant**, **Sarg(e)ant**, **Sarge(au)nt**, **Sargint**, **Sarjant**, **Sarjent**. Fr.: **Sergent**, **Sargent**.

Patrs.: Eng.: **Serjeantson**, **Sarge(a)ntson**, **Sarjantson**, **Sergenson**, **Serginson**, **Sarginson**, **Sargeson**, **Sargi(s)son**, **Surgison**.

Sergio Italian: from the L family name *Sergius* (of uncertain, possibly Etruscan, origin), borne by a 4th-cent. Christian saint martyred in Cappadocia under Diocletian. The given name was hereditary in the ducal houses of Amalfi and Naples between the 11th and 13th cents. In the form *Sergei* it is also extremely popular in Russia.

Var.: **Sergi**.

Patrs.: Russ.: **Sergeev**; **Sergievski** (a clerical name). Beloruss.: **Syarkeev**. Gk: **Sergiou**. Armenian: **Sarkis(s)ian**.

Patrs. (from dims.): Russ.: **Sergevin**, **Serganov**, **Sergachyov**, **Sergun(k)ov**, **Sergunchikov**, **Seryozhechkin**, **Seryozhichev**.

Serier *see* CERISIER

Serle *see* SEARLE

Serlin *see* SORIN

Sermon English: metonymic occupational name for a preacher, or perhaps a nickname for a long-winded and pompous person, from ME *serm(o)un* sermon (OF *sermon*, from L *sermo*, gen. *sermōnis*, speech, discourse). The agent derivs. attested in the Middle Ages do not seem to have survived as modern surnames.

Vars.: **Surmon**, **Surman**, **Sirmon**, **Sirman**, **Sermin**, **Serman**.

Serna Spanish: feudal status name for someone who worked on a plot of land owned by the lord of the manor and cultivated for him as part of the prescribed feudal service, Sp. *serna* (OSp. *senera*, apparently of Celt. origin, composed of the separative prefix *sen-* + *ar* to plough, cultivate). There are several places in Spain named with this word, and the surname could also be a habitation name from any of these.

Sernin *see* SATURNIN

Serpe French: metonymic occupational name for a maker or seller of scythes and other agricultural implements, from OF *sarpe* (hypercorrected to *serpe*) scythe, sickle (LL *sarpa*, from *sarpere* to trim, cut).
Dims.: **Sarpot**, **Serpot**, **Serpeau**, **Serpin(et)**, **Serpy**, **Serpette**.
Eng.: **Serpell**.

Serrat Catalan: topographic name for someone who lived on a wooded upland, Cat. *serrat* (a deriv. of *serra* chain, range of hills; see SERRE).

Serre Provençal: topographic name for someone who lived on or near a ridge or chain of hills, OProv. *serre* (L *serra* saw).
Vars.: **Serres**, **Sarre**; **Sarran**.
Dims.: Prov.: **Serreau**, **Sarreau**, **Serret**, **Sarret**, **Sarrey**, **Sarron**, **Sarrot**, **Sarrin**, **Sarry**. It.: **Serretta**, **Serrini**, **Serrotti**.
Aug.: It.: **Serrone**.

Sertell *see* SHORTALL

Servadio Italian (Jewish): from a given name composed of the It. elements *servare* to serve + *Dio* God, representing a calque of the Hebr. male given name *Ovadya* (Eng. *Obadiah*).

Servis English: metonymic occupational name for a brewer or a tavern-keeper, from ANF *cerveise* ale (OF *cervoise*, of apparently Gaul. origin).
Vars.: **Service**, **Servais**, **Sarvis**.

Sessions English: habitation name from *Soissons* in N France, so called from the Gaul. tribe who once inhabited the area, and whose name is recorded in L documents in the form *Suessiones*, of uncertain derivation.

Šesták Czech: from *šesták*, name of an old coin (literally 'sixer'; it was at one time worth six kreuzers). The surname would have been acquired by someone who had to pay rent of this amount or for some other anecdotal reason. Cf. SHOSTAKOVICH.

Sestini *see* SIX

Seth *see* SHEEHY

Seton *see* SEATON

Setterfield *see* SATTERTHWAITE

Settle English: habitation name from a place in W Yorks., so called from OE *setl* seat, dwelling.

Seuberlich *see* SAUBER

Seuffert *see* SIEGFRIED

Seurat *see* SÉVERIN

Seuss German: habitation name representing a S Ger. pronunciation of *Seis*, a place in the Tyrol.
Vars.: **Seis(er)**.

Seuter *see* SAUTER

Ševčík *see* SZEWC

Seveke *see* SIEGFRIED

Sevène *see* SABIN

Séverin French: from a given name (L *Severīnus*, from the same root as *Severus*; see SEVEROV). This was borne by several early Christian saints, including bishops of Trèves (2nd cent.), Cologne (4th cent.), Bordeaux (5th cent.), and Santempeda (6th cent.), and hermits of Paris (6th cent.) and Tivoli (8th cent.), as well as a 5th-cent. apostle of Austria.
Vars.: **Sévrin**, **Sevrain**, **S(e)urin**.
Dims.: Fr.: **Seuret**, **Seurot**.
Aug.: Fr.: **Seurat**.
Patrs.: Low Ger.: **Vrings**, **Frin(g)s**, **Freins**. Flem., Du.: **Severyns**. Dan., Norw.: **Severinsen**, **Sørens(en)**. Swed.: **Sörensson**. Pol.: **Seweryniak**.

Severn English: **1.** cogn. of Fr. SÉVERIN. **2.** topographic name for someone living on the banks of the river *Severn*, which flows from Wales through much of W England to the Bristol Channel. The river name is recorded as early as the 2nd cent. AD in the form *Sabrina*. This is one of Britain's most ancient river names; the original meaning is uncertain, but it may have been 'Slowmoving'.
Var.: **Severne**.

Severov Russian: surname adopted by Orthodox priests, from the L personal name *Severus* (in L meaning 'Harsh, Austere'). This was the name of several Roman Emperors, including Alexander Severus (d. 235), born in Syria, who was noted for his virtuous and studious character and his tolerance towards Christians. The given name enjoyed some popularity among early Christians. Its adoption as a Russian priestly surname was reinforced by the Russ. vocab. word *sever* North.

Severy *see* SAVORY

Seveter *see* SILVESTER

Sévigné French: habitation name from a place in Ille-et-Vilaine, so called from the Gallo-Roman personal name *Sabinius* (a deriv. of L *Sabinus*; see SABIN) + the local suffix *-ācum*.

Sevilla Spanish: habitation name from the city of this name in SW Spain, the capital of Andalusia. The city is extremely ancient, having reputedly been founded by the Phoenicians. The origin of the name is obscure, presumably Phoenician. It is first recorded in the L form *Hispalis*, which was adopted into Arabic as *Isbilia*, and thence into Sp. as *Sibilia*, now *Sevilla*.
Var.: **Sevillano**.

Seville *see* SAVILLE

Seward **1.** English: from a ME given name representing two originally distinct personal names, *Siward* and *Seward*, OE *Sigeweard* and *Sǣweard*, composed of the elements *sige* victory and *sǣ* sea + *weard* guard, protect. They became confused in the late OE period. **2.** English: occupational name for a swineherd, from OE *sū* pig + *hierde* herdsman (see HEARD). **3.** Irish: Anglicized form of Gael. **Ó Suaird**, **Ó Suairt** 'descendant of *Suart*', a personal name derived from an ON cogn. of OE *Sigeweard*; cf. 1 above.
Vars. (of 3): **O'Swerte**, **O'Sworde**, SWORD.

Sewell English: **1.** from the ME given names *Siwal(d)* and *Sewal(d)*, OE *Sigeweald* and *Sæweald*, composed of the elements *sige* victory and *sæ* sea + *weald* rule. **2.** habitation name from *Sewell* in Beds., *Showell* in Oxon., or *Seawell* or *Sywell* in Northants, all of which are so called from OE *seofon* seven + *wella* spring (cf. CIFUENTES).

Vars.: **Sewall**, **Sewill**, **Sa(y)well**.

Sewer English: **1.** occupational name for a shoemaker or cobbler, an agent deriv. of ME *sew(en)* to sew (OE *si(o)wan)*, reinforced by ANF *suo(u)r* (L *sūtor*; cf. SAUTER. The OE term was also used to denote a tailor; cf. SOUSTER. **2.** occupational name for an official in charge of banqueting arrangements, from ANF *seour*, an aphetic form of OF *asseour* (from *asseoir* to seat, L *adsīdere* to sit down (to)). **3.** occupational name for a sawyer, from ANF *syour* (OF *seior*, L *secātor*, from *secāre* to cut). Compare SAWYER.

Equivs. (of 1, not cogn.): Ger. and Jewish: SCHUSTER. Pol.: SZEWC.

Seweryniak *see* SÉVERIN

Sewter *see* SAUTER

Sexton 1. English: occupational name for a sexton or churchwarden, ME *sexteyn* (OF *secrestein*, from L *sacristānus*). **2.** Irish: Anglicized form of Gael. Ó **Seastnáin** 'descendant of *Seastnán*', a personal name of uncertain origin; it may have been originally a byname meaning 'Bodyguard', from *seasuighim* to resist, defend.

Vars.: (of 1): **Sexten**, **Sex(st)on**, **Seckerson**, **Secretan**, **Saxton**, **Saxon**. (Of 2): **O'Sesnane**, **O'Shesnan**, **Shasnan**.

Equivs. (of 1, not cogn.): Ger.: GLOCKNER, KIRCHNER, KÜSTER, MESNER. Russ.: PONOMARYOV.

Seyerlin *see* SAUER

Seyers *see* SAYER

Seyfahrt *see* SIEGFRIED

Seyler *see* SEILER

Seyman *see* SEAMAN

Seymour English: **1.** Norman habitation name from *Saint-Maur*-des-Fossées in Seine, N France, so called from the dedication of the church there to St *Maur* (see MOORE 3). **2.** habitation name from either of two places in N Yorks. called *Seamer*, from OE *sæ* sea, lake + *mere* lake, pond. Ekwall postulates that the original name in OE was simply *Sæ* 'the Lake', the second element being added when the denotation of the first came to be restricted to a body of salt water. There are also places called *Semer* in Norfolk, Suffolk, and N Yorks., which have the same origin and may lie behind some instances of the surname.

Vars.: **Seymo(u)re**, **Seymer**.

Seyner *see* SENIOR

Shackell English: **1.** metonymic occupational name for a maker of fetters, from ME *schackel* chain, bond (OE *sceacol*). **2.** from the medieval given name *Schackel*, an Anglicized form of the ON byname *Skokull* 'Wagon-pole' (a cogn. of 1), given perhaps to a tall, thin man.

Vars.: **Shackel**, **Shackle**, **Skakle**.

Patr. (from 2): **Shackles**.

Shacklady English (Lancs.): of uncertain origin, probably a bawdy nickname for a man who was suspected of having made love to a lady higher than him in social rank, from ME *schak(k)en*, *schag(g)en* to shake, toss (cf. SHAKESPEARE) + *ladie* lady (OE *hlæfdige*, literally 'loaf kneader').

Var.: **Shakelady**.

Shackleton English: habitation name from a place in the parish of Halifax, W Yorks., so called from OE **scacol* tongue of land (a cogn. of ON *skekill*) + *tūn* enclosure, settlement.

Shacklock English (Derbys.): metonymic occupational name for a jailer, from ME *shaklock* fetter (apparently a cpd of *schackel* (see SHACKELL 1) + LOCK). According to the OED the vocab. word is first found in an isolated instance from the 16th cent.

Shaddick *see* CHADWICK

Shade Scots and English: **1.** local name for someone who lived near a boundary, OE *scēad* (from *scēadan* to divide; cf. SCHEIDT). **2.** nickname for a very thin man, from ME *schade* shadow, wraith (OE *sceadu*, gen. *scead(u)we*).

Var.: **Schade**.

Shadwell English: habitation name from any of the places so called, in London, Norfolk, and W Yorks. The first is named from OE *sceald* shallow + *well(a)* spring, stream (see WELL), the latter two from *scēad* boundary (see SHADE 1) + *well(a)*.

Shafran *see* SAFRAN

Shaftoe English: habitation name from a place in Northumb., probably so called from OE *sceaft* shaft (presumably a post marking a boundary) + *hōh* ridge (see HOE).

Shagalov *see* SEGAL

Shain *see* SCHÖN

Shakespeare English: nickname for a belligerent person or perhaps a bawdy name for an exhibitionist, from ME *schak(k)en* to brandish (OE *sc(e)acan*) + *speer* spear (OE *spere*).

Vars.: **Schakespear**, **Shakspeare**.

Shale English (W Midlands): apparently a nickname from ME *shale* shell (OE *scealu*), perhaps denoting someone considered of little value, as in the ME phrase *vayled not of a schale* 'not worth a shell'.

Shallcross English: habitation name from a place named after an ancient stone cross in the High Peak forest of Derbys., in the parish of Chapel en le Frith, known as the *Shackelcross*. The first element in this name appears to be from OE *sceacol* (see SHACKELL 1), perhaps denoting a cross to which penitents could be fettered.

Vars.: **Shalcross**, **Shallcrass**, **Shellcross**; **Shawcross**.

Shalom *see* SHOLEM

Shand Scots: of uncertain origin, perhaps from a short form of ALEXANDER (see SAND 2), or a Norman habitation name from *Chandai* in Orne, recorded in the early 12th cent. as *Canziacum*, from the Gallo-Roman personal name *Candius* + the local suffix *-ācum*.

Shane Irish: **1.** Anglicized form of Gael. **Mac Seáin** 'son of *Seán*', a form of JOHN. **2.** Anglicized form of Gael. **Ó Seanaigh** 'descendant of *Seanach*', a byname meaning 'Old', 'Wise'.

Vars. (of 1): **McShane**. (Of 2): **O'Shanna**, **O'Shann(e)y**, **O'Sheny**; **Shannagh**, **Shann(e)y**, **Sheeny**.

Dims. (of 2): **O'Sheanaghaine**, **O'Shanahan**, **Shana(g)han**, **Shanghan**, **Shan(ih)an** (Gael. **Ó Seanacháin**); **O'Shenane**, **O'Shennan**, **(O')Shannon**, **(O')Shanan** (Gael. **Ó Seanáin**).

Shanks N English and Scots: nickname for someone with long legs or some peculiarity of gait, from OE *sceanca* shinbone, leg. This vocab. word was preserved in Scotland, whereas in England it was replaced by ON *leggr* (see LEGG). See also CRUIKSHANK and SHEEPSHANKS.

Var.: **Shank**.

Shanley Irish: Anglicized form of the Gael. personal name *Seanlaoch*, composed of the elements *sean* old + *laoch* hero.

Var.: **Shanly**.

Patrs.: **McShanl(e)y**.

'Descendant of S.': **O'Shanley**

Shapcott English (Somerset): topographic name for someone who lived by a sheepcote (from OE *scēap, scīp* sheep + *cot* shelter), no doubt equivalent to an occupational name for a shepherd.

Shaper English: occupational name for a tailor, from an agent deriv. of ME *schap(en)* to form, mould (a back-formation from *schap*, OE *(ge)sceap*, from **sciepan* to create).

Vars.: **Shapster**, **Shipster** (fem. forms).

Shapiro Jewish (Ashkenazic): **1.** possibly an ornamental name, from Hebr. *shapir* fair, lovely. **2.** habitation name from the German town of *Speyer*, which had a large Jewish population in the Middle Ages; cf. SAPIR, SPIER, and SPIRE.

Vars.: **Schapiro**, **Shapero**, **Shapira**; **Chapiro** (a Fr. spelling); **Szapiro**, **Szapira** (Pol. spellings); **Shapir**.

Shápka see CHAPE

Shapley see SHIPLEY

Shapochnikov Russian: patr. from *shapochnik*, occupational name for a hatter, an agent noun from *shapka* hat (from OF *chape, Chapel* hat, via MHG *schäpel* and Pol. *czapka*).

Var.: **Shaposhnikov**.

Shard see SHEARD

Shardlow English: habitation name from a place in Derbys., so called from OE *sceard* notched + *hlāw* hill, tumulus (see LAW 2 and LOW 1), i.e. a hill or tumulus with an indentation in its outline.

Sharer see SHEARER

Sharkey Irish: Anglicized form of Gael. **Ó Searcaigh** 'descendant of *Searcach*', a byname meaning 'Beloved'.

Sharman see SHERMAN

Sharp English: nickname from ME *scharp* keen, active, quick (OE *scearp*).

Vars.: **Sharpe**; **Shairp** (Scots).

Patrs.: Eng.: **Sharps**. Low Ger.: **Scharping**, **Schärping**, **Scherping**.

Cpds (arbitrary elaborations): Jewish: **Scharfherz**, **Szarfherc**, **Szarfharc** ('sharp heart'); **Scharfstein**, **Szarfstein** ('sharp stone').

Sharples English (very common in Lancs.): habitation name from *Sharples* Hall near Bolton, probably so called from OE *scearp* sharp, i.e. steep + *lǣs* pasture.

Var.: **Sharpless**.

Sharratt see SHERRATT

Sharrock see SHORROCK

Shasnan see SEXTON

Shaughnessy Irish: Anglicized form of Gael. **Ó Seachnasaigh** 'descendant of *Seachnasach*', a personal name of uncertain origin, perhaps derived from *seachnach* elusive.

Vars.: **O'Shaughnessy**, **O'Shoughnessy**, **(O')Shannessy**, **O'Shanesy**.

Shaulick see SAUL

Shaw 1. English: topographic name for someone who lived by a copse or thicket, OE *sceaga*, or habitation name from one of the numerous minor places named with this word. **2.** Scots and Irish: Anglicized form of any of various surnames derived from the Gael. personal name *Sithech* 'Wolf'.

Vars. (of 1): **Shawe**, **Shay**, **Shay(e)s**, **Shave(s)**, **Shafe**.

Shcherbakov Russian: patr. from the nickname *Shcherbak* (from *shcherba* hole, tear, scar), denoting a man disfigured by pockmarks or scars.

Var.: **Shcherbatov**.

Shchukin Russian: patr. from the nickname *Shchuka* 'Pike', denoting a sharp or malicious person.

Shea Irish: Anglicized form of Gael. **Ó Séaghdha** 'descendant of *Séaghdha*', a byname meaning 'Fine', 'Fortunate'.

Vars.: **Shee**; **O'Shea** (the most common form), **O'Shee**.

Sheal see SHIELD

Shear English: nickname for a beautiful or radiant person, or one with fair hair, from ME *scher, schir*, OE *scīr* bright, fair.

Vars.: **Sheer**, **She(e)re**, **Sher(r)**.

Patrs.: **Shear(e)s**, **Sheer(e)s**; **Shires** (Yorks.); **Shearing** (E Anglia).

Sheard English (W Yorks.): topographic name for someone who lived by a gap between hills, OE *sceard* (a deriv. of *sceran* to cut, shear).

Vars.: **Shard**, **Sheards**.

Shearer Scots and N English: occupational name for a sheep-shearer or someone who used scissors to trim the surface of finished cloth and remove excessive nap, from an agent deriv. of ME *schere(n)* to shear (OE *sceran*). ME *schere* denoted shears and scissors of all sizes.

Vars.: **Sherer**, **Sharer**, **Shirer**, **She(a)ra**.

Equivs. (not cogn.): Ger.: FUGGER. Fr.: TONDEUR.

Shechter *see* SCHECHTER

Sheddon Scots: of uncertain origin, perhaps a habitation name from *Sheddens* in the former county of Renfrews. This placename contains a first element of uncertain derivation + ME *den* hollow, valley (OE *denu*; see DEAN 1).

Vars.: **Shedden**, **Sheddan**.

Sheedy Irish: Anglicized form of Gael. **Ó Síoda** 'descendant of *Síoda*', a byname meaning 'Silk'.

Vars.: **O'Shydie**, **Shead**; SILK.

Sheehan Irish: Anglicized form of Gael. **Ó Síodhacháin** 'descendant of *Síodhachán*', a personal name representing a dim. of *síodhach* peaceful.

Vars.: **O'Shiegane**, **O'Shehane**, **O'Sheehan**, **(O')Sheahan**, **She(e)an**, **Sheane**, **Sheen**, **Shine**.

Sheehy Scots and Irish: Anglicized form of the Gael. personal name *Sítheach*, probably originally a byname from the adj. *sítheach* relating to fairies, eerie, mysterious.

Vars.: **Sheekey**, **Sheach**, **Shiach**, **Se(a)th**.

Patrs.: **McShee(hy)**, **McShiehie**, **McShihy** (Gael. **Mac Síthigh**); **McKeith**.

Sheeny *see* SHANE

Sheep *see* SHIPMAN

Sheepshanks N English and Scots: nickname for someone with an odd, shambling gait, from Northern ME *schep* sheep + SHANKS.

Shefer *see* SCHÄFER

Sheffield English: habitation name from the city in S Yorks., so called from the river name *Sheaf* (from OE **scēað* boundary, a byform of *scēad*; see SHADE 1) + OE *feld* pasture, open country (see FIELD). There are also minor places of the same name in Sussex (from OE *scēap, scīp* sheep + *feld*) and Berks. (from OE *scēo* shelter, shed + *feld*), which may have contributed to the surname.

Shein *see* SCHÖN

Sheinenson *see* SCHEINIS

Shelby English: of uncertain origin, either a var. of SELBY, or a habitation name from an unidentified place named with the Northern ME elements *schēle* hut (see SHIELD 2) + *by* settlement, farm (ON *býr*). The surname is now more common in the U.S. than in England.

Sheldon English: habitation name from any of the various places so called. The main source is probably the one in Derbys., recorded in Domesday Book as *Scelhadun*, formed by the addition of the OE distinguishing term *scylf* shelf to the placename *Haddon* (from OE *hæð* heath(er) + *dūn* hill). There are also places called *Sheldon* in Devon (from OE *scylf* shelf + *denu* valley) and Birmingham (from OE *scylf* + *dūn* hill).

Sheldrake English (chiefly E Anglia): nickname for a vain or showy person, from a type of brightly coloured duck,

ME *scheldrake* (from the E Anglian dial. term *scheld* variegated (MLG *schelede*, past part. of *schelen* to differ) + *drake* male duck (apparently also of Low Ger. origin)).

Vars.: **Shildrake**, **Sheldrick**, **Shildrick**.

Shellcross *see* SHALLCROSS

Shelley English: habitation name from any of various places, for example in Sussex, Suffolk, Essex, and W Yorks., all so called from OE *scylf* shelf + *lēah* wood, clearing. The surname is now as common in the W Midlands as it is in E Anglia and London.

Var.: **Shelly**.

Shelton English (most common in Notts.): habitation name from any of various places, for example in Notts., Beds., Norfolk, Shrops., and Staffs., all apparently so called from OE *scylf* shelf + *tūn* enclosure, settlement. See also SHILTON and SKELTON.

Shenton English: habitation name from a place in Leics., originally named as the settlement (OE *tūn*) on the river *Sence*. This river name is a Normanized form of OE *Scenc* 'Drinking Cup', referring to its abundance of potable water.

Sheppard English: occupational name for a shepherd, ME *schepherde*, from OE *scēap, scīp* sheep + *hierde* herdsman (see HEARD) or *weard* guardian (see WARD 1).

Vars.: **Shephe(a)rd**, **Shep(h)ard**, **Shepe(a)rd**, **Shepperd**, **Shippard**.

Patrs.: Eng.: **Sheppardson**, **Shepper(d)son**, **Shep(h)erdson**.

Sheraton English: habitation name from a place in Co. Durham, found in 11th-cent. records as *Scurufatun*, and hence probably of the same origin as SCRUTON.

Sherborne English: habitation name from any of various places, for example in Dorset, Gloucs., Hants, and Warwicks., all so called from OE *scīr* bright (see SHEAR) + *burna* stream (see BOURNE).

Vars.: **Sherbourne**, **Sherborn**; **Sherburn** (Yorks.).

Sheremetyev Russian: patr. from a Turkic given name, from Arab. *Ahmad* (see AKHMATOV), with the addition of the title *Shir* 'Lion' (of Persian origin).

Var.: **Sheremetev**.

Shereshevski *see* SIEROTA

Sheridan Irish: Anglicized form of Gael. **Ó Sirideáin** 'descendant of *Sirideán*', a personal name of uncertain origin, possibly akin to *sirim* to seek.

Vars.: **Sherridan**, **O'Sheridane**, **O'Shiridane**.

Sheriff English: occupational name for a sheriff, a word derived from OE *scīr* shire, administrative district (the original sense being (sphere of) office, duty') + *(ge)rēfa* REEVE. In some cases it may also have arisen as a nickname. In England before the Norman Conquest the sheriff was the king's representative in a county, responsible for every aspect of local administration. Gradually the duties of the office became restricted, until by the 19th cent. they were more or less confined to the administration of county courts and prisons, this being something of a sinecure. In some counties the office was hereditary, a practice which continued in Westmorland until 1850. Similar officials were found in Scotland in the Middle Ages, and from the 16th cent. in Ireland.

Vars.: **Sherriff, Shir(r)eff, Shiriff, Shirra, Shre(e)ve, Sch(r)ieve, Schrive.**

Patrs.: **Sher(r)iffs, Shirref(f)s, Shreeves, Schrieves, Shrives.**

Sherington English: habitation name from a place in Bucks., so called from OE *Scīringtūn* 'settlement associated with *Scīra*', a byname meaning 'Bright', 'Fair' (see SHEAR).

Vars.: **Sherrington** (now found chiefly in Lancs.), **Shrimpton.**

Sherlock English: nickname for someone with fair hair or a lock of fair hair, ME *schirloc*, from OE *scīr* bright, fair (see SHEAR) + *loc* lock (of hair).

Var.: **Shurlock.**

Sherman 1. English: occupational name for a sheep-shearer or someone who used shears to trim the surface of finished cloth and remove excess nap, ME *shereman*; cf. SHEARER. 2. Jewish (Ashkenazic): occupational name for a tailor, from Yid. *sher* scissors + *man* man.

Vars. (of 1): **Sh(e)arman, Sheerman, Shurman.** (Of 2): **Shermann, Szerman, Shermeister.**

Sherratt English: of uncertain origin, apparently a deriv. of ME *shere* bright, fair (see SHEAR) with the addition of the ANF pej. suffix *-ard*.

Vars.: **Sharratt; Sherrett, Sherott, Sherrad, Sherred, Sherr(e)ard, Sherard.**

Sherwin English: nickname for a swift runner, from ME *schere(n)* to shear + *wind*; the Ger. surname **Schneidewin(d)** 'cut wind' provides a semantic parallel. The Eng. surname is sometimes translated in medieval sources into the ANF form *Tranchevent*.

Var.: **Sherwen.**

Sherwood English: habitation name from a place in Notts., around which once stood the famous Sherwood Forest. The place is so called from OE *scīr* shire (see SHERIFF) or *scīr* bright (see SHEAR) + *wudu* WOOD.

Var.: **Shearwood.**

Shettlesworth see SHUTTLEWORTH

Shevchenko see SZEWC

Shiach see SHEEHY

Shick see SCHICK

Shield 1. English: metonymic occupational name for an armourer; cf. SCHILD 1. 2. English: habitation name from places in Northumb. and Co. Durham (now both in Tyne and Wear) called respectively N and S *Shields*, from ME *schēle* shed, hut, shelter (OE *scēol*). Some examples of the surname may be topographic names, derived directly from the vocab. word. 3. English: topographic name for someone who lived near the shallow part of a river, from OE *scieldu* shallows, a deriv. of *sceald* shallow. 4. Irish: Anglicized form of Gael. **Ó Siaghail, Ó Siadhail** 'descendant of *Siadhal*', a well-attested personal name of unknown derivation.

Vars. (mainly of 2): **Shiel(ds); Shiel(l)s** (chiefly Sc.); **Sheil(ds), Sheal(s).** (Of 4): **O'Siegall, O'Shiel(l), O'Sheal, O'Shill, Sheil(d)s.**

Shielman see SCHULER

Shildrake see SHELDRAKE

Shiler see SCHILLER

Shillingford English: habitation name from places so called, in Devon and Oxon., which are of uncertain etymology. The second element is clearly OE *ford* FORD; Ekwall proposes that the first is probably a tribal name, *Scillingas* 'people of *Sciell(a)*', a byname from OE *sciell* resounding.

Shillito English: of uncertain meaning. This surname seems to have a single origin in the parish of Featherstone, W Yorks.

Vars.: **Sillito(e).**

Shilton English: habitation name from any of various places (in Berks., Leics., Oxon., and Warwicks.) which have the same origin as SHELTON.

Shimkevich see SIMON

Shimshon see SAMSON

Shinagh see TINNEY

Shine see SHEEHAN

Shingler English: occupational name for someone who laid wooden tiles (shingles) on roofs, an agent deriv. of ME *schingle* shingle (OE *scingel*, from L *scindula, scandula*).

Var.: **Shingles.**

Equiv.: Pol.: SZKUDLAREK.

Shinn see SKINNER

Shipley English: habitation name from any of the various places, for example in Derbys., Co. Durham, Northumb., Shrops., Sussex, and W Yorks., so called from OE *scēap, scīp* sheep + *lēah* wood, clearing.

Vars.: **Shiplee, Shapley.**

Shipman English: 1. occupational name for a shepherd, ME *schepman*, from OE *scēap, scīp* sheep + *mann* man. See also SHEPPARD. 2. occupational name for a mariner, or occasionally perhaps for a boat-builder, ME *schipman*, from OE *scip* ship + *mann*.

Vars. (of 1): **Sheep.** (Of 2): **Ship(p).**

Shippam English: habitation name from *Shipham* in Somerset, so called from OE *scēap, scīp* sheep + *hām* homestead.

Shippard see SHEPPARD

Shippen English: habitation name from any of various places named from OE *scypen* cattleshed, such as *Shippen* in W Yorks. and *Shippon* in Berks., or topographical name derived directly from the vocab. word. In some cases it may originally have been acquired as an occupational name for a cowman, who in medieval times would often have shared the quarters of his charges.

Shipperbottom see SHUFFLEBOTTOM

Shipside English: of uncertain origin. It may be a habitation name from some unidentified place, perhaps so called from OE *scēap, scīp* sheep + *sīde* slope. The earliest known bearers of the name are found as far apart as Worcs.

and Co. Durham. Another possibility is that it may derive from *Shepshed* in Leics., recorded in Domesday Book as *Scepe(s)hefde*, and derived from OE *scēap* sheep + *hēafod* head, hill.

Var.: **Shipsides**.

Shipster *see* SHAPER

Shipstone English: habitation name, probably from *Shipston* on Stour in Warwicks., which is recorded in Domesday Book as *Shepwestun*, from OE *scēapwæsc* place for washing sheep + *tūn* enclosure, settlement.

Shipton English: habitation name from any of the various places, for example in Dorset, Gloucs., Hants, Oxon., and Shrops., so called from OE *scēap, scīp* sheep + *tūn* enclosure, settlement.

Shipway English (Gloucs.): probably a topographic name for someone who lived by a road along which sheep were regularly driven, from ME *schip* sheep + *way* path, road (see WAY).

Shireff *see* SHERIFF

Shirer *see* SHEARER

Shires *see* SHEAR

Shirley English: habitation name from any of various places, for example in Derbys., Hants, Surrey, and the W Midlands, all so called from OE *scīr* bright + *lēah* wood, clearing; cf. SHERWOOD.

Shkolnik *see* SCHULER

Shleicher *see* SCHLEICHER

Shlemovich *see* SALOMON

Shmil *see* SAMUEL

Shneebaum *see* SNOW

Shneerson *see* SCHNEIR

Shneiderov *see* SCHNEIDER

Shnur *see* SCHNUR

Shochet *see* SHOIKHET

Shoebotham *see* SHUFFLEBOTTOM

Shoemaker *see* SCHUH

Shoen *see* SCHÖN

Shoesmith English: occupational name for a blacksmith who specialized in the shoeing of horses, ME *schosmith*, from OE *scōh* shoe (cf. SCHUH) + *smið* SMITH.

Var.: **Shoosmith**.

Shoikhet Jewish (Southern Ashkenazic): occupational name for a ritual slaughterer, Yid. *shoykhet*.

Vars.: **Shoichet**; **S(c)hochet**, **Shohet** (E Ashkenazic); **Szochet** (a Pol. spelling); **Schauchet** (reflecting a W Yid. pronunciation); **Shohetman**.

Patr.: **Szochatowicz**.

Shol *see* SCHOLL

Sholem Jewish (Ashkenazic): from the Yid. male given name *Sholem* (from Hebr. *shalom* peace).

Vars.: **Shulem** (reflecting a S Yid. pronunciation); **Shalom** (Israeli).

Patrs.: **Shulimson** (reflecting a S Yid. pronunciation); **Sholemoff** (NE Ashkenazic); **Shalomoff** (a partly Hebraicized form).

Sholl 1. Cornish: of uncertain origin. It may perhaps be from Corn. *is* under + *hall* moor. **2.** Anglicized form of Ger. or Jewish SCHOLL.

Sholokhov Russian: patr. from the nickname *Sholokh* 'Stir', 'Bustle' (of imitative origin), denoting an officious or self-important person.

Var.: **Sholokov**.

Shonnagh *see* TINNEY

Shooter English (now chiefly E Midlands): occupational name for a marksman, from an agent deriv. of ME *schoot(en)* to shoot (OE *scēotan*).

Vars.: **Shotter**, **Shut(t)er**; see also SHUTT.

Shor *see* SCHAUER

Shore 1. English: topographic name for someone who lived by the sea-shore, ME *schore* (of uncertain origin, from Low Ger. or the native *scora* below). **2.** English: topographic name for someone who lived by a bank or steep slope, from OE *scora*. There are minor places named with this word in Lancs. and W Yorks., and the surname may also be a habitation name from one of these. **3.** Jewish (Ashkenazic): Anglicized spelling of *S(c)hor(r)* and *Szor*; see SCHAUER 2.

Var. (of 1 and 2): **Shores**.

Shorrock English (Lancs.): habitation name from *Shorrock* Green in Lancs., probably so called from OE *scora* bank + *āc* oak.

Vars.: **Shorrocks**, **Sharrock(s)**, **Shurrock**.

Short 1. English: nickname for a person of low stature, from ME *schort*, OE *sceort* short. **2.** Irish: translation of Gael. *Mac an Ghirr*; see McGIRR.

Vars. (of 1): **Shortman** (Somerset). (Of 2): **Shortt**.

Comparative (of 1): **Shorter**.

Shortall Irish: re-Anglicized form of Gael. *Soirtéil*, itself a Gaelicized form of an Eng. surname, *Shorthals*. This name, which was brought to Ireland in the reign of Edward I, was originally a nickname from ME *schort* SHORT + *halse* neck (see HALS). It survives in England only in the form SHORTHOUSE.

Vars.: **Scorthals**, **Shorthall**, **Shortle**, **Sertell**, **Sertill**, **Surtill**, **Shorten** (Gael. **Seartáin**; an altered form common in Co. Cork).

Shorthouse English (now chiefly W Midlands): **1.** nickname from a peculiarity of dress, from ME *schort* SHORT + *hose* (OE *hosa*; cf. HOSIER). Hose were the regular medieval leg covering, varying in kind from a garment rather like a pair of tights to *half hose*, which reached only to the knee. Compare CURTIS 2. **2.** nickname for someone with a short neck, a var. of SHORTALL.

Vars.: (chiefly of 1): **Shorthose**, **Shorters**, **Shortis**.

Shoshin Jewish (E Ashkenazic): metr. from the Yid. female given name *Shoshe* (from the Hebr. name *Shoshana*, from *shoshan* lily) + the Slav. metr. suffix *-in*.

Vars.: **Sosin**; **Sosis** (Ashkenazic); **Shoshkin**, **Soskin**, **Shoshkes** (E Ashkenazic, from a dim. form, *Shoshke*, of the given name).

Shostakovich Belorussian: patr. from the nickname *Shastak*, a deriv. of *shast* six. The application of the nickname is uncertain; it may have denoted a person with six fingers on one hand, or it may have had some anecdotal reference to the coin (worth three copeks) so called. The surname has been given a Great Russ. form by the substitution of (unstressed) *o* for *a* in the first syllable.

Shotton English (chiefly Northumb.): habitation name from any of various places in Co. Durham and Northumb., so called from OE *Scotta-tūn* 'settlement of the Scots' (from *Scotta* Scots), or *Scēot-tūn* 'settlement at a steep place' (from *scēot* quick, steep, a deriv. of *scēotan* to shoot), or *Scēat-tūn* 'settlement in a projection of a parish or other administrative division' (from *scēat* projection, corner, promontory). *Shotton* in the parish of Glendale, Northumb., is 'hill of the Scots', with the second element OE *dūn* hill (see DOWN 1). There are also two minor places in the W Midlands—*Shotten* on the Welsh border and *Shotton* in Hadnall, Shrops—that may lie behind some instances of the surname in this area. There is also a *Shotton* in Clwyd.

Shovell English: metonymic occupational name for a maker or seller of shovels, or for someone who regularly used a shovel in his work, from ME *schovel* (OE *scofl*, a deriv. of *scūfan* to push, shove).

Vars.: **Shovel**, **Showell**, **Showl**; **Shoveller**, **Showler**, **Shouler**.

Shpitz *see* SPITZ

Shpringer *see* SPRINGER

Shrapnel *see* CARBONELL

Shreeve *see* SHERIFF

Shreier *see* SCHREIER

Shrimpton *see* SHERINGTON

Shroff English: although this is for the most part an Asian name (from a Hindi word for a money-changer or moneylender), it was already well established in England in the 19th cent. (see below), and may also be of Eng. origin. The etymology is unknown; it may be connected with *shroffe (metal)* old copper or brass (a term first recorded in the 16th cent., perhaps derived from Ger. *Schroff* fragment).

Shterenglass *see* STARR

Shtivel *see* STIEFEL

Shtolzer *see* STOLZ

Shtrauss *see* STRAUSS

Shtrom *see* STRÖM

Shtul Jewish (Ashkenazic): **1.** apparently a metonymic occupational name for a maker of chairs, from Ger. *Stuhl*, Yid. *shtul* chair. **2.** possibly also from a S Yid. pronunciation of Yid. *shtol* STEEL.

Vars.: **Shtull**, **Shtulman**.

Shturm *see* STORM

Shuchmacher *see* SCHUH

Shufflebottom English: habitation name from *Shipperbottom* in Lancs., which derives its name from OE *scēpwælla* spring where sheep are washed + *boðm* valley (see BOTTOM).

Vars.: **Shufflebot(h)am**, **Shovelbottom**, **Shipperbottom**, **Shoebottom**, **Shoebotham**, **Shubotham**.

Shugg Cornish: of unknown origin.

Shugrue *see* SUGRUE

Shulem *see* SHOLEM

Shunnagh *see* TINNEY

Shurlock *see* SHERLOCK

Shurman *see* SHERMAN

Shurrock *see* SHORROCK

Shuster *see* SCHUSTER

Shute English: habitation name from *Shute* in Devon, so called from OE **scīete*, a var. form of *scēat* projection. There are minor places in Wilts. and Berks. named with this word; their modern forms are *Shute* and *Shoot* respectively.

Shuter *see* SHOOTER

Shutt English: occupational name for an archer, ME *schut(te)*, *schit(te)*, OE *scytta*, a primary deriv. of *scēotan* to shoot.

Vars.: **Shut(te)**. See also SHOOTER.

Patr.: Eng.: **Shutts**.

Shuttleworth English: habitation name from any of several places so called (in Lancs., Derbys., and W Yorks.), which derive their name from OE *scyttel(s)* bar, bolt + *worð* enclosure (see WORTH).

Var.: **Shettlesworth**.

Shvanenfeld *see* SWAN

Shvetsov *see* SZEWC

Shynn *see* SKINNER

Sibbald Scots and N English: from the ME given name *Sybald*, OE *Sigebeald*, composed of the elements *sige* victory + *beald* bold, brave, reinforced in the early Middle Ages by the Norman introduction of a Continental cogn.

Patr.: Fris.: **Siebels**.

Sibbe *see* SIEBERT

Sibbett Scots and English: from the early mod. Eng. given name *Sebode*, probably from an unattested OE personal name **Sigeboda*, composed of the elements *sige* victory + *boda* messenger. However, there has been some confusion with SIBBALD.

Vars.: **Sibbit(t)**.

Sibley English: from the popular medieval female given name *Sibley*, a vernacular form of L *Sibilla*, from Gk *Sibylla*, a title (of obscure origin) borne by various oracular priestesses in Classical times. In Christian mythology the sibyls came to be classed as pagan prophets, and hence the name was a respectable one to be bestowed on a child.

Vars.: **Sibly**, **Sebley**; **Sibble**.

Dims.: Fr.: **Sibilleau**, **Sibillot**, **Sébilleau**, **Sébillot**, **Sébillon**, **Sébline**, **Subileau**.

Aug.: Fr.: **Sibillat**.

Metrs.: Eng.: **Sibbles**; **Sibson** (from a pet form).

Sicely *see* SISLEY

Sich *see* SYKES

Šich *see* SIMON

Sichardt *see* SIEGHARD

Sicilia Italian and Spanish: name for someone from the island of Sicily, which formed part of the kingdom of Aragon from 1282 to 1713.

Vars.: It.: **Siciliano**, **Siciliani**.

Sick *see* SIEGEL

Siddall N English: habitation name from places in Lancs. (in the parish of Middleton) and W Yorks. (part of Halifax) called *Siddal*, from OE *sīd* wide + *halh* nook, recess (see HALE 1).

Vars.: **Siddle**, **Sidell**.

Siddenham *see* SYDENHAM

Sidebottom N English: habitation name from a place in Ches., so called from OE *sīd* wide + *boðm* valley (see BOTTOM).

Var.: **Sidebotham**.

Sidgewick *see* SEDGWICK

Sidney English: 1. habitation name from *Sidney* in Surrey and Lincs., so called from OE *sīd* wide + *ēg* island, dry land in a fen, with the adj. retaining traces of the weak dat. ending, originally used after a preposition and def. art. Two places in Ches. called *Sydney* are from OE *sīd* + *halh* nook, recess (see HALE 1) and may also be partial sources of the surname. 2. possibly also a habitation name from a place in Normandy called *Saint-Denis*, from the dedication of its church to St *Dionysius* (see DENNIS). There is, however, no evidence to support this derivation beyond occasional early mod. Eng. forms such as *Seyndenys*, which may equally well be the result of folk etymology.

Var.: **Sydney**.

Sidorchik *see* ISIDORE

Sidwell *see* SITWELL

Siebels *see* SIBBALD

Siebert German: from a Gmc personal name composed of the elements *sigi* victory + *berht* bright, famous. There has

been some confusion between forms of this name and those of the more common SIEGFRIED.

Vars.: **Siegbert**; **Segebrecht**, **Sägebrecht**, **Siebrecht**, **Zieprecht**, **Zyprecht**.

Dims.: Low Ger.: **Sieb(e)**, **Sibbe**, **Sipp**, **Siebeck(e)**, **Sieb(e)ke**, **Seibicke**. Fris.: **Segelke**.

Patrs.: Low Ger.: **Segbers**, **Siebers**, **Siebertz**, **Seibers**, **Seibertz**, **Zeiberts**, **Sibbers(en)**. Flem., Du.: **Sebrechts**, **Sibers**.

Patrs. (from dims.): Low Ger.: **Siebs**, **Sieben(s)**, **Siebken**.

Sieczkowski Polish: habitation name from a place called *Sieczków* (named from Pol. *sieczka* chaff + the possessive suffix *ów*), with the addition of the suffix of local surnames *-ski* (see BARANOWSKI).

Siedlecki Polish and Jewish (Ashkenazic): habitation name from the town of *Siedlce* in E Poland, which gets its name from OPol. **siedlo* abode, dwelling place.

Sieff Jewish (W Ashkenazic): said to be from the Yid. male given name *Zev* (from Hebr. *Zeev*, literally 'Wolf', the symbolic animal associated with the tribe of BENJAMIN), but this explanation is problematic because the Yid. given name has /ε/, whereas *Sieff* and *Seef* have /i/ and *Ziff* has /ɪ/. Only *Zevin* is clearly from the given name.

Vars.: **Seef**, **Ziff**.

Patr. (E Ashkenazic): **Zevin**.

Siegel 1. German: metonymic occupational name, a cogn. of SEAL 2. 2. German: from a medieval given name, a dim. of a short form of the various Gmc cpd personal names with the first element *sigi* victory; cf., e.g., SIEBERT, SIEGFRIED, SIEGHARD, SIEGMUND, and SIEMER. 3. Jewish (Ashkenazic): var. of SEGAL 1.

Vars. (of 2): **Siegl**, **Sigle**, **Sick(el)**; **Siedl**, **Seidl**. (Of 3): **Siegelman**.

Patrs. (from 2): Ger.: **Sicks**, **Seggeling**. Fris.: **Segelken**.

Siegers *see* SAYER

Siegfried German: from a Gmc personal name composed of the elements *sigi* victory + *fridu* peace. The Ger. surname has also occasionally been adopted by Ashkenazic Jews.

Vars.: **Seefried**, **Seifer(t)**, **S(e)iffert**, **Sey(f)fahrt**, **Seifart(h)**, **Seuffert**.

Dims.: Ger.: **Seiferlin**. Low Ger.: **S(i)efke**, **S(i)eveke**. Fris.: **Süfke**.

Patrs.: Low Ger.: **Siever(t)s**, **Siefers**, **Siewers**, **Seevers**, **Seffers**; **Siever(t)sen**, **Siewertsen**; **Siever(d)ing**. Dan., Norw.: **Sivertsen**.

Patrs. (from dims.): Low Ger.: **Siefken**; **Söf(f)ker**; **Sieveking**, **Söffing**.

Sieghard German: from a Gmc personal name composed of the elements *sigi* victory + *hard* hardy, brave, strong.

Vars.: **Sichardt**, **Si(e)ghart**, **Siehard**.

Siegmund German: from a Gmc personal name composed of the elements *sigi* victory + *mund* protection.

There has also been some confusion in the vars. and cogns. with SIMON.

Vars.: **S(i)egemund**; **Sigismund**; **Siemund, Seemund, Simond**.

Pol.: **Zygmunt, Zygmański**. Hung.: **Zsigmond**.

Dims.: It.: **Simondini**. Czech: **Zich, Zika, Zíka, Zýka, Zikán, Zykán**; **Žižka**. Pol.: **Zygmuńczyk**; **Zych, Zychoń**.

Patr.: Pol.: **Zygmuntowicz**.

Patr. (from a dim.): Pol.: **Zychowicz**.

Habitation name (from a dim.): Pol.: **Zychowski**.

Siekiera Polish: metonymic occupational name for a wood-cutter or axeman, one who wielded an axe, from Pol. *siekiera* axe, hatchet. It may also in part represent a nickname.

Vars.: **Sierkierski**; **Skierski**.

Sielski Polish: regional name for someone from *Sioło* eastern Poland, or nickname for a rural or rustic person, from Pol. *sielski* rural, pastoral.

Siemandl *see* SIMON

Siemer German: from the Gmc personal name *Siegmar*, composed of the elements *sigi* victory + *mari, meri* famous.

Dims.: Low Ger.: **Siem(ann)**.

Patr.: Low Ger.: **Siemers**.

Patrs. (from dims.): Low Ger.: **Siems, Siem(s)sen, Siemen(s), Siemensen**.

Siemiński Polish: from a short form of any of various OPol. personal names such as *Siemisław, Siemomysł, Siemirad* (see SEMRÁD), having OSlav. *sěmъ* person as a first element.

Var.: **Simiński**.

Patr. (from a dim.): Pol.: **Sienkiewicz**.

Sieradzki Polish: habitation name from the town of *Sieradz* in W central Poland, which gets its name from a OPol. personal name, *Sie(mi)rad* (see SEMRÁD).

Sierota Polish and Jewish (E Ashkenazic): nickname for an orphan, Pol. *sierota*.

Vars.: Pol.: **Sierocki, Sieroń, Sierant**. Jewish: **Sirota**; **Sieroszewski, Szereszewski, Sher(e)shevski, Shershevsky, Scherschewski**.

Dims.: Czech: **Sirotek**. Ukr.: **Sirotyuk, Sirotenko**.

Patrs.: Russ.: **Sirot(in)in**.

Patr. (from a dim.): Russ.: **Sirotkin**.

Habitation names: Pol.: **Sieroszewski, Sieroczewski, Sierociński**.

Sieur *see* SEIGNEUR

Siffert *see* SIEGFRIED

Sigal *see* SEGAL

Sighart *see* SIEGHARD

Sigismund *see* SIEGMUND

Sigle *see* SIEGEL

Signoraccio *see* SEIGNEUR

Sigsworth English (Yorks.): habitation name from *Sigsworth* Moor, near Pately Bridge, so called from the gen. case of the ON personal name *Síkr* + OE *ford* FORD.

Siguret *see* SÉGUR

Sijmons *see* SIMON

Sikes *see* SYKES

Sikora Polish and Jewish (Ashkenazic): nickname for a small, dark person, from Pol. *sikora* titmouse, coalmouse, or, in the case of the Jewish name, an ornamental name.

Var.: **Sikorski**.

Šilhavý Czech: nickname for a boss-eyed person, Czech *šilhavý* (adj.).

Var.: **Šilhan**.

Dim.: **Šilhánek**.

Silk 1. English: metonymic occupational name for a merchant dealing in silk, OE *seolc* (L *sēricum*). **2.** English: from a medieval given name, a back-formation from *Silkin*; see SILL. **3.** Irish: translation of Gael. *Ó Síoda*; see SHEEDY.

Var.: **Silke**.

Silkstone English: habitation name from a place in S Yorks., so called from the gen. case of the OE personal name *Sigelāc* (composed of the elements *sigi* victory + *lāc* play, sport) + OE *tūn* enclosure, settlement.

Sill English: from a medieval given name, a short form of SILVESTER or *Silvanus* (see SELWYN 1).

Dims.: **Sillett** (E Anglia), **Silkin, Silcock**.

Patr.: **Sills**.

Patrs. (from dims.): **Silcocks, Silcox**.

Silley *see* SEALEY

Sillito *see* SHILLITO

Sillman *see* SELMAN

Silva Spanish and Portuguese: topographic name for someone who lived in a wood, OSp., OPort. *silva* (L *silva*). During the Middle Ages the Sp. term was replaced by *bosque* (see BOIS), but in the west of the Peninsula it survived with the altered sense 'bramble bush', 'thicket', and in some cases this may have been the meaning of the surname.

Collective: Port.: **Silveira**.

Silver 1. English: nickname for a rich man or for someone with silvery grey hair, from ME *silver*, OE *seolfor* silver. Sometimes, too, it may have originated as a metonymic occupational name for a silversmith. **2.** English: topographic name from any of the various streams in different parts of England named with this word, from the silvery appearance of the water. **3.** Jewish (Ashkenazic): Anglicized form of **Silber** (from Ger. *Silber*, Yid. *zilber* silver), an ornamental name.

Patr.: Eng.: **Silvers**.

Cpds (ornamental): Jewish: **Silberbach** ('silver stream'); **Silberbaum, Zylberbaum** ('silver tree'); **Silberberg, Zylberberg** ('silver hill'; partly Anglicized **Silverberg**); **Silberblatt** ('silver leaf'); **Silberbusch** ('silver bush'); **Silberfaden** ('silver thread'); **Silberfarb, Zylberfarb** ('silver colour'); **Silberfeld** ('silver field'); **Silberfreund** ('silver friend'); **Silberher(t)z** ('silver heart'); **Silberlicht** ('silver light'); **Silbermin(t)z, Zylbermin(t)z** ('silver coin'); **Silbernadel** ('silver needle'); **Silberpfennig, Silberfenig, Silberphenig** ('silver penny'); **Zylbering** ('silver ring'); **Silbers(c)hatz** ('silver treasure'); **Silbershein** ('silver shine');

Silberschlag ('silver stroke'); **Silberso(h)n** ('son of silver'); **Silberspitz**, **Zylberspic** ('silver point'); **Silberstein**, **Zylbers(z)tein**, **Zylbersztejn**, **Zylbersztajn** ('silver stone'; partly Anglicized **Silverstein**; see also SILVERSTONE); **Zylberstrom** ('silver stream'); **Silberwasser** ('silver water'); **Silberzahn** ('silver tooth'); **Silberzweig** ('silver twig').

Silvério Portuguese: from a medieval given name (L *Silverius*, a deriv. of *silva* wood; cf. SELWYN 1 and SILVESTER), borne in honour of a 6th-cent. pope, who met a premature end as the result of the enmity of the Empress Theodora, but was subsequently revered as a saint.

Silverstone 1. English: habitation name from a place in Northants, recorded in Domesday Book as *Silvetone* and *Selvestone*, from the gen. case of an OE personal name, either *Sǣwulf* (see SELF) or *Sigewulf* ('victory wolf') + OE *tūn* enclosure, settlement. 2. Jewish (Ashkenazic): Anglicized form of *Silberstein*; see SILVER.

Vars. (of 1): **Silverston**, **Silveston**.

Silverthorne English (Bristol): apparently a habitation name from some unidentified minor place deriving its name from OE *seolfor* SILVER + *þorn* thorn bush (see THORN).

Silverton English: of uncertain origin, apparently a habitation name. The surname is first recorded in Kent and Suffolk in the 17th cent., which lends no support to the theory that it is a var. of SILVERSTONE.

Silverwood English (Yorks.): apparently a habitation name, perhaps from *Silver Wood* in Ravenfield, W Yorks. (although that is not recorded until 1764). The placename may be referring to a wood of silver birches.

Silvester English and German: from a given name (L *Silvester*, a deriv. of *silva* wood; cf. SELWYN 1 and SILVÉRIO). This was borne by three popes, including a contemporary of Constantine the Great.

Vars.: Eng.: **Selvester**, **Sylvester**; **Siviter** (W Midlands), **Seveter**. Ger.: **Ve(h)ster**, **Fe(h)ster** (aphetic forms).

Dims.: It.: **Silvestrelli**, **Silvestrini**, **Vestrini**, **Vestrucci**. Pol.: **Symbestyrek**.

Aug.: It.: **Silvestroni**.

Patrs.: Low Ger.: **Festersen**. It.: **De Silvestri**, **(De) Silvestris**, **Vestris**. Russ.: **Silvestrov**, **Silverstov**, **Seliverstov**. Beloruss.: **Silvestrovich**. Pol.: **Sylwestrowicz**, **Sylwestrzak**.

Habitation name: Pol.: **Sylwestrowski**.

Sim Scots and N English: from the ME given name *Sim(me)*, a short form of SIMON.

Vars.: **Simm** (Lancs. and Northumb.); **Sime**, **Syme**.

Dims.: **Simmie** (chiefly Scots); SIMKIN; **Simcock**, **Sincock**, **Sincoe** (chiefly W Midlands).

Patrs.: SIMSON, McKIMM.

Patrs. (from dims.): **Simcocks**, **Simcox**, **Symcox**.

Simble see SEMPLE

Simel see SEMMEL

Simiński see SIEMIŃSKI

Simkin 1. English (W Midlands): from the ME given name of this form, a dim. of SIM. 2. Jewish (E Ashkenazic): metr. from *Simke*, a pet form of the Yid. female given name

Sime, from Hebr. *Simcha* 'Joy', with the Slav. metr. suffix *-in*.

Vars. (of 1): **Simpkin**, **Sinkin**, **Semkin**. (Of 2): **Simkovic(h)**, **Simkovitz**, **Simkievitz**, **Simkovits**.

Patrs. (from 1): **Sim(p)kins**, **Sim(p)kiss**, **Sinkin(g)s**, **Sempkins**, **Simpkinson**, **Sinkinson**.

Simmer see SUMMER

Simon English, French, German, Flemish/Dutch, Czech, Hungarian, and Jewish (Ashkenazic): from the Hebr. personal name *Shim'on*, which is probably derived from the verb *sham'a* to hearken. In the Vulgate and in many vernacular versions of the Old Testament, this is usually rendered as *Simeon*. In the New Testament, however, the name is normally rendered *Simōn*, partly as a result of association with the pre-existing Gk byname *Sīmōn* (from *sīmos* snub-nosed). Both *Simon* and *Simeon* were in use as given names in W Europe from the Middle Ages onwards. However, the former was far more popular, no doubt because of its associations with the apostle Simon Peter, the brother of Andrew. In Britain there was also confusion from an early date with Anglo-Scandinavian forms of *Sigmund* (see SIEGMUND), a name whose popularity was reinforced at the Conquest by the Norman form *Simund*. This confusion is also found in other languages, e.g. Italian.

Vars.: Eng.: **Simeon**, **Simion**; **Symon** (Scots); **Simmen**. Fr.: **Simeon**. Ger.: **Simmon**, **Siemon**. Jewish: **S(c)himon**, **Szymon**, **Szimon**; **S(h)imoni**, **S(h)imony**, **Schimoni**, **Szimoni**, **Szymoni** (with the Hebr. suffix *-i*).

Dims.: Eng.: SIM, **Sim(o)nett**, **Sim(m)onite**, **Simnel(l)**. Fr.: **Simonel**, **Sim(e)nel**, **Simoneau**, **Simon(n)et**, **Simounet**, **Simenet**, **Simon(et)on**, **Simonou**, **Simenon**, **Simon(n)ot**, **Simenot**, **Simon(n)in**, **Simony**, **Sémonin**. It.: **Simonetti**, **Simonetto**, **Simonitto**, **Simonutti**, **Simon(c)elli**, **Simoncello**, **Scimonelli**, **Simon(c)ini**, **Simeoli**, **Simioli**, **Monetti**, **Monelli**, **Monini**. Ger.: **Siemandl**, **Siemantel** (Bavaria). Low Ger.: **Simmgen**. Fris.: **Zie(h)m**, **Ziemke**. Ger. (of Slav. origin): **Schimonek**, **Schimank**, **Schimmang**, **Simmank**, **Schimek**, **Simmig**, **Schim(p)ke**, **Schimaschke**, **Zima**, **Zimek**; **Manske**, **Manntschke**. Czech: **Šimek**, **Šimeček**, **Šimáček**, **Šimánek**, **Šimůnek**; **Ších(a)**. Pol.: **Szymczyk**, **Szymanek**, **Szymanczyk**. Ukr.: **Simchenko**, **Senchenko**, **Semechik**. Beloruss.: **Shimuk**. Jewish: **Simanenko**, **Simko**. Hung.: **Simó**, **Simka**, **Simkó**.

Pejs.: Fr.: **Simonard**. It.: **Simonazzi**, **Simonassi**, **Sim(i)onato**.

Patrs.: Eng.: **Sim(m)on(d)s**, **Simeons**; **Sym(m)ons** (Devon); **Symonds** (chiefly E Anglia); **Simmens**, **Simmins**, **Sim(m)ans**, **Simmance**; **Simonson**, **Symondson**, **Simison**, **Simyson**; **Fitzsimmons**. It.: **De Simone**, **De Simoni**, **Simoneschi**. Port.: **Simões**. Rum.: **Simionescu**. Low Ger.: **Simons(en)**. Flem.: **Simo(e)ns**, **Moens**. Du.: **Si(e)mons**, **Sijmons**. Norw., Dan.: **Simonsen**. Swed.: **Simonsson**. Ger. (of Slav. origin): **Schiemen(t)z**. Pol.: **Szymanowicz**, **Szymonowicz**, **Szymaniak**. Ukr.: **Simonich**, **Semenovich**. Beloruss.: **Simonich**, **Shimonov**, **Semyanovich**. Russ.: **Sim(e)onov**, **Semyonov**, **Semanov**. Lithuanian: **Simonaitis**, **Semenas**. Hung.: **Simonf(f)y**. Croatian: **Sim(on)ović**, **Simić**, **Šimić**. Armenian: **Simonian**. Jewish: **Simons**, **Simonso(h)n** (Ashkenazic); **Simonov**, **Simonof**, **Simonow**, **Simonovitch**, **Simonowicz**, **Simonowitz**, **Simon(ov)itz**, **Shimonoff**, **Shimonov(ich)**, **Shimonovitz**, **S(c)himonowitz**, **Szymonowicz** (E Ashkenazic); **Simonovici** (a Rum. spelling).

Patrs. (from dims.): Eng.: **Syson** (Notts.). Sc.: **McKimmie** (Gael. **Mac Shimidh**). Fris.: **Zie(h)ms**, **Ziemens**, **Ziemsen**. Russ.: **Simonin**, **Sim(ak)ov**, **Simukov**, **Simushin**, **Simulin**, **Sim(y)agin**, **Simarov**, **Semyonychev**, **Semichev**, **Semakin**, **Semyashkin**,

Semchishchev, **Sem(en)ischev**, **Semen(n)ikov**, **Semenyutin**, **Sementsov**, **Semendyaev**, **Senyagin**, **Senyavin**, **Sentyurin**, **Syomin**. Pol.: **Szymankiewicz**, **Szymczykiewicz**; **Szymczak**. Lithuanian: **Schimkat**, **Schimkus**. Jewish (E Ashkenazic): **Simkovic(h)**, **Simkovitz**, **Szymkiewicz**, **Shimkevicz**, **Shimkevich**, **Shimkewitz**, **Shimkevitz** (based on the E Yid. pet form *Shimke*).

'Son of the wife of S.': Russ.: **Semyonikhin**.

'Son of the wife of S. (dim.)': Russ.: **Semchikhin**, **Sentyurikhin**. Ukr.: **Semchishin**.

Habitation names: Pol.: **Szymanowski**, **Szymczewski**, **Szymczyński**. Czech: **Šimononský**.

Simond *see* SIEGMUND

Simper *see* SAMPER

Simson 1. English: patr. from the medieval given name SIM. 2. German and Jewish (Ashkenazic): var. of SAMSON. Vars. (of 1): **Simpson**; **Sim(m)s**, **Sym(m)s**; **Simes**, **Symes**.

Simulev *see* SAMUEL

Sinatra Italian: from a given name borne by both men and women in Sicily and S Calabria. The name was apparently in origin a nickname from L *senātor* member of the Roman senate (L *senātus*, a deriv. of *senex* old), which later came to be used as a title of magistrates in various It. states.

Var.: **Sinatora**.

Sinclair 1. Scots and English (Norman): habitation name from *Saint-Clair*-sur-Elle in La Manche or *Saint-Clair*-l'Évêque in Calvados, so called from the dedication of their chuches to St *Clarus* (see CLARE 1). 2. French: habitation name from the same places as in 1 above or from others of the same name in other parts of France.

Vars.: Eng.: **Sinclaire**, **Saint-Clair**, **Saint-Clare**. Fr.: **Sainclair**, **Saint-Clair**.

Sincock *see* SIM

Singers *see* SANGER

Singleton English: habitation name from places in Lancs. and Sussex. The former seems from the present-day distribution of the surname to be the major source, and is named from OE *scingel* shingle(s) + *tūn* enclosure, settlement; the latter gets its name from OE *sengel* burnt clearing + *tūn*.

Sinisbury *see* SAINSBURY

Sinkin *see* SIMKIN

Sinnott English and Irish: from the ME given name *Sinod*, OE *Sigenōð*, composed of the elements *sige* victory + *nōð* brave.

Vars.: **Synot**, **Synnot(t)**, **Sinnett**, **Sinnatt**, **Senet**, **Sennett**, **Sennitt**.

Sinton Scots: habitation name from a place near Selkirk, also spelled *Synton*. In the 12th and 13th cents. it is recorded several times as *Sintun*. The origin of the first element is uncertain; the second is clearly OE *tūn* enclosure, settlement.

Sinyard *see* SENIOR

Siosbrick *see* SCARISBRICK

Šíp Czech: from Czech *šíp* arrow, perhaps applied as a nickname for a thin man or a swift runner, or as a metonymic occupational name for an archer.

Dim.: **Šípek** (as a vocab. word, this also means 'dogrose' or 'briar', the thorns being likened to little arrows; the surname may therefore also be topographic for someone who lived by a briar patch).

Sipp *see* SIEBERT

Sippings *see* SEPPINGS

Sircutt *see* CIRCUIT

Sire *see* SEIGNEUR

Sired *see* SYRETT

Sirkes *see* SORIN

Sirman *see* SERMON

Sirota *see* SIEROTA

Siskin *see* ZISIN

Siskind *see* SÜSSKIND

Sisley English: from the medieval female given name *Sisley, Cecilie* (L *Caecilia*, fem. form of the Roman family name *Caecilius*, originally a deriv. of *caecus* blind). This was the name of a Roman virgin martyr of the 2nd or 3rd cent., who came to be regarded as the patron saint of music.

Var.: **Sicely**.

Dim.: Eng.: **Sisson**.

Metrs. (from dims.): Eng.: **Sissons**, **Sissens**; **Sisterson** (Northumb.; from earlier *Sissotson*, altered by folk etymology).

Sissmilch *see* SWEET

Sitarz Polish: occupational name for a maker or seller of sieves, Pol. *sitarz* (from *sito* sieve).

Var.: **Sitarski**.

Dim.: **Sitarek**.

Sitch *see* SYKES

Sittart, van Dutch: habitation name from a place in the province of Limburg.

Sittich German: 1. nickname for a courteous person, from Ger. *sittig* demure, well-behaved (MHG *sitec*, a deriv. of *site* custom, use, OHG *situ*). 2. nickname for someone supposedly resembling a parrot, from Ger. *Sittich* parakeet (MHG, OHG *sitich*, L *psittacus*, from Gk).

Sitwell English: of uncertain origin. It would appear to be a habitation name from an unidentified place with a second element from OE *well(a)* spring, stream, but on the other hand early forms are found without prepositions, so it may be a phrasal nickname.

Var.: **Sidwell**.

Sivertsen *see* SIEGFRIED

Siviter *see* SILVESTER

Siwek *see* SIWIEC

Siwiec Polish: nickname for a grey-haired man, Pol. *siwiec*, from *siwy* grey.

Dim.: **Siwek**.

Habitation name: Pol.: **Siwiński**.

Six 1. French and German: from a given name (L *Sixtus*, a var. of *Sextus* 'Sixth(-born)'), borne by various saints and popes in the early cents. of the Christian era, and subsequently adopted in their honour. **2.** French: nickname from OF *six* six (L *sex*), given for some anecdotal reason now lost (cf. SHOSTAKOVICH); the surnames **Deux** ('Two'), **Huit** ('Eight'), and **Dix** ('Ten') also exist, but all are rare. In English, the surname **Eighteen** is attested, of similarly obscure anecdotal origin.

Vars. (of 1): Ger.: **Sixt(us)**.

Dims. (of 1): Ger.: **Sixl** (Bavaria). It.: **Sestini**.

Sixsmith English (Lancs.): apparently an occupational name for a SMITH, but with a first element of obscure origin. It may conceivably be from ME *sikel* sickle (OE *sicel*, *sicol*), in which case it denotes a maker of sickles. The surname is first attested in 1590.

Sizebrick *see* SCARISBRICK

Sjöberg *see* SEE

Skaife *see* SCAIFE

Skakle *see* SHACKELL

Skally *see* SCULLY

Skalski Polish: topographic name for someone who lived by a rock or crag, Pol. *skała*.

Var.: **Skałecki**.

Škarda Czech: nickname for a sullen individual, from Czech *škaredý* sullen, sour-faced.

Skate *see* SKEAT

Skeat N English: from the ON byname *Skjótr* 'Swift'.

Vars.: **Skeate**, **Skeet(e)**, **Skate**; **Skett** (W Midlands).

Patrs.: **Skeat(e)s**, **Skates**.

Skeffington English: habitation name from a place in Leics., so called from OE *Scēaftingtūn* 'settlement (OE *tūn*) associated with *Scēaft*', a byname meaning 'Shaft', 'Spear'. The initial consonant cluster has been modified from /ʃ/ to /sk/ as a result of Scandinavian influence.

Vars.: **Skiffington**, **Skevington**, **Skivington**.

Skegg N English: from the ON byname *Skegg* 'Beard'.

Patr.: **Skeggs**.

Skelding English: habitation name from a place in W Yorks., near Ripon, also known as *Skelden*. It is so called from the river name *Skell* (ON *Skjallr* 'Resounding'; cf. SHILLINGFORD) + OE *denu* valley (see DEAN 1).

Skeldon Scots and N English: habitation name from a place in Ayrs., probably so called from OE *scylf* shelf, ledge + *dūn* hill, with later change of /ʃ/ to /sk/ under Scandinavian influence; cf. SHELDON.

Skelly *see* SCULLY

Skelton N English: habitation name from places in Cumb. and Yorks., originally named with the same elem-

ents as SHELTON, but with later change of /ʃ-/ to /sk-/ under Scandinavian influence.

Var.: **Skilton** (N England and Yorks., also N Ireland).

Skene Scots: habitation name from a place in the former county of Aberdeens., so called from Gael. *sceathin* bush.

Vars.: **Skeen(e)**.

Skepper *see* SKIPPER

Skermer *see* SCRIMGEOUR

Skevington *see* SKEFFINGTON

Skewes *see* SKUSE

Skiba Polish: topographic name from Pol. *skiba* ridge.

Var.: **Skibicki**.

Habitation name: **Skibiński**.

Skidmore *see* SCUDAMORE

Skierski *see* SIEKIERA

Skiffington *see* SKEFFINGTON

Skilton *see* SKELTON

Skinner English: occupational name for someone who stripped the hide from animals, to be used in the production of fur garments or to be tanned for leather, from an agent deriv. of ME *skin* hide, pelt (ON *skinn*). The much rarer var. **Shinner** is from the OE cogn. *scinn*, displaced in the ME period by the Scandinavian form.

Vars.: **Skyn(n)er**, **Skin**; **Shinn**, **Shynn**.

Skipper English (chiefly Norfolk): **1.** occupational name for the master of a ship, ME *skipper* (from MLG, MDu. *schipper*; cf. SHIPMAN 2). **2.** occupational name for an acrobat or professional tumbler, or nickname for a high-spirited person, from an agent deriv. of ME *skip(en)* to jump, spring (apparently of Scandinavian origin). **3.** occupational name for a basket-maker, from an agent deriv. of ME *skipp(e)*, *skepp(e)* basket, hamper (ON *skeppa*; cf. SCHÄFFLER).

Vars. (of 3): **Skepper**; **Skipp**.

Skipsey English (Northumb.): habitation name from *Skipsea* in N Yorks., so called from Northern ME *skip* ship (ON *skip*) + *see* lake, pond (OE *sǣ*).

Skipwith English (Yorks.): habitation name from a place in Yorks., recorded in Domesday Book as *Schipwic*, from OE *scēap*, *scīp* sheep + *wīc* outlying settlement (see WICK). Under later Scandinavian influence the initial /ʃ-/ became /sk-/ and the second element was changed to *-with* (ON *viðr* wood).

Var.: **Skipworth** (Lincs.).

Skirmer *see* SCRIMGEOUR

Skitt *see* SCUTT

Skoczylas Polish: topographic name for someone who lived by a dam on a stream or river in a forest, from an OPol. word composed of the elements *skok-* dam (akin to *skoczy-* to leap) + *las* forest.

Škoda Czech: from the vocab. word *skoda* damage, loss; apparently a nickname denoting someone whose property had been damaged or who had a financial claim on someone else.

Skoler *see* SCHULER

Skoneczny *see* KONIECZNY

Skóra Polish: metonymic occupational name for a leather-worker or tanner, from Pol. *skóra* leather.
Vars.: **Skórski**, **Skórnik**.
Dims.: **Skórka**, **Skórek**, SKOREK.
Habitation name: **Skórzewski**.

Skorek Polish: **1.** var. of *Skórek*, dim. of SKÓRA. **2.** nickname from Pol. *skory* eager. **3.** offensive nickname meaning 'Earwig'.

Skorokhodov Russian: patr. from the nickname *Skorokhod*, denoting a runner or messenger, from *skoro* swiftly + *khodit* to go, walk.

Skorupa Polish: nickname for someone with a rough skin or a skin disease, or for a 'crusty' individual, from Pol. *skorupa* crust, shell.
Var.: **Skorupski**.

Skovgård Danish: habitation name from a place so called from the elements *scov* copse (cf. SHAW) + *gård* enclosure, farm (cf. GARTH).

Skowron Polish: nickname for a happy, cheerful person, from Pol. *skowronek* skylark.
Var.: **Skowroński**.
Dim.: Czech: **Skřivánek**.

Skrimshire *see* SCRIMGEOUR

Skřivánek *see* SKOWRON

Skrzydlewski Polish: habitation name from some place named with Pol. *skrzydło* wing, probably in the sense of a 'wing-shaped' piece of land + *-ew* possessive suffix, with the addition of *-ski*, suffix of local surnames (see BARANOWSKI).

Skrzypek Polish: occupational name for a violinist or fiddler, Pol. *skrzypek* (from *skrzypieć* to creak, groan, ultimately cogn. with Eng. *scrape*).
Var.: **Skrzypczak**.
Habitation names: **Skrzypiński**, **Skrzypczyński**.

Skulnik *see* SCHULER

Skupień Polish: apparently from Pol. *skupić* to buy up (perhaps a nickname for a shrewd businessman), or from another word of the same form, meaning 'to mass or concentrate in one place'.
Var.: **Skupiński**.

Skuse Cornish: habitation name from any of various minor places named with Corn. *skaw* elder bush + the suffix of location *-es*.
Vars.: **Scuce**, **Skew(e)s**, **Skewis**.

Skvortsov Russian: patr. from the nickname *Skvorets* 'Starling' (of apparently imitative origin).

Skwara Polish: apparently a nickname from OPol. *skwara* scorching heat, *skwarny* scorching, although the applica-

tion is not clear. It may have been applied to a 'hot-tempered' person.
Vars.: **Skwarski**, **Skwarnecki**.
Dim.: **Skwarnek**.

Skyner *see* SKINNER

Słaby Polish: nickname for a weak and feeble individual, from Pol. *słaby* weak.
Vars.: **Słabicki**, **Słabiak**.

Slack English (chiefly N Midlands): **1.** topographic name for someone who lived in a shallow valley, Northern ME *slack* (ON *slakki*) or habitation name from one of the places named with this term, for example near Stainland and near Hebden Bridge in W Yorks. **2.** nickname for an idle or indolent person, from ME *slack* lazy, careless (OE *slæc*).
Var.: **Slacke**.

Slade S English: topographic name for someone who lived in a small valley, OE *slæd*, or habitation name from any of the minor places named with this word, for example in Devon and Somerset, or *Slad* in Gloucs.
Var.: **Slader**.

Sládek Czech: occupational name for a maltster, from Czech *slad* malt.
Vars.: **Sladovník**, **Sladovský**.

Sladen English: probably a habitation name from an unidentified place. The original form is *Sloden*, perhaps from OE elements *slōh* slough (see SLOW 1) + *denu* valley (see DEAN 1).
Var.: **Sladden**.

Slater English: occupational name for someone who covered roofs with slate, from an agent deriv. of ME *s(c)late* slate (OF *esclate*, a var. of *esclat* splinter, slat, of Gmc origin, akin to OHG *sleizen* to tear).
Vars.: **Slator**, **Sclater**, **Slatter**, **Slate**.

Slatin *see* ZLATIN

Slattery Irish: Anglicized form of Gael. **Ó Slat(ar)ra** 'descendant of *Slatra*', a byname meaning 'Robust', 'Strong', 'Bold'.
Vars.: **O'Slattery**, **O'Slattra**.

Slaughter English: **1.** occupational name for a slaughterer of animals, ME *slahter* (a agent deriv. of *slaht* killing, OE *slēaht*). **2.** topographic name for someone who lived by a muddy spot, ME *sloghtre* (OE **slōhtre*, a deriv. of *slōh*; see SLOW 1), or habitation name from a place named with this term, for example Upper and Lower *Slaughter* in Gloucs. **3.** topographic name for someone who lived by a sloe tree, OE *slāhtrēow* (cf. SLOW 3).
Vars.: **Slagter**, **Slafter**. (Of 1 only): **Slayter**, **Slaytor**, **Sleator**.

Slavíček *see* SŁOWIK

Slavin Jewish (E Ashkenazic): metr. from the Yid. female given name *Slave* (from the Slav. word *slava* glory, fame, praise) + the Slav. metr. suffix *-in*.
Vars.: **Slawin**; **Slovin**, **Slowes** (from the variant given name *Slove*).

Slawin *see* SLAVIN

Sławiński Polish: from any of the numerous Pol. given names containing the element *sław* glory, fame, praise. The surname has the form of a habitation name.

Slay English: 1. metonymic occupational name for someone who made slays, instruments used in weaving to push the weft thread that had just been laid tightly against the thread of the preceding pass of the shuttle. The name is from ME *slaye* (OE *slege*, from *slēan* to strike). 2. topographic name for someone who lived by a grassy slope, ME *slay* (OE *slēa*).

Var. (of 1): **Slaymaker**.

Slazenger see SCHLESSINGER

Sleath see SLY

Sleator see SLAUGHTER

Slechten see SCHLECHT

Slesinger see SCHLESSINGER

Slevin Irish: Anglicized form of Gael. **Ó Sléibhín** 'descendant of *Sléibhín*', a personal name representing a dim. of *sliabh* mountain (perhaps originally a short form of *Dunnshléibhe*; see DUNLEAVY).

Sleymovich see SALOMON

Sligh see SLY

Slight Scots: 1. nickname from Northern ME *sleght, slyght* smooth, sleek, slender, slim (apparently of ON origin). 2. nickname from ME *sleghth* craft, cunning, dexterity, adroitness (ON *slǽgð*, a deriv. of *slǽgr* SLY).

Slim English: topographic name for someone who lived in a muddy area, from OE *slīm* slime, mud. The mod. Eng. adj. *slim* slender (from Low Ger. or Du.) is not found before the 17th cent.

Slinger N English: occupational name for a soldier or hunter armed with a sling, or nickname for someone who was a particularly good shot with this weapon, from an agent deriv. of ME *sling* strap for hurling stones (of Low Ger. origin).

Slingsby English: habitation name from a place in N Yorks., so called from the gen. case of the ON byname *Slengr* 'Idle' + ON *býr* farm, settlement.

Śliwa Polish: metonymic occupational name for a grower or seller of plums, from Pol. *śliwa* plum, or possibly a nickname from the same word.

Habitation name: Pol.: **Śliwiński**.

Sloan Scots and N Irish: Anglicized form of the Gael. personal name *Sluaghadhán*, a dim. of *Sluaghadh* (see SLOWEY).

Vars.: **Sloane**, **Slo(y)ne**, **Slowan**, **Sloyan**.

Slocombe English (W Country): habitation name from a place, as for example *Slocum* on the Isle of Wight and in Devon, named with the OE elements *slāh* sloe (see SLOW 3) + *cumb* valley (see COOMBE).

Vars.: **Slocom**, **Slocum**.

Słodski Polish: nickname meaning 'Sweet, Lovely', with the addition of the surname suffix *-ski* (see BARANOWSKI).

Var.: **Słodak**.

Patr. (from a dim.): Pol.: **Słodkiewicz**.

Słomka see SALOMON

Słomkowski Polish: habitation name from a place named with Pol. *słomka* woodcock + *-ów* possessive suffix, with the addition of *-ski*, suffix of local surnames (see BARANOWSKI).

Słomski Polish: from Pol. *słoma* straw + *-ski* suffix of surnames (see BARANOWSKI). The application as a surname is not clear; it may be an occupational name for a dealer in straw or a nickname for someone with straw-coloured hair (cf. STRAW).

Habitation names: **Słomiński**; **Słomczewski**, **Słomczyński** (the latter two could also be vars. of SŁOMKOWSKI).

Sloper English: occupational name for a maker of loose overgarments, from an agent deriv. of ME *slop(e)* overall (apparently of OE origin, akin to *slūpan* to slip, reinforced by a MLG cogn.).

Slough see SLOW

Slovák Czech: ethnic name for someone from Slovakia (Czech *Slovensko*); the name is possibly derived from the Slav. element *slov-* speak, talk.

Dim.: **Slováček**.

Slovin see SLAVIN

Slow English: 1. topographic name for someone who lived near a swamp or bog, from OE *slōh* slough, or habitation name from one of the various places, for example *Slough* in Berks., named with this word. 2. nickname for a sluggish or stupid person, from ME *slōw* (OE *slāw*; for the change of vowel, cf. ROPER). 3. topographic name for someone who lived by a sloe tree, ME *slōh* (OE *slāh*).

Vars.: **Slowe**, SLOWMAN. (Of 1 only): **Slough**.

Slowey Irish: Anglicized form of Gael. **Ó Sluaghadhaigh** 'descendant of *Sluaghadhach*', a personal name derived from *sluaghadh* expedition, raid.

Vars.: **O'Slowey**, **Slo(e)y**.

Słowik Polish: nickname for a good singer, or else a nighttime reveller, from Pol. *słowik* nightingale.

Dim.: Czech: **Slavíček**.

Habitation names: Pol.: **Słowikowski**; **Słowiński** (there are cases on record of the Ger. surname *Nachtigall* (see NIGHTINGALE) being altered to *Słowiński*).

Slowman 1. English: var. of SLOW. 2. Scots: var. of SLOAN.

Vars. (of 1): Eng.: **Sloman**, **Sluman**.

Sluis Dutch: topographic name for someone who lived by a lock or weir, MDu. *sluis* (OF *escluse*, from LL *exclūsa (aqua)*, past part. of *exclūdere* to dam, keep out). Some examples of the name may derive from a town in the province of Zeeland, founded in the 13th cent. and named with this word.

Vars.: **Van der Sluis**, **Van (der) Sluijs**, **Van (der) Sluys**, **Verslui(j)s**, **Versluys**.

Sluman *see* SLOWMAN

Ślusarski Polish: occupational name for an ironworker or locksmith, Pol. *ślusarz*, with the addition of -*ski*, suffix of surnames (see BARANOWSKI).
Dims.: Pol.: **Ślusarczyk, Ślusarek**.

Slutsky Jewish (NE Ashkenazic): habitation name from *Slutsk*, a city in the province of Minsk, Belorussia.
Vars.: **Slutski, Slutzk(y), Slucky, Slucki; Slutzker**.

Sly English (chiefly W Midlands): nickname for a cunning or crafty individual, from Midland and Southern ME *sligh* sly (earlier *slegh*, from ON *slægr*).
Vars.: **Sligh, Slyman, Sliman, Slimmon, Slimming; Slee(man); Slemming** (N England); **Sleith, Sleath** (Yorks.).
Patrs.: **Slemmings, Slemmonds**.

Small English: nickname for a person of slender build or diminutive stature, from ME *smal* thin, narrow, small (OE *smæl*).
Vars.: **Smale** (Cornwall), **Smaile** (Scotland); **Smeal(l)**.
Patrs.: Eng.: **Small(e)s, Smales; Smailes** (Northumb.), **Smiles** (Scotland). Low Ger.: **Schmeling**.

Smallen *see* SPILLANE

Smalley English: habitation name from places in Derbys. and Lancs, so called from OE *smæl* narrow (see SMALL) + *lēah* wood, clearing.
Var.: **Smally**; SMILEY.

Smallman English: ostensibly a nickname for a small man, but the vocab. word was also used as a technical term of feudalism to denote an inferior tenant, and so the surname may in fact be a status name with this origin.
Var.: **Smalman**.

Smallshaw English (Lancs.): habitation name from a place in W Yorks., so called from OE *smæl* narrow (see SMALL) + *sceaga* copse (see SHAW).

Smallwood English (chiefly W Midlands): habitation name from a place in Ches., so called from OE *smæl* narrow (see SMALL) + *wudu* WOOD.

Smart English: nickname for a brisk or active person, from ME *smart* quick, prompt (OE *smeart* stinging, painful, from *smeortan* to sting, hurt).
Var.: **Smartman**.

Smeal *see* SMALL

Smeaton English and Scots: habitation name from any of various places, notably *Smeaton* near Edinburgh and in N and W Yorks., or *Smeeton* in Leics., all so called from OE *Smiðatūn* 'settlement (OE *tūn*) of the smiths'.
Vars.: **Smeeton, Smieton**.

Smeder *see* SMITH

Smedley English (Notts): apparently a habitation name from an unidentified place, perhaps so called from OE *smēðe* smooth (see SMEETH) + *lēah* wood, clearing.

Smeesters *see* MASTER

Smeeth English: ostensibly a topographic name for someone who lived on a piece of smooth, level ground, from ME *smethe* smooth (OE *smēðe*), or a nickname from the same word used in a transferred sense for someone of an amiable disposition. However, it is more probably simply a spelling var. of SMITH.
Vars.: **Smee(d), Smead, Smeath(man)**.

Šmejkal Czech: apparently a deriv. of Czech *smýkat* to drag, perhaps a nickname for someone with a bad limp.

Smellie *see* SMILLIE

Smerdon English (Devon): habitation name from *Smeardon* Down in the parish of Petertavy, so called from OE *smeoru* butter + *dūn* hill.

Smetana Czech and Jewish (E Ashkenazic): nickname from Czech *smetana* soured cream, given perhaps to someone who was particularly fond of this food. It may also have been a metonymic occupational name for a trader in dairy products.
Var.: Jewish: **Smetanka**.

Smethurst English (Lancs.): habitation name from a minor place near Manchester, so called from OE *smēðe* smooth (see SMEETH) + *hyrst* (wooded) hill (see HURST).

Smeyers *see* MAYER

Śmiałkowski Polish: habitation name from a place named with Pol. *śmiałek* brave man, hero (from *śmiały* brave) + -*ów* possessive suffix, with the addition of -*ski*, suffix of local surnames (see BARANOWSKI).

Śmiech Polish: nickname for a cheerful person who was always laughing, from Pol. *śmiech* laughter.
Patr.: Pol.: **Śmiechowicz**.
Habitation name: Pol.: **Śmiechowski**.

Smieton *see* SMEATON

Śmigielski *see* SZMIGIEL

Smiles *see* SMALL

Smiley Scots: of uncertain origin, probably a var. of SMILLIE, but perhaps a habitation name representing a var. of SMALLEY, or a nickname from ME *smile* smile, grin (probably of Scand. origin).
Var.: **Smylie**.

Smillie Scots: nickname for someone notorious for giving off a smell that was obnoxious even by medieval standards, or for someone who made great use of perfumes and pomanders to counteract this tendency in an age when such measures were not generally considered necessary. The word is a deriv. of ME *smil, smel* odour.
Var.: **Smellie**.

Smirnyagin Russian: patr. from the nickname *Smirnyaga*, denoting a quiet, humble person (from the adj. *smirnoi*, a deriv. of the Slav. element *mera* measure, restraint, but early associated by folk etymology with *mir* peace, quiet).
Var.: **Smirnov**.

Smith English: occupational name for a worker in metal, ME *smith*, OE *smið* (probably a deriv. of *smītan* to strike, hammer). Metal-working was one of the earliest occupations for which specialist skills were required, and its importance ensured that this term and its cogns. and equivalents were perhaps the most widespread of all occupational surnames in Europe. Medieval smiths were important not only in making horseshoes, ploughshares, and other domestic articles, but above all for their skill in forging swords, other weapons, and armour. Brett has calculated that there are about 187,000 subscribers named *Smith* in British telephone directories; his regional study shows that the name is most common in the Aberdeen area, with a distribution of 184 per 10,000, and that it is also common throughout the Midlands and again in E Anglia. It is least common in Wales and the W Country.

Vars.: **Smyth**, Smythe; **Smither** (with the ME agent suffix -*er*).

Dims.: Ger.: **Schmiedel**, **Schmiedle**. Low Ger.: **Schmedeke**, **Schmädicke**, **Schmedtje**. Czech: **Šmídek**.

Patrs.: Eng.: **Smithson**, **Smythson**, **Smisson**; **Smithers**. Ger.: **Schmitz**. Low Ger.: **Smets**, **Smuts**, **S(ch)meder**; **Schmedding**. Flem., Du.: **Smits**, **Smets**.

Patrs. (from a dim.): Flem.: **Smeken(s)**.

'Servant of the smith': Eng.: **Smidman**, **Smitherman**.

Cpds: Eng.: **Blacksmith**, Shoesmith (working in iron, usually for domestic purposes); **Brownsmith**, Coppersmith; **Greensmith** (working in lead); **Redsmith**, Goldsmith; Sixsmith; **Whitesmith** (working in tin).

Equivs. (of 1, not cogn.): Celtic: Gough. Fr.: Fèvre. Pol.: Kowalski. Russ.: Kuznetsov. Finn.: Seppänen. Lithuanian: Kálvaitis.

Smithe see Smythe

Smolarek Polish: occupational name for a distiller of pitch, from a dim. of Pol. *smolarz* pitch-burner, from *smoła* pitch.

Dim.: Czech: **Smolík**.

Smolders see Miller

Smoleński Polish: habitation name from the city of *Smolensk* in Russia, which was a great trade centre in medieval times. The placename probably derives from Slav. *smola* pitch, because of tar pits in the region.

Smollan see Spillane

Smollett English and Scots: nickname for a person with delicate features or of meagre intelligence, from ME *smal* Small + *heved* head (OE *hēafod*).

Smrček Czech: topographic name for someone who lived by a clump of spruce trees, Czech *smrček* (a deriv. of *smrk* spruce), or habitation name from a place named with this word.

Var.: **Smrčka**.

Smulczyk see Samuel

Smulders see Miller

Smullen see Spillane

Smutný Czech: nickname for a person with a gloomy disposition, from Czech *smutný* sad.

Smuts see Smith

Smylie see Smiley

Smyth see Smith

Smythe English: 1. topographic name for someone who lived by a forge, ME *smithe* (OE *smiððe*), or occupational name for someone employed at a forge. 2. spelling var. of Smith.

Vars.: **Smithe**. (Of 1 only): **Smithies**, **Smithyes**, **Smythyes**; **Athersmith**.

Snadden see Snowden

Snaith English: habitation name from a place in Humberside near Goole (formerly in W Yorks.), so called from ON *sneið* piece of land, or from the same word used independently in other minor place names. The surname is commonest in the Newcastle and Sunderland areas.

Vars.: **Sneath**; **Snee(d)**, **Snead**, **Sneyd** (apparently from a cogn. OE **snǣd*); **Snoad**, **Snode** (from OE **snād*).

Snape 1. N English and Scots: habitation name from any of various places in N England and S Scotland, for example in N Yorks. near Bedale and in the Lowlands near Biggar, so called from ON *snap* poor grazing, winter pasture. 2. habitation name from any of various minor places in S England named with the cogn. OE word *snæp*. In Sussex the dial. term *snape* is still used of boggy uncultivable land.

Snead see Snaith

Snedden see Snowden

Snell English: nickname for a brisk or active person, from ME *snell* quick, lively, in part representing a survival of the OE personal name *Snell* or the cogn. ON *Snjallr*.

Vars.: **Snel(l)man** (also 'servant of S.').

Patrs.: Eng.: **Snelling**; **Snelson**.

Snellgrove English: apparently a habitation name from an unidentified place, perhaps so called from OE *snæg(e)l* snail (cf. Schneck) + *grāf* grove.

Vars.: **Snelgrove**, **Snellgrave**.

Sneyders see Schneider

Śniady Polish: nickname for a person with dark hair or a dark complexion, from Pol. *śniady* tawny, swarthy.

Snider see Schneider

Snoad see Snaith

Snoddy Scots and N Irish: nickname from Northern ME *snod* neat, trim, smart (probably of Scand. origin; cf. Snodgrass) + a dim. suffix.

Var.: **Snoddie**.

Snodgrass Scots: habitation name from a minor place near Irvine in the former county of Ayrs., so called from Northern ME *snod* smooth, sleek, even (probably of Scand. origin; cf. ON *snoðinn* bald) + *grass* grass.

Var.: **Snodgers**.

Snook English: topographic name for someone who lived on a projecting piece of land, ME *snoke* (OE **snōc*). It is possible that this term was also used as a nickname for someone with a long nose.

Patr.: Eng.: **Snooks**.

Snow 1. English: nickname denoting someone with very white hair or an exceptionally pale complexion, from OE *snāw* snow. **2.** Jewish (Ashkenazic): Anglicized and shortened form of any of the ornamental cpds listed below.

Dims.: Eng.: **Snowling**. Ger.: **Schneele**, **Schnelli** (Swiss).

Cpds (ornamental): Jewish: **Shneebaum**, **Schneibaum**, **Schneubaum** ('snow tree'); **Schneeberg**, **Sznejberg** ('snow hill', the latter a Pol. spelling); **Schneeweiss** ('snow white').

Snowball English (Northumb.): apparently a nickname from ME *snawball* snowball, given either for some anecdotal reason now irrecoverable, or (as Reaney suggests) with reference to a white streak or bald spot in dark hair.

Snowden English: habitation name from a place in W Yorks., so called from OE *snāw* SNOW + *dūn* hill (see DOWN 1), i.e. a hill where snow lies long.

Vars.: **Snawdon**; **Snowdon** (a place in Devon, and the name of the highest mountain in Wales, as well as the former name of *Snow End* in Herts. and *Snow Hill* in Windsor, Berks.); **Snoddon**, **Sneddon**, **Snedden**, **Snadden** (Scots, from a place near Dumfries).

Snyders see SCHNEIDER

Soal see SOLE

Soame English: habitation name from places in Cambs. and Suffolk called *Soham*, from OE *sā* sea, lake (a byform of *sǣ*) + *hām* homestead.

Vars.: **So(a)mes**.

Soane English: distinguishing epithet for a son (ME *sone*, OE *sunu*) who shared the same given name as his father.

Vars.: **Son(n)**, **Sone**, **Soan**.

Dims.: Ger.: **Söhnlein**, **Söhndl**. Low Ger.: **Söhnchen**, **Söhngen**, **Söhnke**.

Patrs.: Eng.: **Soan(e)s** (Norfolk), **Sones**. Low Ger.: **Sohns**, **Söhns**.

Patrs. (from dims.): Low Ger.: **Sohnker**, **Sönnecken**, **Sönnischen**, **Sönksen**.

Soaper see SOPER

Soar English (chiefly Notts.): **1.** topographic name for someone who lived by the river *Soar*, which is of Brit. origin, probably from a root **sar-* to flow. **2.** nickname for a person with reddish hair, from ANF *sor* chestnut (of Gmc origin, apparently referring originally to the colour of dry leaves).

Dims. (of 2): Eng.: **Sorrel(l)**, **Sorrill**. Fr.: **Sorel**, **Soreau**, **Saurel**, **Soret**, **Sauret**, **Sorin**, **Saurin**, **Saury**.

Aug. (of 2): Fr.: **Saurat**.

Patrs. (from 2): Eng.: **Soar(e)s**.

Soares see SUERO

Sobel Jewish (E Ashkenazic): nickname from Pol. *sobol*, a type of marten with handsome fur. The Eng. word *sable* derives from this source, via OHG *zobel* and OF *soble*, *sable*. In some cases the surname may have arisen as a metonymic occupational name for a trader in furs, but the name is too frequent and the number of Ashkenazic furriers too low at the time when surnames were taken for this explanation to be plausible in most cases. It is, rather, for the most part ornamental.

Vars.: **Sobol**, **Zobel**; **Sobelman**; **Soibelman** (from Yid. *soybl*).

Patrs.: Jewish: **Soboliev**, **Sobolewitz**.

Sobieraj Polish: anecdotal nickname for someone who coped well in difficult circumstances, from Pol. *sobie radzić* to manage, make shift.

Var.: **Sobierajski**.

Sobota 1. Polish and Czech: from Pol., Czech *Sobota* Saturday, a name bestowed on or taken by someone who was born, baptized, or registered on a Saturday, esp. a new convert to Christianity. **2.** Czech: deriv. of the personal name *Soběslav*, composed of elements meaning 'take for oneself', 'appropriate', 'usurp' + 'glory'.

Dims.: Czech: **Sobotka**. (Of 2 only): Pol.: **Sobek**, **Sobczyk**, **Sobieszek**.

Patrs. (from 2): Pol.: **Sobusiak**; **Sob(iesz)czak**, **Sobkiewicz** (from dims.).

Habitation name (from 2): Pol.: **Sobczyński**.

Sobral Portuguese: topographic name for someone who lived by a grove of cork oaks, Port. *sobral*, a collective of *sobro* cork oak (L *sūber*).

Sobrino Spanish: nickname from Sp. *sobrino*, a term of relationship applied to nephews and, in the Middle Ages, also to second and third cousins (L *sobrīnus* second cousin; cf. *consobrīnus* first COUSIN). The name was probably originally applied to someone who was related in this way to an important member of the community.

Socha 1. Polish and Czech: metonymic occupational name for a ploughman, from Pol., Czech *socha* a kind of simple plough. **2.** Czech: nickname for a strong man, from *socha* bar, column (var. of SOCHOR).

Vars. (of 1): Pol.: **Sochacki**, **Sochala**.

Sochor Czech: nickname for a man of exceptional strength, from a metaphorical use of the vocabulary word *sochor* strong pole, crowbar.

Dim.: **Sochůrek**.

Socol see SOKOL

Socquet see SUCH

Soden see SOWDEN

Söderbäck see SOUTH

Søegaard see SØGÅRD

Sofer Jewish: occupational name for a scribe, Hebr. *sofer*.

Vars.: **Soffer**; **Soferman** (Ashkenazic); **Soifer** (S Ashkenazic).

Söffing see SIEGFRIED

Søgård Danish: habitation name from a placename composed of the elements *sø* sea + *gård* enclosure, farm.

Vars.: **Søegård**, **Sø(e)gaard**.

Sohnker see SOANE

Soibelman see SOBEL

Soiberman see SAUBER

Soifer see SOFER

Soikin Russian: patr. from the nickname *Soika*, a dim. of *soya* jay, presumably denoting a garrulous or garishly dressed person.

Sokol 1. Czech: nickname from *sokol* falcon, or metonymic occupational name for a falconer. 2. Jewish (E Ashkenazic): from Slav. *sokol* falcon, one of the many Ashkenazic ornamental surnames taken from animal names.

Vars.: Jewish: **Sokoll**, **Sokole**, **Socol**; **Sokolski**, **Sokolsky**.

Dim.: Jewish: **Sokolik**.

Patrs.: Russ.: **Sokolov**. Pol.: **Sokołowicz**. Jewish: **Sokolov**, **Socolov**, **Sokolow**, **Socolow**, **Sokolof(f)**, **Socolof(f)**. Croatian: **Sokolović**, **Sokić**.

Habitation name: Pol.: **Sokołowski**.

Sol 1. Provençal: topographic name for someone who lived by a communal threshing-floor, OProv. *sol* (from L *solum* bottom, floor, ground). 2. Spanish and Catalan: nickname for someone with a sunny personality, from *sol* sun (L *sōl*). This was also sometimes used as a female given name in medieval Spain, and some examples of the surname may derive from this use. 3. Catalan: nickname from OCat. *sàul* saved (L *salvus*; cf. SAUVÉ). 4. Jewish: of unknown origin.

Var. (of 1): **Delsol**.

Solano Spanish: habitation name from any of various places, for example in the provinces of Burgos and Malaga, so called from OSp. *solano* place exposed to the sun (LL *sōlānum*, a deriv. of *sōl* sun; cf. SOL 2).

Var.: **Solana**.

Dim.: Prov.: **Soulanet**.

Solarek *see* SALTER

Soldan *see* SOWDEN

Soldevila Catalan: topographic name for someone who lived in the lower part of a settlement, from Cat. *sòl* bottom (L *solum*) + *de* of (L *de* from) + *vila* village, settlement (L *villa* country house, estate).

Var.: **Soldevilla**.

Söldner *see* SELD

Sole English: 1. topographic name from OE *sol* muddy place, or habitation name from one of the places named with this word, as for example *Soles* in Kent. 2. nickname for an unmarried man, from ME, OF *soul* single, unmarried (L *sōlus* alone).

Vars.: **Soal(l)**. (Of 1 only): **Soles**.

Soler Provençal and Catalan: habitation name from any of numerous minor places so called, from *soler* site, plot (LL *solārium*, a deriv. of *solum* bottom, ground).

Vars.: Prov.: **Sol(l)ier**. Cat.: **Solé**.

Dims.: It.: **Solarino**, **Solaroli**.

Solignac French: habitation name from any of the various places, for example in Haute-Vienne and Haute-Loire, so called from the Gallo-Roman personal name *Sollemnius* (a deriv. of L *sollemnis* solemn, sacred) + the local suffix *-ācum*.

Var.: **Solinhac** (Prov. spelling).

Solis 1. English: from a medieval given name bestowed on a child born after the death of a sibling, from ME *solace* comfort, consolation (OF *solas*, from L *sōlācium*). The word also came to have the sense 'delight', 'amusement', and so the surname may in some cases have been originally

given as a nickname to a playful or entertaining person. 2. Jewish (Sefardic): of unknown origin.

Vars.: **Soliss**, **Solass**.

Solmon *see* SALMON

Solomon *see* SALOMON

Solovey Jewish (E Ashkenazic): ornamental name from Yid. *solevey* nightingale (of Slav. origin, probably referring originally to the colour of the bird, 'yellowish brown'). This is one of the large class of Ashkenazic surnames taken from the names of birds; in some cases it may have been chosen as a nickname by a cantor.

Vars.: **Solovei**, **Solovej**; **Soloway** (an Anglicized form); **Solvay**.

Dims.: **Solov(ei)chik**, **Soloveitshik**, **Soloweiczyk**, **Solowieczyk**, **Solovieczyk**, **Solovitzik**.

Solsona Catalan: habitation name from a place in the province of Lérida. The placename is of pre-Roman origin and unknown meaning.

Sołtysik *see* SCHULTZ

Solzhenitsyn Russian: of uncertain origin. Unbegaun suggests that it may be connected with *solod* malt. The Soviet writer of this name is of Cossack descent.

Somer *see* SUMMER

Somerlad *see* SUMMERLAD

Somerscales N English: topographic name for someone who lived in a shelter (on upland pastures) inhabited only in the summer, from ON *sumar* SUMMER + *skáli* hut, shelter (see SCHOLES).

Vars.: **Somerscale**, **Summerscale(s)**, **Summerskill**, **Summersgill**.

Somerset English: regional name from the county of this name, so called from OE *Sumor(tūn)sǣte* 'dwellers at the summer settlement'.

Vars.: **Som(m)ersett**, **Summersett**.

Somerville 1. Scots (Norman): habitation name, probably from (Graveron) *Sémerville* in Nord, so called from the Gmc personal name *Sigimar* (see SIEMER) + OF *ville* settlement (see VILLE). 2. Irish: Anglicized form of Gael. *Ó Somacháin*; see SUMMERLY.

Vars. (of 1): **Sommerville**, **Summerville**, **Somervail(le)**, **Somervell**; **Summerfield** (see also SUMMER).

Somes *see* SOAME

Somoza Spanish: habitation name from any of various places so called, in the provinces of La Coruña, Orense, and Pontevedra.

Son *see* SOANE

Søndergård Danish: habitation name from a place named with the elements *sønder* southern + *gård* enclosure, farm.

Var.: **Søndergaard**.

Sønderup Danish: habitation name from a place named with the elements *sønder* southern + *rup* settlement.

Songer *see* SANGER

Sonnenschein 1. German: nickname for a person of a friendly or cheerful temperament, from Ger. *Sonnenschein*, composed of the MHG elements *sunne* sun (OHG *sunna*) + *schīn* shine (OHG *skīn*). It may also in part be a topographic name for someone who lived at a place which caught the sun, or a house name from a house marked with the sign of the sun. **2.** Jewish (Ashkenazic): ornamental name from the Ger. word meaning 'sunshine'; cf. the less frequent **Sonnenstein** ('sun stone') and **Mondschein** ('moonshine'). According to Kaganoff, it was selected because of a supposed phonetic association with SAMSON, or a semantic one with the various Hebr. given names referring to light, such as *Uri* and *Meir*. There is no evidence to support either of these speculations.

Vars. (of 2): **Sonschein**, **Sunshine**, **Zonens(c)hein**, **Zonenshine**.

Sonnier French: occupational name for a bell-ringer, OF *sonnier* (LL *sonārius*, an agent deriv. of *sonāre* to sound, ring).

Vars.: **Son(n)eur**.

Sonntag German and Jewish (Ashkenazic): nickname for someone who had some particular connection with Sunday, Ger. *Sonntag* (MHG *sun(nen)tac*, OHG *sunnūn tag* day of the sun). The Ger. word was sometimes used as a given name for a child born on a Sunday, for this was considered as lucky as Friday (see FREITAG) was unlucky. Among Jews, it seems to have been one of the group of names referring to days of the week that were distributed at random by government officials.

Var.: **Sontag**.

Soolivan *see* SULLIVAN

Soonhouse *see* SOUNESS

Soord *see* SWORD

Sopeña Spanish: topographic name for someone who lived at the foot of a cliff, from OSp. *so* below, under, hard by (L *sub*) + *peña* cliff, rock (L *pinna* pinnacle, battlements).

Soper English (chiefly Cornwall): occupational name for someone who manufactured soap, by boiling oil or fat together with potash or soda. The name is from an agent deriv. of ME *sōpe* (OE *sāpe*, apparently of Celt. origin).

Vars.: **Soaper**, **Sopper**.

Soquet *see* SUCH

Sorbie *see* SOWERBY

Sorbier French: topographic name for someone who lived near a sorb or service tree, OF *sorbier* (L *sorbārium*, a deriv. of *sorbus* service berry), or habitation name from a place named with this word.

Dims.: Fr.: **Sorbet**, **Sorbon**.

Sordet *see* SOURD

Soreau *see* SOAR

Soref *see* ZOREF

Sørens *see* SÉVERIN

Sorge German: nickname for a careworn individual, from Ger. *Sorge* care, concern, worry, anxiety (MHG *sorge*, OHG *sor(a)ga*).

Var.: **Sorg**.

Dim.: Ger.: **Sörgel**.

Soria Spanish and Jewish (Sefardic): habitation name from a city of this name in Castile, of uncertain etymology.

Vars.: **Soriano**, **Soreano**; **Soriyano** (Jewish only).

Sorin 1. Jewish (NE Ashkenazic): metr. from the Yid. female given name *Sore* Sarah (from the Hebr. female given name *Sara* 'Princess'), with the Slav. metr. suffix *-in*. **2.** French: dim. of *sor*; see SOAR.

Vars. (of 1): **Sorenson** (with a double suffix, Slav. *-in* + mod. Ger. *-sohn*); **Surin**, **Suris**, **Surizon** (S Ashkenazic).

Dims. (of 1): **Sorkin**, **Surkin**, **Sirkin**, **Zirkin**, **Sarkin**; **Zirlin**, **Serlin**, **Cerlin**; **S(o)urkes**, **Surkis**, **Sorkis**, **Sirkes**, **Zerkus**.

Sorkin *see* SORIN

Sorley Scots: Anglicized form of the Gael. personal name *Somhairle*, itself a Gael. form of the ON name discussed at SUMMERLAD.

Vars.: **Sorlie**, **Sorrie**.

Patr.: **McSorley**.

Sornin *see* SATURNIN

Soroff Jewish (NE Ashkenazic): apparently a metr. from the Yid. female given name *Sore*; see SORIN. It may also be an ornamental name deriving from the NE Ashkenazic pronunciation of Hebrew *saraf* seraph (cf. SERAFIM).

Sorokin Russian and Jewish (E Ashkenazic): patr. from the nickname *Soroka* 'Magpie', denoting a garrulous or thievish person, or someone with a streak of white among black hair. In the case of the Jewish surname it is normally an ornamental name, one of the many taken from bird names.

Vars. (not patrs.): Jewish: **Soroka**, **Soroko**; **Soroker** (elaborated with an agentive suffix).

Sorribas Catalan: topographic name for someone who lived on the bank of a river, from Cat. *so* below, hard by (L *sub*) + *ribas* banks (L *ripae*).

Var.: **Sorribes** (the name of two places in the province of Lérida).

Sosin *see* SHOSHIN

Sosnin Russian: patr. from the nickname *Sosna* 'Pine', given perhaps to a tall, thin person.

Sotelo *see* SAULT

Sotham *see* SOUTHAM

Sotheby N English: topographic name for someone who lived in the southern part of a settlement, from ON *suðr í bý* south in the village.

Vars.: **Sutherby**, **Suddaby**.

Sotheran *see* SOUTH

Soubeyre Provençal: topographic name for someone who lived in an elevated position, from OProv. *soubeyre* (L *superior*, comp. of *super* above).

Vars.: **Soubrier**; **Soub(e)iran**, **Soub(ey)ran**; **Soubeyrol**, **Soubayrol**, **Soubirou(s)**.

Souček see SUK

Souch see SUCH

Soukup Czech (a common Czech surname): occupational name for a merchant or dealer, Czech *soukup*, from Slav. *sou-* with + *kup-* buy (from Gmc *kaupjan* (mod. Ger. *kaufen*), which is from L *caupō* shopkeeper). The Czech word also acquired the sense 'one who aids or abets a thief', but this probably did not affect the development of the surname.

Soul French: **1.** nickname for a habitual drunkard, from OF *soul* drunk, satiated (LL *salullus*, a dim. form of *salur* full, class. L *satur*). **2.** habitation name from places in Cantal and Lorrèze, so called because they catch the sun (OF, L *sol*; cf. SOL 2 and SOLANO).

Var. (of 1): **Saoul**.

Pej. (of 1): **Soulard**.

Soulanet see SOLANO

Soulier French: **1.** topographic name for someone who lived in a house with more than one storey, something of a rarity in the Middle Ages, from a deriv. of OF *soule* platform, storey (L *solium* throne, dais). **2.** metonymic occupational name for a shoemaker, from OF *soulier* shoe, sandal (LL *sublelārius* open sandal, from *sublel* arch of the foot).

Vars.: **Soullier**, **Soul(i)é**.

Soulsby English (Northumb.): of uncertain origin, perhaps a habitation name from either of two places called *Soulby*, one near Penrith and the other near Kirkby Stephen. These are probably named from ON *súl* post + *býr* farm, settlement. There is, however, no reason why either of the placenames should have developed an *s* in it.

Soult French: probably a nickname for a man who had separated from his wife, from OF *soult* free, detached (L *solūtus*, past part. of *solvere* to loose, untie).

Souness Scots: habitation name from a locality near Blainslie in the former county of Roxburghs.

Vars.: **Sounness**, **Soonhouse**.

Sourd French: nickname for a deaf man, from OF *sourd* deaf (L *surdus* muffled).

Var.: **Lesourd**.

Dims.: Fr.: **Sourdeau**, **So(u)rdet**, **Sourdin**, **Sourdou**, **Sourdillon**. It.: **Sordini**.

Augs.: Fr.: **Sourdat**. It.: **Sordon(i)**.

Sourkes see SORIN

Sousa Portuguese: habitation name from any of various minor places so called. The placename is of uncertain origin; it was probably applied originally to a salt-marsh, a var. of *sausa* (fem.) salty (L *salsa*), with the word *agua* water (L *aqua*) understood.

Vars.: **Souza** (also a Sefardic name); **De Souza**, **D'Souza**.

Souster English: occupational name for a tailor, from ME *soustere* sewer, from OE *si(o)wan* to sew (see SEWER) + *-ster* agent suffix. The *-ster* ending was originally feminine, but by the Middle English period it was applied equally to both sexes. See also SEWER.

Soutar see SAUTER

South English: topographic name for someone who lived to the south of a settlement, or regional name for someone who had migrated from the south, from ME *s(o)uth* (OE *sūð*).

Vars.: **Sowman**; **Southern**, **S(o)uther(i)n**, **Suthren**, **Sother(a)n**, **Sotheron**, **Southorn**; **Southan**, **Southon**; **Sudran**, **Sudron**.

Cpds (mostly arbitrary elaborations rather than genuine habitation names): Swed.: **Söderbäck** ('south stream'); **Söderberg** ('south hill'); **Söderblom** ('south flower'); **Södergren** ('south branch'); **Söderholm** ('south island'); **Söderlind(h)** ('south lime'); **Söderlund** ('south grove'); **Söderqvist** ('south twig'); **Söderstöm** ('south river').

Southall English (chiefly W Midlands): habitation name from any of the various places so called, from OE *sūð* SOUTH + *halh* nook, recess (see HALE 1). This might be the town that is now a district of W London, but the distribution of the surname makes a Warwicks. origin more likely. Places called *Southall* in Doverdale, Worcs., and Billingsley, Shrops., are also possible sources.

Southam English: habitation name from places in Gloucs. and Warwicks., so called from OE *sūð* SOUTH + *hām* homestead.

Var.: **Sotham**.

Southcott English (W Country): habitation name from any of various places, for example *Southcot* in Devon or *Southcott* in Devon (of which spelling there are three occurrences) and Cornwall, named with the OE elements *sūð* SOUTH + *cot* cottage, shelter (see COATES).

Southerland see SUTHERLAND

Southey English: habitation name from any of various places, for example *Southey* in the parish of Culmstock, Devon, in Ecclesford, W Yorks., *Southey* Green in Essex, or *Southey* Wood in Ufford, Northants. All of these get their names from OE *sūð* SOUTH + *(ge)hæg* enclosure (see HAY 1).

Var.: **Southee** (mainly Kent, centred on Canterbury).

Southgate English: **1.** habitation name from a place in Norfolk, so called from OE *sūð* SOUTH + *geat* gate; the village was situated near the southern entrance to a large medieval enclosed forest. **2.** topographic name for someone who lived near the south gate of a medieval walled town or other enclosed place.

Vars. (of 2): **Suggate**; **Suggett**, **Suggitt** (chiefly Yorks.).

Southwell English: habitation name from a place in Notts., so called from OE *sūð* SOUTH + *well(a)* spring, stream (see WELL), or topographic name from the same vocab. elements used independently.

Southwood English: habitation name from a place in Norfolk, so called from OE *sūð* SOUTH + *wudu* WOOD, or topographic name from the same vocab. elements used independently.

Southworth English (Lancs.): habitation name from a place in Ches. (formerly S Lancs.), so called from OE *sūð* SOUTH + *worð* enclosure (see WORTH).

Var.: **Southward**.

Sowa Polish: nickname meaning 'Owl', perhaps denoting a bookish or knowledgeable person, or arising out of some fancied physical resemblance.

Vars.: **Sowała**, **Sowiak**.

Habitation name: Pol.: **Sowiński**.

Sowden English: nickname from ME, OF *soudan* sultan (Arabic *sultān* ruler), either for someone who behaved in an outlandish and autocratic manner, or for someone who had played the part of a sultan in a pageant.

Vars.: **Soden**, **Soldan**, **Sultan**.

Sowerby English: habitation name from any of various places in N England named with the ON elements *saurr* sour ground + *býr* farm, settlement.

Vars.: **Sowersby**, **Sor(s)bie**, **Sor(s)by**, **Surby**.

Sowman *see* SOUTH

Spaak Dutch: metonymic occupational name for someone who made spokes for wheels, from MDu. *spaak* spoke (OSax. *spēce*; cf. OE *spāca*).

Var.: **Spock** (Anglicized).

Špaček Czech: nickname from a vocab. word meaning 'starling'.

Spackman *see* SPEAKMAN

Spadazzi *see* ESPADA

Spagnoleto *see* PAGNOL

Spahn *see* SPOONER

Spaight *see* SPEIGHT

Spain English and Irish (Norman): **1.** habitation name from *Épaignes* in Eure, recorded in the L form *Hispānia* in the 12th cent. It seems to have been so called because it was established by colonists from Spain during the Roman Empire. **2.** habitation name from *Espinay* in Ille-et-Vilaine, Brittany, so called from a collective of OF *espine* thorn bush. **3.** (rarely) ethnic name for a Spaniard; see PAGNOL.

Spalane *see* SPILLANE

Spalding English: habitation name from a place in Lincs., so called from the OE tribal name *Spaldingas* 'people of the district called *Spald*'. The district name probably means 'Ditches', referring to drainage channels in the fenland.

Vars.: **Spaulding**, SPAUGHTON.

Spanton English (Norfolk): habitation name from *Spaunton* in E Yorks., so called from ON *spánn* shingle, wooden tile (cf. SPOONER) + OE *tūn* settlement, i.e. 'settlement with shingled roofs'.

Spargo Cornish: habitation name from Higher or Lower *Spargo*, in the parish of Mabe, so called from Corn. *spern* thorn bushes + **cor* enclosure.

Spark **1.** English: from the ON byname *Sparkr* 'Sprightly', 'Vivacious'. **2.** Low German: cogn. of SPARROW.

Vars. (of 1): **Sparke**; **Sprake**, **Sprague**, **Spragg(e)** (metathesized forms). (Of 2): **Spahr**, **Spaar**.

Patrs. (from 1): Eng.: **Spark(e)s**.

Sparrow English: nickname, perhaps for a small, chirpy person, or else for someone bearing some fancied physical resemblance to a sparrow, ME *sparewe*, OE *spearwa*.

Var.: **Sparrowe**.

Dims.: Eng.: **Sparling**, **Sperling**, **Spurling**. Ger.: **Sperl(ing)**, **Spierling**, **Sperlich**; **Spörl** (Bavaria). Jewish (Ashkenazic): **Sperling** (an ornamental name).

Patr.: Flem., Du.: **Verspreeuwen**.

Spasski Russian: **1.** habitation name from any of the numerous places called *Spasskoe*, from the dedication of their churches to the Saviour, ORuss. *Spas(itel)* (from *spasti* to save, a calque of Gk *sōtēr*, from *sōzein* to save). **2.** surname adopted by Orthodox priests, affirming their dedication to Jesus Christ as Saviour.

Spath German: nickname for a tardy person, from Ger. *spät* late (MHG *spæte*, OHG *spāti*).

Vars.: **Späth(e)**, **Späthmann**, **Speth(mann)**.

Spaughton English: of uncertain origin, from its form apparently a habitation name. The suggestion has been put forward that it is a var. of SPALDING, assimilated by folk etymology to the common placename ending -*ton*. The name *de Spotton* is well established in the Malden-Tolworth-Chessington area of Surrey from the 13th cent. onwards, so perhaps a local Surrey origin should be sought. However, no suitable placename in this area is known.

Vars.: **Spawton**, **Sporton**, **Spotton**, **Spolton**, **Spalton**.

Spawforth *see* SPOFFORTH

Speak English: nickname from the woodpecker, ME *spek(e)* (an aphetic form of OF *espeche(e)*, of Gmc origin; cf. SPEIGHT).

Vars.: **Spe(a)ke**, **Speek**; SPECK, **Spick**.

Patrs.: **Speaks**, **Speeks**.

Speakman English (chiefly Lancs.): nickname or occupational name for someone who acted as a spokesman, from ME *spekeman* advocate, spokesman (from OE *specan* to speak + *mann* man).

Var.: **Spackman**.

Spear English: nickname for a tall, thin person, or else for a skilled user of the hunting spear, from ME, OE *spere* spear. In part it may also have been a metonymic occupational name for a maker of spears.

Vars.: **Speare**; **Speir**, SPIER (Scotland); **Speer** (N Ireland).

Patrs.: Eng.: **Spearing**, **Spear(e)s**; **Speirs**, **Spiers** (Scotland); **Speers** (N Ireland).

Spearman English: **1.** occupational name for a soldier armed with a spear, from ME *spere* SPEAR + *man*. **2.** from a ME, OE personal name *Spereman*, of the same origin as the occupational name above.

Speck **1.** German: metonymic occupational name for a seller of bacon or a pork butcher, from Ger. *Speck* bacon (MHG *spec* bacon, OHG *spek*), or nickname for someone who was particularly fond of this food. **2.** English: var. of SPEAK.

Var. (of 1): **Speckesser** ('bacon eater').

Dim. (of 1): Ger.: **Speckle**.

Spector Jewish (E Ashkenazic): of uncertain origin. It is possibly an occupational name for someone who inspected meat to ensure that it conformed with Jewish dietary laws; the Yid. name for this officer was *mazhgiekh* (Hebr. *mashgiach*). According to Kaganoff the name was taken by a tutor in the household of a rich Jew who had special permission to reside in the large cities of Russia where other Jews could not live, but this is unlikely since 'inspector' and 'tutor' are semantically distinct.
Vars.: **Spektor, Inspektor, Spectorman**.

Spedding N English and Scots: of uncertain origin, possibly a patr. from the OE byname *Spēd* 'Success', 'Prosperity' (cf. SPEED). However, Black is not able to quote forms earlier than 1502, which makes this hypothesis very doubtful.

Spedracci see PETER

Speed 1. English: nickname for a fortunate person, from ME *sped* (OE *spēd*) success, good fortune, smooth progress (hence the mod. meaning 'swiftness'). **2.** English: nickname for a swift runner, from the derived sense of ME *sped* mentioned above. **3.** Irish: translation of Gael. *Ó Fuada*; see FOODY.
Dim. (of 2): **Speedie** (Scotland).

Speer 1. N Irish: var. of SPEAR. **2.** German: cogn. of SPEAR, from Ger. *Speer* spear (MHG *sper, spar(e)*, OHG *sper*). **3.** German: cogn. of SPARROW, from MHG *spar(e)* (OHG *sparo*). **4.** Jewish (Ashkenazic): of unknown origin, probably an adoption of the German name.

Spehr see SPOHRER

Speight English (now chiefly Yorks.): nickname from ME *speght* woodpecker (presumably from an unrecorded OE **speoht*, apparently akin to OE *specan* to speak, talk, chatter).
Vars.: **Sp(e)aight, Spieght**.

Speiser 1. German: occupational name for a steward in charge of the supply and distribution of provisions in a great house or monastery, from an agent deriv. of Ger. *Speise* food, supplies (MHG *spīse*, OHG *spīsa*, from an aphetic form of LL *expe(n)sa (pecunia)* (money) expended). Cf. SPENCE and SPENDER. **2.** Jewish (Ashkenazic): occupational name for a grocer, from a later semantic development of the same word as in 1.
Vars. (of 2): **Spieser, Speis(man), Speizman; Szpajzer** (a Pol. spelling).

Spellane see SPILLANE

Speller English: occupational name for a reciter, from an agent deriv. of ME *spell(en)* to tell, relate (OE *spellian*). There has probably been some confusion with SPILLER.
Vars.: **Spelar, Spel(l)man**.

Spence English: metonymic occupational name for a servant employed in the pantry of a great house or monastery, from ME *spense* larder, storeroom (an aphetic form of OF *despense*, from a LL deriv. of *dispendere*, past part. *dispensus*, to weigh out, dispense). Cf. SPEISER and SPENDER.
Vars.: **Spens** (Scots); **Spencer, Spenser; Despenser**.

Spender English: occupational name for a steward in charge of the supply of necessities in a great house or monastery, from an aphetic form of ME, OF *despendeour* dispenser (L *dispenditor*, from *dispendere* to weigh out, dispense). Cf. SPEISER and SPENCE.

Spendlove English: nickname for someone who was free with his affections, from ME *spend(en)* to spend, squander (OE *spendan*) + *love* love (OE *lufu*).
Vars.: **Spen(d)low**.

Spengler German: occupational name for a metalworker, from an agent deriv. of a dim. form of MHG *spange* clasp, buckle, ornamental fastening. In S Germany, Austria, and Switzerland the mod. Ger. vocab. word *Spengler* means 'plumber', but in earlier times it had a wider range of meanings.
Var.: **Spengel**.

Sperber 1. German: nickname for a small but pugnacious person, from Ger. *Sperber* sparrowhawk (MHG *sperwære*, OHG *sparwāri*, a cpd of *sparw* SPARROW + *āri* 'eagle'; cf. ADLER and EARNSHAW). **2.** Jewish (Ashkenazic): ornamental name from the mod. Ger. bird name.
Var. (of 2): **Sperberg** (influenced by the many Ashkenazic surnames ending in the element -*berg* hill).

Sperelli see KASPAR

Sperl see SPARROW

Sperrin English: metonymic occupational name for a maker of spurs, from ME *sperun* spur (OF *(e)speron*, of Gmc origin; cf. SPOHRER and SPURR).
Vars.: **Sperryn, Spurren, Spearon, Sperring, Spurring**.

Speth see SPATH

Spicer English: occupational name for a seller of spices, ME *spic(i)er* (an aphetic form of OF *espicier*, LL *speciārius*, an agent deriv. of *speciēs* spice, groceries, merchandise).
Var.: **Spice**.
Equivs. (not cogn.): Prov.: SABRIER. Jewish (Ashkenazic): GEWIRTZ.

Spick see SPEAK

Spieght see SPEIGHT

Spiegler German and Jewish (Ashkenazic): occupational name for a maker or seller of mirrors, from an agent deriv. of Ger. *Spiegel*, Yid. *shpigl* (OHG *spiagal*, from L *speculum*, a deriv. of *specere* to look, see).
Vars.: Ger.: **Spieg(e)l, Spiegelmann**. Jewish: **Spigler, Spi(e)gel(man)**.

Spielberg German and Jewish (Ashkenazic): habitation name from any of the various places so called, from a contracted form of MHG *spiegel* look-out point (L *speculum*; cf. SPIEGLER) + *berg* hill.
Vars.: Jewish: **Spielberger; Szpilberg** (a Pol. spelling).

Spier 1. English: occupational name for a lookout or watchman, or nickname for a nosy person, from an agent deriv. of ME *(e)spi(en)* to watch, observe (OF *espier*, of Gmc origin). **2.** Scots: var. of SPEAR. **3.** Jewish (Ashkenazic): of uncertain origin, possibly a habitation name from the Ger. city of *Speyer*; cf. SPIRE 2.

Var. (of 3): **Spierer**.

Spierling *see* SPARROW

Spiers *see* SPEAR

Spieser *see* SPEISER

Spillane Irish: Anglicized form of Gael. **Ó Spealáin** 'descendant of *Spealán*', a personal name representing a dim. of *speal* scythe.

Vars.: **O'Spillane**, **O'Spallane**, **(O')Spollane**, **Spellane**, **Spalane**, **Spollan**, **Spollen**; **Spla(i)ne**; **Smallen**, **Smollan**, **Smullen**.

Spiller English: **1.** occupational name for a tumbler or jester, from an agent deriv. of ME *spill(en)* to play, jest, sport (OE *spilian*). **2.** nickname for a destructive or wasteful person, from an agent deriv. of the homonymous ME *spill(en)* to spoil, waste, squander (OE *spillan*).

Spilling English (Norfolk): of uncertain origin, apparently from a medieval given name, perhaps from an OE patr., *Spilling*, of a personal name *Spill(a)*. Evidence for an ON byname *Spilli*, from *spillir* squanderer, profligate (cf. SPILLER 2), may be found in the placename *Spilsby* (Lincs.).

Patr.: **Spillings**.

Spillman English: from a ME given name Spileman, which was originally an OE byname meaning 'Juggler', 'Tumbler', 'Actor' (cf. SPILLER).

Spilsbury English: habitation name from *Spelsbury* in Oxon., apparently so called from the gen. case of an OE byname *Spēol* 'Watchful' + OE *burh* town, fortress.

Spindler English, German, and Jewish (Ashkenazic): occupational name for a maker or user of spindles, from an agent deriv. of ME *spindle*, Ger. *Spindel*, Yid. *shpindl* (OE *spinel*, MHG *spinnele*, OHG *spin(n)ila*, all derived from a Gmc verb meaning 'to spin').

Var.: Jewish: **Spindel**.

Spinella *see* ÉPINE

Spink English: nickname from ME *spink* chaffinch (of uncertain, probably imitative, origin), bestowed on account of some fancied resemblance to the bird.

Var.: **Spinke**.

Patr.: **Spinks**.

Spire 1. English: nickname for a tall, thin man, from ME *spir* stalk, stem (OE *spīr*). This was apparently used as a personal name or byname, in view of the fact that there are patr. derivs. In some ME dialects this word also denoted reeds, and the surname may in part have been originally a topographic name for someone who lived in a marshy area. The application to a church steeple is not attested before the 16th cent., and is not a likely source of the surname. **2.** Jewish (Ashkenazic): Anglicized form of **Speyer**, a habitation name from the German town so called, which had a large Jewish population in the Middle Ages; cf. SAPIR, SHAPIRO, and SPIER 3.

Vars. (of 2): **Spiro**, **Spira**, **Spirer**.

Dims. (of 1): Eng.: **Spirett**, **Spirit**.

Patrs. (from 1): Eng.: **Spiring**; **Spires**.

Spittle English: occupational name for someone who was employed at a lodging house, ME *spital* (an apheticform of OF *hospital*, LL *hospitāle*, from *hostis*, gen. *hospitis*, guest).

Vars.: **Spittel**, **Spital(l)**, **Spittles**; **Spitt(e)ler**.

Spitz 1. German: topographic name for someone who lived by a pointed hill or by a field with an acute angle, from Ger. *spitz* pointed (OHG *spizzi*). There are numerous minor places throughout Germany named with this word, and the surname may also be a habitation name from any of these. **2.** Jewish (Ashkenazic): of uncertain origin, perhaps of similar derivation to the German name, or from Yid. *shpitsn* lace.

Vars.: Ger.: **Spitz(l)er**. Jewish: **S(c)hpitz**, **S(h)pitzer**, **Spitzman**.

Spitzweg German: metonymic occupational name for a baker who specialized in a particular type of pastry baked in a pointed shape, MHG *spitzweck* (from SPITZ + *wecke* wedge).

Spivak Jewish (E Ashkenazic): occupational name from Ukr. *spivák* singer, used as a translation of KAZAN.

Vars.: **Spivack**; **Spi(e)wak**, **Spievak** (from the cogn. Pol. *śpiewak*; **Spivakovsky**.

Spjut Swedish: nickname from Swed. *spjut* spear, lance, pike, javelin; this is one of the 'soldiers' names' assumed during military service in the 17th and 18th cents. before surnames came into regular use in Sweden.

Var.: **Spjuth**.

Splaine *see* SPILLANE

Spock *see* SPAAK

Spode English: habitation name from *Spoad* in Shrops., the name of which is of obscure origin.

Spofforth English: habitation name from a place in N Yorks., recorded in Domesday Book as *Spoford* and perhaps so called from OE *splott* spot, plot of land + *ford* FORD.

Vars.: **Spofford**, **Spoffard**, **Spawforth**.

Spohrer German: occupational name for a maker of spurs, from an agent deriv. of MHG *spor* spur (OHG *sporo*; mod. Ger. *Sporn*).

Vars.: **Spör(n)er**, **Spehrer**, **Sperner**; **Spohr**, **Spehr** (metonymic); **Spo(h)rmann**.

Spollan *see* SPILLANE

Spolton *see* SPAUGHTON

Spooner English: occupational name for someone who covered roofs with wooden shingles, from an agent deriv. of ME *spoon* chip, splinter (OE *spōn*). However, from the 14th cent., under Scandinavian influence, the word had also begun to acquire its modern sense denoting the eating utensil, and the surname may therefore in some cases have been acquired by someone who made these articles from wood or horn.

Spoor *see* SPURR

Spörl *see* SPARROW

Sporran Irish: Anglicized form of Gael. **Mac Sparáin** 'son of *Sparán*', a byname meaning 'Purse' (ultimately from L *bursa*; cf. PURSER). The main family of this name held the hereditary post of purse-bearers to the McDonnells of the Isles.
Vars.: **McSporran**; **McSparran** (Ulster).

Sposito *see* ESPOSITO

Spottiswoode Scots: habitation name from a place in the parish of Gordon, Berwicks., first recorded in 1249 as *Spottiswode*. The second element is ME *wode* WOOD; the first appears to derive from a personal name.
Vars.: **Spottiswood**, **Spotswood**.

Spragg *see* SPARK

Spratt English: nickname for a small and insignificant person, from ME *sprat* sprat (of uncertain origin, possibly a deriv. of OE *spryt, sprot* sprout, young shoot; see SPROTT).

Spray English (Notts. and Derbys.): nickname for a thin person, from ME *spray* slender branch (of uncertain origin).
Patr.: **Sprason**.

Sprigg English: nickname for a tall, thin, bony person, from ME *sprigge* twig, branch (apparently of ON or Low Ger. origin, first recorded as a vocab. word in Eng. in the 15th cent.).
Patr.: **Spriggs**.

Spring English: of uncertain origin. Early examples, as for example William *Spring* (Yorks. 1280), all point to a personal name or nickname, perhaps going back to an OE by-name derived from the verb *springan* to jump, leap (see SPRINGER 1). Reaney derives the surname from the season, but there is a difficulty in that the word is not attested in this sense until the 16th cent., the usual ME word being *lenten* (cf. LENZ).
Dims.: **Springett**, **Springate**.

Springall English: 1. nickname from ME *springal(d)* youth, stripling (of uncertain origin, perhaps from SPRING with the addition of the OF suffix *-ald*). 2. nickname for a violent and destructive individual or metonymic occupational name for an operator of the medieval siege-engine known in ME as a *springalde* (OF *espringalle*, apparently from a Gmc root cogn. with OE *springan* to jump, leap). The engine worked like a giant catapult, hurling missiles against fortifications.
Vars.: **Springhall**, **Springell**, **Springle**.

Springer 1. English, German, Dutch, and Jewish (Ashkenazic): nickname for a lively person, from an agent deriv. of ME, Ger. *springen*, MDu. *springhen*, Yid. *shpringen* to jump, leap (OE, OHG, OSax. *springan*). 2. English: topographic name for someone who lived by a fountain or the source of a stream, from ME *spring* (OE *spring, spryng*, a deriv. of the verb given above). The word *spring* was also

used of a plantation of young trees, and this may in some cases be the source of the surname.
Vars. (of 1): Ger.: **Spranger**. Jewish: **Shpringer**.

Springfield English: habitation name from a place in Essex, recorded in Domesday Book as *Springinghefelda* as well as *Springafelda*, apparently from OE *Springingafeld* 'pasture (see FIELD) of the people who live by a spring'.

Sprott Scottish and N English: from the ME, OE personal name *Sprot*, of uncertain origin. It may be derived from OE *sprot* sprout, young shoot.
Var.: **Sproat**.

Spruce English: ethnic name for someone from Prussia, the ME name for which was *Spruce* or *Sprewse*; cf. PREUSS. The adj. *spruce* neat, dapper, which probably derives from an attrib. use of the name of the country, is not recorded until the late 16th cent., too late for it to be a likely source of the surname. The tree (earlier *Spruce fir*) has likewise only come to be known by this name in the last couple of cents.

Spry English: apparently a nickname for an active, brisk, or smart person. Although *spry* is not recorded in OED until the 18th cent., it was probably in colloquial use in the W Country dialect and in Scots much earlier. The word is of obscure origin. The surname is found mainly in Devon, but there is also a modest concentration of bearers in NE England.

Spurling *see* SPARROW

Spurr English (now chiefly Yorks.): metonymic occupational name for a maker of spurs, from ME *spore, spure* spur (OE *spora, spura*). Cf. SPERRING.
Vars.: **Spurrs**; **Spore**, **Spoor(s)** (Northumb.); **Spurrier** (from a ME agent deriv.).

Spurren *see* SPERRIN

Spurway English: habitation name from a place in Devon, apparently so called from OE *spræg* brushwood + *weg* path, way.

Spychalski Polish: nickname for an idle worker, a 'buck passer', Pol. dial. *spychacz*, from *spychać* to push down. 2. topographic name for someone living by a precipice, Pol. dial. *spych*, also from *spychać*.
Var.: **Spychała**.

Squeers *see* SQUIRE

Squibb English: perhaps a nickname for a sarcastic, witty, or spiteful person, from early mod. Eng. *squibbe* lampoon, satirical attack. The word, which is probably of imitative origin, is not recorded until the 16th cent.; the original sense was 'firework'.

Squire English: status name for a man belonging to the social rank immediately below that of knight, from ME *squyer*, an aphetic form of OF *esquier* shield-bearer (L *scūtārius*, a deriv. of *scūtum* shield). At first it denoted a young man of good birth attendant on a knight, or by extension any attendant or servant, but by the 14th cent. the meaning had been generalized, and referred to social status rather than age. By the 17th cent., the term denoted any member of the landed gentry, but this is unlikely to have influenced the development of the surname.

Vars.: **Squier**, **Swire**, **Swyer**.

Patrs.: Eng.: **Squires**, **Squiers**, **Squeers**, **Swires**, **Swiers**.

Squirrel English: nickname from ME *squirel* squirrel, an aphetic form of OF *esquirel* (LL *scūriŏlus*, a dim. from Gk *skiouros*, from *skia* shadow + *oura* tail). This was presumably bestowed on someone bearing some resemblance to a squirrel, such as puffy cheeks and big eyes.

Vars.: **Squir(rel)l**, **Scurrell**.

Šrámek see SCHRAMM

Srbek see SERBINOV

Sroka Polish: nickname for a thievish or insolent person, from Pol. *sroka* magpie.

Habitation name: Pol.: **Sroczyński**.

Srol see ISRAEL

Srul see ISRAEL

Stabe German: nickname for a tall, thin person, or metonymic occupational name for anyone who carried a staff of office, a reminder of his right to inflict physical discipline, from Ger. *Stab* rod, staff (MHG *stap*, OHG *stab*).

Vars.: **Staab**, **Staap**.

Dim.: Ger.: **Stäble**.

Stables English: topographic name for someone who lived by a stable, or occupational name for someone employed in one, from ME *stable* (an aphetic form of OF *estable*, from L *stabulum*, a deriv. of *stāre* to stand). In ME the term was used of the quarters occupied by cattle as well as those reserved for horses.

Vars.: **Stable**, **Stab(e)ler**.

Stace English: from the medieval male given name *Stace*, an aphetic vernacular form of *Eustace* (L *Eustacius*, from Gk *Eustakhios* 'Fruitful', crossed with the originally distinct *Eustathios* 'Orderly'). The name was born by various genuine minor saints, but nothing of historical value is known of the most famous St Eustace, said to have been converted by the vision of a crucifix between the antlers of a hunted stag.

Var.: **Eustace**.

Dims.: Eng.: **Stacey**, **Eustie**. Ger.: **Stachl**, **Stächelin**.

Patrs.: Low Ger.: **Staasen**, **Staats**. Flem., Du.: **Staesen**.

Stach Polish and Czech: from the given name *Stach*, a pet form of Pol. *Stanisław*, Czech *Stanislav* (see STANISŁAWSKI).

Vars.: Pol.: **Stachura**, **Stachurski**.

Patrs.: Pol.: **Stachowicz**; **Stachowiak**.

Habitation names: Pol.: **Stachowski**, **Stachlewski**.

Stächelin see STACE

Stachvanyonok see STEPHEN

Stack English: nickname for a large, well-built man, from ME *stack* haystack (ON *stakkr*).

Vars.: **Stak(e)** (Ireland).

Stackpoole Irish: habitation name from a place called *Stackpole* 'Pool by the Rock' in the former county of

Pembrokes., Wales, from which settlers of Norman descent made their way into Ireland. The name is recorded in Dublin as early as 1200, and has been Gaelicized as **de Stacapúl**; bearers were also known as **Galldubh** ('Black Stranger'; see also STAPLETON).

Vars.: **Stackpole**, **Stacpoole**.

Staddon English (W Country): habitation name from any of half a dozen places in Devon, all earlier found as *Stoddon*, from OE *stod* stud or *stott* bullock + *dūn* hill.

Var.: **Stadden**.

Stadler German: topographic name for someone who lived near a barn or granary, or occupational name for an official who was responsible for receiving tithes into the manorial storehouse, from a deriv. of MHG *stadel* barn, granary (OHG *stadal*). Cf. SCHAUER. The surname is also occasionally borne by Ashkenazic Jews, apparently as an adoption of the Ger. surname.

Vars.: Ger. only: **Stadel(mann)**, **Stadtler**, **Städtler**.

Stafford English: habitation name from any of the various places so called, which do not all share the same etymology. The county town of Staffs. (which is probably the main source of the surname) gets its name from OE *stæð* landing place + *ford* FORD. Examples in Devon seem to have as their first element OE *stān* STONE, and one in Sussex is probably named with OE *stēor* STEER.

Var.: **Staffurth**.

Stagg English: nickname from OE *stagga* male deer, stag. In N dials. of ME the term was also used of a young horse, perhaps under Scandinavian influence, and in some cases this meaning may lie behind the original application of the name.

Stäheli see STEEL

Staiger see STEIGER

Stain see STEIN

Stainburn N English: habitation name from a place in Cumb., so called from ON *steinn* or OE *stān* STONE + OE *burna* stream (see BOURNE).

Stainer English: occupational name for a dyer, particularly of glass rather than fabrics, from an agent deriv. of ME *steyn(en)*, an aphetic form of *disteyn(en)* (OF *disteindre*, L *distingere*, from *tingere* to dye; cf. TEINTURIER).

Vars.: **Steiner**, **Steinor**.

Staines English: habitation name from a place on the Thames west of London, apparently so called from OE *stān* stone. The reference may be to a milestone on the Roman road that ran through the town, while the vocalic development seems to be the result of Norman influence.

Stainmetz see STEINMETZ

Stainsby English: habitation name from either of two places, one in Derbys. (*Steinesbi* in Domesday Book) and one in Lincs. (*Stafnebi* in 12th-cent. records). The former is so called from the ON personal name *Steinn* 'Stone' + ON *býr* farm, settlement, the latter from the ON personal name *Stafn* 'Stem' + *býr*.

Var.: **Stansbie**.

Stainthorpe English: habitation name from *Staindrop* in Co. Durham, which Ekwall derives from OE *stǣner* stony ground + *hop* enclosed valley (see HOPE). If this is correct, the second syllable has been assimilated by folk etymology to the common habitation element THORPE.

Stait English (W Midlands): topographic name for someone who lived by a landing stage, ME *sta(i)the* (OE *stæð*; cf. STATHAM).

Stakes English: apparently a topographic name for someone who lived by a prominent post or stake, ME *stake* (OE *staca*). The stake in question may well have been a boundary marker.

Stakhanov Russian: patr. from the given name *Stakhan* (from Gk *Stakhys* 'Bunch of Grapes', with the addition of the suffix from *Stepan* STEPHEN). *Stakhys* was the name of a 1st-cent. Christian, traditionally regarded as the first bishop of Byzantium, and so an important figure in the Orthodox Church.
Vars.: **Stakheev**, **Stasov**; **Stashinin** (from a dim.).

Stalder German: topographic name for someone who lived on a steep slope, MHG *stalde*, or habitation name for someone from a place named with this word, as for example *Stalden* in Switzerland.

Stalker Scots and N English: occupational name for a trapper or nickname for a stealthy person, from an agent deriv. of ME *stalk(en)* to stalk, approach stealthily (OE **stealcian*, a deriv. of *stelan* to steel).

Stallard English: nickname for a valiant or resolute person, from ME *stalward, stalworth* (OE *stælwierðe*, a cpd of *stæl* place + *wierðe* worthy).
Vars.: **Stollard**, **Stallwood**; **Stal(l)worthy**, **Stolworthy**; **Stal(l)ey**.

Stallmach *see* STELLMACHER

Stamm Jewish (Ashkenazic): 1. ornamental name from Ger. *Stamm* stem, stock (MHG, OHG *stam*), or perhaps in some cases a short form of names such as *Aronstam* 'stock of AARON' (the first high priest), **Kohenstam** 'stock of the kohenim' (see COHEN), and **Löwenstam** 'stock of the Levites' (see LEVI and LÖWE 2). 2. acronym of the Hebr. phrase *(sofer) Sifre-tora, Tefilim uMezuzot*, an occupational title for a scribe (see SOFER) who wrote scrolls of the law, phylacteries, and mezuzas.
Var.: **Stam**.

Stammer 1. English: from the OE personal name *Stānmǣr*, composed of the elements *stān* stone + *mǣr* famous. 2. English: habitation name from *Stanmer* in Sussex, so called from OE *stān* STONE + *mere* lake. 3. Jewish (Ashkenazic): of unknown origin.
Var. (of 2): **Stanmore** (a place in the former county of Middlesex).
Patr. (from 1): **Stammers**.

Stamp English (Norman): habitation name from *Étampes* in Seine-et-Oise, a placename apparently of Celt. origin; the meaning is uncertain.
Var.: **Stamps**.

Stanbridge English: habitation name from any of various places, for example in Beds. and Hants, so called from OE

stān STONE + *brycg* BRIDGE, i.e. a bridge built of stone rather than wood.

Stanbury English (Devon): habitation name from *Stanborough* in Devon, so called from OE *stān* STONE + *beorg* hill, tumulus. There is a place called *Stanbury* in W Yorks. near Haworth, but it does not seem to have given rise to the surname.
Vars.: **Stanborough**, **Stanberry**, **Stanbra**.

Stancliffe English (W Yorks.): habitation name, probably from a minor place such as *Stonecliff* or *Stancliffe* in Agbrigg, W Yorks., so called from OE *stān* STONE + *clif* slope (see CLIVE).

Standen English: habitation name from any of various places, for example in Berks., Lancs., and Wilts., so called from OE *stān* STONE + *denu* valley (see DEAN 1), or from another on the Isle of Wight, the second element of which is OE *dūn* hill (see DOWN 1).
Var.: **Standing** (chiefly Sussex; also Lancs., where it is a place name).

Standeven English: one of the several ME nicknames for an independent and resolute person, derived from the verb *stand(en)* to stand (OE *standan*) + *even* firm, balanced (OE *efen*). Others include **Standfast** and **Standwell**.

Standish English: habitation name from a place in Lancs. (now part of Greater Manchester), so called from OE *stān* STONE + *edisc* pasture. There is another place so named in Gloucs., but it does not seem to be the source of the surname.
Vars.: **Standage**, **Standidge**.

Stanford English: habitation name from any of the various places, for example in Beds., Berks., Essex, Herts., Kent, Norfolk, Northants, Notts., and Worcs., so called from OE *stān* STONE + *ford* FORD.
Vars.: **Stamford**, **Standford**, **Staniford**, **Staniforth**, **Stanyforth**.

Stanger 1. English (Newcastle and Durham): of uncertain origin, probably a deriv. of Northern ME *stang* pole (ON *stǫngr*). Possible meanings include a topographic name for someone who lived by a pole or stake (cf. STAKES) or an occupational name for someone armed with one. It may alternatively be a nickname for someone who had 'ridden the stang', i.e. been carried on a pole through the streets as an object of derision, in punishment for some misdemeanour. However, this custom is of uncertain antiquity. 2. Jewish (Ashkenazic): of unknown origin.

Stanhope English: habitation name from a place in Co. Durham, so called from OE *stān* STONE + *hop* enclosed valley (see HOPE).

Stanier English (chiefly Staffs.): occupational name for a stonecutter, one who cut and dressed stone, ME *stanyer* (from *stan* stone (OE *stān*) + a reduced form of *hewer*, agent deriv. of *hew(en)* to cut, chop (OE *hēawan*), assimilated to the agent suffix -*(i)er*).
Vars.: **Stanyer**, **Stonier**.

Stanisław ski Polish: from the given name *Stanisław* (composed of the Slav. elements *stan* become + *slav* glory, fame, praise) + the surname suffix *-ski* (see BARANOWSKI).

Dims.: Pol.: **Stanek, Stan(i)ecki, Stańczyk, Staniaszek, Staniaszczyk, Stanisz**; STACH, **Staszczyk**. Czech: **Staněk**, STACH. Jewish (E Ashkenazic): **Stashevsky, Stashevski, Stas(h)ewsky, Stas(h)ewski** (probably adoptions of the Pol. surnames, but also possibly habitation names from *Staszów* in Poland, whose Yid. name is *Stashev*).

Patrs.: Pol.: **Staniak**; **Stasiak, Staszak; Stanilewicz**. Croatian: **Stanisavljević, Stanić**.

Patrs. (from dims.): Pol.: **Stankiewicz** (also adopted as an E Ashkenazic surname); **Staszkiewicz, Staśkiewicz; Stańczak**. Croatian: **Stanković, Stanišić**.

Habitation names: Pol.: **Staniszewski, Staszewski, Stasiński, Stan(i)kowski, Stańczykowski**.

Stanley English: habitation name from any of the various places, for example in Derbys., Co. Durham, Gloucs., Staffs., Wilts., and W Yorks., so called from OE *stān* STONE + *lēah* wood, clearing.

Vars.: **Stanly, Standley, Stanleigh**.

Stannard English (E Anglia): from the ME given name *Stanhard*, OE *Stānheard*, composed of the elements *stān* stone + *heard* hardy, brave, strong.

Vars.: **Ston(h)ard, Stannett**.

Stansfield English: habitation name from a place in W Yorks., so called either from the gen. case of the OE personal name *Stān* (a byname or short form of the various cpd names with this first element; cf., e.g., STAMMER 1 and STANNARD) + OE *feld* pasture, open country (see FIELD), or else from a cpd meaning 'open land of the stone', with reference to a monolith. There are other places so called, e.g. in Suffolk, but the distribution suggests that the Yorks. one is the source of the surname.

Var.: **Stansfeld**.

Stanton English: habitation name from any of the extremely numerous places throughout England so called from OE *stān* STONE + *tūn* enclosure, settlement. Most of them get the name from their situation on stony ground, but in the case of *Stanton* Harcourt in Oxon. and *Stanton* Drew in Avon the reference is to the proximity of prehistoric stone monuments. The name has also sometimes been chosen by Ashkenazic Jews as an Anglicization of various like-sounding Jewish surnames.

Vars.: **Staunton** (places in Gloucs., Herefords., Leics., Notts., Somerset and Worcs.); **Stainton** (from various places in N England, where the first element has been influenced by the cogn. ON *steinn* stone); **Stenton** (see also STENSON).

Staple English: topographic name for someone who lived near a boundary post, ME *staple* (OE *stapol*), or habitation name from some place named with this word, as for example *Staple* in Kent or *Staple* Fitzpaine in Somerset.

Var.: **Staples**.

Stapleton English and Irish: habitation name from any of the various places, as for example in Cumb., Gloucs., Herefords., Leics., Shrops., Somerset, and N and W Yorks., so called from OE *stapol* post (see STAPLE) + *tūn* enclosure, settlement.

Var.: **Stapylton**.

Stapley English: habitation name from *Stapeley* in Ches. or *Stapely* in Hants, so called from OE *stapol* post (see STAPLE) + *lēah* wood, clearing. The reference may have been to a place where timber was got for posts.

Starikov Russian: patr. from the nickname *Starik* 'Old Man' (from *stary* old).

Dims.: Pol.: **Starek, Starzyk, Starczyk**. Czech: **Stárek**. Ukr.: **Starshenko**. Croatian: **Starčević** (patr.). Ger. (of Slav. origin): **Staroske**.

Habitation names: Pol.: **Starzyński, Starczewski**.

Stark N English and Scots: nickname for a stern, determined, or physically strong person, from ME *stark* firm, unyielding (OE *stearc*, ON *sterkr*). The Continental cogns. have the sense 'strong', 'brave'.

Dims.: Eng.: **Starkie, Starkey**. Ger.: **Stärkel, Stärkle**.

Patrs.: Eng.: **Starcks; Starkings**. Flem.: **Stercken(s), Sterckx, Ster(c)kmans**.

Starling English: nickname from some fancied resemblance to the bird, ME *starling* (OE *stær(ling)*; for the suffix, cf. CHAMBERLAIN).

Starosta Polish and Czech: status name for the headman of a village or district, a deriv. of *stary* old (cf. STARIKOV).

Var.: Pol.: **Starostecki**.

Starr English: nickname from ME *sterre, starre* star (OE *steorra*). The word was also used in a transferred sense of a patch of white hair on the forehead of a horse, and so perhaps the name denoted someone with a streak of white hair. It is possibly also a house name, for someone who lived at a house distinguished by the sign of a star.

Var.: **Starman** (also 'servant of S.').

Cpds (ornamental, except where indicated): Swed.: **Stjernqvist** ('star twig'); **Stjernström** ('star river'). Jewish: **Sternbach, Sternbuch** ('star stream'); **Sternbaum, Szterenbojm** ('star tree'); **S(h)ternberg, Sterenberg, Sternberger** ((dweller on a) star hill'); **Sternblitz** ('star lightning'); **Sternfeld** ('star field'); **S(z)ternfinkel, Sternfinkiel** ('star sparkle'); **Sternglanz** ('star radiance'); **Sternglass, Shterenglass** ('star glass'); **Sternheim** ('star homestead'); **Sternhell** ('star bright'); **Sternhertz, Shterngartz** ('star heart', the latter from Slav. regions lacking /h/); **Sternklar** ('star clear'); **Sternkuker** ('star gazer', apparently a nickname based on some now irrecoverable minor incident); **Sternli(e)b** ('star love'); **Sternlicht** ('star light'); **Sternschein** ('star shine'); **Sternschuss, Shternshuss, Sternshos** ('star shot'); **Sternt(h)al, Sterental** ('star valley'); **Ster(e)nzis, Szternzys** ('star sweet').

Start English: habitation name from any of the various minor places, for example in Devon, so called from OE *steort* tail, apparently in the transferred sense of a promontory or a spur of a hill.

Vars.: **Starte, Stert, Sturt; Starrett, Sterritt** (N Ireland).

Dim.: Ger.: **Stertzel**.

Startifant *see* STURTIVANT

Startin Scots (Aberdeen): habitation name from *Stirton* near Cupar in the former county of Fife. The placename is of unknown origin.

Var.: **Stirton**.

Šťastný Czech: from a given name representing a Czech vocab. word meaning 'happy', 'fortunate', or 'lucky', used as a translation of L FELIX.

Patrs.: Pol.: **Szczęsnowicz**; **Szczęśniak**, **Szcześniak** (also nicknames meaning 'lucky fellow').

Patr. (from a dim.): Pol.: **Szczęścikowicz**.

Stassen see ANSTICE

Statham English: habitation name from a place in Ches., so called from the dat. pl. *stæðum* of OE *stæð* landing stage (see STAIT), i.e. 'at the landing stages'.

Stauche German: nickname for someone who was distinguished by some peculiarity of dress, from MHG *stûche*, a term used to denote both a type of wide sleeve and a headcovering (OHG *stûhha*, denoting any wide, flat object).

Vars.: **Stauch**, **Steichen**.

Staude German: topographic name for someone who lived by a patch of uncleared dense undergrowth, from MHG *stûde* thicket, wilderness (OHG *stûda*).

Vars.: **Staudt**, **Stäuder**, **Stüde(r)**.

Dims.: Ger.: **Stäudle**, **Stüdle**, **Steidle**, **Steudle**.

Stauffer German: **1.** occupational name for a maker or seller of beakers or mugs, from an agent deriv. of Ger. *Stauf* beaker, stoop (MHG, OHG *stouf*). **2.** habitation name from any of the various minor places named with this word; the reference is to hills thought to resemble a beaker in shape.

Vars.: **Staufer(t)**.

Stawski Polish: topographic name for someone who lived by a pond, from Pol. *staw* pond + *-ski* suffix of local surnames (see BARANOWSKI).

Vars.: **Stawicki**, **Stawiak**.

Habitation names: **Stawiński**, **Stawowski**, **Stawiszyński**.

Staziker see STIRZAKER

Stead English (chiefly W Yorks.): **1.** habitation name from *Stead* in W Yorks., or from some other place taking its name from OE *stede* estate, farm, place. **2.** from ME *steed* stud horse, stallion (OE *stēda*), applied as a nickname to a lusty person or as an occupational name to someone responsible for looking after stallions.

Vars.: **Steed(e)**, **Stede**, **Steeds**. (Of 2 only): **Ste(a)dman**; **Steedman** (chiefly Scotland); **Stedmont**.

Stebbing English (E Anglia): topographic name for someone who lived in a clearing in woodland, from ME *stebbing*, *stubbing* clearing (OE *stybbing*, a deriv. of *stubb* tree stump; see STUBBE), or habitation name from some minor place deriving its name from this element.

Vars.: **Stebbings**, **Stubbin(g)s**.

Štěch see STEPHEN

Steckel see STYLES

Steckler Jewish (Ashkenazic): occupational name for a glass worker or glazier, from Russ. *steklo* glass (cf. SZKLAR) + the Ger., Yid. agent suffix *-er*.

Vars.: **Stekler**, **Steckl**, **Steckelman**, **Steckelmacher**.

Steel English and Scots: nickname for someone considered as hard and durable as steel, or metonymic occupational name for a foundry worker, from ME *stele* steel (OE *stȳle*). The name has also been used as an Anglicization of the Jewish forms listed below.

Var.: **Steele**.

Dims.: Ger.: **Stählin**, **Stäheli(n)**.

Patr.: Eng.: **Steels**.

Cpd (ornamental): Swed.: **Stå(h)lberg** ('steel hill').

Steenke see STONE

Steeples English (E Midlands): topographic name for someone who lived by a tall tower, ME *stepel* (OE *stēpel*). The term was first used of a church spire in the 15th cent.; this sense is unlikely to lie behind many examples of the surname.

Steer English: nickname for a truculent person or metonymic occupational name for someone who was responsible for tending bullocks, from ME *steer* bullock (OE *stēor*).

Vars.: **Steere**, **Stear**; **Ste(a)rman** (occupational only).

Dim.: Ger.: **Stierle**.

Patrs.: Eng.: **Steers**, **Stears**.

Steichen see STAUCHE

Steidle see STAUDE

Steiger German: **1.** topographic name for someone who lived by a path running up a hillside, from an agent deriv. of Ger. *Steig* steep path or track (MHG, OHG *stîc*, from OHG *stîgan* to climb). **2.** topographic name for someone who lived by a plank bridge, from a deriv. of MHG *stec* (OHG *steg*, from the same verb as in 1).

Vars.: **Staiger**, **Steg(n)er**; **Steg(e)mann**.

Stein **1.** German and Jewish (Ashkenazic): cogn. of STONE. **2.** Scots: from a contracted form of the given name STEPHEN.

Vars. (of 2): Sc.: **Steen**, **Stain**.

Patr. (from 2): Sc.: **Steenson**. See also STENSON.

Cpds (of 1): See STONE.

Steiner see STAINER

Steinhouse see STONEHOUSE

Steinmetz German and Jewish (Ashkenazic): occupational name for a mason or worker in stone, Ger. *Steinmetz* stonemason (MHG *steinmetze*, OHG *steinmezzo*, a cpd of *stein* STONE and *mezzo* MASON).

Vars.: Ger.: **Stainmetz**, **Stamitz**. Jewish: **Stienmetz**, **Stienmets**.

Dims.: Ger.: **Steinmetzel**, **Steinmeissel**, **Steinmassel**.

Steinweg German: habitation name from an unidentified place named with the OHG elements *stein* STONE + *weg* path (see WAY).

Var.: **Steinway** (Anglicized).

Stejskal Czech: nickname for a miserable, unhappy, or complaining person, a deriv. of the verb *stejskat, stýskat* to be unhappy, lonely, or grumpy.

Stekel see STYLES

Stell see STILL

Stella Italian: from It. *stella* star (L *stella*). In most cases it probably derives from a medieval given name or nickname, but it may also have been a house name for someone who lived at a house distinguished by this sign, or a topographic name for someone who lived at a place from which roads radiated out in various different directions.

Vars.: It.: **Stelli**; **La Stella** (Apulia).

Port.: **Estrela**.

Dims.: It.: **Stellin(i)**, **Stellino**.

Augs.: It.: **Stellon(i)**.

Pej.: It.: **Stellacci**.

Stellmacher German: occupational name for a cart-wright, Ger. *Stellmacher*, from MHG *stelle* carriage (originally 'frame', 'chassis') + *macher* maker. The term originated in Silesia and spread across northern Germany during the Middle Ages, though it never displaced WAG-NER in the south.

Vars.: **Stellmach**, **Stallmach**.

Dims.: Pol.: **Stelmaszczyk**. Ukr.: **Stelmashenko**. Beloruss.: **Stelmashonok**.

Stendal Jewish (Ashkenazic): probably a habitation name from a place near Magdeburg so called from MLG *steen* STONE + *dal* valley (see DALE).

Vars.: **Stendahl**, **Stendhal**, **Stendel**.

Stenhouse Scots: habitation name from a former barony near Falkirk, whose name has the same origin as STONEHOUSE.

Stenning English: habitation name from *Steyning* in Sussex, so called from OE *Stēningas* 'people of *Stān*', a byname or short form of the various cpd personal names with the first element *stān* stone.

Stenson English: **1.** patr. from a contracted form of the given name STEPHEN (cf. STEIN 2). **2.** habitation name from a place in Derbys., recorded in Domesday Book as *Steintune*, later as *Steineston*, from the ON personal name *Steinn* 'Stone' + OE *tūn* enclosure, settlement.

Vars. (of 1): **Stinson**, **Stim(p)son**. (Of 2): **Stenton** (see also STANTON).

Stenton see STANTON

Stephen English: from the ME given name *Stephen, Steven* (Gk *Stephanos* 'Crown'). This was a popular name throughout Christendom in the Middle Ages, having been borne by the first Christian martyr, stoned to death at Jerusalem three years after the death of Christ.

Vars.: **Steven**, **Stiven**, **Steffen**, **Steffan**. See also STEIN 2.

Dims.: Fr.: **Stevenet**, **Thévenet**, **Theuvenet**, **Thouv(en)et**, **Thevet**, **Thivet**, **Touvet**, **Étiennet**, **Thenet**; **Theuveney**, **Étienney**; **Thévenot**, **Thouvenot**, **Thevot**, **Thieblot**, **Étiennot**, **T(h)ienot**, **Thénot**, **Tenot**; **Thevenon**, **Thouvignon**, **T(h)enon**; **Stevenin**, **Thévenin**, **Thouvenin**, **Thiévin**, **Thevin**, **Thieblin**; **The(u)veny**, **Théveny**; **Stevenel**, **Théveneau**, **Thouvenel**. It.: **Stefanelli**, **Stifanelli**, **Stephanelli**, **Stevanelli**, **Stivanelli**, **Stephanello**, **Stef(f)anini**, **Stevanini**, **Stivanini**, **Stef(an)utti**, **Stefanutto**. Ger.: **Steff(l)**, STIEFEL. Flem., Du.: **Sties**. Ger. (of Slav. origin): **Stepke**, **Steffke**, **Steffek**, **Staffke**, **Stief(ke)**, **Schep(p)e**, **Scheppe**, **Tschepe**, **Tschäpe**, **Schäp(k)e**, **Zschäpe**, **Schepke**, **Schip(p)ke**, **Schipek**, **Schippig**, **Schoppe**, **Schoppa**, **Schöpe**, **Tschöp(p)e**. Czech: **Štěpánek**; **Štefek**; **Štěpnicka**, **Štěch**; **Šticha**. Pol.: **Stefanek**, **Stefanczyk**; **Szczepanik**,

Szczepanek. Ukr.: **Stepanenko**, **Steshenko**, **Stepyuk**, **Stetsyuk**, **Stepura**, **Stetsyura**. Beloruss.: **Stepanets**, **Stachvanyonok**.

Aug.: It.: **Stefanoni**.

Pejs.: Fr.: **Estévenard**, **Stiévenard**, **Stiévenart**, **Thév(en)ard**, **Thénard**, **Thénau(l)t**.

Patrs.: Eng.: **Stephens**, **Stevens**, **Steffens**; **Stephenson**, **Stephinson**, **Stevenson**, **Stevinson**, **Steverson**; STENSON. It.: **De Stefani(s)**. Sp.: **Estébanez**. Cat.: **Estévez**. Port.: **Esteves**. Rum.: **Stefanescu**. Low Ger.: **Stevens**, **Steffens(en)**. Fris.: **Stevinga**. Flem., Du.: **Stevens**. Dan., Norw.: **Steffensen**, **Stefansen**, **Stephensen**, **Stephansen**. Russ.: **Stepanov**. Bulg.: **Stefanov**. Pol.: **Stefanowicz**; **Stefaniak**; **Szczepanowicz**; **Szczepaniak**. Lithuanian: **Stepanaitis**. Armenian: **Stapanian**. Croatian: **Stepanović**, **Stefanović**, **Stevanović**; **Šćepanović**.

Patrs. (from dims.): Russ.: **Stepanchikov**, **Stepanychev**, **Step(an)ichev**, **Step(an)ishchev**, **Stepunin**, **Stepynin**, **Stepurin**, **Stepykin**, **Stepyryov**, **Stepulev**, **Styopushkin**, **Styokhin**. Ukr.: **Stepovich**, **Stetskiv**. Pol.: **Stefankiewicz**; **Szczepankiewicz**. Bulg.: **Penev**. Croatian: **Stev(ov)ić**.

Habitation names: Pol.: **Stefanowski**; **Szczepanowski**.

Stępień Polish: of uncertain origin, possibly an occupational name for a herbalist or other user of a pestle and mortar, from Pol. *stępor* mortar.

Vars.: **Stępiński**, **Stępni(a)k**.

Habitation names: **Stępniewski**, **Stępczyński**, **Stęp(k)owski**, **Stęplewski**.

Štěrba Czech: probably a nickname for someone with a front tooth missing, from Czech *štěrba* gap.

Stercken see STARK

Sterenberg see STARR

Sterling see STIRLING

Stern **1.** German and Jewish (Ashkenazic): cogn. of STARR. **2.** English: nickname for a severe person, from ME *stern(e)* strict, austere (OE *styrne*).

Vars. (of 2): Eng.: **Sterne**, **Stearn(e)**.

Patrs. (from 2): Eng.: **Ste(a)rns**.

Sterritt see START

Stersaker see STIRZAKER

Stert see START

Štětina Czech: **1.** nickname for a shoemaker, from the vocab. word *štětina* bristle, thread (i.e. the thread used to sew shoes with, which was made from bristles). **2.** nickname for a person with thick, spiky hair (from the same word as in 1).

Steuben see STUBBE

Steventon English: habitation name from *Steventon* in Berks., Hants, and Shrops., or *Stevington* in Beds. and Essex, probably all originally meaning 'settlement associated with *Stīf(a)*'. The surname is most common in Birmingham, where it probably derives from the Shrops. placename.

Stewart Scots: occupational name for an administrative official, from ME *stiward*, OE *stigweard*, *stīweard*, a cpd of *stig* house(hold) + *weard* guardian (see WARD). In OE times this title was used of an officer controlling the domestic affairs of a household, esp. of the royal household; after the Conquest it was also used more widely as the native equivalent of SENESCHAL for the steward of a manor or manager of an estate.

Vars.: **St(e)uart**; **Steward** (England).

Patrs.: **Stewartson**, **Stewardson**.

Stibor Czech: from an OCzech given name composed of the elements *cti*, gen. of *čest* honour + *bor* warrior.

Var.: **Ctibor**.

Štícha *see* STEPHEN

Stickel *see* STYLES

Stiddard *see* STODDART

Stiddolph English (Northumb.): from the OE personal name *Stīðwulf*, composed of the elements *stīð* stiff, hard + *wulf* wolf.

Var.: **Stidolph**.

Stiefel **1.** German and Jewish (Ashkenazic): metonymic occupational name for a maker of boots or nickname for someone who wore boots, from Ger. *Stiefel*, Yid. *shtivl* boot (MHG *stivel*, OHG *stival*, from LL *aestivale* light shoe, a deriv. of *aestas* summer). **2.** German: from a given name, a dim. of STEPHEN.

Vars. (of 1): Jewish: **Shtivel**; **Stiefler**, **Stiffelman**, **Stivelman** (occupational).

Stieger *see* STEIGER

Stienen *see* AUSTIN

Stienfeld *see* STONE

Stienmets *see* STEINMETZ

Stierle *see* STEER

Stiff English: nickname for someone who had difficulty in bending, from ME *stif* rigid, inflexible (OE *stīf*). The term was also used in a transferred sense of character (generally in the approving sense 'resolute', 'steadfast') from the 12th cent., and this use may lie behind many examples of the surname.

Stigand English: from an ON personal name composed of the element *stigr* path, way + the suffix *-and* (cf. WIGGIN).

Vars.: **Stigant**; **Styan**.

Patrs.: **Stiggants**, **Stiggins**; **Styants**, **Styance**.

Still **1.** English and German: nickname for a placid person, from ME, MHG *still* calm, quiet (OE *stille*, OHG *stilli*). **2.** English: topographic name for someone who lived by a fish trap in a river, ME *still*, *stell* (OE *stiell*).

Vars. (of 1 and 2): Eng.: **Stille**, **Stillman**. (Of 1 only): Ger.: **Stille**, **Stiller(t)**. (Of 2 only): Eng.: **Stiller**, **Stell**.

Stillingfleet English: habitation name from a place in E Yorks., recorded in Domesday Book as *Steflingefled* 'stream (OE *flēot*; see FLEET) of the people of **Stȳfel*', a dim. of the attested byname *Stūf* (of uncertain origin).

Stimpson *see* STENSON

Stinchcombe English: habitation name from a village in Gloucs., recorded in the 12th cent. as *Stintescombe*, from

the dial. term *stint* sandpiper + *cumb* narrow valley (see COOMBE).

Stirk English: nickname for someone resembling a bullock or metonymic occupational name for someone who had charge of bullocks, from ME *stirk* bullock (OE *styr(i)c*, *steorc*).

Stirland *see* STRICKLAND

Stirling Scots: habitation name from the city in central Scotland, recorded in the 12th cent. as *Strevelin*. The name is of problematic etymology, perhaps from a river name.

Var.: **Sterling**.

Stirrup English (Lancs.): **1.** possibly a metonymic occupational name for a maker of stirrup irons or stirrup leathers (or both), from OE *stīgrāp* stirrup (a cpd of *stīgan* to rise + *rāp* rope). However, there is no evidence that stirrup-making had any special status as an occupation in the Middle Ages. **2.** habitation name from *Styrrup* in Northants, which is probably so called from OE *stīgrāp* stirrup because of a stirrup-shaped ridge near which it stands.

Stirton *see* STARTIN

Stirzaker English (Lancs.): habitation name from *Stirzacre* in the parish of Garstang, N Lancs., so called from the gen. case of the ON personal name *Styrr* + OE *æcer* cultivated land (see ACKER) or the ON cogn. *akr*.

Vars.: **Stirsacre**, **Sturzaker**, **Stursaker**, **Stersaker**, **Sturraker**, **Staziker**.

Stitt *see* STUDD

Stivanelli *see* STEPHEN

Stjernqvist *see* STARR

Stobbart English (Northumb.): from a medieval given name. This is first recorded in Domesday Book as *Stubart*. It is probably a late OE formation from *stubb* stump, which seems to have been in use as a byname (see STUBBE), + *-heard* hardy, brave, strong.

Vars.: **Stobart**, **Stubbert**.

Stobbe *see* STUBBE

Stobie Scots: habitation name from *Stobo* near Peebles in S Scotland, so called from OE *stubb* tree stump + *holh* hollow (see HOLE) or *halh* nook, recess (see HALE 1).

Var.: **Stobo**.

Stock English: probably for the most part a topographic name for someone who lived near the uprooted trunk or stump of a large tree, OE *stocc*. In some cases the reference may be to a primitive foot-bridge over a stream consisting of a felled tree trunk. Some early examples without prepositions may point to a nickname for a stout, 'stocky' man or a metonymic occupational name for a keeper of punishment stocks.

Vars.: **Stocke**, **Stocks**; **Stocker**; **Stockman**.

Dims.: Ger.: **Stökel**, **Stöckle**.

Stockdale English: habitation name from a valley in Cumb. and N Yorks., so called from OE *stocc* tree trunk (see STOCK) + *dæl* valley (see DALE).

Vars.: **Stogdale**, **Stockdill**.

Stockley English: habitation name from any of various places, for example in Devon, Co. Durham, and Staffs., called *Stockleigh* or *Stockley*, from OE *stocc* tree trunk (see STOCK) + *lēah* wood, clearing.

Vars.: **Stockleigh**, **Stokel(e)y**.

Stockton English: habitation name from any of the places, for example in Ches., Co. Durham, Herts., Norfolk, Shrops., Warwicks., Wilts., Worcs., and N and W Yorks., so called from OE *stocc* tree trunk (see STOCK) or *stoc* dependent settlement (see STOKE) + *tūn* enclosure, settlement. It is not possible to distinguish between the two first elements on the basis of early forms.

Stockwell English: habitation name from a place now in S London, so called from OE *stocc* tree trunk, plank bridge (see STOCK) + *well(a)* spring, stream (see WELL).

Stoddart English (Northumb.): occupational name for a breeder or keeper of horses, from OE *stōd* stud (see STUDD) or *stott* inferior kind of horse (see STOTT) + *hierde* herdsman, keeper (see HEARD). There is a difficulty in deriving this name from OE *stōd* in that *stud* is not recorded in the sense 'collection of horses bred by one person' until the 17th cent.; before that it denoted a place where horses were kept for breeding, but that sense does not combine naturally with 'herdsman'.

Vars.: **Stod(h)art**, **Stoddard**, **Studart**, **Studd(e)ard**, **Studdert**, **Stiddard**, **Stothard**, **Stothart**, **Stothert**, **Stuttard**.

Stoffer see CHRISTOPHER

Stoke English: habitation name from any of the numerous places throughout England named from ME *stoke* (OE *stoc*). The exact sense in individual cases is not clear; it seems to have meant originally merely 'place', and to have been used mainly for an outlying hamlet or dependent settlement.

Vars.: **Stokes**, **Stoak(s)**, **Stook(es)**, STOKER.

Stoker 1. English: habitation name, a var. of STOKE. 2. Flemish and Dutch: cogn. of STOCK. 3. Scots: occupational name for a trumpeter, from Gael. *stocaire*, an agent deriv. of *stoc* Gaelic trumpet. The name is borne by a sept of the McFarlanes.

Patrs. (from 3): **McInstocker**, **McStoker** (Gael. **Mac an Stocaire**).

Stokoe English: habitation name from *Stockhow* in Cumb. The placename is first attested in 1581 as *Stackay*; in the absence of earlier forms it is not possible to suggest an etymology with any confidence.

Stokowski Polish: habitation name from a place named with Pol. *stok* hillside, slope + *-ów* possessive suffix, with the addition of *-ski* suffix of local surnames (see BARANOWSKI). It may also be a topographic name for someone who lived on a hillside.

Stolarski Polish and Jewish (E Ashkenazic): occupational name for a joiner, Pol. *stolarz* (a calque of Ger. TISCHLER, from Pol. *stół* table), with the addition of the surname suffix *-ski* (see BARANOWSKI).

Vars.: Pol.: **Stolarz**. Jewish: **Stol(i)ar**; **Stol(l)er**, **Stolersky** (from E Yid. *stolyer*).

Dims.: Pol.: **Stolarek**, **Stolarczyk**.

Stollard see STALLARD

Stolworthy see STALLARD

Stolz German and Jewish (Ashkenazic): nickname for a proud or haughty person, from Ger. *stolz*, Yid. *shtolts* proud.

Vars.: Ger.: **Stoltz(e)**, **Stolze**. Jewish: **Shtolzer**; **Sztolc** (a Pol. spelling).

Dims.: Ger.: **Stöl(t)zel**.

Patrs.: Low Ger.: **Stolten**, **Stolting**, **Stölting**.

Stonard see STANNARD

Stone English: from OE *stān* stone, in any of several uses. It is most commonly a topographic name, for someone who lived either on stony ground or by a notable outcrop of rock or a stone boundary-marker or monument, but it is also found as a metonymic occupational name for someone who worked in stone, a mason or stonecutter. There are various places in S and W England named with this word, for example in Bucks., Gloucs., Hants, Kent, Somerset, Staffs., and Worcs., and the surname may also be a habitation name from any of these. The form *Stone* is also found as an Anglicization of the various Jewish surnames listed below, including compounds.

Vars.: **Stones**; **Stoner**, **Stenner**; **Stoneman** (Devon); ASTON.

Dims.: Ger.: **Steinl(e)**, **Steindl**. Low Ger.: **Steinchen**, **Steinke**, **Steine(c)ke**, **Steinicke**, **Steenke(n)**, **Stehnke**.

Cpds (ornamental): Swed.: **Stenbäck** ('stone stream'); **Stenberg** ('stone hill'); **Stenholm** ('stone island'); **Stenmark** ('stone territory'); **Stenqvist** ('stone twig'); **Stenström** ('stone river'). Jewish: **Steinbach** ('stone stream'); **Steinbaum**, **Sztajnbaum**, **Sztejnbaum** ('stone tree'); **S(z)teinberg**, **Sztajnberg**, **Sztejnberg**, **Steinberger** ((dweller on a) stone hill'); **Steinfeld**, **Stienfeld** ('stone field'); **Steingart(en)** ('stone garden'); **Steingold** ('stone gold'; cf. GOLDSTEIN); **Steinhard(t)** ('stone hard'); **Steinher(t)z** ('stone heart'); **Steinhorn** ('stone horn'); **Steinreich** ('stone rich'); **Steinwurzel**, **Steinwercel** ('stone root').

Stoneham English: habitation name from a pair of villages in Hants, so called from OE *stān* STONE + *hām* homestead.

Var.: **Stonham** (a place in Suffolk).

Stonehouse 1. English: topographic name (from OE *stān* STONE + *hūs* HOUSE for someone who lived in a house built of stone, something of a rarity in the Middle Ages, or habitation name from a place so named, for example in Devon and Gloucs. See also STENHOUSE. 2. Jewish (Ashkenazic): Anglicized form of **Steinhaus** 'stone house', a topographic name for someone who lived in a house made of this material; see STONE.

Var. (of 2): **Steinhouse**.

Stonier see STANIER

Stonor English: habitation name from a place in Oxon., so called from OE *stān* STONE + *ōra* slope (see ORR 3).

Stopford English: habitation name from *Stockport* in Greater Manchester, which used to be locally pronounced /ˈstɒpfɔːd/. The placename is recorded in the 12th cent. as *Stokeport*, probably from OE *stoc* hamlet, dependent settlement (see STOKE) + *port* market place (see PORT).

The confusion of the second element with *ford* appears in 1288, and the form *Stopford* is recorded in 1347.

Vars.: **Stopforth**, **Stop(p)ard**, **Stopper**.

Stordy *see* STURDY

Storer English: occupational name for an official in charge of dispensing provisions in a great house or monastery, or who collected rents paid in kind, from an agent deriv. of ME *stor* provisions, supplies (an aphetic form of OF *estor*, from the verb *estorer* to lay in, store, L *instaurāre* renew, replace). The word *stor* was also used in the Middle Ages for livestock, and the surname may sometimes have denoted a keeper of animals.

Vars.: **Storrar**, **Storah**, **Storror**, **Storrow**; **Stores**.

Storey N English: from the ON byname *Stóri* (from *storr* big, large), also used as a given name in N England in the early Middle Ages.

Vars.: **Story**; **Stor(r)ie** (Scotland); **Storr** (from *storr* 'big' used as a nickname).

Stork English: nickname for a thin man with long legs, from the bird (OE *storc*), or perhaps occasionally a house name from a house distinguished by the sign of a stork.

Dims.: Ger.: **Störchel**, **Störkel**.

Storm English, Low German, Flemish/Dutch, and Danish/Norwegian: nickname for a man of blustery temperament, from OE, OSax. *storm*, ON *stormr* storm.

Vars.: Eng.: **Storme**. Flem., Du.: **Van den Storm**.

Dims.: Ger.: **Stürmle**; **Sturm(l)i** (Switzerland).

Patrs.: Eng.: **Stormes**. Flem., Du.: **Storms**.

Stortone *see* TORT

Stott English: nickname from ME *stott* steer, bullock (OE *stott* inferior kind of horse), or metonymic occupational name for a keeper of the animals. The term was also occasionally used in ME of a horse or of a heifer (and so as a term of abuse for a woman), and these senses may also lie behind some examples of the surname.

Stourton English: habitation name from any of various places, in Staffs., Warwicks., and Wilts., so called from their situation on different rivers *Stour* + OE *tūn* enclosure, settlement. The river name is of Gmc origin, and seems to have originally meant 'Strong', 'Powerful'.

Stout English: 1. nickname for a brave or powerfully built man, from ME *stout* steadfast (an aphetic form of OF *estout*, from a Gmc cogn. of STOLZ). 2. from the ON byname *Stútr* 'Gnat', denoting a small and insignificant person. 3. possibly also a habitation name from a minor place named with the OE element *stūt* stumpy hillock, which is found as a component in various Devon placenames.

Vars.: **Stoute**, **St(o)utt**.

Stow 1. English: habitation name from any of the numerous places, for example in Cambs., Essex, Gloucs., Lincs., Norfolk, Shrops., and Suffolk, so called from OE *stōw*, a word akin to *stoc* (see STOKE), with the specialized meaning 'meeting place', frequently referring to a holy place or church. Places in Bucks., Cambs., Lincs., Northants, and Staffs. having this origin use the spelling *Stowe*, but the spelling difference cannot be relied on as an indication of locality of origin. The final *-e* in part represents a trace of the OE dat. inflection. 2. Jewish (Ashkenazic): Anglicized form of various like-sounding Jewish surnames.

Var.: **Stowe**.

Strachan Scots: habitation name from a place in the parish of Banchory, near Kincardine, which is first recorded in 1153 in the form *Strateyhan*, and perhaps gets its name from Gael. *srath* valley + *eachain*, gen. case of *eachan* foal (dim. of *each* horse; cf. KEOGH). The pronunciation is traditionally /strɔːn/.

Vars.: **Strahan**; **Straughan** (Northumb.); **Strain** (N Ireland).

Strack *see* ASTRUC

Stradivari Italian: topographic name for someone who lived in a street with many bends, from It. *strada* STREET + *vara* (fem.) bent, crooked (L *vāra*). Both parts of the name have been assimilated to the most common surname ending *-i*.

Strahl Jewish (Ashkenazic): ornamental name from Yid. *shtral* or Ger. *Strahl* ray of light, sunbeam (MHG *strāle* flash of lightning, arrow, OHG *strāla*). It is possible that the name was adopted as a translation of any of the various Hebr. given names referring to light, such as *Uri* and *Meir*, but there is no evidence for this.

Var.: **Strahler**.

Strand Danish, Norwegian, and Swedish: topographic name for someone who lived by the sea-shore, or arbitrarily chosen ornamental surname, from Dan., Swed. *strand* shore (ON *strond*).

Var.: Swed.: **Strandh**.

Cpds: Swed.: **Strandberg**, **Strindberg** ('shore hill').

Strange English: nickname for a newcomer to the area, from ME *strange* foreign (an aphetic form of OF *estrange*, L *extrāneus*, from *extra* outside).

Vars.: **Strainge**, **Lestrange**, **Stranger**.

Strangeways English: habitation name from a place near Manchester, so called from OE *strang* STRONG + *(ge)wæsc* wash, current.

Vars.: **Strangways**, **Strangeway**, **Strangewick**.

Stránský Czech: topographic name for someone living on a hillside, Czech *stráň*, or habitation name from a place named with this element, for example *Strán, Strana*, or *Stránka*.

Stratfield English: habitation name from places in Berks. and Hants, so called from OE *strēt* (Roman) road (see STREET) + *feld* pasture, open country (see FIELD).

Vars.: **Stre(a)tfield**.

Stratford English: habitation name from any of various places, for example in Greater London, Beds., Bucks., Northants, Suffolk, Wilts., and Warwicks., so called from OE *strēt* (Roman) road (see STREET) + *ford* FORD.

Var.: **Strafford**.

Stratton English: habitation name from any of various places, for example in Beds., Dorset, Hants, Norfolk, Oxon., Somerset, Suffolk, Surrey, and Wilts., so called from OE *strēt* (Roman) road (see STREET) + *tūn* enclosure, settlement. A place of the same name in Cornwall, which may also be a partial source of the surname, probably has as its first element Corn. *stras* valley.

Var.: **Stretton** (the name of places in Ches., Derbys., Herefords., Leics., Shrops., Staffs., and Warwicks.).

Straub German: nickname for a shock-headed man, from MHG *strūp* rough, unkempt (OHG *strūb*).

Dims.: Ger.: **Sträuble, Strubel, Strobel.**

Patrs.: Low Ger.: **Strübing, Strüwing, Strüfing.**

Strauss 1. German: nickname for an awkward or belligerent person, from Ger. *Strauss* quarrel, complaint (MHG *strūz*; cf. STRUTT). **2.** German: house name from a house distinguished by the sign of an ostrich, Ger. *Strauss* (MHG *strūze*, OHG *strūz*, from L *strūthio*, Gk *srouthion*), or nickname for someone who wore a hat decorated with an ostrich feather. **3.** Jewish (Ashkenazic): ornamental name from Ger. *Strauss* ostrich, one of the many Ashkenazic surnames taken from bird names.

Var.: **Straus.** (Of 3 only): **Shtrauss; Strausz** (a Hung. spelling); **Straussman(n), Strusman.**

Dims.: Ger.: **Sträussle, Streissle.** Low Ger.: **Strussgen.**

Straw English (chiefly Notts.): metonymic occupational name for a dealer in straw (OE *strēaw*), or nickname for an exceptionally thin man or someone with straw-coloured hair.

Dim.: Ger.: **Ströhlein.**

Streatley English: habitation name from any of various places, for example in Beds. and Berks., so called from OE *strǣt* (Roman) road (see STREET) + *lēah* wood, clearing.

Vars.: **Streetley** (a place in Essex); **Streetly** (places in Cambs. and Warwicks.); **Strelley** (a place in Notts.).

Streek English: nickname for a stern or obstinate person, from ME *streke* severe, unyielding (OE *strǣc, strec*).

Var.: **Streake.**

Streep Dutch: nickname for someone marked in some way with a stripe or streak, MDu. *strīpe.*

Street English: habitation name from any of the various places, for example in Herts., Kent, and Somerset, so called from OE *strǣt* Roman road (L *strāta (via)*, from the past part. of *sternere* to strew, cover, surface). In the Middle Ages the word also came to denote the main street in a village, and so the surname may also have been a topographic name for someone who lived on the main street.

Vars.: **Streat** (a place in Sussex); **Strete** (places in Devon); **Streete, Streets; Streeter, Streater.**

Dims. (topographic): It.: **Stradella.** Flem.: **Straetje(s).**

Streltsov Russian: patr. from the occupational term *strelets* marksman, musketeer (a deriv. of *strelyat* to shoot, originally with arrows, from *strela* arrow, an ultimate cogn. of STRAHL).

Habitation names: Pol.: **Strzelecki** (from either of two towns called *Strzelce*). Jewish (E Ashkenazic): **Strelec.**

Strettell English: probably a habitation name from an unidentified place named with the OE elements *strǣt* (Roman) road (see STREET) + *hyll* HILL.

Strickland English: habitation name from a place in Cumb., so called from OE *styr(i)c, steorc* bullock (see STIRK) + *land* land, pasture.

Var.: **Stirland** (common in Notts.; perhaps from a different (unidentified) place of the same etymology).

Stride English: apparently a nickname for someone with long legs or whose gait had a purposeful air, from ME *stride* (long) pace (from *stride(n)* to walk with long steps, OE *strīdan* to straddle).

Striker English: occupational name for someone whose job was to fill level measures of corn by passing a flat stick over the brim of the measure, thus removing any heaped excess, from an agent deriv. of ME *strike(n)* to stroke, smooth (OE *strīccan*).

Vars.: **Strike** (a metonymic name from the stick used); **Straker** (from the OE byform *strācian*).

Stringer English: occupational name for a maker of string, from an agent deriv. of ME *string* string (OE *streng*).

Var.: **String** (metonymic).

Stringfellow English (Lancs.): nickname for a powerful man, from ME *streng* mighty, STRONG + *felaw* FELLOW.

Strnad Czech: nickname for someone bearing some fancied resemblance to a bunting, Czech *strnad*.

Stroev Russian: patr. from the ORuss. term of relationship *stroi* uncle. The word was also used as an affectionate nickname and even as a given name in some parts of Russia, whereas in others it was used to describe a cripple or beggar, and the surname may also derive from either of these senses.

Stroganov Russian: patr. from the nickname *Strogan*, which may derive either from the adj. *strogi* stern, severe, or from the past part. *stroganni* of the verb *strogat* to shave.

Vars.: **Strogonov; Stroganoff** (a Fr. spelling).

Strohane Irish: Anglicized form of Gael. **Ó Sruthåin** 'descendant of *Sruthån*', a personal name from a dim. of *sruth* sage, elder (or, less likely, of the homonymous *sruth* stream).

Ström Swedish: topographic name for someone who lived by a river, or arbitrarily adopted ornamental name, from *ström* river (ON *straumr*, a cogn. of OE *strēam*, mod. Eng. *stream*).

Cpds (ornamental): **Strömbäck** ('river stream'); **Strömberg** ('river hill'); **Strömblad** ('river leaf'); **Strömblom** ('river flower'); **Strömbom** ('river tree'); **Strömgren** ('river branch'); **Strömqvist** ('river twig'); **Strömwall, Strömvall** ('river bank').

Stronach Scots: nickname for an interfering person, from Gael. *sronach* nosey.

Strong English: nickname for a strong man, or perhaps sometimes ironically for a weakling, from ME, OE *strong, strang* strong.

Vars.: **Stronge; Strang** (Scots; according to Black a var. of STRANGE); **Strangman.**

Strongitharm *see* ARMSTRONG

Stroud English: habitation name from places in Gloucs. and Middx, so called from an OE element *strōd*, used to describe marshy ground overgrown with brushwood.

Strood in Kent is named with the same word, and some examples of the surname are no doubt derived from this term in independent use.

Vars.: **Strood**, **Strode**.

Stróżyński Polish: habitation name referring to a place where a gate-keeper lived, from Pol. *stróż* gatekeeper + *-yn* possessive suffix + *-ski* suffix of local surnames (see BARANOWSKI). In effect, it is normally an occupational name for a gate-keeper or watchman.

Strudwick English: habitation name from an unidentified minor place, so called from OE *strōd* damp land (see STROUD) + *wīc* dairy farm (see WICK). *Strudgewick* in the parish of Kirdford, Sussex, was earlier *Strodwike*, and may be a partial source of the surname.

Strumiłło Polish: topographic name for someone who lived by a stream, from Pol. *strum-* (cf. mod. Pol. *strumień*), with the Lithuanian ending *-i(e)łło* (cf. RADZIWIŁŁ).

Var.: **Strumiński**.

Struthers Scots: topographic name from Northern ME *strother* damp land (from OE *strōd*, the same word as in STROUD), or habitation name from any of the various places named with this element, as for example *Struther* near Stonehouse, Lanarks., *Sruthers* in Fife, or *Srother* in Northumb.

Strutt English: of uncertain origin, probably from the ON byname *Strútr* (from a vocab. word referring to a cone-like ornament on a headdress or cap). Alternatively it may be a nickname for an argumentative person, from ME *strut(t)* quarrel (cf. STRAUSS 1).

Strzałkowski Polish: habitation name referring to a place where an archer or musketeer lived, from a dim. of Pol. *strzał* shot, archery (cf. STRELTSOV) + *-ów* possessive suffix + *-ski* suffix of local surnames (see BARANOWSKI). In effect, it is probably an occupational name for an archer or musketeer.

Stuart *see* STEWART

Stubbe English: topographic name for someone who lived near the stump of a large felled tree, or nickname for a short, stout man, from OE *stub(b)* tree stump.

Vars.: **Stubber** (local); **Stobbe**.

Patrs. (from the nickname): Eng.: **Stubbs**, **Stobbs** (also vars. of the topographic name). Low Ger.: **Steuben**, **Stüven**.

Stubbert *see* STOBBART

Stubbings *see* STEBBING

Stubley English: habitation name from any of several places so called, from OE *stub(b)* tree stump (see STUBBE) + *lēah* wood, clearing, i.e. a patch where the trees had been felled, leaving only stumps; cf. STUKELEY. The surname is commonest in Yorks., and the source is probably most often *Stubley* in Heckmondwike.

Studart *see* STODDART

Studd English: topographic name for someone who lived on a stud farm, or occupational name for someone who was employed on one, from ME *stode, stud(d)e* stud (OE *stōd*; cf. STODDART).

Vars.: **Stitt** (Scotland and N Ireland); **Studman**.

Stüde *see* STAUDE

Studley English: habitation name from any of various places, in Oxon., Warwicks., Wilts., and W Yorks., so called from OE *stōd* stud farm + *lēah* wood, clearing, pasture.

Studziński Polish: topographic name for someone who lived beside a well, from Pol. *studzień* well + *-ski* suffix of local surnames (see BARANOWSKI).

Vars.: **Studzieński**; **Studnicki**.

Dim.: **Studniarek** (occupational name for a well-sinker).

Stukeley English: habitation name from a place in the former county of Hunts., now part of Cambs., so called from OE *styfic* stump + *lēah* wood, clearing; cf. STUBLEY. *Stewkley* IN BUCKS. HAS THE SAME ORIGIN AND MAY ALSO BE A PARTIAL SOURCE OF THE SURNAME.

Vars.: **Stukely**, **Stucley**.

Stümbke N German: habitation name from the village of *Steimbke*, near Sachsenhagen, Hesse.

Vars.: **Stümbcke**, **Stümpke**, **Stüm(c)ke**.

Stump English: of similar meaning to STUBBE, from ME *stump* tree stump (a borrowing from MLG *stump(e)*, obscurely related to OE *stub(b)*).

Sturdy English: nickname for an impetuous or hot-headed man, from ME *st(o)urdi* reckless, rash (an aphetic form of OF *est(o)urdi*, past part. of *estourdir* to daze, stupify, LL *exturdīre*, a deriv. of *turdus* thrush, which was thought to be a stupid bird, dazed and drunken from its diet of grapes).

Vars.: **Sturdee**, **Stordy**.

Sturgeon English: metonymic occupational name for a fishmonger, or possibly a nickname, from ME *sturgeon* (an aphetic form of OF *estourgeon*, of Gmc origin, which replaced the native cogn. *styrga*).

Sturgess English: apparently from the ON personal name *Þorgils*, composed of the divine name *Þorr* + *gils* hostage, pledge. However, the inorganic initial *S-* is not easily explained; it may be the result of OF influence.

Vars.: **Sturges**, **Sturgis**, **Sturge**; **Turgoose**.

Sturman 1. English: occupational name for a navigator, from ON *stýrimaðr* steersman (a cpd of *stýra* to steer + *maðr*, gen. *manns*, man). 2. English: from a OF dim. form **Esturmin* of a Gmc byname meaning STORM'. 3. Jewish (Ashkenazic): of unknown origin.

Sturmi *see* STORM

Sturraker *see* STIRZAKER

Sturrock Scots (Dundee): Black comments that this name is an occupational name for a sheep-farmer or store-master, but he gives no further explanation. The connection, if any, with ME *stor*, OF *estor* (see STORER) is by no means clear.

Patr.: **Sturrocks**.

Sturt *see* START

Sturtivant English: apparently a nickname for a hasty individual, from ME *stert(en)* to start, leap (OE *styrtan*) +

ANF *avaunt* forward (LL *abante*, a cpd of class. L *ab* away + *ante* in front).

Vars.: **Sturtevant, Sturdevant, Startifant**.

Stutt *see* STOUT

Stüven *see* STUBBE

Stuyvesant Dutch: probably a nickname for a blustering person or for a keen horseman, from MDu. *stūven* to stir up (cf. MHG *stieben*, OHG *stioban*) + *sant* sand.

Styan *see* STIGAND

Styczyński Polish: from Pol. *styczeń* January, a name taken by or bestowed on someone who was born or baptized in January, esp. a convert to Christianity.

Styles English: 1. topographic name for someone who lived near a steep ascent, OE *stigol* (a deriv. of *stīgan* to climb; cf. STEIGER). 2. topographic name for someone who lived near a stile, OE *stigel* (from the same verb).

Vars.: **Style, Stile(s), Stileman; Stiggles, Stygal(l), Stickel, Stickel(l)s, Stickles, Stegel(l), Steggle(s), Steggall(s), Steggals, Ste(c)kel, Stekles**.

Styokhin *see* STEPHEN

Suárez *see* SUERO

Suc Provençal: topographic name for someone who lived on a hillock or mound, OProv. *suc*.

Var.: **Delsuc**.

Dims.: **Suquet, Suchet**.

Aug.: **Suchat**.

Such English: from ME, OF *s(o)uche* tree stump (probably of Gaul. origin, apparently ultimately related to Eng. STOCK). The original application of this word as a surname is not clear; it may be a topographic name for someone who lived by a tree stump, or else a nickname for a man of stumpy build.

Vars.: **Souch, Sutch, Zouch; Chuck(s)** (from the Norman form *chouque*).

Dims.: Fr.: **Souchet, Dusouchet, Souchon**. Prov.: **So(u)quet, Socquet, Socquin**. It.: **Zoccoli**.

Augs.: It.: **Zocconi, Zoccone**.

Suchý Czech: nickname for a thin man, from Czech *suchý*, the original meaning of which is 'dry'.

Var.: **Suchan**.

Dim.: Czech: **Suchánek**.

Suckling English: nickname for a person who was childish in appearance or behaviour, from ME *suckling* infant at the breast (from OE *sūcan* to suck + the Gmc suffix *-ling* (cf. CHAMBERLAIN), probably under the influence of MDu. *sūgeling*). The surname is attested from the 13th cent., although the vocab. word does not appear until the 15th cent.

Suddaby *see* SOTHEBY

Sudell N English: probably a habitation name from an unidentified place, possibly *Sud Hill* in Hunmanby, E Yorks. (*Suddale* in the 12th cent.), which is named with OE *sūð* or ON *suðr* SOUTH + OE *dæl* or ON *dalr* valley (see DALE).

Sudran *see* SOUTH

Sudworth English (Lancs.): habitation name from the depopulated village of *Southworth* near Winwick in Ches., so called from OE *sūð* SOUTH + *worð* enclosure (see WORTH).

Suero Spanish: from a medieval given name of Gmc origin, attested in the Latinized form *Suerius*. The first element is of obscure origin, the second is *heri, hari* army.

Patrs.: Sp.: **Suárez**. Port.: **Soares**.

Süfke *see* SIEGFRIED

Sugarman *see* ZUCKER

Sugden English: habitation name from a place in W Yorks., so called from OE *sucga* sparrow (or other small bird) + *denu* valley (see DEAN 1).

Var.: **Sugdon**.

Suggate *see* SOUTHGATE

Sugrue Irish: Anglicized form of Gael. **Ó Siochfhradha** 'descendant of *Siochfhradh*', a personal name representing a Gaelicized form of an ON cogn. of SIEGFRIED. The surname is largely confined to Co. Kerry.

Var.: **Shugrue**.

Suikermans *see* ZUCKER

Suk Czech: from the vocab. word *suk* knot, knar, applied either as a topographic name for someone who lived by a tree with a knotty trunk, or as a nickname for a powerful, unyielding man or a stubborn, awkward one, from the same word in a transferred sense.

Dim.: Czech: **Souček**.

Habitation names: Pol.: **Sękowski; Sęczkowski** (from a dim., *sęczek*).

Suliman *see* SALOMON

Sulley English (Notts.): habitation name from an unidentified place named with the OE elements *sūð* SOUTH + *lēah* wood, clearing.

Sullivan Irish: Anglicized form of Gael. **Ó Súileabháin** 'descendant of *Súileabhán*', a personal name composed of the elements *súil* eye + *dubh* black, dark + the dim. suffix *-án*.

Vars.: **O'Sullivan, Sullevan, Soolivan**.

Sully 1. French: habitation name from any of various places, for example in Calvados, Loiret, and Oise. The first of these is recorded in 1180 as *Silleium*, from the Gallo-Roman personal name *Silius* or *Cilius* + the local suffix *-ācum*. The others are from a personal name *Sol(l)ius* + *-ācum*. 2. S English: of uncertain origin; possibly a habitation name imported from France and so identical with 1, or alternatively a var. of SULLEY. It may also be from the parish of *Sully* in the former county of Glamorgan, Wales, so called either from ON *sul* cleft + *ey* island or from the Norman family name *de Sulley* (as in 1), which is found in Glamorgan in the 12th cent.

Sultan *see* SOWDEN

Summer 1. English: nickname for someone of a warm or sunny disposition, or for someone associated with the season of summer in some other way, from ME *sum(m)er* summer (OE *somer*); cf. WINTER. 2. English: assimilated var. of SUMNER. 3. English: assimilated var. of SUMPTER. 4.

Irish: translation of Gael. **Ó Samhraidh** 'descendant of *Samhradh*', a byname meaning 'Summer'.

Vars.: **Som(m)er**; **Simmer** (Scots). (Of 4 only): **O'Sawrie**, **O'Sawra**.

Patrs. (from 1): Eng.: **Summers**, **Som(m)ers**, **Simmers**, **Sym(m)ers**; **Summerson**.

Cpds (of 1): Jewish: **Somerfreund** ('summer friend'); **Sommerfeld(t)** ('summer field'; Anglicized **Summerfield**, see also SOMERVILLE); **Somerschein** ('summer sunshine'); **Som(m)erstein** ('summer stone').

Summerfield *see* SOMERVILLE

Summerhayes S English: probably a topographic name referring to an enclosure (on upland pasture), where animals were kept in summer; for the second element (from OE *(ge)hæg* enclosure) see HAY 1.

Summerhill S English: probably a habitation name from an unidentified minor place named with the OE elements *somer* SUMMER + *hyll* HILL, i.e. hill used for summer grazing.

Summerlad English: from an ON personal name composed of the elements *sumar* summer + *liðr* warrior; the second element has been variously altered by folk etymology.

Vars.: **Summerland**, **Sommerlat**, **Som(m)erlad**.

Summerly Irish: Anglicized form of Gael. **Ó Somacháin** 'descendant of *Somachán*', a byname originally denoting a soft, fat person.

Var.: SOMERVILLE.

Summerscale *see* SOMERSCALES

Summersett *see* SOMERSET

Sumner English (now common mainly in Lancs.): occupational name for an official who was responsible for ensuring the appearance of witnesses in court, ME *sumner*, *sumnor* summoner (OF *sumoneor*, L *submonitor*, from *submonēre* to remind discreetly).

Vars.: **Sumpner**, **Somner**, **Simner**, **Simnor**, SUMMER.

Sumpter English: occupational name for a carrier, from ME *sum(p)ter* (driver of a) pack animal (OF *som(m)etier*, from LL *sagmatārius*, a deriv. of *sagma*, gen. *sagmatis*, pack saddle, from Gk).

Vars.: **Sunter**, SUMMER.

Sund Swedish: arbitrarily adopted or ornamental surname from the Swed. vocab. word *sund* sound, strait (ON *sund*), perhaps in some cases adopted as a topographic name by someone who lived by a strait.

Vars.: **Sundh**, **Sundén**, **Sundin**, **Sundell**, **Sundelius**, **Sundelin**, **Sundman**.

Cpds (ornamental): **Sundberg** ('strait hill'); **Sundblad** ('strait leaf'); **Sundgren** ('strait branch'); **Sundqvist** ('strait twig'); **Sundstedt** ('strait homestead'); **Sundström** ('strait river'); **Sundwall**, **Sundvall** ('strait slope').

Sunderland English: habitation name from any of various places so called, especially the city at the mouth of the river Wear. This, like other places so called in Cumb., Lancs., and S Scotland, derives its name from OE *sundor* separate + *land* land; a further example in Northumb. has the same origin as SUTHERLAND.

Sunshine *see* SONNENSCHEIN

Sunter *see* SUMPTER

Sunyer Catalan: from a Gmc personal name composed of the elements *sunj* truth + *heri*, *hari* army.

Vars.: **Suñer**, **Sunyé**, **Suñé**.

Suominen Finnish: ostensibly a patr. from the word meaning 'Finn', this surname was apparently adopted in a spirit of patriotism. *Suomi* Finland is a deriv. of *suomaa* marshland.

Suquet *see* SUC

Surby *see* SOWERBY

Surcoate *see* CIRCUIT

Sureau French: topographic name for someone who lived by an elder tree, from a dim. of OF *seür* elder (originally *seü*, *saü*, from L *sa(m)būcus*, but apparently altered by association with the adj. *sur* sour, of Gmc origin).

Vars.: **Surel**; **Saüc**, **Sahuc**, **Sahut**; **Sahu(c)quet**.

Surgeon English: occupational name for a person who performed operations, mostly amputations, ME, OF *sur(ri)gien* (LL *chirurgiānus*, from *chirurgia* handiwork, Gk *kheirourgia*, a cpd of *kheir* hand + *ourgia* work, from *ergein* to perform, do). Before the advent of anaesthetics, only crude surgery was possible, and the calling was often combined with that of the BARBER or bath-house attendant (cf. BADER).

Vars.: **Surgey**; **Surge(o)ner**, **Surgenor** (with ME agent suffixes).

Surgison *see* SERGEANT

Surin *see* SÉVERIN, SORIN

Surman *see* SERMON

Surowiec Polish: nickname for a serious, grim, or unrefined person, from a deriv. of Pol. *surowy* raw, serious. The word *surowiec* also means 'raw material'.

Var.: **Surowiecki**.

Surridge English: 1. from a ME given name, *Seric*, which represents a coalescence of two OE personal names, *Sǣrīc* (composed of the elements *sǣ* sea + *rīc* power) and *Sigerīc* (composed of the elements *sige* victory + *rīc* power). This would normally have given mod. Eng. *Serrich*, but the form has been altered under the influence of OF *surreis* southerner (see 2 below). 2. regional name for someone who had migrated from the South, from OF *surreis* southerner; cf. NORRIS. 3. habitation name from a place in the parish of Morebath, Devon, so called from OE *sūð* SOUTH + *hrycg* RIDGE.

Vars. (of 1): **Surrage**, **S(e)arch**, **Sarge**, **Ser(ri)ck**, **Sark**, **Sea(w)right**.

Surtees English (Northumb.): topographic name from ANF *sur* on, by (L *super* on, over) + *Tees* (a river in N England, so called from a Brit. term cogn. with Gael. *teas* heat, and so probably meaning 'boiling', 'surging'). Some early forms, as for example Randulf *de Super Teise* (Northants 1174), seem to point to a lost placename composed of these elements.

Surtill *see* SHORTALL

Susin *see* ZISIN

Sussapfel *see* SWEET

Süsskind Jewish (Ashkenazic): **1.** ornamental name from Ger. *süss* SWEET + *kind* child. **2.** metr. from the Yid. dim. female given name *Ziske* (see ZISIN), altered by folk etymology to conform to 1. Many Jewish surnames ending in -*kin* (actually from the dim. given name ending -*k(e)* + the Slav. possessive ending -*in*) acquired an excrescent -*d* as a result of folk-etymological association with Yid. *kind* child.
Vars.: **Susskind**; **Siskind**; **Zusskind, Zyskind, Zis(s)kind**.

Sutcliffe English: habitation name from any of the three places in W Yorks. so called from OE *sūð* SOUTH + *clif* riverbank, slope, cliff (see CLIVE).
Var.: **Sutcliff**.

Sutherby *see* SOTHEBY

Sutherin *see* SOUTH

Sutherland Scots: regional name from the former county of this name, so called from ON *suðroen* southern + *land* land; the territory was so named because it lay south of Scandinavia and the earlier Norse colonies in the Orkney and Shetland Islands.
Vars.: **Southerland, Sutherlan**.

Sutter *see* SAUTER

Sutton English: habitation name from any of the extremely numerous places so called, from OE *sūð* SOUTH + *tūn* enclosure, settlement.

Suwalski Polish: habitation name from the town of *Suwałki* in NE Poland.

Svanberg *see* SWAN

Svanetti *see* JOHN

Svatoš Czech: from any of the Czech personal names with a first element *svat-* holy (cf. ŚWIĄTEK), for example *Svatomír* ('holy' + 'great'), *Svatoslav* ('holy' + 'glory'), and *Svatobor* ('holy' + 'warrior').
Vars.: **Svatoň, Svačina; Švanda** (altered by folk etymology to conform with the vocab. word *švanda* joke, fun).
Dims.: **Svátek, Svášek, Sváček; Svach**.

Svedin Swedish: ornamental name, ostensibly from Swed. *sved* (burnt) clearing (past. part. of *svedja* to singe, scorch). This was perhaps sometimes chosen as a topographic name by someone who lived in or near such a clearing, but far more often no doubt it was adopted, on the basis of folk etymology, for patriotic reasons, because of the similarity of this vocab. word to L *Suedia* Sweden. The Swed. name of Sweden is *Sverige*, from *Sve(ar)* Swede(s) + *rige* kingdom. In LL the name of the country occurs variously as *Suedia, Sueonia*, and *Suecia*.
Cpds: **Svedberg, Swedberg** ('clearing hill'); **Swedenborg** ('clearing town'); **Swedlund** ('clearing grove').

Svehla Czech: nickname for a twittering person, from a deriv. of OCzech *švehlat* to twitter.
Var.: **Švehlák**.
Dims.: **Švehlík, Švehelka**.

Svendsen *see* SWAIN

Svoboda Czech: the third most common Czech surname, from a noun literally meaning 'freedom'. This was a technical term in the feudal system for a freeman, i.e. a peasant who was not a serf.

Swaby English: habitation name from a place in Lincs., so called from the ON ethnic byname *Sváfi* 'Swabian' + ON *býr* farm, settlement.

Swain English: **1.** occupational name for a servant or attendant, ME *swein* (ON *sveinn*, a cogn. of OE *swān*; cf. SWAN 2). Not until the 16th cent. did the word *swain* develop the senses 'young rustic' and hence 'rustic lover', 'wooer'. **2.** from the ON personal name *Sveinn*, originally a byname meaning 'Boy', 'Servant' (cf. 1 above).
Vars.: **Swaine, Swayn(e)**.
Patrs.: Eng.: **Swe(y)nson, Swainson**. Low Ger.: **Schwennen, Schwenn(e)sen**. Dan., Norw.: **Svendsen, Svenningsen**. Swed.: **Svensson**.

Swallow English: **1.** nickname for someone thought to resemble a swallow, perhaps in swiftness and grace, from ME *swal(e)we, swalu* (OE *swealwe*). **2.** habitation name from a place in Lincs., so called from the river *Swallow* on which it stands, whose name is apparently ultimately akin to that of the bird, presumably with some transferred meaning such as 'swirling' or 'rushing'.
Dim. (of 1): Ger.: **Schwälble**.
Patr. (from 1): Flem.: **Swaelus**.

Swan English: **1.** nickname for a person noted for purity or excellence (which were taken to be attributes of the swan), or resembling a swan in some other way, from OE *swan, swon* swan. In some cases it may be a house name for someone who lived at a house with the sign of a swan. **2.** occupational name for a servant or retainer; cf. SWAIN 1. In part it may be from an OE byname, preserved into the Middle Ages as a given name.
Var.: **Swann**.
Dims. (of 1): Low Ger.: **Schwan(e)ke, Schwank, Schwen(e)ke**. (Of 2): Sc.: **Swanie, Swanney**.
Patr. (from 2): Eng.: **Swanson**.
Cpds (of cogns. of 1, ornamental): Swed.: **Svanberg** ('swan hill'); **Svanström** ('swan river'). Jewish (Ashkenazic): **Schwanenfeld, Shvanenfeld** ('swan field').

Swannell English: from an ON female personal name, *Svanhildr*, composed of the elements *svanr* swan + *hild* battle.
Var.: **Swonnell**.

Swansborough English: probably a habitation name from an unidentified place, named from the gen. case of the OE byname *Swān* (see SWAN 2) + OE *burh* fortress, town.
Var.: **Swansbury**.

Swanston **1.** Scots: habitation name from a place near Edinburgh, probably so called from the gen. case of the OE byname *Swān* (see SWAN 2) + OE *tūn* enclosure, settlement. **2.** English: var. of SWANTON.

Swanton English: habitation name from one of the places, in Kent and Norfolk, so called from OE *Swānatūn* 'settlement (OE *tūn*) of the retainers (see SWAN 2)'; cf. CHARLTON and KNIGHTON.

Var.: SWANSTON.

Swanwick English: habitation name from a place in Derbys., so called from OE *Swānawīc* 'outlying settlement (see WICK) of the retainers (see SWAN 2)'.

Swarbrick English (Lancs.): habitation name from a place in the parish of Kirkham, Lancs., so called from the ON byname *Svartr* 'Black' + ON *brekka* slope.

Swatkins *see* WATT

Swatman *see* SWEET

Sweatman *see* SWEET

Swedberg *see* SVEDIN

Sweeney Irish: Anglicized form of Gael. **Mac Suibhne** 'son of *Suibhne*', a byname meaning 'Pleasant'.

Vars.: **McSeveny**, **McSween(ey)**, **(Mc)Swiney**, **McSwine**; **McQueenie**, McQUEEN, **McQueyn**, **McQuine**, **Maguen**, **(Mc)Whin**, **McWhan** (Gael. **Mac Shuibhne**).

Sweet English (most common in the W Country): nickname for a popular person, from ME *swete* sweet, pleasant, agreeable (OE *swēte*, cogn. with MHG *süeze*, Ger. *süss*); cf. SWEETING. The OE bynames *Swēt(a)* (masc.) and *Swēte* (fem.) derived from this word survived into the early ME period, and may also be sources of the surname.

Vars.: **Swett**; **Swe(e)tman**, **Sweatman**; **Swatman** (Norfolk).

Patrs.: Jewish (from the Yid. male given name *Zusman*): **Zusmans**; **Zusmanovitch, Zusmanovitz, Zusmanovics, Sussmanowitz** (E Ashkenazic).

Cpds (ornamental): Jewish (Ashkenazic): **Sussapfel, Zisapel** ('sweet apple'); **Zisberg** ('sweet hill'); **Zuserblum** ('sweet flower'); **Sussholz, Zishol(t)z** ('sweet wood'); **Sissmilch** ('sweet milk').

Sweeting English: **1.** from a medieval given name, originally an OE patr. from *Swēt(a)*; see SWEET. **2.** nickname for a popular and attractive person, or for somebody who habitually addressed people with the ME term *sweting* darling, sweetheart.

Sweetsir English: nickname from ME *swete* pleasant, agreeable (see SWEET) + *sire* lord, master (see SEIGNEUR). The name was probably ironical in tone and given either to someone of condescending manner or to someone who habitually used this form of address.

Vars.: **Sweetsur, Sweetzer, Switsur, Switzer**.

Swenerton *see* SWINNERTON

Swenson *see* SWAIN

Swerts *see* SCHWARZ

Świątek Polish: name taken by someone, esp. a convert to Christianity, who was baptized on a holy day or feast day, Pol. *świątek* (from *święty* saint (n.), holy (adj.)).

Var.: **Świątczak**.

Habitation names: **Świątkowski**; **Święcicki** (from *Święcice* in Mazovia, named as a 'holy' place).

Swibel *see* ZWIEBEL

Świderski Polish: nickname for a boss-eyed person, from Pol. *świder* drill, gimlet + the surname suffix -*ski* (see BARANOWSKI).

Dim.: **Świderek**.

Świercz Polish: nickname for a diminutive, chirpy person, from Pol. *śwircz* cricket (the insect).

Habitation name: **Świerczyński**.

Swiers *see* SQUIRE

Swift 1. English: nickname for a rapid runner, from ME, OE *swift* fleet. **2.** Irish: translation of Gael. *Ó Fuada*; see FOODY.

Swinburn English: habitation name from a place in Northumb., so called from OE *swīn* pig, wild boar + *burna* stream (see BOURNE).

Vars.: **Swinburne, Swinbourn(e)**.

Swindells English (Lancs.): of uncertain origin, in spite of being a very common name in Lancs. It is possibly a habitation name from *Swindale* in Skelton, N Yorks., so called from OE *swīn* pig, wild boar + *dæl* valley (see DALE).

Var.: **Swindell**.

Swindlehurst English (Lancs.): probably a habitation name from *Swinglehurst* in Bowland Forest, W Yorks., so called from OE *swīn* pig, wild boar + *hyll* hill + *hyrst* wooded ridge.

Var.: **Swinglehurst**.

Swiney *see* SWEENEY

Swingler English (W Midlands): occupational name for someone who made or used a certain type of wooden instrument used for beating hemp, ME *swingle* (MDu. *swinghel*, from the verb 'to swing').

Swinley English: habitation name from a place in Lancs., near Manchester, so called from OE *swīn* pig, wild boar + *lēah* wood, clearing.

Swinnerton English: habitation name from *Swynnerton* in Staffs., so called from OE *swīn* pig, wild boar + *ford* FORD + *tūn* enclosure, settlement.

Vars.: **Swinerton, Swyn(n)erton, Swinarton, Swenerton, Swinnington**.

Swinscoe English: habitation name from a place in Staffs., so called from ON *svín* pig, wild boar + *skógr* copse (cf. SHAW).

Swinton English and Scots: habitation name from any of various places, for example in Lancs. and N and S Yorks., so called from OE *swīn* pig, wild boar + *tūn* enclosure, settlement.

Swithenbank English (Yorks.): habitation name from an unidentified place, so called from ME *swithen* land cleared by burning (from ON *suiðinn* burnt) + *bank* slope (see BANKS).

Switser *see* SCHWEITZER

Switsur *see* SWEETSIR

Swonnell *see* SWANNELL

Sword 1. English and Scots: metonymic occupational name for an armourer, from ME *swerd, sword*, OE *sweord* sword. 2. Irish: Anglicized form of Gael. *Ó Suaird*; see SEWARD 3.

Vars. (of 1): **Soord**; **Sworder** (largely concentrated in E Herts. and W Essex). (Of 2): **Sworde**.

Dim.: Ger.: **Schwertl**.

Swyer *see* SQUIRE

Swynerton *see* SWINNERTON

Syarkeev *see* SERGIO

Sydenham English: habitation name from any of various places, for example in Devon, Oxon., and Somerset, so called from OE *sīd* wide + *hamm* water meadow, with the adj. retaining traces of the weak dat. ending originally used after a preposition and def. art. A further example in S London is a late alteration of *Chippenham* 'homestead of *Cippa*', and is not likely to have contributed to the surname.

Vars.: **Syddenham**, **Sid(d)enham**.

Sydney *see* SIDNEY

Sykes N English: topographic name for someone who lived by a marshy stream or damp gully, ME *syke* (from OE *sīc* or the cogn. ON *sík*).

Vars.: **Sikes**; **Si(t)ch**, **Seach** (S Eng. forms, with palatalization of the OE final consonant).

Sylvaine *see* SELWYN

Sylvester *see* SILVESTER

Symber *see* SAMPER

Symbestyrek *see* SILVESTER

Symcox *see* SIM

Symers *see* SUMMER

Symes *see* SIMSON

Symington Scots: habitation name from either of two places, one near Glasgow and the other near Ayr, so called from the given name SIMON + ME *toun* settlement (OE *tūn*). Both places were held in the late 12th cent. by a certain Simon Loccard or Lockhart, from whom they presumably derive their name.

Symmons *see* SIMON

Synnot *see* SINNOTT

Syomin *see* SIMON

Sypniewski Polish: habitation name from a place named *Sypniewo*, from Pol. *sypn-* heap up, build (an embankment or dike) + the possessive suffix *-ew*, with the addition of -*ski*, suffix of local surnames (see BARANOWSKI).

Syrett English: 1. from the ME male given name *Syred*, OE *Sigerǣd*, composed of the elements *sige* victory + *rǣd* counsel. 2. from the ME female personal name *Sigerith*, ON *Sigríðr*, a contraction of *Sigfríðr*, composed of the elements *sige* victory + *fríðr* lovely.

Vars.: **Sirett(e)**, **Sired**, **Syred**, **Syrad**, **Syratt**.

Syson *see* SIMON

Szablewski Polish: habitation name from a place named with Pol. *szabla* sabre + the possessive suffix *-ew*, with the addition of -*ski*, suffix of local surnames (see BARANOWSKI). The name would have been applied either to a sabre-shaped piece of land or to a place where a noted swordsman lived.

Vars.: **Szabłowski**, **Szabliński**.

Szabó Hungarian (partly Ashkenazic Jewish): occupational name for a tailor, Hung. *szabó*.

Szadkowski Polish: habitation name from a place called *Szadków* or *Szadkowo*, from *szady* grey.

Szainfeld *see* SCHÖN

Szántó Hungarian (partly Ashkenazic Jewish): occupational name for a ploughman or farmer, Hung. *szántó* (from *szánt* to plough).

Szapira *see* SHAPIRO

Szarfharc *see* SHARP

Szatz *see* SCHATZ

Szczeciński Polish (partly Ashkenazic Jewish): 1. habitation name from the great seaport of *Szczecin* in NW Poland (Ger. *Stettin*), which probably gets its name either from Pol. *szczeć*, a species of sharp spiky grass, or from *szczecina* pine needles or bristles. 2. habitation name derived directly from either of the two vocab. words mentioned above.

Szczepanek *see* STEPHEN

Szczęścikowicz *see* ST'ASTNÝ

Szczygieł Polish: nickname for a person with bright yellow hair, from Pol. *szczygieł* goldfinch.

Var.: **Szczygielski**.

Szechter *see* SCHECHTER

Szefer *see* SCHÄFER

Szeinfeld *see* SCHÖN

Széll Hungarian (partly Ashkenazic Jewish): topographic name for someone who lived in a spot exposed to the wind, from Hung. *szél* wind.

Var.: **Szeles**.

Szenes *see* SCHEINIS

Szepe *see* JOSEPH

Szereszewski *see* SIEROTA

Szerman *see* SHERMAN

Szewc Polish: occupational name for a shoemaker, from a deriv. of Pol. *szewać* to sew (*szew* seam). The word is ultimately cogn. with MHG *sūtære* sewer (see SAUTER, SCHUSTER).

Dims.: Pol.: **Szewczyk**. Czech: **Ševčík**. Ukr.: **Shevchenko**, **Shevchuk**. Beloruss.: **Shevchik**.

Patrs.: Russ.: **Shvetsov**, **Shevtsov**.

Szigeti Hungarian: topographic name for someone who lived on or near an island, Hung. *sziget*, or habitation name from a place named with this word.

Szimon *see* SIMON

Szimszewicz *see* SAMSON

Szklar Polish (partly E Ashkenazic Jewish): occupational name for a glazier, Pol. *szklarz*, an agent deriv. of *szkło* glass.

Var.: **Szklarski**.

Dim.: Pol.: **Szklarek**.

Szkoler *see* SCHULER

Szkudlarek Polish: occupational name for a maker of shingles (wooden roof tiles), from a dim. of Pol. *szkudlarz* SHINGLER, a deriv. of *szkudła* shingle.

Szlomowicz *see* SALOMON

Szlosberg *see* SCHLOSSBERG

Szmigiel Polish: 1. nickname for a fast and furious driver of a horse-drawn vehicle, from Pol. *śmigać* to crack the whip. 2. nickname for a tall, thin man, from Pol. dial. *śmigły* tall and thin, gangly.

Vars.: **Szmigielski**, **Śmigielski**.

Szmuel *see* SAMUEL

Sznajderman *see* SCHNEIDER

Sznejberg *see* SNOW

Sznejor *see* SCHNEIR

Szochatowicz *see* SHOIKHET

Szor *see* SCHAUER

Szpajzer *see* SPEISER

Szpilberg *see* SPIELBERG

Szrayer *see* SCHREIER

Szreiber *see* SCHREIBER

Sztajnbaum *see* STONE

Szterenbojm *see* STARR

Sztolc *see* STOLZ

Szuba Polish: from Pol. *szuba* fur-lined coat, a nickname for someone who habitually wore one or a metonymic occupational name for a dealer in fur-lined coats.

Var.: **Szubski**.

Szulezewski *see* SCHULTZ

Szulman *see* SCHULER

Szurgot Polish: nickname for a dirty, untidy person, or one who talked nonsense, from Pol. *szurgot* ragamuffin, buffoon.

Szürke Hungarian: nickname for a grey-haired man or for someone who habitually dressed in grey, from Hung. *szürke* grey.

Szwedziński *see* SCHWEDER

Szweitzer *see* SCHWEITZER

Szydłowski Polish: in form, a habitation name referring to a place where a worker in leather lived, especially a shoemaker, from Pol. *szydło* awl + *-ów* possessive suffix + *-ski* suffix of local surnames (see BARANOWSKI). In practice this would often have amounted to an occupational name for a shoemaker.

Var.: **Szydłowiecki**.

Szymanczyk *see* SIMON

T

Taaffe see DAVID

Tabak German and Jewish (Ashkenazic): metonymic occupational name for a seller of tobacco, from Ger. *Tabak*, Yid. *tabik* (both ultimately from Sp. *tabaco*, of Caribbean origin). As a Ger. surname, this is of relatively late formation, since tobacco was not introduced into Europe until the 16th cent.

Vars.: Jewish: **Tabakman**, **Tabekman**; **Tabatchnik**, **Tabacznik**, **Tabatznik** (E Ashkenazic); **Tabakero** (Sefardic).

Patrs.: Jewish: **Tabatchnikov**, **Tabashnikov** (E Ashkenazic).

Tabard English and French: nickname for a habitual wearer of a *tabard*, a long sleeveless coat of heavy material, or occupational name for a maker or seller of such garments. Originally the normal outdoor wear of peasants and soldiers, the tabard was later adopted by knights as an outer garment emblazoned with armorial bearings, and hence by the 16th cent. had become specialized as the official coat of a herald.

Vars.: Eng.: **Tabbitt**. Fr.: **Tabart**.

Dims.: Fr.: **Tabarel**, **Tabareau**, **Tabarin**, **Tabary**.

Taboada Spanish (Galicia): habitation name from any of various places, for example in the province of Lugo, so called from the dial. term *taboada* plot of land marked out with drainage channels (Sp. *tablada*, L *(terra) tabulāta*, a deriv. of *tabula* board, writing tablet, record; the reference is to the division of the land into strips like the columns of accounts or lists).

Tabor 1. English: metonymic occupational name for a drummer, from ME, OF *tabo(u)r* drum (of uncertain origin, perhaps ultimately from Pers. *tabīr*). 2. Jewish (Israeli): ornamental name taken from Mount *Tabor* (Hebr. *Tavor*), in Israel.

Vars. (of 1): **Taber**, **Tabah**; **Tab(b)erer**, **Tabborah**, **Tabrar** (with the addition of ME agent suffixes); **Tab(b)erner**, **Tab(i)ner** (from the ME verb *tabourn(en)* to drum, OF *tabourner*). (Of 2): **Tavor**; **Tabori**, **Tabory**, **Tavori**, **Tavory** (all with the Hebr. adj. ending *-i*, but among Hung. Jews adopted under the influence of the Hung. surname *Tábori*; see TABORSKI).

Dims. (of 1): Fr.: **Tabourel**, **Taboureaux**, **Ta(m)bourin**, **Tab(o)uret**, **Tabourot**. It.: **Tamburelli**, **Tamburello**, **Tammurello**, **Tambur(l)ini**, **Tamburino**, **Tamborino**.

Taborski Polish: topographic name for someone who lived at a minor settlement, from Pol. *tabor* camp, encampment + *-ski* suffix of local surnames (see BARANOWSKI).

Tache French: nickname for someone with a birthmark or scar, from OF *tache*, *teche* spot, stain (probably of Gmc origin). The word also had different technical meanings in various medieval crafts and trades, and in some cases the surname may have originated as an occupational name connected with one of these.

Vars.: **Taché**; **Taque** (Normandy).

Dims.: **Tachet**, **Tacheau**, **Tachon**, **Tachot**; **Taquet** (Normandy).

Tadié French: from a vernacular form of the given name *Thaddeus*. This is the name given in St Mark's Gospel to one of Christ's disciples, referred to elsewhere as Judas son of James. It represents an Aramaic form *Thaddai*, of uncertain origin; it may be of Hebr. origin and mean 'Beloved', 'Desired', but it is also possible that it is an adaptation of the Gk name *Theodōros* (see THÉODORE).

Var.: **Thaddée**.

Dims.: It.: **Taddeini**, **Tad(ol)ini**, **Taddeucci**. Pol.: **Tadeusik**.

Patrs.: Pol.: **Tadeusiewicz**; **Tadeusiak**. Russ.: **Fad(n)eev**, **Fadeichev**, **Khadeev**.

Patrs. (from dims.): Russ.: **Fadyshin**. Croatian: **Tadić**.

Taffee see DAVID

Tafintsev see OSTAPOV

Taft see TOFT

Taggart Scots and N Irish: Anglicized form of Gael. **Mac an t-Sagairt** 'son of the priest', from *sagart* priest. Marriage by members of the clergy was illegal and invalid after the 12th cent., but was frequently practised nevertheless.

Vars.: **McEntaggart**, **McIntaggart**, **McTaggart**, **(Mc)Taggert**, **Taggairt**, **Tagart**, **Taggard**, **Target**.

Tagliavini Italian: apparently a nickname for an alleged adulterator of wine, from It. *taglia(re)* to cut (see TAILLANT) + *vino* wine (L *vīnum*).

Tague see TIGHE

Taigman see TEIG

Taillant French: occupational name for a tailor or nickname for a good swordsman, from *taillant* cutting, pres. part. of OF *tailler* to cut (LL *taliāre*, from *talea* (plant) cutting; cf. TALLIS and TAYLOR).

Pejs.: Fr.: **Ta(i)llard**.

Taillefer see TELFER

Tailour see TAYLOR

Tainturier see TEINTURIER

Tait Scots and N English: nickname for a cheerful person, from ON *teitr* cheerful, gay. This surname is quite distinct in origin from TATE.

Var.: **Teyte**.

Taitel see TEITELBAUM

Taitz see DEUTSCH

Tajchman see TEICH

Tajtelbaum *see* TEITELBAUM

Taks *see* DACHS

Talavera Spanish: habitation name from any of several places, in the provinces of Badajóz, Cáceres, Lérida, and Toledo, all of which seem to be so called from the (attested) pre-Roman personal name *Talavus, Talevus* + the L local suffix *-āria*; cf. TÀVARES.

Talbot English (Norman): of much disputed origin, but probably from a Gmc personal name composed of the elements *tal* destroy (cf. TALLEYRAND) + *bod* message, tidings (cf. BOTHA), i.e. 'messenger of destruction'.
Vars.: **Talbott**, **Talbut(t)**, **Taulbut**.

Talboys English: **1.** occupational name for a woodcutter, from OF *taille(r)* to cut (see TAILLANT) + *bosc, bois* wood (see BOIS). **2.** habitation name from *Taillebois* in Orne, Normandy, so called from OF *taille* clearing (see TALLIS) + *bosc, bois* wood.
Vars.: **Tallboy(s)**.

Talfourd *see* TELFORD

Tall English: nickname for a respectable or decent person, or else a good-looking one, both these senses belonging to ME *tall* (OE *getæl* swift, prompt). The mod. sense 'of high stature' did not develop until the end of the 16th cent.; the usual ME equivalents were LONG and HIGH.

Tallamach *see* TOLLEMACHE

Tallard *see* TAILLANT

Talleyrand French: of uncertain origin, perhaps from a Gmc personal name composed of the elements *tal* destroy (cf. TALBOT) + *rand* (shield) rim, shield.

Tallis **1.** English (Norman): habitation name from some minor locality named with ANF *taillis* clearing in an area of woodland (a deriv. of *tailler* to cut; cf. TAILLANT). **2.** Jewish (Ashkenazic): from Yid. *tales* prayer shawl (from Hebr. *talit*).
Vars. (of 2): **Talis(man)**; **Talisnik** (E Ashkenazic); **Talit(man)** (Israeli).

Tallon English and Irish (Norman), and French: **1.** from a Gmc personal name derived from the element *tal* destroy, either as a short form of a cpd name with this first element (cf. TALBOT and TALLEYRAND) or as an independent byname. **2.** metonymic nickname for a swift runner or for someone with a deformed heel, from OF *talon* heel (a dim. of *tal*, L *tālus*).
Vars.: Ir.: **Talún** (a Gaelicized form). Fr.: **Talon**.

Tally *see* TULLY

Talma French: habitation name from *Talmas* in Somme, Picardy, so called from L *templum Martis* temple of *Mars*, the Roman god of war.

Talmachev *see* TOLMACHEV

Tamblyn English (chiefly Devon and Cornwall): from the ME given name *Tamlin*, a double dim., with the ANF suffixes *-el* and *-in*, of *Tam, Tom*, itself a short form of THOMAS.
Vars.: **Tamblin(g)**, **Tamplin**; **Tamlin**, **Tamlyn**.

Tamborino *see* TABOR

Tamcke *see* DANKMAR

Tame English: **1.** nickname for a quiet and gentle person, from ME *tame* tame, domesticated (OE *tam*). **2.** habitation name from *Thame* in Oxon., so called from a Brit. river name, meaning possibly 'dark'.

Tammage *see* TOLLEMACHE

Tamminen Finnish: ornamental name from Finn. *tammi* oak + the genitive suffix *-nen*, perhaps sometimes chosen as a topographic name by someone who lived by an oak tree.

Tanasković *see* AFANASYEV

Tanck *see* DANKMAR

Tancock *see* ANDREW

Tancred English: from an OF personal name, *Tancred*, composed of the Gmc elements *þank* thought + *rēd* counsel. This was introduced to Britain by the Normans. There has been some confusion with TANKARD.

Taneev *see* TONEY

Taney English (Norman): habitation name from Saint-Aubin-du-Thennay or Saint-Jean-du-Thennay in Eure, Normandy, both so called from an uncertain first element (possibly a Gallo-Roman personal name or the Gaul. element *tann* oak, holly; cf. TANNER 1) + the local suffix *-ācum*.
Var.: **Tawney**.

Tanguy Breton, English (Norman), and French: from a Bret. personal name composed of the elements *tān* fire + *ci* dog, borne by a 6th-cent. Christian saint associated with Paul Aurelian. The name was introduced into England at the time of the Norman Conquest, and was reintroduced into Cornwall independently at a later date.
Vars.: Eng.: **Tangye**, **Tingay**, **Tingey**, **Tengue**; **Tangney** (Ireland). Fr.: **Tanneguy**, **Tinguy**.

Tani *see* GAETANO

Tankard English: **1.** from a Norman personal name, *Tancard*, composed of the Gmc elements *þank* thought + *hard* hardy, brave, strong. See also TANCRED. **2.** metonymic occupational name for a maker of barrels and drinking vessels, or nickname for a hardened drinker, from ME *tankard* tub, cup (apparently a borrowing from MDu.).

Tann **1.** German: topographic name for someone who lived in a forest, Ger. *Tann* (MHG *tan*). This was originally a distinct word from TANNE pine tree, and denoted a forest of any kind. Inevitably, however, the two became confused, with the result that *Tann* now denotes only coniferous forests; it is a rather rare and literary word. **2.** English (E Anglia): occupational name, a var. of TANNER.

Tanne German: topographic name for someone who lived near a conspicuous pine tree or among pine trees, Ger. *Tanne* pine (MHG *tanne*, OHG *tanna*).
Cpds (ornamental): Jewish (Ashkenazic): **Tan(n)enbaum**, **Tanenboim** ('pine tree'); **Tanenholz** ('pine timber'); **Tannenwald** ('pine forest'); **Tanenwurzel** ('pine root').

Tanner **1.** English: occupational name for a tanner of skins, ME *tanner* (OE *tannere*, from LL *tannārius*, reinforced by OF *taneor*, from LL *tannātor*; both LL forms derive from a verb *tannāre*, possibly from a Celt. word for the oak, whose bark was used in the process). **2.** German: topographic name, a var. of TANN and TANNE. **3.** Finnish: ornamental name from Finn. *tanner* open field, or topographic name chosen by someone who lived by an open field, Finn. *tanner*. **4.** Jewish (Ashkenazic): of unknown origin.

Vars. (of 2): **Thanner**, **T(h)enner**.

Dims. (of 1): Fr.: **Tan(ne)ret**, **Tanron**.

Equivs. (of 1, not cogns.): Prov.: ESCOFFIER. It.: SCORZA. Ger.: GERBER, LAUER. Hung.: TIMÁR.

Tansey Irish and Scots: Anglicized form of Gael. **Mac an Tánaiste** 'son of the *tanist*' (*tanist* denoted the heir presumptive to a throne).

Tansini *see* CONSTANT

Tansley English: habitation name from a place in Derbys., so called from OE *tān* branch(ing valley) + *lēah* wood, clearing.

Tanzer **1.** German: nickname for a skilled or enthusiastic dancer, or occupational name for a professional acrobat, from Ger. *Tanzer* dancer, an agent deriv. of MHG *tanzen* to dance (from OF *danser*, of disputed origin; the initial *t*- is the result of hypercorrection of a presumed Low Ger. form). **2.** Jewish (Ashkenazic): apparently of similar origin to the German name. There were, however, no Jewish acrobats, and Jews generally danced only at weddings. The name may have been taken by Chasidim, since members of this branch of Jewry (which arose in the 18th cent.) do place great emphasis on dancing.

Vars. (of 1): **Tänz(l)er**, **Tenzer**; **Dantzer**, **Dentz(ler)**. (Of 2): **Tantzer**, **Ten(t)zer**, **Tantzman**; **Tanc(man)** (Polish spelling).

Dims.: Ger.: **Denzel**, **Denzle**. Fr.: **Danset(te)**, **Dancet(te)**, **Dansin**.

Tänzler *see* TANZER

Tapia Spanish: topographic name for someone who lived by a mud wall, Sp. *tapia* (of uncertain origin), or, more commonly, a habitation name from one of the places named with this word, in the provinces of Burgos, León, and Oviedo.

Var.: **Tapias**.

Tapp English: from an OE personal name *Tæppa*, of uncertain origin and meaning.

Var.: **Tappe**.

Dims.: **Tap(l)in**.

Patrs.: **Tapping** (Bucks.); **Tapps(on)**.

Tappenden English: habitation name from an unidentified place, probably so called from the gen. case of the OE personal name *Tæppa* (see TAPP) + OE *denu* valley (see DEAN 1).

Tapster English: **1.** occupational name for a wine merchant, tavern keeper, or hostess in a tavern, ME *tapster* (an agent deriv. (formally fem.) of *tappen* to draw off, from *tap* tap). **2.** occupational name for a weaver or seller of carpets or figured cloths, from ANF *tap(is)ser* (LL *tapetiārius*, an agent deriv. of *tapetium* carpet, Gk *tapetion*, dim. of *tapēs*, gen. *tapētis*).

Var. (of 1): **Tapper**.

Taque *see* TACHE

Tarasov Russian: patr. from the given name *Taras* (Gk *Tarasios* 'Native of *Taras*', a place in S Italy now known as *Taranto*), which was borne by an 8th-cent. patriarch of Constantinople much venerated in the Eastern Church.

Vars.: **Tarasyev**, **Taranov**.

Dims.: Russ.: **Tarasikov** (patr.). Ukr.: **Tarasyuk**. Beloruss.: **Tarasenya**, **Tarasyonok**; **Tarashkevich** (patr.).

Tarbin *see* THORBURN

Tarbock English: habitation name from a place in Lancs., so called from OE *þorn* thorn bush (see THORN 1) + *brōc* BROOK; in Domesday Book it is already *Torboc*, but the form *Thornebrooke* occurs as late as the mid-13th cent., when Sir Henry *de Torbok*, bailiff of the territory between the Ribble and Mersey, is recorded also as Henry *de Thornebrooke*.

Vars.: **Tarbuck**, **Tarbox**, **Terbocke**.

Tarczyński Polish: habitation name from a place called *Tarczyn* (there is one SW of Warsaw, and another is now in the Soviet Union), named from Pol. *tarcz* shield + *-yn* possessive suffix, with the addition of *-ski* suffix of local surnames (see BARANOWSKI).

Tarde French: habitation name from *Tardes* in Creuse, probably so called from LL *Tarda* (*villa*) 'settlement (see VILLE) of *Tardus*', a byname meaning 'Slow' (cf. TARDIF).

Tardif English and French: nickname for a sluggish person, from ME, OF *tardif* slow (LL *tardīvus*, for class. L *tardus*).

Vars.: Eng.: **Tardew**. Fr.: **Tardy**, **Tardieu**.

Dims.: Fr.: **Tardiveau**, **Tardivel**, **Tard(iv)on**.

Target *see* TAGGART

Targownik Polish: occupational name for a merchant or trader, Pol. *targownik* (from *targ* market, trade).

Var.: **Targowski**.

Tarkowski Polish: habitation name, probably from a place named with OPol. *tarkać* to rattle, chatter, whirr + *-ów* possessive suffix, with the addition of *-ski* suffix of local surnames (see BARANOWSKI).

Tarleton English: **1.** habitation name from *Tarleton* in Lancs., near Croston, so called from the ON personal name *Þórvaldr* (see THOROLD) + OE *tūn* enclosure, settlement. **2.** habitation name from *Tarlton* in Gloucs., recorded in Domesday Book as *Tornentone* and *Torentune*, and of the same origin as THORNTON 1.

Var.: **Tarlton**.

Tarling English: habitation name from *Terling* in Essex, apparently so called from the OE tribal name *Tyrhtelingas* 'people of *Tyrhtel*'.

Tarn N English: topographic name for someone who lived by a tarn, a small lake or pool, Northern ME *tarne* (ON *tarnu*).

Tarnowski Polish and Jewish (E Ashkenazic): habitation name from one of the places called *Tarnów*, named with Pol. *tarn* blackthorn + *-ów* possessive suffix, with the addition of *-ski* suffix of local surnames. There are at least two places so named; in the case of the Jewish surname, the source is usually, if not exclusively, the city in Galicia.

Vars.: Jewish: **Tarnovski**, **Tarnovsky**; Turner.

Tarpey Irish: Anglicized form of Gael. **Ó Tarpaigh** 'descendant of *Tarpach*', a byname originally denoting a sturdy person.

Var.: **Torpy**.

Tarr English (Bristol): apparently from the vocab. word *tar* (OE *te(o)ru*), and applied perhaps to someone who worked with tar or bitumen in waterproofing ships.

Tarragó Catalan: habitation name from the city of *Tarragona* in NE Spain. The placename is first recorded in L as *Tarraco* (gen. *Tarracōnis*), but the meaning is unknown. It is an extremely ancient city, captured by the Romans from the Carthaginians in the Second Punic War (218 BC).

Tarrant 1. English: topographic name for someone living on the banks of the river *Tarrant* in Dorset, which is of the same origin as Trent. As well as giving rise to a surname, it has been added as a distinguishing epithet to several Dorset placenames. **2.** Irish: Anglicized form of Gael. **Ó Toráin** 'descendant of *Torán*', a personal name from a dim. of *tor* hero, champion.

Tarrés Catalan: habitation name from a place in the province of Lérida, of uncertain origin. It is probably from the pl. form of a var. of Cat. *terrer* plot of land (LL *terrārium*, a deriv. of *terra* land).

Tarry *see* Terry

Tartaglia Italian: nickname for a stammerer, from It. *tartagliare* to stammer, stutter.

Tartakowski Polish: habitation name from a place named with Pol. *tartak* sawmill + *-ów* possessive suffix, with the addition of *-ski* suffix of local surnames (see Baranowski).

Tartarelli *see* Tatarinov

Tartier French: occupational name for a baker or seller of filled pastries, from an agent deriv. of OF *tarte* pastry, pie (of unknown origin).

Var.: **Tartière** (a fem. form).

Augs.: **Tart(e)rat**.

Tash English: topographic name for someone who lived by an ash tree, from the ME phrase *at(te) asche* at (the) Ash.

Vars.: **Tasche**, **Tesh(e)**.

Tasker English: occupational name for someone who did piece-work, from an agent deriv. of ANF *tasque* task (OF *tasche*, LL *taxa*, of uncertain origin), applied particularly to someone who threshed corn with a flail.

Dim.: Fr.: **Taschereau**.

Tasse French: metonymic occupational name for a maker or seller of purses and bags, or nickname for a rich man or a miser, from OF *tasse* purse (apparently of Arabic origin).

Vars.: **Tassier**, **Tassié** (agent derivs.).

Dims.: Fr.: **Tasset**, **Tassin**, **Tasson**, **Tassot**.

Pejs.: Fr.: **Tassard**, **Tassaud**.

Tasso Italian: **1.** topographic name for someone who lived near a prominent yew tree, It. *tasso* (L *taxus*, gen. *taxi*). **2.**

nickname for a person thought to resemble a badger in some way, for example in his nocturnal habits, from It. *tasso* badger (LL *taxo*, gen. *taxōnis*, of Gmc origin; cf. Dachs). **3.** from a Gmc personal name derived from the obscure element *tāt* (possibly akin to OHG *tāt* deed; see also Tate).

Var.: **Tassi**.

Dims.: It.: **Tasselli**, **Tassetto**, **Tassino**, **Tassotto**; **Tasin(i)** (Venetia). (Of 2 only): Fr.: **Tessel**.

Collectives (of 1): Sp.: **Tejeda** (the name of places in the provinces of Cáceres and Salamanca). Port.: **Teixeira**.

Tatarinov Russian: patr. from the name *tatarin* Tatar (apparently ultimately from a Turkic word meaning 'Stammerer'). The word came to be used in languages outside Russia (e.g. Czech and Italian) as a nickname for a wild or uncontrolled person. However, in English, this use did not develop until the late 16th or early 17th cent., and there are no surnames derived from it.

Var.: **Tatarintsev**.

Dims.: Czech: **Tatárek**. It.: **Tartarini**, **Tartarino**, **Tarterini**, **Tartarelli**.

Aug.: It.: **Tartaroni**.

Tate English: from the OE personal name *Tāta*, possibly a short form of various cpd names with the obscure first element *tāt*, or else a nursery formation.

Tatelbaum *see* Teitelbaum

Tatford *see* Titford

Tatham English: habitation name from a place in N Lancs., so called from the OE personal name *Tāta* (see Tate) + OE *hām* homestead.

Vars.: **Tatam**, **Tatem**, **Tatum**.

Tatishchev Russian: patr. from the ORuss. nickname *Tatishche*, a dim. of *tat* thief. Family tradition, however, prefers to derive the name from the phrase *tat ishchi* 'seek out the thief', allegedly a nickname denoting a minor official who pursued a vigorous policy of law and order.

Tatler English: of uncertain origin. It would seem to be a nickname for someone who was unsteady in either his gait or his speech, from ME *tatelen* to falter, stammer (from MDu., of imitative origin). The sense 'gossip' did not develop until the 16th cent.

Vars.: **Tattler**, **Tatlar**, **Tatlor**.

Tattersall English: habitation name from *Tattershall* in Lincs., so called from the gen. of the OE personal name *Tāthere* (composed of an obscure element *tāt* + *here* army) + OE *halh* nook, recess (see Hale 1). The surname has been common in Lancs. from an early period.

Vars.: **Tattershall**, **Tattershaw**, **Tattersill**, **Tettersell**, **Tetsall**.

Tattersfield English: probably a habitation name from *Tatsfield* in Surrey, so called from the gen. case of an OE personal name *Tātel* + OE *feld* pasture, open country (see Field).

Tatton English: habitation name from places in Ches. and Dorset, so called from the OE personal name *Tāta* (see Tate) + OE *tūn* enclosure, settlement.

Taube 1. German and Jewish (Ashkenazic): 1. from Ger. *Taube* pigeon, dove (MHG *tūbe*, OHG *tūba*; cogn. of Eng. Dove). This is either a metonymic occupational name for a keeper of doves or pigeons, a nickname for a mild and gentle person, or, in the case of the Jewish surname, an ornamental adoption of the vocab. word or its Yid. cogn. *toyb*. **2.** Jewish (Ashkenazic): from the Yid. female given name *Toybe* (from Yid. *toyb* dove).

Vars. (of 1): Ger.: **Tauber**, **Taubner**, **Taubert**, **Täuber(t)**, **Teuber(t)**, **Taubner**, **Teubner**; **Daube**, **Dauber(t)**, **Däubler**, **Deubler**, **Deibler**, **Deubner**, **Deibner**. Jewish: **Taubman** (see also **Tauber** 2). (Of 2): **Daube**.

Metrs. (from 2): **Toibin** (E Ashkenazic, with the Slavic suffix *-in*), **Tojbin** (Pol. spelling); **Tobis** (S Ashkenazic, from a regional pronunciation of *Toybe*, with Yid. possessive *-s*); **Taubes**, **Taubin** (Germanized forms).

Metr. (from a dim. of 2): **Taubkin** (from the Yid. dim. female given name *Toybke*).

Cpds (ornamental): Jewish: **Tauberg** ('dove hill'); **Taubenblat(t)** ('dove leaf'); **Taubenfeld** ('dove field'); **Taubenhaus** ('dove house', partly Anglicized as **Taubenhouse**); **Taubenschlag** ('dovecot').

Tauber 1. German and Jewish (Ashkenazic): var. of **Taube** 1, from an agent noun deriv. ending in *-er*. **2.** German and Jewish (Ashkenazic): nickname for a deaf person, from Ger. *taub* deaf (MHG *toup*), with the strong inflectional ending *-er*, originally used before a male given name. The adj. also had the sense 'stupid', and this may lie behind some examples of the Ger. name. **3.** German: occupational name for a player of the horn or a similar musical instrument, MHG *toubære*.

Vars. (of 1 and 2): Ger.: **Taub(mann)**, **Daub(mann)**. Jewish: **Taub(man)** (see also **Taube**).

Patr. (from 2): Flem., Du.: **Den Dooven**.

Taufer German: name for a member of the Anabaptist sect, who believed in adult rebaptism, from an agent deriv. of Ger. *taufen* to baptize (MHG *toufen*, a cogn. of mod. Eng. *dip* and a calque of LL *baptizāre*, from Gk *baptein* to dip).

Vars.: **Tauffer**, **Täufer**.

Taulbut *see* Talbot

Taupin French: nickname for a short-sighted or stupid person, or for someone who habitually dressed in a brownish grey colour, from a dim. of OF *taupe* mole (L *talpa*).

Var.: **Taupeau**.

Dims.: **Taupenot**, **Taupeneau**.

Pej.: **Taupinard**.

Taureau *see* Toro

Tavares Portuguese: habitation name from any of at least seven minor places so called, first recorded in the forms *Taavares* and *Thalavares*. It is probably a deriv. of the personal name *Talavus* (see Talavera).

Taverner English: occupational name for an innkeeper, ANF *taverner* (OF *tavernier*, LL *tabernārius* from *taberna* shop, inn). OIt. *taverna* was also used of a stable, and in Tuscany of a slaughterhouse, and the It. cogns. may have referred to someone employed at one of these places.

Vars.: **Tavernor**, **Taven(n)er**, **Tavenor**, **Tav(i)ner**, **Tavender**.

Tavor *see* Tabor

Tawney *see* Taney

Tawyer English: occupational name for a dresser of white leather, cured with alum rather than tanned with bark, from an agent deriv. of ME *taw(en)* (OE *tawian* to prepare, make ready). See also Whittier.

Var.: **Tower**.

Tax *see* Dachs

Taylor English: occupational name for a tailor, from OF *tailleur* (LL *tāliātor*, from *tāliāre* to cut; cf. Taillant). The surname is extremely common and widespread, and its numbers have been swelled by its adoption as an Anglicized form of various equivalent names such as Schneider, Szabó, and Portnov.

Vars.: **Tayler**, **Tailour**, **Taylour**.

Patrs.: Eng.: **Taylorson**, **Taylerson**.

Equivs. (not cogn.): Fr.: Sartre, Couturier. Ger. and Jewish: Schneider. Ger.: Schröder. Pol. and Jewish: Krawiec. Hung. and Jewish: Szabó. Russ. and Jewish: Portnov. Jewish: Chait.

Taytel *see* Teitelbaum

Tchernichovsky *see* Chernyakov

Tchernovitz Jewish (E Ashkenazic): habitation name from *Czernowitz*, the Ger. name of the city of *Chernovtsy* in the Ukraine, which is named from Slav. *cherny* black (see Chernyakov).

Teacher English: occupational name for an instructor in any branch of learning, or nickname for a wise or a pompous man, from an agent deriv. of ME *teche(n)* to teach (OE *tǣcan*).

Teage *see* Tighe

Teague 1. Cornish: nickname for a handsome person, from Corn. *tek* fair, beautiful (cf. Tegg 1). **2.** Irish: var. of Tighe.

Teale English: nickname for a person considered to resemble the water-bird in some way, from ME *tele* teal (of uncertain origin).

Vars.: **Teal(l)**.

Tear *see* McIntyre

Tearall *see* Tyrrell

Tearle English: of uncertain origin, probably a var. of Tyrrell.

Tearney *see* Tierney

Teasdale English: regional name from *Teesdale* in Co. Durham and N Yorks., so called from the river name *Tees* (see Surtees) + OE *dæl* valley (see Dale).

Tebaldeschi *see* Theobald

Tech *see* Tess

Tedd English: of uncertain origin, perhaps from a medieval given name, but not the short form of Edward represented in mod. Eng. *Ted*. It may have been a short form of an OE or Norman name beginning with the Gmc element **þeudō-* people. An OE name *Teoda* is on record, but there is some controversy whether any of the pre-Conquest *Theod-* names are really OE or whether they are Continental importations. More probably, given the early distribution, it is a habitation name from *Tydd* in Lincs., south of the Wash, which is named from OE *titt* teat, with reference to a small hill.

Patr.: **Teds**.

Tedesco Italian and Jewish: name for someone of Ger. origin or who spoke German, from It. *tedesco* German (OHG *diutisc*; see DEUTSCH). As a Jewish name, it was given to or taken by Ashkenazic Jews in Italy, or is based on a nickname given to a Jew who had been to Italy.

In Lucca the vars. **Todesco** and **To(d)eschi** were also nicknames for a stammerer; in Naples the var. **Todisco** was a nickname for a tippling simpleton.

Vars. (in addition to those mentioned above): Italian and Jewish: **Tedeschi**. Italian only: **Tudisco** (Sicily, Calabria).

Dims.: Italian and Jewish: **Todeschini**. Italian only: **Tedeschini**.

Tedoradze *see* THÉODORE

Tedstone English: habitation name from a pair of places (*Tedstone* Delamere and *Tedstone* Wafre) in NE Herefords. The placename is recorded in Domesday Book as *Tedesthorne*, from the gen. case of an OE personal name of uncertain form (see TEDD) + *þorn* thorn bush (see THORN 1).

Tee *see* TYE

Teehan *see* TIGHE

Teewen *see* THIESS

Tegg 1. Welsh: nickname for a handsome person, from W *teg* fair, beautiful (cf. TEAGE 1). **2.** English: occupational name for a shepherd, from ME *tegge* sheep in its second year (OE *tegga*).

Var. (of 2): **Tigg**.

Teggart English: occupational name for a shepherd, from ME *tegge* young sheep (see TEGG 2) + HEARD herdsman.

Var.: **Tegart**.

Teich German and Jewish (Ashkenazic): topographic name for someone who lived by a pond or lake, Ger. *Teich* (MHG *tīch*, a cogn. of DITCH). See also WEIHER, the equivalent term used in S and W Germany during the Middle Ages. The Jewish name also denoted someone who lived near a river: in Yid. *taykh* means 'river'.

Vars.: Ger.: **Teicher(t)**, **Teichner**, **Teichler**, **Teichmann**. Jewish: **Teich(n)er**, **Teichman(n)**; **Tajchman** (Pol. spelling).

Teig Jewish (Ashkenazic): metonymic occupational name for a baker, from mod. Ger. *Teig* dough, Yid. *teyg*.

Vars.: **Teigman**, **Taigman**; **Teigfeld** ('dough field', an ornamental elaboration).

Teige *see* TIGHE

Teil French: topographic name for someone who lived near a lime tree, OF *teil* (L *tilia*).

Vars.: **Theil**, **Thil(l)**, **Til**; **Dut(h)(e)il**, **Dut(h)euil**, **Duteille**; **Tilleul** (from the LL dim. *tiliōlus*); **Dut(h)illeul**, **Dutilleux**; **T(h)illier**.

Dims.: Fr.: **Teillet**, **T(h)illet**, **T(e)illon**, **Tillou**, **Til(le)quin**; **Dut(h)(e)illet**.

Pejs.: Fr.: **Te(i)lhard**, **Teillard**, **T(h)illard**, **Teillaud**.

Collectives: Fr.: **Thillaye**, **Theilley**, **Tilloy**; **Dutillay**, **Dutilloy**. Sp.: **Tejada** (the name of places in the provinces of Burgos and Salamanca).

Teinturier French: occupational name for a dyer, from OF *teint(e)ur* (L *tinctor*, from *tingere*, past part. *tinctus*, to dye, stain), with the later addition of the OF agent suffix *-ier* (L *-ārius*).

Vars.: **Tainturier**; **Leteinturier**, **Letainturier**.

Dims.: It.: **Tintorello**, **Tintoretto**.

Teissier *see* TISSIER

Teitelbaum Jewish (Ashkenazic): ornamental name from Yid. *teytlboym* date palm (from MHG *tahtel* date (OHG *dahtil*, from Gk *daktylos* finger) + *boum* tree). The name may sometimes have been chosen in reference to Psalm 92: 12 'the righteous shall flourish like the palm tree'.

Vars.: **Teitelbo(i)m**, **Tejtelbaum**, **Taitelbaum**, **Taytelboim**, **Ta(j)telbaum**; **Teitel(man)**, **Taitel(man)**, **Deitel**, **Tatelman**; **T(a)ytel**.

Teitz *see* DEUTSCH

Teixeira *see* TASSO

Tejada *see* TEIL

Tejeda *see* TASSO

Tejtelbaum *see* TEITELBAUM

Tekach *see* TKACH

Telegin Russian: patr. from the nickname *Telega* 'Cart', 'Waggon', given presumably as an occupational name to a carter.

Dim.: Russ.: **Telezhkin** (patr.).

Telemann *see* TERRY

Telfer English (chiefly Northumb.) and Scots: nickname for a strong man or ferocious warrior, from OF *taille(r)* to cut (see TAILLANT) + *fer* iron (L *ferrum*).

Vars.: **Taillefer**, **Telfair**, **Tulliver**, **Tolver**; TELFORD.

Telford Scots and English (Northumb.): not, as its form would imply, a habitation name, even though there is a town in Shrops. so called, but a var. of TELFER, assimilated to the pattern of habitation names in *-ford*. The Shrops. place is a 'new town', named after the celebrated Scottish civil engineer Thomas Telford (1757–1834).

Vars.: **Tilfo(u)rd**, **Talfourd**.

Telhard *see* TEIL

Tell 1. Low German: dim. of *Dietrich*; see DERRICK and TERRY 1. **2.** Low German: habitation name from any of the various minor places so called from MLG *telg(e)* branch, twig. **3.** Jewish: of unknown origin.

Vars. (of 2): **Telle**, **Telge**; TELLER; **Tellmann**, **Telgmann**.

Teller 1. Low German: habitation name, a var. of TELL 2.
2. Jewish (Ashkenazic): of uncertain origin, possibly an
occupational name for a barber-surgeon, derived from
the sign of the platter (Ger. *Teller*, Yid. *teler*), with
which barber-surgeons' shops were distinguished in central Europe.

Var. (of 2): **Teler**.

Tello Spanish: from a medieval given name, which is
probably of Gmc origin, and may be akin to the Gmc personal name represented by OE *Tila* (cf. TILBROOK, TIL-
BURY, and TILDEN).

Patrs.: Sp.: **Téllez**. Port.: **Teles**.

Teml *see* THOMAS

Tempany *see* TIMPANY

Tempest English: nickname for someone of blustery temperament, from ME, OF *tempest(e)* storm (L *tempestas* weather, season, a deriv. of *tempus* time).

Dim.: It.: **Tempestini**.

Temple 1. English and French: occupational name or
habitation name for someone who was employed at or
lived near one of the houses ('temples') maintained by
the Knights Templar, a crusading order so named because
they claimed to occupy in Jerusalem the site of the old
temple (ME, OF *temple*, L *templum*, a deriv. of *temere* to
cut, referring originally to a sacred enclosure). The order
was founded in 1118 and flourished for 200 years, but was
suppressed as heretical in 1312. **2.** English: name given to
foundlings baptized at the Temple Church, London, so
called because it was originally built on land belonging
to the Templars. **3.** Scots: habitation name from the parish
of *Temple* in Edinburgh, likewise so called because it was
the site of the local headquarters of the Knights Templar.

Vars.: Eng.: **Templar**, **Templer** (Somerset); **Templeman**. Fr.:
Templier.

Templeton Scots: habitation name from a place near
Dundonald, in the former county of Ayrs. (now part of
Strathclyde region), so called from ME *temple* house of
the Knights Templar + *toun* settlement (OE *tūn*). There
are also places in Wales, Berks. and Devon so called, but
these do not seem to be the source of any surnames.

Tena 1. Spanish: topographic name from the dial. term
tena rough farm building (e.g. a cattle-shed or barn). The
word is probably from L *tigna*, pl. of *tignum* beam, plank.
There is a place so named in the province of Huesca, and
the surname may in part be a habitation name from this. **2.**
Catalan: metonymic occupational name for a shopkeeper,
from OCat. *tena* shop (LL *tenda*). **3.** Jewish: of unknown
origin.

Tenbrinck *see* BRINK

Tendler German and Jewish (Ashkenazic): occupational
name for a dealer in second-hand goods, Ger. *Tändler*,
MHG *tendelære*, an agent deriv. of MHG *tändeln* to
deal, trade, ultimately from LL *tantum* price (originally
meaning 'so much', correlative to *quantum* 'how much';
cf. GANTER). The Ger. vocab. word and the surname are
restricted largely to Bavaria, Austria, and the Sudeten Germans.

Vars.: **Tandler**, **Dandler**.

Tengel *see* DENGLER

Tengue *see* TANGUY

Tennant English: status name for a farmer who held his
land from an overlord by obligations of rent or service,
from OF, ME *tenant* (pres. part. of OF *tenir* to hold, L
tenere). This was the normal situation for landholders in
the Middle Ages, since under the feudal system all land
belonged ultimately to the king and use of it was granted
in return for financial or military support.

Vars.: **Tennent**; **Tenner** (from an agent noun).

Patr.: Eng.: **Tennents**.

Tenner *see* TANNER

Tenney English (Yorks.): from a medieval given name, a
dim. of DENNIS 1. The variation in initial seems to have
been occasioned by the model of Gmc personal names with
initial Þ-, which were often introduced to England in
doublet forms with initial *D*- and *T*-; cf., e.g., DERRICK
and TERRY 1.

Patrs.: **Tennyson**, **Tennison**, **Tenneson**.

Tenniel English: of uncertain origin; it may be a var. of
DANIEL (cf. the form *Denial* quoted there, and, for the
altered initial, TENNEY).

Tenon *see* STEPHEN

Tenpenny *see* TIMPANY

Tentzer *see* TANZER

Teodorczyk *see* THÉODORE

Teperson *see* TÖPFER

Teplý Czech: nickname for an eager or enthusiastic person, from the Czech adj. *teplý* warm.

Terbeck *see* BACH

Terbocke *see* TARBOCK-

Tereshkov Russian: patr. from the given name *Tereshko*,
a dim. form of *Terenti* (L *Terentius*, an old Roman family
name). This name was borne by numerous early Christian
saints.

Ter Haar *see* HAAR

Terkel *see* TURK

Terkelsen *see* THIRKILL

Termeer *see* MEER

Ternan *see* TIERNEY

Ternoster *see* PATERNOSTER

Terrall *see* TYRRELL

Terrance *see* McTERRELLY

Terrón Spanish: topographic name for someone who lived
by a plot of agricultural land, Sp. *terrón* (a deriv. of L *terra*
land; cf. TARRÉS).

Terry 1. English: from the common Norman personal name, *T(h)erry* (OF *Thierri*), composed of the Gmc elements **þeudō-* people, race + *rīc* power. Theodoric was the name of the Ostrogothic leader (*c.*454–526) who invaded Italy in 488 and established his capital at Ravenna in 493. His name was often taken as a deriv. of Gk *Theodōros* (see THÉODORE). 2. Irish: Anglicized form of Gael. *Mac Toirdhealbhaigh*; see McTERRELLY and CURLEY. 3. Provençal: occupational name for a potter, from OProv. *terrin* earthenware vase (a dim. of *terre* earth, L *terra*).

Vars. (of 1): **Terrey**, **Tarry**, **Torr(e)y**, **Torrie**, **Todrick**. See also DERRICK.

Dims. (of 1): Fr.: **Thiriet**, **Thiriez**, **Theuriet**, **Thiriot**, **Thériot**, **Thirion**, **Thir(i)eau**. Ger.: **Tietze(l)**, **Thielsch**, **Tilke**, **Tillich**. Low Ger.: **T(h)iede**, **Tiedmann**, **Thie(de)mann**, **Theimann**, **The(d)e**; **Thieke**, **Tieck(e)**, **Theeck**; **Tietz(e)**, **Tietzmann**, **Titze**, **Tetze**; **Thiel(e)**, **Tiel**, **Thielmann**, **Theil(e)**, **Theilemann**, **Theel(e)**, **Thele(mann)**, **Telemann**, **Thälmann**, TELL, TILL; **Thieleke**, **Thieleck**, **Tilke**. Fris.: **T(h)ode**, **Thöl(e)**, **T(h)ölke**; **Thede**; **Thade**.

Pejs. (of 1): Fr.: **Thierrard**, **Thiérard**, **Thierrart**, **Thiérart**.

Patrs. (from 1): Eng.: **Torris**. Fris.: **Tiarks**, **Tjarcks**, **Jarcks**.

Patrs. (from dims. of 1): Ger.: **Thielscher**. Low Ger.: **The(e)den(s)**, **Th(i)elen(s)**, **Tillmanns**; **The(e)ding**, **Thielking**; **Theeder**, **Tielker**. Fris.: **Thoden**, **Tholen**, **Thölen**, **T(h)ölken**; **Todsen**; **Thedinga**. Flem.: **Tits**.

Terschüren *see* SCHEUER

Teruel Spanish: habitation name from the city of this name in E Spain, so called from L *Turiolum*, a dim. formation from the pre-Roman element *tur* hill (found also in Fr. placenames, and akin to OE *torr*, of Brit. origin). See also THÉRON.

Tesárek *see* CIEŚLAK

Tesh *see* TASH

Tesler *see* TISCHLER

Tess German (of Slav. origin): short form of the various Slav. personal names with a first element *tech* comfort, consolation, e.g. *Techomir* (with a second element meaning 'great', 'famous'), which has itself given the Ger. surname **Tes(s)mer**.

Vars.: **Tessmann**, **Tetzmann**, **Tech**, **Teck**.

Dims.: **Teske**, **Tetzke**, **Tetzel**, **Techel**, **Teckel**.

Patrs.: **Tessen**, **Techen**.

Tessel *see* TASSO

Teste French: nickname for someone with a large or ugly head, from OF *teste* head (LL *testa*, originally used to describe an earthenware pot).

Vars.: **Tête**; **Testu**, **Tétu**.

Dims.: Fr.: **Testot**, **Tétot**, **Teston**. It.: **Testini**, **Testino**.

Augs.: It.: **Testoni**, **Testone**.

Pejs.: Fr.: **Testard**, **Tétard**, **Testart**, **Tétart**, **Testaud**, **Têtaud**. Eng.: **Tester**, **Testar**.

Tétard *see* TESTE

Tetley English (Yorks.): apparently a habitation name from an unidentified place, perhaps named from the OE byname *Tǣta* or its ON cogn. *Teitr* (cf. TAIT) + OE *lēah* wood, clearing.

Tetsall *see* TATTERSALL

Tetze *see* TERRY

Teuber *see* TAUBE

Teunisse *see* THON

Tevelov *see* DAVID

Tew 1. English: habitation name from a place in Oxon., named from an OE element *tīewe* row, ridge. 2. Welsh: nickname for a fat man, from W *tew* plump.

Tewelson *see* DAVID

Tewes *see* THIESS

Tewson *see* TUSON

Texereau *see* TISSIER

Tey *see* TYE

Teysédou *see* TISSIER

Teyte *see* TAIT

Thacker English (W Midlands): occupational name for a THATCHER, from an agent deriv. of Northern ME *thack* thatch (ON *þak*).

Vars.: **Thak(k)er**, **Thakkar**, **Thackore**; **Thaxter** (formally fem., largely confined to Norfolk).

Thackeray English: habitation name from *Thackray* in the parish of Great Timble, W Yorks., now submerged in Fewston reservoir. It was named with the ON elements *þak* thatching, reeds + *(v)rá* nook, corner. The surname is found principally in Yorks. and Cumb.

Vars.: **Thacker(e)y**, **Thack(w)ray**, **Thack(a)ra**, **Thackrah**.

Thaddée *see* TADIÉ

Thade *see* TERRY

Thain Scots and English: occupational name for a noble retainer or attendant, ME *thayn* (OE *þeg(e)n*). In Scotland the term was used in the later Middle Ages to denote someone who held land directly from the king.

Vars.: **Thaine**, **Thayne**.

Thake English: occupational name for a THATCHER, or habitation name for someone who lived in a house with a thatched roof when this was something of a rarity in the neighbourhood. The name is from ME *thake* thatch (OE *ðæc*).

Thaker *see* THACKER

Thämel *see* THOMAS

Thamm *see* DANKMAR

Thanner *see* TANNER

Tharp *see* THORPE

Thatcher English: occupational name for a thatcher, someone who covered roofs in straw, from an agent deriv. of ME *thach(en)* to thatch (OE *þæccan* to cover, roof). See also THACKER and THEAKER, and DECKER 1 for cogns.

Thaysen *see* THIESS

Theaker English (Yorks.): occupational name for a THATCHER, from an agent deriv. of Northern ME *theke(n)* to thatch (ON *þekja* to cover, roof).

Thede *see* TERRY

Theesinga *see* THIESS

Theil *see* TEIL

Theinel *see* DEINHARD

Thelwall English: habitation name from a place in Ches., so called from OE *þel* plank (bridge) + *wǣl* pool, deep part of a river.
Var.: **Thelwell**.

Themann *see* THOMAS

Thenet *see* STEPHEN

Theng *see* THON

Thenner *see* TANNER

Theobald English: learned form, re-created from Fr. *Théobald*, of the common medieval given name *Tebald*, *Tibalt* (OF *Teobaud*, *Tibaut*), from a Gmc personal name composed of the elements *þeudō*- people, race + *bald* bold, brave.
Vars.: **Theobold, Tudbald, Tudball, Tidbold, Ti(d)bald, Ti(d)ball, Tibble, Tippell, Tipple, Tebbell, Tebble, Dybald, Dyball, Diboll, Dybell, Dib(b)le, Dyble, Dipple; Tibbett, Tibbitt, Tibbott, Tebbet(t), Tebbit(t), Tebbut(t), Debutt, Teboth; Tippett** (Cornwall).
Dims.: Eng.: **Tebb, Tibb, Tipp**. Fr.: **Thibaudeau, Thibaudet, Thibaudin**. It.: **Tebaldini**.
Aug.: Fr.: **Thibaudat**.
Patrs.: Eng.: **Theobalds, Tibballs, Tibbles, Tipples; Tibbat(t)s, Tibbet(t)s, Tippetts, Tibbit(t)s, Tibbotts**. It.: **Fittipaldi, Fittipoldi; Tebaldeschi**. Low Ger.: **Diepolder, Diebels**. Flem.: **Dibbauts**.
Patrs. (from dims.): Eng.: **Tebbs, Tibb(in)s, Tippins, Tipson**.

Théodore French: from the given name *Théodore* (Gk *Theodōros*, a cpd of *theos* God + *dōron* gift), relatively popular in the Middle Ages because of its auspicious meaning; cf. DIEUDONNÉ. There has been considerable confusion with the Gmc personal name *Theodoric*; see TERRY. Gk *Th*- regularly gives Russ. *F*-, hence the common Russ. given name *Fyodor*.
Dims.: Fr.: **Doret, Dorot, Dorin**. It.: **Toderini, Todarini, Todarello**. Ger.: **Jöderli** (Swiss). Ukr.: **Tedorenko, Fedoronko, Fedorchenko, Fedorchik, Fesenko, Fedko, Khvedko**. Beloruss.: **Fedorinchik, Fedchonok**. Pol.: **Teodorczyk, Fedorczyk, Fedorko, Fedyszyn; Chwedko, Chodźko**.
Patrs.: Russ.: **Fyodorov(ykh)**. Ukr.: **Khodorovich**. Beloruss.: **Teodorovich**. Pol.: **Teodorowicz; F(i)edorowicz**. Croatian: **T(e)odorović**. Bulg.: **Todorov**. Georgian: **Tedoradze**. Armenian: **Torosian**. Rum.: **Teodorescu, Theodoresco**. Greek: **Theodoridis, Theodorakis**.
Patrs. (from dims.): Russ.: **Fedorushov, Fedorishchev, Fedorintsev, Fed(k)in, Fed(i)kov, Fedyakin, Fedyakov, Fedyanin, Fedyash(k)in, Fedya(sh)ev, Fedyukin, Fedyukov, Fedyun(k)in, Fedunov, Fedyunyaev, Fedyush(k)in, Fedichkin,**

Fedinin, Fedyshin, Fed(e)nev, Fedchin, Fedishchev. Beloruss.: **Fedorkevich, Khodasevich, Khadkevich**. Pol.: **Chodkiewicz**.
Habitation name: Pol.: **Fedorowski**.
Habitation name (from a dim.): Pol.: **Chwedkowski**.

Thériot *see* TERRY

Therkelsen *see* THIRKILL

Théron French: habitation name from a place in the Massif Central, apparently named with a Gaul. element *turon* height, hill (see TERUEL). There seems to have been some confusion with **Thirion**, which is derived from a medieval given name of uncertain origin. Both surnames were borne by Huguenot refugees to England in the 17th–18th cents.
Var.: **Thérond**.

Thewlis English (chiefly Yorks.): nickname for an illmannered person, from the northern ME adj. *thewless* badly behaved, immoral (OE *þēawlēas*, a cpd of *þēaw* custom, correct behaviour + -*lēas* lacking, without).
Vars.: **Thewles(s); Thowless** (Scotland).

Thibaudat *see* THEOBALD

Thicks *see* DICK

Thieblin *see* STEPHEN

Thiede *see* TERRY

Thieme *see* DIETMAR

Thiemeke *see* TIMM

Thiendl *see* DEINHARD

Thiers *see* TIERS

Thiess Low German: from an aphetic short form of the given name *Mathiess*; see MATTHEW.
Vars.: **Thies(e), Dies(s); Theuss, Deuss; T(h)ew(e)s, Thevs; Theis(s)**.
Dims.: Low Ger.: **Theismann, Deissmann**.
Patrs.: Low Ger.: **Thies(s)en, Tiessen, Th(i)esing, Diesing; The(u)ssen, Deussen, Deesen, Deus(s)ing; The(u)vissen, Thewissen, Thywissen, Thevessen, Devissen; Theissen, T(h)yssen, Thaysen**. Fris.: **Theesinga**. Flem., Du.: **T(h)ijssen, Diessens, Teewen**. Dan., Norw.: **Thiesen, Theisen, Thuesen, Thygesen**.

Thijssen *see* THIESS

Thil *see* TEIL

Thin English: nickname for a slender man, from ME *thinne* thin (OE *þynne*).
Vars.: **Thynn(e)**.

Thirkill English: from the ON personal name *Þorkell*, a contracted form of a name composed of the divine name *Þórr* (see THOR 2) + *ketill* cauldron. The given name *Thurkill* or *Thirkill* was in use throughout England in the Middle Ages; in N England it had been introduced directly by Scandinavian settlers, whereas in the South it was the result of Norman influence. Surnames of this group are especially common in E Anglia, where Norman-French settlement was heavy.

Vars.: **Thurkettle**, **Thurkittle**, **Thirkettle**; **Thurtell**, **Turtill**, **Thurtle**, **Thirtle**, **Turtle**, **Tuttle**; **Thurkell**, **Thirkell**, **Turkel**, **T(h)urgell**, **Turkill**, **Thirkhill**, **Turgill**, **Thorkell**, **Toghill**.

Patrs.: Sc.: **McCorquodale**, **McCorkindale**; **McCorkell**, **McCork(h)ill**, **McCorkle**. Dan.: **T(h)erkelsen**, **T(h)erkildsen**.

Thirwell English (Northumb.): probably a habitation name from *Thirlwall* in Northumb., so called from OE *þerel* hollow, perforated + *weall* WALL. The placename apparently referred to a gap in the Roman wall, which passes through the settlement.

Thistlewaite English (Lancs.): habitation name from a minor place in the parish of Lancaster called *Thistlethwaite*, from ME *thistle* (OE *þistel*) + *thwaite* meadow (see THWAITE), i.e. a meadow overgrown with thistles.

Thistlewood English: habitation name from *Thistleworth* farm in the parish of W Grinstead, Sussex, so called from OE *þistel* thistle (cf. DISTEL) + *worð* enclosure (see WORTH).

Thode *see* TERRY

Thoinet *see* TONEY

Thomas English (and Welsh and Cornish), French, German, Dutch/Flemish, and Danish/Norwegian: from the popular medieval given name, of biblical origin. The *-h-* is organic, the initial letter of the name in the Gk New Testament being a theta. The universal Eng. pronunciation as /t/ rather than /θ/ is the result of Fr. influence from an early date. The biblical name was originally an Aramaic byname meaning 'Twin', borne by one of the disciples of Christ, best known for his scepticism about Christ's resurrection (John 20: 24–9). This disciple is stated by Eusebius, on no scriptural authority, to have borne the given name *Judah*. Aphetic forms are common in most European languages; see MAAS.

Vars.: Eng.: **Tomas**. Fr.: **Thoumas**. It.: **Tom(m)asi**, **Tommaseo**, **Tom(m)ei**, **Tom(m)eo**, **Toma**, **Tome**. Ger.: **Thoma**, **Thome**.

Dims.: Eng.: **Thomazin**; **T(h)om(p)sett**; **Thom** (Scotland); **Tom(a)lin**, **Tomblin(g)**, TAMBLYN; **Tom(p)kin**, **Tonkin** (W Country). Fr.: **Thomasset**, **Thom(az)et**, **Thomé**; **Thomassin**, **Thomelin**; **Tho(u)masson**, **Thomazon**, **Thom(es)son**; **Thomasseau**, **Thomazeau**. It.: **Tomas(s)ini**, **Tommasini**, **Tom(m)asino**, **Tom(ad)ini**, **Tomaini**, **Tomaino**, **Tumini**; **Tom(m)aselli**, **Tom(m)asello**, **Tomaelli**, **Tomaello**, **Tuminelli**; **Tomas(s)etti**, **Tommasetti**, **Tumiotto**, **Tomasutti**, **Tom(m)asuzzi**, **Tomasicchio**. Ger.: **Thömel**, **Dömel**, **Theml** (Bavaria); **Teml** (Austria); **Dehmel**, **Demel(t)**, **Thämel(t)**, **Dähmel**, **Thümnel**. Low Ger.: **Thomann**, **Do(h)mann**, **Themann**, **Demann**, **Thumann**, **Thome**, **Domke**, **Demke**, **Demchen**, **Dumke**. Ger. (under Slav. influence): **Tom(as)ek**, **Domaschek**, **Tomaschke**, **Domaschke**, **Damaschke**, **Demschke**, **Tomisch**. Pol.: **Tomaszczyk**, **Tomaszek**, **Tomasik**, **Tomalczyk**, **Tomanek**, **Tomczyk**, **Tomik**. Ukr.: **Khomik**. Czech: **Tomášek**, **Tománek**, **Tomeček**; **Tomek**.

Augs.: It.: **Tomas(s)oni**, **Tommasoni**, **Tomadoni**.

Patrs.: Eng.: **Thomas(s)on**, **Thomerson**. Sc.: McTAVISH, McOMISH. Dan., Norw.: **Thoma(s)sen**. Swed.: **Thomasson**. Beloruss.: **Tomashov**, **Tomashevich**. Pol.: **Tomaszewicz**, **Tomasiewicz**; **Tomowicz**. Lithuanian: **Tomaskunas**,

Tomaskaitis. Czech: **Tomšů**. Croatian: **Tomašević**, **Tom(ov)ić**. Armenian: **Tomasian**, **Tumasian**.

Patrs. (from dims.): Eng.: **Toms** (chiefly W Country); **Thoms** (chiefly Scots); **Tombs**, **Toomb(e)s**, **Tomes**, **Tommis**; **Tomlins**; **Tomblings**; **Tom(p)kins**, **Tom(p)kiss**, **Tomkies**, **Tomkys**; **Tonks** (Midlands); **T(h)om(p)son**, **Tomsen**, **Thombleson**, **T(h)omlinson**, **Tom(p)kinson**, **Townson**. Sc.: McCOMB. Low Ger.: **Thoms(en)**, **Thömen**, **Dohms**, **Dohmer**. Fris.: **Thöminga**. Flem.: **Tommen**. Dan., Norw.: **Thomsen**. Swed.: **Thomsson**. Russ.: **Fominov**, **Fom(ush)kin**, **Fomichkin**, **Fomichyov**. Beloruss.: **Tomich**, **Khomich**, **Khomin**, **Tomashkov**. Pol.: **Tomaszkiewicz**, **Tomkowicz**, **Tomczykiewicz**, **Tomankiewicz**; **Chomicz**; **Tomczak**. Armenian: **Tumayan**.

'Son of the wife of T.': Ukr.: **Khomishin**.

Habitation names: Pol.: **Tomaszewski**, **Tomaszyński**, **Tomicki**, **Chomicki**, **Chomiński**, **Chomiszewski**.

Habitation names (from dims.): Pol.: **Tomczyński**, **Tomczykowski**; **Tomankowski**.

Thon 1. German: from an aphetic form of the given name *Ant(h)on*; see ANTHONY and TONEY. 2. Jewish (E Ashkenazic): of unknown origin.

Vars. (of 1): **Toni**, **Thön**; **Theng**, **Deng** (Switzerland, Swabia).

Dim. (of 1): Low Ger.: **Dohnke**.

Patrs. (from 1): Low Ger.: **Thönes**, **Tön(is)sen**. **Tönsing**. Du.: **Teunisse(n)**, **Theunissen**.

Patrs. (from dims. of 1): Low Ger.: **T(h)onjes**, **Thönges**, **Dönges**.

Thor 1. German: habitation name for someone who lived near the gates of a town or metonymic occupational name for someone responsible for guarding them, from MHG *thor*, OHG *tor* gate (mod. Ger. *Tor*). 2. Swedish: from a given name, a short form of any of the various Scand. personal names containing as their first element *Thor* (ON *Þórr*), the name of the god of thunder in Scandinavian mythology (cf. names such as THORBURN and THOROGOOD).

Vars. (of 1): **Thormann**; **Thorwart(h)** (for the second element cf. WARD 1).

Dims. (of 1): **Thörl**; **Dörl** (Franconia, Thuringia).

Patrs. (from 2): Swed.: **T(h)or(e)sson**, **T(h)uresson**. Dan., Norw.: **Thorsen**.

Thorburn Scots and N English: from a Northern ME given name (ON *Þórbjörn*, composed of the divine name *Þórr* (see THOR 2) + *björn* bear, warrior).

Vars.: **Thoburn**, **Thurburn**, **Thurbon**, **Thurban**, **Thubron**, **Turbin**, **Tarbun**, **Tarbin**.

Thorel French: 1. nickname for a strong or violent individual, from OF *t(h)or(el)* bull; see TORO. 2. from a dim. of an aphetic short form of the given name MATURIN.

Vars.: **Thoreau**, **Thoret**, **Thoré**, **Thorez**.

Thorkell *see* THIRKILL

Thorley N English: habitation name. There are places called *Thorley* in Herts. (near Bishop's Stortford) and in the Isle of Wight. However, the surname almost certainly derives from *Thornley* in Lancs. The origin of all of these is OE *þorn* thorn bush (see THORN 1) + *lēah* wood, clearing.

Var.: **Thornley**.

Thorman *see* THURMAN

Thörmer *see* THURN

Thorn 1. English and Danish: topographic name for someone who lived by a thorn bush or hedge (OE, ON *þorn*), or habitation name from a place named with this word, for example *Thorne* in Somerset or *Thorns* in Suffolk. **2.** Low German and Danish: topographic name for someone who lived near a tower, from MLG *torn* tower (see THURN). **3.** German: habitation name from the city of *Thorn*, now *Toruń* in Poland, the name of which is from MHG *torn* tower (see THURN).

Vars. (of 1): Eng.: **Thorne, Thorn(e)s.** (Of 3): **Thörner.**

Thornber English: habitation name from *Thornborough* in N Yorks. (*Thornebergh* in 12th-cent. records) or *Thornbrough* in Northumb. and N Yorks. (*T(h)orneburg* in 13th-cent. records). The former is probably so called from OE *þorn* thorn bush + *berg* hill; the latter from *þorn* + *burh* fort. There are other places in England bearing these names, but they are less likely to be the source of the surname.

Vars.: **Thornberry, Thornbury, Thornburgh, Thornborough, Thornborrow.**

Thorndike English: habitation name from some minor place so called from OE *þorn* thorn bush + *dīc* ditch, dyke, or topographic name for someone who lived by a defence-work consisting of a thorn hedge and a ditch.

Vars.: **Thorndyke, Thorndick.**

Thornhill English: habitation name from any of various places, for example in Dorset, Wilts., Derbys., and W Yorks., so called from OE *þorn* thorn bush + *hyll* HILL.

Var.: **Thornell** (Wilts.).

Thornton 1. English and Scots: habitation name from any of the numerous places throughout England and Scotland so called, from OE *þorn* thorn bush + *tūn* enclosure, settlement. **2.** Irish: translation of Gael. **Mac Sceacháin** 'son of *Sceachán*', a personal name from a dim. of *sceach* thorn-bush. **3.** Irish: Anglicized form of Gael. *Ó Draighneáin*; see DRENNAN.

Thorogood English: from the Northern ME given name *Thurgod* (ON *Þorgautr*, composed of the divine name *Þórr* (see THOR 2) + the ethnic name *Gautr*; see JOCELYN). The derivation from ME *thur(og)h* completely (OE *þur(u)h*) + *gode* good (OE *gōd*), supported by Ekwall among others, is less plausible.

Vars.: **Thorou(gh)good, Thor(r)owgood; Thorgood, Thurgood, Thurgate.**

Thorold English: from the ME given name *Turold* (ON *Þorvaldr*, composed of the divine name *Þórr* (see THOR 2) + *valdr* rule).

Vars.: **Thorrold, Thourault, Torode.**
Dims.: Fr.: **Trudon, Trudeau.**
Patr.: Dan.: **Thorvaldsen.**

Thorpe English: habitation name from any of the numerous places in England named with the ON element *þorp* hamlet, village, or the rarer OE cogn. *þrop*.

Vars.: **Thorp, Tharp, Turp; Thro(u)p, T(h)rupp, Thripp.** See also TROUP.
Dims.: Ger.: **Dörfle(in).** Jewish: **Derfler** (from Yid. *derfl*, dim. of *dorf* village).

Thorstensson see THURSTON

Thouvenel see STEPHEN

Thowless see THEWLIS

Thoytes see THWAITE

Thrane Danish: nickname for someone who was thought to resemble a crane (Dan. *trane*, ON *trani*) in some way, most probably in having long spindly legs.

Threadgold English: occupational nickname for someone who embroidered fine clothes with gold thread, from ME *thred(en)* to thread (from OE *þrǣd* thread) + *gold* GOLD.

Vars.: **Threadgould, Threadgill, Threadgall, Thridgould, Tre(a)dgold.**

Threapleton English (Yorks.): apparently a habitation name from an unidentified place, the etymology of which is unclear. The last element is OE *tūn* enclosure, settlement; the first may represent a personal name *Þrýðbeald* (composed of the elements *þrýð* might + *beald* bold, brave), or it may be akin to OE *þrēapland* land over which there was some dispute (from *þrēapian* to quarrel).

Var.: **Thrippleton.**

Threlfall English (Lancs.): habitation name from a place near Kirkham, so called from ME *thrall* serf (ON *þráll*) + *fall* clearing, place where the trees had been felled.

Var.: **Trelfall.**

Thridgould see THREADGOLD

Thrift see FIRTH

Thripp see THORPE

Thrippleton see THREAPLETON

Throssell see THRUSSELL

Thrower S English: occupational name for someone who made silk thread from raw silk, from an agent deriv. of ME *thrōw(en)* (OE *þrāwan* to twist). From the 13th cent. the verb began to be used in its mod. sense, including throwing clay in pottery, and so the surname may also have originated as an occupational name for a potter.

Var.: **Trower.**

Thrussell English: nickname from ME *throstle* thrush (OE *þrostle*), given probably to a cheerful person, the bird being noted for its cheerful song.

Vars.: **Thrustle, Throssell; Thrush** (OE *þrysce*).

Thubron see THORBURN

Thuesen see THIESS

Thumann see THOMAS

Thumb 1. English: nickname for someone with a missing or deformed thumb, or for someone of very small size, from ME *thum* thumb (OE *þūma*; cf. DAUM). **2.** German: nickname for a foolish person, from MHG *tump* ignorant, stupid (OHG *tumb* dumb).

Vars. (of 1): **Thum.** (Of 2): **Thumm, Dummer, Dummann.**

Thureau see ARTHUR

Thuresson see THOR

Thurgate see THOROGOOD

Thurgell see THIRKILL

Thurlow English: habitation name from a place in Suffolk, recorded in Domesday Book as *Tritlawa* and *Tridlauua*, and apparently named from the OE elements *þrȳð* troop, assembly + *hlāw* hill.
Var.: **Thurloe**.

Thurman English: from the ME given name *Thurmond*, ON *Þormundr*, composed of the divine name *Þórr* (see THOR 2) + *mundr* protection.
Vars.: **Thurmand**, **Thorman**.

Thurn German: topographic name for someone who lived near a watch tower or metonymic occupational name for someone responsible for manning it, from MHG *turn, torn* tower (from OF *torn*, a byform of *torz*; see TOWER). Some examples may derive from the town of *Thurn* in Austria, named with this word. See also THORN 3.
Vars.: **Thurm; Thurner, Thurmer, Thörmer**.

Thursfield English (W Midlands): habitation name from *Thursfield* (now New Chapel) near Newcastle in Staffs., so called from the ON personal name *Þorvaldr* (see THOROLD) + OE *feld* pasture, open country (see FIELD).

Thurston English: 1. from a medieval given name (ON *Þorsteinn*, composed of the divine name *Þórr* (see THOR 2) + *steinn* stone). 2. habitation name from a place in Suffolk, so called from the gen. case of the ON personal name *Þori* (see THOR 2) + OE *tūn* enclosure, settlement.
Vars. (of 1): **Thurstan, Thursting; Tustain, Tustian, Tustin(g), Dusting; Tutin(g), Tut(t)on**.
Patrs. (from 1): Eng.: **Thurstans**. Swed.: **T(h)orstensson**.
Dan., Norw.: **Torstensen**.

Thwaite N English: topographic name for someone who lived by a clearing or patch of pasture land, ME *thwaite* (ON *þveit*), or habitation name from any of the various places named with this word, in N England and in Norfolk and Suffolk.
Vars.: **Thwaites, Thwaytes, Thoytes; Twaite, Twatt, Twait(e)s, Tweats, Twite**.

Thygesen see THIESS

Thynn see THIN

Tiago see SANTIAGO

Tiarks see TERRY

Tibald see THEOBALD

Ticháček see CICHY

Tichborne English: habitation name from a place in Hants, so called from OE *ticce(n)* goat, kid + *burna* stream (see BOURNE).
Vars.: **Tichbourne, Tichbon, Tichband**.

Tichner see TITCHENER

Tickle English: habitation name from *Tickhill* in S Yorks., so called from the OE personal name or byname *Tica* (of uncertain origin) or *ticce(n)* kid + *hyll* HILL.
Vars.: **Tickel(l)**.

Tidbald see THEOBALD

Tidman English: 1. status name for the head of a tithing, OE *tēoðingmann* (from *tēoðing* tithing, group of households, originally ten households, + *mann* man). According to the medieval system of frankpledge, every member of a tithing was responsible for every other, so that for example if one of them committed a crime the others had to help pay for it. 2. from the ME, OE given name *Tideman*, composed of the OE elements *tīd* time, season + *mann* man.
Vars.: **Tiddeman, Tydeman, Tit(t)man**.

Tidmarsh English: habitation name from a place in Berks., whose name means 'marsh of the people', from OE *þeōd* nation + *mersc* MARSH.

Tidy English: nickname for a handsome or admirable person, from ME *tīdi* fine, excellent (a deriv. of OE *tīd* (due) season).

Tieck see TERRY

Tienke see AUSTIN, MARTIN

Tienot see STEPHEN

Tier see MCINTYRE

Tierney Irish (esp. common in Galway): Anglicized form of Gael. Ó Tíghearnaigh 'descendant of *Tighearnach*', a byname meaning 'Lord', 'Master'.
Vars.: **Tierny, O'Tiern(e)y, (O')Te(a)rney; LORD**.
Dims.: **(O')Tiernan, O'Ternane, Ternan** (Gael. Ó Tíghearnáin).

Tiers French: 1. name for a third-born son, from OF *tiers* third (L *tertius*). 2. habitation name from any of various places named from OF *tierce* third part (L *tertia (pars)*), either because they formed part of estates divided into three, or because they were subject to a rent of one-third of the produce raised.
Var.: **Thiers**.

Tiessen see THIESS

Tiévant see STEPHEN

Tiffin English: from the medieval female given name *Tiffania* (OF *Tiphaine*, from Gk *Theophania*, a cpd of *theos* God + *phainein* to appear). This name was often given to girls born around the feast of Epiphany.
Vars.: **Tiffen, Tiffany, Tiffney**.
Dims.: Fr.: **Tif(f)en(n)eau, Tipheneau, Tifon, Tiphon**.

Tigg see TEGG

Tighe Irish: Anglicized form of Gael. Ó Taidhg 'descendant of *Tadhg*', a byname meaning 'Bard', 'Poet', 'Philosopher'. See also MCCAIG.
Vars.: **TEAGUE, Tague, T(e)igue, Teige, Teage, Teek**.
Dims.: **Teahan, Teehan** (Gael. Ó Tadhgán).

Tijssen see THIESS

Tikhonov Russian: patr. from a given name, *Tikhon* (Gk *Tykhōn*, a deriv. of *tynkhanein* to hit, succeed). This was borne by a 5th-cent. bishop of Cyprus, who finally suppressed the cult of Aphrodite. The popularity of the given name in Russia may have been enhanced by folk-etymological associations with *tikh* quiet, calm, a common element in Slav. cpd personal names.

Var.: **Tikhanov**.

Dims.: Russ.: **Tishutkin**, **Tiseev** (patrs.). Ukr.: **Tishchenko**.

Til *see* TEIL

Tilbrook English: habitation name from a place in the former county of Hunts. (now part of Cambs.), so called from the OE byname *Tila* (from *til* capable) + OE *brōc* BROOK.

Tilbury English: habitation name from the port on the Thames in Essex, so called from the OE byname *Tila* (cf. TILBROOK) + OE *burh* fortress (see BURY).

Tilden English: probably a habitation name from an unidentified place, apparently so called from the OE byname *Tila* (cf. TILBROOK) + OE *denu* valley (see DEAN 1).

Tildesley *see* TYLDESLEY

Tiler English: occupational name for a maker or layer of tiles, from an agent deriv. of ME *tile* tile (OE *tigele*, from L *tēgula*, a deriv. of *tegere* cover). In the Middle Ages tiles were widely used in floors and pavements, and to a lesser extent in roofing, where they did not really come into their own until the 16th cent.

Vars.: **Tyler**, **Tylor**. See also TILLER.

Tilford *see* TELFORD

Tilke *see* TERRY

Till 1. English: from a common medieval female given name, a short form of *Matilda* (see MOULT 1). 2. Low German: dim. of *Dietrich*; see DERRICK and TERRY 1.

Var.: **Tille**. (Of 2 only): **Tillmann**.

Dims. (of 1): TILLEY, **Tillet(t)**, **Tillot(t)**, **Til(l)cock**.

Metrs. (from 1): TILSON.

Tiller English: occupational name for a husbandman, from ME *til(l)er*, a secondary deriv. of OE *tilian* to till, cultivate (cf. TILLEY 3). There has been some confusion with TILLER.

Vars.: **Tillier**, **Til(l)yer**, **Tillyard**; **Tillman**.

Tilley English: 1. Norman habitation name from any of various places in N France called *Tilly* (*Tiliācum* in medieval records). Examples in Eure and Calvados are so called from a Gallo-Roman personal name *Tilius* (perhaps from L *tilia* lime tree; cf. TEIL) + the local suffix *-ācum*; one in Seine-et-Oise gets its name from the personal name *Attilius* (a deriv. of *Attalus*, a hereditary name of uncertain origin used by the kings of Pergamum and adopted occasionally in the Roman Empire) + *-ācum*. 2. habitation name from *Tilley* in Shrops., so called from OE *telg(e)* branch, bough (cf. TELL 2) + *lēah* wood, clearing. 3. occupational name for a husbandman, ME *tilie* (OE *tilia*, a primary deriv. of *tilian* to till, cultivate; cf. TILLER). 4. from a medieval female given name, a dim. of TILL.

Vars.: **Tilly** (see also TULLY), **Tillie**, **Til(e)y**, **Tyley**.

Tilling English: from a medieval given name, possibly a dim. (originally in *-in*) of TILL, but more probably a patr. deriv. of the OE byname *Tila* (see TILBROOK).

Tilly *see* TULLY

Tilson 1. English: metr. from the medieval female given name TILL. 2. Jewish (Ashkenazic): metr. from the Yid. female given name *Tile* (from the Hebr. name *Tehila* 'Splendour').

Vars. (of 1): **Tills(on)**. (Of 2): **Til(l)es**, **Tillis**, **Tilas**, **Till(e)son**.

From dims. (of 1): **Tillotson**. (Of 2): **Tilkin**.

Timár Hungarian: occupational name for a tanner, Hung. *timár* (a deriv. of *tim(só)* alum).

Timberlake English: habitation name from a lost place in the parish of Bayton, Worcs., so called from OE *timber* timber, wood + *lacu* stream (see LAKE).

Var.: **Timblick**.

Timbrell English: from ME *tumbrel* cart typically used for carting away and tipping out dung (OF *tomberel*, from *tomber* to fall, let fall), and so a metonymic occupational name for a maker of tip-up carts or for someone who had the job of collecting and transporting dung.

Timm 1. English: probably from an otherwise unrecorded OE personal name, cogn. with the attested Continental Gmc form *Timmo*. This is of uncertain origin, perhaps a short form of DIETMAR. The given name *Timothy* (see TIMOFEEV) was not in use in England until Tudor times, and is therefore not a likely source of this group of surnames. 2. Low German: from a short form of the medieval given name DIETMAR.

Vars. (of 1): **Timme**, **Tym(m)**. (Of 2): **Thimm**, **Timme**.

Dims. (of 1): **Timblin**, **Timkin**. (Of 2): **Thimmann**, **Thiemeke**.

Patrs. (from 1): **Tim(m)s**, **Timmes**, **Tymms**, **Tim(p)son**.

Patrs. (from 1) (dims.): TIMMONS; **Timmins**, **Timmi(e)s** (chiefly W Midlands); **Timkiss**.

Timmerman *see* ZIMMERMANN

Timmons 1. English: patr. from a dim. of the given name TIMM. 2. Irish: Anglicized form of Gael. **Mac Toimín** 'son of *Toimín*', a dim. form of *Tomás* THOMAS. 3. Irish: Anglicized form of Gael. **Ó Tiomáin** 'descendant of *Tiomán*', a personal name from a dim. of *tiom* pliant, soft. 4. Irish: Anglicized form of Gael. *Ó Tiománaidhe*; see TIMONY.

Timofeev Russian: patr. from the given name *Timofei* Timothy (Gk *Timotheos*, from *timān* to honour + *theos* God), which was bestowed in honour of various early saints, notably the companion of St Paul and first bishop of Ephesus.

Dims.: Ukr.: **Timoshchuk**, **Timoshenko**, **Timchenko**. Hung.: **Timkó**.

Patrs. (from dims.): Russ.: **Timoshkov**, **Timosh(k)in**, **Timochin**, **Timonin**, **Tim(k)in**, **Timshin**, **Timakov**, **Timachyov**, **Tim(y)ashaev**, **Timu(sh)ev**, **Timeshov**. Pol.: **Tymkiewicz**.

'Son of the wife of T. (dim.)': Ukr.: **Timchishin**.

Timony Irish: Anglicized form of Gael. **Ó Tiománaidhe** 'descendant of *Tiománaidhe*', a byname meaning 'Driver'.

Vars.: **Tymmany**, **(Mc)Timney**, TIMMONS.

Timothy *see* TOMELTY

Timpany English: metonymic occupational name for a player on the tympany (ME *timpan(e)*, OE *timpana*, from L *tumpanon*, from Gk), a kind of drum or tambourine.

Vars.: **Tympany, Tumpany, Tempany, Tempeny, Tenpen(n)y**.
Dim.: It.: **Timpanelli**.

Timperley English: habitation name from *Timperley* in N Ches., which is so called from OE *timber* timber, wood + *lēah* wood, clearing, i.e. a clearing where timber for building was obtained.

Tindale English: regional name for someone who lived in *Tynedale*, the valley of the river Tyne, or habitation name from a place so called in Cumb., situated on a tributary of the S *Tyne*. The name derives from a Brit. river name *Tina* (apparently from a Celt. root meaning 'to flow') + OE *dæl* valley (see DALE).

Vars.: **Tyndale, Tindal(l), Tyndall, Tindell, Tindle, Tindill**.

Tingay see TANGUY

Tingle English: metonymic occupational name for a maker of nails or pins, or nickname for a small, thin man, from ME *tingle*, a kind of very small nail (of Low Ger. origin).

Var.: **Tingler** (an agent deriv.).

Tinker English: occupational name for a mender of pots and pans, ME *tink(l)er* (of uncertain origin).

Var.: **Tinkler**.

Tinney Irish: Anglicized form of Gael. **Mac an tSionnaigh** 'son of the fox', from *sionnach* fox.

Vars.: **McAsinagh; Shin(n)agh, Shinnock, Shinnick, Shinwick, Shonnagh, Shunnagh, Shunny**.

Tinot see MARTIN

Tinsley English: habitation name from a place in S Yorks. near Rotherham, so called from the gen. case of the unattested OE personal name *Tynni* (a byform of the attested *Tunne*, of uncertain origin) + OE *hlāw* hill, mound, barrow (see LAW 2 and LOW 1).

Tintorello see TEINTURIER

Tinu see CONSTANTINE

Tioli Italian (Venetia): from an aphetic dim. of the given name *Matio*; see MATTHEW.

Vars.: **Tiozzi, Tiosso, Tiussi**.

Tipheneau see TIFFIN

Tiplady English: nickname for a lecherous man or one who was reputed to have achieved sexual success with a woman of higher rank, from ME *tȳpe(n)* to knock over (of obscure origin) + *lady*; cf. SHACKLADY.

Vars.: **Toplady, Topley**.

Tipp see THEOBALD

Tipper English: probably an occupational name for a maker of arrowheads, from an agent deriv. of ME *tippe* tip, head. On the other hand it may possibly be a bawdy nickname comparable to TIPLADY.

Tipping English: from a medieval given name, originally an OE patr. from a personal name or byname *Tippa*, for

which there is evidence in placenames such as *Tiptree*, but which is of uncertain origin.

Patrs.: **Tippings**.

Tipton English: habitation name from a place in the W Midlands, recorded in Domesday Book as *Tibintone*, from the gen. case of an unrecorded OE personal name *Tibba* (of obscure origin, possibly akin to *Tippa*; see TIPPING) + *tūn* enclosure, settlement.

Tirado Spanish: probably a nickname for someone with long limbs, from Sp. *tirado* stretched (past part. of *tirar* to pull; cf. TYRRELL). The nickname may also have had the sense of Sp. *estirado* lofty, haughty, difficult.

Tirial see TYRRELL

Tirpitz German: habitation name from *Tirpitz* near Küstrin, Brandenburg, or from *Türpitz* in Silesia, recorded in the 13th cent. as *Tirpiz*. Both placenames are of Slav. origin.

Var.: **Türpitz**.

Tischbein German: metonymic occupational name for a furniture maker, from Ger. *Tischbein* table leg, a cpd formed from MHG *tisch* table (see TISCHLER) + *bein* leg.

Tischler German and Jewish (Ashkenazic): occupational name for a joiner, from an agent deriv. of Ger. *Tisch* table (MHG *tisch*, OHG *tisc*). This was the normal term for the craftsman in N and E Germany and in Austria and Switzerland during the Middle Ages; in the W, from Bavaria to the Dutch border, the equivalent was SCHREINER.

Vars.: **Tischmann**. Ger.: **Tisch(n)er**. Jewish: **Tishler, Tishman(n), Tischman, Teszler, Tes(s)ler**.

Tisdall English: apparently a habitation name from an unidentified place, perhaps named with the OE personal name *Tissi* (contracted form of *Tīdsige*, composed of the elements *tīd* season + *sige* victory) + OE *dæl* valley (see DALE).

Tishchenko see TIKHONOV

Tissier French: occupational name for a weaver, OF *tissier* (LL *texārius*, a deriv. of *texere* to weave).

Vars.: **Te(i)ssier, Teyssier, Tixier, Te(i)xier, Letessier; Tisserand, Tesserand**.
Dims.: Fr.: **Tessereau, Texereau; Tissot**. Prov.: **Teysédou**. It.: **Tesserin(i), Tessarin(i), Tessarotto, Tessarolo, Tessaroli**.
Patrs.: Fr.: **Autissier, Autixier, Autessier**.

Titchener English: topographic name for someone who lived at a crossroads or a fork in the road, OE *twicen(e)* (a deriv. of *twā* two).

Vars.: **Tutchener, Tichner, Tickner; Twitchen, Twitching(s), Tutchings**.

Titford English: habitation name from an unidentifed place. This may well be *Tetford* in Lincs., so called from OE *þeōd* people + *ford* FORD, i.e. the public ford that everybody used. However, the surname is associated chiefly with Wilts., and a connection with early Lincs. bearers has not been established.

Var.: **Tatford** (an altered form first occurring in Hants in the late 18th cent.).

Titley English: habitation name from a place in Herefords., so called from the OE personal name *Titta* (apparently a short form of the various cpd names with the first element *tīd* season) + OE *lēah* wood, clearing.

Titman *see* TIDMAN

Titmus English: nickname for a small person, from ME *titmōse* titmouse (composed of the prefix *tit-*, probably of ON origin, indicating small size, + OE *māse*, the original name of the bird).
Vars.: **Titmuss**, **Titmas**.

Tito 1. Italian: from a medieval given name (L *Titus*, probably Etruscan in origin). The name was popular in the Middle Ages since it had been borne by a disciple of St Paul who became bishop of Crete. **2.** Jewish: of unknown origin, possibly an adoption of the Italian name.
Var.: **Titi**.
Dim.: It.: **Titolo**.
Aug.: It.: **Titone**.
Patrs.: Russ.: **Titov, Titaev, Titanov; Kitov, Kitaev, Kit(m)anov** (forms found from the late 15th cent.; the reason for the substitution of initial *K-* for *T-* is unknown; there may have been some association with Russ. *kit* whale, from Gk *kētos*). Beloruss.: **Tsitov(ich)**.
Patrs. (from dims.): Russ.: **Titkov, Titkin, Titushin**.

Tits *see* TERRY

Titterington English: habitation name from *Tytherington* in Ches., so called from OE *Tydringtūn* 'settlement (OE *tūn*) associated with *Tydre*', a personal name of uncertain meaning.

Tittoni *see* BAPTISTE

Tiussi *see* TIOLI

Tixier *see* TISSIER

Tiziano Italian: from a medieval given name (LL *Titiānus*, a deriv. of *Titus*; cf. TITO). The name was popular in the Middle Ages as it had been borne by a 6th-cent. bishop of Brescia and a 7th-cent. bishop of Oderzo. The surname is particularly common in Naples.
Vars.: **Tizziano, Tiz(z)iani**.
Dim.: **Tizzanini**.

Tjarcks *see* TERRY

Tjellander *see* KÄLL

Tkach Ukrainian and Jewish (E Ashkenazic): occupational name for a weaver, Ukr. *tkach*, a deriv. of *tkaty* to weave (cogn. with Pol. *tkać*, Czech *tkát*, etc.).
Vars.: Jewish: **Tkatsh, Tekach, Tkacz**.
Dims.: Ukr.: **Tkachuk**. Pol.: **Tkaczyk**. Czech: **Kadleček**.

Toal *see* TOOLE

Tobel German and Jewish (Ashkenazic): topographic name for someone who lived near a ravine or gorge, from MHG southern dial. *tobel* gorge.
Vars.: Ger.: **Tobler** (esp. Swiss); **Zumtobel**; DOBEL.

Tobias English, French, German, and Jewish: from a Gk form of the Hebr. male given name *Tovya* 'Jehovah is good', which, together with various deriv. forms, have been popular among Jews for generations. Other derivs. were occasionally used by Christians in the Middle Ages.
Vars.: Eng.: **Tob(e)y, Tooby**. Fr.: **Tobie**. Ger.: **Tobis**; **Töbi** (Switzerland). Jewish: **Tovia(s); Tuvia, Tuvya(hu)**.
Dims.: Eng.: TOBIN. Ger.: **Döbl** (Bavaria). Ger. (of Slav. origin): **Tob(i)sch, Tobusch, Topsch, Dobisch, Dopsch**.
Patrs.: Pol.: **Tobiasewicz, Tobolewicz**.

Tobin 1. English: dim. of the given name TOBIAS. **2.** Irish: Anglicized form of Gael. *Tóibín*, which is itself an aphetic Gaelicized version of a Norman habitation name from *Saint-Aubin* in Brittany (so called from the dedication of its church to St ALBIN).

Tobis *see* TAUBE

Tocqueville French: habitation name from any of the places, in Eure, Manche, and Seine-Maritime, so called from the ON personal name *Tóki* (see TOOKE) + OF *ville* settlement (see VILLE).

Todarello *see* THÉODORE

Todd English: nickname for someone thought to resemble a fox in some way, for example in cunning or slyness, or perhaps more obviously in having red hair, from Northern ME *tod(de)* fox (of unknown origin).
Var.: **Tod** (Scots).

Tode *see* TERRY

Todeschini *see* TEDESCO

Todhunter English (Cumb.): nickname for a keen hunter of foxes, from Northern ME *tod(de)* fox (see TODD) + HUNTER.

Todt *see* TOTH

Tofanelli *see* CHRISTOPHER

Toft English: habitation name from any of the various places, for example in Cambs., Lincs., Norfolk, and Warwicks., so called from ME *toft* homestead (ON *topt, tomt*).
Vars.: **Tofts; Taft**.

Toghill *see* THIRKILL

Tognacci *see* TONEY

Tohall *see* TOOLE

Toibin *see* TAUBE

Toinet *see* TONEY

Toivonen Finnish: patr. from the OFinn. personal name *Toivo* 'Hope'.

Tojbin *see* TAUBE

Tokarz Polish: occupational name for a turner, Pol. *tokarz*.
Var.: **Tokarski**.
Dims.: Pol.: **Tokarczyk, Tokarek**.
Patrs.: Pol.: **Tokarzewicz**. Beloruss.: **Tokarevich**.

Toke *see* TOOKE

Tolbert French and English (Norman): from a Continental Gmc personal name composed of a first element of uncertain meaning + *berht* bright, famous.

Tolces *see* DUCE

Tole *see* TOWLE

Toledo Spanish and Jewish (Sefardic): habitation name from the city in central Spain, which was the capital of the Visigothic state and afterwards of the kingdom of Castile between the 11th and 16th cents. It was a major cultural and political centre throughout the Middle Ages, and was also the home of an important Jewish community. The placename, first recorded in L as *Tolētum*, is of obscure etymology, possibly connected with *Toleto* in Piedmont; Jewish tradition connects it with Hebr. *toledot* generations, but this is no more than folk etymology.

Var.: **Toledano**.

Tölke *see* TERRY

Tollemache English: apparently a metonymic occupational name for an itinerant merchant, from OF *talemasche* knapsack (of uncertain origin).

Vars.: **Tallemach**, **Tallamach**, **Talma(d)ge**, **Tammage**. (The form *Talmadge* has also been used as an Anglicized form of one or more like-sounding Jewish surnames.)

Toller 1. English: occupational name for a toll taker or tax gatherer, from an agent deriv. of ME *toll* tax, payment (OE *toln*, from LL *tolōneum, telōneum*, a deriv. of Gk *telos* tax). 2. habitation name from *Toller* in Dorset, so called from a Brit. river name, apparently composed of elements akin to W *toll* hollow, pierced + *dw(f)r* stream.

Vars. (of 1): **Towler**, **Towner**; **Towlard**.

Tolmachev Russian: patr. from the occupational term *tolmach* interpreter, a word of Turkic origin.

Var.: **Talmachev**.

Tolomelli *see* BARTHOLOMEW

Tolstoy Russian and Jewish (E Ashkenazic): nickname for a plump man, from Russ. *tolstoi*, a dial. var. of *tolsty* fat.

Patrs.: Russ.: **Tolst(yak)ov**, **Tolstenev**, **Tolstykh**.

Tolver *see* TELFER

Tombrinck *see* BRINK

Tombrock *see* BROCK

Tomdieck *see* DITCH

Tomelty Irish: Anglicized form of Gael. **Mac Tomhaltaigh** and **Ó Tomhaltaigh** 'son' and 'descendant of *Tomaltach*', a byname apparently meaning 'Glutton'.

Vars.: **Tumelty**, **Timothy**.

Tondeur French: occupational name for a sheep-shearer, OF *tondeur* (L *tonditor*, from *tondere* to shear; cf. TIJERINA).

Toner 1. English: topographic name for someone who lived in a village, as opposed to an outlying farm or hamlet, from ME *tune, tone* (OE *tūn*, which originally meant 'fence' and then 'enclosure', although the sense 'settlement, village' was already firmly established in the OE period). The

Ger. cogns. (see ZAUNER) retain the sense 'fence', whereas the Du. ones (see below) have the meaning 'garden'. 2. Irish: Anglicized form of Gael. **Ó Tomhrair** 'descendant of *Tomhrar*', a personal name from *tomhra(r)* protection.

Vars. (of 1): Eng.: **Town(e)**, **Toon(e)**, **Tune**, **Town(e)s**; **Towning**.

Toney English: from the medieval given name *Ton(e)y*, an apheretic form of ANTHONY.

Dims.: Fr.: **T(h)oinet**, **Tonet**, **T(h)oinot**, **Tonin**, **Tony**. It.: **Tone(ll)i**, **Tognello**, **Ton(i)celli**; **Ton(i)etti**, **Tognetti**, **Tugnetti**, **Tonitto**; **To(g)nini**; **Tonicchi**; **Ton(i)olo**, **Tognoli**, **Tunioli**, **Tugnoli**, **Ton(i)olli**; **Tonizzo**, **Tonizzi**, **Tonissi**, **Tonussi**, **Ton(i)utti**, **Ton(ell)otto**.

Pejs.: It.: **Toniacci**, **Tognacci**, **Toniazzi**, **Tognazzi**, **Tonassi**.

Patrs.: It.: **De Toni**. Russ.: **Toneev**, **Taneev**.

Tong English: 1. metonymic occupational name for a maker or user of tongs (OE *tang(e)*). 2. habitation name from any of the various places, for example in Lancs., Shrops., and W Yorks., called *Tong* from their situation by a fork in a road or river. 3. nickname for a chatterbox or a scold or for someone with some deformity of the tongue, ME, OE *tunge*. 4. topographic name for someone who lived on a tongue of land, or habitation name from a place named with this word, for example *Tonge* in Leics.

Vars.: **Tong(u)e**, **Tongs**.

Toni *see* THON

Tonkin *see* THOMAS

Tonnellier French: occupational name for a cooper, OF *tonnellier* (LL *tunnellārius*, from *tunnella*, dim. of *tunna* cask, vat, of Celt. origin).

Var.: **Tonelier**.

Tooby *see* TOBIAS

Tooey *see* TUOHY

Toogood English: apparently a nickname from ME *to* exceedingly + *gode* GOOD, perhaps ironic in application.

Vars.: **Towgood**, **Tugwood**.

Tooke English (Norfolk): from the ON personal name or byname *Tóki*, of uncertain origin, perhaps a short form of THIRKILL.

Vars.: **Took**, **Tuck**, **Toke**, **Tuke**; **Tookey**, **Tuckey**.

Toole 1. Irish: Anglicized form of Gael. **Ó Tuathail** 'descendant of *Tuathal*', an old Celt. personal name composed of elements meaning 'people', 'tribe' + 'rule'. 2. English: var. of TOWLE.

Vars. (of 1): **O'Toole**, **O'Tuale**, **(O')Tou(g)hill**, **(O')Twohill**, **To(o)hill**, **Tohall**, **Toal(e)**.

Tooley *see* TOWLE

Toombes *see* THOMAS

Toomey *see* TWOMEY

Toon *see* TONER

Toop English: from the ON personal name *Tópi*, *Túpi*, probably a short form of a personal name with a first element consisting of the divine name *Þórr* (see THOR 2) + a second element with initial *b-*, for example *björn* bear, warrior (see THORBURN).

Var.: **Toope**.

Tootell English (Lancs.): topographic name for someone who lived by a hill used as a look-out station, from OE **tōt*-look-out (apparently akin to *tōtian* to protrude, peep, or peer) + *hyll* HILL, or habitation name from some place named with these elements, e.g. *Tootle* Heights in Lancs.

Vars.: **Tootill**, **Tootal**, **Tootle**, **Tottle**; **Tothill**.

Tooth 1. English (W Midlands): nickname for someone with a prominent tooth or teeth, from ME *tōth* (OE *tōð*). 2. Irish: Anglicization of Gael. *Mac Confhiaclaigh*; see TUITE.

Toovey *see* TOVEY

Töpfer German: occupational name for a maker of metal or earthenware pots, from Ger. *Töpfer* potter, an agent deriv. of *Topf* pot, vessel (MHG *topf(e)*, first attested in the 12th cent., and at first confined to the E Ger. dialects). See also EULER, HAFNER, KACHLER, and POTTER.

Vars.: **Töpper**, **Tepfer**, **Döpfner**, **Döp(p)ner**, **Döpfler**.

Patr.: Jewish: **Teperson**.

Topham English: habitation name from a place in Yorks., near Snaith. The final element is probably OE *hām* homestead, and the first may be the personal name *Toppa* (see TOPP).

Toplady *see* TIPLADY

Topol 1. Czech: topographic name for someone who lived by a poplar tree, Czech *topol* (Pol. *topola*). 2. Jewish (E Ashkenazic): ornamental name from the tree.

Vars. (of 2): **Topiol**; **Topol(i)ansky**, **Topolski**, **Topolsky**.

Topp English: from the OE byname *Topp* 'Tuft', 'Crest', or the cogn. ON *Toppr*.

Patr.: **Topping** (common in Lancs. and N Ireland).

Töppler *see* DOPPLER

Topsch *see* TOBIAS

Torbeck *see* BACH

Toresson *see* THOR

Toretta *see* TOWER

Toribio Spanish: from a medieval given name, *Toribio* (L *Turibius*, of apparently Gmc (Visigothic) origin, but uncertain derivation), bestowed in honour of two Spanish saints. St Turibius of Astorga was a 5th-cent. bishop who championed Catholic doctrine against the Priscillianist heresy. St Turibius of Palencia was the 6th-cent. founder of the famous abbey of Liébana in Asturias.

Torley *see* McTERRELLY

Tormo Catalan: topographic name for someone who lived by a crag or boulder, OCat. *tormo* (of uncertain, probably pre-Roman, origin). There are various places named with forms of this word, for example *Tormos* in Alicante, *El Tormo* in Castellón, and *Torms* in Lérida, and the surname may also be a habitation name from any of these.

Toro 1. Italian and Spanish: nickname for a lusty person or metonymic occupational name for a tender of bulls, from It., Sp. *toro* bull (L *taurus*). 2. Italian: from a medieval given name, an aphetic short form of various names such as VICTOR and SALVADOR.

Var.: It.: **Tori**.

Dims.: It.: **Toretto**, **Toritto**; **Torelli**, **Torello** (Tuscany); **Toriello**, **Turiello**. (Of 1 only): Fr.: **Taurel**, **Taureau**, THOREL.

Torode *see* THOROLD

Torosian *see* THÉODORE

Torpy *see* TARPEY

Torquemada Spanish: habitation name from a place in the province of Logroño, so called from Sp. *torre* TOWER + *quemada* (fem.) burnt (from the past part. of *quemar* to burn, L *cremāre*).

Torr English: 1. topographic name for someone who lived by a tor or rocky hilltop (OE *torr*, of Celt. origin; cf. TERUEL and THÉRON). 2. nickname for someone thought to resemble a bull, ANF *tor* (see TORO).

Torrado Spanish and Portuguese: nickname for an exceptionally dark-skinned person, from Sp., Port. *torrado* toasted, roasted (past part. of *torrar*, LL *torrāre*, for class. L *torrēre* to burn, parch; cf. TORRENTE).

Torralba Spanish and Catalan: habitation name from any of the numerous places so called from Sp., Cat. *torre* TOWER + OSp., OCat. *alba* (fem.) white.

Torrance Scots and N Irish: habitation name from either of two places (one near E Kilbride, the other north of Glasgow under the Campsie Fells), so called from Gael. *torran* hillock, mound, with the later addition of the Eng. pl. /s/.

Vars.: **Torrence**, **Torrens**.

Torrecilla *see* TOWER

Torrente Spanish: topographic name for someone who lived by a flood stream, Sp. *torrente* (L *torrens*, gen. *torrentis*, from the pres. part. of *torrēre* to rush, seethe (originally 'to burn, parch'; cf. TORRADO)).

Torrey *see* TERRY

Torstensen *see* THURSTON

Tort French, Provençal, and Catalan: nickname for a crippled or deformed man, from OF, Prov., Cat. *tort* twisted, crooked (L *tortus*, past part. of *torquēre* to turn, twist). The Cat. word also has the sense 'one-eyed'.

Var.: Fr.: **Letort**.

Dim.: Fr.: **Torteau**.

Augs.: Fr.: **Tortat**. It.: **Stortone**.

Tortel *see* TOURTE

Tortorella *see* TURTLE

Tortosa Catalan: habitation name from a place in the province of Tarragona, recorded in L as *Dertosa*, but of pre-Roman origin and unknown meaning.

Tosato *see* TOUS

Toscano Italian: regional name for someone from Tuscany, It. *Toscana*.

Vars.: **Toscan(i)**, **Tuscano**; **Toscanese**, **Toscanesi**; **Tosco**, **Toschi**.

Dims.: **Toscanello**, **Toscanelli**, **Toscanino**, **Toscanini**.

Toschach see MCINTOSH

Tosh see MCINTOSH

Toth German: **1.** nickname from MHG *tōt* DEATH. **2.** nickname from MHG *tote* godfather (OHG *toto*, in origin apparently a nursery word).

Vars.: **Todt**, **Tott**.

Dim.: **Töttel**.

Tóth Hungarian: name for a Slavonian, Slovak, or Slovene, from Hung. *tót* Slav, ultimately related to DEUTSCH German.

Var.: **Tót**.

Tothill see TOOTELL

Touche French: topographic name for someone who lived by a grove or thicket, OF *touche* (of unknown origin).

Vars.: **Latouche**, **Letouche**, **Delatouche**, **Destouches**.

Dims.: **Touchet**, **Touchon**.

Collectives: **Tou(c)quoy**, **To(c)quoy** (Picardy).

Tough **1.** Scots: topographic name for someone who lived on a hillside, from Gael. *tulach* hill, mound, or habitation name from a minor place named with this word. The Scots surname is pronounced /tu:x/. **2.** English: nickname for a valiant or stubborn person, from ME *togh* steadfast (OE *tōh*).

Vars. (of 2): **Tow(e)**.

Patr. (from 2): **Towes**.

Toughill see TOOLE

Toulouse French: habitation name from the city in Haute-Garonne, whose name is of uncertain, apparently Celt., etymology.

Vars.: **de Toulouse**, **Toul(ou)ze**; **Toulousa(i)n**, **Toulousy**, **Toulza(n)**.

Toulson see TOWLE

Touret see TOWER

Tournay see TURNEY

Tourpin see TURPIN

Tourte French: metonymic occupational name for a baker, or nickname for a short, dumpy man, from OF *tourte* round loaf (of uncertain origin).

Vars.: **Tourtier**; **Tourtel(l)ier**, **Tortellier**.

Dims.: **To(u)rtel**, **Tourteau**.

Tous French: nickname from OF *tous* clean-shaven, close-cropped (L *tonsus*, past part. of *tondere* to cut, shear; cf. TONDEUR). In the later Middle Ages it was for some time the fashion for young men to cut their hair close, while their elders preferred a longer style.

Dims.: Fr.: **Touzel**, **Touzeau**, **Letouzel**, **Touzet**, **Touzé**, **Letouzé**, **Letouzey**, **Touz(el)in**. It.: **Toselli**, **Tosetti**, **Tosetto**, **Tos(ol)ini**, **Tositti**.

Aug.: It.: **Tosoni**.

Pejs.: Fr.: **Touzard**. It.: **Tosat(t)o**, **Tosatti**.

Toussaint French: from a nickname or given name composed of the elements *tous* (pl.) all + *saints* saints. The name was given to someone who was born on All Saints' Day (1 November), or chosen as an invocation of the protection of all the saints of the calendar. Cf. SANTORO.

Touvet see STEPHEN

Tovar Spanish: topographic name for someone who lived by a quarry of pumice stone, OSp. *tovar* (LL *tōfāre*, a deriv. of *tōfus* tufa, porous stone).

Tovell English (E Anglia): from a Scandinavian female personal name of an unusual type, *Tōfa-Hildr* 'Hildr the daughter of *Tōfi*' (see TOVEY).

Tovey English: from the ON personal name *Tófi*, a short form of any of various cpd names whose first element is the divine name *Þórr* (see THOR 2), while the second begins with *f* or *v*, for example *valdr* rule (see THOROLD).

Vars.: **Toovey**, **Tuvey**, **Tovee**.

Tovia see TOBIAS

Tow see TOUGH

Toward N English (Northumb.) and Scots: nickname for a meek, obedient person, from ME *toward* docile, biddable.

Tower English: **1.** topographic name for someone who lived near a tower, usually a defensive fortification or watchtower, from ME, OF *tūr* (L *turris*). **2.** occupational name for a maker of white leather, a var. of TAWYER.

Dims. (of 1): Fr.: **Touret(te)**, **Tourot**, **Tourry**. It.: **Toretta**, **Toretti**, **Torritti**, **Torrini**, **Turrini**, **Torricina**, **Torricella**. Sp.: **Torrecilla(s)**, **Torrijos**, **Torrejón**.

Towers English: **1.** var. of TOWER, with later -*s*. **2.** habitation name from *Tours* in Eure-et-Loire, N France, so called from the Gaul. tribal name *Turones*, of uncertain etymology.

Towey see TUOHY

Towgood see TOOGOOD

Towlard see TOLLER

Towle English (Notts.): from the ME given name *Toll*, OE *Toll*, or ON *Tóli*, the latter being derived from a short form of some cpd name such as *Þórleifr* (composed of the divine name *Þórr* (see THOR 2) + *leifr* relic) or *Þórleikr* (composed of the elements *Þórr* + *leikr* sport, play).

Vars.: **Tow(e)ll**, **Toole**, **Tole**, **Toll**.

Dims.: **Tol(l)ey** (chiefly W Midlands), **Tooley**.

Patrs.: **Towlson** (Notts.), **Tolson** (Yorks.), **Toulson**.

Towmey see TWOMEY

Town see TONER

Townley English: habitation name from *Towneley* near Burnley in Lancs., which is named with the OE elements *tūn* enclosure, settlement + *lēah* wood, clearing.
Vars.: **Towneley**, **Townsley**.

Townsend English: topographic name for someone who lived at the extremity of a village, from ME *tone, tune* village, settlement (see TONER) + *end* end (OE *ende*).
Vars.: **Townshend** (Norfolk), **Townend** (Yorks.), **Townen**.

Townson see THOMAS

Toy English: nickname for a light-hearted or frivolous person, from ME *toy* play, sport (of uncertain origin).
Var.: **Toye**.

Tozer English: occupational name for a comber or carder of wool, from an agent deriv. of ME *tōse(n)* to tease (OE *tāsian*, a byform of *tǣsan*). For the change of -*ā*- to -*ō*-, cf. ROPER.

Tozzetti see DODD

Tracey 1. English (Norman): habitation name from *Tracy*-Bocage or *Tracy*-sur-Mer in Calvados, both so called from the Gallo-Roman personal name *Thracius* (a deriv. of L *Thrax*, gen. *Thracis*, 'Thracian') + the local suffix -*eium*. 2. Irish: var. of TREACY.
Var.: **Tracy**.

Trachtenberg Jewish (Ashkenazic): of unknown origin. The less common **Trachtenbroit** and **Trachtengot**, **Trachtingot** would seem to be related. -*berg* hill is a very common ornamental ending of Yiddish surnames; -*broit* clearly reflects the S Yiddish pronunciation of Yid. *broyt* bread; and -*got* is presumably Yid. *got* or Ger. *Gott* God. *Trachten*-, however, is unclear. The following vocab. words have been considered, but none of them seems appropriate: Yid. *trakhtn* to think, Ger. *trachten* to endeavour, Ger. *Trachten* endeavours, Ger. *Trachten* loads.

Tracz Polish: occupational name for a sawyer, Pol. *tracz*.
Dim.: **Traczyk** (also Jewish (E Ashkenazic)).

Tradescant English: of unknown origin. The names *Tradeskin* and *Tredeskin*, found as early as the 11th cent. in the parishes of Walberswick and Harleston, Suffolk, are apparently early forms of this name.

Tradewell see TREADWELL

Trafford English: habitation name from any of various places so called. One in Northants is named with the OE elements *trceppe* (fish-)trap + *ford* FORD. The places called *Trafford* in Ches. have as their first element OE *trog* trough, valley (see TROW 3); while *Trafford* in Lancs. was originally called STRATFORD. Nevertheless, most cases of the surname probably derive from the last of these places; a landowning family can be traced there to the 13th cent.

Trager German and Jewish (Ashkenazic): occupational name for someone who carried a load, a pedlar or porter, from Ger. *Träger*, Yid. *treger*, agent derivs. of Ger. *tragen* to carry (OHG *tragan*).
Vars.: Ger.: **Trage**, **Träger**. Jewish: **Treger(man)**.

Traherne see TREHEARNE

Trahms see BERTRAM

Trainor 1. N English, Scots, and N Irish: occupational name for a trapper, from an agent deriv. of ME *train(e)* trap, snare (from OF *trainer* to draw, allure, LL *tragināre*, a deriv. of class. L *trahere*). 2. Irish: Anglicized form of Gael. **Mac Thréinfhir** 'son of *Thréinfhear*', a byname meaning 'Champion' (from *tréan* strong + *fear* man).
Vars.: **Trainer**. (Of 2 only): **Traynor**, **Treanor**, **McCranor**.

Traister see TROST

Tranchant French: occupational name for a butcher, or nickname for a violent person, from the pres. part. of OF *trenchier* to cut, hack, slice (L *truncāre*, a deriv. of *truncus* lopped, short).
Vars.: **Tranchand**, **Trenchant**; **Tranchaire**.
Dims.: **Tranch(ill)on**.
Pejs.: **Tranchard**, **Trenchard**; **Tranquard**, **Trincard** (Normandy).

Tranter English: occupational name for a pedlar or hawker, esp. one equipped with a horse and cart, ME *traunter*, *traventer* (LL *trāvetārius*, of uncertain origin, possibly derived from L *transvehere* to convey).
Var.: **Trenter**.

Trappe 1. English: metonymic occupational name for a trapper, from a deriv. of ME *trapp* trap (OE *trceppe*, reinforced by MDu. *trappe*). 2. German: nickname for a stupid person, from MHG *trappe* bustard (of Slav. origin).
Var.: **Trapp**.

Trassy see TREACY

Traub 1. German: metonymic occupational name for a wine-grower, from Ger. *Traube* grape (MHG *trūbe* bunch of grapes, OHG *t(h)rūba*). In some cases it may originally have been a house name, for someone who lived at a house marked with the sign of a bunch of grapes. 2. Jewish (Ashkenazic): ornamental name or, occasionally perhaps, metonymic occupational name for a wine-grower, from Ger. *Traube*.
Vars.: Ger.: **Traube**; **Trübner** (Switzerland). Jewish: **Traube**, **Traubner**, **Traubnik**, **Traubmann**.
Dims.: Ger.: **Traubel**, **Treibel**, **Träuble**.

Travers 1. English and French: topographic name for someone who lived by a bridge or ford, or occupational name for a gatherer of tolls exacted for the right of passage, from ME, OF *travers* passage, crossing (from OF *traverser* to cross, LL *transversāre*). 2. Irish: Anglicized form of Gael. **Ó Treabhair**; see TREVOR 2.
Vars. (of 1): Eng.: **Traves**, **Travis(s)**, **Trevis**. Fr.: **Traverse**, **Traver(t)**.
Dim. (of 1): It.: **Traversini**.

Travor see TREVOR

Trawiński Polish: habitation name from some place named for its fine grass, from Pol. *trawa* grass, lawn + -*in* possessive suffix + -*ski* suffix of local surnames (see BARANOWSKI).
Var.: **Trawczyński**.

Traxler see DRECHSLER

Trazzi *see* PETER

Treacher English: nickname for a devious or unreliable person, from OF *tricheor* trickster, cheat (from *trichier* to cheat, trick, of uncertain origin). See also TRICK.

Treacy Irish: Anglicized form of Gael. **Ó Treasaigh** 'descendant of *Treasach*', a personal name meaning 'Warlike', 'Fierce'.
Vars.: TRACEY, **Treasey**, **O'Trasey**, **(O')Trassy**, **(O')Tressy**.

Treadgold *see* THREADGOLD

Treadwell English (chiefly W Midlands): occupational nickname for a fuller, from ME *tred(en)* to tread (OE *tredan*) + *well* well (OE *wel(l)*).
Vars.: **Tredwell**, **Tretwell**, **Trad(e)well**.

Treanor *see* TRAINOR

Treasure English: **1.** metonymic occupational name for a treasurer or person in charge of financial administration, from ME *tresor* treasure, wealth, riches (OF *trésor*, from L *thēsaurus* hoard). **2.** affectionate nickname for a loved or valued person, from ME *tresor* used as a term of endearment.

Trebilcock Cornish: habitation name from a place in the parish of Roche, apparently so called from Corn. *tre* homestead, settlement + a mutated form of the ME term of endearment *pilicock* darling.

Tredinnick Cornish: habitation name from any of various places, for example near Bodmin, Liskeard, and St Issey. Some of these get the name from Corn. *tre* homestead, settlement + **dynek* fortified (a deriv. of *dyn* fort; cf. DOWN 1); in other cases the second element is **eythynek* overgrown with gorse or **redenek* overgrown with bracken.

Tredwell *see* TREADWELL

Tree *see* TROW

Treen Cornish: habitation name from places in the parishes of Zennor and St Levan, both of which appear earlier in the form *Trethyn*, from Corn. *tre* homestead, settlement + *dyn* fort (cf. DOWN 1).

Trefus *see* DREYFUSS

Trefusis Cornish: habitation name from a place in the parish of Mylor, recorded in 1346 as *Trevusus*, from Corn. *tre* homestead, settlement + a second element of unknown form and meaning.

Tregear Cornish: habitation name from any of various places so called, from Corn. *tre* homestead, settlement + a mutated form of **ker* farmstead encircled by a hedge.
Vars.: **Tregeare**, **Tregears**, **Tregair**, **Tregare**.

Tregenza Cornish: habitation name from a place in the parish of Creed, so called from Corn. *tre* homestead, settlement + a second element **kensyth* of unknown meaning (possibly a personal name).

Treger *see* TRAGER

Tregoning Cornish: habitation name from any of various places so called, from Corn. *tre* homestead, settlement + a mutated form of the personal name CONAN.
Vars.: **Tregonning**, **Tregon(n)an**.

Tregunna Cornish: habitation name, probably from a place in the parish of St Breock, so called from Corn. *tre* homestead, settlement + a second element of unknown form and meaning (possibly *gonyow*, pl. of *goon* down). This name, or its vars., may also be from various places called *Tregon(na)* or *Tregenna*, which are likewise from *tre* + an unknown second element.
Vars.: **Tregunno** (a place in the parish of Breage), **Tregonnowe**, **Tregon(n)a**.

Trehearne Welsh: from the personal name *Trahaearn*, composed of the elements *tra* most, very + *haearn* iron. This personal name has also given rise to a placename, spelled *Trehaearn* as if containing the element *tre(f)* homestead, settlement, and so in some cases the surname may be a habitation name with this origin.
Var.: **Traherne**.

Treibel *see* TRAUB

Treille French: topographic name for someone who lived near a vineyard or in a house with an ornamental vine, from OF *treille* lattice used to support vines (LL *trichila* arbour, bower).
Vars.: **Treilles**, **Trille**, **Latr(e)ille**.
Dims.: Fr.: **Tr(e)illet**.
Aug.: Fr.: **Trillat**.

Treinen *see* CATLIN

Treister *see* TROST

Trelawney Cornish: habitation name from *Trelawny* in the parish of Altarnun, so called from Corn. *tre* homestead, settlement + a second element of unknown form and meaning.
Var.: **Trelawny**.

Treleaven Cornish: habitation name from a place in the parish of Mevagissey, so called from Corn. *tre* homestead, settlement + a second element of unknown form and meaning (possibly *leven* level, flat).
Var.: **Treleven**.

Trelfall *see* THRELFALL

Tremaine Cornish: habitation name from any of various places so called, from Corn. *tre* homestead, settlement + *men* stone.
Vars.: **Tremayne**; **Tremain** (also Welsh, from a place in the former county of Cardigan named with W *tre* homestead, settlement + *main* stones).

Trembath Cornish: habitation name from a place in the parish of Madron, so called from Corn. *tre an bagh* 'homestead of the corner'.

Trembeth Cornish: habitation name from *Trembleath* in the parish of St Mawgan in Pydar, recorded in 1327 as *Trenbeth*, from Corn. *tre an beth* 'homestead of the grave'.

Tremble 1. French: topographic name for someone who lived near an aspen, OF *tremble* (from *trembler* to quiver, LL *tremulāre*, a deriv. of *tremulus*, from class. L *tremere*). **2.** English: var. of TRUMBULL.
Vars. (of 1): **Trémo(u)ille**, **Trimouille**.
Dims. (of 1): **Tremblet**, **Tremblot**.
Collective (of 1): Fr.: **Tremblay**.

Tremenheere Cornish: habitation name from any of various places named with the Corn. elements *tre* homestead, settlement + **menhyr* menhir, standing stone (a cpd of *men* stone + *hyr* long).

Vars.: **Tremenhere, Tremenheer**.

Tremlett English (Norman): habitation name from Les *Trois Minettes* in Calvados, apparently so called from three mines of some sort.

Vars.: **Trimlett, Tremblet**.

Trench English (of French origin): habitation name from La *Tranche* in Poitou, so called from the OF topographical term *trenche*, a deriv. of the verb *trenchier* to cut (LL *truncāre*; cf. TRANCHANT). The noun denoted both a ditch and a track cut through a forest.

Trenchant *see* TRANCHANT

Trenerry Cornish: habitation name from a place in the parish of St Allen, so called from Corn. *tre* homestead, settlement + a second element of uncertain form and meaning.

Trent English: topographic name for someone living on the banks of any of the several rivers so called. The river name is of Brit. origin; it may be composed of the elements **tri* through, across + **sant-* travel, journey (cogn. with W *hynt* road); alternatively it may mean 'traveller' or 'trespasser', a reference to frequent flooding. There is also a village in Dorset of this name, on the river *Trent* or Piddle, and the surname may therefore also be a habitation name derived from this.

Trenter *see* TRANTER

Trépard *see* TRIPP

Trepat Catalan: presumably a nickname for someone who was scarred with pock-marks or else one who dressed in rags, from Cat. *trepat* full of holes (past part. of *trepar* to pierce, LL *trepāre*). It may also be a topographic name for someone who lived in a house with some form of openwork decoration.

Trerise 1. Cornish: habitation name from any of various places so called. Most get the name from Corn. *tre* homestead, settlement + *rid*, **rys* ford; in some cases the second element may be the personal name **Rys*, equivalent to W RHYS. 2. Welsh: habitation name from W *tre(f)* homestead, settlement + the personal name RHYS.

Var.: **Trerice**.

Trescher *see* DRESCHER

Tresidder Cornish: habitation name from places in the parishes of St Buryan and Constantine, so called from Corn. *tre* homestead, settlement + a second element of uncertain form and meaning.

Třešňák Czech: habitation name from *Třešně*, near Písek in S Bohemia. The placename means 'cherries' or 'cherry trees'; it is a Slav. borrowing from Old Bavarian **chersia*, which is from LL *ceresia*.

Trethewey Cornish: habitation name from any of various places so called, from Corn. *tre* homestead, settlement + a mutated form of the personal name *Dewi* DAVID.

Vars.: **Trethewy; Trethevy**.

Trethowan Cornish: habitation name from a place in the parish of Constantine, recorded in 1195 in the form *Treðewen* and in 1327 as *Trethouen*, from Corn. *tre* homestead, settlement + what is perhaps a mutated form of a personal name **Dewin*, equivalent to W *Dewin* 'Magician', 'Wizard'.

Tretyakov Russian: patr. from *Tretyak*, presumably originally a byname for a third child or third son, from Russ. *treti* third.

Vars.: **Tretnikov, Tretilov, Tretyukhin; Tryoshnikov**.

Trevail Cornish: habitation name from places in the parishes of Cubert, Ladock, and Zennor called *Treveal(e)*, from Corn. *tre* homestead, settlement + a mutated form of a personal name equivalent to Bret. *Mael* 'Chief', 'Leader'.

Trevaldwyn Welsh: habitation name from the town and former county of Montgomery, known in Welsh as *Trefaldwyn*, from *tre(f)* homestead, settlement + *Faldwyn*, a mutated form of the personal name BALDWIN. Montgomery was granted to Baldwin de Bollers in 1102 and the castle of Montgomery became known as *Castell Baldwin* in Welsh. The town was called *Trefaldwyn* by the 16th cent.

Trevarthen 1. Cornish: habitation name from places in the parishes of St Hilary and Newlyn East, so called from Corn. *tre(v)* homestead, settlement + a personal name equivalent to W *Arthen*. 2. Welsh: habitation name from W *tre(f)* homestead, settlement + the personal name *Arthen*.

Trevaskis Cornish: habitation name from *Trevaskis* in the parish of Gwinear or *Trevascus* in the parish of Goran, both so called from Corn. *tre* homestead, settlement + a mutated form of a personal name equivalent to Bret. *Maelscuet*.

Vars.: **Tregaskis(s)**.

Trevelyan Cornish: habitation name from a place in the parish of St Veep, apparently so called from Corn. *tre* homestead, settlement + a mutated form of *melin* mill.

Vars.: **Trevell(y)an; Trevellion** (a place near Bodmin, in the parish of Luxulian).

Trevena Cornish: habitation name from any of various places so called, from Corn. *tre* homestead, settlement + a mutated form of *meneth* mountain, hill.

Vars.: **Trevenna, Treven(n)er**.

Treverrow Cornish: habitation name from *Trevarra* in the parish of St Minver, recorded in 1233 in the form *Treveru*, from Corn. *tre(v)* homestead, settlement + *erw* acre, ploughed land.

Treves *see* DREYFUSS

Trevethan Cornish: habitation name from places in the parishes of Budock, St Eval, and Gwennap, all so called from Corn. *tre* homestead, settlement + a second element of uncertain form and meaning (possibly a mutated form of *budin*, **buthyn* meadow).

Trevis *see* DREYFUSS, TRAVERS

Trevithick Cornish: habitation name from any of various places, in the parishes of St Columb Major, St Columb

Minor, Perranzabuloe, and St Ewe, so called from Corn. *tre* homestead, settlement + various personal names; in the case of the last-mentioned place, the second element may be from a mutated form of *methek* doctor.

Var.: **Trevethick**.

Trevor 1. Welsh: habitation name from any of the numerous places, for example in the former counties of Denbigh and Cardigan, so called from W *tre(f)* homestead, settlement + a mutated form of *mawr* large. **2.** Irish: Anglicized form of Gael. **Ó Treabhair** 'descendant of *Treabhar*', a byname meaning 'Industrious', 'Prudent'.

Vars. (of 2): **O'Trevir**, **O'Trover**, **Treyor**, **Trower**, **Trevors**, **Travor(s)**, Travers.

Trevorrow Cornish: habitation name from a place in the parish of Ludgvan, so called from Corn. *tre* homestead, settlement + a second element of uncertain form and meaning.

Trewhella Cornish: habitation name from *Trewhella* in the parish of St Hilary or *Trewhela* in the parish of St Enoder, both apparently so called from Corn. *tre* homestead, settlement + a deriv. of *hwilen* beetle.

Var.: **Trewheela**.

Trewin Cornish: habitation name from any of the various places called *Trewen*; most get their names from Corn. *tre* homestead, settlement + various second elements, for example the vocabulary word *gwynn* white, fair and the personal name *Gwen*.

Trewman *see* Trueman

Trezise Cornish: habitation name from *Trezise* in the parish of St Martin in Meneage or *Tresayes* in the parish of Roche, both so called from Corn. *tre* homestead, settlement + **Seys* Englishman.

Vars.: **Trezize**, **Tresize**, **Tresise**.

Tribus *see* Dreyfuss

Trick English: metonymic nickname for a cunning or crafty person, from ME *trick* strategem, device (from a Norman form of OF *triche*; cf. Treacher).

Var.: **Tricker** (an agent deriv.).
Dim.: **Trickett**.

Triene *see* Catlin

Triffault *see* Truffault

Trigg English: from the ON byname *Triggr* 'Trustworthy', 'Faithful', a cogn. of Trow 1.
Var.: **Trigge**.
Patr.: Eng.: **Triggs**.

Trigo Spanish and Portuguese: occupational name for a grower or seller of wheat, Sp., Port. *trigo* (L *trīticum*, from *terere* to grind, past part. *trītus*).
Var.: Sp.: **Triguero** (an agent deriv.).

Trillat *see* Treille

Trillo Spanish: **1.** metonymic occupational name for a thresher, from Sp. *trillo* threshing-sledge (L *tribulum*). **2.**

habitation name from a place in the province of Guadalajara, presumably so called from some similarity of shape.
Dims. (of 1): Fr.: **Triboulet**, **Triboulot**.
Pej. (of 1): Fr.: **Tribouillard**.

Trim English: apparently a nickname for a well-turned-out person, from the adj. *trim* well-equipped, neatly made. The word is first attested in the early 16th cent. (cf. Trimmer), but may well have been in colloquial use much earlier.

Trimble *see* Trumbull

Trimlett *see* Tremlett

Trimmer English: occupational name, probably for a trimmer of cloth. The verb *trim* is not attested in its mod. sense before the early 16th cent., but the surname form William *le Trymmere* is found in the 14th cent., and this seems to be continuous with OE *trymian, trymman* to strengthen, confirm (from *trum* strong, firm).

Trimouille *see* Tremble

Trincard *see* Tranchant

Trindade Portuguese: religious byname adopted in honour of the Holy Trinity, and given in particular to children born on Trinity Sunday. The name is from Port. *trindade* trinity (LL *trīnitās*, gen. *trīnitātis*, a deriv. of *trēs* three).

Trinder English: occupational name for a braider or a spinner, from an agent deriv. of ME *trend(en)* to twist, plait (OE *trendan* to turn round, roll).

Tripconey Cornish: habitation name from a place in the parish of St Columb Major, now known as *Trekenning*. The placename is recorded in 1294 in the form *Trehepkenyn*, probably from Corn. *tre* homestead, settlement + a personal name **Hepkenyn*. The form of the surname has been affected by folk etymology: the family arms registered in 1573 by John *Tripconie* of Gulval, fifth in descent from Ralph *Tripcony* who lived in the reign of Edward III (1327–77), feature three black conies (rabbits).

Tripp English: **1.** metonymic occupational name for a dancer, or nickname for someone with an odd gait, from ME *trip(p)(en)* to step lightly, skip, hop (OF *triper*, of Gmc origin; cf. OE *treppan* to tread). **2.** metonymic occupational name for a butcher or tripedresser, from ME, OF *trip(p)e* tripe (of unknown origin).

Vars.: **Tripper**. (Of 2 only): **Tripe**.
Dims. (of 2): Fr.: **Tripet(te)**, **Tripon**, **Tripeau**.
Pejs. (of 1): Fr.: **Trépard**, **Trépaud**.

Trishkin *see* Trofimov

Tříska Czech: nickname for a thin man, one who was 'as thin as a splinter', from Czech *tříska* splinter.
Var.: **Tříška**.

Trnka Czech: **1.** topographic name for someone living by a sloe or blackthorn, Czech *trnka*. **2.** nickname for someone with eyes as dark as sloes, from the same word in a transferred sense.

Trock Jewish (E Ashkenazic): habitation name from *Trok*, the Yid. name of a town in Lithuania (Lithuanian *Trakai*, Russ. *Troki*), which had a large Jewish population.

Vars.: **Trocker** (from Yid. *troker* inhabitant of *Trok*); **Trocki**, **Trotski**, **Trotsky** (from Russ. *trotskii*, adj., relating to *Troki*).

Trofimov Russian: patr. from the given name *Trofim* (Gk *Trophimos* 'Nursling', from *trophein* to raise, rear). The personal name was borne by various early Christian saints martyred at Rome and in the East under the emperors Probus and Diocletian.

Dims.: Russ.: **Tronyaev**, **Trishkin** (patrs.). Ukr.: **Troshchenko**. Beloruss.: **Trokhinchik**; **Atrakhovich**, **Atrashkevich** (patrs.).

Troitski Russian: surname originally adopted by Orthodox priests in honour of the Holy Trinity, from ORuss. *troitsa* group of three (a calque of Gk *trias*; cf. TRINDADE) + the (originally local) suffix *-ski*. In recent years it has also been adopted in the Soviet Union by bearers of the name *Trotski* (see TROCK), which was felt to be politically undesirable.

Trojan Czech: from an OSlav. personal name, *Trojan*, apparently a form of L *Traiānus*, the name of a Roman emperor (53–117), who extended the Roman Empire east into Dacia (mod. Rumania). In early Slav. records the name is also found denoting a mythical creature or deity.

Dims.: **Trojánek**, **Trojášek**, **Trojančík**, **Trojek**.

Trokhinchik *see* TROFIMOV

Trollope English: habitation name from the former name of Troughburn in Northumb., from ON *troll* imp, supernatural being (cf. TROUILLET) + OE *hop* enclosed valley (see HOPE).

Var.: **Trollop**.

Troman *see* TRUEMAN

Troni *see* PETER

Tronson *see* TRUNCHION

Trösch *see* DRESCHER

Trossier French: occupational name for a pedlar, from an agent deriv. of OF *tro(u)sse* pack, bundle (of uncertain origin).

Var.: **Troussié**.

Trost 1. German: from a medieval given name or byname often bestowed on a child born after the death of a sibling, from Ger. *Trost* comfort, consolation (MHG *trōst*, OHG *trōst* confidence, trust); cf. SOLIS. 2. Jewish (Ashkenazic): ornamental name from mod. Ger. *Trost* comfort, consolation.

Vars.: Ger.: **Tröster**. Jewish: **Treister**, **Traister**, **Trejster** (from Yid. *treyster* comforter, consoler); **Trostman**, **Treistman**, **Traistman**, **Trajstman** (coined from Yid. *treyst* comfort, consolation + *-man* man).

Troth English (Worcs., centred on Bromsgrove): nickname from ME *trowthe*, *trouthe* good faith, loyalty (OE *trēowð* truth, a deriv. of *trēow* true; cf. TROW 1). *By my troth* was a common phrase emphasizing the veracity of an assertion, and the nickname may have been bestowed on someone who used it habitually or to excess.

Trotter 1. English and Scots: occupational name for a messenger, from an agent deriv. of ME *trot(en)* to walk fast (OF *troter*, of Gmc origin, akin to 2 below). 2. German: occupational name for a grape-treader, from an agent deriv. of MHG *trot(t)e* winepress (OHG *trot(t)a*, from *trottōn* to tread, trample). The vocab. word and the surname are confined largely to Alsace, Lorraine, Switzerland, and Swabia.

Vars. (of 1): **Trott**, **Trotman**. (Of 2): **Trott**, **Trot(t)mann**.

Dims. (of 1): Fr.: **Trottereau**, **Trotteleau**; **Trotot**, **Trotin**, **Trotignon**.

Troughton English: habitation name from *Troughton* Hall in the parish of Kirkby Ireleth, Lancs., so called from OE *trog* trough, hollow (see TROW 3) + *tūn* enclosure, settlement.

Var.: **Trouton**.

Trouillet French: metonymic nickname for a devious character, from a dim. of OF *trouille* trickery, sorcery (of Gmc origin, apparently akin to ON *troll* imp, supernatural being).

Vars.: **Trouillot**, **Trouillon**.

Pej.: Fr.: **Trouillard**.

Troup Scots: habitation name from a place in the parish of Gamrie, near Banff. The place is situated on a headland affording some sheltered anchorage, and may get its name from ME *true hope*; however, when first recorded in 1296 it already appears as *Trup*, and so is more likely to be of the same origin as THORPE.

Vars.: **Troupe**, **Troop**.

Trout English: metonymic occupational name for a fisherman, or nickname for someone supposedly resembling this freshwater fish, ME *trowte* (OE *trūht*).

Trouvé French: nickname for a foundling, from the past part. of OF *trouver* to find (of uncertain origin, probably from L *turbāre* to disturb, the semantic development being a result of the practice of disturbing water to catch fish).

Dims.: Fr.: **Trouvin**. It.: **Trovatello**, **Trovatelli**.

Trovatelli *see* TROUVÉ

Trow English (chiefly W Midlands): 1. nickname for a trustworthy person, from ME *trow(e)*, *trew(e)* faithful, steadfast (OE *trēowe*). 2. topographic name for someone who lived near a conspicuous tree, ME *trow*, *trew* (OE *trēow*). 3. topographic name for someone who lived near a depression in the ground, from ME *trow* trough, hollow (OE *trog*).

Vars. (mostly of 1): **Trew**, **True**. See also TRUEMAN. (Of 2 only): **Tree(s)**, **Treece**.

Trowbridge English: habitation name from a place in Wilts., so called from OE *trēow* tree (see TROW 2) + *brycg* BRIDGE; the name probably referred to a felled trunk serving as a rough-and-ready bridge.

Vars.: **Tro(u)bridge**, **Trubridge**.

Trower *see* THROWER, TREVOR

Troy 1. Irish: Anglicized form of Gael. **Ó Troighthigh** 'descendant of *Troightheach*', a byname meaning 'Foot Soldier'. 2. Jewish (E Ashkenazic): presumably an Anglicized form of some like-sounding Jewish surname or an Anglicized spelling of *Treu* (see TROW).

Var. (of 1): **O'Trehy**.

Trübner see TRAUB

Trubridge see TROWBRIDGE

Truc Provençal: topographic name for someone who lived near or on a hill or elevation, OProv. *t(r)uc* (a word of Gaul. origin commonly found in placenames).

Vars.: **Tuc**; **Dut(r)u(c)**, **Dutrut**, **Duthu**; **Tusse** (SE France).

Dims.: **T(r)uquet**, **Truchet(et)**, **Truchon**, **Truchot**, **Truchy**; **Tusseau**, **Tussaud**.

Trudeau see THOROLD

Trudgeon English (Cornwall): habitation name from *Tregian* in the parish of St Ewe, earlier *Trudgeon*. The placename is recorded in 1331 in the form *Trehydian*, from Corn. *tre* homestead, settlement + a personal name similar in form to the attested *Hedyn*.

Var.: **Trudgian**.

Trudgill English (Norfolk): of uncertain origin. According to Barber it is from an OE personal name composed of the elements *prȳð* might + *hild* battle.

True see TROW

Trueman English (common esp. in the Midlands): nickname for a trustworthy man, from ME *trew(e)*, *trow(e)* faithful (see TROW 1) + *man* man. This was apparently also used as a given name during the Middle Ages, and some instances of the surname may derive from this use. The name is also found among Ashkenazic Jews as an Anglicization of any of the various Jewish surnames listed at TROW.

Vars.: **Truman**, **Trewman**; **Tro(w)man** (W Midlands, esp. Staffs.).

Patrs.: Eng.: **Tro(w)mans** (Staffs.).

Truett see TYRWHITT

Truffault French: nickname for a joker or a trickster, from a pej. deriv. of OF *trufe* deceit, abuse, teasing (of uncertain origin).

Vars.: **Truffaut**, **Truffot**, **Triffault**; **Truffaudier** (with an agent suffix).

Truhlář Czech: occupational name for a joiner, Czech *truhlář*, agent noun from *truhla* chest, coffer, a borrowing from Ger. *Truhe* chest.

Trujillo Spanish: habitation name from places in the provinces of Cáceres and Seville, first recorded in L as *Turgalium* and of unknown, presumably pre-Roman, origin.

Trumbull English and Scots: from an OE personal name, *Trumbeald, composed of the elements *trum* strong, firm + *beald* bold, brave. See also TURNBULL, which is thought by some to be a var. of this.

Vars.: **Trumble**, TREMBLE; **Trimble** (N Ireland).

Trunchion English: nickname for a short, fat man, from ME, OF *tronchon* piece broken off (LL *trunciō*, gen. *trunciōnis*, from *truncus* lopped, cut short). It is just possible that the nickname also denoted someone who carried

a staff or cudgel as a symbol of office, but this sense of the word is not attested in Eng. before the 16th cent.

Vars.: **Tro(u)nson**.

Trupin see TURPIN

Trupp see THORPE

Truscott Cornish: habitation name from a place in the parish of St Stephens by Launceston, so called from Corn. *dres* beyond + *cuit* wood.

Trussell English (E Midlands): of uncertain origin, perhaps a metonymic occupational name for a pedlar, from a dim. of ME *truss* bundle, package (cf. TROSSIER), or else a nickname representing a var. of THRUSSELL.

Vars.: **Trussel**, **Truswell**.

Tryon English, of Dutch origin and uncertain derivation.

Tryoshnikov see TRETYAKOV

Trzciński Polish: habitation name from a place called *Trzcian(a)* or another called *Trzcin*, both of which are named from Pol. *trzcina* reed.

Var.: **Trzcieński**.

Trzepałkowski Polish: habitation name from a place named from the nickname *Trzepałek*, meaning either 'Thrasher' or 'Chatterer', from Pol. *trzepać* to beat, thrash, or chatter.

Var.: **Trzepiński**.

Tsaddik see ZADIK

Tsadok Jewish: from the Hebr. male given name *Tsadok* (from Hebr. *tsadik* pious, saintly man, whence Yid. *tsadik*; see ZADIK). The Eng. word *Sadducee* is related.

Vars.: **Tzadok**, **Zadok**; **Tsodek** (NE Ashkenazic; from the Yid. form, *Tsodek*, of the given name); **Tzudick** (S Ashkenazic). name).

Patr.: **Zudkevitz** (S Ashkenazic).

Tsaplin see CHAPLIN

Tschäpe see STEPHEN

Tscharnke see CHERNYAKOV

Tschierschke see GEORGE

Tseder see CEDER

Tshernichov see CHERNYAKOV

Tsigler see ZIEGLER

Tsin see ZINN

Tsitov see TITO

Tsodek see TSADOK

Tsvetkov see KWIATEK

Tsybulkin see ZWIEBEL

Tsyganov Russian: patr. from the name *tsygan* Gipsy. The vocab. word is of uncertain origin; it may have come from India at the same time as the Gipsies themselves. In any event, it reached Russ. by way of Byzantine Gk, where it had been associated by folk etymology with *athinganos* untouchable.

Tubb English: from the ME given name *Tubbe*, apparently derived from either ON *Tubbi* or OE **Tubba* (evidence for which is found in the placename *Tubney*, Berks.). There is no evidence to support the suggestion that it might be a metonymic occupational name or nickname from ME *tub* barrel (of Low Ger. origin).

Var.: **Tubby** (Norfolk, of ON origin).

Patr.: **Tubbs**.

Tuc see TRUC

Tuček Czech: nickname for a plump person, from a dim. form of Czech *tučný* fat.

Tuchmann German and Jewish (Ashkenazic): occupational name for a maker or seller of cloths, from Ger. *Tuch* cloth (MHG *tuoch*) + *mann* man.

Vars.: Ger.: **Tucher(t)**. Jewish: **Tuchman, Tuchler**; **Tuchmacher** ('cloth maker'); **Tuchschneider, Tuchsznajder** ('cloth cutter'; the second form is a Pol. spelling (E Ashkenazic)).

Tuck see TOOKE

Tucker 1. English (chiefly W Country): occupational name for a fuller, from an agent deriv. of ME *tuck(en)* to full cloth (OE *tūcian* to torment). This was the term used for the process in the Middle Ages in SW England, and the present-day distribution of the surname still reflects this (see also FULLER and WALKER). 2. English: occasionally perhaps a nickname for a brave or generous man, from OF *tout* all (L *tōtus*) + *coeur* heart (L *cor*). 3. Jewish (Ashkenazic): Anglicized form of *To(c)ker*; see TOKARZ.

Tuckwell English: apparently an occupational nickname for a TUCKER; cf. TREADWELL.

Var.: **Tugwell**.

Tudbald see THEOBALD

Tuddenham English (E Anglia): habitation name from a group of places in Norfolk and Suffolk, so called from the gen. case of the OE personal name *Tudda* + OE *hām* homestead.

Var.: **Tudman**.

Tudela Spanish and Catalan: habitation name from any of various places, for example in the provinces of Lérida, Navarre, Oviedo, and Valladolid. The placename is of pre-Roman origin and unknown meaning.

Tudisco see TEDESCO

Tugnetti see TONEY

Tugwell see TUCKWELL

Tugwood see TOOGOOD

Tuháček Czech: nickname for a stiff or unbending person, from Czech *tuhý* stiff, rigid.

Tuhy see TUOHY

Tuite Irish: in origin apparently a Norman habitation name, from an unknown place (see below), but from an early date it was taken as an Anglicization of Gael. **Mac Confhiaclaigh** 'son of *Cú Fhiaclach*', a personal name meaning 'Large-toothed Hound', the essential element of which was translated into Eng. as TOOTH, of which *Tuite* came to be taken as a variant.

Tuke see TOOKE

Tull English: of uncertain origin, possibly from an unrecorded late survival of the OE personal name *Tula*.

Tulliver see TELFER

Tulloch Scots: habitation name from a place near Dingwall on the Firth of Cromarty, so called from Gael. *tulach* hillock, or from any of various other minor places named with this element.

Vars.: **Tullock, Tulloh**. See also TOUGH 1.

Tully Irish: 1. Anglicized form of Gael. **Ó Taithlagh** 'descendant of *Taithleach*', a byname meaning 'Quiet', 'Peaceable'. 2. Anglicized form of Gael. **Ó Maol Tuile** 'descendant of the devotee of (St) *Tuile*', a personal name derived from *toil* will (of God).

Vars.: **Tilly** (see also TILLEY). (Of 1 only): **Tally**. (Of 2 only): **O'Multully, O'Multilly**; FLOOD (the result of erroneous association with the vocab. word *tuile* flood).

Tumanov Russian: patr. from the nickname *Tuman* 'Mist', 'Fog' (a Turkic borrowing), perhaps denoting a dim-witted person.

Tumasian see THOMAS

Tumelty see TOMELTY

Tumpany see TIMPANY

Tune see TONER

Tungate English (Norfolk): habitation name from a minor place near N Walsham, so called from ME *tune*, *tone* village, settlement (OE *tūn*) + *gate* GATE.

Tunik Jewish (E Ashkenazic): habitation name from a town so called near Minsk in Belorussia.

Var.: **Tunick**.

Tunney Irish: Anglicized form of Gael. **Ó Tonnaigh** 'descendant of *Tonnach*', a personal name meaning either 'Billowy' (from *tonn* wave) or 'Shining' or 'Swamp'.

Tunnicliffe English: habitation name from *Tonacliffe* in Lancs., recorded in 1246 as *Tunwal(e)clif*, from OE *tūn* enclosure, settlement + *wæll(a)* spring, stream + *clif* bank, slope.

Vars.: **Tunnicliff, Dunnicliff(e)**.

Tunstall English: habitation name from any of the numerous places, for example in Lancs., N Yorks., Co. Durham, Humberside, Kent, Norfolk, Shrops., Staffs., and Suffolk, so called from OE *tūn* enclosure, settlement + *st(e)all* site. The surname is found chiefly in Lancs. and Yorks.

Vars.: **Tunstell, Tunstill**. See also DUNSTALL.

Tuohy Irish: Anglicized form of Gael. **Ó Tuathaigh** 'descendant of *Tuathach*', a byname meaning 'Chief', 'Lord' (i.e. ruler over a *tuath* tribe, territory).

Vars.: **O'Towie, (O')Twohy, T(w)oohy, Tuhy, Tooey, Towey**.

Tuominen Finnish: ornamental name from Finn. *tuomi* bird cherry (*Prunus padus*) + the gen. suffix *-nen*. Cf. Swed. HÄGG.

Tuomy see TWOMEY

Tupper 1. English: occupational name for a herdsman who had charge of rams, from an agent deriv. of ME *to(u)pe* ram (of uncertain origin). 2. German: of uncertain origin, possibly a cogn. of 1.

Tuquet *see* TRUC

Tura *see* VENTURA

Turbin *see* THORBURN

Tureau *see* ARTHUR

Turella *see* VENTURA

Turesson *see* THOR

Turgell *see* THIRKILL

Turgenev Russian: patr. from the Mongol nickname *Türgen* 'Swift'.

Turgoose *see* STURGESS

Turiello *see* TORO

Turk 1. English: nickname for a rowdy or unruly person, from ME, OF *turc* Turk (of unknown ultimate origin). The non-Jewish Continental cogns. listed below are also house names, derived from the use of a picture of a Turk as a house sign, and nicknames for someone who had taken part in the wars against the Turks. The Jewish names mean 'Jew from Turkey'. 2. English: from a medieval given name, apparently a back-formation from THIRKILL, misanalysed as containing the OF dim. suffix *-el*. 3. Scots: Anglicized form of Gael. *Mac Torc*; see MCTURK.

Dims. (of 1): Fr.: **Turquet**, **Turquin**. It.: **Turchelli**, **Turchetti**, **Turchetto**, **Turchini**. Ger. and Jewish (Ashkenazic): **Terkel**. Czech: **Tureček**.

Patrs. (from 1): It.: **Del Turco**, **Turcheschi**. Pol.: **Turkiewicz**; **Turczak**.

Habitation name: Pol.: **Turkowski**.

Turkheim *see* DURKHEIM

Turkington N Irish: of uncertain origin, apparently a habitation name from *Torkington* in Ches., but now much more common in N Ireland than anywhere else. It may have been used as an Anglicized form of Sc. MCTURK.

Turley *see* MCTERRELLY

Turnbull N English (chiefly Northumb.) and Scots: apparently a nickname for a man thought to be strong and brave enough to turn back a charging bull, from ME *turn(en)* to turn (OE *turnian*, reinforced by OF *torner*, both from L *tornāre*, a deriv. of *tornus* lathe; cf. TURNER) + *bul(l)e* BULL.

Var.: **Turnbill**.

Turner 1. English and Scots (extremely common and widespread): occupational name for a maker of small objects of wood, metal, or bone by turning on a lathe, from ANF *torner* (OF *tornier*, L *tornārius*, a deriv. of *tornus* lathe). The surname may also derive from various other senses of ME *turn* and have originally described a turnspit, translator or interpreter, or tumbler. 2. English and Scots (rarely): nickname for a fast runner, from ME *turnen* to turn + HARE; cf. TURNBULL. 3. English and Scots: occupational name for an official in charge of a tournament, OF

tornei (in origin akin to 1). 4. Jewish (Ashkenazic): habitation name from a S Yid. pronunciation of Yid. *Torner*, denoting a native or inhabitant of the city of *Tarnów* (Yid. *Torne*), in Galicia (see TARNOWSKI). 5. Jewish (Ashkenazic): translation or Anglicized form of any of various other Jewish surnames.

Vars. (of 1): **Turno(u)r**.

Equivs. (not cogn.): Ger. and Jewish: DRECHSLER. N Ger.: DREIER. Pol.: TOKARZ.

Turney English (Norman): habitation name from any of various places in N France called *Tournai* (Orne), *Tournay* (Calvados), or *Tourny* (Eure), all from the pre-Roman personal name *Turnus* (probably meaning 'Height', 'Eminence'; cf. TERUEL and THÉRON) + the local suffix *-ācum*.

Var.: **Tournay**.

Turnham English: habitation name from *Turnham* in E Yorks or *Turnham* Green in W London, both of which are so called from OE *trun* circular + *hamm* water meadow or *hām* homestead.

Turov Russian: patr. from the nickname *Tur* 'Aurochs' (ultimately cogn. with L *taurus* bull; see TORO).

Dim.: Pol.: **Turajczyk**.

Turp *see* THORPE

Turpin English and French: from a Norman French form of the ON personal name *Þorfinnr*, composed of the divine name *Þórr* (see THOR 2) + the ethnic name *Finnr*. This may have absorbed another name, *Turpius*, *Turpinus* (from L *turpis* ugly, base), one of the self-abasing names adopted as a mark of humility by the early Christians. It was borne by the archbishop of Rheims in the Charlemagne legend.

Vars.: Fr.: **Tourpin**, **Trupin**.

Dim.: Scots: **Turpie**.

Türpitz *see* TIRPITZ

Turrell *see* TYRRELL

Turrini *see* TOWER

Turtle English: 1. var. of THIRKILL. 2. nickname for a mild and gentle or affectionate person, from ME *turtel* turtle dove (OE *turtla*, *turtle*, from L *turtur*, apparently of imitative origin). 3. nickname for a crippled or deformed person, from OF *tourtel*, a dim. of *tourt* crooked (L *tortus*, past part. of *torquere* to twist).

Dims. (of 2): It.: **Tortorella**, **Tortorello**, **Tortorelli**; **Torturiello**, **Turturiello** (Naples).

Turton English: habitation name from a place in Lancs., so called from the ON personal name *Þóri* (see THOR 2) + OE *tūn* enclosure, settlement. The surname is now as common in the Midlands as it is in Lancs. and Yorks.

Turvey English: habitation name from a place in Beds., so called from OE *turf* turf, grass + *ēg* island, low-lying land.

Tuscano *see* TOSCANO

Tuson English (Lancs.): apparently a patr. from the given name *Tuwe* or *Tywe*, which occurs in Lancs. in the 14th cent., but is of unknown origin.

Var.: **Tewson**.

Tussaud *see* TRUC

Tustain *see* THURSTON

Tutchener *see* TITCHENER

Tutin *see* THURSTON

Tutt English: from an OE personal name or byname *Tutta*, preserved in placenames such as *Tutnall* (Worcs.) and *Tuttington* (Norfolk), and apparently persisting into the Middle Ages. Its origin and meaning are unclear.

Tuttle *see* THIRKILL

Tutty Irish: Anglicized form of Gael. **Ó Tuataigh** 'descendant of *Tuatach*', a byname meaning 'Rustic', 'Boorish'.

Tuvey *see* TOVEY

Tuvia *see* TOBIAS

Tverdashov *see* TVRDÍK

Tvrdík Czech: nickname for an obstinate or severe person, from a deriv. of Czech *tvrdý* hard.
Patrs.: Russ.: **Tvyordyshev, Tverdashov, Tverdyukov.**
Habitation name: Pol.: **Twardowski.**
Cpd: Jewish (E Ashkenazic): **Twardogora** ('hard hill'; reason for adoption unknown).

Tvyordyshev *see* TVRDÍK

Twaddell *see* TWEDDLE

Twaite *see* THWAITE

Twardogora *see* TVRDÍK

Tweats *see* THWAITE

Tweddle N English and Scots: regional name for someone who lived in the valley (see DALE) of the river TWEED.
Vars.: **Tweddell, Tweed(a)le, Twaddle, Twaddell.**

Tweed N English and Scots: topographic name for someone living on the banks of the river *Tweed*, which flows between NE England and SE Scotland, and bears a Brit. name of uncertain meaning. It may be akin to W *twyad* hemming in (from *twy* check, bound), with reference to the deep and narrow valley at points along its course, or it may derive from a lost Brit. word cogn. with an Indo-European root meaning 'to swell, be powerful'.

Tweedie Scots: habitation name from a place in the parish of Stonehouse, south of Glasgow, the name of which is of uncertain origin.
Var.: **Tweedy.**

Twell *see* ATTWELL

Twigg English: nickname for a thin person, from ME, OE *twigge* twig, shoot. Since the word occurs only late in the OE period and was initially confined to Northern dialects, it may be a borrowing from ON. The surname is found mainly in the Midlands.
Var.: **Twigge.**
Dims.: Ger.: **Zweigle.** Jewish: **Zweig(e)l.**
Cpds (ornamental): Jewish: **Zweigenbaum** ('twig tree'); **Zweigenberg, Cwajgenberg** ('twig hill').

Twin English: name for one of a pair of twins, from ME *twinn* (OE *(ge)twinn* twofold, double, a deriv. of *twā* two).
Var.: **Twinn.**

Twist English (chiefly Lancs. and W Midlands): of uncertain origin, possibly a metonymic occupational name for someone in the cotton-spinning industry, whose responsibility was to combine threads into a strong cord, a sense of *twist* recorded from the 16th cent.
Var.: **Twiss.**

Twitchen *see* TITCHENER

Twite *see* THWAITE

Twohill *see* TOOLE

Twohy *see* TUOHY

Twomey Irish: Anglicized form of Gael. **Ó Tuama** 'descendant of *Tuama*', a personal name probably derived from *tuaim* hill, small mountain.
Vars.: **Twoomy, Tuomy, Towmey, O'Twomey, (O')Toomey.**

Twyford English: habitation name from any of the numerous places, for example in Berks., Bucks., Derbys., Hants, Leics., Lincs., Middx, and Norfolk, so called from OE *twī-* double (cf. TWIN) + *ford* FORD.

Tyas English: ethnic name of early date (12th cent. onwards) for someone from Germany or the Low Countries, from ANF *tieis, tiois* German (OHG *tiutisc*; cf. DEUTSCH and TEDESCO).
Var.: **Tyers.**

Tydeman *see* TIDMAN

Tydsley *see* TYLDESLEY

Tye English: 1. topographic name for someone who lived by a common pasture, ME *tye* (OE *tēag*). 2. topographic name for someone who lived by a river or on an island, from a misdivision of ME *at(te)ye, at(te)ey*; cf. NYE and RYE.
Vars.: **Tey, Tee.**

Tyers *see* TYAS

Tyldesley English: habitation name from a place in Lancs., near Leigh, so called from the gen. case of the OE personal name *Tilweald* (composed of the elements *til* good + *weald* rule) + OE *lēah* wood, clearing. The surname has been common in the surrounding area since the 14th cent.
Vars.: **Tyldeslegh, Tydsley, Tild(e)sley, Til(l)sley, Tilzey.**

Tyler *see* TILER

Tyley *see* TILLEY

Tym *see* TIMM

Tymkiewicz *see* TIMOFEEV

Tymmany *see* TIMONY

Tympany *see* TIMPANY

Tynan Irish: Anglicized form of Gael. **Ó Teimhneáin** 'descendant of *Teimhneán*', a dim. form of the OIr. personal name *Teimhean* 'Dark'.

Tyndale see TINDALE

Tyre see MCINTYRE

Tyrer English (Lancs.): of unknown origin. It is possible that it arose as an occupational name for an official in charge of the wardrobe of a great personage, from an agent deriv. of ME *tire(n)* to equip, dress (an aphetic form of OF *atir(i)er*, from the phrase *a tire* in order, which is itself of uncertain origin). However, there is no early evidence for this.

Tyringham English: habitation name from a place in Bucks., probably so called from OE *Tīdheringahām* 'homestead (OE *hām*) of the people of *Tīdhere*', a personal name composed of the elements *tīd* time + *here* army. Alternatively, the proprietor may have borne the shorter name of *Tīr(a)*, a short form of the rare cpd names with the first element *tīr* glory.

Tyrrell English and Irish: of uncertain origin, probably a Norman nickname for a stubborn person, from OF *tirel*, used of an animal which pulls on the reins, a deriv. of *tirer* to pull (cf. TIRADO).
Vars.: **Tyrell**, **Tirrell**, **Terrill**, **Terrell**, **Terrall**, **Turrell**, **Tearall**; **Tirial** (a Gaelicized form).

Tyrwhitt English: habitation name from *Trewhitt* in Northumb., so called from ON *tyri* dry resinous wood + *þvít* meadow, piece of land (see THWAITE).
Var.: **Truett**.

Tyson English: 1. var. of *Dyson*; see DYE. 2. nickname for someone of a fiery temperament, from OF *tison* firebrand (L *titio*, gen. *titiōnis*).

Tyssen see THIESS

Tytel see TEITELBAUM

Tyzack English (of French origin): habitation name from *Tizac* in Gironde, Aquitaine, so called from the L personal name *Titius* (a deriv. of *Titus*; see TITO) + the local suffix *-ācum*.

Tzadik see ZADIK

Tzadok see TSADOK

Tzarkov see KAISER

Tzeitlin see ZEITLIN

Tzin see ZINN

Tzudick see TSADOK

Tzuker see ZUCKER

U

Ubach see BACH

Uccello Italian: metonymic occupational name for a bird-catcher or a nickname for a small birdlike person, from It. *uccello* bird (LL *avicellus*, a dim. of class. L *avis*).
Vars.: **Uccelli**, **Ulcelli**, **Uzielli**; **Auc(i)ello**, **Aucelli**, **Augello**, **Ausielli**; **Oselli**.
Dims.: It.: **Uccelletti**; **Augelluzzi**; **Oseletti**. Fr.: **Loiselet**, **Loisillon**, **Loizillon**.

Uceda Spanish: habitation name from a place in the province of Guadalajara, so called from a collective deriv. of the Sp. dial. term *uz*, denoting a kind of heather (L *ulex*, gen. *ulicis*).

Uciński Polish: habitation name from a place probably named from Pol. *ucinać* to cut off, dock, with the addition of *-ski*, suffix of local surnames (see BARANOWSKI).

Udall English: habitation name from *Yewdale* in Lancs., so called from OE *īw* yew tree + *dæl* valley (see DALE).
Vars.: **Udell**, **Uvedale**.

Uddin English: of uncertain origin, probably a dim. of the given name HUDD. The name is relatively common in the London area, but rare elsewhere.

Ude see ULRICH

Udovchik see WIDDOW

Ufer German: topographic name for someone who lived on a riverbank, Ger. *Ufer*, MHG *uover* (not attested in OHG, but cf. OVER), or habitation name from one of the various places named with this word, of which there are two in Austria and one near Cologne.
Vars.: **Ufert**, **Ufermann**.

Ufford English: habitation name from places in Northants and Suffolk, so called from the OE personal name *Uffa* (of uncertain origin) + OE *worð* enclosure (see WORTH).

Ugalde Basque: topographic name for someone who lived near water, from Basque *ur* water + *alde* place, direction, side. In the dialect of Navarre the combination has the sense 'river', and this may sometimes lie behind the surname.

Ugarte Basque: topographic name for someone who lived on an island or piece of land between two rivers, Basque *ugarte* (from *ur* water + *arte* intervening space). There are places so named in the provinces of Álava and Biscay, and the surname may also be a habitation name from one of these.

Ughelli see HUGH

Uhde see ULRICH

Uhl see ULRICH

Uhlíř Czech: occupational name for a coal merchant or, at an earlier date, a charcoal burner, an agent deriv. of Czech *uhlí* coal, charcoal.
Dim.: **Uhlík**.

Uijs see UYS

Uken see ULRICH

Ukraintsev Russian: patr. from the name *ukrainets* Ukrainian. The Ukraine (Russ. *Ukraina*) gets its name from the Slav. elements *u* at + *kraina* boundary, edge, i.e. 'border territory'.
Dim.: Ukr.: **Ukraïnko**.

Ulanov Russian: **1.** patr. from the occupational term *ulan* lancer, uhlan (from a Turkic word meaning 'youth'). **2.** Russianized form of the Mongol (Kalmuck) byname *Ulan*, meaning 'Red'.
Habitation name: Pol.: **Ulanowski**.

Ulatowski Polish: apparently a habitation name, of uncertain origin, perhaps from a place deriving its name from OPol. *ulatać* to yield, defer (meaning 'to fly away' in mod. Pol.).

Ulcelli see UCCELLO

Uli see ULRICH

Uliot see WOLFIT

Uliva see OLIVA

Ulke see ULRICH

Ullerich see ULRICH

Ullett see WOLFIT

Ullman see ULMAN

Ulman Jewish (Ashkenazic): habitation name from the city of *Ulm* in Baden-Württemberg, with the suffix *-man* man, which is occasionally found as a surname-forming element with placenames, denoting a native or inhabitant of a place.
Var.: **Ullman**.

Ulph see WOLF

Ulrich German: from the given name *Ulrich*, OHG *Odalrīc*, composed of the elements *odal* prosperity, fortune + *rīc* power. The name was borne by a 10th-cent. saint, bishop of Augsburg, whose fame contributed greatly to the popularity of the given name in German- and Slavic-speaking areas in the Middle Ages.

Vars.: **Ull(e)rich**; **Uhlich, Uhlig, Urich, Urech, U(h)rig** (under Slav. influence).

Dims.: Ger.: **U(h)de, Uhl(e), Uli, Ühl(e)in; Utz, Ützle; Ullmann**. Ger. (under Slav. influence): **Ulisch, Ul(t)sch, Ulusch; Jedele**. Low Ger.: **Ullmann, Uhl(e)mann, Utzmann; Ulke, Jehle**. Czech: **Volek**.

Patrs.: Ger.: **Ulrici** (Latinized). Low Ger.: **Öhlrichs**.

Patrs. (from dims.): Low Ger.: **Öhlerking, Öllerking; Ulkes, U(l)ken**. Fris.: **Ukena**.

Ulsch *see* ULRICH

Ultsch *see* ULRICH

Ulusch *see* ULRICH

Ulyachin *see* JULIAN

Ulyate *see* WOLFIT

Umfreville English and Scots (Norman): habitation name from a place in La Manche, so called from the OF personal name *Umfroi* (see HUMPHREY) + OF *ville* settlement (see VILLE).

Vars.: **Umfraville, Umphraville**.

Umpleby English (Yorks.): habitation name from *Anlaby* in E Yorks., recorded 1234 as *Anlaweby* but in Domesday Book as *Umloueby*. The place is named from the ON personal name *Anláfr, Óláfr* (see OLIFF) + ON *býr* farm, settlement.

Unbehauen German: nickname for an ill-mannered or boorish individual, from the MHG adj. *unbehouwen*, lit. 'not hewn into shape', i.e. rough, crude.

Vars.: **Unbehaun**; **Unbegaun** (in regions such as Russia, where the local Slav. language substitutes /g/ for /h/).

Uncle English: **1.** nickname for an avuncular man, from the term of relationship, ME *uncle* (OF *oncle*, L *avunculus*), which eventually displaced the native EAME. **2.** from the ON personal name *Úlfketill*, composed of the elements *úlfr* wolf + *ketill* cauldron. This was reasonably common as a given name in N England in the early Middle Ages, especially in the contracted form *Úlfkell*.

Dim. (of 1): Flem.: **Onckelet**.

Patrs. (from 1): Eng.: **Uncles, Ungles(s)**. Rom.: **Onciulesco**.

Underhill English (most common in the W Midlands, but also found in the W Country and elsewhere): topographic name for someone who lived at the foot of a hill, from ME *under* + HILL, or habitation name from a place named with these elements, for example in Devon.

Var.: **Undrell**.

Underwood English and Scots: topographic name for someone who lived at the edge of a wood, from ME *under* + WOOD, or habitation name from a place named with these elements, for example in Derbys., Notts., and the former county of Ayrs.

Unger German, Czech, and Jewish (Ashkenazic): name for a Magyar or someone from Hungary (Ger. *Ungarn*, Yid. *Ungern*), perhaps also in some cases a nickname for

someone who had some trading or other connection with Hungary.

Vars.: Ger. and Jewish: **Ungar, Hunger, Hungar; Ungerer, Ungermann**. Jewish only: **Ungerland** (from Yid.), **Ungerman**; INGER; **Hungerer, Hungerland** (the initial *H*- generally added under Eng. influence).

Dims.: Ger.: **Hüngerle**. It.: **Ongarelli, Ungarelli, Ungherelli, Ungaretti**.

Patrs.: Jewish: **Ungerson**; **Ingerov** (S Ashkenazic). It.: **Dell'Ongaro**.

Ungles *see* UNCLE

Unruh German: nickname for a restless or quarrelsome person, from Ger. *Unruhe* disturbance, unrest (MHG *unrou(we)*, *unrāwa*, OHG *unrāwa*, from the negative prefix *un-* + *ruowa* rest, calm).

Unsworth English (Lancs.): habitation name from a place in Greater Manchester, so called from the gen. case of the OE byname *Hund* 'Dog' + OE *worð* enclosure (see WORTH).

Unwin English: from the OE personal name *Hūnwine*, composed of the elements *hūn* bearcub + *wine* friend. Later in the OE or early ME period, this name came to be confused with the word *unwine* enemy (from the negative prefix *un-* + *wine* friend), and this is no doubt the source of the surname in some cases.

Var.: **Hunwin**.

Upjohn Welsh: patr. from JOHN, with the prefix *ap* son of.

Upton English: habitation name from any of the numerous places so called. The majority of them get the name from OE *up-* upper + *tūn* enclosure, settlement. One in Essex, however, was originally named with the phrase *upp in tūne* up in the settlement, i.e. the higher part of the settlement; and one in Worcs. is probably so called from the OE personal name *Ubba* (of uncertain origin) + *tūn*.

Uran *see* UREN

Urban English, French, Czech, Polish, Belorussian, and Jewish (E Ashkenazic): from a medieval given name (L *Urbānus* 'City-dweller', a deriv. of *urbs* town, city). The name was borne by a 4th-cent. saint, the patron of vines, and by seven early popes. The Jewish names are adoptions of the Polish or Belorussian surname.

Vars.: Eng.: **Urben**. Fr.: **Urb(a)in**. Pol.: **Urbański; Urbaniec**.

Dims.: It.: **Urbaniello**. Ger. (under Slav. influence): **Urbanek, Urbanke, Hurbank, Wurbank; Urbasch, Urbisch, Horbasch**. Czech: **Urbánek**. Pol.: **Urbańczyk, Urbanek**.

Aug.: Czech: **Urbanec**.

Patrs.: Pol.: **Urbanowicz; Urbaniak**. Beloruss.: **Urbanovich**. Russ.: **Urbanov**. Jewish: **Urbanovsky**.

Patrs. (from dims.): Russ.: **Urbantsov, Urbantsev, Urmantsov, Urmantsev**.

Habitation name: Pol.: **Urbanowski**.

Ure Scots: from the Older Scots given name *Ure*, a var. of IVOR.

Patr.: **McUre**.

Urech see ULRICH

Uren Cornish: from the Brittonic personal name recorded as *Urbgen* in OW and as *Urbien* and *Urien* in OBret. The first element is unexplained; the second represents the root *gen* birth, born. In Cornwall the name may be a survival from the Celtic period or, more probably, an import from Brittany.

Vars.: **Urien, Urren, Urene, Urion, Ur(r)on, Urian, Ur(r)an, Urane, Urrin, Urin(e), Uring, Uryn, Urne, Youren, Youron, Yourn(e), Euren, Eweren**.

Patrs.: **Yourenson, Youronson**.

Ureña Spanish: habitation name from any of various places, for example in the provinces of Salamanca and Segovia, called *Urueña*. These are first recorded in the L form *Oronia*, and are of uncertain, presumably pre-Roman, origin.

Urevich see HOROWITZ

Urey see WOOLDRIDGE

Uría Spanish form of Basque **Uria**: topographic name for someone who lived in a village rather than the open countryside, from Basque *uri* settlement (a western dial. var. of *iri*; cf. IRIGOYEN) + the def. art. *-a*.

Urian see UREN

Uriarte Basque: topographic name for someone who lived between two settlements, from *uri* settlement (see URIA) + *arte* intervening space.

Var.: **Iriarte**.

Uribarri Basque: habitation name from any of various places, for example in the provinces of Álava, Biscay, and Guipúzcoa, so called from *uri* settlement (see URIA) + *barri* new.

Uribe Basque: topographic name for someone who lived in the lower part of a village, from *uri* settlement (see URIA) + *be(h)e* lower part.

Urich see ULRICH

Urie see WOOLDRIDGE

Urlin see HARLING

Urmantsev see URBAN

Urne see UREN

Uron see UREN

Urquhart Scots: habitation name from a place in the former county of Inverness, on Loch Ness, apparently named with cogns. of W *ar* on, upon + *cardden* thicket.

Urquijo Spanish form of Basque **Urkiza, Urkizu**: topographic name for someone who lived by a group of birch trees, from Basque *urki* birch tree + the suffix of abundance *-zo, -zu*.

Urran see UREN

Urrutia Basque: topographic name for someone who lived at some distance from the main settlement, from *urruti* distant + the def. art. *-a*.

Urry see WOOLDRIDGE

Urshalimi see YERUSHALMI

Ursi see ORSO

Urvine see IRVINE

Urwin see IRVINE

Urwitz see HOROWITZ

Ury see WOOLDRIDGE

Uryn see UREN

Urzędowski Polish: habitation name from the town of *Urzędów* SW of Lublin (so called from Pol. *urząd* office + *-ów* possessive suffix), with the addition of *-ski*, suffix of local surnames (see BARANOWSKI).

Var.: **Urzędowicz** (patr. in form, probably meaning 'son of the official').

Usatchov see WĄSIK

Usborne see OSBORN

Ushakov Russian: patr. from the nickname *Ushak*, a deriv. of *ukh* ear, pl. *ushi*. The nickname may have been used for a man with large or conspicuous ears, or perhaps for someone who had good hearing or who was given to eavesdropping.

Usher 1. English, Scots, and Irish: occupational name for a janitor or gate-keeper, ME *usher* (ANF *usser*, OF *ussier*, *huissier*, from LL *ustiārius*, a deriv. of class. L *ostium* door, gate). The term was also used in the Middle Ages of a court official charged with accompanying a person of rank on ceremonial occasions, and this may be a partial souce of the surname. 2. Jewish (S Ashkenazic): from a S Yid. pronunciation of the Yid. male given name OSHER (Hebr. ASHER).

Vars. (of 1): **Ussher, Husher; Lusher** (with the OF def. art.).

Patrs. (from 2): **Usherov(itz), Usherowicz; Uszerowicz** (Pol. spelling).

Usherwood see ISHERWOOD

Ussher see USHER

Ustimenko see JUSTIN

Uszerowicz see USHER

Utley N English: habitation name from a place in Yorks., near Keighley, so called from the OE personal name *Utta* (see UTTING) + OE *lēah* wood, clearing.

Var.: **Uttley**.

Utridge see UTTRIDGE

Utting English (Norfolk): from the OE personal name *Utting*, in origin a patr. from the attested *Utta*, which is of uncertain origin. The name is also discussed by Black as Scots, though it does not now seem to be common north of the border.

Var.: **Uttin**.

Uttley see UTLEY

Uttridge English: from the OE personal name *Ūhtrīc*, composed of the elements *ūht* dawn + *rīc* power.
Vars.: **Ut(te)ridge**; **Out(te)ridge**, **Ou(gh)tright**.

Utz *see* ULRICH

Uvedale *see* UDALL

Uys Flemish and Dutch: nickname for a belligerent individual or occupational name for a professional champion, from MDu. *huys* fighter.
Var.: **Uijs**.

Uzielli *see* UCCELLO

V

Vaamonde see BAAMONDE

Vaandrager Dutch: occupational name for a standard bearer, from MDu. *vann* flag (cf. GONFALONIERI) + *draghen* to carry (OSax. *dragan*).
Patr.: **Vendricks**.

Vabre see VAUR

Vacca Italian: nickname from It. *vacca* cow (L *vacca*), denoting a cowherd (see VACCARO) or a gentle person.
Var.: **Vacchi**.
Dims.: It.: **Vacchelli**. Fr.: **Vachet(te)**; **Vachey** (Burgundy); **Vachez** (N France); **Vachon**, **Vachot**, **Vachoux** (E France); **Vacquez**, **Vacquin** (Normandy).

Vaccaro Italian: occupational name for a cowherd, It. *vaccaro* (LL *vaccārius*, a deriv. of *vacca* cow; see VACCA).
Vars.: **Vaccari**; **Vaccai** (Tuscany); **Vaccher**, **Vaguer** (Venetia).
Dims.: It.: **Vaccarino**, **Vaccarini**, **Vaccar(i)ello**, **Vaccarelli**. Fr.: **Vacheret**, **Vache(y)ron**, **Vacherot**; **Vacquerel**.
Augs.: Fr.: **Vacherat**. It.: **Vaccaroni**.

Vacelet see VASS

Vachrameev see BARTHOLOMEW

Václav Czech: from the Czech given name *Václav*, OCzech *Vęceslav* (cogn. with Pol. *Więcław*, *Wacław*; Anglicized as *Wenceslas*). It is composed of the elements *vęce* greater + *slav* glory. It was borne by a 10th-cent. duke of Bohemia who fought against a revival of paganism in his territory, and after his death became patron saint of Bohemia.
Vars.: **Vacula**, **Vácha(l)**, **Vach(e)l**; **Vása**, **Vašák**, **Vaňa**, **Vaňáč**, **Vančata**, **Vančura**, **Vaniš**, **Vaňous**.
Dims.: Czech: **Vacek**, **Vacík**; **Václavek**, **Václavík**, **Vacuík**; **Vachek**; **Vašek**, **Vašíček**, **Vaško**; **Vaňek**, **Vaníček**, **Vaněček**, **Vaňásek**.
Patrs.: Czech: **Václavů**. Pol.: **Więclawicz**.
Habitation name: Czech: **Václavovský**.

Vadé see WADE

Vadimov Russian: patr. from the given name *Vadim*, a shortened form of the Slav. personal name *Vadimir*, composed of the elements *vad-* to tame + *mir* peace or *mer* great. This name was not accepted by the Orthodox Church as a baptismal name, but it was commonly used in the Middle Ages as a familiar name borne in addition to an official given name.

Vagedes see VOGT

Vagg see FAGG

Vaguer see VACCARO

Vaida see VAJDA

Vail see VEIL

Vainberg see WEINBERG

Vainer see WEIN

Vaines see FANE

Vainio Finnish: ornamental name from Finn. *vainio* field, in some cases perhaps chosen as a topographic name by someone who lived by a field.

Vair French: nickname for someone with a blotchy complexion, or who made a habit of dressing in clothes of different colours, from OF *vair* variegated (L *varius*). The same word was also used in the Middle Ages of a type of variegated fur, probably that of the Russian squirrel (cf. the Czech word VEVERKA 'Squirrel'), and the surname may also have denoted someone who traded in furs. According to an early version of the fairy tale, Cinderella's slippers were made of this fur, but when the word fell out of use and was no longer understood, it was changed to the less plausible *verre* glass (cf. VERRIER).
Var.: **Ver**.
Dims.: **Vairel**, **Vérel**, **Vairet**, **Vér(el)et**, **Verlet**, **Vairon**, **Veyron**.

Vairow see FARRAR

Vaisey English: nickname for a cheerful person, from an aphetic form of ANF *enveisié* playful, merry (OF *envoisié*, past part. of *envoisier* to sport, enjoy oneself, from LL *invitiāre*, a deriv. of *vitium* pleasure (originally 'vice', 'fault')).
Vars.: **Vaizey**, **Vasey**, **Veas(e)y**, **Veazey**, **Ve(y)sey**, **Vezey**, **Voisey**, **Voizey**, **Voysey**, **Voyzey**; **F(e)asey**, **F(e)acey**, **Feazy**, **Feesey**, **Foizey**; **Pha(i)sey**, **Phazey**, **Pheasey**, **Pheazey**, **Pheysey**; **Lenfestey**.

Vaisfeld see WHITE

Vaissade see VAYSSE

Vaitl see VITO

Vaivre see VAUR

Vajda 1. Hungarian: status name from Hung. *vajda* leader, governor, a word of Slav. origin (cf. VEJVODA). 2. Jewish (Ashkenazic): adoption of the Hung. name, presumably taken by a rabbi; cf. HAUPTMANN.
Var. (of 2): **Vaida**.

Vajselfisz see WEISSELFISCH

Vakhlov see BARTHOLOMEW

Valadéz see BAUD

Valbuena Spanish: habitation name from any of various places, for example in the provinces of Palencia, Salamanca, and Valladolid, so called from OSp. *val* valley (see VALE) + *buena* (fem.) good, pleasant, attractive (see BON).
Vars.: **Balbuena**; **Balboa** (Galicia).

Valcárcel Spanish: habitation name from a place in the province of León now called *Valcarce*, from OSp. *val* valley (see VALE) + *cárcel* prison (L *carcer*), the second element being used in the transferred sense of a confined space, i.e. a narrow gorge.

Var.: **Valcarce**.

Vald *see* WALD

Valderrama Spanish: habitation name from a place in the province of Burgos, first recorded as *Val de Rama* 'valley (see VALE) of *Rama*'; it is not clear whether the final element represents Sp. *rama* branch (see RAM 2) or a personal name.

Vale English (chiefly S England and Midlands): topographic name for someone who lived in a valley, ME *vale* (OF *val*, from L *vallis*). The surname is now also common in Ireland, where it has been Gaelicized as **de Bhál** (see also WALL 3). The Fr. cogn. was originally fem., as in L, but later became masc., perhaps under the influence of MONT.

Dims.: Fr.: **VALLET**, **Val(l)ette**, **Lavallette**, **Duvallet**, **Delavalette**, **Vallon**. It.: **Valetta**, **Valletti**; **Val(l)otto** (Venetia); **Vallillo** (Campania); **Vallarino**, **Vallarini**. Sp.: **Vallejo**.

Augs.: It.: **Vallone**, **Valloni**.

Valencia Spanish: habitation name from any of various places so called, principally the major city in E Spain, which was formerly the capital of an independent Moorish kingdom of the same name. The city was named by the Romans as *Valentia*, a deriv. of the personal name *Valens* (see VALENTE).

Var.: **Valenciano**.

Dim.: Sp.: **Valenzuela** (places in the provinces of Ciudad Real and Córdoba).

Valente Italian and Portuguese: from the medieval given name *Valente* (L *Valens*, gen. *Valentis*, pres. part. of *valēre* to be strong, healthy). The name was especially popular in medieval Italy, in honour of a 6th-cent. bishop of Verona.

Valentine English and Scots: from a medieval given name (L *Valentīnus*, a deriv. of *Valens*; see VALENTE), which was never common in England, but is occasionally found from the end of the 12th cent., probably as the result of Fr. influence. The name was borne by a 3rd-cent. saint and martyr, whose chief claim to fame is that his feast falls on 14 February, the date of a traditional celebration of spring going back to the Roman fertility festival of Juno Februata. A 5th-cent. missionary bishop of Rhaetia of this name was venerated esp. in S Germany, being invoked as a patron against gout and epilepsy.

Vars.: **Valentin**, **Vallentin(e)**, **Val(l)intine**, **Vallantine**.

Dims.: It.: **Valentinelli**, **Valentinetti**, **Valentinuzzi**. Ger.: **Valtl**, **Veltl**. Low Ger.: **Velte**. Czech: **Válek**; **Valášek**. Pol.: **Walaszczyk**, **Walasik**, **Waliszek**.

Patrs.: Pol.: **Walentynowicz**, **Walewicz**.

Patrs. (from dims.): Low Ger.: **Velten**, **Felten**. Fris.: **Veltjes**. Pol.: **Walentkiewicz**, **Walkiewicz**; **Walczak**, **Walisiak**.

Habitation names: Pol.: **Walewski**, **Walczyński**, **Waliszewski**, **Walkowski**.

Valera Spanish: habitation name from any of various places so called from LL *Valēria (villa)* 'homestead of

Valērius' (cf. VALERIO), for example in the province of Cuenca.

Valeriano Italian: from a medieval given name (L *Valēriānus*, a deriv. of *Valērius*; see VALERIO). The name was borne by various minor Christian saints, most notably 4th-cent. bishops of Aquileia and Auxerre.

Var.: **Valeriani**.

Patr.: Russ.: **Valerianov**.

Valerio Italian: from a medieval given name (L *Valērius*, a Roman family name probably connected with L *valēre* to flourish, be strong, healthy; cf. VALENTE). The name was borne by several minor Christian saints, among them 4th-cent. bishops of Trier and Saragossa and 5th-cent. bishops of Sorrento and of Antibes in S France.

Vars.: **Valeri**; **Valleri** (Tuscany); **Val(i)er** (Venetia).

Dim.: It.: **Valerini**. Hung.: **Valkó**.

Valiant English: nickname for a stalwart or courageous person, from ME *vailaunt, valiaunt* sturdy, brave (OF *vail(l)ant*, pres. part. of *vail(l)ir* to be strong, healthy, L *valēre*; cf. VALENTE).

Vall Catalan: 1. topographic name for someone who lived in a valley (a cogn. of VALE). 2. topographic name for someone who lived by a ditch (in form a cogn. of WALL 1, but for the meaning cf. VALLAT).

Var.: **Valls**.

Vallance English and Scots (Norman): habitation name from *Valence* in Drôme, which probably has the same origin as VALENCIA.

Vars.: **Valance**, **Vallans**.

Vallat Provençal: topographic name for someone who lived by a ditch, OProv. *vallat* (LL *vallātum*, a deriv. of *vallum* palisade, fortification composed of both a mound and a ditch).

Vars.: **Valat**, **Val(l)adier**, **Val(l)ayer**; **Balat**, **Albalat**, **Delbalat** (Gascony).

Dim.: **Valadon**.

Vallender German: habitation name from *Valandar* near Koblenz, which according to Bahlow is so called from a prehistoric river name *Val-andra* 'stagnant water'.

Vallès Catalan: regional name for someone from a region of Catalonia centred on Granollers in the province of Barcelona, called *El Vallès*. In a few cases the surname may be a habitation name from a village of the same name in the province of Valencia. In both cases the placename is from L *vallēnsis*, an adj. deriv. of *vallis* valley; cf. VALE and VALOIS.

Vallet 1. French and English: occupational name for a manservant, ME, OF *vaslet, val(l)et* (a dim. of *vassal* serf; see VASS, VASSALL and VAVASOUR). 2. French: dim. of *val* valley (see VALE).

Vars. (of 1): Eng.: **Valet(t)**. Fr.: **Va(y)let**, **Leval(l)et**, **Val(l)ot**, **Vaslet**, **Vaslot**, **Varlet**, **Levarlet**, **Varlot**.

Dims.: Fr.: **Val(le)teau**, **Val(e)ton**, **Valtot**, **Valtin**.

Vallverdú Catalan: local name composed of the elements VALL valley + the placename *Verdú* (see VARDON).

Valois French: topographic name for someone who lived in a valley, or habitation name from any of the various places called *Val(l)ois*, or regional name from the district in N France so called, which was once an independent duchy. In all cases the source is an adj. deriv. of OF *val* valley (see VALE).

Var.: **Levallois**.

Valverde Spanish: habitation name from any of the numerous places so called from OSp. *val* valley (see VALE) + *verde* green (see VERDE). The reference is to particularly lush pastures in a well-watered valley.

Vámbéry see BAMBERGER

Vaňa see VÁCLAV

Van Beek see BACH

Van Boven see OBER

Vance see FENN

Vanchakov see JOHN

Van Dam see DAM

Van Dantzig see DANZIG

Van de Brinck see BRINK

Van de Loo see LOO

Van de Meij see MAY

Van den Brinck see BRINK

Van den Oever see OVER

Van den Pol see POL

Van den Storm see STORM

Van der Beek see BACH

Van der Geest see GEEST

Van der Haar see HAAR

Van der Kooi see KOOY

Van der Meer see MEER

Van der Most see MOST

Van der Schueren see SCHEUER

Van der Sluijs see SLUIS

Van der Werff see WERF, VAN DER

Van der Zyl see ZYL, VAN

Van de Veer see VEERMAN

Van Deventer see DEVENTER

Van Duijn see DUIN

Vane see FANE

Van Geest see GEEST

Van Gheest see GEEST

Van Kooi see KOOY

Van Loo see LOO

Vannar see FANNER

Vannier French: occupational name for a winnower, or more often, since this was a highly seasonal activity, for a maker and seller of winnowing fans, from an agent deriv. of OF *vanne* winnowing fan (L *vannus*) or the verb *van(n)ier* to winnow. Cf. FANNER.

Vars.: **Vanier**, **Levannier**; **Vanneur**, **Levanneur**.
Dim.: **Vannereau**.

Van Praag see PRAGER

Van Sluijs see SLUIS

Van Zijl see ZYL, VAN

Vara Spanish: nickname from Sp. *vara* rod, stick (LL *vāra* forked stick, probably a deriv. of *vārus* bent, twisted). The nickname may have been given to a keeper of animals, who used a rod to urge his charges on, or to an official who carried a rod as a symbol of his office, but it is also possible that it had a sexual connotation (cf., e.g., HARDSTAFF and WAGSTAFF).

Var.: **Varas**.
Dim.: **Varela** (also Port.).

Varah see FARRAR

Varder see VERDIER

Vardon English (Norman): habitation name from any of various places in France called *Verdun*. The placename is probably of Gaul. origin, and probably derives from the elements *ver(n)* alder (see VER 1) + *dūn* hill, fortress. Some early bearers of the name certainly came from a place of this name in La Manche, others possibly from one in Eure. For the ME change of *-er-* to *-ar-*, cf. MARCHANT.

Vars.: **Varden**; **Verdon**, **Verden**, **Verd(u)in**, **Verduyn**.

Varfalameev see BARTHOLOMEW

Varga Hungarian: occupational name from Hung. *varga* cobbler, shoemaker.

Vargas Spanish and Portuguese: topographic name from Sp., Port. *varga*, a dial. term used in the northern part of the Peninsula in various senses: hut, slope, fenced pasture-land which becomes waterlogged in winter. These different senses were apparently originally represented by two or three distinct pre-Roman words, but they fell together too early for their history to be reconstructed. Cf. BÁRCENA.

Varlet see VALLET

Varley English: of uncertain origin, probably a habitation name from *Verly* in Aisne, Picardy, so called from the Gallo-Roman personal name *Virilius* (a deriv. of *virilis* male, from *vir* man) + the local suffix *-ācum*. For the ME change of *-er-* to *-ar-*, cf. MARCHANT. The surname is now most common in W Yorks.

Vars.: **Verley**, **Virley**.

Varnerin see WARNER

Varnes see FERN

Varney English (Norman): habitation name from Saint-Paul-du-Vernay in Calvados or any of various other places in N France of the same name. All are apparently so called from the Gaul. element *ver(n)* alder (see VER 1) + the local suffix *-ācum*. For the ME change of *-er-* to *-ar-*, cf. MARCHANT.

Vars.: **Vernay**, **Vern(e)y**.

Varnon *see* VERNON

Varran *see* FARREN

Varty *see* VERITY

Varvarin *see* BARBARY

Vása *see* VÁCLAV

Vasari Italian: occupational name for a potter, It. *vasaro* (LL *vāsārius*, a deriv. of *vās* vessel, jar, pot).

Vásári Hungarian: topographic name for someone who lived by a market-place or in a market town, or occupational name for a trader, from Hung. *vásár* market.

Var.: **Vásáry**.

Vasco 1. Italian: ethnic name for someone from the Basque region in S France and N Spain. The inhabitants of this region are first recorded in L sources as the *Vascōnes*, a word of unknown origin (see also GASCOIGNE). The Basques' own name for themselves is *Euskaldun*. **2.** Jewish: of unknown origin.

Var.: **Lo Vasco** (Sicily).

Dims.: It.: **Vaschetti**, **Vaschini**. Fr.: **Basquet**, **Basquin**. Prov.: **Bascou(l)**.

Vasconcelos Portuguese: habitation name from a place near Braga, so called because it was originally settled by Basques. The placename is from the pl. of a dim. form of the adj. *vasconço* Basque (see VASCO).

Vasechkin *see* BASIL

Vasey *see* VAISEY

Vaslet *see* VALLET

Vaslin *see* JARVIS

Vasques *see* VELASCO

Vass 1. English: status name for a serf, ME, OF *vass(e)* (LL *vassus*, of Celt. origin; cf. W *gwas* boy, Gael. *foss* servant). **2.** English: var. of VAUSE. **3.** Swedish: var. of WASS (2 and 3).

Var. (of 1): **Vasse**.

Dims. (of 1): Fr.: **Vacelet**, **Vasselin**, **Vasselot**.

Pej. (of 1): Fr.: **Vassard**.

Vassall English: status name for a servant or retainer, ME, OF *vassal* (LL *vassallus*, a deriv. of *vassus*; see VASS).

Vassberg *see* WASS

Vasserot *see* VAVASOUR

Vatel *see* WADE

Vatini *see* ABBÉ

Vattiato Italian (Sicily): nickname for a devout Christian, from the Sicilian dial. form, *vattiatu*, of It. *battezzato* baptized (L *baptizātus*, past part. of *baptizāre* to baptize, from Gk *baptizein*, a deriv. of *baptein* to dip).

Vars.: **Battiato**, **Battiati**.

Vaubel *see* VOLPERT

Vaughan 1. Welsh: dim. of BAUGH, with mutation of the initial consonant to *f*. **2.** Irish: Anglicized form of various Gael. surnames, such as Ó *Mocháin* (see MOHAN), Ó *Macháin*, and Ó *Beacháin*.

Vars.: **Vaughn**, **Vaugham**.

Vauquelin French: of uncertain origin. Dauzat derives it from a Gmc personal name *Walklino*, a dim. formation from the element *walk* to full (cf. WALKER). The surname is most common in Normandy, especially in the *département* of Calvados.

Var.: **Gauquelin** (Picardy).

Vaur French: habitation name from any of various minor places that derive their names from the Gaul. element *vober*, *vaber* stream, watercourse, ravine.

Vars.: **Vaure**, **Vaurs**, **Vabre**, **Vaivre**, **Voivre**; **Duvaur**, **Delavaivre**, **Desvoivres**.

Vause English and Scots (Norman): habitation name from any of various places in N France called *Vaux*, from the OF pl. of *val* valley (see VALE). Reaney explains a few early English examples with arts. rather than preps. as being from a southern form of ME *faus* false, untrustworthy (late OE *fals*, from L *falsus*, reinforced by OF *fals*, *faus* from the same source).

Vars.: **Vaus(s)**, **Vaux**; VASS; **Waus(s)**.

Vauth *see* VOGT

Vauthrin *see* WALTER

Vavasour English: from ME, OF *vavasour*, a technical term of the feudal system for a tenant ranking immediately below a baron. Such a tenant would have been a prosperous man, and the surname may have been used for someone in his service more often than for the man himself. The term is probably derived from med. L *vassus vassorum* 'vassal of vassals', i.e. vassal-in-chief; cf. VASS and VASSALL.

Var.: **Vavasseur**.

Dim.: Fr.: **Vasserot**.

Vavilin *see* BABEL

Vavřička *see* LAWRENCE

Vaylet *see* VALLET

Vayne *see* FANE

Vaynzof *see* WEIN

Vaysse French: habitation name from any of the various minor places, mainly in the Massif Central, that get their names from the Gaul. element *vas* hazel.

Vars.: **Vaisse**; **Vayssier**, **Vaissier**, **Veyssier**, **Vayssié**, **Vaissié**, **Veyssié**.

Dims.: **Vayset(te)**, **Vaisset(te)**, **Veyset(te)**, **Voisset**.

Aug.: **Vaissat**.

Collectives: **Vayssière**, **Vaissière**, **Veyssière**. Prov.: **Vayssade**, **Vaissade**, **Veyssade**.

Vaz *see* VELASCO

Vdovenko *see* WIDDOW

Veail *see* VEIL

Veal English (Norman): **1.** nickname for an old man, or for the elder of two bearers of the same given name, from ANF *viel* old (OF *vieil*, from LL *vetulus*, a dim. of class. L *vetus*). **2.** metonymic occupational name for a calf-herd or nickname for a docile, calf-like person, from ANF *ve(e)l* calf (OF *veel*, from LL *vitellus*, a dim. of class. L *vitulus*).

Vars.: **Veall**, **Veel**.

Dims. (of 1): Fr.: **Vieillot**. It.: **Vecchini**, **Vecchiett(in)i**, **Vecchiotto**, **Vecchiotti**, **Vecchiuzzo**. (Of 2): Fr.: **Vellet**, **Vélo(t)**.

Augs. (of 1): It.: **Vecchioni**, **Vecchione**.

Patrs. (from 1): It.: **De Vecchi**; **Del Vecchio** (in part borne by Jews; according to tradition this name was taken by various Jewish families long established in Italy (allegedly since the capture of Jerusalem by the Romans in AD 70) to distinguish themselves from later arrivals who migrated there on being expelled from the Iberian Peninsula after 1492).

Veasey see VAISEY

Vécard see BISHOP

Vecchietti see VEAL

Veck see LEVICK

Vedekhin see BENNETT

Vedovelli see WIDDOW

Veel see VEAL

Veerman Dutch: **1.** occupational name for a trader in feathers, from MDu. *veder(e)* FEATHER + *man* man. The omission of dentals between vowels is a common development in Low Ger. and Du. **2.** occupational name for a ferryman, from MDu. *vēre* ferry + *man* man.

Var.: **Van de Veer**.

Vega Spanish: topographic name for someone who lived by a meadow, Sp. *vega* (of pre-Roman origin, apparently originally denoting irrigated land, and perhaps akin to the Basque elements *ibai* river + the gen. suffix *-ko*, *-ka*).

Vars.: **Vegas**, **Veiga**.

Végh Hungarian: topographic name for someone who lived at the end of a village, from Hung. *vég* end.

Vehster see SILVESTER

Veil **1.** English: occupational name for a watchman, from ANF *veil(le)* watch, guard (L *vigilia* watch, wakefulness). **2.** Jewish (W Ashkenazic): of uncertain origin, according to Kaganoff perhaps chosen as an anagram of LEVI. See also WEIL 2.

Vars. (of 1): **V(e)ail**.

Dims. (of 1): Fr.: **Veillet(et)**, **Veillon**, **Veillot**.

Veinbaum see WEIN

Veinberg see WEINBERG

Veisbein see WHITE

Veitle see VITO

Vejvoda Czech: status name for the administrative head of a district, Czech *Vojevoda*, originally the commander of an army, from Czech *voj* army + *vodič* leader (see VODIČKA).

Vela Spanish: **1.** from a medieval given name, of Gmc (Visigothic) origin. The name represents a reduced from of *Vigila*, from a short form of the various cpd names with a first element *wīg* war. **2.** occupational name for a watchman, a cogn. of VEIL 1.

Patrs. (from 1): Sp.: **Vélez**. Port.: **Velez**.

Velasco Spanish: from a very common medieval given name of Basque origin, from *bela* crow + the dim. suffix *-sko*.

Patrs.: Sp.: **V(el)ázquez**. Port.: **Vasques**, **Vaz**.

Velden see FIELD

Velekhov see BENJAMIN

Velík Czech: from a dim. given name, derived from a short form of any of the OCzech personal names containing the first element *veli-* great (see VELIKOV), for example *Velislav* 'great glory' or *Velimir* 'great fame' (or 'great peace').

Vars.: **Velek**, **Velíšek**.

Velikov **1.** Russian and Bulgarian: patr. from the nickname *Veliki* 'Great', denoting a large man. **2.** Jewish (E Ashkenazic): adoption of the Slav. name. Kaganoff suggests that was it was used as a translation of the Hebr. male given name *Gedalya* 'God is great', but offers no evidence in support of this hypothesis.

Vars. (Jewish): **Velikovski**, **Velkovics**, **Welkovitz**, **Welkovitch**.

Velkel see VOLK

Vellacott English: habitation name from a place in Devon, so called from the OE personal name *Willa* (a short form of the various cpd names containing the first element *will* will, desire) + OE *cot* cottage, dwelling (see COATES).

Vellet see VEAL

Veloso Portuguese: nickname for a hirsute individual, from Port. *veloso* hairy (L *villōsus*, a deriv. of *villus* (shaggy) hair).

Velte see VALENTINE

Venables English (Norman): habitation name from a place in Eure, probably so called from LL *vēnābulum* hunting ground (a deriv. of *vēnāri* to hunt; cf. VENÂNCIO and VENNER 2).

Venâncio Portuguese: from a medieval given name (L *Vēnantius*, a deriv. of *vēnans*, gen. *vēnantis*, pres. part. of *vēnari* to hunt, chase), borne in honour of various early saints of the 3rd–6th cents.

Venc see WENZEL

Vendrell Catalan: habitation name from a place in the province of Tarragona, which derives its name from the OCat. personal name *Venrello* (LL *Venerellus*, a dim. of *Venereus* 'of Venus'). The personal name seems usually to have denoted someone born or baptized on a Friday (LL *Veneris dies* 'Venus' day').

Vendricks see VAANDRAGER

Vendryes French: habitation name from a place in Quercy, apparently so called from LL *Veneriānus (fundus)* '(estate) of *Venerius*', a personal name derived from that of the goddess Venus (cf. VENDRELL).

Venediktov see BENNETT

Venezia Italian (partly Jewish): habitation name or regional name from the city of Venice or the region of Venetia, both called *Venezia* in It., from L *Venetia*. The name derives from the tribal name, of obscure origin, of the *Veneti*, a probably Celt. tribe who inhabited this area before the Roman expansion.
Vars.: It.: **Veneziano**, **Venezian(i)**.

Venezkey *see* WINNICK

Venn *see* FENN

Venner English: **1.** topographic name for someone who lived in a fen or marsh; see FENN. **2.** occupational name for a huntsman, from OF *veneo(u)r* (L *venātor*, a deriv. of *venāri* to hunt).
Var. (of 2): **Venour**.

Venter *see* DEVENTER

Venton *see* FENTON

Ventosa Spanish and Catalan: habitation name from any of various places, for example in the provinces of Burgos, Cuenca, and Salamanca, so called from their exposed and windy situation; the placename is from LL *ventōsa*, a deriv. of *ventus* wind.

Ventre French: nickname for a man with a large paunch, from OF *ventre* belly (L *venter*).
Dim.: **Ventrillon**.

Ventris English: probably a nickname for a daring person, from an aphetic form of ME *aventurous* bold, venturesome (a deriv. of ME, OF *aventure*; see VENTURE). The vocab. word *aventurous* is attested from the 14th cent. onwards, the aphetic form *venturous* from the 16th.
Vars.: **Ventress**; **Venters** (Scots: Fife).

Ventura 1. Italian (partly Jewish): cogn. of VENTURE. **2.** Italian, Spanish, Catalan, and Portuguese: from a medieval given name, a short form of *Bonaventura* 'Good Fortune'. The name was borne in honour of a saint (1221–74) who was given this nickname by St Francis of Assisi when he cured him miraculously as a child.
Vars.: It.: **Venturi**; **Tura**.
Dims.: It.: **Venturella**, **Venturelli**, **Venturino**, **Venturin(i)**, **Venturoli**, **Venturucci**; **Turella**, **Turello**, **Turelli**.

Venture English: nickname for a bold or venturesome person, from an aphetic form of ME, OF *aventure* chance, hazard, exploit (LL *adventūra* chance happening, a deriv. of *advenīre* to happen, come about, lit. arrive, come on the scene). The normal vocab. word in ME was *aventure*, found from the 13th cent.; the aphetic form *venture* occurs from the 15th, shortly before the reintroduction of the L root as mod. Eng. *adventure*.
Var.: **Ventur**.

Venus English (Norman): habitation name from *Venoix* in Calvados, the name of which is of uncertain origin. The surname in this spelling is now found principally in NE England.
Vars.: **Venes(s)**, **Venis(e)**.

Venutelli *see* BENVENUTI

Venzi *see* VINCENT

Véquaud *see* BISHOP

Ver French: **1.** habitation name from any of the numerous places named with the Gaul. element *ver(n)* alder; cf. VARDON, VARNEY, and VERNON. **2.** from the medieval given name *Ver* (L *Vērus* 'True'), which enjoyed some slight currency in honour of a 4th-cent. bishop of Vienne. **3.** var. of VAIR. **4.** var. of *Vert*; see VERDE.
Vars. (of 1): **Verne(s)**, **Vergne**, **Vernhe**; **Lavergne**; **Duverne**; **Vernier**.
Dims. (of 1): Fr.: **Vernet**, **Vergnol(le)**.
Collective (of 1): Fr.: **Vernière**.

Vera Spanish: topographic name for someone who lived on a river bank, Sp. *vera* (of pre-Roman origin), or habitation name from one of the several places named with this word.
Var.: **Veras**.

Verbeek *see* BACH

Verdaguer Catalan: topographic name for someone who lived by a meadow or grassy spot, OCat. *verdeguer* (LL *viridicārium*, a deriv. of *viridis* green; cf. VERDIER).
Var.: **Verdeguer**.

Verde Italian: from It. *verde* green (L *viridis*, akin to *virēre* to bloom, flourish), presumably a nickname for someone who habitually dressed in this colour.
Vars.: **Verdi**; **Virde**, **Virdi** (Sicily); **Lo Verde** (S Italy).
Dims.: It.: **Verdelli**, **Verdini**, **Verdicchio**. Fr.: **Verdel**, **Verd(el)et**, **Verdin**, **Verdon(net)**.
Aug.: It.: **Verdone**.
Pej.: It.: **Verdacci**.
Patr.: It.: **Virdis** (Sicily).

Verden *see* VARDON

Verdier 1. English (Norman) and French: occupational name for a forester, OF *verdier* (LL *viridārius*, a deriv. of *viridis* green; see VERDE). The officials were so called from their green costumes, which may be regarded as an early example of camouflage. **2.** Provençal: topographic name for someone who lived near an orchard or garden, or occupational name for someone who was employed in one, from OProv. *verdier* orchard (LL *virid(i)ārium*).
Vars. (of 1): Eng.: **Varder**. (Of 2): **Verdié**; **Vergès**, **Bergès** (Gascony).

Verdugo Spanish: occupational name for an officer of justice or public executioner, Sp. *verdugo*. The name has been transferred to denote an individual from the rod or staff of office he held, OSp. *verdugo* (LL *vir(i)dūcum* switch, shoot, a deriv. of *viridis* green; cf. VERDE).

Veres *see* VÖRÖS

Vergara Spanish form of Basque **Bergara**: habitation name from places so called (earlier *Virgara*) in the provinces of Guipúzcoa and Navarre, which are of uncertain derivation. The second element is *gara* hill, height, eminence, but the first has not been satisfactorily identified.

Vergeest *see* GEEST

Vergin *see* VIRGO

Verhaar *see* HAAR

Veríssimo Portuguese: from a medieval given name (L *Vērissimus*, superlative of *vērus* true; cf. VER 2), borne in honour of a saint who was martyred at Lisbon at the beginning of the 4th cent. AD in the persecution instigated by the emperor Diocletian.

Verity English (Yorks.): nickname for a truthful person, or perhaps rather for someone who was in the habit of insisting repeatedly on the truth of the stories he told, from ME *verite* truth(fulness) (OF *verité*, from L *vēritās*, a deriv. of *vērus* true; cf. VER 2). The surname may also sometimes have been acquired by someone who had acted the part of the personified quality of Truth in a mystery play or pageant.
Var.: **Varty**.

Verlaine Belgian: of uncertain origin, perhaps a Gallicized form of Flem. *Verlaen*; see LANE 1.

Verlet see VAIR

Verley see VARLEY

Vermaas see MAAS

Vermeer see MEER

Vermette see MOULT

Vern see FERN

Vernay see VARNEY

Verner Scots: of uncertain origin, probably a var. of WARNER (cf. VERNIER 2). Another possibility is that it may be a habitation name from *Vernours* in the former county of Midlothian, but it seems more likely that this placename is derived from the family name.

Vernier French: **1.** topographic name for someone who lived near an alder tree; see VER 1. **2.** hypercorrected form of *Varnier*, the version of WARNER found in E France.

Vernon 1. English (Norman): habitation name from *Vernon* in Eure, so called from the Gaul. element *ver(n)* alder (see VER 1) + the Gallo-Roman local suffix *-o* (gen. *ōnis*). **2.** French: habitation name from the same place as in 1 or from one of the numerous other places in France with the same name and etymology.
Vars.: Eng.: **Vernum, Varnon**. Fr.: **Vernou**.

Verona Italian: habitation name or regional name from the city and province in NE Italy, L *Vērōna*. The town was an important settlement long before its capture by the Romans in 89 BC; its name is of uncertain origin.
Vars.: **Veronese, Veronesi**.

Verpillat see GOUPIL

Verran Cornish: of uncertain origin, possibly a habitation name from *Treverran* in the parish of Tywardreath, so called from Corn. *tre* homestead, settlement + a second element of unknown original form and meaning. Alternatively it may derive from *Veryan* near Tregony. This latter placename is a shortened version of *St Veryan*, itself the result of a misinterpretation of the form *Symphorianus* recorded from 1278 onwards. The church there was dedicated to a certain St Symphorianus, probably the 2nd-cent. martyr of Autun revered in France.

Verrier English (Norman) and French: occupational name for a maker of glass objects, OF *verrie(o)r* (from *verre, voir(r)e* glass, L *vitrum*).
Vars.: Eng.: **Verriour**. Fr.: **Veyrier, Leverrier**.

Verschoor see SCHEUER

Vershinin Russian: patr. from the nickname *Vershina* 'Mountain Peak', given presumably to a particularly tall person or to someone who lived at the top of a hill.

Versluijs see SLUIS

Verspreeuwen see SPARROW

Verty see VIRTUE

Very English: habitation name from an unidentified place in N France named with the Gaul. element *ver(n)* alder (see VER 1, and cf. VARNEY) or the Gallo-Roman personal name *Vērus* (see VER 2) + the local suffix *-ācum*.

Vescovini see BISHOP

Veselov Russian: patr. from the nickname *Vesyoly* 'Cheerful'.
Var.: **Veselago** (for the ending, cf. ZHIVAGO).
Dim.: Pol.: **Wesołek**.
Habitation name: Pol.: **Wesołowski**.

Vesey see VAISEY

Vespucci Italian: nickname for a waspish individual, from a dim. form of It. *vespa* wasp (L *vespa*).

Vessey English (Norman): habitation name from a place in La Manche, so called from the Gallo-Roman personal name *Vessius* or *Vettius* (of uncertain origin) + the local suffix *-ācum*.
Var.: **Vessie** (Scotland).

Vester see SILVESTER

Vetrov Russian: patr. from the nickname *Veter* 'Wind' (earlier also 'Storm'), perhaps denoting someone with a blustery or an inconstant temperament (cf. the Czech vocab. word *větroplach* madcap, devil-may-care).

Vetter German: nickname from MHG *veter(e)* uncle, nephew (i.e. father's brother or brother's son). The word is from OHG *fetiro* (a deriv. of *fater* father), which was used more generally of various male relatives; the meaning of the mod. Ger. word *Vetter* is 'cousin'. In N Germany the vocab. word was sometimes used as a given name, and this may lie behind some cases of the surname.
Var.: **Vötter** (Bavaria).
Dims.: **Vetterle**; **Vötterl** (Bavaria).

Vettorel see VICTOR

Veughelen see VOGEL

Veverka Czech: nickname meaning 'squirrel', applied either to someone who bore a fancied resemblance to a squirrel, or perhaps to someone who habitually dressed in squirrel fur (cf. Fr. VAIR).

Vexelbaum see WECHSLER

Veyrier see VERRIER

Veyron see VAIR

Veyset *see* VAYSSE

Veysey *see* VAISEY

Vezey *see* VAISEY

Vezin *see* VOISIN

Vial *see* VITALE

Viana Portuguese: habitation name from *Viana* do Castelo, a city in the province of Minho, or *Viana* do Alentejo, a town in the province of Alto Alentejo.

Vianelli *see* VIVIAN

Vicario Italian: occupational name for a parish priest (see VICKAR), or for any ecclesiastical or civil official who carried out duties on behalf of an absentee office-holder or who deputized for a magistrate.

Vars.: **Vicaro**, **Vicari**.

Vicars *see* VICKERS

Viceconte *see* VISCONTE

Vicedomini *see* VISDOMINI

Vićentijević *see* VINCENT

Vích *see* VICTOR

Vicinelli *see* VOISIN

Vick *see* FREDERICK, LEVICK

Vickar **1.** English: occupational name for a parish priest, ME *vica(i)re, vikere* (OF *vicaire*, from L *vicārius* substitute, deputy, a deriv. of *vices* place, turn). The word was originally used to denote someone who carried out pastoral duties on behalf of the absentee holder of a benefice. It became a regular word for a parish priest because in practice most benefice-holders were absentees. See also VICARIO. **2.** Irish: surname used as an approximate translation of Gael. *Mac an Abadh* 'son of the abbot'; see ABBÉ.

Vars. (of 1): **Vicker**, **Vicar**; **Vicar(e)y**, **Viccary**, **Vickary**, **Vickery** (S and W English, from a ME var. *vicarie*, derived directly from L *vicārius*).

Patrs. (from 1): Eng.: **VICKERS**. Sc.: **McVicar**, **McVicker** (Gael. **Mac Bhiocair**).

Vickers English: patr. for the son of a vicar or, perhaps in most cases, occupational name for the servant of a vicar, from ME *vicare* (see VICKAR) + the possessive ending *-s*. In many cases it may also represent an elliptical form of a topographic name; cf. PARSONS.

Vars.: **Vic(c)ars**, **Vickars**; **Vickarman** (occupational name only).

Vickmann *see* WIK

Vico Italian: **1.** topographic name for someone who lived in a village as opposed to an outlying farmstead, from OIt. *vico* settlement, village (L *vīcus*). **2.** aphetic short form of the medieval given name *Lodovico*; see LEWIS 1.

Vars.: **Vigo**, **Vig(g)hi** (N Italy). (Of 1 only): **Da Vico**; **Vig(i)ano**, **Vigiani**, **Vigato**.

Dims.: **Vigetti**, **Vigotti**, **Vigutto**, **Viguzzi**, **Vigolo**.

Augs.: **Vigone**, **Vigoni**.

Patr. (from 2 only): **De Vico**.

Victor French: from a medieval given name (L *Victor* 'Conqueror', an agent deriv. of *vincere* to win, defeat).

Early Christians often bore this name in reference to Christ's victory over sin and death, and there are a large number of saints so called. Some of the principal ones, who contributed to the popularity of the given name in the Middle Ages, are a 2nd-cent. pope, a 3rd-cent. Mauritanian martyr, and a 5th-cent. bishop of Cologne. See also AVIGDOR.

Dims.: Prov.: **Victouron**. It.: **Vittorelli**, **Vettorello**, **Vettorel(li)**, **Vettoretti**, **Vettoretto**. Port.: **Vitorino**. Czech: **Vích**. Pol.: **Wiktorczyk**.

Patrs.: It.: **De Vettori**. Swed.: **Victorsson**. Pol.: **Wiktorowicz**. Beloruss.: **Viktorevich**. Croatian: **Vitorović**.

Habitation name: Pol.: **Wiktorowski**.

Vida *see* GUY, VITA

Vidaković *see* VITO

Vidal *see* VITALE

Videan *see* VIVIAN

Videira Portuguese: topographic name for someone who lived by a vineyard or in a house distinguished by an ornamental vine, from Port. *videira* vine (LL *vītāria*, a deriv. of class. L *vītis*).

Videll *see* WEIDE

Videneev *see* BENNETT

Vidler English: **1.** var. of *Fidler* (see FIEDLER), with the voiced initial consonant characteristic of S dialects of ME. **2.** nickname from the ANF phrase *vis de leu* 'Wolf-face' (from *vis* face, L *vīsus* appearance + *de* of, L *de* from + *leu* wolf, L *lupus*).

Viebig *see* FIEBACK

Viegas Portuguese: of uncertain derivation, probably a macaronic name, the first letter representing a reduced form of the Arabic prefix *ibn* son of, the remainder being the medieval given name *Egas*, patr. from the personal name *Egga*. The source of this is not clear; it may be of Gmc origin (cf. ECK 2).

Vieillot *see* VEAL

Vieira Portuguese: **1.** religious byname from Port. *veiria* scallop (LL *veneria*, a deriv. of the name of *Venus* (cf. VENDRELL and VENDRYES); the goddess was often depicted riding on a scallop). The scallop was a symbol of the pilgrim who had been to the shrine of Santiago de Compostela. **2.** habitation name from any of various minor places so called because they were situated in scallop-shaped depressions.

Viel *see* VITO

Vielmetti *see* WILLIAM

Viennet *see* VIVIAN

Vierin *see* OLIVER

Vietze *see* VINCENT

Vigano *see* VICO

Vigder *see* AVIGDOR

Vigeon *see* VIVIAN

Viggars English: nickname for a sturdy person, from ME *vigrus* strong, lusty (OF *vigoro(u)s*, a deriv. of *vigour* strength, vitality, L *vigor*, from *vigēre* to flourish). There may have been some confusion with VICKERS.

Vars.: **Vigars**, **Vig(g)ers**, **Vigo(u)rs**, **Vigu(r)s**, **Vigrass**.

Viglia *see* WILLIAM

Vigne *see* VINE

Vignodolli *see* BENVENUTI

Vikmann *see* WIK

Viktorevich *see* VICTOR

Vilagrassa Catalan: habitation name from a place in the province of Lérida, so called from Cat. *vila* settlement (see VILLE) + *grassa* (fem.) lush, fertile (L *grassa*).

Var.: **Villagrasa**.

Vilalta Catalan: habitation name from any of various places, for example in the province of Lérida, so called from Cat. *vila* settlement (see VILLE) + *alta* (fem.) high (L *alta*).

Vilaplana Catalan: habitation name from a place in the province of Tarragona, so called from Cat. *vila* settlement (see VILLE) + *plana* (fem.) flat (L *plāna*).

Vilaseca Catalan: habitation name from places in the provinces of Barcelona and Tarragona, so called from Cat. *vila* settlement (see VILLE) + *seca* (fem.) dry (L *sicca*).

Vilhelmsen *see* WILLIAM

Villain English and French: from ME, OF *vilein, vilain* feudal serf, peasant owing personal service to his lord (LL *villānus*, a deriv. of *villa* estate; see VILLE). The low status of such serfs led to the semantic decline of the vocab. word to mod. Eng. *villain* rogue, evildoer, mod. Fr. *vilain* ugly, naughty, but these sense developments occurred late and are unlikely to lie behind any cases of the surname.

Vars.: Eng.: **Vilain**, **Villin**. Fr.: **Vilain**, **Vil(l)an**, **Levillain**.

Dims.: Fr.: **Villaneau**. It.: **Villanelli**, **Villanello**, **Villanetti**.

Villalba Spanish: habitation name from any of the numerous places so called from Sp. *villa* settlement (see VILLE) + *alba* (fem.) white (L *alba*).

Villalobos Spanish: habitation name from a place in the province of Zamora, so called from LL *villa* settlement (see VILLE) + the personal name *Lupus* 'Wolf'.

Villanueva Spanish: habitation name from any of the numerous places so called, which get their name from Sp. *villa* settlement (see VILLE) + *nueva* (fem.) new (L *nova*).

Villarreal Spanish: habitation name from any of various places, for example in the province of Badajoz, so called from Sp. *villa* settlement (see VILLE) + *real* royal (L *rēgālis*). The places were so named from having some particular connection with the Crown.

Villarrubia Spanish: habitation name from places in the provinces of Ciudad Real, Cuenca, and Toledo, so called from Sp. *villa* settlement (see VILLE) + *rubia* (fem.) red(dish) (L *rubea*).

Villate Basque: habitation name composed of the elements *villa* settlement (a Romance borrowing; see VILLE) + *ate* door; the name seems to have referred to a settlement situated by a pass between hills.

Villaverde Spanish: habitation name from any of the numerous places so called, from Sp. *villa* settlement (see VILLE) + *verde* green (see VERDE).

Ville French: topographic name for someone who lived in a village as opposed to an isolated farmhouse, or in the town as opposed to the countryside, from OF *ville* settlement (L *villa* country house, estate, later used of a group of houses forming a settlement).

Vars.: **Laville**, **De(la)ville**, **Desvilles**.

Cat.: **Vila(s)**; **Vilà**.

Dims.: Fr.: **Vil(l)ette**, **Devillette**, **Desvillettes**; **Villon**, **Villot**. It.: **Villetti**, **Villino**, **Villotta**, **Villotti**. Cat.: **Vilella**. Port.: **Vilela**.

Villefranche French: habitation name from any of various places, in more than a dozen *départements*, so called from OF *ville* settlement (see VILLE) + *franche* (fem.) free (see FRANK 2). The settlements were so named because they were exempt from certain feudal taxes or obligations, normally as a reward for some special service.

Villegas Spanish: habitation name from places in the provinces of Albacete and Burgos, so called from Sp. *villa* settlement (see VILLE) + the personal name *Egas* (see VIEGAS).

Villena Spanish: habitation name from a place in the province of Alicante, so called from LL *Belliēna*, a deriv. of the personal name *Bellius*, of uncertain origin.

Villiers English (Norman) and French: habitation name from any of the numerous places in France called *Vill(i)er(s)*, from LL *villāre* outlying farm, dependent settlement, a deriv. of *villa* village, settlement (see VILLE, and cf. CASA and CASALE).

Vars.: Eng.: **Villers**, **Villar(s)**, **Villis**. Fr.: **Villers**; **Devilliers**, **Deviller**, **Divill(i)er**.

Dims.: Prov.: **Vil(l)aret**, **Villarel**, **Villaron**. Cat.: **Vilardell**, **Vilaró**.

Villsson *see* WILL

Vilnai *see* WILLNER

Vinagre Portuguese: nickname for a man of sour temperament, from Port. *vinagre* vinegar (L *vīnum acre* sour wine).

Viñals *see* VINYALS

Vinblad *see* WEIN

Vincent 1. English and French: from a medieval given name (L *Vincentius*, a deriv. of *vincens*, gen. *vincentis*, pres. part. of *vincere* to conquer; cf. VICTOR). The name was borne by a 3rd-cent. Sp. martyr widely venerated in the Middle Ages and by a 5th-cent. monk and writer of Lérins, as well as various other early saints. In E Europe the name was popular in honour of Wincenty Kadłubek (d. 1223), a bishop of Cracow and an early chronicler; he was venerated especially in Silesia and his head was believed to rest in Wrocław. 2. Irish: Anglicized form of Gael. *Mac Dhuibhinse*; see McAVINCHY.

Vars. (of 1): Eng.: **Vincett**; **Vinsen**, **Vinson**, **Vinsun**. Fr.: **Vincens**; **Vinson**, **Vinçon**.

Dims. (of 1): Eng.: **Vince** (E Anglia). Fr.: **Vincendeau**, **Vincendet**, **Vincendon**, **Vincenot**, **Vinçonneau**, **Vinsonneau**,

Vincot. It.: **Vinci**, **Venzi**; **Vincenzot(to)**. Ger.: **Vinz(el)**, **Finzel**; **Zen(t)z**. Ger. (under Slav. influence): **Vietze**, **Fietz(e)**; **Wien(t)zek**, **Fietzek**, **Fietzke**. Pol.: **Więcek**; **Winceniuk**. Hung.: **Vinc(z)e**.

Aug. (of 1): It.: **Cenzon**.

Patrs. (from 1): It.: **De Vincenzo** (S Italy). Pol.: **Wincentowicz**. Croatian: **Vićentijević**.

Patrs. (from dims. of 1): It.: **Da Vinci**. Low Ger.: **Zensen**. Pol.: **Wi(ę)czkiewicz**, **Węcewicz**, **Węczkowicz**.

Habitation names: Pol.: **W(i)ęckowski**.

Vine English: topographic name for someone who lived near a vineyard, or metonymic occupational name for a vine dresser, from ME *vine* vine(yard) (OF *vi(g)ne*, from L *vīnea*, a deriv. of *vīnum* wine). Vine growing was formerly more common in England than it is now, and there are several minor places in S England named from their vineyard, any of which may be partial sources of the surname. See also WINYARD.

Vars.: **Vines**, **Vigne(s)**; **Viner**, **Vyner** (agent derivs.).

Dims.: Fr.: **Vigneau**, **Vignon**, **Vignol(le)**. It.: **Vignini**, **Vignola**, **Vignol(in)i**, **Vignolo**, **Vignot(t)o**, **Vignozzi**.

Augs.: It.: **Vignone**, **Vignoni**.

Habitation names: Czech: **Vinecký**, **Vinický** (from places named *Vinec* and *Vinice* respectively, both from the vocab. word *vinice* vineyard).

Viney English: apparently a habitation name from some place in N France named from LL *vīnētum* vineyard, a deriv. of *vīnea* vine (see VINE).

Vinitzky *see* WINNICK

Vinnick *see* FENWICK

Vinogradov Russian and Jewish (E Ashkenazic): patr. from Russ. *vinograd* grape(s), raisin(s) (a collective singular, ultimately a borrowing from a Gmc cogn. of WINYARD; an earlier meaning was 'vine' and before that 'vineyard'). The name may occasionally have been taken as an occupational name, but for the most part it is ornamental (cf. WEIN).

Vars.: Jewish: **Winogradow**; **Winograd**, **Vinogradski**; **Weingrod** (influenced by Ger. *Wein* or Yid. *vayn* wine); **Wajngrod** (Pol. spelling).

Vinokur Jewish (E Ashkenazic): occupational name for a distiller, Russ. *vinokur* (from *vino* wine, earlier used also of spirits (L *vīnum*, borrowed by way of a Gmc intermediary; cf. VINOGRADOV) + *kurit* to distil (in mod. Russ. 'to smoke')).

Vars.: **Winokur**, **Winocur**; **Winocour** (a Fr. spelling).

Vinter *see* WINTER

Vinuesa Spanish: habitation name from a place in the province of Soria. The name is probably of Italic origin, identical with that of *Venosa* in Italy (L *Venusia*), a town on the borders of Apulia and Lucania, birthplace of the poet Horace.

Vinyals Catalan: habitation name from any of various minor places so called from a pl. form of Cat. *vinyal* land planted with vines (LL *vineāle*, a deriv. of *vinea* vineyard; cf. VINE).

Var.: **Viñals** (Spanish spelling).

Vio *see* VITO

Viola Italian and Spanish: **1.** from a medieval female given name, originally an affectionate nickname, from It., Sp. *viola* violet (L *viola*). **2.** metonymic occupational name for a player of the musical instrument of this name (from LL *vītula*; see FIEDLER).

Vars.: It.: **Violi**; **La Viola** (Apulia).

Dims.: It.: **Violetta**, **Violetti**, **Violino**, **Violin(i)**. Fr.: **Violleau**, **Viol(l)et**, **Viol(l)ot**.

Virde *see* VERDE

Virgili Catalan: from a medieval given name (L *Virgilius*, *Vergilius*, a Roman family name of unknown derivation; perhaps from *virga* stick or *virgo* virgin, or of Etruscan origin). This was the name of the most famous of all Roman poets, who in the Middle Ages was considered to have been a fount of all kinds of wisdom and virtue, and thus almost an honorary Christian. However, the given name may also have been bestowed in honour of a 7th-cent. Christian saint, Virgilius of Arles.

Virgo English: of uncertain origin. The surname coincides in form with L *virgo*, gen. *virginis*, maiden, from which is derived (via OF) mod. Eng. *virgin*. It is possible that the surname was originally a nickname for someone who had played the part of the Blessed Virgin Mary in a mystery play. This, and the vernacular vars. listed below, may also have been nicknames for shy young men, or possibly ironically for notorious lechers.

Vars.: **Virgoe**, **Vergo**; **Virgin**, **Vergin(e)**.

Virley *see* VARLEY

Virtanen Finnish: ornamental name from Finn. *virta* stream + the gen. suffix *-nen*, perhaps in some cases chosen as a topographic name by someone who lived by a stream. This is the most common Finnish surname.

Virtue English and Scots: nickname from ME, OF *vertu* moral worth or goodness (L *virtūs* manliness, valour, worth, a deriv. of *vir* man). This may have been bestowed on a good or pious person, it may alternatively have been a sarcastic nickname for a prig, or it may have been borne by someone who had played the part of Virtue in a medieval mystery play.

Var.: **Verty** (Scots).

Visconte Italian: from It. *visconte*, a title of rank (med. L *vicecomes* deputy of a COUNT). Unusually (since most noble families took their surnames from their estates), the surname was sometimes of literal application, but it is also no doubt in part a nickname for someone who gave himself airs and graces, and in part an occupational name for someone employed by a viscount.

Vars.: **Visconti**; **Bisconti** (S Italy); **Viceconte**, **Viceconti** (learned alterations).

Visdomini Italian: occupational name for the steward of an estate or the headman of a village, from med. L *vicedominus* deputy, local representative of the lord.

Vars.: **Bisdomini**; **Vicedomino**, **Vicedomini**, **Vicidomini** (learned alterations).

Víšek *see* VITO

Vissers *see* FISHER

Vita 1. Italian: from a medieval female given name, originally an affectionate nickname, from It. *vita* life (L *vita*). **2.** Jewish (Ashkenazic): from the Yid. female given name *Vite* (of Romance origin, adopted as a translation of the Hebr. name *Chaya* 'Life'; cf. VITALE 2).

Var. (of 1): It.: **Vida** (N Italy).

Metrs. (from 1): **De Vita**. (From 2): **Vitas, Vites, Wit(t)es; Vitin** (E Ashkenazic).

Metrs. (from dims. of 2): **Wittels, Vitelson, Witelson, Witelzon, Vitalzon, Vit(t)lin, Vitlov** (from the Yid. dim. given name *Vitl*; the last two are E Ashkenazic); **Vitkes** (from the E Yid. dim. given name *Vitke*), **Vitkin(d), Witkin(d)** (showing influence of Yid. *kind* child; see SÜSSKIND). See also VITO.

Vitale 1. Italian: from a medieval given name (L *Vitālis*, a deriv. of *vita* life; cf. VITA). The name was popular with Christians as a symbol of their belief in eternal life, and was borne by a dozen early saints. **2.** Jewish: borrowing of the It. name, adopted as a translation of the Hebr. male given name *Chayim* 'Life'; cf. HYAM.

Vars.: It.: **Vitali; Vidale, Vidali** (N Italy); **Vidal, Viale, Vial(i)** (Venetia); **Biale** (Liguria). Jewish: **Vitalis**.

Dims.: It.: **Vitaletti, Vitalitti, Vitalini; Vialetto**. Fr.: **Vidalin, Vi(d)alet, Vid(al)on, Vialon, Vid(al)ot, Vialot**.

Augs.: It.: **Vitalone, Vitaloni**.

Patr.: Eng.: **Vials**.

Vitet *see* GUY

Vito Italian: from a medieval given name (L *Vitus*, from *vita* life; cf. VITA). The name was popular in the Middle Ages as the result of the cult of an early Christian martyr in S Italy, about whom very little of historical value is known. He was regarded as a patron against epilepsy and the nervous tremor named after him, 'St Vitus' dance'. His cult spread into Germany and thence through E Europe, where the name was reinforced by native Slav. names such as *Vitoslav* and *Vitomír*, with a first element derived from OSlav. *vitati* inhabit or welcome.

Vars.: It.: **Vit(t)i; Vidi, Vi(d)o** (N Italy; see also GUY); **Bitto, Bit(t)i** (S Italy).

Dims.: It.: **Vitelli, Vitello** (see also VEAL); **Vitillo, Vitullo, Vitulli, Vitolo, Vitucci, Vitussi, Vitt(u)ozzo; Vidollo, Vidos(si), Vidusso, Vi(d)us(si), Vidotti, Vidotto** (N Italy); **Viel(li)** (Venetia); **Vietti, Vietto, Viotti, Viotto** (NW Italy); **Bitelli, Bitetti, Bitetto, Bittini, Bittolo** (S Italy). Ger.: **Veitle; Vaitl** (Bavaria). Czech: **Vítek, Vitáček, Vitášek, Vitoušek; Víšek**. Pol.: **Witek, Witaszek**.

Augs.: It.: **Vitone, Vitoni, Vidoni**.

Patrs.: It.: **De Vito, De Viti; De Vit, De Vio** (Venetia). Ger.: **Vix, F(e)ix**. Low Ger.: **Vieten, Viets(en)**. Pol.: **Witasiak, Witczak**. Czech: **Vitů**. Croatian: **Vit(ov)ić, Vid(ov)ić**.

Patrs. (from dims.): It.: **Vitelleschi**. Low Ger.: **Vietken, Vietjen**. Pol.: **Witkiewicz**. Croatian: **Vidaković**. Jewish (E Ashkenazic): **Witkovitz, Witkowitz, Vitkovski, Vitkovsky, Wit(t)kowski, Wit(t)kowsky, Witkowsky** (in part adoptions of the non-Jewish surname, but more often derivs. of VITA 2).

Habitation names: Pol.: **Witkowski**. Czech: **Vítovec, Vítovský**.

Vitry French: habitation name from any of various places, for example in Aube, Loiret, Marne, and Seine, so called from the Gallo-Roman personal name *Victorius* (a deriv. of VICTOR) + the local suffix -*ācum*.

Var.: **Vitrey** (places in Haute-Saône and Meurthe-et-Moselle).

Vittor *see* VICTOR

Vius *see* VITO

Vivaldi Italian: from a Gmc personal name composed of the elements *wīg* war + *wald* rule.

Vivar *see* WEIHER

Vivas Catalan: from a medieval given name or byname bestowed on children for the sake of a good omen, from the expression *vivas* 'may you live', found in Catalan, Spanish, and in Latin.

Var.: **Vives**.

Vivian English and French: from a medieval given name (L *Viviānus*, a deriv. of *vivus* living, alive; cf. VITO and VITALE). The name was borne by a 5th-cent. bishop of Saintes, and was popular among the Normans, by whom it was introduced to England.

Vars.: Eng.: **Vivien, Vyvyan; Videan, Vidge(o)n, Vigeon; Fiddian, Fidge(o)n; Phyt(h)ian, Phethean**. Fr.: **Vivien, Viviand, Vivant, Vivie**.

Dims.: Eng.: **Fidkin, Fitkin**. Fr.: **Viennet, Viénet, Vianey, Viennot, Viénot**. It.: **Vianello, Vianelli, Vianini**.

Patr.: Eng.: **Vivians**.

Vix *see* VITO

Vizard *see* WISHART

Vizcaíno Spanish: habitation name or regional name for someone from the town or province of Biscay (Sp. *Vizcaya*) in N Spain. The placename derives from Basque *bizkai* ridge + the def. art. -*a*.

Vlach Czech: from *vlach* Italian. This vocab. word originally meant 'foreigner'; it is cogn. with Ger. *welsch* Latin, Romance-speaking, and ultimately with OE *wælisc* foreign and mod. Eng. *Welsh*; see WALSH. At the time when surnames were formed, the Czech word was applied chiefly to Italians, but also to the Rumanians (Walachians).

Dims.: Czech: **Vlášek, Vlašánek, Vlašín**. Pol.: **Włoszek**.

Patrs.: Croatian: **Vlahović, Vlašić, Vlajić**. Pol.: **Włochowicz**. Russ.: **Volokhov, Volosh(en)inov**.

Patr. (from a dim.): Croatian: **Vlajković**.

Habitation name: Czech: **Vlachovský**.

Vladimirov Russian and Bulgarian: patr. from the given name *Vladimir*, which is composed of the Slav. elements *vlad*- wealth, rule + *mer* famous, glorious. This was one of the very few Slav. names acceptable for baptism in the Orthodox Church, due to the acceptability to the Church of the immensely popular St Vladimir (d. 1015), the first Christian Grand Duke of Kiev (who, as a matter of fact, himself bore the baptismal name *Vasili*).

Var.: Russ.: **Volodimerov**.

Dims. (not patrs.): Ukr.: **Volodko**. Beloruss.: **Volodzhko**. Pol.: **Włodek, Wołodko**. Ger. (of Slav. origin): **Wlodasch, Wlotzka, Wlotzke**.

Dims. (patrs.): Russ.: **Volodin, Volodichev**. Ukr.: **Volodich**. Pol.: **Wołodkiewicz, Włodkowicz**. Rumanian (of Slav. origin): **Vladescu**.

Vladyka Czech: occupational name approximately equivalent to Eng. *steward* (see STEWART). The Czech vocab. word *vladyka* also came to denote a minor rank of aristocracy, while in the larger cities it was a term for an alderman, and the surname in many cases is probably a status name from one of these.

Vlasák Czech: nickname for a man with thick or long hair, from Czech *vlas* hair + *-ák* suffix denoting human nouns, or occupational name for a buyer of hair, where the suffix is agentive.

Var.: **Vlas**.

Dim.: **Vlásek**.

Vlášek *see* VLACH

Vlasenko *see* BLAISE

Vlček *see* WILK

Vleminckx *see* FLEMING

Vluchkov *see* WILK

Voak *see* FOULKES

Vobora Czech: **1.** topographic name for someone who lived by an enclosure, Czech *(v)obora*. The vocab. word came to denote specifically an enclosed forest in which red deer were kept for hunting, and the surname may also be a metonymic occupational name for a gamekeeper. **2.** habitation name from a place called *Obora*, named with Czech *(v)obora* enclosure.

Vars. (of 1): **Voborník**. (Of 2): **Voborský**.

Vobořil Czech: nickname for an irritable person, from Czech *(v)obořit se* to speak angrily or gruffly.

Vodička Czech: topographic name for someone living by a body of water, or a nickname for a teetotaller, from a dim. of Czech *voda* water. The name was also used as a humorous nickname for an innkeeper.

Vodopyanov Russian: patr. from the nickname *Vodopyan* 'Water-drinker' (from *voda* water + *pit* to drink), presumably denoting a teetotaller. Cf. BOILEAU and DRINKWATER.

Vogel **1.** German and Dutch/Flemish: metonymic occupational name for a bird-catcher or nickname for a timid person, from Ger. *Vogel* bird (MHG, MLG *vogel*, OHG *fogul*; cf. FOWLE). **2.** Jewish (Ashkenazic): ornamental name from mod. Ger. *Vogel* bird.

Vars.: Du., Flem.: **De Vogel**, **(De) Voogel**. Flem. only: **(De) Voghel**. Jewish: **Fogiel** (a Pol. spelling); **Vogelman**, **Fogel(man)**; **Feigelman** (from Yid. *feygl* birds, which in NE Yid. also had a sing. meaning); **Fogelmanas** (with Lithuanian nom. sing. ending *-as*).

Dims.: Ger.: **Vögele(in)**; **Vögeli** (Switzerland).

Patrs.: Du.: **Vogels**. Flem.: **Voghels**, **Veughelen**.

Cpds (ornamental): Swed.: **Fogelberg** ('bird hill'); **Fogelström** ('bird river'). Jewish: **Fogelbaum** ('bird tree'); **Vogelblat** ('bird leaf'); **Vogelfang** ('bird claw'); **Fogelfuss**, **Feigelfuss** ('bird foot'); **Fogelhut** ('bird hat'); **Fogelnest** ('bird nest'); **Vogelsang**, **Fogelsang** ('bird song'); **Fogelstein**, **Feigelstein** ('bird stone'); **Feigelstock** ('bird stick').

Vogt German: occupational name for a bailiff or farm manager, MHG *voget* (LL *advocātus*, past part. of *advocāre* to call up (to help); cf. AVOGADRO). The term originally described someone who appeared before a court on behalf of some party not permitted to make direct representa-

tions, often an ecclesiastical body which was not supposed to have any dealings with temporal authorities.

Vars.: **Vögt**, **Voi(g)t**, **Voigh(t)**; **Vauth**, **Faut(h)**, **Fath(mann)** (Franconia, Hesse).

Dims.: Ger.: **Vögtle**; **Voitl** (Bavaria).

Patrs.: Low Ger.: **Vogts**, **Vögting**. Flem., Du.: **Vagts**, **Vagedes**.

Voiello *see* BOEUF

Voigh *see* VOGT

Voisey *see* VAISEY

Voisin English (Norman) and French: from OF *voisin* (ANF *veisin*) neighbour (L *vicīnus*, a deriv. of *vicus* village, district; cf. VICO). The application is uncertain; it may be a nickname for a 'good neighbour', or for someone who used this word as a frequent term of address.

Var.: Eng.: **Vezin**.

Dim.: It.: **Vicinelli**.

Patr.: Fr.: **Duvoisin** (with fused prep. and article *du* 'of the').

Voisset *see* VAYSSE

Voitekhov *see* VOJTĚCH

Voivre *see* VAUR

Vojtěch Czech: from a Czech personal name, *Vojtěch*, composed of the elements *voi* soldier + *tech* comfort, consolation. This, along with its Pol. cogn. *Wojciech* and the Ger. form *Wozzek*, was a popular given name among Christians in E Europe, mainly because of the cult of St Vojtěch (*c* 955–97). The latter was bishop of Prague from 982 onwards. In 995 he was expelled from Bohemia and in 996 he went to Poland on a mission to the Prussians (members of a heathen Baltic-speaking people, not the German-speakers who later took their name). He was killed by the Prussians in 997, and was canonized in 999. He is regarded as the first Polish saint; in Polish he is known as St Wojciech, in German as St Adalbert (or Albert) of Prague.

Vars.: **Vojtek**, **Vojtěk**, **Vojtík**, **Vojta(s)**, **Vojtaš**; **Vojka**.

Dims.: Czech: **Vojtíšek**, **Vojtášek**, **Vojtárek**. Pol.: **Wojcieszek**, **Wojtczyk**, **Wojtasik**, **Wojtylak**; **Woś**, **Wosik**, **Woszczyk**. Ger. (of Slav. origin): **Wuttschke**, **Wutzke**, **Woitke**.

Patrs.: Pol.: **Wojciechowicz**, **Wojtowicz**, **Wojtanowicz**, **Wojtczak**, **Wojtysiak**. Beloruss.: **Voit(s)ekhov**.

Patrs. (from dims.): Pol.: **Wojtkiewicz**; **Wojtkowiak**; **Woszczak**. Habitation names: Pol.: **Wojciechowski**, **Wojtaszewski**, **Wojtanowski**, **Wojtkowski**. Czech: **Vojtěchovský**.

Vokes *see* FOULKES

Vokoun Czech: **1.** nickname for someone supposedly bearing some resemblance to a perch (the fish), from Czech *(v)okoun* perch. **2.** nickname for someone with prominent eyes, from a deriv. of Czech *oko* eye.

Volák Czech: occupational name for a keeper of or dealer in oxen, from Czech *vůl* ox (cogn. with Pol. *wół*).

Habitation name: Pol.: **Wołowski**.

Volchik *see* WILK

Volchonsky *see* OLSZEWSKI

Volek *see* ULRICH

Volfing *see* WOLF

Völgyi Hungarian: topographic name for someone who lived in a valley, Hung. *völgy*.

Volk 1. German: from a medieval given name, a short form of various Gmc personal names with the first element *folk* people (cf. FOULKES). **2.** Jewish (Ashkenazic): apparently from the mod. Ger. vocab. word *Volk* people or an adoption of the Ger. surname, but perhaps also influenced by Pol. *wilk* wolf, Czech *vlk* (see WILK).

Vars. (of 1): **Folk**, **Volke**, **Voll(e)**, **Völke**. (Of 2): **Volkman(n)**, **Folk(man)**.

Dims. (of 1): Ger.: **Völkel**, **Velkel**, **Fölkel**, **Felkel**; **Vol(t)z**, **Völ(t)z**, **Völzle** (Swabia). Low Ger.: **Volkmann**. Fris.: **Fokema**. Ger. (of Slav. origin): **Völsch**, **Vözke**, **Fölsch**, **Fölske**.

Patrs. (from 1): Low Ger.: **Focken(s)**, **Focks**, Fox. Fris.: **Focken**, **Focken(g)a**.

Patrs. (from 1) (dims.): Ger.: **Völser**, **Fölser**.

Volk *see* FOULKES

Volkering *see* FULCHER

Volkerts *see* FOLKARD

Voller *see* FULLER

Volmer German: from the Gmc personal name *Folkmar*, composed of the elements *folk* people, race + *meri, mari* famous.

Vars.: **Vollmer**, **Vol(l)mert**, **Völlmer**, **Volk(a)mer**, **Völkmer**, **Vollmar**, **Völlmar**, **Volkmar**; **Volkmeier**.

Dims.: **Völm(le)**; **Völmy**; **Felmy** (Switzerland). Low Ger.: **Völlmeke**.

Volodich *see* VLADIMIROV

Volokhov *see* VLACH

Volpe 1. Italian: nickname for a crafty person, from It. *volpe* fox (L *vulpes*, an ultimate cogn. of WOLF; see also GOUPIL). **2.** Jewish (E Ashkenazic): habitation name from a town in Belorussia, SE of Grodno, the Yid. name of which is *Volp(e)* (Beloruss., Russ. *Volpa*, Pol. *Wołpa*).

Vars. (of 1): **Volpi**, **Vulpi**, **La Volpe**. (Of 2): **Volper**, **Wolpe(r)**.

Dims. (of 1): **Volpino**, **Volpin(i)**, **Volp(ic)ella**, **Volp(ic)elli**.

Augs. (of 1): **Volpone**, **Volponi**.

Patrs. (from 1): **Volpis**, **Vulpis**; **Della Volpe**, **Dalla Volpe**.

Volpert 1. Low German: from the Gmc personal name *Folkberht*, composed of the elements *folk* people, race + *berht* bright, famous. **2.** Jewish (Ashkenazic): adoption of the name in 1 above, or possibly a var., with excrescent *-t*, of *Volper* (see VOLPE 2).

Vars. (of 1): **Volber(t)**. (Of 2): **Wolpert**.

Dims.: Ger.: **Völpel**, **Vopel**, **Vaupel**, **Vaubel**.

Patrs.: Low Ger.: **Volper(t)s**, **Volbers**; **Volberding**, **Volb(e)ring**. Fris.: **Völpts**.

Volta Italian: habitation name from any of the numerous minor places so called from their situation on a bend in a road or a river. The name is from It. *volta* curve, bend (LL *volūta*, a deriv. of *volvere* to turn).

Vars.: **Della Volta**, **Dalla Volta**.

Vonášek *see* ANDREW

Von der Dunk *see* DUNG

Voogel *see* VOGEL

Voorzanger Dutch (Jewish): name taken by a cantor. See KAZAN and SANGER 2.

Vopel *see* VOLPERT

Vorchheimer *see* FORCHHEIMER

Vorlíček *see* ORLOV

Vorobyov Russian: patr. from the nickname *Vorobei* 'Sparrow', denoting a small, chirpy individual.

Habitation name: Pol. **Wróblewski** (also a Jewish ornamental name).

Voronin Russian: patr. from the nickname *Vorona* 'Crow', denoting a raucous person or someone with very dark hair. The stress is on the second syllable.

Dims.: Ger. (of Slav. origin): **Wronka**, **Wronek**.

Habitation name: Pol.: **Wronowski**.

Voronov Russian: patr. from the nickname *Voron* 'Raven', denoting someone with very dark hair. The stress is on the first syllable.

Vörös Hungarian: nickname for a man with red hair, from Hung. *vörös* red.

Vars.: **Veres(s)**, **Weöres**.

Vorotnikov Russian: patr. from the occupational term *vorotnik* gatekeeper (a deriv. of *vorota* gates, ultimately a cogn. of OE *worð* fence, enclosure; see WORTH).

Vortman *see* WORTMAN

Vos *see* FOSSE

Vosátka Czech: status name for the leader of a new settlement, from a dim. of Czech *osada* settlement (originally meaning 'people').

Voss *see* FOSSE

Vostrý Czech: nickname for a quick-minded person, from Czech *(v)ostrý* sharp, keen, acute.

Vars.: **Ostrý**; **Vostřák** (also means 'hobby', a kind of falcon).

Dim.: **Vostárek**.

Votava Czech: **1.** topographic name for someone living by the river *Otava*. **2.** from the Czech vocab. word *(v)otava*, lit. 'aftermath', i.e. a second crop of grass from the same field, after a first crop has been mown in early summer. As a surname, this may be a topographic name or an anecdotal nickname. The vocab. word also means 'convalescence', and this meaning may alternatively lie behind the surname.

Var.: **Otava**.

Votruba Czech: nickname for a stupid person, from Czech *(v)otruby* bran, husks of corn, which has the figurative sense 'blockhead'.

Vötter *see* VETTER

Vouls *see* FOWLE

Vovchenko *see* WILK

Vowell *see* FOWLE

Vowler *see* FOWLER

Voysey *see* VAISEY

Vözke *see* VOLK

Vrba Czech: **1.** topographic name for someone who lived by a conspicuous willow tree or among willow trees, from Czech *vrba* willow. **2.** nickname for a timid person, with reference to the trembling leves of the willow tree.

Dims. (of 2): Czech: **Vrbík**, **Vrbka**.

Habitation names: Czech: **Vrb(en)ský**. Pol.: WIERZBICKI. Ger.: FRÖBE.

Vreede see FIRTH

Vriens see FRIEND

Vrings see SÉVERIN

Vroome see FROOME

Vršecký Czech: habitation name from any of several places named with Czech *vršek*, dim. of *vrch* hill.

Vučenović see WILK

Vuillaumet see WILLIAM

Vuillin see WILL

Vuittet see GUY

Vukčević see WILK

Vulfov see WOLF

Vulkov see WILK

Vulpi see VOLPE

Vuorinen Finnish: ornamental name from Finn. *vuori* mound, hill + the gen. suffix *-nen*, perhaps sometimes chosen as a topographic name by someone who lived on a hillock.

Výborný Czech: nickname for a good person, from Czech *výborný* good, excellent, or more probably for a habitual user of the exclamation *výborně* 'Excellent!', 'Well done!'

Vyner see VINE

Vyskočil Czech: from the past tense of the verb *vyskočit* to jump up. The application of this word as a surname is uncertain; it may be a nickname for one who had risen in social status.

Vyvyan see VIVIAN

W

Waage *see* WÄGER

Wabbel *see* WALBURG

Wace **1.** Scots and English: from the Norman personal name *Wazo*, apparently derived from a compound Gmc name with a first element *wad* to go (cf. WADE 1). **2.** Welsh: status name for a servant, W *(g)was* (cf. VASS).

Vars.: WASE, WASS. (Of 1 only): **Waison, Wayson, Was(s)on** (from the OF oblique case); **Gaze** (E Anglia), GASS, **Ga(i)sh**, **Gas(s)on, Gashion** (from central Fr. forms).

Dims. (of 1): **Was(se)lin, Wastling**.

Wach *see* LAWRENCE, WENZEL

Wachsmann German: occupational name for a gatherer or seller of beeswax, from Ger. *Wachs* wax (MHG, OHG *wahs*) + *Mann* man. Wax was important in former times, being used for example to make candles and for sealing letters.

Vars.: **Wachs, Was(s)mann**.

Wachtel **1.** German: nickname for a timorous or stupid person, from Ger. *Wachtel* quail (MHG *wachtele*, OHG *wahtala*, of imitative origin; cf. QUAIL). **2.** Jewish (Ashkenazic): ornamental name taken from Ger. *Wachtel* or Yid. *vakhtl* quail. According to Kaganoff the name was adopted in reference to the quails miraculously provided for the Israelites in the wilderness (Exod. 16: 13), but the name is more likely to be simply one of the large number of Jewish ornamental names derived from words for animals and birds, or, in view of the connotations of the Ger. word, it may have been one of the derogatory surnames imposed on Jews by non-Jewish government officials in central Europe.

Wachter **1.** German: occupational name for a watchman, Ger. *Wachter*, an agent deriv. of MHG *wachte* watch, guard (OHG *wahta*; cf. WAITE). **2.** Jewish (Ashkenazic): from Ger. *Wachter* watchman, possibly adopted as an occupational name by a synagogue beadle (Yid. *shames*).

Vars.: Ger.: **Wächter, Wachtmann**. Jewish: **Wachtman(n)**.

Wackley *see* WAKELEY

Waddell Scots: habitation name from *Wedale* (now Stow) near Edinburgh. The origins of this placename are uncertain. The second element is evidently OE *dæl* or ON *dalr* valley (see DALE). The first element might conceivably be OE *wedd* pledge, security or its ON cogn. *veð* (although this is not found elsewhere as a placename element). In Scotland the stress normally falls on the first syllable of the surname, but elsewhere the name is often accented on the second syllable to avoid association with the vocabulary word *waddle*.

Vars.: **Waddel, Waddle, Weddel(l), Woddell; Weddle** (Northumb.).

Waddingham English: habitation name from a place in Lincs., recorded in Domesday Book as *Wadingeham*, i.e. 'homestead (OE *hām*) of the people of *Wada*' (see WADE 1).

Waddington N English: habitation name from any of various places. One near Clitheroe in Lancs. and another in Lincs. (*Wadintune* in Domesday Book) were originally named in OE as the 'settlement (OE *tūn*) associated with *Wada*' (see WADE 1); cf. WADDINGHAM.

Var.: **Wadington**.

Waddy *see* WALTHEW

Wade English: **1.** from the ME given name *Wade*, OE *Wada*, from the verb *wadan* to go. (*Wada* was the name of a legendary sea-giant.) **2.** topographic name for someone who lived near a ford, OE *(ge)wæd* (of cogn. origin to 1), or habitation name from a place named with this word, as for example *Wade* in Suffolk.

Var.: **Waide**.

Dims. (of 1): Fr.: **Vadet, Vadé, Vadez, Vadon, Vadel; Vatel(ot), Vat(t)in, Vaton; Wat(t)el, Watteau, Watelet, Watelot, Wat(t)in**. (Of 2): Sp.: **Vadillo**.

Patrs. (from 1): Eng.: **Wądeson, Waidson**.

Wader English: occupational name for a gatherer or seller of woad, from an agent deriv. of ME *wade* woad (OE *wād*, reinforced by OF *waisde*, likewise of Gmc origin). This plant produces a powerful blue dye, which was widely used in the Middle Ages.

Var.: **Waider; Wad(e)man, Wodeman**.

Wadham English: apparently a habitation name from an unidentified place, perhaps so called from the OE personal name *Wada* (see WADE 1) + OE *hām* homestead. It may be a contracted form of WADDINGHAM.

Wadley English: habitation name from a place in Berks., so called from OE *wād* woad (see WADER) or the personal name *Wade* (see WADE 1) + *lēah* wood, clearing.

Wadsworth *see* WORDSWORTH

Wäger German: occupational name for an official responsible for weighing produce, esp. that offered as rent in kind, or else for one who was in charge of checking weights and measures used by merchants. The vocab. word is an agent deriv. of MHG *wegen* to weigh (OHG *wegan*).

Vars.: **Waage** (from MHG *wāge* scales); **Wag(e)mann**.

Waghorn English and Scots: according to Reaney, this is an occupational nickname for a hornblower or trumpeter, from ME *wag(gen)* to brandish, shake (OE *wagian*) + *horn* HORN. It is also quite possible that it was originally an obscene nickname with *horn* in the sense 'penis'; cf. WAGSTAFF. Black states that the name, recorded in Scotland in the 14th cent., is of local origin, with *horn* in a topographical sense.

Var.: **Waghorne**.

Wagner German and Jewish (Ashkenazic): occupational name for a carter or cartwright, from an agent deriv. of Ger. *Wagen* cart, waggon (MHG *wagen*, OHG *wagan*).

Vars.: Ger.: **Wagener**, **Wahner**, **Wähner(t)**, **Wehner(t)**, **Wainer**, **Woiner**; **Wag(g)oner** (a recently Anglicized form; mod. Eng. *waggon* was borrowed in the 16th cent. from Du.).

Habitation name: Pol.: **Wojnarowski**.

Wągrowski Polish: habitation name from *Wągrowiec*, a town SW of Poznań (which probably derives its name from Pol. *wągroda* enclosed pasture), with the addition of *-ski*, suffix of local surnames (see BARANOWSKI).

Wagstaff English (chiefly Midlands and Yorks.): 1. occupational nickname for some official who carried a staff of office, from ME *wag(gen)* to brandish, shake (OE *wagian*) + *staff* staff, rod (OE *stæf*). 2. obscene nickname for a medieval 'flasher', one who brandished his 'staff' publicly; cf. WAGHORN.

Var.: **Wagstaffe**.

Wahl 1. Jewish (Ashkenazic): according to Jewish tradition, this name is taken from Ger. *Wahl* election (MHG *wal(e)*, OHG *wala* choice), and was adopted by people who claimed descent from Saul Katzenellenbogen (1541–c.1617), who according to a Jewish legend was elected king of Poland for a single day at the time when Poland was an elective monarchy (hence *Wahl* election). 2. Swedish: var. of WALL 4.

Wahlberg *see* WALL

Wahncke *see* JOHN

Wahner *see* WAGNER

Waide *see* WADE, WEIDE

Waider *see* WADER

Waigh *see* WAY

Wailer *see* WHEELER

Wailes *see* WALE

Wain English: metonymic occupational name for a carter or cartwright, from ME *wain* cart, waggon (OE *wægen*). Occasionally it may have been a house name for someone who lived at a house distinguished with this sign, probably from the constellation of the Plough, known in the Middle Ages as *Charles's Wain*, the reference being to Charlemagne.

Vars.: **Waine(s)**, **Wayne**; **Wane** (Lancs.); **Wainman**, **W(h)enman**.

Wainapel *see* WEIN

Wainberg *see* WEINBERG

Wainer *see* WAGNER

Wainrauch *see* WEINREICH

Waintraub *see* WEINTRAUB

Wainwright English (chiefly Lancs. and Yorks.): occupational name for a maker of carts or waggons; see WAIN + WRIGHT.

Vars.: **Wainewright**, **Wainrig(h)t**.

Waisblat *see* WHITE

Waison *see* WACE

Waistcoat *see* WESTCOTT

Waistell *see* WASTELL

Waite English: occupational name for a watchman, ANF *waite* (of Gmc origin; cf. WACHTER), or from the same word in its original abstract/collective sense, 'the watch'. There may also have been some late confusion with WHITE.

Vars.: **Wait**, **Wayt(e)**, **Waight(e)**.

Patrs.: Eng.: **Wait(e)s**, **Wa(y)tes**, **Whait(e)s**; **Gaites**.

Wajdenbaum *see* WEIDE

Wajnbaum *see* WEIN

Wajnberg *see* WEINBERG

Wajngrod *see* VINOGRADOV

Wajnszelbaum *see* WEINSCHEL

Wajntraub *see* WEINTRAUB

Wajsbaum *see* WHITE

Wake N English: apparently from the ON byname *Vakr* 'Wakeful', 'Vigilant' (from *vaka* to remain awake), or perhaps from a cogn. OE *Waca* (apparently attested in placenames such as WAKEFORD, WAKEHAM, and WAKELEY). In the case of the noble family of this name, however, it is apparently of Continental origin; see below.

Wakefield English: habitation name from the city in W Yorks., and perhaps also from a place of the same name in Northants. Both are so called from OE *wacu* vigil, festival (a deriv. of *wac(i)an* to watch, wake; cf. WAKEMAN) + *feld* pasture, open country, i.e. a patch of open land where a fair was held.

Wakeford English: habitation name from an unidentified place, presumably so called from the OE byname *Waca* 'Watchful' (see WAKE) + OE *ford* FORD. There was one place of this name (now lost) near WAKEHAM in Sussex.

Wakeham English: habitation name from places in Devon and Sussex, both so called from the OE byname *Waca* 'Watchful' (see WAKE) + OE *hām* homestead.

Var.: **Wakem**.

Wakeley English: habitation name from a place in Herts., so called from the OE byname *Waca* 'Watchful' (see WAKE) + OE *lēah* wood, clearing.

Vars.: **Wakely**, **Wa(c)kley**.

Wakeling English: from the medieval given name *Walquelin*, an ANF dim. of the Gmc byname *Walho* 'Foreigner' (cf. WALLACE).

Vars.: **Wakelin**, **Wa(l)kling**, **Walklin**, **Walklyn**, **Wakelam**.

Wakeman English: occupational name for a watchman, from ME *wake* watch, vigil (OE *wacu*; see WAKEFIELD) +

man man (OE *mann*). This was the title of the mayor of Ripon until the 16th cent.

Wakenshaw *see* WALKINGSHAW

Walasik *see* VALENTINE

Walburg German: from a Gmc female personal name composed of the elements *wald* rule + *burg* fortress. St Walburga (d. 779) was an Eng. missionary who accompanied St Boniface on his mission to Germany, and became abbess of Heidenheim. Her cult became very popular in N Germany in the early Middle Ages, with consequent effects on the frequency of the given name. Her bodily remains were later transferred to Eichstätt, according to legend on 1 May, which thus came to be known as *Walpurgisnacht*. This is also the date of an extremely ancient pagan fertility festival, welcoming the return of summer, and associated with witchcraft and revelry.

Vars.: **Wallburg**, **Wolburg**.

Dims.: Ger.: **Walpl**, **Wabbel**. Low Ger.: **Wobbe**, **Wöbb**, **Wöb(c)ke**.

Metrs. (from dims.): Low Ger.: **Wobben**, **Wöbken**, **Wöbbeking**.

Walcot English: habitation name from any of various places, for example in Berks., Lincs., Northants, Oxon., Shrops., Warwicks., and Wilts., all so called from OE *wealh* foreigner, Briton, serf (see WALLACE) + *cot* cottage, shelter (see COATES).

Vars.: **Walcott** (places in Norfolk and Worcs.); **Walcote** (a place in Leics.).

Wald 1. English and German: topographic name for someone who lived in or near a forest (OE *w(e)ald*, OHG *wald*). After the extensive clearances of forests in England before the Norman Conquest, the OE term *w(e)ald* also came to be used in ME to denote open uplands (*wolds*) and waste land not brought into cultivation. **2.** Jewish (Ashkenazic): in most cases, an ornamental name from the Ger. vocab. word *Wald* forest. Very few Jews would have been living in or near forests at the time when they acquired surnames. However, the forms ending in -*man(n)* or -*ner* are more probaby explained as in 1 or as metonymic occupational names for someone whose job was connected with wood, such as a woodcutter or lumber merchant.

Vars.: Eng.: **Walde**, **Waud**; **Wo(u)ld(e)**, **Wo(u)lds**; **We(a)ld**, **Weild**; **Waldman**, **Walder**, **Walding**. Ger.: **Walde**, **Waldmann**, **Wald(n)er**, **Wallner**. Jewish: **Waldman(n)**, **Waldner**, **Vald(man)**.

Cpds (ornamental): Jewish: **Valdberg** ('forest hill'); **Valdboim** ('forest tree'); **Waldfogel** ('forest bird'); **Waldhorn** ('forest horn'); **Waldstein** ('forest stone').

Waldeck German and Jewish (Ashkenazic): habitation name from a place in Hesse, on the river Eder, apparently so called from OHG *wald* wood + *ecka*, *egga* corner, recess. However, Bahlow interprets the earliest recorded forms of the name, *Waldegg* and *Waldei*, as pointing to an ancient term for a stretch of water.

Waldegrave English: habitation name from *Walgrave* in Northants, recorded in Domesday Book as *Waldgrave* 'grove (OE *grāf*) belonging to *Old*'. *Old* is a nearby place, so called from OE *w(e)ald* forest (see WALD 1). The surname is often pronounced /ˈwɔlɡreɪv/, as though it had the same spelling as the modern form of the place name.

Walden English: habitation name from any of the places, in Essex, Herts., and N Yorks., so called from OE *wealh* foreigner, Briton, serf (see WALLACE) + *denu* valley (see DEAN 1).

Waldorf German: habitation name from any of at least three places, all apparently so called from OHG *wald* forest + *dorf* village, settlement (see THORPE).

Waldron English: **1.** from a Gmc personal name composed of the elements *walh* foreigner + *hrafn* raven. **2.** habitation name from a place in Sussex, so called from OE *w(e)ald* forest + *ærn* house, dwelling. The surname is now also common in Ireland, esp. in Connacht.

Vars. (of 1): **Waldren**, **Waldram**, **Waldrum**, **Walrand**, **Walrond**, **Wallraven**.

Wale English: **1.** from a Gmc personal name *Walo*, either a byname meaning 'Foreigner' (see WALLACE), or else a short form of the various cpd names with this first element (cf., e.g., WALDRON 1). See also WAKELING and GALE 2. **2.** nickname for a well-liked person, from ME *wale* good, excellent (originally 'choice'; cf. WAHL 1). **3.** topographic name for someone who lived near an embankment, ME *wale* (OE *walu*).

Patrs. (from 1): **Wa(i)les**.

Waley *see* WHALLEY

Walford English: habitation name from any of various places so called. Examples in Herefords. and Shrops. are so called from OE (W Midlands) *wæll(a)* spring, stream (see WALL 2) + *ford* FORD. A second place in Herefords. of the same name originally had as its first element OE *w(e)alh* foreigner, Briton, serf (see WALLACE), and one in Dorset had OE *wealt* unsteady, difficult.

Walkden English (Lancs.): habitation name from a place near Rochdale, probably so called from an OE stream-name *Wealce* (from *wealcan* to roll along) + *denu* valley (see DEAN 1).

Walker English and Scots: **1.** occupational name for a fuller, ME *walkere*, OE *wealcere*, an agent deriv. of *wealcan* to walk, tread. This was the regular term for the occupation during the Middle Ages in W and N England (cf. FULLER and TUCKER), but now the surname is fairly widespread. The highest concentrations are in a patch of NW England centred on Leeds, and in the Grampian region of Scotland. As a Scots surname it has also been used as a translation of Gael. *Mac an Fhucadair*; see McNUCATOR. **2.** habitation name from a place in Northumb., so called from ME *wall* (Roman) wall (see WALL 1) + *kerr* marsh (see KERR).

Walkingshaw Scots: habitation name from *Walkinshaw* in the former county of Renfrews., which is probably named from OE *wealcere* fuller (see WALKER) + *sceaga* copse (see SHAW).

Vars.: **Walkinshaw**; **Wakenshaw** (Northumb.).

Walklin *see* WAKELING

Wall 1. English: topographic name for someone who lived by a stone-built wall, e.g. one used to fortify a town or to keep back the encroachment of the sea (OE *w(e)all*, from L *vallum* rampart, palisade). **2.** N English: topographic name for someone who lived by a spring or stream, Northern ME *wall(e)* (OE (W Midlands) *wæll(a)*; cf. WELL). **3.** Irish: var. of VALE, a re-Anglicized form of Gael. *de Bhál.* **4.** Swedish: ornamental name from Swed. *wall, vall* grassy bank, pasture, or grazing ground, perhaps adopted in some cases as a topographic name by someone who lived by a grassy bank.

Vars. (of 1 and 2): Eng.: **Walle, Walls, WALLER, Wallman.** (Of 4): Swed.: WAHL; **Wallén, Wallin, Wallenius; Wallner, Wallman, Wallander.**

Cpds (of 4, mainly ornamental): Swed.: **Wall(en)berg, Wahlberg** ('pasture hill'); **Wallgren, Wahlgren** ('pasture branch'); **Wahlquist** ('pasture twig'); **Wahlsted** ('pasture homestead'); **Wallström, Wahlström** ('pasture river').

Wallace Scots, Irish, and English: name for a Celt, from ANF *waleis* (from a Gmc cogn. of OE *wealh* foreign). In different parts of Britain this term was used to denote variously Scotsmen, Welshmen, and Bretons, as well as the small pocket of Strathclyde Britons who persisted into the Middle Ages. English placenames containing *wealh* (as for example WALCOT, WALDEN, WALFORD, and WALLINGTON) are believed to refer to enclaves of Welsh-speaking people noted by the Anglo-Saxons. The surname has also been adopted in the 19th and 20th cents. as an Anglicized form of various Ashkenazic Jewish surnames.

Vars.: **Wallice, Wallis, Walles, Wallas.** See also WALSH and WAUGH.

Wallbank N English: apparently a topographic name for someone who lived by a bank with a wall on it, from ME *wall* (see WALL 1) + *bank* (see BANKS). Alternatively, the first element may be Northern ME *wall(e)* spring, stream (see WALL 2), in which case the surname would denote someone who lived on the banks of a stream.

Vars.: **Wallbanks, Walbank, Walbanck(e).**

Wallburg see WALBURG

Waller English: **1.** topographic name, a var. of WALL 1, or occupational name for a mason. **2.** topographic name, a var. of WALL 2; see also WELL. **3.** occupational name for someone who boiled sea water to extract the salt, from an agent deriv. of ME *well(en)* to boil (OE *weallan*). **4.** nickname for a good-humoured person, ANF *wall(i)er* (an agent deriv. of OF *galer* to make merry, of Gmc origin; cf. GALE 1 and GAILLARD).

Vars. (of 4): **Gall(i)er, Gallear** (from central Fr. forms).

Wallington English: habitation name from any of various places so called, with perhaps as many as four different origins. Those in Berks., Hants, and Surrey are probably all so called from the gen. pl. of OE *wealh* foreigner, Briton (see WALLACE) + OE *tūn* enclosure, settlement. One in Northumb. was originally OE *Wealingtūn* 'settlement associated with *Wealh*', a personal name or byname (cf. WALE 1). One in Herts. was named as the 'settlement of the people of *Wændel*', while one in Norfolk was probably the 'settlement of the dwellers by the wall'; see WALL 1.

Wallop English: **1.** habitation name from a place in Hants, so called from OE (W Midlands) *wæll(a)* spring, stream (see WALL 2) + *hop* enclosed valley (see HOPE). There are also minor places of the same name and etymology in Gloucs. and Shrops., and these may be partial sources of the surname. **2.** var. of GALLOP.

Wallwork English (Lancs.): habitation name of uncertain origin. Thomas *de Wallerwork* was living in Lancs. *c.*1324, and throughout the Middle Ages forms in *-work* alternate with ones in *-worth*. No similarly named place in Lancs. has been identified, and it is possible that the surname derives from places in Co. Durham or Greater London called *Walworth*, from OE *w(e)alh* foreigner, Briton (see WALLACE) + *worð* enclosure (see WORTH).

Walmsley English: habitation name from *Walmersley* near Bury in Lancs., which according to Ekwall is so called from OE *wald* wood + *mere* lake or *(ge)mǣre* boundary + *lēah* wood, clearing. However, it is perhaps more plausibly from the gen. case of an OE personal name *Wealhmǣr* 'Foreign-famous' or *Wealdmǣr* 'Rule-famous' + OE *lēah*.

Vars.: **Walmesley, Walmisley, Wa(r)msley, Waumsley.**

Walpole English: habitation name from either of two places, in Norfolk and Suffolk. The first element of the former is OE *w(e)all* wall (see WALL 1), while the first element of the latter is *wealh* foreigner, Briton (see WALLACE); they share the second element OE *pōl* pool.

Vars.: **Wolpole, Waple(s).**

Walsh **1.** English: name for a Celt, from ME *walsche* Celtic, foreign (OE *wælisc*, a deriv. of *wealh* foreign; cf. WALLACE and WAUGH). This word is cogn. with Ger. *welsch* foreign, southern European, Romance-speaking, so ultimately with Czech *Vlach*. **2.** Irish: translation of the Gael. name *Breathnach* 'British', 'Welsh'; cf. BRANNICK.

Vars. (mostly of 1): **Walshe, Welsh, Walch, Welch, Wals(h)man.**

Walshaw English (Yorks.): habitation name from a place in W Yorks., near Hebden Bridge, so called from OE *w(e)alh* foreigner, Briton (see WALLACE) + *sceaga* copse (see SHAW).

Walsingham English: habitation name from a place in Norfolk, so called from OE *Wælsingahām* 'homestead (OE *hām*) of the people of *Wæls*', a personal name of uncertain origin, which occurs in *Beowulf*.

Walter English: from a Gmc personal name composed of the elements *wald* rule + *heri, hari* army, introduced into England by the Normans in the form *Walt(i)er, Waut(i)er.* The normal vernacular pronunciation of the Middle Ages reflected the latter of these forms.

Vars.: WATER; **Gualter** (from the central Fr. form).

Dims.: Fr.: **Gaut(h)ereau, Gautreau, Gaudr(i)eau, Gautr(el)et, Gaut(h)eron, Gautron, Gaud(e)ron, Gaut(h)erot, Gautrot, Vautrot, Gaut(h)erin, Vaut(h)rin, Vautrin(ot).** It.: **Galtierotti.** Ger.: **Wal(t)z, Wäl(t)z, Walzel, Welz(el); Wälti, Welti** (Switzerland). Low Ger.: **Wolterke, Wöldeke, Wöhlk(e), Wölke, Wöhl(e).**

Patrs.: Eng.: **Walters, Walterson; Fitzwa(l)ter.** Sc.: **McWalter, McWatters** (Gael. **Mac Uaitéir**). Low Ger.: **Welters, Wo(h)lters, Wolders, Wohlers; Woltering, Woldering, Wollring.** Flem., Du.: **Wauters, Wouters(en).**

Patrs. (from dims.): Low Ger.: **Wolterkes, Wölterges, Wöhlken(s), Wölken, Wöhl(k)ing.** Fris.: **Wöltjes, Wöljen.** Flem., Du.: **Wouts.**

Walthew English: from a widespread Anglo-Scandinavian personal name *Wælþēof* (ON *Valþiófr*), composed of the elements *val* battle + *þiofr* thief, i.e. one who snatched victory out of battle.

Vars.: **Waltho**, **Waldy**, **Waldo**; **Waddy**.

Walton English: habitation name from any of the numerous places so called. The first element in these names was variously OE *wealh* foreigner, Briton (see WALLACE), *w(e)ald* wood (see WALD), *w(e)all* wall (see WALL 1), or *wæll(a)* spring, stream (see WALL 2).

Vars.: **Walten**, **Wauton**.

Wamsley *see* WALMSLEY

Wancke *see* JOHN

Wander 1. German: occupational name for a builder, one who built walls, from an agent deriv. of Ger. *Wand* wall (MHG, OHG *want* wall, from OHG *wenten* to wind, weave; the earliest domestic walls were of wattle and daub construction, made from woven hurdles packed with clay). 2. German: occupational name for a maker or seller of cloth, from an agent deriv. of an aphetic form of Ger. *Gewand* cloth, garment (MHG *gewant*, OHG *giwant*, likewise a deriv. of *wenten* to weave). 3. Jewish (Ashkenazic): of uncertain origin, possibly a cogn. of 1 or 2.

Vars. (of 1): **Wand(t)**. (Of 2): **Wand**.

Wanderschek *see* ANDREW

Wane *see* WAIN

Wang 1. German: topographic name for someone who lived near a meadow, from the Low Ger. and Austrian/Bavarian dial. term *wang*. 2. Jewish (Ashkenazic): either a cogn. of 1, or else a habitation name for a Jew from Hungary (cf. Russ. *Vengria* Hungary).

Vars. (of 1): **Wang(n)er**, **Wäng(l)er**.

Wanner German: occupational name for a maker or seller of winnowing fans, from an agent deriv. of MHG *wanne* (OHG *wanna*, from L *vannus*; cf. FANNER).

Wanzel *see* WENZEL

Waple *see* WALPOLE

Waplington English: habitation name from a place in E Yorks. (now Humberside), so called from OE *Wapolingtun* 'settlement (OE *tūn*) associated with a pond or march', from OE *wapol* pond, marsh.

Warboys English: 1. occupational name for a forester, from ANF *warde(r)* to guard (see WARDEN) + *bois* wood (see BOIS). 2. habitation name from a place in the former county of Hunts. (now part of Cambs.), so called from ON *varði* beacon + *buski* brushwood, bushes. Both elements are cogn. with those in 1.

Vars.: **Warboy**, **Worboys**.

Warburton English: habitation name from a place in Ches., so called from the OE female personal name *Wǣrburh* (composed of the elements *wǣr* pledge + *burh* fortress) + OE *tūn* enclosure, settlement.

Var.: **Warbutton** (Bristol).

Ward 1. English: occupational name for a watchman or guard, from OE *weard* guard (used as both an agent noun and an abstract noun). 2. Irish: Anglicized form of

Gael. *Mac an Bhaird*; see BARD. 3. Jewish (Ashkenazic): Anglicization of *Warszawczyk* (see WARSZAWSKI).

Vars. (of 1): Eng.: **Warde**, **Wardman**, **Wordman**.

Patr. (from 1): Eng.: **Wards**.

Warden English: 1. occupational name for a watchman or guard, from ANF *wardein* (a deriv. of *warder* to guard, of Gmc origin; cf. WARD 1 and GUARD). 2. habitation name from any of various places, for example in Beds., Co. Durham, Kent, Northumb., and Northants, so called from OE *weard* watch + *dūn* hill; cf. WARDHAUGH, WARDLAW, and WARDLE 1.

Dim. (of 1): Fr.: **Gardiennet**.

Wardhaugh English (Northumb.) and Scots: habitation name from some minor place so called, presumably from ON *varða* beacon + *haugr* hill; cf. WARDEN 2, WARDLAW, and WARDLE 1.

Wardlaw Scots: habitation name from any of several minor places so called, from OE *weard* watch + *hlāw* hill; cf. WARDEN 2, WARDHAUGH, and WARDLE 1.

Wardle English: 1. habitation name from places in Ches. and Lancs., so called from OE *weard* watch + *hyll* hill; cf. WARDEN 2, WARDHAUGH, and WARDLAW. 2. regional name from *Weardale* in Co. Durham, so called from the river *Wear* (named with a Brit. word apparently meaning 'liquid', 'water') + OE *dæl* valley (see DALE).

Vars.: **Wardel(l)**, **Wardill**, **Wardall**, **Wardale**.

Wardley English: habitation name from a place in the former county of Rutland (now part of Leics.), apparently so called from OE *wǣr* weir (see WARE 1) + *lēah* wood, clearing; the -d- does not appear before the late 13th cent., and is apparently excrescent.

Wardrop English and Scots: metonymic occupational name for someone who was in charge of the garments worn by a feudal lord and his household, from ANF *warde(r)* to keep, guard (cf. WARDEN and GUARD) + *robe* garment (cf. ROPERO).

Vars.: **Wardrope**, **Wardrupp**, **Whatrup**, **Wardrobe**; **Wardrop(p)er**, **Waredraper**.

Ware English: 1. topographic name for someone who lived by a dam or weir on a river (OE *wǣr*, *wer*), or habitation name from a place named with this word, such as *Ware* in Herts. 2. nickname for a cautious person, from ME *war(e)* wary, prudent (OE *(ge)wær*).

Vars. (of 1): **Wares**, **Wear**, **Weir**, **W(h)ere**.

Wareham English: habitation name from a place in Dorset, so called from OE *wǣr* weir (see WARE 1) + *hām* homestead.

Var.: **Warham** (places in Herefords. and Norfolk).

Warfield English: habitation name from a place in Berks., recorded in Domesday Book as *Warwelt*, from OE *wǣr* weir (see WARE 1) + *feld* pasture, open land (see FIELD).

Waring English: from the Norman personal name *Warin*, derived from the Gmc element *war(in)* guard, and used as a short form of various cpd names with this first element (cf., e.g., WARNER 2). The name was popular in France and among the Normans, partly as a result of the fame of the Carolingian lay *Guérin de Montglave*.

Vars.: **Wareing**, **Warring**, **Wearing**, **Werring**, **W(h)arin**, **Werren**; **Guerin** (Ireland, from a central Fr. form; sometimes Gaelicized **Geran**).

Dims.: Fr.: **Guérineau**, **Guérinet**, **Guérinon**, **Guérinot**. It.: **Guariniello** (Naples).

Aug.: It.: **Guarinoni** (Venetia).

Patrs.: Eng.: **Fitzwarin**. It.: **Gaureschi**.

Wark English (Northumb.) and Scots: habitation name from *Wark* on the river Tweed, which gets its name from OE *(ge)weorc* (earth)works, fortification.

Var.: **Warke**.

Warman English: **1.** occupational name for a merchant or trader, from ME *ware* wares, articles of trade (OE *waru*, a collective noun, apparently from the root *war-* guard; cf. WARD 1 and WARING) + *man* man. **2.** from the OE personal name *Wǣrmund*, composed of the elements *wǣr* pledge + *mund* protection. **3.** Jewish (Ashkenazic): probably an ornamental name from Ger. *wahr* true + *Mann* man.

Warmington English: habitation name from either of two places so called. The one in Warwicks. was originally named in OE as *Wǣrmundingtūn* 'settlement (OE *tūn*) associated with *Wǣrmund*' (see WARMAN 2). That in Northants was *Wyrmingtūn* 'settlement associated with *Wyrm*', a byname meaning 'Serpent', 'Dragon'.

Warmoll *see* WORMALD

Warmsley *see* WALMSLEY

Warne English: habitation name from a place in Devon, first recorded in 1194 as *Wagefen*, apparently from an OE deriv. of *wagian* to shake, quiver (cf. WAGHORN and WAGSTAFF) + *fen* bog, marsh (see FENN).

Vars.: **Warn**, **Wearne**.

Warner English (Norman): **1.** from a Gmc personal name composed of the Gmc elements *war(in)* guard + *heri, hari* army, introduced into England by the Normans in the form *Warnier*. See also GARNER. **2.** contracted form of *Warrener*; see WARREN 2.

Dims. (of 1): Fr.: **GARNON**, **Garnot(el)**, **Garnotin**. It.: **Varnerin(i)** (Venetia). Ger.: **Wer(n)lein**, **Wernle**, **We(h)rle**, **Werndl**, **We(r)n(t)z**, **Wertz**; **Wöhrle(in)**, **Wörlin**, **Wörn(d)le**, **Wörn(z)** (Bavaria); **Wehrli** (Switzerland). Low Ger.: **Warn(e)(c)ke**, **Werne(c)ke**, **Warremann**. Fris.: **Warntje**, **Wessel(mann)**.

Patrs. (from 1): Low Ger.: **Warn(d)ers**.

Patrs. (from 1) (dims.): Low Ger.: **Warn(ke)s**; **Warnken**; **Warn(ek)ing**, **Warninck**, **Wern(ek)ing**, **Warnkönig**. Fris.: **Warrentjes**, **Werntjes**, **Wessels**; **Warntjen**, **Werntjen**; **Wesseling**.

Warnes English (E Anglia): of uncertain origin. In one modern family of this name there is a tradition that it is of Low Ger. origin, and it is possibly in origin a patr. from a short form of WARNER 1. There was fairly extensive migration from the Low Countries to E Anglia during the Middle Ages in connection with the wool trade.

Warnock Scots: Anglicized form of Gael. **Mac Gille Mheàrnaig** 'son of the servant of (St) *Meàrnag*', a per-

sonal name possibly representing a dim. form of *mear* wild, solitary.

Vars.: **Warnoch**; **McGilvernock**, **McIlvernock**, **McVarnock**.

Warr English: nickname for a belligerent person or for a valiant soldier, from ANF *werr(e)* war (OF *guerre*, of Gmc origin); for the change of *-er-* to *-ar-*, cf. MARCHANT.

Vars.: **Warre**; **W(h)arrier**, **Warrior**.

Dims.: Fr.: **Guerreau**, **Guerrin**, **Guerry**.

Pej.: It.: **Guerrazzi**.

Warren English: **1.** Norman habitation name from *La Varrenne* in Seine-Maritime, so called from a Gaul. element probably descriptive of alluvial land or sandy soil. **2.** topographic name for someone who lived by a gamepark, or occupational name for someone employed in one, from ANF *warenne* warren, piece of land for breeding game (of uncertain origin, perhaps akin to 1, or to the Gmc element *war(in)-* guard, preserve).

Vars.: Eng.: **Warran(d)**, **Warrant**, **Warrenne**. (Of 2 only): **Warren(d)er**, **Warriner**, WARNER.

Warrington English: habitation name from the town in Lancs., probably named in OE as *Wǣringtun* 'settlement by the weir', from OE *wǣring*, a deriv. of *wǣr* (see WARE 1) + *tūn* settlement.

Warsop English: habitation name from the town of Market *Warsop* in Notts., recorded in Domesday Book as *Wareshope*, from the gen. case of the OE name *Wǣr* or *Wǣr* + OE *hop* enclosed valley (see HOPE).

Warszawski Polish and Jewish (E Ashkenazic): habitation name from the city of Warsaw (Pol. *Warszawa*), which became the capital of Poland at the end of the 16th cent., after the destruction of Cracow by fire.

Vars.: Pol.: **Warszakowski**. Jewish: **Warszavski**, **Wars(c)haw(ski)**, **Wars(c)hawsky**, **Wars(c)havski**, **Wars(c)havsky**; **Warszawiak**, **Warshawiak**, **Warshaviak**; **Warschauer** (a Ger. form); **Warscher** (from W Yid. *varsher* 'native or inhabitant of Warsaw'); **Warschawer**, **Warszawer** (from E Yid. *varshever* 'native or inhabitant of Warsaw', the *a* in the second syllable being the result of the influence of the Pol. form).

Dim.: Jewish: **Warszawczyk**.

Warters *see* WATER

Warth **1.** English: habitation name from any of various minor places named with the ON term *varða* beacon (a deriv. of *varða* to guard; cf. WARD 1). **2.** German: habitation name from any of various minor places named with an OHG cogn. of this element.

Vars. (of 2): Ger.: **Warthe(r)**.

Warwick English: **1.** habitation name from the county town of Warwicks., or regional name from the county itself. The town was originally named as the 'outlying settlement (see WICK) by the weir'; cf. WARRINGTON. **2.** habitation name from a much smaller place of the same name in Cumb., so called from OE *waroð* slope, bank + *wīc*.

Vars.: **W(h)arrick**.

Wase **1.** Scots and English: var. of WACE. **2.** German: topographic name for someone who lived on a patch of reclaimed marshland (which generally provided rich pasture land), MHG *wase* (from OHG *waso* marsh; cf. OE *wāse* mud).

Vars. (of 2): Ger.: **Was(n)er, Wasmer**.

Washbourne English: **1.** habitation name from *Washbourne* in Devon, so called from OE *wæsce* washing (an abstract noun from *wæscan* to wash; cf. WASHER) + *burna* stream (see BOURNE), i.e. stream where washing was done. **2.** habitation name from *Washbourne* in Gloucs., so called from OE *wæsse* alluvial land (cf. WASE 2) + *burna*. See also WASHBURN.

Var.: **Washbourn**.

Washbrook English: habitation name from any of various places, for example in Lancs., Somerset, and Suffolk, so called from OE *wæsce* washing + *brōc* BROOK; cf. WASHBOURNE 1.

Washburn N English: topographic name for someone living on the banks of the river *Washburn* in W Yorks., so called from the OE personal name *Walc* + OE *burna* stream (see BOURNE). The river name is first recorded as *Walke(s)burna* in the early 12th cent. There is no evidence of any confusion with the S English name WASHBOURNE, although this is of course possible.

Var.: **Washburne**.

Washer English: occupational name for a laundryman, or for someone who washed raw wool before spinning, from an agent deriv of ME *wasch(en)* to wash (OE *wæscan*). In some cases it may have denoted a man who washed or dipped sheep; some tenants on the manor of Burpham, near Worthing, in Sussex (where the surname is found from an early date), had as part of their feudal service to wash the flocks of their master.

Washington English: habitation name from either of the places so called, in Tyne and Wear and in W Sussex. The latter is from OE *Wassingatūn* 'settlement (OE *tūn*) of the people of *Wassa*', a personal name apparently representing a short form of some cpd name such as *Wāðsige*, composed of the elements *wāð* hunt + *sige* victory. Washington in Tyne and Wear is from OE *Wassingtūn* 'settlement associated with *Wassa*'.

Washtell *see* WASTELL

Wasiak *see* LAWRENCE

Wasiela *see* BASIL

Wąsik Polish: nickname for a man with a particularly fine or noticeable moustache, from Pol. *wąs* moustache + *-ik* dim. suffix.

Patrs.: Pol.: **Wąs(ik)iewicz, Wąsowicz**. Russ.: **Usatchov, Usatych**.

Habitation name: Pol.: **Wąs(ik)owski**.

Waslin *see* WACE

Wasmann *see* WACHSMANN

Wass 1. Scots and English: var. of WACE. **2.** Swedish: from Swed. *vass* sharp, keen. This is a 'soldier's name', one of the identifying names adopted by Swed. soldiers in the 17th and 18th cents., before the use of surnames became general in Scandinavia. **3.** Swedish: ornamental name from Swed. *vass* reed, marsh (cf. WASE 2), one of

the many Swed. surnames derived from vocab. words denoting features of the natural landscape.

Var. (of 2 and 3): Vass.

Cpds (of 3, ornamental): **Wassberg, Vassberg** ('marsh hill').

Wastell English: **1.** metonymic occupational name for a baker of fancy breads, from ANF *wastel* cake (mod. Fr. *gâteau*, apparently of Gmc origin). **2.** habitation name from *Wasthills* in Worcs., so called from OE *weardsetl* guardhouse.

Vars.: **Wastall, Waistell, Washtell, Wassell, Wassall**. (Of 1 only): **Gastall** (from the central Fr. form).

Waszczyk *see* JOHN

Watel *see* WADE

Water 1. English: var. of WALTER, representing the normal medieval pronunciation of the name. **2.** English: topographic name for someone who lived by a stretch of water (OE *wæter*). **3.** Irish: Anglicized form of Gael. *Ó Fuarisc(e)*; see FOURISH.

Var.: **Waters** (commonly a patr. from 1 as well as a var. of 2 and 3).

Patrs. (from 1): Eng.: **Wat(t)ers, Warters, Worters; Wat(t)erson; Fitzwater**.

Waterfield English (Norman): habitation name from *Vatierville* in Seine-Maritime, so called from the personal name WALTER + OF *ville* settlement (see VILLE).

Waterhouse English (chiefly Yorks., Lancs., and Midlands): topographic name for someone who lived in a house by a stretch of water.

Waterman 1. English: occupational name for the servant of a bearer of the given name *Wa(l)ter*; see WATER 1. **2.** English and Flemish/Dutch: occupational name for a boatman or a water-carrier, or topographic name for someone who lived by a stretch of water; see WATER 2. **3.** Jewish (Ashkenazic): Anglicized form of **Wasserman**, occupational surname given to a water-carrier; cf. 2 above.

Waterton English: habitation name from *Waterston* in Dorset, recorded in the early 13th cent. as *Walterton*, named from the ME personal name *Wa(l)ter* + ME *tone, tune* settlement.

Waterworth English (chiefly Lancs.): ostensibly a habitation name from a place deriving its name from OE *wæter* water + *worð* enclosure, but in fact, as McKinley has shown, an occupational name for a water bailiff, earlier **Waterward**, from ME *water* + WARD 1. All the early examples occur on the banks of Martin Mere, a large freshwater lake (now drained) in W Lancs.

Wates *see* WAITE

Watford English: habitation name from the town in Herts. or from the much smaller one in Northants. Both derive their name from OE *wāð* hunt + *ford* FORD.

Watley *see* WHEATLEY

Watman 1. English: occupational name for the servant of someone called *Wat(t)*; see WATT. **2.** English: from a ME given name, *W(h)atman, Wheteman*, a survival of OE *Hwætmann*, composed of the elements *hwæt* bold, brave + *mann* man. **3.** Jewish (Ashkenazic): of unknown origin.

Vars. (of 2): **Wh(e)atman, W(h)eetman**.

Watmoor see WHATMORE

Watmough English (chiefly Yorks.): name for someone who was related to a bearer of the given name *Wat(t)*; see WATT. The ME term *maugh, mough* was used of various relatives, normally those connected by marriage rather than by blood.
Vars.: **Whatmough**, **W(h)atmaugh**, **W(h)atmuff**, **Wha(r)tmouth**; WHATMORE.

Watt English and Scots: from an extremely common ME given name, *Wat(t)*, a short form of WALTER.
Dims.: **Watkin(g)**; **Watlin(g)**, **Whatling**.
Patrs.: **Watt(i)s**, **Watson**.
Patrs. (from dims.): **W(h)atkins**, **Watkiss**, **Watkeys**; **Gwatkins** (Wales); **Swatkins** (Gloucs.); **Watkinson** (widespread, but commonest in Lancs. and S Yorks.).

Wätzold see WENZEL

Waud see WALD

Waugh Scots and N English: of disputed origin. It is most likely from OE (Anglian) *walh* foreign (see WALLACE), perhaps applied originally to the Strathclyde Britons who survived as a separate group in Scotland well into the Middle Ages.

Waumsley see WALMSLEY

Waus see VAUSE

Wauters see WALTER

Wauton see WALTON

Wavell English (Norman): habitation name from *Vauville* in Calvados and La Manche, both so called from the Gmc personal name *Walo* (see WALE 1) + OF *ville* settlement (see VILLE).
Vars.: **Wevell**, **We(a)vill**.

Wawn see GAVIN

Wawrzeńczyk see LAWRENCE

Way English (chiefly Southern): topographic name for someone who lived near a road or path, OE *weg* (cogn. with ON *vegr*, OHG *weg*), or habitation name from some minor place named with this word.
Vars.: **Waye**, **Whay**, **Wey**, **Waigh**, **Weigh**; **Attaway**, **Byway**, **Bytheway**, **Bythway**, **Bidaway**.

Wayler see WHEELER

Wayman see WYMAN

Waymark see WYMER

Wayne see WAIN

Waysberg see WHITE

Wayson see WACE

Wayt see WAITE

Wąż see WĘŻYK

Wdowczak see WIDDOW

Weake English: **1.** topographic or habitation name, a var. of WICK. **2.** nickname for a poor physical specimen, from ME *wayke* weak, feeble (ON *veikr*).
Vars.: **Week**. (Of 1 only): **Week(e)s**, **Wheeker**.

Weald see WALD

Wear English (Northumb.): **1.** topographic name for someone who lived by the N English river of this name. The river name occurs in the form *Vedra* in Ptolemy's *Geographia*. It is probably a Celt. word meaning simply 'water'. **2.** topographic name for someone who lived near a dam or weir, a var. of WARE 1.
Vars.: **Weare**, **Wears**.

Wearden English (Lancs.): habitation name from *Worden* in Lancs, so called from OE *wær, wer* weir (see WARE 1) + *denu* valley (see DEAN 1).

Wearing see WARING

Wearne English: habitation name from a place so called in Somerset, which gets its name from the river that runs through it. The river name is of Brit. origin, from the element *ver(n)* alder; cf. VER 1.

Wearne see WARNE

Weate see WHEAT

Weather English: nickname from ME *wether* wether, (castrated) ram (OE *weðer*), denoting a man supposedly resembling a wether in some way, esp. in lacking sexual prowess. In some cases, however, it may be no more than a metonymic occupational name for a shepherd.
Patr.: **Weathers**.

Weatherall English: habitation name from *Wetheral* in Cumb., so called from OE *weðer* wether, ram (see WEATHER) + *halh* nook, recess (see HALE 1).
Vars.: **Wetherall**, **Wetherald**, **We(a)therell**, **Wetheril(l)**, **Weather(h)ill**, **We(a)therilt**, **Weatheritt**, **Weathrall**, **Wealthall**, **Wederell**.

Weatherburn see WEDDERBURN

Weatherhead English and Scots: according to Reaney this is an occupational name for a shepherd, from ME *wether* wether, ram (see WEATHER) + *herd* herdsman (see HEARD). His only evidence for this interpretation of the final syllable is alternation in the late 15th cent. between *Weydurherd* and *Wedirhed*. Black quotes numerous later forms that undoubtedly belong to this name; they divide fairly evenly between endings in *-heid* (representing the normal Scots pronunciation of mod. Eng. *head*) and *-at*. He supposes that the name derives from an unidentified minor hill in the former county of Berwicks.
Vars.: **Wetherhead**, **Wethered**.

Weatherley Scots and English: habitation name, probably from *Wedderlie* in the former county of Berwicks., so called from OE *weðer* wether, ram (see WEATHER) + *lēah* wood, clearing.
Var.: **Weatherly**.

Weathersby English: habitation name from *Wetherby* in W Yorks., so called from ON *veðr* wether, ram (cf. WEATHER) + *býr* farm, settlement.

Vars.: **We(a)therby**, **Witherby**, **Wetherbee**.

Weatherspoon *see* WITHERSPOON

Weaver English: **1.** occupational name, from an agent deriv. of ME *weven* to weave (OE *wefan*); cf. WEBB. **2.** habitation name from a place on the river *Weaver* in Ches., now called *Weaver* Hall (recorded simply as *Weuere* in the 13th and 14th cents.). The river name is from OE *wēfer(e)* winding stream.

Var.: **Weafer**.

Patrs. (from 1): Eng.: **Weavers**. Low Ger.: **Wewers**, **Wevers**, **We(i)fers**, **Weverinck**. Flem., Du.: **Web(b)ers**, **Wevers**.

Equivs.: Scot.: McNIDDER. Fr.: TISSIER. Ukr. and Jewish: TKACH.

Weavill *see* WAVELL

Webb 1. English: occupational name for a weaver, early ME *webbe*, from OE *webba* (a primary deriv. of *wefan* to weave; cf. WEAVER 1). This word survived into ME long enough to give rise to the surname, but was already obsolescent as an agent noun; hence the secondary forms with the (redundant) agent suffixes *-(st)er*. **2.** Jewish (Ashkenazic): Anglicizations of the various Jewish names given at WEAVER.

Vars. (of 1): **Webbe**; **Webber** (chiefly W Country); **Webster** (chiefly Yorks., Lancs., and Midlands). (Of 2): **Web**.

Webbers *see* WEAVER

Webley English (Gloucs.): of uncertain origin, perhaps a habitation name from *Weobley* in Herefords. (*Webbeley* 1242, *Wibelai* in Domesday Book), in which the first element is probably from a byform, *Weobba* or *Wiobba*, of the attested personal name *Wibba* (of uncertain origin).

Websdale English: of uncertain origin, apparently a habitation name from a place whose name contains as its second element ME DALE. The first element, however, has not been identified.

Węcewicz *see* VINCENT

Wechsler German and Jewish (Ashkenazic): occupational name for a money-changer, Ger. *Wechsler*, an agent deriv. of Ger. *wechseln* to exchange (MHG *wehseln*, OHG *wehsalōn*).

Vars.: Jewish: **Weksler** (Pol. spelling); **Wexler** (Anglicized spelling); **Vexler**; **Wechselman(n)**, **Wekselman**, **Vexelman**.

Cpds (ornamental): Jewish: **Wexelbaum**, **Vexelbaum** ('exchange tree'); **Wechselberg** ('exchange hill'); **Wechselfis(c)h** ('exchange fish').

Weck *see* WEDEKIND

Wedberg *see* WOOD

Weddel *see* WADDELL

Wedderburn Scots: habitation name from a place in the former county of Berwicks., so called from OE *weðer* wether, ram (see WEATHER) + *burna* stream (see BOURNE), i.e. probably a place where sheep were washed.

Var.: **Weatherburn**.

Wedderspoon *see* WITHERSPOON

Wedekind Low German: from a Gmc personal name composed of the elements *widu* wood + *kind* child. The name became famous as that of a Duke of Lower Saxony who was an opponent of Charlemagne, and was consequently popular in N Germany as a given name throughout the Middle Ages.

Vars.: **Widdekind**, **Witekind**, **Wehkind**.

Dims.: **Weck(e)**, **Weckl(e)in**.

Patrs. (from dims.): **Weckes**, **Wecken**, **Wecking**, **Wekking**.

Wederell *see* WEATHERALL

Wedge English: of uncertain origin, possibly from ME *wegge* wedge (OE *wecg*) used as a topographic name for someone who lived on a wedge-shaped (i.e. triangular) piece of land. However, this suggestion must be regarded as extremely doubtful since *wecg* is not recorded as an element in English placenames.

Var.: **Wegg** (Norfolk).

Wedgewood English: apparently a habitation name from an unidentified place, perhaps named with the OE elements *wice* wych elm (see WICH 2) + *wudu* WOOD.

Var.: **Wedgwood**.

Wedlock *see* WOODLOCK

Weech *see* WICH

Weedon English: habitation name from places in Bucks. and Northants, so called from OE *wēoh* pagan temple + *dūn* hill (see DOWN 1).

Var.: **Weeden**.

Week *see* WEAKE

Weekley English: habitation name from a place in Northants, so called from OE *wīc* settlement (perhaps in this case a Roman *vīcus*; see WICKHAM) + *lēah* wood, clearing.

Var.: **Weekly**.

Weems *see* WEMYSS

Weet *see* WHEAT

Weetman *see* WATMAN

Wefers *see* WEAVER

Wegg *see* WEDGE

Weggin *see* KEOGH

Wehkind *see* WEDEKIND

Wehner *see* WAGNER

Wehrle *see* WARNER

Weide 1. German: topographic name for someone who lived by a conspicuous willow or by a group of willow trees, from Ger. *Weide* willow (MHG *wīde*, OHG *wīda*; cf. WITHEY, WYTHE). **2.** German: topographic name for someone who lived by a patch of pasture land or by a hunting ground, Ger. *Weide* (MHG *weide*, OHG *weida* feeding, grazing, hunting; cf. OE *wāð*). **3.** Jewish (Ashkenazic): ornamental name from Ger. *Weide* willow tree.

Vars.: Jewish: **Weid(en)**, **Waide**, **Weid(l)er**, **Weidman(n)**. (Of 2 only): Ger.: **Weidner**, **Weid(t)ler**, **W(e)idmann** (also occupational names for a huntsman).

Dims.: Ger.: **Weidel**, **Weidle**.

Cpds (ornamental): Swed.: **Wid(e)gren** ('willow branch'); **Widerberg** ('willow hill'); **Widholm** ('willow island'); **Widlund** ('willow grove'); **Widmark** ('willow land'); **Widerström** ('willow river'). Jewish: **Weidenbaum**, **Wajdenbaum** ('willow tree'; the second form is a Pol. spelling); **Weidberg** ('willow hill'); **Weidenfeld**, **Waidenfeld** ('willow field'); **Weidhorn** ('willow horn'); **Weidenkopf** ('willow head'); **Weidwasser** ('willow water').

Weifers *see* WEAVER

Weigel *see* WIGGIN

Weigh *see* WAY

Weightman *see* WIGHT

Weiher German: topographic name for someone who lived by a fish pond, Ger. *Weiher* (MHG *wīher*, *wī(w)er*, OHG *wī(w)āri*, from L *vīvārium*, a deriv. of *vīvus* alive).

Weil 1. German: habitation name from any of various places, in Baden, Württemberg, and Bavaria, so called from L *villa* (see VILLE). **2.** Jewish (Ashkenazic): according to Kaganoff, this name was sometimes selected as an anagram of *Lewi*, but there does not seem to be any evidence supporting this conjecture, and it is far more likely that it is a habitation name as in 1, esp. in view of the fact that the vars. ending in *-er* (see below) are clearly habitational.

Vars.: Ger.: **Weill**, **Weile**. Jewish: **Weill**, **Weil(l)er**.

Weiland *see* WIELAND

Weild *see* WALD

Wein 1. German: metonymic occupational name for a producer or seller of wine, from Ger. *Wein* wine, vine (MHG *wīn*; cf. VINE). **2.** Jewish (Ashkenazic): largely an ornamental name, reflecting the prominence of wine in the Jewish Scriptures and its use in several Jewish ceremonies. It has been suggested that the surname has been adopted because of the symbolic association of the vine with the Hebr. personal name ISRAEL ('they shall thoroughly glean the remnant of Israel as a vine', Jer. 6: 9), but since wine is mentioned over nine hundred times in the Jewish Scriptures it is unwise to try to find one passage to explain all the ornamental occurrences of this name.

Vars.: Ger.: **Weiner**, **Wei(n)mann**. Jewish: **Weiner(man)**, **Wainer(man)**, **Veiner**, **Vainer(man)**, **Weinman(n)**, **Veinman**, **Wainman**, **Wajner(man)** (occupational, the last being a Pol. spelling); **Weinbren(n)** (occupational name for a distiller; cf. BRENNER 1); **Weinschenk(er)**, **Wainshenker** (occupational names for an innkeeper; cf. SCHENKE); **Weinis(c)h** (an adj. deriv.).

Cpds (mostly ornamental): Jewish: **Weinapel**, **Wainapel** ('wine apple'); **Weinbach** ('wine stream'); **Weinbaum**, **Veinbaum**, **Wainbaum**, **Wajnbaum** ('wine tree'); WEINBERG; **Weinblatt**, **Weinblot** ('wine leaf'); **Weinblum** ('wine flower'); **Weinblut** ('wine blood', or perhaps 'wine blossom', from Ger. *Blüte*); **Weindorf** ('wine village'); **Weinfeld**, **Wainfeld** ('wine field'); **Waingart(en)**, **Waingarten** ('wine garden' or 'vineyard'); **Weingold** ('wine gold'); **Weingrub** ('wine dig'); **Weinhaus** ('wine house'); **Weinhol(t)z** ('wine wood'); **Weinkeller** ('wine cellar'); **Winekran(t)z** ('wine garland'); **Weinlager** ('wine store');

Weinpres ('wine press'); **Weinreb(e)**, **Weinrib**, **Wainryb**, **Wajnryb**, **Weinraub**, **Weinrieber**, **Weinrober**, **Wainrober** ('wine branch'); **Weinrot** ('wine red'); **Weinsaft**, **Wainsaft** ('wine juice'); **Weinshnabel** ('wine snout'); **Weinstein(er)**, **Veinstein**, **Vainstein**, **Wainshtein**, **Wajnsztajn** ('wine stone'); **Weinsto(c)k**, **Weinshtock**, **Wainshtok**, **Wajnsztok** ('grape vine'); **Weint(h)al**, **Waintal**, **Vaintal** ('wine valley'); **Vaynzof** ('wine guzzle', presumably a nickname for a heavy drinker of wine); **Weinzweig** ('wine twig'). Swed.: **Winblad(h)**, **Vinblad(h)** ('vine leaf'); **Winquist** ('vine twig').

Weinberg 1. German: topographic name for someone who lived near a vineyard on a hillside, or occupational name for someone who worked in one, from Ger. *Weinberg* vineyard (MHG *wīnberc*, a cpd of *wīn* vine + *berc* hill; vineyards were normally built on hillsides). **2.** Jewish (Ashkenazic): ornamental combination of the elements WEIN + BERG, or topographic or ornamental name as in 1.

Vars.: Jewish: **Weinberger**, **Veinberg**, **Wainberg(er)**, **Vainberg(er)**, **Wajnberg**; **Wijnbergen** (Dutch).

Weingrod *see* VINOGRADOV

Weinreich Jewish (Ashkenazic): ornamental name, either a combination of the Ger. elements WEIN wine + *Reich* kingdom, or from mod. Ger. *weinreich* abounding in wine, vines, or a modification of Yid. *vayrekh* incense (Ger. *Weihrauch*).

Vars.: **Weinrich**, **Weinrauch**, **Wainrauch**.

Weinschel Jewish (Ashkenazic): ornamental name, from Yid. *vaynshl* sour cherry (a deriv. of *vayn* wine; cf. WEIN).

Vars.: **Weinshel**, **Weinschal(l)**; **Weins(c)helbaum**, **Wajnszelbaum** ('sour cherry tree', the latter form being a Pol. spelling).

Weintraub Jewish (Ashkenazic): ornamental name, representing a Germanized form of Yid. *vayntroyb* grape (Ger. *Weintraub*).

Vars.: **Weintrob**, **Waintraub**, **Waintrob**; **Wajntraub**, **Wajntrob** (Pol. spellings).

Weir 1. English: topographic name for someone who lived by a dam or weir on a river, a var. of WARE 1. **2.** Irish: Anglicized form of Gael. *Mac an Mhaoir* 'son of the steward'; see McNAIR. **3.** Irish: Anglicized form, based on an erroneous translation (as if from Gael. *core* weir, stepping stones), of various Gael. names such as *Ó Corra* and *Ó Comhraidhe* (see CORR and CORY 2). **4.** Scots: according to Black this name is of Norman origin, from various places in Calvados, Manche, Eure-et-Loire, and Orne called *Vere*, from ON *ver* dam, which makes it ultimately cogn. with 1 above. However, cf. VER 1.

Weisbecker *see* WHITE

Weisselfisch Jewish (E Ashkenazic): either an ornamental name or an anecdotal nickname based on some now irrecoverable event, composed of the Yid. elements *Vaysl* Vistula (the river that flows through Poland) + *fish* fish.

Var.: **Vajselfisz** (Pol. spelling).

Weissgerber German and Jewish (Ashkenazic): occupational name for a dresser of white leather, one whose job was to cure the fine leather from the hide of goats and kids with alum salts; cf. ROTGERBER. The word is a cpd of Ger.

weiss white + *Gerber* leather-dresser (see GERBER); cf. WHITTIER.

Weiter 1. German: occupational name for a gatherer or seller of woad, from an agent deriv. of MHG, OHG *weit* woad; cf. WADER. 2. Jewish (Ashkenazic): apparently an anecdotal nickname, commemorating some now forgotten incident, from mod. Ger. *weiter* farther, or its Yid. cogn. *vayter*.

Weitzberg *see* WHEAT

Wekking *see* WEDEKIND

Wekselman *see* WECHSLER

Weland Scots: of uncertain origin, apparently from a personal name. According to Black it is a form of VALENTINE, but it seems more likely that it is a var. of Wieland.
Var.: **Welland**.

Welbourne English: habitation name from *Welbourn* in Lincs., *Welborne* in Norfolk, or *Welburn* in N Yorks., all so called from OE *well(a)* spring (see WELL) + *burna* stream (see BOURNE).
Var.: **Welburn**.

Welch *see* WALSH

Welcome English: 1. habitation name from places in Devon and Warwicks. called *Welcombe*, from OE *well(a)* spring, stream (see WELL) + *cumb* broad, straight valley (see COOMBE). 2. nickname for a well-liked person or one noted for his hospitality, from ME *welcume*, a calque of OF *bienvenu* or ON *velkominn*.
Vars.: **Welcomme**, **Wellcome**.

Weld *see* WALD

Weldon English: habitation name from a place in Northants, so called from OE *well(a)* spring, stream (see WELL) + *dūn* hill (see DOWN 1).
Vars.: **Welldon**, **Wel(l)den**.

Welford English: habitation name from any of the places so called, of which there are instances in Berks., Gloucs., Northants, and elsewhere. The first is so called from OE *welig* willow + *ford* FORD; the latter two seem to have the first element *well(a)* spring, stream (see WELL). The surname is now found chiefly on Tyneside.

Welham English: habitation name from any of the places so called, of which there are instances in Leics., Notts., and E Yorks. The first gets its name from OE *well(a)* spring, stream (see WELL) + *hām* homestead; the latter two from the dat. pl. *wellum*, originally used after a preposition.
Vars.: **Wellam**, **Wellum**.

Welkovitch *see* VELIKOV

Well English: topographic name for someone who lived near a spring or stream, ME *well(e)* (OE *well(a)*).
Vars.: **Wells**, **Weller**, **Welling(s)**, **Wel(l)man**; WALL, WILL, WOOL.

Wellesley English: apparently a habitation name from an unidentified place, so called from the gen. case of the OE byname *Wealh* 'Foreigner' (cf. WALE 1) + OE *lēah* wood, clearing.

Welliam *see* WILLIAM

Wellington English: habitation name from any of the three places so called, in Herts., Shrops., and Somerset. All are considered by Ekwall to have been originally named in OE as *Wēolingatūn* 'settlement (OE *tūn*) of the *Wēolingas*', a tribal name apparently derived from OE *wēoh* (pagan) temple + *lēah* wood, clearing. This origin is disputed, however, and the meaning is actually quite uncertain.

Welters *see* WALTER

Welton English: habitation name from any of various places, for example in Cumb., Lincs., Northants, and E Yorks., so called from OE *well(a)* spring, stream (see WELL) + *tūn* enclosure, settlement.

Wemyss Scots: habitation name from places in the former counties of Fife and Argylls., so called from OGael. *uaim* cave, with the addition of the ME pl. suffix *-s*. The pronunciation is /wiːmz/.
Vars.: **Weems**, **Wemes**.

Wendt German: name for a Wend, MHG *wind(e)* (OHG *winida*, of unknown origin). The Wends once occupied a large area of NE Germany, and many Ger. placenames and surnames are of Wendish origin. Their Slav. language is still spoken in the SE part of E Germany, around Bautzen and Cottbus.
Vars.: **Wend(e)**, WIND; **Wendisch**; **Windisch** (the name of an Austrian noble family, also sometimes adopted by Ashkenazic Jews); **Winsch**, **Wündisch**, **Wünsch(e)**; **Wentscher**, **Wintscher**, **Wünscher**; **Win(di)schmann**, **Wünschmann**; **Wendland(t)**, **Wendländer**.

Wenham English: habitation name from places so called in Suffolk and Sussex, both of which seem to have as their first element OE *wenn* tumour, used of a tumulus or hill. The former is probably 'homestead (OE *hām*) by a hill', the latter 'watermeadow (OE *hamm*) with tumuli'.

Wenig German and Jewish (Ashkenazic): nickname for a small or insignificant man, from Ger. *wenig* little or, in the case of the Ger. name, from MHG *wēnec, weinec* puny, pitiable (OHG *wēnag, weinag*, from *weinōn* to weep).
Var.: **Weniger** (an inflected form).

Wenman *see* WAIN

Went English: topographic name for someone who lived by a road or path, ME *went* (a deriv. of OE *wendan* to turn).
Var.: **Whent**.

Wentworth English: habitation name from places in Cambs. and S Yorks., probably so called from the OE byname *Wintra* 'WINTER' + OE *worð* enclosure (see WORTH). It is, however, also possible that the name referred to a settlement inhabited only in winter; cf. WINTERBOTTOM and SOMERSCALES.

Wentz *see* WARNER

Wenzel German (of Slav. origin): from the given name *Wenzel*, a dim. (with the Ger. dim. suffix *-el*) of the MHG given name *Wenze*, a borrowing from Slavic representing a short form of the OCzech personal name *Vęceslav* (see VÁCLAV); the borrowing took place before Czech lost its nasal vowels.

Vars.: **Wentzel, Wanzel, Fenzl(ein); Wetzel, Wötzel, Wätzold; Wen(t)zke, Wen(t)zig, Wetz(ig)**.

Dims.: Ger.: **Wenz, Wach(e), Fach(e), Fech(e)**. Czech: **Venclik; Venc**.

Patrs.: Ger.: **Wen(t)zler; Fech(t)ner, Fechler**.

Weöres see VÖRÖS

Wepner German: occupational name for a maker or seller of offensive and defensive weaponry, or for an armed official or a shield-bearer, from an agent deriv. of MHG *wāpen* weapon, shield (a borrowing from Low Ger., used alongside the original High Ger. byform *wāfen*).

Vars.: **Weppner, Weppler**.

Were see WARE

Werf, Van der Dutch: topographic name for someone who lived by a wharf, MDu. *werf* (cf. OE *hwearf*; in mod. Du. the word means 'shipyard').

Var.: **Van der Werff**.

Werfel see WÜRFEL

Werle see WARNER

Werren see WARING

Werth 1. German: topographic name for someone who lived on an island in a river, or on a riverbank, or on a patch of dry land in a fen, all of which were senses of the MHG term *wert, werder* (OHG *werid* island, a cogn. of OE *waroð* shore, bank, apparently from the Gmc root *war-* guard). 2. English: var. of WORTH.

Vars. (of 1): **Werder**.

Wertheim Jewish (W Ashkenazic): habitation name from a place on the Main, so called from OHG *werid* island (see WERTH) + *heim* homestead.

Vars.: **Werthajm** (Pol. spelling); **Wertheimer, Werthaimer, Werthammer**.

Wesker 1. Scots: var. of WISHART. 2. English: topographic name for someone who lived on a patch of damp land to the west of a settlement, from ME *west* WEST + *kerr* marshland (see KERR). The name has also been adopted as a Jewish surname.

Wesley English: habitation name from any of various places named with the OE elements *west* WEST + *lēah* wood, clearing, as for example *Westley* in Cambs. and Suffolk, and *Westleigh* in Devon and Greater Manchester.

Vars.: **Westl(e)y**.

Wesołek see VESELOV

Wessel see WARNER

West English and German: topographic name for someone who lived to the west of a settlement, or regional name for one who had migrated from further west, from ME, MHG *west* west.

Vars.: Eng.: **Western, Westren, Westron** (from the OE adj. *westerne*); **Westman, Wester; Westerman** (chiefly Yorks.). Ger.: **Weste(r), Westermann, West(erl)ing**.

Cpds (mostly ornamental elaborations rather than habitation names): Swed.: **West(er)berg** ('western hill'); **Westerdahl** ('west-ern valley'); **Westergren** ('western branch'); **West(er)holm** ('western island'); **Westerlind** ('western lime'); **West(er)lund** ('western grove'); **Westermark** ('western land').

Westbrook English: habitation name from any of various places, for example in Berks., Kent, and the Isle of Wight, so called from OE *west* WEST + *brōc* BROOK.

Vars.: **Westbrooke, Westbrock**.

Westbury English: habitation name from any of various places, for example in Bucks., Gloucs., Hants, Shrops., Somerset, and Wilts., so called from OE *west* WEST + *burh* fortress, town (see BURY).

Westby English: habitation name from any of various places, for example in Lancs., Lincs., and W Yorks., so called from ON *vestr* WEST + *býr* settlement.

Westcott English: habitation name from any of various minor places, for example *Westcott* in Surrey and Berks., named with the OE elements *west* WEST + *cot* cottage, shelter (see COATES).

Vars.: **Westcot** (another place in Berks.), **Westacott, Westicott, Wescot(t), Weskett, Waistcoat; Westcote** (places in Gloucs., Hants, and Warwicks.), **Westcoate**.

Westgate English: 1. topographic name for someone who lived by the west gate of a city, from ME *west* WEST + *gate* GATE. From the present-day distribution of the surname, the city in question in many if not all cases was probably Norwich. 2. habitation name from any of various places, for example in Co. Durham, Kent, and Northumb., named with these elements.

Westhead English (Lancs.): habitation name from a minor place near Ormskirk, Lancs., presumably so called from ME *west* WEST + *heved* headland (see HEAD 2).

Westhuizen, Van der Dutch: habitation name from places in the provinces of Gelderland and Overijssel, so called from the MDu. elements *west* WEST + *huis* HOUSE.

Westlake English: topographic name for someone who lived to the west of a streamlet, from ME *by weste lake* (see LAKE). The place of this name in Devon derives from the surname, rather than the other way about.

Var.: **Weslake**.

Westmorland N English: regional name for someone from the former county of this name, originally named in OE as *Westmōringaland* 'territory of the people living west of the moors' (i.e. the Pennines).

Var.: **Westmoreland**.

Weston English and Scots: habitation name from any of the very many places so called, from OE *west* WEST + *tūn* enclosure, settlement. In some cases (see below), it may be from the Leics. or Middlesex villages called *Whetstone* or the Derbys. village of *Wheston*, all of which are so called from OE *hwetstān* whetstone. This supposition is supported by forms of the Leics. placename recorded in the 13th and 14th cents., although in Domesday Book it is called *Westham*.

Var.: **Wesson** (Midlands).

Westray 1. English: regional name for someone who migrated from the west, from the ANF adj. *westreis*. 2. Scots:

local name from one of the islands in the Orkneys, so called from ON *vestr* west + *ey* island.

Westrop English: probably a habitation name from *Westrip* in Gloucs. or *Westrop* in Wilts., both originally named with ME *west* WEST + *thorp, throp* village (see THORPE). However, see also below.

Westwood English and Scots: habitation name from any of various places so called, from OE *west* WEST + *wudu* WOOD.

Wetherald *see* WEATHERALL

Wetherbee *see* WEATHERSBY

Wethered *see* WEATHERHEAD

Wetherspoon *see* WITHERSPOON

Wettin German: the noble family of this name (see WINDSOR) trace their descent from Burkhard, Count in the Grabfeld (d. 908). The castle of *Wettin*, on the river Saale near Halle, was acquired by his descendants in the 11th cent., but sold to the Archbishop of Magdeburg in 1288.

Wetton English: habitation name from a place in Staffs., so called from OE *wēt* wet + *dūn* hill (see DOWN 1).

Wetz *see* WENZEL

Wevell *see* WAVELL

Weverinck *see* WEAVER

Wewers *see* WEAVER

Wexelbaum *see* WECHSLER

Wey *see* WAY

Weyman *see* WYMAN

Wężyk Polish: unflattering nickname from a dim. of Pol. *wąż* snake, applied presumably to an astute, cunning, or untrustworthy person.
Var.: **Wąż**.

Whaites *see* WAITE

Whale English: nickname for a large, ungainly person, from ME *hwal* whale (OE *hwæl*).
Var.: **Whall**.
Patr.: **Whales**.

Whalen *see* WHELAN

Whaler *see* WHEELER

Whalley English: habitation name from *Whalley* in Lancs. or *Whaley* in Derbys., both so called from OE *hwealf* vault, arch, hill + *lēah* wood, clearing. In some cases it may also be from *Waley* in Ches., which has as its first element OE *weg* path, road (see WAY).
Vars.: **Whaley**, **Wal(l)ey**.

Whamond *see* WYMAN

Whannell *see* MCCONNELL

Wharin *see* WARING

Wharmby English (E Midlands): habitation name from *Quarmby* in W Yorks., recorded in Domesday Book as

Cornebi, apparently from ON *kvern* handmill + *býr* farm, settlement.
Var.: **Quarmby**.

Wharrick *see* WARWICK

Wharrier *see* WARR

Whartmouth *see* WATMOUGH

Wharton English: habitation name from any of various places so called. Examples in Ches. and Herefords. are from an OE river name *Wæfer* (derived from *wæfre* wandering, winding) + OE *tūn* settlement; another in Lincs. has as its first element OE *wearde* beacon or *waroð* shore, bank; one in the former county of Westmorland (now in Cumb.) is from OE *hwearf* wharf, embankment + *tūn*.

Whate *see* WHEAT

Whateley *see* WHEATLEY

Whatkins *see* WATT

Whatman *see* WATMAN

Whatmore English: 1. var. of WATMOUGH. 2. habitation name from *Whatmoor* in Shrops., apparently so called from OE *wēt* wet + *mōr* marsh.
Vars.: **Watmore**, **W(h)atmoor**.

Whatrup *see* WARDROP

Whay *see* WAY

Wheat English (chiefly Notts.): metonymic occupational name for a grower or seller of wheat, from OE *hwǣte* wheat (a deriv. of *hwīt* white, because of its use in making white flour).
Vars.: **W(h)eate**, **Whate**, **Weet**.
Cpds: Jewish (ornamental, possibly adopted by or assigned to millers or bakers): **Weitzberg** ('wheat hill'); **Weitzfeld** ('wheat field').

Wheatcroft English: habitation name from some place so called from OE *hwǣte* WHEAT + *croft* paddock, smallholding (see CROFT). There is one such place in Derbys.; the surname is most common in Notts.
Var.: **Whitcroft**.

Wheatley English: habitation name from any of various places, for example in Essex, Lancs., Notts., Oxon., and W Yorks., so called from OE *hwǣte* WHEAT + *lēah* wood, clearing.
Vars.: **Wheatly**, **Wheatleigh**; **Whately** (a place in Warwicks.), **Whateley**; **Whatley** (a place in Somerset), **Whatly**, **Watley**.

Wheatman *see* WATMAN

Wheaton English: of uncertain origin, apparently a habitation name, perhaps from an unidentified place named with the OE elements *hwǣte* WHEAT + *tūn* enclosure, settlement.

Wheeker *see* WEAKE

Wheel English: from ME *whele* wheel (OE *hwēol*, *hweowol*), generally no doubt a metonymic occupational name for a maker of wheels (cf. WHEELER), but perhaps occasionally a topographic name for someone who lived near a water-wheel.
Vars.: **Wheele**, **Wheels**, **Wheal(e)**, **Wheals**, **While**, **Whewell**.

Wheeldon English: habitation name from *Wheeldon* in Derbys. or *Whielden* in Bucks. The former is so called from OE *hwēol* WHEEL (referring perhaps to a rounded shape) + *dūn* hill (see DOWN 1), the latter from *hwēol* + *denu* valley (see DEAN 1).

Vars.: **Wh(i)eldon**, **W(he)ildon**, **Wheelden**.

Wheeler English: occupational name for a maker of wheels (for vehicles or for use in spinning or various other manufacturing processes), from an agent deriv. of ME *whele* WHEEL.

Vars.: **Wheeller**, **Whe(al)ler**, **Whaler**, **Wailer**, **Wayler**, **W(h)iler**, **Wyler**; **Wheelwright** (see WRIGHT); **W(h)ilesmith** (see SMITH).

Equivs.: Low Ger. and Du.: RADEMAKER. Pol.: KOŁODZIEJ.

Wheelhouse English (Yorks. and E Midlands): habitation name, composed of the ME elements *whele* WHEEL + *hous* HOUSE. According to Reaney, the reference is often to a house near a dammed-up stream where a cutler ground his knives on a small water-wheel. The cpd is not attested as a vocab. word in this or any other sense before the 19th cent., although the surname William *de Whelehous* is found in 1379.

Whelan Irish: Anglicized form of Gael. **Ó Faoláin** 'descendant of *Faolán*', a personal name representing a dim. of *faol* wolf.

Vars.: **Wheelan**, **Whelehan**, **O'Whealane**, **(O')Whalen**; **O'F(e)olane**, **(O')Fylan**; **O'Phelane**, **Phelan**, **Philan**; **Heelan**; **Wolf**.

Whenman *see* WAIN

Whent *see* WENT

Where *see* WARE

Whick *see* WICK

Whieldon *see* WHEELDON

Whiffen *see* WIFFEN

Whild *see* WILD

While *see* WHEEL

Whiler *see* WHEELER

Whimster *see* FEMISTER

Whin *see* SWEENEY

Whineray *see* WINROW

Whipp English: of uncertain origin, perhaps a metonymic occupational name for someone who carried out judicial floggings, from ME *whip* (probably of Low Ger. origin, from a Gmc root indicating quick movement).

Whipple English: of uncertain origin, perhaps a topographic name for someone who lived by a whipple tree. Chaucer lists the *whippletree* together with the maple, thorn, beech, hazel, and yew; the word apparently denotes the cornel tree, and is a cogn. of MLG *wipelbōm*.

Whiscard *see* WISHART

Whistler English: occupational name for a player on a pipe or flute, from an agent deriv. of ME *whistle* (OE *hwistle*, of imitative origin). Alternatively, it may be a nick-name for someone noted for his habit of whistling cheerfully.

Var.: **Wissler**.

Whiston English: habitation name from any of various places so called. Examples in Lancs. and W Yorks. are named from OE *hwīt* white + *stān* stone, while one in Staffs. is from the gen. case of the OE byname *Hwīt* 'White' + OE *tūn* enclosure, settlement. Another place of the same name, in Northants, was probably named as the settlement associated with *Hwicce*, an OE personal name from the tribal name *Hwicce*.

Whitbread English: metonymic occupational name for a baker of the finer sorts of bread, from ME *whit* WHITE or *whete* WHEAT + *bred* bread (OE *brēad*). For the confusion between the two first elements, cf. WHITTAKER.

Whitby English: habitation name from the port in N Yorks., so called from ON *hvítr* white + *býr* farm, settlement, or from a place of the same name in Ches., originally named with OE *hwīt* white (i.e. stone-built) + *burh* manor-house, fortified place.

Whitchurch English: habitation name from any of several places so named from having a 'white' church, i.e. one built of stone.

Whitcombe English: habitation name from any of various places so called, for example in Dorset and the Isle of Wight. The former means 'wide valley' (see WITCOMB), the latter 'white valley', from OE *hwīt* + *cumb*.

Vars.: **Whitcomb** (used in S Fermanagh as an Anglicized form of Gael. *Mac Thighearnáin* (see TIERNEY), perhaps because the contracted form *Kiernáin* was associated with *cíor* comb); **Witcomb(e)**.

Whitcroft *see* WHEATCROFT

White English, Scots, and Irish: nickname for someone with white hair or an unnaturally pale complexion, from ME *whit* white (OE *hwīt*). In some cases it may represent the ME use as a given name of an OE byname, *Hwīt(a)*, of this origin. As a Sc. and Ir. surname it has been widely used as a translation of various Gael. names derived from the elements *bán* white (see BAIN 1) or *fionn* fair (see FINN 1). There has also been some confusion with WIGHT. It has also been adopted by Ashkenazic Jews as an Anglicization of any of the various Jewish surnames listed below.

Vars.: **Whyte** (esp. Sc. and Ir.); **Whitt(e)** (Notts.), **Witt(e)**.

Dims.: Low Ger.: **Wittke**, **Wittje**, **Wittgen**. Pol.: **Wajsczyk**.

Patrs.: Eng.: **Whit(e)ing**, **W(h)itting**; **Whites**, **Witts**; **Whit(e)son**, **Whitsun** (chiefly Sc.). Low Ger.: **Witten**, **Witting**.

Patr. (from a dim.): Low Ger.: **Wittgens**.

Cpds (mostly ornamental elaborations): Jewish: **Weissadler** ('white eagle'); **Weissbaum**, **Weisbom**, **Waissbaum**, **Wajsbaum** ('white tree'); **Weissbecher** ('white goblet'); **Weis(s)becker**, **Wajsbecker** (occupational name from Ger. *Weissbäcker* fancy baker); **Weis(s)bein**, **Veisbein** ('white bone'); **Wajsberg**, **Waysberg**, **Weiszberger** ('white hill'); **Weissblat(t)**, **Weisblat**, **Waisblat** ('white leaf'); **Weissblech** ('white tin'); **Weis(s)blum**, **Weissbloom** ('white flower'); **Weissbluth** ('white blossom'); **Weis(s)brem** ('white eyebrow'); **Weissbrod**, **Weisbrod(t)**, **Waisbrot**, **Waysbrot** ('white bread', occupational name for a baker); **Weissbrun** ('white brown'); **Weis(s)buch**, **Veisbuch** ('white book', or perhaps from mod. Ger. *Weissbuche* hornbeam); **Weissburg** ('white town'); **Weis(s)feld**, **Vaisfeld**,

Wajsfeld ('white field', partly Anglicized as **Weisfield**); **Weis(s)fisch** ('white fish'); **Wajsfogiel** ('white bird'); **Weisgarten** ('white garden'); **Weis(s)glas, Weisglass, Wajsglus** ('white glass'); **Wajsgras** ('white grass'); **Weishaus** ('white house'); **Weisshaut** ('white skin'); **Weisshof, Wajshof** ('white court'); **Weisskirch** ('white church'); **Weis(s)kopf, Weiszkopf** ('white head'); **Weissmel, Wajsmehl** ('white flour'); **Weisrosen** ('white roses'); **Weissalz** ('white salt'); **Waissztein** ('white stone'); **Weistuch, Waistuch** ('white cloth'); **Weiswasser** ('white water'); **Waiswohl** ('white wool', or perhaps from Yid. *veys voyl* knows well).

Whitecross Scots: habitation name from any of various minor places that get their names from a cross of white stone, perhaps principally *Whitecross* in the parish of Chapel in the former county of Aberdeens.

Whiteford Scots: habitation name from a place named with the elements WHITE + FORD, in most cases apparently from *Whitefoord* near Paisley, outside Glasgow.

Whitehead **1.** English and Scots: nickname for someone with fair or prematurely white hair, from ME *whit* WHITE + *heved* HEAD. **2.** Irish (Connacht): erroneous translation of CANAVAN, as if it were from Gael. *ceann* head + *bán* white.

Var.: **Whytehead**.

Whitehorn Scots: habitation name from *Whithorn* near Wigtown, so called from OE *hwīt* WHITE + *ærn* house. The settlement is said to have been established in the 5th cent. by St Ninian, and named from the white stone church built by him.

Vars.: **Whitehorne, Whithorn**.

Whitehouse English (widespread, but especially common in the W Midlands): topographic name for someone who lived in a white house, from ME *whit* WHITE + *hous* HOUSE, or habitation name from a place named with these elements, as for example *Whittus* in Cumb.

Vars.: **Whithous, Whitters**.

Whitelaw Scots and N English: habitation name from any of various places in the Borders so called, from OE *hwīt* WHITE + *hlāw* hill (see LAW 2).

Vars.: **Whitlaw, Whyt(e)law**.

Whiteley English (chiefly Yorks.): habitation name from any of various places, mostly now spelled *Whitley*, named with the OE elements *hwīt* WHITE + *lēah* wood, clearing.

Vars.: **Whitely, Whit(t)ley, Whit(t)la, Witley**.

Whiter English: occupational name for a bleacher or a whitewasher, from an agent deriv. of ME *whit* WHITE.

Vars.: **Whitter** (Lancs.), **Whitta**.

Whiteside English (Lancs.) and Scots (also N Ireland): probably a habitation name from any of various minor places so called, from OE *hwīt* WHITE + *sīde* slope of a hill. Reaney, however, quotes early forms without prepositions and derives the surname from a nickname.

Var.: **Whitesides**.

Whitesmith *see* SMITH

Whitfield English: habitation name from any of various places, for example in Derbys., Kent, Northants, and Northumb., so called from OE *hwīt* WHITE + *feld* pasture, open country (see FIELD), because of their chalky soil.

Var.: **Whitefield** (places in Lancs. and the Isle of Wight).

Whitford English: habitation name from a place in Devon, so called from OE *hwīt* WHITE + *ford* FORD, or possibly also from some other place similarly named.

Whitgift English: habitation name from a place in Humberside, so called from the ON byname *Hvíti* 'White' + ON *gipt* gift, dowry.

Whitlam English: nickname for an inoffensive individual, from ME *whit* WHITE + *lam* LAMB. Some examples may be house names from houses marked with such a sign, in origin a reference to the paschal lamb.

Vars.: **Whitelam, Whit(e)lum**.

Whitlock English: **1.** nickname for someone with white or fair hair, from ME *whit* WHITE + *lock* tress, curl; cf. SHERLOCK. **2.** from an OE personal name composed of the elements *wiht* creature, demon + *lāc* play, sport.

Vars.: (of 1): **Whitelock(e)**.

Whitman English: from ME *whit* white + *man* man, either a nickname with the same sense as WHITE, or else an occupational name for a servant of a bearer of the nickname WHITE.

Vars.: **Whiteman, Wittman**.

Whitmarsh English: habitation name from a place in the parish of Sedgehill, Wilts., so called from OE *hwīt* WHITE (i.e. phosphorescent) + *mersc* MARSH; cf. WHITMORE.

Whitmore English: **1.** habitation name from any of various places, for example in Staffs., so called from OE *hwīt* WHITE + *mōr* moor (see MOORE 1). **2.** in some cases, bearers of the name are apparently descended from John of *Whytenmere*, Shrops., who lived in the 13th cent. This form may represent a poor spelling for *Whittimere* on the Staffs.-Shrops. border, the name of which perhaps means 'pool associated with someone called *Hwīta*'.

Vars. (of 1): **Whitemore; Whittemore, Whit(t)amore, Whittimore, Wittamore** (Devon forms, probably from *Whitmoor* in that county). (Of 2): **Whitmer**.

Whitney English: habitation name from a place in Herefords., the etymology of which is uncertain. The second element is OE *ēg* island, low-lying land; the first appears to be *hwītan*, which is either the gen. sing. of an OE byname *Hwīta* 'White', or the weak dat. case (originally used after a preposition and article) of the adj. *hwīt* white.

Whittaker English: habitation name from any of various places named from OE *hwīt* WHITE or *hwǣte* WHEAT + *æcer* cultivated land (see ACKER), as for example *Whitaker* in Lancs. and *Whitacre* in Warwicks. (both 'white field') or *Whiteacre* in Kent and *Wheatacre* in Norfolk (both 'wheat field').

Vars.: **Whit(e)aker; Whitticase**.

Whittier English: occupational name for a white-leather dresser, from ME *whit* WHITE + *taw(i)er* TAWYER (cf. WEISSGERBER).

Vars.: **Whit(t)ear, Whit(e)hair, Whithear**.

Whittingham English and Scots: habitation name from places in Lancs., Northumb., and the former county of E Lothian, originally named in OE as *Hwītingahām* 'homestead (OE *hām*) of the people of *Hwīta*', a byname meaning WHITE'.

Whittington English: habitation name from any of a large number of places so called, for example in Gloucs., Worcs., Warwicks., Shrops., Staffs., Derbys., Lancs., and Northumb. The placename could mean *Hwīta*'s settlement' (OE *Hwītantūn*), 'settlement associated with *Hwīta*' (OE *Hwītingtūn*), or (at the) white settlement' (OE *(æt ðǽm) hwītan tūne*).

Var.: **Whitington**.

Whittle English (chiefly Lancs.): **1.** habitation name from any of various places, especially one in Lancs., so called from OE *hwīt* WHITE + *hyll* HILL. **2.** var. of WHITWELL.

Whitton Scots and English: habitation name from any of various places, for example in the former county of Roxburghs., Co. Durham, Northumb., Shrops., Suffolk, and SW London, so called from the OE byname *Hwīta* WHITE' (or the adj. *hwīt* white) + OE *tūn* enclosure, settlement.

Whitty English: of uncertain origin, possibly: **1.** habitation name from an unidentified place named with the OE elements *hwīt* WHITE + *(ge)hæg* enclosure (see HAY 1). **2.** nickname for someone with unusually pale eyes, from ME *whit* WHITE + *eye* eye (OE *ēaga*).

Vars.: **Whit(t)ey**, **Whitie**.

Whitwell English: habitation name from any of various places, for example in Dorset, Herts., Leics. (formerly Rutland), Norfolk, and N Yorks., so called from OE *hwīt* WHITE + *well(a)* spring, stream (see WELL).

Vars.: **Whit(t)ell**, WHITTLE.

Whitworth English: habitation name from any of several places so called, from the OE byname *Hwīta* WHITE' (or the adj. *hwīt* white) + OE *worð* enclosure (see WORTH). The chief places of this name are in Co. Durham and Lancs., but the surname is fairly evenly distributed throughout N England and the Midlands.

Whooley see HOOLEY

Whorall see WORRALL

Whorisky see FOURISH

Why see GUY

Whyard see WYATT

Whybrow English: from the ME female given name *Wyburgh*, OE *Wīgburh*, composed of the elements *wīg* war + *burh* fortress.

Vars.: **Whybro**, **Wybrow**, **Wibrow**, **Wibroe**.

Whyman see WYMAN

Whyte see WHITE

Whytehead see WHITEHEAD

Whytelaw see WHITELAW

Wiarda see GUICHARD

Wibroe see WHYBROW

Wich **1.** English: topographic or habitation name, from a palatalized form of OE *wīc*; see WICK. **2.** English: topographic name for someone who lived by a wych elm tree, OE *wice*. **3.** Polish: from the given name *Wich*, shortened form of the given names *Wincenty* (see VINCENT) and *Węcesław* (see VÁCLAV).

Vars.: (of 1 and 2): **Wych**, **Wee(t)ch**. (Of 3): **Wichan**; **Wiech**.

Wicharz see GUICHARD

Wick English: topographic name for someone who lived in an outlying settlement dependent on a larger village, OE *wīc* (L *vīcus*; cf. VICO 1), or habitation name from a place named with this word, of which there are examples in Berks., Gloucs., Somerset, and Worcs. The term seems to have been used especially of an outlying dairy farm or a salt works.

Vars.: **Whick**, **Wi(c)ke**, **Wyke**, WEAKE; **Wick(e)s**, **Wix**, **Wykes**; **Wicken(s)**, **Wickins** (from the OE dat. pl. *wīcum*, with the addition of the ME pl. suffix -*s*); **W(h)icker**, **W(h)ickman**; **Att(w)ick**.

Wickberg see WIK

Wickham English: habitation name from any of various places so called, for example in Cambs., Suffolk, Essex, Herts., Kent, Hants, Berks., and Oxon. It has been established that *wīchām* was an OE term for a settlement (OE *hām*) associated with a Romano-British town, *wīc* in this case being an adaptation of L *vīcus*. Childs Wickham in Gloucs. bears a British name with a different etymology.

Vars.: **Wykeham**; **Wigham** (Northumb. and Scotland).

Wiczkiewicz see VINCENT

Widdecombe see WITHYCOMBE

Widdekind see WEDEKIND

Widdow English: nickname for a widow or widower, both described in ME by the term *widow(e)* (OE *widewe* fem., *widewa* masc.).

Pol.: **Wdowiak** (masc.).

Dims.: It.: **Vedovelli**, **Vedovetto**, **Vedovotto**. Pol.: **Wdowczak**. Ukr.: **Udov(ich)enko**, **Vdovenko**. Beloruss.: **Udovchik**. Metrs. (or patrs.): Eng.: **Widdow(e)s**, **Widders**, **Widdess**, **Widdas**; **Wid(d)owson**, **Widde(r)son**, **Widdison**. It. (metr. only): **Della Vedova**. Russ. (metr. only): **Vdovin**.

Widdrington English (Northumb.): habitation name from a place in Northumb., so called from OE *Wuduheringatūn* 'settlement (OE *tūn*) of the people of *Wuduhere*', a personal name composed of the elements *wudu* wood + *here* army.

Widegren see WEIDE

Wiech see WICH

Wiechers see GUICHARD

Więclawicz see VÁCLAV

Wieczorek Polish: nickname for someone supposedly resembling a bat, from Pol. dial. *wieczorek* bat, dim. of *wieczor* evening (cogn. with Czech (Moravian) *večeřek*, dim. of *večer* evening).

Patr.: Pol.: **Wieczorkiewicz**.

Habitation name: Pol.: **Wieczorkowski**.

Wieland 1. German: from a Gmc personal name composed of the elements *wīg* war + *land* land, territory. This name was borne by the supernaturally skilled smith of Gmc folk legend, and for this reason it may in part have been given as a nickname to smiths. **2.** Jewish (Ashkenazic): presumably an adoption of the Ger. surname.

Var.: **Weiland**.

Wien German and Jewish (Ashkenazic): habitation name from the city of Vienna (Ger. *Wien*, Yid. *Vin*). The placename is first recorded in the L form *Vindobona*, and is of Celt. origin. Before the Holocaust there was a large Jewish population in Vienna; from the 17th cent. onwards the Leopoldstadt district was officially designated as a Jewish quarter, and many families bearing this surname no doubt originated there.

Var.: **Wiener**.

Wientzek *see* VINCENT

Wierzbicki Polish: habitation name from *Wierzbica*, a town in Poland S of Radom (the name of which is derived from Pol. *wierzba* willow; cf. Czech VRBA), or topographic name for someone who lived among willow trees.

Var.: **Wierzbowski**.

Wiese German: topographic name for someone who lived by a patch of meadowland, Ger. *Wiese* (MHG *wise*, OHG *wisa*).

Vars.: **Wieser, Wies(e)ner, Wiesemann**.

Cpds (ornamental): Jewish: **Wiesenberg** ('meadow hill'); **Wiesenfeld** ('meadow field'); **Wiesengrund** ('meadow ground'); **Wiesenthal** ('meadow valley'); **Wiesenstern** ('meadow star').

Wiestner *see* WÜST

Wiffen English: of uncertain origin, possibly a habitation name from an unidentified place named with the OE elements *hwīt* white, i.e. phosphorescent + *fen* marsh; cf. WHITMARSH and WHITMORE 1.

Vars.: **Whiffen, Whiffin**.

Wigder *see* AVIGDOR

Wigg English (E Anglia): **1.** nickname from ME *wigge* beetle, bug (OE *wicga*; cf. mod. Eng. *earwig*). **2.** metonymic occupational name for a maker of fancy breads baked in rounds and then divided up into wedge-shaped slices, ME *wigge* (from MDu. *wigge* wedge(-shaped cake); cf. SPITZWEG).

Var. (of 2): **Wigger**.

Patr. (from 1): **Wiggs**.

Wiggers *see* GUICHARD

Wiggin English: **1.** from the Bret. personal name *Wiucon*, composed of elements meaning 'worthy' + 'high', 'noble', which was introduced into England by followers of William the Conqueror. **2.** from the Gmc personal name *Wīgant*, originally a byname meaning 'Warrior', from the pres. part. of *wīgan* to fight, likewise introduced to England in the wake of the Conquest.

Vars.: **Wigin, Wigan(d)**.

Dims. (of 2): Ger.: **Weigel(t), Weigl; Witzel**.

Patrs.: Eng.: **Wiggins, Wiggans, Wigens**.

Wigglesworth English (W Yorks.): habitation name from a place in Ribblesdale, recorded in Domesday Book as *Winchelesuuorde*, from the gen. case of the OE byname *Wincel* 'Child' + OE *worð* enclosure (see WORTH).

Wigham *see* WICKHAM

Wight Scots and N English: **1.** nickname for a strong-willed or brave man, from ME *wigt* valiant, stalwart (ON *vígt*). **2.** topographic name for someone who lived by a bend or curve in a river or road, OE *wiht* (a deriv. of *wican* to bend). There does not seem to be any connection between modern bearers of this surname and the Isle of *Wight* (the name of which is apparently of Brit. origin, perhaps meaning 'watershed').

Vars. (of 1): **W(e)ightman**.

Wigley English: habitation name from places in Derbys. and Hants, so called from the OE byname *Wicga* 'Beetle', 'Bug' (cf. WIGG 1) + *lēah* wood, clearing.

Wigmore English: habitation name from a place in Herefords., so called from OE *wicga* (see WIGG 1) in the sense 'something moving' + *mōr* marsh (see MOORE 1).

Wignal English (Lancs.): habitation name from a minor place near Holmes in the parish of Croston, so called from the gen. case of the OE byname *Wicga* 'Beetle', 'Insect' (cf. WIGG 1) + OE *h(e)alh* nook, corner, recess (see HALE 1). The surname occurs in the surrounding area from the 14th cent., and had already become frequent there by the 16th.

Wijnbergen *see* WEINBERG

Wik Swedish: ornamental name from Swed. *vik* bay (ON *vík*), perhaps sometimes chosen as a topographic name by someone who lived by a bay.

Vars.: **Wi(c)kmann, Vi(c)kmann** (of which **Wikander** is a Graecized form); **Wikner**.

Cpds: **Wi(c)kberg** ('bay hill'); **Wi(c)klund** ('bay grove'); **Wi(c)kström, Vi(c)kström** ('bay river').

Wike *see* WICK

Wiktorczyk *see* VICTOR

Wilberfoss English: habitation name from a place in Humberside, so called from the OE female personal name *Wilburh* (composed of the elements *wil* will, desire + *burh* fortress) + OE *foss* ditch (see FOSS).

Var.: **Wilberforce**.

Wilbert English: from a Gmc personal name composed of the elements *wil* will, desire + *berht* bright, famous. The native form, *Wilbeorht*, is attested before the Conquest, but was greatly reinforced in the early Middle Ages by the introduction of the Continental cogn. by the Normans.

Dims.: Fr.: **Guilbon, Guilbot**.

Patrs.: Low Ger.: **Wilbertz, Wilbers; Wilberding**.

Wilby English: habitation name from any of various places so called. One in Norfolk probably represents a contracted form of WILLOUGHBY; one in Suffolk is from OE *wilig* willow + *bēag* ring, circle; and one in Northants is from the ON personal name *Vili* (a short form of various cpd names with the first element *vil* will, desire) + ON *býr* settlement. The surname is found in E Anglia, but is most common in W Yorks.

Wilcock English (chiefly Lancs. and Yorks.): from a medieval given name, a dim. of WILL 1 with the addition of the hypocoristic suffix -*cock* (see COCK 1).

Vars.: **Willcock** (Devon), **Wilcocke**.

Patrs.: **Wil(l)cocks**, **Wil(l)cox** (widespread throughout England); **Wil(l)cockson**, **Wil(l)cox(s)on**.

Wild English: **1.** nickname for a man of violent and undisciplined character, from ME *wild* wild, uncontrolled (OE *wilde*). **2.** topographic name for someone who lived on a patch of uncultivated land left in a state of nature.

Vars.: **Wilde**, **Whild(e)**, **Wyld(e)**; **Wilder**, **Wildman**.

Patrs. (from 1): Eng.: **Wyld(e)s**.

Wildig English: of uncertain origin, possibly a var. of WILDING. The name has not been found in records before the late 16th cent.; John *Wildigge* was married at Wybunbury, Ches., in 1581, and the name is still concentrated in that area.

Vars.: **Wildigg**, **Willdig(g)**.

Wilding English (now chiefly Lancs.): from the OE personal name *Wilding, a deriv. of OE *wilde* wild, savage (see WILD 1). It is also possible that it may be from a topographical term derived from the same vocab. word (cf. WILD 2), but early forms with prepositions are not found.

Var.: **Wilden**.

Wildish English: topographic name for someone who lived in an area of wooded land, from OE *wealdisc*, an adj. deriv. of *weald* wood (see WALD).

Var.: **Wildash**.

Wildon see WHEELDON

Wildy English: of uncertain origin. Reaney claims that it is a var. of WALTHEW, but this is by no means certain.

Var.: **Willday**.

Wileman English: occupational name for a trapper or hunter, or nickname for a devious person, from ME *wile* trap, snare (late OE *wīl* contrivance, trick, possibly of Scandinavian origin) + *man* man (OE *mann*).

Vars.: **Wiles**, **Wyles**.

Wiler see WHEELER

Wilk **1.** English: from a medieval given name, a back-formation from WILKIN, as if that contained the ANF dim. suffix -*in*. **2.** Polish: from Pol. *wilk* WOLF, probably from an OSlav. personal name containing this element, but perhaps also applied as a nickname for someone thought to resemble a wolf or connected with wolves in some other way.

Vars. (of 1): **Wilck**, **Wilke**.

Dims. (of 1): Eng.: **Wilkie** (Scotland). (Of 2): Pol.: **Wilczek**. Ukr.: **Vovchenko**. Beloruss.: **Volchik**. Czech: **Vlček**.

Patrs. (from 1): Eng.: **Wilk(e)s**. (From 2): Pol.: **Wilkowicz**, **Wilczak**. Ukr.: **Vovkovich**. Russ.: **Volkov**. Bulg.: **Vulkov**, **Vluchkov**. Croatian: **Vuk(ov)ić**, **Vukotić**.

Patrs. (from dims. of 1): Eng.: **Wilkieson** (Scotland). (From dims. of 2): Croatian: **Vuk(i)č(ev)ić**, **Vukelić**, **Vučić**, **Vučković**, **Vučinić**, **Vučenović**, **Vučetić**, **Vučićević**.

Habitation name (from 2): Pol.: **Wilczyński**.

Wilkin English: from a medieval given name, a short form of WILL with the addition of the hypocoristic suffix -*kin* (of Low Ger. origin).

Var.: **Wilken**.

Patrs.: **Wilkins**, **Wilkens**; **Wilkinson**, **Wilkenson**, **Wilkerson**.

Will **1.** Scots and N English: from the medieval given name *Will*, a dim. of WILLIAM. In a few cases it may be from one of the other medieval given names with this first element; cf., e.g., WILBERT and WILLARD. **2.** S and SW English: topographic name for someone who lived by a spring or stream, ME *will* (from the W Saxon form, *wiell(a)*, of OE *well(a)*; see WELL).

Dims. (of 1): Eng.: WILCOCK, WILKIN; **Willet(t)**, **Willitt**, **Willott**, GILLET. Fr.: **Guillet(on)**, **Willet**; **Guillot(eau)**, **Guilloton**, **Will(i)ot**, **Vuillot**, **Vuillod**; **Guillon(eau)**, **Guillou(x)**, **Guilloud**, **Guill(a)in**, **Guilly**, **Vuillin**. Low Ger.: **Wil(l)mann**, **Wilke**. Flem., Du.: **Wilman**, **Willeke**. Pol.: **Wilmański**, **Wilmanowski**.

Patrs. (from 1): Eng.: **Will(e)s**, **Willis**, **Wyllis**; **Wilson**, **Will(e)son**, **Willison**. Low Ger.: **Willing(s)**. Flem., Du.: **Wils(ens)**. Swed.: **Wil(l)sson**, **Vil(l)sson**.

Patrs. (from 1) (dims.): Eng.: **Willetts** (esp. W Midlands), **Wilets**, **Willats**. Low Ger.: **Willmanns**, **Wilken(s)**. Flem., Du.: **Willekens**.

Willard English: from a Gmc personal name composed of the elements *wil* wil, desire + *hard* brave, hardy, strong.

Var.: **Wyllarde**.

Patrs.: Low Ger.: **Willers**, **Willerding**.

Willerton English: habitation name from *Willoughton* in Lincs., so called from OE *wilig* willow + *tūn* enclosure, settlement; cf. WILTON.

Willey English: habitation name from any of various places so called. Those in Ches., Herefords., Shrops., and Warwicks. are named from OE *wilig* willow + *lēah* wood, clearing; one in Devon probably has as its first element OE *wīdig* willow, while one in Surrey has OE *wēoh* pagan temple.

Willgress English (E Anglia): apparently a nickname from ME *wild* WILD + *grise* pig (see GRICE 2).

Vars.: **Wilgress**, **Wilgrass**, **Willgross**.

William English: from the Norman form of an OF personal name composed of the Gmc elements *wil* will, desire + *helm* helmet, protection. This was introduced into England at the time of the Conquest, and within a very short period it became the most popular given name in England, mainly no doubt in honour of the Conqueror himself. The given name has also enjoyed considerable popularity in Germany (as *Wilhelm*), France (as *Guillaume*), Spain (as *Guillermo*), and Italy (as *Guglielmo*, with numerous dims.).

Vars.: **Welliam**; **Gill(i)am**, **Gil(l)ham**, **Gillum** (from central Fr. forms).

Dims.: Eng.: **Willmett**, **Wil(l)mot(t)**, **Willimott**, **Willmutt**, **Wil(l)min**, **Will(i)ment**, **Willament**, **Willimont** (from OF forms; see WILL for native derivs., and also WYATT). Fr.: **Guillaumet**, **Guil(le)met**, **Willemet**, **Vuillaumet**, **Vuille(r)met**; **Guillaumot**, **Guil(le)mot**, **Willemot**, **Vuille(r)mot**; **Guillaumin**, **Guil(le)min(ot)**, **Willemin**, **Vuillaumin**, **Vuillem(a)in**, **Vuilleminet**, **Vuilleminot**, **Vuillemenot**; **Guillaumeau**, **Guillermou**, **Guillermic** (Brittany). It.: **Guglielmin(ett)i**, **Guglielmino**, **Gelmini**, **Vielmini**, **Ghiglino**, **Viglini**;

G(ugli)elmetti, **Vielmetti**, **Viglietto**, **Viglietti**, **Biglietto**, **Biglietti**; **Guglielmotti**, **Ghilgliotti**, **Vigliotto**, **Vigliotti**, **Guglielmelli**; **Guglielmucci**; **Memoli** (Campania). Cat.: **Guillemet**. Port.: **Guilhermino**. Czech: **Vilímek**.

Augs.: Fr.: **Guillaumat**. It.: **Guglielmoni**, **Guglielmone**, **Ghiglione**, **Viglione**; **Memon** (Venetia).

Patrs.: Eng.: **Williams** (also very common in Wales); **Willems**; **Wiliems** (Wales); **Williamson**; **Fitzwilliam(s)**. Sc.: McWILLIAM. Fr.: **Aguillaume**. It.: **De Guglielmo**. Ger.: **Wilhelmer**; **Wilhelmi** (Latinized). Low Ger.: **Wil(he)lms(en)**. Flem., Du.: **Willems**, **Wil(l)ms**, **Willemse(n)**. Dan., Norw.: **Wilhelmsen**, **Vilhelmsen**, **Willumsen**, **Villumsen**. Swed.: **Wilhelmsson**, **Vilhelmsson**.

Patrs. (from dims.): Eng.: **Willmetts**, **Willmotts**.

Habitation names: Pol.: **Wilimowski**, **Wiliński**. Czech: **Vilímovský**.

Willmore English: habitation name from *Wildmore* in Lincs. or the *Weald Moors* in Shrops., both named with the OE elements *wild* wild, uncultivated (see WILD 2) + *mōr* moor, marsh (see MOORE 1).

Var.: **Wilmore**.

Willner 1. German: habitation name from any of various places, for example in Saxony, Upper Franconia, the Upper Palatinate, and Upper Austria, called *Wildenau*, from OHG *wildi* wild, uncultivated (with the adj. retaining the weak dat. ending originally used after a preposition and article) + *ouwa* wet land, marsh. 2. Jewish (E Ashkenazic): habitation name from Yid. *vilner* native or inhabitant of the Lithuanian city of Vilnius (Yid. *Vilne*).

Vars. (of 1): **Wil(d)ner**. (Of 2): **Wilner**, **Vilner**; **Vilnai** (Israeli, a Hebr. form).

Willock Scots and English: from the ME and OE personal name *Willoc*, dim. from a short form of the various cpd names with the first element *willa* will, desire. In the Middle Ages it was used as a dim. of the given name WILLIAM.

Patrs.: **Willocks**, **Willox**.

Willoughby English: habitation name from any of the various places, for example in Leics., Lincs., Notts., and Warwicks., so called. This is from OE *wilig* willow + ON *býr* farm, settlement, or perhaps in some cases from *wilig* + OE *bēag* ring (cf. WILBY).

Wilton English: habitation name from any of various places so called. Most, including those in Cumb., Herefords., Norfolk, and E and N Yorks., are named from OE *wilig* willow + *tūn* enclosure, settlement. One in Somerset and another in Wilts. have as their first element OE *wiell(a)* spring, stream (see WILL 2), and the one that has given its name to WILTSHIRE derives its name from that of the river *Wylye*, on which it stands (an ancient Brit. river name, perhaps meaning 'Capricious').

Wiltshire English: regional name from the county of Wiltshire in SW central England, which gets its name from WILTON, once its principal town, + OE *scīr* district, administrative division.

Vars.: **Wiltsh(i)er**, **Wiltshear**, **Will(i)shire**, **Wilshire**, **Wil(l)sher(e)**, **Willshear**, **Wilcher**, **Wiltshaw**, **Wil(l)shaw**.

Wimmers *see* WYMER

Wimpenny English: nickname for an acquisitive person, from ME *winn(en)* to gain (OE *winnan* to conquer, defeat) + *penny* PENNY.

Var.: **Winpenny**.

Wimpey English: of uncertain origin. Sir Elijah IMPEY, a well-known 18th-cent. judge, had an illegitimate son who used this name, but it may simply have been selected as an existing surname approximating to his father's.

Winblad *see* WEIN

Winceniuk *see* VINCENT

Winch English: 1. in examples such as William *de la Winche* (Worcs. 1275) evidently a topographic name, perhaps for someone who lived at a spot where boats were hauled up onto the land by means of pulleys, from ME *winche* reel, roller (OE *wince*). 2. in examples such as William *le Wynch* (Sussex 1327) it appears to be a nickname, perhaps from the lapwing, OE *(hlēap)wince*.

Vars.: **Wynch**; **Wink**.

Winchester English: habitation name from the city in Hants, so called from the addition of OE *ceaster* Roman town (L *castra* legionary camp) to the Romano-British name *Venta*, of disputed etymology.

Winckel German: metonymic occupational name for someone who kept a corner shop, especially one that dealt in second-hand items, or topographic name for someone who lived on a corner of land in the countryside or on a street corner in a town, from Ger. *Winkel* corner (MHG *winkel*, OHG *winkil*).

Vars.: **Winkel**, **Win(c)kler**, **Win(c)kelmann**, **Zumwinkel**.

Wind 1. English: topographic name for someone who lived near a pathway, alleyway, or road, OE *(ge)wind* (from *windan* to go, proceed). 2. English: nickname for a swift runner, from ME, OE *wind* wind (cf. SHERWIN). 3. German: var. of WENDT.

Vars. (of 3): **Winde**, **Windt**.

Winder English: 1. occupational name for a winder of wool, from an agent deriv. of ME *wind(en)* to wind (OE *windan* to go, proceed; cf. WIND 1). The verb was also used in the Middle Ages of various weaving and plaiting processes, so that in some cases the name may have referred to a maker of baskets or hurdles. 2. habitation name from any of the various minor places in N England so called, from OE *vindr* wind + *erg* hut, shelter, i.e. a shelter against the wind.

Winderlich *see* WUNDERLICH

Windham *see* WYNDHAM

Windisch *see* WENDT

Windle English (Lancs. and Yorks.): habitation name from *Windhill* in W Yorks. or *Windle* in Lancs., both so called from OE *wind* wind + *hyll* HILL, i.e. a mound exposed to fierce gusts.

Var.: **Wintle** (Gloucs.).

Windsor English: habitation name from places in Berks. and Dorset, named from OE *windels* windlass + *ōra* bank.

Vars.: **Winsor** (places in Devon and Hants); **Winser**, **Winzor**, **Winzer**, **Winzar**.

Winfield English: habitation name from any of various places now called *Wingfield*. N and S Wingfield in Derbys. seem to be named from OE *wynn* meadow, pasture + *feld* pasture, open country (see FIELD); an example in Beds. may have as it first element a topographical term or bird name *wince* (see WINCH); and one in Suffolk was probably either the 'field of the people of *Wīga*', a short form of the various cpd names with a first element *wīg* war, or else derives its first element from OE *wēoh* pagan temple.

Var.: **Wingfield**.

Wing English: habitation name from places in Bucks. and Leics. (formerly Rutland). The former is probably a drastically contracted form of OE *Wihthūningas* 'people of *Wihthūn*', a personal name composed of the elements *wiht* creature + *hūn* bearcub; the latter is from ON *vengi*, a deriv. of *vangr* field (cf. WANG).

Wingate Scots and N English: habitation name from places so called, for example in Northumb. and Co. Durham, from OE *wind* wind + *geat* gate, i.e. a place where the wind howls through a narrow pass.

Vars.: **Wingett**, **Wynniatt**, **Wynyates**.

Wingrove English: habitation name from *Wingrave* in Bucks., so called from the nearby village of WING + OE *grāf* GROVE.

Winn English: from the OE personal name and byname *Wine* 'Friend', in part a short form of various cpd names with this first element.

Vars.: **Wynn(e)**.

Patrs.: Eng.: **Wyn(n)es**, **Wyness**.

Winnick Jewish (E Ashkenazic): occupational name for a distiller of brandy, Yid. *vinik*, Ukr. *vinnik*, from the Slav. element *vino* wine (cf. WEIN) + the agent suffix *-nik*.

Vars.: **Winnik**, **Wini(c)k(man)**, **Vinnik**; **Winitzky**, **Winicki**, **Vinitzky**, **Venezkey**.

Patrs.: **Winikov**, **Winnikow**, **Winikoff**.

Winocour see VINOKUR

Winograd see VINOGRADOV

Winpenny see WIMPENNY

Winrow English (Lancs.): of uncertain origin, perhaps a habitation name from an unidentified minor place named with the ON elements *hvin* whin, gorse + *vrá* nook, corner.

Vars.: **Whinrow**, **Whin(w)ray**, **Whiner(a)y**, **Whinnerah**.

Winsch see WENDT

Winslow English: habitation name from a place in Bucks., so called from the gen. case of the OE personal name or byname *Wine* (see WINN) + OE *hlāw* hill, mound, barrow (see LAW 2 and LOW 1).

Winstanley English (Lancs.): habitation name from a place near Manchester, so called from the OE personal name *Wynnstān* (see WINSTON 1) + OE *lēah* wood, clearing.

Winston 1. English: from an OE personal name composed of the elements *wynn* joy + *stān* stone. **2.** English: habitation name from any of various places called *Winston* or *Winstone*, from various OE personal names + OE *tūn* enclosure, settlement, or, in the case of *Winstone* in Gloucs., OE *stān* stone. **3.** Jewish (Ashkenazic): Anglicized form of *Weinstein*; see WEIN.

Var. (of 1 and 2): **Winstone**.

Winter 1. English, German, and Danish/Norwegian: nickname or byname for someone of a frosty or gloomy temperament, variously from ME, MHG, or Dan./Norw. *winter* (OE *winter*, OHG *wintar*, ON *vetr*). **2.** Jewish (Ashkenazic): from Ger. *Winter* winter, either an ornamental name or one of the group of names denoting the seasons, which were distributed at random by government officials; cf. SUMMER, FRULING, and HERBST. **3.** Irish: translation of Gael. *Mac Giolla-Gheimhridh*; see MCALIVERY.

Vars.: Eng.: **Wynter**, **Wintour**. Dan., Norw.: **Vinter**.

Dims.: Ger.: **Winterl(e)**, **Winterlein**.

Patrs.: Eng.: **Winters**, **Wynters**; **Winterson**. Flem., Du.: **Winters**.

Cpds (ornamental elaborations): Jewish: **Winterberg**, **Winterstein**.

Winterbottom English: topographic name, esp. in the hilly regions of Lancs. and Yorks., for someone whose principal dwelling was in a valley inhabited only in winter (the summer being spent in temporary shelters on the upland pasture), from ME *winter* WINTER + *bottom* valley (see BOTTOM). In many cases, the surname is a habitation name from the place of this name in Ches.

Var.: **Winterbotham**.

Winterbourne English: habitation name from any of the various places, for example in Berks., Dorset, Sussex, and Wilts., so called from OE *winter* WINTER + *burna* stream (see BOURNE), i.e. a watercourse which dried up in summer.

Vars.: **Winterborne** (places in Dorset); **Winterburn** (a place in W Yorks.); **Winterbo(u)rn**.

Winterton English: habitation name from places in S Humberside and Norfolk, so called from OE *winter* winter + *tūn* enclosure, settlement, referring perhaps to a place inhabited only in winter (cf. WINTERBOTTOM), or named from a proprietor who bore this byname (see WINTER 1).

Winthrop English: habitation name from places in Lincs. and Notts. called *Winthorpe*. The former is so called from the OE personal name or byname *Wina* (see WINN) + OE *þorp* settlement (see THORPE). In the latter the first element represents a contracted form of the OE personal name *Wīgmund*, composed of the elements *wīg* war + *mund* protection.

Winton English and Scots: habitation name from any of various places so called. Those in N Yorks. and near Edinburgh are so called from the OE byname or personal name *Wine* (see WINN) + OE *tūn* enclosure, settlement; one in Westmorland (now Cumb.) probably has as its first element OE *wynn* pasture; and one in Lancs. has OE *wiðigen* 'growing with willows'. In S England it is the name of a place just outside Bournemouth.

Winyard English: topographic name for someone who lived by a vineyard, or occupational name for someone who worked in one, from ME *winyard* (a cpd of OE *wīn* wine, vine + *geard* yard, enclosure). Wine growing was formerly more common in England than it is now.

Vars.: **Wynyard**, **Wingard**; **Winnard** (Lancs.).

Wirth 1. German and Jewish (Ashkenazic): occupational name for an innkeeper, from Ger. *Wirt* host (MHG *wirt*). **2.** German: status name for a man who was the head of a family and the master of his own household, from the same word in the sense 'provider'.

Var.: Ger.: **Würth**.

Dims.: Ger.: **Würthle**. Low Ger.: **Wirthgen**.

Patrs.: Low Ger.: **Wirtz**, **Wirths**.

Wise 1. English: nickname for a wise or learned person, or in some cases a nickname for someone suspected of being acquainted with the occult arts, from ME *wise* wise (OE *wīs*). **2.** U.S.: Anglicized form of Ger. and Jewish (Ashkenazic) *Weiss*; see WHITE.

Vars. (of 1): **Wyse**; **Wiseman**; **Wisdom**.

Wishart Scots: from the Norman form, *Wischard*, of the OF personal name *Guiscard*. This was formed in Normandy from the ON elements *viskr* wise + *hard* hardy, brave, bold (or possibly the OF suffix *-ard*).

Vars.: **Whiscard**, **Wysard**, **Vizard**; **Wiskar**, **W(h)isker**, WESKER.

Wiśniak Polish: topographic name for someone who lived by a cherry tree, from Pol. *wiśnia* cherry tree (see WIŚNIEWSKI) + *-ak* suffix of agent nouns. The Pol. vocab. word *wiśniak* also means 'cherry brandy', and in some cases the surname may be an occupational name for a seller of this or a nickname for a habitual drinker of it.

Wiśniewski 1. Polish: habitation name from a place called *Wiśniewo* (named with Pol. *wiśnia* cherry tree), with the addition of *-ski*, suffix of local surnames (see BARANOWSKI). **2.** Jewish (E Ashkenazic): ornamental name from Pol. *wiśnia* cherry tree, or habitation name as in 1.

Vars.: **Wiszniewski**, **Wiśniowski**, **Wiśniowiecki**.

Wisser *see* FISHER

Wissler *see* WHISTLER

Witasiak *see* VITO

Witcomb *see* WHITCOMBE

Witekind *see* WEDEKIND

Witelson *see* VITA

With *see* WYTHE

Witham English: habitation name from any of various places so called. N and S *Witham* in Lincs. derive the name from the river on which they stand, which is of ancient Brit. origin and uncertain meaning. *Witham* on the Hill in Lincs., along with other examples in Essex and Somerset, was probably originally named with an OE byname *Wit(t)a* (presumably from *wit(t)* wits, mind) + OE *hām* homestead. However, the first element may instead have been OE *wiht* bend (see WIGHT 2).

Vars.: **Withams**, **Wittams**.

Wither English: **1.** from the ON personal name *Viðarr*, composed of the elements *víð* wide + *árr* messenger. **2.** topographic name for someone who lived near a willow tree, a deriv. of ME *wyth(e)*; see WYTHE.

Patr. (from 1): **Withers**.

Witherby *see* WEATHERSBY

Witherspoon Scots: of uncertain origin, perhaps a habitation name from an unidentified place named with ME *wether* sheep, ram (see WEATHER) + *spong, spang*, a dial. term for a narrow strip of land.

Vars.: **We(a)therspoon**, **Wedderspoon**, **Wotherspoon**.

Withey English: topographic name for someone who lived by a willow tree, ME *withy* (OE *wīðig*; cf. WEIDE 1 and WYTHE).

Var.: **Withy**.

Withington English: habitation name from any of several places so called. The majority, including those in Ches., Herefords., Lancs., and Shrops., get the name from derivs. of OE *wīðig* willow (see WITHEY) + *tūn* enclosure, settlement; *Withington* in Gloucs. appears in Domesday Book as *Widindune*, from the gen. case of an OE personal name *Widia* + OE *dūn* hill (see DOWN 1).

Withnell English (Lancs.): habitation name from a place near Blackburn, so called from OE *wīðegn* willow wood + *hyll* HILL.

Withycombe English: habitation name from any of various places, for example in Devon and Somerset, so called from OE *wīðig* willow (see WITHEY) + *cumb* valley (see COOMBE).

Vars.: **Withecombe**, **Withacombe**, **Widdicombe**, **Widdecombe**.

Witley *see* WHITELEY

Witney English: habitation name from a place in Oxon., so called from the gen. case, *Wit(t)an*, of the OE personal name *Wit(t)a* (cf. WITHAM) + OE *ēg* island, raised land in a marsh.

Witt *see* WHITE

Wittamore *see* WHITMORE

Witte *see* WHITE

Wittelsbach German: habitation name from the village and former castle of *Wittelsbach* in Upper Bavaria.

Wittman *see* WHITMAN

Witty English: nickname for a bright or inventive person, from ME *witty* clever, ingenious (OE *(ge)wittig* learned, from *wit(t)* wits, mind). It is possible that some early examples may represent a survival into ME of OE *wītega* soothsayer, and there may also have been some confusion with WHITTY.

Var.: **Wittey**.

Witzel *see* WIGGIN

Wix *see* WICK

Włochowicz see VLACH

Włodarski Polish: occupational name for a steward, from Pol. *włodarz* (a deriv. of *włodać* to govern, rule, order), with the addition of the (originally local) suffix of surnames -*ski* (see BARANOWSKI).

Dims.: **Włodarczyk**, **Włodarek**.

Wlodasch see VLADIMIROV

Wnuk Polish: from Pol. *wnuk* grandson, presumably a name either for the grandson of an important personage or for someone who was brought up by his grandparents after being left an orphan.

Wobbe see WALBURG

Woddell see WADDELL

Wodehouse see WOODHOUSE

Wodeman see WADER

Wodhams see WOODHAM

Wodzyński Polish: habitation name from Pol. *wódz* military commander + -*yn* possessive suffix, with the addition of -*ski*, suffix of local surnames (see BARANOWSKI).

Woffenden see WOLFENDEN

Woffit see WOLFIT

Wogan Welsh: from the OW personal name (still used as a given name during the Middle Ages) *Gwgan*, *Gwgon*, originally a byname (probably a dim. of *gwg* scowl, i.e. 'Little Scowler'). The name was taken early on from Wales to Ireland, where it is common.

Wohl Jewish (Ashkenazic): ornamental name adopted in a spirit of optimism, from mod. Ger. *Wohl* wellbeing.

Vars.: **Wohlman(n)**.

Cpds (mostly ornamental, although some may be based on now irrecoverable minor events and anecdotes): **Wohlberg** ('good hill'); **Wohlfarth** ('good journey'); **Wohlfeld** ('good field'); **Wohlfinger** ('good finger'); **Wohlgemueth** ('good mood'); **Wohlspiegel** ('good mirror'); **Wohlsta(e)dter** ('good city'); **Wohlstein** ('good stone').

Wohlers see WALTER

Wohlfromm see WOLFRAM

Wöhrle see WARNER

Woiner see WAGNER

Woitke see VOJTĚCH

Wojciechowicz see VOJTĚCH

Wójcik Polish: status name from a dim. of Pol. *wójt* village headman, a borrowing of Ger. VOGT. There has probably been some confusion with derivs. of the given name *Wojciech* (see VOJTĚCH).

Vars.: **Wójcicki**, **Wójt**.

Patrs.: **Wójcikiewicz**; **Wójtowicz**.

Habitation names: **Wójcikowski**, **Wójciński**.

Wojnarowski see WAGNER

Wolburg see WALBURG

Wolcott see WOOLCOTT

Wold see WALD

Woldering see WALTER

Wolf 1. English and German: from a short form of the various Gmc cpd names with a first element *wolf* wolf, or a byname or nickname with this meaning. The wolf was native throughout the forests of Europe, including Britain, until comparatively recently, and played an important role in Gmc mythology, being regarded as one of the sacred beasts of Woden. **2.** Jewish (Ashkenazic): from the Yid. male given name *Volf* 'Wolf', which is associated with the Hebr. given name *Binyamin* (see BENJAMIN). This association stems from Jacob's dying words 'Benjamin shall ravin as a wolf: in the morning he shall devour the prey, and at night he shall divide the spoil' (Gen. 49: 27). **3.** Irish: translation of Gael. *Ó Faoláin*; see WHELAN.

Vars. (of 1): Eng.: **Wo(u)lfe** (also an Ir. var. of 3); **Woolf(e)**, **Woof(f)**; **Ulph** (Norfolk, from the ON byname *Úlfr*). Ger.: **Wolff**. (Of 2): Jewish: **Wolff**, **Wulf(f)**, **Volf**; **Wolfman(n)**, **Volfman**.

Dims.: Ger.: **Wölfel**, **Wölfle**, **Wölf(f)lin**. Low Ger.: **Wülfke**, **Wolfgen**.

Patrs.: Eng.: **Wolfes**, **Wolfson**. Low Ger.: **Wulfen**, **Wolfen**, **Wolfsen**, **Wulfing**. Dan., Norw. **Volfing**. Jewish: **Wolf(f)sohn**, **Wolfenso(h)n**, **Wolfson**, **Wulfsohn**; **Wolfin**, **Wolfowitch**, **Wolfowi(t)ch**, **Wolfowicz**, **Wulfowicz**, **Wolfowitz**, **Wolfovitz**, **Wolfovits**, **Volfovich**, **Wolfovsky**, **Volfovski**, **Volfovsky**, **Vulfov(ich)** (E Ashkenazic); **Volfovici** (Rumanian spelling).

Patr. (from a dim.): Low Ger.: **Wülfken**.

Cpds (ornamental elaborations): Jewish: **Wolfberg** ('wolf hill'); **Wolfheim** ('wolf home'); **Wolfstein** ('wolf stone').

Wolfenden English: habitation name from a place in the parish of Newchurch-in-Rossendale, Lancs., apparently so called from the OE personal name *Wulfhelm* (composed of the elements *wulf* wolf + *helm* helmet, protection) + OE *denu* valley (see DEAN 1).

Vars.: **Woolfenden**, **Woffenden**, **Woffendon**, **Woffindon**, **Woffindin**, **Woofinden**.

Wolfit English: from the ME given name *Wolfet, Wolfat*, OE *Wulfgēat*, composed of the element *wulf* wolf + the ethnic name *Gēat* (see JOCELYN).

Vars.: **Woolfit(t)**, **Woffit**, **Wool(v)ett**, **Wo(o)llett**, **Woolatt**; **Ul(l)yett**, **Ulyet**, **Ullett**, **Ul(l)yatt**, **Ullyat(e)**, **Ulyate**, **Ullyott**, **Ulyot**, **Uliot** (found in Notts. and Lincs., and to a lesser extent in Yorks. and Derbys., where there was Scandinavian influence; cf. *Ulph* at WOLF).

Wolfner see WOOLNOUGH

Wolford see WOOLFORD

Wolfram English and German: from the Gmc personal name *Wolfram*, composed of the elements *wolf* wolf + *hrafn* raven. Both these creatures played an important role in Gmc mythology. They are usually represented in battle poetry as scavengers of the slain, while Woden (Odin) is generally accompanied by the wolves Geri and Freki and the ravens Hugin and Munin.

Vars.: Ger.: **Wolfrum**, **Wolfrom**, **Wohlfromm**, **Wolfgram**, **Wulfgram**.

Wolichman see VLACH

Woll see WOOL

Wollaston English: habitation name from any of various places so called. Those in Northants (Domesday Book *Wilavestone*) and Shrops. (Domesday Book *Willavestune*) get the name from the gen. case of the OE personal name *Wīglāf* (composed of the elements *wīg* war + *lāf* relic) + OE *tūn* enclosure, settlement. The one in Worcs. (first recorded in 1275 as *Wollaueston*) has as its first element the gen. case of the OE personal name *Wulflāf* (composed of the elements *wulf* wolf + *lāf* relic).

Var.: **Woollaston**.

Wolley *see* WOOLLEY

Wolniak Polish: status name for a freedman, one who had been released from the feudal obligations of serfdom, from Pol. *wolny* free + *-ak* suffix of animate nouns. The vocab. word *wolniak* also denoted an unmarried man, but this is less likely to lie behind the surname.

Var.: **Wolnicki**.

Patr.: Pol.: **Wolniewicz**.

Wołodkiewicz *see* VLADIMIROV

Wołowski *see* VOLÁK

Wolpe *see* VOLPE

Wolpert *see* VOLPERT

Wolpole *see* WALPOLE

Wolrich *see* WOOLDRIDGE

Wolsey English: from the ME given name *Wulsi*, OE *Wulfsige*, composed of the elements *wulf* wolf + *sige* victory.

Vars.: **Woo(l)sey**.

Wolski *see* ZWOLSKI

Wolstenholme English: habitation name from a place in Lancs., so called from the OE personal name *Wulfstān* (see WOOLSTON 1) + ON *holmr* island, dry land in a fen (see HOLME 2).

Vars.: **Wolstonholm(e)**, **Wolstanholme**, **Wo(o)lstenhulme**, **Worstenholme**, **Wostenholm**, **Wusteman**, **Woosnam**, **Woosman**, **Worsman**.

Wolston *see* WOOLSTON

Wolstonecraft English: habitation name from *Woolstencroft* in Ches., so called from the OE personal name *Wulfstān* (see WOOLSTON 1) + OE *croft* paddock, smallholding (see CROFT).

Vars.: **Wollstonecraft**, **Wolstoncraft**, **Wo(o)lstencroft**, **Wors(t)encroft**, **Wosencroft**, **Wozencroft**.

Wombwell English: habitation name from a place in S Yorks., so called from the OE byname *Wamba* 'Belly' (or this vocab. word used in a transferred topographical sense) + OE *well(a)* spring, stream (see WELL).

Vars.: **Womwell**, **Wo(o)mbell**, **Woombill**, **Woomble**.

Womersley English (Yorks.): habitation name from a place near Pontefract, recorded in Domesday Book as *Wilmereslege*, probably from the gen. case of the OE personal name *Wilmǣr* (composed of the elements *willa* will, desire + *mǣr* famous) + OE *lēah* wood, clearing. However, since this personal name is not definitely instanced in England before the Conquest, Ekwall suggests that the first part may alternatively be composed of the elements *wil(i)g* willow + *mere* pond, lake.

Wondraschek *see* ANDREW

Wońicko *see* WOŹNIAK

Wood English and Scots: 1. in the overwhelming majority of cases a topographic name for someone who lived in or by a wood or a metonymic occupational name for a woodcutter or forester, from ME *wode* wood (OE *wudu*). 2. nickname for a mad, eccentric, or violent person, from ME *wōd* mad, frenzied (OE *wād*), as in Adam *le Wode* 'Adam the Mad', Worcs. 1221.

Vars. (of 1): **Woode**, **Woods**; **Wooder**, WOODMAN; **Wooding(s)**, **Wood(d)in**; ATTWOOD, **Bywood**.

Cpd (of a cogn. of 1): Swed.: **Wedberg** ('wood hill').

Woodard English: 1. from the ME given name *Wodard*, *Udard*, *Hudard*, OE **Wuduheard*, composed of the elements *wudu* wood + *heard* hardy, brave, strong. 2. occupational name for someone who tended pigs feeding on mast in a wood, from OE *wudu* WOOD + *hierde* herdsman (see HEARD). 3. var. of WOODWARD.

Var.: **Huddart**.

Woodbridge English: habitation name from a place in Suffolk, so called from OE *wudu* WOOD + *brycg* BRIDGE, i.e. a bridge made of timber or one near a wood.

Woodburn Scots and N English: habitation name from places in the former counties of Ayrs., Kincardines., and Midlothian, and in Northumb., so called from OE *wudu* WOOD + *burna* stream (see BOURNE), i.e. a stream flowing through a wood.

Var.: **Woodburne**.

Woodcock English: 1. nickname for a guileless or stupid person, from ME *woodcock* (a cpd of OE *wudu* wood + *cocc* cock, bird), a bird easily caught. 2. habitation name from any of various places named with the OE elements *wudu* WOOD + *cot* cottage, shelter (see COATES), as for example *Woodcott* in Ches. and Hants or *Woodcote* in Hants, Surrey, Oxon., and Warwicks., and Shrops.

Var. (of 2): **Woodcott**.

Patr. (from 1): **Woodcocks**.

Woodfield 1. English: topographic name that originated in the parish of Napton-on-the-Hill, Warwicks. In the earliest parish registers it is found as *Woodhull* (with minor variations), from OE *wudu* WOOD + *hyll* HILL. By 1620, however, the change to *Woodfield* was established. The surname has always been largely confined to Warwicks., but is now found also in Australia and New Zealand. 2. Scots: Black derives this name from a place near Annan in the former county of Dumfries, citing a certain Roger *Wodyfelde* who held land in Dumfries in 1365.

Woodford English and Scots: habitation name from any of various places, as far apart as Essex, Wilts., Cornwall, Northants, Ches., and Roxburghs., so called from OE *wudu* WOOD + *ford* FORD.

Vars.: **Woodforde**, **Woodfords**.

Woodgate English: topographic name for someone who lived by a gate leading into an enclosed wood, from ME *wode* WOOD + *gate* GATE.

Vars.: **Woodgates**, **Woodget(t)**, **Woodjetts**, **Woodyatt**.

Woodhall English and Scots: habitation name from any of various places, for example in Herts., Lincs., N Yorks., Dumfries, and E Lothian, so called from OE *wudu* WOOD + *hall* HALL.

Var.: **Woodall** (chiefly Staffs.).

Woodham English: habitation name from any of various places so called. Most, as for example those in Essex and Surrey, are named from OE *wudu* WOOD + *hām* homestead; one in Bucks., however, probably has as its second element OE *hamm* water meadow, and one in Co. Durham is from *wudum*, the dat. pl. of *wudu*, originally used after a preposition.

Vars.: **Wo(o)dhams**.

Woodhatch English: topographic name for someone who lived by a gate into an enclosed forest (cf. WOODGATE), from OE *wudu* WOOD + *hæcc* gate (see HATCH), or habitation name from any of the places, for example in Essex and Surrey, named with these elements.

Woodhead English and Scots: habitation name from any of various minor places, for example in W Yorks. and Strathmore, so called from OE *wudu* WOOD + *hēafod* head(land), top, extremity.

Woodhouse English and Scots: habitation name from any of numerous places, for example in Leics., Peebles., and W Yorks., so called from OE *wudu* WOOD + *hūs* HOUSE.

Vars.: **Wodehouse**, **Wooders**, **Woodus**.

Woodland English: topographic name for someone living in an area of woodland, from OE *wudu* WOOD + *land* land, or habitation name from any of the numerous places, for example in Devon, named with these elements.

Var.: **Woodlands** (the name of places in Kent, Dorset, and Somerset).

Woodley English: habitation name from *Woodleigh* in Devon, *Woodley* in Berks., or some other place named with the OE elements *wudu* WOOD + *lēah* clearing, pasture.

Var.: **Woodleigh**.

Woodlock Irish and English: from an OE personal name, *Wudlāc*, composed of the elements *wudu* wood + *lāc* play, sport.

Vars.: **Woodlake**, **Wedlock**.

Woodman English and Scots: topographic name, a var. of WOOD 1, or specifically occupational name for a woodcutter or a forester (cf. WOODWARD). In a few cases, it is possible that it derives from the OE personal name *Wudumann*.

Woodrow English: habitation name for someone who lived in a row of cottages near a wood, from OE *wudu* WOOD + *rāw* row, line. There are places bearing this name in Dorset, Wilts., Bucks., and Worcs., but the surname is found mainly in Norfolk.

Woodruff English: topographic name for someone who lived on a patch of land thickly grown with woodruff, OE *wudurofe* (apparently a cpd of *wudu* wood with a second

element of unknown origin). The leaves of the plant have a sweet smell and the surname may also have been a nickname for one who used it as a perfume, or perhaps an ironical nickname for a malodorous person.

Vars.: **Woodruffe**, **Woodrup**, **Woodroff(e)**, **Woodroof(e)**, **Woodrooffe**, **Woodrough**.

Woodside Scots and N Irish: habitation name for any of various minor places, for example in the former county of Ayrs., so called from OE *wudu* WOOD + *sīde* slope of a hill.

Woodward English: 1. occupational name for a forester employed to look after the trees and game, ME *woodward* (a cpd of OE *wudu* WOOD + *weard* guardian, protector; see WARD 1). 2. occasionally perhaps from an OE personal name *Wuduweard*, composed of the vocab. elements mentioned in 1.

Var.: WOODARD.

Woof *see* WOLF

Woofinden *see* WOLFENDEN

Wookey English (Somerset): habitation name from a place in the Mendip Hills, apparently named with the rare OE word *wōcig* snare, trap.

Wool English: 1. metonymic occupational name for a worker in wool, ME *woll* (OE *wull*). 2. in SW England, a topographic name for someone who lived by a spring or stream, from ME *woll, wull* spring, stream, a western dial. development of OE (W Saxon) *wiell(a)* (see WILL 2).

Vars.: **Wo(o)ll**, **Wool(l)er**, **Woller**, **Woolman**, **Wol(l)man**.

Woolatt *see* WOLFIT

Woolcott English: habitation name from *Woolcot* in Somerset, which is named from ME *woll* spring, stream (see WOOL 2) + *cot* cottage, shelter (see COATES).

Vars.: **Woolcot**, **Wolcott**, **Woollcott**, **Woolcock**.

Wooldridge English: from the ME given name *Wol(f)rich*, OE *Wulfrīc*, composed of the elements *wulf* wolf + *rīc* power.

Vars.: **Wo(o)lveridge**, **Woolridge**, **Wo(o)lrich**, **Woolright**; **Ur(r)y**, **Urey**, **Urie**, **Ourry**, **Orr(e)y**, **Hurr(e)y**, **Hurrie**, **Horr(e)y** (from Norman forms).

Woolford English: 1. from the ME given name *Wol(f)ward*, OE *Wulfweard*, composed of the elements *wulf* wolf + *weard* guardian, protector. 2. habitation name from *Wolford* in Warwicks., apparently named with the same two elements as in 1, perhaps in the sense of an enclosure to protect livestock from marauding wolves.

Vars.: **Wolford**, **Woolforde**, **Woolforth**, **Woolfarth**, **Woolfoot**, **Woolward**, **Wool(l)ard**, **Wollard**.

Woolgar English: from the ME given name *Wol(f)gar*, OE *Wulfgār*, composed of the elements *wulf* wolf + *gār* spear.

Vars.: **Woolgard**, **Woolger**.

Woollaston *see* WOLLASTON

Woolley English: habitation name from any of various places so called. Most, including those in Berks., Cambs. (formerly Hunts.), and W Yorks., get the name from OE *wulf* wolf (or perhaps the personal name or byname *Wulf*; see WOLF) + *lēah* wood, clearing; one example in Somerset, however, has as its first element ME *woll, wull* spring, stream (see WOOL 2).

Vars.: **Wooley, Wolley**.

Woollin English (W Yorks.): of uncertain origin. Reaney derives a large number of similar names (**Woollan, Woollon(s), Wool(l)en**) from minor places named with the OE elements *wōh* curved, crooked + *land* land. The surname is found mainly in Wakefield.

Woolnough English (chiefly E Anglia): from the ME given name *Wo(o)lnoth, Wulnaugh, Wulnod*, OE *Wulfnōð*, composed of the elements *wulf* wolf + *nōð* daring.

Vars.: **Woolnoth, Woolner, Wolfner**.

Woolsey *see* WOLSEY

Woolstencroft *see* WOLSTONECRAFT

Woolstenhulme *see* WOLSTENHOLME

Woolston English (chiefly E Anglia): **1.** from the ME given name *Wol(f)stan*, OE *Wulfstān*, composed of the elements *wulf* wolf + *stān* stone. **2.** habitation name from any of a large number of places called *Woolston(e)* or *Wollston*, all of which are named from OE personal names containing the first element *Wulf* (*Wulfhēah, Wulfhelm, Wulfrīc, Wulfsige*, and *Wulfweard*) + OE *tūn* enclosure, settlement.

Vars.: **Woolstone, Woollston, Wolston**.

Woombell *see* WOMBWELL

Wooster English: habitation name from the city of *Worcester*, so called from the addition of OE *ceaster* Roman fort (L *castra* legionary camp) to a Brit. tribal name of uncertain origin.

Vars.: **Wostear, Wor(ce)ster**.

Wootton English: habitation name from any of the extremely numerous places so called from OE *wudu* WOOD + *tūn* enclosure, settlement.

Vars.: **Wooton, Woot(t)en, Wotton**.

Worboys *see* WARBOYS

Worcester *see* WOOSTER

Worden English (Lancs.): habitation name from a place near Chorley. Early forms consistently show the first syllable as *Wer-*, and the name is probably derived from OE *wer* weir (see WARE 1) + *denu* valley (see DEAN 1).

Wordman *see* WARD

Wordsworth English: habitation name from *Wadsworth* near Halifax, W Yorks., so called from the OE personal name *Wæddi* (related to *Wada*; see WADE 1) + *worð* enclosure (see WORTH).

Var.: **Wadsworth**.

Worgan Welsh: from the personal name *Gorgan, Gwrgan*, of uncertain origin.

Workman English: ostensibly an occupational name for a labourer, from ME *work* (OE *weorc*) + *man* (OE *mann*). According to a gloss cited by Reaney the term was used in the Middle Ages to denote an ambidextrous person, and the surname may also be a nickname in this sense.

Worley English: apparently a habitation name, from a place that has not been identified with certainty. It is perhaps a var. of WORTLEY, or is from places in Essex and Somerset called *Warley*, from OE *wær, wer* weir (see WARE 1) + *lēah* wood, clearing, or from *Warley* in the West Midlands, which is from OE *weorf* yoke oxen + *lēah*.

Wörlin *see* WARNER

Wormald English (Yorks.): habitation name from places so called in the parishes of Barkisland and Rishworth, both so called from the OE female personal name *Wulfrūn* (composed of the elements *wulf* wolf + *rūn* secret) + northern OE *wæll(a)* spring, stream (see WALL 2); the excrescent *-d* is not found before the middle of the 17th cent. Some of the vars. may also derive from *Wormill* in Derbys., so called from OE *wyrm* serpent, reptile (perhaps a byname) + *hyll* HILL.

Vars.: **Wormal, Wormhall, Wormell, Wormull, Warmoll**.

Wörmbke *see* ORME

Worrall English: habitation name from a place in S Yorks., so called from OE *wīr* bog myrtle + *halh* nook, recess (see HALE). The *Wirrall* peninsula in Ches. has the same origin and may well be the source of the surname in some cases. The surname is now especially common in Lancs. and the W Midlands as well as in S Yorks.

Vars.: **Worral, Whorall, Worrell, Worril**.

Worsencroft *see* WOLSTONECRAFT

Worsfold English: of uncertain origin, probably a habitation name from an unidentified place.

Var.: **Worsfield**.

Worsley English: habitation name from places in Lancs. and Worcs. The former, which appears to be the main source of the surname, is probably named from the gen. case of an OE personal name of uncertain form (probably with a first element *weorc* work, fortification) + OE *lēah* wood, clearing. The latter apparently gets its first element from the gen. case of OE *weorf* draught cattle (a collective noun).

Worsman *see* WOLSTENHOLME

Worsthorne English: habitation name from a place in Lancs., so called from the gen. case of the OE byname *Wurð* 'Worthy' + OE *þorn* thorn bush (see THORN).

Worswick English (Lancs.): habitation name from *Urswick* in Lancs., so called from OE *ūr* wild ox, bison, aurochs + *sæ* lake + *wīc* (dependent) settlement.

Var.: **Worsick**.

Wort English: metonymic occupational name for a grower or seller of vegetables or of medicinal herbs and spices, from ME *wurt, wort* plant (OE *wyrt*; cf. OHG *wurz*).

Vars.: **Wortt, Worts**; WORTMAN.

Worters *see* WATER

Worth English: habitation name from any of the various places, for example in Ches., Dorset, Sussex, and Kent, so called from OE *worð* enclosure, settlement. The vocab. word probably survived into the Middle English period in the sense of a subsidiary settlement dependent on a main village, and in some cases the surname may be a topographic name derived from this use.

Var.: WERTH.

Worthington English: habitation name from places in Lancs. and Leics.; both may have originally been named in OE as *Wurðingtūn* 'settlement (OE *tūn*) associated with *Wurð*' (cf. WORSTHORNE), but it is also possible that the first element was OE *worðign*, a deriv. of *worð* enclosure (see WORTH and WORTHY 1).

Worthy English: **1.** habitation name from any of various minor places so called from OE *worðig*, a deriv. of *worð* enclosure (see WORTH). **2.** nickname for a respected member of the community, from ME *worthy* valuable (a deriv. of *worth* value, merit, OE *weorð*).

Wortley English: habitation name from either of two places so called in W Yorks. The one near Barnsley gets its name from OE *wyrt* plant, vegetable (see WORT) + *lēah* wood, clearing; the one near Leeds probably has as its first element an OE personal name *Wyrca, perhaps a short form of a cpd name with a first element *weorc* work, fortification (cf. WORSLEY).

Wortman **1.** English: var. of WORT. **2.** Jewish (Ashkenazic): nickname for a reliable person who could be trusted to keep his word, from Yid. *vort*, mod. Ger. *Wort* word + *man, Mann* man.

Vars. (of 2): **Vortman**; **Vortsman**, **Vortzman** ('man of his word'); **Worthalter** (based on Yid. *haltn vort* to keep one's word).

Worton English: habitation name from any of various places so called. Most get the name from OE *wyrt* plant, vegetable (see WORT) + *tūn* enclosure, i.e. a kitchen garden, but in some cases the first element may be OE *worð* enclosure (see WORTH), and in the case of Nether and Over *Worton* in Oxon (*Hortone* in Domesday Book, *Orton* in other early sources), it is OE *ōra* bank, slope.

Woś *see* VOJTĚCH

Wosencroft *see* WOLSTONECRAFT

Wosik *see* VOJTĚCH

Wostear *see* WOOSTER

Wostenholm *see* WOLSTENHOLME

Wotherspoon *see* WITHERSPOON

Wotton *see* WOOTTON

Wötzel *see* WENZEL

Would *see* WALD

Woulfe *see* WOLF

Wouts *see* WALTER

Wozencroft *see* WOLSTONECRAFT

Woźniak Polish: **1.** occupational name for a coachman, driver, or carter, Pol. *woźnica* (from *wozić* to convey, carry). **2.** occupational name for a bailiff, Pol. *woźny* (like-

wise from *wozić*, in the transferred sense 'carry out (a magistrate's decisions)'.

Vars.: **Woźni(a)cki**, **Wońicko**. (Of 2 only): **Woźny**.

Patr.: Pol.: **Woźniakiewicz**.

Habitation name: Pol.: **Woźniakowski**.

Wraight *see* WRIGHT

Wraith N English: nickname for someone with a violent temper, from Northern ME *wrath* angry (OE *wrāð*). Reaney cites John *Wrayth*, recorded in 1587 as the son of Thomas *Wrath*. The S English forms **Wro(a)th** are far less common (for the vowel, cf. ROPER).

Wray N English: habitation name from any of various minor places in N England, so called from ON *vrá* nook, corner, recess.

Vars.: **Wra**, **Wrey**, **Wroe**, RAY.

Wreight *see* WRIGHT

Wren **1.** English: nickname from the bird (ME *wrenne*, OE *wrenna, wrænna*), probably in reference to its small size. **2.** Irish: Anglicized form of Gael. **Ó Rinn** 'descendant of *Rinn*', a personal name from *rinn* star, constellation.

Vars.: **Wrenn**. (Of 2 only): **(O')Rinne**, **Rynn(e)**, **Wrynn**.

Wrey *see* WRAY

Wrigglesworth English: habitation name from a place in W Yorks., now called *Woodlesford* but recorded in the 12th cent. as *Wridelesford*, apparently from OE *wrīdels*, a deriv. of *wrīd* bush, thicket + *ford* FORD. The change of the final element in the surname is a relatively late development.

Vars.: **Wriglesworth**, **Rigglesford**, **Riggulsford**.

Wright English and Scots: common occupational name for a maker of machinery or objects, mostly in wood, of any of a wide range of kinds, from OE *wyrhta, wryhta* craftsman (a deriv. of *wyrcan* to work, make). The term is found in several combinations (cf., e.g., CARTWRIGHT and WAINWRIGHT), but when used in isolation it generally referred to a builder of windmills or watermills.

Vars.: **Wrighte**, **Wraight(e)**, **Wreight**, **Wrate**.

Patrs.: **Wrightson**, **Wrixon**.

Wrigley English (Lancs.): habitation name from *Wrigley* Head near Salford, the second element of which is presumably OE *lēah* wood, clearing; the first may be a personal name or topographical term from OE *wrigian* to strive, bend, turn.

Var.: **Rigley** (Notts.).

Wring English (Bristol): topographic name for someone living on the river in Somerset formerly known as the *Wring* (now called the Yeo). The river name is of uncertain derivation, perhaps from a Brit. word meaning 'twisted', 'crooked'.

Wriottesley *see* WROTTESLEY

Wróblewski *see* VOROBYOV

Wrocławski Polish: habitation name from the city of *Wrocław* in W Poland (Ger. BRESLAU), with the addition of the surname suffix *-ski* (see BARANOWSKI). The placename is attested in the 11th cent. as *Wortizlaua*, i.e.

castle of *Wortislav*, a Slav. personal name. Later this became *Wrocisław*, and eventually contracted to *Wrocław*.

Wroe *see* WRAY

Wronek *see* VORONIN

Wrottesley English: habitation name from a place in Staffs., apparently so called from the gen. case of an OE personal name **Wrott* + OE *lēah* wood, clearing.

Vars.: **Wriottesley**, **Wrothesley**.

Wrynn *see* WREN

Wrzesiński Polish: from Pol. *wrzesień* September + *-ski* suffix of surnames (see BARANOWSKI). The name was generally acquired by someone born or baptized in September, in particular a convert who adopted Christianity in that month.

Vars.: **Wrzesieński**.

Habitation name: **Wrześniewski**.

Wulf *see* WOLF

Wunderlich 1. German: nickname for an eccentric or moody person, from Ger., MHG *wunderlich* odd, capricious, unpredictable (a deriv. of *wunder*, OHG *wundar* puzzle, marvel). 2. Jewish (Ashkenazic): probably an anecdotal nickname from Yid. *vunderlekh* wonderful, marvellous, based on some now irrecoverable event, but possibly also a descriptive nickname from Ger. *wunderlich* odd, strange.

Vars. (of 1): **Wünderlich**, **Winderlich**.

Wündisch *see* WENDT

Wundt German: nickname for a maimed or crippled person, from MHG, OHG *wunt* wounded, disabled.

Wurbank *see* URBAN

Würfel German: nickname for an enthusiastic gambler, from Ger. *Würfel* die, dice (MHG *würfel*, OHG *wurfil*, a deriv. of *werfan* to throw). In some cases it may have originated as a metonymic occupational name for a maker of dice.

Var.: **Werfel** (Bohemia; also Jewish).

Würmeling *see* ORME

Wurst German: from Ger. *Wurst* sausage (MHG, OHG *wurst*, a collective noun), either a metonymic occupational name for a butcher who specialized in the production of spiced sausages, or a nickname for a plump person or someone who was particularly fond of such sausages.

Vars.: **Wurst(n)er**, **Wurstler** (agent derivs.).

Dim.: Ger.: **Würstl(e)**.

Würth *see* WIRTH

Württemberg German: habitation name from a castle and town in S Germany, which gave its name to the state of which Stuttgart was the capital. The surname may also be a regional name from this state. The castle is first recorded as *Wirteneberg*; the final element is clearly OHG *berg* hill, and Bahlow suggests that the first may represent an ancient element meaning 'reeds', 'rushes'.

Wüst German: topographic name for someone who lived on a piece of waste land, from Ger. *Wüste* empty, uncultivated land (MHG *wüeste*, OHG *wuosti*).

Vars.: **Wüst(n)er**, **Wiestner**; **Wüstemann**, **Wustmann**.

Wusteman *see* WOLSTENHOLME

Wuttschke *see* VOJTĚCH

Wyatt English: from the medieval given name *Wiot*, *Wyot*, *Gyot*, which derives from the OE personal name *Wīgheard*, composed of the elements *wīg* war + *heard* hardy, brave, strong. Under Norman influence it was also adopted as a dim. of both GUY 1 and WILLIAM.

Vars.: **Whyatt**, **W(h)yard**; **Guyat(t)**, **Gyatt**.

Dim.: Fr.: **Guyardeau**.

Wybrow *see* WHYBROW

Wych *see* WICH

Wycliffe English: habitation name from a place in N Yorks., situated on a bend in the Tees, and probably named from OE *wiht* bend (see WIGHT 2) + *clif* slope, bank (see CLIVE).

Wyd *see* GUY

Wye English: 1. habitation name from a place in Kent, so called from the dat. case (originally used after a preposition) of OE *wēoh* pagan temple. 2. var. of GUY.

Wyerda *see* GUICHARD

Wygodarz Polish: occupational name for an innkeeper, Pol. *wygodarz* (an agent deriv. of *wygoda* comfort, convenience, inn).

Wyke *see* WICK

Wykeham *see* WICKHAM

Wyld *see* WILD

Wyler *see* WHEELER

Wyles *see* WILEMAN

Wyllarde *see* WILLARD

Wyllis *see* WILL

Wyman English: from the ME given name *Wymund*, OE *Wīgmund* (composed of the elements *wīg* war + *mund* protection), reinforced by the cogn. ON form *Vígmundr*, introduced by Scandinavian settlers in N England.

Vars.: **Wymann**, **Whyman(t)**, **W(h)ayman**, **Whaymand**, **W(h)aymont**, **Whamond**, **Weyman**, **Weymont**.

Patr.: **Wymans**.

Wymer English: 1. from the ME given name *Wymer*, OE *Wīgmǣr* (composed of the elements *wīg* war + *mǣr* famous), reinforced by the cogn. Continental Gmc form *Wigmar*, introduced into England by the Normans. 2. from the OBret. personal name *Wiumarch*, composed of the elements *uuiu* worthy + *march* horse. The name was borne by both men and women and became relatively popular in E Anglia during the early Middle Ages as a result of the influence of Bretons who settled there in the wake of the Conquest.

Vars. (of 1): GUYMER. (Of 2): **W(a)ymark**.

Patr. (from 1): Du.: **Wimmers**.

Wynch *see* WINCH

Wyndham 1. English: habitation name from a place in W Sussex, near W Grinstead, apparently so called from an OE personal name *Winda* + OE *hamm* water meadow; or from *Wymondham* in Leics. and Norfolk, so called from the OE personal name *Wīgmund* (see WYMAN) + OE *hām* homestead. The name *de Wyndem* is found in Westmorland as early as 1284, and the surname may additionally derive from some unidentified place in N England. 2. Irish: Anglicized form of various Gael. names derived from *gaoith* wind; cf. e.g. GAHAN 2.

Var.: **Windham**.

Wynes *see* WINN

Wynniatt *see* WINGATE

Wynter *see* WINTER

Wynyard *see* WINYARD

Wyon *see* GUY

Wypych Polish: occupational name for a judicial investigator or a spy, from OPol. *wypych*, a deriv. of *wypytać* to find out (from *wy-* out + *pytać* to ask).

Wyrębski Polish: topographic name for someone who lived in a clearing in a wood, from Pol. *wyrąb* clearing (a deriv. of *wyrąbeć* to fell, cut down) + *-ski* suffix of surnames (see BARANOWSKI).

Wyrzkowski Polish: habitation name from a place called *Wyrzeka*, from Pol. *wyrzek* source (of a river), with the addition of *-ski*, suffix of local surnames (see BARANOWSKI).

Wysard *see* WISHART

Wyse *see* WISE

Wysocki Polish and Jewish (E Ashkenazic): habitation name from a placename such as *Wysocko* or *Wysoko* (named from Pol. *wysoki* high), with the addition of *-ski*, suffix of local surnames (see BARANOWSKI).

Var.: Pol.: **Wysokiński**.

Wyszyński Polish: occupational name for an innkeeper or seller of alcoholic drinks, from Pol. *wyszynk* sale of alcoholic drinks + *-ski* suffix of surnames (see BARANOWSKI).

Wythe English: topographic name for someone who lived by a willow tree, ME *wythe* (OE *wiððe*, a byform of *wīðig*; cf. WITHEY).

Vars.: **Wyth**, **With(e)**.

X

Xenakis Greek: patr. from the nickname *Xenos* 'Stranger', denoting a newcomer to a locality.

Ximénez *see* JIMENO

Y

Yaakov *see* JACOB

Yaglom *see* JAGLOM

Yagodin Russian: patr. from the nickname *Yagoda* 'Berry', given perhaps to a small, wizened man, or to someone who gathered and sold berries, or to someone who lived by a tree that produced them.
Dim.: Russ.: **Yagodkin** (patr.).

Yagüe Spanish: apparently a religious byname for someone who was born on St James' Day, from OSp. *Santi Yague*, a frequent medieval form of SANTIAGO.

Yakhnin *see* JACOB

Yakimishin *see* JOACHIM

Yale Welsh: habitation name for someone who lived in the commote of *Iâl* (near Wrexham in NE Wales), so called from W *iâl* fertile or arable upland.

Yalin *see* JELEN

Yallop English (Norfolk): of unknown origin. According to Barber it derives from the ON personal name or byname *Hjálpr* 'Help', whereas Harrison believes that it is a topographic name composed of the ME elements *yelow, yalow* yellow + *hop(e)* enclosed valley (see HOPE).

Yankelevitz *see* JANKOFF

Yankishin *see* JOHN

Yapp English (chiefly W Midlands): nickname for a clever or cunning person, from the ME adj. *yap* devious (OE *gēap*). The OE word, which seems to have meant originally 'open', 'wide', also had the sense 'curved', 'bent', but this does not appear to have survived into the period of surname formation.
Var.: **Yap**.

Yarbrough English: habitation name from places in Lincs. called *Yarborough* and *Yarburgh*, from OE *eorðburg* earthworks, fortifications (a cpd of *eorð* earth, soil + *burh* fortress, stronghold).
Var.: **Yarborough**.

Yard English: **1.** topographic name for someone who lived by an enclosure of some kind, ME *yard(e)* (OE *geard*; cf. GARTH). **2.** nickname from ME *yard* rod, stick (OE (Anglian) *gerd*), probably with reference to a rod or staff carried as a symbol of authority. **3.** from the same word as in 2, used to denote a measure of land. The surname probably denoted someone who held this quantity of land, and as it was quite a large amount (varying at different periods and in different places, but generally approximately 30 acres, a quarter of a hide), such a person would have been a reasonably prosperous farmer.
Var.: **Yarde**.

Yarden *see* JORDAN

Yardley English (W Midlands): habitation name from any of various places, for example *Yardley* in the W Midlands, Essex, Northants, etc., or *Yarley* in Somerset, so called from OE *gerd* pole, stick (see YARD 2) + *lēah* wood, clearing. The cpd apparently referred to a forest where timber could be gathered.
Vars.: **Year(d)ley**.

Yarham English (Norfolk): apparently a habitation name from some unidentified minor place, perhaps on the river *Yare*. If so, it would be named from the river (a Brit. river name of uncertain meaning; possibly, according to Ekwall, 'Babbling') + OE *hām* homestead or *hamm* water meadow.

Yarmus *see* JEREMY

Yarrow English: **1.** topographic name for someone who lived by a river of this name in Lancs. or by one in the Border region of Scotland, both apparently so called from a Brit. cogn. of W *garw*, Gael. *garbh* rough. The one in Scotland has also given its name to a town that stands by it. **2.** topographic name for someone who lived in a place overgrown with the plant yarrow, OE *gearwe*.

Yarwood English (Lancs.): habitation name, probably from *Yarwood* in Ches. Despite its modern frequency and concentration, the surname does not seem to be recorded in Lancs. before the 17th cent., when it is found as *Ye(a)rwood*.
Var.: **Yearwood**.

Yashaev *see* JACOB

Yastrebov Russian: patr. from the nickname *Yastreb* 'Hawk', given perhaps to a cruel or rapacious man. The vocab. word derives from an element meaning originally 'swift'.
Var.: **Yastrebtsov**.

Yate N English: topographic name for someone who lived near a gate or metonymic occupational name for a gatekeeper, from OE *geat* gate; cf. GATES.
Vars.: **Yates**, **Yeat(e)s**, **Yetts**; **Y(e)atman**, **Yetman**.

Yaxley English (E Anglia): habitation name from a place so called, of which there is one in Suffolk and another in Cambs. (formerly Hunts.). The name is derived from the gen. case of OE *gēac* cuckoo (perhaps a byname) + *lēah* wood, clearing.

Yea *see* YEO

Yeadon English (Yorks.): habitation name from a place in W Yorks. Ekwall suggests that the placename may come from OE *hēah* high + *dūn* hill.

Yealland *see* YELLAND

Yeaman *see* YEOMAN

Yeardley see YARDLEY

Yearwood see YARWOOD

Yeates see YATE

Yecheskel see EZEKIEL

Yefimov Russian: patr. from the given name *Yefim*, a Russ. form of Gk *Euthumios* 'Cheerful' or 'Bold' (composed of the elements *eu* good, well + *thumos* heart, mind, spirit). This name was borne by various early saints, among them Euthumios the Great (378–473), an Armenian monk highly revered in the Orthodox Church.

Vars.: **Yevfimov**, **Yefimyev**, **Yefimanov**, **Nefimanov**, **Nefimonov**.

Dims.: **Yefimychev**, **Yefimochkin**, **Yefimtsev**, **Yefintsov**, **Fimichev**, **Khimichev** (all patrs.).

Yefremov Russian: patr. from the given name *Yefrem*, a Russ. form of Hebr. *Efrayim* Efraim (lit., 'Meadows'). In the Bible this name is borne by the younger son of Joseph. In W Europe the given name is found mainly among Jews. In the Orthodox Church, however, it is much more widespread, as a result of having been borne by a 4th-cent. Syrian saint famous for his biblical commentaries and mariological hymns.

Var.: **Afremov**.

Dims. (patrs.): Russ.: **Yefremushkin**. Jewish (E Ashkenazic): **Fromc(h)enko**; **Froikin** (from the Yid. dim. given name *Froyke*).

Yegorchenkov see GEORGE

Yekaterinin see CATLIN

Yekel see JACOB

Yelen see JELEN

Yeliashev see ELLIS

Yelland English (Devon): habitation name from any of several places called *Yelland* (from OE *ēald* old + *land* land), or conceivably from *Yealand* in Lancs. (so called from OE *hēah* high + *land* land).

Var.: **Yealland**.

Yeman see YEOMAN

Yemelyanchikov see ÉMILIEN

Yental see JENTEL

Yeo English (chiefly Devon and Somerset): topographic name for someone who lived near a stream, from OE *ēa* stream, river (cf. NYE, RYE 1, and TYE 1), which became *ya* or *yo* in the ME dials. of Somerset and Devon, and gave rise to several river names and minor placenames in this region.

Vars.: **Yeoh**, **Yea**; **Attyea**; YEOMAN.

Yeoman English: 1. status name, from ME *yoman, yeman*, used of an attendant of relatively high status in a noble household, ranking beween a SERGEANT and a GROOM, or between a SQUIRE and a PAGE. The word appears to derive from a cpd of OE *geong* YOUNG + *mann* man. Later in the ME period it came to be used of a modest independent freeholder, and this latter sense may well lie behind some examples of the surname. 2. topographic name, a var. of YEO.

Vars. (of 1): **Youngman**, **Younkman** (Norfolk; also simply a nickname). (Of 2): **Ye(a)man**.

Patr. (from 1): **Yeomans** (chiefly Midlands).

Yeoward see EWART

Yeowell see YULE

Yepifanov Russian: patr. from the given name *Yepifan*, a Russ. form of Gk *Epiphanios* (from *epiphanē* epiphany, manifestation, from *epiphainein* to show, display). This name was borne by a 4th-cent. bishop of Salamis, venerated in the Orthodox Church.

Var.: **Yepifanyev**.

Dims.: **Yepish(ch)ev**, **Yepishin**, **Yepikhin** (all patrs.).

Yepiskopov see BISHOP

Yerasov see JEREMY

Yerburgh English: habitation name from a place in Lincs., probably so called from OE *g(i)erd*, a land measure (see YARD 3) + *burh* fortress, town.

Yernmonger see IRONMONGER

Yerushalmi Jewish: from the Hebr. habitational name *Yerushalmi* Jerusalemite, from Hebr. *Yerushalayim* Jerusalem. The name may have been adopted by Jews in exile as a symbol of the longed-for homeland, or have referred to someone who had made a pilgrimage to the Holy Land, or have been adopted by someone who was born there and later migrated elsewhere.

Vars.: **Yero(u)shalmi**, **Yerushalmy**, **Jerushalmi**, **Jerushalmy**, **Ieroushalmi**, **Urshalimi**; **Yerushamsky**; **Jerozolimski** (from the Pol. adj. derived from the placename).

Yesenev see JOSEPH

Yestifeev see YEVTIKHIEV

Yetman see YATE

Yeuell see YULE

Yevdokimov Russian: patr. from the given name *Yevdokim*, a Russ. form of Gk *Eudokimos* 'Respected' (from *eu* good, well + *dokein* to seem). The name was borne by a 9th-cent. saint, governor of Cappodocia, much revered in the Orthodox Church.

Var.: **Ovdkimov**.

Dims.: **Evdakov**, **Evdonin**, **Evdoshin**, **Avdakov**, **Aldakov**, **Avdon(k)in**, **Aldonin**, **Aldoshin** (all patrs.). Beloruss.: **Evdokinchik**.

Yevfimov see YEFIMOV

Yevseev see EUSÉBIO

Yevtikhiev Russian: patr. from the given name *Yevtikhi*, a Russ. form of Gk. *Eutykhios* 'Fortunate' (from *eu* good, well + *tykhē* chance, fortune). This name was borne by various early Christian saints, notably a 6th-cent. bishop of Constantinople much revered in the Orthodox Church.

Vars.: **Yevtikhov**, **Yev(s)tikheev**, **Yev(s)tifeev**, **Yestifeev**, **Yevtyukhov**, **Ovtukhov**, **Oltukhov**, **Avtukhov**, **Altukhov**, **Altufyev**, **Antifeev**.

Dims.: Russ.: **Yevteev**, **Yevtyugin** (patrs.). Ukr.: **Yevtushenko**.

Yewen *see* EWAN

Yezafovich *see* JOSEPH

Yezhov Russian: patr. from the nickname *Yozh* 'Hedge-hog', presumably denoting a man of prickly, shy, or un-approachable temperament.

Dims.: Czech: **Ježek**.

Habitation names: Pol.: **Jeżewski**, **Jeżowski** (either 'place of the hedgehog' or 'place where a man nicknamed Hedgehog lived').

Yisrael *see* ISRAEL

Yisraeli *see* ISRAELER

Yitschaky *see* ISAAC

Yizhak *see* ISAAC

Yoachimsohn *see* JOACHIM

Yockelman *see* JACOB

Yoel Jewish: from the Hebr. male given name *Yoel* (Eng. *Joel*), borne by a biblical prophet.

Vars.: **Joel** (see also JEKYLL); **Yoeli**, **Joeli**, **Joely** (with the Hebr. suffix *-i*).

Dim.: **Yolleck** (E Ashkenazic).

Patrs.: **Joels(on)**, **Yoelson**, **Yolles**, **Jol(l)es** (Ashkenazic).

Yoell *see* YULE

Yokel *see* JACOB

Yolkin Russian: **1.** patr. from the given name *Yolka*, dim. of any of the various Russ. names beginning with the syl-lable *Yel-*. None of these names is individually very frequent; they include *Yelevferi* (Gk *Eleutherios* 'Free') and *Yelizar* (Hebr. *Eliezer*; see LAZAR). **2.** patr. from the nickname *Yolka* 'Fir' (a dim. of the common noun *yel*, cogn. with Pol. *jodła* fir, spruce), given perhaps to a tall, thin man, or to someone who lived by a fir tree.

Habitation name (cogn. with 2): Pol.: **Jodłowski**.

Yolleck *see* YOEL

Yong *see* YOUNG

Yonis *see* JONAS

York English: habitation name from the city of York in N England, or perhaps in some cases regional name from the county of Yorkshire. The surname is now widespread throughout England. Originally, the town bore the Brit. name *Eburācum*, which probably meant 'yew-tree place'. This was altered by folk etymology into OE *Eoforwīc* (from the elements *eofor* wild boar + *wīc* outlying settlement (see WICK)). This name was taken over by Scandinavian set-tlers in the area, who altered it back to opacity in the form *Iorvík* and eventually *Iork*, in which form it was finally settled by the 13th cent. The surname has also been ad-opted by Jews as an Anglicization of various like-sounding Jewish surnames.

Var.: Eng.: **Yorke**.

Yorkston Scots (Edinburgh): habitation name from a place near the village of Corstorphine, recorded in 1354 as *Yokistoun*, in 1374 as *Yorkeston*, apparently from the

gen. case of the ON personal name *Jórek* + ME *toun* settle-ment.

Vars.: **Yo(u)rston**, **Yorstoun**, **Yorkson**.

Yoselevitch *see* JOSEPH

Youat *see* EWART

Youel *see* YULE

Youens *see* EWAN

Young English: distinguishing name, from ME *yunge*, *yonge* young (OE *geong*), for the younger of two bearers of the same given name, usually a son who bore the same name as his father. In ME this name is often found with the ANF def. art., e.g. Robert *le Yunge*.

Vars.: **Younge**, **Yong(e)**.

Patrs.: Eng.: **Youngs** (common in Norfolk). Flem., Du.: **Jongen**.

Younger English: **1.** distinguishing name, a var. of YOUNG, from the comparative of OE *geong* young. **2.** An-glicized form of MDu. *jonghheer* young nobleman (a cpd of *jong(h)* young + *herr* master, lord; cf. Ger. *Junker*). The term was used of a member of the European nobility who had not yet assumed knighthood.

Patrs. (from 2): Ger.: **Junkers**. Flem., Du.: **Jonkers**.

Youngman *see* YEOMAN

Youren *see* UREN

Yourston *see* YORKSTON

Yubero Spanish: occupational name for an oxherd or muleteer, from Sp. *yubero*, a dial. var. of *yuguero* (LL *iugārius*, an agent deriv. of *iugum* yoke).

Yudayov *see* JUDE

Yuell *see* YULE

Yuile *see* YULE

Yukhin *see* GEORGE

Yule Scots and English: nickname for someone who was born on Christmas Day or had some other connection with this time of year, from ME *yule* Christmastide (OE *gēol*, reinforced by the cogn. ON *jól*). This was originally the name of a pagan midwinter festival, which was later ap-propriated by the Christian Church for celebration of the birth of Christ. Its further etymology is unknown.

Vars.: **Youle**, **Youel**, **You(hi)ll**, **Yoell**, **Yeowell**, **Y(e)uell**, **Yuile**, **Yuill(e)**.

Patrs.: Eng.: **Youles**, **Youels**.

Yuranov *see* GEORGE

Yushachkov *see* GEORGE

Yust *see* JUST

Yusupov *see* JOSEPH

Yvelin *see* IVE

Yvonnet *see* IVE

Ywersen *see* IVOR

Z

Zabala Spanish: habitation name from a place in the province of Biscay, so called from Basque *zabal* small square + the def. art. *-a*. In some cases the surname may derive directly from the vocab. word.

Var.: **Zaballa** (places in the provinces of Burgos and Logroño).

Zabatino *see* SABBATO

Zaborowski Polish: habitation name from a place near Leszno called *Zaborowo* (probably named with the Pol. elements *za* beyond + *bór* forest + *-owo* suffix of placenames, but alternatively perhaps from *zabór* sequestration). It could alternatively be a topographic name for someone who lived 'on the other side of the forest'.

Var.: **Zaborski**.

Zábranský Czech: topographic name for someone who lived 'behind the gate' (*za branou*) of a town, or at a place named *Zábraní*, from these elements.

Var.: **Zábrana**.

Zac *see* SATZ

Zacchetti *see* JACK

Žáček *see* ZAK

Zachary Jewish, Polish, and English: from the Hebr. male given name *Zecharya*, composed of the elements *zachar* to remember + *ya* God. This name was borne by a biblical prophet and by the father of John the Baptist, and for that reason it achieved a modest popularity among Gentiles during the Middle Ages. The given name has always been popular among Jews.

Vars.: Jewish: **Za(c)haria**, **Zachari(a)s** (Ashkenazic); **Zachariasz**, **Zachari(a)sh**, **Sachariasch** (E Ashkenazic). Pol.: **Zachara**, **Zachariasz**; **Zacharski**.

Dims.: Ger.: **Zacherl**, **Sacherl**, **Zecherle**, **Zechel**. Czech: **Zach**. It.: **Zaccariello**, **Zaccarielli**, **Zaccarino**, **Zaccarini**, **Zaccherini**, **Zacchiroli**.

Aug.: It.: **Zaccheroni**.

Patrs.: Eng.: **Ackery**, **Ackary** (apparently the result of misdivision of the extinct *FitzZackery*). Dan., Norw.: **Zachariessen**.

Swed.: **Za(c)krisson**, **Zachrisson**. Jewish: **Zacharin**, **Zacharovitch**, **Zaharovich**, **Zacharowicz**, **Zacharowitz**, **Zacharovitz**, **Zacharovits** (E Ashkenazic); **Zahareanu**, **Zaharianu** (among Rumanian Jews). Russ.: **Zakharov**, **Sakharov**, **Zakharyev**, **Zakharyin**. Bulg.: **Zakhariev**. Gk: **Zachariou**, **Zachariades**.

Zadik Jewish: from Yid. *tsadik* pious, saintly man (cf. TSADOK).

Vars.: **Tzadik**, **Tsaddik**, **Zadek**; **Zadiki** (with the Hebr. suffix *-i*).

Patrs.: **Zadikov**, **Zadikoff**, **Zadickoviz**; **Tzadikian** (among Iranian Jews).

Zadok *see* TSADOK

Zaffren *see* SAFRAN

Zafra Spanish: habitation name from any of various places so called, notably one in the province of Extremadura. The placename is from OSp. *zafra*, *çafra* rock, crag (of Arabic origin). In some cases the surname may be a topographic name derived directly from the vocab. word.

Zaghetti *see* DEAKIN

Zagone *see* JACK

Zagórski Polish and Jewish (E Ashkenazic): topographic name composed of the Pol. elements *za* beyond, on the other side of + *góra* hill (see GÓRSKI) + the local surname suffix *-ski* (see BARANOWSKI), or habitation name from a place named with the elements *za* + *góra*.

Vars.: Pol.: **Zagórny**, **Zagórowski**. Jewish: **Zagorsky**, **Zagursky**.

Zahareanu *see* ZACHARY

Zahn German and Jewish (Ashkenazic): nickname for someone with a large or peculiar tooth or a remarkable or defective set of teeth, from Ger. *Zahn* tooth (MHG *zan(t)*).

Var.: Ger.: **Zandt**.

Dims.: Ger.: **Zähnle**, **Zehnle**.

Zahradník Czech: occupational name for a person who farmed on a small scale, from *zahrada* smallholding, orchard, or garden. A *zahradník* held lands larger than those of a cotter (*chalupník*) but smaller than those of a farmer (*sedlák*).

Dim.: **Zahradníček**.

Habitation name: **Zahrádka** (from a place named with this word in its earlier sense 'enclosure').

Zähringen German: habitation name from a place so called near Freiburg in Breisgau.

Zaiss *see* ZEISS

Zaitsev Russian: patr. from the nickname *Zayats* (gen. *Zaitsa*) 'Hare', denoting a swift runner. (The Slav. term meant originally 'jumper', 'leaper'.)

Dims.: Pol.: **Zajączek**. Czech: **Zajíček**. Jewish: **Zaicik**, **Zajczyk**. Ger. (of Slav. origin): **Zajacek**, **Zajecek**.

Habitation name (from a dim.): Pol.: **Zajączkowski** (also borne by Karaites in Poland, presumably an adoption of the Pol. surname).

Zajacek *see* ZAITSEV

Zajdensznir *see* SEIDE

Żak Polish: nickname for a youthful or studious person, from Pol. *żak* student, schoolboy. The original meaning of this word was 'novice, candidate for the priesthood', and so in some cases it is perhaps a nickname for one who had been destined for holy orders.

Dim.: Czech: **Žáček**.

Aug.: Czech: **Žákovec**.

Patr.: Pol.: **Żakiewicz**.

Habitation names: Pol.: **Żakowski**. Czech: **Žákovský**.

Zakhariev *see* ZACHARY

Zakheim *see* SACK

Zákostelecký Czech: topographic name for someone who lived 'behind the church', from Czech *za* behind + *kostel* church + *-ec* suffix of animate nouns + *-ský* adjectival suffix applied used in forming local names.

Zakrzewski Polish: habitation name from a place called *Zakrzewie* (from Pol. *za* beyond + *krzewie* thicket, collective noun from *kierz* bush), with the addition of *-ski*, suffix of local surnames (see BARANOWSKI).

Var.: **Zakrzeski**.

Zaks *see* SACHS

Zalcstein *see* SALT

Załęcki Polish: topographic name for someone who lived 'on the other side of the meadow', from Pol. *za* beyond + *łąka* meadow + *-ski* suffix of local surnames (see BARANOWSKI).

Var.: **Załęski**.

Zaleski Polish: 1. topographic name for someone who lived 'on the other side of the wood', from Pol. *za* beyond + *les, las* wood, with the addition of *-ski*, suffix of local surnames (see BARANOWSKI), or habitation name from a place, *Zalesie*, named with the elements *za* + *les*. 2. var. of ZALEWSKI.

Vars. (of 1): **Zalasa**, **Zalasik**.

Zalewski Polish: topographic name for someone who lived by a flood plain or bay, Pol. *zalew*, or habitation name from a place named with this element, with the addition of *-ski*, suffix of local surnames (see BARANOWSKI). There has been considerable confusion with ZALESKI.

Zaliznyak Ukrainian: occupational name for an ironmonger or, less commonly, a blacksmith. The vocab. word is an agentive deriv. from Ukr. *zalizo* iron.

Var.: **Zheleznyak**.

Habitation name: Pol.: **Żelazowski**.

Zalman *see* SALMON

Zámečník Czech: occupational name for a locksmith, Czech *zámečník*, agent noun derived from *zámek* lock (which also means 'castle').

Var.: **Zámek** (also a topographic name for someone who lived in or by a castle).

Zammit Jewish (E Ashkenazic): regional name from *Zamet*, the Yid. name of Samogitia, an area of Lithuania.

Zamora Spanish: habitation name from a city in NW Spain, the name of which is of Arabic origin, apparently from *azemur* wild olive.

Var.: **Zamorano**.

Zanardi *see* JOHN

Zandberg *see* SAND

Zandt *see* ZAHN

Zanger *see* ZENGER

Zangers *see* SANGER

Zangwill Jewish (Ashkenazic): ornamental name from Hebr. *zangvil* ginger.

Var.: **Zangvil**.

Zanobelli *see* ZINOVYEV

Zappa Italian: metonymic occupational name for an agricultural worker, from It. *zappa* mattock.

Var.: **Zappi**.

Dims.: **Zappell(in)i**, **Zappetta**, **Zappett(in)i**, **Zappini**, **Zappino**; **Zapp(ar)oli** (Emilia); **Zapulla**, **Zappulli** (Sicily).

Zaragoza Spanish: habitation name from *Zaragoza*, Sp. name of the city of Saragossa in NE Spain, the ancient capital of the kingdom of Aragon. The name derives, via Arabic, from L *Caesarea Augusta*, the name bestowed in the 1st cent. AD by the Emperor Augustus, from two of the names belonging to the imperial house (cf. CESARE and AGOSTI).

Zárate Spanish form of Basque **Zarate**: habitation name from a place in the province of Álava, so called from the elements *zara* (oak) wood + *ate* pass, defile.

Zaremba Polish: occupational name for a woodcutter, a deriv. of Pol. *zarębać* to hack, chop.

Vars.: **Zaręba**; **Zarębski**, **Zarembski**.

Zarfati *see* SARFATTI

Zarges *see* NAZAIRE

Zarncke *see* CHERNYAKOV

Zarraga Basque: topographic name for someone who lived by a slag heap, from *zarra* slag + the local suffix *-aga*.

Zarza Spanish: topographic name for someone who lived on a patch of land overgrown with brambles, from Sp. *zarza* bramble (of pre-Roman origin).

Zarzecki Polish and Jewish (E Ashkenazic): topographic name for someone who lived 'on the other side of the river', from Pol. *za* beyond + *rzek(a)* river, with the addition of *-ski*, suffix of local surnames (see BARANOWSKI). The Jewish surname may possibly also be a habitation name from the city of *Shklov Zaretski* in the Ukraine, which bore the distinguishing epithet to differentiate it from *Shklov Dneprovski*, a town of the same name situated on the banks of the Dnieper. However, this is only conjecture: when Ashkenazic surnames are based on compound placenames, it is as a rule only the first element of the placename that forms the basis for the surname.

Vars.: Pol.: **Zarzycki**. Jewish: **Zarecki**, **Zarecky**, **Zaretski**, **Zare(t)zki**.

Zasada Polish: status name for a person who organized a new settlement, OPol. *zasadźca*. The name has been altered by folk etymology to conform to the mod. Pol.

word *zasada* principle, basis (which formerly meant 'trap' or 'ambush').

Habitation name: **Zasadziński**.

Zatorski Polish: habitation name from the town of *Zator* near Oświęcim in S Poland.

Zatz *see* SATZ

Zauner German: occupational name for a fence-builder, from an agent deriv. of Ger. *Zaun* fence, hedge, enclosure (MHG, OHG *zūn*, a cogn. of OE *tūn* enclosure, settlement). The vocab. word denoted in particular the enclosure built surrounding a village as a defence against marauding animals and strangers. In some cases the surname may also be a topographic name for someone who lived by such a fence.

Vars.: **Zäuner**, **Zeuner**.

Zavadzki *see* ZAWADZKI

Zavetaev Russian: patr. from the nickname *Zavetai* 'Heir' (a deriv. of *zavet* will, testament), denoting someone who had inherited or was due to inherit a substantial estate or fortune.

Zawadzki Polish and Jewish (E Ashkenazic): nickname for a troublesome or troubled person, from Pol. *zawada* difficulty, obstacle, with the addition of the surname suffix *-ski* (see BARANOWSKI). In some cases it may be a topographic name for someone who lived by a physical obstruction.

Vars.: **Zawada**, **Zawadski**. Jewish only: **Zavadzki**, **Zavatzky**, **Zawacki**; **Zawader**.

Habitation name: Pol.: **Zawadowski**.

Zawierucha Polish and Jewish (E Ashkenazic): nickname or, as a Jewish name, ornamental name from Pol. *zawierucha* snowstorm, blizzard.

Zawiślak Polish: **1.** topographic name for someone who lived on the 'far side' of the River Vistula, from Pol. *za* beyond + *wiśl-* (from *Wisła* Vistula) + *-ak* suffix denoting animate nouns. **2.** nickname for a hanger-on, from Pol. *zawisły* dependent.

Zayas Jewish (Ashkenazic): ornamental name, derived from the Ashkenazic pronunciation, *zayis*, of Hebr. *zayit* olive.

Zazo Spanish: nickname for someone with a lisp. The adj. is of imitative origin, representing the pronunciation of /s/ as /θ/ (written in Sp. as *z*).

Zdanowicz *see* ZDENĚK

Zdeněk Czech: from the OSlav. personal name *Zdeněk*, pet form of *Zdeslav*, composed of the elements *zde* here + *slav* glory, i.e. bringer of glory.

Vars.: **Zděnek**; **Zděnovec**.

Patr.: Pol.: **Zdanowicz**.

Habitation name: Pol.: **Zdanowski**.

Zdrojewski Polish: habitation name from a place naemd with Pol. *zdrój* spring, source + *-ew* possessive suffix, with the addition of *-ski* suffix of local surnames (see BARANOWSKI). It may also be a habitation name from a place named with this word.

Zduniak Polish: **1.** habitation name from the town of *Zduny*, SW of Kalisz. **2.** occupational name for a potter or maker of stoves, from Pol. *zdun* potter + the redundant agent suffix *-iak*.

Dims.: **Zduńczyk**, **Zdunek**.

Patr. (from a dim.): **Zdunkiewicz**.

Zeal *see* SEAL

Zealey *see* SEALEY

Żebrowski Polish: **1.** habitation name from some place named with Pol. *żebry* penury, poverty, perhaps because of its poor soil. **2.** nickname for a beggar, Pol. *żebrak* (from the same root as in 1).

Zecchetti *see* FRANCIS

Zechel *see* ZACHARY

Zeder *see* CEDER

Zedník Czech: occupational name for a mason, Czech *zedník*.

Dim.: Czech: **Zedníček**.

Patr.: Bulg.: **Zidarov**.

Zeggiato *see* LILLY

Zehender German: occupational name for an official responsible for collecting, on behalf of the lord of the manor, tithes of agricultural produce owed as rent. The more prosperous tenants had to contribute wine and corn, those with smaller holdings fruit, vegetables, milk, cheese, beer, and poultry. The MHG term for this official was *zehendære*, a deriv. of *zehende* tenth part, tithe (OHG *zehanto*, from *zehan* ten). The surname is most common in Bavaria, Austria, Switzerland, and Württemberg.

Vars.: **Zehe(n)tner**, **Zehner**, **Zent(n)er**, **Center**.

Zehnle *see* ZAHN

Zehrer German: unflattering nickname for a sponger, spendthrift, or prodigal, from an agent deriv. of Ger. *zehren* to live off, feed on, sap (MHG *(ver)zern* to consume, use up, OHG *zeren*).

Zeiberts *see* SIEBERT

Zeiss German: nickname for a gentle person, from MHG *zeiss* tender, kind.

Vars.: **Zeisse**, **Zaiss**.

Dim.: **Zaissle**.

Zeitlin Jewish (E Ashkenazic): metr. from the Yid. female given name *Tseytl*, which is of uncertain origin, with the addition of the Slav. metr. suffix *-in*.

Vars.: **Tzeitlin**; **Ceitlin** (a Pol. spelling).

Zelaya *see* CELAYA

Żelazowski *see* ZALIZNYAK

Zeldes Jewish (Ashkenazic): metr. from the Yid. female given name *Zelde* (from MHG *sælde* fortunate, blessed) + the Yid. possessive suffix *-s*.

Vars.: **Zeldis**, **Seldes**, **Seldis**; **Zeldin**, **Seldin**, **Zeld(ov)ich** (E Ashkenazic).

Zelichovsky *see* SELIG

Zell *see* SELL

Zeller German and Jewish (Ashkenazic): topographic name for someone who lived by a shrine or at the site of a hermit's cell, Ger. *Zelle* (MHG *zelle*, from L *cella* small room), or habitation name from any of the various places named with this word, most notably the town of *Celle* near Hanover. In some cases it may also have been an occupational name for someone who owned or was employed at a small workshop, and this is the most likely source of the Jewish surname.

Vars.: **Zellmann**. Jewish only: **Zelman**.

Zelley *see* SEALEY

Zelli *see* AIELLO

Zeman Czech: status name for a yeoman farmer or small landowner, Czech *zeman* (a deriv. of *zem* land). This is one of the most common Czech surnames.

Dims.: **Zemánek**, **Zemek**.

Zemel *see* SEMMEL

Zenger German: nickname for a lively or active person, from MHG *zenger*, *zanger* sharp, biting.

Vars.: **Zenker** (also Jewish), **Zanger**, **Zänger**.

Dims.: **Zengerle**, **Zangerl**, **Zängerle**; **Zingerle** (Tyrol).

Zensen *see* VINCENT

Zenter *see* ZEHENDER

Zeppelin German: habitation name from the town of *Zepelin* in Mecklenburg, so called from a Slav. word cogn. with Pol. *Czaplin* 'place of herons' (cf. CHAPLIN 2).

Var.: **Zeplin**.

Zerges *see* NAZAIRE

Zerkus *see* SORIN

Zerndl *see* ZORN

Zetto *see* FRANCIS

Zeuner *see* ZAUNER

Zeuthen Danish: habitation name from the town of *Søften* in Jutland.

Zevin *see* SIEFF

Žežulka Czech: nickname from the vocab. word *žežulka* cuckoo.

Vars.: **Zezulka**, **Zezulák**, **Zezula**.

Zhavoronkov Russian: patr. from the nickname *Zhavoronok* 'Lark' (probably from a dim. of the same stem as in *voron* raven (see VORONOV) and *vorona* crow (see VORONIN), with the addition of an obscure prefix). The nickname probably denoted an early riser or else someone with a fine singing voice.

Zheleznyak *see* ZALIZNYAK

Zhidovinov Russian: patr. from the ORuss. name *zhidovin* Jew.

Var.: **Zhidovtsev**.

Dim.: Czech: **Žídek**.

Zhivago Russian: nickname from Russ. *zhivoi* lively, brisk, quick. The ending is unusual; it perhaps represents an OSlav. gen. case of this word, or it may be an alteration of a deriv. in -*aga*, under the influence of Beloruss. and Ukr. dims. in -*o*.

Vars.: **Zhivagin** (patr.); **Zhivchikov** (patr., from a dim.).

Zhukov Russian: patr. from the nickname *Zhuk* 'Beetle', presumably denoting someone bearing some supposed resemblance to a beetle.

Dims.: Ukr.: **Zhuchenko**.

Patr. from a dim.: Beloruss.: **Zhuchkevich**.

Habitation names: Pol.: **Żukowski**. Ukr., Beloruss.: **Zhukovski**.

Zibell *see* ZWIEBEL

Zich *see* SIEGMUND

Zidarov *see* ZEDNÍK

Žídek *see* ZHIDOVINOV

Zieboll *see* ZWIEBEL

Zieger German: metonymic occupational name for a preparer or seller of goat's curd cheese, MHG *ziger(kæse)*. The word is of problematic etymology, apparently being of neither Gmc nor Romance origin; it may derive from one of the Celt. elements preserved in the Alpine region.

Vars.: **Ziegert**, **Ziegerer**.

Ziegler German and Jewish (Ashkenazic): occupational name for a tiler, from an agent deriv. of Ger. *Ziegel* roof tile (MHG *ziegel*, OHG *ziagal*, from L *tēgula*). In the Middle Ages the term came to denote bricks as well as tiles, and so in some cases the term may have denoted a brickmaker or bricklayer rather than a tiler. Cf. CEGIELSKI.

Vars.: Jewish: **Tsigler**, **Cigler**, **Cygler**, **Cygel**, **Ziegel(man)**, **Cygielman** (from Yid. *tsigl* brick or mod. Ger. *Ziegel* tile).

Ziehm *see* SIMON

Zielak Polish: **1.** var. of ZIELIŃSKI. **2.** occupational name for a herbalist, from a deriv. of Pol. *ziele* herb (related to *zielony* green; see ZIELIŃSKI).

Var.: **Ziołek** (from the var. vocab. word *ziółko*).

Patr.: **Ziółkiewicz**.

Habitation names: **Ziółkowski**, **Zielewski**.

Zieliński Polish and Jewish (E Ashkenazic): from the vocab. word *zielony* green, in various applications. As a Pol. name it seems primarily to have been a nickname for a person with a sickly 'greenish' complexion. It may also have been a nickname for someone who habitually dressed in green, or who was 'green' in the sense of being immature or inexperienced. Additionally, it may be a habitation name from a place named with this word. As a Jewish name it is mainly an ornamental name.

Vars.: **Zielonka**; **Zieleniewski**; ZIELAK.

Patrs.: Pol.: **Zielen(k)iewicz**.

Zieprecht *see* SIEBERT

Ziff *see* SIEFF

Zigliotti *see* LILLY

Zika *see* SIEGMUND

Zilbermintz *see* SILVER

Zilioli *see* GILES

Zima Czech: **1.** from the vocab. word *zima* winter, cold, probably a nickname from someone with a gloomy or un-approachable personality, but possibly also a topographic name for someone living in a particularly cold spot. **2.** from a short form of the given name *Erazim* ERASMUS.

Zima *see* SIMON

Zimbalist German and Jewish (Ashkenazic): occupational name for a player on the cymbals, from an agent deriv. of Ger. *Zimbal* cymbal (MHG *zymbel(e)*, OHG *zymbala*, from Gk *kymbala* (pl.)). As a Jewish surname it refers specifically to a cymbalist in a band that provided music at a wedding feast.

Vars.: Jewish (E Ashkenazic): **Cymbalist(a)**, **Cimbalist(a)**, (Pol. spellings); **Zimbalista**, **Zymbalist(a)**; **Cimbal**, **Zimbal(er)**.

Zimler *see* SEMMEL

Zimmermann German and Jewish (Ashkenazic): occupational name for a carpenter, Ger. *Zimmermann* (MHG *zimbermann*, a cpd of *zimber, zimmer* timber, wood + *mann* man).

Vars.: Ger.: **Zimmer(er)**. Jewish: **Zim(m)erman**; **Cimerman**, **Cymerman** (Pol. spellings); **Cymmermann**, **Cimmermann**, **Timmerman(n)**.

Patr.: Flem., Du.: **Timmermans**.

Zinger *see* SANGER

Zingerle *see* ZENGER

Zingg *see* ZINK

Zingler German and Jewish (Ashkenazic): topographic name for someone who lived by the outermost defensive wall of a town or city, from MHG *zingel* (from L *cingula* belt, from *cingere* to surround, encompass) + *-er* suffix denoting human nouns.

Vars.: Ger.: **Zingel(mann)**. Jewish: **Zingel** (but this may also be a deriv. of Yid. *tsingl* 'little tongue'; see TONG).

Zini *see* FRANCIS

Zinichev *see* ZINOVYEV

Zink German: from Ger. *Zinke* tip, point, prong (MHG *zinke*, OHG *zinko*), acquired either as a topographic name by someone who lived on a pointed piece of land or as a nickname for a man with a singularly pointed nose (cf. mod. Ger. slang *Zinken* 'hooter'). The same word was used to denote the cornet, although the semantic development is not clear, and the surname may sometimes have been metonymic for a player of this instrument. It was not until the 16th cent. that the metal *zinc* was discovered and named (apparently from its jagged appearance in the furnace), so this is unlikely to lie behind the surname.

Vars.: **Zinke**, **Zingg**.

Zinn German and Jewish (Ashkenazic): metonymic occupational name for a worker in tin, Ger. *Zinn*, Yid. *tsin* (MHG, OHG *zin*). In medieval times the metal was used to make cups and vessels for use in the more pros-

perous households, while the majority of the population had to make do with wooden utensils.

Vars.: Ger.: **Zinner(t)**. Jewish: **Zin**, **Tzin**, **Tsin**, **Zin(n)er**.

Zinovyev Russian: patr. from the given name *Zinovi*, a Russ. form of Gk *Zēnobios*, composed of the elements *Zeus*, gen. *Zēnos*, the name of the principal god in the ancient Gk pantheon + *bios* life. In spite of its pagan overtones, the name was borne by several early Christian saints, including a 4th-cent. bishop of Florence. Its popularity in E Europe is largely due to the veneration in the Orthodox Church of an early Christian martyr, a priest and physician who was killed in Asia Minor at the end of the 3rd cent.

Var.: **Zinovichev**.

Dims.: Russ.: **Zinkov**, **Zinichev**, **Zinyukhin** (all patrs.). Ukr.: **Zin(chen)ko**, **Zinchuk**. It.: **Zanobelli**, **Zanobetti**; **Zobin(i)**, **Zob(b)oli**, **Zob(b)olo**, **Zobele**.

Ziołek *see* ZIELAK

Zirkin *see* SORIN

Zirkler German: occupational name for a town watchman, from an agent deriv. of MHG *zirk(e)len* to do the rounds (OHG *zirkilan*, from L *circulāre*, a deriv. of *cīrculus* circle, dim. of *circus* ring).

Vars.: **Zirkel**; **Zürcklert** (Saxony).

Zisapel *see* SWEET

Zisin Jewish (E Ashkenazic): metr. from the Yid. female given name *Zise* (from Yid. *zis* sweet) + the Slav. metr. suffix *-in*.

Vars.: **Zissin**, **Susin**, **Zisovich**, **Ziszovics**.

Dims. (metrs.): **Ziske**, **Ziskis**, **Ziskin**, **Zyskin**, **Siskin**, **Suskin**, **Süsskin**, **Ziskovi(t)ch**, **Ziskovitz**, **Zuscovitch**, **Susskovitch**, **Suskovitz** (all from the Yid. dim. female given name *Ziske*; see also the derivs. listed at SÜSSKIND); **Zislis**, **Zislin**, **Sislin**, **Zisslowicz** (from the Yid. dim. female given name *Zisl*). Forms with *ü* show the influence of mod. Ger. *süss* sweet; forms with *u* are derivs. of *süss* or are S Yid. hypercorrections.

Ziskind *see* SÜSSKIND

Zistler German: occupational name for a basket-maker, from an agent deriv. of MHG *zistel* small basket (from L *cistella*, a dim. of *cistis* bag, box, basket, from Gk *kystis* pouch, bladder).

Zito S Italian: from the medieval given name *Zito*, originally a nickname from the S It. dial. term *zito, zite, zitu* young bachelor.

Vars.: **Lozito**, **Losito**, **Loseto** (nicknames, with fused def. art.).

Dims.: **Zitello**, **Zitelli**.

Žižka *see* SIEGMUND

Zlatanović Croatian: patr. from a Croat. given name, *Zlatan* 'Golden', from Croat. *zlato* gold, cogn. with Russ. *zoloto*; cf. ZOLOTARYOV.

Var.: **Zlatić**.

Patr. from a dim.: **Zlatković**.

Zlatin Jewish (E Ashkenazic): metr. from the Yid. female given name *Zlate* (from the Czech word meaning 'gold'; cf. ZOLOTARYOV) + the Slav. metr. suffix *-in*.

Vars.: **Slatin(e)**.

Metrs. (from dims.): **Zlatkin**, **Slatkin(e)**, **Zlatkes**, **Zlatkis**.

Zlatníček *see* ZOLOTARYOV

Zmitrichenko *see* DMITRIEV

Zoanetti *see* JOHN

Zobboli *see* ZINOVYEV

Zobel *see* SOBEL

Zobrist *see* OBER

Zoccoli *see* SUCH

Zoiberman *see* SAUBER

Zola 1. Italian: habitation name from any of various minor places called *Zol(l)a*, named with a dial. term for a mound or bank of earth. 2. Jewish: of unknown origin.
Vars. (of 1): **Zolla**, **Zol(l)i**; **Zolese**, **Zolesi**.

Zolini *see* FRANCIS

Zolotaryov Russian: patr. from the occupational term *zolotar* goldsmith (a deriv. of *zoloto* gold).
Dims.: Ukr.: **Zolotarenko**. Beloruss.: **Zolotarenko**, **Zolotaryonok**. Czech: **Zlatníček**.

Zonenschein *see* SONNENSCHEIN

Zoppo Italian: nickname for a lame man, from It. *zoppo* lame.
Var.: **Zoppi**.
Dims.: **Zopetti**, **Zoppetto**, **Zoppini**, **Zoppino**.

Zoref Jewish: occupational name for a goldsmith, Hebr. *tsoref*.
Vars.: **Zoreff**, **Soref(f)**.

Zorn German and Jewish (Ashkenazic): nickname for a short-tempered man, from Ger. *Zorn* anger (MHG *zorn*).
Var.: Ger.: **Zorndt**.
Dims.: Ger.: **Zörnle**, **Zerndl**. Low Ger.: **Zörnchen**.

Zörneke *see* CHERNYAKOV

Zorrilla Spanish: nickname for a crafty or devious person, from a dim. of Sp. *zorra* vixen. The Sp. name of the fox means literally 'the lazy one', from OSp. *zorro* lazy (from *zorrar* to drag, apparently of imitative origin), and it is likely that the nickname was sometimes given in this original sense.

Zorzenoni *see* GEORGE

Zotti *see* FRANCIS

Zoubek *see* ZUBAKOV

Zouch *see* SUCH

Zoyer *see* SAUER

Zschäpe *see* STEPHEN

Zuanazzi *see* JOHN

Zuazo Basque: topographic name for someone who lived by a group of trees, from *zuaitz* tree + the suffix of abundance -*zo*, -*zu*. There are several places in the Basque country so called, and the surname may also derive from any of them.

Zubakov Russian: patr. from the nickname *Zubak* 'Toothy' (a deriv. of *zub* tooth), denoting someone with something odd or noticeable about his teeth.
Vars.: **Zubin**; **Zubarev**, **Zubavin**.
Dims.: Russ.: **Zubkin**. Ukr.: **Zubko**. Czech: **Z(o)ubek**. Beloruss.: **Zubashkevich**.

Zubiaur Basque: habitation name from either of two places in the province of Biscay, so called from the elements *zubi* bridge + *aurre* front part, i.e. a settlement in front of a bridge.

Zuccheri Italian: metonymic occupational name for a dealer in sugar or for a confectioner or seller of sweatmeets, from It. *zucchero* sugar (of Arabic and probably ultimately of Skt origin).
Vars.: **Zuccari**, **Zuccaro** (S Italy); **Zucaro** (Naples).
Dims.: It.: **Zuccherini**, **Zuccherino**, **Zuccarini**, **Zuccarino**, **Zuccarelli**, **Zuccarello**.

Zucchi Italian: in part a metonymic occupational name for a grower and seller of gourds (squashes or marrows), from It. *zucca* gourd (LL *cucutia*, for class. L *cucurbita*). More often, however, it is a nickname from the same word used in its colloquial transferred sense 'head'.
Vars.: **Zucca**, **Zucco**.
Dims.: **Zucchelli**, **Zucchello**, **Zucchetti**, **Zucchetto**, **Zucchetta**, **Zucchini**, **Zucchino**, **Zuccol(in)i**, **Zuccolo**, **Zuccotti**, **Zuccotto**.
Aug.: **Zucconi**.

Zucker 1. German: metonymic occupational name for a dealer in sugar or a confectioner, from MHG *zucker* sugar (cf. ZUCCHERI). 2. Jewish (Ashkenazic): generally an ornamental surname from mod. Ger. *Zucker*, Yid. *zuker* sugar, but possibly also an occupational name as in 1. 3. German: offensive nickname for someone thought to be a thief, from MHG *zuckære* thief, an agent deriv. of *zucken* to snatch, grab (OHG *zucchen*, an intensive formation from *ziohan* to pull, draw).
Vars.: Jewish (those ending in -*man* and -*nik* are occupational; the rest may be ornamental): **Zuker**, **Tzuker**; **Zuckerman(n)**, **Zuk(i)erman**, **Czukerman** (Anglicized **Sugarman**); **Cuk(i)er(man)** (Pol. spellings); **Zukernik**, **Cukiernik** (E Ashkenazic); **Zukerovitz** (patr. in form).
Dim. (of 2): Jewish: **Cukerl**.
Patr. (from 1): Flem.: **Suikermans**.
Cpds (of 2, ornamental): Jewish: **Zuckerbaum** ('sugar tree'); **Zuckerberg(er)**, **Zukerberg** ('sugar hill'); **Zuckerblum** ('sugar flower'); **Zuckerbrot** ('sugar bread'; also a metonymic occupational name for a fancy baker); **Zuckerfein** ('sugar fine'); **Zu(c)kerkandel** ('sugar candy'); **Zuckerstein**, **Cukierstein** ('sugar stone'); **Zukerwasser** ('sugar water').

Zudkevitz *see* TSADOK

Zuenelli *see* JOHN

Żukowski *see* ZHUKOV

Zulin *see* JÚLIO

Zulueta Basque: habitation name from a place in the province of Navarre, so called from *zulo* hole + the suffix of abundance -*eta*, i.e. presumably an area where the ground was full of pits and indentations.

Zumbichl *see* BÜHLER

Zumbrink *see* BRINK

Zumloh *see* LOO

Zumtobel *see* TOBEL

Zumwinkel *see* WINCKEL

Zunder German and Jewish (Ashkenazic): metonymic occupational name for a seller of kindling wood, from Ger. *Zunder* tinder (MHG *zunder*, OHG *zuntara*, a cogn. of OE *tynder*).
Dims.: Ger.: **Zundel**, **Zündel**; **Zundler**, **Zündler**.

Zunz Jewish: probably a habitation name from *Zons*, a town situated on the Rhine not far from Cologne and Düsseldorf, although the reason for the change in the vowel is not clear. The placename is of uncertain origin, traced by Bahlow to an ancient element *san, sen, sin, son, sun*, meaning (stagnant) water'.
Vars.: **Zuntz**; **Zunser** (with the habitational ending *-er*).

Żuraw Polish: nickname for a tall, gangling person, from Pol. *żuraw* crane (cogn. with Czech *jeřáb*). The term was also used as a nickname for a chimney-sweep, referring to the crane's habit of nesting on chimneys.
Var.: **Żurawski**.

Zürcklert *see* ZIRKLER

Zurdo Spanish: nickname for a left-handed person, Sp. *zurdo* (of pre-Roman origin, apparently related to Basque *zurrun* heavy, sluggish, clumsy).

Zurita Spanish: habitation name from any of several places so called. The placename is of uncertain origin; it may have some connection with Basque *zuri* white, or with Sp. *zurita* dove (allegedly of imitative origin).

Zuscovitch *see* ZISIN

Zuserblum *see* SWEET

Zusskind *see* SÜSSKIND

Zvezdochyotov Russian: patr. from the ORuss. occupational term *zvezdochyot* astrologer (from *zvezda* star + *chet* to read).

Zwartjes *see* SCHWARZ

Zweigel *see* TWIGG

Zwiebel 1. German: metonymic occupational name for a grower or seller of onions, Ger. *Zwiebel* onion (MHG *z(w)ibolle*, *zwifel* from LL *cēpulla*, dim. of class. L *cēpa*). In the Pomeranian dialect the word and the surname were accented on the second syllable. 2. Jewish (Ashkenazic): metonymic occupational name for a grower or seller of on-

ions, or unflattering surname bestowed at random by non-Jewish government officials, or just one of the large number of Jewish ornamental names referring to plants.
Vars.: Ger.: **Zwibel**, **Swibel**; **Zieboll**, **Zibell**, **Zibill**; **Zwiebler**, **Zwiebelmann**; **Zwiefel**, **Zwiefler** (Bavaria). Jewish: **Zwibel**; **Cibula**, **Cybula**; **Zibulsky**, **Cibulski** (E Ashkenazic).
Dim.: Russ.: **Tsybulkin** (patr.). Jewish (E Ashkenazic): **Zibulkin** (patr. in form).

Zwierzchowski Polish: habitation name from a place named with Pol. *zwierzchni* upper + *-ów* possessive suffix, with the addition of *-ski* suffix of local surnames (see BARANOWSKI), or else a topographic name for someone who lived on an upper storey.

Zwierzyński Polish: habitation name from *Zwierzyna*, a district of Cracow, named with Pol. *zwierzę* animal, or from some other place named with this element.

Zwilling German and Jewish (Ashkenazic): nickname for a twin, Ger. *Zwilling*, Yid. *tsviling* (MHG *zwillinc*, OHG *zwiniling*, a deriv. of *zwinal* double, from *zwēne* two).
Dim.: Ger.: **Zwingli** (Switzerland).
Patr.: Ger.: **Zwillinger**.

Zwolski Polish: probably a habitation name from any of the various places in Poland called *Wola*, with fused preposition *z*; *z Woli* means 'from Wola'.
Vars.: **Wolski**; **Zwoliński**.

Zyablikov Russian: patr. from the nickname *Zyablik* 'Finch', given perhaps to a cheerful or birdlike man. The word itself is said to derive from an element meaning 'to freeze', because the finch appears as soon as the winter snows begin to melt, and disappears again when ice and frost return.

Zych *see* SIEGMUND

Zygmuńczyk *see* SIEGMUND

Zýka *see* SIEGMUND

Zyl, van Dutch: topographic name for someone who lived by a patch of stagnant water, i.e. a lake or canal.
Vars.: **Van der Zyl**, **Van Zijl**, **Zylman**.

Zylberbaum *see* SILVER

Zymbalist *see* ZIMBALIST

Zyprecht *see* SIEBERT

Zyskin *see* ZISIN

Zyskind *see* SÜSSKIND

A DICTIONARY OF
FIRST NAMES

PATRICK HANKS · FLAVIA HODGES

INTRODUCTION

Scope of the work

What is a 'first name'? Strictly, it is the first of a sequence of one or more given names borne by an individual. A given name is one that is bestowed on a child by its parents or guardians at birth, as opposed to an inherited surname. More loosely, the term is used with much the same significance as 'given name'. All the names listed in this book can, of course, be used both as first names and as second or subsequent given names. But the range of names used as second, third, or fourth given names is somewhat wider. Typically, for example, a mother's maiden surname, or an unusual personal name with some special family significance, may be found used in this way. In many cases, this has been a first stage in the transfer of a surname to use as a common conventional given name. Those names that have clearly completed the transfer are included in this dictionary. Other, less usual secondary given names are not included here.

A person's given name is a badge of cultural identity. Cultural identity is closely allied to religious identity: religious affiliation and native language are often key factors, overtly or subliminally, in the choice of an appropriate name for a new member of a family. Even agnostics and atheists typically choose names for their children that are common among the sect or religion which they may have rejected but in whose midst they live, rather than totally alien or invented names.

It is difficult to imagine a human culture without personal names. The names that people bear are determined in large part by the culture that they belong to. A woman called *Niamh* can be presumed to be Irish; at the very least, her parents, in choosing this name for her, were announcing some sort of cultural identification with Ireland and Irish culture.

Even the commonest names are to some extent culture-specific in form. *John* is one of the commonest first names in Europe, but it is still a reasonable guess that a man called *John* is English-speaking and Christian. If he is German, we expect him to be called *Johann* or *Hans*: the choice of the form *John* for a German is unusual and suggestive of Anglophilia. At the very least, it would invite comment or explanation. Names such as *Maria*, which are shared in the same form by several languages, are the exception rather than the rule in Europe, despite the shared cultural history and the cross-fertilization that are characteristic of Europe and that have played such an important part in determining choices of names.

For underlying the differences are deeper unities, connecting naming practices across linguistic boundaries. *John, Seán, Ia(i)n, Giovanni, Johann, Jean, Jan, Ivan*, and so on are in one sense all variants of the same name, with the same 'meaning'. A description that is relevant to one will be in large part relevant to another.

The purpose of this dictionary is to record and explain these similarities and differences in the names of Europe and the English-speaking world, giving the forms, linguistic origins, cultural peculiarities, and cognate relationships of each. Where a name that is essentially 'the same name' is found in many different forms in the different languages of Europe, the main entry is placed under the usual English spelling. There are cross-references, in small capitals, where differences in spelling mean that two names are more than a few entries apart.

Also included are two supplements on naming traditions that up to now have been largely independent of the European tradition, but that are of increasing interest among English speakers and others. The first of these describes the most frequent given names in the Arab world. These are important not only in their own right, but also because they are the source of the most common Islamic names in every part of the globe where Islam is practised. They provide a striking parallel to the Judaeo-Christian tradition. The other supplement records and explains the most common Indian names. The ancient religions and culture of India have long attracted interest in the West, and the need for summary information on the names from this rich and varied culture is reinforced now by immigration. Each of the supplements is preceded by a short introduction explaining the principal features of naming practices in the two cultures.

A

Aaltje (f.) Low German, Dutch, and Frisian: pet form derived from *Aalt*, a contracted form of ADELHEID.

Aaltruide (f.) Dutch form of ADELTRAUD.

Aaron (m.) Biblical: name of the brother of Moses, who was appointed by God to be Moses' spokesman, and became the first high priest of the Israelites (Exodus 4: 14–16;7: 1–2). It is of uncertain origin and meaning but most probably, like MOSES, of Egyptian rather than Hebrew origin. The traditional derivation from Hebrew *har-on* 'mountain of strength' is no more than a folk etymology. The name has been used fairly infrequently by Christians, rather more commonly by Jews.
Variants: Jewish: **Aharon** (Hebrew); **Arn** (Yiddish).
Pet form: Yiddish: **Arke**.

Aatami (m.) Finnish form of ADAM.

Abbie (f.) 1. English: pet form of ABIGAIL, now used as an independent given name. 2. Irish: Anglicized form of GOBNAIT.
Variant: **Abbey**.

Abbondio (m.) Italian: from Late Latin *Abundius*, a derivative of *abundans* abundant, copious (genitive *abundantis*). The name was borne by a 5th-century bishop of Como, who is the subject of a local cult. The name is still most common in the Como region.

Abe (m.) 1. Jewish (two syllables): Yiddish name, from Aramaic *abba* father, which was used as a personal name in Talmudic times instead of ABRAHAM. 2. Jewish and English (one syllable): short form of ABRAHAM.

Abel (m.) Biblical: name of the younger son of Adam and Eve, who was murdered out of jealousy by his brother Cain (Genesis 4: 1–8). The Hebrew form is *Hevel*, ostensibly representing the vocabulary word *hevel* breath, vapour, and so taken to imply vanity or worthlessness. Abel is considered by the Christian Church to have been a pre-Christian martyr (cf. Matthew 23: 35), and is invoked as a saint in the litany for the dying. Nevertheless, his name has not been much used either before or after its brief vogue among the Puritans.

Abelone (f.) Danish form of APOLLONIA.

Abigail (f.) Biblical: name (meaning 'father of exaltation' in Hebrew) borne by one of King David's wives, who had earlier been married to Nabal (I Samuel 25: 3), and by the mother of Absalom's captain Amasa (2 Samuel 1: 25). The name was popular in the 17th century under Puritan influence. It was a common name in literature for a lady's maid, for example in Beaumont and Fletcher's play *The Scornful Lady* (1616), partly no doubt because the biblical Abigail refers to herself as 'thy servant'. In Ireland this name has traditionally been used as an Anglicized form of GOBNAIT, although the reasons for this are not clear.
Pet forms: English, Irish: **Abbie**, **Abbey**.

Abilene (f.) English (U.S.): a comparatively rare name. In the New Testament, Abilene is a region of the Holy Land (Luke 3:

1), whose name is of uncertain origin, but may be derived from a Hebrew element meaning 'grass'. Several places in America have been named from this reference, notably a city in Kansas, which was the boyhood home of President Dwight D. Eisenhower. Its adoption as a female given name was probably encouraged partly by its resemblance to ABBIE and partly by the productive suffix of female names *-lene* (cf. e.g. CHARLENE).

Abishag (f.) Biblical: name (possibly meaning 'wise, educated' in Hebrew) borne by a beautiful Shunammite virgin who was brought to the dying King David in a vain attempt to restore him to health and vigour. She was later used by David's son and successor Solomon as a reason for executing his half-brother and rival Adonijah (I Kings 1–2): Adonijah had wanted to marry Abishag.
Variant: Jewish: **Avishag**.

Abner (m.) Biblical: name (meaning 'father of light' in Hebrew) of a relative of King Saul, who was in command of Saul's army (I Samuel 14: 50; 26: 5). It is not common as a given name in England, but has enjoyed a steady, modest popularity in America, where it was brought in at the time of the earliest Puritan settlements.
Variant: Jewish: **Avner**.

Abraham (m.) Biblical: name of the first of the Jewish patriarchs, who entered into a covenant with God that his descendants should possess the land of Canaan. The Hebrew form is *Avraham*, of uncertain derivation. In Genesis 17: 5 it is explained as 'father of a multitude (of nations)' (Hebrew *av hamon (goyim)*). It has always been a popular given name among Jews, and was also chosen by Christians, especially among 17th-century Puritans and other fundamentalists. Various early saints of the Eastern Roman Empire also bore this name. Its currency in the United States was greatly enhanced by the fame of President Abraham Lincoln (1809–65).
Variants: Jewish: **Avraham** (Hebrew); **Avrom** (Yiddish).
Short form: English: **Abe**.

Abram (m.) Biblical: variant of ABRAHAM. It was probably originally a distinct name (meaning 'high father' in Hebrew). According to Genesis 17: 5, the patriarch's name was changed by divine command from *Abram* to *Abraham*. From the Middle Ages, however, if not before, it was taken to be a contracted version.

Absalom (m.) Biblical: name (probably meaning 'father of peace' in Hebrew) of the third son of King David, who rebelled against him and was eventually killed when he was caught by the hair in an oak tree as he fled, to the great grief of his father (2 Samuel 15–18). The name has never been particularly common in the English-speaking world, but the Scandinavian form AXEL is familiar in the United States.

Achilles (m.) From Greek mythology. Achilles, son of the sea nymph Thetis and the mortal Peleus, was the leading warrior of the Greek army attacking Troy. In the *Iliad*, Homer relates how he withdrew from the siege as a result of a slight to his honour, until his lover Patroclus was killed wearing his armour, whereupon he rejoined the fray in order to avenge him. The Greek form of his name is *Akhilleus*, and is of unknown, possibly pre-Greek, origin; it may be connected with that of the River *Akheloös*. The name has been used only rarely in the English-speaking world, usually as a result of recent Continental influence. Although there were various minor early saints so named, it has normally been chosen by parents who wished to take advantage of the licence given by the Catholic Church to select names borne by classical heroes as well as those of saints.

Derivatives: French: **Achille**. Italian: **Achilleo**. Spanish: **Aquiles**.

Achim (m.) A German short form of JOACHIM.

Acke (m.) Swedish: pet form of AXEL.

Ada (f.) English: of uncertain origin, apparently not generally bestowed before the late 18th century. In part, this is a pet form of ADELE and ADELAIDE, and so it may go back to a Germanic female personal name, a short form of various compound names with the first element *adal* noble. Ada was the name of a 7th-century abbess of Saint-Julien-des-Prés at Le Mans. Alternatively, it may represent a variant of ADAH.

Adah (f.) Biblical: Authorized Version spelling of the name (meaning 'adornment' in Hebrew) borne by the wives of Lamech (Genesis 4: 19) and of Esau (Genesis 36: 2). See also ADA.

Adalgisa (f.) Italian: of Germanic origin, composed of the elements *adal* noble + *gisil* pledge or hostage. It died out in the Middle Ages, but has undergone a minor revival since the 19th century as a result of the popularity of Bellini's opera *Norma* (1831), in which it is borne, inappropriately enough, by a Celtic priestess.

Adam (m.) Biblical: name of the first man (Genesis 2–3). It probably derives from Hebrew *adama* earth; it is a common feature of creation legends that the god responsible fashioned the first human beings from earth or clay and breathed life into them. The name was subsequently borne by a 7th-century Irish abbot of Fermo in Italy. It has enjoyed something of a resurgence in the English-speaking world since the 1960s. In Hebrew it is a generic term for 'man' (Genesis 5: 2) and has never been considered a personal name, although *Hava* 'Eve' has enjoyed popularity among Jews.

Derivatives: Irish Gaelic: **Ádhamh**. Scottish Gaelic: **Adhamh**. Italian: **Adamo**. Spanish: **Adán**. Portuguese: **Adão**. Finnish: **Aatami**. Pet form: Scottish: ADIF.

Adda (f.) German: pet form of ADELHEID.

Addolorata (f.) Italian equivalent of DOLORES, from Italian *Madonna Addolorata* 'Our Lady of Sorrows'.

Adela (f.) English: Latinate form of ADELE, especially popular in the late 19th century

Adelaide (f.) English (from French **Adélaïde**): of Germanic origin, composed of the elements *adal* noble + *heid* kind, sort. It was borne in the 10th century by the wife of the Holy Roman Emperor Otto the Great. She became regent after his death and was revered as a saint. The given name increased in popularity in England during the 19th century, when it was borne by the wife of King William IV; she was the daughter of the ruler of the German duchy of Saxe-Meiningen. The Australian city of Adelaide was named in her honour.

Pet form: **Addie** (esp. Irish).

Adele (f.) English (from French **Adèle**): of Germanic origin, representing a short form of various compound names with the first element *adal* noble. It was popular among the Normans as a result of the fame of a 7th-century saint, a daughter of the Frankish king Dagobert II. It was also the name of William the Conqueror's youngest daughter (*c*.1062–1137), who became the wife of Stephen of Blois and was likewise revered as a saint. It was revived in England in the late 19th century, being the name of a character in Johann Strauss's opera *Die Fledermaus*. Its popularity was further reinforced in the 1930s as the name of a character in the novels of Dornford Yates.

Adelheid (f.) German, Dutch, and Scandinavian form of ADELAIDE.

Pet forms: German: **Adda**, **Heidi**. Frisian, Dutch: ELKF

Adeline (f.) French: diminutive of *Adèle* (see ADELE). The Latinate form **Adelina** is also found. Both enjoyed a brief vogue in the 19th century.

Adeltraud (f.) German: cognate of ETHELDREDA and AUDREY. It enjoyed some popularity in the 19th century, but has now fallen back into disuse.

Variants: **Adeltrud**, **Edeltr(a)ud**.
Cognate: Dutch: **Aaltruide**.

Adie (m.) Scottish: pet form of ADAM or, less commonly, of AIDAN. **Adaidh** is a Gaelic spelling of *Adie*, hence the surname *Mac Adaidh*, Anglicized as *McCadie*.

Adina (f., m.) Mainly Jewish: in the Bible a male name, derived from Hebrew *adin* slender. It is borne by a soldier in the army of King David, 'Adina the son of Shiza the Reubenite, a captain of the Reubenites, and thirty with him' (1 Chronicles 11: 42). In modern times it was revived as a male name among Zionists, but is now more commonly a female name, no doubt because of the characteristically feminine *-a* ending.

Adlai (m.) Biblical: name of a very minor character, the father of one of King David's herdsmen (1 Chronicles 27: 29). It represents an Aramaic contracted form of the Hebrew name *Adaliah* 'God is just'. In recent times, it is particularly associated with the American statesman and Democratic presidential candidate Adlai Stevenson (1900–65), in whose family the name was traditional: it was also borne by his grandfather (1835–1914), who was vice-president in 1893–7.

Adolf (m.) German: composed of the Germanic elements *adal* noble + *wolf* wolf. This form of the name was first introduced into Britain by the Normans, displacing the Old English cognate *Æthelwulf*, but it did not become at all common until it was reintroduced by the Hanoverians in the 18th century. The association with Adolf Hitler (1889–1945) has meant that the name has hardly been used since the Second World War.

Adolphus (m.) Latinized form of ADOLF (the *ph* a result of hypercorrection). This has been a recurring name in the Swedish royal family, and this form has also been used occasionally in the English-speaking world.

Adria (f.) English: modern feminine form of ADRIAN.

Adrian (m.) Usual English form of the Latin name *Hadriānus* 'man from Hadria'. Hadria was a town in northern Italy which has given its name to the Adriatic Sea; it is of unknown derivation, and the initial *H*-has always been very volatile. The name was borne by the Roman emperor Publius Aelius Hadrianus, during whose reign (AD 117–38) Hadrian's Wall was built across northern England. The name was later taken by several early popes, including the only English pope, Nicholas Breakspeare (Adrian IV). It has become particularly popular in the English-speaking world during the past thirty years.

Cognates: French: **Adrien**. Italian: **Adriano**. Spanish: **Adrián**. Portuguese: **Adrião**. Hungarian: **Adorjan**.

Adrianne (f.) English: modern feminine form of ADRIAN, less common than ADRIENNE.

Variants: **Adrianna**, **Adriana**.

Adrienne (f.) French: feminine form of ADRIAN, now also used in the English-speaking world.

Aegidius (m.) Original Latin form of GILES, sometimes used in Germany.

Aegle (f.) From Latin: the name borne in classical mythology by various characters—a daughter of the Sun and sister of Phaeton; one of the Hesperides; and a nymph, daughter of Jupiter and Neaera. It derives from the Greek word *aiglē* brightness, splendour.

Aeneas (m.) British (rare): from the Latin name of the Trojan hero who, according to classical legend, fled after the sack of Troy and sailed eventually to Italy, where he founded the Roman state. This, in essence, is the subject of Virgil's *Aeneid*. The name is of unknown derivation; it appears in Homer as *Aineas*, and was associated by the Romans themselves with Greek *ainein* to praise. As a given name, it used to be quite common in Scotland as an Anglicized form of Gaelic AONGHAS, and in Ireland as an Anglicized form of Gaelic **Éigneachán**, a personal name representing a diminutive of *éigneach* violent fate or death.

Aeron (f.) Welsh: name borne in early Celtic mythology by the goddess of battle and slaughter, *Agrona*. Her name is probably a derivative of the element represented in modern Welsh *aer* battle. In modern use this name may have been selected because of its homonymy with the vocabulary word *aeron* fruit, berries. The extended forms **Aeronwy** (using a name suffix of ancient origin and uncertain derivation) and **Aeronwen** (with Welsh *(g)wen* white, fair, blessed, holy) are also in common use.

Afanasi (m.) Russian form of ATHANASIUS.

Pet form: **Afonya**.

Afonso (m.) Portuguese form of ALFONSO.

Afonya (m.) Russian: pet form of AFANASI.

Africa (f.) English: name adopted in the 20th century among American Blacks, conscious of their ancestral heritage in the continent of Africa. It was also formerly used in Scotland as an Anglicized form of the Gaelic name OIGHRIG, but this use is now completely obsolete.

Agafya (f.) Russian: from Greek *Agapia*, a derivative of *agapē* love. The masculine form *Agapius* was borne by several early saints.

Agatha (f.) English: Latinized version of the Greek name *Agathē*, from the feminine form of the adjective *agathos* good, honourable. This was the name of a Christian saint popular in the Middle Ages; she was a Sicilian martyr of the 3rd century who suffered the fate of having her breasts cut off. According to the traditional iconography, she is depicted holding them on a platter. In some versions they look more like loaves, leading to the custom of blessing bread on her feast day

(5 February). The name was revived in the 19th century, but has faded again since.

Cognates: French, German: **Agathe**. Italian, Scandinavian, Polish: **Agata**. Spanish: **Águeda**. Czech: **Agáta**. Hungarian: **Ágota**. Norwegian also: **Ågot**. Swedish also: **Agda**.

Pet form: English: **Aggie**.

Åge (m.) Danish: variant of ÅKE.

Aggie (f.) Scottish and English: pet form of AGNES and AGATHA.

Ägid (m.) German form of the Latin name AEGIDIUS; see GILES.

Aglaia (f.) Russian: from Greek. This was the name in classical mythology of one of the three Graces, but its acceptability for the Orthodox Church was due to the fact that it was also the name of a companion of St Boniface. It is of uncertain derivation, but is probably connected with AEGLE.

Agna (f.) Scandinavian and German: pet form of AGNETHE, also used as an independent given name.

Agnes (f.) English, German, Dutch, and Scandinavian: Latinized version of the Greek name *Hagnē*, from the feminine form of the adjective *hagnos* pure, holy. This was the name of a young Roman virgin martyred in the persecutions instigated by the Roman emperor Diocletian. She became a very popular saint in the Middle Ages. Her name was early associated with Latin *agnus* lamb, leading to the consistent dropping of the initial *H-* and to her representation in art accompanied by a lamb. The name was strongly revived in the 19th century, and has become especially popular in Scotland. In Ireland it has traditionally been used as a 'translation' of ÚNA.

Cognates: Irish Gaelic: **Aignéis**. French: **Agnès**. Italian: **Agnese**. Spanish: **Inés**. Portuguese: **Inês**. Polish: **Agnieszka**. Czech: **Anežka**. Finnish: **Aune**. See also ANNIS.

Pet form: Scottish: **Aggie**.

Agnethe (f.) German and Scandinavian form of AGNES, derived from the Latin genitive case *Agnētis*. It has occasionally been used in the English-speaking world during the 20th century

Variant: Swedish: **Agneta**.

Short form: Swedish: **Neta**.

Pet form: **Agna**.

Agostinho (m.) Portuguese form of AUGUSTINE.

Agostino (m.) Italian form of AUGUSTINE.

Ågot (f.) Norwegian form of AGATHA.

Ágota (f.) Hungarian form of AGATHA.

Agrafena (f.) Russian: vernacular form of *Agrippina*, the name of several prominent women in the Roman imperial family, most notably the mother of Nero, who was murdered by order of her son. As a Russian given name it has been adopted in honour of an early Christian saint of the same name, martyred under the Emperor Valerian. The given name is derived from the old Roman family name *Agrippa*, which is probably of Etruscan origin.

Pet forms: **Grunya**, **Grusha**.

Águeda (f.) Spanish form of AGATHA.

Agurtzane (f.) Basque equivalent of ROSARIO. The contracted form **Agurne** is also used.

Agustí (m.) Catalan form of AUGUSTINE.

Agustín (m.) Spanish form of AUGUSTINE.

Aharon (m.) Jewish: modern Hebrew form of AARON.

Ahuva (f.) Jewish: modern Hebrew name, coined from the vocabulary word meaning 'beloved'. The Yiddish name LIBE no doubt provided a stimulus for the coining of the Hebrew name.

Aidan (m.) Irish: Anglicized form of the Gaelic name **Aodán**, a diminutive of AODH. This was borne by various early Irish saints, among them the 7th-century apostle of Northumbria. It has been revived in the 20th century, in particular during the past couple of decades, by parents conscious of their Irish ancestry.

Variant: **Edan**.
Cognate: Welsh: **Aeddan**.

Ailbeart (m.) Scottish Gaelic form of ALBERT.

Ailbhe (m., f.) Irish Gaelic: traditional name of uncertain origin, perhaps from an Old Celtic element cognate with Latin *albus* white (cf. ALBINA). It has been Anglicized as **Alby** and, as a male name, ALBERT.

Ailean (m.) Scottish Gaelic form of ALAN.

Aileen (f.) Scottish and English: variant spelling of EILEEN.

Ailie (f.) Scottish: pet form of AILEEN or an Anglicized spelling of EILIDH.

Ailís (f.) Irish Gaelic form of ALICE.

Ailsa (f.) Scottish: modern name derived from that of *Ailsa Craig*, a high rocky islet in the Clyde estuary off the Ayrshire coast, near the traditional estates of the Scottish Kennedys. Its name is derived from Old Norse *Alfsigesey* 'island of *Alfsigr*', a personal name composed of the elements *alf* elf, supernatural being + *sigi* victory. Adoption as a given name probably represents an Anglicized form of EALASAID. Ailsa Craig is known in Gaelic as *Allasa*, or popularly *Creag Ealasaid*.

Aimée (f.) French: originally a vernacular nickname meaning 'beloved', from the past participle of French *aimer* to love (Latin *amāre*; cf. AMY). It has been in use, although never very common, since the Middle Ages. It is now also sometimes used, with or without the accent, as a given name in the English-speaking world.

Aindrea (m.) Scottish Gaelic form of ANDREW; See also ANNDRA.

Aindréas (m.) Irish Gaelic form of ANDREW.

Variants: **Aindrias, Aindriú**.

Áine (f.) Irish Gaelic: traditional name meaning originally 'brightness' or 'radiance'. It is the traditional name of the queen of the fairies, who plays an important and varied role in Celtic mythology. It has also been used as an Irish form of ANNE.

Aingeal (f.) Irish Gaelic form of ANGELA, from the Gaelic vocabulary word *aingeal* angel. The word is masculine in gender but it is used as a female given name.

Aingeru (m.) Basque form of the male name ANGEL; See also GOTZON.

Ainsley (m., occasionally f.) Scottish and English: transferred use of the surname, which is borne by a powerful and ancient family long established in the Scottish borders. It was probably originally a local name, taken north from either *Annesley* in Nottinghamshire or *Ansley* in Warwickshire. The former gets its name from the genitive case of the Old English

name *Ān* (a short form of any of various compounds containing as a first element *ān* one, only) + Old English *lēah* wood or clearing. The latter is from Old English *ānsetl* hermitage + *lēah*.

Variant: **Ainslee**.

Aisling (f.) Irish Gaelic: from the vocabulary word meaning 'dream, vision'. This was not in use as a given name during the Middle Ages, but was adopted as part of the Irish revival in the 20th century.

Variants: **Aislinn; Ashling** (Anglicized form).

Aisone (f.) Basque equivalent of ASUNCIÓN.

Aitor (m.) Basque: of unknown origin. It was the name of the legendary founder of the Basque people, and is still bestowed in his honour.

Aizik (m.) Jewish: Yiddish form of *Yitzhak* (see ISAAC).

Åke (m.) Scandinavian: related to the medieval Germanic name *Anicho* (a derivative of the element *ano* ancestor, which is not common as a name element). It has also been associated with the Latin names *Achatius* or *Acacius* (from Greek words meaning 'agate' and 'blameless' respectively).

Variant: Danish: **Åge**.

Akilina (f.) Russian: from the Late Latin woman's personal name *Aquilīna*, a derivative of *Aquila* 'eagle', which had been used as a family name in the classical period. St Aquilina is revered in the Orthodox Church as a young virgin martyr beheaded in Syria at the end of the third century.

Variant: **Akulina** (a vernacular form).
Cognate: Ukrainian: **Kilina**.
Pet forms: Russian: **Akulya; Kilya, Kulya**.

Akim (m.) Scandinavian and Russian form of JOACHIM, traditional in the villages of the Russian countryside, but now rare among city-dwellers. It has become familiar in the English-speaking world through the film actor Akim Tamaroff (1899–1972).

Pet form: **Kima**.

Al (m.) English: short form of any of the English male names beginning with this syllable.

Ala (f.) Polish: pet form of ALICJA.

Variant: **Alinka**.

Alain (m.) French form of ALAN, which originated in Brittany and is now common in all parts of France.

Alan (m.) English and Scottish: of Celtic origin and uncertain derivation (possibly a diminutive of a word meaning 'rock'). It was introduced into England by Breton followers of William the Conqueror, most notably Alan, Earl of Brittany, who was rewarded for his services with vast estates in the newly conquered kingdom.

In Britain the variants **Allan** and **Allen** are considerably less frequent, and generally represent transferred uses of surname forms, whereas in America all three forms of the name are approximately equally common. See also ALUN.

Cognates: Scottish Gaelic: **Ailean**. French: **Alain**.

Alana (f.) English: feminine form of ALAN, a comparatively recent coinage.

Variants: **Alanna, ALANNAH**.

Alanda (f.) English: a recent coinage, a feminine form of ALAN influenced by AMANDA.

Alannah (f.) English (esp. U.S.): respelling of ALANA, possibly influenced by names of Hebrew origin such as HANNAH and *Susannah* (see SUSANNA) and by the Anglo-Irish term of endearment *alannah* (Gaelic a *leanbh* O child).

Alaric (m.) English (rare): from a Germanic personal name composed of the elements *ala* all or *ali* stranger + *rīc* power, ruler, which was introduced to Britain in this form by the Normans. The first element may also in part derive from a contracted form of the element *adal* noble. The Blessed Alaricus or Adalricus (d. 975) was a Swabian prince who became a monk at the monastery of Einsiedeln in Switzerland.

Alasdair (m.) Scottish Gaelic form of ALEXANDER, often Anglicized as ALISTAIR.

Variants: **Alastair**, **Alaster**.

Alastar (m.) Irish Gaelic form of ALEXANDER.

Alazne (f.) Basque equivalent of MILAGROS.

Alba (f.) Italian, occasionally used in the English-speaking world. It seems to represent the feminine form of the Latin adjective *alba* white, but may in fact be a derivative of Germanic *alb* elf, supernatural being.

Alban (m.) Mainly English: name of the first British Christian martyr, the Latin form of which is *Albānus*. This may be an ethnic name from one of the numerous places in the Roman Empire called *Alba*. Alternatively, it may represent a Latinized form of a British name derived from the Celtic element *alp* rock, crag. The 3rd- or 4th-century Romano-British saint was executed at the place now known as St Albans, from the Benedictine abbey founded there in his memory by King Offa. The name was in use in the Middle Ages, and was revived in the 19th century. In some people's minds it may have been associated with *Albion*, a poetic name for Britain.

Alberic (m.) English: learned form of AUBREY, derived from the Latin *Albericus* in the 14th century. It enjoyed a slight and brief vogue in the 19th century, but is now once again very rare.

Albert (m.) French and English (Norman): of Germanic origin, composed of the elements *adal* noble + *berht* bright, famous. The Norman form displaced the Old English cognate *Æþelbeorht*. The name is popular in a variety of forms in Western Europe, and has been traditional in a number of European princely families. Its great popularity in England in the 19th century was due largely to Queen Victoria's consort, Prince Albert of Saxe-Coburg-Gotha. In Ireland, it has been used as an Anglicized form of the male name AILBHE.

Cognates: Scottish Gaelic: **Ailbeart**. Italian, Spanish: **Alberto**. German: **Albrecht**.
Short forms: English: **Al**, **Bert**.
Pet form: English: **Bertie**.

Albina (f.) Latin feminine form of *Albinus*, a derivative of the Roman family name *Albius*, which is from *albus* white. It is the name of a minor saint: St Albina was a young woman martyred at Caesarea in 250. She is particularly venerated in Campania, where her relics are preserved to this day.

Short form: BINA.

Albrecht (m.) German form of ALBERT.

Alby (m., f.) Irish: Anglicized form of AILBHE.

Aldo (m.) Italian: of Germanic origin, possibly from the element *ald* old. More probably it is from a metathesized form of *adal* noble, or rather from any of the two-element names of which this forms the first element (cf. e.g. ALBERT).

Aldous (m.) English: of uncertain origin; probably a short form of any of various Norman names, such as, *Aldebrand*, *Aldemund*, and *Alderan*, containing the Germanic element *ald* old. It was relatively common in East Anglia during the Middle Ages, but is now rare, known mainly as the given name of the novelist Aldous Huxley (1894–1963).

Alec (m.) English and Scottish: short form of ALEXANDER, now somewhat less popular in England than ALEX, possibly because of the colloquial pejorative term *smart alec*. See also ALICK.

Aleida (f.) German (esp. N. Germany): form of ADELHEID, influenced by the Low German form ALEIT.

Aleit (f.) Low German: contracted form of ADELHEID.

Aleix (m.) Catalan form of ALEXIUS.

Aleixandre (m.) Catalan form of ALEXANDER.

Aleixo (m.) Portuguese form of ALEXIUS.

Alejandra (f.) Spanish form of ALEXANDRA; feminine of ALEJANDRO.

Alejandro (m.) Spanish form of ALEXANDER.

Alejo (m.) Spanish form of ALEXIUS.

Aleksander (m.) Polish form of ALEXANDER.

Aleksandr (m.) Usual spelling in the Roman alphabet of the Russian form of ALEXANDER.
Feminine form: **Aleksandra**.

Aleksei (m.) Russian form of ALEXIUS.
Pet form: **Alyosha**.

Aleksy (m.) Polish form of ALEXIUS.

Alena (f.) German and Czech: aphetic short form of *Magdalena* (see MAGDALENE).

Aleš (m.) Czech: pet form of ALEXEJ.

Alessandra (f.) Italian form of ALEXANDRA; feminine of ALESSANDRO.

Alessandro (m.) Italian form of ALEXANDER.

Alessia (f.) Italian form of ALEXIA.

Alessio (m.) Italian form of ALEXIUS.

Alethea (f.) English: a learned coinage, not found before the 17th century. It represents the Greek word *alētheia* truth, and seems to have arisen as a result of the Puritan enthusiasm for using terms for abstract virtues as female names. See also ALTHEA.

Alette (f.) French: Gallicized form of the Middle Low German name ALEIT, which is a contracted form of ADELHEID.

Alex (m., f.) English: short form of ALEXANDER, ALEXANDRA, or ALEXIS; also commonly used as a given name in its own right. It is now also sometimes used in France and Germany.
Variant: English: **Alix** (f.).
Short form: English: **Lex**.

Alexa (f.) English: short form of ALEXANDRA or variant of ALEXIS as a female name.

Alexander (m.) English, Dutch, German, and Hebrew: from the Latin form of the Greek name *Alexandros*, which is composed of the elements *alexein* to defend + *anēr* man, warrior (genitive *andros*). The compound was probably coined originally as a title of the goddess Hera, consort of Zeus. It was also borne as a byname by the Trojan prince Paris. The name became extremely popular in the post-classical period, and was borne by several characters in the New Testament and some early Christian saints. Its use as a common given name throughout Europe, however, derives largely from the fame of Alexander the Great, King of Macedon (356–23 BC), around whom a large body of popular legend grew up in late antiquity, much of which came to be embodied in the medieval 'Alexander romances'. It also became a popular Hebrew name under Alexander the Great's benign rule of Palestine.

Cognates: Scottish Gaelic: **Alasdair** (Anglicized as ALISTAIR). Irish Gaelic: **Alastar**. French: **Alexandre**. Italian: **Alessandro**. Spanish: **Alejandro**. Catalan: **Aleixandre**. Portuguese: **Alexandre**. Romanian: **Alexandru**. Russian: **Aleksandr**. Ukrainian: **Oleksander**. Polish: **Aleksander**. Czech: **Alexandr**. Hungarian: **Sándor**. Yiddish: **Sender**.
Short forms: English: **Alex, Alec, Alick**. Italian: **Sandro**.
Pet forms: English, Scottish: **Sandy** (Gaelic **Sandaidh**). Scottish: **Sawney**. Russian: **Sasha, Sanya, Shura**. Polish: **Oleś, Olech, Olek**. Czech: **Olexa**.

Alexandra (f.) Latinate feminine form of ALEXANDER. It was very little used in the English-speaking world before the 20th century, when it was brought in from Scandinavia and Eastern Europe. It owes its sudden rise in popularity in Britain at the end of the 19th century to Queen Alexandra, Danish wife of Edward VII.
Derivatives: Italian: **Alessandra**. Spanish: **Alejandra**. Russian: **Aleksandra**.
Short forms: English: **Alex, Alexa**; SANDRA.
Pet forms: English, Scottish: **Sandy**; **Lexy**. Russian: **Sasha, Sanya, Shura**.

Alexandrina (f.) Latinate derivative of ALEXANDRA. It was most common in the 19th century, and was in fact the first name of Queen Victoria.

Alexej (m.) Czech form of ALEXIUS, or pet form of ALEXANDER.
Pet form: **Aleš**.

Alexia (f.) English and German: variant of ALEXIS as a female name.
Cognate: Italian: **Alessia**.

Alexina (f.) Scottish (Highland): elaborated feminine form of the male name ALEX, used as an unambiguously female name.

Alexis (f., m.) English and German: variant (or female derivative) of ALEXIUS. It was originally a male name, but is now more commonly given to girls.

Alexius (m.) Latin spelling of Greek *Alexios*, derived from a short form of various compound personal names with the first element *alexein* to defend. St Alexius was a 5th-century saint of Edessa, venerated particularly in the Orthodox Church as a 'man of God'. In Eastern European languages there has been some confusion between derivatives of this name and pet forms of ALEXANDER.
Variant: ALEXIS.
Derivatives: Italian: **Alessio**. Spanish: **Alejo**. Catalan: **Aleix**. Portuguese: **Aleixo**. Polish: **Aleksy**. Czech: **Alexej**. Russian: **Aleksei**.

Aleydis (f.) Dutch: from a contracted form of the medieval name *Adalheidis* (see ADELAIDE).

Alf (m.) English: short form of ALFRED.
Pet form: **Alfie**.

Alfa (m., f.) English: variant spelling of ALPHA.

Alfio (m.) Italian: a typically Sicilian name, borne in honour of a saint martyred under the Emperor Decius in 251, together with his brothers Philadelphus and Cyrinus. The name may represent Greek *Alphios*, from *alphos* wheat, or it may be from the Roman family name *Alfius*; this is from an Italic dialectal form, *alfus*, of Latin *albus* white, and is in fact distantly connected with the Greek word.

Alfonso (m.) Spanish: of Germanic (Visigothic) origin, probably composed of the elements *adal* noble + *funs* ready, prompt. Alternatively, the first element may be *ala* all, *hadu* struggle, or *hild* battle; forms are found to support each derivation, so it is possible that several names that were originally distinct in Visigothic have fallen together. St Alphonsus was a 9th-century bishop of Astorga, who spent the last years of his life at the abbey of St Stephen de Ribas de Sil in Galicia. The major influence on the spread and popularity of the name, however, was the fact that it was established as a traditional name in various royal families of the Iberian peninsula from a very early date. Alfonso I (*c*.693–757), King of Asturias, played an important part in establishing Christianity in Spain. By the 14th century, eleven Alfonsos had sat on the throne of Leon and Castile, four on the throne of Aragon, and four *Afonsos* on the throne of Portugal.
Variant: **Alonso**.
Cognates: French: **Alphonse**. Portuguese: **Afonso**. See also ALPHONSUS.

Alfred (m.) English: from Old English, composed of the elements *ælf* elf, supernatural being + *ræd* counsel. It was a relatively common name before the Norman Conquest of Britain, being borne most notably by Alfred the Great (849–99), King of Wessex. After the Conquest it was adopted by the Normans in a variety of more or less radically altered forms, and provides a rare example (see also EDWARD) of a distinctively Old English name that has spread widely on the Continent. It was strongly revived in the 19th century, along with other names of pre-Conquest historical figures (such as *Hereward*), but has faded since. See also AVERY.
Derivatives: Irish Gaelic: **Ailfrid**. Italian, Spanish: **Alfredo**.
Short forms: English: **Alf, Fred**.

Alger (m.) English: from Old English, composed of the elements *ælf* elf, supernatural being + *gār* spear; it is possible that this form may also have absorbed other names with the first elements *æþel* noble, *ēald* old, and *ēalh* temple. The name was not common either before or after the Norman Conquest, but was revived in the 19th century, along with other Germanic names. It is relatively common in America, where it seems to have been taken up as a more 'manly' short form of ALGERNON.

Algernon (m.) English: of Norman French origin. In Norman French it was a byname meaning 'moustached' (from *grenon*, *gernon* moustache, of Germanic origin). The Normans were as a rule clean-shaven, and this formed a suitable distinguishing nickname when it was applied to William de Percy, a companion of William the Conqueror. In the 15th century it was revived, with a sense of family tradition, as a byname or second given name for his descendant Henry Percy (1478–1527), and thereafter regularly used in that family. It was subsequently adopted into other families connected by marriage with the Percys, and eventually became common property.

Pet forms: **Algy**, **Algie**.

Algot (m.) Scandinavian: from an Old Norse or Old Swedish personal name, *Alfgautr*, composed of the elements *alfr* elf, supernatural being + the tribal name *Gautr* Goth.

Alice (f.) English and French: variant of ADELAIDE, representing an Old French spelling of a greatly contracted version of Germanic *Adalheidis*. It was regarded as a distinct name when it was revived in the 19th century. It was the name of the child heroine of Lewis Carroll's *Alice's Adventures in Wonderland* (1865) and *Through the Looking Glass* (1872), who was based on his child friend Alice Patience Liddell, daughter of the dean of Christ Church, Oxford.

Variant: **Alys**.

Cognate: Irish Gaelic: **Ailís**.

Alicia (f.) Spanish and English: modern Latinate form of ALICE.

Variants: English: **Alissa**, **Alyssa**.

Alicja (f.) Polish form of ALICE.

Pet forms: **Ala**, **Alinka**.

Alick (m.) Scottish and English: variant of ALEC, which has gained some currency as a given name in its own right. In the Highlands the form *Ellic* was also formerly in use; the Gaelic form is **Ailig**.

Feminine form: Scottish (Highland): **Alickina**.

Alida (f.) Hungarian form of ADELAIDE, now also used in German-speaking countries.

Alina (f.) Used in both English- and German-speaking countries, and of uncertain origin. It is probably a variant of ALINE, but could also be of Arabic origin, from a word meaning 'noble' or 'illustrious'. In Scotland it has been used as a feminine form of ALISTAIR.

Alinda (f.) In the English-speaking world this name is of recent origin; apparently it represents an artificial combination of the names ALINA and LINDA. It is, however, also used in German-speaking countries, where it may be derived from the Germanic personal name *Adelinde*, composed of the elements *adal* noble + *lind* soft, tender, weak.

Aline (f.) English and French: in the Middle Ages this represented a contracted form of ADELINE. In modern use it is either a revival of this or a respelling of AILEEN. In Scotland and Ireland it has sometimes been chosen as representing an Anglicized spelling of the Gaelic vocabulary word *àlainn* (Scottish), *álainn* (Irish) lovely.

Alinka (f.) Polish: pet form of ALICJA

Alirio (m.) Spanish: of uncertain origin. It may possibly derive from a popular form of Latin *Hilarius* (see HILARY) or *Hilarion* (see ILLARION). A saint variously known as *Allyre or Illidius* was a 4th-century bishop of Clermont: his name may be connected with this one.

Alison (f.) Scottish, English, and French: from a very popular medieval Norman diminutive of ALICE, formed by the addition of the diminutive suffix -*on*. In spite of its medieval popularity, the name virtually died out in England in the 15th century. However, it survived in Scotland, with the result that until its revival in England in the 20th century the name had a strongly Scottish flavour.

Pet forms: English: **Allie**, **Ally**.

Alissa (f.) English: variant of ALICIA.

Alistair (m.) Scottish: altered spelling of Gaelic **Alasdair**, a form of ALEXANDER. Alexander has long been a popular name in Scotland, having been borne by three early medieval kings of the country.

Variants: **Alisdair**, **Alastair**, **Alister**, **Al(l)aster**.

Pet form: **Aly**.

Alix (f.) English: variant of ALEX, used only as a feminine name. Its formation has probably been influenced by ALICE.

Aliza (f.) Jewish: modern Hebrew name meaning 'gay'. Its popularity has been influenced by the English names GAY and ALICE, and it has also been used as a translation of the Yiddish name FREYDE.

Alke (m.) Low German: popular pet form used as a given name in its own right, derived from a dramatically shortened version of ADELHEID (cf. AALTJE).

Allan (m.) Scottish and English: variant spelling of ALAN.

Allaster (m.) Scottish: variant spelling of ALISTAIR. It is borne, for example, by a minstrel in Sir Walter Scott's *Rob Roy* (1818), which ensured its 19th-century popularity.

Allegra (f.) Italian and English: from the feminine form of the Italian adjective *allegro* gay, jaunty (familiar in English as a musical tempo). It seems to have been an original coinage when it was given to Byron's illegitimate daughter (1817–22), but since then it has been taken up by parents in many English-speaking countries. It is not commonly used as a given name in Italy.

Allen (m.) Scottish and English: variant spelling of ALAN, in Britain generally found only as a surname, but in the United States equally common as a given name.

Allie (f.) English: pet form of ALISON, occasionally used as a given name in its own right.

Variant: **Ally**.

Allina (f.) English and Scottish: variant of ALINA.

Alma (f.) English: a relatively modern creation, of uncertain origin. It had a temporary vogue following the Battle of Alma (1854), which is named from the river in the Crimea by which it took place; similarly *Trafalgar* had occasionally been used as a female name earlier in the century. Nevertheless, the historical event seems only to have increased the popularity of an existing, if rare, name. *Alma* is also the feminine form of the Latin adjective *almus* nourishing, kind (cf. *alma mater* fostering mother, the clichéd phrase for an educational establishment). In Tennessee Williams's play *Summer and Smoke* (1948), a bearer of the name explains that it is 'Spanish for soul' (Latin *anima*), but this seems to be only coincidental.

Alois (m.) German and Czech form of ALOYSIUS.

Aloisia (f.) German and English: Latinate feminine form of ALOYSIUS.

Cognate: Czech: **Aloisie**.

Alojzy (m.) Polish form of ALOYSIUS.

Alonso (m.) Spanish: popular altered form of ALFONSO, with simplification of the consonantal cluster.

Aloysius (m.) English, German, and Dutch: of unknown origin, possibly a Latinized form of a Provençal version of LOUIS. It was relatively common in Italy in the Middle Ages, and has subsequently enjoyed some popularity among Roman Catholics in honour of St Aloysius Gonzaga (1568–91), who was born in Lombardy.

Variant: German: **Alois**.
Cognates: Polish: **Alojzy**. Czech: **Alois**.

Alpha (m., f.) English: name taken from the first letter of the Greek alphabet (ultimately of Semitic origin; cf. Hebrew *āleph* ox). It seems to have been chosen as a given name in the 19th and 20th centuries as a symbol of primacy and excellence, and is used for both boys and girls.

Variant: **Alfa**.

Alphonse (m.) French form of ALFONSO. The *-ph-* spelling is the result of classical influences (or classical pretensions). It has been occasionally used in the English-speaking world, especially among West Indians and American Blacks, but is now out of fashion.

Alphonsine (f.) French: feminine diminutive of ALPHONSE, now also used in the English-speaking world.

Alphonsus (m.) Irish: Latinized form of ALFONSO, used as an equivalent of the Gaelic name **Anluan**. This is of uncertain origin, but could be composed of an intensive prefix + an element meaning 'hound' or 'warrior'.

Pet forms: **Fonsie**, **Fonso**.

Alpin (m.) Scottish: Anglicized form of Gaelic **Ailpein**, a name widely borne in the Highlands from the time of the earliest historical records. It has no obvious Gaelic etymology, and for that reason, if no other, is often taken to be of Pictish origin.

Variant: **Alpine**.

Alte (f.) Jewish: feminine form of *Alter* (see ALTMAN).

Althea (f.) English: from Greek mythology. Although often considered to be a contracted form of ALETHEA, it is actually a quite distinct name (Greek *Althaia*), of uncertain origin. It was borne in classical legend by the mother of Meleager, who was given a brand plucked from the fire at the instant of her son's birth, with the promise that his life would last as long as the brand did; some twenty years later she destroyed it in a fit of pique. The name was revived by the 17th-century poet Richard Lovelace, as a poetic pseudonym for his beloved.

Althena (f.) English: modern coinage, apparently a blend of ALTHEA and ATHENE.

Altman (m.) Jewish: composed of the Yiddish elements *alt* old + *man* man. Traditionally, it was a name given to children to protect them from the angel of death, who would be confused by the conflict between the name and its infant bearer, or else as an omen name intended to ensure that the bearer would live to a ripe old age. The nominal adjective **Alter** is also used as a given name.

Alton (m.) English: transferred use of the surname, which is of local origin, being derived from any of several places in England so called. These have various origins; the most common is from Old English *ǣwiell* source (of a river) + *tūn* settlement, enclosure. It was borne (but dropped) as a given name by the American bandleader and trombonist Alton Glenn Miller (1904–44).

Alun (m.) Welsh: possibly a cognate of ALAN. It is borne in the *Mabinogi* by Alun of Dyfed, a character mentioned in passing several times. It is also a river name and a regional name in Wales, sometimes spelled *Alyn*. Alun was adopted as a bardic

name by John Blackwell (1797–1840) and became popular as a result of his fame.

Alva (f.) Irish: Anglicized form of the Gaelic name **Almha.** This is of uncertain origin; it is earlier found in the form *Almu* and was borne, according to legend, by a semi-divine heroine who gave her name to the fortress and hill of Almu in Leinster.

Alvar (m.) English: from a medieval English name, representing an Old English personal name, *Ælfhere*, composed of the elements *ælf* elf, supernatural being + *here* army, warrior. In modern use it is either a revival of this (or a transferred use of the surname derived from it) or an Anglicized form of the Spanish ÁLVARO. A name of the same form is also in occasional use in Scandinavia, in which case it derives from an Old Norse personal name cognate with the Old English form quoted above.

Álvaro (m.) Spanish: of Germanic (Visigothic) origin. It is probably composed of the elements *al* all + *war* guard. The name is now also quite common in Italy, where the accent falls on the second syllable. It seems to have been taken up as a result of the influence of Verdi's opera *The Force of Destiny* (1862), in which a Peruvian character of this name appears.

Alvin (m.) English: from an Old English personal name composed of the elements *ælf* elf, supernatural being + *wine* friend. The medieval name was not especially common in Britain either before or after the Norman Conquest, but the modern form has recently become fairly popular in the United States. The reasons for this are not entirely clear; association with CALVIN may be a factor, but a more plausible (though less elevated) reason may be that it was the name given to the naughty chipmunk in a popular American television cartoon series of the 1960s.

Alwyn (m.) English: variant of ALVIN.

Variant: **Aylwin**.

Alyosha (m.) Russian: pet form of ALEKSEI.

Alys (f.) English: variant spelling of ALICE.

Alyssa (f.) English: variant spelling of ALISSA.

Alžběta (f.) Czech form of ELIZABETH.

Short form: **Běta**.
Pet forms: **Bětka**, **Betuška**.

Amabel (f.) English: of Old French origin, from Latin *amābilis* lovable. This name is now very rare in the English-speaking world, but lies behind the much commoner ANNABEL and MABEL. It gained some currency from being borne by the character Amabel Rose Adams in Angela Thirkell's *Barsetshire Chronicles* (1933 onwards).

Amadeus (m.) Original Latin form of AMEDEO, famous chiefly as the second name of the composer Wolfgang Amadeus Mozart (1756–91), for whom it was a Latin version of GOTTLIEB. It is still occasionally bestowed by music-loving parents in his honour.

Amado (m.) Spanish form of AMATO.

Amador (m.) Spanish: from the Latin name *Amātor* 'lover' (an agent derivative of *amāre* to love). It was borne by a 9th-century Cordoban priest who was executed by the Moors for his Christian faith.

Amalia (f.) Latinized form of the Germanic name *Amal*, representing the vocabulary element *amal* work. This was a first element in various names—now more or less obsolete—such as

Amalberta, *Amalfriede*, and *Amalgunde*, for which *Amal* was used as a short form. *Amalia* is chiefly German and Scandinavian, but is also found occasionally in the English-speaking world. Its popularity was enhanced in Germany in the 18th century by the fame of Anna Amalia, Duchess of Saxe-Weimar (1739–1807), a great patron of the arts, whose court attracted Goethe, Schiller, Herder, and many others.

Variant: German: **Amalie**.

Amancio (m.) Spanish: from the Latin name: *Amantius* 'loving', a derivative of the present participle of *amāre* to love. This name was borne by some half-dozen minor early saints, but there has been much confusion in the sources with the name *Amandus* 'lovable'.

Cognates: Catalan: **Amans**, **Mans**.

Amanda (f.) A 17th-century literary coinage from the Latin gerundive (feminine) *amanda* lovable, fit to be loved, from *amāre* to love. This is evidently modelled on MIRANDA. The masculine form *Amandus*, borne by various saints from the 4th to the 7th century, seems not to have been the source of the feminine form, and is itself not now used. The female name enjoyed considerable popularity in the mid-20th century.

Short form: **Manda**.

Pet form: MANDY.

Amans (m.) Catalan form of AMANCIO.

Variant: **Mans**.

Amaryllis (f.) Name borne in classical pastoral poetry, including Virgil's *Eclogues*, by a typical shepherdess or country girl. The name is of Greek origin and uncertain derivation, possibly from *amaryssein* to sparkle. In modern times the name may sometimes have been given because of association with the flower, named in the 19th century from the Arcadian heroine.

Amato (m.) Italian: from the Latin name *Amātus* 'beloved'. There are two saints of this name who have influenced its popularity: the first abbot of Remiremont (*c*.597–*c*.630) and the tenth bishop of Sion (d. *c*.690).

Cognate: Spanish: **Amado**.

Amber (f.) English: from the vocabulary word for the gemstone *amber*, a word derived via Old French and Latin from Arabic *ambar*. This was first used as a given name at the end of the 19th century, but has become particularly popular in the past couple of decades. In part it owes its popularity to Kathleen Winsor's novel *Forever Amber* (1944).

Ambjörn (m.) Swedish: assimilated form of ARNBJÖRN.

Ambrose (m.) English (and Old French) form of the Late Latin name *Ambrosius*, from post-classical Greek *Ambrosios* 'immortal'. This was borne by various early saints, most notably a 4th-century bishop of Milan. The name has never been common in England, but has enjoyed considerably greater popularity in Roman Catholic Ireland, where the surname *Mac Ambrois* is Anglicized as *McCambridge*.

Cognates: Irish Gaelic: **Ambrós**. Welsh: **Emrys**. French: **Ambroise**. Italian: **Ambrogio**. Spanish, Portuguese: **Ambrosio**. Catalan: **Ambròs**. Polish: **Ambrozy**. Czech: **Ambrož**. Hungarian: **Ambróz**.

Short forms: Italian: **Brogio**. Czech: **Brož**. Polish: **Mroz**.

Pet forms: Czech: **Brožek**. Polish: **Mrozek**.

Amedeo (m.) Italian: from the medieval Latin name **Amadeus**, composed of the elements *ama-*, from *amāre* to love, + *Deus* God. It was probably originally a deliberate ca-

ique of Greek *Theophilos* (see THEOPHILUS). The name has been traditional in the royal house of Savoy; bearers include the Blessed Amadeus IX, Duke of Savoy (1435–72). It is also quite common as an Italian Jewish name; recent bearers include the painter Amedeo Modigliani (1884–1920).

Cognate: French: **Amedée**.

Amelia (f.) English: probably the result of a cross between the Latin-origin *Emilia* (see EMILY) and the Latinized Germanic AMALIA. Its first use seems to have been in the English-speaking world, by Henry Fielding for the heroine of his novel *Amelia* (1751)

Amélie (f.) French form of AMELIA, now sometimes also used in the English-speaking world, with or without the accent.

Amerigo (m.) Italian: an early byform of *Enrico* (see HENRY). *Amerigo* is found in Italian sources from *c*.1100, evidently already well established by that time. It was probably introduced into Italy by the Ostrogoths some six centuries earlier; they controlled Italy from 493 to 552, and the name does not seem to have been in use among the Lombards who succeeded them. Its most famous bearer was Amerigo Vespucci (1454–1512), the Italian explorer and geographer who gave his name to the continent of America; it is sometimes used among Italian Americans in his honour.

Amhlaoibh (m.) Irish Gaelic form of OLAF. The Old Norse name was introduced to Ireland by Viking settlers.

Anglicized forms: **Auliffe**, HUMPHREY.

Cognates: Scottish: **Amhla(i)dh** (Gaelic), **Aulay** (Anglicized).

Amias (m.) English: rare, and of uncertain origin, possibly from the surname *Amias*, which is a local name for someone from Amiens in France. However, both surname and given name are rare. The ending *-ias* is found in biblical names (e.g. TOBIAS), where it represents a Greek form of Hebrew *-iyah* 'God'; *Amias* may sometimes have been chosen in the belief that it was a biblical name, reinforced by the fact that *am-* is the Latin root meaning 'love'. See also AMIAZ and AMYAS.

Amiaz (m.) Jewish: modern Hebrew given name, meaning 'my people is strong'.

Amice (f.) English: from a medieval given name derived from Latin *ami(ci)tia* friendship; see AMITY.

Amilcare (m.) Italian: from the name of the Carthaginian general Hamilcar Barca (d. *c*.228 BC), father of Hannibal. Hamilcar led the Carthaginian army against the Romans in the First Punic War, and was chiefly responsible for establishing Carthaginian influence in Spain. His name is composed of the Phoenician elements *hi* friend + the divine name *Melkar*.

Amita (f.) English: apparently a modern creation, representing an altered form of AMITY. In form it coincides with Latin *amita* maternal aunt.

Amittai (m.) Jewish: biblical name (meaning 'true' or 'honest' in Hebrew), borne by the father of Jonah (2 Kings 14: 25).

Amity (f.) English: comparatively recent coinage from the learned, Latinate vocabulary word meaning 'friendship'. The medieval doublet AMICE has also been occasionally revived.

Amnon (m.) Mainly Jewish: name (meaning 'faithful' in Hebrew) borne in the Bible by King David's eldest son, who raped and abandoned his half-sister Tamar and was killed by her brother Absalom.

Amos (m.) Biblical: name of a Hebrew prophet of the 8th century BC, whose sayings are collected in the book of the Bible that bears his name. This is of uncertain derivation, but may be connected with the Hebrew verb *amos* to carry. In some traditions it is assigned the meaning 'borne by God'. The name is used among Christians as well as Jews, and was popular among the Puritans, In Britain it survived well into the 19th century, but is little used today.

Amparo (f.) Spanish: from the vocabulary word *amparo* protection (from the verb *amparar* to help or protect, Late Latin *anteparāre* to prepare in advance). The given name was coined with reference to the role of the Virgin Mary in affording protection to Christians.

Amshel (m.) Jewish (Yiddish): variant of ANTSHEL.

Amund (m.) Scandinavian (esp. Norwegian): from an Old Norse personal name composed of the elements *ag* awe, fear or edge, point + *mundr* protector. The usual modern spelling is with a boll: **Åmund**.

Amy (f.) English: Anglicized form of Old French *Amee* 'beloved'. This originated in part as a vernacular nickname, in pan as a form of Latin *Amāta*. The latter is ostensibly the feminine form of the past participle of *amāre* to love, but in fact it may have had a different, pre-Roman, origin; it was borne in classical mythology by the wife of King Latinus, whose daughter Lavinia married Aeneas and (according to the story in the *Aeneid*) became the mother of the Roman people.

Amyas (m.) English: of uncertain origin; possibly a variant of AMIAS. It first occurs in Spenser's *Faerie Queene*, in which it is the name of a 'squire of low degree'.

Ana (f.) Spanish form of ANNE.
Pet form: ANITA.

Anacleto (m.) Italian, Spanish, and Portuguese: from the Late Latin personal name *Anaclētus*, Greek *Anaklētos*, originally a divine byname meaning 'called on, invoked'. It also seems to have absorbed the personal name *Anengklētos* meaning 'irreproachable'. This was the name of the third pope.
Short form: **Cleto** (also used as a full baptismal name).

Anaïs (f.) Catalan and Provençal derivative of ANA.

Anastasia (f.) Russian: feminine form of the Greek male name *Anastasios* (a derivative of *anastasis* resurrection). It has always been popular in Eastern Europe as a result of the fame of a 4th-century saint who was martyred at Sirmium in Dalmatia, and in the Middle Ages it was in use in England too. One of the daughters of the last tsar of Russia bore this name. She was probably murdered along with the rest of the family by the Bolsheviks in 1918, but in 1920 a woman claiming to be the Romanov princess Anastasia came to public notice in Germany, and a film was subsequently based on this story (1956).
Cognates: Polish: **Anastazja**. Czech: **Anastázie**.
Short form: Russian: **Nastasia**.
Pet forms: Russian: **Nastya**, **Asya**. Polish: **Nastka**, **Nastusia**. Czech: **Nast'a**.

Anatole (m.) French: from the Late Latin personal name *Anatolius*, an adjectival derivative of Greek *anatolē* sunrise, dawn. The name was popular among early Christians because of its optimistic associations. It was borne by an early bishop of

Cahors and by a 9th-century Scottish bishop, who settled as a hermit at Salins.

Anatoli (m.) Russian form of ANATOLE. The popularity of this name in Russia and in the Eastern Church is largely due to the influence of St Anatolius, bishop of Constantinople from 449 to 458.

Anděl (m.) Czech form of the male name ANGEL.
Pet form: **Andělik**.

Anděla (f.) Czech form of ANGELA.
Pet form: **Andělka**.

Anders (m.) Scandinavian form of ANDREW.

Andoni (m.) Basque form of ANTHONY.

Andor (m.) Scandinavian: from an Old Norse name composed of the elements *arn* eagle + a derivative of *Porr* Thor, the god of thunder.

Andra (f., m.) 1. (f.) English: modern feminine form of ANDREW. 2. (m.) Scottish: traditional Lowland Scots form of ANDREW.

Andras (m.) Welsh form of ANDREW.

András (m.) Hungarian form of ANDREW. It has been sometimes bestowed in Hungary in honour of a Benedictine monk of Zobor Abbey, who was killed, along with a companion, St Benedict, by marauders in *c*.1020.

Andre (m.) Portuguese form of ANDREW.

André (m.) French form of ANDREW, which has been borrowed into English recently. It was the twenty-seventh most common male name among American Blacks in 1982.

Andrea (m., f.) 1. (m.) Italian equivalent of ANDREW. 2. (f.) English: of disputed origin. It has been in use since the 17th century, although never common. It is now generally taken as a feminine equivalent of ANDREAS, and this probably represents its actual origin. However, it was not in use in the Middle Ages, and the suggestion has also been made that it represents an independent coinage in English from the Greek vocabulary word *andreia* manliness, virility.

Andreas (m.) The original New Testament Greek form of ANDREW, also found in Latin, and still used in German, and now occasionally in English.

Andrée (f.) French: feminine form of ANDREW, now also occasionally used in the English-speaking world.

Andrei (m.) Russian form of ANDREW. St Andrew is the patron saint of Russia as well as of Greece and Scotland.

Andrej (m.) Czech: 'learned' form of ANDREW. See also ONDŘEJ
Pet forms: **Andráš**, **Androušek**.

Andrés (m.) Spanish form of ANDREW.

Andreu (m.) Catalan form of ANDREW.

Andrew (m.) English form of the Greek name *Andreas*, short form of any of various compound names with the first element *andr*- man or, in particular, warrior. In the New Testament, this is the name of the first disciple to be called by Jesus. After the Resurrection, St Andrew preached in Asia Minor and Greece, and was probably crucified at Patras in Achaia. He was one of the most popular saints of the Middle Ages and was adopted as the patron of Scotland, Russia, and Greece. The name has long been popular in Scotland (in the Lowlands traditionally in the form **Andra**); its popularity in England has been enhanced by its use as a British royal name for Prince Andrew (b. 1960), the Duke of York.

Cognates: Scottish Gaelic: **Aindrea, Anndra**. Irish Gaelic: **Aindrias, Aindréas; Aindriú**. Welsh: **Andras**. French: **André**. Italian: Andrea. Spanish: **Andrés**. Catalan: **Andreu**. Portuguese: **Andre**. German: **Andreas**. Low German, Dutch: **Andries**. Scandinavian: **Anders**. Polish: **Andrzej, Jędrzej**. Czech: **Andrej, Ondřej**. Russian: **Andrei**. Ukrainian: **Andrei**. Hungarian: **András, Endre**. Finnish: **Antero**.

Short forms: Scottish: **Drew**. Low German, Dutch: **Dries**.

Andriana (f.) English: modern coinage, apparently a blend of Andrea and *Adriana* (see Adrianne) or possibly *Arianna* (see Ariadne).

Andries (m.) Low German and Dutch form of Andrew. St Andries Wouters (d. 1572) was a Catholic hanged by Calvinists at Gorkum.

Short form: **Dries**.

Andrine (f.) English: comparatively rare feminine derivative of Andrew with the characteristically feminine ending *-ine*.

Andrzej (m.) Polish form of Andrew. St Andrzej Bobola was a Polish Jesuit murdered by Cossacks at Janów in 1657.

Andula (f.) Czech: pet form of Anna.

Variant: **Andulka**.

Andy (m.) Scottish and English: pet form of Andrew.

Aneirin (m.) Welsh: of uncertain derivation. The original form of the name was *Neirin*, with the initial *A-* developing in the 13th century; it may be derived from an element cognate with Irish Gaelic *nár* noble, modest. This name was borne by the first known Welsh poet, who lived *c*.600. The 'Book of Aneirin' is a 13th-century manuscript which purports to preserve his work, including the *Gododdin*, a long work about the defeat of the Welsh by the Saxons.

Variant: **Aneurin** (A modern form).

Pet form: **Nye** (popularized as a result of the fame of the statesman Aneurin Bevan, 1897–1960).

Anežka (f.) Czech form of Agnes.

Pet forms: **Aneša, Neš(k)a**.

Anfisa (f.) Russian: from Greek *Anthousa*, a name of uncertain derivation. It may be a derivative of *anthos* flower. St Anthousa was a 9th-century abbess who lived near Constantinople.

Short form: **Fisa**.

Angel (f.), formerly also (m.) English: originally a male name, as in the case of Angel Clare, the chief male character in Thomas Hardy's novel *Tess of the D'Urbevilles* (1891), and derived from the Church Latin name *Angelus*, from Greek *angelos*. This meant 'messenger' in classical Greek, but in New Testament Greek it had the specialized meaning 'messenger of God', i.e. an angel. It is now completely out of fashion as a male name in English, but is being increasingly bestowed as a female name, especially among American Blacks. It is no doubt influenced strongly by the use of the English vocabulary word *angel* as an affectionate term of address for a good (or pretty) little girl.

Cognates all (m.): Italian: **Angelo**. Spanish: **Ángel**. Basque: **Aingeru**. Polish: **Aniol**. Czech: **Anděl**. Yiddish: **An(t)shel**.

Angela (f.) English and Italian: from Church Latin, feminine form of the male name *Angelus* (see Angel), which is from

New Testament Greek *angelos* angel, which meant 'messenger' in classical Greek. It has been in use in Britain and America from the 18th century, since when it has increased steadily in popularity.

Cognates: Spanish: **Ángela**. Polish: **Aniela**. Czech: **Anděla**. Irish Gaelic: **Aingeal**.

Pet forms: English: **Angie**. Spanish: **Angelita**. Czech: **Andělka**.

Ángeles (f.) Spanish: from a title of the Virgin Mary, *Maria de los Ángeles*. Mary is revered in Roman Catholic tradition as the Queen of Heaven and mistress of the ranks of angels who wait on the throne of God.

Cognate: French: **Marie-Ange**.

Angelica (f.) English: from Church Latin, from the feminine form of the Latin adjective *angelicus* angelic, or simply a Latinate elaboration of Angela.

Cognates: French: **Angélique**. German: **Angelika, Angelike**.

Angelina (f.) English: Latinate elaboration of Angela.

Cognate: French: **Angeline** (now also used in the English-speaking world).

Angélique (f.) French form of Angelica.

Angelita (f.) Spanish: diminutive pet form of *Ángela* (see Angela).

Angelo (m.) Italian form of the male name Angel.

Angharad (f.) Welsh: composed of the Old Celtic intensive prefix *an-* + the root *cār* love + the noun suffix *-ad*. This was the name of the mother of the 12th-century chronicler Giraldus Cambrensis ('Gerald the Welshman'). In the *Mabinogi*, Angharad Golden Hand at first rejects Peredur's suit, but later falls in love with him when he comes back as the unknown Mute Knight. The name has been strongly revived in Wales since the 1940s.

Angie (f., m.) 1. (f.) English (pronounced /'ændʒɪ/): pet form of Angela. 2. (m.) Scottish (pronounced /'aŋgɪ/): pet form of Angus.

Angosto (f.) Spanish (mainly Galician): from a title of the Virgin Mary, *Nuestra Señora de Angosto* 'Our Lady of Angosto'. Angosto is a place in the province of Álava where the Virgin is supposed to have appeared in a vision. The place derives its name from Late Latin *angustum* narrows or mountain pass.

Angus (m.) Scottish and Irish: Anglicized form of the Gaelic name **Aonghus** or **Aonghas**, composed of Celtic elements meaning 'one' and 'choice'. This is the name of an old Celtic god, and is first recorded as a personal name in Adomnan's 'Life of St Columba', where it occurs in the form *Oinogus(s)ius* as the name of a man for whom the saint prophesied a long life and a peaceful death. This is also almost certainly the name of the 8th-century Pictish king variously recorded as *Onnust* and *Hungus*.

Short form: Gus.
Pet form: Angie.
Feminine form: **Angusina**.

Angustias (f.) Spanish: variant of Angosto, altered by folk etymology as if from the Castilian vocabulary word *angustias*, plural of *angustia* mental or physical anguish or distress. The reference is to a title of the Virgin Mary, *Nuestra Señora de las Angustias*, which enshrines the notion that the Virgin will come to the aid of those who pray to her in their distress.

Aniceto (m.) Italian, Spanish, and Portuguese form of Latin *Anicētus*, a derivative of Greek *Anikētos* 'unconquered' or 'unconquerable', from *a-* not + *nikein* to conquer. This was the name of a 2nd-century pope of Syrian origin; see NIKITA.

Aniela (f.) Polish form of ANGELA. This name is now also occasionally used in the English-speaking world, and is sometimes respelled **Anniela** by association with ANNE. There has also been some confusion with Italian ANIELLA.

Aniella (f.) Italian: feminine form of ANIELLO, rather more popular than the masculine form.

Aniello (m.) Italian: a vernacular variant of the learned form *Agnello*, from Church Latin *Agnellus*, a diminutive of *agnus* lamb. The Paschal Lamb was a particularly important symbol to the early Christians, and so the medieval Latin name was quite common. St Agnellus (d. *c.*596), abbot of San Gaudioso, is one of the patrons of Naples, and this name has enjoyed some currency there as a result, but it is otherwise not common.

Anioł (m.) Polish form of the male name ANGEL.

Anisim (m.) Russian: from the Greek name *Onesimos* 'useful' or 'profitable'. This was a fairly common slave name during the classical and post-classical periods, and was borne by a runaway slave who was converted to Christianity by St Paul. Paul says of him in the Epistle to his master Philemon that 'in time past he was to thee unprofitable, but now profitable to thee and to me' (Philemon II). This early Christian use made it a very acceptable name in the Orthodox Church, quite apart from the connotations that it acquired of 'usefulness to Christ'.
Variant: **Onisim**.

Anita (f.) Originally Spanish: pet form of *Ana*, the Spanish version of ANNE. It is now widely used in English-speaking countries with little awareness of its Spanish origin.

Anitra (f.) Apparently a literary coinage by Henrik Ibsen, who used it as the name of an Eastern princess in *Peer Gynt* (1867). No Arabic original is known, however. It is now occasionally used as a given name, not only in Norway, but also elsewhere in Scandinavia, in Germany, and in the English-speaking world.

Anke (f.) Low German: pet form of ANNE. The name is now quite extensively used in northern Germany.

Anker (m.) Danish: name that has been used since the Middle Ages. It is of uncertain origin, but may derive from the vocabulary word *annkarl* agricultural labourer (from the elements *ann* harvest, busy season + *karl* man), or else from the elements *arn* eagle + *karl* man.

Ann (f.) English: variant spelling of ANNE, *Ann* was the more common of the two spellings in the 19th century, but is now losing ground to the form with final *-e*.

Anna (f.) Latinate variant of ANNE, in common use as a given name in English, Gaelic, Italian, German, Dutch, Scandinavian languages, and Slavonic languages. Among people with a classical education, it has from time to time been associated with Virgil's *Aeneid*, where it is borne by the sister of Dido, Queen of Carthage. This Phoenician name may ultimately be of Semitic origin, and thus cognate with the biblical *Anne*. However, the connection, if it exists, is indirect rather than direct.

Cognate: Spanish: **Ana**.
Pet forms: Scottish Gaelic: **Annag**. Swedish: **Annika**. Polish: **Anula**, **Anusia**. Czech: **Anin(k)a**, **Andul(k)a**, **Anuška**. Russian: **Asya**.

Annabel (f.) English: sometimes taken as an elaboration of ANNA, but more probably a dissimilated form of AMABEL. It has been common in Scotland since the 12th century (often being used as an Anglicized form of Gaelic *Barabal*; see BARBARA) and in the rest of the English-speaking world since the 1940s.
Variants: **Annabella** (Latinized); **Annabelle** (Gallicized, under the influence of BELLE).

Anndra (m.) Scottish Gaelic form of ANDREW; see also AINDREA.

Anne (f.) English, French, and German form (via Old French, Latin, and Greek) of the Hebrew female name *Hanna* 'He (God) has favoured me (i.e. with a child)'. This is the name borne in the Bible by the mother of Samuel (see HANNAH), and according to non-biblical tradition also by the mother of the Virgin Mary. It is the widespread folk cult of the latter that has led to the great popularity of the name in various forms throughout Europe. The simplified form ANN was in the 19th century very much more common, but the form with final *-e* has grown in popularity during the 20th century, partly perhaps due to the enormous popularity of L. M. Montgomery's story *Anne of Green Gables* (1908), and partly due to Princess Anne (b. 1950). In Ireland *Anne* has been used as an Anglicized form of ÁINE. See also ANNA.
Pet forms: English: **Annie**. French: **Annette**, **Ninon**. Breton: **Annick**. Low German: **Anke**, **Antje**. Dutch: **Anneke**.

Anneka (f.) Latinate variant of the Dutch name **Anneke**, a pet form of ANNE, popularized in Britain in the 1980s by the television personality Anneka Rice.

Anneli (f.) Scandinavian: shortened form of the originally German given name ANNELIESE.

Anneliese (f.) German and Scandinavian: compound name composed of the elements ANNE and LIESE.

Annella (f.) English and Scottish: elaborated form, common particularly in the Highlands, of ANNE.

Annetta (f.) English: Latinate elaboration of ANNETTE, not in very common use.

Annette (f.) French: pet form of ANNE, now also widely used in the English-speaking world.

Annfrid (f.) Norwegian: from the Old Norse female personal name *Arnfriðr*, composed of the elements *arn* eagle + *friðr* fair, beautiful.

Annibale (m.) Italian: bestowed in honour of the Carthaginian general Hannibal Barca (247–182 BC), who led a Carthaginian army from Spain across the Alps and into Italy to attack the Romans. He was eventually defeated by Scipio at Zama (202 BC), but not until he had shaken the Roman republic to its core. The name is sometimes chosen by Italians with strong regional loyalties, opposed to the centralizing tendencies of the government in Rome. The name is composed of the Phoenician elements *hann* grace, favour (and so distantly related to HANNAH) + the name of the god *Baal*.

Annice (f.) English: variant spelling of ANNIS, based on the numerous women's names ending in the syllable *-ice*.

Annick (f.) Breton: pet form of ANNE.

Annika (f.) Swedish: pet form of ANNA, apparently derived from the German dialect form *Anniken*.

Annis (f.) Scottish and English: a medieval vernacular form of AGNES, which gave rise to a surname. Its modern use as a given name is probably at least in part a transferred use of the surname as well as a revival of the medieval given name.

Variants: **Annys, Annice**.

Annunziata (f.) Italian: one of the many Roman Catholic names in Italy and Spain that are derived from titles of the Virgin Mary. This one refers to the Annunciation to her of God's favour and the impending birth of Christ (Luke 1: 20–38). The festival of the Annunciation has been celebrated since the 5th century. It was at first kept on Ember Wednesday during Lent, but was later moved to 25 March, exactly nine months before Christmas Day, replacing pagan festivals celebrating the vernal equinox.

Short form: **Nunzia**.

Annwyl (f.) Welsh: from the vocabulary word *annwyl* beloved.

Variant: **Anwyl**.

Annys (f.) Scottish and English: variant of ANNIS, in a deliberately archaic spelling.

Anona (f.) English: of uncertain origin, apparently not recorded before the 1920s. It seems most likely that it arose as an artificial combination of elements from existing names, for example ANNE and FIONA. In form it resembles Latin *annona* corn supply, but this is unlikely to have influenced the formation of the name.

Anraí (m.) Irish Gaelic form of HENRY; see also EINRÍ.

Anselmo (m.) Italian: of Germanic origin, composed of the elements *ans* divinity + *helm* helmet. This name seems to have been largely confined to Italy until brought to England by St Anselm, who was archbishop of Canterbury in the late 11th and early 12th centuries, and is regarded as one of the Doctors of the Church. He was born at Aosta in Piedmont.

Cognates: English: **Anselm** (rare, borne mainly by Roman Catholics). Polish: **Anzelm**.

Anshel (m.) Jewish (Yiddish): variant of ANTSHEL.

Antal (m.) Hungarian form of ANTHONY.

Antero (m.) Finnish form of ANDREW.

Pet form: **Antti**.

Anthea (f.) Latinized spelling of Greek *Antheia*, a personal name derived from the feminine of the adjective *antheios* flowery. This was used in the classical period as a byname of the goddess Hera at Argos, but as a modern given name it was reinvented in the 17th century by English pastoral poets such as Robert Herrick.

Anthony (m.) The usual English form of the old Roman family name *Antōnius*, which is of uncertain (probably Etruscan) origin. The spelling with *-th-* (not normally reflected in the pronunciation) represents a learned but erroneous attempt to associate it with Greek *anthos* flower. In the post-classical period it was a common name, borne by various early saints, most notably a 3rd-century Egyptian hermit monk, who is regarded as the founder of Christian monasticism.

Variant: **Antony**.

Cognates: Irish Gaelic: **Antain(e)**. French: **Antoine**. Italian, Spanish: **Antonio**. Catalan: **Antoni**. Basque: **Andoni**. German: **Anton**.

Polish: **Antoni**. Czech: **Antonin**. Russian: **Anton**. Hungarian: **Antal**.

Short forms: English: **Tony**. Italian: **Tonio**. Spanish: **Toño**. Low German, Frisian: **Tönjes**.

Pet forms: Spanish: **Tonete**.

Antigone (f.) Classical name in occasional modern use. In Greek mythology Antigone was a daughter of Oedipus by his accidental incestuous marriage to his own mother, Jocasta. She tended her father as he wandered through Greece, blinded, disgraced, and suffering mental anguish. After her brothers, Eteocles and Polynices, killed each other, she gave funeral rites to both of them, defying the order of her uncle Creon, King of Thebes, that the rebel Polynices should be left unburied. For this, Creon had her buried alive. Its choice as a modern given name is perhaps made with reference to her strength of character in doing what she perceived as right in terrible circumstances. Her name is composed of the Greek elements *anti* against, contrary + *gen-, gon-* born.

Antioco (m.) Italian: a typically Sardinian name, bestowed in honour of a Christian saint who was martyred under the Emperor Hadrian in *c*.110 on the islet of Sulcis near Sardinia, which is now also known as the Isola di Sant'Antioco ('island of St Antiochus'). The name is from Greek *Antiochos*, composed of the elements *anti* against + *ekhein* to have, i.e. to hold out against, denoting stubborn tenacity of character. It was borne in classical times by the father of the Macedonian general Seleucus I, who in *c*.300 BC named the city of Antioch in Asia Minor after him.

Antip (m.) Russian: from the Greek personal name *Antipas*, a short form of *Antipatēr*, which means 'like a father', from the elements *anti-* like + *patēr* father. This name is mentioned in the Book of Revelation (2: 13), where the bearer is the first bishop of Pergamum, who was martyred there *c*.90. He is greatly revered in the Orthodox Church.

Antje (f.) Low German and Dutch: pet form of ANNE.

Antoine (m.) French form of ANTHONY, now also used in the English-speaking world. It was the thirtieth most common male name among American Blacks in 1982.

Antoinette (f.) French: feminine diminutive of ANTOINE, which has become even more popular in the English-speaking world than the masculine form.

Short form: **Toinette**.

Anton (m.) German and Russian form of ANTHONY, now also used in the English-speaking world.

Antoni (m.) Catalan and Polish form of ANTHONY.

Antonia (f.) English, German, Dutch, Scandinavian, Italian, Spanish, and Portuguese: feminine form of ANTHONY and its cognates, unaltered since classical times, when it was a common Roman feminine family name.

Cognates: Czech: **Antonie**. Finnish: **Toini**.

Pet form: English: **Toni**.

Antonín (m.) Czech form of ANTHONY, actually from the Latin derivative *Antonīnus*.

Antonina (f.) Latin derivative of ANTONIA, common in Poland and occasionally used in the English-speaking world.

Cognate: Czech: **Antonína**.

Antonio (m.) Italian and Spanish form of ANTHONY, from Latin *Antōnius*. It is now also used in parts of the English-speaking world.

Antony (m.) English: variant spelling of ANTHONY.

Antshel (m.) Jewish (Yiddish): ultimately from Latin *angelus* angel.

Variants: **Anshel, Amshel**.

Antti (m.) Finnish: pet form of ANTERO.

Anula (f.) Polish: pet form of ANNA.

Anunciación (f.) Spanish: one of a whole set of names derived from titles of the Virgin Mary. It commemorates the Annuciation to her of God's favour and the forthcoming birth of Christ (cf. ANNUNZIATA).

Short form: **Anuncia**.

Anusia (f.) Polish: pet form of ANNA.

Anuška (f.) Czech: pet form of ANNA.

Anwyl (f.) Welsh: variant of ANNWYL.

Anzelm (m.) Polish form of ANSELMO.

Aodh (m.) Irish and Scottish Gaelic: name, meaning 'fire', of the old Celtic sun god. This was a very common personal name from the earliest times. From the later Middle Ages it was commonly Anglicized as HUGH and more recently as EUGENE, but the Gaelic form has also survived in common use. It has given the surnames *Magee* (Gaelic *Mac Aodha*) in Ireland and *McKay* (Gaelic *Mac Aoidh*) in Scotland.

Aoibheann (f.) Irish Gaelic: traditional name meaning 'beautiful'. It was borne by a number of women in the early history of the royal family of Ireland.

Variant: **Aoibhinn**.

Anglicized form: **Eavan**.

Aoife (f.) Irish Gaelic: of uncertain origin, probably a derivative of *aoibh* beauty (cf. AOIBHEANN). It was borne by a daughter of King Dermot of Leinster, who married Richard de Clare, Earl of Pembroke, the leader of the Anglo-Norman invasion of 1169. The name has sometimes been Anglicized as EVA.

Aonghas (m.) The modern Gaelic form of ANGUS.

Variant: **Aonghus**.

Aparición (f.) Spanish: religious name, referring to Christ's appearance to the apostles after the Resurrection.

Aphra (f.) English: of uncertain origin, perhaps an Anglicization of an Irish name; see AFRICA, EITHRIG. It could also be a hypercorrected spelling of a Late Latin name, *Afra*. This was originally an ethnic name for a woman from Africa (in Roman times meaning the area around Carthage). It was used in the post-classical period as a nickname for someone with dark colouring, and eventually became a given name, being borne, for example, by saints martyred at Brescia under the Roman emperor Hadrian and at Augsburg under Diocletian. The respelling of the name may have been prompted by Micah 1: 10 'in the house of Aphrah roll thyself in the dust', where *Aphrah* is often taken as a personal name, but is in fact a placename meaning 'dust'. The first name has never been frequently used, but is remembered as the name of the English writer Aphra Behn (1640–89).

Apollinare (m.) Italian: a name characteristic of the Romagna region and in particular of Ravenna, where it is borne in honour of St Apollinaris, a 1st-century bishop of the city who was martyred under the Emperor Vespasian. The name is of classical origin, being taken from an adjectival form of the name of the god Apollo (see APOLLONIA).

Apollinaria (f.) Feminine form of Latin *Apollinaris* (see APOLLINARE), influenced by APOLLONIA. It has been used in Russian and occasionally in English.

Pet form: Russian: **Polina**.

Apollonia (f.) Latin feminine form of the Greek masculine name *Apollonios*, an adjectival derivative of the name of the sun god, *Apollo*. This is of uncertain origin, and may be pre-Greek. St Apollonia was an elderly deaconess martyred at Alexandria under the Emperor Decius in the mid-3rd century. The name in this form has been used in both English and German.

Derivatives: French: **Apolline**. Danish: **Abelone**.

April (f.) English: from the month (Latin (*mensis*) *aprīlis*, probably a derivative of *aperīre* open, as the month when buds open and flowers appear). It forms a series with the more common names MAY and JUNE, all taken from months associated with the spring, a time of new birth and growth, and may originally have been intended as an English version of the supposedly French name AVRIL.

Aquiles (m.) Portuguese form of ACHILLES.

Arabella (f.) Scottish and English: of uncertain etymology. It probably represents an alteration of *An(n)abella* (see ANNABEL).

Variant: **Arabel** (now rare, but commoner in earlier centuries, when it was also sometimes found as **Orabel**, apparently altered by folk etymology to conform with Latin *orābilis* invokable (from *orāre* to pray to), i.e. a saint who could be invoked).

Araceli (f.) Spanish (mainly Latin American): apparently a modern coinage from Latin *ara* altar + *c(o)eli* of the sky.

Arailt (m.) Scottish Gaelic form of HAROLD.

Aram (m.) Biblical: name (meaning 'height' in Hebrew) borne by a son of Shem and grandson of Noah mentioned in a genealogy (Genesis 10: 22).

Aranka (f.) Hungarian: originally a pet form derived from Hungarian *arany* gold (cf. *Zlata* at ZLATAN). Later, it came to be regarded as a vernacular form of AURELIA.

Aranrhod (f.) Welsh: name borne in the *Mabinogi* by the mother of Dylan and Lleu Llaw Gyffes. It seems to be composed of Old Celtic elements meaning 'huge, round, humped' + 'wheel'; the legendary heroine may originally have been a moon goddess. See also ARIANRHOD.

Aránzazu (f.) Basque: from the name of a place near Oñate in the province of Guipúzcoa, whose name means 'thornbush' in Basque. It was adopted as a given name because in 1469 the Virgin Mary appeared in a vision to a shepherd at this place.

Pet form: **Arantxa**.

Archibald (m.) Scottish: of Norman French origin, from Continental Germanic, composed of the elements *ercan* genuine + *bald* bold, brave. It has always been largely associated with Scotland, where it is in regular use as the English equivalent of Scottish Gaelic *Gilleasbaig* (see GILLESPIE).

Pet forms: **Archie, Archy** (Gaelic **Eair(r)dsidh**); **Baldie**.

Ardal (m.) Irish: Anglicized form of the traditional Gaelic name *Ard(gh)al*, composed of the elements *and* high or possibly *art* bear + *gal* valour.

Arduino (m.) Italian form of HARTWIN.

Are (m.) Scandinavian: from the Old Norse personal name *Ari*, originally a byname meaning 'eagle', or else a short form of the compound names containing this first element.

Ariadne (f.) From classical mythology: the name of a daughter of the Cretan king Minos. She gave the Athenian hero Theseus a ball of wool to enable him to find his way out of the Labyrinth after killing the Minotaur. He took her with him when he sailed from Crete, but abandoned her on the island of Naxos on the way back to Athens. Greek lexicographers of the Hellenistic period claimed that the name was composed of the Cretan dialect elements *ari*- an intensive prefix + *adnos* holy. The name survived in the Christian era because of St Ariadne (d. *c.*130), an early Phrygian martyr.

Derivatives: French: **Arianne**. Italian: **Arianna**.

Arianrhod (f.) Welsh: altered form of ARANRHOD, made up of the modern Welsh elements *arian* silver + *rhod* wheel.

Arianwen (f.) Welsh: composed of the elements *arian* silver + (*g*)*wen*, feminine of *gwyn* white, fair, blessed, holy. The name was borne in the 5th century by one of the daughters of Brychan, a semi-legendary Welsh chieftain.

Ariel (m., f.) Jewish: from the biblical placename *Ariel*, said to mean 'lion of God' in Hebrew. It is mentioned in the prophecies of Ezra (8: 16) and Isaiah (29: 1–2). It has achieved popularity as a modern Hebrew first name, perhaps as an alternative to ARYE.

Arina (f.) Russian: variant of IRINA.

Pet forms: **Arisha**, **Orya**.

Aristide (m.) French: from the classical Greek name *Aristides*, which is in origin a patronymic from a short form of any of the various compound names having as a first element the word *aristos* best, excellent. In the classical period this was borne by an Athenian statesman known as Aristides the Just, whose probity was such that he helped to vote for his own banishment by writing his own name down when asked to do so by an illiterate citizen. In the Christian era, St Aristides (d. *c.*123) was an Athenian philosopher who presented an *Apologia* for Christianity to the Emperor Hadrian. In recent times, the name is best known as being that of the French socialist statesman Aristide Briand (1862–1932), who advocated the idea of a United States of Europe.

Arkadi (m.) Russian: from Greek *Arkadios*, an adjective referring to the region of Arcadia in the central Peloponnese. This placename was explained in classical mythology as being derived from *Arkas*, the name of a son of Zeus and the nymph Callisto, founder of the Arcadian people. The true origin is unknown. In the later classical period Arcadia became the conventional setting for pastoral idylls, a convention copied in later European literature. The Russian given name owes its existence mainly to St Arkadios, a 4th-century missionary bishop venerated in the Eastern Church.

Cognate: Hungarian: **Árkos**.

Arke (m.) Jewish: Yiddish pet form of AARON.

Arkhip (m.) Russian: from Greek *Arkhippos*, composed of the elements *arkhē* beginning or rule + *hippos* horse. St Arkhippos was one of the earliest Christians, twice mentioned by St Paul in his epistles (Colossians 4: 17; Philemon 2). Tradition has it that he became the first bishop of Colossae in Phrygia.

Pet form: **Khipa**.

Árkos (m.) Hungarian form of ARKADI.

Arlene (f.) English: modern coinage, most common in the United States. It is of unknown origin, probably a fanciful coinage based on MARLENE or CHARLENE or on both.

Arlette (f.) French and English: of ancient but uncertain origin. It seems to represent a Norman French double diminutive form derived from the Germanic name element *arn* eagle. It was the name of the mistress of Duke Robert of Normandy in the 11th century; their son was William the Conqueror.

Armelle (f.) French (of Breton origin): feminine form of the rarer male name *Armel*, originally borne by a Breton saint of the 6th century who founded the abbeys of St-Armel-des-Bascheaux and Plouërmel which still bear his name. According to medieval sources, he was born in Wales and was a cousin of St Samson. His name seems to be composed of the Celtic elements *art* stone + *mael* prince, chief.

Armin (m.) German: a modern revival of an ancient Germanic name, mentioned in the form *Arminius* by the Roman historian Tacitus. Arminius (d. AD 21) was a chief of a Germanic tribe called the Cherusci, who in AD 9 inflicted a tremendous defeat on the Roman armies at the Teutoburgerwald, so that they abandoned any serious further attempts to extend their influence east of the Rhine. The name, which is probably etymologically identical with HERMANN, enjoyed a vogue during the period of National Socialism, with its emphasis on German military achievements.

Armstrong (m.) English and Scottish: transferred use of the surname, which originated in the Borders in the Middle Ages, probably as a nickname for a man with strong arms. Like most given names derived from surnames, it no doubt owes its adoption as a given name to a maternal maiden name, but its choice may also have been influenced by the still transparent etymology.

Arn (m.) **1**. Jewish: Yiddish contracted form of AARON. **2**. English: short form of ARNOLD, of recent origin.

Pet form: **Arnie**.

Arnaldo (m.) Italian form of ARNOLD.

Arnaud (m.) French form of ARNOLD.

Arnbjörn (m.) Swedish: from an Old Norse personal name composed of the elements *arn* eagle + *björn* bear.

Variant: **Ambjörn**.

Cognate: Norwegian: **Arnbjørn**.

Arndt (m.) German (esp. N. Germany): contracted form of ARNOLD.

Variant: **Arnd**.

Pet form: **Arne**.

Arne (m.) **1**. Scandinavian: short form of any of various names derived from Old Norse names containing the first element *arn* eagle, for example ARNBJÖRN, *Arnfinn*, and *Arnsten*. It is now quite widely used as a given name in its own right. **2**. German: pet form of ARNDT.

Arno (m.) German: an old Germanic personal name, a short form of the various compound names beginning with the element *arn* eagle, for example ARNOLD and *Arnulf* ('eagle wolf').

Arnold (m.) English and German: of Continental Germanic origin, composed of the elements *arn* eagle + *wald* ruler. It was introduced to Britain by the Normans. An early saint of this name, whose cult contributed to its popularity, was a musician at the court of Charlemagne. He is said to have been a Greek by birth; it is not clear when and how he acquired his Germanic name. It had died out in England by the end of the Middle Ages and was revived in the 19th century, along with a large number of other medieval Germanic names.

Variant: **Arndt** (N. German).
Cognates: French: **Arnaud**, Italian: **Arnaldo**.
Short form: English: **Arn**.

Arnon (m.) Jewish: modern name taken from that of a river mentioned in the Bible (Numbers 21: 15). The river name means 'swift' in Hebrew.

Arnošt (m.) Czech form of **Ernest**.

Aron (m.) Simplified variant of **Aaron**, also the regular Polish form.

Árpád (m.) Hungarian: apparently from a diminutive of the vocabulary word *árpa* seed, barleycorn. It was the name of the Magyar chieftain who first conquered the territory that is modern Hungary, in the late 9th century, and who led his people to settle there. He is regarded as a national hero in Hungary, and many children are named after him.

Arrigo (m.) Italian: vernacular form of the more learned **Enrico**, a cognate of English **Henry**, German *Heinrich*. *Arrigo* is the older form of the name, and was used throughout the Middle Ages.

Arron (m.) English: altered spelling of **Aron**.

Arseni (m.) Russian: from the Greek name *Arsenios* 'male, virile'. St Arsenius the Great (d. *c*.449) was a Roman deacon who served as tutor to Arcadius and Honorius, the sons of the Emperor Theodosius, who divided the Roman Empire between them. In later life Arsenius became a hermit.

Pet form: **Senya**.

Art (m.) English, Irish, and Scottish: now generally taken as an informal short form of **Arthur**. There is also a traditional Gaelic name of this form (from the vocabulary word *art* bear) which has generally been Anglicized as *Arthur* although in fact has no connection with that name. In the diminutive form *Artan* it has given rise to the Skye surname *Mac Artain*, Anglicized as *McCartan*.

Artair (m.) Scottish Gaelic form of **Arthur**.

Artemas (m.) Of New Testament Greek origin, from a name that in fact represents a short form of various compound names containing that of the goddess **Artemis** (for example, *Artemidoros* 'gift of Artemis' and *Artemisthens* 'strength of Artemis'). It is borne in the Bible by a character mentioned briefly in St Paul's letter to Titus (3: 12). The name enjoyed some popularity among the Puritans in the 17th century, but fell out of use again.

Variant: **Artemus** (Latinized).

Artemi (m.) Russian: from Greek *Artemios*, a derivative of **Artemas**. St Artemius (d. 363) was a powerful official under the Emperor Constantine the Great, and was prefect of Egypt under his successor Constantius Chlorus. However, when Julian the Apostate came to the throne, Artemius was beheaded.

Variant: **Artyom**.
Pet form: **Tyoma**.

Artemis (f.) From the name of the Greek goddess of the moon and of hunting, equivalent to the Latin **Diana**. It is of uncertain derivation, and may well be pre-Greek. As a given name, it is rare in any country, but is chosen occasionally by parents in search of something distinctive. It is borne by a

granddaughter of Lady Diana Cooper, perhaps as an oblique tribute to the grandmother.

Arthur (m.) Of Celtic origin. King Arthur was a British king of the 5th or 6th century, about whom virtually no historical facts are known. He ruled in Britain after the collapse of the Roman Empire and before the coming of the Germanic tribes, and a vast body of legends grew up around him in the literatures of medieval Western Europe. His name is first found in the Latinized form *Artorius* and is of obscure derivation. The spelling with *-th-*, now invariably reflected in the pronunciation of the English name, is not found before the 16th century, and seems to represent no more than an artificial embellishment. The name became particularly popular in Britain in the 19th century, partly as a result of the fame of Arthur Wellesley (1769–1852), Duke of Wellington, partly because of the popularity of Tennyson's *Idylls of the King* (1842–85), and partly because of the enormous Victorian interest in things medieval in general and in Arthurian legend in particular. This interest also accounts for its adoption as a given name in France and elsewhere in Western Europe.

Cognates: Scottish Gaelic: **Artair** (from which derives the surname *Mac Artair*, Anglicized as *McArthur* and *Carter*). Irish Gaelic: **Artúr**. Italian, Spanish: **Arturo**.
Short form: **Art**.

Artyom (m.) Russian: variant of **Artemi**.

Arvid (m.) Scandinavian: from an Old Norse personal name composed of the elements *arn* eagle + *viðr* wood, tree.

Arye (m.) Jewish: meaning 'lion' in Hebrew. The lion is traditionally associated with the name **Judah**, Hebrew **Yehuda**, because of Jacob's words in his dying blessing: 'Judah is a lion's whelp' (Genesis 49: 9). It became common during the Middle Ages when such animal names were popular in Europe and is often used together with the Yiddish name **Leib**.

Asa (m.) Biblical: name of one of the early kings of Judah, who reigned for forty years, as recorded in 1 Kings and 2 Chronicles. It was originally a byname meaning 'doctor, healer' in Hebrew, and is still a common Jewish name. It was first used among English-speaking Christians by the Puritans in the 17th century, and although now far from common, it has never completely dropped out of use. In the 20th century it is largely known as the given name of the historian Asa Briggs and of the footballer Asa Hertford. See also **Åsa**.

Åsa (f.) Scandinavian: short form of any of various Old Norse female personal names containing the first element *áss* god. In Norway and Denmark the form **Åse** is also common.

Asaph (m.) Biblical: from a Hebrew vocabulary word meaning 'collector'. This is found attached to some of the Psalms (50 and 73–83), and may have been the name of the writer or of a cantor. Asaph is also mentioned at 1 Chronicles 6: 39, 9: 15, and 25: 1; and other, apparently unrelated bearers of the name are mentioned at 2 Kings 18: 37 and Isaiah 36: 3 and 36: 22. In more recent times the name was borne by Asaph Hall (1829–1907), the American astronomer who discovered the two satellites of Mars.

Asdrubale (m.) Italian: from the name of the Carthaginian general *Hasdrubal* Barca (d. *c*.207 BC), brother of Hannibal (see **Annibale**). The name is composed of the Phoenician elements *asru* aid (related to **Ezra**) + the divine name *Baal* 'lord'. As a given name in Italy, this is not as common as **Annibale** and **Amilcare**.

Asenath (f.) Biblical: name borne by Joseph's Egyptian wife (Genesis 41: 45), who became the mother of Manasseh and Ephraim. The name seems to have meant 'she belongs to her father' in ancient Egyptian.

Asher (m.) Jewish: meaning 'fortunate' or 'happy' in Hebrew. This was borne in the Bible by one of the sons of Jacob: 'and Leah said, Happy am I, for the daughters will call me blessed; and she called his name Asher' (Genesis 30: 13).
Variant: **Osher**.

Ashley (m., f.) English: an increasingly popular given name for girls, this is a transferred use of the surname, which comes from any of numerous places in England named in Old English with the elements *æsc* ash + *lēah* wood. Its use as a given name may have been first inspired by admiration for the humanitarian work of Anthony Ashley Cooper (1801–85), Earl of Shaftesbury.

Ashling (f.) Irish: Anglicized form of AISLING.

Aslög (f.) Swedish: from an Old Norse female personal name composed of the elements *áss* god + *laug* consecrated, dedicated. The form **Åslög** is also used.
Cognates: Norwegian: **Aslaug**, **Åslaug**. Danish: **Asløg**, **Aslaug**.

Åsmund (m.) Scandinavian: from the Old Norse personal name *Ásmundr*, composed of the elements *áss* god + *mundr* protector.
Cognate: English: OSMOND.

Assumpta (f.) Latin form of ASSUNTA, used especially in Ireland among Roman Catholics.

Assunta (f.) Italian: from a title of the Virgin Mary, *Maria Assunta*, referring to her assumption into heaven. Cf. ASUNCIÓN.

Asta (f.) Scandinavian: short form of ASTRID. There has been much confusion with ÅSTA.

Åsta (f.) Scandinavian: from the Old Norse female personal name *Ásta*, derived from the vocabulary element *ást* love.

Aston (m.) English: transferred use of the surname, which originated in the Middle Ages as a local name, from any of the numerous English places so called, most being named with the Old English elements *ēast* east + *tūn* settlement.

Astrid (f.) Scandinavian: composed of the Old Norse elements *áss* god + *fríðr* fair, beautiful. It has become fairly common in the English-speaking world during the 20th century, in part as a result of the fame of the Queen of the Belgians (1905–35) who bore this name.
Short form: **Asta**.
Pet form: Swedish: **Sassa**.

Asunción (f.) Spanish: another of the many female names bestowed in honour of the Virgin Mary. This one commemorates her assumption into heaven, the festival of which has been celebrated on 15 August since at least the 7th century, although this has been a matter of official dogma since only 1950.
Short form: **Asun**.

Asya (f.) Russian: pet form of both ANASTASIA and ANNA.

Atalanta (f.) From classical mythology. Atalanta was a girl who was a swift runner and who took part in the hunt for the Calydonian boar. Meleager, leader of the hunt, gave her its pelt, for he had fallen in love with her. However, he died as a result of quarrels with his brothers. Atalanta undertook to marry only a man who could defeat her in a race; losers were condemned to death. Eventually, Hippomenes defeated her by dropping three golden apples which she stopped to pick up.

Atarah (f.) Biblical: from a Hebrew word meaning 'crown'. Atarah was one of the wives of Jerahmeel (1 Chronicles 2: 26).
Variant: **Atara** (now a common modern Hebrew name, possibly as a translation of Yiddish KREINE).

Athanasius (m.) Latin: the name of an early Christian saint (*c*.297–373), an Alexandrian theologian venerated particularly in the Eastern Church. His name is derived from the Greek vocabulary word *athanatos* immortal, and was popular among early Christians, since it expressed their confidence in eternal life.
Derivatives: French: **Athanase**. Russian: **Afanasi**. Polish: **Atanazy**.
Pet form: Russian: **Afonya**.

Athene (f.) From classical mythology: the name of the Greek goddess of wisdom and patron of Athens. It is used occasionally in the English-speaking world by parents seeking a distinctive name.

Athol (m., f.) Scottish: transferred use of the name of a district of Perthshire, seat of the dukes of Atholl. The placename is thought to derive from Gaelic *ath Fodla* new Ireland.
Variants: **Atholl**, **Athole**.

Attila (m.) Hungarian: name bestowed occasionally in honour of the great pagan military leader Attila the Hun (d. 453), who struck terror into the hearts of people in the Roman Empire, acquiring the nickname 'the Scourge of God'. The origin of his name is unknown. His exploits were recorded and embroidered in Germanic legend; he lies behind the figure of Etzel in the *Nibelungenlied*, for example. Although the Huns inhabited what is now Hungary, and indeed gave it its modern English name, they were probably a Mongoloid people, and almost certainly unrelated to the Magyars, the modern inhabitants of Hungary.

Attilio (m.) Italian: from the Latin family name *Attilius*, which is generally taken to be of Etruscan origin. The name was taken up in Italy during the Renaissance in honour of the Roman general Marcus Attilius Regulus (d. *c*.250 BC), who fought against Hamilcar during the First Punic War.

Attracta (f.) Irish: Latinized version (as if from *attractus* attracted, drawn) of the Gaelic name **Athracht**. St Athracht or Attracta was a contemporary of St Patrick who lived as a recluse in Sligo.

Auberon (m.) English: of Norman French origin, from Germanic. There is much doubt about the form and meaning of the elements of which it was originally composed; it may be connected with AUBREY, or may derive from the elements *adal* noble + *ber(n)* bear.
Variant: **Oberon**.

Aubrey (m., f.) English: from a Norman French form of the Germanic name *Alberic*, composed of the elements *alb* elf, supernatural being + *ric* power. This was the (appropriate) name, according to Germanic mythology, of the king of the elves. The native Old English cognate, Ælfrīc, borne by a 10th-century archbishop of Canterbury, did not long survive the Conquest. *Aubrey* was a relatively common given name during the Middle Ages, but later fell out of favour. Its occurrence since the 19th century may in part represent a transferred use of the surname derived from the Norman given name, as well as a revival of the latter.

Audrey (f.) English: drastically reduced form of the Old English female name *Æðelpryð*, composed of the elements *æðel* noble + *pryð* strength. This was the name of a 6th-century saint (normally known by the Latinized form of her name, *Etheldreda*), who was a particular favourite in the Middle Ages. According to tradition she died from a tumour of the neck, which she bore stoically as a divine punishment for her youthful delight in fine necklaces. The name went into a decline at the end of the Middle Ages, when it came to be considered vulgar, being associated with *tawdry*, that is, lace and other goods sold at fairs held in her name (the word deriving from a misdivision of *Saint Audrey*). Shakespeare bestowed it on Touchstone's comic sweetheart in *As You Like It*. In the last century such associations have largely been forgotten, and the name has enjoyed some revival of popularity. The form **Audra** is also used, especially in the southern United States in double names such as *Audra jo* and *Audra Rose*.

Audrina (f.) English: recent fanciful elaboration of AUDREY.

August (m.) German and Polish form of AUGUSTUS.

Augusta (f.) Latinate feminine form of AUGUSTUS, which enjoyed a vogue in Britain towards the end of the 19th century.

Auguste (m.) French form of AUGUSTUS.

Augustine (m.) English form of the Latin name *Augustīnus* (a derivative of AUGUSTUS). Its most famous bearer is St Augustine of Hippo (354–430), perhaps the greatest of the Fathers of the Christian Church. He formulated the principles followed by the numerous medieval communities named after him as *Austin* canons, friars, and nuns. Also important in England was St Augustine of Canterbury, who brought Christianity to Kent in the 6th century. See also AUSTIN.
Cognates: Irish Gaelic: **Ághaistin**, **Aibhistin**. Italian: **Agostino**. Spanish: **Agustín**. Catalan: **Agustí**. Portuguese: **Agostinho**. Russian: **Avgustin**. Polish: **Augustyn**. Finnish: **Tauno**.

Augustus (m.) Latin name, from the adjective *augustus* great, magnificent (from *augēre* to increase). This word was adopted as a title by the Roman emperors, starting with Octavian (Caius Julius Caesar Octavianus), the adopted son of Julius Caesar, who assumed it in 27 BC and is now generally known as the Emperor Augustus. This name, together with AUGUSTA, was revived in England in the 18th century, but it has now again declined in popularity.
Derivatives: German, Polish: **August**. French: **Auguste**. Italian, Spanish, Portuguese: **Augusto**. Russian: **Avgust**.
Short form: English, Irish: **Gus**.

Aulay (m.) Scottish: Anglicized form of *Amhla(i)dh* (see AMHLAOIBH).

Auliffe (m.) Irish: Anglicized form of AMHLAOIBH.

Aune (f.) Finnish form of AGNES.

Aurèle (m.) French form of the Roman family name *Aurēlius*, which is derived from *aureus* golden. Its most famous bearer was the 2nd-century emperor Marcus Aurelius Antoninus, also noted as a philosophical writer. It was later borne by various saints, including a 5th-century archbishop of Carthage who was a friend of St Augustine. It did not, however, enjoy much popularity in the Middle Ages, nor has it done so since; the modern use of the feminine form since the 17th

century seems to be the result of its relatively transparent etymology ('golden').
Cognates: Italian, Spanish, Portuguese: **Aurelio**. German: **Aurel**; **Orell** (Switzerland).

Aurelia (f.) Feminine form of Latin *Aurelius* (see AURÈLE), used occasionally in the English-speaking world.
Derivative: French: **Aurélie**.

Aurkene (f.) Basque equivalent of PRESENTACIÓN.

Aurora (f.) From Latin *aurōra* dawn, also used in the classical period as the name of the personified goddess of the dawn. It was not used as a given name in the postclassical or medieval period, but is a reinvention of the Renaissance, and has generally been bestowed as a learned equivalent of DAWN by parents conscious of its etymology.
Derivative: French: **Aurore**.

Austin (m.) English: from a medieval contracted form of the Latin name *Augustīnus* (see AUGUSTINE). The present-day use of this form as a given name is probably a reintroduction from its survival as a surname, for the full forms are rare in the English-speaking world.
Variant: **Austen**.
Cognate: Welsh: **Awstin**.

Auxilio (f.) Spanish: religious name meaning 'help', referring to the feast of *Maria Auxiliadora* 'Mary the Helper' celebrated on 24 May.

Ava (f.) English: of uncertain origin, probably Germanic, from a short form of various female compound names containing the element *av* (cf. AVIS). St Ava or Avia was a 9th-century abbess of Dinart in Hainault and a member of the Frankish royal family. However, evidence for its use between the early Middle Ages and the mid-20th century is lacking, and it may be a modern invention. Its recent popularity is largely due to the film actress Ava Gardner (1922–90).

Avdotya (f.) Russian: vernacular form of the learned name *Evdokia*, from the Greek name *Eudokia* (a compound of *eu* well, good + *dokein* to seem). This was Latinized as *Eudocia*. St Eudocia (98–117) was a Samaritan martyr beheaded by Trajan at Heliopolis in Syria.
Pet forms: **Avdunya**, **Dunya**, **Dunyasha**.

Aveline (f.) English: of Germanic origin, introduced by the Normans. It seems to represent an Old French diminutive form of the Germanic name AVILA, a derivative of AVIS. See also EILEEN.

Averil (f.) English: variant of AVRIL.

Averill (m.) English (esp. U.S.): transferred use of the surname, which originated during the Middle Ages from the Old English female personal name *Eoforhild* (see AVRIL.)
Variant: **Averell**.

Averki (m.) Russian: from the Greek name *Aberkios* (Latin *Abercius*), which is of uncertain, presumably non-classical, origin. It was borne by a 2nd-century bishop of Hieropolis in Phrygia, who is revered as a saint in the Orthodox Church.

Avery (m.) English: transferred use of the surname, which originated in the Middle Ages from a Norman French pronunciation of ALFRED.

Avgust (m.) Russian form of AUGUSTUS.

Avgustin (m.) Russian form of AUGUSTINE.

Avice (f.) English: variant spelling of Avis.

Avila (f.) English: this occurs in the Middle Ages as a Latinized form of a medieval Germanic name related to Avis. In modern use, however, it is borne almost exclusively by Roman Catholics, among whom it is bestowed in honour of St Theresa of Avila (1515–82).

Avis (f.) English: from a Norman French form of the Germanic name *Aveza*, derived from a short form of various female compound names containing the first element *av* (of uncertain meaning). The name probably owes its modest popularity in the later Middle Ages and subsequent centuries to its correspondence in form to the Latin feminine noun *avis* bird.
Variant: **Avice**.

Avishag (f.) Jewish: modern Hebrew form of Abishag.

Avital (f.) Jewish: modern Hebrew form of the biblical name *Abital*, meaning 'dewy', borne by a wife of King David (2 Samuel 3:4).

Aviva (f.) Jewish: recent coinage from a modern Hebrew vocabulary word meaning 'spring'.

Avner (m.) Jewish: modern Hebrew form of Abner.

Avraham (m.) Jewish: modern Hebrew form of Abraham.

Avril (f.) English: although generally taken as the French form of the name of the fourth month (see April), this has also been influenced by the English surname *Everill*, which is from an Old English female personal name composed of the elements *eofor* boar + *hild* battle.

Avrom (m.) Jewish: Yiddish form of Abraham.

Axel (m.) Scandinavian (Danish) form of Absalom, sometimes also used in the United States.
Pet form: **Acke**.

Ayala (f.) Jewish: modern Hebrew name meaning 'hind' or 'doe'; cf. Hinde.

Aylwin (m.) English: variant of Alwyn.

Azaria (f.) English: female name apparently created in the 20th century and modelled on the rare male name Azarias.

Azarias (m.) Biblical: Greek form of the Hebrew name *Azariah* 'helped by God', the name of a prophet who recalled King Asa to a proper observance of religion (2 Chronicles 15: 1–8).

Azriel (m.) Jewish: name (meaning 'God helps' in Hebrew) borne in the Bible by a character briefly mentioned as a leading member of the tribe of Manasseh (1 Chronicles 5: 24).

Azucena (f.) Spanish: from the vocabulary word *azucena* madonna lily (from Arabic *as-susana* the lily; cf. Susanna). The word seems to have been adopted as a given name because of the association of the flower with the Virgin Mary.

B

Babs (f.) English: informal pet form of BARBARA.

Badane (f.) Jewish: Yiddish form of *Bogdana* (see BOGDAN).

Baibín (f.) Irish Gaelic: pet form of BAIRBRE.

Bailey (m.) English: transferred use of the surname, which has various origins. Most commonly it was an occupational name for a bailiff or administrative official; in other cases it apparently originated as a local name for someone who lived near a bailey, i.e. a city fortification, and in others it may be a local name from *Bailey* in Lancashire, which gets its name from Old English *bēg* berry + *lēah* wood, clearing.

Bairbre (f.) Irish Gaelic form of BARBARA.
Pet form: **Baibín**.

Bakarne (f.) Basque equivalent of SOLEDAD.

Balázs (m.) Hungarian form of BLAISE.

Baldassare (m.) Italian cognate of BALTHASAR, occasionally borne in honour of the Blessed Balthasar of Chiavari, venerated in Pavia.

Balder (m.) Swedish: from the name of an Old Norse god, meaning 'prince' or 'ruler', cognate with *bold* brave, strong. According to Norse mythology, this was the name of a son of Odin by his wife Frigg. According to some stories, Balder was the god of light. His mother persuaded everything in the world to swear an oath not to harm him, but she overlooked the mistletoe. The evil and cunning god Loki persuaded the blind god Hoder to aim a dart made of mistletoe at Balder, and it killed him. He is sometimes taken as a personification of doomed purity and beauty.
Cognate: German: **Baldur**.

Baldie (m.) Scottish: pet form of ARCHIBALD.

Baldomero (m.) Spanish: from a Germanic (Frankish) personal name composed of the elements *bald* bold, brave + *mari*, *meri* famous. This name was borne by a 7th-century saint from Lyons, patron of locksmiths.
Cognate: Provençal: **Baldomar**.

Baldur (m.) German cognate of BALDER.

Baldwin (m.) English: Norman name composed of the Germanic elements *bald* bold, brave + *wine* friend. In the Middle Ages this was a comparatively common name, which gave rise to a surname. It was the given name of the Norman crusader (Baldwin of Boulogne) who in 1100 was elected first king of Jerusalem. It was also the name of four further crusader kings of Jerusalem. In modern English use, it normally represents a transferred use of the surname rather than a direct revival of the Norman given name.
Cognate: French (esp. Belgian): **Baudouin**.

Bálint (m.) Hungarian form of VALENTINE.

Balthasar (m.) English: name ascribed in medieval Christian tradition to one of the three wise men of the Orient who brought gifts to the infant Jesus (see also JASPER and MELCHIORRE). The name is a variant of that of the biblical king *Belshazzar* and means 'Baal protect the king'. It has never been a common given name in the English-speaking world.
Variant: **Balthazar**.
Cognates: Italian: **Baldassare**. Spanish: **Baltasar**.

Baptist (m.) English and German form of BAPTISTE. As an English name it is used mainly in the United States by Blacks who are members of evangelical sects.

Baptiste (m.) French: meaning 'baptist' (Late Latin *baptista*, Greek *baptistēs*, from *baphein* to dip), the epithet of the most popular of the numerous saints called JOHN. Although it occurs independently as a given name, it is normally found in combination with *Jean* (see JOHN).
Cognates: German, English: BAPTIST. Italian: **Battista** Spanish: **Bautista**. Portuguese: **Batista**.

Barbara (f.) English, German, and Polish: from Latin, meaning 'foreign woman' (a feminine form of *barbarus* foreign, from **Greek**, referring originally to the unintelligible chatter of foreigners, which sounded to the Greek ear like no more than *bar-bar*). St Barbara has always been one of the most popular saints in the calendar, although there is some doubt whether she ever existed. According to legend, she was imprisoned in a tower and later murdered by her father, who was then struck down by a bolt of lightning; accordingly, she is the patron of architects, stonemasons, and fortifications, and of firework makers, artillerymen, and gunpowder magazines. The name is now occasionally modishly spelled **Barbra**, notably in the case of the actress and singer Barbra Streisand (b. 1942).
Cognates: Irish Gaelic: **Bairbre**. Scottish Gaelic: **Barabal**. Swedish: **Barbro**. Czech: **Barbora**. Russian: **Varvara**. Hungarian: **Borbála**.
Short forms: English: **Barb** (mainly U.S. informal). French: **Barbe**.
Pet forms: English: **Barbie**, **Babs**. Irish Gaelic: **Baibín**. German: **Bärbel**. Polish: **Basia**. Czech: **Bára**, **Bora**, **Bar(čin)ka**, **Barun(k)a**, **Baruška**.

Barclay (m.) Scottish, English, and Irish: generally a transferred use of the Scottish surname, which was taken to Scotland in the 12th century by Walter de Berchelai, who became chamberlain of Scotland in 1165. His name is almost certainly derived from *Berkeley* in Gloucestershire, which is named with the Old English elements *beorc* birch tree + *lēah* wood or clearing. His descendants became one of the most powerful families in Scotland, and the transferred use as a given name probably originated in Scotland with reference to this family. In Ireland it has been pressed into service as an Anglicized form of PARTHALÁN.

Barnabas (m.) English and German: from the New Testament, where *Barnabas* represents a Greek form of the name of a companion of St Paul. The Aramaic original meant 'son of consolation'.
Variant: English: **Barnaby** (from a medieval vernacular form).
Cognates: French: **Barnabé**. Spanish: **Bernabé**. Polish: **Barnaba**.

Czech: **Barnabá**. Hungarian: **Barna**.
Pet forms: English: **Barney**, **Barny**.

Barrett (m.) English: transferred use of the surname, which is of obscure origin. It is probably a nickname from Middle English *baret* dispute, argument. The transferred use as a given name is recent.

Barry (m.) Irish: Anglicized form of the Gaelic name **Barra** (Old Irish *Bairre*), a short form *of Fionnb(h)arr* (see FINBAR). In the 20th century this name has also become very popular in other areas of English-speaking world, particularly Australia.
Informal pet forms: **Baz**, **Bazza** (Australian).

Bart (m.) English: short form of BARTON and BARTHOLO-MEW.

Barthold (m.) Low German form of BERTHOLD.

Bartholomew (m.) English: of New Testament origin, the name of an apostle mentioned in all the synoptic gospels (Matthew, Mark, and Luke) and in the Acts of the Apostles. It is an Aramaic formation meaning 'son of Talmai', and has been assumed by many scholars to be a byname of the apostle Nathaniel. *Talmai* is a Hebrew name, said to mean 'abounding in furrows' (Numbers 13:22).
Cognates: Irish Gaelic: **Bairtliméad**; PARTHALÁN. Scottish Gaelic: **Pàrlan**. French: **Barthélemy**. Provençal: **Barthomieu**. Catalan: **Bartomeu**. Spanish: **Bartolomé**. Portuguese: **Bartolmeu** Italian: **Bartolo(m)meo**. German: **Bartolomäus**. Dutch: **Bartholomeus** (learned); **Bartel** (vernacular). Polish: **Bartlomiej** (learned); **Bartosz** (vernacular). Czech: **Bartoloměj**. Russian: **Varfolomei**. Hungarian: **Bartal**, **Bartos**, **Bartó**. Finnish: **Perttu**.
Short forms: English: **Bart**. Irish: **Bartle**, **Bartley**. Italian: **Bàrtolo**; **Meo**.

Barton (m.) English: transferred use of the surname, originally a local name from any of the numerous places in England so called from Old English *bere* barley + *tūn* enclosure, settlement.
Short form: **Bart**.

Baruch (m.) Jewish: biblical name meaning 'blessed' in Hebrew (cf. BENEDICT). It is borne by a character who appears in the Book of Jeremiah.

Baruna (f.) Czech: pet form of *Barbora* (see BARBARA).
Variants: **Barunka**, **Baruška**.

Bashe (f.) Jewish: Yiddish pet form of BATYAH.

Basia (f.) Polish: pet form of BARBARA.

Basil (m.) English: from the Greek name *Basileios* 'royal' (a derivative of *basileus* king). This name was borne by St Basil the Great (*c*.330–379), bishop of Caesarea, a theologian regarded as one of the Fathers of the Eastern Church. It was also the name of several early saints martyred in the East.
Cognates: Polish: **Bazyli**. Russian: **Vasili**.

Bastien (m.) French: aphetic short from of *Sébastien* (see SEBASTIAN).
Feminine form: **Bastienne**.

Basye (f.) Jewish: Yiddish pet form of BATYAH.

Bathsheba (f.) Biblical name, meaning 'daughter of the oath' in Hebrew. This was the name of the woman who became the wife of King David, after he had disposed of her husband Uriah, and mother of King Solomon (2 Samuel 11–12). It was popular with the Puritans in England, no doubt because of the great beauty attributed to the biblical character.

Variant: Jewish: **Batsheva** (the modern Hebrew form).

Batista (m.) Portuguese form of BAPTISTE.

Battista (m.) Italian form of BAPTISTE.

Batyah (f.) Jewish: modern Hebrew name composed of the elements *bat* daughter + *yah* God. It is also possibly a variant of *Bithiah*, the name of an Egyptian princess mentioned in 1 Chronicles 4:18. The Hebrew spelling of *Batyah* and *Bithiah* is identical.
Pet forms: **Basye**, **Bashe**.

Batzion (f.) Jewish: modern Hebrew name meaning 'daughter of Zion'.

Baudouin (m.) French form of BALDWIN, common especially in Belgium, where it is borne by Baudouin I (b. 1930), King of the Belgians since 1951.

Bautista (m.) Spanish form of BAPTISTE.

Baxter (m.) English: transferred use of the surname, which originated in the Middle Ages as an occupational name for a baker, Old English *bæcestre*. The *-estre* suffix was originally feminine, but by the Middle English period the gender difference had been lost; *Baxter* was merely a regional variant of *Baker*.

Baz (m.) English: informal pet form of BARRY.
Variant: **Bazza** (Australian).

Bazyli (m.) Polish form of BASIL.

Bea (f.) English: informal short form of BEATRICE or BEATRIX.

Bean (m.) Scottish: Anglicized form of the Gaelic name BEATHAN.

Bearnard (m.) Irish and Scottish Gaelic form of BERNARD.

Bearnas (f.) Scottish Gaelic form of BERENICE, often considered as a feminine equivalent of BEARNARD.

Beat (m.) Swiss German: name borne in honour of the apostle of Switzerland, a hermit of uncertain date who established himself at the place now called *Beatenberg*, above the lake of Thun. His name derives from Late Latin *Beātus* 'blessed'; cf. BEATA.

Beata (f.) Late Latin feminine form of *Beātus* 'blessed'. St Beata is the name of an early Christian saint martyred at an unknown date in North Africa. The name is widely used among Roman Catholics in Germany, Poland, and elsewhere; it is less common in the English-speaking world.

Beathan (m.) Scottish Gaelic: traditional name, a derivative of *beatha* life.
Anglicized forms: **Bean**; BENJAMIN.
Feminine form: **Beathag** (often Anglicized as SOPHIA or REBECCA).

Beatrice (f.) Italian and French form of BEATRIX, occasionally used in England during the Middle Ages, and strongly revived in the 19th century. It is most famous as the name of Dante's beloved.
Cognates: Scottish Gaelic: **Beitiris**. Welsh: **Betrys** (a modern Welsh spelling of the English given name).
Short form: English: **Bea**.
Pet forms: English: **Beat(t)ie**. Italian: **Bice**.

Beatrix (f.) English and German: from a Late Latin personal name, which was borne by a saint executed in Rome, together with Faustinus and Simplicius, in the early 4th century. The original form of the name seems to have been *Viātrix*, a feminine version of *Viātōr* 'voyager (through life)', which was common among early Christians. This was then altered by association with Latin *Beātus* 'blessed' (*Via-* and *Bea-* being pronounced very similarly in Late Latin).

Cognate: Spanish: **Beatriz**. See also BEATRICE.

Beau (m.) English: recent coinage as a given name, originally a nickname meaning 'handsome', as borne by Beau Brummell (1778–1840), the dandy who was for a time a friend of the Prince Regent. The word was also used in the 19th century with the meaning 'admirer' or 'sweetheart'. Its adoption as a given name seems to have been due to the hero of P. C. Wren's novel *Beau Gate* (1924) or to the character of Beau Wilks in Margaret Mitchell's *Gone with the Wind* (1936), which was made into an exceptionally popular film in 1939.

Bechor (m.) Jewish: Hebrew name meaning 'firstborn'. This given name is borne particularly by Jews of Sephardic descent.

Becky (f.) English: pet form of REBECCA. It has occasionally been used as an independent given name, and was especially popular in the 18th and 19th centuries. The modern short form **Becca** is also occasionally used, and the form **Beca** is well established in Wales.

Bedřich (m.) Czech form of FREDERICK.

Feminine form: **Bedřiška**.
Pet forms: **Béda** (m., f.); **Bedřišek** (m.); **Bed'ka, Beduna, Řiška** (f.).

Begoña (f.) Spanish (largely confined to the Basque country): name bestowed in honour of our Lady of Begoña, venerated as the patron saint of Bilbao. There is no connection with the flower *begonia*, which was so named in the 18th century after Michel Begon (1630–1710), a French patron of science.

Beile (f.) Jewish (Yiddish): probably derived from the Slavonic element *beli* white (cf. the Czech female name *Běla*). According to others, it is from the Romance element *bella* beautiful (cf. BELLA and SHAYNA).

Variant: **Beyle**.
Pet form: **Beylke**.

Beileag (f.) Scottish Gaelic: pet form of ISEABAIL.

Variants: **Bella(g)** (Anglicized forms).

Beistean (m.) Scottish Gaelic: pet form of *Gille Easbaig* (see GILLESPIE).

Beitidh (f.) Scottish Gaelic form of BETTY.

Beitiris (f.) Scottish Gaelic form of BEATRICE.

Béla (m.) Hungarian: of uncertain origin. There seems to be no linguistic foundation for connecting it with the German name *Albrecht* (see ALBERT). It may be a borrowing from Slavonic, from *belo* white, the first element in such names as *Belo-slav*. Alternatively, it may be from the Hungarian vocabulary word *bél* inner part, or from a Turkic byname meaning 'distinguished'.

Belén (f.) Spanish: chosen in commemoration of Jesus's birthplace at *Bethlehem* in Judea, the Spanish form of which is *Belén*. The placename means 'house of bread' in Hebrew.

Belinda (f.) English: of uncertain origin. It was used by Sir John Vanbrugh for a character in his comedy *The Provok'd Wife* (1697), was taken up by Alexander Pope in *The Rape of the Lock* (1712), and has enjoyed a steady popularity ever since. It is not certain where Vanbrugh got the name from. The

notion that it is Germanic (with a second element *lind* lime tree) does not seem to be well-founded. In Italian literature it is the name ascribed to the wife of Orlando, vassal of Charlemagne, but this use is not supported in Germanic sources. The name may be an Italian coinage from *bella* beautiful (see BELLA) + the feminine name suffix *-inda* (cf. e.g. LUCINDA).

Bella (f.) Italian, Scottish, and English: aphetic short form of *Isabella*, the Italian form of ISABEL, but also associated with the Italian adjective *bella*, feminine of *bello* handsome, beautiful (Late Latin *bellus*).

Bellarmino (m.) Catholic name given in honour of the Italian saint Roberto Bellarmino (1542–1621), a prominent Jesuit. He was canonized in 1930 and declared a Doctor of the Church in 1931; his surname has occasionally been used as a given name in the 20th century.

Belle (f.) English: variant of BELLA, reflecting the French feminine adjective *belle* beautiful.

Beltrán (m.) Spanish form, by dissimilation, of BERTRAM.

Ben (m.) English: short form of BENJAMIN, or less commonly of BENEDICT or BENNETT.

Pet forms: **Benny, Bennie**.

Benedict (m.) English: from Church Latin *Benedictus* 'blessed'. This was the name of the saint (*c*.480–*c*.550) who composed the Benedictine rule of Christian monastic life that is still followed in essence by all Western orders. He was born near Spoleto in Umbria, central Italy. After studying in Rome, he went to live as a hermit at Subiaco, and later organized groups of followers and imitators into monastic cells. In *c*.529 he moved to Monte Cassino, where he founded the great monastery that is still the centre of the Benedictine order. His rule is simple, restrained, and practical. The name is used mainly by Roman Catholics.

Variant: English: BENNETT.
Cognates: Scottish Gaelic: **Benneit**. French: **Benoît**. Italian: **Benedetto**. Spanish: BENITO. Portuguese: **Bento**. Catalan: **Benet**. Provençal: **Bénézet**. German, Dutch: **Benedikt**. Danish: **Bendt, Bent**. Swedish: **Bengt**. Russian: **Venedikt**. Polish: **Benedykt** Czech: **Beneš**. Hungarian: **Benedek**. Finnish: **Pentti**.
Feminine forms: Latin: **Benedicta**. French: **Benoîte**. Italian: **Benedetta**. German, Dutch: **Benedikta**.

Benigno (m.) Italian and Spanish: from the Late Latin name *Benignus* 'kind' (a derivative of Latin *bene* well), which was borne by a large number of early saints. One was the 3rd-century martyr to whom Dijon cathedral is dedicated; another was a 5th-century disciple of St Patrick.

Benito (m.) Spanish form of BENEDICT. In the 20th century it has also been used in Italy, most notably by the dictator Benito Mussolini (1883–1945), who was named after the Mexican revolutionary leader Benito Pablo Juarez (1806–72).

Benjamin (m.) English (also French and German): of biblical origin. Benjamin was one of the founders of the twelve tribes of Israel, the youngest of the twelve sons of Jacob. His mother Rachel died in giving birth to him, and in her last moments she named him *Benoni*, meaning 'son of my sorrow'. His father, however, did not wish him to bear such an ill-omened name, and renamed him *Benyamin* (Genesis 35: 16–18; 42: 4). This means either 'son of the right hand' or more likely 'son of the south' (Hebrew *yamin* can also mean 'south'), since Benjamin was the only child of Jacob born in Canaan and not in Mesopotamia to the north. Another tradition is that the second element of the name is a variant of the Hebrew word *yamim* which means 'days' but is used idiomatically to mean 'year' or 'years'. The name would then mean 'son of (my) old age' and refer to the fact that Benjamin was Jacob's youngest child. In the Middle Ages the name was often given to sons whose mothers had died in childbirth. Today it has no such unfortunate associations, but is still mainly a Jewish name. In the Scottish Highlands it has been used as an Anglicized form of the Gaelic name BEATHAN.

Variant: Jewish: **Binyamin** (the modern Hebrew form).
Cognate: Russian: **Venyamin**.
Short form: English: **Ben**.
Pet forms: English: **Benny, Bennie, Benji(e)**.

Benneit (m.) Scottish Gaelic form of BENEDICT.

Bennett (m.) English: the normal medieval form of BENEDICT, now sometimes used as an antiquarian revival, but more often it is a transferred use of the surname, which is derived from the medieval given name.

Variants: **Benett, Bennet, Benet**.

Benno (m.) German: from a medieval short form of various compound Germanic names containing the first element *bern* bear. By the later Middle Ages it came to be considered and used as a short form of BENEDICT. St Benno (1010–1106) was a bishop of Meissen, who preached to the Wends in what is now East Germany. He is the patron saint of Munich.

Benoît (m.) French form of BENEDICT.

Feminine form: **Benoîte**.

Benson (m.) English: transferred use of the surname, which originated in part as a patronymic from *Ben(n)*, a short form of BENEDICT, and in part as a local name from *Benson* (formerly *Bensington*) in Oxfordshire.

Bent (m.) Danish: simplified form of *Bendt* (see BENEDICT).

Bentley (m.) English: transferred use of the surname, which originated as a local name from any of the dozen or so places in England so called from Old English *beonet* bent grass + *lēah* wood or clearing.

Bento (m.) Portuguese form of BENEDICT.

Benvenuto (m.) Italian: from a medieval given name meaning 'welcome', composed of the elements *bene* well, good + *venuto*, past participle of *venire* to come, arrive. The Italian metalworker, sculptor, and writer Benvenuto Cellini (1500–71) is one of the most vital and engaging figures of the Renaissance, and the name may in some cases be bestowed in his honour, although parts of his autobiography are far from spiritually uplifting. The meaning of the name has remained transparent, however, and in the majority of cases it has no doubt been bestowed as an expression of the parents' joy in the birth of their child.

Benzion (m.) Jewish: modern Hebrew name meaning 'son of Zion' (cf. BATZION).

Beppe (m.) Italian: pet form of GIUSEPPE.
Variant: **Beppo**.

Ber (m.) Jewish: from the Yiddish vocabulary word *ber* bear (cf. modern German *Bär*), probably influenced by the early medieval European practice of giving animal names to people. It is often paired with Dov in order to provide a Hebrew name in certain rituals.

Berenice (f.) English and Italian: from the Greek personal name *Berenikē*, which seems to have originated in the royal house of Macedon. It is almost certainly a Macedonian dialectal form of the Greek name *Pherenīkē* 'victory bringer'. It was introduced to the Egyptian royal house by the widow of one of Alexander the Great's officers, who married Ptolemy I. It was also borne by an early Christian woman mentioned in Acts 25, for which reason it was felt to be acceptable by the Puritans in the 17th century. It has now fallen out of fashion again.

Variant: **Bernice** (the form used in the Authorized Version).
Cognates: Scottish Gaelic: **Bearnas**. French: **Bérénice**.

Berit (f.) Scandinavian: variant of BIRGIT.

Berkley (m.) English and Irish: variant of BARCLAY.

Bernabé (m.) Spanish form of BARNABAS.

Bernadette (f.) French: feminine diminutive of BERNARD. Its use in Britain and Ireland is almost exclusively confined to Roman Catholics;, who take it in honour of St Bernadette Soubirous (1844–79), a French peasant girl who had visions of the Virgin Mary and uncovered a spring near Lourdes where miraculous cures are still sought.

Variant: **Bernardette**.
Cognate: Italian: **Bernardetta**.

Bernard (m.) English and French: from a Germanic personal name composed of the elements *ber(n)* bear + *hard* hardy, brave, strong. This was the name of three famous medieval churchmen: St Bernard of Menthon (923–1008), founder of a hospice on each of the Alpine passes named after him; the monastic reformer St Bernard of Clairvaux (1090–1153); and the scholastic philosopher Bernard of Chartres. In England before the Norman Conquest a native Old English form of the name, *Beornheard*, existed, but it is the Norman form, derived through French from Continental Germanic, that became established as a conventional English given name.

Cognates: Gaelic: **Bearnard**. Italian, Spanish: **Bernardo**. Catalan: **Bernat**. German: **Bernhard(t), Bernd(t)**. Scandinavian: **Bernt**.
Pet form: English: **Bernie**.

Berneen (f.) Irish: diminutive from a shortening of BERNADETTE.

Bernice (f.) French and English: contracted form of BERENICE, now fairly popular in the English-speaking world.

Berry (f.) English: from the vocabulary word (Old English *berie*). This is one of the less common of the names referring to flowers, fruit, and vegetation introduced to the English-speaking world in the 20th century.

Bert (m.) English: short form of any of the various names containing this syllable as a first or second element, for example ALBERT and BERTRAM. See also BURT.

Pet form: **Bertie**.

Bertha (f.) German and English: Latinized version of a Germanic name, a short form of various compound women's personal names containing the element *berht* famous (cognate with Modern English *bright*). It probably existed in England before the Conquest, and was certainly reinforced by Norman use, but fell from currency. It was reintroduced into the English-speaking world from Germany in the 19th century, but has once again fallen out of fashion.

Cognates: French: **Berthe**. Polish, Czech: **Berta**.

Berthold (m.) German: from an old Germanic personal name composed of the elements *berht* bright, famous + *wald* ruler. The second element has been altered by association with German *hold* lovely, splendid.

Cognate: Low German: **Barthold**.

Bertil (m.) Scandinavian: from a Germanic pet form of various compound names containing the first element *berht* bright, famous, with the hypocoristic suffix *-il*. The Blessed Bertilo (d. *c*.878) was an abbot of St Benignus at Dijon in Burgundy, who was murdered by Norman raiders.

Variant: **Bertel**.

Bertram (m.) English: from a Norman French name composed of the Germanic elements *berht* bright, famous + *hramn* raven. Ravens were traditional symbols of wisdom in Germanic mythology; Odin was regularly accompanied by ravens called Hugin and Munin. See also **Bertrand**.

Cognate: Spanish: **Beltrán**.
Short form: English: **Bert**.
Pet form: English: **Bertie**.

Bertrand (m.) French and English: variant of **Bertram**, originating in the Middle Ages. In modern times it has been made famous by the English philosopher Bertrand Russell (1872–1970).

Berwyn (m.) Welsh: from an ancient Welsh personal name composed of the elements *barr* head + *(g)wyn* white, fair.

Beryl (f.) English: one of several women's names that are taken from gemstones and which came into fashion at the end of the 19th century. Beryl is a pale green stone (of which emerald is a variety). Other colours are also found. The word is from Greek, and is ultimately of Indian origin.

Bess (f.) English: short form of **Elizabeth**, in common use in the days of Queen Elizabeth I, who was known as 'Good Queen Bess'.

Pet forms: **Bessie**, **Bessy**.

Bet (f.) English: short form of **Elizabeth**.

Pet form: **Betty**.

Běta (f.) Czech: short form of **Alžběta**.

Pet forms: **Bětka**, **Bětuška**.

Beth (f.) English: short form of **Elizabeth**, not used before the 19th century, when it became popular in America and elsewhere after publication of Louisa M. Alcott's novel *Little Women* (1868), in which Beth March is one of the four sisters who are the central characters.

Pet form: Welsh: **Bethan** (now also popular elsewhere in the English-speaking world).

Bethany (f.) English: of New Testament origin. In the New Testament it is a placename, that of the village just outside Jerusalem where Jesus stayed during Holy Week, before going on to Jerusalem and crucifixion (Matthew 21: 17; Mark 11: 1; Luke 19: 29; John 12: 1). Its Hebrew name may mean 'house of figs' (*beth te'ena or beth te'enimf*). The given name is favoured mainly by Roman Catholics, being bestowed in honour of Mary of Bethany, sister of Martha and Lazarus. She is sometimes identified with Mary Magdalene (see **Madeleine**), although the grounds for this identification are very poor.

Betrys (f.) Welsh form of **Beatrice**.

Betsy (f.) English: pet form of **Elizabeth**, a cross between *Betty* (see **Bet**) and *Bessie* (see **Bess**).

Bettina (f.) 1. English: Latinate elaboration of **Betty**. 2. Italian: contracted elaboration of *Benedetta* (see **Benedict**).

Betty (f.) English: pet form of **Elizabeth**, dating from the 18th century.

Cognate: Scottish Gaelic: **Beitidh**.

Beulah (f.) Biblical: from the name applied to the land of Israel by the prophet Isaiah (Isaiah 62: 4). It means 'married' in Hebrew, but 'the land of Beulah' has sometimes been taken as a reference to heaven. It was taken up as a given name in England at the time of the Reformation and was popular among the Puritans in the 17th century. It is still occasionally used in the United States, largely among Blacks.

Beverley (f.) also (m.) English: transferred use of the surname, which comes from a place in Humberside named in Old English with the elements *beofor* beaver + *lēac* stream. The spelling **Beverly** is apparently used exclusively for girls, and is the usual form of the female name in America. It is not clear why it should have become a comparatively popular female name. In America, association with Beverly Hills in Los Angeles, the district where many film stars live, may have been an influencing factor.

Beynish (m.) Jewish (Yiddish): from the Czech given name *Beneš*, a form of **Benedict**. It was no doubt adopted by Jews on account of its auspicious meaning, 'blessed', and as a translation of **Baruch**.

Bhàtair (m.) Scottish Gaelic form of **Walter**.

Variant: **Bhaltair**.

Bhictoria (f.) Scottish Gaelic form of **Victoria**.

Biagio (m.) Italian form of **Blaise**.

Bianca (f.) Italian: from *bianca* white (i.e. 'pure', but cf. **Blanche**). The name was used by Shakespeare for characters in two of his plays that are supposed to take place in an Italian context: the mild-mannered sister of Katharina, the 'shrew' in *The Taming of the Shrew*, and a courtesan in *Othello*. Recently, it has been borne most famously by Bianca Jagger, the Nicaraguan fashion model, peace worker, and diplomat who was for a time married to the rock singer Mick Jagger.

Cognates: French: **Blanche**. Spanish: **Blanca**. Polish, Czech: **Blanka**.

Bice (f.) Italian: contracted pet form of **Beatrice**.

Biddy (f.) Irish and English: pet form of **Bride** or **Bridget**. It was formerly quite common, but is now seldom used outside Ireland, partly perhaps because the informal expression 'an old biddy' in English has come to denote a tiresome old woman.

Bigge (m.) Swedish: pet form of **Birger**.

Bill (m.) English: altered short form of **William**, not used before the 19th century. The reason for the change in the initial consonant is not clear, but it conforms to the pattern regularly found when English words beginning with *w*- are borrowed into Gaelic; the nickname 'King Billy' for William of Orange is an early example from Ireland which may have influenced English usage.

Pet forms: English: **Billy**, **Billie**. Gaelic: **Builidh**.

Billie (f., m.) English: variant of *Billy* (see **Bill**), now mainly used for girls, and sometimes bestowed at baptism as a feminine equivalent of **William**.

Bina (f.) **1**. Jewish (Yiddish): from the Yiddish vocabulary word *bin(e)* bee. This was used as a translation of the Hebrew name *Devorah* (see DEBORAH), meaning 'bee'. However, it was often taken as being from Hebrew *bina* understanding. **2**. Among Gentiles, it occasionally occurs as an aphetic short form of ALBINA.
Variants: **Binah**, **Bine**.
Pet form: **Binke**.

Binyamin (m.) Jewish: modern Hebrew form of BENJAMIN.

Bionda (f.) Italian: originally a nickname for a woman with fair hair, from the vocabulary word meaning 'blonde' (of Germanic origin).

Birger (m.) Swedish: of Old Norse origin, apparently an agent derivative of the verb *biarga* to help. Earlier forms of the name are *Birghir* and *Byrghir*. It has been in use from the Viking period to the present day, and it may in some cases have been chosen as a masculine form of BIRGIT.
Variant: **BÖRJE**.
Pet forms: **Bigge**, **Birre**.

Birgit (f.) Swedish (also used elsewhere in Scandinavia): borrowing of the Irish Gaelic name *Brighid* (see BRIDGET). This name owes its enormous popularity in Scandinavia, especially in Sweden, to St Birgitta (1304–73), patron saint of Sweden. She was a noblewoman who bore her husband eight children. After his death, she founded an order of nuns, the 'Bridgettines' or Order of the Most Holy Saviour. She also went to Rome, where she attempted to reform religious life.
Variants: **Berit**, **Britt**, **Brit(t)a**; **Birgitta** (now rare). Danish: **Birgitte**, **Birt(h)e**, **Gitte**.

Birre (m.) Swedish: pet form of BIRGER.

Björn (m.) Swedish: from an Old Norse byname meaning 'bear'. It is also in part a short form of compound names such as ARNBJÖRN and TORBJÖRN.
Cognates: Norwegian: **Bjørn**, **Bjarne**.

Blahoslav (m.) Czech: from an old Slavonic personal name composed of the elements *blago* blessed + *slav* glory.
Feminine form: **Blahoslava**.
Pet forms: **Blahoš(ek)** (m.); **Blahuše** (f.).

Blair (m., f.) Scottish: transferred use of the surname, a local name from various places named with Gaelic *blàr* plain, field. In North America, it is now widely used as a female given name.

Blaise (m.) French: the name (Latin *Blasius*, probably from *blaesus* lisping) of a saint popular throughout Europe in the Middle Ages but almost forgotten today. He was a bishop of Sebaste in Armenia, and was martyred in the early years of the 4th century; these bare facts were elaborated in a great number of legends that reached Europe from the East at the time of the Crusades. The name is rare in the English–speaking world; its modern popularity in France is partly due to the 17th-century French philosopher and mathematician Blaise Pascal.
Cognates: Italian: **Biag(g)io**. Spanish: **Blas**. Portuguese: **Bras**, **Braz**. Catalan: **Blai**. Provençal: **Blasi**. Polish: **Blazej**. Czech: **Blažej**. Russian: **Vlas(i)**. Hungarian: **Balázs**.

Blake (m.) English: transferred use of the surname, which has two quite distinct etymologies. It is both from Old English *blæc* black and from Old English *blāc* pale, white; it was thus originally a nickname given to someone with hair or skin that was either remarkably dark or remarkably light. It is now quite popular as a male given name.

Blanche (f.) French and English: originally a nickname for a blonde, from *blanche*, feminine of Old French *blanc* white (of Germanic origin). It came to be associated with the notion of whiteness as indicating purity, and was introduced into England as a given name by the Normans. A pale complexion combined with light hair has long been an ideal of beauty in Europe (cf. modern English *fair*, which at first meant 'beautiful' and then, from the 16th century, 'light in colouring').
Cognates: Italian: BIANCA. Spanish: **Blanca**. Polish, Czech: **Blanka**.

Bláthnaid (f.) Irish Gaelic: originally an affectionate nickname representing a diminutive form of *bláth* flower.
Variants: **Bláithín**, **Bláthnait**.

Bleddyn (m.) Welsh: ancient byname derived from the vocabulary element *blaidd* wolf + the diminutive suffix *-yn*. *Blaidd* was often used in medieval Welsh as a term for a hero.

Blodwedd (f.) Welsh: name borne by a character in the *Mabinogi*. She was conjured up out of flowers as a bride for Lleu Llaw Gyffes, and was originally called *Blodeuedd*, a derivative of *blawd* flowers. After she had treacherously had her husband killed she was transformed into an owl, and her name was changed to *Blodeuwedd* 'flower face', an allusion to the markings round the eyes of the owl.

Blodwen (f.) Welsh: traditional name composed of the elements *blawd* flowers + *(g)wen* white, feminine of *gwyn* white, fair, blessed, holy. The name was a relatively common one in the Middle Ages and has recently been revived.

Blossom (f.) English: 19th-century coinage, from the vocabulary word for flowers on a fruit–tree or ornamental tree (Old English *blōstm*), used as an affectionate pet name for a young girl.

Blume (f.) Jewish: Yiddish name, originally an affectionate nickname meaning 'flower' (from Middle High German *bluome*).
Pet form: **Blumke**.

Bo (m.) Swedish and Danish: originally a byname for a householder, from a derivative of Old Norse *búa* to live, dwell, have a household.
Pet form: Swedish: **Bosse**.

Boaz (m.) Biblical: Hebrew name of uncertain origin, perhaps meaning 'swiftness'. In the Bible it is borne by a distant kinsman of Ruth who treats her generously and eventually marries her. The given name was in occasional use in England in the 17th and 18th centuries but is now very rare. It is sometimes used in Jewish families.
Variant: **Boas**.

Bob (m.) English: altered short form of ROBERT, a later development than the common medieval forms *Hob*, *Dob*, and *Nob*, all of which, unlike *Bob*, have given rise to English surnames.
Pet forms: **Bobby**, BOBBIE.

Boba (m.) Russian: pet form of BORIS.

Bobbie (f., m.) English: variant of *Bobby* (see BOB), now mainly used as a female name, in part as a pet form of *Roberta* (see ROBERT).

Bodek (m.) Polish: pet form of BOGDAN.

Bodil (f.) Scandinavian (originally Danish): from an Old Norse female personal name composed of the elements *bót* bettering, remedy, compensation + *hildr* battle.
Variants: **Botilda** (Latinized). Swedish: **Bothild**.

Bodo (m.) German: from an old Germanic personal name, originally a short form of various compound names containing the first element *bod* tidings, messenger.

Bódog (m.) Hungarian: originally a nickname meaning 'fortunate', used as a loan translation of FELIX.

Bodzio (m.) Polish: pet form of BOGDAN.

Bogdan (m.) Polish and Ukrainian: from an old Slavonic personal name composed of the elements *bog* god + *dan* gift. It is therefore semantically equivalent to THEODORE and DOROTHY as well as to MATTHEW, NATHANIEL, and JONATHAN.
Cognate: Czech: **Bohdan**.
Pet forms: Polish: **Bodek**, **Bodzio**.
Feminine forms: Polish: **Bogdana**, **Bogna**, **Dana**. Czech: **Bohdana**. Ukrainian: **Bohdanna**. Yiddish: **Badane**.

Boguchwał (m.) Polish: vernacular name originating in the Middle Ages, composed of the elements *Bóg* God + *chwała* praise (cf. GOTTLOB). This is a specifically Christian formation, modelled on already existing names of pagan origin such as BOGUMIERZ.
Variant: **Bogufal**. See also CHWALIBÓG.

Bogumierz (m.) Polish: from an old Slavonic personal name composed of the elements *bog* god + *meri* great, famous (see CASIMIR).
Cognates: Czech: **Bohumír**. Ukrainian: **Bohomir**.

Bogumił (m.) Polish: from an old Slavonic personal name composed of the elements *bog* god + *mil* grace, favour. St Bogumił (d. 1182) was an archbishop of Gniezno (Gnesen) who founded the abbey of Koronowa. His cult was not officially approved by the Church until 1925, but it flourished nevertheless during seven centuries of turbulence and repression, sometimes serving as a symbol of Polish national and spiritual aspirations.
Cognate: Czech: **Bohumil**.
Feminine forms: Polish: **Bogumiła**. Czech: **Bohumila**.

Bogusław (m.) Polish: from an old Slavonic personal name composed of the elements *bog* god + *slav* glory.
Cognate: Czech: **Bohuslav**.
Pet forms: Polish: **Bogusz**, **Bohusz**.
Feminine forms: Polish: **Bogusława**. Czech: **Bohuslava**.

Bojan (m.) Czech: from an old Slavonic personal name, a derivative of the element *boi* battle.
Feminine form: **Bojana**.
Pet forms: **Bojánek**, **Bojek**, **Bojík** (m.); **Bojka** (f.).

Boje (m.) Frisian spelling of BOYE.

Bolesław (m.) Polish: from an old Slavonic personal name composed of the elements *bole* large + *slav* glory.
Cognate: Czech: **Boleslav**.
Feminine forms: Polish: **Bolesawa**. Czech: **Boleslava**.
Pet forms: Czech: **Bolek** (m.); **Bolen(k)a** (f.).

Bona (f.) Italian and Polish: from the feminine form of the Late Latin name *Bonus* 'good'. This was a traditional hereditary name in the royal house of Savoy, and in the 16th century it was taken to Poland by Bona Sforza, who married King Sigismund I of Poland. She was noted as a patron of the arts, and was instrumental in bringing the Renaissance to Poland. The name was also borne by a Pisan saint (d. 1207), and also by the first abbess of Rheims (d. c.680). In the latter case, however, an alteration by folk etymology from the Germanic name *Bova* may be in question.

Bonaventura (m.) Italian: common medieval vernacular given name, composed of the elements *b(u)ona* good + *ventura* luck, fortune. It was borne by a follower of St Francis of Assisi, who was so called by the saint in exchange for his baptismal name *Giovanni*.

Bonifacio (m.) Italian, Spanish, and Portuguese: from the Late Latin name *Bonifatius*, derived from the elements *bonum* good + *fatum* fate, bestowed on a child as a hopeful omen. In the early Middle Ages the name came to be alternatively written as *Bonifacius* (with the same pronunciation), and reanalysed as a compound of *bonum* + *facere* to do, i.e. 'doer of good deeds'. The name was borne by several early saints, including a 7th-century pope and an Anglo-Saxon missionary who evangelized extensively in Germany in the 8th century. The latter was originally named *Winfrid*, but took the name *Bonifacius* on entering holy orders.
Cognate: German: **Bonifaz**.

Bonita (f.) English: apparently coined in America in the 1940s, probably from the feminine form of Spanish *bonito* pretty, although this is not used as a given name in Spanish-speaking countries. *Bonita* looks like the feminine form of a medieval Latin male name, *Bonītus* (from *bonus* good), which was borne by an Italian saint of the 6th century and a Provençal saint of the 7th. However, the feminine form is not found in medieval records, and this is an unlikely source of the name.

Bonnie (f.) English (esp. U.S.): originally an affectionate nickname from the Scottish word *bonnie* fine, attractive, pretty. However, it is not—or at any rate has not been until recently—used as a given name in Scotland. Its popularity may be attributed to the character of Scarlett O' Hara's infant daughter Bonnie in the film *Gone With the Wind* (1939), based on Margaret Mitchell's novel of the same name. (Bonnie's name was really Eugenie Victoria, but she had 'eyes as blue as the bonnie blue flag'.) A famous American bearer was Bonnie Parker, accomplice of the bank robber Clyde Barrow; their life together was the subject of the film *Bonnie and Clyde* (1967). The name enjoyed a vogue in the second part of the 20th century, and has also been used as a pet form of BONITA.

Bora (f.) Czech: short form of *Barbora* (see BARBARA), used as a pet name.

Borbála (f.) Hungarian form of BARBARA.

Borghild (f.) Scandinavian (mainly Norwegian): from an Old Norse female personal name composed of the elements *borg* fortification + *hildr* battle. The name is attested from the Viking period, but modern use appears to be the result of a 19th-century revival.

Boris (m.) Russian: apparently in origin not of Slavonic etymology, but from the Tartar nickname *Bogoris* 'small'. It was later, however, taken to be a shortened form of **Borislav**, composed of the elements *bor* battle + *slav* glory. The name was borne in the 9th century by a ruler of Bulgaria who converted his kingdom to Christianity and sheltered disciples of Sts Cyril and Methodius when they were expelled from Moravia. The name was also borne by a 10th-century Russian saint, son of Prince Vladimir of Kiev and brother of St Gleb. It is as a result of his influence that *Boris* is one of the very few non-classical names that the Orthodox Church allows to be taken as baptismal names (although the saint himself bore the baptismal name *Romanus*).

Pet forms: **Borya**, **Boba**.

Bořivoj (m.) Czech: from an old Slavonic personal name composed of the elements *borit* to fight + *voi* warrior.

Pet forms: **Boĭra**, **Bořek**, **Bořik**.

Börje (m.) Swedish: variant of BIRGER, first found in the 14th century in the forms *Byrghe* and *Byrie*.

Cognates: Danish: **Børge**. Norwegian: **Børge**, **Børre**.

Börries (m.) Low German: from the Late Latin personal name *Liborius*. This is of uncertain origin, perhaps an altered form of *Liberius* (see LIBOR), or possibly of Celtic origin. St Liborius was a 4th-century bishop of Le Mans, whose relics were taken to Paderborn in the 9th century.

Borya (m.) Russian: pet form of BORIS.

Bosse (m.) Swedish: pet form of Bo.

Bothild (f.) Swedish form of BODIL.

Variant: **Botilda** (Latinized).

Boye (m.) Dutch: of uncertain origin, found in this form from the early Middle Ages onwards. It may derive from the Germanic personal name *Bodo* (a short form of various compound names containing the element *bod* messenger, tidings), with the loss of *d* between vowels typical of Dutch. Alternatively, it may have been originally a byname cognate with modern English *boy* lad, young man.

Cognate: Frisian: **Boje**.

Bożydar (m.) Polish: from a medieval personal name composed of the vocabulary elements *boży* divine + *dar* gift.

Cognate: Czech: **Božidar**.

Feminine form: Czech: **Božidara**.

Pet forms: Czech: **Boža** (m., f.); **Božek** (m.); **Božka**, **Božena** (f.)

Brad (m.) English (mainly U.S.): short form of BRADFORD and BRADLEY.

Bradford (m.) English (mainly U.S.): transferred use of the surname, in origin a local name from any of the numerous places in England so called from Old English *brād* broad + *ford* ford. The surname was borne most famously by William Bradford (1590–1657), leader of the Pilgrim Fathers from 1621 and governor of Plymouth Colony for some 30 years. It was also the name of another William Bradford (1722–91), a printer who played an important part in the American Revolution.

Bradley (m.) English (mainly U.S.): transferred use of the surname, in origin a local name from any of the numerous places in England so called from Old English *brād* broad + *lēk* wood or clearing. The most famous American bearer of this surname was General Omar N. Bradley (1893–1981).

Brady (m.) Irish and English (mainly U.S.): transferred use of the surname, which is of Irish origin, from Gaelic *O Brádaigh* 'descendant of Brádach'. *Brádach* is an old Irish byname, the meaning of which is not clear. It is unlikely to be connected with Gaelic *bradach* thieving, dishonest, which has a short first vowel; it may represent a contracted form of *Brághadach* 'large-chested', a derivative of *brágha* chest, throat.

Brandon (m.) English (mainly U.S.): transferred use of the surname, in origin a local name from any of various places so called, most of which get their name from Old English *brōm* broom, *gorse* + *dūn* hill. In 1982 this was the seventh commonest male given name among Blacks in the United States, and the twenty-third commonest among Whites. In part it may be regarded as an altered form of BRENDAN. There has probably also been some influence from the surname of the Italian American actor Marlon Brando (b. 1924).

Branislav (m.) Czech: variant of *Bronislav* (see BRONISLAW).

Feminine form: **Branislava**.

Pet forms: **Branek** (m.); **Braňa**, **Branka** (f.).

Branton (m.) English (mainly U.S.): variant of BRANDON or transferred use of the surname *Branton*. This is a local name from places in Northumbria and West Yorkshire so named from Old English *brōm* broom, gorse + *tūn* enclosure, settlement.

Branwen (f.) Welsh: apparently composed of the elements *brân* raven + *(g)wen*, feminine of *gwyn* white, fair, blessed, holy. Alternatively, it is possible that it is a variant of BRONWEN. The story of Branwen, daughter of Llŷr, forms the second chapter or 'branch' of the *Mabinogi*: it tells of her beauty and of the conflict on her account between her brother Bran, King of the 'Island of the Mighty' (Britain), and her husband Matholwch, King of Ireland.

Bras (m.) Portuguese form of *Blaise*.

Variant: **Braz**.

Bratislav (m.) Czech: from an old Slavonic personal name composed of the elements *brat* brother + *slav* glory.

Feminine form: **Bratislava**.

Bratumił (m.) Polish: from an old Slavonic personal name composed of the elements *brat* brother + *mil* grace, favour.

Brayne (f.) Jewish: Yiddish name, a back-formation from **Brayndel**, itself an affectionate diminutive form of Yiddish *broyn* brown (cf. modern German *braun*).

Breeda (f.) Irish: Anglicized form (with the typical feminine name-suffix -*a*) of Gaelic *Bríd*; see BRIDE.

Brenda (f.) Scottish, Irish, and (in the 20th century) English: of uncertain derivation. It seems to be of Scandinavian rather than Celtic origin (in spite of its similarity to BRENDAN), and may be a short form of various compound names containing the element *brand* (flaming) sword.

Brendan (m.) Irish: from the old Irish personal name *Bréanainn*, derived from a Celtic element meaning 'prince'. This was the name of two 6th-century Irish saints, Brendan the Voyager and Brendan of Birr. According to legend, the former was the first European to set foot on North American soil. The modern Irish Gaelic form **Breandán** and the Anglicized *Brendan* are based on the medieval Latin form *Bredanus*.

Brent (m.) English: transferred use of the surname, which is derived from any of several places in Devon and Somerset which are on or near prominent hills, and seem therefore to have been named with a Celtic or Old English term for a hill. The given name has enjoyed considerable popularity in Britain in the 1970s and 1980s, and may have been influenced by BRETT, which has experienced a similar vogue, starting somewhat earlier.

Břetislav (m.) Czech: from an old Slavonic personal name composed of the elements *brech* noise, din (of battle) + *slav* glory.

Feminine form: **Břetislava**.

Pet forms: **Břetík** (m.); **Břeťka**, **Bretička** (f.).

Brett (m.) English: transferred use of the surname, which originated in the Middle Ages as an ethnic name for one of the Bretons who arrived in England in the wake of the Norman Conquest; it is most common in East Anglia, where Breton settlement was particularly concentrated. As a given name, it has enjoyed something of a vogue in the latter half of the 20th century.

Brewster (m.) English (mainly U.S.): transferred use of the surname, in origin an occupational name for a brewer, Middle English *brēowestre*. The *-estre* sufix was originally feminine, but by the Middle English period this grammatical distinction had been lost (cf. BAXTER).

Brian (m.) Irish and English: perhaps from an Old Celtic word meaning 'high' or 'noble'. The name has been perennially popular in Ireland, largely on account of the fame of Brian Boru (Gaelic *Brian Bóroimhe*), a 10th-century high king of Ireland. In the Middle Ages it was relatively common in East Anglia, to which it was introduced by Breton settlers, and in north-west England, to which it was introduced by Scandinavians from Ireland. In Gaelic Scotland it was at first borne exclusively by members of certain professional families of Irish origin.

Variant: **Bryan**.

Brianne (f.) English: recent coinage to create a female equivalent of BRIAN.

Briartach (m.) Irish Gaelic: variant form of MUIRIARTACH, common particularly in Connacht.

Brice (m.) French: from the name of a 5th-century saint who was a disciple and successor of St Martin of Tours. His name is found in the Latinized forms *Bri(c)tius* or *Bricius* and is probably of Gaulish origin, possibly derived from an element meaning 'speckled' (Welsh *brych*).

Cognate: Italian: BRIZIO.

Bride (f.) Irish: Anglicized form of **Bríd**, the modern Gaelic contracted form of *Brighid* (see BRIDGET).

Variant: **Breeda**.

Pet forms: **Bridie** (English); **Brídín** (Gaelic).

Bridget (f.) Irish, Scottish, and English: Anglicized form of the Gaelic name **Brighid**. This was the name of an ancient Celtic goddess, of uncertain origin; it is unlikely to be connected with Gaelic *brigh* strength, force, since this word has a long vowel. St Brigid of Kildare (*c*.450–*c*.525) is one of the patron saints of Ireland. Very few facts are known about her life. She founded a religious house for women at Kildare, and is said to be have been buried at Downpatrick, where St Patrick and St Columba were also buried. Many of the stories of miracles told about St Brigid seem to be Christianized versions of pagan legends concerning the goddess.

Variants: **Brigit**, BRIDE.

Cognates: Welsh: **Ffraid**. German, French: **Brigitte**. Italian: **Brigida**. Scandinavian: BIRGIT. Finnish: **Pirjo**, **Pirkko**.

Pet form: Irish, English: BIDDY.

Brigham (m.) English (mainly U.S.): name adopted in honour of the early Mormon leader, Brigham Young (1801–77). It was originally a surname, a local name from places in Cumbria and North Yorkshire so called from Old English *brycg* bridge + *hām* homestead, settlement. It is not known why the Mormon leader received this given name; he was the son of John and Abigail Young of Whitingham, Vermont.

Briony (f.) English: variant spelling of BRYONY.

Britt (f.) Swedish: contracted form of BIRGIT, made famous in the English-speaking world by the actress Britt Ekland (b. 1942; her surname was originally Eklund).

Variants: **Britta**, **Brita**.

Brizio (m.) Italian: 1. From *Brictius*, an ancient name probably of Gaulish origin (see BRICE). St Brizio (d. *c*.312) was bishop of Martola near Spoleto in Umbria, who suffered in the persecutions instituted by the Emperor Diocletian. His cult is still popular in the region. 2. Short form of *Fabrizio* (see FABRICE).

Broder (m.) Swedish, Danish, and Frisian: from the Old Norse vocabulary word *bróðir* brother. This seems to have been bestowed on younger sons.

Variant: Swedish: **Bror**.

Pet form: Swedish: **Brolle**.

Brogio (m.) Italian: short form of *Ambrogio* (see AMBROSE).

Bronisław (m.) Polish: from an old Slavonic personal name composed of the elements *bron* armour, protection + *slav* glory.

Cognates: Czech: **Bronislav**, **Branislav**.

Pet form: Czech: **Branek**.

Bronisława (f.) Polish: feminine form of BRONISŁAW. The Blessed Bronislava (d. 1259) was a cousin of St Hyacinth of Poland (see JACEK).

Cognates: Czech: **Bronislava**, **Branislava**.

Pet forms: Czech: **Broňa**, **Braňa**, **Bron(ič)ka**, **Branka**.

Bronwen (f.) Welsh: composed of the elements *bron* breast + *(g)wen*, feminine of *gwyn* white, fair, blessed, holy.

Bronya (f.) Polish: pet form of various old Slavonic compound names containing the element *bron* armour, protection (e.g. BRONISŁAWA).

Bror (m.) Swedish: contracted variant of BRODER.

Pet form: **Brolle**.

Brož (m.) Czech: short form of *Ambroz* (see AMBROSE).

Pet form: **Brožek**.

Bruce (m.) Scottish and English: transferred use of the Scottish surname, now used as a given name throughout the English-speaking world, but in recent years particularly popular in Australia. The surname was originally a Norman baronial name, but a precise identification of the place from which it was derived has not been made (there are a large number of possible candidates). The Bruces were an influential Norman family in Scottish affairs in the early Middle Ages; its most famous member was Robert 'the Bruce' (1274–1329), who is said to have drawn inspiration after his defeat at Methven from the perseverance of a spider in repeatedly climbing up again after being knocked down. He ruled Scotland as King Robert I from 1306 to 1329.

Brunella (f.) Latinate feminine formation from BRUNO. Its formation may have been influenced by the existence of the name PRUNELLA.

Brunhilde (f.) German: from an old Germanic female personal name composed of the elements *brun* armour, protection + *hild* battle. In so far as it is found at all in modern use, it is a literary name. In Germanic legend, Brunhilde is a warrior queen, wife of Gunther, who plays a central role in the *Nibelungenlied*. She appears as *Brynhild* in the Icelandic *Volsungasaga*, where she is the chief of the Valkyries, a group of supernatural warrior maidens who collect the slain after a battle and carry them off to Valhalla. She is also a central figure in Richard Wagner's opera cycle *The Ring of the Nibelungs*. Wagner's Brünnhilde is a Valkyrie, daughter of Wotan, chief of the gods, who defies her father to help the lovers Siegmund and Sieglinde. As a punishment she is immolated on a mountain top, surrounded by a wall of fire. Her rescue by Siegfried, the son of Siegmund and Sieglinde, has a tragic outcome, leading to universal destruction. The character of Brunhilde may have a historical basis in the person of Brunhilda (?534–613), a powerful Frankish queen.

Variants: **Brunhild**, **Brünhilde**, **Brünnhilde**.
Cognate: Icelandic: **Brynhildur**.

Bruno (m.) German and English: from the Germanic vocabulary element *brun* brown. This name was in use in many of the ruling families of Germany during the Middle Ages, being borne by a 10th-century saint, son of the Emperor Henry the Fowler, and also by the Saxon duke who gave his name to Brunswick (German *Braunschweig*, i.e. 'Bruno's settlement') Its use in the English-speaking world, which dates from the end of the 19th century, may have been partly influenced by Lewis Carroll's *Sylvie and Bruno* (1889), but more probably it was first used by settlers of German ancestry in the United States.

Bryan (m.) English: variant of BRIAN, influenced by the usual spelling of the associated surname.

Bryant (m.) English: transferred use of the surname, which is derived from the given name BRIAN. The final -*t* seems to have arisen as a result of association with names such as CONSTANT.

Brychan (m.) Welsh: from an Old Welsh byname meaning 'speckled'. A traditional Welsh figure of this name was the father of ten sons and twenty-four daughters (more in one Cornish list), many of whom came to be venerated as saints.

Bryn (m.) Welsh: 20th-century coinage from the Welsh topographical term *bryn* hill, in part as a short form of BRYNMOR.

Brynmor (m.) Welsh: 20th-century coinage from the name of a place in Gwynedd, composed of the Welsh elements *bryn* hill + *mawr* large.

Bryony (f.) English: from the name of the plant (Greek *bryonia*). This is one of a more recently coined (20th-century) batch of names taken from vocabulary words denoting flowers.
Variant: **Briony**.

Buck (m.) English (U.S.): from the English nickname *Buck*, denoting a robust and spirited young man, from the vocabulary word for a male deer (Old English *bucc*) or a he-goat (Old English *bucca*).

Bud (m.) English (U.S.): originally a short form of the nickname or vocabulary word *buddy* friend, which may be an al-

teration, perhaps a nursery form, of *brother* or else derive from the Scottish Gaelic vocative case *a bhodaich* 'old man!'. It is now occasionally used as a given name in its own right, especially in America.

Budzisław (m.) Polish: from an old Slavonic personal name composed of the elements *budit* to arouse, stir + *slav* glory.
Cognate: Czech: **Budislav**.
Pet forms: Polish: **Budzyk**, **Budzisz**. Czech: **Budĕk**.

Buffy (f.) English: pet form of ELIZABETH, based on a child's unsuccessful attempts to pronounce the name.

Bunem (m.) Jewish: Yiddish name derived ultimately from the French phrase *bon homme* 'good man' bestowed as an affectionate nickname.

Bunty (f.) English: nickname and occasional baptismal name, relatively popular in the early 20th century, but of uncertain derivation. It seems most likely that it derives from what was originally a dialectal pet name for a lamb, from the verb to *bunt* to butt gently.

Burgess (m.) English: transferred use of the surname, which is derived from the Old French word *burgeis* freeman of a borough (a derivative of *burg* town, of Germanic origin).

Burkhard (m.) German: from an old Germanic personal name composed of the elements *burg* protection + *hard* hardy, brave, strong. St Burkhard (d. *c*.754) was a companion of St Boniface who became the first bishop of Würzburg and founded several Benedictine monasteries in the area. Like Boniface, he seems to have been an Anglo-Saxon by birth, perhaps originally bearing the cognate Old English personal name *Burgheard*.

Burt (m.) English (U.S.): of various origins. In the case of the film actor Burt Lancaster (b. 1913) it is a short form of BURTON, but it has also been used as a variant spelling of BERT. The pianist and composer Burt Bacharach (b. 1928) was the son of a Bert Bacharach, and his given name is presumably simply a variation of his father's.

Burton (m.) English: transferred use of the surname, which is a local name from any of the numerous places in England so called. In most cases the placename is derived from Old English *burh* fortress, fortified place + *tūn* enclosure, settlement.

Buster (m.) English (U.S.): originally a nickname from the slang term of address *buster*, which is apparently a derivative of the verb *bust* to break, smash (an altered form of *burst*). It was the nickname of the silent movie comedian Joseph Francis 'Buster' Keaton (1895–1966).

Byron (m.) English: transferred use of the surname, first bestowed as a given name in honour of the poet Lord Byron (George Gordon, 6th Baron Byron, 1784–1824). The surname derives from the Old English phrase *æt ðæm bȳrum* 'at the byres or cattlesheds', and was given to someone who lived there because it was his job to look after cattle.

C

Cäcilie (f.) German form of CECILY.

Cade (m.) English: transferred use of the surname, which originated as a nickname from a vocabulary element denoting something round and lumpish. It is one of several given names that owe their origin to their use for a character in Margaret Mitchell's novel *Gone with the Wind* (1936).

Cadell (m.) Welsh: from an Old Welsh personal name composed of the elements *cad* battle + the diminutive suffix *-ell*.

Cadogan (m.) Welsh, Irish, and English: Anglicized form of the Old Welsh personal name **Cadwgan** or **Cadwgawn**, a compound of the elements *cad* battle + *gwogawn* glory, distinction, honour. The name was borne by several Welsh rulers in the early Middle Ages, and is mentioned as the name of two characters in the *Mabinogi*. It has been revived to some extent in the 19th and 20th centuries, probably under the influence of the surname derived from it, which was taken to Ireland in the 17th century.

Cadwalader (m.) Welsh: Anglicized form of **Cadwaladr**, an ancient Celtic name composed of the elements *cad* battle + *gwaladr* leader and commonly given to the sons of kings and princes. St Cadwalader (d. *c*.682) was a British chieftain who died maintaining a stronghold against the pagan Saxon invaders.

Caerwyn (m.) Welsh: altered form of CARWYN, influenced by the many Welsh placenames with the first element *caer* fort.

Caesar (m.) English (esp. U.S.): Anglicized form of Italian *Cesare* or French CÉSAR, or a direct adoption of the Roman imperial family name *Caesar*; cf. DUKE, EARL, KING, and PRINCE.

Caetano (m.) Portuguese form of GAETANO.

Cahal (m.) Irish: Anglicized spelling of CATHAL.

Cahir (m.) Irish: Anglicized spelling of CATHAOIR.

Cainneach (m.) Irish Gaelic form of COINNEACH, generally Anglicized as KENNY. See also CANICE.

Cairistìona (f.) Scottish Gaelic form of CHRISTINE.
Variant: **Cairistine**.
Pet form: **Stineag**.

Cáit (f.) Irish Gaelic form of KATE or short form of CAITRÍONA.

Caitir (f.) Scottish: name derived from Gaelic *Caitriona* (see CATRIONA), by mis-analysis as *Caitir Fhiona*, the second element taken as meaning 'of wine'. This name has sometimes been Anglicized as CLARISSA.

Caitlín (f.) Irish Gaelic form of KATHERINE, derived from the Old French form *Catheline*.

Caitrín (f.) Irish Gaelic form of KATHERINE, derived from the Old French form *Catherine*.

Caitríona (f.) Irish Gaelic: the most usual form of KATHERINE.
Short forms: **Cáit**, **Tríona**. See also RÍONA.

Cajetan (m.) English: Roman Catholic religious name; see GAETANO

Caleb (m.) Biblical: name borne by an early Israelite, one of only two of those who set out with Moses from Egypt to live long enough to enter the promised land (Numbers 26: 65). The name, which is related to the the word for 'dog' in Hebrew, is said in some traditions to symbolize his rabid devotion to God. It was popular among the Puritans and was introduced by them to America, where it is still in use.

Callisto (m.) Italian: from the Late Latin personal name *Callistus*, which is apparently adopted from the Greek vocabulary word *kallistos*, superlative of *kalos* fair, good. The forms *Callixtus* and *Calixtus* are also found in Late Latin, but seem to be later developments. The name was borne by several early saints, including a 3rd-century pope and 6th-century bishop of Todi in central Italy.
Cognate: Spanish: **Calisto**.

Calogero (m.) Italian: characteristically southern Italian and especially Sicilian name. St Calogerus the Anchorite (d. *c*.486) lived as a hermit near Grigenti in Sicily, and is the subject of a local cult. The name is composed of the Greek elements *kalos* fair, good + *gēras* old age; in the Late Greek period it was used as a title of respect for anchorites and monks.

Calum (m.) Scottish Gaelic form of the Late Latin personal name *Columba* 'dove'. This was popular among early Christians because the dove was a symbol of gentleness, purity, peace, and the Holy Spirit. St Columba (see also COLM) was one of the most influential of all the early Celtic saints. He was born in Donegal in 521 into a noble family, and was trained for the priesthood from early in life. He founded monastery schools at Durrow, Derry, and Kells, and then, in 563, sailed with twelve companions to Scotland, to convert the people there to Christianity. He established a monastery on the island of Iona, and from there converted the Pictish and Irish inhabitants of Scotland. He died in 597 and was buried at Downpatrick, along with St Patrick and St Brighid. See also COLIN (2).
Pet forms: **Cally**, **Caley**.
Feminine forms: **Calumina**, **Calaminag**.

Calvin (m.) English (esp. U.S.): from the French surname, used as a given name among Nonconformists in honour of the French Protestant theologian Jean Calvin (1509–64). It has enjoyed a recent vogue as a given name. The surname meant originally 'little bald one', from a diminutive of *calve*, a Norman and Picard form of French *chauve* bald. (The theologian was born in Noyon, Picardy.)
Short form: **Cal**.

Cameron (m.) Scottish: transferred use of the surname, which is borne by one of the great Highland clans. Their name is derived from an ancestor with a 'crooked nose' (Gaelic *cam shron*). There were also Camerons in the Lowlands, apparently the result of an assimilation to this name of a Norman baronial name derived from *Cambernon* in Normandy.

Camilla (f.) English and Italian: feminine form of the old Roman family name *Camillus*, of obscure and presumably non-Roman origin. According to tradition, recorded by the Roman poet Virgil, Camilla was the name of a warrior maiden, Queen of the Volcians, who fought in the army of Aeneas (*Aeneid* 7. 803–17). The masculine form is much less common, except in Italy, where it is bestowed in honour of St Camillo de Lellis (1550–1614), who founded the nursing order of the Ministers of the Sick.

Cognates: French: **Camille** (also (m.)). Polish, Czech: **Kamila**.
Short form: English: **Milla**.
Pet form: English: **Millie**.
Masculine forms: Italian: **Camillo**. Spanish, Portuguese: **Camilo**.
French: **Camille** (also (f.)). Polish, Czech: **Kamil**.

Campbell (m.) Scottish: transferred use of the surname, borne by one of the great Highland clans, whose head is the Duke of Argyll. The name is derived from an ancestor with a 'crooked mouth' (Gaelic *cam beul*).

Candace (f.) English: from the hereditary name of a long line of queens of Ethiopia. One of them is mentioned in the Bible, when the apostle Philip baptizes 'a man of Ethiopia, an eunuch of great authority under Candace queen of the Ethiopians, who had the charge of all her treasure' (Acts 8: 27). This name is now much less common than its presumed derivative CANDICE.

Candelaria (f.) Spanish: religious name referring to the feast of Candlemas (a derivative of *candela* candle). This festival, on 2 February, commemorates the Purification of the Virgin Mary (cf. PURIFICACIÓN) and the Presentation of Christ in the temple (cf. PRESENTACIÓN).

Pet form: **Candela**.

Candice (f.) English: apparently a respelling of CANDACE. The spelling may have been influenced by CLARICE; or more probably by a folk etymology deriving the name from Late Latin *canditia* whiteness.

Candida (f.) English: from Late Latin, meaning 'white'. The colour was associated in Christian imagery with purity and salvation (cf. Revelation 3: 4 'thou hast a few names even in Sardis which have not defiled their garments; and they shall walk with me in white: for they are worthy'). This was the name of several early saints, including a woman supposedly cured by St Peter himself.

Candy (f.) English (esp. U.S.): from an affectionate nickname derived from the vocabulary word *candy* confectionery. The word *candy* is from French *sucre candi* 'candied sugar', i.e. sugar boiled to make a crystalline sweet. The French word is derived from Arabic *qandi*, which is in turn of Indian origin. *Candy* could, in theory, also be a short form of CANDICE and of CANDIDA, but there is no evidence that this is so.

Canice (m.) Irish: from the Latinized form, *Canisius*, of the Old Irish personal name *Cainnech* (modern Gaelic **Cainneach**; cf. COINNEACH). It seems to have been originally a byname meaning 'handsome, fair one', and was borne by a large number of early saints. The most important of these is St Cainnech of Aghaboe, patron of Kilkenny. See also KENNY.

Caoilte (m.) Irish Gaelic: name of uncertain derivation, borne by the legendary hero Caoilte Mac Rónáin, famous as

a swift runner. It has been revived as a given name in the 20th century.

Caoimhe (f.) Irish Gaelic: modern name representing the abstract noun derived from the vocabulary word *caomh* kind, gentle (earlier 'beloved' or 'beautiful'; cf. KEVIN).

Cara (f.) English: 20th-century coinage, from the Italian term of endearment *cara* 'beloved' or the Irish Gaelic vocabulary word *cara* friend. This is not normally used as a given name in Italy, where such innovations are held in check by the hostility of the Roman Catholic Church to baptismal names that have not been borne by saints.

Caradoc (m.) Welsh: respelling of **Caradog**. This represents an ancient Celtic name apparently derived from the root *cār* love. A form of this name was borne by the British chieftain recorded under the Latinized version *Caratacus*, son of Cunobelinos. He rebelled against Roman rule in the 1st century AD, and although the rebellion was swiftly put down he is recorded by the Roman historian Tacitus as having impressed the Emperor Claudius by his proud bearing in captivity.

Careen (f.) English: of recent origin and uncertain derivation. Its first appearance seems to have been in Margaret Mitchell's novel *Gone with the Wind* (1936), where it is borne by one of the sisters of Scarlett O'Hara (the other being Sue Ellen). The name may represent a combination of CARA with the hypocoristic suffix *-een* (of Irish origin; cf. MAUREEN), or it may be an altered form of CARINA.

Carey (f., m.) **1**. Irish: transferred use of the surname *Carey*, which has two origins. It is in part a local name from Carew Castle in Pembrokeshire, and was taken to Ireland in the 12th century by followers of Strongbow, Earl of Pembroke. To this has been assimilated an Irish patronymic, *Ó Ciardha* 'descendant of the dark one'. **2**. English: variant spelling of CARY, used mainly as a female name, under the influence of CARRIE.

Caridad (f.) Spanish form of CHARITY.

Cognate: Portuguese: **Caridade**.

Carina (f.) Scandinavian, German, and English: late 19th-century coinage, apparently representing a Latinate elaboration of CARA; in part it may also have been inspired by KARIN.

Carl (m.) German and English: old-fashioned German spelling variant of KARL, the German version of CHARLES. It is now increasingly used in English-speaking countries, and for some reason is particularly popular in Wales.

Carla (f.) Italian, English, and German: feminine form of CARLO, CHARLES, or CARL. See also *Karla* at KARL.

Carlin (f.) English: elaborated from of CARLA, apparently of German origin.

Carlo (m.) Italian form of CHARLES.

Carlos (m.) Spanish and Portuguese form of CHARLES.

Carlotta (f.) Italian form of CHARLOTTE, occasionally used in the English-speaking world.

Carlton (m.) English: transferred use of the surname, which is of the same origin as CHARLTON, being derived from any of various places (in Beds., Cambs., Co. Durham, Leics., Lincs., Northants, Notts., Suffolk, and Yorks.) named with the Old English elements *ceorl* (free) man + *tūn* settlement, i.e.

'settlement of the free peasants'. The initial /k/ sound is the result of Anglo-Scandinavian influence.

Carly (f.) English: pet form or variant of CARLA.
Variants: **Carlie**, **Carley**.

Carmel (f.) English: of early Christian origin, referring to 'Our Lady of Carmel', a title of the Virgin Mary. *Carmel* is the name (meaning 'garden' or 'orchard' in Hebrew) of a mountain in the Holy Land near modern Haifa, which was populated from very early Christian times by hermits. They were later organized into the Carmelite order of monks. The name is favoured mainly by Roman Catholics.
Cognates: Portuguese: **Carmo**. Spanish: CARMEN; **Carmela** (also S. Italian and Sicilian).
Pet forms: Spanish: **Carmencita**, **Carmelita**; **Menchu**.
Masculine forms: Spanish: **Carmelo**. Italian: **Carmine**.

Carmela (f.) 1. Spanish, S. Italian, and Sicilian form of the given name CARMEL. 2. Jewish: modern Hebrew name derived from the placename CARMEL.

Carmen (f.) Spanish form of CARMEL, altered by folk etymology to the form of the Latin word *carmen* song. It is now sometimes found as a given name in the English-speaking world, in spite of, or perhaps because of, its association with the tragic romantic heroine of Bizet's opera *Carmen* (1875), based on a short story by Prosper Mérimée.

Carol (f.), originally (m.) English: Anglicized form of *Carolus* (see CHARLES), or of its feminine derivative **Carola**. It has never been common as a male name, and has become even less so since its growth in popularity as a female name. This seems to be of relatively recent origin (not being found much before the end of the 19th century) and may have originated as a short form of CAROLINE.

Carole (f.) French form of CAROL, formerly quite commonly used in the English-speaking world in order to make it clear that a female name was in question. Now that *Carol* is used almost exclusively for girls, *Carole* has become slightly less common.

Caroline (f.) English and French: from the French form of Latin or Italian **Carolina**, a feminine derivative of *Carolus* (see CHARLES).
Variant: **Carolyn**.
Cognates: German, Danish: **Karoline**. Scandinavian, Polish, Czech: **Karolina**.
Short forms: English: **Caro** (not normally used as an independent given name); CARRIE.

Carrie (f.) English: pet form of CAROLINE or occasionally of other girls' names beginning with the syllable *Car-*. It was first used in the 19th century and is now popular in its own right, *Caro* having to some extent taken over the role of the short form.

Carroll (m.) Irish: Anglicized form of CEARBHALL.

Carson (m.) Scottish and Northern Irish: transferred use of the surname, which is of uncertain derivation; in spite of its *-son* ending, it does not seem to be a true patronymic. The first known bearer is a certain Robert *de Carsan* (or de Acarson), recorded in 1276; the 'de' in his name suggests derivation from a placename, but no suitable candidates have been identified. Among Protestants in Northern Ireland, it is sometimes bestowed in honour of Edward Carson (1854–1935), the Dublin barrister and politician who was a violent opponent of Home Rule for Ireland. In America the popularity of the name

may have been affected by the legendary Missouri frontiersman Kit Carson (1809–68).

Carsten (m.) Low German form of CHRISTIAN.

Carter (m.) English: transferred use of the surname, which for the most part originated as an occupational name for someone who transported goods in a cart. In Scotland the surname also represents an Anglicized form of the Gaelic surname *MacArtair* 'son of Artair'.

Carwyn (m.) Welsh: modern coinage, composed of the elements *cār* love + *(g)wyn* white, fair, blessed, holy.

Cary (m.), sometimes (f.) English: transferred use of the surname, which comes from one of the places in Devon or Somerset so called from an old Celtic river name. *Cary* became popular as a given name in the middle of the 20th century, due to the fame of the film actor Cary Grant (1904–89), who was born in Bristol and made his first theatrical appearances under his original name of Archie Leach.
Variant: CAREY.

Caryl (f.), occasionally (m.) English: of uncertain origin, probably a variant of CAROL, possibly influenced by BERYL. As a male name it is probably an altered spelling of CARROLL.

Carys (f.) Welsh: modern coinage, from the vocabulary element *cār* love + the ending *-ys*, by analogy with names such as BETRYS and GLADYS.

Casey (m.), now occasionally also (f.) English (esp. U.S.): 1. Bestowed originally in honour of the American engine-driver and folk hero 'Casey' Jones (1863–1900), who saved the lives of passengers on the 'Cannonball Express' at the expense of his own. He was baptized Johnathan Luther Jones in Cayce, Kentucky, and acquired his nickname from his birthplace. 2. From the Irish surname, the Gaelic form of which is *Ó Cathasaigh* 'descendant of *Cathasach*', a byname meaning 'vigilant, wakeful'. 3. As a female name it is probably a variant of *Cassie* (see CASS).

Casilda (f.) Spanish: of uncertain origin. This was the name of an 11th-century saint who was born in Toledo. She was probably of Moorish descent. She lived as an anchorite nun in the province of Burgos, and is particularly venerated in Burgos and Toledo.

Casimir (m.) Anglicized spelling of Polish *Kazimierz*, derived from *kazić* to destroy + the Old Slavonic element *meri* great, famous (later taken as the medieval and modern word *mir* peace or world). This was a traditional name of Polish kings in the Middle Ages. Casimir I succeeded in reuniting Polish lands and restoring Polish power. Casimir III, 'the Great' (1310–70), king from 1333 to 1370, was an effective and able ruler, and also a just and humane one, who presided over a golden age in Polish history. St Casimir (1458–83) was a son of King Casimir IV; his father wished him to seize the crown of Hungary, but instead he retired from the world, eventually dying of consumption.

Caspar (m.) Dutch form of JASPER, also found as an occasional variant in English. According to legend, this was the name of one of the three Magi or 'wise men' who brought gifts to the infant Christ. The Magi are not named in the Bible, but early Christian tradition assigned them the names *Caspar*, *Balthasar*, and *Melchior*.

Variants: **Casper**, **Kaspar**, **Kasper**.
Cognates: German: **Kaspar**. Polish: **Kasper**. Italian: **Gasparo**.
French: **Gaspard**. Hungarian: **Gáspár**.

Cass (f.) English: medieval and modern short form of CAS-SANDRA, now often used as an independent given name.
Pet form: **Cassie** (common in Scotland).

Cassandra (f.) from Greek legend. Cassandra was a Trojan princess blessed with the gift of prophecy but cursed with the fate that nobody would ever believe her. She was brought back to Greece as a captive concubine by Agamemnon, but met her death at the hands of his jealous wife Clytemnestra. This was one of the most popular girls' names in the Middle Ages, and has recently been revived by parents looking to the pages of classical mythology for distinctive girls' names.

Cassia (f.) English: apparently an adoption of the name of the spice (cf. KEZIA). It may also in part have been adopted as a feminine form of CASSIAN.

Cassian (m.) English: from the name (Latin *Cassiānus*) of several early saints, most notably one martyred at Tangier in 298. The name is a derivative of the old Roman family name *Cassius*. It is of uncertain derivation, but may be connected with the Latin vocabulary word *cassus* empty, hollow.

Cassidy (m., f.) English (esp. U.S.): from the Irish surname *Ó Caiside*. Its use as a female name may be due to the *-y* ending, coupled with the fact that it could be taken as an expanded form of CASS.

Catalina (f.) Spanish form of KATHERINE.

Catarina (f.) Portuguese form of KATHERINE.

Catarina (f.) Italian form of KATHERINE.

Cathal (m.) Irish Gaelic: name derived from the Old Celtic vocabulary elements *cath* battle + *val* rule. It was borne by a 7th-century saint who served as head of the monastic school at Lismore, before being appointed bishop of Taranto in south Italy. In Gaelic Scotland the name appears to have been borne only by descendants of the Mac Mhuirichs, a learned family of Irish origin.
Variants: **Cathaldus**; **Cahal**, **Catheld**, **Kathel** (Anglicized forms).

Cathán (m.) Irish Gaelic: traditional name, representing a diminutive form of the element *cath* battle.
Anglicized form: **Kane**.

Cathaoir (m.) Irish Gaelic: from *cathaoir* warrior, a derivative of the Old Celtic vocabulary elements *cath* fight, battle + *vir* man.
Variant: **Cahir** (Anglicized form).

Catherine (f.) English: variant spelling of KATHERINE. This form of the name is also used in France.
Variant: English: **Catharine**.
Short form: English: **Cath**.
Pet form: English: **Cath**.

Cathleen (f.) Irish: variant spelling of KATHLEEN.

Cathy (f.) English: pet form of CATHERINE.

Catraoine (f.) Irish Gaelic form of KATHERINE, less common than *Caitríona*, *Caitrín*, and *Caitlin*.

Catrin (f.) Welsh form of KATHERINE.

Catriona (f.) Scottish and Irish: Anglicized form of the Gaelic names **Ca(i)triona** (Scottish) and **Caitríona** (Irish), which are themselves forms of KATHERINE. The name is now also used elsewhere in the English-speaking world, although it is still especially popular among people of Scottish ancestry. It attracted wider attention as the title of Robert Louis Stevenson's novel *Catriona* (1893), sequel to *Kidnapped*.
Variant: **Catrina**.

Cayetano (m.) Spanish form of GAETANO.

Cayo (m.) Spanish: from the classical Latin personal name *Caius*, *Gaius*, which is of extremely ancient origin and uncertain etymology. It was borne, for example, by the dictator Caius Julius Caesar, and in the early Christian period by numerous saints.

Ceallachán (m.) Irish Gaelic: diminutive form of CEALLAGH.

Ceallagh (m.) Irish Gaelic: of uncertain origin; it is probably a derivative of *ceall* monastery, church.
Anglicized form: **KELLY**.

Cearbhall (m.) Irish Gaelic: name of uncertain derivation; it possibly arose as a nickname for a violent warrior, from *cearbh* hacking. In the Middle Ages it was common among the learned Ó Dálaigh family of traditional poets. In modern times, it has been borne by Cearbhall Ó Dálaigh (1911–78), president of the Irish Republic.
Variant: **Cearúl(l)** (a modern 'reformed' spelling).
Anglicized forms: **Carroll**, **CHARLES**.

Cebrià (m.) Catalan form of CIPRIANO.

Cebrián (m.) Spanish form of CIPRIANO.

Cecil (m.) English: transferred use of the surname of a great noble family, which rose to prominence in England during the 16th century. The Cecils were of Welsh origin, and their surname represents an Anglicized form of the Welsh given name *Seissylt*, apparently a Brittonic or Old Welsh form of the Latin name *Sextilius*, from *Sextus* 'sixth'. In the Middle Ages *Cecil* was occasionally used as an English form of Latin *Caecilius* (an old Roman family name derived from the byname *Caecus* 'blind'), borne by a minor saint of the 3rd century, a friend of St Cyprian.

Cecily (f.) English: from the Latin name *Caecilia*, feminine of *Caecilius* (see CECIL). This was a good deal more common than the masculine form, largely due to the fame of the 2nd- or 3rd-century virgin martyr whose name is still mentioned daily in the Roman Catholic Canon of the Mass. She is regarded as the patron saint of music and has inspired works such as Purcell's 'Ode on St Cecilia's Day', although the reasons for this association are not clear.
Variants: **Cecilia**, **Cicely**.
Cognates: Irish Gaelic: **Síle**. Scottish Gaelic: **Síle**, **Sileas**. French: **Cécile** (sometimes also used in the English-speaking world). German: **Cäcilie**. Finnish: **Silja**.
Pet forms: English: **Sessy**, **Sissy**. Low German, Frisian: **Silke**.

Cedric (m.) English: coined by Sir Walter Scott for the character Cedric of Rotherwood in *Ivanhoe* (1819). It seems to be a metathesized form of *Cerdic*, the name of the traditional founder of the kingdom of Wessex. Cerdic was a Saxon (Scott's novel also has a Saxon setting), and his name is presumably of Germanic origin, but the formation is not clear. The name has acquired something of a 'sissy' image, probably on account of Cedric Errol Fauntleroy, the long-haired, velvet-suited boy hero of Frances Hodgson Burnett's *Little Lord Fauntleroy* (1886).

Cees (m.) Dutch: variant spelling of KEES.

Ceinwen (f.) Welsh: composed of the vocabulary elements *cain* fair, lovely + *(g)wen* white, blessed, holy. The name was borne by a 5th-century saint, daughter of the chieftain Brychan, about whom little is known.

Ceit (f.) Scottish Gaelic spelling of KATE.
Pet form: **Ceiteag**.

Céleste (f.) French, now also quite common in the English-speaking world: from Latin *Caelestis* 'heavenly', a popular name among early Christians.
Variant: English: **Celeste**.

Celia (f.) English and Italian: from Latin *Caelia*, feminine of the old Roman family name *Caelius* (of uncertain origin, probably a derivative of *caelum* heaven). The name was not used in the Middle Ages, but was introduced to the English-speaking world as the name of a character in Shakespeare's *As You Like It*. It is now often regarded as a short form of *Cecilia*.
Cognate: French: **Célie** (not now a common given name).
Pet form: Low German, Frisian: **Silke**.

Céline (f.) French, also found occasionally in the English-speaking world: apparently from Latin *Caelīna*, a feminine form of *Caelīnus*, which is a derivative of *Caelius* (see CELIA). It may alternatively be an aphetic short form of *Marcel(l)ine*, a feminine diminutive of MARCEL.

Celso (m.) Italian and Spanish: from the Latin family name (later a personal name) *Celsus*. This was originally a nickname from the Latin vocabulary word *celsus* tall, high, lofty. The name was borne by various minor early Roman saints, and it has also been used as a Latinized form of several Irish saints called CEALLAGH.

Čenek (m.) Czech: pet form of *Vincenc* (see VINCENT).

Ceri (f.) Welsh: of uncertain origin, probably a short form of CERIDWEN.

Ceridwen (f.) Welsh: name borne in Celtic mythology by the goddess of poetic inspiration. It is apparently composed of the elements *cerdd* poetry + *(g)wen* feminine of *gwyn* white, fair, blessed, holy. This is said to have been the name of the mother of the legendary 6th-century Welsh hero Taliesin, but it is not clear whether in fact it represents a personal name or whether Taliesin is to be regarded as the son of the goddess of poetry.

Césaire (m.) French: from the Late Latin personal name *Caesarius*, a derivative of CAESAR. The name was borne most notably by an early bishop of Arles (470–542). During the siege of that city in 508 he sold the treasures of his church in order to relieve the distress being suffered by the poor.

César (m.) French: from the old Roman family name *Caesar*, of uncertain meaning. It has been connected with Latin *caesaries* head of hair, but this is probably no more than folk etymology; the name may be of Etruscan origin. Its most notable bearer was Gaius Julius Caesar (?102–44 BC) and it also formed part of the full name of his relative Augustus (Gaius Julius Caesar Octavianus Augustus). Subsequently it was used as an imperial title and eventually became a vocabulary word for an emperor (leading to German *Kaiser* and Russian *tsar*).
Cognates: Italian: **Cesare**. English: CAESAR.

Česlav (m.) Czech form of CZESLAW.

Chad (m.) English: modern spelling of Old English *Ceadda*, name of a 7th-century saint who was for a time archbishop of York. This is of uncertain derivation. The name is comparatively rare, even among Roman Catholics, by whom it is chiefly favoured.

Chaim (m.) Jewish: variant spelling of HYAM.

Chandler (m.) English: transferred use of the surname, which originated in the Middle Ages as an occupational name for someone who made and sold candles (a derivative of Old French *chandele*, Latin *candēla*). The extended sense 'retail dealer' (in various goods) arose in the 16th century.

Chantal (f.) French, also sometimes found in the English-speaking world: bestowed in honour of St Jane Frances (Jeanne Françoise) Frémiot (1572–1641). In 1592 she married the Baron de Chantal (a place in Saône-et-Loire, so called from a dialect form of Old Provençal *cantal* stone, boulder) and adopted his family name. After his death she became an associate of St Francis of Sales and founded a new order of nuns.
Variants: English: **Chantale**; **Chantelle**; (influenced by the feminine diminutive suffix *-elle*).

Chapman (m.) English: transferred use of the surname, which originated in the Middle Ages as an occupational name for a merchant or a smaller-scale pedlar, from Old English *cēapmanns* (a compound of *cēapan* to buy, sell, trade + *mann* man).

Charis (f.) English: from Greek *kharis* grace. This was a key word in early Christian thought, but was not used as a name in the early centuries after Christ or in the Middle Ages. As a given name it seems to be an innovation of the 17th century, chosen either to express the original idea of charity, or else as a reference to the three Graces (Greek *kharites*) of classical mythology (Aglaia, Euphrosyne, and Thalia, of which the first and third have also been occasionally used as given names).

Charissa (f.) English: apparently a recent elaboration of CHARIS, perhaps as a result of crossing with CLARISSA.

Charity (f.) English: from the vocabulary word, denoting originally the Christian's love for his fellow man (Latin *caritās*, from *carus* dear). In spite of St Paul's words 'and now abideth faith, hope, charity, these three; but the greatest of these is charity' (1 Corinthians 13: 13), *Charity* is now rarely used as a given name in comparison with the shorter FAITH and HOPE.
Cognates: Spanish: **Caridad**. Portuguese: **Caridade**. Finnish: **Karita**.

Charlene (f.) English (chiefly Australian and southern U.S.): 20th-century coinage, from *Charles* + *-ene* taken as a feminine ending. It may have been influenced by the older but much rarer French name **Charline**, a feminine diminutive of CHARLES.

Charles (m.) English and French: originally from a Germanic word meaning 'free man', cognate with Old English *ceorl* man. (The modern English words *churl* and *churlish* are derived from this, and their unpleasant overtones are a much later accretion.) The name originally owed its popularity in Europe to the Frankish leader Charlemagne (?742–814), who in 800 established himself as Holy Roman Emperor. His name (Latin *Carolus Magnus*) means 'Charles the Great'. *Charles* or KARL (the German form) was a common name among Frankish leaders, including Charlemagne's grandfather Charles Martel (688–741). The name was also borne by a succession of Holy Roman Emperors and ten kings of France. It was hardly used at all among the Normans, and was introduced to Britain by Mary Queen of Scots (1542–87), who had been brought up in France. She chose the names *Charles James* for her son (1566–1625), who later became King James VI of Scotland and, from 1603, James I of England. His son and grandson both reigned as King Charles, and the name thus became established in the 17th century both as a name in the Stuart royal house and as a favoured name among English and Scottish supporters of the monarchy. In the 19th century the popularity of the name was further increased by romanticization of the story of 'Bonnie Prince Charlie', Stuart pretender to the throne in the preceding century and leader of the 1745 rebellion. This popularity continued in the 20th century with the baptism in 1948 of the heir to the British throne as Prince Charles.

In Ireland this name has been used as an Anglicized form of CEARBHALL. and sometimes of CORMAC; in Scotland it has been used for TEÀRLACH.
Cognates: Irish Gaelic: **Séarlas**. Welsh: **Siarl**. Italian: **Carlo**. Spanish, Portuguese: **Carlos**. German: **Karl**, CARL. Dutch: **Karel**. Scandinavian: **Karl**. Polish: **Karol**. Czech: **Karel**. Hungarian: **Károly**. Finnish: **Kaarle**.
Pet form: English: **Charlie**.

Charlie (m., f.) 1. (m.) English and Scottish: pet form of CHARLES. 2. (f.) English: modern pet form of CHARLOTTE.

Charlotte (f.) English and French: feminine diminutive of CHARLES, used in England since the 17th century, but most popular in the 18th and 19th centuries, in part due to the influence of first, Queen Charlotte (1744–1818), wife of George III, and secondly, the novelist Charlotte Brontë (1816–55). In the Scottish Highlands this name has been used as an Anglicized form of *Teàrlag* (see TEÀRLACH).
Cognates: Irish: **Sérlait**. Italian: **Carlotta**. German: **Karlotte**. Scandinavian: **Chrlotta**.
Pet forms: English: **Lottie**, **Tottie**, **Charlie**.

Charlton (m.) English: transferred use of the surname, used as a given name largely as a result of the fame of the film actor Charlton Heston (b. 1924; *Charlton* was his mother's maiden name). The surname originally denoted someone who came from one of the numerous places in England named in Old English as the 'settlement of the free peasants', Old English *ceorlatun*. The first element of the placename is ultimately connected with the source of CHARLES.

Charmaine (f.) English: possibly a variant of CHARMIAN, influenced by names such as GERMAINE, but more probably an invented name based on the vocabulary word *charm* + *-aine* as in LORRAINE. It is not found before 1920, but enjoyed some popularity in the 1960s due to The Bachelors' hit song of this name.

Charmian (f.) English: from the Late Greek name *Kharmion* (a diminutive of *kharma* delight). The name was used by Shakespeare in *Antony and Cleopatra* for one of the attendants of the Egyptian queen; he took it from Sir Thomas North's translation of Plutarch's *Parallel Lives*.

Charna (f.) Jewish: Yiddish name, from a Slavonic element meaning 'dark, black' (cf. Polish *czarny*).
Pet forms: **Charnke**, **Charnele**.

Charo (f.) Spanish: pet form of ROSARIO.

Chase (m.) English (esp. U.S.): transferred use of the surname, which originated in the Middle Ages as a nickname for a huntsman, from Anglo-Norman *chase* chase, hunt.

Chauncey (m.) English: American coinage from a well-known New England surname. It seems to have been originally chosen as a given name in honour of the Harvard College president Charles Chauncy (1592–1672), the New England clergyman Charles Chauncy (1705–87), or the naval officer Isaac Chauncey (1772–1840). All these men were almost certainly descended from a single family; the surname is found in England in the Middle Ages, and probably has a Norman baronial origin, but now seems to be extinct in Britain.

Chaya (f.) Jewish: feminine counterpart of CHAIM, from Hebrew *Hayya* 'alive' or 'animal'. In the first meaning it corresponds to CHAIM and names such as VIDAL, and in the second meaning it parallels animal names such as ARYE, DOV, and ZVI. See also EVE.

Chelle (f.) English: informal short form of MICHELLE. See also SHELL.

Chelo (f.) Spanish: pet form of CONSUELO.

Cherelle (f.) English: apparently a respelling of CHERYL, influenced by the popular name ending *-elle* (originally a French feminine diminutive suffix).

Cherene (f.) English (esp. U.S.): modern coinage, a combination of the popular element *Cher-* (cf. CHERIDA, CHERYL, and CHERYTH) with the productive feminine suffix *-ene*.

Cherida (f.) English: a modern coinage, apparently the result of crossing CHERYL with PHILLIDA.

Cherish (f.) English: modern coinage, apparently an alteration of CHERYTH to match the vocabulary element *cherish* to treasure, care for (borrowed in the Middle Ages from Old French *cherir*, a derivative of *cher* dear).

Cherna (f.) Jewish: Yiddish name, from a Slavonic element meaning 'dark, black' (cf. Russian *cherny*).
Pet forms: **Chernke**, **Chernele**.

Cherry (f.) English: now generally regarded as an Anglicized spelling of the French word *chéries* darling (cf. CARA). However, Dickens used it as a pet form of CHARITY: in *Martin Chuzzlewit* (1844) Mr Pecksniff's daughters Charity and Mercy are known as Cherry and Merry. Nowadays the name is sometimes also taken as referring to the fruit.

Cheryl (f.) English: not found before the 1920s, and not common until the 1940s. It seems to be an artificial creation, perhaps the result of a crossing of CHERRY with BERYL.

Cheryth (f.) English: apparently the result of a crossing of CHERRY with GWYNETH.

Cheslav (m.) Russian form of CZESŁAW

Chester (m.) English: transferred use of the surname, which originally denoted someone from the town of *Chester*, so called from an Old English form of Latin *castra* legionary camp. Use as a given name has become quite common in the 20th century.

Chevonne (f.) Anglicized spelling of SIOBHÁN.

Chiara (f.) Italian form of CLARE.

Chirsty (f.) Scottish: usual spelling in the Highlands of KIRSTIE.

Chita (f.) Spanish: short form of *Conchita* (see CONCHA).

Chloe (f.) From the Late Greek name *Khloē*, originally used in the classical period as an epithet of the fertility goddess Demeter. It seems to be connected with CHLORIS. It occurs only fleetingly in the New Testament (1 Corinthians 1: 11), but its use as a given name in the English-speaking world almost certainly derives from this, having been adopted by 17th-century Puritans. It has survived much better than the majority of the minor biblical names taken up in the 17th century.

Chloris (f.) From Greek mythology. *Khlōris* was a minor goddess of vegetation; her name derives from Greek *khlōros* green. It was used by the Roman poet Horace for one of his loves (*cf.* LALAGE), and was taken up by Augustan poets of the 17th and 18th centuries.

Chole (f.) Spanish: pet form of SOLEDAD.

Chris (m., f.) English: 1. (m.) Short form of CHRISTOPHER. 2. (f.) Short form of CHRISTINE and the group of related female names.

Chrissie (f.) English and Scottish: pet form of CHRISTINE and the group of related women's names. It is especially common in Scotland.

Variants: Scottish: **Criosaidh** (a Gaelic form).

Christa (f.) Latinate short form of CHRISTINE and CHRISTINA. It seems to have originated in Germany, but is now also well established in Scandinavia and the English-speaking world.

Christabel (f.) English: a 19th-century coinage from the first syllable of CHRISTINE, combined with the productive suffix *-bel* (see BELLE). The coinage was apparently made by Samuel Taylor Coleridge (1772–1834) in a poem called *Christabel* (1816). The name was also borne by the suffragette Christabel Pankhurst (1880–1958), in whose honour it is now sometimes bestowed.

Variants: **Christabelle**, **Christabella**.

Christelle (f.) French: altered form of CHRISTINE, derived by replacement of the seemingly feminine diminutive suffix *-ine* with the suffix *-elle* of similar function. The name is now also used in the English-speaking world, where its popularity has been enhanced by that of the similar-sounding CRYSTAL.

Christer (m.) Swedish and Danish form of the male name CHRISTIAN. It is first found in the 15th century, when it began to be borne regularly in a few noble families. It came into more general popularity in the 1940s.

Christhard (m.) German: hybrid religious name based on the name *Christ* (see CHRISTIAN) + the Germanic personal name element *-hard* hardy, brave, strong.

Christian (m.), occasionally (f.) English: from Latin *Christiānus* 'follower of Christ', in use as a given name during the Middle Ages, and sporadically ever since. The name *Christ* itself (Greek *Khristos*) is a translation of the Hebrew term *Messiah* 'anointed'.

Cognates (m.): Low German: **Carsten**. Danish: **Kristen**.

Christiana (f.) English: medieval learned feminine form of CHRISTIAN. As a recent revival it represents an elaborated form of CHRISTINA. It is also sometimes spelled **Christianna** under the influence of the name ANNA.

Christie (m., f.) 1. (m.) Scottish and Irish: pet form of CHRISTOPHER. 2. (f.) English: pet form of CHRISTINE.

Variant: **Christy**.

Christina (f.) English: simplified form of Latin *Christiāna*, feminine of *Christiānus* (see CHRISTIAN), or a Latinized form of Middle English *Christin* 'Christian' (Old English *christen*, from Latin).

Cognates: Scottish Gaelic: **Cairistiona**, **Cairistine**. Irish Gaelic: **Cristiona**. Italian, Spanish, Portuguese: **Cristina**. Polish: **Krystyna**.

Christine (f.) English and French: form of CHRISTINA, not much used in Britain until the end of the 19th century. Until fairly recently it was principally associated with Scotland, but now it is very popular in all parts of the English-speaking world.

Short form: English: **Chris**.

Pet forms: Scottish: **Chrissie**; **Chirsty**, KIRSTIE (Gaelic **Ciorstaidh**, **Curstaidh**; **Ciorstag**; **Ciorsdan**).

Christmas (m.) English: from the festival celebrating the birth of Christ (so called from *Christ* (see CHRISTIAN) + *mass* festival). It is sometimes given to a boy born on Christmas Day. See also NOËL and NATALIE.

Christopher (m.) English: from Greek *Khristophoros*, a name composed of the elements *Khristos* Christ + *pherein* to bear. This was popular among early Christians, conscious of the fact that they were metaphorically bearing Christ in their hearts. A later, over-literal interpretation of the name gave rise to the legend of a saint who actually bore the Christ-child over a stream; he is regarded as the patron of travellers.

Cognates: Irish Gaelic: **Críostóir**. Scottish: **Kester**; See also CRÌSDEAN. French: **Christophe**. Italian: **Cristoforo**. Spanish: **Cristóbal**. Catalan: **Cristòfol**. Portuguese: **Cristovão**. German: **Christoph**. Scandinavian: **Kristoffer**. Polish: **Krzysztof**. Czech: **Kryštof** Finnish: **Risto**.

Short forms: English: **Chris**. Spanish: **Cristo**.

Pet forms: English: **Kit**. German: **Stoffel**.

Christy (m., f.) Scottish, Irish, and English: variant spelling of CHRISTIE.

Chrystal (f.) English: rare variant spelling of CRYSTAL, apparently influenced by the Greek-origin element *khrysos* gold.

Variant: **Chrystalla** (Latinate).

Chucho (m., f.) Spanish: pet form of JESÚS or *María Jesús*.

Chuck (m.) English (almost exclusively U.S.): nickname occasionally used as a given name in its own right. It derives from the English term of endearment, itself probably from Middle English *chukken* to cluck (of imitative origin). It is now often used as a pet form of CHARLES.

Pet form: **Chuckie**.

Chus (m., f.) Spanish: pet form of JESÚS or *María Jesús*.

Chwalibóg (m.) Polish: religious name of medieval origin, composed of the elements *chwata* praise + *bóg* God.

Variant: **Falibog**. See also BOGUCHWAL.

Cian (m.) Irish: traditional Gaelic name, from the Irish vocabulary word meaning 'ancient'. It was borne by a son-in-law of Brian Boru who played a leading role in the Battle of Clontarf (1014).

Anglicized forms: **Kean(e)**.

Ciannait (f.) Irish: Gaelic name representing a feminine diminutive form of CIAN.

Ciara (f.) Irish: modern name created as a feminine form of CIARÁN.

Ciarán (m.) Irish: Gaelic name often Anglicized as KIERAN. It was originally a byname, representing a diminutive form of *ciar* black, and was borne by two Irish saints, of the 5th and 6th centuries.

Cibor (m.) Polish: simplified variant of CZCIBOR.

Cicely (f.) English: variant spelling of CECILY. This was a common form of the name in the Middle Ages.

Cognate: Scandinavian: **Sissel**.

Pet form: English: SISSY.

Cillian (m.) Irish: Gaelic name often Anglicized as KILLIAN. It was originally a byname representing a diminutive form of Gaelic *ceallach* strife, or possibly derived from Gaelic *ceall* monastery, church (*cf.* KELLY), and was borne by various early Irish saints, including the 7th-century author of a life of St Bridget and missionaries to Artois and Franconia.

Variant: **Cillín**.

Cindy (f.) English: pet form of CYNTHIA or, less often, of LUCINDA, now very commonly used as an independent given name, especially in America. It has occasionally also been taken as a short form of the name of the fairy-tale *Cinderella*, which in fact is not related to it (French *Cendrillon*, a derivative of *cendre* cinders).

Cinzia (f.) Italian form of CYNTHIA.

Ciorstaidh (f.) Scottish Gaelic form of KIRSTIE.

Variant: **Ciorstag**.

Cipriano (m.) Italian: from Latin *Cyprianus*, originally an ethnic name for someone from the island of Cyprus. The most famous of several early saints of this name is a 3rd-century bishop of Carthage who was a major theological thinker and writer.

Cognates: Spanish: **Cebrián**. Catalan: **Cebrià**.

Ciriaco (m.) Italian and Spanish (more common in the latter country): from Latin *Cyriācus*, Greek *Kyriakos*, a derivative of *kyrios* lord. This was a very popular name among early Christians, who chose it as a token of their devotion to their Lord, and it was borne by a very large number of minor saints of the first centuries AD.

Ciro (m.) Italian form of CYRUS, commonly used in that country.

Claire (f.) French form of CLARA. It was introduced to Britain by the Normans, but subsequently abandoned. This spelling was revived in the 19th century as a variant of CLARE.

Variant: **Clair**.

Clancy (m.) Irish (esp. U.S.): from the Irish surname, Gaelic *Mac Fhlannchaidh* 'son of *Flannchadh*', a personal name perhaps meaning 'red warrior'.

Variant: **Clancey**.

Clara (f.) English, Italian, and German: post-classical Latin name, from the feminine form of the adjective *clārus* famous. In the modern English-speaking world it represents a re-Latinization of the regular English form CLARE. In the Scottish Highlands it has been used as a translation equivalent of the Gaelic name SORCHA.

Variant: German: **Klara**.

Pet form: English: **Clarrie**.

Clare (f.) English: the normal vernacular form of CLARA during the Middle Ages and since. The name has always been particularly popular in Italy (in the forms *Chiara* and *Clara*) and has been borne by several Italian saints, notably Clare of Assisi (*c*.1193–1253), an associate of Francis of Assisi and founder of the order of nuns known as the Poor Clares. In Britain the given name was probably reinforced by the Anglo-Irish surname, derived from a place in Suffolk. The surname was taken to Ireland by Richard de Clare, 2nd Earl of Pembroke (d. 1176), known as 'Strongbow'.

Clarence (m.) English: in use from the end of the 19th century, but now rare. It was first used in honour of the popular elder son of Edward VII, who was created Duke of Clarence in 1890, but died in 1892. His title (*Dux Clarentiae* in Latin) originated with a son of Edward III, who in the 14th century was married to the heiress of Clare in Suffolk (which is so called from a Celtic river name and has no connection with the given name CLARE). The title has been held by various British royal princes at different periods in history.

Pet form: **Clarrie**.

Clarette (f.) English: rare extended form of CLARE, with the French feminine diminutive suffix -*ette*. The formation may have been influenced by the wine *claret* (Medieval Latin (*vīnum*) *clārātum* clarified wine).

Clarice (f.) English: medieval English and French form of the Latin name *Claritia*. This seems to have meant 'fame' (an abstract derivative of *clārus* famous), but it may simply have been an arbitrary elaboration of CLARA. It was borne by a character who features in some versions of the medieval romances of Roland and the other paladins of Charlemagne.

Clarinda (f.) English: elaboration of CLARA with the suffix -*inda* (*cf.* BELINDA and LUCINDA). *Clarinda* first appears in Spenser's *Faerie Queene* (1596). The formation seems to have been influenced by the name *Clorinda*, which occurs in Torquato Tasso's *Gerusalemme Liberata* (1580), and is probably a similarly arbitrary elaboration of CHLORIS. Robert Burns (1759–96) wrote four poems *To Clarinda*.

Clarissa (f.) English: Latinate form of CLARICE occasionally found in medieval documents. It was revived by Samuel Richardson as the name of the central character in his novel *Clarissa* (1748).

Cognate: Spanish: **Clarisa**. See also CAITIR.

Clark (m.) English: transferred use of the surname, originally an occupational name denoting a *clerk* or secretary, in the Middle Ages a man in minor holy orders, who earned his living by his ability to read and write. It is now quite commonly used as a given name, especially in the United States. The word *clerk* derives from Latin *clericus*, but this more common form of the surname and given name reflects a widespread medieval shift in pronunciation from -*er*- to -*ar*- (preserved in the British but not the American pronunciation of the vocabulary word).

Clarrie (m., f.) English: pet form of CLARENCE, also of CLARA and the various similar womens' names. It is now fairly rare and almost never used as an independent given name.

Claud (m.) English: Anglicized spelling of CLAUDE.

Claude (m.) French and English: from the Latin name *Claudius* (itself occasionally used as a modern given name), which was an old Roman family name derived from the byname *Claudus* 'lame'. It was borne by various early saints, but its popularity in France is largely due to the fame of the 7th-century St Claude of Besan-con. In France, *Claude* also occasionally occurs as a female name (*cf.* CLAUDIA).

Cognates: Italian, Spanish, Portuguese: **Claudio**. Russian: **Klavdii**. Polish: **Klaudiusz**. Hungarian: **Kolos**.

Claudette (f.) French: feminine diminutive form of CLAUDE, now also occasionally used in the English-speaking world.

Claudia (f.) English and German: from the Latin female name, a feminine form of *Claudius* (see CLAUDE). The name receives a fleeting mention in one of St Paul's letters to Timothy (2. 4: 21 'Eubulus greeteth thee, and Pudens, and Linus, and Claudia and all the brethren'), from which it was taken up in the 16th century (cf. CHLOE).
Cognates: Russian: **Klavdia**. Polish: **Klaudia**.

Claudine (f.) French: feminine diminutive form of CLAUDE. It was made popular at the beginning of the 20th century as the name of the heroine of a series of novels by the French writer Colette (1873–1954), and is now also occasionally used in the English-speaking world.

Claudio (m.) Italian, Spanish, and Portuguese form of CLAUDE.

Claus (m.) German: aphetic form of *Niclaus* or *Niklaus*, representing the usual German form of NICHOLAS. In America this name tends to be associated with the figure of *Santa Claus* (originally *Sankt Niklaus*), which inhibits serious use of it.
Variant: German: **Klaus**.
Cognates: Dutch: **Klaas**. Frisian: **Klaes**. Finnish: **Launo**.

Claver (m.) Catholic name given in honour of the Catalan saint Pere Claver (1581–1654), a Jesuit who worked among Black slaves in Central America. He was canonized in 1888. His surname is a Catalan occupational name for a locksmith.

Clay (m.) English: either a shortened form of CLAYTON or a transferred use of the independent surname, which was originally a local name for someone who lived on a patch of land whose soil was predominantly clay (Old English *clæg*).

Clayton (m.) English (esp. U.S.): transferred use of the surname, originally a local name from any of the several places in England (for example, in Lancs., Staffs., Sussex, and W. Yorks.) originally named with the Old English elements *clæg* clay + *tūn* enclosure, settlement.

Cledwyn (m.) Welsh: traditional name, apparently composed of the elements *caled* hard, rough + *(g)wyn* white, fair, blessed, holy.

Clelia (f.) Italian and English: from Latin *Cloelia*, the name borne by a semi-mythological heroine of early Roman history. She was given as a hostage to the Etruscan invader Lars Porsenna, but made an escape back to Rome by swimming the Tiber.

Clem (m.) English: short form of CLEMENT and of women's names such as CLEMENCE. It is occasionally used as an independent given name, especially in the United States.

Clematis (f.) English: from the name of the flower (so named in the 16th century from Greek *klēmatis* climbing plant), perhaps under the influence of names such as CLEMENCE and the ending *-is* found in names such as PHYLLIS.

Clemence (f.) English: medieval French and English form of Latin *Clēmentius* (masculine derivative of *Clēmens*; see CLEMENT) or of *Clēmentia* (feminine version of *Clēmentius* or an abstract noun meaning 'mercy'). It has never been particularly common, but is still occasionally used as a female name.
Short form: **Clem**.
Pet form: **Clemmie**.

Clemency (f.) English: rare variant of CLEMENCE or a direct use of the abstract noun, on the model of CHARITY, FAITH, MERCY, etc.

Clement (m.) English: from the Late Latin name *Clēmens* (genitive *Clēmentis*) meaning 'merciful'. This was borne by several early saints, notably the fourth pope and the early Christian theologian Clement of Alexandria (Titus Flavius Clemens, ?150–?215).
Cognates: Scottish Gaelic: **Cliamain** French: **Clément**. Italian, Spanish, Portuguese: **Clemente**. German, Danish, Swedish, Polish: **Klemens**. Russian, Czech: **Kliment**. Hungarian: **Kelemen**.
Short form: English: **Clem**.
Pet forms: English: **Clemmie**. Polish: **Klimek**.

Clementine (f.) English: feminine form of CLEMENT, created with the French feminine diminutive suffix *-ine*. The name was first used in the 19th century, and for a time it was very popular. It is now largely associated with the popular song with this title. The Latinate form **Clementina** is also found.
Cognate: Polish: **klementyna**.

Clemmie (f., m.) English: diminutive form of CLEM, borne more often by girls than by boys.

Cleo (f.) English: short form of CLEOPATRA (see also CLIO).

Cleopatra (f.) From Greek *Kleopatra*, the name (composed of the elements *kleos* glory + *patēr* father) borne by a large number of women in the Ptolemaic royal family of Egypt. The most famous (?69–30 BC) was the lover of Mark Antony, and has always figured largely in both literature and the popular imagination as a model of a passionate woman of unsurpassed beauty, who 'gave all for love' and in the process destroyed the man she loved. She had previously been the mistress of Julius Caesar. The name is occasionally chosen, especially in Black families.

Cleto (m.) Italian, Spanish, and Portuguese: short form of ANACLETO.

Cliamain (m.) Scottish Gaelic form of CLEMENT.

Cliff (m.) English: short form of CLIFFORD (now also sometimes of CLIFTON). It is commonly used as an independent given name, especially since the rise to fame in the 1950s of the pop singer Cliff Richard (real name Harry Webb). It has sometimes also been associated with CLIVE.

Clifford (m.) English: transferred use of the surname, originally a local name from any of several places (Gloucs., Herefords., Yorks.) named in Old English with the elements *clif* cliff, slope, riverbank + *ford* ford.

Clifton (m.) English: transferred use of the surname, originally a local name from any of the numerous places named in Old English with the elements *clif* cliff, slope, riverbank + *tūn* enclosure, settlement. Use of this as a given name is more recent than that of CLIFFORD, and it may in some cases have been adopted as an expanded form of CLIFF.

Clint (m.) English: short form of the surname *Clinton*, made famous by the actor Clint Eastwood (b. 1930). It was apparently originally used as a given name in America in honour of the Clinton family, whose members included the statesman George Clinton (1739–1812), governor of New York, and his nephew De Witt Clinton (1769–1828), who was responsible for overseeing the construction of the Erie Canal. It was also borne by Sir Henry Clinton (1735–95), British commander-in-chief in America during the Revolution.

Clio (f.) English: from Greek *Kleio*, the name borne in classical mythology both by one of the nymphs and by one of the

Muses. It is probably ultimately connected with, the word *kleos* glory; cf. CLEOPATRA. The name is now sometimes used as a variant of CLEO.

Clíona (f.) Irish: contracted spelling of the Gaelic name **Clíodhna** (Old Irish *Clídna*), borne in Fenian legends by a fairy princess. It has been revived in the 20th century and become a popular given name in Ireland.

Clitus (m.) Mainly U.S.: Latinized form of Greek *Kleitos*, the name of one of Alexander the Great's generals. This name is probably ultimately connected with *Kleio* (see CLIO).

Clive (m.) English: transferred use of the surname, originally a local name from any of the various places (in e.g. Cheshire, Shropshire) so called from Old English *clif* cliff, slope. As a given name it seems to have been originally chosen in honour of 'Clive of India' (Robert Clive, created Baron Clive of Plassey in 1760).

Clodagh (f.) Irish: of recent origin. It is the name of a river in Tipperary, and seems to have been arbitrarily transferred to use as a given name. There may be some association in the minds of givers with the Latin name *Clōdia* (borne by the mistress of the Roman poet Catullus), a variant of CLAUDIA.

Clothilde (f.) French: from a Germanic female personal name, composed of the elements *hlōd* famous + *hild* battle. The most famous bearer of the name (*c*.474–545) was a daughter of the Burgundian king Chilperic who married the Frankish king Clovis and converted him to Christianity.

Clover (f.) English: modern name taken from the flower (Old English *clāfre*). Its popularity may have been influenced by its slight similarity in sound to CHLOE.

Clyde (m.) English (esp. U.S.): apparently from the river in south-west Scotland that runs through Glasgow, perhaps by way of a surname derived from the river name. The name is comparatively popular among West Indian and American Blacks; Dunkling points out that geographical names such as *Aberdeen* and *Glasgow* were bestowed on slaves in the southern United States. A large number of plantation owners were of Scottish origin. *Clyde*, unlike other such names, seems to have survived, and even gained some currency among southern Whites. The bank robber Clyde Barrow became something of a cult figure, especially after the film *Bonnie and Clyde* (1967).

Coinneach (m.) Scottish Gaelic: traditional name, probably originally a byname meaning 'handsome, fair one'. This is one of the two names that have merged in the Anglicized form KENNETH, and it remains in common use in the Highlands. From it is derived the surname *Mackenzie* (Gaelic *Mac Coinnich*).

Cokkie (f.) Dutch: pet form of CORNELIA.

Colbert (m.) English: from a Germanic personal name introduced by the Normans, composed of the element *col* of uncertain meaning + *berht* bright, famous. In modern use it probably represents a transferred use of the surname derived from the given name in the Middle Ages.

Cole (m.) English: transferred use of the surname, itself derived from a medieval given name of uncertain origin. It seems to represent the Old English byname *Cola* 'swarthy, coalblack' (from *col* charcoal). The given name is occasionally used as a short form of NICHOLAS.

Coleman (m.) English and Irish: variant of COLMAN. In part it also represents a transferred use of the surname, which derives in most cases from the Gaelic personal name *Colmán*, but in others may be an occupational term for a charcoal burner.

Colette (f.) French and English: short form of *Nicolette* (pet form of NICOLE) or feminine diminutive of the medieval name *Col(le)* (cf. COLIN). It was given particular currency from the 1920s onwards by the fame of the French novelist Colette (1873–1954).

Colin (m.) **1**. English: diminutive form of the medieval name *Col(le)*, a short form of NICHOLAS. It has been enduringly popular and is now normally regarded as an independent name rather than as a pet form of *Nicholas*. **2**. Scottish: Anglicized form of the Gaelic name **Cailean**, particularly favoured among the Campbells and the MacKenzies. It relates to St Columba (see CALUM) as *Crìsdean* does to Christ and *Moirean* to Mary.

Coll (m.) Scottish: Anglicized form of the Gaelic name **Colla**, perhaps from an Old Celtic root meaning 'high'.

Colleen (f.) Mainly U.S. and Australian: from the Anglo-Irish vocabulary word *colleen* girl, wench (Gaelic *cailín*). The name arose during the period of enthusiasm for Irish names in the 1940s and became especially popular in America, although it is not in fact used as a given name in Ireland. It is sometimes taken as a feminine of COLIN.

Collette (f.) English: variant spelling of COLETTE.

Colm (m.) Irish Gaelic form of Latin Columba; see CALUM. Variant: **Colom** (an older Gaelic form). Pet form: **Cóilín**.

Colman (m.) Irish: Anglicized form of the Gaelic name **Colmán**, from Late Latin *Columbānus*, a derivative of *Columba* (see CALUM and COLOMBE). The name was borne by a large number of early Irish saints, including Colman of Armagh, a 5th-century disciple of St Patrick. St Colman or *Columban* (*c*.540–615) founded the monastery at Bobbio in northern Italy in 614, and became something of a cult figure in central Europe. St Colman of Stockerau (d. 1012) was an Irish pilgrim who was killed at Stockerau near Vienna while on his way to the Holy Land. He is said to have worked numerous miracles after his death, and was particularly venerated in Hungary. Cognates: Czech: **Kolman**. Hungarian: **Kámán**. Italian: **Columbano**. French: **Colombain**.

Colombe (f.) French: from the Late Latin name *Columba* 'dove', borne both by men (see CALUM) and by women. In France the name is borne principally in honour of Conception St Colombe of Sens (d. 273), who fled to France from Spain to avoid persecution but was put to death near Meaux.

Columbine (f.) English: from Italian *Colombitia*, a diminutive of *Colombo* 'dove'. In the tradition of the *commedia dell'arte* this is the name of Harlequin's sweetheart. The modern name, however, was probably coined independently as one of the class of names taken in the 19th century from flowers. The columbine gets its name from the fact that its petals are supposed to resemble five doves clustered together.

Comgal (m.) Irish: Anglicized form of the Gaelic name **Comhghall**, composed of the elements *comh* together, joint + *gall* pledge. It was borne by a 6th-century saint, founder of Bangor Abbey in Northern Ireland and teacher of Columbanus.

Comgan (m.) Irish: Anglicized form of the Gaelic name **Comhghán**, composed of the elements *comh* together, joint + *gan-*, *gen-* born. It seems originally to have been a byname referring to a twin. The name was borne by an 8th-century Irish prince who lived as a monk in Scotland.

Comyn (m.) Irish: Anglicized form of CUIMÍN.

Conall (m.) Irish and Scottish Gaelic: name composed of Old Celtic elements meaning 'wolf' + 'strong'. This name was borne by many early chieftains and warriors of Ireland, including the Ulster hero Conall Cearnach.
Variant: Scottish: **Comhnall**.

Conan (m.) Irish: Anglicized form of the Gaelic name *Cónán*, originally a byname representing a diminutive of *cú* hound. The name was borne by a 7th-century saint, who probably served as a bishop on the Isle of Man. Sir Arthur Conan Doyle (1859–1930), creator of the fictional detective Sherlock Holmes, was of Irish stock.

Concepción (f.) Spanish: name commemorating the Immaculate Conception of the Virgin Mary. This doctrine was officially proclaimed by the Roman Catholic Church only in 1854, but had been debated since the 12th century and reached a peak of popularity in the late Middle Ages.
Pet forms: **Concha**, **Conchita**.
Cognate: Portuguese: **Conceição**.

Concepta (f.) Latin form of CONCETTA, used especially in Ireland among Roman Catholics.

Concetta (f.) Italian: name referring to a title of the Virgin Mary, *Maria Concetta*, that alludes to her Immaculate Conception (cf. CONCEPCIÓN).

Concha (f.) Spanish: pet form of CONCEPCIÓN.
Variant: **Conchita**.

Conleth (m.) Irish: Anglicized form of the obsolete Gaelic personal name *Connlaeth*, apparently composed of the elements *conn* chief + *flaith* lord.
Variant: **Conla**.

Conn (m.) Irish Gaelic: name derived from an Old Celtic element meaning 'chief'. It is now also used as a short form of CONNOR and of various non-Irish names beginning with the syllable *Con-*.

Connie (f.) English: pet form of CONSTANCE.

Connor (m.) Irish: Anglicized form of the Gaelic name **Conchobhar**, possibly meaning 'lover of hounds'. Conchobhar was a semi-legendary Irish king who lived shortly after the time of Christ.
Variant: **Cnochúr** (a modern Gaelic form).

Conrad (m.) English and German: variant spelling of KONRAD, a Germanic personal name composed of the elements *kuon* bold + *rad* counsel. It was used occasionally in Britain in the Middle Ages in honour of a 10th-century bishop of Constance in Switzerland, but modern use in the English-speaking world is a reimportation dating mainly from the 19th century.
Variants: German: **Konrad**, **Kurt**.
Cognates: Dutch: **Koenrad**, **Kort**. Polish: **Konrad**. Italian: **Corrado**.

Conseja (f.) Spanish: religious name referring to the Marian title, *Nuestra Señora del Buen Consejo* 'Our Lady of Good

Counsel'. There is a festival dedicated to this aspect of the Virgin on 26 April.
Cognate: Italian: **Consilia**.

Consolata (f.) Italian: name referring to a title of the Virgin Mary, *Maria Consolata* (cf. CONSUELO).

Constance (f.) English and French: medieval form of the Late Latin name *Constantia*, which is either a feminine form of *Constantius*, a derivative of *Constans* (see CONSTANT), or an abstract noun meaning 'constancy'. This was a popular name among the Normans, and was borne by, amongst others, the formidable Constance of Sicily (1158–98), wife of the Emperor Henry VI.
Pet form: English: **Connie**.

Constant (m.) English and French: medieval form of the Late Latin name *Constans* (genitive *Constantis*) 'steadfast', but not common in the Middle Ages. It was taken up by the Puritans because of its transparent meaning, as an expression of their determination to 'resist stedfast in the faith' (1 Peter 5: 9).
Equivalent: Hungarian: **Szilárd**.

Constantine (m.) English and French: medieval form of the Late Latin name *Constantīnus* (a derivative of *Constans*; see CONSTANT). This was the name of Constantine the Great (?288–337), the first Christian emperor of Rome. It was also born by three kings of Scotland, apparently as an Anglicized form of CONN.
Cognates: Scottish Gaelic: **Còiseam**. Russian, Czech, Hungarian, Scandinavian, German: **Konstantin**. Polish: **Konstantyn**.

Consuelo (m.) Spanish: name referring to a title of the Virgin Mary, *Nuestra Señora del Consuelo* 'Our Lady of Solace' (Spanish *consuelo*, from Latin *consolātus*). Mary is traditionally a comforter of the bereaved and distressed and an intercessor with God.
Cognate: Italian: **Consolata**.
Short form: Spanish: **Suelo**.
Pet form: Spanish: **Chelo**.

Cor (m.) Dutch: short form of CORNELIS.

Cora (f.) English: name apparently coined by James Fenimore Cooper for one of the characters in *The Last of the Mohicans* (1826). It could represent a Latinized form of Greek *Korē* 'maiden'. In classical mythology this was a euphemistic name of the goddess of the underworld, Persephone, and would not have been a well-omened name to take.

Coral (f.) English: late 19th-century coinage. This is one of the group of girls' names taken from the vocabulary of jewellery. Coral is a beautiful pink calcareous material found in warm seas; it actually consists of the skeletons of millions of tiny sea creatures. The word is from Late Latin *corallium* and is probably ultimately of Semitic origin.

Coralie (f.) English: apparently an elaboration of CORA or CORAL on the model of ROSALIE.

Corazón (f.) Spanish: religious name referring to the Sacred Heart of Jesus, from Spanish *corazón* heart (an augmentative formation from Latin *cor*). Devotion to the Sacred Heart is known to some extent from early Christian times, but it became official and public in the 17th century; the feast was formally established in the Roman Catholic Church in 1855.

Cordelia (f.) English: name used by Shakespeare for King Lear's one virtuous daughter. It is not clear where he got it from; it does not seem likely to have a genuine Celtic origin. It may be a fanciful elaboration of Latin *cor* (genitive *cordis*) heart, and certainly this association has been made by many of those who have subsequently chosen it.

Cordula (f.) English and German: apparently a Late Latin diminutive form of *cor* (genitive *cordis*) heart. A saint of this name was, according to legend, one of Ursula's eleven thousand companions.

Coretta (f.) English: elaborated form of CORA, with the addition of the productive feminine suffix *-etta* (originally an Italian diminutive form). This is the name of the widow of the American civil rights campaigner Martin Luther King.

Corey (m.) English (U.S.): a fairly common male name among Blacks in the United States, but the reasons for its popularity are not clear. It is identical in form with the English surname *Corey*, which is derived from the Old Norse personal name *Kori*.

Variant: **Cory**.

Corin (m.) French: from Latin *Quirīnus*, the name of an ancient Roman divinity partly associated with the legendary figure of Romulus. It is of uncertain origin, probably connected with the Sabine word *quiris* or *curis* spear. In the early Christian period the name was borne by several saints martyred for the faith. The name is occasionally also used in the English-speaking world (where it is often regarded as a male equivalent of CORINNA), notably by the actor Corin Redgrave (b. 1939).

Corinna (f.) English and German: from the Greek name *Korinna* (probably a derivative of *Korē*, cf. CORA), borne by a Boeotian poetess of uncertain date, whose works survive in fragmentary form. The name was also used by the Roman poet Ovid for the woman addressed in his love poetry.

Corinne (f.) French form of CORINNA, also used in the English-speaking world.

Cormac (m.) Irish Gaelic: traditional name, apparently composed of the elements *corb* defilement + *mac* son. This has been a very popular name in Ireland from the earliest times. Cormac Ó Cuilleannáin, a 10th-century king and bishop, wrote an important dictionary of the Irish language.

Cognate: Scottish Gaelic: **Cormag**.

Cornelia (f.) English, German, and Dutch: from the Latin feminine form of the old Roman family name CORNELIUS. It was borne most notably in the 2nd century BC by the mother of the revolutionary reformers Tiberius and Gaius Sempronius Gracchus, and is still occasionally bestowed in her honour.

Pet forms: Dutch: **Cokkie, Nelleke**.

Cornelis (m.) Dutch form of CORNELIUS, very common in Holland and South Africa.

Short forms: **Cor, Niels**.
Pet forms: **Kees, Cees**.

Cornelius (m.) From an old Roman family name, *Cornēlius*, which is of uncertain origin, possibly a derivative of Latin *cornu* horn. This was the name of an early Christian who died in Civitavecchia in *c*.253.

Variants: Dutch: CORNELIS. French: **Corneille**. Polish: **Kornel(i), Korneliusz**. Czech: **Kornel**.

Cornell (m.) Medieval vernacular form of CORNELIUS in various languages, including English. In modern use it normally represents a transferred use of the surname, which is of very varied origin.

Corona (f.) German (S. Germany): from a Late Latin name meaning 'crown'. St Corona was a minor saint martyred in Syria in the 2nd century, together with her husband Victor. During the Middle Ages she was venerated in Bavaria, Austria, and Bohemia.

Corrado (m.) Italian form of CONRAD. This was a common name in several of the Italian royal houses during the Middle Ages, and is still used as a result of the fame of St Conrad Confalonieri (1290–1354), a nobleman of Piacenza.

Cosima (f.) English, German, and Italian: feminine form of COSMO, occasionally used in the English-speaking world. The most famous bearer is probably Cosima Wagner (1837–1930), daughter of Franz Liszt and wife of Richard Wagner.

Cosmo (m.) Italian, English, and German: Italian form (also found as **Cosimo**) of the Greek name *Kosmas* (a short form of various names containing the element *kosmos* order, beauty). This was borne by a Christian saint martyred, together with his brother Damian, at Aegea in Cilicia in the early 4th century. It was first brought to Britain in the 18th century by the Scottish dukes of Gordon, who had connections with the ducal house of Tuscany. The name was traditional in that family, having been borne most famously by Cosimo de' Medici (1389–1464), its founder and one of the chief patrons of the Italian Renaissance.

Courtney (m., f.) English (mainly U.S.): transferred use of the surname, originally a Norman baronial name from any of various places in northern France called *Courtenay* ('domain of Curtius'). However, from an early period it was taken as a nickname from Old French *court nez* 'short nose'. It is also used as a female name, especially in America.

Coy (m.) U.S.: of uncertain origin. It is hardly likely to be from the modern English vocabulary word, which has both feminine and pejorative connotations. It probably represents a transferred use of the surname *Coy*, or it may be of Irish origin (from *McCoy*, a variant of *McKay*, meaning 'son of Aodh'; *Aodh* was an old Gaelic name meaning 'fire').

Craig (m.) Scottish and English: transferred use of the surname, originally a local name derived from any of the many places in Scotland named with the Gaelic element *creag* rock. It is now widely fashionable throughout the English-speaking world, and is chosen as a given name by people who have no connection with Scotland.

Creighton (m.) Scottish and English: transferred use of the surname, which is of Scottish origin. It arose as a local name from *Crichton* in Midlothian, so called from Gaelic *crìoch* border, boundary + Middle English *tune* settlement (Old English *tūn*).

Crescentia (f.) German (S. Germany): original Latin form of the vernacular name KRESZENZ.

Cressa (f.) English: modern name, apparently originating as a contracted short form of CRESSIDA.

Cressida (f.) English: from a medieval legend, told by Chaucer and Shakespeare among others, set in ancient Troy. Cressida is a Trojan princess, daughter of Calchas, a priest who has defected to the Greeks. When she is restored to her father, she jilts her Trojan lover Troilus in favour of the Greek Diomedes. The story is not found in classical sources. Chaucer used the name in the form *Criseyde*, getting it from Boccaccio's *Criseida*. This in turn is ultimately based on Greek *Khryseis* (a derivative of *khrysos* gold), the name of a Trojan girl who is mentioned briefly as a prisoner of the Greeks at the beginning of Homer's *Iliad*. Chaucer's version of the name was Latinized by Shakespeare as *Cressida*. In spite of the unhappy associations of the story, the name has enjoyed some popularity in the 20th century.

Críostóir (m.) Irish Gaelic form of CHRISTOPHER.

Crisdean (m.) Scottish Gaelic: name derived from *Críosd* Christ, used as an equivalent of CHRISTOPHER.

Crispian (m.) English: medieval variant of CRISPIN, now very rarely used as a given name.

Crispin (m.) English: from Latin *Crispīnus*, a derivative of the old Roman family name *Crispus* 'curly(-headed)'. St Crispin was martyred with his brother Crispinian in *c*.285, and the pair were popular saints in the Middle Ages.

Cristina (f.) Italian, Spanish, and Portuguese form of CHRISTINA.

Crístíona (f.) Irish Gaelic form of CHRISTINA.

Cristo (m.) Spanish: short form of CRISTÓBAL. It is occasionally also used in the English-speaking world as an informal pet form of CHRISTOPHER.

Cristóbal (m.) Spanish form of CHRISTOPHER

Cristòfol (m.) Catalan form of CHRISTOPHER.

Cristoforo (m.) Italian form of CHRISTOPHER.

Cristovão (m.) Portuguese form of CHRISTOPHER.

Cronan (m.) Irish: Anglicized form of the Gaelic name **Crónán**, originally a byname representing a diminutive form of Gaelic *crón* swarthy.
Variant: **Cronin**.

Cruz (f.) Spanish: religious name referring to the agony of Mary at the foot of the Cross (Spanish *cruz*, from Latin *crux*, genitive *crūcis*).
Pet form: **Crucita**.

Crystal (f.) English: 19th-century coinage. This is one of the group of names taken from or suggestive of gemstones. The word *crystal*, denoting high-quality cut glass, is derived from Greek *krystallos* ice. (As a male name, *Crystal* originated as a Scottish pet form of CHRISTOPHER, but it is hardly, if ever, used today.)
Variant: **Krystle**.

Ctibor (m.) Czech form of CZCIBOR.
Pet form: **Ctik**.

Ctislav (m.) Czech variant of *Česlav* (see CZESLAW).

Cuán (m.) Irish Gaelic: originally a byname representing a diminutive form of Gaelic *cú* hound; cf. CONAN. This name has been strongly revived in the 20th century.

Cuddy (m.) Lowland Scottish: pet form of CUTHBERT. It has also become established as a conventional byname for a donkey.

Cugat (m.) Catalan: from Latin *Cucuphas* (genitive *Cucuphatis*), a name of Carthaginian origin and unknown derivation. It was borne by a 3rd-century saint who was martyred near Barcelona.

Cuimín (m.) Irish Gaelic: originally a byname representing a diminutive form of Gaelic *cam* bent, twisted.
Anglicized form: **Comyn**.

Cuithbeart (m.) Scottish Gaelic form of CUTHBERT.
Variant: **Cuithbrig**.

Curro (m.) Spanish: pet form of *Francisco* (see FRANCIS).

Curstaidh (f.) Scottish Gaelic spelling of KIRSTIE.
Variant: **Curstag**.

Curt (m.) **1.** German: variant spelling of KURT. **2.** English: originally an Anglicized spelling of German KURT, but now also used as a short form of CURTIS. Association with the vocabulary word *curt* 'brusque' does not seem to have harmed its popularity.

Curtis (m.) English: transferred use of the surname, which originated in the Middle Ages as a nickname for someone who was 'courteous' (Old French *curteis*). At an early date, however, it came to be associated with Middle English *curt* short + *hose* leggings; cf. COURTNEY.

Cuthbert (m.) English: from an Old English personal name composed (somewhat tautologously) of the elements *cūð* known + *beorht* bright, famous. It was borne by two pre-Conquest English saints: a 7th-century bishop of Lindisfarne and an 8th-century archbishop of Canterbury who corresponded with St Boniface.
Cognates: Scottish Gaelic: **Cuithbeart**, **Cuithbrig**.
Pet form: Scottish (Lowland): **Cuddy**.

Cy (m.) English: short form of CYRUS, sometimes used in America as an independent given name.

Cynddelw (m.) Welsh: traditional name of uncertain derivation, perhaps from an Old Celtic element meaning 'high, exalted' + Welsh *delw* image, statue, effigy.

Cynthia (f.) English: from Greek *Kynthia*, an epithet applied to the goddess Artemis, who was supposed to have been born on Mount *Kynthos* on the island of Delos. The mountain name is of pre-Greek origin. *Cynthia* was later used by the Roman poet Propertius as the name of the woman to whom he addressed his love poetry. The English given name was not used in the Middle Ages, but dates from the classical revival of the 17th and 18th centuries.
Cognate: Italian: **Cinzia**.

Cyril (m.) English: from the post-classical Greek name *Kyrillos*, a derivative of *kyrios* lord. It was borne by a large number of early saints, most notably the theologians Cyril of Alexandria and Cyril of Jerusalem. It was also the name of one of the Greek evangelists who brought Christianity to the Slavonic regions of Eastern Europe; in order to provide written translations of the gospels for their converts, they devised the alphabet still known as Cyrillic. In Ireland this has been used as an Anglicized form of the Gaelic name **Coireall** or **Caireall** (Old Irish *Cairell*).
Cognate: Russian: **Kirill**.

Cyrille (m., f.) French form of CYRIL, now also occasionally used in the English-speaking world, sometimes as a elaborated spelling variant and sometimes as a feminine form.

Cyrus (m.) U.S.: from the Greek form (*Kyros*) of the name of several kings of Persia, most notably Cyrus the Great (d. 529 BC). The origin of the name is not known, but in the early Christian period it was associated with Greek *kyrios* lord, and borne by various saints, including an Egyptian martyr and a bishop of Carthage.
Cognate: Italian: **Ciro**.
Short form: U.S.: **Cy**.

Czcibor (m.) Polish: from an old Slavonic personal name composed of the elements *chest* honour + *borit* to fight.
Variants: **Ścibor**, **Cibor**.
Cognate: Czech: **Ctibor**.

Czesław (m.) Polish: from an old Slavonic personal name composed of the elements *chest* honour + *slav* glory.
Cognates: Czech: **Česlav**, **Ctislav**. Russian: **Cheslav**.
Pet forms: Polish: **Czech**, **Czesiek**.

D

Daffodil (f.) English: one of the rarer flower names, which perhaps originated as an expanded version of DAFFY. The flower got its name in the 14th century from a run-together form of Dutch *de affodil* 'the asphodel'.

Daffy (f.) English: pet form of DAPHNE, not much used as an independent given name. Its popularity has not been aided by the occurence since the 19th century of the homonymous adjective *daffy* frivolous, absent-minded (from *daff* fool, connected with *daft*).

Dafydd (m.) Welsh form of DAVID; see also DEWI. This form of the name was in widespread use during the Middle Ages. Later it was largely replaced in Wales by the English form *David*, but from the late 19th century it has come into its own again.

Dag (m.) Scandinavian: from the Old Norse vocabulary word *dagr* day.

Dagmar (f.) Scandinavian (now also used in the German-speaking world): of uncertain origin. It would appear to be composed of the Old Scandinavian elements *dag* day + *mār* maid. It is possible that it represents a reworking of the Slavonic name *Dragomira*, composed of the elements *dorog* dear + *meri* great, famous (see CASIMIR). It is now occasionally used also in the English-speaking world.

Dagny (f.) Scandinavian: from an Old Norse female personal name composed of the elements *dag* day + *ný* new. The forms **Dagna** and **Dagne** are also used.

Dahlia (f.) English: from the name of the flower, which was so called in the 19th century in honour of the pioneering Swedish botanist Anders Dahl (1751–89). His surname represents a cognate of English DALE.

Variant: **Dalya**.

Dai (m.) Welsh: now used as a Welsh pet form of DAVID, but originally of distinct origin, probably from an Old Celtic element *dei* to shine.

Daibhidh (m.) Scottish Gaelic form of DAVID.

Daisy (f.) English: from the name of the flower, Old English *dægesēage*, the 'day's eye', so called because it uncovers the yellow disc of its centre in the morning and closes its petals over it again at the end of the day. The name seems to have been used early on as a punning pet form of MARGARET, by association with French *Marguerite*, which is both a version of that name and the word for the flower. However, it was not widespread until taken up at the end of the 19th century as part of the general vogue for flower names.

Dale (m., f.) English: transferred use of the surname, originally a local name for someone who lived in a *dale* or valley. It is now commonly used as a given name, especially in America, along with other monosyllabic surnames of topographical origin (cf. e.g. DELL and HALE). It is for the most part a male name, but occasionally also given to girls.

Daley (m.) Irish and English: from the Irish surname, the Gaelic form of which is *Ó Dálaigh* 'descendant of *Dálach*', a personal name derived from *dál* assembly, gathering.

Variant: **Daly**.

Dalibor (m.) Czech: from an old Slavonic personal name composed of the elements *dal* afar + *borit* to fight.

Feminine form: **Dalibora**.
Pet forms: **Dal(ek)** (m.); **Dal(en)(k)a** (f.).

Dalmazio (m.) Italian: from the Late Latin personal name *Dalmatius*, originally an ethnic name for someone from Dalmatia, across the Adriatic from Italy. The name was borne by an early bishop of Pavia who was martyred in 304.

Cognate: Spanish: **Dalmacio**.

Daly (m.) English: variant spelling of DALEY.

Dalya (f.) English: variant of DAHLIA.

Damaris (f.) New Testament: name of a woman mentioned as being converted to Christianity by St Paul (Acts 17: 34). Its origin is not clear, but it is probably Greek, perhaps a late form of *Damalis* 'calf'. It was taken up in the 17th century, along with the names of other characters fleetingly mentioned in the New Testament, and has been occasionally used ever since.

Damaso (m.) Spanish: name borne in honour of a 4th-century pope, St *Damasus*, who was a close friend of St Jerome. He was apparently of Spanish descent. The name is of Greek origin and is derived from the element *damān* to tame, subdue, kill (cf. DAMON and DAMIAN).

Damian (m.) English and Polish: from Greek *Damianos*, the name of the brother of Cosmas (see COSMO); the two brothers were martyred together at Aegea in Cilicia in the early 4th century. The origin of the name is not certain, but it is probably akin to DAMON.

Cognates: French: **Damien** (sometimes also used in the English-speaking world). Italian: **Damiano**. Spanish: **Damián**. Portuguese: **Damião**. Russian: **Demyan**.

Damon (m.) English: from a classical Greek name, a derivative of *damān* to tame, subdue (often a euphemism for 'kill'). This was made famous in antiquity by the story of Damon and Pythias. In the early 4th century BC Pythias was condemned to death by Dionysius, ruler of Syracuse. His friend Damon offered to stand surety for him, and took his place in the condemned cell while Pythias put his affairs in order. When Pythias duly returned to be executed, rather than absconding and leaving his friend to his fate, Dionysius was so impressed by the trust and friendship of the two young men that he pardoned both of them. The name was not used in the early centuries of the Christian era or during the Middle Ages. Its modern use seems to date from the 1930s and is probably due to the fame of the American short-story writer Damon Runyon (1884–1946). It is sometimes taken as a variant of DAMIAN.

Dan (m.) **1.** Biblical: name (meaning 'he judged' in Hebrew) borne by one of Jacob's twelve sons (Genesis 30: 6). Samson

734

was a member of the tribe which descended from him. **2**. English: short form of DANIEL.

Dana (f., m.) **1**. (f.) E. European: for the most part a feminine form of DAN (1) or DANIEL. In Poland it is also used as a short form of *Bogdana* (see BOGDAN) and a pet form of DARIA. **2**. (f., m) English (esp. U.S.): from the surname, which is relatively common in the United States, but of uncertain derivation. Use as a given name began in honour of Richard Dana (1815–82), author of *Two Years before the Mast*. A lawyer by profession, he supported the rights of fugitive slaves, and lent his backing to the Union during the Civil War.
Pet forms (of 1): Czech: **Danka**, **Danuše**, **Danuška**, **Danička**, **Danul(k)a**.

Danaë (f.) Name borne in Greek mythology by the daughter of Acrisius, who was ravished by Zeus in the form of a shower of gold; as a result she gave birth to the hero Perseus. Her name is of uncertain derivation; she was a great great-granddaughter of *Danaus*, the eponymous founder of the Greek tribe of the *Danai* or Argives.

Dane (m.) English: transferred use of the surname, which was originally a local name representing a dialect variant of DEAN that was common in south-east England.

Daniel (m.) Jewish, English, French, German, Polish, and Czech: biblical name (meaning 'God is my judge' in Hebrew) borne by the prophet whose story is told in the Book of Daniel. He was an Israelite slave of the Assyrian king Nebuchadnezzar, who obtained great favour through his skill in interpreting dreams and the 'writing on the wall' at the feast held by Nebuchadnezzar's son Belshazzar. His enemies managed to get him cast into a lions' den, but he was saved by God. This was a favourite tale in the Middle Ages, often represented in miracle plays. The name is popular among both Jews and Gentiles; in Ireland it has often been used as an Anglicized form of Gaelic *Domhnall* (see DONALD).
Cognates: Welsh: **Deiniol**. Scottish Gaelic: **Dàniel**. Italian: **Daniele**. Russian: **Daniil**. Ukrainian: **Danilo**. Finnish: **Taneli**.
Short form: English: **Dan**.
Pet forms: English: **Danny**. Czech: **Danek**, **Daneš**, **Danoušek**.

Daniela (f.) Polish and Czech: Latinate feminine form of DANIEL, occasionally used also in the English-speaking world.

Danièle (f.) French: feminine form of DANIEL, occasionally used also in the English-speaking world.
Variant: **Danielle** (rather more commonly used in the English-speaking world).
Pet form: **Dany**.

Danika (f.) Eastern European name, now also in occasional use in the English-speaking world. It is derived from a Slavonic element denoting the morning star.

Danny (m.) English: pet form of DANIEL, with the hypocoristic suffix *-y*.

Dante (m.) Italian: name bestowed in honour of the medieval poet Dante Alighieri (1265–1321). The medieval given name *Dante* represents a contracted form of *Durante* 'steadfast, enduring' (from Latin *dūrans*, genitive *dūrantis*, present participle of *dūrāre* to endure).

Danuta (f.) Polish: of uncertain origin, apparently a derivative of DANA. It is also possible that *Danuta* may derive from Latin *Donāta*, feminine of *Donātus* (see DONATO).

Dany (f.) French: pet form of DANIÈLE and its variant *Danielle*.

Daphne (f.) Name borne in Greek mythology by a nymph who was changed into a laurel by her father, a river god, to enable her to escape the attentions of Apollo, who was pursuing her. The name means 'laurel' in Greek. According to the myth, then, the nymph gave her name to the shrub, but in fact of course it was the other way about: her name was taken from the vocabulary word (which seems to be of pre-Greek origin, and may therefore have been thought to need explaining). The name was not used in England until the end of the 19th century, when it seems to have been adopted as part of the vogue for flower names at that time.

Dara (m.) Irish Gaelic: short form of MAC DARA. This name is common in Connemara and now also elsewhere in Ireland. It was formerly often Anglicized as DUDLEY.
Variant: **Darach**.

Darby (m.) English: transferred use of the surname, which originated in the Middle Ages as a local name for someone from the city of Derby or the district of West Derby near Liverpool. These are so called from Old Norse *diur* deer + *býr* settlement. The Middle English change of *-er*-to *-ar-* is normally reflected in the spelling of the given name as well as most cases of the surname, whereas the placename retains a more conservative orthographic form. In Ireland this name has often been used as an Anglicized form of Gaelic *Diarmait* (see DERMOT).

Darcy (m.) English: transferred use of the surname, originally a Norman baronial name (*d'Arcy*) borne by a family who came from Arcy in northern France. It has always retained a somewhat aristocratic flavour, which has enhanced its popularity as a given name. It is the surname of the hero of Jane Austen's novel *Pride and Prejudice* (1813).

Daria (f.) English, Italian, and Polish: feminine form of the much rarer male name *Darius* (see DARIO). St Daria (d. 283) was a Greek woman married to an Egyptian Christian called Chrysanthus; they lived at Rome and were both martyred under the joint emperors Numerian and Carinus.
Cognates: Russian: **Darya**. Czech: **Darie**.
Pet forms: Polish: **Dana**. Russian: **Dasha**. Czech: **Darka**, **Darin(k)a**, **Daruška**.

Dario (m.) Italian: from the Late Latin name *Darius*, Greek *Dareios*, originally a transliterated version of the name of various ancient Persian kings. The original form of the name seems to have been *Darayavahush*, composed of the elements *daraya(miy)* to hold, possess, maintain + *vahu* well, good. A rather obscure saint of this name was martyred at Nicaea with three companions at an uncertain date. The Latin form **Darius** is occasionally used as a given name in the United States.

Darlene (f.) English (esp. Australia and U.S.): modern coinage, apparently representing an alteration of the affectionate nickname *Darling* by fusion with the suffix *-lene*, found as an ending in other female given names.

Darrell (m.) English: transferred use of the surname, originally a Norman baronial name (*d'Airelle*) borne by a family who came from Airelle in Calvados. It was first used as a given name towards the end of the 19th century, and has enjoyed a considerable vogue in the latter part of the 20th century.
Variants: **Darrel**, **Darell**.

Darren (m.) English: recently coined name of uncertain derivation. It may well have been an arbitrary coinage, or from a surname (of obscure origin). It seems to have been first borne by the American actor Darren McGavin (b. 1922). It came to the attention of the public as the name of a character in the popular American television comedy series *Bewitched* (made in the 1960s). In the spelling **Darin**, it is associated with the singer Bobby Darin (1936–73), who was originally called Walden Robert Cassotto and who chose the name he made famous from a telephone directory.

Darrene (f.) English: feminine form of DARREN, formed by fusion with the productive feminine suffix *-ene*.

Darryl (m.), occasionally (f.) English: apparently a variant of DARRELL. Together with the variant **Daryl**, it is occasionally borne by women, perhaps under the influence of names such as CHERYL.

Darya (f.) Russian form of DARIA.

Pet form: **Dasha**.

Dassah (f.) Jewish: aphetic short form of HADASSAH. The shortening may have been assisted by the erroneous association of the first syllable with the Hebrew definite article *ha*.

David (m.) Biblical: name of the greatest of the Israelite kings, whose history is recounted in 1 Samuel and elsewhere. As a boy he killed the giant Philistine, Goliath, with his slingshot; as king of Judah, and later of all Israel, he expanded the power of the Israelites and established their security. He was also noted as a poet, with many of the Psalms being attributed to him. He had many sons and, according to the gospels, Jesus was descended from him. The Hebrew derivation of the name is uncertain; it is said by some to represent a nursery word meaning 'darling'. In America this is mainly a Jewish name, but it has no such weighting in Britain, where it is particularly common in Wales and Scotland, having been borne by the patron saint of Wales (see DEWI) and by two medieval kings of Scotland.

Cognates: Scottish Gaelic: **Dàibhidh**. Irish Gaelic: **Dáibhidh**. Welsh: DAFYDD, DEWI. Polish: **Dawid**. Finnish: **Taavi**.
Short form: English: **Dave**.
Pet forms: English and Scottish: **Davy**, **Davey**, **Davie**. Welsh: DAI.

Davina (f.) Scottish and English: Latinate feminine form of DAVID. The name seems to have originated in Scotland, and is occasionally elaborated to **Davinia**, on the model of LAVINIA. The more straightforward feminine **Davida** is considerably less frequent.

Davy (m.) English and Scottish: pet form of DAVID. It is fairly extensively used as an independent given name, particularly in Scotland.

Variants: **Davey**, **Davie**.

Dawn (f.) English: from the vocabulary word for daybreak, no doubt originally bestowed because of the connotations of freshness and purity of this time of day. It may have originated as a vernacular translation of AURORA. According to Dunkling, it was first used in 1928, after which it quickly became popular. Twin girls are sometimes given the names *Dawn* and EVE, although the latter name does not in fact have anything to do with the time of day.

Dean (m.) English: transferred use of the surname, which has a double origin. In part it is a local name for someone who lived in a valley (Middle English *dene*, Old English *denu*), in part an occupational name for someone who served as a dean, i.e. ec-

clesiastical supervisor (Latin *decanus*). The given name also sometimes represents Italian DINO, as in the case of the American actor and singer Dean Martin (b. 1917).

Variants: **Deane**, **Dene**.

Deanna (f.) English: originally a fanciful respelling of DIANA, now often taken as a feminine form of DEAN. It was made popular by the singing actress Deanna Durbin (b. 1922), whose original given name was EDNA; *Deanna* may have been derived as a partial anagram of this.

Deborah (f.) Jewish and English: biblical name (meaning 'bee' in Hebrew) borne by the nurse of Rebecca (Genesis 35: 8) and by a woman judge and prophet (Judges 4–5), who led the Israelites to victory over the Canaanites. The name has always been popular among Jews. It was taken up among Christians by the Puritans in the 17th century, no doubt in part because the bee was a symbol of industriousness. It has steadily increased in popularity ever since and is currently enjoying a great vogue.

Variants: **Debora**, **Debra**. Jewish: **Devora(h)** (Hebrew); **Dvoire** (Yiddish).
Pet forms: English: **Debbie**, **Debbi**, **Debi**, **Debs**.

Declan (m.) Irish: Anglicized form of Gaelic **Deaglán**, of uncertain derivation. It was borne by a 5th-century disciple of St Colman, who became a bishop in the district of Ardmore. In recent years the name has been strongly revived in Ireland.

Dee (f., m.) English: pet form of any of the given names beginning with the letter D- (cf. KAY), especially DOROTHY. It is also used as an independent name, and may in some cases be associated with the River Dee (cf. CLYDE).

Deforest (m.) U.S.: name apparently adopted in honour of John Deforest (1826–1906), the author of several once popular novels, mostly set during the American Civil War.

Variant: **Deforrest**.

Deiniol (m.) Welsh: apparently a form of DANIEL. The name was borne by a 6th-century Welsh saint.

Deirdre (f.) Irish and English: name borne in Celtic legend by a tragic heroine, sometimes referred to as 'Deirdre of the Sorrows'. The story goes that she was betrothed to Conchobhar, King of Ulster, but instead eloped with her beloved Naoise. Eventually, however, the jilted king murdered Naoise and his brothers, and Deirdre herself died of a broken heart. She is sometimes taken as symbolic of the fate of Ireland under English rule, but this has not stopped her name's being used by English parents with no Celtic blood in them. It became popular in Ireland and elsewhere in the Edwardian era, following retellings of the legend by both the poet W. B. Yeats (1907) and the playwright J. M. Synge (1910). The name itself is of uncertain derivation; the earliest Celtic forms are very variable.

Del (m.) English: colloquial pet form of DEREK, with alteration of the exposed *-r* of the short form to *-l* (cf. SAL and TEL).

Delbert (m.) English (borne mainly by Blacks): apparently a modern coinage, composed of the name elements *Del-* (see DELMAR and DELROY) + *-bert*. In the 1980s it was adopted by the comedian Lenny Henry as the name of one of his comic creations, Delbert Wilkins.

Delfina (f.) Italian and Spanish form of DELPHINE, sometimes also used in the English-speaking world.

Delia (f.) English: from a classical Greek epithet of the goddess Artemis, referring to her birth on the island of *Delos* (*cf.* CYNTHIA). It was taken up by the pastoral poets of the 17th century, and has been moderately popular ever since.

Delice (f.) English: variant of DELICIA, apparently modelled on medieval given names such as AMICE and CLARICE.

Delicia (f.) English: feminine form of the Late Latin name *Delicius*, a derivative of *deliciae* delight. Use as a given name seems to be a modern phenomenon; it is not found in the Middle Ages.

Delilah (f.) Biblical: name (of uncertain origin) of Samson's mistress, who wheedled him into revealing the secret of his strength and then betrayed him to the Philistines (Judges 16: 4–20). Although the biblical Delilah was deceitful and treacherous, the name was taken up quite enthusiastically by the Puritans in the 17th century, perhaps because she was also beautiful and clever. The name fell out of use in the 18th century, but has been occasionally revived as an exotic name.
Variant: **Delila**.

Delite (f.) English: modern coinage, apparently based on the vocabulary word *delight* (from Old French *delit*, cf. DELICIA; the *-gh-* of the modern spelling is not justified by the etymology).

Dell (m.) English: transferred use of the surname, originally a local name for someone who lived in a *dell* or hollow.

Della (f.) English: name which first appeared in the 1870s and has continued to grow steadily in popularity ever since. Its derivation is not clear; if it is not simply an arbitrary creation, it may be an altered form of DELIA or DELILAH, or a short form of ADELA. In modern use it is sometimes taken as a feminine form of DELL.

Delma (f.) Irish: short form of FIDELMA.

Delmar (m.) English: of uncertain derivation, possibly an arbitrary alteration of ELMER (cf. DELROY and ELROY). In form it coincides with Spanish *del mar* 'of the sea', which occurs in various placenames as a distinguishing epithet and also in the Marian title, *Reina del Mar* 'Queen of the Sea'. As a given name, it is popular chiefly among American Blacks.

Delores (f.) English: variant of DOLORES, quite common in the United States.
Variant: **Deloris**.

Delphine (f.) French and English: from Latin *Delphīna* 'woman from Delphi'. The Blessed Delphina (1283–1358) was a Provençal nun, who may herself have been named in honour of the 4th-century St Delphinus of Bordeaux. In modern times the name seems often to have been chosen for its association with the *delphinium* flower.
Cognate: Italian, Spanish: **Delfina**.

Delroy (m.) Apparently an altered form of LEROY, perhaps representing the Old French phrase *del roy* '(son, servant) of the king'. It is used chiefly among West Indians in Britain.

Delwyn (f.) Welsh: modern name composed of the elements *del* pretty, neat + *(g)wyn* white, fair, blessed, holy.

Delyth (f.) Welsh: modern name composed of the vocabulary word *del* pretty, neat + the ending *-yth*, formed on the analogy of names such as GWENYTH.

Demelza (f.) Modern Cornish name that has no history as a Celtic personal name but derives from a place in the parish of St Columb Major. The given name began to be used in the 1950s and was given a boost by the serialization on British television of the 'Poldark' novels by Winston Gráham, in which it is the name of the heroine.

Demetrio (m.) Italian and Spanish form of Latin *Dēmētrius* (see DMITRI).

Demid (m.) Russian: from Greek *Diomēdēs*, composed of a byform of the divine name *Zeus* + the element *mēdesthai* to care for, consider. St Diomedes was born at Tarsus in Cilicia and martyred at Nicaea in Bithynia under the Emperor Diocletian.

Demyan (m.) Russian form of DAMIAN.

Den (m.) English: short form of DENNIS.
Pet form: **Denny**.

Dena (f.) English: modern coinage, representing either a respelling of DINA, or else a form created as a feminine version of DEAN.

Dene (m.) English: variant spelling of DEAN.

Dénes (m.) Hungarian form of DENNIS.

Denice (f.) English: altered form of DENISE, based on the alternative pronunciation of that name.

Denis (m.) French and Russian form of DENNIS, and a variant spelling in the English-speaking world.

Denise (f.) French: feminine form of DENIS, now also widely used in the English-speaking world.

Dennis (m.) English and French: medieval vernacular form of the Greek name *Dionysios*, which was borne by several early Christian saints, including St Denis, a 3rd-century evangelist who converted the Gauls and became a patron saint of Paris. It was on his account that the name was popular among the Normans. In classical times, the word originally denoted a devotee of the god Dionysos. This deity was a relatively late introduction to the classical pantheon; his orgiastic cult seems to have originated in Persia or elsewhere in Asia. His name is of uncertain derivation, although the first part seems to be related to the name of the supreme god *Zeus*.
Cognates: French, Russian: **Denis**. Polish: **Dionizy**. Hungarian: **Dénes**.
Short form: English: **Den**.
Pet form: English: **Denny**.

Denton (m.) English: transferred use of the surname, originally a local name from any of the numerous places so called from Old English *denu* valley + *tūn* enclosure, settlement.

Denzil (m.) English: from the Cornish surname, the original spelling of which was *Denzell*, a local name from a place in Cornwall. It came to be used as a given name in the Hollis family in the 16th century, when the Hollis family and the Denzell family became connected by marriage, and spread from there into more general use.

Deòiridh (f.) Scottish Gaelic: from the vocabulary word meaning 'pilgrim'. This name has been Anglicized as DORCAS.

Deònaid (f.) Scottish Gaelic: dialectal variant of SEÒNAID.

Deòrsa (m.) Scottish Gaelic form of GEORGE; See also SEÒRAS.

Derek (m.) English: from a Low German form of *Theodoric* (see TERRY), introduced to Britain during the Middle Ages by

Flemish settlers connected with the cloth trades. It is a comparatively rare name in the United States.

Cognates: German: **Dietrich**. Low German: **Diederick**. Flemish, Dutch: **Dirk**. E. Frisian: **Tjark**.

Pet form: English: **Del**.

Derick (m.) **1**. English: variant of DEREK. **2**. Scottish: short form of RODERICK.

Dermot (m.) Irish: Anglicized form of the Gaelic name **Diarmaid**. An earlier Gaelic form is *Diarm(u)it*. It occurs in the 7th-century Latin *Life of St Columba* as *Diormitius*. The derivation is uncertain, but it has been suggested that it is composed of the elements *di* without + *airmit* injunction or *airmait* envy.

Cognates: Scottish: **Diarmad** (Gaelic); **Diarmid**, **Dermid** (Anglicized forms).

Derrick (m.) English: variant spelling of DEREK. This is the usual American spelling of the given name, but in Britain it is more common as a surname than as a given name.

Derry (m.) English: of uncertain origin, perhaps a cross between DEREK and the ultimately cognate TERRY.

Dervla (f.) Irish: Anglicized form of the Gaelic name **Deirbhile**, composed of the elements *der* daughter + *file* poet.

Variant: **Dervila**.

Desdemona (f.) English: name chosen occasionally by parents in search of an unusual name, who are no doubt attracted by the sweet nature and innocence of Shakespeare's character and not deterred by her tragic fate. She was murdered by her husband Othello in an ill-founded jealous rage, and her name is in fact particularly appropriate to her destiny, as it probably represents a Latinized form of Greek *dysdaimōn* ill-starred.

Desiderio (m.) Italian, Spanish, and Portuguese form of *Desiderius* (see DIDIER).

Desirée (f.) French (now also used in the English-speaking world): from Latin *Desiderāta* 'desired'. This name was given by early Christians to a longed-for child, but the French form is now often taken as suggesting that the bearer will grow up into a desirable woman.

Desmond (m.) Irish and English: apparently originally a local name for someone who came from south Munster (Gaelic *Deas-Mhumhan*). The form has been influenced by the Norman (Germanic) name ESMOND.

Short form: **Des**.
Pet form: **Desy**.

Desya (m.) Russian: pet form of MODEST.

Detlev (m.) Low German: from an old Germanic personal name composed of the elements *peud* people, race + *leib* relic, inheritance, descendant. The High German form, *Dietleib*, is not current as a given name.

Variant: **Detlef**.
Cognates: E. Frisian: **Tjalf**. Swedish: **Detlof**.

Detta (f.) Italian: short form of various given names such as *Benedetta* (see BENEDICT) and *Bernardetta* (see BERNADETTE).

Devereux (m.) English (esp. U.S.): transferred use of a surname, which was originally a Norman baronial name derived (with fused preposition *de*) from *Evreux* in the *département* of Eure. It was the family name of the 16th-century earls of Essex; Robert Devereux, the 2nd earl, was a favourite of Queen Elizabeth I, later disgraced and executed for treason.

Devorah (f.) Jewish: modern Hebrew form of DEBORAH.

Devorgilla (f.) Scottish: Anglicized form of Gaelic **Diorbhail**, earlier *Diorbhorguil*, apparently meaning 'true testimony'. See also DOROTHY.

Dewey (m.) U.S.: of uncertain origin, perhaps a respelling of DEWI.

Dewi (m.) A Welsh form (earlier *Dewydd*) of DAVID, traditionally associated with the patron saint of Wales. This form of the given name was little used during the Middle Ages, but during the 20th century it has become quite common in Wales, but rare elsewhere. St Dewi was born in South Wales in the 5th century and became the first bishop of Menevia, the tiny cathedral city now known as St Davids.

Dex (m.) Mainly U.S.: short form of DEXTER (cf. LEX and TEX).

Dexter (m.) English (mainly U.S.): transferred use of the surname. Although this is now a male given name, the word that gave rise to the surname originally denoted a female dyer, from Old English *dēag* dye + *-estre* feminine suffix of agent nouns. However, the distinction of gender was already lost in Middle English. The name coincides in form with Latin *dexter* right-handed, auspicious, and may sometimes have been chosen because of this.

Dezsö (m.) Hungarian form of *Desiderius* (see DIDIER).

Dezydery (m.) Polish form of *Desiderius* (see DIDIER).

Diana (f.) English: name borne in Roman mythology by the goddess of the moon and of hunting, equivalent to the Greek Artemis. In mythology she is characterized as both beautiful and chaste. Her name is of ancient and uncertain derivation. It probably contains a first element that is also found in the name of the supreme god *Jupiter* and in Greek *Dionysios* (see DENNIS). It was adopted in Britain during the Tudor period as a learned name, a borrowing from Latin influenced by the French form DIANE. It was not particularly popular until the end of the 19th century, and its increased frequency at that time has been attributed in part to George Meredith's novel *Diana of the Crossways* (1885). However, Dunkling casts doubt on this suggestion. In earlier centuries, some clergymen were reluctant to baptize girls with this pagan name, remembering the riots against St Paul stirred up by worshippers of Diana of the Ephesians (Acts 19: 24-41).

Short form: **Di**.

Diane (f.) French form of DIANA, now also used in the English-speaking world. It was especially popular among the Renaissance aristocracy, who loved hunting and were therefore proud to name their daughters after the classical goddess of the chase.

Variants: **Dianne** (by association with ANNE); **Dyan** (U.S.).
Short form: **Di**.

Diarmad (m.) Scottish Gaelic form of DERMOT. It has sometimes been Anglicized as JEREMIAH.

Variants: **Diarmid**, **Dermid** (Anglicized).

Dick (m.) English: short form of RICHARD (cf. *Rick*). The alteration of the initial consonant is supposed to result from the difficulty that English speakers in the Middle Ages had in pronouncing the trilled Norman *R-*.

Dickie (m.) English: pet form of DICK, with the originally Scottish and northern English hypocoristic suffix *-ie*. This has more or less completely replaced the medieval diminutive *Dickon*, with the Old French suffix -*on*.

Didier (m.) French: from Late Latin *Dēsīderius*, a derivative of *dēsīderium* longing. The name was popular among the early Christians, who chose it to give expression to their longing for Christ. Among the saints who bore it are an early bishop of Langres and 7th-century bishops of Auxerre, Cahors, and Vienne, all of whom are subjects of local cults.
Cognates: Italian, Spanish, Portuguese: **Desiderio**. Polish: **Dezydery**. Hungarian: **Dezsö**.

Diederik (m.) Dutch form of DIETRICH.
Pet form: **Tiede**.

Diego (m.) Spanish: of uncertain origin. Although it is often claimed to be an aphetic form of SANTIAGO, it is clear that its regular Latin form in the Middle Ages was *Didacus*. This may possibly be a derivative of Greek *didakhē* teaching, but it is more likely that is represents a Latinized form of some native Iberian name.
Cognate: Portuguese: **Diogo**.

Dieter (m.) German: from an old Germanic personal name composed of the elements *peud* people, race + *hari, heri* army, warrior. St Theuderius (d. *c*.575) was a monk of Lérins who founded three monasteries near his native city of Vienne.

Dietfried (m.) German: from an old Germanic personal name composed of the elements *peud* people, race + *fred, frid* peace.

Dietlinde (f.) German: from an old Germanic female personal name composed of the elements *peud* people, race + *lind* weak, tender, soft.

Dietmar (m.) German: from an old Germanic personal name composed of the elements *peud* people, race + *māri, mēri* famous. St Theodemar (d. 1152) was a native of Bremen who became a missionary to the Wends. Another St Theodmarus (d. 1102), also known by the short form *Thieme*, was a member of the Bavarian royal family who became archbishop of Salzburg.

Dietrich (m.) German form of DEREK.

Dieudonné (m.) French: medieval given name meaning 'given by God' in the vernacular, from Old French *Dieu* God (Latin *Deus*) + *donné* given (Latin *donātus*). It is thus an equivalent in meaning of such names as MATTHEW, NATHANIEL, THEODORE, and DOROTHY. The name is occasionally used nowadays in a spirit of self-conscious antiquarianism.

Digby (m.) English: transferred use of the surname, originally a local name for someone from Digby in Lincolnshire, so called from the Old Norse elements *diki* ditch + *býr* settlement.

Digna (f.) Spanish: from the Late Latin name *Digna* 'worthy', which was borne by a martyr beheaded in Spain during the 9th century.

Dillon (m.) English: variant spelling of DYLAN, based on an English surname of different origin. The surname *Dillon* or *Dyllon* derives in part from a now extinct Norman French personal name of Germanic origin; in part it is a local name for someone from *Dilwyn* in Hereford.

Dilly (f.) English: pet form of DILYS, DILWEN, and DAFFODIL, now sometimes used as an independent given name.

Dilwen (f.) Welsh: modern name, composed of the elements *dil* from DILYS + *(g)wen* feminine form of *gwyn* white, fair, blessed, holy.

Dilwyn (m.) Welsh: modern name, composed of the elements *dil* from DILYS + *(g)wyn* white, fair, blessed, holy.

Dilys (f.) Welsh: of modern origin, from the vocabulary word *dilys* genuine, steadfast, true.

Dimitri (m.) Russian: variant of DMITRI.

Dina (f.) 1. English: in part a variant spelling of DINAH, with which it often has the same pronunciation. In part, however, it seems to represent the adoption of a feminine form of DINO. 2. Scottish: short form of *Murdina* (see MURDO).

Dinah (f.) Biblical: name (a feminine form derived from Hebrew *din* judgement) borne by a daughter of Jacob. She was raped by Shechem but avenged by her brothers Simeon and Levi (Genesis 34). In modern times it has often been taken as a variant of the much more common DIANA.
Variant: Yiddish: **Dine**.

Dino (m.) Italian: aphetic short form of any of the various names ending in these syllables, as for example *Bernardino* (see BERNARD) and *Leonardino* (see LEONARD).

Diogo (m.) Portuguese form of DIEGO.

Dion (m.) French: from Latin *Dio* (genitive *Diōnis*), a short form of the various names of Greek origin containing as their first element the divine name *Dio*- Zeus, as, for example, *Diodoros* 'gift of Zeus' and *Diogenēs* 'born of Zeus'. The name is also used in the English-speaking world, where it is particularly common among Blacks.

Dionizy (m.) Polish form of DENNIS.

Dionne (f.) English: feminine form of DION, or an altered form of *Dianne* (see DIANE).

Dirk (m.) Flemish and Dutch form of DEREK. Its use in the English-speaking world since the 1960s is largely due to the fame of the actor Dirk Bogarde (b. 1921; originally Derek Niven van den Bogaerde). He is of Dutch descent, although he was actually born in Scotland. The manly image of the name has been reinforced by its coincidence in form with the Scottish vocabulary word *dirk* dagger (from Gaelic *durc*).

Disa (f.) Scandinavian: Latinized version of an aphetic short form of the various women's names of Old Norse origin containing the final element *dis* goddess (cf. e.g. HJÖRDIS and TORDIS).

Dmitri (m.) Russian: from the Greek name *Dēmētrios*, a derivative of the name of the goddess *Dēmētēr*, which in turn seems to be composed of *dē*, a variant of *gē* earth + *mētēr* mother. The most famous St Demetrius was an early 4th-century martyr executed at Sirmium in Dalmatia under the Emperor Diocletian; many legends have grown up around him in the Eastern Church.
Variant: **Dimitri**.
Cognates: Italian, Spanish: **Demetrio**. Romanian: **Dumitru**. Polish: **Dymitr**. Ukrainian: **Dmitro**.
Pet form: Russian: **Mitya** (see also MITROFAN).

Dobre (f.) Jewish (E. Yiddish): from the Slavonic element *dobro* good, kind.
Variant: **Dobe**.
Pet form: **Dobke**.

Dobrila (f.) Slavonic: derivative of the element *dobro* good, kind. This may in origin be an affectionate nickname, or else a short form of the various compound names with this first element.

Variant: Russian: **Dobryna**.

Dobromierz (m.) Polish: from an old Slavonic personal name composed of the elements *dobro* good, kind + *meri* great, famous (see CASIMIR).

Cognate: Czech: **Dobromir**.
Feminine forms: Polish: **Dobromira**. Czech: **Dobromíra**.

Dobromil (m.) Polish: from an old Slavonic personal name composed of the elements *dobro* good, kind + *mil* grace, favour.

Cognate: Czech: **Dobromil**.
Feminine form: Czech: **Dobromila**.

Dobrosław (m.) Polish: from an old Slavonic personal name composed of the elements *dobro* good, kind + *slav* glory.

Cognate: Czech: **Dobroslav**.
Feminine forms: Polish: **Dobrosława**. Czech: **Dobroslava**.

Dodie (f.) English: unusual pet form of DOROTHY, derived from a child's unsuccessful attempts to pronounce the name.

Dolina (f.) Scottish: Latinate formation based on the Gaelic name *Dolag*, a feminine diminutive form of DONALD.

Variant: **Dolanna**.

Dolly (f., m.) **1**. (f.) English: originally (from the 16th century onwards) a pet form of DOROTHY, but now more commonly used as a pet form of DOLORES and as an independent given name (taken as being from the vocabulary word *doll*, although in fact this was derived from the pet name in the 17th century). **2**. (m.) Highland Scottish: pet form of DONALD.

Dolores (f.) Spanish (now also borne in the English-speaking world, mainly by Roman Catholics): from the Marian title, *Maria de los Dolores* 'Mary of Sorrows', a reference to the Seven Sorrows of the Virgin in Christian belief. The feast of Our Lady's Dolours was established in 1423.

Variants: English: **Delores**, **Deloris**.
Cognate: Portuguese: **Dores**.
Pet forms: Spanish: **Lola**, **Lolita**. English: **Dolly**.

Domicela (f.) Polish form of DOMITILLA.

Dominga (f.) Spanish: feminine form of *Domingo* (see DOMINIC).

Dominic (m.) English and Irish: from the Late Latin name *Dominicus* (a derivative of *dominus* lord; cf. CYRIL). It is used mainly by Roman Catholics, in honour of St Dominic (1170–1221), founder of the Dominican order of monks.

Variant: **Dominick** (an old spelling, still in occasional use).
Cognates: French: DOMINIQUE. Italian: **Domenico**. Spanish: **Domingo**. Catalan: **Domenge**. Basque: **Txomin**. Polish, Czech: **Dominik**. Hungarian: **Domonkos**.

Dominica (f.) Latinate feminine form of DOMINIC. This name was borne by a saint martyred in Campania under the Emperor Diocletian and by a wealthy Roman widow who was an associate of St Laurence.

Dominique (f., m.) French form of DOMINICA and DOMINIC. It is used as both a female and a male name, but is now much more commonly used as a female name, and as such has also become widespread in the English-speaking world. In Britain it is found especially among Roman Catholics.

Domitilla (f.) Italian and English: name used by Roman Catholics in honour of a 2nd-century saint, Flavia Domitilla, who was a member of the Roman imperial family. She was the great-niece of the Emperor Domitian, and her name represents

a diminutive form of *Domitius*, the old Roman family name of which *Domitiānus* is a derivative. It is most probably derived from the nickname *Domitus* 'tamed'.

Cognate: Polish: **Domicela**.

Domonkos (m.) Hungarian form of DOMINIC.

Don (m.) English and Scottish: short form of DONALD. It is also a variant of the Irish name DONN.

Pet forms: Scottish: **Donny**, **Donnie** (Gaelic **Donnaidh**).

Donagh (m.) Irish: Anglicized form of the Gaelic name **Donnchadh**; see DUNCAN.

Variants: **Dono(u)gh**.

Donal (m.) Irish: Anglicized form of the Gaelic name **Dónal**, a simplified form of *Domhnall* (see DONALD). The form **Donall** is also used.

Donald (m.) Scottish and English: Anglicized form of the Gaelic name **Domhnall**, composed of the Old Celtic elements *dubno* world + *val* rule. The final -*d* of the Anglicized form derives partly from misinterpretation by English-speakers of the Gaelic devoiced sound (cf. DUGALD), and partly from association with Germanic-origin names such as RONALD. This name is very much associated with clan MacDonald, the clan of the medieval Lords of the Isles. In the Highlands and Islands it now ranks second only to *Iain* (see IAN). *Donald* is now quite commonly also used in Britain and America by families with no Scottish connections.

Short form: **Don**.
Pet forms: Scottish: **Donny**, **Donnie** (Gaelic **Donaidh**); **Dolly** (Gaelic **Dolaidh**).
Feminine forms: Scottish Highland: **Donalda**, **Donella**; **Donna(g)**, **Dol(l)ag**, **Doileag**, **Dolina**, **Dolanna**.

Donat (m.) French, Provençal, Catalan, and Polish form of DONATO.

Donatella (f.) Italian: feminine diminutive form of DONATO. Half a dozen saints of this name were martyred in the early persecutions of the Christians.

Donatien (m.) French: from Late Latin *Dōnātiānus*, a derivative of *Dōnātus* (see DONATO). The name was borne by various early saints, including a 4th-century bishop of Rheims who became the patron of Bruges when his relics were taken there in the 9th century. This was the given name of the Marquis de Sade (1740–1814).

Donato (m.) Italian, Spanish, and Portuguese: from Late Latin *Dōnātus* 'given (by God)' (the past participle of *dōnāre* to give, donate). The name was popular among early Christians and was borne by over twenty saints in the first centuries AD. Among the most famous is a bishop of Arezzo in Tuscany who was beheaded under Julian the Apostate.

Cognate: French, Provençal, Catalan, Polish: **Donat**.

Donella (f.) Scottish: name coined as a feminine equivalent of DONALD.

Donla (f.) Irish: modern spelling of a traditional Gaelic name composed of the elements *donn* brown + *flaith* lady, revived in this form in the 20th century.

Donn (m.) Irish Gaelic: ancient byname meaning either 'brown' or 'king', in use from the earliest times until the 19th century. It is borne in Irish mythology by the king of the underworld. In modern use *Donn* normally represents a short form of any of the various Gaelic names containing the first element *donn* brown.

Donna (f.) English and Scottish: of recent origin (not found before the 1920s). It seems to be taken from the Italian word *donna* lady (cf. MADONNA), but it has often been used as a feminine form of DONALD.

Donnchadh (m.) Gaelic form of DUNCAN.

Donny (m.) English: pet form of DON.

Donough (m.) Irish: variant spelling of **Donagh**.
Variant: **Donogh**.

Donovan (m.) Irish and English: from the Irish surname, Gaelic *Ó Donndubháin* 'descendant of *Donndubhán*', a personal name composed of the elements *donn* brown + *dubh* black, dark, with the addition of the diminutive suffix *-án*. Its use as a given name dates from the early 1900s. The folk-rock singer Donovan may have had some influence on its increase in popularity in the 1960s. It is now also used by people with no Irish connections.

Doortje (f.) Dutch: pet form derived from a contracted version of DOROTHEA.

Dora (f.) English and French: 19th-century coinage, representing a short form of ISIDORA, THEODORA, DOROTHY, and any other name containing the Greek element *dōron* gift. In some cases, it seems to have been taken as actually meaning 'gift', presumably as a Latinate version of the Greek word. Wordsworth's daughter (b. 1804), christened Dorothy, was always known in adult life as Dora. The name's popularity was enhanced by the character of Dora Spenlow in Dickens's novel *David Copperfield* (1850).
Pet form: **Dory**.

Doran (m.) Irish and English: from the Irish surname, in Gaelic *Ó Deoradháin* 'descendant of *Deoradhán*'. *Deoradhán* is an old Irish personal name meaning 'exile, wanderer'.

Dorcas (f.) English: from Greek *dorkas* doe, gazelle. It does not actually seem to have been used as a personal name by the ancient Greeks, but is offered in the Bible as an 'interpretation' of the Aramaic name TABITHA (Acts 9: 36), and was taken up by the early Christians. It was much used among the Puritans in the 16th century, and has remained in occasional use ever since. In Scotland it has been used as an Anglicized form of DEÒIRIDH.

Dorean (f.) Irish: Anglicized form of the Gaelic name **Doireann**, possibly from Gaelic *der* daughter + the name of the legendary hero FINN. This has been revived as a given name in the 20th century, and has become very popular, perhaps in part as a result of the popularity of the similar name DOREEN.

Doreen (f.) English: derivative of DORA, with the addition of the productive suffix *-een* (in origin an Irish diminutive). The name came into use at the beginning of the 20th century, when there was a particular vogue for such names. See also DOREAN.
Variants: **Dorene**, **Dorine**.

Dores (f.) Portuguese form of DOLORES.

Dorete (f.) Danish form of DOROTHEA.

Doria (f.) English: of uncertain origin, probably a back-formation from DORIAN or else an elaboration of DORA on the model of the numerous women's given names ending in *-ia*.

Dorian (m.) English: early 20th-century coinage, apparently invented by Oscar Wilde, as no evidence has been found of its existence before he used it for the central character in *The Portrait of Dorian Gray* (1891). Dorian Gray is a dissolute rake who retains unblemished youthful good looks; in the attic of his home is a portrait which does his ageing for him, gradually acquiring all the outward marks of his depravity. This macabre background has not deterred parents from occasionally bestowing the name on their children. Wilde probably took the name from Late Latin *Dōriānus*, from Greek *Dōrieus*, member of the Greek-speaking people who settled in the Peloponnese in pre-classical times. *Dorian* would thus be a masculine version of DORIS. It may have been selected occasionally by admirers of ancient Sparta and its militaristic institutions, since the Spartans were of Dorian stock.

Dorinda (f.) English: artificial extension of DORA, with the suffix *-inda* (cf. CLARINDA). The name was coined in the 18th century, and has undergone a modest revival of interest in the 20th.

Doris (f.) English and German: from the classical Greek ethnic name meaning 'Dorian woman'. The Dorians were one of the tribes of Greece; their name was traditionally derived from an ancestor, *Dōros* (son of Hellen, who gave his name to the Hellenes), but it is more likely that Doros (whose name could be from *dōron* gift) was invented to account for a tribal name of obscure origin. In Greek mythology, Doris was a minor goddess of the sea, the consort of Nereus and the mother of his daughters, the Nereids or seanymphs, who numbered fifty (in some versions, more). The name was especially popular from about 1880 to about 1930, and was borne by the American film star Doris Day (b. 1924).

Dorofei (m.) Russian: from Greek *Dōrotheus*, composed of the elements *dōron* gift + *theos* god (cf. THEODORE and DOSIFEI). The name was borne by various early saints much venerated in the Eastern Church, including a 4th-century bishop of Tyre and the abbots Dorotheus the Archimandrite (7th century) and Dorotheus the Younger (11th century).

Doron (m.) 1. English: apparently a variant spelling of DORIAN (perhaps influenced by the pair of names DAMIAN and DAMON), although it corresponds in form with the Greek word *dōron* gift. 2. Jewish: modern Hebrew name based on a direct borrowing of the Greek word *doron* gift.

Dorothea (f.) English, German, and Dutch: Latinate form of a post-classical Greek name composed of the elements *dōron* gift + *theos* god (the same elements as in THEODORA, but in reverse order). The masculine form *Dōrotheus* (see DOROFEI) was borne by several early Christian saints, the feminine only by two minor ones, but in Western Europe today it only survives as a female name. In modern use in the English-speaking world it represents a 19th-century Latinization of DOROTHY, or a learned reborrowing.
Cognates: Danish: **Dorete**, **Dort(h)e**. Polish, Czech: **Dorota**. Hungarian: **Dorottya**.
Pet forms: Dutch: **Doortje**. Polish: **Dosia**.

Dorothy (f.) Usual English form of DOROTHEA. The name was not used in the Middle Ages, but was taken up in the 16th century and became common thereafter. In Scotland it has been used as an Anglicized form of the Gaelic name **Diorbhail**, also Anglicized as DEVORGILLA.
Short form: **Dot**.
Pet forms: **Dottie**, **Dodie**, **Dolly**.

Dorte (f.) Danish: contracted variant of DORETE.
Variant: **Dorthe**.

Dory (f.) English: pet form of DORA, now seldom used in that function and even less commonly bestowed as an independent given name.

Dosia (f.) Polish: pet form of *Dorota* (see DOROTHEA).

Dosifei (m.) Russian: from Greek *Dōsitheos*, composed of the elements *dōsis* giving and *theos* god (see also TEODOSIO). St Dositheus (d c.530) was a monk of Gaza who led an unspectacular life but is much venerated in the Eastern Church.

Dot (f.) English: short form of DOROTHY.

Dottie (f.) English: pet form of DOT, with the hypocoristic suffix *-ie*. The form **Dotty** is also used, and its popularity does not seem to have been adversely affected by the fact that it coincides in form with the slang word meaning 'crazy'.

Doug (m.) English: short form of DOUGLAS.

Dougal (m.) Scottish: Anglicized form of the Gaelic name **Dubhghall** or **Dùghall**, composed of the elements *dubh* black, dark + *gall* stranger. This is said to have been a byname applied to Danes, in contrast to the fairer Norwegians and Icelanders (see FINGAL).
Variants: **Dugald**, **Dugal**.
Pet form: **Dougie**.

Douglas (m.) Scottish and English: transferred use of the surname borne by what was one of the most powerful families in Scotland, the earls of Douglas and of Angus, also notorious in earlier times as Border reivers. Today this name is sometimes assumed to be connected with DOUGAL, but it seems more likely that the surname is derived from the place in the Southern Uplands of Scotland where the family had their stronghold. This is probably named with the Gaelic elements *dubh* black + *glas* stream.
Variant: **Dùbhghlas** (Gaelic).
Short form: **Doug**.
Pet form: **Dougie**.

Dov (m.) Jewish: name meaning 'bear' in Hebrew. There is no biblical character of this name: it represents a translation into Hebrew of an animal name that became popular in European languages in the early Middle Ages. The bear is often associated with the name ISSACHAR, although the reason for this is not clear, for in Jacob's dying blessing (Genesis 49: 14) Issachar is referred to as a 'strong ass couching down between two burdens'. There was a famous rabbi named Issachar Dov, but this may have been simply a fortuitous pairing of the two names. Subsequent bearers may then have been named after him.

Doyle (m.) Irish and English: variant of DOUGAL and DUGALD, in part derived from an Anglicized form of the Gaelic surname *Ó Dubhghaill* 'descendant of Dubhghall'.

Drahomír (m.) Czech form of DROGOMIR.
Feminine: **Drahomira**.
Pet forms: **Draha** (m., f.); **Drahoš(ek)** (m.); **Drahuše**, **Drahuška**, **Dráža** (f.).

Dreda (f.) English: short form of ETHELDREDA, quite commonly used as an independent given name in the 19th century, when the longer form was also in fashion. It has survived slightly better than the more cumbersome quadrisyllabic form, but is nevertheless now rare.

Drew (m.) Scottish short form of ANDREW, often used as an independent name in Scotland, and in recent years increasingly popular elsewhere in the English-speaking world.

Dries (m.) Low German and Dutch short form of ANDRIES.

Drogo (m.) English (Norman): of uncertain etymology. Norman given names are most often of Continental Germanic derivation, and this one is possibly ultimately from the Old Saxon word *drog* ghost, phantom, or perhaps from Old High German *tragan* to carry. However, the most plausible suggestion is that it was brought into Germanic from Slavonic, representing a short form of a name containing the element *dorogo* dear (see DROGOMIR). This particular name was revived in the Montagu family in the 19th century, when a fashion grew up for Norman, Old English, and Celtic names.

Drogomir (m.) Polish: from an old Slavonic personal name composed of the elements *dorogo* dear, beloved + *meri* great, famous (see CASIMIR).
Cognate: Czech: **Drahomir**.

Drusilla (f.) From a Late Latin name, a feminine diminutive of the old Roman family name *Dr(a)usus*, which was first taken by a certain Livius, who had killed in single combat a Gaul of this name and, according to a custom of the time, took his victim's name as a cognomen. Of the several women in the Roman imperial family who were called Livia Drusilla, the most notorious was Caligula's sister and mistress. The name is borne in the Bible by a Jewish woman, wife of the Roman citizen Felix, who was converted to Christianity by St Paul (Acts 24: 24). In England it was taken up as a given name in the 17th century as a result of the biblical mention.

Drystan (m.) Welsh and English: variant of TRISTRAM. Drystan son of Tallwch is fleetingly mentioned in the *Mabinogi* as one of the members of King Arthur's council of advisers.

Duald (m.) Irish: Anglicized form of the Gaelic name **Dubhaltach**, possibly meaning 'black-haired', 'black-jointed', or 'dark-limbed'. This name has also formerly been Anglicized as DUDLEY.

Duane (m.) Irish and English: Anglicized form of the Gaelic name **Dubhán**, originally a byname representing a diminutive form of Gaelic *dubh* dark, black. In modern use it may well represent the surname *Ó Dubháin* 'descendant of Dubhán', derived from the personal name. Its popularity since the mid-1950s was no doubt influenced by the fame of the guitarist and singer Duane Eddy.
Variants: **Dwane**, **Dwayne**.

Duarte (m.) Portuguese form of EDWARD.

Dubhdara (m.) Irish Gaelic: name composed of the elements *dubh* black + *dara* of oak. This is a common given name in Connemara; cf. DARA and MAC DARA. It was formerly often Anglicized as DUDLEY.

Dud (m.) English: short form of DUDLEY, in fairly common use (although not normally as an independent name) in spite of its coincidence in form with the modern slang term *dud* meaning 'useless'.

Dudley (m.) English: transferred use of the surname of a noble family, who came originally from Dudley in the West Midlands, named in Old English as the 'wood or clearing of Dudda'. Their most famous member was Robert Dudley, Earl of Leicester (?1532–88), who came closer than any other man to marrying Queen Elizabeth I. In America this given name is much less common than in England. In Ireland it was formerly used as an Anglicized form of DUBHDARA and DARA and of *Dubhaltach* (see DUALD).

Duff (m.) Scottish: short form of various Gaelic compound names containing the element *dubh* dark, black. In modern use it is in part a transferred use of the surname *Duff*, originally a nickname for a person with dark hair or a swarthy complexion.

Dugald (m.) Scottish: variant of DOUGAL. The final consonant is explained by the fact that the devoicing of the final -*ll* of the Gaelic form suggested to English ears that a *d* or *t* followed.

Duggie (m.) English: pet form of DOUG.

Duke (m.) English: in modern use this normally represents a coinage parallel to EARL and KING, but it is also a short form of MARMADUKE. It is especially popular in the United States.

Dulcie (f.) English: learned re-creation in the 19th century of the medieval name *Dowse*, *Duce* (forms that have given rise to surnames), from Late Latin *Dulcia*, a derivative of *dulcis* sweet. See also TOLTSE.

Dumitru (m.) Romanian form of DMITRI.

Duncan (m.) Scottish and English: Anglicized form of the Gaelic name **Donnchadh**, composed of Old Celtic elements meaning 'brown' and 'battle'. The name was borne by a 7th-century Scottish saint, abbot of Iona, and a 10th-century Irish saint, abbot of Clonmacnoise. The Anglicized form of the final syllable seems to be the result of confusion with the Gaelic element *ceann* head during Latinization into *Duncanus*. The oblique case *Donnchaidh* is possibly the origin of the English word *donkey* (cf. CUDDY).

Pet form: **Dunky**.

Dunstan (m.) English: from an Old English personal name composed of the elements *dun* dark + *stān* stone, borne most notably by a 10th-century saint who was archbishop of Canterbury. The name is now used mainly by Roman Catholics.

Dunya (f.) Russian: short form of *Avdunya*, itself a pet form of AVDOTYA.

Pet form (a further derivative): **Dunyasha**.

Dušan (m.) Czech: equivalent of the Russian name SPIRIDON, derived from the element *dusha* spirit, soul.

Feminine form: **Dušana**.

Pet forms: **Duša** (m., f.); **Duš(an)ek** (m.); **Duš(an)ka**, **Dušička** (f.).

Dustin (m.) English: transferred use of the surname, which is of uncertain origin, probably a Norman form of the Old Norse personal name *Þórsteinn*, composed of elements meaning 'Thor's stone'. It is now used fairly commonly as a given name, largely as a result of the fame of the film actor Dustin Hoffman (b. 1937), who is said to have been named in honour of the less well-known silent-film actor Dustin Farnum.

Dusty (m., f.) English: apparently a pet form, or in some cases a feminine form, of DUSTIN. As a female name it was made popular in the 1960s by the singer Dusty Springfield.

Dvoire (f.) Jewish: Yiddish form of DEBORAH (Hebrew *Devorah*).

Variant: **Dvoyre**.

Pet form: **Dvosye**.

Dwane (m.) Irish and English: variant of DUANE.

Variant: **Dwayne**.

Dwight (m.) English: transferred use of the surname, which probably comes from the medieval English female name *Diot*, a pet form of *Dionysia* (see DENNIS). It is especially common in America, where its increase in popularity since the Second World War is mainly a result of the fame of the American general and president Dwight D. Eisenhower (1890–1969). He was apparently named in honour of the New England thinker Timothy Dwight (1752–1817) and his brother Theodore Dwight (1764–1846).

Dyan (f.) English: modern variant spelling of DIANE, especially popular in America.

Dylan (m.) Welsh: of uncertain origin, probably connected with a Celtic element meaning 'sea'. In the *Mabinogi* it is the name of the miraculously born son of Arianrhod, who became a minor divinity of the sea. In the second half of the 20th century the name has become fairly popular outside Wales as a result of the fame of the Welsh poet Dylan Thomas (1914–53) and the American singer Bob Dylan (b. 1941), who changed his surname from Zimmerman as a tribute to the poet.

Dymphna (f.) Irish: Anglicized form of the Gaelic name **Damhnait**, apparently a feminine diminutive form of *damh* fawn. Little is known of the saint of this name, who is regarded as the protector of the deranged and lunatic; her relics are preserved at Gheel, near Antwerp in Belgium.

Variant: **Dympna**.

E

Éabha (f.) Irish Gaelic form of *Eve*; see EVA.

Eachann (m.) Scottish Gaelic: name composed of the elements *each* horse + *donn* brown. It has often been Anglicized as HECTOR.

Éadaoin (f.) Irish Gaelic: modern form of the Old Irish name *Étáin*, borne in Irish mythology by a sun goddess. The name seems to be a derivative of Old Irish *ét* jealousy.

Eairdsidh (m.) Scottish Gaelic form of ARCHIE.
Variant: **Eairrsidh**.

Ealasaid (f.) Scottish Gaelic form of ELIZABETH.

Eamon (m.) Irish and English: from the Gaelic form of ED-MUND. The normal Gaelic spelling is Éamon or Éamonn. Éamon de Valera (1882–1973) was president of Ireland 1959–73.
Cognate: Scottish Gaelic: **Eumann**.

Eanraig (m.) Scottish Gaelic form of HENRY.

Earl (m.) English (mainly U.S.): from the English aristocratic title, originally a nickname parallel to DUKE, KING, etc. The title was first used in England in the 12th century, as an equivalent to the French *comte* count; it is from Old English *eorl* warrior, nobleman, prince. In some cases the given name may have been taken from the surname *Earl*, which was given originally to someone who worked in the household of an earl.
Variants: **Earle**, **Erle**.

Eavan (f.) Irish: Anglicized form of Gaelic AOIBHEANN.

Ebba (f.) **1.** German; probably from the various compound Germanic female names containing the first element *eber* wild boar, as for example *Ebergard* and *Eberhild*. **2.** English: 19th-century revival of an Old English female name, a contracted form of *Eadburga*, composed of the elements *ēad* prosperity, riches, fortune + *burg* fortress. St Ebba the Elder (d. *c.*638) was a sister of Oswald, King of Northumbria, who founded a Benedictine abbey at Coldingham in Berwickshire; St Ebba the Younger (d. *c.*870) was abbess there and was murdered by marauding Danes.

Ebbe (m.) **1.** Scandinavian: pet form of ESBJÖRN. **2.** German: pet form of EBERHARD.

Ebenezer (m.) English: originally the name (meaning 'stone of help' in Hebrew) of a place mentioned in the Bible, where the Israelites were defeated by the Philistines (1 Samuel 4:1). When they took their revenge Samuel set up a memorial stone with this same name (1 Samuel 7:12). It was taken up as a given name by the Puritans in the 17th century, possibly after being misread in the Bible as a personal name, or else because of its favourable etymological connotations. It now has unfavourable connotations because of the miserly character of Ebenezer Scrooge in Charles Dickens's *A Christmas Carol* (1843).

Eberhard (m.) German: from an old Germanic personal name, composed of the elements *eber* wild boar + *hard* hardy, brave, strong. St Eberhard of Salzburg (1085–1164) was a leading ecclesiastical figure of his day.
Cognate: Low German: **Evert**.
Pet form: German: **Ebbe**.

Ebony (f.) English: from the name of the deeply black wood (Late Latin *ebenius*, from Greek *ebenos*; the word seems to be ultimately of Egyptian origin). The name has been adopted very recently (since the 1970s) by Blacks as a symbol of pride in their colour. This was the third commonest name among Black females in the United States in 1982.

Eckehard (m.) German: from an old Germanic personal name composed of the elements *ek, eg* edge, point (of a sword) + *hard* hardy, brave, strong. The Blessed Ekhard (d. 1084) was canon of the cathedral of Magdeburg and first abbot of Huysberg.
Variant: **Eckhard(t)**.
Cognates: Low German: **Eggert**. Frisian: **Edzard**.

Ed (m.) English: short form of the various male names with the first syllable *Ed*-, especially EDWARD. See also TED.

Edan (m.) Scottish and Irish: variant of AIDAN. St Edan was an Irish disciple of St David of Wales who later became bishop of Ferns.

Edda (f.) Italian form of HEDDA.

Eddie (m.) English: pet form of ED, with the addition of the hypocoristic suffix *-ie*.

Edeltraud (f.) German: later form of ADELTRAUD.
Variant: **Edeltrud**.

Eden (m.) English: transferred use of the surname, itself derived in the Middle Ages from a given name *Edun* or *Edon*. This is of Old English origin, composed of the elements *ēad* prosperity, riches, fortune + *hūn* bear cub. Use as a modern given name has probably been encouraged by association with the biblical Garden of Eden, so named from Hebrew '*ēden* place of pleasure.

Edgar (m.) English (also used in France): from an Old English personal name composed of the elements *ēad* prosperity, riches, fortune + *gār* spear. This was the name of an English king and saint, Edgar the Peaceful (d. 975), and of Edgar Atheling (?1060–?1125), the young prince who was chosen to succeed Harold as king in 1066, but who was supplanted by the Normans.
Variant: French: **Edgard** (probably influenced in spelling by the more common ÉDOUARD).

Edith (f.) English (also occasionally used in France, Germany, and Scandinavia): from an Old English female personal name composed of the elements *ēad* prosperity, riches, fortune + *gȳð* strife. This was borne by a daughter (961–84) of Edgar the Peaceful, who was named in accordance with the common Old English practice of repeating name elements within a family. She spent her short life in a convent, and is regarded as a saint.

Variant: **Edythe**.
Cognate: Polish: **Edyta**.
Pet form: English: **Edie**.

Edmé (f.) Scottish: variant of ESMÉ, used as a female name. The reason for the change of *-s-* to *-d-* is not clear, but it may have been due to the influence of the coexisting given names ESMOND. and (commoner) EDMUND. In spite of its accent, it is not found as a French name.

Variant: **Edmée**.

Edmund (m.) English (also used in Germany): from an Old English personal name composed of the elements *ēad* prosperity, riches, fortune + *mund* protector. It was borne by several early royal and saintly figures, including a 9th-century king of East Anglia killed by invading Danes, allegedly for his adherence to Christianity. This story earned him a cult that spread throughout Western and Central Europe.

Cognates: Irish: EAMON. Scottish Gaelic: **Eumann**. French, Dutch: **Edmond**. Italian: **Edmondo**. Spanish, Portuguese: **Edmundo**. Hungarian: **Ödön**.

Edna (f.) Irish and English: in Ireland an Anglicized form of EITHNE, and probably of this origin in England too. However, the name also occurs in the Bible, in the apocryphal Book of Tobit, where it is the name of the mother of Sarah and stepmother of Tobias. This is said to be from Hebrew *'ednah* rejuvenation, pleasure, or delight, and if so it is connected with the name of the Garden of EDEN. It does not occur in the Hebrew Bible or Old Testament, although the variants *'eden* and *'adnah* occur as male names. The earliest known uses of the given name in England are in the 18th century, when it was probably imported from Ireland, rather than taken from the Bible.

Edoardo (m.) Italian form of EDWARD.

Edom (m.) Biblical: byname of Esau, meaning 'red' in Hebrew. The name was given to him because he sold his birthright for a bowl of red lentil soup. It was frequently used in medieval Scotland, where it was taken to represent a variant of ADAM, and is occasionally bestowed in modern times by parents with Scottish connections.

Édouard (m.) French form of EDWARD.

Edsel (m.) In Germanic mythology this name is a variant of ETZEL. In modern times its most famous bearer was Edsel Ford, son of Henry Ford, founder of the Ford Motor Corporation. The family was partly of Dutch or Flemish descent, but the reason for the choice of given name is not known.

Eduard (m.) Czech form of EDWARD.

Eduardo (m.) Spanish form of EDWARD.

Edurne (f.) Basque equivalent of NIEVES.

Edvard (m.) Scandinavian and Czech form of EDWARD.

Edvige (f.) Italian form of HEDWIG.

Edward (m.) English (also Polish in this spelling): from an Old English personal name composed of the elements *ēad* prosperity, riches, fortune + *weard* guard. This has been one of the most successful of all Old English names, surviving from before the Conquest to the present day, and even being exported into other European languages. It was the name of three Anglo-Saxon kings and has been borne by eight kings of England since the Norman Conquest. It is also the name of the youngest son of Queen Elizabeth II. Undoubtedly the most influential bearer was King Edward the Confessor (?1002–66;

ruled 1042–66;). In a troubled period of English history, he contrived to rule fairly and (for a time at any rate) firmly. But in the latter part of his reign he paid more attention to his religion than to his kingdom. He died childless, and his death sparked off conflicting claims to his throne, which were resolved by the victory of William the Conqueror at the Battle of Hastings. His memory was honoured by Normans and English alike, for his fairness and his piety. Edward's mother was Norman; he had spent part of his youth in Normandy; and William claimed to have been nominated by Edward as his successor. Edward was canonized in the 12th century, and came to be venerated throughout Europe as a model of a Christian king.

Derivatives: Scottish Gaelic: **Eideard**; **Eudard** (a dialectal variant). French: **Édouard**. Italian: **Edoardo**. Spanish: **Eduardo**. Portuguese: **Duarte**. German: **Eduard** (influenced by the French form). Scandinavian: **Edvard**. Finnish: **Eetu**. Czech: **Eduard**, **Edvard**. Russian: **Edvard**.
Short forms: English: **Ed**, **Ned**, **Ted**.
Pet form: English: **Eddie**.

Edwige (f.) French form of HEDWIG.

Edwin (m.) English: 19th-century revival of an Old English personal name composed of the elements *ēad* prosperity, riches, fortune + *wine* friend. It was borne by a 7th-century king of Northumbria, who was converted to Christianity by St Paulinus and was killed in battle against pagan forces, a combination of circumstances which led to his being venerated as a martyr.

Edwina (f.) English: 19th-century coinage, representing a Latinate feminine form of EDWIN or, in at least one case, of EDWARD. Edwina Ashley, a descendant of Lord Shaftesbury who became the wife of Earl Mountbatten, was so named in honour of Edward VII; the king had originally wished her to be called *Edwardina*.

Edyta (f.) Polish form of EDITH.

Edythe (f.) English: fanciful respelling of EDITH, popular in the United States during the early part of the 20th century.

Edzard (m.) Frisian form of ECKEHARD.

Eero (m.) Finnish form of ERIC; See also ERKKI.

Eetu (m.) Finnish form of EDWARD.

Effemy (f.) English and Scottish: Older vernacular form of EUPHEMIA.

Effi (f.) German: pet form derived from an assimilated version of **Elfriede**, the German form of ELFREDA.

Effie (f., m.) **1.** (f.) English: pet form of EUPHEMIA, now as rarely used as the full form, but popular in the 19th century. **2.** (f.) Scottish: Anglicized form of the Gaelic name OIGHRIG. **3.** (m.) Jewish: pet form of EPHRAIM.

Efisio (m.) Italian: typically Sardinian name, borne in honour of a martyr allegedly put to death at Cagliari under the Emperor Diocletian in 303. He is greatly venerated on the island and every 1 May a large festival commemorates his intervention in the plague of 1625; nevertheless, there is no mention of him in any sources before the 15th century. The name is from Latin *Ephesius*, originally a local name from the Greek city of Ephesus, where there was a famous temple of Diana in antiquity.

Efraín (m.) Spanish form of EPHRAIM, used mainly in Latin America.

Efric (f.) Scottish: Anglicized form of the Gaelic name OIGHRIG; See also AFRICA.

Egan (m.) Irish: Anglicized form of the Gaelic name **Aogán**, earlier *Aodhagán*, a double diminutive of AODH.

Cognate: Scottish: **Iagan**.

Egbert (m.) English: from an Old English personal name composed of the elements *ecg* edge (of a sword) + *beorht* bright, famous. It was borne by two English saints of the 8th century and by a 9th-century king of Wessex. It survived for a while after the Conquest, but fell out of use by the 14th century. It was briefly revived in the 19th century, but is now again completely out of fashion.

Eggert (m.) Low German form of ECKEHARD.

Egidio (m.) Italian form of GILES.

Egidiusz (m.) Polish: learned form of IDZI, the Polish vernacular form of GILES.

Egil (m.) Scandinavian: from the Old Norse personal name *Egill*, in origin a diminutive of the element *ag, eg* edge, point (cf. e.g. EILERT).

Eglantine (f.) English: flower name, used as a nickname by Chaucer, and occasionally as a given name in the 19th century, but not at present in use. It is from an alternative name for the sweetbrier, derived in the 14th century from Old French *aiglent*, ultimately a derivative of Latin *acus* needle, referring to the prickly stem of the plant.

Egon (m.) German: medieval name derived from the Germanic element *ek, eg* edge, point (of a sword), an element that is found for example in ECKEHARD. St Egon or Egino (d. 1122) was abbot of the monastery of Ulric and Afra in Augsburg.

Eguzki (f.) Basque equivalent of SOL.

Egyed (m.) Hungarian form of GILES.

Ehrenfried (m.) German: apparently a reworking of the old Germanic personal name *Arnfried*, composed of the elements *arn* eagle + *fred, frid* peace. The first element has been assimilated to modern German *Ehre* (combining form *Ehren-*) honour.

Ehud (m.) Jewish: name (probably meaning 'pleasant, sympathetic' in Hebrew) borne in the Bible by a left-handed Benjaminite, who saved the Israelites by stabbing the Moabite king Eglon (Judges 3: 15–26).

Éaibhear (m.) Irish Gaelic: of unknown origin. According to legend, this was the name of the son of Mil, leader of the first Gaels to settle in Ireland.

Anglicized forms: HEBER, IVOR.

Eiddwen (f.) Welsh: modern coinage, apparently derived from the element *eiddun* desirous, fond, with the addition of the common suffix of women's names *(g)wen*, feminine of *gwyn* white, fair, blessed, holy.

Eideard (m.) Scottish Gaelic form of EDWARD.

Eileen (f.) Irish and English: Anglicized form of the Gaelic name **Eibhlín** or *Aibhilín*, derived from Norman-French AVELINE. The combination *bh* is normally pronounced as *v*, but sometimes dropped, as reflected in the Anglicized spelling. This name became tremendously popular in the early part of the 20th century, but the reasons for this sudden rise in favour are not known.

Variant: **Aileen** (esp. Scottish).

Eilert (m.) Frisian and Scandinavian: from an old Germanic personal name composed of the elements *eg(il)* edge, point (of a sword) + *hard* hardy, brave, strong (cf. ECKEHARD). The name is now also quite commonly used in Scandinavia, where it was taken in the 17th century.

Eilidh (f.) Scottish Gaelic form of ELLIE, now normally Anglicized as HELEN.

Variant: **Ailie** (an Anglicized spelling).

Eilif (m.) Norwegian: from an Old Norse personal name composed of the elements *ei* always, ever or *einn* one, alone + *lifr* alive.

Variant: **Eiliv**.

Eilís (f.) Irish Gaelic form of ELIZABETH.

Einar (m.) Scandinavian: from an Old Norse personal name composed of the elements *einn* one, alone + *herr* army, warrior.

Einion (m.) Welsh: traditional name, originally a byname meaning 'anvil'.

Pet form: **Einwys**.

Eino (m.) German: medieval name derived from the Germanic element *eg(in)* edge, point (of a sword), and so a byform of EGON.

Einri (m.) Irish Gaelic form of HENRY; See also ANRAÍ.

Eira (f.) Welsh: modern name, from the vocabulary word *eira* snow.

Eireen (f.) Irish and English: of recent origin, probably a respelling of IRENE under the influence of EILEEN.

Eiric (f.) Scottish Gaelic: variant of OIGHRIG; See also EITHRIG.

Eirik (m.) Norwegian form of ERIC.

Eirwen (f.) Welsh: modern name, composed of the elements *eira* snow + *(g)wen* feminine form of *gwyn* white, fair, blessed, holy.

Eistir (f.) Irish Gaelic form of ESTHER.

Eitan (m.) Jewish: modern Hebrew form of ETHAN.

Eithne (f.) Irish Gaelic: traditional name, apparently from the vocabulary word *eithne* kernel, which was used as a term of praise in old bardic poetry. The name has been Anglicized variously as EDNA, Et(h)na, and ENA. St Ethenia was a daughter of King Laoghaire and one of St Patrick's first converts, together with her sister Fidelmia (see FIDELMA).

Eithrig (f.) Scottish Gaelic: variant of OIGHRIG; See also EIRIC.

Eladio (m.) Spanish: from the Late Latin name *Helladius*, Late Greek *Helladios*, a derivative of *Hellas (genitive Hellados)* Greece. St Helladius of Toledo (d. 632) was a minister at the court of the Visigothic kings, who retired from public life to become a monk, and was eventually appointed archbishop of Toledo.

Elaine (f.) English: originally a version of HELEN, but now generally regarded as an independent name. The Greek and Latin forms of the name had a long vowel in the second syllable, which produced this form (as opposed to ELLEN) in Old French. In Arthurian legend, Elaine is the name of one of the women who fell in love with Lancelot. The name occurs in this form in the 15th-century English *Morte D'Arthur* of Thomas

Malory. In the 19th century it was popularized in one of Tennyson's *Idylls of the King* (1859). Most of the characters in Arthurian legend have names that are Celtic in origin, although subjected to heavy French influence, and it has therefore been suggested that *Elaine* may actually be derived from a Welsh element meaning 'hind' or 'fawn'.

Elda (f.) Italian: not in use before the 20th century. It seems to represent an altered form of HILDA.

Eldon (m.) English: transferred use of the surname, which originated in the Middle Ages as a local name from a place in Co. Durham, so called from the Old English male personal name *Ella* + Old English *dūn* hill.

Eleanor (f.) English: from an Old French respelling of the Old Provençal name *Alienor*, which has been taken as a derivative of HELEN, but is probably of Germanic derivation (with a first element *ali* other, foreign). The name was introduced to England by Eleanor of Aquitaine (1122–1204), who came from south-west France to be the wife of King Henry II. It was also borne by Eleanor of Provence, the wife of Henry III, and Eleanor of Castile, the wife of Edward I.
Variants: **Ellenor**, **Elinor**.
Cognates: Irish Gaelic: **Eileanóra**. French: **Éléonore**. Italian: **Eleonora**. German: **Eleonore**.
Pet forms: English: NELL, **Ellie**.

Eleazar (m.) Biblical: variant of ELIEZER. See also LAZARUS.

Elen (f.) Welsh: probably a Welsh form of HELEN. It is identical with the vocabulary word *elen* nymph, but was used in Welsh texts from an early period as the name of the mother of Constantine, finder of the True Cross.
Variant: **Elin**.

Elena (f.) Italian and Spanish form of HELEN.

Eleonora (f.) Italian form of ELEANOR, now sometimes also used in the English-speaking world.

Eleonore (f.) German form of ELEANOR.

Éléonore (f.) French form of ELEANOR.

Eleri (f.) Welsh: ancient name of uncertain origin. It was borne in the 5th century by a daughter of the semi-legendary chieftain Brychan. *Eleri* is also a Welsh river name; in this case it seems to derive from the element *alar* surfeit.

Elettra (f.) Italian: name of a heroine of classical mythology, in English *Electra*, who, with her brother Orestes, avenged the murder of her father Agamemnon by her stepfather Aegisthus and her mother Clytemnestra. The name is derived from the Greek vocabulary word *ēlektōr* brilliant.

Elfleda (f.) English: Latinized form of the Old English female personal name *Æðelflǣd*, composed of the elements *æðel* noble + *flǣd* beauty. It was revived briefly in the 19th century.

Elfreda (f.) English: 19th-century revival of a Latinized form of the Old English female personal name *Ælfþryð*, composed of the elements *ælf* elf, supernatural being + *þryð* strength. This form may also have absorbed the originally distinct *Æðelþryð* (see AUDREY).
Cognate: German: **Elfriede**.
Short forms: English: **Freda**. German: **Friede**.
Pet forms: German: **Effi**, **Elfi**.

Eli (m.) 1. Biblical: from a Hebrew word meaning 'height'. *Eli* was the name of the priest and judge who brought up the future prophet Samuel (1 Samuel 3). It was especially popular among Puritans in the 17th century. 2. Jewish: short form of any of numerous names containing the first element '*el* God, such as ELIEZER, ELIJAH, and *Elisha* (see ELISEO).

Éliane (f.) French: from Latin *Aeliāna*, feminine form of the Late Latin family name *Aeliānus*. This name seems to represent a hypercorrected form of *Ēliānus* or *Hēliānus*, from Greek *hēlios* sun. St Eliana was an early martyr of Amasea in Pontus.
Cognate: Italian, Spanish, Portuguese: **Eliana**.

Eliezer (m.) Biblical: name (meaning 'God helps' in Hebrew) borne by one of the sons of Aaron (Exodus 6: 23). In the Authorized Version the name is rendered as ELEAZAR.

Eligio (m.) Italian form of ELOY. This form is also used in Spain as a learned byform.

Elijah (m.) Biblical: name (meaning 'Yahweh is God') of an Israelite prophet whose exploits are recounted in the First and Second Book of Kings. Elijah's victory over the prophets of Baal on Mount Carmel played an important part in maintaining the Jewish monotheistic religion. This story, and the other stories in which he figures, including his conflicts with Ahab's queen, Jezebel, and his prophecies of doom, are among the most vivid in the Bible. For some reason it has not been much used as a given name by Christians, although it was among the names used by the early Puritan settlers in New England, and recently it has also been adopted among Black Muslims. See also ELIYAHU.

Elin (f.) Welsh: variant of ELEN.

Elinor (f.) English: variant spelling of ELEANOR.

Eliot (m.) English: variant spelling of ELLIOT.
Variant: **Eliott**.

Elisabet (f.) The usual Scandinavian form of ELIZABETH.

Elisabeth (f.) The spelling of ELIZABETH used in the Authorized Version of the New Testament, and in most modern European languages. This was the name of the mother of John the Baptist (Luke 1: 60). Etymologically, the name means 'God is my oath', and is therefore identical with *Elisheba*, name of the wife of Aaron, according to the genealogy at Exodus 6: 23. The final element seems to have been altered by association with Hebrew *shabbāth* sabbath.

Elisabetta (f.) Italian form of ELIZABETH.

Élise (f.) French: short form of ELISABETH. The name was introduced into the English-speaking world (where it is often written without the accent) in the late 19th century.

Eliseo (m.) Italian and Spanish: name of the biblical prophet normally known in English as *Elisha*, the successor of Elijah. The feast of St *Eliseus*, as he is known in Latin, is liturgically observed (on 14 June) by the Carmelite order of monks, and is also important in the Eastern Church. The Latin form of the name derives from the Greek *Elisaios*, used in the New Testament. The name is composed of the Hebrew elements '*el* God + *sha*' to help, save.
Cognate: Russian: **Yelisei**.

Eliyahu (m.) Jewish: Hebrew name meaning 'Jehovah is God', familiar in the English-speaking world in the form ELIJAH.
Pet form: **Elye** (Yiddish).

Eliza (f.) English: short form of ELIZABETH, first used in the 16th century. It became popular, sometimes as an independent name, in the 18th and 19th centuries. The name was used by

George Bernard Shaw for the main female character, Eliza Dolittle, in his play *Pygmalion* (1913), which was the basis for the musical and film *My Fair Lady*.

Elizabeth (f.) The usual spelling of ELISABETH in English. It was first made popular by being borne by Queen Elizabeth I of England (1533–1603). In the 20th century it became extremely fashionable, partly because it was the name of Elizabeth Bowes-Lyon (b. 1900), who in 1936 became Queen Elizabeth as the wife of King George VI, and, even more influentially, it is the name of her daughter Queen Elizabeth II (b. 1926).

Variant: **Elisabeth**. See also ELSPETH and ISABEL.

Cognates: Irish Gaelic: **Eilis**. Scottish Gaelic: **Ealasaid**. French, German: **Elisabeth**. Italian: **Elisabetta**. Spanish: **Isabel**. Scandinavian: **Elisabet**. Polish: **Elzbieta**. Czech: **Alžběta**. Russian: **Yelizaveta**. Hungarian: **Erzsébet**.

Short forms: English: ELIZA, ELSA; **Liza**, **Lisa**, **Liz**; **Beth**, **Bet**, **Bess**; **Elspeth**; **Lisbet**. French: **Élise**, **Lise**. German: **Elsa**, **Else**, **Ilse**; **Liese**. Scandinavian: **Elsa**, **Else**; **Lisa**, **Lise**, **Lis**. Polish: **Ela**. Pet forms: English: **Elsie**; **Bessie**, **Bessy**, **Betty**, **Betsy**; **Tetty**; **Libby**; **Lizzie**, **Lizzy**. French: **Lisette**. German: **Lil(l)i**; **Elli**.

Elkan (m.) Jewish and English: shortened form of the Hebrew name *Elkanah* 'possessed by God', borne in the Bible by several people, including the father of the prophet Samuel (1 Samuel 1: 1).

Elke (f.) **1**. Frisian and Dutch: pet form derived from a shortened version of ADELHEID. **2**. Jewish: Yiddish name, apparently adopted as a feminine form of ELKAN. The variant **Elkie** is well known as the name of the singer Elkie Brooks.

Ella (f.) English: of Germanic origin, introduced to Britain by the Normans. The name was probably originally a short form of any of various compound names containing the element *ali* other, foreign (cf. ELEANOR and ELVIRA). It is now often taken to be a variant or pet form of ELLEN.

Ellar (m.) Scottish: Anglicized form of the Gaelic name **Eallair**, originally a byname **Ceallair**, referring to someone who was a butler or steward in a monastery (Latin *cellārius*, a derivative of *cella* storeroom, cellar). The initial *C-* was lost through the frequent use of the given name in association with the patronymic surname *Mac Ceallair*.

Ellen (f.) English: originally a variant of HELEN, although now no longer associated with that name. Initial *H-* tended to be added and dropped rather capriciously, leading to many doublets (cf. e.g. ESTHER and *Hester*; ÉLOISE and *Héloïse*).

Pet form: NELL.

Ellenor (f.) English: variant spelling of ELEANOR, the result of blending with ELLEN.

Elli (f.) German: pet form of ELISABETH.

Ellie (f.) English: pet form of any of the numerous female names beginning with the syllable *El-*, in particular ELEANOR.

Cognate: Scottish Gaelic: **EILIDH** (re-Anglicized as HELEN).

Elliot (m.) English: transferred use of the surname, which is itself derived from a medieval (Norman French) masculine given name. This was a diminutive of *Elie*, the Old French version of *Elias* (see ELLIS).

Variants: **Elliott**, **Eliot(t)**.

Ellis (m.) English: transferred use of the surname, which is derived from *Elias*, the Greek version (used in the New Testament) of the name of the Old Testament prophet ELIJAH. In

Wales it is now often taken as an Anglicized form of the Old Welsh name *Elisud*, which is really from *elus* kind, benevolent.

Elmer (m.) English: transferred use of the surname, which is itself derived from an Old English personal name composed of the elements *æðel* noble + *mǣr* famous. This has been used as a given name in America since the 19th century, in honour of the brothers Ebenezer and Jonathan Elmer, leading supporters of the American Revolution.

Elmo (m.) Italian (occasionally used also in the English-speaking world): in origin probably a Germanic name derived from *helm* helmet, protection, either as a byname or else as a short form of any of the various compound names with this first element, as for example HELMUT. Later, however, along with the variant *Ermo*, it came to be used as a pet form of ERASMUS.

Elodia (f.) Spanish: Latinized version of a Visigothic female personal name, composed of the elements *ali* other, foreign + *od* riches, wealth, prosperity. The name was borne by a 9th-century saint, martyred at Huesca together with her sister Nuncilo, at the behest of their Islamic stepfather.

Cognate: French: **Élodie**.

Elof (m.) Swedish: from an Old Norse personal name composed of the elements *ei* ever, always or *einn* one, alone + *lāfr* descendant, heir.

Variant: **Elov**.

Cognate: Danish: **Eluf**.

Pet form: Swedish: **Loffe**.

Eloi (m.) French and Portuguese form of ELOY.

Éloise (f.) French: probably of Germanic origin, although the elements of which it is composed have not been identified. Éloise or Héloïse was the name of the learned and beautiful wife (d. *c*.1164) of the French philosopher and theologian Peter Abelard (1079–1142), whom she married secretly. A misunderstanding with her uncle and guardian, the powerful and violent Canon Fulbert of Notre Dame led to Abelard being set upon, beaten up, and castrated. He became a monk, and Héloïse spent the rest of her days as abbess of a nunnery, but they continued to write to each other. The name has been occasionally revived in modern times in allusion to her fidelity and piety.

Cognate: English: **Eloise**.

Elov (m.) Swedish: variant of ELOF.

Eloy (m.) Spanish: from the Latin name *Eligius*, a derivative of *eligere* to choose, select. St Eligius (588–660) was a bishop of Noyon who evangelized the districts around Antwerp, Ghent, and Courtrai.

Variant: **Eligio**.

Cognates: French, Portuguese: **Eloi**. Italian: **Eligio**.

Elpidio (m.) Italian and Spanish: from the Late Latin name *Elpidius*, Greek *Elpidios*, a derivative of Greek *elpis* (genitive *elpidos*) hope. The name was borne by various early saints, particularly a 4th-century hermit who spent twenty-five years in a cave in Cappadocia. Relics believed to be his were preserved in the Middle Ages at the village of Sant'Elpidio in the marches of Ancona, and the name was most commonly used in that region.

Elroy (m.) English: variant of LEROY. The initial syllable seems to be the result of simple transposition of the first two letters; it may also have been influenced by the Spanish definite article *el* and by the associated name DELROY. This is now a popular name among Blacks.

Elsa (f.) English, German, and Swedish: shortened form of ELISABETH or ELIZABETH. The name was borne by the English-born film actress Elsa Lanchester (1902–86), whose original name was Elizabeth Sullivan. The name is now also associated with the lioness named Elsa featured in the book and film *Born Free*.

Elsdon (m.) English (mainly U.S.): transferred use of the surname, which originated in the Middle Ages as a local name from a place in Northumbria. The place-name is recorded in the 13th century in the forms *Eledene*, *Hellesden*, *Elisden*, and *Ellesden*; it seems to derive from the genitive case of the personal name *Elli* + Old English *denu* valley.

Else (f.) Danish form of ELSA, used also in Germany (particularly in the north of the country).

Elsie (f.) Scottish and English: simplified form of **Elspie**, a pet form of ELSPETH. This came to be used as an independent name, and in the early 20th century proved more popular than *Elspeth*.

Elspeth (f.) Scottish and English: contracted form of ELIZABETH.

Elton (m.) English: transferred use of the surname, which originated in the Middle Ages as a local name from any of numerous places in England so called (mostly from the Old English masculine personal name *Ella* + Old English *tūn* enclosure, settlement). In England it is largely associated with the singer–songwriter Elton John; born Reginald Dwight, he took his adopted given name in honour of the saxophonist Elton Dean.

Eluf (m.) Danish form of ELOF.

Eluned (f.) Welsh: apparently a reformed version of earlier *Luned*, *Lunet*. *Lunete* is the form of the name used by the French writer Chrétien de Troyes; cf LYNETTE.

Elvira (f.) Spanish: of Germanic (Visi-gothic) origin, very common in the Middle Ages and still in use today. The original form and meaning of the elements of which it is composed are far from certain (probably *ali* other, foreign + *wēr* true). The name was not used in the English-speaking world until the 19th century, when it was made familiar as the name of the long-suffering wife of Don Juan, both in Mozart's opera *Don Giovanni* (1789) and Byron's satirical epic poem *Don Juan* (1819–24).

Elvis (m.) English (esp. U.S.): of obscure derivation, made famous by the American rock singer Elvis Presley (1935–77). It may be derived from the surname of an ancestor, or it may have been made up, but it was certainly not chosen for the singer in anticipation of a career in show business, for his father's name was Vernon Elvis Presley. A St Elvis, apparently an Irishman of the 6th century, is also known as *Elwyn*, *Elwin*, *Elian*, and *Allan*.

Elżbieta (f.) Polish form of ELIZABETH.

Emanuel (m.) Scandinavian form of EMMANUEL. This form of the name is also used in Germany, alongside *Emmanuel* and the commoner German form IMMANUEL.

Emanuele (m.) Italian form of EMMANUEL. The name is fairly common in Italy among Gentiles as well as Jews. It was introduced to the royal house of Savoy at the beginning of the 16th century, when a daughter of Manoel I of Portugal married Carlo II of Savoy; the name was given to their son.

Emeny (f.) English: medieval name of uncertain origin. It appears in various forms such as *Emonie* and *Imanie* and seems to be of Germanic origin. It was Latinized as ISMENE.

Emer (f.) Irish Gaelic: traditional name of uncertain derivation. This was the name of Cú Chulainn's beloved, a woman of many talents who was blessed with the gifts of beauty, voice, sweet speech, wisdom, needlework, and chastity. It has been revived as a given name in the 20th century.
Cognates: Scottish Gaelic: **Eamhair**, **Éimhear**.

Emerald (f.) English: from the name of the gemstone, representing a vernacular form of ESMERALDA.

Emerenzia (f.) Italian: from Latin *Emerentia*, a derivative of *ēmerēri* to earn, merit. The name was borne by a Roman martyr of uncertain date, who has become associated with the legend of St Agnes.

Emeterio (m.) Spanish: from Latin *Emeterius* or *Hemiterius*, a name of uncertain (probably Greek) origin. St Hemiterius was martyred together with a certain Cheledonius at Calahorra in Spain in the 4th century.
Cognate: Catalan: **Medir**.

Emidio (m.) Italian: of uncertain origin. The name is borne in honour of St *Emidius* or *Emygdius* (d. *c*.303), the patron saint of Ascoli Piceno. He is said to have come from a noble Gaulish family and to have been born at Trier.

Emil (m.) German and Scandinavian: from the Latin name *Aemilius* (see EMILY).
Cognates: French: **Émile**. Italian, Spanish, Portuguese: **Emilio**.

Émilie (f.) French form of EMILY. Without the accent this form of the name is also used in Germany.

Émilien (m.) French: from Latin *Aemiliānus*, a family name representing a derivative of *Aemilius* (see EMILY). This was made popular as a Christian name by various minor early saints.
Cognate: Catalan: **Millà**.

Emilio (m.) Italian, Spanish, and Portuguese form of EMIL.

Emily (f.) English: from a medieval form of the Latin name *Aemilia*, the feminine version of the old Roman family name *Aemilius* (probably from *aemulus* rival). It was not common in the Middle Ages, and when it was revived in the 19th century there was much confusion between the originally distinct AMELIA and the Latinate form of this name, *Emilia*.
Cognates: French: **Émilie**. German: **Emilie**.

Emlyn (m.) Welsh: of uncertain origin, possibly from Latin *Aemiliānus* (see ÉMILIEN). On the other hand, it may have a Celtic origin; there are Breton and Irish saints recorded as *Aemilianus*, which may be a Latinized form of a lost Celtic name.

Emma (f.) English: of Germanic origin, introduced to Britain by the Normans. It was the name of the mother of Edward the Confessor. It originated as a short form of the medieval versions of compound names such as ERMINTRUDE and IRMGARD, containing the element *erm(en)*, *irm(en)* entire (cf. IRMA). It is now sometimes used as a pet form of EMILY, but this is etymologically unjustified.

Emmanuel (m.) Biblical: the name (meaning 'God is with us' in Hebrew) of the promised Messiah, as prophesied by Isaiah

(7: 14; reported in Matthew 1: 23). The Authorized Version of the Bible uses the Hebrew form IMMANUEL in the Old Testament, *Emmanuel* in the New. Both forms have been used as given names in England. This has always been a comparatively rare name in the English-speaking world, whereas the Hispanic cognate *Manuel* is one of the commonest Spanish given names.

Derivatives: German: **Immanuel**. Scandinavian: **Emanuel**. Italian: **Emanuele**. Spanish: **Manuel**. Portuguese: **Manoel**. Basque: **Imanol**. Pet forms: Jewish: **Man, Manny**.
Feminine form: Spanish: **Manuela**.

Emmarald (f.) English: variant of EMERALD, influenced by the given name EMMA.

Emmeline (f.) English: of Germanic origin, introduced to Britain by the Normans. Even in the Middle Ages it was not clear whether this name was a derivative of EMMA or of AMALIA (the spellings are very varied), and when it was revived in the 19th century there was further confusion with EMILY. A famous bearer was the suffragette Emmeline Pankhurst (1858–1928), mother of Christabel and Sylvia.

Emmet (m.) English: transferred use of the surname, which itself was derived in the Middle Ages from the female given name *Emmet*, a diminutive form of EMMA. It may sometimes be used by parents with Irish connections, in honour of the rebel Robert Emmet (1778–1803), who led a disastrous attempt at rebellion against the English.

Emmy (f.) English: pet form of EMMA, EMILY, and related names. It is occasionally used as an independent given name, especially in the United States and in combinations such as **Emmy Jane** and **Emmy Jo**.

Emrys (m.) Welsh form of AMBROSE. The name has been very commonly used in families of Welsh origin in the 20th century.

Emyr (m.) Welsh: originally a byname meaning 'ruler, king, lord'. The name was borne by a 6th-century Breton saint who settled in Cornwall.

Ena (f.) Irish and English: one of several Anglicized forms of the Gaelic name EITHNE. However, in the case of Queen Victoria's granddaughter Princess Ena (Victoria Eugénie Julia Ena, 1887–1969) it had a different origin: it was apparently a misreading by the minister who baptized her of a handwritten note of the originally intended name EVA. In England, the name is currently out of fashion, and is remembered principally as that of the fearsome Ena Sharples in the television soap opera *Coronation Street*.

Encarnación (f.) Spanish: name commemorating the festival of the Incarnation (Spanish *encarnación*, from Late Latin *incarnātio*, a derivative of *caro* flesh), celebrated on Christmas Day.
Short form: **Encarna**.

Enda (m.) Irish: Anglicized form of the Gaelic name **Éanna**, a derivative of *éan* bird. This name was borne by the famous St Éanna of Aran, and it is still a popular given name in the west of Ireland.

Endre (m.) Hungarian form of ANDREW.

Enfys (f.) Welsh: modern name, taken from the vocabulary word meaning 'rainbow'.

Engelbert (m.) German: from an old Germanic personal name, composed of the ethnic term *Angil* Angle + the element

berht bright, famous. St Engelbert (1186–1255) was an archbishop of Cologne, murdered by a hired assassin.

Engracia (f.) Spanish: from the Latin name *Encratis* or *Encratia*. This is derived from the Greek word *enkratēs* in control, temperate, moderate, but it has been influenced by Latin *grātia* grace. St Encratia (d. *c*.304) was martyred at Saragossa under Diocletian and is commemorated by the poet Prudentius.

Enid (f.) Welsh and English: Celtic name of extemely uncertain derivation, borne by a virtuous character in the Arthurian romances, the long-suffering wife of Geraint. The name was revived in the second half of the 19th century, and enjoyed a great vogue in England in the 1920s.

Ennio (m.) Italian: from Latin *Ennius*, a family name (of uncertain derivation) borne by the early Roman poet Quintus Ennius (239–161 BC).

Enoch (m.) Biblical: name (possibly meaning 'experienced' in Hebrew) of the son of Cain (Genesis 4: 16–22) and father of Methuselah (Genesis 5: 18-24). The latter is said to have lived for 365 years and the apocryphal 'Books of Enoch' are attributed to him.

Enola (f.) English: 20th-century coinage of uncertain derivation. One theory is that it originated as a reversal in spelling of the word *alone*, but this may be no more than coincidental.

Enos (m.) Biblical: name (meaning 'mankind' in Hebrew) borne by a son of Seth and grandson of Adam (Genesis 4: 26) who allegedly lived for nine hundred and five years. In Ireland this name has been used as an Anglicized form of the Gaelic name *Aonghus* (see ANGUS).

Enric (m.) Catalan form of HENRY.

Enrico (m.) Italian form of HENRY (see also AMERIGO and ARRIGO).

Enrique (m.) Spanish form of HENRY.
Pet form: **Quique**.

Enzo (m.) Italian: probably of Germanic origin, but of uncertain derivation. It may have been originally a byname from *ent* giant. Alternatively, it could have originated as a short form of given names such as LORENZO or *Vicenzo* (see VINCENT), or perhaps as an Italianized form of the German name HEINZ.

Eóghan (m.) Irish and Scottish Gaelic: name of great antiquity and disputed derivation. It has been suggested that it may be composed of Old Celtic elements meaning 'yew' and 'born', i.e. 'born of the yew'. It is Anglicized in Ireland as OWEN and EUGENE, in Scotland as EWAN, *Ewen, Euan*, EVAN, and sometimes HUGH.
Variant: Scottish Gaelic: **Eòghann**.

Eoin (m.) Gaelic form of JOHN, used especially to designate the saints of that name. It is also in secular use, especially in Ireland, but also in Scotland (Eòin), where it tends to be Anglicized as JONATHAN.

Ephraim (m.) Biblical: name of one of the sons of Joseph and of one of the tribes of Israel. The name probably means 'fruitful' in Hebrew; it is so explained in the Bible (Genesis 41: 52 'and the name of the second called he Ephraim: For God hath caused me to be fruitful in the land of my affliction'). Unlike many Old Testament names, this was not particularly popular with the Puritans, and was used more in the 18th and

19th centuries than the 17th. It is still a common Jewish given name.

Derivatives: Spanish: **Efrain**. Russian: **Yefrem**. Yiddish: **Evron**, **Froim**.

Pet form: Jewish: **Effie**.

Eppie (f.) English: pet form of EUPHEMIA, fairly common in Victorian times. This is the name of the orphan child adopted by the eponymous hero of George Eliot's novel *Silas Marner*; in this case it represents a pet form of HEPHZIBAH.

Erasmus (m.) English: Latinized form of Greek *Erasmos*, a derivative of *erān* to love. St Erasmus (d. 303) was a bishop of Formiae in Campania, martyred under Diocletian; he is numbered among the Fourteen Holy Helpers and is a patron of sailors. This is a fairly rare given name in the English-speaking world, and is borne mainly by Roman Catholics. It is sometimes bestowed in honour of the great Dutch humanist scholar and teacher Erasmus Rotterodamus (?1466–1536).

Ercole (m.) Italian form of HERCULES. The name is particularly common in the region of Emilia.

Erdmann (m.) German: altered form of HARTMANN. This form seems to have come into use during the 17th century, when the first element was associated with modern German *Erde* earth. The meaning 'earth-man' was seen to be an appropriate one for a Christian, since Adam was made by God from earth.

Erdmut (m.) German: altered form of HARTMUT, in use since the 17th century, although never common.

Variant: **Erdmuth**.

Erdmute (f.) German: feminine form of ERDMUT, for some reason rather more popular than the male name. In the 20th century, however, it too has fallen out of fashion.

Variant: **Erdmuthe**.

Erhard (m.) German: from an old Germanic personal name composed of the elements *ēra* honour, respect + *hard* hardy, brave, strong. It was borne by a 7th-century saint, allegedly of Irish origin, who served as a missionary bishop around the area of Regensburg in Bavaria.

Eric (m.) English: of Old Norse origin, composed of the elements *ei* ever, always or *einn* one, alone + *rīkr* ruler. It was introduced into Britain by Scandinavian settlers before the Conquest and was occasionally used during the Middle Ages and later. The surname *Herrick* derives from it. As a modern given name it was revived in the mid-19th century.

Cognates: German: **Erich**. Swedish: **Erik** (the most common male name given in Sweden in 1973); **Jerk(er)**. Norwegian: **Eirik**. Finnish: **Erkki**, **Eero**.

Erica (f.) English and Scottish: **Latinate** feminine form of ERIC, coined towards the end of the 18th century. It remains common in Gaelic Scotland as an Anglicized form of OIGHRIG (see also EIRIC and EITHRIG). It has no doubt also been reinforced by the fact that *erica* is the Latin word for 'heather'.

Cognate: German, Scandinavian: **Erika**.

Erin (f.) English and Irish: from Gaelic *Éirinn*, dative case of *Éire* Ireland. *Erin* has been used as a poetic name for Ireland for centuries, and in recent years this has become a very popular given name. It has enjoyed particular popularity in the United States, even among people with no Irish ancestry.

Erkki (m.) Finnish form of ERIC (see also EERO).

Erland (m.) Scandinavian: from an Old Norse personal name, originally a byname from the vocabulary word *örlendr* foreigner, stranger.

Variant: **Erlend**.

Erle (m.) English: variant spelling of EARL.

Erline (f.) English: apparently a feminine derivative of ERLE.

Ermanno (m.) Italian form of HERMANN. This is not one of the Germanic personal names that were in use in Italy in the Middle Ages; it seems to have been introduced from Germany relatively recently.

Ermenegildo (m.) Italian form and Spanish variant of HERMENEGILDO.

Ermentraud (f.) German form of ERMINTRUDE.

Variant: **Ermentrud**.

Ermete (m.) Italian: from Latin *Hermēs*, genitive *Hermētis*, the name of the Greek messenger god (of extremely uncertain derivation, perhaps taken from one of the languages of Asia Minor). In spite of its pagan connotations, the name was common among the early Christians and was borne by more than twenty saints of the early centuries AD, most of them rather minor figures. In modern use the name is mainly found in Tuscany and Emilia.

Ermine (f.) English: in origin perhaps a variant of HERMINE, but strongly influenced in popularity by association with the name of the fur (Old French *ermine*, medieval Latin *armēnius* (*mūs*) Armenian mouse).

Ermintrude (f.) English: of Germanic origin, introduced to Britain by the Normans. It is composed of the elements *erm(en)*, *irm(en)* entire + *traut* beloved. The name did not survive long into the Middle Ages, but was occasionally revived in the 18th and 19th centuries. It is now completely out of fashion.

Cognates: German: **Erm(en)tr(a)ud**. See also IRMTRAUD.

Ern (m.) English: short form of ERNEST.

Pet form: **Ernie**.

Erna (f.) German: simplified form of *Ernesta* (see ERNEST).

Ernan (m.) Irish: Anglicized form of the Gaelic name **Earnán**, possibly a derivative of *iarn* iron. St Earnán is the patron saint of Tory Island.

Ernest (m.) English: of Germanic origin, derived from the Old High German vocabulary word *eornost* seriousness, battle (to the death). The name was introduced into England in the 18th century by followers of the Hanoverian Elector who became George I of England. A variant spelling **Earnest** has arisen from the modern English adjective *earnest*, which is only distantly connected with the name.

Cognates: Italian, Spanish, Portuguese: **Ernesto**. German: **Ernst**. Czech: **Arnošt**. Hungarian: **Ernö**.

Short form: English: **Ern**.

Pet form: English: **Ernie**.

Feminine forms: English: **Ernesta**, **Ernestine**. German: **Ernsta**, **Erna**.

Errol (m.) English (borne mainly by Blacks): from the Scottish surname, which derives from a placename. It has been made famous by the film actor Errol Flynn (1909–59), noted for his 'swashbuckling' roles. It is now very popular among Blacks, influenced by such figures as the jazz pianist Errol Garner (1923–77).

Errukiñe (f.) Basque equivalent of PIEDAD.

Erskine (m.) Scottish, Irish, and English: from the Scottish surname, which derives from the name of a place near Glasgow. The surname has also been taken to Ireland by Scottish settlers, and was first brought to public attention as a given name by the half-Irish writer and political activist Erskine Childers (1870–1922).

Erwin (m.) German: from an old Germanic personal name composed of the elements *ēra* honour, respect + *win* friend. During the Middle Ages it was most common in the Rhine region and was borne, for example, by the founder of Strasburg cathedral. In modern times it has been borne most notably by the Second World War field marshal Erwin Rommel (1891–1944). In the United States it is sometimes used as a variant of IRWIN and IRVING.

Erzsébet (f.) Hungarian form of ELIZABETH.

Esa (m.) Finnish form of ISAIAH.

Esau (m.) Biblical: name of the elder twin brother of Jacob, to whom he sold his birthright for a bite to eat when he came home tired and hungry from a hunt. The name seems to have meant 'hairy' in Hebrew (Genesis 25: 25 'and the first came out red, all over like an hairy garment; and they called his name Esau'). It is now rarely used as a given name in the English-speaking world.

Esbjörn (m.) Swedish: from an Old Norse personal name composed of the elements *áss* god, divinity + *björn* bear.
Cognates: Norwegian: **Esbjørn**, **Asbjørn**.
Danish: **Esben**, **Esbern**.
Pet form: **Ebbe**.

Esdras (m.) Biblical: Greek form of the Hebrew name EZRA, used in the Douay Bible as the title of the Books of Ezra (1 Esdras) and Nehemiah (2 Esdras) and of two further books (3 and 4 Esdras) not included in the Protestant canon.

Eskarne (f.) Basque equivalent of MERCEDES.

Eskil (m.) Scandinavian: from an Old Norse personal name composed of the elements *áss* god, divinity + *ketill* sacrificial cauldron.
Variant: **Eskel**.

Esmé (m.) French: from the past participle of the verb *esmer* to love (Latin *aestimāre* to value, esteem). In French this verb was absorbed by *amer* (see AMY) in the modern French form *aimer*, but has survived in a different sense in English *aim* (originally 'estimate, reckon'). The name was introduced to Scotland in the 16th century, and is still occasionally used as a male given name in the English speaking world, where it is often spelled without the accent; it is occasionally also used as a female name. See also EDMÉ.
Feminine form: French, English: **Esmée**.

Esmeralda (f.) English: from the Spanish vocabulary word *esmeralda* emerald. Its occasional modern use as a given name seems to date from Victor Hugo's *Notre Dame de Paris* (1831), in which it is the nickname of the gypsy girl loved by the hunchback Quasimodo; she was given the name because she wore an amulet containing an artificial emerald.
Variant: **Esmerelda**.

Esmond (m.) English: from an Old English personal name composed of the elements *ēast* grace, beauty + *mund* protection. This, or a Continental Germanic cognate, was adopted into Norman French but was not used as a given name between the 14th century and the late 19th century, when it was revived.

Esperanza (f.) Spanish: from the Late Latin name *Sperantia* 'hope' (a derivative of *sperans*, present participle of *sperāre* to hope, replacing the classical Latin noun *spēs*).

Esta (f.) English: Latinate respelling of ESTHER.

Estéban (m.) Spanish form of STEPHEN.

Estefanía (f.) Spanish form of STEPHANIE.

Estelle (f.) English: Old French name meaning 'star' (Latin STELLA), comparatively rarely used during the Middle Ages. It was revived in the 19th century, together with the Latinate form **Estella**, which was used by Dickens for the ward of Miss Havisham in *Great Expectations* (1861).

Ester (f.) Scandinavian and Eastern European form of ESTHER.

Estevão (m.) Portuguese form of STEPHEN.

Esteve (m.) Catalan form of STEPHEN.

Estève (m.) Provençal form of STEPHEN.

Esther (f.) Biblical: name borne in the Bible by a Jewish captive who became the wife of the Persian king Ahasuerus. According to the book of the Bible that bears her name, she managed, by her perception and persuasion, to save large numbers of the Jews from the evil machinations of the royal counsellor Haman. Her Hebrew name was *Hadassah* 'myrtle', and the form *Esther* is said to be a Persian translation of this, although others derive it from Persian *stara* star. It may also be a Hebrew form of the name of the Persian goddess *Ishtar*.
Cognates: Scandinavian and E. European: **Ester**. Hungarian: **Eszter**. Irish Gaelic: **Eistir**.

Estrella (f.) Spanish form of STELLA. The prothetic *E-* before the consonant cluster *-st-* is a regular feature of Spanish, and the intrusive *-r-* in this word is found also in Portuguese and some north Italian dialects.

Estrild (f.) English (rare): from an Old English or Continental Germanic female personal name composed of the divine name *Éastre* (a goddess of spring, whose name lies behind modern English *Easter*) + the element *hild* battle. According to a legend narrated by Geoffrey of Monmouth, *Estrildis* was the name of a German princess who was captured and brought to England. She so enchanted King Locrine that he left his wife Gwendolen for her: in revenge, Gwendolen had both Estrildis and her daughter Sabrina thrown into the River Severn and drowned.

Eszter (f.) Hungarian form of ESTHER.

Ethan (m.) Biblical: name (meaning 'firmness' or 'long-lived' in Hebrew) of an obscure figure, Ethan the Ezrahite, mentioned as a wise man whom Solomon surpassed in wisdom (1 Kings 4: 31). The name was sparingly used even among the Puritans, but became famous in the United States since it was borne by Ethan Allen (1738–89), leader of the 'Green Mountain Boys', a group of Vermont patriots who fought in the American Revolution. It has also been revived as a popular modern Hebrew given name and surname.
Variants: Jewish: **E(i)tan** (Hebrew).

Ethel (f.) English: 19th-century revival of an Old English or Continental Germanic short form of the various female personal names beginning with the Germanic element *ethel* noble, including *Ethelburga* 'noble fortress', ETHELDREDA, and *Ethelgiva* 'noble gift'. All of these are now very rare (and were never common), but *Ethel* itself enjoyed great popularity for a period at the beginning of the 20th century, although it is now out of fashion.

Etheldreda (f.) English: Latinized form of the Old English female personal name *Æðelþryð* (see AUDREY). It was taken up as a given name in the 19th century, but is now rare.

Ethna (f.) Irish: Anglicized form of EITHNE.

Étienne (m.) French form of STEPHEN.

Étiennette (f.) French: feminine form of ÉTIENNE, with the diminutive suffix -*ette*.

Etna (f.) Irish: Anglicized form of EITHNE.

Etta (f.) English and Scottish: short form of the various names ending in this element (originally an Italian feminine diminutive suffix), now sometimes used as an independent given name. In Gaelic Scotland it is used as a pet form of MAIREAD (Anglicized as *Mar(i)etta*).

Ettore (m.) Italian form of HECTOR, sometimes deliberately chosen as a nonsaint's name by anti-clerical parents.

Etzel (m.) German: medieval name apparently derived from the element *adal* noble, or else from the nickname *Atta* 'father'.

Variant: EDSEL.

Euan (m.) Scottish: Anglicized form of Gaelic EÓGHAN, currently much in fashion.

Eubh (f.) Scottish Gaelic form of *Eve*, see EVA.

Variant: **Eubha**.

Eudora (f.) English: ostensibly a Greek name, composed of the elements *eu* well, good + a derivative of *dōron* gift. However, there is no saint of this name, and it is more probably a modern combination of elements which are both common in other given names.

Eufemia (f.) Italian, Spanish, and Portuguese form of EU-PHEMIA.

Eugene (m.) English: from the Old French form of the Greek name *Eugenios* (from *eugenēs* well-born, noble). This was the name of various early saints, notably a 5th-century bishop of Carthage, a 7th-century bishop of Toledo, and four popes. The popularity of the name in Russia is due to the cult of a 4th-century missionary bishop who preached in the Crimea and southern Russia. In Western Europe, the name owes its popularity at least in part to the fame of Prince Eugene of Savoy (1663–1736), a general in the service of Austria who co-operated with Marlborough in defeating the French forces of Louis XIV. He was noted not only for his brilliance as a commander, but also for his strong moral principles. In Ireland the name has been used as an Anglicized form of EÓGHAN and AODH.

Cognates: French: **Eugène**. Italian, Spanish: **Eugenio**. Portuguese: **Eugénio**. German: **Eugen**. Polish: **Eugeniusz**. Czech: **Evžen**. Russian: **Yevgeni**. Hungarian: **Jenő**.
Short form: English (esp. U.S.): **Gene**.

Eugenia (f.) English, Italian, and Spanish: feminine form of Greek *Eugenios* or Latin *Eugenius*; see EUGENE.

Eugénie (f.) French form of EUGENIA. The name was introduced to England as the name of the Empress Eugénie (Eugenia María de Montijo de Guzmán, 1826–1920), wife of Napoleon III, and has since been occasionally used (sometimes without the accent) in the English-speaking world.

Eugenio (m.) Italian and Spanish form of EUGENE.

Eugênio (m.) Portuguese form of EUGENE.

Eugeniusz (m.) Polish form of EUGENE.

Eulalia (f.) English, Italian, and Spanish: from a Late Greek personal name composed of the elements *eu* well, good + *lalein* to talk, chatter. It was very common in the Middle Ages, when it was to a large extent confused with HILARY, but is now rare.
Cognates: French: **Eulalie**. Spanish: OLALLA.

Eumann (m.) Scottish Gaelic form of EDMUND (cf. EAMON).

Euna (f.) Scottish: Anglicized form of the Gaelic name *Ùna* (see ÚNA).

Eunan (m.) Irish and Scottish: Anglicized form of the Gaelic name **Ádhamhnán**. This is possibly a diminutive form of *Ádhamh*, the Gaelic version of ADAM, but is now thought more likely to represent a diminutive form of *adomnae* great fear, hence 'Little Horror'. The name was borne by a 7th-century saint, abbot of Iona and biographer of St Columba.

Eunice (f.) English: from a Late Greek name composed of the elements *eu* well, good + *nikē* victory. It is mentioned in the New Testament as the name of the mother of Timothy, who introduced him to Christianity (2 Timothy 1: 5). This reference led to the name being taken up by the Puritans in the 17th century.

Euphemia (f.) Latin form of a Late Greek name composed of the elements *eu* well, good + *phēmi* I speak. This is the name of various early saints, most notably a virgin martyr supposedly burnt at the stake at Chalcedon in 307. It was particularly popular in England in the Victorian period, especially in the pet form EFFIE. See also OIGHRIG.

Derivatives: French: **Euphémie**. Italian, Spanish, Portuguese: **Eufemia**.
Pet forms: English: **Effie**, **Eppie**.
Masculine form: Russian: **Yefim**.

Eusebio (m.) Spanish, Portuguese, and Italian: from the Late Greek name *Eusebios*, derived from the adjective *eusebēs* respectful, pious (from *eu* well, good + *sebein* to worship, honour). This name was borne by a large number of early saints, including a friend of St Jerome traditionally regarded as the founder of the abbey of Guadalupe in Spain, and a 4th-century bishop of Bologna.

Eustace (m.) English: from the Old French form of the Late Greek names *Eustakhios* and *Eustathios*. These were evidently of separate origin, the former composed of the elements *eu* well, good + *stakhys* grapes, the latter of *eu* + *stēnai* to stand. However, the tradition is very confused. The name was introduced in this form to Britain by the Normans, among whom it was popular as a result of the fame of St Eustace, who was said to have been converted to Christianity by the vision of a crucifix between the antlers of the stag he was hunting. It is at present out of fashion.
Cognates: French: **Eustache**. Italian: **Eustachio**. Spanish: **Eustaquio**.

Eutropio (m.) Spanish: from the Late Greek name *Eutropios*, composed of the elements *eu* well, good + *tropos* way, manner, i.e. 'well-mannered'. Alternatively, it may derive from the classical Greek adjective *eutropos* versatile, in which the second element derives from the root of the verb *trepein* to turn. The name was borne by various minor early saints.

Cognate: French: **Eutrope** (not common).

Eva (f.) Latinate form of EVE, used commonly in English, Italian, Spanish, Portuguese, and Scandinavian languages among others. In Ireland it has sometimes been used as an Anglicized form of AOIFE.

Variants: Polish: **Ewa**. Irish Gaelic: **Ébha**. Scottish Gaelic: **Eubh**, **Eubha**.

Pet forms: Spanish: **Evita**. Czech: **Evka**, **Evuška**, **Evulka**, **Evinka**, **Evička**.

Evadne (f.) English: from a Greek personal name composed of the element *eu* well, good + another element that is of uncertain meaning. It was borne by a minor figure in classical legend who threw herself on to the funeral pyre of her husband, and was regarded as an example of wifely piety. The modern spelling and pronunciation is the result of transmission through Latin sources. The name has never been common, and is now completely out of fashion. It is associated with the character of Dr Evadne Hinge in the British comedy television series *Hinge and Bracket*.

Evan (m.) **1**. Welsh: Anglicized form of *Iefan*, a later development of IEUAN. **2**. Scottish: Anglicized form of EGHAN.

Variant (of 1): **Ifan**.

Evander (m.) Scottish (Highland): classical name used as an Anglicized form of Scottish Gaelic *Ìomhair* (see IVOR). This form is peculiar to the MacIver family, apparently coined to differentiate it from the surname. In classical legend, *Evander* is the name of the Arcadian hero who founded a city in Italy where Rome was later built. It is a Latin form of Greek *Euandros*, composed of the elements *eu* well, good + *anēr* man (genitive *andros*).

Evangeline (f.) English: fanciful name derived from Latin *evangelium* gospel (Greek *euangelion*, from *eu* well, good + *angelma* tidings) + the suffix (in origin a French feminine diminutive) *-ine*. *Evangeline* is the title of a narrative poem (1848) by the American poet Henry Wadsworth Longfellow, in which the central character is called Evangeline Belle-fontaine.

Evaristo (m.) Italian, Spanish, and Portuguese: from the Late Greek personal name *Euarestos*, derived from the elements *eu* well, good + *areskein* to please, satisfy. The second element has been respelled as if from Greek *aristos* best, excellent. This name was borne by an early pope, said to have been martyred under the Roman emperor Hadrian in about 107.

Cognate: French: **Évariste**.

Eve (f.) English and French form of the name borne in the Bible by the first woman, created from one of Adam's ribs (Genesis 2: 22). It derives, via Latin *Ēva*, from Hebrew *Havva*, which is considered to be a variant of the vocabulary word *hayya* living or animal (see CHAYA). Adam gave names to all the animals (Genesis 2: 19–20) and then to his wife, who was 'the mother of all living' (Genesis 3: 20).

Variant: **Eva**.
Pet form: **Evie**.

Evelina (f.) English and Irish: apparently a Latinate form of the female name EVELYN, or perhaps a combination of EVE with the suffix *-lina*.

Evelyn (m., f.) English: modern use of this as both a female and a male given name seems to derive from an English surname, which is in turn derived from a Norman female name (see AVELINE).

Variants: **Evelyne**, **Eveline**.

Everard (m.) English: from an Old English personal name composed of the elements *eofor* boar + *heard* hardy, brave, strong. This was reinforced at the time of the Conquest by a Continental Germanic cognate (see EBERHARD) introduced by the Normans. In modern use this may be a transferred use of the surname, but it was in regular use in the Digby family of Rutland from the 15th to the 17th century, probably as a survival of the Old English or Norman name. It alternated in this family with KENELM.

Cognate: French: **Evrard**.

Everett (m.) English: transferred use of the surname, a variant of EVERARD.

Evert (m.) Low German form of EBERHARD.

Evette (f.) English and French: altered form of YVETTE, influenced by the given name EVE.

Evie (f.) English: pet form of EVE or EVA, occasionally also of EVELYN as a female name.

Evita (f.) Spanish: pet form of EVA. This was the name by which Eva Duarte de Perón (1919–52), wife of the Argentinian dictator Juan Domingo Perón, was affectionately known. Its popularity in the English-speaking world has recently been increased by the musical based on her life.

Evonne (f.) English: altered form of YVONNE, influenced by the given name EVE.

Evrard (m.) French: contracted form of EVERARD.

Evron (m.) Jewish: Yiddish form of EPHRAIM.

Evžen (m.) Czech form of EUGENE.

Feminine form: **Evženie**.
Pet forms: **Evža** (m., f.); **Evženek**, **Evžík** (m.); **Evženka**, **Evžička** (f.).

Ewa (f.) Polish form of EVE.

Pet forms: **Ewka**, **Ewusia**.

Ewald (m.) German: from an old Germanic personal name composed of the elements *ēo* law, right + *wald* rule. This name was borne in the 7th century by a pair of brothers, apparently originally from Northumbria, who evangelized north Germany and Frisia. In order to distinguish them they were known as 'Ewald the Fair' and 'Ewald the Dark'.

Cognate: Dutch: **Ewould**.

Ewan (m.) The usual Anglicized form in Scotland of Gaelic EÓGHAN, also used occasionally in Ireland and elsewhere.

Variant: **Ewen**.

Ewart (m.) Scottish and English: **transferred** use of the surname, probably first used as a given name in honour of the Victorian statesman William Ewart Gladstone (1809–98). The surname has several possible origins: it may represent a Norman form of EDWARD, or an occupational name for a eweherd, or a local name from a place in Northumbria.

Ewould (m.) Dutch form of EWALD.

Eydl (f.) Jewish: Yiddish name, originally an affectionate nickname meaning 'noble' (Yiddish *eydl*, cf. modern German *edel*).

Variant: **Eyde** (a back-formation based on the belief that *Eydl* was a pet form with the hypocoristic suffix -*(e)l*).

Eyolf (m.) Norwegian: of Old Norse origin, composed of the Protoscandinavian elements *anja* luck, gift + *(w)olf*. It was brought to the attention of the public by Henrik Ibsen's play *Little Eyolf* (1894), and has been in occasional use ever since.

Ezekiel (m.) Biblical: name (meaning 'God strengthens' in Hebrew) borne by one of the major prophets. The book of the Bible that bears his name is probably best known for its vision of a field of dry bones, which Ezekiel prophesies will live again (chapter 37). His prophecies were addressed to the Jews in Babylonian exile, after Nebuchadnezzar had seized Jerusalem in 597 BC.

Derivatives: Yiddish: **Heskel**; **Haskel** (U.S.). Short form: English: **Zeke**.

Ezio (m.) Italian: from the Late Latin personal name *Aetius*. This represents a conflation of two originally distinct names: *Aetius*, an old Roman family name of apparently Etruscan origin and unknown meaning, and *Aëstios*, a Late Greek name derived from Greek *a(i)etos* eagle. The name has been popular in Italy since Verdi's opera *Attila* (1846), in which Ezio (the historical character Flavius Aëtius, general of the Emperor Valentinian in his campaign against the Huns) was seen as a prototype Italian revolutionary hero.

Ezra (m.) Biblical: name (meaning 'help' in Hebrew) of a prophet, author of the book of the Bible that bears his name. It was taken up by the Puritans in the 17th century, and has remained in occasional use ever since, especially in America, where it was borne, for example, by the poet Ezra Pound (1885–1972).

Variant: ESDRAS.

Ezzo (m.) Italian: of uncertain derivation. It seems to be of Germanic origin, and may be derived from the element *adal* noble or the rarer *atta* father (cf. ETZEL).

F

Faas (m.) Dutch and Flemish: from the old Germanic personal name *Fastred*, composed of the elements *fast* firm, resolute + *red* counsel. The Blessed Fastred of Cavamiez (d. 1163) was born in Hainault; he was a disciple of Bernard of Clairvaux.

Fabia (f.) Latin feminine form of the old Roman family name *Fabius* (see FABIO).

Fabian (m.) English and Polish form of the Late Latin name *Fabiānus*, a derivative of the family name *Fabius* (see FABIO). It was borne by an early pope (236–50), who was martyred under the Emperor Decius. The name was introduced into Britain by the Normans, but it has never been much used in the English-speaking world.

Cognates: French: **Fabien**. Italian: **Fabiano**.
Spanish: **Fabián**. Portuguese: **Fabião**.
Feminine form: French: **Fabienne**.

Fabio (m.) Italian, Spanish, and Portuguese: from the old Roman family name *Fabius*, said to be a derivative of *faba* bean. Members of this family were prominent in republican Rome. The most famous of them was Quintus Fabius Maximus (d. 203 BC), the Roman general who harassed the invader Hannibal but never joined battle, giving his name to the phrase 'Fabian tactics', implying a policy of gradual attrition as opposed to full-scale confrontation. The name was also used among the early Christians: St Fabius (d. 300) was a Roman soldier beheaded at Caesarea in Mauretania under the Emperor Diocletian.

Fabiola (f.) Late Latin feminine diminutive form of *Fabius* (see FABIO). St Fabiola (d. *c*.400) was a Roman widow who founded the first Western hospital, originally a hostel to accommodate the flood of pilgrims who flocked to Rome, but in which she tended the sick as well as accommodating the healthy.

Fabrice (m.) French: from the old Roman family name *Fabricius*, probably a derivative of *faber* craftsman, smith. There are no saints of this name, but it is permitted as a given name by the Catholic Church in honour of the Roman republican general and statesman Caius Fabricius Luscinus (d. 250 BC), who was noted not only for his skill as a military commander and negotiator of peace treaties, but also for the great simplicity of his lifestyle and for his refusal to take bribes.

Cognates: Italian: **Fabrizio**. Spanish: **Fabricio**.
Short form: Italian: BRIZIO.

Fachtna (m.) Irish Gaelic: traditional name of uncertain origin, possibly meaning 'malicious, hostile'. It has sometimes been Latinized as FESTUS.

Faddei (m.) Russian form of THADDEUS.

Fae (f.) English: variant spelling of FAY.

Faith (f.) English: from the abstract noun denoting the quality of believing and trusting in God. The name began to be used in the 16th century, and was very popular among the Puritans of the 17th.

Faivish (m.) Jewish (Yiddish): probably from Greek *Phoibos*, an epithet of the sun god Apollo. It is said to have been adopted as a learned religious translation equivalent of Hebrew *Shimshon* (see SAMSON), but it is more likely derived directly from the Greek. The Greeks often named captured slaves after gods, and it would thus have been likely for Jews to come to have this name. It was often paired with the Aramaic name SHRAGA meaning 'fire, lantern' as *Shraga Faivish*, since it was important for Jewish men to be called by a Hebrew or Aramaic name in certain religious rites.

Pet forms: **Fayvel**, **Feivel**.

Falibóg (m.) Polish: variant of CHWALIBÓG.

Falk (m.) Jewish: from the Yiddish vocabulary word *falk* falcon (modern German *Falke*). It is sometimes taken as a translation of the Hebrew given name *Yehoshua* (see JOSHUA); there have been many famous rabbis named Joshua Falk. The association between the main Hebrew personal names and various animals is traditional in Jewish culture, and is usually to be explained on the basis of some biblical reference. In this case, however, the connection is far from clear; it has been suggested that Joshua circled the Land of Canaan like a bird of prey before swooping down on it triumphantly.

Fanchon (f.) French: pet form of *Françoise* (see FRANÇOIS).

Fania (f.) Italian: short form of STEFANIA.

Fanny (f.) English: pet form of FRANCES, sometimes used as an independent name in its own right. It was very popular in the 19th century, but is now rarely found, no doubt due to the vulgar sense of the vocabulary word that has been derived from it in the 20th century.

Fardoragh (m.) Irish: Anglicized form of FEARDORCHA.

Farkas (m.) Jewish: name meaning 'wolf' in Hungarian, borne among Hungarian Jews as a translated form of Yiddish VOLF.

Farquhar (m.) Scottish: Anglicized form of the Gaelic name **Fearchar**, composed of Old Celtic elements meaning 'man' + 'dear'.

Farry (m.) Irish: Anglicized form of the Gaelic name FEARADHACH.

Fatima (f.) Usually a Muslim name, given in honour of Muhammad's daughter. However, it is occasionally borne by Roman Catholics in honour of 'Our Lady of Fatima', who in 1917 appeared to three shepherd children from the village of Fatima, near Leiria in western Portugal.

Fay (f.) English: late 19th century coinage, from the archaic word *fay* fairy. It was to some extent influenced by the revival of interest in Arthurian legend, in which Morgan le Fay is King Arthur's half-sister, a mysterious sorceress who both attempts to destroy Arthur and tends his wounds in Avalon after his last battle. She is sometimes identified with the 'Lady of the Lake'.

Variants: **Faye**, **Fae**.

Fayge (f.) Jewish (Yiddish): variant of FEIGE.

Fayvel (m.) Jewish (Yiddish): variant of FEIVEL.

Fearadhach (m.) Irish Gaelic: from a vocabulary word meaning 'manly' or 'masculine', a derivative of *fear* man.
Anglicized forms: **Farry**; FERDINAND, **Ferdie**.

Feardorcha (m.) Irish Gaelic: name composed of the elements *fear* man + *dorcha* dark.
Anglicized forms: **Fardoragh**, FERDINAND, FREDERICK.

Fearghal (m.) Irish Gaelic: name Anglicized as FERGAL.

Fearghas (m.) Scottish and Irish Gaelic: name Anglicized as FERGUS.

Fedele (m.) Italian form of FIDEL.

Fedelma (f.) Irish: variant of FIDELMA.

Federico (m.) Italian and Spanish form of FREDERICK. This Germanic name was introduced to Sicily by the Normans, where it was borne by, amongst others, the son of the Norman queen Constance and the German emperor Henry VI. At the age of three, in 1197, Federico became King of Sicily; he later went on to become King of the Germans and Holy Roman Emperor. He was a patron of the arts and sciences, and in 1224 founded the University of Naples.

Fedosi (m.) Russian form of TEODOSIO.
Variant: **Feodosi**.

Fedot (m.) Russian: from Greek *Theodotos*, composed of the elements *theos* God + *dotos* given. This name, like the related *Theodoros* and *Theodosius*, was popular among early Christians because of its auspicious sense, and was borne by several saints of the first century AD. The most famous (d. 304) was an innkeeper in Ancyra who was executed under Diocletian for having given Christian burial to the seven virgin martyrs Thecusa, Alexandra, Claudia, Phaina, Euphrasia, Matrona, and Julitta.

Fedya (m.) Russian: pet form of FYODOR and of the rarer FEDOSI and FEDOT.

Feel (m.) Dutch form of FELIX.

Feichin (m.) Irish Gaelic: originally a byname representing a diminutive of Gaelic *fiach* raven. It has sometimes been Latinized as FESTUS.

Feige (f.) Jewish: from Yiddish **Feygl** 'bird' (modern German *Vogel*; cf. ZIPPORAH). The present form of the name was arrived at by back-formation, the final -l having been interpreted as a Yiddish hypocoristic suffix rather than an integral part of the word.
Variant: **Fayge**.

Feivel (m.) Jewish (Yiddish): pet form of FAIVISH.
Variant: **Fayvel**.

Felice (m.) Italian form of FELIX.

Felicia (f.) Latinate feminine form of FELIX, of medieval origin.
Derivatives: German: **Felicie**. Hungarian: **Felicia**, **Licia**.

Feliciano (m.) Italian, Spanish, and Portuguese: from the Latin personal name *Feliciānus*, a derivative of *Felicius*, itself a derivative of FELIX. The main saint of this name was a 3rd-century bishop of Foligno in Umbria.

Felicity (f.) English: from the abstract noun denoting luck or good fortune (via Old French from Latin *felicitās*; cf. FELIX). The English vocabulary word was first used as a given name in the 17th century. It also represents the English form of the Late Latin personal name *Felicitas*, which was borne by several early saints, notably a slave who was martyred in 203 together with her mistress Perpetua and several other companions.
Cognates: Italian: **Felicita**. Spanish: **Felicidad**. Portuguese: **Felicidade**.
Pet form: English: **Flick**.

Felip (m.) Catalan form of PHILIP.

Felipe (m.) Spanish form of PHILIP.

Felix (m.) Latin name meaning 'lucky', which has from time to time been popular as a given name in Britain and elsewhere because of its auspicious omen. It was in use as a byname in Latin, being applied for example to the dictator Sulla (138–78 BC). It was very popular among the early Christians, being borne by a large number of early saints.
Derivatives: French: **Félix**. Italian: **Felice**. Dutch: **Feel**. See also SZCZĘSNY.

Fenella (f.) Scottish: Anglicized form of Gaelic **Fionnuala**.
Variants: **Finelia**, **Finola**, **Fionola**. See also NUALA.

Fenton (m.) English: transferred use of the surname, originally a local name from any of the various places (for example, in Cumbria, Lincs., Northumbria, Notts., Staffs., and W. Yorks.) so called from Old English *fenn* marsh, fen + *tūn* enclosure, settlement.

Feodora (f.) Russian form of THEODORA.

Feodosi (m.) Russian: variant of FEDOSI.

Feofil (m.) Russian form of THEOPHILUS.

Feoras (m.) Irish Gaelic form of PIERS.

Ferapont (m.) Russian: from the Greek name *Therapōn* (genitive *Therapontos*) meaning 'attendant, servant', and hence, among the early Christians, 'worshipper'.

Ferdie (m.) 1. English: pet form of FERDINAND. 2. Irish: Anglicized form of the Gaelic name FEARADHACH.

Ferdinand (m.) English, German, and French: from a Spanish name, originally *Ferdinando*, which is of Germanic (Visigothic) origin, being composed of the elements *farð* journey (or possibly a metathesized form of *frið* peace) and *nand* ready, prepared. The name was hereditary in the royal families of Spain from an early date. It was borne, for example, by Ferdinand I (d. 1065) of Castile and Leon, sometimes called Ferdinand the Great, who conducted successful campaigns against the Moors, and by his descendant Ferdinand V (1452–1516), who finally expelled the Moors from Spain altogether. Ferdinand V was the king who gave financial backing to Columbus. Through the marriage in 1496 of his daughter Joan the Mad of Castile to the Habsburg Archduke Philip, the name Ferdinand also became hereditary in the Austrian imperial family. Their younger son was called Ferdinand; he lived from 1503 to 1564, acquiring the succession to the kingdoms of Hungary and Bohemia by marriage in 1521, and becoming Holy Roman Emperor in 1558. Thus the name Ferdinand is intimately associated, not only with the history of Spain, but also with the origins of the Austro-Hungarian Empire.

The Old French contracted form *Ferrand* was sometimes used in England in the Middle Ages, but has not survived. The current form appeared in Britain in the 16th century, probably introduced by Roman Catholic supporters of Queen Mary I, who married Philip II of Spain in 1554.

In Ireland it has been used as an Anglicized form of the Gaelic names FEARADHACH and FEARDORCHA.

Variant: French: **Fernand**.
Cognates: Spanish: **Fernando, Hernando; Fernán, Hernán**. Portuguese: **Fernando, Fernão, Ferrão**. Italian: **Ferdinando**. Romanian: **Nandru**. Hungarian: **Nándor**.

Ferenc (m.) Hungarian form of FRANCIS.

Fergal (m.) Irish: Anglicized form of the Gaelic name *Fearghal*, composed of the elements *fear* man + *gal* valour.

Fergus (m.) Scottish and Irish: Anglicized form of the Gaelic name *Fearghas*, composed of the elements *fear* man + *gus* vigour. This was the name of a shadowy hero in Irish mythology, also of the grandfather of St Columba. It is still used mainly by families in Scotland and Ireland, and those who remain conscious of their Gaelic ancestry.

Pet form: Scottish: **Fergie**.

Fermin (m.) Spanish form of FIRMIN.

Fern (f.) English: from the vocabulary word denoting the plant (Old English *fearn*). Use of this word as a given name is of comparatively recent origin: it is one of several words denoting flowers and plants that have been pressed into service during the past hundred years. Its popularity seems to be increasing.

Fernán (m.) Spanish form of FERDINAND, more common in the Middle Ages than today.

Fernand (m.) French form of FERDINAND.

Fernando (m.) Spanish and Portuguese form of FERDINAND, rather more common in modern use than *Hernando*.

Fernão (m.) Portuguese form of FERDINAND.

Variant: **Ferrão**.

Ferrer (m.) Catholic name given in honour of the Valencian saint, Vicente Ferrer (*c*.1350–1418), who travelled throughout Europe seeking to heal the papal schism. His surname is a Catalan occupational name for a blacksmith.

Ferruccio (m.) Italian: from a medieval diminutive form of the byname *Ferro* 'iron', applied either to someone with grey hair or to a person of stalwart temperament and sturdy physique.

Fester (m.) Low German: variant of VESTER.

Festus (m.) 1. Latin name meaning 'firm, steadfast'. This was the name of the Roman procurator of Judea who refused to bow to pressure from the Jews and condemn St Paul to death for his preaching, although he was totally unconvinced by it (Acts 25; 26: 30–2). It was also borne by some early minor saints. 2. Irish: Latinized form of FACHTNA and FEICHÍN.

Ffraid (f.) Welsh cognate of BRIDGET.

Fiachna (m.) Irish Gaelic: apparently a derivative of *fiach* ravens (cf. FEICHÍN and FIACHRA). It has been revived as a given name in the 20th century.

Fiachra (m.) Irish Gaelic: apparently a derivative of *fiach* raven (cf. FEICHÍN and FIACHRA). A 7th-century St Fiachra settled at Meaux in France, and his cult became popular in that country, where he came to be regarded as the patron of gardeners. Through the Hôtel de Saint Fiacre in Paris he gave his name to the vocabulary word *fiacre*, since these carriages were originally available for hire outside the building.

Fiammetta (f.) Italian: from a diminutive form of the vocabulary word *fiamma* flame, fire, which is also used as a term of endearment.

Fidel (m.) Spanish: from the Late Latin name *Fidelis* 'faithful'. St Fidelis (d. *c*.570) seems to have come from the East, reaching Mérida in the company of merchants; eventually he became bishop of that city. The name is now chiefly associated with that of the left-wing Cuban leader Fidel Castro (b. 1927).

Cognate: Italian: **Fedele**.

Fidelma (f.) Irish: Anglicized form of Gaelic **Feidhelm**, an ancient personal name of uncertain derivation. It may have some connection with the male name *Feidhlimidh*; see PHELIM. St Fidelmia was a daughter of King Laoghaire and one of St Patrick's first converts.

Variant: **Fedelma**.
Short form: **Delma**.

Fidelis (m.) Original Latin form of FIDEL, occasionally used as a given name in the English-speaking world.

Fieke (f.) Low German: pet form of SOFIE.

Fife (m.) Scottish and English: transferred use of the surname, which originated in the Middle Ages as a local name for someone from the kingdom (now region) of Fife. This is said to get its name from that of the legendary Pictish hero *Fib*, one of the seven sons of Cruithne.

Variant: **Fyfe**.

Fifi (f.) French: nursery form of JOSÉPHINE. It may have been influenced by the term of endearment *ma fille* 'my daughter'. In the English-speaking world it now has definite connotations of frivolity.

Filat (m.) Russian: the usual vernacular contracted form of *Feofilakt*, from the Greek personal name *Theophylaktos* 'guarded by God' (from *theos* god + *phylassein* to guard, protect). This was the name of a 9th-century saint, bishop of Nicomedia, venerated in the Orthodox Church. In the Roman Martyrology he is commemorated under the much more common name *Theophilus*.

Filib (m.) Scottish Gaelic form of PHILIP. From this comes the surname *Mac Fhilib*, Anglicized as *MacKillop*.

Filiberto (m.) Italian: from a Germanic personal name composed of the elements *fil* much + *berht* bright, famous. This was a traditional name, of Frankish origin, in the royal house of Savoy. In the present century it has been moderately popular in many parts of Italy.

Filip (m.) Polish and Czech form of PHILIP.

Pet forms: Polish: **Filipek**. Czech: **Filípek, Fil(ouš)ek**.

Filippo (m.) Italian form of PHILIP.

Fima (f.) Russian: short form of *Serafima* (see SERAPHINA).

Pet form: **Fimochka**.

Fina (f.) 1. Irish: Anglicized form of Gaelic FÍONA. 2. English: short form of SERAPHINA.

Finbar (m.) Irish: Anglicized form of the Gaelic name **Fionnb(h)arr**, composed of the elements *fionn* white, fair + *barr* head. This was the name of at least three early Irish saints, one of whom became the first bishop of Cork in the 6th century. He is the subject of many legends, for example that he crossed the Irish Sea on horseback and that he made a pilgrimage to Rome with St David. He gave his name to the Isle of Barra in the Hebrides.

Finella (f.) Scottish: variant of FENELLA.

Fingal (m.) Scottish: Anglicized form of the Gaelic name **Fionnghall**, composed of the elements *fionn* white, fair + *gall* stranger. It was originally a byname applied to Norse settlers (cf. DOUGAL), and was adopted by James Macpherson (1736–96), author of the Ossianic poems, to render the name of the Gaelic hero *Fionn* (see FINN).

Variant: **Fingall**.

Finín (m.) Irish Gaelic: modern form of the Old Irish name *Fingin*, composed of elements meaning 'wine' and 'born'. In the Middle Ages it was commonly Anglicized as the male name FLORENCE.

Finlay (m.) Scottish: Anglicized form of the Gaelic name **Fionnlagh** (dialectally **Fionnla**), composed of the elements *fionn* white, fair + *laogh* warrior or calf. The Gaelic surname *Mac Fhionnlaigh* is Anglicized as *MacKinlay*.

Variant: **Finley**.

Finn (m.) **1**. Irish Gaelic: traditional name meaning 'white, fair'. The modern Gaelic form is **Fionn**. The mythological Irish hero Finn MacCool (*Finn Mac Cumaill* in Irish) was noted for his wisdom and fairness. He was leader of the Fenians or *Fianna*, a band of warriors about whom many stories are told. There may be a basis of fact behind the legends, in that Finn may be identified with an early Irish leader who defended Ireland against Norse raiders. **2**. Scandinavian: from the Old Norse personal name *Finnr*, originally either an ethnic byname for someone from Finland or else a short form of the various compound names containing this element.

Finnian (m.) Irish Gaelic: earlier *Finnén*, a derivative of Old Irish *finn* white, fair. This name was borne by two 6th-century Irish bishops.

Variant: **Finian**.

Finola (f.) Irish and Scottish: Anglicized form of FIONNUALA.

Fio (m.) Italian: short form of FIORENZO.

Fiona (f.) Scottish: Latinate derivative of the Gaelic element *fionn* white, fair. It was first used by James Macpherson (1736–96), author of the Ossianic poems, which were supposedly translations from ancient Gaelic. It was subsequently used as a penname by William Sharp (1855–1905), who produced many romantic works under the name of Fiona Macleod. It has since become extremely popular in England as well as Scotland, and is sometimes used as an Anglicized form of the Irish name FÍONA.

Fíona (f.) Irish Gaelic: traditional name meaning 'vine'. In origin this has no connection with the Scottish name FIONA, which, however, is often now used as an Anglicized form of it.

Variant: **Fina** (Anglicized).

Fionnán (m.) Irish Gaelic: originally a byname representing a diminutive of Gaelic *fionn* white, fair.

Fionnuala (f.) Irish Gaelic: modern form of *Fionnguala*, a traditional name composed of the elements *fionn* white, fair + *guala* shoulder.

Cognate: Scottish Gaelic: **Fionn(a)gh(u)al(a)** (Anglicized as FLORA).

Short form: **Nuala**.

Fionola (f.) Scottish: variant of *Finella* and *Finola*. In the English-speaking world it is now sometimes taken as an elaboration of FIONA.

Fiontan (m.) Irish Gaelic: earlier *Fintan*, apparently representing a derivative of Old Irish *finn* white, fair.

Fiorella (f.) Italian: from a diminutive form of the vocabulary word *fiore* flower, used as a term of endearment.

Fiorenzo (m.) Italian form of the male name FLORENCE.

Short form: **Fio**.

Firmin (m.) French: from Late Latin *Firminus*, a derivative of *firmus* firm, steadfast. This was a popular name among early Christians mindful of St Paul's injunction to 'be stedfast in the faith'. It was borne by several early saints, including the first and third bishops of Amiens (2nd and 3rd centuries); the third bishop of Gévaudon; a 5th-century bishop of Metz; and 6th-century bishops of Viviers, Uzès, and Verdun.

Cognates: Italian, Portuguese: **Firmino**. Spanish: **Fermin**.

Firs (m.) Russian: from Greek *Thyrsos* (see TIRSO).

Fisa (f.) Russian: short form of ANFISA.

Fishl (m.) Jewish (Yiddish): diminutive form of the vocabulary word *fish* fish (modern German *Fisch*). It seems to have been adopted as a given name because of the biblical prophecy that the descendants of Ephraim and Manasseh would multiply as the fish in the sea (Genesis 48: 16).

Variant: **Fishke**.

Flann (m.) Irish Gaelic: originally a byname meaning 'red, ruddy'.

Flannan (m.) Irish: Anglicized form of the Gaelic name **Flannán**, originally a byname representing a diminutive of Gaelic *flann* red, ruddy. St Flannan is the patron of the diocese of Killaloe in Co. Clare, and this is still a popular given name in that area.

Flavia (f.) Italian: feminine form of the old Roman family name *Flāvius* (from *flāvus* yellow, yellow-haired, golden). This was the name of at least five saints, most notably Flavia DOMITILLA.

Cognate: French: **Flavie**.

Flemming (m.) Danish: from a medieval byname, originally an ethnic byname for someone from Flanders. This is now one of the most common of all Danish male given names.

Fletcher (m.) English: transferred use of the surname, which originated as an occupational name for a maker of arrows, from Old French *flech(i)er*, an agent derivative of *fleche* (of Germanic origin). An early bearer of this as a given name was Fletcher Christian, leader of the mutiny on the *Bounty* in 1789.

Fleur (f.) English: from an Old French name meaning 'flower', occasionally used in the Middle Ages. Modern use, however, seems to derive mainly from the character of this name in John Galsworthy's *The Forsyte Saga* (1922). The English vocabulary word, **Flower**, is also occasionally found as a given name, probably as a translation equivalent of *Fleur*. The latter is not, however, in general use as a French given name.

Diminutive: **Fleurette**.

Flick (f.) English: pet form based on the given name FELI-CITY.

Flo (f.) English: short form of FLORENCE and FLORA, common in the early part of the 20th century, but now widely considered somewhat old-fashioned (in contrast to most other short forms in -*o*, e.g. Jo).

Floella (f.) English: name of recent origin, used among British Blacks. It presumably originated as a compound of the independent short names FLO and ELLA.

Flora (f.) Scottish, English, and German: name borne in Roman mythology by the goddess of flowers and the spring (a derivative of Latin *flōs* flower, genitive *flōris*). It is also the feminine form of the old Roman family name *Flōrus*, likewise derived from *flōs*. There were medieval given names for both sexes from this root, but they have mostly died out (see FLORIAN, however). *Flora* was little used in England before the 18th century, when it was imported from Scotland. In 1746 Flora MacDonald (1722–90), daughter of Ranald MacDonald of Milton in South Uist, helped Bonnie Prince Charlie to escape from there to the Island of Skye, disguised as a woman, after his defeat at Culloden. In fact, *Flora* was merely an Anglicized form of her Gaelic name, *Fionnaghal*, a variant of *Fionnghuala* (see FENELLA). However, her fame made the name *Flora* popular in the Highlands as well as elsewhere.
Short form: English: **Flo**.
Pet form: English and Scottish: **Florrie** (Gaelic **Flòraidh**).

Florence (f.), formerly also (m.) English and French: medieval form of the Latin masculine name *Florentius* (a derivative of *florens* blossoming, flourishing) and its feminine form *Florentia*. In the Middle Ages the name was borne by men (for example, the historian Florence of Worcester), but it is now exclusively a female name, except in Ireland, where it has been used as an Anglicized form of *Flaithrí* (see FLORRY) and FÍNÍN. In the second half of the 19th century the female name was revived, being given in honour of Florence Nightingale (1820–1910), the founder of modern nursing, who organized a group of nurses to serve in the Crimean War. She herself received the name because she was born in the Italian city of Florence (Latin *Florentia*, Italian *Firenze*).
Cognates (all m.): Italian: **Fiorenzo**. Spanish, Portuguese: **Florencio**. German: **Florenz**. Dutch: **Floris**. Russian: **Florenti**.
Short form: English: **Flo** (f.).
Pet forms: English: **Florrie**, **Flossie** (f.).

Florentina (f.) Latin: feminine form of *Florentīnus*, an elaborated form of *Florens* (see FLORENCE). The name was borne by a 7th-century Spanish saint, sister of the other saints Fulgentius, Isidore, and Leander.
Cognate: Polish: **Florentyna**.

Florian (m.) German and Polish: from Latin *Flōriānus*, a derivative of *Flōrus* (see FLORA). St Florian is the patron of Upper Austria and Poland; he was a high-ranking Roman officer who was put to death by drowning in the River Enns during the persecutions under the Emperor Diocletian. A second saint of the same name was martyred in Palestine in the 7th century together with sixty companions.

Floris (m.) Dutch form of the male name FLORENCE.

Florrie (f.) English and Scottish: pet form of FLORA and FLORENCE, now little used except in the Highlands.

Florry (m.) Irish: **1**. Anglicized form of the Gaelic name **Flaithrí**, composed of the elements *flaith* prince, leader + *rí* king. **2**. Pet form of the male name FLORENCE, itself used as an Anglicized form of the Gaelic names *Flaithrí* and FÍNÍN.
Variant: **Flurry**.

Flossie (f.) English: pet form from a contraction of FLORENCE, common in the 19th century, but now no longer much used. The popularity of the name was no doubt enhanced by association with the soft downy material known as *floss*.

Floyd (m.) English: variant of LLOYD. This form of the name results from an attempt to represent the sound of the Welsh initial *Ll*- using standard English pronunciation and orthography. In the 20th century it has been particularly common in the southern United States and among American Blacks.

Flurry (m.) Irish: variant of FLORRY.

Foka (m.) Russian: from the Late Greek personal name *Phokas* (apparently a derivative of *phokē* seal (the animal)). This name was borne by several early saints venerated in the Orthodox Church, particularly Phocas the Gardener who was martyred under Diocletian. The name is stressed on the second syllable.

Folant (m.) Welsh form of the male name VALENTINE.

Folke (m.) Scandinavian: from the Old Norse personal name *Folki*, a short form of the various compound names containing the element *folk* people, tribe (as for example *Folkvarðr* 'people guard', which has given rise to the modern forms **Folkvar** and **Falkor**.
Cognate: English: FULK.

Foma (m.) Russian form of THOMAS. It is stressed on the second syllable.

Fonsie (m.) Irish: pet form of ALPHONSUS.
Variant: **Fonso**.

Forbes (m.) Scottish: transferred use of the surname, which originated as a local name from the lands of Forbes in Aberdeenshire. These are so called from the Gaelic element *forba* field, district + the locative suffix *-ais*. In Scotland this name was traditionally pronounced in two syllables, but a monosyllabic pronunciation is now the norm.

Ford (m.) English: transferred use of the common surname, originally a local name for someone who lived near a place where a river could be crossed by wading through it (Old English *ford*).

Forrest (m.) English: transferred use of the surname, which originated as a local name for someone who lived in or by an enclosed wood, Old French *forest*.

Fortunato (m.) Italian, Spanish, and Portuguese: from the Late Latin name *Fortūnātus* 'fortunate', a derivative of *fortūna* fortune, fate. This name was popular because of its good omen and was borne by a large number of early saints.
Feminine form: **Fortunata**.

Foster (m.) English: transferred use of the surname, originally an occupational name with at least four possible derivations—from Middle English *foster* foster-parent, *for(e)ster* forester, *fors(e)ter* shearer, or *fu(y)ster* saddle-tree maker.

Fran (f., m.) English: short form of FRANCES, or less commonly (in Britain at least) of FRANCIS.

Franca (f.) Italian: feminine form of FRANCO.

France (m.) English: either from the name of the country or, in some cases, a short form of FRANCIS that is sometimes used in America as an independent given name.

Frances (f.) English: feminine form of FRANCIS. In the 16th century the two spellings were used indiscriminately for both sexes, the distinction in spelling not being established until the 17th century.
Short form: **Fran**.
Pet form: **Fanny**.

Francesca (f.) Italian: feminine form of FRANCESCO. Originally a vocabulary word meaning 'French', it was bestowed from the 13th century onwards in honour of St Francis of Assisi. It has also been used independently as an English name. Probably its most famous bearer was Francesca di Rimini, daughter of Giovanni da Polenta, Count of Ravenna. A legendary beauty, she was betrothed by her father to the misshapen Giovanni Malatesta, Lord of Rimini, in return for military support. However, when Malatesta's good-looking younger brother, Paolo, acted as proxy in the betrothal, Francesca and he fell in love. They were discovered, and put to death by Malatesta in 1289. Their tragedy is enshrined in the Fifth Canto of Dante's *Inferno*, as well as in several other works of literature and in a symphonic fantasy by Tchaikovsky.
Cognates: English: FRANCES. Irish Gaelic: **Proinséas**. Scottish Gaelic: **Frangag**. French: **Françoise**. Spanish, Portuguese: **Francisca**. German: **Franziska**. Polish: **Franciszka**. Czech: **Františka**.
Pet forms: Spanish: **Frascuela**, **Frasquita**. German: **Zissi**.

Francesco (m.) Italian: originally a vocabulary word meaning 'French' or 'Frenchman' (Late Latin *Franciscus*; cf. FRANK). This was a nickname given to St Francis of Assisi (1181–1226) because of his wealthy father's business connections in France. His baptismal name was GIOVANNI. He had a pleasant, ordinary life as a child and young man, but after two serious illnesses, a period of military service, and a year as a prisoner of war in Perugia, he turned from the world and devoted himself to caring for the poor and the sick. He was joined by groups of disciples, calling themselves 'minor friars' (*friari minores*). The main features of the Franciscan rule are humility, poverty, and love for all living creatures. In his honour the various vernacular forms of *Francesco* came to be commonly used as given names from the 13th century onwards in France, Spain, and elsewhere as well as Italy.
Variant: FRANCO.
Cognates: Irish Gaelic: **Proinsias**. Scottish Gaelic: **Frang**. Spanish, Portuguese: **Francisco**. Catalan: **Francesc**. Basque: **Patxi**. French: FRANÇOIS. English: FRANCIS. German: FRANZ. Polish: **Franciszek**. Czech: **František**. Hungarian: **Ferenc**. Finnish: **Ransu**.
Pet forms: Scottish Gaelic: **Frangan**. Spanish: **Frascuelo**, **Frasquito**, **Paco**, **Pancho**, **Paquito**, **Curro**. Basque: **Patxi**.
Feminine forms: see FRANCESCA, FRANCES.

Francine (f.) French and English: diminutive pet form of *Françoise* (see FRANÇOIS).
Variants: English: **Francene**, **Franceen**.

Francis (m.) English (and Old French) form of Italian FRANCESCO, introduced into England in the early 16th century, when there was a surge of admiration for, and imitation of, Italian Renaissance culture.

Short forms: FRANK, **Fran**, **France**.
Feminine form: FRANCES.

Franco (m.) Italian: contracted form of FRANCESCO, occasionally taken as an Italian version of FRANK.
Feminine form: **Franca**.

François (m.) French: from the Old French word *françois* 'French' (*français* in modern French; See also FRANK). The use of this word as a given name was inspired by the fame of St Francis of Assisi (see FRANCESCO). The popularity of the name has been further enhanced by its patriotic meaning, and, less recently, by the fact that it was borne by two kings of France: François I, otherwise known as François d'Angoulême, who reigned 1515–47, presiding over a rich period of prosperity and cultural activity, and François II, who died in 1560 at the age of 16, having been King of France for a year and married to Mary Queen of Scots for two years.
Feminine form: **Françoise**.

Frank (m.) English: **1**. Of Germanic origin. The name referred originally to a member of the tribe of the Franks, who are said to have got the name from a characteristic type of spear that they used (as the Saxons did from a characteristic knife). When the Franks migrated into Gaul in the 4th century, the country received its modern name of France (Late Latin *Francia*) and the tribal term Frank came to mean 'Frenchman'. **2**. Now quite often taken, especially in America, as a short form of FRANCIS. **3**. Anglicized form of the Italian name FRANCO. The popularity of *Frank* as a given name was greatly enhanced, especially among Italian Americans, by the fame of the singer Frank Sinatra (b. 1915).

Frankie (m., f.) English: **1**. (m.) Pet form of FRANK. **2**. (f.) Pet form of FRANCES, FRANCESCA, or FRANCINE. As a female name, it is perhaps most familiar as the name of the heroine of *The Ballad of Frankie and Johnny*, who ended up in the electric chair, 'with the sweat running through her hair'.

Franklin (m.) English: transferred use of the surname, which derives from Middle English *frankeleyn* freeman, which came to denote a member of a class of freeholders who were not of noble birth. This is derived from the Norman French word *frank*, which means both 'free' and 'Frankish'. The connection between freemen and Franks is reflected in the Late Latin term *francalia*, originally denoting lands held by Franks, which came to mean lands that were not subject to taxes. The given name is now quite common, especially in the United States, having been so used at first in honour of the American statesman and scientist Benjamin Franklin (1706–90), and more recently of President Franklin D. Roosevelt (1882–1945).

František (m.) Czech form of FRANCESCO.
Feminine form: **Františka**.
Pet forms: **Franta**, **Frantik**, **Franek**, **Fanoušek** (m.); **Fráňa** (m., f.).

Franz (m.) German form of FRANCESCO. This name was introduced to the Habsburg family in 1736, when Franz, François, or Francesco, Duke of Lorraine and Grand Duke of Tuscany (1708–65), married Maria Theresa of Austria. In 1740, he became Holy Roman Emperor jointly with her. The name was also borne by the Emperor Franz Josef (reigned 1848–1916) and his great-nephew the Archduke Franz Ferdinand, whose assassination in 1914 sparked off the First World War. The name is still popular in German-speaking countries, especially among Roman Catholics.
Feminine form: **Franziska** (rare).

Frascuelo (m.) Spanish: pet form of *Francisco* (see FRANCIS).

Feminine form: **Frascuela**.

Fraser (m.) Scottish: transferred use of the surname of a leading Highland and Lowland family. The surname is undoubtedly of Norman origin, but its exact derivation is uncertain. The earliest forms are *de Frisselle* and *de Fresel(iere)*, but the name seems to have been altered by association with Old French *fraise* strawberry.

Variant: **Frazer**.

Frasquito (m.) Spanish: pet form of *Francisco* (see FRANCIS).

Feminine form: **Frasquita**.

Frauke (f.) Low German: originally a byname representing a diminutive formation from the vocabulary word *Frau* lady (Middle High German *vrouwe*, Old High German *frouwa*; Old Saxon *frūa*). It has also been used as a pet form of *Veronika* (see VERONICA), because of the similarity in sound. In the 1960s it came to be commonly used as an independent given name in German-speaking countries.

Fred (m.) English: short form of FREDERICK or, occasionally, of ALFRED. It has also been used as an independent given name (cf. BERT).

Pet forms: **Freddie**, **Freddy**.

Freda (f.) English: short form of various names such as ELFREDA and WINIFRED, also, occasionally, of FREDERICA. The name is sometimes spelled Frieda, under the influence of German FRIEDE.

Pet form: **Freddie**.

Freddie (m., f.) English: 1. (m.) Pet form of FRED. 2. (f.) Pet form of FREDA and FREDERICA.

Variant: **Freddy** (m.).

Frédéric (m.) French form of FREDERICK.

Frederica (f.) Latinate feminine form of FREDERICK.

Cognates: French: **Frédérique**. German: **Friederike**. Czech: **Bedřiška**.

Short forms: English: **Freda**. German: **Friede**.

Pet forms: English: **Freddie**. German: **Fritzi**.

Frederick (m.) 1. English: from an old Germanic name, composed of the elements *fred*, *frid* peace + *rīc* power, ruler. It was first introduced into Britain by the Normans at the time of the Conquest, but did not survive long. However, it continued to be popular as a royal name elsewhere in Europe (see FRIEDRICH). Modern use in Britain dates from its reintroduction in the 18th century by followers of the Elector of Hanover, who in 1714 became George I of England, and was reinforced by the vogue for Germanic names in Victorian times. 2. Irish: used as an Anglicized form of the Gaelic name FEARDORCHA.

Variants (of 1): **Fred(e)ric** (becoming increasingly fashionable, no doubt under the influence of French *Frédéric* and perhaps also of English *Dominic*, where the spelling *Dominick* is perceived as distinctly archaic).

Cognates (of 1): French: **Frédéric**. Italian, Spanish: FEDERICO. German: FRIEDRICH. Low German, Danish: FREDERIK. Swedish: FREDRIK. Dutch: **Frerik**, **Freek**. Polish: **Fryderyk**. Czech: **Bedřich**. Hungarian: **Frigyes**. Finnish: **Rieti**.

Short form: English: **Fred**.

Pet forms: English: **Freddie**, **Freddy**. German: **Fritz**.

Frederik (m.) Danish and Low German form of FREDERICK. This has been the name of no less than nine kings of Denmark.

Fredrik (m.) Swedish form of FREDERICK. The name was first used in Sweden in the 14th century, but did not become popular until the 18th century, with the reigns of the kings Fredrik I (1720–51) and Adolf Fredrik (1751–71).

Freja (f.) Swedish form of FREYA, revived in the 19th century.

Frerik (m.) Dutch form of FREDERICK. The omission of dental consonants between vowels is a regular feature of Dutch.

Freya (f.) Scottish: of Old Norse origin. *Freya* or *Fröja* was the goddess of love in Scandinavian mythology, and her name seems to be derived from an element cognate with Old High German *frouwa* lady, mistress. The name was long a traditional one in Shetland, and is still used in Scotland. A notable modern bearer is the explorer and writer Freya Stark.

Cognate: Swedish: **Freja**.

Freyde (f.) Jewish: name meaning 'joy' in Yiddish (modern German *Freude*).

Friede (f.) German form of FREDA.

Friedelinde (f.) German: from an old Germanic female personal name composed of the elements *fred*, *frid* peace + *lind* weak, tender, soft. The name was revived in the 19th century, but has not become common.

Friedemann (m.) German: from an old Germanic personal name composed of the elements *fred*, *frid* peace + *man* man. It is to a large extent borne by Jews as a translation of SHLOMO. One notable non-Jewish bearer was Wilhelm Friedemann Bach (1710–84), the eldest son of Johann Sebastian Bach, and himself a composer.

Friederike (f.) German form of FREDERICA.

Pet form: **Fritzi**.

Friedhelm (m.) German: from an old Germanic personal name composed of the elements *fred*, *frid* peace + *helm* helmet, protection.

Friedrich (m.) German form of FREDERICK. It owes its great popularity in Germany at least in part to having been a royal name from an early date. It was borne by both Hohenstauffens and Habsburgs. Notable bearers include Friedrich Barbarossa (King of Germany 1152–90 and Holy Roman Emperor 1155–90), and Friedrich II (King of Sicily from 1197, when he was three years old, King of Germany 1212–20, and Holy Roman Emperor 1220–50: he called himself 'lord of the world'). The name was later borne by many German princes and princelings, as well as several kings of Prussia. The most famous of these is undoubtedly Friedrich der Grosse (Frederick the Great, reigned 1740–86), noted as a glorious patron of the arts as well as being a decisive statesman and victorious military commander.

Pet form: **Fritz**.

Frigyes (m.) Hungarian form of FREDERICK.

Fritjof (m.) Scandinavian: from an Old Norse personal name composed of the elements *friðr* peace + *þjófr* thief. The spellings **Fridtjof** and **Fri(d)tjov** are also used. The former was borne, for example, by the Norwegian explorer Fridtjof Nansen (1861–1930), who also served as the League of Nations' high commissioner for refugees and was responsible for the issuing of 'Nansen' passports to stateless persons after the First World War.

Fritz (m.) German: pet form of FRIEDRICH. The name is also sometimes used as a given name or nickname in the English-speaking world.

Fritzi (f.) German: pet form of FRIEDERIKE.

Frode (m.) Danish and Norwegian: from the Old Norse personal name *Fróðoi*, originally a byname for a wise or prudent person, from *fróðr* knowing, learned, well-informed. The name was revived *c.*1930 and has become increasingly popular since about 1970.

Froim (m.) Jewish: Yiddish form of EPHRAIM.

Frume (f.) Jewish: Yiddish name, originally a nickname meaning 'pious, devout' (modern German *fromm*).
Pet form: **Frumke**.

Fryderyk (m.) Polish form of FREDERICK.

Fucho (f.) Spanish: pet form of REFUGIO.

Fulgencio (m.) Spanish: from the Latin name *Fulgentius*, a derivative of *fulgens* (genitive *fulgentis*) shining. The name was borne by a 7th-century Spanish saint, brother of Isidore of Seville.

Fulgenzio (m.) Italian form of FULGENCIO. The name was borne by a saint (468–533) who served as bishop of Ruspe but was expelled by the Vandals and retired to Sardinia.

Fulk (m.) English: of Germanic origin, introduced to Britain by the Normans. The name originally represented a short form of various compound names containing the element 'people, tribe' (cf. modern English *folk*). It has gradually died out of general use, but is still used in certain families, such as the Grevilles. Fulke Greville, 1st Baron Brooke, was a leading figure at the court of Elizabeth I.
Variant: **Fulke**.

Fülöp (m.) Hungarian form of PHILIP.

Fulton (m.) Scottish: transferred use of the surname, which seems to have been originally a local name from a lost place in Ayrshire. Robert Fulton (1765–1815) was the American engineer who designed the first commercially successful steamboat.

Fulvia (f.) Italian and English: from the feminine form of the old Roman family name *Fulvius*, a derivative of Latin *fulvus* dusky, tawny (ultimately connected with *flāvus*; cf. FLAVIA). The name does not seem to have been much used among early Christians, and there are no saints Fulvia or Fulvius. In classical times its most famous bearer was the wife of Mark Antony, who opposed Octavian by force on her husband's behalf while he was in Egypt.

Fyfe (m.) Scottish: variant spelling of FIFE.

Fyodor (m.) Russian form of THEODORE.
Pet form: **Fedya**.

G

Gabino (m.) Spanish form of GAVINO.

Gábor (m.) Hungarian form of GABRIEL. It is particularly popular in Hungary because of the legend that in the year 1001 the archangel Gabriel advised Pope Sylvester II to send a holy crown to King (later St) Stephen (ISTVÁN), thus recognizing Hungary as a Christian sovereign state.

Gabriel (m.) Biblical: name (meaning 'man of God' in Hebrew) of one of the archangels. Gabriel appeared to Daniel in the Old Testament (Daniel 8: 16; 9: 21), and in the New Testament to Zacharias (Luke 1: 19; 26: 27) and, most famously, to Mary to announce the impending birth of Christ (Luke 1: 2). *Gabriel* has occasionally been used as a given name in the English-speaking world, mainly as a result of Continental European influence (rather more commonly than RAPHAEL, but much less so than MICHAEL, the names of two other chief archangels).

Cognates: Hungarian: GÁBOR. Italian: **Gabriele**. Finnish: **Kaapo**. Feminine forms: French (now also used in English): **Gabrielle**, **Gaby**. Italian: **Gabriella**. German: **Gabriele**, **Gabi**. Polish: **Gabriela**. Czech: **Gabriele**.
Pet forms: Irish: **Gay**. Polish: **Gabryś**, **Gabrysz** (m.); **Gabrysia** (f.). Czech: **Gába** (m., f.); **Riel**, **Gabek** (m.); **Gabra**, **Gabin-(k)a** (f.).

Gae (f.) English: variant spelling of GAY.

Gaenor (f.) Welsh: apparently a form of GAYNOR adapted to Welsh orthography. It also may have been influenced by the name of the saint commemorated at *Llangeinwyr* in Glamorgan, known popularly as *Llangeinor*. Her name seems to be composed of the Welsh elements *cain* beautiful + (*g*)*wyry*(*f*) maiden.

Gaetano (m.) Italian: from Latin *Caietānus*, originally an ethnic name for someone from *Caieta* (now *Gaeta*) in Latium. According to Roman legend, the town was named in honour of Aeneas' faithful nurse Caieta, who accompanied him from Troy to Italy and died at that spot. St Gaetano (*c*.1480–1547) was a religious reformer who lived in Naples; he is not to be confused with his contemporary Cardinal Gaetano, an active opponent of Martin Luther.

Cognates: French: **Gaétan**. Spanish: **Cayetano**. Portuguese: **Caetano**. German: **Kayetan**. Polish: **Kajetan**. English: **Cajetan** (rarely, if ever, used as a given name, but sometimes adopted as a clerical name by members of Roman Catholic religious orders).

Gaia (f.) From the name borne in classical mythology by the primeval goddess of the earth, who bore Ouranos 'sky' and by him Okeanos 'sea', Kronos 'time', and the Titans. Her name, spelled in Latin *Gaea*, derives from Greek *gē* earth.

Gail (f.) English: aphetic short form of ABIGAIL, now very commonly used as an independent given name, but apparently not in existence before the middle of the 20th century.

Variants: **Gale**, **Gayle**.

Gaitzka (m.) Basque equivalent of SALVADOR.

Gala (f.) Russian: normally a pet form of GALINA. In the case of the wife (1904–84) of the Catalan painter Salvador Dali, it

was a pet name bestowed on her by her first lover Paul Eluard; she was born Yelena Diakonov in Kazan. The name has now also been adopted into English, perhaps influenced by the festive connotations of the vocabulary word.

Gale (f.) English: variant spelling of GAIL.

Galen (m.) English: from the name of the Graeco-Roman medical writer Claudius Galēnus (AD ?130–?200). His name appears to represent a Latinized form of a Greek name derived from *galēnē* calm.

Galia (f.) Jewish: modern Hebrew name, meaning 'wave'.

Galina (f.) Russian: of uncertain origin, probably from Greek *galēnē* calm (cf. GALEN). Another possibility is that it may represent a vernacular form of HELEN, beside the more learned YELENA.

Gamaliel (m.) Biblical: name, apparently meaning 'benefit of God' in Hebrew, borne in the New Testament by a wise Pharisee (Acts 5: 34) and by a teacher of St Paul (Acts 22: 3), possibly the same person. In the Old Testament it is the name of the prince of the tribe of Manasseh at the time of the Exodus (Numbers 1: 10).

Garbikunde (f.) Basque equivalent of PURIFICACIÓN.

Garbiñe (f.) Basque equivalent of INMACULADA. This name shares with the previous one a derivation from the Basque element *garbi* clean, pure.

Gärd (f.) Swedish: variant of GERD.

Gareth (m.) Welsh and English: of Celtic origin, but uncertain ultimate derivation. It first occurs in Malory's *Morte D'Arthur*, as the name of the lover of Eluned and seems to have been heavily altered from its original form, whatever that may have been (possibly the same as GERAINT). It is now very common in Wales, partly because GARY, which is actually an independent name, is often taken to be a pet form of it.

Garfield (m.) English: transferred use of the surname, originally a local name for someone who lived near a triangular field, from Old English *gār* triangular piece of land + *feld* open country.

Garret (m.) Irish and English: transferred use of the surname, which is derived from the given names GERALD and GERARD. In Ireland it often represents a direct Anglicization of GEARÓID.

Variant: **Garrett**.

Garrison (m.) English (mainly U.S.): transferred use of the surname, originally a local name from *Garriston* in North Yorkshire or else a patronymic for the son of someone called GARRET. William Lloyd Garrison (1805–79) was a prominent American anti-slavery campaigner: the given name may originally have been bestowed in honour of him. It is now sometimes given to the sons of fathers who are called GARY or GARRY (cf. JEFFERSON).

Garrit (m.) Frisian: variant of GERRIT.

Garry (m.) English: variant spelling of GARY, influenced in spelling by BARRY.

Garsha (m.) Russian: pet form of GERASIM.

Garth (m.) English and Welsh: from a surname, but often taken to be a contracted form of GARETH. As a surname it originated in the north of England, and originally denoted someone who lived beside an enclosure (Old Norse *garðr*). In modern times its popularity has been influenced by the virile superhero of this name, main character in a long-running strip cartoon in the *Daily Mirror* newspaper.

Gary (m.) English: from a surname, which is probably derived from a Norman personal name of Germanic origin, a short form of any of the various compound names with *gar* spear as a first element. One bearer of this surname was the American industrialist Elbert Henry Gary (1846–1927), who gave his name to the steel town of Gary, Indiana (chartered in 1906). In this town was born the theatrical agent Nan Collins, who suggested *Gary* as a stage name for her client Frank Cooper, who thus became Gary Cooper (1901–61). His film career caused the name to become enormously popular from the 1930s to the present day. Its popularity has been maintained by the cricketer Gary Sobers (b. 1936; in his case it is in fact a pet form of *Garfield*) and the pop singer Gary Glitter (real name Paul Gadd). It is now often taken as a pet form of GARETH. Curiously, in the spelling *Garaidh*, the name is borne by a minor warrior in the Gaelic Finn sagas and hence has been used as a dog's name in the Highlands.

Variant: **Garry**.

Pet form (informal): **Gaz**.

Gáspár (m.) Hungarian form of CASPAR.

Gaspard (m.) French form of CASPAR. The *-d* has been added as a result of association with the many personal names of Germanic origin ending in *-ard* (from the name element *hard* hardy, brave, strong).

Gaspare (m.) Italian form of CASPAR.

Gaston (m.) French: of uncertain derivation. It seems to have originated in the south of France, and in the Middle Ages was a hereditary name among the counts of Foix and viscounts of Béarn. It is probably of Germanic origin, derived from the element *gast* guest, stranger. According to another theory, it was originally an ethnic name for a *Gascon*. There are no grounds for the common association made between this name and *Vedastus* (see VAAST).

Gavin (m.) Scottish and English: of Celtic origin, but uncertain ultimate derivation; it first appears in French sources as *Gauvain*. The name is borne in the Arthurian romances by one of the knights of the Round Table (more familiar in English versions as Sir *Gawain*). It died out in the 16th century except in Scotland, whence it has been reintroduced in the past couple of decades. It is now extremely popular in England, Wales, and elsewhere in the English-speaking world.

Gavino (m.) Italian: characteristically Sardinian name, unrelated to GAVIN. It is probably from Late Latin *Gabīnus*, originally an ethnic name for someone from the city of *Gabium* in Latium. St Gabinus was martyred at Torres in Sardinia, together with his companion Crispulus, under the Roman emperor Hadrian (*c*.130).

Cognate: Spanish: **Gabino**.

Gaweł (m.) Polish: from the old Roman family name *Gallus*, originally a byname meaning 'cock' but later taken to be an ethnic name meaning 'Gaul'. In the Christian period it was borne by an uncle (*c*.489–*c*.554) of Gregory of Tours, and by a 7th-century Irish saint and missionary to central Europe. The latter founded a monastery to the south of Lake Constance, which later became known as St Gall and gave its name to a Swiss town and canton. His name probably represents a Latinization of an Irish name derived from *gall* stranger. The form of the Polish given name has been altered by association with *Paweł* (from Latin *Paulus*; see PAUL).

Cognate: Czech: **Havel**.

Gay (f., m.)**1**. (f., m.) English: from the vocabulary word meaning 'blithe, cheerful' (from Old French, of Germanic origin), chosen as a given name because of its well-omened meaning (cf. HAPPY and MERRY). It was not used before the 20th century, and has fallen out of favour again since the 1960s, since the vocabulary word *gay* has acquired the meaning 'homosexual'. It was generally a female name, but has also been borne by men. **2**. (m.) Irish: pet form of GABRIEL.

Variants (of 1): **Gaye**, **Gae** (f.).

Gayle (f.) English: variant spelling of GAIL. Its popularity has no doubt been increased by the fame of the American film actress Gayle Hunnicutt (b. 1942).

Gaylord (m.) English: from a surname, which is a form, altered by folk etymology, of the Old French nickname *Gaillard* 'dandy'. It may sometimes have been chosen as a given name because parents liked the idea of their son's living as a fine lord, but it now seems likely to suffer the same fate as GAY.

Gaynor (f.) English: a medieval form of the name of Arthur's queen, GUINEVERE, recently undergoing a strong revival in popularity.

Gaz (m.) English: informal pet form of GARY (cf. BAZ and LAZ).

Gearóid (m.) Irish Gaelic form of GERALD, from Old French *Geraud*. The name originated in Ireland at the time of Strongbow's invasion (1170): the constable of Strongbow's castle at Pembroke was called *Gerald*, and his son founded a major Irish family, the Fitzgeralds. The Irish form of the name has been revived in modern times.

Variant: **Gearalt**.

Gebhard (m.) German: from an old Germanic personal name composed of the elements *geb*, *gib* gift + *hard* hardy, brave, strong. St Gebhard was bishop of Constance in the late 10th century, and founded the abbey of Petershausen near there.

Cognate: Low German: **Gebbert**.

Ged (m.) English: short form of GERARD or GERALD.

Gedeon (m.) Russian form of GIDEON.

Geert (m.) Low German and Dutch form of GERHARD.

Geerta (f.) Low German and Dutch: Latinate version of a contracted form of GERTRUDE, or occasionally of *Gerharde*, a rare feminine version of GERHARD.

Pet forms: **Geertke**, **Geertje**.

Gellért (m.) Hungarian form of GERARD. St Gerard Sagredo, born in Venice, was a missionary to Hungary during the 11th century, and became the first bishop of Czanad. He was murdered by being thrown into the Danube by unconverted heathens.

Gemma (f.) English, Irish, and Italian: from a medieval Italian nickname meaning 'gem, jewel'. It has been chosen in modern times mainly because of its transparent etymology. Among Roman Catholics it is sometimes chosen in honour of St Gemma Galgani (1878–1903), who was the subject of many extraordinary signs of grace, such as ecstasies and the appearance of the stigmata.

Variant: English: **Jemma**.

Gene (m.) English: short form of EUGENE, now quite commonly used as an independent given name in America. It has been made familiar especially by film stars such as Gene Autry, Gene Hackman, and Gene Wilder.

Genette (f.) English: variant spelling of JEANNETTE.

Geneva (f.) English: of recent origin and uncertain derivation. In form it coincides with the city in Switzerland (cf. FLORENCE and VENETIA), but it may rather have been intended as a Latinate short form of GENEVIÈVE.

Geneviève (f.) French: the name of the patron saint of Paris, a 5th-century Gallo-Roman nun who encouraged the people of Paris in the face of the occupation of the town by the Franks and threatened attacks by the Huns. Her name seems to have been composed of Celtic elements meaning 'people, tribe' and 'woman', but if so it has been heavily altered by its transmission through French sources. The name was introduced to Britain from France in the 19th century.

Cognates: English: **Genevieve**. Italian: **Genoveffa**, **Ginevra**.

Genista (f.) English: modern name, a learned coinage taken from the Latin name of the broom plant, *genesta*, *genista*. It is from this word that the English royal dynasty of the Plantagenets took its name: the founder, Geoffrey Plantagenet (d. 1151) wore a sprig of broom (Latin *planta genesta*) to distinguish himself in battle.

Gennadi (m.) Russian: from Greek *Gennadios*, a name of very uncertain origin. It may come from a derivative (originally patronymic in form) of a short form of the various Greek names such as *Diogenes* 'born of Zeus' and *Hermogenes* 'born of Hermes'. St Gennadius has been venerated from ancient times in the Eastern Church, together with his companion Felix, but very little is known about them. Another saint of the same name (d. *c*.936) was a bishop of Astorga.

Gennaro (m.) Italian: from Latin *Januārius*, a derivative of (*mensis*) *Januārius* January. The name of the month is derived from that of the god *Janus*, who was associated with doors (*januae*) and new beginnings; he was represented in sculpture as having two faces on a single head, one looking forwards and the other backwards. The name *Januarius* was borne by a large number of early saints, but the one most particularly associated with Italy was a bishop of Benevento beheaded at Pozzuoli under Diocletian in 304. His body was enshrined at Naples and he is the patron of that city. Phials of his blood are preserved at both Naples and Pozzuoli and are believed to liquefy regularly to this day.

Cognate: Spanish: **Jenaro**.

Genoveffa (f.) Italian form of GENEVIÈVE.

Gentzane (f.) Basque equivalent of PAZ.

Geoff (m.) English: short form of GEOFFREY. See also JEFF.

Geoffrey (m.) English: of Germanic (Frankish and Lombard) origin, introduced to Britain by the Normans. It was in regular use among the counts of Anjou, ancestors of the English royal house of Plantagenet, who were descended from Geoffrey Plantagenet, Count of Anjou (1113–51). Godefroy de Bouillon, leader of the First Crusade, is commemorated in Torquato Tasso's *Gerusalemme Liberata* (1581). It was a particularly popular name in England and France in the later Middle Ages; notable bearers in England include the poet Geoffrey Chaucer (*c*.1340–1400) and in Wales the chronicler Geoffrey of Monmouth (Gaufridus Monemutensis; d. 1155). The original form and meaning of the elements of which the name is composed are disputed. According to one theory, the name is merely a variant of GODFREY; others derive the first part from the Germanic elements *gawia* territory, *walah* stranger, or *gisil* pledge. Medieval forms can be found to support all these theories, and it is possible that several names have fallen together, or that the name was subjected to reanalysis by folk etymology at an early date.

Variant: JEFFREY.

Cognates: French: **Geoffroi**. Italian: **Goffredo**. Spanish, Portuguese: **Godofredo**. Welsh: **Sieffre**. Irish Gaelic: **Siothrún**.

Geordie (m.) Pet form of GEORGE, still used in Scotland and the north of England. It is from this name that the generic term *Geordie* for a Tynesider derives.

George (m.) English: from Old French, from Latin *Georgius*, from Greek *Georgios* (from *geōrgos* farmer, a compound of *gē* earth + *ergein* to work). This was the name of several early saints, including the shadowy figure who is now the patron of England (as well as of Germany and Portugal). Gibbon identified him with a Cappadocian leader of this name, but this cannot be right. If the saint existed at all, he was perhaps martyred in Palestine in the persecutions instigated by the Emperor Diocletian at the beginning of the 4th century. The popular legend in which the hero slays a dragon is a medieval Italian invention. He was for a long time a more important saint in the Orthodox Church than in the West, and the name was not much used in England during the Middle Ages, even after St George came to be regarded as the patron of England in the 14th century. The real impulse for its popularity was the accession of the first king of England of this name, who came from Germany in 1714 and brought many German retainers with him. It has been one of the most popular English male names ever since.

Cognates: Irish Gaelic: **Seoirse**. Scottish Gaelic: **Seòras**, **Deòrsa**. Welsh: **Siôr**, **Sior(y)s**. French: **Georges**. Provençal: **Jori**. Italian: **Giorgio**. Spanish, Portuguese: **Jorge**. Catalan: **Jordi**. Basque: **Gorka**. German: **Georg**; **Jörg** (dialectal); **Jürgen** (Low German in origin). Dutch, Frisian: **Joris**, **Joren**, **Jurg**. Danish: **Jørgen**, **Jørn**. Swedish: **Göran**, **Jöran**, **Jörgen**, **Örjan**. Finnish: **Yrjö**. Russian: **Georgi**, **Yuri**, **Yegor**. Polish: **Jerzy**. Czech: **Jiří**. Hungarian: **György**. Romanian: **Gheorghe**, **Iorghu**. See also YORICK.

Pet forms: English: **Georgie**, **Geordie**. Russian: **Goga**, **Gora**, **Gorya**. Polish: **Jurek**.

Feminine forms: English: GEORGIA, GEORGINA, GEORGETTE. Scottish Gaelic: **Seòrdag**.

Georgene (f.) English: altered form of GEORGINE, by association with the productive suffix -*ene*.

Georgette (f.) French: feminine diminutive of *Georges* (see GEORGE), now also used in the English-speaking world. The crêpe material so called derives its name from that of an early 20th-century French dressmaker, Mme Georgette de la Plante.

Georgia (f.) Latinate feminine form of GEORGE. It was borne by a 5th-century saint who became a recluse near Clermont in the Auvergne.

Georgiana (f.) Elaborated Latinate form of GEORGIA or GEORGINA, now sometimes used in the English-speaking world. It seems to take its pattern from Latin names such as JULIANA, a derivative of JULIA. In Latin the suffix *-ānus* was originally a derivative element used in names as a distinguishing feature; for example, on his adoption by Julius Caesar, Caius Octavius (later known as the Emperor Augustus) became Caius Julius Caesar Octavianus.

Georgie (m., f.) English: occasionally used as a pet form of GEORGE, but more commonly as a female name, a pet form of GEORGIA or GEORGINA.

Georgina (f.) Scottish, English, etc.: Latinate feminine derivative of GEORGE. This feminine form originated in Scotland in the 18th century, when *George* itself became common among anti-Jacobites. It has now been borrowed by other European languages, including Dutch, German, Danish, Norwegian, and Swedish.

Cognates: French: **Georgine**. Czech: **Jiřina**.

Georgine (f.) French form of GEORGINA, now also used in the English-speaking world.

Variant: English: **Georgene**.

Geraint (m.) Welsh: of uncertain origin, derived from a British name that first appears in a Greek inscription in the form *Gerontios*, possibly influenced by the Greek vocabulary word *gerōn* (genitive *gerontos*) old man. The story of Geraint (or *Gereint*), son of Erbin of Cornwall, is told in the *Mabinogi*. Geraint is one of the knights of Arthur's Round Table. He wins the love of Enid at a tournament, and marries her. He is infatuated with her to the point of neglecting all else, but comes to suspect her, wrongly, of infidelity. By her submissiveness and loyalty, she regains his trust. The story of Geraint and Enid was used by Tennyson in the *Idylls of the King*. In recent years the name has become extremely popular in Wales.

Gerald (m.) English and Irish: of Germanic origin, composed of the elements *gār*, *gēr* spear + *wald* rule. The name was introduced to Britain by the Normans, but soon became confused with GERARD. It died out in England at the end of the 13th century. However, it continued in Ireland, where it had been brought in the 12th century, at the time of Strongbow's invasion, principally by Maurice *FitzGerald*, 'son of Gerald'. The name was revived in England in the 19th century, along with several other long-extinct names of Germanic and Celtic origin, and is now more common than GERARD, which survived all along as an English 'gentry' name.

Variant: **Jerrold**.
Cognates: Irish Gaelic: **Gearóid**, **Gearalt**. Welsh: **Gerallt**. Dutch: **Gerolt**. German: **Gerhold**. Italian: **Giraldo**. French: **Gérald**, **Géraud**.
Short form: English: **Ged**.
Pet forms: English: **Gerry**, **Jerry**.

Geraldine (f.) English: feminine derivative of GERALD, invented in the 16th century by the English poet the Earl of Surrey, in a poem praising Lady FitzGerald. However, it remained very little used until the 18th century.

Pet form: **Gerry**.

Gerard (m.) English, Irish, and Dutch: of Germanic origin, introduced to Britain by the Normans. It is composed of the elements *gār*, *gēr* spear + *hard* brave, hardy, strong. In the Middle Ages this was a much more common name than GERALD, with which it was sometimes confused, but nowadays is less common. It survives mainly among Roman Catholics.
Variants: **Gerrard**, **Jerrard**.
Cognates: French: **Gérard**. Italian: **Gerardo**. German: **Gerhard**, **Gerhar(d)t**. Low German: **Gerrit**, **Ge(e)rt**. Dutch, Flemish: **Geeraard**, **Geerd**, **Ge(e)rt**. Frisian: **Gerrit**, **Garrit**. Hungarian: **Gellért**.
Short form: English: **Ged**.
Pet forms: English: **Gerry**, **Jerry**.

Gerasim (m.) Russian: from the Late Greek personal name *Gerasimos*, a derivative of *geras* old age (cf. GERAINT and GEREON), or of the homonymous *geras* honour. The name was borne by a 5th-century saint venerated in the Eastern Church; he lived as a hermit in the Holy Land.
Pet form: **Garsha**.

Gerd (f.) Scandinavian: name borne in Old Norse mythology by a beautiful goddess who was the wife of Frey. The pair seem to have been originally fertility gods, and her name is probably connected with the Old Norse word *garðr* enclosure, stronghold.
Variant: **Gärd**.

Gerda (f.) Scandinavian, German, and Dutch: Latinate form of GERD, revived in Scandinavia in the 19th century. In Germany and the Netherlands, it is sometimes taken as a feminine derivative of GERARD. It is now sometimes also found in the English-speaking world.
Variant: German: **Gerde**.
Pet form: German: **Gerdi**.

Gereon (m.) German: confined almost exclusively to the Cologne area, this represents the name of a saint martyred there at the beginning of the 4th century. He was executed together with a band of companions traditionally said to have numbered 318. The name is apparently a derivative of Greek *gerōn* old man.

Gergely (m.) Hungarian form of GREGORY.

Gerhard (m.) German form of GERARD.
Variants: **Gerhart**, **Gerhardt**.

Gerlach (m.) German and Dutch: from an old Germanic personal name composed of the elements *geri*, *gari* spear + *laic* play, sport. St Gerlach was a hermit who lived near Valkenberg in the 12th century.

Gerlinde (f.) German: from an old Germanic female personal name composed of the elements *geri*, *gari* spear + *lind* weak, tender, soft. St Gerlinde lived in the 8th century; she was a member of the royal family of Alsace, sister of St Ottilie.

Germaine (f.) French and English: feminine form of the rarer French male name **Germain** (Late Latin *Germānus* 'brother'; the original reference may have been to the concept of Christian brotherhood). Germaine Cousin (*c.*1579–1601) was a Provençal saint, the daughter of a poor farmer. Her canonization in 1867 gave an additional impulse to the use of the name in Europe and the English-speaking world. It is now particularly known as the name of the Australian feminist writer Germaine Greer (b. 1939). See also JERMAINE.

Gernot (m.) German: from an old Germanic personal name composed of the elements *gār*, *gēr* spear + *nōt* need, want or perhaps *hnod-* crush). The same elements are found in reverse order in the name NOTGER.

Geronimo (m.) Italian: learned form of JEROME, much less common than the vernacular GIROLAMO. In the United States it is known as the name of a famous Apache chief (1829–1909), presumably a phonetic approximation to his native name.

Gerrard (m.) English: variant spelling of GERARD, in part from the modern surname.

Gerrit (m.) Low German and Frisian form of GERHARD, current predominantly in the North Rhine area.
Variants: Low German: **Ge(e)rt**. Frisian: **Garrit**; **Gerritt** (E. Frisian).

Gerry (f., m.) English: 1. (f.) Pet form of GERALDINE; it is also sometimes used as an independent female name. 2. (m.) Pet form of GERALD or GERARD; cf. JERRY.

Gershom (m.) Biblical: name borne by a son of Moses (Exodus 2: 22). The name possibly means 'exile' (i.e. a person in exile) in Hebrew, but it is usually interpreted as 'sojourner', from Hebrew *ger sham* meaning 'a stranger there'.

Gershon (m.) Biblical: byform of GERSHOM, borne by a son of Levi (Genesis 46: 11).

Gert (m., f.) 1. (m.) Dutch and Low German: contracted form of GERARD. 2. (f.) English: short form of GERTRUDE.
Variant (of 1): **Geert**.
Pet form (of 2): **Gertie**.

Gertrude (f.) English, Dutch, and German: from a Germanic personal name composed of the elements *gār*, *gēr* spear + *þrūþ* strength. The name does not appear in England immediately after the Conquest, but only in the later Middle English period: it is probable that it was introduced by migrants from the Low Countries, who came to England in connection with the cloth trade. It was popular in the 19th century, at the time of the revival of many Germanic names, but has now fallen from favour again. In Germany, usually in the form *Gertrud*, it was much more popular than it ever was in England. It was the name of two famous 13th-century nuns of the Cistercian abbey of Helfta near Eisleben, whose spiritual writings had a great influence.
Variants: German: **Gertrud**; **Gertraud**; **Gertraut** (by association with the element *traut* dear, beloved). Dutch: **Ge(e)rtruida**.
Cognates: Spanish: **Gertrudis**. Portuguese: **Gertrudes**. Low German, Dutch: **Geerta**.
Finnish: **Kerttu**.
Short form: English: **Gert**.
Pet forms: English: **Gertie**. German: **Gerda**, **Gerdi**, **Trude**, **Trudi**. Dutch: **Geertke**, **Geertje**. Low German, Frisian: **Gesa**.

Gervaise (m.) English: introduced to Britain by the Normans. It is of unknown derivation: it has been suggested that it might be a dithematic Germanic name, with the first element *gār*, *gēr* spear, but it is difficult to suggest a plausible second element. The use of the name seems to be due entirely to a certain St Gervasius, whose remains, together with those of Protasius, were discovered in Milan in the year 386. Nothing is known about their lives, but St Ambrose, who had ordered the search for their remains, declared that they were martyrs, and a cult soon grew up. Given these circumstances, we might expect their names to be Greek or Latin, but if they are, the elements remain unidentified. The name is in use mainly among Roman Catholics. *Protasius* has not survived as a given name. See also JARVIS.
Variant: **Gervase**.
Cognates: French **Gervais**. Italian, Spanish, Portuguese: **Gervasio**. German: **Gervas**. Dutch: **Gervaas**. Polish: **Gerwazy**. Russian: **Gervasi**.

Gesa (f.) Frisian pet form of GERTRUDE.

Gesualdo (m.) Italian: from a medieval given name of Germanic origin, probably originally composed of the elements *gisil* pledge (see GISELLE) + *wald* ruler. It has been influenced in form by association with *Gesù* Jesus.

Gethin (m.) Welsh: derived from a lenited adjectival form of the byname *Cethin* 'dusky, swarthy'.
Variant: **Gethen**.

Géza (m.) Hungarian: of uncertain derivation, said to be from a medieval honorific title of Turkic origin.

Gheorghe (m.) Romanian form of GEORGE.

Ghislain (f.) English: of recent origin, or at any rate a recent introduction to the English-speaking world. It is apparently a revival of the Old French oblique case of GISELLE. The spelling indicates some Low German influence.
Variant: **Ghislaine**.

Giacobbe (m.) Italian form of JACOB, rather less common than GIACOMO.

Giacomo (m.) Italian form of JAMES.

Giambattista (m.) Italian: contracted form of GIANNI and BATTISTA.

Giammaria (m.) Italian: contracted form of GIANNI and MARIA.

Giampaolo (m.) Italian: contracted form of GIANNI and PAOLO.

Gianni (m.) Italian: contracted form of GIOVANNI, in very common use.
Feminine form: **Gianna**.
Pet forms: **Giannino**, **Nino** (m.); **Giannetta**, **Giannina** (f.).

Gib (m.) English: medieval and modern short form of GILBERT.

Gideon (m.) Biblical name (meaning 'one who cuts down' in Hebrew) borne by an Israelite leader appointed to deliver his people from the Midianites (Judges 6: 14). He did this by getting his army to creep up on them with their torches hidden in pitchers. The name was popular among the 17th-century Puritans, and is still used in America and in modern Hebrew.
Derivatives: Russian: **Gedeon**. Jewish: **Gidon** (Hebrew).

Gigi (f.) French: pet name, originally a nursery reduplication, based on GEORGINE or *Virginie* (see VIRGINIA).

Gil (m.) Spanish and Portuguese form of GILES.

Gilbert (m.) English, French, Flemish, and Dutch: of Germanic origin, introduced to Britain by the Normans. It is composed of the elements *gisil* pledge + *berht* bright, famous. This was the name of the founder of the only native British religious order (abolished at the Dissolution of the Monasteries), St Gilbert of Sempringham (?1083–1189), in whose honour it is still sometimes bestowed, especially among Roman Catholics. It gained a wider currency in the 19th century. In Gaelic Scotland the name was used from an early period to render the name *Gille Brighde* 'servant of St BRIDGET', gradually assuming the form **Gilleabart**.
Short form: English: **Gib**.
Pet forms: Scottish: **Gibby** (Gaelic **Gibidh**).

Gilda (f.) Italian: apparently of Germanic origin, representing a feminine short form of names containing the element *gild* sacrifice (cf. e.g. HERMENEGILDO). Its popularity as a current given name derives in part from its use in Verdi's *Rigoletto*, in which Gilda, the innocent young daughter of the hunchback jester Rigoletto, becomes the object of the Duke of Mantua's affections and is murdered on her father's orders as the result of a series of misunderstandings.

Giles (m.) English: much altered version of the Late Latin name *Aegidius*, from Greek *Aegidios* (a derivative of *aigidion* kid, young goat). The name was very popular in the Middle Ages, as the result of the fame of the 8th-century St Giles. According to tradition, he was an Athenian citizen who fled to Provence because he could not cope with the fame and adulation caused by his power to work miracles, in particular by healing the lame and crippled. He is the patron saint of cripples.

Variant: **Gyles**.

Cognates: French: **Gilles**. Provençal, Spanish, Portuguese: **Gil**. Danish, Dutch: **Gillis**. Italian: **Egidio**. German: **Ägid(ius)**. Polish: **Egidiusz, Idzi**. Hungarian: **Egyed**.

Gill (f.) English: short form of GILLIAN, rather less commonly used as an independent given name than JILL.

Gillanders (m.) Scottish: Anglicized form of Gaelic *Gille Ainndreis* or *Gille Ainndrais* 'servant of St ANDREW'.

Gilleonan (m.) Scottish: Anglicized form of Gaelic *Gille Adhamhnain* 'servant of St Adomnan' (see EUNAN).

Gilles (m.) French form of GILES.

Gillespie (m.) Scottish: Anglicized form of Gaelic *Gille Easbaig* 'bishop's servant'. See also ARCHIBALD.

Pet form: **Beistean**.

Gillian (f.) English: variant of JULIAN, from which it was differentiated in spelling in the 17th century.

Variant: **Jillian**.
Short forms: **Gill, Jill**.
Pet form: **Gilly**.

Gillies (m.) Scottish: Anglicized form of Gaelic *Gille Iosa* 'servant of Jesus'.

Gillis (m.) Danish and Dutch form of GILES.

Gilly (f.) English: pet form of GILL. There may have been some influence from the name of the *gillyflower* (earlier *gilofre, girofle*, from Late Greek *karyophyllon*).

Gilroy (m.) Irish and Scottish: transferred use of the surname, probably influenced to some extent by ELROY, DELROY, and LEROY. The surname is of Gaelic origin (Irish *Mac Giolla Ruaidh*, Scottish *Mac Gille Ruaidh*), meaning 'son of the red-haired lad'.

Gina (f.) Italian and English: short form of GEORGINA and *Giorgina*, now sometimes used as an independent given name. It has been made famous by the Italian actress Gina Lollobrigida (b. 1927). As an Italian name it also represents in part a short form of *Luigina*, a feminine diminutive form of LUIGI.

Ginevra (f.) Italian form of GENEVIÈVE, now also occasionally used in the English-speaking world.

Ginger (m., f.) English: 1. (m., f.) Originally a nickname for someone with red hair (or, occasionally, with a violent temper), sometimes used as a given name in the 20th century, perhaps for a child with ginger hair. 2. (f.) As a female name it may also represent a pet form of VIRGINIA (as in the case of the film actress Ginger Rogers, born in 1911 as Virginia McMath).

Ginny (f.) English: pet form of VIRGINIA, rarely used as an independent given name.

Gino (m.) Italian: short form of any of the many given names ending in *-gino*, for example *Ambrogino* (a diminutive of *Ambrogio*; see AMBROSE), *Biagino* (a diminutive of BIAGIO), *Giorgino* (a diminutive of GIORGIO), and *Luigino* (a diminutive of LUIGI).

Gioacchino (m.) Italian form of JOACHIM, now only fairly rarely used as a given name.

Variant: **Gioachino**.

Gioconda (f.) Italian: name meaning 'happy, jovial' (from Latin *jucunda*). St Jucunda (d. 466) was a virgin of Reggio in Aemilia, associated with St Prosper.

Giorgio (m.) Italian form of GEORGE.

Giosuè (m.) Italian form of JOSHUA.

Giovanni (m.) Most common Italian form of JOHN. There are several others, e.g. *Gianni* and *Vanni*.

Feminine form: **Giovanna**.

Girolamo (m.) Italian: vernacular form of JEROME, much more common than the learned form GERONIMO.

Giselle (f.) French and English: of Germanic origin, derived from the vocabulary element *gisil* pledge. It was a common practice in medieval Europe to leave children as pledges for an alliance, to be brought up at a foreign court, and the name may be derived as a byname from this practice. This was the name by which the wife of Duke Rollo of Normandy (c.860–c.930) was known. She was a daughter of Charles the Simple of France, and may indeed have been offered to Rollo as a pledge for their truce in 911. On her account the name enjoyed considerable popularity in France from an early period. *Gisela* was also the name of the wife (c.995–c.1085) of King Stephen I of Hungary. She was a Bavarian princess, noted for her Christian faith and her good works. Use of the name in English-speaking countries is much more recent, and is due mainly to the ballet *Giselle* (first performed in 1841).

Variant: French: **Gisèle**.
Cognate: German, Dutch: **Gisela**.
Short form: German: **Gisa**.

Gislög (f.) Swedish: from an Old Norse female personal name composed of the elements *gisil* hostage + *laug* consecrated.

Cognate: Norwegian: **Gislaug**.

Gitte (f.) 1. German and Danish: short form of *Brigitte* (see BRIDGET) and *Birgitte* (see BIRGIT). 2. Jewish: of Yiddish origin, originally a nickname meaning 'good' (modern German *gut*).

Pet form (of 2): Jewish: **Gittel**.

Giulia (f.) Italian form of JULIA.

Giulietta (f.) Italian: diminutive of GIULIA.

Giulio (m.) Italian form of JULIUS.

Giuseppe (m.) Italian form of JOSEPH.

Pet forms: **Beppe, Beppo**.

Giuseppina (f.) Italian form of JOSEPHINE.

Gixane (f.) Basque equivalent of ENCARNACIÓN.

Gjord (m.) Swedish: contracted form of an (unattested) Old Norse personal name composed of the elements *guð* god + *friðr* peace, or of the German cognate GOTTFRIED.

Cognate: Norwegian: **Gjurd**.

Gladstone (m.) Scottish and English: transferred use of the surname, originally a local name from *Gledstanes* in Biggar, so called from Old English *glæd* kite + *stān* rock (the final *-s* is a later addition). As a given name it has been adopted in honour of the Victorian Liberal statesman William Ewart Gladstone (1809–98). It is now favoured by West Indians: the Warwickshire and England fast bowler Gladstone Small is of West Indian parentage.

Gladwin (m.) English: transferred use of the surname, itself from a medieval given name composed of the Old English elements *glæd* bright + *wine* friend.

Gladys (f.) Welsh and English: from the Welsh name *Gwladus*, which is of uncertain derivation. It has been quite widely used outside Wales in the 20th century.

Gleb (m.) Russian: of Scandinavian origin, from an Old Norse personal name composed of the elements *guð* god + *leifr* life. St Gleb was a son of Prince Vladimir, first Christian ruler of Kiev, and was assassinated in 1015 together with his brother Boris; his name in the Church was *David*.

Glen (m.) Scottish and English: probably a transferred use of the surname, which was originally a topographic name from the Gaelic element *gleann* valley. It is also possible, however, that the given name is derived directly from the topographic term (compare DEAN). In recent years it has been adopted in England as well as Scotland as a given name. There also appears to have been some confusion with the Welsh name GLYN.
Variant: **Glenn** (borne as a female name by the American actress Glenn Close (b. 1947)).
Feminine form: **Glenna**.

Glenda (f.) Welsh: modern coinage, composed of the vocabulary words *glân* clean, pure, holy + *da* good.

Glenys (f.) Welsh: modern coinage, probably from *glân* clean, pure, holy + the ending *-ys* by analogy with names such as DILYS and GLADYS.

Gloria (f.) English: from the Latin word meaning 'glory', not used as a given name before the 20th century, but now very popular. It first occurs as the name of a character in George Bernard Shaw's play *You Never Can Tell* (1898).

Glory (f.) English: Anglicized form of GLORIA, now occasionally used as a given name, especially among Blacks.

Glyn (m.) Welsh: from the Welsh placename element *glyn* valley. This seems to have been transferred directly from a placename to a given name in the 20th century, as the result of a desire to bestow on Welsh children specifically Welsh names.
Variant: **Glynn**.

Glyndwr (m.) Welsh: adopted in the 20th century in honour of the medieval Welsh patriot Owain Glyndŵr (*c*.1359–1416; known in English as Owen Glendower). In his case it was a byname referring to the fact that he came from a place named with the Welsh elements *glyn* valley + *dŵr* water.

Glynis (f.) English: apparently an altered form of GLENYS.

Gobnait (f.) Irish Gaelic: traditional name, of uncertain derivation. It seems to represent a feminine diminutive form of *goba* smith, apparently a reference to the Celtic god of craftsmanship, *Gobniu*. This was the name of an important Munster saint, and the name is still in use in west Munster. It was formerly often Anglicized as ABBIE and ABIGAIL.

Variant: **Gobnet** (Anglicized).

Goddard (m.) English: from the Old English personal name *Godeheard*, composed of the elements *god* god + *heard* hardy, brave, strong. Modern use as a given name is probably a transferred use of the surname derived from this given name in the Middle Ages, rather than a revival of the Old English name.
Cognate: German: GOTTHARD.

Godelieve (f.) French (Walloon): from a Germanic personal name composed of the elements *god* god or *gōd* good + *liob* dear. It is thus a feminine equivalent of German GOTTLIEB. St *Godleva* or *Godliva* (Latinized forms of the name) was murdered in the 11th century by her husband, Bertulf of Ghistelles; she has a cult in Flanders as a suffering innocent, and the name is still in use there.

Godfrey (m.) English: of Germanic origin, introduced to Britain by the Normans. It is composed of the elements *god* god (or *gōd* good) + *fred*, *frid* peace. The name was very popular in the Middle Ages. It was borne by, among others, a Norman saint (*c*.1066–1115) who became bishop of Amiens. There has been considerable confusion with GEOFFREY.
Cognates: Scottish Gaelic: **Goiridh**, **Goraidh**. German: **Gottfried**.
Dutch: **Godfried**.
Pet form: German: **Götz**.

Godiva (f.) English: Latinized form of an Old English female personal name composed of the elements *god* god + *gyfu* gift. It is thus the equivalent of THEODORA and *Bogdana* (see BOGDAN). The name was borne by an 11th-century Mercian noblewoman who, according to a famous legend, rode naked on horseback through the streets of Coventry to dissuade her husband Earl Leofric from imposing a heavy tax on the townspeople. It is rarely, if ever, used as a modern given name.

Godwin (m.) English: from the Old English personal name *Godwine*, composed of the elements *god* god + *wine* friend. This name was borne in the 11th century by the Earl of Wessex, the most important man in the England after the king. He was an influential adviser to successive kings of England, and father of the King Harold who was defeated at Hastings in 1066. The personal name continued in use after the Norman Conquest long enough to give rise to a surname. Modern use as a given name is probably a transferred use of the surname, rather than a revival of the Old English name.

Goga (m.) Russian: pet form of *Georgi* and *Yegor* (see GEORGE).

Goito (m.) Spanish: variant of GOYO.

Goldie (f.) Jewish: Anglicized form of Yiddish **Golde** or **Golda** (borne, for example, by the former Israeli prime minister, Golda Meir, 1898–1978, who Hebraicized her name from Golda Meyerson). It was originally a nickname meaning 'gold'. Occasionally it is a non-Jewish name, derived from an English nickname for a fair-haired person.

Gomer (m.) Biblical: name (meaning 'complete' in Hebrew) borne by a son of Japheth and grandson of Noah. It was taken up by the Puritans, and is still in occasional use in America, where it has been reinforced by the homophonous English surname *Gomer*. This is derived from an Old English personal name composed of the elements *gōd* good + *mǣr* famous.

Gonçalvo (m.) Portuguese form of GONZALO.

Gonzague (m.) French: name chosen in honour of St Aloysius Gonzaga (1568–91). He was a Jesuit of noble birth, who died at the age of 23 while tending victims of the plague: he is regarded as a special patron of young people.

Gonzalo (m.) Spanish: of Germanic (Visigothic) origin. The name is found in the Middle Ages in the Latin form *Gundisalvus*, composed of the elements *gund* strife + *salv*, of uncertain meaning (it may be a borrowing of Latin *salvus* whole, safe).
Cognate: Portuguese: **Gonçalvo**.

Goodwin (m.) English: tranferred use of the surname, which is derived from the Old English personal name *Gōdwine*. This is composed of the elements *gōd* good + *wine* friend. There has been considerable confusion with GODWIN.

Gora (m.) Russian: pet form of *Georgi* and *Yegor* (see GEORGE).

Göran (m.) Swedish form of GEORGE. The -*n* suggests derivation from a Latinate elaboration *Georgianus* (based on pairs such as *Julius* and *Julianus*), rather than directly from *Georgius*.
Variants: **Jöran**, **Örjan**.

Gordon (m.) Scottish and English: from the Scottish surname, which is derived from a placename. It is a matter of dispute whether it referred originally to the Gordon in Berwickshire or to a similarly named place in Normandy. As a given name it seems to have been taken up in honour of Charles George Gordon (1833–85), the British general who died at Khartoum.

Goretti (f.) English and Irish (borne by Roman Catholics): name bestowed in honour of the 20th-century Italian saint, Maria Goretti. In 1902, at the age of 11, she was savagely assaulted by a neighbour in an attempted rape. She forgave her attacker before expiring in hospital, and was canonized in 1950 as an example to children of a saintly life at an early age.

Gorka (m.) Basque form of GEORGE.

Gormlaith (f.) Irish and Scottish Gaelic: traditional name composed of the elements *gorm* illustrious, splendid + *flaith* lady, princess. This name was borne by the wife of Brian Boru and mother of Sitric, King of Dublin (d. 1030).
Variants: **Gormla** (modern Gaelic spelling); **Gormelia** (an Anglicized form used in Scotland).

Goronwy (m.) Welsh: of uncertain derivation, borne in the *Mabinogi* by Goronwy the Staunch, Lord of Penllyn. He became the lover of the flower-maiden Blodeuedd and murdered her husband Lleu Llaw Gyffes, but Lleu was later restored to life and definitively dispatched Goronwy.

Gorya (m.) Russian: pet form of *Georgi* and *Yegor* (see GEORGE).

Gosia (f.) Polish: short form of *Malgosia*, a pet form of MALGORZATA.

Gösta (m.) Swedish: vernacular form of GUSTAV, used in its own right as a baptismal name, but also as a pet form of the learned version.

Gottfried (m.) German form of GODFREY. This was a common name in medieval Germany, and has been ever since. A famous early bearer was the 13th-century poet Gottfried von Strassburg.
Pet form: **Götz**.

Gotthard (m.) German form of GODDARD. St Gotthard was an 11th-century bishop of Hildesheim in Bavaria.

Gotthelf (m.) German: religious name, dating from the 17th century, composed of the elements *Gott* God + the verbal stem *helf*, *hilf* help.
Variants: **Gotthilf**, **Helfgott**.

Gotthold (m.) German: religious name, dating from the 17th century, composed of the elements *Gott* God + *hold* lovely, splendid. -(*h*)*old* is a common second element in Germanic personal names, but in most cases it derives from -*wald* rule. This given name was borne, for example, by the dramatist and critic Gotthold Lessing (1729–81).

Gottlieb (m.) German: religious name, dating from the 17th century, composed of the elements *Gott* God + the verbal stem *lieb* love (and so an equivalent of THEOPHILUS).
Cognate: Dutch: **Godlef**.

Gottlob (m.) German: religious name, dating from the 17th century, composed of the elements *Gott* God + the verbal stem *lob* praise.

Gottschalk (m.) German: religious name, dating from the early Middle Ages, composed of the elements *god*, *got* God + *scalc* servant. St Gotteschalk (d. 1066) was a Wendish prince who was married to a grand-niece of King Canute of England. An earlier Gotteschalk (d. *c*.868) preached total predestination. In the later Middle Ages the name was for a time characteristically Jewish, used as a translation of the Hebrew names *Abdiel* or OBADIAH. It is now little used by any group.

Götz (m.) German: pet form of GOTTFRIED.

Gotzon (m.) Basque: vernacular equivalent of ANGEL; see also AINGERU.
Feminine form: **Gotzone**.

Goyo (m.) Spanish: pet form of *Gregorio* (see GREGORY).
Variant: **Goito**.

Grace (f.) English, Irish, and Scottish: from the abstract noun (from Latin *grātia*), first used as a given name by the Puritans in the 17th century, and still moderately popular (and to a large extent dissociated from the vocabulary word). Its popularity has increased in the 20th century owing to the fame of the late wife of Prince Rainier of Monaco, the actress Grace Kelly (1928–82). It has always been a popular name in Scotland and northern England (borne, for example, by Grace Darling, the lighthouse keeper's daughter whose heroism in 1838, saving sailors in a storm, caught popular imagination). In Ireland it has often been used as an Anglicized form of GRÁINNE, for example in the case of the famous 16th-century female sea captain Gráinne Ní Mháille, known in English as Grace O'Malley.
Cognates: Italian: **Grazia**. Spanish: **Gracia**. German, Dutch: **Gratia**.
Pet form: English, Scottish: **Gracie**.

Graciano (m.) Spanish and Portuguese form of GRATIEN.

Gracie (f.) English and Scottish: pet form of GRACE. It was made famous by the Lancashire singer and comedienne Gracie Fields (1898–1979), whose original name was Grace Stansfield.

Graham (m.) Scottish and English: from a Scottish surname, which derives from a place that is in neither Scotland nor Normandy, but Lincolnshire. *Grantham*, near the border with Leicestershire and Nottinghamshire, is recorded in Domesday Book not only in its current form but also as *Grandham*, *Granham*, and *Graham*; it seems to have been originally named as the 'gravelly place', from Old English *grand* gravel (unattested) + *hām* homestead. The surname was taken to Scotland in the 12th century by Sir William de Graham, founder of a famous clan. The earls of Montrose were among his descendants.

Variants: **Grahame**, **Graeme**.

Gráinne (f.) Irish Gaelic: of uncertain origin, possibly a derivative of *grán* grain or *gráin* disgust. In Irish legend Gráinne was the daughter of King Cormac; she was beloved by the hero Finn, but eloped with Finn's nephew Diarmait. Finn pursued them over great distances, and eventually brought about the death of Diarmait, after which Gráinne killed herself. The name has sometimes been Anglicized as GRACE.

Grania (f.) English and Irish: Latinized form of GRÁINNE.
Variant: **Granya**.

Grant (m.) Scottish and English: from the Scottish surname, the name of a famous clan, which is nevertheless probably derived from a Norman nickname meaning 'large' (Anglo-Norman *grand*). In America the name is sometimes bestowed in honour of the Civil War general and 18th president, Ulysses S. Grant (1822–85).

Granville (m.) English: from one of the Norman baronial names that subsequently became aristocratic English surnames and are now used intermittently as male given names. This one derives from any of several places in Normandy named with the Old French elements *grand* large + *ville* settlement.

Granya (f.) English and Irish: variant spelling of GRANIA.

Gratia (f.) Latinate form of GRACE, used in Germany and Holland.

Gratien (m.) French: from Latin *Gratiānus*, a derivative of *Gratius*, itself a derivative of *gratus* pleasing, lovely. St Gratian (d. ?*c*.337) was a disciple of St Denis of Paris; he became the first bishop of Tours.
Cognates: Italian: **Graziano**. Spanish, Portuguese: **Graciano**.

Grazia (f.) Italian form of GRACE.

Graziano (m.) Italian form of GRATIEN.

Graziella (f.) Italian: diminutive form of GRAZIA.

Greer (f.) Scottish and English: from the Scottish surname, which originated in the Middle Ages from a contracted form of GREGOR. It has become known as a female name in the English-speaking world through the fame of the actress Greer Garson (b. 1908), whose mother's maiden name it was.
Variant: **Grier**.

Greg (m.) English and Scottish: short form of GREGORY or GREGOR.
Variants: **Gregg**, **Greig** (chiefly Scottish, and generally a transferred use of the surname so spelled, which is itself a derivative of the given name).

Greger (m.) Swedish form of GREGORY.

Gregers (m.) Danish and Norwegian form of GREGORY (from Latin *Gregorius*).

Grégoire (m.) Traditional French form of GREGORY.

Gregor (m.) Scottish form of GREGORY, currently undergoing a revival in popularity. In part it represents an Anglicized form of Gaelic **Griogair**, which gave rise to the Highland surname *MacGregor*. This is derived in turn from the Norman French form of *Gregory* (see GRÉGOIRE).

Gregory (m.) English and Scottish: via Latin *Gregorius* from the post-classical Greek name *Gregōrios* 'watchful' (a derivative of *gregōrein* to watch, be vigilant). The name was an extremely popular one with the early Christians, who were mindful of the instruction 'be sober, be vigilant' (1 Peter 5: 8): it was borne by a number of early saints. The most important, in honour of whom the name was often bestowed from medieval times onwards, were Gregory of Nazianzen (*c*.329–90), Gregory of Nyssa (d. *c*.395), Gregory of Tours (538–94), and Pope Gregory the Great (*c*.540–604). The name has traditionally been particularly popular in Scotland, where it often took the form GREGOR.
Cognates: Irish Gaelic: **Gréagóir**. Scottish Gaelic: **Griogair**. Welsh: **Grigor**. French: **Grégoire**; **Grégory** (Provençal in origin, now more fashionable than the traditional form). Italian, Spanish, Portuguese: **Gregorio**. Dutch, Frisian: **Joris**. Swedish: **Greger**. Danish, Norwegian: **Gregers**. Polish: **Grzegorz**. Czech: **Řehoř**. Russian: **Grigori**. Hungarian: **Gergely**. Finnish: **Reijo**.
Short forms: English: **Greg**. Scottish: **Greg(g)**, **Greig**.
Pet forms: Spanish: **Goyo**, **Goito**. Russian: **Grisha**.

Greville (m.) English: transferred use of the surname, which is a Norman baronial name from *Gréville* in La Manche. The Greville family were earls of Warwick, and held Warwick Castle from the time of Queen Elizabeth I, who granted it to her favourite Fulke Greville (1554–1628).

Greta (f.) Short form of *Margareta* (see MARGARET), used particularly in Sweden, Germany, and Ireland. It became fairly popular in the English-speaking world as a result of the fame of the Swedish-born film actress Greta Garbo (1905–92; b. Greta Louisa Gustafsson).

Grete (f.) German and Danish: short form of *Margarete* (see MARGARET), now also occasionally used as an independent given name in the English-speaking world.
Pet form: German: **Gretel** (made famous by the story of Hansel and Gretel, the 'babes in the wood' in *Grimm's Fairy Tales*).

Gretta (f.) English: variant spelling of GRETA.

Griet (f.) Low German, Dutch, and Frisian: short form of *Margriet* (see MARGARET), now used as an independent given name.
Variants: **Greet**, **Gret**.
Pet forms: **Grietje**, **Greetje**, **Gretje**.

Griff (m.) Welsh: informal short form of GRIFFITH.

Griffin (m.) Welsh: from a medieval Latinized form, *Griffinus*, of GRIFFITH.

Griffith (m.) Welsh: Anglicized form of **Gruffudd** or **Griffudd**, Old Welsh *Grip-(p)iud*. The second element of this means 'lord, prince', but the first is extremely uncertain. Gruffydd ap Llewellyn (d. 1063) was one of the most able rulers of Wales in the Middle Ages, scoring some notable victories over the English until he was eventually defeated by King Harold in 1063.
Short form: **Griff**.
Pet forms: **Guto**; **Gutun**, **Gutyn**.

Grigori (m.) Russian form of GREGORY.
Pet form: **Grisha**.

Griogair (m.) Scottish Gaelic form of GREGOR.
Variant: **Griogal** (a dialectal form).

Griselda (f.) Scottish and English: of uncertain origin, possibly from a Germanic name composed of the elements *gris* grey + *hild* battle. It became popular in the Middle Ages with reference to the tale of 'patient Griselda' (told by Boccaccio and Chaucer), who was taken as a model of the patient, long-suffering wife.

Variant: Scottish: **Grizel**.

Grisha (m.) Russian: pet form of GRIGORI.

Grit (f.) German: short form of *Margrit* (see MARGARET).

Variants: **Gritt**, **Gritta**.

Grizel (f.) Scottish: vernacular form of GRISELDA. The name has now almost or completely died out, no doubt in part because of its similarity to the vocabulary word *grizzle* meaning 'to grumble or whine'.

Gro (f.) Scandinavian (esp. Norwegian): from an Old Norse female personal name of uncertain derivation. It may derive from the Norse verb *gróa* to grow, increase, or possibly be related to the Celtic element *gruach* woman.

Grover (m.) English: transferred use of the surname, which originated as a local name for someone who lived near a grove of trees (Old English *grāf*). Use as a given name may be partly due to the American president Stephen Grover Cleveland (1837–1908), who was generally known as 'Grover Cleveland'.

Grunya (f.) Russian: pet form of AGRAFENA.

Grusha (f.) Russian: pet form of AGRAFENA.

Grzegorz (m.) Polish form of GREGORY.

Guadalupe (f.) Spanish: name reflecting a title of the Blessed Virgin Mary, Our Lady of Guadalupe. Guadalupe is a place in the province of Cáceres, so called from Arabic *wādī al-lubb* river of the wolf; it was the site of a famous Hieronymite convent, founded in the 14th century, which possesses a celebrated image of the Virgin. In 1531 a Mexican peasant saw a vision of the Virgin Mary, in which she allegedly declared herself to be the 'Lady of Guadalupe'; it has been suggested that this choice of title was inspired by the name of a native Mexican goddess, derived from Nahuatl *coatl* serpent.

Pet form: **Lupita**.

Gudrun (f.) Scandinavian: from an Old Norse female personal name composed of the elements *guð* god + *rūn* secret lore. In Norse legend this was the name borne by the heroine of the *Volsungasaga*, sister of Gunnar and wife of Sigurd, whose destruction she brought about. The name was revived in the second part of the 19th century, and is now also used in Germany and to some extent in the English-speaking world, probably under the influence of Wagner, although the character of Gutrune in Wagner's *Götterdämmerung* does not correspond to the Gudrun of the *Volsungasaga*.

Pet form: Norwegian: **Guro** (informal).

Guglielmo (m.) Italian form of WILLIAM.

Guido (m.) Italian form of GUY. Two important saints of this name lived in the 11th century: an abbot of Pomposa, near **Ferrara**, and a bishop of Acqui in Monferrato, Piedmont.

Guilherme (m.) Portuguese form of WILLIAM.

Guillaume (m.) French form of WILLIAM.

Guillem (m.) Catalan form of WILLIAM.

Guillermo (m.) Spanish form of WILLIAM.

Guinevere (f.) English: from the Old French form of the Welsh name *Gwenhwyfar*, composed of the elements *gwen* white, fair, blessed, holy + *hwyfar* smooth, soft. It is famous as the name of King Arthur's beautiful wife, who in most versions of the Arthurian legends is unfaithful to him, having fallen in love with Sir Lancelot. See also GAYNOR and JENNIFER.

Gull (f.) Scandinavian: pet form of the various women's names of Old Norse origin containing the first element *guð* god. It has also been associated with *gull* gold, and is now much used in Swedish compound names such as **Gull-Britt**, **Gull-Lis**, and **Gull-Maj**.

Gumersinda (f.) Spanish: from a Germanic (Visigothic) personal name composed of the elements *guma* man + *sind* path.

Short form: **Sinda**.

Gunder (m.) Danish: variant of GUNNAR.

Guni (m.) Jewish: name (meaning 'painted, coloured' in Hebrew) borne in the Bible by a son of Naphtali and grandson of Jacob (Genesis 46: 24).

Gunilla (f.) Swedish: Latinized form of GUNNHILD, in use from the 16th century to the present day. It enjoyed a vogue of particular popularity in Sweden during the 1940s.

Gunn (f.) Scandinavian: short form of the various women's names of Old Norse origin containing the first element *gunnr* strife, such as GUNNBORG, GUNNHILD, and GUNNVOR.

Variant: **Gun**.

Gunnar (m.) Scandinavian form of GÜNTHER. The name is of West Germanic, not Old Norse, origin but has been used in Scandinavia since the time of the sagas at least.

Variant: Danish: **Gunder**.

Gunnborg (f.) Scandinavian: from an Old Norse female personal name composed of the elements *gunnr* strife + *borg* fortification.

Variant: **Gunborg**.

Gunne (m.) Scandinavian: from Old Norse *Gunni*, a short form of GUNNAR and of the various rarer male names of Old Norse origin containing the first element *gunnr* strife, such as **Gunnbjörn** ('strife + bear') and **Gunnleif** ('strife + descendant'). In Norway it is occasionally used as a female name, from Old Norse *Gunna*, a short form of the various female names containing this same element.

Gunnhild (f.) Scandinavian: from an Old Norse female personal name composed of the nearly synonymous elements *gunnr* strife + *hildr* battle. The name has been in common use since the Viking period. It lies behind the English surnames *Gunnell* and *Cunnell*.

Variant: **Gunhild**.

Gunnvor (f.) Scandinavian: from an Old Norse female personal name composed of the elements *gunnr* strife + *vor* cautious, wary.

Variants: **Gunvor**; **Gunver** (chiefly Danish).

Günther (m.) German: from an old Germanic personal name composed of the elements *gund* strife + *heri*, *hari* army, warrior. According to Germanic legend, as recounted in the *Nibelungenlied*, Günther was the name of a king of Burgundy, brother-in-law of the warrior hero Siegfried. Siegfried obtains the beautiful Brunhild as wife for Günther, but the outcome is tragedy and destruction: Brunhild contrives Siegfried's death; Siegfried's widow Kriemhild, Günther's sister, takes her revenge by destroying Günther, Brunhild, and all their house. This grisly story was taken up by Richard Wagner and adapted for his opera *Götterdämmerung* (1876), and the revival of popularity of the name probably owes something to Wagner. The name has long been popular in German-speaking countries, in spite of the tragic story with which it is associated. On a more historical level, its currency in the Middle Ages probably owed something to the Blessed Günther (955–1045), a Bavarian monk, who was a cousin of St Stephen of Hungary.

Variants: **Gunt(h)er**, **Günter**.

Cognates: Scandinavian: **Gunnar**; **Gunder** (Danish).

Guro (f.) Norwegian: informal pet form of GUDRUN.

Gurutz (m.) Basque: name expressing devotion to the Cross. The vocabulary word *gurutz* is a borrowing from Latin (cf. CRUZ), but in Basque the name is a male one, not female.

Gus (m.) English, Scottish, and Irish: short form of AUGUSTUS, ANGUS, or *Gustave* (see GUSTAV). In the case of Gus the Theatre Cat, a character in T. S. Eliot's *Old Possum's Book of Practical Cats* (1939), it is a short form of *Asparagus!*

Gustav (m.) Scandinavian: from an Old Norse personal name composed of the tribal name *Gautr* + the element *stafr* staff. According to some scholars this name is of Slavonic origin (cf. DAGMAR), and originally had the form *Gostislav* or *Goslav*. It has been borne by various kings of Sweden, beginning with Gustav Vasa (?1496–1560), who was elected king in 1523 after freeing Sweden from Danish rule.

Variants: **Gustavus** (Latinized). Swedish: **Gustaf**, **Gösta**.

Cognates: French: **Gustave** (used also occasionally in the English-speaking world). Finnish: **Kustaa**, **Kyösti**. Dutch: **Gustaaf**, **Staaf**.

Guto (m.) Welsh: pet form of *Gruffudd* (see GRIFFITH).

Variants: **Gutun**, **Gutyn**.

Guy (m.) English and French (of Norman origin): from a short form of a compound Germanic name having as its first element *witu* wood or *wīt* wide. In Norman French initial *w-* regularly became *gu-*, and the usual Norman forms of the name were *Gy* or *Guido*. In medieval Latin the same name occurs as *Wido*. It was a popular name among the Normans, enhanced no doubt by the romance of *Guy of Warwick*, recounting the exploits of a folk hero of the Crusades.

Cognates: Italian: **Guido**. Dutch: **Veit**.

Gwalchmai (m.) Welsh: traditional name composed of the elements *gwalch* hawk + *mai* plain. In the *Mabinogi*, Gwalchmai (or *Gwalchmei*) is the name of one of King Arthur's nine captains, 'the most distinguished for his fighting ability and his noble bearing'.

Gwallter (m.) Welsh form of WALTER.

Gwatcyn (m.) Welsh form of WATKIN.

Gwen (f.) Welsh and English: short form of GWENDOLEN or GWENLLIAN, or an independent name from Welsh *gwen*, the feminine form of *gwyn* white, fair, blessed, holy (see GWYN). It was borne by a 5th-century saint, aunt of St David and mother of the minor saints Cybi and Cadfan, and by a reputed daughter of Brychan.

Gwenda (f.) Welsh and English: of modern origin, composed of the vocabulary words *gwen* white, fair, blessed, holy (see GWEN) + *da* good.

Gwendolen (f.) Welsh and English: apparently composed of the elements *gwen* white, fair, blessed, holy + *dolen* ring, bow. According to Geoffrey of Monmouth, this was the name of the wife of the mythical Welsh king Locrine, who, however, left her for a German princess called Estrildis. Gwendolen in re-

venge had Estrildis and her daughter Sabrina drowned in the River Seven. The name is borne by one of the principal characters in Oscar Wilde's play *The Importance of Being Earnest* (first performed in 1895).

Variants: **Gwendolin**, **Gwendolyn**; **Gwendoline** (formed under the influence of the many female given names ending in *-line*).

Gwenfrewi (f.) Welsh: from *gwen* white, fair, blessed, holy + *frewi* reconciliation. This was borne by a 7th-century Welsh saint around whom a large body of legends grew up. It has been Anglicized as WINIFRED.

Gwenhwyfar (f.) Welsh form of GUINEVERE.

Gwenllian (f.) Welsh: traditional name composed of the elements *gwen*, feminine form of *gwyn* white, fair, blessed, holy + *lliant* flood, flow (probably in the transferred sense 'foamy, white', referring to a pale complexion).

Gwenyth (f.) Welsh and English: variant of GWYNETH. It may alternatively be based on Welsh *gwenith* wheat, a word used in poetry to mean 'the favourite' or 'the pick of the bunch'.

Gwerful (f.) Welsh: traditional name composed of *gwair* bend, ring, circle + the mutated form of *mul* shy, modest.

Variants: **Gweirful**, **Gwerfyl**.

Gwilym (m.) Welsh form of WILLIAM, in use since the Middle Ages, and currently undergoing a revival in popularity.

Gwladus (f.) The original Welsh spelling of GLADYS, occasionally revived in recent years.

Variant: **Gwladys**.

Gwyn (m.). Welsh: originally a byname from Welsh *gwyn* white, fair, blessed, holy. See also WYN.

Gwynedd (m.) Welsh: name taken from a region of medieval North Wales (now resurrected as the name of a new composite county in Wales).

Gwyneth (f.) Welsh: altered form of GWYNEDD, used as a female name. Its popularity from the late 19th century, at first in Wales and then more widely in the English-speaking world, seems to have been due originally to the influence of Annie Harriet Hughes (1852–1910), who adopted the penname Gwyneth Vaughan.

Gwynfor (m.) Welsh: coined in the 20th century, apparently from the elements *gwyn* white, fair, blessed, holy + the mutated unaccented form of *mawr* great, large, found in this form in a number of placenames.

Gwythyr (m.) Welsh: traditional name derived in sub-Roman times from the Latin name VICTOR. A character with this name appears in the *Mabinogi*.

Variant: **Gwydyr**.

Gyles (m.) English: variant spelling of GILES.

György (m.) Hungarian form of GEORGE.

Győző (m.) Hungarian: name meaning 'conqueror', used as a loan translation of VICTOR.

Gytha (f.) English: from an Old English female personal name, a short form of various compound names containing the element *gyð* strife. This name was born in the 11th century by the wife of Godwin, Earl of Wessex. It was revived in Victorian times and has been occasionally used since then.

Gyula (m.) Hungarian form of JULIUS.

H

Habacuc (m.) Biblical name, meaning 'embrace' in Hebrew, borne by one of the twelve minor prophets, author of the book of the Bible that bears his name. The name is hardly, if ever, used in modern times, but was occasionally used by Puritans and Dissenters from the 17th century to the 19th.
Variant: **Habakkuk** (spelling used in the Authorized Version of the Bible).

Hadassah (f.) Jewish: Hebrew name (Esther 2: 7) of the biblical queen more commonly known by her Persian name ESTHER. It is sometimes used as a modern given name by Jews.
Short form: **Dassah**.

Hagen (m.) Danish form of HÅKAN.

Hagar (f.) Biblical name (meaning 'flight' in Hebrew, although the biblical character so called was Egyptian) borne by a handmaid of Abraham's wife Sarah. Sarah let Hagar conceive a child by Abraham since she herself was barren, but she later resented her and treated her so harshly that she fled. Hagar was sent back by an angel, and her son Ishmael became Abraham's first child.

Haidee (f.) English: as the name of a character in Byron's poem *Don Juan* (1819–24), this may have been intended to be connected with the classical Greek adjective *aidoios* modest. In modern use it is taken as a variant of HEIDI.

Håkan (m.) Swedish: from the Old Norse personal name *Hákon*, composed of the elements *hā* horse or high + *konr* son, descendant.
Variant: **Hakon** (an older form).
Cognates: Danish: **Hagen**. Norwegian: **Håkon**.

Hal (m.) English: short form of HARRY, of medieval origin. It was used by Shakespeare in *King Henry IV* as the name of the king's son, the future Henry V. Substitution of -*l* for -*r* has also occurred in derivatives of *Terry* (*Tel*), *Derek* (*Del*), and in girls' names such as Sally (from *Sarah*).

Haldor (m.) Scandinavian: from an Old Norse personal name composed of the element *hallr* rock + a derivative of the divine name *Þórr* Thor, the god of thunder.
Variant: **Halldor** (chiefly Norwegian).

Hale (m.) English: transferred use of the surname, originally a local name for someone living in a nook or recess (Old English *halh*).

Haley (f.) English: variant spelling of HAYLEY.

Halina (f.) Polish: of uncertain derivation. It seems to be a form of either GALINA or HELEN.

Hall (m.) English: transferred use of the surname, originally a local name for someone, usually a servant or retainer, who lived at a manor house (Old English *heall*).

Halle (m.) Scandinavian: short form of the names HALSTEN and HALVARD, or a pet form of HARALD.

Halsten (m.) Swedish: from an Old Norse personal name composed of the nearly synonymous elements *hallr* rock + *steinn* stone.
Variant: **Hallsten**.
Cognate: Norwegian: **Hallstein**.

Halvard (m.) Scandinavian: from an Old Norse personal name composed of the elements *hallr* rock + *varðr* guardian, watcher, defender.
Variants: **Halvor**; **Hallvard**, **Hallvor** (chiefly Norwegian); **Halvar** (Swedish).

Halvdan (m.) Scandinavian: from an Old Norse personal name, originally a byname for someone who was of partly Danish stock (from Old Norse *hálfr* half + the ethnic name *Danr*). The personal name was a relatively common one in the Viking period and lies behind the English surname *Haldane*.

Hamilton (m.) English (mainly U.S.) and Scottish: transferred use of the Scottish and American surname. Use as a given name seems to have begun in America in honour of Alexander Hamilton (?1757–1804), who was Secretary of the Treasury under George Washington and did much to establish the political and financial system on which the industrial growth and prosperity of the United States came to be founded. He was killed in a duel with the irascible Aaron Burr. The surname was brought to Scotland in or before the 13th century from a village (now deserted) called *Hamilton* or *Hameldune*, near Barkby in Leicestershire (named with the Old English elements *hamel* blunt, flat-topped, or crooked + *dun* hill). It became the surname of an enormously widespread and influential family, who acquired many titles, including the dukedom of Hamilton. The town near Glasgow so called is named after the family, not vice versa.

Hamish (m.) Scottish: Anglicized spelling of the vocative case, *Sheumais*, of the Gaelic version of JAMES; see SEUMAS.

Hana (f.) Czech: short form of JOHANA.

Handel (m.) From the surname of the composer, adopted as a given name particularly by the music-loving Welsh (cf. HAYDN). Georg Friedrich Handel (1685–1759), who came to England with George I when he succeeded to the English throne in 1714, is regarded as one of the greatest exponents of the baroque. His surname is derived from a diminutive form of the given name HANS.

Hank (m.) English: originally a medieval back-formation from *Hankin*, which is composed of *Han* (a short form of *Jehan* JOHN) + the Middle English diminutive suffix -*kin*. However, the suffix was mistaken for the Anglo-Norman diminutive -*in*, hence the form *Hank*. *Hank* is now sometimes used as an independent given name in America, where it is usually taken as a pet form of HENRY. It has more or less died out in Britain.

Hanke (m.) Low German: pet form from a short form of JOHAN.

Hannah (f.) Biblical: name of the mother of the prophet Samuel (1 Samuel 1: 2), Hebrew *Hanna*, from a Hebrew word meaning 'He (God) has favoured me (i.e. with a child)' (see ANNE). This form of the name was taken up as a given name by the Puritans in the 16th and 17th centuries, and has always been a common Jewish name.

Derivative: Polish: **Hania**.

Hanne (f.) German: short form of JOHANNA. The name is often used in combinations such as **Hannelore**.

Hannes (m.) Short form of *Johannes*, the Latin form of JOHN. It is found in Dutch, and is a common name in South Africa, where the Latin forms of names (such as *Jacobus*, *Petrus*, and *Stephanus*) are still very much in current use among Afrikaners.

Hanni (f.) Swiss: pet form of HANNE.

Hannibal (m.) English form of ANNIBALE, extremely rarely used as a given name.

Hannu (m.) A Finnish form of JOHN.

Hans (m.) German form of JOHN, derived from a shortened and contracted form of Latin *Johannes*.

Hansi (m.) (f.) German: **1.** (m.) Pet form of HANS. **2.** (f.) Less commonly, a pet form of JOHANNA, occasionally used as an independent given name, in line with other pet forms such as MAXI and MITZI.

Hansine (f.) German and Danish: feminine form of HANS, formed with the suffix seen in names such as *Wilhelmine* see WILHELMINA).

Hanuš (m.) Czech: pet form of JOHAN.

Variants: **Hanušek, Hanek, Nušek**.

Happy (f.) English: from the English vocabulary word, occasionally used in the 20th century for the sake of the good omen of its meaning; cf. MERRY and GAY.

Harald (m.) Scandinavian form of HAROLD. It has been popular in Norway, Sweden, and Denmark uninterruptedly from the time of the very earliest records, and was borne by several medieval kings of Norway and Denmark. Harald Fairhair (?850–933) was the first proper king of Norway, and presided over a remarkable period of Viking civilization. During his reign the first substantial wave of Scandinavian settlers migrated to Iceland.

Pet form: **Halle**.

Harbert (m.) Dutch form of HERBERT.

Variant: **Harbrecht**.

Harding (m.) English: transferred use of the surname, which is derived from a medieval English given name. The Old English form was *Hearding*, a derivative (originally patronymic in form) of *Heard* 'hardy, brave, strong', a byname or short form of the various compound personal names containing this element.

Harlan (m.) English (esp. U.S.): transferred use of the surname, originally a local name from any of various places in England, mostly named with the Old English elements *hara* hare + *land*. Use as a given name honours the American judge John Marshall Harlan (1833–1911), a conservative Republican who was nevertheless a pioneering supporter of civil rights in the Supreme Court.

Variant: **Harland**.

Harold (m.) English: from an Old English personal name composed of the elements *here* army + *weald* ruler, reinforced before the Norman Conquest by the Scandinavian cognate *Haraldr*, introduced by Norse settlers. The name was not common in the later Middle Ages, perhaps because it was associated with King Harold, the loser at the Battle of Hastings in 1066. It was revived in the 19th century, along with a number of other Old English names.

Cognates: Scandinavian: **Harald**. Scottish Gaelic: **Arailt, Haral**.

Harper (m.) (f.) English (mainly U.S.): transferred use of the surname, originally an occupational name for someone who played the harp. As a female name it has been borne in particular by the southern American writer Harper Lee, author of *To Kill a Mockingbird* (1960).

Harriet (f.) English: Anglicized form of French *Henriette*, a feminine diminutive of HENRY (French *Henri*) coined in the 17th century. It was quite common in England in the 18th and early 19th centuries. In Scotland it has been used as an Anglicized form of OIGHRIG.

Pet form: **Hattie**.

Harriette (f.) English: variant of HARRIET, probably coined to look more 'feminine', but it could be a reconstructed form, blending HARRIET with its source *Henriette*.

Harrison (m.) English: transferred use of the surname, which originated as a patronymic, meaning 'son of HARRY'.

Harry (m.) English: pet form of HENRY, sometimes used as an independent name. This was the usual English form of HENRY in the Middle Ages and later, and was the form used by Shakespeare as the familiar name of the mature King Henry V (compare HAL). The intermediate form *Herry* probably arose from the French pronunciation with a nasalized vowel, or it may be the result of straightforward assimilation; the change of *-er-* to *-ar-* was a regular feature of late Middle English.

Pet form: **Hal**.

Hartley (m.) English: transferred use of the surname, originally a local name from any of the numerous places so called. Most (for example, those in Berkshire, Dorset, Hampshire, and Kent) are so called from Old English *heorot* hart, male deer + *léah* wood or clearing. One in Northumbria is from *heorot* + *hlǽw* hill, and one in Cumbria is probably from *haraþ* wood + *clā* claw, i.e. river-fork.

Hartmann (m.) German: from an old Germanic personal name composed of the elements *hard* hardy, brave, strong + *man* man. The Blessed Hartmann (d. 1164) enjoyed a cult in Austria. Hartmann von Aue (*c*.1170–*c*.1220) was an influential writer of chivalric romances. See also ERDMANN.

Hartmut (m.) German: from an old Germanic personal name composed of the elements *hard* hardy, brave, strong + *muot* spirit, courage. See also ERDMUT.

Hartwig (m.) German: from an old Germanic personal name composed of the elements *hard* hardy, brave, strong + *wīg* battle. The Blessed Hartwig was archbishop of Salzburg 991–1023.

Hartwin (m.) German: from an old Germanic personal name composed of the elements *hard* hardy, brave, strong + *wine* friend.

Cognate: Italian: **Arduino**.

Harvey (m.) English: transferred use of the surname, which is of Breton origin, from a personal name composed of the elements *haer* battle + *vy* worthy. It was introduced to Britain by the Bretons who settled in East Anglia and elsewhere in the wake of the Norman Conquest.

Cognate: French: **Hervé** (a direct borrowing of the Breton personal name).

Short form: English: **Harv(e)**.

Haskel (m.) Jewish (U.S.): altered form of HESKEL, made to correspond with the non-Jewish surname *Haskel*, which is a medieval English derivative of the Old Norse personal name *Áskell*, composed of the elements *ás* god, divinity + *ketill* sacrificial cauldron.

Hattie (f.) English: pet form of HARRIET, now rarely used.

Hava (f.) Jewish: modern Hebrew form of EVE.

Havel (m.) Czech form of GAWEL.

Pet forms: **Háva**, **Havelek**, **Havlík**.

Haya (f.) Jewish: name meaning 'life' in Hebrew. It represents a feminine form of HYAM.

Haydn (m.) From the surname of the composer, adopted in his honour particularly by the music-loving Welsh (cf. HANDEL). Josef Haydn (1732–1809) was court composer and kapellmeister to the powerful Count Nicholas Esterhazy, and spent most of his working life at the Esterhazy palace near Vienna. His surname is a respelling of the nickname *Heiden* 'heathen' (Middle High German *heiden*, Old High German *heidano*).

Hayley (f.) English: transferred use of the surname, which derives from a placename, probably *Hailey* in Oxfordshire, which was originally named from Old English *hēg* hay + *lēah* clearing. Its use as a given name began only in the 1960s, inspired by the actress Hayley Mills, daughter of Sir John Mills and Mary Hayley Bell, but it has enjoyed great popularity since then.

Variant: **Haley**.

Hazel (f.) English: from the vocabulary word denoting the tree (Old English *hæsel*), or its light reddish-brown nuts. This is one of the most successful of the names coined in the 19th century from words denoting plants, and it has enjoyed continuous popularity. The fact that it also denotes an eye colour may have influenced its continuing choice.

Heather (f.) English: from the word denoting the hardy, brightly coloured plant (Middle English *hather*; the spelling was altered in the 18th century as a result of folk etymological association with *heath*). The name was first used in the late 19th century; it has been particularly popular since about 1950.

Hebe (f.) English (pronounced as two syllables): from a Greek name, a feminine form of + adjective *hēbos* young. This was borne in Greek mythology by a minor goddess who was a personification of youth. She was a daughter of Zeus and the wife of Hephaistos; it was her duty to act as cup-bearer to the gods. The name was taken up in England in the late 19th century, but it has fallen out of fashion again.

Heber (m.) **1**. Biblical: name, meaning 'enclave' in Hebrew, borne by various minor characters. This name has only occasionally been used outside Ireland (see below). **2**. Irish: from the Gaelic name **Éibhear**, assimilated in form to the biblical name. *Éibhir* was the name of the son of Míl, leader of the Gaelic race that, according to legend, first conquered Ireland. This is still a common given name among the McMahon families.

Hector (m.) **1**. English and Scottish (also French and Spanish): name borne in classical legend by the Trojan champion, who was killed by the Greek Achilles. His name (Greek *Hektōr*) seems to be an agent derivative of Greek *ekhein* to check, restrain. **2**. Scottish: Anglicized form of the Gaelic name EACHANN.

Cognates: Italian: **Ettore**. Portuguese: **Heitor**.
Pet form: Scottish: **Heckie**.
Feminine form: Scottish: **Hectorina**.

Hedda (f.) Scandinavian: pet form of HEDVIG. It is widely known in the English-speaking world as the name of the eponymous heroine of Henrik Ibsen's play *Hedda Gabler* (1890).

Cognate: Italian: **Edda**.

Heddwyn (m.) Welsh: modern coinage, composed of the elements *hedd* peace + *(g)wyn* white, fair, blessed, holy. Use as a given name was popularized by the fame of the young poet Ellis Humphrey Evans who posthumously won the bardic chair at the National Eisteddfod in 1917, having been killed in the First World War; his bardic name was *Hedd Wyn*.

Hedley (m.) English: transferred use of the surname, originally a local name from any of various places in Durham and Northumbria so called from Old English *hæþ* heather + *lēah* wood or clearing.

Hedvig (f.) Scandinavian form of HEDWIG, popular in Denmark, Norway, and Sweden. It is borne by the young girl who is the central character in Henrik Ibsen's play *The Wild Duck* (1886).

Hedwig (f.) German: from an old Germanic female personal name composed of the elements *hadu* contention + *wīg* war. The Blessed Hedwig or Hadwigis (d. *c*.887) was the Benedictine abbess of Herford in Westphalia.

Cognates: French: **Edwige**. Italian: **Edvige**. Scandinavian: **Hedvig**. Polish: JADWIGA.
Czech: **Hedvika**.
Pet form: Scandinavian: **Hedda**.

Heidi (f.) Swiss: pet form of ADELHEID, now also popular in the English-speaking world, as a result of the cult of Johanna Spyri's popular children's classic *Heidi* (1881).

Heike (f.) Low German: contracted pet form of HENRIKE. It has now attained a wider popularity in the German-speaking world as an independent given name.

Heikki (m.) Finnish form of HENRY.

Heiko (m.) Low German and Frisian: pet form of HENRIK.

Heilyn (m.) Welsh: traditional name, originally an occupational byname for a steward or wine-pourer, composed of the stem of the verb *heilio* to prepare, wait on + the diminutive suffix *-yn*. The name is borne in the *Mabinogi* by two characters: Heilyn the son of Gwynn the Old, and Heilyn the Red, son of Cadwgawn.

Heino (m.) German: from an old Germanic personal name, a short form of various names containing the element *heim* home, as for example *Heimbert* ('home famous') and *Heinrad* ('home counsel'). It has been revived in modern times as a pet form of HEINRICH.

Heinrich (m.) German form of HENRY.
Feminine form: **Heinrike**.

Heinz (m.) German: pet form of HEINRICH, used as such since the Middle Ages, and now extremely popular as a given name in its own right.

Heitor (m.) Portuguese form of HECTOR, which enjoys considerable popularity. It was borne, for example, by the Brazilian composer Heitor Villa-Lobos (1887–1959).

Heledd (f.) Welsh: traditional name of uncertain derivation. It was borne by a semi-legendary princess of the 7th century, in whose name a lament for her brother's death was composed in the 9th century.

Variant: **Hyledd**.

Helen (f.) English form of the name (Greek *Hēlénē*) borne in classical legend by the famous beauty, wife of Menelaus, whose seizure by the Trojan prince Paris sparked off the Trojan War. Her name is of uncertain origin; it may be connected with an element meaning 'ray, beam of the sun' cf. Greek *hēlios* sun. It has sometimes been taken as connected with the Greek word for 'Greek', *Hellēn*, but this is doubtful speculation. In the early Christian period the name was borne by the mother of the Emperor Constantine, who is usually known by the Latin version of her name, *Helena*. She is credited with having found the True Cross in Jerusalem. She was born in about 248, probably in Bithynia. However, in medieval England it was thought that she had been born in Britain, which greatly increased the popularity of the name there.

Variant: **Helena** (Latinate form, used also in Germany, the Netherlands, Scandinavia, and E. Europe).

Cognates: Irish Gaelic: **Léan**. Scottish Gaelic: **Eilidh**. French: **Hélène**. Italian, Spanish, Portuguese: **Elena**. German: **Helene**. Romanian: **Ileana**. Russian: **Yelena**. Ukrainian: **Olena**. Hungarian: **Ilona**. See also ELLEN and ELEN.

Short forms: German, Dutch, Scandinavian: **Lena**. German, Dutch: **Lene**.

Helfgott (m.) German: reversed variant of GOTTHELF. Among Jews this given name has been popular as a translation of the Hebrew names AZRIEL or ELIEZER.

Helga (f.) German and Scandinavian: feminine form of HELGE. It was introduced to England before the Conquest, but did not survive long. It has been reintroduced to the English-speaking world in the 20th century from Scandinavia and Germany.

Variant: **Hella**.

Helge (m.) Scandinavian: from an early medieval personal name, a derivative of the adjective *heilagr* prosperous, successful (from Old Norse *heill* hale, hearty, happy). The word later developed the meaning 'blessed, holy', with the result that the name seemed a particularly suitable choice to give expression to pious hopes.

Variant: **Helje** (Danish).

Hella (f.) German and Scandinavian: assimilated variant of HELGA.

Helma (f.) German: short form of HELMINE, or an independently formed Latinate feminine derivative of WILHELM.

Helmfried (m.) German: from an old Germanic personal name composed of the elements *helm* helmet, protection + *fred*, *frid* peace.

Variants: **Helmfrid**, **Helfried**.

Helmine (f.) German: short form of WILHELMINA.

Helmut (m.) German: from an old Germanic personal name composed of the elements *helm* helmet, protection + *muot* spirit, courage. Although both these elements are well attested in other names from the earliest times, this particular combination does not seem to occur before the late Middle Ages. It continues to be an extremely popular and widespread German given name.

Variant: **Helmuth**.

Héloïse (f.) French: variant of ÉLOISE, which enjoyed a revival of popularity in the 18th century after publication of Rousseau's philosophical novel *La Nouvelle Héloïse* (1761).

Hemming (m.) Scandinavian: of disputed origin, probably a derivative of Old Norse *hamr* shape, in which case it could have been a byname for a 'shape changer' or werewolf.

Hendrik (m.) Dutch and Scandinavian form of HENRY.

Henning (m.) Low German and Danish: derivative (originally patronymic in form) of a short form of HENRIK and also of *Johannes* (see JOHN).

Henri (m.) French form of HENRY.

Henrietta (f.) English: Latinate form of French *Henriette*, a feminine diminutive of HENRI. This form of the name enjoyed a vogue from the late 19th century until well into the 20th century. In Scotland it has been used as an Anglicized form of OIGHRIG. See also HARRIET.

Pet forms: **Hettie**, **Hattie**.

Henrik (m.) Low German, Scandinavian, and Hungarian form of HENRY. It has enjoyed great popularity in recent years, especially in Denmark.

Pet forms: Low German: **Heiko**, **Henning**. Danish: **Henning**.

Henrike (f.) German: feminine form of HEINRICH.

Pet form: Low German: **Heike**.

Henry (m.) English: a perennially enduring given name, of Continental Germanic origin, composed of the elements *haim* home + *rīc* power, ruler. It was introduced to Britain by the Normans, and has been borne by eight kings of England. In its various European cognate forms and in the Latin form *Henricus*, it has been borne by kings and princes in many countries of Europe. Henry the Fowler (*c.*876–936), Duke of Saxony, was elected King of the Germans and became the first of a long succession of bearers of the name to rule in central Europe. It was also borne by six kings of France and four kings of Castile and Leon. In England it was not until the 17th century that the form *Henry* (rather than HARRY) became the standard vernacular form, mainly as a result of the influence of Latin *Henricus* and French *Henri*.

Cognates: Irish Gaelic: **Anraí**, **Éinri**. Scottish Gaelic: **Eanraig**. French: **Henri**. Italian: **Enrico**. Spanish: **Enrique**. Catalan: **Enric**. Portuguese: **Henrique**. Romanian: **Henric**. German: **Heinrich**. Low German: **Hinrich**. Dutch: **Hendrik**. Scandinavian: **Hen(d)rik**. Polish: **Henryk**. Czech: **Jindřich**. Finnish: **Heikki**. Hungarian: **Henrik**; See also IMRE.

Pet forms: English: **Hal**, **Hank**, **Harry**. Spanish: **Quique**. German: **Heino**, **Heinz**. Low German: **Heiko**, **Henning**. Danish: **Henning**.

Hephzibah (f.) Biblical name meaning 'my delight is in her (i.e. a new-born daughter)'. This was borne by the wife of Hezekiah, King of Judah; she was the mother of Manasseh (2 Kings 21). It is also used in the prophecies of Isaiah as an allusive name for the land of Israel (cf. BEULAH).

Variant: **Hepzibah**.

Herb (m.) English: short form of HERBERT, used especially in the United States.

Pet form: **Herbie**.

Herbert (m.) English, German, and French: of Continental Germanic origin, introduced to Britain by the Normans. It is composed of the elements *heri, hari* army + *berht* bright, famous. A form of this name (*Herebeorht*) existed in England before the Conquest, at which time it was replaced by the Continental form introduced by the Normans. This gave rise to an important surname. The family were earls of Pembroke in the 16th and 17th centuries, and the poet George Herbert was a member of the family. By the end of the Middle Ages *Herbert* was little used as a given name, and its greater frequency in Britain from the 19th century onwards owes something to the trend for the revival of medieval names of Germanic origin and something to the trend for the transferred use of surnames.

Variant: German: **Heribert**.
Cognate: Dutch: **Harbert**.
Short form: English: **Herb**.
Pet form: English: **Herbie**.

Hercules (m.) Latin form of the name of the Greek mythological hero *Herakles*, whose name means 'glory of Hera'. He was the son of Zeus, king of the gods, by Alcmene, a mortal woman. In many versions of the legend, despite the meaning of the name, Hera, chief goddess in the Greek pantheon and wife of Zeus, is portrayed as the implacable enemy of Hercules, the child of her unfaithful husband. Hercules was noted for his exceptional physical strength; according to the myth, he was set a daunting series of twelve labours, and after successfully completing them he was made a god. The name has occasionally been used in the English-speaking world, under European influence. In the Highlands of Scotland it has been used as an Anglicized form of the rare Gaelic name **Athairne**.

Derivatives: French: **Hercule**. Italian: **Ercole**.

Heribert (m.) German: historical form of HERBERT, currently undergoing a modest revival.

Herleif (m.) Scandinavian: from an Old Norse personal name composed of the elements *herr* army + *leifr* heir, descendant.

Variants: **Härlief**; **Herlof**; **Herluf** (Danish form).

Herlindis (f.) Dutch: of Germanic origin, composed of the elements *heri, hari* army + *lind* weak, tender, soft. St Herlindis (d. *c.*745) was the first abbess of Aldeneyck on the Meuse; she was succeeded by her sister Relindis.

Cognates: German: **Herlinde** (not a common given name). Spanish: **Herlinda**.

Herman (m.) English form of HERMANN. The name was in use among the Normans, and enjoyed a limited revival in Britain in the 19th century, when it also became common in America, most probably as a result of the influence of German settlers.

Hermann (m.) German: from an old Germanic personal name composed of the elements *heri, hari* army + *man* man. The given name was popular in the 19th century, when it was widely believed to have been borne by the early Teutonic national leader *Arminius* the Cheruscan, mentioned by Tacitus (see ARMIN).

Cognate: Italian: **Ermanno**.

Hermenegildo (m.) Spanish and Portuguese: of Germanic (Visigothic) origin, composed of the elements *ermen, irmen* whole, entire + *gild* sacrifice. St Hermenigild (d. 585) was a son of the Visigothic king Leovigild; he is considered a martyr, though the reasons behind the revolt against his father which led to his death were at least as much political as religious.

Variant: **Ermenegildo**.
Cognates: Italian: **Ermenegildo**. French: **Ermenegilde**.

Hermia (f.) Latinate derivative of the name of the Greek god *Hermes* (cf. HERMIONE). This was used by Shakespeare for the name of a character in *A Midsummer Night's Dream* (1595). The name is occasionally also used in Germany, where it is taken as a Latinate version of HERMINE.

Hermine (f.) German: feminine form of HERMANN, formed on the lines of *Wilhelmine* (see WILHELMINA). The name is now also used in France.

Hermione (f.) Name borne in classical mythology by a daughter of Helen and Menelaus, who grew up to marry her cousin Orestes. It is evidently a derivative of *Hermes*, name of the messenger god, but the formation is not clear. The name was used by Shakespeare for one of the main characters in *A Winter's Tale*, and is still occasionally used in the 20th century.

Hernán (m.) Spanish form of FERDINAND, a variant of FERNÁN.

Hernando (m.) Spanish form of FERDINAND, regular in the Middle Ages, but now much less common than FERNANDO.

Hershel (m.) Jewish (Yiddish): pet form of HIRSH, derived from a dialect variant.

Variants: **Herschel**, **Heshel**, **Heshi**.

Hertha (f.) German: apparently the result of a misreading of the name of the Germanic goddess *Nertha* (cf. NJORD), mentioned by the Roman historian Tacitus. For a similar 'accidental' coining, cf. IMOGEN.

Variant: **Herta**.

Hervé (m.) French (originally Breton) form of HARVEY.

Heshel (m.) Jewish (Yiddish): variant of HERSHEL. The form **Heshi** is also found.

Heskel (m.) Jewish: Yiddish form of EZEKIEL. See also HASKEL.

Hesketh (m.) English: transferred use of the surname, originally a local name from any of the various places in northern England named with the Old Norse elements *hestr* horse + *skeiðr* racecourse. Horse racing and horse fighting were favourite sports among the Scandinavian settlers in England.

Hester (f.) English: variant of ESTHER, of medieval origin. For a long while the two forms were interchangeable, the addition or dropping of *h*- being commonplace in a whole range of words, but now they are generally regarded as two distinct names.

Hettie (f.) English: pet form of HENRIETTA and occasionally also of HESTER, now rarely used either as such or as an independent name.

Hewie (m.) Scottish and N. English: variant spelling of HUGHIE.

Hieronymus (m.) Latinate form of JEROME, still used in Germany, especially in Catholic Bavaria and in the north German Rhineland.

Hilary (m., f.) English: from the medieval form of the (post-classical) Latin masculine name *Hilarius* (a derivative of *hilaris* cheerful) and its feminine form *Hilaria*. From the Middle Ages onwards, the name was borne principally by men (in honour of the 4th-century theologian St Hilarius of Poitiers). Now, however, it is more commonly given to girls.

Variant: **Hillary**.

Cognates (all masculine): Welsh: **Ilar**. French: **Hilaire**. Italian: **Ilario**. Spanish, Portuguese: **Hilario**. Russian: **Ilari**. See also VIDOR.

Hilda (f.) English, German, Dutch, and Scandinavian: of Germanic origin, a Latinized short form of any of several female names containing the element *hild* battle (e.g. HILDEGARD). Many of these are found in both Continental Germanic and Old English forms. St Hilda (614–80) was a Northumbrian princess who founded the abbey at Whitby and became its abbess. *Hilda* was a popular name in England both before and after the Norman Conquest. Its popularity waned in Tudor times, but it never quite died out, and was strongly revived in the 19th century.

Variants: English: **Hylda**. German: **Hilde**.

Cognate: Hungarian: **Ildikó**.

Masculine forms: Dutch: **Hild**, **Hildo**.

Hildebrand (m.) German: from an old Germanic personal name composed of the elements *hild* battle + *brand* (flaming) sword. The name was borne by a saint (*c*.1020–85) who became pope under the name of Gregory VII.

Hildegard (f.) German, Scandinavian, and English: from an old Germanic female personal name composed of the elements *hild* battle + *gard* enclosure. It was borne by the second wife of Charlemagne and by the mystical writer Hildegard of Bingen (1098–1179).

Hillel (m.) Jewish: Hebrew name (apparently derived from the Hebrew word meaning 'praise') borne in the Bible by the father of one of the Judges of Israel (Judges 12: 13). It was also the name of an outstanding 1st-century rabbi and has been a popular Jewish name as a result of his fame.

Hillevi (f.) Danish: reworking of the rare German name **Heilwig**, which is composed of the Germanic elements *heil* whole, safe + *wīg* war. The name is now also more widely used in Scandinavia.

Hilppa (f.) Finnish form of PHILIPPA.

Hiltraud (f.) German: from an old Germanic female personal name composed of the elements *hild* battle + *trūd* strength. St Hiltrude (d. *c*.790) was a Benedictine nun who lived as a recluse near Liesses.

Variant: **Hiltrud**.

Hinde (f.) Jewish: from Yiddish *hinde* hind, female deer (modern German *Hinde*), originally an affectionate pet name or female equivalent of HIRSH.

Hinrich (m.) Low German form of HEINRICH.

Hippolyte (m.) French: from Greek *Hippolytos*, composed of the elements *hippos* horse + *lyein* to loose, free. The name was borne by several early saints, including an important 3rd-century ecclesiastical writer. In classical legend it had been borne by an unfortunate youth who was the object of his stepmother's love and met his death in a chariot accident. The popularity of the name in France was increased by the use of the legend as the subject of a tragedy by Racine (1677).

Cognates: Italian: **Ippolito**. Spanish, Portuguese: **Hipolito**. Catalan: **Hipòlit**, **Pòlit**.

Hiram (m.) Biblical name, borne by a king of Tyre who is repeatedly mentioned in the Bible (2 Samuel 2: 11; 1 Kings 5; 9: 11; 10: 11; 1 Chronicles 14: 1; 2 Chronicles 2: 11) as supplying wood, craftsmen, and money to enable David and Solomon to construct various buildings. It was also the name of a craftsman of Tyre who worked in brass for Solomon (1 Kings 7: 13). The name is presumably of Semitic origin, but is probably a Phoenician name; if it is Hebrew, it may be an aphetic form of *Ahiram* 'brother of the exalted'. In England, the name was taken up by the Puritans in the 17th century, but soon dropped out of use again. It is still used in America.

Hirsh (m.) Jewish: from a Yiddish vocabulary word meaning 'hart, deer' (modern German *Hirsch*). See also ZVI.

Variant: **Hirsch**.

Hjalmar (m.) Scandinavian: from an Old Norse personal name composed of the elements *hjálmr* helmet, protection + *herr* army, warrior. The name was revived towards the end of the 18th century, and for this reason it did not undergo the usual Swedish development, which would yield **Hjälmar** (a form which, however, now also occurs).

Hjördis (f.) Scandinavian: from an Old Norse female personal name composed of the elements *hjorr* sword + *dis* goddess.

Holger (m.) Scandinavian: from an Old Norse personal name composed of the elements *hólmr* island + *geirr* spear. The name was borne by a character of medieval romance, one of Charlemagne's generals, known in English as *Ogier* the Dane. One tale about him is that he quarrelled with the emperor after Charlemagne's son Charlot had killed his own son. He was flung into prison, but agreed to lead an army against the attacking Saracens on condition that Charlot was handed over to him. When this request was granted he spared his life, won a great victory, and was reconciled with Charlemagne and richly rewarded by him. This form of the name results from mediation through Old French sources, where it fell together with a different Germanic name having the first element *odal* riches, prosperity, fortune.

Pet form: **Hogge**.

Hollie (f.) English: variant spelling of HOLLY, altered in accordance with the vague convention that spellings in *-ie* are more appropriate for girls.

Holly (f.) English: from the vocabulary word denoting the evergreen shrub or tree (Middle English *holi(n)*, Old English *holegn*). The name was first used at the beginning of the 20th century, and has been particularly popular since about 1960. It is bestowed especially on girls born around Christmas, when sprigs of holly are traditionally taken indoors to decorate rooms.

Variant: HOLLIE.

Homer (m.) English (esp. U.S.): the usual English form of the name of the Greek epic poet *Homēros*, now regularly used as a given name in America (cf. VIRGIL). Many theories have been put forward to explain the ancient Greek name of the poet, but none is conclusive. It is identical in form with the Greek vocabulary word *homēros* hostage.

Honey (f.) English: from the vocabulary word, Old English *huneg*. Honey was used throughout the Middle Ages in place of sugar (which was only introduced from the New World in the 16th century), and the word has long been used as an expression of endearment. Its modern life as a given name was prompted by use as such in Margaret Mitchell's novel *Gone* *with the Wind*, which was made into a film in 1939, the enormous popularity of which yielded several other modern given names, such as SCARLETT and RHETT.

Honore (f.) French form of HO ORIA, also used occasionally in the English-speaking world.

Honoré (m.) French: from the Late Latin name *Hono tus* meaning 'honoured', borne by various early saints, including Honoratus of Toulouse (3rd century), Honoratus of Arles (d. 429), and Honoratus of Amiens (d. *c*.600).

Honoria (f.) Feminine form of the Late Latin male name *Honorius* (a derivative of *honor* honour), which was borne by various early saints, including a 7th-century archbishop of Canterbury. It is occasionally used in the English-speaking world as an elaborated form of HONOUR.

Honorine (f.) French: from the Late Latin name *Honorina*, a derivative of HONORIA. St Honorina was one of the early martyrs of Gaul, but nothing is known of her life.

Honour (f.) English: from the vocabulary word *honour* (via Old French from Latin *honor*). The name was popular with the Puritans in the 17th century and has survived to the present day.

Variants: ono esp. U.S.); **Ho ora** esp. Ireland; cf. NORA.

Hope (f.) English: from the vocabulary word *hope* (Old English *hopa*), denoting the quality, in particular the Christian quality of expectation in the resurrection and in eternal life. The name was created by the Puritans and has been one of their most successful coinages. The given name is still fairly common, and has its existence independently of the vocabulary word. It has probably been reinforced by transferred use of the surname *Hope*, which is derived from the dialect term *hope* meaning 'enclosed valley' (Old English *hop*).

Hopkin (m.) English and Welsh: transferred use of the surname, now found mainly in Wales. It is derived from a medieval given name, a pet form (with the hypocoristic suffix *-kin*) of *Hob*, which is a short form of ROBERT that probably had its origin through English mishearing of the Norman pronunciation of *R-*.

Variant: **Hopcyn** (a Welsh spelling).

Horace (m.) English and French: from the old Roman family name HORATIUS. The name was once widely used among admirers of the Roman poet Horace (Quintus Horatius Flaccus), but it is at present out of fashion. See also HORATIO.

Cognate: Italian: **Orazio**.

Horatia (f.) Feminine form of Latin HORATIUS. It has never been common in the English-speaking world, but was borne, for example, by the daughter of Horatio, Lord Nelson.

Horatio (m.) English: variant of HORACE, influenced by the Latin form HORATIUS and the Italian form *Orazio*. *Horatio* has occasionally been used in the English-speaking world; for example, it was borne by the admiral Horatio Nelson (1758–1805)

Horatius (m.) Latin: an old Roman family name, which is of obscure, possibly Etruscan, origin. Its most famous bearer by far was the Roman poet Quintus Horatius Flaccus (65–8 BC), gene ly nown in English as HORACE. From the mid-19th century, the name has occasionally been used by English speakers in its original Latin form. This probably owes more to the *Lays of Ancient Rome* (1842) by Thomas Babbington Macaulay than to the poet Horace. Macaulay relates, in verse that was once

popular, the exploit of an early Roman hero, recounting 'How Horatius kept the bridge'.

Hořek (m.) Czech: pet form of *Řehoř*, the Czech form of GREGORY.

Variant: **Hořík**.

Horst (m.) Low German: apparently from the vocabulary word *horst* wood, wooded hill (cf. Old English *hyrst*, which lies behind the many English placenames in *-hurst*). It is not clear why this should have given rise to a given name; an alternative suggestion is that it may derive from the Old Saxon personal name *Horsa* 'horse', altered by association with the related *Hengist* 'stallion'. (Hengist and Horsa were 5th-century leaders of the first Germanic settlers in England.) The name *Horst* is first recorded in the 15th century; it is now quite common throughout the German-speaking world.

Hortense (f.) French form of Latin *Hortensia*, the feminine version of the old Roman family name *Hortensius*. This is of uncertain origin, but may be derived from Latin *hortus* garden. The given name began to be used in the English-speaking world in the 19th century, but is not common today.

Howard (m.) English: transferred use of the surname of an English noble family. The surname has a large number of possible origins, but in the case of the noble family early forms often have the spelling *Haward*, and so it is probably from a Scandinavian personal name composed of the elements *hā* high + *ward* guardian. (The traditional derivation from the Old English name *Hereweard* 'army guardian' is untenable.)

Howell (m.) English and Welsh: Anglicized form of the Welsh name HYWEL, or a transferred use of the surname derived from that name.

Hrothgar (m.) Old English cognate form of ROGER. The name is borne in the Old English narrative poem *Beowulf* by the Danish king who suffered the depredations of the monster Grendel for twelve years. In modern times it has been borne by Hrothgar J. Habakkuk (b. 1915), a former vice-chancellor of Oxford University.

Hubert (m.) English, French, German, and Dutch: of Germanic origin, composed of the elements *hug* heart, mind, spirit + *berht* bright, famous. It was popular among the Normans, who introduced it to Britain, where it was later reinforced by settlers from the Low Countries. An 8th-century St Hubert succeeded St Lambert as bishop of Maastricht and is regarded as the patron of hunters, since, like St Eustace, he is supposed to have seen a vision of Christ crucified between the antlers of a stag; he is sometimes called 'the apostle of the Ardennes'. The name is at present somewhat out of fashion.

Variants: German: **Huppert**, **Hupprecht**. Dutch: **Hubrecht**, **Hubertus**.

Short forms: Dutch: **Huub**, **Huib**.

Hugh (m.) English: of Germanic origin, brought to Britain by the Normans. It is derived from the element *hug* heart, mind, spirit. Originally, the name was a short form of various compound names containing this element. Little Hugh of Lincoln was a child supposed in the Middle Ages to have been murdered by Jews in about 1255, a legend responsible for several outbursts of anti-Semitism at various times. The story is referred to by Chaucer in *The Prioress's Tale*. He is not to be confused with St Hugh of Lincoln (1140–1200), bishop of Lincoln (1186–1200), who was noted for his charity and good works, his piety, and his defence of the Church against the State.

In Scotland and Ireland this has been used as an Anglicized form of the Gaelic names AODH, ÙISDEAN, and sometimes EÓGHAN.

Variant: **Hugo** (Latinized; also used in Dutch and German).
Cognates: French: HUGUES. Italian: **Ugo**. Welsh: **Huw**.
Feminine form: Scottish: **Hughina**.

Hughie (m.) **1**. English: pet form of HUGH. **2**. Scottish: Anglicized form of the Gaelic name **Eódhnag**, a derivative of *Adhamhnan* (see EUNAN).

Variant: **Hewie**.

Hugues (m.) French form of HUGH. This name was borne by Hugues Capet (?938–96), ruler of France (987–96) and founder of the Capetian dynasty.

Huguette (f.) French: feminine diminutive form of HUGUES.

Variant: **Huette**.

Hùisdean (m.) Scottish Gaelic: variant of ÙISDEAN.

Hulda (f.) **1**. Biblical name (meaning 'weasel' in Hebrew) borne by a prophetess who foretold to Josiah the destruction of Jerusalem (2 Kings 22). **2**. Swedish: 18th-century derivation from the adjective *huld* sweet, lovable. The name has also been adopted in Denmark, Norway, and Germany.

Variant (of 1): **Huldah**.

Humbert (m.) English, French, and German: of Germanic origin, introduced to Britain by the Normans. It is composed of the elements *hun* bear-cub, warrior + *berht* bright, famous. It was not common in Britain in the Middle Ages, and has always had a Continental flavour. It was used by Vladimir Nabokov for the name of the demented pederast, Humbert Humbert, who is the narrator in his novel *Lolita* (1955). This has no doubt contributed to its demise as a given name in the English-speaking world.

Cognate: Italian: UMBERTO.

Humphrey (m.) English: of Germanic origin, introduced to Britain by the Normans. It is composed of the elements *hun* bear-cub, warrior + *fred*, *frid* peace. A form of this name (*Hunfrith*) existed in England before the Conquest, but it was replaced by the Norman Continental version *Hunfrid*. The spelling with -*ph*- reflects classicizing influence. It has always enjoyed a modest popularity in England. Perhaps its best known bearer was the Duke of Gloucester (1391–1447), youngest son of King Henry IV, known as 'Duke Humphrey'. He was noted as a patron of literature, and founded what is now

part of the Bodleian Library at Oxford. In Ireland this has been used as an Anglicized form of Gaelic AMHLAOIBH.

Variant: **Humphry**.
Cognate: Welsh: **Wmffre**.
Pet form: English: **Huffie**.

Huub (m.) Dutch: short form of HUBERT.

Huw (m.) Welsh form of HUGH, now sometimes also used in other parts of the English-speaking world.

Hyacinth (f.) English form of the name borne in classical mythology by a beautiful youth (*Hyakinthos* in Greek, *Hyacinthus* in Latin) who was accidentally killed by Apollo and from whose blood sprang a flower bearing his name (not the modern hyacinth, but a type of dark lily). The name was later borne by various early saints, principally one martyred in the 3rd century with his brother Protus. This gave encouragement to its use as a male name in Christian Europe, including, occasionally, Britain. However, in Britain at the end of the 19th century there was a vogue for coining new female names from vocabulary words denoting plants and flowers (e.g. DAISY, IVY). *Hyacinth* accordingly came to be regarded as an exclusively female name. It has never been common. However, the Spanish, Portuguese, and Polish cognates given below are still used as male names.

Cognates (masculine): Spanish, Portuguese: **Jacinto**. Polish: JACENTY.
Pet form: Polish: JACEK.

Hyam (m.) Jewish: from the Hebrew word *hayyim* life. Several different transliterations are in use; another common one is CHAIM. This name is sometimes added to the existing name of a seriously ill person during prayers for his recovery.

Hylda (f.) English: variant spelling of HILDA.

Hyledd (f.) Welsh: variant of HELEDD.

Hyman (m.) Jewish: altered form of HYAM, influenced by the common Yiddish name element *man* man.

Variant: **Hymen** (altered form, perhaps under the influence of *Hymen* in Latin and Greek, which was the name of the god of marriage).

Hymie (m.) Jewish: pet form of HYMAN or HYAM.

Hywel (m.) Welsh: traditional name, originally a byname from a vocabulary word meaning 'eminent, conspicuous'. This name was common in the Middle Ages and lies behind the Anglicized surname *Howell*. In the 20th century it has been revived and now enjoys great popularity.

Variants: **Hywell**; **Howell** (Anglicized).

I

Iagan (m.) Scottish Gaelic: modern spelling of *Aodhagán*, a diminutive form of AODH (cf. EGAN). From this given name is derived the surname *Mac Iagain*, Anglicized as *MacKeegan*.

Iaione (f.) Basque equivalent of NATIVIDAD.

Ian (m.) Scottish version of JOHN, now very widely used as an independent given name in the broader English-speaking world, where it has largely lost its connection both with Scotland and with *John*. The Gaelic form **Iain** is popular in Scotland.

Iarlaith (m.) Irish Gaelic: name composed of the elements *ior*, of uncertain meaning, + *flaith* prince, leader.
Anglicized form: JARLATH.

Ib (m.) Danish: relatively common name, attested since the Middle Ages, probably a vernacular development of JACOB (via *Jep*).

Ida (f.) English: originally a Norman name, of Germanic origin, derived from the element *id* work. This died out during the later Middle Ages. It was revived in the 19th century, mainly as a result of its use in Tennyson's *The Princess* (1847) as the name of the central character, who devotes herself to the cause of women's rights and women's education in a thoroughly Victorian way. The name is also associated with Mount Ida in Crete, which was connected in classical times with the worship of Zeus, king of the gods, who was supposed to have been brought up in a cave on the mountainside.

Idony (f.) English: medieval name derived from the Old Norse female personal name *Iðunnr*, which is also the name of a goddess in Old Norse mythology. It is probably a derivative of the element *ið* again: Iðunnr was in charge of the gods' apples of eternal youth. The name has sometimes been Latinized as **Idonea**, as if from the feminine form of the Latin adjective *idoneus* suitable.

Idoya (f.) Spanish: name assumed in honour of the Virgin of *Idoia*, a place in the Basque country so called from an element meaning 'pool' or 'pond'.

Idris (m.) Welsh: traditional name composed of the elements *iud* lord + *rīs* ardent, impulsive. It was common in the Middle Ages and earlier, and has been strongly revived since the late 19th century.

Idwal (m.) Welsh: traditional name composed of the elements *iud* lord, master + *(g)wal* wall, rampart.

Idzi (m.) Polish form of GILES.

Iestyn (m.) Welsh form of JUSTIN, occasionally used in modern times.

Ieuan (m.) The original Welsh form of JOHN, from Latin *Johannes*. Later forms are **Iefan** (Anglicized as EVAN) and **Ifan**.

Ifor (m.) Welsh: traditional name of uncertain derivation. It has sometimes been Anglicized as IVOR, but there is in origin no connection between the two names.

Ignatius (m.) Late Latin name, derived from the old Roman family name *Egnatius* (of uncertain origin, possibly Etruscan). This was altered in the early Christian period by association with Latin *ignis* fire. It was borne by various early saints, and more recently by St Ignatius Loyola (1491–1556), who founded the Society of Jesus (the Jesuits). In the modern English-speaking world it seems to be used exclusively by Roman Catholics. In Ireland it has been used as an Anglicized form of the Gaelic name *Eighneachán* (see AENEAS).
Derivatives: French: **Ignace**. Italian: **Ignazio**. Spanish: **Ignacio**. German: **Ignatz**. Dutch: **Ignaas**. Polish: **Ignacy**. Czech: **Ignác**. Basque: **Iñaki**. See also INIGO.
Short form: Spanish: **Nacio**.
Pet forms: Spanish: **Nacho**. Polish: **Ignacek**, **Nacek**. Czech: **Ignáček**, **Nác(íč)ek**.

Igor (m.) Russian: variant form of IVOR, one of the names taken to Russia at the time of the first Scandinavian settlement of Kiev in the 9th century (cf. OLEG, OLGA, and RURIK).

Ike (m.) English: pet form of ISAAC. However, it was made famous in the 20th century as the nickname of the American general and president Dwight D. Eisenhower (1890–1969), in whose case it was based on the surname.

Ikerne (f.) Basque equivalent of VISITACIÓN.

Ilana (f.) Modern Jewish name, meaning 'tree' in Hebrew.
Masculine form: **Ilan**.

Ilar (m.) Welsh form of the male name HILARY.

Ilari (m.) Russian form of the male name HILARY.

Ilario (m.) Italian form of the male name HILARY.

Ilayne (f.) English: apparently a fanciful respelling of ELAINE.

Ildikó (f.) Hungarian: a derivative of German *Hilde* (see HILDA).

Ileana (f.) Romanian form of HELEN.

Ilene (f.) English: apparently a fanciful respelling of EILEEN.

Ilie (m.) Romanian form of *Elias* (see ELLIS).
Feminine form: **Ilinca**.

Ilka (f.) Hungarian: pet form of ILONA.

Illarion (m.) Russian: from Greek *Hilarion*, a derivative of *Hilarios* (see HILARY). St Hilarion (*c*.291–*c*.371) was a famous hermit born at Gaza in Palestine; he desired to live a solitary, contemplative life, but was continually forced to move on by the crowds that flocked to follow him.

Illtud (m.) Welsh: traditional name composed of the elements *il*, *el* multitude + *tud* land, people. The name was borne by a famous Welsh saint (d. *c*.505) who founded the abbey of Llantwit (originally *Llan-Illtut* 'church of Illtud').
Variant: **Illtyd** (a modern spelling).

Ilona (f.) Hungarian form of HELEN, now also sometimes used in the English-speaking world.
Pet form: **Ilka**.

Ilse (f.) German: short form of ELIZABETH.

Ilya (m.) Russian form of *Elias* (see ELLIS).

Imanol (m.) Basque form of EMMANUEL.

Imelda (f.) Italian and Spanish: of Germanic origin. It seems to be composed of the elements *irm(en)*, *erm(en)* whole, entire + *hild* battle.

Imke (f.) Low German: pet form of **Imma**, an assimilated byform of IRMA. *Imke* is now quite widely used as an independent given name in northern Germany.

Immacolata (f.) Italian: name reflecting a title of the Blessed Virgin Mary, *Maria Immacolata*, referring to the doctrine of her Immaculate Conception; cf. CONCEPCIÓN. The name is also sometimes used by Roman Catholics in the English-speaking world.

Immaculata (f.) Latin form of IMMACOLATA, used in Ireland by Roman Catholics.

Immanuel (m.) Variant of EMMANUEL, used in the Old Testament. This is the usual German form of the name, and was borne, for example, by the philosopher Immanuel Kant (1724–1804). In the English-speaking world this spelling in particular is generally a Jewish name.

Imogen (f.) English: the name owes its existence to a character in Shakespeare's *Cymbeline* (1609), but in earlier accounts of the events on which the play is based this character is named as *Innogen*. The modern form of the name is thus due to a misreading of these sources by Shakespeare, or of the play's text by his printer. The name *Innogen* is of Celtic origin, probably connected with Gaelic *inghean* girl, maiden.

Imre (m.) Hungarian form of the Germanic name *Emeric* or *Emmerich*. This seems to be a byform of HENRY, but it has possibly also absorbed a rarer name composed of the elements *amal* work + *rīc* rule. St Emeric (1007–31) was the son and heir of St Stephen of Hungary. In spite of his comparatively short life, he was canonized together with his father in 1063.

Ina (f.) English and Scottish: short form of any of the various female names ending in this syllable (often a Latinate feminine suffix), for example CHRISTINA, GEORGINA, KATRINA. Scottish examples include DOLINA and *Murdina* (see MURDO); the pronunciation is usually /-aɪnə/ rather than /-iːnə/ as in England.

Iñaki (m.) Basque form of IGNATIUS.

Indalecio (m.) Spanish: from Latin *Indaletius*, a name of obscure derivation. St Indaletius was a 1st-century evangelist of Spain who worked principally at Urci in Almería and is believed to have died a martyr.

India (f.) English: presumably from the name of the subcontinent, and apparently taken into regular use as a result of its occurence in Margaret Mitchell's novel *Gone with the Wind* (1936), which contributed a remarkable number of given names to the English language. In the case of India Hicks, Lord Mountbatten's granddaughter, the name was chosen because of her family's association with, and affection for, India.

Inés (f.) Spanish form of AGNES. The name is now also used, without the accent, in the English-speaking world.

Inês (f.) Portuguese form of AGNES; cf. INÉS.

Inga (f.) Swedish: short form of the various female names of Old Norse origin containing as their first element the name of the fertility god *Ing*, as, for example, INGEBORG, INGEGERD, and INGRID. It is now widely used as an independent given name.

Inge (f., m.) **1.** (f.) German and Danish: short form of INGEBORG or, in the case of Danish, of any of the other female Scandinavian names with *Ing(e)-* as a first element. **2.** (m.) Swedish: short form of various male names, such as INGEMAR and INGVAR, with *Ing(e)-* as a first element.

Ingeborg (f.) Scandinavian and German: from an Old Norse female personal name composed of the name of the fertility god *Ing + borg* fortification.

Ingegerd (f.) Scandinavian: from an Old Norse female personal name composed of the name of the fertility god *Ing + garðr* enclosure, stronghold.

Variant: Swedish: **Ingegärd**.

Ingemar (m.) Scandinavian: from an Old Norse personal name composed of the name of the fertility god *Ing* + the element *mærr* famous. The contracted form **Ingmar** is also used, notably as the name of the Swedish film director, Ingmar Bergman (b. 1918).

Inger (f.) Swedish: variant form of both INGEGERD and INGRID, attested from the 16th century.

Ingram (m.) English: transferred use of the surname, which is derived from a medieval given name. This was probably a contracted form of the Norman name *Engelram*, composed of the Germanic ethnic name *Engel* Angle + *hramn* raven. It is also possible that in some cases the first element was the name of the Old Norse fertility god, *Ing*.

Ingrid (f.) Scandinavian and German: from an Old Norse female personal name composed of the name of the fertility god *Ing + fríðr* fair, beautiful. It was introduced into the English-speaking world in the 20th century and became extremely popular, largely because of the fame of the Swedish film actress Ingrid Bergman (1915–82).

Ingvar (m.) Scandinavian: from an Old Norse personal name composed of the name of the fertility god *Ing(w)-* + *arr* warrior.

Variant: **Yngvar**.

Inigo (m.) English: from the medieval Spanish given name *Íñigo*, a vernacular derivative of IGNATIUS, apparently the result of crossing with a name recorded in the Middle Ages as *Ennecus*. This is of uncertain, possibly Basque, origin. *Íñigo* is now rarely used as a given name in Spain. In the English-speaking world it is mainly associated with the architect and stage designer Inigo Jones (1573–1652). The name had previously been borne by his father, a London clothmaker, who may well have received it at around the time of Queen Mary's marriage to Philip of Spain, when Spanish ways and Spanish names were fashionable, especially among devout Roman Catholics. The architect passed it on to his son, but later occurrences are rare.

Inmaculada (f.) Spanish: name corresponding to Italian IMMACOLATA.

Innes (m., f.) Scottish: Anglicized form based on the pronunciation of the Gaelic name *Aonghas* (see ANGUS). It is also a surname, and use as a female name is in part the result of a regular trend (cf. e.g. LESLEY), but may have been influenced by adoption in the English-speaking world of the Spanish name INÉS.

Innokenti (m.) Russian: from Late Latin *Innocentius*, a derivative of *innocens* innocent, harmless. The name was borne by various early saints venerated in the Eastern Church, including the leader of a group of thirty-two martyrs who were killed at Sirmium, now Mitrovica, in the Balkans.

Cognates: Italian: **Innocenzo**. Spanish: **Inocencio**.
Pet form: Russian: **Kenya**.

Iolanthe (f.) English: modern coinage based on the Greek elements *iolē* violet + *anthos* flower, possibly also influenced by the name YOLANDE. The name is chiefly known as the title of a Gilbert and Sullivan opera.

Iole (f.) English: from the name borne in classical mythology by a daughter of Eurytus of Oechalia. Herakles' infatuation with her led to his murder by his wife Deianeira. It represents the classical Greek vocabulary word meaning 'violet', and may in part have been chosen as a learned response to the 19th-century vogue for given names derived from vocabulary words denoting flowers and plants.

Iolo (m.) Welsh: pet form of IORWERTH.
Variant: **Iolyn**.

Ion (m.) Romanian and Basque form of JOHN.

Iona (f.) Scottish and English: from the name of the tiny island in the Hebrides, off the west coast of Mull, where in 563 St Columba founded a monastery that became an important early centre of Christianity. It is said to result from a misreading of the Latin form of the island's name, *Ioua*, as *Iona*. Its Gaelic name is *Ì*, from Old Norse *ey* island. The given name is most common in Scotland, but is also used elsewhere in the English-speaking world.

Ione (f.) English: 19th-century coinage, apparently with reference to the glories of Ionian Greece in the 5th century BC. No such name exists in classical Greek.

Iorgu (m.) Romanian form of GEORGE.

Iorwerth (m.) Welsh: traditional name composed of the elements *iōr* lord + a mutated form of *berth* handsome. It is borne in the *Mabinogi* by the jealous brother of Madawg, son of Maredudd. *Iorwerth* came to be regarded as a Welsh form of EDWARD, but in origin it had no connection with that name.
Variant: **Yorath**.
Pet forms: IOLO, **Iolyn**.

Iosif (m.) Russian form of JOSEPH (see also OSIP).

Ipati (m.) Russian: from the Late Greek personal name *Hypatios*, a derivative of *hypatos* highest, best, adopted by early Christians because of its symbolic significance. The name was borne by several early saints venerated in the Eastern Church, notably a bishop of Ganyra in Paphlagonia who played a prominent part at the Council of Nicaea.
Pet form: **Patya**.

Ippolito (m.) Italian form of HIPPOLYTE.

Ira (m.) Biblical: name (meaning 'watchful' in Hebrew) borne by a character mentioned very briefly in the Bible, one of the chief officers of King David (2 Samuel 20: 26). In England it was taken up by the Puritans in the 17th century, and is still occasionally used, mainly in America.

Iragarte (f.) Basque equivalent of ANUNCIACIÓN.

Irena (f.) Latinate form of IRENE, used as a female given name in several languages, including Dutch, Polish, and Czech.

Irene (f.) English: name (from Greek *eirēnē* peace) borne in Greek mythology by a minor goddess who personified peace, and by a Byzantine empress (752–803). The name was taken up in the English-speaking world at the end of the 19th century, and became popular in the 20th, partly as a result of being used as the name of a character in John Galsworthy's *The Forsyte Saga* (1922). It was formerly pronounced in three syllables, as in Greek, but is now thoroughly naturalized as an English name and usually pronounced as two syllables.
Cognates: IRENA. French: **Irène**. Russian: IRINA.

Iréné (m.) French: from *Iren(a)eus*, Latin form of Greek *Eirēnaios* 'peaceable' (see IRENE). This was favoured as a given name by the early Christians. St Irenaeus (*c*.125–*c*.202) was bishop of Lyons and a major early father of the Church.
Cognates: Dutch: **Ireneus**. Polish: **Ireneusz**. Russian: IRINEI.

Irial (m.) Irish Gaelic: name of obscure derivation. It was borne by a son of the Ulster hero Conall Cearnach, and has been revived as a given name in the 20th century.

Irina (f.) Russian form of IRENE, one of the commonest of all female names in the Soviet Union.
Variant: **Arina** (much less common).
Pet form: **Orya**.

Irinei (m.) Russian: from Greek *Eirēnaios*, a derivative of *eirēnē* peace (cf. IRENE). The name was borne by several early saints venerated in the Eastern Church. The form Irenei is also used; cf. IRÉNÉ.

Iris (f.) English, German, and Dutch: name (from Greek *iris* rainbow) borne in Greek mythology by a minor goddess, one of the messengers of the gods, who was so named because the rainbow was thought to be a sign from the gods to men. In English her name was used in the 16th century to denote both the flower and the coloured part of the eye, on account of their varied colours. In modern English use the name is often taken as being from the word for the flower, but it is also in use in Germany, where there is no such pattern of flower names.

Irma (f.) German: pet form of various female names beginning with the element *irm(en)*, *erm(en)* whole, entire, such as IRMGARD and IRMTRAUD. Its origins are thus the same as those of EMMA. It was introduced to the English-speaking world at the end of the 19th century.

Irmgard (f.) German: from an old Germanic female personal name composed of the elements *irm(en)*, *erm(en)* whole, entire + *gard* enclosure. The Blessed Irmgard (d. 866), a great-granddaughter of Charlemagne, was abbess of Buchau and later of Chiemsee.

Irmtraud (f.) German: variant of *Ermtraud* (see ERMINTRUDE).
Variant: **Irmtrud**.

Irune (f.) Basque equivalent of TRINIDAD.

Irving (m.) Scottish and English (chiefly U.S.): transferred use of the Scottish surname, which originated as a local name from a place in the former county of Dumfriesshire. The surname variant **Irvine** (which in most cases comes from a place in Ayrshire) is also used as a given name. One of the most famous of modern bearers was the lyricist Irving Berlin

(b. 1888), but in his case the name was adopted: he was of Jewish origin, and was originally called Israel Baline.

Irwin (m.) English: transferred use of the surname, which is derived from the medieval given name *Erwin*, composed of the Old English elements *eofor* boar + *wine* friend. There has also been some confusion with IRVING. See also ERWIN.

Isaac (m.) Biblical name, borne by the son of Abraham, who was about to be sacrificed by his father according to a command of God which was changed at the last moment. A ram, caught in a nearby thicket, was sacrificed instead (Genesis 22: 1–13). Isaac lived on to marry Rebecca and become the father of Esau and Jacob. The derivation of the name is not certain; it has traditionally been connected with the Hebrew verb meaning 'to laugh'. In the Middle Ages it seems to have been borne only by Jews, but it was taken up by the Puritans in the 17th century and has continued in use since then among Christians in the English-speaking world, although it is still more common among Jews.

Cognates: Hebrew: **Yitzhak**. Yiddish: **Aizik**. German: **Izaak**. Swedish: **Isak**.
Pet form: English (esp. U.S.): **Ike**.

Isabel (f.) Spanish, French, and English: originally a Spanish version of ELIZABETH, which was coined by deletion of the first syllable and alteration of the final consonant sound to one that can normally end a word in Spanish. The name was imported into France in the early Middle Ages, and thence into England. It was a royal name, and its popularity may have been enhanced by the fact that it was borne by a queen of England—Isabella (1296–1358), daughter of Philip IV of France—even though she led a turbulent life and eventually had her husband, Edward II, murdered.

Variants: English: **Isobel**, **Isbel**; **Isabella** (Latinate form, which became popular in England in the 18th century).
Cognates: Scottish: **Iseabail** (Gaelic), **Ishbel** (Anglicized). Irish Gaelic: **Isibéal**, **Sibéal**.
Short form: English: **Sabella**.
Pet forms: English: **Izzy**, **Izzie**. Scottish Gaelic: **Beileag**.

Isaiah (m.) English form of a biblical name (meaning 'God is salvation' in Hebrew) borne by the most important of the major prophets. Rather surprisingly perhaps, the name has never been common in the English-speaking world, apart from a brief flicker among the Puritans in the 17th century. In modern use it is either a Jewish name or an Anglicized version of one of the forms in other languages listed below.

Cognates: Italian: **Isaia**. French: **Isaïe**. Finnish: **Esa**.

Isaura (f.) Spanish: from the Late Latin personal name *Isaura*, originally an ethnic byname denoting a woman from *Isauria* in Asia Minor.

Isbel (f.) English and Scottish: contracted form of ISABEL and ISOBEL.

Iseabail (f.) Scottish Gaelic form of ISABEL. The Anglicized spelling **Ishbel**, which is occasionally used, is based on the Gaelic pronunciation.

Pet form: **Beileag**.

Iser (m.) Jewish: back-formation from Yiddish **Iserl** (a metathesized form of ISRAEL), the final -*l* having been taken as a hypocoristic element.

Variant: **Issur**.

Iseult (f.) English: variant of ISOLDE, from the medieval French form of the name.

Ishbel (f.) Scottish: Anglicized form of Gaelic ISEABAIL.

Ishmael (m.) Biblical name borne by Abraham's first son, the offspring of his barren wife's maidservant Hagar. It is composed of Hebrew elements meaning 'to hearken' and 'God'; an angel told Hagar 'Behold, thou art with child, and shalt bear a son, and shalt call his name Ishmael; because the Lord hath heard thy affliction' (Genesis 16: 11). The name is hardly ever used in the English-speaking world. In Islamic tradition, Ishmael or *Ismail* is believed to have been the ancestor of the Arabs.

Isidora (f.) Feminine form of ISIDORE. This name was little used in the Middle Ages, but has recently become more popular as a result of the fame of the American dancer Isadora Duncan (1878–1927).

Variant: **Isadora**.

Isidore (m.) English form (via Old French and Latin) of the Greek name *Isidōros*, composed of the name of the goddess *Isis* (who was Egyptian in origin) + the Greek element *dōron* gift. In spite of its pagan connotations the name was a common one among early Christians, and was borne, for example, by the great encyclopaedist St Isidore of Seville (*c*.560–636). By the late Middle Ages, however, it had come to be considered a typically Jewish name (although originally adopted as a Christianized version of ISAIAH).

Cognates: German: **Isidor**. Polish: **Izydor**.

Isla (f.) Scottish: of recent origin, apparently taken from the usual pronunciation, /'aɪlə/, of the island-name *Islay*.

Masculine form: **Islay** (less common).

Islwyn (m.) Welsh: taken from the name of a mountain in the county of Gwent, the name of which is composed of the elements *is* below + *llwyn* grove.

Ismene (f.) Name borne in classical mythology by a daughter of Oedipus. Like the names of her mother *Jocasta* and her sister *Antigone*, it has been used occasionally in modern times by parents looking for an unusual name, in spite of the grim fate of the house of Oedipus. After Oedipus has blinded himself on discovering that he has killed his father and that Jocasta is not only his wife but also his mother, Ismene deserts her father, while Antigone stays with him and supports him.

Isobel (f.) Variant of ISABEL, found mainly in Scotland. The contracted form **Isbel** also occurs.

Isolde (f.) English: the name of the tragic mistress of Tristram in the Arthurian romances. There are several different versions of the story. The main features are that the beautiful Isolde, an Irish princess, is betrothed to the aged King Mark of Cornwall. However, through accidentally drinking a magic potion, she and the young Cornish knight Tristram fall in love, with tragic consequences. The story has exercised a powerful hold on the European imagination. The name was relatively common in Britain in the Middle Ages, but is much rarer today. The Welsh form **Esyllt** probably originally meant 'fair aspect'.

Variant: **Iseult**.

Israel (m.) Biblical: the byname (meaning 'he who strives with God' in Hebrew) given to Jacob after he had wrestled with an angel: 'Thy name shall be called no more Jacob, but Israel: for as a prince hast thou power with God and with men, and hast prevailed' (Genesis 32: 28). The name was later applied to his descendants, the Children of Israel, and was chosen as the name of the modern Jewish state. The given name was used by the Puritans in the 17th century, but is now once again almost exclusively a Jewish name.

Derivatives: Yiddish: **Sroel**, **Iser**, **Issur**.

Issachar (m.) Biblical: name, probably meaning 'hireling' in Hebrew, borne by one of the sons of Jacob: 'And Leah said, God hath given me my hire, because I have given my maiden to my husband: and she called his name Issachar' (Genesis 30: 18). The name is still borne by Jews, but is rare or unused among Gentiles.

Issur (m.) Jewish: variant of ISER.

István (m.) Hungarian form of STEPHEN. St Stephen of Hungary (975–1038), Duke of Hungary (997–1001) and first King of the Magyars (1001–1038), is the patron saint of Hungary. He continued the Christianization of the country begun by his father Géza, and is remembered as an effective ruler who created a strong and united nation.

Ita (f.) English and Irish: Anglicized form of the Gaelic name **Íde**, of uncertain origin (possibly connected with Old Irish *ítu* thirst). This name was borne by a 6th-century saint who founded a convent in Limerick.

Italo (m.) Italian: from Latin *Italus*, the name borne, according to Roman legend, by the father of the twins Romulus and Remus, founders of Rome. Italy (Latin *Italia*) is said to have got its name from him, but in fact the character was invented to explain the name of the country, which is of very uncertain derivation.

Feminine form: **Itala**.

Itamar (m.) Jewish: Hebrew name (meaning 'palm island') borne in the Bible by a son of Aaron and brother of Eleazar (Exodus 6: 23; Leviticus 10: 1–7).

Itzal (f.) Basque equivalent of AMPARO.

Ivan (m.) Russian, Belorussian, Ukrainian and Czech form of JOHN, sometimes used in the English-speaking world in the 20th century.

Pet form: Russian: **Vanya**.
Feminine forms: Ukrainian: **Ivanna**. Czech: **Ivana**.

Ivo (m.) Form of YVES used in Germany and occasionally in other countries. It represents the nominative case of the Latinized form of the name.

Variant: **Ivon** (derived from the oblique case of the name).

Ivor (m.) **1.** English: of Scandinavian origin, from an Old Norse personal name composed of the elements *ýr* yew, bow + *herr* army, warrior. **2.** Scottish: Anglicized form of the ancient Gaelic name *Éibhear*.

Cognates (of 1): Scandinavian: **Ivar**; **Iver** (Danish). Scottish Gaelic: **Íomhar**, **Ímhear**.

Ivy (f.) English: from the vocabulary word denoting the plant (Old English *īfig*). This given name was coined at the end of the 19th century together with a large number of other female given names derived from words denoting flowers and plants. It is currently somewhat out of fashion.

Iwo (m.) Polish form of YVES (cf. IVO).

Izydor (m.) Polish form of ISIDORE.

Izzy (f.) English: pet form of ISABEL.
Variant: **Izzie**.

J

Jaakko (m.) Finnish form of JACOB.

Jaap (m.) Dutch: pet form of JACOB.

Jabez (m.) Biblical name, possibly meaning 'sorrowful' in Hebrew, borne by a descendant of Judah: 'and his mother called his name Jabez, saying, Because I bare him with sorrow' (1 Chronicles 4: 9). The name is thus metathesized from Hebrew *ya'zeb*, but there are other cases of metathesis in biblical names. His name occurs in a long list of genealogies, and is memorable because of the characterizations given: he was 'more honourable than his brethren', and he called on God for material success and protection: 'Oh that thou wouldest bless me indeed and enlarge my coast, and that thine hand might be with me.' The Puritans found great support for their beliefs in this, especially since the Bible says explicitly that God granted his request. Consequently the name was particularly popular among Puritans and Dissenters from the 17th century onwards. It is out of fashion now.

Jacek (m.) Polish: pet form of JACENTY, now more common than the original from which it is derived.

Short form: JACH.

Jacenty (m.) Polish form of the male name HYACINTH. This was popular in Poland in earlier centuries, and is the source of the modern Polish given name JACEK. It owes less to the early Christian saints called *Hyacinthus* than to the Polish missionary St Jacenty (1185–1257). He was a canon of Cracow and was initiated into the Dominican order by St Dominic himself. He is said to have undertaken missionary journeys to Pomerania, Russia, Denmark, Norway, Sweden, and even China and Tibet.

Jach (m.) Polish and Czech: short form of any of several names beginning with *Ja-*, principally JAN, JAKUB, JOACHIM or JÁCHYM, and JACEK.

Jáchym (m.) Czech form of JOACHIM.

Jacinta (f.) Spanish: feminine form of JACINTO.

Cognate: French: **Jacinthe**.

Jacinto (m.) Spanish form of the male name HYACINTH.

Jack (m.) English: originally a pet form of JOHN, but now well established as a given name in its own right. It is derived from Middle English *Jankin*, later altered to *Jackin*, from *Jan* (a contracted form of *Jehan* John) + the hypocoristic suffix *-kin*. This led to the back-formation *Jack*, as if the name had contained the Old French diminutive suffix *-in*. It is sometimes also taken to be an informal pet form of JAMES, influenced no doubt by French JACQUES. See also JOCK and JAKE.

Jackie (m., f.) English: originally a male name, a pet form of JACK, but now also found as a female name, a pet form of JACQUELINE.

Variant: **Jacky**.

Jackson (m.) English: transferred use of the surname, meaning originally 'son of JACK' and in modern times sometimes bestowed with precisely this meaning. In the United States it

has also been used in honour of President Andrew Jackson (1767–1845) and of the Confederate general Thomas 'Stonewall' Jackson (1824–63).

Jacob (m.) English (and Dutch) form of the biblical Hebrew name *Yaakov*. This was borne by perhaps the most important of all the patriarchs in the Book of Genesis. Jacob was the father of twelve sons, who gave their names to the twelve tribes of Israel. He was the son of Isaac and Rebecca. According to the story in Genesis, he was the cunning younger twin, who persuaded his fractionally older brother Esau to part with his right to his inheritance in exchange for a bowl of soup ('a mess of pottage'). Later, he tricked his blind and dying father into blessing him in place of Esau. The derivation of the name has been much discussed. It is traditionally explained as being derived from Hebrew *akev* heel and to have meant 'heel grabber', because when Jacob was born 'his hand took hold of Esau's heel' (Genesis 25: 26). This is interpreted later in the Bible as 'supplanter'; Esau himself remarks, 'Is he not rightly named Jacob? for he has supplanted me these two times' (Genesis 27: 36).

As a given name, *Jacob* is especially common among Jews, although it has also been used by Christians. The usual Christian form *James* and its cognates in other languages arose from a Late Latin byform, *Iacomus*, of the Latin form *Iacobus*.

Cognates: Italian: **Giacobbe**. German, Scandinavian: **Jakob**. French: JACQUES. Polish, Czech: **Jakub**. Russian: **Yakov**. Finnish: **Jaako**. Hebrew: **Yakov**. See also at JAMES.
Pet forms: Dutch: **Jaap**, **Cobus**, **Coos**. Polish: **Kuba**. Yiddish: **Koppel**.

Jacqueline (f.) English and French: feminine diminutive of the French male name JACQUES. In the 1960s it became very popular in America and elsewhere, no doubt strongly influenced by the fame and stylish image of Jacqueline Kennedy, wife of President John F. Kennedy. She is herself of French extraction.

Variants: English: **Jacquelyn** (influenced by the productive suffix *-lyn*; see LYNN); **Jacklyn** (influenced by the male name JACK).
Pet forms: English: **Jackie**, **Jacky**, **Jacqui** (all now very common).

Jacques (m.) French form of JAMES and JACOB. In French there is no distinction between a form corresponding to *Jacob* and a form corresponding to *James*. This is a perennially popular French given name, and *Jacques* or *Jacques Bonhomme* has been used (like *John Bull* in English) as a typification of the ordinary citizen.

Jacquetta (f.) English: respelling (influenced by JACQUELINE) of the Italian name *Giachetta*, a feminine diminutive of *Giac(om)o*, the Italian version of JAMES.

Jacqui (f.) English: variant spelling of JACKIE, reflecting the influence of the full form JACQUELINE and the increasing tendency to use *-i* as a distinctively feminine suffix (cf. e.g. TONI).

Jade (f.) English: from the name of the precious stone, a word that reached English from Spanish (*piedra de*) *ijada*, which literally means '(stone of the) bowels'. It was so called because it was believed to have the magical power of providing protection against disorders of the intestines. The vogue for this word as a given name developed later than that for other gemstone names, possibly because of the unfortunate etymological associations, or more probably because it sounds the same as the vocabulary word denoting a broken-down old horse or a nagging woman. Its popular appeal received a considerable boost in the early 1970s when the daughter of the English rock singer Mick Jagger was so named.

Jadwiga (f.) Polish form of HEDWIG. St Jadwiga (*c*.1174–1243) was born in Bavaria of Moravian descent, the daughter of the Duke of Croatia and Dalmatia. St Elizabeth of Hungary was her niece. When she was 12 she was married to the Duke of Silesia, head of the Polish royal family. She did much to foster Christianity in Poland. The Blessed Jadwiga (1371–99) was a later queen of Poland who converted many Lithuanians to Christianity, starting with her husband, Władysław Jagiełło, Grand Duke of Lithuania.

Short form: **Wiga**.
Pet form: **Wisia**.

Jael (f.) Jewish: variant of YAEL.

Jaffe (f.) Jewish: Polish and German spelling of a modern Hebrew name from the Hebrew vocabulary word *yafe* lovely, beautiful.

Variant: **Yaffa**.

Jago (m.) Cornish form of JAMES. It has increased in popularity recently, perhaps as a transferred use of the surname *Jago*, which itself derives from the Cornish given name.

Jaime (m., f.) **1**. (m.) Spanish form of JAMES. **2**. (f.) English (esp. Canadian): apparently a respelling of the female name JAMIE.

Jake (m.) Variant of JACK, of Middle English origin, which has now come back into fashion as an independent name. It is also sometimes used as a short form of JACOB.

Jakob (m.) German, Dutch, and Scandinavian form of JACOB.

Jakub (m.) Polish and Czech form of JACOB.

Pet forms: Polish: **Kuba**. Czech: **Jakoubek**; **Kuba**, **Kubíček**, **Kubeš**.

James (m.) English and Scottish form of the name borne in the New Testament by two of Christ's disciples, James son of Zebedee and James son of Alphaeus. This form comes from Late Latin *Iacomus*, a variant of *Iacobus*, Latin form of the New Testament Greek name *Iakobos*. This is the same name as Old Testament JACOB (Hebrew *Yaakov*). For many centuries now it has been thought of in the English-speaking world and elsewhere as a distinct name, but in some other cultures, e.g. French, no distinction is made.

In Britain, *James* is a royal name that from the beginning of the 15th century onwards has been associated particularly with the Scottish house of Stewart: James I of Scotland (1394–1437; ruled 1424–37) was a patron of the arts and a noted poet, as well as an energetic monarch. King James VI of Scotland (1566–1625; reigned 1567–1625) succeeded to the throne of England in 1603. His grandson, James II of England (1633–1701; reigned 1685–8) was a Roman Catholic, deposed in 1688 in favour of his Protestant daughter Mary and her husband William of Orange. From then on he, his son (also called James), and his grandson Charles ('Bonnie Prince Charlie') made various unsuccessful attempts to recover the English throne. Their

supporters were known as Jacobites (from *Jacobus*, Latin form of *James*), and the name James became for a while particularly associated with Roman Catholicism on the one hand, and Highland opposition to the English government on the other. It is now widely used by people of many different creeds and nationalities.

Cognates: French: JACQUES. Italian: **Giacomo**. Spanish: **Jaime**. Catalan: **Jaume**. Galician: **Xaime**. Irish: **Séamas**, **Séamus**, **Seumas**, **Seumus** (Gaelic); **Shamus** (Anglicized). Scottish: **Seumas** (Gaelic); HAMISH (Anglicized). Cornish: **Jago**. See also JEM.
Short form: English: **Jim**.
Pet form: English, Scottish: **Jimmy**, **Jimmie**.
Feminine form: Scottish: **Jamesina**. See also JAMIE.

Jamie (m.), occasionally (f.) **1**. (m.) Scottish: pet form of JAMES, used especially among Lowland Scots, in contrast to the Highland form HAMISH, which is derived from a Gaelic form. **2**. (f.) English (esp. U.S.): recent adoption as a feminine equivalent of *James*, influenced by the fact that *-ie* has come to be regarded as a characteristically feminine ending, except in Scotland.

Jan (m., f.) **1**. (m.); pronounced /jan/ Dutch, Low German, Scandinavian, Polish, and Czech form of JOHN. **2**. (m.); pronounced /dʒæn/) English: a revival of Middle English *Jan*, a byform of JOHN. The forms *Johan* and *Jehan* are found in Old French and Early Middle English, but in Middle English the name was generally shortened to a monosyllable, spelled variously *Jon*, *John*, and *Jan*. It has sometimes been suggested that the latter is an importation from Low German or Dutch, but this seems unnecessary. **3**. (f.); pronounced /dʒæn/) English: an increasingly popular female given name, formed either as an independent feminine form of JOHN (alongside JOAN, JEAN, JANE, etc.) or as a shortened form of names beginning with *Jan-*, principally JANET and JANICE.

Pet forms (of 1): Polish: **Janek**, **Janik**, **Janko**, **Janusz**. Czech: **Janek**, **Janik**, **Janeček**.

Jana (f.) Polish and Czech: feminine form of JAN (1).

Jancis (f.) English: modern blend of JAN (3) and FRANCES, apparently first used in the novel *Precious Bane* (1924) by Mary Webb, for the character of Jancis Beguildy, daughter of Felix and Hephzibah.

Jane (f.) English: originally a feminine form of JOHN, from the Old French form *Je(h)anne*. Since the 17th century it has proved the most common of the feminine forms of *John*, ahead of JOAN and JEAN. It now also commonly occurs as the second element in combinations such as *Sarah-Jane*.

It is not a royal name: the nearest it ever came was as the name of the tragic Lady Jane Grey (1537–54), who was unwillingly proclaimed queen in 1553, deposed nine days later, and executed the following year. Seventy years earlier, the name had come into prominence as that of Jane Shore, mistress of King Edward IV and subsequently of Thomas Grey, 1st Marquess of Dorset, Lady Jane's grandfather. Jane Shore's tribulations in 1483 at the hands of Richard III, Edward's brother and successor, became the subject of popular ballads and plays, which may well have increased the currency of the name in the 16th century. A 19th-century influence was its use as the name of the central character in Charlotte Brontë's novel *Jane Eyre* (1847). In the 20th century it has been used intermittently since the 1940s as the name of a cheerful and scantily clad beauty whose adventures are chronicled in a strip cartoon in the *Daily Mirror*.

Janelle (f.) English: modern elaborated form of JANE, with the feminine ending -elle abstracted from names such as *Danielle*.

Variant: **Jayne**. See also JEAN, JOAN, and JOANNA.
Pet forms: English: **Janey, Janie, Jaynie**.
Cognates: Irish Gaelic: **Sine, Siobhán**. Scottish Gaelic: **Sine, Siubhan**. Welsh: **Siân**. French: **Jeanne**. Spanish: **Juana**. Italian: **Giovanna, Gianna**. German: **Johanna, Hanne, Hansine**. Dutch: **Johanna**. Scandinavian: **Johanna; Jensine** (Danish, Norwegian); **Jonna** (Danish). Polish: **Jana**. Czech: **Johana, Hana, Jana**.

Janelle (f.) English: modern elaborated form of JANE, with the feminine ending-elle abstracted from names such as *Danielle*.

Variant: **Janella** (a Latinate form; for the ending, cf. PRUNELLA).

Janet (f.) English: diminutive of JANE, already in common use in the Middle English period. Towards the end of the Middle Ages the name largely died out except in Scotland. It was revived at the end of the 19th century to much more widespread use, but still retains its popularity in Scotland. See also SEÒNAID, SÍNEAD, and SIONED.

Short form: JAN.

Janette (f.) English: either an elaborated version of JANET, emphasizing the feminine form of the suffix, or a simplified form of JEANNETTE.

Janey (f.) English: pet form of JANE.

Variants: **Janie, Jaynie**.

Janice (f.) English: derivative of JANE, with the addition of the suffix -ice, abstracted from female names such as CANDICE and BERNICE. It seems to have been first used as the name of the heroine of the novel *Janice Meredith* by Paul Leicester Ford, published in 1899.

Variant: **Janis**.
Short form: **Jan**.

Janine (f.) English: simplified form of French JEANNINE.

Variant: **Janina** (Latinate form).

Janis (f.) English: variant spelling of JANICE, made popular in the 1960s and 1970s by the American rock singer Janis Joplin (1943–70).

Janna (f.) English: Latinate elaboration of the female name JAN.

Janne (m., f.) **1**. (m.) Swedish: pet form of the male name JAN (1). **2**. (f.) Danish, Norwegian: contracted form of JOHANNA.

Jannike (f.) Scandinavian: apparently derived from French JEANNE, via the diminutive *Jeannique*.

János (m.) Hungarian form of JOHN.

Janusz (m.) Polish: pet form of JAN (1), now also used as an independent given name.

Jared (m.) Biblical name, probably meaning 'descent' in Hebrew, borne by a descendant of Adam (Genesis 5: 15). According to the Book of Genesis, he became the father of Enoch at the age of 162, and lived for a further eight hundred years. This name was occasionally used by the Puritans; Dunkling records that it was briefly revived in the 1960s, for reasons that are not clear.

Variant: **Yered** (Hebrew).

Jarek (m.) Polish and Czech: pet form of various names of Slavonic origin containing the element *jaro* spring (cf. JAROGNIEW, JAROMIERZ, JAROMIL, JAROPELK, and JAROSLAW).

Feminine form: Czech: **Jarka**.
Pet forms: Czech: **Jaroušek** (m.); **Jaruše, Jaruška** (f.).

Jarlath (m.) Irish: Anglicized form of Gaelic IARLAITH. St Jarlath is the patron of the diocese of Tuam in Co. Galway, and *Jarlath* is still a popular given name in that area.

Jarogniew (m.) Polish: from an old Slavonic personal name composed of the elements *jaro* spring + *gniew* anger.

Jaromierz (m.) Polish: from an old Slavonic personal name composed of the elements *jaro* spring + *meri* great, famous (see CASIMIR).

Cognate: Czech: **Jaromir**.

Jaromil (m.) Polish: from an old Slavonic personal name composed of the elements *jaro* spring + *milo* grace, favour.

Cognates: Czech: **Jar(o)mil**.
Feminine form: Czech: **Jarmila**.

Jaropelk (m.) Polish: from an old Slavonic personal name composed of the elements *jaro* spring + *polk* people, tribe.

Cognates: Czech: **Jaropluk**. Russian: **Yaropolk**.

Jarosław (m.) Polish: from an old Slavonic personal name composed of the elements *jaro* spring + *slav* glory.

Cognates: Czech: **Jaroslav**. Russian: **Yaroslav**.
Feminine forms: Polish: **Jarosawa**. Czech: **Jaroslava**.

Jarvis (m.) English: transferred use of the surname, which is from a Middle English form of the Norman given name GERVAISE. Modern use may in part represent an antiquarian revival of the medieval given name.

Jasmine (f.) English: from the vocabulary word denoting the climbing plant with its delicate, fragrant flowers (from Old French, ultimately from Persian *yasmin*).

Variants: **Jasmin**, YASMIN.

Jason (m.) English form of the name (Greek *Iasōn*) borne in classical mythology by a hero, leader of the Argonauts, who sailed to Colchis in search of the Golden Fleece, enduring many hardships and adventures. The sorceress Medea fell in love with him and helped him to obtain the Fleece; they escaped together and should have lived happily ever after. However, Jason fell in love with another woman (either Creusa or Glauce, daughter of King Creon), and deserted Medea. Medea took her revenge by killing her rival, but Jason himself survived to be killed in old age by one of the rotting timbers of his ship, the *Argo*, falling on his head.

The classical Greek name *Iasōn* probably derives from the Greek vocabulary word *iasthai* to heal. *Iasō* (f.) was the name of a minor goddess of healing. In New Testament Greek, the name probably represents a classicized form of JOSHUA. It was borne by an early Christian in Thessalonica, at whose house St Paul stayed (Acts 17: 5–9; Romans 16: 21). Probably for this reason, it enjoyed some popularity among the Puritans in the 17th century. In the mid-20th century it has enjoyed a considerable increase in its popularity, although, as Dunkling comments, it has also been the subject of some rather surprising hostility. A 20th-century influence has been the film actor Jason Robards (b. 1920); his father, also a film actor, was likewise called Jason Robards. The name has been used for numerous characters in films and television series.

Jasper (m.) English: the usual English form of the name assigned in Christian folklore to one of the three Magi or 'wise men', who brought gifts to the infant Christ at his birth (Matthew 2: 1). The name does not appear in the Bible, and is first found in medieval tradition. It seems to be ultimately of Persian origin, from a word meaning 'treasurer'. There is probably no connection with the English vocabulary word *jasper* denoting a gemstone, which is of Semitic origin. The names assigned by the same folklore tradition to the other Magi, BALTHAZAR and *Melchior* (see MELCHIORRE), have also been used as given names in Europe, but only very rarely in the English-speaking world.

Cognates: Danish: **Jesper**. Dutch: CASPAR. German: **Kaspar**. Polish: **Kasper**. Hungarian: **Gáspár**. French: GASPARD. Italian: **Gaspare**.

Jaume (m.) Catalan form of JAMES.

Javier (m.) Portuguese form (and Spanish variant) of XAVIER.

Jay (m., f.) English: pet form of any of the given names beginning with the letter *J*- (cf. DEE and KAY). It is now also used as an independent name in its own right.

Jayne (f.) English: variant spelling of JANE.

Jean (m., f.) **1**. (f.) English and Scottish: like JANE and JOAN, a medieval variant of Old French *Je(h)anne*. Towards the end of the Middle Ages this form became largely confined to Scotland. In the 20th century it has been more widely used in the English-speaking world, but still retains a Scottish flavour. **2**. (m.) French form of JOHN.
Cognate (of 1): Scottish Gaelic: SÌNE.

Jeane (f.) English: variant spelling of the female name JEAN, common especially in the United States.
Variant: **Jeana**.

Jeanie (f.) Scottish and English: pet form of the female name JEAN, which is more strongly associated with Scotland than *Jean* itself. It is occasionally used as an independent given name.
Variants: **Jeannie**; **Sineag**, **Sìonag** (Gaelic).

Jeanne (f.) French: feminine form of the male name JEAN.

Jeannette (f.) French: diminutive form of JEANNE, now also commonly used in the English-speaking world.
Variants: English: **Jeanette**; **Genette** (rare).

Jeannine (f.) French: diminutive form of JEANNE, now also sometimes used in the English-speaking world.

Jed (m.) English (mainly U.S.): now frequently used as an independent name, although originally a short form of the biblical name **Jedidiah**, which was an alternative name of King Solomon (2 Samuel 12: 25), meaning 'beloved of God'. This was a favourite with the Puritans, who considered themselves, too, to be loved by God, but the full form fell out of favour along with other rare or unwieldy Old Testament names.

Jędrej (m.) Polish form of ANDREW.

Jeff (m.) English: short form of JEFFREY, now commonly used as an independent given name, especially in America.

Jefferson (m.) English: transferred use of the surname, originally meaning 'son of JEFFREY', and now occasionally selected by fathers themselves named JEFFREY or GEOFFREY. It has sometimes been used in honour of the American president Thomas Jefferson (1743–1826; president 1801–9), who was principally responsible for the text of the Declaration of Independence, and who is admired as a scientist, architect, and thinker as well as a statesman.

Jeffrey (m.) English: variant spelling of GEOFFREY, common in the Middle Ages (as reflected in surnames such as *Jefferson*). This is the usual spelling of the name in the United States.
Variant: **Jeffery**.
Short form: **Jeff**.

Jem (m.) English: from a medieval vernacular form of JAMES. In modern use, however, it is often taken as a pet form of JEREMY.

Jemima (f.) Biblical name (meaning 'dove' or 'bright as day' in Hebrew) of the eldest of the daughters of Job, born to him towards the end of his life when his prosperity had been restored (Job 42: 14). The name was common in the first part of the 19th century, and has continued in modest use since then. Recently the name of Job's second daughter, KEZIA, has been taken up by parents looking for an unusual name, but that of the youngest, *Keren-happuch*, meaning 'horn of eyepaint', has remained intractable (see KERENA).

Jemma (f.) English: variant spelling of GEMMA.

Jenaro (m.) Spanish form of GENNARO.

Jenkin (m.) English and Welsh: transferred use of the surname, which is derived from the medieval given name *Jankin*. This was a pet form of JAN (2), with the hypocoristic suffix -*kin* (cf. JACK). The modern given name is comparatively popular in Wales, where the surname *Jenkins* also predominates.
Variant: **Siencyn** (a Welsh spelling).

Jenna (f.) English: fanciful alteration of JENNY, with the Latinate feminine ending -*a*.

Jennet (f.) English: variant spelling of JEANNETTE, or a revival of a medieval diminutive form of the female name JEAN.

Jenni (f.) English: variant spelling of JENNY, now commonly used for the sake of variety or stylishness (-*i* as an ending of female names being in vogue; cf. JACQUI, TONI).

Jennifer (f.) English: of Celtic (Arthurian) origin. This represents a Cornish form of the name of King Arthur's unfaithful wife (see GUINEVERE). At the beginning of the 20th century, the name was merely a Cornish curiosity, but since then it has become enormously popular all over the English-speaking world. One factor in its rise was probably Bernard Shaw's use of it for the character of Jennifer Dubedat in *The Doctor's Dilemma* (1905). See also GAYNOR.

Jenny (f.) English: now universally taken as a short form of JENNIFER, but in fact this name existed during the Middle Ages as a pet form of JEAN.
Variants: **Jenni**, **Jenna**.

Jenö (m.) Hungarian form of EUGENE.

Jens (m.) Scandinavian (mainly Danish) form of JOHN.
Feminine form: **Jensine**.

Jeremiah (m.) Biblical name (meaning 'appointed by God' in Hebrew) borne by the great Hebrew prophet of the 7th–6th centuries BC, whose story, prophecies of judgement, and lamentations are recorded in the book of the Bible that bears his name. The Book of Lamentations is also attributed to him; in this he bewails the destruction of Jerusalem and the temple by the Babylonians in 587 BC. Despite the gloomy subject-matter of these texts, the name enjoyed some popularity among Puritans and Christian fundamentalists, partly perhaps because Jeremiah also preached reconciliation with God after his wrath was assuaged. In Ireland and Scotland it has been used as an Anglicized form of *Diarmaid* and *Diarmad* (see DERMOT).

Jeremy (m.) English: Anglicized form, used in the Authorized Version of the New Testament (Matthew 2: 17; 27: 9), of the biblical name JEREMIAH. It is a vernacular derivative of the Latin (Vulgate) form of the name, *Jeremias*, which in turn is from Greek *Ieremaias*.
Cognate: Finnish: **Jorma**.
Pet forms: English: **Jerry**, **Jem**.

Jerker (m.) Swedish: dialectal form of *Erik* (see ERIC), formerly found mainly in the Uppland region.
Variant: **Jerk**.

Jermaine (m.) English: variant spelling of GERMAINE, popular in particular as a male name among Blacks in the United States.

Jerome (m.) English: Anglicized form of the Greek name *Hieronymos*, composed of the elements *hieros* holy + *onoma* name. St Jerome (*c*.342–420) was a citizen of the Eastern Roman Empire, who bore the Greek names Eusebios Hieronymos Sophronios; he was chiefly responsible for the translation into Latin of the Bible, the Vulgate. He also wrote many works of commentary and exposition on the Bible, and is regarded as one of the Doctors of the Church.
Cognates: French: **Jérôme**. Italian: **Geronimo**, **Girolamo**. Spanish: **Jerónimo**. Dutch: **Jeroen** (the most popular male name of all in Holland in 1981).
Pet form: English: **Jerry**.

Jerrard (m.) English: rare variant of GERARD, probably influenced by the form of the modern surname, if not a transferred use.

Jerrold (m.) English: rare variant of GERALD, probably a transferred use of the modern surname.

Jerry (m., f.) English: 1. (m.) Pet form of JEREMY or GERALD, or occasionally of GERARD and JEROME. 2. (f.) A comparatively rare variant of GERRY.

Jerzy (m.) Polish form of GEORGE.
Pet form: **Jurek**.

Jesper (m.) Danish form of JASPER, still a very popular name in Denmark.

Jess (f., m.) English: usually a female name, a short form of JESSIE or JESSICA. As a male name, it is a simplified form of JESSE.

Jesse (m.) English: name (apparently meaning 'gift' in Hebrew) borne in the Bible by the father of King David (1 Samuel 16), from whose line (according to the New Testament) Jesus was ultimately descended. It was popular among the Puritans, and is still used fairly frequently in the United States, more rarely in Britain.
Variant: JESS.

Jessica (f.) English: apparently of Shakespearian origin. This was the name of the daughter of Shylock in *The Merchant of Venice* (1596). Shakespeare's source has not been discovered, but he presumably intended it to seem like a typically Jewish name. It may be from a biblical name that appeared, in the translations available in Shakespeare's day, as *Jesca* (Genesis 11: 29; *Iscah* in the Authorized Version). This appears in a somewhat obscure genealogical passage; Iscah appears to have been Abraham's niece.
Short form: **Jess**.

Jessie (f.) Scottish and English: apparently originally a Scottish pet form of JEAN, although the derivation is not clear; the Gaelic form is **Teasag**. It is now sometimes used as a given name in its own right, or as a short form of JESSICA.
Short form: **Jess**.

Jesús (m.) Spanish and Portuguese: name taken in honour of Christ. The name *Jesus* is an Aramaic byform (meaning 'saviour') of the earlier Hebrew name JOSHUA. It was suggested to Mary's husband Joseph by the angel of the Lord at the Annunciation: 'she shall bring forth a son, and thou shalt call his name JESUS: for he shall save his people from their sins' (Matthew 1: 21). In many European countries it has been felt impious to give this name to mere mortal children, but there are no such inhibitions in the Hispanic world, where it is regularly bestowed as a token of Christian faith.
Feminine form: **Jesusa**.
Pet forms: **Chus**, **Chucho** (m., f.).

Jethro (m.) English: name borne in the Bible by the father of Moses's wife Zipporah (Exodus 3: 1; 4: 18). It seems to be a variant of the Hebrew name *Ithra*, said to mean 'excellence', which is found at 2 Samuel 17: 25. It was popular among the Puritans, but then fell out of general use. It was borne by the agricultural reformer Jethro Tull (1674–1741). In 1968 a 'progressive rock' group in Britain adopted the name 'Jethro Tull', and shortly afterwards the given name *Jethro* enjoyed a revival of popularity.

Jetta (f.) English: a comparatively recent coinage, a Latinate derivative of the vocabulary word denoting the mineral *jet*. This is in turn derived from Old French *jaiet*, from Latin (*lapis*) *gagātēs* 'stone from *Gagaï*', a town in Lycia, Asia Minor.

Jewel (f.) English: modern coinage from the vocabulary word meaning 'gemstone' (from Old French *jouel*, apparently a diminutive form of *jou* plaything, delight, Latin *iocus*). Use as a given name may derive from its use as a term of affection, or may have been suggested by the vogue in the 19th century for using words denoting particular gemstones as given names, e.g. BERYL, RUBY.

Jill (f.) English: short form (respelled) of GILLIAN, now often used as an independent name in its own right. It was already used as a prototypical female name in the phrase 'Jack and Jill' by the 15th century.

Jim (m.) English and Irish: short form of JAMES, already common in the Middle Ages.

Jimmy (m.) English, Scottish, and Irish: pet form of JIM.
Variant: **Jimmie**.

Jindřich (m.) Czech form of HENRY.
Feminine form: **Jindřiška**.
Pet forms: **Jindra** (m., f.); **Jindřík**, **Jindříšek**, **Jindroušek** (m.); **Jindruška**, **Jindřina** (f.).

Jiří (m.) Czech form of GEORGE.
Pet forms: **Jíra**, **Jirka**, **Jiřík**, **Jiříček**, **Jiroušek**, **Jiran**, **Jiránek**.
Feminine form: **Jiřina**.

Jitka (f.) Czech: pet form of *Judita* (see JUDITH).

Jo (f., m.) English: usually a female name, a short form of JOANNA, JOANNE, JODY, or JOSEPHINE, sometimes used in combination with other names, for example *Nancy Jo* and *Jo Anne* (see JOANNE). Its popularity as a female name was influenced by the character of Jo March in Louisa M. Alcott's *Little Women* (1868). Occasionally it is a male name, a variant of JOE.

Elaborated female form: Scottish (Highland): **Joina** (three syllables).

Joachim (m.) English, French, German, Polish, etc.: from the biblical Hebrew name *Johoiachin*, meaning 'established by God', borne by a king of Judah who was defeated by Nebuchadnezzar and carried off into Babylonian exile (2 Kings 24). Alternatively, it may be a derivative of the name of the father of this king, *Jehoiakim*. The reason for the great popularity of the name in Christian Europe is that in medieval Christian tradition it was the name commonly ascribed to the father of the Virgin Mary. (Other names assigned to him include *Cleopas*, *Eliachim*, *Heli*, *Jonahir*, and *Sadoc*.) He is not named at all in the Bible, but with the growth of the cult of Mary many legends grew up about her early life, and her parents came to be venerated as saints under the names *Joachim* and ANNE.

Cognates: Italian: **Gioac(c)hino**. Spanish: **Joaquin**. Portuguese: **Joaquim**. German: **Jochim, Jochem, Jochen; Achim**. Scandinavian: **Joakim; Jokum** (Danish, Norwegian); **Jockum** (Danish). Czech: **Jáchym**. Russian: **Yackim, Akim**.
Pet form: Russian: **Kima**.

Joan (f., m.) **1**. (f.) English: contracted form of Old French *Jo(h)anne*, from Latin *Jo(h)anna* (see JOANNA). In England this was the usual feminine form of JOHN from the Middle English period onwards, but in the 16th and 17th centuries it was largely superseded by JANE. It was strongly revived in the first part of the 20th century, partly under the influence of George Bernard Shaw's play *St Joan* (1923), based on the life of Joan of Arc (1412–31). In French, her name is *Jeanne D'Arc*; Schiller knew her as *Johanna*. She is also sometimes called 'the maid of Orléans'. Claiming to be guided by the voices of the saints, she persuaded the French dauphin to defy the occupying English forces and have himself crowned, and she led the French army that raised the siege of Orléans in 1429. The following year she was captured by the Burgundians and sold to the English, and a year later she was burned at the stake for witchcraft at the age of 18 or 19. Her story has captured the imagination of many writers, and she is variously portrayed as a national and political hero, a model of apolitical straightforwardness and honesty, and a religious heroine. She was canonized in 1920. **2**. (m.) Catalan form of JOHN.

Cognate (of 1): Scottish Gaelic: SEONAG.
Pet forms (of 1): English: **Joanie, Joni**.

Joanna (f.) Latin form of Greek *Iōanna*, the feminine equivalent of *Iōannēs* (see JOHN). In the New Testament, this name is borne by a woman who was one of Jesus's followers (Luke 8: 3; 24: 10). She was the wife of the steward of the household of King Herod Antipas. The name was regularly used throughout the Middle Ages in most parts of Europe as a feminine equivalent of JOHN, but in England it has only been in common use as a vernacular given name since the 19th century.
Short form: **Jo**.

Joanne (f.) English: from an Old French feminine form of JOHN, *Jo(h)anne*, and so a doublet of JOAN. This too was revived as a given name in its own right in the first half of the 20th century. It has to some extent been influenced by the independently formed combination *Jo Anne*.
Short form: **Jo**.

João (m.) Portuguese form of JOHN.

Joaquim (m.) Portuguese form of JOACHIM.

Joaquin (m.) Spanish form of JOACHIM.

Job (m.) Biblical name, borne by the eponymous hero of the Book of Job, a man of exemplary patience, whose faith was severely tested by God's apparently motiveless maltreatment of him. His name, appropriately enough, means 'persecuted' in Hebrew. His story was a favourite one in the Middle Ages and formed the subject of miracle plays. The name was used among Puritans and Christian fundamentalists, but is currently out of favour.

Jobst (m.) Low German form of *Jodocus*, Latinized form of the Breton name *Iodoc*, meaning 'lord' (cf. JOYCE, JOOST). The Low German form was altered under the influence of the biblical name JOB.

Jocasta (f.) English: name borne in classical legend by the mother of Oedipus, King of Thebes. As the result of a series of misunderstandings, she also became his wife and the mother of his children. The derivation of her name is not known. In spite of its tragic associations, the name has enjoyed a certain vogue in recent years. The names of her daughters, *Antigone* and *Ismene*, have been occasionally used since the Middle Ages, but there has been no move to take up those of her sons, *Eteodes* and *Polynices*.

Jocelyn (f., m.) English: now normally a female name, but in earlier times more often given to boys. It represents a transferred use of the English surname, which in turn is derived from a masculine personal name introduced to Britain by the Normans in the form *Joscelin*. This was originally a derivative, *Gautzelin*, of the name of a Germanic tribe, the *Gauts* (cf. WENDELIN). The spelling of the first syllable was altered because the name was taken as a double diminutive (with the Old French suffixes *-el* and *-in*) of *Josce* (see JOYCE).
Variant: **Josceline** (f.) only.
Short form: **Joss**.

Jochen (m.) German: variant of JOACHIM.
Variants: **Jochim, Jochem**.

Jock (m.) Scottish: variant of JACK, sometimes used as an archetypal nickname for a Scotsman.
Variant: **Seoc** (Gaelic).
Pet forms: **Jockie, Jockey, Jockan; Seocan** (Gaelic).

Jockum (m.) Danish: variant of JOKUM.

Jodene (f.) English: a recent fanciful coinage, formed from JODY plus the productive suffix *-ene*.

Jody (f., m.) English: of uncertain origin. It may be a pet form of JUDITH and JUDE, but if so the reason for the change in the vowel is not clear. Alternatively, it may be a playful elaboration of JO and JOE, with *-d-* introduced for euphony before the hypocoristic suffix *-y*.
Variants: **Jodie, Jodi**.

Joe (m.) English: short form of JOSEPH.
Variant: **Jo**.
Pet form: **Joey**.

Joel (m.) Biblical name, composed of two different Hebrew elements, *Yah(weh)* and *El*, both of which mean 'God'; the implication of the name is that the Hebrew God, *Yahweh*, is the only true god. This is a common name in the Bible, being borne by, among others, one of King David's 'mighty men' (1 Chronicles 11: 38), and by a minor prophet who lived in the 8th century BC. The book of the Bible of which the latter was author interprets a plague of locusts as a punishment from God and uses it as an occasion for a call to repentance. The name has been perennially popular among Jews, and was also very popular among the Puritans and other Christian fundamentalists. It is still used in America, where it seems to be enjoying a modest revival of popularity. In Britain, however, it is not common.

Cognate: French: **Joël** (currently a fashionable given name).

Joelle (f.) English borrowing of the fashionable French name **Joëlle**, a feminine form of JOEL. Its selection as a given name may also have been influenced by the fact that it can be taken as a combination of Jo and the productive suffix -elle (originally a French feminine diminutive ending).

Joey (m.) English: pet form of JOE.

Johan (m., f.) **1.** (m.) Scandinavian and Low German form of JOHN. It is also used as a more learned Czech form of the name, a doublet of JAN. **2.** (f.) Older Scottish spelling of JOAN, which was traditionally pronounced as two syllables.

Pet forms (of 1): Low German: **Hanke**. Czech: **Hanuš**.

Johana (f.) Czech form of JOANNA.

Johann (m.) Common German form of JOHN, representing a more learned form than HANS.

Johanna (f.) Latinate feminine form of *Johannes* (see JOHN), used in Germany, Holland, and Scandinavia.

John (m.) English form of Latin *Johannes*, New Testament Greek *Iōannēs*, a contracted form of the Hebrew name *Johanan* 'God is gracious' (the name of several different characters in the Old Testament, including one of King David's *'mighty men'*). *John* is the spelling used in the Authorized Version of the New Testament. The name is of great importance in early Christianity: it was borne by John the Baptist (the precursor of Christ himself, who baptized sinners in the River Jordan), by one of Christ's disciples (John the Apostle, a fisherman, brother of James), and by the author of the fourth gospel (John the Evangelist, identified in Christian tradition with the apostle, but more probably a Greek-speaking Jewish Christian living over half a century later). The name was also borne by many subsequent Christian saints and by twenty-three popes, including John XXIII (Giuseppe Roncalli, 1881–1963), whose popularity was yet another factor influencing people to choose this given name. It was also a royal name, being born by eight Byzantine emperors and by kings of Hungary, Poland, Portugal, France, and elsewhere. In its various forms in different languages, it has been the most perennially popular of all Christian names.

Cognates: Irish: EOIN, SEÁN. Scottish: IAN, Iain, Eòin, Seathan. Welsh: IEUAN, SIÔN. French: **Jean**. Breton: **Yann**. Italian: **Giovanni, Gianni**. Spanish: **Juan**. Catalan: **Joan**. Galician: **Xoán**. Portuguese: **João**. Basque: **Ion, Yon**. Romanian: **Ion**. German: **Johann, Johannes, Hans**. Low German: **Johan**. Dutch: **Jan**. Danish, Norwegian: **Jens, Johan, Jan**. Swedish: **Johan, Jöns, Jon, Jan**. Polish: **Jan; Iwan** (an E. Polish, Belorussian, or Ukrainian form). Czech: **Johan, Jan**. Russian: **Ivan**. Hungarian: **János**. Finnish: **Juhani, Jussi, Hannu**.
Pet forms: English: **Johnny, Johnnie**; JACK; HANK. Scottish Gaelic: **Seonaidh**. Spanish: **Juanito**. Breton: **Yannic(k)**. German: **Hansi**. Low German: **Hanke, Henning**. Dutch: **Joop**. Danish: **Henning**. Swedish: **Jösse**. Polish: **Janusz**. Czech: **Hanuš**.

Johnathon (m.) English: respelled form of JONATHAN, influenced by JOHN.

Johnny (m., f.) English and Scottish: pet form of JOHN. In America it is occasionally also used as a female name.

Variant: **Johnnie**.

Jokum (m.) Danish and Norwegian form of JOACHIM.

Jolanda (f.) Italian form of YOLANDE. The name was a traditional one in the royal house of Savoy, and was revived in Italy in 1901, when it was given by King Victor Emmanuel III to his first child. This spelling is also commonly used in Holland.

Cognates: Polish: **Jolanta**. Czech: **Jolan(t)a**. Hungarian: **Jolán**.
Pet form: Polish: **Jola**.

Jolene (f.) English: a recent coinage, combining the short form Jo with the productive suffix -lene, extracted from names such as MARLENE. It seems to have originated in America in the 1940s. It was made famous by a hit song with this title, recorded by Dolly Parton in 1979.

Jolyon (m.) English: medieval variant spelling of JULIAN. Its occasional use in modern Britain derives from the name of a character in John Galsworthy's sequence of novels *The Forsyte Saga* (1922), which was serialized on British television in the late 1960s.

Jon (m.) Swedish form of JOHN. This form of the name is also used in the English-speaking world as a variant spelling of JOHN or short form of JONATHAN.

Jonah (m.) Biblical name (meaning 'dove' in Hebrew) borne by a prophet whose adventures are the subject of one of the shorter books of the Bible. God appeared to Jonah and ordered him to go and preach in Nineveh. When Jonah disobeyed, God caused a storm to threaten the ship in which Jonah was travelling. His shipmates, realizing that Jonah was the cause of their peril, threw him overboard, whereupon the storm subsided. A 'great fish' swallowed Jonah and delivered him, willy-nilly, to the coasts of Nineveh. This story was immensely popular in the Middle Ages, and a favourite subject of miracle plays.

Variant: **Jonas** (from the New Testament Greek form, *Iōnas*).

Jonathan (m.) Biblical name, meaning 'God has given', composed of the same elements as those of MATTHEW, but in reverse order. This is the name of several characters in the Bible, most notably a son of King Saul, who was a devoted friend and supporter of the young David, even when David and Saul were themselves at loggerheads (1 Samuel 31; 2 Samuel 1: 19–26). The name is often taken as symbolic of steadfast friendship and loyalty. See also EOIN.

Variants: English: **Jonathon, Johnathan**.
Cognate: Irish Gaelic: **Seonac**.
Short form: **English: Jon**.

Joni (f.) English: modern respelling of *Joanie*, pet form of JOAN. It is particularly associated with the Canadian folk singer Joni Mitchell (b. 1943).

Jonna (f.) Danish: contracted form of JOHANNA.

Jonquil (f.) English: from the name of the flower, which was taken into English from French *jonquille* (a diminutive of Spanish *junco*, Latin *juncus* reed). This is one of the latest and rarest of the flower names, which enjoyed a brief vogue during the 1940s and 1950s.

Jöns (m.) Swedish: variant of JOHAN, from a contracted form of Latin *Johannes*.

Pet form: **Jösse**.

Joop (m.) Dutch: pet form of *Josef* (see JOSEPH) and of *Johannes* (see JOHN).

Joord (m.) Dutch: pet form of *Jordaan* (see JORDAN).

Joost (m.) Dutch form of the Latin name JUSTUS or of *Jodocus*, a Latinized form of the Breton name *Iodoc* (see JOYCE).

Jöran (m.) Swedish: variant of GÖRAN.

Jordan (m.) English and German: originally a name given to a child (of either sex) baptized in holy water that was, purportedly at least, brought from the River Jordan, whose Hebrew name, *ha-yarden*, means 'flowing down'. It was in this river that Christ was baptized by John the Baptist, and medieval pilgrims to the Holy Land usually tried to bring back a flask of its water with them. The modern given name is either a revival of this, or else a transferred use of the surname that was derived from the medieval given name.

Cognates: French: **Jourdain**. Italian: **Giordano**. Dutch: **Jordaan**.
Pet forms: English: **Judd** (rare). Dutch: **Joord**.

Jordi (m.) Catalan form of GEORGE, the patron saint of Catalonia.

Jörg (m.) German: dialectal form of GEORGE, characteristic of the Alemannic and Swabian dialects.

Jorge (m.) Spanish and Portuguese form of GEORGE.

Jørgen (m.) Danish form of GEORGE (cf. GÖRAN).
Variant: **Jørn**.
Cognate: Swedish: **Jörgen**.

Jori (m.) Provençal form of GEORGE.

Joris (m.) Dutch and Frisian form of both *Georgius* (see GEORGE) and *Gregorius* (see GREGORY).

Jorma (m.) Finnish form of JEREMY.

Jørn (m.) Danish: contracted form of JØRGEN.

Josceline (f.) English: variant of JOCELYN as a female name.

José (m.) Spanish form of JOSEPH, also borne by women as the second part of the compound name *María José*. As a male name, it is now also occasionally used in the English-speaking world.

Josée (f.) French: feminine form of JOSEPH, at one time commonly used in the combination **Marie-Josée**.

Joseba (m.) Basque form of JOSEPH.

Josef (m.) German, Dutch, Scandinavian, and Czech form of JOSEPH.

Pet forms: Czech: **Józa**, **Joska**, **Jož(k)a**, **Jožánek**.

Josefa (f.) Feminine form of JOSEPH, used in Spanish, Portuguese, the Scandinavian languages, and Czech.

Pet forms: Spanish: **Pepa**, **Pepita**.

Joseph (m.) English and French form of the biblical Hebrew name *Yosef*, meaning '(God) shall add (another son)'. This was borne by the favourite son of Jacob, whose brothers became jealous of him and sold him into slavery (Genesis 37). He was taken to Egypt, where he rose to become chief steward to Pharaoh, and was eventually reconciled to his brothers when they came to buy corn during a seven-year famine (Genesis 43–7).

In the New Testament *Joseph* is the name of the husband of the Virgin Mary. It is also borne by a rich Jew, Joseph of Arimathea (Matthew 27: 57; Mark 15: 43; Luke 23: 50; John 19: 38), who took Jesus down from the Cross, wrapped him in a shroud, and buried him in a rock tomb. According to medieval legend, Joseph of Arimathea brought the Holy Grail to Britain.

Cognates: Irish Gaelic: **Seosamh**. Scottish Gaelic: **Ìoseph**. Italian: **Giuseppe**. Spanish: **José**. Catalan: **Josep**. Galician: **Xosé**. Basque: **Joseba**. German, Dutch, Scandinavian, Czech: **Josef**. Polish: **Józef**. Hungarian: **József**. Russian: **Iosif**, **Osip**. Hebrew: **Yosef**.
Short forms: English, Irish: **Jo(e)**. German: **Sepp**.
Pet forms: Scottish: **Josie**; **Seòsaidh** (Gaelic). Spanish: **Pepe**, **Pepito**. Dutch: **Joop**.

Josèphe (f.) French: feminine form of JOSEPH, now much less common than JOSÉPHINE.

Josephine (f.) English form of JOSÉPHINE, now widely adopted in the English-speaking world.

Cognates: Irish Gaelic: **Seosaimhín**. Italian: **Giuseppina**.
Short form: English: **Jo**.
Pet forms: English: **Josie**, **Josette**, FIFI, POSY.

Joséphine (f.) French: feminine form of JOSEPH, formed with the addition of the productive hypocoristic suffix *-ine*. The name owes much of its popularity in France to the Empress Joséphine (1763–184), first wife of Napoleon Bonaparte, a charming if somewhat frivolous woman. She presided over a brilliant court until 1809, when Napoleon had the marriage annulled on the grounds that she had not borne him a child. Her original name was Marie Josèphe Rose Tascher de la Pagerie; she had been born in Martinique and, before meeting Napoleon, had been married to Alexandre de Beauharnais, an aristocrat who was guillotined in 1794.

Pet forms: **Josette**, FIFI.

Josette (f.) French: modern pet form of JOSÉPHINE, sometimes also used in the English-speaking world in the 20th century.

Josh (m.) English: short form of JOSHUA, occasionally used as an independent given name.

Joshua (m.) Biblical name (meaning 'God is salvation' in Hebrew) borne by the Israelite leader who took command of the children of Israel after the death of Moses and led them, after many battles, to take possession of the promised land. Other forms of his name include Hebrew *Yehoshua(h)*, *Yeshua*, *Hosea*, *Oshea*, and Greek *Iēsos* (*Jesus*). The name is very popular among Jews, and was also favoured by the Puritans and Nonconformists.

Cognates: Dutch: **Jozua**. Italian: **Giosuè**.

Josiah (m.) Biblical name (meaning 'God heals' in Hebrew) borne by a king of Judah, whose story is recounted in 2 Kings 22–3. This was fairly frequently used as a given name in the English-speaking world, especially among Dissenters, from the 18th to the early 20th century. The most famous English bearer was the potter Josiah Wedgwood (1730–95). In North America this was a recurrent name in the Quincy family of Massachusetts; the best-known Josiah Quincy (1744–75) was a pre-Revolutionary patriot, who died at the age of 31 while returning from arguing the cause of the American colonists in London.

Josiane (f.) French: elaborated form of JOSÉE, now occasionally also used in the English-speaking world.

Josie (f., m.) 1. (f.) English: pet form of JOSEPHINE, occasionally used as an independent given name in the 20th century. 2. (m.) Scottish: pet form of JOSEPH, in Gaelic **Seòsaidh**.

Joss (m., f.) English: short form of JOCELYN, occasionally used as an independent given name. In part it may also represent a revival of a medieval spelling of the male name JOYCE.

Jösse (m.) Swedish: pet form of Jöns.

Josune (f.) Basque form of *Jesusa* (see Jesús).

Joy (f.) English: from the vocabulary word (from Old French *joie*, Late Latin *gaudia*). Being 'joyful in the Lord' was a duty that the Puritans took seriously, so the name became popular in the 17th century under their influence. In modern times, it is generally used as an omen name, with the intention of wishing the child a happy life (cf. Happy and Merry).

Joyce (f.), formerly (m.) English: apparently from the Norman male name *Josce* (Middle English *Josse*), which in turn is from *Jodocus*, a Latinized form of a Breton name, *Iodoc*, meaning 'lord', borne by a 7th-century Breton saint. The name was in use among Breton followers of William the Conqueror. However, although this was fairly common as a male given name in the Middle Ages, it had virtually died out by the 14th century. There is some evidence of its use as a female name in the 17th and 18th centuries, perhaps as a variant of Joy. It was strongly revived in the 19th century under the influence of popular fiction. It is borne by characters in Mrs Henry Wood's *East Lynne* (1861) and Edna Lyall's *In the Golden Days* (1885). Modern use may well have been influenced also by the common Irish surname derived from the medieval Norman male name. See also Joss.

Cognates: Low German: JOBST. Dutch: JOOST, **Joos**.

Jozafat (m.) Polish: from *Josaphat*, a Greek form (used in the New Testament) of Hebrew *Jehoshaphat* 'God has judged'. This was the name in the Bible of a virtuous king of Judah. It owes its popularity as a Polish name to having been borne as a name in religion by a Polish saint (1584–1623), archbishop of Polotsk in Lithuania; his baptismal name was John.

Józef (m.) Polish form of Joseph.

Feminine form: **Józefa**.

József (m.) Hungarian form of Joseph.

Juan (m.) Spanish form of John, now occasionally used as a given name in English-speaking countries, in spite of the unfavourable associations with *Don Juan*, the heartless seducer of Mozart's opera (1788) and libertine hero of Byron's satirical epic (1819–24).

Juana (f.) Spanish: feminine form of Juan.

Juanita (f.) Spanish: feminine pet form of Juan. It is now also occasionally used in the English-speaking world, to which it was introduced mainly by Hispanic settlers in the United States.

Juanito (m.) Spanish: pet form of Juan.

Judah (m.) Biblical name, possibly meaning 'praised' in Hebrew, borne by the fourth son of Jacob (Genesis 29: 35), who gave his name to one of the twelve tribes of Israel and to one of its two kingdoms.

Cognate: Hebrew: **Yehuda**.

Judas (m.) New Testament: Greek form of Judah. This is borne in the New Testament by several characters, but most notably by Judas Iscariot, the apostle who betrayed Christ in the Garden of Gethsemane. There was another apostle called *Judas* (see Jude), and the name was also borne by Judas Maccabaeus, who liberated Judea briefly from the Syrians in 165 BC, but was killed in battle (161). His story was very popular in the Middle Ages. However, the association with Iscariot has ensured that this name has hardly ever been used as a Christian name, and that *Jude* has always been much rarer than other apostles' names.

Judd (m.) English: medieval pet form of Jordan, now restored to use as a given name from the derived surname.

Jude (m.) English: short form of Judas, occasionally adopted in the New Testament and elsewhere in an attempt to distinguish the apostle Jude (Judas Thaddeus), to whom one of the epistles in the New Testament is attributed, from the traitor Judas Iscariot. The name is also borne by the central character in Thomas Hardy's gloomy novel *Jude the Obscure* (1895). More recently it received some support from the Lennon and McCartney song '*Hey Jude*' (1968).

Judith (f.) Biblical name, meaning 'Jewess' or 'woman from Judea', borne by a Jewish heroine whose story is recorded in the Book of Judith in the Apocrypha. Judith is portrayed as a beautiful widow who delivers her people from the invading Assyrians by gaining the confidence of their commander, Holofernes, and cutting off his head while he is asleep; without their commander, the Assyrians are duly routed. The name is also borne by one of the Hittite wives of Esau (Genesis 26: 34). This has been a perennially popular Jewish name. In the English-speaking world it was taken up among Nonconformists in the 18th century, and has enjoyed great popularity in the 20th century. It was in occasional use among Gentiles before this: for example, it was borne by a niece of William the Conqueror. Elsewhere in Europe, it has usually been regarded as a characteristically Jewish name. In Ireland and Scotland it has been used as an Anglicized form of the Gaelic names Siobhán and Siubhan.

Cognates: Hebrew: **Yehudit**. Latinized: **Juditha**. Polish: **Judyta**. Czech: **Judita**.

Pet forms: English: **Judy, Judi, Judie**. German: **Jutta, Jutte**. Dutch: **Jutka, Jutte, Juut**. Danish: **Jytte**. Czech: **Jitka**.

Judy (f.) English: pet form of Judith, now sometimes taken as an independent name in its own right.

Variants: **Judi, Judie**.

Juhani (m.) Finnish form of John.

Juià (m.) Catalan form of Julian.

Jules (m.), now sometimes also (f.) **1**. (m.) French form of Julius. It is a very common given name in France and is occasionally also found in the English-speaking world. **2**. (m.) English: pet form of Julian. **3**. (f.) English: informal pet form of Julie.

Julia (f.) Feminine form of the Roman family name Julius. A woman called Julia is mentioned in Paul's *Epistle* to the Romans (Romans 16: 15), and the name was borne by numerous early saints. Its frequency increased with the vogue for classical names in the 18th century, and it continues to enjoy considerable popularity, although the recent introduction of Julie to the English-speaking world has reduced its popularity somewhat.

Cognates: Italian: **Giulia**. French: Julie.

Julian (m.); occasionally (f.) English: from the common Late Latin given name *Juliānus*, a derivative of Julius. In classical times *Juliānus* was a name borne not only by various minor early saints, but also by the Roman emperor Julian 'the Apostate', who attempted to return the Roman Empire from institutionalized Christianity to paganism. For many centuries the English name *Julian* was borne by women as well as men, for example by the Blessed Julian of Norwich (*c*.1342–after

1413). The differentiation in form of *Julian* and GILLIAN did not occur until the 16th century. *Julian* is still occasionally used as a female name.

Variant: JOLYON (m.).

Cognates: French: **Julien**. Spanish: **Julián**. Catalan: **Juià**.

Juliana (f.) Latin feminine form of *Juliānus* (see JULIAN), which was revived in England in the 18th century and has been used occasionally ever since. The name in this form is also used in Germany, the Netherlands, Scandinavia, Spain, and Portugal.

Variant: German: **Juliane**.

Julianne (f.) English: modern combination of the given names JULIE and ANNE, perhaps sometimes intended as a form of JULIANA.

Julie (f.) French form of JULIA. This was imported to the English-speaking world in the 1920s, and for some reason has become enormously popular. Its popularity was increased in the 1960s by the fame of the actresses Julie Harris (b. 1925) and Julie Andrews (b. 1935 as Julia Wells).

Julien (m.) French form of the male name JULIAN.

Feminine form: **Julienne**.

Juliet (f.) English: Anglicized form of French JULIETTE or Italian GIULIETTA. The name is most famous as that of the 'star-crossed' heroine of Shakespeare's tragedy *Romeo and Juliet*.

Juliette (f.) French: diminutive of JULIE, used also in the English-speaking world.

Cognate: Italian: **Giulietta**.

Julio (m.) Spanish form of JULIUS.

Julitta (f.) Italian and English: of uncertain origin, probably a Late Latin form of JUDITH, influenced by JULIA. This was the name borne by the mother of the infant saint, Quiricus (see QUIRCE); she was martyred with him at Tarsus in 304.

Julius (m.) Roman family name, of obscure derivation, borne most notably by Gaius Julius Caesar (?102–44 BC). It was in use among the early Christians, and was the name of an early and influential pope (337–52), as well as of a later pope (1443–1513) who attempted to combat the corruption of the Renaissance papacy. *Julius* is now sometimes found as a Jewish name, having on occasions been chosen as a substitute for any of the numerous Hebrew names normally transliterated with an initial *J*-.

Cognates: Italian: **Giulio**. Spanish: **Julio**. Polish: **Juliusz**. Hungarian: **Gyula**. See also IOLO.

June (f.) English: the most successful and enduring of the names coined in the early 20th century from the names of months of the year (cf. APRIL and MAY).

Juniper (f.) English: from the name of the plant (derived in the Middle Ages from Late Latin *juniperus*, of uncertain origin). The term is also used in the Authorized Version of the Old Testament as a translation of Hebrew *rothem*, a substantial desert shrub whose wood was used in the building of the temple of Solomon. This is not a particularly common given name; there may have been some influence from JENNIFER (the surname *Juniper* is in part derived from *Jennifer*).

Junita (f.) English: variant of JUANITA, perhaps influenced by the name of the Roman goddess *Juno* or by the given name JUNE, or by both.

Juno (f.) Irish: Anglicized form of ÚNA, assimilated to the name of the Roman goddess *Juno*, consort of Jupiter.

Jurek (m.) Polish: pet form of JERZY.

Jürgen (m.) Low German form of GEORGE.

Jussi (m.) A Finnish form of JOHN.

Justin (m.) English: Anglicized form of the Latin given name *Justīnus*, a derivative of JUSTUS. *Justīnus* was the name borne by various early saints, notably a 2nd-century Christian apologist and a (possibly spurious) boy martyr of the 3rd century. As an English name, *Justin* has enjoyed considerable popularity in the second part of the 20th century.

Cognate: Welsh: **Iestyn**.

Justine (f.) English: feminine form of JUSTIN. Its popularity in Britain since the 1960s is no doubt partly due to the influence of Lawrence Durrell's novel of this name.

Variant: **Justina** (Latin form).

Justus (m.) Latin name meaning 'just' or 'fair'. Because of its transparently well-omened meaning, it has been used occasionally as a given name in several countries, including Germany and the Netherlands.

Cognates: French: **Just(e)**. Dutch: JOOST.

Jutte (f.) German: vernacular form of JUDITH, now well established as an independent given name in its own right.

Variant: **Jutta**.

Jytte (f.) Danish form of JUTTE.

K

Kaapo (m.) Finnish form of GABRIEL.

Kaarle (m.) Finnish form of CHARLES.

Kai (m.) Scandinavian (mainly Danish), N. German, and Frisian: a popular name of uncertain origin. It may be connected with the Old Norse vocabulary word *kaða* hen, chicken. Alternatively, it may come from the Roman name *Gaius* (see CAYO). See also KAY (2).

Variant: **Kaj**.
Cognate: Czech: **Kája, Kájin**.
Pet forms: Czech: **Kajik, Kajíček, Kajínek**.

Kajetan (m.) German and Polish form of GAETANO.

Kajsa (f.) Swedish: pet form of KATARINA.

Kaley (f.) English: variant spelling of KAYLEY.

Variant: **Kaleigh**.

Kalle (m.) Swedish: pet form of KARL. The name is now also used to some extent in Germany.

Kálmán (m.) Hungarian form of COLMAN. It is a common name as a result of the fame of St Colman of Stockerau (d. 1012), an Irish pilgrim who was killed at Stockerau near Vienna while on his way to the Holy Land, and who worked numerous miracles after his death. It was also the name of an early king of Hungary (ruled 1095–1116), remembered as a lawgiver.

Kamil (m.) Polish and Czech form of the Latin name *Camillus* (see CAMILLA).

Feminine form: **Kamila**.

Kane (m.) Irish: Anglicized form of the Gaelic name CATHÁN.

Kapiton (m.) Russian: from the Late Latin name *Capito* (genitive *Capitōnis*), originally a nickname meaning 'bigheaded', from *caput* (genitive *capitis*) head. St Capiton was a 4th-century missionary bishop who preached in the Crimea and south Russia.

Kåre (m.) Scandinavian: from the Old Norse personal name *Kári*, originally a byname meaning 'curly-haired'.

Karel (m.) Dutch and Czech form of CHARLES.

Pet forms: Czech: **Karlí(če)k, Karloušek**.

Karen (f.) Danish form of KATHERINE, first introduced to the English-speaking world by Scandinavian settlers in America. It has been used in Britain only since the 1950s, but has become very popular.

Kari (f.) Norwegian (or dialectal Swedish) form of KATHERINE; cf. KARIN and KAREN.

Karin (f.) Swedish form of KATHERINE, found as a less common variant of KAREN in America and Britain.

Karita (f.) Scandinavian form of CHARITY, from the Late Latin name *Caritas*.

Karl (m.) German and Scandinavian form of CHARLES, now also used to some extent in the English-speaking world. The perennial popularity of this name in the German-speaking world was reinforced by the fact that it was an aristocratic and royal name from an early date, being borne, for example, by no less than seven Austrian emperors. Its status as an imperial name is reflected in the fact that the Polish, Czech, and Hungarian vocabulary words for 'emperor' are derived from the personal name: *król*, *král*, and *király* respectively. See also CARL.

Pet form: **Kalle**.
Cognates: Dutch, Czech: **Karel**. Polish: **Karol**.
Hungarian: **Károly**. See also CHARLES.
Feminine forms: German, Scandinavian: **Karla** See also CARLA.

Karlmann (m.) German: from an old Germanic personal name, an elaboration of KARL with the Old High German element *man* man. The Blessed Carloman (707–55) was a member of the Frankish royal family, being the eldest son of Charles Martel, brother of Pepin the Short, and uncle of Charlemagne.

Karlotte (f.) German form of CHARLOTTE.

Karol (m.) Polish form of CHARLES.

Karolina (f.) Scandinavian, Polish, and Czech form of CAROLINE.

Karoline (f.) German and Danish form of CAROLINE.

Károly (m.) Hungarian form of CHARLES.

Karp (m.) Russian: from the Late Greek personal name *Karpos*, from *karpos* fruit, produce, result. This seems to have been a short form of the name *Karpophoros* 'fruit-bearing', i.e. fruitful, productive. The name is found in the New Testament, when St Paul refers in passing to 'the cloak that I left at Troas with Carpus' (2 Timothy 4: 13); in the Eastern Church this person is believed to have been an early bishop.

Karsten (m.) Low German: variant spelling of CARSTEN.

Kasia (f.) Polish: pet form of *Katarzyna* (see KATHERINE).

Kaspar (m.) The principal German and Scandinavian form of CASPAR.

Kasper (m.) Polish form of CASPAR, also used in Scandinavia.

Katarina (f.) Swedish form of KATHERINE.

Pet forms: **Kata, Kajsa**.

Katarzyna (f.) Polish form of KATHERINE.

Kate (f.) English: short form of KATHERINE (or any of its variant spellings), reflecting the French pronunciation with -t- for -th-, which was also usual in medieval England. This short form has been continuously popular since the Middle Ages. It was used by Shakespeare for two important characters: the daughter of the King of France who is wooed and won by King Henry V, and the 'shrew' in *The Taming of the Shrew*.

Cognates: Irish Gaelic: **Cáit**. Scottish Gaelic: **Ceit**.

Katerina (f.) Russian: popular form of KATHERINE.

Kateřina (f.) Czech form of KATHERINE.

Kath (f.) English: modern short form of KATHERINE and its variants.

Katha (f.) English: altered form of *Kathy* or name formed directly from KATHERINE.

Katharine (f.) Variant of KATHERINE, the preferred form in America. The spelling has been affected by folk-etymological association with Greek *katharos* pure.

Käthe (f.) German: pet form of KATHARINE.

Katherine (f.) English form of the name of a saint martyred at Alexandria in 307. The story has it that she was a brilliant and learned young woman who was condemned to be broken on the wheel for her Christian belief and opposition to paganism. However, the wheel miraculously fell apart, so she was beheaded instead. There were innumerable elaborations on this story, which was one of the most popular in early Christian mythology, and she has been the object of a vast popular cult. The earliest sources that mention her are in Greek and give the name in the form *Aikaterinē* (still the modern Greek form, reflected also in the Russian form, *Yekaterina*). The name is of unknown etymology; the suggestion that it may be derived from *Hecate*, the pagan goddess of magic and enchantment, is not convincing. From an early date, it was associated with the Greek adjective *katharos* pure. This led to spellings with *-th-* and to a change in the middle vowel (see KATHARINE). Several later saints also bore the name, including the mystic St Katherine of Siena (1347–80), who both led a contemplative life and played a role in the affairs of state of her day.

    Katherine is also a royal name: in England it was borne by the formidable and popular Katherine of Aragon (1485–1536), first wife of Henry VIII, as well as by the wives of Henry V and Charles II. In France, it was borne by Catherine de' Medici (1519–89), wife of King Henry II and regent (1560–74). Probably the most famous royal bearer of all was the Russian empress Catherine the Great (1729–96; reigned 1762–96).

Variants: **Katharine**, **Catherine**, **Catharine**, **Kathryn**, **Cathryn**. Cognates: Irish Gaelic: **Caitríona**, **Caitrín**, **Catraoine**, **Caitlin**. Scottish: CATRIONA, **Ca(i)triona**. Welsh: **Catrin**. French: **Catherine**. Italian: **Caterina**. Spanish: **Catalina**. Portuguese: **Catarina**. German: **Kat(h)arine**, **Katrine**. Dutch: **Katrien**, **Katrijn**. Polish: **Katarzyna**. Czech: **Kateřina**. Russian: **Yekaterina**; **Katerina** (popular form). See also KAREN, KARIN, KARI.
Short forms: English: KATE; **Kath**, **Cath**.
Pet forms: English: **Kathy**, **Cathy**; **Katie**, **Katy**, **Kit(ty)**. German: **Käthe**. Polish: **Kasia**. Russian: **Katya**, **Katinka**.

Kathleen (f.) Irish and English: Anglicized form of Gaelic CAITLÍN.
Variant: **Cathleen**.

Kathryn (f.) American form of KATHERINE, now the most common spelling in the United States. It seems to have originated as a deliberate alteration for the sake of distinction, perhaps influenced by the suffix *-lyn* (see LYNN).

Katie English: pet form of KATE, with the hypocoristic suffix *-ie*.
Variant: **Katy**.
Cognate: Scottish Gaelic: **Ceiteag**.

Katinka (f.) Russian: pet form derived from an extended version of KATYA.

Katrien (f.) Dutch form of KATHERINE.
Variant: **Katrijn**.

Katriona (f.) English: variant spelling of CATRIONA.

Katrine (f.) German and Danish: contracted form of KATHARINE, now used occasionally in the English-speaking world, in part as an Anglicized form of Irish Gaelic *Caitrín*.

Katy (f.) English: variant spelling of KATIE.

Katya (f.) Russian: pet form of YEKATARINA, now sometimes used as an independent given name in the English-speaking world.

Kay (f., m.) English: **1**. (f.) Pet form of any of the various female names beginning with the letter *K-* (cf. DEE and JAY), most notably KATHERINE and its variants. **2**. (m.) Comparatively rare male name, which presumably originated in honour of the Arthurian knight so called, although Sir Kay is not a particularly attractive character. His name seems to be a Celticized form of Latin *Gaius*, an old Roman given name of uncertain derivation (cf. CAYO).

Kayla (f.) English: recently coined altered form of KAYLEY.

Kayley (f.) Irish and English: of recent origin and uncertain derivation. *Kayley* is an Irish surname, an Anglicized form of Gaelic *Ó Caollaidhe* 'descendant of *Caolladhe*', an old male personal name derived from the element *caol* slender. Its adoption as a modern given name has probably also been influenced by the popularity of the names KELLY and KYLIE.
Variants: **Kayly**, **Kaley**, **Ka(y)leigh**.

Kazimierz (m.) Polish form of CASIMIR.

Kean (m.) Irish: Anglicized form of the Gaelic name CIAN.
Variant: **Keane**.

Keeley (f.) English and Irish: of recent origin and uncertain etymology, possibly an alteration of KEELIN to fit in with the pattern of female names ending in *-(e)y* or *-ie*. The Irish surname *Keeley* is a variant of KAYLEY.
Variants: **Keely**, **Keeleigh**, KEIGHLEY.

Keelin (f.) Irish: Anglicized form of the Gaelic name **Caoilfhionn**, composed of the elements *caol* slender + *fionn* white.

Kees (m.) Dutch: pet form of CORNELIS, now also used as an independent given name.
Variant: **Cees**.

Keighley (f.) English: fanciful respelling of KEELEY, inspired by the Yorkshire town of *Keighley*, which is, however, pronounced /ki:θlɪ/.

Keir (m.) Scottish: transferred use of the surname, in origin a variant of KERR. In some cases, the name may be chosen in honour of the trade unionist and first Labour MP, James Keir Hardie (1856–1915), whose mother's maiden name was Keir.

Keith (m.) English and Scottish: from a Scottish surname, originally a local name derived from lands so called in East Lothian, probably from a Celtic (Brythonic) word meaning 'wood'. The principal family bearing this surname were hereditary Earls Marischal of Scotland from 1455 to 1715. This is one of a number of Scottish aristocratic surnames that have become well established since the 19th century as male names throughout the English-speaking world, not just in Scotland. Others include BRUCE, GRAHAM, DOUGLAS, and LESLIE.
Feminine form: **Keitha**.

Kelan (m.) Irish: Anglicized form of Gaelic **Caolán**, originally a byname representing a diminutive form of *cool* slender.

Keld (m.) Danish form of KETTIL.

Kelemen (m.) Hungarian form of CLEMENT.

Kelly (m., f.) English: As a male name, an Anglicized form of Irish Gaelic CEALLAGH. In Australia and elsewhere in the English-speaking world it is now more commonly used as a female given name. This use probably derives from the Irish surname (Gaelic *Ó Ceallaigh* 'descendant of Ceallagh'); cf. the similar recent use of CASEY and CASSIDY as female given names.

Variants: **Kelley**, **Kellie** (f.).

Kelsey (m., f.) English: transferred use of the surname, which is derived from the Old English masculine personal name *Céolsige*, composed of the elements *céol* ship + *sige* victory.

Variant: **Kelsie**.

Kelvin (m.) English: modern given name, first used in the 1920s. It is taken from a Scottish river which runs through Glasgow into the Clyde (cf. CLYDE). Its choice as a given name may also have been influenced by the form of such names as MELVIN and CALVIN and the fame of the scientist Lord Kelvin.

Kemp (m.) English: transferred use of the surname, which originated in the Middle Ages as an occupational name or nickname from Middle English *kempe* athlete, wrestler (from Old English *kempa* warrior, champion).

Ken (m.) English: short form of KENNETH, or occasionally of various other male names with this first syllable.

Kendall (m., f.) English, Cornish, and Welsh: transferred use of the surname, which is at least in part a local name, either from *Kendal* in Cumbria (formerly the county town of Westmorland, so named because it stands in the valley of the river *Kent*), or from *Kendale* in Driffield, Humberside, where the first element is Old Norse *keld* spring. The distribution of the surname makes it seem likely that it is also partly derived from the Welsh given name CYNDDELW, or from a Cornish cognate.

Variant: **Kendal**.

Kendra (f.) English: recently coined feminine form of KENDRICK.

Kendrick (m.) English: in modern use a transferred use of the surname, the origins of which are confused. Given its distribution, the most likely source in the majority of cases is the Old Welsh personal name *Cynwrig*. This is of uncertain derivation, but may be composed of Old Celtic elements meaning 'high, exalted' + 'hill, summit'.

The Scottish surname *Ken(d)rick* is a shortened form of *MacKen(d)rick* (Gaelic *Mac Eanraig* 'son of Henry'); Scottish bearers are descended from a certain Henry MacNaughton, and therefore the (Mac)Ken(d)ricks are a sept of Clan MacNaughton.

It is also possible that, as an English surname, *Ken(d)rick* is derived in part from the Old English personal names *Cēnerīc* and *Cyneríc*. The first of these is composed of the elements *cēne* keen or bold + *rīc* power; the second is from *cyne* royal + *rīc* power. Withycombe says that 'the Christian name *Cynric* survived into the 17th century,' but unfortunately does not give any evidence. Without information about the location it is impossible to decide whether it is a survival (and, if so, of what), a revival, or a transferred use.

Variant: **Kenrick**.

Kenelm (m.) English: from an Old English personal name composed of the elements *cēne* keen, bold + *helm* helmet, protection. The name was popular in England during the Middle Ages, when a shadowy 9th-century Mercian prince of this name was widely revered as a saint and martyr, although his death seems to have been rather the result of personal and political motives. It has remained in occasional use ever since, especially in the Digby family, where it tended to alternate with EVERARD. The most famous Sir Kenelm Digby (1603–65) was notable as a writer, scientist, adventurer, diplomat, and lover.

Kennard (m.) English: ultimately from an Old English personal name in which several earlier names have fallen together. The first element is either *cēne* keen, bold, or *cyne* royal; the second is either *weard* guard or *heard* brave, hardy. This name seems to have died out during the Middle Ages, and in modern times *Kennard* probably represents a transferred use of the surname derived from it.

Kennedy (m.) Irish, Scottish, and English: Anglicized form of Irish Gaelic *Cinnéidigh*, a traditional name composed of the elements *ceann* head + *éidigh* ugly. In the Scottish Highlands this form has also been used as an Anglicized equivalent of the Scottish Gaelic name UARRAIG, apparently because that given name was common in kindreds surnamed *Kennedy* (Irish *Ó Cinnéidigh*). In recent years it has sometimes been chosen in the English-speaking world in honour of the assassinated American president John F. Kennedy (1917–63) and his brother Robert (1925–68).

Kenneth (m.) Scottish and English: Anglicized form of two different Gaelic names, *Cinaed* and *Cainnech*. The former seems to have been originally a personal name meaning 'born of fire', the latter a byname meaning 'handsome, fair one'. *Cinaed* was the Gaelic name of Kenneth Mac Alpin, first king of the Picts and Scots; *Cainnech* survives today in Scotland as the common Gaelic name *Coinneach*. In the 20th century *Kenneth* has enjoyed great popularity well beyond the boundaries of Scotland.

Derivatives: Scandinavian: **Kennet**, **Kent**.
Short form: English: **Ken**.
Pet form: Scottish, English: KENNY.
Feminine forms: Scottish: **Kenna**, **Kenina**.

Kenny (m.) **1**. Characteristically Scottish pet form of KENNETH; one of the best-known bearers in modern times is the footballer Kenny Dalglish. **2**. Anglicized form of Irish Gaelic CAINNEACH.

Kent (m.) **1**. English: transferred use of the surname, which originally denoted someone from the county of Kent. This is probably named with a Celtic element meaning 'border'. Its use as a given name is of recent origin, but is now quite popular. **2**. Scandinavian: contracted form of *Kennet*, the Scandinavian form of KENNETH.

Kenton (m.) English: transferred use of the surname, originally a local name from any of various places so called. The one in Devon gets its name from the British river name *Kenn* + Old English *tūn* enclosure, settlement; the one in north-west London is from the Old English personal name *Cēna* 'keen' + *tūn*; the one in Northumberland is from Old English *cyne-* royal + *tūn*; and that in Staffordshire probably from the personal name *Cēna* 'keen' or *Cyna* 'royal' + *tūn*.

Kenya (m.) Russian: pet form of INNOKENTI.

Kepa (m.) Basque equivalent of PETER, taken directly from the Aramaic form *Kephas*.

Kerena (f.) English: Latinate elaboration of **Keren**, itself a version shortened to manageable proportions of the biblical name *Keren-happuch* (meaning 'horn of eye-paint' in Hebrew) borne by the third of Job's daughters (Job 42: 14).

Kermit (m.) English: of Irish and Manx origin, from the Gaelic surname form *Mac Dhiarmaid* 'son of *Diarmad*' (see DERMOT). The name was borne by a son of the American president Theodore Roosevelt, and more recently by a frog puppet on Jim Henson's *Muppet Show*.

Kerr (m.) English: transferred use of the surname, which is a northern English local name for someone who lived by a patch of wet ground overgrown with brushwood (Old Norse *kjarr*).

Kerry (f., m.) English: of recent, Australian, origin, probably from the name of the Irish county. It is now becoming relatively common in Britain as well as Australia, especially as a female name.

Kerstin (f.) Swedish: variant of KRISTINA.

Kerttu (f.) Finnish form of GERTRUDE.

Kester (m.) Medieval Scottish form of CHRISTOPHER, occasionally revived as a modern given name.

Kestrel (f.) English: one of the rarer female names derived from vocabulary words denoting birds that have come into use in the 20th century. The word itself derives from Old French *cresserelle*, apparently a derivative of *cressele* rattle.

Kettil (m.) Swedish: from the Old Norse name *Ketill*, a short form of various compound names containing the second element *ketill* sacrificial cauldron, for example *Thorketill* (see TORKEL) and *Arnketill*.

Variant: **Kjell**.

Cognates: Norwegian: **Kjetil**. Danish: **Kjeld**, **Keld**.

Keturah (f.) Biblical: name (meaning 'incense' in Hebrew) borne by the wife *Abraham* married after *Sarah*'s death (Genesis 25: 1). The name is occasionally chosen in the English-speaking world by parents in search of an unusual name.

Kevin (m.) Irish and English: Anglicized form of the Gaelic name *Caoimhín*, originally a byname representing a diminutive of Gaelic *caomh* comely, beloved. This was the name of a 7th-century saint who is one of the patrons of Dublin.

Variant: **Kevan** (from Gaelic **Caoimheán**, with a different diminutive suffix).

Kezia (f.) Biblical: name of one of Job's daughters, born to him towards the end of his life, after his prosperity had been restored (Job 42: 14). It represents the Hebrew word for the *cassia* tree (named in English, via Latin and Greek, from a similar Semitic source). The name is used in the English-speaking world rather less frequently than JEMIMA, but considerably more so than *Keren-happuch*, the name of Job's third daughter (see KERENA).

Pet forms: **Kizzie**, **Kizzy**.

Khipa (m.) Russian: pet form of ARKHIP.

Kicki (f.) Swedish: pet form of KRISTINA. Derived apparently from a childish pronunciation of the name, this form is found from the late 19th century onwards.

Kiera (f.) Irish and English: recently coined feminine form of KIERAN; cf. CIARA.

Kieran (m.) Irish: Anglicized form of Gaelic CIARÁN.

Variant: **Kyran**.

Kilina (f.) Ukrainian form of AKILINA.

Killian (m.) Irish: Anglicized form of Gaelic CILLIAN. This name was borne by various early Irish saints, including the 7th-century author of a 'Life of St Bridget', and missionaries to Artois and Franconia.

Variant: **Kilian**.

Kilya (f.) Russian: pet form of AKILINA.

Kim (f., m.) 1. (f., m.) English: originally a male name, a short form of KIMBERLEY, but now much more common than the latter and nearly always a female name. It has become established as an independent name in its own right. The hero of Rudyard Kipling's novel *Kim* (1901) bore the name as a short form of *Kimball* (a surname used as a given name). 2. (m.) Scandinavian: aphetic short form of *joakim* (see JOACHIM).

Kima (m.) Russian: pet form of AKIM or YAKIM.

Kimberley (f., m.) English: becoming increasingly common as a female name, being regarded, probably rightly, as the full form of KIM. Its history is complicated, in that it is from a placename, from a surname, from a placename. The immediate source is the town in South Africa, the scene of fighting during the Boer War, which brought it to public notice at the end of the 19th century. The town was named after a certain Lord Kimberley, whose ancestors derived their surname from one of the places in England called Kimberley. The first part of the placename derives from various Old English personal names; the second (from Old English *lēah*) means 'wood' or 'clearing'.

Variants: **Kimberly** (the more common U.S. spelling); **Kimberleigh**.

Kina (f.) Scottish (Highland): short form of *Alickina* (see ALICK).

King (m.) English: from the vocabulary word for a monarch, bestowed, especially in America, with a hint of the notion that the bearer would have kingly qualities; cf. DUKE and EARL. In some cases it may be a transferred use of the surname (originally a nickname or an occupational name given to someone who was employed in a royal household). Its frequency has increased recently among American Blacks, no doubt partly as a result of its being bestowed in honour of the civil rights leader Martin Luther King (1929–68).

Kinge (f.) German: pet form of KUNIGUNDE.

Variant: **Kinga**.

Kingsley (m., f.) English: transferred use of the surname, originally a local name derived from various places (in Cheshire, Hampshire, Staffordshire) named in Old English as *Cyningeslēah* 'king's wood'. It is not clear what was the initial impulse towards use as a given name; the usual pattern in such cases is for a mother's maiden name to be chosen as a given name, but in this case the choice may have been made in honour of the author Charles Kingsley (1819–75).

Kirill (m.) Russian form of CYRIL.

Kirk (m.) Scottish and English: transferred use of the surname, originally a northern English and Scottish local name for someone who lived near a church (from Old Norse *kirkja*). Recent use has probably been influenced to some extent by the film actor Kirk Douglas, who was born in 1916 as Issur Danielovich Demsky.

Kirsten (f.) Danish and Norwegian form of CHRISTINE, now well established in English-speaking countries.

Kirstie (f.) Scottish: pet form of KIRSTIN, now quite commonly used as an independent given name in the rest of the English-speaking world as well as in Scotland.
Variants: **Kirsty**; **Chirsty** (the usual spelling in the Highlands); **Curstaidh**, **Ciorstiadh**, **Curstag**, **Ciorstag** (Gaelic).

Kirstin (f.) Scottish: vernacular form of CHRISTINE, now quite widely used in the English-speaking world.

Kit (m., f.) English: 1. (m.) Pet form of CHRISTOPHER. 2. (f.) Pet form of KATHERINE, an altered form of *Kat*.

Kitty (f.) English: pet form of KATHERINE, derived from the pet form KIT + the hypocoristic suffix *-y*.

Kizzie (f.) English: pet form of KEZIA, now sometimes used as an independent name.
Variant: **Kizzy**.

Kjell (m.) Swedish: contracted form of KETTIL.
Cognates: Norwegian: **Kjetil**. Danish: **Kjeld**, **Keld**.

Klaartje (f.) Dutch: pet form of KLARA.

Klaas (m.) Dutch form of CLAUS.

Klaes (m.) Frisian form of CLAUS.

Klara (f.) German, Dutch, Russian, Polish, and Scandinavian form of CLARA.
Pet form: Dutch: **Klaartje**.

Klaudia (f.) Polish form of CLAUDIA.

Klaudiusz (m.) Polish form of CLAUDE.

Klaus (m.) German: variant spelling of CLAUS.

Klavdia (f.) Russian form of CLAUDIA.

Klavdii (m.) Russian form of CLAUDE.

Klemens (m.) German, Danish, Swedish, and Polish form of CLEMENT.
Pet form: Polish: **Klimek**.

Klementyna (f.) Polish form of *Clementina* (see CLEMENTINE).

Klimek (m.) Polish: diminutive pet form of KLEMENS, now used as an independent given name.

Kliment (m.) Russian and Czech form of CLEMENT.

Knut (m.) Scandinavian: from Old Norse *Knútr* 'knot', originally a byname given to a short, squat man. King Knut (d. 1035) ruled over Denmark, Norway, and England in the 11th century. His great-nephew Knut (d. 1086) was another king of Denmark, who founded churches throughout his realm. He was canonized as a martyr, the main reason apparently being that he was murdered by opponents of the laws enforcing payment of tithes to the Church. The latter's nephew, also Knut (d. 1131), was Duke of Schleswig and is also venerated as a martyr, although the justification for this is not clear. It is still a popular Danish and Norwegian given name.
Variant: Danish: **Knud**.
Anglicized form: **Canute**.

Koenraad (m.) Dutch form of CONRAD.

Koldo (m.) Basque: shortened form of *Koldobika*, a derivative of an Ostrogothic form of the Germanic name *Chlodovik*, and so an equivalent of Spanish *Luis* (see LOUIS).

Kolos (m.) Hungarian form of CLAUDE.

Kolya (m.) Russian: aphetic pet form of NIKOLAI.

Kondrat (m.) Polish form of CONRAD, but there has been considerable confusion between this and the Russian name *Kondrati*, which is officially derived from the Late Greek name *Kodratos*, from the Latin byname *Quadrātus*, meaning 'square', i.e. squat, portly. This was borne by various early saints venerated in the Eastern Church, most notably by the writer of the first apologia for Christianity, addressed to the Emperor Hadrian, and by the leader of a group of forty-three martyrs executed in Anatolia under the Emperor Decius.

Konrad (m.) The usual German and Polish spelling of CONRAD.
Variant: **Kurt**.

Konstantin (m.) German, Scandinavian, Hungarian, Czech, and Russian form of CONSTANTINE.
Pet form: Russian: **Kostya**.

Konstantyn (m.) Polish form of CONSTANTINE.

Koppel (m.) Jewish: Yiddish aphetic pet form of JAKOB.

Korbinian (m.) German (S. Germany): given name bestowed in honour of a Frankish saint (?670–770), who evangelized Bavaria from a base at Freising, near Munich. His name was presumably originally Frankish, but in the form in which it has been handed down it appears to be an adjectival derivative of Latin *corvus* raven, which has a Late Latin variant *corbus*. This may represent a translation of the Germanic personal name *Hraban*.
Pet form: **Körbl**.

Kornel (m.) Polish and Czech form of CORNELIUS.
Variants: Polish: **Korneli**, **Korneliusz**.

Kort (m.) Dutch form of KURT.

Kostya (m.) Russian: pet form of KONSTANTIN, which is often pronounced as *Kostatin* in the vernacular.

Kreine (f.) Jewish: from a dialect form of Yiddish *kroine* crown (equivalent to modern German *Krone*, from Latin *corōna*). See also ATARAH.

Kreszenz (f.) German (S. Germany): from the Late Latin pesonal name *Crescentia*, a feminine form of the male name *Crescens*, genitive *Crescentis*. This represents a participial form of Latin *crescere* to grow. It seems originally to have been used as a name of good omen, in the hope that the child bearing it would grow up strong and healthy.
Variant: **Crescentia**.
Pet form: **Zenzi**.

Kriemhild (f.) German: from an old Germanic female personal name composed of the elements *grim* mask + *hild* battle. In the *Nibelungenlied* this is the name of the sister of Gunther; she marries Siegfried, and later takes vengeance on her brother for her husband's murder.
Variants: **Kriemhilde**, **Krimhilde**.

Kristeen (f.) English: fanciful respelling of CHRISTINE, influenced by the Danish forms KRISTEN and KIRSTEN.
Variants: **Kristene**, **Kristine**.

Kristen (m.) Danish form of CHRISTIAN.

Kristie (f.) English: fanciful respelling of the female name CHRISTIE, under the influence of the Scottish form KIRSTIE.
Variant: **Kristy**.

Kristina (f.) Swedish and Czech form of CHRISTINA. The name is very popular in Sweden. Queen Kristina of Sweden (1626–89) succeeded her father Gustavus Adolphus in 1632. Growing to adulthood, she presided over a glittering court, but in 1654 she abdicated, left Sweden dressed as a man, converted to Roman Catholicism, and lived for most of the rest of her life in Rome. Her character was the subject of a famous but largely fictitious film (1933), in which the part of the queen was played by Greta Garbo.

Variant: Swedish: **Kerstin**.

Pet form: Swedish: **Kicki**.

Kristoffer (m.) Scandinavian form of CHRISTOPHER.

Krystle (f.) English: fanciful respelling of CRYSTAL.

Kryštof (m.) Czech form of CHRISTOPHER.

Pet forms: **Kryša**, **Kryšek**.

Krystyna (f.) Polish form of CHRISTINA.

Krzysztof (m.) Polish form of CHRISTOPHER.

Ksawery (m.) Polish form of XAVIER.

Kuba (m.) Polish and Czech: pet form of JAKUB.

Variants: Polish: **Kubú**. Czech: **Kubeš**, **Kubiček**.

Kukka (f.) Finnish: originally an affectionate nickname meaning 'flower'.

Kulya (f.) Russian: pet form of AKILINA.

Kunigunde (f.) German: from an old Germanic female personal name composed of the elements *kuoni* brave + *gund* strife. St Cunegund (d. 1039) was the wife of the Holy Roman Emperor Henry II, with whom she is said to have lived in 'conjugal virginity'.

Cognates: Dutch: **Kunigonde**, **Cunegonde**.

Pet forms: German: **Kinge**, **Kinga**.

Kurt (m.) German: in origin a contracted form of KONRAD, but now well established as a given name in its own right.

Variant: **Curt**.

Cognate: Dutch: **Kort**.

Kustaa (m.) Finnish form of GUSTAV; See also KYÖSTI.

Kvĕta (f.) Czech. originally an affectionate nickname derived from the vocabulary word *kvĕt* flower, which came to be adopted as a given name.

Pet forms: **Kvĕtka**, **Kvĕtuše**, **Kvĕtuška**.

Kwiatosław (m.) Polish: from an old Slavonic personal name composed of the elements *kviat* flower + *slav* glory.

Cognate: **Czech: Kvĕtoslav**.

Kyla (f.) English: recently coined name, created as a feminine form of KYLE or else a variant of KYLIE.

Kyle (m., f.) English: transferred use of a Scottish surname, which originated as a local name from the region so called in the former county of Ayrshire. *Kyle* is a topographic term referring to a narrow strait or channel, from Gaelic *caol* narrow.

Kylie (f.) English: of Australian origin, said to represent an Aboriginal term for the boomerang. However, in view of the inappropriateness of this meaning, it seems more likely that the name is an artificial invention influenced by KYLE and KELLY. It is extremely popular in Australia and, in part due to the fame of the Australian actress and singer Kylie Minogue (b. 1968), it is gradually coming into use in the rest of the English-speaking world.

Variant: **Kyleigh**.

Kynaston (m.) English: transferred use of the surname, which originated in the Middle Ages as a local name from places in Hereford and Shropshire so called from Old English *Cynefripestūn* 'settlement of *Cynefrip*', a male personal name composed of the elements *cyne* royal + *frip* peace.

Kyösti (m.) Finnish form of GUSTAV; See also KUSTAA.

Kyra (f.) English: apparently a variant spelling of *Cyra*, feminine form of CYRUS, or else a feminine name formed directly from KYRAN.

Kyran (m.) English and Irish: variant spelling of KIERAN.

L

Labhrás (m.) Irish Gaelic form of LAURENCE.

Labhrainn (m.) Scottish Gaelic form of LAURENCE.

Lacey (m., f.) English: transferred use of the surname, originally a Norman baronial name signifying origin in *Lassy*, Calvados. The Lacey family was important in Ireland during the early Middle Ages. As a female name this seems to have been influenced by association with the vocabulary word *lace*, denoting an ornamental trimming (Old French *laz* braid, from Latin *laqueus* noose).

Variant: **Lacy** mainly (m.).

Lachlan (m.) Scottish (Gaelic **Lachlann**, dialectally **Lachann**; earlier *Lochlann*): said to refer originally to a migrant from Norway, the 'land of the lochs'. It is normally used only in families that have some connection with Scotland.

Pet forms: Scottish: **Lachie**. Canadian: **Lockie**.
Feminine form: Scottish (Highland): **Lachina**.

Lachtna (m.) Irish Gaelic: originally a byname meaning 'milk-coloured'. It was borne, according to tradition, by the great-great-grandfather of the legendary king, Brian Boru. It is sometimes found in a Latinized form as LUCIUS.

Ladislao (m.) Italian equivalent of LÁSZLÓ, used mainly in the town of Fiume, which for a long time was under Hungarian control (though since 1947 it has formed part of Yugoslavia, under the name Rijeka).

Ladislas (m.) Latinate form of Polish WLADISLAW, Czech VLADISLAV, or Hungarian LÁSZLÓ, occasionally used in Britain, the Netherlands, and elsewhere, but mainly as a translation name.

Variant: **Ladislaus**.

Ladislav (m.) Czech: variant of VLADISLAV.

Feminine form: **Ladislava**.

Laetitia (f.) Original Latin form of LETTICE. This is currently a moderately fashionable name in France.

Laila (f.) 1. English: variant spelling of LEILA. 2. Scandinavian: ancient name of Saami origin, not uncommon in modern Denmark, Norway, and Sweden.

Lajos (m.) Hungarian form of LOUIS.

Lalage (f.) Classical name, pronounced /ˈlælədʒi/ or /ˈlæləgɪ/. It was used by Horace in one of his *Odes* as the name of his beloved of the moment; without doubt it was not her real name, but a literary pseudonym derived from Greek *lalagein* to chatter or babble. It has enjoyed a modest popularity among classically educated parents since the 19th century. It was the name of the central character in E. Arnot Robertson's *Ordinary Families* (1933) and it also occurs in John Fowles's *The French Lieutenant's Woman* (1969).

Lally (f.) English: pet form of LALAGE.

Variants: **Lallie**, **Lalla**, **Lala**.

Lambert (m.) English, French, German, and Dutch: of Germanic origin, composed of the elements *land* land, territory +

beorht famous. It was introduced to Britain by the Normans. Its frequency in Britain in the later Middle Ages, however, was mainly due to its popularity among immigrants from the Low Countries (who came to England in connection with the cloth trade). St Lambert of Maastricht was a 7th-century saint who aided St Willibrord in his evangelical work.

Variants: Dutch and Low German: **Lammert**. German: **Lamprecht**.

Lana (f.) 1. English (esp. U.S.): of uncertain origin. If not simply an invention, it may have been devised as a feminine equivalent of ALAN (of which it is an anagram), or an aphetic form of ALANA. It seems to have been first used by the film actress Lana Turner (b. 1920), whose original name was *Julia*. 2. Russian: aphetic short form of SVETLANA.

Lance (m.) English: from Old French *Lance*, from the Germanic name *Lanzo*, a pet form of various compound names with the first element *land* land, territory (cf. e.g. LAMBERT), but associated from an early date with Old French *lance*, the weapon (from Latin *lancea*). In modern use the given name seems to have originated as a transferred use of the surname derived from the medieval given name, although it is also commonly taken to be a short form of LANCELOT.

Lancelot (m.) English: the name borne by one of King Arthur's best and most valued knights, who eventually betrayed his trust by becoming the lover of Queen Guinevere. The name is of uncertain origin. It is probably, like other Arthurian names, of Celtic derivation, but has been heavily distorted by mediation through French sources.

Laocadia (f.) Portuguese form of LEOCADIA.

Laoiseach (m.) Irish Gaelic: originally an ethnic name for someone from the region of *Laois* in Leinster (the modern county of Leix).

Anglicized forms: LOUIS, LEWIS.

Lara (f.) Russian: short form of LARISSA, introduced in the early 20th century to the English-speaking world. Here it became popular in particular as the name of one of the principal characters in Boris Pasternak's novel *Dr Zhivago* (1957), which was made into a popular Hollywood film in 1965. The name is associated with 'Lara's theme', from the film score by Maurice Jarre. Occasionally the name also represents a short form of KLARA.

Laraine (f.) English (mainly U.S.): of uncertain origin, perhaps a variant spelling of LORRAINE or derived from the French vocabulary word *la reine* meaning 'the queen' (cf. RAINE). The prefix *La-* has become a popular one in female names in America since the 1970s, particularly among Blacks; the forms **Lakisha**, **Latoya**, LATASHA, and LATISHA were among the top one hundred Black female names in 1982.

Variant: **Lareine**.

Larissa (f.) Russian: of uncertain origin. It is the name of a Greek martyr venerated in the Eastern Church, and may perhaps be derived from the ancient Thessalian town of Larissa.

Variant: **Larisa**.

Lark (f.) English: one of a small set of female names derived from vocabulary words denoting birds, which have achieved some currency during the 20th century. The associations of the lark (Old English *lāwerce*) with early rising, cheerfulness, and sweet song have no doubt contributed to its occasional choice as a given name.

Larry (m.) English: pet form of LAURENCE or LAWRENCE. Informal modern variant: **Laz**.

Lars (m.) Scandinavian form of LAURENCE. This was the second commonest male name in Denmark in 1965 and the third commonest in Sweden in 1973.

Lassarina (m.) Irish: Anglicized form of the Gaelic name **Lasairíona**, composed of the elements *lasair* flame + *fion* wine.

Lasse (m.) Finnish form of LAURENCE, derived from a Scandinavian pet form of the name. It has been borne, for example, by the Finnish runner Lasse Viren (b. 1949).
Variant: **Lassi**.

László (m.) Hungarian form of WLADYSLAW. The name is still very popular in Hungary: its popularity was originally due to St László (1040–95), King of Hungary (1077–95), who is honoured by the Hungarians as a model of chivalry, courage, and Christian virtue, as well as a patriot and lawgiver.

Latasha (f.) English (esp. U.S.): a recent coinage, possibly representing a cross between LATISHA and NATASHA. It was the twenty-second most common female name among American Blacks in 1982.

Latisha (f.) English (esp. U.S.): a recent coinage, probably a respelling of LAETITIA. It enjoys considerable popularity among American Blacks.
Pet form: **Tisha**.

Laughlin (m.) Irish: Anglicized form of Gaelic LOCHLAINN.

Launo (m.) Finnish form of CLAUS.

Laura (f.) Italian, Spanish, and English: feminine form of the Late Latin male name *Laurus* 'Laurel'. St Laura was a 9th-century Spanish nun who met her death in a cauldron of molten lead. Laura is also the name of the woman addressed in the love poetry of the Italian poet Petrarch (Francesco Petrarca, 1304–74), and it owes much of its subsequent popularity to this. There have been various speculations about her identity, but it has not been established with any certainty. He first met her in 1327 while living in Avignon, and she died of the plague in 1348. The current popularity of the given name in the English-speaking world dates from the 19th century, when it was probably imported from Italy.
Cognates: French: **Laure**. Catalan: **Llora**. German: **Lora**, **Lore**.
Pet form: English: **Laurie**.

Laurel (f.) English: 19th-century adoption of the English vocabulary word denoting the tree (Middle English *lorel*, a dissimilated form of Old French *lorer*), probably influenced by LAURA. It may have been taken as a pet form of LAURA.
Variant (elaborated form): **Laurelle**.
Pet form: **Laurie**.

Lauren (f.) English: apparently modelled on LAURENCE, this was first used, or at any rate first brought to public attention, by the film actress Lauren Bacall (born Betty Jean Perske in 1924). She was famous for her partnership with Humphrey Bogart, especially in *To Have and Have Not* (1943) and *The Big Sleep* (1946).

Variant: **Loren** (occasionally used as a male name).

Laurence (m., f.) (m.) 1. English: from a French form of Latin *Laurentius* 'man from Laurentum'. *Laurentum* was a town in Latium, which may have got its name from Latin *laurus* laurel, or may alternatively be of pre-Roman origin. The given name was popular in the Middle Ages as a result of the fame of a 3rd-century saint who was one of the seven deacons of Rome. He was martyred in 258. The legend is that, having been required to hand over the Church's treasures to the civil authorities, he assembled the poor and sick and presented them. For this, he was supposedly roasted to death on a gridiron. In England the name is also associated with St Laurence of Canterbury (d. 619), the second bishop of Canterbury, who fought against pagan backsliding among his flock. See also LAWRENCE. 2. (f.) French: feminine form of *Laurent*.
Cognates: Irish Gaelic: **Labhrás**. Scottish Gaelic: **Labhrainn**. French: **Laurent**. Italian: **Lorenzo**. Spanish: **Lorencio**. Catalan: **Llorenç**. Portuguese: **Laurenço**. German: **Lorenz**. Dutch: **Laurens**. Scandinavian: **Lara**. Finnish: **Lauri**, **Lasse**, **Lassi**. Russian: **Lavrenti**. Polish: **Laurencjusz** (vernacular spelling of Latin *Laurentius*); **Lawrenty**; **Wawrzyniec** (vernacular form). Czech: **Vavřinec**.
Pet forms: English: **Larry**, **Laurie**. German: **Lenz**.

Laurent (m.) French form of LAURENCE.

Lauretta (f.) Italian: diminutive form of LAURA; cf. LORETTA.
Cognate: French: **Laurette**.

Lauri (m.) Finnish: learned form of LAURENCE; See also LASSE.

Laurie (f., m.) English: pet form of LAURA, LAUREL, and LAURENCE.

Lavender (f.) English (rare): from the vocabulary word denoting the herb with sweet-smelling flowers (Old French *lavendre*, from Late Latin *lavendula*).

Lavinia (f.) Name, according to Roman mythology, of the wife of Aeneas, and thus the mother of the Roman people. Legend had it that she gave her name to the Latin town of *Lavinium*, but in fact she was almost certainly invented to explain the placename, which is of pre-Roman origin. She was said to be the daughter of King Latinus, who was similarly invented, to account for the name of *Latium*.

Lavrenti (m.) Russian form of LAURENCE.

Lawrence (m.) English: Anglicized spelling of LAURENCE. This is the usual spelling of the surname, and is now becoming increasingly common as a given name, especially in America.
Pet forms: **Larry**, **Lawrie**.

Laz (m.) English: modern informal pet form of LARRY (cf. *Baz* from *Barry* and *Gaz* from *Gary*).

Lazarus (m.) Name borne in the New Testament by two different characters: the brother of Martha and Mary, who was raised from the dead by Jesus (John 11: 1–44), and the beggar who appears in the parable of Dives and Lazarus narrated by Jesus (Luke 16: 19–31). The form *Lazarus*, used in the Authorized Version, is a Latinate version of Greek *Lazaros*, itself a transliteration of Aramaic *Lazar*, an aphetic short form of Hebrew *Eleazar* 'God is my help'. Because the beggar Lazarus was 'full of sores' the name was often used in the Middle Ages as a generic term for a leper, and so came to be avoided as a given name. It is still not common.

Cognates: French: **Lazare**. Catalan: **Llàtzer**. Italian: **Lazzaro**. Polish: **azarz**.

Leagsaidh (f.) Scottish Gaelic form of LEXY.

Leah (f.) Biblical name (meaning 'languid' in Hebrew) borne by the elder sister of Rachel (Genesis 29: 23). Jacob served her father Laban for seven years in return for the hand of Rachel, but was deceived into marrying Leah first. He was then given Rachel as well, but had to labour seven more years afterwards. The name is common mainly among Jews, although it also enjoyed some popularity among the Puritans in the 17th century.

Variant: **Lea**. See also LIA.
Cognate: French: **Léa**.

Léan (f.) Irish Gaelic form of HELEN.

Leander (m.) Latin form of the Greek name *Leandros*, which is composed of the elements *leōn* lion + *anēr* (genitive *andros*) man. In Greek legend, Leander is the name of a hero who swam across the Hellespont every night to visit his beloved, Hero, and back again in the morning, but was eventually drowned during a violent storm. In Christian times, the name was borne by a 6th-century saint, the brother of Sts Fulgentius, Isidore, and Florentina. He was a leading ecclesiastical figure of his day, a friend of Gregory the Great, and became archbishop of Seville. In modern times, the name has occasionally been used as an elaboration of LEE (as a male name). In addition, Dunkling has recorded at least one instance of its use as a female name.

Cognates: French: **Léandre**. Italian, Spanish, Portuguese: **Leandro**.

Leanne (f.) English: modern combination of LEE and ANNE, or else a respelling of LIANE.

Leão (m.) Portuguese form of LEO.

Leberecht (m.) German: religious name, meaning 'live rightly', coined in the 17th century. It was borne, for example, by the Prussian field marshal, Gebhard Leberecht von Blücher (1742–1819).

Lech (m.) Polish: name of the legendary founder of the Polish race, brother of the *Czech* and *Rus* who gave their names to the Czechs and Russians respectively. All three of these names are of very ancient origin and uncertain derivation.

Pet form: **Leszek**.

Lechosław (m.) Polish: from an old Slavonic personal name composed of the ethnic term *lech* Pole (see LECH) + *slav* glory.

Variant: **Leslaw**.

Leda (f.) Name borne in classical mythology by a queen of Sparta, who was ravished by Zeus in the shape of a swan. She gave birth to two eggs which, when hatched, revealed the two sets of twins: Castor and Pollux, and Helen and Hermione.

Lee (m., f.) English: transferred use of the surname, originally a local name from any of numerous places so called from Old English *lēah* wood or clearing. It is especially popular now in America, where it has sometimes been bestowed in honour of the Confederate general, Robert E. Lee (1807–70). As a female name, it may also be a variant of *Lea* (see LEAH).

Leesa (f.) English: fanciful modern variant spelling of LISA, influenced by the female name LEE.

Léger (m.) French form of LUITGER. This name was borne by a 7th-century bishop of Autun.

Leib (m.) Jewish: Yiddish name, meaning 'lion' (cf. modern German *Löwe*). See also ARYE.

Leif (m.) Scandinavian: from Old Norse *Leifr*, a short form of various compound names containing the second element *leifr* heir, descendant. Leif Ericsson was a Norse navigator who, in around 1000, discovered the New World.

Variant: Norwegian: **Leiv**.

Leighton (m.) English: transferred use of the surname, which originated as a local name from any of several places named with the Old English elements *lēac* leek + *tūm* enclosure, settlement; of these the best known is Leighton Buzzard in Bedfordshire.

Variant: **Layton** (a variant spelling of the surname, reflecting the pronunciation).

Leila (f.) Of Arabic origin, now fairly common in the English-speaking world, having been used as a name for an oriental beauty by both Byron, in *The Giaour* (1813) and *Don Juan* (1819–24), and by Lord Lytton for the heroine of his novel *Leila* (1838). In Arabic it means 'night', apparently alluding to a dark complexion.

Variants: **Laila**, **Lila**.

Leland (m.) English (esp. U.S.): transferred use of the surname, which originated as a local name for someone who lived by a patch of fallow land, from Middle English *lay*, *ley* fallow (Old English *lǣge*) + *land* land (Old English *land*). The surname is not a particularly common or famous one, and it is not clear why it should have been adopted as a given name. In America it is the name of a town in Mississippi, and it was also the surname borne by the humorous writer Charles Leland (1824–1903), author of *The Breitmann Ballads*.

Lelle (m.) Scandinavian: pet form of LENNART.

Lempi (f.) Finnish: meaning 'love', this is a loan translation of the Latin name *Charitas* or the Greek *Agapē*.

Lemuel (m.) Biblical name (possibly meaning 'devoted to God' in Hebrew) borne by an obscure king who was lectured by his mother on the perils of strong drink and the virtues of a dutiful wife (Proverbs 31). He is mentioned by Chaucer in *The Canterbury Tales*, where his name is carefully distinguished from the more familiar SAMUEL. Lemuel Gulliver was the unusual name of the hero of Jonathan Swift's *Gulliver's Travels* (1726).

Len (m.) English: short form of LEONARD, and possibly also of the rarer given name LENNOX. In the case of the British trade-union leader Len Murray (b. 1922) it represents a short form of LIONEL.

Pet form: LENNY.

Lena (f.) English, Scottish, Dutch, German, and Scandinavian: abstracted from various names ending in *-lena* or *-lina*, such as *Helena* (from HELEN) and *Magdalena* (from MAGDALENE), or, in the Scottish Highlands, *Dolina* (from DONALD). In America it is famous as the name of the singer Lena Horne.

Variant: German and Danish: **Lene**.

Lenda (f.) English: apparently an arbitrary alteration of LINDA, originating in the 20th century.

Lene (f.) German and Danish: aphetic short form of both *Helene* (see HELEN) and MAGDALENE. It is very frequently used as an independent given name, not directly connected with either of these full forms, and was the third commonest female name in use in Denmark in 1965.

Leni (f.) German: pet form of LENA and LENE.

Lennard (m.) English: assimilated spelling of LEONARD, perhaps in part representing a transferred use of the surname derived from this given name in the Middle Ages.

Lennart (m.) Scandinavian form of LEONARD.
Pet forms: **Lenne**, **Lelle**.

Lennox (m.) Scottish and English: from the Scottish surname and earldom, originally a local name from a district north of Glasgow formerly known as *The Levenach*. This was the first name borne by the composer Sir Lennox Berkeley (1903–89).

Lenny (m.) English: normally a pet form of LEN, to some extent used as an independent given name.

Lenora (f.) English: originally a contracted form of LEONORA, although sometimes chosen as an expanded version of LENA.
Variants: **Lennora**, **Len(n)orah**.

Lenz (m.) German: contracted short form of LORENZ. This form of the name was formerly common in south and southwest Germany, but is now rare.

Leo (m.) English: from a Late Latin personal name, meaning 'lion', which was borne by a large number of early Christian saints, most notably Pope Leo the Great (?390–461). It is also found as a Jewish name (see LEON). In modern use it seems also to have been given as an omen name by parents who wished for a 'lion-hearted' son.
Cognates: French: LÉON. Italian: **Leone**. Spanish: **León**. Portuguese: **Leão**. Catalan: **Lleó**. Czech: **Leoš**.

Leocadia (f.) Spanish: probably a Latinate derivative of Greek *leukas* (genitive *leukados*), a poetic feminine form of *leukos* light, bright, clear. The first part of the name has subsequently been altered by association with Latin *leo* lion. St Leocadia (d. *c.*303) was a virgin martyr of Toledo, of whose life little is known, but who nevertheless enjoys a considerable cult.
Cognates: Catalan: **Llogaia**. Portuguese: **Laocadia**.
Masculine form: Spanish: **Leocadio**.

Leodegar (m.) French and German: learned form (influenced by the Latin word *leo* lion) of the names found in the vernaculars as LÉGER and LUITGER.

Leon (m.) English, German, and Irish Gaelic form of LEO. This form is common as a Jewish name. The lion is an important symbol among Jews because of Jacob's dying pronouncement that 'Judah is a lion's whelp' (Genesis 49: 9). See also LEIB, ARYE.

Léon (m.) French form of LEO.

Leona (f.) English and German: Latinate feminine form of LEON.

Leonard (m.) English: from an Old French personal name of Germanic origin, composed of the elements *leon* lion (a late borrowing from Romance) + *hard* hardy, brave, strong. This was the name of a 5th-century Frankish saint, who became the patron of peasants and horses. Although it was introduced into Britain by the Normans, *Leonard* was not a particularly common name there during the Middle Ages. It was revived during the 19th century and became very popular. It is now also common as a Jewish name (cf. LEON.

Variant: **Lennard**.
Cognates: French: **Léonard**. Italian, Spanish, Portuguese: LEONARDO. Catalan: **Lleonard**. German: **Leonhard(t)**. Scandinavian: **Lennart**.
Short form: English: **Len**.
Pet forms: English: **Lenny**. Scandinavian: **Lenne**, **Lelle**, **Nenne**.

Leonardo (m.) Italian, Spanish, and Portuguese form of LEONARD. Its most famous bearer was the Renaissance genius Leonardo da Vinci (1452–1519), remembered principally as a painter and sculptor, but also as an architect, engineer, and scientist.

Léonce (m.) French form of LEONZIO.

Leoncio (m.) Spanish form of LEONZIO.

Leone (m.) Italian form of LEO.

Leonid (m.) Russian: from the Greek name *Leonidas*, a Spartan dialectal form of *Leonidēs*, borne by a king of Sparta who, with seven hundred followers, was killed by the invading Persians at the heroic defence of the pass at Thermopylae (480 BC). This action gave the rest of Greece time to arm and prepare to meet the invaders. He was named from his grandfather *Leōn*, the name being a patronymic derivative of *Leōn* 'lion'. Later the name was borne by two early saints venerated especially in the Eastern Church: an Alexandrian, the father of Origen, martyred in 202, and an Egyptian martyred with several companions in 304.

Léonie (m.) French: from Latin *Leonia*, feminine form of *Leonius*, derived from *leo* lion. It is most common among Jews as a feminine equivalent of LEON, but is now also widely used (normally without the accent, Leoni(e)) in the English-speaking world among non-Jews.

Léonne (f.) French: feminine form of LÉON, occasionally also used (normally without the accent) in the English-speaking world.

Leonora (f.) English: aphetic form of ELEONORA.
Cognate: German: **Leonore**.

Leonti (m.) Russian form of the Byzantine Greek name *Leont(e)ios*, Greek equivalent of Latin *Leontius* (see LEONZIO). This was borne by several minor figures venerated in the Eastern Church, including Leontios of Neopolis (d. *c.*630).

Leontina (f.) Italian, from Latin: a feminine derivative of *Leontius* (see LEONZIO).

Léontine (f.) French form of LEONTINA, occasionally also used (normally without the accent) in the English-speaking world.

Leonzio (m.) Italian: from the Late Latin personal name *Leontius*, a derivative of LEO. The name was borne by several early saints, including Leontius the Elder (d. *c.*541) and Leontius the Younger (*c.*510–*c.*565), successive bishops of Bordeaux.
Cognates: French: **Léonce**. Spanish: **Leoncio**. Russian: LEONTI.

Leopold (m.) English: of Germanic origin, composed of the elements *liut* people + *bold* bold, brave. The first element was altered by association with Latin *leo* lion. A name of this origin may have been introduced into Britain by the Normans, but if so it did not survive long. It was reintroduced from the Continent towards the end of the 19th century, partly in honour of King Leopold of the Belgians (1790–1865), the uncle of Queen Victoria, who was an influential adviser to her in her youth, and after whom she named one of her sons. In the 17th and 18th centuries it was also the name of two Austro-Hungarian emperors, who were also kings of Bohemia.

Cognates: French: **Léopold**. Italian, Spanish, Portuguese: **Leopoldo**. German: **Luitpold**.

Leoš (m.) Czech form of LEO. This was the given name borne by the Czech composer Leoš Janáček (1854–1928).

Leroy (m.) English: now considered a typical Black American given name, but formerly also extensively borne by White Americans. It is from a French nickname meaning 'the king', but it is not entirely clear why this particular form should have become such a popular given name in English. See also DELROY.

Les (m.) English: short form of LESLIE.

Lesław (m.) Polish: contracted form of LECHOSŁAW.

Lesley (f., m.) Scottish and English: originally simply a variant of LESLIE, but now specialized in Britain as the female form. Its first recorded use as a female name is in a poem by Robert Burns.

Leslie (m.), occasionally (f.), esp. in the U.S. Scottish and English: transferred use of the Scottish surname derived from the lands of Lesslyn in Aberdeenshire (a placename perhaps from Gaelic *leas cuilinn* meaning 'garden of hollies'). Surnames and clan names have been used as given names more readily and from an earlier date in Scotland than elsewhere, and this is the name of an ancient clan, who in the 14th and 15th centuries were close associates of the Scottish royal house of Stewart. However, in the 17th century their most famous member, the general David Leslie (d. 1682), was a Covenanter who in the Civil War played a major role in defeating the royalists (including James Graham, Earl of Montrose, in 1645). But by 1650 he had switched sides and was the commander of the Scottish royalists who defeated Cromwell at Dunbar. The Leslies have held the earldom of Rothes since 1457.

The British film actor Leslie Howard (1890–1943), who was of Hungarian origin, had a considerable influence on the popularity of the name, especially in the United States, where he appeared in *Gone with the Wind* (1939), the film that has probably had more influence on naming than any other.

Short form: **Les** (m.).

Lester (m.) English: transferred use of the surname, which is a local name from the city of *Leicester*. The placename is recorded in the 10th century as *Ligora cæster*, representing a British name of obscure origin + the Old English term *cæster* 'Roman fort'.

Leszek (m.) Polish: pet form of LECH.

Letizia (f.) Italian form of LETTICE. This was the given name of Napoleon's mother.

Lettice (f.) English: from the medieval English form of the Latin name *Laetitia* 'happiness'. It was popular among the Victorians, but is now regarded as faintly risible (perhaps because of its similarity to the vocabulary word *lettuce*).

Pet forms: **Letty**, **Lettie**.

Lev (m.) Russian: from the Russian vocabulary word *lev* lion, representing an early vernacular calque of LEO.

Variant (informal): **Lyov**.
Cognate: Polish: **Lew**.

Levi (m.) Biblical name (meaning 'associated' in Hebrew) given by Jacob's wife Leah to her third son as an expression of her hope, 'Now this time will my husband be joined unto me, because I have born him three sons: therefore was his name called Levi' (Genesis 29: 34). The priestly caste of the Levites are descended from Levi. In the New Testament, Levi is a byname of the apostle and evangelist Matthew. In modern times the name is borne mostly by Jews, but occasionally also by Black revivalist Christians.

Lew (m.) 1. Polish spelling of LEV. The name is common among Jews; cf. LEIB. 2. English: short form of LEWIS.

Lewie (m.) 1. English: respelling of LOUIS or pet form of LEWIS. 2. Irish: Anglicized form of the Gaelic name LUGHAIDH.

Lewis (m.) 1. Common English form, since the Middle Ages, of the Norman and French name LOUIS. In modern use it is also in part a transferred use of the surname derived from this given name. 2. In Wales, an Anglicized form of LLEWELLYN. 3. In Scotland, a variant of LUDOVIC, or, among families connected with the Isle of Lewis, a transferred use of the placename. 4. In Ireland, an Anglicized form of Gaelic LAOISEACH and LUGHAIDH.

Short form: **Lew**.
Pet forms: **Lewie**, **Louie**.

Lex (m.) English: short form of ALEX. The minor vogue for this name, and the rhyming DEX and TEX, may have been inspired by the now distinctly old-fashioned REX.

Lexine (f.) English and Scottish: apparently an elaboration of LEXY with the addition of the originally French feminine diminutive suffix *-ine*, which has long been productive in forming English female names.

Lexy (f.) English and Scottish: pet form of ALEXANDRA.

Lia (f.) Italian: of uncertain derivation. It is probably either a form of LEAH or, especially in Sicily, a shortened form of *Rosalia* (see ROSALIE).

Liam (m.) Irish: short form of **Uilliam**, Gaelic form of WILLIAM.

Liane (f.) French and English: short form of ÉLIANE.

Variant: **Lianne**.

Libby (f.) English: pet form of ELIZABETH, based originally on a child's unsuccessful attempts to pronounce the name. It is now also occasionally used as an independent name.

Libe (f.) Jewish: Yiddish name, meaning 'love' (cf. modern German *Liebe*).

Liběna (f.) Czech: equivalent of the Russian name LYUBOV, derived from the element *lib* love.

Pet forms: **Liba**, **Liběnka**, **Libuše**, **Libuška**.

Libor (m.) Czech: from the Latin name *Liberius*, a derivative of *liber* free. St Liberius was a 2nd-century bishop of Ravenna.

Pet forms: **Liborek**, **Libek**.

Licerio (m.) Spanish: from the Late Latin personal name *Lycerius*, a derivative of either Greek *lykē* light or *lykos* wolf. St Licerius was born in Lérida, and became bishop of Conserans in France (506–*c*.548). The French form of his name is *Lizier*, but this is not regularly used as a given name.

Lícia (f.) Hungarian: shortened form of *Felicia* (see FELICIA).

Licio (m.) Italian: from the Late Latin personal name *Lycius*, originally an ethnic derivative of the region of *Lycia* in Asia

Minor. The name was borne principally by slaves, some of whom may have come from this region.

Lida (f.) Czech form of LYDIA.

Lidia (f.) Polish form of LYDIA.

Lidmila (f.) The usual Czech form of LUDMILA.
Pet forms: **Lida**; **Lidka, Lidun(k)a, Liduše, Liduška**.

Liduina (f.) Italian form of LIDWINA, used in particular in the Emilian region.

Lidwina (f.) Dutch: name borne in honour of the Blessed *Lidwina* or *Lydwina* of Schiedam (1380–1433), a lifelong invalid and mystic. The name is a feminine form of the Germanic name *Lidwin*, composed of the elements *liut* people, race + *win* friend.

Liese (f.) German: a popular pet form of ELISABETH. It is now also quite widely used as an independent given name in both the German-speaking and the English-speaking world.

Lieselotte (f.) German: 19th-century coinage composed of the elements LIESE + *-lotte*, abstracted from KARLOTTE and treated as a feminine diminutive suffix.
Pet form: **Lilo**.

Life (f.) Irish Gaelic: traditional name, borne, according to legend, by a figure who gave her name to the River *Liffey*.

Ligia (f.) Spanish and Portuguese: of uncertain origin, apparently a shortened form of *Eligia*, the feminine version of ELIGIO (see also ELOY and ELOI).

Lila (f.) English: apparently a variant spelling of LEILA or LAILA.

Lilac (f.) English: a modern adoption of the vocabulary word denoting the shrub with large sprays of heavily scented purple or white flowers. The word is from French, which derived it via Spanish from Arabic *līlak*, from Persian *nīlak* bluish, a derivative of *nil* blue.

Lili (f.) German: pet form, originally a reduplicated nursery form, of ELISABETH. This form is associated in particular with the Second World War popular song *Lili Marlene*.
Variant: **Lilli**.

Lilian (f.) English: of uncertain origin, first recorded in the late 16th century, and probably derived from a nursery form of ELIZABETH. It is now sometimes regarded as a derivative of the flower name LILY, but this was not used as a given name in England until the 19th century.
Variant: **Lillian**.

Lilith (f.) The name borne, according to medieval tradition, by a wife of Adam prior to Eve. She is said to have been turned into an ugly demon for refusing to obey him. *Lilith* occurs in the Bible as a vocabulary word meaning 'night monster' or 'screech owl' (Isaiah 34: 14), and in Jewish folklore is the name of an ugly demon. In spite of its unpleasant connotations, it has occasionally been used as a given name in the 20th century, perhaps in part being taken as an elaborated form of LILY.

Lillian (f.) English: variant spelling of LILIAN, common especially in America.

Lilo (f.) German: pet form of LIESELOTTE.

Lily (f.) English: from the vocabulary word denoting the flower (Latin *lilium*), regarded in Christian imagery as a symbol of purity.

Lincoln (m.) English: transferred use of the surname, a local name derived from the name of the city of Lincoln. This is found in the 7th century as *Lindum colonia*, representing a British name probably meaning 'lake' (cf. Welsh *llyn*) + the Latin defining term *colonia* colony, settlement. As a given name it has sometimes been bestowed in honour of Abraham Lincoln (1809–65), 16th president of the United States, who led the Union to victory in the Civil War and enforced the emancipation of slaves.

Linda (f.) English: of recent and somewhat uncertain origin. It is first recorded in the 19th century, perhaps either as a shortening of BELINDA or as an adoption of the Spanish vocabulary word *linda* pretty (masculine *lindo*). Alternatively, it may be derived from the Latinate form of any of various other Germanic female names ending in the element *-lind* meaning 'weak, tender, soft'. It has become very popular in the 20th century.
Pet form: **Lindie, Lindy**.

Linden (f.) English: ostensibly from the vocabulary word denoting the lime tree (originally the adjectival form, derived from Old English *linde*). However, the given name is of recent, probably 20th-century, origin and it is more likely that this is simply an elaboration of LINDA, along the lines of LAUREN from LAURA.

Lindon (m.) English: variant spelling of LYNDON.

Lindsay (f., m.) Scottish and English: from the Scottish surname, originally borne by Sir Walter de Lindesay, one of the retainers of King David I of Scotland (1084–1153), who took the name to Scotland from Lindsey in Lincolnshire. This place was named in Old English as the 'wetland (Old English *ey*) belonging to Lincoln'. It was at first used as a male name, and this is still the case in Scotland, but elsewhere it is now nearly always used for girls.
Variants: **Lindsey, Lynsey, Linzi**.

Lindy (f.) English: apparently an altered form or pet form of LINDA, by a reversal of the process that derived e.g. JENNA from JENNY.

Linford (m.) English: transferred use of the surname, which originated as a local name from any of various places named with the Old English elements *lin* flax or *lind* lime tree + *ford* ford. In the case of Great and Little Linford in Berkshire, however, the first element seems to have been originally Old English *hlyn* maple. The given name is associated in particular with the athlete Linford Christie.

Linnéa (f.) Swedish: a popular given name first bestowed in honour of the Swedish botanist Carl von Linné (1707–70; Latinized as *Linnaeus*). He gave his name to the now internationally recognized *Linnaean* system of taxonomic classification, and to a type of flower known as *Linnaea*. The female given name was first used in the mid-19th century in the form *Linnaea*, and is now sometimes spelled Linnea (without the accent).
Short form: **Nea**.

Linnet (f.) English: simplified spelling of LINNETTE, strongly influenced in popularity by the vocabulary word denoting a small bird (Old French *linotte*, a derivative of *lin* flax, on the seeds of which it feeds).

Linnette (f.) English: variant spelling of LYNETTE.

Linton (m.) English: from a local surname, now also quite commonly used as a given name, especially among British Blacks. The surname derives from any of numerous places in England so called; most get the name from Old English *lin* flax, cotton or *lind* lime tree + *tūn* enclosure, settlement.

Linus (m.) Latin form of the Greek name *Linos*, which is of uncertain origin. In Greek mythology, Linus is both a famous musician who taught music to Hercules and an infant son of Apollo who had been exposed to die on a mountainside in Argos. The name may have been invented to explain the obscure refrain, '*ailinon*', of the so-called 'Linus song', a lament sung at harvest time in Argos. In the Christian era, *Linus* is the name of the second pope, St Peter's successor, who was martyred in *c*.76. He has been tentatively identified with the Linus to whom Paul sends greetings in 2 Timothy 4: 21. The given name has occasionally been used in America. It is now associated with a character in the extremely popular *Peanuts* strip cartoon series, a little boy inseparable from his security blanket.

Linzi (f.) English: fanciful respelling of LINDSAY.

Liona (f.) English: apparently an altered form of LEONA, influenced by LIONEL.

Lionel (m.) English: from a medieval diminutive of the Old French name LÉON or the Middle English nickname *Lion*.

Lipa (f.) Romanian: short form of *Filipa* (see PHILIPPA).

Lis (f.) **1.** Scandinavian: dramatically shortened form of ELISABET, first used in the early years of the 20th century. It occurs as the second element of numerous compound names, such as *Anne-Lis*, *Ing-Lis*, and *Maj-Lis*. **2.** English: variant spelling of LIZ.

Lisa (f.) English: variant of LIZA, influenced by French *Lise* and German *Liese*..

Lisbet (f.) English and Scandinavian: shortened form of ELIZABETH or *Elisabet*, now in fairly wide use as an independent given name.

Lisette (f.) French: diminutive form of *Lise*, which is itself a shortened form of ELISABETH.

Variant: **Lysette**.

Lisha (f.) English: modern coinage, apparently a respelled shortened form of names such as DELICIA and FELICIA, on the model of TRISHA from PATRICIA.

Lissa (f.) English: short form of MELISSA. See also LYSSA.

Liùsaidh (f.) Scottish Gaelic form of LOUISA or LUCY.

Liv (f.) Scandinavian: from an Old Norse female personal name identical in form with the vocabulary word *hlif* defence, protection. In modern use it is often associated with the Norwegian vocabulary word *liv* life. The name is borne by a character in Nordic legend, and was revived in the late 19th century. It is now sometimes taken as a short form of ELISABETH.

Livia (f.) English: in modern use often taken as a short form of OLIVIA, but originally a distinct name, a feminine form of the Roman family name *Livius*. This is of uncertain derivation, perhaps connected with *lividus* bluish.

Liz (f.) English: the most common of all the various short forms of ELIZABETH.

Liza (f.) English: short form of ELIZA.

Variant: **Lisa**.

Lizzie (f.) English: pet form of LIZ, with the hypocoristic suffix -*ie*.

Variant: **Lizzy**.

Llàtzer (m.) Catalan form of LAZARUS.

Lleó (m.) Catalan form of LEO.

Lleonard (m.) Catalan form of LEONARD.

Lleu (m.) Welsh: traditional name, meaning 'bright, shining', cognate with the name of the Celtic god known in Old Irish as *Lugh*, in Gaulish as *Lugus*. This name was borne in the *Mabinogi* by Lleu Llaw Gyffes 'Lleu Skilful Hand', the son of Aranrhod. It has been revived in modern times.

Llew (m.) Welsh: traditional name meaning 'lion'. It is also used as a short form of LLEWELYN.

Llewelyn (m.) Welsh: altered form (influenced by the vocabulary word *llew* lion) of *Llywelyn*, an ancient name of uncertain derivation. It goes back to an Old Celtic form *Lugobelinos*; the first element seems to be the divine name *Lugu-* (see LLEU), the second is found also in names such as *Cunobelinus* or *Cymbeline*. In historical times the name was borne in particular by Llywelyn ap Iorwerth (1173–1240) and his grandson Llywelyn ap Gruffydd (d. 1282), Welsh princes who for a time united their countrymen in North Wales and led opposition to the power of the Norman barons in South Wales and the borders. It has sometimes been Anglicized as LEWIS.

Short forms: **LLEW**, **LYN**.

Pet form: **Llelo**.

Llogaia (f.) Catalan form of LEOCADIA.

Llora (f.) Catalan form of LAURA.

Llorenç (m.) Catalan form of LAURENCE.

Lloyd (m.) English: from the Welsh surname, originally a nickname meaning 'grey(-haired)' (Welsh *llwyd*); cf. FLOYD.

Lluch (m.) Catalan form of LUKE.

Variant: **Lluc**.

Lluís (m.) Catalan form of LOUIS.

Llywarch (m.) Welsh: traditional name, now only occasionally used, composed of the god's name *Lugu-* (see LLEU) + Old Celtic *marcos* horse.

Lochlainn (m.) Irish Gaelic: a cognate of Scottish *Lachlann*; see LACHLAN.

Anglicized forms: **Loughlin**, **Laughlin**.

Lockie (m.) Canadian: pet form of LACHLAN.

Lodewijk (m.) Dutch form of LOUIS.

Lodovico (m.) Italian: learned form of LOUIS, much rarer than the vernacular LUIGI.

Loffe (m.) Scandinavian: pet form of ELOF.

Logan (m.) Scottish: transferred use of the Scottish surname, a local name derived from a place so called in Ayrshire.

Lois (f.) New Testament: name, of unknown origin, borne by the grandmother of the Timothy to whom St Paul wrote two epistles (see 2 Timothy 1: 5). Both Timothy and his mother Eunice bore common Greek names, but *Lois* is hard to explain. It certainly has no connection with either LOUISE or ELOISE (which are both of Germanic origin), although it has often been taken to be associated with them in modern times.

Lola (f.) Spanish and English: originally a nursery form of DOLORES, now established as a popular name in its own right. It owes some of its popularity to the fame of Lola Montez (1818–61), stage name adopted by Marie Gilbert, an Irish dancer and courtesan who had affairs with Liszt, Dumas, and others. From 1846 to 1848 she so captivated the elderly Ludwig I of Bavaria that she became the virtual ruler of the country, precipitating riots, a constitutional crisis, and the abdication of the king. She arrived in New York in 1851, and spent the last years of her life working to help prostitutes.

Lolicia (f.) English (esp. U.S.): elaborated form of LOLA, with the addition of a suffix derived from names such as DELICIA.

Lolita (f.) Spanish: pet form of LOLA. This was once relatively common as a given name in its own right in America, with its large Hispanic population, but has since been completely overshadowed by its association with Vladimir Nabokov's novel *Lolita* (1955). The Lolita of the title is the pubescent object of the narrator's desires, and the name is now used as a generic term for any under-age sex kitten.

Loman (m.) Irish: Anglicized form of Gaelic **Lomán**, originally a diminutive of the vocabulary word *lomm* bare, used as a byname. The name was borne by various early Irish saints, including one who was a nephew of St Patrick, and who became first bishop of Trim in Meath in the early 5th century.

Lonan (m.) Irish: Anglicized form of Gaelic **Lonán**, originally a diminutive of the vocabulary word *lon* blackbird, used as a byname. This name was borne by several minor early Irish saints.

Lone (f.) Danish: shortened form of ABELONE and *Magdelone* (see MAGDALENE). It is now very commonly used as an independent name.

Lonnie (m.) English: of uncertain origin, possibly an Anglicized or pet form of the Spanish name ALONSO, but just as likely a variant of LENNY. It is chiefly associated in Britain with the skiffle singer Lonnie Donegan, famous in the 1950s and 1960s.

Lope (m.) Spanish: name derived in the Middle Ages from the Late Latin personal name *Lupus*, probably adopted as a calque of the Germanic name WOLF. *Lupus* was the name borne by various early but obscure saints, including bishops of Bayeux, Châlons-sur-Saône, Lyons, Sens, Soissons, Troyes, and Verona, between the 4th and 7th centuries.

Lora (f.) German form of LAURA, occasionally also used in the English-speaking world.
Variant: **Lore**.

Lorane (f.) English: variant spelling of LORRAINE.

Lóránt (m.) Hungarian form of ROLAND.

Lorcan (m.) Irish: Anglicized form of the Gaelic name **Lorcán**, originally a byname representing a diminutive of Gaelic *lorc* fierce (or possibly 'dumb'). This name was borne by St Lorcán Ó Tuathail (1128–80), archbishop of Dublin, known in English as Laurence O'Toole.

Lore (f.) German: of two possible origins. In most cases it represents a dramatically contracted form of *Leonore* (see LEONORA), but it is also sometimes also a variant of LORA.

Loredana (f.) Italian: name apparently invented by Luciano Zuccoli for the heroine of his novel *L'amore de Loredana* (1908). It seems to represent a feminine form of the famous Venetian surname *Loredan*, in origin a dialectal derivative of the placename *Loreo* in Rovigo (earlier *Loredo*, from Latin *laurētum* laurel grove).

Loreen (f.) English: elaboration of LORA, with the addition of the suffix *-een* (originally an Irish diminutive, Gaelic *-ín*).
Variant: **Lorene**.

Lorelle (f.) English: elaboration of LORA, with the addition of the suffix *-elle* (originally a French feminine diminutive).

Loren (f.), occasionally (m.) English: variant spelling of LAUREN.

Lorena (f.) Latinate elaboration of LOREN.

Lorene (f.) English: variant spelling of LOREEN.

Lorenz (m.) German form of LAURENCE.
Short form: **Lenz**.

Lorenzo (m.) Italian form of LAURENCE.

Loreto (f.) English and Irish (borne by *Roman Catholics*): religious name referring to the town in central Italy to which in the 13th century the Holy House of the Virgin is supposed to have been miraculously transported from Nazareth by angels.

Loretta (f.) English: variant of LAURETTA, normally borne by Catholics, among whom it is associated with LORETO.

Lori (f.) English: pet form of LORRAINE or variant of LAURIE.

Lorin (m.) English (esp. U.S.): variant spelling of the male name LOREN.

Lorinda (f.) English: elaboration of LORA, with the addition of the productive feminine suffix *-inda* (cf. e.g. BELINDA, CLARINDA, LUCINDA).

Lorna (f.) English and Scottish: invented by R. D. Blackmore for the heroine of his novel *Lorna Doone* (1869), child captive of the outlawed Doones on Exmoor, who is eventually discovered to be in reality Lady Lorna Dugal, daughter of the Earl of Dugal. Blackmore seems to have derived the name from the Scottish placename *Lorn(e)* (Gaelic *Latharna*), a territory in Argyll. The given name is now popular in Scotland.

Lorne (m.) English (esp. Canadian): of uncertain derivation, presumably from the territory of *Lorne* in Argyll (cf. LORNA). One of the earliest bearers was the Canadian actor Lorne Greene (b. 1915), and the given name is now also fairly common in Scotland.

Lorraine (f.) English and Scottish: transferred use of the surname, denoting a migrant from the province of Lorraine in eastern France. This derives its name from Latin *Lotharingia* 'territory of the people of Lothar' (see LOTHAR). *Lorraine* began to be used as a female given name in the 19th century, and has recently become enormously popular, for reasons which are not clear.
Variant: **Lorane**.
Pet forms: **Lor(r)i**.

Lorri (f.) English: variant spelling of LORI.

Lorrin (m.) English (esp. U.S.): variant spelling of the male name LOREN.

Lothar (m.) German: from an old Germanic personal name composed of the elements *hlud* fame + *heri, hari* army, warrior. St Lotharius was an 8th-century bishop of Séez in Orne, founder of the monastery of Saint-Loyer-des-Champs. *Lothar* was also a Frankish royal name in the Middle Ages, and was borne by two Holy Roman Emperors. Lothar I (795–855) gave his name to the province of LORRAINE, which was all he was able to bequeath to his son (also called Lothar), after his quarrels with his brothers Charles the Bald and Louis the German. Lorraine (Latin *Lotharingia*, German *Lothringen*) was originally a much larger region than the present province.

Anglicized form: **Lothair**.

Lottelore (f.) German: double name composed of the elements *Lotte* (a shortened form of KARLOTTE) and LORE.

Lottie (f.) English: pet form of CHARLOTTE. It was common in the 19th century, but is much less used at the present time.

Variant: **Lotty**.

Lou (m., f.) English: short form of LOUIS or, less commonly, LOUISE.

Louella (f.) English: modern coinage from the first syllable of LOUISE + the productive suffix *-ella* (an Italian or Latinate feminine diminutive; cf. ELLA). It is particularly associated with the Hollywood gossip columnist Louella Parsons (1880–1972).

Variant: **Luella**.

Loughlin (m.) Irish: Anglicized form of Gaelic LOCHLAINN.

Louie (m.) English: Variant spelling of LEWIE.

Louis (m.) French: an extremely common French name, of Germanic origin. It is composed of the elements *hlud* fame + *wīg* warrior, and is thus etymologically the same name as German LUDWIG. From the early Middle Ages onwards, it was very frequently used in French royal and noble families. An archaic Latinized form of the name is *Clovis*, and this is the form generally used for the Frankish leader (?466–511) who ended the Roman domination over Gaul: Clovis defeated rival Germanic tribes, married the Burgundian princess Clothilde, and founded the Frankish monarchy in what is now France. In 496 he and his followers were converted to Christianity. Louis I (778–840) was the son of Charlemagne, who ruled both as King of France and Holy Roman Emperor. Altogether, the name was borne by sixteen kings of France up to the French Revolution, in which Louis XVI perished. Louis XIV, 'the Sun King' (1638–1715), reigned for seventy-two years (1643–1715), presiding in the middle part of his reign over a period of unparalleled French power and prosperity. See also LUDWIG.

In modern times, *Louis* is occasionally used in the English-speaking world (usually pronounced /'luːiː/). In Britain the Anglicized form LEWIS is rather more common, whereas in America the reverse is true. Both forms have been used as Anglicized versions of Gaelic LAOISEACH and LUGHAIDH.

Cognates: Scottish Gaelic: **Luthais**. Italian: **Luigi**, **Lodovico**. Spanish, Portuguese: **Luis**. Catalan: **Lluis**. Basque: **Koldo**. German: LUDWIG.

Short form: English: **Lou**.

Louisa (f.) Latinate feminine form of LOUIS, commonly used as an English given name since the 18th century.

Cognates: French: LOUISE (also used in English). German: **Luise**. Swedish: **Lovisa**. Danish, Norwegian: **Lovise**.
Pet form: German: **Lulu**.

Louise (f.) French and English: feminine form of LOUIS, introduced to England in the 17th century.

Short form: English: **Lou**.

Lourdes (f.) English and Spanish (borne almost exclusively by Roman Catholics): from the name of the place in southern France where a shrine was established after a young peasant girl, Bernadette Soubirous, had visions of the Virgin Mary and uncovered a healing spring in 1858. In recent times, Lourdes has become a major centre for pilgrimage, especially by people suffering from various illnesses or physical handicaps.

Variant: Spanish: **Lurdes**.

Lova (f.) Swedish: pet form of LOVISA.

Lovell (m.) English: transferred use of the surname, which originated in the Middle Ages from the Old (Norman) French nickname *Louvel* 'wolf-cub', a diminutive of *lou* wolf.

Lovisa (f.) Latinate form of LOUISE, much used in Sweden.

Pet form: **Lova**.

Lowell (m.) English (mainly U.S.): transferred use of the surname of a well-known New England family, whose members included the poet Robert Lowell (1917–77). The surname is a variant of LOVELL.

Loyal (m.) English (mainly U.S.): a comparatively recent adoption of the vocabulary word (which is from Old French *leial*, from Latin *legalis* legal).

Luana (f.) English and Italian: first used in King Vidor's 1932 film *The Bird of Paradise* as the name of a Polynesian maiden, and taken up since. It is apparently an arbitrary combination of the syllables *Lu-* and *-ana*. The Vidor film achieved considerable popularity in Italy under the title *Luana, la vergine sacra*, and the name is now also relatively common there.

Variants: English: **Luanna**, **Luanne**.

Lubomierz (m.) Polish: from an old Slavonic personal name composed of the elements *lub* love + *meri* great, famous (see CASIMIR).

Cognates: Czech: **Lubomír**, **Lubor**, **Lumír**.
Feminine form: Czech: **Lubomíra**.
Pet forms: Czech: **Luba** (m., f.); **Lubomírek**, **Lub(or)ek**, **Luboš(ek)** (m.); **Lubka**, **Luběna**, **Lubin(k)a**, **Luboška** (f.).

Lubomił (m.) Polish: from an old Slavonic personal name composed of the elements *lub* love + *mil* grace, favour.

Luc (m.) French form of LUKE.

Luca (m.) Italian form of LUKE.

Lucas (m.) 1. English: in part a learned form of LUKE, in part a transferred use of the surname derived from it. The Latin form *Lucas* was often used in the Middle Ages in written documents in place of the spoken vernacular form *Luke*, hence the common surname. It is also the spelling preferred in the Authorized Version of the New Testament, which has had some influence on its selection as a given name. *Lucas* is now also used as an Anglicized form of various Eastern European equivalents (see the cognates listed at LUKE). 2. Usual Dutch form of *Luke*.

Lucetta (f.) English: fanciful elaboration of LUCIA or LUCY, formed with the productive suffix *-etta*, originally an Italian feminine diminutive suffix. The name is found in Shakespeare, where it is borne by Julia's waiting woman in *Two Gentlemen of Verona*, but it is not much used in Italy and was unusual in England before the 19th century.

Lucia (f.) Feminine form of the old Roman given name LUCIUS, which is probably a derivative of Latin *lux* light. The female name is common in Italy and elsewhere. It is found as a learned, Latinate doublet of *Lucy* in England, where it is much more frequent than its masculine counterpart. St Lucia of Syracuse, who was martyred in 304, was a very popular saint in the Middle Ages; she is often represented in medieval art as blinded and with her eyes on a platter, but the tradition that she had her eyes put out is probably based on nothing more than the association between light and eyes. She still enjoys a considerable cult in southern Italy and Sicily.

Derivatives: Spanish: **Lucía**. English: Lucy.
Pet forms: Italian: **Luciella**. English: **Lucilla**.

Luciano (m.) Italian, Spanish, and Portuguese form of Lucien. The feminine form, *Luciana*, is the name of one of the principal characters in Shakespeare's *Comedy of Errors*.

Feminine form: **Luciana**.

Luciella (f.) Italian: diminutive form of Lucia.

Lucien (m.) French: from Latin *Luciānus*, a derivative of Lucius. Saints Lucian, Maximian, and Julian were three missionaries to Gaul martyred at Beauvais at the end of the 3rd century.

Cognate: Italian, Spanish, Portuguese: **Luciano**.
Feminine form: French: **Lucienne**.

Lucilla (f.) Latin pet form of Lucia, with the diminutive feminine suffix *-illa*. This name was borne by various minor early saints, including one martyred at Rome in *c*.258.

Lucille (f.) French form of Lucilla, used also in the English-speaking world, especially in the southern United States.

Lucinda (f.) Derivative of Lucia, with the addition of the productive suffix *-inda*. The formation is first found in Cervantes's *Don Quixote* (1605), but does not seem to have been much in use in the 17th century except as a literary name. *Lucinde* was used by both Molière (in *Le Médecin malgré lui*, 1665) and Friedrich von Schlegel (in his novel *Lucinde*, 1799). It enjoyed considerable popularity in England in the 18th century, and has been in use ever since.

Cognate: French: **Lucinde**.
Pet forms: **Sinda**, **Sindy**, **Cindy**; Lucy.

Lucio (m.) Italian, Spanish, and Portuguese form of Lucius.

Lucius (m.) Old Roman given name, probably ultimately a derivative of Latin *lux* light. This is occasionally used as a given name in the English-speaking world, especially in America, but it is not as common as its feminine counterpart, Lucia. Lucius was the name of two early Christians mentioned in the New Testament (Acts 13: 1; Romans 16: 21), and it was also borne by three popes.

Lucrece (f.) English: vernacular form of Lucretia, used, for example, in Shakespeare's narrative poem *The Rape of Lucrece*.

Lucretia (f.) Feminine form of the Roman family name *Lucretius*, which is of unknown derivation. In Roman legend, this is the name of a Roman maiden of the 5th century BC who killed herself after being raped by the King of Rome; the resulting scandal led to the end of the monarchy. It was also borne by a Spanish martyr who perished under Diocletian, but is now chiefly remembered as the name of Lucretia Borgia (1480–1519), regarded in legend as a demon poisoner who had incestuous relations with her father, Pope Alexander VI, and her brother Cesare. Although these allegations cannot now be disproved, history records her, after her marriage in 1501 to Alfonso d'Este, Duke of Ferrara, as being in reality a beautiful, intelligent, and fairminded woman, and a generous patron of the arts. In spite of its unfortunate associations, the name is still occasionally used, especially in the United States.

Derivatives: Italian: **Lucrezia**. English: Lucrece.

Lucy (f.) 1. English: from Old French *Lucie*, the vernacular form of Lucia. It is sometimes assumed that *Lucy* is a pet form of Lucinda, but there is no etymological justification for this assumption. It was in fairly widespread use in the Middle Ages, and increased greatly in popularity in the 18th century. 2. Irish: Anglicized form of Gaelic Luíseach.

Ludger (m.) Low German and Dutch form of Luitger. St Ludger (*c*.744–809) was a Frisian who studied at Utrecht and in England, before becoming a missionary in Westphalia and later first bishop of Münster, where he founded a monastery that gave the place its name.

Ludmila (f.) Russian and Czech: from an old Slavonic personal name composed of the elements *lud* people, tribe (apparently a borrowing from Germanic *liut*) + *mil* grace, favour. St Ludmila (d. 921) was a duchess of Bohemia and grandmother of St Wenceslas; she was murdered on the orders of her mother-in-law and came to be regarded as a martyr. The name is now also occasionally used in the English-speaking world, where it is usually spelled **Ludmilla**.

Variant: Czech: **Lidmila**.
Cognate: Polish: **Ludmita**.

Ludo (m.) English and Scottish: short form of Ludovic.

Ludomierz (m.) Polish: from an old Slavonic personal name composed of the elements *lud* people, tribe (cf. Ludmila) + *meri* great, famous (see Casimir).

Cognate: Czech: **Ludomir**.
Pet form: Czech: **Ludĕk** (see also next entry).

Ludosław (m.) Polish: from an old Slavonic personal name composed of the elements *lud* people, tribe (cf. Ludmila) + *slav* glory.

Cognate: Czech: **Ludoslav**.
Pet form: Czech: **Ludĕk** (see also previous entry).

Ludovic (m.) English and Scottish: from Latin *Ludovicus*, the form used in medieval documents to represent the Germanic name *Hludwig* (see Ludwig, Louis). In the Highlands it came to be used as an Anglicized form of the Gaelic name *Maol Dòmhnaich* 'devotee of the Lord', probably because both contained the same succession of sounds: *l-d-o-v-c(h)*. It has survived as a traditional given name in the Grant family, sometimes taking the form Lewis or *Louis*.

Short form: **Ludo**.

Ludovica (f.) German, Dutch, and occasionally English: Latinate feminine form of Ludovic.

Ludvík (m.) Czech form of Ludwig.

Ludwig (m.) German: from an old Germanic personal name composed of the elements *hlud* fame + *wīg* warrior. It is thus etymologically the same as French Louis. *Ludwig* was a royal and imperial name, especially in Bavaria, which Louis the German (Ludwig der Deutsche) had received as his portion of his father's empire when the latter divided it in 817. See also Louis, Ludovic.

Cognates: Scandinavian: **Ludvig**. Dutch: **Lodewijk**. Polish: **Ludwik**. Czech: **Ludvík**. Hungarian: **Lajos**. French: Louis.
Pet form: German: **Lutz**.

Ludwik (m.) Polish form of Ludwig.

Luella (f.) English: variant spelling of Louella.

Lughaidh (m.) Irish Gaelic: a derivative of the divine name *Lugh* (see LLEU).
Anglicized forms: LEWIE, LEWIS, LOUIS.

Luigi (m.) Italian: vernacular form of LOUIS; cf. LODOVICO.

Luis (m.) Spanish form of LOUIS.
Feminine form: **Luisa**.

Luise (f.) German form of LOUISE, now also sometimes used in the English-speaking world as a spelling variant.
Pet form: **Lulu**.

Luíseach (f.) Irish Gaelic: a feminine derivative of the divine name *Lugh*.
Anglicized form: LUCY.

Luitgard (m.) German: from an old Germanic personal name composed of the elements *liut* people + *gard* protection. It was fairly common in the Middle Ages, and is occasionally revived today.

Luitger (m.) German: from an old Germanic personal name composed of the elements *liut* people + *gari, geri* spear. See also LÉGER, LEODEGAR, and LUDGER.

Luitpold (m.) German form of LEOPOLD, rather closer to the original form of the name. This version was common in the Middle Ages, but is now little used except in a few particular families in which its use is traditional. It was associated particularly with the royal house of Bavaria.
Pet form: **Poldi** (chiefly Bavarian).

Luke (m.) English: Middle English form of LUCAS, Latin form of the post-classical Greek name *Loukas* 'man from Lucania'. This owes its perennial popularity throughout Christian Europe to the fact that, from the 2nd century onwards, the third gospel in the New Testament has been ascribed to the Lucas or Luke mentioned at various places in Acts and in the Epistles. He was a doctor, a Gentile, and a friend and convert of St Paul.
Cognates: Scottish Gaelic: **Lùcas**. Irish Gaelic: **Lúcás**. French: **Luc**. Italian: **Luca**. Catalan: **Lluc(h)**. German: **Lukas**. Dutch: **Lucas**. Polish: **Łukasz**. Czech: **Lukáš**. Hungarian: **Lukács**. Russian: **Luka**.

Lulu (f.) German: pet form of LUISE, originally a reduplicated nursery form. It is now also used in the English-speaking world, both as a pet form of LOUISE and as an independent given name.

Lupita (f.) Spanish: pet form of GUADALUPE.

Lurdes (f.) Spanish: variant of LOURDES.

Luthais (m.) Scottish Gaelic form of LOUIS.

Luther (m.) English (esp. U.S.): from the German surname, which is derived from a Germanic personal name composed of the elements *liut* people + *heri* army, warrior. It is most commonly bestowed among evangelical Protestants, in honour of the ecclesiastical reformer and theologian Martin Luther (1483–1546). In recent times it has also become especially popular among American Blacks, partly in honour of the assassinated civil rights leader Martin Luther King (1929–68).

Lutz (m.) German: pet form of LUDWIG.

Luvenia (f.) English: apparently an arbitrary coinage originating in the southern United States

Luz (f.) Spanish: name reflecting a title of the Virgin Mary, 'Our Lady of Light' (Spanish *luz*, from Latin *lux*).

Luzdivina (f.) Spanish: apparently derived from LIDWINA, but altered by popular etymology to mean 'divine light' (cf. LUZ).

Lyall (m.) Scottish: transferred use of the surname, which is probably derived from the Old Norse personal name *Liulfr*, of which the first element is obscure. The second is clearly Old Norse *úlfr* wolf. See also LYLE.

Lydia (f.) English: of Greek origin, meaning 'woman from Lydia', an area of Asia Minor. It is borne in the Bible by a woman of Thyatira who was converted by St Paul and who entertained him in her house (Acts 16: 14–15, 40). It has enjoyed steady popularity in the English-speaking world since the 17th century.
Cognates: French: **Lydie**. Polish: **Lidia**. Czech: **Lida**.

Lyle (m.) English and Scottish: transferred use of the surname, which originated as a local name for someone who came 'from the island' (Anglo-Norman *de l'isle*). The island in question would in many cases have been an area of higher, dry ground in a marsh or fen, rather than in a sea or river. There may have been some confusion with LYALL.

Lyn (m., f.) **1.** (m.) Welsh: short form of LLEWELLYN. **2.** (f.) English: variant of LYNN.

Lyndon (m.) English: transferred use of the surname, derived from the place known as Lyndon in the former county of Rutland (now part of Leicestershire), so called from Old English *lind* linden, lime tree + *dūn* hill. Its modern use as a male given name owes something to the American president Lyndon Baines Johnson (1908–73).
Variant: **Lindon**.

Lynette (f.) English: in modern use a derivative of LYNN, formed with the French feminine diminutive suffix *-ette*. However, this is not the origin for the name as used in Tennyson's *Idylls of the King* (1859–85), through which it first came to public attention. There, it represents an altered form of some Celtic original; cf. Welsh ELUNED.
Variants: **Lynnette**, **Lin(n)ette**.

Lynn (f.) English: apparently a modern short form of LINDA with the spelling arbitrarily altered. There may also be some connection with the French name *Line*, which originated as a short form of various female names ending in this syllable, notably CAROLINE. The element *-lyn(n)* has also been used as a productive suffix in female names since around the middle of the 20th century.

Lynsey (f.) English: variant spelling of LINDSAY.

Lyov (m.) Russian: colloquial variant of LEV.

Lys (f.) English: variant spelling of LIS or LIZ, apparently inspired by medieval French *(fleur de) lys* lily.

Lysette (f.) English: variant spelling of LISETTE.

Lyssa (f.) English: short form of ALYSSA. In form it coincides with the name, in Greek mythology, of the personification of madness or frenzy. See also LISSA.

Lyubov (f.) Russian: from the vocabulary word meaning 'love'. It was originally adopted as a vernacular loan translation of Greek *Agapē* (see AGAFYA). See also LIBĚNA.
Pet form: **Lyuba**.

M

Maarten (m.) Dutch form of MARTIN, now rather less common than *Martijn*.

Maartje (f.) Dutch: feminine form of MAARTEN.

Maas (m.) Dutch: short form of THOMAS.

Mabel (f.) **1**. English: originally a nickname from the Old French vocabulary word *amabel*, *amable* lovely (related to modern English *amiable* friendly, good-humoured). The initial vowel began to be lost as early as the 12th century (the same woman is referred to as both *Mabilia* and *Amabilia* in a document of 1185), but a short vowel in the resulting first syllable was standard, giving a rhyme with *babble*, until the 19th century, when people began to pronounce the name to rhyme with *table*. **2**. Spanish: contracted short form of *Maria Isabel* (cf. MARIBEL).
Variant: English: **Mable**.
Cognate (of I): Irish Gaelic: **Máible**.

Mabelle (f.) English: altered spelling of MABEL, based on French *ma belle* 'my beautiful one'.

Mabon (m.) Welsh: 20th-century revival of an Old Welsh personal name derived from the Old Celtic element *mab* son. This seems to have been originally the name of a divinity; it is also borne by a character in the tale of *'Culhwch and Olwen'*.

Mac Dara (m.) Irish Gaelic: name meaning 'son of oak'. This is the name of the patron saint of a parish in Connemara in which is situated Mac Dara's island, goal of an annual pilgrimage on 16 July. The given name is still common in the surrounding region.

Maciej (m.) Polish form of MATTHEW.
Pet form: **Maciek**.

Madeleine (f.) French and English: the French form of the byname of a character in the New Testament, Mary Magdalene 'Mary of Magdala'. Magdala was a village on Lake Galilee, a few miles north of Tiberias. The woman 'which had been healed of evil spirits and infirmities' (Luke 8: 2) was given this name in the Bible to distinguish her from other bearers of the very common name MARY. It was widely accepted in Christian folk belief that she was the same person as the repentant sinner who washed Christ's feet with her tears in the previous chapter (Luke 7), but there is no support in the text for this identification.
Variants: English: **Madeline** (common esp. in Ireland), **Madoline**; **Madelaine**, **Madlyn**; MAGDALENE.
Cognate: Irish Gaelic: **Madailéin**.
Pet forms: English: **Maddie**, **Maddy**. French: **Madelon**.

Madge (f.) English: pet form of MARGARET, representing a palatalized version of *Mag(g)* (see MAGGIE).

Madonna (f.) English (esp. U.S.): from an Italian title of the Virgin Mary (literally 'my lady'), applied to countless Renaissance paintings of beautiful young women (with and without infants), representing the mother of Christ. Its use as a given name seems to be a fairly recent phenomenon, arising among Americans of Italian descent. In the 1980s, the name became particularly well known as a result of the fame of the American pop star Madonna Ciccone (b. 1958).

Madrona (f.) Jewish: from the Romance name MATRONA. The name was apparently chosen in the hope that the baby would live to become a mother herself.
Masculine form: **Madron**.

Mads (m.) Danish form of MATTHEW.

Madzia (f.) Polish: pet form of *Magdalena* (see MAGDALENE).

Mae (f.) English: variant spelling of MAY, possibly influenced by MAEVE. It has been most notably borne by the American film actress Mae West (1892–1980), whose prominent bust led to her name being given, by members of the RAF, to a type of inflatable life-jacket used in the Second World War. This spelling is now no longer much used.

Maeve (f.) Irish: Anglicized form of Gaelic Meadhbh, an ancient Celtic name meaning 'intoxicating, she who makes drunk'. It is borne by the Queen of Connacht in the Irish epic *Táin Bó Cuailgne*, 'the Cattle Raid of Cooley'. In this, Meadhbh leads a raid on Ulster in order to seize the Brown Bull of Cooley, but she is repulsed single-handed by the hero Cuchulain. The historical events underlying the epic probably took place in about the 1st century AD. Shakespeare's Queen Mab, 'the fairy's midwife' (*Romeo and Juliet* I. iv. 53), may owe her name, if nothing else, to the legendary Queen of Connacht.
Variants: **Mave** (also an informal short form of MAVIS), **Meave**.

Mafalda (f.) Portuguese and Italian: variant of MATILDA, used especially in Portugal. The name was taken there by a princess from the royal house of Savoy, who in 1146 went to marry the Portuguese king. St Mafalda (1203–52) was a daughter of King Sancho II of Portugal. King Victor Emmanuel III of Italy, a member of the house of Savoy, gave it to a daughter of his in 1902.

Magali (f.) French (of Provençal origin): name of uncertain derivation, possibly a form of MARGARET. It has become widely known as a result of its occurrence in a popular Provençal folk song.
Variant: **Magalie**.

Magdalene (f.) Learned form of MADELEINE, used especially in Germany.
Variants: English: **Magdalen**. Latinate: **Magdalena** (used in Spain, Portugal, Germany, Holland, Norway, Sweden, Poland, and Czechoslovakia).
Cognates: Italian: **Maddalena**. Russian: **Magdalina**. Hungarian: **Magdolna**. Danish: **Magdalone**, **Malene**.
Short forms: German, Scandinavian, and E. European: **Magda**. German and Czech: **Alena**.
Pet form: Polish: **Madzia**.

Maggie (f.) English: pet form of MARGARET. In the Middle Ages the short form *Mag(g)* was common, as a result of the early loss in pronunciation of the English preconsonantal *r*. This is not now used as a given name, but has given rise to the surname *Maggs*; *Maggie* is also a derivative of *Mag(g)* formed with the characteristically Scottish hypocoristic suffix *-ie*. Until recently it was most common in Scotland. It is now fashionable elsewhere as well.

Cognate: Scottish Gaelic: **Magaidh**.

Magnus (m.) Scandinavian, Scottish, and English: originally a Latin byname meaning 'great', this was first extracted from the name of *Charlemagne* (recorded in Latin chronicles as *Carolus Magnus* 'Charles the Great') and used as a given name by the Scandinavians. It was borne by seven medieval kings of Norway, including Magnus I (1024–47), known as Magnus the Good, and Magnus VI (1238–80), known as Magnus the Law Mender. There are several early Scandinavian saints called Magnus, including an earl of Orkney (d. 1116), to whom Kirkwall cathedral is dedicated. The name was imported to Scotland and Ireland during the Middle Ages.

Vernacular forms: Danish: **Mogens**. Swedish: **Måns**. Scottish Gaelic: **Mànas**. Irish Gaelic: **Maghnus** (Anglicized as **Manus**). Finnish: **Mauno**.

Mahalia (f.) English: apparently a cross between the two biblical masculine personal names *Mahali* (Exodus 6: 19) and *Mahalah* (1 Chronicles 7: 18), both fleetingly mentioned in genealogies.

Mahon (m.) Irish: Anglicized form of Gaelic **Mathúin**.

Mai (f.) Swedish: pet form of **Maria** and *Margit* (see **Margaret**). It is now used as an independent given name and is common as both the first and the second element of compound names such as *Mai-Britt*, *Mai-Lis*, *Anne-Mai*, and *Britt-Mai*.

Maica (f.) Spanish: contracted pet form of *María Carmen*; cf. **Maite**.

Maidie (f.) Scottish and Irish: apparently a pet form of modern English *maid* young woman (Old English *mæg(den)*), originally given as an affectionate nickname. However, it may also be an altered form of **Maisie**.

Maike (f.) Frisian: pet form of **Maria**. The name now also has a wider currency as an independent given name in the Dutch- and German-speaking world.

Variant: **Maiken** (esp. common in Scandinavia).

Màili (f.) Scottish Gaelic: variant of **Màiri**.

Mainchín (m.) Irish Gaelic: originally a byname representing a diminutive of *manach* monk.

Anglicized form: **Mannix**.

Mair (f.) Welsh form of **Mary**, derived from Latin *Maria* via Old Welsh *Meir*.

Máire (f.) Irish Gaelic form of **Mary**, derived from Old French *Marie*.

Mairéad (f.) Irish Gaelic form of **Margaret**. The name is also used in Scotland, where it is spelled **Mairead** or **Maighread**.

Màiri (f.) Scottish Gaelic form of **Mary**.

Máirín (f.) Irish Gaelic: name Anglicized as **Maureen**.

Mairtin (m.) Irish Gaelic form of **Martin**.

Maisie (f.) Scottish: pet form derived from *Mairead*, the Gaelic form of **Margaret**, with the Scottish and northern English hypocoristic suffix *-ie*. Gaelic palatalized *-r-* sounds to English ears like /z/. The name occurs in Scottish border ballads in the form *Masery*.

Maite (f.) Spanish: contracted pet form of *Maria Teresa*; cf. **Maica**. Coincidentally, the vocabulary word *maite* means 'beloved, dear' in the Basque language.

Maj (f.) Swedish: variant spelling of **Mai**.

Maja (f.) German and Scandianvian: pet form of **Maria**, or else from Latin *Maia* (see **Maya**).

Majella (f.) English and Irish (borne by Roman Catholics): name given in honour of St Gerard Majella (1725–55), an Italian Redemptorist monk who was the focus of a number of miraculous phenomena and who was canonized in 1904.

Makari (m.) Russian: from the Late Greek name *Makarios*, a derivative of *makaros* blessed. This was a very popular name among early Christians, and was borne by a large number of saints, among them Macarius the Elder (*c*.300–90) and Macarius the Younger (d. *c*.408), both of whom lived in Egypt, and a 4th-century bishop of Jerusalem who identified the True Cross found by St Helena. Another St Macarius (d. *c*.350) was originally name *Arius*, but has been renamed in order to distinguish him from the founder of the Arian heresy, which he strongly opposed.

Variant: **Makar**.

Cognates: Italian, Spanish, Portuguese: **Macario**. French: **Macaire**. Polish: **Makary**.

Malachy (m.) Irish: name of an Irish king who defeated the Norse invaders in an important battle. His baptismal name was *Maoileachlainn* 'devotee of St Seachnall' or Secundinus, but in medieval sources telling of his life this has already been altered to coincide with that of the biblical prophet generally known in English as **Malachi**. Malachi was the last of the twelve minor prophets of the Old Testament; he foretold the coming of Christ and his name means, appropriately, 'my messenger' in Hebrew.

Malcolm (m.) Scottish and English: Anglicized form of the Gaelic name *Mael Coluim* 'devotee of St Columba'. Columba, whose name means 'dove' in Latin, was a 6th-century monk of Irish origin who played a leading part in the conversion to Christianity of Scotland and northern England; See also **Calum** and **Colm**. He has always been one of the most popular saints in Scotland, but in the Middle Ages it was felt to be presumptuous to give the names of saints directly to children; instead their blessing was invoked by prefixing the name with *mael* 'devotee of' (cf. **Marmaduke**) or *gille* 'servant of'. In the Highlands *Malcolm* is still used as an Anglicized form of *Calum*.

Feminine forms: **Malcolmina**, **Malina**.

Malene (f.) Danish: contracted form of **Magdalene**.

Małgorzata (f.) Polish form of **Margaret**.

Pet form: **Malgosia**.

Malkah (f.) Jewish: from Hebrew *malkah* queen. This name does not appear in the Hebrew Scriptures, but represents an affectionate nickname used from the Middle Ages onwards.

Mallory (m.) occasionally (f.) English (esp. U.S.): transferred use of the surname, which originated as a Norman French nickname for an unfortunate person, from Old French *malheure* unhappy or unlucky.

Mallt (f.) Welsh form of **Maud**, a common name in the Middle Ages.

Malvina (f.) Scottish, English, and Scandinavian (esp. Danish): apparently a factitious name, based on Gaelic *mala mhin* smoothbrow, invented by James Macpherson (1736–96), the Scottish antiquarian poet who published works allegedly translated from the ancient Gaelic bard Ossian. The name became popular in Scandinavia because of the admiration of the Emperor Napoleon for the Ossianic poems: he was godfather to several of the children of his marshal Jean Baptiste Bernadotte (who ruled Norway and Sweden (1818–44) as Karl XIV Johan) and imposed his own taste in naming practices on them, hence the frequency of 'Ossianic' given names in Scandinavia. *Las Malvinas* is the Argentinian name for the Falkland Islands; the origin of this is disputed, but it appears to have no connection with the Ossianic name.

Cognate: German: **Malwine** (now rare).

Mamie (f.) English: short form of MARGARET or MARY, which has been used occasionally as an independent given name, especially in America, where it was the name by which the wife of President Eisenhower was usually known. It seems to have originated as a nursery form.

Mànas (m.) Scottish Gaelic form of MAGNUS.

Manda (f.) English: short form of AMANDA.

Mandel (m.) Jewish: back-formation from MENDEL, assumed by folk etymology to be from German *Männl*, a diminutive of *Mann* man. It probably has no connection with the Yiddish vocabulary word *mandel* almond.

Mandy (f.) (m.) English: **1**. (f.) Pet form of AMANDA, now sometimes used as a given name in its own right. **2**. (m.) Occasionally it is also found as a Jewish male name, an Anglicized form of MANDEL.

Manfred (m.) German, Dutch, and English: from an old Germanic personal name, usually said to be composed of the elements *man* man + *fred, frid* peace. However, it is more likely that the first element was *magin* strength (the Norman form being normally *Mainfred*; cf. modern English 'might and main') or *manag* much (cf. modern English *many*). This was in use among the Normans, who introduced it to Britain, but it did not become part of the common stock of English given names, and was reintroduced from Germany in the 19th century. It was a traditional name among the Hohenstaufens, and was borne by the last Hohenstaufen king of Sicily (1258–66), who died in battle against papal forces at Benevento. The name was also used by Byron for the central character in his poetic drama *Manfred* (1817), a brooding outcast, tormented by incestuous love for his halfsister.

Variants: German: **Manfried**, **Manfrid**.
Cognate: Italian: **Manfredo**.

Mania (f.) Polish: pet form of MARIA.
Variant: **Maniuta**.

Manley (m.) English: transferred use of the surname, which in most cases originated as a local name from places in Devon and Cheshire, so called from Old English *(ge)mǣne* common, shared + *lēah* wood or clearing. Its choice as a first name may well have been influenced by association with the vocabulary word *manly* and the hope that the qualities denoted by the adjective would be attributes of the bearer. The vocabulary word may also lie behind some cases of the surname, as a nickname for a 'manly' person.

Manlio (m.) Italian: from the Latin name, *Manlius*, of a famous Roman family of staunch republican virtues and heroism. An earlier form of the name was *Manilius*. It appears to be a derivative of the old Roman given name *Manius*, which is probably derived either from *māne* morning or from the archaic root *mān-* good. Marcus Manlius Capitolinus (d. ?384 BC), who saved Rome from the besieging Gauls in 389 BC, is said to have defended plebeian debtors from their patrician creditors, and the following year to have been impeached and executed by being thrown from the Tarpeian Rock. The Italian form of the name was bestowed by Garibaldi on one of his sons.

Mannix (m.) Irish: Anglicized form of Gaelic MAINCHÍN.

Manny (m.) English: aphetic pet form of EMMANUEL, in use mainly among British Jews.

Manoel (m.) Portuguese form of EMMANUEL. The Portuguese king Manoel I (1469–1521; reigned 1495–1521) presided over a glittering period in Portuguese history, at a time when wealth was flowing in from Portugal's new conquests in both the East Indies and South America.

Manon (f.) French: pet form of MARIE, common in the 18th and 19th centuries. For the formation, cf. MANIA and *Madelon* (from MADELEINE). The name is familiar in the English-speaking world through the Abbé Prévost's story *Manon Lescaut* (1731), which was given operatic treatment by both Puccini and Massenet. In it the young Chevalier des Grieux elopes with the heroine, who supports them by becoming a courtesan, and is eventually deported to Louisiana, where she dies.

Mans (m.) Catalan: variant of AMANS.

Måns (m.) Swedish: vernacular form of MAGNUS.

Manuel (m.) Spanish form of EMMANUEL.
Feminine form: **Manuela**.
Pet forms: **Manolo, Manolito, Manolete** (m.); **Manola, Manolita** (f.).

Manus (m.) Irish: Anglicized form of Gaelic *Maghnus* and *Mánus*, forms of MAGNUS.

Manya (f.) Russian: pet form of MARIA.

Maoiliosa (originally (m.) now also (f.)) Irish Gaelic: name meaning 'devotee of Jesus'.
Anglicized form: MELISSA (a modern development).
Cognate ((m.) only): Scottish Gaelic: **Maoilios** (Anglicized as MYLES).

Maolra (m.) Irish Gaelic: modern spelling, common particularly in the west of Ireland, of earlier *Maoil-Mhuire* 'devotee of Mary'.
Anglicized form: MYLES.

Mara (f.) English: of biblical origin, from Hebrew *Mara* 'bitter', a name referred to by Naomi when she went back to Bethlehem because of the famine in the land of Moab and the deaths of her husband and two sons: 'call me not Naomi, call me Mara: for the Almighty hath dealt very bitterly with me' (Ruth 1: 20).

Marc (m.) French form of MARK, now also quite popular in the English-speaking world. It was given some currency in England in the 1960s by the pop singer Marc Bolan.

Marcel (m.) French: from the Latin name *Marcellus*, originally a diminutive of MARCUS. The name has always been popular in France as it was borne by a 3rd-century missionary to Gaul, martyred at Bourges with his companion Anastasius.
Cognates: Italian: **Marcello**. Spanish, Portuguese: **Marcelo**.
Feminine forms: Irish Gaelic: **Mairsile**. Scottish Gaelic: **Marsaili**.

Latin: **Marcella** (used to some extent in the English-speaking world, esp. Ireland, and also in Italy). French: **Marcelle**. Spanish, Polish, Czech: **Marcela**.

Marcellin (m.) French: from the Latin name *Marcellīnus*, a double derivative of MARCUS borne by a dozen early saints, including a pope who died in the persecutions instigated by the Roman emperor Diocletian.

Cognates: Italian: **Marcellino**. Spanish, Portuguese: **Marcelino**.

Marcia (f.) English: often used as a feminine equivalent of MARK, but in fact a feminine form of *Marcius*, itself a derivative of MARCUS. One St Marcia is commemorated in a group with Felix, Luciolus, Fortunatus, and others; another with Zenais, Cyria, and Valeria; and a third with Ariston, Crescentian, Eutychian, Urban, Vitalis, Justus, Felicissimus, Felix, and Symphorosa. None is individually very famous.

Variant: **Marsha**.

Pet forms: **Marcie**, **Marcy** (chiefly U.S.).

Marcin (m.) Polish form of MARTIN.

Marco (m.) Italian and usual Spanish form of MARK.

Marcos (m.) Portuguese form of MARK. It is also used in Spain as a variant form of the more common MARCO.

Marcus (m.) The original Latin form of MARK, of unknown derivation; it may possibly be connected with MARIUS. This is also the form of the name in Scottish Gaelic, whence the surname *Mac Mharrius*, Anglicized as *Marquis*. *Marcus* was rarely used as a given name in the English-speaking world until recent years, when it has been seized on by parents seeking to give a distinctive form to a common and popular name. Among American Blacks it is sometimes bestowed in honour of the Black Consciousness leader Marcus Garvey (1887–1940).

Marea (f.) English: apparently an altered spelling of MARIA.

Mared (f.) Welsh form of MARGARET, a simplified version of *Marged*.

Marek (m.) Polish and Czech form of MARK.

Pet forms: Polish: **Mareczek**, **Maruś**. Czech: **Mareček**, **Maroušek**, **Mareš**, **Mařík**.

Maretta (f.) Scottish: Anglicized form of MAIREAD; See also MARIETTA.

Marga (f.) English: short form of MARGARET or any of the large number of related names beginning with these two syllables.

Margaret (f.) English and Scottish: an extremely common medieval given name, derived via Old French *Marguerite* and Latin *Margarīta* from Greek *Margarītēs*, from *margaron* pearl, a word ultimately of Hebrew origin. The name was always understood to mean 'pearl' throughout the Middle Ages. The first St Margaret was martyred at Antioch in Pisidia during the persecution instigated by the Emperor Diocletian in the early 4th century. However, there seems to be some doubt about her name, as the same saint is venerated in the Orthodox Church as MARINA. There were several other saintly bearers of the name, including St Margaret of Scotland (d. 1093), wife of King Malcolm Canmore and daughter of Edmund Ironside of England. It was also the name of the wife of Henry VI of England, Margaret of Anjou (1430–82), and of Margaret Tudor (1489–1541), sister of Henry VIII, who married James IV of Scotland and ruled as regent there after his death. In Scandinavia, the name was borne by one of the most powerful rulers in Scandinavian history, Queen Margareta (1353–1412),

daughter of the Danish king Waldemar IV, wife of Haakon VI of Norway, and mother of Olaf V of both kingdoms. She effectively ruled Denmark and Norway as regent for her son Olaf and, after his death in 1387, for her greatnephew, Eric of Pomerania, adding Sweden to her empire in 1389. *Margaret* was also well established as a royal name in the Holy Roman Empire, France, Navarre, and Italy. In Britain in 1930 it was selected by the future King George VI and his wife for their second daughter, Princess Margaret Rose. See also MARGERY, MARJORIE.

Cognates: Latinate: **Margaret(t)a**. Irish Gaelic: **Mairéad**. Scottish Gaelic: **Mair(gh)ead**. Welsh: **Mar(g)ed**, **Mererid**. French: MARGUERITE. Italian: **Margherita**. Spanish: **Margarita**. Porruguese: **Margarida**. German and Scandinavian: **Margaret(h)a**. German, Danish: **Margaret(h)e**, **Margrethe**. German (vernacular): **Margrit**, **Margret; Meta**. Dutch, Low German: **Margriet**. Scandinavian (vernacular): **Margit; Marit** (Norwegian, Swedish); **Marete** (Danish). Polish: **Malgorzata**. Czech: **Markéta**. Hungarian: **Margit**. Finnish: **Marketta**. Jewish (modern Hebrew): **Margalit**, **Marganit**, **Marganita**.

Short forms: English: **Meg**, **Peg; Madge; Gretta**. Spanish: **Rita**. German: **Greta**, **Grete**, **Gritt(a)**, **Grit**. Low German, Dutch, Frisian: **Griet**, **Gre(e)t**. Swedish: **Maj**, **Greta**. Danish: **Grete**.

Pet forms: English: MAGGIE, **Meggie**, PEGGY; **Marge**, **Margie** (informal); MAY; See also DAISY. Scottish Gaelic: **Magaidh**, **Peigi**. Welsh: MEGAN. French: **Margot**. German, Danish, Swedish: **Meta**. Low German, Dutch, Frisian: **Grietje**, **Gre(e)tje**. Polish: **Malgosia**, **Gosia**, **Gośka**.

Margery (f.) English: the usual medieval vernacular form of MARGARET (now also commonly spelled MARJORIE). This form of the name is preserved in the nursery rhyme 'See-saw, Margery Daw'.

Margot (f.) French, English, German, and E. European: pet form of MARGUERITE, now used as an independent name. In England it is still usually pronounced in the French way, but in Eastern Europe the final consonant is sounded, and this has had some influence in America. The name of the American actress Margaux Hemingway (b. 1955) represents a fanciful respelling of this name inspired by a village near Bordeaux noted for its red wine.

Marguerite (f.) French form of MARGARET, also used in the English-speaking world, where its use has been reinforced by the fact that the name was adopted in the 19th century for a garden flower, a large cultivated variety of daisy. *Margaret* was earlier used in English as a dialect word denoting the ox-eye daisy, and the French equivalent was borrowed into English just in time to catch the vogue for deriving female given names from vocabulary words denoting flowers. See also DAISY.

Mari (f.) Welsh form of MARY.

Maria (f.) Latin form of MARY, still used in most European languages, either as the main local form of the name, as in Italian, Spanish (**María**), Portuguese, German, Dutch, Scandinavian, Polish, and Czech, or as a learned doublet of a vernacular form. In English it is a learned revival dating from the 18th century, pronounced both /mə'ri:ə/ and, more traditionally, /mə'raiə/. The original Latin name *Maria* arose as a back-formation from the early Christian female name *Mariam*. This was taken as an accusative case, with the usual Latin feminine accusative ending *-am*. In fact, however, it is an indeclinable Aramaic alternative form of the Hebrew name MIRIAM. This form of the name is in common use in most European languages; for example, it was the most common of all female names in Sweden in 1973. In Spain not only is the name *María*

itself enormously common, but a large number of Marian epithets and words associated with the cult of the Virgin are also used as female given names. *Maria* is also used as a male name in combinations such as *Giammaria* (Italian) and *José María* (Spanish).
Short form: **Ria**.
Cognates and pet forms: see MARY.
Masculine forms: MARIUS. Italian, Spanish, Portuguese: MARIO.

Mariamne (f.) The form of MIRIAM used by the Jewish historian Flavius Josephus, writing in Latin in the 1st century BC, as the name of the wife of King Herod. On the basis of this evidence, it has been thought by some to be closer to the original form of the name actually borne by the Virgin MARY, and has therefore been bestowed in her honour.

Marian (f., m.) 1. (f.) English: originally a medieval variant spelling of MARION. However, in the 18th century, when combined names began to come into fashion, it was sometimes understood as a combination of MARY and ANN. 2. (m.) Polish: from the Latin name *Mariānus* (see MARIANO), often bestowed among Roman Catholics in honour of the Virgin Mary.

Marianne (f.) 1. English: extended spelling of MARIAN, reinforcing the association of the second element with ANN(E). 2. French: assimilated form of MARIAMNE. *Marianne* is the name used for the symbolic figure of the French Republic.
Variant: English: **Marianna** (a Latinate form).

Mariano (m.) Italian, Spanish, and Portuguese: from the Latin name *Mariānus*, a derivative of MARIUS. In the early Christian era it came to be taken as an adjective derived from MARIA, and was associated with the cult of the Virgin Mary. It was borne by various early saints, including a 3rd-century martyr of Lambesa in Numidia and a 5th-century hermit of Berry, France.
Cognate: Polish, Czech: **Marian**.
Feminine form: **Mariana**.

Maribel (f.) Spanish: contracted short form of *Maria Isabel* (see also MABEL). The name is also occasionally used in the English-speaking world, where it may represent a simplified form of MARIBELLA.

Maribella (f.) English: Latinate combination of MARIA with the name BELLA or the productive suffix -*bella* (cf. ANNABEL and CHRISTABEL). The name is also occasionally used in Italy.

Marica (f.) Hungarian pet form of MARIA.

Marice (f.) English: respelling of MARIS, or else a combination of the first syllable of MARY or MARGARET with the name suffix -*ice* (cf. e.g. JANICE).

Marie (f.) French form of MARIA. When first introduced to England in the Middle Ages, it was Anglicized in pronunciation and respelled MARY. This French form was reintroduced into the English-speaking world as a separate name in the 19th century, and is still pronounced more or less in the French manner, although sometimes with the stress on the first syllable. The French name is also commonly used as a male name in the combination *Jean-Marie*.
Pet form: MANON.

Marie-Ange (f.) French equivalent of ÁNGELES. The name *Ange* is not used on its own in French.

Marie-France (f.) French: combination of MARIE with the national name *France*, invoking the protection of the Virgin Mary as the special guardian of France.

Mariel (f.) English: 1. Shortened form of MARIELLA. 2. Altered form of MURIEL or MERIEL.

Mariella (f.) Italian: diminutive form of MARIA.

Marielle (f.) French: diminutive form of MARIE, now fairly commonly used as an independent given name in the English-speaking world.

Marietta (f.) Italian: diminutive form of MARIA, now sometimes used as an independent name in the English-speaking world. In Gaelic Scotland *Mar(i)etta* is quite commonly used as an Anglicized form of MAIREAD, and abbreviated to ETTA.
Cognate: Spanish: **Marieta**.

Marigold (f.) English: one of the older of the group of names that were adopted from words for flowers in the late 19th and early 20th centuries. The Old English name of the flower was *golde*, presumably from *gold* (the precious metal), in reference to its colour. At some time before the 14th century the flower became associated with the Virgin Mary, and its name was extended accordingly to *marigold*. Not until the 19th century was this used as a female given name.

Marika (f.) Slavonic: pet form of MARIA, sometimes used as an independent given name in the English-speaking world.

Marilee (f.) English: modern coinage, a combination of MARY and LEE.

Marilene (f.) English: modern coinage, a combination of the name MARY with the productive suffix -*lene*, or else a variant of MARILYN.

Marilyn (f.) English: 20th-century elaboration of MARY, with the addition of the productive suffix -*lyn* (see LYNN).
Variant: **Marylyn**, MARILENE.

Marina (f.) Italian, Spanish, English, Scottish, and German: from a Late Latin name, a feminine form of the family name *Marīnus*. This was in fact a derivative of MARIUS, but even during the early centuries AD it was widely assumed to be identical with the Latin adjective *marīnus* 'of the sea'. The early saints of this name are all of extremely shaky historical identification. In Scotland the name has been used as an Anglicized form of MÀIRI, in place of plain MARY, following the pattern of feminine derivatives in -*ina* (cf. e.g. *Angusina* and *Calumina*).

Mario (m.) Italian, Spanish, and Portuguese form of *Marius*, a very common male name in these languages.

Marion (f., m.) English: 1. (f.) Originally a medieval French diminutive form of MARIE, introduced to Britain in the Middle Ages, and now completely Anglicized in pronunciation. 2. (m.) Altered form of the Continental male name MARIAN.
Elaborated form (of 1): **Marionne**.

Maripepa (f.) Spanish: pet form of the compound name *María Josefa*.

Mariquita (f.) Spanish: pet form of MARIA.

Marirrosa (f.) Spanish: compound name made up of the elements MARIA and ROSA.

Maris (f.) English: modern name of uncertain origin. It may derive from the second word of the Marian epithet *stella maris* 'star of the sea'.

Marisa (f.) Italian, Spanish, and English: 20th-century elaboration of MARIA, the suffix *-isa* apparently being abstracted from such names as LISA and *Luisa* (see LUIS).

Cognate: Dutch: **Marijse**.

Marisol (f.) Spanish: compound name made up of the elements MARIA and SOL.

Marit (f.) Norwegian and Swedish: vernacular form of MARGARET.

Marita (f.) Spanish: pet form of MARIA.

Marius (m.) Latin name, used in English, German, French, and other European languages: from a Roman family name of uncertain derivation. It is probably from *Mars*, the name of the Roman god of war, or from the adjective *mas* (genitive maris) male, virile. A derivation from *mare* sea has been proposed by some writers, but seems unlikely (cf. MARINA). This name and in particular its southern European form *Mario* owe their popularity to having been pressed into service as masculine equivalents of MARY in countries where the cult of the Virgin Mary is strong.

Cognate: Italian, Spanish, Portuguese: **Mario**. See also MARIAN (2).

Marji (f.) English: modern respelling of *Margie* (see MARGARET).

Variant: **Marjie**.

Marjolaine (f.) French: from the French name of the herb *marjoram*; cf. MARJORIE.

Marjorie (f.) English: usual modern spelling of MARGERY. It seems to have arisen as the result of popular etymological association of the name with that of the herb *marjoram* (cf. ROSEMARY). This word is of uncertain origin; its Middle English and Old French form was *majorane*, without the first *-r-*.

Variant: **Marjory** (the usual spelling in Scotland; See also MARSAILI).

Mark (m.) English: from the Latin name *Marcus*, borne by the evangelist, author of the second gospel in the New Testament, and by several other early and medieval saints. St Mark became the patron saint of Venice, and the Italian name *Marco* has long been especially popular in that city. This was one of the extremely limited number of Roman given names in use in the classical period. There were only about a dozen of these in general use, with perhaps another dozen confined to particular families. In Arthurian legend, King Mark is the aged ruler of Cornwall to whom Isolde is brought as a bride by Tristan. *Mark* was not notably borne by royalty and was not a particularly common name in the Middle Ages outside a few centres such as Venice.

Variant: MARCUS.

Cognates: Irish and Scottish Gaelic: **Marcas**. French: **Marc**. Italian, Spanish: **Marco**. Portuguese (also Spanish): **Marcos**. Romanian: **Marku**. German: **Markus**. Polish, Czech: **Marek**. Ukrainian: **Marko**. Finnish: **Markku**.

Markéta (f.) Czech form of MARGARET.

Marketta (f.) Finnish form of MARGARET.

Marla (f.) English: modern creation, representing an altered form of MARLENE, or else a name invented as a feminine equivalent of MARLON.

Marlene (f.) German, now also widely used in the English-speaking world: contracted form of *Maria Magdalene* (see MADELEINE). Probably the first, and certainly the most famous, bearer of the name is Marlene Dietrich, born in 1902 as Maria Magdalene von Losch. The name was further popularized in the 1940s by the wartime German song 'Lili Marlene', which was immensely popular among both German and British troops in North Africa.

Marlon (m.) English: name apparently first brought to public attention by the American actor Marlon Brando (b. 1924) and now sometimes used more widely as a result of his fame. The name was borne also by his father, and is of uncertain origin, possibly derived from MARC with the addition of the French diminutive suffix *-lon* (originally a combination of two separate suffixes, *-el* and *-on*); the family is said to have been of French origin. In America the name is used fairly regularly among Blacks, but in Britain the most notable bearer is the young go-karting enthusiast in the *Perishers* cartoon strip.

Marmaduke (m.) English: of uncertain derivation. It is generally held to be an Anglicized form of the Old Irish name *Mael-Maedóc* 'devotee of Maedóc'. The name *Maedóc* was borne by various early Irish saints, most notably a 6th-century abbot of Clonmore and a 7th-century bishop of Ferns. Mael-Maedóc Ó Morgair (1095–1148) was a reformer of the Church in Ireland and a friend of Bernard of Clairvaux. However, the modern Gaelic form (from *c*.1200) is *Maol-Maodhóg* (pronounced /mʌlˈmɔʊg/), so that the name would have had to have been borrowed into English before this loss of the *d*. *Marmaduke* has never been common except in a small area of North Yorkshire, and is at present almost completely out of fashion.

Short form: DUKE.

Marna (f.) Swedish: vernacular form of MARINA.

Marnie (f.) English (mainly U.S.): Anglicized form of MARNA.

Marsaili (f.) Scottish Gaelic form of MARGERY and of *Marcella* (see MARCEL).

Marsh (m.) English: **1**. Transferred use of the surname, which originated as a local name for someone who lived on a patch of marshy ground, from Middle English *mersche* (Old English *mersc*). **2**. Informal short form of MARSHALL.

Marsha (f.) Phonetic spelling of MARCIA, popular especially among American Blacks.

Marshall (m.) English: transferred use of the surname, derived from a Norman French occupational term that originally denoted someone who looked after horses, ultimately from the Germanic elements *marah* horse + *scale* servant. By the time it became fixed as a surname it had the meaning 'shoeing smith'; later it came to denote an official whose duties were to a large extent ceremonial. The surname is phonetically identical with the English pronunciation of the name of the Roman poet *Martial* (from Latin *Mars*, genitive *Martis*; cf. MARTIN), and this may possibly have contributed something to its use as a given name.

Märta (f.) Danish: contracted form of *Märeta*, an obsolete variant of MERETE. The name is now also very popular in Sweden, where it was the thirty-sixth most common female name in 1973.

Martha (f.) New Testament name, of Aramaic rather than Hebrew origin, meaning 'lady'. It was borne by the sister of Lazarus and Mary of Bethany (John 11: 1). According to Luke 10: 38, when Jesus visited the house of Mary and Martha, Mary sat at his feet, listening to him, while Martha 'was cumbered about much serving', so that she complained to Jesus,

'Lord, dost thou not care that my sister hath left me to serve alone?' For this reason, the name *Martha* has always been associated with hard domestic work, as opposed to the contemplative life.

Other forms: French, German: Marthe. Scandinavian: **Mart(h)a**, **Mart(h)e**. Spanish, Italian, Polish, and Czech: **Marta**. Hungarian: **Márta**. Pet form: Spanish: **Martita**.

Marti (f.) English: short form of MARTINA (or its French equivalent *Martine*). Its best-known bearer in Britain is the English comedienne Marti Caine (b. 1945).

Variants: **Martie**, **Marty**.

Martin (m.) English, French, and German form of the Latin name *Martīnus*. This was probably originally derived from *Mars* (genitive *Martis*), the name of the Roman god of war (and earlier of fertility). MARTIN became very popular in the Middle Ages, especially on the Continent, as a result of the fame of St Martin of Tours. He was born the son of a Roman officer in Upper Pannonia (an outpost of the Roman Empire, now part of Hungary), and although he became a leading figure, in the 4th-century Church, he is chiefly remembered now for having divided his cloak in two and given half to a beggar. The name was also borne by five popes, including one who defended Roman Catholic dogma against Eastern Orthodox theology. He died after suffering imprisonment and privations in Naxos and public humiliation in Constantinople, and was promptly acclaimed a martyr by supporters of the Roman Church. Among Protestants, the name is sometimes bestowed in honour of the German theologian Martin Luther (1483–1546); *Martin* was used as a symbolic name for the Protestant Church in satires by both Dryden and Swift. A further influence, especially among American Blacks, may be its use as the given name of the civil-rights leader Martin Luther King (1929–68).

Variant: English: **Martyn**.
Cognates: Irish Gaelic: **Máirtín**, **Mártan**. Scottish Gaelic: **Màrtainn**. Italian: **Martino**. Spanish: **Martín**. Portuguese: **Martinho**. Catalan: **Martí**. Low German: **Merten**. Dutch: **Maarten**, **Martijn**. Danish, Norwegian: **Morten**. Swedish: **Mårten**. Polish: **Marcin**. Hungarian: **Márton**. Finnish: **Martti**.
Pet form: English: **Marty**.
Feminine forms: MARTINA, **Martine**.

Martina (f.) Feminine form of the Latin name *Martīnus* (see MARTIN). This form is in use in almost all the major languages of Europe, although it is not common in France. It was in use from an early period, being borne by a notorious poisoner mentioned by the historian Tacitus. The 3rd-century saint of the same name is of doubtful authenticity. Modern use of the name in the English-speaking world seems to be the result of German or Eastern European influence, as in the case of the tennis player Martina Navratilova (b. 1956), who was born in Czechoslovakia.

Cognates: French, German, and English: **Martine**. Polish: **Martyna**.

Martirio (f.) Spanish: religious name alluding to the spiritual quality of martyrdom (Spanish *martirio*, from Late Latin *martyrium*, a derivative of Greek *martyr* witness) or suffering for the sake of one's faith.

Martita (f.) Spanish: pet form of *Marta* (see MARTHA), now also sometimes used in the English-speaking world.

Short form: **Tīta**.

Marty (m.) English: short form of MARTIN that has come into favour in the latter part of the 20th century, being associated

particularly with the comedian Marty Feldman (1933–83), the 1960s pop singer Marty Wilde (b. 1938 as Reginald Smith), and the country-and-western singer Marty Robbins (b. 1926). It occurs occasionally as a female name, a variant of MARTI.

Marva (f.) English: modern creation, apparently invented as a feminine form of MARVIN. The fanciful name **Marvalee** represents an elaboration of this.

Marvin (m.) English: from a medieval variant of MERVYN, resulting from the regular Middle English change of *-er-* to *-ar-*. Modern use may represent a transferred use of the surname derived from this in the Middle Ages. It is very popular in the United States, where it is often borne by Blacks and is associated in particular with the American singer Marvin Gaye (1939–84).

Mary (f.) English: originally a Middle English Anglicized form of French MARIE, from Latin MARIA. This is a New Testament form of MIRIAM, which St Jerome derives from elements meaning 'drop of the sea' (Latin *stilla maris*, later altered to *stella maris* 'star of the sea'). *Mary* is the most popular and enduring of all female Christian names, being the name of the Virgin Mary, mother of Jesus Christ, who has been the subject of a cult from earliest times. Consequently, the name was extremely common among early Christians, several saints among them, and by the Middle Ages was well established in every country in Europe at every level of society. It has been enduringly popular ever since, its popularity having been almost completely undisturbed by the vagaries of fashion that affect other names. In Spain and Portugal, the cult of the Virgin is so widespread and important that vocabulary words and placenames associated with aspects of her cult have been pressed into service as female given names, even when the gender of the vocabulary word is actually masculine: see, e.g., DOLORES, MERCEDES, PILAR, and ROSARIO. The Gaels, reluctant as always to put their saints' names to profane use, keep *Muire* (Irish) and *Moire* (Scottish) for the Virgin herself, and use late derivations of *Maria* (cited below) for secular naming purposes.

In the New Testament, *Mary* is also the name of several other women: Mary Magdalene (see MADELEINE); Mary the sister of Martha, who sat at Jesus's feet while Martha served (Luke 10: 38–42; John 11: 1–46; 12: 1–9) and who came to be taken in Christian tradition as symbolizing the value of a contemplative life; the mother of St Mark (Colossians 4: 10); and a Roman matron mentioned by St Paul (Romans 16: 6).

Cognates: In most European languages, including English: MARIA. Irish Gaelic: **Máire** (see also MOIRA, MAURA); **Máiria** (a learned form). Scottish Gaelic: **Màiri**, **Màili**. Welsh: **Mair**, **Mari**. French: MARIE. Basque: **Miren**. Russian: **Marya**.
Pet forms: English: MAY, MOLLY. Irish Gaelic: **Máirín**. Scottish Gaelic: **Màireag**. Italian: **Marietta**, **Mariella**. Spanish: **Mari(qui)ta**, **Maruja**, S. German and Swiss: **Mitzi**. Dutch: **Marieke**, **Micke**, **Miep**. Frisian: **Maike**. Danish: **Mia**. Swedish: **Maj**, **Maja**, **Mia**. Russian: **Masha**, **Manya**. Polish: **Marika** (also found in other Slavonic languages); **Marusia**; **Marzena**; **Mania**.

Marylyn (f.) English: variant spelling of MARILYN.

Maryvonne (f.) French: combination of the names MARIE and YVONNE. This has recently become a fashionable given name.

Masha (f.) Russian: pet form of *Marya* (see MARY).

Masław (m.) Polish: vernacular contracted form of MIECZYSŁAW.

Maso (m.) Italian: short form of TOMMASO.

Mason (m.) English (esp. U.S.): transferred use of the surname, which originated in the early Middle Ages as an occupational name for a worker in stone, Old French *maçon* (of Germanic origin, connected with Old English *macian* to make).

Massimo (m.) Italian form of MAXIM.

Masterman (m.) Scottish and English: transferred use of the surname, which originated in Scotland as a term denoting a retainer or servant: the 'man' of the 'master'. This was used in particular for the eldest sons of barons and the uncles of lords. As a given name it is principally known from the central character of Captain Frederick Marryat's novel *Masterman Ready* (1841).

Matěj (m.) Czech form of MATTHEW.
Pet forms: **Máta, Matejek, Matěji(če)k, Matoušek, Matys, Matýsek.**

Mateusz (m.) Polish form of MATTHEW.
Pet forms: **Matus(ek), Matuszek, Matys(ek).**

Mathúin (m.) Irish Gaelic: modern name meaning 'bear'. It represents a simplified form of the earlier *Mathghamhain*, borne by a brother of Brian Boru, High King of Ireland in the early 11th century.
Anglicized form: **Mahon.**

Matilda (f.) Latinized form of a Germanic personal name composed of the elements *maht, meht* might + *hild* battle. This was the name of an early German queen (895–968), wife of Henry the Fowler, who was noted for her piety and generosity. It was also the name of the wife of William the Conqueror and of the daughter of Henry I of England (see MAUD). The name was introduced into England by the Normans, and this Latinized form is the one that normally occurs in medieval records, although the vernacular form MAUD seems to have been the one in everyday use. *Matilda* was revived in England as a learned form in the 18th century.
Variant: **Mathilda.**
Cognates: French: **Mathilde.** Spanish, Portuguese: **Matilde.** Portuguese, Italian: **Mafalda.** German: **Mechtilde.** Low German: **Mette.** Polish, Czech: **Matylda.**
Short forms: English: **Tilda.** Swedish: **Tilda.** Danish: **Tilde.**
Pet forms: English: **Mattie; Tilly, Tillie.**

Matrona (f.) Russian: from the Late Latin name *Mātrōna* 'lady' (earlier 'married, respectable, noble woman', a derivative of *māter* mother). This name was borne by various early saints martyred for their faith.
Variant: **Matryona** (popular form).
Cognate: Jewish: **Madrona.**
Pet forms: Russian: **Matryosh(k)a, Matyush(k)a,** MOTYA.

Matthew (m.) English form of the name of the Christian evangelist, author of the first gospel in the New Testament. His name is a form of the Hebrew name *Matt thia*, meaning 'gift of God', which is fairly common in the Old Testament, being rendered in the Authorized Version in a number of different forms: *Mattan(i)ah, Mattatha(h), Mattithiah, Mattathias*, and so on. In the Authorized Version, the evangelist is regularly referred to as *Matthew*, while the apostle chosen to replace Judas Iscariot is distinguished as MATTHIAS. A related name from the same Hebrew roots, but reversed, is JONATHAN.

Cognates (also of MATTHIAS): Irish Gaelic: **Maitiú, Maitias.** Scottish Gaelic: **Mata; Matha** (a dialectal variant). French: **Mathieu.** Italian: **Matteo, Mattia.** Spanish: **Mateo.** Portuguese: **Mateus.** Catalan: **Mateu.** German: **Mattäus.** Dutch: **Matthijs.** Swedish, Norwegian: **Mats.** Danish: **Mads, Mathies.** Polish: **Mateusz, Maciej.** Czech: **Matěj, Matyáš.** Russian: **Matvei.** Ukrainian: **Matvi.** Hungarian: **Mátyás, Máté.** Finnish: **Matti.**
Short forms: English: **Matt.** Dutch: **Thijs.**
Pet forms: English: **Mattie.** Polish: **Maciek.** Russian: MOTYA.

Matthias (m.) New Testament Greek form of the Hebrew name *Mattathia* (see MATTHEW), or rather of an Aramaic derivative. The Latin form of the name is *Matthaeus*. In English the form *Matthias* is used in the Authorized Version of the New Testament to distinguish the disciple who was chosen after the treachery of Judas to make up the twelve (Acts 1: 23–6) from the evangelist *Matthew*. However, this distinction is not observed in other languages, where *Matthias* (or a version of it) is often a learned doublet existing alongside a vernacular derivative.
Variant: **Mathias.**
Cognates: see MATTHEW.

Mattie (m.), occasionally (f.) English: **1.** (m.) Pet form of MATTHEW. **2.** (f.) Pet form of MATILDA.

Matyáš (m.) Czech form of MATTHEW.

Matyusha (f.) Russian: pet form of *Matryona* (see MATRONA).
Variant: **Matyushka.**

Maud (f.) English: a medieval vernacular form of MATILDA. This form was characteristically Low German (i.e. including medieval Dutch and Flemish). The wife of William the Conqueror, who bore this name, was the daughter of Baldwin, Count of Flanders. In Flemish and Dutch the letter -*t*- was generally lost when it occurred between vowels, giving forms such as *Ma(h)auld, Maud* or *Matilda* was also the name of the daughter (1102–67) of Henry I of England; she was married early in life to the Holy Roman emperor Henry V, and later disputed the throne of England with her cousin Stephen. In 1128 she married Geoffrey, Count of Anjou. A medieval chronicler commented, 'she was a good woman, but she had little bliss with him.' The name *Maud* became quite common in England in the 19th century, when its popularity was influenced in part by Tennyson's poem *Maud*, published in 1855.

Mauno (m.) Finnish form of MAGNUS.

Maura (f.) **1.** English, Scottish, and Irish: of Celtic origin. St Maura was a 5th-century martyr, of whom very little is known; her companion is variously named as *Britta* (of Celtic origin) and *Baya* (of Latin origin). In Ireland *Maura* is now commonly regarded as a form of MARY (cf. MOIRA and MAUREEN). **2.** Italian and Spanish: feminine form of MAURO.
Cognate (of 2): Russian: **Mavra.**

Maureen (f.) English and Irish: Anglicized form of Irish Gaelic **Máirín**, a pet form of *Máire*. See also MOREEN.
Variants: **Maurene, Maurine.**
Short form: **Mo.**

Maurice (m.) **1.** English and French: from the Late Latin name *Mauricius*, a derivative of *Maurus* (see MAURO), borne by, among others, an early Byzantine emperor (c.539–602). It was introduced to Britain by the Normans, and was popular in the Middle English period, but was not widely adopted by the nobility, and became rare in the 17th century. In Germany it became established as a traditional name among the dukes of Saxony in the 16th century. It is now sometimes believed in Britain and America to be a mainly French name, perhaps because of the enormous popular influence of the French singer and film actor Maurice Chevalier (1888–1972), who, in his public image at least, was the very epitome of Gallic charm. See also MORRIS. **2**. Irish: Anglicized form of the Gaelic name **Muirgheos**, which is composed of the elements *muir* sea + *gus* choice.

Cognates (of 1): Irish Gaelic: **Muiris**. Welsh: **Meurig**. Italian: **Maurizio**. Spanish, Portuguese: **Mauricio**. German and Jewish: **Moritz**. Scandinavian: **Maurits**. Russian: **Mavriki**.

Short form: English: **Mo**.

Mauro (m.) Italian: from Latin *Maurus*, a byname meaning 'Moor', i.e. 'dark, swarthy', borne by a dozen early saints. In the 6th century it was the name of one of the earliest followers of St Benedict, placed in the care of the monk at an early age by his father Eutychius.

Mave (f.) **1**. Irish: variant of MAEVE. **2**. English: informal short form of MAVIS.

Mavis (f.) English: not found before the last decade of the 19th century, and apparently one of the small class of female given names taken from vocabulary words denoting bir s. *Mavis* is another word for the song-thrush, first attested in Chaucer. It is from Old French, and probably ultimately of Breton origin.

Short form (informal): **Mave**.

Mavra (f.) Russian form of MAURA (2).

Max (m.) English and German: short form of MAXIMILIAN and, perhaps now more commonly in the English-speaking world, of MAXWELL. It is also used as an independent given name.

Maxi (m., f.) German: short form of MAXIMILIAN or its feminine equivalent **Maximiliane**. It is now sometimes also used as an independent female given name in the English-speaking world.

Variant: English: **Maxie** (f.).

Maxim (m.) Russian: from the Latin cognomen *Maximus* 'greatest', later used as a given name. This was the name of a very large number of early saints, including a Byzantine theologian and mystic (*c*.580–662) who was persecuted under the Emperor Constans. *Maxim* Gorki was the pseudonym adopted by the Russian writer Alexei Maximovich Peshkov (1868–1936).

Cognates: Italian: **Massimo**. Spanish, Portuguese: **Máximo**. French: **Maxime**.

Maximilian (m.) German and English: from the Latin name *Maximilānus* (a diminutive of *Maximus*; see MAXIM). This was borne by a 3rd-century saint numbered among the 'Fourteen Holy Helpers'. Although already existing, the name was renalysed in the 15th century by the Emperor Friedrich III, who bestowed it upon his first-born son (1459–1519), as a blend of the names *Maximus* and *Aemiliānus*, intending thereby to pay homage to the two classical Roman generals Q. Fabius Maximus 'Cunctator' and P. Cornelius Scipio Aemilianus. The name became traditional in the Habsburg family in Austria-Hungary and also in the royal house of Bav-

aria. It was borne by an ill-fated Austrian archduke (1832–67) who was set up as emperor of Mexico but later overthrown and shot.

Maxine (f.) English: modern coinage, first recorded around 1930; a derivative of MAX by addition of the feminine ending *-ine*.

Maxwell (m.) Scottish and English: from the Scottish surname, which is derived from a placename, *Maxwell*, originally 'the stream (Old English *well(a)*) of *Mack* (a form of MAGNUS)', a minor place on the River Tweed. It was the middle name of the newspaper tycoon William Maxwell Aitken, Lord Beaverbrook (1879–1964), who was born in Canada, and has been used as a given name among his descendants. It is now also frequently taken as an expansion of MAX.

May (f.) English: pet form of both MARGARET and MARY. The popularity of this name, which was at its height in the early 20th century, has been reinforced by the fact that it fits into the series of month names with APRIL and JUNE, and also belongs to the group of flower names, being another word for the hawthorn, whose white flowers blossom in May. It has been out of fashion for a time.

Maya (f.) English: Latinate version of MAY or a respelled form of the name of the Roman goddess *Māia*, influenced by the common English name MAY. The goddess Maia was one of the Pleiades, the daughters of Atlas and Pleione; she was the mother by Jupiter of mercury. Her name seems to be derived from the root *māi*- great, seen also in Latin *māior* larger. In the case of the Black American writer Maya Angelou (b. 1928), *Maya* is a nickname acquired in early childhood as a result of her younger brother's reference to her as 'mya sista'.

Maybelle (f.) English: alteration of MABEL, influenced by the independent names MAY and BELLE.

Maynard (m.) English: transferred use of the surname, which is derived from a Norman given name of Germanic origin, composed of the elements *magin* strength + *hard* hardy, brave, strong.

Cognate: German: **Mein(h)ard**.

Meave (f.) Irish: variant of MAEVE.

Mecheslav (m.) Russian form of MIECZYSŁAW.

Mechtilde (f.) German form of MATILDA.

Medardo (m.) Italian, Spanish, and Portuguese: from an old Germanic personal name composed of a first element of uncertain origin + *hard* hardy, brave, strong. It is borne in honour of St Medard (*c*.470–*c*.558), bishop of Noyon and Tournai. His brother, St Gildard, served as archbishop of Rouen.

Medea (f.) Name borne in classical mythology by a Colchian princess who helped Jason to steal the Golden Fleece from her father. Later, however, she was abandoned by Jason in favour of Creusa (or, in some versions, Glauce). She took her revenge by killing the two children previously born to Jason and herself. The name may derive from the Greek verb *mēdesthai* to reflect, meditate, or ponder.

Medir (m.) Catalan form of EMETERIO.

Mefodi (m.) Russian: from the Late Greek personal name *Methodios* 'fellow traveller' (from *meta* with + *hodos* road, path). St Methodius (d. 885) and his brother Cyril (d. 869) together evangelized the Slavonic region of Moravia in present-day Czechoslovakia. It was Methodius who first translated the Bible into Slavonic, although the cyrillic alphabet devised for this purpose bears his brother's name.

Cognates: Polish: **Metody**. Czech: **Metoděj**.

Pet forms: Russian: **Mefodya**, **Modya**.

Meg (f.) English: short form of MARGARET, an alteration of the obsolete short form *Mag(g)* (as in MAGGIE). Until recently *Meg* was a characteristically Scottish pet form, but it is now used more widely. Its popularity no doubt owes something to Meg March, one of the four sisters who are the main characters in Louisa M. Alcott's novel *Little Women* (1855).

Megan (f.) Welsh: pet form of MEG, nowadays generally used as an independent first name both within and beyond Wales, but nevertheless retaining a strong Welsh flavour.

Variants: **Meghan**, **Meaghan** (pseudo-Irish spellings much used in Australia and Canada).

Meggie (f.) **1**. English: obsolete pet form of MEG. **2**. Australian: pet form of MEGAN, as in the case of the central character of Colleen McCullough's novel *The Thorn Birds* (1977).

Mehalia (f.) English: apparently an altered form of MAHALIA.

Mehitabel (f.) Biblical: from the Hebrew name **Mehetabel** 'God makes happy'. Mehetabel 'the daughter of Matred, the daughter of Mezahab' is mentioned in passing in a biblical genealogy (Genesis 36: 39), and the name achieved some currency among the Puritans in the 17th century. Nowadays, however, the name is chiefly associated with the companion (a cat) of Archy, the cockroach in the poems of Don Marquis (1927).

Meical (m.) Welsh form of MICHAEL.

Short form: **Meic**.

Meilyr (m.) Welsh; traditional name derived from an Old Celtic form *Maglorīx*, composed of the elements *maglos* chief + *rīx* ruler.

Meinard (m.) German form of MAYNARD.

Variant: **Meinhard**.

Meinwen (f.) Welsh: modern coinage composed of the elements *main* slender + *(g)wen*, feminine form of *gwyn* white, fair, blessed, holy.

Meinrad (m.) German: from an old Germanic personal name composed of the elements *magin* strength + *rād* counsel. St Meinrad (d. 861) was a member of the Hohenzollern royal family who became a hermit in Switzerland, at the place where the monastery of Einsiedeln was later built.

Meir (m.) Jewish: traditional name, meaning 'giving light' in Hebrew.

Variants: **Meier**, **Meyer**, **Myer**, **Maier**, **Mayr** (generally assimilations to German surname forms).

Meirion (m.) Welsh: traditional name, derived in the sub-Roman period from Latin *Mariānus* (see MARIANO and MARIAN (2)).

Feminine forms: **Meiriona**, **Meirionwen** (modern creations).

Mel (m., f.) English: short form of MELVIN or MELVILLE, or, in the case of the female name, of MELANIE or the several other female names beginning with this syllable.

Melanie (f.) English and Dutch: from an Old French form of Latin *Melania*, a derivative of the feminine form, *melaina*, of the Greek adjective *melas* black, dark. This was the name of two Roman saints of the 5th century, a grandmother and

granddaughter. St Melania the Younger was a member of an extremely rich patrician family. She led an austere and devout Christian life and, on inheriting her father's wealth, she emancipated her slaves, sold her property, and gave the proceeds to the poor. She also established several contemplative houses, including one on the Mount of Olives to which she eventually retired. The name *Melanie* was introduced to England from France in the Middle Ages, but died out again. It has been reintroduced and has become popular in the late 20th century.

Variants: **Melany**, MELONY.

Cognate: French: **Mélanie**.

Melchiorre (m.) Italian: from the name assigned by medieval tradition to one of the three Magi. It is said to be of Persian origin, composed of the elements *melk* king (cf. MELEK) + *quart* city.

Melek (m.) Jewish: from a vocabulary element meaning 'king' in Hebrew. It originated in part as a nickname, in part as a short form of various compound names containing this element, for example *Elimelek* 'God is king'.

Melinda (f.) English: derived from the first syllable of names such as MELANIE and MELISSA, with the addition of the productive suffix *-inda* (cf. e.g. LUCINDA).

Melissa (f.) **1**. English: from the Greek word *melissa* bee. It is the name of the good witch who releases Rogero from the power of the bad witch Alcina in Ariosto's narrative poem *Orlando Furioso* (1532). The name has recently increased considerably in popularity, together with other female names sharing the same first syllable. **2**. Irish: recently adopted as an Anglicized form of the Gaelic female name MAOILÍOSA.

Variant (of 1): **Melitta** (from an ancient Greek dialectal variant of the same word).

Melody (f.) English: modern transferred use of the vocabulary word (Greek *melōdia* singing of songs, from *melos* song + *aeidein* to sing), chosen partly because of its pleasant associations and partly under the influence of other female names with the same first syllable.

Melony (f.) Variant of MELANIE, perhaps influenced by MELODY.

Variants: **Mellony**, **Mel(l)oney**.

Melor (m.) Russian: modern name composed of the initial letters of the words *Marx, Engels, Lenin, October, Revolution*. The name has been created by Communist parents spurning the traditional stock of Russian na nes derived from the names of saints (see also NINEL and VLADILEN).

Melville (m.) English (esp. U.S.): transferred use of the Scottish surname, which originated as a Norman baronial name borne by the lords of a place in northern France called *Malleville* 'bad settlement', i.e. settlement on infertile land. The name was taken to Scotland as early as the 12th century and became an important surname there; use as a given name seems also to have originated in Scotland.

Melvin (m.) English: a very popular modern name of uncertain origin, probably a variant of the less common MELVILLE.

Variant: **Melvyn**.

Menahem (m.) Jewish: name meaning 'comforter' in Hebrew. It was borne in the Scriptures by an evil king of Israel who massacred pregnant women (2 Kings 15: 14–18), but the name has nevertheless always been a popular one among Jews; in earlier times it was given particularly to a child born after the death of a sibling and seen as a comfort to his parents. See also MENDEL.

Variant: **Menachem.**

Menchu (f.) Spanish: pet form of CARMEN.

Mendel (m.) Jewish: Yiddish form of Hebrew MENAHEM. It seems to have originated as a result of substitution of the Yiddish diminutive suffix -*l* (plus an intrusive -*d*-) for -*hem*, which was taken erroneously as the German diminutive suffix -*chen*.

Menuha (f.) Jewish: name meaning 'peace, stillness, tranquillity' in Hebrew.

Variant: **Menuhah.**

Meo (m.) Italian: short form of *Bartolomeo* (see BARTHOLO-MEW).

Mercedes (f.) Spanish: Marian name, from the liturgical title *Maria de las Mercedes* (literally, 'Mary of Mercies'; in English, 'Our Lady of Ransom'). Latin *mercēdes* originally meant 'wages' or 'ransom'; in Christian theology, Christ's sacrifice is regarded as a 'ransom for the sins of mankind', and hence an 'act of ransom' was seen as identical with an 'act of mercy'. There are special feasts in the Catholic calendar on 10 August and 24 September to commemorate the Virgin under this name. The name is now occasionally used in England, and more commonly in America, but normally only by Roman Catholics.

Pet form: **Merche.**

Mercia (f.) English: Latinate elaboration of MERCY, coinciding in form with the name of the Anglo-Saxon kingdom of Mercia, which dominated England during the 8th century under its king, Offa.

Mercy (f.) English: **1.** From the vocabulary word denoting the quality of magnanimity, and in particular God's forgiveness of sinners, a quality much prized in Christian tradition. The word is derived from Latin *mercēs*, which originally meant 'wages' or 'reward' (see MERCEDES). The name was much favoured by the Puritans; Mercy is the companion of Christiana in the second part of John Bunyan's *Pilgrim's Progress* (1684). Subsequently, it fell out of use as a given name. **2.** In modern use, this is often an Anglicized form of *Mercedes*.

Meredith (m., f.) English: from the Old Welsh personal name *Maredudd*, later *Mereudd*. This is of uncertain origin; the second element is Welsh *iudd* lord. In recent years the name has sometimes been given to girls, presumably being thought of as the formal form of MERRY.

Mererid (f.) Welsh form of MARGARET (see also MARED).

Merete (f.) Danish: vernacular form of MARGARET.

Variants: **Mereta; Märta; Mette.**

Merfyn (m.) Welsh: traditional name composed of the Old Welsh elements *mer*, probably meaning 'marrow' + *myn* eminent. This name was borne by a shadowy 9th-century Welsh king.

Meriel (f.) English: variant of MURIEL; both forms are 19th-century revivals of an older Celtic name. Of the two forms, *Meriel* was never as popular as *Muriel*, but for that reason seems to have escaped the current somewhat old-fashioned image of the latter name.

Merle (f., m.) English: probably a contracted form of MERIEL, but also associated with the small class of female names derived from birds, since it is identical in form with Old French *merle*

blackbird (Latin *merula*). The name came to public notice in the 1930s with the actress Merle Oberon (1911–79); she was born Estelle Merle O'Brien Thompson. In Britain this is still normally a female name; in the United States it is more commonly borne by males.

Merlin (m.) Usual English form of the Welsh name *Myrddin*. The name is most famous as that of the legendary magician who guides the destiny of King Arthur. It seems to have originally been composed of Old Celtic elements meaning 'sea' and 'hill, fort', but it has been distorted by mediation through Old French sources, which associated the second element with the diminutive suffix -*lin*.

Variant: **Merlyn** (occasionally given to girls, as if containing the productive suffix of female names -*lyn*).

Merrill (m.) English: transferred use of the surname, which is derived from the female name MERIEL or MURIEL.

Merrily (f.) English (U.S.): apparently a respelling of MARILEE, reshaped to coincide with the adverb derived from the adjective *merry*.

Merry (f.) English: originally apparently an assimilated form of MERCY. In Dickens's novel *Martin Chuzzlewit* (1844), Mr Pecksniff's daughters CHARITY and *Mercy* are known as *Cherry* and *Merry*. Nowadays the name is usually bestowed because of its association with the adjective denoting a cheerful and jolly temperament (cf. HAPPY). In the accent of the central and northern United States there is no difference in pronunciation between MERRY and MARY.

Merten (m.) Low German form of MARTIN.

Mertice (f.) English: recent coinage, popular in the southern United States. It seems to be an entirely arbitrary invention.

Mervyn (m.) Anglicized form of Welsh MERFYN, now widely popular both in and beyond Wales.

Variant: **Mervin.**

Meryl (f.) English: a recent coinage, owing its current popularity to the fame of the American actress Meryl Streep (b. Mary Louise Streep in 1949). It has also been influenced in part by the ending -*yl* in names such as CHERYL.

Meshulam (m.) Jewish: Hebrew name, apparently meaning either 'paid for' or 'friend'. It is borne by a minor character in the Old Testament (2 Kings 22: 3); the spelling *Meshullam* is used in the Authorized Version.

Meta (f.) German, Danish, and Swedish: contracted pet form of *Margareta* (see MARGARET). It was very popular in the 19th and early 20th centuries, but is now perceived as old-fashioned.

Metoděj (m.) Czech form of MEFODI.

Pet forms: **Metodek, Metoušek.**

Metody (m.) Polish form of MEFODI.

Mette (f.) **1.** Danish: contracted form of MERETE. **2.** Low German: contracted form of *Mechtilde* (see MATILDA).

Meurig (m.) Welsh form of MAURICE, derived from Latin *Mauricius* via Old Welsh *Mouric*.

Mia (f.) Danish and Swedish: pet form of MARIA. It is now also used in the English-speaking world, largely as a result of the fame of the actress Mia Farrow (b. 1945).

Micah (m.) Biblical: Hebrew name meaning 'who is like (Yahweh)?', and thus a doublet of MICHAEL. This was the name of a prophet, author of the book of the Bible that bears his name, and which dates from the late 8th century BC.

Michael (m.) English and German form of a common biblical name (meaning 'who is like God?') borne by one of the archangels, who is also regarded as a saint of the Catholic Church (cf. GABRIEL and RAPHAEL). In the Middle Ages, Michael was regarded as captain of the heavenly host (see Revelation 12: 7–9), symbol of the Church Militant, and patron of soldiers. He was often depicted bearing a flaming sword. Because of its sanctified warlike connotations, *Michael* was a popular name among early Christian military leaders, and was borne by eight Byzantine emperors, as well as by the founder (1596–1645) of the Romanov dynasty in Russia. The name is also borne by a Persian prince and ally of Belshazzar mentioned in the Book of Daniel. See also MICHAL.

Cognates: Irish Gaelic: **Micheál**. Scottish Gaelic: **Micheal**. Welsh: **Meical**, MIHANGEL. French: **Michel**. Italian: **Michele**. Spanish, Portuguese: **Miguel**. Catalan: **Miquel**. Basque: **Mikel**. Romanian: **Mihai**. Swedish: **Mikael**. Danish, Norwegian: **Mikkel**, **Mikael**. Polish: **Michal**. Czech: **Mich(a)el**. Russian: **Mikhail**. Ukrainian: **Mikhailo**. Finnish: **Mikko**. Hungarian: **Mihály**.
Short forms: English: **Mike**, MICK.
Pet forms: English: **Micky**. Russian: **Misha**.
Feminine forms: Latinate: **Michaela** (used in England and Germany); **Micaela** (used in Italy and Spain). French: **Michèle**, **Michelle**. Polish: **Michalina**.

Michal (f.) Biblical name (meaning 'brook' in Hebrew) borne by a daughter of Saul who married King David. It is probably through confusion with this name that MICHAEL has occasionally been used as a female given name in the English-speaking world.

Michelangelo (m.) Italian: compound made up of *Michele* MICHAEL + *angelo* angel. Its best-known bearer was the Florentine painter, sculptor, architect, and poet Michelangelo Buonarroti (1475–1564).

Michèle (f.) French: feminine form of *Michel* (see MICHAEL).

Micheline (f.) French: diminutive form of MICHÈLE, now used as an independent given name, to some extent also in the English-speaking world.

Michelle (f.) French: variant of MICHÈLE. This name is now also used extensively in the English-speaking world (partly influenced by a Beatles song with this name as its title).
Short forms: English: **Chelle**, SHELL.

Mick (m.) English: short form of MICHAEL; now common as a generic, and often derogatory, term for a Catholic Irishman.
Pet form: **Micky**. See also MIKKI.

Micolau (m.) Catalan: variant of *Nicolau* (see NICHOLAS).

Mieczysław (m.) Polish: from an old Slavonic personal name, in which a first element of uncertain form, probably derived from Old Polish *miecz* man or *mieszka* bear, is combined with the regular name-forming element *slav* glory. It was borne by two early rulers of Poland, the first of whom, Mieczysław I (c.922–92), played an important role in opposing Teutonic incursions and securing papal support for the Poles.
Variant: **Masław**.
Cognates: Czech: **Měčislav**. Russian: **Mecheslav**.
Feminine form: Czech: **Měčislava**.
Pet forms: Polish: **Mietek**, **Mieszko** (m.).
Czech: **Měčislavek**, **Meček**, **Měčik** (m.); **Měčka**, **Měčina** (f.)

Mieke (f.) Dutch: pet form of MARIA.
Variant: **Miep**.

Mignonette (f.) English: probably a direct use of the French nickname *mignonette* 'little darling', a feminine diminutive of *mignon* sweet, cute, dainty. Alternatively, it may belong to the class of names derived from vocabulary words denoting flowers (the word in English denotes a species of *Reseda*).

Miguel (m.) Spanish and Portuguese form of MICHAEL.

Mihai (m.) Romanian form of MICHAEL.

Mihály (m.) Hungarian form of MICHAEL.

Mihangel (m.) Older Welsh form of MICHAEL, representing a contraction of the phrase 'Michael the Archangel'.

Mikael (m.) Scandinavian form of MICHAEL.

Mike (m.) English: usual short form of MICHAEL in the English-speaking world. It is also used as an independent given name, particularly in America.
Pet form: **Mikey**.

Mikkel (m.) Danish and Norwegian form of MICHAEL.

Mikki (f.) English: feminine variant of *Micky* (see MICK) or pet form of *Michaela* (see MICHAEL), now sometimes used as an independent given name.
Variants: **Micki**, **Mickie**, **Mickey**.

Mikko (m.) Finnish form of MICHAEL.

Miklós (m.) Hungarian form of NICHOLAS.

Mikołaj (m.) Polish form of NICHOLAS.
Pet forms: **Mikulášek**, **Mikuš**.

Mikoláš (m.) Czech form of NICHOLAS.
Variant: **Mikuláš**.

Milagros (f.) Spanish: from a title of the Virgin Mary, *Nuestra Señora de los Milagros* 'Our Lady of Miracles'. Mary is regarded as the dispenser of miracles above all other saints.

Milan (m.) Czech: masculine equivalent of MILENA.

Mildred (f.) English: 19th-century revival of the Old English female name *Mildþryð*, composed of the elements *mild* gentle + *þryð* strength. This was the name of a 7th-century abbess, who had a less famous but equally saintly elder sister called *Mildburh* and a younger sister called *Mildgyð*; all were daughters of a certain Queen Ermenburh. Their names illustrate clearly the Old English pattern of combining and recombining the same small group of name elements within a single family.

Milena (f.) Czech: from a short form of various compound names containing the element *mil* grace, favour (cf. MILES). The name is now fairly common in Italy, where it is often assumed to be a contraction of *Maria* + *Elena*. In fact it was little known before 1900, when King Victor Emmanuel III married Elena of Montenegro, whose mother was called Milena.
Variants: **Milana**, **Milada**, **Mlad(en)a**.
Pet forms: **Milenka**, **Milanka**, **Miládka**, **Milka**, **Miluše**, **Miluška**, **Mlad(uš)ka**.

Miles (m.) English: of Norman origin but uncertain derivation. Unlike most Norman names, it is, as far as can be ascertained, not derived from any known Germanic name element. It may be a greatly altered pet form of MICHAEL, which came to be associated with the Latin word *miles* soldier because of the military attributes of the archangel Michael. However, the usual Latin form of the name in the Middle Ages was *Milo*. There is a common Slavonic name element *mil* grace, favour, with which it may possibly have some ultimate connection. The name has been modestly popular in England ever since the Conquest. See also MYLES.

Milla (f.) English: short form of CAMILLA.

Millà (m.) Catalan form of ÉMILIEN.

Millicent (f.) English: Norman name of Germanic origin, composed of the elements *amal* labour + *swinth* strength. This was the name of a daughter of Charlemagne. It was first introduced to Britain by the Normans in the form *Melisende*.

Pet form: **Millie** (see also CAMILLA).

Milo (m.) **1**. English: Latinized form of MILES, regularly used in documents of the Middle Ages, and revived as a given name in the 19th century. **2**. Irish: used as a pet form of MYLES.

Milosław (m.) Polish: from an old Slavonic personal name composed of the elements *mil* grace, favour + *slav* glory.

Cognate: Czech: **Miloslav**.
Feminine forms: Polish: **Miloslawa**. Czech: **Miloslava**.

Miłosz (m.) Polish: pet name derived from a short form of various compound names containing the old Slavonic element *mil* grace, favour, e.g. MILOSLAW.

Variant: **Miuś**.
Cognates: Czech: **Miluš**, **Miloň**.

Milton (m.) English: transferred use of the surname, itself derived from any of the numerous places so called, a large number of which get their name from Old English *mylentūn* 'settlement with a mill'. Others were originally named as 'the middle (of three) settlements', from Old English *middel* middle + *tūn* settlement. The surname is most famous as that of the poet John Milton (1608–74), and the given name is sometimes bestowed in his honour.

Miluše (f.) Czech: pet form of MILENA.

Variant: **Miluška**.

Mimi (f.) Italian: pet form of MARIA, originally a nursery name. The heroine of Puccini's opera *La Bohème* (1896) announces 'They call me Mimi', and the name has occasionally been used in the English-speaking world.

Mina (f.) Scottish (Highland): short form of *Calumina* (see CALUM) and *Normina* (see NORMAN).

Mine (f.) **1**. German and Danish: short form of WILHELMINA and *Vilhelmina* respectively. **2**. Jewish: Yiddish spelling of MINNE.

Minette (f.) English: of uncertain origin. Although ostensibly a French name, it is not in fact used in France. It is possibly a contracted form of MIGNONETTE.

Minne (f.) German: originally an affectionate nickname from Middle High German *minne* love (as celebrated by the medieval German lyric poets and musicians known as the minnesingers). It is now also used as a pet form of WILHELMINA.

Variant: **Minna**.

Minnie (f.) English: pet form of WILHELMINA, at its peak of popularity in the latter half of the 19th century, when several names were introduced into Britain from Germany in the wake of Queen Victoria's consort, Prince Albert of Saxe-Coburg-Gotha, whom she married in 1840. It has now largely fallen

out of use, partly because German names in general became unacceptable in Britain during the First World War, partly perhaps also because of association with cartoon characters such as Minnie Mouse (in Walt Disney's animations) and Minnie the Minx (in the *Beano* children's comic).

Miquel (m.) Catalan form of MICHAEL.

Mira (f.) Slavonic: short form of the various Slavonic female names (e.g. *Miroslava*; see MIROSLAW) containing the element *meri* great, famous (see CASIMIR). It is now also occasionally used in the English-speaking world, probably as a result of association with the feminine form of the Latin adjective *mīrus* wonderful, astonishing (cf. MIRANDA).

Pet form: **Mirka**.

Mirabelle (f.) French and English: apparently coined from the Latin word *mīrābilis* wondrous, lovely (a derivative of *mīrāri* to wonder at, admire; cf. MIRANDA). It was quite common in the late Middle Ages, and occasionally the form Mirabel was used for boys as well as girls, but by the 17th century both forms were rare.

Variant: **Latinate**, Italian: **Mirabella**.

Miranda (f.) English: invented by Shakespeare for the heroine of *The Tempest* (1611). It represents the feminine form of the Latin gerundive *mīrandus* admirable, lovely, from *mīrāri* to wonder at, admire; cf. AMANDA.

Short form: **Randa**.
Pet forms: **Randy**, **Randie**.

Mireille (f.) French: apparently first used, in the Provençal form **Mireio**, as the title of a verse romance by the poet Frédéric Mistral (1830–1914). The name is probably a derivative of Provençal *mirar* to admire (cf. MIRANDA), but the poet himself declared it to be a form of MIRIAM; this was in order to overcome the objections of a priest to so baptizing his god daughter with a non-liturgical name.

Mirek (m.) Polish and Czech: pet form of the various old Slavonic personal names (e.g. MIROSLAW, *Miroslav*) containing the element *meri* great, famous (see CASIMIR).

Mirella (f.) Italian form of MIREILLE or a contracted form of *Mirabella* (see MIRABELLE).

Miren (f.) Basque form of MARY.

Pet form: **Mirentxu**.

Miriam (f.) Biblical: the Old Testament form of the Hebrew name *Maryam* (see MARY). Of uncertain ultimate origin, this is first recorded as being borne by the elder sister of Moses (Exodus 15: 20). Since the names of both Moses and his brother Aaron are probably of Egyptian origin, it is possible that this feminine name is too. It was enthusiastically taken up as a given name by the Israelites, and is still borne mainly, but by no means exclusively, by Jews.

Variant: MARIAMNE.

Mirka (f.) Slavonic: pet form of MIRA.

Mirosław (m.) Polish: from an old Slavonic personal name composed of the elements *meri* great, famous (see CASIMIR) + *slav* glory.

Cognate: Czech, Russian: **Miroslav**.
Feminine forms: Polish: **Miroslawa**. Czech: **Miroslava**.

Misha (m.) Russian: pet form of *Mikhail* (see MICHAEL).

Misia (f.) Polish: pet form of *Michalina* (see MICHAEL).

Misty (f.) English: modern name, apparently from the vocabulary word, a derivative of *mist* thin fog (Old English *mist*).

Mitchell (m.) English: transferred use of the surname, itself derived from a common medieval form of MICHAEL, representing an Anglicized pronunciation of Norman French *Michel*.

Short form: **Mitch** (informal).

Mitrofan (m.) Russian: from Greek *Mētrophanēs*, a derivative of *mētēr* (genitive *mētros*) mother (sc. of God) + *phainein* to show, appear. The name was borne by the first bishop of Byzantium.

Pet forms: **Mitroshka**; **Mitya** (see also DMITRI).

Mitzi (f.) S. German and Swiss: pet form of MARIA.

Mladka (f.) Czech: pet form derived from a contracted version of *Milada* (see MILENA).

Variant: **Mladuška**.

Mo (f., m.) English: short form of MAUREEN and, less commonly, of MAURICE.

Modest (f.) Russian: from the Late Latin personal name *Modestus*, originally a byname from a vocabulary word meaning 'moderate, restrained, obedient, modest' (a derivative of *modus* (due) measure, moderation). The name was borne by half a dozen early saints, including a child martyred at Alexandria in Egypt together with his brother Ammonius, and an 8th-century evangelist of Carinthia.

Cognates: Spanish, Portuguese, Italian: **Modesto**. See also SZERÉNY.

Pet form: Russian: **Desya**.

Modya (m.) Russian: pet form of MEFODI.

Mogens (m.) Danish form of MAGNUS.

Moira (f.) Irish, Scottish and English: Anglicized form of Irish Gaelic *Máire* (a form of MARY). This is now an extremely popular name in its own right throughout the English-speaking world.

Variant: **Moyra**.

Moirean (m.) Scottish Gaelic: derivative of *Moire*, the name of the Virgin Mary, just as *Cailean* is based on the name of St Columba and *Crisdean* on that of Christ.

Molly (f.) English and Irish: long-established pet form of MARY, representing an altered version of the earlier pet form *Mally*. The name is chiefly associated with Ireland, although it is not Gaelic. It is at present somewhat out of fashion.

Mona (f.) 1. Irish and English: Anglicized form of the Gaelic name **Muadhnait**, a feminine diminutive of *muadh* noble. It is no longer restricted to people with Irish connections, and has sometimes been taken as connected with Greek *monos* single, only. In Gaelic Scotland it may represent a feminine form of TORMOD, since the latter was used as a Gaelic form of NORMAN. 2. Scandinavian: short form of *Monika* (see MONICA).

Mona is also found as a female name in Arabic.

Moncho (m.) Spanish: pet form of RAMÓN.

Monica (f.) English: of uncertain ultimate origin. This was the name of the mother of St Augustine, as transmitted to us by her famous son. She was a citizen of Carthage, so her name may well be of Phoenician origin, but in the early Middle Ages it was taken to be a derivative of Latin *monēre* to warn, counsel, or advise, since it was as a result of her guidance that her son was converted to Christianity.

Cognates: French: **Monique**. German, Scandinavian, Slavonic: **Monika**.

Monroe (m.) Scottish and English: transferred use of the Scottish surname, usually spelled *Munro*. The ancestors of the Scottish Munros are said to have originally come from Ireland, apparently from a settlement by the River Roe in County Derry; their name is therefore supposed to be derived from Gaelic *bun Rotha* 'mouth of the Roe'. In America the popularity of the given name may have been influenced by the fame of James Monroe (1758–1831), fifth president of the United States and propounder (in 1823) of the Monroe Doctrine, asserting that European powers should not seek to colonize in North or South America and that the United States would not intervene in European affairs. A more recent influence could have been the film star Marilyn Monroe (1926–62), whose original name was Norma-Jean Baker; however, the name is not bestowed on female children, so the influence of her adopted surname does not appear to have been significant.

Variants: **Monro**, **Munro(e)**.

Montague (m.) English: 19th-century transferred use of the English surname. This was originally a Norman baronial name borne by the lords of Montaigu in La Manche. (The placename is composed of the Old French elements *mont* hill (Latin *mons*, genitive *montis*) + *aigu* pointed (Latin *acūtus*).) A certain Drogo of Montaigu is known to have accompanied William the Conqueror in his invasion of England in 1066, and *Montague* thus became established as an aristocratic British family name.

Montgomery (m.) English: transferred use of the surname, originally a Norman baronial name from various places in Calvados. The placename is derived from Old French *mont* hill + the Germanic personal name *Gomeric* 'man power'. It has never been common as a given name, although it was given additional currency by the actor Montgomery Clift (1920–66), and during and after the Second World War by the British field marshal, Bernard Montgomery (1887–1976).

Montmorency (m.) English: transferred use of the surname, originally a Norman baronial name derived from a place in Seine-et-Oise (so called from Old French *mont* hill + the Gallo-Roman personal name *Maurentius*). The given name enjoyed a brief vogue in the 19th century, but is now regarded as affected and so hardly ever used.

Montserrat (f.) Catalan: Marian name, referring to the famous Benedictine monastery of the Virgin Mary founded in 976 on the mountain of Montserrat near Barcelona. The mountain gets its name from Latin *mons serrātus* jagged hill.

Short forms: **Montse**, **Monse**.

Monty (m.) English: short form of MONTAGUE or of the much rarer MONTGOMERY and MONTMORENCY, all of which have gone through the cycle of transformation from French placename to Norman baronial name to noble British surname to modern given name. The full forms of all these names are now rare. *Monty* is now often used as an independent name, especially among Jews.

Mór (f.) Scottish and Irish Gaelic: originally a byname meaning 'large, great'. This was the commonest of all female given names in late medieval Ireland, and has continued in frequent use in both Scotland and Ireland to the present day. In Scotland it has sometimes been Anglicized as SARAH.

Pet forms: MORAG, MOREEN.

Morag (f.) Scottish: Anglicized spelling of Gaelic **Mórag**, a pet form of Mór. In the 20th century this name has become hugely popular in its own right in Scotland, and is also used elsewhere in the English-speaking world.

Moray (m.) Scottish: variant of Murray, and the more usual spelling of the place-name from which the surname is derived.

Mordecai (m.) Biblical: the name of Esther's cousin and foster-father, who secured her introduction to King Ahasuerus (Esther 2–9). The name is of Persian origin and seems to have meant 'devotee of the god Marduk'. It had some currency among English Puritans in the 17th century and Nonconformists in the 18th and 19th centuries, but has always been, and still is, mainly Jewish.

Pet forms: Yiddish: **Motke**, **Motl**.

Moreen (f.) Irish: Anglicized form of Gaelic **Móirín**, a pet form of Mór. It has now been to a large extent confused with Maureen.

Morgan (m., f.) Welsh: traditional name derived from Old Welsh *Morcant*. The first element is of uncertain derivation, the second represents the Old Celtic element *cant* circle, completion. In recent years it has occasionally been used outside Wales as a female name, perhaps with conscious reference to King Arthur's jealous stepsister Morgan le Fay.

Moritz (m.) German and Jewish form of Maurice.

Morley (m.) English: transferred use of the surname, which originated as a local name from any of the numerous places in Britain named with the Old English elements *mōr* moor, marsh + *lēah* wood or clearing.

Morna (f.) Irish and Scottish: variant of Myrna. This is the name borne by Fingal's mother in the Ossianic poems of James Macpherson (cf. Malvina).

Morris (m.) 1. English: variant of Maurice. The spelling *Morris* was quite common as a given name in the Middle Ages, but it fell out of use and was readopted in modern times, in part from the surname earlier derived from the given name. 2. Jewish: adopted as an Anglicized form of Moses, like several other English surnames beginning with M-, such as Mortimer and Morton.

Morten (m.) Danish form of Martin.

Mortimer (m.) 1. English: transferred use of the surname, which is derived from a Norman baronial name, originally borne by the lords of *Mortemer* in Normandy. The placename meant 'dead sea' in Old French, and probably referred to a stagnant marsh. It was not used as a given name until the 19th century. 2. Irish: Anglicized form of Muiriartach. 3. Jewish: Anglicized form of Moses.

Morton (m.) 1. English: transferred use of the surname, originally a local name derived from any of the numerous places so called from Old English *mōrtūn* 'settlement by or on a moor' (cf. Morris). 2. Jewish: adopted as an Anglicized form of Moses.

Short form (mainly U.S.): **Mort**.

Morven (f.) English: this was the name of Fingal's kingdom in the Ossianic poems of James Macpherson. In reality it is a district in north Argyll, Scotland, properly *Morvern*, known in Gaelic as *a' Mhorbhairne* 'the big gap'. *Morven* could alternatively be held to represent Gaelic *mór bheinn* big peak. It has occasionally been used in modern times as a female given name (cf. Selma).

Morwenna (f.) Cornish and Welsh: from an Old Celtic personal name derived from an element cognate with Welsh *morwyn* maiden. It was borne by a somewhat obscure Cornish saint of the 5th century; churches in her honour have named several places in Cornwall. The name was revived in Wales in the mid-20th century as a result of nationalistic sentiment.

Moses (m.) Biblical: English form of the name of the patriarch (Moshe in Hebrew) who led the Israelites out of Egypt (Exodus 4). His name is thought to be of Egyptian origin, most probably from the same root as that found in the second element of names such as *Tutmosis* and *Rameses*, where it means 'born of (a certain god)'. Various Hebrew etymologies have been proposed, beginning with the biblical 'saved (from the water)' (Exodus 2: 10), but none is convincing. It is now mainly Jewish, and has always been tremendously popular among Jews. Up until the 20th century, however, it also enjoyed some popularity among Christians in England, especially among Puritans and Nonconformists.

Cognates: Irish Gaelic: **Maois**. French: **Moïse**. Jewish (Yiddish): **Moishe**.

Moss (m.) 1. English (also Jewish): from the usual medieval form of Moses or, among Gentiles, transferred use of the English surname derived from *Moses*. 2. Welsh: in recent years it has also been used as a short form of Mostyn.

Mostyn (m.) Welsh: from the name of a place in Clwyd, on the Dee estuary. The place in fact derives its name from Old English rather than Welsh elements: it appears in the Domesday Book as *Mostone*, from Old English *mos* moss + *tūn* enclosure, settlement.

Motke (m.) Jewish: Yiddish pet form of Mordecai.

Variant: **Motl**.

Motya (m., f.) Russian: pet form of both *Matvei* (see Matthew) and Matrona.

Mroż (m.) Polish: short form of *Ambroży* (see Ambrose).

Pet form: **Mrozk**.

Mścisław (m.) Polish: from an old Slavonic personal name composed of the elements *mshcha* vengeance + *slav* glory.

Cognate: Czech and Russian: **Mstislav**.
Pet form: Czech: **Mstik**.

Muir (m.) Scottish: transferred use of the surname, in origin a local name representing a Scottish dialect variant of *moor* rough grazing.

Muireall (f.) Scottish Gaelic: traditional name, apparently composed of Old Celtic elements meaning 'sea' + 'bright'. It is often Anglicized as Muriel.

Cognates: Irish Gaelic: **Muirgheal**, **Muiriol**.

Muireann (f.) Irish Gaelic: traditional name, apparently composed of the elements *muir* sea + *fionn* white, fair. The spelling **Muirinn** is also used, and there has been considerable confusion with both Maureen and Moreen.

Cognate: Scottish Gaelic: **Mora(i)nn**.

Muiriartach (m.) Irish Gaelic: a modern form of earlier *Muicheachtach*, originally a byname meaning 'seaman, mariner'.

Variant: **Briartach**.
Anglicized form: MORTIMER.
Pet form: **Murty**.

Muiris (m.) Irish form of MAURICE. In part it also represents a contracted form of Gaelic **Muirgheas**, composed of the elements *muir* sea + *gus* choice.

Muirne (f.) Irish Gaelic: traditional name, originally a byname meaning 'beloved'.
Anglicized forms: **Myrna**, **Morna**,

Mungo (m.) Scottish: of uncertain derivation. It is recorded as the byname of St Kentigern, the 6th-century apostle of south-west Scotland and north-west England, and glossed in Latin by his biographer as *carissimus amicus* 'dearest friend', although it does not correspond to any Gaelic elements with this meaning.
Variant: **Munga** (Gaelic).

Murdo (m.) Scottish (Highland): Anglicized spelling of the Gaelic name *Muireadhach* (now **Murchadh**), apparently a derivative of *muir* sea.
Variant: **Murdoch**.
Pet forms: **Murdy**, **Murdie**, **Murdanie**.
Feminine forms: **Murdag**, **Murdann**, **Murdina**, **Dina**.

Murgatroyd (m.) English: from the Yorkshire surname, in origin a local name from an unidentified place named as 'the clearing (Yorkshire dialect *royd*) belonging to (a certain) *Margaret*'.

Muriel (f.) English: of Celtic origin; see MUIREALL. Forms of the name are found in Breton as well as in Scottish and Irish Gaelic, and in the Middle Ages it was in use even in the heart of England, having been introduced from various sources; the surname *Merrill* is derived from it. See also MERIEL.

Murray (m.) Scottish (now also used in England, America, and elsewhere): **1.** Transferred use of the Scottish surname, originally a local name derived from the region now called *Moray*. **2.** Anglicized form of the Gaelic name **Muireach**, a contracted form of *Muireadhach* (see MURDO).
Variant (of 2): **Moray**.

Murty (m.) Irish: pet form of MUIRIARTACH.

Myfanwy (f.) Welsh: name composed of the Welsh affectionate prefix *my-* + *banwy*, a variant form of *banw*, related to *benyw* or *menyw* woman. Its popularity dates only from relatively recent times, when specifically Welsh names have been sought as tokens of Welsh national identity.
Short forms: **Myf(f)** (in English use); **Myf**.

Myles (m.) **1.** English: variant spelling of MILES. **2.** Irish: Anglicized form of Gaelic MAOLRA. **3.** Scottish: Anglicized form of Gaelic *Maoilios* (see MAOILÍOSA).

Myra (f.) English: invented in the 17th century by the poet Fulke Greville (1554–1628). It is impossible to guess what models he had consciously or unconsciously in mind, but it has been variously conjectured that the name is an anagram of MARY; that it is a simplified spelling of Latin *myrrha* myrrh, unguent; and that it is connected with Latin *mīrāri* to admire or wonder at (cf. MIRANDA). In the Highlands of Scotland this name is now sometimes used as an Anglicized form of *Mairead* (see MAIRÉAD), being almost identical in pronunciation with it.

Myriam (f.) French and English: variant of MIRIAM. This is the usual spelling of the name in France.

Myrna (f.) Irish and English: Anglicized form of Gaelic MUIRNE, now also used elsewhere in the English-speaking world.
Variant: **Morna**.

Myron (m.) English: from a classical Greek name, derived from Greek *myron* myrrh. The name was borne by a famous sculptor of the 5th century BC. It was taken up with particular enthusiasm by the early Christians because they associated it with the gift of myrrh made by the three kings to the infant Christ, and because of the association of myrrh (as an embalming spice) with death and eternal life. The name was borne by various early saints, notably a 3rd-century martyr of Cyzicus and a 4th-century bishop of Crete. Their cult is greater in the Eastern Church than the Western.

Myrtle (f.) English: from the word denoting the plant (Old French *myrtille*, Late Latin *myrtilla*, a diminutive of classical Latin *myrta*). This is one of the group of plant names that became popular as female names in the late 19th century.

Myslik (m.) Czech: pet form of *Přemysl* (see PRZEMYSL).

N

Nacek (m.) Polish: pet form of *Ignacy* (see IGNATIUS).

Nácek (m.) Czech: pet form of *Ignác* (see IGNATIUS).

Nacho (m.) Spanish: pet form of *Ignacio* (see IGNATIUS).

Nacio (m.) Spanish: short form of *Ignacio* (see IGNATIUS).

Nadezhda (f.) Russian: from the vocabulary word meaning 'hope', an important theological virtue.

Cognates: Polish: **Nadzieja**. Czech: **Naděžda**. See also REMÉNYKE
Pet forms: Russian: **Nadya**. Czech: **Naděja**.

Nadia (f.) French and English spelling of Russian *Nadya* (see NADEZHDA). This name has enjoyed a considerable vogue in the English-speaking world in the 20th century.

Variant: **Nadja** (German).

Nadine (f.) French: elaboration of NADIA. Many names of Russian origin became established in France and elsewhere in the early 20th century as a result of the popularity of the Ballet Russe, established in Paris by Diaghilev in 1909.

Nahman (m.) Jewish: an Aramaic-influenced form of NAHUM 'comforter', from the same root as MENAHEM. This name has been in use from the Middle Ages to the present day.

Nahum (m.) Biblical name, meaning 'comforter' in Hebrew, borne by a prophet of the 7th century BC. He was the author of the book of the Bible that bears his name, in which he prophesies the downfall of Nineveh, which fell in 612 BC. This is a well-established Jewish name, which was also popular among 17th-century Puritans in England. It was borne by the minor Restoration dramatist Nahum
Tate (1652–1715), who rewrote Shakespeare's *King Lear* with a happy ending. See also NAHMAN and MENAHEM.

Derivative: Russian: **Naum**.

Naldo (m.) Italian: short form of various given names ending in these syllables, as, for example, RINALDO.

Nan (f.) English: originally a pet form of ANN (for the initial *N-*, cf. NED). It is now generally used as a short form of NANCY.

Pet forms: Scottish: **Nanny** (Gaelic **Nandag**).

Nancy (f.) English: of uncertain origin. From the 18th century it was used as a pet form of ANN (cf. NAN), but it may originally have been a similar formation deriving from the common medieval given name ANNIS. Nowadays it is an independent name, and was especially popular in America between about 1920 and 1960. In the 1980s it came to prominence as the name of President Reagan's wife.

Nando (m.) Italian: short form of various given names ending in these syllables, as, for example, *Ferdinando* (see FERDINAND).

Nándor (m.) Hungarian form of FERDINAND.

Nandru (m.) Romanian form of FERDINAND.

Nanette (f.) English: elaboration of NAN, with the addition of the French feminine diminutive suffix *-ette*.

Nanna (f.) Scandinavian: from the Old Norse mythological woman's name Nanna, a derivative of the element *nanp* daring.

Nanne (m.) Swedish: originally a short form of the Old Norse personal name Nannulf, composed of the elements *nanp* daring + *ulfr* wolf. Nowadays it is used as a pet form of ANDERS.

Naoise (m.) Irish Gaelic: name of uncertain derivation, borne, according to legend, by the lover of Deirdre, who was pursued and murdered by Conchobhar, King of Ulster. The story goes that after Naoise's death, Deirdre died of a broken heart.

Naomi (f.) Biblical name (meaning 'pleasantness' in Hebrew) of the wise mother-in-law of Ruth. The name has long been regarded as typically Jewish, but recently has begun to come into more general use.

Derivatives: French: **Noémie**. Italian: NOEMI.

Naphtali (m.) Biblical: name, probably meaning 'wrestling' in Hebrew, borne by one of the sons of Jacob. The traditional explanation is given in the following quotation: 'and Rachel said, with great wrestlings have I wrestled with my sister, and I have prevailed: and she called his name Naphtali' (Genesis 30: 8). See also ZVI.

Nápla (f.) Irish Gaelic: name derived in the early Middle Ages from Anglo-Norman *Anable, Anaple* (see ANNABEL).

Napoleon (m.) Occasionally bestowed in modern times in honour of the French emperor Napoleon Bonaparte (1769–1821), who was born in Corsica into a family that was ultimately of Italian origin. **Napoleone** is a rare Italian given name, used in the Abruzzo, Latium, Umbria, and Tuscany. It is probably of Germanic origin, perhaps connected with the name of the elvish *Nibelungen* 'sons of the mist' (cf. modern German *Nebel*). It was later altered by association with Italian *Napoli* Naples (Greek *nea polis* new city) and *leone* lion.

Narcissus (m.) Latin form of the Greek name *Narkissos*. In classical mythology, Narcissus was a beautiful youth who fell in love with his own reflection in a pool of water and remained there transfixed until he faded away and turned into a flower. The legend purports to account for the name of the flower, a kind of lily, known in Greek as *narkissos*. The name is almost certainly of pre-Greek origin, but attempts have been made to link it with Greek *narkē* numbness. The vocabulary word in English and horticultural Latin denotes the genus of flowers that includes the daffodil. The name was common among slaves and freedmen in the early Christian era, and a Roman citizen bearing this name is mentioned in St Paul's Epistle to the Romans (16: 11). One St Narcissus was bishop of Jerusalem in 195; another was a Spanish bishop put to death at Gerona under Diocletian in *c*.307.

Derivatives: Italian, Spanish, Portuguese: **Narciso**. Catalan: **Narcís**. French: **Narcisse**. Polish: **Narcyz**.
Feminine form (rare): **Narcissa**.

Nastasia (f.) Eastern European: short form of ANASTASIA.

Nastya (f.) Russian: pet form of ANASTASIA.
Cognates: Polish: **Nastka**, **Nastusia**. Czech: **Nast'a**.

Nat (m.) English: short form of NATHAN and NATHANIEL.

Natalie (f.) French form of NATALYA, adopted from Russian in the early 20th century, probably, like NADINE, under the influence of Diaghilev's Ballet Russe, which was established in Paris in 1909. The name is now very common in France and in the English-speaking world, where it was borne by the actress Natalie Wood (1938–82). She was born Natasha Gurdin, in San Francisco. Her father was of Russian descent, her mother of French extraction.
Variant: **Nathalie**.

Natalya (f.) Russian: from the Late Latin name *Natālia*, a derivative of Latin *natālis* (*diēs*) birthday, especially Christ's birthday, i.e. Christmas; cf. NOËL. St Natalia was a Christian inhabitant of Nicomedia who is said to have given succour to the martyrs, including her husband Adrian, who suffered there in persecutions under Diocletian in 303. She is regarded as a Christian saint, although she was not herself martyred.
Pet forms: **Talya**, NATASHA.

Natasha (f.) Russian: pet form of NATALYA, now widely adopted as an independent name in the English-speaking world and elsewhere. Like *Noëlle* (see NOËL), it is sometimes given to girls born on or about Christmas Day.
Short form (in the English-speaking world): **Tasha**.

Nathan (m.) Biblical name, meaning 'he (God) has given' in Hebrew (cf. NATHANIEL). This was the name of a prophet who had the courage to reproach King David for arranging the death in battle of Uriah the Hittite in order to get possession of the latter's wife Bathsheba (2 Samuel 12: 1–15). It was also the name of one of David's own sons. In modern times this name has often been taken as a short form of *Nathaniel* or of JONATHAN.

Nathaniel (m.) English form of a New Testament name, which is derived from the Greek form of a Hebrew name meaning 'God has given' (cf. NATHAN, which is sometimes taken as a short form of this name). It was borne by one of the less prominent of Christ's apostles (John 1: 45; 21: 2), who in fact is probably identical with BARTHOLOMEW. The spelling used in the Authorized Version of the New Testament is **Nathanael**, but this has never been common as a given name in the English-speaking world. The biblical form of the Old Testament name is *Nethaneel*; it was the name of the prince of the tribe of Issachar at the time of the Exodus (Numbers 1: 8). The name is little used in other European languages.
Cognate: Italian: **Natanaele**.

Natividad (f.) Spanish: religious name name referring to the festival of the Nativity (Spanish *natividad*, from Late Latin *nativitās*, a derivative of *nasci* to be born) of the Virgin Mary. This has been celebrated (on 5 September) since the 5th century in the Eastern Church, since the 7th century in the Western.
Short form: **Nati**.

Naughton (m.) Scottish: Anglicized form of the Gaelic name **Neachdann**, a derivative of *necht* pure. From this personal name comes the surname *Mac Neachdainn*, Anglicized as *MacNaughton*.

Naum (m.) Russian form of NAHUM. Its popularity has been influenced by popular etymological analysis as a compound of the Russian prefix *na* + the adjective *umny* clever, intelligent.

Nazaret (f.) Spanish: religious name, referring to Christ's native village, *Nazareth*. The placename seems to have been derived from a word meaning 'branch' in Hebrew.

Nazario (m.) Italian, Spanish, and Portuguese: from the Late Latin name *Nazarius*, a derivative of *Nazareth* (cf. NAZARET). The name was a relatively common one among early Christians and was borne by several saints, most notably one martyred with Celsus at Milan in the 1st century.
Cognate: French: **Nazaire**.

Nea (f.) Swedish: short form of LINNÉA.

Neacal (m.) Scottish Gaelic form of NICHOLAS.

Neal (m.) English: variant of NEIL, influenced by the surname in this spelling.

Neassa (f.) Irish Gaelic: traditional name of uncertain derivation. In ancient Irish legend, it was borne by the mother of Conchobhar Mac Neassa, King of Ulster.

Ned (m.) English: short form of EDWARD, originating in the misdivision of phrases such as *mine Ed* (cf. NAN). It was common in the Middle Ages and up to the 18th century, but in the 19th was almost entirely superseded in the role of short form by TED. It is now, however, enjoying a modest revival.

Neil (m.) Irish, Scottish, and English: Anglicized form of the enduringly popular Gaelic name **Niall**. Its derivation is disputed, and it may mean 'cloud', 'passionate', or perhaps 'champion'. It was adopted by the Scandinavians in the form *Njal* and soon became very popular among them. From the Middle Ages onwards, this name was found mainly in Ireland and the English-Scottish Border region. However, in the 20th century it has spread to enjoy great popularity in all parts of the English-speaking world.
Variant: **Neal**. See also NIGEL.
Pet form: Scottish (Highland): **Neillie**.
Feminine form: Scottish (Highland): **Neilina**.

Nekane (f.) Basque equivalent of DOLORES.

Nell (f.) English: short form of ELEANOR, ELLEN, and HELEN; of medieval origin, but now also established as a given name in its own right. For an explanation of the initial *N*-, cf. NED. It was the name by which Charles II's mistress Eleanor Gwyn (1650–87) was universally known to her contemporaries, and at about that time it also became established as an independent name.
Cognate: Irish Gaelic: **Neile**.
Pet forms: English: **Nellie**, **Nelly**.

Nelleke (f.) Dutch: pet form derived from a short form of CORNELIA.

Nels (m.) S. Swedish: dialectal form of NILS.

Nelson (m.) English: transferred use of the surname, which originated as a patronymic from either NEIL or NELL. Use as a given name probably began as a tribute to the British admiral Lord Nelson (1758–1805), the victor of the Battle of Trafalgar; cf. HORATIO. It is, however, now much more common in America than in Britain.

Nelya (f.) Russian: pet form of both YELENA and NINEL.

Nena (f.) English: variant spelling of NINA.

Nepomuk (m.) Czech: name bestowed in honour of St John of Nepomuk (*c.*1345–93). Born at Nepomuk in Bohemia, he became chaplain at the court of King Wenceslas IV, and was killed by the king, allegedly for refusing to disclose what the queen had revealed in confession. The given name is also used to some extent among Catholics in Germany and Austria.

Short form: **Pomuk**.

Pet form: **Nepomuček**.

Nereida (f.) Latinate name derived from Greek *nēreis* (genitive *nēreidos*) nymph, sea sprite (in origin a patronymic from *Nēreus* god of the ocean).

Nerina (f.) Italian: of uncertain origin. It seems to have arisen as a feminine form of the obsolete *Nerino*, a diminutive of Nero or possibly of Nerio. Alternatively, it may represent a Latinized form of Greek *Nērinē*, derived from the name of the sea god *Nēreus* (cf. Nereida and Nerissa).

Nerio (m.) Italian: from Greek *Nēreus*, the name (of uncertain derivation) of a divinity of the sea. This was the name in the 1st century of a Roman soldier who was baptized by St Paul and exiled with Sts Achilleus and Flavia.

Nerissa (f.) English: of Shakespearian origin. It is the name of a minor character in *The Merchant of Venice*, Portia's waiting woman, who marries Gratiano. The name seems to represent a Latinate elaboration of Greek *nēreis* nymph, sea sprite (see Nereida).

Nero (m.) Tuscan: short form of Raniero, not connected with the name of the Roman emperor Nero.

Nerys (f.) Welsh: of uncertain derivation, perhaps intended to be from Welsh *nêr* lord, with the suffix *-ys* by analogy with other female names such as Dilys and Gladys. This was not used as a given name in the Middle Ages, and dates only from the recent Welsh cultural revival; this has been accompanied by a spate of modern coinages of Welsh names, enabling Welsh parents to give their children names reflecting their national identity.

Neša (f.) Czech: pet form of Anežka.

Variant: **Neška**.

Nessa (f.) **1.** English: originally a short form of *Agnessa*, a Latinate form of Agnes. In modern use in the English-speaking world it is more often a short form of Vanessa, and is also used as an independent given name. **2.** Irish Gaelic: older form of Neassa. **3.** Jewish: apparently from Hebrew *nes* banner, miracle.

Pet form: **Nessie**.

Nesta (f.) Welsh: Latinized version of **Nest**, a Welsh pet form of Agnes. Nesta was the name of the grandmother of the 12th-century chronicler Giraldus Cambrensis ('Gerald the Welshman').

Nestore (m.) Italian: from the Greek personal name *Nestōr*, possibly a derivative of *nostos* homecoming. In Homer's *Iliad*, Nestor is one of the leaders of the Greeks at Troy, the aged but still vigorous king of Pylos. The name had some currency among early Christians and was borne by several early martyrs.

Neta (f.) Swedish: short form of *Agneta* (see Agnethe).

Netta (f.) English: apparently a Latinate variant of Nettie, though in Gaelic Scotland it is more likely to represent a feminine form of Neil.

Nettie (f.) English: pet form derived from various female names ending in the syllable *-nette*, for example Annette and Jeannette, with the hypocoristic suffix *-ie*. It had a brief vogue in the late 19th and early 20th centuries.

Neves (f.) Portuguese form of Nieves.

Neville (m.) English: transferred use of the surname, which is derived from a Norman baronial name from any of several places in Normandy called *Néville* or *Neuville* 'new settlement'. First used as a given name in the early 17th century, and with increasing regularity from the second half of the 19th, it is now so firmly established as a given name that it has lost touch with its origin as a surname.

Ngaio (f.) New Zealand: from the name of a type of tree cultivated for its wood, originally named in Maori.

Niall (m.) Irish and Scottish Gaelic: original spelling of Neil. It has been strongly revived among non-Gaelic speakers in the 20th century.

Niallghus (m.) Scottish Gaelic: a compound of Niall + *gus* strength. From this derives the surname *Mac Niallghuis*, Anglicized as *MacNeillage*.

Niamh (f.) Irish Gaelic: name meaning 'brightness, beauty'. It was borne in Irish mythology by the daughter of the sea god, who fell in love with the youthful Oisín, son of Finn MacCool, and carried him off over the sea to the land of perpetual youth, Tír na nÓg. It is now a very popular given name in Ireland.

Nicanor (m.) Spanish: from the Late Greek name *Nikanōr*. This is probably a byform of the earlier name *Nikandēr*, which is composed of the elements *nikē* victory + *anēr* man (genitive *andros*). It was the name of one of the Hellenized Jews chosen as deacons by the apostles (Acts 6: 5). One of the gates of the temple in Jesusalem was known as 'Nicanor's Gate', apparently after an official who was governor of Jerusalem in the 2nd century AD.

Nicasio (m.) Spanish: from the Late Greek personal name *Nikasios*. This seems to be a derivative of *Nikasia*, the name of a tiny island near Naxos. St Nicasius was a bishop of Rheims who was martyred either by the Vandals in 407 or by the Huns in 451.

Cognate: Catalan: **Nicasi**.

Nicholas (m.) English and French: from the post-classical Greek personal name *Nikolaos*, composed of the elements *nikē* victory + *laos* people. The spelling with *-ch-* first occurred as early as the 12th century, and became firmly established at the time of the Reformation, although *Nicolas* is still occasionally found. St Nicholas was a 4th-century bishop of Myra in Lycia, about whom virtually nothing factual is known, although a vast body of legend grew up around him, and he became the patron saint of Greece and Russia, as well as of children, sailors, merchants, and pawnbrokers. His feast-day is 6 December, and among the many roles which legend has assigned to him is that of bringer of Christmas presents, in the guise of 'Santa Claus' (an alteration of the Dutch form of his name, *Sinterklaas*).

Variant: **Nicolas**.

Cognates: Scottish: Nicol; **Neacal** (Gaelic). Irish Gaelic: **Nioclas**. Italian: **Nicola**, **Nic(c)olò**. Spanish: **Nicolás**, **Nicolao**. Catalan: **Nicolau**, **Micolau**. Portuguese: **Nicolau**. German: **Nikolaus**, **Niklaus**. Scandinavian: **Niklas**; **Nils** (Swedish, Norwegian); **Niels** (Danish). Finnish: **Launo**. Russian: **Nikolai**. Polish: **Mikolaj**.

Czech: **Mikoláš**. Romanian: **Nicolae**. Hungarian: **Miklós**. Finnish: **Niilo**.

Short forms: English: **Nick**. German: **Klaus**, **Claus**. Dutch: **Claus**.

Pet forms: English: **Nicky**. Swedish: **Nisse**. Russian: **Kolya**.

Feminine forms: English (Latinate): NICOLA. French, English: NICOLE. Spanish: **Nicolasa**.

Nicky (m., f.) English: **1**. (m.) Pet form of *Nick* (see NICHOLAS). **2**. (f.) Variant of NIKKI.

Nico (m., f.) **1**. (m.) Italian: short form of *Nicolò* (see NICHOLAS) or of the rarer *Nicodemo* (see NICODÈME), NICOMEDO, or NICOSTRATO. **2**. (m, f.) English: short form of both NICHOLAS and NICOLA (cf. e.g. *Ludo* and *Caro*).

Nicodème (m.) French: from Greek *Nikodēmos*, composed of the elements *nikē* victory + *dēmos* people, population. This is the name borne in the New Testament by one of the leading Greek Jews who spoke up for Jesus at his trial (John 7: 50) and was present at his burial (John 19: 39).

Cognate: Italian, Spanish, Portuguese: **Nicodemo**.

Nicol (m.) Scottish and English: common medieval form of NICHOLAS, current until a relatively late period in Scotland, and now being revived in more general use. Modern use as a given name may owe something to the character Bailie Nicol Jarvie in Sir Walter Scott's novel *Rob Roy*.

Variants: **Nichol**, **Nic(h)oll**.

Nicola (f., m.) **1**. (f.) English: Latinate feminine form of NICHOLAS. **2**. (m.) Italian form of NICHOLAS; See also NICOLÒ.

Nicole (f.) French: feminine form of NICHOLAS, now increasingly common in the English-speaking world.

Pet form: **Nicolette** (also used as a given name in its own right in both France and the English-speaking world).

Nicolò (m.) Italian: variant form of the male name *Nicola* (see NICHOLAS).

Variant: **Niccolò**.

Nicomedo (m.) Italian: from Greek *Nikomēdēs*, composed of the elements *nikē* victory + *mēdesthai* to ponder, scheme. St Nicomedes was a Roman priest martyred during the 1st century.

Nicostrato (m.) Italian: from Greek *Nikostratos*, composed of the elements *nikē* victory + *stratos* army. St Nicostratos was the leader of a group of Roman soldiers martyred in Palestine under the Emperor Diocletian (*c*.303).

Niels (m.) **1**. Danish form of NICHOLAS (cf. NILS). **2**. Dutch: short form of CORNELIS.

Nieves (f.) Spanish: from a title of the Virgin Mary, *Nuestra Señora de las Nieves* 'Our Lady of the Snows'. The name refers to a miracle alleged to have taken place in the 4th century, when Mary caused it to snow in Rome during August.

Cognate: Portuguese: **Neves**.

Nigel (m.) English: Anglicized form of the medieval name *Nigellus*, a Latinized version (ostensibly representing a diminutive of Latin *niger* black) of the vernacular *Ni(h)el*, i.e. NEIL. Although it is frequently found in medieval records, this form was probably not used in everyday life before its revival by antiquarians such as Sir Walter Scott in the 19th century.

Feminine: **Nigella**.

Niilo (m.) Finnish form of NICHOLAS.

Nikita (m.) Russian: from the Greek name *Anikētos* 'unconquered, unconquerable' (from the negative prefix *a-* + *nikān* to conquer). This was the name of an early pope (*c*.152–60); he was a Syrian by descent and is particularly honoured in the Eastern Church.

Nikki (f.) English: pet form of NICOLA, now sometimes used as an independent given name.

Variants: **Nicki**, **Nickie**, **Nicky**.

Nikolai (m.) Russian form of NICHOLAS.

Pet form: **Kolya**.

Nikolaus (m.) German form of NICHOLAS.

Variant: **Niklaus**.

Nille (f.) Scandinavian (esp. Danish): short form of *Pernille* (see PERNILLA).

Nils (m.) Swedish form of NICHOLAS.

Variant: S. Swedish: **Nels**.

Feminine form: **Nilsine**.

Nina (f.) Russian: short form of ANTONINA, now commonly used as an independent name in the French- and English-speaking worlds, as well as in Russia.

Variant: English: **Nena**.

Ninel (f.) Russian: modern coinage adopted by patriotic Soviet citizens, representing *Lenin* spelled backwards (cf. VLADILEN).

Pet form: **Nelya**.

Ninette (f.) French: diminutive form of NINA. Like NADINE, this was one of the names brought to the English-speaking world from Russian via French in the early 20th century.

Ninian (m.) Scottish and Irish: of uncertain origin. This was the name of a 5th-century British saint who was responsible for evangelizing the northern Britons and the Picts. His name first appears in the Latinized form *Ninianus* in the 8th century; this appears to be the same as the *Nynnyarv* recorded in the *Mabinogi*. The given name was used in his honour until at least the 16th century in Scotland and has recently been revived.

Nino (m.) Italian: short form of *Giannino*, a pet form of GIANNI.

Ninon (f.) French: **1**. Pet form of ANNE. The most famous bearer of this name was the celebrated Parisian beauty Ninon de Lenclos (1620–1705). **2**. Pet form of NINA.

Nioclás (m.) Irish Gaelic form of NICHOLAS.

Nisse (m.) Swedish: pet form of NILS.

Nita (f.) English: short form of various names that end in these syllables, as for example ANITA and *Marganita* (see MARGARET).

Niven (m.) Scottish: Anglicized form of the Gaelic name **Naoimhean** or *Gille Naomh*, a borrowing of Irish *Gille na Naomh* 'servant of the saint'.

Njord (m.) Scandinavian: from the name of a minor Norse divinity, recorded in the form *Nerthus* by the Roman historian Tacitus in the 1st century AD. It is of uncertain derivation, but was revived as a given name in the early 19th century.

Noah (m.) English form of the name of the biblical character whose family was the only one saved from the great Flood ordained by God to destroy mankind because of its wickedness. The origin of the name is far from certain; in the Bible it is implied that it means 'rest' (Genesis 5: 29, 'and he called his name Noah, saying, This same shall comfort us concerning our work and the toil of our hands, because of the ground which the Lord hath cursed'). One tradition indeed explains it as derived from the Hebrew root meaning 'to comfort' (see NAHUM) with the final consonant dropped.

Cognate: French: **Noë**.

Noam (m.) Jewish: modern name, from a Hebrew vocabulary word meaning 'delight, joy, pleasantness' (cf. NAOMI, from the same Hebrew root). Its most famous bearer is the American linguist Noam Chomsky (b. 1928).

Noble (m.) English (esp. U.S.): name derived from the modern English adjective (via Old French from Latin *nobilis*). The idea behind it may have been to hint at high-born origin (cf. DUKE, EARL, KING, and PRINCE) or to suggest qualities of character. In part there may be some influence from the surname, which arose in the Middle Ages as a descriptive nickname in the first sense.

Noël (m.) French: from Old French *noel*, *nael* Christmas, from Latin *natālis diēs* (*Domini*) birthday (of the Lord). The meaning is still relatively transparent, partly because the term occurs as a synonym for 'Christmas' in the refrain of well-known carols. The name is often given to children born at Christmas time. It is also used in the English-speaking world, normally without the diaeresis, **Noel**.

Feminine forms: **Noëlle**, **Noelle**.

Noemi (f.) Italian form of NAOMI, derived from the representation of the Hebrew name used in the Latin translation of the Vulgate.

Cognate: French: **Noémie**.

Noga (f.) Jewish: modern Israeli female name. In the Authorized Version the form *Nogah* occurs as the name of a man, one of David's sons born in Jerusalem (1 Chronicles 3: 7). The name derives from a Hebrew word meaning 'brightness'.

Nola (f.) Irish and Australian: probably a name created as a feminine form of NOLAN. It may also represent a short form of Gaelic *Fionn(gh)uala*; see FENELLA and FINOLA.

Nolan (m.) Australian, Irish, and English: from the Irish surname, Gaelic *Ó Nualláin* 'descendant of Nuallán'. *Nuallán* is an old Gaelic personal name, apparently originally a byname representing a diminutive of *nuall* chariot-fighter, champion.

Nolasco (m.) Italian: name adopted in honour of St Peter Nolasco (*c*.1189–1258), who founded the order of Our Lady of Ransom with the purpose of obtaining the release of Christians captured by the Moors during the Crusades.

Nolene (f.) Mainly Australian: name created as a feminine form of NOLAN.

Variant: **Noleen**.

Noll (m.) English: pet form of OLIVER, frequent in the Middle Ages and occasionally revived in modern times. The initial consonant seems to derive from a misdivision of a vocative phrase; cf. NED.

Nona (f.) English: from the feminine form of the Latin ordinal *nonus* ninth, sometimes used as a given name in Victorian times for the ninth-born child in a family if it was a girl, or even for the ninth-born girl. At the present day, when few people have nine children, let alone nine girls, it has passed into more general, if only occasional, use.

Nonie (f.) English: pet form of IONE or of NORA, also used to a limited extent as an independent given name.

Variant: **Noni**.

Nora (f.) English, Irish, Scottish and Scandinavian: short form of names such as *Eleonara* (see ELEANOR), *Honora* (see HONOUR), and LEONORA. Although these are not Gaelic in origin, *Nora* (Gaelic **Nóra**) was particularly associated with Ireland at one time. In the Scottish Highlands it is used as a feminine form of NORMAN. In Scandinavia the name is known particularly as that borne by the heroine of Henrik Ibsen's play *A Doll's House*.

Variant: **Norah**.

Norbert (m.) English: of Norman origin, and so ultimately Germanic, composed of the elements *nord* north + *berht* bright, famous. Its best-known bearer was an 11th-century saint who founded an order of monks known as Norbertians (also called Premonstratensians from their first home at Premontré near Laon). *Norbert* was one of several names of Germanic origin that were revived in Britain in the late 19th century, but it is now rather more common in America than Britain.

Noreen (f.) Irish and English: originally an Anglicized form of the Gaelic name **Nóirín**, a diminutive of *Nóra* (see NORA). It is now used as an independent given name in the English-speaking world.

Variants: **Norene**, **Norine**.

Norma (f.) Italian and English: apparently invented by Felice Romani in his libretto for Bellini's opera of this name (first performed in 1832). It is identical in form with Latin *norma* rule, standard, but there is no evidence that this word was the actual source of the name. In recent times, it has come to be taken in England and the Scottish Highlands as a feminine equivalent of NORMAN.

Norman (m.) English: of Germanic origin, composed of the elements *nord* north + *man* man, i.e. 'Norseman'. This name was found in England before the Conquest, and was reinforced by its use among the Norman invaders themselves. In the Scottish Highlands it is used as the Anglicized equivalent of TORMOD.

Pet form: Scottish: **Norrie**.
Feminine forms: Scottish (Highland): **Normanna**, **Normina**, **Norma**, **Nora**, **Mona**.

Norris (m.) English: transferred use of the surname, which is derived from Old Norman French *norreis* (in which the stem represents the Germanic element *nord*), originally a local designation for someone who had migrated from the north.

Notger (m.) German: from an old Germanic personal name composed of the elements *nōt* need, want + *gār*, *gēr* spear. The form **Notker** is a variant of this. The Blessed Notker Balbulus ('the Stammerer') was a Benedictine monk at the abbey of St Gall in Switzerland in the 10th century; he composed a biography of Charlemagne.

Nuala (f.) Irish: short form of the Gaelic name FIONNUALA. It is now in general use as an independent given name.

Nunzia (f.) Italian: short form of ANNUNZIATA.
Pet forms: **Nunziatella**, **Nunziatina**.
Masculine form: Italian (characteristic of S. Italy): **Nunzio**.

Nuria (f.) Catalan: from a title of the Virgin Mary, *Nuestra Señora de Nuria* 'Our Lady of Nuria'. Nuria is a place in the province of Gerona, where there is a famous image of the Virgin.

This was long venerated as a 'black madonna', but cleaning in the 1940s removed the grime that had come from centuries of smoking candles, and restored the original bright colours.

Nušek (m.) Czech: pet form of HANUŠ, preserving only a single letter of the base form *Jan*.

Nye (m.) Pet form of the Welsh name ANEIRIN, representing the middle syllable of that name as commonly pronounced.

The name is particularly associated with the Welsh Labour statesman Aneurin Bevan (1897–1960).

Nyree (f.) English spelling of a Maori name usually transcribed as **Ngaire**, the origin of which is obscure. It is relatively common in New Zealand and has been taken up to some extent in Britain due to the fame of the New Zealand-born actress Nyree Dawn Porter (b. 1940).

O

Obadiah (m.) English: from a biblical name meaning 'servant of God' in Hebrew (cf. Arabic *Abdullah*, which has the same meaning). This was the name of a prophet who gave his name to one of the shorter books of the Bible, and of two other minor biblical characters: a porter in the temple (Nehemiah 12: 25), and the man who introduced King Ahab to the prophet Elijah (1 Kings 18).

Variant: Modern Hebrew: **Ovadia**.

Oberon (m.) English: variant spelling of AUBERON.

Octavia (f.) English: of Latin origin, representing a feminine form of OCTAVIUS. It was borne by various female members of the Roman imperial family.

Cognate: Italian: **Ottavia**.

Octavian (m.) Usual English form of the Latin name *Octāviānus*, a derivative of OCTAVIUS. The first Roman emperor, now generally known by the imperial title *Augustus*, was born Caius Octavius; when he was adopted by Julius Caesar he became Caius Julius Caesar Octavianus. Another Octavianus was a 5th-century Carthaginian saint who was put to death with several thousand companions by the Asiatic Vandal king Hunneric.

Octavius (m.) English: from the Roman family name, derived from Latin *octāvus* eighth. The name was fairly frequently given to a male eighth child (or eighth son) in large Victorian families. It is much less common these days, when families rarely extend to eight children, but is occasionally selected for reasons of family tradition or for some other reason without regard to its original meaning.

Cognate: Italian: **Ottavio**.

Odd (m.) Scandinavian: from an Old Norse personal name, originally perhaps a byname, derived from the vocabulary word *oddr* point (of a weapon).

Oded (m.) Jewish: Hebrew name, meaning 'upholder, encourager', borne in the Bible by a prophet who persuaded the Israelites to release the captives that they had taken from the kingdom of Judah (2 Chronicles 28: 9–15). It is a popular modern Hebrew name.

Odette (f.) French: feminine diminutive form of the Old French masculine name *Oda*, which is of Germanic origin (cf. OTTO). Although the original male name has dropped out of use, this feminine derivative has survived and is now used as a given name in its own right.

Odile (f.) French: from the medieval Germanic name *Odila* (a derivative of the vocabulary element *od* riches, prosperity, fortune; cf. OTTO). This was the name of an 8th-century saint who founded a Benedictine convent at what is now Odilienburg in Alsace. She is the patron saint of Alsace. See also OTTILIE.

Ödön (m.) Hungarian form of EDMUND. The infant Anglo-Saxon princes Edward and Edmund, sons of Edmund Ironside, were sent away from England by the usurping Canute.

They eventually settled in Hungary, where they were granted large estates by King Andrew I.

Ofra (f.) Jewish: variant spelling of OPHRAH.

Oighrig (f.) Scottish Gaelic: name of uncertain derivation, apparently from an earlier form *Aithbhreac* meaning 'new speckled one'. It has commonly been Anglicized as ERICA, EFRIC, EFFIE and EUPHEMIA, formerly also as AFRICA. See also EITHRIG and EIRIC.

Okko (m.) Finnish: pet form of *Oskari* (see OSCAR).

Oktyabrina (f.) Russian: name adopted in the Soviet period, in commemoration of the October Revolution of 1917 which brought the Bolsheviks to power.

Olaf (m.) Scandinavian: from an Old Norse personal name composed of the elements *anu* ancestor + *leifr* heir, descendant. St Olaf, King of Norway (995–1030), aided the spread of Christianity in his kingdom. The name was introduced to Britain before the Norman Conquest, but modern use as a given name in the English-speaking world originated in America, where it was taken by recent Scandinavian immigrants.

Variants: Swedish: OLOF, **Olov**, **Oluf**. Norwegian and SW Swedish: **Ola**. Norwegian and Danish: **Olav**, **Ole**. Finnish: **Olavi**. See also AMHLAOIBH.

Olalla (f.) Spanish form of EULALIA. The name was borne by two famous Spanish martyrs, Eulalia of Barcelona (d. 304) and Eulalia of Mérida (d. 364); it is possible that they were identical.

Oldřich (m.) Czech form of ULRICH.

Feminine form: **Oldřiška**.

Pet forms: **Oldra**, **Olda** (m., f.); **Oldřísek**, **Oleček**, **Olik**, **Oloušek**, **Olin** (m.); **Oldřina**, **Olina**, **Oluše**, **Riška** (f.).

Oleg (m.) Russian form of HELGE. This name was introduced to Russia by the earliest Scandinavian settlers, and was borne by Prince Oleg of Kiev (d. 912), the Varangian leader who established Kiev as his capital in place of Novgorod and set up trading links with Byzantium. Since he was not a Christian, the name has never been sanctioned by the Russian Orthodox Church, unlike its feminine equivalent, OLGA.

Oleksander (m.) Ukrainian form of ALEXANDER.

Olena (f.) Ukrainian form of HELEN.

Oleś (m.) Polish: pet form of ALEXANDER.

Variants: **Olech**, **Olek**.
Cognate: Czech: **Olexa**.

Olga (f.) Russian: feminine form of OLEG, and equivalent of HELGA, taken to Russia by the Scandinavian settlers who founded the first Russian state in the 9th century. St Olga of Kiev (d. 969) was a Varangian noblewoman who was baptized at Byzantium in about 957 and set about converting her people. The name was introduced to the English-speaking world in the late 19th century, but retains a distinctively Russian flavour. It is also much in use in Scandinavia.

Pet form: **Olya**.

Olive (f.) English: one of the earliest and most successful of the names coined during the 19th century from vocabulary words denoting plants, no doubt partly because an olive branch has been a symbol of peace since biblical times. The Latinate form **Oliva** was used as a given name in medieval times, but dropped out of use in the English-speaking world after its pronunciation became indistinguishable from that of the male name OLIVER. See also OLIVIA.

Oliver (m.) English: of Norman, and hence ultimately Germanic, origin. It was first used as the name (French *Olivier*) of one of Charlemagne's paladins or retainers, the close companion in arms of Roland in the *Chanson de Roland*. Where Roland is headstrong and rash, Oliver is thoughtful and cautious. Ostensibly this name derives from Late Latin *olivārius* olive tree (cf. OLIVE), but Charlemagne's other paladins all bear solidly Germanic names, so it is more probably an altered form of a Germanic name, perhaps a version of OLAF.
Cognates: French: **Olivier**. Scottish Gaelic: **Olghar**, **Oilbhreis**.
Pet forms: English: **Ollie**, NOLL.

Olivia (f.) English: Latinate name, first used by Shakespeare as the name of the rich heiress wooed by the duke in *Twelfth Night* (1599). Shakespeare may have taken it as a feminine form of OLIVER or he may have derived it from Latin *oliva* olive; it may also have been influenced by the medieval female given name *Oliva*, although this had dropped out of use by the 16th century.

Ollie (m.) English: pet form of OLIVER, associated particularly with the comic film actor Oliver Hardy (1892–1957), the rotund partner of Stan Laurel.

Olof (m.) Swedish form of OLAF. St Olof, King of Sweden (d. *c*.950) was murdered by his rebellious heathen subjects for refusing to sacrifice to idols.
Variants: **Olov**, **Oluf**.

Olwen (f.) Welsh; composed of the elements *ôl* footprint, track + *(g)iven* white, fair, blessed, holy. A character of this name in Welsh legend had the magical property of causing flowers to spring up behind her wherever she went.

Olya (f.) Russian: pet form of OLGA.

Olympe (f.) French: from the Latin name *Olympia*, a feminine form of *Olympius*, from Greek *Olympos*, the home, according to classical mythology, of the gods.

Omar (m.) English: biblical name borne by a character mentioned in a genealogy (Genesis 36: 11). It has been occasionally used from Puritan times down to the present day in America. More often, however, it is of Arabic origin, as in the case of the film actor and international bridge player Omar Sharif (b. 1932 in Egypt).

Omri (m.) Jewish: Hebrew name, possibly derived from an element meaning 'sheaf of grain'. It is borne in the Bible by a king of Israel who built the city of Samaria, but who also 'wrought evil in the eyes of the Lord' (1 Kings 16: 23–8). This has not prevented *Omri* from being used as a modern given name.

Ona (f.) English: apparently an aphetic short form of any of the given names ending in these letters, for example FIONA and ANONA.

Ondřej (m.) Czech form of ANDREW.
Pet forms: **Ondra**, **Ondřejek**, **Ondrášek**, **Ondroušek**.

Onisim (m.) Russian: less common form of ANISIM.

Onóra (f.) Irish Gaelic: name derived in the early Middle Ages from Anglo-Norman HONORE.

Oona (f.) Irish: Anglicized form of the Gaelic name ÚNA.
Variant: **Oonagh**.

Opal (f.) English: one of the rarer female names taken in the late 19th century from vocabulary words for gemstones. This is ultimately derived (via Latin and Greek) from an Indian language (cf. Sanskrit *upala* precious stone).

Opaline (f.) English: a comparatively recent coinage; an elaboration of OPAL with the addition of *-ine*, a productive suffix of feminine names.

Ophelia (f.) English: name of a character in Shakespeare's *Hamlet*, the beautiful daughter of Polonius; she loves Hamlet, and eventually goes mad and drowns herself. In spite of the ill omen of this literary association, the name has enjoyed moderate popularity since the 19th century. Apparently it was first used by the Italian pastoralist Jacopo Sannazzaro (1458–1530), who presumably intended it as a feminine form of the Greek name *Ōphelos* 'help'. Shakespeare seems to have borrowed the name from Sannazzaro, without considering whether it was an appropriate name for a play set in medieval Denmark.

Ophrah (f., m.) Jewish: Hebrew name meaning 'fawn'. It is borne in the Old Testament by a man (1 Chronicles 4: 14), but it is now more commonly given to girls. The spellings **Ophra** and **Ofra** are also used.

Oralie (f.) English: of uncertain origin, possibly an altered form of *Aurélie* (see AURELIA).
Variant: **Oralee**.

Oran (m.) Irish: Anglicized form of Gaelic **Odhrán**, originally a byname representing a diminutive of *odhar* dun, sallow. The name was borne by various early saints, most notably a 6th-century abbot of Meath who accompanied Columba to Scotland.

Orazio (m.) Italian form of HORACE.

Orbán (m.) Hungarian form of URBAN.

Orell (m.) Swiss form of *Aurelius* (see AURÈLE).

Orfeo (m.) Italian: from Greek *Orpheus*, the name in classical mythology of a Thracian musician whose playing on the lyre was so beautiful that he charmed Nature itself. After his wife Eurydice died, he descended in search of her to the underworld, and charmed Hades, the king of the underworld, into allowing him to take her back to the world of the living, on condition that he should not look at her until they had regained the sunlight. He lost her again, because he looked back to check that she was behind him. The name is of very uncertain derivation, and it seems likely that the legend originally concerned a pre-Greek divinity of the natural world.

Oriana (f.) Latinate name first found in the medieval tale of *Amadis of Gaul* as the name of the daughter of Lisuarte, King of England, courted and eventually won by the model knight Amadis. It may be a derivative of Old French *or*, Spanish *oro* gold (Latin *aurum*).
Variant: French: **Oriane**.

Örjan (m.) Swedish: older form of GÖRAN, still in use as a given name.

Orla (f.) Irish: Anglicized form of the Gaelic name **Órla**, earlier *Ór (fh)laith*, composed of the elements *ór* gold + *flaith* lady, princess.

Orlando (m.) Italian form of ROLAND, occasionally used as a given name in the English-speaking world. It is the name of the hero in Shakespeare's comedy *As You Like It*.

Orna (f.) Irish: Anglicized form of the Gaelic name **Odharnait**, a feminine diminutive form of *Odhar* 'dun, sallow' (cf. ORAN). The loss of the final consonant is due to the influence of ORLA.

Ornella (f.) Italian: apparently originated by Gabriele d'Annunzio, who gave the name to one of the characters in his novel *Figlia de Iorio* (1904). It seems to represent a feminine form of the Tuscan dialect word *ornello* flowering ash tree.

Ornetta (f.) Italian: apparently an altered form of ORNELLA, with the substitution of the Italian feminine diminutive suffix *-etta* for the similarly functioning *-ella*. The name is also used in the English-speaking world.
Cognate: French: **Ornette**.

Orson (m.) English: from an Old Norman French nickname meaning 'bear-cub' (a diminutive of *ors* bear, Latin *ursus*), used occasionally in medieval times, but in modern times probably always a transferred use of the associated surname. In the 20th century it has come to public notice as a result of the fame of the American actor Orson Welles (1915–85), who dropped his more prosaic given name, George, in favour of his middle name before embarking on his acting career.

Orville (m.) English: though in appearance a surname of Norman baronial origin, this name seems to have been invented (with the intention of evoking such associations) by the novelist Fanny Burney for the hero, Lord Orville, of her novel *Evelina* (1778).

Orya (f.) Russian: pet form of IRINA and its variant ARINA.

Osane (f.) Basque equivalent of REMEDIOS.

Osbert (m.) English: from an Old English personal name composed of the elements *ōs* god + *beorht* bright, famous. It is not now common in the English-speaking world, but has been borne, for example, by the British cartoonist Osbert Lancaster and the writer Osbert Sitwell.

Osborn (m.) English: from a Late Old English personal name composed of the elements *ōs* god + *beorn* bear, warrior (both of Scandinavian origin). As a modern given name it generally represents a transferred use of the surname that was derived from this name during the Middle Ages.
Variants: **Osborne**, **Osbourne**.

Oscar (m.) English and Irish: name, apparently composed of the Irish Gaelic elements *os* deer + *cara* friend, borne in the Fenian sagas by a grandson of Finn McCool. It was resuscitated by the antiquarian and poet James Macpherson (1736–96). This is now also a characteristically Scandinavian name; it was introduced there because Napoleon, being an admirer of the works of Macpherson, imposed the name on his godson Oscar Bernadotte, who became King Oscar I of Sweden in 1844. In more recent times it has been associated particularly with the Irish writer and wit Oscar Wilde (1854–1900).
Cognates: Scottish Gaelic: **Osgar**. German, Scandinavian, E. European: **Oskar**. Finnish: **Oskari**.

Osheen (m.) Irish: Anglicized form of the Gaelic name **Oisín**, in origin a byname representing a diminutive form of *os* deer. This is the name altered by James Macpherson, author of the *'Ossianic'* poems, to *Ossian*.
Cognate: Scottish Gaelic: **Oisein**.

Osher (m.) Jewish: variant of ASHER, representing an alternative Hebrew pronunciation of the name.

Osip (m.) Russian: vernacular form of JOSEPH.

Osmond (m.) English: 19th-century revival of an Old English personal name composed of the elements *ōs* god + *mund* protector. The name was also in use among the Normans and was borne by an 11th-century saint who was appointed to the see of Salisbury by William the Conqueror. As a modern given name it may be in part a transferred use of the surname derived from this name.
Variant: **Osmund**.
Cognate: Scandinavian: **Åsmund**.

Oswald (m.) English: 19th-century revival of an Old English personal name composed of the elements *ōs* god + *weald* rule. This was the name of two English saints. The first was a 7th-century king of Northumbria, who was killed in battle in 641. He was a Christian, a convert of St Aidan's, and his opponent, Penda, was a heathen, so his death was counted as a martyrdom by the Christian Church. The second St Oswald was a 10th-century bishop of Worcester and archbishop of York, of Danish parentage, who effected reforms in the English Church. The name more or less died out after the Middle Ages, but underwent a modest revival in the 19th century as part of the vogue for pre-Conquest English names.

Oswin (m.) English: 19th-century revival of an Old English personal name composed of the elements *ōs* god + *wine* friend. St Oswin was a 7th-century king of Northumbria, a cousin of King Oswald, who is likewise venerated as a martyr. However, the reasons for his death at the hand of his brother Oswy seem to have been political and personal rather than religious.

Otilie (f.) Czech form of OTTILIE.

Otis (m.) English (esp. U.S.): transferred use of the surname, derived from the genitive case of the medieval given name *Ote* or *Ode* (of Norman, and ultimately Germanic, origin; cf. OTTO). This originally denoted a man who was the 'son of Ote'. It came to be used as a given name in America in honour of the Revolutionary hero James Otis (1725–83); in modern times it has been bestowed in honour of the American soul singer Otis Redding (1941–67).

Otmar (m.) German: from an old Germanic personal name composed of the elements *od*, *ot* prosperity, fortune, riches + *meri*, *mari* famous. This name was borne by an 8th-century saint who refounded the monastery of St Gall in Switzerland.
Pet form: **Otli** (Swiss).

Otokar (m.) Czech form of OTTOKAR.

Ottavia (m.) Italian form of OCTAVIA.

Ottavio (m.) Italian form of OCTAVIUS.

Ottilie (f.) French and German: from the medieval female given name *Odila* (see ODILE), a feminine version of OTTO.
Cognates: Polish: **Otylia**. Czech: **Otilie**.

Otto (m.) German: originally a short form of the various Germanic compound personal names containing the element *od*, *ot* prosperity, fortune, riches (cf. the corresponding Old English *ēad* in names such as EDWARD and EDWIN). St Otto of Bamberg (d. 1139) was a missionary to the Pomeranians. Otto the Great (912–73) is generally regarded as the founder of the Holy Roman Empire, and the name has been borne by several members of German and Austrian royal houses.

Ottokar (m.) German: from an old Germanic personal name composed of the elements *od*, *ot* prosperity, fortune, riches + *wacar* watchful, vigilant. A version of this name was borne by the Gothic king Odo(v)acar (?434–93), who ruled most of Italy from 476–493, in which year he was assassinated by his rival Theodoric. The name was also borne by two 13th-century kings of Bohemia.

Cognate: Czech: **Otokar**.

Ottoline (f.) French and English: originally a diminutive of OTTILIE. It now has independent status in the English-speaking world, partly due to the influence of the literary hostess Lady Ottoline Morrell (1873–1938).

Otylia (f.) Polish form of OTTILIE.

Ovadia (m.) Jewish: modern Hebrew form of OBADIAH.

Ove (m.) Scandinavian: originally a Danish vernacular form of *Aghi*, short form of the various names of Old Norse origin containing the element *ag* edge (of a weapon) or awe, terror. It has long been used as an independent name.

Owen (m.) **1**. Welsh: of uncertain origin. It may have derived in the sub-Roman period from the Latin name *Eugenius* (see EUGENE). Alternatively, it may represent an Old Celtic name meaning 'born of Esos'. *Esos* or *Aesos* was a god with a cult in Gaul. **2**. Irish: Anglicized form of the Gaelic name EÓGHAN.

Oz (m.) English: short form of OSWALD or any of the various other names beginning with *Os-*.

Pet forms: **Ozzy**, **Ozzie**.

P

Paavo (m.) Finnish form of PAUL.

Pablo (m.) Spanish form of PAUL.

Paco (m.) Spanish: pet form of *Francisco* (see FRANCIS).
Variant: **Paquito**.

Paddy (m.) English and Irish: pet form of PATRICK. The formation in *-y* is in origin characteristic of Lowland Scots, and this pet form seems to have arisen in Ulster in the 17th century. Since the 19th century it has come to function in English as a generic nickname for an Irishman.

Pádraig (m.) Irish Gaelic form of PATRICK.
Variant: **Páraic** (found in Connacht).
Cognates: Scottish Gaelic: **Pàdraig** (used as a secular form of PETER); **Pàra**, **Pàdair** (dialectal forms).
Pet forms: Irish Gaelic: **Páidín** (Anglicized as **Paudeen**). Scottish Gaelic: **Pàidean** (from which comes the surname *Mac Phàidein*, Anglicized as *MacFadyen*).

Paige (f.) A modern female given name used regularly in America, but seldom elsewhere. It is evidently a transferred use of the surname *Paige*, a less common variant of *Page*, originally an occupational name given to someone who served as a page to a great lord. It is not clear why this should have been taken up in the 20th century as a female given name. The American film actress Janis Paige (born in 1920 under the name Donna Mae Jaden) may have something to do with it. There are a number of actresses and singers who spell their surname *Page*, but they are unlikely to have directly influenced the choice of the given name in this spelling.

Pál (m.) Hungarian form of PAUL.

Pàl (m.) Scottish Gaelic form of PAUL.

Pål (m.) Swedish form of PAUL.

Palasha (f.) Russian: pet form of *Pelageya*, derived from the older form *Palageya* (see PELAGIA).

Palmiro (m.) Italian: name derived in the Middle Ages from the vocabulary word *palmiere* palmer, pilgrim who had visited the Holy Land (from Latin *palmārius*, a derivative of *palma* palm). The name has been altered by association with the ancient city of *Palmyra* in Syria. In modern times it is sometimes given to boys born on Palm Sunday.

Paloma (f.) Spanish: from the vocabulary word meaning 'dove' (Latin *palumba*, earlier *palumbes*). The given name has originated because of the attractive gentle qualities of the bird; it may in part have a religious significance, as the dove is the symbol of the Holy Spirit.

Pamela (f.) English: invented by the Elizabethan pastoral poet Sir Philip Sidney (1554–86), in whose verse it is stressed on the second syllable. There is no clue to the sources that influenced Sidney in this coinage. It was later taken up by Samuel Richardson for the name of the heroine of his novel *Pamela* (1740). In Henry Fielding's *Joseph Andrews* (1742), which started out as a parody of *Pamela*, Fielding comments that the name is 'very strange'.
Variant: **Pamella** (a modern spelling).

Pancho (m.) Spanish: pet form of *Francisco* (see FRANCIS).

Pancras (m.) English: Middle English form of Greek *Pankratios* (see PANCRAZIO), popular in England during the early Middle Ages because in the 7th century the Pope had sent to an Anglo-Saxon king relics of a saint so called (an obscure 3rd-century martyr, not the more famous Sicilian saint mentioned at *Pancrazio*). It is now very rare, and modern instances are probably adaptations of the Italian name.

Pancrazio (m.) Italian: from the Greek epithet *pankratios* 'all-powerful' (from *pan* all, every + *kratein* to rule). This was a major title of Christ in Byzantine Greek, and was used as a personal name among early Christians. It was borne by a saint of the 1st century, who was stoned to death at Tauromenium (now Taormina) in Sicily, and who is still venerated on the island.
Cognates: Russian: **Pankrati**. German: **Pankraz** (S. Germany). English: PANCRAS.

Pandora (f.) English: name borne in classical mythology by the first woman on earth, created by the fire god Hephaistos as a scourge for men in general, in revenge for Prometheus' act of stealing fire on behalf of mankind. Pandora was given as a wife to Prometheus' foolish brother Epimetheus, along with a box which she was forbidden to open. Being endowed with great curiosity, she nevertheless did open it, and unleashed every type of hardship and suffering on the world, hope alone being left inside the box. The name itself is ironically composed of the Greek elements *pan* all, every + *dōron* gift.

Pansy (f.) English: 19th-century flower name, from the garden flower that got its name from Old French *pensee* thought. This was never especially popular, and is seldom chosen at all now that the word *pansy* has acquired a derogatory slang sense denoting an effeminate man.

Paolino (m.) Italian: a form of PAULINO or a diminutive of PAOLO. It is not a common given name.

Paolo (m.) Italian form of PAUL.
Feminine form: **Paola**.

Paquito (m.) Spanish: diminutive form of PACO.

Páraic (m.) Irish Gaelic: variant of PÁDRAIG, current in Connacht.

Paris (m.) English: apparently an adoption of the name of the character from Greek mythology, the son of Priam who carried off Helen from Sparta to Troy and so caused the Trojan War. The name was borne in the 4th century by a Greek-born bishop of Teano, near Naples, who is venerated as a saint.

Pàrlan (m.) Scottish Gaelic form of PARTHALÁN. From this name derive the surname *Mac Phàrlain*, Anglicized as *MacFarlane*, and the placename *Dùn Phàrlain*, Anglicized as *Dunfermline*.

Parthalán (m.) Irish Gaelic: name of uncertain derivation, possibly from Latin *Bartholomaeus* (see BARTHOLOMEW). It was borne, according to Celtic legend, by an early invader of Ireland, the first to come to those shores after the biblical Flood. It has often been Anglicized as *Bartholomew*, and also as BARCLAY and BERKLEY, but is now being revived in its own right.

Variants: **Párth(h)lán**, **Partnán**.
Cognate: Scottish Gaelic: PÀRLAN.

Parthenope (f.) Name borne in classical mythology by one of the Sirens, who drowned herself in frustration when Odysseus managed to avoid her lures by having himself tied to the mast and ordering his companions to block their ears with wax. Her name seems to be a derivative of Greek *parthenos* maiden (an epithet of Athena) + *ōps* face, form. This name was borne by a sister of Florence Nightingale who was born at Naples, where the body of the Siren is said to have been washed ashore.

Pascal (m.) French: from Late Latin *Paschālis* 'relating to Easter' (Latin *Pascha*, from Hebrew *pesach* Passover). This was taken up by the early Christians as a personal name, partly in honour of the great Christian festival, but mainly as a name for sons born at this time of the year. It was borne by two medieval popes, neither of whom achieved anything particularly notable. Its popularity may have been influenced by the fame of the French philosopher Blaise Pascal (1623–62), whose *Pensées* ('Thoughts') were published posthumously in 1670. The name is now occasionally used in the English-speaking world, mainly by Roman Catholics.

Variant: **Paschal**.
Cognates: Italian: **Pasquale**. Spanish: **Pascual**. Portuguese: **Pascoal**.
Feminine forms: French, also occasionally English: **Pascale**. Spanish: **Pascuala**.

Pasha (m., f.) Russian: pet form of both *Pavel* (see PAUL) and PRASKOVYA.

Pastor (m.) Spanish: from the Late Latin name *Pastōr* 'shepherd', adopted by early Christians because of the parable of the Good Shepherd caring for his flock. St Pastor was a 9-year-old boy martyred at Alcalá at the beginning of the 4th century, together with his 13-year-old brother Justus.

Feminine form: **Pastora**.

Pat (f., m.) English: short form of both PATRICIA and PATRICK.

Pet forms: **Patty**, **Pattie**, **Patti** (f.).

Patience (f.) English: from the vocabulary word denoting one of the Seven Christian Virtues. This name was a favourite with the Puritans, and survived better than many similar names, but now seems somewhat old-fashioned. The word is derived from Latin *pati* to suffer, and was associated by the early Christians with those who endured persecution and misfortune without complaint or loss of faith.

Patricia (f.) English: feminine form of PATRICK, also found in Spanish and Portuguese as a feminine of *Patricio*.

Cognate: Italian: **Patrizia**.
Short forms: English: PAT, **Tricia**, **Trisha**.

Patrick (m.) English and Irish, also very popular in France: name of the apostle and patron saint of Ireland (*c*.389–461). He was a Christian Briton and a Roman citizen, who as a young man was captured and enslaved by raiders from Ireland. He escaped and went to Gaul before returning home to Britain. However, in about 419 he felt a call to do missionary work in Ireland. He studied for twelve years at Auxerre, and in 432

returned to Ireland, where he went to the court of the high kings at Tara, and made some converts. He then travelled about Ireland making further converts until about 445, when he established his archiepiscopal see at Armagh. By the time of his death almost the whole of Ireland was Christian. He codified the laws of Ireland, preserving the social structure of pagan Ireland and grafting Christianity on to it. In his Latin autobiography, as well as in later tradition, his name appears as *Patricius* 'patrician' (i.e. belonging to the Roman senatorial or noble class), but this may actually represent a Latinized form of some lost Celtic (British) name.

Variant: French: **Patrice**.
Cognates: Irish Gaelic: **Pádraig**, **Páraic**. Scottish Gaelic: **Pàdraig** (usually Anglicized as PETER). Italian: **Patrizio**. Spanish, Portuguese: **Patricio**.
Short form: PAT.
Pet form: PADDY.

Patsy (f., m.) Irish and English: pet form of PATRICIA or PATRICK. It is generally a female name; as a male name it is almost completely restricted to Irish communities. Its popularity does not seem to have been seriously affected by its use in derogatory senses in the general vocabulary, in America meaning 'a dupe' and in Australia 'a homosexual'.

Patxi (m.) Basque form of FRANCIS, representing a shortened version of the full form *Pantzeska*.

Patya (m.) Russian: pet form of IPATI.

Paudeen (f.) Irish: Anglicized form of Gaelic *Páidín*, pet form of PÁDRAIG.

Paul (m.) English, French, and German form of *Paulus*, a Latin family name, originally a nickname meaning 'small', used in the post-classical period as a given name. Pre-eminently this is the name of the saint who is generally regarded, with St Peter, as co-founder of the Christian Church. Born in Tarsus, and originally named SAUL, he was both a Roman citizen and a Jew, and at first found employment as a minor official persecuting Christians. He was converted to Christianity by a vision of Christ while on the road to Damascus, and thereafter undertook extensive missionary journeys, converting people, especially Gentiles, to Christianity all over the eastern Mediterranean. His preaching aroused considerable official hostility, and eventually he was beheaded at Rome in about AD 65. He is the author of the fourteen epistles to churches and individuals which form part of the New Testament.

Cognates: Irish Gaelic: **Pól**. Scottish Gaelic: **Pàl** (in secular use, the form *Pòl* being reserved for the name of the saint). Italian: **Paolo**. Spanish: **Pablo**. Catalan: **Pau**. Portuguese: **Paulo**. Danish: **Poul**. Swedish: **Pål**, **Påvel**. Russian: **Pavel**. Polish: **Paweł**. Ukrainian: **Pavlo**. Hungarian: **Pál**. Finnish: **Paavo**.
Pet forms: Russian: **Pava**, **Pasha**, **Pusha**. Czech: **Pavlík**, **Pavlíček**, **Pavloušek**.
Feminine forms: English: **Paula**, PAULINE, PAULETTE. German: **Paula**. French: **Paule**. Czech: **Pavla**.

Paula (f.) English and German: Latinate feminine form of PAUL, borne by various minor early saints and martyrs.

Paulette (f.) French: diminutive feminine form of PAUL. It is widely used in the English-speaking world, where, however, it is a more recent importation than PAULINE.

Paulina (f.) Latin feminine form of *Paulinus* (see PAULINO), borne by several minor early martyrs.

Pauline (f.) French form of PAULINA that has long been common also in the English-speaking world, where it is now established as the most common feminine equivalent of PAUL.
Variants: English: **Paulyne**, **Paulene**, **Pauleen**.

Paulino (m.) Spanish and Portuguese: from the Late Latin name *Paulīnus*, a derivative of *Paulus* (see PAUL). St Paulinus of Nola (Pontius Meropius Anicius Paulinus) was a 5th-century bishop and early Christian poet.

Paz (f.) Spanish: name derived from a title of the Virgin Mary, *Nuestra Señora de la Paz* 'Our Lady of Peace'.

Peadar (m.) Irish Gaelic form of PETER. In Scotland this form is reserved to refer to the saint; in secular use *Pàdraig* (see PÁDRAIG) is used instead.

Pearce (m.) English and Irish: variant of PIERCE. It normally represents a transferred use of the English surname derived from the given name in the Middle Ages. It has been a popular name among Irish nationalists since the rising of 1916, led by the writer and educationist Patrick Henry Pearce; he was executed by the British and is regarded as a martyr to the nationalist cause.

Pearl (f.) English: one of the group of names coined in the 19th century from words for precious and semi-precious stones. It has a longer history as a Jewish name, representing an Anglicized form of Yiddish *Perle*, an affectionate nickname or vernacular equivalent of MARGARET.
Cognates: Italian, Spanish: **Perla**.
Pet form: Spanish: **Perlita**.

Pedr (m.) Welsh form of PETER.

Pedro (m.) Spanish form of PETER.

Peggy (f.) English: variant of MAGGIE, or of the obsolete *Meggie*, both pet forms of MARGARET. The reason for the alternation of *M-* and *P-*, which occurs also in *Molly/Polly*, is not known; it has been ascribed to Celtic influence, but this particular alternation does not correspond to any of the usual mutational patterns in Celtic languages.
Short form: **Peg**.

Peig (f.) Irish Gaelic form of *Peg* (see PEGGY).
Pet form: **Peigín** (Anglicized as **Pegeen**).

Peigi (f.) Scottish Gaelic form of PEGGY.

Pekka (m.) Finnish: vernacular form of PETER (cf. PIETARI).

Pelagia (f.) Polish: from the feminine form of the Greek name *Pelagios* (Latin *Pelagius*), a derivative of Greek *pelagos* open sea. The name was borne by various early saints, including a 15-year-old virgin martyr of the 4th century who died by throwing herself from the top of a building to preserve her chastity.
Derivatives: Russian: **Pelageya**. French: **Pélagie**.

Pelayo (m.) Spanish form of *Pelagius*; see PELAGIA. The name was borne by a 10th-century saint who was martyred at the hands of the Moors in Cordoba, and who is still venerated in Spain.

Peleg (m.) Biblical name, meaning 'division' in Hebrew, borne by a minor figure mentioned in a genealogy (Genesis 10: 25). The name was in use among the Puritans, but has become very rare in the modern English-speaking world. In Israel, however, it has been taken up, and is now both a given name and a surname.

Pelham (m.) English: transferred use of the surname, which originated as a local name from a place in Hertfordshire, so called from the Old English personal name *Pēo(t)la* + *hām* homestead. From 1715 this was the surname of the dukes of Newcastle.

Pella (f.) Swedish: pet form of PERNILLA, representing a dramatically contracted form of the name.

Pelle (m.) Swedish: pet form of *Per*, the Scandinavian form of PETER.

Pellegrino (m.) Italian form of PEREGRINE.

Penelope (f.) English: name borne in Greek mythology by the wife of Odysseus who sat patiently awaiting his return for twenty years, meanwhile, as a supposed widow, fending off by persuasion and guile a pressing horde of suitors for her hand in marriage. Her name would seem to derive from Greek *pēnelops* duck, and play is made with this word in the *Odyssey*, but this may obscure a more complex origin, now no longer known.
Short form: **Pen**.
Pet form: **Penny** (commonly used as a given name in its own right).

Peninnah (f.) Jewish: traditional name meaning 'coral' in Hebrew. It was borne in the Scriptures by the co-wife (with Hannah) of Elkanah, the father of Samuel. In modern Hebrew it means 'pearl' and has become a popular name, substituting for the foreign forms *Perle* and PEARL.
Variants: **Peninna**, **Penina**.

Pentti (m.) Finnish form of BENEDICT.

Pepa (f.) Spanish: pet form of JOSEFA.
Variant: **Pepita**.

Pepe (m.) Spanish: pet form of JOSÉ.
Variant: **Pepito**.

Per (m.) Scandinavian: vernacular form of PETER.

Perce (m.) 1. English: informal short form of PERCY. 2. Irish: variant of PIERCE.
Variant (of 2): **Perse**.

Percival (m.) English: from Arthurian legend in its Old French versions, where the name is spelled *Perceval*. According to Chrétien de Troyes (12th century) and Wolfram von Eschenbach (c.1170–1220), Perceval (German *Parzifal*) was the perfectly pure and innocent knight who alone could succeed in the quest for the Holy Grail (a cup or bowl with supernatural powers, which in medieval legend was identified with the chalice that had received Christ's blood at the Crucifixion). Later versions of the Grail legend assign this role to Sir Galahad. The name *Perceval* probably represents a drastic remodelling of the Celtic name *Peredur*, as if from Old French *perce(r)* to pierce + *val* valley. This may well have been influenced by PERCY, which was similarly analysed as a compound of *perce(r)* + *haie* hedge.

Percy (m.) English: originally a transferred use of a famous surname, but long established as a given name, and now often erroneously taken as a pet or informal form of PERCIVAL. The surname originated as a Norman territorial name, borne by a baronial family who had held a fief in Normandy called *Perci* (from Late Latin *Persiācum*, composed of the Gallo-Roman personal name *Persius* and the local suffix *-ācum*). As a given name it was taken up in the early 18th century in the Seymour family, which had intermarried with the Percy family. The poet Percy Bysshe Shelley (1792–1822) was also distantly connected with this family, and it was partly due to his influence that the given name became more widespread. It is at present out of fashion.

Perdita (f.) English: Shakespearian coinage, borne by a character in *The Winter's Tale* (1610). The feminine form of Latin *perditus* lost, it has a clear reference to the events of the play, and this is explicitly commented on in the text. The name is now more closely associated in some people's minds with a (canine) character in Dodie Smith's *One Hundred and One Dalmatians* (1956), made into a film by Walt Disney.

Pere (m.) Catalan form of PETER.

Peregrine (m.) English: from Latin *Peregrīnus* 'foreigner, stranger', a name borne by various early Christian saints, perhaps referring to the belief that men and women are merely sojourners upon the earth, their true home being in heaven. In modern times the name is rare, borne mostly by Roman Catholics, who choose it in honour of those saints.

Cognate: Italian: **Pellegrino**.

Perico (m.) Spanish: pet form of PEDRO, derived from the archaic variant *Pero*.

Perla (f.) Italian and Spanish form of PEARL.

Pet form: Spanish: **Perlita**.

Pernilla (f.) Swedish form of Latin *Petronilla* (see PETRONEL).

Cognate: **Pernille** (Danish).

Peronel (f.) English: common medieval simplified form of PETRONEL, occasionally revived in modern times as a given name.

Perrine (f.) French: feminine form of *Perrin*, an obsolete diminutive of PIERRE.

Perry (m.) English: pet form of PEREGRINE, or transferred use of the surname *Perry*, which was originally a local name for someone who lived by a pear tree (Old English *pirige*). In modern times, it has been borne by the American singer Perry Como (1912–2001), whose name was originally Nick Perido.

Persis (f.) English: of New Testament origin, from Greek *Persis*, originally an ethnic name meaning 'Persian woman'. This name is borne by a woman mentioned fleetingly by St Paul—'the beloved Persis, which laboured much in the Lord' (Romans 16: 12)—and was taken up from there at the time of the Reformation.

Perttu (m.) Finnish form of BARTHOLOMEW.

Pesah (m.) Jewish: Hebrew name meaning 'Passover' (cf. PASCAL). It has traditionally been given to boys born during this period.

Variant: **Pesach**.

Pet (f.) English: short form of PETULA, in part influenced by the common affectionate term of address 'pet', derived from the vocabulary word for a tame animal kept for companionship.

Peta (f.) English: modern feminine form of PETER, not used before the 1930s.

Peter (m.) English, German, and Scandinavian (learned form): name of the best-known of all Christ's apostles, traditionally regarded as the founder of the Christian Church. The name derives, via Latin, from Greek *petros* stone or rock. This is used as a translation of the Aramaic byname *Cephas*, given to

the apostle Simon son of Jona, to distinguish him from another of the same name (Simon Zelotes). 'When Jesus beheld him, he said, Thou art Simon the son of Jona: thou shalt be called Cephas, which is by interpretation, A stone' (John 1: 42). According to Matthew 16: 17–18, Christ says more explicitly, 'Blessed art thou, Simon Bar-jona ⋯ thou art Peter, and upon this rock I will build my church'. In Scotland this is used as an Anglicized form of the Scottish Gaelic names listed at PÁDRAIG.

Cognates: Gaelic: **Peadar**. Welsh: **Pedr**. French: **Pierre**. Italian: **Pietro**, **Piero**. Spanish: **Pedro**. Catalan: **Pere**. Dutch, Flemish, and Low German: **Piet**. Danish, Norwegian: **Per**. Swedish: **Petter**, **Per**, **Pär** (vernacular forms). Russian: **Pyotr**. Ukrainian: **Petro**. Polish: **Piotr**. Czech: **Petr**. Hungarian: **Péter**. See also KEPA.

Short form (informal): English: **Pete**.

Pet forms: Scottish Gaelic: **Peidearan**. Russian: **Petya**. Czech: **Pét'a**, **Pet'ka**, **Petulka**, **Petunka**, **Petri(če)k**, **Petroušek**.

Feminine forms: Latinate: **Petra**. English (modern): **Peta**. French: **Pierrette**. Italian: **Piera**. Norwegian, Danish: **Petrine**.

Petra (f.) English: modern feminine form of PETER, representing a hypothetical Latin name *Petra*; *petra* is in fact the regular Late Latin word for 'stone' (Greek *petra*), of which *petrus* (see PETER) is a byform.

Petronel (f.) English: from Latin *Petronilla*, originally a feminine diminutive of the Roman family name *Petrōnius* (of uncertain derivation). The name *Petronilla* was borne by a 1st-century martyr, and early in the Christian era came to be connected with PETER, so that in many legends surrounding her she is described as a companion or even the daughter of St Peter.

Variant (Latinate): **Petronella**.

Petula (f.) English: of uncertain origin, not used before the 20th century It is possibly a coinage intended to mean 'supplicant, postulant', from Late Latin *petulāre* to ask, or there may be some connection with the flower name *petunia*. Alternatively, it may be an elaboration of the vocabulary word *pet* used as a term of endearment, with the suffix *-ula* abstracted from names such as *Ursula*.

Short form: **Pet**.

Phelim (m.) Irish: Anglicized form of the old Gaelic name Feidhlim, of obscure derivation. St Phelim or Fidelminus was a 6th-century disciple of St Columba.

Phil (m., f.) English: short form of PHILIP, PHYLLIS, or of any of the various other male and female names beginning with the syllable *Phil-*.

Philbert (m.) English and French (rare): from a Germanic personal name composed of the elements *fila* much + *berht* bright, famous. The first element has later been associated with the Greek name element *phil-* love. St Philibert (*c.*608–84) was a Frankish monk who founded several abbeys.

Philip (m.) English: from the Greek name *Philippos*, composed of the elements *philein* to love + *hippos* horse, which was popular in the classical period and after. It was the name of the father of Alexander the Great. It was also the name of one of Christ's apostles, of a deacon ordained by the apostles after the death of Christ, and of several other early saints. The spelling Phillip is sometimes used, although not etymologically justified; it is in part a result of the influence of the English surname *Phillips*, which is generally spelt with *-ll-*.

Cognates: Irish Gaelic: **Pilib**. Scottish Gaelic: **Filib**. French: **Philippe**. Italian: **Filippo**. Spanish: **Felipe**. Catalan: **Felip**. German: **Philipp**. Polish, Czech, Scandinavian: **Filip**. Hungarian: **Fülöp**. Finnish: **Vilppu**.

Short forms: English: **Phil**, **Pip**.

Feminine form: PHILIPPA.

Philippa (f.) English and German: Latinate feminine form of PHILIP. In England during the Middle Ages the vernacular name *Philip* was borne by women as well as men, but female bearers were distinguished in Latin records by this form. It was not, however, used as a regular given name until the 19th century.

Variants: **Philipa**, **Phillip(p)a**.

Cognates: Russian: **Filipa**. Finnish: **Hilppa**.

Pet forms: English: **Pippa**. Romanian: **Lipa**.

Philippina (f.) English and German: Latinate elaboration of PHILIPPA. In the Middle Ages it was sometimes interpreted as a compound of Greek *philein* to love + *poinē* pain, punishment, since Christians were supposed to rejoice in purging themselves of their sins by pain and punishment, such as flagellation and the wearing of hairshirts.

Variants: **Philipina**, **Phillip(p)ina**.

Cognate: French: **Philippine** (common as a feminine form of *Philippe* in the Middle Ages, and still occasionally used).

Phillida (f.) English: variant of PHYLLIS, derived from the genitive case (Greek *Phyllidos*, Latin *Phyllidis*) with the addition of the Latin feminine ending -*a*.

Variant: **Phyllida**.

Philo (m.) English and German: from the Late Greek personal name *Philōn*, a derivative of the element *phil-* love, in part as a short form of the various compound names containing this element. The name was borne by a 2nd-century saint, a deacon of St Ignatius.

Philomena (f.) English and German: from the name of an obscure saint (probably of the 3rd century) with a local cult in Italy. In 1527 the bones of a young woman were discovered under the church altar at San Severino near Ancona, together with a Latin inscription declaring them to be the body of St Filomena. Her name seems to be a feminine form of Latin *Philomenus*, from Greek *Philomenēs*, composed of the elements *philein* to love + *menos* strength. The name became popular in the 19th century, as a result of the supposed discovery in 1802 of the relics of another St Philomena in the catacombs at Rome. All the excitement, however, resulted from the misinterpretation of the Latin inscription *Filumena pax tecum* 'peace be with you, beloved' (from Greek *philoumena* beloved).

Phineas (m.) Biblical: name borne by two minor characters. One was a grandson of Aaron, who preserved the purity of the race of Israel and deflected God's wrath by killing an Israelite who had taken a Midianite woman to wife (Numbers 25: 6–15); the other, a son of the priest Eli, was killed in combat with the Philistines over the Ark of the Covenant (1 Samuel 1: 3; 4: 6–11). The name is spelled *Phinehas* in the Authorized Version, and has been taken to mean 'serpent's mouth' (i.e. 'oracle') in Hebrew, but this is an incorrect popular etymology. It is in fact derived from the Egyptian name *Panhsj*, originally a byname meaning 'the Nubian' and used as a personal name in ancient Egypt. *Phineas* was popular among the Puritans in the 17th century, and has been occasionally used since, especially in America. Its variants have long been popular Jewish names.

Variants: Yiddish: **Pinhas**, **Pinchas**.

Phoebe (f.) English: Latinized form of the name of a Greek deity, *Phoibē* (from *phoibos* bright), partially identified with Artemis, goddess of the moon and of hunting, sister of the sun god Apollo, who was also known as *Phoibos* (Latin *Phoebus*).

Phyllis (f.) English and German: name of a minor character in Greek mythology who killed herself for love and was transformed into an almond tree; the Greek word *phyllis* means 'foliage', so clearly her name doomed her from the start.

Pia (f.) English, Italian, Scandinavian and Polish: from the feminine form of Latin *pius* pious, respectful, honourable. The name is common in Italy, and is also regularly used in Eastern Europe and Scandinavia, but is a recent introduction to the English-speaking world.

Piaras (m.) Irish Gaelic: name derived in the early Middle Ages from Anglo-Norman PIERS. Piaras Feiritéar (1600–53) was a Kerry chieftain and poet. In the 20th century *Piaras* has been used as a Gaelic form of the popular nationalist name PEARCE.

Piedad (f.) Spanish: religious name celebrating the quality of piety (Latin *pietās*, a derivative of *pius*; see PIA). The Virgin Mary is honoured under the title *Nuestra Señora de la Piedad* on 5 November.

Pierce (f.) English and Irish: variant of PIERS, in use in Ireland from the time of the Norman Conquest up to the present day. In many cases it may represent a transferred use of the English surname derived from the given name in the Middle Ages.

Pierluigi (m.) Italian: compound name made up of the elements *Piero* (see PIETRO) + LUIGI.

Pierre (m.) French form of PETER.

Pierrette (f.) French: feminine diminutive form of PIERRE, used as a female equivalent of that name.

Piers (m.) English: regular Middle English form of PETER (from the Old French nominative case, as against the oblique *Pier*). In the form PIERCE it survived into the 18th century, although in part this may be a transferred use of the surname derived from the medieval given name. *Piers* was revived in the mid-20th century, perhaps partly under the influence of William Langland's great rambling medieval poem *Piers Plowman* (1367–86), in which the character of Piers symbolizes the virtues of hard work, honesty, and fairness.

Piet (m.) Low German, Dutch, and Flemish form of PETER.

Variant: Dutch: **Pieter**.

Pietari (m.) Finnish: learned form of PETER (cf. PEKKA).

Pietro (m.) Italian form of PETER. The simplified form **Piero** was formerly more common, but has declined in frequency during the present century. The feminine form is **Piera**.

Pilar (f.) Spanish: name referring to a title of the Virgin Mary, *Nuestra Señora del Pilar* 'Our Lady of the Pillar'. The story is that in AD 40 the Virgin appeared, standing on a pillar, to St James the Greater at Saragossa. The vocabulary word *pilar* is masculine, but this has not inhibited its use as a feminine given name.

Pet forms: **Pili** (most commonly found in the combination **Maripili**); **Pilita**, **Piluca**.

Pimen (m.) Russian: from the Greek name *Poimēn* 'shepherd'. The name was a popular one among early Christians because of the New Testament parable of the Good Shepherd and his flock (cf. PASTOR). It was borne in the 5th century by a hermit who lived in the Egyptian desert; he is a saint still greatly venerated in the Eastern Church.

Pet form: **Pima**.

Pinchas (m.) Yiddish form of PHINEAS, still in regular use as a Jewish name.

Variant: **Pinhas**.

Pino (m.) Italian: short form of any of various diminutive given names such as *Filippino*, *Giacoppino*, and *Giuseppino*, derived from *Filippo* (PHILIP), *Giacobbe* (JACOB/JAMES), and *Giuseppe* (JOSEPH) respectively.

Pio (m.) Italian, Spanish, and Portuguese: from Latin *Pius* (see PIA).

Piotr (m.) Polish form of PETER.

Pip (m.) English: contracted short form of PHILIP, best known as the name of the main character in Charles Dickens's *Great Expectations* (1861), whose full name was Philip Pirrip.

Pippa (f.) English: contracted pet form of PHILIPPA, now quite commonly used as an independent given name. It was popularized in the 19th century by Browning's narrative poem *Pippa Passes* (1841), in which the heroine is a child worker in an Italian silk-mill, whose innocent admiration of 'great' people is ironically juxtaposed with their sordid lives. The name is presumably supposed to be Italian, but is not in fact used in Italy.

Pirjo (f.) Finnish form of BRIDGET.

Variant: **Pirkko**.

Pirmin (m.) S. German, Austrian, and Swiss (Romansch): name borne by an 8th-century saint who founded numerous Benedictine monasteries, for example at Amorbach, Murbach, and Reichenau. It seems to be an altered form of FIRMIN.

Placido (m.) Italian, Spanish, and Portuguese: from the Late Latin name *Placidus* 'untroubled'. This name was commonly borne by early Christians, to express their serenity in the faith, and there are several minor saints so called.

Poldi (m.) German (esp. Bavarian): pet form of LUITPOLD.

Polina (f.) Russian: pet form of APOLLINARIA.

Pòlit (m.) Catalan: variant form of *Hipòlit* (see HIPPOLYTE).

Polly (f.) English: variant of MOLLY, now established as a given name in its own right. The reason for the interchange of *M-* and *P-* is not clear; cf. PEGGY.

Short form: **Poll**.

Pompeo (m.) Italian: from the old Roman family name *Pompeius*, of uncertain origin. It is probably derived from an Italic dialectal word for 'five', and so is ultimately a doublet of QUINTUS and PONS. The name was borne by a few early saints, but owes its modern use to revival during the Renaissance, in tribute to the Roman general and statesman Pompey the Great (Gnaeus Pompeius Magnus, 106–48 BC).

Pomuk (m.) Czech: short form of NEPOMUK.

Pons (m.) French: from Latin *Pontius*, originally a family name of uncertain origin. It is probably derived from an Italic dialectal word for 'five', and so is ultimately a doublet of QUINTUS and POMPEO. In spite of its unfortunate association with Pontius Pilate, the Roman procurator of Judea who ordered the crucifixion of Jesus, it came to be used occasionally as

a given name in honour of the cult of St Pons of Cimiez (d. 258).

Cognates: Italian: **Ponzio**. Spanish: **Poncio**. Catalan: **Ponç**.

Poppy (f.) English: from the name of the flower, Old English *popæg* (ultimately from Latin *papāver*). It has been used as a given name since the latter years of the 19th century, and reached a peak of popularity in the 1920s.

Porfirio (m.) Italian and Spanish: from Late Latin *Porphyrius*, Greek *Porphyrios*, a derivative of *porphyra* purple dye (apparently of oriental origin). This name was borne by some half dozen saints of the first centuries AD.

Porick (m.) Irish: Anglicized spelling of Gaelic PÁDRAIG, representing a common pronunciation of that name.

Portia (f.) English: name that occurs twice in the works of Shakespeare, once as the name of the wife of Brutus in *Julius Caesar*. The historical Brutus' wife was called *Porcia*, feminine form of the Roman family name *Porcius*, which is apparently a derivative of Latin *porcus* pig. The main influence on the choice of this given name, however, is undoubtedly the other Shakespearian character of this name, an heiress in *The Merchant of Venice* who, disguised as a man, shows herself to be a brilliant advocate.

Posy (f.) English: pet form (originally a nursery version) of JOSEPHINE. It has also been associated with the vocabulary word *posy* bunch of flowers (originally a collection of verses, from *poesy* poetry), and is occasionally used as an independent given name, fitting into the series of names associated with flowers.

Poul (m.) Danish form of PAUL.

Praskovya (f.) Russian: vernacular form of learned *Paraskeva*, from Late Greek (*megalē*) *paraskeuē* (Good) Friday (from classical Greek *paraskeuē* preparation). A saint of this name is venerated in the Eastern Church as having been martyred in the 1st century, together with Photina, Joseph, Victor, Sebastian, Anatolius, Photius, Photis, and Cyriaca.

Pet form: **Pasha**.

Preben (m.) Danish: from medieval *Pridbjørn*, a reworking (with assimilation to the Scandinavian element *bjørn* bear) of the Slavonic personal name *Pritbor*, composed of the elements *prid* foremost, leading + *bor* battle.

Presentación (f.) Spanish: religious name referring to the feast of the Presentation (Spanish *presentación*, from Late Latin *praesentātio*, a derivative of *praesens* present), commemorating the presentation of the Virgin Mary in the temple at Jerusalem after the birth of Christ. This has been celebrated (on 21 November) since the 5th century in the Eastern Church and since the 7th century in the Western. However, since it is largely based on incidents in the apocryphal 'Book of James', its significance has been played down in modern times.

Short form: **Presen**.

Preston (m.) English: transferred use of the surname, which originated as a local name from any of the numerous places in England named with the Old English elements *prēost* priest + *tūn* enclosure, settlement.

Pribislav (m.) Russian form of PRZYBYSŁAW.

Primitivo (m.) Spanish: from the Late Latin name *Prīmitīvus* 'earliest' (a derivative of *prīmus* first; see PRIMO). The name was borne by various early martyrs, most notably one born at

León in Spain and beheaded *c*.300 together with his companion St Facundus.

Primo (m.) Italian, Spanish, and Portuguese: from the Late Latin name *Prīmus* 'first', borne by four minor early saints.
Cognate: Polish: **Prym**.

Primrose (f.) English: one of the several female names taken from words for flowers in the late 19th century. The word is from Latin *prima rosa* first rose, although it does not in fact have any connection with the rose family and does not bloom particularly early.

Prince (m.) English: originally a nickname from the royal title. The Old French title *prince* (Latin *princeps*, from *primus* first + *capere* to take, i.e. one who took the first place) was introduced to Britain by the Normans; before the Conquest young members of the royal house had been known as *æðelingas* (from Old English *æðel* noble). As a given name, *Prince* is common among Blacks in America; it was often bestowed on slaves with cruel irony, but has been perpetuated by their descendants with pride.

Prisca (f.) Of New Testament origin: feminine form of the Roman family name *Priscus* (originally a nickname meaning 'ancient'). Prisca (2 Timothy 4: 19) and Priscilla (Acts 18: 3) are apparently the same person, but it is the diminutive form which became established as a common given name.

Priscilla (f.) Of New Testament origin: from a post-classical Latin personal name, a feminine diminutive of the Roman family name *Priscus* (see PRISCA). *Priscilla* was the name of a woman with whom St Paul stayed at Corinth (Acts 18: 3), referred to elsewhere as *Prisca*. The name was popular among the Puritans in the 17th century and again enjoyed a vogue in the 19th century.

Proinséas (f.) Irish Gaelic form of FRANCES.

Proinsias (m.) Irish Gaelic form of FRANCIS.

Prokhor (m.) Russian: from Greek *Prokhoros*, originally a name given to the leader of a troupe of singers and dancers (from *pro* before, ahead + *khorein* to sing, dance). St Prochorus was one of the seven deacons ordained by the apostles (Acts 6: 5); according to tradition, he later went on to become bishop of Nicomedia and was martyred at Antioch.
Pet forms: **Pronya**, **Prosha**.

Prokopi (m.) Russian: from Greek *Prokopios*, a derivative of *prokopē* success, progress, prosperity (from *pro* before, ahead + *koptein* to cut, hit). The name was borne by the first victim of the Diocletianic persecution in Palestine (beheaded at Caesarea Maritima in 303), and later by the founder (*c*.980–1053) of the Sabaza abbey in Prague.
Variant: **Prokofi** (vernacular form).
Cognate: Polish, Czech: **Prokop**.
Pet forms: Russian: **Pronya**, **Prosha**.

Prosper (m.) French and English: from the Latin name *Prosperus*, derived from the adjective *prosper* fortunate, prosperous (originally 'according to one's wishes', Latin *pro spe*). This was the name of various early saints, including a 5th-century theologian and contemporaneous bishops of Orléans and Reggio. It was a favourite among the English Puritans, partly because of its association with the English vocabulary word *prosper*, but is now rare. In France it is best known as the given name of the writer Prosper Mérimée (1803–70).
Cognate: Italian, Spanish, and Portuguese: PROSPERO.

Prospero (m.) Italian, Spanish, and Portuguese form of PROSPER. This form of the name was used by Shakespeare for the central figure of the magician and Duke of Milan in *The Tempest*, and for this reason it has very occasionally been adopted in the English-speaking world.

Prudence (f.) English: originally a medieval form of the Latin name *Prūdentia*, a feminine form of *Prūdentius*, from *prūdens* provident. The Blessed Prudentia was a 15th-century abbess who founded a new convent at Como in Italy. Later, among the Puritans in 17th-century England, *Prudence* was used as a quality name, taken from the vocabulary word.
Short forms: **Prue**, **Pru**.

Prudencio (m.) Spanish and Portuguese: from Late Latin *Prūdentius*, a derivative of *prūdens* provident, prudent. *Prudentius* was the name of two Spanish saints. One, who lived in the 8th century, was born at Armentia in the province of Álava and became bishop of Tarazona in Aragon. The second (d. 861) was originally called Galindo, but changed his name to Prudentius when he moved to France to escape the Moors; he eventually became bishop of Troyes.
Cognate: Italian: **Prudenzio**.

Prunella (f.) English: Latinate name, probably one of the names coined in the 19th century from vocabulary words for plants and flowers, in this case from a diminutive derived from Late Latin *pruna* plum. The name has enjoyed a minor vogue in the latter part of the 20th century, and is borne by two well-known English actresses, Prunella Scales and Prunella Gee.
Short forms: **Prue**, **Pru**.

Pryderi (m.) Welsh: traditional name meaning 'caring for' (later 'anxiety'). It is borne in the *Mabinogi* by Pryderi, son of Pwyll, who makes several appearances in the narrative.

Prym (m.) Polish form of PRIMO.

Przemysł (m.) Polish: originally a byname from an Old Polish noun meaning 'trick, stratagem', given to a cunning person. This name was borne by two Polish kings of the Middle Ages, Przemysl I (?1220–57) and Przemysl II (1257–96).
Cognate: Czech: **Přemysl**.
Pet forms: Polish: **Przemko**. Czech: **Přem(ouš)ek**, **Myslík**.

Przybysław (m.) Polish: from an old Slavonic personal name composed of the elements *pribit* to be present, help + *slav* glory.
Cognates: Czech: **Přibislav**. Russian: **Pribislav**.
Feminine form: Czech: **Přibislava**.
Pet forms: Czech: **Přiba**, **Přibík**, **Přibišek** (m.); **Přibka**, **Přibena**, **Přibuška** (f.).

Purificación (f.) Spanish: Marian name, taken in honour of the feast of the Purification (Spanish *purificación*, from Late Latin *purificātio*, a derivative of *purus* pure + *facere* to make). This feast is celebrated on 2 February, and commemorates the day when, in accordance with Jewish law, the Virgin Mary took her son Jesus to the temple for the first time to present him to God and be herself purged of the uncleanliness associated with childbirth.
Short form: **Pura**.
Pet form: **Purita**.

Pusha (m.) Russian: pet form of *Pavel* (see PAUL).

Pyotr (m.) Russian form of PETER.

Q

Queenie (f.) English: from the affectionate nickname *Queen* (going back to Old English *cwēn*, related to *cwene* woman, re-spelled as if derived from Latin), with the addition of the hypocoristic suffix *-ie* (originally characteristic of northern England and Scotland). In the Victorian era it was sometimes used as an allusive pet form for VICTORIA. As a Jewish name it represents an Anglicized form of MALKAH.

Quentin (m.) English and French: from the Old French form of the Latin name *Quintīnus*, a derivative of the given name QUINTUS. The name was borne by a 3rd-century saint who worked as a missionary in Gaul.

Variants: English: **Quintin**, QUINTON.
Cognates: Scottish Gaelic: **Caointean**, **Caoidhean**.

Quincy (m.) English (chiefly U.S.): transferred use of the surname, originally a Norman baronial name borne by the family that held lands at *Cuinchy* in Pasde-Calais, Normandy, so called from the Gallo-Roman personal name QUINTUS and the local suffix *-ācum*. This was the surname of a prominent New England family in the colonial era. Josiah Quincy (1744–75) was a lawyer and Revolutionary patriot, a close friend of John Adams (1735–1826), who became second president of the United States (1797–1801). The latter's son, John Quincy Adams (1767–1848), also served as president (1825–9). He may have received his middle name in honour of his father's Josiah Quincy, or it may have been taken from the township of Quincy, Massachusetts, where he was born and where the Adams family had their seat.

Variant: **Quincey**.

Quinton (m.) English: variant of QUENTIN, influenced by the surname of this form, which originated in the Middle Ages as a local name from any of several places named with the Old English vocabulary elements *cwēn* queen + *tūn* enclosure, settlement.

Quintus (m.) English: an old Roman given name meaning 'fifth'. It has been used in the English-speaking world, mainly in the 19th century, for the fifth-born son or male fifth-born child in a family (cf. SEXTUS, SEPTIMUS, OCTAVIUS, and NONA).

Quique (m.) Spanish: pet form of ENRIQUE.

Quirce (m.) Spanish: from Latin *Quiricus*, which apparently represents a variant of *Cyriācus* (see CIRIACO), crossed with *Quirīnus* (see CORIN). The name was borne by a 3-year-old boy martyred at Tarsus in 304 together with his mother Julitta.

Cognate: Catalan: **Quire**.

Quirino (m.) Italian: from Latin *Quirīnus* (see CORIN).

R

Rabbie (m.) Scottish: pet form of ROBERT, from the short form *Rab*, *Rob*. It is now often associated with the poet Robert Burns (1759–96).

Rachel (f.) English, French, and German: biblical name meaning 'ewe' in Hebrew. This was borne by the beloved wife of Jacob and mother (after long barrenness) of Joseph (Genesis 28–35) and of Benjamin, at whose birth she died. In the Middle Ages and later this was a characteristically Jewish name. It is still extremely popular among Jews, but is now widely used among Gentiles as well. In Scotland it has long been used as an Anglicized form of *Raghnaid* (see RAGHNAILT).

Variants: English: RACHELLE; **Rachael** (apparently by association with MICHAEL).
Cognates: Spanish: RAQUEL. Italian: **Rachele**. Scandinavian: **Rakel**.

Rachelle (f.) English: elaborated form of RACHEL, as if from French, but actually a recent coinage in English. The French form of the name is also *Rachel*, but this is not very common.

Racław (m.) Polish: contracted form of RADOSŁAW.

Rada (f.) Slavonic: short form of various female compound names containing the vocabulary element *rad* glad, as for example *Radostława* (see RADOSŁAW).

Radek (m.) Czech: pet form (with the diminutive suffix *-ek*) derived from a short form of any of the various Slavonic compound names containing the element *rad* glad, as for example *Radimír* (see RADZIMIERZ) and *Radoslav* (see RADOSŁAW).
Variants: **Radik**, **Radko**, **Radoš**, **Radan**, **Radeček**, **Radoušek**.

Radosław (m.) Polish: from an old Slavonic personal name composed of the vocabulary elements *rad* glad + *slav* glory.
Cognate: Czech, Russian: **Radoslav**.
Feminine forms: Polish: **Radosawa**. Czech: **Radoslava**.

Radu (m.) Romanian: short form of the various male names of Slavonic origin containing the element *rad* glad (cf. e.g. RADZIMIERZ and RADOSŁAW).

Radzimierz (m.) Polish: from an old Slavonic personal name composed of the elements *rad* glad + *meri* great, famous (see CASIMIR).
Variant: **Radzim**.
Cognates: Czech: **Radimír**, **Radomír**, **Radim**. Russian: **Radimir**.
Feminine form: Czech: **Radomíra**.

Rae (f.) Australian and English: probably originally a short form of RACHEL, but now generally taken as a feminine form of RAY or RAYMOND. It is also possible that in some cases it represents a transferred use of the Scottish surname *Rae*, originally either a short form of *MacRae* (from a Gaelic personal name meaning 'son of grace') or a nickname from the roebuck. It is often used in combinations such as *Rae Ellen and Mary Rae*.

Raelene (f.) Australian: fanciful coinage of recent origin, from RAE + the productive feminine suffix *-lene*.

Rafael (m.) Spanish and Portuguese form (also a German variant) of RAPHAEL.
Pet form: Spanish: **Rafa**.

Rafal (m.) Polish form of RAPHAEL.

Rafe (m.) English: spelling representation of the traditional pronunciation of the name RALPH, a pronunciation now largely restricted to the upper classes in England.

Rafel (m.) Catalan form of RAPHAEL.

Raffaele (m.) Italian form of RAPHAEL.
Variant: **Raffaello**.

Raghnailt (f.) Irish Gaelic: from Norse RAGNHILD. This was a very common woman's given name in medieval Ireland, often rendered in Latin documents as REGINA.
Cognate: Scottish Gaelic: **Raghnaid**.

Raghnall (m.) Irish and Scottish Gaelic: name borrowed from Old Norse *Rögnvaldr* (see RAGNVALD). It is usually Anglicized as *Ronald*, *Ranald*, or *Randal*.
Variant: **Raonull**.

Ragna (f.) Scandinavian: from the Old Norse female personal name *Ragna*, a short form of the various compound names containing the element *regin* advice, decision (also, the gods), as, for example, RAGNBORG and RAGNHILD. The name was used in the Viking period and revived in the late 19th century. In modern use it is to a large extent taken as a feminine form of RAGNAR.

Ragnar (m.) Scandinavian: from an Old Norse personal name cognate with RAYNER.

Ragnborg (f.) Scandinavian: from an Old Norse female personal name composed of the elements *regin* advice, decision (also, the gods) + *borg* fortification. The name was used in the Viking period and revived in the 19th century.
Variant: **Ramborg** (Swedish).

Ragnhild (f.) Scandinavian: from an Old Norse female personal name composed of the elements *regin* advice, decision (also, the gods) + *hildr* battle.
Variant: **Ragnild**.
Cognates: Irish Gaelic: **Raghnailt**. Scottish Gaelic: **Raghnaid**.

Ragnvald (m.) Scandinavian: from the Old Norse personal name *Rögnvaldr*, composed of the elements *regin* advice, decision (also, the gods) + *valdr* ruler. This name is cognate with the West Germanic form REYNOLD. See also RONALD.

Raibeart (m.) Scottish Gaelic form of ROBERT.

Raimondo (m.) Italian form of RAYMOND.

Raimundo (m.) Spanish and Portuguese form of RAYMOND.

Raina (f.) Polish and Czech form of REGINA, also sometimes used in the English-speaking world, to which it was introduced by George Bernard Shaw, as the name of a character in *Arms and the Man* (1894).

Raine (f.) English: of modern origin and uncertain derivation. It is possibly a respelling of the French vocabulary word *reine* queen (cf. REGINA and RAINA), or a transferred use of the surname *Raine* or *Rayne*. The surname is derived from various medieval given names beginning with the Germanic element *ra(g)in* advice, decision. In modern times, this given name is borne by the Countess Spencer, daughter of the romantic novelist Barbara Cartland and stepmother of the Princess of Wales.

Rainer (m.) German form of RAYNER.

Rainerio (m.) Spanish form of RAYNER.

Rainier (m.) French form of RAYNER.

Raisa (f.) Russian: from the Late Greek name *Raisa*, of uncertain derivation. It may be a derivative of *rhaiōn*, comparative of *rhadios* easy-going, adaptable. The name was borne by a Christian martyr executed in 308. It has recently come to prominence as the name of the wife of the Soviet leader Mikhail Gorbachev.

Pet form: **Raya**.

Rakel (f.) Scandinavian form of RACHEL.

Ralph (m.) English: of Norman origin, representing a contracted form of the Germanic name *Radulf*, composed of the elements *rād* counsel + *wulf* wolf. The spelling with *-ph* is the result of classically influenced 'improvement' in the 18th century.

Variants: **Ralf**, **Raff**.
Cognates: French: **Raoul**. Italian: **Raul**. Spanish: **Raúl**.

Ramborg (f.) Swedish: assimilated variant of RAGNBORG.

Ramiro (m.) Spanish: of Germanic (Visigothic) origin. It is probably composed of the elements *ragin* advice, decision + *māri*, *mēri* famous. St Ramirus was a 5th- or 6th-century prior who was martyred at León by the Visigoths, who subscribed to the Arian heresy, which he opposed.

Ramón (m.) Spanish form of RAYMOND. This name is in frequent use in America among people of Hispanic descent, but has not been taken up outside such communities to anything like the same extent as the feminine form RAMONA.

Pet from: **Moncho**.

Ramona (f.) Spanish: feminine form of RAMÓN. This has achieved some popularity in recent decades with non-Hispanic parents in America and, to a lesser extent, in Britain, partly due to the influence of a popular song about a girl called Ramona.

Ramsay (m.) Scottish: transferred use of the Scottish surname, which was originally a local name imported to Scotland from *Ramsey* in Huntingdonshire (so called from Old English *hramsa* wild garlic + *ēg* island). In the 12th century David, brother of King Alexander I of Scotland, was brought up at the English court, and acquired the earldoms of Huntingdon and Northampton. When he succeeded his brother as king, he took many of his retainers and associates with him to Scotland, and some of them took their surnames with them from places in eastern England. This explains why some famous Scottish surnames, such as *Ramsay*, *Lindsay*, *Graham*, etc., are derived from placenames in that part of England. Some of these surnames have in turn gone on to be used as given names.

Variant: **Ramsey**.

Ran (m.) English and Scottish: short form of the various names beginning with this syllable, as, for example, RANDOLF, RANALD, and RANULF.

Ranald (m.) Scottish: Anglicized form of the Gaelic name *Raghnall*, which itself is borrowed from Old Norse *Rögnvaldr* (see RAGNVALD).

Randa (f.) English: short form of MIRANDA. See also RANDY.

Randall (m.) English: a regular medieval form of RANDOLF. This fell out of use, but before it did so gave rise to a surname. Modern use of the given name represents a transferred use of this surname.

Variants: **Randal**, **Randel(l)**, **Randle**.

Randolf (m.) English: of Norman origin, derived from a Germanic personal name composed of the elements *rand* rim, edge (of a shield) + *wulf* wolf.

Variant: **Randolph**.

Randy (m., f.) English (esp. U.S. and Australian): as a male name this originated as a pet form of RANDALL, RANDOLF, or, in some cases, ANDREW. As a female name it may have originated either as a transferred use of the male name or else as a pet form of MIRANDA (cf. RANDA). It is now fairly commonly used as an independent name, mainly by men, in spite of the unfortunate connotations of the slang term *randy* meaning 'lustful'.

Variants: **Randi**, **Randie** (f.).

Raniero (m.) Italian form of RAYNER, a relatively late coinage under French influence.

Short form: NERO.

Ransu (m.) Finnish form of FRANCIS.

Ranulf (m.) Scottish: from an Old Norse personal name, *Reginulfr*, composed of the elements *regin* advice, decision (also, the gods) + *úlfr* wolf. The name was introduced into Scotland by Scandinavian settlers in the early Middle Ages.

Raoul (m.) French form of RALPH, occasionally used in the English-speaking world. The form **Raul** (sometimes pronounced as a single syllable) is either a simplified spelling, or a use of the Italian or Spanish form.

Raphael (m.) English, French, and German: from early Christian tradition, in which it is the name of one of the archangels (see also GABRIEL and MICHAEL). It is composed of Hebrew vocabulary elements meaning 'to heal' and 'God'. Raphael is not named in the canonical text of the Bible, but plays a part in the apocryphal tale of Tobias. The shorter form *Rapha* 'he (God) heals' (cf. NATHANIEL and NATHAN) is borne by several characters in the Old Testament. The name has always been much more common in southern Europe than in Britain, and use in the English-speaking world today generally reflects southern European influence. It has also become a popular modern Hebrew name.

Variant: German: **Rafael**.
Cognates: Italian: **Raffaele**, **Raffaello**. Spanish, Portuguese: **Rafael**. Catalan: **Rafel**. Polish: **Rafal**.
Pet form: Spanish: **Rafa**.

Raquel (f.) Spanish form of RACHEL, brought to public attention by the fame and good looks of the film actress Raquel Welch (b. 1940 as Raquel Tejada, in Chicago). Her father was Bolivian, her mother of English parentage.

Rastus (m.) English: of New Testament origin, where it is a short form of the Latin name *Erastus* (Greek *Erastos*, from *erān* to love). This was the name of the treasurer of Corinth converted to Christianity by St Paul (Romans 16: 23). In the early

20th century *Rastus* came to be regarded as a typically Black name, for reasons which are unclear.

Rathnait (f.) Irish Gaelic: name representing a feminine diminutive form of *rath* grace, prosperity.
Anglicized form: RONIT.

Raúl (m.) Spanish form of RALPH.

Ray (m.) English: short form of RAYMOND, now often used as an independent name. In a few instances it may represent a transferred use of the surname *Ray*, which was normally first acquired as a nickname, from Old French *rei, roi* king (cf. ROY and LEROY).

Raya (f.) Russian: pet form of RAISA.

Raymond (m.) English and French: of Norman origin, derived from a Germanic personal name composed of the elements *ragin* advice, decision + *mund* protector. It dropped out of use, but was revived in the middle of the 19th century, together with several other given names of Anglo-Saxon and Norman Germanic origin.
Cognates: Irish: **Réamann** (Gaelic); **Redmond** (Anglicized). German: **Rei(n)mund**, **Raimund**. Italian: **Raimondo**. Spanish: RAMÓN, **Raimundo**. Portuguese: **Raimundo**.
Short form: English: RAY.
Feminine forms: French, English: **Raymonde** (rare). German: **Raimunde**. Italian: **Raimonda**. Spanish: RAMONA, **Raimunda**.

Rayner (m.) English: of Norman origin, derived from a Germanic personal name composed of the elements *ragin* advice, decision + *heri, hari* army, warrior. As a modern given name it in part represents a transferred use of the surname derived from this given name in the Middle Ages.
Cognates: German: **Rainer**. Scandinavian: **Ragnar**. Danish: **Regner**. French: **Rainier**. Italian: **Raniero**. Spanish: **Rainerio**.

Read (m.) American, Scottish, and English: transferred use of the English surname. In most cases, this originated as a nickname for someone with red hair or a ruddy complexion, from Old English *rēad* red; cf. REID. In other cases, it may have arisen as a local name, from Old English *hrēod* reeds or *rēod* cleared land.

Reanna (f.) English: modern name, apparently an altered form of DEANNA, influenced by the Welsh name RHIANNON. The form **Reanne** is also used.

Rearden (m.) Irish: variant of RIORDAN.

Rebecca (f.) Biblical: from the Latin form of the Hebrew name *Rebekah*, borne by the wife of Isaac, who was the mother of Esau and Jacob (Genesis 24–7). The Hebrew root occurs in the Bible only in the vocabulary word *marbek* cattle stall, and its connection with the name is doubtful. In any case, Rebecca was Aramean, and the name probably has a source in Aramaic. It has always been common among Jews; in England and elsewhere it began to be used also by Christians at the time of the Reformation, when Old Testament names became popular. It was very common among the Puritans in the 17th century, and has enjoyed a further vogue in England in the latter part of the 20th century, among people of many different creeds. In the Scottish Highlands it has been used as an Anglicized form of the Gaelic name *Beathag* (see BEATHAN).
Variants: French: **Rébecca**. Spanish, Portuguese: **Rebeca**. German, Danish, Norwegian: **Rebekka**. Swedish: **Rebecka**. Hebrew: **Rivka**.
Short form: English: **Becca**.
Pet form: English: **Becky**.

Redmond (m.) Irish: apparently an Anglicized form of the Gaelic name **Réamann**, itself a form of RAYMOND. An alternative explanation, which better accounts for the form of the name, derives it from an Old English personal name composed of the elements *rēd* counsel + *mund* protector.

Reenie (f.) English: respelling of *Renée* (see RENÉ), representing the Anglicized pronunciation of the name. It may also occasionally represent a pet form of various names ending in the syllable *-reen*, such as DOREEN and MAUREEN.

Rees (m.) Welsh and English: Anglicized spelling of the Welsh name RHYS, in some cases representing a transferred use of the surname so spelled, which is derived from the Welsh given name.

Refugio (f.) Spanish: religious name referring to the Marian title, *Nuestra Señora de Refugio* 'Our Lady of Refuge'.
Pet form: **Fucho**.

Reg (m.) English: short form of REGINALD, often preferred by bearers of that name for use in almost all situations, but rarely actually bestowed as a baptismal name.

Regan (f.) English: apparently of Shakespearian origin. This is the name of one of the three daughters in *King Lear* (1605), a most unattractive character, who flatters her father into giving her half his kingdom and then turns him out into a raging storm at night. It is not known where Shakespeare got the name; he presumably believed it to be of Celtic origin. Modern use has been reinforced by the Irish surname *Re(a)gan* (Gaelic *Ó Riagáin*).

Reggie (m.) English: pet form of REG, common in the 19th and early 20th century, but now less so.

Regina (f.) English: from the Latin nickname meaning 'queen'. It seems to have been occasionally used among early Christians; a St Regina, probably of the 3rd century, was venerated as a virgin martyr at Autun from an early date. In modern use it is normally borne by Roman Catholics in allusion to the Marian epithet *Regina Coeli* 'Queen of Heaven', a cult title since the 8th century. In Ireland it has sometimes also been used as a Latinized form of RAGHNAILT and RIONA.

Reginald (m.) English: of Norman origin, derived from *Reginaldus*, a Latinized form of REYNOLD influenced by Latin *regina* queen. It is now regarded as very formal, and bearers generally shorten it to REG in ordinary usage.

Régine (f.) French form of REGINA.

Régis (m.) French: name given in honour of St Jean-François Régis (d. 1640) of Narbonne, who strove to reform prostitutes. His surname derives from an Old Provençal word meaning 'ruler'.

Regner (m.) Danish: variant of RAGNAR.

Regula (f.) Mainly Swiss: from Latin *rēgula* rule (of conduct), adopted as a name by early Christians in their zeal for following the precepts laid down by Christ. It was borne by a 3rd-century saint who was martyred near Zurich, together with her brother Felix. She is the patron saint of Zurich.

Řehoř (m.) Czech form of GREGORY.
Pet forms: **Řehořek, Řehůrek, Řehák; Hořek, Hořík**.

Reid (m.) Scottish and N. English: transferred use of the surname, which originated as a nickname for someone with red hair or a ruddy complexion (from Old English *rēad* red; cf. READ).

Reijo (m.) Finnish form of GREGORY.

Reine (f., m.) **1**. (f.) French: vernacular descendant of Latin *rēgina* queen (cf. RÉGINE), probably arising for the most part from a medieval affectionate nickname. **2**. (m.) Swedish: short form of the (originally German) given names REINHARD and REINHOLD.

Reinhard (m.) German form of REYNARD.

Reinhold (m.) German form of REYNOLD.

Reinmund (m.) German form of RAYMOND.
Variants: **Reimund**, **Raimund**.

Reisel (f.) Jewish: Yiddish pet form of **Reise**, itself a Yiddish form of ROSE.
Variant: **Reisl**.

Rella (f.) Jewish: from Yiddish **Rele**, originally a pet form of either RACHEL, REBECCA, or REISEL, but now used as an independent given name.

Rema (m.) Russian: pet form of YEFREM.

Remedios (f.) Spanish: religious name from a title of the Virgin Mary, *Nuestra Señora de los Remedios*, referring to her promised intervention to relieve the suffering of those who pray to her (from Spanish *remedio* remedy, relief, help, from Latin *remedium* cure, remedy, a derivative of *(re)medēre* to cure, restore to health).

Reményke (f.) Hungarian: loan translation of the Russian name NADEZHDA, from Hungarian *remény* hope.

Remus (m.) English: the name, according to ancient Roman tradition, of the brother of Romulus, co-founder with him of the city of Rome. In America this rare given name is associated particularly with the 'Uncle Remus' stories of Joel Chandler Harris (1848–1908), Uncle Remus being a Black who is the narrator of the stories.
Italian form: **Remo** (much less common than ROMOLO).

Rémy (m.) French: from Latin *Rēmigius*, a derivative of *rēmex* (genitive *rēmigis*) oarsman (from *rēmus* oar + *agere* to ply, work). The name was borne by a 6th-century bishop of Rheims who was responsible for the conversion and baptism of Clovis, king of the Franks, and also by an 8th-century bishop of Rouen, the latter being an illegitimate son of King Charles Martel (grandfather of Charlemagne). There has been some confusion with the name *Remedius* (from Latin *(re)medēre* to heal; cf. REMEDIOS), borne by an early bishop of Gap in the French Alps.
Cognates: Italian, Spanish, Portuguese: **Remigio**.

Rena (f.) English: of recent origin, either an altered form of *Renée* (see RENÉ) or else a variant spelling of RINA.

Renata (f.) The original Latin form of *Renée* (see RENÉ). This form of the name is now common in Italy (although it was seldom used there until the mid-19th century), and it is also used in Germany (beside *Renate*), Poland, and Czechoslovakia.

René (m.) French: from the Late Latin name *Renātus* 'reborn', used by early Christians as a baptismal name celebrating spiritual rebirth in Christ. The feminine form is generally commoner than the masculine, especially in Britain.

Cognates: Italian, Spanish, Portuguese: **Renato**. Catalan: **Renat**.
Feminine forms: French and English: **Renée**. Italian, English, German, Polish, and Czech: RENATA. German: **Renate**.

Resi (f.) German: pet form of *Theresia*; see THERESA.
Variants: **Reser** (S. Germany); **Resli** (Switzerland).

Reto (m.) Swiss: originally an ethnic name for someone from the region of *R(h)aetia* in east Switzerland, so called from its original occupaton by a Celtic tribe called the *R(h)aeti*.

Reuben (m.) Biblical: Hebrew name borne by one of the twelve sons of Jacob, and so the name of one of the twelve tribes of Israel. It is said to mean 'behold, a son' in Hebrew. Genesis 29: 32 explains it as follows: 'and Leah conceived, and bare a son, and she called his name Reuben: for she said, Surely the Lord hath looked upon my affliction: now therefore my husband will love me'. In Genesis 30: 14–15, Reuben is depicted as a devoted son to his mother, but he incurred his father's wrath for seducing his concubine Bilhah and on his deathbed Jacob, rather than blessing him, cursed Reuben because of this incident (Genesis 49: 4). Despite this, the name has enjoyed popularity among Jews. Among Christians the name experienced something of a vogue at the Reformation, and again in the 19th century, but it is out of fashion at present.
Variant (esp. Jewish): **Reuven**.
Cognates: Spanish: **Rubén**. Scandinavian: **Ruben**. Finnish: **Ruupeni**, **Ruuppo**.
Short form (informal): U.S.: **Rube**.

Reuel (m.) Biblical: name (meaning 'friend of God' in Hebrew) borne by a character mentioned in a genealogy (2 Chronicles 9: 8).

Rex (m.) English: from Latin *rex* king. This was not used as a personal name in Latin of the classical or Christian periods, and its adoption as a given name seems to have been a 19th-century innovation.

Rexanne (f.) English: apparently an altered form of ROXANE, based on the male given name REX.

Reynard (m.) English: of Norman origin, derived from a Germanic personal name composed of the elements *ragin* advice, decision + *hard* hardy, brave, strong. In French, *renard* (derived from this name) has become the generic name for a fox, as a result of the popularity of medieval beast tales featuring *Re(y)nard le goupil* 'Reynard the fox'.
Cognate: German: **Reinhard**.

Reynold (m.) English: of Norman origin, derived from a Germanic personal name composed of the elements *ragin* advice, decision + *wald* ruler.
Variant: REGINALD. See also RONALD.
Cognates: Welsh: **Rheinallt**. French: **Reynaud**. Italian: **Rinaldo**. German: **Reinhold**. See also RAGNVALD.

Rezsö (m.) Hungarian form of RUDOLF.

Rhea (f.) The name borne, according to ancient Roman tradition, by the mother (Rhea Silvia) of Romulus and Remus, who grew up to be the founders of the city of Rome. It was also a title of the goddess Cybele, introduced to Rome from Phrygia, and its meaning is quite obscure. It is comparatively rarely used as a given name in the modern world.

Rheanna (f.) English: apparently an elaboration of RHEA, perhaps influenced by the names DEANNA and RHIANNON.

Rheinallt (m.) Welsh form of REYNOLD.

Rhett (m.) American English: transferred use of an American surname derived from Dutch *de Raedt*, from Middle Dutch *raet* advice. It was invented for the character of Rhett Butler in Margaret Mitchell's *Gone with the Wind* (1936). Like some of the other names in that novel (cf. ASHLEY, CAREEN, and SCARLETT), it has attained a modest currency in the real world.

Feminine: **Rhetta** (a recent coinage).

Rhiannon (f.) Welsh: name borne in Celtic mythology by a minor deity associated with the moon, and in the *Mabinogi* by a daughter of Hyfeidd the Old. It is probably derived from the Old Celtic title *Rigantona* 'great queen'; it was not used as a given name before the 20th century.

Rhisiart (m.) Welsh form of RICHARD.

Rhoda (f.) English: from the post-classical Greek name *Rhoda*, derived either directly from *rhodon* rose, or else indirectly as an ethnic name meaning 'woman from Rhodes', an island which possibly originally got its name from the same word *rhodon*. In the New Testament Rhoda was a servant in the house of Mary the mother of John, where Peter went after his release from prison by an angel (Acts 12: 13). In the Scottish Highlands *Rhoda* appears to be used as a feminine form of RODERICK.

Rhodri (m.) Welsh: from an Old Welsh personal name composed of the elements *rhod* wheel + *rhi* ruler, borne by a 9th-century Welsh king.

Rhona (f.) Scottish and English: of uncertain derivation, apparently originating in Scotland sometime around 1870. The spelling **Rona** is also found, and it is probable that the name was devised as a feminine form of RONALD or an Anglicized form of *Raghnaid* (see RAGNHILD). It has also been suggested that it may be associated with the Hebridean island name *Rona* (cf. AILSA, IONA, ISLA); the spelling would then have been altered by association with RHODA.

Rhonda (f.) English: of recent origin, apparently a blend of RHODA and RHONA. It is now generally taken to be a Welsh name composed of the elements *rhon* pike, lance, as in RHONWEN, + -*da* good, as in GLENDA. The *Rhondda* valley in South Wales was probably also a factor in making this connection, although it derives from a river name of completely different etymology.

Rhonwen (f.) Welsh: traditional name composed either of the elements *rhon* lance + *(g)wen* white, fair, blessed, holy or of *rhawn* hair + *(g)wen*. It was used by medieval Welsh poets as a form of ROWENA, regarded as the progenitrix of the English nation, and is now fairly common in Wales.

Rhydderch (m.) Welsh: traditional name, originally a by-name meaning 'reddishbrown'. This was a relatively common name in the Middle Ages and in Tudor times, when it gave rise to the surname *Prothero(e)* (Welsh *ap Rhydderch* 'son of Rhydderch'). It has recently been revived by parents proudly conscious of their Welsh roots and culture.

Anglicized form: RODERICK.

Rhys (m.) Welsh: traditional name meaning 'ardour'. The name was borne in the early Middle Ages by various rulers in south-west Wales, such as Rhys ap Tewdur (d. 1093) and Rhys ap Gruffudd (1132–97).

Anglicized form: REES.

Ria (f.) Short form of MARIA, of German origin but now also used occasionally in the English-speaking world.

Rich (m.) English: short form of RICHARD. There was a medieval name *Rich(e)*, but it is connected only indirectly with the modern form: it represents a short form of several medieval names, including not only *Richard* but also other, rarer names of Norman (Germanic) origin with the same first element, as, for example, *Rich(i)er* 'power army' and *Richaud* 'power rule'. It also came to be used as an independent baptismal name in the 15th century.

Richard (m.) English, French, German, and Czech: one of the most enduringly successful of the Germanic personal names introduced into Britain by the Normans. It is composed of the elements *rīc* power + *hard* hardy, brave, strong. It has enjoyed continuous popularity in England from the Conquest to the present day, strongly influenced by the fact that it was borne by three kings of England, in particular Richard I (1157–99). He was king for only ten years (1189–99), most of which he spent in warfare abroad, costing the people of England considerable sums in taxes. Nevertheless, he achieved the status of a folk hero, and was never in England long enough to disappoint popular faith in his goodness and justice. He was also Duke of Aquitaine and Normandy and Count of Anjou, fiefs which he held at a time of maximum English expansion in France. His exploits as a leader of the Third Crusade earned him the nickname 'Cœur de Lion' or 'Lion-heart' and a permanent place in popular imagination, in which he was even more firmly enshrined by Sir Walter Scott's novel *Ivanhoe* (1820).

Cognates: Irish Gaelic: **Ristéard**. Scottish Gaelic: **Ruiseart**. Welsh: **Rhisiart**. Italian: **Riccardo**. Spanish: **Ricardo**. Low German: **Ri(c)kert**. Scandinavian: **Rikard**. Polish: **Ryszard**.
Short forms: English: **Rick**, DICK, RICH.
Pet forms: English: **Ricky**, **Rickie**; **Dicky**, **Dickie**; RICHIE.
Feminine form: **Ricarda** (Latinate, used mainly in Germany).

Richie (m.) Scottish, English, and Australian: pet form of RICHARD. The suffix -*ie* was originally characteristic of Scotland and northern England, but the name is now found elsewhere. In some cases it represents a transferred use of the surname derived from the Scottish pet name.

Variant: **Ritchie** (probably also a transferred use of the surname spelled thus).

Ridley (m.) English: transferred use of the surname, originally a local name from any of various places, in Essex, Kent, Cheshire, Northumbria, and elsewhere. The first two are so called from Old English *hrēod* reeds + *lēah* wood or clearing, the latter two from *rydde* cleared land + *lēah*. The given name may have been chosen in some cases by ardent Protestants to express admiration for Bishop Nicholas Ridley (?1500–55), burnt at the stake for his Protestantism under Mary Tudor.

Riel (m.) Czech: short form of GABRIEL.

Rieti (m.) Finnish form of FREDERICK.

Rigborg (f.) Danish: from an Old High German female personal name composed of the elements *rīc* power + *burg* fortification.

Rigmor (f.) Scandinavian (Danish): from an Old High German female personal name composed of the elements *rīc* power + *muot* spirit, courage. The second element has been replaced by the Scandinavian form *mār* maid.

Rikard (m.) Scandinavian form of RICHARD.

Rike (f.) German: short form of any of the various female names ending thus, for example FRIEDERIKE, *Heinrike* (see HEINRICH), and ULRIKE.

Rikki (f.) English: feminine form of *Ricky* or *Rickie* (pet forms of *Rick*, a short form of RICHARD), modelled on NIKKI and *Vikki* (see VICKY).

Riley (m.) English: in some cases a transferred use of the English surname, originally a local name from a place named with the Old English elements *ryge* rye + *lēah* clearing, meadow. There is one such place in Devon and another in Lancashire. In other cases it probably represents a respelling of the Irish surname *Reilly*, which is from an old Irish personal name, *Raghallach*, of unknown origin.

Rina (f.) English: short form of any of the various female names ending in these syllables or Anglicized form of Irish RÍONA.

Rinaldo (m.) Italian form of REYNOLD.

Ríona (f.) Irish Gaelic: a simplified form of **Rionach**, earlier *Ríoghnach*, which is probably a derivative of *rioghan* queen (cf. RHIANNON). It is now also commonly used as a short form of CAITRÍONA.

Riordan (m.) Irish: Anglicized form of the Gaelic name **Rórdán**, earlier *Ríoghbhardán*, composed of the elements *ríogh* king + a diminutive form of *bard* poet.

Variant: **Rearden**.

Riška (f.) Czech: short form of *Bedřiška* (see BEDŘICH) and *Oldřiška* (see OLDŘICH), used as a pet name.

Ristéard (m.) Irish Gaelic form of RICHARD.

Risto (m.) Finnish form of CHRISTOPHER.

Rita (f.) English and Scandinavian: originally a short form of *Margarita*, the Spanish form of MARGARET, or of *Margherita*, the Italian form. This short form is much more common in England and America than either of the full versions.

Rivka (f.) Jewish: Hebrew form of REBECCA.

Roald (m.) Norwegian: from an Old Norse personal name composed of the elements *hrǫðr* fame + *valdr* ruler.

Roar (m.) Scandinavian form of ROGER.

Robert (m.) English, Scottish, and French (also Scandinavian): one of the many French names of Germanic origin that were introduced into Britain by the Normans. This one is composed of the nearly synonymous elements *hrod* fame + *berht* bright, famous. It had a native Old English predecessor of similar form (*Hreodbeorht*), which was supplanted by the Norman name. It was the name of two dukes of Normandy in the 11th century: the father of William the Conqueror (sometimes identified with the legendary Robert the Devil), and his eldest son. It was borne by three kings of Scotland, notably Robert the Bruce (1274–1329), who freed Scotland from English domination. The altered short form *Bob* is very common, but *Hob* and *Dob*, which were common in the Middle Ages and gave rise to surnames, are extinct. See also RUPERT.

Cognates: Scottish Gaelic: **Raibeart**. Irish Gaelic **Roibéard**. Italian, Spanish, Portuguese: **Roberto**. German: **Rupprecht**. Low German (also English): RUPERT.

Short forms: English: **Bob**, **Rob**. Scottish: **Rob**, **Rab**.

Pet forms: English: **Bobby**, **Robbie**, ROBIN.

Scottish: **Robbie**, **Rabbie**; **Roban** (Gaelic).

Feminine form: English: **Roberta**.

Robin (m., f.) English: originally a pet form of ROBERT, from the short form *Rob* and the diminutive suffix *-in* (of Old French

origin), but now nearly always used as an independent name. In recent years it has been increasingly used as a female name, no doubt partly influenced by the vocabulary word for the bird.

Variant: **Robyn** (f.).

Rocco (m.) Italian: of Germanic origin, derived from the element *hrok* rest. The name was borne by a 14th-century saint, a Frenchman from Montpelier who was on a pilgrimage to Rome when he encountered plague victims in north Italy. He stopped to nurse them, and went from place to place ministering to these unfortunates in many cities. Eventually, at Piacenza, he too was stricken. In his extremity he was comforted by the companionship of a dog (hence his representation in paintings as accompanied by a dog). He is said to have recovered and returned home, but was not recognized by his family and died in prison. He is a patron saint of the sick and his aid is invoked by Roman Catholics against illness.

Cognates: French: **Roch**. Spanish and Portuguese: **Roque**. Catalan: **Roc**.

Rochelle (f.) U.S., French, and English: either a feminine diminutive form of *Roch* (see ROCCO), or else derived from the French fishing port of La Rochelle on the Atlantic coast, which was a stronghold of Protestantism in the 16th and 17th centuries. The given name is little used in France but common in the United States, especially among Blacks. The American name may in part represent a respelling of RACHELLE.

Rocío (f.) Spanish: from a title of the Virgin Mary, *Maria de la Rocío* 'Mary of the Dew' (Spanish *rocío*, from Late Latin *roscidum*, an adjectival derivative of *ros* dew). Dew is closely associated with Mary, and is sometimes symbolically connected in Roman Catholic hagiography with the tears which she sheds for the wickedness of the world.

Rocky (m.) English: of recent American origin, originally a nickname for a tough individual. The name came to public notice through the American heavyweight boxing champion Rocky Marciano (1923–69). He was of Italian extraction, and Anglicized his original name, ROCCO, into a form that seems particularly appropriate for a fighter. It was later taken up in a film as the name of a boxer played by the muscular actor Sylvester Stallone, and it has also been adopted as a nickname among devotees of body-building.

Rod (m.) English: short form of RODERICK and RODNEY.

Pet form: **Roddy**.

Roderick (m.) English: of Germanic origin, composed of the elements *hrōd* fame + *rīc* power. This name was introduced into England in slightly different forms, first by Scandinavian settlers in the Danelaw and later by the Normans. However, it did not survive beyond the Middle English period. It owes its modern use to a poem by Sir Walter Scott, *The Vision of Don Roderick* (1811), where it is an Anglicized form of the cognate Spanish name RODRIGO, borne by the last Visigothic king of Spain, whose vision is the subject of the poem. It is now also very commonly used as an Anglicized form of two unrelated Celtic names: Scottish Gaelic *Ruairidh* (see RUAIDHRÍ) and Welsh RHYDDERCH. See also RURIK.

Pet form: Scottish: **Roddy**.

Feminine forms: Scottish (Highland): **Rodina**, **Rhoda**.

Rodion (m.) Russian: from a short form of the Greek name *Hērōdion*, a diminutive form of *Hērōdēs*, itself a derivative (originally patronymic in form) of *Hēra*, the name of a

Greek goddess, wife of Zeus. The name *Herodion* was borne by a kinsman of St Paul mentioned in the New Testament (Romans 16: 11). According to post-biblical tradition he became bishop of Patras and met a martyr's death.

Pet form: **Rodya**.

Rodney (m.) English: originally a transferred use of the surname, but in independent use as a given name since the 18th century, when it was bestowed in honour of Admiral Lord Rodney (1719–92), who soundly defeated the French navy in 1759–60. The surname probably derives ultimately from a placename, but the location and etymology of this are uncertain. Stoke Rodney in Somerset is probably named from the surname: the manor was held by one Richard de *Rodene* in the early 14th century.

Rodolf (m.) German and Dutch: variant of RUDOLF.

Rodolfo (m.) Italian and Spanish form of RUDOLF.

Rodolphe (m.) French form of RUDOLF.

Rodrigo (m.) Spanish: of Germanic (Visigothic) origin, composed of the elements *hrōd* fame and *rīc* power, and so a cognate of RODERICK, which represents an Anglicized form of it. It was the name of the last king of the Visigoths, who was defeated by the Moors in 711, and of a saint martyred under the Moors at Cordoba in 857. It is now sometimes used in the English-speaking world, but mainly in families of Hispanic descent.

Pet form: **Ruy**.

Rodya (m.) Russian: pet form of RODION.

Roelof (m.) Dutch: vernacular form of RODOLF.

Rogelio (m.) Spanish: from Late Latin *Rogelius* (or *Rogellus*), a name of uncertain derivation. It may be a diminutive form of *Rogātus* 'requested, prayed for'. Sts Rogellus and Servus-Dei were martyred at Cordoba under the Moors in 852.

Roger (m.) English and French: of Germanic origin, composed of the elements *hrōd* fame + *gār*, *gēr* spear. This, the Continental Germanic form, was introduced to Britain by the Normans, replacing the native Old English cognate *Hrōðgār* (see HROTHGAR). Roger, Count of Sicily (c.1031–1101), son of Tancred, recovered Sicily from the Arabs. His son, also called Roger, ruled Sicily as king, presiding over a court noted for its splendour and patronage of the arts.

In modern English usage, the informal short form **Rodge** is occasionally encountered, but the medieval short forms *Hodge* and *Dodge* are extinct.

Variant: English: **Rodger**.
Cognates: Italian: **Rugg(i)ero**. Spanish: **Rogerio**. German: **Rüdiger**. Low German: **Rötger**. Dutch: **Rutger**. Scandinavian: **Roar**.

Roibéard (m.) Irish Gaelic form of ROBERT.

Róisín (f.) Irish Gaelic: pet form of **Róis**, itself the Gaelic form of ROSE.
Variant: **Rosheen** (Anglicized).

Roland (m.) English and French, also German and Scandinavian: derived from a Germanic personal name composed of the elements *hrōd* fame + *land* land, territory. The name was introduced to Britain by the Normans. It was borne by a legendary Frankish hero, a vassal of Charlemagne, whose exploits are related in the *Chanson de Roland*. The subject of the poem is Roland's death at the Battle of Roncesvalles in the Pyrenees in 778, while protecting the rearguard of the

Frankish army on its retreat from Spain. Roland is depicted in literature and legend as headstrong and impulsive. His devoted friendship with the prudent Oliver is also legendary. In Italian literature he appears as ORLANDO.

Variant: English: **Rowland**.
Cognates: Welsh: **Rolant**. Italian: ORLANDO. Spanish: **Roldán**. Portuguese: **Roldao**. Hungarian: **Loránd**.
Feminine form: French and English: **Rolande** (rare).

Rolf (m.) English, German, and Scandinavian: a contracted version of an old Germanic personal name composed of the elements *hrōd* fame + *wulf* wolf. This is found in Old Norse as *Hrólfr*. As an English name, it represents in part a Norman importation of a Continental Germanic form, in part a much more recent (19th-century) importation of the modern German name. See also RUDOLF.

Rollo (m.) Latinized form of *Roul*, the Old French version of ROLF (cf. *Raoul* for *Ralph*). This form appears regularly in Latin documents of the Middle Ages, but does not seem to have been used in everyday vernacular contexts. It is the form by which the first Duke of Normandy (c.860–932) is generally known. He was a Viking who, with his followers, settled at the mouth of the Seine and raided Paris, Chartres, and elsewhere. By the treaty of St Clair he received the duchy of Normandy from Charles III, on condition that he should receive Christian baptism. Use of this name in English families in modern times seems to be a consciously archaistic revival.

Roly (m.) English: pet form of ROLAND. See also ROWLEY.

Roman (m.) Russian, Polish, and Czech: from the Late Latin personal name *Rōmānus*, originally an ethnic name meaning 'Roman' (a derivative of *Rōma*; cf. ROMOLO). This name was borne by a large number of early saints, and in the 10th century was given as a baptismal name to Boris, son of Vladimir, the ruler who Christianized Kievan Russia. Boris and his brother Gleb were murdered by their brother Svyatopolk and canonized as martyrs.

Cognates: French: **Romain**. Italian: **Romano**. Spanish: **Román**. Portuguese: **Romão**.
Feminine forms: Latinate: **Romana**. French: **Romaine** (also used in the English-speaking world).

Romeo (m.) Italian: from the medieval religious name *Romeo* 'pilgrim to Rome' (Late Latin *Rōmaeus*, a derivative of *Rōma* cf. ROMOLO). For his romantic tragedy, Shakespeare derived the name of the hero, the lover of Juliet, from a poem by Arthur Brooke, *The Tragicall Historye of Romeus and Juliet*. This is ultimately derived from a story by the Italian writer Matteo Bandello (1485–1561), whose works are the source of the plots of several Elizabethan and Jacobean plays.

Romilda (f.) N. Italian: from an old Germanic female personal name composed of the elements *hrōm* fame + *hild* battle.

Romolo (m.) Italian (characteristic of the region around Rome): from the Latin name *Rōmulus*, borne by one of the legendary founders of the Roman state. According to the legend, Romulus won a competition with his twin brother Remus to name and rule over the city which they had founded. In fact the derivation is the other way about, and *Rōmulus* comes from *Rōma* Rome, itself of uncertain origin. The Romans themselves often connected it with Greek *rhōmē* strength, but this is no more than a folk etymology.

Feminine form: **Romola** (the name of the heroine of a novel by George Eliot, set in 15th-century Florence).

Romy (f.) German and English: pet form of *Rosemarie* (see ROSEMARY), made famous by the Austrian film actress Romy Schneider (1938–82).

Variant: English: **Romey**.

Rona (f.) English: variant of RHONA.

Ronald (m.) English and Scottish: from the Old Norse personal name *Rögnvaldr*; see RAGNVALD. This name was regularly used in the Middle Ages in northern England and Scotland, where Scandinavian influence was strong. It is now widespread throughout the English-speaking world. See also RANALD and RAGHNALL.

Short form: **Ron**.
Pet form: **Ronnie**.
Feminine form: **Ronalda** (Scottish).

Ronan (m.) Irish: from Gaelic **Rónán**, originally a byname representing a diminutive form of *rón* seal (the animal). The name is recorded as borne by various early Celtic saints, but there has been much confusion in the transmission of their names and most of them are also reliably named as *Ruadhán* (see ROWAN). The most famous is a 5th-century Irish saint who was consecrated as a bishop by St Patrick and subsequently worked as a missionary in Cornwall and Brittany.

Ronit (f.) 1. Irish: Anglicized form of Gaelic RATHNAIT. 2. Jewish: modern Hebrew name meaning 'song'.

Ronnie (m., f.) English: 1. (m.) Pet form of RONALD. 2. (f.) Pet form of VERONICA.

Roque (m.) Spanish and Portuguese form of ROCCO.

Rory (m.) Irish and Scottish: Anglicized form of the Gaelic name RUAIDHRÍ (Irish) or *Ruairidh*, *Ruaraidh* (Scottish). In Scotland this is further Anglicized to RODERICK.

Ros (f.) English: short form of ROSALIND and ROSAMUND.

Rosa (f.) Spanish, Italian, and Latinate form of ROSE, also in use in Scandinavia.

Pet forms: Spanish: **Rosita**. Italian: **Rosetta**. English: **Rosie**.

Rosalba (f.) Italian: from the Latinate elements *rosa* rose + *alba* (feminine) white. This was apparently originally coined as an ornamental name.

Rosaleen (f.) English: variant of ROSALYN, influenced by the suffix *-een* (in origin the Irish Gaelic diminutive *-ín*). 'Dark Rosaleen' was the title of a poem by James Clarence Mangan (1803–49), based on the Gaelic poem *Róisín Dubh*; in it the name is used as a figurative allusion to the Irish nation.

Rosalie (f.) French form of the Latin name *Rosalia* (from *rosa* rose), introduced to the English-speaking world in the latter part of the 19th century. St Rosalia was a 12th-century Sicilian virgin, and is the patron of Palermo.

Cognate: Italian: **Rosalia**.

Rosalind (f.) English: originally an old Germanic female name composed of the elements *hros* horse + *lind* weak, tender, soft, which was introduced to Britain by the Normans. In the Middle Ages it was reanalysed by folk etymology as if from Latin *rosa linda* 'lovely rose'. Its popularity as a given name owes much to its use by Edmund Spenser for the character of a shepherdess in his pastoral poetry, and by Shakespeare as the name of the heroine in *As You Like It* (1599).

Rosaline (f.) English: originally a variant of ROSALIND; cf. ROSALYN and ROSALEEN. It is the name of a minor character in Shakespeare's *Love's Labour's Lost* and is used for another,

who does not appear but is merely mentioned, in *Romeo and Juliet*.

Rosalyn (f.) English: altered form of ROSALIND. **Rosalin** was a common medieval form, since the letter *-d* tended to occur variably with final *-n*. The name has been further influenced by the productive suffix *-lyn* (see LYNN).

Variants: **Rosalynn(e)**.

Rosamund (f.) English: from an old Germanic female personal name composed of the elements *hros* horse + *mund* protection. In the Middle Ages it was reanalysed as Latin *rosa munda* 'pure rose' or *rosa mundi* 'rose of the world', titles given to the Virgin Mary. The spelling **Rosamond** has been common since the Middle Ages, when scribes sometimes used *o* for *u*, to distinguish it from *n* and *m*, all of which consisted of very similar downstrokes of the pen. 'Fair Rosamond' (Rosamond Clifford) was a legendary beauty who lived at Woodstock in Oxfordshire in the 12th century. She is said to have been the mistress of King Henry II, and to have been murdered by the queen, Eleanor of Aquitaine, in 1176.

Rosangela (f.) Italian: combination of the names ROSA and ANGELA.

Rosanne (f.) English: modern coinage from a combination of the names ROSE and ANNE, probably influenced by the popularity of the given name ROXANE.

Variants: **Roseanne**, **Rosanna**; **Rosannagh** (a fanciful respelling).

Rosario (f.) Spanish: from a title of the Virgin Mary, *Nuestra Señora del Rosario* 'Our Lady of the Rosary'. The rosary (from Latin *rosārium*, originally 'rose bower') became an important symbol in Catholic life during the 15th century; the feast of Our Lady of the Rosary was established in 1573 and extended to the whole Church in 1716. In southern Italy and in Sicily this is occasionally used as a male name, influenced no doubt by the fact that the ending *-o* is characteristically masculine.

Pet form: **Charo**.

Rościsław (m.) Polish: from an old Slavonic personal name composed of the elements *rosts* usurp, arrogate + *slav* glory (cf. SOBIESLAW).

Cognate: Russian, Czech: **Rostislav**.
Feminine forms: Polish: **Rościsawa**. Czech: **Rostislava**.
Pet forms: Russian: **Rostya** (m.). Czech: **Rost'a** (m., f.); **Rostek**, **Rosti(če)k** (m.); **Rostin(k)a**, **Rostuška** (f.).

Roscoe (m.) English: transferred use of the surname, which originated as a local name from a place in northern England named with the Old Norse elements *rá* roe-deer + *skógr* wood, copse.

Rose (f.) English: ostensibly from the name of the flower (Latin *rosa*). However, the name was in use throughout the Middle Ages, long before any of the other female names derived from flowers, which are generally of 19th-century origin. In part it may refer to the flower as a symbol of the Virgin Mary, but it seems likely that it also has a Germanic origin, probably as a short form of various female names with the first element *hros* horse or *hrod* fame. The Latinate form *Rohesia* is commonly found in documents of the Middle Ages. As well as being a name in its own right, it is currently used as a short form of ROSEMARY and, less often (because of their different pronunciation), of other names beginning *Ros-*, such as ROSALIND and ROSAMUND.

Cognates: Spanish, Italian, and Latinate: **Rosa**. Irish Gaelic: **Róis**. Yiddish: **Reise**. Polish: **Róza**. Czech: **Růžena**. Hungarian: **Rózsa**. Pet form: English: **Rosie**.

Roselle (f.) English: combination of the given name ROSE with the productive suffix *-elle* (originally a French feminine diminutive suffix).

Rosemary (f.) English: a 19th-century coinage, from the name of the herb (which is from Latin *ros marīnus* sea dew). It is often also assumed to be a combination of the names ROSE and MARY.
Cognate: German, Scandinavian: **Rosemarie**.
Pet forms: English: **Rosie**. German: **Röschen**, **Romy**.

Rosendo (m.) Spanish: of Germanic (Visigothic) origin, composed of the elements *hrōd* fame + *sinþs* path. St *Rudesind* or Rosendo (907–77) was born in Galicia of a noble family, and served as bishop of Mondoñedo.

Rosetta (f.) Italian: pet form of ROSA, sometimes also used in the English-speaking world.

Rosie (f.) English: pet form of ROSE, ROSA, or ROSEMARY. It was first used in the 1860s and is now well established as an independent given name, particularly in America.

Rosita (f.) Spanish: pet form of ROSA, sometimes also used in the English-speaking world and in Scandinavia.

Ross (m.) Scottish and English: transferred use of the Scottish surname, which is the name of a large kindred that has played a major role in Scottish history. The kindred name appears to be derived ultimately from the Gaelic word *ros* headland.

Rostislav (m.) Russian and Czech form of ROŚCISŁAW.
Feminine form: **Rostislava**.
Pet form: Russian: **Rostya**.

Roswitha (f.) German: Latinate form of an old Germanic female personal name composed of the elements *hrōd* fame + *swinþ* strength. The name was borne by a 10th-century nun, Roswitha of Gandersheim, who wrote Latin verse and plays in the manner of Terence.
Variant: **Roswithe**.

Rötger (m.) Low German form of ROGER.

Rowan (m., f.) English: 1. (m.) Transferred use of the surname, which is of Irish origin, being an Anglicized form of the Gaelic byname *Ruadhán* 'little red one' (a diminutive of *ruadh* red; cf. ROY). It was borne by a 6th-century saint who founded the monastery of Lothra, and it is an alternative name of the 5th-century saint also known as RONAN. 2. (f.) From the English vocabulary word (of Scandinavian origin) for the tree, an attractive sight with its clusters of bright red berries.

Rowena (f.) English: apparently a Latinized form of a Saxon name (of uncertain original form and derivation, perhaps composed of the Germanic elements *hrōd* fame + *wynn* joy). It first occurs in the Latin chronicles of Geoffrey of Mon-mouth (12th century) as the name of a daughter of the Saxon invader Hengist, and was taken up by Sir Walter Scott as the name of a Saxon woman, Lady Rowena of Hargottstanstede, who marries the eponymous hero of his novel *Ivanhoe* (1819).

Rowland (m.) English: variant of ROLAND, or a transferred use of the surname derived from that name in the Middle Ages.

Rowley (m.) English: variant of ROLY, or a transferred use of the local surname, which originated in the Middle Ages from any of the various places named with the Old English elements *rūh* rough, overgrown + *lēah* wood or clearing.

Roxane (f.) English and French: from Latin *Roxana*, Greek *Roxanē*, recorded as the name of the wife of Alexander the Great. She was the daughter of Oxyartes the Bactrian, and her name is presumably of Persian origin; it is said to mean 'dawn'. In English literature it is the name of the heroine of a novel by Defoe (1724), a beautiful adventuress who, deserted by her husband, enjoys a glittering career as a courtesan, but eventually dies in a state of penitence, having been thrown into prison for debt.
Variant: **Roxanne**.
Cognate: Russian: **Roksana**.

Roy (m.) Originally a Scottish name, representing an Anglicized spelling of the Gaelic nickname *Ruadh* 'red' (cf. ROWAN). It has since spread to other parts of the English-speaking world, where it is often reanalysed as Old French *roy* king (cf. LEROY).

Royle (m.) English: transferred use of the surname, which originated as a local name from a place in Lancashire, so called from Old English *ryge* rye + *hyll* hill. It may have become popular as a given name because of association with the vocabulary word *royal* (cf. KING) or because of similarity in sound to the name DOYLE.

Royston (m.) English: transferred use of the surname, derived from the name of a place in Hertfordshire, known in the Middle Ages as the 'settlement of *Royce*' (which name is an obsolete variant of ROSE, from its Germanic form). It is now used as a given name especially among British West Indians, although the reasons for its popularity among them are not clear. It may, in some cases, be taken as a version of 'Roy's son'.

Roz (f.) English: variant spelling of ROS, with the final consonant altered to represent the voiced sound of the names from which it derives.

Róża (f.) Polish form of ROSE.

Rozanne (f.) English: variant spelling of ROSANNE or ROXANE.

Rózsa (f.) Hungarian form of ROSE.

Ruaidhrí (m.) Irish Gaelic: traditional name composed of Old Celtic elements meaning 'red' and 'king'. This was the name of the last high king of Ireland, Rory O'Conor, who reigned 1166–70.
Variant: **Ruairí**.
Cognates: Scottish Gaelic: **Ruairi(dh)**, **Ruaraidh**.

Rube (m., f.) English: informal short form of REUBEN and of RUBY.

Ruby (f.) English: from the vocabulary word for the gemstone (Latin *rubīnus*, from *rubeus* red). The name was chiefly common in the late 19th century and up to the middle of the 20th. It is now out of fashion.

Rudi (m.) German: short form of RUDOLF and, occasionally, of RÜDIGER.

Rüdiger (m.) German cognate of ROGER. It was borne by a hero of the medieval *Nibelungenlied*, but is not now a common name.

Rudolf (m.) German, Dutch, Scandinavian, Polish, Czech, and English: from a Latinized version, *Rudolphus*, of the Germanic name *Hrōdwulf* (see ROLF). It was introduced to the English-speaking world from Germany in the 19th century. *Rudolf* was a hereditary name among the Habsburgs, the Holy Roman Emperors and rulers of Austria, from the Emperor Rudolf I (1218–91) to the Archduke Rudolf, Crown Prince of Austria-Hungary, who died in mysterious circumstances at his country house at Meyerling in 1889.

Rudolf Rassendyll was the central character of Anthony Hope's immensely popular adventure stories *The Prisoner of Zenda* (1894) and *Rupert of Hentzau* (1898), in which he is an English gentleman who turns out to be the half-brother of the King of Ruritania, to whom he bears a great physical resemblance and whom he successfully impersonates for reasons of state. In the 20th century the popularity of this name was further enhanced by the American silent-film actor Rudolph Valentino (1895–1926), born in Italy as Rodolpho di Valentina d'Antonguolla. However, it is at present out of fashion.

Variants: German, Dutch: **Rodolf**. Dutch: **Roelof** (vernacular). English: **Rudolph**.
Cognates: French: **Rodolphe**. Italian, Spanish: **Rodolfo**.
Short forms: German: **Rudi**. Dutch: **Ruud**. English: **Rudy**.

Rufino (m.) Italian, Spanish, and Portuguese: from Latin *Rufinus*, a derivative of RUFUS used originally as a Roman family name. The numerous early saints so called include a 5th-century bishop of Capua.

Variant: **Ruffino**.
Cognate: Catalan: **Rufi**.

Rufus (m.) English: from a Latin nickname meaning 'red(-haired)', sometimes used in medieval documents as a translation of various surnames with the same sense. It began to be used as a given name in the 19th century.

Ruggiero (m.) Italian form of ROGER.
Variant: **Ruggero**.

Ruiseart (m.) Scottish Gaelic form of RICHARD.

Runa (f.) Scandinavian: from the Old Norse female personal name *Rúna*, a short form of various female compound names containing the element *rún* secret lore.

Rune (m.) Scandinavian: from the rare Old Norse male personal name *Rúni*, a short form of various male compound names containing the element *rún* secret lore, as, for example, *Rúnólfr*. Its revival in the late 19th century is probably due to the influence of the more frequent female name RUNA. It has become very popular in the 20th century.

Rupert (m.) English, Low German, and Dutch: Low German form of ROBERT, first brought to England by Prince Rupert of the Rhine (1618–92), a dashing military leader who came to help his uncle, Charles I, in the Civil War.

Cognate: German: **Rupprecht**.

Rurik (m.) Russian: from a Scandinavian cognate of RODERICK. This form of the name was borne by a 9th-century Varangian leader who founded the principality of Novgorod and established the Russian monarchy. His descendants held the throne until the 16th century, and the name *Rurik* is still sometimes used in the Soviet Union. This form is also used to some extent in Finland and Sweden.

Russ (m.) English: short form of RUSSELL, now also used as an independent given name. In some cases it may represent a transferred use of the surname *Russ*, from Old French *rous* red.

Russell (m.) English: transferred use of the common surname, itself originally from the Old French nickname *Rousel* 'little red one' (a diminutive of *rous* red, from Latin *russus*). It is now widely used as a given name in its own right and may in some cases have been bestowed in honour of the philosopher Bertrand Russell (1872–1970), who was noted for his liberal agnostic views and his passionate championship of causes such as pacifism (in the First World War), free love, and nuclear disarmament. He was the grandson of the Victorian statesman Lord John Russell (1792–1878).

Rusty (m., f.) English: nickname for someone with reddish-brown hair, from modern English *rust* (Old English *rust*).

Rut (f.) Form of RUTH used in Italy, Spain, Germany, the Netherlands, Scandinavia, and Poland. Only in Sweden is it really common; there it was the twenty-fourth most frequent female name in 1973.

Rutger (m.) Dutch form of ROGER.

Ruth (f.) Biblical: name (of uncertain derivation) of a Moabite woman who left her own people to remain with her mother-in-law Naomi, and afterwards became the wife of Boaz and an ancestress of David. Her story is told in the book of the Bible that bears her name. It was popular among the Puritans, partly because of its association with the term *ruth* meaning 'compassion'. It is now as common among Gentiles as among Jews.

Cognate: Gaelic, Italian, Spanish, German, Dutch, Scandinavian, and Polish: **Rut**.

Ruud (m.) Dutch: short form of RUDOLF.

Ruy (m.) Spanish: pet form of RODRIGO. This form was common in the Middle Ages, being borne, for example, by El Cid, Ruy Diaz de Vivar (?1043–99).

Růžena (f.) Czech form of ROSE.

Ryan (m.) U.S., Australian, Irish, and English: from the Irish Gaelic surname *Ó Riain* 'descendant of Rian'. *Rian* is an old Gaelic personal name of uncertain origin, probably a derivative of *rí* king.

Ryszard (m.) Polish form of RICHARD.

S

Sabella (f.) English: modern name, apparently derived from *Isabella* by the dropping of the initial vowel (see ISABEL).

Sabia (f.) Irish: Latinized form of Gaelic SADHBH, in use during the Middle Ages and occasionally at the present day.

Sabine (f.) French (two syllables) or German (three syllables): from the Latin name *Sabīna* 'Sabine woman'. The Sabines were an ancient Italic race whose territory was early taken over by the Romans. According to tradition, the Romans made a raid on the Sabines and carried off a number of their women, but when the Sabines came for revenge the women succeeded in making peace between the two groups. The name *Sabina* was borne by three minor early Christian saints, in particular a Roman maiden martyred in about 127.
Variant: **Sabina** (used in Ireland as an Anglicized form of Gaelic SADHBH).

Sabrina (f.) English: from the name of a character in Celtic legend, who supposedly gave her name to the River Severn. In fact this is one of the most ancient of all British river names, and its true origins are obscure. Legend, as preserved by Geoffrey of Monmouth, had it that Sabrina was the illegitimate daughter of a Welsh king called Locrine, and was drowned in the river on the orders of the king's wife Gwendolen. The river name is found in the form *Sabrina* in the Latin writings of Tacitus, Gildas, and Bede. Geoffrey of Monmouth comments that in Welsh the name is *Habren* (modern Welsh *Hafren*). The name of the legendary character is almost certainly derived from that of the river, rather than vice versa.

Sacha (m.) French version of SASHA. Many names of Russian origin were introduced to the English-speaking world, via French, at the time when Diaghilev's Ballet Russe made its great impact in Paris (1909–20).

Sachairi (m.) Scottish Gaelic form of ZACHARY.

Sacheverell (m.) English: transferred use of the surname, apparently originally a baronial name of Norman origin (from an unidentified place in Normandy believed to have been called *Saute-Chevreuil*, meaning 'roebuck leap'). It was made familiar as a given name by the writer Sacheverell Sitwell (1897–1985), who was named in honour of his ancestor William Sacheverell (1638–91), a minor Whig statesman.
Pet form: **Sachie**.

Sadhbh (f.) Irish Gaelic: traditional name, said to mean 'sweet'. This was a very common female given name during the Middle Ages.
Anglicized forms: **Sabia**, **Sabina**, **Sive**.

Sadie (f.) English: originally a pet form of SARAH, but now generally treated as an independent name. The exact formation is not clear.

Sal (f., m.) **1.** (f.) English: short form of SALLY. **2.** (m.) U.S.: short form of Spanish SALVADOR or its Italian cognate, *Salvatore*.

Sally (f.) English: in origin a pet form of SARAH, but in the 20th century normally treated as a name in its own right. It is frequently used as the first element in combinations such as *Sally-Anne* and *Sally-Jane*.
Short form: **Sal**.

Salome (f.) English, German, etc.: Greek form of an unrecorded Aramaic name, related to the Hebrew word *shalom* peace. It was common at the time of Christ, and was borne by one of the women who were at his tomb at the time of the Resurrection (Mark 16: 1–8). This would normally have led to its common use as a Christian name, and it is indeed found as such in medieval times. However, according to the Jewish historian Josephus, it was also the name of King Herod's stepdaughter, the daughter of Queen Herodias. In the Bible, a daughter of Herodias, generally identified as this Salome, danced for Herod and so pleased him that he offered to give her anything she wanted. Prompted by her mother, she asked for (and got) the head of John the Baptist, who was in one of Herod's prisons (Mark 6: 17–28). This story so gripped medieval imagination that the name Salome became more or less taboo until the end of the 19th century, when Oscar Wilde wrote a play about her and some unconventional souls began to choose the name for their daughters.
Cognates: French: **Salomé**. Polish: **Salomea**.

Salud (f.) Spanish: religious name referring to the Marian title, *Nuestra Señora de la Salud* 'Our Lady of Salvation' (from Latin *salus*, genitive *salūtis*). The Virgin is venerated under this name in several places, especially in Catalonia and Valencia.

Salvador (m.) Spanish: from the Late Latin word *salvātor* saviour; this is a common epithet of Christ, and the name is borne in his honour.
Cognate: Italian: **Salvatore** (common in the south of Italy, where there has been considerable Spanish influence).
Short form: **Sal** (U.S.).

Sam (m., f.) English: **1.** (m.) Long-established short form of SAMUEL or, less frequently, of SAMSON. **2.** (f.) Short form, which has recently become fashionable, of SAMANTHA.
Pet forms (of 1): **Sammy**. (Of 2): **Sammie**.

Samantha (f.) English: of problematic and much debated origin. It seems to have originated in the southern states of America in the 18th century, possibly as a combination of SAM (from SAMUEL) + a newly coined feminine suffix *-antha* (perhaps suggested by ANTHEA).

Samoyla (m.) Russian: popular form of SAMUEL.

Samson (m.) English form of a biblical name (Hebrew **Shimshon**, probably derived from *shemesh* sun) borne by a Jewish champion and judge famous for his prodigious strength. He was betrayed by his mistress, Delilah, and enslaved and blinded by the Philistines; nevertheless, he was able to bring the pillars of the temple of the Philistines crashing down in a final suicidal act of strength (Judges 13–16). This famous story provided the theme for Milton's poetic drama *Samson Agonistes* (1671), which is modelled on ancient Greek tragedy. In the Middle Ages the popularity of the given name was increased in Celtic areas by the fame of a 6th-century Celtic saint who bore it, probably as a classicized form of some Old Celtic name. He was a Welsh monk who did missionary work in Cornwall and afterwards established a monastery at Dol in Brittany.

Variant: **Sampson** (usually a transferred use of the surname).
Cognate: Italian: **Sansone**.

Samuel (m.) Biblical name (Hebrew **Shemuel**), possibly meaning 'He (God) has hearkened' (presumably to the prayers of a mother for a son). It may also be understood as a contracted form of Hebrew *sha'ul me'el* meaning 'asked of God'. In the case of Samuel the son of Hannah, this would be more in keeping with his mother's statement 'Because I have asked him of the Lord' (1 Samuel 1: 20). Living in the 11th century BC, Samuel was a Hebrew judge and prophet of the greatest historical importance, who established the Hebrew monarchy, anointing as king both Saul and, later, David. In the Authorized Version two books of the Old Testament are named after him, although in Roman Catholic and Orthodox versions of the Bible they are known as the first and second Book of Kings. The story of Samuel being called by God while still a child serving in the house of Eli the priest (1 Samuel 3) is of great vividness and has moved countless generations.

In England and America the name was particularly popular among the 17th-century Puritans and among Nonconformists from the 17th to the 19th century. It has always been a common Jewish name, and in Gaelic Scotland it has sometimes been used as an Anglicized form of Gaelic *Somhairle* (see SOMERLED).

Cognates: Welsh: **Sawyl**. Hebrew: **Shmuel**. Russian: **Samuil; Samoyla** (vernacular form).
Short form: English: SAM.
Pet form: English: **Sammy**.

Sancho (m.) Spanish: of uncertain origin. The vernacular form *Sancho* and the Latin *Sanctius* are used interchangeably in medieval documents, and it is possible that *Sancho* is derived from *Sanctius*, a derivative of *sanctus* holy. On the other hand, the phonetic development is not regular, and it is possible that *Sanctius* is a Latinized form of a name of different origin. St Sancho or Sanctius was martyred at Cordoba by the Moors in 851, but the name is inescapably associated now with Sancho Panza, the dumpy, long-suffering, commonsensical squire of Don Quixote in Cervantes' novel (1605–15).

Feminine forms: **Sanch(i)a**.

Sandalio (m.) Spanish: from Latin *Sandal(i)us*. This seems to be a Latinized form of a Germanic (Visigothic) name composed of the elements *sand* true + *ulf* wolf. A saint of this name was martyred at Cordoba by the Moors in *c*.855.

Sandford (m.) English (U.S.): variant of SANFORD.

Sándor (m.) Hungarian form of ALEXANDER.

Sandra (f.) Italian and English: short form of *Alessandra*, the Italian form of ALEXANDRA. A major influence on its use in English was George Meredith's novel *Sandra Belloni* (1886), originally published as *Emilia* in England (1864); the heroine, Emilia Sandra Belloni, is a beautiful, passionate young singer.

Variant: Scottish: **Saundra**.

Sandro (m.) Italian: short form of *Alessandro* (see ALEXANDER), now common in Italy as a given name in its own right.

Sandy (m., f.) 1. (m.) Scottish and English: pet form, originally Scottish, of ALEXANDER. 2. (f.) English: pet form of ALEXANDRA or SANDRA, now sometimes used as an independent given name. 3. (m., f.) English: nickname for someone with a crop of 'sandy' (light reddish-brown) hair.

Variants: **Sandie** (f.). (Of 1 only): Scottish: **Sandaidh** (Gaelic).

Sanford (m.) English (U.S.): transferred use of the surname, which originated as a local name from any of numerous places in England called *Sandford*, from Old English *sand* sand + *ford* ford. Use as a given name in America honours Peleg Sanford, an early governor (1680–3) of Rhode Island.

Variant: **Sandford**.

Sanna (f.) Scandinavian: short form of SUSANNA. It may be favoured by association with the Swedish and Norwegian adjective *sann* true.

Sansone (m.) Italian form of SAMSON.

Santiago (m.) Spanish: name chosen to invoke the protection of St James on a son. *Iago* is an obsolete Spanish form of JAMES. St James the Greater is the patron saint of Spain; he was one of the twelve disciples of Christ, the brother of John the Baptist, and was martyred under Herod Agrippa. The legend that he visited Spain before his death does not seem to have arisen before the 9th century, but by the 11th century the site of his alleged relics at Compostela in Galicia was a place of pilgrimage from all over Europe. See also DIEGO.

Santos (m.) Spanish and Portuguese: name chosen by parents who wish to invoke the protection of all the saints, without further specification, for their son. It is also often given to a boy born on the feast of All Saints; cf. TOUSSAINT.

Santuzza (f.) Italian: diminutive form, originating in Sicily, of the name *Santa*, a feminine version of *Santo*, from Latin *sanctus* holy. This form of the name has become known through being borne by a character in the opera *Cavalleria Rusticana* (1890) by Mascagni.

Sanya (m.) Russian: pet form of ALEXANDER and ALEXANDRA.

Saoirse (f.) Irish Gaelic: modern name from the vocabulary word meaning 'freedom'.

Sara (f.) Variant of SARAH. This is the form used in the Greek of the New Testament (Hebrews 11: 11).

Sarah (f.) Biblical: name of the wife of Abraham and mother of Isaac. According to the Book of Genesis, she was originally called *Sarai* (possibly meaning 'contentious' in Hebrew), but had her name changed by God to the more auspicious *Sarah* 'princess' in token of a greater blessing (Genesis 17: 15, 'And God said unto Abraham, As for Sarai thy wife, thou shalt not call her name Sarai, but Sarah shall her name be'). In Ireland this has been used as an Anglicized form of SORCHA, in Scotland of MÓR.

Variants: **Sara**, ZARA.
Cognate: Hungarian: **Sára**.
Pet forms: English: SALLY, SADIE. Spanish: **Sarita**. Swedish: **Sassa**. Hungarian: **Sári**.

Sasha (m., f.) English spelling of a Russian pet form of ALEXANDER and ALEXANDRA. It has been used in the English-speaking world as an independent name, introduced in the 20th century via France. Use as a female name in the

English-speaking world is encouraged by the characteristically feminine -*a* ending.

Variants: French spelling: **Sacha**. German spelling: **Sascha**.

Saskia (f.) Dutch: of uncertain derivation. The name has been in use since the Middle Ages, and was borne, for example, by the wife of the artist Rembrandt. It may derive by metathesis and Latinization from the Germanic ethnic name element *sachs* Saxon.

Sassa (f.) Swedish: pet form of both ASTRID and SARA.

Saturnino (m.) Italian, Spanish, and Portuguese: from Latin *Saturnīnus*, a derivative of *Saturnus*, the name of the Roman god of agriculture and vegetation. The divine name was connected by the Romans themselves with Latin *satur* full, but this may be no more than folk etymology. There was a very large number of early saints named Saturninus; the most famous is probably the 3rd-century apostle of Navarre and first bishop of Toulouse.

Saul (m.) Biblical: name (from a Hebrew word meaning 'asked for' or 'prayed for') of one of the first kings of Israel, and also, before his conversion, of St Paul. It was popular among the Puritans, but is now once again mainly a Jewish name.

Saundra (f.) Scottish: variant of SANDRA, reflecting the same development in pronunciation as is shown by surnames such as *Saunders* and *Saunderson*, originally from short forms of ALEXANDER.

Sava (m.) Russian: from Late Greek *Sab(b)as*, a derivative of Hebrew *saba* old man. Two early saints of this name are venerated in the Eastern Church. The first was martyred *c*.372 near Tirgovist in Romania; he seems to have been a Goth in origin. The second (439–532) was a Cappadocian who is regarded as one of the founders of Eastern monasticism.

Saveli (m.) Russian: from the Late Latin personal name *Sabellius*, originally an ethnic name denoting a member of the Italian tribe of the Sabelli, displaced by the Romans. The saint venerated under this name, executed under Julian the Apostate in 362, was Persian, and his original name may have been cognate with that discussed at SAVA.

Saverio (m.) Italian form of XAVIER.

Sawney (m.) Scottish: variant of SANDY, resulting from a pronunciation reflected also in the surname *Saunders*. The name declined in popularity in the 19th and 20th centuries, perhaps as a result of its use as a vocabulary word for a fool.

Sawyl (m.) Welsh form of SAMUEL, a reduced version of earlier *Safwyl*.

Scarlett (f.) English: name popularized by the central character in the novel *Gone With the Wind* (1936) by Margaret Mitchell, later made into a famous film. The characters in the novel bear a variety of unusual given names, which had a remarkable influence on naming practices throughout the English-speaking world in the 20th century. According to the novel, the name of the central character was Katie Scarlett O'Hara (the middle name representing her grandmother's maiden surname), but she was always known as Scarlett.

Variant: **Scarlet**.

Scevola (m.) Italian: name chosen out of admiration for the Roman semi-legendary hero of the 6th century BC, Gaius Mucius Scaevola. He is said to have burnt off his own right hand in an altar fire in order to demonstrate to the Etruscan king, Lars Porsenna, the strength of his willpower. Allegedly as a result of this exploit he received the cognomen *Scaevola*, a derivative of *scaevus* left-handed. This was borne in turn by his descendants, several of whom rose to prominent positions in the Roman republic.

Ścibor (m.) Polish: variant of CZCIBOR.

Scott (m.) Scottish and English: although this was in use as a personal name both before and after the Norman Conquest, modern use in most cases almost certainly represents a transferred use of the surname. This originated as a byname for someone from Scotland or, within Scotland itself, a member of the Gaelic-speaking people who originally came from Ireland. The given name is now often chosen by parents conscious of their Scottish ancestry and heritage, but it is also used more widely.

Seaghdh (m.) Scottish Gaelic: traditional name of uncertain derivation, perhaps meaning 'hawk-like, fine, goodly'. It has been Anglicized as SHAW and SETH.

Cognate: Irish Gaelic: **Séaghdha**.

Séamas (m.) Irish Gaelic: modern form of JAMES. Earlier Gaelic spellings are **Séamus**, **Seumus**, and **Seumas**.

Seán (m.) Irish Gaelic form of JOHN, derived in the early Middle Ages from Anglo-Norman *Jehan*. The name has always been common in Ireland, but is now being increasingly chosen also by parents who have no Irish connections (usually without the accent, **Sean**).

Séarlait (f.) Irish Gaelic form of CHARLOTTE.

Séarlas (m.) Irish Gaelic form of CHARLES.

Seathan (m.) Scottish Gaelic form of JOHN, derived from Old French *Je(h)an*.

Sebastian (m.) English: name of early Christian origin, borne by a 3rd-century saint who was a Roman soldier martyred by the arrows of his fellow officers; his sufferings were a favourite subject for medieval artists. The name means 'man from Sebasta', a town in Asia Minor so called from Greek *Sebastos*, a translation of the Latin imperial title *Augustus*.

Cognates: French: **Sébastien**. Spanish: **Sebastián**. Italian: **Sebastiano**. Dutch: **Sebastiaan**. Russian: **Sevastian**.
Short forms: English: **Seb**. French: **Bastien**. Russian: **Seva**.

Séimí (m.) Irish Gaelic form of the Scottish male name JAMIE, in use in Northern Ireland.

Selig (m.) Jewish: from the Yiddish vocabulary word *selig* happy, fortunate (modern German *selig*), used as a vernacular translation of the Hebrew name ASHER.

Variant: **Zelig**.

Selima (f.) English: of uncertain origin. The name seems to have been first recorded by the poet Thomas Gray (1716–71) as that of Horace Walpole's cat, 'drowned in a tub of gold fishes'. The metre shows that the name was stressed on the first syllable, but there is no clue as to its derivation. Gray was possibly influenced by the Arabic name *Selim* 'peace'.

Selina (f.) English: of uncertain origin. The name first occurs in the 17th century, and it may be an altered form of *Selena* (Greek *Selēnē*), the name of a goddess of the moon, or of *Celina* (Latin *Caelīna*), a derivative of CELIA. The name suddenly became more popular in Britain in the 1980s, partly perhaps because of the familiarity of the television newsreader Selina Scott.

Selma (f.) English: of uncertain origin, probably a contracted form of SELIMA. It has also been occasionally used in Germany and Scandinavia, probably because it occurs as the name of Ossian's castle in Macpherson's poems, once enormously popular there.

Selwyn (m.) English: transferred use of the surname, which is of disputed origin. There was a given name *Selewyn* in use in the Middle Ages, which probably represents a survival of an unrecorded Old English name composed of the elements *sēle* prosperity or *sele* hall + *wine* friend. Alternatively, the surname may be Norman, derived from *Seluein*, an Old French form of Latin *Silvānus* (from *silva* wood; cf. SILAS).

Variant: **Selwin**.

Semyon (m.) Russian form of SIMON (actually from the form *Simeon*).

Pet form: **Senya**.

Senan (m.) Irish: Anglicized form of the Gaelic name **Seanán**, originally a byname representing a diminutive of *sean* old, wise. This name was borne by numerous early Irish saints, including a 6th-century bishop and a 7th-century hermit.

Sender (m.) Jewish: Yiddish form of ALEXANDER.

Senga (f.) Scottish: common in the northeast of Scotland, this name is popularly supposed to represent AGNES spelled backwards (which it undeniably does). However, it is more likely to have originated from the Gaelic vocabulary word *seang* slender.

Senya (m.) Russian: pet form of both ARSENI and SEMYON.

Seocan (m.) Scottish Gaelic: pet form of JOCK.

Seoirse (m.) Irish Gaelic form of GEORGE.

Seonag (f.) Scottish Gaelic form of JOAN.

Seònaid (f.) Scottish Gaelic form of JANET.

Anglicized forms: **Seona**, **Shona**.

Seòras (m.) Scottish Gaelic form of GEORGE.

Variants: **Seòrsa**, **Deòrsa**.

Seòsaidh (m.) Scottish Gaelic form of JOSEPH.

Seosaimhin (f.) Irish Gaelic form of JOSEPHINE.

Seosamh (m.) Irish Gaelic form of JOSEPH.

Sepp (m.) German (esp. Bavarian): short form of JOSEPH.

Septimus (m.) English: from a Late Latin name derived from Latin *septimus* seventh. It was fairly commonly used in large Victorian families for the seventh son or a male seventh child, but is now rare.

Seraphina (f.) Latinate derivative of Hebrew *seraphim* 'burning ones', the name of an order of angels (Isaiah 6: 2). It was borne by a rather shadowy saint who was martyred at the beginning of the 5th century in Italy, Spain, or Armenia.

Variant: **Serafina**.
Cognate: Russian: **Serafima**.
Short form: English: **Fina**.
Pet forms: Russian: **Sima**, **Fima**, **Fimochka**.
Masculine form: Italian: **Serafino**.

Serena (f.) From a Latin name, representing the feminine form of the adjective *serēnus* calm, serene. It was borne by an early Christian saint, about whom little is known. In her *Life* she is described as a wife of the Emperor Domitian (AD 51–

96), but there is no mention of her in any of the historical sources that deal with this period.

Serge (m.) French form of SERGEI, brought into use at the beginning of the 20th century. There is no connection with the type of material called *serge* (Old French *sarge*, from Latin *sericum* silk).

Sergei (m.) Russian: from the old Roman family name *Sergius*, which is of uncertain, though probably Etruscan, origin. (It was borne, for example, by the conspirator denounced by Cicero, Lucius Sergius Catilina.) St Sergius of Radonezh (*c.*1314–92) is one of the most famous of all Russian saints, hence the great popularity of the name.

Pet form: **Seryozha**.

Servaas (m.) Dutch: from the Late Latin name *Servātius*, a derivative of *servātus* saved, i.e. 'redeemed'. This was the name of a 4th-century saint, bishop of Tangres in the Low Countries.

Sessy (f.) English: pet form of CECILY.

Sesto (m.) Italian form of SEXTUS.

Seth (m.) Biblical: name (from a Hebrew word meaning 'appointed, placed') of the third son of Adam, who was born after the murder of Abel (Genesis 4: 25, 'And Adam knew his wife again; and she bare a son, and called his name Seth: For God, said she, hath appointed me another seed instead of Abel, whom Cain slew'). It was popular among the Puritans (particularly for children born after the death of an elder sibling), and has been occasionally used since. By the 20th century it had become rare. It was used for the darkly passionate rural character Seth Starkadder in Stella Gibbons's comic novel *Cold Comfort Farm* (1932). In Scotland it has been used as an Anglicized form of SEAGHDH.

Seumas (m.) Scottish Gaelic form of JAMES, also an older Irish Gaelic form.

Seumus (m.) Irish Gaelic: older spelling of SÉAMAS.

Seva (m.) Russian: pet form of both VSEVOLOD and SEVASTIAN.

Variant: **Syova**.

Sevastian (m.) Russian form of SEBASTIAN.

Variant: **Sevastyan**.

Seve (m.) Spanish: pet form of SEVERIANO and SEVERINO.

Severiano (m.) Italian, Spanish, and Portuguese: from Latin *Sevēriānus*, a further elaboration of *Sevērīnus* (see SEVERINO). The name was borne by several early minor saints, but is not now in common use.

Severino (m.) Italian, Spanish, and Portuguese: from the Latin family name *Sevērīnus*, a derivative of *Sevērus* (see SEVERO). This name was borne by a large number of early saints, including a 5th-century apostle of Austria and a 6th-century bishop of Santempeda (now *Sanseverino*).

Cognates: Polish: **Seweryn**. Danish: **Søren**. Hungarian: **Szörény**.
Feminine forms: Latinate: **Severina**. French: **Séverine**.

Severo (m.) Italian, Spanish, and Portuguese: from Latin *Sevērus*, an old Roman family name, originally a byname meaning 'severe, stern'. This name was borne by a large number of early saints, including bishops of Ravenna (d. *c.*348), Naples (d. 409), and Barcelona (d. 633).

Sextus (m.) Traditional Latin given name, meaning originally 'sixth'. It was taken up in England during the Victorian period, often for a sixth son or a male sixth child, but it is now little used. The form *Sixtus* borne by three early popes is most likely a variant of this name, although it is often associated with the Greek word *xystos* polished.

Cognates: Italian: **Sesto**, **Sisto**.

Seymour (m.) English: transferred use of the surname, originally a Norman baronial name from *Saint-Maur* in Normandy. This place was so called from the dedication of its church to St Maurus, whose Latin name means 'Moor', i.e. North African. The identity of this saint is not known.

Sgàire (m.) Scottish Gaelic: traditional name, probably in origin a borrowing of the Old Norse byname *Skári* 'seamew'. It has sometimes been Anglicized as ZACHARY.

Shabbetai (m.) Jewish: Hebrew name derived from *shabbāth* sabbath (itself a derivative of *shābath* rested). It has been given to boys born on this day of the week.

Variant (contracted form): **Shabtai**.

Shahar (m.) Jewish: modern Hebrew name meaning 'dawn'.

Shalom (m.) Jewish: from the Hebrew vocabulary word *shalom* peace.

Shamus (m.) Anglicized spelling of *Séamus* (see SÉAMAS). It has sometimes been used in Ireland, but is now rare.

Shane (m., f.) English and Irish: early Anglicized form of SEÁN, representing a Northern Irish pronunciation of the Gaelic name. In recent years it has also been used as a female name.

Shanee (f.) English: apparently an Anglicized form of Welsh *Siani* (see SIÂN).

Shannah (f.) English: rare name of uncertain origin. It would seem to represent a short form of *Shoshannah*, the original Hebrew form of SUSANNA. However, the even rarer spelling Shannagh would seem to suggest association with the Irish surname *Shannagh*, from Gaelic *Ó Seanaigh* 'descendant of Seanach'. *Seanach* is a Gaelic personal name derived from *sean* old, wise (cf. SENAN).

Shannon (f.) English (chiefly U.S.): from the name of a river in Ireland. It is not clear why it has become so popular as a given name, but it combines a similar phonetic shape to SHARON, an Irish reference as in ERIN, and a river name as in CLODAGH. It is not used in Ireland itself.

Shari (f.) English (esp. U.S.): Anglicized spelling of *Sári* (see SARAH).

Sharman (f., m.) English: **1**. (f.) Altered form of CHARMIAN. **2**. (m.) Transferred use of the surname, a variant of SHERMAN.

Sharon (f.) English: a 20th-century coinage, from a biblical placename. The derivation is from the phrase 'I am the rose of Sharon, and the lily of the valleys' (Song of Solomon 2: 1). The plant name 'rose of Sharon' is used for a shrub of the genus *Hypericum*, with yellow flowers, and for a species of hibiscus, with purple flowers. *Rosasharn* (Rose of Sharon) is the name of one of the characters in John Steinbeck's novel *The Grapes of Wrath* (1936).

Variant: **Sharron**.

Sharona (f.) Latinate elaborated form of SHARON, now quite often used in the English-speaking world.

Sharonda (f.) English: less frequent elaboration of SHARON, with the suffix *-da* apparently abstracted from names such as GLENDA and LINDA.

Sharron (f.) English: variant spelling of SHARON.

Shaughan (m.) English and Irish: variant spelling of SHAUN, probably influenced by VAUGHAN.

Shaun (m.) Anglicized spelling of SEÁN, somewhat less common than SHAWN in America, but more so in Britain.

Shauna (f.) A feminized form of SHAUN, unknown in Ireland and rare in Britain, but reasonably common in America.

Shaw (m.) **1**. Scottish: Anglicized form of SEAGHDH. **2**. English: transferred use of the surname, which originated as a local name meaning 'wood, copse' (Old English *sceaga*, Old Norse *skógr*).

Shawn (m.) Anglicized spelling of SEÁN, found mainly in America.

Shayna (f.) Jewish: Yiddish name meaning 'beautiful' (modern German *schön*). See also BEILE and YAFFA.

Variant: **Sheine**.

Sheena (f.) Anglicized spelling of *Sìne* (Scottish) or *Síne* (Irish), the Gaelic forms of JANE (see SÍNE).

Sheila (f.) Anglicized spelling of Irish Gaelic SÍLE, now so common that it is hardly felt to be Irish any longer. In Australia since the 19th century it has been a slang generic term for any woman.

Sheine (f.) Jewish (Yiddish): variant of SHAYNA.

Shelagh (f.) Another Anglicized form of SÍLE (see also SHEILA). The final consonants in the written form seem to have been added to restore a Gaelic feel to the name, since they occur at the end of many Gaelic words and are silent. However, they do not have any historically justified place in the name.

Variant: **Sheelagh**.

Sheldon (m.) English: transferred use of the surname, which originated as a local name from any of various places so called. Examples occur in Derbyshire, Devon, and the West Midlands; they all have different origins.

Shell (f.) English: **1**. Normally a short form of MICHELLE. **2**. In some cases it may be a back-formation from SHELLEY (as if this contained the hypocoristic suffix *-(e)y*) or simply a shortened form of SHELLEY.

Shelley (f., occasionally m.) English: transferred use of the surname, the most famous bearer of which was the English Romantic poet Percy Bysshe Shelley (1792–1822). The surname is a local name from one of the various places (in Essex, Suffolk, and Yorkshire) named in Old English as the 'wood (or clearing) on (or near) a slope (or ledge)'. The name is now almost exclusively female, in part no doubt as a result of association with SHIRLEY (the actress Shelley Winters was born in 1922 as Shirley Schrift), and in part due to the characteristically feminine ending *-ie*, *-y*.

Shelomit (f.) Jewish: derived from Hebrew *shalom* peace. It is both a male and a female name in the Bible, but in modern Hebrew it is only used as a female name.

Sheree (f.) English: respelled form of *Chérie* (see CHERRY), used especially in America.

Sheridan (m.) English: transferred use of the surname made famous by the Irish playwright Richard Brinsley Sheridan (1751–1816). The surname is from Gaelic *Ó Sirideáin* 'descendant of *Sirideán*', a personal name of uncertain origin, possibly connected with *sirim* to seek.

Sherman (m.) English: transferred use of the surname, which originated in the Middle Ages as an occupational name for someone who trimmed the nap of woollen cloth after it had been woven. It represents a compound of the Old English elements *scēara* shears + *mann* man.

Sherry (f.) English: probably in origin a respelled form of *Chérie* (see CHERRY). It is now more closely associated with the fortified wine, earlier *sherry wine*, so named from the port of Jérez in southern Spain.
Variant: **Sherrie**.

Sheryl (f.) English: variant of CHERYL.
Variants: **Sherill**, **Sherrill**.

Shevaun (f.) Irish and English: Anglicized form of Gaelic SIOBHÁN.

Shifra (f.) Jewish: from Hebrew *shifra* beauty, grace. Spelled *Shiphrah* in the Authorized Version, it was the name of one of the midwives who defied Pharaoh's order to drown all newborn Hebrew boys (Exodus 1: 15–19).
Variant: **Shiphrah**.

Shilla (f.) English: modern name, apparently an altered spelling of SHEILA.

Shimon (m.) Jewish: modern Hebrew form of SIMON.

Shiphrah (f.) Jewish: variant of SHIFRA.

Shireen (f.) English: variant of SHIRIN, by association with the productive suffix *-een*.

Shirin (f.) Muslim name of Persian or Arabic origin now beginning to be fairly commonly used in the English-speaking world.
Variant: **Shirrin**.

Shirley (f., formerly m.) English: transferred use of the surname, which is a local name from any of the various places (in the West Midlands, Derbyshire, Hampshire, and Surrey) named in Old English from the elements *scīr* county, shire or *scīr* bright + *lēah* wood or clearing. It was given by Charlotte Brontë to the heroine of her novel *Shirley* (1849). According to the novel, her parents had selected the name in prospect of a male child and used it regardless. *Shirley* had earlier been used as a male name (Charlotte Brontë refers to it as a 'masculine cognomen'), but this literary influence fixed it firmly as a female name. It was strongly reinforced during the 1930s and 1940s by the popularity of the child film star Shirley Temple (b. 1928).
Variant: **Shirlee** (rare).

Shlomo (m.) Jewish: modern Hebrew form of SOLOMON.

Shmuel (m.) Jewish: modern Hebrew form of SAMUEL.

Shneur (m.) Jewish: Yiddish name, apparently derived from Latin *senior* elder. Alternatively, it may have a Hebrew origin meaning 'two lights', a reference to illustrious ancestors on both sides of the child's family.

Sholto (m.) Scottish: apparently an Anglicized form of a Gaelic name, **Sioltach**, originally a byname meaning 'sower', i.e. 'fruitful' or 'seed-bearing'. This name is traditional in the Douglas family.

Shona (f.) Scottish: Anglicized form of Gaelic SEONAG or SEÒNAID.

Shprinze (f.) Jewish: of uncertain origin, probably a Yiddish form of ESPERANZA.

Shraga (m.) Jewish: Aramaic name meaning 'fire, lantern'. It is usually paired with the Yiddish equivalent FAIVISH.

Shula (f.) As a Jewish name this is a short form of SHULAMIT. It has been adopted by non-Jews in the English-speaking world as an independent given name.

Shulamit (f.) Jewish: Hebrew name meaning 'peacefulness', a derivative of *shalom* peace. The name occurs as a personification in the Song of Solomon (6: 13): 'Return, return, O Shulamite; return, return, that we may look upon thee'. It is a popular modern Hebrew name.
Variants: **Shulamith**, **Shulamite**.

Shura (m., f.) Russian: short form of *Sashura*, itself an elaborated version of SASHA, a pet form of ALEXANDER. Occasionally it is found as a female name, ultimately from ALEXANDRA.

Siân (f.) Welsh form of JANE, derived from Anglo-Norman *Jeanne*. In the English-speaking world it is often used without the accent (**Sian**).
Pet form: **Siani**.

Siarl (m.) Welsh form of CHARLES.

Sibb (f.) English: short form of SIBYL, popular in the Middle Ages, but now rare.
Pet form: **Sibby** (used in Ireland as an Anglicized form of Gaelic SIBÉAL).

Sibéal (f.) Irish Gaelic form of ISABEL, derived in the early Middle Ages from the Anglo-Norman name.

Sibyl (f.) English: variant spelling of SYBIL. Even in classical times there was confusion between the vowels in this word.
Variants: **Sibylla** (Latinate form, common in Denmark and Sweden); **Sibilla**; **Sibella** (by association with the Italian feminine diminutive suffix *-ella*).

Sidney (m., occasionally f.) English: transferred use of the surname, which is usually said to be a Norman baronial name from *Saint-Denis* in France. However, at least in the case of the family of the poet and soldier Sir Philip Sidney (1554–86), it appears to have a more humble origin, being derived from lands in Surrey named as the 'wide meadow' (Old English *sīdan* wide (dative case) + *ēg* island in a river, riverside meadow). The popularity of the male name increased considerably in the 19th century, probably under the influence of Sidney Carton, hero of Dickens's novel *A Tale of Two Cities* (1859). As a female name it is perhaps in part a contsracted form of SIDONY, and coincidentally represents a metathesized form of SINDY, but this use is quite rare.
Variant: **Sydney**.
Short form: **Sid**.

Sidony (f.) English: from a Latin ethnic name, *Sidōnius* (m.) or *Sidōnia* (f.) 'person from Sidon' (in Phoenicia). This quite early came to be associated with the Greek word *sindon* winding-sheet. Two saints called Sidonius are venerated in the Catholic Church: Sidonius Apollinaris, a 4th-century bishop of Clermont, and a 7th-century Irish monk who was the first abbot of the monastery of Saint-Saëns (named with a much mutilated form of his name). *Sidonius* does not seem to have been used as a given name in the later Middle Ages, but the feminine form *Sidonia* (English *Sidony*) was comparatively popular and has continued in occasional use ever since.

Variant: **Sidonie**.

Sieffre (m.) Welsh form of GEOFFREY.

Siegbert (m.) German (esp. Jewish): from an old Germanic personal name composed of the elements *sige* victory + *berht* bright, famous. The name was borne by a 7th-century French king, regarded as a saint because of his foundation of numerous hospitals, churches, and monasteries. An Old English cognate was borne by a contemporary who was the first Christian king of East Anglia. The reason why the name should have become particularly popular among Jews is not clear.

Siegfried (m.) German: from an old Germanic personal name composed of the elements *sige* victory + *frid*, *fred* peace. This was a relatively common given name in the Middle Ages, but its modern use dates from the latter part of the 19th century, and reflects the revival of interest in Germanic legend, culminating in Wagner's operatic treatment in his *Ring* cycle.

Sieglinde (f.) German: from an old Germanic female personal name composed of the elements *sige* victory + *lind* weak, tender, soft.

Siegmund (m.) Usual modern German form of SIGMUND.

Siemen (m.) Dutch and Low German form of SIMON.

Siencyn (m.) Welsh spelling of JENKIN.

Sigbjörn (m.) Swedish: from an Old Norse personal name composed of the elements *sigr* victory + *björn* bear.

Cognate: Norwegian: **Sigbjørn**.
Pet form: Swedish: **Sigge**.

Sigge (m.) Swedish: pet form of *Sigurd* and, occasionally, of the less common SIGBJÖRN.

Sigi (m.) German: pet form of any of the various male names of Germanic origin containing the first element *sige* victory, as, for example, SIEGBERT, SIEGFRIED, and SIEGMUND.

Sigismund (m.) German: variant of SIGMUND, with the first element representing an extended form of the Germanic element *sige* victory. St Sigismund (d. 523) was a king of the Burgundians, murdered by political enemies but honoured as a martyr because he died in a monk's habit adopted for disguise.

Sigiswald (m.) German: from an old Germanic personal name composed of the elements *sige* victory + *wald* ruler.

Sigmund (m.) English and German: from an old Germanic personal name composed of the elements *sige* victory + *mund* protector. It was introduced to Britain both before and after the Conquest, from Scandinavia and Normandy, but there was much confusion with SIMON (final -*d* being added and dropped in the Middle Ages with great abandon) and it eventually fell out of use. As a modern given name in the English-speaking world, it is a recent reintroduction from Germany.

Variants: German: **Siegmund**, SIGISMUND.
Cognate: Polish: **Zygmunt**.

Signy (f.) Scandinavian: from an Old Norse female personal name composed of the elements *sigr* victory + *ný* new.

Variants: **Signi**, **Signe**.

Sigrid (f.) Scandinavian: from an Old Norse female personal name composed of the elements *sigr* victory + *fríðr* fair, beau-

tiful. The name is now also fairly commonly used in the English-speaking world.

Pet form: **Siri**.

Sigrun (f.) Scandinavian: from an Old Norse female personal name composed of the elements *sigr* victory + *rūn* secret lore. The name was borne in Scandinavian mythology by one of the Valkyries, and was revived as a given name in the late 18th century.

Sigurd (m.) Scandinavian: from an Old Norse personal name composed of the elements *sigr* victory + *vörðr* guardian. According to Scandinavian legend, a character of this name slew the dragon Fafnir, who was guarding an accursed treasure; according to Wagner's treatment in the *Ring* cycle, this role is taken by Siegfried.

Variant: Norwegian: **Sjurd**.
Pet form: Swedish: **Sigge**.

Sikke (m.) Frisian: pet form of any of the various names of Germanic origin containing the first element *sige* victory; cf. SIGI.

Silas (m.) New Testament: Greek name, a short form of *Silouanus* (Latin *Silvānus*, from *silva* wood). This name was borne by a companion of St Paul, who is also mentioned in the Bible in the full form of his name. The Eastern Church recognizes two separate saints, Silas and Silvanus, but honours both on the same day (20 July).

Sile (f.) Irish Gaelic form of CECILY, derived in the early Middle Ages from the Anglo-Norman form *Cecile*.

Anglicized forms: SHEILA, **She(e)lagh**.
Cognates: Scottish Gaelic: **Sile**, **Sileas**, **Silis**.

Silja (f.) Finnish (used also in Denmark, Norway, and Sweden): vernacular form of *Cecilia* (see CECILY). The name was made famous by the novel *The Maid Silja* (1931) by Frans Eemil Sillanpää, winner of the Nobel Prize for literature.

Silke (f.) Low German and Frisian: pet name derived from a short form of CELIA or *Cecilia* (see CECILY). The name is now also more widely popular in the German-speaking world.

Silvana (f.) Italian: feminine form of SILVANO, now also used in Germany and occasionally in the English-speaking world.

Silvano (m.) Italian: from Latin *Silvānus*; see SILAS. The name Silvanus was also borne by over a dozen other early saints, including a 6th-century abbot of Bangor in Ireland. In his case, the name is probably a classicized form of some faintly similar Celtic original.

Cognate: French: **Sylvain**.

Silver (f., m.) English: from the name of the precious metal (Old English *siolfor*), sometimes given to babies born with very fair, silvery white hair.

Silvester (m.) English and German: from a Latin name, meaning 'of the woods'. It was borne by various early saints, most notably by the first pope to govern a Church free from persecution (314–35). His feast is on 31 December, and in various parts of Europe the New Year is celebrated under his name. The name has been continuously, if modestly, used from the Middle Ages to the present day.

Variant: **Sylvester**.
Cognates: Italian: **Silvestro**. Spanish: **Silvestre**. Polish: **Sylwester**.

Silvestra (f.) Latinate feminine form of SILVESTER.

Silvia (f.) Italian and English: from Roman legend. Rhea *Silvia* was, according to mythological tradition, the mother of the twins Romulus and Remus, who founded Rome. Her name probably represents a reworking, by association with Latin *silva* wood, of some pre-Roman form. It was borne by a 6th-century saint, mother of Gregory the Great, and has always been relatively popular in Italy. Shakespeare used it as a typically Italian name in his *Two Gentlemen of Verona*, but it is now completely established in the English-speaking world.
Variant: English, Scandinavian: **Sylvia**.
Cognate: French: **Sylvie**.

Silvio (m.) Italian: from Latin *Silvius*, a masculine form of SILVIA. Several of the legendary kings of Alba Longa bore this name, and a St Silvius was martyred at Alexandria in Egypt in one of the early persecutions of the Christians.

Sima (f.) Russian: pet form of *Serafima* (see SERAPHINA).

Simcha (m., f.) Jewish: Hebrew name meaning 'joy'. It was orignally a female name, but is now more commonly given to males among Ashkenazic Jews.

Simeon (m.) Biblical: from Hebrew, meaning 'hearkening'. It is borne by several Old and New Testament characters, rendered in the Authorized Version variously as *Shimeon*, *Simeon*, and SIMON. In the New Testament, it is the spelling used for the man who blessed the infant Christ (Luke 2: 25).

Simon (m.) Usual English form of SIMEON. This form of the name is borne in the New Testament by various characters: two apostles, a brother of Jesus, a Pharisee, a leper, a tanner, a sorcerer (who offered money for the gifts of the Holy Ghost, giving rise to the term *simony*), and the man who carried Jesus's cross to the Crucifixion.
Cognates: Irish Gaelic: **Siomón**. Scottish Gaelic: **Sim**, **Simidh**. Dutch, Low German: **Siemen**. Polish: **Szymon**. Czech: **Šimon**. Russian: **Semyon**. Hebrew: **Shimon**.
Pet forms: Czech: **Ši(on)ek**, **Simůnek**, **Simeček**.

Simone (f.) French: feminine form of SIMON, now also quite commonly used in the English-speaking world.

Sina (f.) German and Scandinavian: short form of various Latinate female names ending in these syllables, for example *Thomasina* (see THOMAS).
Variant: Danish: **Sine**.

Sinclair (m.) English and Scottish: transferred use of the Scottish surname, which originated as a Norman baronial name borne by a family that held a manor in northern France called *Saint-Clair*, probably Saint-Clair-sur-Elle in La Manche. It is an extremely common Scottish surname: the Norman family received the earldoms of Caithness and Orkney. They merged with the Norse- and Gaelic-speaking inhabitants of their domains to form one of the most powerful of the Scottish Highland families. The name of the novelist Sinclair Lewis (1885–1951) may have had some influence on the choice of this as a twentieth-century given name.

Sinda (f.) **1**. English: variant of SINDY. **2**. Spanish: short form of various names ending in this element, of Visigothic origin, as, for example, GUMERSINDA.

Sindy (f.) English: variant spelling of CINDY that came into use in about 1950 and is most common in America.

Sine (f.) Danish: variant of SINA.

Sine (f.) Irish Gaelic form of JANE, derived from Anglo-Norman *Jeanne*.

Cognate: Scottish Gaelic: **Sìne** (Anglicized as **Sheena**).
Pet form: Scottish Gaelic: **Sineag**.

Sinéad (f.) Irish Gaelic form of JANET, derived from Anglo-Norman *Jeannette*.
Diminutive: **Sinéidín**.

Siobhán (f.) Irish Gaelic form of JANE, derived from the Anglo-Norman disyllabic form *Jehanne*. It became widely known in the English-speaking world as a result of the fame of the actress Siobhán McKenna (1923–86), and has recently come to be a popular given name.
Anglicized forms: **Shevaun**, **Chevonne** (modern).
Cognate: Scottish Gaelic: **Siubhan**.

Siôn (m.) Welsh form of JOHN, derived from Anglo-Norman *Jean*.
Pet form: **Sionyn**.

Sioned (f.) Welsh form of JANET.

Siôr (m.) Welsh form of GEORGE.
Variants: **Sior(y)s**.

Siothrún (m.) Irish Gaelic form of *Geoffrey*.

Siri (f.) Scandinavian: simplified form of SIGRID, often used as a pet form of that name.

Sissel (f.) Scandinavian form of CICELY.

Sissy (f.) English: pet form of CICELY that came into use about 1890 but disappeared again after about 1920, no doubt because of the homonymous slang word *sissy* 'effeminate' (which is probably from the kinship term *sister*). In recent years it has undergone something of a revival.
Variants: **Sissey**, **Sissie**.

Sisto (m.) Italian: variant of *Sesto* (see SEXTUS).

Siubhan (f.) Scottish Gaelic form of JANE, derived from the Old French disyllabic form *Jehanne* (see JEAN). This name is usually Anglicized as JUDITH.

Siùsan (f.) Scottish Gaelic form of *Susan* (see SUSANNA).
Variant: **Siùsaidh**.

Siv (f.) Scandinavian: originally a byname meaning 'bride, wife'. It is borne in Scandinavian mythology by the wife of Thor.

Sive (f.) Irish: Anglicized form of Gaelic SADHBH. *Sive* is the title of a popular contemporary play by John B. Keene.

Sixten (f.) Swedish: from an Old Norse personal name composed of the elements *sigr* victory + *steinn* stone.

Sjurd (m.) Norwegian: contracted form of SIGURD.

Skipper (m.) English: originally a nickname from the vocabulary word *skipper* boss (originally a ship's captain, from Middle Dutch *schipper*), or else representing an agent derivative of *skip* to leap, bound (probably of Scandinavian origin). It is now sometimes used as an independent given name, especially in America.
Short forms: **Skip**, **Skipp**.

Slava (m.) Russian: pet form of the numerous compound names containing the Slavonic element *slav* glory, as, for example, *Mstislav* (see MŚCISŁAW), ROSTISLAV, *Stanislav* (see STANISLAS), and VYACHESLAV.

Sławomierz (m.) Polish: from an old Slavonic personal name composed of the elements *slav* glory + *meri* great, famous (see CASIMIR). The same elements appear in the reverse order in the name MIROSLAW.

Cognate: Czech: **Slavomír**.

Sly (m., f.) English (mainly U.S.): modern name. The reasons for its adoption as a given name are not clear. In the case of the American actor Sylvester Stallone, it is used as a contracted pet form of his given name. The fact that it coincides in form with the vocabulary word *sly* 'cunning, devious' does not seem to have been a bar to its use as a given name.

Sobiesław (m.) Polish: from an old Slavonic personal name composed of the elements *sobi* to appropriate, usurp + *slav* glory (cf. ROŚCISLAW).

Cognate: Czech: **Soběslav**.
Feminine form: Czech: **Soběslava**.
Pet forms: Czech: **Sobík**, **Sobeš** (m.); **Soběna**, **Sobeška** (f.).

Socorro (f.) Spanish: from a title of the Virgin Mary, *Nuestra Señora del Socorro* 'Our Lady of Perpetual Succour', alluding to her readiness to intercede for her devotees in distress.

Sofia (f.) Norwegian and Swedish form of SOPHIA.

Sofie (f.) Low German, Dutch, and Danish form of SOPHIA.

Sol (f., m.) **1**. (f.) Spanish: from Spanish *sol* sun (Latin *sol*), apparently alluding to the beauty and purity of the celestial body. This was a common given name in the Middle Ages, being borne, for example, by one of the daughters of El Cid, and it is still in use today; in part it may now be taken as a short form of SOLEDAD. **2**. (m.) Jewish: short form of SOLOMON used in the English-speaking world. The pet form **Solly** is also used.

Solange (f.) French: vernacular form of the Late Latin name *Sollemnia*, a derivative of *sollemnis* solemn, religious. St Solange was a poor shepherdess from Bourges who was killed in the 9th century by her master for resisting his attempts on her virtue; in consequence she came to be regarded as a martyr for the faith.

Soledad (f.) Spanish: from a title of the Virgin Mary, *María de Soledad* (from Spanish *soledad* solitude, Late Latin *sōlitās*, a derivative of *sōlus* alone). The allusion is to the Christian virtue of solitude, or separation from the distractions of the world.

Pet form: **Chole**.

Solita (f.) Spanish: pet form of the female name SOL.

Solly (m.) Pet form of the male name SOL, used mainly by Jews in the English-speaking world.

Solomon (m.) Biblical: name (Hebrew *Shlomo*, derived from *shalom* peace) of a king of Israel, son of David and Bathsheba, who was legendary for his wisdom (2 Samuel 12–24; 1 Kings 1–11; 2 Chronicles 1–9). The books of Proverbs and Ecclesiastes were ascribed to him, and the Song of Solomon, otherwise known as the Song of Songs, bears his name. It has been sporadically used among Gentiles since the Middle Ages, often by parents who wished wisdom for their child, but is still largely a Jewish name.

Other forms: Jewish: **Shlomo** (Hebrew); **Zalman** (Yiddish). Gaelic: **Solamh**.
Short form: SOL.

Solveig (f.) Norwegian: from an Old Norse female personal name composed of the elements *salr* house, hall + *veig* strength. The usual Swedish spelling of the name is **Solvig**, the Danish **Solvej**. The name Solveig is borne by the heroine of Henrik Ibsen's *Peer Gynt* (1867, first performed 1876); although abandoned by Peer without warning, she patiently waits several years for his return, and at the last redeems him from doom by her love and forgiveness.

Somerled (m.) Scottish (Highland): from the Old Norse personal name *Sumarliðr*, probably originally a byname meaning 'summer traveller'. This was the name of the founder of the powerful and widespread Clan MacDonald, Lords of the Isles from the 12th to the 15th century, and it is still occasionally bestowed on Macdonalds and members of septs of the various branches of the clan. The Somerled in question was Lord of Argyll from about 1130 to 1164. The clan actually takes its name from his grandson.

Variants: **Summerlad** (altered by folk etymology); **Somhairle** (Gaelic form, also used in Ireland; Anglicized as **Sorley**).

Sonya (f.) Russian: pet form of *Sofya* (see SOPHIA), popular as a given name in its own right in Britain and elsewhere since the 1920s.

Variants: **Sonia** (English spelling); **Sonja**, **Sonje** (German and Scandinavian spellings).

Soo (f.) English: fanciful variant spelling of SUE.

Sondra (f.) English: of recent origin, apparently an altered form of SANDRA.

Sophia (f.) From the Greek word meaning 'wisdom'. The Eastern cult of St Sophia seems to be the result of misinterpretation of the phrase *Hagia Sophia* 'holy wisdom' as if it meant 'St Sophia'. The name became popular in England in the 17th and 18th centuries. The heroine of Fielding's novel *Tom Jones* (1749) is called Sophia Weston. In recent years, its popularity has been further increased by the fame of the Italian film actress Sophia Loren (b. 1934). In the Scottish Highlands it has been used as an Anglicized form of the Gaelic name *Beathag* (see BEATHAN).

Derivatives: French, English, German: **Sophie**. Low German, Danish, Dutch: **Sofie**. Norwegian, Swedish: **Sofia**. Polish: **Zofia**. Czech: **Zofie**. Hungarian: **Zsófia**.
Pet forms: Low German: **Fieke**. Russian: **Sonya**. Polish: **Zosia**. Czech: **Žofka**.

Sophie (f.) Variant, of French origin, of SOPHIA. In the English-speaking world, where it has been popular since the 18th century, it is often taken as a pet form of *Sophia*, and is sometimes spelled **Sophy**.

Sorcha (f.) Irish and Scottish Gaelic name derived from an Old Celtic element meaning 'brightness'. In Ireland it has been considered a Gaelic form of SARAH, and Anglicized as *Sarah* and *Sally*, but this is based on no more than a slight phonetic similarity. In Scotland the meaning of the name has resulted in its being translated as *Clara*.

Sören (m.) Scandinavian (Danish) form of *Severinus* (see SEVERINO).

Sorley (m.) Scottish (Highland) and Irish: Anglicized form of Gaelic *Somhairle*; see SOMERLED.

Sorne (f.) Basque equivalent of CONCEPCIÓN.

Sorrel (f.) English: from the plant, so named in the Middle Ages from Old French *surele*, apparently a derivative of *sur* sour (of Germanic origin), alluding to the acid taste of its leaves. The spellings **Sorrell** and **Sorell** also occur; the rare **Sorel** is used in Noel Coward's *Hay Fever* (1925).

Spencer (m.) English: transferred use of the surname, originally an occupational name for a 'dispenser' of supplies in a manor house. This is the name of a great English noble family, traditionally supposed to be descended from someone who performed this function in the royal household. Its popularity as a given name was increased in the mid-20th century by the fame of the American film actor Spencer Tracy (1900–67).

Spike (m.) English: normally a nickname, but occasionally bestowed as an official given name. As a nickname it seems usually to refer to an unruly tuft or 'spike' of hair.

Spiridon (m.) Russian: from the Late Greek personal name *Spiridion*, a diminutive formation from Latin *spiritus* spirit, soul. This name was borne by a 4th-century saint much venerated in the Eastern Church. He was a bishop of Tremithus in Cyprus and was persecuted under the Emperor Diocletian, but survived to play a major role at the Council of Nicaea (325). See also DUŠAN.

Sroel (m.) Jewish: Yiddish form of ISRAEL.

Staaf (m.) Dutch: short form of *Gustaaf* (see GUSTAV).

Staas (m.) Frisian: derived from a short form of *Anastasius* (see ANASTASIA), and perhaps also the rarer *Eustasius* (see EUSTACE).

Stacey (f.) English: of uncertain derivation, perhaps originating as a pet form of ANASTASIA, and respelled as a result of association with EUSTACE. It is not clear why this name, together with its variants **Stacy** and **Stacie**, should have become so common in the 1970s and 1980s. It is now also occasionally used as a male name.

Staffan (m.) Swedish form of STEPHEN, now rather less common than STEFAN.

Stafford (m.) English: transferred use of the aristocratic surname, which originated as a local name from any of various places, so called from Old English *staò* landing place + *ford* ford, most notably the county town of Staffordshire. This was the surname of the family that held the dukedom of Buckingham in the 15th and 16th centuries.

Stan (m.) English: short form of STANLEY, not commonly used as an independent given name.

Stanislas (m.) Latinized form of an old Slavonic personal name composed of the elements *stan* government + *slav* glory. St Stanislas Szczepanowski (1030–79) was a bishop of Cracow who was killed by King Bolesław the Cruel of Poland.
Variant: **Stanislaus**.
Cognates: Polish: **Stanisaw**. Czech, Russian: **Stanislav**.
Feminine forms: Polish: **Stanisawa**. Czech: **Stanislava**.
Pet forms: Polish: **Stasiak** (m.). Czech: **Stáňa** (m., f.); **Stanek, Stanko, Staní(če)k, Stanouš(ek)** (m.); **Stáníčka, Stanuška** (f.).

Stanley (m.) English: transferred use of the surname, derived from any of numerous places (in Derbys., Durham, Gloucs., Staffs., Wilts., and Yorks.) named in Old English from *stān* stone + *lēah* wood or clearing. This is well established as a given name, and has been widely used as such since the 1880s. It had been in occasional use earlier. Its popularity seems to have stemmed at least in part from the fame of the explorer Sir Henry Morton Stanley (1841–1904), who was born in Wales as John Rowlands but later took the name of his adoptive father, a New Orleans cotton dealer.
Short form: **Stan**.

Star (f.) English: modern given name, a vernacular equivalent of STELLA.

Stasiak (m.) Polish: pet form of *Stanisław* (see STANISLAS).

Steaphan (m.) Scottish Gaelic form of STEPHEN.

Stefan (m.) German and Scandinavian form of STEPHEN. This form is also in use in Russia and Poland, beside the more common respective forms STEPAN and SZCZEPAN.

Stefania (f.) Italian form of STEPHANIE. This form of the name is also used in Poland.
Short form: Italian: **Fania**.

Stefano (m.) Italian form of STEPHEN.

Steffan (m.) Welsh form of STEPHEN.

Steffany (f.) English: variant spelling of STEPHANIE.

Steffen (m.) Low German form of STEPHEN.

Steffi (f.) German: pet form of STEPHANIE.

Stella (f.) English: from Latin *stella* star. This was not used as a given name before the 16th century, when Sir Philip Sidney seems to have been the first to use it (as a name deliberately far removed from the prosaic range of everyday names) in his sonnets supposedly addressed by Astrophel to his lady, Stella.
Cognate: Spanish: **Estrella**. See also ESTELLE.

Sten (m.) Swedish: from an Old Norse personal name, originally a short form of the various compound names containing the element *steinn* stone (cf. e.g. TORSTEN). Numerous names of Old Norse origin containing this as a first element are still in limited used today, as, for example, **Stenbjörn, Stenfinn, Stenkil**, and **Stenulf**.
Cognates: Norwegian: **Stein**. Danish: **Ste(e)n**.

Stenya (m.) Russian: pet form of STEPAN. The form **Styopa** is also used.

Stepan (m.) The usual Russian form of STEPHAN.

Štěpán (m.) Czech form of STEPHEN.
Pet forms: **Štěpanek, Štěp(k)a, Štěpek, Štěpík, Stepoušek**.
Feminine form: **Stěpánka** (formally a diminutive).

Steph (f.) English: informal short form of STEPHANIE.

Stephan (m.) German and English: variant of STEPHEN, preserving the vowels of the Greek name.

Stéphane (m.) French: learned form of STEPHEN, in occasional use beside the vernacular ÉTIENNE.

Stephanie (f.) English and German: from French *Stéphanie*, vernacular form of Latin *Stephania*, a variant of *Stephana*, which was in use among early Christians as a feminine form of *Stephanus* (see STEPHEN).
Variant: English: **Steffany**.
Cognates: Italian, Polish: **Stefania**. Spanish: **Estefania**.
Pet form: English: **Stevie**.

Stephen (m.) Usual English spelling of the name of the first Christian martyr (Acts 6–7), whose feast is accordingly celebrated next after Christ's own (26 December). His name is derived from the Greek word *stephanos* garland, crown.
Variants: **Steven, Stephan**.
Cognates: Irish Gaelic: **Stiofán, Stiana**. Scottish Gaelic: **Steaphan**. Welsh: **Steffan**. French: **Étienne, Stéphane**. Provençal: **Esteve**. Italian: **Stefano**. Spanish: **Estéban**. Catalan: **Esteve**. Portuguese: **Estévao**. German: **Stefan, Stephan**. Low German: **Steffen**. Scandinavian: **Stefan; Staffan** (Swedish). Polish: **Szczepan, Stefan**. Czech: **Stěpan**. Russian: **Stepan, Stefan**. Hungarian: **István**.
Short form: English: **Steve**.
Pet form: English: **Stevie**.

Sterling (m.) English: transferred use of the surname, which may represent a hypercorrected form of the nickname *Starling* (referring to the bird). As a given name, however, *Sterling* is likely to have been chosen because of its association with the vocabulary word occurring in such phrases as 'sterling qualities' and 'sterling worth'. This word is derived from the Middle English word *sterrling* 'little star': some Norman coins had a little star on them.

Variant: **Stirling** (respelled as if derived from the Scottish placename, which is of uncertain derivation, possibly from **Welsh** *ystre Velyn* 'dwelling of Melyn').

Steve (m.) English: short form of STEPHEN and STEVEN.

Steven (m.) English: variant of STEPHEN, reflecting the normal pronunciation of the name in the English-speaking world.

Stevie (m., f.) English: pet form of STEPHEN and of STEPHANIE. A well-known recent female bearer was the poet Stevie Smith (1902–71), whose baptismal name was Florence Margaret Smith.

Variant: **Stevi** (f.).

Stewart (m.) English: variant of STUART, less common as a given name, although more common as a surname.

Stian (m.) Scandinavian: from the Old Norse personal name *Stígandr*, originally a byname meaning 'wanderer'. This is currently a very popular given name in Norway.

Stiana (m.) Irish Gaelic form of STEPHEN (see also STIOFÁN).

Stig (m.) Scandinavian: from the Old Norse personal name *Stígr*, a short form of *Stígandr* (see STIAN).

Stina (f.) German and Scandinavian: short form of any of the Latinate female given names that end in these two syllables, principally CRISTINA.

Stìneag (f.) Scottish Gaelic form of CHRISTINA.

Stiofán (m.) Irish Gaelic form of STEPHEN.

St John (m.) English: name expressing devotion to St John; it has been in use in the English-speaking world, mainly among Roman Catholics, from the last two decades of the 19th century up to the present day.

Stoffel (m.) German: pet form of *Christoph* (see CHRISTOPHER), with the addition of the hypocoristic suffix *-(e)l*.

Storm (m., f.) English: apparently a 20th-century coinage, although it may have been in use slightly earlier. The name is presumably derived from the climatic phenomenon, although it is hard to see why it should be chosen. It derives perhaps from the Romantic commitment to emotional drama, and may sometimes have been given in the hope that a child would have a dramatic personality. In other cases, it may have been used for a child born during a storm.

Stuart (m.) Scottish and English: from the French version of the surname *Stewart*. This form was introduced to Scotland in the 16th century by Mary Stuart, Queen of Scots, who was brought up in France. The surname originated as an occupational or status name for someone who served as a *steward* in a manor or royal household. The Scottish royal family of this name are traditionally supposed to be descended from a family who were hereditary stewards in Brittany before the Conquest. Use as a given name originated in Scotland, but is now widespread throughout the English-speaking world.

Variant: **Stewart**.
Short forms: **Stu**, **Stew**.

Sture (m.) Scandinavian (Swedish): from a medieval byname derived from the verb *stura* to be contrary, self-willed. This is now a common given name in Sweden as it has been borne by several great personalities in Swedish history.

Sue (f.) English: short form of SUSAN and, less commonly, of SUSANNA and SUZANNE. In the past couple of decades it has sometimes been used as an independent name.

Variants: **Su**, **Soo**.

Suelo (f.) Spanish: short form of CONSUELO.

Sukie (f.) English: pet form of SUSAN, very common in the 18th century, but now rare.

Variant: **Sukey**.

Summer (f.) English (esp. U.S.): from the name of the season (Old English *sumor*), used in modern times as a given name because of its pleasant associations.

Summerlad (m.) Scottish: variant spelling of SOMERLED, being taken by folk etymology as derived from the words *summer* and *lad*.

Sunniva (f.) Scandinavian: Latinized form of the Old English female name *Sunngifu*, composed of the elements *sunne* sun + *gifu* gift. According to legend, St Sunniva was a 10th-century British princess who was shipwrecked off the coast of Norway and murdered by the inhabitants as she struggled ashore.

Cognates: Swedish: **Synnöve**. Danish, Norwegian: **Synnøve**.

Susan (f.) English: Anglicized form of SUSANNA, and always the most common of this group of names.

Variant: **Suzan**.
Short form: **Sue**.
Pet forms: **Susie**, **Sukie**.

Susanna (f.) New Testament form (Luke 8: 3) of the Hebrew name *Shoshana* (from *shoshan* lily, in modern Hebrew also 'rose'). The name is also spelled **Susannah**, a transliteration used in the Old Testament. The tale of Susannah, wife of Joachim, and the elders who falsely accused her of adultery, is to be found in the apocryphal book that bears her name, and was popular in the Middle Ages and later.

Variant: **Suzanna**.
Cognates: English: **Susan**. Scottish Gaelic: **Siùsan**, **Siùsaidh**. French: **Suzanne**. German: **Susanne**. Polish: **Zuzanna**. Czech: **Zuzana**. Hungarian: **Zsuzsanna**.
Short form: Scandinavian: **Sanna**.

Susie (f.) English: pet form of SUSAN and SUSANNA.

Variants: **Suzie**, **Suzy**.

Suzanne (f.) French version of SUSANNA, now also used in the English-speaking world.

Suzette (f.) French: pet form of SUZANNE.

Svanhild (f.) Scandinavian spelling of SWANHILD. This is the name borne by the daughter of Sigurd and Gudrun in the Edda.

Svante (m.) Swedish: short form, dating from the Middle Ages, of the Slavonic name ŚWIĘTOPEŁK; cf. DAGMAR and GUSTAV.

Svatomír (m.) Czech form of ŚWIĘTOMIERZ.

Svatopluk (m.) Czech form of ŚWIĘTOPEŁK.

Svatoslav (m.) Czech form of ŚWIĘTOSŁAW.

Svea (f.) Swedish: patriotic name formed in the 19th century from the former name of Sweden, *Svearike* (now *Sverige*). The second element of the national name is from Old Norse *ríki* kingdom; the first is of uncertain derivation.

Sven (m.) Swedish: from the Old Norse byname *Sveinn* 'boy, lad'. It is now also used in the German-speaking world and to some extent in the United States.
Cognates: Danish: **Svend**. Norwegian: **Svein**.

Sverre (m.) Norwegian: from the Old Norse personal name *Sverrir*, originally apparently a byname for a wild or restless person, and connected with the dialectal term *sverra* to spin, swing, swirl about.

Svetlana (f.) Russian: vernacular loan translation (from the Slavonic element *svet* light) of the Greek name *Phōtinē* (from Greek *phōtos* light). St Photine was an early saint martyred at Rome in the 1st century; in the Eastern Church she has been identified with the 'Samaritan woman' mentioned in St John's gospel, chapter 4.
Cognate: Czech: **Světlana**.
Pet forms: Czech: **Světla**, **Světlanka**, **Světluše**, **Světluška**.

Svyatopolk (m.) Russian form of ŚWIĘTOPEŁK. This was the name of the brother of St Boris and St Gleb at whose behest they were murdered in 1015.

Svyatoslav (m.) Russian form of ŚWIĘTOSŁAW.

Swanhild (f.) Low German: from an Old Saxon female personal name composed of the elements *swan* swan + *hild* battle.
Variants: **Swanhilda**, **Swanhilde**.
Cognate: Scandinavian: **Svanhild**.

Świętomierz (m.) Polish: from an old Slavonic personal name composed of the elements *svyanto* bright, holy + *meri* great, famous (see CASIMIR).
Cognate: Czech: **Svatomír**.

Świętopełk (m.) Polish: from an old Slavonic personal name composed of the elements *svyanto* bright, holy + *polk* people, race.
Cognates: Czech: **Svatopluk**. Russian: **Svyatopolk**.

Świętosław (m.) Polish: from an old Slavonic personal name composed of the elements *svyanto* bright, holy + *slav* glory.
Cognates: Czech: **Svatoslav**. Russian: **Svyatoslav**.

Sybil (f.) English: from the name (Greek *Sibylla* or *Sybilla*, with confusion over the vowels from an early period) of a class of ancient prophetesses inspired by Apollo. According to medieval theology, they were pagans denied the knowledge of Christ but blessed by God with some insight into things to come and accordingly admitted to heaven. It was thus regarded as a respectable name to be borne by Christians. The classical form **Sybilla** and the French form **Sybille** are also occasionally used in the English-speaking world.
Variants: **Sibyl**, SIBILLA.

Sydney (m., occasionally f.) English: variant of SIDNEY. It was a medieval practice to write *y* for *i*, for greater clarity since *i* was easily confused with other letters.

Sylvain (m.) French form of *Silvanus* (see SILVANO).

Sylvester (m.) English: variant of SILVESTER.

Sylvia (f.) English: variant, respelled for elegance, of SILVIA. It is now rather more common than the plain form.

Sylvie (f.) French form of SILVIA, now also used in the English-speaking world.

Sylwester (m.) Polish form of SILVESTER.

Synnöve (f.) Swedish: vernacular form of SUNNIVA. In Denmark and Norway the form **Synnøve** is used.

Szczepan (m.) The usual Polish form of STEPHEN.

Szczęsny (m.) Polish: name meaning 'happy, fortunate', used as a vernacular equivalent of FELIX.

Szerény (m.) Hungarian: name representing a loan translation of MODEST.

Szilárd (m.) Hungarian: from the vocabulary word *szilárd* firm, steadfast. The name is used as a loan translation of CONSTANT.

Szörény (m.) Hungarian form of *Severinus*; see SEVERINO.

Szymon (m.) Polish form of SIMON.

T

Taavi (m.) Finnish form of DAVID.

Tabitha (f.) Aramaic name, meaning 'doe' or 'roe', borne in the New Testament by a woman who was restored to life by St Peter (Acts 9: 36–41). In the biblical account this form of the name is given together with its Greek equivalent, DORCAS. It was one of the names much favoured by Puritans and Dissenters from the 17th to the 19th century, and is still occasionally used as a girl's name in the English- and German-speaking world. However, in Britain it is more commonly bestowed on cats.
Pet forms: English: **Tabby** (obsolete). German: **Tabea** (at present a fashionable name in German-speaking countries).

Tad (m.) English and Irish: normally an Anglicized form of TADHG, but sometimes a short form of THADDEUS. It is fairly commonly used as an independent given name, in particular in America.

Taddeo (m.) Italian form of THADDEUS.

Tadeo (m.) Spanish form of THADDEUS.

Tadeu (m.) Portuguese form of THADDEUS.

Tadeusz (m.) Polish form of THADDEUS.

Tadhg (m.) Irish and Scottish Gaelic: traditional name, originally a byname meaning 'poet, philosopher'. This was a very common given name throughout the Middle Ages, and Protestants in modern Northern Ireland use *Taig* or *Teague* as a generic derogatory term for a Catholic Irishman.
Variant: Scottish Gaelic: **Taogh**.
Anglicized forms (Irish): **Tad**, **Teague**, **Teigue**, THADDEUS, **Thady**, **Tim**.

Tadzio (m.) Polish: pet form of TADEUSZ.

Tage (m.) Scandinavian (Danish): from Old Danish *Taki*, originally a byname meaning 'guarantor, surety' or 'receiver' (from *taka* to take).

Talfryn (m.) Welsh: modern given name, originally a local name, from Welsh *tal* high, end of + a mutated form of *bryn* hill.

Taliesin (m.) Welsh: composed of the elements *tâl* brow + *iesin* shining. This was the name of a legendary 6th-century Welsh poet, and has been revived in recent times.

Talitha (f.) New Testament: from an Aramaic word meaning 'little girl'. Jesus raised a child from the dead with the words 'Talitha cumi; which is, being interpreted, Damsel, I say unto thee, arise' (Mark 5: 41).

Tallulah (f.) English: rare name, chosen occasionally as a result of the fame of the American actress Tallulah Bankhead (1903–68). In spite of its exotic appearance, her given name was not adopted for the sake of her career but inherited from her grandmother. It may be a variant of TALULLA; or it may be taken from the placename Tallulah Falls, Georgia, which is of American Indian origin.

Talulla (f.) Irish: Anglicized form of the Gaelic name Tuilelaith, composed of elements meaning 'abundance' and 'lady, princess'. This name was borne by at least two Irish saints of the 8th and 9th centuries.

Talya (f.) Russian: pet form of NATALYA.
Variant: **Talia** (an Anglicized spelling).

Tam (m.) Scottish: short form of THOMAS.

Tamar (f.) Jewish: very popular modern Hebrew name; see TAMARA.
Variant: **Tama**.

Tamara (f.) Russian: probably derived from the Hebrew name *Tamar* 'date palm', with the addition of the feminine suffix -*a*. The name Tamar is borne in the Bible by two female characters: the daughter-in-law of Judah, who is involved in a somewhat seamy story of sexual intrigue (Genesis 38), and a daughter of King David (2 Samuel 13), the full sister of Absalom, who is raped by her half-brother Amnon, for which Absalom kills him. It is rather surprising, therefore, that it should have given rise to such a popular given name. However, Absalom himself later has a daughter named Tamar, who is referred to as 'a woman of a fair countenance' (2 Samuel 14: 27), and the name may derive its popularity from this reference.

Tammaro (m.) Italian: of Germanic origin, composed of the elements *thank* thought + *mār*, *mēr* fame. St Tammarus was an African priest who, together with St Priscus, landed in southern Italy in the 5th century after being cast adrift in a rudderless boat by the Arian Vandals.

Tammy (f.) English: pet form of TAMARA and TAMSIN.

Tamsin (f.) English: contracted form of *Thomasina* (see THOMAS), relatively common throughout Britain in the Middle Ages, but confined to Cornwall immediately before its recent revival.

Tancredo (m.) Italian: of Germanic origin, composed of the elements *thank* thought + *rād* counsel. The name has become known in Italy through Torquato Tasso's *Gerusalemme Liberata* (1581), in which a prominent part is played by Tancred, hero of the *First Crusade* (1199).

Taneli (m.) Finnish form of DANIEL.

Tansy (f.) English: a flower name, derived from Greek *athanasia* immortal. It has enjoyed some popularity as a given name in the 20th century.

Tanya (f.) Russian: pet form of TATIANA, now quite commonly also used as an independent given name in the English-speaking world.
Variants: **Tania** (an English spelling); **Tanja** (a German spelling).

Tara (f.) English: from the name (meaning 'hill') of a place in Meath, seat of the high kings of Ireland. It has been used as a female given name in America since around 1940, probably as a result of the success of the film *Gone with the Wind*, in which the estate of this name has great emotional significance. In Britain it was not much used before the 1960s, and its popularity since then seems to be the result of its use for the character Tara King in the television series *The Avengers*.

Taras (m.) Russian: from Greek *Tarasios* or *Tharasios*, a name of uncertain origin, possibly connected with the town or river of *Taras* (Latin *Tarentum*) in southern Italy. St Tarasius (d. 806) was bishop of Constantinople during a period of considerable religious and political upheaval, and he is much venerated in the Orthodox Church. The form *Tarasi* is less common.

Tárlach (m.) Irish Gaelic: a modern shortened form of TOIRDHEALBHACH.

Tarquin (m.) The name borne by two early kings of Rome, Tarquinius Priscus 'the Old' (616–578 BC) and Tarquinius Superbus 'the Proud' (534–510 BC). It is of uncertain, probably Etruscan, origin; many of the most ancient Roman institutions and the vocabulary associated with them, as well as many Roman family names, were borrowed from the Etruscans. The name is now occasionally used in the English-speaking world.

Tasgall (m.) Scottish Gaelic: traditional name, originally a borrowing of the Old Norse personal name *Ásketill*, composed of the elements *fás* god + *ketill* sacrificial cauldron. This name is in use among the MacAskills in the Isle of Berneray, whose surname derives from a patronymic form of the same name. It is sometimes Anglicized as Taskill.

Tasha (f.) Short form of NATASHA, now quite commonly used in the English-speaking world (especially in America) as an independent given name.

Tatiana (f.) Russian: of early Christian origin. This was the name of various early saints honoured particularly in the Eastern Church. In origin it is a feminine form of Latin *Tatiānus*, apparently a derivative of *Tatius*, a Roman family name of obscure origin. Titus Tatius was, according to tradition, a king of the Sabines who later shared with Romulus the rule over a united population of Sabines and Latins.

Pet form: **Tanya**.

Tauno (m.) Finnish form of AUGUSTINE.

Tawny (f.) English: from the vocabulary word descriptive of hair colour (Anglo-Norman *tauné*, Old French *tané* tanned). This is a modern name created on the lines of examples such as GINGER and SANDY.

Variant: **Tawney**.

Taylor (m.) English: transferred use of the surname, which originated as an occupational name for a tailor, from Anglo-Norman French *taillour*, a derivative of *taillier* to cut (Late Latin *tāleāre*).

Teague (m.) Irish: Anglicized form of Gaelic TADHG.

Variant: **Teigue**.

Teal (f.) English: one of the female names taken from birds in the past couple of decades. The teal is a kind of small duck; its name is attested since the 14th century and seems to be connected with Middle Low German *tēlink*, Middle Dutch *tēling*.

Variant: **Teale**.

Teàrlach (m.) Scottish Gaelic: a modern shortened form of TOIRDHEALBHACH.

Feminine form: **Teàrlag**.

Teasag (f.) Scottish Gaelic form of JESSIE.

Techomír (m.) Czech: from an old Slavonic personal name composed of the elements *tech* consolation + *meri* great, famous (see CASIMIR).

Techoslav (m.) Czech: from an old Slavonic personal name composed of the elements *tech* consolation + *slav* glory.

Ted (m.) English: short form of EDWARD, also used for THEODORE.

Pet form: **Teddy**.

Teda (f.) Polish: pet form of TEODORA.

Teddy (m.) English: pet form of TED. Teddy bears were so named from the American president Theodore Roosevelt (1858–1919).

Tegwen (f.) Welsh: modern name composed of the elements *teg* fair, lovely + *(g)wen*, feminine form of *gwyn* white, fair, blessed, holy.

Teigue (m.) Irish: variant of TEAGUE.

Teive (m.) Jewish (Yiddish): variant of TEVYE.

Tekla (f.) Scandinavian form of THECLA.

Tel (m.) English: altered short form of TERRY or TERENCE, of recent origin. For the substitution of *-l* for *-r*, cf. HAL.

Teleri (f.) Welsh: extension of the name ELERI, with the addition of the honorific prefix *ty-* your. Teleri, daughter of Peul, is mentioned in the *Mabinogi*.

Telesforo (m.) Italian and Spanish: from Greek *Telesphoros*, a compound derived from *telos* end, completion + *pherein* to bring, bear. This was originally an epithet of Zeus or of the personified abstraction, Justice. Later it came to be understood as the name of an independent deity concerned with health, a companion of Aesculapius and Hygiea. In the Late Greek period it was used as a personal name, and in early Christian times it was borne by an early pope who was martyred under Hadrian in 136; he was a Calabrian Greek by origin.

Cognate: French: **Télesphore** (rare).

Teodora (f.) Italian, Spanish, Portuguese, Swedish, and Polish form of THEODORA.

Pet form: Polish: **Teda**.

Teodosio (m.) Italian, Spanish, and Portuguese: from the Latin name *Theodosius*, Greek *Theodosios*, composed of the elements *theos* god + *dōsis* giving (and so a doublet of THEODORE). The name was borne by several early saints, most notably Theodosius the Cenobiarch (423–529), a Cappadocian who founded several monasteries in Palestine.

Cognate: Russian: **Fe(o)dosi**. See also DOSIFEI.

Teofilo (m.) Italian, Spanish, and Portuguese form of THEOPHILUS.

Tere (f.) Spanish: short form of TERESA.

Terence (m.) English and Irish: from the Latin name *Terentius*, which is of uncertain origin. It was borne by the Roman playwright Marcus Terentius Afer (who was a former slave, and took his name from his master, Publius Terentius Lucanus), and later by various minor early Christian saints. As a modern given name it is a 'learned' back-formation from the supposed pet form TERRY. It has become common in Ireland through being used as an Anglicized form of the Gaelic name TOIRDHEALBHACH 'instigator'.

Variants: **Terrance**, **Terrence**.
Short form: **Tel**. See also TERRY.

Teresa (f.) Italian and Spanish form of THERESA. In the English-speaking world the name is often chosen in this spelling by Roman Catholics, with particular reference to the Spanish saint, Teresa of Ávila (Teresa Cepeda de Ahumada, 1515–82).
Short form: Spanish: **Tere**.
Pet forms: Spanish: **Teresita**, **Tete**.

Terje (m.) Norwegian: vernacular form of *Torgeir* (see TORGER).

Terrance (m.) The most common American spelling of TERENCE. The spelling Terrence is also frequent.

Terri (f.) English (esp. U.S.): name that seems to have originated either as a pet form of THERESA, or directly as a feminine spelling of TERRY.

Terry (m.) English: in the Middle Ages this was a Germanic name (composed of elements meaning 'tribe' and 'power' see DIETRICH) introduced to England by the Normans in the form *T(h)ierri*. (A fuller form is represented by the name of the Emperor *Theodoric*, where the spelling has been influenced by association with THEODORE; See also DEREK and DERRICK.) In modern English use *Terry* seems at first to have been a transferred use of the surname, which is derived from the medieval given name, and later to have been taken as a pet form of TERENCE.
Short form: **Tel**.

Terryl (f.) English: modern coinage, apparently an elaboration of TERRI with the suffix *-yl* seen in names such as CHERYL.

Tessa (f.) English: this name and its shortened form **Tess** are generally considered to be pet forms of THERESA, although now often used independently. However, the formation is not clear, and *Tessa* may be of distinct origin. Literary contexts of the late 19th century show that the name was thought of as Italian, although it is in fact unknown in Italy.
Pet form: **Tessie**.

Tete (f.) Spanish: pet form of TERESA.

Tetty (f.) English: pet form of ELIZABETH, common in the 18th century (when it was borne, for example, by Samuel Johnson's wife) but now little used.
Variant: **Tettie**.

Teunis (m.) Dutch: short form derived from *Antonius* (see ANTHONY).

Tevye (m.) Jewish: Yiddish form of TUVIA.

Tex (m.) English (U.S.): short form of the ethnic name *Texan*, now used as a given name along the lines of DEX, LEX, and REX.

Thaddeus (m.) Latin form of a New Testament name, the byname used to refer to one of Christ's lesser-known apostles, whose given name was *Lebbaeus* (Matthew 10: 3). It is of uncertain origin. It may be a Greek spelling of an Aramaic version of a short form of a Greek name, perhaps *Theodōros* 'gift of God' (see THEODORE) or *Theodotos* 'given by God'. In Ireland this has been used as an Anglicized form of TADHG.
Derivatives: Italian: **Taddeo**. Spanish: **Tadeo**. Portuguese: **Tadeu**. Polish: **Tadeusz**. Russian: **Faddei**.
Short form: English, Irish: **Tad**.
Pet forms: Polish: **Tadzio**. Irish: **Thady**.

Thalia (f.) Name borne in classical mythology by the Muse of comedy; it is derived from Greek *thallein* to flourish, and has occasionally been chosen in recent years by parents in the English-speaking world in search of novelty.

Thea (f.) English: short form of DOROTHEA, now to some extent used as an independent given name.

Thecla (f.) English: contracted form of the Greek name *Theokleia*, composed of the elements *theos* god + *kleia* glory. The name was borne by a 1st-century saint (the first female martyr), who was particularly popular in the Middle Ages because of the lurid details of her suffering recorded in the apocryphal 'Acts of Paul and Thecla'.
Cognate: Scandinavian: **Tekla**.

Theda (f.) German: Latinate short form of the various old Germanic female names containing the element *theod* people, race, as, for example, *Theodelinde* 'people + tender' and *Theodegunde* 'people + strife'. The name enjoyed a brief popularity in America from about 1915 to 1920, due to the popularity of the silent-film actress Theda Bara (1890–1955), the original 'vamp'. Her real name was Theodosia Goodman.

Thelma (f.) English: first used by the novelist Marie Corelli for the heroine of her novel *Thelma* (1887). She was supposed to be Norwegian, but it is not a traditional Scandinavian name. Greek *thelēma* (neuter) means 'wish, (act of) will', and the name could perhaps be interpreted as a contracted form of this.

Thelonius (m.) Latinized form of the name of St Tillo (see TILL). The spelling Thelonious is particularly associated with the American jazz pianist Thelonious Monk (1920–82).

Theo (m.) English: short form of THEODORE and, less commonly, of THEOBALD.

Theobald (m.) English: from a Latinized form, first found in medieval documents, of a Norman name of Germanic origin, composed of the elements *theud* people, race + *bald* bold, brave; the first element has been altered under the influence of Greek *theos* god.
Cognates: Irish Gaelic: **Tiobóid**. Scottish Gaelic: **Tiobaid**.

Theodoor (m.) Dutch form of THEODORE.

Theodor (m.) German form of THEODORE.

Theodora (f.) Feminine form of THEODORE, borne most notably by a 9th-century empress of Byzantium, the wife of Theophilus the Iconoclast. It has frequently been used as an English given name. The elements are the same as those of DOROTHEA, but in reverse order.
Derivatives: Italian, Spanish, Portuguese, Swedish, and Polish: **TEODORA**. Russian: **Feodora**.

Theodore (m.) English: from the French form of the Greek name *Theodōros*, composed of the elements *theos* god + *dōron* gift. The name was popular among early Christians and was borne by several saints.
Cognates: French: **Théodore**. German: **Theodor**. Dutch: **Theodoor**. Hungarian: **Tivadar**. Russian: **Fyodor**. Jewish (Aramaic): **Todos**.
Short forms: English: **Theo**, **Ted**.

Theodosia (f.) Greek: derived from the elements *theos* god + *dōsis* giving. It was borne by several early saints venerated mostly in the Eastern Church, and is only very occasionally used in the English-speaking world today.

Theophilus (m.) New Testament: Latin form of the name of the addressee of St Luke's gospel and the Acts of the Apostles; also borne by various early saints. It is composed of the Greek elements *theos* god + *philos* friend, and was popular among early Christians because of its well-omened meaning: 'lover of God' or 'beloved by God'.

Derivatives: French: **Théophile**. Italian, Spanish, Portuguese: **Teofilo**. Russian: **Feofil**.

Thera (f.) English: of uncertain derivation. It could either represent a shortened form of THERESA, or be derived from the name of the Greek island of *Thēra*.

Theresa (f.) English: of problematic origin. The name seems to have been first used in Spain and Portugal, and, according to tradition, was the name of the wife of St Paulinus of Nola, who spent most of his life in Spain; she was said to have originated (and to have derived her name) from the Greek island of *Thēra*. However, this theory is neither factually nor etymologically reliable.

Cognates: Irish Gaelic: **Treasa**. French: **Thérèse** (also sometimes used in the English-speaking world in honour of St Thérèse of Lisieux, Marie Françoise Thérèse Martin, 1873–97). Spanish, Italian: TERESA. German: **Theresia** (much used in the combination **Maria Theresia** in families claiming connection with the royal Habsburg line; also occasionally used in the English-speaking world).

Short form: Spanish: **Tere**.

Pet forms: English: **Terri**; TESSA, **Tess**. Spanish: **Teresita**, **Tete**. German: **Resi**, **Reserl**, **Resli**.

Thierry (m.) French form of the Germanic name *Theodoric*; See also TERRY, DIETRICH, and DEREK.

Thijs (m.) Dutch: aphetic short form of *Matthijs* (see MATTHEW), now used as an independent given name.

Thomas (m.) New Testament name, borne by one of Christ's twelve apostles, referred to as 'Thomas, called Didymus' (John 11: 16; 20: 24). *Didymos* is the Greek word for 'twin', and the name is the Greek form of an Aramaic byname meaning 'twin'. The given name has always been popular throughout Christendom, perhaps because St Thomas's doubts and reassurance have made him seem a very human character.

Derivatives: Irish Gaelic: **Tomás**. Scottish Gaelic: **Tòmas**; **Tàmhas** (a dialectal variant, from which comes the surname *Mac Thàmhais*, Anglicized as *MacTavish*). Welsh: **Tomos**. Italian: **Tommaso**. Polish: **Tomasz**. Czech: **Tomáš**. Russian: **Foma**. Finnish: **Tuomo**.

Short forms: English: **Tom**. Scottish: **Tam**. Italian: **Maso**. Dutch: **Maas**.

Pet forms: English: **Tommy**. Scottish Gaelic: **Tòmachan**, **Tòmag**.

Feminine forms: English: **Thomasina**, **Thomasine**, TAMSIN.

Tia (f.) English: apparently in origin a short form of the various given names ending thus, as, for example, CRESCENTIA and LAETITIA.

Tibor (m.) Hungarian: from Latin *Tiberius*, a derivative of the name (of obscure origin) of the River Tiber. It was borne by the second Roman emperor and by a martyr who was executed in 303 under the Emperor Diocletian, together with Modestus and Florence.

Tiede (m.) Dutch: pet form of DIEDERIK.

Tiernan (m.) Irish: Anglicized form of the Gaelic name Ti(ghe)arnán, originally a byname representing a diminutive form of *tighearna* lord.

Tierney (m.) Irish: Anglicized form of the Gaelic name Ti(ghe)arnach, a derivative of *tighearna* lord. The name was borne by a 6th-century saint who served as abbot of Clones and later as bishop of Clogher.

Tiffany (f.) Usual medieval English form of Greek *Theophania* 'Epiphany', from *theos* god + *phainein* to appear. This was once a relatively common name, given particularly to girls born on the feast of the Epiphany (6 January), and it gave rise to an English surname. As a given name, it fell into disuse until revived in the 20th century under the influence of the famous New York jewellers, Tiffany's, and the film, starring Audrey Hepburn, *Breakfast at Tiffany's* (1961). In 1982 this was the most popular of all female names in use among American Blacks, and thirty-third most popular among Whites.

Tikhon (m.) Russian form of TYCHO.

Tikvah (f.) Jewish: Hebrew name meaning 'hope'. The name is borne in the Bible by a male character mentioned in passing (2 Kings 22: 14), but is now a female name chosen for the sake of its good omen.

Variant: **Tikva**.

Tilda (f.) English and Swedish: short form of MATILDA.

Cognate: Danish: **Tilde**.

Till (m.) Low German: from a medieval pet form of DIETRICH and other Germanic personal names with the same first element. St Tillol evangelized the district around Tournai and Courtrai in Belgium during the 8th century.

Extended forms: **Til(l)man**; **Thelonius** (Latinized).

Tilly (f.) English: pet form of MATILDA, much used from the Middle Ages to the late 19th century, when it also came to be an independent given name. It is rare in either use nowadays.

Variant: **Tillie**.

Tim (m.) English: short form of TIMOTHY, also used in Ireland as an Anglicized form of TADHG.

Pet form: **Timmy** (normally used only for young boys).

Timothy (m.) English form, used in the Authorized Version of the Bible (alongside the Latin form *Timotheus*), of Greek *Timotheos*, composed of the elements *tīmē* honour + *theos* god. This was the name of a companion of St Paul; according to tradition, he was stoned to death for denouncing the worship of Diana, but there is no historical evidence for this. Surprisingly, the name was not used in England at all before the Reformation.

Cognates: French: **Timothée**. Italian, Spanish, Portuguese: **Timoteo**. Polish: **Tymoteusz**. Russian: **Timofei**.

Pet form: Russian: **Tyoma**.

Tina (f.) Short form of CHRISTINA and, less commonly, of other female names ending in *-tina*. This is a relatively common given name in the English-speaking world, and elsewhere. It was the most common of all female names bestowed in Denmark in the mid-1960s.

Tioboid (m.) Irish Gaelic form of THEOBALD, derived in the early Middle Ages from Anglo-Norman *Thebaud*.

Cognate: Scottish Gaelic: **Tiobaid**.

Tirion (f.) Welsh: modern given name, from the vocabulary word meaning 'kind, gentle'.

Tirso (m.) Spanish: from the Greek name *Thyrsos*. A *thyrsos* was a characteristic vine-decked staff carried by devotees of the god Dionysus; the word seems to have been introduced, together with the cult of Dionysus, from the Orient. St Thyrsos was martyred at Apollonia in Phrygia in *c*.251, together with Lucius and Kallinikos. Their relics were brought to Spain in the early Middle Ages, and Thyrsos was honoured with a full office in the Mozarabic liturgy.

Cognates: Catalan: **Tirs**. Russian: **Firs**.

Tita (f.) English: short form of MARTITA, or else perhaps a feminine form of TITUS.

Titty (f.) English: pet form of LAETITIA that has now become obsolete because of its unfortunate coincidence in form with the slang word for a female breast.

Titus (m.) From an old Roman given name, of unknown origin. It was borne by a companion of St Paul who became the first bishop of Crete, and also by the Roman emperor who destroyed Jerusalem in AD 70. It is not commonly used as a given name in the English-speaking world.

Derivative: Italian, Spanish, Portuguese: **Tito**.

Tivadar (m.) Hungarian form of THEODORE.

Tiziano (m.) Italian: name borne in honour of the famous medieval painter Tiziano Vecellio (?1490–1576), known in English as Titian. The medieval name *Tiziano* derives from Latin *Titiānus*, a double derivative of TITUS that was borne by a 6th-century bishop of Brescia and a 7th-century bishop of Oderzo.

Tjalf (m.) East Frisian form of DETLEV.

Tjark (m.) East Frisian form of DEREK.

Toal (m.) Irish: Anglicized form of TUATHAL.

Tobbe (m.) Swedish and Danish: pet form of TORBJÖRN and *Torbjørn*.

Tobias (m.) Biblical: Greek form of Hebrew *Tobiah* 'God is good'. This name is borne by several characters in the Bible (appearing in the Authorized Version also as *Tobijah*), but in the Middle Ages it was principally associated with the tale of 'Tobias and the Angel'. According to the Book of Tobit in the Apocrypha, Tobias, the son of Tobit, a rich and righteous Jew of Nineveh, was lucky enough to acquire the services of the archangel Raphael as a travelling companion on a journey to Ecbatana. He returned wealthy, married, and with a cure for his father's blindness. A historical St Tobias was martyred (*c*.315) at Sebaste in Armenia, together with Carterius, Styriacus, Eudoxius, Agapius, and five others.

Cognates: Jewish: **Tuvia** (Hebrew); **Tevye**, **Teive** (Yiddish).

Toby (m.) English: vernacular form of TOBIAS.

Todd (m.) English: transferred use of the surname, which was originally a nickname from an English dialect word meaning 'fox'.

Todos (m.) Jewish: Aramaic form of Greek *Theodōros* (see THEODORE). The name has been in use among Jews since the Hellenistic period.

Toinette (f.) English and French: short form of ANTOINETTE.

Toini (f.) Finnish form of ANTONIA.

Toirdhealbhach (m.) Irish Gaelic: probably originally a by-name meaning 'instigator', from *toirdhealbh* prompting + the Gaelic suffix *-ach*. The belief that this is a derivative of the name of the Norse god of thunder, *Porr*, is probably no more than folk etymology.

Cognate: Scottish Gaelic: **Teàrlach**.
Anglicized forms: TURLOUGH, **Turley**; TERENCE.

Toivo (f.) Finnish: meaning 'hope', this is a loan translation of Latin *spes*, Greek *elpis*.

Toltse (f.) Jewish: Yiddish name, probably from the Italian affectionate nickname *Dolce* 'sweet, lovely' (cf. DULCIE).

Tom (m.) English: short form of THOMAS, in use since the Middle Ages, and recorded as an independent name since the 18th century.

Pet form: **Tommy**.

Tòmas (m.) Scottish Gaelic form of THOMAS.

Tomás (m.) Irish Gaelic form of THOMAS.

Tomáš (m.) Czech form of THOMAS.

Pet forms: **Tomášek, Tomoušek, Tomik, Toman**.

Tomasz (m.) Polish form of THOMAS.

Tommaso (m.) Italian form of THOMAS.

Short form: **Maso**.

Tomos (m.) Welsh form of THOMAS.

Tonete (m.) Spanish: pet form of ANTONIO.

Toni (f.) English (mainly U.S.): either a pet form of ANTONIA or a supposedly feminine spelling of TONY.

Variants: **Tonia**, **Tonie** (less common).

Tonio (m.) Italian: short form of ANTONIO.

Tönjes (m.) Low German and Frisian: short form of *Antonius* (see ANTHONY).

Variant: **Tönnies**.

Toño (m.) Spanish: short form of ANTONIO.

Tony (m.) English: short form of ANTHONY, now sometimes used as an independent name in the English-speaking world.

Topaz (f.) English: one of the rarer examples of the class of modern female names taken from vocabulary words denoting gemstones. The topaz gets its name via French and Latin from Greek; it is probably ultimately of oriental origin. In the Middle Ages this was sometimes used as a male name, representing a form of TOBIAS.

Tor (m.) Scandinavian: originally the name of the god of thunder in Norse mythology, Thor (Old Norse *Þórr*). This was not used as a personal name during the Middle Ages. The modern name is either a late 18th-century revival of the divine name or else a vernacular development of TORD.

Variant: **Thor** (chiefly Danish).

Torbjörn (m.) Swedish: from an Old Norse personal name composed of the name of the god Thor (*Þórr*) + Old Norse *björn* bear.

Cognates: Danish: **T(h)orbjørn, Torbe(r)n**.
Norwegian: **Torbjørn**.
Pet form: Swedish, Danish: **Tobbe**.

Torborg (f.) Scandinavian: from an Old Norse female personal name composed of the name of the god Thor (*Þórr*) + Old Norse *borg* fortification.

Variants: **Thorborg**. Norwegian: **Torbjørg**.

Tord (m.) Scandinavian: contracted form of the Old Norse personal name *Þorfriðr*, composed of the name of the god Thor (*Þórr*) + Old Norse *friðr* peace.

Tordis (f.) Scandinavian: from an Old Norse female personal name composed of the name of the god Thor (*Þórr*) + Old Norse *dís* goddess.

Tore (m.) Scandinavian: from the Old Norse personal name *Þórir*, apparently originally composed of the name of the god Thor (*Þórr*) + Old Norse *verr* man. It has also been interpreted as a derivative form from *Þórr*. As early as the Viking period, however, the form *Þóri* was being used as a short form of all the compound names with the first element *Þórr*.

Variant: **Ture**.

Torger (m.) Swedish: from an Old Norse personal name composed of the name of the god Thor (*Þórr*) + Old Norse *geirr* spear.

Cognates: Norwegian: **Torgeir**, **Terje**.

Toribio (m.) Spanish: from Latin *Turibius*, a name of extremely uncertain derivation. It may represent a Latinized form of an indigenous Iberian name. The name was borne by a 5th-century bishop of Astorga and by the 6th-century founder of the abbey of Liébana in Asturias.

Torkel (m.) Swedish: from a contracted form of the Old Norse personal name *Þorketill*, composed of the name of the god Thor (*Þórr*) + Old Norse *ketill* kettle, helmet.

Variants: **Torkil**, **Thorkel**.
Cognates: Norwegian: **Torkjell**. Danish: **Torkil(d)**. See also **Torquil**.

Tormod (m.) Scottish Gaelic: traditional name, originally a borrowing of the Old Norse personal name *Þormóðr*, composed of the name of the god Thor (*Þórr*) + Old Norse *móðr* mind, courage.

Variant: **Tormailt** (a dialectal form).
Anglicized form: **Norman** (chosen because of the similarity in sound and because the Gaelic name is generally known to be of Norse origin).

Torolf (m.) Swedish and Danish: from an Old Norse personal name composed of the name of the god Thor (*Þórr*) + Old Norse *úlfr* wolf.

Variant: **Torulf**.
Cognate: Norwegian: **Torolv**.

Torquil (m.) Scottish: Anglicized form of the traditional Gaelic name **Torcall**, originally a borrowing of the Old Norse personal name *Þorketill* (see **Torkel**). The earlier uncontracted form of the Gaelic name is preserved in the surname *Mac Thorcadail*, Anglicized as *MacCorquodale*.

Torsten (m.) Swedish and Danish: from an Old Norse personal name composed of the name of the god Thor (*Þórr*) + Old Norse *steinn* stone.

Variant: **Thorstein(n)**.
Cognate: Norwegian: **Torstein**.

Torvald (m.) Scandinavian: from an Old Norse personal name composed of the name of the god Thor (*Þórr*) + Old Norse *valdr* ruler.

Variant: **Thorwald**. See also **Tove**.

Tory (f.) English: pet form of **Victoria**.

Totty (f.) English: pet form of **Charlotte**, representing a rhyming variant of **Lottie**. The name was most common in the 18th and 19th centuries, like **Tetty**.

Variant: **Tottie**.

Toussaint (m.) French: name chosen by parents who wish to invoke the blessing and protection of 'all the saints' (French *tous (les) saints*) for their son. The name is also often given to a boy born on the feast of All Saints (cf. **Santos**).

Tova (f.) 1. Jewish: modern Hebrew name meaning 'good' (cf. **Tobias**). 2. Swedish: from the Old Norse female personal name *Tófa*, a short form of *Þorfríðr* (see **Turid**).

Tove (f., m.) 1. (f.) Danish and Norwegian: from the Old Norse female personal name *Tófa*, a short form of *Þorfríðr* (see **Turid**). 2. (m.) Swedish: short form, used as early as the Viking period, of **Torvald**.

Variant (of 2): **Tuve**.

Tracy (f., formerly m.) English: transferred use of the surname, which is derived from a Norman baronial name from places in France called Tracy 'place of Thracius'. In former times, *Tracy* was occasionally used as a male given name, as were the surnames of other English noble families. Later, it was also used as a female name, generally being taken as a pet form of **Theresa**. In recent years, it has become an immensely popular female name. A strong influence was the character of Tracy Lord, played by Grace Kelly in the film *High Society* (1956).

Variants: **Tracey**, **Tracie** (f.).

Trahaearn (m.) Welsh: traditional name composed of the intensive prefix *tra-* + *haearn* iron.

Traolach (m.) Irish Gaelic: a dialectal form of **Toirdhealbhach**.

Travis (m.) English: transferred use of the surname, which is derived from a Norman French occupational name (from *traverser* to cross) for someone who collected a toll from users of a bridge or a particular stretch of road. It is now regularly used as a given name, especially in America and Australia.

Treasa (f.) Irish: Gaelic form of **Theresa**.

Treena (f.) English: modern variant spelling of **Trina**.

Treeza (f.) English: modern contracted spelling of **Theresa**.

Trevelyan (m.) English: transferred use of the surname, which is of Cornish origin, a local name from a place named in the Domesday Book as *Trevelien*, i.e. 'homestead or settlement (Cornish *tref*) of *Elian*'.

Trevor (m.) Welsh and English: transferred use of the Welsh surname, which in turn is from a placename. There are a large number of places in Wales called *Trefor*, from the elements *tref* settlement + *fôr*, mutated and unaccented form of *mawr* large. In recent years, *Trevor* has also become popular as a given name among people who have no connection with Wales.

Welsh form: **Trefor**.
Short form (informal): **Trev**.

Tricia (f.) English: short form of **Patricia**.

Trina (f.) English: short form of **Katrina**.

Trine (f.) Danish: short form of **Katrine**.

Trinette (f.) English: modern elaboration of **Trina**, using the originally French feminine diminutive suffix *-ette*.

Trinidad (f.) Spanish: name taken in honour of the Holy Trinity (Latin *trīnitas*, genitive *trīnitātis*, from *trīni*, a distributive numeral from *trēs* three).

Cognate: Portuguese: **Trindade**.
Short form: Spanish: **Trini**.

Triona (f.) Irish Gaelic: short form of **Caitríona**.

Anglicized form: **Triona**.

Trisha (f.) English: phonetic respelling of TRICIA, comparatively recent in origin. It is currently fairly popular, and sometimes bestowed as a given name in its own right.

Tristan (m.) English, Welsh, and French: variant of TRISTRAM. Both forms of the name occur in medieval and later versions of the legend.
Variant: **Trystan** (mainly Welsh).

Tristram (m.) English: from Celtic legend, the name borne by a hero of medieval romance. There are many different versions of the immensely popular and tragic story of Tristram and his love for Isolde. Generally, they agree that Tristram was an envoy sent by King Mark of Cornwall to bring back his bride, the Irish princess Isolde. Unfortunately, Tristram and Isolde fall in love with each other, having accidentally drunk the love potion intended for King Mark's wedding night. Tristram eventually leaves Cornwall to fight for King Howel of Brittany. Wounded in battle, he sends for Isolde. She arrives too late, and dies of grief beside his bier. The name *Tristram* is of unknown derivation, though it may be connected with Pictish *Drostan*; it has been altered from an irrecoverable original as a result of transmission through Old French sources that insisted on associating it with Latin *tristis* sad, a reference to the young knight's tragic fate.
Variants: **Tristrand**, **Tristan**, **Drystan**.

Trixie (f.) English: pet name derived from a short form of BEATRIX, occasionally used as an independent given name.
Variant: **Trixi**.

Trofim (m.) Russian: from the Greek name *Trophimos*, a derivative of *trophos* nurseling. It was borne by half a dozen early Christian saints, martyred under the Emperors Probus and Diocletian and much venerated in the Eastern Church.

Trond (m.) Scandinavian: originally an ethnic byname for someone who came from the Trøndelag region in central Norway. The name was in use in the Viking period, and was revived in the early 20th century.

Troy (m., f.) English: probably originally a transferred use of the surname, which is derived from *Troyes* in France. Nowadays, however, the given name is principally associated with the ancient city of Troy in Asia Minor, whose fate has been a central topic in epic poetry from Homer onwards. The story tells how Troy was sacked by the Greeks after a siege of ten years; according to classical legend, a few Trojan survivors got away to found Rome (and, according to medieval legend, another group founded Britain).

Trudeliese (f.) German: combination of the names *Trude* (see TRUDI) and LIESE.

Trudi (f.) German (esp. Swiss): pet form of the various female names ending in *-trud*; see, for example, GERTRUDE and ERMINTRUDE. It is now also used to some extent in the English-speaking world, under the influence of the many other female names now spelled with a final *-i*.

Trudy (f.) English: respelling of TRUDI.
Variant: **Trudie**.

Truman (m.) English: in the main, a transferred use of the surname. This is in part of English origin, representing a nickname derived from Old English *trēowe* true, trusty + *mann* man, but in America it is more commonly an Anglicized version of the German cognate *Treumann*. The favourable meaning of the elements has no doubt influenced its choice as a given name to some extent. A further possible influence may have been the fame of Harry S Truman (1884–1972), president of the United States (1945–52), but the given name was in use before he became president.
Variant: **Trueman**.

Tryggve (m.) Scandinavian: from an Old Norse personal name, originally a byname derived from the adjective *tryggr* true, trusty (cf. TRUMAN).
Variant: **Trygve**.

Trystan (m.) Variant (mainly Welsh) of TRISTAN.

Tuathal (m.) Irish Gaelic: name meaning 'ruler of a tribe'.
Anglicized form: **Toal**.

Tudur (m.) Welsh: traditional name derived from the Old Celtic form *Teutorix*, composed of elements meaning 'people, tribe' + 'ruler, king'. The name has been widely believed to be a Welsh form of THEODORE, but there is in fact no connection between the two names.
Variants: **Tudyr** (an earlier spelling); **Tudor** (an Anglicized spelling).

Tullio (m.) Italian: from the old Roman family name *Tullius*, borne, for example, by the orator Marcus Tullius Cicero (106–43 BC).

Tuomo (m.) Finnish form of THOMAS.

Ture (m.) Scandinavian: variant of TORE, formerly used mainly in Denmark and southern Sweden.

Turid (f.) Scandinavian: from an Old Norse female personal name composed of the name of the god Thor (*Þórr*) + Old Norse *fríðr* fair, beautiful.

Turiddu (m.) Italian (Sicilian): local pet form of *Salvatore* (see SALVADOR).

Turlough (m.) Irish: Anglicized form of Gaelic TOIRDHEALBHACH.

Tuvia (m.) Jewish: modern Hebrew form of TOBIAS.
Cognates: Yiddish: **Tevye**, **Teive**.

Tybalt (m.) English: the usual medieval form of THEOBALD, rarely used nowadays. It occurs in Shakespeare's *Romeo and Juliet* as the name of a brash young man who is killed in a brawl.

Tycho (m.) Latinized form of the name of St Tychon (d. *c*.450), bishop of Amathus in Cyprus, who worked to suppress the last remnants of the cult of Aphrodite on the island. The Greek name *Tychōn* means 'hitting the mark', and was chosen for the sake of its good omen. The most famous modern bearer of the given name was the Danish astronomer Tycho Brahe (1546–1601).
Derivatives: Swedish: **Tyko**. Danish: **Tyge** (vernacular). Russian: **Tikhon**.

Tyler (m.) English: transferred use of the surname, which originated as an occupational name borne by someone who tiled roofs.

Tymoteusz (m.) Polish form of TIMOTHY.

Tyoma (m.) Russian: pet form of ARTEMI and of *Timofei* (see TIMOTHY).

Tyrone (m.) English (esp. U.S.): from the name of a county in Northern Ireland and a town in Pennsylvania. Its use as a given name seems to be entirely due to the influence of the two film actors (father and son) called Tyrone Power.

Txomin (m.) Basque form of DOMINIC.

U

Ualan (m.) Scottish Gaelic form of the male name VALEN-TINE.

Variant: **Uailean**.

Uarraig (m.) Scottish Gaelic: traditional name composed of the elements *uall* pride + *garg* fierce. It has been Anglicized as KENNEDY, apparently because it was a common given name in kindreds with that surname.

Udo (m.) German: an old Germanic personal name derived from the element *uod(al)* prosperity, riches, fortune. It probably originated as a short form of the various compound names containing this element. It is still in comparatively common use in Germany.

Ughtred (m.) English: from the rare Old English personal name *Uhtræd*, composed of the elements *uht* dawn + *ræd* counsel, advice. This is a very uncommon given name in the English-speaking world, but remains in use in the Shuttleworth family.

Ugo (m.) Italian form of HUGH.

Uilleam (m.) Scottish Gaelic form of WILLIAM.

Pet forms: **Uilleachan**, **Uillidh**.

Uinseann (m.) Irish Gaelic form of VINCENT.

Uisdean (m.) Scottish Gaelic: traditional name, originally a borrowing of the Old Norse personal name *Eysteinn*, composed of the elements *ei*, *ey* always, for ever + *steinn* stone.

Variant: **Hùisdean**.

Anglicized form: HUGH.

Ulf (m.) Danish and Swedish: cognate of WOLF, from the Old Norse personal name or byname *Úlfr*.

Cognate: Norwegian: **Ulv**.

Ulick (m.) Irish: Anglicized form of Gaelic **Uilleac** or **Uilleag**. This name probably derives from Old Norse *Hugleikr*, composed of the elements *hugr* heart, mind, spirit + *leikr* play, sport. Alternatively, it may represent a diminutive derived from a short form of *Uilleam*, a Gaelic version of WILLIAM (cf. LIAM).

Ulises (m.) Spanish form of ULYSSES.

Ulisse (m.) Italian form of ULYSSES, taken up as a given name during the Renaissance, and permitted as a baptismal name by the Roman Catholic Church even though it had been borne neither by a New Testament character nor by an early saint.

Ulla (f.) Scandinavian: pet form of ULRIKA.

Ulric (m.) English: in the Middle Ages, this represented an Old English name composed of the elements *wulf* wolf + *ríc* power. In its occasional modern use, it is probably an Anglicized spelling of ULRICH.

Variant: **Ulrick**.

Ulrich (m.) German: from an old Germanic personal name composed of the elements *uodal* prosperity, riches, fortune + *ríc* power. This name was borne by two major German saints, Ulrich of Augsburg (d. 973) and Ulrich of Cluny (*c*.1018–93),

as well as by the Blessed Ulrich of Einsiedeln in Switzerland (d. *c*.980).

Cognates: Scandinavian: **Ulrik**. Polish: **Ulryk**.
Czech: **Oldřich**.
Pet form: German: **Utz**.

Ulrika (f.) Scandinavian form and German variant of ULRIKE.

Pet form: Scandinavian: **Ulla**.

Ulrike (f.) German and Danish: feminine form of ULRICH. The name is now also occasionally used in the English-speaking world.

Cognate: Czech: **Oldřiška**.

Ultan (m.) Irish: Anglicized form of the Gaelic name *Ultán*, a diminutive form of the ethnic name *Ultach* 'Ulsterman'.

Ulysses (m.) Latin form of the Greek name *Odysseus*, borne by the famous wanderer of Homer's *Odyssey*. The name is of uncertain derivation (it was associated by the Greeks themselves with the verb *odyssesthai* to hate); moreover, it is not clear why the Latin form should be so altered (mediation through Etruscan has been one suggestion). As an English given name it has occasionally been used in the 19th and 20th centuries, especially in America (like other names of classical origin such as HOMER and VIRGIL). It was the name of the 18th president of the United States, Ulysses S. Grant (1822–85). It has also been used in Ireland as a classicizing form of ULICK.

Derivatives: Italian: **Ulisse**. Spanish: **Ulises**.

Umberto (m.) Italian form of HUMBERT. The former Italian royal family is descended from the Blessed Umberto of Savoy (1136–88).

Úna (f.) Irish Gaelic: traditional name of uncertain derivation. It is identical in form with the vocabulary word *úna* hunger, famine, but may rather be connnected with *uan* lamb. The Anglicized form *Una* is sometimes taken to be from the feminine of Latin *unus* one, and therefore a doublet of UNITY. It is the name used by Edmund Spenser as that of the lady of the Red Cross Knight in *The Faerie Queene*: he almost certainly had Latin rather than Irish in mind, even though he worked in Ireland for a while.

Cognate: Scottish Gaelic: **Úna**.
Anglicized forms: **Una**; **Oona(gh)** (Irish); **Euna** (Scottish); UNITY, JUNO, WINIFRED, AGNES.

Unity (f.) English: from the quality (**Latin** *unitás*, a derivative of *unus* one). It achieved some currency among the Puritans, but has been mainly used in Ireland as a kind of Anglicized extended form of ÚNA.

Urban (m.) English, Danish, Swedish, Polish, and Czech: from the Latin name *Urbānus* 'city-dweller'. This was borne by numerous early saints, and was adopted by several popes (who may have felt it to be particularly appropriate since they ruled from the city of Rome).

Cognate: Hungarian: **Órban**.
Pet forms: Czech: **Ur(b)a**, **Ur(b)ek**.

Uri (m.) Jewish: from a Hebrew word meaning 'light' (cf. URIAH and URIEL). There is no connection with the Russian name YURI.

Uriah (m.) Biblical: name (from Hebrew, meaning 'God is light') borne by a Hittite warrior treacherously disposed of by King David after he had made Uriah's wife Bathsheba pregnant (2 Samuel 11). The Greek form *Urias* occurs in the New Testament (Matthew 1: 6). The name was popular in the 19th century, but is now most closely associated with the character of the obsequious Uriah Heep in Dickens's *David Copperfield* (1850) and has consequently undergone a sharp decline in popularity.

Uriel (m.) Biblical: Hebrew name composed of the elements *uri* light (cf. URI) + *'el* God, and so a doublet of URIAH. It is borne by two minor characters mentioned in genealogies (1 Chronicles 6: 24; 2 Chronicles 13: 2), and is relatively common among modern Jews.

Urien (m.) Welsh: name borne by a character in the *Mabinogi*, Urien of Rheged. He is probably identical with the historical figure Urien who fought against the Northumbrians in the 6th century. The name may be composed of the Old Celtic elements *ōrbo* privileged + *gen* birth.

Urs (m.) German (esp. Swiss): vernacular form of the Latin name *Ursus* 'bear'. Victor and Ursus were two soldiers of the Theban legion who were martyred in 286 and are particularly venerated in Switzerland.

Ursula (f.) English, German, and Scandinavian: from the Latin name *Ursula*, a diminutive of *ursa* (she-)bear (cf. URS). This was the name of a 4th-century saint martyred at Cologne with a number of companions, traditionally said to have been eleven thousand, but more probably just eleven, the exaggeration being due to a misreading of a diacritic mark in an early manuscript.

Uschi (f.) German: common pet form of URSULA.

Usko (f.) Finnish: meaning 'faith', this is a loan translation of the Latin name *Fides* or the Greek *Pistis*.

Ute (f.) German: from a medieval given name derived from the Germanic element *uod(al)* prosperity, riches, fortune. It is therefore a feminine equivalent of UDO.
Variants: **Ude**, **Ode** (both rare).

Utz (m.) German: pet form of ULRICH.

Uwe (m.) Low German and Frisian: equivalent form of OVE.

Uzi (m.) Mainly Jewish: name, meaning 'power' or 'might' in Hebrew, borne in the Bible by six minor characters mentioned in genealogies. In the Authorized Version the spelling **Uzzi** is used. The name seems to represent a short form of the theophoric names UZZIAH and UZZIEL.

Uzziah (m.) Biblical: Hebrew name meaning 'power of Yahweh (God)'. It is borne by several characters in the Old Testament, including one of the kings of Judea.
Variant: **Uziah**.

Uzziel (m.) Biblical: Hebrew name meaning 'power of God'. It is borne by several minor characters mentioned in Old Testament genealogies and has enjoyed some popularity as a given name among Jews.
Variant: **Uziel**.

V

Vaast (m.) Flemish: borne by a 6th-century saint, bishop of Arras-Cambrai. His name appears in medieval sources in the Latinized form *Vedastus*, and is of uncertain origin. It is probably a contracted form of the name *Widogast* (or *Widigast*), which is also found in medieval documents; it is composed of the Germanic elements *widu* wood + *gast* guest.

Václav (m.) Czech form of WENCESLAS.

Feminine form: **Václava**.

Vadim (m.) Russian: of uncertain origin. The name has been in use since the Middle Ages, and would seem to represent a reduced form of VLADIMIR, but this may be too simple an explanation.

Val (f., occasionally m.) English: **1**. (f.) Short form of VALERIE. **2**. (m.) Short form of VALENTINE.

Valda (f.) English: a 20th-century coinage, representing a fanciful elaboration of VAL with the suffix *-da*, extracted from names such as GLENDA and LINDA.

Valdemar (f.) Scandinavian: variant spelling of WALDEMAR.

Valene (f.) English: a 20th-century coinage, apparently of Australian origin, representing a fanciful elaboration of VAL with the productive feminine suffix *-ene*.

Valentine (m., occasionally f.) English form of the Latin name *Valentīnus*, a derivative of *valens* healthy, strong. This was the name of a Roman martyr of the 3rd century, whose feast is celebrated on 14 February. This was the date of a pagan fertility festival marking the first stirrings of spring, which has survived in an attenuated form under the patronage of the saint.
Cognates: Scottish Gaelic: **Ualan**, **Uailean**. Welsh: **Folant**. French, Danish, Swedish: **Valentin**. Italian: **Valentino**. Spanish: **Valentín**. Portuguese: **Valentim**. German: **Valentin**. S. German: **Velten**. Polish: **Walenty**. Czech: **Valentin**. Hungarian: **Bálint**.
Short form: English: **Val**.
Feminine forms: Latinate: **Valentina** (used esp. in Eastern Europe). Polish: **Walentyna**.

Valère (m.) French form of the Latin name *Valērius* (see VALERIE). There are several early saints of this name who have connections with France: a Roman missionary martyred at Soissons in 287, the first bishop of Conserans, an early bishop of Trèves, and a 5th-century bishop of Antibes.

Valeri (m.) Russian form of the Latin name *Valērius* (see VALERIE).

Valerie (f.) English: from the French form of the Latin name *Valēria*, the feminine form of the old Roman family name *Valērius*, which was apparently derived from *valēre* to be healthy, strong. The name was popular in France in the Middle Ages as a result of the cult of a 3rd-century saint (probably spurious) converted by Martial of Limoges.
Cognate: French: **Valérie**.
Short form: English: **Val**.

Valéry (m.) French: often taken to be a variant of VALÈRE, but in fact of Germanic rather than Latin origin. It is composed of the Germanic elements *walh* foreign, strange + *rīc* power. St Valéry or Walericus was the 7th-century founder of the abbey of Lencone at the mouth of the Somme.

Valetta (f.) English: a 20th-century coinage, representing an elaboration of VAL with the suffix *-etta*, originally an Italian feminine diminutive suffix. Valetta or Valletta is coincidentally the name of the capital of Malta.

Valter (m.) Scandinavian: variant spelling of WALTER.

Vanessa (f.) English: name invented by Jonathan Swift (1667–1745) for his intimate friend Esther Vanhomrigh. It seems to have been derived from the first syllable of her (Dutch) surname, with the addition of the suffix *-essa* (perhaps influenced by the first syllable of her given name).
Short form: **Nessa**.

Vanja (f.) Scandinavian: from the Russian name VANYA, but used as a girl's name because in the Scandinavian languages the ending *-a* is typical of female names.

Vanya (m.) Russian: pet form of IVAN.

Varda (f.) Jewish: modern name meaning 'rose' in Hebrew.
Variant: **Vardah**.

Varfolomei (m.) Russian form of BARTHOLOMEW.

Varvara (f.) Russian form of BARBARA.
Pet form: **Varya**.

Vasco (m.) Spanish, Portuguese, and Italian: contracted form of the medieval Spanish given name *Velasco* or *Belasco*, from which is derived the Spanish surname *Velázquez*. The medieval name is of uncertain origin; it may be connected with a Basque element meaning 'crow'. In form the modern given name coincides with the Spanish adjective *vasco* Basque (cf. GASTON).

Vasili (m.) Russian form of BASIL.

Vaughan (m.) Welsh and English: transferred use of the Welsh surname, which derives from the mutated form (*fychan* in Welsh orthography) of the Welsh adjective *bychan* small. This was originally a nickname or descriptive name.

Vavřinec (m.) Czech form of LAURENCE.
Short form: **Vavro**.
Pet forms: **Vavřik**, **Vavřiniček**.

Veerle (f.) Belgian: vernacular Flemish form of the old Germanic female personal name *Farahilda*, composed of the elements *fara* to go, travel + *hild* battle. The 8th-century St Farahilda, who was mistreated by her husband because of her extreme Christian zeal, has long been venerated as a patron saint of Ghent.

Veit (m.) **1**. German: vernacular form of VITUS. **2**. Dutch form of GUY.

Veleslav (m.) Czech form of WIELISŁAW.
Feminine form: **Veleslava**.
Pet forms: **Vela** (m., f.); **Velek**, **Veloušek** (m.); **Velka**, **Veluška**, **Velin(k)a** (f.).

Velma (f.) English (esp. U.S.): of modern origin and uncertain derivation, possibly based on SELMA or THELMA.

Velten (m.) South German form of VALENTINE.

Venceslao (m.) Italian form of WENCESLAS, occasionally borne in honour of the Bohemian saint.
Cognates: Spanish: **Venceslás**. Portuguese: **Venceslau**.

Věnceslav (m.) Older Czech form of WENCESLAS; cf. VÁCLAV.
Feminine form: **Věnceslava**.
Pet forms: **Věna** (m., f.); **Věnek, Venoušek** (m.); **Venka, Venuška** (f.).

Vendelín (m.) Czech form of WENDELIN.

Venedikt (m.) Russian form of BENEDICT.

Venessa (f.) English: modern altered form of VANESSA.

Venetia (f.) English: of uncertain origin, used occasionally since the late Middle Ages. In form the name coincides with that of the region of northern Italy.

Venyamin (m.) Russian form of BENJAMIN.
Pet form: **Venya**.

Vera (f.) Russian name, meaning 'faith', introduced to Britain at the beginning of the 20th century. It coincides in form with the feminine form of the Latin adjective *vērus* true, and this has no doubt enhanced its popularity as a given name in the English-speaking world and in Scandinavia.
Cognates: Polish: **Wera, Wiera**. Czech: **Věra**.
Pet forms: Czech: **Věrka, Veruška**.

Vere (m.) English: transferred use of the surname, which originated as a Norman French baronial name, from any of the numerous places in northern France so called from the Gaulish element *ver(n)* alder.

Verena (f.) Characteristically Swiss name, first borne by a 3rd-century saint who lived as a hermit near Zurich. She is said to have come originally from Thebes in Egypt, and the origin of her name is obscure.
Pet form: **Vreni**.

Vergil (m.) English (esp. U.S.): variant of VIRGIL.

Verina (f.) English: variant of VERENA, with the common feminine name ending *-ina*.

Verity (f.) English: from the archaic abstract noun meaning 'truth' (coming via Old French from Latin *vēritās*, a derivative of *vērus* true; cf. VERA). It was a popular Puritan name, and is still occasionally used in the English-speaking world.

Verna (f.) English: a name that originated in the latter part of the 19th century, perhaps as a contracted form of VERENA or VERONA, or as a deliberately formed feminine equivalent of VERNON.

Verner (m.) Scandinavian: variant spelling of WERNER.

Vernon (m.) English: transferred use of the surname, which originated as a Norman French baronial name, from any of various places in Normandy so called from Gaulish elements meaning 'place of alders' (cf. VERE).

Verona (f.) English: of uncertain origin. It seems to have come into use towards the end of the 19th century, and may either represent a shortened form of VERONICA or be taken from the name of the Italian city. It became more widely known from Sinclair Lewis's novel *Babbitt* (1923), in which it is borne by the daughter of the eponymous hero.

Veronica (f.) Latin form, somewhat garbled, of BERENICE, influenced from an early date by association with the Church Latin phrase *vera icon* 'true image', of which this form is an anagram. The legend of the saint who wiped Christ's face on the way to Calvary and found an image of his face imprinted on the towel seems to have been invented to account for this derivation.
Cognates: French: **Véronique** (sometimes also used in the English-speaking world). German: **Veronike**. Scandinavian: **Veronika**.
Pet form: English: **Ronnie**.

Vessa (f.) English: modern creation, representing a contracted form of VENESSA or an assimilated form of VESTA.

Vesta (f.) English: from the Latin name of the Roman goddess of the hearth, cognate with that of a Greek goddess with similar functions, *Hestia*, but of uncertain derivation. It is only rarely used as a given name in the English-speaking world, but was borne as a stage name by the Victorian music-hall artiste Vesta Tilley (1864–1952).

Vester (m.) German: short form of SILVESTER.

Vi (f.) English: short form of VIOLET or VIVIAN/VIVIEN as a female name.

Vibeke (f.) Danish and Norwegian form of WIBEKE, also in use in Sweden.

Vicenc (m.) Catalan form of VINCENT.

Vicente (m.) Spanish form of VINCENT.

Vicky (f.) English: pet form of VICTORIA.
Variants: **Vickie, Vicki, Vikki**.

Victoire (f.) French form of VICTORIA.

Victor (m.) English: from a Late Latin personal name meaning 'conqueror'. This was popular among early Christians as a reference to Christ's victory over death and sin, and was borne by several saints.
Cognates: German, Scandinavian, Polish, Czech: **Viktor**. Italian: **Vittore**. See also GWYTHYR.
Equivalent: Hungarian: **Győző**.

Victoria (f.) English and Spanish: feminine form of the Latin name *Victōrius* (see VITTORIO), also perhaps a direct use of Latin *victōria* victory. It was little known in England until the accession in 1837 of Queen Victoria (1819–1901), who got it from her German mother, Mary Louise Victoria of Saxe-Coburg. It did not begin to be a popular name among commoners in Britain until the 1940s, reaching a peak in the 1970s.
Cognates: German, Scandinavian: **Viktoria**. Italian: **Vittoria**. French: **Victoire**; **Victorine** (an elaborated form). Scottish Gaelic: **Bhictoria**.
Pet form: English: **Vicky**.

Vidal (m.) Spanish form of VITALE that has been adopted in particular by Sefardic Jews as a translation of the Hebrew name *Hayyim* 'life' (see CHAIM and HYAM).

Vidkun (m.) Scandinavian: from an Old Norse personal name composed of the elements *viðr* wide + *kunnr* wise, experienced. It was borne by Vidkun Quisling (1887–1945), the Norwegian collaborator with the Nazis, whose surname has become a by-word for treachery. Consequently, it is now completely out of fashion.

Vidor (m.) Hungarian: name representing a loan translation of HILARY.

Vigdis (f.) Scandinavian: from an Old Norse female personal name composed of the elements *vig* war + *dis* goddess.

Viggo (m.) Scandinavian: Latinized form of the Old Danish personal name *Vigge*, a short form of various compound names with the first element *vig* war.

Vigilio (m.) Italian (characteristic of the Trentino region): borne in honour of the local saint, *Vigilius*, bishop of Trent (d. 405), who was stoned to death for overturning a statue of Saturn. The name is probably a derivative of Latin *vigil* wakeful, watchful (cf. GREGORY).

Viktoria (f.) German and Scandinavian form of VICTORIA.

Vilém (m.) Czech form of WILLIAM.
Pet forms: **Vilémek, Vile(če)k, Vilík, Viloušek**.

Vilfred (m.) Scandinavian form of WILFRID.

Vilhelm (m.) Scandinavian form of WILLIAM.

Vilhelmina (f.) Swedish form of WILHELMINA.
Cognate: Danish, Norwegian: **Vilhelmine**.
Pet form: Danish: **Mine**.

Vilmos (m.) Hungarian form of WILLIAM.
Feminine form: **Vilma**.

Vilppu (m.) Finnish form of PHILIP.

Vince (m.) 1. English: short form of VINCENT, in use at least from the 17th century, and probably earlier, since it has given rise to a surname. 2. Hungarian form of VINCENT.

Vincent (m.) English, French, Dutch, Danish, and Swedish: from the Old French form of the Latin name *Vincens* 'conquering' (genitive *Vincentis*), from *vincere* to conquer. This name was borne by various early saints particularly associated with France, most notably the 5th-century St Vincent of Lérins.
Cognates: Irish Gaelic: **Uinseann**. Italian: **Vincente**; **Vi(n)cenzo** (from the elaborated form *Vincentius*). Spanish: **Vicente**. Catalan: **Vicenç**. German: **Vinzenz** (from *Vincentius*). Polish: **Wincenty** (from *Vincentius*). Czech: **Vincenc** (from *Vincentius*). Hungarian: **Vince**.
Short form: English: **Vince**.
Pet forms: Czech: **Vinca, Vinc(en)ck, Čenck**.

Viola (f.) English, Italian, and Scandinavian: from Latin *viola* violet. The name is relatively common in Italy and was used by Shakespeare in *Twelfth Night* (where most of the characters have Italianate names). However, in England it seems to have been used in modern times mainly as a result of its association with the somewhat larger flower so called in English (a single-coloured pansy).

Violet (f.) English: from the name of the flower (Old French *violette*, Late Latin *violetta*, a diminutive of *viola*). This was one of the earliest flower names to become popular in Britain, being well established before the middle of the 19th century, but it is now out of favour.
Cognates: French: **Violette**. Italian: **Violetta**.
Short form: English: **Vi**.

Virág (m.) Hungarian: originally an affectionate nickname meaning 'flower', now a given name in its own right.

Virgil (m.) Usual English form of the name of the most celebrated of Roman poets, Publius Vergilius Maro (70–19 BC). The correct Latin spelling is *Vergilius*, but it was early altered to *Virgilius* by association with *virgo* maiden or *virga* stick. Today the name is almost always given with direct reference

to the poet, but medieval instances may have been intended to honour instead a 6th-century bishop of Arles or an 8th-century Irish monk who evangelized Carinthia and became archbishop of Salzburg, both of whom also bore the name. In the case of the later saint, it was a classicized form of the Gaelic name *Fearghal*; see FERGAL.
Variant: **Vergil**.
Cognate: Italian, Spanish: **Virgilio**.

Virginia (f.) English, Italian, Spanish, Portuguese, Danish, and Swedish: from the feminine form of Latin *Virginius* (more correctly *Verginius*; cf. VIRGIL), a Roman family name. It was borne by a Roman maiden killed, according to legend, by her own father to spare her the attentions of an importunate suitor. It does not seem to have been used as a given name in the Middle Ages. It was bestowed on the first American child of English parentage, born at Roanoke, Virginia, in August 1587. It has since become very popular. Both child and province were named in honour of Elizabeth I, the 'Virgin Queen'.
Cognate: French: **Virginie** (sometimes also used in the English-speaking world).
Pet form: English: **Ginny**. See also GINGER.

Virtudes (f.) Spanish: name given as a reference to the Seven Christian Virtues (Spanish *virtudes* virtues, Latin *virtūtes*, originally a derivative of *vir* man, meaning 'manly qualities').

Visitación (f.) Spanish: name recalling the New Testament story of the visit by the Virgin Mary to her cousin Elizabeth, the mother of John the Baptist (Luke 1: 39–56). This event is commemorated in the Catholic Church with a feast on 2 July, recognized since 1389.
Cognate: Portuguese: **Visitação**.

Vissarion (m.) Russian: from Greek *Bessarion*, a name of extremely uncertain derivation (probably a transliteration of a non-Greek original). A 2nd-century saint of this name lived as a hermit in the Egyptian desert, and he is still greatly venerated in the Orthodox Church.

Vit (m.) Czech form of VITUS.

Vita (f.) English and Danish: 19th-century coinage, either directly from Latin *vita* life, or else as a feminine form of VITUS. It has been borne most notably by the English writer Vita Sackville-West (1892–1962), in whose case it was a pet form of the given name *Victoria*.

Vitale (m.) Italian: from the Late Latin name *Vitālis*, a derivative of *vita* life. There are over a dozen early saints of this name, including Vitalis of Milan, the father of Gervasius and Protasius.
Cognate: Russian: **Vitali**.

Vittore (m.) Italian form of VICTOR.

Vittoria (f.) Italian form of VICTORIA.

Vittorio (m.) Italian: from the Latin name *Victōrius*, a derivative of VICTOR borne by a 5th-century bishop of Le Mans and by two obscure early martyrs.

Vitus (m.) The name of a child saint martyred in Sicily at an unknown (but early) date, together with his nurse Crescentia and her husband Modestus. His name seems to derive from Latin *vita* life (cf. VITA), and his two companions bear unmistakably Latin names, but there has been some confusion with forms of GUY.
Derivatives: German: **Veit**. Polish: **Wit**. Czech: **Vit**.

Viv (f., m.) English: short form, usually feminine, of VIVIAN and VIVIEN.

Viveka (f.) Swedish form of WIBEKE.
Variants: **Viveca**, **Vivica**.

Vivi (f.) English and Scandinavian: feminine pet form of VIVIAN or VIVIEN.

Vivian (m., occasionally f.) English: from an Old French form of the Latin name *Viviānus* (probably a derivative of *vivus* alive). The name was borne by a 5th-century bishop of Saintes in western France, who protected his people during the invasion of the Visigoths. As a woman's name it has sometimes been used as an Anglicized form of the Irish Gaelic name **Béibhinn** meaning 'white lady'.
Variant: **Vyvyan**.
Short forms: **Vi**, **Viv**, **Vivi**.

Vivien (f., formerly m.) Originally the more common Old French form of VIVIAN, but used by Tennyson in his poem *Merlin and Vivien* (1859) as a female name in place of the usual feminine form VIVIENNE; in this case, it may represent an altered form of some Celtic name. The actress Vivien Leigh (1913–67) was originally christened *Vivian*.
Variants: **Viviann(e)** (also used in Scandinavia), **Vivean**.
Short forms: **Vi**, **Viv**, **Vivi**.

Vivienne (f.) French: feminine form of VIVIEN, popular also in the English-speaking world.

Vladilen (m.) Russian: modern name constructed from that of the founder of the Soviet state, Vladimir Ilyich Lenin (1870–1924). Cf. NINEL and MELOR.
Variant: **Vladlen**.
Feminine form: **Vladilena**.

Vladimir (m.) Russian: from an old Slavonic personal name composed of the elements *volod* rule (cognate with Germanic *wald*) + *meri* great, famous (see CASIMIR). The stress is on the second syllable. St Vladimir (956–1015) was Great Prince of Kievan Russia and the father of St Boris and St Gleb; he is honoured as the ruler, 'equal to the apostles', who brought Russia into the Christian Church. See also VADIM.
Cognates: Polish: **Wlodzimierz**. Czech: **Vladimir**. German, Dutch: **Waldemar**. Scandinavian: **Waldemar**, **Valdemar**.
Pet forms: Russian: **Volodya**, **Volya**.
Feminine forms: Russian: **Vladimira**. Czech: **Vladimira**.

Vladislav (m.) Czech form of WLADYSLAW.
Variant: **Ladislav**.
Feminine forms: **Vladislava**, **Ladislava**.

Vlas (m.) Russian form of BLAISE. The learned variant **Vlasi** is also used.

Vojtěch (m.) Czech form of WOJCIECH.
Pet forms: **Vojta**, **Vojtek**, **Vojtik**, **Vojtíšek**.

Volf (m.) Jewish: Yiddish form of WOLF.

Volker (m.) German: from an old Germanic personal name composed of the elements *folk* people + *heri*, *hari* army, warrior. The English surname *Fulcher* derives from a Norman form of this.

Volkmar (m.) German: from an old Germanic personal name composed of the elements *folk* people + *māri*, *mēri* famous.

Volodya (m.) Russian: pet form of VLADIMIR (via the colloquial form *Volodimir*) and of VSEVOLOD.

Volya (m.) Russian: contracted form of VOLODYA.

Vreni (f.) Swiss: contracted pet form of VERENA.

Vsevolod (m.) Russian: from an old Slavonic personal name composed of the elements *vse* all + *volod* rule, representing a loan translation of Greek *Pankratios* (see PANCRAZIO and PANCRAS).
Pet forms: **Volodya**, **Volya**, **Seva**.

Vyacheslav (m.) Russian form of WENCESLAS.

Vyvyan (m.) English: fanciful respelling of the male name VIVIAN.

W

Wacław (m.) Polish form of WENCESLAS.
Variants: **Więcesław**, **Wieńczysław**, **Wenczeslaw** (all archaic).

Wade (m.) English: transferred use of the surname, which is derived either from a medieval given name or from the medieval vocabulary word *wade* ford. The former represents an Old English personal name, derived from *wadan* to go, which according to legend was borne by a great sea-giant.

Walburg (f.) German: from a Germanic personal name composed of the elements *wald* rule or *wal* foreign, strange + *burg* fortress. St Walburg was of Anglo-Saxon origin, the sister of St WILLIBALD, and the original form of her name was *Wealdburh* or *Wealburh*. She became abbess of Heidenheim and her relics are preserved at Eichstätt.

Waldemar (m.) German, Scandinavian, and Dutch: from an old Germanic personal name composed of the elements *wald* rule + *māri*, *mēri* famous. This was the name of four kings of Denmark, in particular Waldemar the Great (ruled 1157–82). The name itself is ultimately a cognate of VLADIMIR and has been used as a Germanic equivalent or translation of that name.
Variants: Scandinavian: **Valdemar**; German, Dutch, Danish: **Woldemar**.

Waldo (m.) English and German: a short form of any of several old Germanic personal names containing *wald* rule as a first element (possibly also as a second element). This gave rise in the early Middle Ages to a surname, borne notably by Peter Waldo, a 12th-century merchant of Lyons, who founded a reformist Catholic sect known as the Waldensians, which in the 16th century joined the Reformation movement. In America the name is particularly associated with the poet and essayist Ralph Waldo Emerson (1803–82), whose father was a Lutheran clergyman.

Walenty (m.) Polish form of VALENTINE.
Feminine form: **Walentyna**.

Wallace (m.) Scottish and English: transferred use of the surname, which was originally an ethnic byname from Old French *waleis* meaning 'foreign, Celtic', used by the Normans to denote members of various Celtic races in areas where they were in the minority—Welshmen in the Welsh Marches, Bretons in East Anglia, and surviving Britons in the Strathclyde region. The given name seems to have been first used in Scotland, being bestowed in honour of the Scottish patriot William Wallace (?1272–1305).

Wally (m.) English: informal pet form of WALTER or, less commonly, of WALLACE. It has dropped almost completely out of fashion, especially since the slang word *wally* is used in Britain for a stupid or incompetent person.

Walter (m.) English, German, and Scandinavian: from an old Germanic personal name composed of the elements *wald* rule + *heri*, *hari* army, warrior. There was a native Old English form of the name, *Wealdhere*, but it was replaced at the time of the Conquest by the Continental forms in use among the Normans. In medieval Germany, the most famous bearer was the minnesinger Walther von der Vogelweide (*c*.1170–*c*.1230).
Variants: German: **Walther**. Scandinavian: **Valter**.
Cognates: Scottish Gaelic: **Bhàtair**, **Bhaltair**. Welsh: **Gwallter**. Dutch: **Wouter**, **Wolter**. Low German: **Wolter**. French: **Gaut(h)ier**. Italian, Spanish: **Gualtiero**.
Short forms: English: **Wat** (medieval, occasionally revived); **Walt** (esp. U.S.). Dutch: **Weit**. Pet form: English: **Watkin**.

Waltraud (f.) German: from an old Germanic female personal name composed of the elements *wald* rule or *walh* foreigner, stranger + *thrūd* strength. St Waltraud was a 7th-century nun who founded a convent at the place that grew to be the town of Mons in Belgium.
Variants: **Waltrud(e)**.

Wanda (f.) English: of uncertain origin. Attempts have been made to derive it from various Germanic and Slavonic roots: it was certainly in use in Poland in the 19th century, and is found in Polish folk-tales as the name of a princess. The derivation may well be from the ethnic term *Wend*, denoting the Slavonic people who inhabited what is now northern East Germany in the Middle Ages. The name was introduced to the English-speaking world by Ouida (Marie Louise de la Ramée), who used it for the heroine of her novel *Wanda* (1883).

Wandelin (m.) Polish: variant of WENDELIN.

Ward (m.) English: transferred use of the surname, originally an occupational name from Old English *weard* guard or watchman.

Warner (m.) English: transferred use of the surname derived from the medieval English given name corresponding to WERNER.

Warren (m.) English: transferred use of the English surname, which is of Norman origin, derived partly from a place in Normandy called *La Varenne* 'the game-park' and partly from a Germanic personal name (cf. WERNER). In America it has sometimes been bestowed in honour of General Joseph Warren, the first hero of the American Revolution, who was killed at Bunker Hill (1775).

Warwick (m.) English: transferred use of the surname, which is taken from the town in the West Midlands. The placename is probably from Old English *wær(ing)*, *wer(ing)* weir, dam + *wīc* dairy farm.

Washington (m.) English (esp. U.S.): from the surname of the first president of the United States, George Washington (1732–99), whose family came originally from Northamptonshire in England. They had been established in Virginia since 1656. The surname in this case is derived from the village of Washington in Co. Durham (now Tyne and Wear), so called from Old English *Wassingtūn* 'settlement associated with Wassa'. Use as a given name is well established, especially in the United States, where it was borne, for example, by the writer Washington Irving (1783–1859).

Wat (m.) English: the usual medieval short form of WALTER, based on the normal vernacular pronunciation, *Water*, with a short 'a'.

Watkin (m.) English: either a revival of the medieval pet name (WAT + the hypocoristic suffix *-kin*), or a transferred use of the surname derived from it.

Wawrzyniec (m.) Polish form of LAURENCE.

Wayne (m.) English: transferred use of the surname, originally an occupational name for a carter or cartwright, from Old English *wægen* cart, wagon. It was adopted as a given name in the second half of the 20th century, mainly as a result of the popularity of the American film actor John Wayne (1907–82), who was born Marion Michael Morrison; his screen name was chosen in honour of the American Revolutionary general Anthony Wayne (1745–96).

Webster (m.) English: transferred use of the surname, which originated as an occupational name for a weaver, Old English *webbestre* (a derivative of *webb* web). The *-estre* suffix was originally feminine, but by the Middle English period the gender distinction had been lost. Use as a given name in America no doubt owes something to the politician and orator Daniel Webster (1782–1852) and the lexicographer Noah Webster (1758–1843).

Wenceslas (m.) Latinized form of an East European Slavonic name, composed of the elements *ventie* more, greater + *slav* glory. St Wenceslas was a 10th-century duke of Bohemia noted for his piety, the grandson of St Ludmilla. He is regarded as the patron of Bohemia, which now forms part of Czechoslovakia. This was also the name of four kings of Bohemia in the period covering the 13th to the 15th century.

Cognates: German: **Wenzeslaus**, WENZEL. Polish: WACŁAW. Czech: **Vĕnceslav**, **Václav**. Russian: **Vyacheslav**. Italian: **Venceslao**. Spanish: **Venceslás**. Portuguese: **Venceslau**.

Wenda (f.) English: apparently an altered form of WENDY (cf. e.g. *Jenna* from *Jenny*), since it does not appear in modern use until the vogue for that name. In the early Middle Ages, however, a name of identical form was in occasional use on the Continent as a short form of various female names (such as *Wendelburg* and *Wendelgard*) containing as their first element the ethnic name of the Wends (cf. WENDEL). It may well have been partly influenced by WANDA.

Wendel (m.) German: from an old Germanic personal name, in origin an ethnic byname for a Wend, a member of the Slavonic people living in the area between the Elbe and the Oder, who were overrun by Germanic migrants in the 12th century. In part it was also used as a short form of various compound names with that first element (cf. WENDA). St Wendel was a 6th- or 7th-century shepherd and confessor, who is venerated especially at Sanktwendel on the River Nahe.

Wendelin (m.) German and Polish: from an old Germanic personal name, a derivative of the ethnic byname *wend* Wend (see WENDEL).

Variant: Polish: **Wandelin**.
Cognate: Czech: **Vendelín**.

Wendell (m.) English (esp. U.S.): from the surname derived in the Middle Ages from the Continental Germanic personal name WENDEL. It has been adopted as a given name as a result of the fame of the American writer Oliver Wendell Holmes (1809–94) and his jurist son, also Oliver Wendell Holmes (1841–1935), members of a leading New England family.

Wendy (f.) English: invented by J. M. Barrie for the 'little mother' in his play *Peter Pan* (1904). He took it from the nickname *Fwendy-Wendy* (i.e. 'friend') used for him by a child acquaintance, Margaret Henley. It has achieved widespread popularity in its short lifespan.
Variant: **Wendi** (rare).

Wenzel (m.) German: medieval pet form of *Wenzeslaus*, the German version of WENCESLAS. This was in common use in the heavily Slavonic regions of eastern Germany and is still occasionally chosen today as an independent given name.

Wera (f.) Polish form of VERA.

Werner (m.) German, Dutch, and Scandinavian: from an old Germanic personal name composed of the tribal name *Warin* + the element *heri*, *hari* army, warrior. See also WARNER.
Variant: Scandinavian: **Verner**.
Pet forms: German: **WETZEL**. Low German, Dutch, Frisian: **Wessel**.

Werther (m.) German: found in the early Middle Ages in the Latinized form *Wertharius*. It probably derives from the Germanic elements *wert* worthy + *heri*, *hari* army, warrior. The name had become comparatively rare in Germany by the later Middle Ages, but was chosen by Goethe for the hero of his early novel *Die Leiden des jungen Werther* ('The Sorrows of Young Werther', 1774), since when it has been quietly popular.

Wesley (m.) English: from the surname of the founder of the Methodist Church, John Wesley (1703–91), and his brother Charles (1707–88), who was also influential in the movement. Their family must have come originally from one or other of the various places in England called *Westley*, the 'western wood, clearing, or meadow'. The given name was at first confined to members of the Methodist Church, but is now very widely used among English-speaking people of many different creeds, often without reference to its religious connotations.
Short form: **Wes**.

Wessel (m.) Low German and Frisian: pet form of WERNER.

Wetzel (m.) German: from a medieval pet form of WERNER, now occasionally chosen as an independent given name.

Whiltierna (f.) Irish: Anglicized form of the Gaelic name Faoiltiarna, composed of the elements *faol* wolf + *tighearna* lord.

Whitney (f., m.) English (mainly U.S.): transferred use of the surname, originally a local name from any of various places in England named with the Middle English phrase *atten whiten ey* 'by the white island'. In the 1980s its popularity as a female name has been increased by the fame of the American singer Whitney Houston.

Wiara (f.) Polish form of VERA.

Wibeke (f.) Low German, Dutch, and Frisian: pet form derived from the medieval given name *Wibe*, in origin a short form of various Germanic compound names, such as *Wigburg*, composed of the elements *wig* war + *burg* fortress.
Variants: **Wi(e)bke**.
Cognates: Danish, Norwegian: **Vibeke**. Swedish: **Viveka**, **Viveca**, **Vivica**.

Więceslaw (m.) Archaic Polish form of WACŁAW. See WENCESLAS.

Wieland (m.) German: from an old Germanic personal name of uncertain derivation. It was borne in Germanic legend by Wieland the Smith, king of the elves, and was revived to a limited extent as a result of the 19th-century interest in this group of tales. The name was borne by a grandson of the composer Richard Wagner.

Wielisław (m.) Polish: from an old Slavonic personal name composed of the elements *vele* great + *slav* glory.
Variant: **Wieslaw**.
Cognate: Czech: **Veleslav**.
Pet forms: Polish: **Wiesi(ul)ek**. Czech: **Vela, Velek, Veloušek**.

Wiera (f.) Polish form of VERA.

Wiga (f.) Polish: short form of JADWIGA.
Pet form: **Wisia**.

Wilberforce (m.) English: transferred use of the surname, which originated as a local name from *Wilberfoss* in North Yorkshire. This place is so called from the Old English female personal name *Wilburg* (see WILBUR) + Old English *foss* ditch (from Latin *fossa*). It may have been taken up as a given name in honour of the antislavery campaigner William Wilberforce (1759–1833), or perhaps because it is thought of as an extended form of *Wilbur*.

Wilbur (m.) English: transferred use of a comparatively rare surname, which is now a fairly common given name, especially in America. The surname probably derives from a medieval female name composed of the Old English elements *will* will, desire + *burh* fortress.

Wilfrid (m.) English: from an Old English personal name composed of the Germanic elements *wil* will, desire + *frid, fred* peace. This name was borne by two saints. There is some doubt about the exact form of the name of the more famous, who played a leading role at the Council of Whitby (664); it may have been *Walfrid* 'stranger peace' or 'peace to the Welsh', from Old English *walh* stranger, Welshman. Wilfrid the Younger was an 8th-century bishop of York. The name was not used in the Middle Ages, but was revived in the 19th century, and enjoyed great popularity then and in the first part of the 20th century.
Variant: **Wilfred**.
Cognates: German: **Wilfried**. Scandinavian: **Vilfred**.
Short form: English: **Wilf**.

Wilhelm (m.) German form of WILLIAM.

Wilhelmina (f.) German: feminine version of WILHELM, formed with the Latinate suffix *-ina*. This name was introduced to the English-speaking world from Germany in the 19th century. It is now very rarely used.
Variant: **Wilhelmine**.
Cognates: Swedish: **Vilhelmina**. Danish, Norwegian: **Vilhelmine**.
Short forms: German: **Wilma, Helmine, Helma, Mine**. Danish: **Mine**.
Pet forms: German: **Minna, Minne**. English: **Minnie**.

Will (m.) English: short form of WILLIAM, in use since the early Middle Ages, when it was occasionally used also for various other given names containing as their first element Germanic *wil* will, desire (e.g. *Wilbert* and WILMER).

Willa (f.) English: a feminine form of WILLIAM, created by appending the characteristically feminine final letter *-a* to the short form WILL.

Willard (m.) English (esp. U.S.): transferred use of the surname, which seems itself to have derived from the Old English personal name *Wilheard*, composed of the elements *will* will, desire + *heard* hardy, brave, strong. The modern given name is sometimes taken as an elaborated form of WILL.

Willem (m.) Low German and Dutch form of WILLIAM.

Willi (m.) German: pet form of WILHELM.

William (m.) English: the most successful of all the Germanic names introduced to England by the Normans. It is composed of the elements *wil* will, desire + *helm* helmet, protection. The fact that it was borne by the Conqueror himself does not seem to have inhibited its favour with the 'conquered' population: in the first century after the Conquest it was the commonest male name of all, not only among Normans. In the later Middle Ages it was overtaken by JOHN, but continued to run second to that name until the 20th century, when the picture became more fragmented. It was a royal name not only in England, but also in Germany and the Netherlands.
Cognates: Irish Gaelic: **Liam**. Scottish Gaelic: **Uilleam**. Welsh: **Gwilym**. French: **Guillaume**. Italian: **Guglielmo**. Spanish: **Guilermo**. Catalan: **Guillem**. Portuguese: **Guilherme**. German: **Wilhelm**. Low German, Dutch: **Willem**. Scandinavian: **Vilhelm**. Czech: **Vilem**. Hungarian: **Vilmos**. Finnish: **Vilppu**.
Short forms: English: **Will**, BILL. German: **Wim**.
Pet forms: English and Scottish: **Willy, Willie**. German: **Willi**.
Feminine forms: English: **Willa, Wilma**, BILLIE. German: **Wilhelmina, Wilhelmine, Helmine, Helma, Mine**. Hungarian: **Vilma**.

Willibald (m.) German: from an old Germanic personal name composed of the elements *wil* will, desire + *bald* bold, brave. St Willibald (*c.*700–*c.*786) was of Anglo-Saxon origin, and aided his cousin Boniface in evangelical missions in Germany.

Willoughby (m.) English: transferred use of the surname, which was originally a local name from any of various places in northern England so called from Old English *welig* willow + Old Norse *býr* settlement.

Willow (f.) English: from the tree, Old English *welig*, noted for its grace and the pliancy of its wood.

Wilma (f.) **1**. German: contracted form of WILHELMINA. **2**. English: either a borrowing of the German name, or an independent coinage, formed as a feminine equivalent of WILLIAM.

Wilmer (m.) English: formally it is possible that this could represent an old Germanic personal name composed of the elements *wil* will, desire + *mēri, māri* famous, but it is more likely to have arisen as a masculine form of the similarly pronounced WILMA (cf. *Peta*, derived from *Peter* by the reverse process).

Wilmette (f.) English (esp. U.S.): a recent coinage, originating as an elaborated form of WILMA with the productive feminine ending (originally a French diminutive) *-ette*.
Variant: **Wilmetta**.

Wilmot (m.) English: transferred use of the surname, which is derived from a medieval pet form of WILLIAM. It is possible from the form of the medieval name that it could represent an old Germanic personal name composed of the elements *wil* will, desire + *muot* mind, courage, but this is no evidence for the existence of such a name.

Wim (m.) German: contracted form of WILHELM.

Win (f.) English: short form of WINIFRED.

Wincenty (m.) Polish form of VINCENT.

Windsor (m.) English: transferred use of the surname, which is derived from a place in Berkshire, originally named in Old English as *Windels-ōra* 'landing place with a windlass'. It is the site of a castle that is in regular use as a residence of the royal family. Its use as a given name dates from the mid-19th century and was reinforced by its adoption in 1917 as the surname of the British royal family (from their residence at Windsor in Berkshire). It was felt necessary to replace the German name *Wettin*, which had been introduced by Queen Victoria's husband Albert, in deference to anti-German feeling during the First World War.

Winifred (f.) English and Welsh: from the Welsh personal name GWENFREWI, altered by association with the Old English name elements *wynn* joy + *frið* peace. In Ireland and Scotland it has been used as an Anglicized form of ÚNA and ÙNA.

Short forms: **Win**, **Freda**.
Pet form: **Winnie**.

Winston (m.) English: transferred use of the surname. Although there was an Old English personal name, *Wynnstan*, composed of the elements *wynn* joy + *stān* stone, which would have had this form if it had survived, the modern given name originated in the Churchill family. The first Winston Churchill (b. 1620) was christened with the surname of his mother's family, who had come originally from the hamlet of Winston in Gloucestershire. The name has continued in this family ever since, and has recently been more widely used in honour of the statesman Winston Spencer Churchill (1874–1965).

Winthrop (m.) English (esp. U.S.): from the surname of a leading American pioneering family, and still more or less completely confined to America. John Winthrop (1588–1649) was one of the first governors of the Massachusetts Bay Colony, and his son (1606–76) and grandson (1638–1707), who bore the same name, were also colonial governors. Their family probably came originally from one of the places in England called *Winthorpe* (named in Old English as the 'village of Wynna').

Winton (m.) English: transferred use of the surname, which originated as a local name from any of the various places so called. One in Cumbria gets its name from Old English *winn* pasture + *tūn* enclosure, settlement; another in the same county is from *wiðig* willow + *tūn*; the one in North Yorkshire is from the Old English personal name *Wina* + *tūn*.

Wisia (f.) Polish: pet form of *Wiga*, a short form of JADWIGA.

Wit (m.) Polish form of VITUS.

Witold (m.) German, Polish: as a German name, this derives from the Germanic elements *wīda* wide or *witu* wood + *wald* ruler. As a Polish name, it represents an assimilation to this form of the Lithuanian name *Vytautas*, borne in the 14th century by the first Christian ruler of Lithuania.
Variant: Polish: **Witołd**.

Władysław (m.) Polish: from an old Slavonic personal name composed of the elements *volod* rule + *slav* glory. This was the name of four kings of Poland, and was an aristocratic name long before it was a royal name. The Blessed Władysław (1440–1505) is revered as an evangelist.

Variant: **Włodzisław**.
Cognates: Czech: **Vladislav**, **Ladislav**. Latinate: LADISLAS. Hungarian: LÁSZLÓ. Italian: **Ladislao**.

Włodzimierz (m.) Polish form of VLADIMIR.

Wmffre (m.) Welsh form of HUMPHREY.

Wojciech (m.) Common Polish name, from an old Slavonic personal name composed of the elements *voi* soldier, warrior + *tech* consolation.
Cognate: Czech: **Vojtěch**.
Pet forms: Polish: **Wojtek**, **Wojteczek**. Czech: **Vojta**, **Vojtek**, **Vojtik**, **Vojtišek**.

Wojsław (m.) Polish: from an old Slavonic personal name composed of the elements *voi* soldier, warrior + *slav* glory.

Wojtek (m.) Polish: pet form of WOJCIECH.
Variant: **Wojteczek**.

Woldemar (m.) German, Dutch, and Danish: variant of WALDEMAR.

Wolf (m.) German and Jewish: short form of WOLFGANG and WOLFRAM, or else an independent given name going back to an old Germanic byname meaning 'wolf' (Old High German *wolf*). Wolves were plentiful in the forests of northern Europe throughout the Middle Ages, and played an important part in Germanic folklore. As a Jewish name it has been used as an equivalent to ZEEV.
Cognates: Danish, Swedish: **Ulf**. Norwegian: **Ulv**.

Wolfgang (m.) German: common name from an old Germanic personal name composed of the elements *wolf* wolf + *gang* going. The name is often bestowed, sometimes even in the English-speaking world, in honour of the composer Wolfgang Amadeus Mozart (1756–91).

Wolfram (m.) German: from an old Germanic personal name composed of the elements *wolf* wolf + *hramn* raven. The name was borne in the Middle Ages by the poet Wolfram von Eschenbach (*c*.1170–*c*.1220).

Wolter (m.) Low German and Dutch form of WALTER.

Woodrow (m.) English: transferred use of the surname, originally a local name given to someone who lived in a row of houses by a wood. It is occasionally bestowed as a given name in the English-speaking world in honour of the American president Woodrow Wilson (1856–1924).

Woody (m.) English (chiefly U.S.): pet form of WOODROW, or in some cases perhaps a nickname bestowed because of some imagined similarity to the cartoon character Woody Woodpecker. It has been borne by the American folk singer Woody (Woodrow Wilson) Guthrie (1912–67) and the 1940s band leader Woody (Woodrow Charles) Herman (1913–87). The American humorist Woody Allen was born Allen Stewart Konigsberg in 1935.

Wouter (m.) Dutch form of WALTER.

Wyn (m.) Welsh: originally a byname from the Welsh vocabulary word *(g)wyn* white, fair, blessed, holy. The name is found in this form from the early Middle Ages. It is at present extremely popular in Wales.

Wyndham (m.) English: transferred use of the surname, which is derived from a contracted form of the placename *Wymondham* in Norfolk, originally named in Old English as the 'homestead of Wigmund'.

Wynne (m., f.) **1.** (m.) English: transferred use of the surname, which is derived from the Old and Middle English personal name *Wine* 'friend'. **2.** (m.) Welsh: elaborated spelling of WYN. **3.** (f.) English: apparently an 'elegant' respelling of *Win*, a short form of WINIFRED.

Variant (of 1): **Wynn**.

Wystan (m.) English: from an Old English personal name composed of the elements *wīg* battle + *stān* stone. St Wistan was a 9th-century prince of Mercia, murdered by his nephew Bertulf. The modern given name is rare, being best known in the name of the poet Wystan Hugh Auden (1907–73).

X

Xaime (m.) Galician form of JAMES; See also JAIME.

Xanthe (f.) English: from the feminine form of the classical Greek adjective *xanthos* yellow, bright. The name was borne by various minor figures in classical mythology and is occasionally chosen by parents in search of an unusual given name for a daughter.

Xavier (m.) From the surname of the Spanish soldier-saint Francis Xavier (1506–52), one of the founding members of the Society of Jesus (the Jesuits). He was born on the ancestral estate at Xavier (now Javier) in Navarre, which in the early Middle Ages was an independent Basque kingdom. *Xavier* probably represents a Hispanicized form of the Basque place-name *Etcheberria* 'the new house' (x was pronounced in the Middle Ages as *sh*, now as *h*). The given name is used almost exclusively among Roman Catholics.

Other forms: Italian: **Saverio**. Spanish, Portuguese: **Javier**. German: **Xaver**. Polish: **Ksawery**.

Xaviera (f.) Feminine form of XAVIER.

Xenia (f.) English: comparatively rare given name, coined from the Greek vocabulary word *xenia* hospitality, from *xenos* stranger, foreigner.

Xoán (m.) Galician form of JOHN; See also JUAN.

Xosé (m.) Galician form of JOSEPH; See also JOSÉ.

Y

Yael (f.) Jewish: from a Hebrew word denoting a female wild goat. The name is borne in the Bible by a Kenite woman who killed Sisera, the Canaanite general and an enemy of the Israelites (Judges 4: 17–22). It has remained extremely popular among Jews to the present day.
Variant: **Jael**.

Yaffa (f.) Jewish: variant of JAFFE. It has become very popular as a modern Hebrew translation of SHAYNA.

Yakim (m.) The usual Russian form of JOACHIM; See also AKIM.
Pet form: **Kima**.

Yakov (m.) Jewish: the modern Hebrew form of JACOB. This is also the form of the name in Russian.
Variant: Jewish: **Yaakov**.
Pet forms: Jewish: **Yankel** (Yiddish). Russian: **Yasha**.
Feminine form: Jewish: **Yakova**.

Yann (m.) Breton form of JOHN.
Pet form: **Yannic(k)**.

Yaropolk (m.) Russian form of JAROPELK.

Yaroslav (m.) Russian form of JAROSLAW.

Yasha (m.) Russian: pet form of YAKOV.

Yasmin (f.) English: variant of JASMINE, representing a 'learned' re-creation of the Persian form.

Yayone (f.) Basque: variant spelling of IAIONE.

Yefim (m.) Russian: from the Greek name *Euphēmios*, composed of the elements *eu* well, good + *phēnai* to speak, say; cf. EUPHEMIA

Yefrem (m.) Russian form of EPHRAIM.
Pet form: **Rema**.

Yegor (m.) Russian: popular form of GEORGE.

Yehiel (m.) Jewish: Hebrew name, meaning 'God lives', borne in the Bible by an early Levite appointed to play the psaltery in sacred processions (1 Chronicles 15: 20). In the Authorized Version the name is transliterated *Jehiel*. It is a popular modern Hebrew name.

Yehuda (m.) Jewish: modern Hebrew form of JUDAH.

Yehudi (m.) Jewish: modern Hebrew name, originally an ethnic byname meaning 'Jew'.

Yehudit (f.) Jewish: modern Hebrew form of JUDITH.

Yekatarina (f.) Russian form of KATHERINE.
Pet form: **Katya**.

Yelena (f.) Russian form of HELEN.
Pet form: **Nelya**.

Yelisaveta (f.) Russian form of ELIZABETH.

Yelisei (m.) Russian form of ELISEO.

Yente (f.) Jewish: Yiddish name, probably a back-formation from Yentl (apparently from the French nickname *Gentille*

'kind, nice'), the *-l* being interpreted as a Yiddish hypocoristic suffix. The Yiddish vocabulary word *yente*, derived from the name, denotes a gossipy woman.

Yered (m.) Jewish: Hebrew form of JARED.

Yermolai (m.) Russian: from the Greek name *Hermolaos*, composed of the elements *Hermēs* (the name of the messenger god; cf. ERMETE) + *lāos*, *leōs* people, tribe. St Hermolaos (d. *c*.300) was martyred in Nicomedia together with his brothers Hermippos and Hermocrates, who shared the first element of his name (combined respectively with *hippos* horse and *kratein* to rule), according to a pattern common in the classical period and later.

Yetta (f.) Jewish: of uncertain origin, possibly a variant of ETTA originating in dialects of Yiddish subject to Slavonic influence, or else a derivative of YEHUDIT or ESTHER.

Yevgeni (m.) Russian form of EUGENE.

Yigael (m.) Jewish: traditional Hebrew name of uncertain derivation, probably meaning 'he shall be redeemed'.

Yitzhak (m.) Jewish: modern Hebrew form of ISAAC.

Yngvar (m.) Scandinavian: variant of INGVAR.

Ynyr (m.) Welsh: traditional name of uncertain derivation, probably from Latin *Honōrius* (see HONORIA). There is a passing reference in the *Mabinogi* to 'the battle between the two Ynyrs'.

Yolande (f.) English and French: of uncertain origin. It is found in Old French in this form, and seems to be ultimately of Germanic origin, but if so it has been changed beyond recognition by attempted associations with various Greek and Latin elements. It is also sometimes identified with the name of St Jolenta (d. 1298), daughter of the king of Hungary; her name is also occasionally rendered as HELEN.
Variant: English: **Yolanda**.
Cognates: Italian: **Jolanda**. Polish: **Jolanta**.
Czech: **Jolan(t)a**. Hungarian: **Jolán**.
Pet form: Polish: **Jola**.

Yon (m.) Basque: variant spelling of ION.

Yoram (m.) Jewish: Hebrew name, meaning 'Yahweh is high', borne in the Bible by an evil king of Israel. This has not stopped it from becoming a moderately popular given name in modern Israel.

Yorath (m.) English and Welsh: Anglicized form of the Welsh personal name IORWERTH or, in some cases, a transferred use of the surname derived from it.

Yorick (m.) English: the name of the (defunct) court jester in Shakespeare's *Hamlet*. It is apparently a respelling of *Jorck*, a Danish form of GEORGE.

York (m.) English: in most cases, probably a transferred use of the surname, which originated as a local name for someone who came from the city of York in northeastern England. The placename was originally *Eburacon*, a derivative of a British element meaning 'yew'. The Anglo-Saxon settlers changed this to Old English *Eofor-wīc* 'boar farm', which in Old Norse became *Iorvik* or *Iork*. The given name may also have been influenced by Scandinavian forms of GEORGE (e.g. Danish *Jorck*).

Yosef (m.) Jewish: modern Hebrew form of JOSEPH.

Yrjö (m.) Finnish form of GEORGE.

Ysanne (f.) English: of uncertain origin, apparently composed of *Ys-* (as in YSEULT) + *Anne*.

Yseult (f.) Medieval French form of ISOLDE, still occasionally used as a given name in the English-speaking world.

Yuri (m.) The usual Russian form of GEORGE, beside *Georgi*. This form is also found in Poland, with the spelling Juri.

Yves (m.) French: from a Germanic personal name representing a short form of various compound names containing the element *iv-* 'yew' (cf. Old Norse *ýr*, as in IVOR). The final *-s* is the mark of the Old French nominative case. The name was introduced to Britain from France at the time of the Norman Conquest, and again in the 20th century.

Cognates: German: **Ivo**. Polish: **Iwo**.

Yvette (f.) French: feminine diminutive form of YVES, now also used in the English-speaking world.

Yvonne (f.) French: feminine diminutive form of YVES (or simply a feminine form based on the Old French oblique case *Yvon*), now also widely used in the English-speaking world and in Scandinavia.

Z

Zachary (m.) English form (pre-dating the Authorized Version) of the New Testament Greek name *Zacharias*, a form of Hebrew ZECHARIAH. In the New Testament it is the name of the father of John the Baptist, who underwent a temporary period of dumbness for his lack of faith (Luke 1), and of a more obscure figure, Zacharias son of Barachias, who was slain 'between the temple and the altar' (Matthew 23: 35; Luke 11: 51). Like many biblical names, it is now out of fashion, although in the United States it is familiar as the name of a 19th-century president, Zachary Taylor. In the Highlands of Scotland it has been used as an Anglicized form of the Gaelic name SGÀIRE.

Variants: **Zacharias**, **Zachariah**, ZECHARIAH.
Cognate: Scottish Gaelic: **Sachairi**.

Zack (m.) English (esp. U.S.): short form of ZACHARY, also occasionally used as an independent given name.

Variant: **Zak**.

Zadok (m.) Jewish: Hebrew name meaning 'just' or 'righteous'. It was borne in the Bible by one of the chief priests of King David, who later anointed Solomon king of Israel (1 Kings 1: 39), and it has been used ever since, no doubt partly because of its auspicious meaning.

Zahava (f.) Jewish: modern Hebrew name, from the vocabulary word *zahav* gold.

Zalman (m.) Jewish: Hebraicized form of *Zalmen*, itself a Yiddish form of SOLOMON.

Zanna (f.) English: modern coinage, apparently originating as a short form of *Suzanna* (see SUSANNA).

Zara (f.) Name occasionally used in the 20th century in Britain, and to a lesser extent in Italy, Spain, and Portugal. It is said to be of Arabic origin, from *zahr* flower. It was given by Princess Anne and Mark Philips to their second child (b. 1981), which aroused considerable comment at the time as a departure from the traditional patterns of royal nomenclature. It has no doubt been influenced by SARAH.

Zaylie (f.) English: rare name of uncertain derivation, perhaps a respelling of ZÉLIE.

Zbigniew (m.) Common Polish name, from an old Slavonic personal name composed of the elements *zbit* to get rid of + *gniew* anger.

Cognate: Czech: **Zbyhněv**.
Feminine form: Czech: **Zbyhněva**.
Pet forms: Czech: **Zbyňa** (m., f.); **Zbyněk**, **Zbyšek** (m.); **Zbyhně(uš)ka**, **Zbyša** (f.).

Zdeněk (m.) Common Czech name, in origin a diminutive derived from a much contracted form of Latin *Sidōnius* (see SIDONY).

Feminine forms: **Zdeňka**, **Zdenka**, **Zdena**.
Pet forms: **Zdenko**, **Zdeněček**, **Zdení(če)k**, **Zdenoušek** (m.); **Zdenička**, **Zdenuška**, **Zdenin(k)a** (f.).

Zdzislaw (m.) Polish: from an old Slavonic personal name composed of the elements *zde* here, present + *slav* glory.

Cognates: Czech: **Zdislav**, **Zdeslav**.
Feminine forms: Polish: **Zdzislawa**. Czech: **Zdislava**, **Zdeslava**.
Pet forms: Polish: **Zdziś**, **Zdzi(e)ch**, **Zdzisiek**, **Zdziesz(ko)** (m.). Czech: **Zdík**, **Zdíšek** (m.); **Zdíš(k)a** (f.).

Zeb (m.) English (esp. U.S.): short form of the much rarer full name Zebulun, borne in the Bible by the sixth son of Leah and Jacob. The name may mean 'exaltation', although Leah derives it from another meaning of the Hebrew root *zabal*, namely 'to dwell': 'now will my husband dwell with me, because I have borne him six sons' (Genesis 30: 20). It appears in the New Testament (Matthew 4: 13) in the form *Zabulon*.

Zechariah (m.) Biblical: name (meaning 'God has remembered' in Hebrew) of several figures in the Bible, most notably one of the twelve 'minor' prophets, author of the book that bears his name. It was also the name of an earlier prophet, who was stoned by the people because of his preaching (2 Chronicles 24: 20–3), and of the last Israelite king of the race of Jehu, who was overthrown by Shallum the son of Jabesh (2 Kings 15: 8–10). See also ZACHARY.

Zed (m.) English (esp. U.S.): short form of the much rarer full name Zedekiah. This name, meaning 'justice of Yahweh' in Hebrew, is borne in the Bible by three separate characters.

Zeev (m.) Jewish: Hebrew name meaning 'wolf'. It has become popular as a translation of European names with this meaning. The wolf is traditionally associated with the tribe of *Binyamin* or BENJAMIN, because in his dying blessing the patriarch Jacob said 'Benjamin shall ravin as a wolf' (Genesis 49: 27).

Zeke (m.) English (esp. U.S.): short form of EZEKIEL, still occasionally used as an independent given name.

Zelah (f.) Biblical: name (meaning 'side' in Hebrew) of one of the fourteen cities of the tribe of Benjamin (Joshua 18: 28). It is far from clear why it should have come to be used, albeit rarely, as a female given name in the English-speaking world. It may simply be a variant of ZILLAH under the influence of the placename. However, for evidence that biblical placenames did yield English given names, cf. EBENEZER.

Zelda (f.) English: modern name of uncertain origin, possibly a short form of GRISELDA. It came to prominence in the 1920s as the name of the wife of the American writer F. Scott FitzGerald (1896–1940). Zelde, however, is a traditional Yiddish given name, derived from a Middle High German vocabulary word meaning 'happiness, good fortune' (cf. SELIG).

Zélie (f.) French and English: apparently an altered form of *Célie* (see CELIA).

Zelig (m.) Jewish: variant of SELIG.

Żelisław (m.) Polish: from an old Slavonic personal name composed of the elements *zhelit* to desire + *slav* glory.

Cognate: Czech: **Želislav**.

Pet forms: Polish: **Zelek, Zelusz**. Czech: **Želek, Želí(če)k, Želoušek**.

Zelma (f.) English: altered form of SELMA.

Zena (f.) 1. English: of uncertain origin. It may be a variant spelling of ZINA, a coinage as a feminine equivalent of ZENO, a shortened form of ZENOBIA, or a simplified variant of XENIA. 2. Scottish (Highland): short form of ALEXINA.

Zeno (m.) From the classical Greek name *Zēnōn*, a short form of any of several names having as their first element *Zēn-*, the stem form of the name of Zeus, king of the gods, for example *Zēnodōros* 'gift of Zeus'. Zeno was the name of two major Greek philosophers and a Christian Eastern Roman emperor (d. 491). Zeno of Elea (*c*.490–430 BC) was an original thinker who challenged common-sense notions like motion and number with sophisticated logical arguments. Zeno of Citium (*c*.334–262 BC) was the founder of the Stoics.

Zenobia (f.) Classical Greek name: feminine form of *Zēnobios*, a personal name composed of the elements *Zēn-* (see ZENO) + *bios* life. This was the name of a queen of Palmyra (*fl.* AD 267–72), who expanded her empire in the eastern Mediterranean and Asia Minor, but eventually came into conflict with Rome and was deposed by Aurelian. She was noted for her beauty and intelligence, but was also ruthless: she appears to have had her husband and his eldest son murdered.

Derivative: Russian: ZINOVIA.

Zenzi (f.) South German: pet form of KRESZENZ.

Zeph (m.) English (esp. U.S): short form of the much rarer full name Zephaniah, meaning 'hidden by God' in Hebrew. This was the name of one of the minor biblical prophets, author of the book of the Bible that bears his name.

Zephyrine (f.) English: Anglicized form of French Zéphyrine, an elaborated name derived from Latin *Zephyrus*, Greek *Zephyros* west wind (apparently a derivative of Greek *zoohos* darkness). St Zephyrinus was pope 199–217, but there is no equivalent female saint, so it is rather surprising that this name should occur only in a female form.

Zhenya (m., f.) Russian: pet form of both YEVGENI and its rarer feminine form *Yevgenia*.

Zillah (f.) Biblical: name (from a Hebrew word meaning 'shade') of one of the two wives of Lamech (Genesis 4: 19). The name was taken up in the first place by the Puritans, and again by fundamentalist Christian groups in the 19th century, partly because Zillah is only the third woman to be mentioned by name in the Bible, and her name was therefore prominent to readers of the Book of Genesis. She is not remarkable for any special qualities of character. ADAH, the name of Lamech's other wife, may in part lie behind ADA, which was also a popular 19th-century female name.

Zina (f.) Russian: short form of ZINAIDA and of ZINOVIA. This name is also occasionally used in the English-speaking world.

Zinaida (f.) Russian: from the Greek name *Zēnais* (genitive *Zēnaidos*), derived from the name of *Zeus* (genitive *Zēnos*), king of the gods. At least two saints of this name are revered in the Orthodox Church as 1st-century martyrs.

Zinovia (f.) Russian form of ZENOBIA. A St Zenobia was martyred in Asia Minor, together with her brother Zenobios, probably at the beginning of the 3rd century.

Zipporah (f.) Jewish: common female form of the rare Hebrew male name Zippor meaning 'bird'. The female name is borne in the Bible by the wife of Moses and mother of Gershom and Eliezer (Exodus 18: 2–4).

Zissi (f.) German: pet form of *Franziska* (see FRANZ).

Zita (f.) Italian and English: from the name of a 13th-century saint from Lucca in Tuscany, who led an uneventful life as a domestic servant; she was canonized in 1696, and is regarded as the patroness of domestic servants. Her name was probably a nickname from the medieval Tuscan dialect word *zit(t)a* girl, although efforts have been made to link it with Greek *zētein* to seek.

Žitomír (m.) Czech: from an old Slavonic personal name composed of the elements *zhit* to live + *meri* great, famous (see CASIMIR).

Feminine form: **Žitomira**.

Pet forms: **Žit(ouš)ek** (m.); **Žitka, Žituše** (f.).

Živan (m.) Czech: from an old Slavonic byname derived from the element *zhiv* living.

Feminine form: **Živ(an)ka**.

Pet forms: **Živ(an)ek, Živko** (m.); **Živuše, Živuška** (f.).

Zlatan (m.) Czech: derivative of the element *zlato* gold, used as a vernacular loan translation of the Latin name *Aurēlius* (see AURÈLE).

Feminine form: **Zlata**.

Pet forms: **Zlatek, Zlatko, Zlatí(če)k, Zlatoušek** (m.); **Zlat(uš)ka, Zlatuše, Zlatin(k)a, Zlatun(k)a** (f.).

Zoë (f.) English: from the Greek name meaning 'life'. This was already in use in Rome towards the end of the classical period (at first as an affectionate nickname), and was popular with the early Christians, who bestowed it with reference to their hopes of eternal life. It was borne by martyrs of the 2nd and 3rd centuries, but was taken up as an English given name only in the 19th century.

Variant: **Zoe**.

Zofia (f.) Polish form of SOFIA.

Pet form: **Zosia**.

Žofie (f.) Czech form of SOFIA.

Zola (f.) English: apparently a late 20th-century creation, formed from the first syllable of ZOË with the ending -*la* common in female names. It coincides in form with the surname of the French novelist Émile Zola (1840–1902), who was of Italian descent, but it is unlikely that he had any influence on the popularity of the name.

Zoltán (m.) Hungarian: of uncertain derivation, possibly from an honorific title of Turkic origin and ultimately connected with modern English *sultan*.

Zosia (f.) Polish: pet form of ZOFIA.

Zsófia (f.) Hungarian form of SOFIA.

Zsuzsanna (f.) Hungarian form of SUSANNA.

Zula (f.) English: modern name, apparently derived from the tribal name of the Zulus. The Zulu people of Southern Africa formed a powerful warrior nation under their leader Chaka in the 19th century, and controlled an extensive empire. In 1838, under the leadership of their ruler Dingaan, they ambushed and slaughtered a group of some 500 Boers. Not surprisingly, this given name is chosen mainly, if not exclusively, by Blacks proud of their African origins.

Zuzana (f.) Czech form of SUSANNA.

Zuzanna (f.) Polish form of SUSANNA.

Zvi (m.) Jewish: Hebrew name meaning 'hart, deer'. It has become a popular modern Hebrew name as a translation of Yiddish HIRSH and HERSHEL. The deer is traditionally associated with the name NAPHTALI, because in his dying blessing the patriarch Jacob says 'Naphtali is a hind let loose' (Genesis 49: 21). In this verse the Hebrew word for 'hind' is *ayala*, but since this is a feminine noun (see AYALA and HINDE), the masculine noun *zvi* is substituted as a male given name.
Variant: **Zwi** (German, Dutch, and Polish spelling).

Zwaante (f.) Frisian: pet derivative of a short form of any of various old Germanic female personal names containing the first element *swan* swan, such as SWANHILD and *Swanburg*.

Zygmunt (m.) Polish form of SIGMUND.

A DICTIONARY OF
BRITISH PLACE-NAMES

A. D. MILLS · ADRIAN ROOM

INTRODUCTION

Place-Names and their Meanings

Place-names, those familiar but often curious labels for places that feature in all their rich diversity on map and signpost, fulfil such an essential function in our daily lives that we take them very much for granted. Yet English place-names are as much part of England's cultural heritage as the English language and the English landscape from which they spring, and almost every place-name has an older original meaning behind its modern form.

Most people will have wondered at some time or other about the original meaning of a place-name— the name of their home town or of the other familiar places encountered *en route* to work by road or rail, the names of stations and destinations and those seen on roadsigns and signposts, and the more unusual names discovered on trips into the countryside or on holiday. Why Eccles, Stoke Poges, Great Snoring, or Leighton Buzzard? What is the meaning of a name like Strangeways or Chiswick? How did Croydon, Liverpool, and Windsor get their names? What does Crick or Bootle mean?

In fact all these names, like the vast majority of the names included in this dictionary, have original meanings that are not at all apparent from their modern forms. That is because most place-names today are what could be termed 'linguistic fossils'. Although they originated as living units of speech, coined by our distant ancestors as descriptions of places in terms of their topography, appearance, situation, use, ownership, or other association, most have become, in the course of time, mere labels, no longer possessing a clear linguistic meaning. This is perhaps not surprising when one considers that most place-names are a thousand years old or more, and are expressed in vocabulary that may have evolved differently from the equivalent words in the ordinary language, or that may now be completely extinct or obscure.

Of course some place-names, even very old ones, have apparently changed very little through the many centuries of their existence, and may still convey something of their original meaning when the words from which they are composed have survived in the ordinary language (even though the features to which they refer may have changed or disappeared).

Names such as Claybrooke, Horseheath, Marshwood, Nettlebed, Oxford, Saltmarshe, Sandford, and Woodbridge are shown by their early spellings to be virtually self-explanatory, having undergone little or no change in form or spelling over a very long period.

But even a casual glance at the alphabetical list of English place-names will show that such instant etymologies are usually a delusion. The modern form of a name can never be assumed to convey its original meaning without early spellings to confirm it, and indeed many names that look equally obvious and easy to interpret prove to have quite unexpected meanings in the light of the evidence of early records. Thus Easter is 'the sheep-fold', Slaughter 'the muddy place', Swine 'the creek or channel', and Wool 'the spring or springs'—the inevitable association of such names with well-known words in the ordinary vocabulary is understandable but quite misleading, for they all derive from old words which survive in fossilized form in place-names but which are no longer found in the language.

Names then can never be taken at their face value, but can only be correctly interpreted after the careful scrutiny of the earliest attested spellings in the light of the dialectal development of the sounds of the language, after wide comparisons have been made with similar or identical names, and after other linguistic, historical, and geographical factors have been taken into account. These fundamental principles of place-name etymology are most clearly illustrated by the names which now have identical forms but which prove to have quite distinct origins: for example, the name Broughton occurs several times but has no less than three different origins ('brook farmstead', 'hill farmstead', and 'fortified farmstead'), the various places called Hinton fall into two distinct groups ('high farmstead' or 'farmstead belonging to a religious community'), and even a place-name like Ashford can be deceptive and means something other than 'ash-tree ford' in two instances. On the other hand, names now with different spellings can turn out to have identical origins: thus Aldermaston and Alderminster are both 'nobleman's farmstead', Chiswick and Keswick are both 'cheese farm', Hatfield and Heathfield are both 'heathy open land', and Naunton, Newington, Newnton, Newton, and Niton are all 'new farmstead'. It goes without saying that guesswork on the basis of a modern form is of little use, and that each name must be the subject of individual scrutiny. For the same reason it should be remembered that the interpretation offered for a particular name in the list may not apply to another name with identical modern spelling occurring elsewhere, which might well have a quite different origin and meaning on the evidence of its early spellings and of other information.

Scope and Arrangement

The main object of this dictionary is simple—to explain the most likely meanings and origins of over 12,000 English place-names in a clear, concise, and easily accessible form, based on the evidence and information so far available. The names included have been selected because they appear in all or several of the popular touring atlases, containing maps on a scale of three or four miles to the inch, produced by the Ordnance Survey and by the motoring organizations and other publishers. Thus the names of all the better-known places have been included: the names of England's towns and cities, of a good number of its villages and hamlets and city suburbs, together with the names of counties and districts (old and new) and of many rivers and coastal features.

The entries are strictly alphabetical, each name being referred to the post-1974 county in which the place is located. Priority in the entries is given to what the individual name 'means'. Thus wherever possible the suggested original meaning, that thought most likely as deduced from the evidence of early spellings and other information and from the fuller discussions of the name available in more detailed studies, is presented as a 'translation' into a modern English phrase of the old words or 'elements' that make up the name. The elements themselves are usually then cited in their original spelling and language, Celtic, Old English, Old Scandinavian, or other as the case may be (a Glossary of some of the most common elements being provided at the end of the book).

Most names can be satisfactorily explained with respect to the elements from which they are derived, although the precise shades of meaning of the individual elements or of a particular compound may not always be easy to ascertain. For some names the evidence so far available is not decisive, and explan-

ations may be somewhat provisional. A few remain doubtful or obscure or partly so. It is of course possible that earlier or better evidence may still come to light for some names, especially for places in those counties like Durham, Hampshire, Kent, Lancashire, Somerset, and Suffolk for which there is as yet no English Place-Name Society survey.

Alternative explanations have often been given for names where two or more interpretations seem possible. For instance it is often difficult to say whether the first element of a compound name is a personal name or a significant word, as in names like Eversden, Hauxley, Hinxhill, Ranskill, and Yearsley. However for reasons of space some alternative explanations considered rather unlikely, problematical, or controversial have been omitted from the entries, in favour of those judged most plausible. Alternative interpretations of this kind are of course more fully rehearsed and discussed in the detailed surveys and monographs.

It should perhaps be pointed out that although the explanations suggested are considered to be the most likely, and are as accurate and reliable as possible within the limitations of scope and space imposed, final certainty in establishing the original meanings of many older place-names is unlikely to be achieved because of the nature of the materials. Given the archaic character of many place-names, and the fact that we can rarely know precisely when and by whom they were originally coined or came into use (as opposed to when they first appear in written records), there will always be an element of conjecture in their interpretation. However the study of place-names is a continually developing and evolving field, as the last few decades have shown, and further revision and refinement of etymologies is bound to come out of current and future research.

Inevitably the rather concise explanations of meaning and origin attempted in this dictionary, although based on the latest research, have meant leaving aside other important considerations. It has not been possible to enter into the complexities of philological argument, or to explore questions as to the precise nature or location of a topographical or habitative feature, or to examine the identity and status of a person associated with a place and the precise significance of that association. Such matters as these, and many other considerations bearing on the significance of a place-name in its historical, archaeological, and geographical context, are of course explored more fully in the various county surveys and studies of name-groups listed in the Bibliography, and they should be consulted by the interested reader wanting further information.

The Chronology and Languages of English Place-Names

Place-names show an astonishing capacity for survival, as the dates alone of most of the earliest spellings testify, even though it should be remembered that every name will of course be older than its earliest occurrence in the records, often a good deal older. In general it might be claimed that most of the names included in this book are about a thousand years old, and that a good many are older than that. The various strata of English place-names reflect all the great historical migrations, conquests, and settlements of the past and the different languages spoken by successive waves of inhabitants.

Some river-names, few in number but the most ancient of all, seem to belong to an unknown early Indo-European language which is neither Celtic nor Germanic. Such pre-Celtic names, sometimes termed 'Old European', may have been in use among the very early inhabitants of these islands in Neolithic times, and it is assumed that they were passed on to Celtic settlers arriving from the Continent about the fourth century BC. Among the ancient names that possibly belong to this small but important group are Colne, Humber, Itchen, and Wey.

During the last four centuries BC there took place the invasions and settlements of the Iron-Age Celts, peoples speaking various Celtic dialects which can be divided into two main groups, Goidelic or Gaelic (later differentiated into Irish, Scots, and Manx) and Brittonic or British (later differentiated into Welsh and Cornish). Celtic place-names coined in British (really the language of the ancient Britons) were in use for several centuries and some have survived from the period when this Celtic language was spoken over the whole of what is now England as well as further west. These early place-names of Celtic or British origin were borrowed by the Anglo-Saxons when they came to Britain from the 5th century AD onwards and are found all over England, only sporadically in the east but increasing in numbers further west towards Cornwall and Wales where they are of course still predominant. Celtic place-names belong for the most part to several well-defined categories: names of tribes or territories like Devon and Leeds, names of important towns and cities like Carlisle, York, and Dover, names of hills and forests (now often transferred to places) like Crick, Mellor, Penge, and Lytchett, and most fre-

quent of all, river-names like Avon, Exe, Frome, Thames, and Trent. There are also a good many hybrid names, consisting of a Celtic name to which an Old English element has been added, like Lichfield, Chatham, Bredon, and Manchester. Some places, important at a very early date, had Celtic names in Romano-British times which were later replaced, for instance Cambridge was *Duroliponte*, Canterbury was *Durovernum*, and Leicester was *Ratae*: for these, reference should be made to the fuller treatments of individual names in the county surveys or to the specialized study by Rivet and Smith (see Bibliography).

The Roman occupation of Britain during the first four centuries AD left little mark on place-names, for it is clear that Latin was mainly the official written language of government and administration rather than the spoken language of the countryside. Thus Celtic names, though usually Latinized in written sources, continued to be used throughout this period and were not replaced. However a few early names like Catterick and Lincoln contain Latin elements, and others like Eccles and Caterham were coined from Celtic elements that were borrowed from Latin during this early period. The small part played by Latin in place-name formation during the Romano-British period should be distinguished from the later influence of Latin on English place-names during the medieval period. In the Middle Ages, Latin was again the language of the church and administration, and this Medieval Latin was widely used in affixes like *Forum* 'market', *Magna* 'great', and *Regis* 'of the king' to distinguish places with identical names, as well as occasionally in the formation of names like Bruera, Dacorum, and Pontefract.

The Anglo-Saxon conquest and settlement of Britain began in the 5th century AD, spreading from east to west and culminating in the occupation of the whole of what is now England, except for Cornwall and some areas along the Welsh border, by the 9th century. These new settlers were the Angles, Saxons, and Jutes, Germanic tribes from Northern Europe whose language was Anglo-Saxon, now usually called Old English to emphasize its continuity with Middle and Modern English. It is in this language, Old English, that the great majority of the place-names now in use in England were coined. This dominant stratum in English place-names (apart from those of Cornwall) is a result of the political domination by the Anglo-Saxons of the Celtic-speaking Britons and the gradual imposition of the Old English language on them. Many Celtic names were borrowed by the incomers as already mentioned (important evidence for the survival of a British population and for continuity and contact between the two peoples), but thousands of new names were coined in Old English during the Anglo-Saxon period between the fifth and eleventh centuries. Thus the majority of English towns and villages, and a good many hamlets and landscape features, have names of Old English origin that predate the Norman Conquest. These names vary in age, and it is not always easy to tell which names belong to the earlier phases of the settlement and which to the later part of the Anglo-Saxon period, although detailed studies have shown that many of the names containing the elements *hām*, *-ingas*, *-inga*, *ēg*, *feld*, *ford*, and *dūn* are among the earliest. It should in any case be remembered that all names are older than their earliest recorded spelling, so that names first mentioned in, for example, Domesday Book (1086) or even in a twelfth-century source usually have their origins in this period.

The Scandinavian invasions and settlements took place during the 9th, 10th, and 11th centuries and resulted in many place-names of Scandinavian origin in the North and East of England. The Vikings came to Britain from two Scandinavian countries, Denmark and Norway, the Danes settling principally in East Anglia, the East Midlands, and a large part of Yorkshire, whilst the Norwegians were mainly concentrated in the North-West, especially Lancashire and Cumbria. The Germanic languages spoken by these Vikings, Old Danish and Old Norse (in this book referred to jointly as Old Scandinavian), were similar in many ways to Old English, but there were also striking differences in sound system and vocabulary which reveal themselves in the early spellings of many place-names from the areas mentioned. Although names of Scandinavian origin are rare to the south of Watling Street (because that formed the boundary of the Danelaw, which was the area subject to Danish law, established in the late 9th century), the distribution of Scandinavian names in the North and East varies greatly, parts of Norfolk, Leicestershire, Lincolnshire, and Yorkshire being among the areas with the thickest concentration. To explain such large numbers of Scandinavian place-names in these areas, recent scholarship has suggested that in addition to settlements made by Viking warriors and their descendants there was probably a large-scale migration and colonization from the Scandinavian homelands in the wake of the invasion.

Many hundreds of names in the areas mentioned are completely of Scandinavian origin (Kirkby, Lowestoft, Scunthorpe, Braithwaite), others are hybrids, a mixture of Scandinavian and English (Grimston, Durham, Welby), and some (on account of the similarity of some Old English and Old Scandinavian words) could be from either language (Crook, Kettleburgh, Lytham, Snape). In addition many place-names of Old English origin were modified by Scandinavian speech in these areas, for example by the substitution of *sk* and *k* sounds for *sh* and *ch* in names like Skidbrooke, Skipton, Keswick, and Kippax.

The number of English place-names of French origin is relatively small, in spite of the far-reaching effects of the Norman Conquest on English social and political life and on the English language in general. It is clear that by 1066, most settlements and landscape features already had established names, but the new French-speaking aristocracy and ecclesiastical hierarchy often gave distinctively French names to their castles, estates, and monasteries (Battle, Belvoir, Grosmont, Montacute, Richmond), some of them transferred directly from France, and there are a few names of French origin referring to landscape and other features (Devizes, Malpas). However the French influence on English place-names is perhaps most evident in the way the names of the great French-speaking feudal families were affixed to the names of the manors they possessed. These manorial additions result in a great many hybrid 'double-barrelled' names which contribute considerable variety and richness to the map of England. Most of them serve to distinguish one manor from another with an identical name, and of course the surnames of the more powerful landowning families occur in a good many different place-names (Kingston Lacy, Stanton Lacy, Sutton Courtenay, Hirst Courtney, Drayton Bassett, Wootton Bassett, and so on). Some place-names of this type are not easily recognizable from their modern spellings, since the manorial affixes are now compounded with the original elements (Herstmonceux, Owermoigne, Stogursey). A further important aspect of the French influence on English place-names is the way it affected their spelling and pronunciation. Norman scribes had difficulty with some English sounds, often substituting their own (as seen for instance in the spellings of Domesday Book and other early medieval sources). Some of these Norman spellings have had a permanent effect on the names in question and have remained in use, disguising the original forms (Cambridge, Cannock, Diss, Durham, Nottingham, Salop, Trafford).

Of course not all of the names on the modern map, even names of sizeable settlements or well-known features, are as old as most of those so far mentioned. Other names besides the French names already noted originated in the Middle English period, that is between the twelfth and fifteenth centuries inclusive. These include settlement names incorporating post-Conquest personal names and surnames like Bassenthwaite, Forston, and Vauxhall, names containing old elements but not on early record like Bournemouth and Paddock Wood, and various other names such as Broadstairs, Forest Row, Poplar, and Sacriston.

Finally there are some place-names, perhaps surprisingly few, which originate in the post-medieval period or even in quite recent times. Many of course are names of new industrial towns or of suburban developments, others are names of coastal resorts or ports or of new administrative districts. Most of these 'modern' names seem rather artificial creations compared with the earlier place-names that began life as actual descriptions of habitations or natural features. Some are in fact simply straight transfers of older names without any change of form (like the post-1974 county name Tyne & Wear, or the 'revived' district names Bassetlawe and Dacorum), some are based on rather fanciful identifications of ancient names made by early antiquarians (like Adur and Morecambe), and others are new adaptations of existing old names with some sort of addition (like Devonport, Thamesmead, and New Brighton). Of the newly formed modern names, some are straightforwardly descriptive of a local feature whether natural (Highcliffe) or man-made (Ironbridge), others are named from a building around which the settlement developed (the pub in Nelson and Queensbury, the chapel in St Helens and Chapel St Leonards), some are named from fields (Hassocks and Whyteleafe), others refer to local products (Coalville, Port Sunlight), commemorate a famous historical event (Peacehaven, Vigo, Waterloo) or even a famous novel (Westward Ho!). In addition a good number of the names coined in more recent times commemorate entrepreneurs or other notable individuals, some consisting simply of their names (Fleetwood, Peterlee, Telford), others incorporating these into a sort of spurious form that looks older than it is (Carterton, Maryport, Stewartby), others referring to landowners (Camden Town) or local families (Burgess Hill, Gerrards Cross).

Some Different Types of Place-Name Formation

All English place-names, whether of Celtic, Old English, or Scandinavian origin, can be divided into three main groups: folk-names, habitative names, and topographical names.

Of the three, **folk-names** form the smallest group though nevertheless a very important and interesting one. Place-names in his category were originally the names of the inhabitants of a place or district. Thus tribal names came to denote the district occupied by the tribe, as with Essex and Sussex (both old Anglo-Saxon kingdoms), and Norfolk and Suffolk (divisions of the Anglo-Saxon kingdom of East Anglia). The names Jarrow, Hitchin, and Ripon also represent tribes (later their territories) from Anglo-Saxon times, and names like Clewer and Ridware must represent the settlements of smaller groups. Of particular interest, because they are to be associated with the early phases of the Anglo-Saxon settlement, are the names formed with the suffix -ingas ('people of', 'dwellers at') like Hastings, Reading, and Spalding, all of them originally denoting family or tribal groups, later their settlements.

Habitative names form a much larger group. They denoted inhabited places from the start, whether homesteads, farms or enclosures, villages or hamlets, strongholds, cottages, or other kinds of building or settlement. In names of this type the second element describes the kind of habitation, and among others the Old English elements hām 'homestead', tūn 'farm', worth 'enclosure', wīc 'dwelling', cot 'cottage', burh 'stronghold', and the Old Scandinavian elements bý 'farmstead' and thorp 'outlying farmstead' are particularly common, as in names like Streatham, Middleton, Lulworth, Ipswich, Didcot, Aylesbury, Grimsby, and Woodthorpe. Detailed studies of the various habitative elements have shown that they had a wide range of meanings which varied according to their use at different periods or in different parts of the country or in combination with other elements. For example Old English tūn may have its original meaning 'enclosure' in some names, whereas in others 'farmstead', 'village', 'manor', or 'estate' may be more appropriate. The reader is recommended to consult the Glossary at the end of the book to discover some of the alternative meanings evidenced for other habitative elements like beretūn, burh, thorp, wīc, wīc-hām, and so on.

Topographical names also form a very large and diverse group. They consisted originally of a description of some topographical or physical feature, either natural or man-made, which was then transferred to the settlement near the feature named, probably at a very early date. Thus names for rivers and streams, springs and lakes, fords and roads, marshes and moors, hills and valleys, woods and clearings, and various other landscape features became the names of inhabited places. Typical examples of the type are Sherborne, Fulbrook, Bakewell, Tranmere, Oxford, Breamore, Stodmarsh, Swindon, Goodwood, Bromsgrove, Bexley, and Hatfield—all have second elements that originally denoted topographical features. Indeed our early ancestors made use of a vast topographical vocabulary, applied with precision and subtlety in any one period or locality to the natural and artificial features they depended upon for their subsistence and survival. However, the meanings of topographical terms can vary a good deal from name to name, for some elements used over a long period in the formation of English place-names underwent considerable changes of meaning during medieval times, for instance Old English *feld* originally 'open land' developed a later sense 'enclosed plot', Old English *wald* 'forest' came to mean 'open upland', and Old English *lēah* 'wood' became 'woodland clearing' and then 'meadow'. The choice of the most likely meaning for one of these elements in an individual name is therefore a matter of judgement, based among other things on locality, the nature of the compound, and assumptions about the age of the name. Moreover recent research has increasingly shown that what seem to be similar terms for hills or valleys, woodland or marshland, or agricultural land, had fine distinctions of meaning in early times. For instance the different Old English terms for 'hill' like *dūn, hyll, hrycg, hōh, hēafod*, and **ofer*, far from being synonymous, seem to have had their own specialized meanings. In addition these and other common topographical elements like *ēg* 'island', *hamm* 'enclosure', and *halh* 'nook' were each capable of a wide range of extended meanings according to date, region, and the character of the landscape itself. Indeed the meanings suggested for names containing these elements can often be checked and refined by those with a close knowledge of the local topography of the places in question. The Glossary at the end of the book provides a selection of the meanings found for some of these topographical elements and gives an idea of the great range and variety of this vocabulary.

A.D. MILLS

Irish Place-Names

A glance at a map of Ireland will show a preponderance of anglicized Irish place-names, both in the Republic and in Northern Ireland. Most of them are descriptive of some kind of settlement, building, or natural feature and include such frequently found elements as *Bally-* (Irish *baile*, 'farmstead, townland') *Carrick-* or *Carrig-* (*carraig*, 'rock'), *Derry-* (*doire*, 'oak grove'), *Drum-* (*droim*, 'ridge'), *Inch-* or *Inish-* (*inis*, 'island'), *Kil-* or *Kill-* (*cill*, 'church', but sometimes *coill*, 'wood'), *Knock-* (*cnoc*, 'hill'), *Letter-* (*leitir*, 'hillside'), and *Slieve-* (*sliabh*, 'mountain'). Both *Lis-* (*lios*) and *Rath-* (*ráth*) are usually translated 'ring fort', the former word denoting the fort as a whole and the latter usually implying the presence of a church or monastery. *Dun-* (*dún*), on the other hand, usually rendered 'fort' or 'fortress', denotes the dwelling of a king or chieftain. The commonly occurring *Ballin-* or *Ballina-* may represent either *baile na*, 'homestead of the …', or *béal átha na*, 'ford-mouth of the …'. Examples of such names and their respective Irish forms are *Ballyshrule* (*Baile Sruthail*), 'homestead of the stream', *Carrickfergus* (*Carraig Fhearghasa*), 'Fergus's rock', *Derryboy* (*Doire Buí*), 'yellow oak grove', *Drumahoe* (*Droim na hUamha*), 'ridge of the cave', *Kilteele* (*Cill Tíle*), 'Tíl's church', *Killadangan* (*Coill an Daingin*), 'wood of the fortress', *Knockmoyle* (*Cnoc Maol*), 'bald hill', *Letterbrick* (*Leitir Bruic*), 'hillside of the badger', *Slieveardagh* (*Sliabh Ardachaidh*), 'mountain of the high field', *Lismore* (*Lios Mór*), 'big fort', *Rathfeigh* (*Ráth Faiche*), 'fort of the green', *Dungannon* (*Dún Geanainn*), 'Geanann's fort', *Ballinderreen* (*Baile an Doirín*, 'homestead of the little oak grove'), and *Ballingar* (*Béal Átha na gCarr*), 'ford-mouth of the carts'.

Other common Irish place-name words include *achadh*, 'field', *aird*, 'promontory', *beag*, 'small', *beann* or *binn*, 'peak', *bóthar*, 'road', *caol*, 'narrow (place)', *cloch*, 'stone', *cluain*, 'meadow', *craobh*, 'tree', *domhnach*, 'church' (from Latin *dominicum*), *glas*, 'grey-green', *gleann*, 'valley', *loch*, 'lake', *mainistir*, 'monastery' (from Latin *monasterium*), *ros*, 'promontory', or sometimes 'grove', *teach*, 'house', often implying a saint's house, *teampall*, 'church' (from Latin *templum*), *tobar*, 'well', and *tóchar*, 'causeway'. Examples of names incorporating these are *Aghabog* (*Achadh Bog*), 'soft field', *Ardmore* (*Aird Mhór*), 'great promontory', *Beginish* (*Beaginis*), 'small island', *Benbane* (*Beann Bán*), 'white peak', *Boherard* (*Bóthar Ard*), 'high road',

Kealkill (*Caolchoill*), 'narrow wood', *Clonakilty* (*Cloch na Coillte*), 'stone of the woods', *Clonmore* (*Cluain Mór*), 'large pasture', *Crewbane* (*Craobh Bán*), 'white tree', *Donaghmore* (*Domhnach Mór*), 'big church', *Glaslough* (*Glasloch*), 'grey-green lake', *Glendowan* (*Gleann Domhain*), 'deep valley', *Loughrea* (*Loch Ria*), 'grey lake', *Monasterevin* (*Mainistir Eimhín*), 'Eimhín's monastery', *Rosslare* (*Ros Láir*), 'middle promontory', *Timolin* (*Tigh Moling*), 'St Moling's house', *Templemichael* (*Teampall Mhichil*), 'St Michael's church', *Tobercurry* (*Tobar an Choire*), 'well of the cauldron', and *Ballintogher* (*Baile an Tóchair*), 'homestead of the causeway'.

Caiseal and *caisleán* both mean 'castle' (from Latin *castellum*), but the former word is normally used of a ring fort with stone walls, while the latter is used specifically of a medieval or post-medieval castle. *Caiseal* is mostly found in the northwest of the country. Examples are *Cashelgarran* (*Caiseal an Ghearráin*), 'castle of the horses', and *Castlederg* (*Caisleán na Deirge*), 'castle on the (river) Derg'.

Viking settlers introduced Scandinavian names to the east and south coasts of Ireland from the 9th century. Many end in *-ford*, which is not 'ford' but 'sea inlet' (OScand. *fjǫrthr*, English *fjord*), as for *Carlingford*, 'inlet of the hag', *Strangford*, 'inlet with a strong current', and *Waterford*, 'inlet where wethers are loaded'. *Wicklow* is 'Vikings' meadow' (*víkingr* + *ló*), while Dublin's *Howth* is *hǫfuth*, 'headland'. *Wexford* combines OIrish *escir*, 'sandbank', and OScand. *fjǫrthr*. Inland, *Leixlip* is 'salmon leap' (*leax* + *hlaup*). Most places with Scandinavian names have unrelated Irish names, so Waterford is *Port Láirge*, 'bank of the haunch', and Wexford *Loch Garman*, 'lake of the (river) Garma'. The province names *Leinster*, *Munster*, and *Ulster* have an OScand. genitive *-s* before Irish *tír*, 'territory'. The name of *Dublin* is Irish (*dubh* + *linn*, 'black pool'), but was used by the Vikings for the town they built by the River Liffey. The city's official Irish name is *Baile Átha Cliath*, 'town of the hurdle ford'.

Anglo-Norman place-names appeared in the 12th century. Few now remain, but examples are *Mitchelstown*, 'Mitchel's homestead', and *Pomeroy*, 'apple orchard'. Some Anglo-Norman names were subsequently gallicized, such as *Ballylanders* (Irish *Baile an Londraigh*), 'de Londra's homestead', presumably denoting an English family from London. The Plantations of the 16th and 17th centuries brought an influx of more directly English names, such as *Cookstown*, *Draperstown*, and *Jamestown*. The Irish names are often unrelated, as *An Chorr Chríochach*, 'the boundary hill', for Cookstown, and *Baile na Croise*, 'town of the cross', for Draperstown. *Maryborough*, named for Queen Mary I of England, is now known by its Irish name of *Port Laoise*, 'port of the people of Laeighis', while *Queen's County*, after the same monarch, is now again *Laois*, earlier anglicized as *Leix*. *Offaly* (*Uibh Fhailí*), '(place of the) descendants of Failge', was similarly *King's County*, after Mary's husband, King Philip II of Spain, but *Kingstown*, now again *Dun Laoghaire*, 'Laoghaire's fort', was a later renaming, after King George IV.

Scottish Place-Names

Scotland's earliest Celtic names are British (Cumbric), in a language akin to Welsh spoken by the 'Ancient' Britons, or Pictish, in a similar language spoken by the Picts. Names such as *Glasgow*, 'green hollow', and *Melrose*, 'bare moor', are British, while Pictish produced the distinctive *Pit-* names found in the northeast of Scotland, Fife, and Angus, such as *Pitcairn*, *Pitlochry*, and *Pittenweem*. The element represents Pictish *pett*, 'portion (of land)', a word ultimately related to English *piece*.

The majority of Scotland's names are Gaelic, however, in the language of the original Scots from Ireland. They incorporate such common words as *achadh*, 'field' (*Achlean*, 'broad field'), *ard*, 'high' (*Ardnamurchan*, 'height of the sea otters'), *baile*, 'town' (*Ballinluig*, 'township in the hollow'), *beinn*, 'mountain' (*Ben Dearg*, 'red mountain'), *cill*, 'church' (*Kilmore*, 'great church'), *druim*, 'ridge' (*Drumbeg*, 'little ridge'), *dùn*, 'fort' (*Dunoon*, 'river fort'), *inis*, 'island' (*Inchcolm*, 'St Columba's island'), *inbhir*, 'river mouth' (*Inverness*, 'mouth of the River Ness'), *loch*, 'lake' (*Lochinvar*, 'lake on the height'), *ros*, 'promontory' (*Rosemarkie*, 'point of land by the horse stream'), and *srath*, 'valley' (*Strathallan*, 'valley of the Allan Water').

South-eastern Scotland has a number of English names, introduced by the Northumbrian Angles from the 7th century. Examples are *Haddington*, 'farm associated with Hada', *Prestwick*, 'outlying farm of the priests', and *Whithorn*, 'white building'. From the 8th century, Scandinavian names began to appear, especially in northern and north-western Scotland. Among them are *Dingwall*, 'field of the assembly', *Kirkwall*, 'church bay', *Lerwick*, 'mud inlet', *Scalloway*, 'bay by the shielings', and *Storno-*

way, 'steerage bay'. OScand. *bólstathr*, 'homestead', lies behind a number of names in the north, and especially in Orkney and Shetland, such as *Isbister*, 'Ine's dwelling', *Kirkabister*, 'church farm', *Lybster*, 'dwelling place by the sheltered spot', and *Scrabster*, 'rocky homestead'. The word is greatly reduced in *Skibo*. 'Skithi's farm'. OScand. *kirkja*, 'church', the source of Scottish *kirk*, gave such names as *Kirkcudbright*, 'St Cuthbert's church', *Kirkoswald*, 'St Oswald's church', and the common *Kirkton*, 'village with a church'. In the first two of these, the word order is Celtic, not Scandinavian.

More recent names include Norman French names such as *Beauly* ('beautiful place'), 'military' names of the 17th and 18th centuries, such as *Fort Augustus*, *Fort George*, and *Fort William*, and names dating from this same period that commemorate a settlement's founder or his wife or daughter, such as *Bettyhill*, *Campbeltown*, *Fraserburgh*, *Grantown*, *Helensburgh*, and *Jemimaville*. *Edinburgh*, popularly derived from St Edwin, 7th-century king of Northumbria, in fact dates from before his time.

Welsh Place-Names

The majority of place-names in Wales are Welsh and descriptive of a natural feature or location, such as *Moelfre*, 'bare hill', or *Penmaenmawr*, 'head of the great rock'. Common Welsh words in place-names include *aber*, 'river-mouth' (*Aberystwyth*, 'mouth of the Ystwyth'), *caer*, 'fort' (*Caerphilly*, 'Ffili's fort'), *cwm*, 'valley' (*Cwmfelin*, 'valley of the mill'), *llan*, 'church' (*Llanfair*, 'St Mary's church'), *llyn*, 'lake' (*Tal-y-llyn*, 'end of the lake'), *nant*, 'stream' (*Nantyglo*, 'stream of the coal'), *tre* or *tref*, 'farm' (*Trefeglwys*, 'church farm'), *pont*, 'bridge' (*Pontnewydd*, 'new bridge'), and *porth*, 'harbour' (*Porthcawl*, 'harbour of the sea kale').

Viking raids on the coasts of Wales from the 9th century have left their imprint in distinctive Scandinavian names, especially those of islands such as *Anglesey*, 'Ongull's island', *Caldy*, 'cold island', *Ramsey*, 'wild garlic island', and *Skomer*, 'cloven island'. Coastal towns with Viking names include *Fishguard*, 'fish yard', *Milford Haven*, 'harbour at the sandy inlet', and *Swansea*, 'Sveinn's sea place'. Norman names followed from the 11th century, such as *Beaumaris*, 'beautiful marsh', *Grosmont*, 'great hill', and *Malpas*, 'bad passage'. English names became established from the 12th century, such as *Chepstow*, 'market place', *Haverfordwest*, 'western ford of the goats', *Holyhead*, 'holy headland', and *Wrexham*, 'Wryhtel's river meadow'. *Snowdon*, 'snow hill', is recorded in 1095.

Distinctive names of the 18th and 19th centuries are those adopted from biblical places, such as *Bethel*, *Bethlehem*, *Carmel* and *Hebron*. They are mainly of small villages that arose around a Nonconformist chapel. The slate quarries of *Bethesda* made it a town with a name of this type. Mine owners, ironmasters, or other industrial or commercial entrepreneurs gave their names to such places as *Griffithstown*, *Morriston*, *Port Talbot*, and *Tredegar*. Such names are mostly found in South Wales.

A number of places in Wales have a name that is an anglicized form of the Welsh original, such as *Cardiff* (*Caerdydd*) and *Denbigh* (*Dinbych*), while several places with Scandinavian or English names have an unrelated Welsh name, such as *Abergwaun*, 'mouth of the (river) Gwaun', for Fishguard, *Abertawe*, 'mouth of the (river) Tawe', for Swansea, and *Caergybi*, 'Cybi's fort', for Holyhead. *Montgomery*, named for its Norman lord, is Welsh *Trefaldwyn*, 'town of Baldwin', another Norman.   ADRIAN ROOM

ABBREVIATIONS

The English Counties and Unitary Authorities

B. & NE. Som.	Bath & North East Somerset	Lincs.	Lincolnshire
Beds.	Bedfordshire	Mersey.	Merseyside
Berks.	Berkshire	Middlesbr.	Middlesbrough
Brist.	City of Bristol	Norfolk	
Bucks.	Buckinghamshire	NE. Lincs.	North East Lincolnshire
Cambs.	Cambridgeshire	N. Lincs.	North Lincolnshire
Ches.	Cheshire	N. Som.	North Somerset
Cornwall		N. Yorks.	North Yorkshire
Cumbria		Northants.	Northamptonshire
Derbys.	Derbyshire	Northum.	Northumberland
Devon		Notts.	Nottinghamshire
Dorset		Oxon.	Oxfordshire
Durham		Red. & Cleve.	Redcar & Cleveland
E R. Yorks.	East Riding of Yorkshire	Rutland	
E. Sussex	East Sussex	Shrops.	Shropshire
Essex		Somerset	
Glos.	Gloucestershire	S. Glos.	South Gloucestershire
Gtr.London	Greater London	S. Yorks.	South Yorkshire
Gtr. Manch.	Greater Manchester	Staffs.	Staffordshire
Hants.	Hampshire	Stock. on T.	Stockton on Tees
Hartlepl.	Hartlepool	Suffolk	
Heref. & Worcs.	Herefordshire and Worcestershire	Surrey	
		Tyne & Wear	
Herts.	Hertfordshire	Warwicks.	Warwickshire
I. of Wight	Isle of Wight	W. Mids.	West Midlands
Kent		W. Sussex	West Sussex
K. upon Hull	City of Kingston upon Hull	W. Yorks.	West Yorkshire
Lancs.	Lancashire	Wilts.	Wiltshire
Leics.	Leicestershire	York	City & County of York

The Welsh Counties and Unitary Authorities

Angl	Anglesey	Mer T.	Merthyr Tydfil
Blae	Blaenau Gwent	Mon	Monmouthshire
Bri	Bridgend	Neat	Neath Port Talbot
Cphy	Caerphilly	Newpt	Newport
Card	Cardiff	Pemb	Pembrokeshire
Carm	Carmarthenshire	Rhon	Rhondda, Cynon, Taff
Cergn	Ceredigion	Swan	Swansea
Denb	Denbighshire	Torf	Torfaen
Flin	Flintshire	Vale Glam	Vale of Glamorgan
Gwyd	Gwynedd	Wrex	Wrexham

The Scottish Counties and Unitary Authorities

Abdn	Aberdeen City	Midloth	Midlothian
Aber	Aberdeenshire	N. Ayr	North Ayrshire
Ang	Angus	N. Lan	North Lanarkshire
Arg	Argyll and Bute	Orkn	Orkney
Edin	City of Edinburgh	Perth	Perth and Kinross
Clac	Clackmannanshire	Renf	Renfrewshire
Dumf	Dumfries and Galloway	Sc. Bord	Scottish Borders
Dund	Dundee City	Shet	Shetland
E. Ayr	East Ayrshire	S. Ayr	South Ayrshire
E. Dunb	East Dunbartonshire	S. Lan	South Lanarkshire
E. Loth	East Lothian	Stir	Stirling
E. Renf	East Renfrewshire	W. Dunbar	West Dunbartonshire
Falk	Falkirk	W. Isles	Western Isles (Eilean Siar)
Glas	Glasgow City	W. Loth	West Lothian
Invclyd	Inverclyde		

A

Ab Kettleby Leics., *see* KETTLEBY.

Abbas Combe Somerset, *see* COMBE.

Abberley Heref. & Worcs. *Edboldelege* 1086 (DB). 'Woodland clearing of a man called Ēadbeald'. OE pers. name + *lēah*.

Abberton Essex. *Edburgetuna* 1086 (DB). 'Farmstead or estate of a woman called Ēadburh'. OE pers. name + *tūn*.

Abberton Heref. & Worcs. *Eadbrihtincgtun* 972, *Edbretintune* 1086 (DB). 'Estate associated with a man called Ēadbeorht'. OE pers. name + *-ing-* + *tūn*.

Abberwick Northum. *Alburwic* 1170. 'Dwelling or (dairy) farm of a woman called Aluburh or Alhburh'. OE pers. name + *wīc*.

Abbess Roding Essex, *see* RODING

Abbey Dore Heref. & Worcs., *see* DORE.

Abbey Hulton Staffs., *see* HULTON.

Abbey Town Cumbria. *Abbey Towne* 1649. 'Estate by the abbey', with reference to the former abbey of Holme Cultram.

Abbeydorney (*Mainistir Ó dTorna*) Kerry. 'Abbey of Uí Thorna'.

Abbeyfeale (*Mainistir na Féile*) Limerick. 'Abbey of the River Feale'.

Abbeylara (*Mainistir Leathrátha*) Longford. 'Abbey of the half ring-fort'.

Abbeyleix (*Mainistir Laoise*) Laois. 'Abbey of Laois'.

Abbeyshrule (*Mainistir Shruthla*) Longford. 'Abbey of the stream'.

Abbeystead Lancs. *Abbey* 1323. '(Deserted) site of the abbey', with reference to the abbey of Wyresdale. ME *abbeye* + *stede*.

Abbots as affix, see main name, e.g. for **Abbots Bickington** (Devon) *see* BICKINGTON.

Abbotsbury Dorset. *Abbedesburie* 946, *Abedesberie* 1086 (DB). 'Fortified house or manor of the abbot'. OE *abbod* + *burh* (dative *byrig*). With reference to early possession by the abbot of Glastonbury.

Abbotsford Sc. Bord. '(Place of the) abbot's ford'. The mansion was built by Sir Walter Scott in 1816 on land owned by the Abbot of Melrose by a ford over the Tweed.

Abbotsham Devon. *Hama* 1086 (DB), *Abbudesham* 1238. OE *hamm* 'enclosure' with the later addition of *abbod* 'abbot' (referring to early possession by the abbot of Tavistock).

Abbotskerswell Devon. *Cærswylle* 956, *Carsuella* 1086 (DB). *Karswill Abbatis* 1285. 'Spring or stream where water-cress grows'. OE *cærse* + *wella*. Affix from early possession by the abbot of Horton.

Abbotsley Cambs. *Adboldesle* 12th cent. 'Woodland clearing of a man called Ealdbeald'. OE pers. name + *lēah*.

Abdon Shrops. *Abetune* 1086 (DB). 'Farmstead or estate of a man called Abba'. OE pers. name + *tūn*.

Aberaeron Cergn. *ad ostium Ayron* 1184. 'Mouth of the River Aeron'. Welsh *aber*. The Celtic river name means 'battle'.

Aberafan. *See* ABERAVON.

Aberavon (*Aberafan*) Neat. *Abberauyn* c.1400, *Aberavan* 1548. 'Mouth of the River Afan'. Welsh *aber*. The river name is probably derived from a pers. name.

Abercraf Powys. *Abercraven* 1680. 'Mouth of the River Craf'. Welsh *aber*. The river name means 'garlic' (Welsh *craf*).

Aberdâr. *See* ABERDARE.

Aberdare (*Aberdâr*) Rhon. *Aberdar* 1203. 'Mouth of the River Dâr'. Welsh *aber*. The Celtic river name means 'oak river'.

Aberdaron Gwyd. 'Mouth of the River Daron'. Welsh *aber*. The Celtic river name means 'oak river'.

Aberdaugleddau. *See* MILFORD HAVEN.

Aberdeen Abdn. *Aberdon* c.1187, *Aberden* c.1214. 'Mouth of the River Don'. Pictish *aber*. The river is named after *Devona*, a Celtic goddess. Modern Aberdeen is at the mouth of the DEE, but the name relates to Old Aberdeen, at the mouth of the Don.

Aberdour Fife. *Abirdaur* 1226. 'Mouth of the River Dour'. Pictish *aber*. The river name means 'waters'.

Aberdovey. *See* ABERDYFI.

Aberdyfi Gwyd. *Aberdewi* 12th cent., *aber dyfi* 14th cent. 'Mouth of the River Dyfi'. Welsh *aber*. The river name probably means 'dark one'.

Aberfeldy Perth. 'Confluence of Peallaidh'. Pictish *aber*. *Peallaidh* is the name of a water sprite said to haunt the place where the Moness Burn enters the Tay.

Aberford W. Yorks. *Ædburford* 1176. 'Ford of a woman called Ædburh'. OE pers. name + *ford*.

Aberfoyle Stir. *Abirfull* 1481. 'Confluence of the streams'. Pictish *aber* + Gaelic *poll* (genitive *phuill*). The two headstreams of the river Forth unite near here, and are joined by the river Foyle.

Abergafenni. *See* ABERGAVENNY.

Abergavenny (*Abergafenni* or *Y Fenni*) Mon. *Gobannio* 4th cent., *Abergavenni* 1175. 'Mouth of the River Gafenni'. Welsh *aber*. The river name probably means 'the smith', referring to the ironworks exploited here by the Romans, whose fort was *Gobannum*, from the same Celtic source.

Abergele Conwy. *Opergelei* 9th cent., *Abergele* 1257. 'Mouth of the River Gele'. Welsh *aber*. The river name means 'blade' (OWelsh *gelau*).

Abergwaun. *See* FISHGUARD.

Aberhonddu. *See* BRECON.

Aberlour Moray. 'Confluence of the Lour Burn'. Pictish *aber*. The river name means 'babbling brook'. The town's formal name is *Charlestown of Aberlour*, after Charles Grant, who laid the original village out in 1812.

Abermo. *See* BARMOUTH.

Abernethy Perth. *Aburnethige* c.970. 'Confluence of the River Nethy'. Pictish *aber*. The river name means 'pure' (Pictish *nectona*). Nectonus is also the name of a Celtic water divinity.

Aberpennar. *See* MOUNTAIN ASH.

Abersychan Torf. *Aber Sychan* c.1850. 'Mouth of the River Sychan'. Welsh *aber*. The river name is based on Welsh *sych*, 'dry', implying a river that dries up in summer.

Abertawe. *See* SWANSEA.

Aberteifi. *See* CARDIGAN.

Aberteleri. *See* ABERTILLERY.

Abertillery (*Abertyleri* or *Aberteleri*) Blae. *Teleri* 1332, *Aber-Tilery* 1779. 'Confluence of the River Teleri'. Welsh *aber*. The river name derives from a pers. name.

Abertporth Cergn. *Aberporth* 1284. 'Estuary in the bay'. Welsh *aber* + *porth*.

Abertsoch Gwyd. *Absogh* 1350, *Avon Soch* 1598. 'Mouth of the River Soch'. Welsh *aber*. The river name meaning 'nosing one', referring to the way the river 'roots' its course through the land.

Abertyleri. *See* ABERTILLERY.

Aberystwyth Cergn. *Aberestuuth* 1232, *aber ystwyth* 14th cent., *Aberystwith, or Aberrheidol* 1868. 'Mouth of the River Ystwyth'. Welsh *aber*. The river name means 'winding one' (Welsh *ystwyth*). Aberystwyth is now at the mouth of the *Rheidol*, but the name relates to the *Ystwyth*, to the south, where a Norman castle was built in 1110.

Abingdon Oxon. *Abbandune* 968, *Ab(b)endone* 1086 (DB). 'Hill of a man called Æbba or of a woman called Æbbe'. OE pers. name (genitive *-n*) + *dūn*.

Abinger Surrey. *Abinceborne* |sic| 1086 (DB), *Abingewurd* 1191. 'Enclosure of the family or followers of a man called Abba', or 'enclosure at Abba's place'. OE pers. name + *-inga-* or *-ing* + *worth*. **Abinger Hammer** is named from the former iron foundry here, called *The Hammer Mill* 1600.

Abington, 'estate associated with a man called Abba', OE pers. name + *-ing-* + *tūn*: **Abington, Great** & **Abington, Little** Cambs. *Abintone* 1086 (DB). **Abington Pigotts** Cambs. *Abintone* 1086 (DB), *Abington Pigots* 1635. Manorial affix from the Pykot family, here from the 15th cent.

Abington (*Mainistir Uaithne*) Limerick. 'Abbey of (the district of) Uaithne'.

Ablington Glos. *Eadbaldingtun* 855. 'Estate associated with a man called Ēadbeald'. OE pers. name + *-ing-* + *tūn*.

Ablington Wilts. *Alboldintone* 1086 (DB). 'Estate associated with a man called Ealdbeald'. OE pers. name + *-ing-* + *tūn*.

Aboyne Aber. *Obyne* 1260. The full formal name is *Charleston of Aboyne*, after Charles Gordon, 1st Earl of Aboyne (d.1681), who erected a burgh of barony here in 1670.

Abram Gtr. Manch. *Adburgham* late 12th cent. 'Homestead or enclosure of a woman called Ēadburh'. OE pers. name + *hām* or *hamm*.

Abridge Essex. *Affebrigg* 1203. 'Bridge of a man called Æffa'. OE pers. name + *brycg*.

Abthorpe Northants. *Abetrop* 1190. 'Outlying farmstead or hamlet of a man called Abba'. OE pers. name + OE *throp* or OScand. *thorp*.

Aby Lincs. *Abi* 1086 (DB). 'Farmstead or village on the stream'. OScand. *á* + *bý*.

Acaster Malbis (York) & **Acaster Selby** (N. Yorks). *Acastre* 1086 (DB), *Acaster Malebisse* 1252, *Acastre Seleby* 1285. 'Fortification on the river'. OScand. *á* (perhaps replacing OE *ēa*) + OE *ceaster*. Manorial affixes from lands here held by the Malbis family and by Selby Abbey.

Accrington Lancs. *Akarinton* 12th cent. 'Farmstead or village where acorns are found or stored'. OE *æcern* + *tūn*.

Achabog (*Achadh Bog*) Monaghan. *Aghabog* 1665. 'Soft field'.

Acharacle Highland. 'Torquil's ford'. OScand. pers. name + Gaelic *ath*.

Achnashellach Forest Highland. *Auchnashellicht* 1543. 'Forest by the field of the willows'. Gaelic *achadh* + *na* + *seileach*.

Achonry (*Achadh Conaire*) Sligo. 'Field of Conaire'.

Achray Forest Stir. *Achray* 1791. Probably 'shaking ford'. Gaelic *àth* + *chrathaidh*. A 'shaking ford' is a quagmire. Forest was added by the Forestry Commission.

Achurch Northants. *Asencircan* c.980, *Asechirce* 1086 (DB). 'Church of a man called *Asa or Ási'. OE or OScand. pers. name + OE *cirice*.

Acklam, '(place at) the oak woods or clearings', OE *āc* + *lēah* (in a dative plural form *lēagum*): **Acklam** Middlesbr. *Aclum* 1086 (DB). **Acklam** N. Yorks. *Aclun* 1086 (DB).

Acklington Northum. *Eclinton* 1177. Probably 'estate associated with a man called Ēadlāc'. OE pers. name + *-ing-* + *tūn*.

Ackton W. Yorks. *Aitone* |sic| 1086 (DB), *Aicton* c.1166. 'Oak-tree farmstead'. OScand. *eik* + OE *tūn*.

Ackworth, High & *Ackworth, Low* W. Yorks. *Aceuurde* 1086 (DB). 'Enclosure of a man called Acca'. OE pers. name + *worth*.

Aclare (*Áth an Chláir*) Sligo. 'Ford of the plain'.

Acle Norfolk. *Acle* 1086 (DB). 'Oak wood or clearing'. OE *āc* + *lēah*.

Acol Kent. *Acholt* 1270. 'Oak wood'. OE *āc* + *holt*.

Acomb, '(place at) the oak-trees', OE *āc* in a dative plural form *ācum*: **Acomb** Northum. *Akum* 1268. **Acomb** York. *Akum* 1222.

Aconbury Heref. & Worcs. *Akornebir* 1213. 'Old fort inhabited by squirrels'. OE *ācweorna* + *burh* (dative *byrig*).

Acre, Castle, *Acre, South* & *Acre, West* Norfolk. *Acre* 1086 (DB), *Castelacr* 1235, *Sutacra* 1242, *Westacre* 1203. 'Newly cultivated land'. OE *æcer*. Distinguishing affixes from OFrench *castel* (with reference to the Norman castle here), OE *sūth* and *west*.

Acton, a common name, usually 'farmstead or village by the oak-tree(s)' or 'specialized farm where oak timber is worked', OE *āc* + *tūn*; examples include: **Acton** Gtr. London. *Acton* 1181. **Acton Beauchamp** Heref. & Worcs. *Aactune* 727. Manorial affix from the Beauchamp family, here from the 12th cent. **Acton Burnell** & **Acton Pigott** Shrops. *Actune, Æctune* 1086 (DB), *Akton Burnell* 1198, *Acton Picot* 1242. Manorial affixes from the Burnell and Picot families, here in the 12th cent. **Acton, Iron** S. Glos. *Actune* 1086 (DB), *Irenacton* 1248. Affix is OE *īren* 'iron', referring to old iron-workings here. **Acton Round** Shrops. *Achetune* 1086 (DB), *Acton la Runde* 1284. Affix is ME *ro(u)nd* 'round in shape' or from its early possession by the Earls of *Arundel* (perhaps falsely interpreted as containing the word *ro(u)nd*). **Acton Scott** Shrops. *Actune* 1086 (DB), *Scottes Acton* 1289. Manorial affix from the Scot family, here in the 13th cent. **Acton Trussell** Staffs. *Actone* 1086 (DB), *Acton Trussel* 1481. Manorial affix from the Trussell family, here in the 14th cent.
However some Actons have a different origin: **Acton** Dorset. *Tacatone* 1086 (DB). Probably 'farmstead or village where young sheep are reared'. OE **tacca* + *tūn*. Initial *T*- was dropped in the 16th cent. due to confusion with the preposition *at*. **Acton** Suffolk. *Acantun* c.995, *Achetuna* 1086 (DB). 'Farmstead or village of a man called Ac(c)a'. OE pers. name + *tūn*. **Acton Turville** S. Glos. *Achetone* 1086 (DB), *Acton Torvile* 1284. Identical in origin with the previous name. Manorial affix from the Turville family, here from the 13th cent.

Acton Armagh. *Acton* 1619. The village was founded by Charles Poyntz in 1600 and named after his native *Iron Acton*, Glos.

Adare (*Áth Dara*) Limerick. 'Ford of the oak'.

Adbaston Staffs. *Edboldestone* 1086 (DB). 'Farmstead or village of a man called Ēadbald'. OE pers. name + *tūn*.

Adber Dorset. *Eatan beares* 956, *Ateberie* 1086 (DB). 'Grove of a man called Ēata'. OE pers. name + *bearu*.

Adderbury, East & *Adderbury, West* Oxon. *Eadburggebyrig* c.950, *Edburgberie* 1086 (DB). 'Stronghold of a woman called Ēadburh'. OE pers. name + *burh* (dative *byrig*).

Adderley Shrops. *Eldredelei* 1086 (DB). 'Woodland clearing of a woman called Althrȳth. OE pers. name + *lēah*.

Adderstone Northum. *Edredeston* 1233. 'Farmstead or village of a man called Ēadrēd'. OE pers. name + *tūn*.

Addingham W. Yorks. *Haddincham* c.972, *Odingehem* 1086 (DB). Probably 'homestead associated with a man called Adda'. OE pers. name + *-ing-* + *hām*.

Addington, 'estate associated with a man called Eadda or Æddi', OE pers. name + *-ing-* + *tūn*: **Addington** Bucks. *Edintone* 1086 (DB). **Addington** Gtr. London. *Eddintone* 1086 (DB). **Addington** Kent. *Eddintune* 1086 (DB). **Addington, Great** & **Addington, Little** Northants. *Edintone* 1086 (DB).

Addiscombe Gtr. London. *Edescamp* 1229. 'Enclosed land of a man called Ǣddi'. OE pers. name + *camp*.

Addlestone Surrey. *Attelesdene* 1241. 'Valley of a man called **Ættel*'. OE pers. name + *denu*.

Addlethorpe Lincs. *Ardluetorp* 1086 (DB). 'Outlying farmstead or hamlet of a man called Eardwulf'. OE pers. name + OScand. *thorp*.

Adel W. Yorks. *Adele* 1086 (DB). From OE *adela* 'dirty, muddy place'.

Adeney Shrops. *Eduney* 1212. 'Island, or dry ground in marsh, of a woman called Ēadwynn'. OE pers. name + *ēg*.

Aderavoher (*Eadar dhá Bhóthair*) Sligo. 'Place between two roads'.

Adisham Kent. *Adesham* 616, *Edesham* 1086 (DB). 'Homestead of a man called **Ēad* or *Ǣddi*'. OE pers. name + *hām*.

Adlestrop Glos. *Titlestrop |sic|* 714, *Tedestrop* 1086 (DB). 'Outlying farmstead or hamlet of a man called **Tǣtel*'. OE pers. name + *throp*. Initial *T*- disappeared from the 14th cent. due to confusion with the preposition *at*.

Adlingfleet E. R. Yorks. *Adelingesfluet* 1086 (DB). 'Water-channel or stream of the prince or nobleman'. OE *ætheling* + *flēot*.

Adlington, 'estate associated with a man called Ēadwulf', OE pers. name + *-ing-* + *tūn*; **Adlington** Ches. *Eduluintune* 1086 (DB). **Adlington** Lancs. *Edeluinton* c.1190.

Admaston Staffs. *Ǣdmundeston* 1176. 'Farmstead or village of a man called Ēadmund'. OE pers. name + *tūn*.

Admington Warwicks. *Edelmintone* 1086 (DB). 'Estate associated with a man called Æthelhelm'. OE pers. name + *-ing-* + *tūn*.

Adrigole (*Eadargóil*) Cork. 'Place between forks'.

Adrivale (*Eadargóil*) Cork. 'Place between forks'.

Adstock Bucks. *Edestoche* 1086 (DB). 'Outlying farmstead or hamlet of a man called Ǣddi or Eadda'. OE pers. name + *stoc*.

Adstone Northants. *Atenestone* 1086 (DB). 'Farmstead or village of a man called **Ǣttīn*'. OE pers. name + *tūn*.

Adur W. Sussex, district name from the River **Adur**, a late back-formation from *Portus Adurni* 'Adurnos's harbour', said to be at the mouth of this river by the 17th cent. antiquarian poet Drayton.

Adwell Oxon. *Advelle* 1086 (DB). 'Spring or stream of a man called Ead(d)a'. OE pers. name + *wella*.

Adwick le Street, *Adwick upon Dearne* S. Yorks. *Adeuuic* 1086 (DB). 'Dwelling or (dairy) farm of a man called Adda'. OE pers. name + *wīc*. Distinguishing affixes from the situation of one Adwick on a Roman road (OE *strǣt*) and of the other on the River Dearne (*see* BOLTON UPON DEARNE).

Affpuddle Dorset. *Affapidele* 1086 (DB). 'Estate on the River Piddle of a man called Æffa'. OE pers. name + river-name (*see* PIDDLEHINTON).

Agangarrive Hill (*Aigeán Garbh*) Antrim. 'Rough hill'.

Agglethorpe N. Yorks. *Aculestorp* 1086 (DB). 'Outlying farmstead or hamlet of a man called Ācwulf'. OE pers. name + OScand. *thorp*.

Agha (*Achadh*) Carlow. 'Field'.

Aghaboe (*Achadh Bó*) Laois. 'Field of the cows'.

Aghabrack (*Achadh Breac*) Westmeath. 'Speckled field'.

Aghabullogue (*Achadh Bolg*) Cork. 'Field of the bulges'.

Aghacashel (*Achadh an Chaisil*) Limerick. 'Field of the stone fort'.

Aghacommon (*Achadh Camán*) Armagh. *Aghcamon* 1617. 'Field of the little bends'.

Aghada (*Achadh Fada*) Cork. 'Long field'.

Aghadarragh (*Achadh Darach*) Tyrone. 'Field of the oak tree'.

Aghadaugh (*Achadh Damh*) Westmeath. 'Field of the oxen'.

Aghadoe (*Achadh dá Eo*) Kerry. 'Field of the two yews'.

Aghadowey (*Achadh Dubhthaigh*) Derry. *Achad Dubthaig c.*1170. 'Dubhthach's field'.

Aghadown (*Achadh Dúin*) Cork. 'Field of the fort'.

Aghafatten (*Achadh Pheatáin*) Antrim. *Aghafatten* 1780. Possibly 'Peatán's field'.

Aghagallon (*Achadh Gallan*) Tyrone, Antrim. 'Field of the standing stone'.

Aghagower (*Achadh Ghobair*) Mayo. 'Field of the spring'.

Aghalane (*Achadh Leathan*) Fermanagh. *Aghalane* 1622. 'Broad field'.

Aghalee (*Achadh Lí*) Antrim. *Acheli* 1306. 'Field'. The second element is obscure.

Aghamore (*Achadh Mór*) Mayo. 'Big field'.

Aghanacliff (*Achadh na Cloiche*) Louth. 'Field of the stones'.

Aghanloo (*Áth Lú*) Derry. *Athlouge* 1397. 'Lú's ford'.

Aghatubrid (*Achadh Tiobraid*) Kerry. 'Field of the well'.

Aghavannagh (*Achadh Bheannach*) Wicklow. 'Hilly field'.

Aghavea (*Achadh beithe*) Fermanagh. 'Birch field'.

Aghawoney (*Achadh Mhóna*) Donegal. 'Field of the bog'.

Agher (*Achair*) Meath. 'Space'.

Aghern (*Áth Chairn*) Cork. 'Ford of the cairn'.

Aghery Lough (*Loch Eachraí*) Down. 'Lake of the horses'.

Aghintain (*Achadh an tSéin*) Tyrone. *Aghityan* 1613. 'Field of the good luck'.

Aghinver (*Achadh Inbhir*) Fermanagh. 'Field of the river mouth'.

Aghleam (*Eachléim*) Mayo. 'Horse leap'.

Aghlish (*Eaglais*) Kerry. 'Church'.

Aghnabohy (*Achadh na Boithe*) Westmeath. 'Field of the huts'.

Aghnahily (*Achadh na hAille*) Laois. 'Field of the cliff'.

Aghnamullen (*Achadh na Muileann*) Monaghan. *Aughamullen* 1530. 'Field of the mills'.

Aghnaskeagh (*Achadh na Scéithe*) Louth. 'Field of the shields'.

Aghory (*Áth Óraí*) Armagh. *Aghoorier* 1610. 'Ford of the boundary'.

Aghowla (*Achadh Abhla*) Limerick. 'Field of the apple tree'.

Aghowle (*Achadh Abhla*) Limerick, Wicklow. 'Field of the apple tree'.

Aghyaran (*Achadh Uí Áráin*) Tyrone. *Agharan* 1666. 'Field of Uí Árán'.

Aghyowle (*Achadh Abhla*) Fermanagh. 'Field of the apple tree'.

Agivey (*Áth Géibhe*) Derry. *Athgeybi* 1492. Possibly 'ford of the fetter'.

Aglish (*An Eaglais*) Waterford. 'The church'.

Agola (*Áth Gobhlach*) Antrim. 'Ford of the fork'.

Ahafona (*Áth an Phóna*) Kerry. 'Ford of the pound'.

Ahakista (*Áth an Chiste*) Kerry. 'Ford of the box'.

Ahalia, Lough (*Loch an tSáile*) Galway. 'Lake of the salt water'.

Ahascragh (*Áth Eascrach*) Galway. 'Ford of the gravel ridge'.

Ahenny (*Áth Eine*) Tipperary. 'Ford of the fire'.

Ahoghill (*Áth Eochaille*) Antrim. *Achochill* 1306. 'Ford of the yew wood'.

Aikton Cumbria. *Aictun c.*1200. 'Oak-tree farmstead'. OScand. *eik* + OE *tūn*.

Aille (*Aille*) Clare, Mayo. 'Cliffs'.

Aillenaveagh (*Aill na bhFiach*) Galway. 'Cliff of the ravens'.

Ailsa Craig (island) S. Ayr. Possibly 'Fairy rock'. Gaelic *allasa* + *creag*. The final element is obscure.

Ailsworth Cambs. *Ægeleswurth* 948, *Eglesworde* 1086 (DB). 'Enclosure of a man called *Ægel*'. OE pers. name + *worth*.

Ainderby Steeple N. Yorks. *Eindrebi* 1086 (DB), *Aynderby wyth Stepil* 1316. 'Farmstead or village of a man called Eindrithi'. OScand. pers. name + *bý*. Affix is OE *stēpel* 'church steeple, tower'.

Ainsdale Mersey. *Einuluesdel* 1086 (DB). 'Valley of a man called *Einulfr*'. OScand. pers. name + *dalr*.

Ainstable Cumbria. *Ainstapillith c.*1210. 'Slope where bracken grows'. OScand. *einstapi* + *hlíth*.

Ainsworth Gtr. Manch. *Haineswrthe c.*1200. 'Enclosure of a man called *Ægen*'. OE pers. name + *worth*.

Aintree Mersey. *Ayntre* 1220. 'Solitary tree'. OScand. *einn* + *tré*.

Airdrie N. Lan. *Airdrie* 1584. 'High slope'. Gaelic *ard* + *ruigh*.

Airmyn E. R. Yorks. *Ermenie* 1086 (DB). 'Mouth of the River Aire'. River-name + OScand. *mynni*. The river-name **Aire** is possibly from OScand. *eyjar* 'islands', but may be of Celtic or pre-Celtic origin with a meaning 'strongly flowing'.

Airton N. Yorks. *Airtone* 1086 (DB). 'Farmstead on the River Aire'. Old river-name (*see* AIRMYN) + *tūn*.

Aisby, 'farmstead or village of a man called Ási', OScand. pers. name + *bý*: **Aisby** Lincs., near Blyton. *Asebi* 1086 (DB). **Aisby** Lincs., near Sleaford. *Asebi* 1086 (DB).

Aisholt, Lower Somerset. *Æscholt* 854. 'Ash-tree wood'. OE *æsc* + *holt*.

Aiskew N. Yorks. *Echescol* |sic| 1086 (DB), *Aykescogh* 1235. 'Oak wood'. OScand. *eik* + *skógr*.

Aislaby N. Yorks., near Pickering. *Aslache(s)bi* 1086 (DB). 'Farmstead or village of a man called Áslákr'. OScand. pers. name + *bý*.

Aislaby N. Yorks., near Whitby. *Asulue(s)bi* 1086 (DB). 'Farmstead or village of a man called Ásulfr'. OScand. pers. name + *bý*.

Aisthorpe Lincs. *Estorp* 1086 (DB). 'East outlying farmstead or hamlet'. OE *ēast* + OScand. *thorp*.

Akeld Northum. *Achelda* 1169. 'Oak-tree slope'. OE *āc* + *helde*.

Akeley Bucks. *Achelei* 1086 (DB). 'Oak wood or clearing'. OE *ācen* + *lēah*.

Akeman Street (Roman road from Bath to St Albans). *Accemannestrete* 12th cent. 'Roman road associated with a man called *Acemann*, from OE pers. name + *strǣt* (an early alternative name for BATH was *Acemannes ceastre* 10th cent., named after the same man with OE *ceaster* 'Roman town or city').

Akenham Suffolk. *Acheham* 1086 (DB). 'Homestead of a man called Aca'. OE pers. name + *hām*.

Alberbury Shrops. *Alberberie* 1086 (DB). 'Stronghold or manor of a woman called Aluburh'. OE pers. name + *burh* (dative *byrig*).

Albourne W. Sussex. *Aleburn* 1177. 'Stream where alders grow'. OE *alor* + *burna*.

Albrighton Shrops., near Shifnal. *Albricstone* 1086 (DB). 'Farmstead or village of a man called Æthelbeorht'. OE pers. name + *tūn*.

Albrighton Shrops., near Shrewsbury. *Etbritone* 1086 (DB). 'Farmstead or village of a man called Ēadbeorht'. OE pers. name + *tūn*.

Alburgh Norfolk. *Aldeberga* 1086 (DB). 'Old mound or hill', or 'mound or hill of a man called Alda'. OE (*e*)*ald* or OE pers. name + *beorg*.

Albury, 'old or disused stronghold', OE (*e*)*ald* + *burh* (dative *byrig*): **Albury** Herts. *Eldeberie* 1086 (DB). **Albury** Surrey. *Ealdeburi* 1062, *Eldeberie* 1086 (DB).

Alby Hill Norfolk. *Alebei* 1086 (DB). 'Farmstead or village of a man called Áli'. OScand. pers. name + *bý*.

Alcaston Shrops. *Ælmundestune* 1086 (DB). 'Farmstead or village of a man called Ealhmund'. OE pers. name + *tūn*.

Alcester Warwicks. *Alencestre* 1138. 'Roman town on the River Alne'. Celtic river-name (*see* ALNE) + OE *ceaster*.

Alciston E. Sussex. *Alsistone* 1086 (DB). 'Farmstead or village of a man called Ælfsige or Ealhsige'. OE pers. name + *tūn*.

Alconbury Cambs. *Acumesberie* |sic| 1086 (DB), *Alcmundesberia* 12th cent. 'Stronghold of a man called Ealhmund'. OE pers. name + *burh* (dative *byrig*).

Aldborough, 'old or disused stronghold', OE (*e*)*ald* + *burh*: **Aldborough** Norfolk. *Aldeburg* 1086 (DB). **Aldborough** N. Yorks. *Burg* 1086 (DB), *Aldeburg* 1145. Here referring to a Roman fort.

Aldbourne Wilts. *Ealdincburnan* c.970, *Aldeborne* 1086 (DB). 'Stream associated with a man called Ealda'. OE pers. name + *-ing-* + *burna*.

Aldbrough, 'old or disused stronghold', OE (*e*)*ald* + *burh*: **Aldbrough** E. R. Yorks. *Aldenburg* 1086 (DB). **Aldbrough** N. Yorks. *Aldeburne* |sic| 1086 (DB), *Aldeburg* 1247.

Aldbury Herts. *Aldeberie* 1086 (DB). 'Old or disused stronghold'. OE (*e*)*ald* + *burh* (dative *byrig*).

Aldeburgh Suffolk. *Aldeburc* 1086 (DB). 'Old or disused stronghold'. OE (*e*)*ald* + *burh*. The river-name **Alde** is a 'back-formation' from the place-name.

Aldeby Norfolk. *Aldebury* 1086 (DB), *Aldeby* c.1180. 'Old or disused stronghold'. OE (*e*)*ald* + *burh* (dative *byrig*) replaced by OScand. *bý* 'farmstead'.

Aldenham Herts. *Ældenham* 785, *Eldeham* 1086 (DB). 'Old homestead', or 'homestead of a man called Ealda'. OE (*e*)*ald* (dative *-an*) or OE pers. name (genitive *-n*) + *hām*.

Alderbury Wilts. *Æthelware byrig* 972, *Alwarberie* 1086 (DB). 'Stronghold of a woman called *Æthelwaru*'. OE pers. name + *burh* (dative *byrig*).

Alderford Norfolk. *Alraforda* 1163. 'Ford where alders grow'. OE *alor* + *ford*.

Alderholt Dorset. *Alreholt* 1285. 'Alder wood'. OE *alor* + *holt*.

Alderley Glos. *Alrelie* 1086 (DB). 'Woodland clearing where alders grow'. OE *alor* + *lēah*.

Alderley Edge Ches. *Aldredelie* 1086 (DB). 'Woodland clearing of a woman called Althrȳth'. OE pers. name + *lēah*. The 19th cent. addition *Edge* is taken from the abrupt escarpment here, itself called Alderley Edge (from OE *ecg*).

Aldermaston Berks. *Ældremanestone* 1086 (DB). 'Farmstead of the chief or nobleman'. OE (*e*)*aldormann* + *tūn*.

Alderminster Warwicks. *Aldermanneston* 1167. Identical in origin with the previous name.

Aldershot Hants. *Halreshet* 1171. 'Projecting piece of land where alders grow'. OE *alor* + *scēat*.

Alderton, usually 'estate associated with a man called Ealdhere', OE pers. name + *-ing-* + *tūn*: **Alderton** Glos. *Aldritone* 1086 (DB). **Alderton** Northants. *Aldritone* 1086 (DB). **Alderton** Wilts. *Aldrintone* 1086 (DB).

However two Aldertons have a different origin, 'farmstead where alders grow', OE *alor* + *tūn*: **Alderton** Shrops. *Olreton* 1309. **Alderton** Suffolk. *Alretuna* 1086 (DB).

Alderwasley Derbys. *Alrewaseleg* 1251. 'Clearing by the alluvial land where alders grow'. OE *alor* + **wæsse* + *lēah*.

Aldfield N. Yorks. *Aldefeld* 1086 (DB). 'Old (i.e. long used) stretch of open country'. OE *ald* + *feld*.

Aldford Ches. *Aldefordia* 1153. 'The old (i.e. formerly used) ford'. OE *ald* + *ford*.

Aldham, 'the old homestead', or 'homestead of a man called Ealda', OE *eald* or OE pers. name + *hām*: **Aldham** Essex. *Aldeham* 1086 (DB). **Aldham** Suffolk. *Aldeham* 1086 (DB).

Aldingbourne W. Sussex. *Ealdingburnan* c.880, *Aldingeborne* 1086 (DB). 'Stream associated with a man called Ealda'. OE pers. name + *-ing-* + *burna*.

Aldingham Cumbria. *Aldingham* 1086 (DB). Probably 'homestead of the family or followers of a man called Alda'. OE pers. name + *-inga-* + *hām*.

Aldington, 'estate associated with a man called Ealda', OE pers. name + *-ing-* + *tūn*: **Aldington** Heref. & Worcs. *Aldintona* 709, *Aldintone* 1086 (DB). **Aldington** Kent. *Aldintone* 1086 (DB).

Aldreth Cambs. *Alrehetha* 1170. 'Landing-place by the alders'. OE *alor* + *hȳth*.

Aldridge W. Midlands. *Alrewic* 1086 (DB). 'Dwelling or farm among alders'. OE *alor* + *wīc*.

Aldringham Suffolk. *Alrincham* 1086 (DB). 'Homestead of the family or followers of a man called Aldhere'. OE pers. name + *-inga-* + *hām*.

Aldsworth Glos. *Ealdeswyrthe* 1004, *Aldeswrde* 1086 (DB). 'Enclosure of a man called **Ald*'. OE pers. name + *worth*.

Aldwark, 'old fortification', OE *(e)ald* + *weorc*: **Aldwark** Derbys. *Aldwerk* 1140. **Aldwark** N. Yorks. *Aldeuuerc* 1086 (DB).

Aldwick W. Sussex. *Aldewyc* 1235. 'Old dwelling', or 'dwelling of a man called Ealda'. OE *eald* or OE pers. name + *wīc*.

Aldwincle Northants. *Eldewincle* 1086 (DB). 'River-bend of a man called Ealda'. OE pers. name + **wincel*.

Aldworth Berks. *Elleorde* |sic| 1086 (DB), *Aldewurda* 1167. 'Old enclosure', or 'enclosure of a man called Ealda'. OE *eald* or OE pers. name + *worth*.

Alexandria W. Dunb. (Place of) Alexander'. The town arose in the mid-18th cent. and the name was given in c.1760 for *Alexander* Smollett (d.1799), MP for Bonhill.

Alfington Devon. *Alfinton* 1244. 'Estate associated with a man called Ælf'. OE pers. name + *-ing-* + *tūn*.

Alfold Surrey. *Alfold* 1227. 'Old fold or enclosure'. OE *eald* + *fald*.

Alford Aber. *Afford* c.1200, *Afurd* 1654. Traditionally thought to mean 'High ford'. Gaelic *ath* + *ard*. But unverified.

Alford Lincs. *Alforde* 1086 (DB). Probably 'ford where eels are found'. OE *æl* + *ford*.

Alford Somerset. *Aldedeford* 1086 (DB). 'Ford of a woman called Ealdgȳth'. OE pers. name + *ford*.

Alfreton Derbys. *Elstretune* |sic| 1086 (DB), *Alferton* 12th cent. 'Farmstead or village of a man called Ælfhere'. OE pers. name + *tūn*.

Alfrick Heref. & Worcs. *Alcredeswike* early 13th cent. 'Dwelling or farm of a man called Ealhræd'. OE pers. name + *wīc*.

Alfriston E. Sussex. *Alvricestone* 1086 (DB). 'Farmstead or village of a man called Ælfrīc'. OE pers. name + *tūn*.

Alhampton Somerset. *Alentona* 1086 (DB). 'Estate on the River Alham'. Celtic river-name (of uncertain meaning) + OE *tūn*.

Alkborough N. Lincs. *Alchebarge* 1086 (DB), *Alchebarua* 12th cent. Probably 'wood or grove of a man called Alca'. OE pers. name + *bearu*.

Alkerton Oxon. *Alcrintone* 1086 (DB). 'Estate associated with a man called Ealhhere'. OE pers. name + *-ing-* + *tūn*.

Alkham Kent. *Ealhham* c.1100. 'Homestead in a sheltered place, or used as a sanctuary'. OE *ealh* + *hām*.

Alkington Shrops. *Alchetune* 1086 (DB), *Alkinton* 1256. 'Estate associated with a man called Ealha'. OE pers. name + *-ing-* + *tūn*.

Alkmonton Derbys. *Alchementune* 1086 (DB). 'Farmstead or village of a man called Ealhmund'. OE pers. name + *tūn*.

All Cannings Wilts., see CANNINGS.

All Stretton Shrops., see STRETTON.

Allendale Town Northum. *Alewenton* 1245. 'Settlement by (in the valley of) the River Allen'. Celtic or pre-Celtic river-name (of uncertain meaning) + OE *tūn*, with the later insertion of OScand. *dalr* 'valley'.

Allenheads Northum. '(Place by) the source of the River Allen'. Celtic or pre-Celtic river-name + OE *hēafod*.

Allensmore Heref. & Worcs. *More* 1086 (DB), *Aleinesmor* 1220. 'Marshy ground of a man called Ala(i)n'. OFrench pers. name + OE *mōr*.

Aller Somerset. *Alre* late 9th cent., 1086 (DB). '(Place at) the alder-tree'. OE *alor*.

Allerby Cumbria. *Aylwardcrosseby* 1260, *Aylewardby* c.1275. 'Farmstead (with crosses) of a man called Ailward (Æthelweard)'. OE pers. name + OScand. *bý* (earlier *krossa-bý*).

Allerford Somerset, near Minehead. *Alresford* 1086 (DB). 'Alder-tree ford'. OE *alor* + *ford*.

Allerston N. Yorks. *Alurestan* 1086 (DB). 'Boundary stone of a man called Ælfhere'. OE pers. name + *stān*.

Allerthorpe E. R. Yorks. *Aluuarestorp* 1086 (DB). 'Outlying farmstead or hamlet of a man called Ælfweard or **Alfvarthr*'. OE or OScand. pers. name + OScand. *thorp*.

Allerton, usually 'farmstead or village where alder-trees grow', OE *alor* + *tūn*: **Allerton** Mersey. *Alretune* 1086 (DB). **Allerton** W. Yorks. *Alretune* 1086 (DB). **Allerton Bywater** W. Yorks. *Alretune* 1086 (DB), *Allerton by ye water* 1430. Affix 'by the water' (OE *wæter*) refers to its situation on the

River Aire. **Allerton, Chapel** W. Yorks. *Alretun* 1086 (DB), *Chapel Allerton* 1360. Affix is ME *chapele* 'a chapel'.

However some Allertons have a different origin: **Allerton, Chapel** Somerset. *Alwarditone* 1086 (DB). 'Farmstead of a man called Ælfweard'. OE pers. name + *tūn*. Affix as in previous name. **Allerton Mauleverer** N. Yorks. *Aluertone* 1086 (DB), *Aluerton Mauleuerer* 1231. 'Farmstead of a man called Ælfhere'. OE pers. name + *tūn*. Manorial affix from the Mauleverer family, here from the 12th cent.

Allesley W. Mids. *Alleslega* 1176. 'Woodland clearing of a man called Ælle'. OE pers. name + *lēah*.

Allestree Derbys. *Adelardestre* 1086 (DB). 'Tree of a man called Æthelheard'. OE pers. name + *trēow*.

Allexton Leics. *Adelachestone* 1086 (DB). 'Farmstead or village of a man called *Æthellāc*'. OE pers. name + *tūn*.

Allhallows Kent. *Ho All Hallows* 1285. Named from the 12th cent. church of All Saints here. For *Ho* in the early form, see HOO.

Allihies (*Na hAilichí*) Cork. 'The cliff fields'.

Allington, a common name, has a number of different origins: **Allington** Kent, near Lenham. *Alnoitone* 1086 (DB), *Eilnothinton* 1242. 'Farmstead associated with a man called Æthelnōth'. OE pers. name + *-ing-* + *tūn*. **Allington** Kent, near Maidstone. *Elentun* 1086 (DB). 'Farmstead associated with a man called Ælla or Ælle'. OE pers. name + *-ing-* + *tūn*. **Allington** Lincs. *Adelingetone* 1086 (DB). 'Farmstead of the princes'. OE *ætheling* + *tūn*. **Allington** Wilts., near Amesbury. *Aldintona* 1178. 'Farmstead associated with a man called Ealda'. OE pers. name + *-ing-* + *tūn*. **Allington** Wilts., near Devizes. *Adelingtone* 1086 (DB). 'Farmstead of the princes'. OE *ætheling* + *tūn*. **Allington, East** Devon. *Alintone* 1086 (DB). 'Farmstead associated with a man called Ælla or Ælle'. OE pers. name + *-ing-* + *tūn*.

Allistragh (*An tAileastrach*) Armagh. *Tallastagh* 1609. 'Place of the wild irises'.

Allithwaite Cumbria. *Hailiuethait* c.1170. 'Clearing of a man called Eilífr'. OScand. pers. name + *thveit*.

Alloa Clac. *Alveth* 1357. 'Rocky plain'. Gaelic *allmhagh*.

Allonby Cumbria. *Alayneby* 1262. 'Farmstead or village of a man called Alein'. OFrench pers. name + OScand. *bý*.

Allow (*Abhainn Alla*) (river) Cork. 'River of (the district of) Ealla'.

Alloway S. Ayr. *Auleway* 1324. 'Rocky plain'. Gaelic *allmhagh*.

Allt Melyd. *See* MELIDEN.

Allweston Dorset. *Alfeston* 1214. 'Farmstead or village of a woman called Ælfflæd or Ælfgifu'. OE pers. name + *tūn*.

Almeley Heref. & Worcs. *Elmelie* 1086 (DB). 'Elm wood or clearing'. OE *elm* + *lēah*.

Almer Dorset. *Elmere* 943. 'Eel pool'. OE *æl* + *mere*.

Almington Staffs. *Almentone* 1086 (DB). 'Farmstead or village of a man called Alhmund'. OE pers. name + *tūn*.

Almondbury W. Yorks. *Almaneberie* 1086 (DB). 'Stronghold of the whole community'. OScand. **almenn* (genitive plural *almanna*) + OE *burh* (dative *byrig*).

Almondsbury S. Glos. *Almodesberie* 1086 (DB). 'Stronghold of a man called Æthelmōd or Æthelmund'. OE pers. name + *burh* (dative *byrig*).

Alne N. Yorks. *Alna* c.1050, *Alne* 1086 (DB). A Celtic name of uncertain meaning.

Alne, Great & *Alne, Little* Warwicks. *Alne* 1086 (DB). Named from the River Alne, a Celtic river-name probably identical in origin with the River Aln (see ALNHAM).

Alness Highland. *Alenes* 1226. '(Place on the) River Alness'. The river name is of pre-Celtic origin meaning 'flowing water'. Gaelic *Alanais*. 'Allan Station.' Gaelic *Fas*.

Alnham Northum. *Alneham* 1228. 'Homestead on the River Aln'. Celtic river-name (earlier *Alaunos*, of uncertain meaning) + OE *hām*.

Alnmouth Northum. *Alnemuth* 1201. 'Mouth of the River Aln'. Celtic river-name (see ALNHAM) + OE *mūtha*.

Alnwick Northum. *Alnewich* 1178. 'Dwelling or farm on the River Aln'. Celtic river-name (see ALNHAM) + OE *wīc*.

Alperton Gtr. London. *Alprinton* 1199. 'Estate associated with a man called Ealhbeorht'. OE pers. name + *-ing-* + *tūn*.

Alphamstone Essex. *Alfelmestuna* 1086 (DB). 'Farmstead or village of a man called Ælfhelm'. OE pers. name + *tūn*.

Alpheton Suffolk. *Alflede(s)ton* 1204. 'Farmstead or village of a woman called Ælfflæd or Æthelflæd'. OE pers. name + *tūn*.

Alphington Devon. *Alfintune* c.1060, *Alfintone* 1086 (DB). 'Estate associated with a man called Ælf' OE pers. name + *-ing-* + *tūn*.

Alport Derbys. *Aldeport* 12th cent. 'Old town'. OE *(e)ald* + *port*.

Alpraham Ches. *Alburgham* 1086 (DB). 'Homestead of a woman called Alhburh'. OE pers. name + *hām*.

Alresford Essex. *Ælesford* c.1000, *Eilesforda* 1086 (DB). 'Ford of a man called **Ægel*'. OE pers. name + *ford*.

Alresford, New & *Alresford, Old* Hants. *Alresforda* 701, *Alresforde* 1086 (DB). 'Alder-tree ford'. OE *alor* (genitive *alres*) + *ford*. The river-name **Alre** is a 'back-formation' from the place-name.

Alrewas Staffs. *Alrewasse* 942, *Alrewas* 1086 (DB). 'Alluvial land where alders grow'. OE *alor* + **wæsse*.

Alsager Ches. *Eleacier* |*sic*| 1086 (DB), *Allesacher* 13th cent. 'Cultivated land of a man called Ælle'. OE pers. name + *æcer*.

Alsh, Loch. *See* KYLE OF LOCHALSH.

Alsop en le Dale Derbys. *Elleshope* 1086 (DB), *Alsope in le dale* 1535. 'Valley of a man called Ælle'. OE pers. name + *hop*. Later affix means 'in the valley'.

Alston Cumbria. *Aldeneby* 1164–71, *Aldeneston* 1209. 'Farmstead or village of a man called Halfdan'. OScand. pers. name + OE *tūn* (earlier OScand. *bý*).

Alstone Glos. *Ælfsigestun* 969. 'Farmstead or village of a man called Ælfsige'. OE pers. name + *tūn*.

Alstonefield Staffs. *Ænestanefelt* |*sic*| 1086 (DB), *Alfstanesfeld* 1179. 'Open country of a man called Ælfstān'. OE pers. name + *feld*.

Altagowlan (*Alt an Ghabhláin*) Roscommon. 'Hillside of the fork'.

Altamuskin (*Alt na Múscán*) Tyrone. *Altmuskan* 1611. 'Hillside of the loose clay'.

Altan (*Altán*) Donegal. 'Little height'.

Altan, Lough (*Loch Allltáin*) Donegal. 'Lake of the flocks'.

Altarnun Cornwall. *Altrenune c*.1100. 'Altar of St Nonn'. Cornish *alter* 'altar of a church' + female saint's name.

Altavilla (*Alta a' Bhile*) Limerick. 'Hillside of the sacred tree'.

Altcar, Great (Lancs.) & *Altcar, Little* (Mersey.). *Acrer* |*sic*| 1086 (DB), *Altekar* 1251. 'Marsh by the River Alt'. Celtic river-name (meaning 'muddy river') + OScand. *kjarr*.

Altham Lancs. *Elvetham c*.1150. 'Enclosure or river-meadow where there are swans'. OE *elfitu* + *hamm*.

Althorne Essex. *Aledhorn* 1198. '(Place at) the burnt thorn-tree'. OE *ǣled* + *thorn*.

Althorp Northants. *Olletorp* 1086 (DB), *Olethorp* 1208. 'Outlying farmstead or hamlet of a man called *Olla*'. OE pers. name + OScand. *thorp*.

Althorpe N. Lincs. *Aletorp* 1086 (DB). 'Outlying farmstead or hamlet of a man called Áli'. OScand. pers. name + *thorp*.

Altinure (*Alt an Iúir*) Cavan, Derry. 'Height of the yew tree'.

Altishahane (*Alt Inse Uí Chatháin*) Tyrone. *Altonisechan c*.1655. 'Hillside of the island of Uí Chatháin'.

Altnamachin (*Alt na Meacan*) Armagh. 'Hillside of the root vegetables'.

Altnaveagh (*Alt na bhFiach*) Tyrone. 'Hillside of the ravens'.

Altofts W. Yorks. *Altoftes c*.1090. Probably 'the old homesteads'. OE *ald* + OScand. *toft*.

Alton, usually 'farmstead at the source of a river', OE *ǣwiell* + *tūn*: **Alton** Hants. *Aultone* 1086 (DB). **Alton Pancras** Dorset. *Awultune* 1012, *Altone* 1086 (DB), *Aweltone Pancratii* 1226. Affix from the dedication of the church to St Pancras. **Alton Priors** Wilts. *Aweltun* 825, *Auuiltone* 1086 (DB), *Aulton Prioris* 1199. Affix from its early possession by the Priory of St Swithin at Winchester.
    However other Altons have a different origin: **Alton** Derbys. *Alton* 1296. 'Old farmstead'. OE *ald* + *tūn*. **Alton** Staffs. *Elvetone* 1086 (DB). 'Farmstead of a man called *Ælfa*'. OE pers. name + *tūn*.

Altore (*Altóir*) Roscommon. 'Altar'.

Altrincham Gtr. Manch. *Aldringeham* 1290. 'Homestead of the family or followers of a man called Aldhere', or 'homestead at the place associated with Aldhere'. OE pers. name + *-inga-* or *-ing* + *hām*.

Alum Bay I. of Wight, first recorded in 1720 and so called from the large quantities of alum mined here as early as the 16th cent. **Alum Chine** Dorset, also on record from the 18th cent., alludes to mining of the same mineral, used in paper-making and leather-tanning.

Alva Clac. *Alweth* 1489. 'Rocky plain'.

Alvah Aber. *Alveth* 1308. 'Rocky plain'. The name applies to both *Bridge of Alvah* and *Kirktown of Alvah*.

Alvanley Ches. *Elveldelie* 1086 (DB). 'Woodland clearing of a man called Ælfweald'. OE pers. name + *lēah*.

Alvaston Derbys. *Alewaldestune c*.1002, *Alewoldestune* 1086 (DB). 'Farmstead or village of a man called Æthelwald or Ælfwald'. OE pers. name + *tūn*.

Alvechurch Heref. & Worcs. *Ælfgythe cyrcan* 10th cent., *Alvievecherche* 1086 (DB). 'Church of a woman called Ælfgȳth'. OE pers. name + *cirice*.

Alvecote Warwicks. *Avecote c*.1160. 'Cottage(s) of a man called Afa'. OE pers. name + *cot*.

Alvediston Wilts. *Alfwieteston* 1165. Probably 'farmstead or village of a man called Ælfgeat'. OE pers. name + *tūn*.

Alveley Shrops. *Alvidelege* 1086 (DB). 'Woodland clearing of a woman called Ælfgȳth'. OE pers. name + *lēah*.

Alverdiscott Devon. *Alveredescota* 1086 (DB). 'Cottage of a man called Ælfrēd'. OE pers. name + *cot*.

Alverstoke Hants. *Stoce* 948, *Alwarestoch* 1086 (DB). 'Outlying farmstead or hamlet of a woman called Ælfwaru or *Æthelwaru*'. OE pers. name + *stoc*.

Alverstone I. of Wight. *Alvrestone* 1086 (DB). 'Farmstead or village of a man called Ælfrēd'. OE pers. name + *tūn*.

Alverton Notts. *Aluriton* 1086 (DB). 'Estate associated with a man called Ælfhere'. OE pers. name + *-ing-* + *tūn*.

Alvescot Oxon. *Elfegescote* 1086 (DB). 'Cottage of a man called Ælfhēah'. OE pers. name + *cot*.

Alveston S. Glos. *Alwestan* 1086 (DB). 'Boundary stone of a man called Ælfwīg'. OE pers. name + *stān*.

Alveston Warwicks. *Eanulfestun* 966, *Alvestone* 1086 (DB). 'Farmstead or village of a man called Ēanwulf'. OE pers. name + *tūn*.

Alvingham Lincs. *Aluingeham* 1086 (DB). 'Homestead of the family or followers of a man called Ælf'. OE pers. name + *-inga-* + *hām*.

Alvington Glos. *Eluinton* 1220. Probably identical in origin with the next name.

Alvington, West Devon. *Alvintone* 1086 (DB). 'Estate associated with a man called Ælf'. OE pers. name + *-ing-* + *tūn*.

Alwalton Cambs. *Æthelwoldingtun* 955, *Alwoltune* 1086 (DB). 'Estate associated with a man called Æthelwald'. OE pers. name + *-ing-* + *tūn*.

Alwinton Northum. *Alwenton* 1242. 'Farmstead or village on the River Alwin'. Celtic or pre-Celtic river-name (of uncertain meaning) + OE *tūn*.

Alwoodley W. Yorks. *Aluuoldelei* 1086 (DB), *Adelwaldesleia* 1166. 'Woodland clearing of a man called Æthelwald'. OE pers. name + *lēah*.

Alyth Perth. *Alicht c.*1249, *Alyth* 1327. Perhaps 'rocky place'. Gaelic *eileach*.

Ambergate Derbys., a recent name, first recorded in 1836, referring to a toll-gate near the River **Amber** (a pre-Celtic river-name of uncertain meaning) which also gives name to the district of **Amber Valley**.

Amberley, probably 'woodland clearing frequented by a bird such as the bunting or yellow-hammer'. OE *amer* + *lēah*: **Amberley** Glos. *Unberleia |sic|* 1166, *Omberleia, Amberley c.*1240. **Amberley** W. Sussex. *Amberle* 957, *Ambrelie* 1086 (DB).

Ambersham, South W. Sussex. *Æmbresham* 963. 'Homestead or river-bend land of a man called *Æmbre'. OE pers. name + *hām* or *hamm*.

Amble Northum. *Ambell* 1204, *Anebell* 1256. Probably 'promontory of a man called *Amma or Anna'. OE pers. name + *bile*.

Amblecote W. Mids. *Elmelecote* 1086 (DB). Probably 'cottage of a man called *Æmela'. OE pers. name + *cot*.

Ambleside Cumbria. *Ameleseta c.*1095. 'Shieling or summer pasture by the river sandbank'. OScand. *á* + *melr* + *sætr*.

Ambleston (*Treamlod*) Pemb. *Amleston* 1230. 'Amelot's farm'. OFrench pers. name + OE *tūn* (Welsh *tref*).

Ambrosden Oxon. *Ambresdone* 1086 (DB). Possibly 'hill of a man called *Ambre', OE pers. name + *dūn*. Alternatively 'hill of the bunting' if the first element is rather OE *amer*.

Amcotts N. Lincs. *Amecotes* 1086 (DB). 'Cottages of a man called *Amma'. OE pers. name + *cot*.

Amersham Bucks. *Agmodesham* 1066, *Elmodesham* 1086 (DB). 'Homestead or village of a man called Ealhmund'. OE pers. name + *hām*.

Amesbury Wilts. *Ambresbyrig c.*880, *Ambreserie* 1086 (DB). Possibly 'stronghold of a man called *Ambre', OE pers. name + *burh* (dative *byrig*). Alternatively '(disused) stronghold frequented by buntings' if the first element is rather OE *amer*.

Amington Staffs. *Ermendone |sic|* 1086 (DB), *Aminton* 1150. Probably 'estate associated with a man called *Earma'. OE pers. name + -*ing*- + *tūn*.

Amlwch Angl. *Anulc* 1254, *Amelogh* 1352. (Place) near the swamp'. Welsh *am* + *llwch*.

Ammanford (*Rhydaman*) Carm. *Amman* 1541. 'Ford over the River Aman'. OE *ford* (Welsh *rhyd*). The river name means 'pig' (Welsh *banw*), for a river that 'roots' its way through the ground.

Amotherby N. Yorks. *Aimundrebi* 1086 (DB). 'Farmstead or village of a man called Eymundr'. OScand. pers. name + *bý*.

Ampleforth N. Yorks. *Ampreforde* 1086 (DB). 'Ford where dock or sorrel grows'. OE *ampre* + *ford*.

Ampney Crucis, Ampney *St Mary*, & *St Peter*, Ampney *Down Ampney* Glos. *Omenie* 1086 (DB), *Ameneye Sancte Crucis* 1287, *Ammeneye Beate Marie* 1291, *Amenel Sancti Petri c.*1275, *Dunamenell* 1205. Named from **Ampney Brook**, 'stream of a man called *Amma', OE pers. name (genitive -*n*) + *ēa*. Distinguishing affixes from the dedica-

tion of the churches to the Holy Rood (Latin *crucis* 'of the cross'), St Mary and St Peter, and from OE *dūne* 'lower downstream'.

Amport Hants. *Anna de Port c.*1270. 'Estate on the River Ann held by a family called de Port'. Celtic river-name (meaning 'ash-tree stream') + manorial affix (from its Domesday owner), *see* ANDOVER.

Ampthill Beds. *Ammetelle* 1086 (DB). 'Anthill, hill infested with ants'. OE *æmette* + *hyll*.

Ampton Suffolk. *Hametuna* 1086 (DB). 'Farmstead or village of a man called *Amma'. OE pers. name + *tūn*.

Amwell, Great & *Amwell, Little* Herts. *Emmewelle* 1086 (DB). 'Spring or stream of a man called *Æmma'. OE pers. name + *wella*.

Anascaul (*Abhainn an Scáil*) (river) Kerry. 'River of the phantom'.

Ancaster Lincs. *Anecastre* 12th cent. Probably 'Roman fort or town associated with a man called Anna'. OE pers. name + *cæster*.

Ancroft Northum. *Anecroft* 1195. 'Lonely or isolated enclosure'. OE *āna* + *croft*.

Anderby Lincs. *Andreby c.*1135. Possibly 'farmstead or village of a man called Arnthórr'. OScand. pers. name + *bý*. Alternatively the first element may be OScand. *andri* 'snow-shoe' perhaps in the sense 'billet of wood'.

Andersonstown (*Baile Andarsan*) Antrim. *Anderson's Town Village* 1832. 'Anderson's town'.

Anderton Ches. *Anderton* 1184. 'Farmstead or village of a man called Ēanrēd or Eindrithi'. OE or OScand. pers. name + *tūn*.

Andover Hants. *Andeferas* 955, *Andovere* 1086 (DB). '(Place by) the ash-tree waters'. Celtic river-name *Ann* (an earlier name for the River Anton and Pillhill Brook) with the Celtic word also found in DOVER.

Andoversford Glos. *Onnan ford* 759. 'Ford of a man called Anna'. OE pers. name + *ford*.

Angersleigh Somerset. *Lega* 1086 (DB), *Aungerlegh* 1354. OE *lēah* 'woodland clearing' with manorial addition from the Aunger family, here in the 13th cent.

Anglesey (*Môn*) (island) Angl. *ynys uon* 815, *Anglesege* 1098, *Ongulsey* 13th cent., *Anglesey, or Anglesea* 1868. 'Ongull's island'. OScand. pers. name + *ey*. The Welsh name cannot satisfactorily be explained. Hence the Roman name, *Mona*.

Angmering W. Sussex. *Angemæringum c.*880, *Angemare* 1086 (DB). '(Settlement of) the family or followers of a man called *Angenmær'. OE pers. name + -*ingas* (dative -*ingum*).

Angram, '(place at) the pastures or grasslands', OE *anger* in a dative plural form *ang(e)rum*: **Angram** N. Yorks., near Keld. *Angram* late 12th cent. **Angram** N. Yorks., near York. *Angrum* 13th cent.

Angus (the unitary authority). *Enegus* 12th cent. '(Place of) *Angus'. *Angus*, 8th-cent. king of the Picts.

Ankail (*Eing Caol*) Kerry. 'Narrow strip'.

Anlaby E. R. Yorks. *Unlouebi* |*sic*| 1086 (DB), *Anlauebi* 1203. 'Farmstead or village of a man called Óláfr'. OScand. pers. name + *bý*.

Anmer Norfolk. *Anemere* |*sic*| 1086 (DB), *Anedemere* 1291. 'Duck pool'. OE *æned* + *mere*.

Ann, Abbots Hants. *Anne* 901, 1086 (DB), *Anne Abbatis* c.1270. 'Estate on the River *Ann* belonging to the abbot'. Celtic river-name (meaning 'ash-tree stream') with manorial affix referring to early possession by Hyde Abbey at Winchester.

Anna Valley Hants., a recent name, coined from the old river-name *Ann* as in previous name, *see* ANDOVER.

Annabella (*Eanach Bile*) Cork. 'Marsh of the sacred tree'.

Annacarty (*Áth na Cairte*) Tipperary. 'Ford of the cart'.

Annaclone (*Eanach Cluana*) Down. *Enaghluan* 1422. 'Marsh of the haunch-like hill'.

Annacloy (*Áth na Cloiche*) Down. *Annacloy* 1621. 'Ford of the stone'.

Annacotty (*Áth an Choite*) Limerick. 'Ford of the boat'.

Annacurragh (*Eanach Churraigh*) Wicklow. 'Marsh of the bog'.

Annadorn (*Áth na nDorn*) Down. *Annaghdorney* 1627. 'Ford of the fists'.

Annaduff (*Eanach Dubh*) Leitrim. 'Black marsh'.

Annagassan (*Áth na gCasán*) Louth. 'Ford of the paths'.

Annagh (*Eanach*) Mayo. 'Marsh'.

Annaghdown (*Eanach Dúin*) Galway. 'Marsh of the fortress'.

Annaghmore (*Eanach Mór*) Armagh, Laois, Offaly. 'Big marsh'.

Annahilt (*Eanach Eilte*) Down. (*Molibae*) *Enaig Elti* c.830. 'Marsh of the doe'.

Annakisha (*Áth na Cise*) Cork. 'Ford of the wicker causeway'.

Annalee (*Abhainn Eanach Lao*) (river) Cavan. 'River of the marsh of the calf'.

Annalong (*Áth na Long*) Down. *Analong* c.1655. 'Ford of the ships'.

Annalore (*Áth na Lobhar*) Monaghan. 'Ford of the leper'.

Annamoe (*Áth na mBó*) Wicklow. 'Ford of the cows'.

Annan Dumf. *Annava* 7th cent., *Estrahanent* 1124, *Stratanant* 1152, *Annandesdale* 1179. '(Place by the) River Annan'. The Celtic river name means 'water'. The last three forms of the name above have added an element meaning 'valley' (Cumbric *ystrad*, Gaelic *srath*, OScand. *dalr*).

Annaveagh (*Áth na bhFiada*) Monaghan. 'Ford of the deer'.

Annesley Woodhouse Notts. *Aneslei* 1086 (DB), *Anseleia* c.1190, *Annesley Wodehouse* 13th cent. Possibly 'woodland clearing of a man called *Ān*'. OE pers. name + *lēah*. Alternatively perhaps identical with ANSLEY Warwicks. The 13th cent. addition denotes 'woodland hamlet'.

Annsborough (*Baile Anna*) Down. *Anne-borough* 1823. After *Annsborough House*, itself perhaps named after the *Annesley* family.

Ansford Somerset. *Almundesford* 1086 (DB). 'Ford associated with a man called Ealhmund'. OE pers. name + *ford*.

Ansley Warwicks. *Hanslei* 1086 (DB), *Anesteleye* 1235. Probably 'woodland clearing with a hermitage'. OE *ānsetl* + *lēah*.

Anslow Staffs. *Eansythelege* 1012. 'Woodland clearing of a woman called Ēanswīth'. OE pers. name + *lēah*.

Anstey, *Ansty*, a name found in various counties, from OE *ānstīg* 'narrow or lonely track', or 'track linking other routes'; examples include: **Anstey** Leics. *Anstige* 1086 (DB). **Anstey, East** & **Anstey, West** Devon. *Anesti(n)ga* 1086 (DB). **Ansty** Warwicks. *Anestie* 1086 (DB). **Ansty** Wilts. *Anestige* 1086 (DB). **Ansty Cross**, **Higher Ansty** Dorset. *Anesty* 1219.

Anston, North & *Anston, South* S. Yorks. *Anestan*, *Litelanstan* 1086 (DB), *Northanstan, Suthanstan* 1297. 'The single or solitary stone'. OE *āna* + *stān*.

Anstruther Fife. *Anestrothir* c.1205. *Ainestrooder* 1178–88. Perhaps 'stream of Etthernan'. Gaelic *sruthair*.

Anthorn Cumbria. *Eynthorn* 1279. 'Solitary thorn-tree'. OScand. *einn* + *thorn*.

Antingham Norfolk. *Antingham* 1044–7, 1086 (DB). 'Homestead of the family or followers of a man called *Anta*'. OE pers. name + *-inga-* + *hām*.

Antonine Wall Dumf, Falk. The wall from the Forth to the Clyde was built in AD 142 for the Roman emperor *Antoninus* Pius.

Antony Cornwall. *Antone* 1086 (DB). 'Farmstead of a man called Anna or *Anta*'. OE pers. name + *tūn*.

Antrim (*Aontroim*, earlier *Aontreibh*) Antrim. (*Fiontan*) *Oentreibh* 612. 'Single house'.

Anwick Lincs. *Amuinc* |*sic*| 1086 (DB), *Amewic* 1218. 'Dwelling or farm of a man called Amma'. OE pers. name + *wīc*.

Anyalla (*Eanaigh Gheala*) Monaghan. *Anyalle* 1591. 'White marshes'.

Apethorpe Northants. *Patorp* |*sic*| 1086 (DB), *Apetorp* 1162. 'Outlying farmstead or hamlet of a man called Api'. OScand. pers. name + *thorp*.

Apley Lincs. *Apeleia* 1086 (DB). 'Apple wood'. OE *æppel* + *lēah*.

Apperknowle Derbys. *Apelknol* 1317. 'Apple-tree hillock'. OE *æppel* + *cnoll*.

Apperley Glos. *Apperleg* 1210. 'Wood or clearing where apple-trees grow'. OE *apuldor* + *lēah*.

Appin (district) Highland. 'Abbey land'. Gaelic *apainn*.

Appleby, 'farmstead or village where apple-trees grow'. OE *æppel* (perhaps replacing OScand. *epli*) + OScand. *bý*: **Appleby** Cumbria. *Aplebi* 1130. **Appleby** N. Lincs. *Aplebi* 1086 (DB). **Appleby Magna** & **Appleby Parva** Leics. *Æppelby* 1002, *Aplebi* 1086 (DB). Distinguishing affixes are Latin *magna* 'great' and *parva* 'little'.

Applecross Highland. *Aporcrosan c.*1080. 'Mouth of the River Crosan'. Pictish *aber*. The river name means 'little cross' (Gaelic *cros* + diminutive suffix -*an*).

Appledore, '(place at) the apple-tree', OE *apuldor*: **Appledore** Devon. *le Apildore* 1335. **Appledore** Kent. *Apuldre* 10th cent., *Apeldres* 1086 (DB).

Appleford Oxon. *Æppelford c.*895, *Apleford* 1086 (DB). 'Ford where apple-trees grow'. OE *æppel* + *ford*.

Appleshaw Hants. *Appelsag* 1200. 'Small wood where apple-trees grow'. OE *æppel* + *sceaga*.

Appleton, 'farmstead where apples grow, apple orchard', OE *æppel-tūn*; examples include: **Appleton** Ches. *Epletune* 1086 (DB). **Appleton** Oxon. *Æppeltune* 942, *Apletune* 1086 (DB). **Appleton, East** N. Yorks. *Apelton* 1086 (DB). **Appleton-le-Moors** N. Yorks. *Apeltun* 1086 (DB). Affix means 'near the moors'. **Appleton-le-Street** N. Yorks. *Apletun* 1086 (DB). Affix means 'on the main road'. **Appleton Roebuck** N. Yorks. *Æppeltune c.*972, *Apleton* 1086 (DB), *Appleton Roebucke* 1664. Manorial affix from the Rabuk family, here in the 14th cent. **Appleton Wiske** N. Yorks. *Apeltona* 1086 (DB). Affix refers to its situation on the River Wiske (from OE *wisc* 'marshy meadow').

Appletreewick N. Yorks. *Apletrewic* 1086 (DB). 'Dwelling or farm by the apple-trees'. OE *æppel-trēow* + *wīc*.

Appley Bridge Lancs. *Appelleie* 13th cent. 'Apple-tree wood or clearing'. OE *æppel* + *lēah*.

Apsley End Beds. *Aspele* 1230. 'Aspen-tree wood'. OE *æspe* + *lēah*.

Apuldram W. Sussex. *Apeldreham* 12th cent. 'Homestead or enclosure where apple-trees grow'. OE *apuldor* + *hām* or *hamm*.

Aran Islands (*Árainn*) Galway. 'Islands of the ridge'.

Aranmore (*Árainn Mhór*) Donegal. 'Big ridge'.

Arberth. *See* NARBERTH.

Arboe (*Ard Bó*) Tyrone. (*Colman*) *Airdi Bó c.*830. 'Height of the cows'.

Arborfield Berks. *Edburgefeld c.*1190, *Erburgefeld* 1222. Probably 'open land of a woman called Hereburh'. OE pers. name + *feld*.

Arbroath Ang. *Aberbrothok* 1178, *Arbroath, or Aberbrothwick* 1868. 'Mouth of the River Brothock'. Pictish *aber*. The river name means 'seething one' (Gaelic *brothach*).

Ardagh (*Ardach*) Longford. 'High field'.

Ardaghy (*Ardachadh*) Monaghan. 'High field'.

Ardakillen (*Ard an Choillín*) Roscommon. 'Height of the little wood'.

Ardanleagh (*Ardán Liath*) Limerick. 'Little grey height'.

Ardara (*Ard an Rátha*) Donegal. *Árd an Rátha c.*1854. 'Height of the fort'.

Ardaragh (*Ard Darach*) Down. *Ardarre* 1549. 'Height of the oak tree'.

Ardattin (*Ard Aitinn*) Carlow. 'Height of the gorse'.

Ardavagga (*Ard a' Mhagaidh*) Offaly. 'Height of merriment'.

Ardballymore (*Ardvhaile Mór*) Westmeath. 'Big high homestead'.

Ardcath (*Ard an Chatha*) Meath. 'Height of the battle'.

Ardcolm (*Ard Coilm*) Wexford. 'Height of Colm'.

Ardcrony (*Ard Cróine*) Tipperary, Wexford. 'Cróne's height'.

Ardee (*Baile Átha Fhirdhia*) Louth. 'Ferdia's ford'.

Ardeen (*Ardín*) Cork, Kerry. 'Little height'.

Ardeley Herts. *Eardeleage* 939, *Erdelei* 1086 (DB). 'Woodland clearing of a man called *Earda*. OE pers. name + *lēah*.

Arden (old forest) Warwicks., *see* HENLEY-IN-ARDEN.

Arderin (*Ard Éireann*) Laois, Offaly. 'Height of Ireland'.

Ardersier Highland. *Ardrosser* 1227, *Arderosseir* 1257. 'Height of the eastern promontory'. Gaelic *ard* + *ros* + *ear*, or 'Promontory of the Artisan'. Gaelic ard-na-suor.

Ardfert (*Ard Fhearta*) Kerry. 'Height of the grave'.

Ardfield (*Ard Ó bhFicheallaigh*) Cork. 'Height of Uí Fhicheallaigh'.

Ardfinnan (*Ard Fhíonáin*) Tipperary. 'Fíonán's height'.

Ardgarvan (*Ard an Garbháin*) Derry. *Ardagarnen* 1616. 'Height of the gravel'.

Ardgivna (*Ard Goibhne*) Sligo. 'Height of the smith'.

Ardglass (*Aird Ghlais*) Down. (*go*)*hAird Glais* 1433. 'Grey point'.

Ardglass (*Ard Glas*) Cork. 'green height'.

Ardgroom (*Dhá Dhrom*) Cork. 'Two ridges'.

Ardingary (*Ard an Gháire*) Donegal. 'Height of shouting'.

Ardingly W. Sussex. *Erdingelega* early 12th cent. 'Woodland clearing of the family or followers of a man called *Earda*. OE pers. name + -*inga*- + *lēah*.

Ardington Oxon. *Ardintone* 1086 (DB). Probably 'estate associated with a man called *Earda*. OE pers. name + -*ing*- + *tūn*.

Ardivaghan (*Ard Uí Mhocháin*) Westmeath. 'Ó Mocháin's height'.

Ardkearagh (*Ard Caorach*) Kerry. 'Height of sheep'.

Ardkeen (*Ard Caoin*) Down. *Ardkene* 1306. 'Pleasant height'.

Ardlea (*Ard Liath*) Laois. 'Grey height'.

Ardleigh Essex. *Erleiam |sic|* 1086 (DB), *Ardlega* 12th cent. Probably 'woodland clearing with a dwelling place'. OE *eard* + *lēah*.

Ardley Oxon. *Eardulfes lea* 995, *Ardulveslie* 1086 (DB). 'Woodland clearing of a man called Eardwulf'. OE pers. name + *lēah*.

Ardlougher (*Ard Luachra*) Cavan. *Ardloagher* 1611. 'Height of the rushes'.

Ardmillan (*Ard an Mhuilinn*) Down. 'Height of the mill'.

Ardmore (*Aird Mhór*) Armagh, Derry, Galway, Mayo, Waterford. 'Big height'.

Ardmore Point Highland (Islay). 'Large point'. Gaelic *ard* + *mór*, and English *point*.

Ardmorney (*Ard Murnaigh*) Westmeath. 'Morna's height'.

Ardnacrohy (*Ard na Croiche*) Limerick. 'Height of the gallows'.

Ardnacrusha (*Ard na Croise*) Clare. 'Height of the cross'.

Ardnaglug (*Ard na gClog*) Westmeath. 'Height of the bell'.

Ardnagroghery (*Ard na gCrochaire*) Cork. 'Height of the hangmen'.

Ardnamoghill (*Ard na mBuachaill*) Donegal. 'Height of the boys'.

Ardnamurchan (peninsula) Highland. *Art Muirchol* c.700, *Ardnamurchin* 1309. 'Point of the otters (literally "sea dogs")'. Gaelic *ard* + *na* + *muir* + *cù* (genitive plural *chon*). The first form of the name above seems to suggest a final element *chol*, 'sin', with 'sea sins' implying piracy.

Ardnapreaghaun (*Ard na bPréachán*) Limerick. 'Height of the crows'.

Ardnaree (*Ard na Ria*) Mayo. 'Height of the executions'.

Ardnurcher (*Áth an Urchair*) Westmeath. 'Ford of the cast'.

Ardpatrick (*Ard Pádraig*) Limerick. 'Patrick's height'.

Ardrahan (*Ard Raithin*) Galway. 'Height of ferns'.

Ardress (*An tArdriasc*) Armagh. *Tardresk* 1609. 'High bog'.

Ardrishaig Arg. 'Height of the brambles'. Gaelic *ard* + *dris*.

Ardroe (*Aird Rua*) Galway. 'Red point'.

Ardross Highland. 'Height of the moorland'. Gaelic *ard* + *ros*. Alternatively, 'height of the headland', from the same elements.

Ardrossan N. Ayr. *Ardrossene* c.1320. 'Height of the little headland'. Gaelic *ard* + *ros* + diminutive suffix -*an*.

Ards Peninsula (*Aird Uladh*) Down. (*i*) *nAird Ulad* c.830. 'Peninsula of the Ulstermen'.

Ardscull (*Ard Scol*) Kildare. 'Height of schools'.

Ardsheelane (*Ard Síoláin*) Kerry. 'Height of Síolán'.

Ardsley S. Yorks. *Erdeslaia* 12th cent. 'Woodland clearing of a man called Eorēd or Ēanrēd'. OE pers. name + *lēah*.

Ardsley East W. Yorks. *Erdeslawe* 1086 (DB). 'Mound of a man called Eorēd or Ēanrēd'. OE pers. name + *hlāw*.

Ardstraw (*Ard Sratha*) Tyrone. (*muintir*) *Aird Sratha* c.900. 'Height of the river island'.

Ardtole (*Ard Tuathail*) Down. 'Tuathal's height'.

Areley Kings Heref. & Worcs. *Erneleia* c.1138, *Kyngges Arley* 1405. 'Wood or clearing frequented by eagles'. OE *earn* + *lēah*. Affix *Kings* because it was part of a royal manor.

Argideen (*Airgidín*) (river) Cork. 'Silver (river)'.

Argyll (district) Arg. *Arregaithel* c.970, *Argail* 1292. 'Coastland of the Gaels'. Gaelic *oirthir Ghaideal*.

Arkendale N. Yorks. *Arghendene* 1086 (DB). Probably 'valley of a man called *Eorcna*'. OE pers. name + *denu* (replaced from the 14th cent. by OScand. *dalr*).

Arkesden Essex. *Archesdana* 1086 (DB). Possibly 'valley of a man called Arnkel'. OScand. pers. name + OE *denu*.

Arkholme Lancs. *Ergune* 1086 (DB). '(Place at) the shielings or hill-pastures'. OScand. *erg* in a dative plural form *ergum*.

Arkley Gtr. London, *Arkeleyslond* 1332, *Arkeley* 1547. Originally, it seems, a manorial name, 'land of a family called Arkeley'.

Arklow (*An tInbhear Mór*) Wicklow. *Herketelou* 1177. 'Arnkell's meadow'. OScand. pers. name + *ló*. The Irish name means 'the big estuary'.

Arksey S. Yorks. *Archeseia* 1086 (DB). 'Island, or dry ground in marsh, of a man called Arnkel'. OScand. pers. name + OE *ēg*.

Arlecdon Cumbria. *Arlauchdene* c.1130. 'Valley of the stream frequented by eagles'. OE *earn* + *lacu* + *denu*.

Arlescote Warwicks. *Orlavescote* 1086 (DB). 'Cottage(s) of a man called Ordlāf'. OE pers. name + *cot*.

Arlesey Beds. *Alricheseia* 1062, 1086 (DB). 'Island or well-watered land of a man called Ælfrīc'. OE pers. name + *ēg*.

Arless (*Ardlios*) Laois. 'High fort'.

Arleston Shrops. *Erdelveston* 1180. 'Farmstead or village of a man called Eardwulf'. OE pers. name + *tūn*.

Arley, usually 'wood or clearing frequented by eagles', OE *earn* + *lēah*: **Arley** Warwicks. *Earnlege* 1001, *Arlei* 1086 (DB). **Arley, Upper** Heref. & Worcs. *Earnleie* 996, *Ernlege* 1086 (DB).
　　However the following may have a different origin: **Arley** Ches. *Arlegh* 1340. Possibly 'grey wood', or 'wood on a boundary'. OE *hār* + *lēah*.

Arlingham Glos. *Erlingeham* 1086 (DB). 'Homestead or enclosure of the family or followers of a man called *Eorl(a)*'. OE pers. name + -*inga*- + *hām* or *hamm*.

Arlington Devon. *Alferdintona* 1086 (DB). 'Estate associated with a man called Ælffrith'. OE pers. name + -*ing*- + *tūn*.

Arlington E. Sussex. *Erlington* 1086 (DB). 'Estate associated with a man called Eorl(a)'. OE pers. name + -*ing*- + *tūn*.

Arlington Glos. *Ælfredincgtune* 1004, *Alvredintone* 1086 (DB). 'Estate associated with a man called Ælfrēd'. OE pers. name + -*ing*- + *tūn*.

Armadale Highland (Skye). *Armidill* 1723. 'arm-shaped valley'. OScand. *armr* + *dalr*.

Armadale W. Loth. The town arose in the mid-19th cent. and was named for William Honeyman, Lord Armadale, who took his title from *Armadale*, Highland, near Melvich. Its own name has the same origin as ARMADALE, Skye.

Armagh (*Ard Mhacha*) Armagh. *Ard Macha* 444. 'Macha's height' or 'height of the plain'.

Armathwaite Cumbria. *Ermitethwait* 1212. 'Clearing of the hermit'. ME *ermite* + OScand. *thveit*.

Arminghall Norfolk. *Hameringahala* 1086 (DB). Possibly 'nook of land of the family or followers of a man called *Ambre or Ēanmær'. OE pers. name + *-inga-* + *halh*.

Armitage Staffs. *Armytage* 1520. '(Place at) the hermitage'. ME *ermitage*.

Armoy (*Oirthear Maí*) Antrim. *Airther Maigi* c.900. 'East of the plain'.

Armscote Warwicks. *Eadmundescote* 1042. 'Cottage(s) of a man called Ēadmund'. OE pers. name + *cot*.

Armthorpe S. Yorks. *Ernulfestorp* 1086 (DB). 'Outlying farmstead or hamlet of a man called Earnwulf or Arnulfr'. OE or OScand. pers. name + OScand. *thorp*.

Arncliffe N. Yorks. *Arneclif* 1086 (DB). 'Cliff of the eagles'. OE *earn* + *clif*.

Arncott, Upper & *Arncott, Lower* Oxon. *Earnigcote* 983, *Ernicote* 1086 (DB). 'Cottage(s) associated with a man called *Earn'. OE pers. name + *-ing-* + *cot*.

Arne Dorset. *Arne* 1268. Probably OE *ærn* 'house or building'. Alternatively '(place at) the heaps of stones or tumuli', from OE *hær* in a dative plural form *harum*.

Arnesby Leics. *Erendesbi* 1086 (DB). 'Farmstead or village of a man called Iarund or *Erendi'. OScand. pers. name + *bý*.

Arnold, 'nook of land frequented by eagles', OE *earn* + *halh*: **Arnold** E. R. Yorks. *Ærnhale* 1190. **Arnold** Notts. *Ernehale* 1086 (DB).

Arnside Cumbria. *Harnolvesheuet* 1184–90. 'Hill or headland of a man called Earnwulf or Arnulfr'. OE or OScand. pers. name + OE *hēafod*.

Arra Mountain (*Sliabh Āra*) Tipperary. 'Mountain of (the district of) Āra'.

Arram E. R. Yorks. *Argun* 1086 (DB). '(Place at) the shielings or hill-pastures'. OScand. *erg* in a dative plural form *ergum*.

Arran (island) N. Ayr. Meaning uncertain. Ancient name.

Arranmore (*Árainn Mhór*) Donegal. *hAruinn Uí Dhomhnuill* c.1600. 'Great ridge'.

Arrathorne N. Yorks. *Ergthorn* 13th cent. 'Thorn-tree by the shieling or hill-pasture'. OScand. *erg* + *thorn*.

Arreton I. of Wight. *Eaderingtune* c.880, *Adrintone* 1086 (DB). 'Estate associated with a man called Ēadhere'. OE pers. name + *-ing-* + *tūn*.

Arrington Cambs. *Earnningtone* c.950, *Erningtune* 1086 (DB). Probably 'farmstead of the family or followers of a man called *Earn(a)'. OE pers. name + *-inga-* + *tūn*.

Arrow (river) Heref. & Worcs., *see* STAUNTON ON ARROW.

Arrow Warwicks. *Arne |sic|* 710, *Arue* 1086 (DB). Named from the River **Arrow**, a Celtic or pre-Celtic river-name meaning simply 'stream'.

Arryheernabin (*Áirí Thír na Binne*) Donegal. 'Shieling of the country of the peak'.

Arthington W. Yorks. *Hardinctone* 1086 (DB). 'Estate associated with a man called *Earda'. OE pers. name + *-ing-* + *tūn*.

Arthingworth Northants. *Arningvorde* 1086 (DB). 'Enclosure associated with a man called *Earn(a)'. OE pers. name + *-ing-* + *worth*.

Articlave (*Ard an Chléibh*) Derry. *Ard Cleibh* c.1680. 'Height of the basket'.

Artiferrall (*Ard Tighe Fearghail*) Antrim. 'Height of Fearghal's house'.

Artigarvan (*Ard Tí Garbháin*) Tyrone. *Ordogarvan* c.1655. 'Height of Garbhán's house'.

Artnagross (*Ard na gCros*) Antrim. *Artnagross* 1780, 'Height of the crosses'.

Artrea (*Ard Tré*) Tyrone. (*airchindeach*) *Arda Trea* 1127. 'Tré's height'.

Arundel W. Sussex. *Harundel* 1086 (DB). 'Valley where the plant horehound grows'. OE *hārhūne* + *dell*. The river-name **Arun** is a 'back-formation' from the place-name.

Arvagh (*Ármhach*) Cavan. *Arvaghbeg*, *Arvaghmore* 1630. 'Battlefield'.

Asby, 'farmstead or village where ash-trees grow', OScand. *askr* + *bý*: **Asby** Cumbria, near Arlecdon. *Asbie* 1654. **Asby, Great** & **Asby, Little** Cumbria. *Aschaby* c.1160.

Ascot, *Ascott*, 'eastern cottage(s)', OE *ēast* + *cot*: **Ascot** Berks. *Estcota* 1177. **Ascott under Wychwood** Oxon. *Estcot* 1220. Affix means 'near the forest of Wychwood' (an OE name, *Huiccewudu* 840, meaning 'wood of a tribe called the Hwicce').

Asdee (*Eas Daoi*) Kerry. 'Dark waterfall'.

Asenby N. Yorks. *Æstanesbi* 1086 (DB). 'Farmstead or village of a man called Eysteinn'. OScand. pers. name + *bý*.

Asfordby Leics. *Osferdebie* 1086 (DB). 'Farmstead or village of a man called Ásfrøthr or Ásfrithr'. OScand. pers. name + *bý*.

Asgarby, 'farmstead or village of a man called Ásgeirr', OScand. pers. name + *bý*: **Asgarby** Lincs., near Sleaford. *Asegarby* 1201. **Asgarby** Lincs., near Spilsby. *Asgerebi* 1086 (DB).

Ash, '(place at) the ash-tree(s)', OE *æsc*; examples include: **Ash** Kent, near Sandwich. *Æsce* c.1100. **Ash** Surrey. *Essa* 1170. **Ash Magna** Shrops. *Magna Asche* 1285. Affix is Latin *magna* 'great'. **Ash Priors** Somerset. *Æsce* 1065, *Esse Prior* 1263. Affix from its early possession by the Prior of Taunton.

Ashampstead Berks. *Essamestede* 1155–8. 'Homestead by the ash-tree(s)'. OE *æsc* + *hām-stede*.

Ashbocking Suffolk. *Assa* 1086 (DB), *Bokkynge Assh* 1411. '(Place at) the ashtree(s)'. OE *æsc* + manorial affix from the de Bocking family, here in the 14th cent.

Ashbourne Derbys. *Esseburne* 1086 (DB). 'Stream where ash-trees grow'. OE *æsc* + *burna*.

Ashbrittle Somerset. *Aisse* 1086 (DB), *Esse Britel* 1212. '(Place at) the ash-tree(s)'. OE *æsc* + manorial affix from its possession by a man called Bretel in 1086.

Ashburnham E. Sussex. *Esseborne* 1086 (DB), *Esburneham* 12th cent. 'Meadow by the stream where ash-trees grow'.

OE *æsc* + *burna* with the later addition of *hamm*. The river here is still called **Ashburn**.

Ashburton Devon. *Essebretone* 1086 (DB). 'Farmstead or village by the stream where ash-trees grow'. OE *æsc* + *burna* + *tūn*.

Ashbury, 'stronghold where ash-trees grow', OE *æsc* + *burh* (dative *byrig*): **Ashbury** Devon. *Esseberie* 1086 (DB). **Ashbury** Oxon. *Eissesberie* |*sic*| 1086 (DB), *Æsseberia* 1187.

Ashby, a common name in the North and Midlands, usually 'farmstead or village where ash-trees grow', OE *æsc* or OScand. *askr* + OScand. *bý*; however 'farmstead of a man called Aski', OScand. pers. name + *bý*, is a possible alternative for some names; examples include: **Ashby** N. Lincs. *Aschebi* 1086 (DB). **Ashby by Partney** Lincs. *Aschebi* 1086 (DB). *See* PARTNEY. **Ashby, Canons** Northants. *Ascebi* 1086 (DB), *Essheby Canons* 13th cent. Affix from the priory here, founded in the 12th cent. **Ashby, Castle** Northants. *Asebi* 1086 (DB), *Castel Assheby* 1361. Affix from the former castle here. **Ashby, Cold** Northants. *Essebi* 1086 (DB), *Caldessebi* c.1150. Affix is OE *cald* 'cold, exposed'. **Ashby cum Fenby** NE. Lincs. *Aschebi* 1086 (DB). Fenby is *Fen(de)bi* 1086 (DB), 'farmstead in a fen or marsh', OE *fenn* + OScand. *bý*; Latin *cum* is 'with'. **Ashby de la Launde** Lincs. *Aschebi* 1086 (DB). Manorial affix from the de la Launde family, here in the 14th cent. **Ashby de la Zouch** Leics. *Ascebi* 1086 (DB), *Esseby la Zusche* 1241. Manorial affix from the de la Zuche family, here in the 13th cent. **Ashby Folville** Leics. *Ascbi* 1086 (DB). Manorial affix from the de Foleuilla family, here in the 12th cent. **Ashby Magna** & **Ashby Parva** Leics. *Essebi* 1086 (DB). Affixes are Latin *magna* 'great', *parva* 'little'. **Ashby, Mears** Northants. *Asbi* 1086 (DB), *Esseby Mares* 1281. Manorial affix from the de Mares family, here in the 13th cent. **Ashby Puerorum** Lincs. *Aschebi* 1086 (DB). Latin affix means 'of the boys', in allusion to a bequest for the support of the choir-boys of Lincoln Cathedral. **Ashby St Ledgers** Northants. *Ascebi* 1086 (DB), *Esseby Sancti Leodegarii* c.1230. Affix from the dedication of the church to St Leger. **Ashby St Mary** Norfolk. *Ascebei* 1086 (DB). Affix from the dedication of the church. **Ashby, West** Lincs. *Aschebi* 1086 (DB).

Ashcombe Devon. *Aissecome* 1086 (DB). 'Valley where ash-trees grow'. OE *æsc* + *cumb*.

Ashcott Somerset. *Aissecote* 1086 (DB). 'Cottage(s) where ash-trees grow'. OE *æsc* + *cot*.

Ashdon Essex. *Æstchendune* c.1036, *Ascenduna* 1086 (DB). 'Hill overgrown with ash-trees'. OE *æscen* + *dūn*.

Ashdown Forest Sussex. *Essendon* 1207. Identical in origin with the previous name.

Asheldham Essex. *Assildeham* c.1130. 'Homestead of a woman called *Æschild*'. OE pers. name + *hām*.

Ashen Essex. *Asce* 1086 (DB), *Asshen* 1344. '(Place at) the ash-trees'. OE *æsc* in a dative plural form *æscum*.

Ashendon Bucks. *Assedune* 1086 (DB). 'Hill overgrown with ash-trees'. OE *æscen* + *dūn*.

Ashfield, 'open land where ash-trees grow', OE *æsc* + *feld*: **Ashfield** Notts. *Esfeld* 1216. An old name now revived as a district name. **Ashfield** Suffolk. *Assefelda* 1086 (DB). **Ashfield, Great** Suffolk. *Eascefelda* 1086 (DB).

Ashford, usually 'ford where ash-trees grow', OE *æsc* + *ford*: **Ashford** Devon. *Aiseforda* 1086 (DB). **Ashford Bowdler** & **Ashford Carbonel** Shrops. *Esseford* 1086 (DB), *Asford Budlers, Aysford Carbonel* 1255. Manorial affixes from the de Boulers and Carbunel families, here at an early date. **Ashford in the Water** Derbys. *Æscforda* 926, *Aisseford* 1086 (DB). Affix 'in the Water' occurs from the late 17th cent., no doubt with reference to the meandering course of the River Wye here

However two Ashfords have a different origin: **Ashford** Kent. *Essetesford* 1086 (DB). 'Ford by a clump of ash-trees'. OE **æcset* + *ford*. **Ashford** Surrey. *Ecclesford* 969, *Exeforde* 1086 (DB). Possibly 'ford of a man called **Eccel*', from OE pers. name + *ford*, or the first element may be an old river-name **Ecel*.

Ashill Norfolk. *Asscelea* 1086 (DB). 'Ash-tree wood'. OE *æsc* + *lēah*.

Ashill Somerset. *Aisselle* 1086 (DB). 'Hill where ash-trees grow'. OE *æsc* + *hyll*.

Ashingdon Essex. *Assandun* 1016, *Nesenduna* |*sic*| 1086 (DB). 'Hill of the ass, or of a man called **Assa*'. OE *assa* or OE pers. name (genitive -*n*) + *dūn*.

Ashington Northum. *Essenden* 1205. 'Valley where ash-trees grow'. OE *æscen* + *denu*.

Ashington W. Sussex. *Essingetona* 1073. 'Farmstead of the family or followers of a man called *Æsc*'. OE pers. name + -*inga*- + *tūn*.

Ashleworth Glos. *Escelesuuorde* 1086 (DB). 'Enclosure of a man called **Æscel*'. OE pers. name + *worth*.

Ashley, a common name, 'ash-tree wood or clearing', OE *æsc* + *lēah*; examples include: **Ashley** Cambs. *Esselie* 1086 (DB). **Ashley** Ches. *Ascelie* 1086 (DB). **Ashley** Devon. *Esshelegh* 1238. **Ashley** Dorset. *Asseleghe* 1246. **Ashley** Hants., near Lymington. *Esselie* 1086 (DB). **Ashley** Hants., near Winchester. *Asselegh* 1275. **Ashley** Northants. *Ascele* 1086 (DB). **Ashley** Staffs. *Esselie* 1086 (DB). **Ashley Green** Bucks. *Essleie* 1227, *Assheley grene* 1468.

Ashling, East & *Ashling, West* W. Sussex. *Estlinges* 1185. Probably '(settlement of) the family or followers of a man called **Æscla*'. OE pers. name + -*ingas*.

Ashmansworth Hants. *Æscmæreswierthe* 909. 'Enclosure by the ash-tree pool'. OE *æsc* + *mere* + *worth*.

Ashmore Dorset. *Aisemare* 1086 (DB). 'Pool where ash-trees grow'. OE *æsc* + *mere*.

Ashorne Warwicks. *Hassorne* 1196. 'Horn-shaped hill where ash-trees grow'. OE *æsc* + *horn*.

Ashover Derbys. *Essovre* 1086 (DB). 'Ridge or slope where ash-trees grow'. OE *æsc* + **ofer*.

Ashow Warwicks. *Asceshot* |*sic*| 1086 (DB), *Essesho* 12th cent. 'Hill spur of the ash-tree or of a man called *Æsc*'. OE *æsc* or OE pers. name + *hōh*.

Ashperton Heref. & Worcs. *Spertune* |*sic*| 1086 (DB), *Aspretonia* 1144. Probably 'farmstead or village of a man called *Æscbeorht* or *Æscberon*'. OE pers. name + *tūn*.

Ashprington Devon. *Aisbertone* 1086 (DB). 'Estate associated with a man called *Æscbeorht* or *Æscbeorn*'. OE pers. name + -*ing*- + *tūn*.

Ashreigney Devon. *Aissa* 1086 (DB), *Esshereingni* 1238. '(Place at) the ash-tree(s)'. OE *æsc* + manorial affix from the de Regny family, here in the 13th cent.

Ashtead Surrey. *Stede* 1086 (DB), *Estede* c.1150. 'Place where ash-trees grow'. OE *æsc* + *stede*.

Ashton, a common name, usually 'farmstead where ash-trees grow', OE *æsc* + *tūn*; examples include: **Ashton** Ches. *Estone* 1086 (DB). **Ashton** Heref. & Worcs. *Estune* 1086 (DB). **Ashton** Northants., near Oundle. *Ascetone* 1086 (DB). **Ashton-in-Makerfield** Gtr. Manch. *Eston* 1212. Affix is an old district name (*Macrefeld* 1121), from a Celtic word meaning 'wall, ruin' + OE *feld* 'open land'. **Ashton Keynes** Wilts. *Æsctun* 880–5, *Essitone* 1086 (DB), *Aysheton Keynes* 1572. Manorial affix from the de Keynes family, here from the 13th cent. **Ashton, Long** N. Som. *Estune* 1086 (DB), *Longe Asshton* 1467. Affix from the length of the village. **Ashton, Steeple** & **Ashton, West** Wilts. *Æystone* 964, *Aistone* 1086 (DB), *Westaston* 1248, *Stepelaston* 1268. Distinguishing affixes from OE *stīepel* 'church steeple' and *west*. **Ashton under Hill** Heref. & Worcs. *Æsctun* 991, *Essetone* 1086 (DB), *Assheton Underhill* 1544. Affix 'under the hill' refers to BREDON Hill. **Ashton-under-Lyne** Gtr. Manch. *Haistune* c.1160, *Asshton under Lyme* 1305. Affix is from an old Celtic district name Lyme, possibly meaning 'elm-tree region'. **Ashton upon Mersey** Gtr. Manch. *Asshton* 1408. On the River Mersey, 'boundary river' from OE *mǣre* (genitive -*s*) + *ēa*.

However some Ashtons have a different origin: **Ashton** Northants., near Northampton. *Asce* 1086 (DB), *Asshen* 1296. '(Place at) the ash-trees'. OE *æsc* in a dative plural form *æscum*. **Ashton, Higher** & **Ashton, Lower** Devon. *Aiserstone* 1086 (DB). 'Farmstead of a man called Æschere'. OE pers. name + *tūn*.

Ashurst, 'wooded hill growing with ash-trees', OE *æsc* + *hyrst*: **Ashurst** Kent. *Aeischerste* c.1100. **Ashurst** W. Sussex. *Essehurst* 1164.

Ashurstwood W. Sussex. *Foresta de Esseherst* 1164. Identical in origin with the previous names.

Ashwater Devon. *Aissa* 1086 (DB), *Esse Valteri* 1270. '(Place at) the ash-tree(s)'. OE *æsc* + manorial affix from its possession by a man called Walter in the 13th cent.

Ashwell, 'spring or stream where ash-trees grow', OE *æsc* + *wella*: **Ashwell** Herts. *Asceuuelle* 1086 (DB). **Ashwell** Rutland. *Exewelle* 1086 (DB).

Ashwellthorpe Norfolk. *Aescewelle, Thorp* c.1066. 'Hamlet belonging to a place called *Ashwell* ("ash-tree spring or stream")'. OE *æsc* + *wella* + OScand. *thorp*.

Ashwick Somerset. *Escewiche* 1086 (DB). 'Dwelling or farmstead where ash-trees grow'. OE *æsc* + *wīc*.

Ashwicken Norfolk. *Wiche* 1086 (DB), *Askiwiken* 1275. '(Place at) the dwellings or buildings'. OE *wīc* in a dative plural form *wīcum* or a ME plural form *wiken*. Later addition may be OE *æsc* 'ash-tree' or a pers. name.

Askam in Furness Cumbria. *Askeham* 1535. Possibly '(place at) the ash-trees'. OScand. *askr* in a dative plural form *askum*. For the affix, *see* BARROW IN FURNESS.

Askamore (*An Easca Mhór*) Wexford. 'The big bog'.

Askanagap (*Easca na gCeap*) Wicklow. 'Bog of the stumps'.

Askeaton (*Eas Géitine*) Limerick. *Eas-Gephtine* n.d. 'Géitine's waterfall'.

Askern S. Yorks. *Askern* c.1170. 'House near the ash-tree'. OScand. *askr* + OE *ærn*.

Askerswell Dorset. *Oscherwille* 1086 (DB). 'Spring or stream of a man called Ōsgār'. OE pers. name + *wella*.

Askham, 'homestead or enclosure where ash-trees grow', OE *æsc* (replaced by OScand. *askr*) + OE *hām* or *hamm*: **Askham** Notts. *Ascam* 1086 (DB). **Askham Bryan** & **Askham Richard** York. *Ascam* 1086 (DB), *Ascam Bryan* 1285, *Askham Ricardi* 1291. Manorial additions from early possession by men called Brian and Richard.

Askham Cumbria. *Askum* 1232. '(Place at) the ash-trees'. OScand. *askr* in the dative plural form *askum*.

Askrigg N. Yorks. *Ascric* 1086 (DB). Probably 'ash-tree ridge'. OScand. *askr* + OE **ric*.

Askwith N. Yorks. *Ascvid* 1086 (DB). 'Ash-tree wood'. OScand. *askr* + *vithr*.

Aslackby Lincs. *Aslachebi* 1086 (DB). 'Farmstead or village of a man called Áslákr'. OScand. pers. name + *bý*.

Aslacton Norfolk. *Aslactuna* 1086 (DB). 'Farmstead or village of a man called Áslákr'. OScand. pers. name + OE *tūn*.

Aslockton Notts. *Aslachetune* 1086 (DB). Identical in origin with the previous name.

Aspatria Cumbria. *Aspatric* c.1160. 'Ash-tree of St Patrick'. OScand. *askr* + Celtic pers. name. The order of elements is Celtic.

Aspenden Herts. *Absesdene* 1086 (DB). 'Valley where aspen-trees grow'. OE *æspe* + *denu*.

Aspley Guise Beds. *Æpslea* 969, *Aspeleia* 1086 (DB), *Aspeleye Gyse* 1363. 'Aspen-tree wood or glade'. OE *æspe* + *lēah*, with manorial affix from the de Gyse family, here in the 13th cent.

Aspull Gtr. Manch. *Aspul* 1212. 'Hill where aspen-trees grow'. OE *æspe* + *hyll*.

Assaroe (*Easa Rua*) Donegal. 'Red waterfall'.

Asselby E. R. Yorks. *Aschilebi* 1086 (DB). 'Farmstead or village of a man called Áskell'. OScand. pers. name + *bý*.

Assendon, Lower & *Assendon, Middle* Oxon. *Assundene* late 10th cent. 'Valley of the ass, or of a man called *Assa*'. OE *assa* or OE pers. name + *denu*.

Assington Suffolk. *Asetona* 1086 (DB), *Assintona* 1175. 'Estate associated with a man called *As(s)a*'. OE pers. name + -*ing*- + *tūn*.

Assolus (*Áth Solais*) Cork. 'Ford of light'.

Astbury Ches. *Astbury* 1093. 'East manor or stronghold'. OE *ēast* + *burh* (dative *byrig*).

Astcote Northants. *Aviescote* 1086 (DB). 'Cottage(s) of a man called Ǣfic'. OE pers. name + *cot*.

Asterley Shrops. *Estrelega* 1208. 'More easterly woodland clearing'. OE *ēasterra* + *lēah*.

Asterton Shrops. *Esthampton* 1255. 'Eastern home farm'. OE *ēast* + *hām-tūn*.

Asthall Oxon. *Esthale* 1086 (DB). 'East nook(s) of land'. OE *ēast* + *h(e)alh*.

Asthall Leigh Oxon. *Estallingeleye* 1272. 'Woodland clearing of the people of Asthall'. ASTHALL + OE *-inga-* + *lēah*.

Astley, 'east wood or clearing', OE *ēast* + *lēah*: **Astley** Gtr. Manch. *Asteleghe* c.1210. **Astley** Heref. & Worcs. *Eslei* 1086 (DB). **Astley** Shrops. *Hesleie* 1086 (DB). **Astley** Warwicks. *Estleia* 1086 (DB). **Astley Abbots** Shrops. *Estleia* c.1090, *Astleye Abbatis* late 13th cent. Affix alludes to early possession by Shrewsbury Abbey.

Aston, a common name, usually 'eastern farmstead or estate', OE *ēast* + *tūn*; examples include: **Aston** S. Yorks. *Estone* 1086 (DB). **Aston** W. Mids. *Estone* 1086 (DB). **Aston Blank** or **Cold Aston** Glos. *Eastunæ* 716–43, *Estone* 1086 (DB). Affix may be OFrench *blanc* 'white, bare'. **Aston Cantlow** Warwicks. *Estone* 1086 (DB), *Aston Cantelou* 1273. Manorial affix from the de Cantilupe family, here in the 13th cent. **Aston, Chetwynd** Shrops. *Estona* 1155, *Greate Aston alias Chetwynde Aston* 1619. For affix, see CHETWYND. **Aston Clinton** Bucks. *Estone* 1086 (DB), *Aston Clinton* 1237–40. Manorial affix from the de Clinton family, here in the late 12th cent. **Aston Fields** Heref. & Worcs. *Eastun* 767, *Estone* 1086 (DB), *Aston Fields* 1649. **Aston Ingham** Heref. & Worcs. *Estune* 1086 (DB), *Estun Ingan* 1242. Manorial affix from the Ingan family, here in the 13th cent. **Aston Rowant** Oxon. *Estone* 1086 (DB), *Aston Roaud* 1318. Manorial affix from Rowald de Eston, here in 1236. **Aston, Steeple** Oxon. *Estone* 1086 (DB), *Stipelestun* 1220. Affix is OE *stīepel* 'church steeple'. **Aston upon Trent** Derbys. *Estune* 1086 (DB). For the river-name, see TRENTHAM. **Aston, Wheaton** Staffs. *Estone* 1086 (DB), *Wetenaston* 1248. Affix is OE *nwæten* 'growing with wheat'. **Aston, White Ladies** Heref. & Worcs. *Eastune* 977, *Estun* 1086 (DB), *Whitladyaston* 1481. Affix from its possession by the Cistercian nuns of Whitstones.

However the following has a different origin: **Aston on Clun** Shrops. *Assheston* 1291. 'Ash-tree farmstead'. OE *æsc* + *tūn*. For the river-name, see CLUN.

Aston Flin. 'Eastern farmstead'. *Estone* 1086 (DB). OE *ēast* + *tūn*.

Astrop Northants. *Estrop* 1200. 'East hamlet'. OE *ēast* + *throp*.

Astwood, 'east wood', OE *ēast* + *wudu*: **Astwood** Bucks. *Estwode* 1151–4. **Astwood** Heref. & Worcs. *Estwode* 1182.

Aswardby Lincs. *Asuuardebi* 1086 (DB). 'Farmstead or village of a man called Ásvarthr'. OScand. pers. name + *bý*.

Aswardby Lincs. *Asewrdeby* c.1155. Identical in origin with the previous name.

Atch Lench Heref. & Worcs., *see* LENCH.

Atcham Shrops. *Atingeham* 1086 (DB). 'Homestead of the family or followers of a man called Ætti or Ēata', or 'homestead at the place associated with Ætti or Ēata'. OE pers. name + *-inga-* or *-ing* + *hām*. Alternatively the final element may be *hamm* 'land in a river-bend'.

Athboy (*Baile Átha Buí*) Meath. 'Town of the yellow ford'.

Athcarne (*Áth Chairn*) Meath. 'Ford of the cairn'.

Athea (*Áth an tSléibhe*) Limerick. 'Ford of the mountain'.

Athelhampton Dorset. *Pidele* 1086 (DB), *Pidele Athelamston* 1285. Originally named from the River Piddle on which it stands (*see* PIDDLEHINTON), later 'farmstead of a man called Æthelhelm', OE pers. name + *tūn*.

Athelington Suffolk. *Alinggeton* 1219. 'Farmstead or village of the princes'. OE *ætheling* + *tūn*.

Athelney Somerset. *Æthelingaeigge* 878, *Adelingi* 1086 (DB). 'Island, or dry ground in marsh, of the princes'. OE *ætheling* + *ēg*.

Athenboy (*Aiteann Buí*) Westmeath. 'Yellow gorse'.

Athenry (*Baile Átha an Rí*) Galway. 'Town of the ford of the kings'.

Atherfield, Little I. of Wight. *Aderingefelda* 959, *Avrefel* 1086 (DB). 'Open land of the family or followers of a man called Ēadhere or Æthelhere'. OE pers. name + *-inga-* + *feld*.

Atherington Devon. *Hadrintone* 1272. 'Estate associated with a man called Ēadhere or Æthelhere'. OE pers. name + *-ing-* + *tūn*.

Atherstone Warwicks. *Aderestone* 1086 (DB), *Atheredestone* 1221. 'Farmstead or village of a man called Æthelrēd'. OE pers. name + *tūn*.

Atherstone on Stour Warwicks. *Eadrichestone* 710, *Edricestone* 1086 (DB). 'Farmstead or village of a man called Ēadrīc'. OE pers. name + *tūn*. Affix from its situation on the River Stour, a Celtic or OE river-name probably meaning 'the strong one'.

Atherton Gtr. Manch. *Aderton* 1212. 'Farmstead or village of a man called Æthelhere'. OE pers. name + *tūn*.

Athgarvan (*Áth Garbháin*) Kildare. 'Garbhán's ford'.

Athgreany (*Áth Gréine*) Wicklow. 'Grian's ford'.

Athlacca (*An tÁth Leacach*) Limerick. 'The ford with flagstones'.

Athleague (*Áth Liag*) Roscommon. 'Ford of the boulders'.

Athlone (*Baile Áth Luain*) Westmeath. 'Town of Luan's ford'.

Athnid (*Áth Nid*) Tipperary. 'Ford of the nest'.

Atholl. *See* BLAIR ATHOLL.

Athy (*Baile Áth Í*) Kildare. 'Town of the yew ford'.

Atlow Derbys. *Etelawe* 1086 (DB). 'Burialmound of a man called Eatta'. OE pers. name + *hlāw*.

Attanagh (*Áth Tanaí*) Laois. 'Shallow ford'.

Attatantee (*Áit a' tSean Tighe*) Donegal. 'Place of the old house'.

Attenborough Notts. *Adinburcha* 12th cent. 'Stronghold associated with a man called Adda or Æddi'. OE pers. name + *-ing-* + *burh*.

Attical (*Áit Tí Chathail*) Down. *Atty Caell* c.1659. 'Place of Cathal's house'.

Atticonor (*Áit Tí Chonuir*) Westmeath. 'Place of Conor's house'.

Attleborough Norfolk. *Atleburc* 1086 (DB). 'Stronghold of a man called Ætla'. OE pers. name + *burh*.

Attleborough Warwicks. *Atteleberga* 12th cent. 'Hill or mound of a man called Ætla'. OE pers. name + *beorg*.

Attlebridge Norfolk. *Atlebruge* 1086 (DB). 'Bridge of a man called Ætla'. OE pers. name + *brycg*.

Attymachugh (*Áit Tí Mhic Aodha*) Mayo. 'Place of Mac Aodha's house'.

Attymass (*Áit Tí an Mheasaigh*) Mayo. 'Place of the church of the Measach'.

Attymon (*Áth Tíomáin*) Galway. 'Tíomán's ford'.

Atwick E. R. Yorks. *Attingwik* 12th cent. 'Dwelling or dairy-farm of a man called Atta'. OE pers. name + *-ing-* + *wīc*.

Atworth Wilts. *Attenwrthe* 1001. 'Enclosure of a man called Atta'. OE pers. name + *worth*.

Aubourn Lincs. *Aburne* 1086 (DB), *Alburn* 1275. 'Stream where alder-trees grow'. OE *alor* + *burna*.

Auchinleck E. Ayr. *Auechinlec* 1239. 'Field of the flat stones'. Gaelic *achadh* + *leac*.

Auchterarder Perth. *Vchterardouere* c.1200. 'Upland of high water'. Gaelic *uachdar* + *ard* + *dobhar*.

Auchtermuchty Fife. *Vchtermuckethin* c.1210. 'Upland of the pig place'. Gaelic *uachdar* + *muccatu*.

Auckland, Bishop, *Auckland, St Helen* & *Auckland, West* Durham. *Alclit* c.1040. Probably a Celtic name meaning 'rock or hill on a river called Clyde ("the cleansing one")'. Clyde was probably the original name of the River Gaunless (from OScand. **gagnlauss* 'unprofitable one'). Later distinguishing affixes from possession by the bishop of Durham and from the church dedication to St Helen.

Auckley S. Yorks. *Alchelie* 1086 (DB). 'Woodland clearing of a man called Alca or *Alha'. OE pers. name + *lēah*.

Aucloggeen (*Áth Cloigín*) Galway. 'Ford of the little bell'.

Audenshaw Gtr. Manch. *Aldwynshawe* c.1200. 'Copse of a man called Aldwine'. OE pers. name + *sceaga*.

Audlem Ches. *Aldelime* 1086 (DB). 'Old *Lyme*', or 'the part of *Lyme* belonging to a man called Alda'. OE *ald* or OE pers. name + old Celtic district name *Lyme* probably meaning 'elm-tree region'.

Audley Staffs. *Aldidelege* 1086 (DB). 'Woodland clearing of a woman called Aldgȳth'. OE pers. name + *lēah*.

Aughall (*Eochaill*) Tipperary. 'Yew wood'.

Aughamullen (*Achadh Ó Maoláin**) Tyrone. *Aghmoylan* 1609. 'Ó Maoláin's field'.

Augher (*Eochair*) Tyrone. *Ogher* c.1655. 'Border'.

Aughil (*Eochaill*) Derry. 'Yew wood'.

Aughinish Island (*Eachinis*) Galway, Limerick. 'Horse island'.

Aughnacloy (*Achadh na Cloiche*) Tyrone. *Aghenecloy* c.1655. 'Field of the stone'.

Aughnagomaun (*Achadh na gComán*) Tipperary. 'Hurling field'.

Aughnahoy (*Achadh na hÁithe*) Antrim. 'Field of the kiln'.

Aughnanure (*Achadh an Iúr*) Galway. 'Field of the yew'.

Aughnasheelan (*Achadh na Síleann*) Leitrim. 'Field of the withies'.

Aughrim (*Eachroim*) Derry, Galway, Wexford. 'Horse ridge'.

Aughris Head (*Ceann Eachrois*) Sligo. 'Horse promontory'.

Aughton, 'farmstead where oak-trees grow', OE *āc* + *tūn*: **Aughton** E. R. Yorks. *Actun* 1086 (DB). **Aughton** Lancs., near Lancaster. *Acheton* 1212. **Aughton** Lancs., near Ormskirk. *Achetun* 1086 (DB). **Aughton** S. Yorks. *Actone* 1086 (DB).

Aughvolyshane (*Áth Bhuaile Shéain*) Tipperary. 'Ford of Seán's milking place'.

Ault Hucknall Derbys., *see* HUCKNALL.

Aultbea Highland. 'Stream where birch trees grow'. Gaelic *allt* + *beithe*.

Aunsby Lincs. *Ounesbi* 1086 (DB), *Outhenby* 1281. Probably 'farmstead or village of a man called Authunn'. OScand. pers. name + *bý*. Alternatively the first element may be OScand. *authn* 'uncultivated land, deserted farm'.

Aust S. Glos. *Austan* 794. Possibly from Latin *Augusta*, perhaps alluding to the crossing of the River Severn here used by the Roman Second Legion, the *Legio Augusta*. Alternatively from the Latin pers. name *Augustinus*.

Austerfield S. Yorks. *Eostrefeld* c.715, *Oustrefeld* 1086 (DB). 'Open land with a sheepfold'. OE *eowestre* + *feld*.

Austrey Warwicks. *Alduluestreow* 958, *Aldulvestreu* 1086 (DB). 'Tree of a man called Ealdwulf'. OE pers. name + *trēow*.

Austwick N. Yorks. *Ousteuuic* 1086 (DB). 'East dwelling or dairy-farm'. OScand. *austr* + OE *wīc*.

Authorpe, 'outlying farmstead or hamlet of a man called Ag(g)i', OScand. pers. name + *thorp*: **Authorpe** Lincs. *Agetorp* 1086 (DB). **Authorpe Row** Lincs. *Aghetorp* c.1115.

Avaghon, Lough (*Loch an Meatháin*) Monaghan. 'Lake of the saplings'.

Avalbane (*Abhall Bán*) Monaghan. 'White orchard'.

Avebury Wilts. *Aureberie* 1086 (DB), *Aveberia* c.1180. Probably 'stronghold of a man called Afa'. OE pers. name + *burh* (dative *byrig*).

Aveley Essex. *Aluitheleam* 1086 (DB). 'Woodland clearing of a woman called Ælfgȳth'. OE pers. name + *lēah*.

Avening Glos. *Æfeningum* 896, *Aveninge* 1086 (DB). '(Settlement of) the people living by the River *Avon*'. Celtic river-name (perhaps the original name of the stream here, meaning simply 'river') + OE *-ingas*.

Averham Notts. *Aigrun* 1086 (DB). Probably '(place by) the floods or high tides' (with reference to the Trent bore). OE *ēgor* in a dative plural form *ēgrum*.

Aveton Gifford Devon. *Avetone* 1086 (DB), *Aveton Giffard* 1276. 'Farmstead on the River *Avon*'. Celtic river-name (meaning simply 'river') + OE *tūn* + manorial affix from the Giffard family, here in the 13th cent.

Aviemore Highland. 'Big hill face'. Gaelic *aghaid* + *mór*.

Avington Berks. *Avintone* 1086 (DB). 'Estate associated with a man called Afa'. OE pers. name + *-ing-* + *tūn*.

Avoca (*Abhóca*) (river) Wicklow. The name was adopted from Ptolemy's *Oboka* (2nd cent.) for a length of the AVONMORE.

Avon, old river-name found several times in England, from a Celtic word meaning simply 'river'. Of these, the Bristol or Lower **Avon** gives name to AVONMOUTH; the Wilts./Hants. **Avon** to AVON, NETHERAVON, and UPAVON; the Devon **Avon** to AVETON GIFFORD; the Glos./Warwicks. **Avon** to STRATFORD UPON AVON.

Avon Hants. *Avere* 1086 (DB). Named from the River Avon, see previous entry.

Avon Dassett Warwicks., *see* DASSETT.

Avonbeg (*An Abhainn Bheag*) (river) Wicklow. 'The little river'. The name contrasts with the AVONMORE.

Avonmore (*An Abhainn Mhór*) Cork, Sligo, Wicklow. 'The big river'.

Avonmouth Brist., a modern port at the mouth of the River Avon (*Afenemuthan* 10th cent.). Celtic river-name (*see* AVON) + OE *mūtha*.

Awbeg (*Abha Bheag*) Cork, Limerick. 'Little river'.

Awbridge Hants. *Abedric* 1086 (DB). 'Ridge of the abbot'. OE *abbod* + *hrycg*.

Awe, Loch Arg. *Aba* 700. 'Loch of (the River) Awe'. Gaelic *loch*. The Celtic river name means 'river'.

Awliscombe Devon. *Aulescome* 1086 (DB). Probably 'valley near the fork of a river'. OE *āwel* + *cumb*.

Awre Glos. *Avre* 1086 (DB). Probably '(place at) the alder-tree'. OE *alor*.

Awsworth Notts. *Ealdeswyrthe* 1002, *Eldesvorde* 1086 (DB). 'Enclosure of a man called *Eald*'. OE pers. name + *worth*.

Axbridge Somerset. *Axanbrycg* 10th cent. 'Bridge over the River Axe'. Celtic river-name (meaning uncertain) + OE *brycg*.

Axford Wilts. *Axeford* 1184. 'Ford by the ash-trees'. OE *æsc* + *ford*.

Axminster Devon. *Ascanmynster* late 9th cent., *Aixeministra* 1086 (DB). 'Monastery or large church by the River Axe'. Celtic river-name + OE *mynster*.

Axmouth Devon. *Axanmuthan* c.880, *Alsemuda* 1086 (DB). 'Mouth of the River Axe'. Celtic river-name + OE *mūtha*.

Aycliffe Durham. *Aclea* c.1085. 'Oak-tree wood or clearing'. OE *āc* + *lēah*.

Aylburton Glos. *Ailbricton* 12th cent. 'Farmstead or village of a man called Æthelbeorht'. OE pers. name + *tūn*.

Ayle Northum., named from the river on which it stands, Ayle Burn (*Alne* 1347), a Celtic river-name of uncertain meaning.

Aylesbeare Devon. *Ailesberga* 1086 (DB). 'Grove of a man called Ægel'. OE pers. name + *bearu*.

Aylesbury Bucks. *Ægelesburg* late 9th cent., *Eilesberia* 1086 (DB). 'Stronghold of a man called *Ægel'. OE pers. name + *burh* (dative *byrig*).

Aylesby NE. Lincs. *Alesbi* 1086 (DB). 'Farmstead or village of a man called Áli'. OScand. pers. name + *bý*.

Aylesford Kent. *Æglesforda* 10th cent., *Ailesford* 1086 (DB). 'Ford of a man called *Ægel'. OE pers. name + *ford*.

Aylesham Kent. *Elisham* 1367. Possibly 'homestead or enclosure of a man called Ægel'. OE pers. name + *hām* or *hamm*.

Aylestone Leics. *Ailestone* 1086 (DB). 'Farmstead or village of a man called *Ægel'. OE pers. name + *tūn*.

Aylmerton Norfolk. *Almartune* 1086 (DB). 'Farmstead or village of a man called Æthelmǣr'. OE pers. name + *tūn*.

Aylsham Norfolk. *Ailesham* 1086 (DB). 'Homestead of a man called *Ægel'. OE pers. name + *hām*.

Aylton Heref. & Worcs. *Aileuetona* 1138. 'Farmstead or village of a woman called Æthelgifu'. OE pers. name + *tūn*.

Aymestrey Heref. & Worcs. *Elmodestreu* 1086 (DB). 'Tree of a man called Æthelmund'. OE pers. name + *trēow*.

Aynho Northants. *Aienho* 1086 (DB). 'Hillspur of a man called *Æga'. OE pers. name (genitive *-n*) + *hōh*.

Ayot *St Lawrence* & *Ayot St Peter* Herts. *Aiegete* c.1060, *Aiete* 1086 (DB). 'Gap or pass of a man called *Æga'. OE pers. name + *geat*. Distinguishing affixes from the dedications of the churches at the two places.

Ayr S. Ayr. *Ar* 1177. '(Mouth of the river) Ayr'. The Celtic river name means simply 'river'. Ayr was formerly known as *Inverayr*, but the 'mouth' element (Gaelic *inbhir*) was dropped.

Aysgarth N. Yorks. *Echescard* 1086 (DB). 'Gap or open place where oak-trees grow'. OScand. *eiki* + *skarth*.

Ayston Rutland. *Æthelstanestun* 1046. 'Farmstead or village of a man called Æthelstān'. OE pers. name + *tūn*.

Aythorpe Roding Essex, *see* RODING.

Ayton, 'farmstead or estate on a river', OE *ēa* (modified by OScand. *ā*) + *tūn*: **Ayton, East** & **Ayton, West** N. Yorks. *Atune* 1086 (DB). **Ayton, Great** & **Ayton, Little** N. Yorks. *Atun* 1086 (DB).

Azerley N. Yorks. *Asserle* 1086 (DB). 'Woodland clearing of a man called Atsurr'. OScand. pers. name + OE *lēah*.

B

Babbacombe Devon. *Babbecumbe c.*1200. 'Valley of a man called Babba'. OE pers. name + *cumb*.

Babcary Somerset. *Babba Cari* 1086 (DB). 'Estate on the River Cary held by a man called Babba'. OE pers. name + Celtic or pre-Celtic river-name (*see* CARY FITZPAINE).

Babraham Cambs. *Badburgham* 1086 (DB). 'Homestead or village of a woman called *Beaduburh'. OE pers. name + *hām*.

Babworth Notts. *Baburde* 1086 (DB). 'Enclosure of a man called Babba'. OE pers. name + *worth*.

Backbarrow Cumbria. *Bakbarowe* 1537. 'Hill with a ridge'. OE *bæc* + *beorg*.

Backford Ches. *Bacfort* 1150. 'Ford by a ridge'. OE *bæc* + *ford*.

Backwell N. Som. *Bacoile |sic|* 1086 (DB), *Bacwell* 1202. 'Spring or stream near a ridge'. OE *bæc* + *wella*.

Backworth Tyne & Wear. *Bacwrth* 12th cent. 'Enclosure of a man called Bacca'. OE pers. name + *worth*.

Baconsthorpe Norfolk. *Baconstorp* 1086 (DB). 'Outlying farmstead or hamlet of a family called Bacon'. Norman surname + OScand. *thorp*.

Bacton, 'farmstead of a man called Bacca', OE pers. name + *tūn*: **Bacton** Heref. & Worcs. *Bachetone* 1086 (DB). **Bacton** Norfolk. *Baketuna* 1086 (DB). **Bacton** Suffolk. *Bachetuna* 1086 (DB).

Bacup Lancs. *Fulebachope c.*1200, *Bacop* 1324. 'Valley by a ridge'. OE *bæc* + *hop* (prefixed by OE *fūl* 'foul, muddy' in the early spelling).

Badbury Wilts. *Baddeburi* 955. Probably 'stronghold of a man called Badda'. OE pers. name + *burh* (dative *byrig*).

Badby Northants. *Baddanbyrig* 944, *Badebi* 1086 (DB). Identical in origin with the previous name, though the second element was replaced at an early date by OScand. *bý* 'farmstead, village'.

Baddeley Green Staffs. *Baddilige* 1227. 'Woodland clearing of a man called Badda'. OE pers. name + *lēah*.

Baddesley, 'woodland clearing of a man called *Bæddi', OE pers. name + *lēah*: **Baddesley Ensor** Warwicks. *Bedeslei* 1086 (DB), *Baddesley Endeshouer* 1327. Manorial affix from the de Edneshoure family (from EDENSOR), here in the 13th cent. **Baddesley, North** Hants. *Bedeslei* 1086 (DB).

Baddow, Great & *Baddow, Little* Essex. *Beadewan c.*975, *Baduuen* 1086 (DB). Probably a Celtic river-name (an old name for the River Chelmer), of uncertain origin and meaning.

Badenoch (district) Highland. *Badenach* 1229. 'Submerged land'. Gaelic *bàithteanach*. The region lies to the south of the river Spey, which is liable to flood.

Badger Shrops. *Beghesovre* 1086 (DB). 'Hillspur of a man called *Bæcg'. OE pers. name + *ofer*.

Badgeworth, *Badgworth*, 'enclosure of a man called *Bæcga', OE pers. name + *worth*: **Badgeworth** Glos. *Beganwurthan* 862, *Beiewrda* 1086 (DB). **Badgworth** Somerset. *Bagewerre* 1086 (DB).

Badingham Suffolk. *Badincham* 1086 (DB). 'Homestead or village associated with a man called *Bēada'. OE pers. name + *-ing-* + *hām*.

Badlesmere Kent. *Badelesmere* 1086 (DB). Probably 'pool of a man called *Bæddel'. OE pers. name + *mere*.

Badminton, Great & *Badminton, Little* S. Glos. *Badimyncgtun* 972, *Madmintune |sic|* 1086 (DB). 'Estate associated with a man called Baduhelm'. OE pers. name + *-ing-* + *tūn*.

Badsey Heref. & Worcs. *Baddeseia* 709, *Badesei* 1086 (DB). 'Island, or dry ground in marsh, of a man called *Bæddi'. OE pers. name + *ēg*.

Badsworth W. Yorks. *Badesuuorde* 1086 (DB). 'Enclosure of a man called Bæddi'. OE pers. name + *worth*.

Badwell Ash Suffolk. *Badewell* 1254, *Badewelle Asfelde* 13th cent. 'Spring or stream of a man called Bada'. OE pers. name + *wella* + later affix from shortened form of ASHFIELD.

Bae Cinmel. *See* KINMEL BAY.

Bae Colwyn. *See* COLWYN BAY.

Bag Enderby Lincs., *see* ENDERBY.

Bagborough, West Somerset. *Bacganbeorg* 904, *Bageberge* 1086 (DB). Probably 'hill of a man called Bacga'. OE pers. name + *beorg*.

Bagby N. Yorks. *Baghebi* 1086 (DB). 'Farmstead or village of a man called Baggi'. OScand. pers. name + *bý*.

Bagendon Glos. *Benwedene |sic|* 1086 (DB), *Baggingeden* 1220. 'Valley of the family or followers of a man called *Bæcga'. OE pers. name + *-inga-* + *denu*.

Baginton Warwicks. *Badechitone* 1086 (DB). 'Estate associated with a man called Badeca'. OE pers. name + *-ing-* + *tūn*.

Baglan Neat. *Bagelan* 1199. '(Church of) Baglan'. From the dedication of the church to St Baglan.

Bagley Shrops. *Bageleia c.*1090. Probably 'wood or clearing frequented by badgers'. OE **bagga* + *lēah*.

Bagnall Staffs. *Badegenhall* 1273. Probably 'nook of land of a man called Badeca'. OE pers. name (genitive *-n*) + *halh*.

Bagshot Surrey. *Bagsheta* 1164. 'Projecting piece of land frequented by badgers'. OE **bagga* + *scēat*.

Bagshot Wilts. *Bechesgete* 1086 (DB). 'Gate or gap of a man called *Beocc'. OE pers. name + *geat*.

Bagthorpe Norfolk. *Bachestorp* 1086 (DB). Probably 'outlying farmstead or hamlet of a man called Bakki or Bacca'. OScand. or OE pers. name + OScand. *thorp*.

Bagworth Leics. *Bageworde* 1086 (DB). 'Enclosure of a man called *Bæcga*. OE pers. name + *worth*.

Baildon W. Yorks. *Bægeltune*, *Bældune* c.1030, *Beldune* 1086 (DB). 'Circle hill'. OE *bægel* + *dūn*.

Baile Átha Cliath. See DUBLIN.

Bailehaise (*Béal Átha hÉis*) Cavan. (*go*) *Béal Átha Haeis* 1644. 'Ford-mouth of the track'.

Baileysmill (*Muileann Bháille*) Down. *Bailey's Mill* 1814. 'Bailey's mill'.

Bailieborough (*Coill an Chollaigh*) Cavan. *Kilcothie al. Bailie-Borrow* 1629. 'Bailie's town'. William *Bailie* built Bailieborough Castle here in 1610. The Irish name means 'wood of the boar'.

Bainbridge N. Yorks. *Bainebrigg* 1218. 'Bridge over the River Bain'. OScand. river-name ('the short or helpful one') + OE *brycg*.

Bainton Cambs. *Badingtun* c.980. 'Estate associated with a man called Bada'. OE pers. name + *-ing-* + *tūn*.

Bainton E. R. Yorks. *Bagentone* 1086 (DB). 'Estate associated with a man called Bǣga'. OE pers. name + *-ing-* + *tūn*.

Bakewell Derbys. *Badecanwelle* 949, *Badequella* 1086 (DB). 'Spring or stream of a man called Badeca'. OE pers. name + *wella*.

Bala Gwyd. 'Outlet'. *la Bala* 1331, *the Bala* 1582. Welsh *bala*. The town is at the point where the Dee leaves Bala Lake, whose Welsh name is *Llyn Tegid*, 'Tegid's lake' (pers. name + Welsh *llyn*).

Balbane (*Baile Bán*) Donegal. 'White townland'.

Balboru (*Béal Boromha*) Clare. 'Mouth of the (river) Borumha'.

Balbriggan (*Baile Brigín*) Dublin. 'Brigín's townland'.

Balcombe W. Sussex. *Balecumba* late 11th cent. Possibly 'valley of a man called Bealda'. OE pers. name + *cumb*. Alternatively the first element may be OE *bealu* 'evil, calamity'.

Balcomie Fife. *Balcolmie* 1253. 'Estate of (Gille) Colm'. Gaelic *baile*.

Baldersby N. Yorks. *Baldrebi* 1086 (DB). 'Farmstead or village of a man called Baldhere'. OE pers. name + OScand. *bý*.

Balderstone Lancs. *Baldreston* 1323. 'Farmstead of a man called Baldhere'. OE pers. name + *tūn*.

Balderton Notts. *Baldretune* 1086 (DB). Identical in origin with the previous name.

Baldock Herts. *Baldoce* c.1140. This place was founded in the 12th cent. by the Knights Templars, who called it *Baldac*, the OFrench form for the Arabian city of Baghdad.

Baldon, Marsh & *Baldon, Toot* Oxon. *Balde(n)done* 1086 (DB), *Mersse Baldindon* 1241, *Totbaldindon* 1316. 'Hill of a man called Bealda'. OE pers. name + *dūn*. Distinguishing affixes from OE *mersc* 'marsh' and *tōt(e)* 'look-out hill'.

Baldoyle (*Baile Dúill*) Dublin. 'Dúghall's townland'.

Baldwinholme Cumbria. *Baldewinholme* 1278. 'Island or water-meadow of a man called Baldwin'. OGerman pers. name + OScand. *holmr*.

Bale Norfolk. *Bathele* 1086 (DB). 'Woodland clearing where there are springs used for bathing'. OE *bæth* + *lēah*.

Balemartine Arg (Tiree). *Balmartin* 1654. 'Martin's village'. Gaelic *baile*.

Balerno Edin. *Belhernoch* 1280. 'Townland where sloe trees grow'. Gaelic *baile* + *airneach*.

Balfeddock (*Baile Feadóg*) Louth. 'Townland of the plover'.

Balfour Orkn (Shapinsay). 'Farm with pasture'. Gaelic *baile* + *pór*.

Balgowan Highland. 'Farm of the smith'. Gaelic *baile* + *gobhan*.

Balgown Highland (Skye). 'Farm of the smith'. Gaelic *baile* + *gobhan*.

Balham Gtr. London. *Bælgenham* 957, *Belgeham* 1086 (DB). Probably 'smooth or rounded enclosure'. OE *bealg* + *hamm*.

Balintore Highland. 'Village where bleaching is done'. Gaelic *baile* + *todhair*.

Balkholme E. R. Yorks. *Balcholm* 1199. 'Island with a low ridge', or 'island of a man called Balki'. OE *balca* or OScand. pers. name + OScand. *holmr*.

Balla (*Balla*) Mayo. 'Spring'.

Ballachulish Highland. 'Townland by the strait'. Gaelic *baile* + *caolas* (genitive *chaolais*).

Ballacolla (*Baile Cholla*) Laois. 'Colla's townland'.

Balladian (*Bealach an dá Éan*) Monaghan. 'Pass of the two birds'.

Ballagan Point (*Gob Bhaile Uí Ágáin*) Louth. 'Point of the townland of Ó Ágán'.

Ballagh (*Bealach*) Fermanagh, Galway, Limerick, Tipperary. 'Pass'.

Ballaghaderreen (*Bealach an Doirín*) Roscommon. 'Pass of the little oak grove'.

Ballaghanery (*Bealach an Aoire*) Down. 'Pass of the shepherd'.

Ballaghkeen (*Bealach Caoin*) Wexford. 'Smooth pass'.

Ballaghmoon (*Bealach Mughna*) Carlow. 'Mughan's pass'.

Ballanagare (*Béal Átha na gCarr*) Roscommon. 'Ford-mouth of the carts'.

Ballanruan (*Baile an Ruáin*) Clare. 'Townland of the red area'.

Ballantrae S. Ayr. 'Village on the shore'. Gaelic *baile* + *traigh*.

Ballard (*Baile Ard*) Offaly. 'High townland'.

Ballater Aber. *Balader* 1704, *Ballader* 1716. Origin obscure, but traditionally 'Water pass'. Gaelic *bealach* + *dobhar*. The name originally applied to the pass where the Ballater Burn flows through the mountains.

Balleen (*Bailín*) Kerry. 'Little townland'.

Ballickmoyler (*Baile Mhic Mhaoilir*) Laois. 'Townland of Mac Maoilir'.

Balliggan (*Baile Uí Uiginn*) Down. *Ballyhiggin* 1623. 'Townland of Ó hUiginn'.

Ballina (*Béal an Átha*) Mayo, Tipperary. 'Ford-mouth'.

Ballinaboy (*Béal Átha na Bá[ighe]*) Galway. 'Ford-mouth of the bay'.

Ballinabrackey (*Buaile na Bréachmhaí*) Meath. 'Milking place of the wolf plain'.

Ballinabranagh (*Baile na mBreatnach*) Carlow. 'Townland of the Breatnachs'.

Ballinacarriga (*Béal na Carraige*) Cork. 'Mouth of the rocks'.

Ballinacarrow (*Baile na Cora*) Sligo. 'Townland of the weir'.

Ballinaclash (*Baile na Claise*) Wicklow. 'Townland of the ravine'.

Ballinaclashet (*Baile na Claise*) Cork. 'Townland of the ravine'.

Ballinaclough (*Baile na Cloiche*) Tipperary. 'Townland of the stone'.

Ballinacor (*Baile na Cora*) Wicklow. 'Townland of the weir'.

Ballinacurra (*Baile na Cora*) Cork, Limerick. 'Townland of the weir'.

Ballinadee (*Baile na Daibhche*) Cork. 'Townland of the well'.

Ballinafad (*Béal an Átha Fada*) Sligo. 'Mouth of the long ford'.

Ballinafid (*Baile na Feide*) Westmeath. 'Townland of the end'.

Ballinagar (*Béal Átha na gCarr*) Offaly. 'Ford-mouth of the carts'.

Ballinaglerach (*Baile na gCléireach*) Leitrim. 'Townland of the clerics'.

Ballinagree (*Baile na Graí*) Cork. 'Townland of the stud'.

Ballinahinch (*Baile na hInse*) Tipperary. 'Townland of the water meadow'.

Ballinakill (*Baile na Coille*) Laois. 'Townland of the wood'.

Ballinalack (*Béal Átha na Leac*) Westmeath. 'Ford-mouth of the flagstones'.

Ballinalea (*Buaile na Lao*) Wicklow. 'Milking place of the calves'.

Ballinalee (*Béal Átha na Lao*) Longford. 'Ford-mouth of the calves'.

Ballinamallard (*Béal Átha na Mallacht*) Fermanagh. 'Ford-mouth of the curses'.

Ballinamara (*Baile na Marbh*) Kilkenny. 'Townland of the dead'.

Ballinameen (*Béal an Átha Mín*) Roscommon. 'Mouth of the smooth ford'.

Ballinamuck (*Béal Átha na Muc*) Longford. 'Ford-mouth of the pigs'.

Ballinard (*Baile an Aird*) Tipperary. 'Townland of the height'.

Ballinascarty (*Béal na Scairte*) Cork. 'Mouth of the thicket'.

Ballinascorny (*Baile na Scórnad*) Dublin. 'Townland of the gullet'.

Ballinaskeagh (*Baile na Sceach*) Down. 'Townland of the thorns'.

Ballinasloe (*Béal Átha na Sluaighe*) Galway. 'Ford-mouth of the hostings'.

Ballinaspick (*Baile an Easpaig*) Waterford. 'Townland of the bishop'.

Ballinattin (*Baile na Aiteann*) Tipperary, Waterford. 'Townland of the gorse'.

Ballinchalla (*Baile an Chaladh*) Mayo. 'Townland of the landing place'.

Ballinclashet (*Baile na Claise*) Cork. 'Townland of the ravine'.

Ballincloher (*Baile an Cloichir*) Kerry. 'Townland of the stony place'.

Ballincollig (*Baile an Chollaigh*) Cork. 'Townland of the boar'.

Ballincrea (*Baile an Chraoibh*) Kilkenny. 'Townland of the sacred tree'.

Ballincurrig (*Baile an Churraigh*) Cork. 'Townland of the marsh'.

Ballindaggan (*Baile an Daingin*) Waterford. 'Townland of the fortress'.

Ballindangan (*Baile an Daingin*) Cork. 'Townland of the fortress'.

Ballindarragh (*Baile na Dara*) Fermanagh. 'Townland of the oak'.

Ballinderreen (*Baile an Doirín*) Galway. 'Townland of the little oak grove'.

Ballinderry (*Baile an Doire*) Antrim, Tipperary. 'Townland of the oak wood'.

Ballindrait (*Baile an Droichid*) Donegal. *Ballendraite* c.1655. 'Townland of the bridge'.

Ballinea (*Béal an Átha*) Westmeath. 'Ford-mouth'.

Ballineddan (*Baile an Fheadáin*) Wicklow. 'Townland of the little stream'.

Ballineen (*Béal Átha Fhinín*) Cork. 'Ford-mouth of Finín'.

Ballinenagh (*Baile an Aonaigh*) Limerick. 'Townland of the assembly'.

Ballinfull (*Baile an Phoill*) Sligo. 'Townland of the pool'.

Ballingaddy (*Baile an Ghadaí*) Limerick. 'Townland of the thief'.

Ballingar (*Béal Átha na gCarr*) Offaly. 'Ford-mouth of the carts'.

Ballingarrane (*Baile an Gharráin*) Limerick. 'Townland of the grove'.

Ballingarry (*Baile an Gharraí*) Limerick, Tipperary. 'Townland of the garden'.

Ballingeary (*Béal Átha an Ghaorthaidh*) Cork. 'Ford-mouth of the wooded valley'.

Ballingham Heref. & Worcs. *Badelingeham* 1215. 'Homestead of the family or followers of a man called *Badela*', or 'homestead at the place associated with *Badela*'. OE pers. name + -*inga*- or -*ing* + *hām*. Alternatively the second element may be OE *hamm* 'land in a river-bend'.

Ballinglen (*Baile an Ghleanna*) Wicklow. 'Townland of the valley'.

Ballingurteen (*Baile an Ghoirtín*) Cork. 'Townland of the little tilled field'.

Ballinhassig (*Béal Átha an Cheasaigh*) Cork. 'Ford-mouth of the wicker causeway'.

Ballinkelleen (*Baile an Chillín*) Carlow. 'Townland of the little church'.

Ballinleeny (*Baile an Laighnigh*) Limerick. 'Townland of the Laighneach'.

Ballinlough (*Baile an Locha*) Meath, Roscommon. 'Townland of the lake'.

Ballinlug (*Baile an Loig*) Galway. 'Townland of the hollow'.

Ballinluska (*Baile an Loiscthe*) Cork. 'Townland of the burnt ground'.

Ballinran (*Baile an Raithin*) Down. *Ballynynranny* 1540. 'Townland of the ferns'.

Ballinridderra (*Baile an Ridire*) Westmeath. 'Townland of the knight'.

Ballinrobe (*Baile an Róba*) Mayo. 'Town of the (river) Róba'.

Ballinskelligs (*Baile an Sceilg*) Kerry. 'Townland of the rocks'.

Ballinspittle (*Béal Átha an Spidéil*) Cork. 'Mouth of the fort of the hospital'.

Ballintaggart (*Baile an tSagairt*) Armagh, Down, Kerry. 'Townland of the priest'.

Ballintannig (*Baile an tSeanaigh*) Cork. 'Townland of the fox'.

Ballinteean (*Baile a' tSiodháin*) Mayo. 'Townland of the fairy hill'.

Ballinteer (*Baile an tSaoir*) Derry, Dublin. 'Townland of the craftsman'.

Ballintemple (*Baile an Teampaill*) Cork. 'Townland of the church'.

Ballintlieve (*Baile an tSléibhe*) Down, Meath. 'Townland of the mountain'.

Ballintober (*Baile an Tobair*) Mayo, Roscommon. 'Townland of the well'.

Ballintogher (*Baile an Tóchair*) Sligo. 'Townland of the causeway'.

Ballintoy (*Baile an Tuaighe*) Antrim. *Ballenatoy* 1603. Possibly 'townland of the ruler of the tuath'. A *tuath* was a petty Irish kingdom.

Ballintra (*Baile an tSratha*) Donegal. *Baile an tSrátha* 1934. 'Townland of the river meadow'.

Ballintrillick (*Béal Átha an Trí Liag*) Sligo. 'Ford-mouth of the three flagstones'.

Ballintubbert (*Baile na Tiobrad*) Laois. 'Townland of the well'.

Ballinturly (*Baile an Turlaigh*) Roscommon. 'Townland of the fen'.

Ballinunty (*Baile an Fhantaigh*) Tipperary. 'Fant's townland'.

Ballinure (*Baile an Iúir*) Galway, Tipperary. 'Townland of the yew'.

Ballinvana (*Baile an Bhána*) Limerick. 'Townland of the green field'.

Ballinvinny (*Baile an Mhuine*) Cork. 'Townland of the thicket'.

Ballinvonear (*Baile an Mhóinéir*) Cork. 'Townland of the meadow'.

Ballinwully (*Baile an Mhullaigh*) Roscommon. 'Townland of the summit'.

Ballisk (*Baile Uisce*) Down. 'Townland of the water'.

Ballitore (*Béal Átha an Tuair*) Kildare. 'Ford-mouth of the bleach green'.

Ballivor (*Baile Íomhair*) Meath. 'Íomhar's townland'.

Ballmacoda (*Baile Mhac Óda*) Cork. 'Mac Códa's townland'.

Ballnaclogh (*Baile na Cloiche*) Tipperary. 'Townland of the stone'.

Balloo (*Baile Aodha*) Down. *Ballow* 1605. 'Aodh's townland'.

Balloughmore (*Bealach Mór*) Laois. 'Big pass'.

Balloughter (*Baile Uachtair*) Wexford. 'Upper townland'.

Ballougry (*Baile Dhúdhoire*) Derry. *Ballidowgry* 1637. 'Townland of the black oak wood'.

Ballsmill (*Baile na gCléireach*) Armagh. *Ballinaglera* 1838. 'Ball's mill'. Thomas Ball was granted land here in the 17th cent. The Irish name means 'townland of the clerics'.

Ballyaghlis (*Baile na hEachlaisce*) Down. *Ballyhaghliske* 1625. 'Townland of the horse enclosure'.

Ballyagran (*Béal Átha Grean*) Limerick. 'Ford-mouth of the gravel'.

Ballyallaght (*Baile Uí Allachta*) Antrim. 'Townland of Ó Allacht'.

Ballyallinan (*Baile Uí Áilleanáin*) Limerick. 'Townland of Ó hÁilleanáin'.

Ballyalton (*Baile Altúin*) Down. *Ballyawlton* 1547. 'Alton's townland'.

Ballyandreen (*Baile Aindrín*) Cork. 'Aindrín's townland'.

Ballyanne (*Baile Anna*) Wexford. 'Anna's townland'.

Ballyardle (*Baile Ardghail*) Down. *Bally Ardell* 1661. 'Ardel's townland'.

Ballybay (*Béal Átha Beithe*) Monaghan. *Balloghnebegh* 1591. 'Ford-mouth of the birch tree'.

Ballybeen (*Baile Bín*) Down. *Ballibeine* 1605. 'Bean's townland'.

Ballybeg (*Baile Beag*) Tipperary. 'Small townland'.

Ballyboden (*Baile Baodáin*) Dublin. 'Baodán's townland'.

Ballybofey (*Bealach Féich*) Donegal. *Srath Bó Diaich* 1548. 'Fiach's pass'.

Ballybogey (*Baile an Bhogaigh*) Antrim. *Ballyboggy* 1669. 'Townland of the swamp'.

Ballyboghal (*Baile Bachaille*) Dublin. 'Townland of the crozier'.

Ballybought (*Baile Bocht*) Antrim. 'Poor townland'.

Ballyboy (*Baile Átha Buí*) Offaly. 'Townland of the yellow ford'.

Ballyboyland (*Baile Uí Bhaolláin*) Antrim. *Bellebolan* c.1659. 'Townland of Ó Baollán'.

Ballybrack (*Baile Breac*) Dublin, Kerry, Tyrone. 'Speckled townland'.

Ballybrittas (*Baile Briotáis*) Laois. 'Townland of the wooden palisade'.

Ballybrood (*Baile Bhrúid*) Limerick. 'Townland of the ashes'.

Ballybrophy (*Baile Uí Bhróithe*) Laois. 'Townland of Ó Bróithe'.

Ballybunion (*Baile an Bhuinneánaigh*) Kerry. 'Buinnéan's townland'.

Ballycahill (*Bealach Achaille*) Tipperary. 'Pass of Achall'.

Ballycallan (*Baile Uí Challáin*) Kilkenny. 'Townland of Ó Calláin'.

Ballycanew (*Baile Uí Chonnmhaí*) Wexford. 'Townland of Ó Connmhaí'.

Ballycarnahan (*Baile Uí Chearnacháin*) Kerry. 'Ó Cearnacháin's townland'.

Ballycarny (*Baile Uí Chearnaigh*) Wexford. 'Townland of Ó Cearnaigh'.

Ballycarra (*Baile na Cora*) Mayo. 'Townland of the weir'.

Ballycarry (*Baile Cora*) Antrim. *Ballycarry* 1669. 'Townland of the weir'.

Ballycashin (*Baile Uí Chaisín*) Waterford. 'Ó Caisín's townland'.

Ballycassidy (*Baile Uí Chaiside*) Fermanagh. *Ballicashedy* 1659. 'Ó Caiside's townland'.

Ballycastle (*Baile an Chaisil*) Mayo. 'Townland of the stone fort'.

Ballycastle (*Baile Chaisleáin*) Antrim. *Baile Caislein* 1565. 'Townland of the castle'.

Ballyclare (*Bealach Cláir*) Antrim. *Balleclare* 1620. 'Pass of the plain'.

Ballyclerahan (*Baile Uí Chléireacháin*) Tipperary. 'Townland of Ó Cléireacháin'.

Ballyclery (*Baile Uí Chléirigh*) Galway. 'Townland of Ó Cléirigh'.

Ballyclogh (*Baile Cloch*) Cork. 'Townland of the stones'.

Ballycommon (*Baile Uí Chomáin*) Offaly, Tipperary. 'Townland of Ó Comán'.

Ballyconneely (*Baile Conaola*) Galway. 'Townland of Conaola'.

Ballyconnell (*Béal Átha Conaill*) Cavan. *Beallaconnell* 1630. 'Ford-mouth of Conall'.

Ballyconree (*Baile Con Raoi*) Galway. 'Townland of Cú Ruí'.

Ballycooge (*Baile Chuag*) Wicklow. 'Townland of the cuckoo'.

Ballycopeland (*Baile Chóplainn*) Down. *Ballicoppland* 1605. 'Copeland's townland'.

Ballycorick (*Béal Átha Chomhraic*) Clare. 'Ford-mouth of the confluence'.

Ballycotton (*Baile Choitín*) Cork. 'Coitín's townland'.

Ballycraddock (*Baile Chreadóig*) Waterford. 'Townland of the clay'.

Ballycrissane (*Baile Crosáin*) Galway. 'Townland of the cross'.

Ballycroghan (*Baile Cruacháin*) Down. 'Townland of the little rick'.

Ballycrossaun (*Baile Crosáin*) Galway. 'Townland of the cross'.

Ballycroy (*Baile Chruaiche*) Mayo. 'Townland of the rick'.

Ballycullane (*Baile Uí Choileáin*) Wexford. 'Ó Coileáin's townland'.

Ballyculter (*Baile Uí Choltair*) Down. *Balinculter* 1183. 'Ó Coltair's townland'.

Ballycumber (*Béal Átha Chomair*) Offaly. 'Ford-mouth of the confluence'.

Ballydaheen (*Baile Dáithín*) Cork. 'Dáthín's townland'.

Ballydangan (*Baile Daighean*) Roscommon. 'Townland of the stronghold'.

Ballydavid (*Baile Dháibhí*) Galway. 'Dóibhí's townland'.

Ballydavid (*Baile Dáibhí*) Kerry. 'Dáith's townland'.

Ballydehob (*Béal an dá Chab*) Cork. 'Mouth of the two openings'.

Ballydesmond (*Baile Deasumhan*) Cork. 'Town of south Munster'.

Ballydonegan (*Baile Uí Dhonnagáin*) Cork. 'Ó Donnagáin's townland'.

Ballydonohoe (*Baile Uí Dhonnchadha*) Kerry. 'Ó Donnchadha's townland'.

Ballydooley (*Baile Uí Dhúlaoich*) Roscommon. 'Townland of Ó Dūlaoich'.

Ballyduff (*An Baile Dubh*) Kerry, Waterford. 'The black townland'.

Ballydugan (*Baile Uí Dhúgáin*) Down. *Boile Í Dhubhagán* 1646. 'Ó Dúgáin's townland'.

Ballyeaston (*Baile Uistín*) Antrim. *Austin's town* 1306. 'Austin's townland'.

Ballyeighter (*Baile Íochtair*) Clare. 'Lower townland'.

Ballyengland (*Baile an Aingleontaigh*) Limerick. 'Townland of the Aingleontach'.

Ballyfarna (*Bealach Fearna*) Mayo. 'Pass of the alder'.

Ballyfarnon (*Béal Átha Fearnáin*) Roscommon. 'Ford-mouth of the alders'.

Ballyfeard (*Baile Feá Aird*) Cork. 'Townland of the high wood'.

Ballyfermot (*Baile Formaid*) Dublin. 'Townland of Formad'.

Ballyferriter (*Baile an Fheirtéaraigh*) Kerry. 'Ferriter's townland'.

Ballyfin (*An Baile Fionn*) Laois. 'The white townland'.

Ballyforan (*Béal Átha Feorainne*) Roscommon. 'Ford-mouth of the brink'.

Ballyfore (*Baile Fuar*) Offaly. 'Cold town'.

Ballyfoyle (*Baile an Phoill*) Kilkenny. 'Townland of the pool'.

Ballygalley (*Baile Geithligh*) Antrim. *Ballegelly* 1635. Possibly 'Geithleach's townland'.

Ballygar (*Béal Átha Ghártha*) Galway. 'Ford-mouth of the garden'.

Ballygarrett (*Baile Ghearóid*) Wexford. 'Gearóid's townland'.

Ballygarvan (*Baile Garbháin*) Cork. 'Garbhán's townland'.

Ballygawley (*Baile Uí Dhálaigh*) Sligo, Tyrone. 'Ó Dálaigh's townland'.

Ballyginniff (*Baile Gainimh*) Antrim. 'Sandy townland'.

Ballyglass (*Béal Átha Glas*) Westmeath. 'Ford-mouth of the streams'.

Ballyglass (*An Baile Glas*) Mayo. 'The grey townland'.

Ballyglunin (*Béal Átha Glúinín*) Galway. 'Ford-mouth of the little bend'.

Ballygomartin (*Baile Gharraí Mhairtín*) Antrim. 'Homestead of Martin's garden'.

Ballygorey (*Baile Guaire*) Kilkenny. 'Guaire's townland'.

Ballygormani (*Baile Uí Ghormáin*) Donegal. *Balligorman* c.1660. 'Ó Gormáin's townland'.

Ballygowan (*Baile Mhic Gabhann*) Down. *Balle-McGowen* 1623. 'Mac Gabhann's townland'.

Ballygrainey (*Baile na Gréine*) Down. *Ballinegrene* 1630. 'Townland of the sun'.

Ballygub (*Baile Gob*) Kilkenny. 'Townland of the snout'.

Ballyhack (*Baile Chac*) Wexford. 'Townland of excrement'.

Ballyhackamore (*Baile Hacamar*) Down. *Ballcakamer* 1620. 'Townland of the slob land'.

Ballyhaght (*Baile an Chéachta*) Limerick. 'Townland of the plough'.

Ballyhahill (*Baile dhá Thuile*) Limerick. 'Townland of the two floods'.

Ballyhalbert (*Baile Thalbóid*) Down. (*Ecclesia de*) *Talbetona* 1306. 'Talbot's townland'.

Ballyhale (*Baile Héil*) Kilkenny. 'Howel's townland'.

Ballyhar (*Baile Uí Aichir*) Kerry. 'Ó hAichir's townland'.

Ballyhean (*Béal Átha hÉin*) Mayo. 'Ford-mouth of the bird'.

Ballyheelan (*Bealach an Chaoláin*) Cavan. *Ballagheelan* 1734. 'Pass of the marshy stream'.

Ballyheerin (*Baile Uí Shírín*) Donegal. *Ballyherrinmore, Ballyherrinbegg* c.1660. 'Ó Sírín's townland'.

Ballyheige (*Baile Uí Thaidhg*) Kerry. 'Ó Taidhg's townland'.

Ballyhisky (*Bealach Uisce*) Tyrone. 'Pass of water'.

Ballyholme (*Baile Hóm*) Down. *Ballehum* 1603. 'Hóm's townland'.

Ballyhooly (*Baile Átha hÚlla*) Cork. 'Pass of the ford of the apple trees'.

Ballyhornan (*Baile Uí Chornáin*) Down. *Ballyhornan* 1636. 'Ó Cornáin's townland'.

Ballyhoura (*Bealach Abhradh*) Cork, Limerick. 'Pass of Feabhra'.

Ballyhugh (*Bealach Aodha*) Cavan. *Bellaghea* 1610. 'Aodh's pass'.

Ballyjamesduff (*Baile Shéamais Dhuibh*) Cavan. *Bally James Doough or Black James' town* c.1744. 'Townland of James Duff'. James Duff, Earl of Fife, was granted land here in the early 17th cent.

Ballykean (*Baile Uí Chéin*) Offaly. 'Ó Céin's townland'.

Ballykeel (*An Baile Caol*) Down. *Ballikeeleloghaghery* 1632. 'The narrow townland'.

Ballykeeran (*Bealach Caorthainn*) Westmeath. 'Pass of the rowan tree'.

Ballykelly (*Baile Uí Cheallaigh*) Derry. *Ballykellye* 1613. 'Ó Ceallaigh's townland'.

Ballykilbeg (*Baile na gCeall Beag*) Down. *Ballenagallbee* 1512. 'Townland of the little churches'.

Ballykillare (*Baile Cille Láir*) Down. 'Townland of the central church'.

Ballykinler (*Baile Coinnleora*) Down. *Ballicanlor* 1542. 'Townland of the candlestick'. Lands here were granted in c.1200 to Christchurch Cathedral, Dublin, for the upkeep of a perpetual light before the crucifix there.

Ballykinsella (*Baile an Chinsealaigh*) Waterford. 'Ó Cinsealaigh's townland'.

Ballyknockan (*Buaile an Chnocáin*) Wicklow. 'Milking place of the hillock'.

Ballylanders (*Baile an Londraigh*) Limerick. 'de Londra's townland'.

Ballylaneen (*Baile Uí Laithnín*) Waterford. 'Ó Laithnín's townland'.

Ballylar (*Baile Láir*) Donegal. 'Townland of the threshing floor'.

Ballyleny (*Baile Léana*) Armagh. *Ballylaney* 1661. 'Townland of the wet meadow'.

Ballylesson (*Baile na Leasán*) Down. *Ballenelassan*. 'Townland of the little forts'.

Ballylickey (*Béal Átha Leice*) Cork. 'Ford-mouth of the flagstone'.

Ballyliffin (*Baile Lifín*) Donegal. *Ballylaffin* 1608. 'Townland of the halfpenny'. The reference is perhaps to a land division.

Ballylinan (*Baile Uí Laigheanáin*) Laois. 'Ó Laigheanán's townland'.

Ballylintagh (*An Baile Linnteach*) Derry. *Bellylintach* 1663. 'The townland of pools'.

Ballylongford (*Béal Átha Longfoirt*) Kerry. 'Ford-mouth of the fortress'.

Ballylooby (*Béal Átha Lúbaigh*) Tipperary. 'Ford-mouth of the winding (river)'.

Ballyloughbeg (*Baile an Locha Beag*) Antrim. 'Townland of the small lake'.

Ballylumford (*Baile an Longfoirt*) Antrim. *Ballylemford* 1669. 'Townland of the fortress'.

Ballymacarbry (*Baile Mhac Cairbre*) Waterford. 'Mac Carbre's townland'.

Ballymacarret (*Baile Mhic Gearóid*) Down. *Bally McCarritt* 1623. 'Mac Gearóid's townland'.

Ballymacart (*Baile Mhac Airt*) Waterford. 'Mac Art's townland'.

Ballymacaw (*Baile Mhac Dháith*) Waterford. 'Mac Dáith's townland'.

Ballymacelligott (*Baile Mhic Eileagóid*) Kerry. 'Mac Eileagód's townland'.

Ballymackey (*Baile Uí Mhacaí*) Tipperary. 'Ó Macaí's townland'.

Ballymaconnelly (*Baile Mhic Conaíle*) Antrim. *Ballymaconnally* 1635. 'Mac Conaíle's townland'.

Ballymacurly (*Baile Mhic Thorlaigh*) Roscommon. 'Mac Thorlaigh's townland'.

Ballymacward (*Baile Mhic an Bhaird*) Galway. 'Townland of Mac an Bhard'.

Ballymadog (*Baile Mhadóg*) Cork. 'Madóg's townland'.

Ballymagan (*Baile MhicCionaoith*) Donegal. *Ballimcganny c.*1635. 'Mac Cionaoith's townland'.

Ballymagarry (*Baile mo Gharraí*) Antrim. 'Townland of my garden'.

Ballymagorry (*Baile Mhic Gofraidh*) Tyrone. *Ballemagorie* 1616. 'Mac Gofraidh's townland'.

Ballymagrorty (*Baile Mhic Robhartaigh*) Derry. *Ballym'roartie* 1604. 'Mac Robhartaigh's townland'.

Ballymaguigan (*Baile Mhic Guaigín*) Derry. *Ballymccuggin c.*1659. 'Mac Guaigín's townland'.

Ballymahon (*Baile Uí Mhatháin*) Longford. 'Ó Matháin's townland'.

Ballymakeery (*Baile Mhic Íre*) Cork. 'Mac Íre's townland'.

Ballymartin (*Baile Mhic Giolla Mhártain*) Down. *Ballymicgyll Mertyn* 1552. 'Townland of Mac Giolla Mhártain'.

Ballymartle (*Baile Mhairtéal*) Cork. 'Mairtéal's townland'.

Ballymascanlan (*Baile Mhic Scanláin*) Louth. 'Mac Scanlán's townland'.

Ballymena (*An Baile Meánach*) Antrim. *Ballymeanagh* 1626. 'The middle townland'.

Ballymoe (*Béal Átha Mó*) Galway, Roscommon. 'Ford-mouth of Mogh'.

Ballymoney (*Baile Monaidh*) Antrim. *Bali Monaid* 1412. 'Townland of the bog'.

Ballymoon (*Baile Móin*) Carlow. 'Townland of the bog'.

Ballymore (*Baile Mór*) Cork, Donegal, Kildare, Westmeath. 'Big townland'.

Ballymorris (*Baile Mhuiris*) Waterford. 'Muiris's townland'.

Ballymote (*Baile an Mhóta*) Sligo. 'Townland of the castle mound'.

Ballymoyle (*Baile Maol*) Wicklow. 'Bald townland'.

Ballymullen (*Baile an Mhuilinn*) Kerry. 'Townland of the mill'.

Ballymurn (*Baile Uí Mhurúin*) Wexford. 'Ó Murúin's townland'.

Ballymurphy (*Baile Uí Mhurchú*) Carlow. 'Ó Murchú's townland'.

Ballymurragh (*Baile Mhurchadha*) Limerick. 'Murchadh's townland'.

Ballymurray (*Baile Uí Mhuirigh*) Roscommon. 'Ó Muireadhaigh's townland'.

Ballynabola (*Baile na Buaile*) Wexford. 'Townland of the milking place'.

Ballynabrackey (*Buaile na Bréamhaí*) Meath. 'Milking place of the wolf plain'.

Ballynabragget (*Baile na Brád*) Down. *Ballynebrade* 1612. 'Townland of the valley'.

Ballynacally (*Baile na Caillí*) Clare. 'Townland of the hag'.

Ballynacargy (*Baile na Carraige*) Westmeath. 'Townland of the rock'.

Ballynacarriga (*Béal na Carraige*) Cork. 'Mouth of the rock'.

Ballynacarrigy (*Baile na Carraige*) Westmeath. 'Townland of the rock'.

Ballynacole (*Baile Niocóil*) Cork. 'Niocól's townland'.

Ballynacorr (*Baile na Cora*) Armagh. *Ballinecorrowe* 1610. 'Townland of the weir'.

Ballynacorra (*Baile na Cora*) Cork. 'Townland of the weir'.

Ballynacourty (*Baile na Cúirte*) Waterford. 'Townland of the mansion'.

Ballynadrumny (*Baile na Droimní*) Kildare. 'Townland of the ridge'.

Ballynafa (*Baile na Faiche*) Kildare. 'Townland of the green'.

Ballynafeigh (*Baile na Faiche*) Down. *Ballinefeigh* 1605. 'Townland of the green'.

Ballynafey (*Baile na Faiche*) Antrim. 'Townland of the green'.

Ballynafid (*Baile na Feide*) Westmeath. 'Townland of the runnel'.

Ballynafie (*Baile na Faiche*) Antrim. 'Townland of the green'.

Ballynagarrick (*Baile na gCarraig*) Down. *Bally-negaricke* 1611. 'Townland of the rocks'.

Ballynagaul (*Baile na nGall*) Waterford. 'Townland of the stones'.

Ballynageeragh (*Baile na gCaorach*) Down. 'Townland of the sheep'.

Ballynagore (*Béal Átha na nGabhar*) Westmeath. 'Ford-mouth of the goats'.

Ballynagree (*Baile na Graí*) Cork. 'Townland of the stud'.

Ballynaguilkee (*Baile na Giolcaí*) Waterford. 'Townland of the reeds'.

Ballynahatinna (*Baile na hAitinn*) Galway. 'Townland of the gorse'.

Ballynahatten (*Baile na hAitinn*) Down, Louth. 'Townland of the gorse'.

Ballynahinch (*Baile na hInse*) Down, Galway, Tipperary. 'Townland of the river meadow'.

Ballynahow (*Baile na hAbha*) Kerry. 'Townland of the river'.

Ballynahowen (*Buaile na hAbhann*) Westmeath. 'Milking place of the river'.

Ballynahown (*Buaile na hAbhann*) Galway, Westmeath. 'Milking place of the river'.

Ballynakill (*Baile na Cille*) Carlow. 'Townland of the church'.

Ballynamallaght (*Béal Átha na Mallacht*) Tyrone. 'Ford-mouth of the curses'.

Ballynameen (*Baile na Míne*) Derry. 'Townland of the smooth place'.

Ballynamona (*Baile na Móna*) Cork. 'Townland of the bog'.

Ballynamult (*Béal na Molt*) Waterford. 'Estuary of the wether'.

Ballynanty (*Baile Uí Neachtain*) Limerick. 'Ó Neachtain's townland'.

Ballynascreen (*Baile na Scrín*) Derry. 'Townland of the shrine'.

Ballynashannagh (*Baile na Seanach*) Donegal. *Ballysheany* 1612. Possibly 'townland of the fox'.

Ballynaskreena (*Bbaile na Scríne*) Kerry. 'Townland of the shrine'.

Ballyneaner (*Baile an Aonfhir*) Tyrone. *Baile an Aoinfhir c.*1675. 'Townland of the lone man'.

Ballynease (*Baile Naosa*) Derry. *Bellinees* 1654. 'Naois's townland'.

Ballyneety (*Baile an Fhaoitigh*) Limerick. 'de Faoite's townland'.

Ballyneill (*Baile Uí Néill*) Tipperary. 'Ó Néill's townland'.

Ballyness (*Baile an Easa*) Derry. 'Townland of the waterfall'.

Ballynoe (*An Baile Nua*) Cork. 'The new townland'.

Ballynure (*Baile an Iúir*) Antrim. *Ballinower* 1605. 'Townland of the yew tree'.

Ballyoran (*Baile Uaráin*) Armagh. *B:uoran* 1609. 'Townland of the spring'.

Ballyorgan (*Baile Uí Argáin*) Limerick. 'Ó hArgáin's townland'.

Ballyote (*Baile Fhóid*) Westmeath. 'Townland of the sod'.

Ballypatrick (*Baile Phádraig*) Tipperary. 'Pádraig's townland'.

Ballyphehane (*Baile Féitheán*) Cork. 'Townland of the osiers'.

Ballyphilip (*Baile Philib*) Waterford. 'Philip's townland'.

Ballyporeen (*Béal Átha Póirín*) Tipperary. 'Ford-mouth of the round stones'.

Ballyquin (*Baile Uí Choinn*) Waterford. 'Ó Coinn's townland'.

Ballyquirk (*Baile Uí Chuirc*) Tipperary. 'Ó Cuirc's townland'.

Ballyragget (*Béal Átha Ragad*) Kerry. 'Ford-mouth of the churl'.

Ballyrashane (*Baile Ráth Singean*) Derry. *Singayton al. Rathsyne* 1542. 'Townland of St John's fort'.

Ballyrawer (*Baile Ramhar*) Down. 'Fertile townland'.

Ballyreagh (*An Baile Riabhach*) Tyrone. 'The grey townland'.

Ballyree (*Baile an Fhraoigh*) Down. 'Townland of the heather'.

Ballyrobert (*Baile Roibeaird*) Antrim. *Ballyrobert c.*1659. 'Robert's townland'.

Ballyronan (*Baile Uí Rónáin*) Derry. *Two Ballioronans* 1654. 'Ó Rónáin's townland'.

Ballyroney (*Baile Uí Ruanaí*) Down. *Ballyronowe* 1611. 'Ó Ruanaí's townland'.

Ballyroosky (*Baile Rusgaidh*) Donegal. 'Townland of the marsh'.

Ballysadare (*Baile Easa Dara*) Sligo. 'Townland of the waterfall of the oak'.

Ballysakeery (*Baile Easa Caoire*) Mayo. 'Townland of the waterfall of the berry'.

Ballysallagh (*Baile Sealbhach*) Down. *Ballyshallagh* 1614. 'Townland of herds'.

Ballysally (*Baile Uí Shalaigh*) Derry. *Ballyosallye* 1543. 'Ó Salaigh's townland'.

Ballyscullion (*Baile Uí Scoillín*) Derry. *Balle Oskullyn* 1397. 'Ó Scoillín's townland'.

Ballyshannon (*Béal Átha Seanaidh*) Donegal. (*for*) *Bhel Atha Senaigh* 1398. 'Ford-mouth of the slope'.

Ballyshrule (*Baile Sruthail*) Galway. 'Townland of the stream'.

Ballysillan (*Baile na Saileán*) Antrim. *Ballynysillan* 1604. 'Townland of the willow grove'.

Ballysimon (*Béal Átha Síomoin*) Limerick. 'Mouth of Síomon's ford'.

Ballyskeagh (*Baile na Sceiche*) Down. 'Townland of the thorn'.

Ballysteen (*Baile Stiabhna*) Limerick. 'Stiabhna's townland'.

Ballystrew (*Baile Sruth*) Down. 'Townland of the stream'.

Ballystrudder (*Baile Strudair*) Antrim. *Ballytredder* 1669. 'Strudar's townland'.

Ballytarsna (*Baile Trasna*) Roscommon, Tipperary. 'Townland across'.

Ballyvade (*Baile Bháid*) Westmeath. 'Townland of the boat'.

Ballyvaghan (*Baile Uí Bheacháin*) Clare. 'Ó Beacháin's townland'.

Ballyvaldon (*Baile Bhalduin*) Wexford. 'Baldwin's townland'.

Ballyvaltron (*Baile Bhaltairín*) Wicklow. 'Little Walter's townland'.

Ballyvangour (*Baile Bheanna Gabhar*) Carlow. 'Townland of the peaks of the goats'.

Ballyvary (*Béal Átha Bhearaigh*) Mayo. 'Ford-mouth of the heifer'.

Ballyvoge (*Baile Uí Bhuaigh*) Cork. 'Ó Buaigh's townland'.

Ballyvourney (*Baile Bhuirne*) Cork. 'Townland of the stony place'.

Ballyvoy (*Baile Bhuí*) Antrim. *Ballyvoy c.*1657. 'Yellow townland'.

Ballyvoyle (*Baile Uí Bhaoil*) Waterford. 'Ó Baoill's townland'.

Ballywalter (*Baile Bháltair*) Down. *Ballywalter* 1661. 'Walter's townland'.

Ballyward (*Baile Mhic an Bhaird*) Down. *Ballymc-Ewarde* 1611. 'Mac an Bhaird's townland'.

Ballywater (*Baile Uachtar*) Wexford. 'Upper townland'.

Ballywee (*Baile Uaimh*) Antrim. 'Townland of the cave'.

Ballywildrick (*Baile Ualraic*) Derry. *Ba:Wolrick* 1613. 'Ualrac's townland'.

Ballywilliam (*Baile Liam*) Wexford. 'Liam's townland'.

Balmoral (*Baile Mhoireil*) Antrim. The name was adopted from *Balmoral*, Scotland.

Balmoral Aber. *Bouchmorale* 1451. Gaelic *both* 'hut': second element uncertain.

Balnakeil Highland. Gaelic *Baile na Cill*.

Balnamore (*Béal an Átha Móir*) Antrim. 'Mouth of the big ford'.

Balne N. Yorks. *Balne* 12th cent. Probably from Latin *balneum* 'a bathing place'.

Balrath (*Baile na Rátha*) Meath. 'Townland of the fort'.

Balroe (*Baile Rua*) Westmeath. 'Red townland'.

Balrothery (*Baile an Ridire*) Dublin. 'Townland of the knight'.

Balsall W. Mids. *Beleshale* 1185. 'Nook of land of a man called *Bæll(i)'. OE pers. name + *halh*. **Temple Balsall** is so called because it belonged to the Knights Templars from 1185.

Balscott Oxon. *Berescote |sic|* 1086 (DB), *Belescot c.*1190. 'Cottage(s) of a man called Bæll(i)'. OE pers. name + *cot*.

Balsham Cambs. *Bellesham* 974, *Belesham* 1086 (DB). 'Homestead or village of a man called Bæll(i)'. OE pers. name + *hām*.

Balterley Staffs. *Baltrytheleag* 1002, *Baltredelege* 1086 (DB). 'Woodland clearing of a woman called *Baldthrȳth'. OE pers. name + *lēah*.

Baltimore (*Dūn na Sēad*) Cork. 'Townland of the big house'. The English name represents Irish *Baile na Tighe Mór*, while the present Irish name means 'fort of the jewels'.

Baltinglass (*Bealach Conglais*) Dublin. 'Pass of Conglas'.

Baltonsborough Somerset. *Balteresberghe* 744, *Baltunesberge* 1086 (DB). 'Hill or mound of a man called Bealdhūn'. OE pers. name + *beorg*.

Bamber Bridge Lancs. *Bymbrig* in an undated medieval document. Probably 'tree-trunk bridge'. OE *bēam* + *brycg*.

Bamburgh Northum. *Bebbanburge c.*710–20. 'Stronghold of a queen called Bebbe'. OE pers. name + *burh*.

Bamford Derbys. *Banford* 1086 (DB). 'Treetrunk ford'. OE *bēam* + *ford*.

Baming, East Kent. *Bermelinge, Bermelie* 1086 (DB). Origin and meaning uncertain.

Bampton, usually 'farmstead made of beams or by a tree', OE *bēam* + *tūn*: **Bampton** Cumbria. *Bampton c.*1160. **Bampton** Oxon. *Bemtun* 1069, *Bentone* 1086 (DB). **Bampton, Little** Cumbria. *Parua Bampton* 1227.
However the following has a different origin: **Bampton** Devon. *Badentone* 1086 (DB). 'Farmstead of the dwellers by the pool'. OE *bæth* + *hæme* + *tūn*.

Banada (*Muine na Fede*) Sligo. 'Thicket of the whistle'.

Banagher (*Beannchar*) Derry, Offaly. 'Place of peaks'.

Banbridge Down. *Bann Br.* 1743. 'Bridge over the (river) Bann'. The equivalent Irish name is *Droichead na Banna*.

Banbury Oxon. *Banesberie* 1086 (DB). 'Stronghold of a man called *Ban(n)a'. OE pers. name + *burh* (dative *byrig*).

Banchory Aber. 'Horn-cast'. Gaelic *beannchar*.

Bandon (*Droichead na Bandan*) Cork. The Irish name of the town means 'bridge on the Bandon', while the river name itself may mean 'goddess'.

Banemore (*An Bán Mór*) Kerry. 'The large pasture land'.

Banff Aber. *Banb c.*1150. (Place on the) River Banff'. The river name means 'piglet' (Gaelic *banbh*), as a nickname for the present River Deveron, seen as 'rooting' its way to the coast.

Bangor (*Beannchar*) Down. *Bennchuir* 555. 'Place of points'. The name probably refers to a pointed wattle enclosure around the original monastic settlement.

Bangor Gwyd. *Benchoer* 634. 'Wattled fence'. Welsh *bangor*. The reference is probably to the wattled fence that enclosed the monastery founded in 525.

Bangor Erris (*Beannchar Iorrais*) Mayo. 'Peaked hill of Iorrais'.

Bangor Is-coed. *See* BANGOR ON DEE.

Bangor on Dee (*Bangor Is-coed*) Wrex. *Bancor* 8th cent., *Bangor* 1277, *Bangor monachorum* 1607. '(Place of the people of) Bangor on the River Dee'. The monastery is said to have been founded by St Deiniol, founder of BANGOR, with the river name ('goddess') added for distinction. The Welsh name means 'Bangor below the wood'. The third form of the name is Latin for 'Bangor of the monks'.

Banham Norfolk. *Benham* 1086 (DB). 'Homestead or enclosure where beans are grown'. OE *bēan* + *hām* or *hamm*.

Bann (*An Bhanna*) (river) Antrim, Armagh, Derry, Down. *Banda c.*800. 'The goddess'.

Banna (*Beanna*) Kerry. 'Peaks'.

Bannau Brycheiniog. *See* BRECON BEACONS.

Banningham Norfolk. *Banincham* 1086 (DB). 'Homestead or village of the family or followers of a man called *Ban(n)a'. OE pers. name + *-inga-* + *hām*.

Bannockburn Stir. *Bannockburn* 1314, *Bannokburne* 1654. (Place on the) Bannock Burn'. OE *burna*. The Celtic river name means 'peaked, horned', referring to the hill from which the stream flows.

Bannow Bay (*Cuan Bhanú*) Wexford. 'Bay of the sucking pig'.

Banogue (*An Bhánog*) Limerick. 'The small green plot'.

Bansha (*An Bháinseach*) Tipperary. 'The green'.

Banstead Surrey. *Benestede* 1086 (DB). 'Place where beans are grown'. OE *bēan* + *stede*.

Banteer (*Bántír*) Cork. 'White land'.

Bantry (*Beanntraí*) Cork. (District of) Beanntraí'. The district name probably means 'Beann's people', from a tribal name.

Banwell N. Som. *Bananwylle* 904, *Banwelle* 1086 (DB). 'Spring or stream of the murderer, or containing water thought to be poisonous'. OE *bana* 'killer' + *wella*.

Bapchild Kent. *Baccancelde* 696–716. 'Spring of a man called Bacca'. OE pers. name + *celde*.

Barbon Cumbria. *Berebrune* 1086 (DB). 'Stream frequented by bears or beavers'. OE *bere* + *burna* or OScand. *bjórr* + *brunnr*.

Barby Northants. *Berchebi* 1086 (DB). 'Farmstead or village on the hill(s)'. OScand. *berg* + *bý*.

Barcheston Warwicks. *Berricestone* 1086 (DB), 'Farmstead of a man called Beaduríc'. OE pers. name + *tūn*.

Barcombe E. Sussex. *Bercham* |*sic*| 1086 (DB), *Berecampe* 12th cent. 'Enclosed land used for barley'. OE *bere* + *camp*.

Bard Head Shet (Bressay). 'Headland of the extremity'. OScand. *barth*. Bard Head is the southernmost point of Bressay. *Cp.* BURWICK.

Barden N. Yorks., near Leyburn. *Bernedan* 1086 (DB). Probably 'valley where barley is grown'. OE *beren* + *denu*.

Bardfield, Great & *Bardfield, Little, Bardfield Saling* Essex. *Byrdefelda* 1086 (DB), *Berdeford Saling* 13th cent. 'Open land by a bank or border'. OE **byrde* + *feld*. Affix from the neighbouring parish of GREAT SALING.

Bardney Lincs. *Beardaneu* 731, *Bardenai* 1086 (DB). 'Island, or dry ground in marsh, of a man called **Bearda'. OE pers. name (genitive -*n*) + *ēg*.

Bardsea Cumbria. *Berretseige* 1086 (DB). 'Island of a man called Beornrǣd'. OE pers. name + *ēg* or OScand. *ey*.

Bardsey W. Yorks. *Berdesei* 1086 (DB). Probably 'island (of higher land) of a man called Beornrǣd'. OE pers. name + *ēg*.

Bardsey Island (*Ynys Enlli*) Gwyd. 'Bardr's island'. OScand. pers. name + *ey*. The Welsh name has been popularly associated with a legendary giant, *Benlli*, but is more likely to be 'island of currents' (welsh *ynys* + *an* + *lli*).

Bardsley Gtr. Manch. *Berdesley* 1422. 'Woodland clearing of a man called Beornrǣd'. OE pers. name + *lēah*.

Bardwell Suffolk. *Berdeuuella* 1086 (DB). Probably 'spring or stream of a man called **Bearda'. OE pers. name + *wella*.

Barford, usually 'barley ford', i.e. 'ford used at harvest time', OE *bere* + *ford*; examples include: **Barford** Norfolk. *Bereforda* 1086 (DB). **Barford** Warwicks. *Bereforde* 1086 (DB). **Barford, Great** Beds. *Bereforde* 1086 (DB). **Barford St Martin** Wilts. *Bereford* 1086 (DB), *Berevord St Martin* 1304. Affix from the dedication of the church. **Barford St Michael** Oxon. *Bereford* 1086 (DB), *Bereford Sancti Michaelis c.*1250. Affix from the dedication of the church.
  However the following has a different origin: **Barford, Little** Beds. *Bereforde* |*sic*| 1086 (DB), *Berkeford* 1202. 'Ford where birch-trees grow'. OE *beorc* + *ford*.

Barfreston Kent. *Berfrestone* 1086 (DB). Probably 'farmstead of a man called Beornfrith'. OE pers. name + *tūn*.

Bargoed Cphy. '(Place on the) River Bargoed'. The river name means 'boundary' (Welsh *bargod*).

Barham Cambs. *Bercheham* 1086 (DB). 'Homestead or enclosure on a hill'. OE *beorg* + *hām* or *hamm*.

Barham Kent. *Bioraham* 799, *Berham* 1086 (DB). 'Homestead or village of a man called **Be(o)ra'. OE pers. name + *hām*.

Barham Suffolk. *Bercham* 1086 (DB). Identical in origin with BARHAM (Cambs.).

Barholm Lincs. *Berc(a)ham* 1086 (DB). 'Homestead or enclosure on a hill'. OE *beorg* + *hām* or *hamm*.

Barkby Leics. *Barchebi* 1086 (DB). 'Farmstead or village of a man called Bǫrkr or Barki'. OScand. pers. name + *bý*.

Barkestone Leics. *Barchestone* 1086 (DB). 'Farmstead of a man called Barkr or Bǫrkr'. OScand. pers. name + OE *tūn*.

Barkham Berks. *Beorchamme* 952, *Bercheham* 1086 (DB). 'Enclosure or river-meadow where birch-trees grow'. OE *beorc* + *hamm*.

Barking, '(settlement of) the family or followers of a man called *Berica*'. OE pers. name + *-ingas*: **Barking** Gtr. London. *Berecingum* 731, *Berchinges* 1086 (DB). **Barking** Suffolk. *Berchinges* c.1050, *Berchingas* 1086 (DB).

Barkisland W. Yorks. *Barkesland* 1246. 'Cultivated land of a man called Barkr'. OScand. pers. name + *land*.

Barkston, 'farmstead of a man called Barkr or Bǫrkr', OScand. pers. name + OE *tūn*: **Barkston** Lincs. *Barchestune* 1086 (DB). **Barkston** N. Yorks. *Barcestune* c.1030, *Barchestun* 1086 (DB).

Barkway Herts. *Bercheuuei* 1086 (DB). 'Birch-tree way'. OE *beorc* + *weg*.

Barkwith, East & *Barkwith, West* Lincs. *Barcuurde* 1086 (DB). Possibly 'enclosure of a man called Barki'. OScand. pers. name + OE *worth*.

Barlaston Staffs. *Beorelfestun* 1002, *Bernulvestone* 1086 (DB). 'Farmstead of a man called Beornwulf'. OE pers. name + *tūn*.

Barlavington W. Sussex. *Berleventone* 1086 (DB). Probably 'estate associated with a man called Beornlāf'. OE pers. name + *-ing-* + *tūn*.

Barlborough Derbys. *Barleburh* c.1002, *Barleburg* 1086 (DB). Probably 'stronghold near the wood frequented by boars'. OE *bār* + *lēah* + *burh*.

Barlby N. Yorks. *Bardulbi* 1086 (DB). 'Farmstead or village of a man called *Beardwulf* or Bardulf'. OE or OGerman pers. name + OScand. *bý*.

Barlestone Leics. *Berulvestone* 1086 (DB). Probably 'farmstead of a man called Beornwulf or Berwulf'. OE pers. name + *tūn*.

Barley Herts. *Beranlei* c.1050, *Berlai* 1086 (DB). Probably 'woodland clearing of a man called *Be(o)ra*'. OE pers. name + *lēah*.

Barley Lancs. *Bayrlegh* 1324. 'Woodland clearing frequented by boars, or where barley is grown'. OE *bār* or *bere* + *lēah*.

Barling Essex. *Bærlingum* 998, *Berlinga* 1086 (DB). '(Settlement of) the family or followers of a man called *Bærla*'. OE pers. name + *-ingas*.

Barlow Derbys. *Barleie* 1086 (DB). 'Woodland clearing frequented by boars, or where barley is grown'. OE *bār* or *bere* + *lēah*.

Barlow N. Yorks. *Bernlege* c.1030, *Berlai* 1086 (DB). 'Woodland clearing with a barn, or where barley is grown'. OE *bere-ærn* or *beren* + *lēah*.

Barmby, probably 'farmstead of the children, i.e. one held jointly by a number of heirs' from OScand. *barn* + *bý*; alternatively 'farmstead of a man called Barni or Bjarni' from OScand. pers. name + *bý*: **Barmby Moor** E. R. Yorks. *Barnebi* 1086 (DB), *Barneby in the More* 1371. Affix is

OE *mōr* 'moor'. **Barmby on the Marsh** E. R. Yorks *Bærnabi* c.1050, *Barnebi* 1086 (DB). Affix is OE *mersc* 'marsh'.

Barmer Norfolk. *Benemara* |*sic*| 1086 (DB), *Beremere* 1202. 'Pool frequented by bears', or 'pool of a man called *Bera*'. OE *bera* or pers. name + *mere*.

Barmouth (*Y Bermo*) Gwyd. *Abermowth* 1410. 'Mouth of the River Mawddach'. Welsh *aber*. The river name, originally *Mawdd*, probably derives from a pers. name. Its estuary was *Abermawdd*, giving the Welsh name (with *y*, 'the'). The English name has been influenced by *mouth*.

Barmston E. R. Yorks. *Benestone* 1086 (DB). 'Farmstead of a man called Beorn'. OE pers. name + *tūn*.

Barna (*Bearna*) Galway, Limerick, Offaly. 'Gap'.

Barnack Cambs. *Beornican* c.980, *Bernac* 1086 (DB). Probably '(place at) the oaktree(s) of the warriors'. OE *beorn* + *āc*.

Barnacle Warwicks. *Bernhangre* 1086 (DB). 'Wooded slope by a barn'. OE *bere-ærn* + *hangra*.

Barnacullia (*Barr na Coille*) Dublin. 'Top of the wood'.

Barnaderg (*Bearna Dhearg*) Galway. 'Red gap'.

Barnageeha (*Bearna Gaoithe*) Limerick. 'Windy gap'.

Barnakillew (*Barr na Coille*) Mayo. 'Top of the wood'.

Barnakilly (*Barr na Coille*) Derry. 'Top of the wood'.

Barnard Castle Durham. *Castellum Bernardi* 1200. 'Castle of a baron called Bernard'. He was here in the 12th cent.

Barnardiston Suffolk. *Bernardeston* 1194. 'Farmstead of a man called Beornheard'. OE pers. name + *tūn*.

Barnatra (*Barr na Trá*) Mayo. 'Top of the strand'.

Barnby, probably 'farmstead of the children, i.e. one held jointly by a number of heirs', OScand. *barn* + *bý*; alternatively the first element of some name may be the OScand. pers. name *Barni* or *Bjarni*; examples include: **Barnby** Suffolk. *Barnebei* 1086 (DB). **Barnby Dun** S. Yorks. *Barnebi* 1086 (DB), *Barneby super Don* 1285. Affix means 'on the River Don'. **Barnby, East** & **Barnby, West** N. Yorks. *Barnebi* 1086 (DB). **Barnby in the Willows** Notts. *Barnebi* 1086 (DB). Affix means 'among the willow-trees'. **Barnby Moor** Notts. *Barnebi* 1086 (DB). Affix means 'on the moor'.

Barnes Gtr. London. *Berne* 1086 (DB). '(Place by) the barn or barns'. OE *bere-ærn*.

Barnes (*Bearnas*) Tyrone. 'Gap'.

Barnesmore (*An Bearnas Mór*) Donegal. 'The great gap'.

Barnet, Chipping, *Barnet, East* & *Barnet, Friern* Gtr. London. *Barneto* c.1070, *Chepyng Barnet* 1321, *Est Barnet* c.1275, *Frerenbarnet* 1274. 'Land cleared by burning'. OE *bærnet*. Distinguishing affixes are OE *cīeping* 'market', *ēast* 'east' and ME *freren* 'of the brothers' (referring to early possession by the Knights of St John of Jerusalem). Chipping Barnet has also been known as *High Barnet* since the 17th cent.

Barnetby le Wold N. Lincs. *Bernedebi* 1086 (DB). 'Farmstead or village of a man called Beornnōth or *Beornede*'. OE pers. name + OScand. *bý*. Affix means 'on the wold(s)', referring to its situation at the northern edge of the Lincolnshire WOLDS.

Barney Norfolk. *Berlei |sic|* 1086 (DB), *Berneie* 1198. Possibly 'island, or dry ground in marsh, of a man called *Bera'. OE pers. name (genitive *-n*) + *ēg*.

Barnham Suffolk. *Byornham c*.1000, *Bernham* 1086 (DB). 'Warrior homestead', or 'homestead of a man called Beorn'. OE *beorn* or OE pers. name + *hām*.

Barnham W. Sussex. *Berneham* 1086 (DB). 'Homestead or enclosure of the warriors, or of a man called Beorna'. OE *beorn* or OE pers. name + *hām* or *hamm*.

Barnham Broom Norfolk. *Bernham* 1086 (DB). Identical in origin with BARNHAM (Suffolk). Affix is OE *brōm* 'broom'.

Barningham, 'homestead or village of the family or followers of a man called Beorn', OE pers. name + *-inga-* + *hām*: **Barningham** Durham. *Berningham* 1086 (DB). **Barningham** Suffolk. *Bernincham* 1086 (DB). **Barningham, Little** Norfolk. *Berningeham* 1086 (DB).

Barnmeen (*Bearn Mhín*) Down. *Ballybarnemyne* 1612. 'Smooth gap'.

Barnoldby le Beck NE. Lincs. *Bernulfbi* 1086 (DB). 'Farmstead or village of a man called Bjǫrnulfr'. OScand. pers. name + OScand. *bý*. Affix means 'on the stream' from OScand. *bekkr*.

Barnoldswick Lancs. *Bernulfesuuic* 1086 (DB). 'Dwelling or (dairy) farm of a man called Beornwulf or Bjǫrnulfr'. OE or OScand. pers. name + OE *wīc*.

Barnsbury Gtr. London. *Bernersbury* 1406. 'Manor of the de Berners family', from ME *bury*. This family held land in Islington from the 13th cent.

Barnsley Glos. *Bearmodeslea c*.802, *Bernesleis* 1086 (DB). 'Woodland clearing of a man called Beornmōd'. OE pers. name + *lēah*.

Barnsley S. Yorks. *Berneslai* 1086 (DB). 'Woodland clearing of a man called Beorn'. OE pers. name + *lēah*.

Barnstaple Devon. *Beardastapol* late 10th cent., *Barnestaple* 1086 (DB). 'Post or pillar of the battle-axe', probably signifying the site of a meeting-place. OE *bearde* (genitive *-an*) + *stapol*.

Barnston Essex. *Bernestuna* 1086 (DB). 'Farmstead of a man called Beorn'. OE pers. name + *tūn*.

Barnston Mersey. *Bernestone* 1086 (DB). 'Farmstead of a man called Beornwulf'. OE pers. name + *tūn*.

Barnstone Notts. *Bernestune* 1086 (DB). 'Farmstead of a man called Beorn'. OE pers. name + *tūn*.

Barnton Ches. *Bertintune* 1086 (DB), *Bertherton* 1313, *Berneton* 1319. 'Farmstead of a woman called Beornthrȳth'. OE pers. name + *tūn*.

Barnwell All Saints Northants. *Byrnewilla c*.980, *Bernewelle* 1086 (DB). Probably 'spring or stream of the warriors, or of a man called Beorna'. OE *beorn* or OE pers. name + *wella*. Affix from the dedication of the church.

Barnwood Glos. *Berneuude* 1086 (DB). 'Wood of the warriors, or of a man called Beorna'. OE *beorn* or OE pers. name + *wudu*.

Barnycarroll (*Bearna Chearúill*) Mayo. 'Cearúll's gap'.

Barr, Great W. Mids. *Bearre* 957, *Barre* 1086 (DB). Celtic *barr* 'hill-top'.

Barra (island) W. Isles. *Barru c*.1090, *Barey c*.1200. 'Rough island'. OScand. *barr* + *ey*. Probably pre-Celtic name.

Barraduff (*Barra Dubh*) Kerry. 'Black ridge'.

Barrasford Northum. *Barwisford* 1242. 'Ford by a grove'. OE *bearu* (genitive *bearwes*) + *ford*.

Barrhead E. Renf. 'Head headland'. Gaelic *barr* + Modern English *head*. The English word would have been added when the Gaelic original was no longer understood.

Barri, Y. *See* BARRY.

Barrington Cambs. *Barentone* 1086 (DB). Probably 'farmstead of a man called *Bāra'. OE pers. name (genitive *-n*) + *tūn*.

Barrington Somerset. *Barintone* 1086 (DB). Probably 'estate associated with a man called *Bāra'. OE pers. name + *-ing-* + *tūn*.

Barrington, Great & **Barrington, Little** Glos. *Berni(n)tone* 1086 (DB). 'Estate associated with a man called Beorn(a)'. OE pers. name + *-ing-* + *tūn*.

Barrow, usually '(place at) the wood or grove', OE *bearu* (in a dative form *bearwe*); examples include: **Barrow** Suffolk. *Baro* 1086 (DB). **Barrow, Great** & **Barrow, Little** Ches. *Barue* 958, *Bero* 1086 (DB). **Barrow Gurney** N. Som. *Berue* 1086 (DB), *Barwe Gurnay* 1283. Affix from possession by *Nigel de Gurnai* in 1086. **Barrow, North** & **Barrow, South** Somerset. *Berue, Berrowene* 1086 (DB). **Barrow upon Humber** N. Lincs. *Ad Baruae* 731, *Barewe* 1086 (DB). For the river-name, *see* HUMBER. *Ad* in the early form is Latin 'at'. **Barrow upon Soar** Leics. *Barhou* 1086 (DB). Soar is a Celtic or pre-Celtic river-name probably meaning 'flowing one'. **Barrow upon Trent** Derbys. *Barewe* 1086 (DB). For the river-name, *see* TRENTHAM.

However some Barrows have a different origin: **Barrow** Rutland, near Oakham. *Berc* 1197. '(Place at) the hill or burial mound'. OE *beorg*. **Barrow in Furness** Cumbria. *Barrai* 1190. 'Promontory island'. Celtic *barr* + OScand. *ey*. The old district name Furness (*Fuththernessa c*.1150) means 'headland by the rump-shaped island', OScand. *futh* (genitive *-ar*) + *nes*.

Barrowby Lincs. *Bergebi* 1086 (DB). 'Farmstead or village on the hill(s)'. OScand. *berg* + *bý*.

Barrowden Rutland. *Berchedone* 1086 (DB). 'Hill with barrows or tumuli'. OE *beorg* + *dūn*.

Barrowford Lancs. *Barouforde* 1296. 'Ford by the grove'. OE *bearu* + *ford*.

Barry (*Y Barri*) Vale Glam. *Barri c*.1190. 'Hill'. Welsh *barr*. The name properly refers to Barry Island. The Welsh name has Welsh *y*, 'the'.

Barryroe (*Barraigh Rua*) Cork. '(District of the) Red Barraigh'.

Barsby Leics. *Barnesbi* 1086 (DB). 'Farmstead or village of the child or young heir, or of a man called Barn'. OScand. *barn* or pers. name + *bý*.

Barsham, 'homestead or village of a man called Bār', OE pers. name + *hām*: **Barsham** Norfolk. *Barseham* 1086 (DB). **Barsham** Suffolk. *Barsham* 1086 (DB).

Barston W. Mids. *Bertanestone* 1086 (DB), *Berestanestona* 1185. Probably 'farmstead or estate of a man called Beorhtstān'. OE pers. name + *tūn*.

Bartestree Heref. & Worcs. *Bertoldestreu* 1086 (DB). 'Tree of a man called Beorhtwald'. OE pers. name + *trēow*.

Barthomley Ches. *Bertemeleu* |*sic*| 1086 (DB), *Bertamelegh* 13th cent. Possibly 'woodland clearing of the dwellers at a place called *Brightmead* or *Brightwell* or the like'. The first element of an older place-name (possibly OE *beorht* 'bright') + *hǣme* + *lēah*.

Bartley, 'birch-tree wood or clearing', OE *beorc* + *lēah*: **Bartley** Hants. *Berchelai* 1107. **Bartley Green** W. Mids. *Berchelai* 1086 (DB).

Bartlow Cambs. *Berkelawe* 1232. 'Mounds or tumuli where birch-trees grow'. OE *beorc* + *hlāw*.

Barton, a common name, usually OE *bere-tūn*, *bær-tūn* 'barley farm, outlying grange where corn is stored'; examples include: **Barton** Cambs. *Barton* 1060, *Bertone* 1086 (DB). **Barton** Devon, near Torquay. *Bertone* 1333. **Barton** Glos., near Guiting. *Berton* 1158. **Barton** Lancs., near Preston. *Bartun* 1086 (DB). **Barton Bendish** Norfolk. *Bertuna* 1086 (DB), *Berton Binnedich* 1249. Affix means 'inside the ditch' (OE *binnan* + *dīc*) referring to Devil's Dyke. **Barton, Earls** Northants. *Bartone* 1086 (DB), *Erlesbarton* 1261. Affix from the Earl of Huntingdon who held the manor in the 12th cent. **Barton, Great** Suffolk. *Bertuna* 945, 1086 (DB), *Magna Bertone* 1254. Early affix is Latin *magna* 'great'. **Barton in Fabis** Notts. *Bartone* 1086 (DB), *Barton in le Benes* 1388. Latin affix means 'where beans are grown'. **Barton le Clay** Beds. *Bertone* 1086 (DB), *Barton-in-the-Clay* 1535. Affix means 'on clay soil'. **Barton Mills** Suffolk. *Bertona* 1086 (DB), *Parva Bertone* 1254. Early affix is Latin *parva* 'little'. **Barton Seagrave** Northants. *Bertone* 1086 (DB), *Barton Segrave* 1321. Manorial affix from the de Segrave family, here in the 13th cent. **Barton Stacey** Hants. *Bertune* c.1000, *Bertune* 1086 (DB), *Berton Sacy* 1302. Manorial affix from the de Saci family, here in the 12th cent. **Barton Turf** Norfolk. *Bertuna* 1086 (DB), *Berton Turfe* 1394. Affix is ME *turf*, presumably because good turf was cut here. **Barton under Needwood** Staffs. *Barton* 942, *Bertone* 1086 (DB). Affix means 'near or within the forest of NEEDWOOD'. **Barton upon Humber** N. Lincs. *Bertune* 1086 (DB). For the river-name, *see* HUMBER.
However the following has a different origin: **Barton on Sea** Hants. *Bermintune* 1086 (DB). 'Estate associated with a man called *Beorma'. OE pers. name + *-ing-* + *tūn*.

Barugh, Great & *Barugh, Little* N. Yorks. *Berg, Berch* 1086 (DB). '(Place at) the hill'. OE *beorg*.

Barway Cambs. *Bergeia* 1155. 'Island, or dry ground in marsh, with barrows or tumuli on it'. OE *beorg* + *ēg*.

Barwell Leics. *Barewelle* 1086 (DB). 'Spring or stream frequented by boars'. OE *bār* + *wella*.

Barwick, 'barley farm, outlying part of an estate'. OE *bere-wīc*: **Barwick** Somerset. *Berewyk* 1219. **Barwick in Elmet** W. Yorks. *Bereuuith* 1086 (DB). *Elmet* is an ancient district name, obscure in origin and meaning, first recorded in the 7th cent. as *Elmed*.

Baschurch Shrops. *Bascherche* 1086 (DB). 'Church of a man called Bas(s)a'. OE pers. name + *cirice*.

Bascote Warwicks. *Bachecota* 1174. Probably 'cottage(s) of a man called *Basuca'. OE pers. name + *cot*.

Basford Staffs. *Bechesword* |*sic*| 1086 (DB), *Barkeford* 1199. Probably 'ford of a man called Beorcol'. OE pers. name + *ford*.

Bashall Eaves Lancs. *Bacschelf* 1086 (DB). 'Ridge shelf'. OE *bæc* + *scelf*. Later addition *Eaves* (from 16th cent.) is from OE *efes* 'edge of a wood'.

Bashley Hants. *Bageslucesleia* 1053, *Bailocheslei* 1086 (DB). 'Woodland clearing of a man called Bægloc'. OE pers. name + *lēah*.

Basildon Essex. *Berlesduna* |*sic*| 1086 (DB), *Bertlesdon* 1194. 'Hill of a man called Beorhtel'. OE pers. name + *dūn*.

Basing Hants. *Basengum* 871, *Basinges* 1086 (DB). '(Settlement of) the family or followers of a man called *Basa'. OE pers. name + *-ingas*. The same tribal group is referred to in the next name.

Basingstoke Hants. *Basingastoc* 990, *Basingestoches* 1086 (DB). 'Secondary settlement or outlying farmstead of the family or followers of a man called Basa'. OE pers. name + *-inga-* + *stoc*.

Baslick (*Baisleac*) Monaghan. 'Church'.

Baslickane (*Baisleacán*) Kerry. 'Small church'.

Baslow Derbys. *Basselau* 1086 (DB). 'Burial mound of a man called Bassa'. OE pers. name + *hlāw*.

Bassenthwaite Cumbria. *Bastunthuait* c.1175. 'Clearing or meadow of a family called Bastun'. ME surname + OScand. *thveit*.

Bassetlaw (district) Notts. *Bernesedelaue* 1086 (DB). Possibly 'mound or hill of the dwellers on land cleared by burning'. OE *bærnet* + *sǣte* + *hlāw*.

Bassingbourn Cambs. *Basingborne* 1086 (DB). 'Stream of the family or followers of a man called Bas(s)a'. OE pers. name + *-inga-* + *burna*.

Bassingfield Notts. *Basingfelt* 1086 (DB). 'Open land of the family or followers of a man called Bas(s)a'. OE pers. name + *-inga-* + *feld*.

Bassingham Lincs. *Basingeham* 1086 (DB). 'Homestead or village of the family or followers of a man called Bas(s)a'. OE pers. name + *-inga-* + *hām*.

Bassingthorpe Lincs. *Torp* 1086 (DB), *Basewinttorp* 1202. 'Outlying farmstead or hamlet'. OScand. *thorp* + later manorial addition from possession by the Basewin family.

Baston Lincs. *Bacstune* 1086 (DB). 'Farmstead of a man called Bak'. OScand. pers. name + OE *tūn*.

Bastwick Norfolk. *Bastwic* 1044-7, *Bastuuic* 1086 (DB). 'Farm or building where bast (the bark of the lime-tree used for rope-making) is stored'. OE *bæst* + *wīc*.

Batcombe, 'valley of a man called Bata', OE pers. name + *cumb*: **Batcombe** Dorset. *Batecumbe* 1201.

Batcombe Somerset, near Bruton. *Batancumbæ* 10th cent., *Batecumbe* 1086 (DB).

Bath B. & NE. Som. *Bathum* 796, *Bade* 1086 (DB). '(Place at) the (Roman) baths'. OE *bæth* in a dative plural form. *See also* AKEMAN STREET.

Bathampton B. & NE. Som. *Hamtun* 956, *Hantone* 1086 (DB). OE *hām-tūn* 'home farm, homestead' with later addition from its proximity to BATH.

Bathealton Somerset. *Badeheltone* 1086 (DB). Possibly 'farmstead of a man called Beaduhelm'. OE pers. name + *tūn*.

Batheaston B. & NE. Som. *Estone* 1086 (DB), *Batheneston* 1258. 'East farmstead or village'. OE *ēast* + *tūn* with later addition from its proximity to BATH.

Bathford B. & NE. Som. *Forda* 957, *Forde* 1086 (DB), *Bathford* 1575. '(Place at) the ford'. OE *ford* with later addition from its proximity to BATH.

Bathgate W. Loth. *Batket* c.1160. 'Boar wood'. Cumbric **badd* + **ceto-*.

Bathley Notts. *Badeleie* 1086 (DB). 'Woodland clearing with springs used for bathing'. OE *bæth* + *lēah*.

Batley W. Yorks. *Bathelie* 1086 (DB) 'Woodland clearing of a man called Bata'. OE pers. name + *lēah*.

Batsford Glos. *Bæccesore* 727–36, *Beceshore* 1086 (DB). 'Hill-slope of a man called **Bæcci*'. OE pers. name + *ōra*.

Battersby N. Yorks. *Badresbi* 1086 (DB). 'Farmstead or village of a man called Bothvarr'. OScand. pers. name + *bý*.

Battersea Gtr. London. *Badrices ege* 11th cent., *Patricesy* 1086 (DB). 'Island, or dry ground in marsh, of a man called Beadurīc'. OE pers. name + *ēg*.

Batterstown (*Baile an Bhóthair*) Meath. 'Homestead of the road'.

Battisford Suffolk. *Betesfort* 1086 (DB). 'Ford of a man called **Bætti*'. OE pers. name + *ford*.

Battle E. Sussex. *La Batailge* 1086 (DB). '(Place of) the battle'. OFrench *bataille*. The abbey here was founded to commemorate the battle of Hastings in 1066.

Battlefield Shrops. *Batelfeld* 1415. 'Field of battle'. OFrench *bataille*. A college of secular canons was founded here to commemorate the battle of Shrewsbury in 1403.

Battlesden Beds. *Badelesdone* 1086 (DB). 'Hill of a man called **Bæddel*'. OE pers. name + *dūn*.

Baughurst Hants. *Beaggan hyrste* 909. 'Wooded hill of a man called **Beagga*'. OE pers. name + *hyrst*. Alternatively the first element may be OE **bagga* 'a badger'.

Baumber Lincs. *Badeburg* 1086 (DB). 'Stronghold of a man called Badda'. OE pers. name + *burh*.

Baunton Glos. *Baudintone* 1086 (DB). 'Estate associated with a man called Balda'. OE pers. name + *-ing-* + *tūn*.

Bauteogue (*Báiteog*) Laois. 'Morass'.

Bautregaum (*Barr Trí gCom*) Kerry. 'Top of three hollows'.

Bavan (*Bádhún*) Donegal, Down. 'Cow fortress'.

Baverstock Wilts. *Babbanstoc* 968, *Babestoche* 1086 (DB). 'Outlying farmstead or hamlet of a man called Babba'. OE pers. name + *stoc*.

Bavington, Great & **Bavington, Little** Northum. *Babington* 1242. 'Estate associated with a man called Babba'. OE pers. name + *-ing-* + *tūn*.

Bawburgh Norfolk. *Bauenburc* 1086 (DB). 'Stronghold of a man called **Bēawa*'. OE pers. name + *burh*.

Bawdeswell Norfolk. *Baldereswella* 1086 (DB). 'Spring or stream of a man called Baldhere'. OE pers. name + *wella*.

Bawdrip Somerset. *Bagetrepe* 1086 (DB). 'Place where badgers are trapped or snared'. OE **bagga* + *træppe*.

Bawdsey Suffolk. *Baldereseia* 1086 (DB). 'Island, or dry ground in marsh, of a man called Baldhere'. OE pers. name + *ēg*.

Bawnboy (*An Bábhún Buí*) Cavan. *Bawnboy* 1664. 'The yellow fortified enclosure'.

Bawtry S. Yorks. *Baltry* 1199. Probably 'tree rounded like a ball'. OE **ball* + *trēow*.

Baxenden Lancs. *Bastanedenecloch* 1194. 'Valley where flat stones for baking are found'. OE **bæc-stān* + *denu*, with OE **clōh* 'ravine' in the early form.

Baxterley Warwicks. *Basterleia* c.1170. 'Woodland clearing belonging to the baker'. OE *bæcestre* + *lēah*.

Baycliff Cumbria. *Belleclive* 1212. Possibly 'cliff where a signal-fire is lit'. OE *bēl* + *clif*.

Baydon Wilts. *Beidona* 1146. 'Hill where berries grow'. OE *beg* + *dūn*.

Bayford Herts. *Begesford* |sic| 1086 (DB), *Begeford* c.1090. 'Ford of a man called Bæga'. OE pers. name + *ford*.

Baylham Suffolk. *Beleham* 1086 (DB). Probably 'homestead or enclosure at a river-bend'. OE **bēgel* + *hām* or *hamm*.

Baylin (*Béal Linne*) Westmeath. 'Mouth of the pool'.

Bayston Shrops. *Begestan* 1086 (DB). 'Stone of a woman called Bēage or of a man called Bæga'. OE pers. name + *stān*. **Bayston Hill** is *Beystaneshull* 1301, from OE *hyll*.

Bayswater Gtr. London. *Bayards Watering Place* 1380. 'Watering place for horses, or belonging to a family called Bayard'. ME *bayard* (or ME surname from this word) + *water*.

Bayton Heref. & Worcs. *Betune* 1086 (DB). 'Farmstead of a woman called Bēage or of a man called Bæga'. OE pers. name + *tūn*.

Beachampton Bucks. *Bechentone* 1086 (DB). 'Home farm by a stream'. OE *bece* + *hām-tūn*.

Beachley Glos. *Beteslega* 12th cent. 'Woodland clearing of a man called Betti'. OE pers. name + *lēah*.

Beachy Head E. Sussex. *Beuchef* 1279. 'Beautiful headland'. OFrench *beau* + *chef*, with the (tautological) addition of *head* in recent times.

Beaconsfield Bucks. *Bekenesfelde* 1184. 'Open land near a beacon or signal-fire'. OE *bēacen* + *feld*.

Beadlam N. Yorks. *Bodlum* 1086 (DB). '(Place at) the buildings'. OE *bōthl* in a dative plural form *bōthlum*.

Beadnell Northum. *Bedehal* 1161. 'Nook of land of a man called Bēda'. OE pers. name (genitive -*n*) + *halh*.

Beaford Devon. *Baverdone* |*sic*| 1086 (DB), *Beuford* 1242. 'Ford infested with gadflies'. OE *bēaw* + *ford*.

Beagh (*Beitheach*) Leitrim. 'Birch land'.

Beaghmore (*Beatheach Mór*) Tyrone. 'Large birch land'.

Beal Northum. *Behil* 1208–10. 'Hill frequented by bees'. OE *bēo* + *hyll*.

Beal N. Yorks. *Begale* 1086 (DB). 'Nook of land in a river-bend'. OE *bēag* + *halh*.

Bealadangan (*Béal an Daingin*) Galway. 'Opening of the stronghold'.

Bealaha (*Béal Átha*) Clare. 'Ford-mouth'.

Bealings, Great & *Bealings, Little* Suffolk. *Belinges* 1086 (DB). Possibly '(settlement of) the dwellers in the glade, or by the funeral pyre'. OE **bel-* or *bēl* + *-ingas*.

Beaminster Dorset. *Bebingmynster* 862, *Beiminstre* 1086 (DB). 'Large church of a woman called Bebbe'. OE pers. name + *mynster*.

Beamish Durham. *Bewmys* 1288. 'Beautiful mansion'. OFrench *beau* + *mes*.

Beamsley N. Yorks. *Bedmesleia* 1086 (DB), *Bethmesleia* 1185. 'Pasture or meadow at or by the valley bottom'. OE *lēah* with an OE **bethme* (a side-form of **bothm*).

Beane (river) Herts., *see* BENINGTON.

Beanley Northum. *Benelega* c.1150. 'Clearing where beans are grown'. OE *bēan* + *lēah*.

Bearley Warwicks. *Burlei* 1086 (DB). 'Woodland clearing near a fortified place'. OE *burh* + *lēah*.

Bearpark Durham. *Beaurepayre* 1267. 'Beautiful retreat'. OFrench *beau* + *repaire*.

Bearsden E. Dunb. Said to be 'Valley inhabited by wild boars', but doubtful. OE *bar* + *denu*.

Bearsted Kent. *Berghamstyde* 695. 'Homestead on a hill'. OE *beorg* + *hām-stede*.

Beauchief S. Yorks. *Beuchef* 12th cent. 'Beautiful headland or hill-spur'. OFrench *beau* + *chef*.

Beaufort (*Cendl*) Blae. The Duke of *Beaufort* owned lands here in the 18th cent. The Welsh name is from Edward *Kendall*, the ironmaster who was granted a lease of the site by the Duke in 1780.

Beaulieu Hants. *Bellus Locus Regis* 1205, *Beulu* c.1300. 'Beautiful place (of the king)'. OFrench *beau* + *lieu* (often rendered in Latin, as in the first spelling).

Beauly Highland. *Prioratus de bello loco* 1230. 'Beautiful place'. OFrench *beau* + *lieu*.

Beaumaris (*Biwmares*) Angl. *Bello Marisco* 1284. 'Beautiful marsh'. OFrench *beau* + *marais*.

Beaumont, 'beautiful hill', OFrench *beau* or *bel* + *mont*: **Beaumont** Cumbria. *Beumund* c.1240. **Beaumont** Essex. *Fulepet* 1086 (DB), *Bealmont* 12th cent. The earlier name means 'foul pit' from OE *fūl* + *pytt*!

Beausale Warwicks. *Beoshelle* |*sic*| 1086 (DB), *Beausala* 12th cent. 'Nook of land of a man called Bēaw'. OE pers. name + *halh*.

Beaworthy Devon. *Begeurde* 1086 (DB). 'Enclosure of a woman called Bēage or of a man called Bǣga'. OE pers. name + *worth*.

Bebington Mersey. *Bebinton* c.1100. 'Estate associated with a woman called Bebbe or a man called **Bebba*'. OE pers. name + *-ing-* + *tūn*.

Bebside Northum. *Bibeshet* 1198. Probably 'projecting piece of land of a man called **Bibba*'. OE pers. name + *scēat*.

Beccles Suffolk. *Becles* 1086 (DB). Probably 'pasture by a stream'. OE *bece* + *lǣs*.

Becconsall Lancs. *Bekaneshou* 1208. 'Burial mound of a man called Bekan'. OIrish pers. name + OScand. *haugr*.

Beckbury Shrops. *Becheberie* 1086 (DB). 'Stronghold or manor of a man called Becca'. OE pers. name + *burh* (dative *byrig*).

Beckenham Gtr. London. *Beohha hammes gemǣru* 973, *Bacheham* 1086 (DB). 'Homestead or enclosure of a man called **Beohha*'. OE pers. name (genitive -*n*) + *hām* or *hamm*. The early form contains OE (*ge*)*mǣre* 'boundary'.

Beckford Heref. & Worcs. *Beccanford* 803, *Beceford* 1086 (DB). 'Ford of a man called Becca'. OE pers. name + *ford*.

Beckham Norfolk. *Beccheham* 1086 (DB). 'Homestead or village of a man called Becca'. OE pers. name + *hām*.

Beckhampton Wilts. *Bachentune* 1086 (DB). 'Home farm near the ridge'. OE *bæc* + *hām-tūn*.

Beckingham, 'homestead or enclosure of the family or followers of a man called Becca or **Beohha*', OE pers. name + *hām* or *hamm*: **Beckingham** Lincs. *Bekingeham* 1177. **Beckingham** Notts. *Bechingeham* 1086 (DB).

Beckington Somerset. *Bechintone* 1086 (DB). 'Estate associated with a man called Becca'. OE pers. name + *-ing-* + *tūn*.

Beckley, 'woodland clearing of a man called Becca', OE pers. name + *lēah*: **Beckley** E. Sussex. *Beccanlea* c.880. **Beckley** Oxon. *Beccalege* 1005–12, *Bechelie* 1086 (DB).

Becontree Gtr. London. *Beuentreu* |*sic*| 1086 (DB), *Begintre* 12th cent. 'Tree of a man called **Beohha*'. OE pers. name (genitive -*n*) + *trēow*. The tree marked the Hundred meeting-place.

Bedale N. Yorks. *Bedale* 1086 (DB). 'Nook of land of a man called Bēda'. OE pers. name + *halh*.

Bedburn Durham. *Bedburn* 1291. 'Stream of a man called Bēda'. OE pers. name + *burna*.

Beddgelert Gwyd. *Bedkelert* 1281. 'Celert's grave'. Irish pers. name + Welsh *bedd*. Local legend derives the pers. name from *Gelert*, a hound slain by its master, Prince Llewellyn, when he thought it had killed his baby son, although it had actually killed a wolf that threatened the child.

Beddingham E. Sussex. *Beadyngham* c.800, *Bedingeham* 1086 (DB). 'Promontory of the family or followers of a man called Bēada'. OE pers. name + *-inga-* + *hamm*.

Beddington Gtr. London. *Beaddinctun* 901–8, *Beddintone* 1086 (DB). 'Estate associated with a man called **Beadda*'. OE pers. name + *-ing-* + *tūn*.

Bedfield Suffolk. *Berdefelda |sic|* 1086 (DB). *Bedefeld* 12th cent. 'Open land of a man called Bēda'. OE pers. name + *feld*.

Bedfont, East (Gtr. London) & *Bedfont, West* (Surrey.) *Bedefunt* 1086 (DB). Probably 'spring provided with a drinking-vessel'. OE *byden* + **funta*.

Bedford Beds. *Bedanford* 880, *Bedeford* 1086 (DB). 'Ford of a man called Bīeda'. OE pers. name + *ford*. **Bedfordshire** (OE *scīr* 'district') is first referred to in the 11th cent.

Bedhampton Hants. *Betametone* 1086 (DB). Possibly 'farmstead of the dwellers where beet is grown'. OE *bēte* + *hǣme* + *tūn*.

Bedingfield Suffolk. *Bedingefelda* 1086 (DB). 'Open land of the family or followers of a man called Bēda'. OE pers. name + *-inga-* + *feld*.

Bedlington Northum. *Bedlingtun* c.1050. Probably 'estate associated with a man called **Bēdla* or **Bētla*'. OE pers. name + *-ing-* + *tūn*.

Bednall Staffs. *Bedehala* 1086 (DB). 'Nook of land of a man called Bēda'. OE pers. name (genitive *-n*) + *halh*.

Bedstone Shrops. *Betietetune* 1086 (DB), *Bedeston* 1176. Probably 'farmstead of a man called **Bedgēat*'. OE pers. name + *tūn*.

Bedwas Cphy. *Bedewas* c.1102. 'Grove of birch trees'. Welsh *bedwos*.

Bedworth Warwicks. *Bedeword* 1086 (DB). 'Enclosure of a man called Bē(a)da'. OE pers. name + *worth*.

Bedwyn, Great & *Bedwyn, Little* Wilts. *Bedewinde* 778, *Bedvinde* 1086 (DB). Probably 'place where bindweed or convolvulus grows'. OE **bedwinde*.

Beeby Leics. *Bebi* 1086 (DB). 'Farmstead or village where bees are kept'. OE *bēo* + OScand. *bý*.

Beech Staffs. *Le Bech* 1285. '(Place at) the beech-tree'. OE *bēce*.

Beech Hill Berks. *Le Bechehulle* 1384. 'Hill where beech-trees grow'. OE *bēce* + *hyll*.

Beechingstoke Wilts. *Stoke* 941, *Bichenestoch* 1086 (DB). 'Outlying farmstead where bitches or hounds are kept'. OE *bicce* (genitive plural *-na*) + *stoc*.

Beeding, Lower & *Beeding, Upper* W. Sussex. *Beadingum* c.880, *Bedinges* 1086 (DB). '(Settlement of) the family or followers of a man called Bēada'. OE pers. name + *-ingas*.

Beedon Berks. *Bydene* 965, *Bedene* 1086 (DB). '(Place at) the tub-shaped valley'. OE *byden*.

Beeford E. R. Yorks. *Biuuorde* 1086 (DB). '(Place) by the ford', or 'ford where bees are found'. OE *bī* or *bēo* + *ford*.

Beeley Derbys. *Begelie* 1086 (DB). 'Woodland clearing of a woman called Bēage or a man called **Bēga*'. OE pers. name + *lēah*.

Beelsby NE Lincs. *Belesbi* 1086 (DB). 'Farmstead or village of a man called Beli'. OScand. pers. name + *bý*.

Beenham Berks. *Benham* 12th cent. 'Homestead or enclosure where beans are grown'. OE *bēan* + *hām* or *hamm*.

Beer Devon. *Bera* 1086 (DB). '(Place by) the grove'. OE *bearu*.

Beer Crocombe Somerset. *Bere* 1086 (DB). 'The grove', or 'the woodland pasture'. OE *bearu* or *bǣr* + manorial affix from the Craucombe family, here in the 13th cent.

Beer Hackett Dorset. *Bera* 1176, *Berehaket* 1362. 'The grove', or 'the woodland pasture'. OE *bearu* or *bǣr* + manorial affix from a 12th cent. owner called Haket.

Beesby Lincs. *Besbi* 1086 (DB). Probably 'farmstead or village of a man called Besi'. OScand. pers. name + *bý*.

Beeston, usually 'farmstead where bent-grass grows', OE **bēos* + *tūn*: **Beeston** Beds. *Bistone* 1086 (DB). **Beeston** Norfolk. *Bestone* 1254. **Beeston** Notts. *Bestune* 1086 (DB). **Beeston** W. Yorks. *Bestune* 1086 (DB). **Beeston Regis** Norfolk. *Besetune* 1086 (DB). Affix is Latin *regis* 'of the king'.
  However the following has a different origin: **Beeston** Ches. *Buistane* 1086 (DB). Probably 'stone or rock where commerce takes place'. OE *byge* + *stān*.

Beetham Cumbria. *Biedun* 1086 (DB). Probably '(place by) the embankments'. OScand. **beth* in a dative plural form **bjǫthum*.

Beetley Norfolk. *Betellea* 1086 (DB). Possibly 'clearing where beet is grown'. OE *bēte* + *lēah*.

Begbroke Oxon. *Bechebroc* 1086 (DB). 'Brook of a man called Becca'. OE pers. name + *brōc*.

Beginish (*Beag Inis*) Kerry. 'Little island'.

Beglieve (*Beagshliabh*) Cavan. *Begleive* 1586. 'Little mountain'.

Behaghane (*Beitheachán*) Kerry. 'Little place of birches'.

Behy (*Beitheach*) Donegal. 'Birch land'.

Beighton Norfolk. *Begetuna* 1086 (DB). 'Farmstead of a woman called Bēage or of a man called Bǣga'. OE pers. name + *tūn*.

Beighton S. Yorks. *Bectune* c.1002, 1086 (DB). 'Farmstead by the stream'. OE *bece* + *tūn*.

Beith N. Ayr. Probably '(Place of) birches'. Gaelic *beith*.

Bekesbourne Kent. *Burnes* 1086 (DB), *Bekesborne* 1280. 'Estate on the river called *Burna* (from OE *burna* 'stream' referring to the Little Stour), with later manorial affix from the de Beche family, here in the late 12th cent.

Belaugh Norfolk. *Belaga* 1086 (DB). Possibly 'enclosure where the dead are cremated'. OE *bēl* + *haga*.

Belbroughton Heref. & Worcs. *Beolne*, *Broctun* 817, *Bellem*, *Brocton* 1086 (DB), *Bellebrocton* 1292. Originally two distinct names. *Bell* is an old river-name, probably from OE *beolone* 'henbane'; *Broughton* is 'farmstead on the brook', OE *brōc* + *tūn*.

Belchamp Otten, *Belchamp St Paul* & *Belchamp Walter* Essex. *Bylcham* c.940, *Belcham*, *Belcamp* 1086 (DB), *Belcham Otes* 1256, *Belchampe of St Paul* 1451, *Waterbelcham* 1297. Probably 'homestead with a beamed or vaulted roof'. OE **belc* + *hām*. Distinguishing affixes from early possession by a man called Otto, by St Paul's Cathedral, and by a man called Walter.

Belchford Lincs. *Beltesford* 1086 (DB). Probably 'ford of a man called **Belt*'. OE pers. name + *ford*.

Belclare (*Béal Chláir*) Galway. 'Mouth of the plain'.

Belcoo (*Béal Cú*) Fermanagh. *Beallacoungamore, Beallacoungabegg* 1607. 'Mouth of the narrow'.

Belderg (*Béal Deirg*) Mayo. 'Mouth of the (river) Derg'.

Belfast (*Béal Feirste*) Antrim. (*bellum*) *Fertsi* 668. 'Ford-mouth of the sandbank'.

Belford Northum. *Beleford* 1242. Possibly 'ford by the bell-shaped hill'. OE *belle* + *ford*.

Belgooly (*Béal Guala*) Cork. 'Mouth of the ridge'.

Bellacorick (*Béal Átha Chomraic*) Mayo. 'Ford-mouth of the confluence'.

Bellaghy (*Baile Eachaidh*) Derry. *Baile Eachaidh* c.1645. 'Eochadh's homestead'.

Bellahy (*Béal Lathaí*) Sligo. 'Mouth of the miry place'.

Bellanagare (*Béal Átha na gCarr*) Roscommon. 'Ford-mouth of the carts'.

Bellanaleck (*Bealach na Leice*) Fermanagh. *Bellanaleck* 1837. 'Pass of the flagstone'.

Bellanamallard (*Béal Átha na Mallacht*) Fermanagh. *Béal Átha na Mallacht* 1645. 'Ford-mouth of the curses'. St Columba is said to have cursed some cocks here in the 6th cent.

Bellanamore (*Béal an Átha Móir*) Donegal. *Beallanaymore* 1621. 'Mouth of the big ford'.

Bellananagh (*Béal Átha na nEach*) Cavan. *Ballinenagh* c.1657. 'Ford-mouth of the horses'.

Bellaneeny (*Béal Átha an Aonaigh*) Roscommon. 'Ford-mouth of the fair'.

Bellanode (*Béal Átha an Fhóid*) Monaghan. *Ballynode* 1835. 'Ford-mouth of the sod'.

Bellarena (*Baile an Mhargaidh*) Derry. *Bellarena* 1835. Possibly 'beautiful strand'. French *belle* + Latin *arena*. The Irish name means 'townland of the market'.

Bellavary (*Béal Átha Bhearaigh*) Mayo. 'Ford-mouth of Bearach'.

Belleau Lincs. *Elgelo* 1086 (DB). 'Meadow of a man called Helgi'. OScand. pers. name + *ló*. The modern form, as if from a French name meaning 'beautiful water', is unhistorical.

Belleek (*Béal Leice*) Fermanagh. *Bel-leice* 1409. 'Mouth of the flagstone'.

Belleeks (*Béal Leice*) Armagh. *Bellick* 1657. 'Mouth of the flagstone'.

Bellerby N. Yorks. *Belgebi* 1086 (DB). 'Farmstead or village of a man called Belgr'. OScand. pers. name + *bý*.

Bellew (*Bile*) Meath. 'Sacred tree'.

Bellia (*Bile*) Clare. 'Sacred tree'.

Bellingham Gtr. London. *Beringaham* 998, *Belingeham* 1198. 'Homestead or enclosure of the family or followers of a man called *Bera*'. OE pers. name + *-inga-* + *hām* or *hamm*.

Bellingham Northum. *Bellingham* 1254. 'Homestead of the dwellers at the bell-shaped hill', or simply 'homestead at the bell-shaped hill'. OE *belle* + *-inga-* or *-ing* + *hām*.

Belmesthorpe Rutland. *Beolmesthorp* c.1050, *Belmestorp* 1086 (DB). 'Outlying farmstead or hamlet of a man called Beornhelm'. OE pers. name + OScand. *thorp*

Belmont Down. *Bellmount* 1834. 'Beautiful hill'. OFrench *bel* + *mont*. The Irish name of Belmont is *An Cnoc Álainn*, 'the beautiful hill'.

Belmont Gtr. London, near Sutton, not on record before the early 19th cent., 'beautiful hill' from OFrench *bel* + *mont*. The same name occurs in other counties, for example **Belmont** Lancs. which is *Belmunt* 1212.

Belmullet (*Béal an Mhuirthead*) Mayo. 'Sea loop'.

Belper Derbys. *Beurepeir* 1231. 'Beautiful retreat'. OFrench *beau* + *repaire*.

Belsay Northum. *Bilesho* 1163. 'Hill-spur of a man called Bil(l)'. OE pers. name + *hōh*.

Belses Sc. Bord. 'Beautiful seat'. OFrench *bel* + *assis*.

Belsize Herts., not on record before the mid 19th cent., but a common name-type found as **Bellasis**, **Bellasize**, etc. in other counties and meaning 'beautiful seat or residence', from OFrench *bel* + *assis*.

Belstead Suffolk. *Belesteda* 1086 (DB). 'place in a glade' or 'place of a funeral pyre'. OE **bel* or *bēl* + *stede*.

Belstone Devon. *Bellestam* |*sic*| 1086 (DB), *Belestan* 1167. '(Place at) the bell-shaped stone'. OE *belle* + *stān*.

Beltany (*Bealtaine*) Donegal. 'Summer festival'.

Beltoft N. Lincs. *Beltot* 1086 (DB). Possibly 'homestead near a funeral pyre, or on dry ground in marsh'. OE *bēl* or **bel* + OScand. *toft*.

Belton, meaning uncertain, 'farmstead in a glade or on dry ground in marsh', or 'farmstead near a beacon or funeral pyre', OE **bel* or *bēl* + *tūn*; **Belton** Leics., near Shepshed. *Beltona* c.1125. **Belton** Lincs. *Beltone* 1086 (DB). **Belton** Norfolk. *Beletuna* 1086 (DB). **Belton** N. Lincs. *Beltone* 1086 (DB). **Belton** Rutland. *Belton* late 11th cent., *Bealton* 1167.

Beltra (*Béal Trá*) Mayo, Sligo. 'Mouth of the strand'.

Belturbet (*Béal Tairbirt*) Cavan. *Bél Tarbert* 1621. 'Mouth of the isthmus'.

Belvelly (*Béal an Bhealaigh*) Cork. 'Mouth of the pass'.

Belvoir Down. *Belvoir* 1744. 'Beautiful view'. OFrench *bel* + *voir*.

Belvoir Leics. *Belveder* 1130. 'Beautiful view'. OFrench *bel* + *vedeir*.

Bembridge I. of Wight. *Bynnebrygg* 1316. '(Place lying) inside (i.e. this side of) the bridge'. OE *binnan* + *brycg*.

Bemerton Wilts. *Bimertone* 1086 (DB). 'Farmstead of the trumpeters'. OE *býmere* + *tūn*.

Bempton E. R. Yorks. *Bentone* 1086 (DB). 'Farmstead made of beams, or by a tree'. OE *bēam* + *tūn*.

Ben Cruachan (mountain) Arg. *Crechanben* c.1375. 'Mountain of the stacks'. Gaelic *beinn* + *cruach*.

Ben Glas (mountain) Stir. 'Grey mountain'. Gaelic *beinn* + *glas*.

Ben Gorm (*An Bhinn Ghorm*) (mountain) Mayo. 'The blue peak'.

Ben Lomond. *See* LOMOND.

Ben More (mountain) Stir. 'Big mountain'. Gaelic *beinn + mór*.

Ben Nevis (mountain) Highland. *Gleann Nibheis* 16th cent. 'Mountain by the River Nevis'. Gaelic *beinn*. The river name derives from an early Celtic word *nebh* 'moist, water'.

Ben Rhydding W. Yorks., not recorded until 1858, from the pers. name *Ben* and **rydding* 'a clearing'.

Ben Vorlich (mountain) Arg. 'Mountain of the sea bag'. Gaelic *beinn* + obscure element.

Benacre Suffolk. *Benagra* 1086 (DB). 'Cultivated plot where beans are grown'. OE *bēan + æcer*.

Benagh (*Beitheanach*) Down. 'Place of birch trees'.

Benbane Head (*An Bhinn Bhán*) Antrim. 'The white headland'.

Benbecula W. Isles. *Beanbeacla* 1449. Possibly 'hill of the fords'. Gaelic *beinn-na-fhaodla*.

Benbeg (*Beann Beag*) Galway. 'Little peak'.

Benbo (*Beann Bó*) Leitrim. 'Peak of the cow'.

Benbrack (*Beann Breac*) Cavan. 'Speckled peak'.

Benbrack (mountain) Dumf. 'Speckled mountain'. Gaelic *beinn + breac*.

Benbulbin (*Beann Ghulbain*) Sligo. 'Gulban's peak'.

Benburb (*An Bhinn Bhorb*) Tyrone. *Beunn Bhoruib* 1621. 'The bold peak'.

Benderloch Arg. *Bintaloch* 1654. 'Hill between two lochs'. Gaelic *beann + eader + da + loch*.

Bendooragh (*Bun Dúraí*) Antrim. *Bun Dubhroighe* c.1645. 'Bottom of black soil'.

Benefield, Upper & *Benefield, Lower* Northants. *Beringafeld* 10th cent., *Benefeld* 1086 (DB). 'Open land of the family or followers of a man called Bera'. OE pers. name + *-inga- + feld*.

Benenden Kent. *Bingdene* 993, *Benindence* 1086 (DB). 'Woodland pasture associated with a man called Bionna'. OE pers. name + *-ing- + denn*.

Benfleet Essex. *Beamfleote* 10th cent., *Benflet* 1086 (DB). 'Tree-trunk creek', perhaps referring to a bridge. OE *bēam + flēot*.

Bengore (*Beann Gabhar*) Antrim. 'Peak of the goats'.

Benhall Green Suffolk. *Benenhala* 1086 (DB). 'Nook of land where beans are grown'. OE *bēanen + halh*.

Beningbrough N. Yorks. *Benniburg* 1086 (DB). 'Stronghold associated with a man called Beonna'. OE pers. name + *-ing- + burh*.

Benington Herts. *Benington* 1086 (DB). 'Farmstead by the River Beane'. Pre-English river-name (of uncertain origin and meaning) + OE *-ing- + tūn*.

Benington Lincs. *Benington* 1166. 'Farmstead associated with a man called Beonna'. OE pers. name + *-ing- + tūn*.

Benllech Angl. 'Head of the stone'. Welsh *pen + llech*. The name refers to the capstone of a cromlech.

Benmore (*Beann Mór*) Antrim. 'Large peak'.

Bennington, Long Lincs. *Beningtun* 1086 (DB). Identical in origin with the previous name.

Benniworth Lincs. *Beningurde* 1086 (DB). 'Enclosure of the family or followers of a man called Beonna'. OE pers. name + *-inga- + worth*.

Benone (*Bun Abhann*) Derry. *Bunowne* 1654. 'Foot of the river'.

Benson Oxon. *Bænesingtun* c.900, *Besintone* 1086 (DB). 'Estate associated with a man called *Benesa'. OE pers. name + *-ing- + tūn*.

Benthall Shrops., near Broseley. *Benethala* 12th cent. 'Nook of land where bent-grass grows'. OE *beonet + halh*.

Bentham, 'homestead or enclosure where bent-grass grows', OE *beonet + hām* or *hamm*: **Bentham** Glos. *Benetham* 1220. **Bentham, High** & **Bentham, Lower** N. Yorks. *Benetain |sic|* 1086 (DB), *Benetham* 1214.

Bentley, a common name, 'woodland clearing where bent-grass grows', OE *beonet + lēah*: examples include: **Bentley** Hants., near Alton. *Beonetleh* c.965, *Benedlei* 1086 (DB). **Bentley** E. R. Yorks. *Benedlage* 1086 (DB). **Bentley** S. Yorks. *Benedleia* 1086 (DB). **Bentley, Fenny** Derbys. *Benedlege* 1086 (DB), *Fennibenetlegh* 1272. Affix is OE *fennig* 'marshy'. **Bentley, Great** & **Bentley, Little** Essex. *Benetleye* c.1040, *Benetlea* 1086 (DB).

Bentworth Hants. *Bintewonda* 1130. Probably 'enclosure of a man called *Binta'. OE pers. name + *worth*.

Benwee Head (*An Bhinn Bhuí*) Mayo. 'The yellow peak'.

Benwick Cambs. *Beymwich* 1221. 'Farm where beans are grown', or 'farm by a tree-trunk'. OE *bēan* or *bēam + wīc*.

Beoley Heref. & Worcs. *Beoleah* 972, *Beolege* 1086 (DB). 'Wood or clearing frequented by bees'. OE *bēo + lēah*.

Bepton W. Sussex. *Babintone* 1086 (DB). 'Estate associated with a woman called Bebbe or a man called *Bebba'. OE pers. name + *-ing- + tūn*.

Beragh (*Bearach*) Tyrone. *Berhagh* 1631. 'Place of peaks'.

Berden Essex. *Berdane* 1086 (DB). Probably 'valley with a woodland pasture'. OE *bær + denu*.

Bere Alston Devon. *Alphameston* 1339, *Berealmiston* c.1450. 'Farmstead of a man called Ælfhelm'. OE pers. name + *tūn*, with *Bere* from BERE FERRERS.

Bere Ferrers Devon. *Birlanda |sic|* 1086 (DB), *Ber* 1242, *Byr Ferrers* 1306. 'Woodland pasture', or 'wood, grove', OE *bær* or *bearu* (in the first spelling with *land* 'estate'). Manorial affix from the de Ferers family, here in the 13th cent.

Bere Regis Dorset. *Bere* 1086 (DB), *Kyngesbyre* 1264. 'Woodland pasture', or 'wood, grove', OE *bær* or *bearu*. Affix is Latin *regis* 'of the king'.

Bergholt, 'Wood on or by a hill', OE *beorg + holt*: **Bergholt, East** Suffolk. *Bercolt* 1086 (DB). **Bergholt, West** Essex. *Bercolt* 1086 (DB).

Berkeley Glos. *Berclea* 824, *Berchelai* 1086 (DB). 'Birch-tree wood or clearing'. OE *beorc + lēah*.

Berkhamsted, Great Herts. *Beorhthanstædæ* 10th cent., *Berchehamstede* 1086 (DB). Probably 'homestead on or near a hill'. OE *beorg* + *hām-stede*.

Berkhamsted, Little Herts. *Berchehamstede* 1086 (DB). Probably 'homestead where birch-trees grow'. OE *beorc* + *hām-stede*.

Berkley Somerset. *Berchelei* 1086 (DB). 'Birch-tree wood or clearing'. OE *beorc* + *lēah*.

Berkshire (the county). *Berrocscire* 893. An ancient Celtic name meaning 'hilly place' + OE *scīr* 'shire, district'.

Berkswell W. Mids. *Berchewelle* 1086 (DB). 'Spring or stream of a man called Beorcol'. OE pers. name + *wella*.

Bermo, Y. *See* BARMOUTH.

Bermondsey Gtr. London. *Vermundesei |sic| c.*712, *Bermundesye* 1086 (DB). 'Island, or dry ground in marsh, of a man called Beornmund'. OE pers. name + *ēg*.

Bernera, Great (island) W. Isles. *Bjarnarey c.*1250. 'Bjarni's island'. OScand. pers. name + *ey*.

Berrick Salome Oxon. *Berewiche* 1086 (DB), *Berwick Sullame* 1571. 'Barley farm', or 'outlying part of an estate'. OE *bere-wīc* + manorial affix from early possession by the de Suleham family.

Berrier Cumbria. *Berghgerge* 1166. 'Shieling or pasture on a hill'. OScand. *berg* + *erg*.

Berrington Northum. *Berigdon* 1208–10. 'Hill with a fortification'. OE *burh* (genitive or dative *byrig*) + *dūn*.

Berrington Shrops. *Beritune* 1086 (DB). 'Farmstead associated with a fortification'. OE *burth* (genitive or dative *byrig*) + *tūn*.

Berrow Somerset. *Burgh* 973, *Berges* 1196. '(Place at) the hill(s) or mound(s)'. OE *beorg*, with reference to the sand-dunes here.

Berrow Green Heref. & Worcs. *Berga* 1275. '(Place at) the hill or mound'. OE *beorg*.

Berry Pomeroy Devon. *Beri* 1086 (DB), *Bury Pomery* 1281. Identical in origin with the previous name. Manorial affix from the de Pomerei family, here from the 11th cent.

Berrynarbor Devon. *Biria c.*1150, *Bery Narberd* 1244. '(Place at) the fortification'. OE *burh* (dative *byrig*) + manorial affix from the Nerebert family, here in the 13th cent.

Bersted W. Sussex. *Beorganstede* 680. Probably 'homestead by a tumulus'. OE *beorg* + *hām-stede*.

Berwick, a common name, from OE *bere-wīc* 'barley farm, outlying part of an estate'; examples include: **Berwick Bassett** Wilts. *Berwicha* 1168, *Berewykbasset* 1321. Manorial affix from the Basset family, here in the 13th cent. **Berwick St James** Wilts. *Berewyk Sancti Jacobi c.*1190. Affix *St James* (Latin *Jacobus*) from the dedication of the church. **Berwick St John** Wilts. *Berwicha* 1167, *Berewyke S. Johannis* 1265. Affix from the dedication of the church. **Berwick St Leonard** Wilts. *Berewica* 12th cent., *Berewyk Sancti Leonardi* 1291. Affix from the dedication of the church. **Berwick upon Tweed** Northum. *Berewich* 1167, *Berewicum super Twedam* 1229. For the river-name, *see* TWEEDMOUTH.

Besford Heref. & Worcs. *Bettesford* 972, *Beford |sic|* 1086 (DB). 'Ford of a man called Betti'. OE pers. name + *ford*.

Bessacarr S. Yorks. *Beseacra* 1182. 'Cultivated plot where bent-grass grows'. OE **bēos* + *æcer*.

Bessbrook Armagh. *Bessbrook* 1888. 'Bess's brook'. The name is that of Elizabeth (Bess) Nicholson, wife of Joseph Nicholson, whose family carried on a linen business here in the early 19th cent. The Irish name of Bessbrook is *An Sruthán*, 'the stream'.

Bessels Leigh Oxon., *see* LEIGH.

Bessingham Norfolk. *Basingeham* 1086 (DB). 'Homestead of the family or followers of a man called **Basa*'. OE pers. name + *-inga-* + *hām*.

Besthorpe, 'outlying farmstead or hamlet of a man called Bōsi, or where bent-grass grows', OScand. pers. name or OE **bēos* + OScand. *thorp*: **Besthorpe** Norfolk. *Besethorp* 1086 (DB). **Besthorpe** Notts. *Bestorp* 1147.

Beswick E.R. Yorks. *Basewic* 1086 (DB). 'Dwelling or (dairy) farm of a man called Bōsi or Bessi'. OScand. pers. name + OE *wīc*.

Betchworth Surrey. *Becesworde* 1086 (DB). 'Enclosure of a man called **Becci*'. OE pers. name + *worth*.

Bethersden Kent. *Baedericesdaenne c.*1100. 'Woodland pasture of a man called Beadurīc'. OE pers. name + *denn*.

Bethesda Gwyd. The town arose around a Welsh Non-conformist chapel built in 1820 that was named after the biblical pool of *Bethesda*, where Jesus healed the sick (John 5:1–10).

Bethnal Green Gtr. London. *Blithehale* 13th cent., *Blethenalegrene* 1443. 'Nook of land of a man called **Blītha*'. OE pers. name (genitive *-n*) + *halh*, with the later addition of grēne 'village green'. Alternatively the first element may be an OE stream-name *Blīthe* meaning 'the gentle one'.

Betley Staffs. *Betelege* 1086 (DB). 'Woodland clearing of a woman called **Bette*'. OE pers. name + *lēah*.

Betteshanger Kent. *Betleshangre* 1176. Probably 'wooded slope by a house or building'. OE *(ge)bytle* + *hangra*.

Bettiscombe Dorset. *Bethescomme* 1129. 'Valley of a man called Betti'. OE pers. name + *cumb*.

Betton, probably 'farmstead or estate where beech-trees grow', OE *bēce* + *tūn*: **Betton** Shrops. near Binweston. *Betune* 1086 (DB). **Betton** Shrops., near Market Drayton. *Baitune* 1086 (DB), *Bectona* 1121.

Bettyhill Highland. 'Betty's hill'. The settlement arose in *c.*1820 and was named for Elizabeth (*Betty*), Countess of Sutherland and Marchioness of Stafford (1765–1839).

Betws-y-coed Conwy. *Betus* 1254, *Bettws y Coed* 1727. 'Chapel in the wood'. Welsh *betws* + *y* + *coed*. Welsh *betws* is borrowed from OE *bed-hūs*, 'oratory' (literally 'bead house').

Bevercotes Notts. *Beurecote* 1165. 'Place where beavers have built their nests'. OE *beofor* + *cot*.

Beverley E. R. Yorks. *Beferlic c.*1025, *Bevreli* 1086 (DB). Probably 'stream frequented by beavers'. OE *beofor* + **licc*.

Beverstone Glos. *Beurestane* 1086 (DB). Probably '(boundary) stone of a man called *Beofor'. OE pers. name + *stān*.

Bewaldeth Cumbria. *Bualdith* 1255. 'Homestead or estate of a woman called Aldgȳth'. OScand. *bú* + OE pers. name. The order of elements is Celtic.

Bewcastle Cumbria. *Bothecastre* 12th cent. 'Roman fort within which shelters or huts were situated'. OScand. *búth* + OE *ceaster*.

Bewdley Heref. & Worcs. *Beuleu* 1275. 'Beautiful place'. OFrench *beau* + *lieu*.

Bewerley N. Yorks. *Beurelie* 1086 (DB). 'Woodland clearing frequented by beavers'. OE *beofor* + *lēah*.

Bewholme E. R. Yorks. *Begun* 1086 (DB). '(Place at) the river-bends'. OE *bēag* or OScand. **bjúgr* in a dative plural form *bēagum* or **bjúgum*.

Bexhill E. Sussex. *Bixlea* 772, *Bexelei* 1086 (DB). 'Wood or clearing where box-trees grow'. OE **byxe* + *lēah*.

Bexington Dorset. *Bessintone* 1086 (DB). 'Farmstead or village where box-trees grow'. OE *byxen* + *tūn*.

Bexley Gtr. London. *Byxlea* 814. 'Wood or clearing where box-trees grow'. OE **byxe* + *lēah*. **Bexleyheath** is a more recent name with the addition *heath*.

Bexwell Norfolk. *Bekeswella* 1086 (DB). 'Spring or stream of a man called *Bēac'. OE pers. name + *wella*.

Beyton Suffolk. *Begatona* 1086 (DB). Probably 'farmstead of a woman called Bēage or of a man called Bǣga'. OE pers. name + *tūn*.

Bibury Glos. *Beaganbyrig* 8th cent., *Begeberie* 1086 (DB). 'Stronghold or manor house of a woman called Bēage'. OE pers. name + *burh* (dative *byrig*). Bēage is named as leasing the estate in a document dated 718–45.

Bicester Oxon. *Bernecestre* 1086 (DB). 'Fort of the warriors, or of a man called Beorna'. OE *beorn* or OE pers. name + *ceaster*.

Bickenhall Somerset. *Bichehalle* 1086 (DB). Probably 'hall of a man called Bica'. OE pers. name (genitive -*n*) + *heall*.

Bickenhill W. Mids. *Bichehelle* 1086 (DB), *Bikenhulle* 1202. Probably 'hill with a point, projecting hill'. OE **bica* (genitive -*n*) + *hyll*.

Bicker Lincs. *Bichere* 1086 (DB). Probably 'village marsh', from OScand. *bý* + *kjarr*. Alternatively '(place) by the marsh', with OE *bī* as first element.

Bickerstaffe Lancs. *Bikerstad* late 12th cent. 'Landing-place of the bee-keepers'. OE **bīcere* + *stæth*.

Bickerton, 'farmstead of the bee-keepers', OE **bīcere* + *tūn*: **Bickerton** Ches. *Bicretone* 1086 (DB). **Bickerton** N. Yorks. *Bicretone* 1086 (DB).

Bickington, 'estate associated with a man called Beocca', OE pers. name + -*ing*- + *tūn*: **Bickington** Devon, near Ashburton. *Bechintona* 1107. **Bickington, Abbots** Devon. *Bicatona* 1086 (DB), *Abbots Bekenton* 1580. Affix from early possession by Hartland Abbey. **Bickington, High** Devon. *Bichentona* 1086 (DB), *Heghebuginton* 1423. Affix is OE *hēah* 'high'.

Bickleigh, *Bickley*, probably 'woodland clearing on or near a pointed ridge', OE **bica* + *lēah*: **Bickleigh** Devon, near Plymouth. *Bicheleia* 1086 (DB). **Bickleigh** Devon, near Tiverton. *Bicanleag* 904, *Bichelia* 1086 (DB). **Bickley** Gtr. London. *Byckeleye* 1279. **Bickley Moss** Ches. *Bichelei* 1086 (DB). Later addition is OE *mos* 'peat-bog'.

Bicknacre Essex. *Bikenacher* 1186. Probably 'cultivated plot of a man called Bica'. OE pers. name (genitive -*n*) + *æcer*.

Bicknoller Somerset. *Bykenalre* 1291. 'Alder-tree of a man called Bica'. OE pers. name (genitive -*n*) + *alor*.

Bicknor Kent. *Bikenora* 1186. Probably 'slope below the pointed hill'. OE **bica* (genitive -*n*) + *ōra*.

Bicknor, English Glos. *Bicanofre* 1086 (DB), *Englise Bykenore* 1248. Probably 'ridge with a point'. OE **bica* (genitive -*n*) + **ofer*. Affix from its situation on the *English* side of the River Wye.

Bicknor, Welsh Heref. & Worcs. *Bykenore Walens* 1291. Identical in origin with the previous name, with distinguishing affix from its situation on the *Welsh* side of the River Wye.

Bickton Hants. *Bichetone* 1086 (DB). Probably 'farmstead of a man called Bica'. OE pers. name + *tūn*.

Bicton Shrops., near Shrewsbury. *Bichetone* |sic| 1086 (DB), *Bikedon* 1204. Probably 'hill with a pointed ridge'. OE **bica* + *dūn*.

Bidborough Kent. *Bitteberga* c.1100. 'Hill or mound of a man called *Bitta'. OE pers. name + *beorg*.

Biddenden Kent. *Bidingden* 993. 'Woodland pasture associated with a man called *Bida'. OE pers. name + -*ing*- + *denn*.

Biddenham Beds. *Bidenham* 1086 (DB). 'Homestead, or land in a river-bend, of a man called Bīeda'. OE pers. name (genitive -*n*) + *hām* or *hamm*.

Biddestone Wilts. *Bedestone* 1086 (DB), *Bedeneston* 1187. Probably 'farmstead of a man called *Bīedin or *Bīede'. OE pers. name + *tūn*.

Biddisham Somerset. *Biddesham* 1065. 'Homestead or enclosure of a man called *Biddi'. OE pers. name + *hām* or *hamm*.

Biddlesden Bucks. *Betesdene* |sic| 1086 (DB), *Bethlesdena* 12th cent. Probably 'valley with a house or building'. OE **bythle* + *denu*. Alternatively the first element may be an OE pers. name *Byttel.

Biddlestone Northum. *Bidlisden* 1242. Probably identical in origin with the previous name.

Biddulph Staffs. *Bidolf* 1086 (DB). '(Place) by the pit or quarry'. OE *bī* + **dylf*.

Bideford Devon. *Bedeford* 1086 (DB). Possibly 'ford at the stream called Bȳd'. Celtic river-name (of uncertain origin and meaning) + OE *ēa* + *ford*.

Bidford on Avon Warwicks. *Budiford* 710, *Bedeford* 1086 (DB). Probably identical in origin with the previous name, but alternatively the first element may be an OE **bydic* 'trough, deep place'.

Bidston Mersey. *Budeston, Bediston* 1260, *Budestan* 1286. Probably 'rocky hill with a house or building'. OE **bythle + stān*.

Bielby E. R. Yorks. *Belebi* 1086 (DB). 'Farmstead or village of a man called Beli'. OScand. pers. name + *bý*.

Bierley W. Yorks. *Birle* 1086 (DB). 'Woodland clearing by the stronghold'. OE *burh* (genitive *byrh*) + *lēah*.

Bierton Bucks. *Bortone* 1086 (DB). 'Farmstead near the stronghold'. OE *byrh-tūn*.

Big Mancot Flin. *Manecote* 1284, *Great Mancott* 1547. 'Mana's cottage'. OE pers. name + *cot*. *Big* for distinction from adjoining *Little Mancot*.

Bigbury Devon. *Bicheberie* 1086 (DB). 'Stronghold of a man called Bica'. OE pers. name + *burh* (dative *byrig*).

Bigby Lincs. *Bechebi* 1086 (DB). Probably 'farmstead or village of a man called **Bekki*'. OScand. pers. name + *bý*.

Biggar S. Lan. *Bigir* 1170. Meaning uncertain, but traditionally thought to be 'Triangular plot of land where barley is grown'. OScand. *bygg* + *geiri*.

Biggin Hill Gtr. London. *Byggunhull* 1499. 'Hill with or near a building'. ME *bigging* + OE *hyll*.

Biggleswade Beds. *Pichelesuuade* |sic| 1086 (DB), *Bicheleswada* 1132. 'Ford of a man called **Biccel*'. OE pers. name + *wæd*.

Bighton Hants. *Bicincgtun* 959, *Bighetone* 1086 (DB). 'Estate associated with a man called Bica'. OE pers. name + *-ing-* + *tūn*.

Bignor W. Sussex. *Bigenevre* 1086 (DB). 'Hill brow of a man called **Bicga*'. OE pers. name (genitive *-n*) + *yfer*.

Bilborough Notts. *Bileburch* 1086 (DB). 'Stronghold of a man called **Bila* or **Billa*'. OE pers. name + *burh*.

Bilbrook Staffs. *Bilrebroch* 1086 (DB). 'Brook where watercress grows'. OE *billere* + *brōc*.

Bilbrough N. Yorks. *Mileburg* |sic| 1086 (DB), *Billeburc* 1167. Identical in origin with BILBOROUGH.

Bildeston Suffolk. *Bilestuna* 1086 (DB). Identical in origin with BILSTONE.

Billericay Essex. *Byllyrica* 1291. Probably from a medieval Latin word **bellerīca* meaning 'dyehouse or tanhouse'.

Billesdon Leics. *Billesdone* 1086 (DB). 'Hill of a man called Bill'. OE pers. name + *dūn*. Alternatively the first element may be OE *bill* 'sword' used of a pointed hill.

Billesley Warwicks. *Billeslæh* 704–9, *Billeslei* 1086 (DB). 'Woodland clearing of a man called Bill'. OE pers. name + *lēah*. Alternatively the first element may be OE *bill* 'pointed hill'.

Billing, Great & **Billing, Little** Northants. *Bel(l)inge* 1086 (DB). Probably '(settlement of) the family or followers of a man called Bill or **Billa*'. OE pers. name + *-ingas*.

Billingborough Lincs. *Billingeburg* 1086 (DB). Probably 'stronghold of the family or followers of a man called Bill or **Billa*'. OE pers. name + *-inga-* + *burh*.

Billinge Mersey. *Billing* 1202. Probably OE **bil(l)ing* 'a hill, a sharp ridge'.

Billingham Stock. on T. *Billingham* c.1050. 'Homestead of the family or followers of a man called Bill or **Billa*, or

'homestead at the place associated with Bill(a)'. OE pers. name + *-inga-* or *-ing* + *hām*. Alternatively the first element may be OE **bil(l)ing* 'a hill'.

Billinghay Lincs. *Belingei* 1086 (DB). 'Island, or dry ground in marsh, of the family or followers of a man called Bill or **Billa*'. OE pers. name + *-inga-* + *ēg*.

Billingley S. Yorks. *Bilingeleia* 1086 (DB). 'Woodland clearing of the family or followers of a man called Bill or **Billa*'. OE pers. name + *-inga-* + *lēah*.

Billingshurst W. Sussex. *Bellingesherst* 1202. Probably 'wooded hill of a man called Billing'. OE pers. name + *hyrst*. Alternatively the first element may be OE **bil(l)ing* 'a hill, a sharp ridge'.

Billington Beds. *Billendon* 1196. 'Hill of a man called **Billa*'. OE pers. name (genitive *-n*) + *dūn*.

Billington Lancs. *Billingduna* 1196. 'Hill with a sharp ridge'. OE **bil(l)ing* + *dūn*.

Billockby Norfolk. *Bithlakebei* 1086 (DB). Possibly 'farmstead or village of a man called **Bithil-Áki*'. OScand. pers. name + *bý*.

Bilney, 'island near a ridge', or 'island of a man called Bil(l)a', OE *bile* or OE pers. name (genitive *-n*) + *ēg*: **Bilney, East** Norfolk. *Billneye* 1254. **Bilney, West** Norfolk. *Bilenei* 1086 (DB).

Bilsborrow Lancs. *Billesbure* 1187. 'Stronghold of a man called Bill'. OE pers. name + *burh*.

Bilsby Lincs. *Billesbi* 1086 (DB). 'Farmstead or village of a man called Bildr'. OScand. pers. name + *bý*.

Bilsington Kent. *Bilsvitone* 1086 (DB). 'Farmstead of a woman called Bilswīth'. OE pers. name + *tūn*.

Bilsthorpe Notts. *Bildestorp* 1086 (DB). 'Outlying farmstead or hamlet of a man called Bildr'. OScand. pers. name + *thorp*. Alternatively the first element may be OScand. *bildr* 'angle' used figuratively for 'hill, promontory'.

Bilston W. Mids. *Bilsetnatun* 996, *Billestune* 1086 (DB). 'Farmstead of the dwellers at the sharp ridge'. OE *bill* + *sǣte* (genitive plural *sǣtna*) + *tūn*.

Bilstone Leics. *Bildestone* 1086 (DB). Probably 'farmstead of a man called Bildr'. OScand. pers. name + OE *tūn*. Alternatively the first element may be OScand. *bildr* 'angle' used figuratively for 'hill, promontory'.

Bilton, usually 'farmstead of a man called Bill or **Billa*', OE pers. name + *tūn*: **Bilton** E. R. Yorks. *Bil(l)etone* 1086 (DB). **Bilton** Northum. *Bylton* 1242. **Bilton** N. Yorks. *Biletone* 1086 (DB).
   However with a different origin is: **Bilton** Warwicks. *Beltone, Bentone* 1086 (DB). Possibly 'farmstead where henbane grows'. OE *beolone* + *tūn*.

Binbrook Lincs. *Binnibroc* 1086 (DB). '(Place) enclosed by the brook', or 'brook of a man called Bynna'. OE *binnan* or OE pers. name + *brōc*. OE *binn(e)* 'manger, stall', perhaps used in a figurative sense 'valley', would also be a possible first element.

Bincombe Dorset. *Beuncumbe* 987, *Beincome* 1086 (DB). Probably 'valley where beans are grown'. OE *bēan* + *cumb*.

Binegar Somerset. *Begenhangra* 1065. Probably 'wooded slope of a woman called Bēage'. OE pers. name (genitive *-n*) + *hangra*. Alternatively the first element may be OE **begen* 'growing with berries'.

Binevenagh (*Binn Fhoibhne*) Derry. 'Foibhne's peak'.

Binfield Berks. *Benetfeld c.*1160. 'Open land where bent-grass grows'. OE *beonet* + *feld*.

Binfield Heath Oxon. *Benifeld* 1177. Probably identical in origin with the previous name, but possibly 'open land of a man called **Beona*'. OE pers. name + *feld*. The addition *heath* is found from the 16th cent.

Bingfield Northum. *Bingefeld* 1181. Probably 'open land of the family or followers of a man called Bynna'. OE pers. name + *-inga-* + *feld*. Alternatively in this and the following two names the first element may be an OE **bing* 'a hollow'.

Bingham Notts. *Bingheham* 1086 (DB). Probably 'homestead of the family or followers of a man called Bynna'. OE pers. name + *-inga-* + *hām*. But *see* BINGFIELD.

Bingley W. Yorks. *Bingelei* 1086 (DB). Probably 'woodland clearing of the family or followers of a man called Bynna'. OE pers. name + *-inga-* + *lēah*. But see BINGFIELD.

Binham Norfolk. *Binneham* 1086 (DB). 'Homestead or enclosure of a man called Bynna'. OE pers. name + *hām* or *hamm*.

Binley W. Mids. *Bilnei* 1086 (DB). 'Island near a ridge', or 'island of a man called Bil(l)a'. OE *bile* or pers. name (genitive *-n*) + *ēg*.

Binstead I. of Wight. *Benestede* 1086 (DB). 'Place where beans are grown', OE *bēan* + *stede*.

Binsted Hants. *Benestede* 1086 (DB). Identical in origin with the previous name.

Binton Warwicks. *Bynningtun c.*1005, *Beninton* 1086 (DB). 'Estate associated with a man called Bynna'. OE pers. name + *-ing-* + *tūn*.

Bintree Norfolk. *Binnetre* 1086 (DB). 'Tree of a man called Bynna'. OE pers. name + *trēow*.

Binweston Shrops. *Binneweston* 1292. Probably 'west farmstead of a man called Bynna'. OE pers. name + *west* + *tūn*.

Birch Essex. *Bric(ce)iam* 1086 (DB). OE *bryce* 'land newly broken up for cultivation'.

Birch, Much & *Birch, Little* Heref. & Worcs. *Birches* 1252. '(Place at) the birch-tree(s).' OE *birce*. The affix *Much* is from OE *micel* 'great'.

Bircham, Great, *Bircham Newton*, *Bircham Tofts* Norfolk. *Brecham* 1086 (DB). 'Homestead by newly cultivated ground'. OE *brēc* + *hām*. Bircham Newton is *Niwetuna* 1086 (DB), 'new farmstead', OE *nīwe* + *tūn*. Bircham Tofts is *Toftes* 1205, OScand. *toft* 'homestead'.

Birchanger Essex. *Bilichangra* |*sic*| 1086 (DB), *Birichangre* 12th cent. 'Wooded slope growing with birch-trees'. OE *birce* + *hangra*.

Bircher Heref. & Worcs. *Burchoure* 1212. 'Ridge where birch-trees grow'. OE *birce* + **ofer*.

Birchington Kent. *Birchenton* 1240. 'Farmstead where birch-trees grow'. OE **bircen* + *tūn*.

Birchover Derbys. *Barcovere* |*sic*| 1086 (DB), *Birchoure* 1226. 'Ridge where birch-trees grow'. OE *birce* + **ofer*.

Birdbrook Essex. *Bridebroc* 1086 (DB). 'Brook frequented by birds'. OE *bridd* + *brōc*.

Birdham W. Sussex. *Bridham* 683, *Brideham* 1086 (DB). 'Homestead or enclosure frequented by birds'. OE *bridd* + *hām* or *hamm*.

Birdlip Glos. *Bridelepe* 1221. Probably 'steep place frequented by birds'. OE *bridd* + **hlēp*.

Birdsall N. Yorks. *Brideshala* 1086 (DB). 'Nook of land of a man called Bridd'. OE pers. name + *halh*.

Birkby N. Yorks. *Bretebi* 1086 (DB). 'Farmstead or village of the Britons'. OScand. *Bretar* + *bý*. The same name occurs in W. Yorks. and Cumbria.

Birkdale Mersey. *Birkedale c.*1200. 'Valley where birch-trees grow'. OScand. *birki* + *dalr*.

Birkenhead Mersey. *Bircheveth c.*1200. 'Headland where birch-trees grow'. OE *birce*, **bircen* (with Scand. *-k-*) + *hēafod*.

Birkenshaw W. Yorks. *Birkenschawe* 1274. 'Small wood or copse where birch-trees grow'. OE **bircen* (with Scand. *-k-*) + *sceaga*.

Birkin N. Yorks. *Byrcene c.*1030, *Berchine* 1086 (DB). 'Place growing with birch-trees'. OE **bircen* (with Scand. *-k-*).

Birley Heref. & Worcs. *Burlei* 1086 (DB). 'Woodland clearing near a stronghold'. OE *burh* + *lēah*.

Birling, probably '(settlement of) the family or followers of a man called **Bærla*', OE pers. name + *-ingas*: **Birling** Kent. *Boerlingas* 788, *Berlinge* 1086 (DB). **Birling** Northum. *Berlinga* 1187.

Birlingham Heref. & Worcs. *Byrlingahamm* 972, *Berlingeham* 1086 (DB). 'Land in a river-bend of the family or followers of a man called **Byrla*'. OE pers. name + *-inga-* + *hamm*.

Birmingham W. Mids. *Bermingeham* 1086 (DB). 'Homestead of the family or followers of a man called **Beorma*', or 'homestead at the place associated with **Beorma*'. OE pers. name + *-inga-* or *-ing* + *hām*.

Birnie Moray. *Brennach c.*1190. 'Marshy place'. Gaelic *braonach*.

Birr (*Biorra*) Offaly. 'Stream'.

Birra (*Biorra*) Donegal. 'Stream'.

Birstall Leics. *Burstelle* 1086 (DB). OE *burhstall* 'the site of a stronghold'.

Birstall W. Yorks. *Birstale* 12th cent. Identical in meaning with the previous name, but from OE *byrh-stall*.

Birstwith N. Yorks. *Beristade* 1086 (DB). Probably 'farm built on the site of a lost farm'. OScand. *býjar-stathr*.

Birtley, 'bright clearing'. OE *beorht* + *lēah*: **Birtley** Northum. *Birtleye* 1229. **Birtley** Tyne & Wear. *Britleia* 1183.

Bisbrooke Rutland. *Bitlesbroch* 1086 (DB). Possibly 'brook of a man called **Bitel* or **Byttel*', OE pers.

name + *brōc*. Alternatively 'brook infested by water-beetles', from an OE *bitel* 'beetle'.

Bisham Berks. *Bistesham* 1086 (DB), *Bistlesham* 1199. 'Homestead or enclosure of a man called *Byssel'. OE pers. name + *hām* or *hamm*.

Bishampton Heref. & Worcs. *Bisantune* 1086 (DB). Possibly 'homestead of a man called *Bisa'. OE pers. name + *hām-tūn*.

Bishop, *Bishops* as affix, see main name, *e.g.* for **Bishop Auckland** (Durham) *see* AUCKLAND.

Bishop's Castle Shrops. *Castrum Episcopi* 1255, *Bisshopescastel* 1282. Named from the castle (Latin *castrum*, ME *castel*) erected *c*.1127 by the Bishop of Hereford.

Bishopsbourne Kent. *Burnan* 799, *Burnes* 1086 (DB), *Biscopesburne* 11th cent. 'Estate on the river called *Burna*' (from OE *burna* 'stream' referring to the Little Stour), with later affix (OE *biscop*) from its possession by the Archbishop of Canterbury.

Bishopsteignton Devon. *Taintona* 1086 (DB), *Teynton Bishops* 1341. 'Farmstead on the River Teign'. Celtic river-name (*see* TEIGNMOUTH) + OE *tūn*, with manorial affix from its possession by the Bishop of Exeter in 1086.

Bishopstoke Hants. *Stoches* 1086 (DB), *Stoke Episcopi* *c*.1270. 'Outlying farmstead or hamlet (of the bishop)'. OE *stoc* with later addition from its possession by the Bishop of Winchester.

Bishopstone, 'the bishop's estate', OE *biscop* + *tūn*; examples include: **Bishopstone** Bucks. *Bissopeston* 1227. **Bishopstone** E. Sussex. *Biscopestone* 1086 (DB). **Bishopstone** Heref. & Worcs. *Biscopestone* 1166. **Bishopstone** Wilts., near Swindon. *Bissopeston* 1186. **Bishopstone** Wilts., near Wilton. *Bissopeston* 1166.

Bishopsworth Brist. *Biscopewrde* 1086 (DB). 'The bishop's enclosure'. OE *biscop* + *worth*.

Bishopthorpe York. *Torp* 1086 (DB), *Biscupthorp* 1275. 'Outlying farmstead or hamlet held by the bishop'. OE *biscop* + OScand. *thorp*.

Bishopton Durham. *Biscoptun* 1104–8. 'The bishop's estate'. OE *biscop* + *tūn*.

Bisley Glos. *Bislege* 986, *Biselege* 1086 (DB). 'Woodland clearing of a man called *Bisa'. OE pers. name + *lēah*.

Bisley Surrey. *Busseleghe* 933. 'Woodland clearing of a man called *Byssa'. OE pers. name + *lēah*.

Bispham, 'the bishop's estate', OE *biscop* + *hām*: **Bispham** Lancs. *Biscopham* 1086 (DB). **Bispham Green** Lancs. *Biscopehaim* *c*.1200.

Bisterne Close Hants. *Betestre* |sic| 1086 (DB), *Budestorn* 1187. Probably 'thorn-tree of a man called *Bytti'. OE pers. name + *thorn*.

Bitchfield Lincs. *Billesfelt* 1086 (DB). 'Open land of a man called Bill'. OE pers. name + *feld*. Alternatively the first element may be OE *bill* 'sword' used figuratively for 'hill, promontory'.

Bittadon Devon. *Bedendone* |sic| 1086 (DB), *Bettenden* 1205. 'Valley of a man called *Beotta'. OE pers. name + *denu*.

Bittering Norfolk. *Britringa* 1086 (DB). '(Settlement of) the family or followers of a man called Beorhthere'. OE pers. name + *-ingas*.

Bitterley Shrops. *Buterlie* 1086 (DB). 'Pasture which produces good butter'. OE *butere* + *lēah*.

Bitterne Hants. *Byterne* *c*.1090. Possibly 'house near a bend'. OE *byht* + *ærn*.

Bitteswell Leics. *Betmeswelle* 1086 (DB). Probably 'spring or stream in a broad valley'. OE *bytm* + *wella*.

Bitton S. Glos. *Betune* 1086 (DB). 'Farmstead on the River Boyd'. Celtic river-name (of uncertain origin and meaning) + OE *tūn*.

Biwmares. *See* BEAUMARIS.

Bix Oxon. *Bixa* 1086 (DB). '(Place at) the box-tree wood'. OE *byxe*.

Blaby Leics. *Bladi* |sic| 1086 (DB), *Blabi* 1175. Probably 'farmstead or village of a man called Blár'. OScand. pers. name + *bý*.

Black as affix, *see* main name, e.g. for **Black Bourton** (Oxon.) *see* BOURTON.

Black Mountains (*Y Mynydd Du*) Powys. 'Dark mountains'. The Welsh name corresponds to the English but is singular.

Blackawton Devon. *Auetone* 1086 (DB), *Blakeauetone* 1281. 'Farmstead of a man called Afa'. OE pers. name + *tūn*. Affix is OE *blæc* 'dark-coloured' (referring to soil or vegetation).

Blackborough, 'dark-coloured hill', OE *blæc* + *beorg*: **Blackborough** Devon. *Blacaberga* 1086 (DB). **Blackborough End** Norfolk. *Blakeberge* *c*.1150.

Blackburn Lancs. *Blacheburne* 1086 (DB). 'Dark-coloured stream'. OE *blæc* + *burna*.

Blackden Heath Ches. *Blakedene* 1287. 'Dark valley'. OE *blæc* + *denu*.

Blackfield Hants., a recent name, self-explanatory.

Blackford Somerset, near Wedmore. *Blacford* 1227. 'Dark ford'. OE *blæc* + *ford*.

Blackfordby Leics. *Blakefordebi* *c*.1125. 'Farmstead at the dark ford'. OE *blæc* + *ford* + OScand. *bý*.

Blackgang I. of Wight, first recorded in 1781, 'the dark path or track', from dialect *gang*.

Blackheath Gtr. London. *Blachehedfeld* 1166. 'Dark-coloured heathland'. OE *blæc* + *hǣth* (with *feld* 'open land' in the early form).

Blackland Wilts. *Blakeland* 1194. 'Dark-coloured cultivated land'. OE *blæc* + *land*.

Blackley Gtr. Manch. *Blakeley* 1282. 'Dark wood or clearing'. OE *blæc* + *lēah*.

Blacklion Cavan. *Black Lion Inn* 1778. The former Irish name was *An Leargaidh*, 'the slope'.

Blackmoor Hants. *Blachemere* 1168. 'Dark-coloured pool'. OE *blæc* + *mere*.

Blackmore Essex. *Blakemore* 1213. 'Dark-coloured marshland'. OE *blæc* + *mōr*.

Blackpool Lancs. *Pul c*.1260, *Blackpoole* 1602. 'Dark-coloured pool'. OE *blæc* + **pull*.

Blackrod Gtr. Manch. *Blacherode c*.1189. 'Dark clearing'. OE *blæc* + **rodu*.

Blackskull Antrim. *Blackskull* 1898. The name originated from an inn with a negro-head sign.

Blackstaff (*Abhainn Bheara*) (river) Antrim. 'River of the staff'. English *black* presumably describes the *staff* or beam that formed a primitive bridge over the river.

Blackthorn Oxon. *Blaketorn* 1190. '(Place at) the blackthorn or sloe-tree'. OE **blæc-thorn*.

Blacktoft E. R. Yorks. *Blaketofte c*.1160. 'Dark-coloured homestead'. OE *blæc* + OScand. *toft*.

Blackwater (*An Abhainn Mór*) (river) Armagh, Cork, Tyrone. 'The big river'.

Blackwatertown Armagh. The village lies on the river BLACKWATER. Its Irish name is *An Port Mór*, 'the big landing-place'.

Blackwell, 'dark-coloured spring or stream', OE *blæc* + *wella*: **Blackwell** Derbys., near Buxton. *Blachewelle* 1086 (DB). **Blackwell** Durham. *Blakewell* 1183. **Blackwell** Warwicks. *Blacwælle* 964, *Blachewelle* 1086 (DB).

Blackwood (*Coed-duon*) Cphy. *Coed-dduon* 1833, *Blackwood* 1856. 'Dark wood'. The Welsh name corresponds to the English.

Blacon Ches. *Blachehol* |*sic*| 1086 (DB), *Blachenol* 1093. 'Dark-coloured hill'. OE *blæc* + *cnoll*.

Bladon Oxon. *Blade* 1086 (DB). A pre-English river-name of uncertain origin and meaning, an old name of the River EVENLODE.

Blaenafon. *See* BLAENAVON.

Blaenau. *See* BLAINA.

Blaenau Ffestiniog Gwyd. *Festynyok c*.1420. 'Uplands of Ffestiniog'. Welsh *blaen* (plural *blaenau*). *Ffestiniog* means 'territory of Ffestin' or possibly 'defensive (place)' (Welsh *ffestiniog*). The town is a 19th-cent. industrial development.

Blaenavon (*Blaenafon*) Torf. *Blaen Avon* 1532, *Blaen-Avon, or Avon* 1868. 'Headstream of the river'. Welsh *blaen* + *afon*. The river is the Sychan.

Blagdon, 'dark-coloured hill', OE *blæc* + *dūn*: **Blagdon** N. Som. *Blachedone* 1086 (DB). **Blagdon** Devon. *Blakedone* 1242. **Blagdon** Somerset. *Blakedona* 12th cent.

Blaina (*Blaenau*) Blae. 'Uplands'. Welsh *blaen* (plural *blaenau*).

Blair Atholl Perth. *Athochlach c*.970, *Athfoithle c*.1050. 'Plain in Atholl'. Gaelic *blàr*. *Atholl* means 'New Ireland' (Gaelic *ath* + *Fótla*, a poetic name for Ireland). The name was given by the Gaels when they came from Ireland to settle in this part of Scotland.

Blairgowrie Perth. *Blare* 13th cent., *Blair in Gowrie* 1604. 'Plain in *Gowrie*'. Gaelic *blàr*. *Gowrie* is (territory of) Gabran', after a 6th-cent. Gaelic king, for distinction from BLAIR ATHOLL.

Blaisdon Glos. *Blechedon* 1186. 'Hill of a man called **Blæcci*'. OE pers. name + *dūn*.

Blakemere Heref. & Worcs. *Blakemere* 1249. 'Dark-coloured pool'. OE *blæc* + *mere*.

Blakeney, 'dark-coloured island or dry ground in marsh', OE *blæc* (dative *blacan*) + *ēg*: **Blakeney** Glos. *Blakeneia* 1196. **Blakeney** Norfolk. *Blakenye* 1242.

Blakenhall Ches. *Blachenhale* 1086 (DB). 'Dark nook of land'. OE *blæc* (dative *blacan*) + *halh*.

Blakenham, Great & *Blakenham, Little* Suffolk. *Blac*(*he*)*ham* 1086 (DB). Probably 'homestead or enclosure of a man called Blaca'. OE pers. name (genitive *-n*) + *hām* or *hamm*.

Blakesley Northants. *Blaculveslei* 1086 (DB). 'Woodland clearing of a man called **Blæcwulf*'. OE pers. name + *lēah*.

Blanchardstown (*Baile Bhlainséir*) Dublin. 'Blanchard's town'.

Blanchland Northum. *Blanchelande* 1165. 'White woodland glade'. OFrench *blanche* + *launde*.

Blandford Forum, *Blandford St Mary* Dorset. *Blaneford* 1086 (DB), *Blaneford Forum* 1297, *Blaneford St Mary* 1254. Probably 'ford where blay or gudgeon are found'. OE *blæge* (genitive plural *blægna*) + *ford*. Distinguishing affixes from Latin *forum* 'market' and from the dedication of the church.

Blaney (*Bléinigh*) Fermanagh. *Bleny* 1659. 'Inlet'.

Blankney Lincs. *Blachene* |*sic*| 1086 (DB), *Blancaneia* 1157. 'Island, or dry ground in marsh, of a man called **Blanca*'. OE pers. name (genitive *-n*) + *ēg*.

Blantyre S. Lan. Possibly 'edge land'. Gaelic *tir* with uncertain first element.

Blaris (*Blárás*) Down. 'Place of open fields'.

Blarney (*An Bhlarna*) Cork. 'The small field'.

Blaston Leics. *Bladestone* 1086 (DB). Possibly 'farmstead of a man called **Blēath*'. OE pers. name + *tūn*.

Blatchington, 'estate associated with a man called Blæcca', OE pers. name + *-ing-* + *tūn*: **Blatchington, East** E. Sussex. *Blechinton* 1169. **Blatchington, West** E. Sussex. *Blacinctona* 1121.

Blatherwycke Northants. *Blarewiche* 1086 (DB). Possibly 'farm where bladder-plants grow'. OE *blædre* + *wīc*.

Blawith Cumbria. *Blawit* 1276. 'Dark wood'. OScand. *blár* + *vithr*.

Blaxhall Suffolk. *Blaccheshala* 1086 (DB). 'Nook of land belonging to a man called **Blæc*'. OE pers. name + *halh*.

Blaxton S. Yorks. *Blacston* 1213. 'Black boundary stone'. OE *blæc* + *stān*.

Blaydon Tyne & Wear. *Bladon* 1340. Probably 'cold or cheerless hill'. OScand. *blár* + OE *dūn*.

Bleadon N. Som. *Bleodun* 956, *Bledone* 1086 (DB), 'Variegated hill'. OE **blēo* + *dūn*.

Blean Kent. *Blean* 724, *Blehem* |*sic*| 1086 (DB), Probably '(place in) the rough ground'. OE **blēa* (dative *-n*).

Bleasby Notts. *Blisetune* 956, *Blesby* 1268. Probably 'farmstead or village of a man called Blesi'. OScand. pers. name + *bý* (OE *tūn* in the earliest form).

Bledington Glos. *Bladintun* 1086 (DB). 'Farmstead on the River *Bladon*'. Pre-English river-name of uncertain origin and meaning (an old name of River EVENLODE) + OE *tūn*.

Bledlow Bucks. *Bleddanhlæw* 10th cent., *Bledelai* 1086 (DB). 'Burial-mound of a man called *Bledda*'. OE pers. name + *hlāw*.

Blencarn Cumbria. *Blencarn* 1159. 'Cairn or rock summit'. Celtic *blain* + *carn*.

Blencogo Cumbria. *Blencoggou* c.1190. 'Cuckoos' summit'. Celtic *blain* + *cog* (plural *cogow*).

Blencow, Great & *Blencow, Little* Cumbria. *Blenco* 1231, *Blenkhaw* 1255. Celtic *blain* 'summit' with an obscure second element, to which OScand. *haugr* 'hill' has been added.

Blendworth Hants. *Blednewrthie* c.1170. Probably 'enclosure of a man called *Blædna*'. OE pers. name + *worth*.

Blennerhasset Cumbria. *Blennerheiseta* 1188. Celtic *blain* 'summit' with an obscure second element, to which OScand. *hey* 'hay' and *sætr* 'shieling' have been added.

Blessington (*Baile Coimhín*) Wicklow. The Irish name, meaning 'Ó Comaín's homestead', was originally anglicized as *Ballycomin*. This was taken to represent *baile comaoine*, 'homestead of favour', and was accordingly misrendered in English as *Blessington*, 'town of blessing'.

Bletchingdon Oxon. *Blecesdone* 1086 (DB). 'Hill of a man called *Blecci*'. OE pers. name + *dūn*.

Bletchingley Surrey. *Blachingelei* 1086 (DB). 'Woodland clearing of the family or followers of a man called Blæcca'. OE pers. name + -*inga*- + *lēah*.

Bletchley Bucks. *Blechelai* 12th cent. 'Woodland clearing of a man called Blæcca'. OE pers. name + *lēah*.

Bletchley Shrops. *Blecheslee* 1222. 'Woodland clearing of a man called Blæcca or *Blecci*'. OE pers. name + *lēah*.

Bletsoe Beds. *Blechesho* 1086 (DB). 'Hillspur of a man called *Blecci*'. OE pers. name + *hōh*.

Blewbury Oxon. *Bleobyrig* 944, *Blidberia* |sic| 1086 (DB). 'Hill-fort with variegated soil'. OE *blēo* + *burh* (dative *byrig*).

Blickling Norfolk. *Blikelinges* 1086 (DB). '(Settlement of) the family or followers of a man called *Blicla*'. OE pers. name + -*ingas*.

Blidworth Notts. *Blideworde* 1086 (DB). 'Enclosure of a man called *Blītha*'. OE pers. name + *worth*.

Blindcrake Cumbria. *Blenecreyc* 12th cent. 'Rock summit'. Celtic *blain* + *creig*.

Blisland Cornwall. *Bleselonde* 1284. OE *land* 'estate' with an obscure first element.

Blisworth Northants. *Blidesworde* 1086 (DB). 'Enclosure of a man called *Blīth*'. OE pers. name + *worth*.

Blithbury Staffs. *Blidebire* 1200. 'Stronghold on the River Blythe'. OE river-name (from *blīthe* 'gentle, pleasant') + *burh* (dative *byrig*). The same river gives name to **Blithfield**, **Blythe Bridge**, and **Blythe Marsh**.

Blo Norton Norfolk, *see* NORTON.

Blockley Glos. *Bloccanleah* 855, *Blochelei* 1086 (DB). 'Woodland clearing of a man called *Blocca*'. OE pers. name + *lēah*.

Blofield Norfolk. *Blafelda* 1086 (DB). Possibly 'exposed open country'. OE *blāw* + *feld*.

Bloody Foreland (*Cnoc Fola*) Donegal. 'Hill of blood'. The name is said to describe the red sunsets seen here.

Bloomsbury Gtr. London. *Blemondesberi* 1291. 'Manor held by the de Blemund family'. OE *burh* (dative *byrig*).

Blore Staffs., near Ilam. *Blora* 1086 (DB). Possibly '(place at) the swelling or hill'. OE *blōr*.

Bloxham Oxon. *Blochesham* 1086 (DB). 'Homestead of a man called *Blocc*'. OE pers. name + *hām*.

Bloxholm Lincs. *Blochesham* 1086 (DB). Identical in origin with the previous name.

Bloxwich W. Mids. *Blocheswic* 1086 (DB). 'Dwelling or (dairy) farm of a man called *Blocc*'. OE pers. name + *wīc*.

Bloxworth Dorset. *Blacewyrthe* 987, *Blocheshorde* 1086 (DB). 'Enclosure of a man called *Blocc*'. OE pers. name + *worth*.

Blubberhouses N. Yorks. *Bluberhusum* 1172. '(Place at) the houses by the bubbling spring'. ME *bluber* + OE *hūs* (dative plural -*um*).

Blue Stack Mountains (*Cruacha Gorma*) Donegal. *Blue Stack* 1837, 'Blue stacks'. The original (singular) name, Irish *An Chruach Ghorm*, 'the blue stack', was that of the highest peak

Blundeston Suffolk. *Blundeston* 1203. 'Farmstead of a man called *Blunt*'. OE pers. name + *tūn*.

Blunham Beds. *Blunham* 1086 (DB). Possibly 'homestead, or land in a river-bend, of a man called *Blūwa*'. OE pers. name (genitive -*n*) + *hām* or *hamm*.

Blunsdon St Andrew, *Broad Blunsdon* Wilts. *Bluntesdone* 1086 (DB), *Bluntesdon Seynt Andreu* 1281, *Bradebluntesdon* 1234. 'Hill of a man called *Blunt*'. OE pers. name + *dūn*. Affixes from the dedication of the church and from OE *brād* 'broad, great'.

Bluntisham Cambs. *Bluntesham* c.1050, 1086 (DB). 'Homestead or enclosure of a man called *Blunt*'. OE pers. name + *hām* or *hamm*.

Blyborough Lincs. *Bliburg* 1086 (DB). Probably 'stronghold of a man called Blígr'. OScand. pers. name + OE *burh*.

Blyford Suffolk. *Blitleford* |sic| c.1060, *Blideforda* 1086 (DB). 'Ford over the River Blyth'. OE river-name ('the gentle or pleasant one' from OE *blīthe*) + *ford*.

Blymhill Staffs. *Brumhelle* |sic| 1086 (DB), *Blumehil* 1167. Possibly 'hill where plum-trees grow'. OE *plȳme* + *hyll*.

Blyth Northum. *Blida* 1130. Named from the River Blyth (OE *blīthe* 'the gentle or pleasant one').

Blyth Notts. *Blide* 1086 (DB). Identical in origin with the previous name, *Blyth* being the old name of the River Ryton.

Blythburgh Suffolk. *Blideburh* 1086 (DB). 'Stronghold on the River Blyth'. OE river-name ('the gentle or pleasant one' from OE *blīthe*) + *burh*.

Blythe Bridge & *Blythe Marsh* Staffs., *see* BLITHBURY.

Blyton Lincs. *Blitone* 1086 (DB). Probably 'farmstead of a man called Blígr'. OScand. pers. name + OE *tūn*.

Boa Island (*Inis Badhbha*) Fermanagh. *Badhba* 1369. 'Badhbh's island'.

Boardmills Antrim. *Boardmills* 1904. The reference is to former wooden corn mills here. The equivalent Irish name is *An Muileann Adhmaid*, 'the timber mill'.

Boarhunt Hants. *Byrhfunt* 10th cent., *Borehunte* 1086 (DB). 'Spring of the stronghold or manor'. OE *burh* (genitive *byrh*) + **funta*.

Boarstall Bucks. *Burchestala* 1158. OE *burh-stall* 'the site of a stronghold'.

Boasley Cross Devon. *Borslea* c.970, *Bosleia* 1086 (DB). 'Woodland clearing where spiky plants grow'. OE **bors* + *lēah*.

Boat of Garten Highland. 'Ferry by the corn field'. English *boat* boat, + Gaelic *gairtean*.

Bobbing Kent. *Bobinge* c.1100. '(Settlement of) the family or followers of a man called Bobba'. OE pers. name + *-ingas*.

Bobbington Staffs. *Bubintone* 1086 (DB). 'Estate associated with a man called Bubba'. OE pers. name + *-ing-* + *tūn*.

Bocking Essex. *Boccinge(s)* c.995, *Bochinges* 1086 (DB). '(Settlement of) the family or followers of a man called *Bocca*, or '*Bocca's place'. OE pers. name + *-ingas* or *-ing*.

Boddington Glos. *Botingune* 1086 (DB). 'Estate associated with a man called Bōta'. OE pers. name + *-ing-* + *tūn*.

Boddington Northants. *Botendon* 1086 (DB). 'Hill of a man called Bōta'. OE pers. name (genitive *-n*) + *dūn*.

Bodenham Heref. & Worcs. *Bodeham* 1086 (DB). 'Homestead or river-bend land of a man called Boda'. OE pers. name (genitive *-n*) + *hām* or *hamm*.

Bodenham Wilts. *Boteham* 1249. 'Homestead or enclosure of a man called Bōta'. OE pers. name (genitive *-n*) + *hām* or *hamm*.

Boderg (*Both Derg*) Leitrim, Roscommon. 'Red hut'.

Bodham Norfolk. *Bodenham* 1086 (DB). 'Homestead or enclosure of a man called Boda'. OE pers. name (genitive *-n*) + *hām* or *hamm*.

Bodiam E. Sussex. *Bodeham* 1086 (DB). Identical in origin with the previous name.

Bodicote Oxon. *Bodicote* 1086 (DB). 'Cottage(s) associated with a man called Boda'. OE pers. name + *-ing-* + *cot*.

Bodmin Cornwall. *Bodmine* c.975, 1086 (DB). Probably 'dwelling by church-land'. OCornish **bod* + **meneghi*.

Bodney Norfolk. *Budeneia* 1086 (DB). 'Island, or dry ground in marsh, of a man called *Beoda*. OE pers. name (genitive *-n*) + *ēg*.

Bodoney (*Both Domhnaigh*) Tyrone. *Bodony* 1613. 'Hut of the church'.

Bofeenaun (*Both Faonáin*) Mayo. 'Faonán's hut'.

Bogare (*Both Chearr*) Kerry. 'Crooked hut'.

Bogay (*Both Ghé*) Donegal. 'Goose hut'.

Bognor Regis W. Sussex. *Bucganora* c.975. 'Shore of a woman called Bucge'. OE pers. name + *ōra*. Latin affix *regis* 'of the king' is only recent, alluding to the stay of George V here in 1929.

Bohacogram (*Both an Chograim*) Kerry. 'Hut of the whispering'.

Bohacullia (*Botha Coille*) Kerry. 'Huts of the wood'.

Bohaun (*Bothán*) Mayo. 'Little hut'.

Boheeshil (*Both Íseal*) Kerry. 'Low hut'.

Boher (*Bóthar*) Limerick. 'Road'.

Boheraphuca (*Bóthar an Phúca*) Offaly. 'Road of the sprite'.

Boherard (*Bóthar Ard*) Cork, Waterford. 'High road'.

Boherboy (*Bóthar Buí*) Cork. 'Yellow road'.

Boherbue (*Bóthar Buí*) Cork. 'Yellow road'.

Bohereen (*Bóithrín*) Limerick. 'Little road'.

Boherlahan (*Bóthar Leathan*) Tipperary. 'Broad road'.

Bohermeen (*An Bóthar Mín*) Meath. 'The smooth road'.

Bohermore (*An Bóthar Mór*) Galway. 'The big road'.

Boho (*Botha*) Fermanagh. *Botha* 1432. 'Huts'.

Bohoge (*Bothóg*) Mayo. 'Little hut'.

Bohola (*Both Chomhla*) Mayo. 'Comla's hut'.

Bolam, '(place at) the tree-trunks', OE **bola* or OScand. *bolr* in a dative plural form *bolum*: **Bolam** Durham. *Bolom* 1317. **Bolam** Northum. *Bolum* 1155.

Bolas, Great Shrops. *Belewas* 1198, *Boulewas* 1199 (1265). OE **wæsse* 'riverside land liable to flood' with an uncertain first element, possibly an OE **bogel* 'small river-bend or meander' in a genitive plural form.

Bold Heath Mersey. *Bolde* 1204. OE *bold* 'a special house or building'.

Boldon Tyne & Wear. *Boldun* c.1170. Probably 'rounded hill'. OE **bol* + *dūn*.

Boldre Hants. *Bovre* |sic| 1086 (DB), *Bolre* 1152. Origin and meaning uncertain, possibly an old name of the Lymington river.

Boldron Durham. *Bolrum* c.1180. 'Clearing used for bulls'. OScand. *boli* + *rúm*.

Bole Notts. *Bolun* 1086 (DB). '(Place at) the tree-trunks'. OE **bola* or OScand. *bolr* in a dative plural form *bolum*.

Bolea (*Both Liath*) Derry. *Boleah* 1613. 'Grey hut'.

Boleran (*Baile Uí Shírín*) Derry. *Ballyirin* 1613. 'Ó Sírín's townland'.

Bolingbroke, Old & *Bolingbroke, New* Lincs. *Bolinbroc* 1086 (DB), *Bulingbroc* 1202. Probably 'brook at Bula's or Bola's place'. OE pers. name + *-ing* + *brōc*.

Bollington, 'farmstead on the River Bollin', old river-name of uncertain origin and meaning + OE *tūn*: **Bollington** Ches., near Altrincham. *Bolinton* c.1222. **Bollington** Ches., near Macclesfield. *Bolynton* 1270.

Bolney E. Sussex. *Bolneye* 1263. 'Island, or dry ground in marsh, of a man called Bola'. OE pers. name (genitive -*n*) + *ēg*.

Bolnhurst Beds. *Bulehestre* |*sic*| 1086 (DB), *Bollenhirst* 11th cent. 'Wooded hill where bulls are kept'. OE **bula* (genitive plural **bulena*) + *hyrst*.

Bolsover Derbys. *Belesovre* |*sic*| 1086 (DB), *Bolesoura* 12th cent. Probably 'ridge of a man called Boll or *Bull'. OE pers. name + **ofer*.

Bolsterstone S. Yorks. *Bolstyrston* 1398. 'Stone on which criminals are beheaded'. OE *bolster* + *stān*.

Bolstone Heref. & Worcs. *Boleston* 1193. 'Stone of a man called Bola'. OE pers. name + *stān*.

Boltby N. Yorks. *Boltebi* 1086 (DB). 'Farmstead or village of a man called Boltr or *Bolti'. OScand. pers. name + *bý*.

Bolton, a common name in the North, from OE **bōthl-tūn* 'settlement with a special building'; examples include: **Bolton** Gtr. Manch. *Boelton* 1185. **Bolton by Bowland** Lancs. *Bodeltone* 1086 (DB). The district-name Bowland (*Boelanda* 1102) means 'district characterized by bends', OE *boga* + *land*. **Bolton, Castle** N. Yorks. *Bodelton* 1086 (DB). Affix from the castle built here in 1379. **Bolton le Sands** Lancs. *Bodeltone* 1086 (DB). Affix means 'on the sands'. **Bolton Percy** N. Yorks. *Bodeltune* 1086 (DB), *Bolton Percy* 1305. Manorial affix from its possession by the de Percy family (from 1086). **Bolton upon Dearne** S. Yorks. *Bodeltone* 1086 (DB). The river-name Dearne is possibly from OE *derne* 'hidden', but may be of Celtic origin.

Bonby N. Lincs. *Bundebi* 1086 (DB). 'Farmstead or village of the peasant farmers'. OScand. *bóndi* + *bý*.

Bonchurch I. of Wight. *Bonecerce* 1086 (DB). 'Church of *Bona'. OE pers. name + *cirice*. The pers. name may be a short-form of (St) Boniface, to whom the church here is dedicated.

Bondleigh Devon. *Bolenei* |*sic*| 1086 (DB), *Bonlege* 1205. Probably 'woodland clearing of a man called Bola'. OE pers. name (genitive -*n*) + *lēah*.

Bonehill Staffs. *Bolenhull* 1230. Probably 'hill where bulls graze'. OE **bula* (genitive plural **bulena*) + *hyll*.

Bo'ness Falk. *Berwardeston* c.1335, *Nes* 1494, *Burnstounnes* 1532, *Borrowstownness, or Bo'ness* 1868. 'Promontory of *Borrowstoun*'. OE *næss*. Borrowstoun is 'Beornweard's farm' (OE pers. name + *tūn*).

Bonhill W. Dunb. *Buchlul* 1225, *Buthelulle* c.1270, *Buchnvl* c.1320. 'House by the stream'. Gaelic *bot* + *an* + *allt* (genitive *uillt*).

Boningale Shrops. *Bolynghale* 12th cent. Probably 'nook of land associated with a man called Bola'. OE pers. name + -*ing*- + *halh*.

Bonnington Kent. *Bonintone* 1086 (DB). 'Estate associated with a man called Buna'. OE pers. name + -*ing*- + *tūn*.

Bonnybridge Falk. 'Bridge over Bonny Water'. The river name, recorded in 1682 as *aquae de Boine*, is said to derive from Scottish English *bonny*, 'beautiful'.

Bonnyrigg Midloth. *Bannockrig* 1773. 'Bannock-shaped ridge'. Modern English *bannock* + Scottish *rig*.

Bonsall Derbys. *Bunteshale* 1086 (DB). 'Nook of land of a man called *Bunt'. OE pers. name + *halh*.

Bont-faen, Y. *See* COWBRIDGE.

Bonvilston (*Tresimwn*) Vale Glam. *Boleuilston* c.1160, *Bonevillestun* c.1206. 'de Bonville's farm'. OE *tun* (Welsh *tref*). The Welsh name comes from *Simon* de Bonville.

Bookham, Great & *Bookham, Little* Surrey. *Bocheham* 1086 (DB). 'Homestead where beech-trees grow'. OE *bōc* + *hām*.

Boola (*Buaile*) Waterford. 'Milking place'.

Boolakennedy (*Buaile Uí Chinnéide*) Tipperary. 'Ó Cinnéide's milking place'.

Boolananave (*Buaile na nDamh*) Kerry. 'Milking place of the oxen'.

Boolavogue (*Baile Mhaodhóg*) Wexford. 'Maodóg's townland'.

Booterstown (*Baile an Bhóthair*) Dublin. 'Town of the road'.

Boothby, 'farmstead or village with booths or shelters', OScand. *bōth* + *bý*: **Boothby Graffoe** Lincs. *Bodebi* 1086 (DB). Affix is an old district name of uncertain origin. **Boothby Pagnell** Lincs. *Bodebi* 1086 (DB). Manorial affix from the Paynel family, here in the 14th cent.

Boothferry E. R. Yorks. *Booth's Ferry* 1651. 'Ferry at Booth (near Howden)', from OScand. *ferja*. The place-name **Booth** (originally *Botheby* 1550) was named from a family who came from one of the places called BOOTHBY (*see* previous names).

Bootle, 'the special building', OE *bōtl*: **Bootle** Cumbria. *Bodele* 1086 (DB). **Bootle** Mersey. *Boltelai* |*sic*| 1086 (DB), *Botle* 1212.

Boraston Shrops. *Bureston* 1188, *Buraston* 1256. Possibly 'eastern farmstead or estate', OE *ēast* + *tūn*, with the addition of OE *burh* 'fortification'.

Borden Kent. *Bordena* 1177. 'Valley or woodland pasture by a hill'. OE **bor* + *denu* or *denn*.

Bordley N. Yorks. *Borelaie* |*sic*| 1086 (DB), *Bordeleia* c.1140. Probably 'woodland clearing where boards are got'. OE *bord* + *lēah*.

Boreham, probably 'homestead or enclosure on or by a hill', OE **bor* + *hām* or *hamm*: **Boreham** Essex. *Borham* c.1045, 1086 (DB). **Boreham Street** E. Sussex. *Borham* 12th cent.

Borehamwood Herts. *Borham* 1188, *Burhamwode* 13th cent. Identical in origin with the previous names + OE *wudu* 'wood'.

Borley Essex. *Barlea* 1086 (DB). 'Woodland clearing frequented by boars'. OE *bār* + *lēah*.

Bornacoola (*Barr na Cúile*) Leitrim. 'Top of the hollow'.

Borough Green Kent. *Borrowe Grene* 1575. From OE *burh* 'manor, borough' or *beorg* 'hill, mound'.

Boroughbridge N. Yorks. *Burbrigg* 1220. 'Bridge near the stronghold'. OE *burh* + *brycg*.

Borris (*An Bhuiríos*) Carlow. 'The borough'.

Borris-in-Ossory (*Buiríos Mór Osraí*) Laois. 'Big borough of Osraí'. Osraí (Ossory) is an ancient territory here.

Borrisbeg (*Buiríos Beag*) Kilkenny. 'Small borough'.

Borrisnoe (*Buiríos Nua*) Tipperary. 'New borough'.

Borrisokane (*Buiríos Uí Chéin*) Tipperary. 'Borough of Ó Céin'.

Borrisoleigh (*Buiríos Ó Luigheach*) Tipperary. 'Borough of Uí Luigheach'.

Borrowby N. Yorks., near Leake, *Bergebi* 1086 (DB). 'Farmstead or village on the hill(s)'. OScand. *berg* + *bý*.

Borrowdale Cumbria, near Keswick. *Borgordale* c.1170. 'Valley of the fort river'. OScand. *borg* (genitive *-ar*) + *á* + *dalr*.

Borth Cergn. '(Place of the) ferry'. Welsh *porth*.

Borth-y-gest Gwyd. *Gest harbour* 1748. 'Harbour of the paunch'. Welsh *porth* + *y* + *cest*. The village takes its name from nearby *Moel y Gest*, 'bare hill of the paunch', a mountain so named for its shape.

Borwick Lancs. *Bereuuic* 1086 (DB). 'Barley farm' or 'outlying part of an estate'. OE *bere-wīc*.

Bosbury Heref. & Worcs. *Bosanbirig* early 12th cent., *Boseberge* 1086 (DB). 'Stronghold of a man called Bōsa'. OE pers. name + *burh* (dative *byrig*).

Boscastle Cornwall. *Boterelescastel* 1302. 'Castle of a family called Boterel'. OFrench surname + *castel*.

Boscombe, probably 'valley overgrown with spiky plants', OE **bors* + *cumb*: **Boscombe** Dorset. *Boscumbe* 1273. **Boscombe** Wilts. *Boscumbe* 1086 (DB).

Bosham W. Sussex. *Bosanham(m)* 731, *Boseham* 1086 (DB). 'Homestead or promontory of a man called Bōsa'. OE pers. name + *hām* or *hamm*.

Bosherston Pemb. *Stakep' bosser* 1291, *Bosherston* (*alias Stacpoll Bosher*) 1594. 'Bosher's farm'. OFrench pers. name + OE *tūn*. The village was originally *Stackpole Bosher*, the manorial name distinguishing it from *Stackpole Elidor*, an alternative name for nearby CHERITON.

Bosley Ches. *Boselega* 1086 (DB). 'Woodland clearing of a man called Bōsa or Bōt'. OE pers. name + *lēah*.

Bossall N. Yorks. *Bosciale* 1086 (DB). Probably 'nook of land of a man called Bōt or *Bōtsige'. OE pers. name + *halh*.

Bossiney Cornwall. *Botcinnii* 1086 (DB). 'Dwelling of a man called Kyni'. OCornish **bod* + pers. name.

Bostock Green Ches. *Botestoch* 1086 (DB). 'Outlying farmstead or hamlet of a man called Bōta'. OE pers. name + *stoc*.

Boston Lincs. *Botuluestan* 1130. 'Stone (marking a boundary or meeting-place) of a man called Bōtwulf'. OE pers. name + *stān*. Identification of Bōtwulf with the 7th cent. missionary St Botulf is quite probable.

Boston Spa W. Yorks. *Bostongate* 1799. A recent name, perhaps so called from a family called Boston from BOSTON (Lincs.). The affix *Spa* refers to the mineral spring discovered here in 1744.

Bosworth, Husbands Leics. *Baresworde* 1086 (DB). Probably 'enclosure of a man called Bār'. OE pers. name + *worth*. Affix probably means 'of the farmers or husbandmen' (from late OE *hūsbonda*).

Bosworth, Market Leics. *Boseworde* 1086 (DB). 'Enclosure of a man called Bōsa'. OE pers. name + *worth*. Affix (found from the 16th cent.) alludes to the important market here.

Botesdale Suffolk. *Botholuesdal* 1275. 'Valley of a man called Bōtwulf'. OE pers. name + *dæl*.

Bothal Northum. *Bothala* 12th cent. 'Nook of land of a man called Bōta'. OE pers. name + *halh*.

Bothamsall Notts. *Bodmescel* 1086 (DB). Etymology obscure, but possibly 'Shelf by a broad river-valley'. OE **bothm* + *scelf*.

Bothel Cumbria. *Bothle* c.1125. OE *bōthl* 'a special house or building'.

Bothenhampton Dorset. *Bothehamton* 1268. 'Home farm in a valley'. OE **bothm* + *hām-tūn*.

Bothwell S. Lan. *Botheuill* c.1242, *Bothvile* c.1300. Etymology obscure, but possibly 'Shelter by the stream'. ME *bothe* + OE *wella*.

Botley Bucks. *Bottlea* 1167. 'Woodland clearing of a man called Botta'. OE pers. name + *lēah*.

Botley Hants. *Botelie* 1086 (DB). 'Woodland clearing of a man called Bōta, or where timber is obtained'. OE pers. name or OE *Bōt* + *lēah*.

Botley Oxon. *Boteleam* 12th cent. Identical in origin with the previous name.

Botolph Claydon Bucks., *see* CLAYDON.

Botolphs W. Sussex. *Sanctus Botulphus* 1288. From the dedication of the parish church to St Botolph.

Bottesford, 'ford by the house or building', OE *Bōtl* + *ford*: **Bottesford** N. Lincs. *Budlesforde* 1086 (DB). **Bottesford** Leics. *Botesford* 1086 (DB).

Bottisham Cambs. *Bodekesham* 1060, *Bodichessham* 1086 (DB). 'Homestead or enclosure of a man called *Boduc'. OE pers. name + *hām* or *hamm*.

Bottlehill Antrim. *Botle hill* c.1657. 'Bottle hill'. *Bottle* ('bundle of straw') implies a good hay harvest.

Botusfleming Cornwall. *Bothflumet* 1259. OCornish **bod* 'dwelling' with an obscure second element.

Boughadoon (*Both an Dúin*) Mayo. 'Hut of the fort'.

Boughton, found in various counties, has two distinct origins. Some are 'farmstead of a man called Bucca, or where bucks (male deer) or he-goats are kept'. OE pers. name or OE *bucc* or *bucca* + *tūn*; examples include: **Boughton** Northants., near Moulton. *Buchetone* 1086 (DB). **Boughton** Notts. *Buchetone* 1086 (DB).

Other Boughtons are either 'farmstead where beech-trees grow' or 'farmstead held by charter', OE *bōc* + *tūn*; examples include: **Boughton Aluph** Kent. *Boltune* |sic| 1086 (DB), *Boctun* c.1020, *Botun Alou* 1237. Manorial affix from a 13th cent. owner called *Alulf*. **Boughton Malherbe** Kent. *Boltune* |sic| 1086 (DB), *Boctun Malerbe* 1275. Manorial affix from early possession by the Malherbe family. **Boughton Monchelsea** Kent. *Boltone* |sic| 1086 (DB), *Bocton Monchansy* 1278. Manorial affix from the de Montchensie family, here in the 13th cent.

Bouladuff (*An Bhuaile Dhubh*) Tipperary. 'The black milking place'.

Bouldon Shrops. *Bolledone* 1086 (DB), *Bullardone* 1166. OE *dūn* 'hill' with an uncertain first element.

Boulge Suffolk. *Bulges* 1086 (DB), *Bulge* 1254. From OFrench *bouge* 'uncultivated land covered with heather'.

Boulmer Northum. *Bulemer* 1161. 'Pond used by bulls'. OE **bula* + *mere*.

Boultham Lincs. *Buletham* 1086 (DB). 'Enclosure where ragged robin or the cuckoo flower grows'. OE *bulut* + *hamm*.

Bourn, *Bourne*, '(place at) the spring(s) or stream(s)', OE *burna* or OScand. *brunnr*: **Bourn** Cambs. *Brune* 1086 (DB). **Bourne** Lincs. *Brune* 1086 (DB). **Bourne, St Mary** Hants. *Borne* 1185, *Maryborne* 1476. Affix from the original dedication of the chapel here.

Bourne End Bucks. *Burnend* 1236. 'End of the stream' (here where the River Wye meets the Thames). OE *burna* + *ende*.

Bournemouth Dorset. *La Bournemowthe* 1407. 'The mouth of the stream'. OE *burna* + *mūtha*.

Bournville W. Mids. 'Town on a river called Bourne' (from OE *burna* 'stream'). A recent name incorporating French *ville* for the estate built 1879 by George Cadbury.

Bourton, usually OE *burh-tūn* 'fortified farmstead' or 'farmstead near a fortification'; examples include: **Bourton** Dorset. *Bureton* 1212. **Bourton, Black** Oxon. *Burtone* 1086 (DB). Affix possibly refers to the black habits of the canons of Osney Abbey who had lands here. **Bourton-on-the-Water** Glos. *Burchtun* 714, *Bortune* 1086 (DB). In this name reference is to the nearby hill-fort. Affix refers to the River Windrush which flows through the village.

Bovedy (*Both Mhíde*) Derry. *Bovidie* 1654. 'Míde's hut'.

Bovevagh (*Boith Mhéabha*) Derry. (*derteach*) *Bothe Medba* 1100. 'Maeve's hut'.

Bovey Tracey, *North Bovey* Devon. *Bovi* 1086 (DB), *Bovy Tracy* 1276, *Northebovy* 1199. Named from the River Bovey, a pre-English river-name of uncertain origin and meaning. Manorial affix from the de Tracy family, here in the 13th cent.

Bovingdon Herts. *Bovyndon* c.1200. Probably 'hill associated with a man called Bōfa'. OE pers. name + *-ing-* + *dūn*.

Bovington Dorset. *Bovintone* 1086 (DB). 'Estate associated with a man called Bōfa'. OE pers. name + *-ing-* + *tūn*.

Bow, '(place at) the arched bridge', OE *boga*: **Bow** Devon. *Limet* |sic| 1086 (DB), *Nymetboghe* 1270, *la Bogh* 1281. *Nymet* is the old name of the River Yeo, *see* NYMET. **Bow** Gtr. London. *Stratford* 1177, *Stratford atte Bowe* 1279. Its earlier name means 'ford on a Roman road', OE *strǣt* + *ford*. ME *atte* means 'at the'.

Bow Brickhill Bucks., *see* BRICKHILL.

Bowcombe I. of Wight. *Bovecome* 1086 (DB). 'Valley of a man called Bōfa', or '(place) above the valley'. OE pers. name or OE *bufan* + *cumb*.

Bowden, Great & *Bowden, Little* Leics. *Bugedone* 1086 (DB). 'Hill of a woman called Bucge or of a man called Bugga'. OE pers. name + *dūn*.

Bowdon Gtr. Manch. *Bogedone* 1086 (DB). 'Curved hill'. OE *boga* + *dūn*.

Bowerchalke Wilts., *see* CHALKE.

Bowers Gifford Essex. *Bure* 1065, *Bura* 1086 (DB), *Buresgiffard* 1315. 'The dwellings or cottages'. OE *būr* + manorial affix from the Giffard family, here in the 13th cent.

Bowes Durham. *Bogas* 1148. 'The river-bends'. OE *boga* or OScand. *bogi*.

Bowland (old district and forest) Lancs./N. Yorks., *see* BOLTON BY BOWLAND.

Bowley Heref. & Worcs. *Bolelei* 1086 (DB). 'Woodland clearing of a man called Bola, or where there are tree-trunks'. OE pers. name or **bola* + *lēah*.

Bowling W. Yorks. *Bollinc* 1086 (DB). 'Place at a hollow'. OE *bolla* + *-ing*.

Bowness-on-Solway Cumbria. *Bounes* c.1225. 'Rounded headland'. OE *boga* + *nǣss*, or OScand. *bogi* + *nes*. Solway (*Sulewad* 1218) probably means 'ford of the pillar or post'. OScand. *súla* + *vath*, perhaps referring to the Lochmaben Stone at the Scottish end of the ford across the Solway Firth (Scottish *firth* 'estuary').

Bowness-on-Windermere Cumbria. *Bulnes* 1282. 'Bull headland'. OE **bula* + *nǣss*. *See* WINDERMERE.

Bowsden Northum. *Bolesdon* 1195. Probably 'hill of a man called **Boll*'. OE pers. name + *dūn*.

Bowthorpe Norfolk. *Boethorp* 1086 (DB). 'Outlying farmstead or hamlet of a man called Búi'. OScand. pers. name + *thorp*.

Box, '(place at) the box-tree', OE *box*: **Box** Glos. *la Boxe* 1260. **Box** Wilts. *Bocza* 1144.

Boxford Berks. *Boxora* 821, *Bousore* 1086 (DB). 'Slope where box-trees grow'. OE *box* + *ōra*.

Boxford Suffolk. *Boxford* 12th cent. 'Ford where box-trees grow'. OE *box* + *ford*. The river-name **Box** is a 'back-formation' from the place-name.

Boxgrove W. Sussex. *Bosgrave* 1086 (DB). 'Box-tree grove'. OE *box* + *grāf*.

Boxley Kent. *Boseleu* |sic| 1086 (DB), *Boxlea* c.1100. 'Wood or clearing where boxtrees grow'. OE *box* + *lēah*.

Boxted Essex. *Bocstede* 1086 (DB). 'Place where beech-trees grow'. OE *bōc* + *stede*.

Boxted Suffolk. *Boesteda* |sic| 1086 (DB), *Bocstede* 1154. 'Place where beech-trees or box-trees grow'. OE *bōc* or *box* + *stede*.

Boxworth Cambs. *Bochesuuorde* 1086 (DB). 'Enclosure of a man called **Bucc*'. OE pers. name + *worth*.

Boyd (river) S. Glos., *see* BITTON.

Boyle (*Mainistir na Búille*) Roscommon. 'Monastery of the river Búill'.

Boylestone Derbys. *Boilestun* 1086 (DB). Probably 'farmstead at the rounded hill'. OE *boga* + *hyll* + *tūn*.

Boynton E. R. Yorks. *Bouintone* 1086 (DB). 'Estate associated with a man called Bōfa'. OE pers. name + *-ing-* + *tūn*.

Boyounagh (*Buíbheanach*) Galway. 'Yellow marsh'.

Boyton, 'farmstead of a man called Boia' or 'farmstead of the boys or servants', OE pers. name or OE **boia* + *tūn*: **Boyton** Cornwall. *Boietone* 1086 (DB). **Boyton** Suffolk. *Boituna* 1086 (DB). **Boyton** Wilts. *Boientone* 1086 (DB).

Bozeat Northants. *Bosiete* 1086 (DB). 'Gate or gap of a man called Bōsa'. OE pers. name + *geat*.

Brabourne Kent. *Bradanburna* c.860, *Bradeburne* 1086 (DB). '(Place at) the broad stream'. OE *brād* + *burna*.

Brabstermire Highland. *Brabustare* 1492, *Brabastermyre* 1538. 'Marsh at Brabster'. OScand. *mýrr*. Brabster is 'broad dwelling' (OScand. *breithr* + *bólstathr*).

Braceborough Lincs. *Braseborg* 1086 (DB). Possibly 'strong fortress', or 'fortress of a man called *Bræsna'. OE *bræsen* or pers. name + *burh*.

Bracebridge Lincs. *Brachebrige* 1086 (DB). Possibly 'bridge or causeway made of small branches or brushwood'. OE **bræsc* + *brycg*.

Braceby Lincs. *Breizbi* 1086 (DB). 'Farmstead or village of a man called Breithr'. OScand. pers. name + *bý*.

Bracewell Lancs. *Braisuelle* 1086 (DB). 'Spring or stream of a man called Breithr'. OScand. pers. name + OE *wella*.

Brackaharagh (*Brá Chatrach*) Kerry. 'Neck of the stone fort'.

Brackenfield Derbys. *Brachentheyt* 1269. 'Bracken clearing'. OScand. **brækni* + *thveit*.

Brackley Northants. *Brachelai* 1086 (DB). Probably 'woodland clearing of a man called *Bracca'. OE pers. name + *lēah*.

Brackloon (*Breac Chluain*) Kerry, Mayo. 'Speckled pasture'.

Bracklyn (*Breaclainn*) Westmeath. 'Speckled place'.

Bracknagh (*Breacánach*) Offaly. 'Speckled place'.

Bracknahevla (*Breacach na hAibhle*) Westmeath. 'Speckled land of the orchard'.

Bracknell Berks. *Braccan heal* 942. 'Nook of land of a man called *Bracca'. OE pers. name (genitive -*n*) + *halh*.

Bracon Ash Norfolk. *Brachene* 1175. '(Place amid) the bracken'. ON **brækni* or OE **bræcen* with the later addition of *ash* 'ash-tree'.

Bradbourne Derbys. *Bradeburne* 1086 (DB). '(Place at) the broad stream'. OE *brād* + *burna*.

Bradden Northants. *Bradene* 1086 (DB). 'Broad valley'. OE *brād* + *denu*.

Braddock Cornwall. *Brodehoc* 1086 (DB). 'Broad oak', or 'broad hook of land'. OE *brād* + *āc* or *hōc*.

Bradenham, 'broad homestead or enclosure', OE *brād* (dative -*an*) + *hām* + *hamm*: **Bradenham** Bucks. *Bradeham* 1086 (DB). **Bradenham** Norfolk. *Bradenham* 1086 (DB).

Bradenstoke Wilts. *Bradenestoche* 1086 (DB). 'Settlement dependent on Braydon forest'. Pre-English forest-name of obscure origin and meaning + OE *stoc*.

Bradfield, 'broad stretch of open land', OE *brād* + *feld*; examples include: **Bradfield** Berks. *Bradanfelda* 990–2, *Bradefelt* 1086 (DB). **Bradfield** Essex. *Bradefelda* 1086 (DB). **Bradfield** Norfolk. *Bradefeld* 1177. **Bradfield** S. Yorks. *Bradesfeld* 1188. **Bradfield Combust**, **Bradfield St Clare**, & **Bradfield St George** Suffolk. *Bradefelda* 1086 (DB). Distinguishing affixes from ME *combust* 'burnt', from early possession by the Seyncler family, and from dedication of the church to St George.

Bradford, a fairly common name, '(place at) the broad ford', OE *brād* + *ford*; examples include: **Bradford** W. Yorks. *Bradeford* 1086 (DB). **Bradford Abbas** Dorset. *Bradanforda* 933, *Bradeford* 1086 (DB), *Braddeford Abbatis* 1386. Affix is Latin *abbas* 'abbot', alluding to early possession by Sherborne Abbey. **Bradford on Avon** Wilts. *Bradanforda be Afne* c.900, *Bradeford* 1086 (DB). Avon is a Celtic river-name meaning simply 'river'. **Bradford Peverell** Dorset. *Bradeford* 1086 (DB), *Bradeford Peuerel* 1244. Manorial affix from the Peverel family, here in the 13th cent.

Brading I. of Wight. *Brerdinges* 683, *Berardinz* 1086 (DB). '(Settlement of) the dwellers on the hill-side'. OE *brerd* + -*ingas*.

Bradley, a common name, usually 'broad wood or clearing', OE *brād* + *lēah*; examples include: **Bradley** Derbys. *Braidelei* 1086 (DB). **Bradley, Maiden** Wilts. *Bradelie* 1086 (DB), *Maydene Bradelega* early 13th cent. Affix means 'of the maidens' and refers to the nuns of Amesbury who had a cell here. **Bradley, North** Wilts. *Bradlega* 1174.

However the following has a different origin: **Bradley in the Moors** Staffs. *Bretlei* 1086 (DB), 'Wood where boards or planks are got'. OE *bred* + *lēah*.

Bradmore Notts. *Brademere* 1086 (DB). 'Broad pool'. OE *brād* + *mere*.

Bradninch Devon. *Bradenese* 1086 (DB). '(Place at) the broad ash-tree or oak-tree'. OE *brād* (dative -*an*) + *æsc* or *āc* (dative *ǣc*).

Bradnop Staffs. *Bradenhop* 1219. 'Broad valley'. OE *brād* (dative -*an*) + *hop*.

Bradoge (*Bráideog*) Donegal. 'Little throat'.

Bradox (*Na Bráideoga*) Monaghan. 'The little throats'.

Bradpole Dorset. *Bratepolle* 1086 (DB). 'Broad pool'. OE *brād* + *pōl*.

Bradshaw Gtr. Manch. *Bradeshaghe* 1246. 'Broad wood or copse'. OE *brād* + *sceaga*.

Bradstone Devon. *Bradan stane* c.970, *Bradestana* 1086 (DB). '(Place at) the broad stone'. OE *brād* + *stān*.

Bradwell, '(place at) the broad spring or stream', OE *brād* + *wella*; examples include: **Bradwell** Bucks. *Bradewelle* 1086 (DB). **Bradwell** Derbys. *Bradewelle* 1086 (DB). **Bradwell** Essex. *Bradewell* 1238. **Bradwell** Norfolk. *Bradewell* 1211. **Bradwell** Staffs. *Bradewull* 1227. **Bradwell-on-Sea** Essex. *Bradewella* 1194.

Bradworthy Devon. *Brawardine* |sic| 1086 (DB), *Bradewurtha* 1175. 'Broad enclosure'. OE *brād* + *worthign* or *worthig*.

Braemar Aber. *the Bray of Marre* 1560. 'Upper part of Mar'. Gaelic *braigh*. *See* MAR.

Brafferton, 'farmstead by the broad ford', OE *brād* + *ford* + *tūn*: **Brafferton** Durham. *Bradfortuna* 1091. **Brafferton** N. Yorks. *Bradfortune* 1086 (DB).

Brafield-on-the-Green Northants. *Bragefelde* 1086 (DB). 'Open country by higher ground'. OE **bragen* + *feld*. The affix dates from the 16th cent.

Braid (*Braghad*) (river) Antrim. 'Throat'.

Brailes Warwicks. *Brailes* 1086 (DB). Possibly from an OE **brægels* 'burial place, tumulus'. Alternatively a Celtic name 'hill court' from **breʒ* + **lis*.

Brailsford Derbys. *Brailesford* 1086 (DB). Possibly 'ford by a burial place'. OE **brægels* + *ford*. Alternatively the first part of this name may be Celtic, *see* the previous name.

Braintree Essex. *Branchetreu* 1086 (DB). 'Tree of a man called **Branca*'. OE pers. name + *trēow*. The river-name **Brain** is a 'back-formation' from the place-name.

Braiseworth Suffolk. *Briseworde* 1086 (DB). 'Enclosure infested with gadflies or belonging to a man called **Brīosa*'. OE *brīosa* or pers. name + *worth*.

Braishfield Hants. *Braisfelde* c.1235. OE *feld* 'open land' with an uncertain first element, possibly an OE **bræsc* 'small branches or brushwood'.

Braithwaite, 'broad clearing', OScand. *breithr* + *thveit*: **Braithwaite** Cumbria, near Keswick. *Braithait* c.1160. **Braithwaite** S. Yorks. *Braytweyt* 1276. **Braithwaite, Low** Cumbria. *Braythweyt* 1285.

Braithwell S. Yorks. *Bradewelle* 1086 (DB). '(Place at) the broad spring or stream'. OE *brād* (replaced by OScand. *breithr*) + *wella*.

Bramber W. Sussex. *Bremre* 956, *Brembre* 1086 (DB). OE *brēmer* 'bramble thicket'.

Bramcote Notts. *Brunecote* |*sic*| 1086 (DB), *Bramcote* c.1156. 'Cottage(s) where broom grows'. OE *brōm* + *cot*.

Bramdean Hants. *Bromdene* 824, *Brondene* 1086 (DB). 'Valley where broom grows'. OE *brōm* + *denu*.

Bramerton Norfolk. *Brambretuna* 1086 (DB). Possibly 'farmstead by the bramble thicket'. OE *brēmer* + *tūn*.

Bramfield Herts. *Brandefelle* |*sic*| 1086 (DB), *Brantefeld* 12th cent. Probably 'steep open land'. OE *brant* + *feld*.

Bramfield Suffolk. *Brunfelda* |*sic*| 1086 (DB), *Bramfeld* 1166. 'Open land where broom grows'. OE *brōm* + *feld*.

Bramford Suffolk. *Bromford* 1040, *Branfort* 1086 (DB). 'Ford where broom grows'. OE *brōm* + *ford*.

Bramhall Gtr. Manch. *Bramale* 1086 (DB). 'Nook of land where broom grows'. OE *brōm* + *halh*.

Bramham W. Yorks. *Bram(e)ham* 1086 (DB). 'Homestead or enclosure where broom grows'. OE *brōm* + *hām* or *hamm*.

Bramhope W. Yorks. *Bramhop* 1086 (DB). 'Valley where broom grows'. OE *brōm* + *hop*.

Bramley, 'woodland clearing where broom grows', OE *brōm* + *lēah*: **Bramley** Hants. *Brumelai* 1086 (DB). **Bramley** S. Yorks. *Bramelei* 1086 (DB). **Bramley** Surrey. *Bronlei* 1086 (DB).

Brampford Speke Devon. *Branfort* 1086 (DB), *Bramford Spec* 1275. Possibly 'ford where broom grows'. OE

brōm + *ford*. Manorial affix from the Espec family, here in the 12th cent.

Brampton, a fairly common name, 'farmstead where broom grows', OE *brōm* + *tūn*; examples include: **Brampton** Cambs. *Brantune* 1086 (DB). **Brampton** Cumbria, near Irthington. *Brampton* 1169. **Brampton Bryan** Heref. & Worcs. *Brantune* 1086 (DB), *Bramptone Brian* 1275. Manorial affix from a 12th cent. owner called *Brian*. **Brampton, Chapel** & **Brampton, Church** Northants. *Brantone* 1086 (DB). The distinguishing affixes occur from the 13th cent.

Bramshall Staffs. *Branselle* |*sic*| 1086 (DB), *Bromschulf* 1327. 'Shelf of land where broom grows'. OE *brōm* + *scelf*.

Bramshaw Hants. *Bramessage* 1086 (DB). Probably 'wood or copse where brambles grow'. OE *brǣmel* + *sceaga*.

Bramshill Hants. *Bromeselle* 1086 (DB). 'Hill of the broom', i.e. 'hill where broom grows'. OE *brōm* (genitive -*es*) + *hyll*.

Bramshott Hants. *Brenbresete* 1086 (DB). 'Projecting piece of land where brambles grow'. OE *brǣmel* + *scēat*.

Bramwith, Kirk S. Yorks. *Branuuet* |*sic*| 1086 (DB), *Branwyth* 1200, *Kyrkbramwith* 1341. 'Wood overgrown with broom'. OE *brōm* + OScand. *vithr*. Affix is OScand. *kirkja* 'church'.

Brancaster Norfolk. *Bramcestria* c.960, *Broncestra* 1086 (DB). 'Roman station at Branodunum'. Reduced form of ancient Celtic name (probably 'crow fort') + OE *ceaster*.

Brancepeth Durham. *Brantespethe* c.1170. 'Path or road of a man called Brandr'. OScand. pers. name + OE *pæth*.

Brandesburton E. R. Yorks. *Brantisburtone* 1086 (DB). 'Fortified farmstead of a man called Brandr'. OScand. pers. name + OE *burh-tūn*.

Brandeston Suffolk. *Brantestona* 1086 (DB). 'Farmstead of a man called **Brant*'. OE pers. name + *tūn*.

Brandiston Norfolk. *Brantestuna* 1086 (DB). Identical in origin with the previous name.

Brandon, usually 'hill where broom grows', OE *brōm* + *dūn*: **Brandon** Durham. *Bromdune* c.1190. **Brandon** Northum. *Bremdona* c.1150, *Bromdun* 1236. Here the first element alternates with OE **brēmen* 'broomy'. **Brandon** Suffolk. *Bromdun* 11th cent., *Brandona* 1086 (DB). **Brandon** Warwicks. *Brandune* 1086 (DB). **Brandon Parva** Norfolk. *Brandun* 1086 (DB).
  However the following may have a different origin: **Brandon** Lincs. *Branthon* 1060–6, *Brandune* 1086 (DB). Probably 'hill by the River Brant'. OE river-name (from OE *brant* 'steep, deep') + *dūn*.

Brandon (*Cé Bhréanainn*) Kerry. 'Quay of Bréanann'.

Brandsby N. Yorks. *Branzbi* 1086 (DB). 'Farmstead or village of a man called Brandr'. OScand. pers. name + *bý*.

Branksome Dorset, a 19th cent. name taken from a house called *Branksome Tower* (built 1855) which in turn was probably named from the setting of Sir Walter Scott's *Lay of the Last Minstrel* (1805).

Branscombe Devon. *Branecescumbe* 9th cent., *Branchescome* 1086 (DB). 'Valley of a man called Branoc'. Celtic pers. name + OE *cumb*.

Bransford Heref. & Worcs. *Bregnesford* 963, *Bradnesford* 1086 (DB). Probably 'ford by the hill'. OE *brægen* + *ford*.

Branston, 'farmstead of a man called Brant', OE pers. name + *tūn*: **Branston** Leics. *Brantestone* 1086 (DB). **Branston** Staffs. *Brontiston* 942, *Brantestone* 1086 (DB).
However the following may have a different origin: **Branston** Lincs. *Branztune* 1086 (DB). Probably 'farmstead of a man called Brandr'. OScand. pers. name + OE *tūn*.

Brant Broughton Lincs., *see* BROUGHTON.

Brantham Suffolk. *Brantham* 1086 (DB). Possibly 'homestead or enclosure of a man called *Branta*'. OE pers. name + *hām* or *hamm*.

Branthwaite Cumbria, near Workington. *Bromthweit* 1210. 'Clearing where broom grows'. OE *brōm* + OScand. *thveit*.

Brantingham E. R. Yorks. *Brentingeham* 1086 (DB). 'Homestead of the family or followers of a man called *Brant*', from OE pers. name + *-inga-* + *hām*. Alternatively 'homestead of those dwelling on the steep slopes', from OE *brant* + *-inga-* + *hām*.

Branton Northum. *Bremetona* c.1150. 'Farmstead overgrown with broom'. OE *brēmen* + *tūn*.

Branton S. Yorks. *Brantune* 1086 (DB). 'Farmstead where broom grows'. OE *brōm* + *tūn*.

Branxton Northum. *Brankeston* 1195. 'Farmstead of a man called Branoc'. Celtic pers. name + OE *tūn*.

Brassington Derbys. *Branzinctun* 1086 (DB). 'Estate associated with a man called *Brandsige*'. OE pers. name + *-ing-* + *tūn*.

Brasted Kent. *Briestede* |sic| 1086 (DB), *Bradestede* c.1100. 'Broad place'. OE *brād* + *stede*.

Bratoft Lincs. *Breietoft* 1086 (DB). 'Broad homestead'. OScand. *breithr* + *toft*.

Brattleby Lincs. *Brotulbi* 1086 (DB). 'Farmstead or village of a man called *Brotulfr*'. OScand. pers. name + *bý*.

Bratton, usually 'farmstead by newly cultivated ground', OE *brēc* + *tūn*: **Bratton** Wilts. *Bratton* 1177. **Bratton Clovelly** Devon. *Bratona* 1086 (DB), *Bratton Clavyle* 1279. Manorial affix from the de Clavill family, here in the 13th cent. **Bratton Fleming** Devon. *Bratona* 1086 (DB). Manorial affix from the Flemeng family, here in the 13th cent.
However the following have a different origin, 'farmstead by a brook', OE *brōc* + *tūn*: **Bratton** Shrops. *Brochetone* 1086 (DB). **Bratton Seymour** Somerset. *Broctune* 1086 (DB). Manorial affix from the Saint Maur family, here c.1400.

Braughing Herts. *Breahingas* 825–8, *Brachinges* 1086 (DB). '(Settlement of) the family or followers of a man called *Breahha*'. OE pers. name + *-ingas*.

Braunston, *Braunstone*, 'farmstead of a man called *Brant*', OE pers. name + *tūn*: **Braunston** Rutland. *Branteston* 1167. **Braunston** Northants. *Brantestun* 956, *Brandestone* 1086 (DB). **Braunstone** Leics. *Brantestone* 1086 (DB).

Braunton Devon. *Brantona* 1086 (DB). 'Farmstead where broom grows'. OE *brōm* + *tūn*.

Brawby N. Yorks. *Bragebi* 1086 (DB). 'Farmstead or village of a man called Bragi'. OScand. pers. name + *bý*.

Braxted, Great Essex. *Brachestedam* 1086 (DB). Probably 'place where fern or bracken grows'. OE *bracu* + *stede*.

Bray Berks. *Brai* 1086 (DB). Probably OFrench *bray(e)* 'marsh'.

Bray (*Bré*) Wicklow. *Bree* n.d. 'Hill'.

Braybrooke Northants. *Bradebroc* 1086 (DB). '(Place at) the broad brook'. OE *brād* + *brōc*.

Brayfield, Cold Bucks. *Bragenfelda* 967. 'Open land by higher ground'. OE *bragen* + *feld*. Affix means 'bleak, exposed'.

Braystones Cumbria. *Bradestanes* 1247. 'Broad stones'. OE *brād* (replaced by OScand. *breithr*) + *stān*.

Brayton N. Yorks. *Breithe-tun* c.1030, *Bretone* 1086 (DB). 'Broad farmstead' or 'farmstead of a man called Breithi'. OScand. *breithr* or pers. name + OE *tūn*.

Breadalbane (district) Perth, Stir. *Bredalban* c.1600. 'Upper part of Alba'. Gaelic *bràghad*. *Alba*, the old name for Scotland.

Breadsall Derbys. *Brægdeshale* 1002, *Braideshale* 1086 (DB). 'Nook of land of a man called *Brægd*'. OE pers. name + *halh*.

Breadstone Glos. *Bradelestan* |sic| 1236, *Bradeneston* 1273. '(Place at) the broad stone'. OE *brād* (dative *-an*) + *stān*.

Bready (*An Bhréadaigh*) Tyrone. 'The (place of) broken ground'.

Breage Cornwall. *Egglosbrec* c.1170. 'Church of St Breage'. From the female patron saint of the church (with Cornish *eglos* 'church' in the early form).

Breaghwy (*Bréachmhaigh*) Mayo, Sligo. 'Wolf plain'.

Breamore Hants. *Brumore* 1086 (DB). 'Moor or marshy ground where broom grows'. OE *brōm* + *mōr*.

Brean Somerset. *Brien* 1086 (DB). Possibly a Celtic name containing a derivative of *bre3* 'hill'.

Brearton N. Yorks. *Braretone* 1086 (DB). 'Farmstead amongst the briars'. OE *brēr* + *tūn*.

Breaston Derbys. *Braidestune* 1086 (DB). 'Farmstead of a man called *Brægd*'. OE pers. name + *tūn*.

Brechin Ang. *Brechin* c.1145. '(Place of) Brychan'. Brychan also gave the name of BRECON.

Breckland (district) Norfolk. 'Area in which ground has been broken up for cultivation', from dialect *breck*, a name first used in the 19th cent.

Breckles Norfolk. *Brecchles* 1086 (DB). 'Meadow by newly-cultivated land'. OE *brēc* + *lǣs*.

Brecknock. See BRECON.

Brecon (*Aberhonddu*) Powys. *Brecheniauc* 1100. '(Place of) Brychan'. Brychan was a 5th-cent. prince. The Welsh name means 'mouth of the River Honddu' (OWelsh *aber*), the river name meaning 'pleasant' (Welsh *hawdd*). In the variant form *Brecknock*, the second element represents the Welsh 'territorial' suffix *-iog*.

Brecon Beacons (*Bannau Brycheiniog*) (mountains) Pemb, Powys. 'Beacons of Brecon'. The mountains were used for signal fires in medieval times. The Welsh name means 'peaks of Brycheiniog' i.e. 'territory of Brychan' (*see* BRECON).

Bredagh (*Brédach*) Westmeath. 'Broken ground'.

Bredbury Gtr. Manch. *Bretberie* 1086 (DB). 'Stronghold or manor-house built of planks'. OE *bred* + *burh* (dative *byrig*).

Brede E. Sussex. *Brade* 1161. 'Broad stretch of land'. OE *brǣdu*.

Bredfield Suffolk. *Bredefelda* 1086 (DB). 'Broad stretch of open country'. OE *brǣdu* + *feld*.

Bredgar Kent. *Bradegare* c.1100. 'Broad triangular plot'. OE *brād* + *gāra*.

Bredhurst Kent. *Bredehurst* 1240. 'Wooded hill where boards are obtained'. OE *bred* + *hyrst*.

Bredon Heref. & Worcs. *Breodun* 772, 1086 (DB). 'Hill called *Bre*'. Celtic **breʒ* 'hill' + explanatory OE *dūn*.

Bredon's Norton Heref. & Worcs., *see* NORTON.

Bredwardine Heref. & Worcs. *Brocheurdie* |*sic*| 1086 (DB), *Bredewerthin* late 12th cent. OE *worthign* 'enclosure', probably with *bred* 'board, plank' or *brǣdu* 'broad stretch of land'.

Bredy, Long & *Littlebredy* Dorset. *Bridian* 987, *Langebride*, *Litelbride* 1086 (DB). Named from the River Bride, a Celtic river-name meaning 'gushing or surging stream'. Distinguishing affixes are OE *lang* 'long' and *lȳtel* 'little'.

Bree (*Brí*) Wexford. 'Hilly place'.

Breedoge (*Bráideog*) Roscommon. 'Little throat'.

Breedon on the Hill Leics. *Briudun* 731. 'Hill called *Bre*'. Celtic **breʒ* 'hill' + explanatory OE *dūn* 'hill'. With the more recent affix the name thus contains three different words for 'hill'.

Breighton E. R. Yorks. *Bricstune* 1086 (DB). Possibly 'bright farmstead' or 'farmstead of a man called **Beorhta*'. OE *beorht* or pers. name + *tūn*.

Bremhill Wilts. *Bre(o)mel* 937, *Breme* |*sic*| 1086 (DB). 'Bramble thicket'. OE *brēmel*.

Brenchley Kent. *Braencesle* c.1100. Probably 'woodland clearing of a man called **Brænci*'. OE pers. name + *lēah*.

Brendon Devon. *Brandone* 1086 (DB). 'Hill where broom grows'. OE *brōm* + *dūn*.

Brenkley Tyne & Wear. *Brinchelawa* 1178. Possibly 'hill or mound of a man called Brynca'. OE pers. name + *hlāw*. Alternatively the first element may be OE **brince* 'brink or edge'.

Brent, probably a Celtic name meaning 'high place': **Brent, East** Somerset. *Brente* 663, *Brentemerse* 1086 (DB). With OE *mersc* 'marsh' in the Domesday form. **Brent Knoll** Somerset. *Brenteknol* 1289, sometimes known as South Brent, *Sudbrente* 1196. With OE *cnoll* 'hill-top', *sūth* 'south'. **Brent, South** Devon. *Brenta* 1086 (DB).

Brent Eleigh Suffolk, *see* ELEIGH.

Brent Pelham Herts., *see* PELHAM.

Brentford Gtr. London. *Breguntford* 705. 'Ford over the River Brent'. Celtic river-name (meaning 'holy one') + OE *ford*. The London borough of **Brent** takes its name from the river.

Brentor Devon. *Brentetor* 1232. 'Rocky hill called *Brente*'. Celtic hill-name + OE *torr*.

Brentwood Essex. *Boscus arsus* 1176, *Brendewode* 1274. 'The burnt wood'. OE **berned* (ME *brende*) + *wudu*. In the earliest form the name has been translated into Latin.

Brenzett Kent. *Brensete* 1086 (DB). 'The burnt fold or stable'. OE **berned* + (*ge*)*set*.

Brereton Ches. *Bretone* |*sic*| 1086 (DB), *Brereton* c.1100. 'Farmstead amongst the briars'. OE *brēr* + *tūn*.

Brereton Staffs. *Breredon* 1279. 'Hill where briars grow'. OE *brēr* + *dūn*.

Bressay (island) Shet. *Bressa* 1654. Originally 'broad island'. OScand. *breithr* + *ey*.

Bressingham Norfolk. *Bresingaham* 1086 (DB). 'Homestead of the family or followers of a man called **Briosa*'. OE pers. name + *-inga-* + *hām*.

Bretford Warwicks. *Bretford* early 11th cent. Probably 'ford provided with planks'. OE *bred* + *ford*.

Bretforton Heref. & Worcs. *Bretfertona* 709, *Bratfortune* 1086 (DB). 'Farmstead near the plank ford'. OE *bred* + *ford* + *tūn*.

Bretherdale Head Cumbria. *Britherdal* 12th cent. 'Valley of the brother(s)'. OScand. *bróthir* + *dalr*.

Bretherton Lancs. *Bretherton* 1190. 'Farmstead of the brother(s)'. OE *brōthor* or OScand. *bróthir* + OE *tūn*.

Brettenham, 'homestead of a man called **Bretta* or **Beorhta*'. OE pers. name (genitive *-n*) + *hām*: **Brettenham** Norfolk. *Bretham* 1086 (DB). **Brettenham** Suffolk. *Bretenhama* 1086 (DB). The name of the River **Brett**, which rises near here, is a 'back-formation' from the place-name.

Bretton, 'farmstead of the Britons'. OE *Brettas* (genitive *Bretta*) + *tūn*: **Bretton, Monk** S. Yorks. *Brettone* 1086 (DB), *Munkebretton* 1225. Affix from OE *munuc* 'monk' referring to the monks of Bretton Priory. **Bretton, West** W. Yorks. *Bretone* 1086 (DB), *West Bretton* c.1200.

Bretton Flin. *Bretton* c.1310. 'Farmstead of the Britons'. OE *Brettas* (genitive *Bretta*) + *tūn*.

Brewham Somerset. *Briweham* 1086 (DB). 'Homestead or enclosure on the River Brue'. Celtic river-name (*see* BRUTON) + OE *hām* or *hamm*.

Brewood Staffs. *Breude* 1086 (DB). 'Wood by the hill called *Bre*'. Celtic **breʒ* 'hill' + OE *wudu*.

Briantspuddle Dorset. *Pidele* 1086 (DB), *Brianis Pedille* 1465. 'Estate on the River Piddle held by a man called Brian'. OE river-name (*see* PIDDLEHINTON) with manorial affix from 14th cent. lord of manor.

Bricett, Great Suffolk. *Brieseta* 1086 (DB). Possibly 'fold or stable infested with gadflies'. OE *brīosa* + (*ge*)*set*.

Bricket Wood Herts. *Bruteyt* 1228. 'Bright-coloured small island or piece of marshland'. OE *beorht* + *ēgeth*.

Brickhill, Bow, *Brickhill, Great* & *Brickhill, Little* Bucks. *Brichelle* 1086 (DB), *Bolle Brichulle, Magna Brikehille, Parua Brichull* 1198. 'Hill called *Brig*'. Celtic **brig* 'hill top' + explanatory OE *hyll*. Distinguishing affixes from OE pers. name *Bolla* (no doubt an early tenant), Latin *magna* 'great' and *parva* 'little'.

Bricklehampton Heref. & Worcs. *Bricstelmestune* 1086 (DB). 'Estate associated with a man called Beorhthelm'. OE pers. name + *-ing-* + *tūn*.

Bricklieve (*Bricshliabh*) Sligo. 'Speckled mountain'.

Bride (river) Dorset, *see* BREDY.

Bridekirk Cumbria. *Bridekirke c.* 1210. 'Church of St Bride or Brigid'. Irish saint's name + OScand. *kirkja*.

Bridestowe Devon. *Bridestou* 1086 (DB). 'Holy place of St Bride or Brigid'. Irish saint's name + OE *stōw*.

Bridford Devon. *Brideforda* 1086 (DB). 'Ford suitable for brides', i.e. a shallow ford easy to cross. OE *brȳd* + *ford*.

Bridge Kent. *Brige* 1086 (DB). '(Place at) the bridge'. OE *brycg*.

Bridge Hewick N. Yorks., *see* HEWICK.

Bridge of Allan Stir. 'Bridge over the River Allan'. The Celtic river name means 'flowing water'.

Bridge of Alvah. *See* ALVAH.

Bridge of Weir Renf. 'Bridge by the weir'. The weir is on the River Gryfe.

Bridge Sollers Heref. & Worcs. *Bricge* 1086 (DB), *Bruges Solers* 1291. '(Place at) the bridge'. OE *brycg* + manorial affix from the de Solers family, here in the 12th cent.

Bridgend (*Ceann an Droichid*) Donegal. 'End of the bridge'.

Bridgend (*Pen-y-bont ar Ogwr*) Bri. *Byrge End* 1535. 'End of the bridge'. OE *brycg* + *ende*. A Norman castle is said to have protected the crossing here over the River Ogmore. The Welsh name means 'head of the bridge on the Ogmore' (Welsh *pen* + *y* + *pont*). For the river name, *see* OGMORE.

Bridgerule Devon. *Brige* 1086 (DB), *Briggeroald* 1238. '(Place at) the bridge held by a man called Ruald'. OE *brycg* + manorial affix from OScand. *Róaldr* (tenant in 1086).

Bridgford, 'ford by the bridge', OE *brycg* + *ford*: **Bridgford, East** Notts. *Brugeford* 1086 (DB). **Bridgford, West** Notts. *Brigeforde* 1086 (DB).

Bridgham Norfolk. *Brugeham c.* 1050. 'Homestead or enclosure by a bridge'. OE *brycg* + *hām* or *hamm*.

Bridgnorth Shrops. *Brug* 1156, *Brugg North* 1282. '(Place at) the bridge'. OE *brycg* + later affix *north*.

Bridgwater Somerset. *Brugie* 1086 (DB), *Brigewaltier* 1194. '(Place at) the bridge held by a man called Walter'. OE *brycg* + manorial affix from an early owner.

Bridlington E. R. Yorks. *Bretlinton* 1086 (DB). 'Estate associated with a man called Berhtel'. OE pers. name + *-ing-* + *tūn*.

Bridport Dorset. *Brideport* 1086 (DB). 'Harbour or market town belonging to (Long) BREDY'. OE *port*. The river-name **Brit** is a 'back-formation' from the place-name.

Bridstow Heref. & Worcs. *Bridestowe* 1277. 'Holy place of St Bride or Brigid'. Irish saint's name + OE *stōw*.

Brierfield Lancs., a self-explanatory name of 19th cent. origin, no doubt influenced by the nearby **Briercliffe** (*Brerecleve* 1193) which is 'bank where briars grow', OE *brēr* + *clif*.

Brierley, 'woodland clearing where briars grow', OE *brēr* + *lēah*: **Brierley** S. Yorks. *Breselai |sic|* 1086 (DB), *Brerelay* 1194. **Brierley Hill** W. Mids. *Brereley* 14th cent.

Brigg N. Lincs., earlier *Glanford Brigg* 1235. 'Bridge at the ford where people assemble for revelry or games'. OE *glēam* + *ford* + *brycg*.

Brigh (*Brīoch*) Tyrone. *Breigh* 1633. 'Hilly place'.

Brigham, 'homestead or enclosure by a bridge', OE *brycg* + *hām* or *hamm*: **Brigham** Cumbria, near Cockermouth. *Briggham c.*1175. **Brigham** E. R. Yorks. *Bringeham |sic|* 1086 (DB), *Brigham* 12th cent.

Brighouse W. Yorks. *Brighuses* 1240. 'Houses by the bridge'. OE *brycg* + *hūs*.

Brighstone I. of Wight. *Brihtwiston* 1212. 'Farmstead of a man called Beorhtwīg'. OE pers. name + *tūn*.

Brighthampton Oxon. *Byrhtelmingtun* 984, *Bristelmestone* 1086 (DB). 'Farmstead of a man called Beorhthelm'. OE pers. name + *tūn*.

Brightling E. Sussex. *Byrhtlingan* 1016–20, *Brislinga* 1086 (DB). '(Settlement of) the family or followers of a man called Beorhtel'. OE pers. name + *-ingas*.

Brightlingsea Essex. *Brictriceseia* 1086 (DB). 'Island of a man called Beorhtrīc or *Beorhtling'. OE pers. name + *ēg*.

Brighton E. Sussex. *Bristelmestune* 1086 (DB). 'Farmstead of a man called Beorhthelm'. OE pers. name + *tūn*.

Brighton, New Mersey., 19th cent. resort named after BRIGHTON.

Brightwalton Berks. *Beorhtwaldingtune* 939, *Bristoldestone* 1086 (DB). 'Estate associated with a man called Beorhtwald'. OE pers. name (+ *-ing-*) + *tūn*.

Brightwell, 'bright or clear spring', OE *beorht* + *wella*: **Brightwell** Oxon. *Beorhtawille* 854, *Bricsteuuelle* 1086 (DB). **Brightwell** Suffolk. *Brithwelle c.* 1050, *Brithtewella* 1086 (DB). **Brightwell Baldwin** Oxon. *Berhtanwellan* 887, *Britewelle* 1086 (DB). Manorial affix from possession by Sir Baldwin de Bereford in the late 14th cent.

Brignall Durham. *Bring(en)hale* 1086 (DB). Possibly 'nook of the family or followers of a man called Brȳni'. OE pers. name + *-inga-* + *halh*.

Brigsley NE. Lincs. *Brigeslai* 1086 (DB). 'Woodland clearing by a bridge'. OE *brycg* + *lēah*.

Brigsteer Cumbria. *Brigstere* early 13th cent. 'Bridge of a family called Stere, or one used for bullocks'. OScand. *bryggja* + ME surname or OE *stēor*. The order of elements is Celtic.

Brigstock Northants. *Bricstoc* 1086 (DB). Probably 'outlying farm or hamlet by a bridge'. OE *brycg* + *stoc*.

Brill Bucks. *Bruhella* 1072, *Brunhelle |sic|* 1086 (DB). 'Hill called *Bre*'. Celtic **breȝ* 'hill' + explanatory OE *hyll*.

Brilley Heref. & Worcs. *Brunlege* 1219. Probably 'woodland clearing where broom grows'. OE *brōm* + *lēah*.

Brimfield Heref. & Worcs. *Bromefeld* 1086 (DB). 'Open land where broom grows'. OE *brōm* + *feld*.

Brimington Derbys. *Brimintune* 1086 (DB). 'Estate associated with a man called Brēme'. OE pers. name + *-ing-* + *tūn*.

Brimpsfield Glos. *Brimesfelde* 1086 (DB). 'Open land of a man called Brēme'. OE pers. name + *feld*.

Brimpton Berks. *Bryningtune* 944, *Brintone* 1086 (DB). 'Estate associated with a man called Bryni'. OE pers. name + *-ing-* + *tūn*.

Brims Ness Highland. *Brymmis* 1559. Probably 'Headland of the surf'. OScand. *brim* + *nes*.

Brind E. R. Yorks. *Brende* 1188. OE **brende* 'place destroyed or cleared by burning'.

Brindle Lancs. *Burnhull* 1206. Probably 'hill by a stream'. OE *burna* + *hyll*.

Brineton Staffs. *Brunitone* 1086 (DB). Probably 'estate associated with a man called Bryni'. OE pers. name + *-ing-* + *tūn*.

Bringhurst Leics. *Bruninghyrst* 1188. Probably 'wooded hill of the family or followers of a man called Bryni'. OE pers. name + *-inga-* + *hyrst*.

Brington, 'estate associated with a man called Bryni', OE pers. name + *-ing-* + *tūn*: **Brington** Cambs. *Brynintune* 974, *Breninctune* 1086 (DB). **Brington, Great** & **Brington, Little** Northants. *Brinintone* 1086 (DB).

Briningham Norfolk. *Bruningaham* 1086 (DB). 'Homestead of the family or followers of a man called Bryni'. OE pers. name + *-inga-* + *hām*.

Brinkhill Lincs. *Brincle* 1086 (DB). 'Woodland clearing of a man called Brynca, or on the brink of a hill'. OE pers. name or OE **brince* + *lēah*.

Brinkley Cambs. *Brinkelai* late 12th cent. 'Woodland clearing of a man called Brynca'. OE pers. name + *lēah*.

Brinklow Warwicks. *Brinckelawe c*.1155. 'Burial mound of a man called Brynca, or on the brink of a hill'. OE **brince* + *hlāw*.

Brinkworth Wilts. *Brinkewrtha* 1065, *Brenchewrde* 1086 (DB). 'Enclosure of a man called Brynca'. OE pers. name + *worth*.

Brinlack (*Bun na Leaca*) Donegal. 'Foot of the flagstones'.

Brinscall Lancs. *Brendescoles c*.1200. 'Burnt huts'. ME *brende* + OScand. *skáli*.

Brinsley Notts. *Brunesleia* 1086 (DB). 'Woodland clearing of a man called Brūn'. OE pers. name + *lēah*.

Brinsop Heref. & Worcs. *Hope* 1086 (DB), *Bruneshopa c*.1130. 'Enclosed valley of a man called Brūn or Bryni'. OE pers. name + *hop*.

Brinsworth S. Yorks. *Brinesford* 1086 (DB). 'Ford of a man called Bryni'. OE pers. name + *ford*.

Brinton Norfolk. *Bruntuna* 1086 (DB). 'Estate associated with a man called Bryni'. OE pers. name + *-ing-* + *tūn*.

Briska (*Brioscach*) Waterford. 'Brittle land'.

Brisley Norfolk. *Bruselea c*.1105. 'Woodland clearing infested with gadflies'. OE *brīosa* + *lēah*.

Brislington Brist. *Brihthelmeston* 1199. 'Farmstead of a man called Beorhthelm'. OE pers. name + *tūn*.

Bristol Brist. *Brycg stowe* 11th cent., *Bristou* 1086 (DB). 'Assembly place by the bridge'. OE *brycg* + *stōw*.

Briston Norfolk. *Burstuna* 1086 (DB). 'Farmstead by a landslip or broken ground'. OE *byrst* + *tūn*.

Britannia Bridge (railway bridge) Gwyd. The bridge opened in 1850 and took its name from the *Britannia* Rock here.

Britford Wilts. *Brutford* 826, *Bredford* 1086 (DB). Possibly 'ford of the Britons'. OE *Bryt* + *ford*.

British (*Briotás*) Antrim. 'Wooden palisade'.

Briton Ferry (*Llansawel*) Neat. *Brigeton* 1201, *Brytton* 1315, *Britan Ferry caullid in Walsche Llanisauel* 1536. 'Ferry at the farm by the bridge'. OE *brycg* + *tūn* + Modern English *ferry*. The Welsh name means 'church of Sawel' (Welsh *llan*). *Cp.* LLANSAWEL.

Brittas (*An Briotás*) Dublin, Wicklow. 'The wooden palisade'.

Britway (*Breachmhaí*) Cork. 'Wolf plain'.

Britwell Salome Oxon. *Brutwelle* 1086 (DB), *Brutewell Solham* 1320. Possibly 'spring or stream of the Britons'. OE *Bryt* + *wella*. Manorial affix from the de Suleham family, here in the 13th cent.

Brixham Devon. *Briseham |sic|* 1086 (DB), *Brikesham* 1205. 'Homestead or enclosure of a man called Brioc'. Celtic pers. name + OE *hām* or *hamm*.

Brixton Devon. *Brisetona |sic|* 1086 (DB). *Brikeston* 1200. Probably 'farmstead of a man called Brioc'. Celtic pers. name + OE *tūn*.

Brixton Gtr. London. *Brixiges stan* 1062, *Brixiestan* 1086 (DB). 'Stone (probably marking a Hundred meeting-place) of a man called Beorhtsige'. OE pers. name + *stān*.

Brixton Deverill Wilts. *Devrel* 1086 (DB), *Britricheston* 1229. 'Estate on the River *Deverill* held by a man called Beorhtrīc'. OE pers. name + *tūn* with Celtic river-name (meaning 'watery'), an old name for the River Wylye.

Brixworth Northants. *Briclesworde* 1086 (DB). 'Enclosure of a man called Beorhtel or *Bricel'. OE pers. name + *worth*.

Brize Norton Oxon., *see* NORTON.

Broad as affix, see main name, e.g. for **Broad Blunsdon** (*Wilts.*) see BLUNSDON.

Broad Haven Pemb. *Brode Hauen* 1578. 'Wide harbour'. *Broad* distinguishes the village from nearby LITTLE HAVEN.

Broad Town Wilts. *Bradetun* 12th cent. 'Broad or large farmstead'. OE *brād* + *tūn*.

Broadbottom Gtr. Manch. *Brodebothem* 1286. 'Broad valley-bottom'. OE *brād* + **bothm*.

Broadford (*Áth Leathan*) Clare. 'Broad ford'.

Broadford Highland (Skye). 'Broad ford'. The name translates Gaelic *an t-àth leathan*.

Broadheath, Upper & *Broadheath, Lower* Heref. & Worcs. *Hethe* 1240, *Broad Heath* 1646. '(Place at) the broad heath'. OE *hǣth* with the later addition of *broad*.

Broadhembury Devon. *Hanberia* 1086 (DB), *Brodehembyri* 1273. 'High or chief fortified place'. OE *hēah* (dative *hēan*) + *burh* (dative *byrig*). Later affix is OE *brād* 'broad, great'.

Broadhempston Devon. *Hamistone* 1086 (DB), *Brodehempstone* 1362. 'Farmstead of a man called *Hǣme or Hemme'. OE pers. name + *tūn*. Affix is OE *brād* 'large' to distinguish this place from LITTLEHEMPSTON.

Broadmayne Dorset. *Maine* 1086 (DB), *Brademaene* 1202. Celtic *main* 'a rock, a stone', with later affix from OE *brād* 'broad, great'.

Broads, The (district) Norfolk, named from over thirty 'broads', i.e. extensive pieces of fresh water formed by the broadening out of rivers.

Broadstairs Kent. *Brodsteyr* 1435. 'Broad stairway or ascent'. OE *brād* + *stǣger*.

Broadstone Dorset, a recent name for a parish formed in 1906, self-explanatory.

Broadwas Heref. & Worcs. *Bradeuuesse* 779, *Bradewesham* 1086 (DB). 'Broad tract of alluvial land'. OE *brād* + *wæsse* (with *hām* 'homestead' in the 1086 form).

Broadwater W. Sussex. *Bradewatre* 1086 (DB). '(Place at) the broad stream'. OE *brād* + *wæter*.

Broadway, '(place at) the broad way or road', OE *brād* + *weg*: **Broadway** Heref. & Worcs. *Bradanuuege* 972, *Bradeweia* 1086 (DB). **Broadway** Somerset. *Bradewei* 1086 (DB).

Broadwell, '(place at) the broad spring or stream', OE *brād* + *wella*: **Broadwell** Glos. *Bradewelle* 1086 (DB). **Broadwell** Oxon. *Bradewelle* 1086 (DB). **Broadwell** Warwicks. *Bradewella* 1130.

Broadwey Dorset. *Wai(a)* 1086 (DB), *Brode Way* 1243. Named from the River Wey, *see* WEYMOUTH. Affix is OE *brād* 'broad, great', referring either to the width of the river here or to the size of the manor.

Broadwindsor Dorset. *Windesore* 1086 (DB), *Brodewyndesore* 1324. 'River-bank with a windlass'. OE *windels* + *ōra*, with *brād* 'great'.

Broadwoodkelly Devon. *Bradehoda* |sic| 1086 (DB), *Brawode Kelly* 1261. 'Broad wood'. OE *brād* + *wudu* + manorial affix from the de Kelly family, here in the 13th cent.

Broadwoodwidger Devon. *Bradewode* 1086 (DB), *Brodwode Wyger* 1310. Identical in origin with the previous name. Manorial affix from the Wyger family, here in the 13th cent.

Brobury Heref. & Worcs. *Brocheberie* 1086 (DB). 'Stronghold or manor near a brook'. OE *brōc* + *burh* (dative *byrig*).

Brockagh (*Brocach*) Westmeath. 'Badger den'.

Brockdish Norfolk. *Brodise* |sic| 1086 (DB), *Brochedisc* c.1095. 'Pasture by the brook'. OE *brōc* + *edisc*.

Brockenhurst Hants. *Broceste* |sic| 1086 (DB), *Brocheherst* 1158. Probably 'wooded hill of a man called *Broca'. OE pers. name (genitive -*n*) + *hyrst*. Alternatively the first element may be OE *brocen* 'broken up, undulating'.

Brockford Street Suffolk. *Brocfort* 1086 (DB). 'Ford over the brook'. OE *brōc* + *ford*.

Brockhall Northants. *Brocole* 1086 (DB). OE *brocc-hol* 'a badger hole, a sett'.

Brockham Surrey. *Brocham* 1241. 'River-meadow by the brook, or frequented by badgers'. OE *brōc* or *brocc* + *hamm*.

Brockhampton, 'homestead by the brook', OE *brōc* + *hām-tūn*: **Brockhampton**, Glos., near Sevenhampton. *Brochamtone* 1166. **Brockhampton** Heref. & Worcs., near Bromyard. *Brockampton* 1251.

Brocklesby Lincs. *Brochelesbi* 1086 (DB). 'Farmstead or village of a man called *Bróklauss'. OScand. pers. name + *bý*.

Brockley N. Som. *Brochelie* 1086 (DB). 'Woodland clearing of a man called *Broca, or frequented by badgers'. OE pers. name or *brocc* + *lēah*.

Brockley Gtr. London. *Brocele* 1182. Identical in origin with the previous name.

Brockley Suffolk. *Broclega* 1086 (DB). 'Woodland clearing by a brook'. OE *brōc* + *lēah*.

Brockton, *Brocton*, 'farmstead by a brook', OE *brōc* + *tūn*: **Brockton** Shrops., near Lilleshall. *Brochetone* 1086 (DB). **Brockton** Shrops., near Madeley. *Broctone* 1086 (DB). **Brockton** Shrops., near Worthen. *Brockton* 1272. **Brocton** Staffs., near Stafford. *Broctone* 1086 (DB).

Brockweir Glos. *Brocwere* c.1145. 'Weir by the brook'. OE *brōc* + *wer*.

Brockworth Glos. *Brocowardinge* 1086 (DB). 'Enclosure by the brook'. OE *brōc* + *worthign*.

Brocton Staffs., *see* BROCKTON.

Brodick N. Ayr (Arran). *Brathwik* 1306, *Bradewik* 1450. 'Broad bay'. OScand. *breithr* + *vík*. The town is on the bay of the same name.

Brodie Moray. *Brothie* 1380. 'Muddy place'. Gaelic *brothaith*.

Brodsworth S. Yorks. *Brodesworde* 1086 (DB). 'Enclosure of a man called Broddr or Brord'. OScand. or OE pers. name + *worth*.

Brokenborough Wilts. *Brokene beregge* 956, *Brocheneberge* 1086 (DB). 'Broken barrow' (probably referring to a tumulus that had been broken into). OE *brocen* + *beorg*.

Bromborough Mersey. *Brunburg* early 12th cent. 'Stronghold of a man called Brūna'. OE pers. name + *burh*.

Brome Suffolk. *Brom* 1086 (DB). 'Place where broom grows'. OE *brōm*.

Bromeswell Suffolk. *Bromeswella* 1086 (DB). 'Rising ground where broom grows'. OE *brōm* + *swelle*.

Bromfield Cumbria. *Brounefeld* c.1125. 'Brown open land, or open land where broom grows'. OE *brūn* or *brōm* + *feld*.

Bromfield Shrops. *Bromfelde* 1061, *Brunfelde* 1086 (DB). 'Open land where broom grows'. OE *brōm* + *feld*.

Bromham, 'homestead or enclosure where broom grows', OE *brōm* + *hām* or *hamm*: **Bromham** Beds. *Bruneham* 1086 (DB). Alternatively the first element in this name may be the OE pers. name *Brūna*. **Bromham** Wilts. *Bromham* 1086 (DB).

Bromley, usually 'woodland clearing where broom grows', OE *brōm* + *lēah*: **Bromley** Herts. *Bromlegh* 1248. **Bromley** Gtr. London, near Beckenham. *Bromleag* 862, *Bronlei* 1086 (DB). **Bromley, Abbots** Staffs. *Bromleage* 1002. Affix from its early possession by Burton Abbey. **Bromley, Great** & **Bromley, Little** Essex. *Brumleiam* 1086 (DB). **Bromley, Kings** Staffs. *Bromelei* 1086 (DB), *Bramlea Regis* 1167. Affix is Latin *regis* 'of the king', alluding to a royal manor.
However the following has a different origin: **Bromley** Gtr. London, near Bow. *Bræmbelege* c.1000. 'Woodland clearing where brambles grow'. OE *bræmbel* + *lēah*.

Brompton, usually 'farmstead where broom grows', OE *brōm* + *tūn*: **Brompton** N. Yorks., near Northallerton. *Bromtun* c.1050, *Bruntone* 1086 (DB). **Brompton** N. Yorks., near Snainton. *Bruntun* 1086 (DB). **Brompton on Swale** N. Yorks. *Bruntun* 1086 (DB). On the River Swale (probably OE **swalwe* 'rushing water'). **Brompton, Patrick** N. Yorks. *Brunton* 1086 (DB), *Patricbrunton* 1157. Manorial affix from its early possession by a man called Patric (an OIrish pers. name). **Brompton, Potter** N. Yorks. *Brunetona* 1086 (DB). Affix probably alludes to early potmaking here.
However the following has a different origin: **Brompton Ralph** & **Brompton Regis** Somerset. *Burnetone, Brunetone* 1086 (DB), *Brompton Radulphi* 1274, *Brompton Regis* 1291. 'Farmstead by the brown hill'. OE *Brūna* (referring to Brendon Hills) + *tūn*. Manorial affixes from early possession by a man called Ralph (Latin *Radulphus*) and by the king (Latin *regis* 'of the king').

Bromsgrove Heref. & Worcs. *Bremesgrefan* 804, *Bremesgrave* 1086 (DB). 'Grove or copse of a man called Brēme'. OE pers. name + *græfe, grāf*.

Bromwich, 'dwelling or farm where broom grows', OE *brōm* + *wīc*: **Bromwich, Castle** W. Mids. *Bramewice* 1168, *Castelbromwic* 13th cent. Affix refers to a 12th cent. earthwork. **Bromwich, West** W. Mids. *Bromwic* 1086, *Westbromwich* 1322.

Bromyard Heref. & Worcs. *Bromgeard* c.840, *Bromgerde* 1086 (DB). 'Enclosure where broom grows'. OE *brōm* + *geard*.

Brondesbury Gtr. London. *Bronnesburie* 1254. 'Manor of a man called Brand'. ME pers. name or surname + *bury* (from OE *byrig*, dative of *burth*).

Brook, *Brooke*, '(place at) the brook', OE *brōc*: **Brook** I. of Wight. *Broc* 1086 (DB). **Brook** Kent. *Broca* 11th cent. **Brooke** Norfolk. *Broc* 1086 (DB). **Brooke** Rutland. *Broc* 1176.

Brookeborough Fermanagh. *Brookeborough* 1835. The village arose in the 19th cent. on land granted to Sir Henry Brooke in 1666.

Brookland Kent. *Broklande* 1262. 'Cultivated land by a brook'. OE *brōc* + *land*.

Brookmans Park Herts. *Brokemanes* 1468. Named from a local family called Brokeman.

Brookthorpe Glos. *Brostorp* |*sic*| 1086 (DB), *Brocthrop* 12th cent. 'Outlying farmstead or hamlet by a brook'. OE *brōc* + *throp*.

Brookwood Surrey. *Brocwude* 1225. 'Wood by a brook'. OE *brōc* + *wudu*.

Broom, *Broome*, 'place where broom grows', OE *brōm*; examples include: **Broom** Beds. *Brume* 1086 (DB). **Broom** Durham. *Brom* c.1170. **Broom** Warwicks. *Brome* 710, 1086 (DB). **Broom** *Brom* 1169. **Broome** Norfolk. *Brom* 1086 (DB).

Broom, Loch Highland. *Braon* 1227. 'Loch of (the river) Broom'. Gaelic *loch* + *braon* 'drop shower'.

Broomfield, 'open land where broom grows', OE *brōm* + *feld*: **Broomfield** Essex. *Brumfeldam* 1086 (DB). **Broomfield** Kent, near Maidstone. *Brunfelle* |*sic*| 1086 (DB), *Brumfeld* c.1100. **Broomfield** Somerset. *Brunfelle* 1086 (DB).

Broomfleet E. R. Yorks. *Brungareflet* 1150–4. 'Stretch of river belonging to a man called Brūngār'. OE pers. name + *flēot*.

Brooms, High Kent, earlier *Bromgebrug* 1270, *Bromelaregg* 1318, from OE *brōm* 'broom' with either *brycg* 'bridge' or *hrycg* 'ridge'.

Brora Highland. *Strabroray* 1499. 'River of the bridge'. OScand. *brú* (genitive *brúar*) + *á*. The bridge, at the mouth of the river of the same name, was long the only one in Sutherland. The form of the name above has Gaelic *srath*, 'valley'.

Broseley Shrops. *Burewardeslega* 1177. 'Woodland clearing of the fort-keeper, or of a man called Burgweard'. OE *burh-weard* or pers. name + *lēah*.

Brotherton N. Yorks. *Brothertun* c.1030. 'Farmstead of the brother, or of a man called Bróthir'. OE *bróthor* or OScand. pers. name + OE *tūn*.

Brotton Red. & Cleve. *Broctune* 1086 (DB). 'Farmstead by a brook'. OE *brōc* + *tūn*.

Brough, 'stronghold or fortification', OE *burh*; examples include: **Brough** Cumbria. *Burc* 1174. **Brough** Derbys. *Burc* 1195. **Brough** E. R. Yorks. *Burg* c.1200. **Brough** Notts. *Burgh* 1525.

Broughderg (*Bruach Dearg*) Tyrone. *Brugh Derge* 1666. 'Red bank'.

Broughnamaddy (*Bruach na Madadh*) Down. 'Bank of the dogs'.

Broughshane (*Bruach Sheáin*) Antrim. *Bruaghshane* c.1655. 'Séan's bank'.

Broughton, a common name, usually 'farmstead by a brook', OE *brōc* + *tūn*; examples include: **Broughton Astley** Leics. *Broctone* 1086 (DB), *Broghton Astley* 1423. Manorial affix from the de Estle family, here in the 13th cent. **Broughton Gifford** Wilts. *Broctun* 1001, *Broctone* 1086 (DB), *Brocton Giffard* 1288. Manorial affix from the Giffard family, here in the 13th cent. **Broughton, Great** &

Broughton, Little Cumbria. *Broctuna* 12th cent. **Broughton Hackett** Heref. & Worcs. *Broctun* 972, *Broctune* 1086 (DB), *Broctone Haket* 1275. Manorial affix from the Hackett family, here in the 12th cent. **Broughton in Furness** Cumbria. *Brocton* 1196. For the district name Furness, *see* BARROW. **Broughton Poggs** Oxon. *Brotone* 1086 (DB), *Broughton Pouges* 1526. Manorial affix from early possession of lands here by the Pugeys family.

However other Broughtons have a different origin: **Broughton** Hants. *Brestone* 1086 (DB), *Burchton* 1173. 'Farmstead by a hill or mound'. OE *beorg* + *tūn*. **Broughton** N. Lincs. *Bertone* 1086 (DB). Identical in origin with previous name. **Broughton** Northants. *Burtone* 1086 (DB). 'Fortified farmstead' or 'farmstead near a fortification'. OE *burh-tūn*. **Broughton, Brant** Lincs. *Burtune* 1086 (DB), *Brendebrocton* 1250. Identical in origin with the previous name. Affix is ME *brende* 'burnt, destroyed by fire'.

Broughton (*Brychdyn*) Flin. *Brochetune* 1086 (DB). 'Farmstead by the brook'. OE *brōc* + *tūn*.

Brown Candover Hants., *see* CANDOVER.

Brown Edge Lancs. *Browneegge* 1551. 'Brown edge or ridge'. OE *Brūn* + *ecg*.

Brownhills Staffs., a recent self-explanatory name.

Brownsea Island Dorset. *Brunkeseye* 1241. 'Island of a man called *Brūnoc*'. OE pers. name + *ēg*.

Brownston Devon. *Brunardeston* 1219. 'Farmstead of a man called *Brūnweard*'. OE pers. name + *tūn*.

Broxbourne Herts. *Brochesborne* 1086 (DB). 'Stream frequented by badgers'. OE *brocc* + *burna*.

Broxburn W. Loth. *Broxburne* 1638. 'Stream frequented by badgers'. OE *brocc* + *burna*.

Broxted Essex. *Brocheseued* c.1050, *Brocchesheuot* 1086 (DB). 'Badger's head', i.e. 'hill frequented by badgers', or 'hill resembling a badger's head'. OE *brocc* + *hēafod*.

Broxton Ches. *Brosse* 1086 (DB), *Brexin, Broxun* 13th cent. An obscure name, possibly from an OE *burgæsn* 'burial place'. In any case the later *-ton* (found from 1260) is unhistorical.

Bruera Ches. *Bruera* c.1150. Latin *bruer(i)a* 'heath'.

Bruff (*An Brú*) Limerick. 'The palace'.

Bruisyard Suffolk. *Buresiart* 1086 (DB). 'Peasant's enclosure'. OE (ge)*būr* + *geard*.

Brumby N. Lincs. *Brunebi* 1086 (DB). 'Farmstead or village of a man called *Brúni*'. OScand. pers. name + *bý*. Alternatively the first element may be OScand. *brunnr* 'spring'.

Brundall Norfolk. *Brundala* 1086 (DB). Possibly 'broomy nook of land'. OE *brōmede* + *halh*.

Brundish Suffolk. *Burnedich* 1177. 'Pasture on a stream'. OE *burna* + *edisc*.

Brunton Northum. *Burneton* 1242. 'Farmstead by a stream'. OE *burna* + *tūn*.

Bruree (*Brú Rí*) Limerick. 'Palace of the king'.

Brushford, 'ford by the bridge', OE *brycg* + *ford*: **Brushford** Devon. *Brigeford* 1086 (DB). **Brushford** Somerset. *Brigeford* 1086 (DB).

Bruton Somerset. *Briwetone* 1086 (DB). 'Farmstead on the River Brue'. Celtic river-name (meaning 'brisk') + OE *tūn*.

Bryansford (*Áth Bhriain*) Down. *Bryansford* 1743. 'Brian's ford'.

Bryanston Dorset. *Blaneford Brian, Brianeston* 1268. 'Brian's estate', from OE *tūn*. Brian de Insula held this manor (originally called *Blaneford* = BLANDFORD) in the early 13th cent.

Brychdyn. *See* BROUGHTON.

Bryher Isles of Scilly, Cornwall. *Braer* 1319. Probably 'the hills'. Cornish *bre* in a plural form.

Brymbo Wrex. *Brynbawe* 1391, *Brinbawe* 1412, *Brymbo* 1480. 'Hill of dirt'. Welsh *bryn* + *baw*.

Brympton Somerset. *Brunetone* 1086 (DB), *Brimpton* 1264, *Bromton* 1331. Probably 'farmstead where broom grows'. OE *brōm* + *tūn*.

Bryn Shrops. *Bren* 1272. Celtic *brinn* 'hill'.

Bryn-mawr Blae. *Bryn-mawr* 1832. 'Big hill'. Welsh *bryn* + *mawr*. Until the early 19th cent. Bryn-Mawr was known as *Gwaun-helygen*, 'moorland of the willow tree' (Welsh *gwaun* + *helygen*).

Brynamman Carm. *Bryn Amman* 1844. 'Hill of the River Amman'. Welsh *bryn*. For the river name, *see* AMMANFORD.

Brynbuga. *See* USK.

Bubbenhall Warwicks. *Bubenhalle* |*sic*| 1086 (DB), *Bubenhull* 1211. 'Hill of a man called Bubba'. OE pers. name (genitive *-n*) + *hyll*.

Bubwith E. R. Yorks. *Bobewyth* 1066–9, *Bubvid* 1086 (DB). 'Wood (or dwelling) of a man called Bubba'. OE pers. name + OScand. *vithr* (perhaps replacing OE *wīc*).

Buccleuch Sc. Bord. *Bockcleugh* c.1590. 'Valley frequented by bucks'. OE *bucc* + *clōh*.

Buchan (district) Aber. *Buchan* c.1150, *Bouwan* c.1295. Said to be 'Place of cows', OWelsh *buwch*, but doubtful.

Buchanhaven Aber. *Thaw* 1775. 'Harbour in Buchan'. *See* BUCHAN.

Buck's Cross Devon. *Bochewis* 1086 (DB). 'Measure of land granted by charter'. OE *bōc* + *hīwisc*.

Buckby, Long Northants. *Buchebi* 1086 (DB), *Longe Bugby* 1565. 'Farmstead or village of a man called Bukki or Bucca'. OScand. or OE pers. name + OScand. *bý*. Affix refers to the length of the village.

Buckden Cambs. *Bugedene* 1086 (DB). 'Valley of a woman called Bucge'. OE pers. name + *denu*.

Buckden N. Yorks. *Buckeden* 12th cent. 'Valley frequented by bucks (male deer)'. OE *bucc* + *denu*.

Buckenham, 'homestead of a man called Bucca', OE pers. name (genitive *-n*) + *hām*: **Buckenham** Norfolk. *Buc(h)anaham* 1086 (DB). **Buckenham, New** & **Buckenham, Old** Norfolk. *Buc(he)ham* 1086 (DB).

Buckerell Devon. *Bucherel* 1165. Obscure in origin and meaning.

Buckfast Devon. *Bucfæsten* 1046, *Bucfestre* 1086 (DB). 'Place of shelter for bucks (male deer)'. OE *bucc* + *fæsten*.

Buckfastleigh Devon. *Leghe Bucfestre* 13th cent. 'Wood or woodland clearing near BUCKFAST'. OE *lēah*.

Buckhaven Fife. *Bukavim* 1549, *Bukhavin* 1556. 'Harbour where bucks are found'. OE *bucc* + *hæfen*.

Buckhorn Weston Dorset, *see* WESTON.

Buckhurst Hill Essex. *Bocherst* 1135. 'Wooded hill growing with beeches'. OE *bōc* + *hyrst*.

Buckie Moray. *Buky* 1362. 'Buck River'. Gaelic *boc*. The name was originally that of the stream here, the *Burn of Buckie*.

Buckingham Bucks. *Buccingahamme* early 10th cent., *Bochingeham* 1086 (DB). 'River-bend land of the family or followers of a man called Bucca'. OE pers. name + *inga-* + *hamm*. **Buckinghamshire** (OE *scīr* 'district') is first referred to in the 11th cent.

Buckland, a common name, from OE *bōc-land* 'charter land', i.e. 'estate with certain rights and privileges created by an Anglo-Saxon royal diploma'; examples include: **Buckland** Surrey. *Bochelant* 1086 (DB). **Buckland Brewer** Devon. *Bochelanda* 1086 (DB), *Boclande Bruere* 1290. Manorial affix from the Briwerre family, here in the 13th cent. **Buckland Dinham** Somerset. *Boclande* 951, *Bochelande* 1086 (DB), *Bokelonddynham* 1329. Manorial affix from the de Dinan family, here in the 13th cent. **Buckland, Egg** Devon. *Bochelanda* 1086 (DB), *Eckebokelond* 1221. Manorial affix from its possession by a man called Heca in 1086. **Buckland Filleigh** Devon. *Bochelan* 1086 (DB), *Bokelondefilleghe* 1333. Manorial affix from the de Fyleleye family, here in the 13th cent. **Buckland in the Moor** Devon. *Bochelanda* 1086 (DB), *Bokelaund in the More* 1318. Affix from its situation on the edge of DARTMOOR. **Buckland Monachorum** Devon. *Boclande c.970*, *Bochelanda* 1086 (DB), *Boclonde Monachorum* 1291. Latin affix 'of the monks', referring to an abbey founded here in 1278. **Buckland Newton** Dorset. *Boclonde* 941, *Bochelande* 1086 (DB), *Newton Buckland* 1576. Relatively late addition Newton is from STURMINSTER NEWTON.

Bucklebury Berks. *Borgeldeberie* 1086 (DB). 'Stronghold of a woman called Burghild'. OE pers. name + *burh* (dative *byrig*).

Bucklers Hard Hants., first so recorded in 1789, named from the Buckler family here in 1664, with dialect *hard* 'firm landing-place'.

Bucklesham Suffolk. *Bukelesham* 1086 (DB). 'Homestead of a man called *Buccel*'. OE pers. name + *hām*.

Buckley (*Bwcle*) Flin. *Bokkeley* 1294, *Bukkelee* 1301. 'Woodland clearing where bucks graze'. OE *bucc* + *lēah*.

Buckminster Leics. *Bucheminstre* 1086 (DB). 'Large church of a man called Bucca'. OE pers. name + *mynster*.

Buckna (*Bocshnámh*) Antrim. *Boughna* 1669. 'Ford used by stags'.

Bucknall, 'nook of land of a man called Bucca, or where he-goats graze', OE pers. name or *bucca* (genitive *-n*) + *halh*: **Bucknall** Lincs. *Bokenhale* 806, *Buchehale* 1086 (DB). **Bucknall** Staffs. *Bucenhole* 1086 (DB).

Bucknell, 'hill of a man called Bucca, or where he-goats graze', OE pers. name or *bucca* (genitive *-n*) + *hyll*:

Bucknell Oxon. *Buchehelle* 1086 (DB). **Bucknell** Shrops. *Buchehalle* [*sic*] 1086 (DB), *Bukenhull* 1209.

Buckode (*Bocóid*) Leitrim. 'Spot'.

Buck's Cross Devon. *Bochewis* 1086 (DB). 'Measure of land granted by charter'. OE *bōc* + *hīwisc*.

Buckton, 'farmstead of a man called Bucca, or where bucks (male deer) or he-goats are kept', OE pers. name or OE *bucc* or *bucca* + *tūn*: **Buckton** E. R. Yorks. *Bochetone* 1086 (DB). **Buckton** Heref. & Worcs. *Buctone* 1086 (DB). **Buckton** Northum. *Buketun* 1208–10.

Buckworth Cambs. *Buchesworde* 1086 (DB). 'Enclosure of a man called *Bucc*'. OE pers. name + *worth*.

Budbrooke Warwicks. *Budebroc* 1086 (DB). 'Brook of a man called Budda'. OE pers. name + *brōc*.

Budby Notts. *Butebi* 1086 (DB). 'Farmstead or village of a man called Butti'. OScand. pers. name + *bý*.

Bude Cornwall. *Bude* 1400. Perhaps originally a river-name, of uncertain origin and meaning.

Budle Northum. *Bolda* 1166. 'The special house or building'. OE *bōthl*.

Budleigh Salterton Devon, *see* SALTERTON.

Budleigh, East Devon. *Bodelie* 1086 (DB). 'Woodland clearing of a man called Budda'. OE pers. name + *lēah*.

Budock Water Cornwall. 'Church of *Sanctus Budocus*' 1208. From the patron saint of the church, St Budock. Later affix is *water* in the sense 'stream'.

Budworth, 'enclosure of a man called Budda', OE pers. name + *worth*: **Budworth, Great** Ches. *Budewrde* 1086 (DB). **Budworth, Little** Ches. *Bodeurde* 1086 (DB).

Buerton Ches., near Audlem. *Burtune* 1086 (DB). 'Enclosure belonging to a fortified place'. OE *byrh-tūn*.

Bugbrooke Northants. *Buchebroc* 1086 (DB). Probably 'brook of a man called Bucca'. OE pers. name + *brōc*.

Buggan (*Bogán*) Fermanagh. 'Soft place'.

Bugthorpe E. R. Yorks. *Bugetorp* 1086 (DB). 'Outlying farmstead or hamlet of a man called Buggi'. OScand. pers. name + *thorp*.

Buildwas Shrops. *Beldewas* 1086 (DB). OE *wæsse* 'alluvial land' with an uncertain first element.

Builth Wells (*Llanfair-ym-Muallt*) Powys. *Buelt* 10th cent. 'Cow pasture with springs'. Welsh *bu* + *gellt* (later *gwellt*). *Wells* was added in the 19th cent. when chalybeate springs were discovered. The Welsh name means 'St Mary's church in *Buallt*' (Welsh *llan* + *Mair* + *yn*), *Buallt* giving *Builth*.

Bulby Lincs. *Bolebi* 1086 (DB). Probably 'farmstead or village of a man called Boli or Bolli'. OScand. pers. name + *bý*.

Bulford Wilts. *Bulte(s)ford* 12th cent. Possibly 'ford by the island where ragged robin or the cuckoo flower grows'. OE *bulut* + *īeg* + *ford*.

Bulkeley Ches. *Bulceleia* 1170. 'Clearing or pasture where bullocks graze'. OE *bulluc* + *lēah*.

Bulkington, 'estate associated with a man called *Bulca*', OE pers. name + *-ing-* + *tūn*: **Bulkington** Warwicks.

Bochintone 1086 (DB). **Bulkington** Wilts. *Boltintone* 1086 (DB).

Bulkworthy Devon. *Buchesworde* 1086 (DB). 'Enclosure of a man called *Bulca'. OE pers. name + *worth*.

Bullaun (*Ballán*) Galway. 'Round hillock'.

Bullers of Buchan (rocky coastal recess) Aber. 'Roaring place of Buchan'. Scottish English *buller*. *See* BUCHAN.

Bulley Glos. *Bulelege* 1086 (DB). 'Woodland clearing where bulls graze'. OE *bula* + *lēah*.

Bullingham, Lower Heref. & Worcs. *Boninhope |sic|* 1086 (DB), *Bullingehope* 1242. 'Marsh enclosure associated with a man called *Bulla', or 'marsh enclosure at *Bulla's place'. OE pers. name + *-ing-* or *-ing* + *hop* (later replaced by *hamm*).

Bulmer, 'pool where bulls drink', OE *bula* (genitive plural *bulena*) + *mere*: **Bulmer** Essex. *Bulenemera* 1086 (DB). **Bulmer** N. Yorks. *Bolemere* 1086 (DB).

Bulphan Essex. *Bulgeuen* 1086 (DB). 'Fen near a fortified place'. OE *burh* + *fenn*. The spelling with *-l-* is due to Norman influence.

Bulverhythe E. Sussex. *Bulwareheda* 12th cent. 'Landing-place of the town-dwellers (of Hastings)'. OE *burh-ware* + *hȳth*.

Bulwell Notts. *Buleuuelle* 1086 (DB). 'Spring or stream of a man called *Bula, or where bulls drink'. OE pers. name or OE *bula* + *wella*.

Bulwick Northants. *Bulewic* 1162. 'Farm where bulls are reared'. OE *bula* + *wīc*.

Bumpstead, Helions & *Bumpstead, Steeple* Essex. *Bumesteda* 1086 (DB), *Bumpsted Helyun* 1238, *Stepilbumstede* 1261. 'Place where reeds grow'. OE *bune* + *stede*. Distinguishing affixes from *Tihel de Helion* who held one manor in 1086, and from OE *stēpel* 'steeple, tower'.

Bun (*Bun*) Offaly. 'Bottom'.

Bunaw (*Bun Abha*) Kerry. 'River mouth'.

Bunbeg (*An Bun Beag*) Donegal. 'The little river mouth'.

Bunbrusna (*Bun Brosnaí*) Westmeath. 'Mouth of the (river) Brosna'.

Bunbury Ches. *Boleberie |sic|* 1086 (DB), *Bonebury* 12th cent. 'Stronghold of a man called *Būna'. OE pers. name + *burh* (dative *byrig*).

Bunclody (*Bun Clóidí*) Carlow, Wexford. 'Mouth of the (river) Clóideach'.

Buncrana (*Bun Cranncha*) Donegal. *Boncranagh* 1601. 'Mouth of the (river) Crannach'.

Bundoran (*Bun Dobhráin*) Donegal. *Bundorin* 1802. 'Mouth of the little water'. The *Dobhrán* was probably an earlier name for the present river *Bradoge*.

Bundorragha (*Bun Dorcha*) Mayo. 'Mouth of the dark river'.

Bunduff (*Bun Dubh*) Leitrim. 'Mouth of the black (river)'.

Bungay Suffolk. *Bunghea* 1086 (DB). Probably 'island of the family or followers of a man called *Būna'. OE pers. name + *-inga-* + *ēg*.

Bunmahon (*Bun Machan*) Waterford. 'Mouth of the (river) Machain'.

Bunnacurry (*Bun an Churraigh*) Mayo. 'Foot of the swamp'.

Bunnahowen (*Bun na hAbhna*) Mayo. 'Mouth of the river'.

Bunnanaddan (*Bun an Fheadáin*) Sligo. 'Mouth of the stream'.

Bunny Notts. *Bonei* 1086 (DB). Probably 'island, or dry ground in marsh, where reeds grow'. OE *bune* + *ēg*.

Bunnyconnellan (*Muine Chonalláin*) Mayo. 'Conallán's thicket'.

Bunowen (*Bun Abhann*) Mayo. 'Mouth of the river'.

Bunratty (*Bun Raite*) Clare. 'Mouth of the (river) Raite'.

Bunree (*Bun Rí*) Mayo. 'Mouth of the (river) Rí'.

Buntingford Herts. *Buntingeford* 1185. 'Ford frequented by buntings or yellow-hammers'. ME *bunting* + *ford*.

Bunwell Norfolk. *Bunewell* 1198. 'Spring or stream where reeds grow'. OE *bune* + *wella*.

Burbage Derbys. *Burbache* 1417. 'Stream or ridge by a fortified place'. OE *burh* + *bece* or *bæc* (dative *bece*).

Burbage Leics. *Burhbeca* 1043, *Burbece* 1086 (DB). Probably 'ridge by a fortified place'. OE *burh* + *bæc* (dative *bece*).

Burbage Wilts. *Burhbece* 961, *Burbetce* 1086 (DB). Probably 'stream by a fortified place'. OE *burh* + *bece*.

Burcombe Wilts. *Brydancumb* 937, *Bredecumbe* 1086 (DB). Probably 'valley of a man called *Brȳda'. OE pers. name + *cumb*.

Burcot Oxon. *Bridicote* 1198. Probably 'cottage(s) associated with a man called *Brȳda'. OE pers. name (+ *-ing-*) + *cot*.

Burdale N. Yorks. *Bredhalle* 1086 (DB). 'Hall or house made of planks'. OE *bred* + *hall*.

Bures & *Mount Bures* Essex. *Bura* 1086 (DB), *Bures* 1198, *Bures atte Munte* 1328. 'The dwellings or cottages'. OE *būr* with later affix 'at the hill' from ME *munt*.

Burford, 'ford by the fortified place', OE *burh* + *ford*: **Burford** Oxon. *Bureford* 1086 (DB). **Burford** Shrops. *Bureford* 1086 (DB).

Burgess Hill W. Sussex. *Burges Hill* 1597. Named from a family called Burgeys, here in the 13th cent.

Burgh, a common name, usually OE *burh* 'fortification, stronghold, fortified manor'; examples include: **Burgh** Suffolk. *Burc* 1086 (DB). **Burgh-by-Sands** Cumbria. *Burch* c.1180, *Burg en le Sandes* 1292. This is an old Roman fort on the coast. **Burgh le Marsh** Lincs. *Burg* 1086 (DB). Affix means 'in the marshland'.

However the following has a different origin: **Burgh, Great** & **Burgh, Heath** Surrey. *Berge* 1086 (DB), *Borow heth* 1545. '(Place at) the barrow(s)', from OE *beorg*, with the later addition of *hǣth* 'heath'.

Burghclere Hants. *Burclere* 1171. OE *burh* in one of its meanings 'fortification, manor, borough, market-town' added to the original name found also in HIGHCLERE.

Burghfield Berks. *Borgefel* 1086 (DB). 'Open land by the hill'. OE *beorg* + *feld*.

Burghill Heref. & Worcs. *Burgelle* 1086 (DB). 'Hill with a fort'. OE *burh* + *hyll*.

Burghwallis S. Yorks. *Burg* 1086 (DB), *Burghwaleys* 1283. 'The stronghold or fortified manor', OE *burh*, with later manorial affix from the Waleys family, here from the 12th cent.

Burham Kent. *Burhham* 10th cent., *Borham* 1086 (DB). 'Homestead near the fortified place'. OE *burh* + *hām*.

Buriton Hants. *Buriton* 1227. 'Enclosure near or belonging to a fortified place'. OE *byrh-tūn*.

Burland Ches. *Burlond* 1260. 'Cultivated land of the peasants'. OE *(ge)būr* + *land*.

Burlescombe Devon. *Berlescoma* |sic| 1086 (DB), *Burewoldescumbe* 12th cent. 'Valley of a man called Burgweald'. OE pers. name + *cumb*.

Burleston Dorset. *Bordelestone* 934. 'Farmstead of a man called Burdel'. OE pers. name + *tūn*.

Burley, 'woodland clearing by or belonging to a fortified place', OE *burh* + *lēah*: **Burley** Hants. *Burgelea* 1178. **Burley** Rutland. *Burgelai* 1086 (DB). **Burley** W. Yorks. *Burcheleia* c.1200. **Burley in Wharfedale** W. Yorks. *Burhleg* c.972, *Burghelai* 1086 (DB). Affix is 'valley of the River Wharfe', Celtic river-name (meaning 'winding one') + OScand. *dalr*.

Burleydam Ches. *Burley* c.1130, *Burleydam* 1643. 'Woodland clearing of the peasants'. OE *(ge)būr* + *lēah* with the later addition of ME *damme* 'a milldam'.

Burlingham Norfolk. *Berlingeham* 1086 (DB). 'Homestead of the family or followers of a man called *Bærla or *Byrla'. OE pers. name + *-inga-* + *hām*.

Burlton Shrops. *Burghelton* 1241. 'Farmstead by a hill with a fort'. OE *burh* + *hyll* + *tūn*.

Burmarsh Kent. *Burwaramers* 7th cent., *Burwarmaresc* 1086 (DB). 'Marsh of the town-dwellers (of Canterbury)'. OE *burh-ware* + *mersc*.

Burmington Warwicks. *Burdintone* |sic| 1086 (DB), *Burminton* late 12th cent. 'Estate associated with a man called Beornmund or *Beorma'. OE pers. name + *-ing-* + *tūn*.

Burn N. Yorks. *Byrne* c.1030. Probably 'place cleared by burning'. OE *bryne*.

Burnaston Derbys. *Burmulfestune* 1086 (DB). 'Farmstead of a man called *Brūnwulf or Brynjólfr'. OE or OScand. pers. name + OE *tūn*.

Burnby E. R. Yorks. *Brunebi* 1086 (DB). 'Farmstead or village by a spring or stream'. OScand. *brunnr* + *bý*.

Burncourt (*An Chúirt Dóite*) Tipperary. 'The burnt court'. The house *Clogheen* ('small stones'), built here in 1641, was burnt down by Cromwell in 1650.

Burneside Cumbria. *Brunoluesheued* c.1180. 'Headland or hill of a man called *Brūnwulf or Brunulf'. OE or OGerman pers. name + OE *hēafod*.

Burneston N. Yorks. *Brennigston* 1086 (DB). Probably 'farmstead of a man called Brýningr'. OScand. pers. name + *tūn*.

Burnett B. & NE. Som. *Bernet* 1086 (DB). 'Land cleared by burning'. OE *bærnet*.

Burnfoot (*Bun n hAbhainn*) Donegal. *Burnfoot Bridge* 1762. 'Foot of the stream'.

Burnham, usually 'homestead or village on a stream', OE *burna* + *hām*: **Burnham** Bucks. *Burneham* 1086 (DB). **Burnham Deepdale** & **Burnham Market**, **Burnham Norton** & **Burnham Overy**, **Burnham Thorpe** Norfolk. *Brun(e)ham*, *Depedala* 1086 (DB), *Brunham Norton* 1457, *Brunham Overhe* 1457, *Brunhamtorp* 1199. Distinguishing affixes are 'deep valley' (OE *dē op* + *dæl*), 'market', 'north farm' (OE *north* + *tūn*), 'over the river' (OE *ofer* + *ēa*) and 'outlying farmstead' (OScand. *thorp*). **Burnham on Crouch** Essex. *Burneham* 1086 (DB). Affix is from the River Crouch (not recorded before 16th cent., probably from OE *crūc* 'a cross').

However two Burnhams have a different origin: **Burnham** N. Lincs. *Brune* |sic| 1086 (DB), *Brunum* c.1115. '(Place at) the springs or streams'. OScand. *brunnr* in a dative plural form *brunnum*. **Burnham on Sea** Somerset. *Burnhamm* c.880, *Burneham* 1086 (DB). 'Enclosure by a stream'. OE *burna* + *hamm*.

Burniston N. Yorks. *Brinnistun* 1086 (DB). 'Farmstead of a man called Brýningr'. OScand. pers. name + OE *tūn*.

Burnley Lancs. *Brunlaia* 1124. 'Woodland clearing by the River Brun'. OE river-name (from *brūn* 'brown' or *burna* 'stream') + *lēah*.

Burnsall N. Yorks. *Brineshale* 1086 (DB). 'Nook of land of a man called Brýni'. OE pers. name + *halh*.

Burnswark Dumf. *Burniswarke* 1542. 'Bruna's fortified place'. OE pers. name + *weorc*.

Burntisland Fife. *Brynt Hand* 1540. 'Burnt island'. OE *brende* + Modern English *island*. A 'burnt island' is one where buildings were destroyed by fire or land cleared for cultivation by burning.

Burpham, 'homestead near the stronghold or fortified place', OE *burh* + *hām*: **Burpham** Surrey. *Borham* 1086 (DB). **Burpham** W. Sussex. *Burhham* c.920, *Bercheham* 1086 (DB).

Burradon, 'hill with a fort', OE *burh* + *dūn*: **Burradon** Northum. *Burhedon* early 13th cent. **Burradon** Tyne & Wear. *Burgdon* 12th cent.

Burren (*Boirinn*) Clare, Down. 'Stony district'.

Burrenbane (*Boireann Bán*) Down. 'White stony district'.

Burrenreagh (*Boireann Riabhach*) Down. 'Grey stony district'.

Burrill N. Yorks. *Borel* 1086 (DB). Probably 'hill with a fort'. OE *burh* + *hyll*.

Burringham N. Lincs. *Burringham* 1199. Probably 'homestead of the dwellers on the stream'. OE *burna* + *-inga-* + *hām*.

Burrington Devon. *Bernintone* 1086 (DB). 'Estate associated with a man called Beorn'. OE pers. name + *-ing-* + *tūn*.

Burrington Heref. & Worcs. *Boritune* 1086 (DB). 'Farmstead by a fortified place'. OE *burh* (genitive or dative *byrig*) + *tūn*.

Burrington N. Som. *Buringtune* 12th cent. 'Farmstead by a fortified place'. OE *burh* (genitive or dative *byrig*) + *tūn*.

Burrough Green Cambs. *Burg* c.1045, *Burch* 1086 (DB), *Boroughegrene* 1571. 'The fortified place'. OE *burh* with the later addition of *grēne* 'village green'.

Burrough on the Hill Leics. *Burg* 1086 (DB). 'The fortified place'. OE *burh*, referring to an Iron Age hill-fort.

Burrow Bridge Somerset. *Æt tham Beorge* 1065. '(Place) at the hill'. OE *beorg*.

Burrow, Nether & *Burrow, Over* Lancs. *Borch* 1086 (DB). 'The fortified place', here referring to a Roman fort. OE *burh*.

Burry Port Carm. *Pembrey ... also called Burry Port* 1897. 'Port of the sand dune'. Modern English dialect *burry* + Modern English *port*.

Burscough Lancs. *Burscogh* c.1190. 'Wood by the fort'. OE *burh* + OScand. *skógr*.

Burshill E. R. Yorks. *Bristehil* 12th cent. 'Hill with a landslip or rough ground'. OE *byrst* + *hyll*.

Bursledon Hants. *Brixendona* c.1170. Probably 'hill associated with a man called Beorhtsige'. OE pers. name + *-ing-* + *dūn*.

Burslem Staffs. *Barcardeslim* |*sic*| 1086 (DB), *Borewardeslyme* 1242. 'Estate in *Lyme* belonging to the fort-keeper, or to a man called Burgweard'. OE *burh-weard* or pers. name with old Celtic district name *Lyme* probably meaning 'elm-tree region'.

Burstall Suffolk. *Burgestala* 1086 (DB). 'Site of a fort or stronghold'. OE *burh-stall*.

Burstead, Great & *Burstead, Little* Essex. *Burgestede* c.1000, *Burghesteda* 1086 (DB). 'Site of a fort or stronghold'. OE *burh-stede*.

Burstock Dorset. *Burewinestoch* 1086 (DB). 'Outlying farmstead or hamlet of a woman called Burgwynn or of a man called Burgwine'. OE pers. name + *stoc*.

Burston Norfolk. *Borstuna* 1086 (DB). Possibly 'farmstead by a landslip or rough ground'. OE *byrst* + *tūn*.

Burston Staffs. *Burouestone* 1086 (DB). Possibly 'farmstead of a man called Burgwine or Burgwulf'. OE pers. name + *tūn*.

Burstow Surrey. *Burestou* 12th cent. 'Place by a fort or stronghold'. OE *burh* (genitive *byrh*) + *stōw*.

Burstwick E. R. Yorks. *Brostewic* 1086 (DB). Probably 'dwelling or farm of a man called Bursti'. OScand. pers. name + OE *wīc*.

Burt (*An Beart*) Donegal. *Droma Bertach* c.830. Possibly 'the heaped ridge'.

Burton, a common name, usually OE *burh-tūn* 'fortified farmstead', or 'farmstead near a fortification'; examples include: **Burton Agnes** E. R. Yorks. *Bortona* 1086 (DB), *Burton Agneys* 1231. Manorial affix from its possession by Agnes de Percy in the late 12th cent. **Burton, Bishop** E. R. Yorks. *Burton* 1086 (DB), *Bisshopburton* 1376. Manorial affix from its early possession by the Archbishops of York.

Burton, Cherry E. R. Yorks. *Burtone* 1086 (DB), *Cheriburton* 1444. Affix is ME *chiri* 'cherry', no doubt referring to cherry-trees growing here. **Burton, Constable** N. Yorks. *Bortone* 1086 (DB), *Burton Constable* 1301. Manorial affix from its possession by the Constables of Richmond Castle in the 12th cent. **Burton Dassett** Warwicks., *see* DASSETT. **Burton Fleming** E. R. Yorks. *Burtone* 1086 (DB), *Burton Flemeng* 1234. Manorial affix from the Fleming family, here in the 12th cent. **Burton Hastings** Warwicks. *Burhtun* 1002, *Bortone* 1086 (DB), *Burugton de Hastings* 1313. Manorial affix from the de Hasteng family, here in the 13th cent. **Burton Latimer** Northants. *Burtone* 1086 (DB), *Burton Latymer* 1482. Manorial affix from the le Latimer family, here in the 13th cent. **Burton upon Stather** N. Lincs. *Burtone* 1086 (DB), *Burtonstather* 1275. Affix means 'by the landing-places' from OScand. *stǫth* in a plural form *stǫthvar*.

However the following have a different origin: **Burton Bradstock** Dorset. *Bridetone* 1086 (DB). 'Farmstead on the River Bride'. Celtic river-name (*see* BREDY) + OE *tūn*. The later addition Bradstock is from the Abbey of BRADENSTOKE which held the manor from the 13th cent. **Burton Joyce** Notts. *Bertune* 1086 (DB), *Birton Jorce* 1327. OE *byrh-tūn* 'farmstead of the fortified place or stronghold'. Manorial affix from the de Jorz family, here in the 13th cent. **Burton Salmon** N. Yorks. *Brettona* c.1160, *Burton Salaman* 1516. 'Farmstead of the Britons'. OE *Brettas* (genitive *Bretta*) + *tūn*. Manorial affix from a man called Salamone who had lands here in the 13th cent. **Burton upon Trent** Staffs. *Byrtun* 1002, *Bertone* 1086 (DB). Identical in origin with BURTON JOYCE. For the river-name, *see* TRENTHAM.

Burtonport Donegal. 'Burton's port'. *Burton Port* 1835. The village arose by a fishing port founded in 1785 by William Burton. The Irish name is *Ailt an Chorráin*, 'ravine of the curve'.

Burtonwood Ches. *Burtoneswod* 1228. 'Wood by the fortified farmstead'. OE *burh-tūn* + *wudu*.

Burwardsley Ches. *Burwardeslei* 1086 (DB). 'Woodland clearing of the fort-keeper, or of a man called Burgweard'. OE *burh-weard* or pers. name + *lēah*.

Burwarton Shrops. *Burertone* |*sic*| 1086 (DB), *Burwardton* 1194. 'Farmstead of the fort-keeper, or of a man called Burgweard'. OE *burh-weard* or pers. name + *tūn*.

Burwash E. Sussex. *Burhercse* 12th cent. 'Ploughed field by the fort'. OE *burh* + *ersc*.

Burwell, 'spring or stream by the fort', OE *burh* + *wella*: **Burwell** Cambs. *Burcwell* 1060, *Buruuella* 1086 (DB). **Burwell** Lincs. *Buruelle* 1086 (DB).

Burwick Orkn (South Ronaldsay). *Bardvik* c.1225. 'Bay of the extremity'. OScand. *bar* + *vík*. Burwick is at the southernmost point of the island.

Bury, '(place by) the fort or stronghold', OE *burh* (dative *byrig*): **Bury** Cambs. *Byrig* 974. **Bury** Gtr. Manch. *Biri* 1194. **Bury** W. Sussex. *Berie* 1086 (DB).

Bury St Edmunds Suffolk. *Sancte Eadmundes Byrig* 1038. 'Town associated with St Ēadmund'. OE saint's name (a 9th cent. king of East Anglia) + OE *burh* (dative *byrig*).

Burythorpe N. Yorks. *Bergetorp* 1086 (DB). Probably 'outlying farmstead or hamlet of a woman called Bjǫrg'. OScand. pers. name + *thorp*.

Busby, Great N. Yorks. *Buschebi* 1086 (DB). 'Farmstead or village of a man called *Buski, or among the bushes or shrubs'. OScand. pers. name or *buskr, *buski + *bý*.

Buscot Oxon. *Boroardescote* 1086 (DB). 'Cottage(s) of the fort-keeper, or of a man called Burgweard'. OE *burh-weard* or pers. name + *cot*.

Bushbury W. Mids. *Byscopesbyri* 996, *Biscopesberie* 1086 (DB). 'The bishop's fortified manor'. OE *biscop* + *burh* (dative *byrig*).

Bushey Herts. *Bissei* 1086 (DB). 'Enclosure near a thicket, or hedged with box-trees'. OE *bysce or *byxe + *hæg*.

Bushley Heref. & Worcs. *Biselege* 1086 (DB). 'Woodland clearing with bushes, or of a man called *Byssa'. OE *bysce or pers. name + *lēah*.

Bushmills Antrim. *Bushmills* 1636. 'Mills on the (river) Bush'. The equivalent Irish name is *Muileann na Buaise*.

Bushton Wilts. *Bissopeston* 1242. 'The bishop's farmstead'. OE *biscop* + *tūn*.

Buston, High & *Buston, Low* Northum. *Buttesdune* 1166, *Butlesdon* 1249. Possibly 'hill of a man called *Buttel', OE pers. name + *dūn*. Alternatively the first element may be OE *butt 'stumpy hill'.

Butcombe N. Som. *Budancumb c*.1000, *Budicome* 1086 (DB). 'Valley of a man called Buda'. OE pers. name + *cumb*.

Bute (island) Arg. *Bot* 1093, *Boot* 1292. '(Island of) fire'. Gaelic *bód*. The name may refer to signal fires.

Butleigh Somerset. *Budecalech* 725, *Boduchelei* 1086 (DB). 'Woodland clearing of a man called *Budeca'. OE pers. name + *lēah*.

Butlers Bridge Cavan. *Butlers Br*. 1728. 'Butler's bridge'. The bridge over the Annalea River is named from the *Butler* family, whose ancestor Sir Stephen Butler was granted land here in 1610. The equivalent Irish name is *Droichead an Bhuitléaraigh*.

Butley Suffolk. *Butelea* 1086 (DB). 'Woodland clearing of a man called *Butta'. OE pers. name + *lēah*. Alternatively the first element may be an OE *butte 'mound, hill'.

Butterleigh Devon. *Buterlei* 1086 (DB). 'Clearing with good pasture'. OE *butere* + *lēah*.

Buttermere, 'lake or pool with good pasture', OE *butere* + *mere*: **Buttermere** Cumbria. *Butermere* 1230. **Buttermere** Wilts. *Butermere* 863. *Butremere* 1086 (DB).

Butterton Staffs., near Leek. *Buterdon* 1200. 'Hill with good pasture'. OE *butere* + *dūn*.

Butterwick, 'dairy farm where butter is made', OE *butere* + *wīc*: **Butterwick** Durham. *Boterwyk* 1131.

Butterwick Lincs. *Butrvic* 1086 (DB). **Butterwick** N. Yorks., near Foxholes. *Butruid |sic|* 1086 (DB), *Butterwic c*.1130. **Butterwick** N. Yorks., near Hovingham. *Butruic* 1086 (DB). **Butterwick, East** & **Butterwick, West** N. Lincs. *Butreuuic* 1086 (DB).

Buttevant (*Cill na Mallach*) Cork. 'Defensive outwork'. OFrench *botavant*. The Irish name means 'church of the summits'.

Buxhall Suffolk. *Bucysheale c*.995, *Buckeshala* 1086 (DB). 'Nook of land of a man called *Bucc'. OE pers. name + *halh*.

Buxted E. Sussex. *Boxted* 1199. 'Place where beech-trees or box-trees grow'. OE *bōc* or *box* + *stede*.

Buxton Derbys. *Buchestanes c*.1100. Probably 'the rocking stones or loganstones'. OE *būg-stān*.

Buxton Norfolk. *Bukestuna* 1086 (DB). 'Farmstead of a man called *Bucc'. OE pers. name + *tūn*.

Buxworth Derbys. *Buggisworth* 1275. 'Enclosure of a man called *Bucg'. OE pers. name + *worth*.

Bwcle. See BUCKLEY.

Bweeng (*Na Boinn*) Cork. 'The swelling'.

Byers Green Durham. *Bires* 1345. 'The byres or cowsheds'. OE *býre*.

Byfield Northants. *Bifelde* 1086 (DB). '(Place) by the open country'. OE *bī* + *feld*.

Byfleet Surrey. *Biflete* 933, *Biflet* 1086 (DB). Probably '(place) by the stream', OE *bī* + *flēot*. Alternatively from an OE compound *bī-flēot 'small area of land cut off by the changing course of a stream'.

Byford Heref. & Worcs. *Buiford* 1086 (DB). 'Ford near the river-bend'. OE *byge* + *ford*.

Bygrave Herts. *Bigravan* 973, *Bigrave* 1086 (DB). '(Place) by the grove or by the trench'. OE *bī* + *grāfa* or *grafa*.

Byker Tyne & Wear. *Bikere* 1196. Identical in origin with BICKER.

Byley Ches. *Bevelei* 1086 (DB). 'Woodland clearing of a man called Bēofa'. OE pers. name + *tūn*.

Bytham, Castle & *Bytham, Little* Lincs. *Bytham c*.1067 *Bitham* 1086 (DB). 'Valley bottom'. OE *bythme*.

Bythorn Cambs. *Bitherna c*.960, *Bierne |sic|* 1086 (DB). '(Place) by the thorn-bush'. OE *bī* + *thyrne*.

Byton Heref. & Worcs. *Boitune* 1086 (DB). 'Farmstead by the river-bend'. OE *byge* + *tūn*.

Bywell Northum. *Biguell* 1104–8, *Biewell* 1195. 'Spring by the river-bend'. OE *byge* + *wella*.

Byworth W. Sussex. *Begworth* 1279. 'Enclosure of a woman called Bēage or a man called Bǣga'. OE pers. name + *worth*.

C

Cabinteely (*Cábán tSíle*) Dublin. 'Síle's cabin'.

Cabourne Lincs. *Caburne* 1086 (DB). 'Stream frequented by jackdaws'. OE *cā* + *burna*.

Cabra (*An Chabrach*) Down. *Ballinecabre* 1605. 'The bad land'.

Cabragh (*An Chabrach*) Dublin, Tyrone. 'The bad land'.

Cadamstown (*Baile Mhic Ádaim*) Kildare, Offaly. 'Mac Ádaim's homestead'.

Cadboll Highland. *Kattepol* 1281. 'Farm frequented by wildcats'. OScand. *köttr* + *ból*(*stathr*).

Cadbury, 'fortified place or stronghold of a man called Cada', OE pers. name + *burh* (dative *byrig*): **Cadbury** Devon. *Cadebirie* 1086 (DB). **Cadbury, North** & **Cadbury, South** Somerset. *Cadanbyrig* c.1000, *Cadeberie* 1086 (DB).

Caddington Beds. *Caddandun* c.1000, *Cadendone* 1086 (DB). 'Hill of a man called Cada'. OE pers. name (genitive -*n*) + *dūn*.

Caddy (*Cadaigh*) Antrim. *Cady* c.1657. Possibly 'land held by treaty'.

Cadeby, 'farmstead or village of a man called Káti', OScand. pers. name + *bý*: **Cadeby** Leics. *Catebi* 1086 (DB). **Cadeby** S. Yorks. *Catebi* 1086 (DB).

Cadeleigh Devon. *Cadelie* 1086 (DB). 'Woodland clearing of a man called Cada'. OE pers. name + *lēah*.

Cader Idris (mountain) Gwyd. 'Seat of Idris'. Celtic pers. name + OWelsh *cadeir*. Idris is a legendary giant and magician.

Cadian (*Céidín*) Tyrone. 'Little hill'.

Cadishead Gtr. Manch. *Cadewalesate* 1212. 'Dwelling or fold by the stream of a man called Cada'. OE pers. name + *wælla* + *set*.

Cadmore End Bucks. *Cademere* 1236. 'Estate boundary or pool of a man called Cada'. OE pers. name + *mǣre* or *mere*.

Cadnam Hants. *Cadenham* 1272. 'Homestead or enclosure of a man called Cada'. OE pers. name (genitive -*n*) + *hām* or *hamm*.

Cadney N. Lincs. *Catenai* 1086 (DB). 'Island, or dry ground in marsh, of a man called Cada'. OE pers. name (genitive -*n*) + *ēg*.

Cadoxton (*Tregatwg*) Vale Glam. *Caddokeston* 1254, *Cadoxston* 1535. 'Cadog's farmstead'. OE *tun* (Welsh *tref*). From the dedication of the church to St Cadog. The Welsh name is the equivalent.

Caenby Lincs. *Couenebi* 1086 (DB). Probably 'farmstead or village of a man called *Cāfna* or *Kafni*'. OE or OScand. pers. name + OScand. *bý*.

Caerdydd. *See* CARDIFF.

Caerffili. *See* CAERPHILLY.

Caerfyrddin. *See* CARMARTHEN.

Caergwrle Flin. *Caergorlei* 1327. 'Fort by the clearing where cranes are seen'. Welsh *caer* + OE *corn* + *lēah*. The 'fort' was a Roman station.

Caergybi. *See* HOLYHEAD.

Caerleon (*Caerllion-ar-Wysg*) Newpt. *castra Legionis* c.150, *Caerleion* 1086 (DB). 'Fort of the legion'. Welsh *caer* + Latin *legio* (genitive *legionis*). The reference is to the Second Legion, stationed here after moving from *Glevum* (Gloucester). The Roman fort was *Isca Legionis*, 'Isca of the legion', *Isca* being the River USK. The Welsh name means 'Caerleon on the Usk'.

Caerllion-ar-Wysg. *See* CAERLEON.

Caernarfon Gwyd. *Kairarvon* 1191, *Kaer yn Arvon* 1258. 'Fort in Arfon'. Welsh *caer* + *yn*. The district name *Arfon* is Welsh *ar Fôn*, 'opposite Môn', i.e. ANGLESEY.

Caerphilly (*Caerffili*) Cphy. *Kaerfili* 1271, *Kaerphilly* 1314. 'Ffili's fort'. Welsh *caer* + Celtic pers. name.

Caersŵs Powys. *Caerswys* 14th cent. 'Swys's fort'. Welsh *caer* + Celtic pers. name.

Caer-went Mon. *Cair Guent* c.800. 'Fort of *Gwent*'. Welsh *caer. See* GWENT. The Roman station here was *Venta Silurum*, 'Venta of the Silures'.

Caher (*An Chathair*) Clare, Tipperary. 'The stone fort'.

Caheragh (*Cathrach*) Cork. 'Abounding in stone forts'.

Caherbarnagh (*An Chathair Bhearnach*) Cork. 'The gapped stone fort'.

Caherconlish (*Cathair Chinn Lis*) Limerick. 'Stone fort of the head of the ford'.

Caherconree (*Cathair Conraoi*) Kerry. 'Stone fort of Cúrí'.

Caherdaniel (*Cathair Dónall*) Kerry. 'Dónall's stone fort'.

Caherelly (*Cathair Ailí*) Limerick. 'Stone fort of the boulder'.

Cahergal (*Cathair Geal*) Kerry. 'White stone fort'.

Caherloughlin (*Cathair Lochlainn*) Clare. 'Stone fort of Lochlann'.

Cahermore (*Cathair Mhór*) Cork, Galway. 'Big stone fort'.

Cahernageeha Mountain (*Cathair na Gaoithe*) Kerry. 'Stone fort of the wind'.

Cahersiveen (*Cathair Saidhbhín*) Kerry. 'Stone fort of Saidhbhín'.

Caime (*Céim*) Wexford. 'Gap'.

Cainscross Glos., not on record until 1776, probably from *cross* 'cross-roads' with the surname *Cain*.

Cairngorm (mountains) Moray. 'Blue rocky hill'. Gaelic *carn* + *gorm*. The name is properly that of *Cairn Gorm*, the highest peak in the group.

Caister, *Caistor*, 'Roman camp or town', OE *cæster*: **Caister-on-Sea** Norfolk. *Castra* 1044–7, 1086 (DB). **Caistor** Lincs. *Castre* 1086 (DB). **Caistor St Edmund** Norfolk. *Castre* c.1025, *Castrum* 1086 (DB), *Castre Sancti Eadmundi* 1254. Affix from its early possession by the Abbey of Bury St Edmunds.

Caistron Northum. *Cers* c.1160, *Kerstirn* 1202. 'Thornbush by the fen'. ME kers + OScand. *thyrnir*.

Caithness (district) Highland. *Kathenessia* c.970. 'Promontory of the Cats'. OScand. *nes*. It is not known why the early Celtic tribe here were called 'cats', the cat may have been their token animal.

Calbourne I. of Wight. *Cawelburne* 826, *Cavborne* 1086 (DB). 'Stream called *Cawel*', or 'stream where cole or cabbage grows'. Celtic river-name (of uncertain meaning) or OE *cawel* + *burna*.

Calceby Lincs. *Calesbi* 1086 (DB). 'Farmstead or village of a man called Kalfr'. OScand. pers. name + *bý*.

Calcethorpe Lincs. *Cheilestorp* c.1115. 'Outlying farmstead or hamlet of a man called *Cægel*'. OE pers. name + OScand. *thorp*.

Calcot Row Berks., not on record before the 18th century, but probably identical in origin with CALDECOTE.

Calcutt Wilts. *Colecote* 1086 (DB). Probably 'cottage of a man called Cola'. OE pers. name + *cot*.

Caldbeck Cumbria. *Caldebek* 11th cent. 'Cold stream'. OScand. *kaldr* + *bekkr*.

Caldbergh N. Yorks. *Caldeber* 1086 (DB). 'Cold hill'. OScand. *kaldr* + *berg*.

Caldecote, *Caldecott*, a place-name found in various counties, meaning 'cold or inhospitable cottage(s), or shelter(s) for travellers', from OE *cald* + *cot*; examples include: **Caldecote** Cambs. *Caldecote* 1086 (DB). **Caldecote** Herts. *Caldecota* 1086 (DB). **Caldecote** Northants. *Caldecot* 1202. **Caldecote Hill** Warwicks. *Caldecote* 1086 (DB). **Caldecott** Northants. *Caldecote* 1086 (DB). **Caldecott** Rutland. *Caldecote* 1086 (DB).

Calder Bridge & *Calder Hall* Cumbria. *Calder* 1178. Named from the River Calder, an old Celtic river-name meaning 'rapid stream'.

Calder Vale Lancs., named from a stream, identical in origin with the previous name.

Calder Water S. Lan. *Caldouer* 1265. 'Hard water'. British **caleto-* + **dubro-*.

Caldicot Mon. *Caldecote* 1086 (DB), *Caldicote* 1268. 'Cold shelter'. OE *cald* + *cot*.

Caldragh (*Cealtragh*) Fermanagh. 'Graveyard'.

Caldwell N. Yorks. *Caldeuuella* 1086 (DB). 'Cold spring or stream'. OE *cald* + *wella*.

Caldy Mersey. *Calders* 1086 (DB), *Caldei* 1182. 'Cold island', earlier 'cold rounded hill'. OE *cald* + *ēg* (replacing *ears*).

Caldy Island (*Ynys Byr*) Pemb. *Caldea* c.1120. 'Cold island'. OScand. *kald* + *ey*. The Welsh name means 'Pyr's island' (Welsh *ynys* + Celtic pers. name).

Cale (river) Dorset, Somerset, *see* WINCANTON.

Caledon Tyrone. *Chind Aird* 1500. The original name of the village was *Kinaird* (*Cionn Aird*), 'head of the hill'. The present name is from James Alexander, who bought land here in 1778 and was created Earl of Caledon in 1800.

Caledonian Canal Highland. 'Canal in *Caledonia*'. The canal and name date from 1803.

Calf of Flotta (island) Orkn. 'Small island next to Flotta'. OScand. *kalfr*. The allusion is to a calf's dependence on its mother cow. *See* FLOTTA.

Calke Derbys. *Calc* 1132. '(Place on) the limestone'. OE *calc*.

Callaly Northum. *Calualea* 1161. 'Clearing where calves graze'. OE *calf* (genitive plural *calfra*) + *lēah*.

Callander Stir. *Kalentare* 1504. '(Place by) hard-flowing water'. British **caleto-* + **dubro-*. The river name may have been that of the present River Teith.

Callater Burn Aber. *Callendar* 1652. 'Hard water'. British **caleto-* + **dubro-*.

Callender Highland. *Kalenter* c.1150. '(Place by) hard-flowing water'. British **caleto-* + **dubro-*.

Callerton, 'hill where calves graze', OE *calf* (genitive plural *calfra*) + *dūn*: **Callerton, Black** Northum. *Calverdona* 1212. Affix is OE *blæc* 'dark-coloured'. **Callerton, High** Northum. *Calverdon* 1242.

Callington Cornwall. *Calwetone* 1086 (DB). Probably 'farmstead by the bare hill'. OE *calu* (in a dative form) + *tūn*.

Callow Heref. & Worcs. *Calua* 1180. 'The bare hill'. OE *calu* in a dative form.

Callow (*An Caladh*) Mayo, Roscommon. 'The riverside land'.

Calmsden Glos. *Kalemundesdene* 852. 'Valley of a man called *Calumund*'. OE pers. name + *denu*.

Calne Wilts. *Calne* 955, 1086 (DB). A pre-English river-name of uncertain meaning.

Calow Derbys. *Calehale* 1086 (DB). 'Bare nook of land', or 'nook of land at a bare hill'. OE *calu* + *halh*.

Calshot Hants. *Celcesoran* 980, *Celceshord* 1011. OE *ord* 'point or spit of land' (replacing *ōra* 'shore' in the earliest spelling) with an uncertain first element, possibly OE *cælic* 'cup, chalice' used in some topographical sense.

Calstock Cornwall. *Kalestoc* 1086 (DB). The second element is OE *stoc* 'outlying farm, secondary settlement', the first is uncertain.

Calstone Wellington Wilts. *Calestone* 1086 (DB), *Caulston Wellington* 1568. Probably 'farmstead or village by CALNE', from OE *tūn*. The manorial addition is from a family called de Wilinton, here from the 13th century.

Calthorpe Norfolk. *Calethorp* 1044–7, *Caletorp* 1086 (DB). 'Outlying farmstead or hamlet of a man called Kali'. OScand. pers. name + *thorp*.

Calthwaite Cumbria. *Caluethweyt* 1272. 'Clearing where calves are kept'. OE *calf* or OScand. *kalfr* + *thveit*.

Calton, 'farm where calves are reared', OE *calf* + *tūn*: **Calton** N. Yorks. *Caltun* 1086 (DB). **Calton** Staffs. *Calton* 1238.

Caltra (*An Chealtrach*) Galway. 'The graveyard'.

Caltraghlea (*Cealtrach Lia*) Galway. 'Grey graveyard'.

Calveley Ches. *Calueleg* c.1235. 'Clearing where calves are pastured'. OE *calf* + *lēah*.

Calver Derbys. *Calvoure* 1086 (DB). 'Slope or ridge where calves graze'. OE *calf* + **ofer*.

Calverhall Shrops. *Cavrahalle* 1086 (DB), *Caluerhale* 1256. 'Nook of land where calves graze'. OE *calf* (genitive plural *calfra*) + *halh*.

Calverleigh Devon. *Calodelie* |*sic*| 1086 (DB), *Calewudelega* 1194. 'Clearing in the bare wood'. OE *calu* + *wudu* + *lēah*.

Calverley W. Yorks. *Caverleia* 1086 (DB). 'Clearing where calves are pastured'. OE *calf* (genitive plural *calfra*) + *lēah*.

Calverton, 'farm where calves are reared', OE *calf* (genitive plural *calfra*) + *tūn*: **Calverton** Bucks. *Calvretone* 1086 (DB). **Calverton** Notts. *Caluretone* 1086 (DB).

Cam Glos. *Camma* 1086 (DB). Named from the River Cam, an old Celtic river-name meaning 'crooked'.

Cam Beck (river) Cumbria, see KIRKCAMBECK.

Camaross (*Camros*) Wexford. 'Crooked grove'.

Camber E. Sussex. *Camere* 1375, *Portus Camera* 1397, *Caumbre* 1442. From OFrench *cambre*, Latin *camera* 'a room, an enclosed space', perhaps originally with reference to a small harbour here before the silting up of the Rother estuary.

Camberley Surrey, an arbitrary name of recent origin, altered from *Cambridge Town* which was named in 1862 from the Duke of Cambridge.

Camberwell Gtr. London. *Cambrewelle* 1086 (DB). OE *wella* 'spring or stream' with an obscure first element.

Camblesforth N. Yorks. *Camelesforde* 1086 (DB). Possibly 'ford associated with a man called **Camel(e)*'. OE pers. name + *ford*.

Cambo Northum. *Camho* 1230. 'Hill-spur with a crest or ridge'. OE *camb* + *hōh*.

Cambois Northum. *Cammes* c.1050. A Celtic name, a derivative of Celtic **camm* 'crooked' and originally referring to the bay here.

Camborne Cornwall. *Camberon* 1182. 'Crooked hill'. Cornish *camm* + *bronn*.

Cambrian Mountains Wales. 'Mountains of Cambria'. *Cambria*, the Roman name for Wales, came from the people's name for themselves, Modern Welsh *Cymry*.

Cambridge Cambs. *Grontabricc* c.745, *Cantebrigie* 1086 (DB). 'Bridge on the River Granta'. Celtic river-name (see GRANTCHESTER) + OE *brycg*. The change from *Grant-* to *Cam-* is due to Norman influence. **Cambridge-shire** (OE *scīr* 'district') is first referred to in the 11th cent. The later river-name **Cam** is a 'back-formation' from the place-name.

Cambridge Glos. *Cambrigga* 1200–10. 'Bridge over the River Cam'. Celtic river-name (see CAM) + OE *brycg*.

Cambus O'May Aber. *Cames i maye* 1600. '(River) bend of the plain'. Gaelic *camus* + *magh*.

Cambuskenneth Stir. *Cambuskynneth* 1147. 'Cinaed's (river) bend'. Gaelic *camus* + Celtic pers. name.

Cambuslang S. Lan. *Camboslanc* 1296. '(River) bend of the ship'. Gaelic *camus* + *long*. The river is the Clyde.

Camden Town Gtr. London, so named in 1795 from Earl Camden (died 1794) who came into possession of the manor of KENTISH TOWN of which this formed part.

Camel, Queen & *Camel, West* Somerset. *Cantmæl* 995, *Camelle* 1086 (DB). Possibly a Celtic name from **canto-* 'border or district' and **mēl* 'bare hill'. Affix *Queen* from its possession by Queen Eleanor in the 13th cent.

Camelford Cornwall. *Camelford* 13th cent. 'Ford over the River Camel'. Celtic river-name (possibly 'crooked one' from a derivative of Celtic **camm*) + OE *ford*.

Camerton B. & NE. Som. *Camelartone* 954, *Camelertone* 1086 (DB). 'Farmstead or estate on Cam Brook'. Celtic river-name (earlier *Cameler*, probably a derivative of **camm* 'crooked') + OE *tūn*.

Camerton Cumbria. *Camerton* c.1150. OE *tūn* 'farmstead, estate' with an obscure first element.

Camlough (*Camloch*) Armagh. *Loch Chamloch* c.1840, 'Crooked lake'.

Cammeringham Lincs. *Camelingeham* |*sic*| 1086 (DB), *Cameryngham* c.1115. Possibly 'homestead of the family or followers of a man called **Cāfmær* or **Cantmær*'. OE pers. name + *-inga-* + *hām*.

Camowen (*Camabhainn*) Tyrone. 'Crooked river'.

Camp (*An Com*) Kerry. 'The hollow'.

Campbeltown Arg. 'Campbell's town'. Archibald Campbell, Earl of Argyle, was granted the site here in 1667 for the erection of a burgh of barony.

Campden, Broad & *Campden, Chipping* Glos. *Campedene* 1086 (DB), *Bradecampedene* 1224, *Chepyng Campedene* 1287. 'Valley with enclosures'. OE *camp* + *denu*. Affixes are OE *brād* 'broad' and OE *cēping* 'market'.

Campile (*Ceann Poill*) Wexford. 'Head of the creek'.

Camport (*Camport*) Mayo. 'Crooked shore'.

Camps, Castle & *Camps, Shudy* Cambs. *Canpas* 1086 (DB), *Campecastel* 13th cent., *Sudekampes* 1219. 'The fields or enclosures', from OE *camp*, plural *campas*. The affix *Castle* is from a medieval castle, *Shudy* is probably an OE **scydd* 'shed, hovel'.

Campsall S. Yorks. *Cansale* |*sic*| 1086 (DB), *Camshale* 12th cent. Possibly 'nook of land of a man called Cam'. OE pers. name + *halh*. Alternatively the first element may be a derivative of Celtic **camm* 'crooked' used in some topographical sense.

Campsey (*Camsan*) Derry. *Camsan* 1613. 'River bends'.

Campsey Ash Suffolk. *Campeseia* 1086 (DB). 'Island, or dry ground in marsh, with a field or enclosure'. OE *camp* + *ēg*. *Ash* was originally a separate place, mentioned as *Esce* in 1086 (DB), from OE *æsc* 'ash-tree'.

Campsie Fells Stir. 'Hills of *Campsie*'. Northern English *fell* from OScand. *fjall*. The range is named from the single hill *Campsie*, traditionally thought to mean 'crooked fairy mountain' (Gaelic *cam* + *sith*) but etymologically unsound.

Campton Beds. *Chambeltone* 1086 (DB). Probably 'farmstead by a river called *Camel*'. Lost Celtic river-name (possibly 'crooked one' from a derivative of Celtic **camm*) + OE *tūn*.

Camross (*Camros*) Laois. 'Crooked copse'.

Candlesby Lincs. *Calnodesbi* 1086 (DB). Probably 'farmstead or village of a man called **Cal(u)nōth*'. OE pers. name + OScand. *bý*.

Candover, Brown & *Candover, Preston* Hants. *Cendefer* c.880, *Candovre* 1086 (DB), *Brunkardoure* 1296, *Prestecandevere* c.1270. Named from the stream here, a Celtic river-name meaning 'pleasant waters'. Distinguishing affixes are manorial, from early possession by a family called Brun and by priests (ME genitive plural *prestene*).

Canewdon Essex. *Carenduna* |*sic*| 1086 (DB), *Canuedon* 1181. Probably 'hill of the family or followers of a man called Cana'. OE pers. name + *-inga-* + *dūn*.

Canfield, Great Essex. *Canefelda* 1086 (DB). 'Open land of a man called Cana'. OE pers. name + *feld*.

Canford Magna, *Little Canford* Dorset. *Cheneford* |*sic*| 1086 (DB), *Kaneford* 1195, *Lytel Canefford* 1381, *Greate Canford* 1612. 'Ford of a man called Cana'. OE pers. name + *ford*.

Canisbay Highland. *Cananesbi* c.1240. 'Conan's farm'. Gaelic pers. name + OScand. *bý*.

Cann Dorset. *Canna* 12th cent. OE *canne* 'a can, a cup', used topographically for 'a hollow, a deep valley'.

Canna (island) Highland. *Kannay* 1549. Possibly 'porpoise island'. Gaelic *cana* + OScand. *ey*. But doubtful.

Cannings, All & *Cannings, Bishops* Wilts. *Caninge* 1086 (DB), *Aldekanning* 1205, *Bisshopescanyngges* 1314. '(Settlement of) the family or followers of a man called Cana'. OE pers. name + *-ingas*. Affixes are OE *eald* 'old' and *biscop* 'bishop' (referring to early possession by the Bishop of Salisbury).

Cannington Somerset. *Cantuctun* c.880, *Cantoctona* 1086 (DB). 'Estate or village by the QUANTOCK HILLS'. Celtic hill-name + OE *tūn*.

Cannock Staffs. *Chenet* |*sic*| 1086 (DB), *Canoc* 12th cent. 'The small hill, the hillock'. OE *cnocc*. It gives name to **Cannock Chase**, from ME *chace* 'tract of land for breeding and hunting wild animals'.

Canon Frome Heref. & Worcs., *see* FROME.

Canonbury Gtr. London. *Canonesbury* 1373. 'Manor of the canons', from ME *canoun* and *bury*, referring to the canons of St Bartholomew's Smithfield who were granted land in ISLINGTON in the early 12th cent.

Canons Ashby Northants., *see* ASHBY.

Canterbury Kent. *Cantwaraburg* c.900, *Canterburie* 1086 (DB). 'Stronghold or fortified town of the people of KENT'. Ancient Celtic name + OE *-ware* + *burh*.

Cantley, probably 'woodland clearing of a man called **Canta*', OE pers. name + *lēah*: **Cantley** Norfolk. *Cantelai* 1086 (DB). **Cantley** S. Yorks. *Canteleia* 1086 (DB).

Cantlop Shrops. *Cantelop* 1086 (DB). OE *hop* 'enclosed place' with an obscure first element.

Cantsfield Lancs. *Cantesfelt* 1086 (DB). Probably 'open land by the River Cant'. Celtic river-name (of uncertain meaning) + OE *feld*.

Canvey Essex. *Caneveye* 1255. Possibly 'island of the family or followers of a man called Cana'. OE pers. name + *-inga-* + *ēg*.

Canwick Lincs. *Canewic* 1086 (DB). 'Dwelling or dairy-farm of a man called Cana'. OE pers. name + *wīc*.

Cape Wrath (headland) Highland. *Wraith* 1583. 'Turning-point'. OScand. *hvarf*. The cape marks the point where ships altered course to follow the coast.

Capel, a place-name found in several counties, from ME *capel* 'a chapel': **Capel** Surrey. *Capella* 1190. **Capel le Ferne** Kent. *Capel ate Verne* 1377. The addition means 'at the ferny place' from OE **(ge)ferne*. **Capel St Andrew** Suffolk. *Capeles* 1086 (DB). Addition from the dedication of the chapel. **Capel St Mary** Suffolk. *Capeles* 1254. Addition from the dedication of the chapel.

Capel Curig Conwy. *Capel Kiryg* 1536, *Capel Kerig* 1578. 'Curig's chapel'. Welsh *capel* + Celtic pers. name. From the dedication of the church to St Curig.

Capenhurst Ches. *Capeles* |*sic*| 1086 (DB), *Capenhurst* 13th cent. Probably 'wooded hill at a look-out place'. OE **cape* (genitive *-an*) + *hyrst*.

Capernwray Lancs. *Coupmanwra* c.1200. 'The merchant's nook or corner of land'. OScand. *kaupmathr* + *vrá*.

Capheaton Northum. *Magna Heton* 1242, *Cappitheton* 1454. 'High farmstead, farmstead situated on high land'. OE *hēah* + *tūn*. The affix *Cap-* is from Latin *caput* 'head, chief'.

Cappagh (*An Cheapaigh*) Waterford. 'The plot of land'.

Cappamore (*An Cheapach Mhór*) Limerick. 'The big plot of land'.

Cappanacush (*Ceapach na Coise*) Kerry. 'Plot of land at the foot'.

Capparoe (*An Cheapach Rua*) Tipperary. 'The red plot of land'.

Cappataggle (*Ceapaigh an tSeagail*) Galway. 'Plot of rye'.

Cappeen (*Caipín*) Cork. 'Cap'.

Cappoquin (*Ceapach Choinn*) Waterford. 'Conn's plot of land'.

Capton Devon. *Capieton* 1278. Probably 'estate of a family called Capia'. ME surname + OE *tūn*.

Car Colston Notts., *see* COLSTON.

Carbis Bay Cornwall, a 19th cent. village named from a farm called Carbis, recorded as *Carbons* 1391, from OCornish **car-bons* 'causeway' (literally 'cart-bridge').

Carbrook S. Yorks. *Kerebroc* 1200–18. Probably 'stream in the marsh'. OScand. *kjarr* + OE *brōc*. Alternatively the first element may be an old Celtic river-name.

Carbrooke Norfolk. *Cherebroc* 1086 (DB). Identical in origin with the previous name.

Carburton Notts. *Carbertone* 1086 (DB). OE *tūn* 'farmstead, village' with an obscure first element.

Carcroft S. Yorks. *Kercroft* 12th cent. 'Enclosure near the marsh'. OScand. *kjarr* + OE *croft*.

Cardenden Fife. *Cardenane* 14th cent., *Cardwane* 1516. 'Hollow by *Carden*'. OE *denu*. *Carden* is a name of Celtic origin meaning 'thicket' (Welsh *cardden*).

Cardeston Shrops. *Cartistune* 1086 (DB). Probably 'farm or estate of a man called *Card*'. OE pers. name + *tūn*.

Cardiff (*Caerdydd*) Card. *Kairdif* 1106, *o gaer dydd* 1566, *Caer Didd* 1698. 'Fort on the River Taf'. Welsh *caer*. For the river name (here in the genitive case), *see* LLANDAFF.

Cardigan (*Aberteifi*) Cergn. *Kerdigan* 1194. 'Ceredig's land'. *See also* CEREDIGION. The Welsh name means 'mouth of the River Teifi' (OWelsh *aber*), the river name being of uncertain origin.

Cardington Beds. *Chernetone* |sic| 1086 (DB), *Kerdinton* c.1190. Probably 'estate associated with a man called *Cærda*'. OE pers. name + *-ing-* + *tūn*.

Cardington Shrops. *Cardintune* 1086 (DB). Probably 'estate associated with a man called *Card(a)*'. OE pers. name + *-ing-* + *tūn*.

Cardinham Cornwall. *Cardinan* c.1180. Both parts of the name mean 'fort', Cornish *ker* + *dinan*.

Cardurnock Cumbria. *Cardrunnock* 13th cent. A Celtic place-name, from *cair* 'fortified town' + *durnōg* 'pebbly'.

Careby Lincs. *Careby* 1199. 'Farmstead or village of a man called Kári'. OScand. pers. name + *bý*.

Cargan (*An Carraigín*) Antrim. *Carrigan* c.1655. 'The little rock'.

Cargo Cumbria. *Cargaou* c.1178. Celtic *carreg* 'rock' + OScand. *haugr* 'hill'.

Carham Northum. *Carrum* c.1050. '(Place) by the rocks'. OE *carr* in a dative plural form *carrum*.

Carhampton Somerset. *Carrum* 9th cent., *Carentone* 1086 (DB). 'Farm at the place by the rocks'. OE *carr* (dative plural *carrum*) + *tūn*.

Carisbrooke I. of Wight. *Caresbroc* 12th cent. Possibly 'the brook called *Cary*'. Lost Celtic river-name + OE *brōc*.

Cark Cumbria. *Karke* 1491. Celtic *carreg* 'a stone, a rock'.

Cark (*Cearc*) Donegal. 'Hen'.

Carlby Lincs. *Carlebi* 1086 (DB). Probably 'homestead or village of the peasants or freemen'. OScand. *karl* + *bý*.

Carlecotes Derbys. *Carlecotes* 13th cent. 'Cottages of the freemen'. OScand. *karl* + OE *cot*.

Carlesmoor N. Yorks. *Carlesmore* 1086 (DB). 'Moorland of the freeman or of a man called Karl'. OScand. *karl* or pers. name + *mór*.

Carleton, Carlton, a common place-name in the old Danelaw areas of the Midlands and the North, usually 'farmstead or estate of the freemen or peasants', from OScand. *karl* (often no doubt replacing OE *ceorl*) + OE *tūn*; examples include: **Carleton** Cumbria. *Karleton* 1250. **Carleton** N. Yorks. *Carlentone* 1086 (DB). **Carleton Forehoe** Norfolk. *Carletuna* 1086 (DB), *Karleton Fourhowe* 1268. Affix from the nearby Forehoe Hills, from OE *fēower* 'four' and OScand. *haugr* 'hill'. **Carleton Rode** Norfolk. *Carletuna* 1086 (DB), *Carleton Rode* 1201. Manorial addition from the de Rode family, here in the 14th cent. **Carlton** Beds. *Carlentone* 1086 (DB). **Carlton** N. Yorks., near Snaith. *Carletun* 1086 (DB). **Carlton** Notts. *Karleton* 1182. **Carlton Colville** Suffolk. *Carletuna* 1086 (DB), *Carleton Colvile* 1346. Manorial addition from the de Colevill family, here in the 13th cent. **Carlton Curlieu** Leics. *Carletone* 1086 (DB), *Carleton Curly* 1273. Manorial addition from the de Curly family, here in the 13th cent. **Carlton Husthwaite** N. Yorks. *Carleton* 1086 (DB), *Carlton Husthwat* 1516. Affix from its proximity to HUSTHWAITE. **Carlton in Lindrick** Notts. *Carletone* 1086 (DB), *Carleton in Lindric* 1212. Affix from the district called Lindrick, which means 'strip of land where lime-trees grow', from OE *lind* + **ric*. **Carlton le Moorland** Lincs. *Carletune* 1086 (DB). Affix from its situation 'in the moorland'. **Carlton Miniott** N. Yorks. *Carletun* 1086 (DB), *Carleton Mynyott* 1579. Manorial addition from the Miniott family, here in the 14th cent. **Carlton on Trent** Notts. *Carletune* 1086 (DB). For the river-name, *see* TRENTHAM. **Carlton Scroop** Lincs. *Carletune* 1086 (DB). Manorial addition from the Scrope family, here in the 14th cent.

Carlingcott B. & NE. Som. *Credelincote* 1086 (DB). 'Cottage associated with a man called *Cridela*'. OE pers. name + *-ing-* + *cot*.

Carlingford (*Cairlinn*) Louth. 'Bay of the hag'. *an Carrlongphort* 1213. OScand. *kerling* + *fjorthr*. The 'hag' is probably the three mountain tops here known as *The Three Nuns*.

Carlisle Cumbria. *Luguvalio* 4th cent., *Carleol* c.1106. An old Celtic name meaning '(place) belonging to a man called **Luguvalos*', to which Celtic *cair* 'fortified town' was added after the Roman period.

Carlow (*Ceatharlach*) Carlow. 'Quadruple lake'.

Carlton, *see* CARLETON.

Carluke S. Lan. *Carlug* 1304, *Cerneluke* c.1320. British *cair* 'stockaded name' + obscure element.

Carmarthen (*Caerfyrddin*) Carm. *Cair Mirdin* 1130. 'Fort at Maridunum'. Welsh *caer*. The Roman town of *Maridunum* has a Celtic name meaning 'fort by the sea' (British **mari-* + **duno-*).

Carmavy (*Carn Méibhe*) Antrim. 'Maeve's cairn'.

Carmel Gwyd. The Welsh Nonconformist chapel here was named after the biblical Mount *Carmel* (1 Kings 18:19, etc).

Carn (*Carn*) Westmeath. 'Cairn'.

Carna (*Carna*) Galway, Wexford. 'Cairns'.

Carnaby E. R. Yorks. *Cherendebi* 1086 (DB). Possibly 'homestead or village of a man called **Kærandi* or **Keyrandi*'. OScand. pers. name + *bý*.

Carnagh (*Carranach*) Armagh. 'Place of cairns'.

Carnalbanagh (*Carn Albanach*) Antrim. *Carnalbanagh* 1780. 'Cairn of the Scotsmen'.

Carnanmore (*Carnán Mór*) Antrim. 'Big little cairn'.

Carncastle (*Carn an Chaistéil*) Antrim. *Carlcastel* 1279. 'Cairn of the castle'.

Carndonagh (*Carn Domhnach*) Donegal. *Carnedony* 1620. 'Cairn of the church'.

Carnew (*Carn an Bhua*) Wicklow. 'Cairn of the victory'.

Carney (*Fearann Uí Chearnaigh*) Sligo. 'Territory of Ó Ciarnaigh'.

Carnforth Lancs. *Chreneforde* 1086 (DB). Probably 'ford frequented by cranes or herons'. OE *cran* + *ford*.

Carnkenny (*Carn Cainnech*) Tyrone. 'Cainnech's cairn'.

Carnlough (*Carnlach*) Antrim. *Carnalloch* 1780. 'Place of cairns'.

Carnmoney (*Carn Monaidh*) Antrim. (*Ecclesia de*) *Coole of Carnmonie* 1615. 'Cairn of the bog'.

Carnoneen (*Carn Eoghainín*) Galway. 'Eoghainín's cairn'.

Carnoustie Ang. *Donaldus Carmusy* 1493. Meaning uncertain. The first element may be Gaelic *cathair*, 'fort', *càrr*, 'rock', or *carn*, 'cairn'. The second has not been satisfactorily explained.

Carnteel (*Carn tSiail*) Tyrone. (cath) *Cairn tSiadhail* 1239. 'Sial's cairn'.

Carntierna (*Carn Tighernaigh*) Cork. 'Tighernach's cairn'.

Carntogher (*Carn Tóchair*) Derry. (mullach) *an Cháirn* c.1740. 'Cairn of the causeway'.

Carperby N. Yorks. *Chirprebi*. Possibly 'homestead or village of a man called Cairpre'. OIrish pers. name + OScand. *bý*.

Carra (*Cairthe*) Mayo. 'Standing stone'.

Carracastle (*Ceathrú an Chaisil*) Roscommon. 'Quarter of the stone fort'.

Carraroe (*Ceathrú Rua*) Galway. 'Red quarter'.

Carrauntoohil (*Corrán Tuathail*) Kerry. 'Inverted crescent'.

Carreg yr Esgob (island) Pemb. *Bishops rock* 1602. 'Bishop's rock'. Welsh *carreg* + *yr* + *esgob*. The name was translated from the English.

Carrichue (*Carraig Aodha*) Derry. 'Aodh's rock'.

Carrick (*An Charraig*) Donegal, Wexford. 'The rock'.

Carrick (district) S. Ayr. *karrio* c.1140. '(Region of) rocks'. Gaelic *carraig*, from British *carrecc* 'rock'.

Carrick-on-Suir (*Carraig na Siúre*) Tipperary. 'Rock on the (river) Suir'.

Carrickaboy (*Carraighigh Buí*) Cavan. *Careghaboy* 1629. 'Yellow rocky place'.

Carrickahorig (*Carraig an Chomhraic*) Tipperary. 'Rock of the confluence'.

Carrickanoran (*Carraig an Uardáin*) Kilkenny, Monaghan. 'Rock of the spring'.

Carrickart (*Carraig Airt*) Donegal. *Carrowfiggart* 1609. 'Art's rock'. The name probably developed from an original Irish form *Ceathrú Fhiodhghoirt*, 'quarter of the field of the wood'.

Carrickbeg (*Carraig Bheag*) Waterford. 'Little rock'.

Carrickfergus (*Carraig Fhearghais*) Antrim. (*go*) *Carraic Ferghusa* 1204. 'Rock of Fergus'.

Carrickmacross (*Carraig Mhachaire Rois*) Monaghan. *Rosse als. Machair Roysse* 1541. 'Rock of the plain of the grove'.

Carrickmore (*An Charraig Mhór*) Tyrone. 'The big rock'.

Carrickroe (*An Charraig Rua*) Monaghan. 'The red rock'.

Carrig (*Carraig*) Tipperary. 'Rock'.

Carrigafoyle (*Carraig an Phoill*) Tipperary. 'Rock of the pool'.

Carrigaholt (*Carraig an Chabhaltaigh*) Clare. 'Rock of the fleet'.

Carrigahorig (*Carraig an Chomhraic*) Tipperary. 'Rock of the confluence'.

Carrigaline (*Carraig Uí Leighin*) Cork. 'Ó Leighin's rock'.

Carrigallen (*Carraig Álainn*) Leitrim. 'Beautiful rock'.

Carrigan (*An Carraigín*) Cavan. *Carrigin* 1699. 'The little rock'.

Carriganimmy (*Carraig an Ime*) Cork. 'Rock of the butter'.

Carrigans (*An Carraigín*) Donegal. *Cairrccín* 1490. 'The little rock'.

Carriganurra (*Carraig an Fhoraidh*) Kilkenny. 'Rock of the mound'.

Carrigatogher (*Carraig an Tóchair*) Tipperary. 'Rock of the causeway'.

Carrigcannon (*Carraig Cheannann*) Kerry. 'White-headed rock'.

Carrigfada (*Carraig Fhada*) Cork. 'Long rock'.

Carrigkerry (*Carraig Chiarraí*) Limerick. 'Rock of Ciarraí'.

Carrignavar (*Carraig na bhFear*) Cork. 'Rock of the men'.

Carrigtogill (*Carraig Thuathail*) Cork. 'Tuathal's rock'.

Carrington Gtr. Manch. *Carrintona* 12th cent. Possibly 'estate associated with a man called *Cāra*'. OE pers. name + *-ing-* + *tūn*. Alternatively the first element may be an OE *caring* 'tending, herding' or an OE *cæring* 'river-bend'.

Carrington Lincs. First recorded in 1812, and named after Robert Smith, Lord Carrington (1752–1838), who had lands here.

Carrock, Castle Cumbria. *Castelcairoc* c.1165. 'Fortified castle'. Celtic *castel* + a derivative of Celtic *cair* 'fort'.

Carron (*Carn*) Clare. 'Cairn'.

Carrowbeg (*An Ceathrú Bheag*) Mayo. 'The small quarter'.

Carrowbehy (*Ceathrú Bheithí*) Roscommon. 'Quarter of the birches'.

Carrowdoan (*Ceathrú Domhain*) Donegal. 'Deep quarter'.

Carrowdore (*Ceathrú Dobhair*) Down. *Kerrowe Dorne* 1627. 'Quarter of the water'.

Carrowholly (*Ceathrú Chalaidh*) Mayo. 'Quarter of the landing place'.

Carrowkeel (*An Cheathrú Chaol*) Donegal. *Carrowkeele* 1639. 'The narrow quarter'.

Carrowmena (*Ceathrú Meánach*) Donegal. 'Middle quarter'.

Carrowmore (*Ceathrú Mhór*) Galway, Mayo, Sligo. 'Big quarter'.

Carrowmoreknock (*Ceathrú Mhór an Chnoic*) Galway. 'Big quarter of the hill'.

Carrownacon (*Ceathrú na Con*) Mayo. 'Quarter of the hound'.

Carrownedan (*Ceathrú an Éadain*) Sligo. 'Quarter of the brow'.

Carrownisky (*Ceathrú an Uisce*) Mayo. 'Quarter of the water'.

Carrowreagh (*Ceathrú Riabhach*) Roscommon. 'Striped quarter'.

Carrowtawy (*Ceathrú an tSamhaidh*) Sligo. 'Quarter of the sorrel'.

Carrowteige (*Ceathrú Thaidhg*) Mayo. 'Taidg's quarter'.

Carryduff (*Ceathrú Aodha Dhuibh*) Down. *Carow-Eduffe al. Carow-Hugh-Duffe al. Tyduffe* 1623. 'Black Aodh's quarter'.

Carse of Gowrie (district) Perth. *Carse de Gowrie* c.1200. 'Alluvial plain of the goat place'. Scots *carse* + Gaelic *gabhar* (genitive *gaibhre*).

Carshalton Gtr. London. *Aultone* 1086 (DB), *Cresaulton* 1235. 'Farm by the river-spring where watercress grows'. OE *æwiell* + *tūn* with the later addition of OE *cærse*.

Carsington Derbys. *Ghersintune* 1086 (DB). Probably 'farmstead where cress grows'. OE **cærsen* + *tūn*.

Carstairs S. Lan. *Casteltarres* 1170. 'Tarres's castle'. ME *castel* + Celtic pers. name.

Carswell Marsh Oxon. *Chersvelle* 1086 (DB), *Carsewell Merssh* 1467. '(Marsh at) the spring or stream where watercress grows'. OE *cærse* + *wella* with the later addition of OE *mersc*.

Carterton Oxon., a recent name for the village founded by one William Carter in 1901.

Carthorpe N. Yorks. *Caretorp* 1086 (DB). 'Outlying farmstead or hamlet of a man called Kári'. OScand. pers. name + *thorp*.

Cartington Northum. *Cretenden* 1220. Probably 'hill associated with a man called **Certa*'. OE pers. name + *-ing-* + *dūn*.

Cartmel Cumbria. *C(e)artmel* 12th cent. 'Sandbank by rough stony ground'. OScand. **kartr* + *melr*.

Cartronlahan (*Cartúr Leathan*) Galway. 'Broad quarter'.

Cary Fitzpaine & **Castle Cary** Somerset. *Cari* 1086 (DB), *Castelkary* 1237. Named from the River Cary, an ancient Celtic or pre-Celtic river-name. Distinguishing affixes from the Fitz Payn family, here in the 13th cent., and from ME *castel* with reference to the Norman castle.

Cas-Gwent. *See* CHEPSTOW.

Cas-wis. *See* WISTON.

Cashel (*Caiseal*) Galway, Tipperary. 'Stone fort'.

Cashelbane (*Caiseal Bán*) Tyrone. 'White stone fort'.

Cashelgarran (*Caiseal an Ghearráin*) Sligo. 'Stone fort of the horse'.

Cashelmore (*An Caiseal Mór*) Donegal. 'The large stone fort'.

Cashla (*Caisle*) Galway. 'Stream'.

Caslai. *See* HAYSCASTLE.

Casllwchwr. *See* LOUGHOR.

Cas-mael. *See* PUNCHESTON.

Casnewydd-ar-Wysg. *See* NEWPORT (Newpt).

Cassagh (*Ceasach*) Wexford. 'Wicker causeway'.

Cassington Oxon. *Cersetone* 1086 (DB), *Kersinton* 12th cent. 'Farmstead where cress grows'. OE **cærsen* + *tūn*.

Cassop Durham. *Cazehope* 1183. Possibly 'valley or enclosure frequented by wild-cats'. OE *catt* + *hop*.

Castell-nedd. *See* NEATH.

Castellhaidd. *See* HAYSCASTLE.

Castellnewydd Emlyn. *See* NEWCASTLE EMLYN.

Casterton, 'farmstead near the (Roman) fort', OE *cæster* + *tūn*: **Casterton** Cumbria. *Castretune* 1086 (DB). **Casterton, Great** & **Casterton, Little** Rutland. *Castretone* 1086 (DB).

Castle as affix, *see* main name, e.g. for **Castle Bolton** (N. Yorks) *see* BOLTON.

Castle Douglas Dumf. 'Douglas's castle'. The castle is Threave Castle. In 1789 Sir William Douglas bought the village of Carlingwerk and developed it into a burgh of barony.

Castlebar (*Caisleán an Bharraigh*) Mayo. 'de Barra's castle'.

Castlebay W. Isles (Barra). (Town by) Castle Bay'. The bay takes its name from Kiessimul Castle. The town arose in the 19th cent. as a fishing port. The name is a translation of Gaelic *Bàgh a' Chaisteal*.

Castleblayney (*Baile na Lorgan*) Monaghan. *Castleblayney* 1663. 'Blayney's castle'. Sir Edward Blayney built a castle here on land granted him by James I in the early 17th cent. The Irish name means 'town of the strip of land'.

Castlecat (*Caiseal Cait*) Antrim. *Castlecat* 1780. 'Stone fort of the cat'.

Castlecaulfield (*Baile Uí Dhonnáile*) Tyrone. *Castle-Caufield* 1618. 'Caulfield's castle'. Sir Toby Caulfield built a castle here in *c*.1612. The Irish name means 'townland of Ó Donnaíle'.

Castlecomer (*Caisleán an Chomair*) Kilkenny. 'Castle of the confluence'.

Castleconnell (*Caisleán Uí Chonaill*) Limerick. 'Ó Conaill's castle'.

Castleconnor (*Caisleán MhicChonchobhair*) Sligo. 'Mac Conchuir's castle'.

Castlecor (*Caisleán na Cora*) Cork. 'Castle of the weir'.

Castledawson Derry. *Castledawson al. Dawson's Bridge* 1677. 'Dawson's castle'. Sir Joshua Dawson founded the village in 1710 on land owned by his family since 1622. Its Irish name is *An Seanmhullach*, 'the old hilltop'.

Castlederg (*Caisleán na Deirge*) Tyrone. *Caislén na Deirce* 1497. 'Castle of the (river) Derg'.

Castledermot (*Caisleán Díseart Diarmada*) Kildare. 'Castle of the hermitage of Diarmaid'.

Castlefinn (*Caisleán na Finne*) Donegal. *Castleffynne* 1617. 'Castle of the (river) Finn'.

Castleford W. Yorks. *Ceaster forda* late 11th cent. 'Ford by the Roman fort'. OE *cæster* + *ford*.

Castlegal (*Caisle Geala*) Sligo. 'White inlet'.

Castlegar (*Caisleán Gearr*) Galway. 'Short castle'.

Castleknock (*Caisleán Cnucha*) Dublin. 'Castle of the hill'.

Castlelyons (*Caisleán Ó Liatháin*) Cork. 'Uí Liatháin's castle'.

Castlemaine (*Caisleán na Mainge*) Kerry. 'Castle of the (river) Maine'.

Castlemartin Pemb. *Castro Sancti Martini* 1290, *Castlemartin* 1341. 'Fort by St Martin's church'. ME *castel*.

Castlemartyr (*Caisleán na Martra*) Cork. 'Castle of the relics'.

Castlemorton Heref. & Worcs. *Mortun* 1235, *Castell Morton* 1346. 'Farmstead in the marshy ground'. OE *mōr* + *tūn*, with the later addition of *castel* 'castle'.

Castlepollard (*Baile na gCros*) Westmeath. Walter Pollard was granted a licence to hold a weekly market here in 1674. The Irish name means 'town of the crosses'.

Castleraghan (*Caisleán Rathain*) Cavan. 'Castle of ferns'.

Castlereagh (*Caisleán Riabhach*) Down, Roscommon. 'Striped castle'.

Castlerock (*Carraig Ceasail*) Derry. 'Castles' rock'. Robert Castles and his crew perished on a nearby rock in 1826. The Irish name gives the meaning as 'castle rock'.

Castleshane (*Caisleán an tSiáin*) Monaghan. 'Castle of the fairy hill'.

Castleton, 'farmstead or village by a castle', from OE *castel* + *tūn*: **Castleton** Derbys. *Castelton* 13th cent. **Castleton** Gtr. Manch. *Castelton* 1246. **Castleton** N. Yorks. *Castleton* 1577.

Castletown Kinneigh (*Baile Chaisleáin Chinn Eich*) Cork. 'Town of the castle of the horse's head'.

Castlewellan (*Caisleán Uidhilín*) Down. *Ballycaslanwilliam* 1605. 'Uidhilín's castle'.

Castley N. Yorks. *Castelai* 1086 (DB). 'Wood or clearing by a heap of stones'. OE *ceastel* + *lēah*.

Caston Norfolk. *Catestuna* 1086 (DB). 'Farmstead or estate of a man called *Catt or *Káti'. OE or OScand. pers. name + OE *tūn*.

Castor Cambs. *Cæstre* 948, *Castre* 1086 (DB). 'The Roman fort'. OE *cæster*.

Catcleugh Northum. *Cattechlow* 1279. 'Deep valley or ravine frequented by wild-cats'. OE *catt* + **clōh*.

Catcott Somerset. *Cadicote* 1086 (DB). 'Cottage of a man called Cada'. OE pers. name + *cot*.

Caterham Surrey. *Catheham* 1179. Probably 'homestead or enclosure at the hill called *Cadeir*', from Celtic **cadeir* (literally 'chair' but used of lofty places) + OE *hām* or *hamm*. Alternatively 'homestead or enclosure of a man called *Catta', with an OE pers. name as first element.

Catesby Northants. *Catesbi* 1086 (DB). 'Farmstead or village of a man called Kátr or Káti'. OScand. pers. name + *bý*.

Catfield Norfolk. *Catefelda* 1086 (DB). Possibly 'open land frequented by wild-cats', OE *catt* + *feld*. Alternatively 'open land of a man called Káti', from an OScand. pers. name.

Catford Gtr. London. *Catford* 1254. 'Ford frequented by wild-cats'. OE *catt* + *ford*.

Catforth Lancs. *Catford* 1332. Identical in origin with the previous name.

Cathays Card. *Catt Hays* 1699. 'Enclosure inhabited by wildcats'. OE *catt* + *haga*.

Catherington Hants. *Cateringatune* |*sic*| *c*.1015. Possibly 'farmstead of the people living by the hill called *Cadeir*', from Celtic **cadeir* 'chair' + *-inga-* + *tūn*. Alternatively 'farmstead of the family or followers of a man called *Cat(t)or*', from OE pers. name + *-inga-* + *tūn*.

Catherston Leweston Dorset. *Chartreston* 1268, *Lesterton* 1316. Originally names of adjacent estates belonging to families called Charteray and Lester respectively, from OE *tūn*.

Catherton Shrops. *Carderton* 1316. OE *tūn* 'farmstead, village' with an obscure first element.

Catmore Berks. *Catmere* 10th cent., 1086 (DB). 'Pool frequented by wild-cats'. OE *catt* + *mere*.

Catmose, Vale of (district) Rutland. *The Val of Catmouse* 1576. 'Bog or marsh frequented by wild-cats'. OE *catt* + *mos*, with ME *vale* 'valley'.

Caton Lancs. *Catun* 1086 (DB). 'Farmstead or village of a man called Káti'. OScand. pers. name + OE *tūn*.

Catsfield E. Sussex. *Cedesfeld* |*sic*| 1086 (DB), *Cattesfeld* 12th cent. 'Open land of a man called *Catt or frequented by wild-cats'. OE pers. name or OE *catt* + *feld*.

Catshill Heref. & Worcs. *Catteshull* 1199. 'Hill of a man called *Catt or frequented by wild-cats'. OE pers. name or OE *catt* + *hyll*.

Cattal N. Yorks. *Catale* 1086 (DB). Probably 'nook of land frequented by wild-cats'. OE *catt* + *halh*.

Cattawade Suffolk. *Cattiwad* 1247. 'Ford or crossing-place frequented by wild-cats'. OE *catt* + *(ge)wæd*.

Catterall Lancs. *Catrehala* 1086 (DB). Possibly OScand. *kattar-hali* 'cat's tail' with reference to the shape of some lost feature. Alternatively OE *halh* 'nook of land' with an obscure first element.

Catterick N. Yorks. *Katouraktónion* c.150, *Catrice* 1086 (DB). From Latin *cataracta* 'waterfall', though apparently through a misunderstanding of the original Celtic place-name meaning '(place of) battle ramparts'.

Catterlen Cumbria. *Kaderleng* 1158. Celtic **cadeir* 'chair' (here 'hill') with an obscure second element, possibly a pers. name.

Catterton N. Yorks. *Cadretune* 1086 (DB). Probably 'farmstead at the hill called *Cadeir*'. Celtic **cadeir* 'chair' + OE *tūn*.

Catthorpe Leics. *Torp* 1086 (DB), *Torpkat* 1276. OScand. *thorp* 'outlying farmstead or hamlet', with a manorial addition from a family called le Cat(t).

Cattishall Suffolk. *Catteshale* 1187. Probably 'nook of land of a man called **Catt* or frequented by wild-cats'. OE pers. name or OE *catt* + *halh*.

Cattistock Dorset. *Stoche* 1086 (DB), *Cattestok* 1288. OE *stoc* 'outlying farm buildings, secondary settlement', with a manorial addition from a person or family called Cat(t).

Catton, usually 'farmstead of a man called Catta or Káti', OE or OScand. pers. name + OE *tūn*: **Catton** Norfolk. *Catetuna* 1086 (DB). **Catton** N. Yorks. *Catune* 1086 (DB). **Catton, High** & **Catton, Low** E. R. Yorks. *Caton, Cattune* 1086 (DB).
However the following has a different origin: **Catton** Northum. *Catteden* 1229. 'Valley frequented by wild-cats'. OE *catt* + *denu*.

Catwick E. R. Yorks. *Catingeuuic* 1086 (DB). 'Dwelling or (dairy) farm associated with a man called Catta'. OE pers. name (+ *-ing-*) + *wīc*.

Catworth Cambs. *Catteswyrth* 10th cent., *Cateuuorde* 1086 (DB). 'Enclosure of a man called **Catt* or Catta'. OE pers. name + *worth*.

Caulcott Oxon. *Caldecot* 1199. Identical in origin with CALDECOTE.

Cauldon Staffs. *Celfdun* 1002, *Caldone* 1086 (DB). 'Hill where calves graze'. OE *cælf* + *dūn*.

Cauldwell Derbys. *Caldewællen* 942, *Caldewelle* 1086 (DB). 'Cold spring or stream'. OE *cald* + *wella*.

Caundle, Bishop's, Purse & Stourton Dorset, *Candel* 1086 (DB), *Purscaundel* 1241, *Caundel Bishops* 1294, *Sturton Candell* 1569–74. Meaning of Caundle is obscure, though it may have been a name for the range of hills here. Affix *Bishop's* is from the possession of this manor by Bishop of Salisbury. *Purse* is probably a manorial affix from a family of this name. *Sturton* refers to possession by the Lords Stourton from 15th–18th cent.

Caunton Notts. *Calnestune* 1086 (DB). Probably 'farmstead of a man called **Cal(u)nōth*'. OE pers. name + *tūn*.

Causey Park Northum. *La Chauce* 1242. ME *cauce* 'embankment, raised way'.

Cavan (*An Cabhán*) Cavan. (*i mainistir in*) *Cabhain* 1330. 'The hollow'.

Cavanagarden (*Cabhán an Gharraí*) Donegal. 'Hollow of the garden'.

Cave, North & *Cave, South* E. R. Yorks. *Cave* 1086 (DB). Probably from the stream here, 'the fast flowing one', from OE *cāf* 'quick'.

Cavendish Suffolk. *Kauanadisc* 1086 (DB). 'Enclosure or enclosed park of a man called **Cāfna*'. OE pers. name + *edisc*.

Cavenham Suffolk. *Kanauaham* |sic| 1086 (DB), *Cauenham* 1198. 'Homestead or enclosure of a man called **Cāfna*'. OE pers. name + *hām* or *hamm*.

Caversfield Oxon. *Cavrefelle* 1086 (DB). 'Open land of a man called **Cāfhere*'. OE pers. name + *feld*.

Caversham Oxon. *Caueresham* 1086 (DB). 'Homestead or enclosure of a man called **Cáfhere*'. OE pers. name + *hām* or *hamm*.

Caverswall Staffs. *Cavreswelle* 1086 (DB). 'Spring or stream of a man called **Cāfhere*'. OE pers. name + *wella*.

Cavil E. R. Yorks. *Cafeld* 959, *Cheuede* 1086 (DB). 'Open land frequented by jackdaws'. OE **cā* + *feld*.

Cawdor Highland. *Kaledor* 1280. '(Place by) hard water'. British **caleto-* + **dubro-*.

Cawkwell Lincs. *Calchewelle* 1086 (DB). 'Chalk spring or stream'. OE *calc* + *wella*.

Cawood N. Yorks. *Kawuda* 963. 'Wood frequented by jackdaws'. OE **cā* + *wudu*.

Cawston, 'farmstead or village of a man called Kalfr', OScand. pers. name + OE *tūn*: **Cawston** Norfolk. *Cau(p)stuna* 1086 (DB). **Cawston** Warwicks. *Calvestone* 1086 (DB).

Cawthorne S. Yorks. *Caltorne* 1086 (DB). 'Cold (i.e. exposed) thorn-tree'. OE *cald* + *thorn*.

Cawthorpe, 'outlying farmstead or hamlet of a man called Kali', OScand. pers. name + *thorp*: **Cawthorpe** Lincs. *Caletorp* 1086 (DB). **Cawthorpe, Little** Lincs. *Calthorp* 1241.

Cawton N. Yorks. *Caluetun* 1086 (DB). 'Farm where calves are reared'. OE *calf* + *tūn*.

Caxton Cambs. *Caustone* |sic| 1086 (DB), *Kakestune* c.1150. Probably 'farmstead of a man called **Kakkr*'. OScand. pers. name + OE *tūn*.

Caynham Shrops, *Caiham* 1086 (DB), *Cainham* 1255. Probably 'homestead or enclosure of a man called **Cæga*'. OE pers. name (genitive *-n*) + *hām* or *hamm*.

Caythorpe, 'outlying farmstead or hamlet of a man called Káti', OScand. pers. name + *thorp*: **Caythorpe** Lincs. *Catorp* 1086 (DB). **Caythorpe** Notts. *Cathorp* 1177.

Cayton N. Yorks. *Caitun(e)* 1086 (DB). 'Farmstead of a man called **Cæga*'. OE pers. name + *tūn*.

Cefn-mawr. Wrex. 'Big ridge'. Welsh *cefn* + *mawr*.

Ceinewydd. See NEW QUAY.

Cemaes Angl. *Kemmeys* 1291. The village is frequently referred to as Cemaes Bay '(place of) bends' (Welsh *camas*, plural *cemais*). 1291 *Kemmeys*.

Cendl. See BEAUFORT.

Ceredigion (the unitary authority). *Cereticiaun* 12th cent. 'Ceredig's land'. *Ceredig* was one of the sons of Cunedda, who gave the name of GWYNEDD. His name is followed by the Welsh territorial suffix *-ion*. Ceredigion itself gave the name of CARDIGAN.

Cerne Abbas Dorset. *Cernel* 1086 (DB), *Cerne Abbatis* 1288. Named from the River Cerne, an old Celtic river-name from Celtic **carn* 'cairn, heap of stones'. Affix is Latin *abbas* 'an abbot', with reference to the abbey here.

Cerne, Nether & *Cerne, Up* Dorset. *Nudernecerna* 1206, *Obcerne* 1086 (DB). Named from the same river as Cerne Abbas. OE *neotherra* 'lower down' and OE *upp* 'higher up' with reference to their situation on the river.

Cerney, North & *Cerney, South, Cerney Wick* Glos. *Cyrnea* 852, *Cernei* 1086 (DB), *Northcerneye* 1291, *Suthcerney* 1285, *Cernewike* 1220. Named from the River Churn (an old Celtic river-name derived from the same root as the first element of CIRENCESTER) + OE *ēa* 'stream'. Wick is from OE *wīc* 'farm, dairy farm'.

Cerrigydrudion Conwy. *Kericdrudion* 1254. 'Stones of the heroes'. Welsh *carreg* (plural *cerrig*) + *y* + *drud* (plural *drudion*).

Chaceley Glos. *Ceateweslean* 972. Possibly a derivative of Celtic **cēd* 'wood' + OE *lēah* 'wood, clearing'.

Chackmore Bucks. *Chakemore* 1241. Possibly 'marshy ground of a man called *Ceacca'. OE pers. name + *mōr*. Alternatively the first element may be OE **ceacce* 'hill'.

Chacombe Northants. *Cewecumbe* 1086 (DB). 'Valley of a man called *Ceawa'. OE pers. name + *cumb*.

Chadderton Gtr. Manch. *Chaderton* c.1200. Possibly 'farmstead at the hill called *Cadeir*'. Celtic **cadeir* 'chair' (here 'hill') + OE *tūn*.

Chaddesden Derbys. *Cedesdene* 1086 (DB). 'Valley of a man called *Ceadd'. OE pers. name + *denu*.

Chaddesley Corbett Heref. & Worcs. *Ceadresleahge* 816, *Cedeslai* 1086 (DB). Possibly 'wood or clearing at the hill called *Cadeir*'. Celtic **cadeir* 'chair' + OE *lēah*, with manorial addition from the Corbet family here in the 12th cent.

Chaddleworth Berks. *Ceadelanwyrth* 960, *Cedeledorde* |sic| 1086 (DB). 'Enclosure of a man called *Ceadela'. OE pers. name + *worth*.

Chadlington Oxon. *Cedelintone* 1086 (DB). 'Estate associated with a man called *Ceadela'. OE pers. name + *-ing- + tūn*.

Chadshunt Warwicks. *Ceadles funtan* 949, *Cedeleshunte* 1086 (DB). 'Spring of a man called *Ceadel'. OE pers. name + **funta*.

Chadwell, 'cold spring or stream', OE *c(e)ald + wella*: **Chadwell** Leics. *Caldeuuelle* 1086 (DB). **Chadwell St Mary** Essex. *Celdeuuella* 1086 (DB). Affix from the dedication of the church.

Chadwick Green Mersey. *Chaddewyk* c.1180. '(Dairy) farm of a man called Ceadda'. OE pers. name + *wīc*.

Chaffcombe Somerset. *Caffecome* 1086 (DB). Probably 'valley of a man called *Ceaffa'. OE pers. name + *cumb*.

Chaffpool (*Lochán na Cáithe*) Sligo. 'Little lake on the chaff'.

Chagford Devon. *Chagefont* 1086 (DB). 'Ford where broom or gorse grows'. OE **ceacga + ford*.

Chailey E. Sussex. *Cheagele* 11th cent. 'Clearing where broom or gorse grows'. OE **ceacga + lēah*.

Chalbury Dorset. *Cheoles burge* 946. 'Fortified place associated with a man called Cēol'. OE pers. name + *burh*.

Chaldon, 'hill where calves graze', OE *cealf + dūn*: **Chaldon** Surrey. *Calvedone* 1086 (DB). **Chaldon Herring or East Chaldon** Dorset. *Celvedune* 1086 (DB), *Chaluedon Hareng* 1243. Manorial affix from the Harang family, here from the 12th cent.

Chale I. of Wight. *Cela* 1086 (DB). OE *ceole* 'throat' used in a topographical sense 'gorge, ravine'.

Chalfont St Giles & *Chalfont St Peter* Bucks. *Celfunte* 1086 (DB), *Chalfund Sancti Egidii* 1237, *Chalfhunte Sancti Petri* 1237–40. 'Spring frequented by calves'. OE *cealf + *funta*, with distinguishing affixes from the dedications of the churches at the two places.

Chalford, 'chalk or limestone ford', OE *cealc + ford*: **Chalford** Glos. *Chalforde* c.1250. **Chalford** Oxon. *Chalcford* 1185–6.

Chalgrave Beds. *Cealhgræfan* 926, *Celgraue* 1086 (DB). 'Chalk pit'. OE *cealc + græf*.

Chalgrove Oxon. *Celgrave* 1086 (DB). Identical in origin with the previous name.

Chalk, *Chalke*, '(place on) the chalk', OE *cealc*: **Chalk** Kent. *Cealca* 10th cent., *Celca* 1086 (DB). **Chalke, Broad** & **Chalke, Bowerchalk** Wilts. *Ceolcum* 955, *Chelche* 1086 (DB), *Brode Chalk* 1380, *Burchelke* 1225. Distinguishing affixes are OE *brād* 'great' and *(ge)būra* 'of the peasants' or *burh* 'fortified place'.

Chalk Farm Gtr. London. *Chaldecote* 1253. 'Cold cottage(s)'. OE *ceald + cot*. The 'worn-down' form *Chalk* first appears 1746.

Challacombe Devon, near Lynton. *Celdecomba* 1086 (DB). 'Cold valley'. OE *ceald + cumb*.

Challock Lees Kent. *Cealfalocum* 824. 'Enclosure(s) for calves'. OE *cealf + loca*, with the later addition of *lǣs* 'pasture'.

Challow, East & *Challow, West* Oxon. *Ceawanhlǣwe* 947, *Ceveslane* |sic| 1086 (DB). 'Tumulus of a man called *Ceawa'. OE pers. name + *hlǣw, hlāw*.

Chalton Beds., near Toddington. *Chaltun* 1131. 'Farm where calves are reared'. OE *cealf + tūn*.

Chalton Hants. *Cealctun* 1015, *Ceptune* 1086 (DB). 'Farmstead on chalk'. OE *cealc + tūn*.

Chalvington E. Sussex. *Calvintone* 1086 (DB). 'Estate associated with a man called *Cealf(a)'. OE pers. name + *-ing- + tūn*.

Chandler's Ford Hants., on record from 1759, named from the Chaundler family, in the area from the 14th cent.

Chanonrock (*Carraig na gCanónach*) Louth. 'Rock of the canons'.

Chapel as affix, *see* main name, e.g. for **Chapel Allerton** (W. Yorks.) *see* ALLERTON.

Chapel en le Frith Derbys. *Capella de le Frith* 1272. 'Chapel in the sparse woodland'. ME *chapele* + OE *fyrhth*, with retention of OFrench preposition and definite article.

Chapelizod (*Séipéal Iosóid*) Dublin. 'Iseult's chapel'.

Chapeltown Down. *Chapeltown* 1886. The village is named for the Roman Catholic chapel erected here in 1791. The equivalent Irish name is *Baile an tSéipéil*.

Chapeltown S. Yorks. *Le Chapel* 13th cent., *Chappeltown* 1707. '(Hamlet by) the chapel'. ME *chapel*.

Chapmanslade Wilts. *Chepmanesled* 1245. 'Valley of the merchants'. OE *ceap-mann* + *slæd*.

Chard, *South Chard* Somerset. *Cerdren* 1065, *Cerdre* 1086 (DB). Possibly 'house or building in rough ground'. OE *ceart* + *ærn*.

Chardstock Devon. *Cerdestoche* 1086 (DB). 'Secondary settlement belonging to CHARD'. OE *stoc*.

Charfield S. Glos. *Cirvelde* 1086 (DB). 'Open land by a bending road, or with a rough surface'. OE **cearr(e)* or *ceart* + *feld*.

Charford, North Hants. *Cerdicesford* late 9th cent., *Cerdeford* 1086 (DB). 'Ford associated with the chieftain called Cerdic'. OE pers. name + *ford*.

Charing Kent. *Ciorrincg* 799, *Cheringes* 1086 (DB). Probably OE **cerring* 'a bend in a road'. Alternatively 'place associated with a man called Ceorra', OE pers. name + *-ing*.

Charing Cross Gtr. London. *Cyrringe* c.1000, *La Charryngcros* 1360. From OE **cerring* (see previous name), with reference either to a bend in the Roman road to the West or in the River Thames. There was a 'Queen Eleanor cross' here in the 14th cent., *see* WALTHAM CROSS.

Charingworth Glos. *Chevringavrde* 1086 (DB). 'Enclosure of the family or followers of a man called **Ceafor*'. OE pers. name + *-inga-* + *worth*.

Charlbury Oxon. *Ceorlingburh* c.1000. 'Fortified place associated with a man called Ceorl'. OE pers. name + *-ing-* + *burh* (dative *byrig*).

Charlcombe B. & NE. Som. *Cerlecume* 1086 (DB). 'Valley of the freemen or peasants'. OE *ceorl* + *cumb*.

Charlecote Warwicks. *Cerlecote* 1086 (DB). 'Cottage(s) of the freemen or peasants'. OE *ceorl* + *cot*.

Charlemont Armagh. *Achadh in dá Charad* c.1645. The village is named for Charles Blount, 8th baron Mountjoy, for whom a fort was erected here in 1602. The original Irish name was *Achadh an dá Chora*, 'field of the two weirs'.

Charles Devon. *Carmes* |*sic*| 1086 (DB), *Charles* 1244. Possibly 'rock-court'. Cornish *carn* + **lys*.

Charlestown Armagh. The village is named for *Charles* Brownlow, who built houses here in c.1830.

Charlestown Cornwall, first so recorded from 1800, a small china-clay port named after its sponsor Charles Rashleigh, a local industrialist.

Charlesworth Derbys. *Cheuenwrde* |*sic*| 1086 (DB), *Chauelisworth* 1286. Probably 'enclosure of a man called **Ceafl*', OE pers. name + *worth*. Alternatively the first element may be OE *ceafl* 'jaw' here used in the sense 'ravine'.

Charleton Devon. *Cherletone* 1086 (DB). 'Farmstead of the freemen or peasants'. OE *ceorl* + *tūn*.

Charlinch Somerset. *Cerdeslinc* 1086 (DB). Possibly 'ridge of a man called Cēolrēd'. OE pers. name + *hlinc*.

Charlton, a common place-name, usually 'farmstead of the freemen or peasants', from OE *ceorl* (genitive plural *-a*) + *tūn*; examples include: **Charlton** Gtr. London. *Cerletone* 1086 (DB). **Charlton** Hants. *Cherletone* 1192. **Charlton** Wilts., near Malmesbury. *Ceorlatunæ* 10th cent., *Cerletone* 1086 (DB). **Charlton Abbots** Glos. *Cerletone* 1086 (DB), *Charleton Abbatis* 1535. Affix from its possession by Winchcomb Abbey. **Charlton Adam** Somerset. *Cerletune* 1086 (DB), *Cherleton Adam* 13th cent. Manorial addition from the fitz Adam family, here in the 13th cent. **Charlton Horethorne** Somerset. *Ceorlatun* c.950. Affix from the old Hundred of Horethorne, meaning 'grey thorn-bush' from OE *hār* + *thyrne*. **Charlton Kings** Glos. *Cherletone* 1160, *Kynges Cherleton* 1245. Affix 'Kings' because it was ancient demesne of the Crown. **Charlton Mackerell** Somerset. *Cerletune* 1086 (DB), *Cherletun Makerel* 1243. Manorial affix from the Makerel family. **Charlton Marshall** Dorset. *Cerletone* 1086 (DB), *Cherleton Marescal* 1288. Manorial addition from the Marshall family, here in the 13th cent. **Charlton Musgrove** Somerset. *Cerletone* 1086 (DB), *Cherleton Mucegros* 1225. Manorial addition from the Mucegros family, here in the 13th cent. **Charlton, North** & **Charlton, South** Northum. *Charleton del North, Charleton del Suth* 1242. **Charlton on Otmoor** Oxon. *Cerlentone* 1086 (DB), *Cherleton upon Ottemour* 1314. Affix from nearby Ot Moor, 'marshy ground of a man called **Otta*', from OE pers. name + *mōr*. **Charlton, Queen** B. & NE. Som. *Cherleton* 1291. Affix because given to Queen Catherine Parr by Henry VIII.

However the following has a different origin: **Charlton** Surrey. *Cerdentone* 1086 (DB). Probably 'estate associated with a man called Cēolrēd'. OE pers. name + *-ing-* + *tūn*.

Charlwood Surrey. *Cherlewde* 12th cent. 'Wood of the freemen or peasants'. OE *ceorl* + *wudu*.

Charminster Dorset. *Cerminstre* 1086 (DB). 'Church on the River Cerne'. Celtic river-name (*see* CERNE) + OE *mynster*.

Charmouth Dorset. *Cernemude* 1086 (DB). 'Mouth of the River Char'. Celtic river-name (identical in origin with CERNE) + OE *mūtha*.

Charndon Bucks. *Credendone* |*sic*| 1086 (DB), *Charendone* 1227. Probably 'hill called *Carn*'. Celtic hill-name (from **carn* 'cairn, heap of stones') + OE *dūn*.

Charney Bassett Oxon. *Ceornei* 821, *Cernei* 1086 (DB). 'Island on a river called *Cern*'. Lost Celtic river-name (identical in origin with CERNE) + OE *ēg*, with manorial addition from a family called Bass(es).

Charnock Richard Lancs. *Chernoch* 1194, *Chernok Richard* 1288. Possibly a derivative of Celtic **carn* 'cairn, heap of stones' + manorial addition from a certain *Richard* here in the 13th cent.

Charnwood Forest Leics. *Cernewoda* 1129. 'Wood in rocky country'. Celtic **carn* + OE *wudu*.

Charsfield Suffolk. *Ceresfelda* 1086 (DB). OE *feld* 'tract of open country', possibly with a Celtic river-name *Char* as first element.

Chart Sutton Kent. *Cært* 814, *Certh* 1086 (DB), *Chert juxta Suthon* 1280. OE *cert* 'rough ground'. Affix from nearby SUTTON VALENCE.

Chart, Great & *Chart, Little* Kent. *Cert* 762, *Certh, Litelcert* 1086 (DB), *Magna Chert* 13th cent. OE *cert* 'rough ground'.

Charterhouse Somerset. *Chartuse* 1243. OFrench *chartrouse* 'a house of Carthusian monks'.

Chartham Kent. *Certham* c.871, *Certeham* 1086 (DB). 'Homestead in rough ground'. OE *cert* + *hām*.

Chartridge Bucks. *Charderuge* 1191–4. Possibly 'ridge of a man called **Cærda*'. OE pers. name + *hrycg*.

Charwelton Northants. *Cerweltone* 1086 (DB). 'Farmstead on the River Cherwell'. River-name (probably 'winding stream' from OE **cearr(e)* + *wella*) + OE *tūn*.

Chastleton Oxon. *Ceastelton* 777, *Cestitone* 1086 (DB). 'Farmstead by the ruined prehistoric camp'. OE *ceastel* + *tūn*.

Chatburn Lancs. *Chatteburn* 1242. 'Stream of a man called Ceatta'. OE pers. name + *burna*.

Chatcull Staffs. *Ceteruille* |*sic*| 1086 (DB), *Chatculne* 1199. 'Kiln of a man called Ceatta'. OE pers. name + *cyln*.

Chatham, 'homestead or village in or by the wood', Celtic **cēd* + OE *hām*: **Chatham** Kent. *Cetham* 880, *Ceteham* 1086 (DB). **Chatham Green** Essex. *Cetham* 1086 (DB).

Chatsworth Derbys. *Chetesuorde* 1086 (DB), *Chattesworth* 1276. 'Enclosed settlement of a man called **Ceatt*'. OE pers. name + *worth*.

Chattenden Kent. *Chatendune* c.1100. Possibly 'hill of a man called Ceatta'. OE pers. name (genitive -*n*) + *dūn*.

Chatteris Cambs. *Cæateric* 974, *Cietriz* 1086 (DB). Probably 'raised strip or ridge of a man called Ceatta'. OE pers. name + **ric*. However the first element may be Celtic **cēd* 'wood'.

Chattisham Suffolk. *Cetessam* 1086 (DB). Probably 'homestead or enclosure of a man called **Ceatt*'. OE pers. name + *hām* or *hamm*.

Chatton Northum. *Chetton* 1178. 'Farmstead of a man called Ceatta'. OE pers. name + *tūn*.

Chatwell, Great Staffs. *Chattewell* 1203. 'Well or spring of a man called Ceatta'. OE pers. name + *wella*.

Chawleigh Devon. *Calvelie* 1086 (DB). 'Clearing where calves are pastured'. OE *cealf* + *lēah*.

Chawston Beds. *Calnestorne* |*sic*| 1086 (DB), *Caluesterne* 1167. 'Thorn-tree of a man called **Cealf*'. OE pers. name + *thyrne*.

Chawton Hants. *Celtone* 1086 (DB). 'Farmstead where calves are reared', or 'farmstead on chalk'. OE *cealf* or *cealc* + *tūn*.

Cheadle, from Celtic **cēd* 'wood' to which an explanatory OE *lēah* 'wood' has been added: **Cheadle** Gtr. Manch. *Cedde* 1086 (DB), *Chedle* c.1165. **Cheadle** Staffs. *Celle* 1086 (DB).

Cheadle Hulme Gtr. Manch. *Hulm* 12th cent. 'Water-meadow belonging to CHEADLE'. OScand. *holmr*.

Cheam Gtr. London. *Cegham* 967, *Ceiham* 1086 (DB). Probably 'homestead or village by the tree-stumps'. OE **ceg* + *hām*.

Chearsley Bucks. *Cerdeslai* 1086 (DB). 'Wood or clearing of a man called Cēolrēd'. OE pers. name + *lēah*.

Chebsey Staffs. *Cebbesio* 1086 (DB). 'Island, or dry ground in marsh, of a man called **Cebbi*'. OE pers. name + *ēg*.

Checkendon Oxon. *Cecadene* 1086 (DB). 'Valley of a man called **Ceacca*', or 'valley by the hill'. OE pers. name or OE **ceacce* (genitive -*an*) + *denu*.

Checkley Ches. *Chackileg* 1252. 'Wood or clearing of a man called **Ceaddica*'. OE pers. name + *lēah*.

Checkley Heref. & Worcs. *Chakkeleya* 1195. 'Wood or clearing of a man called **Ceacca*', or 'wood or clearing on or near a hill'. OE pers. name or OE **ceacce* + *lēah*.

Checkley Staffs. *Cedla* |*sic*| 1086 (DB), *Checkeleg* 1196. Identical in origin with the previous name.

Chedburgh Suffolk. *Cedeberia* 1086 (DB). 'Hill of a man called Cedda'. OE pers. name + *beorg*.

Cheddar Somerset. *Ceodre* c.880, *Cedre* 1086 (DB). Probably OE **cēodor* 'ravine', with reference to Cheddar Gorge.

Cheddington Bucks. *Cete(n)done* 1086 (DB). 'Hill of a man called **Cetta*'. OE pers. name (genitive -*n*) + *dūn*.

Cheddleton Staffs. *Celtetone* 1086 (DB), *Chetilton* 1201. 'Farmstead in a valley'. OE *cetel* + *tūn*.

Cheddon Fitzpaine Somerset. *Succedene* |*sic*| 1086 (DB), *Chedene* 1182. OE *denu* 'valley', possibly with Celtic **cēd* 'wood'. Manorial addition from the Fitzpaine family, here in the 13th cent.

Chedgrave Norfolk. *Scatagraua* 1086 (DB), *Chategrave* 1165–70. Probably 'pit of a man called Ceatta'. OE pers. name + *græf*. The river-name **Chet** is a 'back-formation' from the place-name.

Chedington Dorset. *Chedinton* 1194. 'Estate associated with a man called **Cedd* or Cedda'. OE pers. name + -*ing*- + *tūn*.

Chediston Suffolk. *Cedestan* 1086 (DB). 'Stone of a man called **Cedd*'. OE pers. name + *stān*.

Chedworth Glos. *Ceddanwryde* |*sic*| 862, *Cedeorde* 1086 (DB). 'Enclosure of a man called Cedda'. OE pers. name + *worth*.

Chedzoy Somerset. *Chedesie* 729. 'Island, or dry ground in marsh, of a man called **Cedd*'. OE pers. name + *ēg*.

Cheekpoint (*Pointe na Síge*) Waterford. 'Streak point'.

Cheetham Gtr. Manch. *Cheteham* late 12th cent. 'Homestead or village by the wood called *Chet*'. Celtic *cēd* 'forest' + OE *hām*.

Cheetwood Gtr. Manch. *Chetewode* 1489. Near CHEETHAM; an explanatory *wudu* 'wood' has been added to the same first element.

Chelborough Dorset. *Celberge* 1086 (DB). Probably 'hill of a man called Cēola'. OE pers. name + *beorg*. Alternatively the first element may be OE *ceole* 'throat, gorge' or *cealc* 'chalk'.

Cheldon Barton Devon. *Chadeledona* 1086 (DB). 'Hill of a man called *Ceadela*'. OE pers. name + *dūn*. Barton is from OE *bere-tūn* 'barley-farm, demesne farm'.

Chelford Ches. *Celeford* 1086 (DB). Probably 'ford of a man called Cēola'. OE pers. name + *ford*. Alternatively the first element could be OE *ceole* 'throat', used in a topographical sense 'channel, gorge'.

Chell Heath Staffs. *Chelle* 1227. Probably 'wood of a man called Cēola'. OE pers. name + *lēah*.

Chellaston Derbys. *Celerdestune* 1086 (DB). 'Farmstead of a man called Cēolheard'. OE pers. name + *tūn*.

Chellington Beds. *Chelewentone* 1219. 'Farmstead of a woman called Cēolwynn'. OE pers. name + *tūn*.

Chelmarsh Shrops. *Celmeres* 1086 (DB). 'Marsh marked out with posts or poles'. OE *cegel* + *mersc*.

Chelmondiston Suffolk. *Chelmundeston* 1174. 'Farmstead of a man called Cēolmund'. OE pers. name + *tūn*.

Chelmorton Derbys. *Chelmerdon(e)* 12th cent. Probably 'hill of a man called Cēolmær'. OE pers. name + *dūn*.

Chelmsford Essex. *Celmeresfort* 1086 (DB). 'Ford of a man called Cēolmær'. OE pers. name + *ford*. The river-name **Chelmer** is a 'back-formation' from the place-name.

Chelsea Gtr. London. *Celchyth* 789, *Chelchede* 1086 (DB). Possibly 'landing-place for chalk or limestone'. OE *cealc* + *hȳth*. Alternatively the first element may be OE *cælic* 'cup, chalice' used in some topographical sense.

Chelsfield Gtr. London. *Cillesfelle* 1086 (DB). 'Open land of a man called Cēol'. OE pers. name + *feld*.

Chelsworth Suffolk. *Ceorleswyrthe* 962, *Cerleswrda* 1086 (DB). 'Enclosure of the freeman or of a man called Ceorl'. OE *ceorl* or OE pers. name + *worth*.

Cheltenham Glos. *Celtanhomme* 803, *Chinteneham* |sic| 1086 (DB). Probably 'enclosure or river-meadow by a hill-slope called *Celte*'. OE or pre-English hill-name + *hamm*. Alternatively the first element may be an OE pers. name *Celta*. The river-name **Chelt** is a 'back-formation' from the place-name.

Chelveston Northants. *Celuestone* 1086 (DB). 'Farmstead of a man called Cēolwulf'. OE pers. name + *tūn*.

Chelvey N. Som. *Calviche* 1086 (DB). 'Farm where calves are reared'. OE *cealf* + *wīc*.

Chelwood B. & NE. Som. *Celeworde* 1086 (DB). 'Enclosure of a man called Cēola'. OE pers. name + *worth*.

Chenies Bucks. *Isenhamstede* 12th cent., *Ysenamstud Cheyne* 13th cent. Probably 'homestead of a man called *Īsa*'. OE pers. name + *hām-stede* + manorial addition (which is now used alone) from the Cheyne family, here in the 13th cent. Alternatively the first element may be an old river-name.

Chepstow (*Cas-gwent*) Mon. *Strigull* |sic| 1224, *Chepstowe* 1308, *Chapestowe* 1338. 'Market place'. OE *cēap* + *stōw*. The Welsh name means 'castle in Gwent' (Welsh *cas*). *See* GWENT.

Cherhill Wilts. *Ciriel* 1155. Possibly Celtic *ial* 'fertile upland' with a Celtic river-name as first element.

Cherington, probably 'village with a church', OE *cirice* + *tūn*: **Cherington** Glos. *Cerintone* 1086 (DB). **Cherington** Warwicks. *Chiriton* 1199.

Cheriton, 'village with a church', OE *cirice* + *tūn*: **Cheriton** Devon. *Ciretone* 1086 (DB). **Cheriton** Hants. *Cherinton* 1167. **Cheriton, North** & **Cheriton, South** Somerset. *Ciretona*, *Cherintone* 1086 (DB). **Cheriton Bishop** Devon. *Ceritone* 1086 (DB), *Bishops Churyton* 1370. Affix from the Bishop of Exeter, granted land here in the 13th cent. **Cheriton Fitzpaine** Devon. *Cerintone* 1086 (DB), *Cheriton Fitz Payn* 1335. Manorial addition from the Fitzpayn family, here in the 13th cent.

Cheriton Pemb. *Cheriton* 1813. 'Village with a church'. OE *cirice* + *tūn*. Cheriton is also known as *Stackpole Elidor*, 'Elidir's (estate by the) pool near the rock' (OScand. *stakkr* + *pollr*).

Cherrington Shrops. *Cerlintone* 1086 (DB), *Cherington* 1230. Possibly 'estate associated with a man called Ceorra', OE pers. name + *-ing-* + *tūn*. Alternatively 'settlement by a river-bend', from OE *cerring* + *tūn*.

Cherry Burton E. R. Yorks., *see* BURTON.

Cherry Hinton Cambs., *see* HINTON.

Cherry Willingham Lincs. *see* WILLINGHAM.

Chertsey Surrey. *Cerotaesei* 731, *Certesy* 1086 (DB). 'Island of a man called *Cerot*'. Celtic pers. name + OE *ēg*.

Cherwell (river) Northants.–Oxon., *see* CHARWELTON.

Cheselbourne Dorset. *Chiselburne* 869, *Ceseburne* 1086 (DB). 'Gravel stream'. OE *cisel* + *burna*.

Chesham, *Chesham Bois* Bucks. *Cæstæleshamme* 1012, *Cestreham* 1086 (DB), *Chesham Boys* 1339. 'River-meadow by a heap of stones'. OE *ceastel* + *hamm*, with manorial affix from the de Bois family, here in the 13th cent. The river-name **Chess** is a 'back-formation' from the place-name.

Cheshire (the county). *Cestre Scire* 1086 (DB). 'Province of the city of CHESTER'. OE *scīr* 'district'.

Cheshunt Herts. *Cestrehunt* 1086 (DB). Probably 'spring by the old (Roman) fort'. OE *ceaster* + *funta*.

Chesil Beach Dorset. *Chisille bank* c.1540. From OE *cisel* 'shingle'. It gives name to the village of **Chesil**, *Chesill* 1608.

Cheslyn Hay Staffs. *Haya de Chistlin* 1236. Probably 'coffin ridge', i.e. 'ridge where a coffin was found'. OE *cest* + *hlinc*, with *hæg* 'enclosure'.

Chessington Gtr. London. *Cisendone* 1086 (DB). 'Hill of a man called Cissa'. OE pers. name (genitive *-n*) + *dūn*.

Chester Ches. *Deoua* c.150, *Legacæstir* 735, *Cestre* 1086 (DB). OE *ceaster* 'Roman town or city'. Originally called *Deoua* from its situation on the River DEE, later *Legacæstir* meaning 'city of the legions'.

Chester le Street Durham. *Cestra* c.1160, *Cestria in Strata* 1400. 'Roman fort on the Roman road'. OE *ceaster* + *strǣt* (Latin *strata*). The French definite article *le* remains after loss of the preposition.

Chesterblade Somerset. *Cesterbled* 1065. OE *ceaster* 'old fortification', possibly with OE *blæd* 'blade' in a topographical sense 'ledge'.

Chesterfield Derbys. *Cesterfelda* 955, *Cestrefeld* 1086 (DB). 'Open land near a Roman fort or settlement'. OE *ceaster* + *feld*.

Chesterford, Great & *Chesterford, Little* Essex. *Ceasterford* 1004, *Cestreforda* 1086 (DB). 'Ford by a Roman fort'. OE *ceaster* + *ford*.

Chesterton, 'farmstead or village by a Roman fort or town', OE *ceaster* + *tūn*: **Chesterton** Cambs. *Cestretone* 1086 (DB). **Chesterton** Oxon. *Cestertune* 1005, *Cestretone* 1086 (DB). **Chesterton** Staffs. *Cestreton* 1214. **Chesterton** Warwicks. *Cestretune* 1043, *Cestretone* 1086 (DB).

Cheswardine Shrops. *Ciseworde* 1086 (DB), *Chesewordin* 1160. Probably 'enclosed settlement where cheese is made'. OE *cēse* + *worthign*.

Cheswick Northum. *Chesewic* 1208–10. 'Farm where cheese is made'. OE *cēse* + *wīc*.

Chetnole Dorset. *Chetenoll* 1242. 'Hill-top or hillock of a man called Ceatta'. OE pers. name + *cnoll*.

Chettiscombe Devon. *Chetelescome* 1086 (DB). Probably OE *cetel* 'deep valley' + explanatory OE *cumb* 'valley'.

Chettisham Cambs. *Chetesham* c.1170. Probably 'enclosure of a man called *Ceatt*'. OE pers. name + *hamm*. Alternatively the first element may be Celtic *cēd* 'wood'.

Chettle Dorset. *Ceotel* 1086 (DB). Probably OE *ceotol* 'deep valley'.

Chetton Shrops. *Catinton* 1086 (DB), *Chetintone* 1210–12. Probably 'estate associated with a man called Ceatta'. OE pers. name + *-ing-* + *tūn*.

Chetwode Bucks. *Cetwuda* 949, *Ceteode* 1086 (DB). Celtic *cēd* 'wood' to which has been added an explanatory OE *wudu* 'wood'.

Chetwynd Shrops. *Catewinde* 1086 (DB). Probably 'winding ascent of a man called Ceatta'. OE pers. name + *(ge)wind*.

Chetwynd Aston Shrops. *See* ASTON.

Cheveley Cambs. *Cæafle* c.1000, *Chauelai* 1086 (DB). 'Wood full of fallen twigs'. OE *ceaf* + *lēah*.

Chevening Kent. *Chivening* 1199. Possibly '(settlement of) the dwellers at the ridge'. Celtic *cevn* + OE *-ingas*.

Cheverell, Great & *Cheverell, Little* Wilts. *Chevrel* 1086 (DB). An unexplained name, obscure in origin and meaning.

Chevington, West Northum. *Chiuingtona* 1236. 'Estate associated with a man called *Cifa*'. OE pers. name + *-ing-* + *tūn*.

Cheviot (Hills) Northum. Sc. Bord. *Chiuet* 1181. Meaning uncertain. The pre-English name is that of the single mountain here called *The Cheviot*.

Chevithorne Devon. *Cheuetorna* 1086 (DB). 'Thorn-tree of a man called Ceofa'. OE pers. name + *thorn*.

Chew Magna B. & NE. Som. *Ciw* 1065, *Chive* 1086 (DB). Named from the River Chew, which is a Celtic river-name, with affix from Latin *magna* 'great'.

Chew Stoke B. & NE. Som. *Stoche* 1086 (DB). 'Secondary settlement belonging to CHEW', from OE *stoc*.

Chewton Mendip Somerset. *Ciwtun* c.880, *Ciwetune* 1086 (DB), *Cheuton by Menedep* 1313. 'Estate on the River Chew'. Celtic river-name (*see* CHEW) + OE *tūn* + affix from the MENDIP HILLS.

Chicheley Bucks. *Cicelai* 1086 (DB). 'Wood or clearing of a man called *Cicca*'. OE pers. name + *lēah*.

Chichester W. Sussex. *Cisseceastre* 895, *Cicestre* 1086 (DB). Probably 'Roman town of a chieftain called Cissa', OE pers. name + *ceaster*. Alternatively the first element could be an OE word *cisse* (genitive *-an*) 'a gravelly feature'.

Chickerell Dorset. *Cicherelle* 1086 (DB). This name remains obscure in origin and meaning.

Chicklade Wilts. *Cytlid* c.912. Possibly 'gate or slope by the wood'. Celtic *cēid* + OE *hlid* or *hlid*.

Chidden Hants. *Cittandene* 956. 'Valley of a man called *Citta*'. OE pers. name + *denu*.

Chiddingfold Surrey. *Chedelingefelt* |sic| 1130, *Chidingefaud* 12th cent. Possibly 'fold of the family or followers of a man called *Cid(d)el* or *Cid(d)a*'. OE pers. name + *-inga-* + *fald*.

Chiddingly E. Sussex. *Cetelingei* |sic| 1086 (DB). *Chitingeleghe* c.1230. Probably 'wood or clearing of the family or followers of a man called *Citta*'. OE pers. name + *-inga-* + *lēah*.

Chiddingstone Kent. *Cidingstane* c.1110. Possibly 'stone associated with a man called *Cidd* or *Cidda*'. OE pers. name + *-ing-* + *stān*.

Chideock Dorset. *Cidiho* c.1086 (DB). 'Wooded place', from a derivative of Celtic *cēd* 'wood'. The river-name **Chid** is a 'back-formation' from the place-name.

Chidham W. Sussex. *Chedeham* 1193. Probably 'homestead or peninsula near the bay'. OE *cēod(e)* + *hām* or *hamm*.

Chieveley Berks. *Cifanlea* 951, *Civelei* 1086 (DB). 'Wood or clearing of a man called *Cifa*'. OE pers. name + *lēah*.

Chignall St James & *Chignall Smealy* Essex. *Cingehala* 1086 (DB), *Chikenhale Iacob* 1254, *Chigehale Smetheleye* 1279. Probably 'nook of land of a man called *Cicca*'. OE pers. name (genitive *-n*) + *halh*. Affixes from the dedication of the church to St James (Latin *Jacobus*), and from a nearby place meaning 'smooth clearing' from OE *smēthe* + *lēah*.

Chigwell Essex. *Cingheuuella* 1086 (DB). *Chiggewell* 1187. Possibly 'spring or stream of a man called *Cicca'. OE pers. name + *wella*.

Chilbolton Hants. *Ceolboldingtun* 909. *Cilbode(n)tune* 1086 (DB). 'Estate associated with a man called Cēolbeald'. OE pers. name + *-ing-* + *tūn*.

Chilcombe Dorset. *Ciltecombe* 1086 (DB). Possibly 'valley at a hill-slope called *Cilte'. OE or pre-English hill-name + OE *cumb*.

Chilcompton Somerset. *Comtuna* 1086 (DB). *Childecumpton* 1227. 'Valley farmstead (or village) of the young men'. OE *cild* + *cumb* + *tūn*.

Chilcote Leics. *Cildecote* 1086 (DB). 'Cottage(s) of the young men'. OE *cild* + *cot*.

Child Okeford Dorset. *See* OKEFORD.

Child's Ercall Shrops., *see* ERCALL.

Childer Thornton Ches., *see* THORNTON.

Childrey Oxon. *Cillarthe* 950, *Celrea* 1086 (DB). Named from Childrey Brook which probably means 'stream of a man called *Cilla or of a woman called Cille'. OE pers. name + *rīth*. Alternatively the first element may be an OE *cille 'a spring'.

Childswickham Heref. & Worcs. *Childeswicwon* 706, *Wicvene* 1086 (DB). Possibly OWelsh *guic 'lodge, wood' + *guoun 'plain, meadow, moor', with OE *cild 'young man'.

Childwall Mersey. *Cildeuuelle* 1086 (DB). 'Spring or stream where young people assemble'. OE *cild* + *wella*.

Chilfrome Dorset. *Frome* 1086 (DB), *Childefrome* 1206. 'Estate on the River Frome belonging to the young men'. Celtic river-name (*see* FROME) with OE *cild*.

Chilgrove W. Sussex. *Chelegrave* 1200. 'Grove in a gorge or gulley', or 'grove of a man called Cēola'. OE *ceole* or OE pers. name + *grāf*.

Chilham Kent. *Cilleham* 1032, 1086 (DB). 'Homestead or village of a man called *Cilla or of a woman called Cille'. OE pers. name + *hām*. Alternatively the first element may be an OE *cille 'a spring'.

Chillenden Kent. *Ciollandene* c.833. *Cilledene* 1086 (DB). 'Valley of a man called Ciolla'. OE pers. name (genitive *-n*) + *denu*.

Chillerton I. of Wight. *Celertune* 1086 (DB). 'Farmstead of a man called Cēolheard' or 'enclosed farmstead in a valley'. OE pers. name + *tūn*, or OE *ceole* + *geard* + *tūn*.

Chillesford Suffolk. *Cesefortda* 1086 (DB), *Chiselford* 1211. 'Gravel ford'. OE *ceosol* + *ford*.

Chillingham Northum. *Cheulingeham* 1187. 'Homestead or village of the family or followers of a man called *Ceofel'. OE pers. name + *-inga-* + *hām*.

Chillington Devon. *Cedelintone* 1086 (DB). 'Estate associated with a man called *Ceadela'. OE pers. name + *-ing-* + *tūn*.

Chillington Somerset. *Cheleton* 1261. 'Farmstead of a man called Cēola'. OE pers. name + *tūn*.

Chilmark Wilts. *Cigelmerc* 984, *Chilmerc* 1086 (DB). 'Boundary mark consisting of a pole'. OE *cigel* + *mearc*.

Chilson Oxon. *Cildestuna* c.1200. 'Farmstead of the young man'. OE *cild* + *tūn*.

Chilsworthy Devon. *Chelesworde* 1086 (DB). 'Enclosure of a man called Cēol'. OE pers. name + *worth*.

Chiltern Hills Bucks. *Ciltern* 1009. Probably identical in origin with the following name, here used of a district.

Chilthorne Domer Somerset. *Cilterne* 1086 (DB), *Chilterne Dunmere* 1280. Possibly a derivative of an OE or pre-English word *celte or *cilte which may have meant 'hill-slope'. Manorial addition from the Dummere family, here in the 13th cent.

Chiltington, East E. Sussex. *Childetune* 1086 (DB). Probably identical with the following name.

Chiltington, West W. Sussex. *Cillingtun* 969, *Cilletone* 1086 (DB). Possibly 'farmstead at a hill-slope called *Cilte'. OE or pre-English hill-name + *-ing* or *-ing-* + *tūn*. Alternatively the first element may be an ancient district-name *Ciltine* derived from the same word.

Chilton, a place-name found in various counties, usually 'farm of the young (noble)men', from OE *cild* + *tūn*; for example: **Chilton** Bucks. *Ciltone* 1086 (DB). **Chilton** Durham. *Ciltona* 1091. **Chilton** Oxon. *Cylda tun* c.895, *Cilletone* 1086 (DB). **Chilton Cantelo** Somerset. *Childeton* 1201, *Chiltone Cauntilo* 1361. Manorial addition from the Cantelu family, here in the 13th cent. **Chilton Foliat** Wilts. *Cilletone* 1086 (DB), *Chilton Foliat* 1221. Manorial addition from the Foliot family, here in the 13th cent. **Chilton Street** Suffolk. *Chilton* 1254. Affix *street* probably has the sense 'straggling village'. **Chilton Trinity** Somerset. *Cildetone* 1086 (DB), *Chilton Sancte Trinitatis* 1431. Affix from the dedication of the church.
    However the following Chilton has a different origin: **Chilton Polden** Somerset. *Ceptone* 1086 (DB), *Chauton* 1303. Possibly 'farmstead on chalk or limestone', from OE *cealc* + *tūn*, with affix from the nearby Polden Hills (*Poeldune* 725, from OE *dūn* 'hill added to a Celtic name *Bouelt* 705 which probably means 'cow pasture').

Chilvers Coton Warwicks., *see* COTON.

Chilwell Notts. *Chideuuelle* 1086 (DB). 'Spring or stream where young people assemble'. OE *cild* + *wella*.

Chilworth, 'enclosure of a man called Cēola'. OE pers. name + *worth*: **Chilworth** Hants. *Celeorde* 1086 (DB). **Chilworth** Surrey. *Celeorde* 1086 (DB).

Chimney Oxon. *Ceommanyg* 1069. 'Island, or dry ground in marsh, of a man called *Ceomma'. OE pers. name (genitive *-n*) + *ēg*.

Chineham Hants. *Chineham* 1086 (DB). 'Homestead or enclosure in a deep valley'. OE *cinu* + *hām* or *hamm*.

Chingford Gtr. London. *Cingefort* |sic| 1086 (DB), *Chingelford* c.1243. 'Shingle ford'. OE *cingel* + *ford*.

Chinley Derbys. *Chynleye* 1285. 'Wood or clearing in a deep valley'. OE *cinu* + *lēah*.

Chinnock, East & *Chinnock, West* Somerset. *Cinnuc* c.950, *Cinioch* 1086 (DB). Possibly a derivative of OE *cinu* 'deep valley', but perhaps an old hill-name of Celtic origin.

Chinnor Oxon. *Chennore* 1086 (DB). 'Slope of a man called *Ceonna'. OE pers. name + *ōra*.

Chipnall Shrops. *Ceppacanole* 1086 (DB), *Chippeknol* c.1250. 'Knoll of a man called *Cippa', or 'knoll where logs are got'. OE pers. name or OE *cipp* (genitive plural *cippa*) + *cnoll*.

Chippenham, probably 'river-meadow of a man called *Cippa', OE pers. name (genitive -*n*) + *hamm*: **Chippenham** Cambs. *Chipeham* 1086 (DB). **Chippenham** Wilts. *Cippanhamme* c.900, *Chipeham* 1086 (DB).

Chipperfield Herts. *Chiperfeld* 1375. Probably 'open land where traders or merchants meet'. OE *cēapere* + *feld*.

Chipping Lancs. *Chippin* 1203. OE *cēping* 'a market, a market-place'.

Chipping as affix, *see* main name, e.g. for **Chipping Barnet** (Gtr. London) *see* BARNET.

Chipstead, 'market-place', OE *cēap-stede*: **Chipstead** Kent. *Chepsteda* 1191. **Chipstead** Surrey. *Tepestede* |*sic*| 1086 (DB), *Chepstede* 1100–29.

Chirbury Shrops. *Cyricbyrig* mid 11th cent., *Cireberie* 1086 (DB). 'Fortified place or manor with or near a church'. OE *cirice* + *burh* (dative *byrig*).

Chirk (*Y Waun*) Wrex. *Chirk* 1295, *Cheyrk* 1309. '(Place on the) River Ceiriog'. The Celtic river name may mean 'favoured one'. The Welsh name means 'the moorland' (Welsh *y* + *gwaun*).

Chirton Wilts. *Ceritone* 1086 (DB). 'Village with a church'. OE *cirice* + *tūn*.

Chisbury Wilts. *Cissanbyrig* early 10th cent., *Cheseberie* 1086 (DB). Possibly 'pre-English earthwork associated with a man called Cissa'. OE pers. name + *burh* (dative *byrig*). Alternatively the first element could be an OE word **cisse* (genitive -*an*) 'a gravelly feature'.

Chiselborough Somerset. *Ceoselbergon* 1086 (DB). 'Gravel mound or hill'. OE *cisel* + *beorg*.

Chiseldon Wilts. *Cyseldene* c.880, *Chiseldene* 1086 (DB). 'Gravel valley'. OE *cisel* + *denu*.

Chisenbury Wilts. *Chesigeberie* 1086 (DB), *Chisingburi* 1202. Possibly 'stronghold of the dwellers on the gravel'. OE **cis* + -*inga*- + *burh* (dative *byrig*). Alternatively the first element could be an OE word **cising* 'gravelly place'.

Chishill, Great & *Chishill, Little* Cambs. *Cishella* 1086 (DB). 'Gravel hill'. OE **cis* + *hyll*.

Chisholme Sc. Bord. *Chesehome* 1254. 'Cheese barn'. OE *cēse* + *helm*. The name implies a rich pasture.

Chislehampton Oxon. *Hentone* 1086 (DB), *Chiselentona* 1147. Originally 'high farm, farm situated on high land'. OE *hēah* (dative *hean*) + *tūn*, with the later addition of OE *cisel* 'gravel'.

Chislehurst Gtr. London. *Cyselhyrst* 973. 'Gravelly wooded hill'. OE *cisel* + *hyrst*.

Chislet Kent. *Cistelet* 605, 1086 (DB). Possibly OE **cistelet* 'a chestnut copse'. Alternatively the name may be a compound of OE **cist* 'chestnut tree' or *cist, cyst* 'chest, container' with (*ge*)*lǣt* 'water-conduit'.

Chiswellgreen Herts., first recorded in 1782, but possibly 'the gravelly spring or stream', from OE **cis* + *wella*, with the later addition of green.

Chiswick Gtr. London. *Ceswican* c.1000. 'Farm where cheese is made'. OE **cīese* + *wīc*.

Chisworth Derbys. *Chisewrde* 1086 (DB). Possibly 'enclosure of a man called Cissa'. OE pers. name + *worth*. Alternatively the first element could be an OE word **cisse* (genitive -*an*) 'a gravelly feature'.

Chithurst W. Sussex. *Titesherste* |*sic*| 1086 (DB), *Chyteherst* 1279. Possibly 'wooded hill of a man called *Citta'. OE pers. name + *hyrst*. Alternatively the first element may be Celtic **cēd* 'wood'.

Chitterne Wilts. *Chetre* 1086 (DB), *Chytterne* 1268. Possibly a derivative of Celtic **cēd* 'wood'.

Chittlehamholt Devon. *Chitelhamholt* 1288. 'Wood of the dwellers in the valley'. OE *cietel* + *hǣme* + *holt*.

Chittlehampton Devon. *Citremetona* 1086 (DB), *Chitelhamtone* 1176. 'Farmstead of the dwellers in the valley'. OE *cietel* + *hǣme* + *tūn*.

Chittoe Wilts. *Chetewe* 1167. Possibly a derivative of Celtic **cēd* 'wood'.

Chivelstone Devon. *Cheueletona* 1086 (DB). 'Farmstead of a man called *Ceofel'. OE pers. name + *tūn*.

Chobham Surrey. *Cebeham* 1086 (DB). 'Homestead or enclosure of a man called *Ceabba'. OE pers. name + *hām* or *hamm*.

Cholderton Wilts. *Celdretone* 1086 (DB). 'Estate associated with a man called Cēolhere or Cēolrēd'. OE pers. name + -*ing*- + *tūn*.

Chollerton Northum. *Choluerton* c.1175. Probably 'farmstead of a man called Cēolferth'. OE pers. name + *tūn*.

Cholmondeley Ches. *Calmundelei* 1086 (DB), *Chelmundeleia* c.1200. 'Woodland clearing of a man called Cēolmund'. OE pers. name + *lēah*.

Cholsey Oxon. *Ceolesig* c.895, *Celsei* 1086 (DB). 'Island, or dry ground in marsh, of a man called Cēol'. OE pers. name + *īeg*.

Cholstrey Heref. & Worcs. *Cerlestreu* 1086 (DB). 'Tree of the freeman or of a man called Ceorl'. OE *ceorl* or OE pers. name + *trēow*.

Choppington Northum. *Cebbington* c.1050. 'Estate associated with a man called *Ceabba'. OE pers. name + -*ing*- + *tūn*.

Chopwell Tyne & Wear. *Cheppwell* c.1155. Probably 'spring where trading takes place'. OE *cēap* + *wella*.

Chorley, 'clearing of the freemen or peasants', OE *ceorl* (genitive plural -*a*) + *lēah*: **Chorley** Ches., near Nantwich. *Cerlere* 1086 (DB). **Chorley** Lancs. *Cherleg* 1246. **Chorley** Staffs. *Cherlec* 1231.

Chorleywood Herts. *Cherle* 1278, *Charlewoode* 1524. 'Clearing of the freemen or peasants'. OE *ceorl* (genitive plural -*a*) + *lēah*, with the later addition of *wood*.

Chorlton, usually 'farmstead of the freemen or peasants', OE *ceorl* (genitive plural -*a*) + *tūn*: **Chorlton** Ches., near Nantwich. *Cerletune* 1086 (DB). **Chorlton Lane** Ches. *Cherlton* 1283. **Chorlton, Chapel** Staffs. *Cerletone* 1086 (DB).
However the following Chorlton has a different origin: **Chorlton cum Hardy** Lancs. *Cholreton* 1243. 'Farmstead of a

man called Cēolfrith'. OE pers. name + *tūn*. Now united
with Hardy (*Hardey* 1555, possibly 'hard island' from OE
heard + *ēg*) as indicated by the Latin preposition *cum*
'with'.

Chowley Ches. *Celelea* 1086 (DB). 'Wood or clearing of a
man called Cēola'. OE pers. name + *lēah*.

Chrishall Essex. *Cristeshala* 1086 (DB). 'Nook of land
dedicated to Christ'. OE *Crist* + *halh*.

Christchurch Dorset. *Christecerce* c.1125. 'Church of
Christ'. OE *Crist* + *cirice*. Earlier called *Twynham*, 'place
between the rivers'. OE *betwēonan* + *ēa* (dative plural
ēam).

Christchurch (*Eglwys y Drindod*) Newpt. *Christi Ecclesia*
1290, *Christeschurche* 1291. 'Church of Christ'. The Welsh
name means 'church of the Trinity', a more recent church
dedication.

Christian Malford Wilts. *Cristemaleford* 937,
Cristemeleford 1086 (DB). 'Ford by a cross'. OE *cristel-
mǣl* + *ford*.

Christleton Ches. *Cristetone* 1086 (DB). *Cristentune* 12th
cent. 'Christian farmstead', or 'farmstead of the
Christians'. OE *Cristen* (as adjective or noun) + *tūn*.

Christmas Common Oxon., hamlet recorded as *Christmas* (*Green*) in the early 18th cent., so called from *Christmas Coppice* 1617 which may have been a coppice where
holly trees (traditionally associated with Christmas) were
abundant. The similar **Christmaspie** Surrey is so called
from *Christmas Pie Farm* 1823, a whimsical name probably
to be associated with the Christmas family mentioned in
16th cent. records.

Christon N. Som. *Crucheston* 1197. 'Farmstead at the
hill'. Celtic **crūg* + OE *tūn*.

Christow Devon. *Cristinestowe* 1244. 'Christian place'.
OE *Cristen* + *stōw*.

Chudleigh Devon. *Ceddelegam* c.1150. 'Clearing of a man
called Ciedda', or 'clearing in a hollow'. OE pers. name or
OE *cēod(e)* + *lēah*.

Chulmleigh Devon. *C(h)almonleuga* 1086 (DB). 'Clearing
of a man called Cēolmund'. OE pers. name + *lēah*.

Chunal Derbys. *Ceolhal* 1086 (DB). 'Nook of land of a man
called Cēola'. or 'nook of land near the ravine', OE pers.
name or OE *ceole* + *halh*.

Church Lancs. *Chirche* 1202. '(Place at) the church'. OE
cirice.

Church as affix, *see* main name, e.g. for **Church Fenton** (N.
Yorks.) *see* FENTON.

Church Hill Fermanagh. *Church-Hill* 1837. The village
was founded in the early 17th cent. and named after a
Church of Ireland church.

Church Knowle Dorset. *Cnolle* 1086 (DB). *Churchecnolle*
1346. OE *cnoll* 'hill-top' with the later addition of *cirice*
'church'.

Churcham Glos. *Hamme* 1086 (DB), *Churchehamme* 1200.
OE *hamm* 'river meadow' with the later addition of *cirice*
'church'.

Churchdown Glos. *Circesdune* 1086 (DB). Celtic **crūg*
'hill' with explanatory OE *dūn* 'hill'.

Churchill, usually from Celtic **crūg* 'hill' with explanatory OE *hyll* 'hill' examples include: **Churchill** Devon, near
Barnstaple. *Cercelle* 1086 (DB). **Churchill** Heref. & Worcs.,
near Kidderminster. *Cercehalle |sic|* 1086 (DB), *Circhul* 11th
cent. **Churchill** Oxon. *Cercelle* 1086 (DB). **Churchill** N. Som.
Cherchille 1201.

Churchover Warwicks. *Wavre* 1086 (DB), *Chirchewavre*
12th cent. Originally a river-name (an earlier name for the
River Swift) meaning 'winding stream' from OE *wæfre*
'wandering', with the later addition of *cirice* 'church'.

Churchstanton Somerset. *Stantone* 1086 (DB),
Cheristontone 13th cent. 'Farmstead on a stony ground'.
OE *stān* + *tūn*, with later addition of OE *cirice* 'church'.

Churchstow Devon. *Churechestowe* 1242. 'Place with a
church'. OE *cirice* + *stōw*.

Churn (river) Glos., *see* CERNEY.

Churt Surrey. *Cert* 685–7. OE *cert* 'rough ground'.

Churton Ches. *Churton* 12th cent. 'Village with a church'.
OE *cirice* + *tūn*.

Churwell W. Yorks. *Cherlewell* 1226. 'Spring or stream of
the freemen or peasants'. OE *ceorl* + *wella*.

Cilgerran Pemb. *Kilgerran* 1165, *Chilgerran* 1166.
'Cerran's corner of land'. Welsh *cil* + Celtic pers. name.

Cilgeti. *See* KILGETTY.

Cinderford Glos. *Sinderford* 1258. 'Ford built up with
cinders or slag (from iron-smelting)'. OE *sinder* + *ford*.

Cirencester Glos. *Korinion* c.150, *Cirenceaster* c.900,
Cirecestre 1086 (DB). 'Roman camp or town called
Corinion'. OE *ceaster* added to the reduced form of a Celtic
name of uncertain origin and meaning.

Clabby (*Clabaigh*) Fermanagh. *Clabby* 1611. Possibly
'place of pock-marked land'.

Clackmannan Clac. *Clacmanan* 1147. 'Stone of Manau'.
Welsh *clog*. *Manau* is the name of the district. The 'stone'
is a glacial rock preserved in the middle of the town.

Clacton on Sea, Great & *Little Clacton* Essex.
Claccingtune c.1000, *Clachintune* 1086 (DB). 'Estate associated with a man called **Clacc*'. OE pers. name + -*ing*-
+ *tūn*.

Claddach Kirkibost W. Isles (North Uist). *Kirkabol*
1654. 'Shore by the homestead of the church'. Gaelic
claddach + OScand. *kirkja* + *bólstathr*.

Claddagh (*Cladach*) Galway, Kerry. 'Shore'.

Claddaghduff (*An Cladach Dubh*) Galway. 'The black
shore'.

Clady (*Cladach*) Donegal, Tyrone. 'Shore'.

Claggan (*Cloigeann*) Donegal. 'Head'.

Claines Heref. & Worcs. *Cleinesse* 11th cent. 'Clay
headland'. OE *clǣg* + *næss*.

Clanabogan (*Cluain Uí Bhogáin*) Tyrone. *Clonyboggan*
c.1655. 'Ó Bogáin's pasture'.

Clandeboy (*Clann Aodha Buí*) Down. *Cloinn Aedha
buidhe* 1319. 'Clan of yellow Aodh'.

Clandon, East & *Clandon West* Surrey. *Clanedun* 1086 (DB). 'Clean hill', i.e. 'hill free from weeds or other unwanted growth'. OE *clǣne* + *dūn*.

Clane (*Claonadh*) Kildare. 'Slanted ford'.

Clanfield, 'clean open land', i.e. 'open land free from weeds or other unwanted growth', OE *clǣne* + *feld*: **Clanfield** Hants. *Clanefeld* 1207. **Clanfield** Oxon. *Chenefelde* |*sic*| 1086 (DB). *Clenefeld* 1196.

Clanville Hants. *Clavesfelle* |*sic*| 1086 (DB), *Clanefeud* 1259. Identical in origin with the previous names.

Clapham, usually 'homestead or enclosure near a hill or hills', OE **clopp(a)* + *hām* or *hamm*: **Clapham** Beds. *Cloppham* 1060, *Clopeham* 1086 (DB). **Clapham** Gtr. London. *Cloppaham* c.880, *Clopeham* 1086 (DB). **Clapham** W. Sussex. *Clopeham* 1086 (DB).
   However the following Clapham has a different origin: **Clapham** N. Yorks. *Clapeham* 1086 (DB). 'Homestead or enclosure by the noisy stream'. OE **clæpe* + *hām* or *hamm*.

Clappersgate Cumbria. *Clappergate* 1588. 'Road or gate by the rough bridge'. ME *clapper* + OScand. *gata* or OE *geat*.

Clapton, 'farmstead or village near a hill or hills', OE **clopp(a)* + *tūn*; examples include: **Clapton** Glos. *Clopton* 1171–83. **Clapton** Northants. *Cloptun* c.960, *Clotone* 1086 (DB). **Clapton** Somerset, near Crewkerne. *Clopton* 1243. **Clapton in Gordano** N. Som. *Clotune* |*sic*| 1086 (DB), *Clopton* 1225. Gordano is an old district name (*Gordeyne* 1270), probably 'dirty or muddy valley', OE *gor* + *denu*.

Clara (*Clóirtheach*) Offaly. 'Level place'.

Clarborough Notts. *Claureburg* 1086 (DB). 'Old fortification overgrown with clover'. OE *clǣfre* + *burh*.

Clare (*Clár*) Armagh, Down, Tyrone. 'Plain'.

Clare Suffolk. *Clara* 1086 (DB). Perhaps originally an old river-name of Celtic origin, identical with that found in HIGHCLERE.

Clare Island (*Cliara*) Mayo. 'Clergy island'.

Clareen (*An Cláirín*) Offaly. 'The little plain'.

Claregalway (*Baile Chláir*) Galway. 'Plain of Galway'.

Claremorris (*Clár Chlainne Muiris*) Mayo. 'Plain of the children of Muiris'.

Clarina (*Clár Aidhne*) Limerick. 'Plank bridge of Aidhne'.

Clarinbridge (*Droichead an Chláirín*) Galway. 'Bridge of the little plank'.

Clas-ar-Wy. *See* GLASBURY.

Clash (*Clais*) Tipperary, Wicklow. 'Ravine'.

Clashmore (*Clais Mhór*) Waterford. 'Big ravine'.

Clatford, Goodworth & *Clatford, Upper* Hants. *Cladford, Godorde* 1086 (DB). 'Ford where burdock grows'. OE *clāte* + *ford*. Goodworth (originally a separate name) means 'enclosure of a man called Gōda', OE pers. name + *worth*.

Clatworthy Somerset. *Clateurde* 1086 (DB), *Clatewurthy* 1243. 'Enclosure where burdock grows'. OE *clāte* + *worth* (replaced by *worthig*).

Claudy (*Clóidigh*) Derry. *Cládech* c.1680. 'Strong-flowing one'. The name probably refers to a section of the River Faughan here.

Claughton, 'farmstead on or by a hill', OE **clacc* + *tūn*: **Claughton** Lancs., near Garstang. *Clactune* 1086 (DB). **Claughton** Lancs., near Lancaster. *Clactun* 1086 (DB).

Claverdon Warwicks. *Clavendone* |*sic*| 1086 (DB), *Claverdona* 1123. 'Hill where clover grows'. OE *clǣfre* + *dūn*.

Claverham N. Som. *Claveham* 1086 (DB). 'Homestead or enclosure where clover grows'. OE *clǣfre* + *hām* or *hamm*.

Clavering Essex. *Clǣfring* c.1000, *Clauelinga* 1086 (DB). 'Place where clover grows'. OE *clǣfre* + *-ing*.

Claverley Shrops. *Claverlege* 1086 (DB). 'Clearing where clover grows'. OE *clǣfre* + *lēah*.

Claverton B. & NE. Som. *Clatfordtun* c.1000, *Claftertone* 1086 (DB). 'Farmstead by the ford where burdock grows'. OE *clāte* + *ford* + *tūn*.

Clawdd Offa. *See* OFFA'S DYKE.

Clawson, Long Leics. *Clachestone* 1086 (DB). 'Farmstead on a hill, or of a man called Klakkr'. OE **clacc* or OScand. pers. name + OE *tūn*.

Clawton Devon. *Clavetone* 1086 (DB). 'Farmstead at the tongue of land'. OE *clawu* + *tūn*.

Claxby, 'farmstead of a man called Klakkr', OScand. pers. name + *bý*: **Claxby** Lincs., near Alford. *Clachesbi* 1086 (DB). **Claxby** Lincs., near Market Rasen. *Cleaxbyg* 1066–8, *Clachesbi* 1086 (DB).

Claxton, 'farmstead on a hill, or of a man called Klakkr', OE **clacc* or OScand. pers. name + OE *tūn*: **Claxton** Norfolk. *Clakestona* 1086 (DB). **Claxton** N. Yorks. *Claxtorp* 1086 (DB), *Clakeston* 1176. Second element originally OScand. *thorp* 'outlying farmstead'.

Clay Coton Northants. *Cotes* 12th cent., *Cleycotes* 1284. 'Cottages in the clayey district'. OE *cot* (dative plural *cotum* or a ME plural *coten*) with the later addition of *clǣg*.

Clay Cross Derbys., a late name, first recorded in 1734, probably named from a local family called Clay.

Claybrooke Magna Leics. *Claibroc* 1086 (DB). 'Clayey brook'. OE *clǣg* + *brōc*, with Latin affix *magna* 'great'.

Claydon, 'Clayey hill', OE *clǣgig* + *dūn*: **Claydon** Oxon. *Cleindona* 1109. **Claydon** Suffolk. *Clainduna* 1086 (DB). **Claydon, Botolph**, & **Claydon, East**, & **Claydon, Middle** Bucks. *Claindone* 1086 (DB), *Botle Cleidun* 1224, *Est Cleydon* 1247, *Middelcleydon* 1242. Affixes from OE *bōtl* 'house, building', *ēast* 'east', and *middel* 'middle'. **Claydon, Steeple** Bucks. *Claindone* 1086 (DB), *Stepel Cleydon* 13th cent. Affix from OE *stēpel* 'steeple, tower'.

Claygate Surrey. *Claigate* 1086 (DB). 'Gate or gap in the clayey district'. OE *clǣg* + *geat*.

Clayhanger W. Mids. *Cleyhungre* 13th cent. 'Clayey wooded slope'. OE *clǣg* + *hangra*. The same name occurs in Ches. and Devon.

Clayhidon Devon. *Hidone* 1086 (DB), *Cleyhidon* 1485. 'Hill where hay is made'. OE *hī(e)g* + *dūn*, with the later addition of OE *clǣg* 'clay'.

Claypole Lincs. *Claipol* 1086 (DB). 'Clayey pool'. OE *clǣg* + *pōl*.

Clayton, 'farmstead on clayey soil', OE *clǣg* + *tūn*; examples include: **Clayton** S. Yorks. *Claitone* 1086 (DB). **Clayton** Staffs. *Claitone* 1086 (DB). **Clayton** W. Sussex. *Claitune* 1086 (DB). **Clayton** W. Yorks. *Claitone* 1086 (DB). **Clayton-le-Moors** Lancs. *Cleyton* 1243. Affix 'on the moorland' from OE *mōr*, the French definite article *le* remaining after loss of the preposition. **Clayton-le-Woods** Lancs. *Cleitonam* 1160. Affix 'in the woodland' from OE *wudu*, with French *le* as in previous name. **Clayton West** W. Yorks. *Claitone* 1086 (DB).

Clayworth Notts. *Clauorde* 1086 (DB). 'Enclosure on the low curving hill'. OE *clawu* + *worth*.

Cleadon Tyne & Wear. *Clyvedon* 1280. 'Hill of the cliffs'. OE *clif* (genitive plural *clifa*) + *dūn*.

Clearwell Glos. *Clouerwalle* c.1282. 'Spring or stream where clover grows'. OE *clāfre* + *wella*.

Cleasby N. Yorks. *Clesbi* 1086 (DB). 'Farmstead or village of a man called Kleppr or *Kleiss*'. OScand. pers. name + *bý*.

Cleatlam Durham. *Cletlinga* c.1050, *Cletlum* 1271. '(Place at) the clearings where burdock grows'. OE *clǣte* + *lēah* (dative plural *lēaum*), with *-ingas* 'dwellers at' in the earliest form.

Cleator (Moor) Cumbria. *Cletergh* c.1200. Probably 'hill pasture where burdock grows'. OE *clǣte* + OScand. *erg*.

Cleckheaton W. Yorks. *Hetun* 1086 (DB), *Claketon* 1285. 'High farmstead, farmstead situated on high land'. OE *hēah* + *tūn*. The affix *Cleck-* is from OScand. *klakkr* 'a hill'.

Clee St Margaret Shrops. *Cleie* 1086 (DB), *Clye Sancte Margarete* 1285. Named from the Clee Hills, probably an OE *clēo* 'ball-shaped, rounded hill'. Affix from the dedication of the church.

Cleethorpes NE. Lincs., not recorded before the 17th cent., meaning 'hamlets (OScand. *thorp*) near Clee'. The latter, now **Old Clee**, is *Cleia* in 1086 (DB), from OE *clǣg* 'clay' with reference to the soil.

Cleeton St Mary Shrops. *Cleotun* 1241. 'Farmstead by the hills called Clee', *see* CLEE ST MARGARET. OE *tūn*.

Cleeve, *Cleve*, '(place) at the cliff or bank', OE *clif* (dative *clife*); examples include: **Cleeve** N. Som. *Clive* 1243. **Cleeve, Bishop's** Glos. *Clife* 8th cent., *Clive* 1086 (DB), *Bissopes Clive* 1284. Affix from its early possession by the Bishops of Worcester. **Cleeve, Old** Somerset. *Clive* 1086 (DB). **Cleeve Prior** Heref. & Worcs. *Clive* 1086 (DB), *Clyve Prior* 1291. Affix from its early possession by the Prior of Worcester.

Cleggan (*An Cloigeann*) Galway. 'The head'.

Clehonger Heref. & Worcs. *Cleunge* 1086 (DB). 'Clayey wooded slope'. OE *clǣg* + *hangra*.

Clench Wilts. *Clenche* 1289. OE *clenc* 'hill'.

Clenchwarton Norfolk. *Ecleuuartuna* |*sic*| 1086 (DB), *Clenchewarton* 1196. Probably 'farmstead or village of the dwellers at the hill'. OE *clenc* + *-ware* + *tūn*.

Clent Heref. & Worcs. *Clent* 1086 (DB). OE *clent* 'rock, rocky hill'.

Cleobury Mortimer & *Cleobury North* Shrops. *Cleberie*, *Claiberie* 1086 (DB), *Clebury Mortimer* 1272, *Northclaibiry* 1222. 'Fortified place or manor near the hills called Clee', *see* CLEE ST MARGARET. OE *burh* (dative *byrig*). Manorial addition from the Mortemer family, here in the 11th cent., the other distinguishing affix being ME *north*.

Clerkenwell Gtr. London. *Clerkenwell* c.1150. 'Well or spring frequented by students'. ME *clerc* (plural *-en*) + OE *wella*.

Clevancy Wilts. *Clive* 1086 (DB), *Clif Wauncy* 1231. '(Place) at the cliff', from OE *clif* (dative *clife*), with manorial addition from the de Wancy family, here in the 13th cent.

Clevedon N. Som. *Clivedon* 1086 (DB). 'Hill of the cliffs'. OE *clif* (genitive plural *clifa*) + *dūn*.

Cleveland (district) Red. & Cleve. *Clivelanda* c.1110. 'District of cliffs, hilly district'. OE *clif* (genitive plural *clifa*) + *land*.

Cleveleys Lancs., not on record before early this cent., probably a manorial name from a family called Cleveley who may have come from Cleveley near Garstang (*Cliueleye* c.1180, 'woodland clearing near a cliff or bank', OE *clif* + *lēah*).

Clewer Somerset. *Cliveware* 1086 (DB). 'The dwellers on a river-bank'. OE *clif* + *-ware*. The same name occurs in Berks.

Cley next the Sea Norfolk. *Claia* 1086 (DB). OE *clǣg* 'clay, place with clayey soil'.

Cliburn Cumbria. *Clibbrun* c.1140. 'Stream by the cliff or bank'. OE *clif* + *burna*.

Cliddesden Hants. *Cleresden* |*sic*| 1086 (DB), *Cledesdene* 1194. Possibly 'valley of the rock or rocky hill'. OE *clȳde* + *denu*.

Cliff, *Cliffe*, *Clyffe*, '(place at) the cliff or bank', OE *clif*; examples include: **Cliffe** Kent. *Cliua* 10th cent., *Clive* 1086 (DB). **Cliffe** N. Yorks. *Clive* 1086 (DB). **Cliffe, King's** Northants. *Clive* 1086 (DB), *Kyngesclive* 1305. A royal manor in 1086. **Cliffe, North** & **Cliffe, South** E. R. Yorks. *Cliue* 1086 (DB). **Cliffe, West** Kent. *Wesclive* 1086 (DB). With OE *west* 'west'. **Clyffe Pypard** Wilts. *æt Clife* 983, *Clive* 1086 (DB), *Clive Pipard* 1291. Manorial affix from the Pipard family, here in the 13th cent.

Cliffony (*Cliafuine*) Sligo. 'Hurdle thicket'.

Clifford, 'ford at a cliff or bank', OE *clif* + *ford*: **Clifford** Heref. & Worcs. *Cliford* 1086 (DB). **Clifford** W. Yorks. *Cliford* 1086 (DB). **Clifford Chambers** Warwicks. *Clifforda* 922, *Clifort* 1086 (DB), *Chaumberesclifford* 1388. Affix from the chamberlain (ME *chamberere*) of St Peter's Gloucester, given the manor in 1099.

Clifton, a common place-name, 'farmstead on or near a cliff or bank', OE *clif* + *tūn*; examples include: **Clifton** Beds. *Cliftune* 10th cent., *Cliftone* 1086 (DB). **Clifton** Brist. *Clistone* 1086 (DB). **Clifton** Cumbria. *Clifton* 1204. **Clifton** Derbys. *Cliftune* 1086 (DB). **Clifton** Notts. *Cliftone* 1086 (DB). **Clifton Campville** Staffs. *Clyfton* 942, *Cliftune* 1086 (DB). Manorial addition from the de Camvill family, here in the 13th cent. **Clifton Hampden** Oxon. *Cliftona* 1146. The affix first occurs in 1836, and may be from a family called Hampden. **Clifton, North** & **Clifton, South** Notts. *Cliftone* 1086 (DB), *Nort Clifton* c.1160, *Suth Clifton* 1280. **Clifton Reynes** Bucks. *Cliftone* 1086 (DB), *Clyfton Reynes* 1383. Manorial addition from the de Reynes family, here in the early 14th cent. **Clifton upon Dunsmore** Warwicks. *Cliptone* 1086 (DB), *Clifton super Donesmore* 1306. For the affix, *see* RYTON-ON-DUNSMORE. **Clifton upon Teme** Heref. & Worcs. *Cliftun ultra Tamedam* 934, *Clistune |sic|* 1086 (DB). Teme is an old Celtic river-name, *see* TENBURY WELLS.

Cliftonville Kent, a modern name invented for this 19th cent. resort.

Climping W. Sussex. *Clepinges |sic|* 1086 (DB), *Clympinges* 1228. '(Settlement of) the family or followers of a man called *Climp'. OE pers. name + *-ingas*.

Clint N. Yorks. *Clint* 1208. OScand. *klint* 'a rocky cliff, a steep bank'.

Clippesby Norfolk. *Clepesbei* 1086 (DB). 'Farmstead or village of a man called Klyppr or *Klippr'. OScand. pers. name + *bý*.

Clipsham Rutland. *Kilpesham* 1203. Probably 'homestead or enclosure of a man called *Cylp'. OE pers. name + *hām* or *hamm*.

Clipston(e), 'farmstead of a man called Klyppr or *Klippr', OScand. pers. name + OE *tūn*: **Clipston** Northants. *Clipestune* 1086 (DB). **Clipston** Notts. *Cliston* 1198. **Clipstone** Notts. *Clipestune* 1086 (DB).

Clitheroe Lancs. *Cliderhou* 1102. 'Hill with loose stones'. OE *clȳder, *clider + OE *hōh* or OScand. *haugr*.

Clive Shrops. *Clive* 1255. '(Place) at the cliff or bank'. OE *clif* (dative *clife*).

Clodock Heref. & Worcs. *Ecclesia Sancti Clitauci* c.1150. '(The church of) St. Clydog'. From the patron saint of the church.

Clogh (*An Chloch*) Antrim, Kilkenny. 'The stone castle'.

Clogh Mills (*Muileann na Cloiche*) Antrim. 'Mill of the stone'.

Cloghan (*An Clochán*) Donegal, Offaly, Westmeath. 'The stony place'.

Cloghane (*An Clochán*) Kerry. 'The stony place'.

Cloghaneely (*Cloich Chionnaola*) (district) Donegal. *Cloíche Chinnfhaoladh* 1284. 'Cionnaola's stone'.

Cloghboley (*Clochbhuaile*) Sligo. 'Stone of the milking place'.

Cloghbrack (*An Chloch Bhreac*) Mayo. 'The speckled stone'.

Clogheen (*An Chloichín*) Tipperary, Waterford. 'The little stone'.

Clogher (*An Chlochar*) Mayo, Tyrone. 'The stony place'.

Cloghernach (*Clocharnach*) Waterford. 'Stony place'.

Cloghjordan (*Cloch Shiurdáin*) Tipperary. 'Jordan's stone castle'.

Cloghmore (*An Chloch Mhór*) Mayo, Monaghan. 'The big stone'.

Cloghore (*Cloich Óir*) Donegal. 'Gold stone'.

Cloghran (*Clochrán*) Dublin. 'Stepping-stones'.

Cloghroe (*Cloch Rua*) Cork. 'Red stone'.

Cloghy (*Clochaigh*) Down. *Cloghie* 1623. 'Stony place'.

Clohamon (*Cloch Amainn*) Wexford. 'Hamon's stone castle'.

Clomantagh (*Cloch Mhantach*) Kilkenny. 'Gapped stone'.

Clonadacasey (*Cluain Fhada Uí Chathasaigh*) Laois. 'Ó Cathasaigh's long pasture'.

Clonakenny (*Cluain Uí Chionaoith*) Tipperary. 'Ó Cionaoith's pasture'.

Clonakilty (*Cloich na Coillte*) Cork. 'Stone of the woods'.

Clonalvy (*Cluain Ailbhe*) Meath. 'Ailbhe's pasture'.

Clonard (*Cluain Ioraird*) Meath. 'Iorard's pasture'.

Clonard (*Cluain Ard*) Wexford. 'High pasture'.

Clonaslee (*Cluain na Slí*) Laois. 'Pasture of the path'.

Clonbanin (*Cluain Báinín*) Cork. 'Pasture of the white tweed'.

Clonbern (*Cluain Bheirn*) Galway. 'Bearn's pasture'.

Clonbulloge (*Cluain Bolg*) Offaly. 'Pasture of the bulges'.

Cloncagh (*Cluain Cath*) Limerick. 'Pasture of battles'.

Cloncreen (*Cluain Crainn*) Offaly. 'Pasture of the tree'.

Cloncurry (*Cluain Curraigh*) Kildare. 'Pasture of the marsh'.

Clondalkin (*Cluain Dolcáin*) Dublin. 'Dolcán's pasture'.

Clondarragh (*Cluain Darach*) Wexford. 'Pasture of the oak tree'.

Clondaw (*Cluain Dáith*) Wexford. 'Dáith's pasture'.

Clondrohid (*Cluain Droichead*) Cork. 'Pasture of the bridges'.

Clondulane (*Cluain Dalláin*) Cork. 'Dallán's pasture'.

Clonea (*Cluain Fhia*) Waterford. 'Pasture of the deer'.

Clonee (*Cluain Aodha*) Meath. 'Aodh's pasture'.

Cloneen (*An Cluainín*) Tipperary. 'The little pasture'.

Clonegall (*Cluain na nGall*) Carlow. 'Pasture of the stones'.

Clonenagh (*Cluain Eidhneach*) Laois. 'Ivied pasture'.

Clones (*Cluain Eois*) Monaghan. (*abb*) *Cluana hEois* 701. 'Pasture of Eos'.

Cloney (*Cluanaidh*) Kildare. 'Pasture'.

Cloneygowan (*Cluain na nGamhan*) Offaly. 'Pasture of the calves'.

Clonfert (*Cluain Fearta*) Galway. 'Pasture of the grave'.

Clonfinlough (*Cluain Fionnlocha*) Offaly. 'Pasture of the white lake'.

Clongorey (*Cluain Guaire*) Kildare. 'Guaire's pasture'.

Clonkeen (*Cluain Chaoin*) Kerry. 'Pleasant pasture'.

Clonleigh (*Cluain Lao*) Donegal. 'Pasture of the calf'.

Clonlost (*Cluain Loiste*) Westmeath. 'Burnt meadow'.

Clonmacnoise (*Cluain Mic Nois*) Offaly. 'Pasture of the descendants of Noas'.

Clonmany (*Cluain Maine*) Donegal. *Clonmane* 1397. 'Maine's meadow'.

Clonmel (*Cluain Meala*) Tipperary. 'Pasture of honey'.

Clonmellon (*Cluain Mileáin*) Westmeath. 'Mileán's meadow'.

Clonmore (*Cluain Mhór*) Carlow, Tipperary. 'Large pasture'.

Clonmult (*Cluain Molt*) Cork. 'Pasture of wethers'.

Clonoe (*Cluain Eo*) Tyrone. *Clondeo* c.1306. 'Meadow of the yew tree'.

Clonoulty (*Cluain Ultaigh*) Tipperary. 'Pasture of the Ulstermen'. The official Irish name is *Cluain Abhla*, 'meadow of the apple tree'.

Clonroche (*Cluain an Róistigh*) Wexford. 'Roches' pasture'.

Clonroosk (*Cluain Rúisc*) Offaly. 'Pasture of the bark'.

Clonsilla (*Cluain Saileach*) Dublin. 'Pasture of the willow'.

Clontallagh (*Cluain tSalach*) Donegal. 'Dirty pasture'.

Clontarf (*Cluain Tarbh*) Dublin. 'Pasture of bulls'.

Clontibret (*Cluain Tiobrad*) Monaghan. (*Mocumae cruimthir*) *Clúana Tiprat* c.830. 'Pasture of the well'.

Clontoe (*Cluain Tó*) Tyrone. 'Tó's pasture'.

Clontuskert (*Cluain Tuaiscirt*) Galway. 'North pasture'.

Clontygora (*Cluainte Ó gCorra*) Armagh. *Clontegora* 1609. 'Pastures of the descendants of Corra'.

Clonygowan (*Cluain na nGamhan*) Offaly. 'Pasture of the calves'.

Cloon (*Cluain*) Clare, Mayo. 'Pasture'.

Cloonacool (*Cluain na Cúile*) Sligo. 'Pasture of the nook'.

Cloonagh (*Cluanach*) Westmeath. 'Meadowland'.

Cloonaghmore (*Cluaineach Mór*) Mayo. 'Large horse meadow'.

Cloondaff (*Cluain Damh*) Mayo. 'Ox meadow'.

Cloondara (*Cluain dá Ráth*) Longford. 'Pasture of the two forts'.

Cloone (*An Chluain*) Leitrim. 'The pasture'.

Clooney (*An Chluanaidh*) Donegal. 'The pasture land'.

Cloonfad (*Cluain Fhada*) Roscommon. 'Long pasture'.

Cloonkeavy (*Cluain Chiabhaigh*) Sligo. 'Hazy pasture'.

Cloonlara (*Cluain Lára*) Clare. 'Pasture of the mare'.

Cloonlough (*Cluain Lua*) Sligo. 'Lua's pasture'.

Cloontia (*Na Cluainte*) Mayo. 'The meadows'.

Cloonymorris (*Cluain Uí Mhuiris*) Galway. 'Ó Muiris's pasture'.

Clophill Beds. *Clopelle* 1086 (DB). 'Lumpy hill'. OE *clopp(a) + hyll*.

Clopton Suffolk. *Clop(e)tuna* 1086 (DB). 'Farmstead or village near a hill or hills'. OE *clopp(a) + tūn*.

Clorhane (*Clochrán*) Offaly. 'Stepping-stones'.

Closkelt (*Cloch Scoilte*) Down. 'Cleft rock'.

Clothall Herts. *Clatheala* c.1060, *Cladhele* 1086 (DB). 'Nook of land where burdock grows'. OE *clāte + healh*.

Clotton Ches. *Clotone* 1086 (DB). 'Farmstead at a dell or deep valley'. OE **clōh + tūn*.

Cloud, Temple B. & NE. Som. *La Clude* 1199. 'The (rocky) hill'. OE *clūd*. Affix probably refers to lands here held by the Knights Templars.

Clough (*Cloch*) Down. *Cloghmagherechat* 1634. 'Stone castle'. An earlier Irish name was *Cloch Mhachaire Cat*, 'stone castle of the plain of the cats'.

Cloughmore (*Cloch Mhór*) Down. 'Big stone'.

Cloughoge (*Clochóg*) Armagh. *Claghoge* 1661. 'Stony place'.

Cloughton N. Yorks. *Cloctune* 1086 (DB). 'Farmstead at a dell or deep valley'. OE **clōh + tūn*.

Clovelly Devon. *Cloveleia* 1086 (DB), *Clofely* 1296. Probably 'earthworks associated with a man called Fele(c)'. Cornish *cleath* 'dyke, bank' (referring to the ancient earthworks of Clovelly Dykes) + pers. name (which may also survive in the name of nearby **Velly**, *Felye* 1287).

Clowne Derbys. *Clune* c.1002, 1086 (DB). Named from the river which rises nearby; it is an old river-name identical with that in the following name.

Cloyfin (*An Chloich Fhionn*) Derry. *Illannecloghfynny* 1637. 'The white stone'.

Cloyne (*Cluain*) Cork. 'Pasture'.

Clun Shrops. *Clune* 1086 (DB). Named from the River Clun, which is an ancient pre-English river-name of uncertain meaning.

Clunbury Shrops. *Cluneberie* 1086 (DB). 'Fortified place on the River Clun'. Pre-English river-name + OE *burh* (dative *byrig*).

Clungunford Shrops. *Clone* 1086 (DB), *Cloune Goneford* 1242. 'Estate on the River Clun held by a man called Gunward'. Pre-English river-name + manorial addition from the name of the lord of the manor in the time of Edward the Confessor.

Clunton Shrops. *Clutone* |sic| 1086 (DB), *Cluntune* 12th cent. 'Farmstead or village on the River Clun'. Pre-English river-name + OE *tūn*.

Clutton, 'farmstead or village at a hill', from OE *clūd + tūn*: **Clutton** B. & NE. Som. *Cluttone* 851, *Clutone* 1086 (DB). **Clutton** Ches. *Clutone* 1086 (DB).

Clwyd (the historic county). *Cloid fluvium* 1191. '(District of) River Clwyd'. The river name means 'hurdle' (Welsh *clwyd*), perhaps referring to a ford or causeway made of hurdles.

Clydach Swan. *Cleudach* 1208. '(Place on the) River Clydach'. The Celtic river name means 'cleansing one' (British **clouta*).

Clyde. *See* CLYDEBANK.

Clydebank W. Dunb. *Burgh* in 1886. '(Place on the) bank of the River Clyde'. The Celtic river name means 'cleansing one'.

Clyffe Pypard Wilts., *see* CLIFF.

Clynnog-fawr Gwyd. *Kelynnauk c.*1291, *Kellynawc* 1346. 'Greater (place) abounding in holly'. Welsh *celyn* + *-og* + *mawr*. The name contrasts with *Clynnog Fechan* (Welsh *fechan*, 'small'), Angl.

Clyst Honiton Devon, see HONITON.

Clyst Hydon Devon. *Clist* 1086 (DB), *Clist Hydone* 1268. 'Estate on the River Clyst held by the de Hidune family' (here in the 13th cent.). Celtic river-name + manorial addition.

Clyst St George Devon. *Clisewic* 1086 (DB), *Clystwik Sancti Georgii* 1327. Originally 'dairy farm on the River Clyst'. Celtic river-name + OE *wīc*, with addition from the dedication of the church.

Clyst St Lawrence Devon. *Clist* 1086 (DB), *Clist Sancti Laurencii* 1203. 'Estate on the River Clyst', with addition from the dedication of the church.

Clyst St Mary Devon. *Clist Sancte Marie* 1242. Identical in origin with the previous name.

Clyst, Broad Devon. *Clistone* 1086 (DB), *Clistun c.*1100, *Brodeclyste* 1372. Like the following Devon places, named from the River Clyst, a Celtic river-name probably meaning 'clean stream'. Originally 'farmstead on the River Clyst' from OE *tūn*, later 'large estate on the River Clyst' from OE *brād*.

Coa (*Cuach*) Fermanagh. *Coagh* 1609. 'Hollow'.

Coachford (*Áth an Chóiste*) Cork. 'Ford of the coach'. The Irish name appears to have been devised to match the English, which itself may be a corruption of some other Irish name.

Coagh (*An Cuach*) Tyrone. *Coagh* 1639. 'The hollow'.

Coalbrookdale Shrops. *Caldebrok* 1250. '(Valley of) the cold brook'. OE *cald* + *brōc* with the later addition of *dale*.

Coalbrookvale. See NANTYGLO.

Coaley Glos. *Couelege* 1086 (DB). 'Clearing with a hut or shelter'. OE *cofa* + *lēah*.

Coalisland Tyrone. *Coal Island* 1837. The town was the inland port for the local coalfield. The equivalent Irish name is *Oileán an Ghuail*.

Coalville Leics., a name of 19th cent. origin, so called because it is in a coal-mining district.

Coan (*An Cuan*) Kilkenny. 'The recess'.

Coatbridge N. Lan. *Coittis* 1584. 'Bridge at Coats'. *Coats* is '(place with) cottages' (OE *cot*).

Coate Wilts., near Devizes. *Cotes* 1255. 'The cottage(s) or hut(s)'. OE *cot*.

Coates, 'the cottages or huts', from OE *cot*; examples include: **Coates** Cambs. *Cotes c.*1280. **Coates** Glos. *Cota* 1175. **Coates** Notts. *Cotes* 1200. **Coates, Great** NE. Lincs. *Cotes* 1086 (DB). **Coates, North** Lincs. *Nordcotis c.*1115. 'Cottages to the north (of FULSTOW)', OE *north*.

Coatham Red. & Cleve. *Cotum* 1123–8. '(Place) at the cottages or huts'. OE *cot* in a dative plural form *cotum*.

Coatham Mundeville Durham. *Cotum* 12th cent., *Cotum Maundevill* 1344. Identical in origin with the previous name. Manorial affix from the de Amundevilla family, here in the 13th cent.

Coberley Glos. *Culberlege* 1086 (DB). 'Wood or clearing of a man called Cūthbeorht'. OE pers. name + *lēah*.

Cobh (*Cóbh*) Cork. *Cove* 1659. 'Cove'. The Irish name is an adoption of English *cove*.

Cobham Kent. *Cobba hammes mearce* 939, *Cobbeham* 1197. 'Enclosure or homestead of a man called *Cobba*. OE pers. name + *hamm* or *hām*. The early form contains OE mearc 'boundary'.

Cobham Surrey. *Covenham* 1086 (DB). 'Homestead or enclosure of a man called *Cofa, or with a hut or shelter'. OE pers. name or OE *cofa* + *hām* or *hamm*.

Cockayne Hatley Beds., see HATLEY.

Cockenzie N. Ayr. *Cowkany* 1590. Meaning unknown. A pers. name may be involved.

Cockerham Lancs. *Cocreham* 1086 (DB). 'Homestead or enclosure on the River Cocker'. Celtic river-name (with a meaning 'crooked') + OE *hām* or *hamm*.

Cockerington, North & *Cockerington, South* Lincs. *Cocrintone* 1086 (DB). Possibly 'farmstead by a stream called *Cocker*'. Celtic river-name (perhaps an earlier name for the River Lud) + *-ing-* + *tūn*.

Cockermouth Cumbria. *Cokyrmoth c.*1150. 'Mouth of the River Cocker'. Celtic river-name (with a meaning 'crooked') + *mūtha*.

Cockfield Durham. *Kokefeld* 1223. 'Open land frequented by cocks (of wild birds), or belonging to a man called *Cocca'. OE *cocc* or OE pers. name + *feld*.

Cockfield Suffolk. *Cochanfelde* 10th cent. 'Open land of a man called *Cohha'. OE pers. name + *feld*.

Cockfosters Gtr. London. *Cokfosters* 1524. 'House or estate of the chief forester'. ME *for(e)ster*.

Cocking W. Sussex. *Cochinges* 1086 (DB). 'Dwellers at the hillock', or '(settlement of) the family or followers of a man called *Cocc(a)'. OE *cocc* or OE pers. name + *-ingas*.

Cockington Devon. *Cochintone* 1086 (DB). Probably 'estate associated with a man called *Cocc(a)'. OE pers. name + *-ing-* + *tūn*.

Cockley Cley Norfolk. *Cleia* 1086 (DB), *Coclikleye* 1324. OE *clǣg* 'clay, place with clayey soil' + affix which may be manorial from a family called Cockley or a local name meaning 'wood frequented by woodcocks' from OE *cocc* + *lēah*.

Cockshutt Shrops. *La Cockesete* 1270. From OE *cocc-scyte* 'a woodland glade where nets were stretched to catch woodcock'.

Cockthorpe Norfolk. *Torp* 1086 (DB), *Coketorp* 1254. Originally OScand. *thorp* 'secondary settlement, outlying farmstead' + affix which may be manorial from a family called Co(c)ke, or indicate 'where cocks are reared' from OE *cocc*.

Coddenham Suffolk. *Codenham* 1086 (DB). 'Homestead or enclosure of a man called *Cod(d)a'. OE pers. name (genitive *-n*) + *ham* or *hamm*.

Coddington, 'estate associated with a man called Cot(t)a', from OE pers. name + *-ing-* + *tūn*: **Coddington** Ches. *Cotintone* 1086 (DB). **Coddington** Heref. & Worcs.

Cotingtune 1086 (DB). **Coddington** Notts. *Cotintone* 1086 (DB).

Codford St Mary & *Codford St Peter* Wilts. *Codan ford* 901, *Coteford* 1086 (DB), *Codeford Sancte Marie, Sancti Petri* 1291. 'Ford of a man called *Cod(d)a'*. OE pers. name + *ford*. Affixes from the dedications of the churches.

Codicote Herts. *Cutheringcoton* 1002, *Codicote* 1086 (DB). 'Cottage(s) associated with a man called Cūthhere'. OE pers. name + *-ing-* + *cot*.

Codnor Derbys. *Cotenoure* 1086 (DB). 'Ridge of a man called *Cod(d)a'*. OE pers. name (genitive *-n*) + *ofer*.

Codrington Glos. *Cuderintuna* 12th cent. 'Estate associated with a man called Cūthhere'. OE pers. name + *-ing-* + *tūn*.

Codsall Staffs. *Codeshale* 1086 (DB). 'Nook of land of a man called *Cōd'*. OE pers. name + *halh*.

Coed-duon. *See* BLACKWOOD.

Coed-poeth Wrex. *Coid poch* 1391, *Coed Poeth* 1412. 'Burnt wood'. Welsh *coed* + *poeth*.

Coffinswell Devon. *Willa* 1086 (DB), *Coffineswell* 1249. '(Place at) the spring or stream'. OE *w(i)ella* + manorial addition from the Coffin family, here in the 12th cent.

Cofton Hackett Heref. & Worcs. *Coftune* 8th cent., *Costune |sic|* 1086 (DB), *Corfton Hakett* 1431. 'Farmstead with a hut or shelter'. OE *cofa* + *tūn* + manorial addition from the Haket family, here in the 12th cent.

Cogan Vale Glam. *Cogan c.*1139. Meaning uncertain. The origin may lie in a stream name.

Cogenhoe Northants. *Cugenho* 1086 (DB). 'Hill-spur of a man called *Cugga'*. OE pers. name (genitive *-n*) + *hōh*.

Cogges, *High Cogges* Oxon. *Coges* 1086 (DB). 'The hills', from OE *cogg*.

Coggeshall Essex. *Cogheshala* 1086 (DB). 'Nook of land of a man called *Cogg'*. OE pers. name + *halh*.

Coker, East, *Coker, North*, & *Coker, West* Somerset. *Cocre* 1086 (DB). Originally the name of the stream here, a Celtic river-name with a meaning 'crooked, winding'.

Colaboll Highland. 'Kol's homestead'. OScand. pers. name + *bólstathr*.

Colan Cornwall. *Sanctus Colanus* 1205. 'Church of St Colan'. From the patron saint of the church.

Colaton Raleigh Devon. *Coletone* 1086 (DB), *Coleton Ralegh* 1316. 'Farmstead of a man called Cola'. OE pers. name + *tūn* + manorial addition from the de Ralegh family, here in the 13th cent.

Colbost Highland (Skye). 'Kol's homestead'. OScand. pers. name + *bólstathr*.

Colburn N. Yorks. *Corburne |sic|* 1086 (DB), *Coleburn* 1198. 'Cool stream'. OE *cōl* + *burna*.

Colby Cumbria. *Collebi* 12th cent. Farmstead of a man called Kolli', or 'hill farmstead'. OScand. pers. name or *kollr* + *bý*.

Colby Norfolk. *Colebei* 1086 (DB). 'Farmstead or village of a man called Koli'. OScand. pers. name + *bý*.

Colchester Essex. *Colneceastre* early 10th cent., *Colecestra* 1086 (DB). 'Roman town on the River Colne'.

Ancient pre-English river-name (see COLNE ENGAINE) + OE *ceaster*. Alternatively the first element may be a reduced form of Latin *colonia* 'Roman colony for retired legionaries' (the Romano-British name of Colchester being *Colonia Camulodunum*, this last being a British name meaning 'fort of the Celtic war-god Camulos').

Cold as affix, *see* main name, e.g. for **Cold Brayfield** (Bucks.) *see* BRAYFIELD.

Coldham Cambs. *Coldham* 1251. 'Cold enclosure'. OE *cald* + *hamm*.

Coldred Kent. *Colret* 1086 (DB). 'Clearing where coal is found, or where charcoal is made'. OE *col* + *ryde*.

Coldridge Devon. *Colrige* 1086 (DB). 'Ridge where charcoal is made'. OE *col* + *hrycg*.

Coldstream Sc. Bord. *Kaldestrem c.*1178, *Caldestream c.*1207, *Coldstreme* 1290. '(Place on the) cold stream'. Coldstream is on the Tweed, but the smaller Leet Water, which joins it here, may have been the original 'cold stream'.

Coldwaltham W. Sussex. *Waltham* 10th cent., *Cold Waltham* 1340. 'Homestead or village in a forest'. OE *w(e)ald* + *hām*, with later affix meaning 'bleak, exposed'.

Cole Somerset. *Colna* 1212. Originally the name of the stream here, a pre-English river-name of uncertain meaning.

Colebatch Shrops. *Colebech* 1176. Probably 'stream-valley of a man called Cola'. OE pers. name + *bece*. Alternatively the first element may be OE *col* 'charcoal'.

Colebrook Devon, near Cullompton. *Colebroca* 1086 (DB). 'Cool brook'. OE *cōl* + *brōc*.

Colebrooke Devon. *Colebroc* 12th cent. Identical in origin with the previous name.

Coleby N. Lincs. *Colebi* 1086 (DB). 'Farmstead or village of a man called Koli'. OScand. pers. name + *bý*.

Coleford Devon. *Colbrukeforde* 1330. 'Ford at COLEBROOKE'. OE *ford*.

Coleford Glos. *Coleforde* 1282. 'Ford across which coal is carried'. OE *col* + *ford*.

Coleford Somerset, near Frome. *Culeford* 1234. 'Ford across which coal or charcoal is carried'. OE *col* + *ford*.

Colehill Dorset. *Colhulle* 1431. OE *hyll* 'hill' with either *col* 'charcoal' or *coll* 'hill'.

Coleman's Hatch E. Sussex. *Colmanhacche* 1495. 'Forest gate (OE *hæcc*) associated with a family called Coleman' (recorded in this area from the 13th cent.).

Colemere Shrops. *Colesmere |sic|* 1086 (DB), *Culemere* 1203. Probably 'pool of a man called *Cūla'*. OE pers. name + *mere*.

Coleorton Leics. *Ovretone* 1086 (DB), *Cole Orton* 1571. Probably 'higher farmstead'. OE *uferra* + *tūn*. Affix is OE *col* 'coal' with reference to mining here.

Coleraine (*Cúil Raithin*) Derry. *Cuile Raithin c.*630. 'Nook of the ferns'.

Colerne Wilts. *Colerne* 1086 (DB). 'Building where charcoal is made or stored'. OE *col* + *ærn*.

Colesbourne Glos. *Col(l)esburnan* 9th cent., *Colesborne* 1086 (DB). 'Stream of a man called *Col or Coll'. OE pers. name + *burna*.

Coleshill Bucks. *Coleshyll* 1507. Possibly identical in origin with the following name. Its earlier name in medieval times was *Stoke* 1175, *Stokke* 1224, from OE *stoc* 'secondary settlement'.

Coleshill Oxon. *Colleshylle* 10th cent., *Coleselle* 1086 (DB). Probably OE *coll* 'hill' with the addition of explanatory OE *hyll*, alternatively 'hill of a man called Coll', from OE pers. name + *hyll*.

Coleshill Warwicks. *Colleshyl* 799, *Coleshelle* 1086 (DB). Possibly identical in origin with the previous names, but more likely 'hill on the River Cole', Celtic river-name (of uncertain meaning) + OE *hyll*.

Colkirk Norfolk. *Colechirca* 1086 (DB). 'Church of a man called Cola or Koli'. OE or OScand. pers. name + *kirkja*.

Coll (island) Arg. '(Place of) hazels'. Probably a pre-Celtic name.

Collaton St Mary Devon. *Coletone* 1261. 'Farmstead of a man called Cola'. OE pers. name + *tūn* + affix from the dedication of the church.

Collinamuck (*Caladh na Muc*) Galway. 'Riverside meadow of the pigs'.

Collingbourne Ducis & *Collingbourne Kingston* Wilts. *Colengaburnam* 903, *Colingeburne* 1086 (DB). Probably 'stream of the family or followers of a man called *Col or Cola'. OE pers. name + *-inga-* + *burna*. Manorial additions from possession by the Dukes of Lancaster (Latin *ducis* 'of the duke') and the king (OE *cyning* + *tūn*).

Collingham, 'homestead or village of the family or followers of a man called *Col or Cola', OE pers. name + *-inga-* + *hām*: **Collingham** Notts. *Colingeham* 1086 (DB). **Collingham** W. Yorks. *Col(l)ingeham* 1167.

Collington Heref. & Worcs. *Col(l)intune* 1086 (DB). 'Estate associated with a man called *Col or Cola'. OE pers. name + *-ing-* + *tūn*.

Collingtree Northants. *Colentreu* 1086 (DB). 'Tree of a man called Cola'. OE pers. name (genitive *-n*) + *trēow*.

Collon (*Collon*) Louth. 'Place of hazels'.

Collooney (*Cúil Mhuine*) Sligo. 'Nook of the thicket'.

Collyweston Northants. *Westone* 1086 (DB), *Colynveston* 1309. 'West farmstead'. OE *west* + *tūn* + manorial affix from Nicholas (of which Colin is a pet-form) de Segrave, here in the 13th cent.

Colmworth Beds. *Colmeworde* 1086 (DB). Possibly 'enclosure of a man called *Culma'. OE pers. name + *worth*.

Coln Rogers, *St Aldwyns*, & *St Dennis* Glos. *Cungle* 962, *Colne* 1086 (DB), *Culna Rogeri* 13th cent., *Culna Sancti Aylwini* 12th cent., *Colne Seint Denys* 1287. '(Places by) the River Coln'. Pre-English river-name of uncertain origin. Additions from possession by Roger de Gloucester (died 1106), from church dedication to St Athelwine, and from possession by the church of St Denis of Paris (in the 11th cent.).

Colnbrook Bucks. *Colebroc* 1107. 'Cool brook', or 'brook near the River Colne'. OE *cōl* or pre-English river-name + OE *brōc*.

Colne Cambs. *Colne* 1086 (DB). Originally the name (now lost) of the stream here, a pre-English river-name of uncertain meaning.

Colne Lancs. *Calna* 1124. '(Place by) the River Colne'. A pre-English river-name of uncertain meaning, identical with River CALNE in Wilts.

Colne Engaine, *Earls Colne, Wakes Colne & White Colne* Essex. *Colne* c.950, *Colun* 1086 (DB), *Colum Engayne* 1254, *Erlescolne* 1358, *Colne Wake* 1375, *Whyte Colne* 1285. '(Places by) the River Colne', an ancient pre-English river-name of uncertain meaning. Manorial additions from possession in medieval times by the Engayne family, the Earls of Oxford, and the Wake family. White Colne was held by Dimidius Blancus in 1086 (DB).

Colney Norfolk. *Coleneia* 1086 (DB). 'Island, or dry ground in marsh, of a man called Cola'. OE pers. name (genitive *-n*) + *ēg*.

Colney, London Herts. *Colnea* 1209–35, *London Colney* 1555. 'Island by the River Colne'. Pre-English river-name + OE *ēg*, with affix from its situation on the main road to London.

Colonsay (island) Arg. *Colyunsay* 14th cent. 'Kolbein's island'. OScand. pers. name + *ey*.

Colsterdale N. Yorks. *Colserdale* 1301. 'Valley of the charcoal burners'. OE *colestre* + OE *dæl* or ON *dalr*.

Colsterworth Lincs. *Colsteuorde* 1086 (DB). 'Enclosure of the charcoal burners'. OE *colestre* + *worth*.

Colston, 'farmstead of a man called Kolr', OScand. pers. name + OE *tūn*: **Colston, Car** Notts. *Colestone* 1086 (DB), *Kyrcoluiston* 1242. Affix from OScand. *kirkja* 'church'. **Colston Bassett** Notts. *Coletone* 1086 (DB), *Coleston Bassett* 1228. Manorial addition from the Basset family, here in the 12th cent.

Coltishall Norfolk. *Coketeshala* 1086 (DB). 'Nook of land of a man called *Cohhede or *Coccede'. OE pers. name + *halh*.

Colton Cumbria. *Coleton* 1202. 'Farmstead on a river called *Cole*'. Celtic river-name (of uncertain meaning) + OE *tūn*.

Colton Norfolk. *Coletuna* 1086 (DB). 'Farmstead of a man called Cola or Koli'. OE or OScand. pers. name + OE *tūn*.

Colton N. Yorks. *Coletune* 1086 (DB). Probably identical in origin with the previous name.

Colton Staffs. *Coltone* 1086 (DB). Probably 'farmstead of a man called Cola'. OE pers. name + *tūn*.

Colwall Heref. & Worcs. *Colewelle* 1086 (DB). 'Cool spring or stream'. OE *cōl* + *wælla*.

Colwell Northum. *Colewel* 1236. 'Cool spring or stream'. OE *cōl* + *wella*.

Colwich Staffs. *Colewich* 1240. Probably 'building where charcoal is made or stored'. OE *col* + *wīc*.

Colworth W. Sussex. *Coleworth* 10th cent. 'Enclosure of a man called Cola'. OE pers. name + *worth*.

Colwyn Bay (*Bae Colwyn*) Conwy. *Coloyne* 1334. 'Bay of the River Colwyn'. The river name means 'puppy' (Welsh *colwyn*), alluding to its small size. The Welsh name corresponds to the English (Welsh *bae*).

Colyford Devon. *Culyford* 1244. 'Ford over the River Coly'. Celtic river-name (possibly 'narrow') + OE *ford*.

Colyton Devon. *Culintona* 946, *Colitone* 1086 (DB). 'Farmstead by the River Coly'. Celtic river-name + OE *tūn*.

Combe, *Coombe*, 'the valley', from OE *cumb*, a common place-name, especially in the South West; examples include: **Combe** Oxon. *Cumbe* 1086 (DB). **Combe, Abbas** Somerset. *Cumbe* 1086 (DB), *Coumbe Abbatisse* 1327. Manorial addition from Latin *abbatisse* 'of the abbess', alluding to early possession by Shaftesbury Abbey. **Combe, Castle** Wilts. *Come* 1086 (DB), *Castelcumbe* 1270. Affix *castel* referring to the Norman castle here. **Combe Florey** Somerset. *Cumba* 12th cent., *Cumbeflori* 1291. Manorial addition from the de Flury family, here in the 12th cent. **Combe Hay** B. & NE. Som. *Come* 1086 (DB), *Cumbehawya* 1249. Manorial addition from the family of de Haweie, here in the 13th cent. **Combeinteignhead** Devon. *Comba* 1086 (DB), *Cumbe in Tenhide* 1227. Affix from a district called Tenhide because it contained 'ten hides of land' (OE *tēn* + *hīd*). **Combe Martin** Devon. *Comba* 1086 (DB), *Cumbe Martini* 1265. Manorial addition from one Martin whose son held the manor in 1133. **Combe, Monkton** B. & NE. Som. *Cume* 1086 (DB). Affix means 'estate of the monks' (OE *munuc* + *tūn*). **Combe Raleigh** Devon. *Cumba* 1237, *Comberalegh* 1383. Manorial addition from the de Ralegh family, here in the 13th cent. **Combe St Nicholas** Somerset. *Cumbe* 1086 (DB). Affix from its possession by the Priory of St Nicholas in Exeter. **Combe, Temple** Somerset. *Come* 1086 (DB), *Cumbe Templer* 1291. Affix from its possession by the Knights Templars at an early date. **Coombe** Hants. *Cumbe* 1086 (DB). **Coombe Bissett** Wilts. *Come* 1086 (DB), *Coumbe Byset* 1288. Manorial addition from the Biset family, here in the 12th cent. **Coombe Keynes** Dorset. *Cume* 1086 (DB), *Combe Kaynes* 1299. Manorial addition from the de Cahaignes family, here in the 12th cent.

Comber (*An Comar*) Down. (*ab*) *Comair* 1221. 'The confluence'.

Comberbach Ches. *Combrebeche* 12th cent. 'Valley or stream of the Britons or of a man called Cumbra'. OE **Cumbre* or OE pers. name + *bece*.

Comberford Staffs. *Cumbreford* 1187. 'Ford of the Britons'. OE **Cumbre* + *ford*.

Comberton Cambs. *Cumbertone* 1086 (DB). 'Farmstead of a man called Cumbra'. OE pers. name + *tūn*.

Comberton, Great & *Comberton, Little* Heref. & Worcs. *Cumbrincgtun* 972, *Cumbrintune* 1086 (DB). 'Estate associated with a man called Cumbra'. OE pers. name + *-ing-* + *tūn*.

Combrook Warwicks. *Cumbroc* 1217. 'Brook in a valley'. OE *cumb* + *brōc*.

Combs Derbys. *Cumbes* 1251. 'The valleys'. OE *cumb*.

Combs Suffolk. *Cambas* 1086 (DB). 'The hill-crests or ridges'. OE *camb*.

Commeen (*An Coimín*) Donegal. *Cuimin* 1835. 'The common land'.

Commondale N. Yorks. *Colemandale* 1272. 'Valley of a man called Colman'. OIrish pers. name + OScand. *dalr*.

Compton, a common place-name, 'farmstead or village in a valley', from OE *cumb* + *tūn*; examples include: **Compton** Berks. *Contone* 1086 (DB). **Compton** Hants. *Cuntone* 1086 (DB). **Compton** Surrey, near Guildford. *Contone* 1086 (DB). **Compton Abbas** Dorset. *Cumtune* 956, *Cuntone* 1086 (DB), *Cumpton Abbatisse* 1293. Manorial addition from Latin *abbatisse* 'of the abbess', alluding to early possession by Shaftesbury Abbey. **Compton Abdale** Glos. *Contone* 1086 (DB), *Apdale Compton* 1504. Affix probably manorial from a family called Apdale. **Compton Bassett** Wilts. *Contone* 1086 (DB), *Cumptone Basset* 1228. Manorial addition from the Basset family, here in the 13th cent. **Compton Beauchamp** Oxon. *Cumtune* 955, *Contone* 1086 (DB), *Cumton Beucamp* 1236. Manorial addition from the de Beauchamp family, here in the 13th cent. **Compton Bishop** Somerset. *Cumbtune* 1067, *Compton Episcopi* 1332. Affix *Bishop* (Latin *episcopus*) from its early possession by the Bishop of Wells. **Compton Chamberlayne** Wilts. *Contone* 1086 (DB), *Compton Chamberleyne* 1316. Manorial affix from a family called Chamberlain, here from the 13th cent. **Compton Dando** B. & NE. Som. *Contone* 1086 (DB), *Cumton Daunon* 1256. Manorial addition from the de Auno or Dauno family, here in the 12th cent. **Compton, Fenny** Warwicks. *Contone* 1086 (DB), *Fennicumpton* 1221. The affix is OE *fennig* 'muddy, marshy'. **Compton, Little** Warwicks. *Contone parva* 1086 (DB). The affix *Little* (Latin *parva*) distinguishes it from Long Compton. **Compton, Long** Warwicks. *Cuntone* 1086 (DB), *Long Compton* 1299. The affix *Long* refers to the length of the village. **Compton Martin** B. & NE. Som. *Comtone* 1086 (DB), *Cumpton Martin* 1228. Manorial addition from one Martin de Tours, whose son held the manor in the early 12th cent. **Compton, Nether** & **Compton, Over** Dorset. *Cumbtun* 998, *Contone* 1086 (DB), *Nethercumpton* 1288, *Ouerecumton* 1268. The additions *Nether* and *Over* are from OE *neotherra* 'lower' and *uferra* 'higher'. **Compton Pauncefoot** Somerset. *Cuntone* 1086 (DB), *Cumpton Paunceuot* 1291. Manorial addition from a family called Pauncefote. **Compton Valence** Dorset. *Contone* 1086 (DB), *Compton Valance* 1280. Manorial addition from William de Valencia, Earl of Pembroke, here in the 13th cent. **Compton, West** Dorset. *Comptone* 934, *Contone* 1086 (DB). Earlier called Compton Abbas but now called West Compton to distinguish it from the other Dorset place of this name.

Comrie Perth. *Comry* 1268. 'Confluence'. Gaelic *comar*. The village stands at the junction of three rivers.

Conair (*Conair*) Kerry. 'Path'.

Conderton Heref. & Worcs. *Cantuaretun* 875, *Canterton* 1201. 'Farmstead of the Kent dwellers or Kentishmen'. OE *Cantware* + *tūn*.

Condicote Glos. *Cundicotan* c.1052, *Condicote* 1086 (DB). 'Cottage associated with a man called Cunda'. OE pers. name + *-ing-* + *cot*.

Condover Shrops. *Conedoure* 1086 (DB). 'Flat-topped ridge by Cound Brook'. Celtic river-name (*see* COUND) + OE **ofer*.

Coney Island (*Coiní*) Clare, Down. 'Rabbit island'.

Coney Weston Suffolk. *Cunegestuna* 1086 (DB). 'The king's manor, the royal estate'. OScand. *konungr* + OE *tūn*.

Coneysthorpe N. Yorks. *Coningestorp* 1086 (DB). 'The king's farmstead or hamlet'. OScand. *konungr* + *thorp*.

Cong (*Conga*) Mayo. 'Narrow stretch of water between two larger stretches'.

Congerstone Leics. *Cuningestone* 1086 (DB). Identical in origin with the previous name.

Congham Norfolk. *Congheham* 1086 (DB). Possibly 'homestead or village at the hill'. OE **cung* + *hām*.

Congleton Ches. *Cogeltone* |sic| 1086 (DB), *Congulton* 13th cent. Probably 'farmstead at the round-topped hill'. OE **cung* + *hyll* + *tūn*.

Congresbury N. Som. *Cungresbyri* 9th cent., *Cungresberie* 1086 (DB). 'Fortified place or manor associated with a saint called Congar'. Celtic pers. name + OE *burh* (dative *byrig*).

Coningsby Lincs. *Cuningesbi* 1086 (DB). 'The king's manor or village'. OScand. *konungr* + *bý*.

Conington, 'the king's manor, the royal estate', OScand. *konungr* + OE *tūn*: **Conington** Cambs., near St Ives. *Cunictune* 10th cent., *Coninctune* 1086 (DB). **Conington** Cambs., near Sawtry. *Cunningtune* 10th cent., *Cunitone* 1086 (DB).

Conisbrough S. Yorks. *Cunugesburh* c.1003, *Coningesburg* 1086 (DB). 'The king's fortification'. OScand. *konungr* + OE *burh*.

Coniscliffe, High & *Coniscliffe, Low* Durham. *Cingcesclife* 1050. 'The king's cliff or bank'. OE *cyning* + *clif*.

Conisholme Lincs. *Cuninggesolm* 1195. 'Island, or dry ground in marsh, belonging to the king'. OScand. *konungr* + *holmr*.

Coniston, *Conistone*, 'the king's manor, the royal estate', OScand. *konungr* + OE *tūn*: **Coniston** Cumbria. *Coningeston* 12th cent. **Coniston** E. R. Yorks. *Coningesbi* |sic| 1086 (DB), *Cuningeston* 1190. OE *tūn* replaced OScand. *bý* 'village' as second element. **Coniston Cold** N. Yorks. *Cuningestone* 1086 (DB), *Calde Cuningeston* 1202. Affix *Cold* (from OE *cald*) from its exposed situation. **Conistone** N. Yorks. *Cunestune* 1086 (DB).

Conlig (*An Choinleac*) Down. (*feall*) *na Coinnleice* 1744. 'The hound stone'. The sense of 'hound' is uncertain.

Connacht (*Cúige Chonnacht*) (the province). 'Province of the Connachta people'.

Connah's Quay Flin. *Connas Quay* 1791. 'Connah's quay'. *Connah* may have been the local innkeeper.

Connaught. *See* CONNACHT.

Connemara (*Conamara*) (district) Galway. *Conmaicnemara* n.d. 'Conmaicne of the sea'. Irish tribal name + *muir*.

Connor (*Coinnire*) Antrim. (*espoc*) *Condere* 514. 'Dog oak wood'.

Cononley N. Yorks. *Cutnelai* 1086 (DB), *Conanlia* 12th cent. OE *lēah* 'wood, clearing' with an uncertain first element, possibly an old Celtic river-name or an OIrish pers. name.

Consett Durham. *Covekesheued* 1183, *Conekesheued* 1228. Probably 'headland or promontory of a hill called *Conek*'. Celtic or pre-Celtic **cunāco-* + OE *hēafod*.

Constable Burton N. Yorks., *see* BURTON.

Constantine Cornwall. *Sanctus Constantinus* 1086 (DB). 'Church of St Constantine'. From the patron saint of the church.

Contin Highland. *Conten* 1226. 'Confluence'. Precise origin unknown, but possibly Gaelic *cointin*.

Convoy (*Conmhaigh*) Donegal. *Convoigh* 1610. 'Hound plain'.

Conwal (*Congbháil*) Donegal, Leitrim. 'Foundation'.

Conwy Conwy. *Conguoy* 12th cent., *Aberconuy* 12th cent., *Conway als. Aberconway* 1698, *Conway, or Conwy* 1868. '(Place on the) River Conwy'. The Celtic river name, meaning, 'reedy one', gave the name of *Canovium*, the Roman town at nearby Caerhun. Conwy was formerly known as *Aberconwy*, 'mouth of the Conwy' (OWelsh *aber*).

Cookbury Devon. *Cukebyr* 1242. 'Fortification of a man called **Cuca*'. OE pers. name + *burh* (dative *byrig*).

Cookham Berks. *Coccham* 798, *Cocheham* 1086 (DB). Possibly 'cook village', i.e. 'village noted for its cooks'. OE *cōc* + *hām*. However the first element may be an OE *cōc(e)* 'hill'.

Cookham Dean Berks. *la Dene* 1220. 'The valley (at COOKHAM)'. OE *denu*.

Cookhill Heref. & Worcs. *Cochilla* 1156. OE **cōc(e)* 'hill' with explanatory OE *hyll*.

Cookley Heref. & Worcs. *Culnan clif* 964, *Culleclive* 11th cent. 'Cliff of a man called **Cūlna*'. OE pers. name + *clif*.

Cookley Suffolk. *Cokelei* 1086 (DB), *Kukeleia* late 12th cent. Possibly 'wood or clearing of a man called **Cuca*', OE pers. name + *lēah*, but the first element may rather be an OE **cucu* 'cuckoo'.

Cookstown Tyrone. *a' Corr Críochach* c.1645. 'Cook's town'. Alan *Cook* founded a settlement here in 1609. The town's Irish name is *An Chorr Chríochach*, 'the boundary hill'.

Coolaney (*Cúil Mhaine*) Sligo. 'Nook of the thicket'.

Coolattin (*Cúl Aitinn*) Limerick, Wexford, Wicklow. 'Hill of gorse'.

Coolbaun (*An Cúl Bán*) Kilkenny, Tipperary. 'The white hill'.

Coolboy (*An Cúl Buí*) Donegal, Wicklow. 'The yellow hill'.

Coolcarrigan (*Cúil Charraigín*) Kildare. 'Nook of the little rock'.

Coolcor (*Cúil Chorr*) Offaly. 'Nook of the hills'.

Coolcullen (*Cúl an Chuillinn*) Kilkenny. 'Back of the steep slope'.

Coolderry (*Cúl Doire*) Monaghan, Offaly. 'Back of the oak wood'.

Coole (*An Chúil*) Westmeath. 'The nook'.

Coolea (*Cúil Aodha*) Cork. 'Aodh's nook'.

Cooley Point (*Cuailnge*) Louth. 'Cooley Point'.

Coolgrange (*Cúil Ghráinseach*) Kilkenny. 'Nook of the monastic farm'.

Coolgreany (*Cúil Ghréine*) Wexford. 'Nook of the sun'.

Cooligrain (*Cúl le Gréin*) Leitrim. 'Nook of the sun'.

Cooling Kent. *Culingas* 808, *Colinges* 1086 (DB). '(Settlement of) the family or followers of a man called *Cūl or *Cūla'. OE pers. name + -*ingas*.

Coolkeeragh (*Cúil Chaorach*) Derry. 'Nook of the sheep'.

Coolkenna (*Cúil Uí Chionaoith*) Wicklow. 'Nook of the Ó Cionaoith'.

Coolmeen (*Cúil Mhín*) Clare. 'Smooth nook'.

Coolmore (*Cúl Mór*) Donegal. 'Big hill'.

Coolock (*An Chúlóg*) Dublin. 'The little corner'.

Coolrain (*Cúil Ruáin*) Laois. 'Nook of the red ground'.

Coolsallagh (*Cúil Saileach*) Down. 'Nook of the willows'.

Coomatloukane (*Com an tSleabhcáin*) Kerry. 'Hollow of the edible seaweed'.

Coombe, *see* COMBE.

Coomnagoppul (*Com na gCapall*) Kerry. 'Hollow of the horses'.

Cooneen (*An Cúinnín*) Fermanagh. *Cunen* 1659. 'The little corner'.

Cooraclare (*Cuar an Chláir*) Clare. 'Curve of the plain'.

Cootehill Cavan. *Coote Hill* 1725. The town is named for Thomas *Coote*, who acquired lands here in the early 17th cent., and his future wife, Frances *Hill*. The Irish name is *Muinchille*, 'sleeve'.

Copdock Suffolk. *Coppedoc* 1195. 'Pollarded oak-tree, i.e. oak-tree with its top removed'. OE *coppod + āc*.

Copeland Island Down. *Kaupmanneyjar* 1230. 'Merchants' island'. OScand. *kaupmathr* (genitive plural *kaupmanna*). Alternatively 'Kaupman's island', with an OScand. surname, later influenced by the Anglo-Norman surname *Copeland*. The equivalent Irish name is *Oileán Chóplainn*.

Copford Green Essex. *Coppanforda* 995, *Copeforda* 1086 (DB). 'Ford of a man called *Coppa'. OE pers. name + *ford* with the later addition of *grēne* 'a village green'.

Cople Beds. *Cochepol* 1086 (DB). 'Pool of a man called *Cocca', or 'pool frequented by cocks (of wild birds)'. OE pers. name or *cocc + pōl*.

Copmanthorpe York. *Copeman Torp* 1086 (DB). 'Outlying farmstead or hamlet belonging to the merchants'. OScand. *kaup-mathr* (genitive plural -*manna*) + *thorp*.

Coppeen (*An Caipín*) Cork. 'Cap'.

Coppenhall Staffs. *Copehale* 1086 (DB). 'Nook of land of a man called *Coppa'. OE pers. name (genitive -*n*) + *halh*.

Coppingford Cambs. *Copemaneforde* 1086 (DB). 'Ford used by merchants'. OScand. *kaup-mathr* (genitive plural -*manna*) + OE *ford*.

Copplestone Devon. *Copelan stan* 974. 'Peaked or towering stone'. OE *copel + stān*.

Coppull Lancs. *Cophill* 1218. 'Hill with a peak'. OE *copp + hyll*.

Copt Hewick N. Yorks., *see* HEWICK.

Copthorne W. Sussex. *Coppethorne* 1437. 'Pollarded thorn-tree, i.e. thorn-tree with its top removed'. OE *coppod + thorn*.

Corballa (*An Corrbhaile*) Sligo. 'The odd homestead'.

Corbally (*Corrbhaile*) Clare. 'Odd homestead'.

Corbet (*Carbad*) Down. *Corbudd* 1609. 'Jaw', referring to some unidentified feature.

Corbo (*Corr Bhó*) Tyrone. 'Round hill of the cow'.

Corbridge Northum. *Corebricg c.*1050. 'Bridge near Corchester'. OE *brycg* 'bridge' with a shortened form of the old Celtic name of Corchester (*Corstopitum*) which is near here.

Corby Northants. *Corbei* 1086 (DB). 'Farmstead or village of a man called Kori'. OScand. pers. name + *bý*.

Corby Glen Lincs. *Corbi* 1086 (DB). Identical in origin with previous name. The affix is from the River Glen, a Celtic river-name meaning 'the clean one'.

Corby, Great Cumbria. *Chorkeby c.*1115. 'Farmstead or village of a man called Corc'. OIrish pers. name + OScand. *bý*.

Corclogh (*Corr Cloch*) Mayo. 'Snout of the stone'.

Corcreaghy (*An Chorr Chríochach*) Louth. 'The snout of the boundary'.

Coreley Shrops. *Cornelie* 1086 (DB). 'Woodland clearing frequented by cranes or herons'. OE *corn + lēah*.

Corfe, 'the cutting, the gap or pass', from OE *corf*: **Corfe** Somerset. *Corf* 1243. **Corfe Castle** Dorset. *Corf* 955, *Corffe Castell* 1302. The affix refers to the Norman castle here. **Corfe Mullen** Dorset. *Corf* 1086 (DB), *Corf le Mulin* 1176. The affix is from OFrench *molin* 'a mill'.

Corfton Shrops. *Cortune* 1086 (DB), *Corfton* 1222. 'Settlement by the River Corve'. OE river-name (from *corf* 'a pass') + *tūn*.

Corglass (*Corr Ghlas*) Leitrim. 'Grey-green hill'.

Corhampton Hants. *Cornhamton* 1201. 'Home farm or settlement where grain is produced'. OE *corn + hām-tūn*.

Cork (*Corcaigh*) Cork. 'Swamp'.

Corkey (*Corcaigh*) Antrim. 'Swamp'.

Corlead (*Corr Liath*) Longford. 'Grey rounded hill'.

Corlesmore (*Corrlios Mór*) Cavan. 'Big rounded hill of the fort'.

Corley Warwicks. *Cornelie* 1086 (DB). 'Clearing frequented by cranes or herons'. OE *corn + lēah*.

Cornafanog (*Corr na bhFeannóg*) Fermanagh. *Cornafenoge* 1751. 'Round hill of the crows'.

Cornafean (*Corr na Féinne*) Cavan. 'Hill of the Fianna'.

Cornafulla (*Corr na Fola*) Roscommon. 'Hill of the blood'.

Cornamona (*Corr na Móna*) Galway. 'Hill of the bog'.

Cornard, Great Suffolk. *Cornerda* 1086 (DB). 'Cultivated land used for corn'. OE *corn* + *erth*.

Corndarragh (*Carn Darach*) Offaly. 'Heap of the oak tree'.

Corney Cumbria. *Corneia* 12th cent. 'Island frequented by cranes or herons. OE *corn* + *ēg*.

Cornforth Durham. *Corneford* 1196. 'Ford frequented by cranes or herons'. OE *corn* + *ford*.

Cornhill-on-Tweed Northum. *Cornehale* 12th cent. 'Nook of land frequented by cranes or herons'. OE *corn* + *halh*. For the river-name, *see* TWEEDMOUTH.

Cornsay Durham. *Corneshowe* 1183. 'Hill-spur frequented by cranes or herons'. OE *corn* + *hōh*.

Cornwall (the county). *Cornubia* c.705, *Cornwalas* 891, *Cornualia* 1086 (DB). '(Territory of) the Britons or Welsh of the *Cornovii* tribe'. Celtic tribal name (meaning 'peninsula people') + OE *walh* (plural *walas*).

Cornwell Oxon. *Cornewelle* 1086 (DB). 'Stream frequented by cranes or herons'. OE *corn* + *wella*.

Cornwood Devon. *Cornehuda* |sic| 1086 (DB), *Curnwod* 1242. Probably 'wood frequented by cranes'. OE *corn* + *wudu*.

Cornworthy Devon. *Corneorda* 1086 (DB). 'Enclosure frequented by cranes, or where corn is grown'. OE *corn* + *worth, worthig*.

Corofin (*Cora Finne*) Clare. 'Weir of the white (water)'.

Corpusty Norfolk. *Corpestih* 1086 (DB). 'Raven path', or 'path of a man called Korpr'. OScand. *korpr* or pers. name + *stígr*.

Corracullin (*Corr an Chuillinn*) Offaly, Westmeath. 'Hill of the steep slope'.

Corrandulla (*Cor an Dola*) Galway. 'Hill of the loop'.

Corranny (*Corr Eanaigh*) Fermanagh. *Corroney* 1659. 'Hill of the bog'.

Corraun (*Corrán*) Mayo. 'Crescent-shaped place'.

Corrib, Lough (*Loch Coirib*) Galway. 'Lake of Oirbse'.

Corriga (*Carraigigh*) Leitrim. 'Abounding in rocks'.

Corrigeenroe (*Carraigín Rua*) Roscommon. 'Little red rock'.

Corringham Essex. *Currincham* 1086 (DB). 'Homestead of the family or followers of a man called *Curra*'. OE pers. name + -*inga*- + *hām*.

Corringham Lincs. *Coringeham* 1086 (DB). 'Homestead of the family or followers of a man called *Cora*'. OE pers. name + -*inga*- + *hām*.

Corrofin (*Cora Finne*) Clare, Galway. 'Weir of the white (water)'.

Corry (*An Choraigh*) Leitrim. 'The pleasant place'.

Corscombe Dorset. *Corigescumb* 1014, *Coriescumbe* 1086 (DB). Possibly 'valley of the road in the pass'. OE *corf* + *weg* + *cumb*. Alternatively the first element may be an old name of the stream here.

Corsham Wilts. *Coseham* 1001, *Cosseham* 1086 (DB). 'Homestead or village of a man called *Cosa* or *Cossa*'. OE pers. name + *hām*.

Corsley Wilts. *Corselie* 1086 (DB). 'Wood or clearing by the marsh'. Celtic *cors* + OE *lēah*.

Corston B. & NE. Som. *Corsantune* 941, *Corstune* 1086 (DB). 'Farmstead or estate on the River Corse'. Old river-name (from Celtic *cors*; 'marsh') + OE *tūn*.

Corston Wilts. *Corstuna* 1065, *Corstone* 1086 (DB). 'Farmstead or estate on Gauze Brook'. Old river-name (from Celtic *cors* 'marsh') + OE *tūn*.

Corstorphine Edin. *Crostorfin* c.1140. 'Thorfinn's crossing'. OScand. *kros* + pers. name.

Corton Suffolk. *Karetuna* 1086 (DB). 'Farmstead of a man called Kári'. OScand. pers. name + OE *tūn*.

Corton Wilts. *Cortitone* 1086 (DB). 'Estate associated with a man called *Cort(a)*'. OE pers. name + -*ing*- + *tūn*.

Corton Denham Somerset. *Corfetone* 1086 (DB). 'Farmstead or village at a pass'. OE *corf* + *tūn* + manorial affix from the de Dinan family, here in the early 13th cent.

Cortown (*An Baile Corr*) Meath. 'The homestead of the twist'.

Cortubber (*Corr Tobair*) Monaghan. 'Hill of the well'.

Corvally (*Cor an Bhealaigh*) Monaghan. 'Twist of the pass'.

Corwen Denb. *Corvaen* 1254, *Korvaen* 14th cent., *Corwen* 1443. 'Sanctuary stone'. Welsh *côr* + *maen*. The church has a reputedly ancient stone called *Carreg-y-Big* ('pointed stone') built into the porch, and this may be the 'sanctuary stone'.

Coryton Devon. *Cur(r)itun* c.970, *Coriton* 1086 (DB). Probably 'farmstead on the River *Curi*'. Pre-English river-name (an old name for the River Lyd) + OE *tūn*.

Coryton Essex, a modern name from the oil refinery established here by Cory & Co. in 1922.

Cosby Leics. *Cossebi* 1086 (DB). 'Farmstead or village of a man called *Cossa*'. OE pers. name + OScand. *bý*.

Coseley W. Mids. *Colseley* 1357. Possibly 'clearing of the charcoal burners'. OE *colestre* + *lēah*.

Cosgrove Northants. *Covesgrave* 1086 (DB). 'Grove of a man called *Cōf*'. OE pers name + *grāf*.

Cosham Hants. *Cos(s)eham* 1086 (DB). 'Homestead or enclosure of a man called *Cossa*'. OE pers. name + *hām* or *hamm*.

Cossall Notts. *Coteshale* 1086 (DB). 'Nook of land of a man called *Cott*'. OE pers. name + *halh*.

Cossington, 'estate associated with a man called *Cosa* or *Cusa*', OE pers. name + -*ing*- + *tūn*: **Cossington** Leics. *Cosintone* 1086 (DB). **Cossington** Somerset. *Cosingtone* 729, *Cosintone* 1086 (DB).

Costessey Norfolk. *Costeseia* 1086 (DB). 'Island, or dry ground in marsh, of a man called *Cost'. OE (or OScand.) pers. name + OE *ēg*.

Costock Notts. *Cortingestoche* 1086 (DB). 'Outlying farmstead of the family or followers of a man called *Cort'. OE pers. name + *-inga-* + *stoc*.

Coston Leics. *Castone* 1086 (DB). Probably 'farmstead of a man called Kátr'. OScand. pers. name + OE *tūn*.

Cotes, 'the cottages or huts', from OE *cot*: **Cotes** Leics. *Cothes* 12th cent. **Cotes** Staffs. *Cota* 1086 (DB).

Cotesbach Leics. *Cotesbece* 1086 (DB). 'Stream or valley of a man called *Cott'. OE pers. name + *bece*, *bæce*.

Cotgrave Notts. *Godegrave* |sic| 1086 (DB), *Cotegrava* 1094. 'Grove or copse of a man called Cotta'. OE pers. name + *grāf*.

Cotham Notts. *Cotune* 1086 (DB). '(Place at) the cottages or huts'. OE *cot* in a dative plural form *cotum*.

Cothelstone Somerset. *Cothelestone* 1327. 'Farmstead of a man called Cūthwulf'. OE pers. name + *tūn*.

Cotherstone Durham. *Codrestune* 1086 (DB). 'Farmstead of a man called Cūthhere'. OE pers. name + *tūn*.

Cotleigh Devon. *Coteleia* 1086 (DB). 'Clearing of a man called Cotta'. OE pers. name + *lēah*.

Coton, '(place at) the cottages or huts', from OE *cot* in the dative plural form *cotum* (though some may be from a ME plural *coten*): **Coton** Cambs. *Cotis* 1086. **Coton** Northants. *Cote* 1086. **Coton** Staffs., near Milwich. *Cote* 1086 (DB). **Coton Clanford** Staffs. *Cote* 1086 (DB). Affix from a local place-name, probably 'clean ford' from OE *clǣne* + *ford*. **Coton in the Elms** Derbys. *Cotune* 1086 (DB). Affix from the abundance of elm-trees here.

Coton, Chilvers Warwicks. *Celverdestoche* 1086 (DB), *Chelverdescote* 1185. 'Cottage(s) of a man called Cēolfrith'. OE pers. name + *cot* (ME plural *coten*). The DB form contains an alternative element OE *stoc* 'hamlet'.

Cotswolds Glos./Worcs. *Codesuualt* 12th cent. 'High forest land of a man called *Cōd'. OE pers. name + *wald*.

Cottam, '(place at) the cottages or huts', from OE *cot* in a dative plural form *cotum*: **Cottam** E.R. Yorks. *Cottun* 1086 (DB). **Cottam** Lancs. *Cotun* 1227. **Cottam** Notts. *Cotum* 1274.

Cottenham Cambs. *Cotenham* 948, *Coteham* 1086 (DB). 'Homestead or village of a man called Cot(t)a'. OE pers. name (genitive *-n*) + *hām*.

Cottered Herts. *Chodrei* |sic| 1086 (DB), *Codreth* 1220. OE *rīth* 'stream' with an uncertain first element, possibly a pers. name or an OE *cōd* 'spawn of fish'.

Cotterstock Northants. *Codestoche* 1086 (DB), *Cotherstoke* 12th cent. Probably from an OE *corther-stoc* 'dairy farm'.

Cottesbrooke Northants. *Cotesbroc* 1086 (DB). 'Brook of a man called *Cott.' OE pers. name + *brōc*.

Cottesmore Rutland. *Cottesmore c.*976, *Cotesmore* 1086 (DB). 'Moor of a man called *Cott'. OE pers. name + *mōr*.

Cottingham, 'homestead of the family or followers of a man called *Cott or Cotta', OE pers. name + *-inga-* + *hām*: **Cottingham** E. R. Yorks. *Cotingeham* 1086 (DB). **Cottingham** Northants. *Cotingeham* 1086 (DB).

Cottingwith E. R. Yorks. *Coteuuid* |sic| 1086 (DB), *Cotingwic* 1195. 'Dairy-farm associated with a man called *Cott or Cotta'. OE pers. name + *-ing-* + *wīc* (replaced by OScand. *vithr* 'wood').

Cottisford Oxon. *Cotesforde* 1086 (DB). 'Ford of a man called *Cott'. OE pers. name + *ford*.

Cotton, Far Northants. *Cotes* 1196. 'The cottages or huts'. OE *cot* in a plural form, *see* COTON. Affix *Far* to distinguish it from other places with this name.

Cotwalton Staffs. *Cotewaltun* 1002, *Cotewoldestune* 1086 (DB). Possibly 'farmstead at the wood or stream of a man called Cotta' OE pers. name + *wald* or *wælla* + *tūn*.

Coughton Warwicks. *Coctune* 1086 (DB). Probably 'farmstead near the hillock'. OE **cocc* + *tūn*.

Coulsdon Gtr. London. *Cudredesdune* 967, *Colesdone* 1086 (DB). 'Hill of a man called Cūthrǣd'. OE pers. name + *dūn*.

Coulston, East & *Coulston, West* Wilts. *Covelestone* 1086 (DB). 'Farmstead of a man called *Cufel'. OE pers. name + *tūn*.

Coulton N. Yorks. *Coltune* 1086 (DB). Probably 'farmstead where charcoal is made'. OE *col* + *tūn*.

Cound Shrops. *Cuneet* 1086 (DB). Named from Cound Brook, a Celtic river-name of uncertain meaning.

Coundon Durham. *Cundun* 1196. Probably 'hill where cows are pastured'. OE *cū* (genitive plural *cūna*) + *dūn*.

Countesthorpe Leics. *Torp* 1209–35, *Cuntastorp* 1242. 'Outlying farmstead or hamlet belonging to a countess'. OScand, *thorp* with manorial affix from ME *contesse*.

Countisbury Devon. *Contesberie* 1086 (DB). 'Fortified place at a hill called *Cunet'. Celtic name (of uncertain meaning) + OE *burh* (dative *byrig*).

Coupar Angus Perth. Meaning unknown but traditionally held to be 'Community in *Angus*'. Gaelic *comh-phàirt*. The name locates the place in ANGUS for distinction from CUPAR in Fife.

Coupland Northum. *Coupland* 1242. 'Purchased land'. OScand. *kaupa-land*.

Courteenhall Northants. *Cortenhale* 1086 (DB). 'Nook of land of a man called *Corta or *Curta'. OE pers. name (genitive *-n*) + *halh*.

Courtmacsherry (*Cúirt Mhic Shéafraidh*) Cork. 'Mansion of Mac Shéafraidh'. The personal name is the Irish form of Geoffrey.

Cove, from OE *cofa* which meant 'hut or shelter', also 'recess or cove': **Cove** Devon. *La Kove* 1242. **Cove** Hants. *Coue* 1086 (DB). **Cove, North** Suffolk. *Cove* 1204. **Cove, South** Suffolk. *Coua* 1086 (DB).

Covehithe Suffolk. *Coveheith* 1523. 'Harbour near (South) COVE', from OE *hȳth*.

Coven Staffs. *Cove* 1086 (DB). '(Place at) the huts or shelters'. OE *cofa* in the dative plural form *cofum*.

Coveney Cambs. *Coueneia c.*1060. 'Island of a man called *Cofa', or 'cove island'. OE pers. name or OE *cofa* (genitive -*n*) + *ēg*.

Covenham St Bartholomew & *Covenham St Mary* Lincs. *Covenham* 1086 (DB). 'Homestead of a man called *Cofa', or 'homestead with a hut or shelter'. OE pers. name or OE *cofa* (genitive -*n*) + *hām*. Affixes from the dedications of the churches.

Coventry W. Mids. *Couentre* 1043, *Couentreu* 1086 (DB). 'Tree of a man called *Cofa'. OE pers. name (genitive -*n*) + *trēow*.

Coverack Cornwall. *Covrack* 1588. Probably originally the name of the stream here, meaning unknown.

Coverham N. Yorks. *Covreham* 1086 (DB). 'Homestead or village on the River Cover'. Celtic river-name + OE *hām*.

Covington Cambs. *Covintune* 1086 (DB). 'Estate associated with a man called *Cofa'. OE pers. name + -*ing*- + *tūn*.

Cow Honeybourne Heref. & Worcs., *see* HONEYBOURNE.

Cowarne, Much & *Cowarne, Little* Heref. & Worcs. *Cuure |sic|* 1086 (DB), *Couern* 1255. 'Cow house, dairy farm'. OE *cū* + *ærn*. Affix *Much* is from OE *mycel* 'great'.

Cowbit Lincs. *Coubiht* 1267. 'River-bend where cows are pastured'. OE *cū* + *byht*.

Cowbridge (*Y Bont-faen*) Vale Glam. *Coubrugge* 1263, *Bontvaen c.*1500. 'Cattle bridge'. OE *cu* + *brycg*. The Welsh name means 'the stone bridge', referring to another bridge nearby.

Cowden Kent. *Cudena c.*1100, 'Pasture for cows'. OE *cū* + *denn*.

Cowden, Great E. R. Yorks. *Coledun* 1086 (DB). 'Hill where charcoal is made'. OE *col* + *dūn*.

Cowdenbeath Fife. *terris de Baithe-Moubray alias Cowdounes-baithe* 1626. 'Cowden's Part of Beath', 'birch trees'. Gaelic *beith*.

Cowes, *East Cowes* I. of Wight, settlements on either side of the River Medina estuary named from two former sandbanks referred to as *Estcowe* and *Westcowe* in 1413, so called like other coastal features from their fancied resemblance to animals. OE *cū* 'a cow'.

Cowesby N. Yorks. *Cahosbi* 1086 (DB). 'Farmstead or village of a man called Kausi'. OScand. pers. name + *bý*.

Cowfold W. Sussex. *Coufaud* 1232. 'Small enclosure for cows. OE *cū* + *fald*.

Cowick, East & *Cowick, West* E. R. Yorks. *Cuwich* 1197, 'Cow farm, dairy farm'. OE *cū* + *wīc*.

Cowley Devon, near Exeter. *Couelegh* 1237. 'Clearing of a man called *Cofa or Cufa'. OE pers. name + *lēah*.

Cowley Glos. *Kulege* 1086 (DB). 'Clearing where cows are pastured'. OE *cū* + *lēah*.

Cowley Gtr. London. *Cofenlea* 959, *Covelie* 1086 (DB). 'Clearing of a man called *Cofa'. OE pers. name + *lēah*.

Cowley Oxon. *Couelea* 1004, *Covelie* 1086 (DB). 'Clearing of a man called *Cofa or Cufa'. OE pers. name + *lēah*.

Cowling N. Yorks., near Glusburn. *Torneton* 1086 (DB), *Thornton Colling* 1202. Originally 'farmstead where thorn-

trees grow' from OE *thorn* + *tūn*, with manorial affix from a person or family called Colling. The first part of the name went out of use in the 15th cent.

Cowling N. Yorks., near Bedale. *Collinghe* 1086 (DB). 'Place characterized by a hill'. OE *coll* + -*ing*.

Cowlinge Suffolk. *Culinge* 1086 (DB). Probably 'place associated with a man called *Cūl or *Cūla'. OE pers. name + -*ing*.

Cowpen Bewley Stock. on T. *Cupum c.*1150. '(Place by) the coops or baskets (for catching fish)'. OE *cūpe* in a dative plural form *cūpum*. Affix from its possession by the manor of Bewley ('beautiful place', OFrench *beau* + *lieu*).

Cowplain Hants, recorded from 1859, self-explanatory.

Cowton, East & *Cowton, North* N. Yorks. *Cudtone, Cotun* 1086 (DB). Probably 'cow farm, dairy farm'. OE *cū* + *tūn*.

Coxhoe Durham. *Cockishow* 1277. Possibly 'hill-spur of a man called *Cocc'. OE pers. name + *hōh*.

Coxley Somerset. *Cokesleg* 1207. 'Wood or clearing belonging to the cook'. OE *cōc* + *lēah*. The wife of a cook in the royal household is recorded as holding lands near Wells in 1086 (DB).

Coxwell, Great & *Coxwell, Little* Oxon. *Cochesvelle* 1086 (DB), *Cokeswell* 1227. Probably 'spring or stream of a man called *Cocc'. OE pers. name + *wella*.

Coxwold N. Yorks. *Cuhawalda |sic|* 758, *Cucualt* 1086 (DB), *Cukewald* 1154–89. Probably 'woodland haunted by the cuckoo'. OE *cucu* + *wald*.

Craanford (*Áth an Chorráin*) Wexford. 'Ford of the crescent'.

Crackenthorpe Cumbria. *Cracantorp* late 12th cent. 'Outlying farmstead or hamlet of a man called *Krakandi, or one frequented by crows or ravens'. OScand. pers. name or OE *crāca* (genitive plural -*ena*) + OScand. *thorp*.

Cracoe N. Yorks. *Crakehou* 12th cent. 'Spur of land or hill frequented by crows or ravens'. OScand. *kráka* + OE *hōh* or OScand. *haugr*.

Cradley Heref. & Worcs. *Credelaie* 1086 (DB). 'Woodland clearing of a man called Creoda'. OE pers. name + *lēah*.

Craggagh (*An Chreagach*) Clare. 'The rocky place'.

Craig (*An Chreig*) Tyrone. 'The rock'.

Craigatuke (*Creig an tSeabhaic*) Tyrone. 'Rock of the hawk'.

Craigavad (*Creig an Bháda*) Down. 'Rock of the boat'.

Craigavon Armagh. Craigavon was designated a New Town in 1965 and named after James *Craig*, first prime minister of Northern Ireland, whose title was Viscount *Craigavon*.

Craigban (*Creig Bán*) Antrim. 'White rock'.

Craigbane (*Creig Bán*) Derry. 'White rock'.

Craigboy (*Creig Buî*) Galway. 'Yellow rock'.

Craigbrack (*Creig Breac*) Derry. 'Speckled rock'.

Craigdoo (*Creig Dubh*) Donegal. 'Black rock'.

Craigie Perth. *Cragyn* 1266. '(Place) by the rock'. Gaelic *creag*.

Craiglea (*Creig Liath*) Derry. 'Grey rock'.

Craigmore (*Creig Mór*) Antrim, Derry. 'Big rock'.

Craigmore Stir (Bute). 'Big rock'. Gaelic *creag* + *mór*.

Craignagat (*Creig na gCat*) Antrim. 'Rock of the cats'.

Craigs (*Na Creaga*) Antrim. 'The rocks'.

Crail Fife. *Cherel* c.1150, *Caraile* 1153. May contain British *caer* 'fortified place'.

Crakehall, Great & **Crakehall, Little** N. Yorks. *Crachele* 1086 (DB). 'Nook of land frequented by crows or ravens'. OScand. *kráka* or *krákr* + OE *halh*.

Crambe N. Yorks. *Crambom* 1086 (DB). '(Place at) the river-bends'. OE **cramb* in a dative plural form **crambum*.

Cramlington Northum. *Cramlingtuna* c.1130. Possibly 'farmstead of the people living at the cranes' stream'. OE *cran* + *wella* + *-inga-* + *tūn*.

Cran (*Crann*) Cavan, Fermanagh. 'Tree'.

Crana (*Crannach*) (river) Donegal. 'Abounding in trees'.

Cranage Ches. *Croeneche* |*sic*| 1086 (DB), *Cranlach* 12th cent. 'Boggy place or stream frequented by crows'. OE *crāwe* (genitive plural *crāwena*) + **læc(c)*.

Cranagh (*An Chrannóg*) Tyrone. 'The place abounding in wood'.

Cranborne Dorset. *Creneburne* 1086 (DB). 'Stream frequented by cranes or herons'. OE *cran* + *burna*. It gives name to **Cranborne Chase**, first recorded in the 13th cent., from ME *chace* 'tract of land for breeding and hunting wild animals'. The river-name **Crane** is a 'back-formation' from the place-name.

Cranbrook Kent. *Cranebroca* 11th cent. 'Brook frequented by cranes or herons'. OE *cran* + *brōc*. The river-name **Crane** is a 'back-formation' from the place-name.

Crancam (*Crann Cam*) Roscommon. 'Crooked tree'.

Cranfield Beds. *Crangfeldæ* 1060, *Cranfelle* 1086 (DB). 'Open land frequented by cranes or herons'. OE *cran*, *cranuc* + *feld*.

Cranford, 'ford frequented by cranes or herons', OE *cran* + *ford*: **Cranford** Gtr. London. *Cranforde* 1086 (DB). **Cranford St Andrew** & **Cranford St John** Northants. *Craneford* 1086 (DB), *Craneford Sancti Andree*, *Craneford Sancti Iohannis* 1254. Affixes from the dedications of the churches.

Cranford (*Creamhgort*) Donegal. *Crawarte* 1603. 'Garlic field'.

Cranham Glos. *Craneham* 12th cent. 'Enclosure or river-meadow frequented by cranes or herons'. OE *cran* + *hamm*.

Cranham Gtr. London. *Craohv* |*sic*| 1086 (DB), *Crawenho* 1201. 'Spur of land frequented by crows'. OE *crāwe* (genitive plural *crāwena*) + *hōh* (the later spelling perhaps reflecting a dative plural *hōum*).

Cranleigh Surrey. *Cranlea* 1166. 'Woodland clearing frequented by cranes or herons' OE *cran* + *lēah*.

Cranmore, East & **Cranmore, West** Somerset. *Cranemere* 10th cent., *Crenemelle* |*sic*|1086 (DB). 'Pool frequented by cranes or herons'. OE *cran* + *mere*.

Crann (*Crann*) Armagh. 'Tree'.

Crannagh (*Crannach*) Galway, Laois, Mayo, Roscommon, Tyrone. 'Abounding in trees'.

Crannogue (*Crannóg*) Tyrone. 'Artificial island'.

Crannogueboy (*Crannóg Buí*) Donegal. 'Yellow artificial island'.

Cranny (*Crannach*) Clare, Derry, Donegal, Tyrone. 'Abounding in trees'.

Cranoe Leics. *Craweho* 1086 (DB). 'Spur of land frequented by crows'. OE *crāwe* (genitive plural *crāwena*) + *hōh*.

Cransford Suffolk. *Craneforda* 1086 (DB). 'Ford frequented by cranes or herons'. OE *cran* + *ford*.

Cransley, Great Northants. *Cranslea* 956, *Craneslea* 1086 (DB). 'Woodland clearing frequented by cranes or herons'. OE *cran* + *lēah*.

Cranswick E. R. Yorks., *see* HUTTON CRANSWICK.

Crantock Cornwall, *Sanctus Carentoch* 1086 (DB). 'Church of St Carantoc'. From the patron saint of the church.

Cranwell Lincs. *Craneuuelle* 1086 (DB). 'Spring or stream frequented by cranes or herons'. OE *cran* + *wella*.

Cranwich Norfolk. *Cranewisse* 1086 (DB). 'Marshy meadow frequented by cranes or herons'. OE *cran* + *wisc*.

Cranworth Norfolk. *Cranaworda* 1086 (DB). 'Enclosure frequented by cranes or herons'. OE *cran* + *worth*.

Craster Northum. *Craucestre* 1242. 'Old fortification or earthwork haunted by crows'. OE *crāwe* + *ceaster*.

Craswall Heref. & Worcs. *Cressewell* 1231. 'Spring or stream where water-cress grows'. OE *cærse* + *wella*.

Cratfield Suffolk. *Cratafelda* 1086 (DB). 'Open land of a man called **Cræta*'. OE pers. name + *feld*.

Crathie Aber. Origin unknown, possibly 'place amid brushwood'. Gaelic *creathach*.

Crathorne N. Yorks. *Cratorne* 1086 (DB). Possibly 'thorn-tree in a nook of land'. OScand. *krá* + *thorn*.

Cratloe (*An Chreatalach*) Clare. 'The place of frames'.

Craughwell (*Creachmhaoil*) Galway. 'Garlic wood'.

Craven (district) N. Yorks. *Crave* 1086 (DB), *Cravena* 12th cent. Probably an old Celtic name meaning 'garlic place'.

Craven Arms Shrops., a 19th cent. name for the town that grew up at this important railway junction, taken from the Craven Arms inn built c.1800 and itself named from the Earls of Craven.

Crawcrook Tyne & Wear. *Cravecroca* 1130. 'Bend (in a road) or nook of land frequented by crows'. OE *crāwe* + OScand. *krókr* or OE **crōc*.

Crawford S. Lan. *Crauford* c.1150. 'Ford frequented by crows'. OE *crawe* + *ford*.

Crawfordsburn Down. *Crawford's Burn* 1744. 'Crawford's stream'. The Crawford family settled here in the early 17th cent. The equivalent Irish name is *Sruth Chráfard*.

Crawley, usually 'wood or clearing frequented by crows' OE *crāwe* + *lēah*; examples include: **Crawley** Hants. *Crawanlea* 909, *Crawelie* 1086 (DB). **Crawley** Oxon. *Croule* 1214. **Crawley** W. Sussex. *Crauleia* 1203. **Crawley Down**, *Crauledun* 1272, has the addition of OE *dūn* 'hill, down'. **Crawley, North** Bucks. *Crauelai* 1086 (DB).

Crawshaw Booth Lancs. *Croweshagh* 1324. 'Small wood or copse frequented by crows'. OE *crāwe* + *sc(e)aga*, with the later addition of OScand. *bōth* 'cowhouse, herdsman's hut'.

Cray, Foots, *Cray, North, Cray, St Mary*, & *Cray, St Pauls* Gtr. London. *Crǣga(n)* 10th cent., *Crai(e)* 1086 (DB), *Fotescrai, Northcraei* c.1100, *Creye sancte Marie* 1257, *Creypaulin* 1291. Named from the River Cray, a Celtic river-name meaning 'fresh, clean'. Foots Cray was held by a man called Fot at the time of Domesday. The affixes in St Mary & St Pauls Cray are from the dedications of the churches to St Mary and St Paulinus.

Crayford Gtr. London. *Creiford* 1199. 'Ford over the River Cray'. Celtic river-name (*see* CRAY) + OE *ford*.

Crayke N. Yorks. *Creic* 10th cent., 1086 (DB). Celtic **creig* 'a rock, a cliff'.

Creacombe Devon. *Crawecome* 1086 (DB). 'Valley frequented by crows'. OE *crāwe* + *cumb*.

Creagh (*Créach*) Fermanagh. *Creagh* 1752. 'Coarse pasture'.

Creake, North & *Creake, South* Norfolk. *Creic, Suthcreich* 1086 (DB), *Northcrec* 1211. Celtic **creig* 'a rock, a cliff'.

Creaton Northants. *Cretone* 1086 (DB). Probably 'farmstead at the rock or cliff'. Celtic **creig* + OE *tūn*.

Crecora (*Craobh Chomhartha*) Limerick. 'Palace of the sign'.

Credenhill Heref. & Worcs. *Cradenhille* 1086 (DB). 'Hill of a man called Creoda'. OE pers. name (genitive *-n*) + *hyll*.

Crediton Devon. *Cridiantune* 930. *Chritetona* 1086 (DB). 'Farmstead or estate on the River Creedy'. Celtic river-name (meaning 'the winding river') + OE *tūn*.

Creech, from Celtic **crūg* 'a mound or hill': **Creech, East** Dorset. *Criz* 1086 (DB). Referring originally to Creech Barrow. **Creech St Michael** Somerset. *Crice* 1086 (DB). Affix from the dedication of the church.

Creed Cornwall. *Sancta Crida* c.1250. 'Church of St Cride'. From the patron saint of the church.

Creedy (river) Devon, *see* CREDITON.

Creegh (*Críoch*) Clare. 'Boundary'.

Creenagh (*Críonach*) Antrim. 'Things dry and rotten with age'.

Creeslough (*An Craoslach*) Donegal. *Creslagh* 1610. 'The gullet lake'.

Creeting St Mary Suffolk. *Cratingas* 1086 (DB), *Creting Sancte Marie* 1254. '(Settlement of) the family or followers of a man called **Crǣta*'. OE pers. name + *-ingas*, with affix from the dedication of the church.

Creeton Lincs. *Cretone* 1086 (DB). Probably 'farmstead of a man called **Crǣta*'. OE pers. name + *tūn*.

Creevagh (*Craobhach*) Clare, Donegal, Galway, Mayo, Offaly, etc. 'Place of sacred trees'.

Creeve (*Craobh*) Antrim, Armagh, Donegal, Down, Longford, Mayo, Monaghan, etc. 'Sacred tree'.

Creevelea (*Craobh Liath*) Leitrim. 'Grey sacred tree'.

Creeveroe (*Craobh Ruadh*) Armagh. 'Red branch'.

Creeves (*Craobha*) Limerick. 'Sacred trees'.

Cregagh (*An Chreagaigh*) Down. *Craigogh* c.1659. 'The rocky place'.

Cregboy (*Creig Buí*) Galway. 'Yellow rock'.

Cregduff (*Creig Dubh*) Mayo. 'Black rock'.

Cregg (*Creig*) Sligo. 'Rock'.

Creggan (*Creagán*) Armagh, Derry, Westmeath. 'Little rocky place'.

Cregganbaun (*An Creagán Bán*) Mayo. 'The white rocky place'.

Creggs (*Na Creaga*) Galway, Roscommon. 'The rocks'.

Cremorne (*Críoch Mughdorn*) (district) Monaghan. *Crioch-Mughdhorn* n.d. 'Territory of the Mughdorna tribe'. The tribal name means 'people of Mughdorn', meaning the descendants of this man.

Crendon, Long, Bucks. *Credendone* 1086 (DB). 'Hill of a man called Creoda'. OE pers. name (genitive *-n*) + *dūn*. Affix (in use since 17th cent.) refers to length of village.

Cressage Shrops. *Cristesache* 1086 (DB). 'Christ's oak-tree'. OE *Crist* + *āc* (dative *ǣc*), probably with reference to a spot where preaching took place.

Cressing Essex. *Cressyng* 1136. 'Place where water-cress grows'. OE **cærsing*.

Cressingham, Great & *Cressingham, Little* Norfolk. *Cressingaham* 1086 (DB). Possibly 'homestead of the family or followers of a man called **Cressa*'. OE pers. name + *-inga-* + *hām*. Alternatively 'homestead with cress-beds', with a first element OE **cærsing*.

Cresswell, *Creswell*, 'spring or stream where water-cress grows', from OE *cærse* + *wella*: **Cresswell** Northum. *Kereswell* 1234. **Cresswell** Staffs. *Cressvale* 1086 (DB). **Creswell** Derbys. *Cressewella* 1176.

Cretingham Suffolk. *Gretingaham* 1086 (DB). 'Homestead of the people from a gravelly district'. OE *grēot* + *-inga-* + *hām*.

Crew (*Craobh*) Antrim, Derry, Tyrone. 'Sacred tree'.

Crew Hill (*Craobh*) Tyrone. 'Hill of the sacred tree'.

Crewe Ches. *Creu* 1086 (DB). Celtic **criu* 'a fish-trap, a weir'.

Crewe Ches., near Farndon. *Creuhalle* 1086 (DB). Identical in origin with the previous name + OE *hall* 'a hall, a manor-house'.

Crewkerne Somerset. *Crucern* 9th cent., *Cruche* 1086 (DB). Probably 'house or building at the hill', Celtic **crūg* + OE *ærn*, although *-ern* may rather represent a Celtic suffix.

Crich Derbys. *Cryc* 1009, *Crich* 1086 (DB). Celtic *crūg* 'a mound or hill'.

Cricieth (*Cricieth*) Gwyd. *Crukeith* 1273. 'Mound of the captives'. Welsh *crug + caith*. The name refers to the Norman castle, built in 1230 on a headland ('mound').

Crichel, Long & *Crichel, Moor* Dorset. *Circel* 1086 (DB), *Langecrechel* 1208, *Mor Kerchel* 1212. 'Hill called *Crich*'. Celtic *crŭg* 'hill' + explanatory OE *hyll*. Affixes are OE *lang* 'long' and OE *mōr* 'marshy ground'.

Cricieth. *See* CRICIETH.

Crick Northants. *Crec* 1086 (DB). Celtic **creig* 'a rock, a cliff'.

Crickadarn (*Crucadarn*) Powys. *Kruc kadarn* 1550, *Crucadarne* 1566, *Crickadarne* 1578, *Crickadarn* 1727, *Crickadarn, or Cerrigcadarn* 1868. 'Strong mound'. Welsh *crug + cadarn*.

Cricket St Thomas Somerset. *Cruche* 1086 (DB), *Cruk Thomas* 1291. Celtic **crŭg* 'a mound or hill' with the later addition of OFrench *-ette* 'little'. Affix from the dedication of the church.

Crickheath Shrops. *Gruchet* 1272. Probably Celtic **crŭg* 'hill' + OE *hēth* 'heath'.

Crickhowell (*Crucywel*) Powys. *Crichoel* 1263, *Crukhowell* 1281. 'Hywel's mound'. Welsh *crug* + pers. name.

Cricklade Wilts. *Cracgelade* 10th cent., *Crichelade* 1086 (DB). 'River-crossing at the rock or hill'. Celtic **creig* or **crŭg* + OE (*ge*)*lād*.

Cricklewood Gtr. London. *Le Crikeldwode* 1294. 'The curved wood'. ME *crikeled + wode*.

Cridling Stubbs N. Yorks. *Credeling* 12th cent., *Credlingstubbes* 1480. 'Place of a man called **Cridela*'. OE pers. name + *-ing*, with the later addition of Stubbs, 'tree-stumps', from OE *stubb*.

Crieff Perth. *Craoibh* n.d. '(Place among the) trees'. Gaelic *craobh*.

Criffell (mountain) Dumf. *Crefel* 1330. Possibly '(split) mountain'. OScand. (*kryfja*) + *fjall*; first element doubtful.

Crigglestone W. Yorks. *Crigestone* 1086 (DB). 'Farmstead at the hill called *Crik*'. Celtic **crŭg* 'hill' + explanatory OE *hyll* + OE *tūn*.

Crilly (*Crithligh*) Tyrone. *Crelly* 1608. 'Quaking bog'.

Crimplesham Norfolk. *Crepelesham* |*sic*| 1086 (DB), *Crimplesham* 1200. 'Homestead of a man called **Crympel*'. OE pers. name + *hām*.

Cringleford Norfolk. *Kringelforda* 1086 (DB). 'Ford by the round hill'. OScand. *kringla* + OE *ford*.

Crinkle (*Críonchoill*) Offaly. 'Withered wood'.

Croagh (*Cruach*) Donegal, Limerick. 'Rick'.

Croaghan (*Cruachán*) Donegal. 'Little rick'.

Croaghanmoira (*Cruach na Machaire*) Wicklow. 'Rock of the plain'.

Croaghbeg (*Cruach Beag*) Donegal. 'Little rick'.

Croaghpatrick (*Cruach Phádraig*) Mayo. 'Pádraig's rick'.

Crockerton Wilts. *Crokerton* 1249. 'Estate of the potters or of a family called Crocker'. OE **croccere* or ME surname + OE *tūn*.

Crocknagapple (*Cnoc na gCapall*) Donegal. 'Hill of the horses'.

Croft, usually from OE *croft* 'a small enclosed field'; examples include: **Croft** Lincs. *Croft* 1086 (DB). **Croft** N. Yorks. *Croft* 1086 (DB).
However the following has a different origin: **Croft** Leics. *Craeft* 836, *Crebre* |*sic*| 1086 (DB). OE *craeft* 'a machine, an engine', perhaps referring to some kind of mill.

Crofton Gtr. London. *Croptun* 8th cent. 'Farmstead near a hill'. OE *crop(p) + tūn*.

Crofton W. Yorks. *Scroftune* |*sic*| 1086 (DB), *Croftona* 12th cent. 'Farmstead with a croft or enclosure'. OE *croft + tūn*.

Croghan (*Cruachán*) Offaly, Roscommon, Wicklow. 'Little rick'.

Croglin Cumbria. *Crokelyn* c.1140. 'Torrent with a bend in it'. OE **crōc + hlynn*.

Crohane (*Cruachán*) Kerry. 'Little rick'.

Crom (*Crom*) Fermanagh. 'Bend'.

Cromane (*An Cromán*) Kerry. 'The hip'.

Cromarty Highland. *Crumbathyn* 1264. 'Crooked (place). OGaelic *crumb* + doubtful element.

Crombie Aber. '(Place) at the crooked place'. Gaelic *crombach* (locative *crombaich*).

Cromer Norfolk. *Crowemere* 13th cent. 'Lake frequented by crows'. OE *crāwe + mere*.

Cromford Derbys. *Crunforde* 1086 (DB). 'Ford by the river bend'. OE **crumbe + ford*.

Cromhall S. Glos. *Cromhal* 1086 (DB). 'Nook of land in the river bend'. OE **crumbe + halh*.

Cromkill (*Cromchoill*) Antrim. 'Bent wood'.

Cromwell Notts. *Crunwelle* 1086 (DB). 'Crooked stream'. OE *crumb + wella*.

Crondall Hants. *Crundellan* c.880, *Crundele* 1086 (DB). '(Place at) the chalk-pits or quarries'. OE *crundel* in a dative plural form.

Cronton Mersey. *Crohinton* 1242. Possibly 'farmstead at the place with a nook'. OE **crōh + -ing + tūn*.

Crook Cumbria. *Croke* 12th cent. OScand. *krókr* or OE **crōc* 'land in a bend, secluded corner of land'.

Crook Durham. *Cruketona* 1267, *Crok* 1304. Identical in origin with the previous name, originally with OE *tūn* 'farmstead, estate'.

Crookham Berks. *Crocheham* 1086 (DB). Probably 'homestead or village by the river bends'. OE **crōc + hām*.

Crookham Northum. *Crucum* 1244. '(Place) at the river bends'. OScand. *krókr* in a dative plural form.

Crookham, Church Hants. *Crocham* 1248. Identical in origin with CROOKHAM (Berks.).

Crookhaven (*An Cruachán*) Cork. 'The haven of the little rick'.

Croom (*Cromadh*) Limerick. 'Crooked ford'.

Croome, Earls Heref. & Worcs. *Cromman* 10th cent., *Crumbe* 1086 (DB), *Erlescrombe* 1495. Originally the name of the stream here, a Celtic river-name meaning 'the crooked or winding one'. Manorial affix from its early possession by the Earls of Warwick.

Cropredy Oxon. *Cropelie* |*sic*| 1086 (DB), *Croprithi* c.1275. 'Small stream of a man called *Croppa, or near a hill'. OE pers. name or *crop(p)* + *rīthig*.

Cropston Leics. *Cropeston* 12th cent. 'Farmstead of a man called *Cropp or Kroppr'. OE or OScand. pers. name + OE *tūn*. Alternatively the first element may be OE *crop(p)* 'hill'.

Cropthorne Heref. & Worcs. *Croppethorne* 8th cent., *Cropetorn* 1086 (DB). 'Thorn-tree near a hill'. OE *crop(p)* + *thorn*.

Cropton N. Yorks. *Croptune* 1086 (DB). 'Farmstead near a hill'. OE *crop(p)* + *tūn*.

Cropwell Bishop & *Cropwell Butler* Notts. *Crophille* 1086 (DB), *Bischopcroppehill* 1280, *Croppill Boteiller* 1265. 'Rounded hill'. OE *crop(p)* + *hyll*. Manorial additions from possession by the Archbishop of York and by the Butler family, here from the 12th cent.

Crory (*Cruaire*) Wexford. 'Hard land'.

Crosby, usually 'village where there are crosses'. from OScand. *krossa-bý*; examples include: **Crosby** Cumbria, near Maryport. *Croseby* 12th cent. **Crosby, Great** & **Crosby, Little** Mersey. *Crosebi* 1086 (DB), *Magna Crossby* c.1190, *Parva Crosseby* 1242. Affixes are Latin *magna* 'great', and *parva* 'little'. **Crosby Garrett** Cumbria. *Crosseby* 1200, *Crosebi Gerard* 1206. Manorial affix from a person or family called Gerard. **Crosby, Low** Cumbria. *Crosebi* c.1200. **Crosby Ravensworth** Cumbria. *Crosseby Raveneswart* 12th cent. Manorial affix from the OScand. pers. name *Rafnsvartr*.
　　However the following has a different origin: **Crosby** N. Lincs. *Cropesbi* |*sic*| 1086 (DB), *Crochesbi* 12th cent. 'Farmstead or village of a man called Krókr, or in a nook'. OScand. pers. name or *krókr* + *bý*.

Croscombe Somerset. *Correges cumb* 705, *Coriscoma* 1086 (DB). Identical in origin with CORSCOMBE Dorset.

Cross (*Crois*) Clare, Mayo. 'Cross'.

Cross Keys Cavan. *Crosskeys* 1728. The name was that of an inn here. The Irish name of the village is *Carraig an Tobair*, 'rock of the well'.

Crossabeg (*Na Crosa Beaga*) Wexford. 'The little crosses'.

Crossakeel (*Crosa Caoil*) Meath. 'Crosses of Caol'.

Crossbarry (*Crois an Bharraigh*) Cork. 'Cross of the Barries'.

Crosscanonby Cumbria. *Crosseby Canoun* 1285. 'Village where there are crosses'. OScand. *krossa-bý*. Canon refers to lands here given to the canons of Carlisle.

Crossdoney (*Cros Domhnaigh*) Cavan. *Crossdony* c.1660. 'Cross of the church'.

Crossens Mersey. *Crossenes* c.1250. 'Headland or promontory with crosses'. OScand. *kross* + *nes*.

Crosserlough (*Crois ar Loch*) Cavan. *Croserlagh* 1601. 'Cross on the lake'.

Crossgar (*An Chrois Ghearr*) Down. 'The short cross'.

Crossmaglen (*Crois Mhic Lionnáin*) Armagh. *Crosmoyglan* 1609. 'Mac Lionnáin's cross'.

Crossmolina (*Crois Mhaoilíona*) Mayo. 'Maoilíona's cross'.

Crossooha (*Crois Uathaidh*) Galway. 'Single cross'.

Crosspatrick (*Crois Phádraig*) Kilkenny, Wicklow. 'Pádraig's cross'.

Crossreagh (*An Chros Riabhach*) Cavan. 'The grey cross' or 'the brindled cross'.

Crosthwaite Cumbria. *Crosthwait* 12th cent. 'Clearing with a cross'. OScand. *kross* + *thveit*.

Croston Lancs. *Croston* 1094. 'Farmstead or village with a cross'. OScand. *kross* or OE *cros* + *tūn*.

Crostwick Norfolk. *Crostueit* 1086 (DB). 'Clearing with a cross'. OScand. *kross* + *thveit*.

Crostwight Norfolk. *Crostwit* 1086 (DB). Identical in origin with the previous name.

Crouch (river) Essex, *see* BURNHAM ON CROUCH.

Croughton Northants. *Creveltone* 1086 (DB). 'Farmstead or village on the fork of land'. OE *creowel* + *tūn*.

Crow Hants. *Croue* 1086 (DB). Possibly Celtic *crīu* 'a fish-trap, a weir'.

Crowan Cornwall. *Eggloscrauuen* c.1170. 'Church of St Cravenna'. From the patron saint of the church (in the early spelling with Cornish *eglos* 'church').

Crowbane (*Cruach Bán*) Donegal. 'White rick'.

Crowborough E. Sussex. *Cranbergh* (*sic*, for *Craubergh*) 1292. 'Hill or mound frequented by crows'. OE *crāwe* + *beorg*.

Crowcombe Somerset. *Crawancumb* 10th cent., *Crawecumbe* 1086 (DB). 'Valley frequented by crows'. OE *crāwe* + *cumb*.

Crowdecote Derbys. *Crudecote* 13th cent. 'Cottage of a man called *Crūda'. OE pers. name + *cot*.

Crowfield Suffolk. *Crofelda* 1086 (DB). Probably 'open land near the nook or corner'. OE *crōh* + *feld*.

Crowhurst E. Sussex. *Croghyrste* 772, *Croherst* 1086 (DB). Probably 'wooded hill near the nook or corner'. OE *crōh* + *hyrst*.

Crowhurst Surrey. *Crouhurst* 12th cent. 'Wooded hill frequented by crows'. OE *crāwe* + *hyrst*.

Crowland Lincs. *Cruwland* 8th cent., *Croiland* 1086 (DB). Possibly 'estate or tract of land at the river bend'. OE *crūw* + *land*.

Crowle Heref. & Worcs. *Crohlea* 9th cent., *Croelai* 1086 (DB). 'Woodland clearing by the nook or corner'. OE *crōh* + *lēah*.

Crowle N. Lincs. *Crule* 1086 (DB). Originally the name of a river here (now gone through draining), from OE *crull* meaning 'winding'.

Crowmarsh Gifford Oxon. *Cravmares* 1086 (DB), *Cromershe Giffard* 1316. 'Marsh frequented by crows'.

OE *crāwe* + *mersc*, with manorial affix from a man called Gifard who held the manor in 1086.

Crownthorpe Norfolk. *Congrethorp, Cronkethor* 1086 (DB). OScand. *thorp* 'outlying farmstead or hamlet' with an uncertain first element, possibly a pers. name.

Crowthorne Berks., first recorded in 1607, 'thorn-tree frequented by crows'.

Crowton Ches. *Crouton* 1260. 'Farmstead frequented by crows'. OE *crāwe* + *tūn*.

Croxall Staffs. *Crokeshalle* 942, *Crocheshalle* 1086 (DB). 'Nook of land of a man called Krókr, or near a bend'. OScand. pers. name or OE **crōc* + OE *halh*.

Croxdale Durham. *Crokesteil* 1195. 'Projecting piece of land of a man called Krókr. OScand. pers. name + OE *tægl*.

Croxden Staffs. *Crochesdene* 1086 (DB). Possibly 'valley of a man called Krókr'. OScand. pers. name + OE *denu*. Alternatively the first element may be OE **crōc* 'nook, bend'.

Croxley Green Herts. *Crokesleya* 1166. 'Woodland clearing of a man called Krókr'. OScand. pers. name + OE *lēah*.

Croxton, 'farmstead in a nook, or of a man called Krókr', from OE **crōc* or OScand. pers. name + OE *tūn*: **Croxton** Cambs. *Crochestone* 1086 (DB). **Croxton** N. Lincs. *Crochestune* 1086 (DB). **Croxton** Norfolk, near Thetford. *Crokestuna* 1086 (DB). **Croxton** Staffs. *Crochestone* 1086 (DB). **Croxton Kerrial** Leics. *Crohtone* 1086 (DB), *Croxton Kyriel* 1247. Manorial addition from the Kyriel family, here in the 13th cent. **Croxton, South** Leics. *Crochestone* 1086 (DB), *Sudcroxton* 1212. OE *sūth* 'south'.

Croyde Devon. *Crideholda* |*sic*| 1086 (DB), *Crideho* 1242. 'The headland', from OE **crȳde* referring to the promontory called Croyde Hoe (with explanatory OE *hōh* 'hill-spur').

Croydon Cambs. *Crauuedene* 1086 (DB). 'Valley frequented by crows'. OE *crāwe* + *denu*.

Croydon Gtr. London. *Crogedene* 809, *Croindene* 1086 (DB). 'Valley where wild saffron grows'. OE *croh, *crogen* + *denu*.

Crucadarn. *See* CRICKADARN.

Cruckmeole Shrops. *Mele* 1255, *Crokemele* 1292. Named from Meole Brook (*see* MEOLE BRACE), first element as in following name.

Cruckton Shrops. *Crokton, Crukton* 1272. Probably 'farmstead or estate by the river-bend'. OE **crōc* + *tūn*.

Crucywel. *See* CRICKHOWELL.

Crudgington Shrops. *Crugetone* |*sic*| 1086 (DB), *Crugelton* 12th cent. Probably 'farmstead by a hill called *Cruc*'. Celtic **crūg* + explanatory OE *hyll* + OE *tūn*.

Crudwell Wilts. *Croddewelle* 9th cent., *Credvelle* 1086 (DB). 'Spring or stream of a man called Creoda'. OE pers. name + *wella*.

Cruit (*An Chruit*) (island) Donegal. 'The hump'.

Crumlin (*Cromghlinn*) Antrim, Dublin. 'Crooked valley'.

Crundale Kent. *Crundala* c.1100. OE *crundel* 'a chalk-pit, a quarry'.

Crusheen (*Croisín*) Clare. 'Little cross'.

Cruwys Morchard Devon, *see* MORCHARD.

Crux Easton Hants., *see* EASTON.

Crymych Pemb. *Crymmych* 1584, *Nant Crymich* 1652. '(Place by the) crooked stream'. Welsh *crwm*. The village probably took its name directly from the Crymych Arms inn here.

Crystal Palace Gtr. London, district named from the spectacular building, originally erected in Hyde Park for the Great Exhibition of 1851 but moved here later that year and destroyed by fire in 1936. The structure was first dubbed Crystal Palace by the magazine Punch on account of its large areas of glass.

Cubbington Warwicks. *Cobintone* 1086 (DB). 'Estate associated with a man called **Cubba*'. OE pers. name + *-ing-* + *tūn*.

Cubert Cornwall. *Sanctus Cubertus* 1269. 'Church of St Cuthbert'. From the patron saint of the church.

Cublington Bucks. *Coblincote* |*sic*| 1086 (DB), *Cubelintone* 12th cent. 'Estate associated with a man called **Cubbel*'. OE pers. name + *-ing-* + *tūn* (with alternative *cot* 'cottage' in the Domesday spelling).

Cuckfield W. Sussex. *Kukefeld, Kukufeld* c.1095. Probably 'open land haunted by the cuckoo'. OE **cucu* + *feld*.

Cucklington Somerset. *Cocintune* |*sic*| 1086 (DB), *Cukelingeton* 1212. 'Estate associated with a man called **Cucol* or **Cucola*'. OE pers. name + *-ing-* + *tūn*.

Cuddesdon Oxon. *Cuthenesdune* 956, *Codesdone* 1086 (DB). 'Hill of a man called **Cūthen*'. OE pers. name + *dūn*.

Cuddington, 'estate associated with a man called Cud(d)a', OE pers. name + *-ing-* + *tūn*: **Cuddington** Bucks. *Cudintuna* 12th cent. **Cuddington** Ches. *Codynton* c.1235. **Cuddington Heath** Ches. *Cuntitone* 1086 (DB), *Cudyngton Hethe* 1532.

Cudham Gtr. London. *Codeham* 1086 (DB). 'Homestead or village of a man called Cuda'. OE pers. name + *hām*.

Cudworth Somerset. *Cudeworde* 1086 (DB). 'Enclosure of a man called Cuda'. OE pers. name + *worth*.

Cudworth S. Yorks. *Cuthewurthe* 12th cent. 'Enclosure of a man called Cūtha'. OE pers. name + *worth*.

Cuffley Herts. *Kuffele* 1255. Probably 'woodland clearing of a man called **Cuffa*'. OE pers. name + *lēah*.

Cuilmore (*An Choill Mhór*) Mayo. 'The big wood'.

Culcavy (*Cúil Chéibhe*) Down. *Cowlecavy* 1632. 'Corner of the long grass'.

Culcheth Ches. *Culchet* 1201. Probably 'narrow wood'. Celtic **cūl* + **cēd*.

Culcrum (*An Choill Chrom*) Antrim. 'The crooked wood'.

Culdaff (*Cúil Dabhcha*) Donegal. *Culldavcha* 1429. 'Corner of the vat'.

Culfadda (*Coill Fhada*) Sligo. 'Long wood'.

Culford Suffolk. *Culeforda* 1086 (DB). 'Ford of a man called **Cūla*'. OE pers. name + *ford*.

Culgaith Cumbria. *Culgait* 12th cent. Identical in origin with CULCHETH.

Culham Oxon. *Culanhom* 821. 'River-meadow of a man called *Cūla'. OE pers. name + *hamm*.

Culkeeny (*Cúil Chaonaigh*) Donegal. 'Wood of the moss'.

Culkerton Glos. *Cvlcortone* 1086 (DB). 'Farmstead with a water-hole, or belonging to a man called *Culcere'. OE *culcor* or OE pers. name + *tūn*.

Culky (*Cuilcigh*) Fermanagh. *Colkie* 1609. 'Abounding in reeds'.

Cullahill (*An Chúlchoill*) Laois. 'The back of the wood'.

Culleens (*Na Coillíní*) Mayo. 'The small hazel woods'.

Cullen (*Cuilleann*) Cork, Tipperary. 'Steep slope'.

Cullentra (*An chuil eanntrach*) 'the holly place'. Tyrone.

Cullercoats Tyne & Wear. *Culvercoats* c.1600. 'Dove-cots'. OE *culfre* + *cot*.

Cullingworth W. Yorks. *Colingauuorde* 1086 (DB). 'Enclosure of the family or followers of a man called *Cūla'. OE pers. name + *-inga-* + *worth*.

Cullion (*Cuilleann*) Tyrone. 'Steep slope'.

Cullompton Devon. *Columtune* c.880, *Colump* |sic| 1086 (DB). 'Farmstead on the Culm river'. Celtic river-name (meaning 'winding stream') + OE *tūn*.

Culloville (*Baile Mhic Cullach*) Armagh. *Cullovill* 1766. 'Mac Cullach's townland'.

Cullybackey (*Cúil na Baice*) Antrim. *Ballycholnabacky* 1607. 'Corner of the river bend'.

Cullyhanna (*Coilleach Eanach*) Armagh. *Collyhanagh* 1640. 'Wood of the swamp'.

Culmington Shrops. *Comintone* |sic| 1086 (DB), *Culminton* 1197. Probably 'estate associated with a man called Cūthhelm'. OE pers. name + *-ing-* + *tūn*.

Culmore (*An Chúil Mhór*) Derry. (*isin*) *Chúil móir* 1600. 'The big corner'.

Culmore (*Coill Mhór*) Mayo. 'Big wood'.

Culmstock Devon. *Culumstocc* 938, *Culmestoche* 1086 (DB). 'Outlying farmstead on the Culm river'. Celtic river-name (*see* CULLOMPTON) + OE *stoc*.

Culnady (*Cúil Chnáidí*) Derry. (*go*) *Cúil Cnáimhdidhe* c.1740. 'Nook of the place of burrs'.

Culross Fife. *Culenross* 12th cent. Probably 'holly point'. Gaelic *cuileam* + *ros*.

Cults Abdn. *Qhylt* 1450, *Cuyltis* 1456. '(Place in the) woods'. Gaelic *cùillhe* + English plural *s*.

Culverthorpe Lincs. *Torp* 1086 (DB), *Calewarthorp* 1275. Originally simply 'outlying farmstead or hamlet' from OScand. *thorp*, later with the name of an owner added, form uncertain.

Culworth Northants. *Culeorde* 1086 (DB). 'Enclosure of a man called *Cūla'. OE pers. name + *worth*.

Cumberland (old county). *Cumbra land* 945. 'Region of the Cymry or Cumbrian Britons'. OE *Cumbre* + *land*.

Cumbernauld N. Lan. *Cumbrenald* c.1295, *Cumyrnald* 1417. 'Meeting of the streams'. Gaelic *comar-nan-allt*.

Cumberworth, 'enclosure of a man called Cumbra, or of the Britons', OE pers. name or OE *Cumbre* + *worth*:

Cumberworth Lincs. *Combreuorde* 1086 (DB). **Cumberworth, Lower** & **Cumberworth, Upper** W. Yorks. *Cumbreuurde* 1086 (DB).

Cumbrae (island) N. Ayr. *Cumberays* 1264. 'Island of the Cymry'. OScand. *ey*. *Great Cumbrae* and *Little Cumbrae* are probably named after the Welsh (Cumbrian) inhabitants of southern Scotland, *Cymry* being the name of the Welsh for themselves (*see* WALES).

Cumbria (new county). *Cumbria* 8th cent. 'Territory of the *Cymry* or Cumbrian Britons'. A latinization of the Primitive Welsh form of *Cymry* 'the Welsh'.

Cummer (*Comar*) Galway. 'Confluence'.

Cummersdale Cumbria. *Cumbredal* 1227. 'Valley of the Cumbrian Britons'. OE *Cumbre* (genitive plural *-a*) + OScand. *dalr*.

Cumnock E. Ayr. *Comnocke* 1297, *Comenok* 1298, *Cumnock* 1300. Meaning uncertain.

Cumnor Oxon. *Cumanoran* 931, *Comenore* 1086 (DB). 'Hill-slope of a man called *Cuma'. OE pers. name (genitive *-n*) + *ōra*.

Cumrew Cumbria. *Cumreu* c.1200. 'Valley by the hill-slope'. Celtic *cumm* + *riu*.

Cumwhinton Cumbria. *Cumquintina* c.1155. 'Valley of a man called Quintin'. Celtic *cumm* + OFrench pers. name.

Cumwhitton Cumbria. *Cumwyditon* 1278. 'Valley at a place called *Whytington* (estate associated with a man called Hwīta)'. Celtic *cumm* added to an English place-name (from OE pers. name + *-ing-* + *tūn*).

Cunard (*Cionn Ard*) Dublin. 'High head'.

Cundall N. Yorks. *Cundel* 1086 (DB). Probably originally OE *cumb* 'valley', later with the addition of an explanatory OScand. *dalr* 'valley'.

Cunnister Shet (Yell). *Cynnyngsitter* 1639. 'King's summer pasture'. OScand. *konungr* + *sætr*.

Cupar Fife. *Cupre* 1183, *Coper* 1294. Meaning uncertain. The name is British. *Cp.* COUPAR ANGUS.

Curbridge Oxon. *Crydan brigce* 956. 'Bridge of a man called Creoda'. OE pers. name + *brycg*.

Curdridge Hants. *Cuthredes hricgæ* 901. 'Ridge of a man called Cūthræd'. OE pers. name + *hrycg*.

Curland Somerset. *Curiland* 1252. Probably 'cultivated land belonging to CURRY'. OE *land*.

Curlew Mountains (*An Corrshliabh*) Roscommon, Sligo. 'The pointed mountains'.

Curr (*Corr*) Tyrone. *Corr* 1666. 'Round hill'.

Currabeha (*An Chorr Bheithe*) Cork. 'The round hill of the birch'.

Curracloe (*Currach Cló*) Wexford. 'Marsh of the impression'.

Curragh (*Currach*) Kildare. 'Marsh'.

Curragh (*Currach*) Waterford. 'Marsh'.

Curraghboy (*An Currach Buí*) Roscommon. 'The yellow marsh'.

Curraghlawn (*Currach Leathan*) Wexford. 'Broad marsh'.

Curraghmore (*Currach Mór*) Waterford. 'Big marsh'.

Curraghroe (*An Currach Rua*) Roscommon. 'The red marsh'.

Curraglass (*Cora Ghlas*) Cork. 'Green weir'.

Curraglass (*Currach Glas*) Cork. 'Grey marsh'.

Curran (*Corrán*) Antrim, Derry. 'Crescent-shaped place'.

Currandrum (*Corr an Droma*) Galway. 'Pointed hill of the ridge'.

Currane (*An Corrán*) Mayo. 'The crescent-shaped place'.

Currans (*Corráin*) Kerry. 'Crescent-shaped places'.

Curreeny (*Na Coirríní*) Tipperary. 'The little pointed hills'.

Currie Edin. *Curey* 1210, *Curry* 1213, *Curri* 1246. '(Place) in the marshland'. Gaelic locative of *currach*.

Currow (*Corra*) Kerry. 'Round hills'.

Curry (*An Choraidh*) Sligo. 'The place of the weir'.

Curry Mallet & *Curry Rivel*, *North Curry* Somerset. *Curig* 9th cent., *Curi*, *Nortcuri* 1086 (DB), *Curi Malet*, *Curry Revel* 1225. 'Estates on the river called *Curi*'. Pre-English river-name (of uncertain origin and meaning), with distinguishing affixes from families called Malet and Revel, here from the late 12th cent., and from OE *north*.

Curryglass (*Currach Glas*) Cork. 'Grey marsh'.

Curthwaite, East & *Curthwaite*, *West* Cumbria. *Kyrkthwate* 1272. 'Clearing near or belonging to a church'. OScand. *kirkja* + *thveit*.

Cury Cornwall. *Egloscuri* 1219. 'Church of St Cury' (a pet-form of St Corentin). From the patron saint of the church, with Cornish *eglos* 'church' in the early form.

Cush (*Cois*) Limerick. 'Foot'.

Cushendall (*Cois Abhann Dalla*) Antrim. *Bun an Dalla* c.1854. 'Foot of the river Dall'. The village was earlier *Bun Abhann Dalla*, 'foot of the river Dall', the present name being an anglicized form of the alternative Irish name.

Cushendun (*Cois Abhann Duinne*) Antrim. *Bun-abhann Duine* 1567. 'Foot of the river Dun'. The village was earlier *Bun Abhann Duinne*, 'foot of the river Dun', the present name being an anglicized form of the alternative Irish name.

Cushina (*Cois Eidhní*) Offaly. 'Beside the ivy (river)'.

Cusop Heref. & Worcs. *Cheweshope* 1086 (DB). OE *hop* 'small enclosed valley', first element possibly a lost Celtic river-name *Cyw*.

Cutsdean Glos. *Codestune* 10th cent., 1086 (DB), *Cottesdena* 12th cent. 'Farmstead and/or valley of a man called *Cōd*'. OE pers. name + *tūn* and/or *denu*.

Cuxham Oxon. *Cuces hamm* 995, *Cuchesham* 1086 (DB). 'River-meadow of a man called *Cuc*'. OE pers. name + *hamm*.

Cuxton Kent. *Cucolanstan* 880, *Coclestane* 1086 (DB). '(Boundary) stone of a man called *Cucola*'. OE pers. name + *stān*.

Cuxwold Lincs. *Cucuwalt* 1086 (DB), *Cucuwald* c.1115. Probably 'woodland haunted by the cuckoo'. OE *cucu* + *wald*.

Cwmafan Neat. 'Valley of the River Afan'. Welsh *cwm*. The Afan flows through the town to enter the sea at ABERAVON.

Cwmbrân Newpt. *Cwmbran* 1707. 'Valley of the River Brân'. Welsh *cwm*. The Celtic river name means 'raven' (Welsh *brân*), referring to its dark waters. Cwmbran was developed as a New Town in 1949.

Cydweli. *See* KIDWELLY.

Cymru. *See* WALES.

D

Daar (*Abhainn na Darach*) (river) Limerick. 'River of the oak tree'.

Daars (*Dairghe*) Kildare. 'Oaks'.

Dacorum (district) Herts. *Danais* 1086 (DB), *hundredo Dacorum* 1196. '(Hundred) belonging to the Danes', from the genitive plural of Latin *Daci* 'the Dacians' (erroneously used of the Danes in medieval times).

Dacre Cumbria. *Dacor* c.1125. Named from the stream called Dacre Beck, a Celtic river-name meaning 'the trickling one'.

Dacre N. Yorks. *Dacre* 1086 (DB). Originally a Celtic river-name for the stream here, identical in origin with the previous name.

Dadford Bucks. *Dodeforde* 1086 (DB). 'Ford of a man called Dodda'. OE pers. name + *ford*.

Dadlington Leics. *Dadelintona* c.1190. Probably 'estate associated with a man called *Dæd(d)el*'. OE pers. name + *-ing-* + *tūn*.

Dagenham Gtr. London. *Dæccanhaam* c.690. 'Homestead or village of a man called *Dæcca*'. OE pers. name (genitive *-n*) + *hām*.

Daglingworth Glos. *Daglingworth* c.1150. 'Enclosure of the family or followers of a man called *Dæggel* or *Dæccel*', or 'enclosure associated with the same man'. OE pers. name + *-inga-* or *-ing-* + *worth*.

Dagnall Bucks. *Dagenhale* 1196. 'Nook of land of a man called *Dægga*'. OE pers. name (genitive *-n*) + *healh*.

Daingean (*Daingean*) Offaly. 'Fortress'.

Dalbeattie Dumf. *Dalbaty* 1469. 'Haugh by the birch wood'. Gaelic *dal* + *beithigh* (gen. of *beilheach*).

Dalby, 'farmstead or village in a valley', OScand. *dalr* + *bý*; examples include: **Dalby, Great** & **Dalby, Little** Leics. *Dalbi* 1086 (DB). **Dalby, Low** N. Yorks. *Dalbi* 1086 (DB).

Dalderby Lincs. *Dalderby* c.1150. Possibly 'farmstead or village in a small valley', from OScand. *dæld* (genitive *-ar*) + *bý*. Alternatively 'valley farmstead where deer are kept', from OScand. *dalr* + *djúr* + *bý*.

Dale Derbys. *La Dale* late 12th cent. '(Place in) the valley'. OE *dæl*.

Dalgleish Sc. Bord. 'Green alluvial valley'. Gaelic *dail* + *ghlais*.

Dalham Suffolk. *Dalham* 1086 (DB). 'Homestead or village in a valley'. OE *dæl* + *hām*.

Dalkeith Midloth. *Dolchet* 1144. 'Meadow by a wood'. British **dol* + **ced*.

Dalkey (*Deilginis*) Dublin. 'Thorn island'. OScand. *dalkr* + *ey*.

Dallas Moray. *Dolays* 1232. 'Meadow'. British **dol* + **foss*.

Dalling, Field & *Dalling, Wood* Norfolk. *Dallinga* 1086 (DB), *Fildedalling* 1272, *Wode Dallinges* 1198. '(Settlement of) the family or followers of a man called Dalla'. OE pers. name + *ingas*. The distinguishing affixes are *feld* or **filden* (denoting 'in the open country') and *wudu* (denoting 'in the woodland').

Dallinghoo Suffolk. *Dallingahou* 1086 (DB). 'Hill-spur of the family or followers of a man called Dalla'. OE pers. name + *-inga-* + *hōh*.

Dallington E. Sussex. *Dalintone* 1086 (DB). 'Estate associated with a man called Dalla'. OE pers. name + *-ing-* + *tūn*.

Dalry N. Ayr. *Dalry* 1315. 'Heather meadow'. Gaelic *daíl fhraoich* (genitive of travel).

Dalston Cumbria. *Daleston* 1187. Probably 'farmstead of a man called **Dall*'. OE pers. name + *tūn*.

Dalston Gtr. London. *Derleston* 1294. 'Farmstead of a man called Dēorlāf'. OE pers. name + *tūn*.

Dalton, a common place-name in the northern counties of England, 'farmstead or village in a valley', from OE *dæl* + *tūn*; examples include: **Dalton** Lancs. *Daltone* 1086 (DB). **Dalton** Northum., near Hexham. *Dalton* 1256. **Dalton** Northum., near Stamfordham. *Dalton* 1201. **Dalton** N. Yorks., near Richmond. *Daltun* 1086 (DB). **Dalton** N. Yorks., near Thirsk. *Deltune* 1086 (DB). **Dalton** S. Yorks. *Daltone* 1086 (DB). **Dalton in Furness** Cumbria. *Daltune* 1086 (DB), *Dalton in Fournais* 1332. For the district name Furness, *see* BARROW IN FURNESS. **Dalton-le-Dale** Durham. *Daltun* 8th cent. The addition means 'in the valley', from OE *dæl*. **Dalton, North** E. R. Yorks. *Dalton* 1086 (DB), *Northdaltona* c.1155. **Dalton-on-Tees** N. Yorks. *Dalton* 1204. On the River Tees. **Dalton Piercy** Hartlepl. *Daltun* c.1150. *Dalton Percy* 1370. Manorial affix from the Percy family, here up to the 14th cent. **Dalton, South** E. R. Yorks. *Delton* 1086 (DB), *Suthdalton* 1260.

Dalton Dumf. *Delton* c.1280. 'Village in a valley'. OE *dæl* + *tūn*.

Dalua (*Abhainn dá Lua*) (river) Cork. 'River of two waters'.

Dalwhinnie Highland. 'Valley of the champions'. Gaelic *dail* + *chuinardh* (genitive).

Dalwood Devon. *Dalewude* 1195. 'Wood in a valley'. OE *dæl* + *wudu*.

Dalziel N. Lan. 'White meadow'. Gaelic *dail* + *ghil* (dative of *geal*).

Damerham Hants. *Domra hamme* c.880, *Dobreham* [*sic*] 1086 (DB). 'Enclosure or river-meadow of the judges'. OE *dōmere* + *hamm*.

Damma (*Dá Mhagh*) Kerry. 'Two plains'.

Danbury Essex. *Danengeberiam* 1086 (DB). Probably 'stronghold of the family or followers of a man called Dene'. OE pers. name + *-inga-* + *burh* (dative *byrig*).

Danby N. Yorks. *Danebi* 1086 (DB). 'Farmstead or village of the Danes'. OScand. *Danir* (genitive plural *Dana*) + *bý*.

Danby Wiske N. Yorks. *Danebi* 1086 (DB), *Daneby super Wiske* 13th cent. Identical in origin with the previous name. Situated on the River Wiske (*see* APPLETON WISKE).

Dane (river) Ches., *see* DAVENHAM.

Danehill E. Sussex. *Denne* 1279. *Denhill* 1437. 'Hill by the woodland pasture'. OE *denn* with the later addition of *hyll*.

Darcy Lever Gtr. Manch., *see* LEVER.

Darenth Kent. *Daerintan* 10th cent., *Tarent* 1086 (DB). '(Estate on) the River Darent'. Darent is a Celtic river-name meaning 'river where oak-trees grow'.

Daresbury Ches. *Deresbiria* 12th cent. 'Stronghold of a man called Dēor'. OE pers. name + *burh* (dative *byrig*).

Darfield S. Yorks. *Dereuueld* 1086 (DB). 'Open land frequented by deer or other wild animals'. OE *dēor* + *feld*.

Darkley (*Dearclaigh*) Armagh. *Darkeley* 1657. 'Place of caves'.

Darlaston W. Mids. *Derlaveston* 1262. 'Farmstead or village of a man called Dēorlāf'. OE pers. name + *tūn*.

Darley, 'woodland clearing frequented by deer or wild animals', OE *dēor* + *lēah*: **Darley Abbey** Derbys. *Derlega* 12th cent. **Darley Dale** Derbys. *Dereleie* 1086 (DB).

Darlingscott Warwicks. *Derlingescot* 1210. 'Cottage(s) of a man called *Dēorling*'. OE pers. name + *cot*.

Darlington Durham. *Dearthingtun* c.1009. 'Estate associated with a man called Dēornōth'. OE pers. name + *-ing- + tūn*.

Darliston Shrops. *Derloueston* 1199. 'Farmstead of a man called Dēorlāf'. OE pers. name + *tūn*.

Darlton Notts. *Derluuetun* 1086 (DB). 'Farmstead of a woman called *Dēorlufu*'. OE pers. name + *tūn*.

Darragh (*An Darach*) Clare. 'The oak tree'.

Darraragh (*Dairbhre*) Mayo. 'Oak wood'.

Darrery (*Dairbhre*) Cork, Galway, Limerick. 'Oak wood'.

Darrington W. Yorks. *Darni(n)tone* 1086 (DB). Probably 'estate associated with a man called Dēornōth'. OE pers. name + *-ing- + tūn*.

Darrynane (*Doire Fhíonáin*) Kerry. 'Fíonán's oak wood'.

Darsham Suffolk. *Dersham* 1086 (DB). 'Homestead or village of a man called Dēor'. OE pers. name + *hām*.

Dartford Kent. *Tarentefort* 1086 (DB). 'Ford over the River Darent'. Celtic river-name (see DARENTH) + OE *ford*.

Dartington Devon. *Dertrintona* 1086 (DB). 'Farmstead on the River Dart'. Celtic river-name (meaning 'river where oak-trees grow') + *-ing- + tūn*.

Dartmoor Devon. *Dertemora* 1182. 'Moor in the Dart valley'. Celtic river-name (*see* DARTINGTON) + OE *mōr*.

Dartmouth Devon. *Dertamuthan* 11th cent. 'Mouth of the River Dart'. Celtic river-name (*see* DARTINGTON) + OE *mūtha*.

Darton S. Yorks. *Dertun* 1086 (DB). 'Enclosure for deer, deer park'. OE *dēor-tūn*.

Darwen Lancs. *Derewent* 1208. '(Estate on) the River Darwen'. Darwen is a Celtic river-name meaning 'river where oak-trees grow'.

Dassett, Avon & *Dassett, Burton* Warwicks. *Derceto(ne)* 1086 (DB). *Afnedereceth* 1185, *Burton Dassett* 1604. Probably 'fold or shelter for deer or other animals'. OE *dēor* + (*ge*)*set* or *cēte*. The distinguishing affixes are from the old Celtic name of the stream here (*Avon* meaning 'river, water') and from a nearby place (*Burton* is from OE *burh-tūn* 'fortified farmstead').

Datchet Berks. *Deccet* 10th cent., *Daceta* 1086 (DB). Probably an old Celtic name of uncertain meaning.

Datchworth Herts. *Dacewrthe* 969, *Daceuuorde* 1086 (DB). 'Enclosure of a man called *Dæcca*'. OE pers. name + *worth*.

Dauntsey Wilts. *Dometsig* 850, *Dantesie* 1086 (DB). Probably 'island or well-watered land of a man called *Dōmgeat*'. OE pers. name + *īeg*.

Davenham Ches. *Deveneham* 1086 (DB). 'Homestead or village on the River Dane'. Celtic river-name (meaning 'trickling stream') + OE *hām*.

Daventry Northants. *Daventrei* 1086 (DB). 'Tree of a man called *Dafa*'. OE pers. name (genitive *-n*) + *trēow*.

Davidson's Mains Edin. 'Davidson's home farm'. William Davidson acquired the home farm ('mains') of the Muirhouse estate here in 1776.

Davidstow Cornwall. 'Church of *Sanctus David* (*alias Dewstow*)' 1269. 'Holy place of St David'. Saint's name (Cornish *Dewy*) + OE *stōw*.

Dawley Shrops. *Dalelie* 1086 (DB), *Dalilea* c.1200. Probably 'woodland clearing associated with a man called *Dealla*'. OE pers. name + *-ing- + lēah*.

Dawlish Devon. *Douelis* 1086 (DB). Originally the name of the stream here, a Celtic river-name meaning 'dark stream'.

Dawros Head (*Ceann Dhamrois*) Donegal. 'Headland of the oxen'.

Daylesford Glos. *Dæglesford* 718, *Eilesford* |*sic*| 1086 (DB). 'Ford of a man called *Dægel*'. OE pers. name + *ford*.

Deal Kent. *Addelam* |*sic*| 1086 (DB), *Dela* 1158. '(Place at) the hollow or valley', from OE *dæl* (with Latin preposition *ad* 'at' prefixed in the earliest spelling).

Dean, *Deane*, a common place-name, '(place in) the valley', from OE *denu*: **Dean** Cumbria. *Dene* c.1170. **Deane** Gtr. Manch. *Dene* 1292. **Deane** Hants. *Dene* 1086 (DB). **Dean, East** & **Dean, West** Hants. *Dene* 1086 (DB). **Dean, East** & **Dean, West** W. Sussex. *Dene* 8th cent., *Estdena, Westdena* 1150. **Dean, Forest of** Glos. *foresta de Dene* 12th cent. **Dean, Lower** & **Dean, Upper** Beds. *Dene* 1086 (DB), *Netherdeane, Overdeane* 1539. OE *neotherra* 'lower' and *uferra* 'upper'. **Dean Prior** Devon. *Denu* 1086 (DB),

Dene Pryour 1415. Affix from its possession by Plympton Priory from the 11th cent.

Dearham Cumbria. *Derham c.*1160. 'Homestead or enclosure where deer are kept'. OE *dēor* + *hām* or *hamm*.

Dearne (river) S. Yorks., *see* BOLTON UPON DEARNE.

Debach Suffolk. *Depebecs* 1086 (DB). 'Valley or ridge near the river called *Dēope* (the deep one)'. OE river-name (*see* DEBENHAM) + *bece* or *bæc* (dative **bece*).

Debden Essex. *Deppedana* 1086 (DB). 'Deep valley'. OE *dēop* + *denu*.

Debden (Green) Essex. *Tippedene* 1062, *Tippedana* 1086 (DB). 'Valley of a man called **Tippa*'. OE pers. name + *denu*, with the addition of *green* from the 18th cent.

Debenham Suffolk. *Depbenham* 1086 (DB). 'Homestead or village by the river called *Dēope* (the deep one)'. OE river-name (now the River **Deben**) + *hām*.

Deddington Oxon: *Dædintun* 1050–2, *Dadintone* 1086 (DB). 'Estate associated with a man called Dæda'. OE pers. name + *-ing-* + *tūn*.

Dedham Essex. *Delham* |*sic*| 1086 (DB), *Dedham* 1166. 'Homestead or village of a man called **Dydda*'. OE pers. name + *hām*.

Dee (river) Ches. *Deoua c.*150. An ancient Celtic river-name meaning 'the goddess, the holy one'.

Dee (river) Abdn, 'Goddess'. British *deva*.

Deehommed (*Deachoimheád*) Down. *Dycovead* 1583. 'Good view'.

Deel (*Daoil*) (river) Limerick, Mayo, Westmeath. 'Black one'.

Deele (*Daoil*) (river) Donegal. 'Black one'.

Deene Northants. *Den* 1065, *Dene* 1086 (DB). '(Place in) the valley'. OE *denu*.

Deenethorpe Northants. *Denetorp* 1169. 'Outlying farmstead or secondary settlement dependent on DEENE'. OScand. *thorp*.

Deenish Island (*Duibhinis*) Kerry. 'Black island'.

Deepdale Cumbria. *Depedale* 1433. 'Deep valley'. OE *dēop* + *dæl*.

Deeping Gate Cambs. *Depynggate* 1390. 'Road to DEEPING' (*see* next name). OScand. *gata*.

Deeping St James & *Deeping St Nicholas*, *Deeping Market* & *West Deeping* Lincs. *Estdepinge*, *West Depinge* 1086 (DB). 'Deep or low place'. OE **dēoping*. Distinguishing affixes from the dedications of the churches, and from *market*, *east*, and *west*.

Deerhurst Glos. *Deorhyrst* 804, *Derheste* |*sic*| 1086 (DB). 'Wooded hill frequented by deer'. OE *dēor* + *hyrst*.

Defford Heref. & Worcs. *Deopanforda* 972, *Depeford* 1086 (DB). 'Deep ford'. OE *dēop* + *ford*.

Deganwy Conwy. *Arx Decantorum* 812, *Dugannu* 1191, *Diganwy* 1254. '(Place of the) Decantae'. The *Decantae* (perhaps 'noble ones') were a British tribe who occupied this region of north Wales.

Deighton, 'farmstead surrounded by a ditch', from OE *dīc* + *tūn*: **Deighton** N. Yorks., near Northallerton. *Dictune* 1086 (DB). **Deighton** York. *Distone* |*sic*| 1086 (DB). *Dicton* 1176. **Deighton, Kirk** & **Deighton, North** N. Yorks. *Distone* |*sic*| 1086 (DB), *Kirke Dighton* 14th cent., *Northdictun* 12th cent. Distinguishing affixes are OScand. *kirkja* 'church' and OE *north*.

Deiniolen Gwyd. '(Church of) St Deiniolen'. The village was originally *Ebeneser*, after the Welsh Nonconformist chapel here, from biblical *Eben-ezer*, where the Israelites were defeated by the Philistines (1 Samuel 4:1). The present name was adopted in the early 20th cent. from the parish name *Llanddeiniolen* (Welsh *llan*, 'church').

Delabole Cornwall. *Deliou* 1086 (DB), *Delyou Bol* 1284. The name of the Domesday manor *Deliou* (possibly from a Cornish word meaning 'leaves' and surviving as nearby **Deli**) with the later addition of Cornish *pol* 'pit' referring to the great slate quarry here.

Delamere Ches., named from the ancient Forest of Delamere, *foresta de la Mare* 13th cent., 'forest of the lake', from OE *mere* with the OFrench preposition and article *de la*.

Delgany (*Deilgne*) Wicklow. 'Thorny place'.

Delph, *New Delph* Gtr. Manch. *Delfe* 1544. From OE (*ge*)*delf* 'a quarry'.

Delvin (*Dealbhna*) Westmeath. '(Territory of the) descendants of Dealbaeth'.

Dembleby Lincs. *Dembelbi* 1086 (DB). 'Farmstead or village with a pool'. OScand. **dembil* + *bý*.

Denbigh (*Dinbych*) Denb. *Dinbych* 1269. 'Little fortress'. Welsh *din* + *bach*. The 'little fortress' would have stood where the the ruins of the 12th-cent. castle now lie. *Cp.* TENBY.

Denbury Devon. *Deveneberie* 1086 (DB). 'Earthwork or fortress of the Devon people'. OE *Defnas* (from Celtic *Dumnonii*) + *burh* (dative *byrig*).

Denby Derbys. *Denebi* 1086 (DB). 'Farmstead or village of the Danes'. OE *Dene* (genitive plural *Dena*) + OScand. *bý*.

Denby Dale W. Yorks. *Denebi* 1086 (DB). Identical in origin with the previous name, with the later addition of *dale* 'valley'.

Denchworth Oxon. *Deniceswurthe* 947, *Denchesworde* 1086 (DB). 'Enclosure of a man called **Denic*'. OE pers. name + *worth*.

Denford Northants. *Deneforde* 1086 (DB). 'Ford in a valley'. OE *denu* + *ford*.

Denge Marsh Kent, *see* DUNGENESS.

Dengie Essex. *Deningei c.*707, *Daneseia* 1086 (DB). Probably 'island or well-watered land associated with a man called Dene, or of Dene's people'. OE pers. name + *-ing-* or *-inga-* + *ēg*.

Denham, 'homestead or village in a valley', OE *denu* + *hām*: **Denham** Bucks. *Deneham* 1066, *Daneham* 1086 (DB). **Denham** Suffolk, near Bury St Edmunds. *Denham* 1086 (DB). **Denham** Suffolk, near Eye. *Denham* 1086 (DB).

Denholme W. Yorks. *Denholme* 1252. 'Water-meadow in the valley'. OE *denu* + OScand. *holmr*.

Denmead Hants. *Denemede* 1205. 'Meadow in the valley'. OE *denu* + *mēd*.

Dennington Suffolk. *Dingifetuna* 1086 (DB). 'Farmstead of a woman called *Denegifu*'. OE pers. name + *tūn*.

Denny Falk. *Litill Dany* 1510. Meaning unknown.

Denston Suffolk. *Danerdestuna* 1086 (DB). 'Farmstead of a man called Deneheard'. OE pers. name + *tūn*.

Denstone Staffs. *Denestone* 1086 (DB). 'Farmstead of a man called Dene'. OE pers. name + *tūn*.

Dent Cumbria, near Sedbergh. *Denet* 1202–8. Possibly an old river-name, origin and meaning uncertain. **Dentdale** (recorded from 1577) contains OScand. *dalr* 'valley'.

Denton, a common place-name, usually 'farmstead or village in a valley', from OE *denu* + *tūn*; examples include: **Denton** Cambs. *Dentun* 10th cent., *Dentone* 1086 (DB). **Denton** Durham. *Denton* 1200. **Denton** E. Sussex. *Denton* 9th cent. **Denton** Gtr. Manch. *Denton* c.1220. **Denton** Kent, near Dover. *Denetun* 799, *Danetone* 1086 (DB). **Denton** Lincs. *Dentune* 1086 (DB). *Dentuna* 1086 (DB). **Denton** N. Yorks. *Dentun* c.972, 1086 (DB). **Denton** Oxon. *Denton* 1122. **Denton, Upper** & **Denton, Nether** Cumbria. *Denton* 1169.
However the following Denton has a different origin: **Denton** Northants. *Dodintone* 1086 (DB). 'Estate associated with a man called Dodda or Dudda'. OE pers. name + *-ing-* + *tūn*.

Denver Norfolk. *Danefella |sic|* 1086 (DB), *Denever* 1200. 'Ford or passage used by the Danes'. OE *Dene* (genitive plural *Dena*) + *fær*.

Denwick Northum. *Den(e)wyc* 1242. 'Dwelling or dairy-farm in a valley'. OE *denu* + *wīc*.

Deopham Norfolk. *Depham* 1086 (DB). 'Homestead or village near the deep place or lake'. OE *Dēope* + *hām*.

Depden Suffolk. *Depdana* 1086 (DB). 'Deep valley'. OE *dēop* + *denu*.

Deptford, 'deep ford', OE *dēop* + *ford*: **Deptford** Gtr. London. *Depeforde* 1293. **Deptford** Wilts. *Depeford* 1086 (DB).

Derby Derbys. *Deoraby* 10th cent., *Derby* 1086 (DB). 'Farmstead or village where deer are kept'. OScand. *djúr* + *bý*. **Derbyshire** (OE *scīr* 'district') is first referred to in the 11th cent.

Derby, West Mersey. *Derbei* 1086 (DB), *Westderbi* 1177. Identical in origin with the previous name.

Dereham, East & *Dereham, West* Norfolk. *Der(e)ham* 1086 (DB), *Estderham* 1428, *Westderham* 1203. 'Homestead or enclosure where deer are kept'. OE *dēor* + *hām* or *hamm*.

Derg (*Dearg*) (river) Tyrone. *The Red river al. Dearg*. 'Red one'.

Derg, Lough (*Loch Dearg*) Clare, Donegal, Galway, Tipperary. 'Red lake'.

Dernagree (*Doire na Graí*) Clare. 'Oak grove of the stud of horses'.

Dernish (*Dair Inis*) Clare, Fermanagh, Sligo. 'Oak island'.

Derrad (*Doire Fhada*) Westmeath. 'Long oak grove'.

Derradda (*Doire Fhada*) Leitrim. 'Long oak wood'.

Derragh (*Darach*) Clare, Longford, Mayo. 'Oak'.

Derrane (*Doireán*) Roscommon. 'Little grove'.

Derravaragh, Lough (*Loch Dairbhreach*) Westmeath. *Logh Dervaragh* 1412. 'Lake of the oakwood'.

Derreen (*Doirín*) (river) Carlow. '(River of the) little oak grove'.

Derreen (*Doirín*) Galway. 'Oak grove'.

Derreenacarrin (*Doire an Chairn*) Clare. 'Oak grove of the cairn'.

Derreenaclaurig (*Doirín an Chláraigh*) Kerry. 'Oak grove of the planking'.

Derreenafoyle (*Doirín an Phoill*) Kerry. 'Oak grove of the pool'.

Derreenavurrig (*Doirín an Mhuirigh*) Kerry. 'Oak grove of the mariner'.

Derreendrislagh (*Doirín Drisleach*) Kerry. 'Brambly oak grove'.

Derreennamucklagh (*Doirín na Muclach*) Kerry. 'Oak grove of the swineherds'.

Derreensillagh (*Doirín Saileach*) Kerry. 'Oak grove of willows'.

Derries (*Doirí*) Offaly. 'Oak woods'.

Derrington Staffs. *Dodintone* 1086 (DB). 'Estate associated with a man called Dod(d)a or Dud(d)a'. OE pers. name + *-ing-* + *tūn*.

Derrinlaur (*Doire an Láir*) Waterford. 'Middle oak grove'.

Derry (*Doire*) Derry. *Doire Calgaigh* 535. 'Oak grove'. The original Irish name was *Doire Chalgaigh*, 'Calgach's oak grove'. A later name was *Doire Cholm Cille*, 'Columcille's oak grove', after a monastery founded by St Columba in 546. In 1613 Derry was renamed *Londonderry* by a group of merchants from *London*.

Derry (*Doire an Bhile*) Down. 'Oak grove of the sacred tree'.

Derryadd (*Doire Fhada*) Armagh. *Derriada* 1609. 'Long oak grove'.

Derryaghy (*Doire Achaidh*) Antrim. *Ardrachi* 1306. 'Oak grove of the field'. An earlier Irish name was *Ard Achaidh*, 'height of the field'.

Derryanvil (*Doire Chonamhail*) Armagh. *Derrehanavile*. 'Oak grove of Conamhail'.

Derrybawn (*Doire Bán*) Wicklow. 'White oak grove'.

Derrybeg (*Doirí Beaga*) Donegal. 'Small oak groves'.

Derryboy (*Doire Buí*) Down. *Dirryboy* 1634. 'Yellow oak grove'.

Derrycaw (*Doire an Chatha*) Armagh. 'Oak wood of the battle'.

Derrychrier (*Doire an Chriathair*) Derry. *Derkreayr* 1397. 'Oak wood of the quagmire'.

Derrycoffey (*Doire Uí Chofaigh*) Offaly. 'Oak wood of Ó Cofaigh'.

Derrycoogh (*Doire Cuach*) Tipperary. 'Oak grove of the cuckoos'.

Derrycooly (*Doire Cúile*) Offaly. 'Oakwood of the nook'.

Derrydamph (*Doire Damh*) Cavan. 'Oak grove of the oxen'.

Derryfubble (*Doire an Phobail*) Tyrone. *Dirripuble* 1609. 'Oak wood of the people'.

Derrygarrane (*Doire an Ghearráin*) Kerry. 'Oak wood of the gelding'.

Derrygarrane North (*Doire an Ghearráin Thuaidh*) Kerry. 'Northern oak wood of the gelding'.

Derrygarrane South (*Doire an Ghearráin Theas*) Kerry. 'Southern oak wood of the gelding'.

Derrygolan (*Doire an Ghabláin*) Westmeath. 'Oak grove of the fork'.

Derrygrath (*Deargráth*) Tipperary. 'Red fort'.

Derrygrogan (*Doire Grógáin*) Offaly. 'Oak wood of the little heap'.

Derryharney (*Doire Charna*) Fermanagh. *Derriharne* 1659. 'Oak wood of the cairn'.

Derryhaw (*Doire an Chatha*) Armagh. *Derricah* 1661. 'Oak wood of the battle'.

Derryhowlaght (*Doire Thaimleacht*) Fermanagh. 'Oak grove of the grave'.

Derrykeevan (*Doire Uí Chaomháin*) Armagh. *Derrykivyn* 1657. 'Ó Caomhán's oak grove'.

Derrykeighan (*Doire Chaocháin*) Antrim. *Daire Chaechain c.*800. 'Caochán's oak grove'.

Derrylahard (*Doire Leath Ard*) Cork. 'Oak grove of the half height'.

Derrylane (*Doire Leathan*) Cavan. 'Broad oak wood'.

Derrylaney (*Doire Léana*) Fermanagh. 'Oak grove of the meadow'.

Derrylard (*Doire Leath Ard*) Armagh. 'Oak grove of the half height'.

Derryleagh (*Doire Liath*) Kerry. 'Grey oak wood'.

Derrylester (*Doire an Leastair*) Fermanagh. 'Oak wood of the small boat'.

Derrylicka (*Doire Lice*) Kerry. 'Oak wood of the flagstone'.

Derrylin (*Doire Fhlainn*) Fermanagh. *Derrelin* 1609. 'Flann's oak grove'.

Derrymihin (*Doire Mheithean*) Cork. 'Oak wood of saplings'.

Derrymore (*Doire Mór*) Armagh. 'Large oak wood'.

Derrynablaha (*Doire na Blátha*) Kerry. 'Oak wood of flowers'.

Derrynacaheragh (*Doirín na Cathrach*) Cork. 'Oak grove of the stone fort'.

Derrynacleigh (*Doire na Cloiche*) Galway. 'Oak grove of the stone'.

Derrynafeana (*Doire na bhFiann*) Kerry. 'Oak grove of the Fianna'.

Derrynafunsha (*Doire na Fuinse*) Kerry. 'Oak grove of the ash'.

Derrynagree (*Doire na Graí*) Kerry. 'Oak grove of the stud'.

Derrynanaff (*Doire na nDamh*) Mayo. 'Oak grove of the oxen'.

Derrynasaggart Mountains (*Cnoic Dhoire na Sagart*) Kerry. 'Mountains of the oak grove of the priests'.

Derrynashaloge (*Doire na Sealg*) Tyrone. 'Oak grove of the hunt'.

Derryness (*Doirinis*) Donegal. 'Oak island'.

Derryrush (*Doire Iorrais*) Galway. 'Oak grove of the headland'.

Derrythorpe N. Lincs. *Dodithorp* 1263. Probably 'outlying farmstead or hamlet of a man called Dod(d)ing'. OE pers. name + OScand. *thorp*.

Derrytrasna (*Doire Trasna*) Armagh. *Derrytrasney* 1661. 'Transverse oak grove'.

Derryveagh Mountains (*Sléibhte Dhoire Bheitheach*) Donegal. 'Mountains of the oak grove of the birches'.

Derryvohy (*Doire Bhoithe*) Mayo. 'Oak grove of the hut'.

Derrywillow (*Doire Bhaile*) Leitrim. 'Oak grove of the homestead'.

Derrywinny (*Doire Bhainne*) Cavan. 'Oak grove of the milk'.

Dersingham Norfolk. *Dersincham* 1086 (DB). 'Homestead of the family or followers of a man called Dēorsige'. OE pers. name + *-inga-* + *hām*.

Dervock (*Dearbhóg*) Antrim. *Deroogg c.*1659. 'Oak plantation'.

Derwent (river), four examples, in Cumbria, Derbys., Durham, and Yorks.; a Celtic river-name recorded from the 8th cent. in the form *Deruuentionis fluvii* 'river where oak-trees grow abundantly'.

Desborough Northants. *Dereburg* 1086 (DB), *Deresburc* 1166. 'Stronghold or fortress of a man called Dēor'. OE pers. name + *burh*.

Desert (*Díseart*) Monaghan. 'Hermitage'.

Desertcreat (*Díseart dá Chríoch*) Tyrone. 'Hermitage of two territories'.

Desertegny (*Díseart Éignigh*) Donegal. 'Éigneach's hermitage'.

Desertmartin (*Díseart Mhártain*) Derry. *Dísiort Mhártain c.*1645. 'Mártan's hermitage'.

Desertoghill (*Díseart Uí Thuathail*) Derry. 'Ó Tuathal's hermitage'.

Desford Leics. *Deresford* 1086 (DB). 'Ford of a man called Dēor'. OE pers. name + *ford*.

Detchant Northum. *Dichende* 1166. 'End of the ditch or dike'. OE *dīc* + *ende*.

Dethick Derbys. *Dethec* 1154–9. 'Death oak-tree', i.e. 'oak-tree on which criminals were hanged'. OE *dēath* + *āc*.

Detling Kent. *Detlinges* 11th cent. '(Settlement of) the family or followers of a man called *Dyttel*'. OE pers. name + *-ingas*.

Devenish (*Daimhinis*) (island) Fermanagh. (*Molassi*) *Daminsi c.*830. 'Island of oxen'.

Deveron (river) Banff. *Douern* 1273. Gaelic *dubh* 'black' + pre-Celtic 'river'.

Devizes Wilts. *Divises* 11th cent. '(Place on) the boundaries'. OFrench *devise*.

Devlin (*Duibh Linn*) Donegal, Mayo, Monaghan. 'Black pool'.

Devon (the county). *Defena, Defenascir* late 9th cent. '(Territory of) the Devonians, earlier called the *Dumnonii*'. OE tribal name *Defnas* (from Celtic *Dumnonii*) + *scīr* 'district'.

Devonport Devon, a modern self-explanatory name only in use since 1824.

Dewchurch, Much & *Dewchurch, Little* Heref. & Worcs. *Lann Deui* 7th cent., *Dewischirche c.*1150. 'Church of St Dewi'. Saint's name (the Welsh form of David) + OE *cirice* (with OWelsh *lann* in the early form). Distinguishing affixes are OE *micel* 'great' and *lȳtel* 'little'.

Dewlish Dorset. *Devenis |sic|* 1086 (DB), *Deueliz* 1194. Originally the name of the stream here, a Celtic river-name meaning 'dark stream'.

Dewsbury W. Yorks. *Deusberia* 1086 (DB). 'Stronghold of a man called Dewi'. OWelsh pers. name + OE *burh* (dative *byrig*).

Dian (*Daingean*) Monaghan, Tyrone. 'Fortress'.

Dibden (Purlieu) Hants. *Depedene* 1086 (DB). 'Deep valley'. OE *dēop* + *denu*. The addition is from ME *purlewe* 'outskirts of a forest'.

Dicker, Lower & *Dicker, Upper* E. Sussex. *Diker* 1229. From ME *dyker* 'ten', probably alluding to a plot of land for which this number of iron rods was paid in rent.

Dickleburgh Norfolk. *Dicclesburc* 1086 (DB). Possibly 'stronghold of a man called *Dicel* or *Dicla*'. OE pers. name + *burh*.

Didbrook Glos. *Duddebrok* 1248. 'Brook of a man called *Dyd(d)a*'. OE pers. name + *brōc*.

Didcot Oxon. *Dudecota* 1206. 'Cottage(s) of a man called Dud(d)a'. OE pers. name + *cot*.

Diddington Cambs. *Dodinctun* 1086 (DB). 'Estate associated with a man called Dod(d)a or Dud(d)a'. OE pers. name + *-ing-* + *tūn*.

Diddlebury Shrops. *Dodeleberia c.*1090. 'Stronghold or manor of a man called *Dud(d)ela*'. OE pers. name + *burh* (dative *byrig*).

Didley Heref. & Worcs. *Dodelegie* 1086 (DB). 'Woodland clearing of a man called Dod(d)a or Dud(d)a'. OE pers. name + *lēah*.

Didmarton Glos. *Dydimeretune* 972, *Dedmertone* 1086 (DB). 'Boundary farmstead of a man called Dyd(d)a', or 'farmstead by Dyd(d)a's pool'. OE pers. name + *mǣre* or *mere* + *tūn*.

Didsbury Gtr. Manch. *Dedesbiry* 1246. 'Stronghold of a man called *Dyd(d)i*'. OE pers. name + *burh* (dative *byrig*).

Diffreen (*Dubh Thrian*) Leitrim. 'Black third'.

Diffwys (mountain) Gwyd. 'Steep slope'. Welsh *diffwys*.

Digby Lincs. *Dicbi* 1086 (DB). 'Farmstead or village at the ditch'. OE *dīc* or OScand. *diki* + *bý*.

Dilham Norfolk. *Dilham* 1086 (DB). 'Homestead or enclosure where dill grows'. OE *dile* + *hām* or *hamm*.

Dilhorne Staffs. *Dulverne* 1086 (DB). 'House or building by a pit or quarry'. OE **dylf* + *ærn*.

Dilston Northum. *Deuelestune* 1172. 'Farmstead by the dark stream'. Celtic river-name + OE *tūn*.

Dilton Marsh Wilts. *Dulinton* 1190. Probably 'farmstead of a man called **Dulla*'. OE pers. name (genitive *-n*) + *tūn*.

Dilwyn Heref. & Worcs. *Dilven* 1086 (DB). '(Settlement at) the shady or secret places'. OE *dīgle* in a dative plural form *dīglum*.

Dinas Powys Vale Glam. *Dinaspowis* 1187, *Dinas Powis c.*1262. 'Fort of Powis'. Welsh *dinas*. *Powys* apparently has the same origin as POWYS.

Dinbych. See DENBIGH.

Dinbych-y-pysgod. See TENBY.

Dinchope Shrops. *Doddinghop* 12th cent. 'Enclosed valley associated with a man called Dudda', or 'valley at Dudda's place'. OE pers. name + *-ing-* or *-ing* + *hop*.

Dinder Somerset. *Dinre* 1174. Probably 'hill with a fort'. Celtic **din* + **breʒ*.

Dinedor Heref. & Worcs. *Dunre* 1086 (DB). Identical in origin with the previous name.

Dingin (*Daingean*) Cavan. 'Fortress'.

Dingle (*An Daingean*) Kerry. 'The fortress'.

Dingley Northants. *Dinglei* 1086 (DB). Possibly 'woodland clearing with hollows'. OE *lēah* with ME *dingle*.

Dingwall Highland. *Dingwell* 1227. 'Field of the assembly'. OScand. *thing-vollr*. The assembly was the Scandinavian 'parliament'. *See also* THINGWALL.

Dinis (*Duibhinis*) Cork. 'Black island'.

Dinmore Heref. & Worcs., *see* HOPE.

Dinnington Somerset. *Dinnitone* 1086 (DB). 'Estate associated with a man called Dynne'. OE pers. name + *-ing-* + *tūn*.

Dinnington S. Yorks. *Dunintone* 1086 (DB). 'Estate associated with a man called Dunn(a)'. OE pers. name + *-ing-* + *tūn*.

Dinnington Tyne & Wear. *Donigton* 1242. Probably identical in origin with the previous name.

Dinorwic. See PORT DINORWIC.

Dinsdale, Low Durham. *Ditneshall c.*1185. 'Nook of land belonging to DEIGHTON (N. Yorks)'. OE *halh*.

Dinton, 'estate associated with a man called Dunn(a)', OE pers. name + *-ing-* + *tūn*: **Dinton** Bucks. *Danitone |sic|* 1086 (DB), *Duninton* 1208. **Dinton** Wilts. *Domnitone |sic|* 1086 (DB), *Dunyngtun* 12th cent.

Diptford Devon. *Depeforde* 1086 (DB). 'Deep ford'. OE *dēop* + *ford*.

Dipton Durham. *Depeden* 1339. 'Deep valley'. OE *dēop* + *denu*.

Diptonmill Northum. *Depeden* 1269. Identical in origin with the previous name, with the later addition of *mill*.

Disert (*Díseart*) Donegal. 'Hermitage'.

Diserth. See DYSERTH.

Diseworth Leics. *Digtheswyrthe c.*972, *Diwort* 1086 (DB). 'Enclosure of a man called *Digoth*'. OE pers. name + *worth*.

Dishforth N. Yorks. *Disforde* 1086 (DB). 'Ford across a ditch'. OE *dīc* + *ford*.

Disley Ches. *Destesleg c.*1251. OE *lēah* 'wood, woodland clearing' with an obscure first element, possibly an OE *dystels* 'mound or heap'.

Diss Norfolk. *Dice* 1086 (DB). '(Place at) the ditch or dike'. OE *dīc*.

Distington Cumbria. *Dustinton c.*1230. OE *tūn* 'farmstead, estate' with an obscure first element, possibly a pers. name.

Ditchburn Northum. *Dicheburn* 1236. 'Ditch stream'. OE *dīc* + *burna*.

Ditcheat Somerset. *Dichesgate* 842, *Dicesget* (DB). 'Gap in the dyke or earthwork'. OE *dīc* + *geat*.

Ditchingham Norfolk. *Dicingaham* 1086 (DB). 'Homestead of the dwellers at a ditch or dyke', or 'homestead of the family or followers of a man called *Dic(c)a* or *Dīca*'. OE *dīc* or OE pers. name + *-inga-* + *hām*.

Ditchling E. Sussex. *Dicelinga* 765, *Dicelinges* 1086 (DB). '(Settlement of) the family or followers of a man called *Dīcel*'. OE pers. name + *-ingas*.

Dittisham Devon. *Didasham* 1086 (DB). 'Enclosure or promontory of a man called *Dyddi*'. OE pers. name + *hamm*.

Ditton, usually 'farmstead by a ditch or dike', OE *dīc* + *tūn*: **Ditton** Ches. *Ditton* 1194. **Ditton** Kent. *Dictun* 10th cent., *Dictune* 1086 (DB). **Ditton, Fen** Cambs. *Dictunæ c.*975, *Fen Dytton* 1286. Affix is OE *fenn* 'fen, marshland'. **Ditton, Long** & **Ditton, Thames** Surrey. *Dictun* 1005, *Ditune* 1086 (DB), *Longa Dittone* 1242, *Temes Ditton* 1235. Distinguishing affixes are OE *lang* 'long' (alluding to the length of the village) and THAMES from the river.

However the following has a different origin: **Ditton Priors** Shrops. *Dodintone* 1086 (DB). 'Estate associated with a man called *Dod(d)a* or *Dud(d)a*'. OE pers. name + *-ing-* + *tūn*. Manorial affix from its possession by Wenlock Priory.

Dixton Glos. *Dricledone* 1086 (DB), *Diclisdon* 1169. Probably 'down of the hill with dikes or earthworks'. OE *dīc* + *hyll* + *dūn*. Alternatively the first element may be an OE pers. name *Dīcel* or *Diccel*.

Doagh Beg (*Dumhaigh Bhig*) Donegal. *Dowaghbegg c.*1655. 'Little sandbank'.

Doagh Isle (*Dumhachoileán*) Donegal. 'Sandhill island'.

Dobcross Gtr. Manch., a late name, first recorded as *Dobcrosse* 1662. 'Cross (or cross-roads) associated with a man called Dobbe'. ME pers. name (a pet-form of *Robert*) or surname + *cross*.

Docking Norfolk. *Doccynge c.*1035, *Dochinga* 1086 (DB). 'Place where docks or water-lilies grow'. OE *docce* + *-ing*.

Docklow Heref. & Worcs. *Dockelawe* 1291. 'Mound or hill where docks grow'. OE *docce* + *hlāw*.

Dockray Cumbria. *Docwra* 1278. 'Nook of land where docks or water-lilies grow'. OE *docce* + OScand. *vrá*.

Doddinghurst Essex. *Doddenhenc |sic|* 1086 (DB), *Duddingeherst* 1218. 'Wooded hill of the family or followers of a man called Dudda or Dodda'. OE pers. name + *-inga-* + *hyrst*.

Doddington, *Dodington*, 'estate associated with a man called Dud(d)a or Dod(d)a', OE pers. name + *-ing-* + *tūn*: **Doddington** Cambs. *Dundingtune |sic| c.*975, *Dodinton* 1086 (DB). **Doddington** Kent. *Duddingtun c.*1100. **Doddington** Lincs. *Dodin(c)tune* 1086 (DB). **Doddington** Northum. *Dodinton* 1207. **Doddington** Shrops. *Dodington* 1285. **Doddington, Dry** Lincs. *Dodintune* 1086 (DB). Affix from OE *drýge* 'dry'. **Doddington, Great** Northants. *Dodintone* 1086 (DB), *Great Dodington* 1290. **Dodington** S. Glos. *Dodintone* 1086 (DB).

Doddiscombsleigh Devon. *Leuga* 1086 (DB), *Doddescumbeleghe* 1309. Originally 'the woodland clearing', OE *lēah*. Later addition from the Doddescumb family, here in the 13th cent.

Dodford, 'ford of a man called Dodda', OE pers. name + *ford*: **Dodford** Heref. & Worcs. *Doddeford* 1232. **Dodford** Northants. *Doddanford* 944, *Dodeforde* 1086 (DB).

Dodington S. Glos., *see* DODDINGTON.

Dodleston Ches. *Dodestune |sic|* 1086 (DB), *Dodleston* 1153. 'Farmstead of a man called *Dod(d)el*'. OE pers. name + *tūn*.

Dodworth S. Yorks. *Dodesuu(o)rde* 1086 (DB). 'Enclosure of a man called Dod(d) or Dod(d)a'. OE pers. name + *worth*.

Doe Castle (*Caislean na dTuath*) Donegal. 'Castle of the territories'.

Dogdyke Lincs. *Dockedic* 12th cent. 'Ditch where docks or water-lilies grow'. OE *docce* + *dīc*.

Dolgarrog Conwy. *Dolgarrog* 1534. 'Water meadows of the fast-flowing stream'. Welsh *dôl* + *carrog*.

Dolgellau Gwyd. *Dolkelew* 1254, *Dolgethly* 1338. 'Water meadow of cells'. Welsh *dôl* + *cell* (plural *cellau*). The 'cells' were possibly monastic cells or perhaps they were merchants' booths.

Dolla (*Dolla*) Tipperary. 'Loops'.

Dollar Clac. *Doler* 1461. 'Meadow'. Celtic *dol* + *ar*.

Dollingstown Down. 'Dolling's town'. Apparently from the Revd Boghey *Dolling*, a local rector early in the 19th cent.

Dollymount (*Cnocán Doirinne*) Dublin. 'Doireanne's mount'.

Dolphinholme Lancs. *Dolphineholme* 1591. 'Island or water-meadow of a man called Dolgfinnr'. OScand. pers. name + *holmr*.

Dolton Devon. *Duueltone* 1086 (DB). Possibly 'farmstead in the open country frequented by doves'. OE *dūfe* + *feld* + *tūn*.

Donabate (*Domhnach Bat*) Dublin. 'Church of the boat'.

Donacarney (*Domhnach Cearnaigh*) Meath. 'Cearnach's church'.

Donadea (*Domhnach Dheá*) Kildare. 'Deadha's church'.

Donagh (*Domhnach*) Fermanagh. *Donagh* 1659. 'Church'.

Donaghadee (*Domhnach Daoi*) Down. *Donanachti* 1204. Possibly 'Daoi's church'.

Donaghanie (*Domhnach an Eich*) Tyrone. *Domhach an Eich* 1518. 'Church of the horse'.

Donaghcloney (*Domhnach Cluana*) Down. *Domhnach Cluana c.*1645. 'Church of the meadow'.

Donaghedy (*Domhnach Caoide*) Tyrone. 'Caoide's church'.

Donaghey (*Dún Eachaidh*) Tyrone. 'Eachaidh's fort'.

Donaghmore (*Domhnach Mór*) Laois, Meath, Tipperary. 'Large church'.

Donaghmoyne (*Domhnach Maighean*) Monaghan. 'Church of the little plain'.

Donaghpatrick (*Domhnach Phádraig*) Meath. 'Pádraig's church'.

Donaghrisk (*Domhnach Riascadh*) Tyrone. 'Church of the marsh'.

Donamon (*Dún Iomain*) Roscommon. 'Ioman's fort'.

Donard (*Dún Ard*) Wexford, Wicklow. 'High fort'.

Donaskeagh (*Dún na Sciath*) Tipperary. 'Fort of the shields'.

Doncaster S. Yorks. *Doneceastre* 1002, *Donecastre* 1086 (DB). 'Roman fort on the River Don'. Celtic river-name (meaning simply 'water, river') + OE *ceaster*.

Donegal (*Dún na nGall*) Donegal. (*mainistir*) *Dúin na nGall* 1474. 'Fort of the foreigners', referring to the Danes active here in the 9th cent. The county of Donegal is sometimes known by the Irish name *Tír Chonaill*, 'Conaill's territory'.

Doneraile (*Dún ar Aill*) Cork. 'Fort on the cliff'.

Donhead St Andrew & *Donhead St Mary* Wilts. *Dunheved* 871, *Duneheve* 1086 (DB), *Dounheved Sanct Andree* 1302, *Donheved Sancte Marie* 1298. 'Head or end of the down'. OE *dūn* + *hēafod*. Affixes from the dedications of the churches.

Donibristle Fife. *Donibrysell c.*1165. 'Breasal's fort'. Gaelic *dúnadh* + pers. name.

Donington, *Donnington*, usually 'estate associated with a man called Dun(n) or Dun(n)a', OE pers. name + -*ing*- + *tūn* (possibly in some cases 'estate at the hill-place', OE **dūning* + *tūn*); examples include: **Donington** Lincs. *Duninctune* 1086 (DB). **Donington, Castle** Leics. *Duni(n)tone* 1086 (DB), *Castel Donyngton* 1428. Affix refers to a former castle here. **Donington le Heath** Leics. *Duntone* 1086 (DB), *Donyngton super le heth* 1462. Affix means 'on the heath', from OE *hǣth*. **Donington on Bain** Lincs. *Duninctune* 1086 (DB), *Donygton super Beyne* 13th cent. Affix from its situation on the River Bain ('the short one', from OScand. *beinn*). **Donnington** Berks. *Deritone* |*sic*| 1086 (DB), *Dunintona* 1086 (DB). **Donnington** Glos. *Doninton c.*1195. **Donnington** Heref. & Worcs. *Dunninctune* 1086 (DB). **Donnington** Shrops., near Eaton Constantine. *Dunniton* 1180. **Donnington** Shrops., near Oakengates. *Donnyton* 1272.

However the following has a different origin: **Donnington**

W. Sussex. *Dunketone* 966, *Cloninctune* |*sic*| 1086 (DB). 'Farmstead of a man called *Dunnuca'. OE pers. name + *tūn*.

Donisthorpe Leics. *Durandestorp* 1086 (DB). 'Outlying farmstead or hamlet of a man called Durand'. OFrench pers. name + OScand. *thorp*.

Donnington, see DONINGTON.

Donnybrook (*Domhnach Broc*) Dublin. 'Broc's church'.

Donnycarney (*Domhnach Cearna*) Dublin. 'Cearnach's church'.

Donohill (*Dún Eochaille*) Tipperary. 'Fort of the yew wood'.

Donore (*Dún Uabhair*) Meath. 'Fort of pride'.

Donoughmore (*Domhnach Mór*) Cork. 'Big church'.

Donyatt Somerset. *Duunegete* 8th cent., *Doniet* 1086 (DB). Probably 'gate or gap of a man called Dun(n)a'. OE pers. name + *geat*.

Doo, Lough (*Loch Dúlocha*) Clare, Mayo. 'Black lake'.

Dooagh (*Dumha Acha*) Mayo. 'Mound of the field'.

Doocastle (*Caisleán an Dumha*) Mayo. 'Mound castle'.

Doochary (*An Dúchoraidh*) Donegal. 'The black weir'.

Doocreggaun (*Dubh Creagán*) Mayo. 'Little black crag'.

Doogary (*An Dúgharraí*) Cavan. 'The black garden'.

Dooghbeg (*Dumha Beag*) Mayo. 'Small mound'.

Doogort (*Dumha Gort*) Mayo. 'Salty mound'.

Doohamlet (*Dúthamhlacht*) Monaghan. 'Black burial mound'.

Doohat (*Dútháite*) Monaghan. 'Black site'.

Doohoma (*Dumha Thuama*) Mayo. 'Mound of the tomb'.

Dooish (*Dubhais*) Donegal, Tyrone. 'Black ridge'.

Dooleeg (*Dumha Liag*) Mayo. 'Black flagstone'.

Doolin (*Dúlainn*) Clare. 'Black pool'.

Doon (*Dún*) Galway, Limerick. 'Fort'.

Doon (river) E. Ayr. *Don* 1197. '(River of the) river goddess'. British *Deuona*.

Doonaha (*Dún Átha*) Clare. 'Fort of the ford'.

Doonally (*Dún Aille*) Sligo. 'Fort of the cliff'.

Doonbeg (*An Dún Beag*) Clare. 'The small fort'.

Doonfeeny (*Dún Fine*) Mayo. 'Fine's fort'.

Dooraheen (*Dubhrathain*) Westmeath. 'Black ferny ground'.

Dorchester Dorset. *Durnovaria* 4th cent., *Dornwaraceaster* 864, *Dorecestre* 1086 (DB). 'Roman town called *Durnovaria*'. Reduced form of Celtic name (perhaps meaning 'place with fist-sized pebbles') + OE *ceaster*.

Dorchester Oxon. *Dorciccaestræ* 731, *Dorchecestre* 1086 (DB). 'Roman town called *Dorcic*'. Celtic name (obscure in origin and meaning) + OE *ceaster*.

Dordon Warwicks. *Derdon* 13th cent. 'Hill frequented by deer or other wild animals'. OE *dēor* + *dūn*.

Dore S. Yorks. *Dore* late 9th cent., 1086 (DB). '(Place at) the gate or narrow pass'. OE *dor*.

Dore, Abbey Heref. & Worcs. *Dore* 1147. Named from the River Dore, a Celtic river-name meaning simply 'the waters'. Affix from the former Cistercian Abbey here.

Dorking Surrey. *Dorchinges* 1086 (DB). '(Settlement of) the family or followers of a man called *Deorc*'. OE pers. name + *-ingas*.

Dormansland Surrey. *Deremanneslond* 1263. 'Cultivated land or estate of the Dereman family'. OE *land*, with the surname of a local family.

Dormanstown Red. & Cleve., a modern name for a new town planned in 1918 for the employees of the manufacturing firm Dorman Long.

Dormington Heref. & Worcs. *Dorminton* 1206. 'Estate associated with a man called Dēormōd or Dēormund'. OE pers. name + *-ing-* + *tūn*.

Dorney Bucks. *Dornei* 1086 (DB). 'Island, or dry ground in marsh, frequented by bumble-bees'. OE *dora* (genitive plural *dorena*) + *ēg*.

Dornoch Highland. *Durnach* 1145. 'Place of fist-stones'. Gaelic *dornach*.

Dornock Dumf. *Durnack* 1182. 'Place of fist-stones'. OWelsh *durnauc*.

Dorridge W. Mids. *Derrech* 1400. 'Ridge frequented by deer or wild animals' OE *dēor* + *hrycg*.

Dorrington Lincs. *Derintone* 1086 (DB). 'Estate associated with a man called Dēor(a)'. OE pers. name + *-ing-* + *tūn*.

Dorrington Shrops., near Condover. *Dodinton* 1198. 'Estate associated with a man called Dod(d)a'. OE pers. name + *-ing-* + *tūn*.

Dorset (the county). *Dornsætum* late 9th cent. '(Territory of) the people around *Dorn*'. Reduced form of *Dornwaraceaster* (*see* DORCHESTER) + OE *sǣte*.

Dorsey (*Na Doirse*) Armagh. 'The gateways'. The present name is a short form of Irish *Doirse Eamhna*, 'gateways of Navan', after *Navan*, the ancient capital of Ulster.

Dorsington Warwicks. *Dorsintune* 1086 (DB). 'Estate associated with a man called Dēorsige'. OE pers. name + *-ing-* + *tūn*.

Dorstone Heref. & Worcs. *Dodintune* |*sic*| 1086 (DB), *Dorsington* c.1138. Possibly identical in origin with the previous name.

Dorton Bucks. *Dortone* 1086 (DB). 'Farmstead or village at the narrow pass'. OE *dor* + *tūn*.

Dosthill Staffs. *Dercelai* |*sic*|. 1086 (DB), *Dercetehill* 1242. Possibly 'hill with a fold or shelter for deer or other animals'. OE *dēor* + (*ge*)*set* or *cēte* + *hyll*.

Doughton Glos. *Ductune* 775–8. 'Duck farmstead'. OE *dūce* + *tūn*.

Douglas (*Dúglas*) Cork, Laois. 'Black stream'.

Douglas S. Lan. *Duuelglas* c.1150. '(Place on the) Douglas Water'. The Celtic river name means 'black stream' (OGaelic *dub* + *glais*).

Doulting Somerset. *Dulting* 725, *Doltin* 1086 (DB). Originally the old name of the River Sheppey on which Doulting stands, probably of Celtic origin but of unknown meaning.

Dove (river) Derbys., an old Celtic river-name first recorded as *Dufan* in the 10th cent. and meaning 'black, dark'. It gives name to **Dovedale** (*Duvesdale* 1269), from OScand. *dalr* 'valley'. The two rivers called **Dove** in Yorkshire are identical in origin.

Dovea (*An Dubhfhéith*) Tipperary. 'The black bog'.

Dovenby Cumbria. *Duuaneby* 1230. 'Farmstead or village of a man called Dufan'. OIrish pers. name + OScand. *bý*.

Dover Kent. *Dubris* 4th cent., *Dofras* c.700, *Dovere* 1086 (DB). Named from the stream here, now called the Dour, a Celtic river-name **dubrās* meaning simply 'the waters'.

Dovercourt Essex. *Douorcortae* c.1000, *Druurecurt* |*sic*| 1086 (DB). Possibly 'enclosed farmyard by the river called *Dover*'. Celtic river-name (meaning 'the waters') + OE **cort(e)* (perhaps from Latin *cohors, cohortem*).

Doverdale Heref. & Worcs. *Douerdale* 706, *Lunvredele* 1086 |*sic*| (DB). 'Valley of the river called *Dover*'. Celtic river-name (meaning 'the waters') + OE *dæl*.

Doveridge Derbys. *Dubrige* 1086 (DB), *Duuebruge* 1252. 'Bridge over the River Dove'. Celtic river-name (meaning 'the dark one') + OE *brycg*.

Dowdeswell Glos. *Dogodeswellan* 8th cent., *Dodesuuelle* 1086 (DB). 'Spring or stream of a man called **Dogod*'. OE pers. name + *wella*.

Dowlais Mert. '(Place by the) black stream'. Welsh *du* + *glais*.

Dowland Devon. *Duuelande* 1086 (DB). Possibly 'estate in the open country frequented by doves'. OE *dūfe* + *feld* + *land*.

Dowlish Wake Somerset. *Duuelis* 1086 (DB), *Duueliz Wak* 1243. Named from the stream here, a Celtic river-name meaning 'dark stream'. Manorial addition from the Wake family, here in the 12th cent.

Down (*An Dún*) (the county). 'The fort'. The fort in question is that of DOWNPATRICK.

Down, *Downe*, '(place at) the hill', OE *dūn*: **Down, East** & **Down, West** Devon. *Duna* 1086 (DB), *Estdoune* 1260, *Westdone* 1273. **Down St Mary** Devon. *Done* 1086 (DB), *Dune St Mary* 1297. Affix from the dedication of the church. **Downe** Gtr. London. *Doune* 1316.

Down Ampney Glos., *see* AMPNEY.

Down Hatherley Glos., *see* HATHERLEY.

Downend S. Glos. *Downe ende* 1573. Self-explanatory, 'end of the down', OE *dūn*.

Downham, usually 'homestead on or near a hill', OE *dūn* + *hām*: **Downham** Cambs. *Duneham* 1086 (DB). **Downham** Essex. *Dunham* 1168. **Downham Market** Norfolk. *Dunham* c.1050, 1086 (DB). Affix from the market here, referred to as early as the 11th cent.

However the following have a different origin, '(place at) the hills', from OE *dūn* in the dative plural form *dūnum*: **Downham** Lancs. *Dunum* 1194. **Downham** Northum. *Dunum* 1186.

Downhead Somerset. *Duneafd* 851, *Dunehefde* 1086 (DB). 'Head or end of the down'. OE *dūn* + *hēafod*.

Downhill (*Dún*) Derry. (*go*) *Dún Bó* 1182. 'Fort of the hill'. The original name was *Dún Bó*, 'fort of the cows', but English *hill* then replaced the second word of this.

Downholme N. Yorks. *Dune* 1086 (DB), *Dunum* 12th cent. '(Place at) the hills'. OE *dūn* in a dative plural form *dūnum*.

Downings (*Dúnaibh*) Donegal. *Na nDuini* 1603. 'Forts'.

Downpatrick (*Dún Pádraig*) Down. (*expugnatio*) *Dúin Lethghlaisse* 496. 'Pádraig's fort'. The town's original Irish name was *Dún Lethglaise*, possibly 'fort of the side of the stream'. The present name is not recorded before the 17th cent.

Downton, 'farmstead on or by the hill or down', OE *dūn* + *tūn*: **Downton** Wilts. *Duntun* 672, *Duntone* 1086 (DB). **Downton on the Rock** Heref. & Worcs. *Duntune* 1086 (DB). Affix from ME *rokke* 'a rock or peak'.

Dowra (*Damhshraith*) Cavan, Leitrim. 'River meadow of the ox'.

Dowsby Lincs. *Dusebi* 1086 (DB). 'Farmstead or village of a man called Dúsi'. OScand. pers. name + *bý*.

Doxey Staffs. *Dochesig* 1086 (DB). 'Island, or dry ground in marsh, of a man called *Docc'. OE pers. name + *ēg*.

Doynton S. Glos. *Didintone* 1086 (DB). 'Estate associated with a man called *Dydda'. OE pers. name + *-ing-* + *tūn*.

Draperstown Derry. *Cross* 1813. 'Drapers' town'. The name was originally applied to the town of *Moneymore*, founded by the Drapers' Company of London in the early 17th cent. Draperstown was founded in 1798 and took its current name in 1818. Its Irish name is *Baile na Croise*, 'town of the cross', referring to the crossroads here.

Draughton, 'farmstead on a slope used for dragging down timber and the like', OScand. *drag* + OE *tūn*: **Draughton** Northants. *Dractone* 1086 (DB). **Draughton** N. Yorks. *Dractone* 1086 (DB).

Drax N. Yorks. *Drac* 1086 (DB), *Drachs* 11th cent. 'The portages, or places where boats are dragged overland or pulled up from the water'. OScand. *drag*.

Drax, Long N. Yorks. *Langrak* 1208. 'Long stretch of river'. OE *lang* + *racu*.

Draycote, *Draycott*, a common place-name, probably 'shed where drays or sledges are kept', OE *dræg* + *cot*; examples include: **Draycote** Warwicks. *Draicote* 1203. **Draycott** Derbys. *Draicot* 1086 (DB). **Draycott** Somerset, near Cheddar. *Draicote* 1086 (DB). **Draycott in the Clay** Staffs. *Draicote* 1086 (DB). Affix 'in the clayey district', from OE *clǣg*. **Draycott in the Moors** Staffs. *Draicot* 1251. Affix 'in the moorland', from OE *mōr*.

Drayton, a common place-name, 'farmstead at or near a portage or slope used for dragging down loads', or 'farmstead where drays or sledges are used', OE *dræg* + *tūn*; examples include: **Drayton** Norfolk. *Draituna* 1086 (DB). **Drayton** Oxon., near Banbury. *Draitone* 1086 (DB). **Drayton** Oxon., near Didcot. *Draitune* 958, *Draitone* 1086 (DB). **Drayton** Somerset, near Curry Rivel. *Drayton* 1243. **Drayton Bassett** Staffs. *Draitone* 1086 (DB), *Drayton Basset* 1301. Manorial affix from the Basset family, here in the 12th cent. **Drayton Beauchamp** Bucks. *Draitone* 1086 (DB), *Drayton Belcamp* 1239. Manorial affix from the Beauchamp family, here in the 13th cent. **Drayton, Dry**

Cambs. *Draitone* 1086 (DB), *Driedraiton* 1218. Affix from OE *drȳge* to distinguish it from FEN DRAYTON. **Drayton, East & Drayton, West** Notts. *Draitone*, *Draitun* 1086 (DB), *Est Draiton* 1276, *West Draytone* 1269. **Drayton, Fen** Cambs. *Drægtun* 1012, *Draitone* 1086 (DB), *Fendreiton* 1188. Affix from OE *fenn* 'marshland' in contrast to DRY DRAYTON. **Drayton, Fenny** Leics. *Draitone* 1086 (DB), *Fenedrayton* 1465. Affix is OE *fennig* 'muddy, marshy'. **Drayton, Market** Shrops. *Draitune* 1086 (DB). Affix from the important market here. **Drayton Parslow** Bucks. *Draitone* 1086 (DB), *Drayton Passelewe* 1254. Manorial affix from the Passelewe family, here in the 11th cent. **Drayton, West** Gtr. London. *Drægtun* 939, *Draitone* 1086 (DB), *Westdrayton* 1465.

Dreen (*Draighean*) Derry. *Drien* 1613. 'Place of blackthorn'.

Drehid (*Droichead*) Kildare. 'Bridge'.

Drenewydd, Y. *See* NEWTOWN.

Drewsteignton Devon. *Taintone* 1086 (DB), *Teyngton Drue* 1275. 'Farmstead or village on the River Teign'. Celtic river-name (*see* TEIGNMOUTH) + OE *tūn* + manorial affix from a man called Drew, here in the 13th cent.

Driby Lincs. *Dribi* 1086 (DB). 'Dry farmstead or village'. OE *drȳge* + OScand. *bý*.

Driffield, 'open land characterized by dirt, or by stubble', OE *drit* or *drīf* + *feld*: **Driffield** Glos. *Drifelle* |sic| 1086 (DB), *Driffeld* 1190. **Driffield, Great** & **Driffield, Little** E. R. Yorks. *Drifeld* 1086 (DB).

Drigg Cumbria. *Dreg* 12th cent. 'The portage, or place where boats are dragged overland or pulled up from the water'. OScand. *drǣg*.

Drighlington W. Yorks. *Dreslin(g)tone* |sic| 1086 (DB), *Drichtlington* 1202. 'Estate associated with a man called *Dryhtel or *Dyrhtla', OE pers. name + *-ing-* + *tūn*.

Drimfries (*Droim Fraoigh*) Donegal. 'Heather ridge'.

Driminidy (*Droim Inide*) Cork. 'Shrovetide ridge'.

Drimnagh (*Droimeanach*) Dublin. 'Ridged land'.

Drimoleague (*Drom dhá Liag*) Cork. 'Ridge of two flagstones'.

Drimpton Dorset. *Dremeton* 1244. 'Farmstead of a man called *Drēama'. OE pers. name + *tūn*.

Drinagh (*Draighneach*) Cork, Wexford. 'Place of blackthorn'.

Drinan (*Draighneán*) Dublin. 'Place of blackthorn'.

Drinkstone Suffolk. *Drincestune* c.1050, *Drencestuna* 1086 (DB). 'Farmstead of a man called Drengr'. OScand. pers. name + OE *tūn*.

Droghed (*Droichead*) Derry. 'Bridge'.

Drogheda (*Droichead Átha*) Louth. 'Bridge of the ford'.

Droichead Nua (*Droichead Nua*) Kildare. 'New bridge'.

Droimlamph (*Droim Leamh*) Derry. 'Elm ridge'.

Drointon Staffs. *Dregetone* |sic| 1086 (DB), *Drengeton* 1199. Probably 'farmstead of the free tenants'. OScand. *drengr* + OE *tūn*.

Droitwich Heref. & Worcs. *Wich* 1086 (DB), *Drihtwych* 1347. 'Dirty or muddy salt-works', OE *wīc* with the later addition of OE *drit* 'dirt'.

Drom (*Drom*) Kerry, Tipperary. 'Ridge'.

Dromacomer (*Drom an Chomair*) Limerick. 'Ridge of the confluence'.

Dromada (*Droim Fhada*) Limerick, Mayo. 'Long ridge'.

Dromahair (*Drom dhá Thiar*) Leitrim. 'Ridge of two demons'.

Dromalivaun (*Drom Leamháin*) Kerry. 'Elm ridge'.

Dromara (*Droim Bearach*) Down. *Drumberra* 1306. 'Ridge of heifers'.

Dromard (*An Droim Ard*) Sligo. 'The high ridge'.

Drombane (*Drom Bán*) Tipperary. 'White ridge'.

Drombofinny (*Droim Bó Fnne*) Cork. 'Ridge of the white cow'.

Dromcolliher (*Drom Collachair*) Limerick. 'Ridge of the hazel wood'.

Dromin (*Droim Ing*) Limerick, Louth. 'Ridge of the difficulty'.

Dromina (*Drom Aithne*) Cork. 'Ridge of the commandment'.

Dromindoora (*Drom an Dúdhoire*) Clare. 'Ridge of the dark oak grove'.

Dromineer (*Drom Inbhir*) Tipperary. 'Ridge of the estuary'.

Dromiskin (*Droim Ineasclainn*) Louth. 'Ridge of the torrent'.

Dromkeen (*Drom Caoin*) Limerick. 'Beautiful ridge'.

Dromlusk (*Droim Loiscthe*) Kerry. 'Burnt ridge'.

Drommahane (*Drom Átháin*) Cork. 'Ridge of the little ford'.

Dromod (*Dromad*) Leitrim. 'Ridge'.

Dromore (*Droim Mór*) Cork, Down, Tyrone, etc. 'Big ridge'.

Dronfield Derbys. *Dranefeld* 1086 (DB). 'Open land infested with drones'. OE *drān* + *feld*.

Droxford Hants. *Drocenesforda* 826, *Drocheneford* 1086 (DB). OE *ford* 'ford', with an obscure first element, possibly an OE **drocen* 'dry place'.

Droylsden Gtr. Manch. *Drilisden* c.1250. Possibly 'valley of the dry spring or stream'. OE *drȳge* + *well*(*a*) + *denu*.

Druidston Pemb. *Drewyston* 1393. 'Drew's farm'. Anglo-Norman pers. name + OE *tūn*.

Druim Fada (mountain ridge) Highland. 'Long ridge'. Gaelic *druim* + *fada*.

Drum (*Droim*) Monaghan. *Driyme* 1591. 'Ridge'.

Drumacrib (*Droim Mhic Roib*) Monaghan. 'Mac Rob's ridge'.

Drumadrihid (*Droim an Droichid*) Clare. 'Ridge of the bridge'.

Drumahoe (*Droim na hUamha*) Derry. *Dromhoghs* 1622. 'Ridge of the cave'.

Drumakill (*Droim na Coille*) Monaghan. 'Ridge of the wood'.

Drumanee (*Droim an Fhiaidh*) Derry. 'Ridge of the deer'.

Drumanespic (*Droim an Easpaig*) Cavan. 'Ridge of the bishop'.

Drumaness (*Droim an Easa*) Down. *Drumenessy* c.1710. 'Ridge of the waterfall'.

Drumaney (*Droim Eanaigh*) Tyrone. 'Ridge of the bog'.

Drumannon (*Droim Meannáin*) Armagh. 'Ridge of the kid'.

Drumantee (*Dromainn Tí*) Armagh. 'Ridge of the house'.

Drumaroad (*Droim an Róid*) Down. *Ballydromerode* 1635. 'Ridge of the route'.

Drumarraght (*Droim Arracht*) Fermanagh. 'Ridge of the apparition'.

Drumatober (*Droim an Tobair*) Galway. 'Ridge of the well'.

Drumbane (*An Drom Bán*) Tipperary. 'The white ridge'.

Drumbeg (*Drom Beag*) Down. 'Little ridge'.

Drumbo (*Droim Bó*) Down. (*ab*) *Dromma Bó* c.830. 'Ridge of cows'.

Drumboy (*Drom Buí*) Donegal. 'Yellow ridge'.

Drumbrughas (*Droim Brughas*) Cavan, Fermanagh. 'Ridge of the mansion'.

Drumcar (*Droim Chora*) Louth. 'Ridge of the weir'.

Drumcliff (*Droim Cliabh*) Sligo. 'Ridge of the baskets'.

Drumcollogher (*Drom Collachair*) Limerick. 'Ridge of the hazel wood'.

Drumcondra (*Droim Conrach*) Dublin, Meath. 'Ridge of the path'.

Drumconrath (*Droim Conrach*) Meath. 'Ridge of the path'.

Drumcose (*Droim Cuas*) Fermanagh. *Drumcoose* 1609. 'Ridge of hollows'.

Drumcree (*Droim Cria*) Westmeath. 'Ridge of the clay'.

Drumcroone (*Droim Cruithean*) Derry. *Drim Crum* 1813. 'Ridge of the Cruithin'. The tribal name is related to *Briton*.

Drumcullen (*Droim Cuilinn*) Offaly. 'Holly ridge'.

Drumdeevin (*Droim Diomhaoin*) Donegal. 'Idle ridge'.

Drumderaown (*Droim 'ir dhá Abhainn*) Cork. 'Ridge between two rivers'.

Drumenny (*Droim Eanaigh*) Tyrone. *Dromany* 1615. 'Ridge of the marsh'.

Drumfad (*Droim Fhada*) Donegal, Down, Sligo, Tyrone. 'Long ridge'.

Drumfadda (*Droim Fhada*) Cork, Kerry. 'Long ridge'.

Drumfea (*Droim Féich*) Carlow. 'Ridge of the raven'.

Drumfin (*Droim Fionn*) Sligo. 'White ridge'.

Drumfree (*Droim Fraoigh*) Donegal. *Druim freigh* 1620. 'Ridge of the heather'.

Drumgath (*Droim gCath*) Down. *Drumgaa* 1435. 'Ridge of battles'.

Drumgoose (*Droim gCaas*) Armagh, Monaghan, Tyrone. 'Ridge of the cave'.

Drumhawan (*Droim Shamhuin*) Monaghan. 'Ridge of the winter festival'.

Drumhuskert (*Droim Thuaisceart*) Mayo. 'Northern ridge'.

Drumkeen (*Droim Caoin*) Donegal. 'Smooth ridge'.

Drumkeeran (*Droim Caorthainn*) Leitrim. 'Ridge of the rowans'.

Drumlane (*Droim Leathan*) Cavan. 'Wide ridge'.

Drumlea (*Droim Léith*) Tyrone. *Dromma Leithi* 1391. 'Grey ridge'.

Drumlee (*Droim Lao*) Down. *Dromlee* 1659. 'Ridge of the calf'.

Drumleevan (*Droim Leamháin*) Leitrim. 'Elm ridge'.

Drumlegagh (*Droim Liagach*) Tyrone. *Dromlegah* 1609. 'Ridge of stones'.

Drumlish (*Droim Lis*) Longford. 'Ridge of the fort'.

Drumloose (*Droim Lus*) Westmeath. 'Ridge of herbs'.

Drummin (*An Dromainn*) Mayo. 'The little ridge'.

Drummond (*Dromainn*) Laois. 'Ridge'.

Drummond Perth. *Droman* 1296. 'Ridge'. Gaelic *drumainn*.

Drummullin (*Droim an Mhuilinn*) Roscommon. 'Ridge of the mill'.

Drumnacarra (*Droim na Chairthe*) Louth. 'Ridge of the pillar stone'.

Drumnadrochit Highland. 'Ridge of the bridge'. Gaelic *druim + na + drochaid*.

Drumnafinnagle (*Droim na Fionghal*) Donegal. 'Ridge of the fratricide'.

Drumnafinnila (*Droim na Fionghal*) Leitrim. 'Ridge of the fratricide'.

Drumnaheark (*Droim na hAdhairce*) Donegal. 'Ridge of the horn'.

Drumnahoe (*Droim na hUamha*) Antrim, Tyrone. 'Ridge of the cave'.

Drumnakilly (*Droim na Coille*) Tyrone. *Dromnekillye* 1613. 'Ridge of the wood'.

Drumnanaliv (*Droim na nDealbh*) Monaghan. 'Ridge of the phantoms'.

Drumnashaloge (*Droim na Sealg*) Tyrone. 'Ridge of the hunt'.

Drumquin (*Droim Caoin*) Tyrone. *Druimchaoin* 1212. 'Smooth ridge'.

Drumragh (*Droim Rátha*) Tyrone. 'Ridge of the ring fort'.

Drumralla (*Droim Rálach*) Fermanagh. 'Ridge of oak'.

Drumraney (*Droim Raithne*) Westmeath. 'Ridge of ferns'.

Drumree (*Droim Rí*) Meath. 'Ridge of the king'.

Drumshanbo (*Droim Seanbhó*) Leitrim. 'Ridge of the old cow'.

Drumskinny (*Droim Scine*) Fermanagh. *Dromskynny* 1639. 'Ridge of the knife'.

Drumsna (*Drom ar Snámh*) Leitrim. 'Ridge of the swimming place'.

Drumsru (*Droim Sruth*) Kildare. 'Ridge of the streams'.

Drumsurn (*Droim Sorn*) Derry. *Drumsoren* 1613. 'Ridge of the furnace'.

Drung (*Drong*) Cavan. 'Folk'.

Dry Doddington Lincs., *see* DODDINGTON.

Dry Drayton Cambs., *see* DRAYTON.

Drybeck Cumbria. *Dribek* 1256. 'Stream which sometimes dries up'. OE *drȳge* + OScand. *bekkr*.

Drybrook Glos. *Druybrok* 1282. 'Brook which sometimes dries up'. OE *drȳge* + *brōc*.

Dryburgh Sc. Bord. *Drieburh c.*1160. 'Dry fortress'. OE *drȳge* + *burh*. The reference is presumably to a former dried-up stream, or a position unreachable by flood.

Duagh (*Dubháth*) Kerry. 'Black ford'.

Duarrigle (*Dubh Aireagal*) Cork. 'Black oratory'.

Dublin (*Dubh Linn*) Dublin. 'Black pool'. *Eblana c.*150, *Dyflin c.*1000, *Duibh-linn* 12th cent. The official Irish name of Dublin is *Baile Átha Cliath*, 'town of the hurdle ford'. Both names refer to the River Liffey.

Duckington Ches. *Dochintone* 1086 (DB). 'Estate associated with a man called *Ducc(a)*'. OE pers. name + *-ing-* + *tūn*.

Ducklington Oxon. *Duclingtun* 958, *Dochelintone* 1086 (DB). Probably 'estate associated with a man called *Ducel*'. OE pers. name + *-ing-* + *tūn*.

Duckmanton, Long Derbys. *Ducemannestune c.*1002, *Dochemanestun* 1086 (DB). 'Farmstead of a man called *Ducemann*'. OE pers. name + *tūn*.

Duddenhoe End Essex. *Dudenho* 12th cent. 'Spur of land or ridge of a man called Dudda'. OE pers. name (genitive *-n*) + *hōh*, with the addition of *end* 'district' from the 18th cent.

Duddington Northants. *Dodintone* 1086 (DB). 'Estate associated with a man called Dud(d)a or Dod(d)a'. OE pers. name + *-ing-* + *tūn*.

Duddo Northum. *Dudehou* 1208–10. 'Spur of land or ridge of a man called Dud(d)a'. OE pers. name + *hōh*.

Duddon Ches. *Dudedun* 1185. 'Hill of a man called Dud(d)a'. OE pers. name + *dūn*.

Duddon (river) Lancs., Cumbria, *see* DUNNERDALE.

Dudleston Shrops. *Dodeleston* 1267. 'Farmstead of a man called Dud(d)el or *Dod(d)el*'. OE pers. name + *tūn*.

Dudley W. Mids. *Dudelei* 1086 (DB). 'Woodland clearing of a man called Dud(d)a'. OE pers. name + *lēah*.

Duffield, 'open land frequented by doves', OE *dūfe* + *feld*: **Duffield** Derbys. *Duvelle |sic|* 1086 (DB), *Duffeld* 12th cent. **Duffield, North** & **Duffield, South** N. Yorks. *Dufeld, Nortdufelt, Suddufeld* 1086 (DB).

Dufftown Moray. 'Duff's town'. The town was founded in 1817 by James Duff, 4th Earl of Fife (1776–1857).

Dufton Cumbria. *Dufton* 1256. 'Farmstead where doves are kept'. OE *dūfe* + *tūn*.

Duggleby N. Yorks. *Difgelibi* 1086 (DB). 'Farmstead or village of a man called Dubgall or Dubgilla'. OIrish pers. name + OScand. *bý*.

Dugort (*Dumha Goirt*) Mayo. 'Black field'.

Duhallow (*Duthaigh Ealla*) Cork. 'District of the (river) Ealla'.

Dukestown Blae. 'Duke's town'. The township arose in the 19th cent. around the Duke's Pit coalmine, opened on land owned by the Duke of Beaufort.

Dukinfield Gtr. Manch. *Dokenfeld* 12th cent. 'Open land where ducks are found'. OE *dūce* (genitive plural *dūcena*) + *feld*.

Dulane (*Tulán*) Meath. 'Little hill'.

Duleek (*Damhliag*) Meath. 'Stone church'.

Dullingham Cambs. *Dullingham* c.1045, *Dullingeham* 1086 (DB). 'Homestead of the family or followers of a man called *Dull(a)*'. OE pers. name + *-inga-* + *hām*.

Duloe Cornwall. *Dulo* 1283. 'Place between the two rivers called Looe'. Cornish *dew* 'two' + river-names from Cornish *logh* 'pool'.

Dulverton Somerset. *Dolvertune* 1086 (DB). Possibly 'farmstead near the hidden ford'. OE *dīegel* + *ford* + *tūn*.

Dulwich Gtr. London. *Dilwihs* 967. 'Marshy meadow where dill grows'. OE *dile* + *wisc*.

Dumbarton W. Dunb. *Dumbrethan* c.1290. 'Fort of the Britons'. Gaelic *dùn*. The name was applied by the neighbouring Gaels to the stronghold occupied from the 5th cent. by the Britons, who called their fortress *Alclut*, 'rock of the Clyde'.

Dumbleton Glos. *Dumbeltun* 995, *Dubentune* |sic| 1086 (DB). Probably 'farmstead near a shady glen or hollow'. OE *dumbel* + *tūn*.

Dumfries Dumf. *Dunfres* c.1183. 'Woodland stronghold'. Gaelic *dùn* + *preas*.

Dummer Hants. *Dunmere* 1086 (DB). 'Pond on a hill'. OE *dūn* + *mere*.

Dummoher (*Droim Mothar*) Limerick. 'Ridge of the ruined fort'.

Dun Laoghaire (*Dún Laoghaire*) Dublin. 'Laoghaire's fort'.

Dunadry (*Dún Eadradh*) Antrim. 'Middle fort'.

Dunaff (*Dún Damh*) Donegal. *Duneffe* c.1659. 'Fort of oxen'.

Dunany (*Dún Áine*) Louth. 'Áine's fort'.

Dunbar E. Loth. *Dynbaer* 709. 'Summit fort'. Gaelic *dùn* + *barr*, based on Burhse dim-bar.

Dunbarton Down. 'Dunbar's town'. Linen mills were founded here in c.1838 by Hugh *Dunbar*.

Dunbeg (*Dún Beag*) Galway. 'Small fort'.

Dunbell (*Dún Bile*) Kilkenny. 'Fort of the sacred tree'.

Dunblane Stir. *Dumblann* c.1200. 'Blaan's hill'. Gaelic *dùn*. Blaan was a 6th-cent. bishop who had a monastery here.

Dunboyne (*Dún Búinne*) Meath. 'Báethán's fort'.

Duncannon (*Dún Canann*) Wexford. 'Canainn's fort'.

Duncansby Head Highland. *Dungalsbaer* c.1225. 'Headland by Dungal's farm'. OScand. *bý*.

Dunchurch Warwicks. *Donecerce* |sic| 1086 (DB), *Duneschirche* c.1150. Probably 'church of a man called Dun(n)'. OE pers. name + *cirice*.

Duncormick (*Dún Chormaic*) Wexford. 'Cormac's fort'.

Duncote Northants. *Dunecote* 1227. 'Cottage(s) of a man called Dun(n)a'. OE pers. name + *cot*.

Duncrun (*Dún Cruithen*) Derry. 'Fort of the Cruithin'.

Duncton W. Sussex. *Donechitone* 1086 (DB). 'Farmstead of a man called *Dunnuca*'. OE pers. name + *tūn*.

Dundalk (*Dún Dealgan*) Louth. 'Dealga's fort'.

Dundareirke (*Dún dá Radharc*) Cork. 'Fort of two prospects'.

Dundaryark (*Dún dá Rhadharc*) Kilkenny. 'Fort of two prospects'.

Dundee Dund. *Dunde* c.1180. 'Daigh's fort'. Gaelic *dùn*.

Dunderry (*Dún Doire*) Meath. 'Fort of the oak grove'.

Dundon Somerset. *Dondeme* |sic| 1086 (DB), *Dunden* 1236. 'Valley by the hill'. OE *dūn* + *denu*.

Dundonald (*Dún Dónaill*) Down. *Dondouenald* c.1183. 'Dónall's fort'.

Dundraw Cumbria. *Drumdrahrigg* 1194. 'Slope of the ridge'. Celtic *drum* + OScand. *drag* (with OScand. *hryggr* 'ridge' in the 12th cent. form).

Dundrod (*Dún dTreodáin*) Antrim. *Doonkilltroddon* c.1672. 'Fort of Treodán'. The present name is a shortened form of *Dún Cille Treodáin*, 'fort of the church of St Treodán'.

Dundrum (*Dún Droma*) Down, Dublin, Laois, Tipperary. 'Fort of the ridge'.

Dundry N. Som. *Dundreg* 1065. Possibly 'slope of the hill (used for dragging down loads)', OE *dūn* + *dræg*. Alternatively perhaps a Celtic name for Dundry Hill from *din* 'fort' with another element.

Duneane (*Dún dá Éan*) Antrim. 'Fort of two birds'.

Duneel (*Dún Aoil*) Westmeath. 'Lime fort'.

Duneight (*Dún Echdach*) Down. 'Eochaid's fort'.

Dunfanaghy (*Dún Fionnachaidh*) Donegal. *Dunfenoghy* 1679. 'Fort of the white field'.

Dunfermline Fife. *Dumfermelyn* 11th cent., *Dumferlin* 1124. Meaning uncertain. The first element is Gaelic *dùn*, 'hill'. The rest is unexplained.

Dunfore (*Dún Fuar*) Sligo. 'Cold fort'.

Dungall (*Dún Gall*) Antrim. 'Fort of the strangers'.

Dungannon (*Dún Geanainn*) Tyrone. (*caislén*) *Dúingenainn* 1505. 'Geanann's fort'.

Dunganstown (*Baile Uí Dhonnagáin*) Wexford. 'Donnagán's homestead'.

Dungarvan (*Dún Garbháin*) Kilkenny, Waterford. 'Garbhán's fort'.

Dungeness Kent. *Dengenesse* 1335. 'Headland (OE *næss*) near Denge Marsh', the latter being *Dengemersc* 774, possibly 'marsh of the valley district' from OE *denu* + **gē* + *mersc*, alternatively 'marsh with manured land' from OE *dyncge* (Kentish *dencge*).

Dungiven (*Dún Geimhin*) Derry. (*o*) *Dún Geimin* c.830. Possibly 'Geimhean's fort'.

Dunglow (*An Clochán Liath*) Donegal. *Dougloo* 1600. 'The grey stepping stones'. The present name represents Irish *Dún gCloiche*, 'fort of stone'.

Dungourney (*Dún Guairne*) Cork. 'Guairne's fort'.

Dunham, 'homestead or village at a hill', OE *dūn* + *hām*: **Dunham** Notts. *Duneham* 1086 (DB). **Dunham, Great** & **Dunham, Little** Norfolk. *Dunham* 1086 (DB). **Dunham on the Hill** Ches. *Doneham* 1086 (DB), *Dunham on the Hill* 1534. Affix from OE *hyll*. **Dunham Town** Gtr. Manch. *Doneham* 1086 (DB).

Dunhampton Heref. & Worcs. *Dunhampton* 1222. 'Homestead or home farm by the hill'. OE *dūn* + *hām-tūn*.

Dunhill (*Dún Aill*) Waterford. 'Fort cliff'.

Dunholme Lincs. *Duneham* 1086 (DB). 'Homestead or village at a hill'. OE *dūn* + *hām*.

Dunineny (*Dún an Aonaigh*) Antrim. 'Fort of the assembly'.

Duniry (*Dún Doighre*) Galway. 'Fort of the blast'.

Dunkeld Perth. *Duncalden* 10th cent. 'Fort of the Caledonians'. Gaelic *dùn*. The 'Caledonians' are the Picts who occupied this region.

Dunkerrin (*Dún Cairin*) Offaly. 'Caire's fort'.

Dunkerron (*Dún Ciaráin*) Kerry. 'Ciarán's fort'.

Dunkeswell Devon. *Doducheswelle |sic|* 1086 (DB), *Dunekeswell* 1219. 'Spring or stream of a man called Duduc or **Dunnuc*'. OE pers. name + *wella*.

Dunkineely (*Dún Cíonnaola*) Donegal. *Duncanally* c.1659. 'Cionnaola's fort'.

Dunkirk Kent, first recorded in 1790, a transferred name from Dunkerque in France. There are examples of the same name, originally given to places considered lawless or remote, in Ches., Notts., S. Glos., Staffs., and Wilts.

Dunlavin (*Dún Luáin*) Wicklow. 'Luán's fort'.

Dunleer (*Dún Léire*) Louth. 'Léire's fort'.

Dunlewy (*Dún Lúiche*) Donegal. *Dunluy* 1654. 'Lughaidh's fort'.

Dunloy (*Dún Lathaí*) Antrim. *Dunlogh* c.1672. 'Fort of the mire'.

Dunluce (*Dúnlios*) Antrim. *Dhúinlis* 1513. 'Fortified residence'.

Dunmanus (*Dún Mánais*) Cork. 'Mánas's fort'.

Dunmoon (*Dún Móin*) Waterford. 'Món's fort'.

Dunmore (*Dún Mór*) Donegal, Galway, Waterford. 'Big fort'.

Dunmow, Great & *Dunmow, Little* Essex. *Dunemowe* 951, *Dommawa* 1086 (DB). 'Meadow on the hill'. OE *dūn* + **māwe*.

Dunmoyle (*An Dún Maol*) Tyrone. *Dunmoyle* c.1655. 'The bald fort'.

Dunmurry (*Dún Muirígh*) Antrim. *Ballydownmory* 1604. 'Muiríoch's fort'.

Dunnalong (*Dún na Long*) Derry. 'Fortress of the ships'.

Dunnamaggan (*Dún na mBogán*) Kildare, Kilkenny. 'Fort of the soft ground'.

Dunnamanagh (*Dún na Manach*) Tyrone. *Downeamannogh* c.1655. 'Fort of the monks'.

Dunnamark (*Dún na mBarc*) Kerry. 'Fort of the boats'.

Dunnamore (*Domhnach Mór*) Tyrone. *Donach Mór* c.930. 'Big church'.

Dunnerdale, Hall Cumbria. *Dunerdale* 1293. 'Valley of the River Duddon'. River-name of uncertain origin and meaning + OScand. *dalr*. Affix probably *hall* 'manor-house'.

Dunnet Head. See THURSO.

Dunnington E. R. Yorks. *Dodintone* 1086 (DB). 'Estate associated with a man called Dud(d)a'. OE pers. name + *-ing-* + *tūn*.

Dunnington York. *Donniton* 1086 (DB). 'Estate associated with a man called Dun(n)a'. OE pers. name + *-ing-* + *tūn*.

Dunnockshaw Lancs. *Dunnockschae* 1296. 'Small wood or copse frequented by hedge-sparrows'. OE **dunnoc* + *sceaga*.

Dunoon Arg. *Dunnon* c.1240, *Dunhoven* 1270. 'Fort by the river'. Gaelic *Dùn Obhaim*. The river is the Clyde.

Dunquin (*Dún Chaoin*) Kerry. 'Pleasant fort'.

Dunraymond (*Dún Réamainn*) Monaghan. 'Réamann's fort'.

Dunree (*Dún Riabhach*) Donegal. 'Striped fort'.

Duns Sc. Bord. *Duns* 1150. '(Place by the) hills'. OE *dun* or Gaelic *dún* + English *-s*.

Duns Tew Oxon., see TEW.

Dunsallagh (*Dún Salach*) Clare. 'Dirty fort'.

Dunsby Lincs., near Rippingale. *Dunesbi* 1086 (DB). 'Farmstead or village of a man called Dun(n)'. OE pers. name + OScand. *bý*.

Dunsden Green Oxon. *Dunesdene* 1086 (DB), *Donsden grene* 1589. 'Valley of a man called Dyn(n)e'. OE pers. name + *denu*, with *grēne* 'village green' added from the 16th cent.

Dunseverick (*Dún Sobhairce*) Antrim. *Dun Sobhairce* 351. 'Sobhairce's fort'.

Dunsfold Surrey. *Duntesfaude* 1259. 'Fold or small enclosure of a man called **Dunt*'. OE pers. name + *fald*.

Dunsford Devon. *Dun(n)esforda* 1086 (DB). 'Ford of a man called Dun(n)'. OE pers. name + *ford*.

Dunsforth, Lower & *Dunsforth, Upper* N. Yorks. *Doneford(e), Dunesford* 1086 (DB). Identical in origin with the previous name.

Dunshaughlin (*Dún Seachlainn*) Meath. 'Seachlann's fort'.

Dunsley N. Yorks. *Dunesle* 1086 (DB). 'Woodland clearing of a man called Dun(n)'. OE pers. name + *lēah*.

Dunsmore (old district) Warwicks., *see* RYTON-ON-DUNSMORE.

Dunstable Beds. *Dunestaple* 1123. 'Boundary post of a man called Dun(n)a'. OE pers. name + *stapol*.

Dunstall Staffs. *Tunstall* 13th cent. 'Site of a farm, a farmstead'. OE **tūn-stall*.

Dunstan Northum. *Dunstan* 1242. 'Stone or rock on a hill'. OE *dūn* + *stān*.

Dunster Somerset. *Torre* 1086 (DB), *Dunestore* 1138. 'Craggy hill-top of a man called Dun(n)'. OE pers. name + *torr*.

Dunston, 'farmstead of a man called Dun(n)', OE pers. name + *tūn*: **Dunston** Lincs. *Dunestune* 1086 (DB). **Dunston** Norfolk. *Dunestun* 1086 (DB). **Dunston** Staffs. *Dunestone* 1086 (DB).

Dunterton Devon. *Dondritone* 1086 (DB). OE *tūn* 'farmstead', possibly added to an old Celtic name meaning 'fort village' (**din* + *tre*).

Duntinny (*Dún Teine*) Donegal. 'Fort of the fire'.

Duntisbourne Abbots, *Duntisbourne Leer*, & *Duntisbourne Rouse* Glos. *Duntesburne* 1055, *Dantesborne*, *Tantesborne*, *Duntesborne* 1086 (DB), *Duntesbourn Abbatis* 1291, *Duntesbourn Lyre* 1307, *Duntesbourn Rus* 1287. 'Stream of a man called **Dunt*'. OE pers. name + *burna*. Manorial affixes from possession in medieval times by the Abbot of St Peter's Abbey at Gloucester, by the Abbey of Lire in Normandy, and by the family of le Rous.

Duntish Dorset. *Dunhethis* 1249. 'Pasture on a hill'. OE *dūn* + **etisc*.

Dunton Beds. *Donitone* 1086 (DB). Probably 'farmstead on a hill'. OE *dūn* + *tūn*.

Dunton Bucks. *Dodintone* 1086 (DB). 'Estate associated with a man called Dud(d)a or Dod(d)a'. OE pers. name + *-ing-* + *tūn*.

Dunton Norfolk. *Dontuna* 1086 (DB). 'Farmstead on a hill'. OE *dūn* + *tūn*.

Dunton Bassett Leics. *Donitone* 1086 (DB), *Dunton Basset* 1418. Probably identical with the previous name. Manorial affix from the Basset family, here in the 12th cent.

Dunton Green Kent. *Dunington* 1244. 'Estate associated with a man called Dun(n) or Dun(n)a'. OE pers. name + *-ing-* + *tūn*.

Dunwich Suffolk. *Domnoc* 731, *Duneuuic* 1086 (DB). An old Celtic name possibly meaning 'deep water' to which OE *wīc* 'harbour, trading centre' was later added.

Durdle Door Dorset. *Dirdale Door* 1811. In spite of the lack of early spellings the first element may be OE *thyrelod* 'pierced' with *duru* 'door, opening'.

Durham Durham. *Dunholm* c.1000. 'Island with a hill'. OE *dūn* + OScand. *holmr*.

Durleigh Somerset. *Derlege* 1086 (DB). 'Wood or clearing frequented by deer'. OE *dēor* + *lēah*.

Durley Hants. *Deorleage* 901, *Derleie* 1086 (DB). Identical in origin with the previous name.

Durness Highland. *Dyrnes* 1230. 'Promontory frequented by deer'. OScand **dyr* + *nes*.

Durnford, Great Wilts. *Diarneford* 1086 (DB). 'Hidden ford'. OE *dierne* + *ford*.

Durrington, 'estate associated with a man called Dēor(a)'. OE pers. name + *-ing-* + *tūn*: **Durrington** W. Sussex. *Derentune* 1086 (DB). **Durrington** Wilts. *Derintone* 1086 (DB).

Durrow (*Darú*) Laois. 'Oak plain'.

Durrus (*Dúras*) Cork. 'Black grove'.

Dursley Glos. *Dersilege* 1086 (DB). 'Woodland clearing of a man called Dēorsige'. OE pers. name + *lēah*.

Durston Somerset. *Derstona* 1086 (DB). 'Farmstead of a man called Dēor'. OE pers. name + *tūn*.

Durweston Dorset. *Derwinestone* 1086 (DB). 'Farmstead of a man called Dēorwine'. OE pers. name + *tūn*.

Duston Northants. *Dustone* 1086 (DB). 'Farmstead on a mound', or 'farmstead with dusty soil'. OE **dus* or *dūst* + *tūn*.

Dutton Ches. *Duntune* 1086 (DB). 'Farmstead at a hill'. OE *dūn* + *tūn*.

Duxford Cambs. *Dukeswrthe* c.950, *Dochesuuorde* 1086 (DB). 'Enclosure of a man called **Duc(c)*'. OE pers. name + *worth*.

Dwygyfylchi Conwy: 'Two circular forts'. Welsh *dwy* + *cyfylchi*.

Dyan (*Daingean*) Tyrone. *Dingan* 1613. 'Stronghold'.

Dyce Abdn. *Dys* 1329. Meaning unknown.

Dyfed (the historic county). '(District of the) Demetae'. The *Demetae*, with name of unknown meaning, were a pre-Roman people who inhabited the part of Wales corresponding to modern Pembrokeshire.

Dyffryn Vale Glam. *The Differin* 1596. '(Place in the) valley'. Welsh *dyffryn*.

Dyke Lincs. *Dic* 1086 (DB). '(Place at) the ditch or dike'. OE *dīc*.

Dymchurch Kent. *Deman circe* c.1100. Probably 'church of the judge'. OE *dēma* + *cirice*.

Dymock Glos. *Dimoch* 1086 (DB). Possibly from Celtic **din* 'fort' + adjectival suffix.

Dyrham S. Glos. *Deorhamme* 950, *Dirham* 1086 (DB). 'Enclosed valley frequented by deer'. OE *dēor* + *hamm*.

Dysart Fife. *Disard* c.1210. 'Hermitage'. Gaelic *diseart*.

Dysart (*An Díseart*) Roscommon, Westmeath. 'The hermitage'.

Dysert (*Díseart*) Clare. 'Hermitage'.

Dyserth (*Diserth*) Denb. *Dissard* 1086 (DB), *Dyssart* 1320. 'Hermitage'. Welsh *diserth*.

E

Eagle Lincs. *Aclei, Aycle* 1086 (DB). 'Wood where oak-trees grow'. OE *āc* (replaced by OScand. *eik*) + OE *lēah*.

Eaglesfield Cumbria. *Eglesfeld c.*1170. 'Open land near a Romano-British Christian church'. Celtic **eglēs* + OE *feld*.

Eakring Notts. *Ecringhe* 1086 (DB). 'Ring or circle of oak-trees'. OScand. *eik* + *hringr*.

Ealand N. Lincs. *Aland* 1316. 'Cultivated land by water or by a river'. OE *ēa-land*.

Ealing Gtr. London. *Gillingas c.*698. '(Settlement of) the family or followers of a man called *Gilla'. OE pers. name + *-ingas*.

Eamont Bridge Cumbria. *Eamotum* 11th cent., *Amotbrig* 1362. 'Bridge at the river-confluences'. OE *ēa-mōt* (replaced by OScand. *á-mót*) + *brycg*.

Earby Lancs. *Eurebi* 1086 (DB). 'Upper farmstead', or 'farmstead of a man called Jǫfurr'. OScand. *efri* or pers. name + *bý*.

Eardington Shrops. *Eardigtun c.*1030, *Ardintone* 1086 (DB). 'Estate associated with a man called *Earda'. OE pers. name + *-ing-* + *tūn*.

Eardisland Heref. & Worcs. *Lene* 1086 (DB), *Erleslen* 1230. 'Nobleman's estate in *Leon*'. OE *eorl* added to old Celtic name for the district (*see* LEOMINSTER).

Eardisley Heref. & Worcs. *Herdeslege* 1086 (DB). 'Woodland clearing of a man called Ægheard'. OE pers. name + *lēah*.

Eardiston Heref. & Worcs. *Eardulfestun c.*957, *Ardolvestone* 1086 (DB). 'Farmstead of a man called Eardwulf'. OE pers. name + *tūn*.

Earith Cambs. *Herheth* 1244. 'Muddy or gravelly landing place'. OE *ēar* + *hýth*.

Earl or *Earl's* as affix, see main name, e.g. for **Earl's Barton** (Northants.) *see* BARTON.

Earle Northum. *Yherdhill* 1242. 'Hill with a fence or enclosure'. OE *geard* + *hyll*.

Earlham Norfolk. *Erlham* 1086 (DB). Possibly 'homestead of a nobleman'. OE *eorl* + *hām*.

Earlston Sc. Bord. *Erchildun c.*1144, *Ercildune c.*1180, *Earlston, or Ercildon* 1868. 'Earcil's hill'. OE *dūn*.

Earn (river) Perth. *Erne* 1190. 'Flowing one'. Pre-Celtic.

Earnley W. Sussex. *Earneleagh* 8th cent. 'Wood or woodland clearing where eagles are seen'. OE *earn* + *lēah*.

Earsdon Tyne & Wear. *Erdesdon* 1233. Probably 'hill of a man called Ēanrǣd or Ēorǣd'. OE pers. name + *dūn*.

Earsham Norfolk. *Ersam* 1086 (DB). Possibly 'homestead or village of a man called Ēanhere'. OE pers. name + *hām*.

Earswick York. *Edresuuic |sic|* 1086 (DB), *Ethericewyk* 13th cent. 'Dwelling or farm of a man called Æthelrīc'. OE pers. name + *wīc*.

Eartham W. Sussex. *Ercheham |sic|* 12th cent., *Ertham* 1279. 'Homestead or enclosure with ploughed land'. OE *erth* + *hām* or *hamm*.

Easby N. Yorks., near Stokesley. *Esebi* 1086 (DB). 'Farmstead or village of a man called Ēsi'. OScand. pers. name + *bý*.

Easebourne W. Sussex. *Eseburne* 1086 (DB). 'Stream of a man called Ēsa'. OE pers. name + *burna*.

Easenhall Warwicks. *Esenhull* 1221. 'Hill of a man called Ēsa'. OE pers. name (genitive *-n*) + *hyll*.

Eashing Surrey. *Æscengum* late 9th cent., *Essinge* 1272. '(Settlement of) the ash-tree folk, or (settlement of) the family or followers of a man called Æsc'. OE *æsc* or pers. name + *-ingas*.

Easington, usually 'estate associated with a man called Ēsa', OE pers. name + *-ing-* + *tūn*: **Easington** Bucks. *Hesintone* 1086 (DB). **Easington** Durham. *Esingtun c.*1050. **Easington** E. R. Yorks. *Esintone* 1086 (DB). **Easington** Red. & Cleve. *Esingetun* 1086 (DB).

However the following have different origins: **Easington** Northum. *Yesington* 1242. Possibly an old name for the stream here + OE *tūn* 'farmstead'. **Easington** Oxon., near Cuxham. *Esidone* 1086 (DB). 'Hill of a man called Ēsa'. OE pers. name (genitive *-n*) + *dūn*.

Easingwold N. Yorks. *Eisincewald* 1086 (DB). 'High forest-land of the family or followers of a man called Ēsa'. OE pers. name + *-inga-* + *wald*.

Easky (*Iascach*) Sligo. 'Abounding in fish'.

Easole Street Kent. *Oesewalum* 824, *Eswalt* 1086 (DB). Possibly 'ridges or banks associated with a god or gods'. OE *ēs, ōs* + *walu*.

East as affix, see main name, e.g. for **East Allington** (Devon) *see* ALLINGTON.

East Kilbride S. Lan. *Kellebride* 1180. 'Eastern (place by) St Brigid's church'. Gaelic *cill*. *East* distinguishes the town from *West Kilbride*, Ayr.

East Linton E. Loth. *Lintun* 1127. 'Eastern flax farm'. OE *lin* + *tun*. *East* distinguishes the place from *West Linton*, Peebles.

East Lothian. See MIDLOTHIAN.

East Wemyss Fife. *Wemys* 1239, *Easter Weimes* 1639. 'Eastern (place by) caves'. ME *east* + Gaelic *uaim* + English plural *-s*.

East Williamston Pemb. *Williamston* 1541. 'Eastern (place called) William's farm'. OE *tun*. *East* distinguishes the village from *West Williamston*.

Eastbourne E. Sussex. *Burne* 1086 (DB), *Estbourne* 1310. '(Place at) the stream'. OE *burna*, with the later addition of *ēast* 'east' to distinguish it from WESTBOURNE.

Eastburn W. Yorks. *Estbrune* 1086 (DB). 'East stream', or '(land lying) east of the stream'. OE *ēast* or *ēastan* + *burna*.

Eastbury Berks. *Eastbury* c.1090. 'East manor'. OE *ēast* + *burh* (dative *byrig*).

Eastchurch Kent. *Eastcyrce* c.1100. 'East church'. OE *ēast* + *cirice*.

Eastcote, *Eastcott*, 'eastern cottage(s)', OE *ēast* + *cot*; examples include: **Eastcote** Gtr. London. *Estcotte* 1248. **Eastcott** Wilts., near Potterne. *Estcota* 1167.

Eastcourt Wilts., near Crudwell. *Escote* 901. Identical in origin with the previous two names.

Eastdean E. Sussex. *Esdene* 1086 (DB). 'East valley'. OE *ēast* + *denu*. 'East' in relation to WESTDEAN.

Easter Ardross Highland. 'Eastern promontory of the height'. English *easter* + Gaelic *àird* + *ros*.

Easter Quarff Shet. *Quharf* 1569. 'Eastern nook'. English *easter* + OScand. *hvarf*. The name contrasts with nearby *Wester Quarff*.

Easter Ross (district) Highland. 'Eastern Ross'. English *easter*. See ROSS.

Easter, Good & *Easter, High* Essex. *Estre* 11th cent., *Estra* 1086 (DB), *Godithestre* 1200, *Heyestre* 1254. '(Place at) the sheep-fold'. OE *eowestre*. Distinguishing affixes from possession in Anglo-Saxon times by a woman called Gōdgȳth or Gōdgifu, and from OE *hēah* 'high'.

Eastergate W. Sussex. *Gate* 1086 (DB), *Estergat* 1263. '(Place at) the gate or gap'. OE *geat*, with the later addition of *ēasterra* 'more easterly' to distinguish it from WESTERGATE.

Easterton Wilts. *Esterton* 1348. 'More easterly farmstead'. OE *ēasterra* + *tūn*.

Eastham Mersey. *Estham* 1086 (DB). 'East homestead or enclosure'. OE *ēast* + *hām* or *hamm*.

Easthampstead Berks. *Lachenestede* 1086 (DB), *Yethamstede* 1176. 'Homestead by the gate or gap'. OE *geat* + *hām-stede*.

Easthope Shrops. *Easthope* 901, *Stope* |sic| 1086 (DB). 'Eastern enclosed valley'. OE *ēast* + *hop*.

Easthorpe Essex. *Estorp* 1086 (DB). 'Eastern outlying farmstead or hamlet'. OE *ēast* + OScand. *thorp*.

Easthouses Midloth. *Esthus* 1241, *Esthouse* 1345, *Eisthousis* 1590. 'Eastern house'. ME *east* + *hūs*. The plural *s* is a recent development.

Eastington Glos., near Stonehouse. *Esteueneston* 1220. 'Farmstead of a man called Ēadstān'. OE pers. name + *tūn*.

Eastleach Martin & *Eastleach Turville* Glos. *Lecche* 862, *Lec(c)e* 1086 (DB), *Estleche Sancti Martini* 1291, *Estleche Roberti de Tureuill* 1221. 'Eastern estate on the River Leach'. OE *ēast* + river-name from OE **læc(c)*, **lece* 'stream flowing through boggy land'. Affixes from the dedication of the church and from the de Turville family, here from the 13th cent.

Eastleigh Hants. *East lea* 932, *Estleie* 1086 (DB). 'East wood or clearing'. OE *ēast* + *lēah*.

Eastling Kent. *Eslinges* 1086 (DB). '(Settlement of) the family or followers of a man called Ēsla'. OE pers. name + *-ingas*.

Eastney Hants. *Esteney* 1242. '(Place in) the east of the island'. OE *ēastan* + *ēg*.

Eastnor Heref. & Worcs. *Astenofre* 1086 (DB). '(Place to) the east of the ridge'. OE *ēastan* + **ofer*.

Eastoft N. Lincs. *Eschetoft* c.1170. 'Homestead or curtilage where ash-trees grow'. OScand. *eski* + *toft*.

Easton, a very common place-name, usually 'east farmstead or village', i.e. one to the east of another settlement, OE *ēast* + *tūn*; examples include: **Easton** Cambs. *Estone* 1086 (DB). **Easton** Cumbria, near Netherby. *Estuna* 12th cent. **Easton** Hants., near Winchester. *Eastun* 825, *Estune* 1086 (DB). **Easton** I. of Wight. *Estetune* 1244. **Easton** Lincs. *Estone* 1086 (DB). **Easton** Norfolk. *Estuna* 1086 (DB). **Easton** Suffolk, near Framlingham. *Estuna* 1086 (DB). **Easton, Crux** Hants. *Eastune* 801, *Estune* 1086 (DB), *Eston Croc* 1242. Manorial addition from a family called Croc(h), here in the 11th cent. **Easton, Great** Leics. *Estone* 1086 (DB). **Easton Grey** Wilts. *Estone* 1086 (DB), *Eston Grey* 1281. Manorial addition from the de Grey family, here in the 13th cent. **Easton in Gordano** N. Som. *Estone* 1086 (DB), *Eston in Gordon* 1293. Affix is an old district name, *see* CLAPTON. **Easton Maudit** Northants. *Estone* 1086 (DB), *Estonemaudeut* 1298. Manorial affix from the Mauduit family, here in the 12th cent. **Easton on the Hill** Northants. *Estone* 1086 (DB). Affix from its situation on the brow of a hill. **Easton Royal** Wilts. *Estone* 1086 (DB). Affix from OFrench *roial* 'royal' referring to its situation on the edge of an old royal forest. **Easton, Ston** Somerset. *Estone* 1086 (DB), *Stonieston* 1230. Affix from OE *stānig* 'stony' referring to stony ground.

However some Eastons have a different origin, among them: **Easton, Great** & **Easton, Little** Essex. *E(i)stanes* 1086 (DB). Probably 'stones by the island or well-watered land'. OE *ēg* + *stān*.

Eastrea Cambs. *Estereie* c.1020. 'Eastern part of the island (of WHITTLESEY)'. OE **ēastor* + *ēg*.

Eastriggs Dumf. 'Eastern arable land'. OE *ēast* + OScand. *hryggr*, or OE *hryog* 'ridge'.

Eastrington E. R. Yorks. *Eastringatun* 959, *Estrincton* 1086 (DB). Probably 'farmstead of those living to the east (of HOWDEN)'. OE **ēastor* + *-inga-* + *tūn*.

Eastry Kent. *Eastorege* 9th cent., *Estrei* 1086 (DB). 'Eastern district or region'. OE **ēastor* + **gē*.

Eastwell Leics. *Estwelle* 1086 (DB). 'Eastern spring or stream'. OE *ēast* + *wella*.

Eastwick Herts. *Esteuuiche* 1086 (DB). 'East dwelling or (dairy) farm'. OE *ēast* + *wīc*.

Eastwood Essex. *Estuuda* 1086 (DB). 'Eastern wood'. OE *ēast* + *wudu*.

Eastwood Notts. *Estewic* |sic| 1086 (DB), *Estweit* 1165. 'East clearing'. OE *ēast* + OScand. *thveit*.

Eathorpe Warwicks. *Ethorpe* 1232. 'Outlying farmstead or hamlet on the river'. OE *ēa* + OScand. *thorp*.

Eaton, a common place-name with two different origins. Most are 'farmstead by a river', from OE *ēa* + *tūn*, among them: **Eaton** Ches., near Congleton. *Yeiton* c.1262. **Eaton** Norfolk. *Ettune* 1086 (DB). **Eaton** Notts. *Etune* 1086 (DB). **Eaton** Oxon. *Eatun* 9th cent., *Eltune* |sic| 1086 (DB). **Eaton** Shrops., near Bishop's Castle. *Eton* 1252. **Eaton** Shrops., near Ticklerton. *Eton* 1227. **Eaton Bishop** Heref. & Worcs. *Etune* 1086 (DB), *Eton Episcopi* 1316. Affix from its possession by the Bishop (Latin *episcopus*) of Hereford. **Eaton, Castle** Wilts. *Ettone* 1086 (DB). The affix is found from the 15th cent. **Eaton Constantine** Shrops. *Etune* 1086 (DB), *Eton Costentyn* 1285. Manorial affix from the de Costentin family, here in the 13th cent. **Eaton Hastings** Oxon. *Etone* 1086 (DB), *Eton Hastinges* 1298. Manorial affix from the de Hastinges family, here in the 12th cent. **Eaton Socon** Cambs. *Etone* 1086 (DB). Affix from OE *sōcn* 'district with a right of jurisdiction'. **Eaton upon Tern** Shrops. *Eton* c.1223. On the River Tern, a Celtic river-name meaning 'the strong one'.

However other Eatons have a different origin, 'farmstead on dry ground in marsh, or on well-watered land', from OE *ēg* + *tūn*, among them: **Eaton** Ches., near Tarporley. *Eyton* 1240. **Eaton** Leics. *Aitona* c.1125. **Eaton Bray** Beds. *Eitone* 1086 (DB). Manorial affix from the Bray family, here in the 15th cent. **Eaton, Little** Derbys. *Detton* |sic| 1086 (DB), *Little Eton* 1392. **Eaton, Long** Derbys. *Aitune* 1086 (DB), *Long Eyton* 1288. Affix refers to length of village.

Ebberston N. Yorks. *Edbriztune* 1086 (DB). 'Farmstead of a man called Ēadbeorht'. OE pers. name + *tūn*.

Ebbesbourne Wake Wilts. *Eblesburna* 826, *Eblesborne* 1086 (DB), *Ebbeleburn Wak* 1249. Probably 'stream of a man called *Ebbel*'. OE pers. name + *burna*, with manorial affix from the Wake family, here in the 12th cent.

Ebbw Vale (*Glynebwy*) Blae. 'Valley of the River Ebwy'. The river name means 'colt' (Welsh *ebol*), perhaps because horses regularly drank or forded the river here or because the water was 'frisky'. The Welsh name is the equivalent of the English (Welsh *glyn*, 'valley').

Ebchester Durham. *Ebbecestr* 1230. 'Roman fort of a man called Ebba or Ebbe'. OE pers. name + *ceaster*.

Ebrington Glos. *Bristentune* |sic| 1086 (DB), *Edbrihttona* 1155. 'Farmstead of a man called Ēadbeorht'. OE pers. name + *tūn*.

Ecchinswell Hants. *Eccleswelle* 1086 (DB). Possibly 'stream of a man called *Eccel*'. OE pers. name + *wella*. Alternatively the first element may be Celtic *eglēs* 'Romano-British Christian church'.

Ecclefechan Dumf. *Eglesfeghan* 1303. 'St Fechin's church'. British *egles*.

Eccles, from Celtic *eglēs* 'Romano-British Christian church'; examples include: **Eccles** Gtr. Manch. *Eccles* c.1200. **Eccles** Kent. *Æcclesse* c.975, *Aiglessa* 1086 (DB).

Ecclesfield S. Yorks. *Eclesfeld* 1086 (DB). 'Open land near a Romano-British Christian church'. Celtic *eglēs* + OE *feld*.

Eccleshall Staffs. *Ecleshelle* |sic| 1086 (DB), *Eccleshale* 1227. 'Nook of land near a Romano-British Christian church'. Celtic *eglēs* + OE *halh*.

Eccleston, 'farmstead by a Romano-British Christian church', Celtic *eglēs* + OE *tūn*: **Eccleston** Ches. *Eclestone* 1086 (DB). **Eccleston** Lancs. *Aycleton* 1094. **Eccleston** Mersey. *Ecclistona* 1190. **Eccleston, Great** & **Eccleston, Little** Lancs. *Eglestun* 1086 (DB), *Great Eccleston* 1285, *Parua Eccliston* 1261.

Eccup W. Yorks. *Echope* 1086 (DB). 'Enclosed valley of a man called Ecca'. OE pers. name + *hop*.

Eckington, 'estate associated with a man called Ecca or Ecci', OE pers. name + *-ing-* + *tūn*: **Eckington** Derbys. *Eccingtune* c.1002, *Eckintune* 1086 (DB). **Eckington** Heref. & Worcs. *Eccyncgtun* 972, *Aichintune* 1086 (DB).

Ecton Northants. *Echentone* 1086 (DB). 'Farmstead of a man called Ecca'. OE pers. name + *tūn*.

Edale Derbys. *Aidele* 1086 (DB). 'Valley with an island or well-watered land'. OE *ēg* + *dæl*.

Edburton W. Sussex. *Eadburgeton* 12th cent. 'Farmstead of a woman called Ēadburh'. OE pers. name + *tūn*.

Eden (*Éadan*) Antrim. *Eden or Edengrenny* 1837. 'Brow'. The earlier full Irish name was *Éadan Gréine*, 'sunny brow'.

Eden, Castle Durham. *Iodene* c.1050. Named from Eden Burn, a Celtic river-name meaning simply 'water' (with OE *burna* 'stream'). The later affix presumably refers to the 18th cent. mansion here.

Edenbridge Kent. *Eadelmesbregge* c.1100. 'Bridge of a man called Ēadhelm'. OE pers. name + *brycg*. The river-name Eden is a 'back-formation' from the place-name.

Edenderry (*Éadan Doire*) Antrim, Offaly. 'Brow of the oak wood'.

Edendork (*Éadan na dTorc*) Tyrone. *Adanadorg* 1609. 'Hill brow of the pigs'.

Edenfield Gtr. Manch. *Aytounfeld* 1324. 'Open land by the island farmstead, or by the farmstead on well-watered land'. OE *ēg* + *tūn* + *feld*.

Edenhall Cumbria. *Edenhal* 1159. 'Nook of land by the River Eden'. Celtic river-name (meaning simply 'water') + OE *halh*.

Edenham Lincs. *Edeneham* 1086 (DB). 'Homestead or enclosure of a man called Ēada'. OE pers. name (genitive *-n*) + *hām* or *hamm*.

Edensor Derbys. *Edensoure* 1086 (DB). 'Sloping bank or ridge of a man called *Ēadin*'. OE pers. name + **ofer*.

Edentrillick (*Éadan Trilic*) Down. *Balliedentrillicke* 1585. 'Hill brow of the megalithic tomb'.

Ederney (*Eadarnaidh*) Fermanagh. *Edernagh* 1610 'Middle place'.

Edgbaston W. Mids. *Celboldeston* |sic| 1086 (DB), *Egbaldestone* 1184. 'Farmstead of a man called Ecgbald'. OE pers. name + *tūn*.

Edgcott Bucks. *Achecote* 1086 (DB). Probably 'cottage(s) made of oak'. OE *æcen* + *cot*.

Edge Shrops. *Egge* 1255. '(Place at) the edge or escarpment'. OE *ecg*.

Edgefield Norfolk. *Edisfelda* 1086 (DB). 'Open land by an enclosure or enclosed park'. OE *edisc* + *feld*.

Edgeworthstown (*Meathas Troim*) Longford. 'Edgeworth's town'. The *Edgeworth* family were here from the 16th cent., Richard Edgeworth building Edgeworthstown House in the late 18th cent. The Irish name means 'frontier of the elder tree'.

Edgmond Shrops. *Edmendune* |*sic*| 1086 (DB), *Egmundun* 1155. 'Hill of a man called Ecgmund'. OE pers. name + *dūn*.

Edgton Shrops. *Egedune* 1086 (DB). Probably 'hill of a man called Ecga'. OE pers. name + *dūn*.

Edgware Gtr. London. *Ægces wer* c.975. 'Weir or fishing-enclosure of a man called Ecgi'. OE pers. name + *wer*.

Edgworth Lancs. *Eggewrthe* 1212. Probably 'enclosure on an edge or hillside'. OE *ecg* + *worth*.

Edinburgh Edin. *Eidyn* c.600, *Edenburge* 1126. 'Fortification at Eidyn'. OE *burh*. The meaning of *Eidyn* is unknown.

Edingale Staffs. *Ednunghale* 1086 (DB). 'Nook of land of the family or followers of a man called *Ēadin'. OE pers. name + *-inga-* + *halh*.

Edingley Notts. *Eddyngleia* c.1180. 'Woodland clearing associated with a man called Eddi'. OE pers. name + *-ing-* + *lēah*.

Edingthorpe Norfolk. *Ædidestorp* 1177, *Edinestorp* (probably for *Ediuestorp*) 1198. 'Outlying farmstead or hamlet of a woman called Ēadgȳth'. OE pers. name + OScand. *thorp*.

Edington Somerset. *Eduuintone* 1086 (DB). 'Farmstead of a man called Ēadwine or of a woman called Ēadwynn'. OE pers. name + *tūn*.

Edington Wilts. *Ethandune* late 9th cent., *Edendone* 1086 (DB). 'Uncultivated hill', or 'hill of a man called Ētha'. OE *ēthe* (genitive *-an*) or OE pers. name (genitive *-n*) + *dūn*.

Edith Weston Rutland, *see* WESTON.

Edlesborough Bucks. *Eddinberge* |*sic*| 1086 (DB), *Eduluesberga* 1163. 'Hill or barrow of a man called Ēadwulf'. OE pers. name + *beorg*.

Edlingham Northum. *Eadwulfincham* c.1050. 'Homestead of the family or followers of a man called Ēadwulf', or 'homestead at Ēadwulf's place'. OE pers. name + *-inga-* or *-ing* + *hām*.

Edlington, 'estate associated with a man called *Ēdla', OE pers. name + *-ing-* + *tūn*: **Edlington** Lincs. *Ellingetone* |*sic*| 1086 (DB), *Edlingtuna* c.1115.

Edlington S. Yorks. *Ellintone* |*sic*| 1086 (DB), *Edelington* 1194–9.

Edmondsham Dorset. *Amedesham* 1086 (DB). 'Homestead or enclosure of a man called *Ēadmōd or Ēadmund'. OE pers. name + *hām* or *hamm*.

Edmondthorpe Leics. *Edmerestorp* 1086 (DB). 'Outlying farmstead or hamlet of a man called Ēadmǣr'. OE pers. name + OScand. *thorp*.

Edmonton Gtr. London. *Adelmetone* 1086 (DB). 'Farmstead of a man called Ēadhelm'. OE pers. name + *tūn*.

Edstaston Shrops. *Stanestune* |*sic*| 1086 (DB), *Edestaneston* 1256. 'Farmstead of a man called Ēadst&amac;n'. OE pers. name + *tūn*.

Edstone, Great N. Yorks. *Micheledestun* 1086 (DB). 'Farmstead of a man called *Ēadin'. OE pers. name + *tūn*. Affix in the early form is OE *micel* 'great'.

Edvin Loach Heref. & Worcs. *Gedeuen* 1086 (DB), *Yedefen Loges* 1242. 'Fen or marshland of a man called *Gedda'. OE pers. name + *fenn*. Manorial affix from the de Loges family, here in the 13th cent.

Edwalton Notts. *Edvvoltone* 1086 (DB). 'Farmstead of a man called Ēadweald'. OE pers. name + *tūn*.

Edwardstone Suffolk. *Eduardestuna* 1086 (DB). 'Farmstead of a man called Ēadweard'. OE pers. name + *tūn*.

Edwinstowe Notts. *Edenestou* 1086 (DB). 'Holy place of St Ēadwine'. OE pers. name + *stōw*.

Effingham Surrey. *Epingeham* |*sic*| 1086 (DB), *Effingeham* 1180. 'Homestead of the family or followers of a man called *Effa'. OE pers. name + *-inga-* + *hām*.

Egerton Kent. *Eardingtun* |*sic*| c.1100, *Egarditon* 1203. 'Estate associated with a man called Ecgheard'. OE pers. name + *-ing-* + *tūn*.

Egerton Green Ches. *Eggerton* 1259. Probably 'farmstead of a man called Ecghere'. OE pers. name + *tūn*. Green is added from the 18th cent.

Egg Buckland Devon, *see* BUCKLAND.

Eggborough, High & *Eggborough, Low* N. Yorks. *Egeburg* 1086 (DB). 'Stronghold of a man called Ecga'. OE pers. name + *burh*.

Eggington Beds. *Ekendon* 1195. Probably 'hill of a man called Ecca'. OE pers. name (genitive *-n*) + *dūn*.

Egginton Derbys. *Ecgintune* 1012, *Eghintune* 1086 (DB). 'Estate associated with a man called Ecga'. OE pers. name + *-ing-* + *tūn*.

Egglescliffe Stock. on T. *Eggascliff* 1085. Probably 'cliff or bank near a Romano-British Christian church'. Celtic *egl̄es* + OE *clif*.

Eggleston Durham. *Egleston* 1196. Probably 'farmstead of a man called *Ecgel'. OE pers. name + *tūn*.

Egham Surrey. *Egeham* 933, 1086 (DB). 'Homestead or village of a man called Ecga'. OE pers. name + *hām*.

Egleton Rutland. *Egoluestun* 1218. 'Farmstead of a man called Ecgwulf'. OE pers. name + *tūn*.

Eglingham Northum. *Ecgwulfincham* c.1050. 'Homestead of the family or followers of a man called Ecgwulf', or 'homestead at Ecgwulf's place'. OE pers. name + *inga-* or *-ing* + *hām*.

Eglinton Derry. The original name of the village was *Muff*, from Irish *An Mhagh*, 'the plain'. The present name was adopted in 1858 when the Earl of Eglinton was Lord Lieutenant of Ireland.

Eglish (*Eaglais*) Tyrone. 'Church'.

Egloshayle Cornwall. *Egloshail* 1166. 'Church on an estuary'. Cornish *eglos* + *heyl*.

Egloskerry Cornwall. *Egloskery c.*1145. 'Church of St Keri'. Cornish *eglos* + saint's name.

Eglwys Lwyd, Yr. *See* LUDCHURCH.

Eglwys y Drindod. *See* CHRISTCHURCH.

Egmanton Notts. *Agemuntone* 1086 (DB). 'Farmstead of a man called Ecgmund'. OE pers. name + *tūn*.

Egremont Cumbria. *Egremont c.*1125. 'Sharp-pointed hill'. OFrench *aigre* + *mont*.

Egton N. Yorks. *Egetune* 1086 (DB). 'Farmstead of a man called Ecga'. OE pers. name + *tūn*. **Egton Bridge** is named from the 19th cent. railway bridge here.

Eigg (island) Highland. *Egg* 1654. '(Island with an) indentation'. Gaelic *Eilean Eige*.

Eighter (*Íochtar*) Cavan. 'Lower portion'.

Eightercua (*Íochtar Cua*) Kerry. 'Lower hollow'.

Eilean Donnan (island) Highland. *Elandonan c.*1425. 'St Donan's island'. Gaelic *eilean*.

Eilean Siar. *See* WESTERN ISLES.

Eirk (*Adharc*) Kerry. 'Peak'.

Elberton S. Glos. *Eldbertone* |*sic*| 1086 (DB), *Albricton* 1186. 'Farmstead of a man called Æthelbeorht'. OE pers. name + *tūn*.

Elburton Devon. *Aliberton* 1254. Identical in origin with the previous name.

Elcombe Wilts. *Elecome* 1086 (DB). 'Valley where elder-trees grow', or 'valley of a man called Ella'. OE *elle(n)* or OE pers. name + *cumb*.

Eldersfield Heref. & Worcs. *Yldresfeld* 972, *Edresfelle* |*sic*| 1086 (DB). 'Open land of the elder-tree, or of a man called Ealdhere'. OE *elle(n)* or pers. name + *feld*.

Eldwick W. Yorks. *Helguic* 1086 (DB). 'Dwelling or (dairy) farm of a man called Helgi'. OScand. pers. name + OE *wīc*.

Eleigh, Brent & *Eleigh, Monks* Suffolk. *Illanlege c.*995, *Illeleia* 1086 (DB), *Brendeylleye* 1312, *Monekesillegh* 1304. 'Woodland clearing of a man called *Illa'. OE pers. name + *lēah*. Affixes are from ME *brende* 'burnt, destroyed by fire' and OE *munuc* 'a monk' (alluding to possession by St Paul's in London).

Elford, 'ford where elder-trees grow', or 'ford of a man called Ella', OE *elle(n)* or OE pers. name + *ford*: **Elford** Northum. *Eleford* 1256. **Elford** Staffs. *Elleford* 1002, *Eleford* 1086 (DB).

Elgin Moray. *Elgin* 1136. Meaning unknown. *cp.* **Glenelg**.

Elham Kent. *Alham* 1086 (DB). 'Homestead or enclosure where eels are found'. OE *ǣl* + *hām* or *hamm*.

Elie Fife. *Elye* 1491, *The Alie c.*1600. '(Place of the) tomb'. Gaelic *ealaidh*, nature of *ealadh*.

Eling Hants. *Edlinges* 1086 (DB). '(Settlement of) the family or followers of a man called *Ēadla or Æthel'. OE pers. name + *ingas*.

Elkesley Notts. *Elchesleie* 1086 (DB). 'Woodland clearing of a man called Ēadlāc'. OE pers. name + *lēah*.

Elkington, North & *Elkington, South* Lincs. *Alchinton* 1086 (DB). *Northalkinton* 12th cent., *Sudhelkinton* early 13th cent. 'Estate associated with a man called Ēadlāc'. OE pers. name + *-ing-* + *tūn*.

Elkstone Glos. *Elchestane* 1086 (DB). 'Boundary stone of a man called Ēalāc'. OE pers. name + *stān*.

Elkstone, Lower & *Elkstone, Upper* Staffs. *Elkesdon* 1227. 'Hill of a man called Ēalāc'. OE pers. name + *dūn*.

Ella, Kirk & *Ella, West* E. R. Yorks. *Aluengi* |*sic*| 1086 (DB), *Kirk Elley* 15th cent., *Westeluelle* 1305. 'Woodland clearing of a man called Ælf(a)'. OE pers. name + *lēah*. Distinguishing affixes are from OScand. *kirkja* 'church' and *west*.

Elland W. Yorks. *Elant* 1086 (DB). 'Cultivated land, or estate, by the river'. OE *ēa-land*.

Ellastone Staffs. *Edelachestone* 1086 (DB). 'Farmstead of a man called Ēadlāc'. OE pers. name + *tūn*.

Ellenhall Staffs. *Linehalle* |*sic*| 1086 (DB), *Ælinhale c.*1200. Possibly 'nook of land associated with a man called Ælle or Ella', from OE pers. name + *-ing-* + *halh*. Alternatively 'nook (by the river) where flax is grown', from OE *līn* + *halh* with the later addition of *ēa*.

Ellerbeck N. Yorks. *Elrebec* 1086 (DB). 'Stream where alders grow'. OScand. *elri* + *bekkr*.

Ellerby N. Yorks. *Elwordebi* 1086 (DB). 'Farmstead or village of a man called Ælfweard'. OE pers. name + OScand. *bý*.

Ellerdine Heath Shrops. *Elleurdine* 1086 (DB). 'Enclosure of a man called Ella'. OE pers. name + *worthign*, with the later addition of *heath*.

Ellerker E. R. Yorks. *Alrecher* 1086 (DB). 'Marsh where alders grow'. OScand. *elri* + *kjarr*.

Ellerton E. R. Yorks. *Elreton* 1086 (DB). 'Farmstead by the alders'. OScand. *elri* + OE *tūn*.

Ellerton Shrops. *Athelarton* 13th cent. 'Farmstead of a man called Æthelheard'. OE pers. name + *tūn*.

Ellesborough Bucks. *Esenberge* |*sic*| 1086 (DB), *Eselbergh* 1195. Probably 'hill where asses are pastured'. OE *esol* + *beorg*.

Ellesmere Shrops. *Ellesmeles* |*sic*| 1086 (DB), *Ellismera* 1177. 'Lake or pool of a man called Elli'. OE pers. name + *mere*.

Ellesmere Port Ches., a modern name, only in use since the early 19th cent., so called because the Ellesmere Canal (from the previous name) joins the Mersey here.

Ellingham, 'homestead of the family or followers of a man called Ella', or 'homestead at Ella's place', OE pers. name + *-inga-* or *-ing* + *hām*: **Ellingham** Norfolk. *Elincham* 1086 (DB). **Ellingham, Great** & **Ellingham, Little** Norfolk. *Elin(c)gham* 1086 (DB), *Magna Elingham, Parva Elingham* 1242. Distinguishing affixes are Latin *magna* 'great' and *parva* 'little'. **Ellingham** Northum. *Ellingeham c.*1130.
  However the following contains a different pers. name:
Ellingham Hants. *Adelingeham* 1086 (DB). 'Homestead of the family or followers of a man called Æthel'. OE pers. name + *-inga-* + *hām*.

Ellingstring N. Yorks. *Elingestrengge* 1198. 'Water-course at the place where eels are caught', or 'water-course at the place associated with a man called Ella or Eli'.

OScand. *strengr* with either OE *ǣl*, *ēl* + *-ing* or OE pers. name + *-ing*.

Ellington, 'farmstead at the place where eels are caught', or 'farmstead associated with a man called Ella or Eli', OE *tūn* with either OE *ǣl*, *ēl* + *-ing* or OE pers. name + *-ing-*: **Ellington** Cambs. *Elintune* 1086 (DB). **Ellington** Northum. *Elingtona* 1166. **Ellington, High** & **Ellington, Low** N. Yorks. *Ellintone* 1086 (DB).

Ellisfield Hants. *Esewelle* |sic| 1086 (DB), *Elsefeld* 1167. Probably 'open land of a man called *Ielfsa*'. OE pers. name + *feld*.

Ellon Aber. *Eilan* c.1150. Meaning unknown.

Ellough Suffolk. *Elga* 1086 (DB). '(Place at) the heathen temple'. OScand. *elgr*.

Elloughton E. R. Yorks. *Elgendon* 1086 (DB). 'Hill with a heathen temple', or 'hill of a man called Helgi'. OScand. *elgr* or pers. name + OE *dūn*.

Elm, '(place at) the elm-tree(s)', OE *elm* (dative plural *elmum*): **Elm** Cambs. *Elm*, *Eolum* 10th cent. **Elm, Great** Somerset. *Telma* 1086 (DB). *T-* in the early form is from the OE preposition *æt* 'at'.

Elmbridge Heref. & Worcs. *Elmerige* 1086 (DB). 'Ridge where elm-trees grow'. OE *elm*, *elmen* + *hrycg*.

Elmdon Essex. *Elmenduna* 1086 (DB). 'Hill where elm-trees grow'. OE *elmen* + *dūn*.

Elmdon W. Mids. *Elmedone* 1086 (DB). 'Hill of the elm-trees'. OE *elm* + *dūn*.

Elmesthorpe Leics. *Ailmerestorp* 1207. 'Outlying farmstead or hamlet of a man called æthelmær'. OE pers. name + OScand. *thorp*.

Elmet (old district) W. Yorks, *see* BARWICK IN ELMENT.

Elmham, 'homestead or village where elm-trees grow', OE *elm*, *elmen* + *hām*: **Elmham, North** Norfolk. *Ælmham* c.1035, *Elmenham* 1086 (DB). **Elmham, South** Norfolk. *Almeham* 1086 (DB). The parishes of All Saints, St James, St Margaret and St Michael South Elmham are named from the dedications of the churches. However the affix in St Cross South Elmham is from *Sancroft* 1254, 'sandy enclosure', OE *sand* + *croft*.

Elmley, 'elm-tree wood or clearing', OE *elm* + *lēah*: **Elmley Castle** Heref. & Worcs. *Elmlege* 780, *Castel Elmeleye* 1327. Affix from the former castle here. **Elmley Lovett** Heref. & Worcs *Ælmeleia* 1086 (DB), *Almeleye Lovet* 1275. Manorial addition from the Lovett family, here in the 13th cent.

Elmore Glos. *Elmour* 1176. 'River-bank or ridge where elm-trees grow'. OE *elm* + *ōfer* or **ofer*.

Elmsall, North & *Elmsall, South* W. Yorks. *Ermeshale* |sic| 1086 (DB), *North Elmesale* 1320, *Suthelmeshal* 1230. 'Nook of land by the elm-tree'. OE *elm* + *halh*.

Elmsett Suffolk. *Ylmesæton* c.995, *Elmeseta* 1086 (DB). '(Settlement of) the dwellers among the elm-trees'. OE **elme* + *sǣte*.

Elmstead Gtr. London. *Elmsted* 1320. 'Place by the elm-trees'. OE *elm* + *stede*.

Elmstead Market Essex. *Elmesteda* 1086 (DB), *Elmested Market* 1475. 'Place where elm-trees grow'. OE **elme* or

*elmen + *stede*. Affix *market* from the important early market here.

Elmsted Kent. *Elmanstede* 811. 'Homestead by the elm-trees'. OE *elm* + *hām-stede*.

Elmstone Kent. *Ailmereston* 1203. 'Farmstead of a man called Æthelmær'. OE pers. name + *tūn*.

Elmstone Hardwicke Glos. *Almundestan* 1086 (DB). 'Boundary stone of a man called Alhmund'. OE pers. name + *stān*. Hardwicke has been added from a nearby place, *see* HARDWICKE.

Elmswell Suffolk. *Elmeswella* 1086 (DB). 'Spring or stream where elm-trees grow'. OE *elm* + *wella*.

Elmton Derbys. *Helmetune* 1086 (DB). 'Farmstead where elm-trees grow'. OE *elm*, **elmen* + *tūn*.

Elphin (*Ail Finn*) Roscommon. 'Fionn's stone'.

Elsdon Northum. *Eledene* 1226. Probably 'valley of a man called El(l)i'. OE pers. name + *denu*.

Elsenham Essex. *Elsenham* 1086 (DB). 'Homestead or village of a man called Elesa'. OE pers. name (genitive *-n*) + *hām*.

Elsfield Oxon. *Esefelde* 1086 (DB), *Elsefeld* c.1130. 'Open land of a man called Elesa'. OE pers. name + *feld*.

Elsham N. Lincs. *Elesham* 1086 (DB). 'Homestead or village of a man called El(l)i'. OE pers. name + *hām*.

Elsing Norfolk. *Helsinga* 1086 (DB). '(Settlement of) the family or followers of a man called Elesa'. OE pers. name + *-ingas*.

Elslack N. Yorks. *Eleslac* 1086 (DB). 'Stream or valley of a man called El(l)i'. OE pers. name + *lacu* or OScand. *slakki*.

Elstead Surrey. *Helstede* 1128. 'Place where elder-trees grow'. OE *elle(n)* + *stede*.

Elsted W. Sussex. *Halestede* |sic| 1086 (DB), *Ellesteda* 1180. Identical in origin with the previous name.

Elston Notts. *Elvestune* 1086 (DB). Probably 'farmstead of a man called Eiláfr'. OScand. pers. name + *tūn*.

Elstow Beds. *Elnestou* 1086 (DB). 'Assembly place of a man called **Ællen*'. OE pers. name + *stōw*.

Elstree Herts. *Tithulfes treow* 11th cent. 'Boundary tree of a man called Tīdwulf'. OE pers. name + *trēow*. Initial *T-* disappeared in the 13th cent. due to confusion with the preposition *at*.

Elstronwick E. R. Yorks. *Asteneuuic* |sic| 1086 (DB), *Elstanwik* c.1265. 'Dwelling or (dairy) farm of a man called Ælfstān'. OE pers. name + *wīc*.

Elswick Lancs. *Edelesuuic* 1086 (DB). 'Dwelling or (dairy) farm of a man called Æthelsige'. OE pers. name + *wīc*.

Elsworth Cambs. *Eleswurth* 974, *Elesuuorde* 1086 (DB). 'Enclosure of a man called El(l)i'. OE pers. name + *worth*.

Elterwater Cumbria. *Heltewatra* c.1160. 'Lake frequented by swans'. OScand. *elptr* + OE *wæter*.

Eltham Gtr. London. *Elteham* 1086 (DB). 'Homestead or river-meadow frequented by swans', or 'of a man called **Elta*'. OE *elfitu* or OE pers. name + *hām* or *hamm*.

Eltisley Cambs. *Hecteslei* |*sic*| 1086 ·(DB), *Eltesle* 1228. 'Woodland clearing of a man called Elti'. OE pers. name + *lēah*.

Elton, sometimes probably 'farmstead where eels are got', OE *ǣl* + *tūn*: **Elton** Ches., near Ellesmere Port. *Eltone* 1086 (DB). **Elton** Derbys. *Eltune* 1086 (DB). **Elton** Stock. on T. *Eltun* *c*.1090.

However other Eltons have a different origin: **Elton** Cambs. *Æthelingtun* 10th cent., *Adelintune* 1086 (DB). 'Farmstead of the princes', or 'farmstead associated with a man called Æthel'. OE *Ætheling* + *tūn*, or OE pers. name + *-ing-* + *tūn*. **Elton** Heref. & Worcs. *Elintune* 1086 (DB).. Probably 'farmstead of a man called Ella'. OE pers. name + *tūn*. **Elton** Notts. *Ailetone* |*sic*| 1086 (DB), *Elleton* 1088. Probably identical with the previous name.

Elvaston Derbys. *Ælwoldestune* 1086 (DB). 'Farmstead of a man called Æthelweald'. OE pers. name + *tūn*.

Elveden Suffolk. *Eluedena* 1086 (DB). 'Swan valley' or 'valley haunted by elves or fairies'. OE *elfitu* or *elf* (genitive plural *-a*) + *denu*.

Elvington York. *Aluuintone* 1086 (DB). 'Farmstead of a man called Ælfwine or a woman called Ælfwynn'. OE pers. name + *tūn*.

Elwick Hartlepl. *Ailewic* *c*.1150. 'Dwelling or (dairy) farm of a man called *Ægla or Ella'. OE pers. name + *wīc*.

Elwick Northum. *Ellewich* 12th cent. 'Dwelling or (dairy) farm of a man called Ella'.

Elworth Ches. *Ellewrdth* 1282. 'Enclosure of a man called Ella'. OE pers. name + *worth*.

Elworthy Somerset. *Elwrde* 1086 (DB). 'Enclosure of a man called Ella'. OE pers. name + *worth* (later replaced by *worthig*).

Ely Cambs. *Elge* 731, *Elyg* 1086 (DB). 'District where eels are to be found'. OE *ǣl*, *ēl* + **gē*.

Emberton Bucks. *Ambretone* 1086 (DB), *Emberdestone* 1227. 'Farmstead of a man called Ēanbeorht'. OE pers. name + *tūn*.

Embleton Cumbria. *Emelton* 1195. 'Farmstead of a man called Ēanbald'. OE pers. name + *tūn*.

Embleton Northum. *Emlesdone* 1212. 'Hill infested by caterpillars', or 'hill of a man called Æmele'. OE *emel* or OE pers. name + *dūn*.

Emborough Somerset. *Amelberge* |*sic*| 1086 (DB), *Emeneberge* 1200. 'Flat-topped mound or hill'. OE *emn* + *beorg*.

Embsay N. Yorks. *Embesie* 1086 (DB). Probably 'enclosure of a man called Embe'. OE pers. name + *hæg*.

Emlagh (*Imleach*) Mayo. 'Borderland'.

Emlaghfad (*Imleach Fada*) Sligo. 'Long borderland'.

Emlaghmore (*An tImleach Mór*) Kerry. 'The large borderland'.

Emley W. Yorks. *Ameleie* 1086 (DB). 'Woodland clearing of a man called *Em(m)a'. OE pers. name + *lēah*.

Emly (*Imleach*) Tipperary. 'Borderland'.

Emmington Oxon. *Amintone* 1086 (DB). 'Estate associated with a man called Eama'. OE pers. name + *-ing-* + *tūn*.

Emneth Norfolk. *Anemetha* 1170. Possibly 'river-confluence of a man called Ēana'. OE pers. name + (*ge*)*mȳthe*. Alternatively the second element may be OE *mǣth* 'mowing grass, meadow'.

Emo (*Ioma*) Laois. 'Image'.

Empingham Rutland. *Epingeham* |*sic*| 1086 (DB), *Empingeham* 12th cent. 'Homestead of the family or followers of a man called *Empa'. OE pers. name + *-inga-* + *hām*.

Empshott Hants. *Hibesete* |*sic*| 1086 (DB), *Himbeset* *c*.1170. 'Corner of land frequented by swarms of bees'. OE *imbe* + *scēat* or ** scīete*.

Emsworth Hants. *Emeleswurth* 1224. 'Enclosure of a man called Æmele'. OE pers. name + *worth*.

Emyvale (*Ioma*) Monaghan. 'Bed of the saint'. *Emyvale* or *Skernagerragh* 1779. Irish *ioma* + English *vale*. A saint of unknown name is said to have lived and slept here. An alternative name was *Scarnageeragh*, from Irish *Scairbh na gCaorach*, 'shallow ford of the sheep'.

Enborne Berks. *Aneborne* |*sic*| 1086 (DB), *Enedburn* 1220. 'Duck stream'. OE *ened* + *burna*.

Enderby Leics. *Endrebie* 1086 (DB). Probably 'farmstead or village of a man called Eindrithi'. OScand. pers. name + *bý*.

Enderby, *Bag*, *Enderby*, *Mavis*, & *Enderby*, *Wood* Lincs. *Andrebi*, *Endrebi* 1086 (DB), *Bagenderby* 1291, *Enderby Malbys* 1302, *Wodenderby* 1198. Probably identical in origin with the previous name. The affix *Mavis* is manorial, from the Malebisse family here in the 13th cent. *Bag* may also be a manorial affix, or from OE **bagga* 'bag' in some topographical sense. *Wood* (from OE *wudu* 'wood') indicates a situation in a once wooded area.

Endon Staffs. *Enedun* 1086 (DB). 'Hill of a man called Ēana, or where lambs are reared'. OE pers. name or OE **ēan* + *dūn*.

Enfield Gtr. London. *Enefelde* 1086 (DB). 'Open land of a man called Ēana, or where lambs are reared'. OE pers. name or OE **ēan* + *feld*.

Enford Wilts. *Enedford* 934, *Enedforde* 1086 (DB). 'Duck ford'. OE *ened* + *ford*.

England *Englaland* *c*.890. 'Land of the Angles'. OE *Engle* (genitive plural *Engla*) 'the Angles' (i.e. the people from the Continental homeland of *Angel* in Schleswig) + *land*.

Englefield Berks. *Englafelda* *c*.900, *Englefel* 1086 (DB). 'Open land of the Angles'. OE *Engle* + *feld*.

Englefield Green Surrey. *Ingelfeld* 1282. Possibly 'open land of a man called *Ingel or Ingweald'. OE pers. name + *feld*. *Green* is added from the 17th cent.

English Bicknor Glos., *see* BICKNOR.

English Frankton Shrops., *see* FRANKTON.

Englishcombe B. & NE. Som. *Ingeliscuma* 1086 (DB). Probably 'valley of a man called *Ingel or Ingweald'. OE pers. name + *cumb*.

Enham Alamein Hants. *Eanham* early 11th cent., *Etham* |*sic*| 1086 (DB). 'Homestead or enclosure where lambs are reared'. OE **ēan* + *hām* or *hamm*. Affix from 1945, commemorating the battle of El Alamein and referring to the centre for disabled ex-servicemen here. Formerly called **Knight's Enham**, *Knyghtesenham* 1389, from the knight's fee held here by Matthew de Columbers in the mid-13th cent.

Enmore Somerset. *Animere* 1086 (DB). 'Duck pool'. OE *ened* + *mere*.

Ennell, Lough (*Loch Ainnínne*) Westmeath. 'Ainneann's lake'.

Ennerdale Bridge Cumbria. *Anenderdale* c.1135, *Eghnerdale* 1321. 'Valley of a man called Anundr'. OScand. pers. name (genitive -*ar*) + *dalr*. Later the first element was replaced by the river-name Ehen (of obscure origin).

Ennis (*Inis*) Clare. 'Island'.

Enniskean (*Inis Céin*) Cork. 'Cian's island'.

Enniskerry (*Áth na Sceire*) Wicklow. 'Ford of the rocky place'.

Enniskillen (*Inis Ceithleann*) Fermanagh. (*Caislén*)*Insi Ceithlenn* 1439. 'Ceithleann's island'.

Ennistimmon (*Inis Díomáin*) Clare. 'Díomán's island'.

Enoch Dumf. '(Place by the) marsh'. Gaelic *eanach*.

Enstone Oxon. *Henestan* 1086 (DB). 'Boundary stone of a man called Enna'. OE pers. name + *stān*.

Enville Staffs. *Efnefeld* 1086 (DB). 'Smooth or level open land'. OE *efn* + *feld*.

Epperstone Notts. *Eprestone* 1086 (DB). Probably 'farmstead of a man called Eorphere'. OE pers. name + *tūn*.

Epping Essex. *Eppinges* 1086 (DB). Probably '(settlement of) the people of the ridge used as a look-out place'. OE *yppe* + -*ingas*.

Eppleby N. Yorks. *Aplebi* 1086 (DB). 'Farmstead where apple-trees grow'. OE *æppel* or OScand. *epli* + *bý*.

Epsom Surrey. *Ebbesham* c.973, *Evesham* |*sic*| 1086 (DB). 'Homestead or village of a man called Ebbe or Ebbi'. OE pers. name + *hām*.

Epwell Oxon. *Eoppan wyllan* 956. 'Spring or stream of a man called Eoppa'. OE pers. name + *wella*.

Epworth N. Lincs. *Epeurde* 1086 (DB). 'Enclosure of a man called Eoppa'. OE pers. name + *worth*.

Ercall, Child's & *Ercall, High* Shrops. *Arcalun* |*sic*|, *Archelov* 1086 (DB), *Childes Ercalewe, Magna Ercalewe* 1327. Possibly an old hill-name *Earcaluw* from OE *ēar* 'gravel, mud' and *calu(w)* 'bare hill', first applied to a settlement and then to a district (the two Ercalls are some 6 miles apart). Affixes are OE *cild* 'son of a noble family' and Latin *magna* 'great'.

Erdington W. Mids. *Hardintone* 1086 (DB). 'Estate associated with a man called *Earda*'. OE pers. name + -*ing*- + *tūn*.

Eriboll Highland. *Eribull* 1499. 'Farm on a gravel bank'. OScand. *eyri* + *ból* (*staþr*).

Ericht, Loch Highland. 'Loch of assemblies'. Gaelic *loch* + *eireachd*.

Eridge Green E. Sussex. *Ernerigg* 1202. 'Ridge frequented by eagles'. OE *earn* + *hrycg*.

Eriskay (island) W. Isles. *Eriskeray* 1549. 'Erikr's island'. OScand. pers. name + *ey*, 'island'.

Eriswell Suffolk. *Hereswella* 1086 (DB). Possibly 'spring or stream of a man called *Here*'. OE pers. name + *wella*.

Erith Gtr. London. *Earhyth* 677, *Earhith* c.960, *Erhede* 1086 (DB). 'Muddy or gravelly landing place'. OE *ēar* + *hȳth*.

Erlestoke Wilts. *Erlestoke* 12th cent. 'Outlying farmstead belonging to the nobleman'. OE *eorl* + *stoc*.

Ermine Street (Roman road from London to the Humber). *Earninga strǣt* 955. 'Roman road of the family or followers of a man called *Earn(a)*'. OE pers. name + -*inga*- + *strǣt*. No doubt originally applied to a stretch of the road near ARRINGTON (Cambs.) before the name was extended to the whole length. The name Ermine Street was later transferred to another Roman road, that from Silchester to Gloucester.

Ermington Devon. *Ermentona* 1086 (DB). Probably 'estate associated with a man called *Earma*'. OE pers. name + -*ing*- + *tūn*.

Erne, Lough (*Loch Éirne*) Fermanagh. 'Érann's lake'. The name is that of a goddess.

Erpingham Norfolk. *Erpingaham* 1086 (DB). 'Homestead of the family or followers of a man called *Eorp*'. OE pers. name + -*inga*- + *hām*.

Errigal (*Earagail*) (mountain) Donegal. 'Oratory'.

Errigal Keerogue (*Earagail Do Chiaróg*) Tyrone. 'Do Chiaróg's oratory'.

Erris (*Iorras*) Mayo. 'Promontory'.

Errislannan (*Iorras Fhlannáin*) Galway. 'Flannan's head'.

Erskine Renf. *Erskin* 1225, *Yrskin* 1227, *Ireskin* 1262, *Harskin* c.1300. Meaning uncertain. The name may be Celtic, but early forms are inconsistent.

Erwarton Suffolk. *Eurewardestuna* 1086 (DB). 'Farmstead of a man called *Eoforweard*'. OE pers. name + *tūn*.

Eryholme N. Yorks. *Argun* 1086 (DB). '(Place at) the shielings or summer pastures'. OScand. *erg* in a dative plural form *ergum*.

Eryri. *See* SNOWDONIA.

Escomb Durham. *Ediscum* 10th cent. '(Place at) the enclosed parks or pastures'. OE *edisc* in a dative plural form.

Escrick N. Yorks. *Ascri* |*sic*| 1086 (DB), *Eskrik* 1169. 'Strip of land or narrow ridge where ash-trees grow'. OScand. *eski* + OE *ric*.

Esh Durham. *Esse* 12th cent. '(Place at) the ash-tree'. OE *æsc*.

Esher Surrey. *Æscæron* 1005, *Aissele* |*sic*| 1086 (DB). 'District where ash-trees grow'. OE *æsc* + *scearu*.

Eshnadarragh (*Ais na Darrach*) Fermanagh. 'Ridge of the oak'.

Eshnadeelada (*Ais na Diallaite*) Fermanagh. 'Ridge of the saddle'.

Eshott Northum. *Esseta* 1187. 'Clump of ash-trees' from OE *æscet*, or 'corner of land growing with ash-trees' from OE *æsc* + *scēat*.

Eshton N. Yorks. *Estune* 1086 (DB). 'Farmstead by the ash-tree(s)'. OE *æsc* + *tūn*.

Esk (river) Dumf. *Ask* c.1200. 'Water'. British **isca*.

Eskdale Green Cumbria. *Eskedal* 1294. 'Valley of the River Esk'. Celtic river-name (meaning simply 'the water') + OScand. *dalr*.

Eske, Lough (*Loch Iasc*) Donegal. 'Lake abounding in fish'.

Esker (*Eiscir*) Dublin, Longford. 'Gravel ridge'.

Eskerridge (*Eiscir*) Tyrone. 'Gravel ridge'.

Eskine (*Eisc Dhoimnin*) Kerry. 'Deep fissure'.

Eskra (*Eiscrach*) Tyrone. 'Place of gravel ridges'.

Esnadarra (*Ais na Darach*) Fermanagh. 'Side of the place abounding in oaks'.

Esprick Lancs. *Eskebrec* c.1210. 'Hill slope where ash-trees grow'. OScand. *eski* + *brekka*.

Essendine Rutland. *Esindone* |sic| 1086 (DB), *Esenden* 1230. 'Valley of a man called Ēsa'. OE pers. name (genitive *-n*) + *denu*.

Essendon Herts. *Eslingadene* 11th cent. 'Valley of the family or followers of a man called **Ēsla*'. OE pers. name + *-inga-* + *denu*.

Essex (the county). *East Seaxe* late 9th cent., *Exsessa* 1086 (DB). '(Territory of) the East Saxons'. OE *ēast* + *Seaxe*.

Essington Staffs. *Esingetun* 996, *Eseningetone* 1086 (DB). 'Farmstead of the family or followers of a man called Esne'. OE pers. name + *-inga-* + *tūn*.

Eston Red. & Cleve. *Astun* 1086 (DB). 'East farmstead or village'. OE *ēast* + *tūn*.

Etal Northum. *Ethale* 1232. Probably 'nook of land used for grazing'. OE *ete* + *halh*.

Etchilhampton Wilts. *Echesatingetone* 1086 (DB), *Ehelhamton* 1196. Possibly 'farmstead of the dwellers at the oak-tree hill'. OE *āc* (genitive *ǣc*) + *hyll* + *hǣme* (earlier *sǣte*) + *tūn*.

Etchingham E. Sussex. *Hechingeham* 1158. 'Homestead or enclosure of the family or followers of a man called Ecci'. OE pers. name + *-inga-* + *hām* or *hamm*.

Etive, Loch Arg. 'Eite's loch'. Gaelic *loch*. Eiteag 'the little horrid one' is the goddess of the loch.

Eton Berks. *Ettone* 1086 (DB). 'Farmstead by the river'. OE *ēa* + *tūn*.

Etruria Staffs., named from a house called *Etruria Hall* built by Josiah Wedgwood, who founded his famous pottery here in 1769, the allusion being to pottery from ancient Etruria (modern Tuscany).

Ettington Warwicks. *Etendone* 1086 (DB). Probably 'hill of a man called Ēata', OE pers. name (genitive *-n*) + *dūn*. Alternatively the first element may be OE *eten* 'grazing, pasture'.

Etton, probably 'farmstead of a man called Ēata', OE pers. name + *tūn*: **Etton** Cambs. *Ettona* 1125–8. **Etton** E. R. Yorks. *Ettone* 1086 (DB).

Ettrick Forest Sc. Bord. *Ethric* c.1235. 'Forest of Ettrick Water'. The river name is of uncertain meaning.

Etwall Derbys. *Etewelle* 1086 (DB). Probably 'spring or stream of a man called Ēata'. OE pers. name + *wella*.

Euston Suffolk. *Euestuna* 1086 (DB). 'Farmstead of a man called Efe'. OE pers. name + *tūn*.

Euxton Lancs. *Eueceston* 1187. 'Farmstead of a man called Æfic'. OE pers. name + *tūn*.

Evanton Highland. 'Evan's village'. The village was founded in the early 19th cent. by *Evan* Fraser of Balconie.

Evedon Lincs. *Evedune* 1086 (DB). 'Hill of a man called Eafa'. OE pers. name + *dūn*.

Evenley Northants. *Evelaia* |sic| 1086 (DB), *Euenlai* 1147. 'Level woodland clearing'. OE *efen* + *lēah*.

Evenlode Glos. *Euulangelade* 772, *Eunilade* 1086 (DB). 'Water-course or river-crossing of a man called **Eowla*'. OE pers. name (genitive *-n*) + (*ge*)*lād*. The river-name **Evenlode** is a 'back-formation' from the place-name; the old name of the river was *Bladon*, *see* BLADON and BLEDINGTON.

Evenwood Durham. *Efenwuda* c.1050. 'Level woodland'. OE *efen* + *wudu*.

Evercreech Somerset. *Evorcric* 1065, *Evrecriz* 1086 (DB). Celtic **crūg* 'hill' with an uncertain first element, possibly OE *eofor* 'wild boar' or a Celtic word meaning 'yew-tree'.

Everdon, Great Northants. *Eferdun* 944, *Everdone* 1086 (DB). 'Hill frequented by wild boars'. OE *eofor* + *dūn*.

Everingham E. R. Yorks. *Yferingaham* c.972, *Evringham* 1086 (DB). 'Homestead of the family or followers of a man called Eofor'. OE pers. name + *-inga-* + *hām*.

Everleigh Wilts. *Eburleagh* 704. 'Wood or clearing frequented by wild boars'. OE *eofor* + *lēah*.

Everley N. Yorks. *Eurelai* 1086 (DB). Identical in origin with the previous name.

Eversden, Great & *Eversden, Little* Cambs. *Euresdone* 1086 (DB), *Everesdon Magna, Parva* 1240. 'Hill of the wild boar, or of a man called Eofor'. OE *eofor* or OE pers. name + *dūn*. Affixes are Latin *magna* 'great', *parva* 'little'.

Eversholt Beds. *Eureshot* |sic| 1086 (DB), *Euresholt* 1185. 'Wood of the wild boar'. OE *eofor* + *holt*.

Evershot Dorset. *Teversict* |sic| 1202, *Evershet* 1286. Probably 'corner of land frequented by wild boars'. OE *eofor* + *scēat* or **sciete*. Initial *T-* in the first form may be from the preposition *at*.

Eversley Hants. *Euereslea* c.1050, *Evreslei* 1086 (DB). 'Wood or clearing of the wild boar, or of a man called Eofor'. OE *eofor* or OE pers. name + *lēah*.

Everton, 'farmstead where wild boars are seen', OE *eofor* + *tūn*: **Everton** Beds. *Euretone* 1086 (DB). **Everton** Mersey. *Evretona* 1094. **Everton** Notts. *Evretone* 1086 (DB).

Evesham Heref. & Worcs. *Eveshomme* 709, *Evesham* 1086 (DB). 'Land in a river-bend belonging to a man called Ēof'. OE pers. name + *hamm*.

Evington Leics. *Avintone* 1086 (DB). 'Estate associated with a man called Eafa'. OE pers. name + *-ing-* + *tūn*.

Ewell Surrey. *Euuelle* 933, *Etwelle* |sic| 1086 (DB). '(Place at) the river-source'. OE *ǣwell*.

Ewell Minnis & Temple Ewell Kent. *Æwille c.*772, *Ewelle* 1086 (DB). Identical in origin with the previous name. The affix *Minnis* is from OE *mǣnnes* 'common land', *Temple* alludes to possession by the Knights Templars from the 12th cent.

Ewelme Oxon. *Auuilme* 1086 (DB). '(Place at) the river-source'. OE *ǣwelm*.

Ewen Glos. *Awilme* 931. Identical in origin with the previous name.

Ewerby Lincs. *Ieresbi* 1086 (DB). 'Farmstead or village of a man called Ívarr'. OScand. pers. name + *bý*.

Ewhurst Surrey. *Iuherst* 1179. 'Yew-tree wooded hill'. OE *īw* + *hyrst*.

Ewloe Flin. *Ewlawe* 1281. 'Hill with a river source'. OE *ǣwell* + *hlāw*.

Ewyas Harold Heref. & Worcs. *Euwias c.*1150, *Euuiasharold* 1176. A Welsh name meaning 'sheep district'. Affix from a nobleman called Harold who held the manor in the 11th cent.

Exbourne Devon. *Hechesburne* |sic| 1086 (DB), *Yekesburne* 1242. 'Stream of the cuckoo, or of a man called *Gēac'. OE *gēac* or OE pers. name + *burna*.

Exbury Hants. *Teocreberie* |sic| 1086 (DB), *Ykeresbirie* 1196. 'Fortified place of a man called *Eohhere'. OE pers. name + *burh* (dative *byrig*).

Exe, Nether & *Exe, Up* Devon. *Niresse* |sic|, *Ulpesse* |sic| 1086 (DB), *Nitherexe* 1196, *Uphexe* 1238. Named from the River Exe, a Celtic river-name meaning simply 'the water'. Affixes are OE *neotherra* 'lower (down river)' and *upp* 'higher (up river)'.

Exebridge Somerset. *Exebrigge* 1255. 'Bridge over the River Exe'. Celtic river-name + OE *brycg*.

Exelby N. Yorks. *Aschilebi* 1086 (DB). 'Farmstead or village of a man called Eskil'. OScand. pers. name + *bý*.

Exeter Devon. *Iska c.*150, *Exanceaster c.*900, *Execestre* 1086 (DB). 'Roman town on the River Exe'. Celtic river-name (see EXE) + OE *ceaster*.

Exford Somerset. *Aisseford* |sic| 1086 (DB), *Exeford* 1243. 'Ford over the River Exe'. Celtic river-name + OE *ford*.

Exminster Devon. *Exanmynster c.*880, *Esseminstre* 1086 (DB). 'Monastery by the River Exe'. Celtic river-name + OE *mynster*.

Exmoor Devon. *Exemora* 1204. 'Moorland on the River Exe'. Celtic river-name + OE *mōr*.

Exmouth Devon. *Exanmutha c.*1025. 'Mouth of the River Exe'. Celtic river-name + OE *mūtha*.

Exning Suffolk. *Essellinge* |sic| 1086 (DB), *Exningis* 1158. '(Settlement of) the family or followers of a man called *Gyxen'. OE pers. name + *-ingas*.

Exton Devon. *Exton* 1242. 'Farmstead on the River Exe'. Celtic river-name + OE *tūn*.

Exton Hants. *East Seaxnatune* 940, *Essessentune* 1086 (DB). 'Farmstead of the East Saxons'. OE *Ēastseaxe* + *tūn*.

Exton Rutland. *Exentune* 1086 (DB). Probably 'farmstead where oxen are kept'. OE *oxa* (genitive plural *exna*) + *tūn*.

Exton Somerset. *Exton* 1216. 'Farmstead on the River Exe'. Celtic river-name + OE *tūn*.

Eyam Derbys. *Aiune* 1086 (DB). '(Place at) the islands, or the pieces of land between streams'. OE *ēg* in a dative plural form *ēgum*.

Eydon Northants. *Egedone* 1086 (DB). 'Hill of a man called *Æga'. OE pers. name + *dūn*.

Eye, '(place at) the island, or well-watered land, or dry ground in marsh', OE *ēg*: **Eye** Cambs. *Ege* 10th cent. **Eye** Heref. & Worcs. *Eia c.*1175. **Eye** Suffolk. *Eia* 1086 (DB).

Eyemouth Sc. Bord. *Aymouthe* 1250. 'Mouth of the Eye Water'. OE *mūtha*. The river name means simply 'river' (OE *ēa*).

Eyke Suffolk. *Eik* 1185. '(Place at) the oak-tree'. OScand. *eik*.

Eynesbury Cambs. *Eanulfesbyrig c.*1000, *Einuluesberie* 1086 (DB). 'Stronghold of a man called Ēanwulf'. OE pers. name + OE *burh* (dative *byrig*).

Eynsford Kent. *Æinesford c.*960. 'Ford of a man called *Ægen'. OE pers. name + *ford*.

Eynsham Oxon. *Egenes homme* 864, *Eglesham* 1086 (DB). Possibly 'enclosure or river-meadow of a man called *Ægen'. OE pers. name + *hamm*.

Eype Dorset. *Yepe* 1365. 'Steep place'. OE *gēap*.

Eythorne Kent. *Heagythethorne* 9th cent. 'Thorn-tree of a woman called *Hēahgȳth'. OE pers. name + *thorn*.

Eyton upon the Weald Moors Shrops. *Etone* 1086 (DB), *Eyton super le Wildmore* 1344. 'Farmstead on dry ground in marsh, or on well-watered land'. OE *ēg* + *tūn*. The affix means 'in the wild moorland', from OE *wilde* + *mōr*.

F

Faccombe Hants. *Faccancumb* 863, *Facumbe* 1086 (DB). 'Valley of a man called *Facca'. OE pers. name + *cumb*.

Faceby N. Yorks. *Feizbi* 1086 (DB). 'Farmstead or village of a man called Feitr'. OScand. pers. name + *bý*.

Fad, Lough (*Loch Fada*) Donegal. 'Long lake'.

Fada, Loch Highland. 'Long loch'. Gaelic *loch* + *fada*.

Faddiley Ches. *Fadilee* c.1220. 'Woodland clearing of a man called *Fad(d)a'. OE pers. name + *lēah*.

Fadmoor N. Yorks. *Fademora* 1086 (DB). 'Moor of a man called *Fad(d)a'. OE pers. name + *mōr*.

Faes (*Féá*) Limerick. 'Wood'.

Faha (*Faiche*) Kerry, Waterford. 'Green'.

Fahamore (*Faiche Mhór*) Kerry. 'Big green'.

Fahan (*Fathain*) Donegal. *Fathunmurra* 1311. 'Burial place'.

Fahanasoodry (*Faiche na Súdaire*) Limerick. 'Green of the tanners'.

Faheeran (*Faiche Chairáin*) Offaly. 'Ciarán's green'.

Fahy (*Faiche*) Offaly. 'Green'.

Faiaflannan (*Faiche Flannáin*) Donegal. 'Flannan's green'.

Failsworth Gtr. Manch. *Fayleswrthe* 1212. Possibly 'enclosure with a special kind of fence'. OE *fēgels* + *worth*.

Fair Isle Shet. *Fridarey* n.d., the earlier name was reinterpreted as 'Island of sheep'. *Fároy* 1350.

Fairburn N. Yorks. *Farenburne* c.1030, *Fareburne* 1086 (DB). 'Stream where ferns grow'. OE *fearn* + *burna*.

Fairfield Heref. & Worcs. *Forfeld* 817. 'Open land where hogs are pastured'. OE *fōr* + *feld*.

Fairford Glos. *Fagranforda* 862, *Fareforde* 1086 (DB). 'Fair or clear ford'. OE *fæger* + *ford*.

Fairlie N. Ayr. Unexplained.

Fairlight E. Sussex. *Farleghe* c.1175. 'Woodland clearing where ferns grow'. OE *fearn* + *lēah*.

Fairstead Essex. *Fairstedam* 1086 (DB). 'Fair or pleasant place'. OE *fæger* + *stede*.

Fakenham, 'homestead of a man called *Facca', OE pers. name (genitive -*n*) + *hām*: **Fakenham** Norfolk. *Fachenham* 1086 (DB). **Fakenham, Little** Suffolk. *Litla Fachenham* 1086 (DB). Affix is OE *lȳtel* 'little'.

Fala Midloth. *Faulawe* 1250. 'Variegated hill'. OE *fāg* + *hlāw*.

Falcarragh (*Fál Carrach*) Donegal. *Fál Carrach* 1835. 'Rough enclosure'.

Faldingworth Lincs. *Falding(e)urde* 1086 (DB). 'Enclosure for folding livestock'. OE *falding* + *worth*.

Falfield S. Glos. *Falefeld* 1227. 'Pale brown or fallow open land'. OE *fealu* + *feld*.

Fali, Y. *See* VALLEY.

Falkenham Suffolk. *Faltenham* 1086 (DB). Probably 'homestead of a man called *Falta'. OE pers. name (genitive -*n*) + *hām*.

Falkirk Falk. *Egglesbreth* 1065, *varia capella* 1166, *Varie Capelle* 1253, *Faukirke* 1298. '(Place with a) speckled church'. OE *fāg* + *cirice*. A 'speckled church' is one with mottled stone. The first three forms above, respectively Gaelic, Latin, and OFrench, have the same meaning.

Falkland Fife. *Falleland* 1128, *Falecklen* 1160. The first element is obscure.

Fallagloon (*Fáladh Lúan*) Derry. *Fallow Lowne* 1613. 'Enclosure of the lambs'.

Falleenadatha (*Faillín an Deatha*) Limerick. 'Little cliff of the smoke'.

Falmer E. Sussex. *Falemere* 1086 (DB). Probably 'fallow-coloured pool'. OE *fealu* + *mere*.

Falmouth Cornwall. *Falemuth* 1235. 'Mouth of the River Fal'. River-name (of uncertain origin and meaning) + OE *mūtha*.

Fambridge, North & *Fambridge, South* Essex. *Fanbruge* 1086 (DB), *North Fambregg, Suthfambregg* 1291. 'Bridge by a fen or marsh'. OE *fenn* + *brycg*.

Fangdale Beck N. Yorks. *Fangedala* 12th cent. 'Stream in the valley good for fishing'. OScand. *fang* + *dalr* + *bekkr*.

Fangfoss E. R. Yorks. *Frangefos* |*sic*| 1086 (DB), *Fangefosse* 12th cent. Possibly 'ditch used for fishing'. OScand. *fang* + OE *foss*.

Far Cotton Northants, *see* COTTON.

Far Sawrey Cumbria, *see* SAWREY.

Fara (island) Orkn. 'Island of sheep'. OScand. *faar* + *ey*.

Faraid Head Highland. Gaelic *An Fharaird* 'projecting headland'.

Farcet Cambs. *Faresheued* 10th cent. 'Bull's headland or hill'. OE *fearr* + *hēafod*.

Fardrum (*Fordroim*) Westmeath. 'Ridge top'.

Fareham Hants. *Fearnham* c.970, *Fernham* 1086 (DB). 'Homestead where ferns grow'. OE *fearn* + *hām*.

Farewell Staffs. *Fagerwell* 1200. 'Pleasant spring or stream'. OE *fæger* + *wella*.

Fargrim (*Fordroim*) Fermanagh, Leitrim. 'Ridge top'.

Faringdon, *Farringdon*, 'fern-covered hill', OE *fearn* + *dūn*: **Faringdon** Oxon. *Færndunæ* c.971, *Ferendone* 1086 (DB). **Farringdon** Devon. *Ferhendone* 1086 (DB). **Farringdon** Hants. *Ferendone* 1086 (DB).

Farington Lancs. *Farinton* 1149. 'Farmstead where ferns grow'. OE *fearn* + *tūn*.

Farleigh, 'woodland clearing growing with ferns', OE *fearn* + *lēah*: **Farleigh** Gtr. London. *Ferlega* 1086 (DB). **Farleigh, East** & **Farleigh, West** Kent. *Fearnlege* 9th cent., *Ferlaga* 1086 (DB). **Farleigh Hungerford** Somerset. *Fearnlæh* 987, *Ferlege* 1086 (DB), *Farlegh Hungerford* 1404. Affix from the Hungerford family, here in the 14th cent. **Farleigh, Monkton** Wilts. *Farnleghe* 1001, *Farlege* 1086 (DB), *Monekenefarlegh* 1321. Affix means 'of the monks' from OE *munuc*, alluding to a priory founded here in 1125. **Farleigh Wallop** Hants. *Ferlege* 1086 (DB). Affix from the Wallop family, here in the 14th cent.

Farlesthorpe Lincs. *Farlestorp* 1190. 'Outlying farmstead or hamlet of a man called Faraldr'. OScand. pers. name + *thorp*.

Farleton Cumbria. *Farelton* 1086 (DB). 'Farmstead of a man called *Færela* or *Faraldr*'. OE or OScand. pers. name + OE *tūn*.

Farley, 'woodland clearing growing with ferns', OE *fearn* + *lēah*; examples include: **Farley** Staffs. *Fernelege* 1086 (DB). **Farley** Wilts. *Farlege* 1086 (DB). **Farley Hill** Berks. *Ferlega* 1167.

Farlington N. Yorks. *Ferlintun* 1086 (DB). Probably 'estate associated with a man called *Færela*'. OE pers. name + *-ing-* + *tūn*.

Farlow Shrops. *Ferlau* 1086 (DB), *Farnlawe* 1222. 'Fern-covered mound or hill'. OE *fearn* + *hlāw*.

Farmborough B. & NE. Som. *Fearnberngas* |*sic*| 901, *Ferenberge* 1086 (DB). 'Hill(s) or mound(s) growing with ferns'. OE *fearn* + *beorg*.

Farmcote Glos. *Fernecote* 1086 (DB). 'Cottage(s) among the ferns'. OE *fearn* + *cot*.

Farmington Glos. *Tormentone* |*sic*| 1086 (DB), *Tormerton* 1182. Probably 'farmstead near the pool where thorn-trees grow'. OE *thorn* + *mere* + *tūn*.

Farnagh (*Farnocht*) Westmeath. 'Bare hill'.

Farnaght (*Farnocht*) Leitrim. 'Bare hill'.

Farnalore (*Fearann an Lobhair*) Westmeath. 'Land of the leper'.

Farnanes (*Na Fearnáin*) Cork. 'The place producing alders'.

Farnaught (*Farnocht*) Sligo. 'Bare hill'.

Farnborough, 'hill(s) or mound(s) growing with ferns', OE *fearn* + *beorg*: **Farnborough** Berks. *Fearnbeorgan* c.935, *Fermeberge* 1086 (DB). **Farnborough** Gtr. London. *Ferenberga* 1180. **Farnborough** Hants. *Ferneberga* 1086 (DB). **Farnborough** Warwicks. *Feornebeorh* c.1015, *Ferneberge* 1086 (DB).

Farncombe Surrey. *Fernecome* 1086 (DB). 'Valley where ferns grow'. OE *fearn* + *cumb*.

Farndon, 'hill growing with ferns', OE *fearn* + *dūn*: **Farndon** Ches. *Fearndune* 924, *Ferentone* |*sic*| 1086 (DB). **Farndon** Notts. *Farendune* 1086 (DB). **Farndon, East** Northants. *Ferendone* 1086 (DB).

Farne Islands Northum. *Farne* c.700. Possibly a derivative of the OE word *fearn* 'fern', but perhaps more probably of Celtic origin.

Farney (*Fearnmhagh*) Monaghan. 'Alder plain'.

Farnham, 'homestead or enclosure where ferns grow', OE *fearn* + *hām* or *hamm*: **Farnham** Dorset. *Fernham* 1086 (DB). **Farnham** Essex. *Phernham* 1086 (DB). **Farnham** N. Yorks. *Farneham* 1086 (DB). **Farnham** Suffolk. *Farnham* 1086 (DB). **Farnham** Surrey. *Fernham* c.686, *Ferneham* 1086 (DB). The second element of this name is probably OE *hamm* in the sense 'river-meadow'. **Farnham Royal** Bucks. *Ferneham* 1086 (DB), *Fernham Riall* 1477. Affix (from OFrench *roial*) because it was held by the grand serjeanty of supporting the king's right arm at his coronation.

Farningham Kent. *Ferningeham* 1086 (DB). Possibly 'homestead of the dwellers among the ferns'. OE *fearn* + *-inga-* + *hām*.

Farnley, 'woodland clearing growing with ferns', OE *fearn* + *lēah*: **Farnley** N. Yorks. *Fernleage* c.1030, *Fernelai* 1086 (DB). **Farnley** W. Yorks. *Ferneleia* 1086 (DB). **Farnley Tyas** W. Yorks. *Fereleia* |*sic*| 1086 (DB), *Farnley Tyas* 1322. Manorial affix from the family of le Tyeis, here in the 13th cent.

Farnsfield Notts. *Fearnesfeld* 958, *Farnesfeld* 1086 (DB). 'Open land where ferns grow'. OE *fearn* + *feld*.

Farnworth, 'enclosure where ferns grow', OE *fearn* + *worth*: **Farnworth** Ches. *Farneword* 1324. **Farnworth** Gtr. Manch. *Farnewurd* 1185.

Farra (*Farrach*) Armagh. 'Meeting place'.

Farragh (*Farrach*) Cavan. 'Meeting place'.

Farraghroe (*Farracha Ruadha*) Westmeath. 'Red meeting places'.

Farran (*Fearann*) Cork, Kerry, Westmeath. 'Territory'.

Farranboley (*Fearann Buaile*) Dublin. 'Territory of the milking place'.

Farranfadda (*Fearann Fada*) Cork. 'Long territory'.

Farranfore (*Fearann Fuar*) Kerry. 'Cold land'.

Farranmacbride (*Fearann Mhic Bhride*) Donegal. 'Mac Bride's land'.

Farringdon, *see* FARINGDON.

Farrington Gurney B. & NE. Som. *Ferentone* 1086 (DB). 'Farmstead where ferns grow'. OE *fearn* + *tūn*. Manorial affix from the de Gurnay family, here in the 13th cent.

Farsetmore (*Fearsad Mór*) Donegal. 'Large sandbank'. .

Farsid (*Fearsad*) Cork. 'Sandbank'.

Farsley W. Yorks. *Ferselleia* 1086 (DB). Possibly 'clearing used for heifers'. OE *fers* + *lēah*.

Farta (*Fearta*) Galway. 'Grave mounds'.

Fartagh (*Feartach*) Cavan, Fermanagh. 'Place of grave mounds'.

Farthinghoe Northants. *Ferningeho* 1086 (DB). Probably 'hill-spur of the dwellers among the ferns'. OE *fearn* + *-inga-* + *hōh*.

Farthingstone Northants. *Fordinestone* 1086 (DB). Probably 'farmstead of a man called Farthegn'. OScand. pers. name + OE *tūn*.

Farway Devon. *Farewei* 1086 (DB). Probably '(place at) the road way'. OE *fær* + *weg*. Alternatively the first element may be OE *fær* 'danger'.

Fasnakyle Highland. Gaelic *Fas na Coille*. 'Level place by a wood'. Gaelic *fas* + *coille*.

Fauldhouse W. Loth. *Fawlhous* 1523, *Falhous* c.1540, *Faldhous* 1559. 'House on fallow land'. OE *falh* + *hus*.

Faulkand Somerset. *Fouklande* 1243. 'Folk-land', i.e. 'land held according to folk-right'. OE *folc-land*.

Faulkbourne Essex. *Falcheburna* 1086 (DB). 'Stream frequented by falcons'. OE **falca* + *burna*.

Faversham Kent. *Fefresham* 811, *Faversham* 1086 (DB). 'Homestead or village of the smith'. OE **fæfer* + *hām*.

Fawkham Green Kent. *Fealcnaham* 10th cent., *Fachesham* |sic| 1086 (DB). 'Homestead or village of a man called **Fealcna*'. OE pers. name + *hām*.

Fawler Oxon. *Fauflor* 1205. 'Variegated floor', i.e. 'tessellated pavement'. OE *fāg* + *flōr*.

Fawley Berks. *Faleslei* 1086 (DB). Probably 'wood frequented by the fallow deer'. OE *fealu* (used as noun) + *lēah*.

Fawley Bucks. *Falelie* 1086 (DB). 'Fallow-coloured woodland clearing', or 'clearing with ploughed land'. OE *fealu* or *fealg* + *lēah*.

Fawley Hants. *Falegia, Falelei* 1086 (DB). Probably identical in origin with the previous name.

Fawley Chapel Heref. & Worcs. *Falileiam* 1142. 'Woodland clearing where hay is made'. OE *fælethe* + *lēah*.

Faxfleet E. R. Yorks. *Faxflete* 1190. 'Stream of a man called Faxi', or 'stream near which coarse grass grows'. OScand. pers. name or OE *feax* + *flēot*.

Fazeley Staffs. *Faresleia* c.1142. 'Clearing used for bulls'. OE *fearr* + *lēah*.

Feagarrid (*Féith Ghairid*) Waterford. 'Short stream'.

Feakle (*Fiacall*) Clare. 'Tooth'.

Feale (*Feil*) (river) Kerry, Limerick. 'Fial's river'.

Fearby N. Yorks. *Federbi* 1086 (DB). OScand. *bý* 'farmstead, village' with a doubtful first element, possibly OE *fether*, OScand. *fjøthr* 'feather' (perhaps referring to a place frequented by flocks of birds).

Fearn Highland. *Ferne* 1529. '(Place of) alders'. Gaelic *fearna*. The Gaelic name is *Manachaimn Rois* 'the monastery of Ross'.

Fearn Hill (*Fearn*) Donegal. 'Alder hill'.

Fearnhead Ches. *Ferneheued* 1292. 'Fern-covered hill'. OE *fearn* + *hēafod*.

Featherstone, '(place at) the four stones, i.e. a tetralith', OE *feother-* + *stān*: **Featherstone** Staffs. *Feother(e)stan* 10th cent., *Ferdestan* 1086 (DB). **Featherstone** W. Yorks. *Fredestan* 1086 (DB).

Feckenham Heref. & Worcs. *Feccanhom* 804, *Fecheham* 1086 (DB). 'Enclosure or water-meadow of a man called **Fecca*'. OE pers. name + *hamm*.

Fedamore (*Feadamair*) Limerick. 'Place of streams'.

Fedany (*Feadanach*) Down. 'Place of streams'.

Feeagh, Lough (*Loch Fíoch*) Mayo. 'Wooded lake'.

Feebane (*Fioda Bán*) Monaghan. 'White wood'.

Feenagh (*Fíonach*) Limerick. 'Wooded place'.

Feenish (*Fiodh-Inis*) Clare. 'Woody island'.

Feeny (*Na Fíneadha*) Derry. *Nefenne* 1613. 'The woods'.

Feering Essex. *Feringas* 1086 (DB). '(Settlement of) the family or followers of a man called **Fēra*'. OE pers. name + *-ingas*.

Feetham N. Yorks. *Fytun* 1242. '(Place at) the riverside meadows'. OScand. *fit* in a dative plural form *fitjum*.

Felbridge Surrey. *Feltbruge* 12th cent. 'Bridge by the open land'. OE *feld* + *brycg*.

Felbrigg Norfolk. *Felebruge* 1086 (DB). 'Bridge made of planks'. OScand. *fjǫl* + OE *brycg*.

Felinheli, Y. *See* PORT DINORWIC.

Felixkirk N. Yorks. *Felicekirke* 13th cent. 'Church dedicated to St Felix'. Saint's name + OScand. *kirkja*.

Felixstowe Suffolk. *Filchestou* 1254. Probably 'holy place or meeting place of a man called **Filica*'. OE pers. name + *stōw*. The pers. name was later associated with that of St Felix, first Bishop of East Anglia.

Felling Tyne & Wear. *Fellyng* c.1220. OE **felling* 'woodland clearing' or *felging* 'fallow land'.

Felmersham Beds. *Falmeresham* 1086 (DB). 'Homestead or enclosure by a fallow-coloured pool, or of a man called **Feolomær*'. OE *fealu* + *mere* or OE pers. name + *hām* or *hamm*.

Felmingham Norfolk. *Felmincham* 1086 (DB). 'Homestead of the family or followers of a man called **Feolma*'. OE pers. name + *-inga-* + *hām*.

Felpham W. Sussex. *Felhhamm* c.880, *Falcheham* 1086 (DB), 'Enclosure with fallow land'. OE **felh* + *hamm*.

Felsham Suffolk. *Fealsham* 1086 (DB). 'Homestead or village of a man called **Fæle*'. OE pers. name + *hām*.

Felsted Essex. *Felstede* 1086 (DB). 'Open-land place'. OE *feld* + *stede*.

Feltham Gtr. London. *Feltham* 969, *Felteham* 1086 (DB). Probably 'homestead or enclosure where mullein or a similar plant grows'. OE *felte* + *hām* or *hamm*. Alternatively the first element may be OE *feld* 'open land'.

Felthorpe Norfolk. *Felethorp* 1086 (DB). Probably 'outlying farmstead or hamlet of a man called **Fæla*'. OE pers. name + OScand. *thorp*.

Felton, usually 'farmstead or village in open country', OE *feld* + *tūn*; examples include: **Felton** Heref. & Worcs. *Felton* 1086 (DB). **Felton** Northum. *Feltona* 1167. **Felton Butler** Shrops. *Feltone* 1086 (DB), *Felton Butler* 13th cent. Manorial affix from the Buteler family, here in the 12th cent. **Felton, West** Shrops. *Feltone* 1086 (DB).

Feltrim (*Fealdruim*) Down. 'Wolf ridge'.

Feltwell Norfolk. *Feltuuella* 1086 (DB). Probably 'spring or stream where mullein or a similar plant grows'. OE *felte* + *wella*.

Fen Ditton Cambs., *see* DITTON.

Fen Drayton Cambs., *see* DRAYTON.

Fenagh (*Fiodhnach*) Leitrim. 'Wooded place'.

Fenby, *Ashby cum* NE. Lincs., *see* ASHBY.

Fenham Northum., near Fenwick. *Fennum c.*1085. '(Place in) the fens'. OE *fenn* in a dative plural form *fennum*.

Fenit (*An Fhianait*) Kerry. 'The wild place'.

Feniton Devon. *Finetone* 1086 (DB). 'Farmstead by Vine Water'. Celtic river-name (meaning 'boundary stream') + OE *tūn*.

Fennagh (*Fionnmhach*) Carlow. 'White plain'.

Fenni, Y. *See* ABERGAVENNY.

Fennor (*Fionnúir*) Waterford. 'Place by white water'.

Fenny as affix, see main name, e.g. for **Fenny Bentley** (Derbys.) *see* BENTLEY.

Fenrother Northum. *Finrode* 1189. 'Clearing by a mound or heap'. OE *fīn* + **rother*.

Fenstanton Cambs. *Stantun* 1012, *Stantone* 1086 (DB), *Fenstanton* 1260. 'Farmstead on stony ground in a marshy district'. OE *fenn* + *stān* + *tūn*.

Fenton, 'farmstead or village in a fen or marshland', OE *fenn* + *tūn*; examples include: **Fenton** Cambs. *Fentun* 1236. **Fenton** Lincs., near Claypole. *Fentun* 1212. **Fenton** Lincs., near Kettlethorpe. *Fentuna c.*1115. **Fenton** Staffs. *Fentone* 1086 (DB). **Fenton, Church** & **Fenton, Little** N. Yorks. *Fentune* 963, *Fentun* 1086 (DB), *Kirkfenton* 1338. Affix from OE *cirice*, OScand. *kirkja*. **Fenton Town** Northum. *Fenton* 1242.

Fenwick, 'dwelling or (dairy) farm in a fen or marsh', OE *fenn* + *wīc*: **Fenwick** Northum., near Kyloe. *Fenwic* 1208. **Fenwick** Northum., near Stamfordham. *Fenwic* 1242. **Fenwick** S. Yorks. *Fenwic* 1166.

Fenwick E. Ayr. 'Dairy farm by a bog'. Probably OE *fen* + *wic*.

Feock Cornwall. *Lanfioc* 12th cent. 'Church of St Fioc'. From the patron saint of the church, with Cornish **lann* in the early form.

Feohanagh (*An Fheothanach*) Limerick. 'The windy place'.

Ferbane (*An Féar Bán*) Offaly. 'The white grass'.

Fermanagh (*Fear Manach*) (the county). (*tigherna*) *Fermanach* 1010. '(Place of the) men of the Manaigh tribe'. The tribe took their name from their chief.

Fermoy (*Mainistir Fhear Maighe*) Cork. 'Monastery of the district of Fir Mhaí'. The district name means 'men of the plain'.

Fermoyle (*Formael*) Kerry. 'Round hill'.

Fern Ang. '(Place of) alders'. Gaelic *fearn*.

Fern, Lough (*Loch Fearna*) Donegal. 'Lake of alders'.

Ferndown Dorset. *Fyrne* 1321. OE *fergen* 'wooded hill' or **fierne* 'ferny place', with the later addition of *dūn* 'down, hill'.

Fernham Oxon. *Fernham* 9th cent. 'River-meadow where ferns grow'. OE *fearn* + *hamm*.

Fernhurst W. Sussex. *Fernherst c.*1200. 'Fern-covered wooded hill'. OE *fearn* + *hyrst*.

Fernilee Derbys. *Ferneley* 12th cent. 'Woodland clearing where ferns grow'. OE *fearn* + *lēah*.

Ferns (*Fearna*) Wexford. 'Place of alders'.

Ferrensby N. Yorks. *Feresbi |sic|* 1086 (DB), *Feringesby* 13th cent. Probably 'farmstead or village of the man from the Faroe Islands'. OScand. *færeyingr* + *bý*.

Ferriby, North (E. R. Yorks.) & **Ferriby, South** (N. Lincs.) *Ferebi* 1086 (DB), *North Feribi* 1284, *Suthferebi c.*1130. 'Farmstead or village near the ferry'. OScand. *ferja* + *bý*. *North* and *South* with reference to their situation on opposite banks of the Humber.

Ferring W. Sussex. *Ferring* 765, *Feringes* 1086 (DB). Probably '(settlement of) the family or followers of a man called **Fēra*'. OE pers. name + *-ingas*.

Ferrybridge W. Yorks. *Ferie* 1086 (DB), *Ferybrig* 1198. 'Bridge by the ferry'. OScand. *ferja* + OE *brycg*. The first bridge here across the River Aire was built in the late 12th cent.

Ferryhill Durham. *Feregenne* 10th cent., *Ferye on the Hill* 1316. OE *fergen* 'wooded hill', with the later addition of *hyll* 'hill'.

Fersfield Norfolk. *Fersafeld c.*1035, *Ferseuella |sic|* 1086 (DB). Possibly 'open land where heifers graze'. OE **fers* + *feld*.

Ferta (*Fearta*) Kerry. 'Grave mounds'.

Fertagh (*Feartach*) Leitrim, Meath. 'Place of graves'.

Fetcham Surrey. *Fecham* 10th cent., *Feceham* 1086 (DB). Probably 'homestead or village of a man called **Fecca*'. OE pers. name + *hām*.

Fethard (*Fiodh Ard*) Tipperary, Wexford. 'High wood'.

Fetlar (island) Shet. *Fœtilar c.*1250. Pre-Norse island name of unknown meaning.

Fettercairn Aber. *Fotherkern c.*970, *Fettercairn c.*1350. 'Slope by a thicket'. Gaelic *foithir* + Pictish *carden*.

Fews (*Feá*) Armagh, Waterford. 'Woods'.

Fewston N. Yorks. *Fostune* 1086 (DB). 'Farmstead of a man called Fótr'. OScand. pers. name + OE *tūn*.

Ffestiniog. *See* BLAENAU FFESTINIOG.

Fflint, Y. *See* FLINT.

Ffontygari. *See* FONT-Y-GARY.

Fforest Fawr (district) Powys. 'Great forest'. Welsh *fforest* + *mawr*.

Fiddington Glos. *Fittingtun* 1004, *Fitentone* 1086 (DB). 'Estate associated with a man called **Fita*'. OE pers. name + *-ing-* + *tūn*.

Fiddington Somerset. *Fitintone* 1086 (DB). Probably identical in origin with the previous name.

Fiddleford Dorset. *Fitelford* 1244. 'Ford of a man called Fitela'. OE pers. name + *ford*.

Fiddown (*Fiodh Dúin*) Kilkenny. 'Wood of the fort'.

Field Staffs. *Felda* 1130. '(Place at) the open land'. OE *feld*.

Field Dalling Norfolk, *see* DALLING.

Fieries (*Foidhrí*) Kerry. 'Slopes'.

Fife (the unitary authority). *Fib* c.1150, *Fif* 1165. '(Territory of) Fib'. *Fib* was one of the seven sons of Cruithe, legendary father of the Picts. But the pers. name dates later than the territory associated with it, so some earlier name must be involved.

Fifehead, Magdalen & *Fifehead, Neville* Dorset. *Fifhide* 1086 (DB), *Fifyde Maudaleyne* 1388, *Fyfhud Neuyle* 1287. '(Estate of) five hides of land'. OE *fīf* + *hīd*. Affix *Magdalen* from the dedication of the church, *Neville* from the de Nevill family, here in the 13th cent.

Fifield, '(estate of) five hides of land', OE *fīf* + *hīd*: **Fifield** Berks. *Fifhide* 1316. **Fifield** Oxon. *Fifhide* 1086 (DB), **Fifield Bavant** Wilts. *Fifhide* 1086 (DB), *Fiffehyde Beaufaunt* 1436. Manorial affix from the de Bavent family, here in the 14th cent.

Figheldean Wilts. *Fisgledene* |sic| 1086 (DB), *Figelden* 1227. 'Valley of a man called *Fygla*'. OE pers. name + *denu*.

Figile (*Abhainn Fhiodh Gaibhle*) (river) Offaly. 'River of the wood of the fork'.

Filby Norfolk. *Filebey* 1086 (DB). 'Farmstead or village of a man called *Fili* or *Fila*'. OScand. or OE pers. name + *bý*. Alternatively the first element may be OScand. *fili* 'planks' (perhaps referring to a bridge or other structure).

Filey N. Yorks. *Fiuelac* |sic| 1086 (DB), *Fivelai* 12th cent. Possibly 'promontory shaped like a sea monster'. OE *fīfel* + *ēg*. The allusion would be to Filey Brigg (OScand. *bryggja* 'jetty'), a ridge of rock, half a mile long, projecting into the sea. Alternatively 'the five clearings', from OE *fīf* + *lēah*.

Filgrave Bucks. *Filegrave* 1241. 'Pit or grove of a man called *Fygla*'. OE pers. name + *græf* or *grāf*.

Filkins Oxon. *Filching* 12th cent. Probably '(settlement of) the family of followers of a man called *Filica*'. OE pers. name + *-ingas*.

Filleigh Devon, near Barnstaple. *Filelei* 1086 (DB). Probably 'woodland clearing where hay is made'. OE *filethe* + *lēah*.

Fillingham Lincs. *Figelingeham* 1086 (DB). 'Homestead of the family or followers of a man called *Fygla*'. OE pers. name + *-inga-* + *hām*.

Fillongley Warwicks. *Filingelei* 1086 (DB). 'Woodland clearing of the family or followers of a man called *Fygla*'. OE pers. name + *-inga-* + *lēah*.

Filton S. Glos. *Filton* 1187. 'Farm or estate where hay is made'. OE *filethe* + *tūn*.

Fimber E. R. Yorks. *Fym(m)ara* 12th cent. 'Pool by a wood pile, or amidst the coarse grass'. OE *fīn* or *finn* + *mere*.

Fin, Lough (*Loch Fionn*) Clare. 'White lake'.

Finaghy (*An Fionnachadh*) Antrim. *Ballyfinnaghey* 1780. 'The white field'.

Finborough Suffolk. *Fineberga* 1086 (DB). 'Hill or mound frequented by woodpeckers'. OE *fīna* + *beorg*.

Fincham Norfolk. *P(h)incham* 1086 (DB). 'Homestead or enclosure frequented by finches'. OE *finc* + *hām* or *hamm*.

Finchampstead Berks. *Finchamestede* 1086 (DB). 'Homestead frequented by finches'. OE *finc* + *hām-stede*.

Finchingfield Essex. *Fincingefelda* 1086 (DB). 'Open land of the family or followers of a man called Finc'. OE pers. name + *-inga-* + *feld*.

Finchley Gtr. London. *Finchelee* c.1208. 'Woodland clearing frequented by finches'. OE *finc* + *lēah*.

Findern Derbys. *Findre* 1086 (DB). An obscure name, still not satisfactorily explained.

Findhorn Moray. '(Place on the river) Findhorn'. Gaelic *fionn* 'white' + a pre-Celtic river-name; *cp.* Deveron.

Findlater Aber. *Finletter* 1266. 'White slope'. Gaelic *fionn* + *leitir*.

Findon W. Sussex. *Findune* 1086 (DB). 'Hill with a mound or heap of wood on it'. OE *fīn* + *dūn*.

Findrum (*Fionn Droim*) Donegal, Tyrone. 'White ridge'.

Finea (*Fiodh an Átha*) Westmeath. 'Wood of the ford'.

Finedon Northants. *Tingdene* 1086 (DB). 'Valley where assemblies meet'. OE *thing* + *denu*.

Fingal's Cave Arg (Staffa). *Fingal* is the legendary Irish giant Fionn Mac Cumhail. The Gaelic name of the cave is *An Uamh Binn*, 'the melodious cave', referring to the eery sound made by the sea among the basalt pillars.

Fingest Bucks. *Tingeherst* 12th cent. 'Wooded hill where assemblies are held'. OE *thing* + *hyrst*.

Finghall N. Yorks. *Finegala* |sic| 1086 (DB), *Finyngale* 1157. Probably 'nook of land of the family or followers of a man called *Fin(a)*'. OE pers. name + *-inga-* + *halh*.

Finglas (*Fionnghlas*) Dublin. 'Bright stream'.

Finglesham Kent. *Thenglesham* 832, *Flengvessam* |sic| 1086 (DB). 'Homestead or village of the prince, or of a man called *Thengel*'. OE *thengel* or pers. name + *hām*.

Fingringhoe Essex. *Fingringaho* 10th cent. Possibly 'hill-spur of the dwellers on the finger of land'. OE *finger* + *-inga-* + *hōh*.

Finisk (*Fionnuisce*) (river) Waterford. 'White water'.

Finmere Oxon. *Finemere* 1086 (DB). 'Pool frequented by woodpeckers'. OE *fīna* + *mere*.

Finn, Lough (*Loch Finne*) Donegal. 'White lake'.

Finnart Perth. *Fynnard* 1350. 'White or holy headland'. Gaelic *fionn* + *àrd*.

Finnea (*Fiodh an Átha*) Cavan, Westmeath. 'Wood of the ford'.

Finningham Suffolk. *Finingaham* 1086 (DB). 'Homestead of the family or followers of a man called *Fīn(a)*'. OE pers. name + *-inga-* + *hām*.

Finningley S. Yorks. *Feniglei* |sic| 1086 (DB), *Feningelay* 1175. 'Woodland clearing of the dwellers in the fen'. OE *fenn* + *-inga-* + *lēah*.

Finny (*Fionnaithe*) Mayo. 'White kiln'.

Finsbury Gtr. London. *Finesbire* 1235. 'Manor of a man called Finn'. OScand. pers. name + ME *bury* (from OE *byrig*, dative of *burh*).

Finsthwaite Cumbria. *Fynnesthwayt* 1336. 'Clearing of a man called Finn'. OScand. pers. name + *thveit*.

Finstock Oxon. *Finestochia* 12th cent. 'Outlying farmstead frequented by woodpeckers'. OE *fīna* + *stoc*.

Fintona (*Fionntamhnach*) Tyrone. (*hi f*)*fionntamhnach* 1488. 'White clearing'.

Fintown (*Baile na Finne*) Donegal. *Fintown* 1835. 'Homestead of the (river) Finn'.

Fintra (*Fionn traigh*) Clare. 'White strand'.

Fintragh (*Fionn traigh*) Donegal. 'White strand'.

Finvoy (*An Fhionnbhoith*) Antrim. *Le Fynmaugh* 1333. 'The white hut'.

Firbeck S. Yorks. *Fritebec* 12th cent. 'Woodland stream'. OE *fyrhth* + OScand. *bekkr*.

Firle, West E. Sussex. *Ferle* 1086 (DB). 'Place where oak-trees grow'. OE **fierel*.

Firsby Lincs., near Spilsby. *Frisebi* 1202. 'Farmstead or village of the Frisians'. OScand. *Frísir* (genitive *Frísa*) + *bý*.

Firth of Forth (sea inlet) Fife, E. Loth. *Forthin* c.970. 'Estuary of the River Forth'. ME *firth*. The Celtic river name probably means 'the slow flowing one'.

Fishbourne, *Fishburn*, 'fish stream, stream where fish are caught', OE *fisc* + *burna*: **Fishbourne** I. of Wight. *Fisseburne* 1267. **Fishbourne** W. Sussex. *Fiseborne* 1086 (DB). **Fishburn** Durham. *Fisseburne* c.1190.

Fishguard (*Abergwaun*) Pemb. *Fissigart* 1200, *Fissegard, id est, Aber gweun* 1210. 'Fish yard'. OScand. *fiskr* + *garthr*. A 'fish yard' is an enclosure for catching fish or for keeping them in when caught. The Welsh name means 'mouth of the River Gwaun' (OWelsh *aber*), the river name meaning 'marsh' (Welsh *gwaun*).

Fishlake S. Yorks. *Fiscelac* 1086 (DB). 'Fish stream'. OE *fisc* + *lacu*.

Fishtoft Lincs. *Toft* 1086 (DB). OScand. *toft* 'building site, curtilage'. The later addition *Fish-* may be a surname or indicate a connection with fishing.

Fiskerton, 'farmstead or village of the fishermen', OE *fiscere* (replaced by OScand. *fiskari*) + *tūn*: **Fiskerton** Lincs. *Fiskertuna* 1060, *Fiscartone* 1086 (DB). **Fiskerton** Notts. *Fiscertune* 956, *Fiscartune* 1086 (DB).

Fittleton Wilts. *Viteletone* 1086 (DB). 'Farmstead of a man called Fitela'. OE pers. name + *tūn*.

Fittleworth W. Sussex. *Fitelwurtha* 1168. 'Enclosure of a man called Fitela'. OE pers. name + *worth*.

Fitz Shrops. *Witesot* |*sic*| 1086 (DB), *Fittesho* 1194. 'Hill-spur of a man called **Fitt*'. OE pers. name + *hōh*.

Fitzhead Somerset. *Fifhida* 1065. '(Estate of) five hides'. OE *fīf* + *hīd*.

Fivehead Somerset. *Fifhide* 1086 (DB). Identical in origin with the previous name.

Fivemiletown Tyrone. *Fivemiletown* 1831. The town is said to be five miles from Clogher, Brookeborough, and Tempo respectively. Its original Irish name was *Baile na Lorgan*, 'homestead of the long low ridge'.

Flackwell Heath Bucks. *Flakewelle* 1227. Possibly 'spring or stream of a man called **Flæcca*'. OE pers. name + *wella*.

Fladbury Heref. & Worcs. *Fledanburg* late 7th cent., *Fledebirie* 1086 (DB). 'Stronghold or manor-house of a woman called **Flǣde*'. OE pers. name + *burh* (dative *byrig*).

Flagg Derbys. *Flagun* 1086 (DB). Probably 'place where turfs are cut'. OScand. *flag* in a dative plural form *flagum*.

Flagstaff Armagh. The name is said to refer to a flag raised on a hill nearby as a guide to shipping. The Irish name of the hamlet was *Barr an Fheadáin*, 'top of the watercourse'.

Flamborough E. R. Yorks. *Flaneburg* 1086 (DB). 'Stronghold of a man called Fleinn'. OScand. pers. name + OE *burh*. Flamborough Head (from OE *hēafod* 'headland') is first recorded in the 14th cent.

Flamstead Herts. *Fleamstede* 990, *Flamestede* 1086 (DB). 'Place of refuge'. OE *flēam* + *stede*.

Flannan Isles W. Isles. 'Islands of St Flannan'.

Flansham W. Sussex. *Flennesham* 1220. OE *hām* 'homestead' or *hamm* 'enclosure' with an obscure first element, probably a pers. name.

Flasby N. Yorks. *Flatebi* 1086 (DB). 'Farmstead or village of a man called Flatr'. OScand. pers. name + *bý*.

Flat Holm (island) Vale Glam. *Les Holmes* 1358, *Flotholm* 1375. 'Fleet island'. OScand. *floti* + *holmr*. The island was used as a Viking naval base.

Flaunden Herts. *Flawenden* 13th cent. Probably 'flag-stone valley'. OE **flage* + *denu*.

Flawborough Notts. *Flodberge* |*sic*| 1086 (DB), *Flouberge* 12th cent. 'Hill with stones'. OE *flōh* + *beorg*.

Flawith N. Yorks. *Flathwayth* c.1190. Possibly 'ford of the female troll or witch'. OScand. *flagth* + *vath*. Alternatively the first element may be OScand. **flatha* 'flat meadow' or OE **fleathe* 'water-lily'.

Flaxby N. Yorks. *Flatesbi* 1086 (DB). 'Farmstead or village of a man called Flatr'. OScand. pers. name + *bý*.

Flaxley Glos. *Flaxlea* 1163. 'Clearing where flax is grown'. OE *fleax* + *lēah*.

Flaxton N. Yorks. *Flaxtune* 1086 (DB). 'Farmstead where flax is grown'. OE *fleax* + *tūn*.

Fleckney Leics. *Flechenie* 1086 (DB). Possibly 'well-watered land of a man called **Flecca*'. OE pers. name (genitive *-n*) + *ēg*.

Flecknoe Warwicks. *Flechenho* 1086 (DB). Possibly 'hill-spur of a man called **Flecca*'. OE pers. name (genitive *-n*) + *hōh*.

Fleet, '(place at) the stream, pool, or creek', OE *flēot*; examples include: **Fleet** Hants. *Flete* 1313. **Fleet** Lincs. *Fleot* 1086 (DB).

Fleetwood Lancs., a modern name, from Sir Peter Fleetwood who laid out the town in 1836.

Flempton Suffolk. *Flemingtuna* 1086 (DB). Possibly 'farmstead of the Flemings (people from Flanders)'. OE *Fleming* + *tūn*.

Fletching E. Sussex. *Flescinge(s)* 1086 (DB). '(Settlement of) the family or followers of a man called *Flecci'. OE pers. name + *-ingas*.

Fletton, Old Cambs. *Fletun* 1086 (DB). 'Farmstead on a stream'. OE *flēot* + *tūn*.

Flimby Cumbria. *Flemyngeby* 12th cent. 'Farmstead or village of the Flemings (people from Flanders)'. OScand. *Flǽmingr* + *bý*.

Flint (*Y Fflint*) Flin. *Le Chaylou* 1277, *le Fflynt* 1300. '(Place of) hard rock'. ME *flint*. The name refers to the stone platform on which Flint Castle was built in 1277. The first form above is the French equivalent.

Flintham Notts. *Flintham* 1086 (DB). 'Homestead or enclosure of a man called *Flinta'. OE pers. name + *hām* or *hamm*.

Flinton E. R. Yorks. *Flintone* 1086 (DB). 'Farmstead where flints are found'. OE *flint* + *tūn*.

Flitcham Norfolk. *Flicham* 1086 (DB). 'Homestead or village where flitches of bacon are produced'. OE *flicce* + *hām*.

Flitton Beds. *Flittan* c.985, *Flictham* |sic| 1086 (DB). Obscure in origin and meaning.

Flitwick Beds. *Flicteuuiche* 1086 (DB). OE *wīc* 'dwelling, (dairy) farm' with an uncertain first element.

Flixborough N. Lincs. *Flichesburg* 1086 (DB). 'Stronghold of a man called Flík'. OScand. pers. name + OE *burh*.

Flixton, 'farmstead or village of a man called Flík', OScand. pers. name + OE *tūn*: **Flixton** Gtr. Manch. *Flixton* 1177. **Flixton** N. Yorks. *Fleustone* |sic| 1086 (DB), *Flixtona* 12th cent. **Flixton** Suffolk, near Bungay. *Flixtuna* 1086 (DB).

Flockton W. Yorks. *Flochetone* 1086 (DB). 'Farmstead of a man called Flóki'. OScand. pers. name + OE *tūn*.

Flodden Northum. *Floddoun* 1517. Possibly 'hill with stones'. OE *flōh* + *dūn*.

Flookburgh Cumbria. *Flokeburg* 1246. Probably 'stronghold of a man called Flóki'. OScand. pers. name + OE *burh*.

Flordon Norfolk. *Florenduna* 1086 (DB). Probably 'hill with a floor or pavement'. OE *flōre* + *dūn*.

Flore Northants. *Flore* 1086 (DB). '(Place at) the floor', probably with reference to a lost tessellated pavement. OE *flōr(e)*.

Florence Court (*Mullach na Seangán*) Fermanagh. The mansion was originally owned by Lord Mount Florence, crated Earl of Enniskillen in 1784. The Irish name means 'height of the ants'.

Flotta (island) Orkn. *Flotey* c.1250. 'Flat island'. OScand. *flatr* + *ey*.

Flotterton Northum. *Flotweyton* 12th cent. Possibly 'farmstead by the road liable to flood'. OE *flot* + *weg* + *tūn*.

Flowton Suffolk. *Flochetuna* 1086 (DB). 'Farmstead of a man called Flóki'. OScand. pers. name + OE *tūn*.

Flushing Cornwall. Recorded from 1698, so named after the port of Flushing (Vlissingen) in Holland, probably because it was founded by Dutch settlers.

Flyford Flavell Heref. & Worcs. *Fleferth* 10th cent. OE *fyrhth* 'sparse woodland' with an uncertain first element. The affix *Flavell* is simply a Normanized form of Flyford, added to distinguish this place from GRAFTON FLYFORD.

Fobbing Essex. *Phobinge* 1086 (DB). '(Settlement of) the family or followers of a man called *Fobba', or '*Fobba's place'. OE pers. name + *-ingas* or *-ing*.

Fochabers Moray. *Fochoper* 1124, *Fochabyr* 1238, *Fochabris* 1514. Second element may be Pictish *aber* 'confluence'.

Fockerby N. Lincs. *Fulcwardby* 12th cent. 'Farmstead or village of a man called Folcward'. OGerman pers. name + OScand. *bý*.

Fofannybane (*Fofannaigh Bhán*) Down. 'White thistle land'.

Fofannyreagh (*Fofannaigh Riabhach*) Down. 'Striped thistle land'.

Foggathorpe E. R. Yorks. *Fulcartorp* 1086 (DB). 'Outlying farmstead or hamlet of a man called Folcward'. OGerman pers. name + OScand. *thorp*.

Foilnaman (*Faill na mBan*) Tipperary. 'Cliff of the women'.

Foleshill W. Mids. *Focheshelle* |sic| 1086 (DB). *Folkeshulla* 12th cent. 'Hill of the people', or 'hill of a man called *Folc'. OE *folc* or OE pers. name + *hyll*.

Folke Dorset. *Folk* 1244. '(Land held by) the people'. OE *folc*.

Folkestone Kent. *Folcanstan* c.697, *Fulchestan* 1086 (DB). Probably 'stone (marking a hundred meeting-place) of a man called *Folca'. OE pers. name + *stān*.

Folkingham Lincs. *Folchingeham* 1086 (DB). 'Homestead of the family or followers of a man called *Folc(a)'. OE pers. name + *-inga-* + *hām*.

Folkington E. Sussex. *Fochintone* |sic| 1086 (DB), *Folkintone* c.1150. 'Estate associated with a man called *Folc(a)'. OE pers. name + *-ing-* + *tūn*.

Folksworth Cambs. *Folchesworde* 1086 (DB). 'Enclosure of a man called *Folc'. OE pers. name + *worth*.

Folkton N. Yorks. *Fulcheton* 1086 (DB). 'Farmstead of a man called Folki or *Folca'. OScand. or OE pers. name + *tūn*.

Follifoot N. Yorks. *Pholifet* 12th cent. '(Place of) the horse-fighting' (alluding to a Viking sport). OE *fola* + *feoht*.

Font-y-gary (*Ffontygari*) Vale Glam. *Fundygary* 1587. Origin uncertain. The first element may be English *font*, referring to Font-y-gary Well here.

Fonthill Bishop & *Fonthill Gifford* Wilts. *Funtial* 901, *Fontel* 1086 (DB), *Fontel Episcopi, Fontel Giffard* 1291. Possibly a Celtic river-name (meaning 'stream in fertile upland'). Manorial affixes from possession by the Bishop

(Latin *episcopus*) of Winchester and the Gifard family at the time of Domesday.

Fontmell Magna Dorset. *Funtemel* 877, *Fontemale* 1086 (DB), *Magnam Funtemell* 1391. Originally a Celtic river-name (meaning 'stream by the bare hill'). Affix is Latin *magna* 'great'.

Foolow Derbys. *Foulowe* 1269. Probably 'hill frequented by birds'. OE *fugol* + *hlāw*.

Foots Cray Gtr. London. *see* CRAY.

Forcett N. Yorks. *Forset* 1086 (DB). Probably 'fold by a ford'. OE *ford* + *set*.

Ford, a common name, '(place by) the ford', from OE *ford*; examples include: **Ford** Northum. *Forda* 1224. **Ford** Shrops. *Forde* 1086 (DB). **Ford** W. Sussex. *Fordes* c.1194. In this name the form was originally plural.

Fordham, 'homestead or enclosure by a ford', OE *ford* + *hām* or *hamm*: **Fordham** Cambs. *Fordham* 10th cent., *Fordeham* 1086 (DB). **Fordham** Essex. *Fordeham* 1086 (DB). **Fordham** Norfolk. *Fordham* 1086 (DB).

Fordingbridge Hants. *Fordingebrige* 1086 (DB). 'Bridge of the people living by the ford'. OE *ford* + *-inga-* + *brycg*.

Fordon E. R. Yorks. *Fordun* 1086 (DB). '(Place) in front of the hill'. OE *fore* + *dūn*.

Fordwich Kent. *Fordeuuicum* 675, *Forewic* |*sic*| 1086 (DB). 'Trading settlement at the ford'. OE *ford* + *wīc*.

Fore ([*Baile*] *Fhobhair*) Westmeath. '(Townland of the) spring'.

Foreland, North Kent. *Forland* 1326. 'Promontory', OE *fore* + *land*. **South Foreland** near Dover has the same origin.

Foremark Derbys. *Fornewerche* 1086 (DB). 'Old fortification'. OScand. *forn* + *verk*.

Forest Hill Oxon. *Fostel* |*sic*| 1086 (DB), *Forsthulle* 1122. 'Hill with a ridge'. OE **forst* + *hyll*.

Forest Row E. Sussex. *Forstrowe* 1467. 'Row (of trees or houses) in ASHDOWN FOREST'. ME *forest* + *row*.

Forfar Ang. *Forfare* c.1200. Unexplained.

Forkill (*Foirceal*) Armagh. (*i*)*nOircel* c.1350. 'Hollow'.

Formal (*Formael*) Meath. 'Bear round hill'.

Formby Mersey. *Fornebei* 1086 (DB). 'Old farmstead', or 'farmstead of a man called Forni'. OScand. *forn* or OScand. pers. name + *bý*.

Formil (*Formael*) Tyrone. 'Round hill'.

Formweel (*Formael*) Galway. 'Round hill'.

Forncett St Mary & *Forncett St Peter* Norfolk. *Fornesseta* 1086 (DB). 'Dwelling or fold of a man called Forni'. OScand. pers. name + OE (*ge*)*set*. Affixes from the dedications of the churches.

Fornham All Saints & *Fornham St Martin* Suffolk. *Fornham* 1086 (DB), *Fornham Omnium Sanctorum*, *Fornham Sancti Martini* 1254. 'Homestead or village where trout are caught'. OE *forne* + *hām*. Affixes from the church dedications.

Forres Moray. *Forais* c.1195. '(Place) below a copse'. Gaelic *fo* + *ras*, or 'Little shrubbery'.

Forsbrook Staffs. *Fotesbroc* 1086 (DB). 'Brook of a man called Fótr'. OScand. pers. name + OE *brōc*.

Forston Dorset. *Fosardeston* 1236. 'Estate of the Forsard family'. ME *toun*. This family was here from the early 13th cent.

Fort Augustus Highland. The village grew up around the garrison enlarged by General Wade in the 1730s and named after William Augustus, Duke of Cumberland (1721–65). The gaelic name is *Cuille Chuimeim* 'Cuimein's Church'.

Fort George Highland. The fortress was established after the 1745 Jacobite rising and named after George II (1683–1760). The Gaelic name is *An Gearasdam* 'the garrison'.

Fort William Highland. The fortress was originally built in 1655 then rebuilt in 1690 as a garrison and named after the reigning monarch, *William* III (1650–1702). The Gaelic name is *An Gearasdam*, cp. Fort George.

Forteviot Perth. *Fothuirtabaicht* c.970. 'Slope of Torbacht'. Gaelic *fothir*.

Forth. *See* FIRTH OF FORTH.

Forthampton Glos. *Forhelmentone* 1086 (DB). 'Estate associated with a man called Forthhelm'. OE pers. name + *-ing-* + *tūn*.

Forton, 'farmstead or village by a ford'. OE *ford* + *tūn*: **Forton** Hants. *Forton* 1312. **Forton** Lancs. *Fortune* 1086 (DB). **Forton** Shrops. *Fordune* |*sic*| 1086 (DB), *Forton* 1240. **Forton** Staffs. *Forton* 1198.

Fortrose Highland. *Forterose* 1455. '(Place) beneath the headland'. Gaelic *foter* + *ros*. The Gaelic name is *A Chananaiel*.

Fortwilliam (*Dún Liam*) Antrim. 'William's fort'. A former fort here was perhaps named after William de Burgh, Earl of Ulster, murdered nearby in 1333.

Fosbury Wilts., near Tidcombe. *Fostesberge* 1086 (DB). 'Stronghold of the ridge'. OE **forst* + *burh* (dative *byrig*).

Fosdyke Lincs. *Fotesdic* 1183. 'Ditch of a man called Fótr'. OScand. pers. name + OE *dīc*.

Fosse Way (Roman road from Lincoln to Bath). *Foss* 8th cent. From OE **foss* 'ditch'. so called from its having had a prominent ditch on either side.

Foston, 'farmstead or village of a man called Fótr'. OScand. pers. name + OE *tūn*: **Foston** Derbys. *Fostun* 12th cent. Recorded as *Farulveston* 1086 (DB), 'farmstead of a man called Farulfr', OScand. pers. name + OE *tūn*. **Foston** Lincs. *Foztun* 1086 (DB). **Foston** N. Yorks. *Fostun* 1086 (DB). **Foston on the Wolds** E. R. Yorks. *Fodstone* 1086 (DB), *Foston on le Wolde* 1609. For the affix, *see* WOLDS.

Fotherby Lincs. *Fodrebi* 1086 (DB). 'Farmstead of a man called Fótr'. OScand. pers. name + *bý*.

Fotheringhay Northants. *Fodringeia* 1086 (DB). Probably 'island or well-watered land used for grazing'. OE **fōdring* + *ēg*.

Foula Shet. 'Bird island'. OScand. *fugl* + *ey*.

Foulden Norfolk. *Fugalduna* 1086 (DB). 'Hill frequented by birds'. OE *fugol* + *dūn*.

Foulness Essex. *Fughelnesse* 1215. 'Promontory frequented by birds'. OE *fugol* + *næss*.

Foulridge Lancs. *Folric* 1219. 'Ridge where foals graze'. OE *fola* + *hrycg*.

Foulsham Norfolk. *Folsham* 1086 (DB). 'Homestead of a man called Fugol'. OE pers. name + *hām*.

Fountains Abbey N. Yorks. *Fonteyns* 1275. 'The fountains or springs', from OFrench *fontein*, referring to the six springs within the 12th cent. abbey site.

Four Marks Hants. *Fowremerkes* 1548. From OE *mearc* 'boundary', so called because the boundaries of four ancient parishes meet here.

Fourstones Northum. *Fourstanys* 1236. 'Four stones', here describing a tetralith. OE *fēower* + *stān*.

Fovant Wilts. *Fobbefunte* 901, *Febefonte* |sic| 1086 (DB). 'Spring of a man called *Fobba*'. OE pers. name + **funta*.

Foveran Aber. *Furene c.*1150. '(Place with a) little spring'. Gaelic *fuaran*.

Fowey Cornwall. *Fawi c.*1223. Named from the River Fowey, a Cornish name probably meaning 'beech-tree river'.

Fowlmere Cambs. *Fuglemære* 1086 (DB). 'Mere or lake frequented by birds'. OE *fugol* + *mere*.

Fownhope Heref. & Worcs. *Hope* 1086 (DB), *Faghehope* 1242. OE *hop* 'small enclosed valley' with the later addition of *fāg* (dative *fāgan*) 'variegated, multi-coloured'.

Foxearth Essex. *Focsearde* 1086 (DB). 'The fox's earth, the fox-hole'. OE *fox* + *eorthe*.

Foxham Wilts. *Foxham* 1065. 'Homestead or enclosure where foxes are seen'. OE *fox* + *hām* or *hamm*.

Foxholes N. Yorks. *Fox(o)hole* 1086 (DB). 'The fox-hole(s), the fox's earth(s)'. OE *fox-hol*.

Foxley, 'woodland clearing frequented by foxes', OE *fox* + *lēah*: **Foxley** Norfolk. *Foxle* 1086 (DB). **Foxley** Wilts. *Foxelege* 1086 (DB).

Foxt Staffs. *Foxwiss* 1176. 'The fox's den'. OE *fox* + *wist*.

Foxton, usually 'farmstead where foxes are often seen', OE *fox* + *tūn*: **Foxton** Cambs. *Foxetune* 1086 (DB). **Foxton** Leics. *Foxtone* 1086 (DB).
However the following has a different second element: **Foxton** Durham. *Foxedene c.*1170. 'Valley frequented by foxes'. OE *fox* + *denu*.

Foxwist Green Ches. *Foxwyste* 1475. 'The fox's den'. OE *fox* + *wist*, with *Green* added from the 19th cent.

Foy Heref. & Worcs. *Lann Timoi c.*1150. '(Church of) St Moi'. From the patron saint of the church, originally with Welsh *llan* 'church'.

Foyers Highland. *Fyers* 1769. 'Terraced slope'. Gaelic *foithir* + an English plural *-s*.

Foyfin (*Faiche Fionn*) Donegal. 'White lawn'.

Foyle, Lough (*Loch Feabhail*) Donegal. Possibly 'lake of the lip'.

Foynes (*Faing*) Limerick. Possibly (raven).

Fradswell Staffs. *Frodeswelle* 1086 (DB). 'Spring or stream of a man called Frōd'. OE pers. name + *wella*.

Fraisthorpe E. R. Yorks. *Frestintorp* 1086 (DB). 'Outlying farmstead or hamlet of a man called **Freistingr* or **Freysteinn*'. OScand. pers. name + *thorp*.

Framfield E. Sussex. *Framelle* |sic| 1086 (DB), *Fremefeld* 1257. 'Open land of a man called **Frem(m)a* or **Fremi*'. OE pers. name + *feld*.

Framilode Glos. *Framilade* 1086 (DB). 'Crossing over the River Frome', Celtic river-name (meaning 'fair, fine') + OE *gelād*.

Framingham Earl & *Framingham Pigot* Norfolk. *Framingaham* 1086 (DB), *Framelingham Comitis*, *Framelingham Picot* 1254. 'Homestead of the family or followers of a man called Fram'. OE pers. name + *-inga-* + *hām*. Manorial affixes from early possession by the Earl of Norfolk (Latin *comitis* 'of the earl') and by the Picot family.

Framlingham Suffolk. *Fram(e)lingaham* 1086 'Homestead of the family or followers of a man called **Framela*'. OE pers. name + *-inga-* + *hām*.

Framlington, Long Northum. *Fremelintun* 1166. 'Estate associated with a man called Framela'. OE pers. name + *-ing-* + *tūn*. Affix from the length of the village.

Frampton, usually 'farmstead or village on the River Frome' (of which there are several), Celtic river-name (meaning 'fair, fine') + OE *tūn*: **Frampton** Dorset. *Frantone* 1086 (DB). **Frampton Cotterell** S. Glos. *Frantone* 1086 (DB), *Frampton Cotell* 1257. Manorial affix from the Cotel family, here in the 12th cent. **Frampton Mansell** Glos. *Frantone* 1086 (DB), *Frompton Maunsel* 1368. Manorial affix from the Maunsel family, here in the 13th cent. **Frampton on Severn** Glos. *Frantone* 1086 (DB), *Fromton upon Severne* 1311.
However the following has a different origin: **Frampton** Lincs. *Franetone* 1086 (DB). Probably 'farmstead of a man called **Fráni*'. OScand. pers. name + *tūn*.

Framsden Suffolk. *Framesdena* 1086 (DB). 'Valley of a man called Fram'. OE pers. name + *denu*.

Framwellgate Moor Durham. *Framwelgat* 1352. 'Street by the strongly gushing spring'. OE *fram* + *wella* + OScand. *gata*.

Franche Heref. & Worcs. *Frenesse* 1086 (DB). 'Ash-tree of a man called **Frēa*'. OE pers. name (genitive *-n*) + *æsc*.

Frankby Mersey. *Frankeby* 13th cent. 'Farm belonging to a Frenchman or to a man called **Franki*'. OE *Franca* or OScand. pers. name + *bý*.

Frankley Heref. & Worcs. *Franchelie* 1086 (DB). 'Woodland clearing of a man called Franca'. OE pers. name + *lēah*.

Frankton, 'farmstead or village of a man called Franca', OE pers. name + *tūn*: **Frankton** Warwicks. *Franchetone* 1086 (DB). **Frankton, English** & **Frankton, Welsh** Shrops. *Franchetone* 1086 (DB), *Englyshe Frankton*, *Welsch Francton* 1577. The distinguishing affixes are self-explanatory, Welsh Frankton being some five miles nearer to the Welsh border.

Fransham Norfolk. *Frandesham* 1086 (DB). OE *hām* 'homestead' or *hamm* 'enclosure' with a pers. name of uncertain form.

Frant E. Sussex. *Fyrnthan* 956. 'Place overgrown with fern or bracken'. OE **fiernthe*.

Fraserburgh Aber. *The toun and burghe of Faythlie, now callit Fraserburghe* 1597. 'Fraser's chartered town'. ME *burh*. Alexander Fraser, 7th Laird of Philorth, was granted a charter to raise the town of Faithlie into a burgh of barony here in 1546.

Frating Green Essex. *Fretinge* c.1060, *Fratinga* 1086 (DB). '(Settlement of) the family or followers of a man called *Fræt(a)', or '*Fræt(a)'s place'. OE pers. name + *-ingas* or *-ing*.

Fratton Hants. *Frodin(c)gtune* 982, *Frodinton* 1086 (DB). 'Estate associated with a man called Frōda'. OE pers. name + *-ing-* + *tūn*.

Freaghduff (*Fraech Dubh*) Tipperary. 'Black heathery place'.

Freaghmore (*Fraech Mór*) Westmeath. 'Large heathery place'.

Freckenham Suffolk. *Frekeham* 895, *Frakenaham* 1086 (DB). 'Homestead or village of a man called *Freca'. OE pers. name (genitive *-n*) + *hām*.

Freckleton Lancs. *Frecheltun* 1086 (DB). Probably 'farmstead of a man called *Frecla'. OE pers. name + *tūn*.

Freeby Leics. *Fredebi* 1086 (DB). 'Farmstead or village of a man called Fræthi'. OScand. pers. name + *bý*.

Freeduff (*Fraech Dubh*) Armagh, Cavan. 'Black heathery place'.

Freethorpe Norfolk. *Frietorp* 1086 (DB). 'Outlying farmstead or hamlet of a man called Fræthi'. OScand. pers. name + *thorp*.

Freiston Lincs., near Boston. *Fristune* 1086 (DB). 'Farmstead or village of the Frisians'. OE *Frīsa* + *tūn*.

Fremington, 'estate associated with a man called *Fremi* or *Frem(m)a*', OE pers. name + *-ing-* + *tūn*: **Fremington** Devon. *Framintone* 1086 (DB). **Fremington** N. Yorks. *Fremington* 1086 (DB).

Frensham Surrey. *Fermesham* 10th cent. 'Homestead or village of a man called *Fremi'. OE pers. name + *hām*.

Freshfield Mersey., a recent name, apparently called after a man named *Fresh* who reclaimed the land after encroachment by sand.

Freshford B. & NE. Som. *Ferscesford* c.1000. 'Ford over the freshwater stream'. OE *fersc* 'fresh' (here used as a noun) + *ford*.

Freshford (*Achadh Úr*) Kilkenny. 'Fresh field'. The English name mistranslates the Irish, confusing *achadh*, 'field', with *áth*, 'ford'.

Freshwater I. of Wight. *Frescewatre* 1086 (DB). 'River with fresh water'. OE *fersc* + *wæter*.

Fressingfield Suffolk. *Fessefelda* |sic| 1086 (DB), *Frisingefeld* 1185. Possibly 'open land of the family or followers of a man called *Frīsa ("the Frisian")'. OE pers. name + *-inga-* + *feld*.

Freston (Suffolk). *Fresantun* 1000–2, *Fresetuna* 1086 (DB). 'Farmstead or village of the Frisian'. OE *Frīsa* + *tūn*.

Frettenham Norfolk. *Fretham* 1086 (DB). 'Homestead or village of a man called *Fræta'. OE pers. name (genitive *-n*) + *hām*.

Fridaythorpe E. R. Yorks. *Fridagstorp* 1086 (DB). Probably 'outlying farmstead or hamlet of a man called *Frīgedæg'. OE pers. name + OScand. *thorp*.

Friern Barnet Gtr. London, *see* BARNET

Frilford Oxon. *Frieliford* 1086 (DB). 'Ford of a man called *Frithela'. OE pers. name + *ford*.

Frilsham Berks. *Frilesham* 1086 (DB). 'Homestead or village of a man called *Frithel'. OE pers. name + *hām*.

Frimley Surrey. *Fremle* 1203. 'Woodland clearing of a man called *Frem(m)a'. OE pers. name + *lēah*.

Frindsbury Kent. *Freondesberiam* 764, *Frandesberie* 1086 (DB). 'Stronghold of a man called *Frēond'. OE pers. name + *burh* (dative *byrig*).

Fring Norfolk. *Frainghes* 1086 (DB). Probably '(settlement of) the family or followers of a man called *Frēa'. OE pers. name + *-ingas*.

Fringford Oxon. *Feringeford* 1086 (DB). Probably 'ford of the family or followers of a man called *Fēra'. OE pers. name + *-inga-* + *ford*.

Frinsted Kent. *Fredenestede* 1086 (DB). 'Place of protection'. OE *frithen* + *stede*.

Frinton on Sea Essex. *Frientuna* 1086 (DB). 'Farmstead of a man called *Fritha', or 'protected farmstead'. OE pers. name (genitive *-n*) or OE *frithen* + *tūn*.

Frisby on the Wreake Leics. *Frisebie* 1086 (DB). 'Farmstead or village of the Frisians'. OScand. *Frísir* (genitive *Frísa*) + *bý*. Wreake is an OScand. river-name meaning 'twisted, winding'.

Friskney Lincs. *Frischenei* 1086 (DB). 'River with fresh water'. OE *fersc* (dative *-an*, with Scand. *-sk-*) + *ēa*.

Friston E. Sussex. *Friston* 1200. Possibly 'farmstead of a man called *Frēo'. OE pers. name + *tūn*.

Friston Suffolk. *Frisetuna* 1086 (DB). 'Farmstead or village of the Frisians'. OE *Frīsa* + *tūn*.

Fritham Hants. *Friham* 1212. Probably 'enclosure in sparse woodland'. OE *fyrhth* + *hamm*.

Frithelstock Devon. *Fredeletestoc* 1086 (DB). 'Outlying farmstead of a man called *Frithulāc'. OE pers. name + *stoc*.

Frithville Lincs. *Le Frith* 1331. OE *fyrhth* 'sparse woodland' with the later addition of *-ville* (from French *ville* 'village, town').

Frittenden Kent. *Friththingden* 9th cent. 'Woodland pasture associated with a man called Frith'. OE pers. name + *-ing-* + *denn*.

Fritton, 'farmstead offering safety or protection', or 'farmstead of a man called Frithi', OE *frith* or OScand. pers. name + OE *tūn*: **Fritton** Norfolk, near Gorleston. *Fridetuna* 1086 (DB). **Fritton** Norfolk, near Morningthorpe. *Fridetuna* 1086 (DB).

Fritwell Oxon. *Fertwelle* 1086 (DB). 'Spring used for divination'. OE *freht* + *wella*.

Frizington Cumbria. *Frisingaton* c.1160. Probably 'estate of the family or followers of a man called *Frīsa ("the Frisian")'. OE pers. name + *-inga-* + *tūn*.

Frobost W. Isles (South Uist). 'Fróthi's homestead'. OScand. pers. n. Fróthi + *bólstathr*.

Frocester Glos. *Frowecestre* 1086 (DB). 'Roman town on the River Frome'. Celtic river-name (meaning 'fair, fine') + OE *ceaster*.

Frodesley Shrops. *Frodeslege* 1086 (DB). 'Woodland clearing of a man called Frōd'. OE pers. name + *lēah*.

Frodingham, 'homestead of the family or followers of a man called Frōd(a)', OE pers. name + *-inga-* + *hām*: **Frodingham** N. Lincs., near Scunthorpe. *Frodingham* 12th cent. **Frodingham, North** E. R. Yorks. *Frotingham* 1086 (DB), *North Frothyngham* 1297.

Frodsham Ches. *Frotesham* 1086 (DB). 'Homestead or promontory of a man called Frōd'. OE pers. name + *hām* or *hamm*.

Froghanstown (*Baile Fraocháin*) Westmeath. 'Homestead of bilberries'.

Frogmore, usually 'pool frequented by frogs', OE *frogga* + *mere*; for example **Frogmore** Hants. *Frogmore* 1294.

Frome, named from the River Frome (of which there are several), a Celtic river-name meaning 'fair, fine, brisk': **Frome** Somerset. *Froom* 8th cent. **Frome, Bishop's**, **Frome, Canon**, & **Frome, Castle** Heref. & Worcs. *Frome* 1086 (DB), *Frume al Evesk* 1252, *Froma Canonicorum*, *Froma Castri* 1242. Affixes 'Bishop's' (OFrench *eveske*) and 'Canon' (Latin *Canonicorum* 'of the canons') refer to possession by the Bishop of Hereford and the canons of Lanthony in medieval times, 'Castle' refers to a Norman castle. **Frome St Quintin** Dorset. *Litelfrome* 1086 (DB), *Fromequintin* 1288. At first called 'little' (OE *lȳtel*) to distinguish it from other manors on the same river, later given a manorial affix from the St Quintin family, here in the 13th cent.

Frosses (*Na Frosa*) Antrim. *Frasses* c.1657. 'Marshy place' (literally 'the showers').

Frostenden Suffolk. *Froxedena* 1086 (DB). Probably 'valley frequented by frogs'. OE *frosc* + *denu*.

Frosterley Durham. *Forsterlegh* 1239. 'Woodland clearing or pasture of the forester'. ME *forester* + OE *lēah*.

Froxfield, 'open land frequented by frogs', OE *frosc* + *feld*: **Froxfield** Wilts. *Forscanfeld* 9th cent. **Froxfield Green** Hants. *Froxafelda* 10th cent.

Fryerning Essex. *Inga* 1086 (DB), *Friering* 1469. Originally '(settlement of) the people of the district'. OE **gē* + *-ingas*. Later distinguished from other manors so called by the affix *Freren-* 'of the brethren' (from ME *frere*) referring to possession by the Knights Hospitallers in the 12th cent.

Fryston, Monk N. Yorks. *Fristun* c.1030, *Munechesfryston* 1166. 'Farmstead of the Frisians'. OE *Frīsa* + *tūn*. Affix from OE *munuc* 'monk' referring to possession by Selby Abbey in the 11th cent.

Fryton N. Yorks. *Frideton* 1086 (DB). 'Farmstead offering safety or protection', or 'farmstead of a man called Frithi'. OE *frith* or OScand. pers. name + OE *tūn*.

Fuerty (*Fiodharta*) Roscommon. 'Wooded place'.

Fulbeck Lincs. *Fulebec* 1086 (DB). 'Foul or dirty stream'. OE *fūl* + OScand. *bekkr*.

Fulbourn Cambs. *Fuulburne* c.1050, *Fuleberne* 1086 (DB). 'Stream frequented by birds'. OE *fugol* + *burna*.

Fulbrook Oxon. *Fulebroc* 1086 (DB). 'Foul or dirty brook'. OE *fūl* + *brōc*.

Fulford, 'foul or dirty ford', OE *fūl* + *ford*: **Fulford** Somerset. *Fuleforde* 1327. **Fulford** Staffs. *Fuleford* 1086 (DB). **Fulford** York. *Fuleford* 1086 (DB).

Fulham Gtr. London. *Fulanham* c.705, *Fuleham* 1086 (DB). 'Land in a river-bend of a man called **Fulla*'. OE pers. name + *hamm*.

Fulking W. Sussex. *Fochinges* |*sic*| 1086 (DB), *Folkinges* c.1100. '(Settlement of) the family or followers of a man called **Folca*'. OE pers. name + *-ingas*.

Full Sutton E. R. Yorks., see SUTTON.

Fullerton Hants. *Fugelerestune* 1086 (DB). 'Farmstead or village of the fowlers or bird-catchers'. OE *fuglere* + *tūn*.

Fulletby Lincs. *Fullobi* 1086 (DB). OScand. *bý* 'farmstead, village' with an obscure first element, possibly a pers. name.

Fulmer Bucks. *Fugelmere* 1198. 'Mere or lake frequented by birds'. OE *fugol* + *mere*.

Fulmodeston Norfolk. *Fulmotestuna* 1086 (DB). 'Farmstead of a man called Fulcmod'. OGerman pers. name + *tūn*.

Fulnetby Lincs. *Fulnedebi* 1086 (DB). OScand. *bý* 'farmstead, village' with an uncertain, first element, possibly OScand. **full-nautr* 'one who has a full share'.

Fulstow Lincs. *Fugelestou* 1086 (DB). 'Holy place or meeting place of a man called Fugol'. OE pers. name + *stōw*. Alternatively the first element may be OE *fugol* 'bird', hence 'place where birds abound'.

Fulwell Tyne & Wear. *Fulewella* 12th cent. 'Foul or dirty spring or stream'. OE *fūl* + *wella*.

Fulwood, 'foul or dirty wood', OE *fūl* + *wudu*: **Fulwood** Lancs. *Fulewde* 1199. **Fulwood** Notts. *Folewode* 13th cent.

Funshion (*Fuinseann*) (river) Cork, Limerick. 'Ash-producing one'.

Funtington W. Sussex. *Fundintune* 12th cent. Possibly 'farmstead at the place with a spring'. OE **funta* + *-ing* + *tūn*.

Furness (old district) Cumbria, see BARROW IN FURNESS.

Furneux Pelham Herts., see PELHAM.

Furraleigh (*Foradh Liath*) Waterford. 'Grey mound'.

Fybagh (*An Fhadhbach*) Kerry. 'The lumpy place'.

Fyfield, '(estate of) five hides of land', OE *fīf* + *hīd*: **Fyfield** Essex. *Fifhidam* 1086 (DB). **Fyfield** Glos. *Fishide* 12th cent. **Fyfield** Hants. *Fifhidon* 975, *Fifhide* 1086 (DB). **Fyfield** Oxon. *Fif Hidum* 956, *Fivehide* 1086 (DB). **Fyfield** Wilts. *Fifhide* 1086 (DB).

Fyfin (*Faiche Fionn*) Tyrone. *Foifin* 1609. 'White green'.

Fylde, The (district) Lancs., see POULTON-LE-FYLDE.

Fyne, Loch. Arg. 'Loch of the River Fyne'. The river name means 'wine'. Gaelic *fiòn*.

G

Gaddesby Leics. *Gadesbi* 1086 (DB). 'Farmstead or village of a man called Gaddr'. OScand. pers. name + *bý*. Alternatively the first element may be OScand. *gaddr* 'spur of land'.

Gaddesden, Great & *Gaddesden, Little* Herts. *Gætesdene* 10th cent., *Gatesdene* 1086 (DB). 'Valley of a man called **Gæte(n)*'. OE pers. name + *denu*. The river-name **Gade** is a 'back-formation' from the place-name.

Gaggin (*Géagánach*) Cork. 'Arm'.

Gagingwell Oxon. *Gadelingwelle c.*1173. 'Spring or stream of the kinsmen or companions'. OE *gædeling* + *wella*.

Gaick Forest Highland. 'Forest in a cleft'. Gaelic *gàg* (dative *gàig*).

Gailey Staffs. *Gageleage c.*1002, *Gragelie |sic|* 1086 (DB). 'Woodland clearing where bog-myrtle grows'. OE *gagel* + *lēah*.

Gaineamhach, Loch Highland. 'Sandy lake'. Gaelic *loch* + *gaineamh* + *-ach*.

Gainford Durham. *Geg(e)nforda c.*1040. 'Direct ford', i.e. 'ford on a direct route'. OE *gegn* + *ford*.

Gainsborough Lincs. *Gainesburg* 1086 (DB). 'Stronghold of a man called **Gegn*'. OE pers. name + *burh*.

Gairloch Highland. *Gerloth* 1275, *Gerloch* 1366. '(Place on) Gair Loch'. The loch name means 'short inlet of the sea' (Gaelic *geàrr* + *loch*).

Gairsay (island) Orkn. 'Garek's island'. OScand. *ey*.

Gaisgill Cumbria. *Gasegille* 1310. 'Ravine frequented by wild geese'. OScand. *gás* + *gil*.

Gala Water. *See* GALASHIELS.

Galashiels Sc. Bord. *Galuschel* 1237. 'Huts by Gala Water'. ME *schele*. The river name is of uncertain origin.

Galbally (*Gallbhaile*) Limerick, Tyrone, Wexford, etc. 'Foreigner's homestead'.

Galbooly (*Gallbhuaile*) Tipperary. 'Stone milking place'.

Galgate Lancs. *Galwaithegate c.*1190. Possibly '(place by) the Galloway road', i.e. 'the road used by cattle drovers from Galloway'. Scottish place-name (meaning 'territory of the stranger-Gaels') + OScand. *gata*.

Galhampton, *Galmpton*, 'farmstead of rent-paying peasants', OE **gafol-mann* + *tūn*: **Galhampton** Somerset. *Galmeton* 1199. **Galmpton** Devon, near Brixham. *Galmentone* 1086 (DB). **Galmpton** Devon, near Salcombe. *Walementone* 1086 (DB).

Gallan (*Gallán*) Tyrone. 'Standing stone'.

Gallan Head W. Isles (Lewis). 'Pillar headland'. Gaelic *gallan*.

Gallane (*Gallán*) Cork. 'Standing stone'.

Gallen (*Gailenga*) Mayo. '(Territory of the) descendants of Gaileng'.

Galliagh (*Baile na gCailleach*) Derry. *Ballinecalleagh* 1604. 'Settlement of the nuns'.

Galloway (district) Dumf. *Galweya c.*970. '(Territory among the) stranger Gaels'. Gaelic *gall* + *Ghaidel*. The 'stranger Gaels' were people of mixed Irish and Scand. descent who settled here in the 9th cent.

Galmoy (*Gabhalmhaigh*) Tipperary. 'Fork of the plain'.

Galphay N. Yorks. *Galghagh* 12th cent. 'Enclosure where a gallows stands'. OE *galga* + *haga*.

Galston E. Ayr. *Gauston* 1260. 'Village of the strangers'. Gaelic *gall* + OE *tūn*.

Galtrim (*Cala Trium*) Meath. 'River meadow of the elder'.

Galty Mountains (*Na Gaibhlte*) Limerick, Tipperary. Perhaps 'forted valleys'.

Galway (*Gaillimh*) Galway. 'Stony (river)'.

Galwolie (*Gallbhuaile*) Donegal. 'Milking place of the foreigner'.

Gamallt (mountain) Cergn. 'Crooked hillside'. Welsh *cam* + *allt*.

Gamblesby Cumbria. *Gamelesbi* 1177. 'Farmstead or village of a man called Gamall'. OScand. pers. name + *bý*.

Gamlingay Cambs. *Gamelingei* 1086 (DB). 'Enclosure or well-watered land associated with a man called **Gamela*, or of **Gamela*'s people'. OE pers. name + *-ing-* or *-inga-* + *hæg* or *ēg*.

Gamston, 'farmstead of a man called Gamall', OScand. pers. name + OE *tūn*: **Gamston** Notts., near East Retford. *Gamelestune* 1086 (DB). **Gamston** Notts., near Nottingham. *Gamelestune* 1086 (DB).

Ganarew Heref. & Worcs. *Genoreu c.*1150. 'Opening or pass of the hill'. Welsh *genau* + *rhiw*.

Ganstead E. R. Yorks. *Gagenestad* 1086 (DB). Probably 'homestead of a man called **Gagni* or **Gagne*'. OScand. pers. name + *stathr*.

Ganthorpe N. Yorks. *Gameltorp |sic|* 1086 (DB), *Galmestorp* 1169. 'Outlying farmstead or hamlet of a man called Galmr'. OScand. pers. name + *thorp*.

Ganton N. Yorks. *Galmeton* 1086 (DB). Probably 'farmstead of a man called Galmr'. OScand. pers. name + OE *tūn*.

Gara, Lough (*Loch Uí Gadhra*) Sligo. 'Ó Gadhra's lake'.

Garadice (*Garbhros*) Leitrim. 'Rough copse'.

Garbally (*Gearrbhaile*) Galway. 'Short homestead'.

Garboldisham Norfolk. *Gerboldesham* 1086 (DB). 'Homestead or village of a man called *Gærbald'. OE pers. name + *hām*.

Gardrum (*Gearrdroim*) Fermanagh, Tyrone. 'Short ridge'.

Garelochhead Arg. *Gerloch* 1272, *Keangerloch* c.1345. 'Head of the short lake'. Gaelic *gearr* + *loch* + English *head* (translating Gaelic *cearn* 'head'.)

Garford Oxon. *Garanforda* 940, *Wareford |sic|* 1086 (DB). 'Ford of a man called *Gāra', or 'ford at the triangular plot of ground'. OE pers. name or *gāra* + *ford*.

Garforth W. Yorks. *Gereford* 1086 (DB). 'Ford of a man called *Gæra', or 'ford at the triangular plot of ground'. OE pers. name or *gāra* (influenced by OScand. *geiri*) + *ford*.

Gargrave N. Yorks. *Geregraue* 1086 (DB). 'Grove in a triangular plot of ground'. OScand. *geiri* (replacing OE *gāra*) + OE *grāf*.

Garnavilla (*Garrán an Bhile*) Tipperary. 'Grove of the sacred tree'.

Garnish (*Gar-inis*) Cork. 'Rough island'.

Garrabost W. Isles (Lewis). 'Farmstead'. OScand. *garthr* + *bólstathr*.

Garranamanagh (*Garrán na Manach*) Kerry. 'Grove of the monks'.

Garranard (*Garrán Ard*) Mayo. 'High grove'.

Garrane (*Garrán*) Tipperary. 'Grove'.

Garranlahan (*An Garrán Leathan*) Roscommon. 'The broad grove'.

Garraun (*Garrán*) Clare, Galway. 'Grove'.

Garrigill Cumbria. *Gerardgile* 1232. 'Deep valley of a man called Gerard'. OGerman pers. name + OScand. *gil*.

Garriskil (*Garascal*) Westmeath. 'Rough nook'.

Garrison (*An Garastún*) Fermanagh. The village is named from a barrack erected here by William III after the battle of Aughrim in 1691.

Garroch Head Arg. *Garrach* 1449. 'Rough place (headland)'. Gaelic *garbh-ach* + English *head*.

Garron (river) Heref. & Worcs., *see* LLANGARRON.

Garron Point (*Gearrán*) Antrim. 'Horse point'.

Garry (*Garraí*) Antrim. 'Garden'.

Garryduff (*Garraí Dubh*) Cork. 'Black garden'.

Garryhill (*An Gharbhchoill*) Carlow. 'The rough wood'.

Garrynafela (*Garraí na Féile*) Westmeath. 'Garden of the hospitality'.

Garryowen (*Garraí Eoghain*) Limerick. 'Eoghan's garden'.

Garryspillane (*Garraí Uí Spealáin*) Limerick. 'Ó Spealáin's garden'.

Garsdale Cumbria. *Garcedale* c.1240. 'Valley of a man called Garthr', or 'grass valley'. OScand. pers. name + *dalr*, or OE *gærs* + *dæl*.

Garsdon Wilts. *Gersdune* 701, *Gardone* 1086 (DB). 'Grass hill'. OE *gæers* + *dūn*.

Garshall Green Staffs. *Garnonshale* 1310. Possibly 'nook of land of a family called Garnon'. ME surname + OE *halh*.

Garsington Oxon. *Gersedun* 1086 (DB). 'Grassy hill'. OE *gærsen* + *dūn*.

Garstang Lancs. *Cherestanc |sic|* 1086 (DB), *Gairstang* c.1195. 'Spear post', probably signifying the site of a meeting-place. OScand. *geirr* + *stong*.

Garston Mersey. *Gerstan* 1094. Possibly 'the great stone'. OE *grēat* + *stān*.

Garston, East Berks. *Esgareston* 1180. 'Estate of a man called Esgar'. OScand. pers. name + OE *tūn*. The modern form is a 'folk etymology' that completely disguises the original meaning of the name.

Garswood Mersey. *Grateswode* 1367. OE *wudu* 'wood' with an obscure first element, possibly a pers. name.

Gartan (*Gartán*) Donegal. *nGartan* c.1630. 'Little field'.

Garthorpe N. Lincs. *Gerulftorp* 1086 (DB). 'Outlying farmstead or hamlet of a man called Geirulfr or Gairulf'. OScand. or OGerman pers. name + OScand. *thorp*.

Garthorpe Leics. *Garthorp* 12th cent. Possibly 'outlying farmstead or hamlet of a man called *Gāra'. OE pers. name + OScand. *thorp*. Alternatively the first element may be OE *gāra* 'triangular plot of ground'.

Garton, 'farmstead in or near the triangular plot of ground', OE *gāra* + *tūn*: **Garton** E. R. Yorks. *Gartun* 1086 (DB). **Garton on the Wolds** E. R. Yorks. *Gartune* 1086 (DB), *Garton in Wald* 1347. For the affix, *see* WOLDS.

Garvagh (*Garbhachadh*) Derry. *Garvaghy* 1634. 'Rough field'.

Garvaghey (*Garbhachadh*) Tyrone. *Garaghye* 1629. 'Rough field'.

Garvaghy (*Garbhachadh*) Down. *Garwaghadh* 1428. 'Rough field'.

Garvellachs (islands) Arg. *Garbeallach* 1390. 'Rough rocks'. Gaelic *garbh* + *eileach*, + English plural -*s*.

Garvellan Rocks Dumf. *Garvellan* 1580. 'Rough island'. Gaelic *garbh* + *eilean*, + English *rocks*.

Garvery (*Garbhaire*) Fermanagh. *Garvorey* 1659. 'Rough land'.

Garvestone Norfolk. *Gerolfestuna* 1086 (DB). 'Farmstead or village of a man called Geirulfr or Gairulf'. OScand. or OGerman pers. name + OE *tūn*.

Garway Heref. & Worcs. *Garou* 1137, *Langarewi* 1189. Probably 'church of a man called Guoruoe'. Welsh *llan* + pers. name.

Gastard Wilts. *Gatesterta* 1154. 'Tail of land where goats are kept'. OE *gāt* + *steort*.

Gasthorpe Norfolk. *Gadesthorp* 1086 (DB). 'Outlying farmstead or hamlet of a man called Gaddr'. OScand. pers. name + *thorp*.

Gatcombe I. of Wight. *Gatecome* 1086 (DB). 'Valley where goats are kept'. OE *gāt* + *cumb*.

Gate Helmsley N. Yorks., *see* HELMSLEY.

Gateforth N. Yorks. *Gæiteford* c.1030. 'Goats' ford', i.e. 'ford used when moving goats'. OScand. *geit* + OE *ford*.

Gateholm (island) Pemb. *Goteholme* 1480. 'Island where goats graze'. OScand. *geit* + *holmr*.

Gatehouse of Fleet Dumf. 'Gatehouse by the River Fleet'. A 'gatehouse' is a roadside house. The river name means simply 'stream' (OScand. *fljót* or OE *flēot*).

Gateley Norfolk. *Gatelea* 1086 (DB). 'Clearing or pasture where goats are kept'. OE *gāt* + *lēah*.

Gatenby N. Yorks. *Ghetenesbi* 1086 (DB). Possibly 'farmstead or village of a man called Gaithan'. OIrish pers. name + OScand. *bý*.

Gateshead Tyne & Wear. *Gatesheued* 1196. 'Goat's headland or hill'. OE *gāt* + *hēafod*.

Gathabawn (*An Geata Bán*) Kilkenny. 'The white gate'.

Gathurst Gtr. Manch. *Gatehurst* 1547. Probably 'wooded hill where goats are kept'. OE *gāt* + *hyrst*.

Gatley Gtr. Manch. *Gateclyve* 1290. 'Cliff or bank where goats are kept'. OE *gāt* + *clif*.

Gatwick Surrey. *Gatwik* 1241. 'Farm where goats are kept'. OE *gāt* + *wīc*.

Gaunless (river) Durham, *see* AUCKLAND.

Gautby Lincs. *Goutebi* 1196. 'Farmstead or village of a man called Gauti'. OScand. pers. name + *bý*.

Gawber S. Yorks. *Galgbergh* 1304. 'Gallows hill'. OE *galga* + *beorg*.

Gawcott Bucks. *Chauescote* |sic| 1086 (DB), *Gauecota* 1090. 'Cottage(s) for which rent is payable'. OE *gafol* + *cot*.

Gawley's Gate Antrim. The hamlet is named from a 17th-cent. tollgate, manned by one Gawley. The equivalent Irish name is *Geata Mhic Amhlaí*.

Gawsworth Ches. *Govesurde* 1086 (DB). Probably 'enclosure of the smith'. Welsh *gof* + OE *worth*.

Gay Island (*Inis na nGédh*) Fermanagh. 'Goose island'.

Gaydon Warwicks. *Gaidone* 1194. 'Hill of a man called *Gǣga*'. OE pers. name + *dūn*.

Gayhurst Bucks. *Gateherst* 1086 (DB). 'Wooded hill where goats are kept'. OE *gāt* + *hyrst*.

Gayles N. Yorks. *Gales* 1534. '(Place at) the ravines'. OScand. *geil*.

Gayton, usually 'farmstead where goats are kept', from OScand. *geit* + *tūn*: **Gayton** Mersey. *Gaitone* 1086 (DB). **Gayton** Norfolk. *Gaituna* 1086 (DB). **Gayton le Marsh** Lincs. *Geiton* 1206. Affix means 'in the marsh' from OE *mersc* with loss of preposition. **Gayton le Wold** Lincs. *Gettone* 1086 (DB). Affix means 'on the wold(s)' with loss of preposition, *see* WOLDS.
However the following have a different origin, 'farmstead of a man called *Gǣga*', from OE pers. name + *tūn*: **Gayton** Northants. *Gaiton* 1162. **Gayton** Staffs. *Gaitone* 1086 (DB).

Gayton Thorpe Norfolk. *Torp* 1086 (DB), *Geytonthorp* 1402. 'Outlying farmstead or hamlet dependent on GAYTON'. OScand. *thorp*.

Gaywood Norfolk. *Gaiuude* 1086 (DB). 'Wood of a man called *Gǣga*'. OE pers. name + *wudu*.

Gazeley Suffolk. *Gaysle* 1219. 'Woodland clearing of a man called *Gǣgi*'. OE pers. name + *lēah*.

Gearha (*Gaortha*) Kerry. 'Wooded valley'.

Gearhameen (*Gaortha Mín*) Kerry. 'Smooth wooded valley'.

Gearhasallagh (*Gaortha Sailech*) Kerry. 'Wooded valley of willows'.

Gedding Suffolk. *Gedinga* 1086 (DB). '(Settlement of) the family or followers of a man called *Gydda*'. OE pers. name + *-ingas*.

Geddington Northants. *Geitentone* 1086 (DB). Possibly 'estate associated with a man called *Gǣte* or Geiti'. OE or OScand. pers. name + OE *-ing-* + *tūn*.

Gedling Notts. *Ghellinge* |sic| 1086 (DB), *Gedlinges* 1187. '(Settlement of) the family or followers of a man called *Gēdel*'. OE pers. name + *-ingas*.

Gedney Lincs. *Gadenai* 1086 (DB). Probably 'island or well-watered land of a man called *Gǣda* or *Gydda*'. OE pers. name (genitive -n) + *ēg*.

Geldeston Norfolk. *Geldestun* 1242. 'Farmstead or village of a man called *Gyldi*'. OE pers. name + *tūn*.

Gelli Gandryll, Y. See HAY-ON-WYE.

Gelston Lincs. *Cheuelestune* 1086 (DB). Probably 'farmstead or village of a man called *Gjǫfull*'. OScand. pers. name + OE *tūn*.

George Nympton Devon, *see* NYMPTON.

Georgeham Devon. *Hama* 1086 (DB), *Hamme Sancti Georgii* 1356. Originally 'the well-watered valley' from OE *hamm*. Later affix from the dedication of the church to St George.

Georgemas Highland. 'St George's mass'. OE *mæsse*. The allusion is to an annual fair on St George's Day (23 April).

Germansweek Devon. *Wica* 1086 (DB), *Wyke Germyn* 1458. Originally 'the dwelling or (dairy) farm' from OE *wīc*. Later affix from the dedication of the church to St Germanus.

Germoe Cornwall. 'Chapel of *Sanctus Germoch*' 12th cent. From the patron saint of the chapel.

Gerrans Cornwall. 'Church of *Sanctus Gerentus*' 1202. 'Church of St. Gerent'. From the patron saint of the church.

Gerrards Cross Bucks. *Gerards Cross* 1692. Named from a local family called Jarrard or Gerrard.

Gestingthorpe Essex. *Gyrstlingathorpe* late 10th cent., *Ghestingetorp* 1086 (DB). 'Outlying farmstead of the family or followers of a man called *Gyrstel*'. OE pers. name + *-inga-* + *throp*.

Giant's Causeway (*Clochán na bhFomhórach*) (columnar rock formation) Antrim. *Clochán na bhfogmharach* c.1675. 'Causeway of the Fomorians'. The English name appears to be a loose translation of the Irish, while the modern Irish name, *Clochán an Aifir*, is apparently a corruption of the earlier name. The Fomorians were legendary giant sea rovers.

Gidding, Great *Gidding, Little,* & *Gidding, Steeple* Cambs. *Geddinge* 1086 (DB), *Magna Giddinge* 1220, *Gydding Parva* 13th cent., *Stepelgedding* 1260. Probably '(settlement of) the family or followers of a man called *Gydda'. OE pers. name + -*ingas*. Distinguishing affixes are Latin *magna* 'great', *parva* 'little' and OE *stēpel* 'steeple, tower'.

Gidea Park Gtr. London. *La Gidiehall* 1258, *Guydie hall parke* 1668. Literally 'the foolish or crazy hall', from ME *gidi* + *hall*, perhaps alluding to a building of unusual design or construction.

Gidleigh Devon. *Gideleia* 1156. 'Woodland clearing of a man called *Gydda'. OE pers. name + *lēah*.

Giggleswick N. Yorks. *Ghigeleswic* 1086 (DB). 'Dwelling or (dairy) farm of a man called Gikel or Gichel'. OE or ME pers. name (probably a short form of the biblical name *Judichael*) + *wīc*.

Gigha (island) Arg. *Gug* 1309, *Gya* c.1400. God's isle or good isle. OScand. *Guith* + *ey*.

Gilberdyke E. R. Yorks. *Dyc* 1234, *Gilbertdike* 1376. '(Place at) the ditch or dike'. OE *dīc* with manorial addition from a person or family called Gilbert.

Gilcrux Cumbria. *Killecruce* c.1175. Probably 'retreat by a hill'. Celtic *cil + *crūg*.

Gildersome W. Yorks. *Gildehusum* 1181. '(Place at) the guild-houses'. OScand. *gildi-hús* in a dative plural form.

Gildingwells S. Yorks. *Gildanwell* 13th cent. Probably 'gushing spring'. OE *gyldande + wella*.

Gilford (*Átha Mhic Giolla*) Down. 'Magill's ford'. *Gilford* 1678. The village is named for Captain John Magill, who acquired lands here in the 17th cent.

Gill, Lough (*Loch Gile*) Kerry, Leitrim, Sligo. 'Lake of brightness'.

Gillamoor N. Yorks. *Gedlingesmore* |sic| 1086 (DB), *Gillingamor* late 12th cent. 'Moorland belonging to the family or followers of a man called *Gȳthla or *Gētla'. OE pers. name + -*inga- + *mōr*.

Gilling '(settlement of) the family or followers of a man called *Gȳthla or *Gētla', OE pers. name + -*ingas*: **Gilling East** N. Yorks. *Ghellinge* 1086 (DB). **Gilling West** N. Yorks. *Ingetlingum* 731, *Ghellinges* 1086 (DB).

Gillingham, 'homestead of the family or followers of a man called *Gylla', OE pers. name + -*inga- + *hām*: **Gillingham** Dorset. *Gelingeham* 1086 (DB). **Gillingham** Kent. *Gyllingeham* 10th cent., *Gelingeham* 1086 (DB). **Gillingham** Norfolk. *Kildincham* |sic| 1086 (DB), *Gelingeham* 12th cent.

Gilmorton Leics. *Mortone* 1086 (DB), *Gilden Morton* 1327. 'Farmstead in marshy ground'. OE *mōr + *tūn*, with later affix from OE *gylden* 'wealthy, splendid'.

Gilsland (Northum.), **Gilsland Spa** (Cumbria). *Gillesland* 12th cent. 'Estate of a man called Gille or Gilli'. OIrish or OScand. pers. name + *land*.

Gilston Herts. *Gedeleston* 1197. 'Farmstead or village of a man called *Gēdel or *Gydel'. OE pers. name + *tūn*.

Gimingham Norfolk. *Gimingeham* 1086 (DB). 'Homestead of the family or followers of a man called *Gymi or *Gymma'. OE pers. name + -*inga- + *hām*.

Ginge, East & *Ginge, West* Oxon. *Gæging* 10th cent., *Gainz* 1086 (DB), *Estgeyng, Westgenge* 13th cent. Originally an OE river-name meaning 'one that turns aside', from the stem of OE *gǣgan + -ing*.

Girsby N. Yorks. *Grisebi* 1086 (DB). 'Farmstead of a man called Gríss', or 'farmstead where young pigs are reared'. OScand. pers. name or OScand. *gríss + bý*.

Girton, 'farmstead or village on gravelly ground', OE *grēot + *tūn*: **Girton** Cambs. *Grittune* c.1060, *Gretone* 1086 (DB). **Girton** Notts. *Gretone* 1086 (DB).

Girvan S. Ayr. *Girven* 1275 Derived from the Water of *Girvan*, of unknown origin.

Gisburn Lancs. *Ghiseburne* |sic| 1086 (DB), *Giselburn* 12th cent. Probably 'gushing stream'. OE *gysel + burna*.

Gisleham Suffolk. *Gisleham* 1086 (DB). 'Homestead or village of a man called *Gysla'. OE pers. name + *hām*.

Gislingham Suffolk. *Gyselingham* c.1060, *Gislingaham* 1086 (DB). 'Homestead of the family or followers of a man called *Gysla'. OE pers. name + -*inga- + *hām*.

Gissing Norfolk. *Gessinga* 1086 (DB). '(Settlement of) the family or followers of a man called *Gyssa or *Gyssi'. OE pers. name + -*ingas*.

Gittisham Devon. *Gidesham* 1086 (DB). 'Homestead or enclosure of a man called Gyddi'. OE pers. name + *hām* or *hamm*.

Givendale, Great E. R. Yorks. *Ghiuedale* 1086 (DB). Probably 'valley of a river called *Gǣvul'. OScand. river-name (meaning 'good for fishing') + *dalr*.

Glaisdale N. Yorks. *Glasedale* 12th cent. 'Valley of a river called *Glas'. Celtic river-name (meaning 'grey-green') + OScand. *dalr*.

Glamis Ang. *Glames* 1187. Meaning unknown.

Glamorgan (*Morgannwg*) (the historic county). 'Morgan's shore'. Welsh *glan*. *Morgan* was a 7th-cent. prince of Gwent. The Welsh name means 'Morgan's territory'.

Glanaman Carm. 'Bank of the River Aman'. Welsh *glan*. For the river name, see AMMANFORD.

Glanaruddery Mountains (*Sléibhte Ghleann an Ridire*) Kerry. 'Mountains of the valley of the knight'.

Glandford Norfolk. *Glamforda* 1086 (DB). Probably 'ford where people assemble for revelry or games'. OE *glēam + ford*.

Glandore (*Gleann Dor*) Cork. 'Valley of the doors'.

Glanmire (*Gleann Maghair*) Cork. 'Valley of the plain'.

Glanmore (*Gleann Mór*) Kerry. 'Big valley'.

Glannavaddoge (*Gleann na bhFeadóg*) Galway. 'Valley of the plovers'.

Glantane (*An Gleanntán*) Cork. 'The little valley'.

Glanton Northum. *Glentendon* 1186. 'Hill frequented by birds of prey or used as a look-out place'. OE *glente + dūn*.

Glanvilles Wootton Dorset, see WOOTTON.

Glanworth (*Gleannúir*) Cork. 'Valley of the yew'.

Glapthorn Northants. *Glapethorn* 12th cent. 'Thorn-tree of a man called Glappa'. OE pers. name + *thorn*.

Glapwell Derbys. *Glappewelle* 1086 (DB). 'Stream of a man called Glappa', or 'stream where the buckbean plant grows'. OE pers. name or OE *glæppe* + *wella*.

Glasbury (*Clas-ar-Wy*) Powys. *Clastbyrig* 1056, *Glesburia* 1191, *Classebury* 1322. 'Town of the monastic community'. Welsh *clas* + OE *burh*. The Welsh name means 'monastic community on the River Wye' (a name of unknown meaning).

Glascarn (*Glascharn*) Westmeath. 'Green cairn'.

Glascoed Mon. 'Green wood'. Welsh *glas* + *coed*.

Glascote Staffs. *Glascote* 12th cent. 'Hut where glass is made'. OE *glæs* + *cot*.

Glasdrumman (*An Ghlasdromainn*) Down. *Glasedrommyn* 1540. 'The grey-green ridge'.

Glasgow Glas. *Glasgu* 1136. 'Green hollow'. British **glas-* + **cau*.

Glashaboy (*Glaise Buí*) Cork. 'Yellow stream'.

Glaslough (*Glasloch*) Monaghan. *Glaslagh* 1591. 'Grey-green lake'.

Glasnevin (*Glas Naíon*) Dublin. 'Stream of the child'.

Glassavullaun (*Glas an Mhulláin*) Dublin. 'Streamlet of the small summit'.

Glassleck (*Glasleic*) Cavan. 'Grey flagstone'.

Glasson Cumbria. *Glassan* 1259. Probably a Celtic river-name containing a derivative of *glas* 'grey-green'.

Glasson Lancs. *Glassene* c.1265. Perhaps originally a river-name meaning 'clear or bright one' from OE **glæsne* or **glæsen*.

Glassonby Cumbria. *Glassanebi* 1177. 'Farmstead or village of a man called Glassán'. OIrish pers. name + OScand. *bý*.

Glasthule (*Glas Tuathail*) Dublin. 'Tuathal's streamlet'.

Glaston Rutland. *Gladestone* 1086 (DB). Probably 'farmstead of a man called **Glathr*'. OScand. pers. name + OE *tūn*.

Glastonbury Somerset. *Glastingburi* 725, *Glæstingeberia* 1086 (DB). 'Stronghold of the people living at *Glaston*'. Celtic name (possibly meaning 'woad place') + OE *-inga-* + *burh* (dative *byrig*).

Glastry (*Glasrach*) Down. *Balliglassarie* 1604. 'Green grassy place'.

Glatton Cambs. *Glatune* 1086 (DB). 'Pleasant farmstead'. OE *glæd* + *tūn*.

Glazebrook Ches. *Glasbroc* 1227. Named from Glaze Brook, a Celtic river-name (meaning 'grey-green') + OE *brōc*.

Glazebury Ches., a late name of recent origin formed from GLAZEBROOK.

Glazeley Shrops. *Gleslei* 1086 (DB), *Glasele* 1255. Possibly 'bright clearing', OE **glæs* + *lēah*. Alternatively the first element may be a lost stream-name from OE *glæs* 'glass'.

Gleadless S. Yorks. *Gledeleys* 13th cent. Probably 'woodland clearings frequented by kites'. OE *gleoda* + *lēah*.

Gleaston Cumbria. *Glassertun* |*sic*| 1086 (DB), *Gleseton* 1269. Probably 'bright farmstead or village'. OE **glæs* + *tūn*. The first element may be used as a stream-name 'the bright one'.

Glemham, Great & *Glemham, Little* Suffolk. *Glaimham* 1086 (DB). Probably 'homestead or village noted for its revelry or games'. OE *glēam* + *hām*.

Glemsford Suffolk. *Glemesford* c.1050, *Clamesforda* |*sic*| 1086 (DB). Probably 'ford where people assemble for revelry or games'. OE *glēam* + *ford*.

Glen (*Gleann*) Cavan, Kilkenny, Waterford. 'Valley'.

Glen Affric Highland. 'Valley of the River Affric'. Gaelic *gleann*. The river name means 'very dappled' (Gaelic *ath* + *breac*).

Glen Parva & *Great Glen* Leics. *Glenne* 849, *Glen* 1086 (DB), *Parva Glen* 1242, *Magna Glen* 1247. '(Place at) the valley'. OE **glenn* (from Celtic **glinn*). Distinguishing affixes are Latin *parva* 'small' and *magna* 'great'.

Glen of Imail (*Gleann Ó Maoil*) Wicklow. 'Valley of Uí Maoil'.

Glenade (*Gleann Éada*) Sligo. 'Éada's valley'.

Glenageary (*Gleann na gCaorach*) Dublin. 'Valley of the sheep'.

Glenagowr (*Gleann na nGabhar*) Limerick. 'Valley of the goats'.

Glenamaddy (*Gleann na Madadh*) Roscommon. 'Valley of the dogs'.

Glenamoy (*Gleann na Muaidhe*) Mayo. 'Valley of the (river) Moy'.

Glenanne (*Gleann Anna*) Armagh. *Glen Anne* 1828. 'Anne's valley'. The name was originally that of the house owned by George Gray, who named it after his wife, Eliza Anne, née Henry.

Glenard (*Gleann Aird*) Antrim. 'High valley'.

Glenariff (*Gleann Aireamh*) Antrim. *Glenarthac* 1279. 'Valley of arable land'.

Glenarm (*Gleann Arma*) Antrim. 'Valley of arms'.

Glenasmole (*Gleann na Smól*) Dublin. 'Valley of the thrushes'.

Glenavy (*Lann Abhaigh*) Antrim. (*o*) *Lainn abhaich* c.1450. 'Church of the dwarf'. According to legend, St Patrick built a church here and left it in charge of his disciple Daniel, nicknamed 'dwarf' for his small size.

Glenbeg (*Gleann Beag*) Cork. 'Small valley'.

Glenbeigh (*Gleann Beithe*) Kerry. 'Valley of the birch'.

Glenboy (*Gleann Buí*) Sligo. 'Yellow valley'.

Glenbryan (*Gleann Bhriain*) Wexford. 'Brian's valley'.

Glenbush (*Gleann na Buaise*) Antrim. 'Valley of the (river) Bush'.

Glencairn (*Gleann an Chairn*) Waterford. 'Valley of the cairn'. The current Irish name is *Baile an Gharráin*, as for BALLINGARRANE.

Glencar (*Gleann an Chairthe*) Kerry, Sligo. 'Valley of the standing stone'.

Glencoe Highland. *Glenchomure* 1343, *Glencole* 1491. 'Valley of the River Coe'. Gaelic *gleann*. The meaning of the river name is unknown.

Glencolumbkille (*Gleann Cholm Cille*) Donegal. *Glend Colaim Cilli* 1532. 'Valley of Colm Cille'.

Glencovet (*Gleann Coimheada*) Donegal. 'Valley of the lookout post'.

Glencullen (*Gleann Cuilinn*) Dublin. 'Valley of holly'.

Glendalough (*Gleann dá Loch*) Wicklow. 'Valley of two lakes'.

Glendavagh (*Gleann dá Mhaighe*) Tyrone. 'Valley of two plains'.

Glenderry (*Gleann Doire*) Kerry. 'Valley of the oak grove'.

Glendowan (*Gleann Domhain*) (district) Donegal. 'Deep valley'.

Glenduff (*Gleann Dubh*) Cork. 'Black valley'.

Glendun (*Gleann Doinne*) (valley) Antrim. *Glendun* 1832. 'Valley of the (river) Dun'.

Gleneagles Perth. *Gleninglese* c.1165, *Glenegas* 1508. Gaelic *gleann* + unknown second element.

Gleneany (*Gleann Eidneach*) Donegal. 'Valley of the river abounding in ivy'.

Gleneask (*Gleann Iasc*) Sligo. 'Fish valley'.

Gleneely (*Gleann Daoile*) Donegal. (*a*) *nGleann Daoile* c.1630. 'Valley of the (river) Daoil'.

Glenelg Highland. *Glenelg* 1292. Gaelic *Gleann Eilge*. Obscure. *Cp.* ELGIN.

Glenfarne (*Gleann Fearna*) Leitrim, Sligo. 'Valley of alders'.

Glenfield Leics. *Clanefelde* 1086 (DB). 'Clean open land', i.e. 'open land free from weeds or other unwanted growth'. OE *clǣne* + *feld*.

Glenflesk (*Gleann Fleisce*) Kerry. 'Valley of the hoop'.

Glengarriff (*Gleann Garbh*) Cork. 'Rough valley'.

Glengesh (*Gleann Gheise*) Donegal. *Glengeish* c.1655. 'Valley of the taboo'.

Glengevlin (*Gleann Gaibhle*) Cavan. 'Gaibhle's valley'.

Glenhull (*Gleann Choll*) Tyrone. 'Valley of hazels'.

Glenmalure (*Gleann Molúra*) Wicklow. 'Molúra's valley'.

Glenmore (*Gleann Mór*) Kerry, Kilkenny. 'Big valley'.

Glennageragh (*Gleann na gCaorach*) Tyrone. 'Valley of the sheep'.

Glennamaddy (*Gleann na Madadh*) Galway. 'Valley of the dogs'.

Glennascaul (*Gleann an Scáil*) Galway. 'Valley of the phantom'.

Glennawoo (*Gleann na bhFuath*) Sligo. 'Valley of the spectres'.

Glenoe (*Gleann Ó*) Antrim. *Glenoe* 1833. 'Valley of the lump'.

Glenone (*Cluain Eoghain*) Derry. *Cloynon* 1654. 'Eoghan's pasture'.

Glenquin (*Gleann an Chuin*) Limerick. 'Valley of the hollow'.

Glenroe (*An Gleann Rua*) Limerick. 'The red valley'.

Glenrothes Fife. 'Valley of Rothes'. Glenrothes was designated a New Town in 1948 and named after the earl of Rothes, the local laird.

Glensmoil (*Gleann an Smóil*) Donegal. 'Valley of the thrush'.

Glensooska (*Gleann Samhaisce*) Kerry. 'Valley of the heifer'.

Glentane (*Gleanntán*) Galway. 'Little valley'.

Glentham Lincs. *Glentham* 1086 (DB). 'Homestead frequented by birds of prey or at a look-out place'. OE **glente* + *hām*.

Glenties (*Na Gleannta*) Donegal. *Na Gleanntaidh* 1835. 'The valleys'.

Glentogher (*Gleann Tóchair*) Donegal. *ye causeway of Clantogher* c.1655. 'Valley of the causeway'.

Glentworth Lincs. *Glentewrde* 1086 (DB). 'Enclosure frequented by birds of prey or at a look-out place'. OE **glente* + *worth*.

Glenvar (*Gleann Bhairr*) Donegal. *Glinvar* 1796. 'Valley of the top'.

Glenwherry (*Gleann an Choire*) Antrim. 'Valley of the cauldron'.

Glin (*An Gleann*) Limerick. 'The valley'.

Glinton Cambs. *Clinton* 1060, *Glintone* 1086 (DB). Possibly 'fenced farmstead'. OE **glind* + *tūn*.

Glooston Leics. *Glorstone* 1086 (DB). 'Farmstead of a man called Glōr'. OE pers. name + *tūn*.

Glossop Derbys. *Glosop* 1086 (DB), *Glotsop* 1219. 'Valley of a man called **Glott*'. OE pers. name + *hop*.

Gloucester Glos. *Coloniae Glev'* 2nd cent., *Glowecestre* 1086 (DB). 'Roman town called *Glevum*'. Celtic name (meaning 'bright place') + OE *ceaster*. The early form contains Latin *colonia* 'Roman colony for retired legionaries'. **Gloucestershire** (OE *scīr* 'district') is first referred to in the 11th cent.

Glounthaune (*An Gleanntán*) Cork. 'The small valley'.

Glusburn N. Yorks. *Glusebrun* 1086 (DB). '(Place at) the bright or shining stream'. OScand. **glus(s)* + *brunnr*.

Glympton Oxon. *Glimtuna* c.1050, *Glintone* 1086 (DB). 'Farmstead on the River Glyme'. Celtic river-name (meaning 'bright stream') + OE *tūn*.

Glyn Ceiriog Wrex. *Lansanfreit* 1291, *llansanffraid y glyn* 1590, *ll.sain ffred glyn Kerioc* 1566, *Lansantffraid Glynn Ceiriog* 1795, *Llansaintffraid-Glyn-Ceiriog* 1868. 'Valley of the River Ceiriog'. For the river name, *see* CHIRK. The formal name of the village is *Llansanffraid Glynceiriog*. *Cp.* LLANSANFFRAID GLAN CONWY.

Glyn-neath (*Glyn-nedd*) Neat. *Glynneth* 1281, *Glyn Nedd* 15th cent. 'Valley of the River Neath'. Welsh *glyn*. For the river name, *see* NEATH.

Glyn-nedd. *See* GLYN-NEATH.

Glynde E. Sussex. *Glinda* 1165. '(Place at) the fence or enclosure'. OE **glind*.

Glyndebourne E. Sussex. *Burne juxta Glynde* 1288. 'Stream near GLYNDE'. OE *burna*.

Glynebwy. *See* EBBW VALE.

Glynn (*Gleann*) Antrim, Carlow, Wexford. 'Valley'.

Gneevgullia (*Gníomh go Leith*) Kerry. 'A gneeve and a half'. A gneeve is a land measure equal to one-twelfth of a ploughland.

Gnosall Staffs. *Geneshale* |sic| 1086 (DB), *Gnowesala* 1140. OE *halh* 'nook of land' with an uncertain first element, probably an OE or OScand. pers. name.

Goadby, 'farmstead or village of a man called Gauti', OScand. pers. name + *bý*: **Goadby** Leics. *Goutebi* 1086 (DB). **Goadby Marwood** Leics. *Goutebi* 1086 (DB). Manorial affix from the Maureward family, here in the 14th cent.

Goathill Dorset. *Gatelme* |sic| 1086 (DB), *Gathulla* 1176. 'Hill where goats are pastured'. OE *gāt* + *hyll*.

Goathland N. Yorks. *Godelandia* c.1110. 'Cultivated land of a man called Gōda', or 'good cultivated land'. OE pers. name or OE *gōd* + *land*.

Goathurst Somerset. *Gahers* |sic| 1086 (DB), *Gothurste* 1292. 'Wooded hill where goats are kept'. OE *gāt* + *hyrst*.

Gobbins, The (*Na Gobáin*) (cliffs) Antrim. *the Gabbon* 1683. 'The peaks'.

Godalming Surrey. *Godelmingum* c.880, *Godelminge* 1086 (DB). '(Settlement of) the family or followers of a man called **Godhelm*'. OE pers. name + *-ingas*.

Goddington Gtr. London. *Godinton* 1240. 'Estate associated with a man called Gōda'. OE pers. name + *-ing-* + *tūn*.

Godmanchester Cambs. *Godmundcestre* 1086 (DB). 'Roman station associated with a man called Godmund'. OE pers. name + *ceaster*.

Godmanstone Dorset. *Godemanestone* 1166. 'Farmstead of a man called Godmann'. OE pers. name + *tūn*.

Godmersham Kent. *Godmeresham* 822, *Gomersham* 1086 (DB). 'Homestead or village of a man called Godmǣr'. OE pers. name + *hām*.

Godney Somerset. *Godeneia* 10th cent. 'Island or well-watered land of a man called Gōda'. OE pers. name (genitive *-n*) + *ēg*.

Godolphin Cross Cornwall. *Wulgholgan* 1194. An obscure name, origin and meaning uncertain.

Godshill, 'hill associated with a heathen god or with the Christian God', OE *god* + *hyll*: **Godshill** Hants. *Godeshull* 1230. **Godshill** I. of Wight. *Godeshella* 12th cent.

Godstone Surrey. *Godeston* 1248, *Codeston* 1279. Probably 'farmstead of a man called **Cōd*'. OE pers. name + *tūn*.

Gola (*Gabhla*) (island) Donegal. *Goolagh* 1614. 'Place of the fork'.

Golborne Gtr. Manch. *Goldeburn* 1187. 'Stream where marsh marigolds grow'. OE *golde* + *burna*.

Golcar W. Yorks. *Gudlagesarc* 1086 (DB). 'Shieling or hill-pasture of a man called Guthleikr or Guthlaugr'. OScand. pers. name + *erg*.

Golden (*An Gabhailín*) Tipperary. 'The little fork'.

Goldhanger Essex. *Goldhangra* 1086 (DB). Probably 'wooded slope where marigolds or other yellow flowers grow'. OE *golde* + *hangra*.

Golding Shrops. *Goldene* 1086 (DB). 'Gold valley', referring to yellow flowers or to soil colour. OE *gold* + *denu*.

Goldsborough N. Yorks., near Knaresborough. *Godenesburg* |sic| 1086 (DB), *Godelesburc* 1170. 'Stronghold of a man called Godel'. OE (or OGerman) pers. name + *burh*.

Goldthorpe S. Yorks. *Goldetorp* 1086 (DB). 'Outlying farmstead or hamlet of a man called Golda'. OE pers. name + OScand. *thorp*.

Goleen (*An Góilín*) Cork. 'The inlet'.

Golspie Highland. *Goldespy* 1330. Probably 'Gold's farm'. OScand. pers. name + *bý*.

Gomeldon Wilts. *Gomeledona* 1189. 'Hill of a man called **Gumela*'. OE pers. name + *dūn*.

Gomersal W. Yorks. *Gomershale* 1086 (DB). 'Nook of land of a man called **Gūthmǣr*'. OE pers. name + *halh*.

Gomshall Surrey. *Gomeselle* |sic| 1086 (DB), *Gumeselva* 1168. 'Shelf or terrace of land of a man called **Guma*'. OE pers. name + *scelf*.

Gonalston Notts. *Gunnulvestune* 1086 (DB). 'Farmstead of a man called Gunnulf'. OScand. pers. name + OE *tūn*.

Gonerby, Great Lincs. *Gunfordebi* 1086 (DB). 'Farmstead or village of a man called Gunnfrøthr'. OScand. pers. name + *bý*.

Good Easter Essex, *see* EASTER.

Gooderstone Norfolk. *Godestuna* |sic| 1086 (DB), *Gutherestone* 1254. 'Farmstead of a man called Gūthhere'. OE pers. name + *tūn*.

Goodleigh Devon. *Godelege* 1086 (DB). 'Woodland clearing of a man called Gōda'. OE pers. name + *lēah*.

Goodmanham E. R. Yorks. *Godmunddingaham* 731, *Gudmundham* 1086 (DB). 'Homestead of the family or followers of a man called Gōdmund'. OE pers. name + *-inga-* + *hām*.

Goodmayes Gtr. London. *Goodmayes* 1456. Named from the Godemay family who had lands here in the 14th cent.

Goodnestone, 'farmstead of a man called Gōdwine', OE pers. name + *tūn*: **Goodnestone** Kent, near Aylesham. *Godwineston* 1196. **Goodnestone** Kent, near Faversham. *Godwineston*.

Goodrich Heref. & Worcs. *Castellum Godric* 1102. Originally 'castle of a man called Gōdrīc'. OE pers. name (that of a land-holder in 1086 (DB)) with Latin *castellum*.

Goodrington Devon. *Godrintone* 1086 (DB). 'Estate associated with a man called Gōdhere'. OE pers. name + *-ing-* + *tūn*.

Goodworth Clatford Hants., *see* CLATFORD.

Goole E. R. Yorks. *Gulle* 1362. 'The stream or channel'. ME *goule*.

Goosey Oxon. *Goseie* 9th cent., *Gosei* 1086 (DB). 'Goose island'. OE *gōs* + *ēg*.

Goosnargh Lancs. *Gusansarghe* 1086 (DB). 'Shieling or hill-pasture of a man called Gussān'. OIrish pers. name + OScand. *erg*.

Gordano (old district) N. Som., *see* CLAPTON IN GORDANO.

Gordonstoun Moray. 'Gordon's estate'. ME *toun*. The estate was acquired in 1638 by Sir Robert *Gordon*.

Gore Kent. *Gore* 1198. '(Place at) the triangular plot of ground'. OE *gāra*. The same name occurs in other counties.

Gorey (*Guaire*) Wexford. 'Sandbank'.

Goring, '(settlement of) the family or followers of a man called *Gāra*', OE pers. name + *-ingas*: **Goring** Oxon. *Garinges* 1086 (DB). **Goring by Sea** W. Sussex. *Garinges* 1086 (DB).

Gorleston on Sea Norfolk. *Gorlestuna* 1086 (DB). Probably 'farmstead of a man called *Gurl*'. OE pers. name + *tūn*.

Gorran Cornwall. *Sanctus Goranus* 1086 (DB). '(Church of) St Goran'. From the partron saint of the church.

Gorseinon Swan. 'Eynon's marsh'. Welsh *cors*. The identity of the named man is unknown.

Gorsley Glos. *Gorstley* 1228. 'Woodland clearing where gorse grows'. OE *gorst* + *lēah*.

Gort (*Gort*) Galway. 'Tilled field'.

Gortaclare (*Gort an Chláir*) Tyrone. *Gortclare* 1620. 'Tilled field of the plain'.

Gortahill (*Gort an Choill*) Cavan. 'Tilled field of the wood'.

Gortamullin (*Gort an Mhuilinn*) Kerry. 'Tilled field of the mill'.

Gortanear (*Gort an Fhéir*) Westmeath. 'Garden of the grass'.

Gortarevan (*Gort an Riabháin*) Offaly. 'Tilled field of the little stripe'.

Gortatlea (*Gort an tSléibhe*) Kerry. 'Tilled field of the mountain'.

Gortavalla (*Gort an Bhaile*) Limerick. 'Tilled field of the homestead'.

Gortavilly (*Gort an Bhile*) Tyrone. 'Tilled field of the sacred tree'.

Gortavoy (*Gort an Bheathaigh*) Tyrone. *Gortavaghy* 1666. 'Tilled field of the cow'.

Gorteen (*Goirtín*) Galway, Sligo, Waterford, etc. 'Little tilled field'.

Gorteeny (*Goirtíní*) Galway. 'Little tilled fields'.

Gorticastle (*Gort an Chaisil*) Tyrone. *Gorte-Castell* 1666. 'Tilled field of the stone fort'.

Gortin (*Goirtín*) Tyrone. *Goirtín* c.1613. 'Little tilled field'.

Gortinagin (*Gortín na gCeann*) Tyrone. 'Tilled field of the heads'.

Gortinure (*Gort an Iuir*) Derry. 'Field of the yew'.

Gortmore (*Gort Mhór*) Tipperary. 'Large tilled field'.

Gortnagappul (*Gort na gCapall*) Clare, Kerry. 'Field of the horses'.

Gortnagoyne (*Gort na gCadhan*) Galway, Roscommon. 'Field of the ducks'.

Gortnagrour (*Gort na gCreabhar*) Limerick. 'Field of the woodcock'.

Gortnahaha (*Gort na hÁithe*) Clare, Tipperary. 'Field of the kiln'.

Gortnahoe (*Gort na hUamha*) Tipperary. 'Tilled field of the cave'.

Gortnahoimna (*Gort na hOmna*) Cavan. 'Field of the oak'.

Gortnahoo (*Gort na hUamha*) Tipperary. 'Tilled field of the cave'.

Gortnananny (*Gort an Eanaigh*) Galway. 'Field of the marsh'.

Gortnavea (*Gort na bhFiadh*) Galway. 'Field of the deer'.

Gortnaveigh (*Gort na bhFiadh*) Tipperary. 'Field of the deer'.

Gorton Gtr. Manch. *Gorton* 1282. 'Dirty farmstead'. OE *gor* + *tūn*.

Gortreagh (*Gort Riabhach*) Tyrone. *Gortreagh* c.1655. 'Striped field'.

Gortymadden (*Gort Uí Mhadaín*) Galway. 'Ó Madaín's tilled field'.

Gorvagh (*Garbhach*) Sligo. 'Rough place'.

Gosbeck Suffolk. *Gosebech* 1179. 'Stream frequented by geese'. OE *gōs* + OScand. *bekkr*.

Gosberton Lincs. *Gosebertechirche* 1086 (DB). 'Church of a man called Gosbert'. OGerman pers. name + OE *cirice* (replaced by *tūn* 'village').

Gosfield Essex. *Gosfeld* 1198. 'Open land frequented by (wild) geese'. OE *gōs* + *feld*.

Gosford, 'ford frequented by geese', OE *gōs* + *ford*; for example **Gosford** Devon. *Goseford* 1249.

Gosforth, 'ford frequented by geese', OE *gōs* + *ford*; **Gosforth** Cumbria. *Goseford* c.1150. **Gosforth** Tyne & Wear. *Goseford* 1166.

Gosport Hants. *Goseport* 1250. 'Market town where geese are sold'. OE *gōs* + *port*.

Goswick Northum. *Gossewic* 1202. 'Farm where geese are kept'. OE *gōs* + *wīc*.

Gotham Notts. *Gatham* 1086 (DB). 'Homestead or enclosure where goats are kept'. OE *gāt* + *hām* or *hamm*.

Gotherington Glos. *Godrinton* 1086 (DB). 'Estate associated with a man called Gūthhere'. OE pers. name + *-ing-* + *tūn*.

Goudhurst Kent. *Guithyrste* 11th cent. Probably 'wooded hill of a man called Gūtha'. OE pers. name + *hyrst*.

Gougane Barra (*Guagán Barra*) Cork. 'Mountain recess of Barra'.

Goulceby Lincs. *Colchesbi* 1086 (DB). 'Farmstead or village of a man called *Kolkr*'. OScand. pers. name + *bý*.

Gourock Invclyd. *Ouir et Nether Gowrockis* 1661. '(Place by the) rounded hillock'. Gaelic *guireag*.

Govan Glas. *Gvuan c.*1150. Meaning not known.

Gowdall E. R. Yorks. *Goldale* 12th cent. 'Nook of land where marigolds grow'. OE *golde* + *halh*.

Gower (*Gŵyr*) (peninsula) Swan. 'Curved (promontory)'. Welsh *gŵyr*.

Gowerton (*Tre-gŵyr*) Swan. 'Town of the Gower (peninsula)'. *See* GOWER. OE *tūn* (Welsh *tref*).

Gowlane (*Gabhlán*) Kerry. 'Fork'.

Gowlaun (*Gabhlán*) Galway. 'Fork'.

Gowna, Lough (*Loch Gamhna*) Cavan. 'Lake of the calf'.

Gowran (*Gabhrán*) Kerry. '(Pass of) Gobhrán'.

Goxhill, probably from OScand. **gausli* '(place at) the gushing spring': **Goxhill** E. R. Yorks. *Golse |sic|* 1086 (DB), *Gosla, Gousele* 12th cent. **Goxhill** N. Lincs. *Golse |sic|* 1086 (DB), *Gousle, Gousel* 12th cent.

Gracehill Antrim. 'Hill of grace'. *Gracehill* 1835. The village was founded by the Moravians in 1756. Its Irish name is *Baile Uí Chinnéide*, 'homestead of Ó Cinnéide'.

Graffham W. Sussex. *Grafham* 1086 (DB). 'Homestead or enclosure in or by a grove'. OE *grāf* + *hām* or *hamm*.

Grafham Cambs. *Grafham* 1086 (DB). Identical in origin with the previous name.

Grafton, a common name, usually 'farmstead in or by a grove', OE *grāf* + *tūn*; examples include: **Grafton** Heref. & Worcs., near Hereford. *Crafton* 1303. **Grafton** N. Yorks. *Graftune* 1086 (DB). **Grafton** Oxon. *Graptone |sic|* 1086 (DB), *Graftona* 1130. **Grafton, East** & **Grafton, West** Wilts. *Graftone* 1086 (DB). **Grafton Flyford** Heref. & Worcs. *Graftun* 9th cent., *Garstune |sic|* 1086 (DB). Affix from the nearby FLYFORD FLAVELL. **Grafton Regis** Northants. *Grastone |sic|* 1086 (DB), *Graftone* 12th cent. Latin affix *regis* 'of the king' because it was a royal manor. **Grafton Underwood** Northants. *Grastone |sic|* 1086 (DB), *Grafton Underwode* 1367. Affix 'under or near the wood' (OE *under* + *wudu*) refers to Rockingham Forest.
However the following has a different origin: **Grafton, Temple** Warwicks. *Greftone* 10th cent., *Grastone |sic|* 1086 (DB), *Temple Grafton* 1363. 'Farmstead by the pit or trench'. OE *græf* + *tūn*. Affix refers to early possession by the Knights Templars or Hospitallers.

Grageen (*Gráigín*) Wexford. 'Little hamlet'.

Graig (*Gráig*) Cork, Galway, Limerick, Tyrone. 'Hamlet'.

Graigeen (*Gráigín*) Limerick. 'Little hamlet'.

Graignagower (*Gráig na nGabhar*) Kerry. 'Hamlet of the goats'.

Graigue (*Gráig*) Cork, Galway, Sligo, Tipperary. 'Hamlet'.

Graiguecullen (*Gráig Cguillin*) Carlow. 'Hamlet of the steep slope'.

Graiguenamanagh (*Gráig na Manach*) Kerry. 'Hamlet of the monks'.

Grain Kent. *Grean c.*1100. 'Gravelly, sandy ground'. OE **grēon*. **Isle of Grain** (formerly an actual island) is *Ile of Greane* 1610.

Grainsby Lincs. *Grenesbi* 1086 (DB). Probably 'farmstead or village of a man called Grein'. OScand. pers. name + *bý*.

Grainthorpe Lincs. *Germund(s)torp* 1086 (DB). 'Outlying farmstead of a man called Geirmundr or Germund'. OScand. or OGerman pers. name + OScand. *thorp*.

Grampians (mountains) Aber, Highland, Perth. Meaning uncertain. Claimed by some to be the *Mons Grampiles* of the Romans.

Grampound Cornwall. *Grauntpount* 1302. '(Place at) the great bridge'. OFrench *grant* + *pont*.

Granagh (*Greanach*) Limerick. 'Gravelly place'.

Granborough Bucks. *Greneborge c.*1060, *Grenesberga |sic|* 1086 (DB). 'Green hill'. OE *grēne* + *beorg*.

Granby Notts. *Granebi* 1086 (DB). 'Farmstead or village of a man called Grani'. OScand. pers. name + *bý*.

Graney (*Greanach*) Kildare. 'Gravelly place'.

Grange, usually 'outlying farm belonging to a religious house', ME *grange*; examples include: **Grange** Cumbria, near Keswick. *The Grange* 1576. Belonged to the monks of Furness Abbey. **Grange-over-Sands** Cumbria. *Grange* 1491. Belonged to Cartmel Priory, affix meaning 'across the sands of Morecambe Bay'.
However the following has a different origin: **Grange** Kent. *Grenic c.*1100. Probably identical in origin and meaning with GREENWICH.

Grange (*Gráinseach*) Cavan, Dublin, Galway, etc. 'Monastic grange'.

Grangecon (*Gráinseach Coinn*) Wicklow. 'Conn's grange'.

Grangemouth Falk. 'Mouth of the Grange Burn'. OE *mutha*. The river is named from the grange of Newbattle Abbey.

Grangetown Red. & Cleve., 19th cent. iron and steel town, named from nearby ESTON Grange which belonged to Fountains Abbey (for *grange* see previous name).

Grangicam (*Gráinseach Cam*) Down. 'Crooked grange'.

Gransden, Great & *Gransden, Little* Cambs. *Grantandene* 973, *Grante(s)dene* 1086 (DB). 'Valley of a man called **Granta* or **Grante*'. OE pers. name + *denu*.

Gransha (*Gráinseach*) Donegal, Down, etc. 'Monastic grange'.

Gransmoor E. R. Yorks. *Grentesmor* 1086 (DB). 'Marshland of a man called **Grante* or **Grentir*'. OE or OScand. pers. name + OE *mōr* or OScand. *mōr*.

Granston (*Treopert*) Pemb. *Villa Grandi* 1291, *Grandiston* 1535. 'Grand's farm'. French pers. name + OE *tūn*. The Welsh name means 'Robert's farm' (French pers. name + Welsh *tref*).

Grantchester Cambs. *Granteseta* 1086 (DB). 'Settlers on the River Granta'. Celtic river-name (etymology obscure) + OE *sǣte*.

Grantham Lincs. *Grantham* 1086 (DB). Probably 'homestead or village of a man called **Granta*'. OE pers. name + *hām*. Alternatively the first element may be OE **grand* 'gravel'.

Grantley, High N. Yorks. *Grantelege* c.1030, *Grentelai* 1086 (DB). 'Woodland clearing of a man called *Granta or *Grante'. OE pers. name + *lēah*.

Granton Edin. *Grendun* c.1200. 'Farm built on gravel'. OE *grand* + *tūn*.

Grantown-on-Spey Highland. 'Grant's town on the River Spey'. The town arose as a model village planned by James *Grant* in 1765. The river has a pre-Celtic name of unknown meaning.

Grappenhall Ches. *Gropenhale* 1086 (DB). 'Nook of land at a ditch or drain'. OE **grōpe* (genitive *-an*) + *halh*.

Grasby Lincs. *Gros(e)bi* 1086 (DB). Possibly 'farmstead or village on gravelly ground'. OScand. *grjót* + *bý*.

Grasmere Cumbria. *Gressemere* 1245. Probably 'mere called grass lake'. OE *gres* + *sǣ* 'lake' with explanatory *mere*.

Grassendale Mersey. *Gresyndale* 13th cent. 'Grassy valley', or 'valley used for grazing'. OE **gærsen* or **gærsing* + *dæl* or OScand. *dalr*.

Grassholm (island) Pemb. *Insula Grasholm* 15th cent. 'Grassy island'. OScand. *gras* + *holmr*.

Grassington N. Yorks. *Ghersintone* 1086 (DB). 'Grazing or pasture farm'. OE **gærsing* + *tūn*.

Grassthorpe Notts. *Grestorp* 1086 (DB). 'Grass farmstead or hamlet'. OScand. *gres* + *thorp*.

Grately Hants. *Greatteleiam* 929. 'Great wood or clearing'. OE *grēat* + *lēah*.

Gratwich Staffs. *Crotewiche* |sic| 1086 (DB), *Grotewic* 1176. '(Dairy) farm by the gravelly place'. OE **grēote* + *wīc*.

Graveley Herts. *Gravelai* 1086 (DB). 'Clearing by a grove or copse'. OE *grǣfe* or *grāf(a)* + *lēah*.

Gravely Cambs. *Greflea* 10th cent., *Gravelei* 1086 (DB). Possibly 'woodland clearing by the pit or trench'. OE *græf* + *lēah*. Alternatively identical in origin with the previous name.

Graveney Kent. *Grafonaea* 9th cent. '(Place at) the ditch stream'. OE **grafa* (genitive *-n*) + *ēa*.

Gravenhurst Beds. *Grauenhurst* 1086 (DB). 'Wooded hill with a coppice or a ditch'. OE *grāfa* or **grafa* (genitive *-n*) + *hyrst*.

Gravesend Kent. *Gravesham* |sic| 1086 (DB), *Grauessend* 1157. '(Place at) the end of the grove or copse'. OE *grāf* + *ende*.

Grayingham Lincs. *Graingeham* 1086 (DB). 'Homestead of the family or followers of a man called *Grǣg(a)'. OE pers. name + *-inga-* + *hām*.

Grayrigg Cumbria. *Grarigg* 12th cent. 'Grey ridge'. OScand. *grár* + *hryggr*.

Grays Essex. *Turruc* 1086 (DB), *Turrokgreys* 1248. Originally Grays THURROCK, with manorial affix from the de Grai family, here in the 12th cent.

Grayshott Hants. *Grauesseta* 1185. 'Corner of land near a grove'. OE *grāf* + *scēat*.

Grazeley Berks. *Grǣgsole* c.950. Probably 'wolves' wallowing-place'. OE **grǣg* + *sol*.

Greasbrough S. Yorks. *Gersebroc* 1086 (DB). Probably 'grassy brook'. OE *gærs*, **gærsen* + *brōc*.

Greasby Mersey. *Gravesberie* 1086 (DB), *Grauisby* c.1100. 'Stronghold at a grove or copse'. OE *grǣfe* + *burh* (dative *byrig*) (replaced by OScand. *bý* 'farmstead').

Greasley Notts. *Griseleia* 1086 (DB). OE *lēah* 'wood or woodland clearing' with an uncertain first element, possibly OE *grēosn* 'gravel'.

Great as affix, *see* main name, e.g. for **Great Abington** (Cambs.) *see* ABINGTON.

Great Cumbrae. *See* CUMBRAE.

Greatford Lincs. *Greteford* 1086 (DB). 'Gravelly ford'. OE *grēot* + *ford*.

Greatham, 'gravelly homestead or enclosure', OE *grēot* + *hām* or *hamm*: **Greatham** Hants. *Greteham* 1086 (DB). **Greatham** Hartlepl. *Gretham* 1196.

Greatstone-on-Sea Kent, a recent name, taken from a rocky headland called *Great Stone* 1801, a shoreline feature before coastal changes took place.

Greatworth Northants. *Grentevorde* |sic| 1086 (DB), *Gretteworth* 12th cent. 'Gravelly enclosure'. OE *grēot* + *worth*.

Green Hammerton N. Yorks., *see* HAMMERTON.

Greenan (*Grianán*) Antrim, Donegal, Fermanagh, etc. 'Sunny place'.

Greenan Arg (Bute). *Grenan* 1400. 'Sunny spot'. Gaelic *grianan*.

Greenane (*Grianán*) Kerry, Wicklow. 'Sunny place'.

Greenans (*Grianáin*) Donegal. 'Sunny places'.

Greenanstown (*Baile Uí Ghrianáin*) Meath. 'Homestead of Ó Grianáin'.

Greenaun (*Grianán*) Clare, Leitrim. 'Sunny place'.

Greencastle Antrim, Donegal, Down, Tyrone. 'Green castle'. The Irish name for these places varies. A 'green castle' is usually one in verdant countryside.

Greenford Gtr. London. *Grenan forda* 845, *Greneforde* 1086 (DB). '(Place at) the green ford'. OE *grēne* + *ford*.

Greenham Berks. *Greneham* 1086 (DB). 'Green enclosure or river-meadow'. OE *grēne* + *hamm*.

Greenhaugh Northum. *Le Grenehalgh* 1326. 'The green nook of land'. OE *grēne* + *halh*.

Greenhead Northum. *Le Greneheued* 1290. 'The green hill'. OE *grēne* + *hēafod*.

Greenhithe Kent. *Grenethe* 1264. 'Green landing place'. OE *grēne* + *hȳth*.

Greenhow Hill N. Yorks. *Grenehoo* 1540. 'Green mound or hill'. OE *grēne* + OScand. *haugr*, with the later addition of *hill*.

Greenlaw Sc. Bord. *Grenlawe* 1250. 'Green hill'. OE *grēne* + *hlāw*.

Greenock Invclyd. *Grenok* c.1395. 'Sunny hillock'. Gaelic *grianag*.

Greenodd Cumbria. *Green Odd* 1774. 'Green point or tongue of land'. From OScand. *oddi*.

Greenore (*An Grianfort*) Louth. 'The sunny port'.

Greens Norton Northants., *see* NORTON.

Greenstead Essex. *Grenstede* 10th cent., *Grenesteda* 1086 (DB). 'Green place' i.e. 'pasture used for grazing'. OE *grēne* + *stede*.

Greensted Essex. *Gernesteda* 1086 (DB). Identical in origin with the previous name.

Greenwich Gtr. London. *Grenewic* 964, *Grenviz* 1086 (DB). 'Green port or harbour'. OE *grēne* + *wīc*.

Greet Glos. *Grete* 12th cent. 'Gravelly place'. OE *grēote*.

Greete Shrops. *Grete* 1183. Identical in origin with the previous name.

Greetham, 'gravelly homestead or enclosure', OE *grēot* + *hām* or *hamm*: **Greetham** Lincs. *Gretham* 1086 (DB). **Greetham** Rutland. *Gretham* 1086 (DB).

Greetland W. Yorks. *Greland* |*sic*| 1086 (DB), *Greteland* 13th cent. 'Rocky cultivated land'. OScand. *grjót* + *land*.

Greinton Somerset. *Graintone* 1086 (DB). 'Farmstead of a man called *Græga*'. OE pers. name (genitive -*n*) + *tūn*.

Grenagh (*Greanach*) Cork. 'Gravelly place'.

Grendon, usually 'green hill', OE *grēne* + *dūn*: **Grendon** Northants. *Grendone* 1086 (DB). **Grendon** Warwicks. *Grendone* 1086 (DB). **Grendon Underwood** Bucks. *Grennedone* 1086 (DB). Affix means 'in or near the wood'.
  However the following has a different second element: **Grendon** Heref. & Worcs. *Grenedene* 1086 (DB). 'Green valley'. OE *grēne* + *denu*.

Gresffordd. See GRESFORD.

Gresford (*Gresffordd*) Wrex. *Gretford* |*sic*| 1086 (DB), *Gresford* 1273. 'Grassy ford'. OE *græs* + *ford*.

Gresham Norfolk. *Gressam* 1086 (DB). 'Grass homestead or enclosure'. OE *gæl* + *hām* or *hamm*.

Gresley, Castle & *Gresley, Church* Derbys. *Gresele* c.1125, *Castelgresele* 1252, *Churchegreseleye* 1363. OE *lēah* 'woodland clearing' with an uncertain first element, possibly OE *grēosn* 'gravel'. Distinguishing affixes from the former castle and the church here.

Gressenhall Norfolk. *Gressenhala* 1086 (DB). 'Grassy or gravelly nook of land'. OE *gærsen* or *grēosn* + *halh*.

Gressingham Lancs. *Ghersinctune* 1086 (DB), *Gersingeham* 1183. 'Homestead or enclosure with grazing or pasture'. OE *gærsing* + *hām* or *hamm* (replaced by *tūn* 'farmstead' in the Domesday form).

Greta (river), three examples, in Cumbria, Lancs., and N. Yorks.; an OScand. river-name recorded from the 13th cent., 'stony stream', from OScand. *grjót* + *á*.

Gretna Green Dumf. *Gretenho* 1223, *Gretenhou* c.1240, *Gratnay* 1576. 'Green by Gretna'. *Gretna* is 'gravel hill' (OE *grēota*, dative *grēotan* + *hōh*).

Gretton Glos. *Gretona* 1175. 'Farmstead near GREET'. OE *tūn*.

Gretton Northants. *Gretone* 1086 (DB). 'Gravel farmstead'. OE *grēot* + *tūn*.

Gretton Shrops. *Grotintune* 1086 (DB). 'Farmstead on gravelly ground'. OE *grēoten* + *tūn*.

Grewelthorpe N. Yorks. *Torp* 1086 (DB), *Gruelthorp* 1281. OScand. *thorp* 'outlying farmstead' with later manorial affix from a family called Gruel.

Greyabbey (*Mainistir Liath*) Down. *Monasterlech* 1193. 'Grey abbey'. The reference is to a Cistercian abbey founded here in 1193.

Greysouthen Cumbria. *Craykesuthen* c.1187. 'Rock or cliff of a man called Suthán'. Celtic *creig* + OIrish pers. name.

Greystoke Cumbria. *Creistoc* 1167. Probably 'secondary settlement by a river once called *Cray*'. Lost Celtic river-name (meaning 'fresh, clean') + OE *stoc*.

Greywell Hants. *Graiwella* 1167. Probably 'spring or stream frequented by wolves', OE *græg* + *wella*.

Grianan (*Grianán*) Donegal. 'Sunny place'.

Griff Warwicks. *Griva* 12th cent. '(Place at) the deep valley or hollow'. OScand. *gryfja*.

Griffithstown Torf. Henry *Griffiths*, the first stationmaster of Pontypool Road, founded a new settlement here c.1856.

Grimley Heref. & Worcs. *Grimanleage* 9th cent., *Grimanleh* 1086 (DB). 'Wood or glade haunted by a spectre or goblin'. OE *grīma* + *lēah*.

Grimoldby Lincs. *Grimoldbi* 1086 (DB). 'Farmstead or village of a man called Grimald'. OGerman pers. name + OScand. *bý*.

Grimsargh Lancs. *Grimesarge* 1086 (DB). 'Hill-pasture of a man called Grímr'. OScand. pers. name + *erg*.

Grimsby, 'farmstead or village of a man called Grímr', OScand. pers. name + *bý*: **Grimsby** NE. Lincs. *Grimesbi* 1086 (DB). **Grimsby, Little** Lincs. *Grimesbi* 1086 (DB).

Grimscote Northants. *Grimescote* 12th cent. 'Cottage(s) of a man called Grímr'. OScand. pers. name + OE *cot*.

Grimsetter Orkn. 'Grímr's homestead'. OScand. pers. name + *setr*.

Grimshader W. Isles (Lewis). 'Grímr's homestead'. OScand. pers. name + *setr*.

Grimstead, East & *Grimstead, West* Wilts. *Gremestede* 1086 (DB). Probably 'green homestead'. OE *grēne* + *hāmstede*.

Grimsthorpe Lincs. *Grimestorp* 1212. 'Outlying farmstead or hamlet of a man called Grímr'. OScand. pers. name + *thorp*.

Grimston, 'farmstead or estate of a man called Grímr', OScand. pers. name + OE *tūn*; examples include: **Grimston** Leics. *Grimestone* 1086 (DB). **Grimston** Norfolk. *Grimastun* c.1035, *Grimestuna* 1086 (DB). **Grimston, North** N. Yorks. *Grimeston* 1086 (DB).

Grindale E. R. Yorks. *Grendele* 1086 (DB). 'Green valley'. OE *grēne* + *dæl*.

Grindleton Lancs. *Gretlintone* 1086 (DB), *Grenlington* 1251. Probably 'farmstead near the gravelly stream'. OE *grendel* + -*ing* + *tūn*.

Grindley Staffs. *Grenleg* 1251. 'Green woodland clearing'. OE *grēne* + *lēah*.

Grindlow Derbys. *Grenlawe* 1199. 'Green hill or mound'. OE *grēne* + *hlāw*.

Grindon, 'green hill', OE *grēne* + *dūn*: **Grindon** Northum. *Grandon* 1210. **Grindon** Staffs. *Grendone* 1086 (DB).

Gringley on the Hill Notts. *Gringeleia* 1086 (DB). Possibly 'woodland clearing of the people living at the green place'. OE *grēne* + *-inga-* + *lēah*.

Grinsdale Cumbria. *Grennesdale* c.1180. Probably 'valley by the green promontory'. OE *grēne* + *næss* + OScand. *dalr*.

Grinshill Shrops. *Grivelesul* |*sic*| 1086 (DB), *Grineleshul* 1242. OE *hyll* 'hill' with an uncertain first element, possibly, a word **grynel* (genitive *-es*), a derivative of OE *grin*, *gryn* 'a snare for animals'.

Grinstead, 'green place' i.e. 'pasture used for grazing', OE *grēne* + *stede*: **Grinstead, East** W. Sussex. *Grenesteda* 1121, *Estgrenested* 1271. **Grinstead, West** W. Sussex. *Grenestede* 1086 (DB), *Westgrenested* 1280.

Grinton N. Yorks. *Grinton* 1086 (DB). 'Green farmstead'. OE *grēne* + *tūn*.

Gristhorpe N. Yorks. *Grisetorp* 1086 (DB). 'Outlying farmstead or hamlet of a man called Gríss, or where young pigs are reared'. OScand. pers. name or *gríss* + *thorp*.

Griston Norfolk. *Gristuna* 1086 (DB). Possibly 'farmstead of a man called Gríss, or where young pigs are reared'. OScand. pers. name or *gríss* + OE *tūn*. Alternatively the first element may be OE *gres* 'grass'.

Grittenham Wilts. *Gruteham* 850. 'Gravelly homestead or enclosure'. OE **grīeten* + *hām* or *hamm*.

Grittleton Wilts. *Grutelington* 940, *Gretelintone* 1086 (DB). Possibly 'estate associated with a man called **Grytel*'. OE pers. name + *-ing-* + *tūn*.

Grizebeck Cumbria. *Grisebek* 13th cent. 'Brook by which young pigs are kept'. OScand. *gríss* + *bekkr*.

Grizedale Cumbria. *Grysdale* 1336. 'Valley where young pigs are kept'. OScand. *gríss* + *dalr*.

Groby Leics. *Grobi* 1086 (DB). Probably 'farmstead near a hollow or pit'. OScand. *gróf* + *bý*.

Groeslon Gwyd. *Croes-lôn* 1838. 'Crossroads'. Welsh *croes* + *lôn*.

Grogan (*Grógán*) Laois. 'Little heap'.

Gronant Flint. *Gronant* 1086 (DB). 'Gravel brook'. Welsh *gro* + *nant*.

Groombridge Kent. *Gromenebregge* 1239. 'Bridge where young men congregate'. ME *grome* (genitive plural *-ene*) + OE *brycg*.

Groomsport (*Port an Ghiolla Ghruama*) Down. 'Port of the gloomy fellow'. *Mollerytoun* 1333. The name appears to refer to a person surnamed *Mallory*, meaning 'unhappy' (OFrench *malheure*).

Grosmont N. Yorks. *Grosmunt* 1228. Originally the name of the priory here, in turn named from the mother Priory of Grosmont in France ('big hill' from OFrench *gros* + *mont*).

Grosmont (*Y Grysmwnt*) Mon. *Grosse Monte* 1187, *Grosmont* 1232. 'Big hill'. OFrench *gros* + *mont*.

Groton Suffolk. *Grotena* 1086 (DB). Probably 'sandy or gravelly stream'. OE **groten* + *ēa*.

Grove, a common name, '(place at) the grove or copse', OE *grāf(a)*; examples include: **Grove** Notts. *Grava* 1086 (DB). **Grove** Oxon. *la Graue* 1188.

Grundisburgh Suffolk. *Grundesburch* 1086 (DB). 'Stronghold on or near the foundation of a building'. OE *grund* + *burh*.

Grutness Shet. 'Gravel promontory'. OScand. *grjót* + *nes*.

Grysmwnt, Y. *See* GROSMONT (Mon).

Guay Perth. *Guay* 1457. '(Place by the) marsh'. Gaelic *gaoth*.

Gubaveeny (*Gob an Mhianaigh*) Louth. 'Mouth of the mine'.

Gubbacrock (*Gob dhá Chnoc*) Fermanagh. 'Beak of two hills'.

Guestling E. Sussex. *Gestelinges* 1086 (DB). '(Settlement of) the family or followers of a man called **Gyrstel*'. OE pers. name + *-ingas*.

Guestwick Norfolk. *Geghestueit* 1086 (DB). 'Clearing belonging to GUIST'. OScand. *thveit*.

Guilden Morden Cambs., *see* MORDEN.

Guilden Sutton Ches., *see* SUTTON.

Guildford Surrey. *Gyldeforda* c.880, *Gildeford* 1086 (DB). Probably 'ford by the gold-coloured (i.e. sandy) hill', from OE **gylde* + *ford*, *see* HOG'S BACK.

Guileen (*Gaibhlín*) Cork. 'Little fork'.

Guilsborough Northants. *Gildesburh* c.1070, *Gisleburg* |*sic*| 1086 (DB). 'Stronghold of a man called **Gyldi*'. OE pers. name + *burh*.

Guisachan Highland. *Gulsackyn* 1221, *Guisachane* 1578. 'Pine forests'. Gaelic *guithsachan*.

Guisborough Red. & Cleve. *Ghigesburg* 1086 (DB). Probably 'stronghold of a man called Gígr'. OScand. pers. name + OE *burh*.

Guiseley W. Yorks. *Gislicleh* c.972, *Gisele* 1086 (DB). 'Woodland clearing of a man called **Gīslic*'. OE pers. name + *lēah*.

Guist Norfolk. *Gægsæte* c.1035, *Gegeseta* 1086 (DB). Possibly 'dwelling of a man called **Gæga* or **Gægi*'. OE pers. name + *sǣte*.

Guiting Power & *Temple Guiting* Glos. *Gythinge* 814, *Getinge* 1086 (DB), *Gettinges Poer* 1220, *Guttinges Templar* 1221. Originally a river-name, 'running stream, stream with a good current', OE *gyte* + *-ing*. Manorial affixes from early possession by the le Poer family and by the Knights Templars.

Guldeford, East E. Sussex. *Est Guldeford* 1517. Named from the Guldeford family (so called because they came from GUILDFORD).

Gulladoo (*Guala Dhubh*) Leitrim. 'Black shoulder'.

Gulladuff (*Guala Dubh*) Derry. *Galladow* 1609. 'Black shoulder'.

Gulval Cornwall. 'Church of *Sancta Welvela*' 1328. '(Church of) St Gwelvel'. From the patron-saint of the church.

Gumfreston Pemb. *Villa Gunfrid* 1291, *Gonnfreiston* 1364. 'Gunfrid's farm'. OGerman pers. name + OE *tūn*.

Gumley Leics. *Godmundesleah* 8th cent., *Godmundelai* 1086 (DB). 'Woodland clearing of a man called Godmund'. OE pers. name + *lēah*.

Gunby E. R. Yorks. *Gunelby* 1066–9. 'Farmstead or village of a woman called Gunnhildr'. OScand. pers. name + *bý*.

Gunby Lincs. *Gunnebi* 1086 (DB). 'Farmstead or village of a man called Gunni'. OScand. pers. name + *bý*.

Gunnersbury Gtr. London. *Gounyldebury* 1334. 'Manor house of a woman called Gunnhildr'. OScand. pers. name + ME *bury* (from OE *byrig*, dative of *burh*).

Gunnerton Northum. *Gunwarton* 1170. Probably 'farmstead of a woman called Gunnvǫr'. OScand. pers. name + OE *tūn*.

Gunness N. Lincs. *Gunnesse* 1199. 'Headland of a man called Gunni'. OScand. pers. name + *nes*.

Gunnislake Cornwall. *Gonellake* 1485. Probably 'stream of a man called Gunni'. OScand. pers. name + OE *lacu*.

Gunthorpe, usually 'outlying farmstead of a man called Gunni', OScand. pers. name + *thorp*: **Gunthorpe** Cambs. *Gunetorp* 1130. **Gunthorpe** Norfolk. *Gunestorp* 1086 (DB).
However the following has a different origin: **Gunthorpe** Notts. *Gulnetorp* 1086 (DB). 'Outlying farmstead of a woman called Gunnhildr'. OScand. pers. name + *thorp*.

Gunwalloe Cornwall. 'Chapel of *Sanctus Wynwolaus*' 1332. From the patron saint of the church or chapel, St Winwaloe.

Gurranebraher (*Garrán na mBráthar*) Cork. 'Grove of the brothers'.

Gussage All Saints & *Gussage St Michael* Dorset. *Gyssic* 10th cent., *Gessic* 1086 (DB), *Gussich All Saints* 1245, *Gussich St Michael* 1297. Probably 'gushing stream', originally the name of the river here. OE **gyse* + *sīc*. Affixes from the dedications of the churches.

Gusserane (*Ráth na gCosarán*) Wexford. 'Fort of the trampling'.

Guston Kent. *Gocistone* 1086 (DB). 'Farmstead of a man called **Gūthsige*'. OE pers. name + *tūn*.

Guyhirn Cambs. *La Gyerne* 1275. OE *hyrne* 'angle or corner of land' with OFrench *guie* 'a guide' (with reference to controlling tidal flow) or 'a salt-water ditch'.

Guyzance Northum. *Gynis* 1242. A manorial name, 'estate of the family called *Guines*'.

Gwalchmai Angl. *Trefwalkemyth* 1291, *Trefwalghmey* 1350, *Gwalghmey* 1352. '(Place of) Gwalchmai'. The name is that of the Welsh court poet *Gwalchmai* (*fl.*1130–80), whose name is said to mean 'May hawk' (Welsh *gwalch* + *Mai*). The first two forms above have Welsh *tref*, 'township'.

Gwaunysgor Flin. *Wenescol* 1086 (DB). 'Meadow by the fort'. Welsh *gwaun* + *ysgor*.

Gweebarra (*Gaoth Beara*) (district) Donegal. 'Inlet of the water'.

Gweedore (*Gaoth Dobhair*) Donegal. *Gydower al. Lower Dower* 1657. 'Inlet of the water'.

Gweek Cornwall. *Wika* 1201. Cornish **gwig* 'village' or OE *wīc* 'hamlet'.

Gweesalia (*Gaoth Sáile*) Mayo. 'Inlet of the sea'.

Gwenfô. See WENVOE.

Gwennap Cornwall. 'Church of *Sancta Wenappa*' 1269. '(Church of) St Wynup'. From the patron saint of the church.

Gwent (the historic county). 'Trading place'. British **venta*.

Gwithian Cornwall. 'Parish of *Sanctus Goythianus*' 1334. From the patron saint of the church, St Gothian.

Gwynedd (the unitary authority). 'Territory of Venedoti'. The ancient kingdom derives its name from the Venedoti tribe.

Gwyr. See GOWER.

Gyleen (*Gaibhlín*) Cork. 'Little fork'.

H

Haa Shet (Whalsay). 'Hull'. OScand. *há*.

Habblesthorpe Notts. *Happelesthorp* 1154. Probably 'outlying farmstead of a man called *Hæppel'. OE pers. name + OScand. *thorp*.

Habost W. Isles (Lewis). 'High farm'. OScand. *há hallr* + *bólstathr*.

Habrough NE. Lincs. *Haburne* |sic| 1086 (DB), *Haburg* 1202. 'High or chief stronghold'. OE *hēah* (replaced by OScand. *hár*) + *burh*.

Habton, Great N. Yorks. *Habetun* 1086 (DB). 'Farmstead of a man called *Hab(b)a'. OE pers. name + *tūn*.

Haccombe Devon. *Hacome* 1086 (DB), *Hakcumbe* c.1200. Probably 'valley with a hatch or fence'. OE *hæcc* + *cumb*.

Haceby Lincs. *Hazebi* 1086 (DB), *Hathsebi* 1115. 'Farmstead or village of a man called Haddr'. OScand. pers. name + *bý*.

Hacheston Suffolk. *Hacestuna* 1086 (DB). 'Farmstead of a man called Hæcci'. OE pers. name + *tūn*.

Hackford Norfolk, near Wymondham. *Hakeforda* 1086 (DB). 'Ford with a hatch or by a bend'. OE *hæcc* or *haca* + *ford*.

Hackforth N. Yorks. *Acheford* 1086 (DB). Identical in origin with the previous name.

Hackleton Northants. *Hachelintone* 1086 (DB). 'Estate associated with a man called *Hæccel'. OE pers. name + *-ing-* + *tūn*.

Hackness N. Yorks. *Hacanos* 731, *Hagenesse* 1086 (DB). 'Hook-shaped or projecting headland'. OE *haca* + *nose*.

Hackney Gtr. London. *Hakeneia* 1198. 'Island, or dry ground in marsh, of a man called *Haca'. OE pers. name (genitive *-n*) + *ēg*.

Hackthorn Lincs. *Hagetorne* 1086 (DB). '(Place at) the hawthorn or prickly thorn-tree'. OE *hagu-thorn* or *haca-thorn*.

Hackthorpe Cumbria. *Hakatorp* c.1150. Possibly 'outlying farmstead or hamlet of a man called Haki'. OScand. pers. name + *thorp*. Alternatively the first element may be OScand. *haki* or OE *haca* 'hook-shaped promontory'.

Haconby Lincs. *Hacunesbi* 1086 (DB). 'Farmstead or village of a man called Hákon'. OScand. pers. name + *bý*.

Haddenham, 'homestead or village of a man called Hæda', OE pers. name + *hām*: **Haddenham** Bucks. *Hedreham* |sic| 1086 (DB), *Hedenham* 1142. **Haddenham** Cambs. *Hædan ham* 970, *Hadreham* 1086 (DB).

Haddington E. Loth. *Hadynton* 1098. 'Farmstead associated with Hada'. OE pers. name + *-ing-* + *tūn*.

Haddington Lincs. *Hadinctune* 1086 (DB). 'Estate associated with a man called Headda or Hada'. OE pers. name + *-ing-* + *tūn*.

Haddiscoe Norfolk. *Hadescou* 1086 (DB). 'Wood of a man called Haddr or Haddi'. OScand. pers. name + *skógr*.

Haddlesey, Chapel & *Haddlesey, West* N. Yorks. *Hathel-sæ* c.1030, *Chappel Haddlesey* 1605, *Westhathelsay* 1280. Probably 'marshy pool in a hollow'. OE *hathel* + *sæ*. Distinguishing affixes from ME *chapel* and *west*.

Haddon, usually 'heath hill, hill where heather grows', OE *hæth* + *dūn*: **Haddon, East** & **Haddon, West** Northants. *Eddone*, *Hadone* 1086 (DB), *Esthaddon* 1220, *Westhaddon* 12th cent. **Haddon, Nether** & **Haddon, Over** Derbys. *Hadun(e)* 1086 (DB), *Nethir Haddon* 1248, *Uverehaddon* 1206. Distinguishing affixes are OE *neotherra* 'lower' and *uferra* 'higher'.
  However the following may have a different origin: **Haddon** Cambs. *Haddedun* 951, *Adone* 1086 (DB). Probably 'hill of a man called Headda'. OE pers. name + *dūn*.

Hadfield Derbys. *Hetfelt* 1086 (DB). 'Heathy open land, or open land where heather grows'. OE *hæth* + *feld*.

Hadham, Much & *Hadham, Little* Herts. *Hædham* 957, *Hadam*, *Parva Hadam* 1086 (DB), *Muchel Hadham* 1373. Probably 'heath homestead'. OE *hæth* + *hām*. Distinguishing affixes from OE *mycel* 'great' and *lytel* 'little' (Latin *parva*).

Hadleigh, *Hadley*, 'heath clearing, clearing where heather grows', OE *hæth* + *lēah*: **Hadleigh** Essex. *Hæthlege* c.1000, *Leam* |sic| 1086 (DB). **Hadleigh** Suffolk. *Hædleage* c.995, *Hetlega* 1086 (DB). **Hadley** Shrops. *Hatlege* 1086 (DB). **Hadley, Monken** Gtr. London. *Hadlegh* 1248, *Monken Hadley* 1489. Affix means 'of the monks' (from OE *munuc*) referring to early possession by Walden Abbey.

Hadlow Kent. *Haslow* |sic| 1086 (DB), *Hadlou* 1235. Probably 'mound or hill where heather grows'. OE *hæth* + *hlāw*.

Hadlow Down E. Sussex. *Hadleg* 1254. Probably 'woodland clearing where heather grows'. OE *hæth* + *lēah*.

Hadnall Shrops. *Hadehelle* |sic| 1086 (DB), *Hadenhale* 1242. 'Nook of land of a man called Headda'. OE pers. name (genitive *-n*) + *halh*.

Hadrian's Wall Cumbria–Northum.–Tyne & Wear, Roman fortification built AD 122–6, called after Roman Emperor Hadrian and giving name to WALL (Northum.), HEDDON ON THE WALL, and WALLSEND.

Hadstock Essex. *Hadestoc* 11th cent. 'Outlying farmstead of a man called Hada'. OE pers. name + *stoc*.

Hadzor Heref. & Worcs. *Hadesore* 1086 (DB). 'Ridge of a man called *Headd'. OE pers. name + *ofer*.

Hafren Forest Powys. 'Forest of the River Severn'. *See* SEVERN.

Hagbourne, East & *Hagbourne, West* Oxon. *Haccaburna* c.895, *Hacheborne* 1086 (DB). Probably '(place by) the stream of a man called *Hacca'. OE pers. name + *burna*.

Haggerston Gtr. London. *Hergotestane* 1086 (DB). 'Boundary stone of a man called Hærgod'. OE pers. name + *stān*.

Haggerston Northum. *Agardeston* 1196. Probably 'estate of a family called Hagard'. ME (from OFrench) surname + OE *tūn*.

Hagley Heref. & Worcs, near Kidderminster. *Hageleia* 1086 (DB). 'Woodland clearing where haws grow'. OE *hagga* + *lēah*.

Hagworthingham Lincs. *Hacberdingeham* |sic| 1086 (DB), *Hagwrthingham* 1198. 'Homestead of the people from the hawthorn enclosure'. OE *hagga* + *worth* + -*inga*- + *hām*.

Haigh, 'the enclosure', OScand. *hagi* or OE *haga*: **Haigh** Gtr. Manch. *Hage* 1194. **Haigh** S. Yorks. *Hagh* 1379.

Haighton Green Lancs. *Halctun* 1086 (DB). 'Farmstead in a nook of land'. OE *halh* + *tūn*.

Hail Weston Cambs., *see* WESTON.

Hailes Glos. *Heile* 1086 (DB), *Heilis* 1114. Perhaps originally the name of the stream here, a Celtic river-name possibly meaning 'dirty stream'.

Hailey, 'clearing where hay is made', OE *hēg* + *lēah*: **Hailey** Herts. *Hailet* |sic| 1086 (DB), *Heile* 1235. **Hailey** Oxon. *Haylegh* 1241.

Hailsham E. Sussex. *Hamelesham* |sic| 1086 (DB), *Helesham* 1189. 'Homestead or enclosure of a man called *Hægel'. OE pers. name + *hām* or *hamm*.

Hainford Norfolk. *Hanforda* 1086 (DB), *Heinford* 12th cent. 'Ford near an enclosure'. OE *hægen* + *ford*.

Hainton Lincs. *Haintone* 1086 (DB). 'Farmstead in an enclosure'. OE *hægen* + *tūn*.

Haisthorpe E. R. Yorks. *Ascheltorp* 1086 (DB). 'Outlying farmstead of a man called Hǫskuldr'. OScand. pers. name + *thorp*.

Halam Notts. *Healum* 958. '(Place at) the nooks or corners of land'. OE *halh* in a dative plural form *halum*.

Halberton Devon. *Halsbretone* 1086 (DB). Possibly 'farmstead by a hazel wood'. OE *hæsel* + *bearu* + *tūn*.

Halden, High Kent. *Hadinwoldungdenne* c.1100. 'Woodland pasture associated with a man called Heathuwald'. OE pers. name + -*ing*- + *denn*.

Hale, a common name, '(place at) the nook or corner of land', OE *halh* (dative *hale*); examples include: **Hale** Ches. *Halas* 1094. Originally in a plural form. **Hale** Gtr. Manch. *Hale* 1086 (DB). **Hale** Hants. *Hala* 1161. **Hale, Great** & **Hale, Little** Lincs. *Hale* 1086 (DB).

Hales, 'the nooks or corners of land', OE *halh* in a plural form: **Hales** Norfolk. *Hals* 1086 (DB). **Hales** Staffs. *Hales* 1291.

Halesowen W. Mids. *Hala* 1086 (DB), *Hales Ouweyn* 1276. 'Nooks or corners of land'. OE *halh* in a plural form, with manorial affix from the Welsh prince called Owen who held the manor in the early 13th cent.

Halesworth Suffolk. *Healesuurda* 1086 (DB). Probably 'enclosure of a man called *Hæle'. OE pers. name + *worth*.

Halewood Mersey. *Halewode* c.1200. 'Wood near HALE'. OE *wudu*.

Halford Shrops. *Hauerford* 1155, *Haleford* 1221–2. OE *ford* 'a ford' with an uncertain first element, possibly OE *halh* 'nook of land, land in a river-bend'.

Halford Warwicks. *Halchford* 12th cent. 'Ford by a nook or corner of land'. OE *halh* + *ford*.

Halifax W. Yorks. *Halyfax* c.1095. Possibly 'area of coarse grass in a nook of land'. OE *halh* + *gefeaxe*.

Halkyn (*Helygain*) Flin. *Helchene* 1086 (DB), *Helygen* 1315. 'Place of willow trees'. Welsh *helygen*.

Hallam S. Yorks. *Hallun* 1086 (DB). Possibly identical in origin with the next name, but alternatively '(place at) the rocks', from OScand. *hallr* or OE *hall* in a dative plural form *hallum*. **Hallamshire**, *Halumsira* 1161, contains OE *scīr* 'district'.

Hallam, Kirk & *Hallam, West* Derbys. *Halun* 1086 (DB), *Kyrkehallam* 12th cent., *Westhalum* 1230. '(Place at) the nooks of land'. OE *halh* in a dative plural form *halum*. Distinguishing affixes from OScand. *kirkja* 'church' and OE *west*.

Hallaton Leics. *Alctone* 1086 (DB). 'Farmstead in a nook of land or narrow valley'. OE *halh* + *tūn*.

Hallatrow B. & NE. Som. *Helgetrev* 1086 (DB). '(Place by) the holy tree'. OE *hālig* + *trēow*.

Halling Kent. *Hallingas* 8th cent., *Hallinges* 1086 (DB). '(Settlement of) the family or followers of a man called *Heall'. OE pers. name + -*ingas*.

Hallingbury, Great & *Hallingbury, Little* Essex. *Hallingeberiam* 1086 (DB). 'Stronghold of the family or followers of a man called *Heall'. OE pers. name + -*inga*- + *burh* (dative *byrig*).

Hallington Northum. *Halidene* 1247. 'Holy valley'. OE *hālig* + *denu*.

Halloughton Notts. *Healhtune* 958. 'Farmstead in a nook of land or narrow valley'. OE *halh* + *tūn*.

Hallow Heref. & Worcs. *Halhagan* 9th cent., *Halhegan* 1086 (DB). 'Enclosures in a nook or corner of land'. OE *halh* + *haga*.

Halnaker W. Sussex. *Helnache* 1086 (DB). 'Half an acre'. OE *healf* (dative -*an*) + *æcer*.

Halsall Lancs. *Heleshale* 1086 (DB). Probably 'nook of land of a man called *Hæle'. OE pers. name + *halh*.

Halse Northants. *Hasou* |sic| 1086 (DB), *Halsou* c.1160. 'Neck of land forming a ridge'. OE *hals* + *hōh*.

Halse Somerset. *Halse* 1086 (DB). '(Place at) the neck of land'. OE *hals*.

Halsham E. R. Yorks. *Halsaham* 1033, *Halsam* 1086 (DB). 'Homestead on the neck of land'. OE *hals* + *hām*.

Halstead, 'place of refuge or shelter', OE *h(e)ald* + *stede*: **Halstead** Essex. *Haltesteda* 1086 (DB). **Halstead** Kent. *Haltesteda* c.1100. **Halstead** Leics. *Elstede* 1086 (DB).

Halstock Dorset. *Halganstoke* 998. 'Outlying farmstead belonging to a religious foundation'. OE *hālig* + *stoc*.

Halstow, 'holy place', OE *hālig* + *stōw*: **Halstow, High** Kent. *Halgesto* c.1100. **Halstow, Lower** Kent. *Halgastaw* c.1100.

Haltemprice E. R. Yorks. *Hautenprise* 1324. 'High or noble enterprise'. OFrench *haut* + *emprise*, originally with reference to an Augustinian Priory founded here in 1322.

Haltham Lincs. *Holtham* 1086 (DB). 'Homestead by or in a wood'. OE *holt* + *hām*.

Halton, a common name, usually 'farmstead in a nook or corner of land', OE *halh* + *tūn*: **Halton** Bucks. *Healtun* c.1033, *Haltone* 1086 (DB). **Halton** Lancs. *Haltune* 1086 (DB). **Halton** W. Yorks. *Halletune* 1086 (DB). **Halton, East** N. Lincs. *Haltune* 1086 (DB). **Halton East** N. Yorks. *Haltone* 1086 (DB). **Halton Holegate** Lincs. *Haltun* 1086 (DB). Affix means 'road in a hollow', OScand. *holr* + *gata*. **Halton, West** N. Lincs. *Haltone* 1086 (DB). Halton West N. Yorks. *Halctun* 12th cent.
However the following have a different origin: **Halton** Ches. *Heletune* 1086 (DB), *Hethelton* 1174. Possibly 'farmstead at a heathery place'. OE **hāthel* + *tūn*. **Halton** Northum. *Haulton* 1161. Possibly 'farmstead at the look-out hill'. OE **hāw* + *hyll* + *tūn*.

Haltwhistle Northum. *Hautwisel* 1240. OE *twisla* 'junction of two streams', possibly with OFrench *haut* 'high'.

Halvergate Norfolk. *Halfriate* 1086 (DB). Possibly 'land for which a half heriot (a feudal service or payment) is due'. OE *half* + *here-geatu*.

Halwell Devon. *Halganwylle* 10th cent. 'Holy spring'. OE *hālig* + *wella*.

Halwill Devon. *Halgewilla* 1086 (DB). Identical in origin with the previous name.

Ham, a common name, from OE *hamm* which had various meanings, including 'enclosure, land hemmed in by water or higher ground, land in a river-bend'; examples include: **Ham** Glos. *Hamma* 1194. **Ham** Gtr. London. *Hama* c.1150. **Ham** Kent. *Hama* 1086 (DB). **Ham** Wilts. *Hamme* 931, *Hame* 1086 (DB). **Ham, East** & **Ham, West** Gtr. London. *Hamme* 958, *Hame* 1086 (DB), *Est Hammes* c.1250, *Westhamma* 1186. **Ham, High** Somerset. *Hamme* 973, *Hame* 1086 (DB).

Hamar Voe Shet (Yell). *Hafnarvag* 12th cent. 'Inlet of the rocky outcrop'. OScand. *hamarr* + *vágr*.

Hamble Hants. *Hamele* 1165. Named from the River Hamble on which it stands, 'crooked river', i.e. 'river with bends in it', from OE **hamel* + *ēa*.

Hambleden Bucks. *Hamelan dene* 1015, *Hanbledene* 1086 (DB). 'Crooked or undulating valley'. OE **hamel* + *denu*.

Hambledon, 'crooked or irregularly-shaped hill', OE **hamel* + *dūn*: **Hambledon** Hants. *Hamelandunæ* 956, *Hamledune* 1086 (DB). **Hambledon** Surrey. *Hameledune* 1086 (DB).

Hambleton, usually 'farmstead at the crooked hill', OE **hamel* + *tūn*: **Hambleton** Lancs. *Hameltune* 1086 (DB). **Hambleton** N. Yorks., near Selby. *Hameltun* 1086 (DB).
However the following has the same origin as

HAMBLEDON: **Hambleton, Upper** Rutland. *Hameldun* 1086 (DB).

Hambrook S. Glos. *Hanbroc* 1086 (DB). Probably 'brook by the stone'. OE *hān* + *brōc*.

Hamdon Hill Somerset, *see* NORTON SUB HAMDON, STOKE SUB HAMDON.

Hameringham Lincs. *Hameringam* 1086 (DB). Probably 'homestead of the dwellers at the cliff or steep hill'. OE *hamor* + *-inga-* + *hām*.

Hamerton Cambs. *Hambertune* 1086 (DB). 'Farmstead with a smithy', or 'farmstead where a plant such as hammer-sedge grows'. OE *hamor* + *tūn*.

Hamilton S. Lan. *Hamelton* 1291. The name may have been 'imported' here in the 13th cent. by Sir Walter de Hameldone, from *Hamilton*, Leics.; earlier name Cadzow.

Hamiltonsbawn Armagh. 'Hamilton's bawn'. *Hamilton's-Bawn* 1681. John Hamilton built a bawn or fortified mansion here in 1619. The equivalent Irish name is *Bábhún Hamaltún*.

Hammersmith Gtr. London. *Hamersmythe* 1294. '(Place with) a hammer smithy or forge'. OE *hamor* + *smiththe*.

Hammerton, Green & *Hammerton, Kirk* N. Yorks. *Hambretone* 1086 (DB), *Grenhamerton* 1176, *Kyrkehamerton* 1226. Probably identical in origin with HAMERTON (Cambs.). Distinguishing affixes from OE *grēne* 'village green' and OScand. *kirkja* 'church'.

Hammerwich Staffs. *Humeruuich* |*sic*| 1086 (DB), *Hamerwich* 1191. Probably 'building with a smithy'. OE *hamor* + *wīc*.

Hammoon Dorset. *Hame* 1086 (DB), *Hamme Moun* 1280. 'Enclosure or land in a river-bend'. OE *hamm*, with manorial affix from the Moion family which held the manor in 1086.

Hamnavoe Shet (Yell). *Hafnarvag* 12th cent. 'Inlet of the harbour'. OScand. *hafn* + *vágr*.

Hampden, Great & *Hampden, Little* Bucks. *Hamdena* 1086 (DB). Probably 'valley with an enclosure'. OE *hamm* + *denu*.

Hampnett Glos. *Hantone* 1086 (DB), *Hamtonett* 1213. 'High farmstead'. OE *hēah* (dative *hēan*) + *tūn*, with the addition of OFrench *-ette* 'little'.

Hampole S. Yorks. *Hanepole* 1086 (DB). 'Pool of a man called Hana', or 'pool frequented by cocks (of wild birds)'. OE pers. name or OE *hana* + *pōl*.

Hampshire (the county). *Hamtunscir* late 9th cent. 'District based on *Hamtun* (i.e. SOUTHAMPTON)'. OE *scīr*.

Hampstead, *Hamstead*, 'the homestead', OE *hām-stede*: **Hampstead** Gtr. London. *Hemstede* 959, *Hamestede* 1086 (DB). **Hampstead Norris** Berks. *Hanstede* 1086 (DB), *Hampstede Norreys* 1517. Manorial affix from the Norreys family who bought the manor in 1448. **Hamstead** I. of Wight. *Hamestede* 1086 (DB). **Hamstead** W. Mids. *Hamsted* 1227. **Hamstead Marshall** Berks. *Hamestede* 1086 (DB), *Hamsted Marchal* 1284. Manorial affix from the Marshal family, here in the 13th cent.

Hampsthwaite N. Yorks. *Hamethwayt c*.1180. 'Clearing of a man called Hamr or Hamall'. OScand. pers. name + *thveit*.

Hampton, a common name, has no less than three different origins. Some are from OE *hām-tūn* 'home farm, homestead': **Hampton Lovett** Heref. & Worcs. *Hamtona* 716, *Hamtune* 1086 (DB). Manorial affix from the Luvet family, here in the 13th cent. **Hampton, Meysey** Glos. *Hantone* 1086 (DB), *Meseishampton* 1287. Manorial addition from de Meisi family, here from the 12th cent. **Hampton Poyle** Oxon. *Hantone* 1086 (DB), *Hampton Poile* 1428. Manorial affix from the de la Puile family, here in the 13th cent.

Other Hamptons are 'farmstead in an enclosure or riverbend', OE *hamm* + *tūn*: **Hampton** Gtr. London. *Hamntone* 1086 (DB). **Hampton Bishop** Heref. & Worcs. *Hantune* 1086 (DB), *Homptone* 1240. Manorial affix from early possession by the Bishop of Hereford. **Hampton Lucy** Warwicks. *Homtune* 781, *Hantone* 1086 (DB). Manorial affix from its possession by the Lucy family in the 16th cent.

Other Hamptons are 'high farmstead', OE *hēah* (dative *hēan*) + *tūn*: **Hampton** Heref. & Worcs., near Evesham. *Heantune* 780, *Hantun* 1086 (DB). **Hampton** Shrops. *Hempton* 1391. **Hampton in Arden** W. Mids. *Hantone* 1086 (DB). Affix refers to the medieval Forest of Arden, *see* HENLEY-IN-ARDEN. **Hampton on the Hill** Warwicks. *Hamtone* 12th cent.

Hams, South (district) Devon. *Southammes* 1396. Possibly 'cultivated areas of land to the south (of Dartmoor)'. OE sūth + *hamm*.

Hamsey E. Sussex. *Hamme* 961, *Hame* 1086 (DB), *Hammes Say* 1306. 'The enclosure, the land in a riverbend'. OE *hamm* with manorial addition from the de Say family, here in the 13th cent.

Hamstall Ridware Staffs., *see* RIDWARE.

Hamstead, *see* HAMPSTEAD.

Hamsterley Durham. *Hamsteleie c*.1190. 'Clearing infested with corn-weevils'. OE **hamstra* + *lēah*.

Hamworthy Dorset. *Hamme* 1236, *Hamworthy* 1463. OE *hamm* 'enclosure'. Here possibly 'peninsula', with the later addition of *worthig* 'enclosure'.

Hanborough, Church & *Hanborough, Long* Oxon. *Haneberge* 1086 (DB). 'Hill of a man called Hagena or Hana'. OE pers. name + *beorg*.

Hanbury, 'high or chief fortified place', OE *hēah* (dative *hēan*) + *burh* (dative *byrig*): **Hanbury** Heref. & Worcs. *Heanburh c*.765, *Hambyrie* 1086 (DB). **Hanbury** Staffs. *Hambury c*.1185.

Hanchurch Staffs. *Hancese* |*sic*| 1086 (DB), *Hanchurche* 1212. 'High church'. OE *hēah* (dative *hēan*) + *cirice*.

Handa Island Highland. 'Sand island'. OScand. *sandr* + *ey*.

Handbridge Ches, *Bruge* 1086 (DB), *Honebrugge c*.1150. 'Bridge at the rock'. OE *hān* + *brycg*.

Handcross W. Sussex, recorded as *Handcrosse* 1617, perhaps 'cross used as a signpost', or 'cross-roads where five roads meet'.

Handforth Ches. *Haneford* 12th cent. 'Ford frequented by cocks (of wild birds)', or 'ford at the stones (used as markers)'. OE *hana* or *hān* + *ford*.

Handley, 'high wood or clearing', OE *hēah* (dative *hēan*) + *lēah*: **Handley** Ches. *Hanlei* 1086 (DB). **Handley, Sixpenny** Dorset. *Hanlee* 877, *Hanlege* 1086 (DB), *Sexpennyhanley* 1575. Affix added in 16th cent. from an old Hundred name *Sexpene* 'hill of the Saxons', from OE *Seaxe* + Celtic **penn*. **Handley, West** Derbys. *Henleie* 1086 (DB).

Handsacre Staffs. *Hadesacre* |*sic*| 1086 (DB), *Handesacra* 1196. 'Arable plot of a man called **Hand*'. OE pers. name + *æcer*.

Handsworth S. Yorks. *Handesuuord* 1086 (DB). 'Enclosure of a man called **Hand*'. OE pers. name + *worth*.

Handsworth W. Mids. *Honesworde* 1086 (DB). 'Enclosure of a man called Hūn'. OE pers. name + *worth*.

Hanford Staffs. *Heneford* |*sic*| 1086 (DB), *Honeford* 1212. 'Ford frequented by cocks (of wild birds)', or 'ford at the stones'. OE *hana* or *hān* + *ford*.

Hanham S. Glos. *Hanun* 1086 (DB). '(Place at) the rocks'. OE *hān* in a dative plural form *hānum*.

Hankelow Ches. *Honcolawe* 12th cent. 'Mound or hill of a man called **Haneca*'. OE pers. name + *hlāw*.

Hankerton Wilts. *Hanekyntone* 680. 'Estate associated with a man called **Haneca*'. OE pers. name + *-ing-* + *tūn*.

Hankham E. Sussex. *Hanecan hamme* 947, *Henecham* 1086 (DB). 'Enclosure, or dry ground in marsh, of a man called **Haneca*'. OE pers. name + *hamm*.

Hanley, 'high wood or clearing', OE *hēah* (dative *hēan*) + *lēah*: **Hanley** Staffs. *Henle* 1212. **Hanley Castle** Heref. & Worcs. *Hanlege* 1086 (DB). Affix from the early 13th cent. castle here. **Hanley Child** & **Hanley William** Heref. & Worcs. *Hanlege* 1086 (DB), *Cheldreshanle* 1255, *Williames Henle* 1275. Affixes from OE *cild* (plural *cildra*) 'young monk, noble-born son', and from a William de la Mare who held one of the manors in 1242.

Hanlith N. Yorks. *Hangelif* |*sic*| 1086 (DB), *Hahgenlid* 12th cent. 'Slope or hill-side of a man called Hagni or Hǫgni'. OScand. pers. name + *hlíth*.

Hannahstown Antrim. 'Hannah's town'. *Hannahstown* 1780. A family with the Scottish surname *Hanna(h)* were here in the 17th cent. The equivalent Irish name is *Baile Haine*.

Hanney, East & *Hanney, West* Oxon. *Hannige* 956, *Hannei* 1086 (DB). 'Island, or land between streams, frequented by cocks (of wild birds)'. OE *hana* + *ēg*.

Hanningfield, East, *Hanningfield, South*, & *Hanningfield, West* Essex. *Hamningefelde c*.1036, *Haningefelda* 1086 (DB). Probably 'open land of the family or followers of a man called Hana'. OE pers. name + *-inga-* + *feld*.

Hannington Hants. *Hanningtun* 1023, *Hanitune* 1086 (DB). 'Estate associated with a man called Hana'. OE pers. name + *-ing-* + *tūn*.

Hannington Northants. *Hanintone* 1086 (DB). Identical in origin with the previous name.

Hannington Wilts. *Hanindone* 1086 (DB). 'Hill frequented by cocks (of wild birds)', or 'hill of a man called *Hana*'. OE *hana* (genitive plural *hanena*) or OE pers. name (genitive *-n*) + *dūn*.

Hanslope Bucks. *Hamslape* 1086 (DB). 'Muddy place or slope of a man called *Hāma*'. OE pers. name + **slǣp*.

Hanthorpe Lincs. *Hermodestorp* 1086 (DB). 'Outlying farmstead or hamlet of a man called Heremōd or Hermōthr'. OE or OScand. pers. name + OScand. *thorp*.

Hanwell Gtr. London. *Hanewelle* 959, *Hanewelle* 1086 (DB). 'Spring or stream frequented by cocks (of wild birds)'. OE *hana* + *wella*.

Hanwell Oxon. *Hanewege* 1086 (DB), *Haneuell* 1236. 'Way (and stream) of a man called Hana'. OE pers. name + *weg* (replaced by *wella* in the 13th cent.).

Hanwood, Great Shorps. *Hanewde* 1086 (DB). Possibly 'wood frequented by cocks (of wild birds)', OE *hana* + *wudu*. Alternatively the first element could be OE *hān* 'rock, stone' or the OE pers. name Hana.

Hanworth Gtr. London. *Haneworde* 1086 (DB). 'Enclosure of a man called Hana'. OE pers. name + *worth*.

Hanworth Norfolk. *Haganaworda* 1086 (DB), 'Enclosure of a man called Hagena'. OE pers. name + *worth*.

Hanworth, Cold Lincs. *Haneurde* 1086 (DB), *Calthaneworth* 1322. 'Enclosure of a man called Hana'. OE pers. name + *worth*. Affix is OE *cald* 'cold, exposed'.

Happisburgh Norfolk. *Hapesburc* 1086 (DB). 'Stronghold of a man called **Hæp*'. OE pers. name + *burh*.

Hapsford Ches. *Happesford* 13th cent. 'Ford of a man called **Hæp*'. OE pers. name + *ford*.

Hapton Lancs. *Apton* 1242. 'Farmstead by a hill'. OE *hēap* + *tūn*.

Hapton Norfolk. *Habetuna* 1086 (DB). 'Farmstead of a man called **Hab(b)a*'. OE pers. name + *tūn*.

Harberton Devon. *Herburnaton* 1108. 'Farmstead on the River Harbourne'. OE river-name ('pleasant stream' from OE *hēore* + *burna*) + *tūn*.

Harbledown Kent. *Herebolddune* 1175. 'Hill of a man called Herebeald'. OE pers. name + *dūn*.

Harborne W. Mids. *Horeborne* 1086 (DB). 'Dirty or muddy stream'. OE *horu* + *burna*.

Harborough Magna Warwicks. *Herdeberge* 1086 (DB), *Hardeburgh Magna* 1498. 'Hill of the flocks or herds'. OE *heord* + *beorg*. Affix is Latin *magna* 'great'.

Harborough, Market Leics. *Haverbergam* 1153, *Mercat Heburgh* 1312. Probably 'hill where oats are grown'. OScand. *hafri* or OE **hæfera* + OScand. *berg* or OE *beorg*. Alternatively the first element may be OE *hæfer* or OScand. *hafr* 'a he-goat'. Affix (ME *merket*) from the important market here.

Harbottle Northum. *Hirbotle* c.1220. Probably 'dwelling of the hireling'. OE *hȳra* + *bōthl*.

Harbourne (river) Devon, *see* HARBERTON.

Harbury Warwicks. *Hereburgebyrig* 1002, *Erburgeberie* 1086 (DB). 'Stronghold or manor-house of a woman called Hereburh'. OE pers. name + *burh* (dative *byrig*).

Harby, 'farmstead of a man called Herrøthr' or 'farmstead with a herd or flock', OScand. pers. name or OScand. *hjǫrth* + *bý*: **Harby** Leics. *Herdebi* 1086 (DB). **Harby** Notts. *Herdrebi* 1086 (DB).

Harden W. Yorks. *Hareden* late 12th cent. 'Rock valley'. or 'valley frequented by hares'. OE **hær* or hara + *denu*.

Hardham W. Sussex. *Heriedeham* 1086 (DB). 'Homestead or river-meadow of a woman called Heregȳth'. OE pers. name + *hām* or *hamm*.

Hardingham Norfolk. *Hardingeham* 1161. 'Homestead of the family or followers of a man called **Hearda*'. OE pers. name + *-inga-* + *hām*.

Hardingstone Northants. *Hardingestone* 1086 (DB), *Hardingesthorn* 12th cent. 'Thorn-tree of a man called Hearding'. OE pers. name + *thorn*.

Hardington, 'estate associated with a man called **Hearda*', OE pers. name + *-ing-* + *tūn*: **Hardington** Somerset. *Hardintone* 1086 (DB). **Hardington Mandeville** Somerset. *Hardintone* 1086 (DB). Manorial affix from its possession by the de Mandeville family from the 12th cent.

Hardley Hants. *Hardelie* 1086 (DB). 'Hard clearing'. OE *heard* + *lēah*.

Hardley Street Norfolk. *Hardale* 1086 (DB). Probably identical in origin with the previous name.

Hardmead Bucks. *Herulfmede* 1086 (DB). Probably 'meadow of a man called Heoruwulf or Herewulf'. OE pers. name + *mǣd*.

Hardres, Upper Kent. *Haredum* 785, *Hardes* 1086 (DB). '(Place at) the woods'. OE **harad* in a plural form.

Hardstoft Derbys. *Hertestaf |sic|* 1086 (DB), *Hertistoft* 1257. 'Homestead of a man called **Heort or Hjǫrtr*'. OE or OScand. pers. name + OScand. *toft*.

Hardwick, *Hardwicke*, a common name, 'herd farm, farm for livestock', OE *heorde-wīc*: **Hardwick** Bucks. *Harduich* 1086 (DB). **Hardwick** Cambs. *Hardwic* c.1050, *Harduic* 1086 (DB). **Hardwick** Norfolk, near King's Lynn. *Herdwic* 1242. **Hardwick** Northants. *Heordewican* c.1067, *Herdewiche* 1086 (DB). **Hardwick** Oxon., near Bicester. *Hardewich* 1086 (DB). **Hardwick** Oxon., near Witney. *Herdewic* 1199. **Hardwick, East** & **Hardwick, West** W. Yorks. *Harduic* 1086 (DB). **Hardwick, Priors** Warwicks. *Herdewyk* 1043, *Herdewiche* 1086 (DB), *Herdewyk Priour* 1310. Affix from its possession by Coventry Priory in the 11th cent. **Hardwicke** Glos., near Stroud. *Herdewike* 12th cent. **Hardwicke** Glos., near Tewkesbury. *Herdeuuic* 1086 (DB). **Hardwicke** Heref. & Worcs., near Clifford. *La Herdewyk* 14th cent.

Hardy Lancs., *see* CHORLTON.

Hareby Lincs. *Harebi* 1086 (DB). Probably 'farmstead or village of a man called Hāri'. OScand. pers. name + *bý*.

Harefield Gtr. London. *Herefelle |sic|* 1086 (DB), *Herefeld* 1206. Probably 'open land used by an army (perhaps a Viking army)'. OE *here* + *feld*.

Haresfield Glos. *Hersefel* 1086 (DB), *Hersefeld* 1213. 'Open land of a man called **Hersa*'. OE pers. name + *feld*.

Harewood W. Yorks. *Harawuda* 10th cent., *Hareuuode* 1086 (DB). 'Grey wood', or 'wood by the rocks', or 'wood frequented by hares'. OE *hār* or **hær* or *hara* + *wudu*.

Harford Devon, near Ivybridge. *Hereford* 1086 (DB). 'Ford suitable for the passage of an army'. OE **here-ford*.

Hargrave, probably 'hoar grove, or grove on a boundary', OE *hār* + *grāf* or *grǣfe*: **Hargrave** Ches. *Haregrave* 1086 (DB). **Hargrave** Northants. *Haregrave* 1086 (DB). **Hargrave** Suffolk. *Haragraua* 1086 (DB).

Harkstead Suffolk. *Herchesteda* 1086 (DB). Probably 'pasture or homestead of a man called Hereca'. OE pers. name + *stede*.

Harlaston Staffs. *Heorelfestun* 1002, *Horulvestone* 1086 (DB). 'Farmstead of a man called Heoruwulf'. OE pers. name + *tūn*.

Harlaxton Lincs. *Herlavestune* 1086 (DB). 'Farmstead of a man called **Herelāf* or **Heorulāf*'. OE pers. name + *tūn*.

Harlech Gwyd. *Hardelagh* c.1290. 'Fine rock'. Welsh *hardd* + *llech*. The name refers to the prominent crag on which Harlech Castle was built in the 13th cent.

Harlesden Gtr. London. *Herulvestune* 1086 (DB). 'Farmstead of a man called Heoruwulf or Herewulf'. OE pers. name + *tūn*.

Harleston, *Harlestone*, 'farmstead of a man called Herewulf or Herewulf', OE pers. name + *tūn*: **Harleston** Devon. *Harliston* 1252. **Harleston** Norfolk. *Heroluestuna* 1086 (DB). **Harleston** Suffolk. *Heroluestuna* 1086 (DB). **Harlestone** Northants. *Herolvestune* 1086 (DB).

Harley Shrops. *Harlege* 1086 (DB), *Herleia* c.1090. Probably 'rock wood or clearing'. OE **hær* + *lēah*.

Harling, East Norfolk. *Herlinge* c.1060, *Herlinga* 1086 (DB). '(Settlement of) the family or followers of a man called **Herela*', or 'place of a man called **Herela*'. OE pers. name + *-ingas* or *-ing*.

Harlington Beds. *Herlingdone* 1086 (DB). 'Hill of the family or followers of a man called **Herela*'. OE pers. name + *-inga-* + *dūn*.

Harlington Gtr. London. *Hygereding tun* 831, *Herdintone* 1086 (DB). 'Estate associated with a man called **Hygerēd*'. OE pers. name + *-ing-* + *tūn*.

Harlow Essex. *Herlawe* 1045, *Herlaua* 1086 (DB). 'Mound or hill associated with an army (perhaps a Viking army)'. OE *here* + *hlāw*.

Harlow Hill Northum. *Hirlawe* 1242. Possibly identical in origin with the previous name.

Harlsey, East N. Yorks. *Herlesege* 1086 (DB). 'Island, or dry ground in marsh, of a man called **Herel*'. OE pers. name + *ēg*.

Harlthorpe E. R. Yorks. *Herlesthorpia* 1150–60. 'Outlying farmstead of a man called Herleifr or Herlaugr'. OScand. pers. name + *thorp*.

Harlton Cambs. *Herletone* 1086 (DB). 'Farmstead of a man called **Herela*'. OE pers. name + *tūn*.

Harmby N. Yorks. *Hernebi* 1086 (DB). 'Farmstead or village of a man called Hjarni'. OScand. pers. name + *bý*.

Harmondsworth Gtr. London. *Hermondesworde* 1086 (DB). 'Enclosure of a man called Heremōd'. OE pers. name + *worth*.

Harmston Lincs. *Hermodestune* 1086 (DB). 'Farmstead of a man called Heremōd or Hermóthr'. OE or OScand. pers. name + OE *tūn*.

Harnham, East & *Harnham, West* Wilts. *Harnham* 1115. Probably 'enclosure frequented by hares'. OE *hara* (genitive plural *harena*) + *hamm*.

Harnhill Glos. *Harehille* 1086 (DB). 'Grey hill' or 'hill frequented by hares'. OE *hār* (dative *-an*) or *hara* (genitive plural *-ena*) + *hyll*.

Harold Hill Gtr. London, named from HAROLD WOOD.

Harold Wood Gtr. London. *Horalds Wood* c.1237. Named from Earl Harold, king of England until his defeat at Hastings in 1066; he held the nearby manor of Havering.

Haroldston West Pemb. *Haraulddyston* 1307. 'Western (place called) Harold's farm'. OScand. pers. name + OE *tūn*. *West* distinguishes the place from nearby *Haroldston St Issells* ('St Ismael').

Harome N. Yorks. *Harum* 1086 (DB). '(Place at) the rocks or stones'. OE **hær* in a dative plural form **harum*.

Harpenden Herts. *Herpedene* c.1060. 'Valley of the harp'. OE *hearpe* (genitive *-an*) + *denu*. Alternatively the first element may be a reduced form of OE *here-pæth* 'highway or main road'.

Harpford Devon. *Harpeford* 1167. 'Ford on a highway or main road'. OE, *here-pæth* + *ford*.

Harpham E. R. Yorks. *Arpen* |*sic*| 1086 (DB), *Harpam* 1100–15. 'Homestead where the harp is played'. OE *hearpe* + *hām*. Alternatively the first element may have the sense 'salt-harp, sieve for making salt'.

Harpley, 'clearing of the harp', perhaps 'harp-shaped clearing', OE *hearpe* + *lēah*: **Harpley** Norfolk. *Herpelai* 1086 (DB). **Harpley** Heref. & Worcs. *Hoppeleia* |*sic*| 1222, *Harpele* 1275.

Harpole Northants. *Horpol* 1086 (DB). 'Dirty or muddy pool'. OE *horu* + *pōl*.

Harpsden Oxon. *Harpendene* 1086 (DB). 'Valley of the harp'. OE *hearpe* (genitive *-an*) + *denu*.

Harpswell Lincs. *Herpeswelle* 1086 (DB). 'Spring or stream of the harp or harper'. OE *hearpe* or *hearpere* + *wella*.

Harptree, East & *Harptree, West* B. & NE. Som. *Harpetreu* 1086 (DB). Probably 'tree by a highway or main road'. OE *here-pæth* + *trēow*.

Harpurhey Gtr. Manch. *Harpourhey* 1320. 'Enclosure of a man called *Harpour*'. OE *hæg* with the surname of a 14th cent. landowner.

Harrietsham Kent. *Herigeardes hamm* 10th cent., *Hariardesham* 1086 (DB). 'River-meadow of a man called Heregeard, or near army quarters'. OE pers. name (or OE *here* + *geard*) + *hamm*.

Harringay Gtr. London, *see* HORNSEY.

Harrington Cumbria. *Haueringtona* c.1160. 'Estate associated with a man called **Hæfer*'. OE pers. name + *-ing-* + *tūn*.

Harrington Lincs. *Haringtona* 12th cent. Possibly 'farmstead of a man called **Hæring*', from OE pers.

name + *tūn*, or the first element may be an OE **hæring* 'stony place' or **hāring* 'grey wood'.

Harrington Northants. *Arintone* |*sic*| 1086 (DB), *Hederingeton* 1184. Possibly 'estate associated with a man called **Heathuhere*'. OE pers. name + *-ing-* + *tūn*.

Harringworth Northants. *Haringwrth* *c*.1060, *Haringeworde* 1086 (DB). Possibly 'enclosure of the dwellers at a stony place'. OE **hær* + *-inga-* + *worth*.

Harris (island district) W. Isles. *Heradh* *c*.1500, *Harrige* 1542, *Harreis* 1588. Gaelic *na-h-earadhi*, probably from old Norse *heruth* (district).

Harrogate N. Yorks. *Harwegate* 1332. '(Place at) the road to the cairn or heap of stones'. OScand. *horgr* + *gata*.

Harrold Beds. *Hareuuelle* |*sic*| 1086 (DB), *Harewolda* 1163. Probably 'high forest-land on a boundary'. OE *hār* + *weald*.

Harrow Gtr. London. *Hearge* 825, *Herges* 1086 (DB). 'Heathen shrine or temple'. OE *hearg*.

Harrow Weald Gtr. London. *Welde* 1282, *Harewewelde* 1388. 'Woodland near HARROW'. OE *weald*.

Harrowden, Great & *Harrowden, Little* Northants. *Hargedone* 1086 (DB). 'Hill of the heathen shrines or temples'. OE *hearg* + *dūn*.

Harston Cambs. *Herlestone* 1086 (DB). Probably 'farmstead of a man called **Herel*'. OE pers. name + *tūn*.

Harston Leics. *Herstan* 1086 (DB). 'Grey or boundary stone'. OE *hār* + *stān*.

Hart Hartlepl. *Heruteu* 8th cent. 'Island or peninsula frequented by harts or stags'. OE *heorot* + *ēg*.

Hartburn, 'stream frequented by harts or stags', OE *heorot* + *burna*: **Hartburn** Northum. *Herteburne* 1198. **Hartburn, East** Stock. on T. *Herteburna* *c*.1190.

Hartest Suffolk. *Hertest* *c*.1050, *Herterst* 1086 (DB). 'Wooded hill frequented by harts or stags'. OE *heorot* + *hyrst*.

Hartfield E. Sussex. *Hertevel* |*sic*| 1086 (DB), *Hertefeld* 12th cent. 'Open land frequented by harts or stags'. OE *heorot* + *feld*.

Hartford, usually 'ford frequented by harts or stags', OE *heorot* + *ford*: **Hartford** Ches. *Herford* |*sic*| 1086 (DB), *Hartford* late 12th cent. **Hartford, East** Northum. *Hertford* 1198.
   However the following has a different origin: **Hartford** Cambs. *Hereforde* 1086 (DB). 'Ford suitable for the passage of an army'. OE **here-ford*.

Harthill, 'hill frequented by harts or stags', OE *heorot* + *hyll*: **Harthill** Ches. *Herthil* 1259. **Harthill** S. Yorks. *Hertil* 1086 (DB).

Harting, East & *Harting, South* W. Sussex. *Hertingas* 970, *Hertinges* 1086 (DB). '(Settlement of) the family or followers of a man called **Heort*'. OE pers. name + *-ingas*.

Hartington Derbys. *Hortedun* 1086 (DB). Probably 'hill of the harts or stags'. OE *heorot* + *dūn*.

Hartland Devon. *Heortigtun* *c*.880, *Hertitona* 1086 (DB), *Hertilanda* 1130. 'Farmstead (or estate) on the peninsula frequented by harts or stags'. OE *heorot* + *īeg* + *tūn* (later *land*).

Hartlebury Heref. & Worcs. *Heortlabyrig* 817, *Huerteberie* 1086 (DB). 'Stronghold of a man called **Heortla*'. OE pers. name + *burh* (dative *byrig*).

Hartlepool Hartlepl. *Herterpol* *c*.1170. 'Pool or bay near the stag peninsula'. OE *heorot* + *ēg* + *pōl*.

Hartley, usually 'wood or clearing frequented by harts or stags', OE *heorot* + *lēah*; examples include: **Hartley** Kent, near Cranbrook. *Heoratleag* 843. **Hartley** Kent, near Longfield. *Erclei* |*sic*| 1086 (DB), *Hertle* 1253. **Hartley Westpall** Hants. *Harlei* 1086 (DB), *Hertlegh Waspayl* *c*.1270. Manorial addition from early possession by the Waspail family. **Hartley Wintney** Hants. *Hurtlege* 12th cent., *Hertleye Wynteneye* 13th cent. Manorial addition from its possession by the Priory of Wintney in the 13th cent.
   However other Hartleys have different origins: **Hartley** Cumbria. *Harteclo* 1176. Probably 'hard ridge of land'. OE *heard* + *clā*. **Hartley** Northum. *Hertelawa* 1167. 'Mound or hill frequented by harts or stags'. OE *heorot* + *hlāw*.

Hartlip Kent. *Heordlyp* 11th cent. 'Gate or fence over which harts or stags can leap'. OE *heorot* + *hlīep*.

Harton N. Yorks. *Heretune* 1086 (DB). Probably 'farmstead by the rocks or stones'. OE **hær* + *tūn*.

Harton Tyne & Wear. *Heortedun* 1104–8. 'Hill frequented by harts or stags'. OE *heorot* + *dūn*.

Hartpury Glos. *Hardepiry* 12th cent. 'Pear-tree with hard fruit'. OE *heard* + *pirige*.

Hartshill, Warwicks. *Ardreshille* |*sic*| 1086 (DB), *Hardredeshella* 1151. 'Hill of a man called Heardrēd'. OE pers. name + *hyll*.

Hartshorne Derbys. *Heorteshone* 1086 (DB). 'Hart's horn', i.e. 'hill thought to resemble a hart's horn'. OE *heorot* + *horn*.

Hartwell Northants. *Hertewelle* 1086 (DB). 'Spring or stream frequented by harts or stags'. OE *heorot* + *wella*.

Harvington Heref. & Worcs. *Herverton* 709, *Herferthun* 1086 (DB). 'Farmstead near the ford suitable for the passage of an army'. OE **here-ford* + *tūn*.

Harwell Oxon. *Haranwylle* 956, *Harvvelle* 1086 (DB). 'Spring or stream by the hill called *Hāra* (the grey one)'. OE hill-name (from *hār* 'grey') + *wella*.

Harwich Essex. *Herewic* 1248. 'Army camp', probably that of a Viking army. OE *here-wīc*.

Harwood, 'grey wood', 'wood by the rocks', or 'wood frequented by hares', OE *hār* or **hær* or *hara* + *wudu*: **Harwood** Gtr. Manch. *Harewode* 1212. **Harwood Dale** N. Yorks. *Harewode* 1301, *Harwoddale* 1577. With OScand. *dalr* 'valley'. **Harwood, Great** Lancs. *Majori Harewuda* early 12th cent. Affix is Latin *maior* 'greater'.

Harworth Notts. *Hareworde* 1086 (DB). Probably 'enclosure on the boundary'. OE *hār* + *worth*.

Hascombe Surrey. *Hescumb* 1232. Possibly 'the witch's valley'. OE *hægtesse* + *cumb*.

Haselbech Northants. *Esbece* |*sic*| 1086 (DB), *Haselbech* 12th cent. 'Valley-stream where hazels grow'. OE *hæsel* + *bece*.

Haselbury Plucknett Somerset. *Halberge |sic|* 1086 (DB), *Haselbare Ploukenet* 1431. 'Hazel wood or grove'. OE *hæsel + bearu*. Manorial affix from its possession by the de Plugenet family in the 13th cent.

Haseley, Great & *Haseley, Little* Oxon. *Hæseleia* 1002, *Haselie* 1086 (DB). 'Hazel wood or clearing'. OE *hæsel + lēah*.

Haselor Warwicks. *Haseloue* 1086 (DB). 'Slope or hill where hazels grow'. OE *hæsel + *ofer*.

Hasfield Glos. *Hasfelde* 1086 (DB). 'Open land where hazels grow'. OE *hæsel + feld*.

Hasguard Pemb. *Hiscart* c.1200. 'House cleft'. OScand. *hús + skarth*. The name apparently refers to the small valley that cuts into rising ground here.

Hasketon Suffolk. *Haschetuna* 1086 (DB). 'Farmstead of a man called *Haseca'. OE pers. name + *tūn*.

Hasland Derbys. *Haselont* 1129–38. 'Hazel grove'. OScand. *hasl + lundr*.

Haslemere Surrey. *Heselmere* 1221. 'Pool where hazels grow'. OE *hæsel + mere*.

Haslingden Lancs. *Heselingedon* 1241. 'Valley growing with hazels'. OE *hæslen + denu*.

Haslingfield Cambs. *Haslingefeld* 1086 (DB). Probably 'open land of the family or followers of a man called *Hæsel(a)'. OE pers. name + *-inga- + feld*. Alternatively the first element may be the genitive plural of an OE *hæsling* 'place growing with hazels'.

Haslington Ches. *Hasillinton* early 13th cent. 'Farmstead where hazels grow'. OE *hæslen + tūn*.

Hassall Ches. *Eteshale |sic|* 1086 (DB), *Hatishale* 13th cent. 'The witch's nook of land'. OE *hægtesse + halh*.

Hassingham Norfolk. *Hasingeham* 1086 (DB). 'Homestead of the family or followers of a man called *Hasu'. OE pers. name + *-inga- + hām*.

Hassocks W. Sussex, a 19th cent. settlement named from a field called *Hassocks*, from OE *hassuc* 'clump of coarse grass'.

Hassop Derbys. *Hetesope* 1086 (DB). Probably 'the witch's valley'. OE *hægtesse + hop*.

Hastingleigh Kent. *Hæstingalege* 993, *Hastingelai* 1086 (DB). 'Woodland clearing of the family or followers of a man called *Hæsta'. OE pers. name + *-inga- + lēah*.

Hastings E. Sussex. *Hastinges* 1086 (DB). '(Settlement of) the family or followers of a man called *Hæsta'. OE pers. name + *-ingas*. Earlier *Hæstingaceaster* c.915, 'Roman town of *Hæsta's people', from OE *ceaster*.

Haswell Durham. *Hessewella* 1131. Probably 'spring or stream where hazels grow'. OE *hæsel + wella*.

Hatch, a common name, from OE *hæcc* 'a hatch-gate (leading to a forest)' or 'floodgate (in a stream)'; examples include: **Hatch** Beds. *La Hache* 1232. **Hatch** Hants. *Heche* 1086 (DB). **Hatch** Wilts. *Hache* 1200. **Hatch Beauchamp** Somerset. *Hache* 1086 (DB), *Hache Beauchampe* 1243. Manorial affix from its possession by the Beauchamp family in the 13th cent. **Hatch, West** Somerset. *Hache* 1201, *Westhache* 1243.

Hatch End Gtr. London. *Le Hacchehend* 1448. 'District by the gate' (probably a gate to Pinner Park). OE *hæcc + ende*.

Hatcliffe NE. Lincs. *Hadecliue* 1086 (DB). 'Cliff or bank of a man called Hadda'. OE pers. name + *clif*.

Hatfield, a common name, 'heathy open land, or open land where heather grows', OE *hæth + feld*; examples include: **Hatfield** Heref. & Worcs., near Kempsey. *Hadfeld* 1182. **Hatfield** Heref. & Worcs., near Pudlestone. *Hetfelde* 1086 (DB). **Hatfield** Herts. *Haethfelth* 731, *Hetfelle* 1086 (DB). **Hatfield** S. Yorks. *Haethfelth* 731, *Hedfeld* 1086 (DB). **Hatfield Broad Oak** Essex. *Hadfelda* 1086 (DB), *Hatfeld Brodehoke* c.1130. Affix from a large oak-tree, OE *brād + āc*. **Hatfield, Great** & **Hatfield, Little** E. R. Yorks. *Haifeld, Heifeld* 1086 (DB), *Haitefeld* 12th cent. First element influenced by OScand. *heithr* 'heath'. **Hatfield Peverel** Essex. *Hadfelda* 1086 (DB), *Hadfeld Peurell* 1166. Manorial affix from its possession by Ralph Peverel in 1086.

Hatford Oxon. *Hevaford |sic|* 1086 (DB), *Hauetford* 1176. 'Ford near a headland or hill'. OE *hēafod + ford*.

Hatherden Hants. *Hetherden* 1193. Probably 'hawthorn valley'. OE *hagu-thorn + denu*.

Hatherleigh Devon. *Hadreleia* 1086 (DB). Probably identical in origin with the next name.

Hatherley, Down & *Hatherley, Up* Glos. *Athelai* 1086 (DB), *Dunheytherleye* 1273, *Hupheberleg* 1221. 'Hawthorn clearing'. OE *hagu-thorn + lēah*. Distinguishing affixes from OE *dūne* 'lower downstream' and *upp* 'higher upstream'.

Hathern Leics. *Avederne |sic|* 1086 (DB), *Hacthurne* 1230. '(Place at) the hawthorn'. OE *hagu-thyrne*.

Hatherop Glos. *Etherope* 1086 (DB). Probably 'high outlying farmstead'. OE *hēah + throp*.

Hathersage Derbys. *Hereseige |sic|* 1086 (DB), *Hauersegg* c.1220. 'He-goat's ridge', or 'ridge of a man called *Hæfer'. OE *hæfer* or OE pers. name + *ecg*.

Hatherton Ches. *Haretone |sic|* 1086 (DB), *Hatherton* 1262. 'Farmstead where hawthorn grows'. OE *hagu-thorn + tūn*.

Hatherton Staffs. *Hagenthorndun* 996. *Hargedone* 1086 (DB). 'Hill where hawthorn grows'. OE *hagu-thorn + dūn*.

Hatley, probably 'woodland clearing on the hill', OE *hætt + lēah*: **Hatley, Cockayne** Beds. *Hattenleia* c.960, *Hatelai* 1086 (DB), *Cocking Hatley* 1576. Manorial affix from the Cockayne family, here in the 15th cent. **Hatley, East** & **Hatley St George** Cambs. *Hatelai* 1086 (DB), *Esthatteleia* 1199, *Hattele de Sancto Georgio* 1279. Distinguishing affixes from OE *ēast* 'east' and from possession by the family de Sancto Georgio here in the 13th cent.

Hattingley Hants. *Hattingele* 1204. Probably 'woodland clearing at the hill place'. OE *hætt + -ing + lēah*.

Hatton, 'farmstead on a heath', OE *hæth + tūn*; examples include: **Hatton** Ches. *Hattone* c.1230. **Hatton** Derbys. *Hatune* 1086 (DB). **Hatton** Gtr. London. *Hatone* 1086 (DB). **Hatton** Lincs. *Hatune* 1086 (DB). **Hatton** Shrops. *Hatton* 1212. **Hatton, Cold** & **Hatton, High** Shrops. *Hatune, Hetune* 1086 (DB), *Colde Hatton* 1233, *Heye Hatton* 1327. Distinguishing affixes from OE *cald* 'cold, exposed' and *hēah* 'high, chief'. **Hatton Heath** Ches. *Etone |sic|* 1086 (DB), *Hettun* 1185.

Haugham Lincs. *Hecham* 1086 (DB). Probably 'high or chief homestead'. OE *hēah + hām*.

Haughley Suffolk. *Hagele c.*1040, *Hagala* 1086 (DB). 'Wood or clearing with a hedge, or where haws grow'. OE *haga + lēah*.

Haughton, usually 'farmstead in or by a nook of land', OE *halh + tūn*: **Haughton** Shrops., near Oswestry. *Halchton* 1285. **Haughton** Shrops., near Shifnal. *Halghton* 1281. **Haughton** Shrops., near Shrewsbury. *Haustone* 1086 (DB). **Haughton** Staffs. *Haltone* 1086 (DB). **Haughton Green** Gtr. Manch. *Halghton* 1307. **Haughton-le-Skerne** Durham. *Halhtun c.*1050. On the River Skerne (for the origin of this river-name *see* SKERNE with which it is identical in meaning).

However the following has a different origin: **Haughton** Notts. *Hoctun* 1086 (DB). 'Farmstead on a spur of land'. OE *hōh + tūn*.

Haunton Staffs. *Hagnatun* 942. 'Farmstead of a man called Hagena'. OE pers. name + *tūn*.

Hautbois, Little Norfolk. *Hobbesse* 1044–7, *Hobuisse* 1086 (DB). Probably 'marshy meadow with tussocks or hummocks'. OE **hobb + wisc, *wisse*.

Hauxley Northum. *Hauekeslaw* 1204. 'Mound of the hawk, or of a man called *Hafoc'. OE *hafoc* or pers. name + *hlāw*.

Hauxton Cambs. *Hafucestune c.*975, *Hauochestun* 1086 (DB). 'Farmstead of a man called *Hafoc'. OE pers. name + *tūn*.

Hauxwell, East N. Yorks. *Hauocheswelle* 1086 (DB). 'Spring of the hawk, or of a man called *Hafoc'. OE *hafoc* or pers. name + *wella*.

Havant Hants. *Hamanfuntan* 935, *Havehunte* 1086 (DB). 'Spring of a man called Hāma'. OE pers. name + **funta*.

Havenstreet I. of Wight. *Hethenestrete* 1255. Probably 'street (of houses) or hamlet of a man called *le Hethene*', from ME *strete*. A certain Richard le Hethene is recorded in this area *c.*1240. Alternatively perhaps 'heather-covered street', from OE *hǣthen*.

Haverfordwest (*Hwlffordd*) Pemb. *Haverfordia* 1191, *Hareford* 1283, *Heverford West* 1448, *Herefordwest* 1471. 'Western ford used by goats'. OE *hæfer + ford + west*. *West* was added to distinguish the town from HEREFORD, Heref. The Welsh name has developed from the original English.

Haverhill Suffolk. *Hauerhella* 1086 (DB). Probably 'hill where oats are grown'. OScand. *hafri* + OE *hyll*.

Haverigg Cumbria. *Haverig c.*1180. 'Ridge where oats are grown, or where he-goats graze'. OScand. *hafri* or *hafr + hryggr*.

Havering-atte-Bower Gtr. London. *Haueringas* 1086 (DB), *Hauring atte Bower* 1272. '(Settlement of) the family or followers of a man called *Hæfer'. OE pers. name + *-ingas*. Affix means 'at the bower or royal residence' from OE *būr*.

Haversham Bucks. *Hæfæresham* 10th cent., *Havresham* 1086 (DB). 'Homestead or river-meadow of a man called *Haefer'. OE pers. name + *hām* or *hamm*.

Haverthwaite Cumbria. *Haverthwayt* 1336. 'Clearing where oats are grown'. OScand. *hafri + thveit*.

Hawarden (*Penarlâg*) Flin. *Haordine* 1086 (DB), *Haworthyn* 1275. 'High enclosure'. OE *hēah + worthign*. The Welsh name probably means 'high ground rich in cattle' (Welsh *pennardd + alafog*).

Hawes N. Yorks. *Hawes* 1614. '(Place at) the pass between the hills'. OE *hals*.

Hawick Sc. Bord. *Hawic c.*1167. 'enclosed farm'. OE *haga + wīc*.

Hawkchurch Devon. *Hauekechierch* 1196. 'Church of a man called *Hafoc'. OE pers. name + *cirice*.

Hawkedon Suffolk. *Hauokeduna* 1086 (DB). Probably 'hill frequented by hawks'. OE *hafoc + dūn*.

Hawkesbury S. Glos. *Havochesberie* 1086 (DB). 'Stronghold of the hawk, or of a man called *Hafoc'. OE *hafoc* or OE pers. name + *burh* (dative *byrig*).

Hawkhill Northum. *Hauechil* 1178. 'Hill frequented by hawks'. OE *hafoc + hyll*.

Hawkhurst Kent. *Hauekehurst* 1254. 'Wooded hill frequented by hawks'. OE *hafoc + hyrst*.

Hawkinge Kent. *Hauekinge* 1204. 'Place frequented by hawks', or 'place of a man called *Hafoc'. OE *hafoc* or pers. name + *-ing*.

Hawkley Hants. *Hauecle* 1207. 'Woodland clearing frequented by hawks'. OE *hafoc + lēah*.

Hawkridge Somerset. *Hauekerega* 1194. 'Ridge frequented by hawks'. OE *hafoc + hrycg*.

Hawkshead Cumbria. *Hovkesete c.*1200. 'Mountain pasture of a man called Haukr'. OScand. pers. name + *sǽtr*.

Hawkswick N. Yorks. *Hochesuuic |sic|* 1086 (DB), *Haukeswic* 1176. 'Dwelling or (dairy) farm of a man called Haukr'. OScand. pers. name + OE *wīc*.

Hawksworth Notts. *Hochesuorde* 1086 (DB). 'Enclosure of a man called Hōc'. OE pers. name + *worth*.

Hawksworth W. Yorks. *Hafecesweorthe c.*1030, *Hauocesorde* 1086 (DB). 'Enclosure of a man called *Hafoc'. OE pers. name + *worth*.

Hawkwell Essex. *Hacuuella* 1086 (DB). 'Winding stream'. OE *haca + wella*.

Hawley Hants. *Hallee, Halely* 1248. Possibly 'woodland clearing near a hall or large house'. OE *heall + lēah*. Alternatively the first element may be *healh* 'nook or corner of land'.

Hawley Kent. *Hagelei |sic|* 1086 (DB), *Halgeleg* 1203. 'Holy wood or clearing'. OE *hālig + lēah*.

Hawling Glos. *Hallinge* 1086 (DB). '(Settlement of) the people from HALLOW', or '(settlement of) the people at the nook of land'. OE *halh + -ingas*. Alternatively, identical in origin with HALLING (Kent).

Hawnby N. Yorks. *Halm(e)bi* 1086 (DB). 'Farmstead or village of a man called Halmi'. OScand. pers. name + *bý*.

Alternatively the first element may be OScand. *halmr* 'straw'.

Haworth W. Yorks. *Hauewrth* 1209. 'Enclosure with a hedge'. OE *haga + worth*.

Hawsker, High N. Yorks. *Houkesgarth* c.1125. 'Enclosure of a man called Haukr'. OScand. pers. name + *garthr*.

Hawstead Suffolk. *Haldsteda* 1086 (DB). 'Place of refuge or shelter'. OE *h(e)ald + stede*.

Hawthorn Durham. *Hagethorn* 1155. '(Place at) the hawthorn'. OE *hagu-thorn*.

Hawton Notts. *Holtone* 1086 (DB). Probably 'farmstead in a hollow'. OE *hol + tūn*.

Haxby York. *Haxebi* 1086 (DB). 'Farmstead or village of a man called Hákr'. OScand. pers. name + *bý*.

Haxey N. Lincs. *Acheseia* 1086 (DB). 'Island, or dry ground in marsh, of a man called Hákr'. OScand. pers. name + OE *ēg* or OScand. *ey*.

Hay-on-Wye (*Y Gelli Gandryll*) Powys. *Hagan* 958, *Haya* 1144. 'Enclosure on the River Wye'. OE *hæg*. The Welsh name means 'the woodland of a hundred plots' (Welsh *y + celli + candryll*). The river name is of uncertain origin and meaning.

Haydock Mersey. *Hedoc* 1169. Probably a Welsh name from **heiddiog* 'barley place, corn farm'.

Haydon, usually 'hill or down where hay is made', OE *hēg + dūn*: **Haydon** Dorset. *Heydone* 1163. **Haydon Wick** Wilts. *Haydon* 1242, *Haydonwyk* 1249. The addition is OE *wīc* 'dairy farm'. However the following has a different second element: **Haydon Bridge** Northum. *Hayden* 1236. 'Valley where hay is made'. OE *hēg + denu*.

Hayes, 'land overgrown with brushwood', OE **hæs(e)*: **Hayes** Gtr. London, near Bromley. *Hesa* 1177. **Hayes** Gtr. London, near Hillingdon. *Hæse* 831, *Hesa* 1086 (DB).

Hayfield Derbys. *Hedfelt* |sic| 1086 (DB), *Heyfeld* 1285. 'Open land where hay is obtained'. OE *hēg + feld*.

Hayle Cornwall. *Heyl* 1265. Named from the River Hayle, a Celtic name meaning 'estuary'.

Hayling Island Hants. *Heglingaigæ* 956, *Halingei* 1086 (DB). 'Island of the family or followers of a man called *Hægel'. OE pers. name + *-inga- + ēg*.

Hayling, North & *Hayling, South* Hants. *Hailinges* c.1140. '(Settlement of) the family or followers of a man called *Hægel'. OE pers. name + *-ingas*.

Haynes Beds. *Hagenes* 1086 (DB). 'The enclosures'. OE **hægen, *hagen* in a plural form.

Hayscastle (*Cas-lai* Pemb. *Castrum Hey* 1293, *Heyscastel* 1326. 'Hay's castle'. ME pers. name + *castel*. The Welsh name is a development of *castell-hay* which translates into English.

Hayton, 'farmstead where hay is made or stored', OE *hēg + tūn*: **Hayton** Cumbria, near Brampton. *Hayton* c.1170. **Hayton** E. R. Yorks. *Haiton* 1086 (DB). **Hayton** Notts. *Heiton* 1175.

Haywards Heath W. Sussex. *Heyworth* 1261, *Haywards Hoth* 1544. 'Heath by the enclosure with a hedge'. OE *hege + worth*, with the later addition of *hǣth*.

Haywood, 'enclosed wood', OE *hæg* or *hege + wudu*: **Haywood** Heref. & Worcs. *Haywode* 1276 **Haywood, Great** & **Haywood, Little** Staffs. *Haiwode* 1086 (DB). **Haywood Oaks** Notts. *Heywod* 1232. The affix no doubt refers to some notable oak-trees.

Hazel Grove Gtr. Manch. *Hesselgrove* 1690. 'Hazel copse'. OE *hæsel + grāf*.

Hazelbury Bryan Dorset. *Hasebere* 1201, *Hasilbere Bryan* 1547. 'Hazel wood or grove'. OE *hæsel + bearu*. Manorial affix from the Bryene family, here in the 14th cent.

Hazeley Hants. *Heishulla* 1167. 'Brushwood hill'. OE **hǣs + hyll*.

Hazelwood Derbys. *Haselwode* 1306. 'Hazel wood'. OE *hæsel + wudu*.

Hazlemere Bucks. *Heselmere* 13th cent. 'Pool where hazels grow'. OE *hæsel + mere*.

Hazleton Glos. *Hasedene* |sic| 1086 (DB), *Haselton* 12th cent. 'Farmstead where hazels grow'. OE *hæsel + tūn*.

Heacham Norfolk. *Hecham* 1086 (DB). 'Homestead with a hedge or hatch-gate'. OE *hecg* or *hecc + hām*.

Headbourne Worthy Hants., see WORTHY.

Headcorn Kent. *Hedekaruna* c.1100. Possibly 'tree-trunk (used as a footbridge) of a man called *Hydeca'. OE pers. name + *hruna*.

Headingley W. Yorks. *Hedingeleia* 1086 (DB). 'Woodland clearing of the family or followers of a man called Head(d)a'. OE pers. name + *-inga- + lēah*.

Headington Oxon. *Hedenandun* 1004, *Hedintone* 1086 (DB). 'Hill of a man called *Hedena'. OE pers. name (genitive -n) + *dūn*.

Headlam Durham. *Hedlum* c.1190. '(Place at) the woodland clearings where heather grows'. OE *hǣth + lēah* (in a dative plural form *lēaum*).

Headley, 'woodland claring where heather grows', OE *hǣth + lēah*; examples include: **Headley** Hants. *Hallege* 1086 (DB). *Hetliga* c.1190. **Headley** Surrey. *Hallega* 1086 (DB).

Headon Notts. *Hedune* 1086 (DB). Probably 'high hill'. OE *hēah + dūn*.

Heage Derbys. *Heyheg* 1251. 'High edge or ridge'. OE *hēah + ecg*.

Healaugh, *Healey*, 'high clearing or wood', OE *hēah + lēah*: **Healaugh** N. Yorks., near Reeth. *Hale* |sic| 1086 (DB), *Helagh* 1200 **Healey** Northum., near Hexham. *Heley* 1268. **Healey** N. Yorks. *Helagh* c.1280.

Healing NE. Lincs. *Hegelinge* 1086 (DB). '(Settlement of) the family or followers of a man called *Hægel'. OE pers. name + *-ingas*.

Heanish Arg (Tiree). 'High headland'. OScand. Undefined first element + *nes*. Cp. HYNISH.

Heanor Derbys. *Hainoure* 1086 (DB). '(Place at) the high ridge'. OE *hēah* (dative *hēan*) + **ofer*.

Heanton Punchardon Devon. *Hantone* 1086 (DB), *Heanton Punchardun* 1297. 'High (or chief) farm'. OE *hēah* (dative *hēan*) + *tūn*. Manorial affix from its possession by the Punchardon family (from the 11th cent.).

Heapham Lincs. *Iopeham* 1086 (DB). 'Homestead or enclosure where rose-hips or brambles grow'. OE *hēope* or *hēopa* + *hām* or *hamm*.

Heath, a common name, '(place at) the heath', OE *hǣth*; examples include: **Heath and Reach** Beds. *La Hethe* 1276. See REACH. **Heath** Derbys. *Heth* 1257. Earlier called *Lunt* 1086 (DB) from OScand. *lundr* 'small wood, grove'.

Heath Hayes Staffs. *Hethhey* 1570. 'Heathy enclosure(s)'. OE *hǣth* + *hæg*.

Heathcote Derbys. *Hedcote* late 12th cent. 'Cottage(s) on a heath'. OE *hǣth* + *cot*.

Heather Leics. *Hadre* 1086 (DB). 'Place where heather grows'. OE **hǣddre*.

Heathfield, 'heathy open land, open land overgrown with heather', OE *hǣth* + *feld*: **Heathfield** E. Sussex. *Hadfeld* 12th cent. **Heathfield** Somerset. *Hafella |sic|* 1086 (DB), *Hathfeld* 1159.

Heathrow Gtr. London, *La Hetherewe* c.1410. 'Row of houses on or near a heath'. OE *hǣth* + *rǣw*.

Heatley Ches. *Heyteley* 1525. 'Woodland clearing where heather grows'. OE *hǣth* + *lēah*.

Heaton, a common name, 'high farmstead'. OE *hēah* + *tūn*; examples include: **Heaton** Tyne & Wear. *Heton* 1256. **Heaton** W. Yorks. *Hetun* 1160. **Heaton, Castle** Northum. *Heton* 1183. Affix may refer to a hall-house here in medieval times. **Heaton, Earls** W. Yorks. *Etone* 1086 (DB), *Erlesheeton* 1308. Manorial affix from possession by the Earls of Warren.

Hebburn Tyne & Wear. *Heabyrm* 1104–8. 'High burial place or tumulus'. OE *hēah* + *byrgen*.

Hebden, 'valley where rose-hips or brambles grow', OE *hēope* or *hēopa* + *denu*: **Hebden** N. Yorks. *Hebedene* 1086 (DB). **Hebden Bridge** W. Yorks. *Hepdenbryge* 1399. With OE *brycg* 'bridge' (over Hebden Water).

Hebrides (islands) Arg, Highland, W. Isles. *Hæbudes* 77, *Hebudes* 300. Meaning uncertain. The Roman name was *Ebudae* or *Ebudes*, and the present name resulted from a misreading of the latter, with *ri* for *u*. The OScand. name was *Suthreyar*, 'southern islands', as being south of Orkney and Shetland.

Hebron Northum. *Heburn* 1242. Probably identical in origin with HEBBURN.

Heck, Great N. Yorks. *Hech* 1153–5. 'The hatch or gate'. OE *hæcc*.

Heckfield Hants. *Hechfeld* 1207. Possibly 'open land by a hedge or hatch-gate'. OE *hecg* or *hecc* + *feld*.

Heckingham Norfolk. *Hechingheam* 1086 (DB), *Hekingeham* 1245. 'Homestead of the family or followers of a man called Heca'. OE pers. name + *-inga-* + *hām*.

Heckington Lincs. *Hechintune* 1086 (DB). 'Estate associated with a man called Heca'. OE pers. name + *-ing-* + *tūn*.

Heckmondwike W. Yorks. *Hedmundewic |sic|* 1086 (DB), *Hecmundewik* 13th cent. 'Dwelling or (dairy) farm of a man called Hēahmund'. OE pers. name + *wīc*.

Hedderwick E. Loth. *Hatheruuich* 1094. 'Farmstead among heather'. OE **hœddre* + *wīc*.

Heddington Wilts. *Edintone* 1086 (DB). 'Estate associated with a man called Hedde'. OE pers. name + *-ing-* + *tūn*.

Heddon, 'hill where heather grows', OE *hǣth* + *dūn*: **Heddon, Black** Northum. *Hedon* 1271. **Heddon on the Wall** Northum. *Hedun* 1175. Affix from its situation on HADRIAN'S WALL.

Hedenham Norfolk. *Hedenaham* 1086 (DB). 'Homestead of a man called **Hedena*'. OE pers. name + *hām*.

Hedge End Hants. *Cutt Hedge End* 1759. Self-explanatory, with *cut* 'clipped' in the 18th cent. form.

Hedgerley Bucks. *Huggeleg* 1195. 'Woodland clearing of a man called **Hycga*'. OE pers. name + *lēah*.

Hedingham, Castle & *Hedingham, Sible* Essex. *Hedingham* 1086 (DB), *Heyngham Sibille* 1231, *Hengham ad castrum* 1254. Probably 'homestead of the family or followers of a man called **Hyth(a)*, or of the dwellers at the landing-place'. OE pers. name or *hȳth* + *-inga-* + *hām*. Distinguishing affixes from ME *castel* (Latin *castrum*) 'castle' and from the family of a lady called Sibil who held land here in the 13th cent.

Hedley on the Hill Northum. *Hedley* 1242. 'Woodland clearing where heather grows'. OE *hǣth* + *lēah*.

Hednesford Staffs. *Hedenesford* 13th cent. 'Ford of a man called **Heddīn*'. OE pers. name + *ford*.

Hedon E. R. Yorks. *Hedon* 12th cent. 'Hill where heather grows'. OE *hǣth* + *dūn*.

Heigham, Potter Norfolk. *Echam* 1086 (DB), *Hegham Pottere* 1182. Possibly 'homestead or enclosure with a hedge or hatch-gate'. OE *hecg* or *hecc* + *hām* or *hamm*. The affix (from OE *pottere*) must allude to pot-making here at an early date.

Heighington Durham. *Heghyngtona* 1183. Probably 'estate associated with a man called Heca'. OE pers. name + *-ing-* + *tūn*.

Heighington Lincs. *Hictinton* 1242. Probably 'estate associated with a man called **Hyht*'. OE pers. name + *-ing-* + *tūn*.

Heighton, South E. Sussex. *Hectone* 1086 (DB), *Sutheghton* 1327. 'High farmstead'. OE *hēah* + *tūn*, with OE *sūth* 'south'.

Helen's Bay Down. The village was named after *Helen* Selina Sheridan by her son, Frederick Hamilton-Temple-Blackwood, 5th Lord Dufferin (1826–1902). Its equivalent Irish name is *Cuan Héilin*.

Helensburgh Arg. 'Helen's town'. Scottish English *burgh*. A new settlement was founded here in 1776 by Sir James Colquhoun of Luss, who named it after his wife, Lady *Helen* Sutherland.

Helford Cornwall. *Helleford* 1230. 'Estuary crossing-place'. Cornish **heyl* + OE *ford*.

Helhoughton Norfolk. *Helgatuna* 1086 (DB). 'Farmstead of a man called Helgi'. OScand. pers. name + OE *tūn*.

Helions Bumpstead Essex., *see* BUMPSTEAD.

Helland Cornwall. *Hellaunde* 1284. 'Old church-site'. Cornish **hen-lann*.

Hellesdon Norfolk. *Hægelisdun c.*985, *Hailesduna* 1086 (DB). 'Hill of a man called *Hægel'. OE pers. name + *dūn*.

Hellidon Northants. *Elliden* 12th cent. 'Holy, healthy, or prosperous valley'. OE *hǣlig* + *denu*.

Hellifield N. Yorks. *Helgefeld* 1086 (DB). Probably 'open land of a man called Helgi'. OScand. pers. name + OE *feld*.

Hellingly E. Sussex. *Hellingeleghe* 13th cent. 'Woodland clearing of the family or followers of a man called *Hielle, or of the hill dwellers'. OE pers. name or OE *hyll* + -*inga*- + *lēah*.

Hellington Norfolk. *Halgatune* 1086 (DB). 'Farmstead of a man called Helgi'. OScand. pers. name + OE *tūn*.

Helmdon Northants. *Elmedene* 1086 (DB). 'Valley of a man called *Helma'. OE pers. name + *denu*.

Helmingham Suffolk. *Helmingheham* 1086 (DB). 'Homestead of the family or followers of a man called Helm'. OE pers. name + -*inga*- + *hām*.

Helmsdale Highland. *Hjalmunddal* 1225. 'Hjalmund's valley'. OScand. pers. name + *dalr*.

Helmshore Lancs. *Hellshour* 1510. 'Steep slope with a cattle shelter'. OE *helm* + **scora*.

Helmsley N. Yorks. *Elmeslac* |*sic*| 1086 (DB), *Helmesley* 12th cent. 'Woodland clearing of a man called Helm'. OE pers. name + *lēah*.

Helmsley, Gate & *Helmsley, Upper* N. Yorks. *Hamelsec(h)* 1086 (DB), *Gatehemelsay* 1438, *Over Hemelsey* 1301. 'Island, or dry ground in marsh, of a man called Hemele'. OE pers. name + *ēg*. Distinguishing affixes from OScand. *gata* 'road' (here a Roman road) and OE *uferra* 'upper'.

Helperby N. Yorks. *Helperby* 972, *Helprebi* 1086 (DB). 'Farmstead or village of a woman called Hjalp'. OScand. pers. name (genitive -*ar*) + *bý*.

Helperthorpe N. Yorks. *Elpetorp* 1086 (DB). 'Outlying farmstead or hamlet of a woman called Hjalp'. OScand. pers. name (genitive -*ar*) + *thorp*.

Helpringham Lincs. *Helperi(n)cham* 1086 (DB). 'Homestead of the family or followers of a man called Helprīc'. OE pers. name + -*inga*- + *hām*.

Helpston Cambs. *Hylpestun* 948. 'Farmstead of a man called *Help'. OE pers. name + *tūn*.

Helsby Ches. *Helesbe* |*sic*| 1086 (DB), *Hellesbi* late 12th cent. 'Farmstead or village on a ledge'. OScand. *hjallr* + *bý*.

Helston, *Helstone*, 'estate at an old court', Cornish **henlys* + OE *tūn*: **Helston** Cornwall. *Henlistone* 1086 (DB). **Helstone** Cornwall. *Henliston* 1086 (DB).

Helton Cumbria. *Helton c.*1160. Probably 'farmstead on a slope'. OE *helde* + *tūn*.

Helvellyn Cumbria. *Helvillon* 1577. Probably Cumbric **hal* 'moor' + **velyn* 'yellow'.

Helvick Waterford. 'Rock shelf bay'. OScand. *hjalli* + *vik*.

Helygain. *See* HALKYN.

Hemblington Norfolk. *Hemelingetun* 1086 (DB). 'Estate associated with a man called Hemele'. OE pers. name + -*ing*- + *tūn*.

Hemel Hempstead Herts., *see* HEMPSTEAD.

Hemingbrough N. Yorks. *Hemingburgh* 1080–6, *Hamiburg* 1086 (DB). Probably 'stronghold of a man called Hemingr'. OScand. pers. name + OE *burh*.

Hemingby Lincs. *Hamingebi* 1086 (DB). 'Farmstead or village of a man called Hemingr'. OScand. pers. name + *bý*.

Hemingford Abbots & *Hemingford Grey* Cambs. *Hemmingeford* 974, *Emingeford* 1086 (DB), *Hemingford Abbatis* 1276, *Hemingford Grey* 1316. 'Ford of the family or followers of a man called Hemma or Hemmi'. OE pers. name + -*inga*- + *ford*. Distinguishing affixes from early possession by the Abbot of Ramsey and the de Grey family.

Hemingstone Suffolk. *Hamingestuna* 1086 (DB). 'Farmstead of a man called Hemingr'. OScand. pers. name + OE *tūn*.

Hemington, 'estate associated with a man called Hemma or Hemmi', OE pers. name + -*ing*- + *tūn*: **Hemington** Leics. *Aminton c.*1125. **Hemington** Northants. *Hemmingtune* 1077, *Hemintone* 1086 (DB). **Hemington** Somerset. *Hammingtona* 1086 (DB).

Hemley Suffolk. *Helmelea* 1086 (DB). 'Woodland clearing of a man called *Helma'. OE pers. name + *lēah*.

Hempholme E. R. Yorks. *Hempholm* 12th cent. 'Raised ground in marshland where hemp is grown'. OE *hænep* + OScand. *holmr*.

Hempnall Norfolk. *Hemenhala* 1086 (DB). 'Nook of land of a man called Hemma'. OE pers. name (genitive -*n*) + *halh*.

Hempstead, usually 'the homestead', OE *hām-stede*, *hǣm-stede*: **Hempstead** Essex. *Hamesteda* 1086 (DB). **Hempstead** Norfolk, near Lessingham. *Hemsteda* 1086 (DB). **Hempstead, Hemel** Herts. *Hamelamestede* 1086 (DB). Hemel is an old district-name first recorded *c.*705 meaning 'broken, undulating' from OE **hamel*.

However the following has a different origin: **Hempstead** Norfolk, near Holt. *Henepsteda* 1086 (DB). 'Place where hemp is grown'. OE *hænep* + *stede*.

Hempsted Glos. *Hechanestede* 1086 (DB). 'High homestead'. OE *hēah* + *hām-stede*.

Hempton Norfolk. *Hamatuna* 1086 (DB). 'Farmstead or village of a man called Hemma'. OE pers. name + *tūn*.

Hempton Oxon. *Henton* 1086 (DB). 'High farm'. OE *hēah* (dative *hēan*) + *tūn*.

Hemsby Norfolk. *Heimesbei* 1086 (DB). Probably 'farmstead or village of a man called *Hēmer'. OScand. pers. name + *bý*.

Hemswell Lincs. *Helmeswelle* 1086 (DB). 'Spring or stream of a man called Helm'. OE pers. name + *wella*.

Hemsworth W. Yorks. *Hamelesuurde* |*sic*| 1086 (DB), *Hymeleswrde* 12th cent. 'Enclosure of a man called *Hymel'. OE pers. name + *worth*.

Hemyock Devon. *Hamihoc* 1086 (DB). Possibly a Celtic river-name meaning 'summer stream', otherwise 'river-bend of a man called Hemma', from OE pers. name + *hōc*.

Henbury Brist. *Heanburg* 692, *Henberie* 1086 (DB). 'High or chief fortified place'. OE *hēah* (dative *hēan*) + *burh* (dative *byrig*).

Henbury Ches. *Hameteberie* 1086 (DB). 'Stronghold or manor-house where a community lives'. OE *hǣmed* + *burh* (dative *byrig*).

Hendon Gtr. London. *Heandun* c.975, *Handone* 1086 (DB). '(Place at) the high hill'. OE *hēah* (dative *hēan*) + *dūn*.

Hendon Tyne & Wear. *Hynden* 1382. 'Valley frequented by hinds'. OE *hind* + *denu*.

Hendred, East & *Hendred, West* Oxon. *Hennarith* 956, *Henret* 1086 (DB). 'Stream frequented by hens (of wild birds)'. OE *henn* + *rīth*.

Hendy-gwyn. *See* WHITLAND.

Henfield W. Sussex. *Hanefeld* 770, *Hamfelde* 1086 (DB). Probably 'open land characterized by stones or rocks'. OE *hān* + *feld*.

Hengoed Carm. 'Old wood'. Welsh *hen* + *coed*.

Hengrave Suffolk. *Hemegretham* |*sic*| 1086 (DB), *Hemegrede* c.1095. 'Grassy meadow of a man called Hemma'. OE pers. name + *grēd* (with *hām* 'homestead' in the Domesday form).

Henham Essex. *Henham* c.1045, 1086 (DB). 'High homestead or enclosure'. OE *hēah* (dative *hēan*) + *hām* or *hamm*.

Henley, usually 'high (or chief) wood or clearing', OE *hēah* (dative *hēan*) + *lēah*; examples include: **Henley** Somerset. *Henleighe* 973. **Henley** Suffolk. *Henleia* 1086 (DB). **Henley-in-Arden** Warwicks. *Henle* c.1180. Affix refers to the medieval Forest of Arden (*Eardene* 1088), possibly a Celtic name meaning 'high district'. **Henley-on-Thames** Oxon. *Henleiam* c.1140. *See* THAMES.
  However the following has a different origin: **Henley** Shrops. *Haneleu* |*sic*| 1086 (DB), *Hennele* 1242. 'Wood or clearing frequented by hens (of wild birds)'. OE *henn* + *lēah*.

Henlow Beds. *Haneslauue* 1086 (DB). 'Hill or mound frequented by hens (of wild birds)'. OE *henn* + *hlāw*.

Hennock Devon. *Hainoc* 1086 (DB). '(Place at) the high oak-tree'. OE *hēah* (dative *hēan*) + *āc*.

Henny, Great Essex. *Heni* 1086 (DB). 'High island or land partly surrounded by water'. OE *hēah* (dative *hēan*) + *ēg*.

Hensall N. Yorks. *Edeshale* |*sic*| 1086 (DB), *Hethensale* 12th cent. 'Nook of land of a man called *Hethīn* or *Hethinn*'. OE or OScand. pers. name + OE *halh*.

Henshaw Northum. *Hedeneshalch* 12th cent. Identical in origin with the previous name.

Henstead Suffolk. *Henestede* 1086 (DB). Probably 'place frequented by hens (of wild birds)'. OE *henn* + *stede*.

Henstridge Somerset. *Hengstesrig* 956, *Hengest(e)rich* 1086 (DB). 'Ridge where stallions are kept' or 'ridge of a man called Hengest'. OE *hengest* or OE pers. name + *hrycg*.

Henton Oxon. *Hentone* 1086 (DB). 'High (or chief) farmstead'. OE *hēah* (dative *hēan*) + *tūn*.

Henton Somerset. *Hentun* 1065. Identical in origin with previous name, or 'farmstead where hens are kept', OE *henn* + *tūn*.

Hepburn Northum. *Hybberndune* c.1050. Probably identical in origin with HEBBURN (and with the addition of OE *dūn* 'hill' in the early spelling).

Hepple Northum. *Hephal* 1205. 'Nook of land where rose-hips or brambles grow'. OE *hēope* or *hēopa* + *halh*.

Hepscott Northum. *Hebscot* 1242. 'Cottage(s) of a man called *Hebbi*'. OE pers. name + *cot*.

Heptonstall W. Yorks. *Heptonstall* 1253. 'Farmstead where rose-hips or brambles grow'. OE *hēope* or *hēopa* + *tūn-stall*.

Hepworth, probably 'enclosure of a man called *Heppa*', OE pers. name + *worth*: **Hepworth** Suffolk. *Hepworda* 1086 (DB). **Hepworth** W. Yorks. *Heppeuuord* 1086 (DB).

Herbrandston Pemb. *Villa Herbrandi* 13th cent., *Herbraundistone* 1307. 'Herbrand's farm'. OGerman pers. name + OE *tūn*.

Hereford, 'ford suitable for the passage of an army', OE *here-ford*: **Hereford** Heref. & Worcs. *Hereford* 958, 1086 (DB). **Herefordshire** (OE *scīr* 'district') is first referred to in the 11th cent. **Hereford, Little** Heref. & Worcs. *Lutelonhereford* 1086 (DB). Affix is OE *lytlan*, dative of *lytel* 'little'.

Hergest Heref. & Worcs. *Hergest(h)* 1086 (DB). Probably a Welsh name, but obscure in origin and meaning.

Hermiston Edin. *Hirdmannistoun* 1233. 'Herdsman's farmstead'. OE *hirdman* + *tūn*.

Herne, *Herne Bay* Kent. *Hyrnan* c.1100. '(Place at) the angle or corner of land'. OE *hyrne*.

Hernhill Kent. *Haranhylle* c.1100. '(Place at) the grey hill'. OE *hār* (dative *-an*) + *hyll*.

Herriard Hants. *Henerd* |*sic*| 1086 (DB), *Herierda* c.1160. Probably 'army quarters' (perhaps of a Viking army), OE *here* + *geard*. Alternatively this may be a Celtic name meaning 'long ridge' from *hyr* + *garth*.

Herringfleet Suffolk. *Herlingaflet* 1086 (DB). 'Creek or stream of the family or followers of a man called *Herela*'. OE pers. name + *-inga-* + *flēot*.

Herringswell Suffolk. *Hyrningwella* 1086 (DB). 'Spring or stream at the corner of land'. OE *hyrne* + *-ing* + *wella*.

Herrington, *East* Tyne & Wear. *Erinton* 1196. Possibly 'estate associated with a man called *Here*'. OE pers. name + *-ing-* + *tūn*.

Hersham Surrey. *Hauerichesham* 1175. 'Homestead or river-meadow of a man called *Hǣferic*'. OE pers. name + *hām* or *hamm*.

Herstmonceux E. Sussex. *Herst* 1086 (DB), *Herstmonceus* 1287. OE *hyrst* 'wooded hill' + manorial affix from possession by the Monceux family in the 12th cent.

Hertford Herts. *Herutford* 731, *Hertforde* 1086 (DB). 'Ford frequented by harts or stags'. OE *heorot* + *ford*. **Hertfordshire** (OE *scīr* 'district') is first referred to in the 11th cent.

Hertingfordbury Herts. *Herefordingberie* |*sic*| 1086 (DB), *Hertfordingeberi* 1220. 'Stronghold of the people of HERTFORD'. OE *-inga-* + *burh* (dative *byrig*).

Hesket, *Hesketh*, probably 'boundary land where horses graze', but possibly 'race course for horses', OScand. *hestr* + *skeith*; examples include: **Hesket, High** & **Hesket,**

Low Cumbria. *Hescayth* 1285. **Hesketh** Lancs. *Heschath* 1288.

However the following has a different origin: **Hesket Newmarket** Cumbria. *Eskeheued* 1227. 'Hill growing with ash-trees'. OScand. *eski* + OE *hēafod*. Affix first found in the 18th cent. refers to the market here.

Heskin Green Lancs. *Heskyn* 1257. A Welsh name meaning 'wet ground growing with sedge or coarse grass'.

Hesleden Durham. *Heseldene* c.1050. 'Valley where hazels grow'. OE *hæsel* + *denu*.

Heslerton, East & *Heslerton, West* N. Yorks. *Heslerton* 1086 (DB). 'Farmstead where hazels grow'. OE **hæsler* + *tūn*.

Heslington York. *Haslinton* 1086 (DB). 'Farmstead by the hazel wood'. OE **hæsling* + *tūn*.

Hessay York. *Hesdesai |sic|* 1086 (DB), *Heslesaia* 12th cent. 'Marshland, or island, where hazels grow'. OE *hæsel* (influenced by OScand. *hesli*) + *sǣ* or *ēg*.

Hessett Suffolk. *Heteseta |sic|* 1086 (DB), *Heggeset* 1225. 'Fold (for animals) with a hedge'. OE *hecg* + *(ge)set*.

Hessle E. R. Yorks. *Hase |sic|* 1086 (DB), *Hesel* 12th cent. '(Place at) the hazel-tree'. OE *hæsel* (influenced by OScand. *hesli*).

Hest Bank Lancs. *Hest* 1177. OE **hǣst* 'undergrowth, brushwood'.

Heston Gtr. London. *Hestone* c.1125. 'Farmstead among the brushwood'. OE **hǣs* + *tūn*.

Heswall Mersey. *Eswelle |sic|* 1086 (DB), *Haselwell* c.1200. 'Spring where hazels grow'. OE *hæsel* + *wella*.

Hethe Oxon. *Hedha* 1086 (DB). OE *hǣth* 'heath, uncultivated land'.

Hethersett Norfolk. *Hederseta* 1086 (DB). Probably '(settlement of) the dwellers among the heather'. OE **hǣddre* + *sǣte*.

Hett Durham. *Het* c.168. '(Place at) the hat-shaped hill'. OE *hætt* or OScand. *hetti* (dative of *hǫttr*).

Hetton N. Yorks. *Hetune* 1086 (DB). 'Farmstead on a heath'. OE *hǣth* + *tūn*.

Hetton le Hole Tyne & Wear. *Heppedun* 1180. 'Hill where rose-hips or brambles grow'. OE *hēope* or *hēopa* + *dūn*. Affix means 'in the hollow'.

Heugh Northum. *Hou* 1279. '(Place at) the ridge or spur of land'. OE *hōh*.

Heveningham Suffolk. *Heueniggeham* 1086 (DB). 'Homestead of the family or followers of a man called **Hefin*'. OE pers. name + *-inga-* + *hām*.

Hever Kent. *Heanyfre* 814. '(Place at) the high edge or hill-brow'. OE *hēah* (dative *hēan*) + *yfer*.

Heversham Cumbria. *Hefresham* c.1050, *Eureshaim* 1086 (DB). Probably 'homestead of a man called *Hēahfrith*'. OE pers. name + *hām*.

Hevingham Norfolk. *Heuincham* 1086 (DB). 'Homestead of the family or followers of a man called Hefa'. OE pers. name + *-inga-* + *hām*.

Hewelsfield Glos. *Hivoldestone* 1086 (DB), *Hualdesfeld* c.1145. 'Open land of a man called Hygewald'. OE pers. name + *feld* (replacing earlier *tūn* 'farmstead').

Hewick, Bridge & *Hewick, Copt* N. Yorks. *Heawic* 1086 (DB), *Hewik atte brigg* 1309, *Coppedehaiwic* 1208. 'High (or chief) dairy-farm'. OE *hēah* (dative *hēan*) + *wīc*. Distinguishing affixes 'at the bridge' (from OE *brycg*) and 'with a peak or hill-top' (OE *coppede*).

Hewish, 'measure of land that would support a family', OE *hīwisc*: **Hewish** Somerset. *Hywys* 1327. **Hewish, East** & **Hewish, West** N. Som. *Hiwis* 1198.

Hexham Northum. *Hagustaldes ham* 685 (c.1120). 'The warrior's homestead'. OE *hagustald* + *hām*.

Hexton Herts. *Hegestanestone* 1086 (DB). 'Farmstead of a man called Hēahstān'. OE pers. name + *tūn*.

Heybridge Essex. *Heaghbregge* c.1200. 'High (or chief) bridge'. OE *hēah* + *brycg*.

Heydon Cambs. *Haidenam* 1086 (DB). 'Valley where hay is made', or 'valley with an enclosure'. OE *hēg* or *hæg* + *denu*.

Heydon Norfolk. *Heidon* 1196. 'Hill where hay is made'. OE *hēg* + *dūn*.

Heyford, 'hay ford', i.e. 'ford used chiefly at hay-making time', OE *hēg* + *ford*: **Heyford, Lower** & **Heyford, Upper** Oxon. *Hegford* 1086 (DB). **Heyford, Nether** & **Heyford, Upper** Northants. *Heiforde* 1086 (DB).

Heysham Lancs. *Hessam* 1086 (DB). 'Homestead or village among the brushwood'. OE **hǣs* + *hām*.

Heyshott W. Sussex. *Hethsete* c.1100. 'Corner of land where heather grows'. OE *hǣth* + *scēat*.

Heytesbury Wilts. *Hestrebe |sic|* 1086 (DB), *Hehtredeberia* c.1115. 'Stronghold of a woman called **Hēahthrȳth*'. OE pers. name + *burh* (dative *byrig*).

Heythrop Oxon. *Edrope |sic|* 1086 (DB), *Hethrop* 11th cent. 'High hamlet or outlying farmstead'. OE *hēah* + *throp*.

Heywood Gtr. Manch. *Heghwode* 1246. 'High (or chief) wood'. OE *hēah* + *wudu*.

Heywood Wilts. *Heiwode* 1225. 'Enclosed wood'. OE *hæg* + *wudu*.

Hibaldstow N. Lincs. *Hiboldestou* 1086 (DB). 'Holy place where St Hygebald is buried'. OE pers. name + *stōw*.

Hickleton S. Yorks. *Icheltone* 1086 (DB). Probably 'farmstead frequented by woodpeckers'. OE *hicol* + *tūn*.

Hickling, '(settlement of) the family or followers of a man called **Hicel*', OE pers. name + *-ingas*: **Hickling** Norfolk. *Hikelinga* 1086 (DB). **Hickling** Notts. *Hikelinge* c.1000, *Hechelinge* 1086 (DB).

Hidcote Boyce Glos. *Hudicota* 716, *Hedecote* 1086 (DB), *Hudicote Boys* 1327. 'Cottage of a man called **Hydeca* or Huda'. OE pers. name + *cot*. Manorial affix from a family called de Bosco or Bois, here in the 13th cent.

Hiendley, South W. Yorks. *Hindeleia* 1086 (DB). 'Wood or clearing frequented by hinds or does'. OE *hind* + *lēah*.

High as affix, see main name, e.g. for **High Ackworth** (W. Yorks.) *see* ACKWORTH.

High Beach Essex. *Highbeach-green* 1670. Probably named from the beech-trees here.

Higham, 'high (or chief) homestead or enclosure', OE *hēah* + *hām* or *hamm*; examples include: **Higham** Derbys. *Hehham* 1155. **Higham** Kent. *Hegham* 1242. **Higham** Lancs. *Hegham* 1296. **Higham** Suffolk, near Stratford St Mary. *Hecham* c.1050, *Heihham* 1086 (DB). **Higham, Cold** Northants. *Hecham* 1086 (DB), *Colehigham* 1541. Affix is OE *cald* 'cold, exposed'. **Higham Ferrers** Northants. *Hecham* 1086 (DB), *Heccham Ferrar* 1279. Manorial affix from the Ferrers family, here in the 12th cent. **Higham Gobion** Beds. *Echam* 1086 (DB), *Heygham Gobyon* 1291. Manorial affix from the Gobion family, here from the 12th cent. **Higham on the Hill** Leics. *Hecham* 1220–35. The affix is found from the 16th cent. **Higham Upshire** Kent. *Heahhaam* c.765, *Hecham* 1086 (DB). The affix means 'higher district' from OE *upp* + *scīr*.

Highampton Devon. *Hantone* 1086 (DB), *Heghanton* 1303. 'High farmstead'. OE *hēah* (dative *hēan*) + *tūn*, with the later addition of ME *heghe* 'high' after the meaning of the original first element had been forgotten.

Highbridge Somerset. *Highbridge* 1324. 'High (or chief) bridge'. OE *hēah* + *brycg*.

Highbury Gtr. London. *Heybury* c.1375. 'High manor', from ME *heghe* + *bury*.

Highclere Hants. *Clere* 1086 (DB), *Alta Clera* c.1270. Perhaps originally a Celtic river-name meaning 'bright stream', with the later addition of *high* (Latin *alta*).

Highcliffe Dorset. *High Clift* |sic| 1759, earlier *Black Cliffe* 1610. Self-explanatory.

Higher as affix, see main name, e.g. for **Higher Ansty** (Dorset) *see* ANSTY.

Higher Kinnerton Flin. *Kynarton* 1240. 'Higher (place called) Cyneheard's farmstead'. OE pers. name + *tūn*. *Higher* distinguishes the place from nearby *Lower Kinnerton*, Ches.

Highgate Gtr. London. *Le Heighgate* 1354. 'High tollgate'. OE *hēah* + *geat*.

Highland (the unitary authority). *the heland* 1529, *the High-Lands of Scotland* c.1627. 'High land'. The mountainous region of northern Scotland is distinguished from the Lowlands to the south.

Highleadon Glos. *Hineledene* 13th cent. 'Estate on the River Leadon belonging to a religious community'. OE *hīwan* (genitive plural *hīgna*) + Celtic river-name (meaning 'broad stream').

Highley Shrops. *Hugelei* 1086 (DB). 'Woodland clearing of a man called *Hugga*'. OE pers. name + *lēah*.

Highnam Glos. *Hamme* 1086 (DB), *Hinehamme* 12th cent. OE *hamm* 'river-meadow' with the later addition of OE *hīwan* (genitive plural *hīgna*) 'a religious community'.

Hightown Ches., late name, meaning simply 'the high part of the town' (of CONGLETON).

Highway Wilts. *Hiwei* 1086 (DB). 'Road used for carrying hay'. OE *hēg* + *weg*.

Highworth Wilts. *Wrde* 1086 (DB), *Hegworth* 1232. OE *worth* 'enclosure, farmstead' with the later addition of *hēah* 'high'.

Hilborough Norfolk. *Hildeburhwella* 1086 (DB), *Hildeburwrthe* 1242. 'Stream or enclosure of a woman called Hildeburh'. OE *pers. name* + *wella* or *worth*.

Hildenborough Kent. *Hyldenn* 1240. *Hildenborough* 1389. Probably 'woodland pasture on or by a hill'. OE *hyll* + *denn* with the later addition of *burh* 'manor, borough'.

Hildersham Cambs. *Hildricesham* 1086 (DB). 'Homestead of a man called *Hildrīc*'. OE pers. name + *hām*.

Hilderstone Staffs. *Hidulvestune* 1086 (DB). 'Farmstead of a man called Hildulfr or Hildwulf'. OScand. or OE pers. name + *tūn*.

Hilderthorpe E. R. Yorks. *Hilgertorp* 1086 (DB). 'Outlying farmstead of a man called Hildiger or a woman called Hildigerthr'. OScand. pers. name + *thorp*.

Hilfield Dorset *Hylfelde* 934. 'Open land by a hill'. OE *hyll* + *feld*.

Hilgay Norfolk. *Hillingeiæ* 974, *Hidlingheia* 1086 (DB). 'Island, or dry ground in marsh, of the family or followers of a man called *Hȳthla* or *Hydla*'. OE pers. name + *-inga-* + *ēg*.

Hill S. Glos. *Hilla* 1086 (DB). '(Place at) the hill'. OE *hyll*.

Hill Head Hants., a recent name, self-explanatory.

Hill, North & *Hill, South* Cornwall. *Henle* 1238, *Northhindle* 1260, *Suthhulle* 1270, *Suthhynile* 1306. 'High wood or clearing' or 'hinds' wood or clearing'. OE *hēah* (dative *hēan*) or *hind* + *lēah*, with later replacement by *hyll* 'hill'.

Hiliam N. Yorks. *Hillum* 963. '(Place at) the hills'. OE *hyll* in a dative plural form *hyllum*.

Hillesden Bucks. *Hildesdun* 949, *Ilesdone* 1086 (DB). 'Hill of a man called Hild'. OE pers. name + *dūn*.

Hillfarance Somerset. *Hilla* 1086 (DB), *Hull Ferun* 1253. '(Place at) the hill'. OE *hyll*. Manorial addition from the Furon family, here in the 12th cent.

Hillhall Down. 'Hill's hall'. Peter *Hill*, son of Sir Moses Hill of HILLSBOROUGH, built a bawn or fortified mansion here in c.1637.

Hillingdon Gtr. London. *Hildendune* c.1080, *Hillendone* 1086 (DB). 'Hill of a man called *Hilda*'. OE pers. name (genitive *-n*) + *dūn*.

Hillington Norfolk. *Helingetuna* 1086 (DB). 'Farmstead of the family or followers of a man called *Hȳthla* or *Hydla*'. OE pers. name + *-inga-* + *tūn*.

Hillmorton Warwicks. *Mortone* 1086 (DB), *Hulle and Morton* 1247. Originally two distinct names, now combined. *Hill* is '(place at) the hill' from OE *hyll*. *Morton* is 'marshland farmstead' from OE *mōr* + *tūn*.

Hillsborough Down. 'Hill's fortified mansion'. Sir Moses Hill, Provost Marshal of Ulster, built a fortress here in c.1610. The Irish name of Hillsborough is *Cromghlinn*, as for CRUMLIN.

Hillswick Shet. *Hildiswik* c.1250. 'Hildir's bay'. OScand. pers. name *Hildir* + *vík*.

Hilltown Down. 'Hill's town'. Wills *Hill*, 1st Marquis of Downshire, built a church here in 1766.

Hilmarton Wilts. *Helmerdingtun* 962, *Helmerintone* 1086 (DB). 'Estate associated with a man called *Helmheard'. OE pers. name + *-ing-* + *tūn*.

Hilperton Wilts. *Help(e)rinton* 1086 (DB). 'Estate associated with a man called *Hylprīc'. OE pers. name + *-ing-* + *tūn*.

Hilton, usually 'farmstead or village on or near a hill', OE *hyll* + *tūn*: **Hilton** Cambs. *Hiltone* 1196. **Hilton** Derbys. *Hiltune* 1086 (DB). **Hilton** Stock on T. *Hiltune* 1086 (DB).
However other Hiltons have a different origin: **Hilton** Cumbria. *Helton* 1289. Probably 'farmstead on a slope'. OE *helde* + *tūn*. **Hilton** Dorset. *Eltone* 1086 (DB). 'Farmstead on a slope or where tansy grows'. OE *h(i)elde* or *helde* + *tūn*.

Himbleton Heref. & Worcs. *Hymeltun* 816, *Himeltun* 1086 (DB). 'Farmstead where the hop plant (or some similar plant) grows'. OE *hymele* + *tūn*.

Himley Staffs. *Himelei* 1086 (DB). 'Woodland clearing where the hop plant (or some similar plant) grows'. OE *hymele* + *lēah*.

Hincaster Cumbria. *Hennecastre* 1086 (DB). 'Old fortification or earthwork haunted by hens (of wild birds)'. OE *henn* + *ceaster*.

Hinckley Leics. *Hinchelie* 1086 (DB). 'Woodland clearing of a man called Hynca'. OE pers. name + *lēah*.

Hinderclay Suffolk. *Hilderclea* 1086 (DB). 'Tongue of land where elder-trees grow'. OE *hyldre* + *clēa*.

Hinderwell N. Yorks. *Hildrewell* 1086 (DB). Possibly 'spring or well associated with St Hild'. OE pers. name (with Scandinavianized genitive *-ar*) + *wella*. Alternatively the first element may be OE *hyldre* or *hylder* 'elder-tree'.

Hindhead Surrey. *Hyndehed* 1571. 'Hill frequented by hinds or does'. OE *hind* + *hēafod*.

Hindley Gtr. Manch. *Hindele* 1212. 'Wood or clearing frequented by hinds or does'. OE *hind* + *lēah*.

Hindlip Heref. & Worcs. *Hindehlep* 966, *Hindelep* 1086 (DB). 'Gate or fence over which hinds can leap'. OE *hind* + *hlīep*.

Hindolveston Norfolk. *Hidolfestuna* 1086 (DB). 'Farmstead of a man called Hildwulf'. OE pers. name + *tūn*.

Hindon Wilts. *Hynedon* 1268. Probably 'hill belonging to a religious community'. OE *hīwan* (genitive plural *hīgna*) + *dūn*.

Hindringham Norfolk. *Hindringaham* 1068 (DB). Possibly 'homestead of the people living behind (the hills)'. OE *hinder* + *-inga-* + *hām*.

Hingham Norfolk. *Hincham* 1086 (DB), *Heingeham* 1173. Probably 'homestead of the family or followers of a man called Hega'. OE *pers. name* + *-inga-* + *hām*.

Hinksey, North & *Hinksey, South* Oxon. *Hengestesige* 10th cent. 'Island or well-watered land of the stallion or of a man called Hengest'. OE *hengest* or OE pers. name + *ēg*.

Hinstock Shrops. *Stoche* 1086 (DB), *Hinestok* 1242. OE *stoc* 'outlying farmstead, dependent settlement' with the later addition of ME *hine* 'household servants'.

Hintlesham Suffolk. *Hintlesham* 1086 (DB). 'Homestead or enclosure of a man called *Hyntel'. OE pers. name + *hām* or *hamm*.

Hinton, a very common name, has two different origins. Sometimes 'high (or chief) farmstead' from OE *hēah* (dative *hēan*) + *tūn*: **Hinton** S. Glos., near Dyrham. *Heanton* 13th cent. **Hinton Ampner** Hants. *Heantun* 1045, *Hentune* 1086 (DB), *Hinton Amner* 13th cent. Affix is OFrench *aumoner* 'almoner', from its early possession by the almoner of St Swithun's Priory at Winchester. **Hinton Blewett** B. & NE. Som. *Hantone* 1086 (DB), *Hentun Bluet* 1246. Manorial affix from its early possession by the Bluet family. **Hinton, Broad** Wilts. *Hentone* 1086 (DB), *Brodehenton* 1319. Affix is OE *brād* 'large'. **Hinton Charterhouse** B. & NE. Som. *Hantone* 1086 (DB), *Henton Charterus* 1273. Affix is OFrench *chartrouse* 'a house of Carthusian monks' referring to a priory founded in the early 13th cent. **Hinton, Great** Wilts. *Henton* 1216. **Hinton St George** Somerset. *Hantone* 1086 (DB), *Hentun Sancti Georgii* 1246. Affix from the dedication of the church. **Hinton St Mary** Dorset. *Hamtune* 944, *Haintone* 1086 (DB), *Hinton Marye* 1627. Affix from the possession of the manor by the Abbey of St Mary at Shaftesbury. **Hinton Waldrist** Oxon. *Hentone* 1086 (DB), *Hinton Walrush* 1676. Manorial affix from the family de Sancto Walerico, here in the 12th cent.
However many Hintons mean 'farmstead belonging to a religious community', from OE *hīwan* (genitive plural *hīgna*) + *tūn*: **Hinton** Heref. & Worcs., near Peterchurch. *Hinetune* 1086 (DB). **Hinton** Northants. *Hintone* 1086 (DB). **Hinton, Cherry** Cambs. *Hintone* 1086 (DB), *Cheryhynton* 1576. Affix is ME *chiri* 'cherry' from the number of cherry-trees formerly growing here. **Hinton in the Hedges** Northants. *Hintone* 1086 (DB). Affix (meaning 'among the hedges') is from OE *hecg*. **Hinton, Little** Wilts. *Hinneton* 1205. **Hinton Martell** Dorset. *Hinetone* 1086 (DB), *Hineton Martel* 1226. Manorial affix from the Martell family, here in the 13th cent. **Hinton on the Green** Heref. & Worcs. *Hinetune* 1086 (DB). Affix is OE *grēne* 'village green'.

Hints, '(place on) the roads or paths', Welsh *hynt*: **Hints** Shrops. *Hintes* 1242. **Hints** Staffs. *Hintes* 1086 (DB).

Hinwick Beds. *Heneuuic(h)* 1086 (DB). 'Farm where hens are kept'. OE *henn* + *wīc*.

Hinxhill Kent. *Haenostesyle* c.1100. 'Hill of the stallion or of a man called Hengest'. OE *hengest* or OE pers. name + *hyll*.

Hinxton Cambs. *Hestitone* |sic| 1086 (DB), *Hengstiton* 1202. 'Estate associated with a man called Hengest'. OE pers. name + *-ing-* + *tūn*.

Hinxworth Herts. *Haingesteuuorde* 1086 (DB). Probably 'enclosure where stallions are kept'. OE *hengest* + *worth*.

Hipperholme W. Yorks. *Huperun* 1086 (DB). '(Place among) the osiers'. OE *hyper in a dative plural form *hyperum*.

Hirst Courtney, Temple Hirst N. Yorks. *Hyrst* c.1030, *Hirst Courtenay* 1303, *Templehurst* 1316. '(Place at) the wooded hill'. OE *hyrst*. Distinguishing affixes from possession by the Courtney family (here in the 13th cent.) and by the Knights Templars (here in the 12th cent.).

Hirwaun Rhon. 'Long moor'. *Hyrweunworgan* 1203, *Hirwen Urgan* 1536, *Hirwaun Wrgan* 1638. Welsh *hir* + *gwaun*. The forms of the name above include the name of *Gwrgan*, reputedly the last king of Glamorgan.

Histon Cambs. *Histone* 1086 (DB). Possibly 'farmstead of the sons or young men'. OE *hys(s)e* + *tūn*.

Hitcham Suffolk. *Hecham* 1086 (DB). 'Homestead with a hedge or hatch-gate'. OE *hecg* or *hecc* + *hām*.

Hitchin Herts. *Hiccam* c.945, *Hiz* 1086 (DB). '(Place in the territory of) the tribe called *Hicce*'. Old tribal name (possibly derived from a Celtic river-name meaning 'dry') in a dative plural form *Hiccum*.

Hittisleigh Devon. *Hitenesleia* 1086 (DB). 'Woodland clearing of a man called *Hyttīn*'. OE pers. name + *lēah*.

Hixon Staffs. *Hustedone* |sic| 1086 (DB), *Huchtesdona* 1130. 'Hill of a man called *Hyht*. OE pers. name + *dūn*.

Hoar Cross Staffs. *Horcros* 1230. 'Grey or boundary cross'. OE *hār* + *cros*.

Hoarwithy Heref. & Worcs. *La Horewythy* 13th cent. '(Place at) the whitebeam'. OE *hār* + *wīthig*.

Hoath Kent. *La hathe* 13th cent. '(Place at) the heath'. OE *hāth*.

Hoathly, 'heathy woodland clearing' or 'woodland clearing where heather grows', OE *hāth* + *lēah*: **Hoathly, East** E. Sussex. *Hodlegh* 1287. **Hoathly, West** W. Sussex. *Hadlega* 1121.

Hôb, Yr. See HOPE.

Hoby Leics. *Hobie* 1086 (DB). 'Farmstead or village on a spur of land'. OE *hōh* + OScand. *bý*.

Hockering Norfolk. *Hokelinka* |sic| 1086 (DB), *Hokeringhes* 12th cent. '(Settlement of) the people at the rounded hill'. OE *hocer* + *-ingas*.

Hockerton Notts. *Hocretone* 1086 (DB). 'Farmstead at the hump or rounded hill'. OE *hocer* + *tūn*.

Hockham, *Great* Norfolk. *Hocham* 1086 (DB). 'Homestead of a man called Hocca, or where hocks or mallows grow'. OE pers. name or OE *hocc* + *hām*.

Hockley Essex. *Hocheleia* 1086 (DB). 'Woodland clearing of a man called Hocca, or where hocks or mallows grow'. OE pers. name or OE *hocc* + *lēah*.

Hockley Heath W. Mids. *Huckeloweheth* c.1280. 'Heath near the mound or hill of a man called *Hucca*'. OE pers. name + *hlāw* + *hēth*.

Hockliffe Beds. *Hocgan clif* 1015, *Hocheleia* |sic| 1086 (DB). Probably 'steep hill-side of a man called *Hocga*'. OE pers. name + *clif*.

Hockwold cum Wilton Norfolk. *Hocuuella* |sic| 1086 (DB), *Hocwolde* 1242. 'Wooded area where hocks or mallows grow'. OE *hocc* + *wald*. See WILTON.

Hockworthy Devon. *Hocoorde* 1086 (DB). 'Enclosure of a man called Hocca'. OE pers. name + *worth*.

Hoddesdon Herts. *Hodesdone* 1086 (DB). 'Hill of a man called *Hod*'. OE pers. name + *dūn*.

Hoddlesden Lancs. *Hoddesdene* 1296. 'Valley of a man called *Hod* or *Hodel*'. OE pers. name + *denu*.

Hodgeston Pemb. *Villa Hogges* 1291, *Hoggeston* 1376. 'Hodge's farm'. OGerman pers. name + OE *tūn*.

Hodnet Shrops. *Odenet* 1086 (DB), *Hodenet* 1121. Probably a British name meaning 'pleasant valley', from the words which became Welsh *hawdd* and *nant*.

Hoe Norfolk. *Hou* 1086 (DB). '(Place at) the ridge or spur of land'. OE *hōh* (dative *hōe*).

Hoff Cumbria. *Houf* 1179. 'The heathen temple or sanctuary'. OScand. *hof*.

Hog's Back Surrey, first so called (from its shape) in 1823, earlier *Geldedon* 1195, probably 'hill called *Gylde* (the gold-coloured one)', from OE **gylde* + *dūn*, see GUILDFORD.

Hoggeston Bucks. *Hochestone* |sic| 1086 (DB), *Hoggeston* 1200. 'Farmstead of a man called **Hogg*'. OE pers. name + *tūn*.

Hoghton Lancs. *Hoctonam* |sic| c.1160. 'Farmstead on or near a hill-spur'. OE *hōh* + *tūn*.

Hognaston Derbys. *Ochenavestun* 1086 (DB). Possibly 'grazing farm of a man called Hocca'. OE pers. name + *æfēsn* + *tūn*.

Hogsthorpe Lincs. *Hocgestorp* 12th cent. 'Outlying farmstead or hamlet of a man called **Hogg*'. OE pers. name + OScand. *thorp*.

Holbeach Lincs. *Holebech* 1086 (DB). 'Hollow stream' or 'hollow ridge'. OE *hol* + *bece* or *bæc* (locative **bece*).

Holbeck Notts. *Holebek* c.1180. 'Hollow stream, stream in a hollow'. OScand. *holr* or *hol* + *bekkr*.

Holbeton Devon. *Holbouton* 1229. 'Farmstead in the hollow bend'. OE *hol* + *boga* + *tūn*.

Holborn Gtr. London. *Holeburne* 1086 (DB). 'Hollow stream, stream in a hollow'. OE *hol* + *burna*.

Holbrook, 'hollow brook, brook in a hollow', OE *hol* + *brōc*: **Holbrook** Derbys. *Holebroc* 1086 (DB). **Holbrook** Suffolk. *Holebroc* |sic| 1086 (DB).

Holbury Hants., near Fawley. *Holeberi* 1187. 'Hollow stronghold', or 'stronghold in a hollow'. OE *hol* + *burh* (dative *byrig*).

Holcombe, a common name, 'deep or hollow valley', OE *hol* + *cumb*; examples include: **Holcombe** Devon, near Dawlish. *Holacumba* c.1070, *Holcomma* 1086 (DB). **Holcombe** Gtr. Manch. *Holecumba* early 13th cent. **Holcombe** Somerset. *Holecumbe* 1243. **Holcombe Burnell** Devon. *Holecumba* 1086 (DB), *Holecumbe Bernard* 1263. Manorial affix (later modified to the modern form) from a man called Bernard whose son held the manor in 1242. **Holcombe Rogus** Devon. *Holecoma* 1086 (DB), *Holecombe Roges* 1281. Manorial affix from one *Rogo* who held the manor in 1086.

Holcot Northants. *Holecote* 1086 (DB). 'Cottage(s) in the hollow(s)'. OE *hol* + *cot*.

Holden Lancs. *Holedene* 1086 (DB). 'Hollow valley'. OE *hol* + *denu*.

Holdenby Northants. *Aldenesbi* 1086 (DB). 'Farmstead or village of a man called Halfdan'. OScand. pers. name + *bý*.

Holderness (district) E. R. Yorks. *Heldernesse* 1086 (DB). 'Headland ruled by a high-ranking yeoman'. OScand. *holdr + nes*.

Holdgate Shrops. *Castrum Helgoti* 1109–18, *Hologodescastel* 1199, *Holegod* 1294. 'Castle of a man called Helgot'. OFrench pers. name with Latin *castrum*, ME *castel* in the early forms.

Holdingham Lincs. *Haldingeham* 1202. 'Homestead of the family or followers of a man called *Hald'. OE pers. name + *-inga-* + *hām*.

Holford Somerset. *Holeforde* 1086 (DB). 'Hollow ford, ford in a hollow'. OE *hol + ford*.

Holker Cumbria. *Holecher* 1086 (DB). 'Hollow marsh, marsh in a hollow'. OScand. *holr* or *hol + kjarr*.

Holkham Norfolk. *Holcham* 1086 (DB). 'Homestead in or near a hollow'. OE *holc + hām*.

Hollacombe Devon. *Holecome* 1086 (DB). 'Deep or hollow valley'. OE *hol + cumb*.

Holland, 'cultivated land by a hill-spur', OE *hōh + land*: **Holland on Sea** Essex. *Holande* c.1000, *Holanda* 1086 (DB). **Holland, Up** Lancs. *Hoiland* 1086 (DB). Affix is OE *upp* 'higher up'.
   However the following, although an identical compound, may have a somewhat different meaning: **Holland** Lincs. *Hoiland* 1086 (DB). Probably 'district characterized by hill-spurs'.

Hollesley Suffolk. *Holeslea* 1086 (DB). 'Woodland clearing in a hollow, or of a man called *Hōl'. OE *hol* or OE pers. name + *lēah*.

Hollingbourne Kent. *Holingeburna* 10th cent., *Holingeborne* 1086 (DB). 'Stream of the family or followers of a man called *Hōla, or of the people dwelling in the hollow'. OE pers. name or *hol + -inga- + burna*.

Hollington, 'farmstead where holly grows', OE *holegn + tūn*: **Hollington** Derbys. *Holintune* 1086 (DB). **Hollington** E. Sussex. *Holintune* 1086 (DB). **Hollington** Staffs. *Holyngton* 13th cent.

Hollingworth Gtr. Manch. *Holisurde* |sic| 1086 (DB), *Holinewurth* 13th cent. 'Holly enclosure'. OE *holegn + worth*.

Holloway Gtr. London. *Le Holeweye* 1307. 'The road in a hollow'. OE *hol + weg*.

Hollowell Northants. *Holewelle* 1086 (DB). 'Spring or stream in a hollow'. OE *hol + wella*.

Hollym E. R. Yorks. *Holam* 1086 (DB). Probably 'homestead or enclosure in or near the hollow'. OE *hol + hām* or *hamm*. Alternatively '(place at) the hollows', from OE *hol* or OScand. *holr* in a dative plural form *holum*.

Holme, a common place-name, usually from OScand. *holmr* 'island, dry ground in marsh, water-meadow': **Holme** Cambs. *Hulmo* 1167. **Holme** Cumbria. *Holme* 1086 (DB). **Holme** N. Yorks. *Hulme* 1086 (DB). **Holme** Notts. *Holme* 1203. **Holme Chapel** Lancs. *Holme* 1305. **Holme Hale** Norfolk. *Holm* 1086 (DB), *Holmhel* 1267. Second element is OE *halh* (dative *hale*) 'nook of land'. **Holme next the Sea** Norfolk. *Holm* c.1035, 1086 (DB). **Holme Pierrepont** Notts. *Holmo* 1086 (DB), *Holme Peyrpointe* 1571. Manorial affix from the de Perpount family, here

in the 14th cent. **Holme St Cuthbert** Cumbria. *Sanct Cuthbert Chappell* 1538. Named from the dedication of the chapel. **Holme, South** N. Yorks. *Holme* 1086 (DB), *Southolme* 1301. **Holme upon Spalding Moor** E. R. Yorks. *Holme* 1086 (DB), *Holm in Spaldingmor* 1293. Spalding Moor is an old district-name meaning 'moor of the people called Spaldingas', from the tribe who gave their name to SPALDING (Lincs.) + OE *mōr*.
   However some examples of Holme have other origins: **Holme** W. Yorks., near Holmfirth. *Holne* 1086 (DB). '(Place at) the holly tree'. OE *holegn*. **Holme, East** & **Holme, West** Dorset. *Holne* 1086 (DB), *Estholn, Westholn* 1288. Identical in origin with the previous name. **Holme Lacy** Heref. & Worcs. *Hamme* 1086 (DB), *Homme Lacy* 1221. OE *hamm* 'enclosure, land in a river-bend'. Manorial affix from its possession by the de Laci family from 1086. **Holme on the Wolds** E. R. Yorks. *Hougon* 1086 (DB), *Holme super Wolde* 1578. '(Place at) the mounds or hills'. OScand. *haugr* in a dative plural form *haugum*. The affix is from OE *wald* 'high forest-land'.

Holmer, 'pool in a hollow', OE *hol + mere*: **Holmer** Heref. & Worcs. *Holemere* 1086 (DB). **Holmer Green** Bucks. *Holemere* 1208.

Holmes Chapel Ches. *Hulm* 12th cent., *Holme chapell* 1400–5. 'Chapel at the place called *Hulme* or *Holme*'. OScand. *holmr* 'water-meadow' with the later addition of ME *chapel*.

Holmesfield Derbys. *Holmesfelt* 1086 (DB). Probably 'open land near a place called *Holm*'. OE *feld* with a lost place-name *Holm* from OScand. *holmr* 'island, dry ground in marsh'.

Holmfirth W. Yorks. *Holnefrith* 1274. 'Sparse woodland belonging to HOLME'. OE *fyrhth*.

Holmpton E. R. Yorks. *Holmetone* 1086 (DB). 'Farmstead near the shore-meadows'. OScand. *holmr* + OE *tūn*.

Holmwood, North & *Holmwood, South* Surrey. *Homwude* 1241. 'Wood in or near an enclosure or river-meadow'. OE *hamm + wudu*.

Holne Devon. *Holle* |sic| 1086 (DB), *Holna* 1178. '(Place at) the holly tree'. OE *holegn*.

Holnest Dorset. *Holeherst* 1185. 'Wooded hill where holly grows'. OE *holegn + hyrst*.

Holsworthy Devon. *Haldeurdi* 1086 (DB). 'Enclosure of a man called *Heald'. OE pers. name + *worthig*.

Holt, a common name, '(place at) the wood or thicket', OE *holt*; examples include: **Holt** Dorset. *Winburneholt* 1185, *Holte* 1372. Originally 'wood near WIMBORNE [MINSTER]'. **Holt** Heref. & Worcs. *Holte* 1086 (DB). **Holt** Norfolk. *Holt* 1086 (DB). **Holt** Wilts. *Holt* 1242. **Holt End** Hants. *Holt* 1167.

Holt Wrex. *Holte* 1326, *the holt* 1535. '(Place by the) wood'. OE *holt*.

Holtby York. *Holtebi* 1086 (DB). Probably 'farmstead or village of a man called Holti'. OScand. pers. name + *bý*.

Holton, a common name, has a number of different origins: **Holton** Lincs., near Beckering. *Houtune* 1086 (DB). 'Farmstead on a spur of land'. OE *hōh + tūn*. **Holton** Oxon. *Healhtun* 956, *Eltone* 1086 (DB). 'Farmstead in a nook of land'. OE *healh* + *tūn*. **Holton** Somerset. *Healhtun* *c*.1000. Identical in origin with the previous name. **Holton** Suffolk. *Holetuna* 1086 (DB). 'Farmstead near a hollow, or of a man called *Hōla'. OE *hol* or OE pers. name + *tūn*. **Holton Heath** Dorset. *Holtone* 1086 (DB). 'Farmstead near a hollow, or near a wood'. OE *hol* or *holt* + *tūn*. **Holton le Clay** Lincs. *Holtun* |*sic*| 1086 (DB), *Houtona c*.1115. 'Farmstead on a spur of land'. OE *hōh* + *tūn*. Affix means 'in the clayey district' from OE *clǣg*. **Holton le Moor** Lincs. *Hoctune* 1086 (DB). Identical in origin with the previous name. Affix means 'in the moorland' from OE *mōr*. **Holton St Mary** Suffolk. *Holetuna* 1086 (DB). 'Farmstead near a hollow, or of a man called *Hōla'. OE *hol* or OE pers. name + *tūn*. Affix from the dedication of the church.

Holwell, a common name, has several different origins: **Holwell** Dorset, near Sherborne. *Holewala* 1188. 'Ridge or bank in a hollow'. OE *hol* + *walu*. **Holwell** Herts. *Holewelle* 969, 1086 (DB). 'Spring or stream in a hollow'. OE *hol* + *wella*. **Holwell** Leics. *Holwelle* 1086 (DB). Identical in origin with the previous name. **Holwell** Oxon. *Haliwell* 1222. 'Holy spring or stream'. OE *hālig* + *wella*.

Holwick Durham. *Holewyk* 1235. Probably 'dwelling or farm in a hollow'. OE *hol* + *wīc*.

Holworth Dorset. *Holewertthe* 934, *Holverde* 1086 (DB). 'Enclosure in a hollow'. OE *hol* + *worth*.

Holy Island (*Ynys Gybi*) Angl. 'Holy island'. OE *hālig* + *ēg-land*. The Welsh name means 'Cybi's island' (Welsh *ynys*) after the Celtic saint to whom the church at HOLYHEAD is dedicated.

Holy Island Northum. *Halieland* 1195. 'Holy island' (from its association with early Christian missionaries). OE *hālig* + *ēg-land*. *See* LINDISFARNE.

Holybourne Hants. *Haliburne* 1086 (DB). 'Holy stream'. OE *hālig* + *burna*.

Holyhead (*Caergybi*) Angl. *Haliheved* 1315, *Holyhede* 1395. 'Holy headland'. OE *hālig* + *hēafod*. The Welsh name means 'Cybi's fort' (Welsh *caer*), from the Celtic saint to whom the church is dedicated.

Holyport Berks. *Horipord* 1220. 'Muddy or dirty market town'. OE *horig* + *port*. The first element was intentionally changed to *holy* by the late 14th cent.

Holystone Northum. *Halistan* 1242. 'Holy stone' (perhaps one at which the gospel was preached). OE *hālig* + *stān*.

Holywell Cambs. *Haliewelle* 1086 (DB). 'Holy spring or stream'. OE *hālig* + *wella*.

Holywell Fermanagh. *Holywell* 1835. 'Holy well'. A well-preserved holy well here has the Irish name *Dabhach Phádraig*, 'St Patrick's well'.

Holywell (*Treffynnon*) Flin. *Haliwel* 1093. 'Holy well'. OE *hālig* + *wella*. The name refers to the sacred well of St Winifred, who founded a nunnery here in the 7th cent. The Welsh name means 'village of the well' (Welsh *tref* + *ffynnon*).

Holywood Down. 'Holy wood'. The name originated with the Normans, who gave it to woodland adjoining the ancient church here. The Irish name of Holywood is *Ard Mhic Nasca*, 'Mac Nasca's height'.

Holywood Dumf. *de Sacro Nemore* 1252. 'Holy wood'. The earlier name was *Dercongal*, 'Congal's oak wood'. OE *hālig* + *wudu*.

Homersfield Suffolk. *Humbresfelda* 1086 (DB). 'Open land of a man called Hūnbeorht'. OE pers. name + *feld*.

Homerton Gtr. London. *Humburton* 1343. 'Farmstead of a woman called Hūnburh'. OE pers. name + *tūn*.

Homington Wilts. *Hummingtun* 956, *Humitone* 1086 (DB). 'Estate associated with a man called *Humma'. OE pers. name + *-ing-* + *tūn*.

Honeyborough Pemb. *Honyburgh* 1325. 'Manor where honey is produced'. OE *hunig* + *burh*.

Honeybourne, Church & *Honeybourne, Cow* Heref. & Worcs. *Huniburna* 709, *Huniburne*, *Heniberge* |*sic*| 1086 (DB), *Churchoniborne* 1535, *Calewe Honiburn* 1374. '(Places on) the stream by which honey is found'. OE *hunig* + *burna*. Affixes from OE *cirice* 'church' and *calu* 'bare, lacking vegetation'.

Honeychurch Devon. *Honechercha* 1086 (DB). Probably 'church of a man called Hūna'. OE pers. name + *cirice*.

Honiley Warwicks. *Hunilege* 1208. 'Woodland clearing where honey is found'. OE *hunig* + *lēah*.

Honing Norfolk. *Hanninge* 1044–7, *Haninga* 1086 (DB). Probably '(settlement of) the people at the rock or hill'. OE *han* + *-ingas*.

Honingham Norfolk. *Hunincham* 1086 (DB). 'Homestead of the family or followers of a man called Hūn(a)'. OE pers. name + *-inga-* + *hām*.

Honington Lincs. *Hundintone* 1086 (DB). Probably 'estate associated with a man called *Hund'. OE pers. name + *-ing-* + *tūn*.

Honington Suffolk. *Hunegetuna* 1086 (DB). Probably 'farmstead of the family or followers of a man called Hūn(a)'. OE pers. name + *-inga-* + *tūn*.

Honington Warwicks. *Hunitona* 1043, *Hunitone* 1086 (DB). 'Farmstead where honey is produced'. OE *hunig* + *tūn*.

Honiton Devon. *Honetone* 1086 (DB). 'Farmstead of a man called Hūna'. OE pers. name + *tūn*.

Honiton, Clyst Devon. *Hinatune c*.1100, *Clysthynetone* 1281. 'Farmstead (on the River Clyst) belonging to a religious community' (in this case Exeter Cathedral). OE *hīwan* (genitive plural *hīgna*) + *tūn*, to which the Celtic river- name (*see* CLYST) was later added.

Honley W. Yorks. *Haneleia* 1086 (DB). 'Woodland clearing where woodcock abound, or where there are stones and rocks'. OE *hana* or *hān* + *lēah*.

Hoo, *Hooe*, '(place at) the spur of land', OE *hōh* (dative *hōe*): **Hoo, St Mary's Hoo** Kent. *Hoge c*.687, *How* 1086 (DB), *Ho St. Mary* 1272. Affix St Mary from the dedication of the church. **Hoo Green** Suffolk. *Ho c*.1050, *Hou* 1086 (DB). **Hooe** Devon. *Ho* 1086 (DB). **Hooe** E. Sussex. *Hou* 1086 (DB).

Hook, *Hooke*, usually '(place at) the hook of land, or bend in a river or hill', OE *hōc*: **Hook** Gtr. London. *Hoke* 1227. **Hook** Hants., near Basingstoke. *Hoc* 1223. **Hook** Wilts. *La Hok* 1238. **Hooke** Dorset. *Lahoc* 1086 (DB). With the French definite article *la* in the early form.

However the following have a different origin: **Hook** E. R. Yorks. *Huck* 12th cent. OE **hūc* 'river-bend'. **Hook Norton** Oxon. *Hocneratune* early 10th cent. Possibly 'farmstead of a tribe called **Hoccanēre*'. OE tribal name (meaning 'people at Hocca's hill-slope'. from OE pers. name and *ōra*) + *tūn*.

Hoole Ches. *Hole* 1119. '(Place at) the hollow'. OE *hol*.

Hoole, Much Lancs. *Hulle* 1204, *Magna Hole* 1235. OE *hulu* 'a shed, a hovel'. Affix is OE *mycel* 'great'. (earlier Latin *magna*).

Hooton, 'farmstead on a spur of land'. OE *hōh* + *tūn*: **Hooton** Ches. *Hotone* 1086 (DB). **Hooton Levitt** S. Yorks. *Hotone* 1086 (DB). Manorial affix from the Livet family, here in the 13th cent. **Hooton Pagnell** S. Yorks. *Hotun* 1086 (DB), *Hotton Painel* 1192. Manorial affix from its possession by the Painel family from the 11th cent. **Hooton Roberts** S. Yorks. *Hotun* 1086 (DB), *Hoton Robert* 1285. Manorial affix from its possession by a man called Robert in the 13th cent.

Hope, a common name, from OE *hop* 'small enclosed valley, enclosed plot of land'; examples include: **Hope** Derbys. *Hope* 926, 1086 (DB). **Hope** Devon. *La Hope* 1281. **Hope** Shrops. *Hope* 1242. **Hope Bowdler** Shrops. *Fordritishope* 1086 (DB), *Hop* 1201, *Hopebulers* 1273. The DB prefix is probably the OE pers. name Forthræd; the later manorial affix is from the de Bulers family, here from 1201. **Hope Green** Ches. *Hope* 1282. With the later addition of *grēne* 'village green'. **Hope Mansell** Heref. & Worcs. *Hope* 1086 (DB). *Hoppe Maloisel* 12th cent. Manorial affix from early possession by the Maloisel family. **Hope, Sollers** Heref. & Worcs. *Hope* 1086 (DB), *Hope Solers* 1242. Manorial affix from the de Solariis family, here in the 13th cent. **Hope under Dinmore** Heref. & Worcs. *Hope* 1086 (DB), *Hope sub' Dinnemor* 1291. *Dinmore* may be a Welsh name *din mawr* meaning 'great fort', or alternatively 'marsh of a man called **Dynna*'. from OE pers. name + *mōr*.

Hope (*Yr Hôb*) Flin. *Hope* 1086 (DB). 'Enclosed land'. OE *hop*.

Hopeman Moray. 'High hill'. Meaning unknown. The village was founded in 1805 by William Young of Inverugie and took its name from a local estate.

Hopton, 'farmstead in a small enclosed valley or enclosed plot of land', OE *hop* + *tūn*: **Hopton** Shrops., near Hodnet. *Hotune* |*sic*| 1086 (DB), *Hopton* 1242. **Hopton** Staffs. *Hoptuna* 1167. **Hopton** Suffolk, near Thetford. *Hopetuna* 1086 (DB). **Hopton Cangeford** Shrops. *Hopton* 1242, *Hopton Cangefot* 1272. Manorial affix from its early possession by the Cangefot family. **Hopton Castle** Shrops. *Opetune* 1086 (DB). Affix from the Norman castle here. **Hopton Wafers** Shrops. *Hopton* 1086 (DB), *Hopton Wafre* 1236. Manorial affix from its early possession by the Wafre family.

Hopwas Staffs. *Opewas* 1086 (DB). 'Marshy or alluvial land near an enclosure'. OE *hop* + **wæsse*.

Hopwood, 'wood near an enclosure or in a small enclosed valley', OE *hop* + *wudu*: **Hopwood** Gtr. Manch. *Hopwode* 1278. **Hopwood** Heref. & Worcs. *Hopwuda* 849.

Horbling Lincs. *Horbelinge* 1086 (DB). Probably 'muddy settlement of the family or followers of a man called Bill or **Billa*'. OE *horu* + OE pers. name + *-ingas*.

Horbury W. Yorks. *Horberie* 1086 (DB). 'Stronghold on muddy land'. OE *horu* + *burh* (dative *byrig*).

Horden Durham. *Horedene* c.1050. 'Dirty or muddy valley'. OE *horu* + *denu*.

Hordle Hants. *Herdel* |*sic*| 1086 (DB), *Hordhull* 1242. 'Hill where treasure was found'. OE *hord* + *hyll*.

Hordley Shrops. *Hordelei* 1086 (DB). 'Woodland clearing where treasure was found'. OE *hord* + *lēah*.

Horham Suffolk. *Horham* c.950. 'Muddy homestead'. OE *horu* + *hām*.

Horkesley, Great & *Horkesley, Little* Essex. *Horchesleia* c.1130. 'Woodland clearing with a shelter', or 'dirty, muddy clearing'. OE **horc* or *horsc* + *lēah*.

Horkstow N. Lincs. *Horchetou* |*sic*| 1086 (DB), *Horkestowe* 12th cent. Probably 'shelter for animals or people'. OE **horc* + *stōw*.

Horley, probably 'woodland clearing in a horn-shaped piece of land'., OE *horn*, **horna* + *lēah*: **Horley** Oxon. *Hornelie* 1086 (DB). **Horley** Surrey. *Horle* 12th cent.

Hormead, Great Herts. *Horemede* 1086 (DB). 'Muddy meadow'. OE *horu* + *mæd*.

Hornblotton Green Somerset. *Hornblawertone* 851, *Horblawetone* 1086 (DB). 'Farmstead of the hornblowers or trumpeters'. OE *horn-blāwere* + *tūn*.

Hornby, 'farmstead or village on a horn-shaped piece of land, or of a man called Horn or **Horni*', OScand. *horn* or pers. name + *bý*: **Hornby** Lancs. *Hornebi* 1086 (DB). **Hornby** N. Yorks., near Great Smeaton. *Hornebia* 1086 (DB). **Hornby** N. Yorks., near Hackforth. *Hornebi* 1086 (DB).

Horncastle Lincs. *Hornecastre* 1086 (DB). 'Roman station or fortification on a horn-shaped piece of land'. OE **horna* + *ceaster*.

Hornchurch Gtr. London. *Hornechurch* 1233. 'Church with horn-like gables'. OE *horn*, *hornede* + *cirice*.

Horncliffe Northum. *Hornecliff* 1210. 'Slope of the horn-shaped hill or piece of land'. OE **horna* + *clif*.

Horndean Hants. *Harmedene* 1199. 'Dormouse valley', or 'valley of a man called **Hearma*'. OE *hearma* or identical pers. name + *denu*.

Horndon on the Hill Essex. *Horninduna* 1086 (DB). 'Horn-shaped hill'. OE **horning* + *dūn*.

Horne Surrey. *Horne* 1208. '(Place at) the horn-shaped hill or piece of land'. OE *horn* or **horna*.

Horning Norfolk. *Horningga* 1020–2, *Horningam* 1086 (DB). '(Settlement of) the people living at the horn-shaped piece of land, here a river-bend'. OE *horn*, **horna* + *-ingas*. Alternatively 'horn-shaped pieces of land', from the plural of an OE **horning*, is formally possible.

Horninghold Leics. *Horniwale* |*sic*| 1086 (DB), *Horningewald* 1163. 'Woodland of the people living at the horn-shaped piece of land'. OE *horn*, **horna* + *-inga-* + *wald*.

Horninglow Staffs. *Horninglow* 12th cent. 'Mound at the horn-shaped hill or piece of land'. OE **horning* + *hlāw*.

Horningsea Cambs. *Horninges ige* c.975, *Horningesie* 1086 (DB). 'Island, or dry ground in marsh, of a man called

*Horning or by the horn-shaped hill'. OE pers. name or *horning + ēg.

Horningsham Wilts. *Horningesham* 1086 (DB). Probably 'homestead of a man called *Horning'. OE pers. name + *hām*. Alternatively the first element may be OE *horning* 'horn-shaped hill or piece of land'.

Horningtoft Norfolk. *Horninghetoft* 1086 (DB). 'Homestead of the people living at the horn-shaped hill or piece of land'. OE *horn*, *horna* + -inga-. + OScand. *toft*.

Hornsby Cumbria. *Ormesby* c.1210. 'Farmstead or village of a man called Ormr'. OScand. pers. name + *bý*.

Hornsea E. R. Yorks. *Hornessei* 1086 (DB). 'Lake with a horn-shaped peninsula'. OScand. horn + *nes* + *sǽr*.

Hornsey Gtr. London. *Haringeie* 1201, *Haringesheye* 1243. 'Enclosure in the grey wood'. or 'of a man called *Hæring'. OE *hāring* or OE pers. name + *hæg*. Nearby HARRINGAY is a different development of the same name.

Hornton Oxon. *Hornigeton* 1194. 'Farmstead near the horn-shaped piece of land'. OE *horning + tūn, or horn(a) + -ing- + tūn.

Horrabridge Devon. *Horebrigge* 1345. 'Grey or boundary bridge'. OE hār + brycg.

Horringer Suffolk. *Horningeserda* 1086 (DB). 'Ploughed land at the bend or headland' or 'of a man called *Horning'. OE *horning or OE pers. name + erth.

Horrington, East & *Horrington, West* Somerset. *Hornningdun* 1065. Possibly 'horn-shaped hill', OE *horning + dūn. Alternatively 'hill of the people living at the horn-shaped piece of land', OE horn or *horna + -inga- + dūn.

Horseheath Cambs. *Horseda* c.1080, *Horsei |sic|* 1086 (DB). 'Heath where horses are kept'. OE hors + hǽth.

Horsell Surrey. *Horisell* 13th cent. 'Shelter for animals in a muddy place'. OE horu + *(ge)sell.

Horsey Norfolk. *Horseia* 1086 (DB). 'Island, or dry ground in marsh, where horses are kept'. OE hors + ēg.

Horsford Norfolk. *Hosforda* 1086 (DB). 'Ford which horses can cross'. OE hors + ford.

Horsforth W. Yorks. *Horseford* 1086 (DB). Identical in origin with the previous name.

Horsham, 'homestead or village where horses are kept', OE hors + hām: **Horsham** W. Sussex. *Horsham* 947. **Horsham St Faith** Norfolk. *Horsham* 1086 (DB). Affix from the dedication of the church.

Horsington Lincs. *Horsintone* 1086 (DB). 'Estate associated with a man called Horsa'. OE pers. name + -ing- + tūn.

Horsington Somerset. *Horstenetone* 1086 (DB). 'Farmstead of the horsekeepers or grooms'. OE horsthegn + tūn.

Horsley, 'clearing or pasture where horses are kept', OE hors + lēah: **Horsley** Derbys. *Horselei* 1086 (DB). **Horsley** Glos. *Horselei* 1086 (DB). **Horsley** Northum. *Horseley* 1242. **Horsley, East** & **Horsley, West** Surrey. *Horsalæge* 9th cent., *Horslei, Orselei* 1086 (DB).

Horsmonden Kent. *Horsbundenne* c.1100. Probably 'woodland pasture near the stream where horses drink'. OE hors + burna + denn.

Horstead, *Horsted*, 'place where horses are kept', OE hors + stede: **Horstead** Norfolk. *Horsteda* 1086 (DB). **Horsted Keynes** W. Sussex. *Horstede* 1086 (DB), *Horsted Kaynes* 1307. Manorial affix from its possession by William de Cahainges in 1086. **Horsted, Little** E. Sussex. *Horstede* 1086 (DB), *Little Horstede* 1307.

Horton, a common name, usually 'dirty or muddy farmstead', OE horu + tūn; examples include: **Horton** Bucks., near Ivinghoe. *Hortone* 1086 (DB). **Horton** Dorset. *Hortun* 1033, *Hortune* 1086 (DB). **Horton** Northants. *Hortone* 1086 (DB). **Horton** Oxon. *Hortun* 1005–12, *Hortone* 1086 (DB). **Horton** Shrops., near Wem. *Hortune* 1086 (DB). **Horton** Staffs. *Horton* 1239. **Horton** Surrey. *Horton* 1178. **Horton** Wilts. *Horton* 1158. **Horton Green** Ches. *Horton* c.1240. **Horton-in-Ribblesdale** N. Yorks. *Hortune* 1086 (DB), *Horton in Ribbelesdale* 13th cent. Affix means 'valley of the River Ribble', OE river-name (*see* RIBBLETON) + OE dæl or OScand. dalr. **Horton Kirby** Kent. *Hortune* 1086 (DB), *Horton Kyrkeby* 1346. Manorial affix from its possession by the de Kirkeby family in the 13th cent.

However the following has a different origin: **Horton** S. Glos. *Horedone* 1086 (DB). 'Hill frequented by harts or stags'. OE heorot + dūn.

Horwich Gtr. Manch. *Horewic* 1221. '(Place at) the grey wych-elm(s)'. OE hār + wice.

Horwood Devon. *Horewode, Hareoda* 1086 (DB). 'Grey wood or muddy wood'. OE hār or horu + wudu.

Horwood, Great & *Horwood, Little* Bucks. *Horwudu* 792, *Hereworde |sic|* 1086 (DB). 'Dirty or muddy wood'. OE horu + wudu.

Hose Leics. *Hoches, Howes* 1086 (DB). 'The spurs of land'. OE hōh in a plural form hō(h)as.

Hotham E. R. Yorks. *Hode* 963, *Hodhum* 1086 (DB). '(Place at) the shelters'. OE *hōd in a dative plural form *hōdum.

Hothfield Kent. *Hathfelde* c.1100. 'Heathy open land'. OE *hǽth + feld.

Hoton Leics. *Hohtone* 1086 (DB). 'Farmstead on a spur of land'. OE hōh + tūn.

Hough, 'the ridge or spur of land', OE hōh: **Hough** Ches., near Willaston. *Hohc* 1241. **Hough** Ches., near Wilmslow. *Le Hogh* 1289.

Hough-on-the-Hill Lincs. *Hach, Hag* 1086 (DB). OE *haga* 'enclosure'.

Hougham Lincs. *Hacham* 1086 (DB). Probably 'river-meadow belonging to HOUGH-ON-THE-HILL.'. OE hamm.

Houghton, a common name, usually 'farmstead on or near a ridge or hill-spur', OE hōh + tūn: **Houghton** Cambs. *Hoctune* 1086 (DB). **Houghton** Cumbria. *Hotton* 1246. **Houghton** Hants. *Hohtun* 982, *Houstun |sic|* 1086 (DB). **Houghton** W. Sussex. *Hohtun* 683. **Houghton Conquest** Beds. *Houstone* 1086 (DB), *Houghton Conquest* 1316. Manorial affix from the Conquest family, here in the 13th cent. **Houghton, Great** & **Houghton, Little** Northants. *Hohtone* 1086 (DB), *Magna Houtona* 1199, *Parva Houtone* 1233.

Distinguishing affixes are Latin *magna* 'great' and *parva* 'little'. **Houghton le Side** Durham. *Hoctona* 1200. Affix means 'by the hill slope'. from OE *sīde*. **Houghton le Spring** Tyne & Wear. *Hoctun, Houghton Springes* c.1220. Manorial affix from the Spring family, here in the 13th cent. **Houghton on the Hill** Leics. *Hohtone* 1086 (DB). The affix is recorded from the 17th cent. **Houghton Regis** Beds. *Houstone* 1086 (DB), *Kyngeshouton* 1287. Latin affix *regis* 'of the king' because it was a royal manor at an early date. **Houghton St Giles** Norfolk. *Hohttune* 1086 (DB). Affix from the dedication of the church.

However the following have a different origin, 'farmstead in a nook of land', OE *halh* + *tūn*: **Houghton, Great** S. Yorks. *Haltun* 1086 (DB), *Magna Halghton* 1303. Affix is Latin *magna* 'great'. **Houghton, Little** S. Yorks. *Haltone* 1086 (DB), *Parva Halghton* 1303. Affix is Latin *parva* 'little'.

Hound Green Hants. *Hūne* 1086 (DB). 'Place where the plant hoarhound grows'. OE *hūne*.

Hounslow Gtr. London. *Honeslaw* |sic| 1086 (DB), *Hundeslawe* 1217. 'Mound or tumulus of the hound, or of a man called *Hund*'. OE *hund* or OE pers. name + *hlāw*.

Houston Renf. *Villa Hugonis* c.1200, *Huston* c.1230. 'Hugo's village'. Anglo-Norman pers. name + OE *tūn*.

Hove E. Sussex. *La Houue* 1288. OE *hūfe* 'hood-shaped hill' or 'shelter'.

Hoveringham Notts. *Horingeham* |sic| 1086 (DB), *Houeringeham* 1167. 'Homestead of the people living at the hump-shaped hill'. OE *hofer* + *-inga-* + *hām*.

Hoveton Norfolk. *Houetonne* 1044–7, *Houetuna* 1086 (DB). 'Farmstead of a man called Hofa, or where the plant ale-hoof grows'. OE pers. name or OE *hōfe* + *tūn*.

Hovingham N. Yorks. *Hovingham* 1086 (DB). 'Homestead of the family or followers of a man called Hofa'. OE pers. name + *-inga-* + *hām*.

Howden E. R. Yorks. *Heafuddene* 959, *Hovedene* 1086 (DB). 'Valley by the headland or spit of land'. OE *hēafod* (replaced by OScand. *hofuth*) + *denu*.

Howe Highland. '(Place by the) mound'. OScand. *haugr*.

Howe Norfolk. *Hou* 1086 (DB). '(Place at) the hill or barrow'. OScand. *haugr*.

Howell Lincs. *Huuelle* 1086 (DB). Second element OE *wella* 'spring, stream', first element doubtful, possibly OE *hugol* 'mound, hillock' or *hūne* 'hoarhound'.

Howick Northum. *Hewic* c.1100, *Hawic* 1230. Probably 'high (or chief) dairy-farm'. OE *hēah* + *wīc*.

Howle Shrops. *Hugle* 1086 (DB). '(Place at) the mound or hillock'. OE *hugol*.

Howsham, '(place at) the houses or buildings', OE *hūs* or OScand. *hús* in a dative plural form: **Howsham** N. Lincs. *Usun* 1086 (DB). **Howsham** N. Yorks. *Huson* 1086 (DB).

Howth Dublin. 'Headland'. OScand. *hofuth*. The Irish name of Howth is *Binn Éadair*, 'Éadar's peak'.

Howton Heref. & Worcs. *Huetune* c.1184. Probably 'estate of a man called Hugh'. OFrench pers. name + OE *tūn*.

Hoxa (island) Orkn. *Haugaheith* c.1390. 'Island with a mound'. OScand. *haugr* + *ey*.

Hoxne Suffolk. *Hoxne* c.950, *Hoxana* 1086 (DB). Possibly 'hock-shaped spur of land'. OE *hōhsinu*.

Hoxton Gtr. London. *Hochestone* 1086 (DB). 'Farmstead of a man called *Hōc*'. OE pers. name + *tūn*.

Hoy (island) Orkn. *Hoye* 1492. 'High island'. OScand. *há* + *ey*.

Hoylake Mersey. *Hyle Lake* 1687. 'Tidal lake or channel at the hillock or sandbank'. OE *hygel* + ME *lake* or OE *lacu*.

Hoyland, 'cultivated land on or near a hill-spur', OE *hōh* + *land*: **Hoyland, High** S. Yorks. *Holand* 1086 (DB), *Heyholand* 1283. Affix is OE *hēah* 'high'. **Hoyland Nether** S. Yorks. *Ho(i)land* 1086 (DB), *Nether Holand* 1390. Affix is OE *neotherra* 'lower'. **Hoyland Swaine** S. Yorks. *Holande* 1086 (DB), *Holandeswayn* 1266. Manorial affix from possession in the 12th cent. by a man called Swein (OScand. *Sveinn*).

Hubberholme N. Yorks. *Huburgheham* 1086 (DB). 'Homestead of a woman called Hūnburh'. OE pers. name + *hām*.

Hubberston Pemb. *Villa Huberti* 1291. 'Hubert's farm'. OGerman pers. name + OE *tūn*.

Huby N. Yorks., near Easingwold. *Hobi* 1086 (DB). 'Farmstead on the spur of land'. OE *hōh* + OScand. *bý*.

Huby N. Yorks., near Stainburn. *Huby* 1198. 'Farmstead of a man called Hugh'. OFrench pers. name + OScand. *bý*.

Hucclecote Glos. *Hochilicote* 1086 (DB). 'Cottage(s) associated with a man called *Hucel(a)*'. OE pers. name + *-ing-* + *cot*.

Hucking Kent. *Hugginges* 1195. '(Settlement of) the family or followers of a man called *Hucca*'. OE pers. name + *-ingas*.

Hucklow, Great & *Hucklow, Little* Derbys. *Hochelai* 1086 (DB), *Magna Hockelawe* 1251, *Parva Hokelawe* 13th cent. 'Mound or hill of a man called *Hucca*'. OE pers. name + *hlāw*. Affixes are Latin *magna* 'great' and *parva* 'little'.

Hucknall, 'nook of land of a man called *Hucca*', OE pers. name (genitive *-n*) + *halh*: **Hucknall** Notts. *Hochenale* 1086 (DB). **Hucknall, Ault** Derbys. *Hokenhale* 1291, *Haulte Huknall* 1535. Affix is OFrench *haut* 'high'.

Huddersfield W. Yorks. *Odresfeld* 1086 (DB). 'Open land of a man called *Hudrǣd*'. OE pers. name + *feld*. Alternatively the first element may be an OE *hūder* 'a shelter'.

Huddington Heref. & Worcs. *Hudintune* 1086 (DB). 'Estate associated with a man called Hūda'. OE pers. name + *-ing-* + *tūn*.

Hudswell N. Yorks. *Hudreswelle* |sic| 1086 (DB), *Hudeleswell* 12th cent. Probably 'spring or stream of a man called *Hūdel*'. OE pers. name + *wella*.

Huggate E. R. Yorks. *Hughete* 1086 (DB). Possibly 'road to or near the mounds'. OScand. *hugr* + *gata*.

Hugh Town Isles of Scilly, Cornwall. *Hugh Town* 17th cent., named from *the Hew Hill* 1593. Probably OE *hōh* 'spur of land'.

Hughenden Valley Bucks. *Huchedene* 1086 (DB). 'Valley of a man called **Huhha*'. OE pers. name (genitive -*n*) + *denu*. The recent addition *Valley* is strictly tautological.

Hughley Shrops. *Leg'* 1203–4, *Huleye* c.1291. Originally 'the wood or clearing', from OE *lēah*. Later addition from possession by a man called Hugh mentioned in 1203–4.

Huish, a common name, 'measure of land that would support a family', OE *hīwisc*; examples include: **Huish** Wilts. *Iwis* 1086 (DB). **Huish Champflower** Somerset. *Hiwis* 1086 (DB), *Hywys Champflur* 1274. Manorial affix from the Champflur family, here in the 13th cent. **Huish Episcopi** Somerset. *Hiwissh* 973. Affix is Latin *episcopi* 'bishop's', referring to early possession by the Bishop of Wells. **Huish, North & Huish, South** Devon. *Hewis, Heuis* 1086 (DB).

Hulcott Bucks. *Hoccote* 1200, *Hulecote* 1228. Probably 'hovel-like cottages'. OE *hulu* + *cot*.

Hull, *see* KINGSTON UPON HULL.

Hull, Bishop's Somerset. *Hylle* 1033, *Hilla* 1086 (DB), *Hulle Episcopi* 1327. '(Place at) the hill'. OE *hyll*. Affix from its early possession by the Bishops of Winchester.

Hulland Derbys. *Hoilant* 1086 (DB). 'Cultivated land by a hill-spur'. OE *hōh* + *land*.

Hullavington Wilts. *Hunlavintone* 1086 (DB). 'Estate associated with a man called Hūnlāf'. OE pers. name + -*ing-* + *tūn*.

Hullbridge Essex. *Whouluebregg* 1375. Probably 'bridge with arches'. OE *hwalf* + *brycg*.

Hulme, 'the island, the dry ground in marsh, the water-meadow', OScand. *holmr*: **Hulme** Gtr. Manch. *Hulm* 1246. **Hulme, Cheadle** Gtr. Manch. *Hulm* late 12th cent., *Chedle Hulm* 1345. Within the parish of CHEADLE. **Hulme End** Staffs. *Hulme* 1227. **Hulme Walfield** Ches. *Wallefeld et Hulm* c.1262. Walfield was originally a separate manor, 'open land at a spring', OE *wælla* or *wælm* + *feld*.

Hulton, Abbey Staffs. *Hulton* 1235. 'Farmstead on a hill'. OE *hyll* + *tūn*. Affix from the Cistercian abbey founded here in 1223.

Humber (river) E. R. Yorks. *Humbri fluminis* c.720, *Humbre* 9th cent. An ancient pre-English river-name of uncertain origin and meaning which also occurs elsewhere in England (as in next name).

Humber Court Heref. & Worcs. *Humbre* 1086 (DB). Originally the name of Humber Brook, see previous name.

Humberston NE. Lincs. *Humbrestone* 1086 (DB). '(Place by) the boundary stone in the River Humber'. Ancient river-name (*see* HUMBER) + OE *stān*.

Humbleton E. R. Yorks. *Humeltone* 1086 (DB). 'Farmstead by a rounded hillock, or where hops grow', or 'farmstead of a man called Humli'. OE **humol* or *humele* or OScand. pers. name + OE *tūn*.

Humbleton Northum. *Hameldun* 1170. 'Crooked or scarred hill'. OE **hamel* + *dūn*.

Hume Sc. Bord. *Houm* 1127. '(Place at the) hill spurs' OE *hōh* (dative plural *hōum*).

Humshaugh Northum. *Hounshale* 1279. Probably 'nook of land of a man called Hūn'. OE pers. name + *halh*.

Huna Highland. *Hofn* c.1250. 'Harbour river'. OScand. *hafn* + *á*.

Huncoat Lancs. *Hunnicot* 1086 (DB). Possibly 'cottage(s) of a man called Hūna', OE pers. name + *cot*. Alternatively the first element may be OE *hunig* 'honey'.

Huncote Leics. *Hunecote* 1086 (DB). Probably 'cottage(s) of a man called Hūna'. OE pers. name + *cot*.

Hunderthwaite Durham. *Hundredestoit* 1086 (DB). 'Clearing or meadow of a man called Húnrøthr'. OScand. pers. name + *thveit*. Alternatively the first element may be OScand. *hundrath* or OE *hundred* in the sense 'administrative district'.

Hundleby Lincs. *Hundelbi* 1086 (DB). 'Farmstead or village of a man called Hundulfr'. OScand. pers. name + *bý*.

Hundleton Pemb. *Hundenton* 1475. 'Farm where dogs are kept'. OE *hund* + *tūn*.

Hundon Suffolk. *Hunedana* 1086 (DB). 'Valley of a man called Hūna'. OE pers. name + *denu*.

Hungerford Berks. *Hungreford* 1101–18. 'Hunger ford', i.e. 'ford leading to poor or unproductive land'. OE *hungor* + *ford*.

Hunmanby N. Yorks. *Hundemanebi* 1086 (DB). 'Farmstead or village of the houndsmen or dog-keepers'. OScand. **hunda-mann* (genitive plural -*a*) + *bý*.

Hunnigham Warwicks. *Huningeham* 1086 (DB). 'Homestead of the family or followers of a man called Hūna'. OE pers. name + -*inga-* + *hām*.

Hunsdon Herts. *Honesdone* 1086 (DB). 'Hill of a man called Hūn'. OE pers. name + *dūn*.

Hunsingore N. Yorks. *Hulsingoure* |sic| 1086 (DB), *Hunsinghouere* 1194. 'Promontory associated with a man called Hūnsige'. OE pers. name + -*ing-* + **ofer*.

Hunslet W. Yorks. *Hunslet* |sic| 1086 (DB), *Hunesflete* 12th cent. 'Inlet or stream of a man called Hūn'. OE pers. name + *flēot*.

Hunsley, High E. R. Yorks. *Hund(r)eslege* 1086 (DB). 'Woodland clearing of a man called **Hund*'. OE pers. name + *lēah*.

Hunsonby Cumbria. *Hunswanby* 1292. 'Farmstead or village of the houndsmen or dog-keepers'. OScand. *hunda-sveinn* + *bý*.

Hunstanton Norfolk. *Hunstanestun* c.1035, *Hunestanestuna* 1086 (DB). 'Farmstead of a man called Hūnstān'. OE pers. name + *tūn*.

Hunstanworth Durham. *Hunstanwortha* 1183. 'Enclosure of a man called Hūnstān'. OE pers. name + *worth*.

Hunston Suffolk. *Hunterstuna* 1086 (DB). 'Farmstead of the hunter'. OE **huntere* + *tūn*.

Hunston W. Sussex. *Hunestan* 1086 (DB). 'Boundary stone of a man called Hūn(a)'. OE pers. name + *stān*.

Hunter's Quay Arg. 'Hunter's quay'. The *Hunter* family of nearby Hafton House gave the clubhouse here to the Royal Clyde Yacht Club in 1872.

Huntingdon Cambs. *Huntandun* 973, *Huntedun* 1086 (DB). 'Hill of the huntsman, or of a man called Hunta'.

OE *hunta* or pers. name (genitive *-n*) + *dūn*. **Huntingdon-shire** (OE *scīr* 'district') is first referred to in the 11th cent.

Huntingfield Suffolk. *Huntingafelde* 1086 (DB). 'Open land of the family or followers of a man called Hunta'. OE pers. name + *-inga-* + *feld*.

Huntington York. *Huntindune* 1086 (DB). Probably 'hunting hill', i.e. 'hill where hunting takes place'. OE *hunting* + *dūn*.

Huntington Staffs. *Huntendon* 1167. 'Hill of the huntsmen'. OE *hunta* (genitive plural *huntena*) + *dūn*.

Huntley Glos. *Huntelei* 1086 (DB). 'Huntsman's wood or clearing'. OE *hunta* + *lēah*.

Huntly Aber. Transferred from Huntly, Sc. Bord., in feudal times; Earls of HUNTLEY. Applied originally to barony and castle only.

Huntly Sc. Bord. *Huntleie* 1180. 'Wood or clearing of the huntsman'. OE *hunta* + *leah*.

Hunton Kent. *Huntindone* 11th cent. 'Hill of the huntsmen'. OE *hunta* (genitive plural *huntena*) + *dūn*.

Hunton N. Yorks. *Huntone* 1086 (DB). 'Farmstead of a man called Hūna'. OE pers. name + *tūn*.

Huntsham Devon. *Honesham* 1086 (DB). 'Homestead or enclosure of a man called Hūn'. OE pers. name + *hām* or *hamm*.

Huntspill Somerset. *Honspil* 1086 (DB). 'Tidal creek of a man called Hūn'. OE pers. name + *pyll*.

Huntworth Somerset. *Hunteworde* 1086 (DB). 'Enclosure of the huntsman, or of a man called Hūnta'. OE *hunta* or pers. name + *worth*.

Hunwick Durham. *Hunewic* c.1050. 'Dwelling or (dairy) farm of a man called Hūna'. OE pers. name + *wīc*.

Hunworth Norfolk. *Hunaworda* 1086 (DB). 'Enclosure of a man called Hūna'. OE pers. name + *worth*.

Hurdsfield Ches. *Hirdelesfeld* 13th cent. Probably 'open land at a hurdle (fence)'. OE *hyrdel*, **hyrdels* + *feld*.

Hurley, 'woodland clearing in a recess in the hills', OE *hyrne* + *lēah*: **Hurley** Berks. *Herlei* 1086 (DB), *Hurnleia* 1106–21. **Hurley** Warwicks. *Hurle* early 11th cent., *Hurnlee* c.1180.

Hurn Dorset. *Herne* 1086 (DB). '(Place at) the angle or corner of land'. OE *hyrne*.

Hursley Hants. *Hurselye* 1171. Probably 'mare's woodland clearing'. OE **hyrse* + *lēah*.

Hurst Berks. *Herst* 1220. '(Place at) the wooded hill'. OE *hyrst*. The same name occurs in other counties.

Hurst, Old Cambs., see OLD HURST.

Hurstbourne Priors & *Hurstbourne Tarrant* Hants. *Hysseburnan* c.880, *Esseborne* 1086 (DB). 'Stream with winding water-plants', probably referring to green canary-grass. OE *hysse* + *burna*. Distinguishing affixes from early possession of the two manors by Winchester Priory and Tarrant Abbey.

Hurstpierpoint W. Sussex. *Herst* 1086 (DB), *Herst Perepunt* 1279. OE *hyrst* 'wooded hill' + manorial addition from possession by Robert de Pierpoint in 1086.

Hurstwood Lancs. *Hurstwode* 1285. 'Wood on a hill'. OE *hyrst* + *wudu*.

Hurworth Durham. *Hurdewurda* 1158. 'Enclosure made with hurdles'. OE **hurth* + *worth*.

Husabost Highland (Skye). 'Dwelling place at the house'. OScand. *hús* + *bólstathr*.

Husbands Bosworth Leics., see BOSWORTH.

Husborne Crawley Beds. *Hysseburnan* 969, *Crawelai* 1086 (DB), *Husseburn Crouleye* 1276. Originally two separate places. 'Stream with winding water-plants', from OE *hysse* + *burna*, and 'wood or clearing frequented by crows' from OE *crāwe* + *lēah*.

Husthwaite N. Yorks. *Hustwait* 1167. 'Clearing with a house or houses built on it'. OScand. *hús* + *thveit*.

Huthwaite Notts. *Hodweit* 1199. 'Clearing on a spur of land'. OE *hōh* + OScand. *thveit*.

Huttoft Lincs. *Hotoft* 1086 (DB). 'Homestead on a spur of land'. OE *hōh* + OScand. *toft*.

Hutton, a common name, 'farmstead on or near a ridge or hill-spur', OE *hōh* + *tūn*: **Hutton** Cumbria. *Hoton* 1291. **Hutton** Essex. *Atahov* 1086 (DB), *Houton* 1200. In DB it is simply '(place) at the ridge or hillspur'. **Hutton** Lancs., near Penwortham. *Hoton* 12th cent. **Hutton** N.Som. *Hotune* 1086 (DB). **Hutton Buscel** N. Yorks. *Hotun* 1086 (DB), *Hoton Buscel* 1253. Manorial affix from the Buscel family, here in the 12th cent. **Hutton Conyers** N. Yorks, *Hotone* 1086 (DB), *Hotonconyers* 1198. Manorial affix from the Conyers family, here in the early 12th cent. **Hutton Cranswick** E. R. Yorks. *Hottune* 1086 (DB). Distinguishing affix from its proximity to Cranswick (*Cranzuic* 1086 (DB)) which is possibly '(dairy) farm of a man called **Cranuc*', OE pers. name + *wīc*. **Hutton Henry** Durham. *Hoton* c.1050. Affix from its possession by Henry de Essh in the 14th cent. **Hutton-le-Hole** N. Yorks. *Hotun* 1086 (DB). Affix means 'in the hollow' from OE *hol*. **Hutton Lowcross** Red. & Cleve. *Hotun* 1086 (DB). Affix from a nearby place (*Loucros* 12th cent.) which may be 'cross of a man called Logi', OScand. pers. name +*cros*. **Hutton Magna** Durham. *Hotton* 1086 (DB), *Magna Hoton* 1157. Latin *magna* 'great'. **Hutton Roof** Cumbria. *Hotunerof* 1278. Affix is probably manorial from some early owner called *Rolf* (OScand. *Hrólfr*). **Hutton Rudby** N. Yorks. *Hotun* 1086 (DB). *Hoton by Ruddeby* 1310. Affix from a nearby place (*Rodebi* 1086 (DB)) which is 'farmstead of a man called Ruthi', OScand. pers. name + *bý*. **Hutton, Sand** N. Yorks. *Hotone* 1086 (DB), *Sandhouton* 1219. Affix is OE *sand* 'sand'. **Hutton Sessay** N. Yorks. *Hottune* 1086 (DB). Affix from its proximity to SESSAY. **Hutton, Sheriff** N. Yorks. *Hotone* 1086 (DB), *Shirefhoton* c.1200. Affix from the *Sheriff* of York who held this manor from the mid-12th cent., OE *scīr-gerēfa*. **Hutton Wandesley** N. Yorks. *Hoton* c.1200. *Hotun Wandelay* 1253. Affix from a nearby place (*Wandeslage* 1086 (DB)), 'woodland clearing of a man called **Wand* or **Wandel*', OE pers. name + *lēah*.

Hutton Sc. Bord. *Hotun* c.1098. 'Farmstead by a ridge'. OE *hōh* + *tūn*.

Huxley Ches. *Huxelehe* early 13th cent. Probably 'woodland clearing of a man called **Hucc*'. OE pers. name + *lēah*.

Huyton Mersey. *Hitune* 1086 (DB). 'Estate with a landing-place'. OE *hȳh* + *tūn*.

Hwlffordd. *See* HAVERFORDWEST.

Hyde, 'estate assessed at one hide, an amount of land for the support of one free family and its dependants', OE *hīd*; for example **Hyde** Gtr. Manch. *Hyde* early 13th cent.

Hykeham, North & *Hykeham, South* Lincs. *Hicham* 1086 (DB). OE *hām* 'homestead' or *hamm* 'enclosure' with a

doubtful first element, possibly an OE **hīce* 'some kind of small bird'.

Hylton, South Tyne & Wear. *Helton* 1195. 'Farmstead on a slope or hill'. OE *helde* or *hyll* + *tūn*.

Hynish Arg (Tiree). 'High headland'. OScand. Unidentified first element + *nes*. *Cp.* HEANISH.

Hythe, 'landing-place or harbour', OE *hȳth*: **Hythe** Kent. *Hede* 1086 (DB). **Hythe** Hants. *La Huthe* 1248.

I

Ibberton Dorset. *Abristetone* 1086 (DB). 'Estate associated with a man called Ēadbeorht'. OE pers. name + *-ing-* + *tūn*.

Ible Derbys. *Ibeholon* 1086 (DB). 'Hollow(s) of a man called Ibba'. OE pers. name + *hol*.

Ibsley Hants. *Tibeslei* 1086 (DB), *Ibeslehe* 13th cent. 'Woodland clearing of a man called *Tibbi* or *Ibbi*'. OE pers. name + *lēah*.

Ibstock Leics. *Ibestoche* 1086 (DB). 'Outlying farmstead or hamlet of a man called Ibba'. OE pers. name + *stoc*.

Ibstone Bucks. *Ebestan* 1086 (DB). 'Boundary stone of a man called Ibba'. OE pers. name + *stān*.

Ibthorpe Hants. *Ebbedrope* 1236, *Ybethrop* 1269. 'Outlying farmstead of a man called Ibba'. OE pers. name + *throp*.

Ickburgh Norfolk. *Iccheburc* 1086 (DB). 'Stronghold of a man called *Ic(c)a*'. OE pers. name + *burh*.

Ickenham Gtr. London. *Ticeham* 1086 (DB). 'Homestead or village of a man called Tic(c)a'. OE pers. name (genitive *-n*) + *hām*. Initial *T-* was lost in the 13th cent. due to confusion with the preposition *at*.

Ickford Bucks. *Iforde |sic|* 1086 (DB), *Ycford* 1175. 'Ford of a man called *Ic(c)a*'. OE pers. name + *ford*.

Ickham Kent. *Ioccham* 785, *Gecham* 1086 (DB). 'Homestead or village comprising a yoke (some fifty acres) of land'. OE *geoc* + *hām*.

Ickleford Herts. *Ikelineford* 12th cent. 'Ford associated with a man called Icel'. OE pers. name + *-ing-* + *ford*.

Icklesham E. Sussex. *Icoleshamme* 770. 'Promontory or river-meadow of a man called Icel'. OE pers. name + *hamm*.

Ickleton Cambs. *Icelingtune* c.975, *Hichelintone* 1086 (DB). 'Estate associated with a man called Icel'. OE pers. name + *-ing-* + *tūn*.

Icklingam Suffolk. *Ecclingaham* 1086 (DB). 'Homestead of the family or followers of a man called *Ycel*'. OE pers. name + *-inga-* + *hām*.

Icknield Way (prehistoric trackway from Norfolk to Dorset). *Icenhylte* 903. Obscure in origin and meaning. The name was transferred in the 12th cent. to the Roman road from Bourton on the Water to Templeborough near Rotherham, now called **Icknield** or **Ryknild Street**.

Ickwell Green Beds. *Ikewelle* c.1170. 'Beneficial spring or stream', or 'spring or stream of a man called *Gic(c)a*'. OE *gēoc* or OE pers. name + *wella*.

Icomb Glos. *Iccacumb* 781, *Iccumbe* 1086 (DB). 'Valley of a man called *Ic(c)a*'. OE pers. name + *cumb*.

Ida (*Uí Deaghaigh*) Kilkenny. 'Descendants of Deaghadh'.

Iddesleigh Devon. *Edeslege |sic|* 1086 (DB), *Edwislega* 1107. 'Woodland clearing of a man called Ēadwīg'. OE pers. name + *lēah*.

Ide Devon. *Ide* 1086 (DB). Possibly an old river-name of pre-English origin.

Ide Hill Kent. *Edythehelle* c.1250. 'Hill of a woman called Edith (OE Ēadgȳth)'. OE pers. name + *hyll*.

Ideford Devon. *Yudaforda* 1086 (DB). 'Ford of a man called *Giedda*', or 'ford where people assemble for speeches or songs'. OE pers. name or OE *giedd* + *ford*

Iden E. Sussex. *Idene* 1086 (DB). 'Woodland pasture where yew-trees grow'. OE *īg* + *denn*.

Idle W. Yorks. *Idla* c.1190, *Idel* 13th cent. Probably OE *īdel* 'idel, empty' used as a noun in the sense 'uncultivated land'.

Idlicote Warwicks. *Etelincote* 1086 (DB). 'Cottage(s) associated with a man called *Yttel(a)*'. OE pers. name + *-ing-* + *cot*.

Idmiston Wilts. *Idemestone* 947. 'Farmstead of a man called *Idmær* or *Idhelm*'. OE pers. name + *tūn*.

Idridgehay Derbys. *Edrichesei* 1230. 'Enclosure of a man called Ēadrīc. OE pers. name + *hæg*.

Idrigill Highland (Skye). 'Outer gully'. OScand. *ytri* + *gil*.

Idstone Oxon. *Edwineston* 1199. 'Farmstead of a man called Ēadwine'. OE pers. name + *tūn*.

Iffley Oxon. *Gifetelea* 1004, *Givetelei* 1086 (DB). Probably 'woodland clearing frequented by the plover or similar bird'. OE *gīfete* + *lēah*.

Ifield W. Sussex. *Ifelt* 1086 (DB). 'Open land where yew-trees grow'. OE *īg* + *feld*.

Ifold W. Sussex. *Ifold* 1296. Probably 'fold or enclosure in well-watered land'. OE *īeg* + *fald*.

Iford E. Sussex. *Niworde |sic|* 1086 (DB), *Yford* late 11th cent. 'Ford in well-watered land', or 'ford where yew-trees grow'. OE *īeg* or *īg* + *ford*.

Ifton Heath Shrops. *Iftone* 1272. Possibly 'farmstead of a man called Ifa'. OE pers. name + *tūn*.

Ightfield Shrops. *Istefelt* 1086 (DB), *Ychtefeld* 1210–12. 'Open land by the River *Ight*'. Pre-English river-name (of uncertain meaning) + OE *feld*.

Ightham Kent. *Ehteham* c.1100. 'Homestead or village of a man called *Ehta*'. OE pers. name + *hām*.

Iken Suffolk. *Ykene* 1212. Possibly an ancient river-name identical with ITCHEN. This would have been the old name of the River Alde, for which see ALDEBURGH.

Ilam Staffs. *Hilum* 1002. Possibly a Celtic river-name (an early name for River Manifold) meaning 'trickling stream'. Alternatively the name may be '(place at) the pools', from OScand. *hylr* in a dative plural form *hylum*.

Ilchester Somerset. *Givelcestre* 1086 (DB). 'Roman town on the River *Gifl*'. Celtic river-name (meaning 'forked river') + OE *ceaster*. *Gifl* was an earlier name for the River Yeo.

Ilderton Northum. *Ildretona* c.1125. 'Farmstead where elder-trees grow'. OE **hyldre* + *tūn*.

Ilen (*Abhainn Eibhlinn*) (river) Cork. 'Sparkling river'.

Ilford Gtr. London. *Ilefort* 1086 (DB). 'Ford over the river called *Hyle*'. Celtic river-name (meaning 'trickling stream') + OE *ford*. *Hyle* was an early name for the River Roding below ONGER.

Ilfracombe Devon. *Alfreincome* 1086 (DB). 'Valley associated with a man called Ælfrēd'. OE pers. name + *-ing-* + *cumb*.

Ilkeston Derbys. *Tilchestune* |sic| 1086 (DB), *Elkesdone* early 11th cent. 'Hill of a man called Ēalāc'. OE pers. name + *dūn*. ·

Ilketshall St Andrew & **Ilketshall St Margaret** Suffolk. *Ilcheteleshala* 1086 (DB). 'Nook of land of a man called **Ylfketill*'. OScand. pers. name + OE *halh*. Distinguishing affixes from the dedications of the churches.

Ilkley W. Yorks. *Hillicleg* c.972, *Illiclei* 1086 (DB). Possibly 'woodland clearing of a man called **Yllica* or **Illica*'. OE pers. name + *lēah*.

Illanfad (*Oileán Fada*) Donegal. 'Long island'.

Illaunfadda (*Oileán Fada*) Galway. 'Long island'.

Illaunmore (*Oileán Mór*) Tipperary. 'Large island'.

Illaunslea (*Oileán Shléibhe*) Kerry. 'Island of the mountain'.

Illauntannig (*Oileán tSeanaigh*) Kerry. 'Seanach's island'.

Illingworth W. Yorks. *Illingworthe* 1276. 'Enclosure associated with a man called **Illa* or *Ylla*'. OE pers. name + *-ing-* + *worth*.

Illogan Cornwall. 'Church of *Sanctus Illoganus*' 1291. 'Church of St Illogan'. From the patron saint of the church.

Illston on the Hill Leics. *Elvestone* 1086 (DB). Possibly 'farmstead of a man called Iólfr or **Elf*'. OScand. or OE pers. name + OE *tūn*.

Ilmer Bucks. *Imere* |sic| 1086 (DB), *Ilmere* 1161–3. Probably 'pool where leeches are found'. OE *īl* + *mere*.

Ilmington Warwicks. *Ylmandun* 978, *Ilmedone* 1086 (DB). 'Hill growing with elm-trees'. OE **ylme* (genitive *-an*) + *dūn*.

Ilminster Somerset. *Illemynister* 995, *Ileminstre* 1086 (DB). 'Large church on the River Isle'. Celtic river-name (of uncertain meaning) + OE *mynster*.

Ilsington Devon. *Ilestintona* 1086 (DB). 'Estate associated with a man called **Ielfstān*'. OE pers. name + *-ing-* + *tūn*.

Ilsley, East & **Ilsley, West** Berks. *Hildeslei* 1086 (DB). 'Woodland clearing of a man called Hild'. OE pers. name + *lēah*.

Ilton N. Yorks. *Ilcheton* 1086 (DB). 'Farmstead of a man called **Yllica* or **Illica*'. OE pers. name + *tūn*.

Ilton Somerset. *Atiltone* |sic| 1086 (DB), *Ilton* 1243. 'Farmstead on the River Isle'. Celtic river-name (of uncertain meaning) + OE *tūn*.

Imaile (*Uí Mail*) Wicklow. 'Descendants of Mal'.

Immingham NE. Lincs. *Imungeham* |sic| 1086 (DB), *Immingeham* c.1115. 'Homestead of the family or followers of a man called Imma'. OE pers. name + *-inga-* + *hām*.

Impington Cambs. *Impintune* c.1050, *Epintone* 1086 (DB). 'Estate associated with a man called **Empa* or **Impa*'. OE pers. name + *-ing-* + *tūn*.

Inagh (*Eidhneach*) Clare. 'Abounding in ivy'.

Inan (*Eidhneán*) Meath. 'Ivy place'.

Inane (*Eidhneán*) Cork, Tipperary. 'Ivy place'.

Ince, 'the island', OWelsh **inis*: **Ince** Ches. *Inise* 1086 (DB). **Ince** Gtr. Manch. *Ines* 1202. **Ince Blundell** Mersey. *Hinne* |sic| 1086 (DB), *Ins Blundell* 1332. Manorial affix from the Blundell family, here in the early 13th cent.

Inch (*Inis*) Cork, Down, Kerry, Wexford. 'Island, water meadow'.

Inchagoill (*Inis an Ghaill*) Galway. 'Island of the foreigners'.

Inchannon (*Inis Eonáin*) Cork. 'Eonán's island'.

Inchcape Rock Ang. 'Rock of the island'. Gaelic *inis* + unknown element and English *rock*.

Inchcolm (island) Fife. *Insula Sancti Columbae* c.1123, *St Colmes Ynch* 1605. 'St Columba's island'. Gaelic *inis*.

Inchee (*Insí*) Kerry. 'Water meadows'.

Inchenny (*Inis Eanaigh*) Tyrone. 'Island of the marsh'.

Inchfarrannaglerach (*Inse Fhearann na gCléireach*) Kerry. 'Water meadows of the land of the clerics'.

Inchicore (*Inse Chór*) Dublin. 'Islands of the snout'.

Inchicronan (*Inse Cronáin*) Clare. 'Cronán's island'.

Inchideraille (*Inis Idir dá Fhaill*) Cork. 'Island between two cliffs'.

Inchigeelagh (*Inse Geimhleach*) Cork. 'Island of the prisoner'.

Inchinaleega (*Inse na Léige*) Kerry. 'Water meadow of the stone'.

Inchinglanna (*Inse an Ghleanna*) Kerry. 'Water meadow of the valley'.

Inchiquin, Lough (*Loch Inse Uí Chuinn*) Clare, Cork. 'Lake of Ó Cuinn's island'.

Inchkeith (island) Fife. *Insula Ked* c.1200. 'Wooded island'. Gaelic *inis* + British **ceto-*.

Inchnamuck (*Inse na Muc*) Tipperary. 'Island of the pigs'.

Ingatestone Essex. *Gynges Atteston* 1283. 'Manor called *Ing* (for which see FRYERNING) at the stone'. One of a group of places so called, this one distinguished by reference to a Roman milestone. OE *stān*.

Ingbirchworth S. Yorks. *Berceuuorde* 1086 (DB), *Yngebyrcheworth* 1424. 'Enclosure where birch-trees grow'. OE *birce* + *worth* with the later addition of OScand. *eng* 'meadow'.

Ingham, possibly 'homestead or village of a man called Inga', OE pers. name + *hām*, although it has recently been suggested that the first element of these names may be a word meaning 'the Inguione', a member of the ancient Germanic tribe called the Inguiones: **Ingham** Lincs. *Ingeham* 1086 (DB). **Ingham** Norfolk. *Hincham* 1086 (DB). **Ingham** Suffolk. *Ingham* 1086 (DB).

Ingleby, 'farmstead or village of the Englishmen', OScand. *Englar* + *bý*: **Ingleby** Derbys. *Englaby* 1009, *Englebi* 1086 (DB). **Ingleby** Lincs. *Englebi* 1086 (DB). **Ingleby Arncliffe** N. Yorks. *Englebi* 1086 (DB). Affix is from a nearby place (*Erneclive* 1086), 'eagles' cliff', OE *earn* + *clif*. **Ingleby Greenhow** N. Yorks. *Englebi* 1086 (DB). Affix is from a nearby place (*Grenehou* 12th cent.), 'green mound', OE *grēne* + OScand. *haugr*.

Inglesham Wilts. *Inggeneshamme* c.950. 'Enclosure or river-meadow of a man called *Ingen* or *Ingīn*'. OE pers. name + *hamm*.

Ingleton Durham. *Ingeltun* c.1050. Probably 'farmstead of a man called Ingeld'. OScand. pers. name + OE *tūn*.

Ingleton N. Yorks. *Inglestune* 1086 (DB). 'Farmstead near the hill or peak'. OE **ingel* + *tūn*.

Inglewhite Lancs. *Inglewhite* 1662. Probably from OE **wiht* 'river-bend' with an uncertain first element.

Ingoe Northum. *Hinghou* 1229. Probably OE **ing* 'hill, peak' with the addition of *hōh* 'spur of land'.

Ingoldisthorpe Norfolk. *Torp* 1086 (DB), *Ingaldestorp* 1203. 'Outlying farmstead or hamlet of a man called Ingjaldr'. OScand. pers. name + *thorp*.

Ingoldmells Lincs. in *Guldelsmere* |*sic*| 1086 (DB), *Ingoldesmeles* 1180. 'Sand-banks of a man called Ingjaldr'. OScand. pers. name + *melr*.

Ingoldsby Lincs. *Ingoldesbi* 1086 (DB). 'Farmstead or village of a man called Ingjaldr'. OScand. pers. name + *bý*.

Ingram Northum. *Angerham* 1242. 'Homestead or enclosure with grassland'. OE **anger* + *hām* or *hamm*.

Ingrave Essex. *Ingam* 1086 (DB), *Gingeraufe* 1276. 'Manor called *Ing* (for which *see* FRYERNING) held by a man called Ralf (OGerman Radulf)'. He was a tenant in 1086.

Ingworth Norfolk. *Inghewurda* 1086 (DB). Probably 'enclosure of a man called Inga'. OE pers. name + *worth*.

Inishargy (*Inis Cairrge*) Down. *Iniscargi* 1306. 'Island of the rock'.

Inishbarra (*Inis Bearachain*) Galway. 'Island of the heifers'.

Inishbiggle (*Inis Bigil*) Mayo. 'Island of the fasting'.

Inishbofin (*Inis Bó Finne*) Donegal, Galway. 'Island of the white cow'.

Inishcarra (*Inis Cara*) Cork. 'Island of the weir'.

Inishcrone (*Inis Crabhann*) Sligo. 'Island of the gravel ridge of the river'.

Inishdadroum (*Inis dá Drom*) Clare. 'Island of two backs'.

Inishdooey (*Inis Dubhthaigh*) (island) Donegal. 'Dubhthach's island'. The current Irish name is *Oileán Dúiche*, 'Sandbank island'.

Inisheer (*Inis Oírr*) Galway. 'Eastern island'.

Inishfree (*Inis Fraoigh*) Donegal. 'Island of heather'.

Inishirrer (*Inis Oirthir*) Donegal. 'Island of the eastern area'.

Inishkeen (*Inis Caoin*) Limerick, Monaghan. 'Beautiful island'.

Inishkeeragh (*Inis Caorach*) Donegal. 'Island of sheep'.

Inishlackan (*Inis Leacan*) Galway. 'Island of the hilside'.

Inishmaan (*Inis Meáin*) Galway. 'Middle island'.

Inishmacowney (*Inish Mhic Uaithne*) Clare. 'Mac Uaithne's island'.

Inishmeane (*Inis Meáin*) Donegal. *Inismahan* 1830. 'Middle island'.

Inishmore (*Inis Mór*) Galway. 'Big island'.

Inishmurray (*Inis Muiri*) Sligo. 'Muireadhach's island'.

Inishnagor (*Inis na gCorr*) Donegal, Sligo. 'Island of the cranes'.

Inishowen (*Inis Eoghain*) Donegal. (*i*)*nInis Eoghain* 465. 'Eoghan's island'.

Inishrush (*Inis Rois*) Derry. *Inishroisse* 1615. 'Island of the wood'.

Inishshark (*Inis Airc*) Galway. 'Island of hardship'.

Inishsirrer (*Inis Oirthir*) Donegal. 'Eastern island'.

Inishtooskert (*Inis Tuaisceart*) Kerry. 'Northern island'.

Inishturk (*Inis Toirc*) Galway. 'Island of the boar'.

Inistioge (*Inis Tíog*) Kilkenny. 'Tíog's island'.

Inkberrow Heref. & Worcs. *Intanbeorgas* 789, *Inteberge* 1086 (DB). 'Hills or mounds of a man called Inta'. OE pers. name + *beorg* (plural -*as*).

Inkpen Berks. *Ingepenne* c.935, *Hingepene* 1086 (DB). OE **ing* 'hill, peak' with either Celtic **penn* 'hill' or OE *penn* 'enclosure, fold'.

Innerleithen Sc. Bord. *Innerlethan* c.1160. 'Mouth of the Leithen Water'. Gaelic *inbhir lektona* 'the dripping river'.

Innisfallen (*Inis Faithlenn*) Kerry. 'Fathlenn's island'.

Inskip Lancs. *Inscip* 1086 (DB). Probably OWelsh **inis* 'island' with OE *cȳpe* 'osier-basket for catching fish'.

Instow Devon. *Johannesto* 1086 (DB). 'Holy place of St John'. Saint's name + OE *stōw*. The church here is dedicated to St John the Baptist.

Inver (*Inbhear Náile*) Donegal. 'Estuary of Náile'.

Inveran (*Indreabhán*) Galway. 'Little estuary'.

Inveraray Arg. 'Mouth of the River Aray'. Gaelic *inbhir*.

Inverclyde (the unitary authority). A modern administrative formation. 'Mouth of the River Clyde'. Gaelic *inbhir*. For the river name, *see* CLYDEBANK.

Invereela (*Inbhear Daeile*) Wicklow. 'Estuary of the (river) Deel'.

Invergordon Highland. 'Gordon's (place at the) river mouth'. Gaelic *inbhir*. Alexander *Gordon* was landowner here c.1760. Earlier, the place was known as *Inverbreckie*, 'mouth of the Breckie', a river name meaning 'speckled' (Gaelic *breac*).

Inverkeithing Fife. *Hinhirkethy* c.1057, *Innerkethyin* 1114. 'Mouth of the Keithing Burn'. Gaelic *inbhir*. The river name probably means 'wooded stream' (British **ceto-*).

Inverleith Edin. *Inerlet* c.1130. 'Mouth of the Water of Leith'. Gaelic *inbhir*. For the river name, *see* LEITH.

Inverness Highland. *Invernis* 1300. 'Mouth of the River Ness'. Gaelic *inbhir*. The river has a Celtic or pre-Celtic name from a root **ned-* 'moist'.

Inverurie Aber. *Inverurie* 1199, *Innervwry* c.1300. 'Confluence of the River Urie and Don'. Gaelic *inbhir* + unexplained river name.

Inwardleigh Devon. *Lega* 1086 (DB), *Inwardlegh* 1235. 'Woodland clearing'. OE *lēah*, with manorial addition from the man called Inwar (OScand. *Ingvar*) who held the manor in 1086.

Inworth Essex. *Inewrth* 1206. 'Enclosure of a man called Ina'. OE pers. name + *worth*.

Iona (island) Arg. *Hiiensis* 634, *Ioua insula* c.700, *Hiona-Columcille* c.1100. '(Place of) yew trees'. OIrish *eo*. The island is associated with St Columba, Gaelic *I Chaluim Chille* or simply *I*.

Iping W. Sussex. *Epinges* 1086 (DB). '(Settlement of) the family or followers of a man called **Ipa*'. OE pers. name + *-ingas*.

Ipplepen Devon. *Iplanpenne* 956, *Iplepene* 1086 (DB). 'Fold or enclosure of a man called **Ipela*'. OE pers. name + *penn*.

Ipsden Oxon. *Yppesdene* 1086 (DB). 'Valley near the upland'. OE *yppe* + *denu*.

Ipstones Staffs. *Yppestan* 1175. Probably 'stone in the high place or upland'. OE *yppe* + *stān*.

Ipswich Suffolk. *Gipeswic* c.975, 1086 (DB). 'Harbour or trading centre of a man called **Gip*'. OE pers. name + *wīc*.

Irby, *Ireby*, 'farmstead or village of the Irishmen', OScand. *Írar* + *bý*: **Irby** Mersey. *Irreby* c.1100. **Irby in the Marsh** Lincs. *Irebi* c.1115. **Irby upon Humber** NE. Lincs. *Iribi* 1086 (DB). For the river-name, *see* HUMBER. **Ireby** Cumbria. *Irebi* c.1160. **Ireby** Lancs. *Irebi* 1086 (DB).

Irchester Northants. *Yranceaster* 973, *Irencestre* 1086 (DB). 'Roman station associated with a man called Ira or **Yra*'. OE pers. name + *ceaster*.

Ireby, *see* IRBY.

Ireland (*Éire*) 'Land of the Irish'. The name amounts to OIrish *Eriu*, 'Eria' + OE *land*. The country name itself may relate to a fertility goddess.

Ireland's Eye (*Inis Mac Neasáin*) (island) Dublin. 'Island of Mic Neasáin'. The English name is a convoluted version of the earlier Irish name *Inis Ereann*, 'Eria's island'. The female personal name was taken to be the genitive of *Éire*, 'Ireland', while *Eye* represents OScand. *ey*, 'island'.

Ireleth Cumbria. *Irlid* 1190. 'Hill-slope of the Irishmen'. OScand. *Írar* + *hlíth*.

Ireton, Kirk Derbys. *Hiretune* 1086 (DB), *Kirkirton* 1370. 'Farmstead of the Irishmen'. OScand. *Írar* + OE *tūn*. Affix is OScand. *kirkja* 'church'.

Irlam Gtr. Manch. *Urwelham* c.1190. 'Homestead or enclosure on the River Irwell'. OE river-name ('winding stream' from OE *irre + wella*) + OE *hām* or *hamm*.

Irnham Lincs. *Gerneham* 1086 (DB). 'Homestead or village of a man called **Georna*'. OE pers. name + *hām*.

Iron Acton S. Glos., *see* ACTON.

Ironbridge Shrops., a late name, so called from the famous iron bridge built here across the River Severn in 1779.

Irthington Cumbria. *Irthinton* 1169. 'Farmstead on the River Irthing'. Celtic river-name + OE *tūn*.

Irthlingborough Northants. *Yrtlingaburg* 780, *Erdi(n)burne |sic|* 1086 (DB). Probably 'fortified manor belonging to the ploughmen'. OE *erthling, yrthling* + *burh*.

Irton Cumbria. *Yrton* c.1225. 'Farmstead on the River Irt'. OE *tūn* with an old pre-English river-name of uncertain meaning.

Irton N. Yorks. *Iretune* 1086 (DB). 'Farmstead of the Irishmen'. OScand. *Írar* + OE *tūn*.

Irvine N. Ayr. *Hirun* c.1190. '(Place on the) River Irvine'. The Celtic river name is probably the same as the river Irfon in Cardiganshire.

Irvinestown Fermanagh. *Irvinestown or Lowthertown* 1837. The original village here was named *Lowthertown*, after Sir Gerard Lowther, who founded it in 1618. In 1667 the estate was sold to Sir Christopher Irvine, and his name was adopted for the village in the early 19th cent. The equivalent Irish name is *Baile an Irbhinigh*.

Irwell (river) Lancs., *see* IRLAM.

Isbister Shet (Whalsay). 'east from'. OScand. *bólstathr*.

Isertkelly (*Díseart Cheallaigh*) Kilkenny. 'Ceallach's hermitage'.

Isfield E. Sussex. *Isefeld* 1214. 'Open land of a man called **Isa*'. OE pers. name + *feld*.

Isham Northants. *Ysham* 974, *Isham* 1086 (DB). 'Homestead or promontory by the River Ise'. Celtic river-name (meaning 'water') + OE *hām* or *hamm*.

Isis (river) Oxon., recorded as *Isa* c.1350, *Isis* 1577, an artificial formation from *Tamesis*, the early form for THAMES, which was falsely interpreted as THAME + Isis.

Island (*Oileán*) Cork, Mayo. 'Island'.

Island Magee (*Oileán Mhic Aodha*) Antrim. *Rensevin* 1521. 'Mac Aodha's island'. An earlier name for the peninsula here was *Rinn Seimhne*, 'peninsula of (the district of) Seimhne', from a tribal name.

Islandmoyle (*Oileán Maol*) Down. 'Bare island'.

Islandreagh (*Oileán Riabhach*) Antrim. 'Striped island'.

Islay (island) Arg. *Ilea* c.690, *Ile* 800. Possibly 'swelling island'. OCeltic **ili*, but probably pre-Celtic.

Isle Abbotts & *Isle Brewers* Somerset. *Yli* 966, *I(s)le* 1086 (DB), *Ile Abbatis* 1291, *Ile Brywer* 1275. Named from the River Isle, which is a Celtic river-name of uncertain meaning. Distinguishing affixes from early possession by Muchelney Abbey (Latin *abbatis* 'of the abbot') and by the Briwer family.

Isle of Dogs Gtr. London, first recorded as *Isle of Doges Ferm* 1593, probably simply descriptive of a marshy peninsula frequented by (wild or stray) dogs.

Isleham Cambs. *Yselham* 895, *Gisleham* 1086 (DB). 'Homestead of a man called *Gīsla*'. OE pers. name + *hām*.

Isleworth Gtr. London, *Gislheresuuyrth* 677, *Gistelesworde* 1086 (DB). 'Enclosure of a man called Gīslhere'. OE pers. name + *worth*.

Islington Gtr. London. *Gislandune* *c.*1000, *Iseldone* 1086 (DB). 'Hill of a man called *Gīsla*'. OE pers. name (genitive -*n*) + *dūn*.

Islip Northants. *Isslepe* 10th cent., *Islep* 1086 (DB). 'Slippery place by the River Ise'. Pre-English river-name (meaning 'water') + OE *slǣp*.

Islip Oxon. *Githslepe* *c.*1050, *Letelape* |sic| 1086 (DB). 'Slippery place by the River *Ight* (an old name for the River Ray)'. Pre-English river-name (of uncertain meaning) + OE *slǣp*.

Itchen Abbas Hants. *Icene* 1086 (DB), *Ichene Monialium* 1167. Named from the River Itchen, an ancient pre-Celtic river-name of unknown origin and meaning. The Latin affix in the 12th cent. form means 'of the nuns', the later affix *Abbas* is a reduced form of Latin *abbatissa* 'abbess', both referring to possession by the Abbey of St Mary, Winchester.

Itchen Stoke Hants. *Stoche* 1086 (DB), *Ichenestoke* 1185. 'Secondary settlement from ITCHEN [ABBAS]'. OE *stoc*.

Itchenor, East & *Itchenor, West* W. Sussex. *Iccannore* 683, *Icenore* 1086 (DB). 'Shore of a man called *Icca*'. OE pers. name (genitive -*n*) + *ōra*.

Itchington S. Glos. *Icenantune* 967, *Icetune* 1086 (DB). 'Farmstead by a stream called *Itchen*'. Lost pre-Celtic river-name (of unknown meaning) + OE *tūn*.

Itchington, Bishops & *Itchington, Long* Warwicks. *Yceantune* 1001, *Ice(n)tone* 1086 (DB), *Bisshopesychengton* 1384, *Longa Hichenton* *c.*1185. 'Farmstead on the River Itchen'. Pre-Celtic river-name (of unknown meaning) + OE *tūn*. Distinguishing affixes from possession by the Bishop of Coventry and Lichfield and from OE *lang* 'long'.

Itteringham Norfolk. *Utrincham* 1086 (DB). Probably 'homestead of the family or followers of a man called *Ytra* or *Ytri*'. OE pers. name + -*inga*- + *hām*.

Ivegill Cumbria. *Yuegill* 1361. 'Deep narrow valley of the River Ive'. OScand. river-name (meaning 'yew stream') + *gil*.

Ivel (river) Beds., Herts., see NORTHILL.

Iver Bucks. *Evreham* 1086 (DB), *Eura* *c.*1130. '(Place by) the brow of a hill or the tip of a promontory'. OE *yfer* (-*am* in the Domesday spelling is a Latin ending).

Iveston Durham. *Ivestan* 1183. 'Boundary stone of a man called Ifa'. OE pers. name + *stān*.

Ivinghoe Bucks. *Evinghehou* 1086 (DB). 'Hill-spur of the family or followers of a man called Ifa'. OE pers. name + -*inga*- + *hōh*.

Ivington Heref. & Worcs. *Ivintune* 1086 (DB). 'Estate associated with a man called Ifa'. OE pers. name + -*ing*- + *tūn*.

Ivybridge Devon. *Ivebrugge* 1292. 'Ivy-covered bridge'. OE *īfig* + *brycg*.

Ivychurch Kent. *Iuecirce* 11th cent. 'Ivy-covered church'. OE *īfig* + *cirice*.

Iwade Kent. *Ywada* 1179. 'Ford or crossing-place where yew-trees grow'. OE *īw* + (*ge*)*wæd*. The crossing-place is to the Isle of Sheppey.

Iwerne Courtney or *Shroton*, *Iwerne Minster* Dorset. *Ywern* 877, *Werne*, *Evneministre* 1086 (DB), *Iwerne Courteney alias Shyrevton* 1403. Named from the River Iwerne, a Celtic river-name possibly meaning 'yew river' or referring to a goddess. Distinguishing affixes from the Courtenay family, here in the 13th cent., and from OE *mynster* 'church of a monastery' in allusion to early possession by Shaftesbury Abbey. Shroton means 'sheriff's estate', OE *scīr-rēfa* + *tūn*.

Ixworth Suffolk. *Gyxeweorde* *c.*1025, *Giswortha* 1086 (DB). 'Enclosure of a man called *Gicsa* or *Gycsa*'. OE pers. name + *worth*.

Ixworth Thorpe Suffolk. *Torp* 1086 (DB), *Ixeworth thorp* 1305. 'Secondary settlement dependent on IXWORTH'. OScand. *thorp*.

J

Jacobstow, *Jacobstowe*, 'holy place of St James', saint's name (Latin *Jacobus*) + OE *stōw*: **Jacobstow** Cornwall. *Jacobestowe* 1270. **Jacobstowe** Devon. *Jacopstoue* 1331.

Jameston Pemb. *Seint Jameston* 1331. 'St James's farm'. OE *tūn*. A fair was held here annually on St James's day.

Jamestown Dunb. 'James's town'. Original name *Dumhead*, called *Jamestown* when accommodation was needed for those employed at the Levenbank Works.

Jarlshof Shet. 'Jarl's temple'. OScand. *jarl* + *hof*. The site was so called in 1816 by Sir Walter Scott, who used the name for the medieval farmhouse in his novel *The Pirate* (1821). A jarl is a Scand. chief.

Jarrow Tyne & Wear. *Gyruum c.*730. '(Settlement of) the fen people'. OE tribal name *Gyrwe* derived from OE *gyr* 'mud, marsh'.

Jaywick Sands Essex. *Clakyngeywyk* 1438, *Gey wyck* 1584. 'Dwelling or (dairy) farm at the place associated with a man called *Clacc*. OE pers. name + *-ing* + *wīc*. The first part of the name (probably taken to be a local form of CLACTON) was dropped in the 16th cent.

Jedburgh Sc. Bord. *Gedwearde* 800, *Geddewrde c.*1100, *Jeddeburgh c.*1160. 'Enclosure by the River Jed'. OE *worth*.

Jeffreyston Pemb. *Villa Galfrid c.*1214, *Geffreiston* 1362. 'Geoffrey's farm'. OGerman pers. name + OE *tūn*. The church is dedicated to St Jeffry and St Oswald, but the former saint may have been suggested by the place name.

Jemimaville Highland. The village was named by Sir George Munro, 4th Laird of Poyntzfield, after his wife, Jemima Charlotte Graham, whom he married in 1822.

Jerrettspass Armagh. *Gerrard* (*Pass*) 1835. 'Jerrett's pass'. The surname is a form of *Garrett*.

Jervaulx Abbey N. Yorks. *Jorvalle c.*1145. 'Valley of the River Ure'. Ancient pre-English river-name of uncertain origin + OFrench *val*(*s*).

Jevington E. Sussex. *Lovingetone |sic|* 1086 (DB), *Govingetona* 1189. 'Farmstead of the family or followers of a man called *Geofa*. OE pers. name + *-inga-* + *tūn*.

Jodrell Bank Ches., recorded from 1831, 'bank or hillside belonging to the Jodrell family', land-owners here in the 19th cent.

John o'Groats Highland. John o'Groat was appointed bailee to the earls of Caithness in the 15th cent.

Johnby Cumbria. *Johannebi* 1200. 'Farmstead or village of a man called Johan'. OFrench pers. name + OScand. *bý*.

Johnston Pemb. *Villa Johannis* 1296, *Johanneston* 1393. 'John's farm'. OE *tūn*.

Johnstone Renf. *Jonestone* 1292. 'John's farm'. OE *tūn*. Founded in 1781 on the site of Brig ò Johnstone.

Jonesborough Armagh. 'Jones's town'. *Jones Borough* 1714. The village was founded in 1706 by Roth Jones, a local landlord.

Joppa Edin. The name was first mentioned in 1793, itself named after the biblical town of *Joppa* (Acts 9:36, etc).

Jordanston (*Trefwrdan*) Pemb. *Villa Jordahi* (*sic*) 1291, *Jordanyston* 1326. 'Jordan's farm'. OE *tūn* (Welsh *tref*). The Welsh name translates the English.

Jordanstown Antrim. 'Jordan's town'. *Bally Jurdon* 1604. An Anglo-Norman family named Jordan were here in the 12th cent.

Juniper Green Edin. 'Field of Junipers'. Originally a park; first mentioned in 1753.

Jura (island) Arg. *Doirad Eilinn* 678. *Dure* 1336. 'Deer island'. ON *Dŷr-ey*.

K

Kaber Cumbria. *Kaberge* late 12th cent. 'Hill frequented by jackdaws'. OE **ca + beorg*, or OScand. **ká + berg*.

Kale Water Sc. Bord. *Kalne* c.1200. 'Calling one'. British **calauna*.

Kanturk (*Ceann Toirc*) Cork. 'Head of the boar'.

Katesbridge Down. 'Kate's bridge'. *McCay's Bridge* 1744. The name is that of Kate McKay, said to have owned a house here where workmen lodged when building a bridge in the 18th cent. The equivalent Irish name is *Droichead Cháit*.

Katrine, Loch Stir. *Loch Ketyerne* 1463. Gaelic *loch* + obscure element.

Kea, Old Kea Cornwall. *Sanctus Che* 1086 (DB). '(Church of) St Kea'. From the dedication of the church.

Keadeen (*Céidín*) (mountain) Wicklow. *Kedi* c.1238, *Kedyn* c.1310. 'Little flat-topped hill'.

Keadew (*Céideadh*) Roscommon. 'Flat-topped hill'.

Keady (*An Céide*) Armagh. *An Chéideadh* c.1854. 'The flat-topped hill'.

Keadydrinagh (*Céide Draigneach*) Sligo. 'Flat-topped hill of the blackthorn'.

Keal, East & *Keal, West* Lincs. *Estrecale, Westrecale* 1086 (DB). 'The ridge of hills'. OScand. *kjǫlr*. Distinguishing affixes are OE *ēasterra* 'more easterly' and *westerra* 'more westerly'.

Kealariddig (*Caol an Roidigh*) Kerry. 'Marshy stream of the red mire'.

Kealkill (*An Caolchoill*) Cork. 'The narrow wood'.

Kearsley Gtr. Manch. *Cherselawe* 1187, *Kersleie* c.1220. 'Clearing where cress grows'. OE *cærse + lēah*.

Kearstwick Cumbria. *Kesthwaite* 1547. 'Valley clearing'. OScand. *kjóss + thveit*.

Kearton N. Yorks. *Karretan* |sic| 13th cent., *Kirton* 1298. Possibly 'farmstead of a man called Kærir'. OScand. pers. name + OE *tūn*.

Keava (*Céibh*) Roscommon. 'Long grass'.

Keave (*Céibh*) Galway. 'Long grass'.

Keddington Lincs. *Cadinton* |sic| 1086 (DB), *Kedingtuna* 12th cent. Probably 'farmstead associated with a man called Cydda'. OE pers. name + -ing- + tūn.

Kedington Suffolk. *Kydington* 1043–5, *Kidituna* 1086 (DB). Identical in origin with the previous name.

Kedleston Derbys. *Chetestune* 1086 (DB). 'Farmstead of a man called Ketill'. OScand. pers. name + OE *tūn*.

Keel (*An Caol*) Mayo. 'The narrow stream'.

Keelby Lincs. *Chelebi* 1086 (DB). 'Farmstead or village on or near a ridge'. OScand. *kjǫlr + bý*.

Keele Staffs. *Kiel* 1169. 'Hill where cows graze'. OE *cȳ + hyll*.

Keeloges (*Caológa*) Wicklow. *Byllock* |sic| 1619, *Culloges* 1690. 'Narrow ridges'.

Keenagh (*Caonach*) Longford. 'Moss'.

Keenaghbeg (*Caonach Beag*) Mayo. 'Little moss'.

Keeragh Islands (*Oileáin na gCaorach*) Wexford. 'Islands of the sheep'.

Keeraunnagark (*Caorán na gCearc*) Galway. 'Moor of the hens'.

Keeston (*Tregetin*) Pemb. *Villa Ketyng* 1289, *Ketingeston* 1295. 'Keting's farm'. OE *tūn* (Welsh *tref*). The English and Welsh names translate each other.

Keevil Wilts. *Kefle* 964, *Chivele* 1086 (DB). Probably 'woodland clearing in a hollow'. OE *cȳf + lēah*.

Kegworth Leics. *Cacheworde* |sic| 1086 (DB), *Caggworth* c.1125. Possibly 'enclosure of a man called *Cægga'. OE pers. name + *worth*.

Keighley W. Yorks. *Chichelai* 1086 (DB). 'Woodland clearing of a man called *Cyhha'. OE pers. name + *lēah*.

Keimaneigh (*Céim an Fhia*) Cork. 'Gap of the deer'.

Keinton Mandeville Somerset. *Chintune* 1086 (DB), *Kyngton Maundevill* 1280. 'Royal manor'. OE *cyne- + tūn*. Manorial affix from the Maundevill family, here in the 13th cent.

Keisby Lincs. *Chisebi* 1086 (DB). 'Farmstead or village of a man called Kisi'. OScand. pers. name + *bý*. Alternatively the first element may be OScand. **kīs* 'gravel, coarse sand'.

Keith Moray. *Geth* 1187, *Ket* c.1220. '(Place by the) wood'. British **ceto-*.

Kelbrook Lancs. *Chelbroc* 1086 (DB). Probably 'brook flowing in a ravine'. OE *ceole* (with Scand. k-) + *brōc*.

Kelby Lincs. *Chelebi* 1086 (DB). Probably 'farmstead or village on or near a ridge or wedge-shaped piece of land'. OScand. *kjǫlr* or **kæl + bý*.

Keld N. Yorks. *Appeltrekelde* 1301, *Kelde* 1538. 'The spring', from OScand. *kelda*, 'by the apple-tree' in the early form.

Keldholme N. Yorks. *Keldeholm* 12th cent. 'Island or river-meadow near the spring'. OScand. *kelda + holmr*.

Kelfield, 'open land where chalk was spread, or by a cup-shaped feature', OE **celce* or *cælc + feld*: **Kelfield** N. Lincs. *Kelkefeld* 12th cent., **Kelfield** N. Yorks. *Chelchefeld* 1086 (DB).

Kelham Notts. *Calun* |sic| 1086 (DB), *Kelum* 1156. '(Place at) the ridges'. OScand. *kjǫlr* in a dative plural form.

Kelk, Great E. R. Yorks. *Chelche* 1086 (DB). 'Chalky ground'. OE **celce* (with Scand. k-).

Kellet, Nether & *Kellet, Over* Lancs. *Chellet* 1086 (DB). 'Slope with a spring'. OScand. *kelda* + *hlíth*.

Kelleth Cumbria. *Keldelith* 12th cent. Identical in origin with the previous name.

Kelling Norfolk. *Chillinge* c.970, *Kellinga* 1086 (DB). '(Settlement of) the family or followers of a man called *Cylla or Ceolla'. OE pers. name + *-ingas*.

Kellington N. Yorks. *Chellinctone* 1086 (DB). 'Estate associated with a man called Ceolla'. OE pers. name (with Scand. *k-*) + *-ing-* + *tūn*.

Kelloe Durham. *Kelflau* c.1170. 'Hill where calves graze'. OE *celf* + *hlāw*.

Kells (*Cealla*) Antrim, Kerry, Kilkenny. 'Churches'.

Kells (*Ceanannas*) Meath. 'Great residence'.

Kelly Devon. *Chenleie* |sic| 1086 (DB), *Chelli* 1166. Probably Cornish *kelli* 'grove, small wood'.

Kelmarsh Northants. *Keilmerse* 1086 (DB). Probably 'marsh marked out by poles or posts'. OE *cegel (with Scand. *k-*) + *mersc*.

Kelmscot Oxon. *Kelmescote* 1234. 'Cottage(s) of a man called Cēnhelm'. OE pers. name + *cot*.

Kelsale Suffolk. *Keleshala* 1086 (DB). 'Nook of land of a man called *Cēl(i) or Cēol'. OE pers. name + *halh*.

Kelsall Ches. *Kelsale* 1257. 'Nook of land of a man called Kell'. ME pers. name + *halh*.

Kelsey, North & *Kelsey, South* Lincs. *Chelsi, Nortchelesei* 1086 (DB), *Sudkeleseia* 1177. Possibly 'island, or dry ground in marsh, of a man called Cēol'. OE pers. name (with Scand. *k-*) + *ēg*.

Kelshall Herts. *Keleshelle* c.1050, *Cheleselle* 1086 (DB). 'Hill of a man called *Cylli'. OE pers. name + *hyll*.

Kelso Sc. Bord. *Calkou* 1126, *Calcehou* c.1128. 'Chalk hill spur'. OE *calc* + *hōh*.

Kelston B. & NE. Som. *Calveston* 1178. OE *tūn* 'farmstead, estate' with a doubtful first element, possibly an OE pers. name *C(e)alf*.

Kelty Fife. *Quilte* 1250, *Quilt* 1329. Possibly '(place by the) hard water'. British *caleto-* + OGaelic *ailhidh*.

Kelvedon Essex. *Cynlauedyne* 998, *Chelleuedana* 1086 (DB). 'Valley of a man called Cynelāf'. OE pers. name + *denu*.

Kelvedon Hatch Essex. *Kylewendune* 1066, *Keluenduna* 1086 (DB), *Kelwedon Hacche* 1276. 'Speckled hill'. OE *cylu* (dative *cylwan*) + *dūn*, with the later addition of *hæcc* 'gate'.

Kelvinside Glas. '(Place) beside the River Kelvin'. The river name is said to derive from Gaelic *caol abhuinn*, 'narrow water'; but uncertain.

Kemberton Shrops. *Chenbritone* 1086 (DB). 'Farmstead of a man called Cēnbeorht'. OE pers. name + *tūn*.

Kemble Glos. *Kemele* 682, *Chemele* 1086 (DB). Probably a Celtic place-name meaning 'border, edge'.

Kemerton Heref. & Worcs. *Cyneburgingctun* 840, *Chenemertune* 1086 (DB). 'Farmstead associated with a woman called Cyneburg'. OE pers. name + *-ing-* + *tūn*.

Kempley Glos. *Chenepelei* 1086 (DB). Probably 'woodland clearing of a man called *Cenep'. OE pers. name + *lēah*.

Kempsey Heref. & Worcs. *Kemesei* 799, *Chemesege* 1086 (DB). 'Island, or dry ground in marsh, of a man called *Cymi'. OE pers. name + *ēg*.

Kempsford Glos. *Cynemæres forda* 9th cent., *Chenemeresforde* 1086 (DB). 'Ford of a man called Cynemær'. OE pers. name + *ford*.

Kempston Beds. *Kemestan* 1060, *Camestone* 1086 (DB). Possibly 'farmstead at the bend'. A derivative of Celtic *camm* 'crooked' + OE *tūn*.

Kempton Shrops. *Chenpitune* 1086 (DB). 'Farmstead of the warrior or of a man called *Cempa'. OE *cempa* or OE pers. name + *tūn*.

Kemsing Kent. *Cymesing* 822. 'Place of a man called *Cymesa'. OE pers. name + *-ing*.

Kenardington Kent. *Kynardingtune* 11th cent. 'Estate associated with a man called Cyneheard'. OE pers. name + *-ing-* + *tūn*.

Kenchester Heref. & Worcs. *Chenecestre* 1086 (DB). 'Roman fort or town associated with a man called Cēna'. OE pers. name + *ceaster*.

Kencot Oxon. *Chenetone* |sic| 1086 (DB), *Chenicota* c.1130. 'Cottage(s) of a man called Cēna'. OE pers. name + *cot* (in the first form *tūn* 'farmstead').

Kendal Cumbria. *Cherchebi* 1086 (DB), *Kircabikendala* c.1095, *Kendale* 1452. 'Village with a church in the valley of the River Kent'. Originally OScand. *kirkju-bý* with the addition of a district name (Celtic river-name of uncertain meaning + OScand. *dalr*) which now alone survives.

Kenilworth Warwicks. *Chinewrde* |sic| 1086 (DB), *Chenildeworda* early 12th cent. 'Enclosure of a woman called Cynehild'. OE pers. name + *worth*.

Kenley, 'woodland clearing of a man called Cēna', OE pers. name + *lēah*: **Kenley** Gtr. London. *Kenele* |sic| 1255. **Kenley** Shrops. *Chenelie* |sic| 1086 (DB).

Kenmare (*Ceann Mara*) Kerry. 'Head of the sea'. The official Irish name of Kenmare is *Neidín*, 'little nest'.

Kenn, originally the name of the streams on which the places stand, a pre-English river-name of uncertain origin and meaning: **Kenn** Devon. *Chent* 1086 (DB). **Kenn** N. Som. *Chen(t)* 1086 (DB).

Kennerleigh Devon. *Kenewarlegh* 1219. 'Woodland clearing of a man called Cyneweard'. OE pers. name + *lēah*.

Kennett Cambs. *Chenet* 1086 (DB). Named from the River Kennett, a Celtic river-name of doubtful meaning.

Kennett, East & *Kennett, West* Wilts. *Cynetan* 939, *Chenete* 1086 (DB). Named from the River Kennet, a river-name identical in origin with that in the previous name.

Kennford Devon. *Keneford* 1300. 'Ford over the River Kenn'. Pre-English river-name (of uncertain origin and meaning) + OE *ford*.

Kenninghall Norfolk. *Keninchala* 1086 (DB). Probably 'nook of land of the family or followers of a man called Cēna'. OE pers. name + *-inga-* + *halh*.

Kennington Gtr. London. *Chenintune* 1086 (DB). 'Farmstead associated with a man called Cēna'. OE pers. name + *-ing-* + *tūn*.

Kennington Kent. *Chenetone* 1086 (DB). 'Royal manor'. OE *cyne-* + *tūn*.

Kennington Oxon. *Chenitun* 821, 1086 (DB). 'Farmstead associated with a man called Cēna'. OE pers. name + *-ing-* + *tūn*.

Kennoway Fife. *Kennachin* 1183, *Kennachyn* 1250, *Kennoquhy* c.1510. Meaning uncertain.

Kennythorpe N. Yorks. *Cheretorp* |*sic*| 1086 (DB), *Kinnerthorp* c.1180. Probably 'outlying farmstead or hamlet of a man called Cēnhere'. OE pers. name + OScand. *thorp*.

Kensal Green Gtr. London. *Kingisholte* 1253, *Kynsale Green* 1550. 'The king's wood'. OE *cyning* + *holt*, with the later addition of grēne 'village green'.

Kensington Gtr. London. *Chenesitun* 1086 (DB). 'Estate associated with a man called Cynesige'. OE pers. name + *-ing-* + *tūn*.

Kensworth Beds. *Ceagnesworthe* 975, *Canesworde* 1086 (DB). 'Enclosure of a man called *Cægīn*'. OE pers. name + *worth*.

Kent (the county). *Cantium* 51 BC. An ancient Celtic name, often explained as 'coastal district' but possibly 'land of the hosts or armies'.

Kent (river) Lancs., Cumbria, *see* KENDAL.

Kentchurch Heref. & Worcs. *Lan Cein* c.1130, *Keynchirche* 1341. 'Church of St Ceina'. Female saint's name + OE *cirice* (with OWelsh **lann* in the early form).

Kentford Suffolk. *Cheneteforde* 11th cent. 'Ford over the River Kennett'. Celtic river-name (of uncertain origin and meaning) + OE *ford*.

Kentisbeare Devon. *Chentesbere* |*sic*| 1086 (DB), *Kentelesbere* 1242. 'Wood or grove of a man called *Centel*. OE pers. name + *bearu*.

Kentisbury Devon. *Chentesberie* |*sic*| 1086 (DB), *Kentelesberi* 1260. 'Stronghold of a man called *Centel*. OE pers. name + *burh* (dative *byrig*).

Kentish Town Gtr. London. *Kentisston* 1208. Probably 'estate held by a family called Kentish'. ME surname (meaning 'man from Kent') + OE *tūn*.

Kentmere Cumbria. *Kentemere* 13th cent. 'Pool by the River Kent'. Celtic river-name (of uncertain meaning) + OE *mere*.

Kenton Devon. *Chentone* 1086 (DB). 'Farmstead on the River Kenn'. Pre-English river-name (of uncertain origin and meaning) + OE *tūn*.

Kenton Gtr. London. *Keninton* 1232. 'Estate associated with a man called Cēna'. OE pers. name + *-ing-* + *tūn*.

Kenton Suffolk. *Chenetuna* 1086 (DB). Probably 'royal manor'. OE *cyne-* + *tūn*. Alternatively the first element may be the OE pers. name *Cēna*.

Kenwick Shrops. *Kenewic* 1203. 'Dwelling or (dairy) farm of a man called Cēna'. OE pers. name + *wīc*.

Kenwyn Cornwall. *Keynwen* 1259. Probably 'white ridge'. OCornish *keyn* + *gwynn*.

Kenyon Gtr. Manch. *Kenien* 1212. Possibly a shortened form of an OWelsh name *Cruc Einion* 'mound of a man called Einion'.

Kepwick N. Yorks. *Chipuic* 1086 (DB). 'Hamlet with a market'. OE *cēap* (with Scand. *k-*) + *wīc*.

Keresley W. Mids. *Keresleia* c.1144. Possibly 'woodland clearing of a man called Cēnhere'. OE pers. name + *lēah*.

Kerne Bridge Heref. & Worcs. *Kernebrigges* 1272. Probably 'bridge(s) by a mill'. OE *cweorn* + *brycg*.

Kerry (*Ciarraí*) (the county). '(Place of) Ciar's people'.

Kerrykeel (*Ceathrú Chaol*) Donegal. 'Narrow quarter'.

Kersall Notts. *Cherueshale* 1086 (DB), *Kyrneshale* 1196. Possibly 'nook of land of a man called Cynehere'. OE pers. name + *halh*.

Kersey Suffolk. *Cæresige* c.995, *Careseia* 1086 (DB). 'Island (of higher ground) where cress grows'. OE *cærse* + *ēg*.

Kersoe Heref. & Worcs. *Criddesho* 780. 'Hill-spur of a man called *Criddi*'. OE pers. name + *hōh*.

Kesgrave Suffolk. *Gressegraua* |*sic*| 1086 (DB), *Kersigrave* 1231. 'Ditch where cress grows'. OE *cærse* + *græf*.

Kesh (*Ceis*) Fermanagh, Sligo. 'Wicker causeway'.

Keshcarrigan (*Ceis Charraigín*) Leitrim. 'Wicker causeway of the little rock'.

Kessingland Suffolk. *Kessingalanda* 1086 (DB). 'Cultivated land of the family or followers of a man called *Cyssi*'. OE pers. name + *-inga-* + *land*.

Kesteven Lincs. *Ceostefne* c.1000, *Chetsteven* 1086 (DB). Probably 'wood meeting-place'. Celtic **cēd* + OScand. *stefna*.

Keston Gtr. London. *Cysse stan* 973, *Chestan* 1086 (DB). 'Boundary stone of a man called *Cyssi*'. OE pers. name + *stān*.

Keswick, 'farm where cheese is made', OE *cēse* (with Scand. *k-*) + *wīc*: **Keswick** Cumbria. *Kesewic* c.1240. **Keswick** Norfolk, near Bacton. *Casewic* c.1150. **Keswick** Norfolk, near Norwich. *Chesewic*, 1086 (DB). **Keswick, East** W. Yorks. *Chesuic* 1086 (DB).

Kettering Northants. *Cytringan* 956, *Cateringe* 1086 (DB). Probably '(settlement of) the family or followers of a man called *Cytra*'. OE pers. name + *-ingas*.

Ketteringham Norfolk. *Keteringham* c.1060, *Keterincham* 1086 (DB). 'Homestead of the family or followers of a man called *Cytra*'. OE pers. name + *-inga-* + *hām*.

Kettlebaston Suffolk. *Kitelbeornastuna* 1086 (DB). 'Farmstead of a man called Ketilbjǫrn'. OScand. pers. name + OE *tūn*.

Kettleburgh Suffolk. *Ketelbiria* 1086 (DB). 'Hill of a man called Ketil, or hill by a deep valley'. OScand. pers. name or OE *cetel* (with Scand. *k-*) + OE *beorg* or OScand. *berg*.

Kettleby, Ab Leics. *Chetelbi* 1086 (DB), *Abeketleby* 1236. 'Farmstead or village of a man called Ketil'. OScand. pers.

name + *bý*, with manorial affix from early possession by a man called Abba.

Kettleshulme Ches. *Ketelisholm* 1285. 'Island or water-meadow of a man called Ketil'. OScand. pers. name + *holmr*.

Kettlesing N. Yorks. *Ketylsyng* 1379. 'Meadow of a man called Ketil'. OScand. pers. name + *eng*.

Kettlestone Norfolk. *Ketlestuna* 1086 (DB). 'Farmstead of a man called Ketil'. OScand. pers. name + OE *tūn*.

Kettlethorpe Lincs. *Ketelstorp* 1220. 'Outlying farm-stead or hamlet of a man called Ketil'. OScand. pers. name + *thorp*.

Kettlewell N. Yorks. *Cheteleuuelle* 1086 (DB). 'Spring or stream in a deep valley'. OE *cetel* (with Scand. *k*-) + *wella*.

Ketton Rutland. *Chetene* 1086 (DB). An old river-name, possibly a derivative of Celtic **cę̄d* 'wood' + OE *ēa* 'river'.

Kew Gtr. London. *Cayho* 1327. 'Key-shaped spur of land, or spur of land near a quay'. OE *cǣg* or ME *key* + OE *hōh*.

Kewstoke N. Som. *Chivestoch* 1086 (DB). OE *stoc* 'secondary settlement' with the addition of the Celtic saint's name *Kew*.

Kexbrough S. Yorks. *Cezeburg* |sic| 1086 (DB), *Kesceburg* c.1170. Probably 'stronghold of a man called Keptr'. OScand. pers. name + OE *burh*.

Kexby Lincs. *Cheftesbi* 1086 (DB). 'Farmstead or village of a man called Keptr'. OScand. pers. name + *bý*.

Kexby York. *Kexebi* 12th cent. Probably 'farmstead or village of a man called Keikr'. OScand. pers. name + *bý*.

Key, Lough (*Loch Cé*) Roscomon. 'Lake of the quay'.

Keyham Leics. *Caiham* 1086 (DB). Possibly 'homestead or village of a man called *Cǣga', OE pers. name + *hām*. Alternatively the first element may be OE *cǣg* 'key' (used of a place that could be locked) or **cǣg* 'stone, boulder'.

Keyhaven Hants. *Kihavene* c.1170. 'Harbour where cows are shipped'. OE *cū* (genitive *cȳ*) + *hæfen*.

Keyingham E. R. Yorks. *Caingeham* 1086 (DB). 'Homestead of the family or followers of a man called *Cǣga'. OE pers. name + *-inga-* + *hām*.

Keymer W. Sussex. *Chemere* 1086 (DB). 'Cow's pond'. OE *cū* (genitive *cȳ*) + *mere*.

Keynsham B. & NE. Som. *Cægineshamme* c.1000, *Cainesham* 1086 (DB). 'Land in a river-bend belonging to a man called *Cǣgin'. OE pers. name + *hamm*.

Keysoe Beds. *Caissot* 1086 (DB). Probably 'key-shaped spur of land'. OE *cǣg* + *hōh*. Alternatively the first element may be OE **cǣg* 'a stone, a boulder'.

Keyston Cambs. *Chetelestan* 1086 (DB). 'Boundary stone of a man called Ketil'. OScand. pers. name + OE *stān*.

Keyworth Notts. *Caworde* 1086 (DB). OE *worth* 'enclosure' with an uncertain first element, probably a pers. name.

Kibblesworth Tyne & Wear. *Kibleswrthe* 1185. 'Enclosure of a man called *Cybbel'. OE pers. name + *worth*.

Kibworth Beauchamp & *Kibworth Harcourt* Leics. *Chiburde* 1086 (DB), *Kybeworth Beauchamp* 1315,

Kibbeworth Harecourt 13th cent. 'Enclosure of a man called *Cybba'. OE pers. name + *worth*. Affixes from early possession by the de Beauchamp and de Harewecurt families.

Kidbrooke Gtr. London. *Ketebroc* 1202. 'Brook where kites are seen'. OE *cȳta* + *brōc*.

Kidderminster Heref. & Worcs. *Chideminstre* |sic| 1086 (DB), *Kedeleministre* 1154. 'Monastery of a man called *Cydela'. OE pers. name + *mynster*.

Kiddington Oxon. *Chidintone* 1086 (DB). 'Estate associated with a man called Cydda'. OE pers. name + *-ing-* + *tūn*.

Kidlington Oxon. *Chedelintone* 1086 (DB). 'Estate associated with a man called *Cydela'. OE pers. name + *-ing-* + *tūn*.

Kidwelly (*Cydweli*) Carm. *Cetgueli* 10th cent., *Cedgueli* c.1150, *Kedwely* 1191, *Kydwelly* 1458. 'Cadwal's territory'. The identity of *Cadwal* is unknown.

Kielder Northum. *Keilder* 1326. Named from the river here, a Celtic river-name meaning 'rapid stream'.

Kielduff (*An Chill Dubh*) Kerry. 'The black church'.

Kiilinaspick (*Cill an Easpaig*) Kilkenny. 'Church of the bishop'.

Kilanerin (*Coill an Iarainn*) Wexford. 'Wood of the iron'.

Kilavullen (*Cill an Mhuilinn*) Cork. 'Church of the mill'.

Kilbaha (*Cill Bheathach*) Clare. 'Church of the birches'.

Kilballyporter (*Coill an Bhealaigh*) Meath. 'Porter's wood of the pass'.

Kilbane (*An Choill Bhán*) Clare. 'The white wood'.

Kilbarrack (*Cill Bharróg*) Dublin. 'Church of little Barra'.

Kilbarron (*Cill Bharfionn*) Donegal. 'Barfionn's church'.

Kilbarry (*Cill Barra*) Cork. 'Barra's church'.

Kilbeg (*Coill Bheag*) Wicklow. *Kilbege* 1526. 'Little wood'.

Kilbeggan (*Cill Bheagáin*) Westmeath. 'Beagán's church'.

Kilbeheny (*Coill Bheithne*) Limerick. 'Wood of birches'.

Kilbennan (*Cill Bheanáin*) Galway. 'Beanán's church'.

Kilberry (*Cill Bhearaigh*) Kildare, Meath. 'Church of Bearach'.

Kilbirnie N. Ayr. *Kilbyrny* 1413. 'Church of St Brendan'. Gaelic *cill*.

Kilbrickan (*Cill Bhreacáin*) Galway. 'Church of Breacán'.

Kilbricken (*Cill Bhriocáin*) Laois. 'Church of Briocán'.

Kilbride (*Cill Bhríde*) Carlow, Down, Wicklow. 'Church of Bríd'.

Kilbride Arg. 'Church of St Bridget'. Gaelic *cill*.

Kilbrien (*Cill Bhriain*) Waterford. 'Church of Brian'.

Kilbrin (*Cill Bhrain*) Cork. 'Church of Bran'.

Kilbrittain (*Cill Briotáin*) Cork. 'Church of Briotán'.

Kilbrogan (*Cill Brógáin*) Cork. 'Brogan's church'.

Kilburn Derbys. *Kileburn* 1179. Possibly 'stream of a man called *Cylla'. OE pers. name + *burna*.

Kilburn Gtr. London. *Cuneburna c.*1130. Possibly 'cows' stream'. OE *cū* (genitive plural *cūna*) + *burna*.

Kilburn N. Yorks. *Chileburne* 1086 (DB). Perhaps identical in origin with KILBURN (Derbys).

Kilby Leics. *Cilebi* 1086 (DB). Probably 'farmstead or village of the young men'. OE *cild* (with Scand. *k-*) + OScand. *bý*.

Kilcaimin (*Cill Chaimín*) Galway. 'Church of Caimín'.

Kilcar (*Cill Charthaigh*) Donegal. *Cill Carthaigh c.*1630. 'Carthach's church'.

Kilcarn (*Cill an Chairn*) Meath. 'Church of the cairn'.

Kilcash (*Cill Chais*) Tipperary. 'Church of Cas'.

Kilcavan (*Cill Chaomháin*) Laois. 'Church of Caomhán'.

Kilchattan Arg (Bute). *Killecatan* 1449. 'Church of St Catan'. Gaelic *cill*.

Kilchenzie Arg. 'Church of St Kenneth'. Gaelic *cill*.

Kilchreest (*Cill Chríost*) Galway. 'Church of Christ'.

Kilclare (*Coill Chláir*) Leitrim. 'Wood of the plain'.

Kilclief (*Cill Chléithe*) Down. (*i*)*Cill Chlethi c.*1125. 'Church of wattle'.

Kilcloher (*Cill Chloichir*) Clare. 'Church of the stony place'.

Kilclone (*Cill Chluana*) Meath. 'Church of the meadow'.

Kilclonfert (*Cill Chluana Fearta*) Offaly. 'Church of the meadow of the grave'.

Kilclooney (*Cill Chluana*) Donegal. 'Church of the meadow'.

Kilcock (*Cill Choca*) Kildare. 'Church of Coca'.

Kilcogy (*Cill Chóige*) Cavan. *Kilcoaga* 1611. 'Church of the fifth'. The reference is to a land division.

Kilcolgan (*Cill Cholgáin*) Galway. 'Church of Colgán'.

Kilcolman (*Cill Cholmáin*) Cork, Limerick. 'Church of Colmán'.

Kilcomin (*Cill Chuimín*) Offaly. 'Church of Cuimín'.

Kilcommon (*Cill Chuimín*) Tipperary. 'Church of Cuimín'.

Kilconly (*Cil Chonla*) Galway. 'Conla's church'.

Kilconnell (*Cill Chonaill*) Galway. 'Church of Conall'.

Kilcoo (*Cill Chua*) Down. *Killcow* 1609. 'Cua's church'.

Kilcoole (*Cill Chomhghaill*) Wicklow. 'Church of Comhghall'.

Kilcooley (*Cill Chúile*) Tipperary. 'Church of the nook'.

Kilcormac (*Cill Chormaic*) Offaly. 'Church of Cormac'.

Kilcornan (*Cill Chornáin*) Limerick. 'Church of Cornán'.

Kilcorney (*Cill Coirne*) Cork. 'Church of Corne'.

Kilcot Glos. *Chilecot* 1086 (DB). 'Cottage(s) of a man called *Cylla*. OE pers. name + *cot*.

Kilcotty (*Cill Chota*) Wexford. 'Church of Cota'.

Kilcrohane (*Cill Crócháin*) Cork. 'Church of Cróchán'.

Kilcullen (*Cill Chuillinn*) Kildare. 'Church of the steep slope'.

Kilcummin (*Cill Chuimín*) Kerry. 'Church of Cuimín'.

Kilcurry (*Cill an Churraigh*) Louth. 'Church of the marsh'.

Kildale N. Yorks. *Childale* 1086 (DB). Probably 'narrow valley'. OScand. *kill* + *dalr*.

Kildalkey (*Cill Dealga*) Meath. 'Church of the thorn'.

Kildangan (*Cill Daingin*) Kildare. 'Church of the fortress'.

Kildangan (*Coill an Daingin*) Offaly. 'Wood of the fortress'.

Kildare (*Cill Dara*) Kildare. 'Church of the oak tree'.

Kildavin (*Cill Damháin*) Carlow. 'Church of Damhán'.

Kildermody (*Cill Dhiarmada*) Waterford. 'Church of Diatmaid'.

Kildimo (*Cill Díoma*) Limerick. 'Díoma's church'.

Kildonan Highland. *Kelduninach c.*1230. 'Church of St Donan'. Gaelic *cill*.

Kildorough (*Coill Dorcha*) Cavan. 'Dusky wood'.

Kildorrery (*Cill Dairbhre*) Cork. 'Church of the place of oaks'.

Kildreenagh (*Cill Draigneach*) Carlow. 'Church of blackthorns'.

Kildrum (*Coill Droma*) Donegal. 'Wood of the ridge'.

Kildwick W. Yorks. *Childeuuic* 1086 (DB). 'Dairy-farm of the young men or attendants'. OE *cild* (with Scand. *k-*) + *wīc*.

Kildysart (*Cill an Dísirt*) Clare. 'Church of the hermitage'.

Kilfeaghan (*Cill Fhéichín*) Down. 'Féichín's church'.

Kilfeakle (*Cill Fiacal*) Tipperary. 'Church of the teeth'.

Kilfearagh (*Cill Fhiachrach*) Clare. 'Church of Fiachra'.

Kilfenora (*Cill Fionnúrach*) Clare. 'Church of Fionnúir'.

Kilfinane (*Cill Fhionáin*) Limerick. 'Church of Fionán'.

Kilfinny (*Cill na Fiodhnaí*) Limerick. 'Church of the wooded place'.

Kilflynn (*Cill Flainn*) Kerry. 'Church of Flan'.

Kilfree (*Cill Fraoigh*) Sligo. 'Church of the heather'.

Kilfullert (*Coill Fulachta*) Down. *Ballykillyfollyat* 1609. 'Wood of the cooking place'.

Kilgarvan (*Cill Gharbháin*) Kerry. 'Church of Garbhán'.

Kilgetty (*Cilgeti*) Pemb. *Kylketty* 1330. 'Ceti's corner of land'. Welsh *cil*. The identity of Ceti is unknown.

Kilglass (*Cil Ghlas*) Roscommon, Sligo. 'Green church'.

Kilglass (*Coill Ghlas*) Galway, Sligo. 'Green wood'.

Kilgobnet (*Cill Ghobnait*) Kerry, Waterford. 'Church of Gobnait'.

Kilgowan (*Coill Ghabann*) Kildare. 'Wood of the smith'.

Kilham, '(place at) the kilns', OE *cyln* in a dative plural form *cylnum*: **Kilham** E. R. Yorks. *Chillun* |sic| 1086 (DB). **Kilham** Northum. *Killum* |sic| 1177.

Kilkea (*Cill Chathaig*) Kildare. 'Church of Cathach'.

Kilkeasy (*Cill Chéise*) Kildare. 'Church of Céis'.

Kilkee (*Cill Chaoi*) Clare. 'Church of Caoi'.

Kilkeel (*Cill Chaoil*) Down. *Kylkeyl* 1369. 'Church of the narrow place'.

Kilkelly (*Cill Cheallaigh*) Mayo. 'Church of Ceallach'.

Kilkenneth Arg. 'Church of St Kenneth'. Gaelic *cill*.

Kilkenny (*Cill Chainnigh*) Kilkenny. 'Church of Cainneach'.

Kilkerin (*Cill Chéirín*) Clare. 'Church of Céirín'.

Kilkerrin (*Cill Chiaráin*) Galway. 'Ciarán's church'.

Kilkerrin (*Cill Choirín*) Galway. 'Church of the little turn'.

Kilkhampton Cornwall. *Chilchetone* 1086 (DB). Probably Cornish **kylgh* 'a circle' (perhaps referring to a lost archaeological feature) with the additon of OE *tūn* 'farmstead'.

Kilkieran (*Cill Chiaráin*) Galway, Kilkenny. 'Church of Ciarán'.

Kilkinlea (*Cill Chinn Sléibhe*) Limerick. 'Church of the head of the mountain'.

Kilkishen (*Cill Chisín*) Clare. 'Church of the wicker causeway'.

Kill (*Cill*) Cavan, Kildare, Waterford. 'Church'.

Killachonna (*Cill Dachonna*) Westmeath. 'Church of Dachonna'.

Killacolla (*Cill an Coille*) Limerick. 'Church of the wood'.

Killadangan (*Coill an Daingin*) Mayo. 'Wood of the fortress'.

Killadeas (*Cill Chéile Dé*) Fermanagh. 'Church of the Céle Dé*. A *Céle Dé* (Culdee) ('servant of God') was a member of a group of monastic reformers originating in the 8th cent.

Killadoon (*Coill an Dúin*) Mayo. 'Wood of the fort'.

Killadreenan (*Cill Achaidh Draighnigh*) Wicklow. 'Church of the field of the blackthorns'.

Killadysert (*Cill an Dísirt*) Clare. 'Church of the hermitage'.

Killag (*Cill Laig*) Wexford. 'Church of the hollow'.

Killagan (*Cill Lagáin*) Antrim. (*ecclesia de*) *Killagan* 1622. 'Church of the small hollow'.

Killala (*Cill Ala*) Mayo. 'Church of Ala'.

Killaloe (*Cill Dalua*) Clare. 'Church of Dalua'.

Killaloo (*Coill an Lao*) Derry. *Kille Loy* 1613. 'Wood of the calf'.

Killamarsh Derbys. *Chinewoldemaresc* 1086 (DB). 'Marsh of a man called Cynewald'. OE pers. name + *mersc*.

Killamery (*Cill Lamhraí*) Kilkenny. 'Church of Lamhrach'.

Killane (*Cill Anna*) Offaly. 'Church of Anna'.

Killann (*Cill Ana*) Wexford. 'Church of Anna'.

Killannummery (*Cill an Iomaire*) Leitrim. 'Church of the ridge'.

Killans (*Coillíní*) Antrim. 'Little hills'.

Killaraght (*Cill Adrochtae*) Sligo. 'Adrochta's church'.

Killard Point (*Aird na Cille*) Down. 'Point of the church'.

Killare (*Cill Air*) Westmeath. 'Church of slaughter'.

Killarga (*Cill Fhearga*) Leitrim. 'Church of Fearga'.

Killarney (*Cill Airne*) Kerry. 'Church of the sloes'.

Killary (*Caolaire*) Galway, Mayo. 'Narrow sea'.

Killashandra (*Cill na Seanrátha*) Cavan. *Kylshanra* 1432. 'Church of the old fort'.

Killashee (*Cill Úsaille*) Longford. 'Church of Úsaile'. The official form of the Irish name is *Cill na Sí*, 'church of the fairy hill'.

Killasser (*Cill Lasrach*) Mayo. 'Lasrach's church'.

Killateeaun (*Coill an tSiáin*) Mayo. 'Wood of the fairy hill'.

Killavally (*Coill an Bhaile*) Mayo. 'Wood of the homestead'.

Killavally (*Coill an Bhealaigh*) Westmeath. 'Wood of the pass'.

Killavil (*Cill Fhábhail*) Sligo. 'Church of the journey'.

Killea (*Cill Aodha*) Tipperary, Waterford. 'Church of Aodh'.

Killeagh (*Cill Ia*) Cork. 'Church of Ia'.

Killeany (*Cill Éinne*) Galway. 'Church of Éanna'.

Killeavan (*Cill Laobháin*) Monaghan. 'Church of Laobhán'.

Killeavy (*Cill Shléibhe*) Armagh. *Cille sleibe Cuilinn* 517. 'Church of the mountain'. The church stood at the foot of Slieve Gullion.

Killedmond (*Cill Éamainn*) Carlow. 'Church of Éamonn'.

Killeedy (*Cill Íde*) Limerick. 'Church of Íde'.

Killeen (*Cillín*) Tipperary. 'Little church'.

Killeenadeema (*Cillín a Díoma*) Galway. 'Little church of Díoma'.

Killeenduff (*Cillín Dubh*) Offaly. 'Little black church'.

Killeeshill (*Cill Íseal*) Tyrone. *Killissyll* 1455. 'Low church'.

Killegar (*Coill an Ghairr*) Limerick. 'Wood of the offal'.

Killeigh (*Cill Aichidh*) Offaly. 'Church of the field'.

Killen (*Cillín*) Tyrone. *Killen c.*1655. 'Little church'.

Killenagh (*Cill Éanach*) Waterford. 'Church of the marsh'.

Killenaule (*Cill Náile*) Tipperary. 'Church of Náile'.

Killerby Durham. *Culuerdebi* 1091. Probably 'farmstead or village of a man called **Ketilfrøthr*'. OScand. pers. name + *bý*.

Killerig (*Cill Dheirge*) Carlow. 'Church of the red ground'.

Killeshil (*Cill Íseal*) Offaly. 'Low church'.

Killeter (*Coill Íochtair*) Tyrone. *Keliter* 1613. 'Lower wood'.

Killiecrankie Perth. 'Wood of aspens'. Gaelic *coille* + *critheann*.

Killimer (*Cill Íomar*) Clare. 'Church of Íomar'.

Killimor (*Cill Íomair*) Galway. 'Church of Íomar'.

Killinaboy (*Cill Iníne Baoith*) Clare. 'Church of the daughter of Baoth'.

Killinardrish (*Cill an Ard-dorais*) Cork. 'Church of the high door'.

Killinchy (*Cill Dhuinsí*) Down. (*o*) *Cill Dunsighe c.*1400. 'Church of Duinseach'. Duinseach was a female saint.

Killincooly (*Cillín Cúile*) Wexford. 'Little church of the nook'.

Killiney (*Cill Éinne*) Kerry. 'Church of Éanna'.

Killiney (*Cill Iníon Léinín*) Dublin. 'Church of the daughters of Léinín'.

Killinghall N. Yorks. *Chilingale* 1086 (DB). 'Nook of land of the family or followers of a man called *Cylla'. OE pers. name + *-inga-* + *halh*.

Killingholme Lincs. *Chelvingeholm* 1086 (DB). Probably 'homestead of the family or followers of a man called Cēolwulf'. OE pers. name + *-inga-* + *hām* (replaced by OScand. *holmr* 'island, dry ground in marsh').

Killington Cumbria. *Killintona* 1175. 'Estate associated with a man called *Cylla'. OE pers. name + *-ing-* + *tūn*.

Killingworth Tyne & Wear. *Killingwrth* 1242. 'Enclosure associated with a man called *Cylla'. OE pers. name + *-ing-* + *worth*.

Killinick (*Cill Fhionnóg*) Wexford. 'Church of Fionnóg'.

Killinierin (*Coill an Iarainn*) Wexford. 'Wood of the iron'.

Killinkere (*Cillín Chéir*) Cavan. 'Little church of the wax candles'.

Killisky (*Cill Uisce*) Wicklow. 'Church of the water'.

Killoe (*Cill Eo*) Longford. 'Church of the yew'.

Killogeenaghan (*Coill Ó gCuinneagáin*) Westmeath. 'Wood of Uí Cuinneagáin'.

Killone (*Cill Eoghain*) Clare. 'Eoghan's church'.

Killoneen (*Cill Eoghanín*) Offaly. 'Little Eoghan's church'.

Killoran (*Cill Odhráin*) Galway. 'Oran's church'.

Killorglin (*Cill Orglan*) Kerry. 'Church of Forgla'.

Killoscully (*Cill Ó Scolaí*) Tipperary. 'Ó Scolaí's church'.

Killough (*Cill Locha*) Down. *Killogh* 1710. 'Church of the lake'.

Killour (*Cill Iúir*) Mayo. 'Church of the tower'.

Killowen (*Cill Eoin*) Down. *Kelcone* 1595. 'Eoin's church'.

Killowny (*Cill Uaithne*) Offaly. 'Church of Uaithne'.

Killucan (*Cill Liúcainne*) Westmeath. 'Liúcian's church'.

Killurin (*Cill Liúráin*) Wexford. 'Church of Liúrán'.

Killusty (*Cill Loiscthe*) Tipperary. 'Burnt church'.

Killybegs (*Na Cealla Beaga*) Donegal. (*cuan*) *na cCeall mBicc* 1513. 'The little churches'. The reference is to an early monastic settlement.

Killybrone (*Coillidh Brón*) Monaghan. 'Sad woodland'.

Killycolpy (*Coill an Cholpa*) Tyrone. *Kilcolpy* 1639. 'Wood of the heifer'.

Killycomain (*Coill Mhic Giolla Mhíchíl*) Armagh. *Killykillvehall* 1657. 'Mac Giolla Mhíchíl's wood'.

Killygarn (*Coill na gCarn*) Antrim. *Ballichilnegarne* 1606. 'Wood of the cairn'.

Killygarvan (*Cill Gharbháin*) Clare. 'Church of Garbhán'.

Killyglen (*Cill Ghlinne*) Antrim. 'Church of the glen'.

Killykergan (*Coill Uí Chiaragáin*) Derry. *Killakerrigan* 1654. 'Ó Ciaragáin's wood'.

Killylea (*Coillidh Léith*) Armagh. *Killeleagh* 1657. 'Grey woodland'.

Killyleagh (*Cill Ó Laoch*) Down. *Cill Ó Laoch c.*1645. 'Church of Uí Laoch'.

Killyman (*Cill na mBan*) Tyrone. *Cill na mBan c.*1645. 'Church of the women'.

Killyon (*Cil Liain*) Offaly. 'Church of Lian'.

Kilmacanoge (*Cill Mocheanóg*) Wicklow. 'Mocheanóg's church'.

Kilmacduagh (*Cill Mhic Duach*) Clare. 'Mac Duach's church'.

Kilmacolm Invclyd. *Kilmacolme c.*1205, *Kilmalcolm* (sic) 1868. 'Church of my Colm'. Gaelic *cill* + *mo*. *Colm* is St Columba, 'my' showing a pers. dedication.

Kilmacow (*Cill Mhic Bhúith*) Kilkenny. 'Church of Mac Búith'.

Kilmacrenan (*Cill Mhic Réanáin*) Donegal. (*o*) *cCill mic Némain* 1129. 'Church of Mac Réanán'. The present name evolved from original *Cill Mhac nÉanáin*, 'church of Mac Éanán'.

Kilmacthomas (*Coill Mhic Thomáisín*) Waterford. 'Wood of Mac Thomáisín'.

Kilmactranny (*Cill Mhic Treana*) Sligo. 'Church of Mac Treana'.

Kilmaine (*Cill Mheáin*) Mayo. 'Middle church'.

Kilmainham (*Cill Mhaighneann*) Dublin, Meath. 'Church of Maighne'.

Kilmaley (*Cill Mháille*) Clare. 'Máille's church'.

Kilmalin (*Cill Moling*) Wicklow. 'Church of Moling'.

Kilmallock (*Cill Mocheallóg*) Limerick. 'Church of Mocheallóg'.

Kilmanagh (*Cill Mhanach*) Kilkenny. 'Church of the monks'.

Kilmanahan (*Cill Mainchín*) Waterford. 'Manchan's church'.

Kilmarnock E. Ayr. *Kelmernoke* 1299. 'Church of my little Ernan'. Gaelic *cill* + *mo*. *Ernan* is St Ernan, here with the diminutive suffix *-oc*.

Kilmead (*Cill Míde*) Kildare. 'Middle church'.

Kilmeaden (*Cill Mhiodáin*) Waterford. 'Church of Miodán'.

Kilmeague (*Cill Maodhóg*) Kildare. 'Church of Maodhóg'.

Kilmeedy (*Cill Míde*) Limerick. 'Church of Íde'.

Kilmersdon Somerset. *Kunemersdon* 951, *Chenemeresdone* 1086 (DB). 'Hill of a man called Cynemǣr'. OE pers. name + *dūn*.

Kilmessan (*Cill Mheasáin*) Meath. 'Church of Measán'.

Kilmeston Hants. *Cenelemestune* 961, *Chelmestune* 1086 (DB). 'Farmstead of a man called Cēnhelm'. OE pers. name + *tūn*.

Kilmichael (*Cill Mhichíl*) Cork, Wexford. 'Church of Micheál'.

Kilmihil (*Cill Mhichíl*) Clare. 'Church of Micheál'.

Kilmington, 'estate associated with a man called Cynehelm', OE pers. name + *-ing-* + *tūn*: **Kilmington** Devon. *Chenemetone* 1086 (DB). **Kilmington** Wilts. *Cilemetone* 1086 (DB).

Kilmoganny (*Cill Mogeanna*) Kilkenny. 'Mogeanna's church'.

Kilmore (*Cill Mhór*) Clare, Roscommon, Wexford. 'Big church'.

Kilmoremoy (*Cellola Maghna Muaide*) Mayo. 'Big church of the river Moy'.

Kilmorony (*Cill Maolrunaidh*) Laois. 'Church of Maolrunaidh'.

Kilmovee (*Cill Mobhí*) Mayo. 'Church of Mobhí'.

Kilmoyle (*Cill Maol*) Antrim. 'Dilapidated church'.

Kilmoyly (*Cill Mhaoile*) Kerry. 'Church of the hornless cow'.

Kilmurry (*Cill Mhuire*) Clare, Cork. 'Mary's church'.

Kilmurvy (*Cill Mhuirbhigh*) Galway. 'Church of the beach'.

Kilmyshall (*Cill Mísil*) Wexford. 'Church of the low central place'.

Kilnaboy (*Cill Iníne Baoith*) Clare. 'Church of the daughter of Baoth'.

Kilnacloghy (*Coill na Cloiche*) Roscommon. 'Wood of the stone'.

Kilnagross (*Coill na gCros*) Leitrim. 'Wood of the crosses'.

Kilnalag (*Coill na Lag*) Galway. 'Wood of the hollows'.

Kilnaleck (*Cill na Leice*) Cavan. *Killnalecky* 1609. 'Church of the flagstone'.

Kilnamanagh (*Coill na Manach*) Tipperary. 'Wood of the monks'.

Kilnamona (*Cill na Móna*) Clare. 'Church of the bog'.

Kilnhurst S. Yorks. *Kilnhirst* 12th cent. 'Wooded hill with a kiln'. OE *cyln* + *hyrst*.

Kilnsea E. R. Yorks. *Chilnesse* 1086 (DB). 'Pool near the kiln'. OE *cyln* + *sǣ*.

Kilnsey N. Yorks. *Chileseie* |sic| 1086 (DB), *Kilnesey* 1162. Probably 'marsh near the kiln'. OE *cyln* + **sǣge*.

Kilnwick E. R. Yorks. *Chileuuit* |sic| 1086 (DB), *Killingwic* late 12th cent. 'Farm associated with a man called *Cylla'. OE pers. name + *-ing-* + *wīc*. Alternatively the first element may be OE *cyln* 'a kiln'.

Kilnwick Percy E. R. Yorks. *Chelingewic* 1086 (DB). 'Farm of the family or followers of a man called *Cylla'. OE pers. name + *-inga-* + *wīc*.

Kilpeck Heref. & Worcs. *Chipeete* 1086 (DB). Welsh *cil* 'corner, nook' with an obscure second element.

Kilpedder (*Cill Pheadair*) Wicklow. 'Peadar's church'.

Kilpin E. R. Yorks. *Celpene* 959, *Chelpin* 1086 (DB). Probably 'enclosure for calves'. OE *celf* (with Scand. *k-*) + *penn*.

Kilquiggan (*Cill Chomhgáin*) Wicklow. 'Comhgán's church'.

Kilraine (*Cill Riáin*) Donegal. 'Rián's church'.

Kilranelagh (*Cill Rannaileach*) Wicklow. 'Church of the verses'.

Kilraughts (*Cill Reachtais*) Antrim. (*ecclesia de*) *Kellrethi* 1306. 'Church of the legislation'.

Kilrea (*Cill Ria*) Derry. (*Coeman*) *Chilli Riada* c.900. Perhaps 'Church of the journey'.

Kilreekill (*Cill Rícill*) Galway. 'Rícill's church'.

Kilronan (*Cill Rónáin*) Galway. 'Rónán's church'.

Kilrooskey (*Coill na Rúscaí*) Roscommon. 'Wood of the bark strips'.

Kilroot (*Cill Ruaidh*) Antrim. *Cilli Ruaid* c.830. 'Church of the red land'.

Kilross (*Cill Ros*) Donegal. 'Church of the wood'.

Kilross (*Cill Ros*) Tipperary. 'Church of the promontory'.

Kilrush (*Cill Rois*) Clare. 'Church of the grove'.

Kilsallagh (*Coill Salach*) Galway, Mayo. 'Willow wood'.

Kilsallaghan (*Cill Shalcháin*) Dublin. 'Church of the willows'.

Kilsaran (*Cill Saráin*) Louth. 'Sarán's church'.

Kilsby Northants. *Kildesbig* 1043, *Chidesbi* 1086 (DB). 'Farmstead or village of the young nobleman, or of a man called Cild'. OE *cild* or pers. name (with Scand. *k-*) + OScand. *bý*.

Kilshanchoe (*Cill Seanchua*) Kildare. 'Church of the old hollow'.

Kilshanny (*Cill Seanaigh*) Clare. 'Seanach's church'.

Kilsheelan (*Cill Síoláin*) Tipperary. 'Síolán's church'.

Kilskeer (*Cill Scíre*) Meath. 'Scíre's church'.

Kilskeery (*Cill Scíre*) Tyrone. (*orcain*) *Cille Scire* 951. 'Scíre's church'.

Kilsyth N. Lan. *Kelvesyth* 1210, *Kelnasydhe* 1217, *Kilsyth* 1239. Meaning uncertain.

Kiltamagh (*Coillte Mach*) Mayo. 'Woods of the plain'.

Kiltealy (*Cill Tíle*) Wexford. 'Tíl's church'.

Kilteel (*Cill tSíle*) Kildare. 'Síle's church'.

Kilteely (*Cill Tíle*) Limerick. 'Tíl's church'.

Kiltegan (*Cill Téagáin*) Wicklow. 'Téagán's church'.

Kilternan (*Cill Tiarnáin*) Dublin. 'Tiarnán's church'.

Kiltober (*Coill Tobair*) Westmeath. 'Wood of the well'.

Kilton Somerset. *Cylfantun c*.880, *Chilvetune* 1086 (DB). 'Farmstead near the club-shaped hill'. OE **cylfe + tūn*.

Kiltoom (*Cill Tuama*) Roscommon. 'Church of the burial mound'.

Kiltormer (*Cill Tormóir*) Galway. 'Tormór's church'.

Kiltullagh (*Cill Tulach*) Galway. 'Church of the hills'.

Kilturk (*Coill Torc*) Fermanagh. *Kilturke* 1609. 'Wood of boars'.

Kiltyclogher (*Coillte Clochair*) Leitrim. 'Woods of the stony place'.

Kilve Somerset. *Clive* 1086 (DB), *Kylve* 1243. 'Club-shaped hill'. OE **cylfe*.

Kilvergan (*Cill Uí Mhuireagáin*) Armagh. 'Church of Ó Muireagáin'.

Kilvington, 'estate associated with a man called *Cylfa or Cynelāf', OE pers. name + *-ing- + tūn*: **Kilvington** Notts. *Chelvinctune* 1086 (DB). **Kilvington, North** N. Yorks. *Chelvintun* 1086 (DB). **Kilvington, South** N. Yorks. *Chelvinctune* 1086 (DB).

Kilwaughter (*Cill Uachtair*) Antrim. (*ecclesia de*) *Killochre* 1306. 'Upper church'.

Kilwinning N. Ayr. *Killvinin c*.1160, *Ecclesia Sti Vinini* 1184, *Kynwenyn c*.1300, *Kylvynnyne* 1357. 'Church of St Finnian'. Gaelic *cill*.

Kilworth (*Cill Uird*) Cork. 'Church of the ritual'.

Kilworth, North & *Kilworth, South* Leics. *Chivelesworde* 1086 (DB), *Kiuelingwurda* 1191. 'Enclosure associated with a man called *Cyfel'. OE pers. name + *-ing- + worth*.

Kimberley Norfolk. *Chineburlai* 1086 (DB). 'Woodland clearing of a woman called Cyneburg'. OE pers. name + *lēah*.

Kimberley Notts. *Chinemarleie* 1086 (DB). 'Woodland clearing of a man called Cynemǣr'. OE pers. name + *lēah*.

Kimble, Great & *Kimble, Little* Bucks. *Chenebelle* 1086 (DB). 'Royal bell-shaped hill'. OE *cyne- + belle*.

Kimblesworth Durham. *Kymliswrth* 13th cent. 'Enclosure of a man called Cynehelm'. OE pers. name + *worth*.

Kimbolton, 'farmstead of a man called Cynebald', OE pers. name + *tūn*: **Kimbolton** Cambs. *Chenebaltone* 1086 (DB). **Kimbolton** Heref. & Worcs. *Kimbalton* 13th cent.

Kimcote Leics. *Chenemundescote* 1086 (DB). 'Cottage(s) of a man called Cynemund'. OE pers. name + *cot*.

Kimmeridge Dorset. *Cameric* |*sic*| 1086 (DB), *Kimerich* 1212. 'Convenient track or strip of land, or one belonging to a man called Cȳma'. OE *cyme* or OE pers. name + **ric*.

Kimmerston Northum. *Kynemereston* 1244. 'Farmstead of a man called Cynemǣr'. OE pers. name + *tūn*.

Kimpton, 'farmstead associated with a man called Cȳma' OE pers. name + *-ing- + tūn*: **Kimpton** Hants. *Chementune* 1086 (DB). **Kimpton** Herts. *Kamintone* 1086 (DB).

Kinawley (*Cill Náile*) Fermanagh. *Cell Náile c*.1170. 'Náile's church'.

Kinbane (*An Cionn Bán*) (headland) Antrim. *Keanbaan* 1551. 'The white head'. The headland is also known by the English name *White Head*.

Kincardine (the historic county). *Cincardin* 1195. 'Head of the copse'. Gaelic *cinn* + Pictish *carden*.

Kincardine O'Neil Aber. *Kyncardyn O Nelee* 1337. 'Uí Néill's (estate at the) head of the copse'. Gaelic *cinn* + Pictish *carden*.

Kincasslagh (*Cionn Caslach*) Donegal. *Cancaslough* 1835. 'Head of the inlet'.

Kincora (*Cionn Coradh*) Clare. 'Head of the weir'.

Kincraig Highland. 'Head of the rock'. Gaelic *ceann + creag*.

Kincun (*Cionn Con*) Mayo. 'Head of the dog'.

Kindrum (*Cionn Droma*) Donegal. *Kindrom* 1608. 'Hill of the ridge'.

Kineigh (*Cionn Eich*) Kerry. 'Head of the horse'.

Kineton Glos. *Kinton* 1191. 'Royal manor'. OE *cyne- + tūn*.

Kineton Warwicks. *Cyngtun* 969, *Quintone* 1086 (DB). 'The king's manor'. OE *cyning + tūn*.

King's as affix, see main name, e.g. for **King's Bromley** (*Staffs.*) *see* BROMLEY.

King's Heath W. Mids. *Kyngesheth* 1511. Self-explanatory, 'the king's heath', with reference to the royal ownership of the manor of KING'S NORTON in which the heathland lay.

King's Lynn Norfolk, *see* LYNN.

Kingarrow (*Ceann Garbh*) Donegal. 'Rough head'.

Kingham Oxon. *Caningeham* |*sic*| 1086 (DB), *Keingaham* 11th cent. 'Homestead of the family or followers of a man called *Cǣga'. OE pers. name + *-inga- + hām*.

Kinghorn Fife. *Chingor c*.1136, *Kingornum c*.1140. 'Head of the marsh'. Gaelic *cinn + gorn*.

Kinglassie Fife. *Kinglassin* 1224. Possibly 'head of the stream'. Gaelic *ceann + glais*.

Kingsbridge Devon. *Cinges bricge* 962. 'The king's bridge'. OE *cyning + brycg*.

Kingsbury, 'the king's manor', OE *cyning + burh* (dative *byrig*): **Kingsbury** Gtr. London. *Kynges Byrig* 1044, *Chingesberie* 1086 (DB). **Kingsbury Episcopi** Somerset. *Cyncgesbyrig* 1065, *Chingesberie* 1086 (DB). Latin affix *episcopi* 'of the bishop' from its early possession by the Bishop of Bath.

However the following has a different origin: **Kingsbury** Warwicks. *Chinesberie* 1086 (DB), *Kinesburi* 12th cent. 'Stronghold of a man called Cyne'. OE pers. name + *burh* (dative *byrig*).

Kingsclere Hants. *Kyngeclera* early 12th cent. OE *cyning* 'king' (denoting a royal manor) added to the original name found also in HIGHCLERE.

Kingscourt (*Dún an Rí*) Cavan. *King's Court orw*. *Donnaree* 1767. 'Fort of the king'.

Kingsdon, *Kingsdown* 'the king's hill', OE *cyning + dūn*: **Kingsdon** Somerset. *Kingesdon* 1194. **Kingsdown** Kent, near Deal. *Kyngesdoune* 1318. **Kingsdown, West** Kent. *Kingesdon* 1199.

Kingsey Bucks. *Eya* 1174, *Kingesie* 1197. 'The king's island'. OE *cyning* + *ēg*.

Kingsford Heref. & Worcs. *Cenungaford* 964. 'Ford of the family or followers of a man called Cēna'. OE pers. name + *-inga-* + *ford*.

Kingsgate Kent, so called because it was at this *gate* (in the sense of 'gap in the cliffs') that Charles II landed in 1683.

Kingskerswell Devon. *Carsewelle* 1086 (DB), *Kyngescharsewell* 1270. 'Spring or stream where watercress grows'. OE *cærse* + *wella*. The manor belonged to the king in 1086.

Kingsland Heref. & Worcs. *Lene* 1086 (DB), *Kingeslan* 1213. 'The king's estate in *Leon*'. OE *cyning* with old Celtic name for the district (*see* LEOMINSTER).

Kingsley, 'the king's wood or clearing', OE *cyning* + *lēah*: **Kingsley** Ches. *Chingeslie* 1086 (DB). **Kingsley** Hants. *Kyngesly* c.1210. **Kingsley** Staffs. *Chingeslei* 1086 (DB).

Kingsmill Tyrone. *Kings mills* 1833. 'King's mill'. A man named *King* owned a corn mill here.

Kingsnorth Kent. *Kingesnade* 1226. 'Detached piece of land or woodland belonging to the king'. OE *cyning* + *snād*.

Kingstanding W. Mids., from ME standing 'a hunter's station from which to shoot game', although according to tradition the mound here was where Charles I reviewed his troops in 1642. The same name occurs in other counties.

Kingsteignton Devon. *Teintona* 1086 (DB), *Kingestentone* 1274. 'Farmstead on the River Teign'. Celtic river-name (*see* TEIGNMOUTH) + OE *tūn*, with affix from its possession by the king in 1086.

Kingsthorpe Northants. *Torp* 1086 (DB), *Kingestorp* 1190. 'Outlying farmstead or hamlet belonging to the king'. OE *cyning* + OScand. *thorp*.

Kingston, a common name, usually 'the king's manor or estate', OE *cyning* + *tūn*; examples include: **Kingston** Hants. *Kingeston* 1194. **Kingston Bagpuize** Oxon. *Cyngestun* c.976. *Chingestune* 1086 (DB), *Kingeston Bagepuz* 1284. Manorial affix from the de Bagpuize family who held the manor from 1086. **Kingston Blount** Oxon. *Chingestone* 1086 (DB), *Kyngestone Blont* 1379. Manorial affix from the le Blund family, here in the 13th cent. **Kingston Deverill** Wilts. *Devrel* 1086 (DB), *Deverel Kyngeston* 1249. For the original river-name *Deverill see* BRIXTON DEVERILL. **Kingston Lacy** Dorset. *Kingestune* 1170, *Kynggestone Lacy* 1319. Manorial affix from the de Lacy family who held the manor in the 13th cent. **Kingston Lisle** Oxon. *Kingeston* 1220, *Kyngeston Lisle* 1322. Manorial affix from the del Isle family, here from the 13th cent. **Kingston near Lewes** E. Sussex. *Kyngestona* c.1100. *see* LEWES. **Kingston St Mary** Somerset. *Kyngestona* 12th cent. Affix from the dedication of the church. **Kingston upon Hull** K. upon Hull. *Kyngeston* 1256, alternatively called simply **Hull** from the River Hull from early times (*Hul* 1228), the river-name being either OScand. (meaning 'deep one') or Celtic (meaning 'muddy one'). **Kingston upon Thames** Gtr. London. *Cyninges tun* 838, *Chingestune* 1086 (DB). *see* THAMES.

However the following has a different origin: **Kingston on Soar** Notts. *Chinestan* 1086 (DB). 'The royal stone'. OE *cyne-* + *stān*. For the river-name, see BARROW UPON SOAR.

Kingstone Heref. & Worcs., near Hereford. *Chingestone* 1086 (DB). 'The king's manor or estate'. OE *cyning* + *tūn*.

Kingstone Somerset. *Chingestana* 1086 (DB). 'The king's boundary stone'. OE *cyning* + *stān*.

Kingswear Devon. *Kingeswere* 12th cent. 'The king's weir'. OE *cyning* + *wer*.

Kingswinford W. Mids. *Svinesford* 1086 (DB), *Kyngesswynford* 1322. 'Pig ford'. OE *swīn* + *ford*. Affix from its being a royal manor.

Kingswood, 'the king's wood', OE *cyning* + *wudu*: **Kingswood** Glos. *Kingeswoda* 1166. **Kingswood** S. Glos. *Kingeswode* 1231. **Kingswood** Surrey. *Kingeswode* c.1180.

Kington, 'royal manor or estate', OE *cyne-* (replaced by *cyning*) + *tūn*: **Kington** Heref. & Worcs., near Inkberrow. *Cyngtun* 972, *Chintune* 1086 (DB). **Kington** Heref. & Worcs., near Lyonshall. *Chingtune* 1086 (DB). **Kington Magna** Dorset. *Chintone* 1086 (DB), *Magna Kington* 1243. Affix is Latin *magna* 'great'. **Kington St Michael** Wilts. *Kingtone* 934, *Chintone* 1086 (DB), *Kyngton Michel* 1279. Affix from the dedication of the church. **Kington, West** Wilts. *Westkinton* 1195.

Kingussie Highland. *Kinguscy* c.1210. 'Head of the pinewood'. Gaelic *ceann* + *giuthsach*.

Kinlet Shrops. *Chinlete* 1086 (DB). 'Royal share or lot'. OE *cyne-* + *hlēt*. The manor was held in 1066 by Queen Edith, widow of Edward the Confessor.

Kinloch Highland. 'Head of the loch'. Gaelic *ceann* + *loch*.

Kinlochleven Highland. 'Head of Loch Leven'. Gaelic *ceann* + *loch*. *Leven* is 'elm river' (Gaelic *leamhain*).

Kinlough (*Cionn Locha*) Leitrim. 'Head of the lake'.

Kinmel Bay (*Bae Cinmel*) Conwy. *Kilmeyl* 1331. 'Mael's nook'. Welsh *cil*. Bay is a recent addition.

Kinnea (*Cionn Ech*) Cavan, Donegal. 'Head of the horse'.

Kinnegad (*Ceann Átha Gad*) Westmeath. 'Head of the ford of the withies'.

Kinnerley, *Kinnersley*, 'woodland clearing of a man called Cyneheard', OE pers. name + *lēah*: **Kinnerley** Shrops. *Chenardelei* 1086 (DB). **Kinnersley** Heref. & Worcs., near Malvern. *Chinardeslege* 1123. **Kinnersley** Heref. & Worcs., near Weobley. *Cyrdes leah* c.1030, *Curdeslege* 1086 (DB).

Kinnerton Powys. *Kynardton* 1303. 'Cyneheard's farm'. OE pers. name + *tūn*.

Kinnerton, Lower Ches. *Kynarton* 1240. 'Farmstead of a man called Cyneheard'. OE pers. name + *tūn*.

Kinnity (*Cionn Eitigh*) Offaly. 'Eiteach's headland'.

Kinoulton Notts. *Kinildetune* c.1000, *Chineltune* 1086 (DB). 'Farmstead of a woman called Cynehild'. OE pers. name + *tūn*.

Kinross Perth. *Kynros* c.1144. 'End of the promontory'. Gaelic *ceann* + *ros*.

Kinsale (*Cionn tSáile*) Cork. 'Head of the salt water'.

Kinsalebeg (*Cionn tSáile Beag*) Waterford. 'Little head of the salt water'.

Kinsaley (*Cionn tSáile*) Dublin. 'Head of the salt water'.

Kinsley W. Yorks. *Chineslai* 1086 (DB). 'Woodland clearing of a man called Cyne'. OE pers. name + *lēah*.

Kinson Dorset. *Chinestanestone* 1086 (DB), *Kinestaneston* 1238. 'Farmstead of a man called Cynestān'. OE pers. name + *tūn*.

Kintail Forest Highland. *Keantalle* 1509. 'Forest at the head of the salt water'. Gaelic *ceann t-saile*.

Kintbury Berks. *Cynetanbyrig* c.935, *Cheneteberie* 1086 (DB). 'Fortified place on the River Kennet'. Celtic river-name (*see* KENNETT) + OE *burh* (dative *byrig*).

Kintyre (peninsula) Arg. *Ciunntire* 807. 'End of the land'. Gaelic *ceann* + *tire*.

Kinvarra (*Cinn Mhara*) Galway. 'Head of the sea'.

Kinver Staffs. *Cynibre* 736, *Chenevare* 1086 (DB). Celtic **brez* 'hill' with an obscure first element.

Kippax W. Yorks. *Chipesch* 1086 (DB). 'Ash-tree of a man called **Cippa* or **Cyppa*'. OE pers. name (with Scand. *K-*) + OE *æsc* (replaced by OScand. *askr*).

Kippure (*Cipiúr*) (mountain) Wicklow. *Kippoore* 1604. Perhaps 'Big place of rough grass'.

Kirby, a common name in the Midlands and North, usually 'village with a church', OScand. *kirkju-bý*; examples include: **Kirby Bedon** Norfolk. *Kerkebei* 1086 (DB), *Kirkeby Bydon* 1291. Manorial affix from the de Bidun family, here in the 12th cent. **Kirby Bellars** Leics. *Chirchebi* 1086 (DB), *Kirkeby Belers* 1428. Manorial affix from the Beler family, here from the 12th cent. **Kirby Grindalythe** N. Yorks. *Chirchebi* 1086 (DB), *Kirkby in Crendalith* 1367. Affix is an old district name meaning 'slope of the valley frequented by cranes', from OE *cran* + *dæl* + OScand. *hlíth*. **Kirby le Soken** Essex. *Kyrkebi* 1181, *Kirkeby in the Sokne* 1385. Affix is from OE *sōcn* 'district with special jurisdiction'. **Kirby, West** Mersey. *Cherchebia* 1081.
However the following have a different origin, 'farmstead or village of a man called Kærir', OScand. pers. name + *bý*: **Kirby, Cold** N. Yorks. *Carebi* 1086 (DB). The affix means 'bleak, exposed'. **Kirby Muxloe** Leics. *Carbi* 1086 (DB). The affix (found from the 17th cent.) is manorial, from lands here held by a family of that name.

Kircubbin (*Cill Ghobáin*) Down. *Ballicarcubbin* 1605. 'Gobán's church'.

Kirdford W. Sussex. *Kinredeford* 1228. 'Ford of a woman called Cynethrȳth or a man called Cynerēd'. OE pers. name + *ford*.

Kirk as affix, see main name, e.g. for **Kirk Bramwith** (S. Yorks.) *see* BRAMWITH.

Kirkabister Shet (Bressay). *Kirkabuster* 1654. 'Homestead of the church'. OScand. *kirkju-bólstathr*.

Kirkandrews upon Eden Cumbria. *Kirkandres* c.1200. 'Church of St Andrew'. OScand. *kirkja*, named from the dedication of the church. Eden is a Celtic river-name.

Kirkbampton Cumbria. *Banton* c.1185, *Kyrkebampton* 1292. 'Farmstead made of beams or by a tree'. OE *bēam* + *tūn*. Later affix is OScand. *kirkja* 'church'.

Kirkbride Cumbria. *Chirchebrid* 1163. 'Church of St Bride or Brigid'. OScand. *kirkja* + Irish saint's name.

Kirkburn E. R. Yorks. *Westburne* 1086 (DB), *Kirkebrun* 1272. '(Place on) the spring or stream'. OE *burna* with OScand. *kirkja* 'church'.

Kirkburton W. Yorks. *Bertone* 1086 (DB). 'Farmstead near or belonging to a fortification'. OE *byrh-tūn*, with affix OScand. *kirkja* 'church' from the 16th cent.

Kirkby, a common name in the Midlands and North, 'village with a church', OScand. *kirkju-bý*; examples include: **Kirkby** Mersey. *Cherchebi* 1086 (DB). **Kirkby in Ashfield** Notts. *Chirchebi* 1086 (DB), *Kirkeby in Esfeld* 1216. The affix is an old district name, *see* ASHFIELD. **Kirkby Lonsdale** Cumbria. *Cherchebi* 1086 (DB), *Kircabi Lauenesdale* 1090–7. The affix means 'in the valley of the River Lune', Celtic river-name (*see* LANCASTER) + OScand. *dalr*. **Kirkby Malzeard** N. Yorks. *Chirchebi* 1086 (DB), *Kirkebi Malesard* c.1105. The affix means 'poor clearing', from OFrench *mal* + *assart*. **Kirkby Overblow** N. Yorks. *Cherchebi* 1086 (DB), *Kirkeby Oreblowere* 1211. The affix is from OE **or-blāwere* 'ore-blower' alluding to the early smelting of iron ore here. **Kirkby, South** W. Yorks. *Cherchebi* 1086 (DB), *Sudkirkebi* c.1124. Affix *south* to distinguish this place from another Kirkby (now lost) in Pontefract. **Kirkby Stephen** Cumbria. *Cherkaby Stephan* c.1094. Affix from the dedication of the church or from the name of an early owner. **Kirkby Thore** Cumbria. *Kirkebythore* 1179. Manorial affix probably from the name (OScand. *Thórir*) of some early owner.

Kirkbymoorside N. Yorks. *Chirchebi* 1086 (DB), *Kirkeby Moresheved* c.1170. Identical in origin with the previous names, with affix meaning 'head or top of the moor', OE *mōr* + *hēafod*.

Kirkcaldy Fife. *Kircalethyn* 12th cent. 'Fort at Caledin'. Welsh *caer*. *Caledin* means 'hard hill' (Welsh *caled* + *din*). *Kirk-* was substituted for the 'fort' element when this was no longer understood.

Kirkcambeck Cumbria. *Camboc* c.1177, *Kirkecamboc* c.1280. 'Place on Cam Beck with a church'. Celtic river-name (meaning 'crooked stream') with the addition of OScand. *kirkja*.

Kirkconnel Dumf. *Kyrkconvelle* 1347, *Kirkconevel* 1354. 'Church of St Conall'. OScand. *kirkja*.

Kirkcudbright Dumf. *Kircuthbright* 1296. 'Church of St Cuthbert'. OScand. *kirkja*. *Kirk-* may have originally been *Kil-* (Gaelic *cill*), since the pers. name follows the generic word, as is usual in Celtic names, rather than preceding it.

Kirkham, 'homestead or village with a church'. OE *cirice* (replaced by OScand. *kirkja*) + OE *hām*: **Kirkham** Lancs. *Chicheham* |*sic*| 1086 (DB), *Kyrkham* 1094. **Kirkham** N. Yorks. *Cherchan* 1086 (DB).

Kirkharle Northum. *Herle* 1177, *Kyrkeherl* 1242. Possibly 'woodland clearing of a man called **Herela*'. OE pers. name + *lēah*.

Kirkheaton, 'high farmstead', OE *hēah* + *tūn* with the later addition of OScand. *kirkja* 'church': **Kirkheaton** Northum. *Heton* 1242. **Kirkheaton** W. Yorks. *Heptone* |*sic*| 1086 (DB), *Kirkheton* 13th cent.

Kirkibost Highland (Skye). 'Homestead with a church'. OScand. *kirkju-bólstathr*.

Kirkintilloch E. Dunb. *Kitkintulach* c.1200. 'Fort at the head of the hillock'. Welsh *caer* + Gaelic *ceann* + *tulach* (genitive *tulaich*), older *cuer-pentaloch*.

Kirkistown Down. *Kirkston* 1631. 'Kirk's town'. A man surnamed *Kirk* owned land here.

Kirkland, 'estate belonging to a church', OScand. *kirkja* + *land*: **Kirkland** Cumbria, near Blencarn. *Kyrkeland* c.1140. **Kirkland** Cumbria, near Lamplugh. *Kirkland* 1586.

Kirkleatham Red. & Cleve. *Westlidum* 1086 (DB), *Kyrkelidun* 1181. '(Place at) the slopes'. OE *hlith* or OScand. *hlíth* in a dative plural form. Affix is OE *west* replaced by OScand. *kirkja* 'church'.

Kirklevington Stock. on T. *Levetona* 1086 (DB). 'Farmstead on the River Leven'. Celtic river-name (possibly meaning 'smooth') + OE *tūn*, with later addition of OScand. *kirkja* 'church'.

Kirkley Suffolk. *Kirkelea* 1086 (DB). 'Woodland clearing near or belonging to a church'. OScand. *kirkja* + OE *lēah*.

Kirklington, 'estate associated with a man called *Cyrtla*', OE pers. name + *-ing-* + *tūn*: **Kirklington** N. Yorks. *Cherdinton |sic|* 1086 (DB), *Chirtlintuna* c.1150. **Kirklington** Notts. *Cyrlingtune* 958, *Cherlinton* 1086 (DB).

Kirklinton Cumbria. *Leuenton* c.1170, *Kirkeleuinton* 1278. 'Farmstead by the River Lyne'. Celtic river-name (possibly 'the smooth one') + OE *tūn*, with later affix from OScand. *kirkja* 'church'.

Kirkness Orkn. 'Promontory with a church'. OScand. *kirkja* + *nes*.

Kirknewton Northum. *Niwetona* 12th cent. 'New farmstead'. OE *nīwe* + *tūn*, with later affix from OScand. *kirkja* 'church'.

Kirkoswald Cumbria. *Karcoswald* 1167. 'Church of St Oswald'. From the dedication of the church (OScand. *kirkja*) to this saint, a 7th cent. king of Northumbria.

Kirkoswald S. Ayr. 'St Oswald's church'. OScand. *kirkja*.

Kirksanton Cumbria. *Santacherche* 1086 (DB), *Kirkesantan* c.1150 'Church of St Sanctán' OScand. *kirkja* with Irish saint's name.

Kirkton of Logie Buchan Aber. 'Village with a church of the hollow (place) in Buchan'. OE *cirice* + *tun* + Gaelic *logach* (dative *logaigh*). *See* BUCHAN.

Kirktown of Alvah. *See* ALVAH.

Kirkwall Orkn. *Kirkiuvagr* c.1225. 'Church by the bay'. OScand. *kirkja* + *vágr*. The bay is the Bay of Kirkwall, and the church the Cathedral of St Magnus.

Kirkwhelpington. Northum. *Welpinton* 1176. 'Estate associated with a man called *Hwelp*'. OE pers. name + *-ing-* + *tūn*, with later affix from OScand. *Kirkja* 'church'.

Kirmington N. Lincs. *Chernitone* 1086 (DB). Possibly 'estate associated with a man called *Cynehere*'. OE pers. name + *-ing-* + *tūn*.

Kirmond le Mire Lincs. *Chevremont* 1086 (DB). 'Goat hill'. OFrench *chèvre* + *mont*. Affix means 'in the marshy ground', from OScand. *mýrr*.

Kirriemuir Ang. *Kerimor* 1250. 'Big quarter'. Gaelic *ceathramh* + *mór*. A *ceathramh* was the fourth part of a *dabhach*, a variable area of land considered large enough to support a single household.

Kirstead Green Norfolk. *Kerkestede* c.1095. 'Site of a church'. OE *cirice* (replaced by OScand. *kirkja*) + OE *stede*.

Kirtling Cambs. *Chertelinge* 1086 (DB). 'Place associated with a man called *Cyrtla*'. OE pers. name + *-ing*.

Kirtlington Oxon. *Kyrtlingtune* c.1000, *Certelintone* 1086 (DB). 'Estate associated with a man called *Cyrtla*'. OE pers. name + *-ing-* + *tūn*.

Kirton, 'village with a church', OScand. *kirkja* (probably replacing OE *cirice*) + OE *tūn*: **Kirton** Lincs. *Chirchetune* 1086 (DB). **Kirton** Notts. *Circeton* 1086 (DB). **Kirton** Suffolk. *Kirketuna* 1086 (DB). **Kirton in Lindsey** N. Lincs. *Chirchetone* 1086 (DB). *See* LINDSEY.

Kishkeam (*Coiscéim na Caillí*) Cork. 'Footstep of the hag'.

Kislingbury Northants. *Ceselingeberie* 1086 (DB). 'Stronghold of the dwellers on the gravel, or of the family or followers of a man called *Cysel*'. OE *cisel* or pers. name + *-inga-* + *burh* (dative *byrig*).

Kiveton Park S. Yorks. *Ciuetone* 1086 (DB). Probably 'farmstead by a tub-shaped feature'. OE *cȳf* + *tūn*.

Knaith Lincs. *Cheneide* 1086 (DB). 'Landing-place by a river-bend'. OE *cnēo* + *hȳth*.

Knaphill Surrey. *La Cnappe* 1225, *Knephull* 1440. 'The hill'. OE *cnæpp*, with later explanatory *hyll*.

Knappagh (*Cnapach*) Mayo. 'Bumpy area'.

Knapton, 'the servant's farmstead', or 'farmstead of a man called *Cnapa*', OE *cnapa* or pers. name + *tūn*: **Knapton** Norfolk. *Kanapatone* 1086 (DB). **Knapton** York. *Cnapetone* 1086 (DB). **Knapton, East** & **Knapton, West** N. Yorks. *Cnapetone* 1086 (DB).

Knapwell Cambs. *Cnapwelle* c.1045, *Chenepewelle* 1086 (DB). 'Spring or stream of the servant, or of a man called *Cnapa*'. OE *cnapa* or pers. name + *wella*.

Knaresborough N. Yorks. *Chenaresburg* 1086 (DB). Probably 'stronghold of a man called *Cēnheard*'. OE pers. name + *burh*.

Knarsdale Northum. *Knaresdal* 1254. 'Valley of the rugged rock'. OE *cnearr* + OScand. *dalr*.

Knayton N. Yorks. *Cheniueton* 1086 (DB). 'Farmstead of a woman called *Cēngifu*'. OE pers. name + *tūn*.

Knebworth Herts. *Chenepeworde* 1086 (DB). 'Enclosure of a man called *Cnebba*'. OE pers. name + *worth*.

Kneesall Notts. *Cheneshale |sic|* 1086 (DB), *Cneshala* 1175. Possibly 'nook of land of a man called *Cynehēah*'. OE pers. name + *halh*.

Kneesworth Cambs. *Cnesworth* c.1218. Possibly 'enclosure of a man called *Cynehēah*'. OE pers. name + *worth*.

Kneeton Notts. *Cheniueton* 1086 (DB). 'Farmstead of a woman called Cēngifu'.OE pers. name + *tūn*.

Knightcote Warwicks. *Knittecote* 1242. 'Cottage(s) of the young retainers'. OE *cniht* + *cot*.

Knighton, a fairly common name, 'farmstead or village of the young thanes or retainers', OE *cniht* + *tūn*; examples include: **Knighton** Leics. *Cnihtetone* 1086 (DB). **Knighton** Staffs., near Eccleshall. *Chnitestone* 1086 (DB). **Knighton, West** Dorset. *Chenistetone* 1086 (DB).

Knighton (*Trefyclo*) Powys. *Chenistetone* 1086 (DB), *Cnicheton* 1193. 'Farmstead of the young men'. OE *cniht* + *tūn*. The Welsh name means 'farm by the dyke' (Welsh *tref* + *y* + *clawdd*), referring to OFFA'S DYKE nearby.

Knightsbridge Gtr. London. *Cnihtebricge* c.1050. 'Bridge of the young men', i.e. where they congregate. OE *cniht* + *brycg*.

Knill Heref. & Worcs. *Chenille* 1086 (DB). '(Place at) the hillock'. OE **cnylle*.

Knipton Leics. *Gniptone* 1086 (DB). 'Farmstead by a steep rock or peak'. OScand. *gnípa* + OE *tūn*.

Knitsley Durham. *Knyhtheley* 1303. 'Woodland clearing of the retainers'. OE *cniht* + *lēah*.

Kniveton Derbys. *Cheniuetun* 1086 (DB). 'Farmstead of a woman called Cēngifu'. OE pers. name + *tūn*.

Knock Cumbria. *Chonoc* 12th cent. OIrish *cnocc* 'a hillock'.

Knock (*Cnoc*) Clare, Down, Mayo. 'Hill'.

Knockaderry (*Cnoc an Doire*) Limerick. 'Hill of the oak wood'.

Knockadoon (*Cnoc an Dúin*) Cork. 'Hill of the fort'.

Knockainy (*Cnoc Áine*) Limerick. 'Áine's hill'.

Knockalough (*Cnoc an Locha*) Clare, Tipperary. 'Hill of the lake'.

Knockananna (*Cnoc an Eanaigh*) Wicklow. 'Hill of the marsh'.

Knockanarrigan (*Cnoc an Aragain*) Wicklow. 'Hill of the conflicts'.

Knockanevin (*Cnocán Aoibhinn*) Cork. 'Pleasant little hill'.

Knockanillaun (*Cnoc an Oileáin*) Mayo. 'Hill of the island'.

Knockanoran (*Cnoc an Uaráin*) Cork, Laois. 'Hill of the spring'.

Knockanore (*Cnoc an Óir*) Waterford. 'Hill of gold'.

Knockatallon (*Cnoc an tSalainn*) Monaghan. 'Hill of the salt'.

Knockaunnaglashy (*Cnocán na Glaise*) Kerry. 'Little hill of the stream'.

Knockboy (*Cnoc Buí*) Cork, Kerry, Waterford. 'Yellow hill'.

Knockbrack (*An Cnoc Breac*) Donegal. 'The speckled hill'.

Knockbreda Down. The present parish was formed in 1658 from the two separate parishes of *Knock* (Irish *An Cnoc*, 'the hill') and *Breda* (Irish *Bréadach*, 'broken land').

Knockcloghrim (*Cnoc Clochdhroma*) Derry. *Knockloghran* 1654. 'Hill of the stony ridge'.

Knockcroghery (*Cnoc an Chrochaire*) Roscommon. 'Hill of the hangman'.

Knockdrin (*Cnoc Droinne*) Westmeath. 'Humpy hill'.

Knockeen (*Cnoicín*) Kerry. 'Little hill'.

Knockerry (*Cnoc Doire*) Clare. 'Hill of the oak wood'.

Knockgraffon (*Cnoc Rafann*) Tipperary. 'Rafainn's hill'.

Knockholt Kent. *Ocholt* 1197, *Nocholt* 1353. '(Place at) the oak wood'. OE *āc* + *holt*, with initial *N*- from the OE definite article.

Knockin Shrops. *Cnochin* 1165. Celtic **cnöccïn* 'a little hillock'.

Knocklayd (*Cnoc Leithid*) Antrim. *Cnoc Leaaid* 1542. 'Hill of the slope'.

Knocklong (*Cnoc Loinge*) Limerick. 'Hill of the ship'.

Knockmealdown Mountains (*Sléibhte Chnoc Mhaoldhomhnaigh*) Tipperary, Waterford. 'Mountains of the hill of Maoldomhnach'.

Knockmore (*An Cnoc Mór*) Mayo. 'The big hill'.

Knockmoyle (*Cnoc Maol*) Galway, Tyrone. 'Bald hill'.

Knocknacarry (*Cnoc na Cora*) Antrim. *Knockenecarry* c.1657. 'Hill of the weir'.

Knocknagashel (*Cnoc na gCaiseal*) Kerry. 'Hill of the stone forts'.

Knocknagoney (*Cnoc na gCoiníní*) Down. *Ballacknocknegonie* 1604. 'Hill of the rabbits'.

Knocknagree (*Cnoc na Graí*) Cork. 'Hill of the horse stud'.

Knocknahorn (*Cnoc na hEorna*) Tyrone. 'Hill of the barley'.

Knocknamuckly (*Cnoc na Muclaí*) Armagh. *Knocknamokally* 1609. 'Hill of the piggery'.

Knockraha (*Cnoc Rátha*) Cork. 'Hill of the fort'.

Knockrath (*Cnoc Rátha*) Wicklow. 'Hill of the fort'.

Knocktopher (*Cnoc an Tóchair*) Kilkenny. 'Hill of the causeway'.

Knockvicar (*Cnoc an Bhiocáire*) Roscommon. 'Hill of the vicar'.

Knodishall Suffolk. *Cnoteseala* 1086 (DB). 'Nook of land of a man called **Cnott*'. OE pers. name + *halh*.

Knook Wilts. *Cunuche* 1086 (DB). Probably OWelsh **cnucc* 'a hillock'.

Knossington Leics. *Nossitone* |sic| 1086 (DB), *Cnossintona* 12th cent. Probably 'estate associated with a man called **Cnossa*'. OE pers. name + *-ing-* + *tūn*.

Knott End on Sea Lancs. *Cnote* 13th cent. ME *knot* 'a hillock'.

Knotting Beds. *Chenotinga* 1086 (DB). Probably '(settlement of) the family or followers of a man called **Cnotta*'. OE pers. name + *-ingas*.

Knottingley W. Yorks. *Notingeleia* 1086 (DB). 'Woodland clearing of the family or followers of a man called *Cnotta'. OE pers. name + -*inga*- + *lēah*.

Knotty Ash Mersey., recorded as simply *Ash.c.*1700, 'the ash-tree', later with the adjective *knotty* 'gnarled'.

Knowle, '(place at) the hill-top or hillock', OE *cnoll*; examples include: **Knowle** Brist. *Canole* 1086 (DB). **Knowle** W. Mids. *La Cnolle* 1221. **Knowle, Church** Dorset. *C(he)nolle* 1086 (DB), *Churchecnolle* 1346. Later addition is OE *cirice* 'church'.

Knowlton Kent. *Chenoltone* 1086 (DB). 'Farmstead by a hillock'. OE *cnoll* + *tūn*.

Knowsley Mersey. *Chenulueslei* 1086 (DB). 'Woodland clearing of a man called Cēnwulf or Cynewulf'. OE pers. name + *lēah*.

Knowstone Devon. *Chenutdestana* 1086 (DB). 'Boundary stone of a man called Knútr'. OScand. pers. name + OE *stān*.

Knoydart (district) Highland. *Knodworath* 1309. 'Knut's inlet'. OScand. pers. name + *fjǫrthr*. The pers. name is identical with that of King Knut (Canute), who invaded Scotland in 1031.

Knoyle, East & *Knoyle, West* Wilts. *Cnugel* 948, *Chenvel* 1086 (DB). '(Place at) the knuckle-shaped hill'. OE **cnugel*.

Knutsford Ches. *Cunetesford* 1086 (DB). Probably 'ford of a man called Knútr'. OScand. pers. name + OE *ford*.

Kyle of Lochalsh Highland. (Place by the) Kyle of Lochalsh'. *Kyle* is Gaelic *caol*, 'strait'. The name of the loch may mean 'foaming one' (Gaelic *aillseach*).

Kyleakin Highland (Skye). '(Place on) Kyle Akin'. The name of the strait means 'Haakon's strait' (Gaelic *caol*), apparently referring to Haakon IV of Norway, who is said to have sailed through it in 1263 after his defeat at Largs.

Kylebrack (*An Choill Bhreac*) Galway. 'The speckled wood'.

Kylemore (*An Choill Mhóir*) Galway. 'The big wood'.

Kyles of Bute (sea channel) Arg. 'Straits of Bute'. Gaelic *caolas. See* BUTE.

Kyloe Northum. *Culeia* 1195. 'Clearing or pasture for cows'. OE *cū* + *lēah*.

Kyme, North & *Kyme, South* Lincs. *Chime* 1086 (DB). '(Place at) the hollow'. OE **cymbe*.

Kyre Magna Heref. & Worcs. *Cuer* 1086 (DB). Named from the stream here, a pre-English river-name of uncertain origin and meaning.

L

Labasheeda (*Leaba Shíoda*) Clare. 'Grave of Síoda'.

Labbacallee (*Leaba Caillighe*) Cork. 'Hag's bed'.

Labbamolaga (*Leaba Molaga*) Cork. 'Molaga's bed'.

Labby (*Leaba*) Derry, Donegal, Sligo. 'Grave'.

Labbyfirmore (*Leaba an Fhir Mhóir*) Monaghan. 'Grave of the big man'.

Laceby NE. Lincs. *Levesbi* 1086 (DB). 'Farmstead or village of a man called Leifr'. OScand. pers. name + *bý*.

Lach Dennis Ches. *Lece* 1086 (DB), *Lache Deneys* 1260. 'The boggy stream'. OE **lece*, with manorial affix from ME *danais* 'Danish' referring to a man called Colben who held the manor in 1086.

Lachtcarn (*Leacht Chairn*) Tipperary. 'Grave of the cairn'.

Lack (*An Leac*) Fermanagh. *Lack* 1834. 'The flagstone'.

Lackagh (*Leacach*) Kildare. 'Abounding in flagstones'.

Lackamore (*An Leaca Mhór*) Tipperary. 'The big hillside'.

Lackan (*An Leacain*) Wicklow. 'The hillside'.

Lackaroe (*Leaca Rua*) Cork, Offaly. 'Red hillside'.

Lackford Suffolk. *Lecforda* 1086 (DB). 'Ford where leeks grow'. OE *lēac* + *ford*. The river-name **Lark** is a 'back-formation' from the place-name.

Lacock Wilts. *Lacok* 854, *Lacoc* 1086 (DB). 'The small stream', OE **lacuc*.

Ladbroke Warwicks. *Hlodbroc* 998, *Lodbroc* 1086 (DB). Possibly 'brook used for divination'. OE *hlod* + *brōc*.

Ladock Cornwall. 'Church of *Sancta Ladoca*' 1268. From the patron saint of the church.

Ladybank Fife. Late 19th-cent. development; perhaps connection with the works of Limdores.

Lagan (*Abhainn an Lagáin*) (river) Antrim, Down. *Logia* c.150. 'River of the low-lying district'.

Lagan (*Lagán*) Donegal. 'Little hollow'.

Lagg N. Ayr. '(Place by a) hollow'. Gaelic *lag*.

Laggan N. Ayr. '(Place by a) little hollow'. Gaelic *lagan*.

Laghil (*Leamhchoill*) Donegal. 'Elm wood'.

Laghile (*Leamhchoill*) Clare, Tipperary. 'Elm wood'.

Laght (*Leacht*) Cork. 'Grave'.

Laghtane (*Leachtán*) Limerick. 'Little grave'.

Laghtgeorge (*Leacht Sheoirse*) Limerick. 'Seoirse's grave'.

Laghtneill (*Leacht Néill*) Cork. 'Néill's grave'.

Laghy (*An Lathaigh*) Donegal. 'The mire'.

Lagnamuck (*Lag na Muc*) Mayo. 'Hollow of the pigs'.

Lagore (*Loch Gabhra*) Meath. 'Lake of the goat'.

Laharan (*Leath Fhearann*) Cork, Kerry. 'Half a measure of land'.

Lahardaun (*Leathardán*) Mayo. 'Side of a plateau'.

Lahesseragh (*Leath Sheisreach*) Tipperary. 'Half ploughland'.

Laindon Essex. *Ligeandune* c.1000, *Leienduna* 1086 (DB). Probably 'hill by a stream called *Lea*'. Lost Celtic river-name (possibly meaning 'light river') + OE *dūn*.

Lairg Highland. *Larg* c.1230. '(Place of the) shank'. Gaelic *lorg*.

Lake Wilts. *Lake* 1289. OE *lacu* 'small stream'.

Lakenham, Old & *Lakenham, New* Norfolk. *Lakemham* 1086 (DB). Probably 'homestead or village of a man called **Lāca*'. OE pers. name (genitive -*n*) + *hām*.

Lakenheath Suffolk. *Lacingahith* 945, *Lakingahethe* 1086 (DB). 'Landing-place of the people living by streams'. OE *lacu* + -*inga*- + *hȳth*.

Laleham Surrey. *Laeleham* 1042–66, *Leleham* 1086 (DB). 'Homestead or enclosure where twigs or brushwood are found'. OE *lǣl* + *ham* or *hamm*.

Laleston (*Trelales*) Bri. *Lagelestun* c.1165, *Laweleston* 1268. 'Legeles' farm'. OE *tūn* (Welsh *tref*). Thomas and Walter Legeles ('Lawless') are recorded in the 13th cent. as members of an Anglo-Scand. family.

Lamarsh Essex. *Lamers* 1086 (DB). 'Loam marsh'. OE *lām* + *mersc*.

Lamas Norfolk. *Lamers* 1086 (DB). Identical in origin with the previous name.

Lambay (*Reachrainn*) (island) Dublin. 'Lamb island'. OScand. *lamb* + *ey*. The meaning of the Irish name is obscure.

Lambeg (*Lann Bheag*) Antrim. *Landebeg* c.1450. 'Little church'.

Lamberhurst Kent. *Lamburherste* c.1100. 'Wooded hill where lambs graze'. OE *lamb* (genitive plural *lambra*) + *hyrst*.

Lambeth Gtr. London. *Lamhytha* 1088. 'Landing-place for lambs'. OE *lamb* + *hȳth*.

Lambley, 'clearing or pasture for lambs', OE *lamb* + *lēah*: **Lambley** Northum. *Lambeleya* 1201. **Lambley** Notts. *Lambeleia* 1086 (DB).

Lambourn, *Lambourne*, probably 'stream where lambs are washed', OE *lamb* + *burna*: **Lambourn, Upper Lambourn** Berks. *Lambburnan* c.880, *Lamborne* 1086 (DB), *Uplamburn* 1182. Distinguishing affix is OE *upp* 'higher upstream'. **Lambourne** Essex. *Lamburna* 1086 (DB).

Lambrook, East Somerset. *Landbroc* 1065. OE *brōc* 'brook' with OE *land* 'cultivated ground, estate'.

Lambston Pemb. *Villa Lamberti* 1291, *Lamberteston* 1321. 'Lambert's farm'. Flemish pers. name + OE *tūn*.

Lamerton Devon. *Lambretona* 1086 (DB). 'Farmstead on the lamb stream or loam stream'. OE *lamb* or *lām* + *burna* + *tūn*.

Lamesley Tyne & Wear. *Lamelay* 1297. 'Clearing or pasture for lambs'. OE *lamb* + *lēah*.

Lammermuir (district) Sc. Bord. 'Moor where lambs graze'. OE *lamb* (genitive plural *lambra*) + *mor*.

Lammermuir Hills E. Loth. *Lombormore* 800. 'Hills by the moor where lambs graze'. OE *lamb* (genitive plural *lambra*) + *mōr*.

Lammy (*Leamhach*) Fermanagh, Tyrone. 'Abounding in elms'.

Lamonby Cumbria. *Lambeneby* 1257. 'Farmstead or village of a man called Lambin'. ME pers. name + OScand. *bý*.

Lamorran Cornwall. *Lannmoren* 969. 'Church-site of St Moren'. From Cornish **lann* with the patron saint of the church.

Lampeter (*Llanbedr Pont Steffan*) Cergn. *Lanpeder* 1284, *Lampeter Pount Steune* 1301. 'Church of St Peter'. Welsh *llan* + *Pedr*. The Welsh name means 'church of St Peter by Stephen's bridge' (Welsh *llan* + *Pedr* + *pont* + *Steffan*).

Lamplugh Cumbria. *Lamplou* c.1150. 'Bare valley'. Celtic *nant* + **bluch*.

Lamport Northants. *Langeport* 1086 (DB). 'Long village or market-place'. OE *lang* + *port*.

Lamyatt Somerset. *Lambageate* late 10th cent., *Lamieta* 1086 (DB). 'Gate for lambs'. OE *lamb* (genitive plural *-a*) + *geat*.

Lanaglug (*Lann na gClog*) Tyrone. 'Church of the bells'.

Lanark S. Lan. *Lannarc* 1188. '(Place in the) glade'. OWelsh *lannerch*.

Lancaster Lancs. *Loncastre* 1086 (DB). 'Roman fort on the River Lune'. Celtic river-name (probably meaning 'healthy, pure') + OE *cæster*. **Lancashire** (the county) is a reduced form of *Lancastreshire* 14th cent., from Lancaster + OE *scīr* 'district'.

Lanchester Durham. *Langecestr* 1196. Apparently 'long Roman fort or stronghold'. OE *lang* + *ceaster*. The first element may however preserve a reduced form of its old Romano-British name *Longovicium* (probably 'place of the ship-fighters' from Celtic **longo* 'ship').

Lancing W. Sussex. *Lancinges* 1086 (DB). '(Settlement of) the family or followers of a man called **Wlanc*'. OE pers. name + *-ingas*.

Land's End Cornwall. *Londeseynde* 1337. 'End of the mainland'. OE *land* + *ende*.

Landbeach Cambs. *Bece* 1086 (DB), *Landebeche* 1218. OE *bece* 'stream, valley' or *bæc* (locative **bece*) 'low ridge', with the later addition of *land* 'dry land' to distinguish it from WATERBEACH.

Landcross Devon. *Lanchers* 1086 (DB). Possibly OE *ears* 'buttock-shaped hill' with OE *hlanc* 'long, narrow'. Alternatively a Celtic name meaning 'church by the fen', from **lann* + **cors*.

Landford Wilts. *Langeford* |sic| 1086 (DB), *Laneford* 1242. 'Ford crossed by a lane'. OE *lanu* + *ford*.

Landkey Devon. *Landechei* 1166. 'Church-site of St Ke'. Cornish **lann* + saint's name.

Landore Swan. '(Place by the) river bank'. Welsh *glan* + *dŵr*.

Landrake Cornwall. *Landerhtun* late 11th cent. Cornish *lannergh* 'a clearing' (with OE *tūn* 'farmstead' in the early spelling).

Landulph Cornwall. *Landelech* 1086 (DB). 'Church-site of Dilic'. Cornish **lann* + saint's name.

Landwade Cambs. *Landuuade* 11th cent. Probably 'estate or district ford'. OE *land* + *wæd*.

Laneast Cornwall. *Lanast* 1076. Cornish **lann* 'church-site' with an obscure second element, probably a pers. name.

Laneham, *Church Laneham* Notts. *Lanun* 1086 (DB). '(Place at) the lanes'. OE *lanu* in a dative plural form *lanum*.

Lanercost Cumbria. *Lanrecost* 1169. Celtic **lannerch* 'glade, clearing', perhaps with the pers. name Aust (from Latin *Augustus*).

Lanesborough (*Béal Átha Liag*) Longford. 'Lane's borough'. The name is apparently that of the English landowner. The original Irish name means 'ford-mouth of the standing stone'.

Langar Notts. *Langare* 1086 (DB). 'Long gore or point of land'. OE *lang* + *gāra*.

Langcliffe N. Yorks. *Lanclif* 1086 (DB). 'Long cliff or bank'. OE *lang* + *clif*.

Langdale, Little Cumbria. *Langedenelittle* c.1160. 'Long valley'. OE *lang* + *denu* (replaced by OScand. *dalr*), with *lȳtel* 'little'.

Langdon, 'long hill or down', OE *lang* + *dūn*: **Langdon, East** & **Langdon, West** Kent. *Langandune* 861, *Estlangedoun*, *Westlangedone* 1291. **Langdon Hills** Essex. *Langenduna* 1086 (DB), *Langdon Hilles* 1485.

Langenhoe Essex. *Langhou* 1086 (DB). 'Long hill-spur'. OE *lang* (dative *-an*) + *hōh*.

Langford, usually 'long ford', OE *lang* + *ford*; examples include: **Langford** Beds. *Longaford* 944–6, *Langeford* 1086 (DB). **Langford** Essex. *Langeford* 1086 (DB). **Langford** Oxon. *Langefort* 1086 (DB). **Langford Budville** Somerset. *Langeford* 1212, *Langeford Budevill* 1305. Manorial affix from the de Buddevill family, here in the 13th cent.
   However the following has a different origin: **Langford** Notts. *Landeforde* 1086 (DB). Possibly 'ford of a man called **Landa*', OE pers. name + *ford*; alternatively the first element may be OE *land* in a sense such as 'boundary or district'.

Langham, usually 'long homestead or enclosure', OE *lang* + *hām* or *hamm*: **Langham** Norfolk. *Langham* 1086 (DB). **Langham** Rutland. *Langham* 1202. **Langham** Suffolk. *Langham* 1086 (DB).
   However the following has a different origin: **Langham** Essex. *Laingaham* 1086 (DB). Possibly 'homestead of the family or followers of a man called **Lahha*'. OE pers. name + *-inga-* + *hām*.

Langho Lancs. *Langale* 13th cent. 'Long nook of land'. OE *lang* + *halh*.

Langholm Dumf. *Langholm* 1376. 'Long island'. OE *lang* + OScand. *holmr*. The 'island' is the strip of land by the River Esk.

Langley, a fairly common name, 'long wood or clearing', OE *lang* + *lēah*; examples include: **Langley** Berks., near Slough. *Langeley* 1208, *Langele Marais* 1316. Manorial affix (later *Marish*) from the Mareis family, here in the 13th cent. **Langley** Derbys., near Heanor. *Langeleie* 1086 (DB). **Langley** Kent. *Longanleag* 814, *Langvelei* 1086 (DB). **Langley, Abbots** & **Langley, Kings** Herts. *Langalege* c.1060, *Langelai* 1086 (DB), *Abbotes Langele* 1263, *Kyngeslangeley* 1436. Distinguishing affixes refer to early possession by the Abbot of St Albans and the King. **Langley Burrell** Wilts. *Langelegh* 940, *Langhelei* 1086 (DB), *Langele Burel* 1309. Manorial affix from the Burel family, here from the 13th cent. **Langley, Kington** Wilts. *Langhelei* 1086 (DB). Affix *Kington*, first added in the 17th cent., is from KINGTON ST MICHAEL nearby. **Langley, Kirk** Derbys. *Langelei* 1086 (DB), *Kyrkelongeleye* 1269. Affix is OScand. *kirkja* 'church'. **Langley Park** Durham. *Langeleye* 1232.

Langney E. Sussex. *Langelie |sic|* 1086 (DB), *Langania* 1121. 'Long island, or long piece of dry ground in marsh'. OE *lang* (dative *-an*) + *ēg*.

Langold Notts. *Langalde* 1246. 'Long shelter or place of refuge'. OE *lang* + *hald*.

Langport Somerset. *Longport* 10th cent., *Lanport* 1086 (DB). 'Long market-place'. OE *lang* + *port*.

Langrick Lincs. *Langrak* 1243. 'Long stretch of river'. OE *lang* + **racu*.

Langridge B. & NE. Som. *Lancheris |sic|* 1086 (DB), *Langerig* 1225. 'Long ridge'. OE *lang* + *hrycg*.

Langrigg Cumbria. *Langrug* 1189. 'Long ridge'. OScand. *langr* + *hryggr*.

Langrish Hants. *Langerishe* 1236. 'Long rush-bed'. OE *lang* + **rysce*.

Langsett S. Yorks. *Langeside* 12th cent. 'Long hill-slope'. OE *lang* + *sīde*.

Langstone Hants. *Langeston* 1289. 'Long (or tall) stone'. OE *lang* + *stān*.

Langstone Newpt. *Langestone* c.1280, *Llangstone* 1868. '(Place by the) long stone'. OE *lang* + *stān*.

Langthorne N. Yorks. *Langetorp |sic|* 1086 (DB), *Langethorn* c.1100. 'Tall thorn-tree'. OE *lang* + *thorn*.

Langthorpe N. Yorks. *Torp* 1086 (DB), *Langliuetorp* 12th cent. 'Outlying farmstead or hamlet of a woman called Langlif'. OScand. pers. name + *thorp*.

Langthwaite N. Yorks. *Langethwait* 1167. 'Long clearing'. OScand. *langr* + *thveit*.

Langtoft, 'long homestead or curtilage', OScand. *langr* + *toft*: **Langtoft** E. R. Yorks. *Langetou |sic|* 1086 (DB), *Langetoft* c.1165. **Langtoft** Lincs. *Langetof* 1086 (DB).

Langton, a fairly common name, usually 'long farmstead or estate', OE *lang* + *tūn*; examples include: **Langton, Church** & **Langton, East** Leics. *Lang(e)tone* 1086 (DB), *Chirh Langeton* 1316, *Estlangeton* 1327. **Langton, Great** N. Yorks. *Langeton* 1086 (DB). *Great Langeton* 1223. **Langton Herring** Dorset. *Langetone* 1086 (DB), *Langeton Heryng* 1336. Manorial affix from the Harang family, here in the 13th cent. **Langton Matravers** Dorset. *Langeton* 1165, *Langeton Mawtravers* 1428. Manorial addition from the Mautravers family, here from the 13th cent.

However the following have a different origin: **Langton** Durham. *Langadun* c.1050. 'Long hill or down'. OE *lang* + *dūn*. **Langton, Tur** Leics. *Terlintone* 1086 (DB). Probably 'estate associated with a man called Tyrhtel or **Tyrli*'. OE pers. name + *-ing-* + *tūn*. The name was later remodelled under the influence of nearby CHURCH & EAST LANGTON.

Langtree Devon. *Langtrewa* 1086 (DB). 'Tall tree'. OE *lang* + *trēow*.

Langwathby Cumbria. *Langwadebi* 1159. 'Farmstead or village by the long ford'. OScand. *langr* + *vath* + *bý*.

Langwith, 'long ford', OScand. *langr* + *vath*: **Langwith, Nether** Notts. *Languath* c.1179, *Netherlangwat* 1252. Affix is OE *neotherra* 'lower (down-stream)' to distinguish it from the next name. **Langwith, Upper** Derbys. *Langwath* 1208.

Langworth Lincs., near Wragby. *Longwathe* c.1055. Identical in origin with the previous names.

Lanivet Cornwall. *Lannived* 1268. 'Church-site at the pagan sacred place'. Cornish **lann* + *neved*.

Lanlivery Cornwall. *Lanliveri* 12th cent. 'Church-site of **Livri*'. Cornish **lann* + pers. name.

Lanreath Cornwall. *Lanredoch* 1086 (DB). 'Church-site of Reydhogh'. Cornish **lann* + pers. name.

Lansallos Cornwall. *Lansaluus* 1086 (DB). 'Church-site of **Salwys*'. Cornish **lann* + pers. name.

Lanteglos Cornwall, near Fowey. *Lanteglos* 1249. 'Valley of the church'. Cornish *nans* + *eglos*.

Lanton Northum. *Langeton* 1242. 'Long farmstead or estate'. OE *lang* + *tūn*.

Laois (*Laois*) (the county). '(Place of the) people of Laeighseach'. Lughaidh *Laeighseach* was granted lands here after he had driven invading forces from Munster. The name is pronounced 'Leesh', giving the former anglicized form *Leix*.

Lapford Devon. *Slapeforda |sic|* 1086 (DB), *Lapeford* 1107. Possibly 'ford of a man called **Hlappa*', OE pers. name + *ford*. Alternatively the first element may be an OE word **(h)lēape* or **(h)lǽpe* 'lapwing'.

Lapley Staffs. *Lappeley* 1061, *Lepelie* 1086 (DB). Possibly 'woodland clearing at the end of the estate or parish'. OE *lǽppa* + *lēah*.

Lapworth Warwicks. *Hlappawurthin* 816, *Lapeforde |sic|* 1086 (DB). Probably 'enclosure of a man called **Hlappa*'. OE pers. name + *worthign* (replaced by *worth*).

Laracor (*Láithreach Cora*) Meath. 'Site of the weir'.

Laragh (*Láithreach*) Laois, Monaghan, Wicklow. 'Site'.

Laragh (*Leath Ráth*) Longford. 'Half a ring fort'.

Larbert Falk. *Lethbert* 1195. 'Half-wood'. Pictish *lledbert*, *cp.* Perth.

Largan (*Leargain*) Mayo. 'Slope'.

Larganreagh (*Leargan Riabhach*) Donegal. 'Striped slope'.

Largo Fife. *Largauch* 1250. 'Steep (place)'. Gaelic *leargach*.

Largs N. Ayr. *Larghes* 1140. '(Places by) slopes'. Gaelic *learg*.

Largy (*Leargaidh*) Antrim, Derry, Fermanagh, etc. 'Slope'.

Largybrack (*Leargaidh Breac*) Donegal. 'Speckled slope'.

Largydonnell (*Learga Uí Dhónaill*) Sligo. 'Ó Dónaill's slope'.

Largyreagh (*Leargaidh Riabhach*) Derry, 'Striped slope'.

Larkfield Kent. *Lavrochesfel* 1086 (DB). 'Open land frequented by larks'. OE *lāwerce* + *feld*.

Larkhall S. Lan. *Laverockhall* 1620. Meaning uncertain. *Laverock* in the early form of the name represents a Scottish equivalent of English *lark*, but there is no evidence that the bird gave the name.

Larling Norfolk. *Lurlinga* 1086 (DB). '(Settlement of) the family or followers of a man called *Lyrel*'. OE pers. name + *-ingas*.

Larne (*Latharna*) Antrim. 'Descendants of Lathar'. According to legend, Lathar was one of the 25 sons of Úgaine Mór (Hugony), a pre-Christian king of Ireland.

Larnog. *See* LAVERNOCK.

Lartington Durham. *Lyrtingtun* c.1050, *Lertinton* 1086 (DB). 'Estate associated with a man called *Lyrti*'. OE pers. name + *-ing-* + *tūn*.

Lasham Hants. *Esseham* |sic| 1086 (DB), *Lasham* 1175. 'Smaller homestead, or homestead of a man called *Leassa*'. OE *lǣssa* or pers. name + *hām*.

Lasswade Midloth. *Laswade* 1148, *Lesswade* c.1150. 'Pasture ford'. OE *lǣs* (genitive *lǣswe*) + *wæd*.

Lastingham N. Yorks. *Lestingeham* 1086 (DB). 'Homestead of the family or followers of a man called *Lǣsta*'. OE pers. name + *-inga-* + *hām*.

Latchingdon Essex. *Lǣcendune* c.1050, *Lacenduna* 1086 (DB). Probably 'hill by the well-watered ground'. OE *lǣcen* + *dūn*.

Lathbury Bucks. *Lateberie* 1086 (DB). 'Fortification built with laths or beams'. OE *lætt* + *burh* (dative *byrig*).

Latheron Highland. *Lagheryn* 1287. Probably 'miry place'. Gaelic *láthach*. The extended form of the name is *Latheronwheel*, adding Gaelic *a' Phuill*, 'of the pool'.

Latimer Bucks. *Yselhamstede* 1220, *Isenhampstede Latymer* 1389. For its original name, *see* CHENIES. The manorial addition (now used alone) is from the Latymer family, here in the 14th cent.

Latnamard (*Leacht na mBard*) Monaghan. 'Grave of the bards'.

Latteragh (*Leatracha*) Tipperary. 'Hill slopes'.

Latteridge S. Glos. *Laderugga* 1176. Possibly 'ridge by a water course'. OE *lād* + *hrycg*.

Lattiford Somerset. *Lodereforda* 1086 (DB). 'Ford frequented by beggars'. OE *loddere* + *ford*.

Lattin (*Laitean*) Tipperary. 'Valley bottom'.

Latton Wilts. *Latone* 1086 (DB). 'Leek or garlic enclosure, herb garden'. OE *lēac-tun*.

Latton (*Leatón*) Monaghan. 'Valley bottom'.

Lauder Sc. Bord. *Louueder* 1208. '(Place on the) Leader Water'. The Celtic river name may mean 'cleansing river' (British *lou- + *dubro-*).

Laugharne (*Talacharn*) Carm. *Talacharn* 1191, *Laugharne, or Tal-Llacharn* 1868. 'End (of the place)'. Welsh *tâl*. The English form of the name has dropped the *Ta-* of the Welsh equivalent. The second element is of obscure origin.

Laughil (*Leamhchoill*) Galway, Longford, Mayo, etc. 'Elm wood'.

Laughill (*Leamhchoill*) Fermanagh, Laois. 'Elm wood'.

Laughterton Lincs. *Leuggtricdun* c.680, *Lactertun* 1227. 'Hill or farmstead where lettuce grows'. OE *leahtric* + *dūn* or *tūn*.

Laughton, usually 'leek or garlic enclosure, herb garden', OE *lēac-tūn*: **Laughton** E. Sussex. *Lestone* 1086 (DB). **Laughton** Leics. *Lachestone* 1086 (DB). **Laughton en le Morthen** S. Yorks. *Lastone* 1086 (DB), *Latton in Morthing* 1230. Affix means 'in the (district called) Morthen', a name first recorded in the 12th cent. from OE or OScand. *mōr* 'moorland' + *thing* 'assembly'.
  However the following has a different origin: **Laughton** Lincs., near Folkingham. *Loctone* 1086 (DB). 'Enclosure that can be locked'. OE *loc* + *tūn*.

Launcells Cornwall. *Landseu* |sic| 1086 (DB), *Lanceles* 1204. Cornish *lann* 'church-site' with an uncertain second element.

Launceston Cornwall. *Lanscavetone* 1086 (DB). 'Estate near the church-site of St Stephen'. Cornish *lann* + saint's name + OE *tūn*.

Laune River (*Leamháin*) Kerry. 'Elm river'.

Launton Oxon. *Langtune* c.1050, *Lantone* 1086 (DB). 'Long farmstead or estate'. OE *lang* + *tūn*.

Lauragh (*An Láithreach*) Kerry. 'The site'.

Laurelvale Armagh. *Laurel Vale* 1835. The name was invented by Thomas Sinton in c.1830 to apply to his house here. The Irish name is *Tamhnaigh Bhealtaine*, 'cultivated spot of the May festival'.

Laurencekirk Aber. 'St Laurence's church'. The town, founded c.1770, was originally known as *Kirkton of St Laurence*, *Kirkton* being 'village with a church' (OE *cirice* + *tūn*). It later adopted its present name, after St Laurence of Canterbury.

Lavagh (*Leamhach*) Donegal, Sligo. 'Abounding in elms'.

Lavally (*Leth Baile*) Clare, Cork, Galway, etc. 'Half townland'.

Lavant, *East Lavant* W. Sussex. *Loventone* 1086 (DB), *Lavent* 1227. Originally 'farmstead on the River Lavant', with OE *tūn*, later taking name from the river alone, a Celtic river-name meaning 'gliding one'.

Lavendon Bucks. *Lavendene* 1086 (DB). 'Valley of a man called Lāfa'. OE pers. name (genitive *-n*) + *denu*.

Lavenham Suffolk. *Lauanham* c.995, *Lauenham* 1086 (DB). 'Homestead of a man called Lāfa'. OE pers. name (genitive -*n*) + *hām*.

Laver, High, *Laver, Little*, & *Laver, Magdalen* Essex. *Lagefare* c.1010, *Lagafara* 1086 (DB), *Laufar la Magdelene* 1263. 'Water passage or crossing'. OE *lagu* + *fær*. Affix *Magdalen* from the dedication of the church.

Lavernock (*Larnog*) Vale Glam. *Lawernach* 13th cent. 'Lark hill'. OE *lāwerce* + *cnocc*. The Welsh name is a phonetic form of the English.

Laverstock Wilts. *Lavvrecestoches* 1086 (DB). 'Outlying farmstead or hamlet frequented by larks'. OE *lāwerce* + *stoc*.

Laverstoke Hants. *Lavrochestoche* 1086 (DB). Identical in origin with the previous name.

Laverton, usually probably 'farmstead frequented by larks', OE *lāwerce* + *tūn*: **Laverton** Glos. *Lawertune* c.1160. **Laverton** Somerset. *Lavretone* 1086 (DB).
However the following has a different origin: **Laverton** N. Yorks. *Lavretone* 1086 (DB). 'Farmstead on the River Laver'. Celtic river-name (meaning 'babbling brook') + OE *tūn*.

Lavey (*Leamhach*) Cavan, Derry. 'Abounding in elms'.

Lavington, probably 'estate associated with a man called Lāfa', OE pers. name + -*ing*- + *tūn*: **Lavington, East** & **Lavington, West** W. Sussex. *Levitone* 1086 (DB). **Lavington, Market** & **Lavington, West** Wilts. *Laventone* 1086 (DB). Distinguishing affixes *market* and *west* first found in the 17th cent.

Lawford, probably 'ford of a man called *Lealla*', OE pers. name + *ford*: **Lawford** Essex. *Lalleford* 1045, *Laleforda* 1086 (DB). **Lawford, Church** & **Lawford, Long** Warwicks. *Lelleford* 1086 (DB), *Chirche Lalleford, Long Lalleford* 1235. Distinguishing affixes are OE *cirice* 'church' and *lang* 'long'.

Lawhitton Cornwall. *Landuuithan* 10th cent., *Languitetone* 1086 (DB). Probably 'valley or church-site of a man called Gwethen', Cornish *nans* or **lann* + pers. name, with the later addition of OE *tūn* 'farmstead'.

Lawkland N. Yorks. *Laukeland* 12th cent. 'Arable land where leeks are grown'. OScand. *laukr* + *land*.

Lawley Shrops. *Lauelei* 1086 (DB). 'Woodland clearing of a man called Lāfa'. OE pers. name + *lēah*.

Lawrencetown Down. *Laurencetown formerly Hall's Mill* c.1834. 'Lawrence's town'. The *Lawrence* family were here before the 18th cent., when the village was known as *Hall's Mill*, after Francis *Hall*, who leased land from the Lawrences in 1674. The corresponding Irish name is *Baile Labhráis*.

Lawrenny Pemb. *Leurenni* c.1200. '(Place on) low ground'. Welsh *llawr*. The second element is of uncertain origin.

Lawshall Suffolk. *Lawessela* 1086 (DB). 'Dwelling or shelter by a hill or mound'. OE *hlāw* + *sele* or **sell*.

Lawton, 'farmstead by a hill or mound', OE *hlāw* + *tūn*: **Lawton** Heref. & Worcs. *Lavtune* 1086 (DB). **Lawton, Church** Ches. *Lautune* 1086 (DB), *Church Laughton* 1331.

Laxay W. Isles (Lewis). '(Place by the) salmon river'. OScand. *lax* + *á*.

Laxfield Suffolk. *Laxefelda* 1086 (DB). 'Open land of a man called **Leaxa*'. OE pers. name + *feld*.

Laxton, 'estate associated with a man called **Leaxa*', OE pers. name + -*ing*- + *tūn*: **Laxton** E. R. Yorks. *Laxinton* 1086 (DB). **Laxton** Notts. *Laxintune* 1086 (DB).
However the following may have a slightly different meaning: **Laxton** Northants. *Lastone* 1086 (DB). '**Leaxa's* estate'. OE pers. name + *tūn*.

Laycock W. Yorks. *Lacoc* 1086 (DB). 'The small stream'. OE **lacuc*.

Layer Breton, *Layer de la Haye* & *Layer Marney* Essex. *Legra* 1086 (DB), *Leyre Bretoun* 1254, *Legra de Haya* 1236, *Leyre Marini* 1254. Probably originally a river-name *Leire* of Celtic origin. Distinguishing affixes from early possession by families called Breton, de Haia and de Marinni.

Layham Suffolk. *Hligham* c.995, *Leiham* 1086 (DB). 'Homestead with a shelter'. OE **hlīg* + *ham*.

Laytham E. R. Yorks. *Ladon* 1086 (DB). '(Place at) the barns'. OScand. *hlatha* in a dative plural form *hlathum*.

Layton, East & *Layton, West* N. Yorks. *Latton, Lastun* 1086 (DB). 'Leek enclosure, herb garden'. OE *lēac-tūn*.

Lazenby Red. & Cleve. *Lesingebi* 1086 (DB). 'Farmstead of the freedmen, or of a man called **Leysingr*'. OScand. *leysingi* or pers. name + *bý*.

Lazonby Cumbria. *Leisingebi* 1165. Identical in origin with the previous name.

Lea (river) Beds., Herts., Essex, *see* LEYTON.

Lea, '(place at) the wood or woodland clearing', OE *lēah*; examples include: **Lea** Derbys. *Lede* |*sic*| 1086 (DB), *Lea* c.1155. **Lea** Heref. & Worcs. *Lecce* |*sic*| 1086 (DB), *La Lee* 1219. **Lea** Lincs. *Lea* 1086 (DB). **Lea** Wilts. *Lia* 1190. **Lea Town** Lancs. *Lea* 1086 (DB).

Leabeg (*Liath Beag*) Offaly. 'Small grey place'.

Leach (river) Glos., *see* EASTLEACH.

Leaden Roding Essex, *see* RODING.

Leadenham Lincs. *Ledeneham* 1086 (DB). Probably 'homestead or village of a man called **Lēoda*'. OE pers. name (genitive -*n*) + *hām*.

Leadgate Durham. *Lidgate* 1590. OE *hlid-geat* 'a swing-gate'.

Leadhills S. Lan. '(Place by the) lead hills'. OE *lēad* + *hyll*. Leadmines.

Leadon (river) Glos., Heref. & Worcs., *see* HIGHLEADON.

Leafield Oxon. *La Felde* 1213. 'The open land'. OE *feld* with the OFrench definite article.

Leafin (*Liathmhuine*) Meath. 'Grey thicket'.

Leafonny (*Liathmhuine*) Sligo. 'Grey thicket'.

Leagrave Beds. *Littegraue* 1224. 'Light-coloured, or lightly wooded, grove'. OE *lēoht* + *grāf*.

Leahan (*Leathan*) Donegal. 'Broad space'.

Leahanmore (*Leathan Mór*) Donegal. 'Big broad space'.

Leake, '(place at) the brook', OScand. *lœkr*: **Leake** N. Yorks *Lec(h)e* 1086 (DB). **Leake, East** & **Leake, West**

Notts. *Lec(c)he* 1086 (DB). **Leake, Old** Lincs. *Leche* 1086 (DB).

Lealholm N. Yorks. *Lelun* 1086 (DB). '(Place among) the twigs or brushwood'. OE *lǣl* in a dative plural form *lǣlum*.

Leamington, 'farmstead on the River Leam', Celtic river-name (meaning 'elm river', or 'marshy river') + OE *tūn*: **Leamington Hastings** Warwicks. *Lunnitone* 1086 (DB), *Lemyngton Hasting* 1285. Manorial affix from the Hastinges family, here in the 13th cent. **Royal Leamington Spa** Warwicks. *Lamintone* 1086 (DB). The affix was granted by Queen Victoria in 1838, *Spa* referring to the medicinal springs here.

Leamlara (*Léim Lára*) Cork. 'Leap of the mare'.

Leap (*Léim*) Cork. 'Leap'.

Learmore (*Ladhar Mór*) Tyrone. 'Large fork'.

Learmount (*Ladhar*) Tyrone. 'Mount of the fork'.

Learmouth, East & *Learmouth, West* Northum. *Leuremue* 1177. 'Mouth of the stream where rushes grow'. OE *lǣfer* + *mūtha*.

Leasingham Lincs. *Leuesingham* 1086 (DB). 'Homestead of the family or followers of a man called Lēofsige'. OE pers. name + *-inga-* + *hām*.

Leatherhead Surrey. *Leodridan* c.880, *Leret |sic|* 1086 (DB). 'Grey ford'. Celtic *lēd* + *rïd*.

Leathley N. Yorks. *Ledelai* 1086 (DB). 'Woodland clearing on the slopes'. OE *hlith* (genitive plural *hleotha*) + *lēah*.

Leaton Shrops. *Letone* 1086 (DB). OE *tūn* 'farmstead' with an uncertain first element.

Leaveland Kent. *Levelant* 1086 (DB). 'Cultivated land of a man called Lēofa'. OE pers. name + *land*.

Leavening N. Yorks. *Ledlinghe |sic|* 1086 (DB), *Leyingges* 1242. Possibly '(settlement of) the family or followers of a man called Lēofhēah'. OE pers. name + *-ingas*.

Lebberston N. Yorks. *Ledbeztun* 1086 (DB). 'Farmstead of a man called Lēodbriht'. OE pers. name + *tūn*.

Lecale (*Leath Cathail*) Down. 'Cathal's portion'.

Lecarrow (*An Leithcheathrú*) Galway. 'The half quarter'.

Lechlade Glos. *Lecelade* 1086 (DB). Probably 'river-crossing near the River Leach'. River-name (from OE *lǣc(c)*, *lece* 'boggy stream') + *gelād*.

Leckanvy (*Leacán Mhaigh*) Mayo. 'Hillside of the plain'.

Leckaun (*An Leacán*) Sligo. 'The hillside'.

Leckford Hants. *Leahtforda* 947, *Lechtford* 1086 (DB). 'Ford at or over a channel'. OE *leaht + ford*.

Leckhampstead, 'homestead where leeks are grown', OE *lēac + hām-stede*: **Leckhampstead** Berks. *Lechamstede* 956–9, *Lecanestede* 1086 (DB). **Leckhampstead** Bucks. *Lechamstede* 1086 (DB).

Leckhampton Glos. *Lechametone* 1086 (DB). 'Home farm where leeks are grown'. OE *lēac + hām-tūn*.

Leckwith (*Lecwydd*) Card. *Leocwtha* c.1170. '(Place of) Helygwydd'. The pers. name is apparently that of a local saint.

Leconfield E. R. Yorks. *Lachinfeld* 1086 (DB). OE *feld* 'open land' with an uncertain first element, possibly a derivative of OE *lǣc(c)*. *lece* 'boggy stream'.

Lecwydd. *See* LECKWITH.

Ledburn Bucks. *Leteburn* 1212. 'Stream with a conduit, or by a cross-roads'. OE *(ge)lǣt(e) + burna*.

Ledbury Heref. & Worcs. *Liedeberge* 1086 (DB). Probably 'fortified place on the River Leadon'. Celtic river-name (*see* HIGHLEADON) + OE *burh* (dative *byrig*).

Ledsham Ches. *Levetesham* 1086 (DB). 'Homestead of a man called Lēofede'. OE pers. name + *hām*.

Ledsham W. Yorks. *Ledesham* c.1030, 1086 (DB). 'Homestead within the district of LEEDS'. OE *hām*.

Ledston W. Yorks. *Ledestune* 1086 (DB). 'Farmstead within the district of LEEDS'. OE *tūn*.

Ledwell Oxon. *Ledewelle* 1086 (DB). 'Spring or stream called the loud one'. OE *hlȳde + wella*.

Lee, '(place at) the wood or woodland clearing', OE *lēah*; examples include: **Lee** Gtr. London. *Lee* 1086 (DB). **Lee** Hants. *Ly* 1236. **Lee** Shrops. *Lee* 1327. **Lee Brockhurst** Shrops. *Lege* 1086 (DB), *Leye under Brochurst* 1285. Affix from a nearby place, 'wooded hill frequented by badgers', OE *brocc + hyrst*. **Lee on the Solent** Hants. *Lie* 1212. *See* SOLENT.

Lee (*Laoi*) (river) Cork. Perhaps water.

Leebotwood Shrops. *Botewde* 1086 (DB), *Lega in Bottewode* c.1170–6. 'Wood of a man called Botta', OE pers. name + *wudu*, with the later addition of a place-name Lee from OE *lēah* 'clearing'.

Leece Cumbria. *Lies* 1086 (DB). Probably from Celtic **liss* a hall, a court, the chief house in a district'.

Leeds Kent. *Esledes* 1086 (DB), *Hledes* c.1100. Possibly from a stream-name, OE **hlȳde* 'the loud one'.

Leeds W. Yorks. *Loidis* 731, *Ledes* 1086 (DB). A Celtic name, originally *Lādenses*, meaning 'people living by the strongly flowing river'.

Leeg (*Liag*) Monaghan. 'Pillar stone'.

Leek Staffs. *Lec* 1086 (DB). '(Place at) the brook'. OScand. *lœkr*.

Leek (*Liag*) Monaghan. 'Pillar stone'.

Leek Wootton Warwicks., *see* WOOTTON.

Leeke (*Liag*) Antrim, Derry. 'Pillar stone'.

Leeming N. Yorks. *Leming* 12th cent. Named from Leeming Beck, a river-name possibly of OE origin and meaning 'bright stream'.

Leenaun (*An Líonán*) Galway. 'The shallow sea bed'.

Lees Gtr. Manch. *The Leese* 1604. 'The woods or woodland clearings'. OE *lēah* (plural *lēas*).

Lefinn (*Liathmhuine*) Donegal. 'Grey thicket'.

Legananny (*Liagán Áine*) Down. *Ballyleganangh* 1609. 'Pillar stone of Áine'. The stone in question is the nearby Legananny Dolmen.

Legbourne Lincs. *Lecheburne* 1086 (DB). Probably 'boggy stream'. OE **lǣc(c)*, **lece + burna*.

Leggamaddy (*Lag an Mhadaidh*) Down. *Liggamaddy* 1755. 'Hollow of the dog'.

Leggs (*Na Laig*) Fermanagh. 'The hollows'.

Legland (*Leithghleann*) Tyrone. *Legglan* 1661. 'Side of the valley'.

Legoniel (*Lag an Aoil*) Antrim. *Ballylagaile* 1604. 'Hollow of the lime'. There are several disused lime quarries locally.

Legsby Lincs. *Lagesbi* 1086 (DB). 'Farmstead or village of a man called Leggr'. OScand. pers. name + *bý*.

Legvoy (*Lec Mhagh*) Roscommon. 'Plain full of flagstones'.

Lehinch (*Leath Inse*) Clare. 'Peninsula'. The current Irish name is *An Leacht*, 'the grave'.

Leicester Leics. *Ligera ceaster* early 10th cent., *Ledecestre* 1086 (DB). 'Roman town of the people called Ligore'. Tribal name (of uncertain origin and meaning) + OE *ceaster*. **Leicestershire** (OE *scīr* 'district') is first referred to in the 11th cent.

Leigh, a common name, '(place at) the wood or woodland clearing', OE *lēah*; examples include: **Leigh** Gtr. Manch. *Legh* 1276. **Leigh** Heref. & Worcs. *Beornotheslcah* 972, *Lege* 1086 (DB). 'Belonging to a man called Beornnōth' in the 10th cent. spelling. **Leigh** Kent. *Lega* c.1100. **Leigh** Surrey. *Leghe* late 12th cent. **Leigh, Abbots** N. Som. *Lege* 1086 (DB). Affix from its early possession by the Abbot of St Augustine's Bristol. **Leigh, Bessels** Oxon. *Leie* 1086 (DB), *Bessilles Lee* 1538. Manorial affix from the Besyles family, here in the 15th cent. **Leigh, North** & **Leigh, South** Oxon. *Lege* 1086 (DB), *Northleg* 1225, *Suthleye* early 13th cent. **Leigh-on-Sea** Essex. *Legra* |*sic*| 1086 (DB), *Legha* 1226. **Leigh Sinton** Heref. & Worcs., *see* SINTON. **Leigh-upon-Mendip** Somerset. *Leage* c.1100. *See* MENDIP HILLS.

Leighlin (*Leithghleann*) Carlow. 'Side of a valley'.

Leighmoney (*Liathmhuine*) Cork. 'Grey thicket'.

Leighs, Great & *Leighs, Little* Essex. *Lega* 1086 (DB), *Leyes* 1271. OE *lēah* 'wood, woodland clearing'.

Leighterton Glos. *Lettrintone* 12th cent. 'Farmstead where lettuce grows'. OE *leahtric* + *tūn*.

Leighton, 'leek or garlic enclosure, herb garden', OE *lēac-tūn*: **Leighton** Shrops. *Lestone* 1086 (DB). **Leighton Bromswold** Cambs. *Lectone* 1086 (DB), *Letton super Bruneswald* 1254. Affix is from a nearby place, 'high forest-land of a man called Brūn', OE pers. name + *weald*. **Leighton Buzzard** Beds. *Lestone* 1086 (DB), *Letton Busard* 1254. Manorial affix is from a family called Busard, no doubt landowners here in the 13th cent.

Leinster (*Cúige Laighean*) (the province). *Laynster* 1515. 'District of the Lagin people'. OScand. possessive *s* + Irish *tír*. The tribal name may mean 'spear'.

Leinthall Earls & *Leinthall Starkes* Heref. & Worcs. *Lentehale* 1086 (DB), *Leintall Comites* 1275, *Leinthale Starkare* 13th cent. 'Nook of land by the River *Lent*'. Lost Celtic river-name (meaning 'torrent, stream') + OE *halh*. Manorial affixes from early possession by an earl (Latin *comitis* 'of the earl') and a man called Starker.

Leintwardine Heref. & Worcs. *Lenteurde* 1086 (DB). 'Enclosure on the River *Lent*'. Lost Celtic river-name (see previous name) + *worth* (replaced by *worthign*).

Leire Leics. *Legre* 1086 (DB). Probably an ancient pre-English river-name for the small tributary of the River Soar on which the place stands.

Leiston Suffolk. *Leistuna* 1086 (DB). Possibly 'farmstead near a beacon-fire'. OE *lēg* + *tūn*.

Leith Edin. *Inverlet* c.1130, *Inverlethe* c.1315. Originally Inverleith, mouth of the river Leith. Gaelic *inbhir*, 'river mouth' + *Lekta* 'dripping (water)'.

Leitrim (*Liatroim*) Down, Leitrim. 'Grey ridge'.

Leixlip Kildare. 'Salmon leap'. OScand. *leax* + *hlaup*. The equivalent Irish name is *Léim an Bhradáin*.

Lelant Cornwall. *Lananta* c.1170. 'Church-site of Anta'. Cornish **lann* + female saint's name.

Lelley E. R. Yorks. *Lelle* 1246. 'Wood or clearing where twigs or brushwood are found'. OE *lǣl* + *lēah*.

Lemanaghan (*Liath Mancháin*) Offaly. 'Grey land of Manchán'.

Lemington, Lower Glos. *Limentone* 1086 (DB). Probably 'farmstead near a stream called *Limen*'. Lost Celtic river-name (meaning 'elm river') + OE *tūn*.

Lemlara (*Léim Lára*) Cork. 'Leap of the mare'.

Lemybrien (*Léim Uí Bhriain*) Waterford. 'Leap of Ó Briain'.

Lenaderg (*Láithreach Dhearg*) Down. *Laireachtdyke* 1427. 'Red site'.

Lenadoon Point (*Léana Dúin*) Sligo. 'Meadow of the fort'.

Lench, from OE **hlenc* 'an extensive hill-slope', originally the name of a district and giving name to: **Lench, Abbots** Heref. & Worcs. *Abeleng* 1086 (DB). Manorial affix originally from possession by a man with the OE pers. name *Abba*. **Lench, Atch** Heref. & Worcs. *Achelenz* 1086 (DB). Manorial affix from possession by a man with the OE pers. name *Ǣcci*. **Lench, Church** Heref. & Worcs. *Lench* 9th cent., *Chirichlench* 1054. Affix is OE *cirice* 'church'. **Lench, Rous** Heref. & Worcs. *Lenc* 983, *Biscopesleng* 1086 (DB), *Rous Lench* 1445. Manorial affix from the Rous family, here in the 14th cent. (held by the Bishop of Worcester in 1086).

Lendrick Perth. *Lennerick* 1669. '(Place by the) glade'. OWelsh *lannerch*.

Lene, Lough (*Loch Léibhinn*) Westmeath. 'Léibhinn's lake'.

Lenham Kent. *Leanaham* 858, *Lerham* |*sic*| 1086 (DB). 'Homestead or village of a man called **Lēana*'. OE pers. name + *hām*. The river-name **Len** is a 'back-formation' from the place-name.

Lennoxtown E. Dunb. 'Lennox's town'. The town arose in the 1780s and took its name from the family of the earls and dukes of *Lennox*, whose title comes from the ancient territory of *Lennox* (Gaelic *leamhanach*, 'abounding in elms').

Lenton Lincs. *Lofintun* c.1067, *Lavintone* 1086 (DB). Probably 'estate associated with a man called Lēofa'. OE pers. name + *-ing-* + *tūn*.

Lenwade Norfolk. *Langewade* 1199. 'Ford crossed by a lane'. OE *lanu* + *gewæd*.

Leny (*Léana*) Westmeath. 'Meadow'.

Leominster Heref. & Worcs. *Leomynster* 10th cent., *Leominstre* 1086 (DB). 'Church in *Leon*'. Old Celtic name for the district (meaning 'at the streams') + OE *mynster*.

Leonard Stanley Glos., *see* STANLEY.

Leppington N. Yorks. *Lepinton* 1086 (DB). 'Estate associated with a man called Leppa'. OE pers. name + *-ing-* + *tūn*.

Lepton W. Yorks. *Leptone* 1086 (DB). 'Farmstead on a hill-slope'. OE **hlēp* + *tūn*.

Lerrig (*Leirg*) Kerry. 'Slope'.

Lerwick Shet. *Lerwick* 1625. 'Mud bay'. OScand. *leirr* + *vík*.

Lesbury Northum. *Lechesbiri* c.1190. 'Fortified house of the leech or physician'. OE *lǣce* + *burh* (dative *byrig*).

Leslie Aber. *Lesslyn* c.1180, *Lescelin* c.1232. A difficult name which was transferred to Fife.

Lesmahagow S. Lan. *Lesmahagu* c.1130. 'Enclosure of beloved Fechin'. Gaelic *leas*. The saint's name is in the affectionate diminutive form *Mo-Fhegu* (Gaelic *mo*, 'my').

Lesnewth Cornwall. *Lisniwen |sic|* 1086 (DB), *Lisneweth* 1201. 'New court'. Cornish **lys* + *nowydh*.

Lessingham Norfolk. *Losincham* 1086 (DB). Possibly 'homestead of the family or followers of a man called Lēofsige'. OE pers. name + *-inga-* + *hām*.

Letchworth Herts. *Leceworde* 1086. Probably 'enclosure that can be locked'. OE **lycce* + *worth*.

Letcombe Bassett & *Letcombe Regis* Oxon. *Ledecumbe* 1086 (DB). 'Valley of a man called Lēoda'. OE pers. name + *cumb*. Distinguishing affixes from early possession by the Bassett family and by the Crown.

Letheringham Suffolk. *Letheringaham* 1086 (DB). Probably 'homestead of the family or followers of a man called Lēodhere'. OE pers. name + *-inga-* + *hām*.

Letheringsett Norfolk. *Leringaseta* 1086 (DB). Probably 'dwelling or fold of the family or followers of a man called Lēodhere'. OE pers. name + *-inga-* + *(ge)set*.

Letter (*Leitir*) Fermanagh, Kerry. 'Hillside'.

Letterbarrow (*Leitir Barra*) Donegal. 'Top hillside'.

Letterbreen (*Leitir Bhrúin*) Fermanagh. *Letterbreen* 1751. Possibly 'hillside of the fairy fort'.

Letterbrick (*Leitir Bruic*) Mayo. 'Hillside of the badger'.

Letterfearn Highland. *Letterfearn* 1509. 'Hill slope growing with alders'. Gaelic *leitir* + *fearn*.

Letterfinnish (*Leitir Fionnuisce*) Kerry. 'Hillside of bright water'.

Lettergesh (*Leitir Geis*) Galway. 'Hillside of the taboo'.

Letterkenny (*Leitir Ceanainn*) Donegal. *Latterkeny* 1685. 'Hillside of the white top'.

Lettermacaward (*Leitir Mhic an Bhaird*) Donegal. *Lettermacaward* 1608. 'Mac an Bard's hillside'.

Lettermore (*Leitir Móir*) Galway. 'Big hillside'.

Lettermullan (*Leitir Mealláin*) Galway. 'Hill slope of Meallán'.

Letternadarriv (*Leitir na dTarbh*) Kerry. 'Hillside of the bulls'.

Letterston (*Treletert*) Pemb. *Villa Letardi* 1230, *Lettardston* 1332. 'Letard's farm'. OGerman pers. name + OE *tūn* (Welsh *tref*). The Welsh name translates the English.

Letton, probably 'leek enclosure, herb garden', OE *lēactūn*: **Letton** Heref. & Worcs., near Eardisley. *Letune* 1086 (DB). **Letton** Heref. & Worcs., near Walford. *Lectune* 1086 (DB).

Letwell S. Yorks. *Lettewelle* c.1150. Possibly 'spring or stream with an obstructed flow'. ME *lette* + OE *wella*.

Leuchars Fife. *Locres* 1300. '(Place of) rushes'. Gaelic *luachar* (genitive *luachair*) + English plural *-s*.

Levally (*Leathbhaile*) Galway, Mayo. 'Half townland'.

Leven (river), Stock. on T., *see* KIRKLEVINGTON.

Leven E. R. Yorks. *Leuene* 1086 (DB). Probably originally the name of the stream here, a lost Celtic river-name possibly meaning 'smooth one'.

Leven Fife. *Levin* c.1535. '(Place on the) River Leven'. The river name means 'elm river' (Gaelic *leamhain*).

Levens Cumbria. *Lefuenes* 1086 (DB). Probably 'promontory of a man called Lēofa'. OE pers. name (genitive *-n*) + *næss*.

Levenshulme Gtr. Manch. *Lewyneshulm* 1246. 'Island of a man called Lēofwine'. OE pers. name + OScand. *holmr*.

Lever, Darcy & *Lever, Little* Gtr. Manch. *Parua Lefre* 1212, *Darcye Lever* 1590. 'Place where rushes grow'. OE *læfer*. Distinguishing affixes are from possession by the D'Arcy family, here c.1500, and from Latin *parva* 'little'.

Leverington Cambs. *Leverington* c.1130. 'Estate associated with a man called Lēofhere'. OE pers. name + *-ing-* + *tūn*.

Leverton Lincs. *Leuretune* 1086 (DB). Probably 'farmstead where rushes grow'. OE *læfer* + *tūn*.

Leverton, North & *Leverton, South* Notts. *Legretone* 1086 (DB). Probably 'farmstead on a stream called *Legre*'. Celtic river-name (of uncertain meaning) + OE *tūn*.

Levington Suffolk. *Leuentona* 1086 (DB). Probably 'farmstead of a man called Lēofa', OE pers. name (genitive *-n*) + *tūn*.

Levisham N. Yorks. *Leuecen |sic|* 1086 (DB), *Leuezham* c.1230. Probably 'homestead or village of a man called Lēofgēat', OE pers. name + *hām*.

Lew Oxon. *Hlæwe* 984, *Lewa* 1086 (DB). '(Place at) the mound or tumulus'. OE *hlæw*.

Lewannick Cornwall. *Lanwenuc* c.1125. 'Church-site of Gwenek'. Cornish **lann* + pers. name.

Lewes E. Sussex. *Læwas* 961, *Lewes* 1086 (DB). Probably 'the burial mounds', from OE *hlæw* in a plural form. Other early spellings like (*to*) *Læwe* in the early 10th cent. Burghal Hidage show alternation with a dative singular form.

Lewis (island) W. Isles. *Leodus* c.1100, *Leoghuis* 1449. Pre-Norse name of unknown linguistic origin.

Lewisham Gtr. London. *Levesham* 1086 (DB). 'Homestead or village of a man called *Lēofsa*'. OE pers. name + *hām*. Also referred to earlier in the phrase *Liofshema mearc* 862 'boundary of the people of Lewisham'.

Lewknor Oxon. *Leofecanoran* 990, *Levecanole* |*sic*| 1086 (DB). 'Hill-slope of a man called *Lēofeca*'. OE pers. name (genitive -*n*) + *ōra*.

Lewtrenchard Devon. *Lewe* 1086 (DB), *Lyu Trencharde* 1261. Originally the name of the river here, a Celtic river-name meaning 'bright one'. Manorial affix from the Trenchard family, here in the 13th cent.

Lexham, East & *Lexham, West* Norfolk. *Lecesham* 1086 (DB). 'Homestead or village of the leech or physician'. OE *lǣce* + *hām*.

Leybourne Kent. *Lillanburna* 10th cent., *Leleburne* 1086 (DB). 'Stream of a man called *Lylla*'. OE pers. name + *burna*.

Leyburn N. Yorks. *Leborne* 1086 (DB). OE *burna* 'stream', possibly with *hlēg* 'shelter'.

Leyland Lancs. *Lailand* 1086 (DB). 'Estate with untilled ground'. OE *lǣge* + *land*.

Leysdown on Sea Kent. *Legesdun* c.1100. Probably 'hill with a beacon-fire'. OE *lēg* + *dūn*.

Leyton Gtr. London. *Lugetune* c.1050, *Leintune* 1086 (DB). 'Farmstead on the River Lea'. Celtic river-name (possibly meaning 'light river') + OE *tūn*.

Lezant Cornwall. *Lansant* c.1125. 'Church-site of Sant'. Cornish *lann* + pers. name.

Liafin (*Liathmhuine*) Donegal. 'Grey thicket'.

Libberton S. Lan. *Libertun* c.1186. Probably 'barley farm on a hillside'. OE *hlith* + *bere-tūn*.

Liberton Edin. *Libertun* 1128. Probably 'barley farm on a hillside'. OE *hlith* + *bere-tūn*.

Lichfield Staffs. *Licitfelda* c.710–20. 'Open land near *Letocetum*'. OE *feld* added to a Celtic place-name meaning 'grey wood'.

Lickeen (*Licín*) Kildare. 'Small flagstone'.

Lickowen (*Leic Eoghain*) Cork. 'Eogha's flagstone'.

Liddesdale Sc. Bord. *Lidelesdale* 1179. 'Valley of the River Liddel'. The river name means 'valley of the River Lid', itself meaning 'loud one' (OE *hlȳde* + *dæl*).

Liddington Wilts. *Lidentune* 940, *Ledentone* 1086 (DB). 'Farmstead on the noisy stream'. OE *hlȳde* + *tūn*.

Lidgate Suffolk. *Litgata* 1086 (DB). '(Place at) the swing-gate'. OE *hlid-geat*.

Lidlington Beds. *Litincletone* 1086 (DB). 'Farmstead of the family or followers of a man called *Lȳtel*'. OE pers. name + -*inga*- + *tūn*.

Lifford (*Leifear*) Donegal. (*caislén*) *Leithbhir* 1527. 'Side of the water'.

Lifton Devon. *Liwtune* c.880, *Listone* |*sic*| 1086 (DB). 'Farmstead on the River Lew'. Celtic river-name (see LEWTRENCHARD) + OE *tūn*.

Lighthorne Warwicks. *Listecorne* |*sic*| 1086 (DB), *Litthethurne* 1235. 'Light-coloured thorn-tree'. OE *lēoht* + *thyrne*.

Lilbourne Northants. *Lilleburne* 1086 (DB). 'Stream of a man called Lilla'. OE pers. name + *burna*.

Lilburn Northum. *Lilleburn* 1170. Identical in origin with the previous name.

Lilleshall Shrops. *Linleshelle* |*sic*| 1086 (DB), *Lilleshull* 1162. 'Hill of a man called Lill'. OE pers. name + *hyll*.

Lilley Herts. *Linleia* 1086 (DB). 'Woodland clearing where flax is grown'. OE *līn* + *lēah*.

Lilling, East & *Lilling, West* N. Yorks. *Lilinge* 1086 (DB). '(Settlement of) the family or followers of a man called Lilla'. OE pers. name + -*ingas*.

Lillingstone Dayrell & *Lillingstone Lovell* Bucks. *Lillingestan* 1086 (DB). *Litlingestan Daireli* 1166. 'Boundary stone of the family or followers of a man called *Lȳtel*'. OE pers. name + -*inga*- + *stān*. Manorial affixes from early possession by the Dayrell and Lovell families.

Lillington Dorset. *Lilletone* 1166, *Lullinton* 1200. 'Estate associated with a man called *Lylla*'. OE pers. name + -*ing*- + *tūn*.

Lillington Warwicks. *Lillintone* 1086 (DB). 'Estate associated with a man called Lilla'. OE pers. name + -*ing*- + *tūn*.

Lilstock Somerset. *Lulestoch* 1086 (DB). 'Outlying farmstead or hamlet of a man called *Lylla*'. OE pers. name + *stoc*.

Lim (river) Devon, Dorset, see LYME REGIS.

Limavady (*Léim an Mhadaidh*) Derry. (i) *Leim an Mhadaidh* 1542. 'Leap of the dog'. The present town was founded in the early 17th cent. under the name *Newtown Limavady*.

Limber, Great Lincs. *Lindbeorhge* c.1067, *Lindberge* 1086 (DB). 'Hill where lime-trees grow'. OE *lind* + *beorg*.

Limbury Beds. *Lygeanburg* late 9th cent. 'Stronghold on the River Lea'. Celtic river-name (see LEYTON) + OE *burh* (dative *byrig*).

Limehouse Gtr. London. *Le Lymhostes* 1367. 'The lime oasts or kilns'. OE *līm* + *āst*.

Limerick (*Luimneach*) Limerick. *Luimneach* 11th cent. 'Bare area'.

Limpenhoe Norfolk. *Limpeho* 1086 (DB). 'Hill-spur of a man called *Limpa*'. OE pers. name (genitive -*n*) + *hōh*.

Limpley Stoke Wilts., see STOKE.

Limpsfield Surrey. *Limenesfelde* 1086 (DB). 'Open land at *Limen*'. OE *feld* added to a Celtic place-name meaning 'elm wood'.

Linby Notts. *Lidebi* |*sic*| 1086 (DB), *Lindebi* 1163. 'Farmstead or village where lime-trees grow'. OScand. *lind* + *bȳ*.

Linchmere W. Sussex. *Wlenchemere* 1186. 'Pool of a man called *Wlenca*'. OE pers. name + *mere*.

Lincoln Lincs. *Lindon* c.150, *Lindum colonia* late 7th cent., *Lincolia* 1086 (DB). 'Roman colony (for retired legionaries) by the pool', referring to the broad pool in the River Witham. Celtic **lindo-* + Latin *colonia*. **Lincolnshire** (OE *scīr* 'district') is first referred to in the 11th cent.

Lindal in Furness Cumbria. *Lindale* c.1220. 'Valley where lime-trees grow'. OScand. *lind* + *dalr*. For the old district name Furness, *see* BARROW IN FURNESS.

Lindale Cumbria. *Lindale* 1246. Identical in origin with the previous name.

Lindfield W. Sussex. *Lindefeldia* c.765. 'Open land where lime-trees grow'. OE *linden* + *feld*.

Lindisfarne Northum. *Lindisfarnae* c.700. Possibly 'island of the travellers from LINDSEY', from OE *fara* (genitive plural *-ena*) + *ēg*. Also called HOLY ISLAND.

Lindrick (old district) Notts., *see* CARLTON IN LINDRICK.

Lindridge Heref. & Worcs. *Lynderycge* 11th cent. 'Ridge where lime-trees grow'. OE *lind* + *hrycg*.

Lindsell Essex. *Lindesela* 1086 (DB). 'Dwelling among lime-trees'. OE *lind* + *sele*.

Lindsey Lincs. (*prouincia*) *Lindissi* c.704–14, *Lindesi* 1086 (DB). Ancient district name, probably 'island, or dry ground in marsh, of the tribe called the Lindēs', from OE *īg*, *ēg* added to *Lindēs* ' the people of Lincoln or of the pool', *see* LINCOLN.

Lindsey Suffolk. *Lealeseia* c.1095. 'Island, or dry ground in marsh, of a man called **Lelli*'. OE pers. name + *ēg*. **Lindsey Tye** contains dialect *tye* 'a large common pasture'.

Linford, Great Bucks. *Linforde* 1086 (DB). Probably 'ford where maple-trees grow'. OE *hlyn* + *ford*.

Lingen Heref. & Worcs. *Lingen* 704–9, *Lingham* 1086 (DB). Probably originally the name of the brook here, perhaps a Celtic name meaning 'clear stream'.

Lingfield Surrey. *Leangafelda* 9th cent. Probably 'open land of the dwellers in the wood or clearing'. OE *lēah* + *-inga-* + *feld*.

Lingwood Norfolk. *Lingewode* 1199. 'Wood on a bank or slope'. OE *hlinc* + *wudu*.

Linkenholt Hants. *Linchehou* |*sic*| 1086 (DB), *Lynkeholte* c.1145. 'Wood by the banks or ledges'. OE *hlinc*, **hlincen* + *holt*.

Linkinhorne Cornwall. *Lankinhorn* c.1175. 'Church-site of a man called Kenhoarn'. Cornish **lann* + pers. name.

Linley, probably 'lime-tree wood or clearing', OE *lind* + *lēah*: **Linley** Shrops. near Bridgnorth. *Linlega* c.1135, *Lindleg* 1204. **Linley** Shrops. near Norbury. *Linlega* c.1150, *Lindele* 1209.

Linlithgow W. Loth. *Linlidcu* c.1138. '(Place by) Linlithgow Loch'. The name of the loch means 'lake in the damp hollow' (OWelsh **linn* + Welsh *llaith* + *cau*).

Linns (*Lan*) Louth. 'Church'.

Linshiels Northum. *Lynsheles* 1292. Probably 'shieling(s) where lime-trees grow'. OE *lind* + **scēla*.

Linslade Beds. *Hlincgelad* 966, *Lincelada* 1086 (DB). 'River-crossing near a bank'. OE *hlinc* + *gelād*.

Linstead Magna & *Linstead Parva* Suffolk. *Linestede* 1086 (DB). 'Place where flax is grown, or where maple-trees grow'. OE *līn* or *hlyn* + *stede*. Affixes are Latin *magna* 'great' and *parva* 'little'.

Linstock Cumbria. *Linstoc* 1212. 'Outlying farmstead or hamlet where flax is grown'. OE *līn* + *stoc*.

Linthwaite W. Yorks. *Lindthait* late 12th cent. 'Clearing where flax is grown, or where lime-trees grow'. OScand. *lín* or *lind* + *thveit*.

Linton, usually 'farmstead where flax is grown', OE *līn* + *tūn*; examples include: **Linton** Cambs. *Lintune* 1008, *Lintone* 1086 (DB). **Linton** Derbys. *Lintone* 942, *Linctune* |*sic*| 1086 (DB). **Linton** Heref. & Worcs., near Ross. *Lintune* 1086 (DB). **Linton** N. Yorks. *Lipton* |*sic*| 1086 (DB), *Linton* 12th cent. Alternatively the first element may be OE *hlynn* 'rushing stream'. **Linton** W. Yorks. *Lintone* 1086 (DB). **Linton-on-Ouse** N. Yorks. *Luctone* |*sic*| 1086 (DB), *Linton* 1176. For the river-name, *see* OUSEBURN.
    However the following has a quite different origin: **Linton** Kent. *Lilintuna* c.1100. 'Estate associated with a man called Lill or Lilla'. OE pers. name + *-ing-* + *tūn*.

Linwood 'lime-tree wood', OE *lind* + *wudu*: **Linwood** Hants. *Lindwude* 1200. **Linwood** Lincs., near Market Rasen. *Lindude* 1086 (DB).

Liphook Hants. *Leophok* 1364. Probably 'angle of land by the deer-leap or steep slope'. OE *hlīep* + *hōc*.

Lisacul (*Lios an Choill*) Roscommon. 'Fort of the wood'.

Lisbane (*Lios Bán*) Down, Limerick. 'White fort'.

Lisbeg (*Lios Beag*) Galway. 'Little fort'.

Lisbellaw (*Lios Béal Átha*) Fermanagh. 'Fort of the mouth of the ford'.

Lisboduff (*Lios Bó Dubh*) Cavan. *Lisbodowe* 1610. 'Fort of the black cows'.

Lisboy (*Lios Buí*) Antrim, Cork, Down, etc. 'Yellow fort'.

Lisburn Antrim. *Lysnecarvagh* 1683. The first element is probably from the earlier name *Lisnagarvey*, Irish *Lios na gCearrbhach*, 'fort of the gamblers'. The second element is dubiously derived from the burning of the town and castle in the siege of 1641.

Liscannor (*Lios Ceannúir*) Clare. 'Fort of Ceannúr'.

Liscard Mersey. *Lisnekarke* c.1260. 'Court at the rock'. Celtic **līs* + **en* 'the' + **carreg*.

Liscarney (*Lios Cearnaigh*) Mayo. 'Carnach's fort'.

Liscarroll (*Lios Cearúill*) Cork. 'Fort of Cearúll'.

Liscloon (*Lios Claon*) Tyrone. *Liscleene* 1661. 'Sloping fort'.

Liscolman (*Lios Cholmáin*) Antrim. *Slaightcolminan* 1669. 'Colmán's fort'.

Lisdeen (*Lios Duibhinn*) Clare. 'Fort of the chief'.

Lisdoonvarna (*Lios Dúin Bhearna*) Clare. 'Fort of the gap'.

Lisdowney (*Lios Dúnadhaigh*) Kilkenny. 'Fort of Dúnadhach'.

Lisduff (*Lios Dubh*) Cavan, Mayo. 'Black fort'.

Lisgoole (*Lios Gabhail*) Fermanagh. 'Fort of the fork'.

Liskeard Cornwall. *Lys Cerruyt c.*1010, *Liscarret* 1086 (DB). Probably 'court of a man called Kerwyd'. Cornish **lys* + pers. name.

Lislea (*Lios Liath*) Armagh, Derry. 'Grey fort'.

Lislevane (*Lios Leamháin*) Cork. 'Elm fort'.

Lismacaffry (*Lios Mhic Gofraidh*) Westmeath. 'Fort of Mac Gofraidh'.

Lismahon (*Lios Mócháin*) Down. 'Móchán's fort'.

Lismore (*Lios Mór*) Waterford. 'Big fort'.

Lismoyney (*Lios Maighne*) Westmeath. 'Fort of the precinct'.

Lisnacask (*Lios na Cásca*) Westmeath. 'Easter fort'.

Lisnacree (*Lios na Crí*) Down. *Lisnechrehy* 1613. 'Fort of the boundary'.

Lisnadill (*Lios na Daille*) Armagh. *Lisnedolle* 1609. 'Fort of the blindness'.

Lisnagade (*Lios na gCéad*) Down. 'Fort of the hundreds'.

Lisnageer (*Lios na gCaor*) Cavan. 'Fort of the berries'.

Lisnagelvin (*Lios na nGealbhán*) Derry. *Lisnegellwan* 1663. 'Fort of the sparrows'.

Lisnagry (*Lios na Graí*) Limerick. 'Fort of the stud'.

Lisnakill (*Lios na Cille*) Waterford. 'Fort of the church'.

Lisnalinchy (*Lios Uí Loingsigh*) Antrim. 'Fort of Ó Loingseach'.

Lisnalong (*Lios na Long*) Monaghan. 'Fort of the boats'.

Lisnamuck (*Lios na Muc*) Derry. *Lisnamuc c.*1834. 'Fort of the pigs'.

Lisnarrick (*Lios na nDaróg*) Fermanagh. *Lisnarrogue* 1659. 'Fort of the oaks'.

Lisnaskea (*Lios na Scéithe*) Fermanagh. (*ag*) *Scéith Ghabhra* 1589. 'Fort of the shield'. The final element of the name, the genitive form of Irish *sciath*, 'shield', is from *Sciath Ghabhra*, the name of the inauguration site of the Maguires, perhaps understood as 'fortress of the (white) horses'.

Lisnastrean (*Lios na Srian*) Down. *Ballelisneshrean* 1623. 'Fort of the bridles'.

Lispole (*Lios Póil*) Kerry. 'Fort of the pool'.

Lisrodden (*Lios Rodáin*) Antrim. *Ballylessraddan* 1605. 'Rodán's fort'.

Lisroe (*Lios Ruadh*) Clare, Cork, Kerry, etc. 'Red fort'.

Lisronagh (*Lios Ruanach*) Tyrone. 'Seal fort'.

Lisryan (*Lios Riáin*) Longford. 'Rián's fort'.

Liss Hants. *Lis* 1086 (DB). Celtic **liss* 'a court, chief house in a district'.

Lissacreasig (*Lios an Chraosaigh*) Cork. 'Fort of the glutton'.

Lissalway (*Lios Sealbhaigh*) Roscommon. 'Fort of Sealbhach'.

Lissan (*Leasán*) Tyrone. *Leassan* 1455. 'Little fort'.

Lissaniska (*Lios an Uisce*) Cork, Kerry, Limerick. 'Fort of the water'.

Lissanisky (*Lios an Uisce*) Cork, Roscommon, Tipperary. 'Fort of the water'.

Lissardagh (*Lios Ardachaidh*) Cork. 'Fort of the high field'.

Lissatava (*Lios an tSamhaidh*) Mayo. 'Fort of the sorrel'.

Lisselton (*Lios Eiltín*) Kerry. 'Fort of the little doe'.

Lissett E. R. Yorks. *Lessete* 1086 (DB). Probably 'dwelling near the pasture-land'. OE *læs* + (*ge*)*set*.

Lissinagroagh (*Lisín na gCruach*) Sligo. 'Little fort of the ridges'.

Lissington Lincs. *Lessintone* 1086 (DB). Probably 'estate associated with a man called Lēofsige'. OE pers. name + *-ing-* + *tūn*.

Lissue (*Lios Aedha*) Antrim. 'Aedh's fort'.

Lissycasey (*Lios Uí Chathasaigh*) Clare. 'Ó Cathasaigh's fort'.

Listooder (*Lios an tSudáire*) Down. *Balle-Listowdrie* 1623. 'Fort of the tanner'.

Listowel (*Lios Tuathail*) Kerry. 'Fort of Tuathal'.

Litcham Norfolk. *Licham* 1086 (DB). Possibly 'homestead or village with an enclosure'. OE **lycce* + *hām*.

Litchborough Northants. *Liceberge* 1086 (DB). Probably 'hill with an enclosure'. OE **lycce* + *beorg*.

Litchfield Hants. *Liveselle* |sic| 1086 (DB), *Lieueselva* 1168. Possibly 'shelf of land with a shelter'. OE **hlīf* + *scelf* or *scylf*.

Litherland Mersey. *Liderlant* 1086 (DB). 'Cultivated land on a slope'. OScand. *hlíth* (genitive *-ar*) + *land*.

Litlington Cambs. *Litlingeton* 1183, *Lidlingtone* 1086 (DB). 'Farmstead of the family or followers of a man called Lȳ*tel'. OE pers. name + *-inga-* + *tūn*.

Litlington E. Sussex. *Litlinton* 1191. 'Little farmstead' from OE *lȳtel* (dative *-an*) + *tūn*, or 'farmstead associated with a man called **Lȳtel(a)*' from OE pers. name + *-ing-* + *tūn*.

Little as affix, *see* main name, e.g. for **Little Abington** (Cambs.) *see* ABINGTON.

Little Bridge Antrim. *Little bridge* 1836. The 'little bridge' over the Lissan Water here is so called by contrast with a 'big bridge' to the south.

Little Cumbrae. See CUMBRAE.

Little England Beyond Wales (district) Pemb. *Ynglond be yond Walys* 1519, *Little England beyond Wales* 1594. The southern part of Pembrokeshire has been chiefly English-speaking since the Viking invasion of the 9th cent.

Little Haven Pemb. *the Lytel hauen* 1578. 'Little harbour'. OE *hæfen*. *Little* distinguishes the place from nearby BROAD HAVEN.

Little Mancot. See BIG MANCOT.

Little Minch. See MINCH.

Littleborough, 'little fort or stronghold', OE *lȳtel* + *burh*: **Littleborough** Gtr. Manch. *Littlebrough* 1577. **Littleborough** Notts. *Litelburg* 1086 (DB).

Littlebourne Kent. *Littelburne* 696, *Liteburne* 1086 (DB). 'Little estate on the river called *Burna*' (from OE *burna* 'stream' referring to the Little Stour), with OE *lȳtel*.

Littlebredy Dorset, *see* BREDY.

Littlebury Essex. *Lytlanbyrig* c.1000, *Litelbyria* 1086 (DB). 'Little fort or stronghold'. OE *lȳtel* + *burh* (dative *byrig*).

Littledean Glos. *Dene* 1086 (DB), *Parva Dene* 1220. OE *denu* 'valley', with later affix *little* (Latin *parva*) to distinguish this place from MITCHELDEAN.

Littleham Devon, near Exmouth. *Lytlanhamme* 1042, *Liteham* 1086 (DB). 'Little enclosure or river-meadow'. OE *lȳtel* + *hamm*.

Littlehampton W. Sussex. *Hantone* 1086 (DB). *Lyttellhampton* 1482. OE *hām-tūn* 'home farm, homestead' with the later addition of little perhaps to distinguish it from SOUTHAMPTON.

Littlehempston Devon. *Hamistone* 1086 (DB), *Parua Hæmeston* 1176. 'Farmstead of a man called *Hæme or Hemme*'. OE pers. name + *tūn*. Affix *little* (Latin *parva*) to distinguish this place from BROADHEMPSTON.

Littlehoughton Northum. *Houcton Parva* 1242. 'Farmstead on or near a ridge or hill-spur'. OE *hōh* + *tūn*. Affix *little* (Latin *parva*) to distinguish this place from LONGHOUGHTON.

Littlemore Oxon. *Luthlemoria* c.1130. 'Little marsh'. OE *lȳtel* + *mōr*.

Littleover Derbys. *Parva Ufre* 1086 (DB). '(Place at) the ridge'. OE **ofer* with the affix *little* (Latin *parva*) to distinguish this place from MICKLEOVER.

Littleport Cambs. *Litelport* 1086 (DB). 'Little (market) town'. OE *lȳtel* + *port*.

Littlestone-on-Sea Kent, a 19th cent. name from a rocky headland called *Little Stone* 1801, formerly a coastal feature near here.

Littleton, 'little farmstead or estate', OE *lȳtel* + *tūn*; examples include: **Littleton** Ches. *Litelton* 1435. Earlier *Parva Cristentona* c.1125, 'the smaller part of CHRISTLETON'. **Littleton** Hants., near Winchester. *Lithleton* 1285. **Littleton** Somerset. *Liteltone* 1086 (DB). **Littleton** Surrey. *Liteltone* 1086 (DB), **Littleton Drew** Wilts. *Liteltone* 1086 (DB), *Littleton Dru* 1311. Manorial affix from the Driwe family, here in the 13th cent. **Littleton, High** B. & NE. Som. *Liteltone* 1086 (DB), *Heghelitleton* 1324. Affix is OE *hēah* 'high'. **Littleton, Middle**, **Littleton, North** & **Littleton, South** Heref. & Worcs. *Litletona* 709, *Liteltune* 1086 (DB). **Littleton Pannell** Wilts. *Liteltone* 1086 (DB), *Lutleton Paynel* 1317. Manorial affix from the Paynel family, here in the 13th cent. **Littleton upon Severn** S. Glos. *Lytletun* 986, *Liteltone* 1086 (DB). For the river-name, *see* SEVERN.

Littlewick Green Berks. *Lidlegewik* c.1060. 'Farm by the woodland clearing with a gate or on a slope'. OE *hlid* or **hlid* + *lēah* + *wīc*.

Littleworth Oxon. *Wyrthæ* c.971, *Ordia |sic|* 1086 (DB), *Lytleworth* 1284. OE *worth* 'enclosure', later with the affix *lȳtel* 'little' to distinguish this place from LONGWORTH.

Litton Derbys. *Litun* 1086 (DB). Possibly 'farmstead on a slope'. OE *hlith* + *tūn*.

Litton N. Yorks. *Litone* 1086 (DB). Probably identical in origin with the previous name.

Litton Somerset. *Hlytton* c.1060, *Litune* 1086 (DB). Possibly 'farmstead at a gate or by a slope'. OE *hlid* or **hlid* + *tūn*.

Litton Cheney Dorset. *Lideton* 1204. Probably 'farmstead by a noisy stream'. OE **hlȳde* + *tūn*. Manorial affix from the Cheyne family, here in the 14th cent.

Livermere, Great Suffolk. *Leuuremer* c.1050, *Liuermera* 1086 (DB). 'Liver-shaped pool, or pool with thick or muddy water'. OE *lifer* + *mere*.

Liverpool Mersey. *Liuerpul* c.1190. 'Pool or creek with thick or muddy water'. OE *lifer* + *pōl*.

Liversedge W. Yorks. *Livresec* 1086 (DB). Probably 'edge or ridge of a man called Lēofhere'. OE pers. name + *ecg*.

Liverton Red. & Cleve. *Liuretun* 1086 (DB). 'Farmstead of a man called Lēofhere, or on a stream with thick or muddy water'. OE pers. name or *lifer* + *tūn*.

Livingston W. Loth. *Villa Leuing* c.1128, *Leuinestun* c.1150. 'Leving's farmstead'. ME pers. name + OE *tun*.

Lixnaw (*Leic Snámha*) Kerry. 'Flagstone of the swimming place'.

Lizard Cornwall. *Lisart* 1086 (DB). 'Court on a height'. Cornish **lys* + **ardh*.

Llan Sain Siôr. *See* ST GEORGE'S.

Llanandras. *See* PRESTEIGNE.

Llanasa Flin. *Llanassa* 1254. 'Church of St Asaph'. Welsh *llan*.

Llanbadarn Fawr Cergn. *Lampadervaur* 1181, *Llanbadarn Vawr* 1557. 'Great church of St Padarn'. Welsh *llan* + *mawr*.

Llanbedr Pont Steffan. *See* LAMPETER.

Llanberis Gwyd. *Lanperis* 1283. 'Church of St Peris'. Welsh *llan*.

Llancarfan Vale Glam. *Lancaruan* 1106, *Nant Carban* 1136. Possibly 'valley of the River Carfan'. Welsh *nant*. Early forms of the name confirm that original Welsh *nant* was replaced by *llan*, 'church'.

Llandaff (*Llandaf*) Card. *Lanntaf* c.1150, *Landaph* 1191. 'Church on the River Taf'. Welsh *llan*. The Celtic river name means simply 'stream' (British **tamos*) or possibly 'dark'. The church is the cathedral church of St Teilo, whose name lies behind LLANDEILO. *Cp.* CARDIFF.

Llanddewi Brefi Cergn. *Landewi Brevi* 13th cent. 'Church of St David on the River Brefi'. Welsh *llan* + *Dewi*. The river name means 'noisy one' (Welsh *bref*).

Llanddewi Nant Hoddni. *See* LLANTHONY.

Llanddewi Velfrey Pemb. *Landwei in Wilfrey* 1488. 'Church of St David in Efelffre'. Welsh *llan* + *Dewi*. The name of the commote *Efelffre* is of uncertain origin, although *-fre* may represent Welsh *bre*, 'hill'.

Llanddulas Conwy. *Llan Dhylas* c.1700. 'Church on the River Dulas'. Welsh *llan*. The river name may mean 'black stream' (Welsh *du* + *glais*).

Llandegfan Angl. *Llandegvan* 1254. 'Church of St Tegfan'. Welsh *llan*.

Llandeilo Carm. *Lanteliau Maur* 1130, *Llandilo Vawr* 1656. 'Church of St Teilo'. Welsh *llan*. The second word of the early forms is Welsh *mawr*, 'great'.

Llandeloy Pemb. *Landalee* 1291. 'Tylwyf's church'. Welsh *llan*. The pers. name is that of the owner of the site.

Llandinabo Heref. & Worcs. *Lann Hunapui* c.1130. 'Church-site of a man called Iunapui'. Welsh *llan* + pers. name.

Llandochau. *See* LLANDOUGH.

Llandough (*Llandochau*) Vale Glam. *Landochan* 1106, *Landough* 1427. 'Docco's church'. Welsh *llan*.

Llandovery (*Llanymddyfri*) Carm. *Llanamdewri* 12th cent., *Lanandeveri* 1194, *Lanymdevery* 1383. 'Church near the waters'. Welsh *llan* + *am* + *dwfr* (plural *dyfri*).

Llandrillo-yn-Rhos. *See* RHOS-ON-SEA.

Llandrindod Wells Powys. *Lando* 1291, *Llandrindod* 1554. 'Church of the Trinity with wells'. Welsh *llan* + *trindod*. The original name of the church was *Llanddwy*, 'church of God'. *Wells* was added from the local chalybeate springs, first exploited in the 18th cent.

Llandudno Conwy. *Llandudno* 1291, *Lantudenou* 1376. 'Church of St Tudno'. Welsh *llan*.

Llandudoch. *See* ST DOGMAELS.

Llandysul Cergn. *Landessel* 1291, *Lantissill* 1299. 'Church of St Tysul'. Welsh *llan*.

Llanelli Carm. *Lann elli* c.1173. 'Church of St Elli'. Welsh *llan*. Elli is said to have been one of the daughters of Brychan, who gave the name of BRECON.

Llanelwy. *See* ST ASAPH.

Llanerch-y-medd Angl. *llan'meth* 1445, *Lannerch y medd* 15th cent. 'Glade in which mead is made'. Welsh *llannerch* + *y* + *medd*.

Llanfair Caereinion Powys. *Llanveyr* 1279, *Llanvair in Krynion* 1579. 'Church of St Mary in Caereinion'. Welsh *llan* + *Mair*. The name of the cantref *Caereinion* means 'fort of Einion' (Welsh *caer* + pers. n).

Llanfair Pwllgwyngyll Angl. *Llan Vair y pwll Gwinghill* 1536, *ll.fair ymhwll gwingill* 1566. 'Church of St Mary in Pwllgwyngyll'. Welsh *llan* + *Mair*. The township name *Pwllgwyngyll* means 'pool of the white hazels' (Welsh *pwll* + *gwyn* + *cyll*). A fanciful addition of *gogerychwyrndrobwllllantysiliogogogoch* was further made in the mid-19th cent., meaning 'fairly near the rapid whirlpool by the church of St Tysilio at the red place' (Welsh *go* + *ger* + *y* + *chwyrn* + *trobwll* + *llantysilio* + *coch*), based on local names or features, giving an overall *Llanfairpwllgwyngyllgogerychwyrndrobwllllantysiliogogogoch*.

Llanfair Waterdine Shrops. *Watredene* 1086 (DB), *Thlanveyr* 1284. 'St Mary's church in the watery (or wet) valley'. Welsh *llan* + saint's name, with the addition from OE *wæter* + *denu*.

Llanfair-ym-Muallt. *See* BUILTH WELLS.

Llanfairfechan Conwy. *Lanueyr* 1284, *Llanbayar* 1291, *Llanvair Vechan* 1475. 'Little church of St Mary'. Welsh *llan* + *Mair* + *bechan*. The church is 'little' compared to the 'big' church of St Mary at Conwy.

Llanfihangel-ar-arth Carm. *Llanfihangel Orarth* 1291. 'St Michael's church on the high hill'. Welsh *llan* + *Mihangel* + *ar* + *garth*. The second word of the early form represents Welsh *gor-*, 'super-' + *garth*, 'hill', referring to the height of the hill.

Llanfihangel Dyffryn Arwy. *See* MICHAELCHURCH-ON-ARROW.

Llanfihangel-y-pwll. *See* MICHAELSTON-LE-PIT.

Llanfyllin Powys. *Llanvelig* 1254, *Lanvyllyn* 1291, *Lanvethlyng* 1309. 'Church of St Myllin'. Welsh *llan*.

Llanfyrnach Pemb. *Ecclesia Sancti Bernaci* 1291. 'Church of St Brynach'. Welsh *llan*.

Llangadog Carm. *Lancadauc* 1281, *Lankadoc* 1284. 'Church of St Cadog'. Welsh *llan*.

Llangarron Heref. & Worcs. *Lann Garan* c.1130. 'Church-site on the River Garron'. Welsh *llan* + Celtic river-name meaning 'crane stream'.

Llangefni Angl. *Llangevni* 1254. 'Church on the River Cefni'. Welsh *llan*.

Llangeitho Cergn. *Lankethau* 1284, *Langeytho* 1290. 'Church of St Ceitho'. Welsh *llan*. Ceitho is one of the saints to whom LLANPUMSAINT is dedicated.

Llangollen Denb. *Lancollien* 1234, 'Church of St Collen'. Welsh *llan*.

Llangolman Pemb. *Llangolman* 1394. 'Church of St Colman'. Welsh *llan*.

Llangrove Heref. & Worcs. *Longe grove* 1372. 'Long grove or copse'. OE *lang* + *grāf*.

Llangurig Powys. *Lankiric* 1254. 'Church of St Curig'. Welsh *llan*.

Llangwm Pemb. *Llandegumme* 1301. 'Church in the valley'. Welsh *llan* + *cwm*.

Llangybi Cergn. *Lankeby* 1284. 'Church of St Cybi'. *Cp.* HOLYHEAD. Welsh *llan*.

Llanidloes Powys. *Lanidloes* 1254. 'Church of St Idloes'. Welsh *llan*.

Llanilltud Fawr. *See* LLANTWIT MAJOR.

Llanllyfni Gwyd. *Thlauthleueny* (*sic*) 1352, *Llanllyfne* 1432. 'Church on the River Llyfni'. Welsh *llan*. The river name means 'smooth-flowing one' (Welsh *llyfn*).

Llanpumsaint Carm. 'Church of the five saints'. Welsh *llan* + *pump* + *saint*. The five saints are Ceitho, Celynnen, Gwyn, Gwynno, and Gwynoro.

Llanrothal Heref. & Worcs. *Lann Ridol* c.1130. Welsh *llan* 'church-site', probably with a pers. name.

Llanrug Gwyd. *ll.v'el yn Ruc* 1566, *Llanvihengle in Rug* 1614. 'Church in Rug'. Welsh *llan*. The township name *Rug* means 'heather' (Welsh *grug*). The full name of the village was *Llanfihangel-yn-Rug*, 'church of St Michael in Rug'.

Llanrwst Conwy. *lhannruste* 1254, *Lannwrvst* 1291. 'Church of St Gwrwst'. Welsh *llan*.

Llansanffraid Glan Conwy Conwy. *Llansanfraid* 1535, *Lhan St Ffraid c.*1700, *Llan Sanfraed Glan Conwy* 1713. 'Church of St Ffraid on the bank of the River Conwy'. Welsh *llan* + *sant* + *glan*. *Ffraid* is a Welsh form of Brigid (Bridget). For the river name, *see* CONWY.

Llansanffraid Glynceiriog. *See* GLYN CEIRIOG.

Llansawel Carm. *Lansawyl* 1265, *Lansawel* 1301. 'Church of St Sawel'. The saint's name is a form of Samuel. *Cp.* BRITON FERRY. Welsh *llan*.

Llansawel. *See* BRITON FERRY.

Llanstadwell Pemb. *Lanstadhewal* 12th cent. 'Church of St Tudwal'. Welsh *llan*.

Llanthony Mon. *Lantony* 1160. 'Church on the River Honddi'. Welsh *llan*. The name is usually said to be an abbreviated form of *Llanddewi Nant Hoddni*, 'church of St David on the river Hoddni' (Welsh *llan* + *Dewi* + *nant*), but more likely *Llanthony* is a form of the river name, *Nant Hoddni*, with *llan* replacing *nant*. The river name means 'pleasant' (Welsh *hawdd*).

Llantrisant Mon. *Landtrissen* 1246. 'Church of three saints'. Welsh *llan* + *tri* + *sant*. The three saints are Dyfodwg, Gwynno, and Illtud.

Llantrithyd Vale Glam. *Landrirede c.*1126, *Nantririd* 1545. 'Rhirid's valley'. Welsh *nant*.

Llantwit Major Vale Glam. *Landiltuit* 1106, *Lannyltwyt* 1291, *Lantwyt* 1480. 'Main church of St Illtud'. Welsh *llan*, 'church'. The name is a part translation, part contraction of Welsh *Llanilltud Fawr*, with Welsh *mawr* represented by Latin *major*. The place is 'great' in relation to *Llantwit Fardre* (Welsh *Llanilltud Faerdre*), Rhon., and *Llantwit-juxta-Neath* (Welsh *Llanilltud Nedd*), Neat.

Llantydewi. *See* ST DOGWELLS.

Llanwarne Heref. & Worcs. *Ladgvern |sic|* 1086 (DB), *Lann Guern c.*1130. 'Church by the alder grove'. Welsh *llan* + *gwern*.

Llanwnda Pemb. *Lanwndaph* 1202. 'Church of St Gwyndaf'. Welsh *llan*.

Llanwrda Carm. *Llanwrdaf* 1302. 'Church of St Gwrdaf'. Welsh *llan*.

Llanwrtyd Wells Powys. *Llanwrtid* 1553, *Ll. Wrtyd* 1566. 'Church of St Gwrtud with wells'. Welsh *llan*. The town developed as a spa in the 19th cent.

Llanyblodwel Shrops. *Llanblodwell* 1535. 'Church of *Blodwell*'. Welsh *llan* with an older English name first recorded as *Blodwelle c.*1200, meaning 'blood spring or stream' from OE *blōd* + *wella*, with reference to the colour of the water or to some other quality or superstition.

Llanybydder Carm. *Lannabedeir* 1319, *Llanybyddeyr* 1401. 'Church of the deaf ones'. Welsh *llan* + *y* 'the' *byddar* (plural *byddair*). The name may allude to a congregation who were deaf to the call preached to them, or whose hitherto deaf ears were opened by it.

Llan-y-cefn Pemb. *Llanekevyn* 1499. 'Church on the ridge'. Welsh *llan* + *y* + *cefn*.

Llanychaer Pemb. *Launerwayth* 1291, *Llanerchaeth* 1408. Meaning uncertain. Early forms suggest that the first element may represent Welsh *llannerch*, 'glade'. The rest is obscure.

Llanymddyfri. *See* LLANDOVERY.

Llanymynech Shrops. *Llanemeneych* 1254. 'Church-site of the monks'. Welsh *llan* + *mynach*.

Llanymynech Powys. *Llanemeneych* 1254. 'Church of the monks'. Welsh *llan* + *mynach*.

Lleyn (Peninsula) Gwyd. (Penrhyn Llŷn). Meaning uncertain. The name may have originally been that of a Celtic people 'the Lageni' hence *Lleyn* and later *Llŷn*, their own name perhaps from *Leinster*, Ireland, whence they may have emigrated.

Llwyneliddon. *See* ST LYTHANS.

Llyfni (river) Gwyd. *Lleueni* 1578. 'Smooth-flowing one'. Welsh *llyfn*. *Cp.* LLYNFI.

Llŷn. *See* LLEYN PENINSULA.

Llyn Tegid. *See* BALA.

Llynfi (river) Bri. *Thleweny* 1314. 'Smooth-flowing one'. Welsh *llyfn*. *Cp.* LLYFNI.

Llys-y-frân Pemb. *Lysurane* 1326, *Lysfrane* 1402. 'Brân's court' or brân (crow). Welsh *llys*.

Load, Long Somerset. *La Lade* 1285. 'The watercourse or drainage channel'. OE *lād*.

Loanends Antrim. 'Lane ends'. Scottish *loan* + English *ends*. Three minor roads join the main road to Antrim here.

Loanhead Midloth. *Loneheid* 1618. 'End of a lane'. OE *lane* + *hēafod*. *Loan* is a Scots form of standard English *lane*.

Lochaber (district) Highland. 'Loch at the confluence'. Gaelic *loch* + Pictish *aber*.

Lochalsh. *See* KYLE OF LOCHALSH.

Lochgelly Fife. *Lochgellie* 1606. '(Place by) Loch Gelly'. Gaelic *loch*. The name of the loch means 'white' (Gaelic *geal*).

Lochgilphead Arg. *Lochgilpshead* 1650. 'Head of Loch Gilp'. Gaelic *loch*. The name of the loch may mean 'chisel-shaped lake' (Gaelic *gilb*).

Lochinvar (loch) Dumf. *Lochinvar* 1540. 'Loch of the height'. Gaelic *loch* + *an* + *barr*. *Loch an bharre*.

Lochinver Highland. '(Place by) Loch Inver'. Gaelic *loch*. The loch is a sea inlet at the mouth (Gaelic *inbhir*) of the river of the same name.

Lochmaben Dumf. *Locmaban* 1166, *Lochmalban c.*1320, *Lochmabane* 1502. 'Loch by Maben'. Gaelic *loch*. The meaning of *Maben* is uncertain.

Lochnagar (mountain) Aber. *Loch Garr* 1640, *Loch na Garr* 1807. The name of the mountain has been transferred from the *loch*. The loch has a name of uncertain origin.

Lochy, Loch Highland. 'Loch of the River Lochy'. Gaelic *loch*. The river name means 'dark one' (Gaelic *lochaidh*).

Lockerbie Dumf. *Lockardebie* 1306. 'Locard's farm'. OScand. pers. name + *bý*.

Lockeridge Wilts. *Locherige* 1086 (DB). Possibly 'ridge with folds or enclosures'. OE *loc(a)* + *hrycg*.

Lockerley Hants. *Locherlega* 1086 (DB). Probably 'woodland clearing of a keeper or shepherd'. OE **lōcere* + *lēah*.

Locking N. Som. *Lockin* 1212. 'Place associuated with a man called Locc', OE pers. name + *-ing*, or from an OE **locing* 'fold or enclosure'.

Lockinge, East & *Lockinge, West* Oxon. *Lacinge* 868, *Lachinges* 1086 (DB), *Estloking*, *Westloking* 1327. Originally the name of the stream here (now called Lockinge Brook) meaning 'the playful one', from OE *lāc* 'play', *lācan* 'to play' + *-ing*.

Lockington E. R. Yorks. *Locheton* 1086 (DB). 'Estate associated with a man called **Loca*'. OE pers. name + *-ing-* + *tūn*. Alternatively the first element may be an OE **locing* 'fold, enclosure'.

Lockton N. Yorks. *Lochetun* 1086 (DB). Probably 'farmstead of a man called **Loca*', OE pers. name + *tūn*. Alternatively the first element may be OE *loca* 'enclosure'.

Loddington Leics. *Ludintone* 1086 (DB). Probably 'estate associated with a man called Luda'. OE pers. name + *-ing-* + *tūn*.

Loddington Northants. *Lodintone* 1086 (DB). 'Estate associated with a man called Lod(a)'. OE pers. name + *-ing-* + *tūn*.

Loddiswell Devon. *Lodeswille* 1086 (DB). 'Spring or stream of a man called **Lod*', OE pers. name + *wella*.

Loddon (river) Berks., Hants., *see* SHERFIELD.

Loddon Norfolk. *Lodne* 1043, *Lotna* 1086 (DB). Originally a Celtic river-name (possibly meaning 'muddy stream'), an old name for the River Chet.

Lode Cambs. *Lada* 12th cent. OE *lād* 'watercourse or drainage channel'.

Loders Dorset. *Lodre(s)* 1086 (DB). Probably originally a Celtic river-name (meaning 'pool stream'), an old name for the River Asker.

Lodsworth W. Sussex. *Lodesorde* 1086 (DB). 'Enclosure of a man called **Lod*'. OE pers. name + *worth*.

Lofthouse W. Yorks., near Leeds. *Loftose* 1086 (DB). 'House(s) with a loft or upper floor'. OScand. *loft-hús* in a dative plural form.

Loftus Red & Cleve. *Loctehusum* 1086 (DB). Identical in origin with the previous name.

Loghill (*Leamhchoill*) Limerick. 'Elm wood'.

Logie Buchan. *See* KIRKTON OF LOGIE BUCHAN.

Lolworth Cambs. *Lollesworthe* 1034, *Lolesuuorde* 1086 (DB). 'Enclosure of a man called **Loll* or Lull'. OE pers. name + *worth*.

Loman (river) Devon, *see* UPLOWMAN.

Lomond, Loch Arg. *Lochlomond* c.1340. '(Loch by) the river Leven'. Gaelic *loch*. The loch takes its name from the river LEVEN.

Londesborough E. R. Yorks. *Lodenesburg* 1086 (DB). 'Stronghold of a man called Lothinn'. OScand. pers. name + OE *burh*.

London *Londinium* c.115. An ancient name often explained as 'place belonging to a man called Londinos',

from a Celtic pers. name with adjectival suffix, but now considered obscure in origin and meaning.

London Colney Herts., *see* COLNEY.

Londonderry. *See* DERRY.

Londonthorpe Lincs. *Lundertorp* 1086 (DB). 'Outlying farmstead or hamlet by a grove'. OScand. *lundr* (genitive *lundar*) + *thorp*.

Long as affix, *see* under main name, e.g. for **Long Ashton** (N. Som.) *see* ASHTON.

Long, Loch Arg. 'Ship loch'. Gaelic *loch* + *long*.

Longbenton Tyne & Wear. *Bentune* c.1190, *Magna Beneton* 1256. 'Farmstead where bent-grass grows, or where beans are grown'. OE *beonet* or *bēan* + *tūn*, with later affix *long*.

Longborough Glos. *Langeberge* 1086 (DB). 'Long hill or barrow'. OE *lang* + *beorg*.

Longbridge W. Mids., a self-explanatory name of recent origin.

Longbridge Deverill Wilts. *Devrel* 1086 (DB), *Deverill Langebrigge* 1316. 'Estate on the River *Deverill* with the long bridge'. OE *lang* + *brycg* with Celtic river-name (for which *see* BRIXTON DEVERILL).

Longburton Dorset. *Burton* 1244, *Langebourton* 1460. 'Fortified farm', or 'farm near a fortification'. OE *burh-tūn*. Affix is OE *lang* referring to the length of the village.

Longcot Oxon. *Cotes* 1233, *Longcote* 1332. 'The cottages', from OE *cot*, with the later addition of *lang* 'long'.

Longden Shrops. *Langedune* 1086 (DB). 'Long hill or down'. OE *lang* + *dūn*.

Longdendale Derbys., Gtr. Manch, *see* MOTTRAM.

Longdon, 'long hill or down', OE *lang* + *dūn*: **Longdon** Heref. & Worcs. *Longandune* 969, *Longedun* 1086 (DB). **Longdon** Staffs. *Langandune* 1002. **Longdon upon Tern** Shrops. *Languedune* 1086 (DB). For the river-name, *see* EATON UPON TERN.

Longfield Kent. *Langafelda* 10th cent., *Langafel* 1086 (DB). 'Long stretch of open country'. OE *lang* + *feld*.

Longford, 'long ford', OE *lang* + *ford*: **Longford** Derbys. *Langeford* 1197. **Longford** Glos. *Langeford* 1107. **Longford** Shrops., near Market Drayton. *Langeford* 13th cent. **Longford** Shrops., near Newport. *Langanford* 1002, *Langeford* 1086 (DB).

Longford (*An Longfort*) Longford. 'The fortified place'.

Longham Norfolk. *Lawingham* 1086 (DB). Probably 'homestead of the family or followers of a man called **Lāwa*'. OE pers. name + *-inga-* + *hām*.

Longhirst Northum. *Langherst* 1200. 'Long wooded hill'. OE *lang* + *hyrst*.

Longhope Glos. *Hope* 1086 (DB), *Langehope* 1248. 'The valley'. OE *hop* with the later addition of *lang* 'long'.

Longhorsley Northum. *Horsleg* 1196. 'Woodland clearing where horses are kept'. OE *hors* + *lēah*, with the later affix *long*.

Longhoughton Northum. *Houcton Magna* 1242. 'Farmstead on or near a ridge or hill-spur'. OE *hōh* + *tūn*.

Affix *long* (earlier Latin *magna* 'great') to distinguish this place from LITTLEHOUGHTON.

Longleat Wilts. *Langelete* 1235. 'Long stream or channel'. OE *lang* + (*ge*)*lǣt*.

Longney Glos. *Longanege* 972, *Langenei* 1086 (DB). 'Long island'. OE *lang* (dative -*an*) + *ēg*.

Longnor Shrops. *Longenalra* 1155. 'Tall alder-tree', or 'long alder-copse'. OE *lang* (dative -*an*) + *alor*.

Longnor Staffs., near Buxton. *Langenoure* 1227. 'Long ridge'. OE *lang* (dative -*an*) + **ofer*.

Longparish Hants. *Langeparisshe* 1389. Self-explanatory. Earlier called Middleton, *Middeltune* 1086 (DB), 'middle farmstead or estate', from OE *middel* + *tūn*.

Longridge Lancs. *Langrig* 1246. 'Long ridge'. OE *lang* + *hrycg*.

Longsdon Staffs. *Longesdon* 1242. Probably 'hill called *Lang* ('the long one')'. OE *lang* + *dūn*.

Longstock Hants. *Stoce* 982, *Stoches* 1086 (DB), *Langestok* 1233. OE *stoc* 'outlying farm or hamlet', with the later addition of *lang* 'long'.

Longstone, Great & *Longstone, Little* Derbys. *Langesdune* 1086 (DB). Probably 'hill called *Lang* ("the long one")'. OE *lang* + *dūn*.

Longton, *Longtown* 'long farmstead or estate', OE *lang* + *tūn*: **Longton** Lancs. *Langetuna c.*1155. **Longton** Staffs. *Longeton* 1212. **Longtown** Cumbria. *Longeton* 1267. **Longtown** Heref. & Worcs. *Longa villa* 1540, earlier *Ewias* 1086 (DB), *Ewyas Lascy* 13th cent. (manorial affix from Roger de Laci, owner in 1086, *see* EWYAS HAROLD).

Longville in the Dale Shrops. *Longefewd* 1255. 'Long stretch of open country'. OE *lang* + *feld*, with later affix from *dæl* 'valley'.

Longwitton Northum. *Wttun* 1236, *Langwotton* 1340. 'Farmstead in or by a wood'. OE *wudu* + *tūn*, with later affix *lang* 'long'.

Longworth Oxon. *Wurthe* 958, *Langewrth* 1284. OE *worth* or *wyrth* 'enclosure', with the later addition of *lang* 'long'.

Looe, East & *Looe, West* Cornwall. *Loo c.*1220. Cornish **logh* 'pool, inlet'.

Loop Head (*Ceann Léime*) Clare. 'Head of the leap'. OScand. *hlaup*.

Loose Kent. *Hlose* 11th cent. '(Place at) the pig-sty'. OE *hlōse*.

Loosley Row Bucks. *Losle* 1241. 'Woodland clearing with a pig-sty'. OE *hlōse* + *lēah*.

Lopen Somerset. *Lopen*(*e*) 1086 (DB). Celtic **penn* 'hill' or OE *penn* 'fold, enclosure' with an uncertain first element.

Lopham, North & *Lopham, South* Norfolk. *Lopham* 1086 (DB). 'Homestead or village of a man called **Loppa*'. OE pers. name + *hām*.

Loppington Shrops. *Lopitone* 1086 (DB). 'Estate associated with a man called **Loppa*'. OE pers. name + -*ing*- + *tūn*.

Lorn (district) Arg. *Lorne* 1304. '(Territory of the) people of *Loarn Mór*', 'the great fox', active in the 6th cent.

Lorton, High & *Lorton, Low* Cumbria. *Loretona c.*1150. Probably 'farmstead on a stream called **Hlóra*'. OScand. river-name (meaning 'roaring one') + OE *tūn*.

Loscoe Derbys. *Loscowe* 1277. 'Wood with a lofthouse'. OScand. *loft* + *skógr*.

Loskeran (*Loscreán*) Waterford. 'Burnt ground'.

Losset (*Losad*) Cavan. 'Productive field'.

Lossiemouth Moray. 'Mouth of the River Lossie'. The river name means 'water of herbs' (Gaelic *Uisge Lossa*).

Lostock, 'outlying farmstead with a pig-sty', OE *hlōse* + *stoc*: **Lostock** Gtr. Manch., near Bolton. *Lostok* 1205. **Lostock Gralam** Ches. *Lostoch c.*1100, *le Lostoke Graliam* 1288. Manorial affix from a 12th cent. owner called *Gralam*.

Lostwithiel Cornwall. *Lostwetell* 1194. 'Tail-end of the woodland'. Cornish *lost* + *gwydhyel*.

Lothian. *See* MIDLOTHIAN.

Loudwater Bucks. *La Ludewatere* 1241. Originally a river-name, 'the noisy stream', OE *hlūd* + *wæter*.

Lough. *See* next word as name, e.g. for *Lough Neagh*, *see* NEAGH, LOUGH.

Loughan (*Lochán*) Meath. 'Little lake'.

Loughanavally (*Lochán an Bhealaigh*) Westmeath. 'Little lake of the routeway'.

Loughanure (*Loch an Iúir*) Donegal. 'Lake of the yew tree'.

Loughborough Leics. *Lucteburne* |*sic*| 1086 (DB), *Lucteburga* 12th cent. 'Fortified house of a man called Luhhede'. OE pers. name + *burh*.

Loughbrickland (*Loch Bricleann*) Down. (*ic*) *Loch B*(*r*)*icreann c.*830. 'Lake of Bricle (earlier Bricriu)'.

Loughduff (*An Lathaigh Dhubh*) Cavan. 'The black mire'.

Lougher (*Luachair*) Kerry. 'Rushy place'.

Loughermore (*Luachair Mhór*) Derry. 'Big rushy place'.

Loughgall (*Loch gCál*) Armagh. An ancient name, meaning unknown.

Loughglinn (*Loch Glinne*) Roscommon. 'Lake of the valley'.

Loughguile (*Loch gCaol*) Antrim. *Lochkele* 1262. 'Lake of the narrows'.

Loughil (*Leamhchoill*) Limerick. 'Elm wood'.

Loughinisland (*Loch an Oileáin*) Down. *Loghnellan* 1616. 'Lake of the island'.

Loughlinstown (*Baile Uí Lachnáin*) Dublin. 'Homestead of Ó Lachnán'.

Loughmacrory (*Loch Mhic Ruairí*) Tyrone. 'Mac Ruairí's lake'.

Loughor (*Casllwchwr*) Swan. *Caslougher* 1691. '(Place by the river) Loughor'. The Celtic river name means 'shining one' (Welsh *llychwr*). The Welsh name means 'castle by the Loughor' (Welsh *cas*).

Loughrea (*Loch Riach*) Galway. 'Grey lake'.

Loughros Point (*Pointe Luachrois*) Donegal. (*hi*) *Luachros* 1509. 'Rushy point'.

Loughton Bucks. *Lochintone* 1086 (DB). 'Estate associated with a man called Luhha'. OE pers. name (+ *-ing-*) + *tūn*.

Loughton Essex. *Lukintone* 1062, *Lochetuna* 1086 (DB). 'Estate associated with a man called *Luca*'. OE pers. name (+ *-ing-*) + *tūn*.

Loughton Shrops. *Lochetona* 1138. 'Farmstead by a pool'. OE *luh* + *tūn*.

Lound, 'small wood or grove', OScand. *lundr*: **Lound** Lincs. *Lund* 1086 (DB). **Lound** Notts. *Lund* 1086 (DB). **Lound** Suffolk. *Lunda* 1086 (DB). **Lound, East** N. Lincs. *Lund* 1086 (DB), *Estlound* 1370. Addition is OE *ēast* 'east'.

Loup, The (*An Lúb*) Derry. *The Loop Lodge* 1798. 'The loop'. The reference is presumably to a bend in a stream here.

Louth Lincs. *Lude* 1086 (DB). Named from the River Lud, OE **Hlūde* 'the loud one, the noisy stream'.

Louth (*Lú*) Louth. *Lughmhaigh* n.d. Perhaps 'Lú's penis', referring to a standing stone. Lú is a sun god. The name formerly had a second element, long explained as Irish *magh*, 'plain'.

Lovat Highland. *Loveth* c.1235. 'Swampy place'. Gaelic *lobh* + *-aid*.

Loversall S. Yorks. *Loureshale* 1086 (DB). 'Nook of a man called Lēofhere'. OE pers. name + *halh*.

Loveston Pemb. *Lovelleston* 1362. 'Lovell's farm'. French pers. name + OE *tūn*.

Lovington Somerset. *Lovintune* 1086 (DB). 'Estate associated with a man called Lufa'. OE pers. name + *-ing-* + *tūn*.

Low as affix, *see* main name, e.g. for **Low Ackworth** (W. Yorks.) *see* ACKWORTH.

Lowdham Notts. *Ludham* 1086 (DB). 'Homestead or village of a man called **Hlūda*'. OE pers. name + *hām*.

Lower as affix, *see* main name, e.g. for **Lower Aisholt** (Somerset) *see* AISHOLT.

Lowery (*Leamhraidhe*) Donegal, Fermanagh. 'Place of elms'.

Lowesby Leics. *Glowesbi* |*sic*| 1086 (DB), *Lousebia* c.1125. Possibly 'farmstead or village of a man called Lauss or Lausi'. OScand. pers. name + *bý*.

Lowestoft Suffolk. *Lothu Wistoft* 1086 (DB). 'Homestead of a man called Hlothvér'. OScand. pers. name + *toft*.

Loweswater Cumbria. *Lousewater* c.1160. Named from the lake, 'leafy lake', from OScand. *lauf* + *sǽr* with the addition of OE *wæter* 'expanse of water'.

Lowick Cumbria. *Lofwik* 1202. Probably 'leafy creek or river-bend'. OScand. *lauf* + *vík*.

Lowick Northants. *Luhwic* 1086 (DB). 'Dwelling or (dairy) farm of a man called Luhha or **Luffa*'. OE pers. name + *wīc*.

Lowick Northum. *Lowich* 1181. 'Dwelling or (dairy) farm on the River Low'. River-name (probably from OE *luh* 'pool') + OE *wīc*.

Lowther Cumbria. *Lauder* c.1175. Named from the River Lowther, possibly an OScand. river-name meaning 'foamy river', OScand. *lauthr* + á, but perhaps Celtic in origin.

Lowther Hills Dumf. Meaning uncertain. The name may be related to LAUDER.

Lowthorpe E. R. Yorks. *Log(h)etorp* 1086 (DB). 'Outlying farmstead or hamlet of a man called Lági or Logi'. OScand. pers. name + *thorp*.

Lowton Gtr. Manch. *Lauton* 1202. 'Farmstead by a mound or hill'. OE *hlāw* + *tūn*.

Loxbeare Devon. *Lochesbere* 1086 (DB). 'Wood or grove of a man called Locc'. OE pers. name + *bearu*.

Loxhore Devon. *Lochesore* 1086 (DB). 'Hill-slope of a man called Locc'. OE pers. name + *ōra*.

Loxley Warwicks. *Locheslei* 1086 (DB). 'Woodland clearing of a man called Locc'. OE pers. name + *lēah*.

Loxton N. Som. *Lochestone* 1086 (DB). 'Farmstead on the stream called Lox Yeo'. Celtic river-name (of uncertain meaning) + OE *ēa* + *tūn*.

Lubenham Leics. *Lubanham*, *Lobenho* 1086 (DB). 'Hill-spur(s) of a man called **Lubba*'. OE pers. name (genitive *-n*) + *hōh* (dative plural *hōum*).

Lucan (*Leamhcán*) Dublin. 'Place of elms'.

Luccombe, probably 'valley of a man called Lufa', OE pers. name + *cumb*: **Luccombe** Somerset. *Locumbe* 1086 (DB). **Luccombe Village** I. of Wight. *Lovecumbe* 1086 (DB).

Lucker Northum. *Lucre* 1170. Probably 'marsh with a pool'. OE *luh* + OScand. *kjarr*.

Luckington Wilts. *Lochintone* 1086 (DB). 'Estate associated with a man called **Luca*'. OE pers. name + *-ing- + tūn*.

Lucton Heref. & Worcs. *Lugton* 1185. 'Farmstead on the River Lugg'. Celtic river-name (*see* LUGWARDINE) + OE *tūn*.

Ludborough Lincs. *Ludeburg* 1086 (DB). Probably 'fortified place belonging to or associated with Louth', from OE *burh*, *see* LOUTH. Alternatively 'fortified place of a man called Luda', OE pers. name + *burh*.

Ludchurch (*Yr Eglwys Lwyd*) Pemb. *Ecclesia de Loudes* 1324, *Loudeschirch* 1353. The modern Welsh name means 'the grey church' (Welsh *yr* + *eglwys* + *llwyd*) but is probably a mistranslation of a medieval English personal name Loud.

Luddenden W. Yorks. *Luddingdene* 1284. 'Valley of the stream called **Hlūding* (the loud one)'. OE name for the stream now called Luddenden Brook + *denu*. **Luddenden Foot** is *Luddingdeneforth* 1307, *Luddendenfoote* 1601, 'ford near Luddenden', from OE *ford* (changed to *foot* by folk etymology).

Luddesdown Kent. *Hludesduna* 10th cent., *Ledesdune* 1086 (DB). 'Hill of a man called **Hlūd*'. OE pers. name + *dūn*.

Luddington N. Lincs. *Ludintone* 1086 (DB). 'Estate associated with a man called Luda'. OE pers. name + *-ing- + tūn*.

Ludford Shrops. *Ludeford* 1086 (DB). 'Ford on the noisy stream' (referring to a crossing of the River Teme). OE **hlūde* + *ford*.

Ludgershall, 'nook with a trapping-spear', OE **lutegār* + *halh*: **Ludgershall** Bucks. *Lotegarser* |*sic*| 1086 (DB),

Lutegareshale 1164. **Ludgershall** Wilts. *Lutegaresheale* 1015, *Litlegarsele |sic|* 1086 (DB).

Ludgvan Cornwall. *Luduhan* 1086 (DB). Possibly 'place of ashes, burnt place'. Cornish *lusow, ludw* + suffix.

Ludham Norfolk. *Ludham* 1021–4, 1086 (DB). 'Homestead or village of a man called Luda'. OE pers. name + *hām*.

Ludlow Shrops. *Ludelaue* 1138. 'Hill or tumulus by the noisy stream' (referring to the River Teme). OE *hlūde* + *hlāw*.

Ludwell Wilts. *Luddewell* early 12th cent. 'Loud spring or stream'. OE *hlūd* + *wella*.

Ludworth Durham. *Ludeuurthe* 12th cent. 'Enclosure of a man called Luda'. OE pers. name + *worth*.

Luffenham, North & *Luffenham, South* Rutland. *Luf(f)enham* 1086 (DB). 'Homestead or village of a man called *Luffa'. OE pers. name + *hām*.

Luffincott Devon. *Lughyngecot* 1242. 'Cottage(s) of the family or followers of a man called Luhha'. OE pers. name + *-inga-* + *cot*.

Lugacaha (*Log an Chatha*) Westmeath. 'Hollow of the battle'.

Luggacurren (*Log an Churraigh*) Laois. 'Hollow of the marsh'.

Lugnaquillia (*Log na Coille*) (mountain) Wicklow. *Logney O Nill* 1617, *Lugnaquilla* 1760. 'Hollow of the wood'.

Lugwardine Heref. & Worcs. *Lucvordine* 1086 (DB). 'Enclosure on the River Lugg'. Celtic river-name (meaning 'bright stream') + OE *worthign*.

Lullingstone Kent. *Lolingestone* 1086 (DB). 'Farmstead or estate of a man called Lulling'. OE pers. name + *tūn*.

Lullington, 'estate associated with a man called Lulla', OE pers. name + *-ing-* + *tūn*: **Lullington** Derbys. *Lullitune* 1086 (DB). **Lullington** Somerset. *Loligtone* 1086 (DB).

Lulsley Heref. & Worcs. *Lulleseia* 12th cent. 'Island, or dry ground in marsh, of a man called Lull'. OE pers. name + *ēg*.

Lulworth, East & *Lulworth, West* Dorset. *Lulvorde* 1086 (DB). 'Enclosure of a man called Lulla'. OE pers. name + *worth*.

Lumb Lancs. *Le Lome* 1534. 'The pool'. OE *lumm*.

Lumby N. Yorks. *Lundby* 963. 'Farmstead in or near a grove'. OScand. *lundr* + *bý*.

Lumley, Great Durham. *Lummalea* c.1050. 'Woodland clearing by the pools.' OE *lumm* + *lēah*.

Lund, 'small wood or grove', OScand. *lundr*: **Lund** E. R. Yorks. *Lont* 1086 (DB). **Lund** N. Yorks., near Barlby. *Lund* 1066–9, *Lont* 1086 (DB).

Lundy Island Devon. *Lundeia* 1189. 'Puffin island'. OScand. *lundi* + *ey*.

Lune (river) Lancs., *Cumbria*, *see* LANCASTER.

Lunt Mersey. *Lund* 1251. Identical in origin with LUND.

Luppitt Devon. *Lovapit* 1086 (DB). 'Pit or hollow of a man called *Lufa'. OE pers. name + *pytt*.

Lupton Cumbria. *Lupetun* 1086 (DB). 'Farmstead of a man called *Hluppa'. OE pers. name + *tūn*.

Lurga (*An Lorgain*) Mayo. 'The ridge'.

Lurgan (*Lorgain*) Armagh, Donegal, Westmeath. 'Ridge'.

Lurgangreen (*Lorgain*) Louth. 'Green of the ridge'.

Lurganreagh (*Lorgan Riabhach*) Down. 'Striped ridge'.

Lurgashall W. Sussex. *Lutegareshale* 12th cent. 'Nook with a trapping-spear'. OE *lūte-gār+halh*.

Lusby Lincs. *Luzebi* 1086 (DB). 'Farmstead or village of a man called Lútr'. OScand. pers. name + *bý*.

Lusk (*Lusca*) Dublin. Meaning uncertain.

Luss Arg. *Lus* 1225. '(Place of) plants'. Gaelic *lus*.

Lustleigh Devon. *Leuestelegh* 1242. Probably 'woodland clearing of a man called *Lēofgiest'. OE pers. name + *lēah*.

Luston Heref. & Worcs. *Lustone* 1086 (DB). Probably 'insignificant, or louse-infested, farmstead'. OE *lūs* + *tūn*.

Luton Beds. *Lygetun* 792, *Loitone* 1086 (DB). 'Farmstead on the River Lea'. Celtic river-name (*see* LEYTON) + OE *tūn*.

Luton Devon, near Ideford. *Leueton* 1238. Possibly 'farmstead of a woman called Lēofgifu'. OE pers. name + *tūn*.

Luton Kent. *Leueton* 1240. 'Farmstead of a man called Lēofa'. OE pers. name + *tūn*.

Lutterworth Leics. *Lutresurde* 1086 (DB). Possibly 'enclosure on a stream called *Hlūtre (the clear or pure one)'. OE river-name (perhaps an earlier name for the River Swift) + *worth*.

Lutton Lincs. *Luctone* 1086 (DB). 'Farmstead by a pool'. OE *luh* + *tūn*.

Lutton Northants. *Lundingtun |sic|* c.970 *Luditone* 1086 (DB). 'Estate associated with a man called Luda'. OE pers. name + *-ing-* + *tūn*.

Lutton, East & *Lutton, West* N. Yorks. *Ludton* 1086 (DB). Probably 'estate of a man called Luda'. OE pers. name + *tūn*.

Luxborough Somerset. *Lolochesberie* 1086 (DB). 'Stronghold, or hill, of a man called Lulluc'. OE pers. name + *burh* or *beorg*.

Luxulyan Cornwall. *Luxulian* 1282. 'Chapel of Sulyen'. Cornish *log* + pers. name.

Lybster Highland. *Libister* 1538. 'Dwelling place by a slope'. OScand. *hlitle* + *bólstathr*.

Lydbrook, Upper Glos. *Luidebroc* 1224. 'Brook called *Hlȳde or the loud one'. OE river-name + *brōc*.

Lydbury North Shrops. *Lideberie* 1086 (DB). Probably 'manor house by the stream called *Hlȳde (the noisy one)'. OE river-name + *burh* (dative *byrig*). The affix *north* distinguishes it from LEDBURY which however has a quite different origin.

Lydd Kent. *Hlidum* 774. Possibly '(place at) the gates'. OE *hlid* in a dative plural form.

Lydden (river) Dorset, *see* LYDLINCH.

Lydden Kent, near Dover. *Hleodaena* c.1100. Probably 'valley with a shelter, or sheltered valley'. OE *hlēo* + *denu*.

Lyddington Rutland. *Lidentone* 1086 (DB). Possibly 'farmstead or estate associated with a man called Hlȳda', from OE pers. name + *-ing-* + *tūn*. Alternatively 'farmstead on the noisy stream', OE **hlȳde* + *tūn* as in LIDDINGTON Wilts.

Lyde Heref. & Worcs. *Lude* 1086 (DB). Named from the stream here. OE **Hlȳde* 'the loud one'.

Lydeard St Lawrence & *Bishop's Lydeard* Somerset. *Lidegeard* 854, *Lidiard*, *Lediart* 1086 (DB). Celtic **garth* 'ridge' with an uncertain first element, possibly **lēd* 'grey'. Distinguishing affixes from the dedication of the church and from early possession by the Bishop of Wells.

Lydford Devon. *Hlydanforda c*.1000, *Lideforda* 1086 (DB). 'Ford over the River Lyd'. OE river-name (from **hlȳde* 'noisy stream') + *ford*.

Lydford Somerset. *Lideford* 1086 (DB). 'Ford over the noisy stream'. OE **hlȳde* + *ford*.

Lydham Shrops. *Lidum* 1086 (DB). Possibly '(place at) the gates or the slopes'. OE *hlid* or **hlid* in a dative plural form.

Lydiard Millicent & *Lydiard Tregoze* Wilts. *Lidgeard* 901, *Lidiarde* 1086 (DB), *Lidiard Milisent* 1275, *Lidiard Tregoz* 1196. Identical in origin with LYDEARD. Manorial affixes from a woman called Millisent and from the Tresgoz family, here in the late 12th cent.

Lydiate Lancs. *Leiate* |*sic*| 1086 (DB), *Liddigate* 1202. '(Place at) the swing-gate'. OE *hlid-geat*.

Lydlinch Dorset. *Lidelinz* 1182. 'Ridge by, or bank of, the River Lydden'. Celtic river-name (probably meaning 'the broad one') + OE *hlinc*.

Lydney Glos. *Lideneg c*.853, *Ledenei* 1086 (DB). 'Island or river-meadow of the sailor, or of a man called **Lida*'. OE *lida* or pers. name (genitive *-n*) + *ēg*.

Lye, Lower Heref. & Worcs. *Lege* 1086 (DB). '(Place at) the wood or woodland clearing'. OE *lēah*.

Lyford Oxon. *Linforda* 944, *Linford* 1086 (DB). 'Ford where flax grows'. OE *līn* + *ford*.

Lyme (old district and forest) Lancs., Ches., Staffs., *see* ASHTON-UNDER-LYNE, NEWCASTLE UNDER LYME.

Lyme Regis Dorset. *Lim* 774, *Lime* 1086 (DB), *Lyme Regis* 1285. Named from the River Lim, a Celtic river-name meaning simply 'stream'. Affix is Latin *regis* 'of the king'.

Lyminge Kent. *Liminge* 689, *Leminges* 1086 (DB). 'District around the River *Limen*'. Celtic river-name (*see* LYMPNE) + OE **gē*.

Lymington Hants. *Lentune* |*sic*| 1086 (DB), *Limington* 1186. Probably 'farmstead on a river called *Limen*'. Lost Celtic river-name (meaning 'elm river' or 'marshy river') + OE *tūn*.

Lyminster W. Sussex. *Lullyngmynster c*.880, *Lolinminstre* 1086 (DB). 'Monastery or large church associated with a man called Lulla'. OE pers. name + *-ing-* + *mynster*.

Lymm Ches. *Lime* 1086 (DB). 'The noisy stream or torrent'. OE *hlimme*.

Lympne Kent. *Lemanis* 4th cent. 'Elm-wood place', or 'marshy place'. Celtic place-name related to the River *Limen* (the old name for the East Rother), a Celtic river-name meaning 'elm-wood river' or 'marshy river'.

Lympsham Somerset. *Limpelesham* 1189. OE *hām* 'homestead' or *hamm* 'enclosure' with an uncertain first element, possibly an OE pers. name **Limpel*.

Lympstone Devon *Levestone* |*sic*| 1086 (DB), *Leveneston* 1238. 'Farmstead of a man called Lēofwine'. OE pers. name + *tūn*.

Lynally (*Lann Eala*) Offaly. 'Church of (Colmán) Eala'.

Lyndhurst Hants. *Linhest* 1086 (DB). 'Wooded hill growing with lime-trees'. OE *lind* + *hyrst*.

Lyndon Rutland. *Lindon* 1167. 'Hill where flax is grown, or where lime-trees grow'. OE *līn* or *lind* + *dūn*.

Lyne (river) Cumbria, *see* KIRKLINTON.

Lyne Surrey, near Chertsey. *La Linde* 1208. 'The lime-tree'. OE *lind*.

Lyneham, 'homestead or enclosure where flax is grown', OE *līn* + *hām* or *hamm*: **Lyneham** Oxon. *Lineham* 1086 (DB). **Lyneham** Wilts. *Linham* 1224.

Lynemouth Northum. *Lynmuth* 1342. 'Mouth of the River Lyne'. Celtic river-name (meaning 'stream') + OE *mūtha*.

Lyng Norfolk. *Ling* 1086 (DB). Probably OE *hlinc* 'bank or ridge'.

Lyng Somerset. *Lengen* early 10th cent., *Lege* |*sic*| 1086 (DB). OE **lengen* 'length', that is 'long place', referring to a long narrow settlement.

Lynmouth Devon. *Lymmouth* 1330. 'Mouth of the River Lyn'. OE river-name (from *hlynn* 'torrent') + *mūtha*.

Lynn (*Lann*) Westmeath. 'Church'.

Lynn, King's & *Lynn, West* Norfolk. *Lena*, *Lun* 1086 (DB). 'The pool'. Celtic **linn*. Affix *King's* dates from the 16th cent.

Lynsted Kent. *Lindestede* 1212–20. 'Place where lime-trees grow'. OE *lind* + *stede*.

Lynton Devon. *Lintone* 1086 (DB). 'Farmstead on the River Lyn'. OE river-name (*see* LYNMOUTH) + *tūn*.

Lyonshall Heref. & Worcs. *Lenehalle* 1086 (DB). 'Nook of land in *Leon*'. Celtic district name (meaning 'at the streams') + OE *halh*.

Lyracrumpane (*Ladhar an Chrompáin*) Kerry. 'Fork of the river valley'.

Lyre (*An Ladhar*) Cork. 'The fork'.

Lyrenageeha (*Ladhar na Gaoithe*) Cork. 'Fort of the fork'.

Lyrenagreena (*Ladhar na Gréine*) Limerick. 'Fort of the fork'.

Lytchett Matravers & *Lytchett Minster* Dorset. *Lichet* 1086 (DB), *Lichet Mautrauers* 1280, *Licheminster* 1244. 'Grey wood'. Celtic **lēd* + **cēd*. Distinguishing affixes from the Maltrauers family, here in 1086, and from OE *mynster* 'large church'.

Lytham St Anne's Lancs. *Lidun* 1086 (DB). '(Place at) the slopes or dunes'. OE *hlith* in a dative plural form *hlithum*. Affix from the dedication of the church.

Lythe N. Yorks. *Lid* 1086 (DB). 'The slope'. OScand. *hlíth*.

M

Maam (*Mám*) Galway. 'Mountain pass'.

Maas (*Más*) Donegal. 'Buttock'.

Mabe Burnthouse Cornwall. *Lavabe* 1524, *Mape* 1549. 'Church-site of Mab'. Cornish **lann* + pers. name. Addition *Burnthouse*, no doubt alluding to a fire here, is first found in early 19th cent.

Mablethorpe Lincs. *Malbertorp* 1086 (DB). 'Outlying farmstead of a man called Malbert'. OGerman pers. name + OScand. *thorp*.

Mabrista (*Má Briste*) Westmeath. 'Broken plain'.

Macclesfield Ches. *Maclesfeld* 1086 (DB). Probably 'open country of a man called **Maccel*'. OE pers. name + *feld*.

Macduff Aber. The settlement was rebuilt in 1783 by James *Duff*, 2nd Earl of Fife, who claimed to be descended from the semi-mythical Macduff in Shakespeare's *Macbeth*, and he named it after his father, William Duff, 1st Earl of Fife, who had acquired land here.

Mace (*Más*) Galway, Mayo. 'Buttock'.

Macgillycuddy's Reeks (*Na Cruacha Dubha*) (mountains) Kerry. 'Mac Gilla Chuda's ricks'. The Irish name means 'the black peaks'.

Machars, The (district) Dumf. 'The plains'. Gaelic *machair* + English plural *-s*.

Machen Cphy. *Mahhayn* 1102. 'Cein's plain'. Welsh *ma*.

Machynlleth Powys. *Machenleyd* 1254. 'Cynllaith's plain'. Welsh *ma*.

Mackworth Derbys. *Macheuorde* 1086 (DB). 'Enclosure of a man called **Macca*'. OE pers. name + *worth*.

Macnean, Lough (*Loch Mac nÉan*) Cavan, Fermanagh, Leitrim. 'Mac Nean's lake'.

Macosquin (*Maigh Choscáin*) Derry (abb mainistre) *Mhaighe Coscrain* 1505. 'Coscán's plain'.

Macroom (*Maigh Chromtha*) Cork. 'Plane of the crooked ford'.

Madabawn (*An Maide Bán*) Cavan. 'The white plant'.

Maddadoo (*Maide Dubh*) Westmeath. 'Black plant'.

Madehurst W. Sussex. *Medliers* 1188. *Medhurst* 1255. Possibly 'wooded hill near meadow-land', OE *mǣd* + *hyrst*. Alternatively the first element may be OE *mæthel* 'assembly, meeting'.

Madeley, 'woodland clearing of a man called **Māda*', OE pers. name + *lēah*: **Madeley** Shrops. *Madelie* 1086 (DB). **Madeley** Staffs., near Newcastle. *Madanlieg* 975, *Madelie* 1086 (DB).

Madingley Cambs. *Madingelei* 1086 (DB). 'Woodland clearing of the family or followers of a man called **Māda*'. OE pers. name + *-inga-* + *lēah*.

Madley Heref. & Worcs. *Medelagie* 1086 (DB), *Madele*, *Maddeleia* c.1200. OE *lēah* 'woodland clearing' with an uncertain first element, possibly an OE pers. name **Māda* as in MADELEY.

Madresfield Heref. & Worcs. *Madresfeld* c.1086, *Metheresfeld* 1192. 'Open land of the mower or of a man called Mǣthhere'. OE *mǣthere* or pers. name + *feld*.

Madron Cornwall. '(Church of) *Sanctus Madernus*' 1203. From the patron saint of the church.

Maenclochog Pemb. *Maenclochawc* 1257. 'Stone sounding like a bell'. Welsh *maen* + *clochog*.

Maenorbyr. *See* MANORBIER.

Maentwrog Gwyd. *Mayntwroc* 1292. 'Rock of St Twrog'. Welsh *maen*.

Maer Staffs. *Mere* 1086 (DB). '(Place at) the pool'. OE *mere*.

Maesbrook Shrops. *Meresbroc* 1086 (DB), *Maysbrok* 1272. Possibly 'brook of the boundary', OE *mǣre* (genitive *-s*) + *brōc*, but the first element may rather be Welsh *maes* 'open field'.

Maesbury Shrops. *Meresberie* 1086 (DB). 'Fort or manor house near the boundary'. OE *mǣre* (genitive *-s*) + *burh* (dative *byrig*).

Maesteg Bri. *Maes tege issa* 1543. 'Fair field'. Welsh *maes* + *teg*.

Maesyfed. *See* NEW RADNOR.

Magdalen Laver Essex, *see* LAVER.

Magharee Islands (*Machairí*) Kerry. 'Flat places'.

Maghera (*Machaire Rátha*) Derry. *Rátha Lúiricch* 814. 'Plain of the fort'. An earlier name was *Ráth Lúraigh*, 'Lúrach's fort', after a 6th-cent. saint.

Maghera (*Machaire*) Down. 'Plain'.

Magherabeg (*Machaire Beag*) Donegal. 'Small plain'.

Magheraboy (*Machaire Buí*) Mayo. 'Yellow plain'.

Magheracloone (*Machaire Cluana*) Monaghan. 'Plain of the pasture'.

Magheradernan (*Machaire Ua dTighearnáin*) Westmeath. 'Plain of Uí Tighearnáin'.

Magherafelt (*Machaire Fíolta*) Derry. *Teeoffigalta* 1426. 'Plain of Fíolta'. An earlier name was *Teach Fíolta*, 'Fíolta's house'.

Magheragall (*Machaire na gCeall*) Antrim. *Magheregall* 1661. 'Plain of the churches'.

Magheralin (*Machaire Lainne*) Down. (*ó*) *Lainn Ronain* c.830. 'Plain of the church'. An earlier name was *Lann Rónáin Fhinn*, 'church of fair Rónan'.

Magheramorne (*Machaire Morna*) Antrim. (*Domnach mor*) *Maigi Domóerna c.*900. 'Plain of the Morna'. The tribal name is of obscure origin.

Magheranageeragh (*Machaire na bCaorach*) Fermanagh, Tyrone. 'Plain of the sheep'.

Magheranerla (*Machaire an Iarla*) Westmeath. 'Field of the earl'.

Magheree Islands (*Machairí*) Kerry. 'Flat places'.

Maghery (*An Machaire*) Donegal. 'The plain'.

Maghull Mersey. *Magele |sic|* 1086 (DB), *Maghal* 1219. Probably 'nook of land where mayweed grows'. OE *mægthe + halh*.

Magilligan (*Aird Mhic Ghiollagáin*) Derry, 'Point of Mac Giollagán'.

Maguiresbridge Fermanagh. 'Maguire's bridge'. *Magwyre's bridge* 1639. The village grew up after 1760 when Brian Maguire of the local family of this name was given a grant to hold a market here. The corresponding Irish name is *Droichead Mhig Uidhir*.

Mahoonagh (*Caislean Maí Tamhnach*) Limerick. 'Stone fort of the plain of the fields'.

Maiden as affix, *see* main name, e.g. for **Maiden Bradley** (Wilts.) *see* BRADLEY.

Maiden Wells Pemb. *Mayden Welle* 1336. 'Spring of the maidens'. OE *mægden + wielle*.

Maidenhead Berks. *Maidenhee* 1202. 'Landing-place of the maidens'. OE *mægden + hȳth*.

Maidenwell Lincs. *Welle* 1086 (DB), *Maidenvell* 1212. Originally '(place at) the spring or stream', from OE *wella*, with the later addition of *mægden* 'maiden'.

Maidford Northants. *Merdeford |sic|* 1086 (DB), *Maideneford* 1166. 'Ford of the maidens, i.e. where they gathered'. OE *mægden + ford*.

Maids Moreton Bucks., *see* MORETON.

Maidstone Kent. *Mægthan stan* late 10th cent., *Meddestane* 1086 (DB). Probably 'stone of the maidens, i.e. where they gathered'. OE *mægth, mægden + stān*.

Maidwell Northants. *Medewelle* 1086 (DB). 'Spring or stream of the maidens, i.e. where they gathered'. OE *mægden + wella*.

Maigue (*Maigh*) (river) Limerick. 'River of the plain'.

Main (*An Mhin*) (river) Antrim. 'The water'.

Maine (*Maighin*) (river) Kerry. 'Meaning uncertain'.

Mainland (island) Orkn. *Meginland c.*1150. 'Chief district'. OScand. *megin + land*.

Maisemore Glos. *Mayesmora* 1138. Probably 'the great field'. Welsh *maes + mawr*.

Makerfield (old district) Lancs., *see* ASHTON-IN-MAKERFIELD.

Malahide (*Mullach Íde*) Dublin. 'Íde's summit'.

Malborough Devon. *Malleberge* 1249. 'Hill or mound of a man called *Mǣrla*, or where gentian grows'. OE pers. name or *meargealla + beorg*.

Malden, *New Malden* Gtr. London. *Meldone* 1086 (DB). 'Hill with a crucifix'. OE *mæl + dūn*.

Maldon Essex. *Mældune* early 10th cent., *Malduna* 1086 (DB). Identical in origin with the previous name.

Malham N. Yorks. *Malgun* 1086 (DB). '(Settlement) by the gravelly places'. OScand. **malgi* in a dative plural form.

Malin (*Málainn*) Donegal. 'Brow'.

Malin Beg (*Málainn Bhig*) Donegal. 'Small brow'.

Malin Head (*Cionn Mhálanna*) Donegal. 'Headland of the brow'.

Malin More (*Málainn Mhóir*) Donegal. 'Large brow'.

Mallaig Highland. Perhaps 'Bay of gulls'. OScand. *mar + vágr*.

Mallaranny (*An Mhala Raithní*) Mayo. 'The brow of the ferns'.

Malling, '(settlement of) the family or followers of a man called *Mealla*', OE pers. name + *-ingas*: **Malling, East** & **Malling, West** Kent. *Meallingas* 942–6, *Mellingetes |sic|* 1086 (DB). **Malling, South** E. Sussex. *Mallingum* 838, *Mellinges* 1086 (DB).

Mallow (*Mala*) Cork. 'Plain of the (river) Allow'. *See* ALLOW.

Mallusk (*Maigh Bhloisce*) Antrim. *Manyblos* 1231. 'Blosce's plain'.

Malmesbury Wilts. *Maldumesburg* 685, *Malmesberie* 1086 (DB). 'Stronghold of a man called Maeldub'. OIrish pers. name + OE *burh* (dative *byrig*).

Malone (*Maigh Luain*) Antrim. *Mylon* 1604. 'Luan's plain'.

Malpas Ches. *Malpas c.*1125. 'The difficult passage'. OFrench *mal + pas*. The same name occurs in other counties.

Malpas Newpt. *Malo Passu* 1291. 'Difficult passage'. OFrench *mal + pas*.

Maltby, 'farmstead or village of a man called Malti, or where malt is made', OScand. pers. name or *malt + bý*: **Maltby** S. Yorks. *Maltebi* 1086 (DB). **Maltby** Stock. on T. *Maltebi* 1086 (DB). **Maltby le Marsh** Lincs. *Maltebi* 1086 (DB). Affix 'in the marshland' from OE *mersc*.

Malton N. Yorks. *Maltune* 1086 (DB). Possibly 'farmstead where an assembly was held'. OE *mæthel + tūn*. Alternatively the first element may be OScand. *methal* 'middle'.

Malvern, Great & *Malvern, Little* Heref. & Worcs. *Mælfern c.*1030, *Malferna* 1086 (DB). 'Bare hill'. Celtic **moil + *brinn*. **Malvern Link**, *Link* 1215, is from OE *hlinc* 'ledge, terrace'.

Mamble Heref. & Worcs. *Mamele* 1086 (DB). Probably a derivative of Celtic **mamm* 'breast-like hill'.

Manaccan Cornwall. '(Church of) *Sancta Manaca*' 1309. Probably from the patron saint of the church.

Manaton Devon. *Manitone* 1086 (DB). 'Farmstead held communally, or by a man called Manna'. OE *(ge)mǣne* or pers. name + *tūn*.

Manby Lincs., near Louth. *Mannebi* 1086 (DB). 'Farmstead or village of a man called Manni, or of the men'. OScand. pers. name or *mann* (genitive plural *-a*) + *bý*.

Mancetter Warwicks. *Manduessedum* 4th cent., *Manacestre* 1195. OE *ceaster* 'Roman fort or town' added to a reduced form of the original Celtic name which probably means 'horse chariot' (perhaps alluding to a topographical feature).

Manchester Gtr. Manch. *Mamucio* 4th cent., *Mamecestre* 1086 (DB). OE *ceaster* 'Roman fort or town' added to a reduced form of the original Celtic name (meaning obscure, but possibly containing Celtic *mamm* 'breast-like hill').

Mancot Royal Flin. The hamlet arose as a housing estate built near BIG MANCOT in 1917 for workers in the nearby Royal Ordnance Factory.

Manea Cambs. *Moneia* 1177. OE *ēg* 'island, well-watered land' with a doubtful first element, possibly OE *(ge)mǣne* 'held in common'.

Manfield N. Yorks. *Mannefelt* 1086 (DB). 'Open land of a man called Manna, or held communally'. OE pers. name or OE *(ge)mǣne* + *feld*.

Mangotsfield S. Glos. *Manegodesfelle* 1086 (DB). 'Open land of a man called Mangod'. OGerman pers. name + OE *feld*.

Manley Ches. *Menlie* 1086 (DB). 'Common wood or clearing'. OE *(ge)mǣne* + *lēah*.

Manningford Bohune & *Manningford Bruce* Wilts. *Maningaford* 987, *Maniford* 1086 (DB), *Manyngeford Bon*, *Manyngeford Breuse* 1279. 'Ford of the family or followers of a man called Manna'. OE pers. name + *-inga-* + *ford*. Manorial additions from the Boun and Breuse families, here in the 13th cent.

Mannington Dorset. *Manitone* 1086 (DB). 'Estate associated with a man called Manna'. OE pers. name + *-ing-* + *tūn*.

Manningtree Essex. *Manitre* 1248. 'Many trees', or 'tree of a man called Manna'. OE *manig* or OE pers. name + *trēow*.

Manorbier (*Maenorbyr*) Pemb. *Mainour pir* 1136, *Manerbire* 1331. 'Pyr's manor'. Welsh *maenor*.

Manorcunningham Donegal. *The Manor of Fort Cownyngham* 1629. The village is named after James *Cunningham* of Ayrshire, Scotland, who was granted land here in 1610. The equivalent Irish name is *Mainéar Uí Chuinneagáin*.

Manordeifi Pemb. *Mamardeyvi* 1219, *Menordaun* 1291. 'Estate on the River Teifi'. Welsh *maenor*. The river name means simply 'stream' (British *tamos*).

Manorhamilton Leitrim. Lands here were granted by Charles I to Sir Frederick *Hamilton*. The Irish name is *Cluainín*, short for *Cuainín Uí Ruairc*, 'little meadow of Ó Ruairc'.

Manorowen Pemb. *Maynornawan* 1326. 'Gnawan's manor'. Welsh *maenor*.

Mansell Gamage & *Mansell Lacy* Heref. & Worcs. *Mælueshylle* c.1045, *Malveselle* 1086 (DB), *Maumeshull Gamages*, *Maumeshull Lacy* 1242. Probably 'hill of the gravel ridge'. OE *malu* + *hyll*. Manorial affixes from the de Gamagis family, here in the 12th cent., and from the de Lacy family, here in 1086.

Mansfield Notts. *Mamesfelde* 1086 (DB). 'Open land by the River Maun'. Celtic river-name (from Celtic *mamm* 'breast-like hill') + OE *feld*.

Mansfield Woodhouse Notts. *Wodehuse* 1230, *Mamesfeud Wodehus* 1280. 'Woodland hamlet near MANSFIELD'. OE *wudu* + *hūs*.

Manston, 'farmstead of a man called Mann', OE pers. name + *tūn*: **Manston** Dorset. *Manestone* 1086 (DB). **Manston** Kent. *Manneston* 1254.

Manthorpe Lincs., near Thurlby. *Mannetorp* 1086 (DB). 'Outlying farmstead or village of a man called Manni, or of the men'. OScand. pers. name or *mann* (genitive plural *-a*) + *thorp*.

Manton N. Lincs. *Malmetun* 1060–6, *Mameltune* 1086 (DB). 'Farmstead on sandy or chalky ground'. OE *malm* + *tūn*.

Manton Rutland. *Mannatonam* 1120–9, *Manatona* c.1130. Probably 'farmstead or estate of a man called Manna'. OE pers. name + *tūn*.

Manton Wilts. *Manetune* 1086 (DB). 'Farmstead held communally, or by a man called Manna'. OE *(ge)mǣne* or OE pers. name + *tūn*.

Mantua (*An Móinteach*) Roscommon. 'The moorland'.

Manuden Essex. *Magghedana* [sic] 1086 (DB), *Manegedan* c.1130. Probably 'valley of the family or followers of a man called Manna'. OE pers. name + *-inga-* + *denu*.

Maplebeck Notts. *Mapelbec* 1086 (DB). 'Stream where maple-trees grow'. OE *mapel* + OScand. *bekkr*.

Mapledurham Oxon. *Mapeldreham* 1086 (DB). 'Homestead where maple-trees grow'. OE *mapuldor* + *hām*.

Mapledurwell Hants. *Mapledrewell* 1086 (DB). 'Spring or stream where maple-trees grow'. OE *mapuldor* + *wella*.

Maplestead, Great & *Maplestead, Little* Essex. *Mapulderstede* 1042, *Mapledestedam* 1086 (DB). 'Place where maple-trees grow'. OE *mapuldor* + *stede*.

Mapperley Derbys. *Maperlie* 1086 (DB). 'Maple-tree wood or clearing'. OE *mapuldor* + *lēah*.

Mapperton Dorset, near Beaminster. *Malperetone* 1086 (DB). 'Farmstead where maple-trees grow'. OE *mapuldor* + *tūn*.

Mappleborough Green Warwicks. *Mepelesbarwe* 848, *Mapelberge* 1086 (DB). 'Hill where maple-trees grow'. OE *mapel* + *beorg*.

Mappleton E. R. Yorks. *Mapletone* 1086 (DB). 'Farmstead where maple-trees grow'. OE *mapel* + *tūn*.

Mappowder Dorset. *Mapledre* 1086 (DB). '(Place at) the maple-tree'. OE *mapuldor*.

Mar(r) (district) Aber. '(Land of the) Mar people'. The tribal name probably comes from a pers. name *Marsos*.

Marazion Cornwall. *Marghasbigan* c.1265. 'Little market'. Cornish *marghas* + *byghan*.

Marbury Ches., near Whitchurch. *Merberie* 1086 (DB). 'Fortified place near a lake'. OE *mere* + *burh* (dative *byrig*).

March Cambs. *Merche* 1086 (DB). '(Place at) the boundary'. OE *mearc* in an old locative form.

Marcham Oxon. *Merchamme* 900, *Merceham* 1086 (DB). 'Enclosure or river-meadow where smallage (wild celery) grows'. OE *merece* + *hamm*.

Marchamley Shrops. *Marcemeslei* 1086 (DB), *Marchemeleg* 1227. Possibly 'woodland clearing of a man called Merchelm', OE pers. name + *lēah*. Alternatively 'woodland clearing at the (territory of) the Mercians', with a first element OE *Mierce* in a dative plural form *Miercum*.

Marchington Staffs. *Mæchamtun* 1002, *Merchametone* 1086 (DB). Probably 'farmstead of the dwellers at a homestead where smallage (wild celery) grows'. OE *merece* + *hǣme* + *tūn*.

Marchwood Hants. *Merceode* 1086 (DB). 'Wood where smallage (wild celery) grows'. OE *merece* + *wudu*.

Marcle, Much & *Marcle, Little* Heref. & Worcs. *Merchelai* 1086 (DB). 'Wood or clearing on a boundary'. OE *mearc* + *lēah*. Affix *Much* is from OE *mycel* 'great'.

Marden Heref. & Worcs. *Maurdine* |*sic*| 1086 (DB), *Magewurdin* 1177. 'Enclosed settlement in the district called MAUND'. OE *worthign*.

Marden Kent. *Maeredaen* c.1100. 'Woodland pasture for mares, or near a boundary'. OE *mere* or (*ge*)*mǣre* + *denn*.

Marden Wilts. *Mercdene* 941, *Meresdene* 1086 (DB). Probably 'boundary valley'. OE *mearc* + *denu*.

Marden, East, *Marden, North*, & *Marden, West* W. Sussex. *Meredone* 1086 (DB). 'Boundary hill'. OE (*ge*)*mǣre* + *dūn*.

Marefield Leics. *Merdefelde* 1086 (DB). 'Open land frequented by martens or weasels'. OE *mearth* + *feld*.

Mareham le Fen & *Mareham on the Hill* Lincs. *Marun*, *Meringhe* 1086 (DB), *Marum* c.1200. '(Place at) the pools' from OE *mere* in a dative plural form *merum*, in early sources alternating with '(settlement of) the dwellers by the pools' from OE *mere* + *-ingas*. Affix *le Fen* means 'in the marshland'.

Maresfield E. Sussex. *Mersfeld* 1234. 'Open land by a marsh or pool'. OE *mersc* or *mere* + *feld*.

Marfleet K. upon Hull. *Mereflet* 1086 (DB). 'Pool creek or stream'. OE *mere* + *flēot*.

Margaret Roding Essex, *see* RODING.

Margaretting Essex. *Ginga* 1086 (DB), *Gynge Margarete* 1291. 'Manor called Ing (for which *see* FRYERNING) of St Margaret'. From the dedication of the church.

Margate Kent. *Meregate* 1254. Probably 'gate or gap leading to the sea, or by a pool'. OE *mere* + *geat*.

Marham Norfolk. *Merham* c.1050, *Marham* 1086 (DB). 'Homestead by or with a pond'. OE *mere* + *hām*.

Marhamchurch Cornwall. *Maronecirce* 1086 (DB). 'Church of St Marwen or Merwenn'. Female saint's name + OE *cirice*.

Marholm Cambs. *Marham* c.1060. 'Homestead by or with a pond'. OE *mere* + *hām*.

Mariansleigh Devon. *Lege* 1086 (DB), *Marinelegh* 1238. 'The wood or clearing' from OE *lēah*, with the later addition of the saint's name *Marina* or *Marion* (a diminutive of *Mary*).

Marishes, High & *Marishes, Low* N. Yorks. *Aschilesmares*, *Chiluesmares*, *Ouduluesmersc* 1086 (DB). 'The marshes', from OE *mersc*. Different manors originally distinguished by the names of early owners, OScand. *Ásketill*, *Ketilfrøthr*, and *Authulfr*.

Mark Somerset. *Mercern* 1065. 'House or building near a boundary'. OE *mearc* + *ærn*.

Markby Lincs. *Marchebi* 1086 (DB). Possibly 'farmstead or village of a man called Marki'. OScand. pers. name + *bý*. Alternatively the first element may be OScand. *mǫrk* 'frontier area, wilderness'.

Market as affix, *see* main name, e.g. for **Market Bosworth** (Leics.) *see* BOSWORTH.

Markethill Armagh. 'Hill with a market'. *Markethill* c.1640. The town, with its steep main street and still thriving livestock markets, grew up in the early 17th cent. The equivalent Irish name is *Cnoc an Mhargaigh*.

Markfield Leics. *Merchenefeld* 1086 (DB). 'Open land of the Mercians'. OE *Merce* (genitive plural *Mercna*) + *feld*.

Markham, East & *Markham, West* Notts. *Marcham* 1086 (DB), *Estmarcham* 1192. 'Homestead or village on a boundary'. OE *mearc* + *hām*.

Markinch Fife. *Marchinke* 1055, *Markynchs* c.1290. 'Horse meadow'. Gaelic *marc* + *innis*.

Markington N. Yorks. *Mercingtune* c.1030, *Merchinton* 1086 (DB). Possibly 'farmstead of the Mercians', OE *Merce* (genitive plural *Mercna*) + *tūn*. Alternatively 'farmstead of the boundary-dwellers, or by a boundary'. OE (*ge*)*merce* (with Scand. *-k-*) + *-inga-* or *-ing* + *tūn*.

Marks Tey Essex, *see* TEY.

Marksbury B. & NE. Som. *Merkesburi* 936, *Mercesberie* 1086 (DB). Possibly 'stronghold of a man called *Mǣrec* or *Mearc*'. OE pers. name + *burh* (dative *byrig*). Alternatively the first element may be OE *mearc* 'boundary' (perhaps with reference to the Wansdyke).

Markyate Herts. *Markʒate* 12th cent. 'Gate at the (county) boundary'. OE *mearc* + *geat*.

Marland, *Peters* Devon. *Mirlanda* 1086 (DB). 'Cultivated land by a pool'. OE *mere* + *land*.

Marlborough Wilts. *Merleberge* 1086 (DB). 'Hill or mound of a man called *Mǣrla*, or where gentian grows'. OE pers. name or *meargealla* + *beorg*.

Marlcliff Warwicks. *Mearnanclyfe* 872. 'Cliff of a man called *Mearna*'. OE pers. name + *clif*.

Marldon Devon. *Mergheldone* 1307. 'Hill where gentian grows'. OE *meargealla* + *dūn*.

Marlesford Suffolk. *Merlesforda* 1086 (DB). Probably 'ford of a man called *Mǣrel*'. OE pers. name + *ford*.

Marlingford Norfolk. *Marthingforth* c.1000, *Merlingeforda*, *Marthingeforda* 1086 (DB). Possibly 'ford of the family or followers of a man called *Mearthel*'. OE pers. name + *-inga-* + *ford*.

Marlow Bucks. *Merelafan* 1015, *Merlaue* 1086 (DB). 'Land remaining after the draining of a pool'. OE *mere* + *lāf*.

Marnham, High & *Marnham, Low* Notts. *Marneham* 1086 (DB). 'Homestead or village of a man called *Mearna*'. OE pers. name + *hām*.

Marnhull Dorset. *Marnhulle* 1267. Probably 'hill of a man called *Mearna'. OE pers. name + *hyll*.

Marple Gtr. Manch. *Merpille* early 13th cent. 'Pool or stream at the boundary'. OE (*ge*)*mǣre* + *pyll*.

Marr S. Yorks. *Marra* 1086 (DB). '(Place at) the marsh'. OScand. *marr*.

Marrick N. Yorks. *Marige* 1086 (DB). 'Boundary ridge'. OE (*ge*)*mǣre* + *hrycg*.

Marsco (mountain) Highland (Skye). 'Seagull rock'. OScand. *már* + *sgo*(?).

Marsden W. Yorks. *Marchesden* 12th cent. Probably 'boundary valley'. OE *mercels* + *denu*.

Marsh, '(place at) the marsh', OE *mersc*: **Marsh** Shrops. *Mersse* 1086 (DB). **Marsh Gibbon** Bucks. *Merse* 1086 (DB), *Mersh Gibwyne* 1292. Manorial affix from the Gibwen family, here in the 12th cent.

Marsh Baldon Oxon., *see* BALDON.

Marsham Norfolk. *Marsam* 1086 (DB). 'Homestead or village by a marsh'. OE *mersc* + *hām*.

Marshfield S. Glos. *Meresfelde* 1086 (DB). Probably 'open land on the boundary' OE (*ge*)*mǣre* + *feld*. Alternatively the first element may be OE *mersc* 'marsh'.

Marshwood Dorset. *Merswude* 1188. 'Wood by a marsh'. OE *mersc* + *wudu*.

Marske, '(place at) the marsh', OE *mersc* (with Scand. -*sk*): **Marske** N. Yorks. *Mersche* 1086 (DB). **Marske-by-the-Sea** Red. & Cleve. *Mersc* 1086 (DB).

Marston, a common name, 'farmstead in or by a marsh', OE *mersc* + *tūn*; examples include: **Marston** Oxon. *Mersttune* c.1069. **Marston, Broad** Heref. & Worcs. *Merestvne* 1086 (DB), *Brademerston* 1224. Affix is OE *brād* 'broad' referring to the shape of the village site. **Marston, Long** N. Yorks. *Mersetone* 1086 (DB). **Marston, Long** Warwicks. *Merstuna* 1043, *Merestone* 1086 (DB), *Longa Merston* 1285. Affix refers to the length of the village. Earlier often called *Dry Marston* or *Marston Sicca* (from Latin *sicca* 'dry'). **Marston Magna** Somerset. *Merstone* 1086 (DB), *Great Merston* 1248. Affix is Latin *magna* 'great'. **Marston Meysey** Wilts. *Merston* 1199, *Merston Meysi* 1259. Manorial affix from the de Meysi family, here in the 13th cent. **Marston Moretaine** Beds. *Merestone* 1086 (DB), *Merston Morteyn* 1383. Manorial affix from its early possession by the Morteyn family. **Marston, Priors** Warwicks. *Merston* 1236, *Prioris Merston* 1316. The manor was held by the Prior of Coventry in 1242. **Marston Trussell** Northants. *Mersitone* 1086 (DB), *Merston Trussel* 1235. Manorial affix from the Trussel family, here in the 13th cent.

Marstow Heref. & Worcs. *Lann Martin* c.1130, *Martinestowe* 1291. 'Church or holy place of St Martin'. Saint's name + OE *stōw* (replacing Welsh *llan* in the early form).

Marsworth Bucks. *Mæssanwyrth* 10th cent., *Misseworde* |*sic*| 1086 (DB). 'Enclosure of a man called *Mæssa'. OE pers. name + *worth*.

Marten Wilts. *Mertone* 1086 (DB). 'Farmstead near a boundary, or by a pool'. OE (*ge*)*mǣre* or *mere* + *tūn*.

Marthall Ches. *Marthale* late 13th cent. 'Nook of land frequented by martens or weasels'. OE *mearth* + *halh*.

Martham Norfolk. *Martham* 1086 (DB). 'Homestead or enclosure frequented by martens or weasels'. OE *mearth* + *hām* or *hamm*.

Martin, 'farmstead near a boundary, or by a pool', OE (*ge*)*mǣre* or *mere* + *tūn*: examples include: **Martin** Hants. *Mertone* 946. **Martin** Lincs., near Horncastle. *Mærtune* 1060, *Martone* 1086 (DB). **Martin** Lincs., near Metheringham. *Martona* 12th cent. **Martin Hussingtree** Heref. & Worcs. *Meretun*, *Husantreo* 972, *Husentre* 1086 (DB), *Marten Hosentre* 1535. Originally two separate manors, Hussingtree being 'tree of a man called Hūsa', from OE pers. name (genitive -*n*) + *trēow*.

Martinhoe Devon. *Matingeho* 1086 (DB). 'Hill-spur of the family or followers of a man called *Matta'. OE pers. name + -*inga*- + *hōh*.

Martinscroft Ches. *Martinescroft* 1332. 'Enclosure of a man called Martin'. ME pers. name + *croft*.

Martinstown Dorset. *Wintreburne* 1086 (DB), *Wynterburn Seynt Martyn* 1280, *Martyn towne* 1494. Originally 'estate on the River WINTERBORNE with a church dedicated to St Martin'. The alternative name came into use in the late 15th cent.

Martinstown Antrim. 'Martin's town'. The village takes its name from a man surnamed Martin. The corresponding Irish name is *Baile Uí Mháirtín*.

Martlesham Suffolk. *Merlesham* |*sic*| 1086 (DB), *Martlesham* 1254. Possibly 'homestead by a woodland clearing frequented by martens'. OE *mearth* + *lēah* + *hām*. Alternatively the first element may be an OE pers. name *Mertel*.

Martletwy Pemb. *Martletwye* c.1230. 'Grave of a saint'. Welsh *merthyr*. The second element represents the name of the saint, possibly Tywai or Tyfai.

Martley Heref. & Worcs. *Mærtleag* c.1030, *Mertelai* 1086 (DB). 'Woodland clearing frequented by martens'. OE *mearth* + *lēah*.

Martock Somerset. *Mertoch* 1086 (DB). Possibly 'outlying farmstead or hamlet by a pool'. OE *mere* + *stoc*.

Marton, a common name, usually 'farmstead by a pool', OE *mere* + *tūn*, although some names may be 'farmstead near a boundary' with OE (*ge*)*mǣre* as first element; examples include: **Marton** Lincs. *Martone* 1086 (DB). **Marton** Warwicks. *Mortone* |*sic*| 1086 (DB), *Merton* 1151. **Marton-le-Moor** N. Yorks. *Marton* 1198, *Marton on the Moor* 1292. Affix is from OE *mōr* 'moor'. **Marton, Long** Cumbria. *Meretun* c.1170. Affix refers to the length of the parish.

Martyr Worthy Hants., *see* WORTHY.

Marwood Devon. *Mereuda* 1086 (DB). Probably 'wood near a boundary'. OE (*ge*)*mǣre* + *wudu*.

Mary Tavey Devon, *see* TAVY.

Maryborough. *See* PORTLAOISE.

Marylebone Gtr. London. *Maryburne* 1453. '(Place by) St Mary's stream'. OE *burna*. Named from the dedication of the church built in the 15th cent. The -*le*- is intrusive and dates from the 17th cent.

Maryport Cumbria. *Mary-port* 1762. A modern name, the harbour here built in the 18th cent. by Humphrey Senhouse being named after his wife Mary.

Marystow Devon. *Sancte Marie Stou* 1266. 'Holy place of St Mary'. OE *stōw*.

Masham N. Yorks. *Massan |sic|* 1086 (DB), *Masham* 1153. 'Homestead or village of a man called *Mæssa'. OE pers. name + *hām*.

Mashbury Essex. *Maisseberia* 1068, *Massebirig* 1086 (DB). 'Stronghold of a man called *Mæssa or *Mæcca'. OE pers. name + *burh* (dative *byrig*).

Massingham, Great & *Massingham, Little* Norfolk. *Masingeham* 1086 (DB). 'Homestead of the family or followers of a man called *Mæssa'. OE pers. name + *-inga-* + *hām*.

Mastergeehy (*Máistir Gaoithe*) Kerry. 'Churning wind'.

Matching Essex. *Matcinga* 1086 (DB). '(Settlement of) the family or followers of a man called *Mæcca', or '*Mæcca's place'. OE pers. name + *-ingas* or *-ing*.

Matehy (*Má Teithe*) Cork. 'Smooth plain'.

Matfen Northum. *Matefen* 1159. Probably 'fen of a man called *Matta'. OE pers. name + *fenn*.

Matfield Kent. *Mattefeld* c.1230. 'Open land of a man called *Matta'. OE pers. name + *feld*.

Mathon Heref. & Worcs. *Matham* 1014, *Matma* 1086 (DB). 'The treasure or gift'. OE *māthm*.

Mathry Pemb. *Marthru* c.1150. Possibly 'grave of a saint'. Welsh *merthyr*.

Matlask Norfolk. *Matelasc* 1086 (DB). 'Ash-tree where meetings are held'. OE *mæthel* + *æsc* or OScand. *askr*.

Matlock Derbys. *Meslach |sic|* 1086 (DB), *Matlac* 1196. 'Oak-tree where meetings are held'. OE *mæthel* + *āc*.

Matterdale End Cumbria. *Mayerdale |sic|* c.1250, *Matherdal* 1323. 'Valley where madder grows'. OScand. *mathra* + *dalr*.

Mattersey Notts. *Madressei* 1086 (DB). 'Island, or well-watered land, of a man called Mæthhere'. OE pers. name + *ēg*.

Mattingley Hants. *Matingelege* 1086 (DB). 'Woodland clearing of the family or followers of a man called *Matta'. OE pers. name + *-inga-* + *lēah*.

Mattishall Norfolk. *Mateshala* 1086 (DB). Probably 'nook of land of a man called *Matt'. OE pers. name + *halh*.

Mauchline E. Ayr. *Machline* c.1130, *Mauhhelin* c.1177, *Mauchlyn* c.1200. Said to mean 'Plain by the pool'. Gaelic *magh* + *linn*.

Maugersbury Glos. *Meilgaresbyri* 714, *Malgeresberie* 1086 (DB). 'Stronghold of a man called *Mæthelgār'. OE pers. name + *burh* (dative *byrig*).

Maulagallane (*Meall an Ghalláin*) Kerry. 'Knoll of the standing stone'.

Maulden Beds. *Meldone* 1086 (DB). 'Hill with a crucifix'. OE *mēl* + *dūn*.

Maulds Meaburn Cumbria, *see* MEABURN.

Maulnagower (*Meall na nGabhar*) Kerry. 'Knoll of the goats'.

Maulnahorna (*Meall na hOrna*) Kerry. 'Knoll of the barley'.

Maulyneill (*Meall Uí Néill*) Kerry. 'Ó Néill's knoll'.

Maumakeogh (*Mám an Cheo*) Mayo. 'Pass of the mist'.

Maumtrasna (*Mám Trasna*) Mayo. 'Mountain pass'.

Maumturk (*Mám Tuirc*) Galway. 'Pass of the boar'.

Maun (river) Notts., *see* MANSFIELD.

Maunby N. Yorks. *Mannebi* 1086 (DB). 'Farmstead or village of a man called Magni'. OScand. pers. name + *bý*.

Maund Bryan Heref. & Worcs. *Magene* 1086 (DB), *Magene Brian* 1242. A difficult name, but possibly '(place at) the hollows', from OE *maga* 'stomach' (used in a topographical sense) in a dative plural form. Alternatively *Maund* (also a district-name) may represent the survival of an ancient Celtic name *Magnis* (probably 'the rocks'). Manorial affix from a 12th cent. owner called Brian.

Mausrower (*Más Ramhar*) Kerry. 'Fat haunch-shaped hill'.

Mausrevagh (*Más Riabhach*) Galway. 'Striped thigh'.

Mautby Norfolk. *Malteby* 1086 (DB). 'Farmstead or village of a man called Malti, or where malt is made'. OScand. pers. name or *malt* + *bý*.

Mavis Enderby Lincs., *see* ENDERBY.

Mawddach. *See* BARMOUTH.

Mawdesley Lancs. *Madesle* 1219. 'Woodland clearing of a woman called Maud'. OFrench pers. name (from OGerman *Mahthildis*) + OE *lēah*.

Mawgan Cornwall. *Scanctus Mawan* 1086 (DB). '(Church of) St Mawgan'. From the patron saint of the church.

Mawnan Cornwall. '(Church of) *Sanctus Maunanus*' 1281. From the patron saint of the church.

Maxey Cambs. *Macuseige* c.963. 'Island, or dry ground in marsh, of a man called Maccus'. OScand. pers. name + *ēg*.

Maxstoke Warwicks. *Makestoka* 1169. 'Outlying farmstead or hamlet of a man called *Macca'. OE pers. name + *stoc*.

Maxwelltown Dumf. *Mackeswel* 1144. 'Village at Maxwell'. OE *tun*. Maxwell is 'Maccus's pool' (OE *wella*). The first element may be a surname. Now part of Dumfries.

May, Isle of Fife. *Mai* 1143, *Maeyar* 1250. Origin unknown.

Maybole S. Ayr. *Mayboill* 1275. 'Kinswomen's dwelling': OE *msēge* + *bothl*.

Mayfield E. Sussex. *Magavelda* 12th cent. 'Open land where mayweed grows'. OE *mægthe* + *feld*.

Mayfield Staffs. *Medevelde |sic|* 1086 (DB), *Matherfeld* c.1180. 'Open land where madder grows'. OE *mæddre* + *feld*.

Mayford Surrey. *Maiford* 1212. Possibly 'maidens' ford', or 'ford where mayweed grows'. OE *mægth* or *mægthe* + *ford*.

Mayglass (*Magh Glas*) Wexford. 'Green plain'.

Mayland Essex. *La Mailanda* 1188. Possibly 'land or estate where mayweed grows', from OE *mægthe* + *land*. Alternatively '(place at) the island', from OE *ēg-land*, with *M-* from the dative case of the OE definite article.

Maynooth (*Maigh Nuadhat*) Kildare. *Magh Nuaddat* n.d. 'Plain of Nuadha'. Nuadha was the supreme leader of the gods.

Mayo (*Maigh Eo*) (the county). 'Plain of yew trees'.

Mayobridge Down. 'Bridge of Mayo'. *Droichead Mhuigheó* 1901. The village is named from the townland of *Mayo* (Irish *Maigh Eo*, 'plain of yew trees').

Mayogall (*Maigh Ghuala*) Derry. 'Plain of the shoulder'.

Maze (*An Mhaigh*) Down. *the 5 towns of the Mew* 1585. 'The plain'.

Meaburn, King's & *Meaburn, Maulds* Cumbria. *Maiburne* 12th cent., *Meburne Regis* 1279, *Meburnemaud* 1278. 'Meadow stream'. OE *mǣd* + *burna*. Distinguishing affixes from possession by the Crown (Latin *regis* 'of the king') and by a woman called Maud here in the 12th cent.

Mealaghans (*Maelachán*) Offaly. 'Little bare hills'.

Meall Dearg (mountain) Highland. 'Red mountain'. Gaelic *meall* + *dearg*.

Meall Dubh (mountain) Highland. 'Black mountain'. Gaelic *meall* + *dubh*.

Meall Garbh (mountain) Highland. 'Rough mountain'. Gaelic *meall* + *garbh*.

Meall Gorm (mountain) Highland. 'Blue mountain'. Gaelic *meall* + *gorm*.

Meall Meadhonach (mountain) Highland. 'Middle mountain'. Gaelic *meall* + *meadhon*.

Meall Mór (mountain) Highland. 'Big mountain'. Gaelic *meall* + *mór*.

Meare Somerset. *Mere* 1086 (DB). '(Place at) the pool or lake'. OE *mere*.

Mearns (district) E. Renf. *Moerne* 12th cent. Gaelic *An Mhaoirne* 'the stewartry'; from *maor* 'steward'.

Mears Ashby Northants., *see* ASHBY.

Measham Leics. *Messeham* 1086 (DB). 'Homestead or village on the River Mease'. OE river-name ('mossy river' from OE *mēos*) + *hām*.

Meath (*An Mhí*) (the county). 'The middle (place)'. *Mide* 9th cent. Meath was formerly the fifth province of Ireland.

Meathop Cumbria. *Midhop* c.1185. 'Middle enclosure in marsh'. OE *midd* (replaced by OScand. *mithr*) + *hop*.

Meaux E. R. Yorks. *Melse* 1086 (DB). 'Sand-bank pool'. OScand. *melr* + *sǽr*.

Meavy Devon. *Mǽwi* 1031, *Mewi* 1086 (DB). Named from the River Meavy, probably a Celtic river-name meaning 'lively stream'.

Medbourne Leics. *Medburne* 1086 (DB). 'Meadow stream'. OE *mǣd* + *burna*.

Meddon Devon. *Madone* 1086 (DB). 'Meadow hill'. OE *mǣd* + *dūn*.

Medina I. of Wight, district named from the River Medina, *Medine* 1196, 'the middle one', from OE *medume*.

Medmenham Bucks. *Medmeham* 1086 (DB). 'Middle or middle-sized homestead or enclosure'. OE *medume* (dative -an) + *hām* or *hamm*.

Medstead Hants. *Medested* 1202. 'Meadow place', or 'place of a man called *Mēde*'. OE *mǣd* or pers. name + *stede*.

Medway (river) Sussex–Kent. *Medeuuæge* 8th cent. Ancient pre-English river-name *Wey* (of obscure etymology), possibly compounded with Celtic or OE *medu* 'mead' with reference to the colour or the sweetness of the water.

Meeldrum (*Maoldruim*) Westmeath. 'Bald ridge'.

Meelin (*An Mhaolinn*) Cork. 'The hillock'.

Meenaclady (*Mín an Chladaigh*) Donegal. 'Smooth place of the shore'.

Meenacross (*Mín na Croise*) Donegal. 'Smooth place of the cross'.

Meenagorp (*Mín na gCorp*) Tyrone. 'Smooth place of the corpses'.

Meenaneary (*Mín an Aoire*) Donegal. *Mininarie* 1755. 'Smooth place of the shepherd'.

Meenavean (*Mín na bhFiann*) Donegal. 'Smooth place of the Fianna'.

Meeniska (*Meadhón Uisge*) Westmeath. 'Middle water'.

Meerbrook Staffs. *Merebroke* 1338. 'Boundary brook'. OE (*ge*)*mǣre* + *brōc*.

Meesden Herts. *Mesdone* 1086 (DB). 'Mossy or boggy hill'. OE *mēos* + *dūn*.

Meeth Devon. *Meda* 1086 (DB). OE (*ge*)*mȳthe* 'confluence of rivers' or *mǣth* 'place where corn or grass is cut'.

Megdale Dumf. 'Marshy meadow'. Cumbric *mig-* + *dôl*.

Meigh (*Maigh*) Armagh. *Moye* 1657. 'Plain'.

Meigle Perth. *Migdele* c.1200, *Mygghil* 1378. 'Marshy meadow'. Pictish *mig-* + *dôl*.

Meirionnydd. See MERIONETH.

Melbourn Cambs. *Meldeburna* 970, *Melleburne* 1086 (DB). Possibly 'stream where orach or a similar plant grows'. OE *melde* + *burna*.

Melbourne Derbys. *Mileburne* 1086 (DB). Probably 'mill stream'. OE *myln* + *burna*.

Melbourne E. R. Yorks. *Middelburne* 1086 (DB). 'Middle stream'. OE *middel* (replaced by OScand. *methal*) + OE *burna*.

Melbury, probably 'multi-coloured fortified place', OE *mǣle* + *burh* (dative *byrig*): **Melbury Abbas** Dorset. *Meleburge* 956, *Meleberie* 1086 (DB), *Melbury Abbatisse* 1291. Affix is Latin *abbatissa* 'abbess' from its early possession by Shaftesbury Abbey. **Melbury Bubb, Melbury Osmond**, & **Melbury Sampford** Dorset. *Mele(s)berie* 1086 (DB), *Melebir Bubbe* 1244, *Melebur Osmund* 1283, *Melebury Saunford* 1312. Manorial affixes from the Bubbe family, from a man called Osmund, and from the Saunford family, all here in the 13th cent.

Melchbourne Beds. *Melceburne* 1086 (DB). 'Stream by pastures yielding good milk'. OE **melce* + *burna*.

Melcombe Regis Dorset. *Melecumb* 1223. Probably 'valley where milk is produced'. OE *meoluc* + *cumb*.

Meldon Devon. *Meledon* 1175. 'Multi-coloured hill'. OE *mǣle* + *dūn*.

Meldon Northum. *Meldon* 1242. 'Hill with a crucifix'. OE *mǣl* + *dūn*.

Meldreth Cambs. *Melrede* 1086 (DB). 'Mill stream'. OE *myln* + *rīth*.

Melford, Long Suffolk. *Melaforda* 1086 (DB). Probably 'ford by a mill'. OE *myln* + *ford*.

Meliden (*Allt Melyd*) Denb. *Altmelyden* 1291. 'Hill of St Melydn'. The word for 'hill' is missing in the English form of the name, but present in the Welsh (*allt*).

Melkinthorpe Cumbria. *Melcanetorp* c.1150. 'Outlying farmstead or hamlet of a man called Maelchon'. OIrish pers. name + OScand. *thorp*.

Melkridge Northum. *Melkrige* 1279. 'Ridge where milk is produced'. OE *meoluc* + *hrycg*.

Melksham Wilts. *Melchesham* 1086 (DB). Possibly 'homestead or enclosure where milk is produced'. OE *meoluc* + *hām* or *hamm*.

Mellifont Louth. 'Fountain of honey'. Latin *mel* + *fons* (genitive *fontis*).

Melling, probably '(settlement of) the family or followers of a man called *Mealla', or '*Mealla's place', OE pers. name + *-ingas* or *-ing*: **Melling** Lancs. *Mellinge* 1086 (DB). **Melling** Mersey. *Melinge* 1086 (DB).

Mellis Suffolk. *Melles* 1086 (DB). 'The mills'. OE *myln*.

Mellor, 'bare or smooth-topped hill', Celtic **mēl* + **breʒ*: **Mellor** Gtr. Manch. *Melver* 1283. **Mellor** Lancs. *Malver* c.1130.

Mells Somerset. *Milne* 942, *Mulle* 1086 (DB). 'The mill(s)'. OE *myln*.

Melmerby, 'farmstead or village of a man called Maelmuire', OIrish pers. name + OScand. *bý*: **Melmerby** Cumbria. *Malmerbi* 1201. **Melmerby** N. Yorks., near Coverham. *Melmerbi* 1086 (DB). **Melmerby** N. Yorks., near Ripon. *Malmerbi* 1086 (DB). First element alternatively OScand. *malmr* 'sandy field'.

Melmore (*An Meall Mór*) Donegal. 'The big lump'.

Melplash Dorset. *Melpleys* 1155. Probably 'multi-coloured pool'. OE *mǣle* + **plæsc*.

Melrose Sc. Bord. *Mailros* c.700. 'Bare promontory'. British *mailo-* + *ros*.

Melsonby N. Yorks. *Malsenebi* 1086 (DB). Possibly 'farmstead or village of a man called Maelsuithan'. OIrish pers. name + OScand. *bý*.

Meltham W. Yorks. *Meltham* 1086 (DB). Possibly 'homestead or village where smelting is done'. OE **melt* + *hām*.

Melton, usually 'middle farmstead', OE *middel* (replaced by OScand. *methal*) + *tūn*: **Melton, Great** & **Melton, Little** Norfolk. *Middilton* c.1060, *Meltuna* 1086 (DB). **Melton, High** S. Yorks. *Middeltun* 1086 (DB). **Melton Mowbray** Leics. *Medeltone* 1086 (DB), *Melton Moubray* 1284. Manorial affix from the de Moubray family, here in the 12th

cent. **Melton Ross** N. Lincs. *Medeltone* 1086 (DB), *Melton Roos* 1375. Manorial affix from the de Ros family, here in the 14th cent.

However the following may have a different origin: **Melton** Suffolk. *Meltune* c.1050, *Meltuna* 1086 (DB). Perhaps rather 'farmstead with a crucifix', OE *mæl* + *tūn*. **Melton Constable** Norfolk. *Maeltuna* 1086 (DB), *Melton Constable* 1320. Possibly identical with the previous name. Manorial affix from possession by the constable of the Bishop of Norwich in the 12th cent.

Melverley Shrops. *Meleurlei* |sic| 1086 (DB), *Milverlegh* 1311. Probably 'woodland clearing by the mill ford'. OE *myln* + *ford* + *lēah*.

Melvin, Lough (*Loch Meilbhe*) Fermanagh. 'Lake of Meilbhe'.

Membury Devon. *Manberia* 1086 (DB). OE *burh* (dative *byrig*) 'fortified place' with an uncertain first element, possibly Celtic **main* 'stone' or OE *mǣne* 'common'.

Menai Bridge (*Porthaethwy*) Angl. 'Bridge over the Menai Strait'. A bridge was built across the Menai Strait in 1826 and the town developed soon after. The name of the strait itself is of uncertain origin. The Welsh name means 'ferry of Daethwy' (Welsh *porth*), from a tribal name.

Mendham Suffolk. *Myndham* c.950, *Mendham* 1086 (DB). 'Homestead or village of a man called *Mynda'. OE pers. name + *hām*.

Mendip Hills Somerset. *Menedepe* 1185. Probably Celtic **mönïth* 'mountain, hill' with an uncertain second element, perhaps OE *yppe* in the sense 'upland, plateau'.

Mendlesham Suffolk. *Mundlesham* 1086 (DB). 'Homestead or village of a man called *Myndel'. OE pers. name + *hām*.

Menheniot Cornwall. *Mahiniet* 1260. 'Land or plain of *Hynyed'. Cornish **ma* + pers. name.

Menlough (*Mionlach*) Galway. 'Small place'.

Menlough (*Mionloch*) Galway. 'Small lake'.

Menston W. Yorks. *Mensinctun* c.972, *Mersintone* 1086 (DB). 'Estate associated with a man called *Mensa'. OE pers. name + *-ing-* + *tūn*.

Menstrie Clac. *Mestryn* 1261, *Mestry* 1315. 'Farmstead in the plain'. Welsh *maes* + *tre*.

Mentmore Bucks. *Mentemore* 1086 (DB). 'Moor of a man called *Menta'. OE pers. name + *mōr*.

Meole Brace Shrops. *Mela(m)* 1086 (DB), *Melesbracy* 1273. Named from Meole Brook (the old name of Rea Brook) which may derive from OE *melu*, *meolu* 'meal' perhaps used figuratively of a stream with cloudy water. Manorial affix from the de Braci family, here in the 13th cent.

Meols, Great & *Meols, Little* Mersey. *Melas* 1086 (DB). 'The sandhills'. OScand. *melr*.

Meon, East & *Meon, West* Hants. *Meone* c.880, *Mene*, *Estmeone* 1086 (DB). Named from the River Meon, a Celtic river-name of uncertain origin and meaning, possibly 'swift one'.

Meonstoke Hants. *Menestoche* 1086 (DB). 'Outlying farmstead on the River Meon or dependent on MEON'. OE *stoc*.

Meopham Kent. *Meapaham* 788, *Mepeham* 1086 (DB). 'Homestead or village of a man called *Mēapa'. OE pers. name + *hām*.

Mepal Cambs. *Mepahala* 12th cent. 'Nook of land of a man called *Mēapa'. OE pers. name + *halh*.

Meppershall Beds. *Maperteshale* 1086 (DB). Probably 'nook of the maple-tree'. OE *mæpel-trēow* + *halh*.

Merchiston Edin. *Merchinstoun* 1266, *Merchammeston* 1278, *Merchenstoun* 1371. 'Merchiaun's farm'. British pers. name + OE *tūn*.

Mere, '(place at) the pool or lake', OE *mere*: **Mere** Ches. *Mera* 1086 (DB). **Mere** Wilts. *Mere* 1086 (DB).

Mereworth Kent. *Meranworth* 843. *Marovrde* 1086 (DB). 'Enclosure of a man called *Mæra'. OE pers. name + *worth*.

Meriden W. Mids. *Mereden* 1230. 'Pleasant valley', or 'valley where merry-making takes place'. OE *myrge* + *denu*.

Merioneth (*Meirionnydd*) (the historic county). 'Seat of Meirion'. *Meirion* (Meriaun) is said to be the grandson of Cunedda.

Merrington Shrops. *Muridon* 1254. 'Pleasant hill', or 'hill where merry-making takes place'. OE *myrge* + *dūn*.

Merrington, Kirk Durham. *Mærintun* c.1085. *Kyrke Merington* 1331. 'Estate associated with a man called *Mæra'. OE pers. name + *-ing-* + *tūn*. Affix is OScand. *kirkja* 'church'.

Merriott Somerset. *Meriet* 1086 (DB). Possibly 'boundary gate'. OE *mēre* + *geat*.

Merrow Surrey. *Marewe* 1185. Possibly OE *mearg* 'marrow' in a figurative sense such as 'fertile ground'.

Mersea, East & *Mersea, West* Essex. *Meresig* early 10th cent., *Meresai* 1086 (DB). 'Island of the pool'. OE *mere* (genitive *-s*) + *ēg*.

Merseyside (new county), named from the River Mersey, *Mærse* 1002, 'boundary river' from OE *mēre* (genitive *-s*) + *ēa*.

Mersham Kent. *Mersaham* 858, *Merseham* 1086 (DB). 'Homestead or village of a man called *Mærsa'. OE pers. name + *hām*.

Merstham Surrey. *Mearsætham* 947, *Merstan* 1086 (DB). 'Homestead near a trap for martens or weasels'. OE *mearth* + *sæt* + *hām*.

Merston W. Sussex. *Mersitone* 1086 (DB). 'Farmstead on marshy ground'. OE *mersc* + *tūn*.

Merstone I. of Wight. *Merestone* 1086 (DB). Identical in origin with the previous name.

Merther Cornwall. *Eglosmerthe* 1201. 'Church at the saint's grave'. Cornish *eglos* + *merther*.

Merthyr Dyfan Vale Glam. *Mertherdevan*. 'Dyfan's grave'. Welsh *merthyr*. The identity of the named saint is uncertain.

Merthyr Tydfil Mer T. *Merthir* 1254, *Merthyr Tutuil* 13th cent. 'Tudful's grave'. Welsh *merthyr*. Tudful is said to have been one of the daughters of Brychan, who gave the name of BRECON.

Merton, 'farmstead by the pool', OE *mere* + *tūn*: **Merton** Devon. *Mertone* 1086 (DB). **Merton** Gtr. London. *Mertone* 949, *Meretone* 1086 (DB). **Merton** Norfolk. *Meretuna* 1086 (DB). **Merton** Oxon. *Meretone* 1086 (DB).

Meshaw Devon. *Mauessart* 1086 (DB). Probably 'bad or infertile clearing'. OFrench *mal* + *assart*.

Messing Essex. *Metcinges* 1086 (DB). '(Settlement of) the family or followers of a man called *Mæcca'. OE pers. name + *-ingas*.

Messingham N. Lincs. *Mæssingaham* c.1067, *Messingeham* 1086 (DB). 'Homestead of the family or followers of a man called *Mæssa'. OE pers. name + *-inga-* + *hām*.

Metfield Suffolk. *Medefeld* 1214. 'Open land with meadow'. OE *mǣd* + *feld*.

Metheringham Lincs. *Medricesham* 1086 (DB), *Mederingeham* 1193. Possibly 'homestead of a man called *Mæthelrīc or of his people'. OE pers. name (+ *-inga-*) + *hām*.

Methley W. Yorks. *Medelai* 1086 (DB). 'Clearing where grass is mown', OE *mǣth* + *lēah*, or 'middle land between rivers'. OScand. *methal* + OE *ēg*.

Methven Perth. *Methfen* 1211. 'Middle stone'. Welsh *medd* + *maen*.

Methwold Norfolk. *Medelwolde* c.1050, *Methelwalde* 1086 (DB). 'Middle forest'. OScand. *methal* + OE *wald*.

Methwold Hythe Norfolk. *Methelwoldehythe* 1277. 'Landing-place near METHWOLD'. OE *hȳth*.

Mettingham Suffolk. *Metingaham* 1086 (DB). Probably 'homestead of the family or followers of a man called *Metti'. OE pers. name + *-inga-* + *hām*.

Mevagissey Cornwall. *Meffagesy* c.1400. From the patron saints of the church, Saints Meva and Issey (the medial *-ag-* in the place-name being from Cornish *hag* 'and').

Mexborough S. Yorks. *Mechesburg* 1086 (DB). 'Stronghold of a man called *Mēoc or Mjúkr'. OE or OScand. pers. name + OE *burh*.

Mey Highland. '(Place in the) plain'. Gaelic *magh*.

Meysey Hampton Glos., *see* HAMPTON.

Michaelchurch, 'church dedicated to St Michael', saint's name + OE *cirice*: **Michaelchurch** Heref. & Worcs. *Lann mihacgel* c.1150. Welsh *llan* 'church'. **Michaelchurch Escley** Heref. & Worcs. *Michaeleschirche* c.1257. Affix is from Escley Brook, probably a Celtic river-name Esk ('the water') + OE *hlynn* 'torrent'.

Michaelchurch-on-Arrow (*Llanfihangel Dyffryn Arwy*) Powys. 'St Michael's church by the River Arrow'. OE *cirice*. The Celtic or pre-Celtic river name means simply 'stream'. The Welsh name means 'St Michael's church in the valley of the River Arrow' (Welsh *llan* + *Mihangel* + *dyffryn*).

Michaelston-le-Pit (*Llanfihangel-y-pwll*) Vale Glam. *Michelstowe* c.1291, *Mighelstowe* 1483, *Michaelstown*

1535, *Mighelston in le Pitt* 1567. 'St Michael's holy place in the pit'. OE *stōw* + OFrench *le* + OE *pytt*. The church is dedicated to St Michael, and the 'pit' is the wide depression in which the village lies. The addition distinguishes the place from nearby *Michaelston-super-Ely*, 'Michaelston on the (river) Ely'. The Welsh name means 'St Michael's church in the pit' (Welsh *llan* + *Mihangel* + *y* + *pwll*).

Michaelstow Cornwall. *Mighelestowe* 1302. 'Holy place of St Michael'. Saint's name + OE *stōw*.

Micheldever Hants. *Mycendefr* 862, *Miceldevere* 1086 (DB). Named from the stream here, probably a Celtic name meaning 'boggy waters', the second element being the Celtic word found in DOVER. At an early date, the first element was confused with OE *micel* 'great'.

Michelmersh Hants. *Miclamersce* 985. 'Large marsh'. OE *micel* + *mersc*.

Mickfield Suffolk. *Mucelfelda* 1086 (DB). 'Large tract of open country'. OE *micel* + *feld*.

Mickle Trafford Ches., *see* TRAFFORD.

Mickleby N. Yorks. *Michelbi* 1086 (DB). 'Large farmstead'. OScand. *mikill* + *bý*.

Mickleham Surrey. *Micleham* 1086 (DB). 'Large homestead or river-meadow'. OE *micel* + *hām* or *hamm*.

Mickleover Derbys. *Vfre* 1011, *Ufre* 1086 (DB), *Magna Oufra* c.1100. '(Place at) the ridge'. OE **ofer*, with the affix *micel* 'great' (earlier Latin *magna*) to distinguish this place from LITTLEOVER.

Mickleton, 'large farmstead', OE *micel* + *tūn*: **Mickleton** Durham. *Micleton* 1086 (DB). **Mickleton** Glos. *Micclantun* 1005, *Muceltvne* 1086 (DB).

Mickley Northum. *Michelleie* c.1190. 'Large wood or clearing'. OE *micel* + *lēah*.

Middle as affix, *see* main name, e.g. for **Middle Assendon** (Oxon.) *see* ASSENDON.

Middleham, 'middle homestead or enclosure', OE *middel* + *hām* or *hamm*: **Middleham** N. Yorks. *Medelai* |sic| 1086 (DB), *Midelham* 12th cent. **Middleham, Bishop** Durham. *Middelham* 12th cent. Affix from early possession by the Bishop of Durham.

Middlesbrough Middlesbr. *Midelesburc* c.1165. 'Middlemost stronghold'. OE *midlest* + *burh*.

Middlesex (the county). *Middelseaxan* 704, *Midelsexe* 1086 (DB). '(Territory of) the Middle Saxons', originally a tribal name from OE *middel* + *Seaxe*.

Middlestown W. Yorks. *Midle Shitlington* 1325, *Myddleston* 1551. A contracted form of 'Middle Shitlington' (now SITLINGTON), which is *Schelintone* 1086 (DB), 'estate associated with a man called *Scyttel', OE pers. name + *-ing-* + *tūn*.

Middleton, a very common name, usually 'middle farmstead or estate', OE *middel* + *tūn*; examples include: **Middleton** Gtr. Manch. *Middelton* 1194. **Middleton** Norfolk. *Mideltuna* 1086 (DB). **Middleton Cheney** Northants. *Mideltone* 1086 (DB), *Middleton Cheyndut* 1342. Manorial affix from the de Chendut family, here in the 12th cent. **Middleton in Teesdale** Durham. *Middeltun* c.1164. Affix means 'in the valley of the River Tees', Celtic river-

name ('surging river') + OScand. *dalr*. **Middleton on Sea** W. Sussex. *Middeltone* 1086 (DB). **Middleton on the Wolds** E. R. Yorks. *Middeltun* 1086 (DB). *See* WOLDS. **Middleton St George** Durham. *Middlinton* 1238. Affix from the dedication of the church. **Middleton Scriven** Shrops. *Middeltone* 1086 (DB), *Skrevensmyddleton* 1577. Manorial affix is probably the ME surname Scriven from a family of this name with lands here. **Middleton Tyas** N. Yorks. *Middeltun* 1086 (DB), *Midilton Tyas* 14th cent. Manorial affix from the le Tyeis family who may have had lands here at an early date.

However the following have a different origin: **Middleton on the Hill** Heref. & Worcs. *Miceltune* 1086 (DB). 'Large farmstead or estate'. OE *micel* + *tūn*. **Middleton Priors** Shrops. *Mittilton* c.1200. First element uncertain. Affix from its early possession by Wenlock Priory.

Middletown Armagh. 'Middle settlement'. *Killaninane* 1657. The earlier Irish name was *Coillidh Chanannáin*, 'Canannán's wood'.

Middlewich Ches. *Wich, Mildestuich* 1086 (DB). 'Middlemost salt-works'. OE *midlest* + *wīc*.

Middlezoy Somerset. *Soweie* 725, *Sowi* 1086 (DB), *Middlesowy* 1227 'Island on the River *Sow*'. Lost pre-English river-name (of doubtful etymology) with the later affix *middle*.

Midge Hall Lancs. *Miggehalgh* 1390. 'Nook of land infested with midges'. OE *mycg* + *halh*.

Midgham Berks. *Migeham* 1086 (DB). 'Homestead or enclosure infested with midges'. OE *mycg* + *hām* or *hamm*.

Midgley, 'wood or clearing infested with midges', OE *mycg* + *lēah*: **Midgley** W. Yorks., near Crigglestone. *Migelaia* 12th cent. **Midgley** W. Yorks., near Halifax. *Micleie* 1086 (DB).

Midhurst W. Sussex. *Middeherst* 1186. 'Middle wooded hill'. OE *midd* + *hyrst*.

Midlothian (the unitary authority). *Loonia* c.970, *Lodoneó* 1098, *Louthion* c.1200. 'Middle Lothian'. The name, that of the historic county between *East Lothian* and *West Lothian*, is ultimately that of the district of *Lothian*, named after one Leudonus.

Midsomer Norton B. & NE. Som., *see* NORTON.

Milborne, *Milbourne, Milburn*, 'mill stream'. OE *myln* + *burna*: **Milborne Port** Somerset. *Mylenburnan* c.880, *Meleburne* 1086 (DB), *Milleburnport* 1249. Affix is OE *port* 'market town'. **Milborne St Andrew** Dorset. *Muleburne* 934, *Meleburne* 1086 (DB), *Muleburne St Andrew* 1294. Affix from the dedication of the church. **Milbourne** Northum. *Meleburna* 1158. **Milburn** Cumbria. *Milleburn* 1178.

Milcombe Oxon. *Midelcumbe* 1086 (DB). 'Middle valley'. OE *middel* + *cumb*.

Milden Suffolk. *Mellinga* |sic| 1086 (DB), *Meldinges* c.1130. '(Settlement of) the family or followers of a man called *Melda', OE pers. name + *-ingas*, or 'place where orach grows'. OE *melde* + *-ing*.

Mildenhall Suffolk. *Mildenhale* c.1050, *Mitdenehalla* 1086 (DB). Possibly 'middle nook of land', OE *middel* + *halh*, but perhaps identical in origin with the next name.

Mildenhall Wilts. *Mildanhald* 803–5, *Mildenhalle* 1086 (DB). 'Nook of land of a man called *Milda'. OE pers. name (genitive *-n*) + *halh*.

Mile End, '(place at) the end of a mile', OE *mīl* + *ende*: **Mile End** Essex. *Milende* 1156–80. **Mile End** Gtr. London. *La Mile Ende* 1288.

Milebush Antrim. 'Mile bush'. The name apparently refers to a bush one mile from Carrickfergus.

Mileham Norfolk. *Meleham* 1086 (DB). 'Homestead or village with a mill'. OE *myln* + *hām*.

Milford, 'ford by a mill', OE *myln* + *ford*: **Milford** Derbys. *Muleford* 1086 (DB). **Milford** Surrey. *Muleford* 1235. **Milford on Sea** Hants. *Melleford* 1086 (DB). **Milford. South** N. Yorks. *Myleford* c.1030.

Milford Armagh. 'Ford by a mill'. A linen mill was formerly here by a ford over the River Callan.

Milford Haven (*Aberdaugleddau*) Pemb. *de Milverdico portu* c.1191, *Mellferth* 1207, *Milford* 1219, *Aber Dav Gleddyf* 15th cent. 'Harbour at Milford'. The original site was *Milford*, 'sandy inlet' (OScand. *melr* + *fjǫrthr*). English *Haven* was then added when the meaning of this was forgotten. The Welsh name means 'mouth of the two Rivers Cleddau' (Welsh *aber* + *dau*). The river Cleddau, divided here into the Eastern Cleddau and Western Cleddau, is the Welsh word *cleddau* meaning 'sword'.

Mill Hill Gtr. London. *Myllehill* 1547. Self-explanatory, 'hill with a windmill'.

Millbrook, 'brook by a mill', OE *myln* + *brōc*: **Millbrook** Beds. *Melebroc* 1086 (DB). **Millbrook** Hants. *Melebroce* 956, *Melebroc* 1086 (DB).

Millbrook Antrim. *Millbrook* 1840. 'Brook by a mill'. A cotton mill was formerly here.

Millford Donegal. 'Ford by a mill'. A corn mill formerly stood by the stream here.

Millington E. R. Yorks. *Milleton* 1086 (DB). 'Farmstead with a mill'. OE *myln* + *tūn*.

Millmeece Staffs. *Mess* 1086 (DB), *Mulnemes* 1289. 'Mossy or boggy place'. OE *mēos* with the later addition of *myln* 'mill'.

Millom Cumbria. *Millum* c.1180. '(Place at) the mills'. OE *myln* in a dative plural form *mylnum*.

Millport N. Ayr. 'Port with a mill'.

Milltown Antrim, Armagh, Cavan, Derry, etc. 'Town with a mill'.

Milngavie E. Dunb. '(Place by the) windmill'. Gaelic *muileann gaoithe* or *meall na gaoithe* 'windy hill'.

Milnrow Gtr. Manch. *Mylnerowe* 1554. 'Row of houses by a mill'. OE *myln* + *rāw*.

Milnthorpe Cumbria. *Milntorp* 1272. 'Outlying farmstead or hamlet with a mill'. OE *myln* + OScand. *thorp*.

Milson Shrops. *Mulstone* 1086 (DB). Possibly 'farmstead of a man called *Myndel'. OE pers. name + *tūn*. Alternatively derivation may be from OE *myln-stān* 'millstone'.

Milstead Kent. *Milstede* late 11th cent. Possibly 'middle place'. OE *middel* + *stede*.

Milston Wilts. *Mildestone* 1086 (DB). Probably 'middlemost farmstead'. OE *midlest* + *tūn*.

Milton, a very common name, usually 'middle farmstead or estate', OE *middel* + *tūn*; examples include: **Milton** Cambs. *Middeltune* c.975, *Middeltone* 1086 (DB). **Milton** Oxon., near Didcot. *Middeltun* 956, *Middeltune* 1086 (DB). **Milton Abbas** Dorset. *Middeltone* 934, *Mideltune* 1086 (DB), *Middelton Abbatis* 1268. Latin affix means 'of the abbot' with reference to the abbey here. **Milton Abbot** Devon. *Middeltone* 1086 (DB), *Middelton Abbots* 1297. Affix from its early possession by Tavistock Abbey. **Milton Bryan** Beds. *Middelton* 1086 (DB), *Mideltone Brian* 1303. Manorial affix from a 12th cent. owner called Brian. **Milton Clevedon** Somerset. *Mideltune* 1086 (DB), *Milton Clyvedon* 1408. Manorial affix from a family called de Clyvedon, here c.1200. **Milton Damerel** Devon. *Mideltone* 1086 (DB), *Middelton Aubemarle* 1301. Manorial affix from Robert de Albemarle who held the manor in 1086. **Milton Ernest** Beds. *Middeltone* 1086 (DB), *Middelton Orneys* 1330. Manorial affix from early possessions here of a man called Erneis. **Milton, Great** & **Milton, Little** Oxon. *Mideltone* 1086 (DB). **Milton Keynes** Bucks. *Middeltone* 1086 (DB), *Middeltone Kaynes* 1227. Manorial affix from the de Cahaignes family, here from the 12th cent. **Milton Malsor** Northants. *Mideltone* 1086 (DB), *Milton alias Middleton Malsor* 1781. Manorial affix from the Malsor family, here in the 12th cent. **Milton under Wychwood** Oxon. *Mideltone* 1086 (DB). For the affix, *see* ASCOTT.

However some Miltons have a different origin, 'farmstead or village with a mill' OE *myln* + *tūn*; examples include: **Milton** Cumbria. *Milneton* 1285. **Milton** Staffs. *Mulneton* 1227.

Milverton, 'farmstead or village by the mill ford', OE *myln* + *ford* + *tūn*: **Milverton** Somerset. *Milferton* 11th cent., *Milvertone* 1086 (DB). **Milverton** Warwicks. *Malvertone |sic|* 1086 (DB), *Mulverton* 1123.

Milwich Staffs. *Mulewiche* 1086 (DB). 'Farmstead with a mill'. OE *myln* + *wīc*.

Mimms, North & *Mimms, South* Herts. *Mimes* 1086 (DB). Possibly '(territory of) a tribe called the Mimmas', although this tribal name is obscure in origin and meaning.

Minch (sea strait) W. Isles, Highland. Gaelic *a' Mhaoil*. The strait is divided into North Minch and the more southerly Little Minch.

Minchinhampton Glos. *Hantone* 1086 (DB), *Minchenhamtone* 1221. 'High farmstead'. OE *hēah* (dative *hēan*) + *tūn*, with affix *myncena* 'of the nuns' (with reference to possession by the nunnery of Čaen in the 11th cent.).

Mindrum Northum. *Minethrum* 1050. 'Mountain ridge'. Celtic **mönïth* + **drum*.

Mine Head (*Mionn Ard*) Waterford. 'High crown'.

Minehead Somerset. *Mynheafdon* 1046, *Maneheve* 1086 (DB). Pre-English hill-name (possibly Celtic **mönïth* 'mountain') + OE *hēafod* 'projecting hill-spur'.

Minety Wilts. *Mintig* 844. 'Island, or dry ground in marsh, where mint grows'. OE *minte* + *ēg*.

Minginish (district) Highland (Skye). 'Great headland'. OScand. *megin* + *nes*.

Mingulay (island) W. Isles. *Megala* 1580. 'Great island'. OScand. *mikill + ey*.

Miningsby Lincs. *Melingesbi |sic|* 1086 (DB), Mithingesbia 1142. Probably 'farmstead or village of a man called Mithjungr'. OScand. pers. name + *bý*.

Minshull, Church Ches. *Maneshale |sic|* 1086 (DB), *Chirchemunsulf* late 13th cent. 'Shelf or shelving terrain of a man called Monn'. OE pers. name + *scelf*. Affix is OE *cirice* 'church'.

Minskip N. Yorks. *Minescip* 1086 (DB). OE *(ge)mǣnscipe* 'a community, a communal holding'.

Minstead Hants. *Mintestede* 1086 (DB). 'Place where mint grows or is grown'. OE *minte + stede*.

Minster, 'the monastery or large church', OE *mynster*: **Minster** Kent, near Ramsgate. *Menstre* 694. **Minster** Kent, near Sheerness. *Menstre* 1203. **Minster Lovell** Oxon. *Minstre* 1086 (DB), *Ministre Lovel* 1279. Manorial affix from the Luvel family, here in the 13th cent.

Minsterley Shrops. *Menistrelie* 1086 (DB). 'Woodland clearing near or belonging to a minster church' (probably referring to that at Westbury). OE *mynster + lēah*.

Minsterworth Glos. *Mynsterworthig* c.1030. 'Enclosure of the monastery' (here St Peter's Gloucester). OE *mynster + worth* (*worthig* in the early form).

Minterne Magna Dorset. *Minterne* 987. 'House near the place where mint grows'. OE *minte + ærn*. Affix is Latin *magna* 'great'.

Minting Lincs. *Mentinges* 1086 (DB). '(Settlement of) the family or followers of a man called *Mynta*'. OE pers. name + *-ingas*.

Minto Sc. Bord. *Myntowe* 1296. '(Place by the) mountain'. The village takes its name from the nearby *Minto Hills*, 'mountain hill spur' (OWelsh *minid* + OE *hōh*). The OE word was added when the original was no longer understood.

Minton Shrops. *Munetune* 1086 (DB). 'Farmstead or estate by the mountain (Long Mynd)'. Welsh *mynydd* + OE *tūn*.

Mirfield W. Yorks. *Mirefeld* 1086 (DB). 'Pleasant open land', or 'open land where festivities are held'. OE *myrge* or *myrgen + feld*.

Miserden Glos. *Musardera* 1186. 'Musard's manor'. OFrench surname + suffix *-ere*. In 1086 (DB) the manor (then called *Grenhamstede* 'the green homestead' from OE *grēne + hām-stede*) was already held by the Musard family.

Missenden, Great & *Missenden, Little* Bucks. *Missedene* 1086 (DB). Probably 'valley where water-plants or marsh-plants grow'. OE **mysse + denu*.

Misson Notts. *Misne* 1086 (DB). Possibly 'mossy or marshy place', from a derivative of OE *mos* 'moss, marsh'.

Misterton, 'farmstead or estate with a church or belonging to a monastery', OE *mynster + tūn*: **Misterton** Leics. *Minstretone* 1086 (DB). **Misterton** Notts. *Ministretone* 1086 (DB). **Misterton** Somerset. *Mintreston* 1199.

Mistley Essex. *Mitteslea |sic|* 1086 (DB). *Misteleg* 1225. Probably 'wood or clearing where mistletoe grows'. OE *mistel + lēah*.

Mitcham Gtr. London. *Michelham* 1086 (DB). 'Large homestead or village'. OE *micel + hām*.

Mitcheldean Glos. *Dena* 1220, *Muckeldine* 1224. '(Place at) the valley'. OE *denu* with the later addition of *micel* 'great'.

Mitchell Cornwall. *Meideshol* 1239. Probably 'maiden's hollow'. OE *mægd(en) + hol*.

Mitchelstown (*Baile Mhistéala*) Cork. *Villa Michel* 13th cent. 'Mitchel's townland'. The name is probably that of a Welsh-Norman landowner.

Mitford Northum. *Midford* 1196. 'Ford where two streams join'. OE *(ge)mȳthe + ford*.

Mitton, 'farmstead where two rivers join', OE *(ge)mȳthe + tūn*; examples include: **Mitton, Great** Lancs. *Mitune* 1086 (DB). **Mitton, Upper** Heref. & Worcs. *Myttun* 841, *Mettune* 1086 (DB).

Mixbury Oxon. *Misseberie* 1086 (DB). 'Fortified place near a dunghill'. OE *mixen + burh* (dative *byrig*).

Moate (*An Móta*) Westmeath. 'The mound'.

Mobberley Ches. *Motburlege* 1086 (DB). 'Clearing at the fortification where meetings are held'. OE *mōt + burh + lēah*.

Moccas Heref. & Worcs. *Mochros* c.1130, *Moches* 1086 (DB). 'Moor where swine are kept'. Welsh *moch + rhos*.

Mockerkin Cumbria. *Moldcorkyn* 1208. Probably 'hill-top of a man called Corcán'. OIrish pers. name + OScand. **moldi*.

Modbury Devon. *Motberia* 1086 (DB). 'Fortification where meetings are held'. OE *mōt + burh* (dative *byrig*).

Moddershall Staffs. *Modredeshale* 1086 (DB). 'Nook of a man called Mōdrēd'. OE pers. name + *halh*.

Modelligo (*Má Deilge*) Waterford. 'Plain of the thorn'.

Modreeny (*Má Dreimhne*) Tipperary. 'Plain of fury'.

Moelfre Angl. *Moylvry* 1399, *Moelvre* 1528. 'Bare hill'. Welsh *moel + bre*.

Moffat Dumf. 'Long plain'. *Moffet* 1179, *Moffete* 1296. Of unknown origin.

Mogeely (*Maigh Dhíle*) Cork. 'Díle's plain'.

Mogerhanger Beds. *Mogarhangre* 1216. OE *hangra* 'wooded slope' with an uncertain first element.

Moglass (*Maigh Ghlas*) Tipperary. 'green'.

Mohill (*Maothail*) Leitrim. 'Soft place'.

Moidart (district) Highland. *Muddeward* 1292. 'Mundi's inlet'. OScand. pers. name + *fjǫrthr*.

Moira (*Maigh Ráth*) Down. (*cath*) *Maighe Rath* 634. 'Plain of wheels', perhaps referring to a meeting of routes.

Mold (*Yr Wyddgrug*) Flin. *de Monte alto* 1267, *Montem Altum* 1278, *Moald* 1284. 'High hill'. OFrench *mont + hault*. The reference is to Bailey Hill, where there was a British and Norman fortification and possibly a Roman one. The Welsh name means 'the burial mound' (Welsh *yr + gŵydd + crug*), referring to the same hill.

Molendinar Burn Glas. *Mellindonor* 1185. Obscure name.

Molescroft E. R. Yorks. *Molescroft* 1086 (DB). 'Enclosure of a man called Mūl'. OE pers. name + *croft*.

Molesey, East & *Molesey, West* Surrey. *Muleseg* 672–4, *Molesham |sic|* 1086 (DB). 'Island, or dry ground in marsh, of a man called Mūl'. OE pers. name + *ēg*. The river-name **Mole** is a 'back-formation' from the place-name.

Molesworth Cambs. *Molesworde* 1086 (DB). 'Enclosure of a man called Mūl'. OE pers. name + *worth*.

Molland Devon. *Mollande* 1086 (DB). OE *land* 'cultivated land, estate' with an uncertain first element, possibly a pre-English hill-name.

Mollington, 'estate associated with a man called Moll', OE pers. name + *-ing-* + *tūn*; **Mollington** Ches. *Molintone* 1086 (DB). **Mollington** Oxon. *Mollintune* c.1015, *Mollitone* 1086 (DB).

Molton, North & *Molton, South* Devon. *Nortmoltone*, *Sudmoltone* 1086 (DB). OE *tūn* 'farmstead, estate' with the same first element as in MOLLAND. Distinguishing affixes are OE *north* and *sūth*. The river-name **Mole** is a 'back-formation' from the place-name; the old name of the river was *Nymet*, *see* NYMPTON.

Môn. See ANGLESEY.

Monadhliath Mountains Highland. 'Grey-blue moors'. Gaelic *monadh* + *liath*.

Monaghan (*Muineachán*) Monaghan. *Muineachán* 1462. 'Place of thickets'.

Monamolin (*Muine Moling*) Wexford. 'Thicket of Moling'.

Monard (*Móin Ard*) Tipperary. 'High bog'.

Monaseed (*Móin na Saighead*) Wexford. 'Bog of the arrows'.

Monaster (*An Mhainistir*) Limerick. 'The monastery'.

Monasteraden (*Mainistir Réadáin*) Sligo. 'Réadán's monastery'.

Monasteranenagh (*Mainistir an Aonaigh*) Limerick. 'Monastery of the assembly'.

Monasterboice (*Mainistir Bhuite*) Louth. 'Buite's monastery'.

Monasterevin (*Mainistir Eimhín*) Kildare. 'Eimhín's monastery'.

Monasterleigh (*Mainistir Liath*) Down. 'Grey abbey'.

Monavullagh (*Móin an Mhullaigh*) (mountains) Waterford. 'Bog of the summit'.

Monea (*Maigh Niadh*) Fermanagh. (*Monua*) *Maigi Niad* c.830. 'Plain of warriors'.

Moness Perth. '(Place) at waterfalls'. Gaelic *i mbun eas*.

Monewden Suffolk. *Munegadena* 1086 (DB). Probably 'valley of the family or followers of a man called *Munda'. OE pers. name + *-inga-* + *denu*.

Moneyflugh (*Muine Fliuch*) Kerry. 'West thicket'.

Moneygall (*Muine Gall*) Offaly. 'Thicket of the stones'.

Moneygashel (*Muine na gCaiseal*) Cavan. *Monygashell* 1619. 'Thicket of the stone forts'.

Moneyglass (*Muine Glas*) Antrim. *Ballymoyneglass* 1605. 'Green thicket'.

Moneylea (*Muine Liath*) Westmeath. 'Grey thicket'.

Moneyneany (*Móin na nIonadh*) Derry. *Monaneney* 1622. 'Bog of the wonders'.

Moneynick (*Muine Chnoic*) Antrim. *Ballivonykie* 1605. 'Thicket of the hill'.

Moneyreagh (*Mónaidh Riabhach*) Down. *Ballymoyne-Righ* 1606. 'Grey bog'.

Moneystown (*An Muine*) Wicklow. 'The town of the thicket'.

Mongeham, Great & *Mongeham, Little* Kent. *Mundelingeham* 761, *Mundingeham* 1086 (DB). 'Homestead of the family or followers of a man called *Mundel', or 'homestead at *Mundel's place'. OE pers. name + *-inga-* or *-ing* + *hām*.

Monifieth Ang. *Munifod* 1178. 'Moor'. Gaelic *moine* + unknown element.

Monivea (*Muine Mheá*) Galway. 'Thicket of the mead'.

Monk as affix, see main name, e.g. for **Monk Bretton** (S. Yorks.) *see* BRETTON.

Monkhopton Shrops. *Hopton* 1255, *Munkehopton* 1577. 'Farmstead in a valley'. OE *hop* + *tūn*. Later affix from its possession by Wenlock Priory.

Monkland Heref. & Worcs. *Leine* 1086 (DB), *Munkelen* c.1180. 'Estate in *Leon* held by the monks'. Old Celtic name for the district (*see* LEOMINSTER) with OE *munuc*. The manor belonged before 1086 to Conches Abbey in Normandy.

Monkleigh Devon. *Lega* 1086 (DB), *Munckenelegh* 1244. 'Wood or clearing of the monks'. OE *munuc* + *lēah*, with reference to possession by Montacute Priory from the 12th cent.

Monkokehampton Devon. *Monacochamentona* 1086 (DB). 'Estate on the River Okement held by the monks'. OE *munuc* + Celtic river-name (possibly 'swift stream') + OE *tūn*. It once belonged to Glastonbury Abbey.

Monks as affix, see main name, e.g. for **Monks Eleigh** (Suffolk) *see* ELEIGH.

Monkseaton Tyne & Wear. *Seton Monachorum* 1380. 'Farmstead by the sea'. OE *sǣ* + *tūn*. Affix 'of the monks' (Latin *monachorum* in the early form) from its early possession by the monks of Tynemouth.

Monksilver Somerset. *Selvere* 1086 (DB), *Monkesilver* 1249. Probably an old river-name from OE *seolfor* 'silver', i.e. 'clear or bright stream'. Affix is OE *munuc* alluding to early possession by the monks of Goldcliff Priory.

Monkstown (*Baile na Manach*) Antrim. *Ballynemanagh* 1605. 'Townland of the monks'.

Monkton, 'farmstead of the monks', OE *munuc* + *tūn*; examples include: **Monkton** Devon. *Muneketon* 1244, **Monkton** Kent. *Munccetun* c.960, *Monocstune* 1086 (DB). **Monkton, Bishop** N. Yorks. *Munecatun* c.1030, *Monucheton* 1086 (DB). Affix from its possession by the Archbishops of York. **Monkton, Moor** & **Monkton, Nun** N. Yorks. *Monechetone* 1086 (DB), *Moremonketon* 1402, *Nunmonkton* 1397. Distinguishing affixes are OE *mōr* 'moor' and *nunne* 'nun' (from the nunnery founded here in the 12th cent.). **Monkton, West** Somerset. *Monechetone* 1086 (DB).

Monkton as affix, see main name, e.g. for **Monkton Combe** B. & NE. Som., *see* COMBE.

Monkwearmouth Tyne & Wear. *Uuiremutha* c.730, *Wermuth Monachorum* 1291. 'The mouth of the River Wear'. Celtic or pre-Celtic river-name (probably meaning simply 'water, river') + OE *mūtha*. Affix *Monk-* (Latin *monachorum* 'of the monks') refers to early possession by the monks of Durham.

Monmouth (*Trefynwy*) Mon. *Munwi Mutha* 11th cent., *Munemuda* 1190, *Monmouth* 1267. 'Mouth of the River Monnow'. OE *mutha*. The Celtic river name may mean 'fast-flowing'. The Welsh name means 'homestead on the River Mynwy' (Welsh *tref*).

Monnington on Wye Heref. & Worcs. *Manitune* 1086 (DB). 'Estate held communally, or by a man called Manna'. OE *(ge)mǣne* or pers. name (genitive -*n*) + *tūn*. For the river-name, *see* ROSS ON WYE.

Monroe (*Móin Ruadh*) Westmeath. 'Red bog'.

Montacute Somerset. *Montagud* 1086 (DB). 'Pointed hill'. OFrench *mont* + *aigu*.

Montford Shrops. *Maneford* 1086 (DB), *Moneford* 1204. Possibly 'ford where people gather', from OE *gemāna* 'fellowship, association' + *ford*.

Montgomery (*Trefaldwyn*) Powys. *Montgomeri* 1086 (DB). The Norman lord Roger de Montgomery built a castle here and named it after his other castle at Montgommery, Normandy. In 1102 this castle passed to the Norman Baldwin de Bollers, who gave the Welsh name, 'Baldwin's town' (Welsh *tref*).

Montrose Ang. *Munros* c.1178. 'Moor on the promontory'. Gaelic *moine* + *ros*.

Monxton Hants. *Anna de Becco* c.1270, *Monkestone* 15th cent. 'Estate (on the River *Ann*) held by the monks (of Bec Abbey)'. OE *munuc* + *tūn*, see ANN.

Monyash Derbys. *Maneis* 1086 (DB). 'Many ash-trees'. OE *manig* + *æsc*.

Monzievaird Perth. *Muithauard* c.1200, *Moneward* 1203. 'Plain of the bards'. Gaelic *magh* + *bard*.

Mooncoin (*Móin Choinn*) Kildare. 'Conn's bog'.

Moone (*Maoin*) Kildare. 'Gift'.

Moor Crichel Dorset, *see* CRICHEL.

Moor Monkton N. Yorks., *see* MONKTON.

Moorby Lincs. *Morebi* 1086 (DB). 'Farmstead or village in the moor or marshland'. OScand. *mōr* + *bý*.

Moore Ches. *Mora* 12th cent. 'The marsh'. OE *mōr*.

Moorfoot Hills Sc. Bord. *Morthwait* c.1142. 'Hills by the moorland clearing'. OScand. *mor* + *thveit* + OE *hyll*.

Moorlinch Somerset. *Mirieling* 971. 'Pleasant ledge or terrace'. OE *myrge* + *hlinc*.

Moors, West Dorset. *La More* 1310, *Moures* 1407. 'The marshy ground(s)'. OE *mōr*.

Moorsholm Red & Cleve. *Morehusum* 1086 (DB). '(Place at) the houses on the moor'. OE *mōr* + *hūs*, or OScand. *mór* + *hús*, in a dative plural form in -*um*.

Moorsley, Low Tyne & Wear. *Moreslau* 12th cent. Probably 'hill of the moor'. OE *mōr* + *hlāw*.

Morar (district) Highland. *Morderer* 1292, *Mordhowar* 14th cent. 'Great water'. Gaelic *mor* + *dobhar*.

Moray (the unitary authority). *Moreb* c.970, *Morauia* 1124, *Murewe* c.1185. 'Sea settlement'. OCeltic **mori-* + **treb*.

Morborne Cambs. *Morburne* 1086 (DB). 'Marsh stream'. OE *mōr* +*burna*.

Morchard, 'great wood or forest', Celtic **mōr* + **cēd*: **Morchard Bishop** Devon. *Morchet* 1086 (DB), *Bisschoppesmorchard* 1311. Affix from its possession by the Bishop of Exeter in 1086. **Morchard, Cruwys** Devon. *Morchet* 1086 (DB), *Cruwys Morchard* c.1260. Manorial affix from the de Crues family, here in the 13th cent.

Morcombelake Dorset. *Mortecumbe* 1240, *Morecomblake* 1558. OE *cumb* 'valley' with OE pers. name **Morta* or **mort* 'young salmon' + *lacu* 'stream'.

Morcott Rutland. *Morcote* 1086 (DB). 'Cottage(s) in the marshland'. OE *mōr* + *cot*.

Morden, 'hill in marshland', OE *mōr* + *dūn*: **Morden** Dorset. *Mordune* 1086 (DB). **Morden** Gtr. London. *Mordune* 969, *Mordone* 1086 (DB). **Morden, Guilden & Morden, Steeple** Cambs. *Mordune* 1015, *Mordune* 1086 (DB), *Gildene Mordon* 1204, *Stepelmordun* 1242. Distinguishing affixes are OE *gylden* 'wealthy, splendid' and *stēpel* 'church steeple'.

Mordiford Heref. & Worcs. *Mord(e)ford* 12th cent. OE *ford* 'a ford' with an uncertain first element.

Mordon Durham. *Mordun* c.1050. 'Hill in marshland'. OE *mōr* + *dūn*.

More Shrops. *La Mora* 1181. 'The marsh'. OE *mōr*.

Morebath Devon. *Morbatha* 1086 (DB). 'Bathing-place in marshy ground'. OE *mōr* + *bæth*.

Morecambe Lancs., a modern revival of an old Celtic name for the Lune estuary, *Morikámbē* 'the curved inlet', first recorded c.150 AD.

Moreleigh Devon. *Morlei* 1086 (DB). 'Woodland clearing on or near a moor'. OE *mōr* + *lēah*.

Morenane (*Boirneán*) Limerick. 'Little stony place'.

Moresby Cumbria. *Moreseby* c.1160. 'Farmstead or village of a man called Maurice'. OFrench pers. name + OScand. *bý*.

Morestead Hants. *Morstede* 1172. 'Place by a moor'. OE *mōr* + *stede*.

Moreton, *Morton*, a common name, 'farmstead in moorland or marshy ground', OE *mōr* + *tūn*; examples include: **Moreton** Dorset. *Mortune* 1086 (DB). **Moreton** Mersey. *Moreton* 1278. **Moreton-in-Marsh** Glos. *Mortun* 714, *Mortune* 1086 (DB), *Morton in Hennemersh* 1253. Affix is an old district-name meaning 'marsh frequented by wild hen-birds (moorhens or the like)'. OE *henn* + *mersc*. **Moreton, Maids** Bucks. *Mortone* 1086 (DB), *Maidenes Morton* c.1488. Affix from the tradition that the church here was built by two maiden ladies in the 15th cent. **Moreton Morrell** Warwicks. *Mortone* 1086 (DB), *Merehull* 1279, *Morton Merehill* 1285. Originally two distinct names first combined in the 13th cent. Morrell means 'boundary hill', OE (ge)mǣre + hyll. **Moreton Pinkney** Northants. *Mortone* 1086 (DB). Manorial affix (first used in the 16th cent.) from the de Pinkeny family who held the manor in the 13th cent. **Moreton Say** Shrops. *Mortune* 1086 (DB), *Morton de Say* 1255. Manorial affix from the de Sai family, here in 1199. **Morton** Derbys. *Mortun* 956, *Mortune* 1086 (DB). **Morton** Lincs., near Bourne. *Mortun* 1086 (DB), **Morton** Lincs., near Gainsborough. *Mortune* 1086 (DB). **Morton Bagot** Warwicks. *Mortone* 1086 (DB), *Morton Bagod* 1262. Manorial affix from the Bagod family, here from the 12th cent.

Moretonhampstead Devon. *Mortone* 1086 (DB), *Morton Hampsted* 1493. Identical in origin with the previous names, with a later addition which may be a family name or from a nearby place (from OE hām-stede 'homestead').

Morfa Cergn. 'Plain by the sea'. Welsh *morfa*.

Morgannwg. *See* GLAMORGAN.

Morland Cumbria. *Morlund* c.1140. 'Grove in the moor or marsh'. OScand. *mór* + *lundr*.

Morley, 'woodland clearing in or near a moor or marsh', OE *mōr* + *lēah*: **Morley** Derbys. *Morlege* 1002, *Morleia* 1086 (DB). **Morley** Durham. *Morley* 1312. **Morley** Norfolk. *Morlea* 1086 (DB). **Morley** W. Yorks. *Moreleia* 1086 (DB).

Morningside Edin. 'Morning slope'. The name is first recorded for an estate formed here in 1657 on the amalgamation of two adjoining properties.

Morningthorpe Norfolk. *Torp, Maringatorp* 1086 (DB). Possibly 'outlying farmstead of the dwellers by the lake or by the boundary'. OE *mere* or *mǣre* + *-inga-* + OScand. *thorp*.

Mornington (*Baile Uí Mhornáin*) Meath. 'Ó Mornán's town'.

Moroe (*Maigh Rua*) Limerick. 'Red plain'.

Morpeth Northum. *Morthpath* c.1200. 'Path where a murder took place'. OE *morth* + *pæth*.

Morriston (*Treforys*) Swan. 'Morris's town'. The settlement was built in c.1768 by Sir John Morris to provide housing for local workers. The Welsh name has the same sense (Welsh *tref* + *Morys*).

Morston Norfolk. *Merstona* 1086 (DB). 'Farmstead by a marsh'. OE *mersc* + *tūn*.

Mortehoe Devon. *Morteho* 1086 (DB). Possibly 'hill-spur called *Mort* or the stump'. OE **mort* + *hōh*.

Mortimer Berks., from the manorial affix of STRATFIELD MORTIMER.

Mortlake Gtr. London. *Mortelage* 1086 (DB). Probably 'stream of a man called **Morta*'. OE pers. name + *lacu*. Alternatively the first element may be OE **mort* 'young salmon or similar fish'.

Morton, *see* MORETON.

Morvah Cornwall. *Morveth* 1327. 'Grave by the sea'. Cornish *mōr* + *bedh*.

Morval Cornwall. *Morval* 1238. Probably Cornish *mor* 'sea' with an obscure second element.

Morville Shrops. *Membrefelde* 1086 (DB), *Mamerfeld, Momerfeld* c.1138. OE *feld* 'open land' with an uncertain first element, possibly a derivative of Celtic **mamm* 'breast-like hill'.

Morwenstow Cornwall. *Morwestewe* 1201. 'Holy place of St Morwenna'. Cornish saint's name + OE *stōw*.

Mosborough S. Yorks. *Moresburh* c.1002, *Moresburg* 1086 (DB). 'Fortified place in the moor'. OE *mōr* + *burh*.

Mosedale Cumbria. *Mosedale* 1285. 'Valley with a bog'. OScand. *mosi* + *dalr*.

Moseley Heref. & Worcs. *Museleie* 1086 (DB). 'Woodland clearing infested with mice'. OE *mūs* + *lēah*.

Moseley W. Mids. *Moleslei* 1086 (DB). 'Woodland clearing of a man called Moll'. OE pers. name + *lēah*.

Moss S. Yorks. *Mose* 1416. 'The swamp or bog'. OE *mos* or OScand. *mosi*.

Moss-side Antrim. *Mosside* c.1657. The name may be English, 'side of the peat bog', or represent Irish *Maigh Saighead*, 'plain of arrows', denoting a battle site.

Mossley Gtr. Manch. *Moselegh* 1319. 'Woodland clearing by a swamp or bog.' OE *mos* or OScand. *mosi* + OE *lēah*.

Mossley Antrim. *Mossley* 1839. The name was adopted from *Mossley*, Lancs.

Mosterton Dorset. *Mortestorne* 1086 (DB). 'Thorn-tree of a man called **Mort*'. OE pers. name + *thorn*.

Moston, usually 'moss or marsh farmstead', OE *mos* + *tūn*; for example **Moston** Shrops. *Mostune* 1086 (DB).

Motcombe Dorset. *Motcumbe* 1244. 'Valley where meetings are held'. OE *mōt* + *cumb*.

Mothel (*Maothail*) Waterford. 'Soft place'.

Motherwell N. Lan. *Matervelle* c.1250, *Moydirwal* 1265. 'Our Lady's well'. ME *mōder* + *wella*.

Mottingham Gtr. London. *Modingeham* 1044. 'Homestead or enclosure of the family or followers of a man called **Mōda*. OE pers. name + *-inga-* + *hām* or *hamm*.

Mottisfont Hants. *Mortesfunde* |sic| 1086 (DB), *Motesfont* 1167. 'Spring near a river-confluence', or 'spring where meetings are held'. OE *mōt* + **funta*.

Mottistone I. of Wight. *Modrestan* 1086 (DB). 'Stone of the speaker(s) at a meeting'. OE *mōtere* + *stān*.

Mottram, possibly 'speakers' place' or 'place where meetings are held', OE *mōtere* or *mōt* + *rūm*: **Mottram in Longdendale** Gtr. Manch. *Mottrum* c.1220, *Mottram in Longedenedale* 1308. Affix is a district name, 'dale of the long valley', OE *lang* + *denu* + OScand. *dalr*. **Mottram St Andrew** Ches. *Motre* |sic| 1086 (DB), *Motromandreus* 1351. Affix is probably manorial from some early owner called *Andrew*.

Mouldsworth Ches. *Moldeworthe* 12th cent. 'Enclosure at a hill'. OE *molda* + *worth*.

Moulsecoomb E. Sussex. *Mulescumba* c.1100. 'Valley of a man called *Mūl*'. OE pers. name + *cumb*.

Moulsford Oxon. *Muleforda* c.1110. Probably 'ford of a man called *Mūl*'. OE pers. name + *ford*.

Moulsoe Bucks. *Moleshou* 1086 (DB). 'Hill-spur of a man called Mūl'. OE pers. name + *hōh*.

Moulton, 'farmstead of a man called Mūla, or where mules are kept', OE pers. name or OE *mūl* + *tūn*: **Moulton** Ches. *Moletune* 1086 (DB). **Moulton** Lincs. *Multune* 1086 (DB). **Moulton** Northants. *Multone* 1086 (DB). **Moulton** N. Yorks. *Moltun* 1086 (DB). **Moulton** Suffolk. *Muletuna* 1086 (DB). **Moulton St Michael** Norfolk. *Mulantun* c.1035, *Muletuna* 1086 (DB). Affix from the dedication of the church.

Moulton Vale Glam. *Molton* 1533. Possibly 'Mula's farmstead'. OE pers. name + *tūn*.

Mount Bures Essex, *see* BURES.

Mount Nugent Cavan. *Mount Nugent* 1837. The Nugent family were granted lands here in 1597.

Mountain Ash (*Aberpennar*) Rhon. The town arose as an industrial development in the 19th cent. and took its name from an inn, itself named after a prominent mountain ash (rowan). The Welsh name means 'confluence of the River Pennar' (Welsh *aber*), with the river named after a nearby mountain, *Cefn Pennar*, 'ridge of the height' (Welsh *cefn* + *pennardd*).

Mountbolus (*Cnocán Bhólais*) Offaly. 'Hill of Bolas'.

Mountcharles Donegal. 'Charles's mount', *town* (land) *of Mount Charles* al. Tawnytallan 1676. The village is named after Charles Conyngham, landlord here in the 17th cent.

Mountfield E. Sussex. *Montifelle* |*sic*| 1086 (DB), *Mundifeld* 12th cent. 'Open land of a man called *Munda'. OE pers. name + *feld*.

Mountjoy Tyrone. *Mountjoy forest* 1834. The village grew up in the early 19th cent. on land owned by Charles John Gardiner, 2nd Viscount Mountjoy.

Mountmellick (*Móinteach Mílic*) Laois. 'Moor of the wet ground'.

Mountnessing Essex. *Ginga* 1086 (DB), *Gynges Munteny* 1237. 'Manor called *Ing* (for which *see* FRYERNING) held by the de Mounteney family'.

Mountnorris Armagh. (*fort of*) *Mountnorris orw. Aghnecranchie* 1606. The name is that of Sir John Norris, who built a fort here in the late 16th cent.

Mountrath (*Móin Rátha*) Laois. 'Bog of the fort'.

Mountsorrel Leics. *Munt Sorel* 1152. 'Sorrel-coloured hill', referring to the pinkish-brown stone here. OFrench *mont* + *sorel*.

Mourne Mountains (*Múrna*) Down. 'Mountains of the Múrna'. The Múrna (earlier Mughdhorna) tribe originated in modern Co. Monaghan, where they gave the name of CREMORNE, but migrated to Co. Down in the 12th cent.

Mousa (island) Shet. *Mosey* c.1150 'Moor island'. OScand. *mór* + *ey*.

Mousehole Cornwall. *Musehole* 1284. Self-explanatory. OE *mūs* + *hol*, originally referring to a large cave here.

Moveen (*Má Mhín*) Clare. 'Smooth plain'.

Movilla (*Maigh Bhile*) Down. *Moige Bile* 850. 'Plain of the sacred tree'.

Moville (*Magh Bhile*) Donegal. (*for lár*) *Maighe Bile* 1167. 'Plain of the sacred tree'.

Mow Cop Ches./Staffs. *Mowel* c.1270, *Mowle-coppe* 1621. 'Heap hill'. OE *mūga* + *hyll* with the later addition of *copp* 'hill top'.

Mowhan (*Much Bhán*) Armagh. *Mowhan* 1838. 'White plain'.

Mowsley Leics. *Muselai* 1086 (DB). 'Wood or clearing infested with mice'. OE *mūs* + *lēah*.

Moy (*An Mhaigh*) Tyrone. *Madh* c.1645. 'The plain'.

Moy (*Muaidh*) (river) Mayo, Sligo. 'Stately one'.

Moy Highland. *Muy* 1235. '(Place) in the plain'. Gaelic *magh* (locative *maigh*).

Moyallan (*Maigh Alúine*) Down. *Moynalvin* c.1657. 'Plain of alum'.

Moyard (*Maigh Ard*) Galway. 'High plain'.

Moyarget (*Maigh Airgid*) Antrim. *Myerget* c.1657. 'Plain of silver'.

Moyasta (*Maigh Sheasta*) Clare. 'Upright plain'.

Moycarky (*Maigh Chairce*) Limerick. 'Plain of oats'.

Moycashel (*Magh Chaisil*) Westmeath. 'Plain of the stone fort'.

Moycullen (*Magh Cuilinn*) Galway. 'Plain of holly'.

Moydow (*Maigh Dumha*) Longford. 'Plain of the mound'.

Moydrum (*Magh Droma*) Westmeath. 'Plain of the ridge'.

Moygashel (*Maigh gCaisil*) Tyrone. *Moygashell* 1609. 'Plain of the stone fort'.

Moyle (*Mael*) Tipperary. 'Hill'.

Moylgrove (*Trewyddel*) Pemb. *Ecclesia de grava Matild'* 1291. 'Matilda's grove'. OGerman pers. name + OE *grāfa*, 'grove'. The Welsh name means 'grove farm' (Welsh *tref* + *gwyddel*).

Moylough (*Maigh Locha*) Galway. 'Plain of the lake'.

Moymore (*Má Mhór*) Clare. 'Big plain'.

Moynalty (*Maigh nEalta*) Meath. 'Plain of the flocks of birds'.

Moyne (*Maighean*) Mayo, Tipperary, Wicklow. 'Precinct'.

Moyne (*Maighín*) Mayo, Tipperary. 'Little plain'.

Moyness Highland. 'Meadow in the plain'. Gaelic *magh* + *inis*.

Moyola (*Maigh Fhoghlach*) (river) Derry. 'Plain of plundering'. The original name of the river was *Bior*, 'water'. Later, it was known as *Abhainn na Scríne*, 'river of Ballynascreen', the parish name meaning 'townland of the shrine'.

Moyvally (*Magh Bhealaigh*) Kildare. 'Plain of the pass'.

Moyvore (*Magh Mhora*) Westmeath. 'Mora's plain'.

Moyvoughly (*Má Bhachla*) Westmeath. 'Plain of the crosier'.

Much as affix, *see* main name, e.g. for **Much Birch** (Heref. & Worcs.) *see* BIRCH.

Muck (island) Highland. *Helantmok* 1370. '(Island of) pigs'. Gaelic *muc*. The early form has Gaelic *eilean*, 'island'.

Muckamore (*Maigh Chomair*) Antrim. 'Plain of the confluence'.

Mucking Essex. *Muc(h)inga* 1086 (DB). '(Settlement of) the family or followers of a man called Mucca', or 'Mucca's place'. OE pers. name + *-ingas* or *-ing*.

Muckish (*An Mhucais*) (mountain) Donegal. 'The ridge of the pig'. The ridge is shaped like a pig's back.

Muckle Flugga (island) Shet. 'Cliff island'. OScand. *mikill* + *flugey*.

Mucklestone Staffs. *Moclestone* 1086 (DB). 'Farmstead of a man called Mucel'. OE pers. name + *tūn*.

Muckno, Lough (*Loch Mucshnámha*) Monaghan. 'Lake of the swimming place of the pigs'.

Muckros (*Mucros*) Donegal. 'Wood of the pigs'.

Muckross (*Mucros*) Kerry. 'Wood of the pigs'.

Muckton Lincs. *Machetone* |sic| 1086 (DB), *Muketun* 12th cent. 'Farmstead of a man called Muca'. OE pers. name + *tūn*.

Muddiford Devon. *Modeworthi* 1303. Probably 'enclosure of a man called *Mōda*'. OE pers. name + *worthig* (later replaced by *ford*).

Mudeford Dorset. *Modeford* 13th cent. Probably 'mud ford', ME *mode, mudde* + *ford*. The river-name **Mude** is a 'back-formation' from the place-name.

Mudford Somerset. *Mudiford* 1086 (DB). 'Muddy ford'. OE **muddig* + *ford*.

Mudgley Somerset. *Mudesle* 1157. OE *lēah* 'wood or clearing' with an uncertain first element, possibly a pers. name.

Muff (*Magh*) Donegal. *Mough* 1621. 'Plain'.

Mugginton Derbys. *Mogintun* 1086 (DB). 'Estate associated with a man called **Mogga* or **Mugga*'. OE pers. name + *-ing-* + *tūn*.

Muggleswick Durham. *Muclingwic c.*1170. 'Farmstead of a man called Mucel'. OE pers. name (+ *-ing-*) + *wīc*.

Muine Bheag (*Muine Bheag*) Carlow. 'Little thicket'.

Muir of Ord Highland. 'Moorland of the rounded hill'. OE *mōr* + Gaelic *òrd*.

Muirkirk E. Ayr. 'Moorland church'. OScand. *mór* + *kirkja*.

Muker N. Yorks. *Meuhaker* 1274. 'Narrow cultivated plot'. OScand. *mjór* + *akr*.

Mulbarton Norfolk. *Molkebertuna* 1086 (DB). 'Outlying farm where milk is produced'. OE *meoluc* + *bere-tūn*.

Muldonagh (*Maol Domhnaigh*) Derry. *Meldony* 1613. 'Round hill of the church'.

Mull (island) Arg. *Malaios c.*150. Pre-Celtic island name.

Mull of Oa Arg (Islay). 'Headland of Oa'. Gaelic *maol na h-Otha*.

Mullagh (*Mullach*) Cavan, Galway, Meath. 'Summit'.

Mullaghanattin (*Mullach an Aitinn*) Kerry. 'Summit of the gorse'.

Mullaghareirk (*Mullach an Radhairc*) (mountains) Cork, Limerick. 'Summit of the prospect'.

Mullaghbawn (*An Mullach Bán*) Armagh. 'White summit'.

Mullaghcarn (*Mullach Chairn*) Tyrone. 'Summit of the cairn'.

Mullaghcleevaun (*Mullach Cliabháin*) Wicklow. 'Summit of the cradle'.

Mullaghmore (*Mullach Mór*) Derry, Sligo. 'Big summit'.

Mullan (*An Muileann*) Monaghan. 'The mill'.

Mullan (*Mullán*) Tyrone. 'Little hill'.

Mullenakill (*Muileann na Cille*) Kilkenny. 'Mill of the church'.

Mullinacuff (*Muileann Mhic Dhuibh*) Wicklow. 'Mill of Mac Duibh'.

Mullinahone (*Muileann na hUamhan*) Tipperary. 'Mill of the cave'.

Mullinavat (*Muileann an Bhata*) Kilkenny. 'Mill of the stick'.

Mullingar (*Muileann Cearr*) Westmeath. *Mullin Cirr* 1305, *Muilenn Cearr* 1450. 'Crooked mill'.

Mullinoran (*Muileann an Fhuaráin*) Westmeath. 'Mill of the spring'.

Mullion Cornwall. 'Church of *Sanctus Melanus*' 1262. From the patron saint of the church.

Mulrany (*Mala Raithne*) Mayo. 'Ferny brae'.

Mulroy Bay (*Maol Rua*) Donegal. *Moyroy* 1608. 'Red current'.

Multyfarnham (*Muilte Farannáin*) Westmeath. 'Farannán's mills'.

Mumbles Head Swan. *Mommulls* 1549. '(Place of the) headland'. OScand. *múli*. The first element is obscure.

Mumby Lincs. *Mundebi* 1086 (DB). Possibly 'farmstead or village of a man called Mundi'. OScand. pers. name + *bý*. Alternatively the first element may be OE or OScand. *mund* in the sense 'protection' or 'hedge'.

Mundesley Norfolk. *Muleslai* 1086 (DB). 'Woodland clearing of a man called *Mūl* or **Mundel*'. OE pers. name + *lēah*.

Mundford, Norfolk. *Mundeforda* 1086 (DB). 'Ford of a man called **Munda*'. OE pers. name + *ford*.

Mundham, 'homestead or enclosure of a man called **Munda*', OE pers. name + *hām* or *hamm*: **Mundham** Norfolk. *Mundaham* 1086 (DB). **Mundham** W. Sussex. *Mundhame c.*692, *Mundreham* 1086 (DB).

Mundon Essex. *Munduna* 1086 (DB). 'Protection hill', i.e. probably 'raised ground safe from flooding, or protected by fencing'. OE *mund* + *dūn*.

Mungrisdale Cumbria. *Grisedale* 1285, *Mounge Grieesdell* 1600. 'Valley where young pigs are kept'. OScand. *gríss* + *dalr*, with the later addition of the saint's name Mungo from the dedication of the church.

Munlough (*Móin Loch*) Cavan. 'Lake of the bog'.

Munsley Heref. & Worcs. *Muleslage, Muneslai* 1086 (DB). 'Woodland clearing of a man called Mūl or *Mundel'. OE pers. name + *lēah*.

Munslow Shrops. *Mosselawa* 1167, *Munselowe* 1252. OE *hlāw* 'mound, tumulus', with an uncertain first element.

Munster (*Cúige Mumhan*) (the province). 'District of the Mumu tribe'. OScand. possessive *s* + Irish *tír*.

Munterburn (*Muintir Bhirn*) Tyrone. 'Family of Birn'.

Munterloney (*Muintir Luinigh*) Tyrone. 'Family of Luinigh'.

Murcott Oxon. *Morcot* c.1191. 'Cottage(s) in marshy ground'. OE *mōr* + *cot*.

Murlough (*Murbholg*) Down. 'Sea swell'.

Murragh (*Murbhach*) Cork. 'Salt marsh'.

Murrayfield Edin. 'Murray's field'. Archibald *Murray*, later Lord Henderland, bought an estate here in 1733 and named it after himself.

Murreagh (*Muiríoch*) Kerry. 'Beach'.

Murroe (*Magh Rua*) Limerick. 'Red plain'.

Murroogh (*Murúch*) Clare. 'Beach'.

Murrow Cambs. *Morrowe* 1376, 'Row (of houses) in marshy ground'. OE *mōr* + *rāw*.

Mursley Bucks. *Muselai* |sic| 1086 (DB), *Murselai* 12th cent. Probably 'woodland clearing of a man called *Myrsa'. OE pers. name + *lēah*.

Murton, 'farmstead in moorland or marshy ground', OE *mōr* + *tūn*: **Murton** Cumbria. *Morton* 1235. **Murton** Durham, near Seaham. *Mortun* 1155. **Murton** Northum. *Morton* 1204. **Murton** York. *Mortun* 1086 (DB).

Musbury Devon. *Musberia* 1086 (DB). 'Old fortification infested with mice'. OE *mūs* + *burh* (dative *byrig*).

Muscoates N. Yorks. *Musecote* c.1160. 'Cottages infested with mice'. OE *mūs* + *cot*.

Musgrave, Great & *Musgrave, Little* Cumbria. *Musegrave* 12th cent. 'Grove or copse infested with mice'. OE *mūs* + *grāf*.

Muskham, North & *Muskham, South* Notts. *Muscham, Nordmuscham* 1086 (DB). Possibly 'homestead or village of a man called *Musca'. OE pers. name + *hām*.

Musselburgh E. Loth. *Muselburge* c.1100. 'Mussel town'. OE *musele* + *burh*.

Muston Leics. *Mustun* 12th cent. 'Mouse-infested farmstead'. OE *mūs* + *tūn*.

Muston N. Yorks. *Mustone* 1086 (DB). Identical with previous name, or 'farmstead of a man called *Músi', OScand. pers. name + OE *tūn*.

Muswell Hill Gtr. London. *Mosewella* c.1155. 'Mossy spring'. OE *mēos* + *wella*, with the addition of *hill* from the 17th cent.

Mweelahorna (*Maol na hEorna*) Waterford. 'Hill of the barley'.

Mweelrea (*Cnoc Maol Réidh*) (mountain) Mayo. 'Grey hill'.

Mybster Highland. 'Marshy farmstead'. OScand. *mýrr* + *bólstathr*.

Myddle Shrops. *Mulleht* |sic| 1086 (DB), *Muthla* 1121. Possibly '(place at) the confluence of streams', from a derivative *(ge)mȳthel* of OE *(ge)mȳthe*.

Mylor Bridge Cornwall. 'Church of *Sanctus Melorus*' 1258. From the patron saint of the church.

Myndtown Shrops. *Munete* 1086 (DB), *Myntowne* 1577. 'Place at the mountain (Long Mynd)'. Welsh *mynydd*, with the later addition of *town*.

Mynydd Bach (mountain) Cergn. 'Little mountain'. Welsh *mynydd* + *bach*.

Mynydd Du (mountain) Cergn. 'Black mountain'. Welsh *mynydd* + *du*.

Myroe (*Maigh na Rua*) Derry. *Moyrowe* 1613. 'Plain of the (river) Roe'.

Myshall (*Míseal*) Carlow. 'Low central place'.

Mytholmroyd W. Yorks. *Mithomrode* late 13th cent. 'Clearing at the river-mouths'. OE *(ge)mȳthe* (dative plural *(ge)mȳthum*) + *rodu*.

Myton, *Mytton*, 'farmstead where two rivers join', OE *(ge)mȳthe* + *tūn*: **Myton on Swale** N. Yorks. *Mytun* 972, *Mitune* 1086 (DB). On the River Swale (probably OE *swalwe* 'rushing water') near to where it joins the Ure.
Mytton Shrops. *Mutone* 1086 (DB).

N

Naas (*An Nás*) Kildare. 'The assembly'.

Naburn York. *Naborne* 1086 (DB). Possibly 'stream called the narrow one'. OE *naru* + *burna*.

Nackington Kent. *Natyngdun* late 10th cent. *Latintone* |*sic*| 1086 (DB). 'Hill at the wet place'. OE **næt* + *-ing* + *dūn*.

Nacton Suffolk. *Nachetuna* 1086 (DB). Possibly 'farmstead of a man called Hnaki'. OScand. pers. name + OE *tūn*.

Nacung, Loch (*Loch na Cuinge*) Donegal. 'Lake of the yoke'.

Nad (*Nead an Iolair*) Cork. 'Eagle's nest'.

Nafferton E. R. Yorks. *Nadfartone* 1086 (DB). Probably 'farmstead of a man called Náttfari'. OScand. pers. name + OE *tūn*.

Nailsea N. Som. *Nailsi* 1196. 'Island, or dry ground in marsh, of a man called **Nægl*'. OE pers. name + *ēg*.

Nailstone Leics. *Naylestone* 1225. 'Farmstead of a man called **Nægl*'. OE pers. name + *tūn*.

Nailsworth Glos. *Naillesωurd* 1196. 'Enclosure of a man called **Nægl*'. OE pers. name + *worth*.

Nairn Highland. *Inuernaren* c.1195, *Narne* 1382. 'Mouth of the River Nairn'. The river has a Celtic or pre-Celtic name possibly meaning 'penetrating one'. The first form above has Gaelic *inbhir*, 'river mouth'.

Nantwich Ches. *Wich* 1086 (DB), *Nametwihc* 1194. 'The salt-works'. OE *wīc* with the later addition of ME *named* 'renowned, famous'.

Nant-y-glo Blae. *Nantygloe* 1752. 'Valley of the coal'. Welsh *nant* + *y* + *glo*.

Nappa N. Yorks., near Hellifield. *Napars* |*sic*| 1086 (DB), *Nappai* 1182. Possibly 'enclosure in a bowl-shaped hollow'. OE *hnæpp* + *hæg*.

Napton on the Hill Warwicks. *Neptone* 1086 (DB). Possibly 'farmstead on a hill thought to resemble an inverted bowl'. OE *hnæpp* + *tūn*.

Narberth (*Arberth*) Pemb. *Nerberth* 1291, *la Nerbert* 1331. '(Place) near the hedge'. Welsh *yn* + *ar* + *perth*. The *N*- comes from Welsh *yn Arberth*, 'in Arberth'.

Narborough Leics. *Norburg* c.1220. 'North stronghold'. OE *north* + *burh*.

Narborough Norfolk. *Nereburh* 1086 (DB). Possibly 'stronghold near a narrow place or pass'. OE **neru* + *burh*. The river-name **Nar** is a 'back-formation' from the place-name.

Narraghmore (*An Fhorrach Mhór*) Kildare. 'The big area of land'.

Nart (*An Fheart*) Monaghan. 'Grave mound'.

Naseby Northants. *Navesberie* 1086 (DB). 'Stronghold of a man called Hnæf'. OE pers. name + *burh* (dative *byrig*), replaced by OScand. *bý* 'village' in the 12th cent.

Nash, 'place at the ash-tree', OE *æsc*, with initial *N*- from ME *atten* 'at the'; examples include: **Nash** Bucks. *Esse* 1231. **Nash** Heref. & Worcs. *Nasche* 1239. **Nash** Shrops. *La Esse* 1242, *Nazsche* 1391.

Nassington Northants. *Nassingtona* 1017–34, *Nassintone* 1086 (DB). Probably 'farmstead on the promontory'. OE *næss* + *-ing* + *tūn*.

Nasty Herts. *Nasthey* 1294. '(Place at) the east enclosure'. OE *ēast* + *hæg*, with *N*- from ME *atten* 'at the'.

Nateby, 'farmstead or village where nettles grow, or of a man called **Nati*', OScand. **nata* or pers. name + *bý*: **Nateby** Cumbria. *Nateby* 1242. **Nateby** Lancs. *Nateby* 1204.

Nately, Up Hants. *Nataleie* 1086 (DB), *Upnateley* 1274. 'Wet wood or clearing'. OE **næt* + *lēah*. Affix is OE *upp* 'higher up'.

Natland Cumbria. *Natalund* c.1175. 'Grove where nettles grow, or of a man called **Nati*'. OScand. **nata* or pers. name + *lundr*.

Naughton Suffolk. *Nawelton* c.1150. Possibly 'farmstead of a man called Nagli'. OScand. pers. name + OE *tūn*.

Naul (*An Aill*) Dublin. 'The cliff'.

Naunton, 'new farmstead or estate', OE *nīwe* (dative *nīwan*) + *tūn*: **Naunton** Glos., near Winchcombe. *Niwetone* 1086 (DB). **Naunton** Heref. & Worcs. *Newentone* c.1120. **Naunton Beauchamp** Heref. & Worcs. *Niwantune* 972, *Newentune* 1086 (DB), *Newenton Beauchamp* 1370. Manorial affix from the Beauchamp family, here from the 11th cent.

Navan (*An Eamhain*) Armagh. Meaning uncertain. The name was first applied to Navan Fort, known in Irish as *Eamhain Mhacha*, said to mean 'Macha's brooch' (*eomhuin*, 'neckpin'), referring to the pin used by the goddess Macha to draw a circle around herself marking the outline of the future fort.

Navan (*An Uaimh*) Meath. 'The cave'.

Navenby Lincs. *Navenebi* 1086 (DB). 'Farmstead or village of a man called Nafni'. OScand. pers. name + *bý*.

Navestock Essex. *Nasingestok* 867, *Nassestoca* 1086 (DB). Probably 'outlying farmstead on the promontory'. OE *næss* + *-ing* + *stoc*. Alternatively 'outlying farmstead belonging to the promontory people or to NAZEING'.

Nawton N. Yorks. *Nagletune* 1086 (DB). 'Farmstead of a man called Nagli'. OScand. pers. name + OE *tūn*.

Nayland Suffolk. *Eilanda* 1086 (DB), *Neiland* 1227. '(Place at) the island'. OE *ēg-land*, with *N*- from ME *atten* 'at the'.

Nazeing Essex. *Nassingan* 1062, *Nasinga* 1086 (DB). '(Settlement of) the people of the promontory'. OE *næss* + *-ingas*.

Neagh, Lough (*Loch nEathach*) Antrim, Armagh, Derry, Down, Tyrone. *Loch nEchach c.*600. 'Eochu's lake'.

Neale (*An Éill*) Mayo. 'The flock of birds'.

Near Sawrey Cumbria, *see* SAWREY.

Neasden Gtr. London. *Neosdune c.*1000. 'Nose-shaped hill'. OE **neosu* + *dūn*.

Neasham Durham. *Nesham* 1158. 'Homestead or enclosure by the projecting piece of land in a river bend'. OE **neosu* + *hām* or *hamm*.

Neath (*Castell-Nedd*) Neat. *Neth* 1191, *Neeth* 1306. '(Place on the) River Neath'. The Celtic river name perhaps means 'shining one'. The Welsh name means 'castle on the Nedd' (Welsh *castell*).

Neatishead Norfolk. *Netheshird* 1020–22, *Snateshirda* |*sic*| 1086 (DB). Probably 'household of a retainer'. OE *genēat* + *hīred*.

Necton Norfolk. *Nechetuna* 1086 (DB). Probably 'farmstead by a neck of land'. OE *hnecca* + *tūn*.

Ned (*Nead*) Cavan, Derry, Fermanagh. 'Nest'.

Neddans (*Na Feadáin*) Tipperary. 'The streamlets'.

Nedeen (*Nadín*) Cork, Kerry. 'Little nest'.

Nedging Tye Suffolk. *Hnyddinge c.*995, *Niedinga* 1086 (DB). 'Place associated with a man called *Hnydda'. OE pers. name + *-ing*. Later affix is *tye* 'common pasture'.

Needham, 'poor or needy homestead'. OE *nēd* + *hām*: **Needham** Norfolk. *Nedham* 1352. **Needham Market** Suffolk. *Nedham* 13th cent., *Nedeham Markett* 1511. **Needham Street** Suffolk. *Nedham c.*1185. Affix *street* here means 'hamlet'.

Needingworth Cambs. *Neddingewurda* 1161. 'Enclosure of the family or followers of a man called *Hnydda'. OE pers. name + *-inga-* + *worth*.

Needwood Staffs. *Nedwode* 1248. 'Poor wood', or 'wood resorted to in need (as a refuge)'. OE *nēd* + *wudu*.

Neen Savage & *Neen Sollars* Shrops. *Nene* 1086 (DB), *Nenesauvage* 13th cent., *Nen Solers* 1274. Originally the Celtic or pre-Celtic name of the river here (an old name for the River Rea). Manorial affixes from the le Savage family here in the 13th cent., and from the de Solers family here in the late 12th cent.

Neenton Shrops. *Newentone* |*sic*| 1086 (DB), *Nenton* 1242. 'Farmstead or estate on the River *Neen*', OE *tūn*, see previous name. The Domesday form suggests confusion of the first element with OE *nīwe* (dative *-an*) 'new'.

Nefyn Gwyd. *Newin* 1254, *Nefyn* 1291. Origin uncertain. The name may represent a pers. name.

Nelson Lancs., a 19th cent. name for the new textile town, taken from the Lord Nelson Inn.

Nempnett Thrubwell B. & NE. Som. *Emnet c.*1200, *Trubewel* 1201. Originally two places. Nempnett is '(place at) the level ground' from OE *emnet* with N- from ME *atten* 'at the'. Thrubwell is from OE *wella* 'spring, stream' with an uncertain first element.

Nenagh (*An tAonach*) Tipperary. 'The assembly'.

Nendrum (*Naendruim*) Down. 'Nine ridges'.

Nene (river) Northants–Lincs. *Nyn* 948. An ancient Celtic or pre-Celtic name, of obscure etymology.

Nenthead Cumbria. *Nentheade* 1631. 'Place at the source of the River Nent'. Celtic river-name (from *nant* 'a glen') + OE *hēafod*.

Nesbit Northum., near Doddington. *Nesebit* 1242. 'Promontory river-bend'. OE **neosu* + *byht*.

Ness, '(place at) the promontory or projecting ridge', OE *næss*: **Ness** Ches. *Nesse* 1086 (DB). **Ness, East** & **Ness, West** N. Yorks. *Ne(i)sse* 1086 (DB). **Ness, Great** & **Ness, Little** Shrops. *Nessham, Nesse* 1086 (DB).

Ness, Loch Highland. 'Loch of the River Ness'. *See* INVERNESS.

Neston Ches. *Nestone* 1086 (DB). 'Farmstead near the promontory'. OE *næss* + *tūn*.

Nether as affix, see main name, e.g. for **Nether Broughton** (Leics.) *see* BROUGHTON.

Netheravon Wilts. *Nigravre* |*sic*| 1086 (DB), *Nederauena c.*1150. '(Settlement) lower down the River Avon'. OE *neotherra* + Celtic river-name (meaning simply 'river').

Netherbury Dorset. *Niderberie* 1086 (DB). 'Lower fortified place'. OE *neotherra* +*burh* (dative *byrig*).

Netherfield E. Sussex. *Nedrefelle* 1086 (DB). 'Open land infested with adders'. OE *næddre* + *feld*.

Netherhampton Wilts. *Notherhampton* 1242. 'Lower homestead'. OE *neotherra* + *hām-tūn*.

Netherseal & *Overseal* Derbys. *Scel(l)a* 1086 (DB), *Nether Scheyle, Overe Scheyle* 13th cent. 'Small wood or copse'. OE **scegel*. Distinguishing affixes are OE *neotherra* 'lower' and *uferra* 'upper'.

Netherthong W. Yorks. *Thoying* 13th cent., *Nethyrthonge* 1448. 'Narrow strip of land'. OE *thwang*, with *neotherra* 'lower' to distinguish it from UPPERTHONG.

Netherton, a common name, 'lower farmstead or estate', OE *neotherra* + *tūn*; examples include: **Netherton** Heref. & Worcs., near Evesham. *Neotheretun* 780, *Neotheretune* 1086 (DB). **Netherton** Northum. *Nedertun c.*1050.

Netley Hants. *Lætanlia* 955–8, *Latelei* 1086 (DB). Probably 'neglected clearing, or clearing left fallow'. OE **læte* + *lēah*, with change to initial *N-* only from the 14th cent. perhaps through confusion with the following name.

Netley Marsh Hants. *Natanleaga* late 9th cent., *Nutlei* |*sic*| 1086 (DB). Probably 'wet wood or clearing'. OE **næt* + *lēah*.

Nettlebed Oxon. *Nettlebed* 1246. 'Plot of ground overgrown with nettles'. OE *netele* + *bedd*.

Nettlecombe Dorset. *Netelcome* 1086 (DB). 'Valley where nettles grow'. OE *netele* + *cumb*.

Nettleden Herts. *Neteleydene c.*1200. 'Valley of the woodland clearing where nettles grow'. OE *netele* + *lēah* + *denu*.

Nettleham Lincs. *Netelham* 1086 (DB). 'Homestead or enclosure where nettles grow'. OE *netele* + *hām* or *hamm*.

Nettlestead Kent. *Netelamstyde* 9th cent., *Nedestede* |sic| 1086 (DB). 'Homestead where nettles grow'. OE *netele* + *hāmstede*.

Nettlestone I. of Wight. *Hoteleston* |sic| 1086 (DB), *Nutelastone* 1248. 'Farmstead by the nut pasture or nut wood'. OE *hnutu* + *lǣs* or *lēah* (genitive *lēas*) + *tūn*.

Nettleton Lincs. *Neteltone* 1086 (DB). 'Farmstead where nettles grow'. OE *netele* + *tūn*.

Nettleton Wilts. *Netelingtone* 940, *Niteletone* 1086 (DB). 'Farmstead at the place overgrown with nettles'. OE *netele* + *-ing* + *tūn*.

Nevendon Essex. *Nezendena* |sic| 1086 (DB), *Neuendene* 1218. '(Place at) the level valley'. OE *efen* + *denu*, with N- from ME *atten* 'at the'.

Nevis, Ben. *See* BEN NEVIS.

New as affix, *see* main name, e.g. for **New Alresford** (Hants.) *see* ALRESFORD.

New Birmingham (*Gleann an Ghuail*) Tipperary. The site was exploited for coal in the 18th cent. and named for *Birmingham*, then in a coalmining region. The Irish name means 'valley of the coal'.

New Ferry Mersey., a district named from a ferry across the River Mersey established here in the 18th cent.

New Forest Hants. *Nova Foresta* 1086 (DB). 'The new forest' created by William the Conqueror in the 11th cent. for hunting game.

New Galloway Dumf. 'New Galloway'. The town dates from 1629, when a royal charter was granted by Charles I to Sir John Gordon, who chose a name to mark his family ties with GALLOWAY.

New Inn Cavan. The name was originally that of a stage-coach inn.

New Invention W. Mids., first on record in 1663, of doubtful origin but possibly referring to some contrivance used in the clay-mining industry, or perhaps derived from an inn here so called. Origin as an inn-name is probably more likely for the identical **New Invention** Shrops.

New Mills Derbys. *New Miln* 1625. Self-explanatory, although the plural form is recent. Earlier called *Midelcauel* 1306, 'the middle allotment of land', from ME *cauel*.

New Quay (*Ceinewydd*) Cergn. 'New quay'. A new quay was built here in 1835 to replace an older and smaller harbour. The Welsh name means the same as the English (Welsh *cei* + *newydd*).

New Radnor (*Maesyfed*) Powys. *Raddrenoue* 1086 (DB), *Radenoura* 1191, *Radnore* 1201, *New Radenore* 1298. 'New Radnor'. The original *Radnor*, 'red bank' (OE *rēad* + *ōra*), was the present *Old Radnor*, called in Welsh *Pencraig*, 'head of the rock' (Welsh *pen* + *craig*). In 1064 the present Radnor was granted rights as the new centre of the region. Its Welsh name means 'Hyfaidd's field' (Welsh *maes*).

New Tredegar Cphy. The town arose in the 19th cent. around a colliery which was regarded as 'new' by comparison with the ironworks at TREDEGAR.

Newark, 'new fortification or building', OE *nīwe* + *weorc*: **Newark** Cambs. *Nieuyrk* 1189. **Newark on Trent** Notts.

Niweweorce c.1080, *Neuuerche* 1086 (DB). For the river-name, *see* TRENTHAM.

Newbald, North E. R. Yorks. *Neoweboldan* 972, *Niuuebold* 1086 (DB). 'New building'. OE *nīwe* + *bold*.

Newbiggin, a common name in the North, 'new building or house', OE *nīwe* + ME *bigging*; examples include: **Newbiggin** Cumbria, near Appleby. *Neubigging* 1179. **Newbiggin** Durham, near Middleton. *Neubigging* 1316. **Newbiggin by the Sea** Northum. *Niwebiginga* 1187.

Newbold, a common name in the Midlands, 'new building', OE *nīwe* + *bold*: examples include: **Newbold** Derbys. *Newebold* 1086 (DB). **Newbold** Leics. *Neoboldia* 12th cent. **Newbold on Avon** Warwicks. *Neobaldo* 1077, *Newebold* 1086 (DB). Avon is a Celtic river-name meaning simply 'river'. **Newbold on Stour** Warwicks. *Nioweboldan* 991. Stour is a Celtic or OE river-name probably meaning 'the strong one'. **Newbold Pacey** Warwicks. *Niwebold* 1086 (DB), *Neubold Pacy* 1235. Manorial affix from the de Pasci family, here in the 13th cent.

Newborough Staffs. *Neuboreg* 1280. 'New fortification'. OE *nīwe* + *burh*.

Newborough (*Niwbwrch*) Angl. *Novus Burgus* 1305, *Neuburgh* 1324, *Newborough* 1379. 'New borough'. OE *nīwe* + *burh*. The 'new borough' was established in the late 13th cent. by Edward I.

Newbottle, 'new building', OE *nīwe* + *bōthl*: **Newbottle** Northants. *Niwebotle* 1086 (DB). **Newbottle** Tyne & Wear. *Neubotl* 1196.

Newbourn Suffolk. *Neubrunna* 1086 (DB). 'New stream', i.e. 'stream which has changed course'. OE *nīwe* + *burna*.

Newbrough Northum. *Nieweburc* 1203. 'New fortification'. OE *nīwe* + *burh*.

Newburgh Lancs. *Neweburgh* 1431. 'New market town or borough'. OE *nīwe* + *burh*.

Newburgh Fife. 'New borough'. *Niwanbyrig* c.1130, *Novus burgus* 1266. OE *nīwe* + *burh*. The town dates from at least the 12th cent.

Newburn Tyne & Wear. *Neuburna* 1121–9. 'New stream', i.e. 'stream which has changed course'. OE *nīwe* + *burna*.

Newbury Berks. *Neuberie* c.1080. 'New market town or borough'. OE *nīwe* + *burh* (dative *byrig*).

Newby, a common name in the North, 'new farmstead or village', OE *nīwe* + OScand. *bý*: examples include: **Newby** Cumbria, near Appleby. *Neubi* 12th cent. **Newby East** Cumbria. *Neuby* c.1190. **Newby West** Cumbria. *Neuby* c.1200. **Newby Wiske** N. Yorks. *Neuby* 1157. Affix from the River Wiske, *see* APPLETON WISKE.

Newcastle, 'new castle', OE *nīwe* + *castel* (often in Latin in early spellings): **Newcastle** Shrops. *Novum castrum* 1284. **Newcastle under Lyme** Staffs. *Novum castellum subtus Lymam* 1173. *Lyme* is an old Celtic district name, probably meaning 'elm-tree region'. **Newcastle upon Tyne** Tyne & Wear. *Novem Castellum* 1130. For the river-name, *see* TYNEMOUTH.

Newcastle (*An Caisleán Nua*) Down. (*ag fersait*) *an chaisléin nui* 1433. 'The new castle'.

Newcastle Emlyn (*Castelnewydd Emlyn*) Carm. *Novum castrum de Emlyn c.*1240, *Emlyn with New Castle* 1257, *Newcastle Emlyn* 1295. 'New castle in Emlyn'. OE *nīwe* + *castel*. The cantref name *Emlyn* means 'around the valley' (Welsh *am* + *glyn*).

Newchurch, 'new church', OE *nīwe* + *cirice*: **Newchurch** I. of Wight. *Niechirche* 12th cent. **Newchurch** Kent. *Nevcerce* 1086 (DB).

Newdigate Surrey. *Niudegate c.*1167. 'Gate by the new wood', OE *nīwe* + *wudu* + *geat*.

Newenden Kent. *Newedene* 1086 (DB). 'New woodland pasture'. OE *nīwe* (dative *-an*) + *denn*.

Newent Glos. *Noent* 1086 (DB). Probably a Celtic name meaning 'new place'.

Newhall, 'new hall or manor house', OE *nīwe* + *hall*: **Newhall** Ches. *La Nouehall* 1252. **Newhall** Derbys. *Niewehal* 1197.

Newham Gtr. London, a recent name created for the new London borough comprising EAST HAM & WEST HAM.

Newham Northum., near Bamburgh. *Neuham* 1242 'New homestead or enclosure', OE *nīwe* + *ham* or *hamm*.

Newhaven E. Sussex. *Newehaven* 1587. 'New harbour'. OE *nīwe* + *hæfen*. Its old name was *Mechingas* 1121, *Mecinges* 1204, '(settlement of) the family or followers of a man called *Mēce', from OE pers. name + *-ingas*.

Newhaven Edin. 'Newly built harbour'. Newhaven dates from *c.*1505.

Newholm N. Yorks. *Neueham* 1086 (DB). 'New homestead or enclosure'. OE *nīwe* + *hām* or *hamm*.

Newick E. Sussex. *Niwicha* 1121. 'New dwelling or farm'. OE *nīwe* + *wīc*.

Newington, 'the new farmstead or estate', OE *nīwe* (dative *nīwan*) + *tūn*: **Newington** Kent, near Hythe. *Neventone* 1086 (DB). **Newington** Kent, near Sittingbourne. *Newetone* 1086 (DB). **Newington** Oxon. *Niwantun c.*1045, *Nevtone* 1086 (DB). **Newington, North** Oxon. *Newinton* 1200. **Newington, South** Oxon. *Niwetone* 1086 (DB). **Newington, Stroke** Gtr. London. *Neutone* 1086. *Neweton Stoken* 1274. Affix means 'by the tree-stumps' or 'made of logs', from OE *stoccen*.

Newland, *Newlands*, 'new arable land', OE *nīwe* + *land*: **Newland** Glos. *Nova terra* 1221, *Neveland* 1248. **Newland** Heref. & Worcs. *La Newelande* 1221. **Newland** N. Yorks. *Newland* 1234. **Newlands** Northum. *Neuland* 1343.

Newlyn Cornwall. *Nulyn* 1279, *Lulyn* 1290. Probably 'pool for a fleet of boats'. Cornish *lu* + *lynn*.

Newlyn East Cornwall. 'Church of *Sancta Niwelina*' 1259. From the patron saint of the church.

Newmarket Suffolk. *Novum Forum* 1200, *la Newmarket* 1418. 'New market town'. ME *market* (rendered by Latin *forum* in the earliest form).

Newmills Tyrone. *New Mills* 1837. The reference is to a former corn mill.

Newnham, a fairly common name, 'the new homestead or enclosure', OE *nīwe* (dative *-an*) + *hām* or *hamm*; examples include: **Newnham** Glos. *Nevneham* 1086 (DB). **Newnham**

Herts. *Neuham* 1086 (DB). **Newnham** Kent. *Newenham* 1177. **Newnham** Northants. *Niwanham* 1021–3.

Newnton, North Wilts. *Northniwetune* 892, *Newetone* 1086 (DB). 'New farmstead'. OE *nīwe* (dative *nīwan*) + *tūn*.

Newport, 'new market town', OE *nīwe* + *port*: **Newport** Devon. *Neuport* 1295. **Newport** Essex. *Neuport* 1086 (DB). **Newport** I. of Wight. *Neweport* 1202. **Newport** Shrops. *Novus Burgus* 12th cent., *Newport* 1237. **Newport Pagnell** Bucks. *Neuport* 1086 (DB), *Neuport Paynelle* 1220. Manorial affix from the Paynel family, here in the 12th cent.

Newport (*Casnewydd-ar-Wysg*) Newpt. *Novus Burgus* 1138, *Nova Villa* 1290, *Neuborh* 1291. 'New town'. OE *nīwe* + *port*. The 12th-cent. castle here was regarded as 'new' by comparison with the Roman fort at Caerleon. The Welsh name means 'new castle on the River Usk' (Welsh *cas* + *newydd* + *ar*). *See* USK.

Newport (*Trefdraeth*) Pemb. *Nuport* 1282, *Newburgh* 1296, *Novus Burgus* 1316. 'New town'. OE *nīwe* + *port*. The original town with market rights here may have been regarded as 'new' by comparison with Fishguard. The Welsh name means 'town by the shore' (Welsh *tref* + *traeth*).

Newport-on-Tay Fife. 'New port on the River Tay'. OE *nīwe* + *port*. For the river name, *see* TAYPORT.

Newquay Cornwall *Newe Kaye* 1602. Named from the new quay (ME *key*) built here in the 15th cent.

Newry (*An tIúr*) Down. *Iobhar Chind Trachta* 1089. 'The yew tree'. An earlier name was *Iúr Cinn Trá*, 'yew tree at the head of the strand'.

Newsham, *Newsholme*, a fairly common name in the North, '(place at) the new houses', OE *nīwe* + *hūs* in a dative plural form *niwum hūsum*; examples include: **Newsham** Northum. *Neuhusum* 1207. **Newsham** N. Yorks., near Ravensworth. *Neuhuson* 1086 (DB). **Newsholme** E. R. Yorks. near Howden. *Neuhusam* 1086 (DB). **Newsholme** Lancs., near Barnoldswick. *Neuhuse* 1086 (DB).

Newstead Northum. *Novus Locus* 13th cent., *Newstede* 1339. 'New farmstead'. OE *nīwe* + *stede*.

Newstead Notts. *Novus Locus* 12th cent., *Newstede* 1302. 'New monastic site'. OE *nīwe* + *stede*.

Newstead Sc. Bord. *Novo Loco* 1189. 'New place'. OE *nīwe* + *stede*.

Newthorpe N. Yorks. *Niwan-thorp c.*1030. 'New outlying farm'. OE *nīwe* + OScand. *thorp*.

Newton, a very common name, 'the new farmstead, estate, or village', OE *nīwe* + *tūn*; examples include: **Newton Abbot** Devon *Nyweton c.*1200, *Nyweton Abbatis* 1270. The Latin affix meaning 'of the abbot' refers to its possession by Torre Abbey in the 12th cent. **Newton Arlosh** Cumbria. *Arlosk* 1185, *Neutonarlosk* 1345. Arlosh is probably a Celtic name meaning 'burnt place'. **Newton Blossomville** Bucks. *Niwetone* 1175, *Newenton Blosmevill* 1254. Manorial affix from the de Blosseville family, here in the 13th cent. **Newton Burgoland** Leics. *Neutone* 1086 (DB), *Neuton Burgilon* 1390. Manorial affix from early possession of lands here by the Burgilon family. **Newton Ferrers** Devon. *Niwetone* 1086 (DB), *Neweton Ferers* 1303. Manorial affix from the de Ferers family, here in the 13th cent. **Newton-le-Willows** Mersey. *Neweton* 1086 (DB). Affix means 'by the willow-trees'. **Newton Longville** Bucks. *Nevtone* 1086 (DB), *Newenton Longevile* 1254. Affix from its possession by the church of St Faith of Longueville in France from the mid-12th cent. **Newton, Maiden** Dorset. *Newetone* 1086 (DB), *Maydene Neweton* 1288. Addition means 'of the maidens', perhaps referring to early possession of the manor by nuns. **Newton, North** Somerset. *Newetune* 1086 (DB). **Newton Poppleford** Devon. *Poplesford* 1226, *Neweton Popilford* 1305. Poppleford means 'pebble ford', OE **popel* + *ford*. **Newton St Cyres** Devon. *Niwantune* c.1070, *Nywetone Sancti Cirici* 1330. Affix from the dedication of the church to St Ciricius.

In contrast to the above 'new settlements' of medieval origin, the following makes use of the old name type for a modern development: **Newton Aycliffe** Durham, a recent 'new town' named from AYCLIFFE.

Newton Mearns E. Renf. *Newtoun de Mernis* 1609. 'New town in Mearns'. *See* MEARNS.

Newton Stewart Dumf. 'New village of Stewart'. OE *nīwe* + *tūn*. The village was laid out in 1677 by William *Stewart*, son of the 2nd Earl of Galloway.

Newtongrange Midloth. 'Grange of the new estate'. OE *nīwe* + *tūn* + OFrench *grange*. The grange was so named for distinction from the one at *Prestongrange*, near Prestonpans.

Newtown I. of Wight. *Niwetune* c.1200, *nouum burgum de Francheuile* 1254. 'New town or borough', OE *nīwe* + *tūn*. The alternative name *Francheville*, in use up to the 16th cent., is 'free town', OFrench *franche* + *ville*.

Newtown (*Y Drenewydd*) Powys. *Newentone* 1250, *the Newtown* 1360. 'New village'. OE *nīwe* + *tūn*. The original 'new town' was designated a New Town in 1967. The Welsh name means 'the new town' (Welsh *y* + *tref* + *newydd*).

Newtown Crommelin Antrim. *Newtown Cromlin* 1833. The village was founded in 1824 by the Huguenot Nicholas Crommelin.

Newtown Cunningham Donegal. *Newtowne Cunningham* c.1655. Land here was granted in 1610 to John Cunningham, whose family also gave the name of MANORCUNNINGHAM.

Newtown Forbes Longford. The name comes from the Scotsman Sir Arthur Forbes, who settled here in the early 17th cent.

Newtownabbey Antrim. The town was created in 1958 out of seven existing villages, one of which, *Whiteabbey*, gave the basis of the name.

Newtownards (*Baile Nua na hAirde*) Down. *New Town of Blathewyc* 1333. 'New town of the promontory'. The current name refers to the ARDS PENINSULA. The original name was *New Town of Blathewic*, from *Uí Bhlathmhaic*, 'descendants of Blathmhac', a personal name meaning 'famous son'.

Newtownbreda (*Baile Nua na Bréadaí*) Down. *Newtownbreda* 1832. 'New town of Breda'. The townland name *Breda* represents Irish *Bréadach*, 'broken land'.

Newtownbutler Fermanagh. *Neetowne* 1622. The *Butler* family settled in Ireland in the 17th cent., and the village of

Newtown took its present name when Theophilus Butler was created Baron of Newtownbutler in 1715.

Newtownhamilton Armagh. *Newtown Hamilton* 1792. The village was founded in c.1770 by Alexander Hamilton, a descendant of the John Hamilton who founded HAMILTONSBAWN.

Newtownmountkennedy (*Baile an Chinnéidigh*) Wicklow. 'Kennedy's town'. Sir Robert Kennedy was granted the manor here in the second half of the 17th cent.

Newtownstewart Tyrone. Sir William Stewart was granted extensive lands in Tyrone and Donegal in the early 17th cent.

Neyland Pemb. *Nailand* 1596, *New Milford, or Neyland* 1896. '(Place at the) island'. OE *ēg-land*. N- is from preceding ME *atten*, 'at the'. Neyland was formerly also known as *New Milford*, by contrast with MILFORD HAVEN.

Nibley, 'woodland clearing near the peak', OE **hnybba* + *lēah*: **Nibley** S. Glos. *Nubbelee* 1189. **Nibley, North** Glos. *Hnibbanlege* 940.

Nidd N. Yorks. *Nith* 1086 (DB). Named from the River Nidd, a Celtic or pre-Celtic river-name of uncertain etymology.

Nier (*An Uidhír*) (river) Waterford. 'The dun-coloured one'.

Nigg Highland. *Nig* 1257. '(Place by the) notch'. Gaelic *eig*. N- is from preceding Gaelic *an*, 'the'.

Ninch (*An Inse*) Meath. 'The island'.

Ninebanks Northum. *Ninebenkes* 1228. 'The nine banks or hills'. OE *nigon* + *benc*.

Ninfield E. Sussex. *Nerewelle |sic|* 1086 (DB), *Nimenefeld* 1255. 'Newly taken-in open land'. OE *nīwe* + *numen* + *feld*.

Nithsdale (valley) Dumf. *Stranit* c.1124, *Stranud* 1181, *Niddesdale* 1256. 'Valley of the River Nith'. OScand. *dalr*. The river name means 'new one' (British **nouio-*). The first two forms above have Gaelic *srath*, 'valley'.

Niton I. of Wight. *Neeton* 1086 (DB). 'New farmstead'. OE *nīwe* + *tūn*.

Niwbwrch. *See* NEWBOROUGH.

Noah's Ark Kent, a late name appearing on the first Ordnance Survey map of 1819 and apparently transferred from a house so called built c.1700. Other examples of this fanciful name, perhaps alluding to an abundance or diversity of animals, occur in Cheshire and Derbyshire.

Nobber (*An Obair*) Meath. 'The construction'.

Nobottle Northants. *Neubote |sic|* 1086 (DB), *Neubottle* 12th cent. 'New building'. OE *nīwe* + *bōthl*.

Nocton Lincs. *Nochetune* 1086 (DB). Probably 'farmstead where wether sheep are kept'. OE *hnoc* + *tūn*.

Noke Oxon. *Ac(h)am* 1086 (DB), *Noke* 1382. '(Place at) the oak-tree'. OE *āc*. with N- from ME *atten* 'at the'.

Nolton Pemb. *Noldeton* 1317, *Nolton* 1403. 'Old farm'. OE *ald* + *tūn*. The N- comes from ME *atten*, 'at the'.

Nonington Kent. *Nunningitun* c.1100. 'Estate associated with a man called Nunna'. OE pers. name + *-ing-* + *tūn*.

Norbiton Gtr. London. *Norberton* 1205. 'Northern grange or outlying farm'. OE *north* + *bere-tūn*. See SURBITON.

Norbury, 'northern stronghold or manor-house', OE *north* + *burh* (dative *byrig*): **Norbury** Ches., near Marbury. *Norberie* 1086 (DB). **Norbury** Derbys. *Nortberie* 1086 (DB). **Norbury** Gtr. London. *Northbury* 1359. **Norbury** Shrops. *Norbir* 1237. **Norbury** Staffs. *Nortberie* 1086 (DB).

Nore (*An Fheoir*) (river) Laois, Tipperary. 'The Feoir'.

Norfolk (the county). *Nordfolc* 1086 (DB). '(Territory of) the northern people (of the East Angles)'. OE *north* + *folc*, see SUFFOLK.

Norham Northum. *Northham* c.1050. 'Northern homestead or enclosure'. OE *north* + *hām* or *hamm*.

Norley Ches. *Northleg* 1239. 'Northern glade or clearing'. OE *north* + *lēah*.

Normanby, 'farmstead or village of the Northmen or Norwegian Vikings', OE *Northman* + OScand. *bȳ*: **Normanby** Lincs. *Normanebi* 1086 (DB). **Normanby** N. Lincs. *Normanebi* 1086 (DB). **Normanby** N. Yorks. *Normanebi* 1086 (DB). **Normanby** Red. & Cleve. *Northmannabi* c.1050. **Normanby le Wold** Lincs. *Normane(s)bi* 1086 (DB). Affix means 'on the wolds', from OE *wald* 'high forest land'.

Normandy Surrey, first on record as *Normandie* 1656, apparently taking its name from an inn here called 'The Duke of Normandy'.

Normanton, a fairly common name in the North and North Midlands, 'farmstead of the Northmen or Norwegian Vikings', OE *Northman* + *tūn*; examples include: **Normanton** Derbys. *Normantun* 1086 (DB). **Normanton** W. Yorks. *Normantone* 1086 (DB). **Normanton, South** Derbys. *Normentune* 1086 (DB). **Normanton, Temple** Derbys. *Normantune* 1086 (DB), *Normanton Templer* 1330. Manorial affix from its possession by the Knights Templars in the late 12th cent.

Norrington Common Wilts. *Northinton* 1227. '(Place lying) north in the village'. OE *north* + *in* + *tūn*.

North as affix, *see* main name, e.g. for **North Anston** (S. Yorks.) *see* ANSTON.

North Berwick E. Loth. *Beruvik* c.1225, *Northberwyk* 1250. 'Northern barley farm'. OE *bere-wīc*. The town is 'north' in relation to BERWICK-UPON-TWEED, Northum.

North Minch. See MINCH.

North Ronaldsay (island) Orkn. *Rinarsey* c.1150. 'Northern Ringan's island'. OScand. *ey*. *Ringan* is said to be a form of the name of St Ninian (or Finian), while *North* distinguishes this island from SOUTH RONALDSAY, where the pers. name is different.

North Uist. See UIST.

Northallerton N. Yorks. *Aluretune* 1086 (DB), *North Alverton* 1293. 'Farmstead of a man called Ælfhere'. OE pers. name + *tūn*, with the affix *north* from the 13th cent.

Northam, 'northern enclosure or promontory', OE *north* + *hamm*: **Northam** Devon. *Northam* 1086 (DB). **Northam** Hants. *Northam* 1086 (DB).

Northampton Northants. *Hamtun* early 10th cent., *Northantone* 1086 (DB). 'Home farm, homestead'. OE *hām-tūn*, with prefix *North* to distinguish this place from SOUTHAMPTON (which has a different origin). **Northamptonshire** (OE *scīr* 'district') is first referred to in the 11th cent.

Northaw Herts. *North Haga* 11th cent. 'Northern enclosure'. OE *north* + *haga*.

Northborough Cambs. *Northburh* 12th cent. 'Northern fortification'. OE *north* + *burh*.

Northbourne Kent. *Nortburne* 618, *Norborne* 1086 (DB). 'Northern stream'. OE *north* + *burna*.

Northchurch Herts. *Ecclesia de North Berchamstede* 1254, *le Northcherche* 1347. Self-explanatory, 'the north church' of BERKHAMSTED, from OE *north* + *cirice*.

Northfield W. Mids. *Nordfeld* 1086 (DB), 'Open land lying to the north' (relative to King's Norton). OE *north* + *feld*.

Northfleet Kent. *Flyote* 10th cent., *Norfluet* 1086 (DB). '(Place at) the stream'. OE *flēot* with the addition of *north* to distinguish it from SOUTHFLEET.

Northiam E. Sussex. *Hiham* 1086 (DB), *Nordhyam* c.1200. Probably 'promontory where hay is grown'. OE *hīg* + *hamm*, with the later addition of *north*. Alternatively the original first element may be OE *hēah* 'high'.

Northill Beds. *Nortgiuele* 1086 (DB), 'Northern settlement of the tribe called *Gifle*', *see* SOUTHILL. OE *north* + tribal name derived from the River Ivel, a Celtic river-name meaning 'forked stream'.

Northington Hants. *Northametone* 903. 'Farmstead of the dwellers to the north' (of Alresford or Winchester). OE *north* + *hǣme* + *tūn*.

Northleach Glos. *Lecce* 1086 (DB), *Northlecche* 1200. 'Northern estate on the River Leach'. OE *north* + river-name (*see* EASTLEACH).

Northleigh Devon. *Lege* 1086 (DB), *Northleghe* 1291. '(Place at) the wood or clearing'. OE *lēah*, with *north* to distinguish it from SOUTHLEIGH.

Northlew Devon. *Leuia* 1086 (DB), *Northlyu* 1282. Named from the River Lew, a Celtic river-name meaning 'bright stream'.

Northmoor Oxon. *More* 1059, *Northmore* 1367. 'The marsh'. OE *mōr* with the later addition of *north*.

Northolt Gtr. London. *Northhealum* 960, *Northala* 1086 (DB). 'Northern nook(s) of land'. OE *north* + *halh*, *see* SOUTHALL.

Northowram W. Yorks. *Ufrun* 1086 (DB), *Northuuerum* 1202. '(Place at) the ridges'. OE **ofer*, **ufer* in a dative plural form **uferum*, with *north* to distinguish it from SOUTHOWRAM.

Northrepps Norfolk. *Norrepes* 1086 (DB), *Nordrepples* 1185. Possibly 'north strips of land'. OE *north* + **reopul*.

Northumberland (the county). *Norhumberland* 1130. 'Territory of the *Northhymbre* (i.e. those living north of the River Humber)'. OE tribal name + *land*. In Anglo-Saxon times the territory of the tribe and kingdom of the *Northymbre* was much larger than the present county.

Northwich Ches. *Wich*, *Norwich* 1086 (DB). 'North salt-works'. OE *north* + *wīc*.

Northwick S. Glos. *Northwican* 955–9. 'Northern (dairy) farm'. OE *north* + *wīc*.

Northwold Norfolk. *Northuuold* 970, *Nortwalde* 1086 (DB). 'Northern forest'. OE *north* + *wald*.

Northwood, 'northern wood'. OE *north* + *wudu*: **Northwood** Gtr. London. *Northwode* 1435. **Northwood** I. of Wight. *Northewde* early 13th cent.

Norton, a very common name, 'north farmstead or village', i.e. one to the north of another settlement, OE *north* + *tun*; examples include: **Norton** Heref. & Worcs., near Evesham. *Nortona* 709, *Nortune* 1086 (DB). **Norton** N. Yorks. *Nortone* 1086 (DB). **Norton** Suffolk. *Nortuna* 1086 (DB). **Norton Bavant** Wilts. *Nortone* 1086 (DB), *Nortonbavent* 1381. Manorial affix from the de Bavent family, here in the 14th cent. **Norton, Blo** Norfolk. *Nortuna* 1086 (DB), *Blonorton* 1291. Affix is probably ME *blo* 'bleak, exposed'. **Norton, Bredon's** Heref. & Worcs. *Nortune* 1086 (DB). Affix from nearby Bredon Hill, *see* BREDON. **Norton, Brize** Oxon. *Nortone* 1086 (DB), *Northone Brun* c.1266. Manorial affix from a William le Brun who had land here in 1200. **Norton Canon** Heref. & Worcs. *Nortune* 1086 (DB), *Norton Canons* 1327. Affix from its early possession by the canons of Hereford Cathedral. **Norton, Chipping** & **Norton, Over** Oxon. *Nortone* 1086 (DB), *Chepingnorthona* 1224, *Overenorton* 1302. Distinguishing affixes are OE *cēping* 'market' and *uferra* 'higher'. **Norton Disney** Lincs. *Nortune* 1086 (DB), Norton *Isny* 1331. Manorial affix from the de Isney family, here in the 12th cent. **Norton Fitzwarren** Somerset. *Nortone* 1086 (DB). Manorial affix from lands here held by a family called Fitzwarren. **Norton, Greens** Northants. *Nortone* 1086 (DB), *Grenesnorton* 1465. Manorial affix from the Grene family, here in the 14th cent. **Norton in Hales** Shrops. *Nortune* 1086 (DB), *Norton in Hales* 1291. Affix refers to the district called *Hales*, a name surviving also in HALES Staffs. **Norton-in-the-Moors** Staffs. *Nortone* 1086 (DB), *Norton super le Mores* 1285. Affix is from OE *mōr* 'moor, marshy ground'. **Norton, King's** W. Mids. *Nortune* 1086 (DB), *Kinges Norton* 1221. A royal manor at the time of Domesday Book. **Norton, Midsomer** B. & NE. Som. *Midsomeres Norton* 1248. Affix from the festival of St John the Baptist, patron saint of the church, on Midsummer Day. **Norton St Philip** Somerset. *Nortune* 1086 (DB), *Norton Sancti Phillipi* 1316. Affix from the dedication of the church. **Norton sub Hamdon** Somerset. *Nortone* 1086 (DB), *Norton under Hamedon* 1246. Affix refers to Hamdon Hill, *see* STOKE SUB HAMDON.

Norton, Hook Oxon., *see* HOOK.

Norwell Notts. *Nortwelle* 1086 (DB). 'North spring or stream'. OE *north* + *wella*.

Norwich Norfolk. *Northwic* 10th cent., *Noruic* 1086 (DB). 'North harbour or trading centre'. OE *north* + *wīc*.

Norwick Shet (Unst). 'Northern inlet'. OScand. *north* + *vík*.

Norwood, 'north wood', OE *north* + *wudu*: **Norwood Green** Gtr. London. *Northuuda* 832. **Norwood Hill** Surrey. *Norwode* 1250. **Norwood, South** & **Norwood, West** Gtr. London. *Norwude* 1176.

Noss Head Highland. 'Promontory'. OScand. *nós*.

Nosterfield N. Yorks. *Nostrefeld* 1204. 'Open land with a sheep-fold or by a hillock'. OE *eowestre* or **ōster* + *feld*, with *N-* from ME *atten* 'at the'.

Notgrove Glos. *Natangrafum* 716–43, *Nategraua* 1086 (DB). 'Wet grove or copse'. OE **næt* + *grāf*.

Notley, Black & *Notley, White* Essex. *Hnutlea* 998, *Nutlea* 1086 (DB), *Blake Nuteleye* 1252, *White Nuteleye* 1235. 'Wood or clearing where nut-trees grow'. OE *hnutu* + *lēah*. Distinguishing affixes *blæc* and *hwīt* may refer to soil colour or vegetation.

Notting Hill Gtr. London. *Knottynghull* 1356. Possibly 'hill at the place associated with a man called **Cnotta*'. OE pers. name + *-ing* + *hyll*. Alternatively Notting may be a family name from KNOTTING (Beds.).

Nottingham Notts. *Snotengaham* late 9th cent., *Snotingeham* 1086 (DB). 'Homestead of the family or followers of a man called Snot'. OE pers. name + *-inga-* + *hām*, with loss of *S-* in the 12th cent. due to Norman influence. **Nottinghamshire** (OE *scīr* 'district') is first referred to in the 11th cent.

Nottington Dorset. *Notinton* 1212. 'Estate associated with a man called **Hnotta*'. OE pers. name + *-ing-* + *tūn*.

Notton W. Yorks. *Notone* 1086 (DB). 'Farmstead where wether sheep are kept'. OE *hnoc* + *tūn*.

Notton Wilts. *Natton* 1232. 'Cattle farm'. OE *nēat* + *tūn*.

Noughaval (*Nuachabhail*) Cork. 'New foundation'.

Nuffield Oxon. *Tofeld* c.1181. Probably 'tough open land'. OE *tōh* + *feld*, with change to initial *N-* only from the 14th cent.

Nun Monkton N. Yorks., *see* MONKTON.

Nunburnholme E. R. Yorks. *Brunha'* 1086 (DB), *Nonnebrynholme* 1530. '(Place at) the springs or streams'. OScand. *brunnr* in a dative plural form *brunnum*, with later affix from the Benedictine nunnery here.

Nuneaton Warwicks. *Etone* 1086 (DB), *Nonne Eton* 1247. 'Farmstead by a river'. OE *ēa* + *tūn*, with later affix from the Benedictine nunnery founded here in the 12th cent.

Nuneham Courtenay Oxon. *Neuham* 1086 (DB), *Newenham Courteneye* 1320. 'New homestead or village'. OE *nīwe* (dative *nīwan*) + *hām*. Manorial affix from the Curtenay family, here in the 13th cent.

Nunney Somerset. *Nuni* 954, *Nonin* |*sic*| 1086 (DB). Probably 'island, or dry ground in marsh, of a man called Nunna', OE pers. name + *ēg*. Alternatively the first element may be OE *nunne* 'a nun'.

Nunnington N. Yorks. *Noningtune* 1086 (DB). 'Estate associated with a man called Nunna'. OE pers. name + *-ing-* + *tūn*.

Nunthorpe Middlesbr. *Torp* 1086 (DB), *Nunnethorp* 1240. 'Outlying farmstead or hamlet of the nuns'. OScand. *thorp*, with later affix from the medieval nunnery here.

Nure (*An Iubhar*) Westmeath. 'The yew tree'.

Nurney (*An Urnaí*) Carlow, Kildare. 'The oratory'.

Nursling Hants. *Nhutscelle* c.800, *Notesselinge* 1086 (DB). 'Nutshell place', probably indicating a small abode or settlement. OE *hnutu* + *scell* + *-ing*.

Nutbourne W. Sussex, near Pulborough. *Nordborne* 1086 (DB). 'North stream'. OE *north* + *burna*.

Nutfield Surrey. *Notfelle* 1086 (DB). 'Open land where nut-trees grow'. OE *hnutu* + *feld*.

Nuthall Notts. *Nutehale* 1086 (DB). 'Nook of land where nut-trees grow'. OE *hnutu* + *halh*.

Nuthampstead Herts. *Nuthamstede* c.1150. 'Homestead where nut-trees grow'. OE *hnutu* + *hām-stede*.

Nuthurst W. Sussex. *Nothurst* 1228. 'Wooded hill where nut-trees grow'. OE *hnutu* + *hyrst*.

Nutley E. Sussex. *Nutleg* 1249. 'Wood or clearing where nut-trees grow'. OE *hnutu* + *lēah*.

Nybster Highland. 'New farm'. OScand. *nýr* + *bólstathr*.

Nyetimber W. Sussex, near Pagham. *Neuetunbra* 12th cent. 'New timbered building'. OE *nīwe* + *timbre*.

Nymet Rowland & *Nymet Tracey* Devon. *Nymed* 974, *Limet |sic|* 1086 (DB), *Nimet Rollandi* 1242, *Nemethe Tracy* 1270. Celtic *nimet* 'holy place' (probably also an old name of the River Yeo). Manorial affixes from posses-

sion by a man called Roland in the 12th cent. and by the de Trascy family in the 13th.

Nympsfield Glos. *Nymdesfelda* 862, *Nimdesfelde* 1086 (DB). 'Open land by the holy place'. Celtic *nimet* + OE *feld*.

Nympton, 'farmstead near the river called *Nymet*' (probably an old name for the River Mole), Celtic *nimet* 'holy place' + OE *tūn*: **Nympton, Bishop's** Devon. *Nimetone* 1086 (DB), *Bysshopes Nymet* 1334. Affix from its possession by the Bishop of Exeter in 1086. **Nympton, George** Devon. *Nimet* 1086 (DB), *Nymeton Sancti Georgij* 1291. Affix from the dedication of the church. **Nympton, King's** Devon. *Nimetone* 1086 (DB), *Kyngesnemeton* 1254. Affix from its status as a royal manor in 1066.

Nynehead Somerset. *Nigon Hidon* 11th cent., *Nichehede* 1086 (DB). '(Estate of) nine hides'. OE *nigon* + *hīd*.

Nyton W. Sussex. *Nyton* 1327. Probably 'new farmstead'. OE **nīge* + *tūn*, or 'farmstead on an island of dry ground in marsh' if the first element is *īeg* (with N- from ME *atten* 'at the').

O

Oadby Leics. *Oldebi* |*sic*| 1086 (DB), *Outheby* 1199. Probably 'farmstead or village of a man called Authi'. OScand. pers. name + *bý*.

Oake Somerset. *Acon* 11th cent., *Acha* 1086 (DB). '(Place at) the oak-trees'. OE *āc* in a dative plural form *ācum*.

Oaken Staffs. *Ache* 1086 (DB). Identical in origin with the previous name.

Oakengates Shrops. *Okenyate* 1414. 'The gate or gap where oak-trees grow'. OE **ācen* + *geat*.

Oakenshaw W. Yorks. *Akescahe* 1246. 'Copse where oak-trees grow'. OE **ācen* + *sceaga*.

Oakford Devon. *Alforda* |*sic*| 1086 (DB). *Acford* 1166. 'Ford by the oak-tree(s)'. OE *āc* + *ford*.

Oakham Rutland. *Ocham* 1067, *Ocheham* 1086 (DB). 'Homestead or enclosure of a man called Oc(c)a'. OE pers. name + *hām* or *hamm*.

Oakhanger Hants. *Acangre* 1086 (DB). 'Wooded slope where oak-trees grow'. OE *āc* + *hangra*.

Oakington Cambs. *Hochinton* 1086 (DB). 'Estate associated with a man called Hocca'. OE pers. name + *-ing-* + *tūn*.

Oakle Street Glos. *Acle* c.1270. 'Wood or clearing where oak-trees grow'. OE *āc* + *lēah*. Later affix *street* probably refers to its situation on a Roman road.

Oakley, a fairly common name, 'wood or clearing where oak-trees grow'. OE *āc* + *lēah*; examples include: **Oakley** Beds. *Achelai* 1086 (DB). **Oakley** Dorset. *Ocle* 1327. **Oakley, Great** Essex. *Accleia* 1086 (DB).

Oakmere Ches. *Ocmare* 1277. '(Place at) the lake where oak-trees grow'. OE *āc* + *mere*.

Oaksey Wilts. *Wochesie* 1086 (DB). 'Island, or well-watered land, of a man called **Wocc*'. OE pers. name + *ēg*.

Oakthorpe Leics. *Achetorp* 1086 (DB). 'Outlying farmstead or hamlet of a man called Áki'. OScand. pers. name + *thorp*.

Oakworth W. Yorks. *Acurde* 1086 (DB). 'Oak-tree enclosure'. OE *āc* + *worth*.

Oare, '(place at) the shore or hill-slope', OE *ōra*: **Oare** Kent. *Ore* 1086 (DB). **Oare** Wilts. *Oran* 934.

Oare Somerset. *Are* 1086 (DB). Named from the stream here, now called Oare Water. This is an ancient pre-Celtic river-name identical with the River Ayr in Scotland.

Oban Arg. '(Place by the) little bay'. Gaelic *òban*. The modern Gaelic name *An t-Oban Latharnach* means 'the little bay of Lorn' (*see* LORN).

Oborne Dorset. *Womburnan* 975, *Wocburne* 1086 (DB). '(Place at) the crooked or winding stream'. OE *wōh* + *burna*.

Occlestone Green Ches. *Aculuestune* 1086 (DB). 'Farmstead of a man called Acwulf'. OE pers. name + *tūn*.

Occold Suffolk. *Acholt* c.1050, *Acolt* 1086 (DB). 'Oak-tree wood'. OE *āc* + *holt*.

Ochil Hills Perth. *Oychellis* 1461, *Ocelli montes* 1580. 'High ones'. British *uxello-*.

Ochiltree Dumf. *Ouchiltre* 1232. 'High homestead'. British *uxello-* + Welsh *tref*.

Ockbrook Derbys. *Ochebroc* 1086 (DB). 'Brook of a man called Occa'. OE pers. name + *brōc*.

Ockendon, North (Gtr. London) & **Ockendon, South** (Essex). *Wokendune* c.1070, *Wochenduna* 1086 (DB). 'Hill of a man called **Wocca*'. OE pers. name (genitive *-n*) + *dūn*.

Ockham Surrey. *Bocheham* |*sic*| 1086 (DB), *Hocham* 1170. Possibly 'homestead or enclosure of a man called Occa'. OE pers. name + *hām* or *hamm*.

Ockley Surrey. *Hoclei* 1086 (DB). Probably 'woodland clearing of a man called Occa'. OE pers. name + *lēah*.

Ocle Pychard Heref. & Worcs. *Aclea* c.1030, *Acle* 1086 (DB), *Acle Pichard* 1242. 'Oak-tree wood or clearing'. OE *āc* + *lēah*. Manorial affix from the Pichard family, here in the 13th cent.

Odcombe Somerset. *Udecome* 1086 (DB). Probably 'valley of a man called Uda'. OE pers. name + *cumb*.

Oddingley Heref. & Worcs. *Oddingalea* 816. *Oddunclei* 1086 (DB). 'Woodland clearing of the family or followers of a man called **Odda*'. OE pers. name + *-inga-* + *lēah*.

Oddington Oxon. *Otendone* 1086 (DB). 'Hill of a man called **Otta*'. OE pers. name (genitive *-n*) + *dūn*.

Odell Beds. *Wadehelle* 1086 (DB). 'Hill where woad is grown'. OE *wād* + *hyll*.

Odiham Hants. *Odiham* 1086 (DB). 'Wooded homestead or enclosure'. OE *wudig* + *hām* or *hamm*.

Odstock Wilts. *Odestoche* 1086 (DB). 'Outlying farmstead or hamlet of a man called **Od(d)a*'. OE pers. name + *stoc*.

Odstone Leics. *Odestone* 1086 (DB). Probably 'farmstead of a man called Oddr'. OScand. pers. name + OE *tūn*.

Offaly (*Uíbh Fhailí*) (the county). '(Place of the) descendants of Failge'. Russ Failge was the eldest son of Catháir Már (Cahirmore), King of Ireland from 120 to 123.

Offa's Dyke (linear rampart forming ancient boundary between England and Wales). (*Clawdd Offa*) Denb–Mon. *Offan dīc* 854. 'Offa's earthwork'. *Offedich* 1184. 'Dyke or earthwork traditionally associated with the 8th cent. Mercian king Offa', from OE *dīc*. The Welsh name has the same sense. *See also* KNIGHTON.

Offchurch Warwicks. *Offechirch* 1139. 'Church of a man called Offa'. OE pers. name + *cirice*.

Offenham Heref. & Worcs. *Offeham* 709, *Offenham* 1086 (DB). 'Homestead of a man called Offa or Uffa'. OE pers. name (genitive -*n*) + *hām*.

Offham E. Sussex. *Wocham* c.1092. Probably 'crooked homestead or enclosure'. OE *wōh* + *hām* or *hamm*.

Offham Kent. *Offaham* 10th cent. 'Homestead of a man called Offa'. OE pers. name + *hām*.

Offley, 'woodland clearing of a man called Offa', OE pers. name + *lēah*: **Offley, Bishops** & **Offley, High** Staffs. *Offeleia* 1086 (DB). Affix *Bishops* is from early possession by the Bishop of Lichfield. **Offley, Great** Herts. *Offanlege* 944–6, *Offelei* 1086 (DB).

Offord Cluny & *Offord Darcy* Cambs. *Upeforde, Opeforde* 1086 (DB), *Offord Clunye* 1257, *Offord Willelmi Daci* 1220. 'Upper ford'. OE *upp(e)* + *ford*. Manorial affixes from early possession by the monks of Cluny Abbey in France and by the Dacy (or le Daneys) family.

Offton Suffolk. *Offetuna* 1086 (DB). 'Farmstead of a man called Offa'. OE pers. name + *tūn*.

Offwell Devon. *Offewille* 1086 (DB). 'Spring or stream of a man called Uffa'. OE pers. name + *wella*.

Ogbourne St Andrew & *Ogbourne St George* Wilts. *Oceburnan* 10th cent., *Ocheburne* 1086 (DB), *Okeborne Sancti Andree* 1289, *Okeburne Sancti Georgii* 1332. 'Stream of a man called Occa'. OE pers. name + *burna*. Distinguishing affixes from the church dedications.

Oghil (*Eochill*) Galway. 'Yew wood'.

Ogle Northum. *Hoggel* 1170. Possibly 'hill of a man called Ocga'. OE pers. name + *hyll*.

Ogmore Vale Glam. '(Place on the) River Ogmore'. The river name (Welsh *Ogwr*) means 'harrow' (Welsh *og*). *See also* BRIDGEND.

Ogonnelloe (*Tuath Ó gConaíle*) Clare. 'Territory of Uí Chonaíle'.

Ogwell, East & *Ogwell, West* Devon. *Wogganwylle* 956, *Wogewille* 1086 (DB). 'Spring or stream of a man called *Wocga*'. OE pers. name + *wella*.

Okeford, Child, & *Okeford Fitzpaine* Dorset. *Acford* 1086 (DB), *Childacford* 1227, *Ocford Fitz Payn* 1321. 'Oak-tree ford'. OE *āc* + *ford*. Affixes are from OE *cild* 'noble-born son' (probably with reference to some early owner) and from the Fitz Payn family, here from the 13th cent.

Okehampton Devon. *Ocmundtun* c.970, *Ochenemitona* 1086 (DB). 'Farmstead on the River Okement'. Celtic river-name (possibly 'swift stream') + OE *tūn*.

Old as affix, *see* main name, e.g. for **Old Alresford** (Hants.) *see* ALRESFORD.

Old Northants. *Walda* 1086 (DB). '(Place at) the woodland or forest'. OE *wald*.

Old Hurst Cambs. *Waldhirst* 1227. 'Wooded hill by the wold or forest'. OE *wald* + *hyrst*.

Old Radnor. *See* NEW RADNOR.

Oldberrow Warwicks. *Ulenbeorge* 709, *Oleberge* 1086 (DB). 'Hill or mound of a man called *Ulla*'. OE pers. name + *beorg*.

Oldbury, 'old fortification or stronghold', OE (*e*)*ald* + *burh* (dative *byrig*): **Oldbury** Kent. *Ealdebery* 1302. **Oldbury** Shrops. *Aldeberie* 1086 (DB). **Oldbury** Warwicks. *Aldburia* 12th cent. **Oldbury** W. Mids. *Aldeberia* 1174. **Oldbury on the Hill** Glos. *Ealdanbyri* 972, *Aldeberie* 1086 (DB). Affix 'on the Hill' first used in the 18th cent. **Oldbury upon Severn** S. Glos. *Aldeburhe* 1185.

Oldham Gtr. Manch. *Aldholm* 1226–8. 'Old promontory'. OE *ald* + OScand. *holmr*.

Oldland S. Glos. *Aldelande* 1086 (DB). 'Old or long-used cultivated land'. OE *ald* + *land*.

Ollerton, 'farmstead where alder-trees grow', OE *alor* + *tūn*: **Ollerton** Ches. *Alretune* 1086 (DB). **Ollerton** Notts. *Alretun* 1086 (DB).

Olney Bucks. *Ollanege* 979, *Olnei* 1086 (DB). 'Island, or dry ground in marsh, of a man called *Olla*'. OE pers. name (genitive -*n*) + *ēg*.

Olton W. Mids. *Alton* 1221. Possibly 'old farmstead'. OE *ald* + *tūn*.

Olveston S. Glos. *Ævestune* 955–9, *Alvestone* 1086 (DB). 'Farmstead of a man called Ælf'. OE pers. name + *tūn*.

Omagh (*An Ómaigh*) Tyrone. (*caislen*) *na hOghmaighe* c.1450. 'The virgin plain'.

Ombersley Heref. & Worcs. *Ambreslege* 706. Possibly 'woodland clearing of a man called *Ambre*', OE pers. name + *lēah*. Alternatively 'woodland clearing of the bunting' if the first element is rather OE *amer*.

Omeath (*Ó Méith*) Louth. '(People) of Uí Méith'.

Omey Island (*Iomaí*) Galway. 'Bed (of Feichín)'.

Ompton Notts. *Almuntone* 1086 (DB). 'Farmstead of a man called Alhmund'. OE pers. name + *tūn*.

Onaght (*Eoghanacht*) Galway. '(Place of the) descendants of Eoghan'.

Onecote Staffs. *Anecote* 1199. 'Lonely cottage(s)'. OE *āna* + *cot*.

Ongar, Chipping & *Ongar, High* Essex. *Aungre* 1045, *Angra* 1086 (DB), *Chepyngaungre* 1314, *Heyghangre* 1339. 'Pasture land'. OE *anger*, with distinguishing affixes *cēping* 'market' and *hēah* 'high'.

Onibury Shrops. *Aneberie* 1086 (DB), *Onebur* 1247. River-name (possibly 'single river', i.e. one formed by the uniting of two headwaters, from OE *āna* and *ēa*) + *burh* (dative *byrig*) 'manor'.

Onn, High Staffs. *Otne* |*sic*| 1086 (DB), *Onna* c.1130. Probably Welsh *onn* 'ash-trees'.

Onneley Staffs. *Anelege* 1086 (DB). 'Woodland clearing of a man called Onna', or 'isolated clearing'. OE pers. name or *āna* + *lēah*.

Oola (*Ulla*) Limerick. 'Apple trees'.

Oran (*Uarán*) Roscommon. 'Spring'.

Oranmore (*Órán Mór*) Galway. 'Big spring'.

Orby Lincs. *Heresbi* |*sic*| 1086 (DB), *Orreby* c.1115. 'Farmstead or village of a man called Orri'. OScand. pers. name + *by*.

Orchard Portman Somerset. *Orceard* 854. OE *orceard* 'a garden or orchard'. Manorial affix from the Portman family, here in the 15th cent.

Orchard, East & *Orchard, West* Dorset. *Archet* 939. '(Place) beside the wood'. Celtic *ar* + **cēd*.

Orcheston Wilts. *Orc(h)estone* 1086 (DB). Probably 'farmstead of a man called Ordrīc'. OE pers. name + *tūn*.

Orcop Heref. & Worcs. *Orcop* 1138. 'Top of the slope or ridge'. OE *ōra* + *copp*.

Ord, East Northum. *Horde* 1196. 'Projecting ridge'. OE *ord*.

Ore E. Sussex. *Ora* 1121–5. '(Place at) the hill-slope or ridge'. OE *ōra*.

Orford Ches. *Orford* 1332. Possibly 'upper ford'. OE *uferra* + *ford*.

Orford Suffolk. *Oreford* 1164. Possibly 'ford near the shore'. OE *ōra* + *ford*. The river-name **Ore** is a 'back-formation' from the place-name.

Orgreave Staffs. *Ordgraue* 1195. Probably 'pointed grove or copse'. OE *ord* + *grǣfe*.

Orkney (the unitary authority). *Orkas* 330 BC, *Orcades* 1st cent., *Orkaneya* 970. 'Islands of (the) Orcos'. OScand. *ey*. The islands may have originally had a Celtic tribal name meaning 'boar'. This was then apparently taken by the Vikings to mean 'seal' (OScand. *orkn*).

Orlar (*Orlár*) Mayo. 'Valley floor'.

Orleton Heref. & Worcs., near Leominster. *Alretune* 1086 (DB). 'Farmstead where alder-trees grow'. OE *alor* + *tūn*.

Orlingbury Northants. *Ordinbaro* |*sic*| 1086 (DB), *Ordelinberg* 1202. Probably 'hill associated with a man called **Ordla*'. OE pers. name + *-ing-* + *beorg*.

Ormes Head, Great Conwy. *Ormeshede insula* 15th cent. 'Snake headland'. OScand. *ormr* + *hofuth*. Cp. WORMS HEAD.

Ormesby, *Ormsby*, usually 'farmstead or village of a man called Ormr', OScand. pers. name + *bý*: **Ormesby** Middlesbr. *Ormesbi* 1086 (DB). **Ormesby St Margaret** & **Ormesby St Michael** Norfolk. *Ormesby* c.1020, *Ormesbei* 1086 (DB). **Ormsby, North** Lincs. *Vrmesbyg* 1066–8, *Ormesbi* 1086 (DB).

However the following has a different origin: **Ormsby, South** Lincs. *Ormesbi* 1086 (DB), *Ormeresbi* early 12th cent. 'Farmstead of a man called Ormarr'. OScand. pers. name + *bý*.

Ormside, Great & *Ormside, Little* Cumbria. *Ormesheued* c.1140. 'Headland of a man called Ormr'. OScand. pers. name + OE *hēafod*. Alternatively the first element may be OScand. *ormr* 'snake'.

Ormskirk Lancs. *Ormeshirche* c.1190. 'Church of a man called Ormr'. OScand. pers. name + *kirkja*.

Oronsay (island) Arg. *Orvansay* 1549. OScand. *orfins-ey* 'ebb island'.

Oronsay (island) Highland. *Oransay* 1549. OScand. *orfins-ey* 'ebb island'.

Orphir Orkn. 'Tidal island'. *Orfura* c.1225, *Orfiara* c.1500. OScand. *ór* + *fjara* + *ey*. The name, literally 'out-of-low-water island', relates to the coastline, regarded as an island that appears above the waterline only at low tide.

Orpington Gtr. London. *Orpedingtun* 1032, *Orpinton* 1086 (DB). 'Estate associated with a man called **Orped*'. OE pers. name + *-ing-* + *tūn*.

Orrell, possibly 'hill where ore is dug', OE *ōra* + *hyll*: **Orrell** Gtr. Manch. *Horhill* 1202. **Orrell** Mersey. *Orhul* 1299.

Orsedd, Yr. *See* ROSSETT.

Orsett Essex. *Orseathan* 957, *Orseda* 1086 (DB). '(Place at) the pits where (iron) ore is dug'. OE *ōra* + *sēath* (dative plural -*um*).

Orston Notts. *Oschintone* 1086 (DB). Probably 'estate associated with a man called **Ōsica*'. OE pers. name + *-ing-* + *tūn*.

Orton, usually 'higher farmstead', or 'farmstead by a ridge or bank', OE *uferra* or **ofer* or *ōfer* + *tūn*: **Orton** Cumbria. *Overton* 1239. **Orton** Northants. *Overtone* 1086 (DB). **Orton Longueville** & **Orton Waterville** Cambs. *Ofertune* 958, *Ovretune* 1086 (DB), *Ouerton Longavill* 1247, *Ouertone Wateruile* 1248. Manorial affixes from the de Longauilla and de Waltervilla families, here in the 12th cent. **Orton on the Hill** Leics. *Wortone* |*sic*| 1086 (DB), *Overton* c.1215.

However the following has a different origin: **Orton, Great** & **Orton, Little** Cumbria. *Orreton* 1210. 'Farmstead of a man called Orri'. OScand. pers. name + OE *tūn*.

Orwell Cambs. *Ordeuuelle* 1086 (DB). 'Spring by a pointed hill'. OE *ord* + *wella*.

Orwell (river) Suffolk. *Arewan* 11th cent., *Orewell* 1341. An ancient pre-Celtic river-name of uncertain meaning, to which has been added OE *wella* 'stream'.

Osbaldeston Lancs. *Ossebaldiston* c.1200. 'Farmstead of a man called Ōsbald'. OE pers. name + *tūn*.

Osbaston Leics. *Sbernestun* |*sic*| 1086 (DB), *Osberneston* 1200. 'Farmstead of a man called Ásbjǫrn'. OScand. pers. name + OE *tūn*.

Osborne I. of Wight. *Austeburn* 1316. Probably 'stream at the sheepfold'. OE *eowestre* + *burna*.

Osbournby Lincs. *Osbernebi* 1086 (DB). 'Farmstead or village of a man called Ásbjǫrn'. OScand. pers. name + *bý*.

Osgathorpe Leics. *Osgodtorp* 1086 (DB). 'Outlying farmstead or hamlet of a man called Ásgautr'. OScand. pers. name + *thorp*.

Osgodby, 'farmstead or village of a man called Ásgautr', OScand. pers. name + *bý*: **Osgodby** Lincs., near Market Rasen. *Osgotebi* 1086 (DB). **Osgodby** N. Yorks. *Asgozbi* 1086 (DB).

Osmaston Derbys., near Derby. *Osmundestune* 1086 (DB). 'Farmstead of a man called Ōsmund'. OE pers. name + *tūn*.

Osmington Dorset. *Osmingtone* 934, *Osmentone* 1086 (DB). 'Estate associated with a man called Ōsmund'. OE pers. name + *-ing-* + *tūn*.

Osmotherley N. Yorks. *Asmundrelac* |*sic*| 1086 (DB), *Osmunderle* 1088. 'Woodland clearing of a man called Ásmundr'. OScand. pers. name (genitive -*ar*) + OE *lēah*.

Ospringe Kent. *Ospringes* 1086 (DB). Possibly '(place at) the spring'. OE **or-spring* or **of-spring*.

Ossett W. Yorks. *Osleset* 1086 (DB). 'Fold of a man called **Ōsla*', or 'fold frequented by blackbirds'. OE pers. name or OE *ōsle* + *set*.

Ossington Notts. *Oschintone* 1086 (DB). Probably 'estate associated with a man called **Ōsica*'. OE pers. name + *-ing-* + *tūn*.

Osterley Gtr. London. *Osterle* 1274. 'Woodland clearing with a sheepfold'. OE *eowestre* + *lēah*.

Oswaldkirk N. Yorks. *Oswaldescherca* 1086 (DB). 'Church dedicated to St Ōswald'. OE pers. name + *cirice* (replaced by OScand. *kirkja*).

Oswaldtwistle Lancs. *Oswaldestwisel* 1246. 'River-junction of a man called Ōswald'. OE pers. name + *twisla*.

Oswestry Shrops. *Oswaldestroe* 1191. 'Tree of a man called Ōswald'. OE pers. name + *trēow*. The traditional connection with St Oswald, 7th cent. king of Northumbria, is uncertain.

Otford Kent. *Otteford* 832, *Otefort* 1086 (DB). 'Ford of a man called **Otta*'. OE pers. name + *ford*.

Otham Kent. *Oteham* 1086 (DB). 'Homestead or village of a man called **Otta*'. OE pers. name + *hām*.

Othery Somerset. *Othri* 1225. Probably 'the other or second island'. OE *ōther* + *ēg*.

Otley, 'woodland clearing of a man called **Otta*', OE pers. name + *lēah*: **Otley** Suffolk. *Otelega* 1086 (DB). **Otley** W. Yorks. *Ottanlege* c.972, *Otelai* 1086 (DB).

Otterbourne, *Otterburn*, 'stream frequented by otters', OE *oter* + *burna*: **Otterbourne** Hants. *Oterburna* c.970, *Otreburne* 1086 (DB). **Otterburn** Northum. *Oterburn* 1217. **Otterburn** N. Yorks. *Otreburne* 1086 (DB).

Otterden Kent. *Otringedene* 1086 (DB). 'Woodland pasture of the family or followers of a man called Oter'. OE pers. name + *-inga-* + *denn*.

Otterham Cornwall. *Otrham* 1086 (DB). Probably 'enclosure or river-meadow by the River Ottery'. OE river-name ('otter stream', OE *oter* + *ēa*) + *hamm*.

Otterington, North & *Otterington, South* N. Yorks. *Otrinctun* 1086 (DB). 'Estate associated with a called **Oter*'. OE pers. name + *-ing-* + *tūn*.

Ottershaw Surrey. *Otershaghe* c.890. 'Small wood frequented by otters'. OE *oter* + *sceaga*.

Otterton Devon. *Otritone* 1086 (DB). 'Farmstead by the River Otter'. OE river-name (*see* OTTERY) + *tūn*.

Ottery St Mary Devon. *Otri* 1086 (DB), *Otery Sancte Marie* 1242. Named from the River Otter, 'stream frequented by otters', OE *oter* + *ēa*. Affix from the dedication of the church.

Ottery, Venn Devon. *Fenotri* 1156. 'Marshy land by the River Otter'. OE *fenn*, *see* previous name.

Ottringham E. R. Yorks. *Otringeham* 1086 (DB). 'Homestead of the family or followers of a man called Oter'. OE pers. name + *-inga-* + *hām*.

Oughter, Lough (*Loch Uachtar*) Cavan. 'Upper lake'.

Oughterard (*Uachtar Ard*) Galway, Kildare. 'High upper place'.

Oughtibridge S. Yorks. *Uhtiuabrigga* 1161. Probably 'bridge of a woman called **Ūhtgifu*'. OE pers. name + *brycg*.

Oulart (*An tAbhallort*) Wexford. 'The orchard'.

Oulston N. Yorks. *Uluestun* 1086 (DB). 'Farmstead of a man called Wulf or Ulfr'. OE or OScand. pers. name + OE *tūn*.

Oulton Cumbria. *Ulveton* c.1200. 'Farmstead of a man called **Wulfa*'. OE pers. name + *tūn*.

Oulton Norfolk. *Oulstuna* 1086 (DB). Probably 'farmstead of a man called Authulfr'. OScand. pers. name + OE *tūn*.

Oulton Suffolk. *Aleton* 1203. 'Farmstead of a man called Áli', or 'old farmstead'. OScand. pers. name or OE *ald* + *tūn*. **Oulton Broad** contains *broad* in the sense 'extensive piece of water', *see* BROADS.

Oulton W. Yorks. *Aleton* 1180. Identical in origin with the previous name.

Ounageeragh (*Abha na gCaorach*) Cork. 'River of the sheep'.

Oundle Northants. *Undolum* c.710–20, *Undele* 1086 (DB). '(Settlement of) the tribe called Undalas'. OE tribal name (meaning possibly 'those without a share' or 'undivided').

Ourna, Lough (*Loch Odharna*) Tipperary. 'Dun-coloured lake'.

Ousby Cumbria. *Uluesbi* 1195. 'Farmstead or village of a man called Ulfr'. OScand. pers. name + *bý*.

Ousden Suffolk. *Uuesdana* 1086 (DB). 'Valley frequented by owls'. OE *ūf* + *denu*.

Ouseburn, Great & *Ouseburn, Little* N. Yorks. *Useburne* 1086 (DB). '(Place at) the stream flowing into the River Ouse'. Celtic or pre-Celtic river-name (meaning simply 'water') + OE *burna*.

Ousefleet E. R. Yorks. *Useflete* 1100–8. '(Place at) the channel of the River Ouse'. OE *flēot*, *see* previous name.

Ouston Durham. *Vlkilstan* 1244–9. 'Boundary stone of a man called Ulfkell'. OScand. pers. name + OE *stān*.

Out Rawcliffe Lancs., *see* RAWCLIFFE.

Outwell Norfolk. *Wellan* 963, *Utuuella* 1086 (DB). '(Place at) the spring or stream'. OE *wella*, with affix *ūte* 'outer, lower downstream' to distinguish it from UPWELL.

Outwood, 'outlying wood', that is 'wood on the outskirts of a manor or parish'. OE *ūt* + *wudu*; examples include: **Outwood** Surrey, recorded thus in 1640. **Outwood** W. Yorks. *Outewode* 1436.

Ovenden W. Yorks. *Ovenden* 1219. Probably 'valley of a man called Ōfa'. OE pers. name (genitive *-n*) + *denu*.

Ovens (*Na hUamhanna*) Cork. 'The caves'.

Over as affix, see main name, e.g. for **Over Compton** (Dorset) *see* COMPTON.

Over, '(place at) the ridge or slope'. OE **ofer*: **Over** Cambs. *Ouer* 1060, *Ovre* 1086 (DB). **Over** Ches. *Ovre* 1086 (DB). **Over** S. Glos. *Ofre* 1005.

Overbury Heref. & Worcs. *Uferebiri* 875, *Ovreberie* 1086 (DB). 'Upper fortification'. OE *uferra* + *burh* (dative *byrig*).

Overseal Derbys., *see* NETHERSEAL.

Overstone Northants. *Oveston* 12th cent. Probably 'farmstead of a man called Ufic'. OE pers. name + *tūn*.

Overstrand Norfolk. *Othestranda* |*sic*| 1086 (DB), *Overstrand* 1231. 'Land along the shore'. OE *ōfer* + *strand*.

Overton, a fairly common name, usually 'higher farmstead', OE *uferra* + *tūn*; examples include: **Overton** Hants. *Uferantun* 909, *Ovretune* 1086 (DB). **Overton, West** Wilts. *Uferantune* 939, *Ovretone* 1086 (DB).
   However some Overtons may have a different origin, 'farmstead by a ridge or bank', OE *ofer or *ōfer* + *tūn*; examples include: **Overton** Lancs. *Ouretun* 1086 (DB). **Overton** N. Yorks. *Ovretun* 1086 (DB). **Overton, Market** Leics. *Overtune* 1086 (DB), *Marketesoverton* 1200. Affix is ME *merket* referring to the early market here.

Overton (*Owrtyn*) Wrex. *Overtone* 1201. 'Farmstead by a bank'. OE *ōfer* + *tūn*.

Oving, '(settlement of) the family or followers of a man called Ūfa', OE pers. name + -*ingas*: **Oving** Bucks. *Olvonge* |*sic*| 1086 (DB), *Vuinges* 12th cent. **Oving** W. Sussex. *Uuinges* 956.

Ovingdean E. Sussex. *Hovingedene* 1086 (DB). Probably 'valley of the family or followers of a man called Ūfa'. OE pers. name + -*inga*- + *denu*.

Ovingham Northum. *Ovingeham* 1238. 'Homestead of the family or followers of a man called Ōfa', or 'homestead at Ōfa's place'. OE pers. name + -*inga*- or -*ing* + *hām*.

Ovington, usually 'estate associated with a man called Ūfa', OE pers. name + -*ing*- + *tun*: **Ovington** Essex. *Ouituna* 1086 (DB). **Ovington** Hants. *Ufinctune* c.970. **Ovington** Norfolk. *Uvinton* 1202.
   However the following have a different origin: **Ovington** Durham. *Ulfeton* 1086 (DB). 'Estate associated with a man called Wulfa'. OE pers. name + -*ing*- + *tūn*. **Ovington** Northum. *Ofingadun* 699–705. 'Hill of the family or followers of a man called Ōfa'. OE pers. name + -*inga*- + *dūn*.

Ow (*Abh*) (river) Wicklow. 'River'.

Owel, Lough (*Loch Uair*) Westmeath. 'Uair's lake'.

Owenass (*Abhainn Easa*) (river) Laois. 'River of the waterfall'.

Owenavorragh (*Abhainn an Bhorraidh*) (river) Wexford. 'River liable to flood'.

Owenbeg (*An Abhainn Bheag*) Sligo. 'The little river'.

Owenboy (*Abhainn Bhuí*) Cork. 'Yellow river'.

Owendalulleegh (*Abhainn dá Loilíoch*) (river) Galway. 'River of two milch cows'.

Owenduff (*An Abhainn Dubh*) Mayo. 'The black river'.

Owenea (*Abhainn an Fia*) (river) Donegal. 'River of the deer'.

Owenglin (*Abhainn Ghlinne*) (river) Galway. 'River of the valley'.

Oweniny (*Abhainn Eidhneach*) (river) Mayo. 'Ivied river'.

Owenkillew (*Abhainn Choilleadh*) (river) Tyrone. 'River of the wood'.

Owenmore (*Abhainn Mór*) (river) Cork, Mayo, Sligo. 'Big river'.

Owennacurra (*Abhainn na Cora*) (river) Cork. 'River of the weir'.

Owenrea Burn (*Abhainn Riabhach*) Tyrone. 'Grey river'.

Owentocker (*Abhainn Tacair*) (river) Donegal. 'River of the pickings'.

Owenur (*Abhainn Fhuar*) (river) Roscommon. 'Cold river'.

Owenwee (*Abhainn Bhuí*) Donegal. 'Yellow river'.

Ower Hants, near Copythorne. *Hore* 1086 (DB). '(Place at) the bank or slope'. OE *ōra*.

Ower (*Odhar*) Galway. 'Dun-coloured place'.

Owermoigne Dorset. *Ogre* 1086 (DB), *Oure Moyngne* 1314. Probably 'the wind-gap(s)', from a British (Celtic) *ogrodust-, referring to gaps in the chalk hills which funnel winds off the sea. Manorial affix from the Moigne family, here in the 13th cent.

Owersby, North & *Owersby, South* Lincs. *Aresbi, Oresbi* 1086 (DB). Possibly 'farmstead or village of a man called Ávarr'. OScand. pers. name + *bý*.

Owey Island (*Uaigh*) Donegal. *The Island of Inishowey* 1613. 'Cave'.

Owmby, probably 'farmstead or village of a man called Authunn', OScand. pers. name + *bý*, though alternatively the first element may be OScand. *authn* 'uncultivated land, deserted farm': **Owmby** Lincs. *Odenebi* 1086 (DB). **Owmby-by-Spital** Lincs. *Ounebi* 1086 (DB). *See* SPITAL.

Owrtyn. *See* OVERTON.

Owslebury Hants. *Oselbyrig* c.970. 'Stronghold of a man called *Ōsla', or 'stronghold frequented by blackbirds'. OE pers. name or OE *ōsle* + *burh* (dative *byrig*).

Owston Leics. *Osulvestone* 1086 (DB). 'Farmstead of a man called Ōswulf. OE pers. name + *tūn*.

Owston S. Yorks. *Aust(h)un* 1086 (DB). 'East farmstead'. OScand. *austr* + OE *tūn*.

Owston Ferry N. Lincs. *Ostone* 1086 (DB). Identical in origin with the previous name.

Owstwick E. R. Yorks. *Osteuuic* 1086 (DB). 'Eastern outlying farm'. OScand. *austr* (possibly replacing OE *ēast*) + OE *wīc*.

Owthorpe Notts. *Ovetorp* 1086 (DB). 'Outlying farmstead or hamlet of a man called Úfi or Ūfa'. OScand. or OE pers. name + OScand. *thorp*.

Owvane (*Abh Bhán*) (river) Cork. 'White river'.

Ox Mountains (*Sliabh Gamh*) Sligo. The Irish name, meaning 'storm mountain' (*gamh*), has been taken to mean 'ox mountain' (*damh*).

Oxborough Norfolk. *Oxenburch* 1086 (DB). 'Fortification where oxen are kept'. OE *oxa* + *burh*.

Oxendon, Great Northants. *Oxendone* 1086 (DB). 'Hill where oxen are pastured'. OE *oxa* (genitive plural *oxna*) + *dūn*.

Oxenholme Cumbria. *Oxinholme* 1274. 'River-meadow where oxen are pastured'. OE *oxa* (genitive plural *oxna*) + OScand. *holmr*.

Oxenhope W. Yorks. *Hoxnehop* 12th cent. 'Valley where oxen are kept'. OE *oxa* (genitive plural *oxna*) + *hop*.

Oxenton Glos. *Oxendone* 1086 (DB). 'Hill where oxen are pastured'. OE *oxa* (genitive plural *oxna*) + *dūn*.

Oxford Oxon. *Oxnaforda* 10th cent., *Oxeneford* 1086 (DB). 'Ford used by oxen'. OE *oxa* (genitive plural *oxna*) + *ford*. **Oxfordshire** (OE *scīr* 'district') is first referred to in the 11th cent.

Oxford Island (peninsula) Armagh. *Oxford's Island* 1835. The name is a corruption of *Hawksworth's Island*. Captain Robert Hawksworth is recorded as a tenant here in 1666.

Oxhey Herts. *Oxangehæge* 1007. 'Enclosure for oxen'. OE *oxa* (genitive plural *oxna*) + (*ge*)*hæg*.

Oxhill Warwicks. *Octeselve* 1086 (DB). 'Shelf or ledge of a man called Ohta'. OE pers. name + *scelf*.

Oxley W. Mids. *Oxelie* 1086 (DB). 'Woodland clearing where oxen are pastured'. OE *oxa* + *lēah*.

Oxnam Sc. Bord. *Oxanaham* 1152. 'Farmstead where oxen are kept'. OE *oxa* (genitive plural *oxna*) + *hām*.

Oxshott Surrey. *Okesseta* 1179. 'Projecting piece of land of a man called Ocga'. OE pers. name + *scēat*.

Oxspring S. Yorks. *Ospring* |*sic*| 1086 (DB), *Oxspring* 1154. 'Spring frequented by oxen'. OE *oxa* + *spring*.

Oxted Surrey. *Acstede* 1086 (DB). 'Place where oak-trees grow'. OE *āc* + *stede*.

Oxton Notts. *Oxetune* 1086 (DB). 'Farmstead where oxen are kept'. OE *oxa* + *tūn*.

Oxwick Norfolk. *Ossuic* |*sic*| 1086 (DB), *Oxewic* 1242. 'Farm where oxen are kept'. OE *oxa* + *wīc*.

Oykel (river) Highland. *Okel* 1365. 'High one'. British *uxello-*.

Oystermouth (*Ystumllwynarth*) Swan. 'The Welsh form, involving *ystum* 'bend (of a river)', *llyn* 'grove' and *garh* 'promontory' (of Mumbles Hill), has long been transformed into *Oystermouth*, supposedly interpreted as 'estuary of oysters'.

Ozleworth Glos. *Oslan wyrth* 940, *Osleuuorde* 1086 (DB). 'Enclosure of a man called **Ōsla*', or 'enclosure frequented by blackbirds'. OE pers. name or OE *ōsle* + *worth*.

P

Pabay (island) Highland (Skye). *Paba* 1580. 'Hermit island'. OScand. *pabi* + *ey*.

Packington Leics. *Pakinton* 1043, *Pachintone* 1086 (DB). 'Estate associated with a man called *Pac(c)a*'. OE pers. name + *-ing-* + *tūn*.

Padbury Bucks. *Pateberie* 1086 (DB). 'Fortified place of a man called Padda'. OE pers. name + *burh* (dative *byrig*).

Paddington Gtr. London. *Padington* c.1050. 'Estate associated with a man called Padda'. OE pers. name + *-ing-* + *tūn*.

Paddlesworth Kent, near Folkestone. *Peadleswurthe* 11th cent. 'Enclosure of a man called *Pæddel*'. OE pers. name + *worth*.

Paddock Wood Kent. *Parrok* 1279. OE *pearroc* 'small enclosure, paddock'.

Padiham Lancs. *Padiham* 1251. Possibly 'homestead or enclosure associated with a man called Padda'. OE pers. name + *-ing-* + *hām* or *hamm*.

Padley, Upper & *Padley, Nether* Derbys. *Paddeley* c.1230. 'Woodland clearing of a man called Padda', or 'one frequented by toads'. OE pers. name or OE *padde* + *lēah*.

Padstow Cornwall. *Sancte Petroces stow* 11th cent. 'Holy place of St Petroc'. Cornish saint's name + OE *stōw*.

Padworth Berks. *Peadanwurthe* 956, *Peteorde* 1086 (DB). 'Enclosure of a man called Peada'. OE pers. name + *worth*.

Pagham W. Sussex. *Pecganham* 680, *Pageham* 1086 (DB). 'Homestead or promontory of a man called *Pæcga*'. OE pers. name + *hām* or *hamm*.

Paglesham Essex. *Paclesham* 1066, *Pachesham* |sic| 1086 (DB). 'Homestead or village of a man called *Pæccel*'. OE pers. name + *hām*.

Paignton Devon. *Peintone* 1086 (DB). Probably 'estate associated with a man called Pæga'. OE pers. name + *-ing-* + *tūn*.

Pailton Warwicks. *Pallentuna* 1077. 'Estate associated with a man called *Pægel*'. OE pers. name + *-ing-* + *tūn*.

Painswick Glos. *Wiche* 1086 (DB), *Painswike* 1237. 'The dwelling or dairy farm'. OE *wīc*. Later manorial affix from Pain Fitzjohn who held the manor in the early 12th cent.

Paisley Renf. '(Place with a) church'. *Passeleth* 1161, *Passelek* 1298. MIrish *baslec*, from Latin *basilica*.

Pakefield Suffolk. *Paggefella* 1086 (DB). 'Open land of a man called *Pacca*'. OE pers. name + *feld*.

Pakenham Suffolk. *Pakenham* c.950, *Pachenham* 1086 (DB). 'Homestead or village of a man called *Pacca*'. OE pers. name (genitive *-n*) + *hām*.

Palace (*Pailís*) Cork, Wexford. 'Stockade'.

Palatine (*Baile na bPailitíneach*) Carlow. 'Town of the Palatines'.

Palgrave Suffolk. *Palegrave* 962, *Palegraua* 1086 (DB). Probably 'grove where poles are got'. OE *pāl* + *grāf*.

Palgrave, Great Norfolk. *Pag(g)raua* 1086 (DB). Possibly 'grove of a man called Paga'. OE pers. name + *grāf*.

Pallas (*Pailís*) Galway, Kerry. 'Stockade'.

Pallas Green (*Pailís Ghréine*) Limerick. 'Stockade of Grian'.

Pallasbeg (*Pailís Beag*) Limerick. 'Small stockade'.

Pallasboy (*Pailís Buí*) Westmeath. 'Yellow stockade'.

Pallaskenry (*Pailís Chaonraí*) Limerick. 'Stockade of Caonraí'.

Palling, Sea Norfolk. *Pallinga* 1086 (DB). '(Settlement of) the family or followers of a man called Pælli'. OE pers. name + *-ingas*. Affix from its coastal situation.

Pallis (*Pailís*) Kerry, Wexford. 'Stockade'.

Palmers Green Gtr. London. *Palmers grene* 1608. Village green named from a family called Palmer, known in this area from the 14th cent.

Palterton Derbys. *Paltertune* c.1002, *Paltretune* 1086 (DB). OE *tūn* 'farmstead' with an uncertain first element.

Pamber Hants. *Penberga* 1165. Probably 'hill with a fold or enclosure'. OE *penn* + *beorg*.

Pamphill Dorset. *Pamphilla* 1168. Possibly 'hill of a man called *Pampa* or *Pempa*', OE pers. name + *hyll*, but the first element may be an OE word *pamp* meaning 'hill'.

Pampisford Cambs. *Pampesuuorde* 1086 (DB). Probably 'enclosure of a man called *Pamp*'. OE pers. name + *worth*.

Pancrasweek Devon. *Pancradeswike* 1197. 'Hamlet with a church dedicated to St Pancras'. OE *wīc*.

Pancross Vale Glam. *Pannecrosse* 1605. Probably 'Pain's crossroads'. ME pers. name + *cros*.

Panfield Essex. *Penfelda* 1086 (DB). 'Open land by the River Pant'. Celtic river-name (meaning 'valley') + OE *feld*.

Pangbourne Berks. *Pegingaburnan* 844, *Pangeborne* 1086 (DB). 'Stream of the family or followers of a man called Pæga'. OE pers. name + *-inga-* + *burna*. The river-name **Pang** is a 'back-formation' from the place-name.

Pannal N. Yorks. *Panhal* 1170. 'Pan-shaped nook of land'. OE *panne* + *halh*.

Panton Lincs. *Pantone* 1086 (DB). Possibly 'farmstead near a hill or pan-shaped feature'. OE *pamp* or *panne* + *tūn*.

Panxworth Norfolk. *Pankesford* 1086 (DB). OE *ford* 'a ford' with an uncertain first element, possibly a pers. name.

Papcastle Cumbria. *Pabecastr* 1260. 'Roman fort occupied by a hermit'. OScand. *papi* + OE *cæster*.

Papplewick Notts. *Papleuuic* 1086 (DB). 'Dwelling or (dairy) farm in the pebbly place'. OE **papol* + *wīc*.

Paps, The (*An Dá Chích*) (mountain) Kerry. 'The two breasts'.

Papworth Everard & *Papworth St Agnes* Cambs. *Pappawyrthe* 1012, *Papeuuorde* 1086 (DB), *Pappewrth Everard* 1254, *Anneys Papwrth* 1241. 'Enclosure of a man called **Pappa*'. OE pers. name + *worth*. Manorial affixes from 12th cent. owners called Evrard and Agnes.

Par Cornwall. *Le Pare* 1573. Probably 'the cove or harbour', from Cornish *porth*.

Paradise, a name found in several counties, usually bestowed on a spot considered particularly pleasant, from ME *paradis*; examples include **Paradise** Glos., near Painswick, recorded as *Paradys* 1327.

Parbold Lancs. *Perebold* 1200. 'Dwelling where pears grow'. OE *peru* + *bold*.

Pardshaw Cumbria. *Perdishaw* c.1205. 'Hill or mound of a man called **Perd(i)*'. OE pers. name + OScand. *haugr*.

Parham Suffolk. *Perreham* 1086 (DB). Probably 'homestead or enclosure where pears grow'. OE *peru* + *hām* or *hamm*.

Park (*Páirc*) Derry, Mayo. 'Field'.

Parkgate Antrim. *Parkgate* 1780. The village arose at the entrance to a great park laid out in the early 17th cent. by Sir Arthur Chichester, Lord Deputy of Ireland.

Parkgate Ches., a self-explanatory name for this former port taken from *the Parkgate* 1610, this referring to the gate of the former park at NESTON.

Parkgorm (*Páirc Gorm*) Tyrone. 'Blue field'.

Parkham Devon. *Percheham* 1086 (DB). Probably 'enclosure with paddocks'. OE *pearroc* + *hamm*.

Parkhurst, *Parkhurst Forest* I. of Wight. *Perkehurst* c.1200. 'The wooded hill in the hunting park', from OE *hyrst* with ME *park*. This 'park' was a royal chase or forest from the time of Domesday Book.

Parkmore (*Páirc Mhór*) Antrim, Galway, Tyrone. 'Big field'.

Parkreagh (*Páirc Riabhach*) Tyrone. 'Grey field'.

Parkstone Dorset. *Parkeston* 1326. 'The park (boundary) stone', from OE *stān* with ME *park*, this probably referring to a medieval hunting park in CANFORD.

Parley, West Dorset. *Perlai* 1086 (DB). 'Wood or clearing where pears grow'. OE *peru* + *lēah*.

Parndon, Great Essex. *Perenduna* 1086 (DB). 'Hill where pears grow'. OE **peren* + *dūn*.

Parracombe Devon. *Pedrecumbe, Pedracomba* 1086 (DB), *Parrecumbe* 1238, *Pearecumbe* 1297. Possibly 'valley of the pedlars', from OE **peddere* (genitive plural *peddera*) + *cumb*. Alternatively, if the DB forms are corrupt, the first element may be OE *pearroc* 'an enclosure'.

Parson Drove Cambs. *Personesdroue* 1324. 'Cattle road used by or belonging to a parson'. ME *persone* + *drove*.

Partick Glas. *Perdeyc* c.1136. Origin obscure.

Partington Gtr. Manch. *Partinton* 1260. 'Estate associated with a man called **Pearta*'. OE pers. name + *-ing-* + *tūn*.

Partney Lincs. *Peartaneu* 731, *Partenay* 1086 (DB). 'Island, or dry ground in marsh, of a man called **Pearta*'. OE pers. name (genitive *-n*) + *ēg*.

Parwich Derbys. *Piowerwic* 963, *Pevrewic* 1086 (DB). Possibly 'dairy farm on the River *Pever*'. Lost Celtic river-name (meaning 'bright stream') + OE *wīc*.

Pass of Keimaneigh (*Céim an Fhia*) Cork. 'Pass of the gap of the deer'.

Passenham Northants. *Passanhamme* early 10th cent., *Passeham* 1086 (DB). 'River-meadow of a man called Passa'. OE pers. name (genitive *-n*) + *hamm*.

Paston Norfolk. *Pastuna* 1086 (DB). Possibly 'farmstead of a man called **Pæcci*', OE pers. name + *tūn*. Alternatively the first element may be an OE **pæsc(e)* 'muddy place, pool'.

Patcham E. Sussex. *Piceham* |sic| 1086 (DB), *Peccham* c.1090. Possibly 'homestead of a man called **Pæcca*'. OE pers. name + *hām*.

Patching W. Sussex. *Pæccingas* 960, *Petchinges* 1086 (DB). '(Settlement of) the family or followers of a man called **Pæcc(i)*'. OE pers. name + *-ingas*.

Patchway S. Glos. *Petshagh* 1276. 'Enclosure of a man called *Pēot*'. OE pers. name + *haga*.

Pateley Bridge N. Yorks. *Pathlay* 1202. 'Woodland clearing near the path(s)'. OE *pæth* + *lēah*.

Patney Wilts. *Peattanige* 963. 'Island or well-watered land of a man called **Peatta*'. OE pers. name (genitive *-n*) + *ēg*.

Patrick Brompton N. Yorks., *see* BROMPTON.

Patrington E. R. Yorks. *Patringtona* 1033, *Patrictone* 1086 (DB). OE *tūn* 'farmstead, estate' with an uncertain first element, probably a pers. name or folk-name.

Patrixbourne Kent. *Borne* 1086 (DB), *Patricburn* 1215. 'Estate on the river called *Burna*' (from OE *burna* 'stream' referring to the Little Stour), with later affix from William Patricius who held the manor in the 12th cent.

Patterdale Cumbria. *Patrichesdale* c.1180. 'Valley of a man called Patric'. OIrish pers. name + OScand. *dalr*.

Pattingham Staffs. *Patingham* 1086 (DB). 'Homestead of the family or followers of a man called **P(e)atta*', or 'homestead at **P(e)atta's* place'. OE pers. name + *-inga-* or *-ing* + *hām*.

Pattishall Northants. *Pascelle* |sic| 1086 (DB), *Patesshille* 12th cent. 'Hill of a man called **Pætti*'. OE pers. name + *hyll*.

Paul Cornwall. 'Church of *Beatus Paulus*, or of *Sanctus Paulinus*' 1259. From the patron saint of the church, St Paul or Paulinus.

Paulerspury Northants. *Pirie* 1086 (DB), *Pirye Pavely* c.1280. Originally '(place at) the pear-tree', from OE *pirige*. Manorial affix from the de Pavelli family who held the manor from 1086, thus distinguishing this place from neighbouring POTTERSPURY.

Paull E. R. Yorks. *Pagele* 1086 (DB). '(Place at) the stake (marking a landing-place)'. OE **pagol*.

Paulton B. & NE. Som. *Palton* 1171. 'Farmstead on a ledge or hill-slope'. OE **peall* + *tūn*.

Pavenham Beds. *Pabeneham* 1086 (DB). 'Homestead or river-meadow of a man called **Papa*'. OE pers. name (genitive *-n*) + *hām* or *hamm*.

Paxton, Great & *Paxton, Little* Cambs. *Pachstone* 1086 (DB). Probably 'farmstead of a man called **Pæcc*'. OE pers. name + *tūn*.

Payhembury Devon. *Hanberie* 1086 (DB), *Paihember* 1236. 'High or chief fortified place'. OE *hēah* (dative *hēan*) + *burh* (dative *byrig*). Later manorial affix from possession by a man called Pæga.

Paythorne Lancs. *Pathorme* 1086 (DB). Possibly 'thorn-tree of a man called Pái'. OScand. pers. name + *thorn*.

Peacehaven E. Sussex, a recent name for this new resort, chosen to commemorate the end of the First World War.

Peak District Derbys. *Pecsætna lond* 7th cent., *Pec* 1086. OE **pēac* 'a peak, a pointed hill', once applied to some particular hill but used of a larger area from early times. The first form means 'land of the peak dwellers', with OE *sǣte* + *land*. The medieval hunting forest here is referred to from the 13th cent. (e.g. *foresta de Pecco* 1223), this in turn giving name to the village of **Peak Forest** Derbys. (*Peake Forest* 1577).

Peakirk Cambs. *Pegecyrcan* 1016. 'Church of St Pega'. OE female saint's name + OE *cirice* (replaced by OScand. *kirkja*).

Pease Pottage W. Sussex, recorded as *Peaspottage Gate* 1724, probably a reference to soft muddy ground.

Peasemore Berks. *Praxemere* |*sic*| 1086 (DB), *Pesemere* 1166. 'Pond by which peas grow'. OE *pise* + *mere*.

Peasenhall Suffolk. *Pesehala* 1086 (DB). 'Nook of land where peas grow'. OE **pisen* + *halh*.

Peasmarsh E. Sussex. *Pisemerse* 12th cent. 'Marshy ground where peas grow'. OE *pise* + *mersc*.

Peatling Magna & *Peatling Parva* Leics. *Petlinge* 1086 (DB). '(Settlement of) the family or followers of a man called **Pēotla*'. OE pers. name + *-ingas*.

Pebmarsh Essex. *Pebeners* 1086 (DB). 'Ploughed field of a man called Pybba'. OE pers. name (genitive *-n*) + *ersc*.

Pebworth Heref. & Worcs. *Pebewrthe* 848, *Pebeworde* 1086 (DB). 'Enclosure of a man called **Peobba*'. OE pers. name + *worth*.

Peckforton Ches. *Pevreton* 1086 (DB). 'Farmstead at the ford by a peak or hill'. OE **pēac* + *ford* + *tūn*.

Peckham, 'homestead by a peak or hill', OE **pēac* + *hām*: **Peckham** Gtr. London. *Pecheham* 1086 (DB). **Peckham Rye** (*-Rithe* 1520) is from OE *rīth* 'stream'. **Peckham, East** & **Peckham, West** Kent. *Peccham* 10th cent., *Pecheham* 1086 (DB).

Peckleton Leics. *Pechintone* |*sic*| 1086 (DB), *Petlington* 1180. 'Estate associated with a man called **Peohtel*'. OE pers. name + *-ing-* + *tūn*.

Pedmore W. Mids. *Pevemore* |*sic*| 1086 (DB), *Pubemora* 1176. 'Marsh of a man called Pybba'. OE pers. name + *mōr*.

Peebles Sc. Bord. *Pebles* c.1125. '(Place with) tents'. Welsh *pabell* (plural *pebyll*).

Pegswood Northum. *Peggiswrth* 1242. 'Enclosure of a man called **Pecg*'. OE pers. name + *worth*.

Pelaw Tyne & Wear. *Pellowe* 1242. Possibly 'mound or hill of a man called **Pēola*'. OE pers. name + *hlāw*.

Peldon Essex. *Piltendone* c.950, *Peltenduna* 1086 (DB). Probably 'hill of a man called **Pylta*'. OE pers. name (genitive *-n*) + *dūn*.

Pelham, Brent, *Pelham, Furneux*, & *Pelham, Stocking* Herts. *Peleham* 1086 (DB), *Barndepelham* 1230, *Pelham Furnelle* 1240, *Stokenepelham* 1235. 'Homestead or village of a man called **Pēola*'. OE pers. name + *hām*. Distinguishing affixes from OE *bærned* 'burnt, destroyed by fire', from the de Fornellis family here in the 13th cent., and from OE *stoccen* 'made of logs' or 'by the tree-stumps'.

Pelsall W. Mids. *Peoleshale* 996, *Peleshale* 1086 (DB). 'Nook of land of a man called **Pēol*'. OE pers. name + *halh*.

Pelton Durham. *Pelton* 1312. Possibly 'farmstead of a man called **Pēola*'. OE pers. name + *tūn*.

Pelynt Cornwall. *Plunent* 1086 (DB). 'Parish of Nennyd'. Cornish *plu* + saint's name.

Pembridge Heref. & Worcs. *Penebruge* 1086 (DB). Possibly 'bridge of a man called **Pena* or **Pægna*'. OE pers. name + *brycg*.

Pembroke (*Penfro*) Pemb. *Pennbro* c.1150, *Pembroch* 1191. 'Land at the end'. Welsh **pen-* + **brog-*.

Pembroke Dock Pemb. *Pembroke Dockyard* 1817. The port was established by the government in 1814 near the head of Milford Haven estuary and took the name of nearby PEMBROKE.

Pembury Kent. *Peppingeberia* c.1100. Possibly 'fortified place of the family or followers of a man called **Pepa or the like'. OE (?) pers. name + *-inga-* + *burh* (dative *byrig*).

Pen-y-Bont ar Ogwr. *See* BRIDGEND.

Penally Pemb. (*Penalun*) *Pennalun* 9th cent., *Penn Alun* 1136. 'Alun's headland'. Welsh *pen*.

Penare Cornwall. *Pennarth* 1284. 'The headland'. Cornish **penn-ardh*.

Penarlâg. *See* HAWARDEN.

Penarth Vale Glam. *Penarth* 1254. 'Top of the headland'. Welsh *pen* + *garth*.

Pencombe Heref. & Worcs. *Pencumbe* 12th cent. Probably 'valley with an enclosure'. OE *penn* + *cumb*.

Pencoyd Heref. & Worcs. *Pencoyt* 1291. 'Wood's end'. Celtic **penn* + **coid*.

Pencraig Heref. & Worcs. *Penncreic* c.1150. 'Top of the crag or rocky hill'. Celtic **penn* + **creig*.

Pendlebury Gtr. Manch. *Penelbiri* 1202. 'Manor by the hill called *Penn*'. Celtic **penn* 'hill' + explanatory OE *hyll* + *burh* (dative *byrig*).

Pendleton Lancs. *Peniltune* 1086 (DB). 'Farmstead by the hill called *Penn* (Pendle Hill)'. Celtic **penn* 'hill' + explanatory OE *hyll* + *tūn*.

Pendock Heref. & Worcs. *Penedoc* 875, 1086 (DB). Possibly 'hill where barley is grown'. Celtic **penn* + **heiddiog*.

Penfro. *See* PEMBROKE.

Penge Gtr. London. *Penceat* 1067. 'Wood's end', or 'chief wood'. Celtic **penn* + **cēd*.

Penhurst E. Sussex. *Penehest* |sic| 1086 (DB), *Peneherste* 12th cent. Possibly 'wooded hill of a man called **Pena*'. OE pers. name + *hyrst*.

Penicuik Midloth. *Penikok* 1250. 'Hill of the cuckoo'. OWelsh *penn* + *y* + *cog*.

Penistone S. Yorks. *Pengestone* 1086 (DB), *Peningeston* 1199. Probably 'farmstead by a hill called *Penning*'. Celtic **penn* 'hill' + OE *-ing* + *tūn*.

Penketh Ches. *Penket* 1242. 'Wood's end'. Celtic **penn* + **cēd*.

Penkridge Staffs. *Pennocrucium* 4th cent., *Pancriz* 1086 (DB). 'Chief mound or tumulus'. Celtic **penn* + **crūg*. The river-name **Penk** is a 'back-formation' from the place-name.

Penmaenmawr Conwy. *Penmayne mawre* 1473, *Penmaen mawr* 1795. '(Place by) Penmaen Mawr'. The prominent headland *Penmaen Mawr* has a name meaning 'great stone headland' (Welsh *penmaen* + *mawr*).

Penmark Vale Glam. *Penmarc* 1153, *Penmarch* 13th cent. 'Height of the horse'. Welsh *pen* + *march*.

Penn, '(place at) the hill', Celtic **penn*: **Penn** Bucks. *Penna* 1188. **Penn, Lower** (Staffs.) & **Penn, Upper** (W. Mids.) *Penne* 1086 (DB).

Pennard, East & *Pennard, West* Somerset. *Pengerd* 681, *Pennarminstre* 1086 (DB). Celtic **penn* 'hill' with either **garth* 'ridge' or *ardd* 'high'. The Domesday form contains OE *mynster* 'large church'.

Pennines, The, a name first appearing in the 18th cent. and of unknown origin, perhaps based partly on the Celtic element **penn* 'hill' or an invention influenced by the name Apennines for the Italian mountain range.

Pennington, probably 'farmstead paying a penny rent', OE *pening* + *tūn*: **Pennington** Cumbria. *Pennigetun* 1086 (DB). **Pennington, Lower** Hants. *Peynton* 12th cent.

Penny Bridge Cumbria, a recent name, from a local family called Penny.

Penrhyn Gwyr. *See* WORMS HEAD.

Penrhyn Llŷn. *See* LLEYN PENINSULA.

Penrhyndeudraeth Gwyd. *Penrindeudrait* 1292. 'Promontory between two beaches'. Welsh *penrhyn* + *dau* + *traeth*. The village stands between *Traeth Mawr* ('big beach') and *Traeth Bach* ('little beach').

Penrith Cumbria. *Penrith* c.1100. 'Hill ford' or 'chief ford'. Celtic **penn* + **rïd*.

Penruddock Cumbria. *Penreddok* 1278. Celtic **penn* 'hill' or 'chief', with an uncertain second element.

Penryn Cornwall. *Penryn* 1236. 'The promontory or headland'. Cornish *penn rynn*.

Pensax Heref. & Worcs. *Pensaxan* 11th cent. 'Hill of the Anglo-Saxons'. Celtic **penn* + **Sachson*. The order of elements is Celtic.

Pensby Mersey. *Penisby* c.1229. 'Farmstead or village at a hill called *Penn*'. Celtic **penn* 'hill' + OScand. *bý*.

Penselwood Somerset. *Penne* 1086 (DB), *Penne in Selewode* 1345. Celtic **penn* 'hill' with the later addition 'in SELWOOD'.

Pensford B. & NE. Som. *Pensford* 1400. OE *ford* 'a ford' with an uncertain first element, possibly a pers. name.

Penshurst Kent. *Pensherst* 1072. Possibly 'wooded hill of a man called **Pefen*'. OE pers. name + *hyrst*.

Pentire, *West Pentire* Cornwall. *Pentir* c.1270. 'The headland'. Cornish *penn tir*.

Pentland Firth Highland, Orkn. *Pettaland fjorthr* c.1085. 'Sea inlet in the land of the Picts'. OScand. *Pett* + *land* + *fjorthr*.

Pentlow Essex. *Pentelawe* c.1045, *Pentelauua* 1086 (DB). Probably 'hill or tumulus of a man called **Penta*'. OE pers. name + *hlāw*.

Pentney Norfolk. *Penteleiet* |sic| 1086 (DB), *Pentenay* 1200. Possibly 'island, or dry ground in marsh, of a man called **Penta*'. OE pers. name (genitive *-n*) + *ēg*.

Penton Mewsey Hants. *Penitone* 1086 (DB), *Penitune Meysi* 1264. 'Farmstead paying a penny rent'. OE *pening* + *tūn*. Manorial affix from the de Meisy family, here in the 13th cent.

Pentraeth Angl. *Pentrayth* 1254. 'End of the beach'. Welsh *pen* + *traeth*.

Pentrich Derbys. *Pentric* 1086 (DB). 'Hill of the boar'. Celtic **penn* + **tyrch*.

Pentridge Dorset. *Pentric* 762. 1086 (DB). Identical in origin with the previous name.

Pentyrch Card. *Penntirch* 12th cent. 'Hill of the boar'. **pen-* + Welsh **tyrch*.

Penwith Cornwall. *See* ST JUST.

Penwortham, Higher & *Penwortham, Lower* Lancs. *Peneverdant* |sic| 1086 (DB), *Penuertham* 1149. Probably 'enclosed homestead at a hill called *Penn*'. Celtic **penn* 'hill' + OE *worth* + *hām*.

Pen-y-groes Gwyd. *Pen-y-groes* 1838. 'Top of the cross-roads'.

Penzance Cornwall. *Pensans* 1284. 'Holy headland'. Cornish *penn* + *sans*.

Peopleton Heref. & Worcs. *Piplingctun* 972, *Piplintune* 1086 (DB). Probably 'estate associated with a man called **Pyppel*'. OE pers. name + *-ing* + *tūn*.

Peover, Lower & *Peover, Over* Ches. *Pevre* 1086 (DB). Named from the River Peover, a Celtic river-name meaning 'the bright one'.

Peper Harow Surrey. *Pipereherge* 1086 (DB). Probably 'heathen temple of the pipers'. OE *pīpere* + *hearg*.

Perivale Gtr. London. *Pyryvale* 1508. 'Pear-tree valley'. ME *perie* + *vale*.

Perranarworthal Cornwall. *Arewethel* 1181, 'church of *Sanctus Pieranus* in *Arwothel*' 1388. 'Parish of St Piran (in the place) beside the marsh'. Cornish saint's name + **ar* + **goethel*.

Perranporth Cornwall. *St Perins creeke* 1577, *Perran Porth* 1810. 'Cove or harbour of St Piran's parish', from English dialect *porth*, with reference to PERRANZABULOE.

Perranuthnoe Cornwall. *Odenol* 1086 (DB), 'church of *Sanctus Pieranus* of *Udno*' 1373. 'Parish of St Piran in the manor of *Uthno*' (meaning obscure).

Perranzabuloe Cornwall. *Lanpiran* 1086 (DB), *Peran in Zabulo* 1535. 'Parish of St Piran in the sand'. Cornish saint's name (with **lann* 'church-site' in the first form) + Latin *in sabulo*.

Perrott, named from the River Parrett, a pre-English river-name of obscure origin: **Perrott, North** Somerset. *Peddredan c.*1050, *Peret* 1086 (DB). **Perrott, South** Dorset. *Pedret* 1086 (DB), *Suthperet* 1268.

Perry Barr W. Mids. *Pirio* 1086 (DB). '(Place at) the pear-tree'. OE *pirige*. It is close to GREAT BARR.

Pershore Heref. & Worcs. *Perscoran* 972, *Persore* 1086 (DB). 'Slope or bank where osiers grow'. OE **persc* + *ōra*.

Pertenhall Beds. *Partenhale* 1086 (DB). 'Nook of land of a man called **Pearta*'. OE pers. name (genitive -*n*) + *halh*.

Perth Perth. *Pert c.*1128, *St Johnstoun or Perth* 1220. '(Place by a) thicket'. Pictish **perta*- Formerly also *St Johnstoun*, from the dedication of the church to St John the Baptist.

Perton Staffs. *Pertona* 1167. 'Farmstead where pears grow'. OE *peru* + *tūn*.

Peter Tavy Devon. *See* TAVY.

Peterborough Cambs. *Burg* 1086 (DB), *Petreburgh* 1333. 'St Peter's town'. OE *burh*, with saint's name from the dedication of the abbey. The original monastery here, founded in the 7th cent., was called *Medeshamstede*, 'homestead of a man called **Mēde*', OE pers. name + *hām-stede*. The *Soke* of Peterborough is from OE *sōcn* 'district under a particular jurisdiction'.

Peterchurch Heref. & Worcs. *Peterescherche* 1302. 'Church dedicated to St Peter'. OE *cirice*.

Peterhead Aber. *Petyrheid* 1544. 'St Peter's headland'. OE *hēafod*. The headland is named after the former St Peter's Kirk. An earlier name was *Inverugie*, 'mouth of the River Ugie' (Gaelic *inbhir*).

Peterlee Durham, a recent name, created to commemorate the trade union leader Peter Lee (died 1935).

Peters Marland Devon. *See* MARLAND.

Petersfield Hants. *Peteresfeld* 1182. Probably '(settlement at) the open land with a church dedicated to St Peter'. OE *feld*.

Petersham Gtr. London. *Patricesham* 1086 (DB). 'Homestead or river-bend land of a man called **Peohtrīc*'. OE pers. name + *hām* or *hamm*.

Peterstow Heref. & Worcs. *Peterestow* 1207. 'Holy place of St Peter'. OE *stōw*.

Petham Kent. *Piteham* 1086 (DB). 'Homestead or enclosure in a hollow'. OE *pytt* + *hām* or *hamm*.

Petherick, Little Cornwall. 'Parish of *Sanctus Petrocus Minor*' 1327. From the dedication of the church to St Petrock.

Petherton, 'farmstead on the River Parrett', pre-English river-name of obscure origin + OE *tūn*: **Petherton, North** Somerset. *Nordperet, Peretune* 1086 (DB). **Petherton, South** Somerset, *Sudperetone* 1086 (DB).

Petherwin, '(church of) Padern the blessed', from the Cornish patron saint of the church + *gwynn* 'blessed': **Petherwin, North** Cornwall. *North Piderwine* 1259. **Petherwin, South** Cornwall. *Suthpydrewyn* 1269.

Petrockstow Devon. *Petrochestou* 1086 (DB). 'Holy place of St Petrock', Cornish saint's name + OE *stōw*.

Pett E. Sussex. *Pette* 1195. '(Place at) the pit'. OE *pytt*.

Pettaugh Suffolk. *Petehaga* 1086 (DB). 'Enclosure of a man called *Pēota*'. OE pers. name + *haga*.

Pettigoe (*Paiteago*) Donegal, Fermanagh. 'Lump'.

Pettistree Suffolk. *Petrestre* 1253. 'Tree of a man called Peohtrēd'. OE pers. name + *trēow*.

Petton Devon. *Petetona c.*1150. 'Farmstead of a man called **Peatta*'. OE pers. name + *tūn*.

Petton Shrops. *Pectone* 1086 (DB). 'Farmstead on or by a pointed hill'. OE **pēac* + *tūn*.

Petts Wood Gtr. London, named from a ship-building family called Pett recorded as having a lease of oak woods in Chislehurst in 1577.

Petworth W. Sussex. *Peteorde* 1086 (DB). 'Enclosure of a man called Pēota'. OE pers. name + *worth*.

Pevensey E. Sussex. *Pefenesea* 947, *Pevenesel* 1086 (DB). 'River of a man called **Pefen*'. OE pers. name + *ēa*.

Pewsey Wilts. *Pefesigge c.*880, *Pevesie* 1086 (DB). 'Island or well-watered land of a man called **Pefe*'. OE pers. name + *ēg*.

Pexall, Lower Ches. *Pexhull* 1274. 'Hill called *Pēac*'. OE **pēac* 'hill' + *hyll*.

Pharis (*Fáras*) Antrim. *Faras* 1780. 'Residence'.

Phillack Cornwall. 'Church of *Sancta Felicitas*' |sic| 1259. *Felok* 1388. From the dedication of the church to a St Felek.

Philleigh Cornwall. 'Church of *Sanctus Filius*' 1312. From the dedication of the church to a St Fily.

Phoenix Park (*Páirc an Fhionnuisce*) Dublin. 'Park of the clear water'. The English name, a corruption of the Irish, has been perpetuated by the Phoenix Column (1745), surmounted by a phoenix.

Pickenham, North & *Pickenham, South* Norfolk. *Pichenham* 1086 (DB). Probably 'homestead or village of a man called **Pīca*'. OE pers. name (genitive -*n*) + *hām*.

Pickering N. Yorks. *Picheringa* 1086 (DB). Possibly '(settlement of) the family or followers of a man called **Pīcer*'. OE pers. name + -*ingas*.

Pickhill N. Yorks. *Picala* 1086 (DB). 'Nook of land by the pointed hills', or 'nook of a man called **Pīca*'. OE *pīc* or pers. name + *halh*.

Picklescott Shrops. *Pikelescote* 1204. Probably 'cottage(s) of a man called Pīcel', OE pers. name + *cot*.

Alternatively the first element could be an OE hill-name *Pīcel 'pointed hill', a derivative of OE *pīc* 'point'.

Pickmere Ches. *Pichemere* 12th cent. 'Lake where pike are found'. OE *pīc* + *mere*.

Pickwell Leics. *Pichewell* 1086 (DB). 'Spring or stream by the pointed hill(s)'. OE *pīc* + *wella*.

Pickwick Wilts. *Pykewyke* 1268. Probably 'dairy farm on or by a pointed spur of land'. OE *pīc* + *wīc*.

Pickworth, 'enclosure of a man called *Pīca', OE pers. name + *worth*: **Pickworth** Lincs. *Picheuuorde* 1086 (DB). **Pickworth** Rutland. *Pichewurtha* 1170.

Picton, 'farmstead of a man called *Pīca', OE pers. name + *tūn*: **Picton** Ches. *Picheton* 1086 (DB). **Picton** N. Yorks. *Piketon* 1200.

Piddinghoe E. Sussex. *Pidingeho* 12th cent. 'Hill-spur of the family or followers of a man called *Pyda'. OE pers. name + *-inga-* + *hōh*.

Piddington, 'estate associated with a man called *Pyda', OE pers. name + *-ing-* + *tūn*: **Piddington** Northants. *Pidentone* 1086 (DB). **Piddington** Oxon. *Petintone* 1086 (DB).

Piddle, North & *Piddle, Wyre* Heref. & Worcs. *Pidele*(*t*) 1086 (DB), *Northpidele* 1271, *Wyre Pidele* 1208. Named from Piddle Brook (OE *pidele* 'a marsh or fen'). Affix *Wyre* is probably from WYRE FOREST.

Piddlehinton Dorset. *Pidele* 1086 (DB), *Pidel Hineton* 1244. 'Estate on the River Piddle belonging to a religious community'. OE river-name (*pidele* 'a marsh or fen') + *hīwan* + *tūn*.

Piddletrenthide Dorset. *Uppidelen* 966, *Pidrie* 1086 (DB), *Pidele Trentehydes* 1212. 'Estate on the River Piddle assessed at thirty hides'. OE river-name (see *PIDDLEHINTON*) + OFrench *trente* + OE *hīd*.

Pidley Cambs. *Pydele* 1228. 'Woodland clearing of a man called *Pyda'. OE pers. name + *lēah*.

Piercebridge Durham. *Persebrigc* c.1050. Probably 'bridge where osiers grow'. OE *persc* + *brycg*.

Pigdon Northum. *Pikedenn* 1205. 'Valley of a man called *Pīca, or by the pointed hills'. OE pers. name or OE *pīc* + *denu*.

Pike (*Píce*) Laois, Tipperary, Waterford. 'Pike'.

Pilgrims Hatch Essex. *Pylgremeshacch* 1483. 'Hatch-gate used by pilgrims' (to the chapel of St Thomas). ME *pilegrim* + OE *hæcc*.

Pilham Lincs. *Pileham* 1086 (DB). Probably 'homestead or enclosure made with stakes'. OE *pīl* + *hām* or *hamm*.

Pillaton Cornwall. *Pilatona* 1086 (DB). 'Farmstead made with stakes'. OE *pīl* + *tūn*.

Pillerton Hersey & *Pillerton Priors* Warwicks. *Pilardintone* 1086 (DB), *Pilardinton Hersy*, *Pilardinton Prior* 1247. 'Estate associated with a man called Pīlheard'. OE pers. name + *-ing-* + *tūn*. Manorial affixes from possession by the de Hersy family, here in the 13th cent., and by the *Prior* of Sheen.

Pilley S. Yorks. *Pillei* 1086 (DB). 'Wood or clearing where stakes are obtained'. OE *pīl* + *lēah*.

Pilling Lancs. *Pylin* c.1195. Named from the River Pilling, probably OE *pyll* 'creek' + *-ing*.

Pilning S. Glos. *Pyllyn* 1529. Probably 'district by the creek or stream'. OE *pyll* + *ende*.

Pilsbury Derbys. *Pilesberie* 1086 (DB). 'Fortified place of a man called *Pīl'. OE pers. name + *burh* (dative *byrig*).

Pilsdon Dorset. *Pilesdone* 1086 (DB). Probably 'hill with a peak', or 'hill marked by a stake'. OE *pīl* + *dūn*.

Pilsley Derbys., near Clay Cross. *Pilleslege* c.1002. *Pinneslei* 1086 (DB). Possibly 'woodland clearing of a man called *Pinnel'. OE pers. name + *lēah*.

Pilton Rutland. *Pilton* 1202. Probably 'farmstead by a stream'. OE *pyll* + *tūn*.

Pilton Northants. *Pilchetone* 1086 (DB). 'Farmstead of a man called *Pīleca'. OE pers. name + *tūn*.

Pilton Somerset. *Piltune* 725, *Piltone* 1086 (DB). Identical in origin with PILTON (Rutland).

Piltown (*Baile an Phoill*) Kilkenny. 'Townland of the creek'.

Pimperne Dorset. *Pimpern* 935, *Pinpre* 1086 (DB). Possibly 'five trees' from Celtic *pimp* + *prenn*, or 'place among the hills' from a derivative of an OE word *pimp* 'hill'.

Pinchbeck Lincs. *Pincebec* 1086 (DB). 'Minnow stream', or 'finch ridge'. OE *pinc* or *pinca* + *bece* (influenced by OScand. *bekkr*) or *bæc* (locative *bece*).

Pinhoe Devon. *Peonho* c.1050, *Pinnoc* 1086 (DB). 'Hill-spur called *Pen*'. Celtic *penn* 'hill' + OE *hōh*.

Pinner Gtr. London. *Pinnora* 1232. 'Peg-shaped or pointed ridge or bank'. OE *pinn* + *ōra*. The river-name **Pinn** is a 'back-formation' from the place-name.

Pinvin Heref. & Worcs. *Pendefen* 1187. 'Fen of a man called Penda'. OE pers. name + *fenn*.

Pinxton Derbys. *Penkeston* 1208. Possibly 'farmstead of a man called *Penec'. OE pers. name + *tūn*.

Pipe Heref. & Worcs. *Pipe* 1086 (DB). OE *pīpe* 'a pipe, a conduit', originally referring to the stream here.

Pipe Ridware Staffs., see RIDWARE.

Pipewell Northants. *Pipewelle* 1086 (DB). 'Spring or stream with a pipe or conduit'. OE *pīpe* + *wella*.

Pirbright Surrey. *Perifrith* 1166. 'Sparse woodland where pear-trees grow'. OE *pirige* + *fyrhth*.

Pirton, 'pear orchard, or farmstead where pear-trees grow', OE *pirige* + *tūn*: **Pirton** Heref. & Worcs. *Pyritune* 972, *Peritune* 1086 (DB). **Pirton** Herts. *Peritone* 1086 (DB).

Pishanagh (*Piseánach*) Westmeath. 'Vetches'.

Pishill Oxon. *Pesehull* 1195. 'Hill where peas grow'. OE *pise* + *hyll*.

Pitcairn Perth. *Peticarne* 1247. 'Portion of the mound'. Pictish *pett* + Gaelic *càrn* (genitive *càirn*).

Pitcaple Aber. 'Portion of the mare'. Pictish *pett* + Gaelic *capull* (genitive *capuill*).

Pitchcott Bucks. *Pichecote* 1176. 'Cottage or shed where pitch is made or stored'. OE *pic* + *cot*.

Pitchford Shrops. *Piceforde* 1086 (DB). 'Ford near a place where pitch is found'. OE *pic* + *ford*.

Pitcombe Somerset. *Pidecombe* 1086 (DB). Probably 'marsh valley'. OE **pide* + *cumb*.

Pitcorthie Fife. *Pittecorthin* 1093. 'Portion with a pillar stone'. Pictish **pett* + Gaelic *coirthe*.

Pitcruvie Fife. 'Portion of the tree'. Pictish **pett* + Gaelic *craobh* (genitive *craoibhe*).

Pitfoskie Aber. 'Portion by a shelter'. Pictish **pett* + Gaelic *fosgadh*.

Pitglassie Highland. 'Portion of the meadow'. Pictish **pett* + Gaelic *ghlasaich*.

Pitliver Fife. *Petlyver* 1450. 'Portion of the book'. Pictish **pett* + Gaelic *leabhar* (genitive *leabhair*). The place may have been church property.

Pitlochry Perth. 'Portion of the stones'. Pictish **pett* + Gaelic *cloichreach*. The reference is probably to stepping stones over the River Tummel.

Pitlurg Aber. *Petnalurge* 1232. 'Portion of the shank'. Pictish **pett* + Gaelic *lorg*.

Pitmedden Aber. 'Middle portion'. Pictish **pett* + Gaelic *medon*.

Pitmillan Aber. *Pitmulen c.*1315. 'Portion of the mill'. Pictish **pett* + Gaelic *muileann*.

Pitminster Somerset. *Pipingmynstre* 938, *Pipeminstre* 1086 (DB). 'Church associated with a man called Pippa'. OE pers. name + *-ing-* + *mynster*.

Pitney Somerset. *Petenie* 1086 (DB). 'Island, or dry ground in marsh, of a man called **Pytta* or Pēota'. OE pers. name (genitive *-n*) + *ēg*.

Pitsea Essex. *Piceseia* 1086 (DB). 'Island, or dry ground in marsh, of a man called Pīc'. OE pers. name + *ēg*.

Pitsford Northants. *Pitesford* 1086 (DB). 'Ford of a man called **Peoht*. OE pers. name + *ford*.

Pitsligo Aber. *Petslegach* 1426. 'Portion of the shelly place'. Pictish **pett* + Gaelic *sligeach*.

Pitstone Bucks. *Pincelestorne* |sic| 1086 (DB), *Pichelesthorne* 1220. 'Thorn-tree of a man called Pīcel'. OE pers. name + *thorn*.

Pittendreich Aber. 'Portion on the hill face'. Pictish **pett* + Gaelic *drech*.

Pittenweem Fife. *Petnaweme c.*1150. 'Portion of the cave'. Pictish **pett* + Gaelic *na h-uamha*.

Pittington Durham. *Pittindun c.*1085. 'Hill associated with a man called **Pytta*'. OE pers. name + *-ing-* + *dūn*.

Pitton Wilts. *Putenton* 1165. 'Farmstead of a man called Putta, or one frequented by hawks'. OE pers. name or OE *putta* + *tūn*.

Plaish Shrops. *Plesc, Plæsc* 963, *Plesham* 1086 (DB). '(Place at) the shallow pool. OE **plæsc*.

Plaistow W. Sussex. *La Pleyestowe* 1271. 'Place for play or sport'. OE *pleg-stōw*. The same name occurs in other counties.

Plaitford Hants. *Pleiteford* 1086 (DB). Probably 'ford where play or sport takes place'. OE **pleget* + *ford*.

Plawsworth Durham. *Plauworth* 1297. Possibly 'enclosure for play or sport'. OE *plaga* + *worth*, but the first element might be a pers. name.

Plaxtol Kent. *Plextole* 1386. 'Place for play or sport'. OE *pleg-stōw*.

Playden E. Sussex. *Pleidena* 1086 (DB). 'Woodland pasture where play or sport takes place'. OE *plega* + *denn*.

Playford Suffolk. *Plegeforda* 1086 (DB). 'Ford where play or sport takes place'. OE *plega* + *ford*.

Plealey Shrops. *Pleyle* 1256. 'Woodland clearing where play or sport takes place'. OE *plega* + *lēah*.

Pleasington Lancs. *Plesigtuna* 1196. 'Estate associated with a man called Plēsa'. OE pers. name + *-ing-* + *tūn*.

Pleasley Derbys. *Pleseleia* 1166. 'Woodland clearing of a man called Plēsa'. OE pers. name + *lēah*.

Plenmeller Northum. *Playnmelor* 1279. Probably 'top of the bare hill'. Celtic **blain* + **mēl* + **breȝ*.

Pleshey Essex. *Plaseiz c.*1150. OFrench *plaisseis* 'an enclosure made with interlaced fencing'.

Plowden Shrops. *Plaueden* 1252. 'Valley where play or sport takes place'. OE *plaga* + *denu*.

Pluckley Kent. *Pluchelei* 1086 (DB). 'Woodland clearing of a man called Plucca'. OE pers. name + *lēah*.

Plumbland Cumbria. *Plumbelund c.*1150. 'Plum-tree grove'. OE *plūme* + OScand. *lundr*.

Plumbridge (*Droichead an Phlum*) Tyrone. *Plumb Bridge* 1837. Possibly 'bridge by the deep pool'. Scottish *plum* + English *bridge*. The bridge is in a deep valley of the Glenelly River.

Plumley Ches. *Plumleia* 1119. 'Plum-tree wood or clearing'. OE *plūme* + *lēah*.

Plumpton, 'farmstead where plum-trees grow', OE *plūme* + *tūn*: **Plumpton** Cumbria. *Plumton* 1212. **Plumpton** E. Sussex. *Pluntune* 1086 (DB). **Plumpton, Great** & **Plumpton, Little** Lancs. *Pluntun* 1086 (DB).

Plumstead, 'place where plum-trees grow', OE *plūme* + *stede*: **Plumstead** Gtr. London. *Plumstede* 961–9, *Plumestede* 1086 (DB). **Plumstead** Norfolk, near Holt. *Plumestede* 1086 (DB). **Plumstead, Great** & **Plumstead, Little** Norfolk. *Plumesteda* 1086 (DB).

Plumtree Notts. *Pluntre* 1086 (DB). '(Place at) the plum-tree'. OE *plūm-trēow*.

Plungar Leics. *Plungar c.*1125. 'Triangular plot where plum-trees grow'. OE *plūme* + *gāra*.

Plush Dorset. *Plyssch* 891. '(Place at) the shallow pool'. OE **plysc*.

Plymouth Devon. *Plymmue* 1230. 'Mouth of the River Plym'. OE *mūtha* with a river-name formed from the next name by the process of 'back-formation'.

Plympton Devon. *Plymentun c.*905, *Plintona* 1086 (DB). 'Farmstead of the plum-tree'. OE *plýme* + *tūn*.

Plymstock Devon. *Plemestocha* 1086. Probably 'outlying farmstead or hamlet connected with PLYMPTON'. OE *stoc*.

Plymtree Devon. *Plumtrei* 1086 (DB). '(Place at) the plum-tree'. OE **plýmtrēow*.

Plynlimon (*Pumlumon*) (mountain) Cergn. 'Five beacons'. Welsh *pum* + *llumon*.

Pockley N. Yorks. *Pochelac |sic|* 1086 (DB), *Pokelai* c.1190. 'Woodland clearing of a man called *Poca'. OE pers. name + *lēah*.

Pocklington E. R. Yorks. *Poclinton* 1086 (DB). 'Estate associated with a man called *Pocela'. OE pers. name + -*ing*- + *tūn*.

Podimore Somerset, probably identical in origin with PODMORE.

Podington Beds. *Podintone* 1086 (DB). 'Estate associated with a man called Poda or Puda'. OE pers. name + -*ing*- + *tūn*.

Podmore Staffs. *Podemore* 1086 (DB). 'Marsh frequented by toads or frogs'. ME *pode* + OE *mōr*.

Pointon Lincs. *Pochinton* 1086 (DB). 'Estate associated with a man called Pohha'. OE pers. name + -*ing*- + *tūn*.

Poisoned Glen (valley) Tyrone. The English name translates Irish *Cró Nimhe*, 'glen of poison', perhaps referring to some poisonous plant that grew here.

Polden Hills Somerset, see CHILTON POLDEN.

Polebrook Northants. *Pochebroc* 1086 (DB). 'Brook by a pouch-shaped feature', OE *pohha* + *brōc*. Alternatively the first element may be an OE *poc(c)e* 'frog'.

Polegate E. Sussex, first recorded as *Powlegate Corner* 1563. 'Gate by the pool', from ME *po(o)le*.

Poles (*Pollaí*) Cavan. 'Pools'.

Polesworth Warwicks. *Polleswyrth* c.1000. 'Enclosure of a man called *Poll'. OE pers. name + *worth*.

Polfore (*Poll Fuar*) Tyrone. 'Cold pool'.

Poling W. Sussex. *Palinges* 1199. '(Settlement of) the family or followers of a man called *Pāl'. OE pers. name + -*ingas*.

Pollagh (*Pollach*) Mayo, Offaly. 'Abounding in holes'.

Pollans (*Pollán*) Donegal. 'Little hole'.

Pollatomish (*Poll an Tómais*) Mayo. 'Tómas's hole'.

Pollboy (*Poll Buí*) Galway. 'Yellow hole'.

Pollicott, Upper Bucks. *Policote* 1086 (DB). Possibly 'cottage(s) associated with a man called *Poll'. OE pers. name + -*ing*- + *cot*.

Pollington E. R. Yorks. *Pouelington* c.1185. 'Farmstead associated with a piece of ground called *Pofel*'. OE *pofel* (of uncertain meaning) + -*ing*- + *tūn*.

Pollokshaws Glas. *Pullock* 1158. 'The woods of Pollock'. British *poll* + OE *sceaga*. The place was originally *Pollok*. The second element was then added to distinguish it from nearby Pollokshields, 'The sheds of Pollock'. (ME *schele*). 1158 *Pullock*.

Pollokshields. *See* POLLOKSHAWS.

Pollremon (*Poll Réamainn*) Galway. 'Réamann's hole'.

Pollrone (*Poll Ruadhain*) Kilkenny. 'Ruadhan's hole'.

Polmadie Glas. *Polmacde* c.1185, *Polmadie* 1617. 'Pool of the sons of Daigh'. British *poll* + Gaelic *mac* (genitive plural *mic*).

Polperro Cornwall. *Portpira* 1303. Probably 'harbour of a man called *Pyra'. Cornish *porth* + pers. name.

Polruan Cornwall. *Porthruan* 1284. 'Harbour of a man called Ruveun'. Cornish *porth* + pers. name.

Polsham Somerset. *Paulesham* 1065. 'Enclosure of a man called Paul'. ME pers. name + OE *hamm*.

Polstead Suffolk. *Polstede* c.975, *Polesteda* 1086 (DB). 'Place by a pool'. OE *pōl* + *stede*.

Poltimore Devon. *Pultimore* 1086 (DB). Possibly 'marshy ground of a man called *Pulta'. OE pers. name + *mōr*.

Polyphant Cornwall. *Polefand*, *Polofant* 1086 (DB). 'Toad's pool'. OCornish *pol* + *lefant*.

Pomeroy Tyrone. *Pomeroy Demesne* c.1834. Possibly 'apple orchard'. OFrench *pommeraie*.

Pont Henry (*Pont-henri*) Carm. *Pont Henry* c.1627, *Pont Hendry* 1760. 'Henry's bridge'. Welsh *pont*. The identity of the named man is unknown.

Pont-y-Pwl. *See* PONTYPOOL.

Pontardawe Neat. *Tir penybont ardawe* 1583, *Ty pen y bont ar y Tawe* 1675, *Ty pen y bont ar tawey* 1706. 'Bridge over the River Tawe'. Welsh *pont* + *ar*. For the river name, *see* SWANSEA. The early forms relate to a house (Welsh *tŷ*).

Pontarddulais Swan. *Ponte ar theleys* 1557. 'Bridge over the River Dulais'. Welsh *pont* + *ar*. The river name means 'dark stream' (Welsh *du* + *glais*).

Pontefract W. Yorks. *Pontefracto* 1090. 'Broken bridge'. Latin *pons* + *fractus*.

Ponteland Northum. *Punteland* 1203. 'Cultivated land by the river called Pont'. Celtic river-name (meaning 'valley') + OE *ēa-land*.

Pontesbury Shrops. *Pantesberie* 1086 (DB). Probably 'fortified place of a man called Pant'. OE pers. name + *burh* (dative *byrig*).

Pont-faen Pemb. *Pons Lapideus* 13th cent., *Pontvaen* 13th cent. '(Place by the) stone bridge'. Welsh *pont* + *maen*.

Pontllan-fraith Cphy. *tre penybont llynvraith* 1492, *Pontllynfraith* 1713. 'Bridge by the speckled pool'. Welsh *pont* + *llyn* + *braith*. The first two words of the first form above mean 'farm at the end of the bridge'.

Ponton, Great & *Ponton, Little* Lincs. *Pamptune* 1086 (DB). Probably 'farmstead by a hill'. OE *pamp* + *tūn*.

Pontycymer Bri. 'Bridge at the confluence'. Welsh *pont* + *y* + *cymer*.

Pontypool (*Pont-y-Pŵl*) Torf. *Pont y poole* 1614. 'Bridge by the pool'. Welsh *pont* + *y* + Modern English *pool*.

Pontypridd Rhon. *Pont y Ty Pridd* c.1700. 'Bridge by the earthen house'. Welsh *pont* + *y* + *tŷ* + *pridd*.

Pool, *Poole*, usually '(place at) the pool or creek'. OE *pōl*: **Pool** Dorset. *Pole* 1183. **Poole Keynes** Glos. *Pole* 10th cent., 1086 (DB). **Pool, South** Devon. *Pole* 1086 (DB).
   However the following has a different origin: **Pool** W. Yorks. *Pofle* c.1030, *Pouele* 1086 (DB). From an OE word *pofel* of uncertain meaning.

Poolbeg (*Poll Beag*) Dublin. 'Little pool'.

Pooley Bridge Cumbria. *Pulhoue* 1252. 'Hill or mound by a pool'. OE *pōl* + OScand. *haugr*.

Poorton, North & *Poorton, South* Dorset. *Pourtone* 1086 (DB). OE *tūn* 'farmstead' with an obscure first element which may be an old river-name.

Popham Hants. *Popham* 903, *Popeham* 1086 (DB). OE *hām* 'homestead' or *hamm* 'enclosure' with an uncertain first element, possibly an OE **pop(p)* 'pebble'.

Poplar Gtr. London. *Popler* 1327. '(Place at) the poplar tree'. ME *popler*.

Poppleton, Nether & *Poppleton, Upper* York. *Popeltune* *c*.972, *Popletone* 1086 (DB). 'Farmstead on pebbly soil'. OE **popel* + *tūn*.

Porin Highland. 'Pasture'. Gaelic *pórainn*.

Poringland, East Norfolk. *Porringalanda* 1086 (DB). 'Cultivated land or estate of a tribe called the Porringas'. Obscure first element (probably an OE pers. name) + *-inga-* + *land*.

Porlock Somerset. *Portloca* 10th cent., *Portloc* 1086 (DB). 'Enclosure by the harbour'. OE *port* + *loca*.

Port Dinorwic (*Y Felinheli*) Gwyd. *the port of Dinorwic* 1851, *Port-Dinorwig* 1868. 'Port of Dinorwic'. Modern English *port*. The town arose as a port for the export of slate from the quarries at *Dinorwic*, 'fort of the Ordovices'. The Welsh name means 'the sea mill' (Welsh *y* + *melin* + *heli*). Today, *Y Felinkeli* is the only official name.

Port Ellen Arg. 'Ellen's port'. The name is that of Lady Ellenor (*Ellen*) Campbell of Islay, widow of the Gaelic scholar W. F. Campbell, who planned the settlement in 1821.

Port Gate Northum. *Portyate* 1269. OE *port* 'gate' with explanatory OE *geat* 'gate', referring to the gap in Hadrian's Wall where Watling Street runs through it.

Port Glasgow Invclyd. 'Port for Glasgow'. The town arose on the Firth of Clyde in the 1660s with the aim of becoming a port for GLASGOW.

Port Isaac Cornwall. *Portusek* 1337. From Cornish *porth* 'cove, harbour' with an uncertain second element, possibly an adjective **usek* meaning literally 'characterized by chaff' but perhaps referring to tidal debris.

Port Láirge. *See* WATERFORD.

Port Laoise (*Port Laoise*) Laois. 'Port of the tribe of Laeighis'. *Cp.* LAOIS.

Port Sunlight Mersey., a modern name for the late 19th-cent. model village, called after the brand-name of the soap made here.

Port Talbot Neat. The town dates from 1836, when docks were built on Swansea Bay on land owned by the *Talbot* family of nearby Margam Abbey.

Port William Dumf. 'William's port'. The village was founded in 1770 by Sir William Maxwell of Monreith.

Portacloy (*Port na Cloche*) Mayo. 'Landing place of the stone'.

Portadown (*Port an Dúnáin*) Armagh. *Port a' Dúnáin* 1646. 'Landing place of the little fort'.

Portaferry (*Port an Pheire*) Down. *Port na Peireadh* *c*.1617. 'Landing place of the ferry'.

Portarlington (*Cúil an tSúdaire*) Laois. Lands here were owned in the 17th cent. by Sir Henry Bennet, Lord Arlington. The Irish name means 'nook of the tanner'.

Portavogie (*Port an Bhogaigh*) Down. *Portaboggach* 1605. 'Harbour of the bog'.

Portballintrae (*Port Bhaile an Trá*) Antrim. *Portballentra* 1605. 'Landing place of Ballintrae'. The townland name Ballintrae represents Irish *Baile an Trá*, 'townland of the strand'.

Portbury N. Som. *Porberie* 1086 (DB). 'Fortified place near the harbour'. OE *port* + *burh* (dative *byrig*).

Portchester Hants. *Porteceaster* *c*.960, *Portcestre* 1086 (DB). 'Roman fort by the harbour'. OE *port* + *ceaster*.

Portesham Dorset. *Porteshamme* 1024, *Portesham* 1086 (DB). 'Enclosure belonging to the town' (probably referring to ABBOTSBURY). OE *port* + *hamm*.

Portglenone (*Port Chluain Eoghain*) Antrim. *Portecomeonone* 1593. 'Landing place of Glenone'. The townland name Glenone represents Irish *Cluain Eoghain*, 'Eoghan's meadow'.

Porth Rhon. 'Gateway'. Welsh *porth*. Porth stands at the confluence of the Rhondda and Little Rhondda, a 'gateway' to places further south in the valley.

Porthaethwy. *See* MENAI BRIDGE.

Porthallow Cornwall, near Manaccan. *Worthalaw* |*sic*| 967, *Porthaleu* 1333. 'Cove or harbour by a stream called *Alaw*'. Cornish *porth* + river-name (probably pre-Celtic) of uncertain meaning.

Porth-cawl Bri. *Portcall* 1632, *Porth Cawl* 1825. 'Harbour where seakale grows'. Welsh *porth* + *cawl*.

Porthceri. *See* PORTHKERRY.

Porthkerry (*Porthceri*) Vale Glam. *Portciri* 1254. 'Harbour of Ceri'. Welsh *porth*.

Porthleven Cornwall. *Port-levan* *c*.1605. 'Smooth harbour', Cornish *porth* + *leven*. Alternatively 'harbour of the stream called *Leven* (the smooth one)'.

Porthmadog Gwyd. *Portmadoc* 1838. 'Port of Madocks'. Welsh *porth*. The name is that of William Alexander *Madocks* (1772–1828), MP for Boston, Lincs, who developed nearby TREMADOC.

Portington E. R. Yorks. *Portinton* 1086 (DB). 'Farmstead belonging to a market town'. OE *port* + *-ing-* + *tūn*.

Portinscale Cumbria. *Porqeneschal* *c*.1160. 'Shielings of the townswomen'. OE *port-cwēn(e)* + OScand. *skáli*.

Portishead N. Som. *Portesheve* |*sic*| 1086 (DB), *Portesheved* 1200. 'Headland by the harbour'. OE *port* + *hēafod*.

Portland, Isle of Dorset. *Port* 9th cent., *Portlande* 862, *Porland* 1086 (DB). 'Estate by the harbour'. OE *port* + *land*. **Portland Bill**, recorded from 1649, is from OE *bile* 'a bill, a beak' used topographically for 'promontory'.

Portlaw (*Port Lách*) Waterford. 'Port of the hill'.

Portlemouth, East Devon. *Porlamuta* |*sic*| 1086 (DB), *Porthelemuthe* 1308. Possibly 'harbour estuary', from Cornish *porth* + **heyl* with OE *mūtha* 'mouth'. Alternatively 'mouth of the harbour stream', from OE *port* + *wella* + *mūtha*.

Portloman (*Port Lomáin*) Westmeath. 'Lomán's port'.

Portmadoc. *See* PORTHMADOG.

Portmahomack Highland. *Portmachalmok* 1678. 'Harbour of Machalmac'. Gaelic *port*. *Machalmac* means 'my little Colman' (Gaelic *ma* + saint's name *Colman* + diminutive suffix *-oc*).

Portmarnock (*Port Mearnóg*) Dublin. 'Mearnóg's port'.

Portmeirion Gwyd. 'Port of Meirion'. The name was devised by the architect Clough Williams-Ellis in the 1920s for his Italianate coastal village in Merionethshire. *Cp.* MERIONETH.

Portnablahy (*Port na Bláiche*) Donegal. 'Port of the buttermilk'.

Portnoo (*Port Nua*) Donegal. *Port Noo* 1849. 'New port'.

Portobello Dublin. The name commemorates the Battle of Portobello in 1739.

Portobello Edin. *Porto-Bello* 1753, *Portobello* 1779. The name was originally that of the *Portobello Hut*, a house built in the mid-18th cent., itself named for the capture of Portobello, Panama, by Admiral Vernon in 1739.

Porton Wilts. *Portone* 1086 (DB). Probably identical in origin with POORTON (Dorset).

Portpatrick Dumf. *Portpatrick* 1630. 'Harbour of St Patrick'. From a chapel dedicated to St Patrick.

Portree Highland (Skye). *Portri* 1549, *Portree, or Port a Roi* 1868. 'Harbour of the slope'. Gaelic *port* + *righe*.

Portroe (*An Port Rua*) Tipperary. 'The red port'.

Portrush (*Port Rois*) Antrim. *Portros* 1262. 'Port of the promontory'.

Portsalon (*Port an tSalainn*) Donegal. 'Port of the salt'.

Portsdown Hants. *Portesdone* 1086 (DB). 'Hill by the harbour'. OE *port* + *dūn*.

Portsea Hants. *Portesig* 982. 'Harbour island'. OE *port* + *ēg*.

Portslade by Sea E. Sussex. *Porteslage* |*sic*| 1086 (DB), *Portes Ladda* c.1095. Probably 'crossing-place near the harbour'. OE *port* + *gelād*.

Portsmouth Hants. *Portesmuthan* late 9th cent. 'Mouth of the harbour'. OE *port* + *mūtha*.

Portstewart Derry. 'Stewart's port'. *Portstewart* 1780. The town arose in 1794 on land purchased from the Stewart family, who had held it from 1734. The Irish equivalent name is *Port Stíobhaird*.

Portswood Hants. *Porteswuda* 1045. 'Wood belonging to the market town'. OE *port* + *wudu*.

Portumna (*Port Omna*) Galway. 'Bank of the tree trunk'.

Poslingford Suffolk. *Poslingeorda* 1086 (DB). 'Enclosure of the family or followers of a man called **Possel*'. OE pers. name + *-inga-* + *worth*.

Postling Kent. *Postinges* |*sic*| 1086 (DB), *Postlinges* 1212. Possibly '(settlement of) the family or followers of a man called **Possel*'. OE pers. name + *-ingas*.

Postwick Norfolk. *Possuic* 1086 (DB). 'Dwelling or (dairy) farm of a man called **Possa*'. OE pers. name + *wīc*.

Potsgrove Beds. *Potesgrave* 1086 (DB). 'Grove near a pit or pot-hole'. OE *pott* + *grāf*.

Pott Shrigley Ches., *see* SHRIGLEY.

Potter Brompton N. Yorks., *see* BROMPTON.

Potter Heigham Norfolk, *see* HEIGHAM.

Potter Street Essex. *Potters streete* 1594. Named from a family called le Pottere ('the potmaker') here in the 13th cent.

Potterhanworth Lincs. *Haneworde* 1086 (DB). 'Enclosure of a man called Hana'. OE pers. name + *worth*, the later affix referring to pot-making here.

Potterne Wilts. *Poterne* 1086 (DB). 'Building where pots are made'. OE *pott* + *ærn*.

Potters Bar Herts. *Potterys Barre* 1509. 'Forest-gate of a family called Potter'. ME surname + *barre*.

Potterspury Northants. *Perie* 1086 (DB). *Potterispirye* 1287. Originally '(place at) the pear-tree', from OE *pirige*, with later affix *Potters-* 'of the pot-maker(s)' from the pottery here. *See* PAULERSPURY.

Pottiaghan (*Poiteacháin*) Westmeath. 'Bad ground'.

Potto N. Yorks. *Pothow* 1202, 'Mound or hill by a pit or where pots were found'. OE *pott* + OScand. *haugr*.

Potton Beds. *Pottun* c.960, *Potone* 1086 (DB). 'Farmstead where pots are made'. OE *pott* + *tūn*.

Poughill Cornwall. *Pochehelle* |*sic*| 1086 (DB), *Pochewell* 1227. 'Spring or stream by a feature resembling a pouch or bag', or 'spring or stream of a man called Pohha'. OE *pohha* or pers. name + *wella*.

Poughill Devon. *Pochehille* 1086 (DB). 'Bag-shaped hill', or 'hill of a man called Pohha', OE *pohha* or pers. name + *hyll*.

Poulaphuca (*Poll an Phúca*) Dublin. 'Pool of the sprite'.

Poulargid (*Poll an Airgid*) Cork. 'Silver pool'.

Poulnagat (*Poll na gCat*). Westmeath. 'Hole of the cats'.

Poulshot Wilts. *Paveshou* |*sic*| 1086 (DB), *Paulesholt* 1187. 'Wood of a man called Paul'. ME pers. name + OE *holt*.

Poulton, 'farmstead by a pool or creek', OE **pull* or *pōl* + *tūn*: **Poulton** Glos. *Pultune* 855. **Poulton** Mersey., near Seacombe. *Pulton* 1260. **Poulton-le-Fylde** Lancs. *Poltun* 1086 (DB). Affix means 'in the district called The Fylde', from OE *filde* 'a plain' (recorded as *Filde* 1246).

Poundon Bucks. *Paundon* 1255. OE *dūn* 'hill' with an uncertain first element.

Poundstock Cornwall. *Pondestoch* 1086 (DB). 'Outlying farmstead or hamlet with a pound for animals'. OE **pund* + *stoc*.

Powderham Devon. *Poldreham* 1086 (DB). 'Promontory in reclaimed marshland'. OE **polra* + *hamm*.

Powerstock Dorset. *Povrestoch* 1086 (DB). OE *stoc* 'outlying farmstead' with the same obscure first element as in POORTON.

Powick Heref. & Worcs. *Poincguuic* 972, *Poiwic* 1086 (DB). 'Dwelling or farm associated with a man called Pohha'. OE pers. name + *-ing-* + *wīc*.

Powys (the unitary authority). 'Provincial (place)'. Low Latin *pagensis*. The name implies that those who lived here were 'country folk', inhabiting an open upland tract that was not protected in the same way as the regions to the north and south, with their hills and valleys.

Poxwell Dorset. *Poceswylle* 987, *Pocheswelle* 1086 (DB). 'Steeply rising ground of a man called *Poca', or 'spring of a man called *Poc'. OE pers. name + *swelle* or *wella*.

Poynings W. Sussex. *Puningas* 960, *Poninges* 1086 (DB). '(Settlement of) the family or followers of a man called *Pūn(a)'. OE pers. name + *-ingas*.

Poyntington Dorset. *Ponditone* 1086 (DB). 'Estate associated with a man called *Punt'. OE pers. name + *-ing- + tūn*.

Poynton Ches. *Povinton* 1249. 'Estate associated with a man called *Pofa'. OE pers. name + *-ing- + tūn*.

Poynton Green Shrops. *Peventone* 1086 (DB). 'Estate associated with a man called *Pēofa'. OE pers. name + *-ing- + tūn*.

Poyntz Pass Armagh. *Poyns pass* c.1655. 'Poyntz's pass'. Lieutenant Charles Poyntz had defended the pass here against Hugh O'Neill, Earl of Tyrone, in 1598. The modern village was founded in 1798.

Pratt's Bottom Gtr. London, first recorded in 1779, 'valley associated with a family called Pratt' (known in this area from the 14th cent.), from OE *botm*.

Prawle, East Devon. *Prenla* |sic| 1086 (DB). *Prahulle* 1204. Probably 'look-out hill'. OE *prāw + hyll*.

Prebaun (*Preabán*) Westmeath. 'Patch'.

Preen, Church Shrops. *Prene* 1086 (DB), *Chircheprene* 1256. OE *Prēon* 'a brooch, a pin', perhaps used figuratively of some landscape feature here, with later affix OE *cirice*.

Prees Shrops. *Pres* 1086 (DB). '(Place by) the brushwood or thicket'. OWelsh *pres*.

Preesall Lancs. *Pressouede* 1086 (DB). 'Brushwood headland'. OWelsh *pres* + OScand. *hofuth* or OE *hēafod*.

Prendwick Northum. *Prendewic* 1242. 'Dwelling or farm of a man called Prend'. OE pers. name + *wīc*.

Prenton Mersey. *Prestune* |sic| 1086 (DB), *Prenton* 1260. 'Farmstead of a man called Præn'. OE pers. name + *tūn*.

Prescot(t), 'priests' cottage(s)', OE *prēost + cot*; for example **Prescot** Mersey. *Prestecota* 1178.

Preseli Hills Pemb. *Precelly*, or *Percelly* 1868. The name renders Welsh *Mynydd Preseli* (Welsh *mynydd*), probably from Welsh *prys*, 'wood'.

Prestatyn Denb. *Prestetone* 1086 (DB), *Prestatton* 1301. 'Priests' farmstead'. OE *prēost + tūn*. The name is equivalent to English PRESTON but Welsh stress has preserved the middle syllable.

Prestbury, 'manor of the priests', OE *prēost + burh* (dative *byrig*): **Prestbury** Ches. *Presteberi* 1181. **Prestbury** Glos. *Preosdabyrig* c.900, *Presteberie* 1086 (DB).

Presteigne (*Llanandras*) Powys. *Prestehemed* 1137, *Prestene* 1548, *Presteign*, or *Llan-Andras of the Welsh* 1868. 'Priests' border meadow'. OE *prēost + hǣmed*. The Welsh name means 'church of St Andrew' (Welsh *llan + Andras*).

Presthope Shrops. *Presthope* 1167. 'Valley of the priests'. OE *prēost + hop*.

Preston, a common name, 'farmstead of the priests', OE *prēost + tūn*; examples include: **Preston** Dorset. *Prestun* 1228. **Preston** E. R. Yorks. *Prestone* 1086 (DB). **Preston** E. Sussex. *Prestetone* 1086 (DB). **Preston** Lancs. *Prestune* 1086 (DB). **Preston** Northum. *Preston* 1242. **Preston Bissett** Bucks. *Prestone* 1086 (DB), *Preston Byset* 1327. Manorial affix from the Biset family, holders of the manor from the 12th cent. **Preston Capes** Northants. *Prestetone* 1086 (DB), *Preston Capes* 1300. Manorial affix from the de Capes family, here in the 13th cent. **Preston Gubbals** Shrops. *Prestone* 1086 (DB), *Preston Gobald* 1292. Manorial affix from a priest called Godebold who held the manor in 1086. **Preston, Long** N. Yorks. *Prestune* 1086 (DB). Affix refers to the length of the village. **Preston-under-Scar** N. Yorks. *Prestun* 1086 (DB), *Preston undescar* 1568. Affix means 'under the rocky hill' from OScand. *sker*. **Preston Wynne** Heref. & Worcs. *Prestetune* 1086 (DB). Manorial affix from a family called la Wyne here in the 14th cent.

Preston E. Loth. 'Priests' village'. OE *prēost + tūn*.

Preston Candover Hants., *see* CANDOVER.

Prestonpans E. Loth. *Saltprestoun* 1587, *Prestonpans* 1654. '(Salt) pans by Preston'. OE *panne*. The monks of Newbattle Abbey laid out salt pans here near PRESTON in the early 13th cent.

Prestwich Gtr. Manch. *Prestwich* 1194. 'Dwelling or farm of the priest(s)'. OE *prēost + wīc*.

Prestwick Northum. *Prestwic* 1242. Identical in origin with the previous name.

Prestwick S. Ayr. *Prestwic* c.1170. 'Priests' farm'. OE *prēost + wīc*.

Prickwillow Cambs. *Prickewylev* 1251. Probably 'willow-tree from which skewers or goads were made'. OE *pricca + *wilig*.

Priddy Somerset. *Pridia* 1182. Probably 'earth house'. Celtic *prith + *tiʒ*.

Priestholm. *See* PUFFIN ISLAND.

Primethorpe Leics. *Torp* 1086 (DB), *Prymesthorp* 1316. 'Outlying farmstead or hamlet of a man called Prim'. OE pers. name + OScand. *thorp*.

Princes Risborough Bucks., *see* RISBOROUGH.

Princethorpe Warwicks. *Prandestorpe* 1221. 'Outlying farmstead or hamlet of a man called Præn or Pren'. OE pers. name + OScand. *thorp*.

Princetown Devon, a modern name, called after the Prince Regent, later George IV (1820–30).

Priors Hardwick Warwicks., *see* HARDWICK.

Priors Marston Warwicks., *see* MARSTON.

Priston B. & NE. Som. *Prisctun* 931, *Pristcone* 1086 (DB). 'Farmstead near the brushwood or copse'. OWelsh **prisc* + OE *tūn*.

Prittlewell Essex. *Pritteuuella* 1086 (DB). 'Babbling spring or stream'. OE **pritol* + *wella*.

Privett Hants. *Pryfetes flodan* late 9th cent. '(Place at) the privet copse'. OE *pryfet* (with *flōde* 'channel, gutter' in the early form).

Probus Cornwall. *Sanctus Probus* 1086 (DB). From the dedication of the church to St Probus.

Prudhoe Northum. *Prudho* 1173. 'Hill-spur of a man called **Prūda*'. OE pers. name + *hōh*.

Puckaun (*Pocán*) Tipperary. 'Little heap'.

Puckeridge Herts. *Pucherugge* 1294. 'Raised strip or ridge haunted by a goblin'. OE *pūca* + **ric* or *hrycg*.

Puckington Somerset. *Pokintuna* 1086 (DB). 'Estate associated with a man called **Pūca*'. OE pers. name + *-ing-* + *tūn*.

Pucklechurch S. Glos. *Pucelancyrcan* 950, *Pulcrecerce* 1086 (DB). 'Church of a man called **Pūcela*'. OE pers. name + *cirice*.

Puddington, 'estate associated with a man called *Put(t)a*', OE pers. name + *-ing-* + *tūn*: **Puddington** Ches. *Potitone* 1086 (DB). **Puddington** Devon. *Potitone* 1086 (DB).

Puddletown Dorset. *Pitretone* |*sic*| 1086 (DB), *Pideleton* 1212. 'Farmstead on the River Piddle'. OE river-name (**pidele* 'a marsh or fen') + *tūn*.

Pudleston Heref. & Worcs. *Pillesdune* |*sic*| 1086 (DB), *Putlesdone* 1212. 'Hill of the mouse-hawk or of a man called *Pyttel*'. OE *pyttel* or pers. name + *dūn*.

Pudsey W. Yorks. *Podechesaie* 1086 (DB). Probably 'enclosure of a man called **Pudoc*, or by the hill called "the Wart"'. OE pers. name or *puduc* + *hæg*.

Puffin Island (*Ynys Seiriol*) Angl. 'Island inhabited by puffins'. The island is also known as *Priestholm*, 'priests' island' (OScand. *holmr*). The Welsh name means 'St Seiriol's island' (Welsh *ynys*).

Pulborough W. Sussex. *Poleberge* 1086 (DB). 'Hill or mound by the pools'. OE *pōl*, **pull* + *beorg*.

Pulford Ches. *Pulford* 1086 (DB). 'Ford by a pool or on a stream'. OE *pōl* or **pull* + *ford*.

Pulham, 'homestead or enclosure by the pools or streams'. OE *pōl* or **pull* + *hām* or *hamm*: **Pulham** Dorset. *Poleham* 1086 (DB). **Pulham Market** & **Pulham St Mary** Norfolk. *Polleham* c.1050, *Pullaham* 1086 (DB). Affixes from the important market here and from the dedication of the church.

Pulloxhill Beds. *Polochessele* 1086 (DB). 'Hill of a man called **Pulloc*'. OE pers. name + *hyll*.

Pulverbatch, Church Shrops. *Polrebec* 1086 (DB), *Puluerbach* 1262, *Chyrche Pulrebach* 1272. OE *bæce* 'stream-valley' with an uncertain first element which may be an old stream-name. Affix is ME *churche* 'church' to distinguish this place from **Castle Pulverbatch**, *Castelpolrebache* 1301, with affix ME *castel* 'castle'

Pumlumon. *See* PLYNLIMON.

Puncheston (*Cas-mael*) Pemb. *Pounchardon* 1291. 'Bridge where thistles grow'. OFrench *pont* + *chardon*. The name may have been transferred from *Pontchardon*, Normandy. Alternatively, 'Ponchard's hill' (French pers. name + OE *dūn*). The Welsh name means 'Mael's fort' (Welsh *cas*).

Puncknowle Dorset. *Pomacanole* 1086 (DB). Probably 'hillock of a man called **Puma*'. OE pers. name + *cnoll*.

Purbeck, Isle of Dorset. *Purbicinga* 948, *Porbi* 1086 (DB). 'Beak-shaped ridge frequented by the bittern or snipe'. OE *pūr* + **bic*. In the earliest spelling the name is combined with a form of OE *-ingas* 'dwellers in'.

Purbrook Hants. *Pukebrok* 1248. 'Brook haunted by a goblin'. OE *pūca* + *brōc*.

Purfleet Essex. *Purteflyete* 1285. 'Creek or stream of a man called **Purta*'. OE pers. name + *flēot*.

Puriton Somerset. *Peritone* 1086 (DB). 'Pear orchard, or farmstead where pear-trees grow'. OE *pirige* + *tūn*.

Purleigh Essex. *Purlea* 998, *Purlai* 1086 (DB). 'Wood or clearing frequented by the bittern or snipe'. OE *pūr* + *lēah*.

Purley Berks. *Porlei* 1086 (DB). Identical in origin with the previous name.

Purley Gtr. London. *Pirlee* 1200. 'Wood or clearing where pear-trees grow'. OE *pirige* + *lēah*.

Purse Caundle Dorset, *see* CAUNDLE.

Purslow Shrops. *Possalau* 1086 (DB). 'Tumulus of a man called **Pussa*'. OE pers. name + *hlāw*.

Purston Jaglin W. Yorks. *Preston* 1086 (DB), *Preston Jakelin* 1269. 'Farmstead of the priests'. OE *prēost* + *tūn*. Manorial affix from some early feudal tenant called Jakelyn.

Purton, 'pear orchard, or farmstead where pear-trees grow', OE *pirige* + *tūn*: **Purton** Glos., near Berkeley. *Piritone* 1297. **Purton** Glos., near Lydney. *Peritone* 1086 (DB). **Purton** Wilts. *Puritone* 796, *Piritone* 1086 (DB).

Pusey Oxon. *Pesei* 1086 (DB). 'Island, or dry ground in marsh, where peas grow'. OE *pise* + *ēg*.

Putford, West Devon. *Poteforda* 1086 (DB). 'Ford of a man called *Putta*, or one frequented by hawks'. OE pers. name or OE **putta* + *ford*.

Putley Heref. & Worcs. *Poteslepe* |*sic*| 1086 (DB), *Putelega* c.1180. 'Woodland clearing of a man called *Putta*, or one frequented by hawks'. OE pers. name or OE **putta* + *lēah*.

Putney Gtr. London. *Putelei* |*sic*| 1086 (DB), *Puttenhuthe* 1279. 'Landing-place of a man called *Putta*, or one frequented by hawks'. OE pers. name or OE **putta* (genitive *-n*) + *hȳth*.

Puttenham, 'homestead or enclosure of a man called *Putta*, or one frequented by hawks', OE pers. name or OE **putta* (genitive *-n*) + *hām* or *hamm*: **Puttenham** Herts. *Puteham* 1086 (DB). **Puttenham** Surrey. *Puteham* 1199.

Puxton N. Som. *Pukereleston* 1212. 'Estate of a family called *Pukerel*'. OFrench surname + OE *tūn*.

Pwllheli Gwyd. *Pwllhely* 1292. '(Place by the) brine pool'. Welsh *pwll* + *heli*.

Pyecombe W. Sussex. *Picumba* late 11th cent. 'Valley infested with gnats or other insects'. OE *pīe* + *cumb*.

Pylle Somerset. *Pil* 705, *Pille* 1086 (DB). 'The tidal creek'. OE *pyll*.

Pyon, Canon & *Pyon, Kings* Heref. & Worcs. *Pionie* 1086 (DB), *Pyone canonicorum* 1221, *Kings Pyon* 1285. 'Island infested with gnats or other insects'. OE *pīe* (genitive plural *pēona*) + *ēg*. Distinguishing affixes from early possession by the canons of Hereford and the Crown.

Pyrford Surrey. *Pyrianforda* 956, *Peliforde |sic|* 1086 (DB). 'Ford by a pear-tree'. OE *pirige* + *ford*.

Pyrton Oxon. *Pirigtune* 987, *Peritone* 1086 (DB). 'Pear orchard, or farmstead where pear-trees grow'. OE *pirige* + *tūn*.

Pytchley Northants. *Pihteslea* 956, *Pihteslea* 1086 (DB). 'Woodland clearing of a man called *Peoht*'. OE pers. name + *lēah*.

Pyworthy Devon. *Paorda |sic|* 1086 (DB), *Peworthy* 1239. 'Enclosure infested with gnats or other insects'. OE *pīe* + *worthig*.

Q

Quadring Lincs. *Quedhaveringe* 1086 (DB). 'Muddy settlement of the family or followers of a man called *Hæfer'. OE *cwēad* + OE pers. name + *-ingas*.

Quaich (river) Perth. '(River with) potholes'. Gaelic *cuach*.

Quainton Bucks. *Chentone* |sic| 1086 (DB), *Quentona* 1167. 'The queen's farmstead or estate'. OE *cwēn* + *tūn*.

Quantock Hills Somerset. *Cantucuudu* 682. Celtic hill name, possibly a derivative of an element *canto-* 'border or district', with OE *wudu* 'wood' in the early form.

Quantoxhead, East & *Quantoxhead, West* Somerset. *Cantocheve* 1086 (DB). 'Projecting ridge of the QUANTOCK HILLS'. Celtic hill name + OE *hēafod*.

Quarley Hants. *Cornelea* 1167. Probably 'woodland clearing with a mill or where mill-stones are obtained'. OE *cweorn* + *lēah*.

Quarndon Derbys. *Cornun* |sic| 1086 (DB), *Querendon* c.1200. 'Hill where mill-stones are obtained'. OE *cweorn* + *dūn*.

Quarrington Lincs. *Corninctun* 1086 (DB). Probably 'farmstead at the mill-stone place'. OE *cweorn* + *-ing* + *tūn*.

Quarrington Hill Durham. *Querendune* c.1190. 'Hill where mill-stones are obtained'. OE *cweorn* + *dūn*.

Quatford Shrops. *Quatford* 1086 (DB). 'Ford in a district called *Cwat(t)*'. OE *ford* with an OE name of obscure origin.

Quatt Shrops. *Quatone* 1086 (DB), *Quatte* 1209. From the same unexplained district-name as QUATFORD, with OE *tūn* 'farmstead' in the Domesday form.

Quedgeley Glos. *Quedesleya* c.1140. Possibly 'woodland clearing of a man called *Cwēod'. OE pers. name + *lēah*.

Queen Camel Somerset, *see* CAMEL.

Queen Charlton B. & NE Som., *see* CHARLTON.

Queenborough Kent. *Queneburgh* 1376. 'Borough named after Queen Philippa'. OE *cwēn* + *burh*. Philippa was the wife of Edward III.

Queensbury W. Yorks., a modern name created in 1863; earlier the village was known as *Queen's Head*, the name of an inn here.

Queensferry Edin. *Passagium S. Marg. Regine* 1183, *Queneferie* c.1295. 'Queen's river crossing'. The name honours Queen Margaret, wife of Malcolm Canmore (d. 1093).

Queensferry Flin. *King's Ferry* 1828, *Queensferry* 1837. 'Ferry of the queen'. The name honours Queen Victoria.

Quendon Essex. *Kuenadana* 1086 (DB). Probably 'valley of the women'. OE *cwene* (genitive plural *cwenena*) + *denu*.

Queniborough Leics. *Cuinburg* |sic| 1086 (DB), *Queniburg* 12th cent. 'The queen's fortified manor'. OE *cwēn* + *burh*.

Quenington Glos. *Quenintone* 1086 (DB). 'Farmstead of the women', or 'farmstead associated with a woman called *Cwēn'. OE *cwene* (genitive plural *cwenena*) + *tūn*, or OE pers. name + *-ing-* + *tūn*.

Quernmore Lancs. *Quernemor* 1228. 'Moor where mill-stones are obtained'. OE *cweorn* + *mōr*.

Querrin (*An Cuibhreann*) Clare. 'The tilled field'.

Quethiock Cornwall. *Quedoc* 1201. 'Wooded place'. OCornish *cuidoc*.

Quidenham Norfolk. *Cuidenham* 1086 (DB). 'Homestead or village of a man called *Cwida'. OE pers. name (genitive *-n*) + *hām*.

Quidhampton, 'muddy home farm', or 'home farm with good manure', OE *cwēad* + *hām-tūn*: **Quidhampton** Hants. *Quedementun* 1086 (DB). **Quidhampton** Wilts. *Quedhampton* 1249.

Quilly (*Coillidh*) Derry, Down, Waterford. 'Woodland'.

Quilty (*Coillte*) Clare. 'Woods'.

Quin (*Cuinche*) Clare. 'Nook'.

Quinag (mountain) Highland. 'Churn-shaped'. Gaelic *cuinneag*.

Quinton, Lower & *Quinton, Upper* Warwicks. *Quentone* 848, *Quenintune* 1086 (DB). 'The queen's farmstead or estate.' OE *cwēn* + *tūn*.

Quoile (*Caol*) (river) Down. *Coyle* 1618. 'Narrow water'.

Quorndon Leics. *Querendon* c.1220. 'Hill where mill-stones are obtained'. OE *cweorn* + *dūn*.

Quy Cambs., *see* STOW CUM QUY.

R

Raasay (island) Highland. *Raasa* 1263. 'Island with a ridge frequented by roedeer'. OScand. *rár* + *áss* + *ey*.

Raby Mersey. *Rabie* 1086 (DB). 'Farmstead or village at a boundary'. OScand. *rá* + *bý*.

Rackenford Devon. *Racheneforda* 1086 (DB). Probably 'ford suitable for riding, by a stretch of river'. OE **racu* + **ærne-ford*.

Rackham W. Sussex. *Recham* 1166. Possibly 'homestead or enclosure with a rick or ricks'. OE *hréac* + *hām* or *hamm*.

Rackheath Norfolk. *Racheitha* 1086 (DB). Probably 'landing-place near a gully or water-course'. OE *hraca* or **racu* + *hȳth*.

Radcliffe, *Radclive*, 'the red cliff or bank', OE *réad* + *clif*:
Radcliffe Gtr. Manch. *Radecliue* 1086 (DB). **Radcliffe on Trent** Notts. *Radeclive* 1086 (DB). For the river-name Trent, see NEWARK. **Radclive** Bucks. *Radeclive* 1086 (DB).

Radcot Oxon. *Rathcota* 1163. 'Red cottage' or 'reed cottage' (i.e. with a roof thatched with reeds). OE *réad* or *hréod* + *cot*.

Rademon (*Ráth Déamain*) Down. 'Deamán's fort'.

Radford Semele Warwicks. *Redeford* 1086 (DB), *Radeford Symely* 1314. 'Redford', i.e. where the soil is red. OE *réad* + *ford*. Manorial affix from the Simely family, here in the 12th cent.

Radipole Dorset. *Retpole* 1086 (DB). 'Reedy pool'. OE *hréod* + *pōl*.

Radlett Herts. *Radelett* 1453. 'Junction of roads'. OE *rād* + (*ge*)*lǽt*.

Radley Oxon. *Radelege* c.1180. 'Red wood or clearing'. OE *réad* + *léah*.

Radnage Bucks. *Radenhech* 1162. '(Place at) the red oak-tree'. OE *réad* + *āc* (dative *ǽc*).

Radnor. *See* NEW RADNOR.

Radstock B. & NE. Som. *Stoche* 1086 (DB), *Radestok* 1221. 'Outlying farmstead by the road' (here the Fosse Way). OE *rād* + *stoc*.

Radstone Northants. *Rodestone* 1086 (DB). '(Place at) the rood-stone or stone cross'. OE **rōd-stān*.

Radur. *See* RADYR.

Radway Warwicks. *Radwei, Rodewei* 1086 (DB), *Radewey* 1198. Probably 'red way' from the colour of the soil here, OE *réad* + *weg*. Alternatively 'way fit for riding on', OE *rād-weg*.

Radwell Beds. *Radeuuelle* 1086 (DB). 'Red spring or stream'. OE *réad* + *wella*.

Radwinter Essex. *Redeuuintra* 1086 (DB). Possibly 'red vineyard', from OE *réad* + **winter*. Alternatively 'tree of a woman called **Rædwynn*', OE pers. name + *tréow*.

Radyr (*Radur*) Card. *Radur* 1254, *Rador* 1291. 'Oratory'. Latin *oratorium*. The reference is to a small chapel for private worship.

Ragdale Leics. *Ragendele |sic|* 1086 (DB), *Rachedal* c.1125. Probably 'valley of the gully or narrow pass'. OE *hraca* + OE *dæl*.

Raglan (*Rhaglan*) Mon. *Raghelan* 1254. '(Place) before the bank'. Welsh *rhag* + *glan*. The name refers to the former castle here.

Ragnall Notts. *Ragenehil* 1086 (DB). 'Hill of a man called Ragni'. OScand. pers. name + OE *hyll*.

Rahan (*Raithean*) Offaly. 'Ferny place'.

Rahara (*Ráth Aradh*) Roscommon. 'Noble fort'.

Raharney (*Ráth Fhearna*) Westmeath. 'Fort of the alder'.

Raheen (*Ráithín*) Cork, Westmeath, Wexford. 'Little fort'.

Raheens (*Na Ráithíní*) Mayo. 'The little forts'.

Raheny (*Ráth Eanaigh*) Dublin. 'Fort of the marsh'.

Raholp (*Ráth Cholpa*) Down. *Raith Colptha* c.1170. 'Fort of the heifer'.

Rahugh (*Ráth Aodha*) Westmeath. 'Aodh's fort'.

Rainford Mersey. *Raineford* 1198. 'Ford of a man called **Regna*', or 'boundary ford'. OE pers. name or OScand. *rein* + OE *ford*.

Rainham Gtr. London. *Renaham* 1086 (DB). Possibly identical in origin with the next name. Alternatively 'homestead of a man called **Regna*', OE pers. name + *hām*.

Rainham Kent. *Roegingaham* 811. Probably 'homestead of the Roegingas'. OE tribal name (of uncertain meaning) + *hām*.

Rainhill Mersey. *Raynhull* c.1190. 'Hill of a man called **Regna*', or 'boundary hill'. OE pers. name or OScand. *rein* + OE *hyll*.

Rainow Ches. *Rauenouh* 1285. 'Hill-spur frequented by ravens'. OE *hræfn* + *hōh*.

Rainton, 'estate associated with a man called **Rægen* or **Regna*', OE pers. name + *-ing-* + *tūn*: **Rainton** N. Yorks. *Rainincton* 1086 (DB). **Rainton, East** (Tyne & Wear) & **Rainton, West** (Durham). *Reiningtone* c.1170.

Rainworth Notts. *Reynwath* 1268. 'Clean ford', or 'boundary ford'. OScand. *hreinn* or *rein* + *vath*.

Raithby Lincs., near Louth. *Radresbi* 1086 (DB). 'Farmstead or village of a man called **Hreithi*'. OScand. pers. name + *bý*.

Raithby Lincs., near Spilsby. *Radebi* 1086 (DB). 'Farmstead or village of a man called Hrathi'. OScand. pers. name + *bý*.

Rake W. Sussex. *Rake* 1296. '(Place at) the hollow or pass'. OE *hraca*.

Ram's Island (*Inis Dairgreann*) Antrim. (*primanmeara*) *Innsi Daircairgrenn* 1056. The present name arose from a mistaken resemblance between Irish *reithe*, 'ram', and the final element of Irish *Inis Draicrenn*, a later version of the original name, itself of unknown meaning.

Rame Cornwall, near Plymouth. *Rame* 1086 (DB). Possibly '(place at) the barrier', perhaps alluding to a fortress. OE **hrama*.

Ramore (*Ráth Mór*) Antrim. 'Big fort'.

Ramornie Fife. *Ramorgany* 1512. 'Fort of a man of Clan Morgan'. Gaelic *ràth*.

Rampisham Dorset. *Ramesham* 1086 (DB). 'Wild-garlic enclosure', or 'enclosure of the ram or of a man called Ramm'. OE *hramsa* or *ramm* or pers. name + *hamm*.

Rampside Cumbria. *Rameshede* 1292. 'Headland of the ram', perhaps from a fancied resemblance to the animal. OE *ramm* + *hēafod*.

Rampton Cambs. *Rantone* 1086 (DB). 'Farmstead where rams are kept'. OE *ramm* + *tūn*.

Rampton Notts. *Rametone* 1086 (DB). Probably identical in origin with the previous name.

Ramsbottom Gtr. Manch. *Romesbothum* 1324. 'Valley of the ram, or where wild garlic grows'. OE *ramm* or *hramsa* + **bothm*.

Ramsbury Wilts. *Rammesburi* 947, *Ramesberie* 1086 (DB). 'Fortification of the raven, or of a man called **Hræfn*'. OE *hræfn* or pers. name + *burh* (dative *byrig*).

Ramsden, probably 'valley where wild garlic grows', OE *hramsa* + *denu*: **Ramsden** Oxon. *Rammesden* 1246. **Ramsden Bellhouse** Essex. *Ramesdana* 1086 (DB), *Ramesden Belhous* 1254. Manorial affix from the de Belhus family, here in the 13th cent.

Ramsey, probably 'island where wild garlic grows', OE *hramsa* + *ēg*: **Ramsey** Cambs. *Hramesege* c.1000. **Ramsey** Essex. *Rameseia* 1086 (DB).

Ramsey Island (*Ynys Dewi*) Pemb. *Ramesey* 1326. 'Island where wild garlic grows'. OScand. *hramsa* + *ey*. The Welsh name means 'St David's island' (Welsh *ynys* + *Dewi*).

Ramsgate Kent. *Remmesgate* 1275. 'Gap (in the cliffs) of the raven, or of a man called **Hræfn*'. OE *hræfn* or pers. name *geat*.

Ramsgill N. Yorks. *Ramesgile* 1198. 'Ravine of the ram, or where wild garlic grows'. OE *ramm* or *hramsa* + OScand. *gil*.

Ramshorn Staffs. *Rumesoura* 1197. 'The ram's ridge', or 'ridge where wild garlic grows'. OE *ramm* or *hramsa* + **ofer*.

Ranby Notts. *Ranebi* 1086 (DB). 'Farmstead or village of a man called Hrani'. OScand. pers. name + *bý*.

Rand Lincs. *Rande* 1086 (DB). '(Place at) the border or edge'. OE *rand*.

Randalstown (*Baile Raghnaill*) Antrim. The town is named after Randal MacDonnell, 2nd Earl and 1st Mar-quis of Antrim, who in c.1650 married his second wife Rose O'Neill, who lived at nearby Shane's Castle.

Randwick Glos. *Rendewiche* 1121. Probably 'dwelling or farm on the edge or border'. OE **rend* + *wīc*.

Ranelagh (*Raghnallach*) Dublin. 'Raghnal's place'.

Rangeworthy S. Glos. *Rengeswurda* 1167. 'Enclosure of a man called **Hrencga*', or 'enclosure made of stakes'. OE pers. name or OE **hrynge* + *worthig*.

Rannafast (*Rann na Feirste*) Donegal. 'Point of the sand-bank'.

Rannoch Moor Highland. *Rannach* 1505. '(Place of) bracken'. Gaelic *raineach*.

Ranskill Notts. *Raveschel* |*sic*| 1086 (DB), *Ravenskelf* 1275. 'Shelf or ridge frequented by ravens, or of a man called Hrafn'. OScand. *hrafn* or pers. name + *skjalf*.

Ranton Staffs. *Rantone* 1086 (DB). Possibly 'farmstead where rams are kept'. OE *ramm* + *tūn*.

Ranworth Norfolk. *Randwrthe* c.1045, *Randuorda* 1086 (DB). 'Enclosure by an edge or border', or 'enclosure of a man called Randi'. OE *rand* or OScand. pers. name + OE *worth*.

Ranza, Loch N. Ayr (Arran). *Lockransay* 1433. 'Loch of the rowan-tree river'. Gaelic *loch* + OScand. **raun* + *á*.

Raphoe (*Ráth Bhoth*) Donegal. (*epscop*) *Ratha Bhoth* 813. 'Fort of the huts'.

Rasen, Market, *Rasen, Middle*, & *Rasen, West* Lincs. *æt ræsnan* 973, *Resne* 1086 (DB), *Marketrasyn* 1358, *Middelrasen* 1201, *Westrasen* 1202. '(Place at) the planks', i.e. 'plankbridge'. OE *ræsn* in dative plural form. The river-name **Rase** is a 'back-formation' from the place-name.

Rasharkin (*Ros Earcáin*) Antrim. *Ros Earcáin* c.1400. 'Earcán's grove'.

Raskelf N. Yorks. *Raschel* 1086 (DB). 'Shelf or ridge frequented by roe-deer'. OScand. *rá* + *skjalf*.

Rastrick W. Yorks. *Rastric* 1086 (DB). Probably 'raised strip or ridge with a resting-place'. OScand. *rǫst* + OE **ric*.

Ratby Leics. *Rotebie* 1086 (DB). 'Farmstead or village of a man called Rōta'. OE pers. name + OScand. *bý*.

Ratcliffe, 'red cliff or bank', OE *rēad* + *clif*: **Ratcliffe Culey** Leics. *Redeclive* 1086 (DB). Manorial affix from the de Culy family, here in the 13th cent. **Ratcliffe on Soar** Notts. *Radeclive* 1086 (DB). For the river-name, *see* BARROW UPON SOAR. **Ratcliffe on the Wreake** Leics. *Radeclive* 1086 (DB). For the river-name, *see* FRISBY ON THE WREAKE.

Rath (*Ráth*) Offaly, Waterford. 'Fort'.

Rath Luirc (*Ráth Loirc*) Cork. 'Lorc's fort'. The usual Irish name is now *An Ráth*, 'the fort'.

Rathangan (*Ráth Iomgháin*) Kildare. 'Iomghán's fort'.

Rathbeg (*Ráth Beag*) Antrim. 'Little fort'.

Rathcabban (*Ráth Cabáin*) Tipperary. 'Fort of the cabin'.

Rathcarra (*Ráth Characch*) Westmeath. 'Rocky fort'.

Rathclittagh (*Ráth Cleiteach*) Westmeath. 'Fort of the feathers'.

Rathcogue (*Ráth Cogaidh*) Westmeath. 'Fort of the war'.

Rathconrath (*Ráth Conarta*) Westmeath. 'Fort of the pack of hounds'.

Rathcool (*Ráth Cúil*) Cork. 'Fort of the hill'.

Rathcoole (*Ráth Cúil*) Dublin. 'Fort of the hill'.

Rathcore (*Ráth Cuair*) Meath. 'Fort of Cuar'.

Rathcormack (*Ráth Chormaic*) Cork. 'Cormac's fort'.

Rathdangan (*Ráth Daingin*) Wicklow. 'Fort of the fortress'.

Rathdowney (*Ráth Domhnaigh*) Laois. 'Fort of the church'.

Rathdrishoge (*Ráth Driseog*) Westmeath. 'Fort of the brambles'.

Rathdrum (*Ráth Droma*) Wicklow. 'Fort of the ridge'.

Rathen Aber. *Rathyn* 1300. Origin obscure.

Rathfarnham (*Ráth Fearnáin*) Dublin. 'Fort of the alder'.

Rathfeigh (*Ráth Faiche*) Meath. 'Fort of the green'.

Rathfield (*Páirc na Rátha*) Kerry. 'Field of the ring fort'.

Rathfran (*Ráth Bhrain*) Mayo. 'Bran's fort'.

Rathfriland (*Ráth Fraoileann*) Down. *Raphrylan* 1583. 'Fraoile's fort'.

Rathfylane (*Ráth Fialáin*) Wexford. 'Fialán's fort'.

Rathgall (*Ráth Gall*) Wicklow. 'Fort of the stone'.

Rathganny (*Ráth Ghainmhe*) Westmeath. 'Sandy fort'.

Rathgar (*Ráth Garbh*) Dublin. 'Rough fort'.

Rathgormuck (*Ráth Ó gCormaic*) Waterford. 'Fort of Uí Chormaic'.

Rathillet Fife. *Radhulit* c.1195. 'Fort of the Ulstermen'. Gaelic *ràth*.

Rathkeale (*Ráth Caola*) Limerick. 'Caola's fort'.

Rathkenny (*Ráth Cheannaigh*) Antrim, Meath. 'Ceannach's fort'.

Rathlacken (*Ráth Leacan*) Mayo. 'Fort of the hillside'.

Rathlee (*Ráth Lao*) Sligo. 'Fort of the calf'.

Rathlin Island (*Reachlainn*) Antrim. (*ecclaise*) *Rechrainne* 630. Meaning uncertain.

Rathlin O'Birne Island (*Reachlainn Uí Bhirn*) Donegal. 'Ó Birn's Reachlainn'.

Rathmarega (*Ráth Mharga*) Westmeath. 'Fort of the market'.

Rathmell N. Yorks. *Rodemele* 1086 (DB). 'Red sandbank'. OScand. *rauthr* + *melr*.

Rathmelton (*Ráth Mealtain*) Donegal. *Ramalton* 1601. 'Mealtan's fort'.

Rathmore (*Ráth Mhór*) Antrim, Kerry, Kildare. 'Big fort'.

Rathmoyle (*An Ráth Mhaol*) Kilkenny. 'The dilapidated fort'.

Rathmullan (*Ráth Maoláin*) Donegal. *Ráith Mailáin* 1516. 'Maolán's fort'.

Rathmullan (*Ráth Mhaoláin*) Down. *Rathmoyln* 1306. 'Maolán's fort'.

Rathmullen (*Ráth an Mhuilinn*) Sligo. 'Fort of the mill'.

Rathnamagh (*Ráth na Mach*) Mayo. 'Fort of the plain'.

Rathnamuddagh (*Ráth na mBodach*) Westmeath. 'Fort of the churls'.

Rathnew (*Ráth Naoi*) Wicklow. 'Noé's fort'.

Rathnure (*Ráth an Iúir*) Wexford. 'Fort of the yew tree'.

Rathowen (*Ráth Eoghain*) Westmeath. 'Eoghan's fort'.

Rathruane (*Ráth Ruáin*) Cork. 'Ruán's fort'.

Rathtoe (*Ráth Tó*) Carlow. 'Tó's fort'.

Rathtroane (*Ráth Ruáin*) Meath. 'Ruán's fort'.

Rathvilla (*Ráth Bhile*) Offaly. 'Fort of the sacred tree'.

Rathvilly (*Ráth Bhile*) Carlow. 'Fort of the sacred tree'.

Ratkeevin (*Ráth Chaoimín*) Tipperary. 'Kevin's fort'.

Ratley Warwicks. *Rotelei* 1086 (DB). 'Clearing with tree-roots', or 'clearing of a man called *Rōta*'. OE *rōt* or pers. name + *lēah*.

Ratlinghope Shrops. *Rotelingehope* 1086 (DB). 'Enclosed valley associated with a man called *Rōtel*', or 'valley at *Rōtel's* place'. OE pers. name + *-ing-* or *-ing* + *hop*.

Ratoath (*Ráth Tó*) Meath. 'Tó's fort'.

Rattery Devon. *Ratreu* 1086 (DB). '(Place at) the red tree'. OE *rēad* + *trēow*.

Rattlesden Suffolk. *Ratlesdena* 1086 (DB). OE *denu* 'valley' with an uncertain first element, possibly a pers. name.

Rattoo (*Ráth Tó*) Kerry. 'Tó's fort'.

Rattray Perth. *Rotrefe* 1291. 'Farm by the fort'. Gaelic *ràth* + British **treb*.

Raubaun (*Ráth Bán*) Westmeath. 'White fort'.

Rauceby, North & *Rauceby, South* Lincs. *Rosbi, Roscebi* 1086 (DB). 'Farmstead or village of a man called Rauthr'. OScand. pers. name + *bý*.

Raughton Head Cumbria. *Ragton* 1182, *Raughtonheved* 1367. Probably 'farmstead where moss or lichen grows'. OE *ragu* + OE *tūn*, with the later addition of *hēafod* 'headland, hill'.

Raunds Northants. *Randan* c.980, *Rande* 1086 (DB). '(Place at) the borders or edges'. OE *rand* in a plural form.

Raveley, Great & *Raveley, Little* Cambs. *Ræflea* c.1060. Possibly 'woodland clearing frequented by ravens'. OE *hræfn* + *lēah*.

Ravendale, East & *Ravendale, West* NE. Lincs. *Ravenedal* 1086 (DB). 'Valley frequented by ravens'. OScand. *hrafn* + *dalr*.

Ravenfield S. Yorks. *Rauenesfeld* 1086 (DB). 'Open land of a man called **Hræfn*, or frequented by ravens'. OE pers. name or OE *hræfn* + *feld*.

Ravenglass Cumbria. *Rengles* c.1180. 'Lot or share of a man called Glas'. OIrish *rann* + pers. name.

Raveningham Norfolk. *Rauenicham* 1086 (DB). 'Homestead of the family or followers of a man called *Hræfn'. OE pers. name + *-inga-* + *hām*.

Ravenscar N. Yorks. *Rauenesere* 1312. 'Rock frequented by ravens'. OScand. *hrafn* + *sker*.

Ravensden Beds. *Rauenesden* c.1150. 'Valley of the raven, or of a man called *Hræfn'. OE *hræfn* or pers. name + *denu*.

Ravensthorpe, 'outlying farmstead or hamlet of a man called Hrafn', OScand. pers. name + *thorp*: **Ravensthorpe** Northants. *Ravenestorp* 1086 (DB). **Ravensthorpe** W. Yorks. *Rauenestorp* 1086 (DB).

Ravenstone, 'farmstead of a man called *Hræfn or *Hrafn', OE or OScand. pers. name + *tūn*: **Ravenstone** Bucks. *Raveneston* 1086 (DB). **Ravenstone** Leics. *Ravenestun* 1086 (DB).

Ravenstonedale Cumbria. *Rauenstandale* 12th cent. 'Valley of the raven stone'. OE *hræfn* + *stān* + OScand. *dalr*.

Ravensworth N. Yorks. *Raveneswet* |*sic*| 1086 (DB), *Raveneswad* 1157. 'Ford of a man called Hrafn'. OScand. pers. name + *vath*.

Ravernet (*Ráth Bhearnáin*) Down. *Balliravarnan* 1585. 'Fort of the little gap'.

Rawcliffe, 'red cliff or bank', OScand. *rauthr* + *klif*: **Rawcliffe** E. R. Yorks. *Routheclif* c.1080. **Rawcliffe** York. *Roudeclife* 1086 (DB). **Rawcliffe, Out** Lancs. *Rodeclif* 1086 (DB). Affix is OE *ūte* 'outer'.

Rawdon W. Yorks. *Roudun* 1086 (DB). 'Red hill'. OScand. *rauthr* + OE *dūn*.

Rawmarsh S. Yorks. *Rodemesc* |*sic*| 1086 (DB), *Rowmareis* c.1200. 'Red marsh'. OScand. *rauthr* + OE *mersc*.

Rawreth Essex. *Raggerea* 1177. 'Stream frequented by herons'. OE *hrāgra* + *rīth*.

Rawtenstall Lancs. *Routonstall* 1324. 'Rough farmstead or cow-pasture'. OE *rūh* + **tūn-stall*.

Ray (*An Ráith*) Donegal. *Raghe* 1622. 'The fort'.

Raydon Suffolk. *Reindune* 1086 (DB). 'Hill where rye is grown'. OE *rygen* + *dūn*.

Rayleigh Essex. *Ragheleia* 1086 (DB). 'Woodland clearing frequented by female roe-deer or by she-goats'. OE *rǣge* + *lēah*.

Rayne Essex. *Hrǣgenan* c.1000, *Raines* 1086 (DB). Possibly '(place at) the shelter or eminence'. OE **hrǣgene*.

Raynham Norfolk. *Reineham* 1086 (DB). Possibly 'homestead or village of a man called *Regna'. OE pers. name + *hām*.

Rea, Lough (*Loch Riach*) Galway. 'Grey lake'.

Reacashlagh (*Réidhchaisleach*) Kerry. 'Clearing of the stone forts'.

Reach, '(place at) the raised strip of land or other linear feature', OE **rǣc*: **Reach** Beds. *Reche* c.1220. **Reach** Cambs. *Reche* 1086. Here the reference is to the post-Roman earthwork of Devil's Dyke.

Read Lancs. *Revet* 1202. 'Headland frequented by female roe-deer or by she-goats'. OE *rǣge* + *hēafod*.

Reading Berks. *Readingum* c.900, *Reddinges* 1086 (DB). '(Settlement of) the family or followers of a man called *Rēad(a)'. OE pers. name + *-ingas*.

Reagill Cumbria. *Reuegile* 1176. 'Ravine frequented by foxes'. OScand. *refr* + *gil*.

Reanaclogheen (*Réidh na bCloichín*) Waterford. 'Clearing of the little stones'.

Reanascreena (*Rae na Scríne*) Cork. 'Level place of the shrine'.

Rear (*Rae*) Tipperary. 'Level place'.

Rearsby Leics. *Redresbi* 1086 (DB). 'Farmstead or village of a man called Hreitharr'. OScand. pers. name + *bý*.

Recess (*Sraith Salach*) Galway. 'Dirty river meadow'.

Reculver Kent. *Regulbium* c.425, *Roculf* 1086 (DB). An ancient Celtic name meaning 'great headland'.

Redberth Pemb. *Ridebard* 1361. 'Ford with bushes'. Welsh *rhyd* + *perth*.

Redbourn, *Redbourne*, 'reedy stream', OE *hrēod* + *burna*: **Redbourn** Herts. *Reodburne* c.1060, *Redborne* 1086 (DB). **Redbourne** N. Lincs. *Radburne* 1086 (DB).

Redbridge Gtr. London, borough named from an old bridge across the River RODING first recorded as *Red Bridge* in 1746.

Redcar Red. & Cleve. *Redker* c.1170. 'Red or reedy marsh'. OE *rēad* or *hrēod* + OScand. *kjarr*.

Redcliff Bay N. Som. *Radeclive* c.1180. 'Red cliff or bank'. OE *rēad* + *clif*.

Reddish Gtr. Manch. *Rediche* 1212. 'Reedy ditch'. OE *hrēod* + *dīc*.

Redditch Heref. & Worcs. *La Rededich* 1247. 'Red or reedy ditch'. OE *rēad* or *hrēod* + *dīc*.

Rede Suffolk. *Reoda* 1086 (DB). Probably '(place at) the reed bed'. OE *hrēod*.

Redenhall Norfolk. *Redanahalla* 1086 (DB). Probably 'nook of land where reeds grow'. OE **hrēoden* + *halh*.

Redgorton Perth. *Rothgortanan* c.1250. 'Fort by the little enclosure'. Gaelic *ràth* + *gortain*.

Redgrave Suffolk. *Redgrafe* 11th cent. 'Reedy pit' from OE *hrēod* + *græf*, or 'red grove' from OE *rēad* + *grāf*.

Redhill N. Som. *Ragiol* 1086 (DB). Possibly 'hill at roe-deer edge'. OE *rā* + *ecg* + *hyll*.

Redhill Surrey. *Redehelde* 1301. 'Red slope'. OE *rēad* + *helde*.

Redhills Cavan. *Redhills* 1837. The village is apparently named from the reddish soil of the hills here.

Redisham Suffolk. *Redesham* 1086 (DB). Probably 'homestead or village of a man called *Rēad'. OE pers. name + *hām*.

Redland Brist. *Thriddeland* 1209. Probably 'third part of an estate'. OE *thridda* + *land*.

Redlingfield Suffolk. *Radinghefelda* |*sic*| 1086 (DB), *Radlingefeld* 1166. 'Open land of the family or followers of a man called Rædel or *Rædla'. OE pers. name + *-inga-* + *feld*.

Redlynch Somerset. *Redlisc* 1086 (DB). 'Reedy marsh'. OE *hrēod* + **lisc*.

Redmarley D'Abitot Glos. *Reodemæreleage* 963, *Ridmerlege* 1086 (DB), *Rudmarleye Dabetot* 1324. 'Woodland clearing with a reedy pond'. OE *hrēod* + *mere* + *lēah*. Manorial affix from the d'Abitot family, here in 1086.

Redmarshall Stock. on T. *Rodmerehil* 1208–10. 'Hill by a red (i.e. sandy) pond'. OE *rēad* + *mere* + *hyll*.

Redmire N. Yorks. *Ridemare* 1086 (DB). 'Reedy pool'. OE *hrēod* + *mere*.

Redruth Cornwall. *Ridruth* 1259. 'Red ford'. OCornish *rid* + *rudh*.

Redwick S. Glos. *Hreodwican* 955–9, *Redeuuiche* 1086 (DB). 'Dairy farm among the reeds'. OE *hrēod* + *wīc*.

Redworth Durham. *Redwortha* 1183. 'Enclosure where reeds grow'. OE *hrēod* + *worth*.

Ree, Lough (*Loch Rí*) Longford, Roscommon, Westmeath. 'King's lake'.

Reed Herts. *Retth* 1086 (DB). Probably OE **rȳ(h)th* 'a rough piece of ground'.

Reedham Norfolk. *Redham* 1044–7, *Redeham* 1086 (DB). 'Homestead or enclosure where reeds grow'. OE *hrēod* + *hām* or *hamm*.

Reedness E. R. Yorks. *Rednesse* c.1170. 'Reedy headland'. OE *hrēod* + *næss*.

Reen (*Rinn*) Kerry. 'Point'.

Reens (*Roighne*) Cork. 'Choicest part'.

Reepham, 'manor held or run by a reeve', OE *rēfa* + *hām*: **Reepham** Lincs. *Refam* 1086 (DB). **Reepham** Norfolk. *Refham* 1086 (DB).

Reeth N. Yorks. *Rie* 1086 (DB), *Rithe* 1184. Probably '(place at) the stream'. OE *rīth*.

Reigate Surrey. *Reigata* c.1170. 'Gate for female roe-deer'. OE *rēge* + *geat*.

Reighton N. Yorks. *Rictone* 1086 (DB). 'Farmstead by the straight ridge'. OE **ric* + *tūn*.

Reiss Highland. 'Rising ground', *cp*. lul. *risa* to rise.

Relaghbeg (*Reidhleach Beag*) Cavan. 'Small level place'.

Relick (*Reilig*) Westmeath. 'Graveyard'.

Remenham Berks. *Rameham* 1086 (DB). Probably 'homestead or enclosure by the river-bank'. OE *reoma* (genitive *-n*) + *hām* or *hamm*.

Rempstone Notts. *Rampestune* 1086 (DB). Probably 'farmstead of a man called **Hrempi*'. OE pers. name + *tūn*.

Renanirree (*Rae na nDoirí*) Cork. 'Level place of the oak trees'.

Rendcomb Glos. *Rindecumbe* 1086 (DB). 'Valley of a stream called *Hrinde*'. OE river-name (meaning 'the pusher') + *cumb*.

Rendham Suffolk. *Rimdham, Rindham* 1086 (DB). 'Cleared homestead', or 'homestead by a hill'. OE *rȳmed* or **rind(e)* + *hām*.

Rendlesham Suffolk. *Rendlæsham* c.730, *Rendlesham* 1086 (DB). Possibly 'homestead of a man called **Rendel*', OE pers. name + *hām*. Alternatively the first element could be an OE word **rendel* 'little shore'.

Renfrew Renf. *Reinfry* c.1128, *Renfriu* c.1150. 'Point of the current'. OWelsh *rhyn* + *frwd*. The River Gryfe enters the Clyde here.

Renhold Beds. *Ranhale* 1220. Probably 'nook of land frequented by roe-deer'. OE *rā* (genitive plural *rāna*) + *halh*.

Rennington Northum. *Reiningtun* 12th cent. 'Estate associated with a man called **Regna*'. OE pers. name + *-ing-* + *tūn*.

Renton W. Dunb. The town was founded in 1782 and named after Cecilia *Renton*, daughter-in-law of Jean Telfer, sister of the novelist Tobias Smollett (1721–74), who was born nearby.

Renwick Cumbria. *Rauenwich* 1178. Probably 'dwelling or farm of a man called Hrafn or **Hræfn*'. OScand. or OE pers. name + *wīc*.

Repps Norfolk. *Repes* 1086 (DB), *Repples* 1191. Possibly 'the strips of land'. OE **reopul*.

Repton Derbys. *Hrypadun* 730–40, *Rapendune* 1086 (DB). 'Hill of the tribe called Hrype'. Old tribal name (*see* RIPON) + OE *dūn*.

Reston, North & *Reston, South* Lincs. *Ristone* 1086 (DB). 'Farmstead near or among brushwood'. OE *hrīs* + *tūn*.

Restormel Cornwall. *Rostormel* 1310. Possibly 'moor at the bare hill'. Cornish **ros* + *tor* + **moyl*.

Retford, East & *Retford, West* Notts. *Redforde* 1086 (DB). 'Red ford'. OE *rēad* + *ford*.

Rettendon Essex. *Rettendun* c.1000, *Ratenduna* 1086 (DB). Probably 'hill infested with rats'. OE **rætten* + *dūn*.

Revesby Lincs. *Resuesbi* 1086 (DB). 'Farmstead or village of a man called Refr'. OScand. pers. name + *bý*.

Rewe Devon. *Rewe* 1086 (DB). 'Row of houses'. OE *rǣw*.

Reydon Suffolk. *Rienduna* 1086 (DB). 'Hill where rye is grown'. OE *rygen* + *dūn*.

Reymerston Norfolk. *Raimerestuna* 1086 (DB). 'Farmstead of a man called Raimar'. OGerman pers. name + OE *tūn*.

Reynalton Pemb. *Reynaldeston* 1394. 'Reynald's farm'. OGerman pers. name + OE *tūn*.

Rhaeadr. *See* RHAYADER.

Rhaglan. *See* RAGLAN.

Rhayader (*Rhaeadr* or *Rhaeadr Gwy*) Powys. *Raidergoe* 1191, *Rayadyr Gwy* 14th cent., *Raiadergwy* 1543. '(Place by the) waterfall'. Welsh *rhaeadr*. The Welsh name adds the name of the River Wye (*Gwy*) (*see* HAY-ON-WYE).

Rhisga. *See* RISCA.

Rhiwabon. *See* RUABON.

Rhobell Fawr (mountain) Gwyd. 'Big saddle'. Welsh *rhobell* + *mawr*.

Rhode (*Ród*) Offaly. 'Route'.

Rhondda Rhon. *Rotheni* 12th cent. '(Place on the) River Rhondda'. The river name means 'noisy one' (Welsh *rhoddni*).

Rhoose (*Y Rhws*) Vale Glam. *Rhos* 1533. '(Place on the) moor'. Welsh *rhos*.

Rhos-on-sea (*Llandrillo-yn-Rhos*) Conwy. The Welsh name means 'St Trillo's church in Rhos' (Welsh *llan* + *yn*), Rhos being a cantref.

Rhosllanerchrugog Wrex. *Rose lane aghregog* 1544. 'Moor of the heather glade'. Welsh *rhos* + *llannerch* + *grugog*.

Rhostryfan Gwyd. 'Moor by (Moel) Tryfan'. *Rhos Tryfan* 1827. Welsh *rhos*. The nearby hill *Moel Tryfan* has a name meaning 'bare hill with a distinctive summit' (Welsh *moel* + *tryfan*).

Rhostyllen Wrex. *Rhos Stellan* 1546. 'Moor on a ledge'. Welsh *rhos* + *ystyllen*.

Rhuddlan Denb. *Roelend* 1086 (DB), *Ruthelan* 1191. 'Red bank'. Welsh *rhudd* + *glan*.

Rhum. *See* RUM.

Rhuthun. *See* RUTHIN.

Rhws, Y. *See* RHOOSE.

Rhydaman. *See* AMMANFORD.

Rhyl Denb. *Ryhull* 1301, *Yrhill* 1578, *Rhyll* 1660. '(Place by) the hill'. Welsh *yr* + ME *hull*.

Rhymney (*Rhymni*) Cphy. *Remni* 1101, *Rempny* 1296, *Rymney* 1541. '(Place on the) River Rhymney'. The river name means 'auger' (Welsh *rhwmp* + adjectival ending *-ni*), describing its boring action.

Rhynd Perth. 'Promontory'. Gaelic *rinn*.

Rhynie Aber. *Rhynyn* c.1230. 'Promontory'. Gaelic *rinn*.

Rhynie Highland. *Rathne* 1529. Probably 'little fort'. Gaelic *ràthan*.

Ribbesford Heref. & Worcs. *Ribbedford* 1023, *Ribeford* 1086 (DB). 'Ford by a bed of ribwort or hound's-tongue'. OE *ribbe* + *bedd* + *ford*.

Ribbleton Lancs. *Ribleton* 1201. 'Farmstead on the River Ribble'. OE river-name (from **ripel* 'tearing' or 'boundary') + *tūn*.

Ribchester Lancs. *Ribelcastre* 1086 (DB). 'Roman fort on the River Ribble'. OE river-name (see previous name) + *ceaster*.

Ribigill Highland. *Regeboll* n.d. 'Farm on a ridge'. OScand. *hryggr* + *ból*.

Ribston, Great & *Ribston, Little* N. Yorks. *Ripestan* 1086. Probably 'rock or stone by which ribwort or hound's-tongue grows'. OE *ribbe* + *stān*.

Riby Lincs. *Ribi* 1086 (DB). 'Farmstead where rye is grown'. OE *ryge* + OScand. *bý*.

Riccall N. Yorks. *Richale* 1086 (DB). 'Nook of land of a man called **Rīca*'. OE pers. name + *halh*.

Rich Hill Armagh. The name comes from Edward *Richardson*, who built Richhill Castle here in the 17th cent.

Richards Castle Heref. & Worcs. *Castellum Ricardi* c.1180–6, *Richardescastel* 1349. From OFrench, ME *castel*, alluding to the Frenchman Richard Scrope whose son Osbern held the castle here in 1086 (DB).

Richborough Kent. *Rutupiae* c.150, *Ratteburg* 1197. 'Stronghold called **Repta*'. Reduced form of ancient Celtic name (probably 'muddy waters or estuary') + OE *burh*.

Richmond Gtr. London. *Richemount* 1502. Earlier called *West Sheen* (*see* SHEEN), renamed by Henry VII from the following place.

Richmond N. Yorks. *Richemund* c.1110. 'Strong hill'. OFrench *riche* + *mont*.

Rickinghall Inferior & *Rickinghall Superior* Suffolk. *Rikinghale* 10th cent., *Rikingahala* 1086 (DB). 'Nook of the family or followers of a man called **Rīca*'. OE pers. name + *-inga-* + *halh*.

Rickling Essex. *Richelinga* 1086 (DB). '(Settlement of) the family or followers of a man called **Rīcela* or a woman called *Rīcola*'. OE pers. name + *-ingas*.

Rickmansworth Herts. *Prichemareworde* |sic| 1086 (DB), *Richemaresworthe* c.1180. 'Enclosure of a man called **Rīcmǣr*'. OE pers. name + *worth*.

Riddlesden W. Yorks. *Redelesden* 1086 (DB). 'Valley of a man called **Rēdel* or *Hrēthel*'. OE pers. name + *denu*.

Ridge Herts. *La Rigge* 1248. 'The ridge'. OE *hrycg*.

Ridgewell Essex. *Rideuuella* 1086 (DB). Probably 'spring or stream where reeds grow'. OE *hrēod* + *wella*.

Ridgmont Beds. *Rugemund* 1227. 'Red hill'. OFrench *rouge* + *mont*.

Riding Mill Northum. *Ryding* 1262. OE **ryding* 'a clearing'.

Riding, East, *Riding, North*, & *Riding, West* (tripartite division of Yorkshire). *Estreding, Nortreding, Westreding* 1086 (DB). From OScand. *thrithjungr* 'a third part', the initial *th-* having coalesced with the final consonant of *ēast, north,* and *west* to give *Riding*.

Ridlington, 'estate associated with a man called **Rēdel* or Hrēthel, OE pers. name + *-ing-* + *tūn*: **Ridlington** Norfolk. *Ridlinketuna* 1086 (DB). **Ridlington** Rutland. *Redlinctune* 1086 (DB).

Ridware, Hamstall & *Ridware, Pipe* Staffs. *Rideware* 1004, 1086 (DB), *Hamstal Ridewar* 1242, *Pipe Ridware* 14th cent. Probably '(settlement of) the dwellers at the ford'. Celtic **rïd* + OE *-ware*. Distinguishing affixes are from OE *hām-stall* 'homestead' and from the Pipe family, holders of the manor in the 13th cent.

Rievaulx N. Yorks. *Rievalle* 1157. 'Valley of the River Rye'. Celtic river-name (probably meaning 'stream') + OFrench *val(s)*.

Rillington N. Yorks. *Redlintone* 1086 (DB). 'Estate associated with a man called **Rēdel* or Hrēthel'. OE pers. name + *-ing-* + *tūn*.

Rimington Lancs. *Renitone* |sic| 1086 (DB), *Rimingtona* 1182–5. 'Farmstead on the boundary stream'. OE *rima* + *-ing* + *tūn*.

Rimpton Somerset. *Rimtune* 938, *Rintone* 1086 (DB). 'Farmstead on the boundary'. OE *rima* + *tūn*.

Rimswell E. R. Yorks. *Rimeswelle* 1086 (DB). Possibly 'spring or stream of a man called Hrímr or *Rȳmi'. OScand. or OE pers. name + OE *wella*.

Rinaston (*Tre-Einar*) Pemb. *Villa Reyneri c.*1308, *Reynerhiston* 1315. 'Reyner's farm'. OGerman pers. name + OE *tun* (Welsh *tref*).

Rinawade (*Rinn an Bháid*) Dublin. 'Point of the boat'.

Rindown (*Rinn Dúin*) Roscommon. 'Point of the fort'.

Rine (*Rinn*) Clare. 'Point'.

Rineanna (*Rinn Eanaigh*) Clare. 'Point of the marsh'.

Rineen (*Rinnín*) Clare. 'Little point'.

Ring (*Rinn*) Waterford. 'Point'.

Ringarogy (*Rinn Gearróige*) Cork. 'Point of the small portion'.

Ringaskiddy (*Rinn an Scídigh*) Cork. 'Scídioch's headland'.

Ringcurran (*Rinn Chorráin*) Cork. 'Point of the sickle'.

Ringfad (*Rinn Fhada*) Down. 'Long point'.

Ringland Norfolk. *Remingaland* 1086 (DB). Probably 'cultivated land of the family or followers of a man called *Rȳmi'. OE pers. name + *-inga-* + *land*.

Ringmer E. Sussex. *Ryngemere* 1276. 'Circular pool', or 'pool near a circular feature'. OE *hring* + *mere*.

Ringmore Devon, near Bigbury. *Reimore* |sic| 1086 (DB), *Redmore* 1242. 'Reedy moor'. OE *hrēod* +*mōr*.

Ringrone (*Rinn Róin*) Cork. 'Seal point'.

Ringsend (*An Rinn*) Dublin. 'The point'. English *end* was added to the Irish name to mean 'place at the end of the promontory'.

Ringsfield Suffolk. *Ringesfelda* 1086 (DB). 'Open land of a man called *Hring, or near a circular feature'. OE pers. name or OE *hring* + *feld*.

Ringshall Suffolk. *Ringeshala* 1086 (DB). Possibly 'nook of land of a man called *Hring, or near a circular feature'. OE pers. name or OE *hring* + *halh*.

Ringstead, 'circular enclosure, or place near a circular feature', OE *hring* + *stede*: **Ringstead** Norfolk. *Ringstyde c.*1050, *Rincsteda* 1086 (DB). **Ringstead** Northants. *Ringstede* 12th cent.

Ringwood Hants. *Rimucwuda* 955, *Rincvede* 1086 (DB). Probably 'wood on a boundary'. OE *rimuc* + *wudu*.

Ringwould Kent. *Roedligwealda* 861. Probably 'woodland of the family or followers of a man called *Rēdel or Hrēthel'. OE pers. name + *-inga-* + *weald*.

Rinmore (*Rinn Mhór*) Donegal. 'Large point'.

Rinn (*Rinn*) Leitrim, Longford. 'Point'.

Rinnafaghla (*Rinn na Fochla*) Donegal. 'Point of the cave'.

Rinneen (*Rinnín*) Galway, Kerry. 'Little point'.

Rinns of Galloway (peninsula) Dumf. *Le Rynnys* 1460. 'Headlands of Galloway'. Gaelic *rinn*. See GALLOWAY.

Rinns of Islay (peninsula) Arg. 'Divisions of Islay'. Gaelic *rann*. The name refers to the three districts into which ISLAY was formerly divided.

Rinville (*Rinn Mhíl*) Galway. 'Point of the animal'.

Rinvyle (*Rinn Mhaoile*) Galway. 'Promontory of the hornless cow'.

Ripe E. Sussex. *Ripe* 1086 (DB). '(Place at) the edge or strip of land'. OE *rip*.

Ripley, usually 'strip-shaped woodland clearing', OE *ripel* + *lēah*: **Ripley** Derbys. *Ripelei* 1086 (DB). **Ripley** Hants. *Riple* 1086 (DB). **Ripley** Surrey. *Ripelia* 1204.
   However the following may have a different origin: **Ripley** N. Yorks. *Ripeleia* 1086 (DB). Probably 'woodland clearing of the tribe called Hrype'. Old tribal name (see RIPON) + OE *lēah*.

Riplingham E. R. Yorks. *Ripingham* |sic| 1086 (DB), *Ripplingeham* 1180. 'Homestead associated with a man called *Rip(p)el', or 'homestead by the strip of land'. OE pers. name or OE *ripel* + *-ing-* + *hām*.

Ripon N. Yorks. *Hrypis c.*715, *Ripum* 1086 (DB). '(Place in the territory of) the tribe called Hrype'. Old tribal name (origin and meaning obscure) in a dative plural form Hrypum.

Rippingale Lincs. *Repingale* 806, *Repinghale* 1086 (DB). 'Nook of the family or followers of a man called *Hrepa'. OE pers. name + *-inga-* + *halh*.

Ripple, '(place at) the strip of land', OE *ripel*: **Ripple** Heref. & Worcs. *Rippell* 708, *Rippel* 1086 (DB). **Ripple** Kent. *Ryple* 1087.

Ripponden W. Yorks. *Ryburnedene* 1307. 'Valley of the River Ryburn'. OE river-name ('fierce or reedy stream') + *denu*.

Ripton, Abbot's & *Ripton, King's* Cambs. *Riptone c.*960, *Riptune* 1086 (DB). 'Farmstead by a strip of land'. OE *rip* + *tūn*. Affixes from early possession by the Abbot of Ramsey and the King.

Risborough, Monks & *Risborough, Princes* Bucks. *Hrisanbyrge* 903, *Riseberge* 1086 (DB). 'Hill(s) where brushwood grows'. OE *hrīsen* + *beorg*. Manorial affixes from early possession by the monks of Christchurch, Canterbury and by the Black Prince.

Risbury Heref. & Worcs. *Riseberia* 1086 (DB). 'Fortress among the brushwood'. OE *hrīs* + *burh* (dative *byrig*).

Risby, 'farmstead or village among the brushwood', OScand. *hrís* + *bý*: **Risby** N. Lincs. *Risebi* 1086 (DB). **Risby** Suffolk. *Risebi* 1086 (DB).

Risca (*Rhisga*) Cphy. *Risca* 1330. '(Place of) bark'. Welsh *rhisg*. The reference may be to a house built of bark-covered logs or to bark used as shingles on walls.

Rise E. R. Yorks. *Risun* 1086 (DB). '(Place among) the brushwood'. OE *hrīs* in a dative plural form *hrīsum*.

Riseley, 'brushwood clearing', OE *hrīs* + *lēah*: **Riseley** Beds. *Riselai* 1086 (DB). **Riseley** Berks. *Rysle* 1300.

Rishangles Suffolk. *Risangra* 1086 (DB). 'Wooded slope where brushwood grows'. OE *hrīs* + *hangra*.

Rishton Lancs. *Riston c.*1205. 'Farmstead where rushes grow'. OE *risc* + *tūn*.

Rishworth W. Yorks. *Risseworde* 12th cent. 'Enclosure where rushes grow'. OE *risc* + *worth*.

Rising, Castle Norfolk. *Risinga* 1086 (DB), *Castel Risinge* 1254. Probably '(settlement of) the family or followers of a man called *Risa'. OE pers. name + *-ingas*, with the later addition of *castel* from the Norman castle here. Alternatively 'dwellers in the brushwood', OE *hrīs* + *-ingas*.

Risley, 'brushwood clearing', OE *hrīs* + *lēah*: **Risley** Ches. *Ryselegh* 1284. **Risley** Derbys. *Riselei* 1086 (DB).

Rissington, Great & *Rissington, Little* Glos. *Rise(n)dune* 1086 (DB). 'Hill where brushwood grows'. OE *hrīsen* + *dūn*.

Riston, Long E. R. Yorks. *Ristune* 1086 (DB). 'Farmstead near or among brushwood'. OE *hrīs* + *tūn*.

Rivenhall End Essex. *Reuenhala* 1068, *Ruenhale* 1086 (DB). Probably 'rough or rugged nook of land'. OE *hrēof* (dative *-an*) + *halh*.

Riverhead Kent. *Reddride* 1278. 'Landing-place for cattle'. OE *hrīther* + *hȳth*.

Rivington Lancs. *Revington* 1202. 'Farmstead at the rough or rugged hill'. OE *hrēof* + *-ing* + *tūn*.

Roade Northants. *Rode* 1086 (DB). '(Place at) the clearing'. OE *rod*.

Roberton S. Lan. *Villa Roberti* c.1155, *Robertstun* 1229. 'Robert's farm'. OE *tun*.

Robertsbridge E. Sussex. *Pons Roberti* 1176, *Robartesbregge* 1445. Named from Robert de St Martin, founder of the 12th cent. abbey here. The earliest form has Latin *pons* 'bridge'.

Robeston Wathen Pemb. *Villa Roberti* 1282, *Roberdeston* 1357, *Robertson Wathen* 1545. 'Robert's farm by Llangwathen'. OE *tun*. *Llangwathen* is 'Gwaiddan's grove' (Welsh *llwyn*, 'grove', replaced by *llan*, 'church').

Robin Hood's Bay N. Yorks. *Robin Hoode Baye* 1532. A late name which probably arose from the popular ballads about this legendary outlaw.

Roborough Devon. *Raweberge* 1086 (DB). 'Rough hill'. OE *rūh beorg*.

Roby Mersey. *Rabil |sic|* 1086 (DB). *Rabi* 1185. 'Farmstead or village at a boundary'. OScand. *rá* + *bý*.

Rocester Staffs. *Rowcestre* 1086 (DB). OE *ceaster* 'Roman fort', possibly with *rūh* 'rough' or an unidentified pers. name.

Rochdale Gtr. Manch. *Recedham* 1086 (DB), *Rachedal* c.1195. 'Valley of the River **Roch**'. River-name + OScand. *dalr*. The river-name itself is a 'back-formation' from the old name *Recedham* 'homestead with a hall', OE *reced* + *hām*.

Roche Cornwall. *La Roche* 1233. 'The rock'. OFrench *roche*.

Rochester Kent. *Hrofaescaestir* 731, *Rovecestre* 1086 (DB). Probably 'Roman town or fort called *Hrofi*'. Ancient Celtic name (reduced from *Durobrivis* 4th cent. 'the walled town with the bridges') + OE *ceaster*.

Rochester Northum. *Rucestr* 1242. Possibly 'rough earthwork or fort'. OE *rūh* + *ceaster*.

Rochford, 'ford of the hunting-dog', OE *ræcc* + *ford*: **Rochford** Essex. *Rochefort* 1086 (DB). **Rochford** Heref. & Worcs. *Recesford* 1086 (DB).

Rock Heref. & Worcs. *Ak* 1224, *Roke* 1259. '(Place at) the oak-tree'. OE *āc*, with *R-* from ME *atter* 'at the'.

Rock Northum. *Rok* 1242. Probably ME *rokke* 'a rock, a peak'.

Rock of Dunamase (*Dún Masg*) Laois. 'Rock of the fort of Masg'.

Rock, The Tyrone. *The Rock* c.1835. The reference is to a rocky outcrop nearby.

Rockall (island) W. Isles. *Rocol* 1606. Possibly 'barren place in the stormy sea'. OScand. *rok* + *kollr*.

Rockbeare Devon. *Rochebere* 1086 (DB). 'Grove frequented by rooks'. OE *hrōc* + *bearu*.

Rockbourne Hants. *Rocheborne* 1086 (DB). 'Stream frequented by rooks'. OE *hrōc* + *burna*.

Rockcliffe Cumbria. *Rodcliua* 1185. 'Red cliff or bank'. OScand. *rauthr* + OE *clif*.

Rockcorry (*Buíochar*) Monaghan. *Rockorry* 1778. The village lies on rocky soil and was founded in the second half of the 18th cent. by Thomas Charles Stewart Corry. The Irish name means 'yellow land'.

Rockhampton S. Glos. *Rochemtune* 1086 (DB). 'Homestead by the rock, or frequented by rooks'. OE *rocc* or *hrōc* + *hām-tūn*.

Rockingham Northants. *Rochingeham* 1086 (DB). 'Homestead of the family or followers of a man called *Hrōc(a)'. OE pers. name + *-inga-* + *hām*.

Rockland, 'grove frequented by rooks', OScand. *hrókr* + *lundr*: **Rockland All Saints** & **Rockland St Peter** Norfolk. *Rokelund* 1086 (DB). Distinguishing affixes from the church dedications. **Rockland St Mary** Norfolk. *Rokelund* 1086 (DB). Affix from the church dedication.

Rockley Wilts. *Rochelie* 1086 (DB) 'Wood or clearing frequented by rooks'. OE *hrōc* + *lēah*.

Rodbourne, 'reedy stream', OE *hrēod* + *burna*: **Rodbourne** Wilts., near Malmesbury. *Reodburna* 701. **Rodbourne Cheney** Wilts. *Redborne* 1086 (DB), *Rodburne Chanu* 1304. Manorial affix from Ralph le Chanu, here in 1242.

Rodd Heref. & Worcs. *La Rode* 1220. 'The clearing'. OE *rod*.

Roddam Northum. *Rodun* 1201. '(Place at) the clearings'. OE *rod* in a dative plural form *rodum*.

Rode, 'the clearing', OE *rod*: **Rode Heath** Ches. *Rode* 1086 (DB), *Rodeheze* 1280. With the later addition of OE *hǣth* 'heath'. **Rode, North** Ches. *Rodo* 1086 (DB).

Roden Shrops. *Hrodene* late 10th cent., *Rodene* 1242. Named from the River Roden, a Celtic river-name probably meaning 'swift river'.

Roding, Abbess, *Roding, Aythorpe, Roding, Beauchamp, Roding, High, Roding, Leaden, Roding, Margaret,* & *Roding, White* Essex. *Rodinges* c.1050, 1086 (DB), *Roinges Abbatisse* 1237, *Roeng Aytrop* 1248, *Roynges Beuchamp* 1238, *High Roinges* 1224, *Ledeineroing* 1248, *Roinges Sancte Margaret* c.1245, *White Roeng* 1248. '(Settlement of) the family or followers of a man called *Hrōth(a)'. OE pers. name + -ingas. The affixes Abbess, Aythorpe, and Beauchamp are all manorial, from early possession by the Abbess of Barking, by a man called Aitrop, and by the de Beauchamp family respectively. High Roding refers to its situation. Leaden (OE lēaden) to the lead roof of the church, Margaret to the dedication of the church, and White to the colour of the church walls. The river-name **Roding** is a 'back- formation' from the place-name; the earlier name for the river was Hyle, see ILFORD.

Rodington Shrops. Rodintone 1086 (DB). 'Farmstead on the River Roden'. Celtic river-name (see RODEN) + OE tūn, possibly with medial connective -ing-.

Rodley Glos. Rodele 1086 (DB). 'Clearing amongst the reeds'. OE hrēod + lēah.

Rodley W. Yorks. Rothelaye 1246. Probably 'woodland clearing of a man called Hrōthwulf or *Róthulfr'. OE or OScand. pers. name + OE lēah.

Rodmarton Glos. Redmertone 1086 (DB). Probably 'farmstead by a reedy pool'. OE hrēod + mere + tūn.

Rodmell E. Sussex. Redmelle |sic| 1086 (DB), Radmelde 1202. Probably '(place with) red soil'. OE rēad + *mylde.

Rodmersham Kent. Rodmaeresham c.1100. 'Homestead or village of a man called *Hrōthmǣr'. OE pers. name + hām.

Rodney Stoke Somerset, see STOKE.

Rodsley Derbys. Redeslei 1086 (DB). OE lēah 'woodland clearing', possibly with OE hrēod 'reed bed'.

Roe (Rua) (river) Derry. 'Red one'.

Roehampton Gtr. London. Rokehampton 1350. 'Home farm frequented by rooks'. OE hrōc + hām-tūn.

Roffey W. Sussex. La Rogheye 1281. Probably 'the fence or enclosure for roe-deer', OE rāh-hege, but 'the rough enclosure' if the first element is OE rūh.

Rogart Highland. Rothegorth c.1230. Gaelic ro-ghorst 'by field'.

Rogate W. Sussex. Ragata 12th cent. 'Gate for roe-deer'. OE rā + geat.

Rogerstone Newpt. Rogerston 1535. 'Roger's farm'. OGerman pers. name + OE tūn.

Rogeston Pemb. Villa Rogeri 14th cent., Rogeriston 1370. 'Roger's farm'. OGerman pers. name + OE tūn.

Rohallion Perth. 'Fort of the Caledonians'. Gaelic ràth.

Rollesby Norfolk. Rollesby 1044–7, Rotholfuesby 1086 (DB). 'Farmstead or village of a man called Hrólfr'. OScand. pers. name + bý.

Rolleston Leics. Rovestone 1086 (DB). 'Farmstead of a man called Hrōthwulf or Hrólfr'. OE or OScand. pers. name + OE tūn.

Rolleston Notts. Roldestun 1086 (DB). 'Farmstead of a man called Hróaldr OScand. pers. name + OE tūn.

Rolleston Staffs. Rothulfeston. 941, Rolvestune 1086 (DB). Identical in origin with ROLLESTON (Leics.).

Rollright, Great & Rollright, Little Oxon. Rollandri |sic| 1086 (DB), Rollendricht 1091. Probably 'property of a man called *Hrolla'. OE pers. name + land-riht.

Rolvenden Kent. Rovindene |sic| 1086 (DB), Ruluinden 1185. 'Woodland pasture associated with a man called Hrōthwulf'. OE pers. name + -ing- + denn.

Romaldkirk Durham. Rumoldesc(h)erce 1086 (DB). 'Church dedicated to St Rūmwald'. OE pers. name + OScand. kirkja.

Romanby N. Yorks. Romundrebi 1086 (DB). 'Farmstead or village of a man called Róthmundr'. OScand. pers. name + bý.

Romansleigh Devon. Liega 1086 (DB), Reymundesle 1228. 'The wood or clearing'. OE lēah, with the later addition of the Celtic saint's name Rumon from the dedication of the church.

Romford Gtr. London. Romfort 1177. Probably 'wide or spacious ford'. OE rūm + ford. The river-name **Rom** is a 'back-formation' from the place-name.

Romiley Gtr. Manch. Rumelie 1086 (DB). 'Spacious woodland clearing'. OE rūm + lēah.

Romney, Old & Romney, New Kent. Rumenea 895, 11th cent., Romenel 1086 (DB). Originally a river-name, from OE ēa 'river' and an uncertain first element, perhaps *Rūmen 'the broad one' which may be an old name for **Romney Marsh**. Settlers here are referred to as Merscware as early as the 8th cent., 'the marsh dwellers' from OE mersc + -ware.

Romsey Hants. Rummæsig c.970, Romesy 1086 (DB). 'Island, or dry ground in marsh, of a man called *Rūm'. OE pers. name + ēg.

Romsley, probably 'wood or clearing of the raven', OE hræfn, hremn + lēah: **Romsley** Heref. & Worcs. Romesle 1270. **Romsley** Shrops. Hremesleage 1002, Rameslege 1086 (DB).

Rona (island) W. Isles. 'Rough island'. OScand. hraun + ey.

Rookhope Durham. Rochop 1242. 'Valley frequented by rooks'. OE hrōc + hop.

Rookley I. of Wight. Roclee 1202. 'Wood or clearing frequented by rooks'. OE hrōc + lēah.

Roos E. R. Yorks. Rosse 1086 (DB). Celtic *ros 'moor, heath, promontory'.

Roose Cumbria. Rosse 1086 (DB). Identical in origin with the previous name.

Ropley Hants. Roppele 1172. 'Woodland clearing of a man called *Hroppa'. OE pers. name + lēah.

Ropsley Lincs. Ropeslai 1086 (DB). Probably 'woodland clearing of a man called *Hropp'. OE pers. name + lēah.

Rorrington Shrops. Roritune 1086 (DB). 'Estate associated with a man called *Hrōr'. OE pers. name + -ing- + tūn.

Rosbeg (Ros Beag) Donegal. 'Little point'.

Rosbercon (Ros Ó mBearchón) Kilkenny. 'Uí Bhearchon's grove'.

Roscommon (Ros Comáin) Roscommon. 'Comán's grove'.

Roscor (Ros Corr) Fermanagh. 'Pointed promontory'.

Roscrea (Ros Cré) Tipperary. 'Cré's point'.

Rose Ash Devon. *Aissa* 1086 (DB), *Assherowes* 1281. '(Place at) the ash-tree'. OE *æsc*, with later manorial affix from possession by a man called Ralph in the late 12th cent.

Roseacre Lancs. *Raysacre* 1283. 'Cultivated land with a cairn'. OScand. *hreysi* + *akr*.

Rosedale Abbey N. Yorks. *Russedal* c.1140. 'Valley of the horses, or of a man called Rossi'. OScand. *hross* or pers. name + *dalr*.

Roseden Northum. *Russeden* 1242. 'Valley where rushes grow'. OE **rysc* + *denu*.

Roseland Cornwall, *see* ST JUST.

Rosemarket Pemb. *Rosmarche* c.1230. 'Roose market'. The medieval market was named from the cantref of *Rhos* (Welsh *rhos*, 'moor').

Rosemarkie Highland. *Rosmarkensis* 1128. 'Point of land by the horse stream'. Gaelic *ros* + *marc* + *-nidh*.

Rosenallis (*Ros Fhionnghlaise*) Laois. 'Grove of the bright stream'.

Rosgill Cumbria. *Rossegile* late 12th cent. 'Ravine of the horses'. OScand. *hross* + *gil*.

Rosguil (*Ros Goill*) Donegal. 'Goll's promontory'.

Roslea (*Ros Liath*) Fermanagh. 'Grey grove'.

Rosley Cumbria. *Rosseleye* 1272. 'Woodland clearing where horses are kept'. OScand. *hross* + OE *lēah*.

Rosliston Derbys. *Redlauestun* 1086 (DB). Probably 'farmstead of a man called Hrōthlāf'. OE pers. name + *tūn*.

Rosmuck (*Ros Muc*) Galway. 'Headland of pigs'.

Rosnakill (*Ros na Cille*) Donegal. 'Grove of the church'.

Ross, 'hill-spur, moor, heathy upland', Celtic **ros*: **Ross** Northum. *Rosse* 1208–10. **Ross on Wye** Heref. & Worcs. *Rosse* 1086 (DB). Wye is an ancient pre-English river-name of unknown origin and meaning.

Ross (*Ros*) Meath. 'Grove'.

Ross (the historic county). 'Moorland or promontory'. Gaelic *ros*.

Ross Carbery (*Ros Ó gCairbre*) Cork. 'Uí Chairbre's point'.

Ross, Lough (*Loch Rois*) Armagh, Galway, Monaghan. 'Lake of the grove'.

Rossadrehid (*Ros an Droichid*) Tipperary. 'Grove of the bridge'.

Rosscahill (*Ros Chathail*) Galway. 'Cahill's grove'.

Rosses, The (*Na Rosa*) (district) Donegal. (*do na*) *Rosaibh* 1603. 'The promontories'.

Rossett (*Yr Orsedd*) Wrex. *Rhossedh* c.1700. '(Place by) the hill'. Welsh *yr* + *gorsedd*.

Rossinan (*Ros Fhionáin*) Kilkenny. 'Fionán's grove'.

Rossington S. Yorks. *Rosington* c.1190. Probably 'farmstead at the moor'. Celtic **ros* + OE *-ing-* + *tūn*.

Rossinver (*Ros Inbhir*) Leitrim. 'Grove of the estuary'.

Rosslare (*Ros Láir*) Wexford. 'Middle promontory'.

Rossmore (*Ros Mór*) Cork, Galway. 'Big promontory'.

Rostherne Ches. *Rodestorne* 1086 (DB). 'Thorn-tree of a man called Rauthr'. OScand. pers. name + OE *thorn* or *thyrne*.

Roston Derbys. *Roschintone* 1086 (DB). Possibly 'estate associated with a man called *Hrōthsige'. OE pers. name + *-ing-* + *tūn*.

Rostrevor (*Ros Treabhair*) Down. *Rose Trevor* 1613. 'Trevor's wood'. Edward Trevor, a Welshman, commanded the English garrison at Newry at the end of the Nine Years War (1594–1603) and later acquired land here.

Rosturk (*Ros Toirc*) Mayo. 'Grove of the boar'.

Rosyth Fife. *Rossyth* c.1170, *Westir Rossith* 1363. Meaning uncertain.

Rothbury Northum. *Routhebiria*. c.1125. 'Stronghold of a man called *Hrōtha'. OE pers. name + *burh* (dative *byrig*). Alternatively the first element may be OScand. *rauthr* 'red' (from the colour of the bed-rock in the area).

Rotherby Leics. *Redebi* 1086 (DB). 'Farmstead or village of a man called Hreitharr or *Hreithi'. OScand. pers. name + *bý*.

Rotherfield, 'open land where cattle graze', OE *hrȳther* + *feld*: **Rotherfield** E. Sussex. *Hrytheranfeld* c.880, *Reredfelle* |*sic*| 1086 (DB). **Rotherfield Greys** & **Rotherfield Peppard** Oxon. *Redrefeld* 1086 (DB), *Retherfeld Grey* 1313, *Ruderefeld Pippard* 1255. Manorial affixes from early possession by the de Gray and Pipard families.

Rotherham S. Yorks. *Rodreham* 1086 (DB). 'Homestead or village on the River Rother'. Celtic river-name (meaning 'chief river') + OE *hām*.

Rotherhithe Gtr. London. *Rederheia* c.1105. 'Landing-place for cattle'. OE *hrȳther* + *hȳth*.

Rothersthorpe Northants. *Torp* 1086 (DB), *Retherestorp* 1231. 'Outlying farm or hamlet of the counsellor or advocate'. OScand. *thorp* with the later addition of OE *rǣdere*.

Rotherwick Hants. *Hrytheruuica*. c.1100. 'Cattle farm'. OE *hrȳther* + *wīc*.

Rothes Moray. *Rothes* 1238. '(Place by the) fort'. Gaelic *ràth*. *See also* GLENROTHES. 1238 *Rothes*.

Rothesay Arg (Bute). *Rothersay* 1321. 'Rother's island'. OScand. *ey*. The pers. name is that of *Roderick*, the son of Reginald, to whom Bute was granted in the 13th cent. 1321 *Rothersay*.

Rothley, probably 'wood with clearings', OE **roth* + *lēah*: **Rothley** Leics. *Rodolei* 1086 (DB). **Rothley** Northum. *Rotheley* 1233.

Rothwell, 'spring or stream by the clearing(s)', OE **roth* + *wella*: **Rothwell** Lincs. *Rodowelle* 1086 (DB). **Rothwell** Northants. *Rodewelle* 1086 (DB). **Rothwell** W. Yorks. *Rodewelle* 1086 (DB).

Rotsea E. R. Yorks. *Rotesse* 1086 (DB). 'Pool with scum on it', or 'pool of a man called Rōta'. OE *hrot* or pers. name + *sǣ*.

Rottingdean E. Sussex. *Rotingedene* 1086 (DB). Probably 'valley of the family or followers of a man called Rōta'. OE pers. name + *-inga-* + *denu*.

Rottington Cumbria. *Rotingtona. c.*1125. 'Estate associated with a man called Rōt(a)'. OE pers. name + *-ing-* + *tūn*.

Rougham, probably 'homestead or village on rough ground', OE *rūh* + *hām*: **Rougham** Norfolk. *Ruhham* 1086 (DB). **Rougham Green** Suffolk. *Rucham c.*950, *Ruhham* 1086 (DB).

Roughton Lincs. *Rocstune* 1086 (DB). 'Rough farm', or 'rye farm'. OE *rūh* or OScand. *rugr* (replacing OE *ryge*) + OE *tūn*.

Roughton Norfolk. *Rugutune* 1086 (DB). Identical in origin with the previous name.

Roughton Shrops. *Roughton* 1316. 'Farmstead on rough ground'. OE *rūh* + *tūn*.

Roughty (*An Ruachtach*) (river) Kerry. 'The destructive one'.

Roundhay W. Yorks. *La Rundehaia c.*1180. 'Round enclosure'. OFrench *rond* + OE *hæg*.

Roundstone (*Cloch na Rón*) Galway. 'Stone of the seals'. Irish *rón* gave English *round*.

Roundway Wilts. *Rindweiam* 1149. Probably 'cleared way'. OE *rȳmed* + *weg*.

Rounton, East & *Rounton, West* N. Yorks. *Rontun, Runtune* 1086 (DB), *Rungtune c.*1130. 'Farmstead enclosed with poles, or near a causeway made with poles'. OE *hrung* + *tūn*.

Rous Lench Heref. & Worcs., *see* LENCH.

Rousay (island) Orkn. *Hrolfsey c.*1260. 'Hrólfr's island'. OScand. pers. name + *ey*.

Rousdon Devon. *Done* 1086 (DB), *Rawesdon* 1285. '(Place at) the hill'. OE *dūn*, with manorial affix from the family of Ralph here from the 12th cent.

Routh E. R. Yorks. *Rutha* 1086 (DB). Possibly 'rough shaly ground'. OScand. *hrúthr*.

Rowde Wilts. *Rode* 1086 (DB). Probably '(place at) the reed bed'. OE *hrēod*.

Rower, The (*An Robhar*) Kilkenny. 'The flood'.

Rowhedge Essex. *Rouhegy* 1346. 'Rough hedge or enclosure'. OE *rūh* + *hecg*.

Rowland Derbys. *Ralunt* 1086 (DB). 'Boundary grove', or 'grove frequented by roe-deer'. OScand. *rá* + *lundr*.

Rowlands Castle Hants. *Rolokescastel c.*1315, *Roulandes Castell* 1369. Originally 'castle of a man called Rolok', from ME *castel* and an OFrench pers. name, but later apparently changed through association with the heroic knight Roland of medieval legend.

Rowley, 'rough wood or clearing', OE *rūh* + *lēah*: **Rowley** E. R. Yorks. *Rulee* 12th cent. **Rowley Hill** W. Yorks. *Ruleia c.*1180. **Rowley Regis** W. Mids. *Roelea* 1173. Affix is Latin *regis* 'of the king' from early possession by the Crown.

Rowsham Bucks. *Rollesham* 1170. 'Homestead or village of a man called Hrōthwulf'. OE pers. name + *hām*.

Rowsley Derbys. *Reuslege |sic|* 1086 (DB), *Rolvesle* 1204. 'Woodland clearing of a man called Hrōthwulf or Hrólfr'. OE or OScand. pers. name + OE *lēah*.

Rowston Lincs. *Rouestune* 1086 (DB). Possibly 'farmstead of a man called Hrólfr'. OScand. pers. name + OE *tūn*. Alternatively the first element may be OE *hrōf* 'roof', perhaps in some topographical sense.

Rowton Ches. *Rowa Christletona* 12th cent., *Roweton* 13th cent. 'The rough part of CHRISTLETON'. OE *rūh* + *tūn*.

Rowton Shrops., near High Ercall. *Routone |sic|* 1086 (DB), *Rowelton* 1195. Possibly 'farmstead by a rough hill'. OE *rūh* + *hyll* + *tūn*. Alternatively the first element may be an OE **rūhel* 'small rough place'.

Roxburgh Sc. Bord. *Rocisburc* 1127. 'Hroc's fortress'. OE pers. name + *burh*.

Roxby N. Lincs. *Roxebi* 1086 (DB). 'Farmstead or village of a man called Hrókr'. OScand. pers. name + *bý*.

Roxby N. Yorks., near Hinderwell. *Roscebi* 1086 (DB). 'Farmstead or village of a man called Rauthr'. OScand. pers. name + *bý*.

Roxton Beds. *Rochesdone* 1086 (DB). Probably 'hill of a man called **Hrōc*'. OE pers. name + *dūn*.

Roxwell Essex. *Rokeswelle* 1291. Probably 'spring or stream of a man called **Hrōc*'. OE pers. name + *wella*.

Royal Leamington Spa Warwicks., *see* LEAMINGTON.

Roydon Essex. *Ruindune* 1086 (DB). 'Hill where rye is grown'. OE *rygen* + *dūn*.

Roydon Norfolk, near Diss. *Rygedune c.*1035, *Regadona* 1086 (DB). 'Rye hill'. OE *ryge* + *dūn*.

Royston Herts. *Roiston* 1286. Originally called *Crux Roaisie* 1184 'cross (Latin *crux*) of a woman called Rohesia', later simply *Roeys* to which *tūn* 'village' was added in the 13th cent.

Royston S. Yorks. *Rorestone* 1086 (DB). 'Farmstead of a man called **Hrōr* or **Róarr*'. OE or OScand. pers. name + OE *tūn*.

Royton Gtr. Manch. *Ritton* 1226. 'Farmstead where rye is grown'. OE *ryge* + *tūn*.

Ruabon (*Rhiwabon*) Wrex. *Rywuabon* 1291, *Rhiwvabon* 1394. 'Mabon's hill'. Welsh *rhiw*. The identity of *Mabon* is uncertain.

Ruan, named from the patron saint of the parish, St Ruan or Rumon: **Ruan Lanihorne** Cornwall. *Lanryhorn* 1270, 'parish of *Sanctus Rumonus* of *Lanyhorn*' 1327. The second part of the name means 'church-site of a man called **Rihoarn*', Cornish **lann* + pers. name. **Ruan Minor** Cornwall. 'Church of *Sanctus Rumonus Parvus*' 1277. Affix is Latin *minor* 'smaller' (earlier *parvus* 'small') to distinguish it from the adjacent parish of Ruan Major.

Ruardean Glos. *Rwirdin* 1086 (DB). 'Rye or hill enclosure'. OE *ryge* or Celtic **riu* + OE *worthign*.

Rubane (*Rú Bán*) Down. *Rowbane c.*1615. 'White clearing'.

Rubery Heref. & Worcs. *Robery Hills* 1650. 'Rough mound or hill'. OE *rūh* + *beorg*.

Ruckcroft Cumbria. *Rucroft* 1211. 'Rye enclosure'. OScand. *rugr* + OE *croft*.

Ruckinge Kent. *Hroching* 786, *Rochinges* 1086 (DB). 'Place characterized by rooks', or 'place associated with a man called *Hrōc'. OE *hrōc* or pers. name + *-ing*.

Ruckland Lincs. *Rocheland* |*sic*| 1086 (DB), *Roclund* 12th cent. 'Grove frequented by rooks'. OScand. *hrókr* + *lundr*.

Ruddington Notts. *Roddintone* 1086 (DB). 'Estate associated with a man called Rudda'. OE pers. name + *-ing-* + *tūn*.

Rudford Glos. *Rudeford* 1086 (DB). 'Ford among the reeds'. OE *hrēod* + *ford*.

Rudge Shrops. *Rigge* 1086 (DB). '(Place at) the ridge'. OE *hrycg*.

Rudgwick W. Sussex. *Regwic* 1210. 'Dwelling or farm on a ridge'. OE *hrycg* + *wīc*.

Rudham, East & *Rudham, West* Norfolk. *Rudeham* 1086 (DB). 'Homestead or village of a man called Rudda'. OE pers. name + *hām*.

Rudston E. R. Yorks. *Rodestan* 1086 (DB). '(Place at) the rood-stone or stone cross'. OE *rōd-stān*.

Rudyard Staffs. *Rudegeard* 1002, *Rudierd* 1086 (DB). Probably 'yard or enclosure where rue is grown'. OE *rūde* + *geard*.

Rue Point (*Rubha*) Antrim. 'Clearing'.

Rufford Lancs. *Ruchford* 1212. 'Rough ford'. OE *rūh* + *ford*.

Rufforth York. *Ruford* 1086 (DB). Identical in origin with the previous name.

Rugby Warwicks. *Rocheberie* 1086 (DB), *Rokebi* 1200. 'Fortified place of a man called *Hrōca'. OE pers. name + *burh* (dative *byrig*) replaced by OScand. *bȳ* 'village'. Alternatively 'fort frequented by rooks', with OE *hrōc* as first element.

Rugeley Staffs. *Rugelie* 1086 (DB). 'Woodland clearing on or near a ridge'. OE *hrycg* + *lēah*.

Ruishton Somerset. *Risctun* 9th cent. 'Farmstead where rushes grow'. OE *rysc* + *tūn*.

Ruislip Gtr. London. *Rislepe* 1086 (DB). Probably 'leaping-place (across the river) where rushes grow'. OE *rysc* + *hlȳp*.

Rum (island) Highland. *Ruim* 677. Probably pre-Celtic.

Rumburgh Suffolk. *Romburch* c.1050, *Ramburc* |*sic*| 1086 (DB). 'Wide stronghold, or stronghold built of tree-trunks'. OE *rūm* or *hruna* + *burh*.

Runcorn Ches. *Rumcofan* c.1000. 'Wide bay or creek'. OE *rūm* + *cofa*.

Runcton W. Sussex. *Rochintone* 1086 (DB). 'Estate associated with a man called *Hrōc(a)'. OE pers. name + *-ing-* + *tūn*.

Runcton, North *Runcton, South*, & *Runcton Holme* Norfolk. *Runghetuna* 1086 (DB), *Rungeton Holm* 1276. 'Farmstead enclosed with poles, or near a causeway made with poles'. OE *hrung* + *tūn*. Holme is probably OScand. *holmr* 'island, raised ground in marsh'.

Runfold Surrey. *Hrunigfeall* 974. 'Place where trees have been felled'. OE *hruna* + **(ge)feall*.

Runhall Norfolk. *Runhal* 1086 (DB). Possibly 'nook of land where there are tree-trunks'. OE **hruna* + *halh*.

Runham Norfolk. *Ronham* 1086 (DB). Possibly 'homestead or enclosure of a man called *Rūna', OE pers. name + *hām* or *hamm*. Alternatively the first element may be OE **hruna* 'tree-trunk', perhaps with reference to its use as a footbridge.

Runnington Somerset. *Runetone* 1086 (DB). Probably 'farmstead of a man called *Rūna'. OE pers. name (genitive *-n*) + *tūn*.

Runnymede Surrey. *Ronimede* 1215. 'Meadow at the island where councils are held'. OE *rūn* + *ēg* + *mǣd*.

Runswick N. Yorks. *Reneswike* 1273. Possibly 'creek of a man called Reinn'. OScand. pers. name + *vík*.

Runton, East & *Runton, West* Norfolk. *Runetune* 1086 (DB). 'Farmstead of a man called *Rūna or *Rúni'. OE or OScand. pers. name + OE *tūn*.

Runwell Essex. *Runewelle* c.940, *Runewella* 1086 (DB). 'Council spring', i.e. probably 'wishing-well'. OE *rūn* + *wella*.

Ruscombe Berks. *Rothescamp* 1091. 'Enclosed land of a man called *Rōt'. OE pers. name + *camp*.

Rush (*Ros*) Dublin. 'Promontory'.

Rushall Norfolk. *Riuessala* 1086 (DB). OE *halh* 'nook of land' with an uncertain first element, probably a pers. name.

Rushall Wilts. *Rusteselve* |*sic*| 1086 (DB), *Rusteshala* 1160. Probably 'nook of land of a man called *Rust'. OE pers. name + *halh*.

Rushbrooke Suffolk. *Ryssebroc* c.950, *Ryscebroc* 1086 (DB). 'Brook where rushes grow'. OE **rysc* + *brōc*.

Rushbury Shrops. *Riseberie* 1086 (DB). 'Fortified house or manor among the rushes'. OE **rysc* + *burh* (dative *byrig*).

Rushden, 'valley where rushes grow', OE **ryscen* + *denu*: **Rushden** Herts. *Risendene* 1086 (DB). **Rushden** Northants. *Risedene* 1086 (DB).

Rushford Suffolk. *Rissewrth* c.1060, *Rusceuuorda* 1086 (DB). 'Enclosure where rushes grow'. OE **rysc* + *worth*.

Rushmere, 'pool where rushes grow', OE **rysc* + *mere*: **Rushmere** Suffolk. *Ryscemara* 1086 (DB). **Rushmere St Andrew** Suffolk. *Ryscemara* 1086 (DB). Affix from the dedication of the church.

Rushock Heref. & Worcs. *Russococ* |*sic*| 1086 (DB), *Rossoc* 1166. Probably 'rushy place, rush-bed'. OE **ryscuc*.

Rusholme Gtr. Manch. *Russum* 1235. '(Place at) the rushes'. OE **rysc* in a dative plural form **ryscum*.

Rushton, 'farmstead where rushes grow', OE **rysc* + *tūn*: **Rushton** Ches. *Rusitone* 1086 (DB). **Rushton** Northants. *Risetone* 1086 (DB). **Rushton Spencer** Staffs. *Risetone* 1086 (DB). Manorial affix from early possession by the Spencer family.

Rushwick Heref. & Worcs. *Russewyk* 1275. 'Dairy farm among the rushes'. OE **rysc* + *wīc*.

Ruskey (*Rúscaigh*) Roscommon. 'Morass'.

Ruskington Lincs. *Rischintone* 1086 (DB). 'Farmstead where rushes grow'. OE **ryscen* (with Scand. *-sk-*) + *tūn*.

Rusland Cumbria. *Rolesland* 1336. 'Cultivated land of a man called Hrólfr or Hróaldr'. OScand. pers. name + *land*.

Rusper W. Sussex. *Rusparre* 1219. '(Place at) the rough spar or beam of wood'. OE *rūh* + **spearr*.

Rustington W. Sussex. *Rustinton* 1180. 'Estate associated with a man called **Rust(a)*'. OE pers. name + *-ing-* + *tūn*.

Ruston N. Yorks. *Rostune* 1086 (DB). Possibly 'farmstead distinguished by its roof-beams or rafters'. OE **hrōst* + *tūn*.

Ruston Parva E. R. Yorks. *Roreston* 1086 (DB). 'Farmstead of a man called **Hrōr* or **Róarr*'. OE or OScand. pers. name + OE *tūn*. Affix is Latin *parva* 'little' to distinguish this place from LONG RISTON.

Ruston, East & *Ruston, Sco* Norfolk. *Ristuna* 1086 (DB), *Estriston* 1361, *Scouriston* c.1280. 'Farmstead near or among brushwood'. OE *hrīs* + *tūn*. Distinguishing affixes are OE *ēast* and OScand. *skógr* 'wood'.

Ruswarp N. Yorks. *Risewarp* c.1146. Possibly 'silted land overgrown with brushwood'. OE *hrīs* + *wearp*.

Rutherglen Glas. *Ruthirglen* c.1160. 'Red valley'. Gaelic *gleann*. First element obscure.

Ruthin (*Rhuthun*) Denb. *Ruthin* 1253. 'Red fort'. Welsh *rhudd* + *din*.

Ruthven Highland. 'Red stone'. *Cp*. Welsh *rhuddfaen*.

Ruthwell Dumf. Possibly 'spring by a cross'. OE *rōd* + *wella*.

Rutland (the county). *Roteland* c.1060, 1086 (DB). 'Estate of a man called Rōta'. OE pers. name + *land*.

Rutland Island Donegal. *Rutland* 1837. The original Irish name of the island was *Inis Mhic an Doirn*, 'island of the son of Dorn'. It was renamed as now in 1785 in honour of Charles Manners, 4th Duke of Rutland, appointed Lord Lieutenant of Ireland the previous year.

Ruyton-XI-Towns Shrops. *Ruitone* 1086 (DB). 'Farmstead where rye is grown'. OE *ryge* + *tūn*. The parish was formerly composed of eleven townships.

Ryal Northum. *Ryhill* 1242. 'Hill where rye is grown'. OE *ryge* + *hyll*.

Ryarsh Kent. *Riesce |sic|* 1086 (DB), *Rierssh* 1242. 'Ploughed field used for rye'. OE *ryge* + *ersc*.

Ryburgh, Great & *Ryburgh, Little* Norfolk. *Reie(n)burh* 1086 (DB). Probably 'old encampment used for growing rye'. OE *ryge(n)* + *burh*.

Rydal Cumbria. *Ridale* 1240. 'Valley where rye is grown'. OE *ryge* + OScand. *dalr*.

Ryde I. of Wight. *La Ride* 1257. 'The small stream'. OE *rīth*.

Rye E. Sussex. *Ria* 1130. '(Place at) the island or dry ground in marsh'. OE *īeg*, with initial *R-* from ME *atter* 'at the'.

Rye (river) N. Yorks., *see* RIEVAULX.

Ryehill, *Ryhill*, 'hill where rye is grown', OE *ryge* + *hyll*: **Ryehill** E. R. Yorks. *Ryel* c.1155. **Ryhill** W. Yorks. *Rihella* 1086 (DB).

Ryhall Rutland. *Righale* c.1050, *Riehale* 1086 (DB). 'Land in a river-bend where rye is grown'. OE *ryge* + *halh*.

Ryhope Tyne & Wear. *Reofhoppas* c.1050. Possibly 'rough valleys or enclosures', OE *hrēof* + *hop* (originally in a plural form). Alternatively the first element may be OE *rēfa* 'a reeve, a bailiff'.

Ryknild or *Icknield Street*, *see* ICKNIELD WAY.

Ryle, Great & *Ryle, Little* Northum. *Rihull* 1212. 'Hill where rye is grown'. OE *ryge* + *hyll*.

Rylstone N. Yorks. *Rilestun* 1086 (DB). OE *tūn* 'farmstead' with an uncertain first element, possibly OE *rynel* 'a small stream'.

Ryme Intrinseca Dorset. *Rima* 1160. '(Place at) the edge or border'. OE *rima*. Latin affix means 'inner', distinguishing this place from the former manor of Ryme Extrinseca ('outer').

Ryston Norfolk. *Ristuna* 1086 (DB). 'Farmstead near or among brushwood'. OE *hrīs* + *tūn*.

Ryther N. Yorks. *Ridre* 1086 (DB). '(Place at) the clearing'. OE **ryther*.

Ryton, usually 'farm where rye is grown', OE *ryge* + *tūn*: **Ryton** Shrops. *Ruitone* 1086 (DB). **Ryton** Tyne & Wear. *Ritona* 1183. **Ryton, Great** Shrops. *Ruiton* 1209. **Ryton-on-Dunsmore** Warwicks. *Ruyton* c.1045, *Rietone* 1086 (DB). Dunsmore (*Dunesmore* 12th cent.) is an old district name meaning 'moor of a man called Dunn', OE pers. name + *mōr*.

However the following has a different origin: **Ryton** N. Yorks. *Ritun* 1086 (DB). 'Farmstead on the River Rye'. Celtic river-name (*see* RIEVAULX) + OE *tūn*.

Sabden Lancs. *Sapeden c.*1140. 'Valley where fir-trees grow'. OE *sæppe* + *denu*.

Sacombe Herts. *Sueuecampe* 1086 (DB). 'Enclosed land of a man called *Swæfa*'. OE pers. name + *camp*.

Sacriston Durham. *Segrysteynhogh* 1312. 'Hill-spur of the sacristan (of Durham)'. ME *secrestein* + OE *hōh*.

Sadberge Durham. *Sadberge* 1169. OScand. *set-berg* 'a flat-topped hill'.

Saddington Leics. *Sadintone* 1086 (DB). OE *tūn* 'farmstead, estate' with an uncertain first element, possibly a reduced form of an OE pers. name such as Sægēat or *Sæhæth with *-ing-*, or OE *sēath* 'pit' with *-ing*.

Saddle Bow Norfolk. *Sadelboge* 1198. 'The saddle-bow', referring to some arched or curved feature. OE *sadol* + *boga*.

Saddleworth Gtr. Manch. *Sadelwrth* late 12th cent. 'Enclosure on a saddle-shaped ridge'. OE *sadol* + *worth*.

Saffron Walden Essex, *see* WALDEN.

Sageston Pemb. *Sagerston* 1362. 'Sager's farm'. OE *tūn*.

Saggart (*Teach Sagart*) Dublin. 'Sagra's house'.

Saham Toney Norfolk. *Saham* 1086 (DB), *Saham Tony* 1498. 'Homestead by the pool'. OE *sæ* + *hām*. Manorial affix from the de Toni family, here in the late 12th cent.

Saighton Ches. *Saltone* 1086 (DB). 'Farmstead where willow-trees grow'. OE *salh* + *tūn*.

Sain Nicolas. See ST NICHOLAS (Vale Glam).

St Agnes Cornwall. 'Parish of *Sancta Agnes*' 1327. From the dedication of the church to St Agnes.

St Albans Herts. *Sancte Albanes stow* 1007, *Villa Sancti Albani* 1086 (DB). 'Holy place of St Alban', from the saint martyred here in AD 209. The early spellings contain OE *stōw* 'holy place' and Latin *villa* 'town'. *See also* WATLING STREET.

Saint Andras. See ST ANDREWS MAJOR.

St Andrews Fife. *Sancti Andree c.*1158. '(Place with the shrine of) St Andrew'. The relics of St Andrew are said to have been brought here in the 8th cent.

St Andrews Major (*Saint Andras*) Vale Glam. *Sancti Andree* 1254. '(Church of) St Andrew'. *Major* distinguishes the place from St Andrews Minor.

St Asaph (*Llanelwy*) Denb. *Sancto Asaph* 1291. '(Church of) St Asaph'. The Welsh name means 'church by the River Elwy' (Welsh *llan*), the river name meaning 'driving one'.

St Austell Cornwall. 'Church of *Austol* c.*1150. From the dedication of the parish church to St Austol.

St Bees Cumbria. 'Church of *Sancta Bega* c.*1135. Named from St Bega, a female saint.

St Blazey Cornwall. 'Chapel of *Sanctus Blasius*' 1440. From the dedication of the church to St Blaise.

St Breock Cornwall. 'Church of *Sanctus Briocus*' 1259. From the patron saint of the church, St Brioc.

St Breward Cornwall. 'Church of *Sanctus Brewveredus*' c.*1190. From the patron saint of the church, St Breward.

St Briavels Glos. '(Castle of) *Sanctus Briauel*' 1130. Named from the Welsh saint Briavel.

St Brides Pemb. *Sancta Brigida* 1242. '(Church of) St Bridget'.

St Budeaux Devon. *Seynt Bodokkys* 1520. From the dedication of the church to the Celtic saint Budoc. Earlier *Bucheside* 1086 (DB). 'St Budoc's hide of land', OE *hīd*.

St Buryan Cornwall. 'Church of *Sancta Beriana* c.*939, *Sancta Berriona* 1086 (DB). Named from St Beryan, a female saint.

St Clears (*Sanclêr*) Carm. *Sancto Claro* 1291, *Seint Cler* 1331. '(Church of) St Clear'.

St Cleer Cornwall. 'Church of *Sanctus Clarus*' 1212. From the patron saint of the church, St Cleer.

St Columb Major & *St Columb Minor* Cornwall. 'Church of *Sancta Columba* c.*1240. Named from St Columba, a female saint.

St Cross South Elmham Suffolk, *see* ELMHAM.

St David's (*Tyddewi*) Pemb. *Ty Dewi* 1586. '(Church of) St David'. The Welsh name means 'house of Dewi' (Welsh *tŷ* + *Dewi*). (Dewi being one of the Welsh forms of *David*.)

St Devereux Heref. & Worcs. 'Church of *Sanctus Dubricius*' 1291. Named from St Dyfrig, a male Welsh saint.

St Dogmaels (*Llandudoch*) Pemb. *Sancti Dogmaelis c.*1208. (Church of) St Dogmael'. The Welsh name apparently means 'St Tydoch's church' (Welsh *llan*), although no such saint is known.

St Dogwells (*Llantydewi*) Pemb. *Ecclesia St. Dogmaelis* 1215. '(Church of) St Dogmael'. *Cp.* ST DOGMAELS. The Welsh name apparently means 'church of the house of St David' (Welsh *llan* + *tŷ* + *Dewi*), perhaps by association with ST DAVID´S.

St Endellion Cornwall. 'Church of *Sancta Endelienta*' 1260. Named from St Endilient, a female saint.

St Florence Pemb. *Sanctus Florencius* 1248. '(Church of) St Florence'.

St George's (*Llan Sain Siôr*) Vale Glam. *Sancti Georgii* 1254. '(Church of) St George'. The Welsh name translates the English (Welsh *llan*, 'church').

St Germans Cornwall. 'Church of *Sanctus Germanus*' 1086 (DB). From the patron saint of the church.

St Giles in the Wood Devon. *Stow St Giles* 1330. 'Holy place of St Giles', from OE *stōw* and the patron saint of the church.

St Giles on the Heath Devon. 'Chapel of *Sanctus Egidius*' 1202, *St Gylses en le Hethe* 1585. From the dedication of the church to St Giles (Latin *Egidius*), with affix 'on the heath' from OE *hǣth*.

St Helens I. of Wight. *Sancta Elena* 12th cent. From the dedication of the church to St Helena.

St Helens Mersey., named from the chapel of St Helen, first recorded in 1552.

St Ippollitts Herts. 'Church of *S. Ypollitus*' 1283. From the dedication of the 11th cent. church here to St Hippolytus.

St Ishmael's Pemb. *Ecclesia Sancti Ismael* 1291. '(Church of) St Ishmael'.

St Issey Cornwall. *Sanctus Ydi* 1195. From the dedication of the church to St Idi.

St Ive Cornwall. *Sanctus Yvo* 1201. From the dedication of the church to St Ivo, *see* next name.

St Ives Cambs. *Sancto Ivo de Slepe* 1110. Named from St Ivo whose relics were found here in the 10th cent. The earlier name *Slepe* is from OE **slæp* 'slippery place'.

St Ives Cornwall. *Sancta Ya* 1284. From the dedication of the church to St Ya, a female saint.

St Ives Dorset. *Iuez* 1167. 'Place overgrown with ivy'. OE **īfet*. *Saint* was only added in recent times on the analogy of the previous names.

St John's Point (*Rinn Eoin*) Down. *Ballihione al. Rinchione* 1549. 'Eoin's point'.

Saint Johnston (*Baile Seangean*) Donegal. *St Johnston* c.1655. The village is named after Saint Johnstone, the former name of PERTH, Scotland.

St Just Cornwall. 'Church of *Sanctus Justus*' 1291. From the dedication of the church to St Just. Often called **St Just in Penwith**, this last (*Penwid* 1186, probably 'end-district') being an old Cornish name for the Land's End peninsula.

St Just in Roseland Cornwall. 'Church of *Sanctus Justus*' c.1070. Identical in origin with the previous name. Roseland (*Roslande* 1259) is an old district name meaning 'promontory land', Cornish *ros* + OE *land*.

St Keverne Cornwall. *Sanctus Achebrannus* 1086 (DB). From the patron saint of the church, St Aghevran.

St Kew Cornwall. *Sanctus Cheus* 1086 (DB). From the patron saint of the church, St Kew. **St Kew Highway**, *Highway* 1699, is a hamlet so called from its situation on the main road to Wadebridge.

St Keyne Cornwall. 'Church of *Sancta Keyna*' 1291. Named from St Keyn, a female saint.

St Kilda (island) W. Isles. *Hert* 1370; *St. Kilda* 17th cent. Obscure origin.

St Lawrence, 'place with a church dedicated to St Lawrence': **St Lawrence** I. of Wight. 'Church of *Sanctus Laurencius*' 1255. Originally also called *Wathe* (*Wathe* 1311, *St Laurence de Wathe* 1340), '(place at) the ford' from OE *wæd*. **St Lawrence** Kent. 'Church of *Sanctus Laurencius*' 1253.

St Lawrence Pemb. *Rectoria Sancti Laurentii* 1535. '(Church of) St Lawrence'.

St Leonards E. Sussex. *Villa de Sancto Leonardo juxta Hasting* ('manor of St Leonard near to Hastings') 1288. Named from the dedication of the original church here, destroyed by the sea in the 15th cent.

St Leonards, Chapel Lincs., a late name, from the dedication of the chapel.

St Levan Cornwall. 'Parish of *Sanctus Silvanus*' 1327. From the dedication of the church to St Selevan.

St Lythans (*Llwyneliddon*) Vale Glam. *Luin Elidon* 1160, *Llan Leiddan* 1590. 'Eliddon's grove'. Welsh *llwyn* + pers. name. Original Welsh *llwyn* was later taken to be *llan*, 'church', suggesting a dedication to a St Lythan.

St Margaret's Island Pemb. *Little Caldey alias St Margaretts Island* 1718. 'St Margaret's island'. The island was originally known as *Little Caldy*. *See* CALDY ISLAND.

St Margaret's at Cliffe Kent. *Sancta Margarita* 1086 (DB), *Cliue* c.1100. 'Church dedicated to St Margaret at the place called Cliffe', from OE *clif* 'cliff'.

St Mary Bourne Hants., *see* BOURNE.

St Mary Cray Gtr. London, *see* CRAY.

St Mary's Bay Kent, named from St Mary in the Marsh (*Seyntemariecherche*, 1240), with affix from OE *mersc*.

St Mary's Hoo Kent, *see* HOO.

St Mawes Cornwall. 'Town of *Sanctus Maudetus*' 1284. From the patron saint of the church, St Maudyth.

St Mawgan Cornwall. 'Church of *Sanctus Mauchanus*' 1257. From the dedication of the church to St Mawgan, *see also* MAWGAN. **Mawgan Porth** is from Cornish *porth* 'cove'.

St Mellion Cornwall. 'Church of *Sanctus Melanus*' 1259. From the patron saint of the church, St Melaine.

St Merryn Cornwall. *Sancta Marina* 1259. Apparently named from St Marina (a female saint), but possibly from St Merin (a male).

St Mewan Cornwall. 'Church of *Sanctus Mawanus*' 1291. From the dedication of the church to St Mewan.

St Michael Caerhays Cornwall. 'Chapel of *Sanctus Michael de Karihaes*' 1259. From the dedication of the church to St Michael the Archangel. The distinguishing affix is from the manor of Caerhays, a name obscure in origin and meaning.

St Michael Penkevil Cornwall. 'Church of *Sanctus Michael de Penkevel*' 1261. From the same dedication as previous name. The affix is from the manor of Penkevil, a Cornish name probably meaning 'horse headland'.

St Michael's on Wyre Lancs. *Michelescherche* 1086 (DB). 'Church of St Michael', with OE *cirice* in the early spelling. Wyre is a Celtic river-name meaning 'winding one'.

St Monance Fife. *Sanct Monanis* 1565. '(Church of) St Monans'.

Saint Mullin's (*Tigh Moling*) Kilkenny. 'Moling's house'.

St Neot Cornwall. *Sanctus Neotus* 1086 (DB). From the patron saint of the church, St Neot.

St Neots Cambs. *S' Neod* 12th cent. Also named from St Neot, whose relics were brought here from Cornwall in the 10th cent.

St Nicholas (*Tremarchog*) Pemb. *Villa Camerarii* 1287, *Tremarchoc* 1551, *Saynt Nycolas* 1554. '(Church of) St Nicholas'. The Welsh name means 'knight's farm' (Welsh *tref* + *marchog*), the first form above being the Latin equivalent.

St Nicholas (*Sain Nicolas*) Vale Glam. *Sancto Nicholao* 1153. '(Church of) St Nicholas'.

St Nicholas at Wade Kent. *Villa Sancti Nicholai* 1254, *St Nicholas at Wade* 1458. Named from the dedication of the church. Wade is from OE *wæd* 'a ford, a crossing-place' (leading to the Isle of Thanet).

St Osyth Essex. *Seynte Osithe* 1046. From the dedication of a priory here to St Ōsgȳth, a 7th-cent. princess. Its early name *Cice* 1086 (DB) is from OE **cicc* 'a bend'.

St Paul's Cray Gtr. London, *see* CRAY.

St Peter's Kent. *Borgha sancti Petri* ('borough of St Peter') 1254. Named from the dedication of the church.

St Petrox Pemb. *Ecclesia de Sancto Petroco* 1291, *St Petrocks* 1603. '(Church of) St Petroc'.

St Quivox S. Ayr. '(Church of) St Caemhan'. The saint's name is represented in the form *Mochaemhoc*, with the Gaelic affectionate prefix *mo*, 'my', and the diminutive suffix *-oc*.

St Tudy Cornwall. *Hecglostudic* 1086 (DB). From the dedication of the church to St Tudy, with Cornish *eglos* 'church' in the early spelling.

St Weonards Heref. & Worcs. *Lann Sant Guainerth* c.1130. 'Church of St Gwennarth', with OWelsh **lann* 'church' in the early spelling.

St Winnow Cornwall. *San Winnuc* 1086 (DB). From the dedication of the church to St Winnoc.

Saintbury Glos. *Svineberie* |sic| 1086 (DB), *Seinesberia* 1186. 'Fortified place of a man called Sǣwine'. OE pers. name + *burh* (dative *byrig*).

Saintfield (*Tamhnaigh Naomh*) Down. *Tawnaghnym* 1605. 'Field of saints'.

Salcombe, 'salt valley', OE *sealt* + *cumb*: **Salcombe** Devon. *Saltecumbe* 1244. **Salcombe Regis** Devon. *Sealtcumbe* c.1060, *Selcome* 1086 (DB). Affix is Latin *regis* 'of the king'.

Salcott Essex. *Saltcot* c.1200. 'Building where salt is made or stored'. OE *sealt* + *cot*.

Sale Gtr. Manch. *Sale* c.1205. '(Place at) the sallow-tree'. OE *salh* in a dative form *sale*.

Saleby Lincs. *Salebi* 1086 (DB). Possibly 'farmstead or village of a man called Sali'. OScand. pers. name + *bý*. Alternatively the first element may be OE *salh* 'sallow, willow'.

Saleen (*Sáilín*) Cork. 'Little (arm of the) sea'.

Salehurst E. Sussex. *Salhert* |sic| 1086 (DB), *Salhirst* c.1210. 'Wooded hill where sallow-trees grow'. OE *salh* + *hyrst*.

Salesbury Lancs. *Sale(s)byry* 1246. 'Fortified place or manor where sallow-trees grow'. OE *salh* + *burh* (dative *byrig*).

Salford Beds. *Saleford* 1086 (DB). 'Ford where sallow-trees grow'. OE *salh* + *ford*.

Salford Gtr. Manch. *Salford* 1086 (DB). Identical in origin with the previous name.

Salford Oxon. *Saltford* 777, *Salford* 1086 (DB). 'Ford over which salt is carried'. OE *salt* + *ford*.

Salford Priors & *Abbots Salford* Warwicks. *Saltford* 714. *Salford* 1086 (DB). Identical in origin with the previous name. Affixes from early possession by Kenilworth Priory and Evesham Abbey.

Salfords Surrey. *Salford* 1279. 'Ford where sallow-trees grow'. OE *salh* + *ford*.

Salhouse Norfolk. *Salhus* 1291. Probably 'the sallow-trees'. OE *salh* in a plural form.

Saling, Great Essex. *Salinges* 1086 (DB). Possibly '(settlement of) the dwellers among the sallow-trees', OE *salh* + *-ingas*. Alternatively 'places where sallow-trees grow', from the plural of an OE word **sal(h)ing*.

Salisbury Wilts. *Searobyrg* c.900, *Sarisberie* 1086 (DB). 'Stronghold at *Sorvio*'. OE *burh* (dative *byrig*) added to reduced form of original Celtic name *Sorviodunum* (obscure word + Celtic **dūno-* 'fort'), this referring in the 4th cent. Antonine Itinerary to the Iron Age hill-fort at **Old Sarum**. The form *Sarum*, found from the 14th cent., arises from a misreading of the abbreviated spelling *Sar'* for *Sarisberie* and the like in medieval documents.

Salkeld, Great & *Salkeld, Little* Cumbria. *Salchild* c.1110. 'Sallow-tree wood'. OE *salh* + **hylte*.

Sallahig (*Saileáin*) Kerry. 'Place of willows'.

Salle Norfolk. *Salla* 1086 (DB). 'Wood or clearing where sallow-trees grow'. OE *salh* + *lēah*.

Sallins (*Na Solláin*) Kildare. 'The willow groves'.

Sallynoggin (*An Naigín*) Dublin. 'The Noggin'.

Salmonby Lincs. *Salmundebi* 1086 (DB). 'Farmstead or village of a man called Salmundr'. OScand. pers. name + *bý*.

Salop (the county), *see* SHROPSHIRE.

Salperton Glos. *Salpretune* 1086 (DB). Probably 'farmstead on a salt-way'. OE *salt* + *here-pæth* + *tūn*.

Salt Staffs. *Selte* 1086 (DB). OE **selte* 'a salt-pit, a salt-works'.

Saltaire W. Yorks., a modern name created for the new town founded in the valley of the River *Aire* (for which *see* AIRMYN) for the manufacture of alpaca by Sir Titus Salt in 1850.

Saltash Cornwall. *Esse* 1201, *Saltehasche* 1302. Originally '(place at) the ashtree', OE *æsc*. Later addition *salt* from the production of salt here.

Saltburn-by-the-Sea Red. & Cleve. *Salteburnam* c.1185. '(Place by) the salt stream'. OE *salt* + *burna*.

Saltby Leics. *Saltebi* 1086 (DB). Possibly 'farmstead or village of a man called **Salti* or *Salt*'. OScand. pers.

name + *bý*. Alternatively the first element may be OScand. *salt* 'salt'.

Saltcoats N. Ayr. *Saltcoates* 1548. 'Buildings where salt is made or stored'. OE *sealt* + *cot*.

Saltee Islands (*Oileán an tSalainn*) Wexford. 'Salt island'.

Salter Lancs. *Salterge* c.1150. 'Shieling where salt is found or kept'. OE *salt* + OScand. *erg*.

Salterforth Lancs. *Salterford* 13th cent. 'Ford used by salt-merchants'. OE *saltere* + *ford*.

Salterton, Budleigh Devon. *Saltre* 1210, *Salterne* 1405. OE *salt-ærn* 'building where salt is made or sold'. Affix from nearby BUDLEIGH.

Salterton, Woodbury Devon. *Salterton* 1306. 'Farmstead of the salt-workers or salt-merchants'. OE *saltere* + *tūn*. Affix from nearby WOODBURY.

Saltfleet Lincs. *Salfluet* 1086 (DB). '(Place by) the salt stream'. OE *salt* + *flēot*.

Saltfleetby All Saints, *Saltfleetby St Clements*, & *Saltfleetby St Peter* Lincs. *Salflatebi* 1086 (DB). 'Farmstead or village by the salt stream'. OE *salt* + *flēot* + OScand. *bý*.

Saltford B. & NE. Som. *Sanford* |*sic*| 1086 (DB), *Salford* 1229, *Saltford* 1291. Probably 'salt-water ford', OE *salt* + *ford*, but the first element may originally have been *salh* 'sallow, willow'.

Salthouse Norfolk. *Salthus* 1086 (DB). 'Building for storing salt'. OE *salt* + *hūs*.

Saltmarshe E. R. Yorks. *Saltemersc* 1086 (DB). 'Salty or brackish marsh'. OE *salt* + *mersc*.

Saltney Flin. *Salteney* c.1230. 'Salty marshland'. OE *salt* + *ēg*.

Saltney Ches. *Salteney* c.1230. 'Salty island or dry ground in marsh'. OE *salt* (dative -*an*) + *ēg*.

Salton N. Yorks. *Saletun* 1086 (DB). 'Farmstead where sallow-trees grow'. OE *salh* + *tūn*.

Saltwood Kent. *Sealtwuda* c.1000, *Salteode* 1086 (DB). 'Wood where salt is made or stored'. OE *sealt* + *wudu*.

Salvington W. Sussex. *Saluinton* 1249. 'Estate associated with a man called Sǣlāf or Sǣwulf'. OE pers. name + -*ing*- + *tūun*.

Salwarpe Heref. & Worcs. *Salouuarpe* 817, *Salewarpe* 1086 (DB). Probably 'dark-coloured silted land'. OE *salu* + *wearp*.

Sambourne Warwicks. *Samburne* 714, *Sandburne* 1086 (DB). 'Sandy stream'. OE *sand* + *burna*.

Sambrook Shrops. *Semebre* |*sic*| 1086 (DB), *Sambroc* 1256. Probably 'sandy brook'. OE *sand* + *brōc*.

Samlesbury Lancs. *Samelesbure* 1188. Probably 'stronghold near a shelf or ledge of land'. OE *scamol* + *burh* (dative *byrig*).

Sampford, 'sandy ford', OE *sand* + *ford*: **Sampford Arundel** Somerset. *Sanford* 1086 (DB), *Samford Arundel* 1240. Manorial affix from Roger Arundel, tenant in 1086. **Sampford Brett** Somerset. *Sanford* 1086 (DB), *Saunford Bret* 1306. Manorial affix from the Bret family, here in the 12th cent. **Sampford Courtenay** Devon. *Sanfort*

1086 (DB), *Saunforde Curtenay* 1262. Manorial affix from the Curtenay family, here in the 13th cent. **Sampford Peverell** Devon. *Sanforda* 1086 (DB), *Saunford Peverel* 1275. Manorial affix from the Peverel family, here in the 12th cent. **Sampford Spiney** Devon. *Sanforda* 1086 (DB), *Saundford Spyneye* 1304. Manorial affix from the Spiney family, here in the 13th cent.

Sanclêr. *See* ST CLEARS.

Sancreed Cornwall. 'Church of *Sanctus Sancretus*' 1235. From the patron saint of the church, St Sancred.

Sancton E. R. Yorks. *Santun* 1086 (DB). 'Farmstead with sandy soil'. OE *sand* + *tūn*.

Sand Hutton N. Yorks., *see* HUTTON.

Sandall, Kirk S. Yorks. *Sandala* 1086 (DB), *Kirke Sandale* 1261. 'Sandy nook of land'. OE *sand* + *halh*. Affix is OScand. *kirkja* 'church'.

Sanday (island) Orkn. 'Sandy island'. OScand. *sand* + *ey*.

Sandbach Ches. *Sanbec* 1086 (DB). 'Sandy valley-stream'. OE *sand* + *bæce*.

Sandbanks Dorset, a modern name not recorded before c.1800, and self-explanatory.

Sanderstead Surrey. *Sondenstede* c.880, *Sandestede* 1086 (DB). 'Sandy homestead'. OE *sand* + *hǣm-styde*.

Sandford, 'sandy ford', OE *sand* + *ford*: **Sandford** Cumbria. *Saunford* c.1210. **Sandford** Devon. *Sandforda* 930. **Sandford** Shrops. *Sanford* 1086 (DB). **Sandford on Thames** Oxon. *Sandforda* 1050, *Sanford* 1086 (DB). **Sandford Orcas** Dorset. *Sanford* 1086 (DB), *Sandford Horscoys* 1372. Manorial affix from the Orescuils family, here from the 12th cent. **Sandford St Martin** Oxon. *Sanford* 1086 (DB). Affix from the dedication of the church.

Sandgate Kent. *Sandgate* 1256. 'Gap or gate leading to the sandy shore'. OE *sand* + *geat*.

Sandhoe Northum. *Sandho* 1225. 'Sandy hill-spur'. OE *sand* + *hōh*.

Sandholes (*Clais an Ghainimh*) Tyrone. *Sandholes* 1834. '(Place by) sand pits'.

Sandhurst, 'sandy wooded hill', OE *sand* + *hyrst*: **Sandhurst** Berks. *Sandherst* 1175. **Sandhurst** Glos. *Sanher* |*sic*| 1086 (DB), *Sandhurst* 12th cent. **Sandhurst** Kent. *Sandhyrste* c.1100.

Sandhutton N. Yorks. *Hotune* 1086 (DB), *Sandhoton* 12th cent. 'Farmstead on a sandy spur of land'. OE *sand* + *hōh* + *tūn*.

Sandiacre Derbys. *Sandiacre* 1086 (DB). 'Sandy cultivated land'. OE *sandig* + *æcer*.

Sandon, 'sandy hill', OE *sand* + *dūn*: **Sandon** Essex. *Sandun* 1199. **Sandon** Herts. *Sandune* c.1000, *Sandone* 1086 (DB). **Sandon** Staffs. *Sandone* 1086 (DB).

Sandown I. of Wight. *Sande* |*sic*| 1086 (DB), *Sandham* 1271. 'Sandy enclosure or river-meadow'. OE *sand* + *hamm*.

Sandown Park Surrey. *Sandone* 1235. 'Sandy hill or down'. OE *sand* + *dūn*.

Sandridge Herts. *Sandrige* 1086 (DB). 'Sandy ridge'. OE *sand* + *hrycg*. The same name occurs in Devon.

Sandringham Norfolk. *Santdersincham* 1086 (DB). 'The sandy part of DERSINGHAM'. The affix is OE *sand*.

Sandtoft N. Lincs. *Sandtofte* 1157. 'Sandy building plot or curtilage'. OScand. *sandr* + *toft*.

Sandwell W. Mids. *Saundwell* 13th cent. 'Sandy spring'. OE *sand* + *wella*.

Sandwich Kent. *Sandwicæ* c.710–20. *Sandwice* 1086 (DB). 'Sandy harbour or trading centre'. OE *sand* + *wīc*.

Sandwick Shet. *Sandvik* 1360. 'Sandy inlet'. OScand. *sand* + *vík*.

Sandwith Cumbria. *Sandwath* 1260. 'Sandy ford'. OScand. *sandr* + *vath*.

Sandy Beds. *Sandeie* 1086 (DB). 'Sandy island'. OE *sand* + *ēg*.

Sankey, Great Ches. *Sonchi* c.1180. Named from the River Sankey, a pre-English river-name of uncertain origin and meaning.

Sanquhar Dumf. *Sanchar* 1150. '(Place by the) old fort'. Gaelic *sean* + *cathair*.

Santon, 'farmstead with sandy soil', OE *sand* + *tūn*: **Santon Bridge** Cumbria. *Santon* c.1235. **Santon, Low** N. Lincs. *Santone* 1086 (DB).

Santry (*Seantrabh*) Dublin. 'Old dwelling'.

Sapcote Leics. *Scepecote* 1086 (DB). 'Shed or shelter for sheep'. OE *scēap* + *cot*.

Sapey, Lower & *Sapey, Upper* Heref. & Worcs. *Sapian* 781, *Sapie* 1086 (DB). Probably from OE *sæpig* 'sappy, juicy', originally applied to Sapey Brook.

Sapiston Suffolk. *Sapestuna* 1086 (DB). OE *tūn* 'farmstead' with an uncertain first element, possibly a pers. name.

Sapley Cambs. *Sappele* 1227. 'Wood or clearing where fir-trees grow'. OE *sæppe* + *lēah*.

Sapperton, 'farmstead of the soap-makers or soap-merchants', OE **sāpere* + *tūn*: **Sapperton** Glos. *Sapertun* c.1075, *Sapletorne* |*sic*| 1086 (DB). **Sapperton** Lincs. *Sapretone* 1086 (DB).

Sarclet Highland. 'Gull cliff'. OScand. *saur* 'mud', or *sauthr* 'sleep' + *klettr*.

Sarn Powys. '(Place by the) causeway'. Welsh *sarn*.

Sarnesfield Heref. & Worcs. *Sarnesfelde* 1086 (DB). 'Open land by a road'. OWelsh *sarn* + OE *feld*.

Sarratt Herts. *Syreth* c.1085. Possibly 'dry or barren place'. OE **sīeret*.

Sarre Kent. *Serræ* 761. Obscure in origin and meaning, but possibly an old pre-English name for the River Wantsum.

Sarsden Oxon. *Secendene* |*sic*| 1086 (DB), *Cerchesdena* c.1180. Probably 'valley of the church'. OE *cirice* + *denu*.

Sarum, Old Wilts., *see* SALISBURY.

Satley Durham. *Sateley* 1228. Possibly 'Woodland clearing with a stable or fold'. OE *set* + *lēah*.

Satterleigh Devon. *Saterlei* 1086 (DB). 'Woodland clearing of the robbers'. OE *sætere* + *lēah*.

Satterthwaite Cumbria. *Saterthwayt* 1336. Probably 'clearing by a hut or shieling'. OScand. *sætr* + *thveit*.

Saughall, Great & *Saughall, Little* Ches. *Salhale* 1086 (DB). 'Nook of land where sallow-trees grow'. OE *salh* + *halh*.

Saul (*Sabhall*) Down. *Sabul Patricii* c.670. 'Barn'.

Saul Glos. *Salle* 12th cent. 'Wood or clearing where sallow-trees grow'. OE *salh* + *lēah*.

Saundby Notts. *Sandebi* 1086 (DB). Probably 'farmstead or village of a man called Sandi'. OScand. pers. name + *bý*. Alternatively the first element may be OScand. *sandr* 'sand'.

Saundersfoot Pemb. *Saunders foot* 1602. 'Saunders' foot'. A hill or cliff here must have been owned by one Saunders.

Saunderton Bucks. *Santesdune* 1086 (DB), *Santredon* 1196. OE *dūn* 'hill' with an uncertain first element.

Saval (*Sabhall*) Down. 'Barn'.

Savernake Forest Wilts, *Safernoc* 934. Probably 'district of a river called *Sabrina* or *Severn*', from a derivative of an ancient pre-English river-name (perhaps applied originally to the River Bedwyn) of unknown origin and meaning.

Sawbridgeworth Herts. *Sabrixteworde* 1086 (DB). 'Enclosure of a man called Sæbeorht'. OE pers. name + *worth*.

Sawdon N. Yorks. *Saldene* early 13th cent. 'Valley where sallow-trees grow'. OE *salh* + *denu*.

Sawel (*Samhail*) (mountain) Tyrone. 'Likeness'. *Samhail Phite Meadhbea* c.1680. The full name is *Samhail Phite Méabha*, 'likeness to Maeve's vulva', referring to a hollow on the side of the mountain.

Sawley Derbys. *Salle* |*sic*| 1086 (DB), *Sallawa* 1166. 'Hill or mound where sallow-trees grow'. OE *salh* + *hlāw*.

Sawley Lancs. *Sotleie* |*sic*| 1086 (DB), *Sallaia* 1147. 'Woodland clearing where sallow-trees grow'. OE *salh* + *lēah*.

Sawley N. Yorks. *Sallege* c.1030. Identical in origin with the previous name.

Sawrey, Far & *Sawrey, Near* Cumbria. *Sourer* 1336. 'The sour or muddy grounds'. OScand. *saurr* in a plural form *saurar*.

Sawston Cambs. *Salsingetune* 970, *Salsiton* 1086 (DB). 'Farmstead of the family or followers of a man called **Salse*'. OE pers. name + *-inga-* + *tūn*.

Sawtry Cambs. *Saltreiam* 974, *Saltrede* 1086 (DB). 'Salty stream', OE *salt* + *rīth*.

Saxby, probably 'farmstead or village of a man called Saksi', OScand. pers. name + *bý*, but alternatively the first element may be OScand. *Saksar* 'Saxons': **Saxby** Leics. *Saxebi* 1086 (DB). **Saxby** Lincs. *Sassebi* 1086 (DB). **Saxby All Saints** N. Lincs. *Saxebi* 1086 (DB). Affix from the dedication of the church.

Saxelby Leics. *Saxelbie* 1086 (DB). Probably 'farmstead or village of a man called Saksulfr'. OScand. pers. name + *bý*.

Saxham, Great & *Saxham, Little* Suffolk. *Saxham* 1086 (DB). Probably 'homestead of the Saxons'. OE *Seaxe* + *hām*.

Saxilby Lincs. *Saxebi* |*sic*| 1086 (DB), *Saxlabi* c.1115. Identical in origin with SAXELBY.

Saxlingham, 'homestead of the family or followers of a man called *Seaxel or Seaxhelm', OE pers. name + *-inga-* + *hām*: **Saxlingham** Norfolk. *Saxelingaham* 1086 (DB). **Saxlingham Nethergate** Norfolk. *Seaxlingaham* 1046, *Saiselingaham* 1086 (DB). The affix, first found in the 13th cent., means 'lower gate or street'.

Saxmundham Suffolk. *Sasmundeham* 1086 (DB). 'Homestead of a man called *Seaxmund'. OE pers. name + *hām*.

Saxondale Notts. *Saxeden* 1086 (DB), *Saxendala* c.1130. 'Valley of the Saxons'. OE *Seaxe* + *dæl* (replacing *denu*).

Saxtead Suffolk. *Saxteda* 1086 (DB). Probably 'place of a man called Seaxa'. OE pers. name + *stede*.

Saxthorpe Norfolk. *Saxthorp* 1086 (DB). 'Outlying farmstead or hamlet of a man called Saksi'. OScand. pers. name + *thorp*.

Saxton N. Yorks. *Saxtun* 1086 (DB). 'Farmstead of the Saxons, or of a man called Saksi'. OE *Seaxe* or OScand. pers. name + OE *tūn*.

Scackleton N. Yorks. *Scacheldene* 1086 (DB). Probably 'valley by a point of land'. OE *scacol* (with Scand. *sk-*) + *denu*.

Scaddy (*Sceadaigh*) Down. *Scaddy* 1886. 'Bare place'.

Scaftworth Notts. *Scafteorde* 1086 (DB). Probably 'enclosure of a man called *Sceafta or Skapti', OE or OScand. pers. name + OE *worth*. Alternatively 'enclosure made with poles', OE *sceaft* (with Scand. *sk-*) + *worth*.

Scagglethorpe N. Yorks. *Scachetorp* 1086 (DB). Probably 'outlying farmstead or hamlet of a man called Skakull or Skakli'. OScand. pers. name + *thorp*.

Scalby, 'farmstead or village of a man called Skalli', OScand. pers. name + *bý*: **Scalby** E. R. Yorks, *Scalleby* 1230. **Scalby** N. Yorks. *Scallebi* 1086 (DB).

Scaldwell Northants. *Scaldewelle* 1086 (DB). 'Shallow spring or stream'. OE *scald* (with Scand. *sk-*) + *wella*.

Scaleby Cumbria. *Schaleby* c.1235. 'Farmstead or village near the huts or shielings'. OScand. *skáli* + *bý*.

Scales, a common name in the North, 'the temporary huts or sheds', OScand. *skáli*; examples include: **Scales** Cumbria, near Aldingham. *Scales* 1269. **Scales** Cumbria, near Threlkeld. *Skales* 1323. **Scales** Lancs., near Newton. *Skalys* 1501.

Scalford Leics. *Scaldeford* 1086 (DB). 'Shallow ford'. OE *scald* (with Scand. *sk-*) + *ford*.

Scalloway Shet. 'Bay by the hut'. OScand. *skáli* + *vágr*.

Scalpay (island) Highland (Skye). 'Boat-shaped island'. OScand. *skalpr* + *ey*.

Scamblesby Lines. *Scamelesbi* 1086 (DB). Probably 'farmstead or village of a man called Skammel'. OScand. pers. name + *bý*.

Scampston N. Yorks. *Scameston* 1086 (DB). 'Farmstead of a man called Skammr or Skammel'. OScand. pers. name + OE *tūn*.

Scampton Lincs. *Scantone* 1086 (DB). 'Short farmstead, or farmstead of a man called Skammi'. OScand. *skammr* or pers. name + OE *tūn*.

Scapa Flow Orkn. *Scalpay* 1579. 'Long narrow isthmus'. OScand. *skalpr* + *eith* + *flóa*. The 'isthmus' is the stretch of land south of Kirkwall on the eastern side of Scapa Bay.

Scarborough N. Yorks. *Escardeburg* c.1160. Probably 'stronghold of a man called Skarthi'. OScand. pers. name + OE *burh*.

Scarcliffe Derbys. *Scardeclif* 1086 (DB). 'Cliff or steep slope with a gap'. OE *sceard* (with Scand. *sk-*) + *clif*.

Scarcroft W. Yorks. *Scardecroft* 1166. Probably 'enclosure in a gap'. OE *sceard* (with Scand. *sk-*) + *croft*.

Scardaun (*Scardán*) Mayo. 'Tiny waterfall'.

Scargill Durham. *Scracreghil* 1086 (DB). Probably 'ravine frequented by mergansers or similar seabirds'. OScand. *skraki* + *gil*.

Scarisbrick Lancs. *Scharisbrec* c.1200. Possibly 'hill-side or slope by a hollow'. OScand. *skar* + *brekka*.

Scarle, North (Lincs.) & *Scarle, South* (Notts.). *Scornelei* 1086 (DB). 'Mud or dung clearing'. OE *scearn* (with Scand. *sk-*) + *lēah*.

Scarnageeragh (*Scarbh na gCaorach*) Monaghan. 'Shallow ford of the sheep'.

Scarning Norfolk. *Scerninga* 1086 (DB). Probably 'the muddy or dirty place'. OE *scearn* (with Scand. *sk-*) + *-ing*.

Scarriff (*Scairbh*) Clare, Cork, Galway. 'Shallow ford'.

Scarrington Notts. *Scarintone* 1086 (DB). Possibly 'muddy or dirty farmstead'. OE *scearnig* (with Scand. *sk-*) + *tūn*. Alternatively the first element may be OE *scearning* 'dirty place'.

Scartaglen (*Scairteach an Ghlinne*) Kerry. 'Thicket of the valley'.

Scarteen (*Scairtín*) Kerry. 'Little thicket'.

Scartho NE. Lincs. *Scarhou* 1086 (DB). 'Mound near a gap, or one frequented by cormorants'. OScand. *skarth* or *skarfr* + *haugr*.

Scarva (*Scarbhach*) Down. *the Skarvagh* 1618. 'Place of the shallow ford'.

Scattery Island (*Inis Cathaigh*) Clare. 'Cathach's island'.

Scawby N. Lincs. *Scallebi* 1086 (DB). Probably 'farmstead or village of a man called Skalli'. OScand. pers. name + *bý*.

Scawton N. Yorks. *Scaltun* 1086 (DB). 'Farmstead in a hollow or with a shieling'. OScand. *skál* or *skáli* + OE *tūn*.

Schiehallion (mountain) Perth. 'Fairy hill of the Caledonians'. Gaelic *sidh*.

Scholar Green Ches. *Scholehalc* late 13th cent. 'Nook of land with a hut or shieling'. OScand. *skáli* + OE *halh*.

Scholes, a common name in the North, 'the temporary huts or sheds', OScand. *skáli*; examples include: **Scholes**

W. Yorks., near Holmfirth. *Scholes* 1284. **Scholes** W. Yorks., near Leeds. *Skales* 1258.

Scilly Isles Cornwall. *Sully* 12th cent. An ancient pre-English name first recorded in the first century AD, of unknown origin and meaning.

Sco Ruston Norfolk, *see* RUSTON.

Scole Norfolk. *Escales* 1191. 'The temporary huts or sheds'. OScand. *skáli*.

Scone Perth. *Sgoinde* 1020. 'Mass of rock'. Unknown.

Scopwick Lincs. *Scapeuic* 1086 (DB). 'Sheep farm'. OE *scēap* (with Scand. *sk-*) + *wīc*.

Scorborough E. R. Yorks. *Scogerbud* 1086 (DB). 'Booth or shelter in a wood'. OScand. *skógr* + *būth*.

Scorton, 'farmstead near a ditch or ravine', OScand. *skor* + OE *tūn*: **Scorton** Lancs. *Scourton* c.1550. **Scorton** N. Yorks. *Scortone* 1086 (DB).

Scotby Cumbria. *Scoteby* 1130. 'Farmstead or village of the Scots'. OScand. *Skoti* + *bý*.

Scotch Corner N. Yorks., road junction on the Great North Road so called because the main road to SW Scotland via Carlisle branches off here.

Scotch Street Armagh. *Scotch Street* 1835. The village, with its single street, was founded by Scottish settlers. The equivalent Irish name is *Sráid na hAlbanach*, 'street of the Scotsmen'.

Scotforth Lancs. *Scozforde* 1086 (DB). 'Ford used by the Scot or Scots'. OE *Scot* (with Scand. *sk-*) + *ford*.

Scothern Lincs. *Scotstorne* 1086 (DB). 'Thorn-tree of the Scot or Scots'. OE *Scot* (with Scand. *sk-*) + *thorn*.

Scotland. 'Land of the Scots'. The original 'Scots' were the Celtic 5th- to 6th-century settlers from Ireland. *Scotia* became the name of the whole country in the 9th cent. after the merger of the Scottish and Pictish kingdoms. The meaning of the tribal name is uncertain.

Scotshouse Monaghan. *Scotshouse* 1835. 'Scott's house'. William Scott was granted an estate here in the 17th cent. The present village was founded in the early 19th cent.

Scotter Lincs. *Scot(e)re* 1086 (DB). Possibly 'tree of the Scots'. OE *Scot* (with Scand. *sk-*) + *trēow*.

Scotterthorpe Lincs. *Scaltorp* 1086 (DB). Probably 'outlying farmstead or hamlet of a man called Skalli'. OScand. pers. name + *thorp*.

Scotton, 'farmstead of the Scots', OE *Scot* (with Scand. *sk-*) + *tūn*: **Scotton** Lincs. *Scottun* 1060–6. *Scotone* 1086 (DB). **Scotton** N. Yorks., near Knaresborough. *Scotone* 1086 (DB). **Scotton** N. Yorks., near Richmond. *Scottune* 1086 (DB).

Scottow Norfolk. *Scoteho* 1044–7, *Scotohou* 1086 (DB). 'Hill-spur of the Scots'. OE *Scot* (with Scand. *sk-*) + *hōh*.

Scoulton Norfolk. *Sculetuna* 1086 (DB). 'Farmstead of a man called Skúli'. OScand. pers. name + OE *tūn*.

Scrabo (*Screabach*) Down. *Scraboc* c.1275. 'Rough land'.

Scrabster Highland. *Skarabolstad* 1201. 'Homestead of the young seagull'. OScand. *skairi* + *bólstathr*.

Scrafton, West N. Yorks. *Scraftun* 1086 (DB). 'Farmstead near a hollow'. OE *scræf* (with Scand. *sk-*) + *tūn*.

Scraghan (*Scrathán*) Westmeath. 'Sward'.

Scrahanagnave (*Screathan na gCnámh*) Kerry. 'Scree of the bones'.

Scrainwood Northum. *Scravenwod* 1242. 'Wood frequented by shrewmice or villains'. OE *scrēawa* (genitive plural -*ena* and with Scand. *sk-*) + *wudu*.

Scramoge (*Scramóg*) Roscommon. Meaning uncertain.

Scrane End Lincs. *Screinga* 12th cent. '(Settlement of) the family or followers of a man called *Scīrhēah* from an OE pers. name + -*ingas*, or 'structure(s) made of poles' from an OE *scræging* (with Scand. *sk-*).

Scraptoft Leics. *Scraptoft* 1043, *Scrapentot |sic|* 1086 (DB). Probably 'homestead of a man called Skrápi'. OScand. pers. name + *toft*.

Scratby Norfolk. *Scroutebi* c.1020, *Scroteby* 1086 (DB). 'Farmstead or village of a man called Skrauti'. OScand. pers. name + *bý*.

Scrayingham N. Yorks. *Screngham, Escraingham* 1086 (DB). 'Homestead of the family or followers of a man called *Scīrhēah* from an OE pers. name + -*inga*- + *hām*, or 'homestead with a structure of poles' from an OE *scræging* (with Scand. *sk-*) + *hām*.

Scredington Lincs. *Scredinctun* 1086 (DB). Possibly 'estate associated with a man called Scīrheard'. OE pers. name (with Scand. *sk-*) + -*ing*- + *tūn*.

Screeb (*Scríb*) Galway. 'Furrow'.

Screen (*An Scrín*) Wexford. 'The shrine'.

Screggan (*An Screagán*) Offaly. 'The rough place'.

Scremby Lincs. *Screnbi* 1086 (DB). 'Farmstead or village of a man called *Skræma* OScand. pers. name + *bý*.

Scremerston Northum. *Schermereton* 1196. 'Estate of the Skermer family'. ME surname + OE *tūn*.

Scribbagh (*Scriobach*) Fermanagh. 'Rough land'.

Scriven N. Yorks. *Scrauing(h)e* 1086 (DB). 'Hollow place with pits'. OE *screfen* (with Scand. *sk-*).

Scrooby Notts. *Scrobi* 1086 (DB). Possibly 'farmstead or village of a man called Skropi'. OScand. pers. name + *bý*.

Scropton Derbys. *Scrotun |sic|* 1086 (DB), *Scropton* c.1141. Probably 'farmstead of a man called Skropi'. OScand. pers. name + OE *tūn*.

Scruton N. Yorks. *Scurvetone* 1086 (DB). 'Farmstead of a man called Skurfa'. OScand. pers. name + OE *tūn*.

Sculthorpe Norfolk. *Sculatorpa* 1086 (DB). 'Outlying farmstead or hamlet of a man called Skúli'. OScand. pers. name + *thorp*.

Scunthorpe N. Lincs. *Escumetorp* 1086 (DB). 'Outlying farmstead or hamlet of a man called Skúma'. OScand. pers. name + *thorp*.

Scur, Lough (*Loch an Scuir*) Leitrim. 'Lake of the camp'.

Sea Palling Norfolk, *see* PALLING.

Seaborough Dorset. *Seveberge* 1086 (DB). 'Seven hills or barrows'. OE *seofon* + *beorg*.

Seacombe Mersey. *Secumbe c.*1277. 'Valley by the sea'. OE *sǣ* + *cumb*.

Seacroft W. Yorks. *Sacroft* 1086 (DB). 'Enclosure by a pool or marsh'. OE *sǣ* + *croft*.

Seadavog (*Suí Dabhóg*) Donegal. 'Davóg's seat'.

Seaford E. Sussex. *Saforde* 12th cent. 'Ford by the sea'. OE *sǣ* + *ford*. The River Ouse flowed into the sea here until the 16th cent.

Seaforde Down. *Seaforde* 1837. 'Forde's seat'. Irish *suí* + English surname. The village arose in the 18th cent. and takes its name from the local Forde family.

Seaforth W. Isles (Lewis). 'Inlet of the sea'. OScand. *sǣr* + *fjǫrthr*.

Seaforth Mersey., a recent name, from *Seaforth House* in Litherland which was named after Lord Seaforth in the early 19th cent.

Seagrave Leics. *Setgraue* 1086 (DB). Possibly 'grove with or near a pit'. OE *sēath* + *grāf*.

Seagry, Upper Wilts. *Segrete* 1086 (DB). 'Stream where sedge grows'. OE *secg* + *rīth*.

Seaham Durham. *Sǣham c.*1050. 'Homestead or village by the sea'. OE *sǣ* + *hām*.

Seal Kent. *La Sela* 1086 (DB). Probably 'the hall or dwelling', OE *sele*. Alternatively 'the sallow-tree copse', OE **sele*.

Sealand Flin. *Sealand* 1726. 'Sea land'. The village is on land reclaimed from the sea north of the River Dee.

Seamer, 'lake or marsh pool', OE *sǣ* + *mere*: **Seamer** N. Yorks., near Scarborough. *Semær* 1086 (DB). **Seamer** N. Yorks., near Stokesley. *Semer* 1086 (DB).

Seapatrick (*Suí Phádraig*) Down. *Soyge-Patrick* 1546. 'Patrick's seat'. The church here is dedicated to St Patrick.

Searby Lincs. *Seurebi* 1086 (DB). 'Farmstead or village of the seafarers, or of a man called Sæfari'. OScand. **sǣfari* or pers. name + *bý*.

Seasalter Kent. *Seseltre* 1086 (DB). 'Salt-works on the sea'. OE *sǣ* + *sealt-ærn*.

Seascale Cumbria. *Sescales c.*1165. 'Shieling(s) or hut(s) by the sea'. OScand. *sǣr* + *skáli*.

Seathwaite Cumbria, near Borrowdale. *Seuethwayt* 1292. 'Sedge clearing'. OScand. *sef* + *thveit*.

Seathwaite Cumbria., near Ulpha. *Seathwhot* 1592. 'Lake clearing'. OScand. *sǣr* + *thveite*.

Seaton, usually 'farmstead by the sea or by an inland pool'. OE *sǣ* + *tūn*; examples include: **Seaton** Devon. *Setton* 1238. **Seaton** Cumbria, near Workington. *Setona c.*1174. **Seaton Carew** Hartlepl. *Setona* late 12th cent., *Seton Carrowe* 1345. Manorial affix from the Carou family, here in the 13th cent. **Seaton Delaval** Northum. *Seton de la Val* 1270. Manorial affix from the de la Val family, here in the 13th cent. **Seaton Ross** E. R. Yorks. *Seton* 1086 (DB), *Seaton Rosse* 1618. Manorial affix from the Ross family who held the vill from the 12th cent.

However the following has a different origin: **Seaton** Rutland. *Segentone, Seieton* 1086 (DB). Probably 'farmstead of a man called **Sǣga*. OE pers. name + *tūn*.

Seavington St Michael & *Seavington St Mary* Somerset. *Seofenempton c.*1025, *Sevenehantune* 1086 (DB). 'Village of seven homesteads'. OE *seofon* + *hām-tūn*. Distinguishing affixes from the dedications of the churches here.

Sebergham Cumbria. *Saburgham* 1223. Probably 'homestead of a woman called Sæburh'. OE pers. name + *hām*.

Seckington Warwicks. *Seccandun* late 9th cent., *Sechintone* 1086 (DB). 'Hill of a man called Secca'. OE pers. name (genitive *-an*) + *dūn*.

Sedbergh Cumbria. *Sedberge* 1086 (DB). OScand. *set-berg* 'a flat-topped hill'.

Sedgeberrow Heref. & Worcs. *Segcgesbearuue* 777, *Seggesbarue* 1086 (DB). 'Grove of a man called **Secg*'. OE pers. name + *bearu*.

Sedgebrook Lincs. *Sechebroc* 1086 (DB). 'Brook where sedge grows'. OE *secg* + *brōc*.

Sedgefield Durham. *Ceddesfeld c.*1050. 'Open land of a man called **Cedd* or Secg'. OE pers. name + *feld*.

Sedgeford Norfolk. *Secesforda* 1086 (DB). Possibly 'ford of a man called **Secci*'. OE pers. name + *ford*.

Sedgehill Wilts. *Seghulle* early 12th cent. 'Hill of a man called Secga, or near where sedge grows'. OE pers. name or OE *secg* + *hyll*.

Sedgley W. Mids. *Secgesleage* 985, *Segleslei* |*sic*| 1086 (DB). 'Woodland clearing of a man called **Secg*'. OE pers. name + *lēah*.

Sedgwick Cumbria. *Sigghiswic c.*1185. 'Dwelling or farm of a man called **Sicg*'. OE pers. name + *wīc*.

Sedlescombe E. Sussex. *Selescome* |*sic*| 1086 (DB), *Sedelescumbe c.*1210. Probably 'valley with a house or dwelling'. OE *sedl* + *cumb*.

Seefin (*Suí Finn*) Cork, Down, Mayo, Waterford. 'Fionn's seat'.

Seend Wilts. *Sinda* 1190. Probably 'sandy place'. OE **sende*.

Seer Green Bucks. *La Sere* 1223. 'The dry or barren place'. OE *sēar*.

Seething Norfolk. *Sithinges* 1086 (DB). Probably '(settlement of) the family or followers of a man called **Sīth(a)*'. OE pers. name + *-ingas*.

Sefton Mersey. *Sextone* |*sic*| 1086 (DB), *Sefftun c.*1220. 'Farmstead where rushes grow'. OScand. *sef* + OE *tūn*.

Seghill Northum. *Syghal* 1198. Possibly 'nook of land by a stream called **Sige*'. OE river-name (meaning 'slow-moving') + *halh*.

Seighford Staffs. *Cesteforde* 1086 (DB). 'Ford by an old fortification'. OE *ceaster* + *ford*.

Selattyn Shrops. *Sulatun* 1254. 'Settlement with ploughs or ploughlands', or 'settlement characterized by gullies'. OE *sulh* (genitive plural *sula*) + *tūn*.

Selborne Hants. *Seleborne* 903, *Selesburne* 1086 (DB). 'Stream by (a copse of) sallow-trees'. OE *sealh* or **sele* + *burna*.

Selby N. Yorks. *Seleby* c.1030, *Salebi* 1086 (DB). 'Farmstead or village near (a copse of) sallow-trees'. OE **sele* or OScand. *selja* + OScand. *bý*.

Selham W. Sussex. *Seleham* 1086 (DB). 'Homestead by a copse of sallow-trees'. OE **sele* + *hām*.

Selkirk Sc. Bord. *Selechirche* c.1120, *Seleschirche* c.1190, *Selkirk* 1306. 'Church by a hall'. OE *sele* + *cirice*.

Sellack Heref. & Worcs. *Lann Suluc* c.1130. 'Church of Suluc (a pet-form of Suliau)'. From the dedication of the church (OWelsh **lann*).

Sellafield Cumbria. *Sellofeld* 1576. Probably 'land by the willow-tree mound'. OScand. *selja* + *haugr* + OE *feld*.

Sellindge Kent. *Sedlinges* 1086 (DB). Probably '(settlement of) those sharing a house or building', from OE *sedl* + *-ingas*. Alternatively 'place at a house or building', OE *sedl* + *-ing*.

Selling Kent. *Setlinges* 1086 (DB). Identical in origin with the previous name.

Selloo (*Suí Lú*) Monaghan. 'Lú's seat'.

Selly Oak W. Mids. *Escelie* |*sic*| 1086 (DB), *Selvele* 1204. 'Woodland clearing on a shelf or ledge'. OE *scelf* + *lēah*, with the later addition *oak*.

Selmeston E. Sussex. *Sielmestone* 1086 (DB). 'Farmstead of a man called Sigehelm'. OE pers. name + *tūn*.

Selsdon Gtr. London. *Selesdune* c.880. 'Hill of a man called **Sele* or **Seli*'. OE pers. name + *dūn*.

Selsey W. Sussex. *Seolesiae* c.715, *Seleisie* 1086 (DB). 'Island of the seal'. OE *seolh* + *ēg*. **Selsey Bill**, not recorded until the 18th cent., is from OE *bile* 'a bill, a beak' used topographically for 'promontory'.

Selsley Glos., not recorded before the late 18th cent., origin uncertain without earlier spellings.

Selston Notts. *Salestune* 1086 (DB). Probably 'farmstead of a man called **Sele* or **Seli*'. OE pers. name + *tūn*.

Selwood Somerset. *Seluudu* c.894. 'Wood where sallow-trees grow'. OE *sealh* + *wudu*.

Selworthy Somerset. *Seleuurde* 1086 (DB). 'Enclosure by a copse of sallow-trees'. OE **sele* + *worth(ig)*.

Semer Suffolk. *Seamera* 1086 (DB). 'Lake or marsh pool'. OE *sǣ* + *mere*.

Semington Wilts. *Semneton* 13th cent. 'Farmstead on the stream called *Semnet*'. Pre-English river-name (of uncertain meaning) + OE *tūn*.

Semley Wilts. *Semeleage* 955. 'Woodland clearing on the River Sem'. Pre-English river-name (of uncertain meaning) + OE *lēah*.

Sempringham Lincs. *Sempingaham* 852, *Sepingeham* |*sic*| 1086 (DB), *Sempringham* 1150. 'Homestead of the *Semp(r)ingas*'. OE *hām* with a tribal name of uncertain origin.

Send Surrey. *Sendan* 960–2, *Sande* 1086 (DB). 'Sandy place'. OE **sende*.

Sennen Cornwall. 'Parish of *Sancta Senana*' 1327. From the female patron saint of the church.

Seskilgreen (*Seisíoch Chill Ghrianna*) Tyrone. 'Plot of the church of the sun'.

Seskin (*Seisceann*) Tipperary. 'Marsh'.

Seskinore (*Seisceann Odhar*) Tyrone. *Shaskannoure* 1613. 'Brownish marsh'.

Seskinryan (*Seisceann Ríain*) Carlow. 'Rían's marsh'.

Sessay N. Yorks. *Sezai* 1086 (DB). 'Island or well-watered land where sedge grows'. OE *secg* + *ēg*.

Setchey Norfolk. *Seche* |*sic*| 1086 (DB), *Sechithe* 13th cent. Possibly 'landing-place of a man called **Secci*'. OE pers. name + *hýth*.

Settle N. Yorks. *Setel* 1086 (DB). 'The house or dwelling'. OE *setl*.

Settrington N. Yorks. *Sendriton* |*sic*| 1086 (DB), *Seteringetune* c.1090. Possibly 'estate associated with a robber or with a man called **Sætere*'. OE *sǣtere* or OE pers. name + *-ing-* + *tūn*.

Seven (river) N. Yorks., *see* SINNINGTON.

Seven Sisters Neat. The name was originally that of a colliery begun in 1872 and named after the pit owner's seven daughters.

Sevenhampton, 'village of seven homesteads', OE *seofon* + *hām-tūn*: **Sevenhampton** Glos. *Sevenhamtone* 1086 (DB). **Sevenhampton** Wilts. *Sevamentone* 1086 (DB).

Sevenoaks Kent. *Seouenaca* c.1100. '(Place by) seven oak-trees'. OE *seofon* + *āc*.

Severn (*Hafren*) (river) Powys. *Sabrina* c.116, *Sauerna* 1086 (DB). Origin uncertain.

Severn (river) Shrops.–Somerset. *Sabrina* 2nd cent. AD, *Sauerna* 1086 (DB). An ancient pre-English river-name of doubtful etymology.

Severn Stoke Heref. & Worcs., *see* STOKE.

Sevington Kent. *Seivetone* 1086 (DB). 'Farmstead of a woman called Sǣgifu'. OE pers. name + *tūn*.

Sewerby E. R. Yorks. *Siuuardbi* 1086 (DB). 'Farmstead or village of a man called Sigvarthr'. OScand. pers. name + *bý*.

Sewstern Leics. *Sewesten* |*sic*| 1086 (DB), *Seustern* c.1125. Possibly 'seven properties', OE *seofon* + **sterne*. Alternatively 'pool of a man called Sǣwig', OE pers. name + OScand. *tjǫrn*.

Sezincote Glos. *Ch(i)esnecote* 1086 (DB). 'Gravelly cottage(s)'. OE **cisen* + *cot*.

Shabbington Bucks. *Sobintone* 1086 (DB). 'Estate associated with a man called **Sc(e)obba*'. OE pers. name + *-ing-* + *tūn*.

Shackerstone Leics. *Sacrestone* 1086 (DB). 'The robber's farmstead'. OE *scēacere* + *tūn*.

Shadforth Durham. *Shaldeford* 1183. 'Shallow ford'. OE **sc(e)ald* + *ford*.

Shadingfield Suffolk. *Scadenafella* 1086 (DB). Possibly 'open land by the boundary valley'. OE *scēad* + *denu* + *feld*.

Shadoxhurst Kent. *Schettokesherst* 1239. OE *hyrst* 'wooded hill' with an uncertain first element, probably a pers. name or surname.

Shaftesbury Dorset *Sceaftesburi* 877, *Sceftesberie* 1086 (DB). 'Fortified place of a man called *Sceaft, or on a shaft-shaped hill'. OE pers. name or OE *sceaft + burh* (dative *byrig*).

Shafton S. Yorks. *Sceptun |sic|* 1086 (DB), *Scaftona c.*1160. 'Farmstead marked by a pole, or made with poles'. OE *sceaft + tūn*.

Shalbourne Wilts. *Scealdeburnan* 955, *Scaldeburne* 1086 (DB). 'Shallow stream'. OE **sceald + burna*.

Shalcombe I. of Wight. *Eseldecome* 1086 (DB), 'Shallow valley'. OE **sceald + cumb*.

Shalden Hants. *Scealdeden* 1046, *Seldene* 1086 (DB). 'Shallow valley'. OE **sceald + denu*.

Shaldon Devon, not recorded before the early 17th cent., probably from OE *dūn* 'hill' but first element uncertain without early spellings.

Shalfleet I. of Wight. *Scealdan fleote* 838, *Seldeflet* 1086 (DB). 'Shallow stream or creek'. OE **sceald + flēot*.

Shalford, 'shallow ford', OE **sceald + ford*: **Shalford** Essex. *Scaldefort* 1086 (DB). **Shalford** Surrey. *Scaldefor* 1086 (DB).

Shalstone Bucks. *Celdestone* 1086 (DB). Possibly 'farmstead at the shallow place or stream'. OE **sceald* (used as a noun) *+ tūn*.

Shanagarry (*An Seangharraí*) Cork. 'The old garden'.

Shanagolden (*Seanghualainn*) Limerick. 'Old shoulder'.

Shanahoe (*Seanchua*) Laois. 'Old hollow'.

Shanbally (*An Seanbhaile*) Cork. 'The old townland'.

Shanballymore (*An Seanbhaile Mór*) Cork. 'The big old homestead'.

Shanco (*Seanchua*) Monaghan. 'Old hollow'.

Shandwick Highland. 'Sandy bay'. OScand. *sand + vík*.

Shane's Castle Antrim. *Castel Edaindaubchairrgi* 1490. The townland is named after Shane O'Neill, ruler of Lower Clandeboy from 1595 to 1617 and grandfather of Rose O'Neill, whose husband gave the name of RANDALSTOWN. The castle's original Irish name was *Éadan Dúcharraige*, 'brow of black rock'.

Shangton Leics. *Sanctone* 1086 (DB). 'Farmstead by a hill-spur, or of a man called *Scanca'. OE *scanca* or pers. name *+ tūn*.

Shankill (*Seanchill*) Antrim, Dublin. 'Old church'.

Shanklin I. of Wight. *Sencliz* 1086 (DB). 'Bank by the drinking cup' (referring to the waterfall here). OE *scenc + hlinc*.

Shanlaragh (*Seanlárach*) Cork. 'Old ruins'.

Shannon (*Sionainn*) (river) Clare, Limerick. *Senos c.*150, *Sinand* n.d. 'Old goddess'.

Shanonagh (*Sean dDomhnach*) Westmeath. 'Old church'.

Shanragh (*Seanráth*) Laois. 'Old fort'.

Shanrahan (*Seanraithean*) Tipperary. 'Old ferny place'.

Shantonagh (*Seantonnach*) Monaghan. 'Old quagmire'.

Shanvaus (*An Seanmhás*) Leitrim. 'The old plain'.

Shap Cumbria. *Hep c.*1190. 'The heap of stones' (referring to an ancient stone circle). OE *hēap*.

Shapinsay (island) Orkn. *Hjalpandisay c.*1250. 'Hjalpand's(?) island'. OScand. pers. name *+ ey*.

Shapwick, 'sheep farm', OE *scēap + wīc*: **Shapwick** Dorset. *Scapeuuic* 1086 (DB). **Shapwick** Somerset. *Sapwic* 725, *Sapeswich* 1086 (DB).

Sharavogue (*Searbhóg*) Offaly. 'Bitter place'.

Shardlow Derbys. *Serdelau* 1086 (DB). 'Mound with a notch or indentation'. OE *sceard + hlāw*.

Shareshill Staffs. *Servesed |sic|* 1086 (DB), *Sarueshull* 1213, *Sarushulf* 1298. Probably 'hill (or shelf of land) of a man called *Scearf'. OE pers. name *+ hyll* (alternating with OE *scylf* in the early forms).

Sharlston W. Yorks. *Scharueston c.*1180. Possibly 'farmstead of a man called *Scearf'. OE pers. name *+ tūn*.

Sharnbrook Beds. *Scernebroc* 1086 (DB). 'Dirty or muddy brook'. OE *scearn + brōc*.

Sharnford Leics. *Scearnford* 1002, *Scerneforde* 1086 (DB). 'Dirty or muddy ford'. OE *scean + ford*.

Sharow N. Yorks. *Sharou c.*1130. 'Boundary hill-spur'. OE *scearu + hōh*.

Sharpenhoe Beds. *Scarpeho* 1197. 'Sharp or steep hill-spur'. OE *scearp* (dative *-an*) *+ hōh*.

Sharperton Northum. *Scharberton* 1242. Possibly 'farmstead by the steep hill'. OE *scearp + beorg + tūn*.

Sharpness Glos. *Nesse* 1086 (DB), *Schobbenasse* 1368. 'Headland of a man called *Scobba'. OE pers. name *+ næss*.

Sharrington Norfolk. *Scarnetuna* 1086 (DB). 'Dirty or muddy farmstead'. OE *scearn* (dative *-an*) *+ tūn*.

Shaugh Prior Devon. *Scage* 1086 (DB). 'Small wood or copse'. OE *sc(e)aga*. Affix from its early possession by Plympton Priory.

Shavington Ches. *Santune |sic|* 1086 (DB), *Shawynton* 1260. 'Estate associated with a man called Scēafa'. OE pers. name *+ -ing- + tūn*.

Shaw, 'small wood or copse', OE *sc(e)aga*: **Shaw** Berks. *Essages |sic|* 1086 (DB), *Shage* 1167. **Shaw** Gtr. Manch. *Shaghe* 1555. **Shaw** Wilts. *Schawe* 1256.

Shawbury Shrops. *Sawesberie* 1086 (DB), *Shawberia c.*1165. 'Manor house by a small wood or copse'. OE *sc(e)aga + burh* (dative *byrig*).

Shawell Leics. *Sawelle |sic|* 1086 (DB), *Schadewelle* 1224. 'Boundary spring or stream'. OE *scēath + wella*.

Shawford Hants. *Scaldeforda* 1208. 'Shallow ford'. OE **sceald + ford*.

Sheaf (river) Derbys., S. Yorks., *see* SHEFFIELD.

Shearsby Leics. *Svevesbi* 1086 (DB). Possibly 'farmstead or village of a man called Swæf or Skeifr'. OE or OScand. pers. name *+ OScand. bý*.

Shebbear Devon. *Sceftbeara* 1050–73, *Sepesberie* 1086 (DB). 'Grove where shafts or poles are got'. OE *sceaft + bearu*.

Shebdon Staffs. *Schebbedon* 1267. 'Hill of a man called *Sceobba'. OE pers. name + *dūn*.

Shedfield Hants. *Scidafelda* 956. 'Open land where planks of wood are got, or where they are used as foot-bridges'. OE *scīd* + *feld*.

Sheean (*An Sián*) Mayo. 'The fairy mound'.

Sheefin (*Suí Finn*) Westmeath. 'Finn's seat'.

Sheefry Hills (*Cnoic Shiofra*) Mayo. 'Siofra's hills'.

Sheelin, Lough (*Loch Síleann*) Cavan, Meath, Westmeath. 'Sileann's lake'.

Sheen, 'the sheds or shelters', OE **scēo* in a plural form **scēon*: **Sheen** Staffs. *Sceon* 1002, 1086 (DB). **Sheen, East & North**, Gtr. London. *Sceon* c.950. *West Sheen* (*West Shene* 1258) was the earlier name for RICHMOND.

Sheepstor Devon. *Sitelestorra* 1168. Possibly 'craggy hill thought to resemble a bar or bolt', OE *scytels* + *torr*. Alternatively the first element may be an OE **scitels* 'dung'.

Sheepwash Devon. *Schepewast* 1166. 'Place where sheep are dipped'. OE *scēap-wæsce*.

Sheepy Magna & *Sheepy Parva* Leics. *Scepehe* 1086 (DB). 'Island, or dry ground in marsh, where sheep graze'. OE *scēap* + *ēg*. Distinguishing affixes are Latin *magna* 'great' and *parva* 'little'.

Sheering Essex. *Sceringa* 1086 (DB). Probably '(settlement) of the family or followers of a man called **Scear(a)'*. OE pers. name + *-ingas*.

Sheerness Kent. *Scerhnesse* 1203. Probably 'bright headland'. OE *scīr* + *næss*. Alternatively the first element may be OE *scear* 'plough-share' alluding to the shape of the headland.

Sheet Hants. *Syeta* c.1210. 'Projecting piece of land, corner or nook'. OE **scīete*.

Sheffield S. Yorks. *Scafeld* 1086 (DB). 'Open land by the River Sheaf'. OE river-name (from *scēath* 'boundary') + *feld*.

Sheffield Bottom Berks. *Sewelle* |*sic*| 1086 (DB), *Scheaffelda* 1167. 'Open land with a shelter'. OE **scēo* + *feld*.

Sheffield Green E. Sussex. *Sifelle* |*sic*| 1086 (DB), *Shipfeud* 1272. 'Open land where sheep graze'. OE *scēap* + *feld*.

Shefford, 'ford used for sheep', OE *scēap* or **scīep* + *ford*: **Shefford** Beds. *Sepford* 1220. **Shefford, East** & **Shefford, Great** Berks. *Siford* |*sic*| 1086 (DB), *Schipforda* 1167.

Shehy Mountains (*Cnoic na Seithe*) Cork. 'Hills of the hides'.

Sheinton Shrops. *Sc(h)entune* 1086 (DB), *Sheinton* 1222. Possibly 'farmstead or estate associated with a man called **Scēna'*. OE pers. name + *-ing-* + *tūn*.

Sheldon Derbys. *Scelhadun* 1086 (DB). Probably 'heathy hill with a shelf or ledge'. OE *scelf* + *hǣth* + *dūn*.

Sheldon Devon. *Sildene* 1086 (DB). 'Valley with steeply shelving sides'. OE *scylf* + *denu*.

Sheldon W. Mids. *Scheldon* 1189. 'Shelf hill'. OE *scelf* + *dūn*.

Sheldwich Kent. *Scilduuic* 784. 'Dwelling or farm with a shelter'. OE *sceld* + *wīc*.

Shelf W. Yorks. *Scelf* 1086 (DB). 'Shelving terrain'. OE *scelf*.

Shelfanger Norfolk. *Sceluangra* 1086 (DB). 'Wood on sloping ground'. OE *scelf* + *hangra*.

Shelfield, 'hill with a shelf or plateau'. OE *scelf* + *hyll*: **Shelfield** Warwicks. *Shelfhulle* 1221. **Shelfield** W. Mids. *Scelfeld* |*sic*| 1086 (DB), *Schelfhul* 1271.

Shelford, 'ford at a shallow place', OE **sceldu* + *ford*: **Shelford** Notts. *Scelforde* 1086 (DB). **Shelford, Great** & **Shelford, Little** Cambs. *Scelford* c.1050, *Escelforde* 1086 (DB).

Shelley W. Yorks. *Scelneleie* |*sic*| 1086 (DB), *Shelfleie* 1198. 'Woodland clearing on shelving terrain'. OE *scelf* + *lēah*.

Shellingford Oxon. *Scaringaford* 931, *Serengeford* 1086 (DB). 'Ford of the family or followers of a man called **Scear'*. OE pers. name + *-inga-* + *ford*.

Shellow Bowells Essex. *Scelga* 1086 (DB), *Scheuele Boules* 1303. 'Winding river' (with reference to the River Roding). OE **Sceolge* from *sceolh* 'twisted'. Manorial affix from the de Bueles family, here in the 13th cent.

Shelton, 'farmstead on a shelf of flat or sloping ground', OE *scelf* + *tūn*: **Shelton** Beds. *Eseltone* 1086 (DB). **Shelton** Norfolk. *Sceltuna* 1086 (DB). **Shelton** Notts. *Sceltun* 1086 (DB). **Shelton** Shrops. *Saltone* |*sic*| 1086 (DB), *Shelfton* 1221.

Shelve Shrops. *Schelfe* 1180. 'Shelf of level ground'. OE *scelf*.

Shelwick Heref. & Worcs. *Scelwiche* 1086 (DB). 'Dwelling or farm with a shelter'. OE *sceld* + *wīc*.

Shenfield Essex. *Scenefelda* 1086 (DB). 'Beautiful open land'. OE *scēne* + *feld*.

Shenington Oxon. *Senendone* 1086 (DB). 'Beautiful hill'. OE *scēne* (dative *-an*) + *dūn*.

Shenley, 'bright or beautiful woodland glade', OE *scēne* + *lēah*: **Shenley** Bucks. *Senelai* 1086 (DB). **Shenley** Herts. *Scenlai* 1086 (DB).

Shenstone Staffs. *Seneste* |*sic*| 1086 (DB), *Scenstan* 11th cent. 'Beautiful stone'. OE *scēne* + *stān*.

Shenton Leics. *Scenctun* 1002, *Scentone* 1086 (DB). 'Farmstead on the River Sence'. OE river-name (from *scenc* 'drinking cup') + *tūn*.

Shepley W. Yorks. *Scipelei* 1086 (DB). 'Clearing where sheep are kept'. OE *scēap* + *lēah*.

Shepperton Surrey. *Scepertune* 959, *Scepertone* 1086 (DB). Probably 'farmstead of the shepherd(s)'. OE *scēap-hirde* + *tūn*.

Sheppey, Isle of Kent. *Scepeig* 696–716, *Scape* 1086 (DB). 'Island where sheep are kept'. OE *scēap* + *ēg*.

Shepreth Cambs. *Esceprid* 1086 (DB). 'Sheep stream'. OE *scēap* + *rīth*.

Shepshed Leics. *Scepeshefde* 1086 (DB). 'Sheep headland'. OE *scēap* + *hēafod*.

Shepton, 'sheep farm', OE *scēap* + *tūn*: **Shepton Beauchamp** Somerset. *Sceptone* 1086 (DB), *Septon Belli campi* 1266. Manorial affix from the de Beauchamp

(Latin *de Bello campo*) family, here in the 13th cent. **Shepton Mallet** Somerset. *Sepetone* 1086 (DB), *Scheopton Malet* 1228. Manorial affix from the Malet family, here in the 12th cent. **Shepton Montague** Somerset. *Sceptone* 1086 (DB), *Schuptone Montagu* 1285. Manorial affix from Drogo de Montacute, tenant in 1086.

Sheraton Durham. *Scurufatun* c.1040. Probably 'farmstead of a man called Skurfa'. OScand. pers. name + OE *tūn*.

Sherborne, *Sherbourne, Sherburn*, '(place at) the bright or clear stream', OE *scīr* + *burna*: **Sherborne** Dorset. *Scireburnan* 864, *Scireburne* 1086 (DB). **Sherborne** Glos. *Scireburne* 1086 (DB). **Sherborne St John** & **Monk Sherborne** Hants. *Sireburne, Sireborne* 1086 (DB), *Shireburna Johannis* 1167, *Schireburne Monachorum* c.1270. Distinguishing affixes from possession by Robert de Sancto Johanne in the 13th cent., and from the priory here (Latin *monachorum* 'of the monks'). **Sherbourne** Warwicks. *Scireburne* 1086 (DB). **Sherburn** Durham. *Scireburne* c.1170. **Sherburn** N. Yorks. *Scire(s)burne* 1086 (DB). **Sherburn in Elmet** N. Yorks. *Scirburnan* c.900, *Scireburne* 1086 (DB). For the old district name Elmet, *see* BARWICK.

Shercock (*Searcóg*) Cavan. *Skarkeoge al. Sharcocke* 1629. Meaning uncertain.

Shere Surrey. *Essira* 1086 (DB). '(Place at) the bright or clear stream'. OE *scīr*.

Shereford Norfolk. *Sciraford* 1086 (DB). 'Bright or clear ford'. OE *scīr* + *ford*.

Sherfield, probably 'bright open land', i.e. having sparse vegetation, OE *scīr* + *feld*: **Sherfield English** Hants. *Sirefelle* 1086 (DB). Manorial affix from le Engleis family, here in the 14th cent. **Sherfield on Loddon** Hants. *Schirefeld* 1179. Loddon is a Celtic river-name (possibly meaning 'muddy stream').

Sherford Devon. *Scireford* c.1050, *Sirefort* 1086 (DB). 'Bright or clear ford'. OE *scīr* + *ford*.

Sheriff Hutton N. Yorks., *see* HUTTON.

Sheriffhales Shrops. *Halas* 1086 (DB), *Shiruehales* 1301. 'Nooks of land', OE *halh* in a plural form. Affix is OE *scīrrēfa* from possession by the Sheriff of Shropshire in 1086.

Sheringham Norfolk. *Silingeham* |sic| 1086 (DB), *Scheringham* 1242. 'Homestead of the family or followers of a man called Scīra'. OE pers. name + *-inga-* + *hām*.

Sherington Bucks. *Serintone* 1086 (DB). 'Estate associated with a man called Scīra'. OE pers. name + *-ing-* + *tūn*.

Sherkin Island (*Inis Arcáin*) Cork. 'Arcán's island'.

Shernborne Norfolk. *Scernebrune* 1086 (DB). 'Dirty or muddy stream'. OE *scearn* + *burna*.

Sherrington Wilts. *Scearntune* 968, *Scarentone* 1086 (DB). 'Dirty or muddy farmstead'. OE *scearn* + *tūn*.

Sherston Wilts. *Scoranstan* 896, *Sorestone* 1086 (DB). 'Stone or rock on a steep slope'. OE **scora* + *stān*.

Sherwood Forest Notts. *Scirwuda* 955. 'Wood belonging to the shire'. OE *scīr* + *wudu*.

Sheskinatawy (*Seisceann an tSamhaid*) Donegal. 'Swamp of the sorrel'.

Sheskinshule (*Seisceann Siúil*) Tyrone. 'Moving marsh'.

Shetland (the unitary authority). *Haltland* c.1100, *Shetland* 1289. Various interpretations but probably reshaping of pre-Norse name.

Shevington Gtr. Manch. *Shefinton* c.1225. Probably 'farmstead near a hill called *Shevin*'. Celtic **cevn* 'ridge' + OE *tūn*.

Sheviock Cornwall. *Savioch* 1086 (DB). Possibly 'strawberry place'. Cornish *sevi* + suffix *-ek*.

Shiant Islands W. Isles. 'Hallowed islands'. Gaelic *seunta*.

Shields, 'temporary sheds or huts (used by fisherman)', ME *schele*: **Shields, North** Tyne & Wear. *Chelis* 1268. **Shields, South** Tyne & Wear. *Scheles* 1235.

Shifnal Shrops. *Scuffanhalch* 12th cent. Probably 'nook or hollow of a man called **Scuffa*'. OE pers. name (genitive *-n*) + *halh*.

Shilbottle Northum. *Schipplingbothill* 1242. Probably 'dwelling of the men of SHIPLEY'. Place-name + OE *-inga-* + *bōtl*.

Shildon Durham. *Sciluedon* 1214. 'Shelf hill'. OE *scylfe* + *dūn*.

Shillelagh (*Síol Éalaigh*) Wicklow. *Sil nElathig* 11th cent. *Shilleylle* 1549. 'Descendants of Éalach'.

Shillingford, probably 'ford of the family or followers of a man called **Sciell(a)*', OE pers. name + *-inga-* + *ford*, but an OE stream-name **Scielling* 'the noisy one' may be an alternative first element: **Shillingford** Devon. *Sellingeford* 1179. **Shillingford** Oxon. *Sillingeforda* 1156. **Shillingford St George** Devon. *Selingeforde* 1086 (DB). Affix from the dedication of the church.

Shillingstone Dorset. *Akeford Skelling* 1220, *Shillyngeston* 1444. 'Schelin's estate (in OKEFORD)'. OE *tūn* with the name of the tenant in 1086 (DB).

Shillington Beds. *Scytlingedune* 1060, *Sethlindone* 1086 (DB). 'Hill of the family or followers of a man called **Scyttel*'. OE pers. name + *-inga-* + *dūn*.

Shilton, 'farmstead on a shelf or ledge', OE *scylf(e)* + *tūn*: **Shilton** Oxon. *Scylftune* 1044. **Shilton** Warwicks. *Scelftone* 1086 (DB). **Shilton, Earl** Leics. *Sceltone* 1086 (DB). Affix from its early possession by the Earls of Leicester.

Shimpling, probably '(settlement of) the family or followers of a man called **Scimpel*', OE pers. name + *-ingas*: **Shimpling** Norfolk. *Simplingham* c.1035, *Simplinga* 1086 (DB). Sometimes with OE *hām* 'homestead' in early spellings. **Shimpling** Suffolk. *Simplinga* 1086 (DB).

Shincliffe Durham. *Scinneclif* c.1085. 'Cliff or bank haunted by a phantom or demon'. OE *scinna* + *clif*.

Shinfield Berks. *Selingefelle* |sic| 1086 (DB), *Schiningefeld* 1167. 'Open land of the family or followers of a man called **Scīene*'. OE pers. name + *-inga-* + *feld*.

Shinglis (*Seanlios*) Westmeath. 'Old fort'.

Shinrone (*Suí an Róin*) Offaly. 'Seat of the seal'.

Shipbourne Kent. *Sciburna* |sic| c.1100, *Scipburn* 1198. 'Sheep stream'. OE *scēap* + *burna*.

Shipdham Norfolk. *Scipdham* 1086 (DB). 'Homestead with a flock of sheep'. OE **scīpde + hām*.

Shiplake Oxon. *Siplac* 1163. 'Sheep stream'. OE *scēap + lacu*.

Shipley, 'clearing or pasture where sheep are kept', OE *scēap* or **scīep + lēah*; examples include: **Shipley** Northum. *Schepley* 1236. **Shipley** Shrops. *Sciplei* 1086 (DB). **Shipley** W. Sussex. *Scapeleia* 1073, *Sepelei* 1086 (DB). **Shipley** W. Yorks. *Scipeleia* 1086 (DB).

Shipmeadow Suffolk. *Scipmedu* 1086 (DB). 'Meadow for sheep'. OE *scēap + mæp* (dative *mǣdwe*).

Shippon Oxon. *Sipene* 1086 (DB). OE *scypen* 'a cattle-shed'.

Shipston on Stour Warwicks. *Scepuuæisctune* c.770, *Scepwestun* 1086 (DB). 'Farmstead by the sheep-wash'. OE *scēap-wæsce + tūn*. Stour is a Celtic or OE river-name probably meaning 'the strong one'.

Shipton, usually 'sheep farm', OE *scēap* or **scīep + tūn*; examples include: **Shipton** Shrops. *Scipetune* 1086 (DB). **Shipton Bellinger** Hants. *Sceptone* 1086 (DB), *Shupton Berenger* 14th cent. Manorial affix from the Berenger family, here in the 13th cent. **Shipton Gorge** Dorset. *Sepetone* 1086 (DB), *Shipton Gorges* 1594. Manorial addition from the de Gorges family, here in the 13th cent. **Shipton Moyne** Glos. *Sciptone* 1086 (DB), *Schipton Moine* 1287. Manorial affix from the Moygne family, here from the 13th cent. **Shipton under Wychwood** Oxon. *Sciptone* 1086 (DB). Wychwood is an old forest-name, *see* ASCOTT UNDER WYCHWOOD.
    However the following has a different origin: **Shipton** N. Yorks. *Hipton* 1086 (DB). 'Farmstead where rose-hips grow'. OE *hēope + tūn*.

Shirburn Oxon. *Scireburne* 1086 (DB). 'Bright or clear stream'. OE *scīr + burna*.

Shirebrook Derbys. *Scirebroc* 1202. 'Boundary brook' or 'bright brook'. OE *scīr* (as noun or adjective) + *brōc*.

Shireoaks Notts. *Shirakes* 12th cent. 'Oak-trees on the (county) boundary'. OE *scīr + āc*. In the similar name **Shire Oak** (W. Mids.) the meaning is rather 'oak-tree marking the site of the shire assembly'.

Shirland Derbys. *Sirelunt* 1086 (DB). Probably 'bright or sparsely wooded grove'. OE *scīr* + OScand. *lundr*.

Shirley, 'bright woodland clearing' or perhaps sometimes 'shire clearing', OE *scīr + lēah*: **Shirley** Derbys. *Sirelei* 1086 (DB). **Shirley** Gtr. London. *Shirleye* 1314. **Shirley** Hants. *Sirelei* 1086 (DB). **Shirley** W. Mids. *Syrley* c.1240.

Shirrell Heath Hants. *Scirhiltæ* 826. Probably 'bright or sparsely wooded grove'. OE *scīr + *hylte*, with the addition of *Heath* from the 17th cent.

Shirwell Devon. *Sirewelle* 1086 (DB). 'Bright or clear spring or stream'. OE *scīr + wella*.

Shobdon Heref. & Worcs. *Scepedune |sic|* 1086 (DB), *Scobbedun* 1242. 'Hill of a man called **Sceobba*'. OE pers. name + *dūn*.

Shobrooke Devon. *Sceocabroc* 938, *Sotebroca* 1086 (DB). 'Brook haunted by an evil spirit'. OE *sceocca + brōc*.

Shocklach Ches. *Socheliche* 1086 (DB). 'Boggy stream haunted by an evil spirit'. OE *sceocca + *læcc*.

Shoeburyness, *North Shoebury* Essex. *Sceobyrig* early 10th cent., *Soberia* 1086 (DB), *Shoberynesse* 16th cent. 'Fortress providing shelter'. OE **scēo + burh* (dative *byrig*), with the later addition of *næss* 'promontory'.

Sholden Kent. *Shoueldune* 1176. Possibly 'hill thought to resemble a shovel'. OE *scofl + dūn*.

Sholing Hants. *Sholling* 1251. Possibly 'uneven or sloping place'. OE *sceolh + -ing*.

Shoreditch Gtr. London. *Soredich* c.1148 'Ditch by a steep bank or slope'. OE **scora + dīc*.

Shoreham, 'homestead by a steep bank or slope', OE **scora + hām*: **Shoreham** Kent. *Scorham* 822. **Shoreham by Sea** W. Sussex. *Sorham* 1073, *Soreham* 1086 (DB).

Shorncote Glos. *Schernecote* 1086 (DB). 'Cottage(s) in a dirty or muddy place'. OE *scearn + cot*.

Shorne Kent. *Scorene* c.1100. 'Steep place'. OE **scoren*.

Shorwell I. of Wight. *Sorewelle* 1086 (DB). 'Spring or stream by a steep slope'. OE **scora + wella*.

Shotesham Norfolk. *Shotesham* 1044–7, *Scotesham* 1086 (DB). 'Homestead of a man called Scot'. OE pers. name + *hām*.

Shotley, possibly 'clearing frequented by pigeons, or where shooting takes place', OE **sceote* or *sceot + lēah*: **Shotley** Suffolk. *Scoteleia* 1086 (DB). **Shotley Bridge** Northum. *Schotley* 1242. The important bridge here over the River Derwent spans the two counties of Northumberland and Durham.

Shottermill Surrey. *Shottover* 1537, *Schotouermyll* 1607. Probably 'mill of a family called Shotover'. ME surname + *myln*.

Shottery Warwicks. *Scotta rith* 699–709. Probably 'stream of the Scots'. OE *Scot* (genitive plural *-a*) + *rīth*. Alternatively the first element may be OE *sc(e)ota* 'trout'.

Shottesbrooke Berks. *Sotesbroc* 1086 (DB), *Schottesbroc*, *Schotebroch* 1187. Probably 'brook of a man called Scot'. OE pers. name + *brōc*.

Shotteswell Warwicks. *Soteswell* c.1140. Probably 'spring or stream of a man called Scot'. OE pers. name + *wella*.

Shottisham Suffolk. *Scotesham* 1086 (DB). 'Homestead of a man called Scot or **Scēot*'. OE pers. name + *hām*.

Shottle Derbys. *Sothelle |sic|* 1086 (DB), *Schethell* 1191. Probably 'hill with a steep slope'. OE **scēot + hyll*.

Shotton Flin. *Schotton* 1283. 'Farm on a hill'. OE *scēot + tūn*.

Shotton Durham, near Peterlee. *Sotton* c.1165. Possibly 'farmstead on or near a steep slope'. OE **scēot + tūn*.

Shotton Northum., near Mindrum. *Scotadun* c.1050. 'Hill of the Scots'. OE *Scot* (genitive plural *-a*) + *dūn*.

Shotts N. Lan. *Bertrum Schottis* 1552. '(Place by the) slopes'. OE **sceot*.

Shotwick Ches. *Sotowiche* 1086 (DB). 'Dwelling or farm at a steep promontory'. OE **scēot + hōh + wīc*.

Shouldham Norfolk. *Sculdeham* 1086 (DB). Probably 'homestead owing a debt or obligation'. OE **sculd* + *hām*.

Shoulton Heref. & Worcs. *Scolegeton c.*1220. Possibly 'farmstead at the stream called **Sceolge*'. OE river-name (meaning 'winding') + *tūn*.

Shraheens (*Na Sraithíní*) Mayo. 'The little river meadow'.

Shrawardine Shrops. *Saleurdine* |*sic*| 1086 (DB), *Scrawardin* 1166. Possibly 'enclosure near a hollow or hovel'. OE *scræf* + *worthign*.

Shrawley Heref. & Worcs. *Scræfleh* 804. 'Woodland clearing near a hollow or hovel'. OE *scræf* + *lēah*.

Shrewsbury Shrops. *Scrobbesbyrig* 11th cent., *Sciropesberie* 1086 (DB). 'Fortified place of the scrubland region'. Old district name (from an OE **scrobb*) + OE *burh* (dative *byrig*).

Shrewton Wilts. *Wintreburne* 1086 (DB), *Winterbourne Syreveton* 1232. 'The sheriff's manor on the stream formerly called *Wintreburne*'. OE *scīr-rēfa* + *tūn*. The 'winter stream' (OE *winter* + *burna*) is now called **Till** (a 'backformation' from TILSHEAD).

Shrigley, Pott Ches. *Schriggeleg* 1285, *Potte Shryggelegh* 1354. Two distinct names. Pott is from ME *potte* 'a deep hole'. Shrigley is 'woodland clearing frequented by misselthrushes', OE *scrīc* + *lēah*.

Shrivenham Oxon. *Scrifenanhamme c.*950, *Seriveham* 1086 (DB). 'River-meadow allotted by decree (to the church)'. OE *scrifen* + *hamm*.

Shronowen (*Srón Abhann*) Kerry. 'Snout of the river'.

Shropham Norfolk. *Screpham* 1086 (DB). OE *hām* 'homestead' with an uncertain first element, possibly a pers. name.

Shropshire (the county). *Sciropescire* 1086 (DB). Shortened form of old spelling for SHREWSBURY + OE *scīr* 'district'. The form **Salop** (now adopted as the name of the 'new' county) is a revival of an old Norman contracted spelling of the name Shropshire.

Shroton Dorset, *see* IWERNE COURTNEY.

Shrough (*Sruth*) Tipperary. 'Stream'.

Shroughan (*Sruthán*) Wicklow. 'Stream'.

Shrove (*An tSrúibh*) Donegal. 'The snout'.

Shrue (*Sidh Ruadh*) Westmeath. 'Red fairy hill'.

Shrule (*Sruthair*) Mayo. 'Stream'.

Shuckburgh Warwicks. *Socheberge* 1086 (DB). 'Hill or mound haunted by an evil spirit'. OE *scucca* + *beorg*.

Shucknall Heref. & Worcs. *Shokenhulle* 1377. 'Hill haunted by an evil spirit'. OE *scucca* (genitive -*n*) + *hyll*.

Shudy Camps Cambs., *see* CAMPS.

Shuna (island) Arg. 'Island'. OScand. Unidentified first element + *ey*.

Shurdington Glos. *Surditona c.*1150. Possibly 'estate associated with a man called **Scyrda*'. OE pers. name + -*ing*- + *tūn*.

Shurton Somerset. *Shureveton* 1219. 'The sheriff's manor'. OE *scīr-rēfa* + *tūn*.

Shustoke Warwicks. *Scotescote* |*sic*| 1086 (DB), *Schutestok* 1247. Probably 'outlying farmstead or hamlet of a man called **Scēot*'. OE pers. name + *stoc* (replacing *cot* 'cottage' of the DB form).

Shute Devon. *Schieta c.*1200. 'The corner or angle of land'. OE **scīete*.

Shutford Oxon. *Schiteford c.*1160. Probably 'ford of a man called **Scytta*'. OE pers. name + *ford*.

Shutlanger Northants. *Shitelhanger* 1162. 'Wooded slope where shuttles or wooden bars are obtained'. OE *scytel* + *hangra*.

Shuttington Warwicks. *Cetitone* |*sic*| 1086 (DB), *Schetintuna c.*1160. 'Estate associated with a man called **Scytta*'. OE pers. name + -*ing*- + *tūn*.

Sibbertoft Northants. *Sibertod* |*sic*| 1086 (DB), *Sibertoft* 1198. 'Homestead of a man called Sigebeorht or Sigbjǫrn'. OE or OScand. pers. name + *toft*.

Sibdon Carwood Shrops. *Sibetune* 1086 (DB), *Sipton Carswood* 1672. 'Farmstead of a man called Sibba'. OE pers. name + *tūn*. Affix from a nearby place Carwood, *Carwod* 1307, probably 'rock wood', from OE *carr* + *wudu*.

Sibford Ferris & *Sibford Gower* Oxon. *Sibeford* 1086 (DB), *Sibbard Ferreys* early 18th cent., *Sibbeford Goyer* 1220. 'Ford of a man called Sibba'. OE pers. name + *ford*. Manorial affixes from early possession by the de Ferrers and Guher families.

Sible Hedingham Essex, *see* HEDINGHAM.

Sibsey Lincs. *Sibolci* 1086 (DB). 'Island of a man called Sigebald'. OE pers. name + *ēg*.

Sibson Cambs. *Sibestune* 1086 (DB). 'Farmstead of a man called Sibbi'. OScand. pers. name + OE *tūn*.

Sibson Leics. *Sibetesdone* 1086 (DB). 'Hill of a man called Sigebed'. OE pers. name + *dūn*.

Sibthorpe Notts. *Sibetorp* 1086 (DB). 'Outlying farm of a man called Sibba or Sibbi'. OE or OScand. pers. name + OScand. *thorp*.

Sibton Suffolk. *Sibbetuna* 1086 (DB). 'Farmstead of a man called Sibba'. OE pers. name + *tūn*.

Sicklinghall N. Yorks. *Sidingale* |*sic*| 1086 (DB), *Sicclinhala c.*1150. 'Nook of land of the family or followers of a man called **Sicel*'. OE pers. name + -*inga*- + *halh*.

Sidbury Devon. *Sideberia* 1086 (DB). 'Fortified place by the River Sid'. OE river-name (from *sīd* 'broad') + *burh* (dative *byrig*).

Sidbury Shrops. *Sudberie* 1086 (DB). 'Southern fortified place or manor'. OE *sūth* + *burh* (dative *byrig*).

Sidcup Gtr. London. *Cetecopp* 1254. Probably 'seat-shaped or flat-topped hill'. OE **set-copp*.

Siddington Ches. *Sudendune* 1086 (DB). '(Place) south of the hill'. OE *sūthan* + *dūn*.

Siddington Glos. *Sudintone* 1086 (DB). '(Land) south in the township'. OE *sūth* + *in* + *tūn*.

Sidestrand Norfolk. *Sistran* |*sic*| 1086 (DB), *Sidestrande* late 12th cent. 'Broad shore'. OE *sīd* + *strand*.

Sidford Devon. *Sideford* 1238. 'Ford on the River Sid'. OE river-name (*see* SIDBURY) + *ford*.

Sidlaw Hills Ang. *Seedlaws* 1799. '(Seat) hills'. First element uncertain + OE *hlāw*.

Sidlesham W. Sussex. *Sidelesham* 683. 'Homestead of a man called *Sidel*'. OE pers. name + *hām*.

Sidmouth Devon. *Sedemuda* 1086 (DB). 'Mouth of the River Sid'. OE river-name (*see* SIDBURY) + *mūtha*.

Siefton Shrops. *Sireton* |sic| 1086 (DB), *Siveton* 1257. Possibly 'farmstead of a woman called Sigegifu'. OE pers. name + *tūn*. Alternatively the first element may be an old stream-name *Siven* of unknown origin.

Sigglesthorne E. R. Yorks. *Siglestorne* 1086 (DB). 'Thorn-tree of a man called Sigulfr'. OScand. pers. name + *thorn*.

Silchester Hants. *Silcestre* 1086 (DB). Possibly 'Roman station by a willow copse'. OE **siele* + *ceaster*. Alternatively the first element may be a reduced form of Calleva 'place in the woods', the original Celtic name of this Roman city first recorded in the 2nd cent. AD.

Sileby Leics. *Siglebi* 1086 (DB). 'Farmstead or village of a man called Sigulfr'. OScand. pers. name + *bý*.

Silecroft Cumbria. *Selecroft* 1211. 'Enclosure where willows grow'. OScand. *selja* + OE *croft*.

Sili. *See* SULLY.

Silk Willoughby Lincs., *see* WILLOUGHBY.

Silkstone S. Yorks. *Silchestone* 1086 (DB). 'Farmstead of a man called Sigelāc'. OE pers. name + *tūn*.

Silksworth Tyne & Wear. *Sylceswurthe* c.1050. 'Enclosure of a man called Sigelāc'. OE pers. name + *worth*.

Silloth Cumbria. *Selathe* 1292. 'Barn(s) by the sea'. OScand. *sǽr* or OE *sǣ* + OScand. *hlatha*.

Silpho N. Yorks. *Silfhou* c.1160. 'Flat-topped hill-spur'. OE *scylfe* + *hōh*.

Silsden W. Yorks. *Siglesdene* 1086 (DB). 'Valley of a man called Sigulfr'. OScand. pers. name + OE *denu*.

Silsoe Beds. *Siuuilessou* 1086 (DB). 'Hill-spur of a man called *Sifel*'. OE pers. name + *hōh*.

Silton, Nether & *Silton, Over* N. Yorks. *Silftune* 1086 (DB). 'Farmstead by a shelf or ledge', or 'farmstead of a man called Sylfa'. OE *scylfe* or OScand. pers. name + OE *tūn*.

Silverdale Lancs. *Selredal* |sic| 1199, *Celverdale* 1292. 'Silver-coloured valley' (from the grey limestone here). OE *seolfor* + *dæl*.

Silverstone Northants. *Sulueston* 942, *Silvestone* 1086 (DB). Probably 'farmstead of a man called Sǽwulf or Sigewulf'. OE pers. name + *tūn*.

Silverton Devon. *Sulfretone* 1086 (DB). Probably 'farmstead near the gully ford'. OE *sulh* + *ford* + *tūn*.

Simonburn Northum. *Simundeburn* 1229. 'Stream of a man called Sigemund'. OE pers. name + *burna*.

Simonstone Lancs. *Simondestan* 1278. 'Boundary stone of a man called Sigemund'. OE pers. name + *stān*.

Simpson Bucks. *Siwinestone* 1086 (DB). 'Farmstead of a man called Sigewine'. OE pers. name + *tūn*.

Sinderby N. Yorks. *Senerebi* 1086 (DB). 'Southern farmstead or village', or 'farmstead or village of a man called Sindri'. OScand. *syndri* or pers. name + *bý*.

Sindlesham Berks. *Sindlesham* 1220. Possibly 'homestead or enclosure of a man called *Synnel*'. OE pers. name + *hām* or *hamm*.

Sineirl (*Suí an Iarla*) Antrim. 'Seat of the earl'.

Singleborough Bucks. *Sincleberia* 1086 (DB). 'Shingle hill'. OE **singel* + *beorg*.

Singleton Lancs. *Singletun* 1086 (DB). 'Farmstead with shingled roof'. OE **scingol* + *tūn*.

Singleton W. Sussex. *Silletone* |sic| 1086 (DB), *Sengelton* 1185. Probably 'farmstead by a burnt clearing'. OE **sengel* + *tūn*.

Sinnington N. Yorks. *Siuenintun* 1086 (DB). 'Farmstead near the River Seven'. Pre-English river-name (of uncertain meaning) + OE *-ing-* + *tūn*.

Sinton, Leigh Heref. & Worcs. *Sothyntone in Lega* 13th cent. '(Place) south in the village (of LEIGH)', OE *sūth* + *in* + *tūn*.

Sion Mills (*Muileann an tSiáin*) Tyrone. the 'Sion Mills' 1843. 'Mill of the fairy mound'.

Sipson Gtr. London. *Sibwineston* c.1150. 'Farmstead of a man called Sibwine'. OE pers. name + *tūn*.

Sissinghurst Kent. *Saxingherste* c.1180. 'Wooded hill of the family or followers of a man called Seaxa'. OE pers. name + *-inga-* + *hyrst*.

Siston S. Glos. *Sistone* 1086 (DB). 'Farmstead of a man called *Sige*'. OE pers. name + *tūn*.

Sithney Cornwall. *St Sythyn* 1230. From the patron saint of the parish church, St Sithny.

Sitlington W. Yorks., *see* MIDDLESTOWN.

Sittingbourne Kent. *Sidingeburn* 1200. Probably 'stream of the dwellers on the slope'. OE *sīde* + *-inga-* + *burna*.

Six Mile Bottom Cambs., hamlet so named 1801, from its situation in a valley (OE *botm*) six miles from Newmarket.

Sixhills Lincs. *Sisse* |sic| 1086 (DB), *Sixlei* 1196. 'Six woodland clearings'. OE *six* + *lēah*.

Sixmilecross Tyrone. *na gCorrach* 1930. The village crossroads is roughly six Irish miles from Omagh. The Irish name of the village is *Na Coracha Móra*, 'the big round hills'.

Sixpenny Handley Dorset, *see* HANDLEY.

Sizewell Suffolk. *Syreswell* 1240. Probably 'Spring or stream of a man called Sigehere'. OE pers. name + *wella*.

Skagh (*Sceach*) Cork, Limerick. 'Hawthorn'.

Skahard (*Sceach Ard*) Limerick. 'High hawthorn'.

Skaill Orkn. 'Hut'. OScand. *skáli*.

Skara Brae Orkn. Origin not known, unless linked with ON *skarfr* 'cormorant'.

Skea (*Sceach*) Fermanagh, Tyrone. 'Hawthorn'.

Skeabost Highland (Skye). 'Skith's farm'. OScand. pers. name *skithi* + *bólstathr*.

Skeagh (*Sceach*) Antrim, Cavan, Donegal, Laois, Tipperary. 'Hawthorn'.

Skeaghmore (*Sceath Mhór*) Westmeath. 'Big hawthorn'.

Skeard (*Scéird*) Mayo. 'Bleak hill'.

Skeeby N. Yorks. *Schirebi* |*sic*| 1086 (DB), *Schittebi* 1187. Probably 'farmstead or village of a man called Skíthi'. OScand pers. name + *bý*.

Skeffington Leics. *Sciftitone* 1086 (DB). Probably 'estate associated with a man called *Sceaft*'. OE pers. name (with Scand. *sk-*) + *-ing-* + *tūn*.

Skeffling E. R. Yorks. *Sckeftling* 12th cent. Probably '(settlement of) the family or followers of a man called *Sceaftel*'. OE pers. name (with Scand. *sk-*) + *-ingas*.

Skegby Notts., near Mansfield. *Schegebi* 1086 (DB). 'Farmstead or village of a man called Skeggi, or on a beard-shaped promontory'. OScand. pers. name or *skegg* + *bý*.

Skegness Lincs. *Sceggenesse* 12th cent. 'Beard-shaped promontory', or 'promontory of a man called Skeggi'. OScand. *skegg* or pers. name + *nes*.

Skegoniel (*Sceitheog an Iarla*) Antrim. *Balliskeighog-Inerla* 1605. 'Thorn bush of the earl'.

Skelbo Highland. 'Shell farm'. OScand. *skel* + *bólstathr* (or *ból*).

Skellingthorpe Lincs. *Scheldinchope* 1086 (DB). 'Enclosure in marsh associated with a man called *Sceld*' from OE pers. name + *-ing-* + *hop*, or 'enclosure in marsh by a shield-shaped hill' from OE *sceld* + *-ing* + *hop*. Initial *Sk-* through Scand. influence.

Skellow S. Yorks. *Scanhalle* |*sic*| 1086 (DB), *Scalehale* c.1190. 'Nook of land with a shieling or hut'. OE **scēla* (influenced by OScand. *skáli*) + *halh*.

Skelmanthorpe W. Yorks. *Scelmertorp* 1086 (DB). 'Outlying farmstead of a man called *Skjaldmarr*'. OScand. pers. name + *thorp*.

Skelmersdale Lancs. *Schelmeresdele* 1086 (DB). 'Valley of a man called *Skjaldmarr*'. OScand. pers. name + *dalr*.

Skelpick Highland. 'Shelly place'. Perhaps Gaelic *sgealbach*.

Skelton, 'farmstead on a shelf or ledge', OE *scelf* (with Scand. *sk-*) + *tūn*: **Skelton** Cumbria. *Sheltone* c.1160. **Skelton** E. R. Yorks. *Schilton* 1086 (DB). **Skelton** N. Yorks., near Richmond. *Scelton* 12th cent. **Skelton** Red. & Cleve. *Scheltun* 1086 (DB). **Skelton** York. *Scheltun* 1086 (DB).

Skelwith Bridge Cumbria. *Schelwath* 1246. 'Ford by the waterfall'. OScand. *skjallr* 'resounding' + *vath*. The waterfall referred to is Skelwith Force (from OScand. *fors* 'waterfall'). The addition *Bridge* is found from the 17th cent.

Skenarget (*Sceach Airgid*) Tyrone. 'Silver hawthorn'.

Skendleby Lincs. *Scheueldebi* |*sic*| 1086 (DB), *Schendelebia* c.1150. OScand. *bý* 'farmstead, village' possibly added to a place-name meaning 'beautiful slope' from OE *scēne* (with Scand. *sk-*) + *helde*.

Skerne E. R. Yorks. *Schirne* 1086 (DB). Named from Skerne Beck, 'the clear or pure stream', from OScand. *skírn*, or (perhaps more likely) from OE *scīr* (dative *-an*) + *ēa* with initial *sk-* through Scand. influence.

Skerray Highland. 'Island by a reef'. OScand. *sker* + *ey*.

Skerries (*Ynysoedd y Moelrhoniaid*) (islands) Angl. 'Reefs'. OScand. *sker*. The Welsh name means 'islands of the seals' (Welsh *ynys*, plural *ynysoedd* + *y* + *moelrhon*, plural *moelrhoniaid*).

Skerries, The (*Na Sceirí*) (islands) Antrim. *The Skerries* 1837. 'The rocky islands'.

Sketty Swan. 'Ceti's island'. Welsh *ynys*.

Skewsby N. Yorks. *Scoxebi* 1086 (DB). 'Farmstead or village in the wood'. OScand. *skógr* + *bý*.

Skeyton Norfolk. *Scegutuna* 1086 (DB). 'Farmstead of a man called Skeggi'. OScand. pers. name + *tūn*.

Skibbereen (*An Sciobhairín*) Cork. 'The place of the little boats'.

Skibo Highland. *Schythebol* 1275. 'Skithi's farm'. OScand. pers. name + *bólstathr*.

Skidbrooke Lincs. *Schitebroc* 1086 (DB). 'Dirty brook'. OE *scite* (with Scand. *sk-*) + *brōc*.

Skidby E. R. Yorks. *Scyteby* 972, *Schitebi* 1086 (DB). 'Farmstead or village of a man called Skyti', or 'dirty farmstead or village'. OScand. pers. name or *skítr* + *bý*.

Skiddernagh (*Sciodarnach*) Mayo. 'Place of puddles'.

Skilgate Somerset. *Schiligata* 1086 (DB). Possibly 'stony or shaly gate or gap'. OE **scilig* + *geat*.

Skillington Lincs. *Schillintune* 1086 (DB). Possibly 'estate associated with a man called *Scill(a)*', OE pers. name + *-ing-* + *tūn*. Alternatively the first element may be OE *scilling* 'shilling' alluding to a rent. Initial *Sk-* through Scand. influence.

Skinburness Cumbria. *Skyneburg* 1175, *Skynburneyse* 1298. 'Promontory near the demon-haunted stronghold'. OE *scinna* (with Scand. *sk-*) + *burh* + OScand. *nes*.

Skinningrove Red. & Cleve. *Scineregrive* c.1175. 'Pit used by skinners or tanners'. OScand. *skinnari* + *gryfja*.

Skipsea E. R. Yorks. *Skipse* 1160. 'Lake used for ships'. OScand. *skip* + *sær*.

Skipton, 'sheep farm', OE *scīp* (with Scand. *sk-*) + *tūn*: **Skipton** N. Yorks. *Scipton* 1086 (DB). **Skipton on Swale** N. Yorks. *Schipetune* 1086 (DB). Swale is an OE river-name probably meaning 'rushing water'.

Skipwith N. Yorks. *Schipewic* 1086 (DB). 'Sheep farm'. OE *scīp* (with Scand. *sk-*) + *wīc* (replaced by OScand. *vithr* 'wood').

Skirlaugh, North & *Skirlaugh, South* E. R. Yorks. *Schirelai* 1086 (DB). 'Bright woodland clearing'. OE *scīr* (with Scand. *sk-*) + *lēah*.

Skirmett Bucks. *La Skiremote* c.1307. 'Meeting-place of the shire-court'. OE *scīr* (with Scand *sk-*) + *(ge)mōt*.

Skirpenbeck E. R. Yorks. *Scarpenbec* 1086 (DB). Probably 'stream which sometimes dries up'. OScand. **skerpin* + *bekkr*.

Skirwith Cumbria. *Skirewit* 1205. 'Wood belonging to the shire'. OE *scīr* (with Scand. *sk-*) + OScand. *vithr*.

Skokholm (island) Pemb. *Scogholm* 1219, *Stokholm* 1275. 'Island in a channel'. OScand. *stokkr* + *holmr*. Expected *St-* has become *Sk-* under the influence of neighbouring SKOMER.

Skomer (island) Pemb. *Skalmey* 1324. 'Cloven island'. OScand. *skálm* + *ey*.

Skreen (*Scrín*) Meath, Sligo. 'Shrine'.

Skull (*Scoil*) Cork. 'School'.

Skye (island) Highland. *Scitis* c.150, *Scia* c.700, *Skith* c.1250, *Skye* 1266. Pre-Celtic name, later reinterpreted as 'winged (island)'. Gaelic *sgiath*. The island's great peninsulas thrust out north and south like wings.

Slade (*An Slaod*) Wexford. 'The fall-away of ground'.

Slaggyford Northum. *Slaggiford* 13th cent. 'Muddy ford'. ME **slaggi* + *ford*.

Slaidburn Lancs. *Slateborne* 1086 (DB). 'Stream by the sheep-pasture'. OE **slæget* + *burna*.

Slaithwaite W. Yorks. *Sladweit* 1178, *Sclagtwayt* 1277. Probably 'clearing where timber was felled'. OScand. *slag* + *thveit*.

Slaley Northum. *Slaveleia* 1166. 'Muddy woodland clearing'. OE **slæf* + *lēah*.

Slamannan Falk. *Slethmanin* 1250. 'Moor of Manau'. Gaelic *sliabh*.

Slane (*Baile Shláine*) Meath. 'Homestead of fullness'.

Slanebeg (*Sleamhain Bheag*) Westmeath. 'Small sleek place'.

Slanemore (*Sleamhain Mhór*) Westmeath. 'Big sleek place'.

Slaney (*Sleine*) (river) Carlow, Wexford, Wicklow. 'Healthy one'.

Slapton, 'farmstead by a slippery place' or 'muddy farmstead', OE **slæp* or **slæp* + *tūn*: **Slapton** Bucks. *Slapetone* 1086 (DB). **Slapton** Devon. *Sladone* |sic| 1086 (DB), *Slapton* 1244. **Slapton** Northants. *Slaptone* 1086 (DB).

Slaugham W. Sussex. *Slacham* c.1100. 'Homestead or enclosure where sloe or blackthorn grows'. OE *slāh* + *hām* or *hamm*.

Slaughter, Lower & *Slaughter, Upper* Glos. *Sclostre* 1086 (DB). Probably 'muddy place'. OE **slōhtre*.

Slaughtmanus (*Sleacht Mhánasa*) Derry. *Laghtmanus* 1613. 'Grave mound of Mánas'.

Slawston Leics. *Slagestone* 1086 (DB). Probably 'farmstead of a man called Slagr'. OScand. pers. name + OE *tūn*.

Slea Head (*Ceann Sléibhe*) Kerry. 'Head of the mountain'.

Sleaford Lincs. *Sliowaford* 852, *Eslaforde* 1086 (DB). 'Ford over the River Slea'. OE river-name (meaning 'muddy stream') + *ford*.

Sleagill Cumbria. *Slegill* c.1190. 'Ravine of the trickling stream, or of a man called **Slefa*'. OScand. *slefa* or pers. name + *gil*.

Sleat (peninsula) Highland (Skye). *Slate* c.1400. 'Level place'. OScand. *slétta*.

Sleatygraigue (*Gráig Shléibhte*) Laois. 'Hamlet of the mountains'.

Sledmere E. R. Yorks. *Slidemare* 1086 (DB). 'Pool in the valley'. OE *slæd* + *mere*.

Sleekburn, East & *Sleekburn, West* Northum. *Sliceburne* c.1050. 'Smooth stream, or muddy stream'. OE **slicu* or **slīc* + *burna*.

Sleightholme Durham. *Slethholm* 1234. Probably 'level raised ground'. OScand. *sléttr* + *holmr*.

Sleights N. Yorks. *Sleghtes* c.1223. 'Smooth or level fields'. OScand. *slétta*.

Slemish (*Sliabh Mis*) (mountain) Antrim. *Slébh Mis* 771. 'Mis's mountain'.

Slievaduff (*Sliabh an Daimh*) (mountain) Kerry. 'Mountain of the ox'.

Slieve Anierin (*Sliabh an Iarainn*) (mountain) Leitrim. 'Iron mountain'.

Slieve Bernagh (*Sliabh Bearnach*) (mountain) Clare, Down. 'Gapped mountain'.

Slieve Binnian (*Sliabh Binneáin*) (mountain) Down. *Great Bennyng* c.1568. 'Mountain of the little peak'.

Slieve Bloom (*Sliabh Bladhma*) (mountain) Laois, Offaly. 'Blaze mountain'.

Slieve Commedagh (*Sliabh Coimhéideach*) (mountain) Down. *Slieve Kimedia* c.1830. 'Guarding mountain'.

Slieve Croob (*Sliabh Crúibe*) (mountain) Down. *Crooby Mountaine* c.1657. 'Mountain of the hoof'.

Slieve Donard (*Sliabh Dónairt*) (mountain) Down. *Sliabh-Domha[n]gaird* 1645. 'St Dónart's mountain'.

Slieve Gamph (*Sliabh Gamh*) (mountain) Mayo, Sligo. 'Mountain of storms'.

Slieve Gullion (*Sliabh gCuillinn*) (mountain) Armagh (*moninni*). *Sleibi Culinn* c.830. 'Mountain of the slope'.

Slieve League (*Sliabh Liag*) (mountain) Donegal. *Sleibh Liacc* c.830. 'Mountain of the pillar stones'.

Slieve Mish (*Sliabh Mis*) (mountain) Kerry. 'Mountain of Mis'.

Slieve na Calliagh (*Sliabh na Calliagh*) (mountain) Meath. 'Mountain of the hag'.

Slieve Snaght (*Sliabh Sneachta*) (mountain) Donegal. *Sléibhte Sneachta* 1260. 'Mountain of snow'.

Slieveardagh (*Sliabh Ardach*) (mountain) Kilkenny, Tipperary. 'Mountain of the high field'.

Slieveaughty (*Sliabh Eachtaí*) (mountain) Galway. 'Eachta's mountain'.

Slievecallan (*Sliabh Calláin*) (mountain) Clare. 'Callán's mountain'.

Slievefelim (*Sliabh Eibhlinne*) (mountain) Limerick. 'Eibhlinn's mountain'.

Slievemore (*Sliabh Mór*) (mountain) Tyrone. 'Big mountain'.

Slievenamon (*Sliabh na mBan*) (mountain) Tipperary. 'Mountain of the women'.

Slieveroe (*Sliabh Rua*) (mountain) Kilkenny. 'Red mountain'.

Slievetooey (*Sliabh Tuaidh*) (mountain) Donegal. *Slieve-a-tory* 1835. 'Northern mountain'.

Sligo (*Sligeach*) Sligo. 'Abounding in shells'.

Slimbridge Glos. *Heslinbruge |sic|* 1086 (DB), *Slimbrugia* c.1153. 'Bridge or causeway over a muddy place'. OE *slīm* + *brycg*.

Slindon, probably 'sloping hill', OE **slinu* + *dūn*: **Slindon** Staffs. *Slindone* 1086 (DB). **Slindon** W. Sussex. *Eslindone* 1086 (DB).

Slingsby N. Yorks. *Selungesbi* 1086 (DB). 'Farmstead or village of a man called Slengr'. OScand. pers. name + *bý*.

Slipton Northants. *Sliptone* 1086 (DB). Probably 'muddy farmstead'. OE *slipa* + *tūn*.

Sloley Norfolk. *Slaleia* 1086 (DB). 'Woodland clearing where sloe or blackthorn grows'. OE *slāh* + *lēah*.

Sloothby Lincs. *Slodebi* 1086 (DB). Probably 'farmstead or village of a man called Slóthi'. OScand. pers. name + *bý*.

Slough Berks. *Slo* 1195. 'The slough or miry place'. OE *slōh*.

Slyne Lancs. *Sline* 1086 (DB). from OE **slinu* 'a slope'.

Smaghran (*Smeachrán*) Roscommon. 'Stripe of land'.

Smailholm Sc. Bord. *Smalham* 1246. 'Narrow village'. OE *smæl* + *hām*.

Small Hythe Kent. *Smalide* 13th cent., *Smalhede* 1289. 'Narrow landing-place or harbour'. OE *smæl* + *hȳth*.

Smallburgh Norfolk. *Smaleberga* 1086 (DB). 'Hill or mound on the River *Smale*'. Old name for the River Ant (from OE *smæl* 'narrow' and *ēa* 'river') + OE *beorg*.

Smalley Derbys. *Smælleage* 1009, *Smalei* 1086 (DB). 'Narrow woodland clearing'. OE *smæl* + *lēah*.

Smardale Cumbria. *Smeredal* 1190. Probably 'valley where butter is produced'. OScand. *smjǫr* or OE *smeoru* + OScand. *dalr*.

Smarden Kent. *Smeredaenne* c.1100. 'Woodland pasture where butter is produced'. OE *smeoru* + *denn*.

Smeaton, 'farmstead of the smiths', OE *smith* + *tūn*: **Smeaton, Great** N. Yorks. *Smithatune* 966–72, *Smidetune* 1086 (DB). **Smeaton, Kirk** & **Smeaton, Little** N. Yorks. *Smedetone* 1086 (DB). Distinguishing affix is OScand. *kirkja* 'church'.

Smeeth Kent. *Smitha* 1018. from OE *smiththe* 'a smithy'.

Smethwick W. Mids. *Smedeuuich* 1086 (DB). 'Dwelling or building of the smiths'. OE *smith* (genitive plural **smeotha*) + *wīc*.

Smisby Derbys. *Smidesbi* 1086 (DB). 'The smith's farmstead'. OScand. *smithr* + *bý*.

Smithborough Monaghan. *Smithsborough* 1778. A man named Smith established cattle fairs here in the latter half of the 18th cent. The Irish name is *Na Mullaí*, 'the hilltops'.

Snailwell Cambs. *Sneillewelle* c.1050, *Snelleuuelle* 1086 (DB). 'Spring or stream infested with snails'. OE *snægl* + *wella*.

Snainton N. Yorks. *Snechintune* 1086 (DB). Possibly 'farmstead associated with a man called **Snoc*'. OE pers. name + *-ing-* + *tūn*.

Snaith E. R. Yorks. *Snaith* c.1080, *Esneid* 1086 (DB). 'Piece of land cut off'. OScand. *sneith*.

Snape, from OE **snæp* 'boggy piece of land' or OScand. *snap* 'poor pasture'; examples include: **Snape** N. Yorks. *Snape* 1154. **Snape** Suffolk. *Snapes* 1086 (DB).

Snaresbrook Gtr. London, not recorded before 1599, from OE *brōc* 'brook' with an uncertain first element.

Snarestone Leics. *Snarchetone* 1086 (DB). 'Farmstead of a man called **Snar(o)c*'. OE pers. name + *tūn*.

Snarford Lincs. *Snerteforde* 1086 (DB). 'Ford of a man called Snǫrtr'. OScand. pers. name + OE *ford*.

Snargate Kent. *Snergathe* c.1197. Probably 'gate or gap where snares for animals are placed'. OE *sneare* + *geat*.

Snave Kent. *Snaues* 1182. Possibly 'the spits or strips of land'. OE **snafa*.

Snead Powys. *Sned* 1201. 'Detached plot of land'. OE *snǣd*.

Sneaton N. Yorks. *Snetune* 1086 (DB). 'Farmstead of a man called Snær, or with a detached piece of land'. OScand. pers. name or OE *snǣd* + *tūn*.

Sneem (*An tSnaidhm*) Kerry. 'The knot'. Many roads and rivers meet here.

Snelland Lincs. *Sneleslunt* 1086 (DB). 'Grove of a man called Snjallr'. OScand. pers. name + *lundr*.

Snelston Derbys. *Snellestune* 1086 (DB). 'Farmstead of a man called Snell'. OE pers. name + *tūn*.

Snettisham Norfolk. *Snetesham* 1086 (DB). 'Homestead of a man called **Snæt or Sneti*'. OE pers. name + *hām*.

Snitter Northum. *Snitere* 1176. Possibly 'weather-beaten place' from a word related to ME *sniteren* 'to snow'.

Snitterby Lincs. *Snetrebi* 1086 (DB). Probably 'farmstead or village of a man called **Snytra*'. OE pers. name + OScand. *bý*.

Snitterfield Warwicks. *Snitefeld* 1086 (DB). 'Open land frequented by snipe'. OE *snīte* + *feld*.

Snodhill Heref. & Worcs. *Snauthil* 1195. Probably 'snowy hill'. OE **snāwede* + *hyll*.

Snodland Kent. *Snoddingland* 838, *Esnoiland |sic|* 1086 (DB). 'Cultivated land associated with a man called **Snodd*'. OE pers. name + *-ing-* + *land*.

Snoreham Essex. *Snorham* 1238. Probably 'homestead or enclosure by a rough hill'. OE **snōr* + *hām*. or *hamm*.

Snoring, Great & *Snoring, Little* Norfolk. *Snaringes* 1086 (DB). Probably '(settlement of) the family or followers of a man called **Snear*'. OE pers. name + *-ingas*.

Snowdon (*Yr Wyddfa*) (mountain) Gwyd. *Snawdune* 1095. 'Snow hill'. OE *snāw* + *dūn*. The Welsh name means 'the mound' (Welsh *yr* + *gwyddfa*), referring to the mountain's use as a burial place.

Snowdonia (*Eryri*) (district) Gwyd. 'District of Snowdon'. *See* SNOWDON. The Welsh name means 'highlands' but has long been perceived as 'district of eagles' (Welsh *eryr* eagle) 'eagle'.

Snowshill Glos. *Snawesille* 1086 (DB). 'Hill where the snow lies long'. OE *snāw* + *hyll*.

Soar (river) Warwicks.–Leics.–Notts., *see* BARROW UPON SOAR.

Soay (island) W. Isles. 'Sheep island'. OScand. *sautha* + *ey*.

Soberton Hants. *Sudbertune* 1086 (DB). 'Southern grange or outlying farm'. OE *sūth* + *bere-tūn*.

Sodbury, Chipping & *Sodbury, Old* S. Glos. *Soppanbyrig* 872–915, *Sopeberie* 1086 (DB), *Cheping Sobbyri* 1269, *Olde Sobbury* 1346. 'Fortified place of a man called *Soppa'. OE pers. name + *burh* (dative *byrig*). Distinguishing affixes from OE *cēping* 'market' and *ald* 'old'.

Soham Cambs. *Sægham* c.1000, *Saham* 1086 (DB). 'Homestead by a swampy pool'. OE *sǣge* + *hām*.

Soham, Earl & *Soham, Monk* Suffolk. *Saham* 1086 (DB). 'Homestead by a pool'. OE *sǣ* or *sā* + *hām*. Distinguishing affixes from early possession by the Earl of Norfolk and the monks of Bury St Edmunds.

Soho Gtr. London. *So Ho* 1632. A hunting cry, from the early association of this area with hunting. Another example of this name, **Soho** Somerset (near Vobster), is identical in origin, though legend has it that it recalls the use of the phrase as the Duke of Monmouth's password in the 1685 Rising.

Soldierstown Antrim. *Soldierstown* 1780. The name refers to a former military station here.

Solent, The Hants. *Soluente* 731. An ancient pre-English name of uncertain origin and meaning.

Solfach. *See* SOLVA.

Solihull W. Mids. *Solihull* 12th cent. 'Muddy hill'. OE *sylig, *solig* + *hyll*. Alternatively the first element may be OE *sulig* 'pig-stye'.

Sollers Hope Heref. & Worcs., *see* HOPE.

Sollom Lancs. *Solayn* c.1200. 'Muddy enclosure' from OScand. *sol* + *hegn*, or 'sunny slope' from OScand. *sól* + *hlein*.

Solva (*Solfach*) Pemb. *Saleuuach* c.1200. '(Place on the) River Solfach'. The river name may mean 'poor one' (Welsh *salw*, 'ugly').

Solway Firth Dumf, Cumbria. *Sulewad* 1218. 'Estuary of the pillar ford'. OScand. *súl* + *vath* + *fjorthr*. The 'pillar' is the Lochmaben Stone marking the ford.

Solway Firth Cumbria, *see* BOWNESS-ON-SOLWAY.

Somborne, King's, *Somborne, Little*, & *Somborne, Upper* Hants. *Swinburnan* 909, *Sunburne* 1086 (DB). 'Pig stream'. OE *swīn* + *burna*. Affix *King's* from its having been a royal estate.

Somerby, probably 'farmstead or village of a man called Sumarlithi', OScand. pers. name + *bý*: **Somerby** Leics. *Sumerlidebie* 1086 (DB). **Somerby** Lincs., near Brigg. *Sumertebi* 1086 (DB).

Somercotes, 'huts or cottages used in summer', OE *sumor* + *cot*: **Somercotes** Derbys. *Somercotes* 1276. **Somercotes, North** & **Somercotes, South** Lincs. *Summercotes* 1086 (DB).

Somerford, 'ford usable in summer', OE *sumor* + *ford*: **Somerford, Great** & **Somerford, Little** Wilts. *Sumerford* 937, *Sumreford* 1086 (DB). **Somerford Keynes** Glos. *Sumerford* 685, *Somerford Keynes* 1291. Manorial affix from the de Kaynes family, here in the 13th cent.

Somerleyton Suffolk. *Sumerledetuna* 1086 (DB). 'Farmstead of a man called Sumarlithi'. OScand. pers. name + OE *tūn*.

Somersal Herbert Derbys. *Summersale* 1086 (DB), *Somersale Herbert* c.1300. 'Nook of land of a man called *Sumor*'. OE pers. name + *halh*. Manorial affix from the Fitzherbert family, here in the 13th cent.

Somersby Lincs. *Summerdebi* 1086 (DB). Probably 'farmstead or village of a man called Sumarlithi'. OScand. pers. name + *bý*.

Somerset (the county). *Sumersǣton* 12th cent. '(District of) the settlers around Somerton'. Reduced form of SOMERTON + OE *sǣte*.

Somersham Cambs. *Summeresham* c.1000, *Sumersham* 1086 (DB). Probably 'homestead of a man called *Sumor* or Sunmær'. OE pers. name + *hām*.

Somersham Suffolk. *Sumersham* 1086 (DB). 'Homestead of a man called *Sumor*'. OE pers. name + *hām*.

Somerton, usually 'farmstead used in summer', OE *sumor* + *tūn*: **Somerton** Norfolk. *Sumertonne* 1044–7, *Somertuna* 1086 (DB). **Somerton** Oxon. *Sumertone* 1086 (DB). **Somerton** Somerset. *Sumortun* 901–24, *Summertone* 1086 (DB).

However the following has a different origin: **Somerton** Suffolk. *Sumerledetuna* 1086 (DB). 'Farmstead of a man called Sumarlithi'. OScand. pers. name + OE *tūn*.

Sompting W. Sussex. *Suntinga* 956, *Sultinges* 1086 (DB). '(Settlement of) the dwellers at the marsh'. OE *sumpt* + *-ingas*.

Sonning Berks. *Soninges* 1086 (DB). '(Settlement of) the family or followers of a man called *Sunna*'. OE pers. name + *-ingas*. The same tribal group gives name to SUNNINGHILL and SUNNINGWELL.

Sopley Hants. *Sopelie* 1086 (DB). Possibly 'woodland clearing of a man called *Soppa*'. OE pers. name + *lēah*. Alternatively the first element may be an OE *soppa* 'marsh'.

Sopworth Wilts. *Sopeworde* 1086 (DB). 'Enclosure of a man called *Soppa*'. OE pers. name + *worth*.

Sorn E. Ayr. '(Place with a) kiln'. Gaelic *sorn*.

Sotby Lincs. *Sotebi* 1086 (DB). 'Farmstead or village of a man called Sóti'. OScand. pers. name + *bý*.

Sotterley Suffolk. *Soterlega* 1086 (DB). OE *lēah* 'woodland clearing' with an uncertain first element, possibly a pers. name.

Soudley, Upper Glos. *Suleie* 1221. 'South woodland clearing'. OE *sūth* + *lēah*.

Soulbury Bucks. *Soleberie* 1086 (DB). 'Stronghold by a gully'. OE *sulh* + *burh* (dative *byrig*).

Soulby, 'farmstead of a man called Súla, or one made of posts', OScand. pers. name or *súla* + *bý*: **Soulby** Cumbria, near Brough. *Sulebi* c.1160. **Soulby** Cumbria, near Penrith. *Suleby* 1235.

Souldern Oxon. *Sulethorne* c.1160. 'Thorn-tree in or near a gully'. OE *sulh* + *thorn*.

Souldrop Beds. *Sultrop* 1196. 'Outlying farmstead near a gully'. OE *sulh* + *throp*.

Sourton Devon. *Swurantune* c.970, *Surintone* 1086 (DB). 'Farmstead by a neck of land or col'. OE *swēora* + *tūn*.

South as affix, *see* main name, e.g. for **South Acre** (Norfolk) *see* ACRE.

South Ronaldsay (island) Orkn. *Rögnvalsey* c.1150. 'Southern Rögnvaldr's island'. OScand. pers. name + *ey*. Rögnvaldr was the brother of Sigurd, first Jarl of Orkney in the late 9th cent. The island is *South* in relation to NORTH RONALDSAY, where the pers. name is different.

South Uist. *See* UIST.

Southall Gtr. London. *Suhaull* 1198. 'Southern nook(s) of land'. OE *sūth* + *halh*, *see* NORTHOLT.

Southam, 'southern homestead or land in a river-bend', OE *sūth* + *hām* or *hamm*: **Southam** Glos. *Suth-ham* c.991, *Surham* |sic| 1086 (DB). **Southam** Warwicks. *Suthham* 998, *Sucham* |sic| 1086 (DB).

Southampton Hants. *Homtun* 825, *Suthhamtunam* 962, *Hantone* 1086 (DB). 'Estate on a promontory'. OE *hamm* + *tūn*, with prefix *sūth* to distinguish this place from NORTHAMPTON (which has a different origin).

Southborough Kent. 'Borough of *Suth*' 1270, *la South Burgh* 1450. 'Southern borough' (of TONBRIDGE). OE *sūth* + *burh*.

Southbourne Dorset, like Northbourne and Westbourne, a name of recent creation for a suburb of BOURNEMOUTH.

Southburgh Norfolk. *Berc* |sic| 1086 (DB), *Suthberg* 1291. 'South hill'. OE *sūth* + *beorg*.

Southchurch Essex. *Suthcyrcan* 1042–66, *Sudcerca* 1086 (DB). 'Southern church'. OE *sūth* + *cirice*.

Southease E. Sussex. *Sueise* 966, *Suesse* 1086 (DB). 'Southern land overgrown with brushwood'. OE *sūth* + **hǣs(e)*.

Southend on Sea Essex. *Sowthende* 1481. 'The southern end (of PRITTLEWELL parish)'. ME *south* + *ende*.

Southery Norfolk. *Suthereye* 942, *Sutreia* 1086 (DB). 'Southerly island'. OE *sūtherra* + *ēg*.

Southfleet Kent. *Suthfleotes* 10th cent., *Sudfleta* 1086 (DB). 'Southern place at the stream'. OE *sūth* + *flēot*.

Southgate Gtr. London. *Suthgate* 1370. 'Southern gate' (to Enfield Chase). OE *sūth* + *geat*.

Southill Beds. *Sudgiuele* 1086 (DB). 'Southern settlement of the tribe called *Gifle*'. OE *sūth* + old tribal name, *see* NORTHILL.

Southleigh Devon. *Lege* 1086 (DB), *Suthlege* 1228. '(Place at) the wood or clearing'. OE *lēah* with *sūth* to distinguish it from NORTHLEIGH.

Southminster Essex. *Suthmynster* c.1000, *Sudmunstra* 1086 (DB). 'Southern church'. OE *sūth* + *mynster*.

Southoe Cambs. *Sutham* |sic| 1086 (DB), *Sudho* 1186. 'Southern hill-spur'. OE *sūth* + *hōh*.

Southolt Suffolk. *Sudholda* 1086 (DB). 'South wood'. OE *sūth* + *holt*.

Southorpe Cambs. *Sudtorp* 1086 (DB). 'Southern outlying farmstead'. OScand. *súthr* + *thorp*.

Southowram W. Yorks. *Overe* 1086 (DB), *Sudhouerum* c.1275. '(Place at) the ridges'. OE **ofer*, **ufer* in a dative plural form **uferum*, with *sūth* to distinguish it from NORTHOWRAM.

Southport Mersey., a modern artificial name, first bestowed on the place in 1798.

Southrepps Norfolk. *Sutrepes* 1086 (DB), *Sutrepples* 1209. Possibly 'south strips of land'. OE *sūth* + **reopul*.

Southrey Lincs. *Sutreie* 1086 (DB). 'Southerly island'. OE *sūtherra* + *ēg*.

Southrop Glos. *Sudthropa* c.1140. 'Southern outlying farmstead'. OE *sūth* + *throp*.

Southsea Hants. *Southsea Castle* c.1600. Self-explanatory. The present place grew up round the castle built by Henry VIII in 1540.

Southwaite Cumbria, near Hesket. *Thouthweyt* 1272. 'Clay clearing'. OE *thōh* + OScand. *thveit*.

Southwark Gtr. London. *Sudwerca* 1086 (DB). 'Southern defensive work or fort'. OE *sūth* + *weorc*. Earlier called *Suthriganaweorc* 10th cent., 'fort of the men of SURREY'.

Southwell Notts. *Suthwellan* 958, *Sudwelle* 1086 (DB). 'South spring'. OE *sūth* + *wella*.

Southwick Dumf. *Suchayt* c.1280. *Suthayk* 1289. In spite of the earlier spelling, probably OE *sūth-wic* 'south hamlet'.

Southwick, 'southern dwelling or (dairy) farm', OE *sūth* + *wīc*: **Southwick** Hants. *Sudwic* c.1140. **Southwick** Northants. *Suthwycan* c.980. **Southwick** Tyne & Wear. *Suthewich* 12th cent. **Southwick** W. Sussex. *Sudewic* 1073. **Southwick** Wilts. *Sudwich* 1196.

Southwold Suffolk. *Sudwolda* 1086 (DB). 'South forest'. OE *sūth* + *wald*.

Southwood Norfolk. *Sudwda* 1086 (DB). 'Southern wood'. OE *sūth* + *wudu*.

Sow (river) Somerset, *see* MIDDLEZOY.

Sowe (river) W. Mids., *see* WALSGRAVE.

Sowerby, 'farmstead on sour ground', OScand. *saurr* + *bý*; examples include: **Sowerby** N. Yorks., near Thirsk. *Sorebi* 1086 (DB). **Sowerby, Sowerby Bridge** W. Yorks. *Sorebi* 1086 (DB), *Sourebybrigge* 15th cent. The bridge is across the River Calder. **Sowerby, Brough** Cumbria. *Sowreby* 1235, *Soureby by Burgh* 1314. It is near to BROUGH. **Sowerby, Temple** Cumbria. *Sourebi* 1179, *Templessoureby* 1292. Affix from its early possession by the Knights Templars.

Sowton Devon. *Southton* 1420. 'South farmstead or village'. OE *sūth* + *tūn*. Its earlier name was *Clis* 1086 (DB), one of several places named from the River Clyst, *see* CLYST HYDON.

Spalding Lincs. *Spallinge* 1086 (DB), *Spaldingis* c.1115. '(Settlement of) the dwellers in *Spald*'. Old district name (possibly from OE **spald* 'ditch or trench') + *-ingas*.

Spaldington E. R. Yorks. *Spellinton* 1086 (DB). 'Farmstead of the tribe called *Spaldingas*' (who give name to SPALDING). OE tribal name (genitive plural *-inga-*) + *tūn*.

Spaldwick Cambs. *Spalduice* 1086 (DB). Possibly 'dwelling or farm by a trickling stream or ditch'. OE *spāld* or **spald* + *wīc*.

Spalford Notts. *Spaldesforde* 1086 (DB). Possibly 'ford over a trickling stream or ditch'. OE *spald* or **spald* + *ford*.

Sparham Norfolk. *Sparham* 1086 (DB). 'Homestead or enclosure made with spars or shafts'. OE **spearr* + *hām* or *hamm*.

Sparkford Somerset. *Sparkeforda* 1086 (DB). 'Brushwood ford'. OE **spearca* + *ford*.

Sparkwell Devon. *Spearcanville* c.1070, *Sperchewelle* 1086 (DB). 'Spring or stream where brushwood grows'. OE **spearca* + *wella*.

Sparsholt, 'wood of the spear' (perhaps referring to a spear-trap for wild animals or to a wood where spear-shafts are obtained), OE *spere* + *holt*: **Sparsholt** Berks. *Speresholte* 963, *Spersolt* 1086 (DB). **Sparsholt** Hants. *Speoresholte* 901. Alternatively the first element of this name may be OE **spearr* 'a spar, a rafter'.

Spaunton N. Yorks. *Spantun* 1086 (DB). 'Farmstead with shingled roof'. OScand. *spánn* + OE *tūn*.

Spaxton Somerset. *Spachestone* 1086 (DB). Probably 'farmstead of a man called Spakr'. OScand. pers. name + OE *tūn*.

Speen Berks. *Spene* 821, *Spone* 1086 (DB). Probably 'place where wood-chips are found'. OE **spēne*. This OE name represents an adaptation of the older Latin name *Spinis* 'at the thorn bushes' (recorded in the 4th cent.).

Speenoge (*Spíonóg*) Donegal. '(Place of) gooseberries'.

Speeton N. Yorks. *Specton* 1086 (DB). Possibly 'enclosure where meetings are held'. OE *spēc* + *tūn*.

Speke Mersey. *Spec* 1086 (DB). Possibly OE *spēc* 'branches, brushwood'.

Speldhurst Kent. *Speldhirst* 8th cent. 'Wooded hill where wood-chips are found'. OE *speld* + *hyrst*.

Spelsbury Oxon. *Speolesbyrig* early 11th cent., *Spelesberie* 1086 (DB). 'Stronghold of a man called **Spēol*'. OE pers. name + *burh* (dative *byrig*).

Spen, from ME *spenne* 'a fence, an enclosure': **Spen** W. Yorks., near Gomersal. *Spen* 1308. This gives name to the modern district of **Spenborough. Spen, High** Tyne & Wear. *Le Spen* 1312.

Spennithorne N. Yorks. *Speningetorp* |*sic*| 1086 (DB), *Speningthorn* 1184. Probably 'thorn-tree by the fence or enclosure'. OE or OScand. **spenning* + *thorn*.

Spennymoor Durham. *Spendingmor* c.1336. Probably 'moor with a fence or enclosure'. OE or OScand. **spenning* + *mōr*.

Spetchley Heref. & Worcs. *Spæclea* 967, *Speclea* 1086 (DB). 'Woodland clearing where meetings are held'. OE *spēc* + *lēah*.

Spetisbury Dorset. *Spehtesberie* 1086 (DB). 'Pre-English earthwork frequented by the green woodpecker'. OE **speoht* + *burh* (dative *byrig*).

Spexhall Suffolk. *Specteshale* 1197. 'Nook of land frequented by the green woodpecker'. OE **speoht* + *halh*.

Spey. *See* GRANTOWN-ON-SPEY.

Spiddal (*Spidéal*) Galway, Meath. 'Hospital'.

Spilsby Lincs. *Spilesbi* 1086 (DB). 'Farmstead or village of a man called **Spillir*'. OScand. pers. name + *bý*.

Spindlestone Northum. *Spindlestan* 1187. 'Stone or rock thought to resemble a spindle'. OE *spinele* + *stān*.

Spink (*Spinc*) Laois. 'Pinnacle'.

Spital in the Street Lincs. *Hospitale* 1204, *Spitelenthestrete* 1322. 'The hospital or religious house on the Roman road (Ermine Street)'. ME *spitel* (from OFrench *hospitale*) with OE *strēt*.

Spithead Hants., not recorded before the 17th cent., 'headland of the sand-spit or pointed sandbank'. OE *spitu* + *hēafod*.

Spithurst E. Sussex. *Splytherst* 1296. 'Wooded hill with an opening or gap'. OE *hyrst* with ME *split*.

Spittaltown (*Baile an Ospidéil*) Westmeath. 'Town of the hospital'.

Spixworth Norfolk. *Spikesuurda* 1086 (DB). Probably 'enclosure of a man called **Spic*'. OE pers. name + *worth*.

Spofforth N. Yorks. *Spoford* |*sic*| 1086 (DB), *Spotford* 1218. 'Ford by a small plot of ground'. OE **spot* + *ford*.

Spondon Derbys. *Spondune* 1086 (DB). 'Hill where wood-chips or shingles are got'. OE *spōn* + *dūn*.

Sporle Norfolk. *Sparlea* 1086 (DB). Probably 'wood or clearing where spars or shafts are obtained'. OE **spearr* + *lēah*.

Spratton Northants. *Spretone* 1086 (DB). Probably 'farmstead made of poles'. OE *sprēot* + *tūn*.

Spreyton Devon. *Spreitone* 1086 (DB). 'Farmstead amongst brushwood'. OE **sprǣg* + *tūn*.

Spridlington Lincs. *Spredelintone* 1086 (DB). Probably 'estate associated with a man called **Sprytel*'. OE pers. name + *-ing-* + *tūn*.

Springthorpe Lincs. *Springetorp* 1086 (DB). 'Outlying farmstead by a spring'. OE *spring* + OScand. *thorp*.

Sproatley E. R. Yorks. *Sprotele* 1086 (DB). 'Woodland clearing where young shoots grow'. OE *sprota* + *lēah*.

Sproston Green Ches. *Sprostune* 1086 (DB). 'Farmstead of a man called Sprow'. OE pers. name + *tūn*.

Sprotbrough S. Yorks. *Sproteburg* 1086 (DB). 'Stronghold of a man called **Sprota*', or 'stronghold overgrown with shoots'. OE pers. name or *sprota* + *burh*.

Sproughton Suffolk. *Sproeston* 1191. Probably 'farmstead of a man called Sprow'. OE pers. name + *tūn*.

Sprowston Norfolk. *Sprowestuna* 1086 (DB). 'Farmstead of a man called Sprow'. OE pers. name + *tūn*.

Sproxton, 'farmstead of a man called *Sprok', or 'brushwood farmstead', OScand. pers. name or *sprogh* + OE *tūn*: **Sproxton** Leics. *Sprotone* |sic| 1086 (DB), *Sproxcheston* c.1125. **Sproxton** N. Yorks. *Sprostune* 1086 (DB).

Spurn Head E. R. Yorks. *Ravenserespourne* 1399. From ME *spurn* 'a spur, a projecting piece of land', in the early spelling with the place-name *Ravenser* which means 'sandbank of a man called Hrafn', OScand. pers. name + *eyrr*.

Spurstow Ches. *Spuretone* |sic| 1086 (DB), *Sporstow* c.1200. 'Meeting place on a trackway, or by a spur of land'. OE *spor* or *spura* + *stōw*.

Srah (*An tSraith*) Mayo. 'The river meadow'.

Srahmore (*An Srath Mór*) Mayo. 'The big river meadow'.

Srue (*Sruth*) Galway. 'Stream'.

Sruh (*Sruth*) Waterford. 'Stream'.

Stackallan (*Stigh Colláin*) Meath. 'Collán's house'.

Stackpole Elidor. See CHERITON.

Stacks of Duncansby (rock group) Highland. 'Steep rocks off Duncansby Head'. OScand. *stakkr. See* DUNCANSBY HEAD.

Stadhampton Oxon. *Stodeham* c.1135. 'Enclosure or river-meadow where horses are kept'. OE *stōd* + *hamm*. The *-ton* is a late addition.

Staffa (island) Arg. 'Pillar island'. OScand. *stafr* + *ey*. The reference is to the columns of basaltic rock.

Staffield Cumbria. *Stafhole* c.1225. 'Round hill with a staff or post'. OScand. *stafr* + *hóll*.

Stafford Staffs. *Stæfford* mid 11th cent., *Stadford* 1086 (DB). 'Ford by a landing-place'. OE *stæth* + *ford*. **Staffordshire** (OE *scīr* 'district') is first referred to in the 11th cent.

Stafford, West Dorset. *Stanford* 1086 (DB). 'Stony ford'. OE *stān* + *ford*.

Staffordstown Antrim. The hamlet is named after Martha *Stafford*, daughter of Sir Francis Stafford, who in the early 17th cent. married Sir Henry O'Neill, son of Shane O'Neill of Shane's Castle.

Stagsden Beds. *Stachedene* 1086 (DB). 'Valley of stakes or boundary posts'. OE *staca* + *denu*.

Stainburn N. Yorks. *Stanburne* c.972, *Sta(i)nburne* 1086 (DB). 'Stony stream'. OE *stān* (replaced by OScand. *steinn*) + *burna*.

Stainby Lincs. *Stigandebi* 1086 (DB). 'Farmstead or village of a man called Stígandi'. OScand. pers. name + *bý*.

Staincross S. Yorks. *Staincros* 1086 (DB). 'Stone cross'. OScand. *steinn* + *kros*.

Staindrop Durham. *Standropa* c.1040. Probably 'valley with stony ground'. OE *stǣner* + *hop*.

Staines Surrey. *Stane* 11th cent., *Stanes* 1086 (DB). '(Place at) the stone(s)'. OE *stān*.

Stainfield Lincs., near Bardney. *Steinfelde* 1086 (DB). 'Stony open land'. OE *stān* (replaced by OScand. *steinn*) + *feld*.

Stainfield Lincs., near Rippingale. *Stentvith* 1086 (DB). 'Stony clearing'. OScand. *steinn* + *thveit*.

Stainforth, 'stony ford', OE *stān* (replaced by OScand. *steinn*) + *ford*: **Stainforth** N. Yorks. *Stainforde* 1086 (DB). **Stainforth** S. Yorks. *Steinforde* 1086 (DB).

Staining Lancs. *Staininghe* 1086 (DB). Possibly '(settlement of) the family or followers of a man called *Stān, or the dwellers in a stony district'. OE pers. name or *stān* (with Scand. influence) + *-ingas*. Alternatively 'stony place', OE *stāning*.

Stainland W. Yorks. *Stanland* 1086 (DB). 'Stony cultivated land'. OE *stān* (replaced by OScand. *steinn*) + *land*.

Stainley, 'stony woodland clearing', OE *stān* (replaced by OScand. *steinn*) + *lēah*: **Stainley, North** N. Yorks. *Stanleh* c.972, *Nordstanlaia* 1086 (DB). **Stainley, South** N. Yorks. *Stanlai* 1086 (DB), *Southstainlei* 1198.

Stainmore, North Cumbria. *Stanmoir* c.990. 'Rocky or stony moor'. OE *stān* (replaced by OScand. *steinn*) + *mōr*.

Stainsacre N. Yorks. *Stainsaker* 1090–6. 'Cultivated land of a man called Steinn'. OScand. pers. name + *akr*.

Stainton, a frequent name in the North, usually 'farmstead on stony ground', OE *stān* (replaced by OScand. *steinn*) + *tūn*; examples include: **Stainton** Durham. *Staynton* c.1150. **Stainton** S. Yorks. *Stantone* 1086 (DB). **Stainton, Market** Lincs. *Staintone* 1086 (DB), *Steynton Market* 1286. Affix is ME *merket*.

Stainton le Vale Lincs. *Staintone* 1086 (DB). Affix means 'in the valley' from ME *vale*.
      However the following has a different origin: **Stainton, Great** & **Stainton, Little** Durham. *Staninctona* 1091. 'Farmstead at the stony place'. OE *stāning* (influenced by OScand. *steinn*) + *tūn*.

Staintondale N. Yorks. *Steintun* 1086 (DB), *Staynton Dale* 1562. 'Farmstead on stony ground'. OE *stān* (replaced by OScand. *steinn*) + *tūn*, with the later addition of *dale* 'valley'.

Stair S. Ayr. '(Place by) stepping stones'. Gaelic *stair*.

Staithes N. Yorks. *Setonstathes* 1415. 'The landing-places'. OE *stæth*. Seaton ('sea farmstead') is a nearby place.

Stalbridge Dorset. *Stapulbreicge* 998, *Staplebrige* 1086 (DB). 'Bridge built on posts or piles'. OE *stapol* + *brycg*.

Stalham Norfolk. *Stalham* 1044–6, 1086 (DB). 'Homestead or enclosure by the fishing pool'. OE *stall* + *hām* or *hamm*.

Stalisfield Green Kent. *Stanefelle* |sic| 1086 (DB), *Stealesfelde* c.1100. Probably 'open land with a stall or stable'. OE *steall* + *feld*.

Stalling Busk N. Yorks. *Stalunesbusc* 1218. 'The stallion's bush'. ME *stalun* + OScand. *buski*.

Stallingborough NE. Lincs. *Stalingeburg* 1086 (DB). Possibly 'stronghold of the dwellers near a stall or stable'. OE *stall* + *-inga-* + *burh*. Alternatively the first element may be a tribal name *Stælingas* (genitive plural *Stælinga*) of unknown meaning.

Stalmine Lancs. *Stalmine* 1086 (DB). Probably 'mouth of the stream or pool'. OE *stæll* + OScand. *mynni*.

Stalybridge Gtr. Manch. *Stauelegh* 13th cent., *Stalybridge* 1687. 'Bridge at the wood where staves are got'. OE *stæf* + *lēah*, with the later addition of *bridge*.

Stambourne Essex. *Stanburna* 1086 (DB). 'Stony stream'. OE *stān* + *burna*.

Stambridge, Great Essex. *Stanbruge* 1086 (DB). 'Stone bridge'. OE *stān* + *brycg*.

Stamford, 'stone ford' or 'stony ford', OE *stān* + *ford*: **Stamford** Lincs. *Steanford* 10th cent., *Stanford* 1086 (DB). **Stamford Bridge** E. R. Yorks. *Stanford brycg c.*1075. The ford here was replaced by a bridge at an early date.

Stamford Hill Gtr. London. *Saundfordhull* 1294. 'Hill by a sandy ford'. OE *sand* + *ford* + *hyll*.

Stamfordham Northum. *Stanfordham* 1188. 'Homestead or village at the stone ford'. OE *stān* + *ford* + *hām*.

Stamullen (*Steach Maoilín*) Meath. 'Maoilín's house'.

Stanbridge Beds. *Stanbrugge* 1165. 'Stone bridge'. OE *stān* + *brycg*.

Standish Gtr. Manch. *Stanesdis* 1178. 'Stony pasture or enclosure'. OE *stān* + *edisc*.

Standlake Oxon. *Stanlache c.*1155. 'Stony stream or channel'. OE *stān* + *lacu*.

Standon 'stony hill', OE *stān* + *dūn*: **Standon** Herts. *Standune* 944–6, *Standone* 1086 (DB). **Standon** Staffs. *Stantone |sic|* 1086 (DB), *Standon* 1190.

Stanfield Norfolk. *Stanfelda* 1086 (DB). 'Stony open land'. OE *stān* + *feld*.

Stanford, found in various counties, 'stone ford' or 'stony ford', OE *stān* + *ford*; examples include: **Stanford** Kent. *Stanford* 1035. **Stanford Bishop** Heref. & Worcs. *Stanford* 1086 (DB). Affix from its early possession by the Bishop of Hereford. **Stanford Dingley** Berks. *Stanworde* 1086 (DB), *Staneford Deanly* 1535. Manorial affix from the Dyngley family, here in the 15th cent. **Stanford in the Vale** Oxon. *Stanford* 1086 (DB), *Stanford in le Vale* 1496. Affix from its situation in the VALE OF WHITE HORSE. **Stanford le Hope** Essex. *Staunford* 1267, *Stanford in the Hope* 1361. Affix means 'in the bay' from ME *hope*. **Stanford Rivers** Essex. *Stanford* 1068, *Stanfort* 1086 (DB), *Stanford Ryueres* 1289. Manorial affix from the Rivers family, here in the 13th cent.

Stanhoe Norfolk. *Stanhou* 1086 (DB). 'Stony hill-spur'. OE *stān* + *hōh*.

Stanhope Durham. *Stanhopa* 1183. 'Stony valley'. OE *stān* + *hop*.

Stanion Northants. *Stanere |sic|* 1086 (DB), *Stanerna* 1162. 'Stone house(s) or building(s)'. OE *stān* + *ærn*.

Stanley, 'stony woodland clearing', OE *stān* + *lēah*; examples include: **Stanley** Derbys. *Stanlei* 1086 (DB). **Stanley** Durham. *Stanley* 1297. **Stanley** Staffs. *Stanlega* 1130. **Stanley** W. Yorks. *Stanlei* 1086 (DB). **Stanley, King's** & **Stanley, Leonard** Glos. *Stanlege* 1086 (DB), *Kingestanleg* 1220. *Stanllegh Leonardi* 1285. Affixes from ownership

by the Crown and from the former dedication of the church to St Leonard.

Stanmer E. Sussex. *Stanmere* 765, 1086 (DB). 'Stony pool'. OE *stān* + *mere*.

Stanmore Gtr. London. *Stanmere* 1086 (DB). Identical in origin with the previous name.

Stanney Ches. *Stanei* 1086 (DB). 'Stone or rock island'. OE *stān* + *ēg*.

Stanningfield Suffolk. *Stanfelda* 1086 (DB), *Stanefeld* 1197. 'Stony open land'. OE *stān* (perhaps alternating with **stānen* 'stony') + *feld*.

Stanningley W. Yorks., near Pudsey. *Stannyngley* 1562. Probably 'stony woodland clearing'. OE **stāning* 'stony place' or **stānen* 'stony' + *lēah*.

Stannington Northum. *Stanigton* 1242. 'Farmstead at the stony place'. OE **stāning* + *tūn*.

Stansfield Suffolk. *Stanesfelda* 1086 (DB). Probably 'open land of a man called **Stān*'. OE pers. name + *feld*.

Stanstead, *Stansted*, 'stony place', OE *stān* + *stede*: **Stanstead** Suffolk. *Stanesteda* 1086 (DB). **Stanstead Abbots** Herts. *Stanestede* 1086 (DB), *Stanstede Abbatis de Wautham* 1247. Affix from early possession by the Abbot of Waltham. **Stansted** Kent. *Stansted* 1231. **Stansted Mountfitchet** Essex. *Stanesteda* 1086 (DB), *Stansted Mounfichet c.*1290. Manorial affix from the Muntfichet family, here in the 12th cent.

Stanton, a common name, usually 'farmstead on stony ground', occasionally 'farmstead near standing stones', OE *stān* + *tūn*; examples include: **Stanton** Glos. *Stantone* 1086 (DB). **Stanton** Suffolk. *Stantuna* 1086 (DB). **Stanton Drew** B. & NE. Som. *Stantone* 1086 (DB), *Stanton Drogonis* 1253. Manorial affix from possession by one *Drogo* or *Drew* in 1225. **Stanton Harcourt** Oxon. *Stantone* 1086 (DB), *Stantone Harecurt c.*1275. Manorial affix from the de Harecurt family, here in the 12th cent. **Stanton, Long** Cambs. *Stantune* 1086 (DB), *Long Stanton* 1282. Affix refers to the length of the village. **Stanton St Quintin** Wilts. *Stantone* 1086 (DB), *Staunton St Quintin* 1283. Manorial affix from the de Sancto Quintino family, here in the 13th cent. **Stanton upon Hine Heath** Shrops. *Stantune* 1086 (DB), *Staunton super Hyne Heth* 1327. Affix means 'heath of the household servants', ME *hine* + *hethe*.

Stanwardine Shrops. *Staurdine* 1086 (DB), *Stanwardin* 1194. 'Enclosure made of stones, or on stony ground'. OE *stān* + *worthign*.

Stanway, 'stony road', OE *stān* + *weg*; examples include: **Stanway** Essex. *Stanwægun c.*1000, *Stanvega* 1086 (DB). **Stanway** Glos. *Stanwege* 12th cent.

Stanwell Surrey. *Stanwelle* 1086 (DB). 'Stony spring or stream'. OE *stān* + *wella*.

Stanwick Northants. *Stanwigga* 10th cent., *Stanvige* 1086 (DB). 'The rocking- or logan-stone'. OE *stān* + *wigga*.

Stapeley Ches. *Steple |sic|* 1086 (DB), *Stapeleg* 1260. Probably 'wood or clearing where posts are got'. OE *stapol* + *lēah*.

Stapenhill Staffs. *Stapenhille* 1086 (DB). '(Place at) the steep hill'. OE *stēap* (dative *-an*) + *hyll*.

Staple, '(place at) the pillar of wood or stone', OE *stapol*: **Staple** Kent. *Stapel* 1240. **Staple Fitzpaine** Somerset. *Staple* 1086 (DB). Manorial affix from the Fitzpaine family, here in the 14th cent.

Stapleford, 'ford marked by a post', OE *stapol* + *ford*; examples include: **Stapleford** Cambs. *Stapelforda* 956, *Stapleforde* 1086 (DB). **Stapleford** Notts. *Stapleford* 1086 (DB). **Stapleford Abbots** & **Stapleford Tawney** Essex. *Staplefort* 1086 (DB), *Staplford Abbatis Sancti Edmundi* 1255, *Stapilford Thany* 1291. Distinguishing affixes from early possession by the Abbot of Bury St Edmunds and by the de Tany family.

Staplegrove Somerset. *Stapilgrove* 1327. 'Grove where posts are got'. OE *stapol* + *grāf*.

Staplehurst Kent. *Stapelherst* 1226. 'Wooded hill where posts are got'. OE *stapol* + *hyrst*.

Stapleton, usually 'farmstead by a post or built on posts', OE *stapol* + *tūn*; examples include: **Stapleton** Brist. *Stapleton* 1215. **Stapleton** Leics. *Stapletone* 1086 (DB).
    However the following probably mean 'farmstead by a steep slope', OE *stēpel* + *tūn*: **Stapleton** Heref. & Worcs. *Stepeltone* 1286. **Stapleton** Shrops. *Stepleton* 12th cent.

Staploe Beds. *Stapelho* 1203. 'Hill-spur marked by, or shaped like, a post'. OE *stapol* + *hōh*.

Starbeck N. Yorks., not recorded before 1817, probably 'sedge brook', from OScand. *star* + *bekkr*.

Starbotton N. Yorks. *Stamphotne* |sic| 1086 (DB), *Stauerboten* 12th cent. 'Valley where stakes are got'. OE **stæfer* (replacing OScand. *stafn* in the first form) + OScand. *botn*.

Starcross Devon, first recorded as *Star Crosse* 1689, probably referring to a cross or cross-roads where starlings gather, from dialect *stare* (OE *stær*) and *cross*.

Starston Norfolk. *Sterestuna* 1086 (DB). 'Farmstead or village of a man called Styrr'. OScand. pers. name + OE *tūn*.

Start Point Devon. *La Sterte* 1310. OE *steort* 'tongue of land, promontory'.

Startforth Durham. *Stretford* c.1050, *Stradford* 1086 (DB). 'Ford on a Roman road'. OE *strǣt* + *ford*.

Stathe Somerset. *Stathe* 1233. 'The landing-place'. OE *stæth*.

Stathern Leics. *Stachedirne* 1086 (DB). 'Stake thorn-tree', i.e. 'thorn-tree marking a boundary'. OE *staca* + *thyrne*.

Staughton, Great (Cambs.) & *Staughton, Little* (Beds.). *Stoctun* c.1000, *Tochestone, Estone* |sic| 1086 (DB). 'Farmstead at an outlying hamlet'. OE *stoc* + *tūn*.

Staunton, usually 'farmstead on stony ground, or one near a standing stone', OE *stān* + *tūn*; examples include: **Staunton** Glos., near Hartpury. *Stantun* 972, 1086 (DB). **Staunton on Arrow** Heref. & Worcs. *Stantun* 958, *Stantune* 1086 (DB). Arrow is an ancient pre-Celtic river-name of uncertain meaning.
    However the following has a different origin: **Staunton on Wye** Heref. & Worcs. *Standune* 1086 (DB). 'Stony hill'. OE *stān* + *dūn*. For the river-name, *see* ROSS ON WYE.

Staveley, 'wood or clearing where staves are got', OE *stæf* + *lēah*: **Staveley** Cumbria. *Staueleye* c.1200. **Staveley** Derbys. *Stavelie* 1086 (DB). **Staveley** N. Yorks. *Stanlei* |sic| 1086 (DB), *Staflea* 1167. **Staveley-in-Cartmel** Cumbria. *Stavelay* 1282. *See* CARTMEL.

Staverton, usually 'farmstead made of or marked by stakes', OE *stæfer* + *tūn*: **Staverton** Glos. *Staruenton* 1086 (DB), **Staverton** Northants. *Stæfertun* 944, *Stavertone* 1086 (DB). **Staverton** Wilts. *Stavretone* 1086 (DB).
    However the following has a different origin: **Staverton** Devon. *Stofordtune* c.1070, *Stovretona* 1086 (DB). 'Farmstead by a stony ford.' OE *stān* + *ford* + *tūn*.

Stawell Somerset. *Stawelle* 1086 (DB). 'Stony spring or stream'. OE *stān* + *wella*.

Staxton N. Yorks. *Stacstone* 1086 (DB). 'Farmstead or village of a man called *Stakkr'. OScand. pers. name + OE *tūn*.

Stearsby N. Yorks. *Stirsbi* 1086 (DB). 'Farmstead or village of a man called Styrr'. OScand. pers. name + *bý*.

Stebbing Essex. *Stibinga* 1086 (DB). '(Settlement of) the family or followers of a man called *Stybba, or the dwellers among the tree-stumps'. OE pers. name or *stybb* + *-ingas*.

Stedham W. Sussex. *Steddanham* 960, *Stedeham* 1086 (DB). 'Homestead or enclosure of the stallion, or of a man called *Stedda'. OE *stēda* or pers. name + *hām* or *hamm*.

Steep Hants. *Stepe* 12th cent. 'The steep place'. OE **stīepe*.

Steeping, Great & *Steeping, Little* Lincs. *Stepinge* 1086 (DB). Probably '(settlement of) the family or followers of a man called Stēapa'. OE pers. name + *-ingas*.

Steeple, 'steep place', OE *stēpel*: **Steeple** Dorset. *Stiple* 1086 (DB). **Steeple** Essex. *Stepla* 1086 (DB).

Steeple as affix, *see* main name, e.g. for **Steeple Ashton** (Wilts.) *see* ASHTON.

Steeton W. Yorks., near Keighley. *Stiuetune* 1086 (DB). Probably 'farmstead built of or amongst tree-stumps'. OE **styfic* + *tūn*.

Stella Tyne & Wear. *Stelyngleye* 1183. 'Pasture with a shelter for cattle'. OE **stelling* + *lēah*.

Stelling Minnis Kent. *Stellinges* 1086 (DB). Possibly '(settlement of) the family or followers of a man called *Stealla'. OE pers. name + *-ingas*. Affix is from OE *mǣnnes* 'common land'.

Stemster Highland. *Stambustar* 1557. 'Farmstead with stones'. OScand. *steinn* + *bólstathr*.

Stenhousemuir Falk. *Stan house* c.1200, *Stenhous* 1601. 'Moorland by the stone house'. OE *stān* + *hūs* + *mōr*.

Stenness Shet. *Steinsness* c.970. 'Stone headland'. OScand. *steinn* + *nes*.

Stenton E. Loth. *Steinton* 1150. 'Stone village'. OE *stān* + *tūn*.

Stepaside Pemb. *Stepaside* 1694. The village would have arisen by a wayside cottage or modest alehouse inviting the traveller to 'step aside' for rest and refreshment.

Stepney Gtr. London. *Stybbanhythe* c.1000 *Stibenhede* 1086 (DB). OE *hyth* 'landing place', with OE pers. name *Stybba* or an OE *stybba (genitive -n) 'stump, pile'.

Steppingley Beds. *Stepigelai* 1086 (DB). 'Woodland clearing of the family or followers of a man called Stēapa'. OE pers. name + -inga- + lēah.

Sternfield Suffolk. *Sternesfelda* 1086 (DB). Possibly 'open land of a man called *Sterne'. OE pers. name + feld.

Stert Wilts. *Sterte* 1086 (DB). 'Projecting piece of land'. OE steort.

Stetchworth Cambs. *Steuicheswrthe* c.1050 *Stiuicesuuorde* 1086 (DB). 'Enclosure amongst the tree-stumps, or of a man called *Styfic'. OE *styfic or pers. name + worth.

Stevenage Herts. *Stithenæce* c.1060, *Stigenace* 1086 (DB). Probably '(place at) the strong oak-tree'. OE stīth (dative -an) + āc (dative ǣc).

Stevenston N. Ayr. *Stevenstoun* 1246. 'Steven's farm'. OE tūn.

Steventon, 'estate associated with a man called *Stīf(a)', OE pers. name + -ing- + tūn, or possibly 'farmstead at the tree-stump place', OE *styf(ic)ing + tūn: **Steventon** Hants. *Stivetune* 1086 (DB). **Steventon** Oxon. *Stivetune* 1086 (DB).

Stevington Beds. *Stiuentone* 1086 (DB). Probably identical in origin with the previous two names.

Stewartby Beds., a recent name for a 'new village' built in 1935 for employees in the brick-making industry, named from Halley Stewart, chairman of a local brick company.

Stewarton E. Ayr. *Stewartoun* 1201. 'Steward's estate'. OE tūn. The reference is to Walter, Seneschal (High Steward) to King David I, who owned the estate in the 12th cent.

Stewartstown Tyrone. *Stewartoune* c.1655. Sir Andrew Stewart was granted land here in 1698 on which he built a castle. The Irish name of Stewartstown is *An Chraobh*, 'the branch'.

Stewkley Bucks. *Stiuelai* |sic| 1086 (DB), *Stiuecelea* 1182. 'Woodland clearing with tree-stumps'. OE *styfic + lēah.

Stewton Lincs. *Stivetone* 1086. Probably 'farmstead built of or amongst tree-stumps'. OE *styfic + tūn.

Steyning W. Sussex. *Stæningum* c.880, *Staninges* 1086 (DB). Possibly '(settlement of) the family or followers of a man called *Stān, or the dwellers at the stony place'. OE pers. name or OE stān or *stǣne + -ingas. Alternatively 'stony places', from the plural of an OE word *stāning or *stǣning.

Steynton Pemb. *Steinton* 1291. 'Farm built of stone'. OScand. steinn + OE tūn. 1291 *Steinton*.

Stibbard Norfolk. *Stabyrda* |sic| 1086 (DB), *Stiberde* 1202. 'Bank beside a path, a road-side'. OE stīg + *byrde.

Stibbington Cambs. *Stebintune* 1086 (DB). Probably 'estate associated with a man called *Stybba'. OE pers. name + -ing- + tūn. Alternatively the first element may be OE *stybbing 'tree-stump clearing'.

Stichill Sc. Bord. *Stichele* c.1270. 'Sticky hill'. OE *sticele 'steep place'.

Stickford Lincs. *Stichesforde* 1086 (DB). 'Ford by the long strip of land'. OE sticca + ford.

Sticklepath Devon. *Stikelepethe* 1280. 'Steep path'. OE sticol + pæth.

Stickney Lincs. *Stichenai* 1086 (DB). 'Long strip of land between streams'. OE sticca (genitive -n) + ēg.

Stiffkey Norfolk. *Stiuekai* 1086 (DB). 'Island, or dry ground in marsh, with tree-stumps'. OE *styfic + ēg.

Stifford Essex. *Stithforde* c.1090, *Stiforda* 1086 (DB). Probably 'ford where lamb's cress or nettles grow'. OE stīthe + ford.

Stillingfleet N. Yorks. *Steflingefled* 1086 (DB). 'Stretch of river belonging to the family or followers of a man called *Stȳfel'. OE pers. name + -inga- + flēot.

Stillington, probably 'estate associated with a man called *Stȳfel', OE pers. name + -ing- + tūn: **Stillington** N. Yorks. *Stiuelinctun* 1086 (DB). **Stillington** Stock. on T. *Stilligtune* c.1190.

Stillorgan (*Stigh Lorgan*) Dublin. 'Lorcan's house'.

Stilton Cambs. *Stichiltone* 1086 (DB). 'Farmstead or village at a stile or steep ascent'. OE stigel + tūn.

Stinchcombe Glos. *Stintescombe* c.1155. 'Valley frequented by the sandpiper or dunlin'. OE *stint + cumb.

Stinsford Dorset. *Stincteford* 1086 (DB). 'Ford frequented by the sandpiper or dunlin'. OE *stint + ford.

Stirchley Shrops. *Styrcleage* 1002. 'Clearing or pasture for young bullocks'. OE styrc + lēah.

Stirling Aber. *Strevelin* 1124, *Sterling* c.1470. Meaning uncertain. The name may have originally been that of the river, now the Forth, on which Stirling stands.

Stisted Essex. *Stistede* 1086 (DB), *Stidsted* 1198. Probably 'place where lamb's cress or nettles grow'. OE stīthe + stede.

Stithians Cornwall. *Sancta Stethyana* 1268. From the dedication of the church to St Stithian, a female saint.

Stittenham, High N. Yorks. *Stidnun* |sic| 1086 (DB), *Stiklum* c.1260. Probably '(place at) the steep ascents'. OE *sticel(e) in a dative plural form *sticelum.

Stivichall W. Mids. *Stivichall* c.1144. 'Nook of land with tree-stumps'. OE *styfic + halh.

Stixwould Lincs. *Stigeswalde* 1086 (DB). 'Forest of a man called Stígr'. OScand. pers. name + OE wald.

Stob Dubh (mountain) Arg. 'Black stump'. Gaelic stob + dubh.

Stoborough Dorset. *Stanberge* 1086 (DB). 'Stony hill or barrow'. OE stān + beorg.

Stock Essex. *Herewardestoc* 1234, *Stocke* 1337. 'Outlying farmstead or hamlet of a man called Hereweard'. OE pers. name + stoc. The longer name remained in use until the 17th cent.

Stock Green & *Stock Wood* Heref. & Worcs. *La Stokke* 1271. 'The tree-stump'. OE stocc.

Stockbridge Hants. *Stocbrugge* 1221. 'Bridge made of logs'. OE stocc + brycg. The same name occurs in other counties.

Stockbridge Edin. 'Bridge of tree trunks'. OE *stocc + brycg*.

Stockbriggs S. Lan. 'Bridge of tree trunks'. OE *stocc + brycg*.

Stockbury Kent. *Stochingeberge* 1086 (DB). 'Woodland pasture of the dwellers at the outlying farmstead'. OE *stoc + -inga- + bǣr*.

Stockerston Leics. *Stoctone |sic|* 1086 (DB), *Stocfaston* c.1130. 'Stronghold built of logs'. OE *stocc + fæsten*.

Stocking Pelham Herts., *see* PELHAM.

Stockingford Warwicks. *Stoccingford* 1157. 'Ford by the tree-stump clearing'. OE **stoccing + ford*.

Stockland, 'cultivated land of the outlying farmstead', OE *stoc + land*: **Stockland** Devon. *Stocland* 998. **Stockland Bristol**. Somerset. *Stocheland* 1086 (DB). Manorial affix from its possession by the chamber of Bristol.

Stockleigh English & *Stockleigh Pomeroy* Devon. *Stochelie* 1086 (DB), *Stokeley Engles* 1268, *Stokelegh Pomeray* 1261. Probably 'woodland clearing with tree-stumps'. OE *stocc + lēah*. Manorial affixes from early possession by the Engles and de Pomerei families.

Stockport Gtr. Manch. *Stokeport* c.1170. 'Market-place at an outlying hamlet'. OE *stoc + port*.

Stocksbridge S. Yorks., not on record before 1841, probably identical in origin with STOCKBRIDGE.

Stocksfield Northum. *Stokesfeld* 1242. 'Open land belonging to an outlying hamlet'. OE *stoc + feld*.

Stockton, a name found in several counties, probably 'farmstead at an outlying hamlet', from OE *stoc + tūn*, although some may be 'farmstead built of logs', OE *stocc + tūn*; examples include: **Stockton** Warwicks. *Stocton* 1249. **Stockton Heath** Ches. *Stocton* c.1200, *Stoaken Heath* 1682. **Stockton on Tees** Stock. on T. *Stocton* 1196. Tees is a Celtic or pre-Celtic river-name, possibly meaning 'surging river'.

Stockwell Gtr. London. *Stokewell* 1197. 'Spring or stream by a tree-stump'. OE *stocc + wella*.

Stockwith, East (Lincs.) & *Stockwith, West* (Notts.). *Stochithe* 12th cent. 'Landing-place made of logs or tree-stumps'. OE *stocc + hȳth*.

Stodmarsh Kent. *Stodmerch* 675. 'Marsh where a herd of horses is kept'. OE *stōd + mersc*.

Stoford, 'stony ford', OE *stān + ford*: **Stoford** Somerset, near Yeovil. *Stafford* 1225. **Stoford** Wilts. *Stanford* 943.

Stogumber Somerset. *Stoke Gunner* 1225. 'Outlying farmstead or hamlet'. OE *stoc*, with pers. name or surname *Gumer* of an early owner.

Stogursey Somerset. *Stoche* 1086 (DB), *Stok Curcy* 1212. 'Outlying farmstead or hamlet'. OE *stoc*, with manorial affix from the de Curci family, here in the 12th cent.

Stoke, a very common name, from OE *stoc* 'outlying farmstead or hamlet, secondary settlement'; examples include: **Stoke Bruerne** Northants. *Stoche* 1086 (DB), *Stokbruer* 1254. Manorial affix from the Briwere family, here in the 13th cent. **Stoke-by-Nayland** Suffolk. *Stoke* c.950, *Stokeneylond* 1272. *See* NAYLAND. **Stoke Climsland** Cornwall. *Stoke* 1266, *Stok in Clymeslond* 1302. Affix is

from OE *land* 'estate' with an obscure first element. **Stoke D'Abernon** Surrey. *Stoche* 1086 (DB), *Stokes de Abernun* 1253. Manorial affix from the de Abernun family, here in the 12th cent. **Stoke Ferry** Norfolk. *Stoches* 1086 (DB), *Stokeferie* 1248. Affix is OScand. *ferja*, referring to a ferry over the River Wissey. **Stoke Fleming** Devon. *Stoc* 1086 (DB), *Stokeflemeng* 1270. Manorial affix from the family of le Flemeng, here in the 13th cent. **Stoke Gabriel** Devon. *Stoke* 1307, *Stokegabriel* 1309. Affix from the dedication of the church to St Gabriel. **Stoke Gifford** S. Glos. *Stoche* 1086 (DB), *Stokes Giffard* 1243. Manorial affix from the Gifard family, here from the 11th to the 14th cent. **Stoke, Limpley** Wilts. *Hangyndestok* 1263, *Stoke* 1333, *Lymply Stoke* 1585. Originally with OE *hangende* 'hanging' from its situation below a steep hillside. The later affix is to be associated with the dedication of a former chapel here called 'Our Lady of Limpley's Chapel' in 1578. **Stoke Mandeville** Bucks. *Stoches* 1086 (DB), *Stoke Mandeville* 1284. Manorial affix from the Mandeville family who held the manor in the 13th cent. **Stoke on Trent** Staffs. *Stoche* 1086 (DB). For the river-name, *see* TRENTHAM. **Stoke Poges** Bucks. *Stoches* 1086 (DB), *Stokepogeis* 1292. Manorial affix from the family of le Pugeis, here in the 13th cent. **Stoke, Rodney** Somerset. *Stoches* 1086 (DB). Manorial affix from the de Rodeney family, here in the early 14th cent. **Stoke St Gregory** Somerset. *Stokes* 1225. Affix from the dedication of the church. **Stoke, Severn** Heref. & Worcs. *Stoc* 972, *Stoche* 1086 (DB), *Savernestok* 1212. Affix from its situation on the River SEVERN. **Stoke sub Hamdon** Somerset. *Stoca* 1086 (DB), *Stokes under Hamden* 1248. Affix refers to Hamdon Hill, *Hamedone* c.1100, possibly 'hill of the enclosures' from OE *hamm + dūn*.

Stoke Newington Gtr. London, *see* NEWINGTON.

Stokeham Notts. *Estoches* 1086 (DB), *Stokum* 1242. '(Place at) the outlying farmsteads'. OE *stoc* in a dative plural form *stocum*.

Stokeinteignhead Devon. *Stoches* 1086 (DB), *Stokes in Tynhide* 1279. Originally 'outlying farmstead or hamlet', from OE *stoc*. Affix means 'in the district consisting of ten hides of land', from OE *tēn + hīd*.

Stokenchurch Bucks. *Stockenechurch* c.1200. 'Church made of logs'. OE *stoccen + cirice*.

Stokenham Devon. *Stokes* 1242, *Stok in Hamme* 1276. 'Outlying farmstead or hamlet in the area of cultivated ground'. OE *stoc + in + hamm*.

Stokesay Shrops. *Stoches* 1086 (DB), *Stok Say* 1256. Originally 'outlying farmstead or hamlet', from OE *stoc*. Manorial affix from the de Say family, here in the 12th cent.

Stokesby Norfolk. *Stokesbei* 1086 (DB). 'Village with an outlying farmstead or pasture'. OE *stoc + OScand. bý*.

Stokesley N. Yorks. *Stocheslage* 1086 (DB). 'Woodland clearing belonging to an outlying farmstead or hamlet'. OE *stoc + lēah*.

Ston Easton Somerset, *see* EASTON.

Stondon, 'stony hill', OE *stān + dūn*: **Stondon Massey** Essex. *Staundune* 1062, *Standon de Marcy* 1238. Manorial affix from the de Marci family, here in the 13th cent. **Standon, Upper** Beds. *Standone* 1086 (DB).

Stone, 'place at the stone or stones', OE *stān*; examples include: **Stone** Bucks. *Stanes* 1086 (DB). **Stone** Glos. *Stane* 1204. **Stone** Kent, near Dartford. *Stane* 10th cent., *Estanes* 1086 (DB). **Stone** Staffs. *Stanes* 1187.

Stonegrave N. Yorks. *Staningagrave* 757–8, *Stainegrif* 1086 (DB). 'Quarry of the people living by the stone or rock'. OE *stān* + *-inga-* + *græf* (influenced by OScand. *gryfja*).

Stonehaven Aber. *Stanehyve* 1587, *Steanhyve* 1629. 'Stone landing place'. OE *stān* + *hȳth*.

Stonehenge Wilts. *Stanenges* c.1130. 'Stone gallows' (from a fancied resemblance of the monument to such). OE *stān* + *hengen*.

Stonehouse Glos. *Stanhus* 1086 (DB). 'The stone-built house'. OE *stān* + *hūs*.

Stoneleigh Warwicks. *Stanlei* 1086 (DB). 'Stony woodland clearing'. OE *stān* + *lēah*.

Stonely Cambs. *Stanlegh* 1260. Identical in origin with the previous name.

Stonesby Leics. *Stovenebi* 1086 (DB). Probably 'farmstead or village by a tree-stump'. OE or OScand. *stofn* + *bý*.

Stonesfield Oxon. *Stuntesfeld* 1086 (DB). 'Open land of a man called *Stunt*'. OE pers. name + *feld*.

Stonham Aspal, *Stonham Earl*, & *Little Stonham* Suffolk. *Stonham* c.1040, *Stanham* 1086 (DB). 'Homestead by a stone or with stony ground'. OE *stān* + *hām*. *Aspal* and *Earl* are manorial affixes from the de Aspale family and from Earl Roger Bigod, here in the 13th cent.

Stonnall Staffs. *Stanahala* 1143. 'Stony nook of land'. OE *stān* + *halh*.

Stonor Oxon. *Stanora* late 10th cent. 'Stony hill-slope'. OE *stān* + *ōra*.

Stonton Wyville Leics. *Stantone* 1086 (DB), *Staunton Wyvile* 1265. 'Farmstead on stony ground'. OE *stān* + *tūn*. Manorial affix from the de Wivill family, here in the 13th cent.

Stony Stratford Bucks., *see* STRATFORD.

Stoodleigh Devon. *Stodlei* 1086 (DB). 'Woodland clearing where a herd of horses is kept'. OE *stōd* + *lēah*.

Stopham W. Sussex. *Stopeham* 1086 (DB). 'Homestead or river-meadow of a man called *Stoppa*, or by a hollow'. OE pers. name or OE *stoppa* + *hām* or *hamm*.

Stopsley Beds. *Stoppelee* 1198. 'Woodland clearing of a man called *Stoppa*, or by a hollow'. OE pers. name or OE *stoppa* + *lēah*.

Storeton Mersey. *Stortone* 1086 (DB). 'Large farmstead', or 'farmstead near a young wood'. OScand. *stórr* or *storth* + OE *tūn*.

Stormont Down. *Storm Mount* 1834. Probably 'storm mount', originally the name of an estate here.

Stornoway W. Isles (Lewis). *Stornochway* 1511. 'Steering bay'. OScand. *stjórn* + *vágr*. The name seems to imply that ships had to manoeuvre carefully when entering or leaving the harbour.

Storridge Heref. & Worcs. *Storugge* 13th cent. 'Stony ridge'. OE *stān* + *hrycg*.

Storrington W. Sussex. *Storgetune* 1086 (DB). Probably 'farmstead or village visited by storks'. OE *storc* + *tūn*.

Stortford, Bishop's Herts. *Storteford* 1086 (DB), *Bysshops Stortford* 1587. 'Ford by the tongues of land'. OE *steort* + *ford*. Affix from its early possession by the Bishop of London. The river-name **Stort** is a 'back-formation' from the place-name.

Storth Cumbria. *Storthes* 1349. 'Brushwood, plantation'. OScand. *storth*.

Stotfold Beds. *Stodfald* 1007, *Stotfalt* 1086 (DB). 'The stud-fold or enclosure for horses'. OE *stōd-fald*.

Stottesdon Shrops. *Stodesdone* 1086 (DB). Probably 'hill where a herd of horses is kept'. OE *stōd* + *dūn*.

Stoughton, 'farmstead at an outlying hamlet', OE *stoc* + *tūn*: **Stoughton** Leics. *Stoctone* 1086 (DB). **Stoughton** Surrey. *Stoctune* 12th cent. **Stoughton** W. Sussex. *Estone* |*sic*| 1086 (DB), *Stoctona* 1121.

Stoulton Heref. & Worcs. *Stoltun* 840, 1086 (DB). 'Farmstead or village with a seat (used at meetings of the Hundred)'. OE *stōl* + *tūn*.

Stour Provost Dorset. *Stur* 1086 (DB), *Sture Preauus* 1270. 'Estate on the River Stour held by the Norman Abbey of Préaux' (during the 12th and 13th centuries), *see* STOUR, EAST & WEST.

Stour, East & *Stour, West* Dorset. *Sture* 1086 (DB). Named from the Dorset/Hants. River Stour, *see* STOURBRIDGE.

Stourbridge W. Mids. *Sturbrug* 1255. 'Bridge over the River Stour'. Celtic or OE river-name (probably meaning 'the strong one') + OE *brycg*. There are no less than five major rivers in England called Stour, *see* following names.

Stourmouth Kent. *Sturmutha* late 11th cent. 'Mouth of the River Stour'. Celtic or OE river-name (*see* STOURBRIDGE) + OE *mūtha*.

Stourpaine Dorset. *Sture* 1086 (DB), *Stures Paen* 1243. 'Estate on the River Stour held by the Payn family' (here in the 13th cent.), *see* STOUR, EAST & WEST.

Stourport-on-Severn Heref. & Worcs. *Stourport* c.1775. 'Port at the confluence of the Rivers Stour and Severn'. A recent name.

Stourton, 'farmstead or village on one of the rivers called Stour', Celtic or OE river-name (probably meaning 'the strong one') + OE *tūn*; **Stourton** Staffs. *Sturton* 1227. **Stourton** Warwicks. *Sturton* 1206. **Stourton** Wilts. *Stortone* 1086 (DB).

Stourton Caundle Dorset, *see* CAUNDLE.

Stoven Suffolk. *Stouone* 1086 (DB). '(Place at) the tree-stump(s)'. OE or OScand. *stofn*.

Stow, Stowe, 'assembly place, holy place', OE *stōw*; examples include: **Stow** lincs. *Stou* 1086 (DB). **Stow Bardolf** Norfolk. *Stou* 1086 (DB). Manorial affix from the Bardulf family, here in the 13th cent. **Stow Bedon** Norfolk. *Stou* 1086 (DB), *Stouwebidun* 1287. Manorial affix from the de Bidun family, here in the 13th cent. **Stow cum Quy** Cambs. *Stoua* 1086, *Stowe cum Quey* 1316. Quy is *Coeia* in 1086

(DB), 'cow island' from OE *cū* + *ēg*. Latin *cum* is 'with'. **Stowe** Staffs. *Stowe* 1242. **Stow Maries** Essex. *Stowe* 1222, *Stowe Mareys* 1420. Manorial affix from the Mareys family, here in the 13th cent. **Stow on the Wold** Glos. *Eduuardesstou* 1086 (DB), *Stoua* 1213, *Stowe on the Olde* 1574. Originally 'St Edward's holy place'. Later affix is from OE *wald* 'high ground cleared of forest'. **Stow, West** Suffolk. *Stowa* 1086 (DB), *Westowe* 1254.

Stowell, 'stony spring or stream', OE *stān* + *wella*: **Stowell** Somerset. *Stanwelle* 1086 (DB). **Stowell, West** Wilts. *Stawelle* 1176.

Stowey, Nether & *Stowey, Over* Somerset. *Stawei* 1086 (DB). 'Stone way'. OE *stān* + *weg*.

Stowford, 'stony ford', OE *stān* + *ford*; examples include: **Stowford** Devon, near Portgate. *Staford* 1086 (DB). **Stowford, East** Devon. *Staveford* 1086 (DB).

Stowlangtoft Suffolk. *Stou* 1086 (DB), *Stowelangetot* 13th cent. OE *stōw* 'place of assembly or holy place', with manorial affix from the de Langetot family, here in the 13th cent.

Stowmarket Suffolk. *Stou* 1086 (DB), *Stowmarket* 1268. OE *stōw* as in previous name, here with later addition referring to the important market here.

Stowting Kent. *Stuting* 1044, *Stotinges* 1086 (DB). Probably 'place characterized by a lumpy hillock', OE **stūt* + *-ing*. Alternatively 'place associated with a man called **Stūt*', with an OE pers. name as first element.

Strabane (*An Srath Bán*) Tyrone. *Sraith Bán c*.1616. 'The white riverside land'.

Strachan Aber. *Stratheyhan* 1153. 'Valley'. Gaelic *srath* + unknown element.

Stradbally (*Sráidbhaile*) Kerry, Laois, Waterford. 'Street town'.

Stradbroke Suffolk. *Statebroc* |sic| 1086 (DB), *Stradebroc* 1168. Possibly 'brook by a paved road'. OE *strǣt* + *brōc*.

Stradone (*Sraith an Domhain*) Cavan. *Shraghadoone* 1629. Possibly 'river meadow of the valley floor'.

Stradsett Norfolk. *Strateseta* 1086 (DB). 'Dwelling or fold on a Roman road'. OE *strǣt* + (*ge*)*set*.

Stragglethorpe Lincs. *Stragerthorp* 1242. OScand. *thorp* 'outlying farmstead or hamlet' with an uncertain first element, possibly the pers. name or surname of some early owner.

Stragolan (*Srath Gabhláin*) Fermanagh. *Stragolan* 1751. 'River meadow of the fork'.

Strahart (*Sraith Airt*) Wexford. 'Art's river meadow'.

Straid (*Sráid*) Antrim, Donegal, Mayo. 'Street'.

Straidarran (*Sráidbhaile Uí Áráin*) Derry. *Baile Uí Hárán c*.1680. 'Street town of the Uí Áráin'.

Straiton Midloth. *Stratone* 1296. 'Village on a Roman road'. OE *strǣt* + *tūn*.

Stralongford (*Srath Longfoirt*) Tyrone. *Shralonghert* 1609. 'River meadow of the fortress'.

Stramshall Staffs. *Stagrigesholle* |sic| 1086 (DB), *Strangricheshull* 1227. Possibly 'hill of a man called **Strangrīc*'. OE pers. name + *hyll*.

Stranagalwilly (*Srath na Gallbhuaile*) Tyrone. *Shraghnagallnilly* 1661. 'River meadow of the stone milking place'.

Strangeways Gtr. Manch. *Strangwas* 1322. Probably '(place by) a stream with a strong current'. OE *strang* + (*ge*)*wæsc*.

Strangford Down. *Strangfiord* 1205. 'Strong sea inlet'. OScand. *strangr* + *fjorthr*. The village is named after Strangford Lough, a long sea inlet, whose Irish name is *Loch Cuan*, 'sea inlet of bays'. The Irish name of the village is *Baile Loch Cuan*, 'town on Strangford Loch'.

Stranmillis (*Sruthán Milis*) Antrim. (*bun*) *a' tSrutháin Mhilis* 1644. 'Sweet stream'.

Stranocum (*Sraith Nócam*) Antrim. *Stronokum c*.1659. Irish *srath*, 'river meadow'. The second element is of obscure origin.

Stranorlar (*Srath an Urláir*) Donegal. *Stranhurland* 1590. 'River meadow of the valley floor'.

Stranraer Dumf. *Stranrever* 1320. 'Broad point'. Gaelic *sròn* + *reamhar*. The 'broad point' is presumably that of the Rinns of Galloway nearby.

Stratfield, 'open land by a Roman road', OE *stræt* + *feld*: **Stratfield Mortimer** Berks. *Stradfeld* 1086 (DB), *Stratfeld Mortimer* 1275. Manorial affix from the de Mortemer family, here from 1086. **Stratfield Saye** & **Stratfield Turgis** Hants. *Stratfeld c*.1060, *Stradfelle* 1086 (DB), *Stratfeld Say* 1277 *Stratfeld Turgys* 1289. Manorial affixes from the de Say and *Turgis* families, here in the 13th cent.

Stratford, 'ford on a Roman road', OE *strēt* + *ford*; examples include: **Stratford** Gtr. London. *Strætforda* 1067. **Stratford, Fenny** Bucks. *Fenni Stratford* 1252. Affix is OE *fennig* 'marshy'. **Stratford St Andrew** Suffolk. *Straffort* 1086 (DB). Affix from the dedication of the church. **Stratford, Stony** Bucks. *Stani Stratford* 1202. Affix is OE *stānig* 'stony'. **Stratford Tony** Wilts. *Stretford* 672, *Stradford* 1086 (DB), *Stratford Touny* 14th cent. Manorial affix from the de Touny family, here in the 13th cent. **Stratford upon Avon** Warwicks. *Stretfordæ c*.700, *Stradforde* 1086 (DB). Avon is a Celtic river-name meaning simply 'river'. **Stratford, Water** Bucks. *Stradford* 1086 (DB), *West Watrestretford* 1383. Affix is OE *wæter* 'river, stream'.

Stratford-on-Slaney (*Áth na Sráide*) Wicklow. 'Ford of the street'. The Irish name translates the English surname of Edward Stratford, 2nd Earl of Aldborough, who founded the village on the River *Slaney* in the late 18th cent.

Strath Beag Highland. 'Little valley'. Gaelic *srath* + *beag*.

Strathallan Perth. *Strathalun* 1187. 'Valley of the Allan Water'. Gaelic *srath*. The river has a pre-Celtic name meaning 'flowing water'.

Strathaven S. Lan. *Strathouren c*.1190. 'Valley of the Avon Water'. Gaelic *srath*. The Celtic river name means simply 'river', like the English Avons.

Strathblane Stir. *Strachblachan c*.1200, *Strachblahane* 1335. Perhaps 'valley of little flowers'. Gaelic *srath* + *bláthan*.

Strathbogie (district) Aber. *Strabolgin* 1187, *Strabolgy* 1335. Perhaps 'Valley of the River Bogie'. Gaelic *srath*.

...iver name means 'river with bag-shaped pools' ...elic *bolg*).

...athclyde (district) N. Lan. 'Valley of the River ...yde'. Gaelic *srath*. For the river name, *see* CLYDEBANK.

...trathdon Aber. 'Valley of the River Don'. Gaelic *srath*. The river name means 'goddess'.

Strathearn Perth. *Sraithh'erni c.*950, *Stradearn* 1185. 'Valley of the River Earn'. Gaelic *srath*. *See* EARN.

Strathkinness Fife. *Stradkines* 1144. Gaelic *srath* + obscure second element.

Strathmiglo Fife. *Scradimigglock c.*1200, *Stramygloke* 1294. 'Valley of the River Miglo'. Gaelic *srath*. *Miglo*, 'bog-loch' (Welsh *mign* + *llwch*), was the name of the marshy lake that now forms the upper reach of the River Eden.

Strathmore (valley) Angus, Perth. 'Great valley'. Gaelic *srath* + *mór*. The long valley separates the Scottish Highlands, to the north, from the Central Lowlands, to the south.

Strathnaver Highland. *Strathnauir* 1268. 'Valley of the River Naver'. Gaelic *srath*. The pre- Celtic river name means 'river'.

Strathpeffer Highland. *Strathpefir* 1350. 'Valley of the River Peffery'. Gaelic *srath*. The river name means 'radiant one' (Pictish *pevr*).

Strathwhillan N. Ayr (Arran). *Terequhilane* 1445. Possibly 'land of Cuilean'. Gaelic *tir* or 'holly land'.

Strathy Highland. '(Place in the) valley'. Gaelic *srath*.

Stratton, usually 'farmstead or village on a Roman road', OE *stræt* + *tūn*; examples include: **Stratton Audley** Oxon. *Stratone* 1086 (DB), *Stratton Audeley* 1318. Manorial affix from the de Alditheleg family, here in the 13th cent. **Stratton, East** & **Stratton, West** Hants. *Strattone* 903, *Stratune* 1086 (DB). **Stratton on the Fosse** Somerset. *Stratone* 1086 (DB). On the great Roman road called FOSSE WAY. **Stratton St Margaret** Wilts. *Stratone* 1086 (DB). Affix from the dedication of the church. **Stratton St Michael** & **Long Stratton** Norfolk. *Stratuna, Stretuna* 1086 (DB). Distinguishing affixes from the dedication of the church and from the length of the village. **Stratton Strawless** Norfolk. *Stratuna* 1086 (DB). *Stratton Streles* 1446. The affix means literally 'lacking in straw', from OE *strēaw* + *-lēas*.

However the following has a different origin: **Stratton** Cornwall. *Strætneat c.*880, *Stratone* 1086 (DB). 'Valley of the River Neet'. Cornish *stras* + Celtic river-name (of uncertain meaning), with the later addition of OE *tūn* 'village'.

Streamstown (*Baile an tSrutháin*) Galway. 'Town of the stream'.

Streat E. Sussex. *Estrat* 1086 (DB). '(Place on or near) a Roman road'. OE *stræt*.

Streatham Gtr. London. *Estreham* |*sic*| 1086 (DB), *Streteham* 1247. 'Homestead or village on a Roman road'. OE *stræt* + *hām*.

Streatley, 'woodland clearing by a Roman road', OE *stræt* + *lēah*: **Streatley** Beds. *Strætlea c.*1053, *Stradlei*

1086 (DB). **Streatley** Berks. *Stretlea c.*690, *Estralei* 1086 (DB).

Street, '(place on or near) a Roman road or other paved highway', OE *stræt;* for example **Street** (Somerset, near Glastonbury): *Stret* 725.

Street (*Sráid*) Westmeath. 'Street'.

Streethay Staffs. *Stretheye* 1262. 'Enclosure on a Roman road'. OE *stræt* + *hæg*.

Streetly, 'woodland clearing by a Roman road', OE *stræt* + *lēah*: **Streetly** W. Mids. *Strætlea* 957. **Streetly End** Cambs. *Stradleia* 1086.

Strefford Shrops. *Straford* 1086 (DB). 'Ford on a Roman road'. OE *stræt* + *ford*.

Strensall York. *Strenshale* 1086 (DB). Possibly 'nook of land given as a reward, or one used for love-making'. OE *strēon* + *halh*.

Strensham Heref. & Worcs. *Strengesho* 972, *Strenchesham c.*1086. 'Homestead or enclosure of a man called *Strenge'. OE pers. name + *hām* or *hamm* (alternating with *hōh* 'promontory' in the early spelling).

Strete Devon. *Streta* 1194. '(Place on) the Roman road'. OE *stræt*.

Stretford Gtr. Manch. *Stretford* 1212. 'Ford on a Roman road'. OE *stræt* + *ford*.

Strethall Essex. *Strathala* 1086 (DB). 'Nook of land by a Roman road'. OE *stræt* + *halh*.

Stretham Cambs. *Stratham c.*970, *Stradham* 1086 (DB). 'Homestead or village on a Roman road'. OE *stræt* + *hām*.

Strettington W. Sussex. *Stratone* 1086 (DB), *Estretementona* 12th cent. 'Farmstead or village of the dwellers by the Roman road'. OE *stræt* + *hæme* + *tūn*.

Stretton, 'farmstead or village on a Roman road', OE *stræt* + *tūn*; examples include: **Stretton** Derbys. *Strættune c.*1002, *Stratune* 1086 (DB). **Stretton, All** & **Stretton, Church** Shrops. *Stratun(e)* 1086 (DB), *Aluredestretton, Chirich Stretton* 1262. Distinguishing affixes from the name of an early owner called Alfred and from OE *cirice* 'church'. **Stretton Grandison** Heref. & Worcs. *Stratune* 1086 (DB), *Stretton Graundison* 1350. Manorial affix from the Grandison family, here in the 14th cent. **Stretton-on-Dunsmore** Warwicks. *Stratone* 1086 (DB). For Dunsmore, *see* RYTON. **Stretton Sugwas** Heref. & Worcs. *Stratone* 1086 (DB), *Strattone by Sugwas* 1334. Sugwas is 'alluvial land frequented by sparrows', or 'marshy alluvial land', OE *sugge* or *sugga* + *wæsse*.

Strickland, Great & *Strickland, Little* Cumbria. *Stircland* late 12th cent. 'Cultivated land where young bullocks are kept'. OE *stirc* + *land*.

Stringston Somerset. *Strengestune* 1086 (DB). 'Farmstead or village of a man called *Strenge'. OE pers. name + *tūn*.

Strixton Northants. *Strixton* 12th cent. 'Farmstead or village of a man called Stríkr'. OScand. pers. name + *tūn*.

Stroan (*Sruthán*) Antrim, Cavan, Kilkenny. 'Stream'.

Strokestown (*Béal na mBuillí*) Roscommon. 'Ford-mouth of the strokes'. The name appears to refer to a battle here.

Stroma (island) Highland. *Straumsey* 1150. 'Island in the current'. OScand. *straumr* + *ey*. Stroma lies in the current of the Pentland Firth. *Cp.* STROMNESS.

Stromness Orkn (North Ronaldsay). *Straumsness* 1150. 'Headland of the current'. OScand. *straumr* + *nes*. The name alludes to the strong current off the headland.

Strone Arg. 'Headland'. Gaelic *sròn*.

Stronsay (island) Orkn. *Striónsay* 13th cent. OScand. *strjón* 'wealth' + *ey*; will for the 'herring fishing'.

Strood, *Stroud*, 'marshy land overgrown with brushwood', OE *strōd*; examples include: **Strood** Kent, near Rochester. *Strod* 889. **Stroud** Glos. (*La*) *Strode* 1200. **Stroud Green** Gtr. London, near Highbury. *Strode* 1407.

Struan Perth. '(Place by a) little stream'. Gaelic *sruthan*.

Strubby Lincs., near Alford. *Strobi* 1086 (DB). Probably 'farmstead or village of a man called Strútr'. OScand. pers. name + *bý*.

Struell (*Sruthail*) Down. (*Capella de*) *Strohull* 1306. 'Stream'.

Strumble Head Pemb. *Strumble head*. Probably 'stormy headland'. Modern English *storm* + *bill*. *Head* was added when the sense of 'headland' in the original was forgotten.

Strumpshaw Norfolk. *Stromessaga* 1086 (DB). 'Tree-stump wood or copse'. OE **strump* + *sceaga*.

Stubbington Hants. *Stubitone* 1086 (DB). 'Estate associated with a man called *Stubba', OE pers. name + *-ing-* + *tūn*, or 'farmstead at the tree-stump clearing', OE **stubbing* + *tūn*.

Stubbins Gtr. Manch. *Stubbyng* 1563. OE **stubbing* 'place with tree-stumps, a clearing'.

Stubbs, Walden N. Yorks. *Istop* |sic| 1086 (DB), *Stubbis* *c*.1180, *Stubbes Walding* 1280. 'The tree-stumps'. OE *stubb*. Manorial affix from an early owner called Walding, here in the 12th cent.

Stubton Lincs. *Stubetune* 1086 (DB). 'Farmstead or village of a man called *Stubba, or where there are tree-stumps'. OE pers. name or *stubb* + *tūn*.

Studdal, East Kent. *Stodwalde* 1240. 'Forest where a herd of horses is kept'. OE *stōd* + *weald*.

Studham Beds. *Stodham* 1053–66, *Estodham* 1086 (DB). 'Homestead or enclosure where a herd of horses is kept'. OE *stōd* + *hām* or *hamm*.

Studland Dorset. *Stollant* 1086 (DB). 'Cultivated land where a herd of horses is kept'. OE *stōd* + *land*.

Studley, 'woodland clearing or pasture where a herd of horses is kept', OE *stōd* + *lēah*: **Studley** Oxon. *Stodleya* *c*.1185. **Studley** Warwicks. *Stodlei* 1086 (DB). **Studley** Wilts. *Stodleia* 12th cent. **Studley Roger** N. Yorks. *Stodlege* *c*.1030, *Stollai* 1086 (DB), *Stodelay Roger* 1228. Manorial affix from early possession by Roger de Mowbray or by Archbishop Roger of York.

Stukeley, Great & *Stukeley, Little* Cambs. *Stivecle* 1086 (DB). 'Woodland clearing with tree-stumps'. OE **styfic* + *lēah*.

Stuntney Cambs. *Stuntenei* 1086 (DB). 'Steep island'. OE *stunt* (dative *-an*) + *ēg*.

Sturmer Essex. *Sturmere* *c*.1000, 1086 (DB). 'Pool [by the] River Stour'. Celtic or OE river-name (probably [strong one') + OE *mere*.

Sturminster Marshall Dorset. *Sture minster* 9th cent [*Sturminstre* 1086 (DB), *Sturministre Marescal* 126['Church on the River Stour'. Celtic or OE river-name (*see* STOUR, EAST & WEST) + OE *mynster*. Manorial affix from the Mareschal family, here in the 13th cent.

Sturminster Newton Dorset. *Nywetone, at Stoure* 968, *Newentone* 1086 (DB), *Sturminstr Nyweton* 1291. Originally two separate names for places on opposite sides of the river, 'new farmstead or village' from OE *nīwe* + *tūn*, and 'church on the River Stour' (*see* previous name).

Sturry Kent. *Sturgeh* 678, *Esturai* 1086 (DB). 'District by the River Stour'. Celtic or OE river-name (*see* STOURMOUTH) + OE **gē*.

Sturton, 'village on a Roman road', OE *strǣt* + *tūn*: **Sturton by Stow** Lincs. *Stratone* 1086 (DB). See STOW. **Sturton, Great** Lincs. *Stratone* 1086 (DB). **Sturton le Steeple** Notts. *Estretone* 1086 (DB). Affix *le Steeple*, first found in the 18th cent., refers to the tower of the church.

Stuston Suffolk. *Stutestuna* 1086 (DB). Probably 'farmstead or village of a man called *Stūt. OE pers. name + *tūn*.

Stutton N. Yorks. *Stouetun* 1086 (DB). 'Farmstead of a man called Stúfr', or 'one built of or amongst tree-stumps'. OScand. pers. name or *stúfr* + OE *tūn*.

Stutton Suffolk. *Stuttuna* 1086 (DB). 'Farmstead or village infested with gnats, or where bullocks are kept'. OE *stūt* or OScand. *stútr* + OE *tūn*.

Styal Ches. *Styhale* *c*.1200. 'Nook of land with a pigsty, or by a path'. OE *stigu* or *stīg* + *halh*.

Styrrup Notts. *Estirape* 1086 (DB), *Stirap* 1197. from OE *stīg-rāp* 'a stirrup', probably named from the hill to the east of the village, perhaps thought by early settlers to resemble a stirrup in shape.

Suckley Heref. & Worcs. *Suchelei* 1086 (DB). 'Woodland clearing frequented by sparrows'. OE **succa* + *lēah*.

Sudborough Northants. *Sutburg* 1086 (DB). 'Southern fortification'. OE *sūth* + *burh*.

Sudbourne Suffolk. *Sutborne* *c*.1050, *Sutburna* 1086 (DB). 'Southern stream'. OE *sūth* + *burna*.

Sudbrooke Lincs., near Lincoln. *Sutbroc* 1086 (DB). 'Southern brook'. OE *sūth* + *brōc*.

Sudbury, 'southern fortification', OE *sūth* + *burh* (dative *byrig*): **Sudbury** Derbys. *Sudberie* 1086 (DB). **Sudbury** Gtr. London. *Suthbery* 1292. Here the second element may mean 'manor'. **Sudbury** Suffolk. *Suthbyrig* *c*.995, *Sutberia* 1086 (DB).

Suffield Norfolk. *Sudfelda* 1086 (DB). 'Southern open land'. OE *sūth* + *feld*.

Suffolk (the county). *Suthfolchi* 895, *Sudfulc* 1086 (DB). '(Territory of) the southern people (of the East Angles)'. OE *sūth* + *folc*, see NORFOLK.

Sugnall Staffs. *Sotehelle* |sic| 1086 (DB), *Sugenhulle* 1222. 'Hill frequented by sparrows'. OE **sugge* (genitive plural *-ena*) + *hyll*.

) (river) Tipperary, Waterford. 'Sister'.

e Northants. *Sulgrave* 1086 (DB). 'Grove near a narrow valley'. OE *sulh* + *grāf*.

am Berks. *Soleham* 1086 (DB). Probably 'homestead gully'. OE *sulh* + *hām*.

ilhamstead Berks. *Silamested* 1198. 'Homestead by a gully or narrow valley'. OE *sulh* (genitive *sylh*) + *hām-stede*.

Sullington W. Sussex. *Sillinctune* 959, *Sillintone* 1086 (DB). Possibly 'farmstead or village by a willow copse'. OE **sieling* + *tūn*. Alternatively the first element may be OE **sielling* 'gift', denoting land given as a gift.

Sullom Voe Shet. 'Sullom bay'. OScand. *sólheinr* 'sunny farm' + *vágr*.

Sully (*Sili*) Vale Glam. *Sulie* 1193, *Sulye* 1254. Origin uncertain. The name may be manorial.

Sumburgh Shet. *Swynbrocht* 1506. 'Small fort'. OScand. *sunn* + *borg*.

Summerseat Gtr. Manch. *Sumersett* 1556. 'Hut or shieling used in summer'. OScand. *sumarr* + *sætr*.

Sunbury Surrey. *Sunnanbyrg* 960, *Sunneberie* 1086 (DB). 'Stronghold of a man called **Sunna*'. OE pers. name + *burh* (dative *byrig*).

Sunderland, usually 'detached estate', OE *sundor-land*: **Sunderland** Cumbria. *Sonderland* 1278. **Sunderland** Tyne & Wear. *Sunderland* c.1168.
However the following has a different origin: **Sunderland, North** Northum. *Sutherlannland* 12th cent. 'Southern cultivated land'. OE *sūtherra* + *land*.

Sundon Beds. *Sunnandune* c.1050, *Sonedone* 1086 (DB). 'Hill of a man called **Sunna*'. OE pers. name + *dūn*.

Sundridge Kent. *Sondresse* 1086 (DB). 'Separate or detached ploughed field'. OE *sundor* + *ersc*.

Sunningdale Berks., a parish-name formed in the 19th cent. from the following name.

Sunninghill Berks. *Sunningehull* 1190. 'Hill of the family or followers of a man called **Sunna*'. OE pers. name + *-inga-* + *hyll*. The same tribal group gives name to SONNING and SUNNINGWELL.

Sunningwell Oxon. *Sunningauuille* 9th cent., *Soningeuuel* 1086 (DB). 'Spring or stream of the family or followers of a man called **Sunna*'. OE pers. name + *-inga-* + *wella*.

Surbiton Gtr. London. *Suberton* 1179. 'Southern grange or outlying farm'. OE *sūth* + *bere-tūn*. *See* NORBITON.

Surfleet Lincs. *Sverefelt |sic|* 1086 (DB), *Surfliet* 1167. 'Sour creek or stream'. OE *sūr* + *flēot*.

Surlingham Norfolk. *Sutherlingaham* 1086 (DB). Probably 'homestead of the family or followers of a man called **Herela*', from OE pers. name + *-inga-* + *hām*, with *sūth* 'south'. Alternatively 'homestead of the people living to the south (of Norwich)', OE *sūther* + *-linga-* + *hām*.

Surrey (the county). *Suthrige* 722, *Sudrie* 1086 (DB). 'Southerly district' (relative to MIDDLESEX). OE *sūther* + **gē*.

Sussex (the county). *Suth Seaxe* late 9th cent., *Sudsexe* 1086 (DB). '(Territory of) the South Saxons'. OE *sūth* + *Seaxe*.

Sustead Norfolk. *Sutstede* 1086 (DB). 'Southern place'. OE *sūth* + *stede*.

Sutcombe Devon. *Sutecome* 1086 (DB). 'Valley of a man called **Sutta*'. OE pers. name + *cumb*.

Sutherland (the historic county). *Suthernelande* c.1250. 'Southern territory'. OScand. *suthr* + *land*. The region was a 'southern territory' to the Vikings who settled in Orkney and Shetland.

Sutterton Lincs. *Suterton* 1200. Probably 'farmstead or village of the shoe-maker(s)'. OE *sūtere* + *tūn*.

Sutton, a very common place-name, 'south farmstead or village', i.e. one to the south of another settlement, OE *sūth* + *tūn*: examples include: **Sutton** Cambs. *Sudtone* 1086 (DB). **Sutton** Gtr. London. *Sudtone* 1086 (DB). **Sutton** Suffolk. *Suthtuna* 1086 (DB). **Sutton at Hone** Kent. *Sudtone* 1086 (DB), *Sutton atte hone* 1240. Affix is 'at the (boundary) stone' from OE *hān*. **Sutton Bonington** Notts. *Sudtone*, *Bonniton* 1086 (DB). Originally two separate manors, Bonington being 'estate associated with a man called Buna', OE pers. name + *-ing-* + *tūn*. **Sutton Bridge** Lincs. named from LONG SUTTON. **Sutton Coldfield** W. Mids. *Sutone* 1086 (DB), *Sutton in Colefeud* 1269. Coldfield is 'open land where charcoal is produced', OE *col* + *feld*. **Sutton Courtenay** Oxon. *Suthtun* c.870, *Sudtone* 1086 (DB), *Suttone Curteney* 1284. Manorial affix from the Curtenai family, here in the 12th cent. **Sutton, Full** E. R. Yorks. *Sudtone* 1086 (DB), *Fulesutton* 1234. Affix is OE *fūl* 'dirty'. **Sutton, Great** & **Sutton, Little** Ches. *Sudtone* 1086 (DB). **Sutton, Guilden** Ches. *Sudtone* 1086 (DB), *Guldenesutton* c.1200. Affix is OE *gylden* 'splendid, wealthy'. **Sutton in Ashfield** Notts. *Sutone* 1086 (DB), *Sutton in Essefeld* 1276. Affix is an old district name, *see* ASHFIELD. **Sutton, Kings** Northants. *Sudtone* 1086 (DB), *Kinges Sutton* 1294. The manor was held by King William in 1086. **Sutton, Long** Lincs. *Sudtone* 1086 (DB). Affix refers to the length of the village. **Sutton, Long** Somerset. *Sudton* 878, *Sutune* 1086 (DB), *Langesutton* 1312. Affix from the length of the village. **Sutton on Hull** K. upon Hull. *Sudtone* 1086 (DB), *Sutune iuxta Hul* 1172. See KINGSTON UPON HULL. **Sutton on Sea** Lincs. *Sudtone* 1086 (DB). **Sutton on Trent** Notts. *Sudtone* 1086 (DB). **Sutton Valence** Kent. *Suthtun* 814, *Sudtone* 1086 (DB), *Sutton Valence* 1316. Manorial affix from the Valence family, here in the 13th cent.

Swaby Lincs. *Suabi* 1086 (DB). 'Farmstead or village of a man called Sváfi'. OScand. pers. name + *bý*.

Swadlincote Derbys. *Sivardingescotes* 1086 (DB). Probably 'cottage(s) of a man called **Sweartling* or **Svartlingr*'. OE or OScand. pers. name + OE *cot*.

Swaffham, 'homestead of the Swabians', OE *Swǣfe* + *hām*: **Swaffham** Norfolk. *Suafham* 1086 (DB). **Swaffham Bulbeck** & **Swaffham Prior** Cambs. *Suafham* c.1050, 1086 (DB), *Swafham Bolebek* 1218, *Swafham Prior* 1261. Manorial affixes from early possession by the de Bolebech family and by the Prior of Ely.

Swafield Norfolk. *Suafelda |sic|* 1086 (DB), *Suathefeld* c.1150. 'Open land characterized by swathes or tracks'. OE *swæth* + *feld*.

Swainby N. Yorks., near Whorlton. *Swaneby* 1314. Probably 'farmstead or village of the young men'. OScand. *sveinn* + *bý*.

Swainsthorpe Norfolk. *Sueinestorp* 1086 (DB). 'Outlying farmstead or hamlet of a man called Sveinn'. OScand. pers. name + *thorp*.

Swalcliffe Oxon. *Sualewclive* c.1166. 'Cliff or slope frequented by swallows'. OE *swealwe* + *clif*.

Swale (river), two examples probably identical in origin, from OE **sw(e)alwe* 'rushing water': i) Kent *see* SWALECLIFFE, ii) N. Yorks., *see* BROMPTON ON SWALE.

Swalecliffe Kent. *Swalewanclife* 949, *Soaneclive |sic|* 1086 (DB). 'Swallow's riverbank', OE *swealwe* + *clif*, or 'bank by (the estuary of) the River SWALE' (the latter once a more extensive river before coastal changes took place).

Swallow Lincs. *Sualun* 1086 (DB). Probably '(place on) the rushing stream'. OE **swalwe*.

Swallowcliffe Wilts. *Swealewanclif* 940, *Svaloclive* 1086 (DB). 'Swallow's cliff or slope'. OE *swealwe* + *clif*.

Swallowfield Berks. *Sualefelle* 1086 (DB). 'Open land on the rushing stream'. OE **swealwe* + *feld*.

Swanage Dorset. *Swanawic* late 9th cent., *Swanwic* 1086 (DB). 'Farm of the herdsmen, or farm where swans are reared'. OE *swān* or *swan* + *wīc*.

Swanbourne Bucks. *Suanaburna* 792, *Sueneborne* 1086 (DB). 'Stream frequented by swans'. OE *swan* + *burna*.

Swanland E. R. Yorks. *Suenelund* 1189. 'Grove of a man called Svanr or Sveinn'. OScand. pers. name + *lundr*.

Swanley Kent, near Farningham. *Swanleg* 1203. Probably 'woodland clearing of the herdsmen'. OE *swān* + *lēah*.

Swanmore Hants. *Suanemere* 1205. 'Pool frequented by swans'. OE *swan* + *mere*.

Swannington, probably 'estate associated with a man called **Swan*', OE pers. name + *-ing-* + *tūn*: **Swannington** Leics. *Suaninton* late 12th cent. **Swannington** Norfolk. *Sueningatuna* 1086 (DB).

Swanscombe Kent. *Suanescamp* 695, *Svinescamp* 1086 (DB). 'Enclosed land of the herdsman'. OE *swān* + *camp*.

Swansea (*Abertawe*) Swan. *Sweynesse* c.1165, *Sueinesea* 1190, *Swanesey* 1322. 'Sveinn's island'. OScand. pers. name + *ey*. The Welsh name means 'mouth of the Tawe' (Welsh *aber*), the Celtic river name perhaps meaning simply 'water'.

Swanton, 'farmstead or village of the herdsmen', OE *swān* + *tūn*: **Swanton Abbot** Norfolk. *Suanetuna* 1086 (DB). Affix from early possession by Holme Abbey. **Swanton Morley** Norfolk. *Suanetuna* 1086 (DB). Manorial affix from the de Morle family, here in the 14th cent. **Swanton Novers** Norfolk. *Suanetuna* 1086 (DB). Manorial affix from the de Nuiers family, here in the 13th cent.

Swanwick, '(dairy) farm of the herdsmen', OE *swān* + *wīc*: **Swanwick** Derbys. *Swanwyk* late 13th cent. **Swanwick** Hants. *Suanewic* 1185.

Swarby Lincs. *Svarrebi* 1086 (DB). 'Farmstead or village of a man called Svarri'. OScand. pers. name + *bý*.

Swardeston Norfolk. *Suerdestuna* 1086 (DB). ['...farmstead] or village of a man called **Sweord*'. OE pers. na[me ...]

Swarkestone Derbys. *Suerchestune* 1086 (DB). P[...] 'farmstead or village of a man called Swerkir'. O[Scand.] pers. name + OE *tūn*.

Swarland Northum. *Swarland* 1242. 'Heavy culti[vated] land'. OE *swǣr* + *land*.

Swaton Lincs. *Svavetone* 1086 (DB). 'Farmstead or village of a man called **Swāfa* or Sváfi'. OE or OScand. pers. name + OE *tūn*.

Swatragh (*Suaitreach*) Derry. *Ballitotry* 1613. '(Billeted) soldier'. The full form of the Irish name is *Baile an tSuaitrigh*, 'homestead of the (billeted) soldier'.

Swavesey Cambs. *Suauesye* 1086 (DB). 'Landing-place of a man called **Swǣf*'. OE pers. name ('the Swabian') + *hȳth*.

Sway Hants. *Sueia* 1086 (DB). Possibly an OE river-name meaning 'noisy stream', or from OE *swæth* 'swathe, track'.

Swayfield Lincs. *Suafeld |sic|* 1086 (DB), *Suathefeld* 1206. 'Open land characterized by swathes or tracks'. OE *swæth* + *feld*.

Swaythling Hants. *Swæthelinge* 909. Probably an old name of the stream here, uncertain in origin and meaning but possibly an OE **swætheling* meaning 'misty stream'.

Swefling Suffolk. *Sueflinga* 1086 (DB), *Sueftlinges* c.1150. Probably '(settlement of) the family or followers of a man called **Swiftel*'. OE pers. name + *-ingas*.

Swell, Lower & *Swell, Upper* Glos. *Swelle* 706, *Svelle* 1086 (DB). OE **swellew* 'rising ground or hill'.

Swepstone Leics. *Scopestone |sic|* 1086 (DB), *Swepeston* c.1125. 'Farmstead or village of a man called **Sweppi*'. OE pers. name + *tūn*.

Swerford Oxon. *Surford* 1086 (DB), *Swereford* 1194, 'Ford by a neck of land or col'. OE *svēora* + *ford*.

Swettenham Ches. *Suetenham* late 12th cent. 'Homestead or enclosure of a man called Swēta'. OE pers. name (genitive *-n*) + *hām* or *hamm*.

Swilland Suffolk. *Suinlanda* 1086 (DB). 'Tract of land where pigs are kept, swine pasture'. OE *swīn* + *land*.

Swillington W. Yorks. *Suillintune* 1086 (DB). Possibly 'farmstead near the pig hill (or clearing)'. OE *swīn* + *hyll* (or *lēah*) + *-ing-* + *tūn*.

Swilly (*Súileach*) (river) Donegal. *Suileach* 1258. 'Seeing one'. The name probably has supernatural connotations.

Swimbridge Devon. *Birige* 1086 (DB), *Svimbrige* 1225. '(Place at) the bridge held by a man called Sǣwine'. OE pers. name (of the tenant in 1086) + *brycg*.

Swinbrook Oxon. *Svinbroc* 1086 (DB). 'Pig brook'. OE *swīn* + *brōc*.

Swinderby Lincs. *Sunderby*, *Suindrebi* 1086 (DB). Possibly 'southern farmstead or village', OScand. *sundri* + *bý*. Alternatively 'animal farmstead where pigs are kept'. OScand. *svin* + *djúr* + *bý*.

Swindon, 'hill where pigs are kept', OE *swīn* + *dūn*: **Swindon** Glos. *Svindone* 1086 (DB). **Swindon** Staffs. *Swineduna* 1167. **Swindon** Wilts. *Svindune* 1086 (DB).

Swine E. R. Yorks. *Suuine* 1086 (DB). '(Place at) the creek or channel'. OE **swin*.

Swinefleet E. R. Yorks. *Swyneflet* *c*.1195. Probably 'stretch of river where pigs are kept'. OE *swīn* + *flēot*.

Swineshead, 'pig's headland or hill', OE *swīn* + *hēafod*: **Swineshead** Beds. *Suineshefet* 1086 (DB). **Swineshead** Lincs. *Suinesheabde* 786–96.

Swinford, 'pig ford', OE *swīn* + *ford*: **Swinford** Leics. *Svineford* 1086 (DB). **Swinford** Oxon. *Swynford* 931.

Swingfield Minnis Kent. *Suinafeld* *c*.1100. 'Open land where pigs are kept'. OE *swīn* + *feld*. Affix is OE *mǣnnes* 'common land'.

Swinhoe Northum. *Swinhou* 1242. 'Swine headland'. OE *swīn* + *hōh*.

Swinhope Lincs. *Suinhope* 1086 (DB). 'Secluded valley where pigs are kept'. OE *swīn* + *hop*.

Swinithwaite N. Yorks. *Swiningethwait* 1202. 'Place cleared by burning'. OScand. *svithningr* + *thveit*.

Swinscoe Staffs. *Swyneskow* 1248. 'Swine wood'. OScand. *svín* + *skógr*.

Swinstead Lincs. *Suinhamstede* 1086 (DB). 'Homestead where pigs are kept'. OE **swīn* + *hām-stede*.

Swinton, 'pig farm', OE *swīn* + *tūn*: **Swinton** Gtr. Manch. *Suinton* 1258. **Swinton** N. Yorks., near Masham, *Suinton* 1086 (DB). **Swinton** S. Yorks. *Suintone* 1086 (DB).

Swinton Sc. Bord. *Suineston* *c*.1098. 'Sveinn's farm'. OScand. pers. name + OE *tūn*.

Swithland Leics. *Swithellund* *c*.1215. 'Grove by the burnt clearing'. OScand. *svitha* + *lundr*.

Swords (*Sord*) Dublin. 'Sward'.

Swyncombe Oxon. *Svinecumbe* 1086 (DB). 'Valley where pigs are kept'. OE *swīn* + *cumb*.

Swynnerton Staffs. *Sulvertone* |sic| 1086 (DB), *Suinuerton* 1242. 'Farmstead by the pig ford'. OE *swīn* + *ford* + *tūn*.

Swyre Dorset. *Suere* 1086 (DB). OE *swēora* 'a neck of land, a col'.

Syde Glos. *Side* 1086 (DB). 'Long hill-slope'. OE *sīde*.

Sydenham Down. The name was adopted from *Sydenham*, Greater London.

Sydenham Gtr. London. *Chipeham* 1206. Probably 'homestead or enclosure of a man called **Cippa*'. OE pers. name (genitive *-n*) + *hām* or *hamm*.

Sydenham Oxon. *Sidreham* |sic| 1086 (DB), *Sidenham* 1216. 'Broad or extensive enclosure'. OE *sīd* (dative *-an*) + *hamm*.

Sydenham Damerel Devon. *Sidelham* |sic| 1086 (DB), *Sydenham Albemarlie* 1297. Identical in origin with the previous name. Manorial affix from the de Albemarle family, here in the 13th cent.

Syderstone Norfolk. *Cidesterna* 1086 (DB). Possibly 'broad or extensive property', OE *sīd* + **sterne*. Alternatively 'pool of a man called **Siduhere*', OE pers. name + OScand. *tjǫrn*.

Sydling St Nicholas Dorset. *Sidelyng* 934, *Sidelince* 1086 (DB). 'Broad ridge'. OE *sīd* + *hlinc*. Affix from the dedication of the church.

Sydmonton Hants. *Sidemanestone* 1086 (DB). 'Farmstead or village of a man called Sidumann'. OE pers. name + *tūn*.

Syerston Notts. *Sirestune* 1086 (DB). 'Farmstead or village of a man called Sigehere'. OE pers. name + *tūn*.

Sykehouse S. Yorks. *Sikehouse* 1404. 'House(s) by the stream'. OScand. *sík* + *hús*.

Symington S. Ayr. *Symondstona* 1293. 'Simon's farm'. OE *tūn*. The place is said to have been named after Simon Lockhart (*c*.1150).

Symondsbury Dorset. *Simondesberge* 1086 (DB). 'Hill or barrow of a man called Sigemund'. OE pers. name + *beorg*.

Syresham Northants. *Sigresham* 1086 (DB). 'Homestead or enclosure of a man called Sigehere'. OE pers. name + *hām* or *hamm*.

Syston Leics. *Sitestone* 1086 (DB). Possibly 'farmstead or village of a man called Sigehæth'. OE pers. name + *tūn*.

Syston Lincs. *Sidestan* 1086 (DB). 'Broad stone'. OE *sīd* + *stān*.

Sywell Northants. *Siwella* 1086 (DB). 'Seven springs'. OE *seofon* + *wella*.

T

Tabley, Over Ches. *Stabelei* |*sic*| 1086 (DB), *Thabbelewe* 12th cent. 'Woodland clearing of a man called Tæbba'. OE pers. name + *lēah*.

Tacker, Lough (*Loch Tacair*) Cavan. 'Artificial lake'.

Tackley Oxon. *Tachelie* 1086 (DB). 'Woodland clearing of a man called *Tæcca*, or where young sheep are kept'. OE pers. name or OE *tacca* + *lēah*.

Tacolneston Norfolk. *Tacoluestuna* 1086 (DB). 'Farmstead or village of a man called Tātwulf'. OE pers. name + *tūn*.

Tacumshin, Lough (*Loch Theach Cuimsin*) Wexford. 'Lake of Cuimsin's house'.

Tadcaster N. Yorks. *Tatecastre* 1086 (DB). 'Roman town of a man called Tāta or *Tāda*'. OE pers. name + *cæster*.

Taddington Derbys. *Tadintune*. 1086 (DB). 'Estate associated with a man called *Tāda*'. OE pers. name + *-ing-* + *tūn*.

Tadley Hants. *Tadanleage* 909. Probably 'woodland clearing of a man called *Tāda*'. OE pers. name + *lēah*.

Tadlow Cambs. *Tadeslaue* c.1080, *Tadelai* 1086 (DB). 'Tumulus of a man called *Tāda*'. OE pers. name + *hlāw*.

Tadmarton Oxon. *Tademærtun* 956, *Tademertone* 1086 (DB). Probably 'farmstead by a pool frequented by toads'. OE *tāde* + *mere* + *tūn*.

Tadworth Surrey. *Thæddeuurthe* 1062, *Tadeorde* 1086 (DB). Possibly 'enclosure of a man called *Thædda*'. OE pers. name + *worth*.

Taff. *See* LLANDAFF.

Tafolog (mountain) Powys. 'Place of dock (plants)'. Welsh *tafol* + *-og*.

Tagheen (*Teach Chaoin*) Mayo. 'Pleasant house'.

Taghmon (*Teach Munna*) Westmeath, Wexford. 'Muna's house'.

Taghnafearagh (*Teach na bFiarach*) Westmeath. 'House of the lea fields'.

Taghshinny (*Teach Sini*) Longford. 'Sineach's house'.

Tagoat (*Teach Gót*) Wexford. 'Gót's house'.

Tai-bach Powys. 'Little houses'. Welsh *tŷ* (plural *tai*) + *bach*.

Tain Highland. *Tene* 1226, *Thayn* 1257. '(Place of the) river'. The name may be pre-Celtic, but the sense seems likely for the stream.

Takeley Essex. *Tacheleia* 1086 (DB). 'Woodland clearing of a man called *Tæcca*, or where young sheep are kept'. OE pers. name or OE *tacca* + *lēah*.

Tal-y-llyn Conwy. 'End of the lake'. Welsh *tâl* + *y* + *llyn*.

Talacharn. *See* LAUGHARNE.

Talacre Flin. 'End of the arable land'. Welsh *tâl* + *acer*.

Talaton Devon. *Taletone* 1086 (DB). 'Farmstead or village on the River Tale'. OE river-name (meaning 'the swift one') + *tūn*.

Talbenny Pemb. *Talbenny* 1291. '(Place at the) end'. Welsh *tâl* + an obscure element.

Talbot Village Dorset, model village built in the 1860s and named after the local landowners, the two Talbot sisters.

Talgarth Powys. 'End of the ridge'. Welsh *tâl* + *garth*.

Talisker Highland (Skye). Possibly 'shelf rock'. OScand. *hjalli* + *sker*.

Talke Staffs. *Talc* 1086 (DB). Possibly an old name for the ridge here, but of obscure origin.

Talkin Cumbria. *Talcan* c.1195. Probably a Celtic name meaning 'white brow (of a hill)'.

Talla Bheith Forest Perth. *An t-All a' Bheithe* n.d. 'Crag of birch trees'. Gaelic *all* + *beithe*.

Tallaght (*Tamhlacht*) Dublin. 'Plague burial place'.

Tallentire Cumbria. *Talentir* c.1160. Probably a Celtic name meaning 'end of the land'.

Tallington Lincs. *Talintune* 1086 (DB). Probably 'estate associated with a man called *Tæl* or *Tala*'. OE pers. name + *-ing-* + *tūn*.

Tallow (*Tulach*) Waterford. 'Hill'. The full Irish name is *Tulach an Iarainn*, 'hill of the iron', referring to former iron-ore workings here.

Talmine Highland. Unknown but perhaps 'level land'. Gaelic *talamh* + *min*.

Tal-sarn Gwyd. 'End of the causeway'. Welsh *tâl* + *y* + *sarn*.

Talwrn Wrex. '(Place by the) field'. Welsh *talwrn*.

Tal-y-bont Cergn. 'End of the bridge'. Welsh *tâl* + *y* + *pont*. *Cp.* BRIDGEND.

Talysarn Gwyd. *Talysarn* 1795. 'End of the causeway'. Welsh *tâl* + *y* + *sarn*.

Tame (river), three examples, *see* THAMES.

Tamerton, 'farmstead or village on the River Tamar', Celtic river-name (possibly 'the dark one' or simply 'river') + OE *tūn*: **Tamerton Foliot** Devon. *Tambretone* 1086 (DB), *Tamereton Foliot* 1262. Manorial affix from the Foliot family, here from the 13th cent. **Tamerton, North** Cornwall. *Tamerton* 1180.

Tamlaght (*Tamhlacht*) Derry. 'Plague burial place'.

Tamlaght Finlagan (*Tamhlacht Fionnlugháin*) Derry. 'Fionnlugh's burial place'.

Tamlaght O'Crilly (*Tamlacht Úi Chroiligh*) Derry. 'O'Crilly's burial place'.

Tamnaghbane (*Tamhnach Bán*) Armagh. 'White cultivated spot'.

Tamney (*Tamhnaigh*) Donegal. *Tamenagh* c.1655. 'Cultivated spot'.

Tamnyrankin (*Tamhnaigh*) Derry. 'Rankin's cultivated spot'.

Tamworth Staffs. *Tamouuorthig* 781, *Tamuuorde* 1086 (DB). 'Enclosure on the River Tame'. Celtic river-name (possibly 'the dark one' or simply 'river') + OE *worthig* (replaced by *worth*).

Tandoo Point Dumf. Perhaps 'Black backside'. Gaelic *ton + dubh*.

Tandragee (*Tóin re Gaoith*) Armagh. *Tóin re Gaoith* 1642. 'Backside to the wind'.

Tandridge Surrey. *Tenhric* c.965, *Tenrige* 1086 (DB). OE *hrycg* 'ridge, hill' with an uncertain first element.

Tanfield Durham. *Tamefeld* 1179. 'Open land on the River Team'. Celtic river-name (possibly 'the dark one' or simply 'river') + OE *feld*.

Tanfield, East & *Tanfield, West* N. Yorks. *Tanefeld* 1086 (DB). Possibly 'open land where shoots or osiers grow'. OE *tān + feld*.

Tang (*An Teanga*) Westmeath. 'The tongue'.

Tangley Hants. *Tangelea* 1175. Possibly 'woodland clearing at the spits of land'. OE *tang + lēah*.

Tangmere W. Sussex. *Tangmere* 680, *Tangemere* 1086 (DB). Possibly 'tongs-shaped pool'. OE *tang + mere*.

Tankersley S. Yorks. *Tancresleia* 1086 (DB). 'Woodland clearing of a man called Tancred or T(h)ancrad'. OGerman pers. name + OE *lēah*.

Tankerton Kent. *Tangerton* 1240. Probably 'farmstead or estate of a man called Tancred or T(h)ancrad'. OGerman pers. name + OE *tūn*.

Tannington Suffolk. *Tatintuna* 1086 (DB). 'Estate associated with a man called Tāta'. OE pers. name + *-ing-* + *tūn*.

Tansley Derbys. *Taneslege* 1086 (DB). Probably 'woodland clearing of a man called *Tān*', OE pers. name + *lēah*. Alternatively the first element may be OE *tān* 'branch' (perhaps used of 'a valley branching off from the main valley').

Tansor Northants. *Tanesovre* 1086 (DB). Probably 'promontory or bank of a man called *Tān*', OE pers. name + *ofer* or *ōfer*. Alternatively the first element may be OE *tān* 'branch' as in previous name.

Tanton N. Yorks. *Tametun* 1086 (DB). 'Farmstead or village on the River Tame'. Celtic river-name (possibly 'the dark one' or simply 'river') + OE *tūn*.

Tanworth-in-Arden Warwicks. *Tanewrthe* 1201. Possibly 'enclosure made with branches'. OE *tān + worth*. For Arden, *see* HENLEY-IN-ARDEN.

Taplow Bucks. *Thapeslau* 1086 (DB). 'Tumulus of a man called *Tæppa*'. OE pers. name + *hlāw*.

Tara (*Teamhair*) Meath. 'Conspicuous place'.

Tarbat Ness Highland. 'Headland by a portage'. Gaelic *tairbeart* + OScand. *nes*. Cp. TARBERT, TARBET.

Tarbert Arg. '(Place by a) portage'. Gaelic *tairbeart*.

Tarbert (*Tairbeart*) Kerry. 'Isthmus'.

Tarbet Arg. '(Place by a) portage'. Gaelic *tairbeart*.

Tarbock Green Mersey. *Torboc* 1086 (DB), *Thornebrooke* c.1240. Probably 'thorn-tree brook'. OE *thorn + brōc*.

Tardebigge Heref. & Worcs. *Tærdebicgan* c.1000, *Terdeberie* |sic| 1086 (DB). In spite of early spellings this name is still obscure in origin and meaning.

Tarelton (*Tír Eiltín*) Cork. 'Eiltín's country'.

Tarlton Glos. *Torentune* |sic| 1086 (DB), *Torleton* 1204. Probably 'farmstead at the thorn-tree clearing'. OE *thorn + lēah + tūn*.

Tarporley Ches. *Torpelei* 1086 (DB), *Thorperlegh* 1281. Possibly 'woodland clearing of the peasants or cottagers'. OE **thorpere + lēah*.

Tarrant, Celtic river-name possibly meaning 'the trespasser', i.e. 'river liable to floods', and giving name to the following: **Tarrant Crawford** Dorset. *Tarente* 1086 (DB), *Little Craweford* 1280. Distinguishing affix from *Craveford* 1086 (DB), 'ford frequented by crows', OE *crāwe + ford*. **Tarrant Gunville** Dorset. *Tarente* 1086 (DB), *Tarente Gundevill* 1233. Manorial affix from the Gundeville family, here in the 12th cent. **Tarrant Hinton** Dorset. *Terente* 9th cent., *Tarente* 1086 (DB), *Tarente Hyneton* 1280. 'Estate on the River Tarrant belonging to a religious community (Shaftesbury Abbey)'. OE *hīwan + tūn*. **Tarrant Keyneston** Dorset. *Tarente* 1086 (DB), *Tarente Kahaines* 1225. 'Estate by the Cahaignes family', here from the 12th cent. **Tarrant Launceston** Dorset. *Tarente* 1086 (DB), *Tarente Loueweniston* 1280. 'Estate held by a man called Lēofwine or a family called Lowin'. **Tarrant Monkton** Dorset. *Tarente* 1086 (DB), *Tarent Moneketon* 1280. 'Estate belonging to the monks (of Tewkesbury Abbey)'. OE *munuc + tūn*. **Tarrant Rawston** Dorset. *Tarente* 1086 (DB). *Tarrant Rawston alias Antyocke* 1535. 'Ralph's estate', earlier 'estate held by the Antioch family'. **Tarrant Rushton** Dorset. *Tarente* 1086 (DB), *Tarente Russeus* 1280. 'Estate held by the de Rusceaus family', here in the 13th cent.

Tarring Neville E. Sussex. *Toringes* 1086 (DB), *Thoring Nevell* 1339. Possibly '(settlement of) the family or followers of a man called *Teorra*', OE pers. name + *-ingas*. Alternatively 'dwellers at the rocky hill', OE *torr + -ingas*. Manorial affix from the de Neville family, here in the 13th cent.

Tarring, West W. Sussex. *Teorringas* 946, *Terringes* 1086 (DB). '(Settlement of) the family or followers of a man called *Teorra*'. OE pers. name + *-ingas*.

Tarrington Heref. & Worcs. *Tatintune* 1086 (DB). 'Estate associated with a man called Tāta'. OE pers. name + *-ing- + tūn*.

Tarvie Highland. 'Place of bulls'. Gaelic *tarbhaidh*.

Tarvin Ches. *Terve* |sic| 1086 (DB), *Teruen* 1185. Celtic river-name meaning 'boundary (stream)', the old name of the River Gowy.

Tasburgh Norfolk. *Taseburc* 1086 (DB). Probably 'stronghold of a man called *Tæsa*'. OE pers. name + *burh*. The river-name **Tas** is a 'back-formation' from the place-name.

Tasley Shrops. *Tasseleya c.*1143. OE *lēah* 'wood, clearing' with an uncertain first element.

Tatenhill Staffs. *Tatenhyll* 942. 'Hill of a man called Tāta'. OE pers. name (genitive *-n*) + *hyll*.

Tatham Lancs. *Tathaim* 1086 (DB). 'Homestead of a man called Tāta'. OE pers. name + *hām*.

Tathwell Lincs. *Tadewelle* 1086 (DB). 'Spring or stream frequented by toads'. OE **tāde* + *wella*.

Tatsfield Surrey. *Tatelefelle* 1086 (DB). 'Open land of a man called Tātel'. OE pers. name + *feld*.

Tattenhall Ches. *Tatenale* 1086 (DB). 'Nook of land of a man called Tāta'. OE pers. name (genitive *-n*) + *halh*.

Tatterford Norfolk. *Taterforda* 1086 (DB). 'Ford of a man called Tāthere'. OE pers. name + *ford*.

Tattersett Norfolk. *Tatessete* 1086 (DB). 'Fold of a man called Tāthere'. OE pers. name + *set*.

Tattershall Lincs. *Tateshale* 1086 (DB). 'Nook of land of a man called Tāthere'. OE pers. name + *halh*.

Tattingstone Suffolk. *Tatistuna |sic|* 1086 (DB), *Tatingeston* 1219. Possibly 'farmstead of a man called **Tāting*', OE pers. name + *tūn*. Alternatively 'farmstead at the place associated with a man called Tāta', OE pers. name + *-ing* + *tūn*.

Taughmaconnell (*Teach Mhic Conaill*) Roscommon. 'Mac Conaill's house'.

Taunton Somerset. *Tantun* 737, *Tantone* 1086 (DB). 'Farmstead or village on the River Tone'. Celtic river-name (possibly 'roaring stream') + OE *tūn*.

Taur (*Teamhair*) Cork. 'Conspicuous place'.

Taverham Norfolk. *Taverham* 1086 (DB). 'Red-lead homestead or enclosure', perhaps referring to a red-painted building or to soil colour. OE *tēafor* + *hām* or *hamm*.

Tavistock Devon. *Tauistoce* 981, *Tavestoc* 1086 (DB). 'Outlying farmstead or hamlet by the River Tavy'. Celtic rivername (possibly 'dark stream') + OE *stoc*.

Tavy, Mary & *Tavy, Peter* Devon. *Tavi, Tawi* 1086 (DB), *Tavymarie* 1412, *Petri Tavy* 1270. Named from the River Tavy, see previous name. Distinguishing affixes from the dedications of their churches.

Tawin Island (*Tamhain*) Galway. 'Stump'.

Tawnaghlahan (*Tamhnach Lahan*) Donegal. 'Broad cultivated spot'.

Tawnyeely (*Tamhnaigh Aelaigh*) Leitrim. 'Cultivated spot of lime'.

Tawnyinah (*Tamhnaigh an Eich*) Mayo. 'Clearing of the horse'.

Tawnylea (*Tamhnaí Liatha*) Sligo. 'Grey cultivated spot'.

Tawstock Devon. *Tauestoca* 1086 (DB). 'Outlying farmstead or hamlet on the River Taw'. Celtic river-name (*see* next name) + OE *stoc*.

Tawton, 'farmstead or village on the River Taw', Celtic river-name (possibly 'strong or silent stream') + OE *tūn*: **Tawton, Bishop's** Devon. *Tautona* 1086 (DB), *Tautone Episcopi* 1284. Affix from its possession by the Bishop (Latin *episcopus*) of Exeter in 1086. **Tawton, North** & **Tawton, South** Devon. *Tawetone, Tavetone* 1086 (DB).

Taxal Derbys. *Tackeshale c.*1251. Possibly 'nook of land held on lease'. ME *tak* + OE *halh*.

Tay. *See* TAYPORT.

Tay, Lough (*Loch Té*) Wicklow. 'Lake of Té'. Té is a goddess.

Taynton Glos. *Tetinton* 1086 (DB). 'Estate associated with a man called Tæta'. OE pers. name + *-ing-* + *tūn*.

Tayport Fife. 'Port on the River Tay'. If Celtic, the river name perhaps means 'silent one'; but may be pre-Celtic.

Tealby Lincs. *Tavelesbi* 1086 (DB). Possibly an ancient tribal name OE **Tāflas* or **Tǣflas* (representing the East Germanic *Taifali*) to which OScand. *bý* 'farmstead, village' was later added.

Team (river) Durham, gives name to TANFIELD, *see* THAMES.

Tean, Lower & *Tean, Upper* Staffs. *Tene* 1086 (DB). Named from the River Tean, a Celtic river-name probably meaning simply 'stream'.

Tearaght Island (*An Tiaracht*) Kerry. Perhaps 'the horse's hindquarters'.

Tebay Cumbria. *Tibeia c.*1160. 'Island of a man called Tiba'. OE pers. name + *ēg*.

Tebworth Beds. *Teobbanwyrthe* 962. 'Enclosure of a man called Teobba'. OE pers. name (genitive *-n*) + *worth*.

Tedavnet (*Tigh Damhnata*) Monaghan. *Thechdamnad* 1306. 'Damhnat's house'.

Tedburn St Mary Devon. *Teteborne* 1086 (DB). '(Place at) the stream of a woman called Tette or a man called **Tetta*'. OE pers. name + *burna*.

Teddington Glos. *Teottingtun* 780, *Teotintune* 1086 (DB). 'Estate associated with a man called **Teotta*'. OE pers. name + *-ing-* + *tūn*.

Teddington Gtr. London. *Tudintun* 969. 'Estate associated with a man called Tuda'. OE pers. name + *-ing-* + *tūn*.

Tedstone Delamere & *Tedstone Wafre* Heref. & Worcs. *Tedesthorne* 1086 (DB), *Teddesthorn la Mare, Teddesthorne Wafre* 1249. Probably 'thorn-tree of a man called **Tēod*'. OE pers. name + *thorn*. Manorial affixes from early possession by the de la Mare and le Wafre families.

Teelin (*Teileann*) Donegal. 'Dish'. The reference is to the shape of the small bay nearby.

Teermaclane (*Tír Mhic Calláin*) Clare. 'Mac Callán's country'.

Teermore (*Tír Mór*) Westmeath. 'Large district'.

Teernacreeve (*Tír dá Craebh*) Westmeath. 'District of two sacred trees'.

Tees (river) Cumbria–Durham, *see* STOCKTON ON TEES.

Teeton Northants. *Teche |sic|* 1086 (DB), *Teacne* 1195. '(Hill with) a beacon'. OE **tǣcne*.

Teevurcher (*Taobh Urchair*) Meath. 'Side of the cast'.

Teffont Evias & *Teffont Magna* Wilts. *Tefunte* 860, *Tefonte* 1086 (DB), *Teffunt Ewyas* 1275. 'Boundary spring'.

OE *tēo* + *funta*. Manorial affix from possession by the barons of Ewyas in the 13th cent.; the other affix is Latin *magna* 'great'.

Teigh Rutland. *Tie* 1086 (DB). OE *tēag* 'a small enclosure'.

Teigngrace Devon. *Taigne* 1086 (DB). *Teyngegras* 1331. Named from the River Teign, a Celtic river-name meaning simply 'stream'. Manorial affix from the Gras family, here in the 14th cent.

Teignmouth Devon. *Tengemutha* 1044. 'Mouth of the River Teign'. Celtic river-name (*see* previous name) + OE *mūtha*.

Telford Shrops., a modern name commemorating the engineer Thomas Telford (1757–1834), famous for his bridges, roads, and canals.

Tellisford Somerset. *Tefleford* 1001, *Tablesford* 1086 (DB). Possibly 'ford at a flat or level place'. OE **tefli* + *ford*. Alternatively the first element may be an OE pers. name such as **Thēofol*.

Telscombe E. Sussex. *Titelescumbe* 966. 'Valley of a man called **Titel*'. OE pers. name + *cumb*.

Teme (river) Shrops.–Heref. & Worcs., *see* TENBURY WELLS.

Temple as affix, *see* main name, e.g. for **Temple Cloud** B. & NE. Som. *see* CLOUD.

Temple, The Down. *The Temple* 1858. The name was originally that of a public house used as a meeting place for a freemasons' lodge.

Templeboy (*Teampall Baoith*) Sligo. 'Baoth's church'.

Templebrendan (*Teampall Brendáin*) Mayo. 'Brendan's church'.

Templecronan (*Teampall Crónáin*) Clare. 'Cronan's church'.

Templederry (*Teampall Doire*) Tipperary. 'Church of the oak wood'.

Templeetney (*Teampall Eithne*) Tipperary. 'Eithne's church'.

Templefinn (*Teampall Fionn*) Down. 'White church'.

Templeglentan (*Teampall an Ghleanntáin*) Limerick. 'Church of the valley'.

Templemartin (*Teampall Mártan*) Cork, Wexford. 'Mártan's church'.

Templemichael (*Teampall Mhichil*) Cork. 'Michael's church'.

Templemore (*An Teampall Mór*) Tipperary. 'The big church'.

Templemoyle (*Teampall Maol*) Down. 'Bald church'.

Templenakilla (*Teampall na Cille*) Kerry. 'Church of the church'.

Templenoe (*Teampall Nua*) Kerry. 'New church'.

Templeogue (*Teach Mealóg*) Dublin. 'Mealóg's house'.

Templeoran (*Teampall Fhuaráin*) Westmeath. 'Church of the spring'.

Templeorum (*Teampall Fhothram*) Kilkenny. 'Church of Fothram'.

Templepatrick (*Teampall Phádraig*) Antrim, Mayo. 'Patrick's church'.

Templeshambo (*Teampall Seanbhoth*) Wexford. 'Church of the old huts'.

Templeton Devon. *Templum* 1206, *Templeton* 1334. 'Manor held by the Knights Templars'. ME temple + OE *tūn*.

Templetouhy (*Teampall Tuaithe*) Tipperary. 'Church of the territory'.

Tempo (*An tIompú Deiseal*) Fermanagh. *Tempodessell* 1622. 'The right-hand turn'.

Tenbury Wells Heref. & Worcs. *Tamedeberie* 1086 (DB). 'Stronghold on the River Teme'. Celtic river-name (possibly 'the dark one') + OE *burh*. The addition *Wells* referring to the spa here is only recent.

Tenby (*Dinbych-y-pysgod*) Pemb. *Dinbych* c.1275, *Tynby* 1369. 'Little fort'. Welsh *din* + *bych*. Cp. DENBIGH. The Welsh name means 'little fort of the fish' (Welsh *din* + *bych* + *y* + *pysgod*), referring to the town's importance as a fishing port.

Tendring Essex. *Tendringa* 1086 (DB). Possibly 'place where tinder or fuel is gathered'. OE *tynder* + *-ing*.

Tenterden Kent. *Tentwardene* 1179. 'Woodland pasture of the Thanet dwellers'. THANET + OE *-ware* + *denn*.

Terenure (*Tír an Iúir*) Dublin. 'Territory of the yew'.

Terling Essex. *Terlinges* 1017–35, *Terlingas* 1086 (DB). '(Settlement of) the family or followers of a man called Tyrhtel'. OE pers. name + *-ingas*. The river-name **Ter** is a 'back-formation' from the placename.

Termon (*An Tearmann*) Cavan, Donegal. 'The sanctuary land'.

Termonfeckin (*Tearmann Feichín*) Louth. 'Feichín's sanctuary'.

Termonmaguirk (*Tearmann*) Tyrone. 'Maguirk's sanctuary'.

Tern (river) Shrops., *see* EATON UPON TERN.

Terrington N. Yorks. *Teurinctune* 1086 (DB). Possibly 'estate associated with a man called **Teofer*'. OE pers. name + *-ing-* + *tūn*.

Terrington *St Clement* & **Terrington St John** Norfolk. *Tilinghetuna* 1086 (DB). *Terintona* 1121. 'Farmstead of the family or followers of a man called **Tir(a)*'. OE pers. name + *-inga-* + *tūn*. Distinguishing affixes from the dedications of the churches.

Terryglass (*Tír dhá Ghlas*) Tipperary. 'Territory of two streams'.

Teston Kent. *Terstan* 10th cent., *Testan* 1086 (DB). 'Stone with a gap or hole'. OE *tær* + *stān*.

Testwood Hants. *Lesteorde* |sic| 1086 (DB), *Terstewode* c.1185. 'Wood by the River Test'. Celtic or pre-Celtic river-name (obscure in origin and meaning) + OE *wudu*.

Tetbury Glos. *Tettanbyrg* c.900, *Teteberie* 1086 (DB). 'Fortified place of a woman called Tette'. OE pers. name + *burh* (dative *byrig*).

Tetcott Devon. *Tetecote* 1086 (DB). 'Cottage of a woman called Tette or of a man called *Tetta'. OE pers. name + *cot*.

Tetford Lincs. *Tedforde* 1086 (DB). 'People's or public ford'. OE *thēod* + *ford*.

Tetney Lincs. *Tatenai* 1086 (DB). 'Island of a man called Tǣta'. OE pers. name (genitive *-n*) + *ēg*.

Tetsworth Oxon. *Tetleswrthe* c.1150. 'Enclosure of a man called *Tætel'. OE pers. name + *worth*.

Tettenhall W. Mids. *Teotanheale* early 10th cent., *Totenhale* 1086 (DB). 'Nook of land of a man called *Tēotta'. OE pers. name (genitive *-n*) + *halh*.

Teversal Notts. *Tevreshalt* 1086 (DB). 'Shelter of the painter or sorcerer, or of a man called *Teofer'. OE *tīefrere* or pers. name + *hald*.

Teversham Cambs. *Teuersham* 1086 (DB). 'Homestead of the painter or sorcerer, or of a man called *Teofer'. OE *tīefrere* or pers. name + *hām*.

Tevrin (*Teamhrín*) Westmeath. 'Small conspicuous hill'.

Tew, Great *Tew, Little*, & *Tew, Duns*, Oxon. *Tiwan* 1004, *Tewe, Teowe* 1086 (DB), *Donestiua* c.1210. Possibly an OE *tīewe* 'row or ridge'. Manorial affix from early possession by a man called Dunn.

Tewin Herts. *Tiwingum* 944–6, *Teuuinge* 1086 (DB). Possibly '(settlement of) the family or followers of a man called *Tīwa'. OE pers. name + *-ingas*.

Tewkesbury Glos. *Teodekesberie* 1086 (DB). 'Fortified place of a man called *Tēodec'. OE pers. name + *burh* (dative *byrig*).

Tey, Great & *Tey, Marks* Essex. *Tygan* c.950. *Teia* 1086 (DB), *Merkys Teye* 1475. From OE *tīege* 'enclosure'. Manorial affix from possession by the de Merck family.

Teynham Kent. *Teneham* 798, *Therham* |sic| 1086 (DB). Probably 'homestead of a man called *Tēna'. OE pers. name + *hām*.

Thakeham W. Sussex. *Taceham* 1086 (DB). 'Homestead with a thatched roof'. OE *thaca* + *hām*.

Thame Oxon. *Tame* c.1000, 1086 (DB). Named from the River Thame, a Celtic river-name, *see* THAMES.

Thames (river) Glos.–London. *Tamesis* 51 BC. An ancient Celtic river-name possibly meaning 'dark one' or simply 'river'. The river–names **Tame** (three examples, N. Yorks., Warwicks.–Staffs., W. Yorks.–Ches.), **Team** (Durham), **Thame** (Bucks.–Oxon.), and (with a different ending) **Tamar** (Cornwall–Devon) are from the same root and probably have a similar meaning.

Thames Ditton Surrey, *see* DITTON.

Thamesmead Gtr. London, a recent name for a new development by the Thames.

Thanet Kent. *Tanatus* 3rd cent., *Tanet* 1086 (DB). A Celtic name possibly meaning 'bright island', perhaps with reference to a beacon.

Thanington Kent. *Taningtune* 833. Possibly 'estate associated with a man called *Tān'. OE pers. name + *-ing-* + *tūn*.

Tharston Norfolk. *Therstuna* 1086 (DB). 'Farmstead or village of a man called Therir'. OScand. pers. name + OE *tūn*.

Thatcham Berks. *Thæcham* c.954, *Taceham* 1086 (DB). 'Thatched homestead, or river-meadow where thatching materials are got'. OE *thæcce* + *hām* or *hamm*.

Thatto Heath Mersey. *Thetwall* 12th cent. 'Spring or stream with a water-pipe'. OE *thēote* + *wella*.

Thaxted Essex. *Tachesteda* 1086 (DB). 'Place where thatching materials are got'. OE *thæc* + *stede*.

Theakston N. Yorks. *Eston* |sic| 1086 (DB). *Thekeston* 1157. Probably 'farmstead or village of a man called *Thēodec'. OE pers. name + *tūn*.

Thealby N. Lincs. *Tedulfbi* 1086 (DB). 'Farmstead or village of a man called Thjóthulfr'. OScand. pers. name + *bý*.

Theale, 'the planks' (referring to a bridge or building), OE *thel* in a plural form *thelu*: **Theale** Berks. *Teile* 1208. **Theale** Somerset. *Thela* 1176.

Thearne E. R. Yorks. *Thoren* 1297. 'The thorn-tree'. OE *thorn*.

Theberton Suffolk. *Thewardetuna* |sic| 1086 (DB), *Tiberton* 1176. 'Farmstead or village of a man called Thēodbeorht'. OE pers. name + *tūn*.

Thedden Grange Hants. *Tedena* |sic| 1168. *Thetdene* 1234. 'Valley with a water-pipe'. OE *thēote* + *denu*.

Theddingworth Leics. *Tedingesworde* |sic| 1086 (DB), *Tedingewrth* 1206. Probably 'enclosure of the family or followers of a man called *Thēoda'. OE pers. name + *-inga-* + *worth*.

Theddlethorpe All Saints & *Theddlethorpe St Helen* Lincs. *Tedlagestorp* 1086 (DB). Possibly 'outlying farmstead or hamlet of a man called *Thēodlāc'. OE pers. name + OScand. *thorp*. Distinguishing affixes from the dedications of the churches.

Thelbridge Devon. *Talebrige* 1086 (DB). 'Plank bridge'. OE *thel* + *brycg*.

Thelnetham Suffolk. *Thelueteham* 1086 (DB). Possibly 'enclosure frequented by swans near a plank bridge'. OE *thel* + *elfitu* + *hamm*.

Thelwall Ches. *Thelwæle* 923. 'Pool by a plank bridge'. OE *thel* + *wel*.

Themelthorpe Norfolk. *Timeltorp* 1203. Possibly 'outlying farmstead or hamlet of a man called *Thӯmel or *Thymill'. OE or OScand. pers. name + *thorp*. Alternatively the first element may be OE *thӯmel* 'a thimble' alluding to the small size of the settlement.

Thenford Northants. *Taneford* 1086 (DB). 'Ford of the thegns or retainers'. OE *thegn* + *ford*.

Therfield Herts. *Therefeld* 1060, *Derevelde* 1086 (DB). 'Dry open land'. OE *thyrre* + *feld*.

Thetford, 'people's or public ford', OE *thēod* + *ford*: **Thetford** Norfolk. *Theodford* late 9th cent., *Tedfort* 1086 (DB). **Thetford, Little** Cambs. *Thiutforda* c.972, *Liteltedford* 1086 (DB). Affix is OE *lӯtel*.

Theydon Bois Essex. *Thecdene* 1062, *Teidana* 1086 (DB), *Teidon Boys* 1257. Probably 'valley where thatching materials are got'. OE *thæc* + *denu*. Manorial affix from the de Bosco or de Boys family, here in the 12th cent.

Thimbleby, 'farmstead or village of a man called *Thymill or *Thymli', OScand. pers. name + *bý*: **Thimbleby** Lincs. *Stimblebi* |*sic*| 1086 (DB), *Timblebi* c.1115. **Thimbleby** N. Yorks. *Timbelbi* 1086 (DB).

Thingwall Mersey. *Tinguelle* 1086 (DB). 'Field where an assembly meets'. OScand. *thing-vǫllr*.

Thirkleby N. Yorks. *Turchilebi* 1086 (DB). 'Farmstead or village of a man called Thorkell'. OScand. pers. name + *bý*.

Thirlby N. Yorks. *Trillebia* 1187. 'Farmstead or village of a man called *Thrylli, or of the thralls'. OScand. pers. name or *thræll* + *bý*.

Thirn N. Yorks. *Thirne* 1086 (DB). 'The thorn-tree'. OE *thyrne*.

Thirsk N. Yorks. *Tresch* 1086 (DB). OScand. *thresk* 'a marsh.

Thirston, East Northum. *Thrasfriston* 1242. Possibly 'farmstead or village of a man called *Thræsfrith'. OE pers. name + *tūn*.

Thistleton, 'farmstead or village where thistles grow', OE *thistel* + *tūn*: **Thistleton** Lancs. *Thistilton* 1212. **Thistleton** Rutland. *Tisteltune* 1086 (DB).

Thixendale N. Yorks. *Sixtendale* 1086 (DB). 'Valley of a man called Sigsteinn'. OScand. pers. name + *dalr*.

Tholthorpe N. Yorks. *Turulfestorp* 1086 (DB). 'Outlying farmstead or hamlet of a man called Thórulfr'. OScand. pers. name + *thorp*.

Thomastown Kilkenny. 'Thomas's town'. The Irish name of Thomastown is *Baile Mhic Andáin*, 'Fitzanthony's homestead'. Thomas Fitzanthony had a castle here in the 13th cent.

Thompson Norfolk. *Tomestuna* 1086 (DB). 'Farmstead or village of a man called Tumi'. OScand. pers. name + OE *tūn*.

Thompson's Bridge Fermanagh. A man named *Thompson* owned a bridge over the Sillees River here.

Thong Kent. *Thuange* c.1200. 'Narrow strip of land'. OE *thwang*.

Thonoge (*Tonóg*) (river) Tipperary. 'Little bottom'.

Thoralby N. Yorks. *Turoldesbi* 1086 (DB). Probably 'farmstead or village of a man called Thóraldr'. OScand. pers. name + *bý*.

Thoresby Notts. *Thuresby* 958, *Turesbi* 1086 (DB). 'Farmstead or village of a man called Thúrir'. OScand. pers. name + *bý*.

Thoresby, North Lincs. *Toresbi* 1086 (DB). 'Farmstead or village of a man called Thórir'. OScand. pers. name + *bý*.

Thoresby, South Lincs. *Toresbi* 1086 (DB). Identical in origin with the previous name.

Thoresway Lincs. *Toreswe* 1086 (DB), *Thoresweie* 1187. Possibly 'way or road of a man called Thórir', OScand. pers. name + OE *weg*. Alternatively the DB form may represent OScand. *Thórswæ* 'shrine dedicated to the heathen god Thor' in which the second element *wæ* was later confused with OE *weg*.

Thorganby, 'farmstead or village of a man called Thorgrímr', OScand. pers. name + *bý*: **Thorganby** Lincs. *Turgrimbi* 1086 (DB). **Thorganby** N. Yorks. *Turgisbi* |*sic*| 1086 (DB), *Turgrimebi* 1192.

Thorington Suffolk. *Torentuna* 1086 (DB). 'Thorn-tree enclosure or farmstead'. OE *thorn* or *thyrne* + *tūn*.

Thorlby N. Yorks. *Toreilderebi* 1086 (DB). 'Farmstead or village of a man called Thóraldr, or of a woman called Thórhildr'. OScand. pers. name + *bý*.

Thorley, 'thorn-tree wood or clearing', OE *thorn* + *lēah*: **Thorely** Herts. *Torlei* 1086 (DB). **Thorley** I. of Wight. *Torlei* 1086 (DB).

Thormanby N. Yorks. *Tormozbi* 1086 (DB). 'Farmstead or village of a man called Thormóthr'. OScand. pers. name + *bý*.

Thornaby on Tees Stock. on T. *Tormozbi* 1086 (DB). Identical in origin with the previous name.

Thornage Norfolk. *Tornedis* 1086 (DB). 'Thorn-tree enclosure or pasture'. OE *thorn* + *edisc*.

Thornborough, 'hill where thorn-trees grow', OE *thorn* + *beorg*: **Thornborough** Bucks. *Torneberge* 1086 (DB). **Thornborough** N. Yorks. *Thornbergh* 1198.

Thornbury, 'fortified place where thorn-trees grow', OE *thorn* + *burh* (dative *byrig*): **Thornbury** Devon. *Torneberie* 1086 (DB). **Thornbury** Heref. & Worcs. *Thornbyrig* c.1000, *Torneberie* 1086 (DB). **Thornbury** S. Glos. *Turneberie* 1086 (DB).

Thornby Northants. *Torneberie* 1086 (DB), *Thirnebi* c.1160. 'Farmstead or village where thorn-trees grow'. OScand. *thyrnir* + *bý* (replacing OE *burh* 'stronghold').

Thorncombe, 'valley where thorn-trees grow', OE *thorn* + *cumb*: **Thorncombe** Dorset, near Blandford. *Tornecome* 1086 (DB). **Thorncombe** Dorset, near Holditch. *Tornecoma* 1086 (DB).

Thorndon Suffolk. *Tornduna* 1086 (DB). 'Hill where thorn-trees grow'. OE *thorn* + *dūn*.

Thorne, '(place at) the thorn-tree', OE *thorn*: **Thorne** S. Yorks. *Torne* 1086 (DB). **Thorne St Margaret** Somerset. *Torne* 1086 (DB), *Thorn St Margaret* 1251. Affix from the dedication of the church.

Thorner W. Yorks. *Tornoure* 1086 (DB). 'Ridge or bank where thorn-trees grow'. OE *thorn* + *ofer*.

Thorney, usually 'thorn-tree island', OE *thorn* + *ēg*; examples include: **Thorney** Cambs. *Thornige* c.960, *Torny* 1086 (DB). **Thorney, West** W. Sussex. *Thorneg* 11th cent., *Tornei* 1086 (DB).

However the following has a different origin: **Thorney** Notts. *Torneshaie* 1086 (DB). 'Thorn-tree enclosure'. OE *thorn* + *haga*.

Thornfalcon Somerset. *Torne* 1086 (DB), *Thorn fagun* 1265. '(Place at) the thorn-tree', OE *thorn*. Manorial affix from early possession by a family called Fagun.

Thornford Dorset. *Thornford* 951, *Torneford* 1086 (DB). 'Ford where thorn-trees grow'. OE *thorn* + *ford*.

Thorngumbald E. R. Yorks. *Torne* 1086 (DB), *Thoren Gumbaud* 1297. '(Place at) the thorn-tree'. OE *thorn*. Manorial affix from the Gumbald family, here in the 13th cent.

Thornham, 'homestead or village where thorn-trees grow', OE *thorn* + *hām*: **Thornham** Norfolk. *Tornham* 1086 (DB). **Thornham Magna** & **Thornham Parva** Suffolk. *Thornham* 1086 (DB). Affixes are Latin *magna* 'great' and *parva* 'little'.

Thornhaugh Cambs. *Thornhawe* 1189. 'Thorn-tree enclosure'. OE *thorn* + *haga*.

Thornhill, 'hill where thorn-trees grow', OE *thorn* + *hyll*; examples include: **Thornhill** Derbys. *Tornhull* 1200. **Thornhill** W. Yorks. *Tornil* 1086 (DB).

Thornley Durham, near Crook. *Thornley* 1382. 'Thorn-tree wood or clearing'. OE *thorn* + *lēah*.

Thornley Durham, near Peterlee. *Thornhlawa* 1071–80. 'Thorn-tree hill or mound'. OE *thorn* + *hlāw*.

Thornthwaite, 'thorn-tree clearing', OScand. *thorn* + *thveit*: **Thornthwaite** Cumbria, near Keswick. *Thornthwayt* 1254. **Thornthwaite** N. Yorks. *Tornthueit* 1230.

Thornton, a common name, 'thorn-tree enclosure or farmstead', OE *thorn* + *tūn*; examples include: **Thornton** Lancs. *Torentun* 1086 (DB). **Thornton** W. Yorks. *Torentone* 1086 (DB). **Thornton, Bishop** N. Yorks. *Thorntune* c.1030, *Torentune* 1086 (DB). Affix refers to its early possession by the Archbishop of York. **Thornton, Childer** Ches. *Thorinthun* c.1210, *Childrethornton* 1288. Affix means 'of the young men' (from OE *cild*, genitive plural *cildra*), with reference to the young monks of St Werburgh's Abbey in Chester. **Thornton Dale** N. Yorks. *Torentune* 1086 (DB). Affix is OScand. *dalr* 'valley'. **Thornton Heath** Gtr. London. *Thorneton Hethe* 1511. With OE *hæth* 'heath'.

Thoroton Notts. *Toruertune* 1086 (DB). 'Farmstead or village of a man called Thorfrøthr'. OScand. pers. name + OE *tūn*.

Thorp, *Thorpe*, a common name, from OScand. *thorp* 'outlying farmstead or hamlet, dependent secondary settlement', except for a few South Country instances which are from OE *throp* of similar meaning; examples include: **Thorp Arch** W. Yorks. *Torp* 1086 (DB), *Thorp de Arches* 1272. Manorial affix from the de Arches family, here in the 11th cent. **Thorpe** Norfolk. *Torpe* 1254. **Thorpe** Surrey. *Thorp* 672–4, *Torp* 1086 (DB). **Thorpe-le-Soken** Essex. *Torp* 12th cent., *Thorpe in ye Sooken* 1612. Affix is from OE *sōcn* 'district with special jurisdiction'. **Thorpe on the Hill** Lincs. *Torp* 1086 (DB). **Thorpe St Andrew** Norfolk. *Torp* 1086 (DB). Affix from the dedication of the church. **Thorpe Salvin** S. Yorks. *Torp* 1086 (DB), *Thorpe Saluayn* 1255. Manorial affix from the Salvain family, here in the 13th cent. **Thorpe Willoughby** N. Yorks. *Torp* 1086 (DB), *Thorp Wyleby* 1276. Manorial affix from the de Willeby family, here in the 13th cent.

Thorrington Essex. *Torinduna* |sic| 1086 (DB), *Torritona* 1202. Probably 'thorn-tree enclosure or farmstead'. OE *thorn* or *thyrne* + *tūn*.

Thorverton Devon. *Toruerton* 1182. Probably 'farmstead by the thorn-tree ford'. OE *thorn* + *ford* + *tūn*.

Thrandeston Suffolk. *Thrandeston* c.1035, *Thrandestuna* 1086 (DB). 'Farmstead or village of a man called Thrándr'. OScand. pers. name + OE *tūn*.

Thrapston Northants. *Trapestone* 1086 (DB). 'Farmstead or village of a man called *Thræpst'. OE pers. name + *tūn*.

Threapwood Ches. *Threpewood* 1548. 'Disputed wood'. OE *thrēap* + *wudu*.

Threave Dumf. 'Farm'. Gaelic *treabh*.

Three Bridges W. Sussex. *Le three bridges* 1613. Self-explanatory.

Threekingham Lincs. *Trichingeham* 1086 (DB). 'Homestead of the tribe called 'Tricingas'. Old tribal name (origin obscure) + OE *hām*.

Threepwood Sc. Bord. *Trepewode* c.1230. 'Disputed woodland'. OE *threap* + *wudu*.

Threlkeld Cumbria. *Trellekell* 1197. 'Spring of the thralls or serfs'. OScand. *thréll* + *kelda*.

Threshfield N. Yorks. *Freschefelt* |sic| 1086 (DB), *Threskefeld* 12th cent. 'Open land where corn is threshed'. OE *thresc* + *feld*.

Thrigby Norfolk. *Trikebei* 1086 (DB). 'Farmstead or village of a man called *Thrykki'. OScand. pers. name + *bý*.

Thringstone Leics. *Trangesbi* |sic| 1086 (DB), *Trengeston* c.1200. 'Farmstead or village of a man called *Thræingr'. OScand. pers. name + OE *tūn* (replacing OScand. *bý*).

Thrintoft N. Yorks. *Tirnetofte* 1086 (DB). 'Thorn-tree homestead'. OScand. *thyrnir* + *toft*. Alternatively the first element may be the OScand. man's name Thyrnir.

Thriplow Cambs. *Tripelan* |sic| c.1050, *Trepeslau* 1086 (DB). 'Hill or tumulus of a man called *Tryppa'. OE pers. name + *hlāw*.

Throcking Herts. *Trochinge* 1086 (DB). Possibly 'place where beams are used or obtained'. OE *throc* + *-ing*.

Throckley Tyne & Wear. *Trokelawa* 1177. Possibly 'hill where beams are obtained'. OE *throc* + *hlāw*.

Throckmorton Heref. & Worcs. *Trochemerton* 1176. Possibly 'farmstead by a pool with a beam bridge'. OE *throc* + *mere* + *tūn*.

Throphill Northum. *Trophil* 1166. 'Hamlet hill'. OE *throp* + *hyll*.

Thropton Northum. *Tropton* 1177. 'Estate with an outlying farmstead or hamlet', OE *throp* + *tūn*.

Throston, High Hartlepl. *Thoreston* c.1300. 'Farmstead or village of a man called Thórir or Thórr'. OScand. pers. name + OE *tūn*.

Throwleigh Devon. *Trule* 1086 (DB). 'Woodland clearing with or near a conduit'. OE *thrūh* + *lēah*.

Throwley Kent. *Trevelai* 1086 (DB). Identical in origin with the previous name.

Thrumpton Notts., near Ruddington. *Turmodestun* 1086 (DB). 'Farmstead or village of a man called Thormóthr'. OScand. pers. name + OE *tūn*.

Thrupp, 'outlying farmstead or hamlet', OE *throp*: **Thrupp** Glos. *Trop* 1261. **Thrupp** Oxon. *Trop* 1086 (DB).

Thrushelton Devon. *Tresetone* 1086 (DB). 'Farmstead or village frequented by thrushes'. OE *thryscele* + *tūn*.

Thruxton, 'estate or manor of a man called Thorkell', OScand. pers. name + OE *tūn*: **Thruxton** Hants.

Turkilleston 1167. **Thruxton** Heref. & Worcs. *Torchestone* |*sic*| 1086 (DB), *Turkelestona* 1160–70.

Thrybergh S. Yorks. *Triberge* 1086 (DB). 'Three hills'. OE *thrī* + *beorg*.

Thundersley Essex. *Thunreslea* 1086 (DB). 'Sacred grove of the heathen god Thunor'. OE god-name + *lēah*.

Thurcaston Leics. *Turchitelestone* 1086 (DB). 'Farmstead or village of a man called Thorketill'. OScand. pers. name + OE *tūn*.

Thurcroft S. Yorks. *Thurscroft* 1319. 'Enclosure of a man called Thórir'. OScand. pers. name + OE *croft*.

Thurgarton, 'farmstead or village of a man called Thorgeirr', OScand. pers. name + OE *tūn*: **Thurgarton** Norfolk. *Thurgartun* 1044–7, *Turgartuna* 1086 (DB). **Thurgarton** Notts. *Turgarstune* 1086 (DB).

Thurgoland S. Yorks. *Turgesland* 1086 (DB). 'Cultivated land of a man called Thorgeirr'. OScand. pers. name + *land*.

Thurlaston, 'farmstead or village of a man called Thorleifr', OScand. pers. name + OE *tūn*: **Thurlaston** Leics. *Turlauestona* 1166. **Thurlaston** Warwicks. *Torlauestone* 1086 (DB).

Thurlby, 'farmstead or village of a man called Thórulfr', OScand. pers. name + *bý*: **Thurlby** Lincs., near Bourne. *Turolvebi* 1086 (DB). **Thurlby** Lincs., near Lincoln. *Turolue(s)bi* 1086 (DB).

Thurleigh Beds. *La Lega* 1086 (DB), *Thyrleye* 1372. '(Place at) the wood or clearing'. From OE *lēah* with the remains of the OE definite article *thǣre* (dative).

Thurles (*Durlas*) Tipperary. 'Strong fort'.

Thurlestone Devon. *Thyrelanstane* 847, *Torlestan* 1086 (DB). 'Stone or rock with a hole in it'. OE *thyrel* + *stān*.

Thurlow, Great & *Thurlow, Little* Suffolk. *Tridlauua* 1086 (DB). Probably 'burial mound of the warriors'. OE *thrȳth* + *hlāw*.

Thurloxton Somerset. *Turlakeston* 1195. 'Farmstead or village of a man called Thorlákr'. OScand. pers. name + OE *tūn*.

Thurlstone S. Yorks. *Turulfestune* 1086 (DB). 'Farmstead or village of a man called Thórulfr'. OScand. pers. name + OE *tūn*.

Thurlton Norfolk. *Thuruertuna* 1086 (DB). 'Farmstead or village of a man called Thorfrithr'. OScand. pers. name + OE *tūn*.

Thurmaston Leics. *Turmodestone* 1086 (DB). 'Farmstead or village of a man called Thormóthr'. OScand. pers. name + OE *tūn*.

Thurnby Leics. *Turneby* 1156. 'Farmstead or village of a man called Thyrnir, or where thorn-bushes grow'. OScand. pers. name or *thyrnir* + *bý*.,

Thurnham Lancs. *Tiernun* |*sic*| 1086 (DB), *Thurnum* 1160. '(Place at) the thorn-trees'. OE *thyrne* in a dative plural form *thyrnum*.

Thurning, 'place where thorn-trees grow', OE *thyrne* + -*ing*: **Thurning** Norfolk. *Turninga* 1086 (DB). **Thurning** Northants. *Torninge* 1086 (DB).

Thurnscoe S. Yorks. *Ternusche* 1086 (DB), *Thirnescoh* *c*.1090. 'Thorn-tree wood'. OScand. *thyrnir* + *skógr*.

Thurrock, Little & *Thurrock, West* Essex. *Thurroce* 1040–2, *Thurrucca* 1086 (DB). 'Place where filthy water collects'. OE *thurruc*. Originally applied to a stretch of marshland west of Tilbury. *See also* GRAYS.

Thursby Cumbria. *Thoresby* *c*.1165. 'Farmstead or village of a man called Thórir'. OScand. pers. name + *bý*.

Thursford Norfolk. *Turesfort* 1086 (DB). 'Ford associated with a giant or demon'. OE *thyrs* + *ford*.

Thursley Surrey. *Thoresle* 1292. Probably 'sacred grove of the heathen god Thunor'. OE god-name + *lēah*.

Thurso Highland. *Thorsa* 1152. '(Place on the) River Thurso'. The Celtic river name probably means 'bull river', from the old name of nearby Dunnet Head, known to the Romans as *Tarvedunum*, 'bull fort'.

Thurstaston Mersey. *Turstanetone* 1086 (DB). 'Farmstead or village of a man called Thorsteinn'. OScand. pers. name + OE *tūn*.

Thurston Suffolk, near Bury. *Thurstuna* 1086 (DB). 'Farmstead or village of a man called Thóri'. OScand. pers. name + OE *tūn*.

Thurstonfield Cumbria. *Turstanfeld* *c*.1210. 'Open land of a man called Thorsteinn'. OScand. pers. name + OE *feld*.

Thurstonland W. Yorks. *Tostenland* 1086 (DB). 'Cultivated land of a man called Thorsteinn'. OScand. pers. name + *land*.

Thurton Norfolk. *Tortuna* 1086 (DB). Probably 'thorn-tree enclosure or farmstead'. OE *thorn* or *thyrne* + *tūn*.

Thurvaston Derbys. *Turverdestune* 1086 (DB). 'Farmstead or village of a man called Thorfrithr'. OScand. pers. name + OE *tūn*.

Thuxton Norfolk. *Turstanestuna* 1086 (DB). 'Farmstead or village of a man called Thorsteinn'. OScand. pers. name + OE *tūn*.

Thwaite, 'the clearing, meadow, or paddock', OScand. *thveit*; examples include: **Thwaite** Suffolk. *Theyt* 1228.

Thwaite St Mary Norfolk. *Thweit* 1254. Affix from the dedication of the church.

Thwing E. R. Yorks. *Tuuenc* 1086 (DB). 'Narrow strip of land'. OScand. *thvengr* or OE *thweng*.

Tibberton, 'farmstead or village of a man called Tīdbeorht, OE pers. name + *tūn*: **Tibberton** Glos. *Tebriston* 1086 (DB). **Tibberton** Heref. & Worcs. *Tidbrihtincgtun* 978–92, *Tidbertun* 1086 (DB). **Tibberton** Shrops. *Tetbristone* 1086 (DB).

Tibohine (*Tigh Baoithín*) Mayo. 'Baoithín's church'.

Tibshelf Derbys. *Tibecel* 1086 (DB). *Tibbeshelf* 1179. 'Shelf or ridge of a man called Tibba'. OE pers. name + *scelf*.

Tibthorpe E. R. Yorks. *Tibetorp* 1086 (DB). 'Outlying farmstead or hamlet of a man called Tibbi or Tibba'. OScand. or OE pers. name + OScand. *thorp*.

Ticehurst E. Sussex. *Tycheherst* 1248. 'Wooded hill where young goats are kept'. OE *ticce(n)* + *hyrst*.

Tichborne Hants. *Ticceburna* c.909. 'Stream frequented by young goats'. OE *ticce(n)* + *burna*.

Tickencote Rutland. *Tichecote* 1086 (DB). 'Shed for young goats'. OE *ticcen* + *cot*.

Tickenham N. Som. *Ticaham* 1086 (DB). 'Homestead or enclosure of a man called Tica, or where young goats are kept'. OE pers. name (genitive -*n*) or *ticcen* + *hām* or *hamm*.

Tickhill S. Yorks. *Tikehill* 12th cent. 'Hill of a man called Tica, or where young goats are kept'. OE pers. name or *ticce(n)* + *hyll*.

Ticknall Derbys. *Ticenheale* c.1002. 'Nook of land where young goats are kept'. OE *ticcen* + *halh*.

Tickton E. R. Yorks. *Tichetone* 1086 (DB). 'Farmstead of a man called Tica, or where young goats are kept'. OE pers. name or *ticce(n)* + *tūn*.

Ticloy (*Tigh Cloiche*) Antrim. 'House of stone'.

Tidcombe Wilts. *Titicome* 1086 (DB). Probably 'valley of a man called *Titta*. OE pers. name + *cumb*.

Tiddington Oxon. *Titendone* 1086 (DB). 'Hill of a man called *Tytta*. OE pers. name (genitive -*n*) + *dūn*.

Tiddington Warwicks. *Tidinctune* 969. 'Estate associated with a man called Tīda'. OE pers. name + -*ing*- + *tūn*.

Tideford Cornwall. *Tutiford* 1201. 'Ford over the River Tiddy'. Old river-name (of uncertain origin and meaning) + OE *ford*.

Tidenham Glos. *Dyddanhamme* 956, *Tedeneham* 1086 (DB). 'Enclosure of a man called *Dydda*. OE pers. name (genitive -*n*) + *hamm*.

Tideswell Derbys. *Tidesuuelle* 1086 (DB). 'Spring or stream of a man called Tīdi'. OE pers. name + *wella*.

Tidmarsh Berks. *Tedmerse* 1196. 'People's or common marsh'. OE *thēod* + *mersc*.

Tidmington Warwicks. *Tidelminctune* 977, *Tidelmintun* 1086 (DB). 'Estate associated with a man called Tidhelm'. OE pers. name + -*ing*- + *tūn*.

Tidworth, North (Wilts.) & *Tidworth, South* (Hants.). *Tudanwyrthe* c.990, *Tode(w)orde* 1086 (DB). 'Enclosure of a man called Tuda'. OE pers. name + *worth*.

Tiermaclane (*Tír Mhic Calláin*) Clare. 'Mac Callán's country'.

Tievemore (*Taobh Mór*) Donegal. 'Large side'.

Tiffield Northants. *Tifelde* 1086 (DB). Possibly 'open land with or near a meeting-place'. OE *tīg* + *feld*.

Tilbrook Cambs. *Tilebroc* 1086 (DB). Probably 'brook of a man called Tila'. OE pers. name + *brōc*.

Tilbury Essex. *Tilaburg* 731, *Tiliberia* 1086 (DB). Probably 'stronghold of a man called Tila'. OE pers. name + *burh* (dative *byrig*). Alternatively the first element may be a lost stream-name *Tila* 'the useful one'.

Tilehurst Berks. *Tigelherst* 1167. 'Wooded hill where tiles are made'. OE *tigel* + *hyrst*.

Tilford Surrey. *Tileford* c.1140. 'Useful ford, or ford of a man called Tila'. OE *til* or pers. name + *ford*.

Tillicoultry Clac. *Tulycultri* 1195, *Tullicultre* c.1199. Possibly 'hill at the back of the settlement'. Gaelic *tulach* + *cùl* + *treabh*. Tillicoultry is on the edge of the Ochill Hills.

Tillingham Essex. *Tillingaham* c.1000, *Tillingham* 1086 (DB). 'Homestead of the family or followers of a man called Tilli'. OE pers. name + -*inga*- + *hām*.

Tillington Heref. & Worcs. *Tullinton* c.1180. 'Estate associated with a man called Tulla or *Tylla*. OE pers. name + -*ing*- + *tūn*.

Tillington W. Sussex. *Tullingtun* 960. 'Estate associated with a man called Tulla'. OE pers. name + -*ing*- + *tūn*.

Tilmanstone Kent. *Tilemanestone* 1086 (DB). 'Farmstead or village of a man called Tilmann'. OE pers. name + *tūn*.

Tilney All Saints & *Tilney St Lawrence* Norfolk. *Tilnea* 1170. 'Useful island, or island of a man called Tila'. OE *til* (dative -*an*) or pers. name (genitive -*n*) + *ēg*. Distinguishing affixes from the dedications of the churches.

Tilshead Wilts. *Tidulfhide* 1086 (DB). 'Hide of land of a man called Tīdwulf'. OE pers. name + *hīd*, *see* SHREWTON.

Tilstock Shrops. *Tildestok* 1211. 'Outlying farmstead or hamlet of a woman called Tīdhild'. OE pers. name + *stoc*.

Tilston Ches. *Tilleston* 1086 (DB). 'Stone of a man called Tilli or Tilla'. OE pers. name + *stān*.

Tilstone Fearnall Ches. *Tidulstane* 1086 (DB), *Tilston Farnhale* 1427. 'Stone of a man called Tīdwulf'. OE pers. name + *stān*. Affix is the name of a local place now lost, 'fern nook', OE *fearn* + *halh*.

Tilsworth Beds. *Pileworde* |*sic*| 1086 (DB), *Thuleswrthe* 1202. Probably 'enclosure of a man called *Thȳfel* or *Tyfel*. OE pers. name + *worth*.

Tilton Leics. *Tiletone* 1086 (DB). 'Farmstead or village of a man called Tila'. OE pers. name + *tūn*.

Timahoe (*Tigh Mochua*) Kildare, Laois. 'Mochua's house'.

Timberland Lincs. *Timberlunt* 1086 (DB). 'Grove where timber is obtained'. OE *timber* or OScand. *timbær* + *lundr*.

Timberscombe Somerset. *Timbrecumbe* 1086 (DB). 'Valley where timber is obtained'. OE *timber* + *cumb*.

Timble N. Yorks. *Timmel* c.972, *Timble* 1086 (DB). Possibly from an OE *tymbel* 'a fall of earth' or 'a tumbling stream'.

Timoleague (*Tigh Molaige*) Cork. 'Molaga's house'.

Timolin (*Tigh Moling*) Kildare. 'Moling's house'.

Timperley Gtr. Manch. *Timperleie* 1211–25. 'Wood or clearing where timber is obtained'. OE *timber* + *lēah*.

Timsbury B. & NE. Som. *Timesberua* |*sic*| 1086 (DB), *Timberesberwe* 1233. 'Grove where timber is obtained'. OE *timber* + *bearu*.

Timsbury Hants. *Timbreberie* 1086 (DB). 'Timber or wooden fort or manor'. OE *timber* + *burh* (dative *byrig*).

Timworth Green Suffolk. *Timeworda* 1086 (DB). 'Enclosure of a man called *Tima*. OE pers. name + *worth*.

Tinahely (*Tigh na hÉille*) Wicklow. 'House of the latchet'.

Tincleton Dorset. *Tincladene* 1086 (DB). 'Valley of the small farms'. OE **tynincel* + *denu*.

Tindale Cumbria. *Tindale* late 12th cent. 'Valley of the River South Tyne'. Celtic or pre-Celtic river-name (meaning simply 'river') + OScand. *dalr*.

Tingewick Bucks. *Tedinwiche* 1086 (DB). Probably 'dwelling or (dairy) farm at the place associated with a man called Tīda or Tēoda'. OE pers. name + *-ing* + *wīc*.

Tingrith Beds. *Tingrei |sic|* 1086 (DB), *Tingrith* c.1215. 'Stream by which assemblies are held'. OE *thing* + *rīth*.

Tinnakilla (*Tigh na Coille*) Wexford. 'House of the wood'.

Tinode (*Tigh an Fhóid*) Westmeath. 'House of the sod'.

Tinsley S. Yorks. *Tineslauue* 1086 (DB). 'Mound of a man called *Tynni'. OE pers. name + *hlāw*.

Tintagel Cornwall. *Tintagol* c.1137. Probably 'fort by the neck of land'. Cornish **din* + **tagell*.

Tintern (*Tyndyrn*) Mon. *Dindyrn* c.1150. 'King's fortress'. Welsh *din* + *teyrn*.

Tintinhull Somerset. *Tintanhulle* 10th cent., *Tintenella* 1086 (DB). OE *hyll* 'hill' added to an old Celtic name from **din* 'fort' with an uncertain second element.

Tintwistle Derbys. *Tengestvisie* 1086 (DB). Probably 'river-fork of the prince'. OE *thengel* + *twisla*.

Tinwald Dumf. *Tynwalde* c.1280. 'Place of assembly'. OScand. *thing-vollr*.

Tinwell Rutland. *Tedinwelle |sic|* 1086 (DB), *Tinningewelle* mid-13th cent. Possibly 'spring or stream of the family or followers of a man called *Tȳni'. OE pers. name + *-inga-* + *wella*.

Tipperary (*Tiobraid Árann*) Tipperary. 'Ára's well'.

Tipperty Aber. *Typpertay* 1501. 'Well place'. OGaelic *tiobartach*.

Tiptoe Hants. First on record in 1555, probably a manorial name from the Typetot family mentioned in this area from the 13th cent.

Tipton W. Mids. *Tibintone* 1086 (DB). 'Estate associated with a man called Tibba'. OE pers. name + *-ing-* + *tūn*.

Tiptree Essex. *Tipentrie* 12th cent. Probably 'tree of a man called *Tippa'. OE pers. name + *trēow*.

Tirawley (*Tír Amhalghaidh*) Mayo. 'Amhalghaidh's territory'.

Tirboy (*Tír Buí*) Galway. 'Yellow territory'.

Tiree (island) Arg. *Tir Iath* c.850, *Tiryad* 1343. 'Eth's land'. Gaelic *tìr*. *Eth* has not been identified and is probably pre-Celtic.

Tireragh (*Tír Fhiachrach*) Sligo. 'Fiachra's territory'.

Tirkane (*Tír Chiana*) Derry. *Tír Chiana* c.1740. Possibly 'Cian's territory'.

Tirley Glos. *Trineleie* 1086 (DB). 'Circular woodland clearing'. OE **trind* + *lēah*.

Tirnamona (*Tír na Móna*) Monaghan. 'Territory of the bog'.

Tisbury Wilts. *Tyssesburg* c.800. *Tisseberie* 1086 (DB). 'Stronghold of a man called *Tyssi'. OE pers. name + *burh* (dative *byrig*).

Tissington Derbys. *Tizinctun* 1086 (DB). 'Estate associated with a man called Tīdsige'. OE pers. name + *-ing- + tūn*.

Tisted, East & *Tisted, West* Hants. *Ticcesstede* 932, *Tistede* 1086 (DB). 'Place where young goats are kept'. OE *ticce(n)* + *stede*.

Titchfield Hants. *Ticefelle* 1086 (DB). 'Open land where young goats are kept'. OE *ticce(n)* + *feld*.

Titchmarsh Northants. *Tuteanmersc* 973, *Ticemerse* 1086 (DB). 'Marsh of a man called Tyccea'. OE pers. name + *mersc*.

Titchwell Norfolk. *Ticeswelle* c.1035, *Tigeuuella* 1086 (DB). 'Spring or stream frequented by young goats'. OE *ticce(n)* + *wella*.

Titley Heref. & Worcs. *Titelege* 1086 (DB). Probably 'woodland clearing of a man called *Titta'. OE pers. name + *lēah*.

Titlington Northum. *Titlingtona* 12th cent. Probably 'estate associated with a man called *Titel'. OE pers. name + *-ing- + tūn*.

Titsey Surrey. *Tydices eg* 10th cent., *Ticesei* 1086 (DB). 'Well-watered land of a man called *Tydic'. OE pers. name + *ēg*.

Tittensor Staffs. *Titesovre |sic|* 1086 (DB), *Titneshovere* 1236. 'Ridge of a man called *Titten'. OE pers. name + **ofer*.

Tittleshall Norfolk. *Titeshala |sic|* 1086 (DB), *Titleshal* 1200. 'Nook of land of a man called *Tyttel'. OE pers. name + *halh*.

Tiverton Ches. *Tevreton* 1086 (DB). 'Red-lead farmstead', perhaps denoting a red-painted building or where red-lead was available. OE *tēafor* + *tūn*.

Tiverton Devon. *Twyfyrde* 880–5, *Tovretona* 1086 (DB). 'Farmstead or village at the double ford'. OE **twī-fyrde* + *tūn*.

Tivetshall *St Margaret* & *St Mary* Norfolk. *Teueteshala* 1086 (DB). OE *halh* 'nook of land', possibly with an old form of dialect *tewhit* 'lapwing'. Distinguishing affixes from the dedications of the churches.

Tixall Staffs. *Ticeshale* 1086 (DB). 'Nook of land where young goats are kept'. OE *ticce(n)* + *halh*.

Tixover Rutland. *Tichesovre* 1086 (DB). 'Promontory where young goats are kept'. OE *ticce(n)* + **ofer*.

Toames (*Tuaim*) Cork. 'Mound'.

Tobarmacdugh (*Tobar Mhic Dhuach*) Galway. 'Mac Duach's well'.

Tober (*Tobar*) Cavan. 'Well'.

Toberavilla (*Tobar an Bhile*) Kerry. 'Well of the sacred tree'.

Toberbreedy (*Tobar Bhríde*) Cork. 'Bríd's well'.

Toberbunny (*Tobar Bainne*) Dublin. 'Well of milk'.

Tobercurry (*Tobar an Choire*) Sligo. 'Well of the cauldron'.

Toberdoney (*Tobar Domhnaigh*) Antrim, Louth, etc. 'Sunday's well'.

Tobermogue (*Tobar Mhodóg*) Westmeath. 'Modóg's well'.

Tobermore (*Tobar Mór*) Derry. *Tobarmore* 1613. 'Big well'.

Tobermory Arg (Mull). *Tibbermore* 1540. 'St Mary's well'. Gaelic *tiobar* + *Moire*.

Tockenham Wilts. *Tockenham* 854, *Tocheham* 1086 (DB). 'Homestead or enclosure of a man called *Toca'. OE pers. name + *hām* or *hamm*.

Tockholes Lancs. *Tocholis* c.1200. 'Hollows of a man called *Toca or Tók(i)'. OE or OScand. pers. name + *hol*.

Tockington S. Glos. *Tochintune* 1086 (DB). 'Estate associated with a man called *Toca'. OE pers. name + -ing- + *tūn*.

Tockwith N. Yorks. *Tocvi* 1086 (DB). 'Wood of a man called Tóki'. OScand. pers. name + *vithr*.

Todber Dorset. *Todeberie* 1086 (DB). Probably 'hill or grove of a man called Tota'. OE pers. name + *beorg* or *bearu*.

Toddington Beds. *Totingedone* 1086 (DB). 'Hill of the family or followers of a man called Tuda'. OE pers. name + -inga- + *dūn*.

Toddington Glos. *Todintun* 1086 (DB). 'Estate associated with a man called Tuda'. OE pers. name + -ing- + *tūn*.

Todenham Glos. *Todanhom* 804, *Teodeham* 1086 (DB). 'Enclosed valley of a man called Tēoda'. OE pers. name (genitive -n) + *hamm*.

Todmorden W. Yorks. *Tottemerden* 1246. 'Boundary valley of a man called Totta'. OE pers. name + *mǣre* + *denu*.

Todwick S. Yorks. *Tatewic* 1086 (DB). 'Dwelling or (dairy) farm of a man called Tāta'. OE pers. name + *wīc*.

Toem (*Tuaim*) Tipperary. 'Mound'.

Toft, *Tofts*, from OScand. *toft* 'curtilage or homestead'; examples include: **Toft** Cambs. *Tofth* 1086 (DB). **Toft Monks** Norfolk. *Toft* 1086 (DB). Affix from its possession by the Norman Abbey of Préaux in the 12th cent. **Tofts, West** Norfolk. *Stofftam* |sic| 1086 (DB), *Toftes* 1199.

Toftrees Norfolk. *Toftes* 1086 (DB). Identical in origin with the previous name.

Toghblane (*Teach Bhláin*) Down. 'Bláin's house'.

Togher (*Tóchar*) Cork, Louth, Offaly. 'Causeway'.

Togherbane (*Tóchar Bán*) Kerry. 'White causeway'.

Togherbeg (*Tóchar Beag*) Galway, Wicklow. 'Little causeway'.

Togston Northum. *Toggesdena* 1130. 'Valley of a man called *Tocg'. OE pers. name + *denu*.

Tolland Somerset. *Talanda* 1086 (DB). 'Cultivated land by the River Tone'. Celtic river-name (*see* TAUNTON) + OE *land*.

Tollard Royal Wilts. *Tollard* 1086 (DB), *Tollard Ryall* 1535. 'Hollow hill'. Celtic *tull* + *ardd*. Affix from lands here held c.1200 by King John.

Toller Fratrum & *Toller Porcorum* Dorset. *Tolre* 1086 (DB), *Tolre Fratrum*, *Tolre Porcorum* 1340. Named from the River *Toller*, now the River Hooke. *Toller* is an old Celtic river-name meaning 'hollow stream'. The humorously contrasting affixes are Latin *fratrum* 'of the brethren' (with reference to early possession by the Knights Hospitallers) and *porcorum* 'of the pigs' (with reference to its herds of swine).

Tollerton N. Yorks. *Toletun* 972. *Tolentun* 1086 (DB). 'Farmstead or village of the tax-gatherers'. OE *tolnere* + *tūn*.

Tollerton Notts. *Troclauestune* 1086 (DB). 'Farmstead or village of a man called Thorleifr'. OScand. pers. name + OE *tūn*.

Tollesbury Essex. *Tolesberia* 1086 (DB). 'Stronghold of a man called *Toll'. OE pers. name + *burh* (dative *byrig*).

Tolleshunt D'Arcy & *Tolleshunt Major* Essex. *Tollesfuntan* c.1000, *Toleshunta* 1086 (DB). 'Spring of a man called *Toll'. OE pers. name + *funta*. Manorial affixes from possession by the Darcy family (here in the 15th cent.) and by a tenant called Malger in 1086.

Tolpuddle Dorset. *Pidele* 1086 (DB), *Tollepidele* 1210. 'Estate on the River Piddle belonging to a woman called Tóla'. OE river-name (*see* PIDDLEHINTON) with OScand. pers. name. The Tóla in question is recorded as giving her lands including Tolpuddle to Abbotsbury Abbey before 1066.

Tolsta Head W. Isles (Lewis): ON *Tholfsstathir* 'Tholfr's farm' + English *head*.

Tolworth Gtr. London. *Taleorde* 1086 (DB). 'Enclosure of a man called *Tala'. OE pers. name + *worth*.

Tomhaggard (*Teach Moshagard*) Wexford. 'Moshagra's house'.

Tomich Highland. 'Place of knolls'. Gaelic *tomach*.

Tomintoul Moray. 'Barn knoll'. Gaelic *toman t-sabail*.

Ton (*Tóin*) Monaghan. 'Bottom'.

Tonbridge Kent. *Tonebrige* 1086 (DB). Probably 'bridge belonging to the estate or manor'. OE *tūn* + *brycg*.

Tonduff (*Tóin Dubh*) Donegal. 'Black bottom'.

Tone (river) Somerset, *see* TAUNTON.

Tong, 'tongs-shaped feature', e.g. 'fork of a river', OE *tang*, *twang* (apparently replacing a related form *tweonga* of similar meaning): **Tong** Shrops. *Tweongan* 10th cent., *Tvange* 1086 (DB). **Tong** W. Yorks. *Tuinc* |sic| 1086 (DB), *Tange* 1176.

Tonge Leics. *Tunge* 1086 (DB). 'The tongue of land'. OScand. *tunga*.

Tongham Surrey. *Tuangham* 1189. 'Homestead or enclosure by the fork of a river'. OE *tang* or *twang* + *hām* or *hamm*.

Tongue Highland. *Toung* 1542. '(Place on the) tongue of land'. OScand. *tunga*.

Tonragee (*Tóin re Gaoith*) Mayo. 'Backside to the wind'.

Tonypandy Rhon. 'Grassland of the fulling mill'. Welsh *ton* + *y* + *pandy*.

Toom (*Tuaim*) Tipperary. 'Mound'.

Toomard (*Tuaim Ard*) Galway. 'High mound'.

Toombeola (*Tuaim Beola*) Galway. 'Beola's mound'.

Toome (*Tuaim*) Antrim. 'Burial mound'. (*for*) *Fertais Tuamma c*.900. The earlier name was *Fearsaid Thuama*, 'sandbank ford of Toome'.

Toomebridge (*Droichead Thuama*) Antrim. 'Bridge of the mound'.

Toomyvara (*Tuaim Uí Mheára*) Tipperary. 'Ó Meára's burial mound'.

Toor (*Tuar*) Limerick. 'Bleach green'.

Tooraree (*Tuar an Fraoigh*) Limerick. 'Bleach green of the heather'.

Tooreen (*An Tuairín*) Mayo. 'The little bleach green'.

Tooreennafersha (*Tuairín na Feirste*) Kerry. 'Little bleach green of the sandbank'.

Tooreennahone (*Tuairín na hÓn*) Kerry. 'Little bleach green of the hole'.

Toorevagh (*Tuar Riabhach*) Westmeath. 'Grey bleach green'.

Toormore (*An Tuar Mór*) Cork. 'The big bleach green'.

Toot Baldon Oxon., *see* BALDON.

Tooting Bec & *Tooting Graveney* Gtr. London. *Totinge* 727, *Totinges* 1086 (DB), *Totinge de Bek* 1255, *Thoting Gravenel* 1272. Possibly '(settlement of) the family or followers of a man called Tōta', from OE pers. name + *-ingas*. Alternatively 'people of the look-out place', from OE **tōt* + *-ingas*. Distinguishing affixes from early possession by the Norman Abbey of Bec-Hellouin and by the de Gravenel family.

Topcliffe N. Yorks. *Topeclive* 1086 (DB). 'Cliff or bank of a man called **Toppa*'. OE pers. name + *clif*.

Topcroft Norfolk. *Topecroft* 1086 (DB). 'Enclosure of a man called Tópi'. OScand. pers. name + OE *croft*.

Toppesfield Essex. *Topesfelda* 1086 (DB). 'Open land of a man called **Topp*'. OE pers. name + *feld*.

Topsham Devon. *Toppeshamme* 937, *Topeshant* |*sic*| 1086 (DB). 'Promontory of a man called **Topp*'. OE pers. name + *hamm*.

Torbay Devon. *Torrebay* 1401. 'Bay near TORRE'. ME *bay*.

Torbryan Devon. *Torre* 1086 (DB), *Torre Briane* 1238. 'The rocky hill'. OE *torr*, with manorial affix from the de Brione family, here in the 13th cent.

Torfaen (the unitary authority). 'Stone gap'. Welsh *tor* + *maen*.

Torksey Lincs. *Turecesieg* 11th cent., *Torchesey* 1086 (DB). 'Island of a man called **Turec*'. OE pers. name + *ēg*.

Tormarton S. Glos. *Tormentone* |*sic*| 1086 (DB), *Tormarton* 1166. 'Boundary farmstead where thorn-trees grow', or 'farmstead by the pool where thorn-trees grow'. OE *thorn* + *mǣre* or *mere* + *tūn*.

Torpenhow Cumbria. *Torpennoc* 1163. 'Ridge of the hill with a rocky peak'. OE *torr* + Celtic **penn* + OE *hōh*.

Torpoint Cornwall. *Tor-point* 1746. 'Rocky headland'. OE *torr* + ME *point*.

Torquay Devon. *Torrekay* 1591. 'Quay near TORRE', *see* TORRE. ME *key*.

Torrance E. Dunb. 'Little hills'. Gaelic *torran*.

Torre Devon. *Torre* 1086 (DB). 'The rocky hill'. OE *torr*.

Torridon Highland. *Torvirlane* 1464. 'Place of portage'. Gaelic *tairbheartan*.

Torrington, Black, *Torrington, Great*, & *Torrington, Little* Devon. *Tori(n)tona* 1086 (DB), *Blaketorrintun* 1219. 'Farmstead or village on the River Torridge'. Celtic river-name (meaning 'turbulent stream') + OE *tūn*. Affix is OE *blæc* 'dark-coloured' (referring to the river here).

Torrington, East & *Torrington, West* Lincs. *Terintone* 1086 (DB). 'Estate associated with a man called **Tir(a)*'. OE pers. name + *-ing-* + *tūn*.

Torrisholme Lancs. *Toredholme* 1086 (DB). 'Island of a man called Thóraldr'. OScand. pers. name + *holmr*.

Tortington W. Sussex. *Tortinton* 1086 (DB). 'Estate associated with a man called **Torhta*'. OE pers. name + *-ing-* + *tūn*.

Tortworth S. Glos. *Torteword* 1086 (DB). 'Enclosure of a man called **Torhta*'. OE pers. name + *worth*.

Torver Cumbria. *Thoruergh* 1190–9. 'Turf-roofed shed or shieling', or 'shieling of a man called **Thorfi*'. OScand. *torf* or pers. name + *erg*.

Torworth Notts. *Turdeworde* 1086 (DB). Probably 'enclosure of a man called Thórthr'. OScand. pers. name + OE *worth*.

Tory Island (*Toraigh*) Donegal. (*fasughadh*) *Toraighe* 611. 'Abounding in rocky heights'.

Toseland Cambs. *Toleslund* 1086 (DB). 'Grove of a man called Tóli'. OScand. pers. name + *lundr*.

Tosson, Great Northum. *Tossan* 1205. Possibly 'look-out stone'. OE **tōt* + *stān*.

Tostock Suffolk. *Totestoc* 1086 (DB). 'Outlying farmstead or hamlet by the look-out place'. OE **tōt* + *stoc*.

Totham, Great & *Totham, Little* Essex. *Totham c*.950, *Tot(e)ham* 1086 (DB). 'Homestead or village by the look-out place'. OE **tōt* + *hām*.

Totland I. of Wight. *Totland* 1608. 'Cultivated land or estate with a look-out place'. OE **tōt* + *land*.

Totley S. Yorks. *Totingelei* 1086 (DB). 'Woodland clearing of the family or followers of a man called Tota'. OE pers. name + *inga-* + *lēah*.

Totnes Devon. *Totanæs c*.1000, *Toteneis* 1086 (DB). 'Promontory of a man called Totta'. OE pers. name + *næss*.

Tottenham Gtr. London. *Toteham* 1086 (DB). 'Homestead or village of a man called Totta'. OE pers. name (genitive *-n*) + *hām*.

Tottenhill Norfolk. *Tottenhella* 1086 (DB). 'Hill of a man called Totta'. OE pers. name (genitive *-n*) + *hyll*.

Totteridge Gtr. London. *Taderege c*.1150. 'Ridge of a man called Tāta'. OE pers. name + *hrycg*.

Totternhoe Beds. *Totenehou* 1086 (DB). 'Hill-spur with a look-out house'. OE **tōt* + *ærn* + *hōh*.

Tottington Gtr. Manch. *Totinton* 1212. Probably 'estate associated with a man called Tota'. OE pers. name + *-ing-* + *tūn*. Alternatively the first element may be OE **tōt* 'look-out hill'.

Totton Hants. *Totintone* 1086 (DB). Identical in orgin with the previous name.

Tour (*Tuar*) Limerick. 'Bleach green'.

Tourlestrane (*Tuar Loistreáin*) Sligo. 'Loistreán's bleach green'.

Tourmakeady (*Tuar Mhic Éadaigh*) Mayo. 'Mac Éadaigh's bleach green'.

Tournafulla (*Tuar na Fola*) Limerick. 'Bleach green of the blood'.

Tow Law Durham. *Tollawe* 1423. Possibly 'look-out hill or mound'. OE **tōt* + *hlāw*.

Towcester Northants. *Tofeceaster* early 10th cent., *Tovecestre* 1086 (DB). 'Roman fort on the River Tove'. OE river-name (meaning 'slow') + *ceaster*.

Towednack Cornwall. 'Parish of *Sanctus Tewennocus*' 1327. From the dedication of the church to St Winwaloe (of which name *To-Winnoc* is a pet-form).

Tower Hamlets Gtr. London, term used at least as early as the 17th cent. for 'hamlets under the jurisdiction of the Tower of London'.

Towersey Oxon. *Eie* 1086 (DB), *Turrisey* 1240. 'The island held by the de Turs family' (here from the 13th cent.). OE *ēg* with later manorial affix.

Towthorpe York. *Touetorp* 1086 (DB). 'Outlying farmstead or hamlet of a man called Tófi'. OScand. pers. name + *thorp*.

Towton N. Yorks. *Touetun* 1086 (DB). 'Farmstead or village of a man called Tófi'. OScand. pers. name + *tūn*.

Towy. *See* TYWI VALLEY.

Towyn. *See* TYWYN.

Toxteth Mersey. *Stochestede* |sic| 1086 (DB), *Tokestath* 1212. 'Landing-place of a man called Tóki or **Tōk*'. OScand. pers. name + *stoth*.

Toye (*Tuaith*) Down. 'Territory'.

Toynton All Saints & *Toynton St Peter* Lincs. *Totintun(e)* 1086 (DB). 'Estate associated with a man called Tota'. OE pers. name + *-ing-* + *tūn*. Alternatively the first element may be OE **tōt* 'look-out hill'. Affixes from the dedications of the churches.

Toynton, High Lincs. *Tedin-*, *Todintune* 1086 (DB). 'Estate associated with a man called Tēoda'. OE pers. name + *-ing-* + *tūn*.

Trafford Park Gtr. Manch. *Stratford* 1206. 'Ford on a Roman road'. OE *strǣt* + *ford*.

Trafford, Bridge & *Trafford, Mickle* Ches. *Trosford*, *Traford* 1086 (DB). 'Trough ford'. OE *trog* + *ford*. Distinguishing affixes are OE *brycg* and OScand. *mikill* 'great'.

Trafrask (*Trá Phraisce*) Cork. 'Strand of kale'.

Tralee (*Trá Lí*) Kerry. 'Strand of the (river) Lí'.

Trallwng, Y. *See* WELSHPOOL.

Tramore (*Trá Mhór*) Waterford. 'Big strand'.

Tranarossan (*Trá na Rosán*) Donegal. 'Strand of the Rosses'.

Tranent E. Loth. *Tranent* 1210. 'Farm on the stream'. Welsh *tref* + *nant*. *Cp*. TREFNANT.

Tranmere Mersey. *Tranemul* late 12th cent. 'Sandbank frequented by cranes'. OScand. *trani* + *melr*.

Tranwell Northum. *Trennewell* 1268. 'Spring or stream frequented by cranes'. OScand. *trani* + OE *wella*.

Trasna Island (*Trasna*) Fermanagh. *Trassna* 1610. 'Island across'.

Trawden Lancs. *Trochdene* 1296. 'Trough-shaped valley'. OE *trog* + *denu*.

Trawmore (*Trá Mhór*) Mayo. 'Big strand'.

Trawsfynydd Gwyd. *Trausvenith* 1292. '(Place by a route) across the mountain'. Welsh *traws* + *mynydd*.

Tre-Einar. *See* RINASTON.

Tre-Gwyr. *See* GOWERTON.

Treales Lancs. *Treueles* 1086 (DB). 'Farmstead of a court'. Welsh *tref* + *llys*.

Treamlod. *See* AMBLESTON.

Trearddur Angl. *Tre Iarthur* 1609, *Treyarddur* 1691. 'Iarddur's farm' (Welsh *tref*). *Iarddur* owned one of the largest farms in northwest Anglesey in medieval times.

Treborough Somerset. *Traberge* 1086 (DB). 'Hill or mound growing with trees'. OE *trēow* + *beorg*.

Tredegar Blae. The town arose in the 19th cent. on land owned by Baron Tredegar, whose title came from *Tredegar*, 'Tegyr's farm' (Welsh *tref*, 'farm'), near Newport. *Cp*. NEW TREDEGAR.

Tredington Warwicks. *Tredingctun* 757, *Tredinctun* 1086 (DB). 'Estate associated with a man called Tyrdda'. OE pers. name + *-ing-* + *tūn*.

Treeton S. Yorks. *Tretone* 1086 (DB). Probably 'farmstead built with posts'. OE *trēow* + *tūn*.

Trefaldwyn. *See* MONTGOMERY.

Trefdraeth. *See* NEWPORT (Pemb).

Trefeglwys Powys. 'Farm by the church'. Welsh *tref* + *eglwys*.

Treffynnon. *See* HOLYWELL.

Trefgarn Pemb. *Traueger* 1324, *Trefgarn* 1368. 'Farm by the rock'. Welsh *tref* + *carn*.

Trefnant Denb. *Trevenant* 1661. 'Farm on the stream'. Welsh *tref* + *nant*.

Treforys. *See* MORRISTON.

Trefriw Conwy. *Treffruu* 1254. 'Farm on the hill'. Welsh *tref* + *rhiw*.

Trefwrdan. *See* JORDANSTON.

Trefyclo. *See* KNIGHTON.

Trefynwy. *See* MONMOUTH.

Tregaron Cergn. *tre garon* 1566, *Caron alias Tre Garon* 1763. 'Village on the River Caron'. Welsh *tref*. The river is named from St *Caron*, to whom the church is dedicated.

Tregatwg. *See* CADOXTON.

Tregetin. *See* KEESTON.

Treglemais Pemb. *Trefclemens* ,1326. 'Clement's farm'. Welsh *tref*.

Tregony Cornwall. *Trefhrigoni* 1049, *Treligani* 1086 (DB). Possibly 'farm of a man called *Rigni*'. Cornish *tre* + pers. name.

Trelales. *See* LALESTON.

Treletert. *See* LETTERSTON.

Tremadog Gwyd. 'Village of Madocks'. Welsh *tref*. The name is that of William Alexander *Madocks*, who gave the name of nearby PORTHMADOG.

Tremaine Cornwall. *Tremen* c.1230. 'Farm of the stone'. Cornish *tre* + *men*.

Tremarchog. *See* ST NICHOLAS (Pemb).

Trematon Cornwall. *Tremetone* 1086 (DB). Cornish *tre* 'farm' + unknown word or pers. name + OE *tūn* 'estate'.

Treneglos Cornwall. *Treneglos* 1269. 'Farm of the church'. Cornish *tre* + *an* 'the' + *eglos*.

Trent Dorset. *Trente* 1086 (DB). Originally the name of the stream here, a Celtic river-name possibly meaning 'the trespasser', i.e. 'river liable to floods'.

Trentham Staffs. *Trenham* 1086 (DB). 'Homestead or river-meadow on the River Trent'. Celtic river-name (identical with previous name) + OE *hām* or *hamm*.

Trentishoe Devon. *Trendesholt* |*sic*| 1086 (DB), *Trenlesho* 1203. 'Round hill-spur'. OE *trendel* + *hōh*.

Treopert. *See* GRANSTON.

Treorchy (*Treorci*) Rhon. 'Village on the River Orci'. Welsh *tref*. The meaning of the river name is unknown.

Tresco Isles of Scilly, Cornwall. *Trescau* 1305. 'Farm of elder-trees'. Cornish *tre* + *scaw*.

Tresimwn. *See* BONVILSTON.

Treswell Notts. *Tireswelle* 1086 (DB). 'Spring or stream of a man called *Tīr*'. OE pers. name + *wella*.

Tretire Heref. & Worcs. *Rythir* 1212. 'Long ford'. Welsh *rhyd* + *hir*.

Trevose Head Cornwall, first recorded in the 17th cent., named from a farm called Trevose which is *Trenfos* 1302, 'farm by the bank or dyke' (perhaps referring to an earlier fort), from Cornish *tre* + *an* 'the' + *fos*.

Trewalter. *See* WALTERSTON.

Trewhitt, High Northum. *Tirwit* 1150–62. Possibly 'river-bend where resinous wood is obtained'. OScand. *tyri* + OE *wiht*.

Trewyddel. *See* MOYLGROVE.

Treyford W. Sussex. *Treverde* 1086 (DB). 'Ford marked by a tree or with a tree-trunk bridge'. OE *trēow* + *ford*.

Trien (*An Trian*) Mayo. 'The third portion'.

Trillick (*Trileac*) Tyrone. (*airchindeach*) *Trelecc* 814. 'Megalithic tomb'.

Trim (*Baile Átha Troim*) Meath. 'Town of the ford of the elder tree'.

Trimdon Durham. *Tremeldon* 1196. Probably 'hill with a wooden cross'. OE *trēow* + *mǣl* + *dūn*.

Trimingham Norfolk. *Trimingeham* 1185. 'Homestead of the family or followers of a man called *Trymma*'. OE pers. name + *-inga-* + *hām*.

Trimley Suffolk. *Tremelaia* 1086 (DB). 'Woodland clearing of a man called *Trymma*'. OE pers. name + *lēah*.

Trimpley Heref. & Worcs. *Trinpelei* 1086 (DB). 'Woodland clearing of a man called *Trympa*'. OE pers. name + *lēah*.

Tring Herts. *Treunge* |*sic*| 1086 (DB), *Trehangr* 1199. 'Wooded slope'. OE *trēow* + *hangra*.

Tritlington Northum. *Turthlyngton* c.1170. 'Estate associated with a man called Tyrhtel'. OE pers. name + *-ing-* + *tūn*.

Tromman (*Tromán*) Meath. 'Little place where elders grow'.

Trommaun (*Tromán*) Roscommon. 'Little place where elders grow'.

Troon S. Ayr. *Le Trone* 1371, *Le Trune* 1464. '(Place by the) headland'. Welsh *trwyn*.

Trossachs (hills) Stir. 'Transverse hills'. The name is said to be based on Welsh *traws*, 'across', referring to the hills that divide Loch Katrine from Loch Achray.

Trostan (*Trostán*) (mountain) Antrim. *Trostan* 1780. 'Pole'.

Troston Suffolk. *Trostingtun* c.1000, *Trostuna* 1086 (DB). 'Estate associated with a man called *Trost(a)*'. OE pers. name + *-ing-* + *tūn*.

Trottiscliffe Kent. *Trottes clyva* 788, *Totesclive* |*sic*| 1086 (DB). 'Cliff or hill-slope of a man called *Trott*'. OE pers. name + *clif*.

Trotton W. Sussex. *Traitone* |*sic*| 1086 (DB), *Tratinton* 12th cent. Possibly 'estate associated with a man called *Trætt*'. OE pers. name + *-ing-* + *tūn*. Alternatively the first element may be an OE *trǣding* 'path, stepping-stones'.

Troutbeck, '(place on) the trout stream'. OE *truht* + OScand. *bekkr*: **Troutbeck** Cumbria, near Ambleside. *Trutebek* 1272. **Troutbeck** Cumbria, near Penruddock. *Troutbek* 1332.

Trowbridge Wilts. *Straburg* |*sic*| 1086 (DB), *Trobrigge* 1184. 'Tree-trunk bridge'. OE *trēow* + *brycg*.

Trowell Notts. *Trowalle* 1086 (DB). 'Tree stream', perhaps referring to a treetrunk used as a bridge. OE *trēow* + *wella*.

Trowse Newton Norfolk. *Treus*, *Newotuna* 1086 (DB). Originally two separate names, 'wooden house' from OE *trēow* + *hūs*, and 'new farmstead' from OE *nīwe* + *tūn*.

Trull Somerset, *Trendle* 1225. 'Circular feature'. OE *trendel*.

Trumpington Cambs. *Trumpintune* c.1050, *Trumpintone* 1086 (DB). 'Estate associated with a man called *Trump(a)*'. OE pers. name + *-ing-* + *tūn*.

Trunch Norfolk. *Trunchet* 1086 (DB). Possibly a Celtic name meaning 'wood on a spur of land'.

Truro Cornwall. *Triueru* c.1173. Possibly a Cornish name meaning '(place of) great water-turbulence'.

Trusham Devon. *Trisma* 1086 (DB). Possibly 'place overgrown with brushwood' from a derivative of OE *trūs*.

Trusley Derbys. *Trusselai* 1166. Possibly 'brushwood clearing'. OE *trūs* + *lēah*.

Trusthorpe Lincs. *Dreuistorp* 1086 (DB). 'Outlying farmstead or hamlet of a man called Drjúgr or Dreus'. OScand. or OFrench pers. name + OScand. *thorp*.

Trym (river) Glos., *see* WESTBURY ON TRYM.

Trysull Staffs. *Treslei* 1086 (DB). Named from the River Trysull, possibly a Celtic river-name meaning 'strongly flowing'.

Tuam (*Tuaim*) Galway. 'Mound'.

Tuamgraney (*Tuaim Gréine*) Clare. 'Grian's mound'.

Tubber (*An Tobar*) Galway. 'The well'.

Tubbrid (*Tiobraid*) Kilkenny, Tipperary. 'Well'.

Tubney Oxon. *Tobenie* 1086 (DB). 'Island, or dry ground in marsh, of a man called *Tubba'. OE pers. name (genitive -*n*) + *ēg*.

Tuddenham, 'homestead or village of a man called Tūda', OE pers. name (genitive -*n*) + *hām*: **Tuddenham** Suffolk. *Todenham* 1086 (DB). **Tuddenham, East** & **Tuddenham, North** Norfolk. *East Tudenham, Nord Tudenham* 1086 (DB).

Tudeley Kent. *Tivedele* 1086 (DB). Possibly 'wood or clearing overgrown with ivy'. OE *īfede* + *lēah*, with initial *T*- from the OE preposition *æt* 'at'.

Tudhoe Durham. *Tudhow* 1279. 'Hill-spur of a man called Tūda'. OE pers. name + *hōh*.

Tuesley Surrey. *Tiwesle* 1086 (DB). Possibly 'wood or clearing dedicated to the heathen god Tīw', from OE god-name + *lēah*. Alternatively the first element may be an OE man's name *Tīwhere.

Tuffley Glos. *Tuffelege* 1086 (DB). 'Woodland clearing of a man called Tuffa'. OE pers. name + *lēah*.

Tufnell Park Gtr. London, named from one William Tufnell, lord of the manor of Barnsbury in 1753.

Tufton Hants. *Tochiton* 1086 (DB). 'Estate associated with a man called *Toca or Tucca'. OE pers. name + -*ing*- + *tūn*.

Tugby Leics. *Tochebi* 1086 (DB). 'Farmstead or village of a man called Tóki'. OScand. pers. name + *bý*.

Tugford Shrops. *Dodefort* |sic| 1086 (DB), *Tuggeford* *c*.1138. 'Ford of a man called *Tucga'. OE pers. name + *ford*.

Tulla (*Tulach*) Clare. 'Hill'.

Tullagh (*Tulach*) Donegal. 'Hill'.

Tullaghan (*Tulachán*) Leitrim, Sligo. 'Little hill'.

Tullaghanmore (*Tulachán Mór*) Westmeath. 'Big hillock'.

Tullagher (*Tulachar*) Kilkenny. 'Hilly place'.

Tullaghoge (*Tulach Óg*) Tyrone. (*oe*) *Telach Occ* 913. 'Hillock of the youths'.

Tullaherin (*Tulach Thirim*) Kilkenny. 'Dry hill'.

Tullakeel (*Tulach Chaoil*) Kerry. 'Narrow hill'.

Tullamore (*Tulach Mhór*) Kerry, Offaly. 'Big hill'.

Tullibody Clac. *Tullibotheny* 1195. 'Hill of the hut'. Gaelic *tulach* + *both*.

Tullow (*An Tulach*) Carlow. 'The hill'.

Tullroan (*Tulach Ruáin*) Kilkenny. 'Ruán's hill'.

Tully (*Tulach*) Galway. 'Hill'.

Tullyallen (*Tulaigh Álainn*) Louth. 'Beautiful hill'.

Tullyco (*Tulaigh Chuach*) Cavan. 'Cuckoo hill'.

Tullycrine (*Tulach an Chrainn*) Limerick. 'Hill of the tree'.

Tullylish (*Tulach Lis*) Down. 'Hill of the fort'.

Tullyrone (*Tulaigh Uí Ruáin*) Armagh. *Tulliroan* 1611. 'Ó Ruáin's hill'.

Tullyvin (*Tulaigh Bhinn*) Cavan. *Tullyvin* 1835. Possibly 'hill of the peak'.

Tulrahan (*Tulach Shrutháin*) Mayo. 'Hill of the stream'.

Tulse Hill Gtr. London, named from the Tulse family, recorded as living here in the 17th cent.

Tumby Lincs. *Tunbi* 1086 (DB). Possibly 'farmstead or village of a man called Tumi'. OScand. pers. name + *bý*. Alternatively the first element may be OE *tūn* or OScand. *tún* 'enclosure'.

Tummel (river) Perth. *Abhain Teimheil* n.d. '(River of) darkness'. OGaelic *temel. The name alludes to the river's heavily wooded gorges.

Tunbridge Wells Kent, named from TONBRIDGE, *Wells* referring to the medicinal springs here discovered in the 17th cent. The affix *Royal* was bestowed on the town by Edward VII.

Tunnyduff (*Tonnach Dhubh*) Cavan. 'Black quagmire'.

Tunstall, found in various countries, from OE *tūn-stall* 'the site of a farm, a farmstead'; examples include: **Tunstall** Kent. *Tunestelle* 1086 (DB). **Tunstall** Staffs., near Stoke. *Tunstal* 1212. **Tunstall** Suffolk. *Tunestal* 1086 (DB).

Tunstead Norfolk. *Tunstede* 1044–7, *Tunesteda* 1086 (DB). OE *tūn-stede* 'farmstead'.

Tunworth Hants. *Tuneworde* 1086 (DB). Probably 'enclosure of a man called Tunna'. OE pers. name + *worth*.

Tuosist (*Tuath Ó Síosta*) Kerry. 'Territory of the Uí Síosta'.

Tupsley Heref. & Worcs. *Topeslage* 1086 (DB). Possibly 'ram's woodland clearing'. ME *tup* (or a byname formed from this word) + OE *lēah*.

Tur Langton Leics., *see* LANGTON.

Ture (*An tIúr*) Donegal. 'The yew tree'.

Turkdean Glos. *Turcandene* 716–43, *Turchedene* 1086 (DB). 'Valley of a river called *Turce*'. Lost Celtic river-name (probably meaning 'boar') + OE *denu*.

Turlough (*Turlach*) Mayo. 'Fen'.

Turloughmore (*An Turlach Mór*) Galway. 'The large fen'.

Turnastone Heref. & Worcs. *Thurneistun* 1242. 'Estate of a family called de Turnei'. OE *tūn*, with the name of a family recorded in the area in the 12th cent.

Suir (*Siúr*) **Puddle** Dorset. *Pidele* 1086 (DB), *Tonerespydele* Estate on the River Piddle held by the Toner gully of . OE river-name (**pidele* 'a marsh or fen') with e of family here from 1086.

Sulgrav

Sulh rnhouse Edin. Obscure.
by a

Su rnworth Dorset. *Torneworde* 1086 (DB). 'Thorn-bush nclosure'. OE *thyrne* + *worth*.

Turreagh (*Tor Riabhach*) Antrim. *Torreagh* 1659. 'Grey crag'.

Turriff Aber. *Turrech* 1273, *Turreth* c.1300, *Turreff* c.1500. Obscure.

Turton Bottoms Lancs. *Turton* 1212. 'Farmstead or village of a man called Thóri or Thórr'. OScand. pers. name + OE *tūn*. Affix is from OE *botm* 'valley bottom'.

Turvey Beds. *Torueie* 1086 (DB). 'Island with good turf or grass'. OE *turf* + *ēg*.

Turville Bucks. *Thyrefeld* 796. Dry open land'. OE *thyre* + *feld*.

Turweston Bucks. *Turvestone* 1086 (DB). Possibly 'farmstead or village of a man called Thorfrothr or *Thorfastr'. OScand. pers. name + OE *tūn*.

Tutbury Staffs. *Toteberia* 1086 (DB), *Stutesberia* c.1150. 'Stronghold of a man called Tutta or *Stūt'. OE pers. name + *burh* (dative *byrig*).

Tutnall Heref. & Worcs. *Tothehel* |sic| 1086 (DB), *Tottenhull* 1262. 'Hill of a man called Totta'. OE pers. name (genitive -*n*) + *hyll*.

Tuttington Norfolk. *Tutincghetuna* 1086 (DB). 'Estate associated with a man called Tutta'. OE pers. name + -*ing*- + *tūn*.

Tuxford Notts. *Tuxfarne* |sic| 1086 (DB), *Tukesford* 12th cent. Possibly 'ford of a man called *Tuk', OScand. pers. name + OE *ford*, but the first element may be an early form of *tusk* 'tussock, tuft of rushes'.

Tweed (river) Sc. Bord. *Tuidi fluminis* c.730, *Twiode* c.1025. Possibly 'powerful one'. British **Tuesis*.

Tweedmouth Northum. *Tuedemue* 1208–10. 'Mouth of the River Tweed'. Celtic or pre-Celtic river-name (possibly meaning 'powerful one') + OE *mūtha*.

Twelve Pins, The (*Beanna Beola*) (mountains) Galway. 'Twelve peaks'. English *pin* is Irish *binn*, 'peak'. The Irish name means 'peaks of Beola'.

Twemlow Green Ches. *Twamlawe* 12th cent. '(Place at) the two tumuli'. OE *twēgen* (dative *twǣm*) + *hlāw*.

Twickenham Gtr. London. *Tuicanhom* 704. Probably 'land in a river-bend of a man called *Twicca'. OE pers. name (genitive -*n*) + *hamm*. Alternatively the first element may be OE **twicce* 'river-fork'.

Twigworth Glos. *Tuiggewrthe* 1216. Possibly 'enclosure of a man called Twicga', OE pers. name + *worth*. Alternatively 'enclosure made with twigs', from OE *twigge*.

Twineham W. Sussex. *Tuineam* late 11th cent. '(Place) between the streams'. OE *betwēonan* + *ēa* (dative plural *ēam*).

Twinstead Essex. *Tumesteda* |sic| 1086 (DB), *Twinstede* 1203. Probably 'double homestead'. OE *twinn* + *stede*.

Twitchen Devon. *Twechon* 1442. OE *twicen*(*e*) 'crossroads'.

Twomileborris (*Buiríos Léith*) Tipperary. Twomileborris is two Irish miles from Leighmore (Leamakevoge), whose Irish name is *Liath Mór Mo-Chaomhóg*, 'big grey place of my little Kevin'. Hence its Irish name, meaning 'borough of Liath'.

Twycross Leics. *Tvicros* 1086 (DB). '(Place with) two crosses'. OE *twi*- + *cros*.

Twyford, found in various counties, 'double ford'. OE **twī-ford* or **twī-fyrde*; examples include: **Twyford** Berks. *Tuiford* 1170. **Twyford** Hants. *Tuifyrde* c.970, *Tviforde* 1086 (DB).

Twyning Glos. *Bituinæum* 814, *Tveninge* 1086 (DB). Originally '(place) between the rivers' from OE *betwēonan* + *ēa* (dative *ēam*), later 'settlement of those living there' with the addition of OE -*ingas*.

Twywell Northants. *Twiwel* 1013, *Tuiwella* 1086 (DB). 'Double spring or stream'. OE *twi*- + *wella*.

Ty-nant Conwy. 'House in the valley'. Welsh *tŷ* + *nant*.

Tydd St Giles (Cambs.) & **Tydd St Mary** (Lincs.). *Tid* 1086 (DB). Probably OE **tydd* 'shrubs or brushwood'. Distinguishing affixes from the church dedications.

Tyddewi. See ST DAVID'S.

Tyfarnham (*Teach Farannáin*) Westmeath. 'Farannán's house'.

Tyldesley Gtr. Manch. *Tildesleia* c.1210. 'Woodland clearing of a man called Tilwald'. OE pers. name + *lēah*.

Tyler Hill Kent. *Tylerhelde* 1304. 'Slope of the tile-makers'. OE **tiglere* + *helde*.

Tynagh (*Tíne*) Galway. 'Watercourse'.

Tynan (*Tuínéan*) Armagh. (*airchindeach*) *Tuidnidha* 1072. 'Watercourse'.

Tyndyrn. See TINTERN.

Tyne & Wear (new county), named from the Rivers Tyne and Wear, *see* TYNEMOUTH, MONKWEARMOUTH.

Tyneham Dorset. *Tigeham* 1086 (DB). Probably 'goat's enclosure'. OE **tige* (genitive -*an*) + *hamm*.

Tynemouth Tyne & Wear. *Tinanmuthe* 792. 'Mouth of the River Tyne'. Celtic or pre-Celtic river-name (meaning simply 'river') + OE *mūtha*. The district-name **Tyneside** is named from the same river.

Tyrella (*Teach Riala*) Down. (*o*) *Thigh Riaghla* c.1630. 'Riail's church'.

Tyringham Bucks. *Telingham* |sic| 1086 (DB), *Tringeham* 1130. 'Homestead or river-meadow of the family or followers of a man called *Tīr(a)'. OE pers. name + -*inga*- + *hām* or *hamm*.

Tyrone (*Tir Eoghain*) (the county). (*tighernuis*) *Thíre hEoghain* c.1500. 'Territory of Eoghan'.

Tyrrellspass (*Bealach an Tirialaigh*) Westmeath. In 1597 Captain Richard *Tyrrell* and Piers Lacy ambushed and defeated an English force on the road here. The Irish name means 'Tyrrell's road'.

Tysoe Warwicks. *Tiheshoche* 1086 (DB). Probably 'hill-spur of the heathen god Tīw'. OE god-name + *hōh*.

Tytherington, 'estate associated with a man called
*Tydre', OE pers. name + *-ing-* + *tūn*, or 'stock-breeding
farmstead', with an OE *tȳd(d)ring* as first element:
Tytherington Ches. *Tidderington c.*1245. **Tytherington** S.
Glos. *Tidrentune* 1086 (DB). **Tytherington** Wilts. *Tuderinton*
1242.

Tytherleigh Devon. *Tiderlege* 12th cent. Probably 'young
wood or clearing', referring to new growth. OE
tīedre + *lēah*.

Tytherley, East & *Tytherley, West* Hants. *Tiderlei* 1086
(DB). Identical in origin with the previous name.

Tytherton Lucas & *East Tytherton* Wilts. *Tedrintone*
1086 (DB). Identical in origin with TYTHERINGTON. Manorial affix from the Lucas family, here in the 13th cent.

Tywardreath Cornwall. *Tiwardrai* 1086 (DB). 'House on
the beach'. Cornish *ti* + *war* + *treth*.

Tywi Valley Carm. 'Valley of the River Tywi'. The Tywi
(Towy) has a Celtic name that may mean 'the dark one'.

Tywyn Gwyd. *Thewyn* 1254, *Tewyn* 1291, *Towyn, or
Tywyn* 1868. '(Place by the) seashore'. Welsh *tywyn*.

U

Up as affix, *see* main name, e.g. for **Up Cerne** (Dorset) *see* CERNE.

Uamh Bheag (mountain) Stir. '(Mountain with the) little cave'. Gaelic *uamh* + *beag* (feminine *bheag*).

Ubbeston Green Suffolk. *Upbestuna* 1086 (DB). 'Farmstead or village of a man called Ubbi'. OScand. pers. name + OE *tūn*.

Ubley B. & NE. Som. *Hubbanlege* late 10th cent., *Tumbeli* |*sic*| 1086 (DB). 'Woodland clearing of a man called Ubba'. OE pers. name + *lēah*.

Uckerby N. Yorks. *Ukerby* 1198. 'Farmstead or village of a man called *Úkyrri or *Útkári'. OScand. pers. name + *bý*.

Uckfield E. Sussex. *Uckefeld* 1220. 'Open land of a man called Ucca'. OE pers. name + *feld*.

Uckington Glos. *Hochinton* 1086 (DB). 'Estate associated with a man called Ucca'. OE pers. name + *-ing-* + *tūn*.

Uddingston S. Lan. *Odistoun* 1296, *Odingstoune* 1475. 'Odda's farm'. OE pers. name + *tūn*.

Udimore E. Sussex. *Dodimere* |*sic*| 1086 (DB), *Odumer* 12th cent. Possibly 'woody pond'. OE *wudig* + *mere*.

Ufficulme Devon. *Offecoma* 1086 (DB). 'Estate on the Culm river held by a man called Uffa'. OE pers. name + Celtic river-name (*see* CULLOMPTON).

Uffington, 'estate associated with a man called Uffa', OE pers. name + *-ing-* + *tūn*. **Uffington** Lincs. *Offintone* 1086 (DB). **Uffington** Shrops. *Ofitone* 1086 (DB).

Uffington Oxon. *Uffentune* 10th cent., *Offentone* 1086 (DB). 'Estate of a man called Uffa'. OE pers. name (genitive *-n*) + *tūn*.

Ufford, 'enclosure of a man called Uffa', OE pers. name + *worth*: **Ufford** Cambs. *Uffawyrtha* 948. **Ufford** Suffolk. *Uffeworda* 1086 (DB).

Ufton Warwicks. *Hulhtune* 1043, *Ulchetone* 1086 (DB). Possibly 'farmstead with a shed or hut'. OE * *huluc* + *tūn*.

Ufton Nervet Berks. *Offetune* 1086 (DB), *Offeton Nernut* 1284 'Farmstead or village of a man called Uffa'. OE pers. name + *tūn*. Manorial affix from the Neyrnut family, here in the 13th cent.

Ugborough Devon. *Ulgeberge* |*sic*| 1086 (DB), *Uggeberge* 1200. 'Hill or mound of a man called *Ugga'. OE pers. name + *beorg*.

Uggeshall Suffolk. *Uggiceheala* 1086 (DB). 'Nook of land of a man called *Uggeca'. OE pers. name + *halh*.

Ugglebarnby N. Yorks. *Ugleberdesbi* 1086 (DB). 'Farmstead or village of a man called *Uglubárthr'. OScand. pers. name + *bý*.

Ugley Essex. *Uggele* *c*.1041, *Ugghelea* 1086 (DB). 'Woodland clearing of a man called *Ugga'. OE pers. name + *lēah*.

Ugthorpe N. Yorks. *Ughetorp* 1086 (DB). 'Outlying farmstead or hamlet of a man called Uggi'. OScand. pers. name + *thorp*.

Uig Highland (Skye). *Wig* 1512. '(Place by a) bay'. Gaelic *ùig* (from OScand. *vik*).

Uig W. Isles (Lewis). *Vye* 1549. '(Place by a) bay'. Gaelic *ùig* (from OScand. *vik*).

Uisge Labhair (river) Highland. 'Noisy water'. Gaelic *uisge* + *labhar*.

Uist (island) W. Isles. *Iuist* 1282, *Ouiste* 1373. Scand. 'inner abode'. OScand. *i* + *vist*. This is a Scandinavian re-interpretation of a pre-Celtic name.

Ulbster Highland. *Ulbister* 1538. 'Wolf's dwelling'. OScand. *ulfr* + *bólstathr*.

Ulceby, 'farmstead or village of a man called Ulfr', OScand. pers. name + *bý*: **Ulceby** Lincs. *Ulesbi* 1086 (DB). **Ulceby** N. Lincs. *Ulvesbi* 1086 (DB).

Ulcombe Kent. *Ulancumbe* 946, *Olecumbe* 1086 (DB). 'Valley of the owl'. OE *ūle* + *cumb*.

Uldale Cumbria. *Ulvesdal* 1216. 'Valley of a man called Ulfr, or one frequented by wolves'. OScand. pers. name or *ulfr* + *dalr*.

Uley Glos. *Euuelege* 1086 (DB). 'Yew-tree wood or clearing'. OE *īw* + *lēah*.

Ulgham Northum. *Wlacam* 1139, *Ulweham* 1242 'Valley or nook frequented by owls'. OE *ūle* + *hwamm*.

Ullapool Highland. *Ullabill* 1610. 'Wolf's dwelling'. OScand. *ulfr* + *boelí*.

Ullard (*Ulaidh Ard*) Kilkenny. 'High penitential station'.

Ullauns (*Ulán*) Kilkenny. 'Penitential station'.

Ullenhall Warwicks. *Holehale* 1086 (DB). 'Nook of land of a man called *Ulla'. OE pers. name (genitive *-n*) + *halh*.

Ulleskelf N. Yorks. *Oleschel* |*sic*| 1086 (DB), *Ulfskelf* 1170–7. 'Shelf or bank of a man called Ulfr'. OScand. pers. name + *skjalf* or OE *scelf* (with Scand. *sk-*).

Ullesthorpe Leics. *Ulestorp* 1086 (DB). 'Outlying farmstead or hamlet of a man called Ulfr'. OScand. pers. name + *thorp*.

Ulley S. Yorks. *Ollei* 1086 (DB). Probably 'woodland clearing frequented by owls'. OE *ūle* + *lēah*.

Ullingswick Heref. & Worcs. *Ullingwic* 1086 (DB). 'Dwelling or (dairy) farm associated with a man called *Ulla'. OE pers. name + *-ing-* + *wīc*.

Ullock Cumbria, near Mockerkin. *Uluelaik* 1279. 'Place where wolves play'. OScand. *ulfr* + *leikr*.

Ullswater Cumbria. *Ulueswater* c.1230. 'Lake of a man called Ulfr'. OScand. pers. name + OE *wæter*.

Ulpha Cumbria, near Coniston. *Wolfhou* 1279. 'Hill frequented by wolves'. OScand. *ulfr* + *haugr*.

Ulrome E. R. Yorks. *Ulfram* 1086 (DB). Probably 'homestead or village of a man called Wulfhere or a woman called Wulfwaru'. OE pers. name + *hām*.

Ulster (*Ulaidh*) (the province). 'Land of the Ulstermen'. *Ouolountoi* c.150. OScand. possessive *s* + Irish *tír*. The meaning of the tribal name is obscure.

Ulverston Cumbria. *Ulurestun* 1086 (DB). 'Farmstead or village of a man called Wulfhere or Ulfarr'. OE or OScand. pers. name + OE *tūn*.

Umberleigh Devon. *Umberlei* 1086 (DB), *Wumberlegh* 1270. Possibly 'woodland clearing by the meadow stream'. OE *winn* + *burna* + *lēah*.

Ummamore (*Iomaidh*) Westmeath. 'Contention'.

Ummeraboy (*Iomaire Buí*) Cork. 'Yellow ridge'.

Ummeracam (*Iomaire Cam*) Armagh. 'Crooked ridge'.

Umrycam (*Iomaire Cam*) Derry, Donegal. 'Crooked ridge'.

Underbarrow Cumbria. *Underbarroe* 1517. '(Place) under the hill'. OE *under* + *beorg*.

Underriver Kent. *Sub le Ryver* 1477. '(Place) under the hill-brow'. OE *under* + *yfer*.

Underwood Notts. *Underwode* 1287. '(Place) within or near a wood'. OE *under* + *wudu*.

Unst (island) Shet. *Ornyst* c.1200. Pre-Scand. name.

Unstone Derbys. *Onestune* 1086 (DB). Probably 'farmstead or village of a man called *Ōn*'. OE pers. name + *tūn*.

Unthank Cumbria, near Gamblesby. *Unthank* 1254. '(Land held) without consent', i.e. 'a squatter's holding'. OE *unthanc*. There are other examples of the name in Northumberland and Cumbria.

Upavon Wilts. *Oppavrene* 1086 (DB). '(Settlement) higher up the River Avon'. OE *upp* + Celtic river-name (meaning simply 'river').

Upchurch Kent. *Upcyrcean* c.1100 'Church standing high up'. OE *upp* + *cirice*.

Upham Hants. *Upham* 1201. 'Upper homestead or enclosure'. OE *upp* + *hām* or *hamm*.

Uphill Somerset. *Opopille* 1086 (DB). '(Place) above the creek'. OE *uppan* + *pyll*.

Upleadon Glos. *Ledene* 1086 (DB), *Upleden* 1253. '(Settlement) higher up the River Leadon'. OE *upp* + Celtic river-name (see HIGHLEADON).

Upleatham Red. & Cleve. *Upelider* 1086 (DB), *Uplithum* c.1150. '(Place at) the upper slopes'. OE *upp* + *hlith*, or OScand. *upp(i)* + *hlíth*, in a dative plural form.

Uplowman Devon. *Oppaluma* 1086 (DB). '(Settlement) higher up the River Loman'. OE *upp* + Celtic river-name (probably meaning 'elm river').

Uplyme Devon, *Lim* 1086 (DB), *Uplim* 1238. '(Settlement) higher up the River Lim'. OE *upp* + Celtic river-name (meaning simply 'stream').

Upminster Gtr. London. *Upmunstra* 1086 (DB). 'Higher minster or church'. OE *upp* + *mynster*.

Upottery Devon. *Upoteri* 1005, *Otri* 1086 (DB). '(Settlement) higher up the River Otter'. OE *upp* + river-name (see OTTERY).

Upper as affix, see main name, e.g. for **Upper Arley** (Heref. & Worcs.) see ARLEY.

Upperland (*Áth an Phoirt Leathain*) Derry. *Aghfortlany* 1613. 'Ford of the broad (river) bank'. The English name arose from a garbled pronunciation of the Irish.

Upperthong W. Yorks. *Thwong* 1274, *Overthong* 1286. 'Narrow strip of land'. OE *thwang*, with *uferra* 'upper' to distinguish it from NETHERTHONG.

Uppingham Rutland. *Yppingeham* 1067. 'Homestead or village of the hill-dwellers'. OE *yppe* + *-inga-* + *hām*.

Uppington Shrops. *Opetone* 1086 (DB), *Oppinton* 1195. Possibly 'estate associated with a man called *Uppa*'. OE pers. name + *-ing-* + *tūn*.

Upsall N. Yorks., near Thirsk. *Upsale* 1086 (DB). 'Higher dwelling(s)'. OScand. *upp* + *salr*.

Upton, a common name, usually 'higher farmstead or village', OE *upp* + *tūn*; examples include: **Upton** Berks., near Slough. *Opetone* 1086 (DB). **Upton** Ches., near Birkenhead. *Optone* 1086 (DB). **Upton** Dorset, near Lytchett. *Upton* 1463. **Upton Cheyney** S. Glos. *Vppeton* 1190, *Upton Chaune* 1325. Manorial affix from the Cheyney family. **Upton Grey** Hants. *Upton* 1202, *Upton Grey* 1281. Manorial affix from the de Grey family, here in the 13th cent. **Upton Hellions** Devon. *Uppetone Hyliun* 1270. Manorial affix from the de Helihun family, here in the 13th cent. **Upton Pyne** Devon. *Opetone* 1264, *Uppetone Pyn* 1283. Manorial affix from the de Pyn family, here in the 13th cent. **Upton St Leonards** Glos. *Optune* 1086 (DB), *Upton Sancti Leonardi* 1287. Affix from the dedication of the church. **Upton Scudamore** Wilts. *Uptune* c.990, *Upton* 1086 (DB), *Upton Squydemor* 1275. Manorial affix from the de Skydemore family, here in the 13th cent. **Upton Snodsbury** Heref. & Worcs. *Snoddesbyri* 972, *Snodesbyrie* 1086 (DB), *Upton juxta Snodebure* 1280. Originally two separate names, the earlier being 'stronghold of a man called *Snodd*', OE pers. name + *burh* (dative *byrig*). **Upton upon Severn** Heref. & Worcs. *Uptune* 897, *Uptun* 1086 (DB).

However the following has a different origin: **Upton Lovell** Wilts. *Ubbantun* 957, *Ubbedon Lovell* 1476. 'Farmstead or village of a man called Ubba'. OE pers. name + *tūn*, with manorial affix from the Lovell family, here in the 15th cent.

Upwaltham W. Sussex. *Waltham* 1086 (DB), *Up Waltham* 1371. 'Homestead or village in a forest'. OE *w(e)ald* + *hām*, with *upp* 'higher'.

Upwell Cambs./Norfolk. *Wellan* 963, *Upwell* 1221. '(Place) higher up the stream'. OE *wella* with affix *upp* to distinguish it from OUTWELL.

Upwey Dorset. *Wai(e)* 1086 (DB), *Uppeweie* 1241. '(Settlement) higher up the River Wey'. Pre-English river-name (*see* WEYMOUTH) with OE *upp*.

Upwood Cambs. *Upwude* 974, *Upehude |sic|* 1086 (DB). 'Higher wood'. OE *upp* + *wudu*.

Urbalreagh (*Earball Riabhach*) Derry. 'Grey end piece'.

Urchfont Wilts. *Ierchesfonte* 1086 (DB). 'Spring of a man called *Eohrīc*. OE pers. name + *funta*.

Urishay Heref. & Worcs. *Haya Hurri* 1242. 'Enclosure of a man called Wulfrīc'. OE pers. name + *hæg*.

Urlingford (*Áth na nUrlainn*) Kilkenny. 'Ford of the shafts'.

Urmston Gtr. Manch. *Wermeston* 1194. 'Farmstead or village of a man called *Wyrm* or Urm'. OE or OScand. pers. name + OE *tūn*.

Urquhart Fife. *Petnaurcha* 1128. 'Portion of the cast'. Pictish *pett* + OGaelic *aurchoir*. The reference is perhaps to a method of allocating land.

Urquhart Highland. *Airchardan c*.1100 '(Place by a) thicket'. British *air cardden*.

Urrin (*Urrainn*) (river) Wexford. 'Division'.

Urswick, Great & *Urswick, Little*, Cumbria. *Ursewica c*.1150. 'Dwelling or (dairy) farm by the bison lake'. OE *ūr* + *sǣ* + *wīc*.

Ushaw Moor Durham. *Ulveskahe* 12th cent. Probably 'small wood frequented by wolves'. OE *wulf* + *scaga*.

Usk (*Brynbuga*) Mon. *Uscha* 1100, *Uisc* 1150. '(Place on the) River Usk'. The Celtic river name may mean 'abounding in fish' or alternatively simply 'water'. The Welsh name means 'Buga's hill' (Welsh *bryn*).

Usselby Lincs. *Osoluebi c*.1115. 'Farmstead or village of a man called Ōswulf'. OE pers. name + OScand. *bý*.

Utterby Lincs. *Uthterby* 1150–60. Probably 'farmstead or village of a man called Ūhtrēd'. OE pers. name + OScand. *bý*.

Uttoxeter Staffs. *Wotocheshede* 1086 (DB). Probably 'heath of a man called *Wuttuc*'. OE pers. name + *hæddre*.

Uxbridge Gtr. London. *Wixebrug c*.1145. 'Bridge of the tribe called *Wixan*'. OE tribal name + *brycg*.

Uzmaston Pemb. *Villa Osmundi* 1230. 'Osmund's farm'. OE pers. name + *tūn*.

V

Vale Royal Ches. *Vallis Regalis* 1277, *Valroyal* 1357. 'Royal valley', the site of a monastery founded by Edward I. OFrench *val* + *roial* (in Latin in the first spelling).

Vale of White Horse (district) Oxon. *The vale of Whithors* 1368. Named from the pre-historic figure of a horse cut into the chalk on White Horse Hill.

Valencia (*Dairbhre*) Kerry. 'Place of oaks'. The English name represents Irish *Béal Inse*, 'estuary of the island'.

Valley (*Y Fali*) Angl. 'The valley'. The name refers to the valley-like cutting from which rubble was extracted to build the Stanley Embankment from mainland Anglesey to Holy Island in the 1820s.

Vange Essex. *Fengge* 963, *Phenge* 1086 (DB). 'Fen or marsh district'. OE *fenn* + **gē*.

Vaternish (peninsula) Highland (Skye). *Watternes* 1501. 'Water promontory'. OScand. *vatr* + *nes* probably influenced by English *water*.

Vauxhall Gtr. London. *Faukeshale* 1279. 'Hall or manor of a man called *Falkes*'. OFrench pers. name + OE *hall*.

Velly Devon, *see* CLOVELLY.

Venn Ottery Devon, *see* OTTERY.

Ventnor I. of Wight. '(Farm of) Vintner' 1617. Probably a manorial name from a family called le Vyntener. The old name of Ventnor was *Holeweia* c.1200, 'the hollow way, or the way in a hollow', from OE *hol* + *weg*.

Ventry (*Fionntrá*) Kerry. 'White strand'.

Vernham Dean Hants. *Ferneham* 1210. 'Homestead or enclosure where ferns grow'. OE *fearn* + *hām* or *hamm*, with the later addition of *denu* 'valley'.

Verwood Dorset. *Beuboys* 1288, *Fairwod* 1329. 'Beautiful wood'. OE *fæger* + *wudu* (alternating with OFrench *beu* + *bois* in the earliest spelling).

Veryan Cornwall. *Sanctus Symphorianus* 1281. From the dedication of the church to St Symphorian.

Vexford, Lower Somerset. *Fescheforde* 1086 (DB). Possibly 'fresh-water ford'. OE *fersc* + *ford*.

Victoria Bridge Tyrone. A bridge was built here in 1842 and named after Queen Victoria.

Vigo Village Kent, modern name apparently commemorating the capture of the Spanish port of Vigo by the British fleet in 1719.

Vilanstown (*Baile na Bhileanach*) Westmeath. *Villenston* c.1590. 'Farmstead of the villeins'.

Vine's Cross E. Sussex, a late name from *cross* 'cross-roads', to be associated with a local family called Vyne recorded from the 16th cent.

Virginia Cavan. *Virginia* 1611. The town, founded in 1611 and originally named *Lough Ramor*, was soon after renamed for the newly-established colony of Virginia in America. Its Irish name is *Achad an Iúir*, 'field of the yew tree'.

Virginia Water Surrey, first recorded in 1749, originally a fanciful name for the artificial lake created here in 1748 by the Duke of Cumberland (earlier Governor of Virginia in America).

Virginstow Devon. *Virginestowe* c.1180. 'Holy place of (St Bridget) the Virgin'. Saint's name (from the dedication of the church) + OE *stōw*.

Vobster Somerset. *Fobbestor* 1234. 'Rocky hill of a man called *Fobb'. OE pers. name + *torr*.

Voe Shet. '(Place by a) little bay'. OScand. *vágr*.

Vowchurch Heref. & Worcs. *Fowchirche* 1291. 'Coloured church'. OE *fāh* + *cirice*.

Vyrnwy, Lake (reservoir) Powys. 'Lake of the River Vyrnwy'. The Welsh form of the river name is *Efyrnwy*, possibly a personal name based on *ebur* 'yew-tree' (as well as 'cow-parsnip') (Welsh *efwr*).

W

Wackerfield Durham. *Wacarfeld c.*1050. Probably 'open land where osiers grow'. OE **wācor* + *feld*.

Wacton Norfolk. *Waketuna* 1086 (DB). 'Farmstead or village of a man called *Waca'. OE pers. name + *tūn*.

Wadborough Heref. & Worcs. *Wadbeorgas* 972, *Wadberge* 1086 (DB). 'Hills where woad grows'. OE *wād* + *beorg*.

Waddesdon Bucks. *Votesdone* 1086 (DB). 'Hill of a man called *Weott'. OE pers. name + *dūn*.

Waddingham Lincs. *Wadingeham* 1086 (DB). 'Homestead of the family or followers of a man called Wada'. OE pers. name + *-inga-* + *hām*.

Waddington, 'estate associated with a man called Wada', OE pers. name + *-ing-* + *tūn*: **Waddington** Lancs. *Widitun |sic|* 1086 (DB), *Wadingtun c.*1231. **Waddington** Lincs. *Wadintune* 1086 (DB).

Waddon Gtr. London. *Waddone c.*1115. 'Hill where woad grows'. OE *wād* + *dūn*.

Wadebridge Cornwall. *Wade* 1358, *Wadebrygge* 1478. OE *wǣd* 'a ford' with the later addition of *brycg* from the 15th cent. when a bridge was built.

Wadenhoe Northants. *Wadenho* 1086 (DB). 'Hill-spur of a man called Wada'. OE pers. name (genitive -n) + *hōh*.

Wadhurst E. Sussex. *Wadehurst* 1253. 'Wooded hill of a man called Wada'. OE pers. name + *hyrst*.

Wadshelf Derbys. *Wadescel* 1086 (DB). 'Shelf or level ground of a man called Wada'. OE pers. name + *scelf*.

Wadworth S. Yorks. *Wadewrde* 1086 (DB). 'Enclosure of a man called Wada'. OE pers. name + *worth*.

Wainfleet All Saints Lincs. *Wenflet* 1086 (DB). 'Creek or stream that can be crossed by a wagon'. OE *wægn* + *flēot*. Affix from the dedication of the church.

Waitby Cumbria. *Watebi c.*1170. 'Wet farmstead'. OScand. *vátr* + *bý*.

Wakefield W. Yorks. *Wachefeld* 1086 (DB). 'Open land where wakes or festivals take place'. OE **wacu* + *feld*.

Wakering, Great & *Wakering, Little* Essex. *Wacheringa* 1086 (DB). '(Settlement of) the family or followers of a man called Wacer'. OE pers. name + *-ingas*.

Wakerley Northants. *Wacherlei* 1086 (DB). 'Woodland clearing of the watchful ones, or where osiers grow'. OE *wacor* (genitive plural *wacra*) or **wācor* + *feld*.

Wakes Colne Essex, *see* COLNE.

Walberswick Suffolk. *Walberdeswike* 1199. 'Dwelling or (dairy) farm of a man called Walbert'. OGerman pers. name + OE *wīc*.

Walberton W. Sussex. *Walburgetone* 1086 (DB). 'Farmstead or village of a woman called Wealdburh or Waldburg'. OE or OGerman pers. name + *tūn*.

Walcot, *Walcote*, *Walcott*, 'cottage(s) of the Britons', OE *walh* (genitive plural *wala*) + *cot*; examples include: **Walcot** Lincs., near Folkingham. *Walecote* 1086 (DB). **Walcote** Leics. *Walecote* 1086 (DB). **Walcott** Norfolk. *Walecota* 1086 (DB).

Walden, 'valley of the Britons', OE *walh* (genitive plural *wala*) + *denu*: **Walden** N. Yorks. *Waldene* 1270. **Walden, King's** & **Walden, Paul's** Herts. *Waledene* 888, *Waldene* 1086 (DB). Distinguishing affixes from possession by the King in 1086 and by St Paul's in London from 1544. **Walden, Saffron** Essex. *Wealadene c.*1000, *Waledana* 1086 (DB), *Saffornewalden* 1582. Affix (ME *safron*) refers to the cultivation of the saffron plant here.

Walden Stubbs N. Yorks., *see* STUBBS.

Walderslade Kent. *Waldeslade* 1190. 'Valley in a forest'. OE *weald* + *slæd*.

Walderton W. Sussex. *Walderton* 1168. 'Farmstead or village of a man called Wealdhere'. OE pers. name + *tūn*.

Waldingfield, Great & *Waldingfield, Little* Suffolk. *Wealdingafeld c.*995, *Waldingefelda* 1086 (DB). 'Open land of the forest dwellers'. OE *weald* + *-inga-* + *feld*.

Walditch Dorset. *Waldic* 1086 (DB). 'Ditch with a wall or embankment'. OE *weall* or *walu* + *dīc*.

Waldridge Durham. *Walrigge* 1297. Probably 'ridge with or by a wall'. OE *wall* + *hrycg*.

Waldringfield Suffolk. *Waldringfeld c.*950, *Waldringafelda* 1086 (DB). 'Open land of the family or followers of a man called Waldhere'. OE pers. name + *-inga-* + *feld*.

Waldron E. Sussex. *Waldrene* 1086 (DB). 'House in the forest'. OE *weald* + *ærn*.

Wales S. Yorks. *Wales* 1086 (DB). '(Settlement of) the Britons'. OE *walh* (plural *walas*). This place-name is thus identical in origin with Wales, the name of the principality.

Wales (*Cymru*). '(Land of the) foreigners'. OE *walh* (plural *walas*). The name was used by the Anglo-Saxons of the 'alien' Celts. The Welsh name has a Celtic meaning 'compatriot'.

Walesby, 'farmstead or village of a man called Valr', OScand. pers. name + *bý*: **Walesby** Lincs. *Walesbi* 1086 (DB). **Walesby** Notts. *Walesbi* 1086 (DB).

Walford Heref. & Worcs., near Ross. *Walecford* 1086 (DB). 'Briton ford'. OE *walh* + *ford*.

Walford Heref. & Worcs., near Wigmore. *Waliforde* 1086 (DB). Probably 'ford near a spring'. OE *wælla* + *ford*.

Walford Shrops. *Waleford* 1086 (DB). Identical in origin with the previous name.

Walgherton Ches. *Walcretune* 1086 (DB). 'Farmstead or village of a man called Walhhere'. OE pers. name + *tūn*.

Walgrave Northants. *Waldgrave* 1086 (DB). 'Grove belonging to OLD'. OE *grāf*.

Walkden Gtr. Manch. *Walkeden* 1325. Possibly 'valley of a man called *Walca*. OE pers. name + *denu*.

Walker Tyne & Wear. *Waucre* 1242. 'Marsh by the (Roman) wall'. OE *wall* + OScand. *kjarr*.

Walkerburn Sc. Bord. '(Place by the) fullers' stream'. OE *walcere* + *burna*.

Walkeringham Notts. *Wacheringeham* 1086 (DB). Probably 'homestead of the family or followers of a man called Walhhere'. OE pers. name + *-inga-* + *hām*.

Walkern Herts. *Walchra* |sic| 1086 (DB), *Walkern* 1222. 'Building for fulling cloth'. OE **walc* + *ærn*.

Walkhampton Devon. *Walchentone* 1084, *Wachetona* |sic| 1086 (DB). Probably 'farmstead of the dwellers on a stream called **Wealce*. OE river-name (meaning 'the rolling one') + *hæme* + *tūn*.

Walkington E. R. Yorks. *Walchinton* 1086 (DB). 'Estate associated with a man called **Walca*. OE pers. name + *-ing-* + *tūn*.

Wall, usually '(place at) the wall' from OE *wall*: **Wall** Northum. *Wal* 1166. With reference to the Roman Wall. **Wall** Staffs. *Walla* 1167. With reference to the Roman town here.
  However the following has a different origin: **Wall, East** & **Wall under Heywood** Shrops. *Walle* 1200, *Walle sub Eywode* 1255. '(Place at) the spring or stream' from OE (Mercian) *wælla*. Affix means 'within or near the enclosed wood', OE *hæg* or *hege* + *wudu*.

Wallasey Mersey. *Walea* 1086 (DB), *Waleyesegh* 1351. 'The island of Waley (Britons' island)'. OE *walh* (genitive plural *wala*) + *ēg* with the later addition of a second explanatory *ēg*.

Wallingford Oxon. *Welingaforda* c.895, *Walingeford* 1086 (DB). 'Ford of the family or followers of a man called Wealh'. OE pers. name + *-inga-* + *ford*.

Wallington Gtr. London. *Waletone* 1086 (DB). 'Farmstead or village of the Britons'. OE *walh* (genitive plural *wala*) + *tūn*.

Wallington Hants. *Waletune* 1233. Probably identical in origin with the previous name.

Wallington Herts. *Wallingtone* |sic| 1086 (DB), *Wandelingetona* 1280. 'Farmstead of the family or followers of a man called **Wændel*. OE pers. name + *-inga-* + *tūn*.

Wallop, Middle, *Wallop, Nether*, & *Wallop, Over* Hants. *Wallope* 1086 (DB). Possibly 'valley with a spring or stream'. OE *wella, wælla* + *hop*. Alternatively the first element may be OE *weall* 'a wall' or *walu* 'a ridge, an embankment'.

Wallsend Tyne & Wear. *Wallesende* c.1085. 'End of the (Roman) wall'. OE *wall* + *ende*.

Walmer Kent. *Walemere* 1087. 'Pool of the Britons'. OE *walh* (genitive plural *wala*) + *mere*.

Walmersley Gtr. Manch. *Walmeresley* 1262. Possibly 'woodland clearing of a man called Waldmær or Walhmær'. OE pers. name + *lēah*.

Walmley W. Mids. *Warmelegh* 1232. 'Warm wood or clearing'. OE *wearm* + *lēah*.

Walney, Isle of Cumbria. *Wagneia* 1127. Probably 'killer-whale island', from OScand. *vǫgn* + *ey*. Alternatively the first element may be OE **wagen* 'quaking sands'.

Walpole *St Andrew* & *Walpole St Peter* Norfolk. *Walpola* 1086 (DB). 'Pool by the (Roman) bank'. OE *wall* + *pōl*. Affixes from the dedications of the churches.

Walpole Suffolk. *Walepola* 1086 (DB). 'Pool of the Britons'. OE *walh* (genitive plural *wala*) + *pōl*.

Walsall W. Mids. *Waleshale* 1163. 'Nook of land or valley of a man called Walh'. OE pers. name + *halh*. Alternatively the first element could be OE *walh* 'Welshman'.

Walsden W. Yorks. *Walseden* 1235. Probably 'valley of a man called **Walsa*. OE pers. name + *denu*.

Walsgrave on Sowe W. Mids. *Sowa* 1086 (DB), *Woldegrove* 1411. 'Grove in or near a forest'. OE *wald* + *grāf*. Originally named from the River Sowe itself, a pre-English river-name of unknown meaning.

Walsham, 'homestead or village of a man called Walh', OE pers. name + *hām*: **Walsham le Willows** Suffolk. *Wal(e)sam* 1086 (DB). Affix means 'among the willow-trees'. **Walsham, North** Norfolk. *Northwalsham* 1044–7, *Walsam* 1086 (DB). **Walsham, South** Norfolk. *Suthwalsham* 1044–7, *Walesham* 1086 (DB).

Walsingham, Great & *Walsingham, Little* Norfolk. *Walsingaham* c.1035, 1086 (DB). 'Homestead of the family or followers of a man called Wæls'. OE pers. name + *-inga-* + *hām*.

Walsoken Cambs. *Walsocne* 974, *Walsoca* 1086 (DB). 'Jurisdictional district near the (Roman) bank'. OE *wall* + *sōcn*.

Walterston (*Trewalter*) Vale Glam. *Waltervilla* c.1102, *Walterston* 1540. 'Walter's farm'. OE *tūn* (Welsh *tref*). The Welsh name translates the English.

Walterstone Heref. & Worcs. *Walterestun* 1249. 'Walter's manor or estate'. OE *tūn*. From its possession by Walter de Lacy in the late 11th cent.

Waltham, found in various counties, 'homestead or village in a forest', OE *w(e)ald* + *hām*; examples include: **Waltham** NE. Lincs. *Waltham* 1086 (DB). **Waltham Abbey** Essex. *Waltham* 1086 (DB). Affix from the medieval Abbey of Holy Cross here. **Waltham, Bishops** Hants. *Waltham* 904, 1086 (DB). Affix from its early possession by the Bishop of Winchester. **Waltham Cross** Herts. *Walthamcros* 1365. 'Cross near WALTHAM [ABBEY]'. Named from the 'Eleanor Cross' set up here by Edward I in memory of Queen Eleanor in 1290. **Waltham, Great** & **Waltham, Little** Essex. *Waltham, Waldham* 1086 (DB), *parua Waltam* 1197, *Waltham Magna* 1238. **Waltham on the Wolds** Leics. *Waltham* 1086 (DB). *See* WOLDS. **Waltham St Lawrence** & **White Waltham** Berks. *Wealtham* 940, *Waltham* 1086 (DB), *Waltamia Sancti Laurencii* 1225, *Wytewaltham* 1243. Distinguishing affixes from the dedication of the church and from OE *hwīt* 'white' referring to chalky soil.

Waltham Forest Gtr. London, new London borough recalling old *foresta de Wautham* 1261 (so named from WALTHAM ABBEY.

Walthamstow Gtr. London. *Wilcumestowe c.*1075, *Wilcumestou* 1086 (DB). 'Holy place where guests are welcome', or 'holy place of a woman called Wilcume'. OE *wilcuma* or pers. name + *stōw*.

Walton, a common name, often 'farmstead or village of the Britons', from OE *walh* (genitive plural *wala*) + *tūn*; examples include: **Walton** Derbys. *Waletune* 1086 (DB). **Walton** Suffolk. *Waletuna* 1086 (DB). **Walton, Higher** Ches. *Waletona* 1154–60. **Walton-le-Dale** Lancs. *Waletune* 1086 (DB), *Walton in La Dale* 1304. Affix means 'in the valley' from OScand. *dalr.* **Walton-on-Thames** Surrey. *Waletona* 1086 (DB). **Walton on the Naze** Essex. *Walentonie* 11th cent., *Walton at the Naase* 1545. Affix means 'on the promontory', from OE *næss.* **Walton upon Trent** Derbys. *Waletune* 942, 1086 (DB).

However several Waltons have a different origin; examples include: **Walton in Gordano** N. Som. *Waltona* 1086 (DB). 'Farmstead in a forest or with a wall'. OE *w(e)ald* or *w(e)all* + *tūn.* For the affix, *see* CLAPTON. **Walton on the Hill** Surrey. *Waltone* 1086 (DB). Identical in origin with the previous name. **Walton, West** Norfolk. *Waltuna* 1086 (DB). 'Farmstead or village by the (Roman) bank'. OE *w(e)all* + *tūn.* **Walton, Wood** Cambs. *Waltune* 1086 (DB), *Wodewalton* 1300. Probably 'farmstead in a forest'. OE *w(e)ald* + *tūn*, with the later addition of *wudu* 'woodland'.

Walworth, 'enclosure of the Britons', OE *walh* (genitive plural *wala*) + *worth*: **Walworth** Durham. *Walewrth* 1207. **Walworth** Gtr. London. *Wealawyrth* 1001, *Waleorde* 1086 (DB).

Wambrook Somerset. *Wambrook* 1280. '(Place at) the winding brook'. OE *wōh* (dative *wōn*) + *brōc.*

Wanborough Surrey. *Weneberge* 1086 (DB). Probably 'hill or mound of a man called *Wenna'. OE pers. name + *beorg.*

Wanborough Wilts. *Wænbeorgon* 854, *Wemberge* 1086 (DB). '(Place at) the tumour-shaped mounds'. OE *wenn* + *beorg.*

Wandsworth Gtr. London. *Wendleswurthe* 11th cent., *Wandelesorde* 1086 (DB). 'Enclosure of a man called *Wændel*. OE pers. name + *worth.* The river-name **Wandle** is a 'back-formation' from the place-name.

Wangford Suffolk, near Southwold. *Wankeforda* 1086 (DB). 'Ford by the open fields'. OE *wang* + *ford.*

Wanlip Leics. *Anlepe* 1086 (DB). 'The lonely or solitary place'. OE *ānlīepe.*

Wansdyke (ancient embankment, now district-name in B. & NE. Som.). *Wodnes dic* 903. 'Dyke associated with the heathen war-god Wōden'. OE god-name + *dīc.*

Wansford Cambs. *Wylmesforda* 972. 'Ford by a spring or whirlpool'. OE *wylm, wælm* + *ford.*

Wansford E. R. Yorks. *Wandesford* 1176. 'Ford of a man called *Wand or *Wandel*. OE pers. name + *ford.*

Wanstead Gtr. London. *Wænstede c.*1055, *Wenesteda* 1086 (DB). 'Place by a tumour-shaped mound or where waggons are kept'. OE *wænn* or *wēn* + *stede.*

Wanstrow Somerset. *Wandestreu* 1086 (DB). 'Tree of a man called *Wand or *Wandel*. OE pers. name + *trēow.*

Wantage Oxon. *Waneting c.*880, *Wanetinz* 1086 (DB). '(Place at) the fluctuating stream'. Derivative of OE *wanian* 'to decrease' + *-ing.*

Wapley S. Glos. *Wapelei* 1086 (DB). 'Woodland clearing by the spring'. OE *wapol* + *lēah.*

Wappenbury Warwicks. *Wapeberie* 1086 (DB). 'Stronghold of a man called *Wæppa'. OE pers. name (genitive *-n*) + *burh* (dative *byrig*).

Wappenham Northants. *Wapeham* 1086 (DB). 'Homestead or enclosure of a man called *Wæppa'. OE pers. name (genitive *-n*) + *hām* or *hamm.*

Wapping Gtr. London. *Wapping c.*1220. Probably '(settlement of) the family or followers of a man called *Wæppa', or '*Wæppa's place'. OE pers. name + *-ingas* or *-ing.*

Warbleton E. Sussex. *Warborgetone* 1086 (DB). 'Farmstead or village of a woman called Wǣrburh'. OE pers. name + *tūn.*

Warblington Hants. *Warblitetone* 1086 (DB), *Werblinton* 1186. 'Farmstead or estate associated with a woman called Wǣrblīth'. OE pers. name + *-ing-* + *tūn.*

Warborough Oxon. *Wardeberg* 1200. 'Watch or look-out hill'. OE *weard* + *beorg.*

Warboys Cambs. *Weardebusc* 974. Probably 'bush of a man called *Wearda'. OE pers. name + *busc.* Alternatively the first element may be OE *weard* 'watch, protection'.

Warbstow Cornwall. 'Chapel of *Sancta Werburga*' 1282, *Warberstowe* 1309. 'Holy place of St Wǣrburh'. OE female saint's name + *stōw.*

Warburton Gtr. Manch. *Wareburgetune* 1086 (DB). 'Farmstead or village of a woman called Wǣrburh'. OE pers. name + *tūn.*

Warcop Cumbria. *Warthecopp* 1199–1225. 'Look-out hill', or 'hill with a cairn'. OScand. *vorthr* (genitive *varthar*) or *vartha* + OE *copp.*

Warden, 'watch or look-out hill', OE *weard* + *dūn*: **Warden** Kent. *Wardon* 1207. **Warden** Northum. *Waredun c.*1175. **Warden, Chipping** Northants. *Waredone* 1086 (DB), *Chepyng Wardoun* 1389. Affix is OE *cēping* 'market'. **Warden, Old** Beds. *Wardone* 1086 (DB), *Old Wardon* 1495. Affix is OE *eald* 'old'.

Wardington Oxon. *Wardinton c.*1180. Probably 'estate associated with a man called *Wearda or Wǣrheard'. OE pers. name + *-ing-* + *tūn.*

Wardlaw Highland. *Wardelaue* 1210. 'Watch hill'. OE *weard* + *hlāw.*

Wardle, 'watch or look-out hill', OE *weard* + *hyll*: **Wardle** Ches. *Warhelle |sic|* 1086 (DB), *Wardle* 1184. **Wardle** Gtr. Manch. *Wardhul c.*1193.

Wardley Rutland. *Werlea* 1067. Probably 'wood or clearing near a weir', OE *wer* + *lēah.* Alternatively the first element may be OE *weard* 'watch, protection' if the *-d*-spelling (found from 1241) is original and not intrusive.

Wardlow Derbys. *Wardelawe* 1258. 'Watch or look-out hill'. OE *weard* + *hlāw*.

Ware Herts. *Waras* 1086 (DB). 'The weirs'. OE *wær*.

Wareham Dorset. *Werham* late 9th cent., *Warham* 1086 (DB). 'Homestead or river-meadow by a weir'. OE *wer*, *wær* + *hām* or *hamm*.

Warehorne Kent. *Werahorna* 830, *Werahorne* 1086 (DB). 'Horn-shaped piece of land by the weirs'. OE *wer* + **horna*.

Warenford Northum. *Warneford* 1256. 'Ford over Warren Burn'. Celtic river-name (probably 'alder river' with the later addition of OE *burna* 'stream') + OE *ford*.

Waresley Cambs. *Wederesbi* |*sic*| 1086 (DB), *Wereslea* 1169. Probably 'woodland clearing of a man called **Wether* or **Wær*'. OE pers. name + *lēah*.

Warfield Berks. *Warvelt* |*sic*| 1086 (DB). *Warefeld* 1171. 'Open land by a weir'. OE *wer*, *wær* + *feld*.

Wargrave Berks. *Weregrave* 1086 (DB). Probably 'grove by the weirs', OE *wer* + *grāf*.

Warham Norfolk. *Warham* 1086 (DB). 'Homestead or village by a weir'. OE *wær* + *hām*.

Waringsford Down. *Waringsford* 1743. The village is named from a former house and estate recorded in 1744 as 'the seat of Henry Waring Esq.'

Waringstown Down. The village is named for William *Warren* or *Waring*, who built a house here in 1666.

Wark, from OE *(ge)weorc* 'fortification': **Wark** Northum., near Bellingham. *Werke* 1279. **Wark** Northum., near Cornhill. *Werch* 1158.

Warkleigh Devon. *Warocle* 1100–3, *Wauerkelegh* 1242. Possibly 'spider wood or clearing'. OE **wæferce* + *lēah*.

Warkton Northants. *Wurcingtun* 946, *Werchintone* 1086 (DB). 'Estate associated with a man called **Weorc(a)*'. OE pers. name + *-ing-* + *tūn*.

Warkworth Northum. *Wercewortne* c.1050. 'Enclosure of a man called **Weorca*'. OE pers. name + *worth*.

Warlaby N. Yorks. *Werlegesbi* 1086 (DB). 'Farmstead or village of the traitor or troth-breaker'. OE *wērloga* + OScand. *bý*.

Warley, Great & *Warley, Little* Essex. *Werle* c.1045, *Wareleia* 1086 (DB). 'Wood or clearing near a weir or subject to a covenant'. OE *wer* or *wær* + *lēah*.

Warlingham Surrey. *Warlyngham* 1144. 'Homestead of the family or followers of a man called **Wærla*.' OE pers. name + *-inga-* + *hām*.

Warmfield W. Yorks. *Warnesfeld* 1086 (DB). 'Open land frequented by wrens, or where stallions are kept'. OE *wærna* or **wærna* + *feld*.

Warmingham Ches. *Warmincham* 1259. 'Homestead of the family or followers of a man called *Wærma* or *Wærmund*', or 'homestead at *Wærma*'s or *Wærmund*'s place'. OE pers. name + *-inga-* or *-ing* + *hām*.

Warmington Northants. *Wyrmingtun* c.980, *Wermintone* 1086 (DB). 'Estate associated with a man called **Wyrma*'. OE pers. name + *-ing-* + *tūn*.

Warmington Warwicks. *Warmintone* 1086 (DB). 'Estate associated with a man called *Wærma* or *Wærmund*'. OE pers. name + *-ing-* + *tūn*.

Warminster Wilts. *Worgemynster* c.912, *Guerminstre* 1086 (DB). 'Church on the River Were'. OE river-name (meaning 'winding') + *mynster*.

Warmsworth S. Yorks. *Wermesford* |*sic*| 1086 (DB), *Wermesworth* c.1105. 'Enclosure of a man called **Wærmi* or *Wærmund*'. OE pers. name + *worth*.

Warmwell Dorset. *Warmewelle* 1086 (DB). 'Warm spring'. OE *wearm* + *wella*.

Warnborough, North & *Warnborough, South* Hants. *Weargeburnan* 973–4, *Wergeborne* 1086 (DB). Possibly 'stream where criminals were drowned', OE *wearg* + *burna*, though *wearg* may have an earlier sense 'wolf', hence perhaps 'stream frequented by wolves'.

Warnford Hants. *Wernæford* c.1053, *Warneford* 1086 (DB). 'Ford frequented by wrens or one used by stallions'. OE *wærna* or **wærna* + *ford*. Alternatively the first element may be an OE man's name **Wærna*.

Warnham W. Sussex. *Werneham* 1166. 'Homestead or enclosure of a man called **Wærna*, or where stallions are kept'. OE pers. name or **wærna* + *hām* or *hamm*.

Warrenpoint Down. 'Warren's point'. *Warings's Point* 1744. It is uncertain whether the *Warren* (or *Waring*) here was related to the family who gave the name of WARINGSTOWN.

Warrington Bucks. *Wardintone* c.1175. Probably 'estate associated with a man called **Wearda* or **Wærheard*'. OE pers. name + *-ing-* + *tūn*.

Warrington Ches. *Walintune* |*sic*| 1086 (DB). *Werington* 1246. 'Farmstead or village by the weir or river-dam'. OE **wering* + *tūn*.

Warsash Hants. *Weresasse* 1272. 'Ash-tree by the weir, or of a man called *Wær*'. OE *wer* or pers. name + *æsc*.

Warslow Staffs. *Wereslei* |*sic*| 1086 (DB). *Werselow* 1300. Possibly 'hill with a watch-tower'. OE *weard-seld* + *hlāw*.

Warsop Notts. *Wareshope* 1086 (DB). Probably 'enclosed valley of a man called **Wær*'. OE pers. name + *hop*.

Warter E. R. Yorks. *Wartre* 1086 (DB). 'The gallows for criminals'. OE *wearg-trēow*.

Warthill N. Yorks. *Wardhilla* 1086 (DB). 'Watch or look-out hill'. OE *weard* + *hyll*.

Wartling E. Sussex. *Werlinges* |*sic*| 1086 (DB), *Wertlingis* 12th cent. '(Settlement of) the family or followers of a man called **Wyrtel*'. OE pers. name + *-ingas*.

Wartnaby Leics. *Worcnodebie* 1086 (DB). Possibly 'farmstead or village of a man called **Wærcnōth*'. OE pers. name + OScand. *bý*.

Warton, 'watch or look-out farmstead', OE *weard* + *tūn*: **Warton** Lancs., near Carnforth. *Wartun* 1086 (DB). **Warton** Lancs., near Kirkham. *Wartun* 1086 (DB). **Warton** Northum. *Wartun* 1236.

Warton Warwicks. *Wavertune* c.1155. 'Farmstead by a swaying tree or near marshy ground'. OE *wæfre* + *tūn*.

Warwick Cumbria. *Warthwic* 1131. 'Dwelling or farm on the bank'. OE *waroth* + *wīc*.

Warwick Warwicks. *Wærincwicum* 1001, *Warwic* 1086 (DB). 'Dwellings by the weir or river-dam'. OE **wæring* + *wīc*. **Warwickshire** (OE *scīr* 'district') is first referred to in the 11th cent.

Wasdale Head Cumbria. *Wastedale* 1279, *Wascedaleheved* 1334. 'Valley of the water or lake'. OScand. *vatn* (genitive *-s*) + *dalr*, with the later addition of OE *hēafod* 'head, upper end'.

Wash, The Lincs./Norfolk. *The Wasshes* c.1545. OE *wæsc* 'sandbank washed by the sea', originally used of two stretches fordable at low water.

Washbourne Devon. *Waseborne* 1086 (DB). 'Stream used for washing (sheep or clothes)'. OE *wæsce* + *burna*.

Washbourne, Great & *Washbourne, Little* Glos. *Uassanburnan* 780, *Waseborne* 1086 (DB). 'Stream with alluvial land'. OE **wæsse* + *burna*.

Washfield Devon. *Wasfelte* 1086 (DB). Probably 'open land near a place used for washing (sheep or clothes)'. OE *wæsce* + *feld*.

Washford Somerset. *Wecetford* c.960. 'Ford on the road to WATCHET'. OE *ford*.

Washford Pyne Devon. *Wasforde* 1086 (DB). Probably 'ford at the place for washing (sheep or clothes)'. OE *wæsce* + *ford*. Manorial affix from the de Pinu family, here in the 13th cent.

Washingborough Lincs. *Washingeburg* 1086 (DB). Possibly 'stronghold of the dwellers at the place subject to floods or used for washing'. OE *wæsce* or *wæsce* + *-inga-* + *burh*.

Washington Tyne & Wear. *Wassyngtona* 1183. 'Estate associated with a man called **Wassa*'. OE pers. name + *-ing-* + *tūn*.

Washington W. Sussex. *Wessingatun* 946–55, *Wasingetune* 1086 (DB). 'Estate of the family or followers of a man called **Wassa*'. OE pers. name + *-inga-* + *tūn*.

Wasing Berks. *Walsince* 1086 (DB). Perhaps originally the name of the stream here, with obscure element + OE *-ing*.

Wasperton Warwicks. *Waspertune* 1043, *Wasmertone |sic|* 1086 (DB). Probably 'pear orchard by alluvial land'. OE **wæsse* + *peru* + *tūn*.

Wass N. Yorks. *Wasse* 1541. Probably 'the fords'. OScand. *vath* in a plural form.

Watchet Somerset. *Wæcet* 962, *Wacet* 1086 (DB). Probably 'lower wood' from Celtic **cēd* 'wood' with prefix.

Watchfield Oxon. *Wæclesfeld* 931, *Wachenesfeld* 1086 (DB). 'Open land of a man called **Wæcel* or **Wæccīn*'. OE pers. name + *feld*.

Watendlath Cumbria. *Wattendlane* late 12th cent. Probably 'lane to the end of the lake'. OScand. *vatn* + *endi* with OE *lane* (replaced by OScand. *hlatha* 'barn').

Water Stratford Bucks., *see* STRATFORD.

Waterbeach Cambs. *Vtbech* 1086 (DB). *Waterbech* 1237. OE *bece* 'stream, valley' or *bæc* (locative **bece*) 'low ridge', with the addition of OE *ūt* 'outer' and *wæter* 'water' to distinguish it from LANDBEACH.

Waterden Norfolk. *Waterdenna* 1086 (DB). 'Valley with a stream or lake'. OE *wæter* + *denu*.

Wateresk (*Uachtar Easc*) Down. 'Upper channel'.

Waterfall Staffs. *Waterfal* 1201. OE *wæter-gefall* 'place where a stream disappears into the ground'.

Waterford (*Port Láirge*) Waterford. *Vadrefiord* n.d. 'Wether inlet'. OScand. *vethr* + *fjorthr*. Wethers were loaded onto boats here to be taken to other ports. The Irish name means 'bank of the haunch'.

Wateringbury Kent. *Uotryngebyri* 964–95, *Otringeberge* 1086 (DB). Possibly 'stronghold of the family or followers of a man called Ōhthere'. OE pers. name + *-inga-* + *burh* (dative *byrig*).

Waterloo Mersey., named from the Royal Waterloo Hotel (founded in 1815 and so called after the famous battle of that year). Similar names commemorating the battle are found in other counties, for example **Waterloo** Gtr. London, **Waterlooville** Hants.

Watermillock Cumbria. *Wethermeloc* early 13th cent. 'Little bare hill where wether-sheep graze'. Celtic **mēl* with diminutive suffix, to which OE *wether* has been added.

Waterperry Oxon. *Perie* 1086 (DB), *Waterperi* c.1190. 'Place at the peartree(s)'. OE *pyrige* with the later addition of OE *wæter* to distinguish it from WOODPERRY.

Waterston Pemb. *Walterystone* 1407. 'Walter's farm'. OGerman pers. name + OE *tūn*.

Watford, 'ford used when hunting', OE *wāth* + *ford*: **Watford** Herts. *Watford* c.945. **Watford** Northants. *Watford* 1086 (DB).

Wath, 'the ford', OScand. *vath*; examples include: **Wath** N. Yorks., near Ripon. *Wat* 1086 (DB). **Wath upon Dearne** S. Yorks. *Wade* 1086 (DB). For the river-name, *see* BOLTON UPON DEARNE.

Watling Street (Roman road from Dover to Wroxeter). *Wæclinga stræt* late 9th cent. 'Roman road associated with the family or followers of a man called **Wacol*'. OE pers. name + *-inga-* + *stræt*. An early name for ST ALBANS is *Wæclingaceaster* c.900, 'Roman fort of **Wacol*'s people', and the road-name was no doubt applied to the stretch of road between St Albans and London before it was extended to the whole length. The name Watling Street was later transferred to several other Roman roads.

Watlington Norfolk. *Watlingetun* 11th cent. Possibly 'farmstead of the family or followers of a man called **Hwætel* or **Wacol*'. OE pers. name + *-inga-* + *tūn*.

Watlington Oxon. *Wæclinctune* 887, *Watelintone* 1086 (DB). Probably 'estate associated with a man called **Wæcel*'. OE pers. name + *-ing-* + *tūn*.

Watnall Notts. *Watenot |sic|* 1086 (DB), *Watenho* 1202. 'Hill-spur of a man called **Wata*'. OE pers. name (genitive *-n*) + *hōh*.

Watten Highland. *Watne* 1230. '(Place by a) lake'. OScand. *vatn*.

Wattisfield Suffolk. *Watlesfelda* 1086 (DB). 'Open land of a man called *Wacol or *Hwætel'. OE pers. name + *feld*.

Wattisham Suffolk. *Wecesham* 1086 (DB). 'Homestead or village of a man called *Wæcci'. OE pers. name + *hām*.

Watton E. R. Yorks. *Uetadun* 731, *Wattune* 1086 (DB). 'Wet hill, or hill of the wet places'. OE *wēt* (as adjective or noun) + *dūn*.

Watton Norfolk. *Wadetuna* 1086 (DB). 'Farmstead of a man called Wada'. OE pers. name + *tūn*.

Watton at Stone Herts. *Wattun* 969, *Wodtone* 1086 (DB), *Watton atte Stone* 1311. 'Farmstead where woad is grown'. OE *wād* + *tūn*. Affix 'at the stone' (OE *stān*) from an old stone here.

Wattstown Rhon. Edmund *Watts* was a coal owner here in the 19th cent.

Waun, Y. *See* CHIRK.

Wavendon Bucks. *Wafandun* 969, *Wavendone* 1086 (DB). 'Hill of a man called *Wafa'. OE pers. name (genitive -*n*) + *dūn*.

Waveney (district) Suffolk, named from the River Waveney which is *Wahenhe* 1275, 'the river by a quagmire', OE *wagen* + *ēa*.

Waverton Ches. *Wavretone* 1086 (DB). 'Farmstead by a swaying tree'. OE *wæfre* + *tūn*.

Waverton Cumbria. *Wauerton* 1183. 'Farmstead by the River Waver'. OE river-name (from *wæfre* 'winding') + *tūn*.

Wawne E. R. Yorks. *Wagene* 1086 (DB). 'Quaking bog or quagmire'. OE *wagen*.

Waxham Norfolk. *Waxtonesham* 1044–7, *Wactanesham*, *Wacstenesham* 1086 (DB). Probably 'homestead of a man called *Wægstān', OE pers. name + *hām*. Alternatively 'homestead by the stone where watch was kept', OE *wacu* + *stān* + *hām*.

Waxholme E. R. Yorks. *Waxham* 1086 (DB). 'Homestead where wax (from bees) is produced'. OE *weax* + *hām*.

Wayford Somerset. *Waiford* 1206. 'Ford on a way or road'. OE *weg* + *ford*.

Weald, 'the woodland or forest', OE *weald*: **Weald Bassett, North** Essex. *Walda* 1086 (DB), *Welde Basset* 1291. Manorial affix from the Basset family, here in the 13th cent. **Weald, South** Essex. *Welde* 1062, *Welda* 1086 (DB). **Weald, The** Kent–Hants. *Waldum* (a dative plural form) 1185.

Wealdstone Gtr. London, a late name, 'boundary stone of HARROW WEALD'.

Wear (river) Tyne & Wear, *see* MONKWEARMOUTH.

Weare, '(place at) the weir or fishing enclosure', OE *wer*: **Weare** Somerset. *Werre* 1086 (DB). **Weare Giffard** Devon. *Were* 1086 (DB). *Weregiffarde* 1328. Manorial affix from the Giffard family, here in the 13th cent.

Weasenham Norfolk. *Wesenham* 1086 (DB). Possibly 'homestead or village of a man called *Weosa'. OE pers. name (genitive -*n*) + *hām*.

Weaverham Ches. *Wivreham* 1086 (DB). 'Homestead or village by the River Weaver'. OE river-name (from *wēfer* 'winding stream') + *hām*.

Weaverthorpe N. Yorks. *Wifretorp* 1086 (DB). 'Outlying farmstead or hamlet of a man called Víthfari'. OScand. pers. name + *thorp*.

Weddington Warwicks. *Watitune* 1086 (DB). Possibly 'estate associated with a man called *Hwæt'. OE pers. name + -*ing*- + *tūn*.

Wedmore Somerset. *Wethmor* late 9th cent., *Wedmore* 1086 (DB). Possibly 'marsh used for hunting'. OE *wēthe* + *mōr*.

Wednesbury W. Mids. *Wadnesberie* 1086 (DB). 'Stronghold associated with the heathen god Wōden'. OE god-name + *burh* (dative *byrig*).

Wednesfield W. Mids. *Wodnesfeld* 996, *Wodnesfelde* 1086 (DB). 'Open land of the heathen god Wōden'. OE god-name + *feld*.

Weedon, 'hill with a heathen temple', OE *wēoh* + *dūn*: **Weedon** Bucks. *Weodune* 1066. **Weedon Bec** Northants. *Weodun* 944, *Wedone* 1086 (DB), *Wedon Beke* 1379. Manorial affix from its possession by the Norman Abbey of Bec-Hellouin in the 12th cent. **Weedon Lois** Northants. *Wedone* 1086 (DB), *Leyes Weedon* 1475. The affix is possibly from a 'well of St Loys or Lewis' in the parish, but it may be manorial.

Weeford Staffs. *Weforde* 1086 (DB). Probably 'ford by a heathen temple'. OE *wēoh* + *ford*.

Week, *Weeke*, 'the dwelling, the specialized farm or trading settlement', OE *wīc*; examples include: **Week St Mary** Cornwall. *Wich* 1086 (DB), *Seintemarywyk* 1321. Affix from the dedication of the church. **Weeke** Hants. *Wike* 1248.

Weekley Northants. *Wiclea* 956, *Wiclei* 1086 (DB). Probably 'wood or clearing near an earlier Romano-British settlement'. OE *wīc* + *lēah*.

Weeley Essex. *Wilgelea* 11th cent., *Wileia* 1086 (DB). 'Wood or clearing where willow-trees grow'. OE *wilig* + *lēah*.

Weeting Norfolk. *Watinge* c.1050, *Wetinge* 1086 (DB). 'Wet or damp place'. OE *wēt* + -*ing*.

Weeton, 'farmstead where willow-trees grow', OE *wīthig* + *tūn*: **Weeton** E. R. Yorks. *Wideton* 1086 (DB). **Weeton** Lancs. *Widetun* 1086 (DB). **Weeton** N. Yorks. *Widitun* 1086 (DB).

Weighton, Little E. R. Yorks. *Widetone* 1086 (DB). Identical in origin with the previous names.

Weighton, Market E. R. Yorks. *Wicstun* 1086 (DB). 'Farmstead by an earlier Romano-British settlement'. OE *wīc* + *tūn*. The affix *Market* first occurs in the early 19th cent.

Welborne, *Welbourn*, *Welburn*, 'stream fed by a spring', OE *wella* + *burna*; examples include: **Welborne** Norfolk. *Walebruna* 1086 (DB). **Welbourn** Lincs. *Wellebrune* 1086 (DB). **Welburn** N. Yorks., near Bulmer. *Wellebrune* 1086 (DB).

Welbury N. Yorks. *Welleberge* 1086 (DB). 'Hill with a spring'. OE *wella* + *beorg*.

Welby Lincs. *Wellebi* 1086 (DB). 'Farmstead or village by a spring or stream'. OE *wella* + OScand. *bý*.

Welcombe Devon. *Walcome* 1086 (DB). 'Valley with a spring or stream'. OE *wella* + *cumb*.

Weldon, Great & *Weldon, Little* Northants. *Weledone* 1086 (DB). 'Hill with a spring or by a stream'. OE *wella* + *dūn*.

Welford Berks. *Weligforda* 949, *Waliford* 1086 (DB). 'Ford where willow-trees grow'. OE *welig* + *ford*.

Welford Northants. *Wellesford* 1086 (DB). 'Ford by the spring or over the stream'. OE *wella* + *ford*.

Welford on Avon Warwicks. *Welleford* 1086 (DB), *Welneford* 1177. 'Ford by the springs'. OE *wella* (genitive plural *-ena*) + *ford*.

Welham Leics. *Weleham* 1086 (DB). Possibly 'homestead by the stream', OE *wella* + *hām*. Alternatively the first element may be an OE pers. name *Wēola.

Welham Notts. *Wellun* 1086 (DB). '(Place at) the springs'. OE *wella* in a dative plural form *wellum*.

Welhamgreen Herts. *Wethyngham* c.1315, *Whelamgrene* 1467. 'Willow-tree enclosure'. OE *wīthign* + *hamm*, with later *grēne* 'green'.

Well, '(place at) the spring or stream', OE *wella*; examples include: **Well** Lincs. *Welle* 1086 (DB). **Well** N. Yorks. *Welle* 1086 (DB).

Welland (river) Northants.–Lincs. *Weolud* 921. A Celtic or pre-Celtic river-name of uncertain meaning.

Wellesbourne Hastings & *Wellesbourne Mountford* Warwicks. *Welesburnan* 840, *Waleborne* 1086 (DB). Possibly 'stream with a pool'. OE *wēl* + *burna*. Distinguishing affixes from possession by the de Hastanges family (from the 14th cent.) and the de Munford family (from the 12th cent.).

Welling Gtr. London. *Wellyngs* 1362. A manorial name from the Welling or Willing family, here in the early 14th cent.

Wellingborough Northants. *Wedlingeberie* 1086 (DB), *Wendlingburch* 1178. 'Stronghold of the family or followers of a man called *Wændel'. OE pers. name + *-inga-* + *burh*.

Wellingham Norfolk. *Walnccham* |sic| 1086 (DB), *Uuelingheham* c.1190. 'Homestead of the dwellers by a spring or stream'. OE *wella* + *-inga-* + *hām*.

Wellingore Lincs. *Wellingoure* 1086 (DB). Probably 'promontory of the dwellers by a spring or stream'. OE *wella* + *-inga-* + *ofer*.

Wellington, probably 'estate associated with a man called *Wēola*, OE pers. name + *-ing-* + *tūn*: **Wellington** Heref. & Worcs. *Weolintun* early 11th cent., *Walintone* 1086 (DB). **Wellington** Shrops. *Walitone* 1086 (DB), *Welintun* c.1145. **Wellington** Somerset. *Weolingtun* 904, *Walintone* 1086 (DB).

Wellow B. & NE. Som. *Weleuue* 1084. Originally the name of the stream here, a Celtic river-name possibly meaning 'winding'.

Wellow I. of Wight. *Welig* c.880, *Welige* 1086 (DB). '(Place at) the willow-tree'. OE *welig*.

Wellow Notts. *Welhag* 1207. 'Enclosure near a spring or stream'. OE *wella* + *haga*.

Wellow, East & *Wellow, West* Hants. *Welewe* c.880, *Weleve* 1086 (DB). Identical in origin with WELLOW (B. & NE. Som.).

Wells, 'the springs', OE *wella* in a plural form: **Wells** Somerset. *Willan* c.1050, *Welle* 1086 (DB). **Wells-next-the-Sea** Norfolk. *Guelle* |sic| 1086 (DB), *Wellis* 1291.

Wellsborough Leics. *Wethelesberne* |sic| 1185, *Weulesbergh* 1285. 'Hill of the wheel', i.e. 'hill with a circular shape or feature'. OE *hweowol* + *beorg*.

Welnetham, Great & *Welnetham, Little* Suffolk. *Hvelfiham* |sic| 1086 (DB), *Weluetham* 1170. Possibly 'enclosure frequented by swans near a water-wheel or other circular feature'. OE *hwēol* + *elfitu* + *hamm*.

Welney Norfolk. *Wellenhe.* c.14th cent. 'River called *Welle*'. The earlier name of Old Croft River (from OE *wella* 'stream') + OE *ēa*.

Welsh Bicknor Heref. & Worcs., *see* BICKNOR.

Welsh Frankton Shrops., *see* FRANKTON.

Welshampton Shrops. *Hantone* 1086 (DB), *Welch Hampton* 1649. Originally 'high farmstead or estate', from OE *hēah* (dative *hēan*) + *tūn*. The later affix 'Welsh' refers to its proximity to a detached portion of Flintshire.

Welshpool (*Y Trallwng*) Powys. *Pola* 1253, *Walshe Pole* 1477. '(Place by the) Welsh pool'. OE *welisc* + *pōl*. The name emphasizes the town's position on the Welsh side of the border. The Welsh name means 'the very wet swamp' (Welsh *y* + *tra* + *llwng*), referring to the same pool.

Welton, usually 'farmstead by a spring or stream', OE *wella* + *tūn*; examples include: **Welton** E. R. Yorks. *Welleton* 1086 (DB). **Welton le Marsh** Lincs. *Waletune* 1086 (DB). Affix means 'in the marshland'. **Welton le Wold** Lincs. *Welletune* 1086 (DB). Affix means 'on the wold(s)' with loss of preposition, *see* WOLDS.

Welwick E. R. Yorks. *Welwic* 1086 (DB). 'Dwelling or (dairy) farm near a spring or stream'. OE *wella* + *wīc*.

Welwyn Herts. *Welingum* c.945, *Welge* 1086 (DB). '(Place at) the willow-trees'. OE *welig* in a dative plural form *weligum*.

Wem Shrops. *Weme* 1086 (DB). 'Dirty or muddy place'. OE *wemm.

Wembdon Somerset. *Wadmendune* 1086 (DB). Probably 'hill of the huntsmen'. OE *wǣthe-mann* + *dūn*.

Wembley Gtr. London. *Wembalea* 825. 'Woodland clearing of a man called *Wemba'. OE pers. name + *lēah*.

Wembury Devon. *Wenbiria* late 12th cent. OE *burh* (dative *byrig*) 'fortified place, stronghold' with an uncertain first element, possibly OE *wenn*, *wænn* 'tumour-shaped mound'.

Wembworthy Devon. *Mameorda* |sic| 1086 (DB), *Wemeworth* 1207. 'Enclosure of a man called *Wemba'. OE pers. name + *worth*.

Wendens Ambo Essex. *Wendena* 1086 (DB). Probably 'winding valley'. OE *wende* + *denu*. Affix is Latin *ambo* 'both', referring to the union of the two parishes called Wenden in 1662.

Wendlebury Oxon. *Wandesberie* |*sic*| 1086 (DB), *Wendelberi* c.1175. 'Stronghold of a man called *Wændla*'. OE pers. name + *burh* (dative *byrig*).

Wendling Norfolk. *Wenlinga* 1086 (DB). Possibly '(settlement of) the family or followers of a man called *Wændel*'. OE pers. name + *-ingas*.

Wendover Bucks. *Wændofran*. c.970, *Wendoure* 1086 (DB). Originally the name of the stream here, a Celtic river-name meaning 'white waters'.

Wendron Cornwall. 'Church of *Sancta Wendrona*' 1291. Named from the patron saint of the church, a female saint of whom nothing is known.

Wendy Cambs. *Wandei* 1086 (DB). 'Island at a river-bend'. OE *wende* + *ēg*.

Wenham, Great & *Wenham, Little* Suffolk. *Wenham* 1086 (DB). Possibly 'homestead or enclosure with pastureland'. OE *wynn* + *hām* or *hamm*.

Wenhaston Suffolk. *Wenadestuna* 1086 (DB). 'Farmstead or village of a man called *Wynhæth*'. OE pers. name + *tūn*.

Wenlock, Little & *Wenlock, Much* Shrops. *Wininicas* 675–90, *Wenlocan, Winlocan* 9th cent., *Wenloch* 1086 (DB). Probably OE *loca* 'enclosed place' (hence perhaps 'monastery') added to the first part of old Celtic name *Wininicas* (obscure, but possibly 'white area' or the like referring to limestone of Wenlock Edge, from Celtic *winn* 'white'). Affix is OE *mycel* 'great'.

Wennington Cambs. *Weningtone* c.960. 'Estate associated with a man called *Wenna*'. OE pers. name + *-ing-* + *tūn*.

Wennington Gtr. London. *Winintune* c.1100. 'Estate associated with a man called Wynna'. OE pers. name + *-ing-* + *tūn*.

Wennington Lancs. *Wennigetun* 1086 (DB). 'Farmstead on the River Wenning'. OE river-name (meaning 'dark stream') + *tūn*.

Wensley Derbys. *Wodnesleie* 1086 (DB). 'Sacred grove of the heathen god Wōden'. OE god-name + *lēah*.

Wensley N. Yorks. *Wendreslaga* 1086 (DB), *Wendesle* 1203. 'Woodland clearing of a man called *Wændel*'. OE pers. name + *lēah*. **Wensleydale** is *Wandesleydale* c.1150, from OScand. *dalr* 'valley'.

Wentbridge W. Yorks. *Wentbrig* 1302. 'Bridge across the River Went'. Pre-English river-name of uncertain origin + OE *brycg*.

Wentnor Shrops. *Wantenoure* 1086 (DB), *Wontenoure* c.1200, *Wentenour* 1251. 'Flattopped ridge of a man called *Wonta* or *Wenta*'. OE pers. name (genitive *-n*) + *ofer*.

Wentworth, probably 'enclosure of a man called Wintra', OE pers. name + *worth*: **Wentworth** Cambs. *Winteuuorde* 1086 (DB). **Wentworth** S. Yorks. *Wintreuuorde* 1086 (DB).

Wenvoe (*Gwenfô*) Vale Glam. *Wnfa* 1153, *Wenvo* c.1262. Meaning uncertain.

Weobley Heref. & Worcs. *Wibelai* 1086 (DB), 'Woodland clearing of a man called *Wiobba*'. OE pers. name + *lēah*.

Were (river) Wilts., *see* WARMINSTER.

Wereham Norfolk. *Wigreham* 1086 (DB). Probably 'homestead on a stream called *Wigor* (the winding one)'. Celtic river-name (an old name for the River Wissey) + OE *hām*.

Werrington Cambs. *Witheringtun* 972, *Widerintone* 1086 (DB). 'Estate associated with a man called Wither'. OE pers. name + *-ing-* + *tūn*.

Werrington Cornwall. *Ulvredintone* 1086 (DB). 'Estate associated with a man called Wulfrāed'. OE pers. name + *-ing-* + *tūn*.

Wervin Ches. *Wivrevene* 1086 (DB). 'Cattle fen, or quaking fen'. OE *weorf* or *wifer* + *fenn*.

Wesham Lancs. *Westhusum* 1189. '(Place at) the westerly houses'. OE *west* + *hūs* in a dative plural form.

Wessex (Anglo-Saxon kingdom centred on Winchester). *West Seaxe* late 9th cent. '(Territory of) the West Saxons'. OE *west* + *Seaxe*.

Wessington Derbys. *Wistanestune* 1086 (DB). 'Farmstead or village of a man called Wīgstān'. OE pers. name + *tūn*.

West as affix, *see* main name, e.g. for **West Acre** (Norfolk) *see* ACRE.

West End Hants. *Westend* 1607. Possibly from OE *wēsten* 'waste-land'.

West Kilbride N. Ayr. 'Western (place by) St Brigid's church'. *West* distinguishes this place from EAST KILBRIDE, although there are almost 30 miles between them.

West Lothian. *See* MIDLOTHIAN.

West Williamston. *See* EAST WILLIAMSTON.

Westbere Kent. *Westbere* 1212. 'Westerly woodland pasture'. OE *west* + *bēr*.

Westborough Lincs. *Westburg* 1086 (DB). 'Westerly stronghold'. OE *west* + *burh*.

Westbourne W. Sussex. *Burne* 1086 (DB), *Westbourne* 1305. '(Place at) the stream'. OE *burna*, with the later addition of *west* to distinguish it from EASTBOURNE.

Westbury, 'westerly stronghold or fortified place', OE *west* + *burh* (dative *byrig*); examples include: **Westbury** Shrops. *Wesberie* 1086 (DB). **Westbury** Wilts. *Westberie* 1086 (DB). **Westbury on Severn** Glos. *Wesberie* 1086 (DB). **Westbury on Trym** Brist. *Westbyrig* 791–6, *Hvesberie* |*sic*| 1086 (DB). Trym is an OE river-name (probably 'strong one').

Westby Lancs. *Westbi* 1086 (DB). 'Westerly farmstead or village'. OScand. *vestr* + *bý*.

Westcliffe on Sea Essex, a self-explanatory name of recent origin.

Westcote, *Westcott*, 'westerly cottage(s)', OE *west* + *cot*; examples include: **Westcote** Glos. *Westcote* 1315. **Westcott** Surrey. *Westcote* 1086 (DB).

Westdean E. Sussex. *Dene* 1086 (DB), *Westdene* 1291. 'West valley'. OE *west* + *denu*. 'West' in relation to EASTDEAN.

Westerdale N. Yorks. *Westerdale* c.1165. 'More westerly valley'. OScand. *vestari* + *dalr*.

Westerfield Suffolk. *Westrefelda* 1086 (DB). '(More) westerly open land'. OE *wester* or *westerra* + *feld*.

Westergate W. Sussex. *Westgate* 1230. 'More westerly gate or gap'. OE *westerra* + *geat*. See EASTERGATE.

Westerham Kent. *Westarham* 871–89, *Oistreham |sic|* 1086 (DB). 'Westerly homestead'. OE **wester* + *hām*.

Westerleigh S. Glos. *Westerlega* 1176. 'More westerly woodland clearing'. OE *westerra* + *lēah*.

Western Isles (the unitary authority). The Outer Hebrides, the most westerly island chain in Scotland. The Gaelic name of the islands is *Na h-Eileanan an Iar*, 'The Islands of the West', or for the unitary authority *Eilean Siar*, 'Western Isles'.

Westfield. 'westerly open land', OE *west* + *feld*: **Westfield** E. Sussex. *Westewelle |sic|* 1086 (DB), *Westefelde* c.1115. **Westfield** Norfolk. *Westfelda* 1086 (DB).

Westgate on Sea Kent. *Westgata* 1168. 'Westerly gate or gap'. OE *west* + *geat*.

Westhall Suffolk. *Westhala* 1139. 'Westerly nook of land'. OE *west* + *halh*.

Westham E. Sussex. *Westham* 1222. 'Westerly promontory'. OE *west* + *hamm*.

Westhampnett W. Sussex. *Hentone* 1086 (DB), *Westhamptonette* 1279. Originally 'high farmstead', from OE *hēah* (dative *hēan* + *tūn*, with the later addition of *west* and OFrench *-ette* 'little'.

Westhead Lancs. *Westhefd* c.1190. 'Westerly headland or ridge'. OE *west* + *hēafod*.

Westhide Heref. & Worcs. *Hide* 1086 (DB), *Westhyde* 1242. 'Westerly hide of land'. OE *west* + *hīd*.

Westhope Shrops. *Weshope* 1086 (DB). 'Westerly enclosed valley'. OE *west* + *hop*.

Westhorpe Suffolk. *Westtorp* 1086 (DB). 'Westerly outlying farmstead or hamlet'. OScand. *vestr* + *thorp*.

Westhoughton Gtr. Manch. *Halcton* c.1210, *Westhalcton* c.1240. 'Westerly farmstead in a nook of land'. OE *west* + *halh* + *tūn*.

Westleigh Devon. *Weslega* 1086 (DB). 'Westerly wood or clearing'. OE *west* + *lēah*.

Westleton Suffolk. *Westledestuna* 1086 (DB). 'Farmstead or village of a man called Vestlithi'. OScand. pers. name + OE *tūn*.

Westley, 'westerly wood or clearing', OE *west* + *lēah*: **Westley** Suffolk. *Westlea* 1086 (DB). **Westley Waterless** Cambs. *Westle* c.1045, *Weslai* 1086 (DB), *Westle Waterles* 1285. Affix means 'wet clearings', from OE *wæter* + *lēas* (the plural of *lēah*).

Westlinton Cumbria. *Westlevington* c.1200. 'Farmstead by the River Lyne'. Celtic river-name (possibly 'the smooth one') + OE *tūn*, with *West* to distinguish it from KIRKLINTON.

Westmeath (*An Iarmhí*) (the county). 'Western Meath'. The county was created out of the province of MEATH in 1542.

Westmeston E. Sussex. *Westmæstun* c.765, *Wesmestun* 1086 (DB). 'Most westerly farmstead'. OE *westmest* + *tūn*.

Westmill Herts. *Westmele* 1086 (DB). 'Westerly mill'. OE *west* + *myln*.

Westminster Gtr. London. *Westmynster* c.975. 'West monastery', i.e. to the west of London. OE *west* + *mynster*.

Westmorland (old county). *Westmoringaland* c.1150. 'District of the people living west of the moors' (alluding to the North Yorkshire Pennines). OE *west* + *mōr* + *-inga-* + *land*.

Westnewton Northum. *Niwetona* 12th cent. 'New farmstead'. OE *nīwe* + *tūn*, with *west* to distinguish it from KIRKNEWTON.

Weston, a very common place-name, 'west farmstead or village', i.e. one to the west of another settlement, OE *west* + *tūn*; examples include: **Weston** Herts. *Westone* 1086 (DB). **Weston** Lincs. *Westune* 1086 (DB). **Weston, Buckhorn** Dorset. *Westone* 1086 (DB), *Boukeresweston* 1275. Manorial affix from some medieval owner called *Bouker*. **Weston, Edith** Rutland. *Westona* 1113, *Weston Edith* 1275. Affix probably from its possession by Queen Ēadgȳth, wife of Edward the Confessor, in 1086. **Weston, Hail** Cambs. *Heilweston* 1199. Affix is the original Celtic name (meaning 'dirty stream') of the River Kym. **Weston Rhyn** Shrops. *Westone* 1086 (DB), *Weston Ryn* 1302. Affix refers to nearby Rhyn, from Welsh *rhyn* 'peak, hill'. **Weston Subedge** Glos. *Westone* 1086 (DB), *Weston sub Egge* 1255. Affix means 'under the edge or escarpment' (of the Cotswolds) from Latin *sub* and OE *ecg*. **Weston super Mare** N. Som. *Weston* c.1230, *Weston super Mare* 1349. The Latin affix means 'on the sea'. **Weston Turville** Bucks. *Westone* 1086 (DB), *Westone Turvile* 1302. Manorial affix from the de Turvile family, here in the 12th cent. **Weston under Penyard** Heref. & Worcs. *Westune* 1086 (DB). Affix from nearby Penyard (Hill), *Peniard* 1228, identical with PENNARD Somerset.

Westoning Beds. *Westone* 1086 (DB), *Westone Ynge* 1365. 'West farmstead', OE *west* + *tūn*, with manorial affix from its possession by the Ing family in the 14th cent.

Westonzoyland Somerset. *Sowi* 1086 (DB), *Westsowi* c.1245. 'The westerly manor of the estate called *Sowi*', thus distinguished from MIDDLEZOY and with the later addition of *land* 'estate'.

Westow N. Yorks. *Wiuestou* 12th cent. 'Holy place of the women, or of a woman called **Wīfe*'. OE *wīf* or pers. name + *stōw*.

Westray (island) Orkn. *Vesturey* c.1260. 'Western island'. OScand. *vestr* + *ey*. Westray is the westernmost of the islands in northern Orkney.

Westward Cumbria. *Le Westwarde* 1354. 'Western division (of a forest)'. ME *west* + *warde*.

Westward Ho! Devon, modern name commemorating the novel of this name by Charles Kingsley (published in 1855) largely set in this locality.

Westwell, 'westerly spring or stream', OE *west* + *wella*: **Westwell** Kent. *Welle* 1086 (DB), *Westwell* 1226. **Westwell** Oxon. *Westwelle* 1086 (DB).

Westwick, 'westerly dwelling or (dairy) farm', OE *west* + *wīc*: **Westwick** Cambs. *Westuuiche* 1086 (DB). **Westwick** Durham. *Westewic* 1091. **Westwick** Norfolk. *Westuuic* 1086 (DB).

Westwood Wilts. *Westwuda* 987, *Westwode* 1086 (DB). 'Westerly wood'. OE *west* + *wudu*.

Wetheral Cumbria. *Wetherhala* c.1100. 'Nook of land where wether-sheep are kept'. OE *wether* + *halh*.

Wetherby W. Yorks. *Wedrebi* 1086 (DB). 'Wether-sheep farmstead'. OScand. *vethr* + *bý*.

Wetherden Suffolk. *Wederdena* 1086 (DB). 'Valley where wether-sheep are kept'. OE *wether* + *denu*.

Wetheringsett Suffolk. *Weddreringesete* c.1035, *Wederingaseta* 1086 (DB). Probably 'fold of the people of WETHERDEN.' Reduced form of previous name + *-inga-* + *set*.

Wethersfield Essex. *Witheresfelda* 1086 (DB). 'Open land of a man called Wihthere or *Wether*'. OE pers. name + *feld*.

Wettenhall Ches. *Watenhale* 1086 (DB). 'Wet nook of land'. OE *wēt* (dative *-an*) + *halh*.

Wetton Staffs. *Wettindun* 1252. Possibly 'wet hill'. OE *wēt* (dative *-an*) + *dūn*.

Wetwang N. Yorks. *Wetuuangha* 1086 (DB). Probably 'field for the trial of a legal action'. OScand. *vætt-vangr*.

Wetwood Staffs. *Wetewode* 1291. 'Wet wood'. OE *wēt* + *wudu*.

Wexcombe Wilts. *Wexcumbe* 1167. 'Valley where wax (from bees) is found'. OE *weax* + *cumb*.

Wexford (*Loch Garman*) Wexford. *Weysford* 15th cent. 'Inlet by the sandbank'. OIrish *escir* + OScand. *fjorthr*. The Irish name of Wexford means 'lake of the (river) Garma'.

Weybourne Norfolk. *Wabrune* 1086 (DB). OE *burna* 'spring, stream' with an uncertain first element, possibly an OE or pre-English name of the river from a root **war-* 'water', or an OE **wagu* 'quagmire', or OE *wær* 'weir, river-dam'.

Weybread Suffolk. *Weibrada* 1086 (DB). Probably 'broad stretch of land by a road'. OE *weg* + *brǣdu*.

Weybridge Surrey. *Webruge* 1086. 'Bridge over the River Wey'. Ancient pre-English river-name of unknown origin and meaning + OE *brycg*.

Weyhill Hants. *La Wou* c.1270. Possibly 'the hill-spur climbed by a road'. OE *weg* + *hōh*, with the later addition of *hill*. Alternatively the original name may be from OE *wēoh* '(heathen) temple'.

Weymouth Dorset. *Waimouthe* 934. 'Mouth of the River Wey'. Ancient pre-English river-name of unknown origin and meaning + OE *mūtha*.

Whaddon, usually 'hill where wheat is grown', OE *hwǣte* + *dūn*; examples include: **Whaddon** Bucks. *Hwǣtædun* 966–75, *Wadone* 1086 (DB). **Whaddon** Cambs. *Wadone* 1086 (DB).
　However the following has a different second element: **Whaddon** Wilts., near Salisbury. *Watedene* 1086 (DB). 'Valley where wheat is grown'. OE *hwǣte* + *denu*.

Whale Cumbria. *Vwal* 1178. OScand. *hváll* 'an isolated round hill'.

Whaley Derbys., near Bolsover. *Walley* 1230. Possibly 'woodland clearing by a spring or stream'. OE *wælla* + *lēah*.

Whaley Bridge Derbys. *Weile* c.1250. 'Woodland clearing by a road'. OE *weg* + *lēah*.

Whalley Lancs. *Hwælleage* 11th cent., *Wallei* 1086 (DB). 'Woodland clearing on or near a round hill'. OE **hwæl* + *lēah*.

Whalsay (island) Shet. *Hvalsey* c.1250. 'Whale-shaped island'. OScand. *hvalr* + *ey*.

Whalton Northum. *Walton* 1203. Possibly 'farmstead by a round hill'. OE **hwæl* + *tūn*.

Whaplode Lincs. *Cappelad* 810, *Copelade* 1086 (DB). 'Watercourse or channel where eelpouts are found'. OE **cwappa* + *lād*.

Wharfe N. Yorks. *Warf* 1224. OScand. *hvarf* or *hverfi* 'a bend or corner'.

Wharfe (river) W. Yorks., *see* BURLEY IN WHARFEDALE.

Wharles Lancs. *Quarlous* 1249. Probably 'hills or mounds near a stone circle'. OE *hwerfel* + *hlāw*.

Wharncliffe Side S. Yorks. *Querncliffe* 1406, *Wharnetcliffe Side* 1634. 'Cliff where querns or millstones are obtained'. OE *cweorn* + *clif*, with the later addition of *sīde* 'hill-side'.

Wharram Percy & *Wharram le Street* N. Yorks. *Warran* 1086 (DB), *Wharrom Percy* 1291, *Warrum in the Strete* 1333. Possibly '(place at) the kettles or cauldrons' (perhaps used in some topographical sense). OE *hwer* in a dative plural form. Distinguishing affixes from early possession by the de Percy family and from proximity to an ancient road ('on the street' from OE *strēt*).

Wharton Ches. *Wanetune* |sic| 1086 (DB), *Waverton* 1216. Probably 'farmstead by a swaying tree or near marshy ground'. OE *wæfre* + *tūn*.

Whashton N. Yorks. *Whassingetun* c.1160. Probably 'estate associated with a man called **Hwæssa*'. OE pers. name + *-ing-* + *tūn*.

Whatcombe Dorset. *Watecumbe* 1288. 'Wet valley', or 'valley where wheat is grown'. OE *wēt* or *hwǣte* + *cumb*.

Whatcote Warwicks. *Quatercote* |sic| 1086 (DB), *Whatcote* 1206. 'Cottage(s) near which wheat is grown'. OE *hwǣte* + *cot*.

Whatfield Suffolk. *Watefelda* 1086 (DB). Probably 'open land where wheat is grown'. OE *hwǣte* + *feld*.

Whatley Somerset, near Chard. *Watelege* 1086 (DB). 'Woodland clearing where wheat is grown'. OE *hwǣte* + *lēah*.

Whatlington E. Sussex. *Watlingetone* 1086 (DB). Probably 'farmstead of the family or followers of a man called **Hwætel*'. OE pers. name + *-inga-* + *tūn*.

Whatstandwell Derbys. *Wattestanwell ford* 1390. Named from a certain Wat or Walter Stonewell who had a house near the ford in 1390.

Whatton, probably 'farmstead where wheat is grown', OE *hwǣte* + *tūn*: **Whatton** Notts. *Watone* 1086 (DB). **Whatton, Long** Leics. *Watton* 1190. Affix (recorded from the 14th cent.) refers to the length of the village.

Wheatacre Norfolk. *Hwateaker* 1086 (DB). 'Cultivated land used for wheat'. OE *hwǣte* + *æcer*.

Wheathampstead Herts. *Wathemestede* c.960, *Watamestede* 1086 (DB). 'Homestead where wheat is grown'. OE *hwǣte* + *ham-stede*.

Wheatley, 'clearing where wheat is grown', OE *hwǣte* + *lēah*; examples include: **Wheatley** Oxon. *Hwatelega* 1163. **Wheatley Lane** Lancs. *Watelei* 1086 (DB). **Wheatley, North** & **Wheatley, South** Notts. *Wateleie* 1086 (DB).

Wheaton Aston Staffs., see ASTON.

Wheddon Cross Somerset. *Wheteden* 1243. 'Valley where wheat is grown'. OE *hwǣte* + *denu*.

Wheelock Ches. *Hoiloch* 1086 (DB). Named from the River Wheelock, a Celtic river-name meaning 'winding'.

Wheelton Lancs. *Weltona* c.1160. 'Farmstead with a water-wheel or near some other circular feature'. OE *hwēol* + *tūn*.

Whenby N. Yorks. *Quennebi* 1086 (DB). 'Farmstead or village of the women'. OScand. *kona* (genitive plural *kvenna*) + *bý*.

Whepstead Suffolk. *Wepstede* 942–51, *Huepestede* 1086 (DB). Probably 'place where brushwood grows'. OE *hwip(p)e* + *stede*.

Wherstead Suffolk. *Weruesteda* 1086 (DB). 'Place by a wharf or shore'. OE *hwearf* + *stede*.

Wherwell Hants. *Hwerwyl* 955. Probably 'spring provided with a kettle or cauldron'. OE *hwer* + *wella*.

Wheston, *Whetstone*, from OE *hwet-stān* 'a whetstone', probably referring to places where stone suitable for whetstones was found: **Wheston** Derbys. *Whetstan* 1251. **Whetstone** Gtr. London. *Wheston* 1417. **Whetstone** Leics. *Westham |sic|* 1086 (DB), *Whetestan* 12th cent.

Whicham Cumbria. *Witingham* 1086 (DB). 'Homestead of the family or followers of a man called Hwīta', or 'homestead at Hwīta's place'. OE pers. name + *-inga-* or *-ing* + *hām*.

Whichford Warwicks. *Wicford* 1086 (DB), *Wicheforda* c.1130. Probably 'ford of the tribe called the Hwicce'. OE tribal name + *ford*.

Whickham Tyne & Wear. *Quicham* 1196. 'Homestead or enclosure with a quickset hedge'. OE *cwic* + *hām* or *hamm*.

Whiddy Island (*Faoide*) Cork. 'Bad weather island'.

Whilton Northants. *Woltone* 1086 (DB). 'Farmstead with a water-wheel, or on a round hill'. OE *hwēol* + *tūn*.

Whimple Devon. *Winple* 1086 (DB). Originally the name of the stream here, a Celtic name meaning 'white pool or stream'.

Whinburgh Norfolk. *Wineberga* 1086 (DB). 'Hill where gorse grows'. OScand. *hvin* + OE *beorg*.

Whippingham I. of Wight. *Wippingeham* 735, *Wipingeham* 1086 (DB). 'Homestead of the family or followers of a man called *Wippa'. OE pers. name + *-inga-* + *hām*.

Whipsnade Beds. *Wibsnede* 1202. 'Detached plot of a man called *Wibba'. OE pers. name + *snǣed*.

Whissendine Rutland. *Wichingedene* 1086 (DB), *Wissenden* 1203. Possibly 'valley of the family or followers of a man called *Hwicce or *Wic', OE pers. name + *-inga-* + *denu*. Alternatively 'valley of the tribe called the Hwicce', OE tribal name (genitive plural *-na*) + *denu*.

Whissonsett Norfolk. *Witcingkeseta* 1086 (DB). Probably 'fold of the family or followers of a man called *Wic'. OE pers. name + *-inga-* + *set*.

Whistley Green Berks. *Wisclea* 968, *Wiselei* 1086 (DB). 'Marshy-meadow clearing'. OE *wisc* + *lēah*.

Whiston Mersey. *Quistan* 1190. 'The white stone'. OE *hwīt* + *stān*.

Whiston Northants. *Hwiccingtune* 974, *Wicentone* 1086 (DB). 'Farmstead of the tribe called the Hwicce'. OE tribal name (genitive plural *-na*) + *tūn*.

Whiston S. Yorks. *Witestan* 1086 (DB). 'The white stone'. OE *hwīt* + *stān*.

Whiston Staffs. *Witestun* c.1002, *Witestone* 1086 (DB). 'Farmstead of a man called *Witi'. OE pers. name + *tūn*.

Whitacre, Nether & *Whitacre, Over* Warwicks. *Witacre* 1086 (DB). 'White cultivated land'. OE *hwīt* + *æcer*.

Whitbeck Cumbria. *Witebec* c.1160. 'White stream'. OScand. *hvítr* + *bekkr*.

Whitbun Tyne & Wear. *Hwiteberne* c.1190. 'Tumulus or barn of a man called Hwīta'. OE pers. name + *byrgen* or *bere-ærn*.

Whitburn W. Loth. *Whiteburne* 1296. '(Place by the) white stream'. OE *hwīt* + *burna*.

Whitby Ches. *Witeberia* c.1100. 'White stronghold or manor-house'. OE *hwīt* + *burh* (dative *byrig*).

Whitby N. Yorks. *Witeby* 1086 (DB). 'White farmstead or village, or of a man called Hvíti. OScand. *hvítr* or pers. name + *bý*.

Whitchurch, 'white church', i.e. probably 'stone-built church', OE *hwīt* + *cirice*; examples include: **Whitchurch** B. & NE Som. *Hwitecirce* 1065. **Whitchurch** Hants. *Hwitancyrice* 909. **Whitchurch** Shrops. *Album Monasterium* 1199 (here the name is rendered in Latin), *Whytchyrche* 13th cent. Called *Westune* 'west farmstead' in 1086 (DB). **Whitchurch Canonicorum** Dorset. *Witcerce* 1086 (DB), *Whitchurch Canonicorum* 1262. Latin affix means 'of the canons', referring to early possession by the canons of Salisbury. The dedication of the church here to St Candida (St Wite) may be derived from the place-name rather than vice versa.

White as affix, see main name, e.g. for **White Notley** (Essex) see NOTLEY.

White City Gtr. London, so called from the white colour of the stadium and exhibition centre built c.1908.

White Ladies Aston Heref. & Worcs., see ASTON.

Whiteabbey Antrim. *White-Abbey, in Irish Mainistir Fhionn* c.1700. The name refers to a 13th-cent. abbey of the Premonstratensian Order, popularly known as the 'White Canons'. The English name may translate original Irish *Mainistir Fhionn*, 'white monastery'.

Whitechapel Gtr. London. *Whitechapele* 1340. 'The white chapel', i.e. probably 'stone-built chapel'. OE *hwīt* + ME *chapele*.

Whitecross Armagh. *Whitecross* c.1835. The reference is to whitewashed houses at a crossroads here.

Whitefield Gtr. Manch. *Whitefeld* 1292. 'White open land'. OE *hwīt* + *feld*.

Whitegate Ches. *Whytegate* 1540. 'The white gate'. OE *hwīt* + *geat*, referring to the outer gate of Vale Royal Abbey.

Whitehaven Cumbria. *Qwithofhavene* c.1135. 'Harbour near the white headland'. OScand. *hvítr* + *hǫuth* + *hafn*.

Whitehead Antrim. *the White-Head* 1683. The town takes its name from the headland *White Head*, itself named in contrast to nearby *Black Head*.

Whitehill Fermanagh. *Whitehill* 1837. 'White hill'.

Whitehouse Antrim. 'White house'. The name was originally that of a fortified house built c.1574.

Whiteley Village, Surrey. Named after William Whiteley (of Whiteley's Stores in London) who had this model village with almshouses built in the early 1900s.

Whiteparish Wilts. *La Whytechyrch* 1278, *Whyteparosshe* 1289. Originally 'the white church', later replaced by 'parish'. OE *hwīt* + *cirice* and ME *paroche*.

Whiterock Antrim. *White Rock* c.1830. 'White rock'. The name relates to a nearby limestone quarry.

Whitestaunton Somerset. *Stantune* 1086 (DB), *Whitestaunton* 1337. 'Farmstead on stony ground', OE *stān* + *tūn*, with later affix referring to the limestone quarries here.

Whitestone Devon. *Hwitastane* c.1100, *Witestan* 1086 (DB). '(Place at) the white stone'. OE *hwīt* + *stān*.

Whitewell Antrim. *Whitewell* 1858. 'White well'.

Whitfield, 'white open land', OE *hwīt* + *feld*: **Whitfield** Kent. *Whytefeld* 1228. **Whitfield** Northants. *Witefelle* 1086 (DB). **Whitfield** Northum. *Witefeld* 1254.

Whitford Devon. *Witefort* 1086 (DB). 'White ford'. OE *hwīt* + *ford*.

Whitgift E. R. Yorks. *Witegift* c.1070. Probably 'dowry land of a man called Hvítr'. OScand. pers. name + *gipt*.

Whitgreave Staffs. *Witegraue* 1193. 'White grove or copse'. OE *hwīt* + *grǣfe*.

Whithorn Dumf. *Candida Casa* c.730, *æt Hwitan Ærne* c.890. 'White building', i.e. 'stone-built church'. OE *hwīt* + *ærn*.

Whitland (*Hendy-gwyn*) Carm. *Alba Domus* 1191, *Alba Landa* 1214, *Whitland* 1309. 'White land'. OE *hwīt* + *land*. The Welsh name means 'old white house' (Welsh *hen* + *tŷ* + *gwyn*).

Whitley, 'white wood or clearing', OE *hwīt* + *lēah*; examples include: **Whitley** Berks., near Reading. *Witelei* 1086 (DB). **Whitley Bay** Tyne & Wear. *Wyteleya* 12th cent. **Whitley, Higher** & **Whitley, Lower** Ches. *Witelei* 1086 (DB).

Whitmore Staffs. *Witemore* 1086 (DB). 'White moor or marsh'. OE *hwīt* + *mōr*.

Whitnash Warwicks. *Witenas* 1086 (DB). '(Place at) the white ash-tree'. OE *hwīt* (dative *-an*) + *æsc*.

Whitney Heref. & Worcs. *Witenie* 1086 (DB). 'White island'. OE *hwīt* (dative *-an*) + *ēg*. Alternatively the first element may be the OE pers. name Hwīta (genitive *-n*).

Whitsbury Hants. *Wiccheberia* c.1130. 'Fortified place where wych-elms grow'. OE *wice* + *burh* (dative *byrig*).

Whitstable Kent. *Witestaple, Witenestaple* 1086 (DB). 'White post', or 'post of the councillors'. OE *hwīt* (dative *-an*) or *wita* (genitive plural *-ena*) + *stapol*.

Whitstone Cornwall. *Witestan* 1086 (DB). 'White stone'. OE *hwīt* + *stān*.

Whittingham, Northum. *Hwitincham* c.1050. 'Homestead of the family or followers of a man called Hwīta', or 'homestead at Hwīta's place'. OE pers. name + *-inga-* or *-ing* + *hām*.

Whittingslow Shrops. *Witecheslawe* 1086 (DB). 'Tumulus of a man called Hwittuc'. OE pers. name + *hlāw*.

Whittington, 'estate associated with a man called Hwīta', OE pers. name + *-ing-* + *tūn*; examples include: **Whittington** Shrops. *Wititone* 1086 (DB). **Whittington** Staffs. *Hwituntune* 925. **Whittington, Great** Northum. *Witynton* 1233.

Whittle-le-Woods Lancs. *Witul* c.1160. 'White hill'. OE *hwīt* + *hyll*. Later affix means 'in the woodland'.

Whittlebury Northants, *Witlanbyrig* c.930. 'Stronghold of a man called *Witla*'. OE pers. name + *burh* (dative *byrig*).

Whittlesey Cambs. *Witlesig* 972, *Witesie* 1086 (DB). 'Island of a man called *Wittel*'. OE pers. name + *ēg*.

Whittlesford Cambs. *Witelesforde* 1086 (DB). 'Ford of a man called *Wittel*'. OE pers. name + *ford*.

Whitton, usually 'white farmstead' or 'farmstead of a man called Hwīta', OE *hwīt* or pers. name + *tūn*, for example: **Whitton** Stock. on T. *Wittune* 1208–10. **Whitton** Suffolk. *Widituna |sic|* 1086 (DB), *Witton* 1212.

However the following has a different origin: **Whitton** N. Lincs. *Witenai* 1086 (DB). 'White island'. OE *hwīt* (dative *-an*) + *ēg*.

Whittonstall Northum. *Quictunstal* 1242. 'Farmstead with a quickset hedge'. OE **cwic* + *tūn-stall*.

Whitwell, 'white spring or stream', OE *hwīt* + *wella*'; examples include: **Whitwell** Derbys. *Hwitewylle* c.1002, *Witewelle* 1086 (DB). **Whitwell** I. of Wight. *Quitewell* 1212.

Whitwick Leics. *Witewic* 1086 (DB). 'White dwelling or (dairy) farm', or 'farm of a man called Hwīta'. OE *hwīt* or pers. name + *wīc*.

Whitwood W. Yorks. *Witewde* 1086 (DB). 'White wood' (referring to colour of tree-bark or blossom). OE *hwīt* + *wudu*.

Whitworth Lancs. *Whitewroth* 13th cent. 'White enclosure'. OE *hwīt* + *worth*.

Whixall Shrops. *Witehala |sic|* 1086 (DB), *Whitekeshal* 1241. 'Nook of land of a man called Hwittuc'. OE pers. name + *halh*.

Whixley N. Yorks. *Cucheslage* 1086 (DB). 'Woodland clearing of a man called **Cwic*'. OE pers. name + *lēah*.

Whorlton, Durham. *Queorningtun* c.1050. Probably 'farmstead at the mill-stone place or the mill stream'. OE *cweorn* + *-ing* + *tūn*.

Whorlton N. Yorks. *Wirveltune* 1086 (DB). 'Farmstead near the round-topped hill'. OE *hwerfel* + *tūn*.

Whyteleafe Surrey, named from *White Leaf Field* 1839, so called from the aspens that grew there.

Wibtoft Leics. *Wibbetofte* 1002, *Wibetot* 1086 (DB). 'Homestead of a man called Wibba or Vibbi'. OE or OScand. pers. name + *toft*.

Wichenford Heref. & Worcs. *Wiceneford* 11th cent. 'Ford by the wych-elms'. OE *wice* (genitive plural *-ena*) + *ford*.

Wichling Kent. *Winchelesmere* 1086 (DB), *Winchelinge* 1220–4. Probably '(settlement of) the family or followers of a man called *Wincel*', OE pers. name + *-ingas*. The alternative name used in the 11th and 12th centuries means '*Wincel's pool or boundary', second element OE *mere* or *mǣre*.

Wick, 'the dwelling, the specialized farm or trading settlement', OE *wīc*; examples include: **Wick** Heref. & Worcs., near Pershore. *Wiche* 1086 (DB). **Wick** S. Glos, near Kingswood. *Wike* 1189. **Wick St Lawrence** N. Som. *Wike* 1225. Affix from the dedication of the church.

Wick Highland. *Vik* 1140, *Weke* 1455. '(Place by the) bay'. OScand. *vik*.

Wicken, 'the dwellings, the specialized farm or trading settlement', OE *wīc* in the dative plural form *wīcum* or a ME plural form *wiken*: **Wicken** Cambs. *Wicha* 1086 (DB). *Wiken* c.1200. **Wicken** Northants. *Wiche* 1086 (DB), *Wicne* c.1235. **Wicken Bonhunt** Essex. *Wica* 1086 (DB), *Wykes Bonhunte* 1238. Originally two separate names, Bonhunt (*Banhunta* 1086 (DB)) possibly being 'place where people were summoned for hunting', OE *bann* + *hunte*.

Wickenby Lincs. *Wichingebi* 1086 (DB). 'Farmstead or village of a man called Vikingr, or of the vikings'. OScand. pers. name or *vikingr* + *bý*.

Wickersley S. Yorks. *Wicresleia* 1086 (DB). 'Woodland clearing of a man called Víkarr'. OScand. pers. name + OE *lēah*.

Wickford Essex. *Wicforda* c.975, *Wicfort* 1086 (DB). Probably 'ford by an earlier Romano-British settlement'. OE *wīc* + *ford*.

Wickham, usually 'homestead associated with a *vicus*, i.e. an earlier Romano-British settlement', OE *wīchām*; examples include: **Wickham** Berks. *Wicham* 1167. **Wickham** Hants. *Wicham* 925–41, *Wiceham* 1086 (DB). **Wickham Bishops** Essex. *Wicham* 1086 (DB), *Wykham Bishops* 1313. Affix from its possession by the Bishop of London. **Wickham Market** Suffolk *Wikham* 1086 (DB). Affix from the important medieval market here. **Wickham Skeith** Suffolk *Wichamm* 1086 (DB), *Wicham Skeyth* 1368. Affix is OScand. *skeith* 'a race-course'. **Wickham, West** Gtr. London. *Wichamm* 973, *Wiceham* 1086 (DB). It is possible that in this name the second element is rather OE *hamm* in the sense 'promontory'.

Wickhambreaux Kent *Wicham* 948, *Wiceham* 1086 (DB), *Wykham Breuhuse* 1270. Identical in origin with

the previous names. Manorial affix from the de Brayhuse family, here in the 13th cent.

Wickhambrook Suffolk *Wicham* 1086 (DB), *Wichambrok* 1254. Identical in origin with the previous names, but with the later addition of OE *brōc* 'brook'.

Wickhamford Heref. & Worcs. *Wicwona* 709, *Wiquene* 1086 (DB), *Wikewaneford* 1221. 'Ford at the place called *Wicwon*'. OE *ford*, see CHILDSWICKHAM

Wickhampton Norfolk *Wichamtuna* 1086 (DB). Probably 'homestead with or near a dairy farm'. OE *wīc* + *hām-tūn*.

Wicklewood Norfolk *Wikelewuda* 1086 (DB). Possibly 'wood by the dairy-farm clearing'. OE *wīc* + *lēah* + *wudu*.

Wicklow (*Cill Mhántain*) Wicklow. *Wykynoelo* n.d. 'Vikings' meadow'. OScand. *víkingr* + *ló*. The Irish name means 'Mantán's church'.

Wickmere Norfolk *Wicmera* 1086 (DB). 'Pool by a dwelling or (dairy) farm'. OE *wīc* + *mere*.

Wickwar S. Glos. *Wichen* 1086 (DB), *Wykewarre* 13th cent. Originally 'the dwellings or specialized farm', from OE *wīc* in a plural form. Later manorial affix from the family of la Warre, here from the early 13th cent.

Widcombe, North & *Widcombe, South* B. & NE. Som. *Widecomb* 1303. 'Wide valley', or 'willow-tree valley'. OE *wīd* or *wīthig* + *cumb*.

Widdington Essex *Widintuna* 1086 (DB). 'Farmstead or village where willow-trees grow'. OE *withign* + *tūn*.

Widdrington Northum. *Vuderintuna* c.1160. 'Estate associated with a man called *Widuhere*'. OE pers. name + *-ing-* + *tūn*.

Widecombe in the Moor Devon *Widecumba* 12th cent. Probably 'valley where willow-trees grow'. OE *wīthig* + *cumb*. Affix refers to its situation on DARTMOOR.

Widford, 'ford where willow-trees grow', OE *wīthig* + *ford*: **Widford** Essex *Witford* 1202. **Widford** Herts *Wideford* 1086 (DB).

Widmerpool Notts *Wimarspol* 1086 (DB). 'Wide lake (or willow-tree lake) pool'. OE *wīd* or *wīthig* + *mere* + *pōl*.

Widnes Ches. *Wydnes* c.1200. 'Wide promontory'. OE *wīd* + *næss*.

Wield Hants. *Walde* 1086 (DB), *Welde* 1256. 'The woodland or forest'. OE *weald*.

Wigan Gtr. Manch. *Wigan* 1199. Probably a shortened form of a Welsh name *Tref Wigan* 'homestead of a man called Wigan'.

Wigborough, Great Essex *Wicgheberga* 1086 (DB). 'Hill of a man called Wicga'. OE *pers. name* + *beorg*.

Wiggenhall Norfolk *Wigrehala* 1086 (DB), *Wiggenhal* 1196. 'Nook of land of a man called Wicga'. OE pers. name (genitive *-n*) + *halh*.

Wigginton, 'farmstead of, or associated with, a man called Wicga', OE pers. name (genitive *-n* or + *-ing-*) + *tūn*: **Wigginton** Herts *Wigentone* 1086 (DB). **Wigginton** Oxon *Wigentone* 1086 (DB). **Wigginton** Staffs. *Wigetone* 1086 (DB). **Wigginton** York. *Wichintun* 1086 (DB).

Wigglesworth N. Yorks. *Winchelesuuorde* 1086 (DB). 'Enclosure of a man called Wincel'. OE *pers. name* + *worth*.

Wiggonby Cumbria *Wygayneby* 1278. 'Farmstead or village of a man called Wigan'. Celtic pers. name + OScand. *bý*.

Wighill N. Yorks. *Duas Wicheles* 1086 (DB), *Wikale* 1219. 'Nook of land with a dairyfarm or by an earlier Romano-British settlement'. OE *wīc* + *halh* (in the plural form in 1086, with Latin *duas* 'two').

Wight, Isle of (the county). *Vectis c*.150, *Wit* 1086 (DB). A Celtic name possibly meaning 'place of the division', referring to its situation between the two arms of the Solent.

Wighton Norfolk *Wistune* 1086 (DB). 'Dwelling place, farmstead with a dwelling'. OE *wīc-tūn*.

Wigmore Heref. & Worcs. *Wigemore* 1086 (DB). Probably 'quaking marsh'. OE *wicga* + *mōr*.

Wigmore Kent. *Wydemere* 1275. 'Broad pool'. OE *wīd* + *mere*.

Wigsley Notts *Wigesleie* 1086 (DB). 'Woodland clearing of a man called *Wicg*'. OE pers. name + *lēah*.

Wigsthorpe Northants. *Wykingethorp* 1232. 'Outlying farmstead or hamlet of a man called Vikingr'. OScand. pers. name + *thorp*.

Wigston Magna Leics *Wichingestone* 1086 (DB). 'Farmstead or estate of a man called *Wīcing* or Vikingr'. OE or OScand. pers. name + OE *tūn*. Affix is Latin *magna* 'great' to distinguish this place from **Wigston Parva** (*Wicestan* 1086 (DB)) which has a quite different origin, either 'rocking-stone' from OE *wigga* + *stān*, or 'stone of a man called *Wicg*' from OE pers. name + *stān*.

Wigtoft Lincs *Wiketoft* 1187. Probably 'homestead by a (former) creek'. OScand. *vík* + *toft*.

Wigton Cumbria *Wiggeton* 1163. 'Farmstead or village of a man called Wicga'. OE pers. name + *tūn*.

Wigtown Dumf. *Wigeton* 1266. 'Dwelling place'. OE *wīc* + *tūn*.

Wigwig Shrops. *Wigewic* 1086 (DB). Probably 'dairy farm of a man called Wicga'. OE pers. name + *wīc*.

Wike, 'the dwelling, the specialized farm', OE *wīc*; for example **Wike** W. Yorks., near Harewood. *Wich* 1086 (DB).

Wilbarston Northants. *Wilbertestone* 1086 (DB). 'Farmstead or village of a man called Wilbeorht'. OE pers. name + *tūn*.

Wilberfoss E. R. Yorks. *Wilburcfosa* 1148. 'Ditch of a woman called Wilburh'. OE pers. name + *foss*.

Wilbraham, Great & **Wilbraham, Little** Cambs. *Wilburgeham c*.975, *Wiborgham* 1086 (DB). 'Homestead or village of a woman called Wilburh'. OE pers. name + *hām*.

Wilburton Cambs. *Wilburhtun* 970, *Wilbertone* 1086 (DB). 'Farmstead or village of a woman called Wilburh'. OE pers. name + *tūn*.

Wilby Norfolk. *Willebeih* 1086 (DB). 'Farmstead by the willow-trees', or possibly 'circle of willow-trees'. OE *wilig* + OScand. *bý* or OE *bēag*.

Wilby Northants. *Willabyg c*.1067, *Wilebi* 1086 (DB). 'Farmstead of a man called Willa or Villi'. OE or OScand. pers. name + *bý*.

Wilby Suffolk *Wilebey* 1086 (DB). Probably 'circle of willow-trees'. OE *wilig* + *bēag*.

Wilcot Wilts. *Wilcotum* 940, *Wilcote* 1086 (DB). 'Cottages by the stream or spring'. OE *wiella* + *cot* (dative plural *-um*).

Wildboarclough Ches *Wildeborclogh* 1357. 'Deep valley frequented by wild boar'. OE *wilde-bār* + *clōh*.

Wilden Beds *Wildene* 1086 (DB). Possibly 'willow-tree valley'. OE *wilig* + *denu*.

Wilden Heref. & Worcs. *Wineladuna |sic|* 1182, *Wiveldon* 1299. Probably 'hill of a man called *Wifela*'. OE pers. name + *dūn*.

Wildsworth Lincs. *Winelesworth |sic|* 1199, *Wyveleswurth* 1280. Probably 'enclosure of a man called *Wifel*'. OE pers. name + *worth*.

Wilford Notts. *Wilesford* 1086 (DB). Probably 'willow-tree ford'. OE *wilig* + *ford*.

Wilkesley Ches. *Wiuelesde |sic|* 1086 (DB), *Wivelescle* 1230. 'Tongue of land of a man called *Wifel*'. OE pers. name + *clēa*.

Willand Devon. *Willelanda* 1086 (DB). 'Waste land', or 'cultivated land reverted to waste'. OE *wilde* + *land*.

Willaston, 'farmstead or village of a man called Wīglāf'. OE pers. name + *tūn*: **Willaston** Ches., near Hooton. *Wilaveston* 1086 (DB). **Willaston** Ches., near Nantwich. *Wilavestune* 1086 (DB).

Willen Bucks *Wily* 1189. '(Place at) the willow-trees'. OE *wilig* in a dative plural form.

Willenhall W. Mids., near Coventry. *Wilenhala* 12th cent. 'Nook or small valley where willow-trees grow'. OE *wiligen* + *halh*.

Willenhall W. Mids., near Wolverhampton. *Willanhalch* 732, *Winenhale |sic|* 1086 (DB). 'Nook or small valley of a man called Willa'. OE pers. name (genitive *-n*) + *halh*.

Willerby, 'farmstead or village of a man called Wilheard', OE pers. name + OScand. *bý*: **Willerby** E. R. Yorks. *Wilgardi |sic|* 1086 (DB), *Willardebi* 1196. **Willerby** N. Yorks. *Willerdebi* 1125–30.

Willersey Glos. *Willerseye* 709, *Willersei* 1086 (DB). 'Island of a man called Wilhere or Wilheard'. OE *pers*. name + *ēg*.

Willersley Heref. & Worcs. *Willaveslege* 1086 (DB). Probably 'woodland clearing of a man called Wīglāf'. OE pers. name + *lēah*.

Willesborough Kent. *Wifelesberg* 863. 'Hill or mound of a man called *Wifel*'. OE pers. name + *beorg*.

Willesden Gtr. London. *Willesdone* 939, *Wellesdone* 1086 (DB). 'Hill with a spring'. OE *wiell* + *dūn*.

Willett Somerset *Willet* 1086 (DB). Named from the River Willett, an old river-name of uncertain origin and meaning.

Willey, usually 'willow-tree wood or clearing', OE *wilig* + *lēah*; examples include: **Willey** Shrops. *Wilit |sic|* 1086 (DB), *Wilileg* 1199. **Willey** Warwicks. *Welei* 1086 (DB).

However the following has a different origin: **Willey** Surrey. *Weoleage* 909. 'Sacred grove with a heathen temple'. OE *wēoh* + *lēah*.

Williamscot Oxon *Williamescote* 1166. 'Cottage(s) of a man called Willelm or William'. OGerman pers. name + OE *cot*.

Willingale Doe & *Willingale Spain* Essex *Willinghehala* 1086 (DB), *Willingeshale Doe* 1270, *Wylinghehale Spayne* 1269. 'Nook of land of the family or followers of a man called Willa'. OE pers. name + *-inga-* + *halh*. Manorial affixes from the de Ou family, here in the 12th cent., and from the de Ispania family, here from 1086.

Willingdon E. Sussex. *Willendone* 1086 (DB). Probably 'hill of a man called Willa'. OE pers. name (genitive *-n*) + *dūn*.

Willingham, sometimes 'homestead of the family or followers of a man called *Wifel', OE pers. name + *-inga-* + *hām*: **Willingham** Cambs., near Cambridge. *Vuivlingeham* c.1050, *Wivelingham* 1086 (DB). **Willingham** Lincs. *Wilingeham* 1086 (DB). **Willingham, North** Lincs. *Wiuilingeham* 1086 (DB).
   However the following are 'homestead of the family or followers of a man called Willa', OE pers. name + *-inga-* + *hām*: **Willingham, Cherry** Lincs. *Wilingeham* 1086 (DB), *Chyry Wylynham* 1386. Affix is ME *chiri* 'cherry-tree'. **Willingham, South** Lincs. *Ulingeham* 1086 (DB).

Willington Beds. *Welitone* 1086 (DB). 'Willow-tree farmstead'. OE **wilign* + *tūn*.

Willington Derbys. *Willetune* 1086 (DB). Probably identical in origin with the previous name.

Willington Durham. *Wyvelintun* c.1190. 'Estate associated with a man called *Wifel'. OE pers. name + *-ing-* + *tūn*.

Willington Tyne & Wear. *Wiflintun* c.1085. Identical in origin with the previous name.

Willington Warwicks. *Ullavintone* 1086 (DB). 'Estate associated with a man called Wulflāf'. OE pers. name + *-ing-* + *tūn*.

Willington Corner Ches. *Winfletone* 1086 (DB). 'Farmstead or village of a woman called Wynflǣed'. OE pers. name + *tūn*. Affix, first used in the 19th cent., refers to a corner of Delamere Forest.

Willisham Tye Suffolk. *Willauesham* c.1040. 'Homestead or enclosure of a man called Wīglāf'. OE pers. name + *hām* or *hamm*. *Tye* is dialect *tye* (from OE *tēag*) 'a large common pasture', as in other Suffolk names.

Willitoft E. R. Yorks. *Wilgetot* 1086 (DB). 'Willow-tree homestead'. OE **wilig* + OScand. *toft*.

Williton Somerset. *Willettun* 904, *Willetone* 1086 (DB). 'Farmstead or village on the River Willett'. Old river-name (*see* WILLETT) + OE *tūn*.

Willoughby, usually 'farmstead by the willow-trees', OE **wilig* + OScand. *bý*, although some may be 'circle of willow-trees', OE **wilig* + *bēag*; examples include: **Willoughby** Lincs., near Alford. *Wilgebi* 1086 (DB). **Willoughby** Warwicks *Wiliabyg* 956, *Wilebei* 1086 (DB). **Willoughby, Silk** Lincs. *Wilgebi* 1086 (DB). Affix is a reduced form of a nearby place *Silkebi* 1212, 'farmstead of a man called Silki, or near a gully', OScand. pers. name or OE **sīoluc* + OScand. *bý*.

Willoughton Lincs. *Wilchetone* 1086 (DB). 'Farmstead or village where willow-trees grow'. OE **wilig* + *tūn*.

Wilmcote Warwicks. *Wilmundigcotan* 1016, *Wilmecote* 1086 (DB). 'Cottage(s) associated with a man called Wilmund'. OE pers. name + *-ing-* + *cot*.

Wilmington Devon. *Wilelmitone* 1086 (DB). 'Estate associated with a man called Wilhelm'. OE pers. name + *-ing-* + *tūn*.

Wilmington E. Sussex. *Wilminte* |sic| 1086 (DB), *Wilminton* 1189. 'Estate associated with a man called Wīghelm or Wilhelm'. OE pers. name + *-ing-* + *tūn*.

Wilmington Kent, near Dartford. *Wilmintuna* 1089. 'Estate associated with a man called Wīghelm'. OE pers. name + *-ing-* + *tūn*.

Wilmslow Ches. *Wilmesloe* c.1250. 'Mound of a man called Wīghelm'. OE pers. name + *hlāw*.

Wilnecote Staffs. *Wilmundecote* 1086 (DB). 'Cottage(s) of a man called Wilmund'. OE pers. name + *cot*.

Wilpshire Lancs. *Wlypschyre* 1246. OE *scīr* 'district, estate' with obscure first element, possibly a pers. name or surname formed from OE *wlips, wlisp* 'lisping'.

Wilsford, 'ford of a man called *Wifel', OE pers. name + *ford*: **Wilsford** Lincs. *Wivelesforde* 1086 (DB). **Wilsford** Wilts., near Pewsey. *Wifelesford* 892, *Wivlesford* 1086 (DB). **Wilsford** Wilts., near Salisbury. *Wiflesford* 1086 (DB).

Wilsill N. Yorks. *Wifeleshealh* c.1030, *Wifleshale* 1086 (DB). 'Small valley of a man called *Wifel or Vífill'. OE or OScand. pers. name + OE *halh*.

Wilson Leics. *Wiuelestunia* 12th cent. 'Farmstead or village of a man called *Wifel'. OE pers. name + *tūn*.

Wilstone Herts. *Wivelestorn* 1220. 'Thorn-tree of a man called *Wifel'. OE pers. name + *thorn*.

Wilton, usually 'farmstead or village where willow-trees grow', OE **wilig* + *tūn*; examples include: **Wilton** Norfolk. *Wiltuna* 1086 (DB). **Wilton** Red. & Cleve. *Wiltune* 1086 (DB). **Wilton, Bishop** E. R. Yorks. *Wiltone* 1086 (DB). Affix from its early possession by the Archbishops of York.
   However the following have a different origin: **Wilton** Wilts., near Burbage. *Wulton* 1227. Probably 'farmstead near a spring or stream'. OE *wiella* + *tūn*. **Wilton** Wilts., near Salisbury. *Uuiltun* 838, *Wiltune* 1086 (DB). 'Farmstead or village on the River Wylye'. Pre-English river-name (*see* WYLYE) + OE *tūn*.

Wiltshire (the county). *Wiltunscir* 870, *Wiltescire* 1086 (DB). 'Shire centred on WILTON (near Salisbury)'. OE *scīr*.

Wimbish Essex. *Winebisc, Wimbisc* c.1040, *Wimbeis* 1086 (DB). Possibly 'bushy copse of a man called Wine'. OE pers. name + **(ge)bysce*.

Wimbledon Gtr. London. *Wunemannedune* c.950. Probably 'hill of a man called *Wynnmann'. OE pers. name + *dūn*.

Wimblington Cambs. *Wimblingetune* c.975. Probably 'estate associated with a man called Wynnbald'. OE pers. name + *-ing-* + *tūn*.

Wimborne Minster Dorset. *Winburnan* late 9th cent., *Winburne* 1086 (DB), *Wymburneminstre* 1236. Originally the name of the river here (now called Allen), 'meadow stream' from OE *winn + burna. Affix is OE mynster 'monastery (church)'.

Wimborne St Giles Dorset. Winburne 1086 (DB), Vpwymburn Sancti Egidij 1268, Upwymbourne St Giles 1399. Like WIMBORNE MINSTER, named from the river here. The early affix is OE upp 'higher up (the river)'. St Giles (Latin Egidius) is from the dedication of the church.

Wimbotsham Norfolk. Winebotesham 1086 (DB). 'Homestead of a man called Winebald'. OE pers. name + hām.

Wimpole Cambs. Winepole 1086 (DB). 'Pool of a man called Wina'. OE pers. name + pōl.

Wimpstone Warwicks. Wylmestone 1313. 'Farmstead of a man called Wilhelm or Wīghelm'. OE pers. name + tūn.

Wincanton Somerset. Wincaletone 1086 (DB). 'Farmstead on (an arm of) the River Cale'. Celtic river-name (of uncertain origin, but prefixed by *winn 'white') + OE tūn.

Winch, East & Winch, West Norfolk. Estwinic, Wesuuinic 1086 (DB). 'Farmstead with meadowland'. OE *winn + wīc.

Wincham Ches. Wimundisham 1086 (DB). 'Homestead of a man called Wīgmund'. OE pers. name + hām.

Winchcombe Glos. Wincelcumbe c.810, 1086 (DB). 'Valley with a bend in it'. OE *wincel + cumb.

Winchelsea E. Sussex. Winceleseia 1130. 'Island by a river-bend'. OE *wincel + ēg.

Winchendon Bucks. Wincandone 1004, Wichendone 1086 (DB). Possibly 'hill at a bend'. OE wince (genitive -an) + dūn.

Winchester Hants. Ouenta c.150, Uintancæstir c.730, Wincestre 1086 (DB). 'Roman town called Venta'. Pre-Celtic name (possibly 'favoured or chief place') + OE ceaster.

Winchfield Hants. Winchelefeld 1229. 'Open land by a nook or corner'. OE *wincel + feld.

Winchmore Hill Gtr. London. Wynsemerhull 1319. Probably 'boundary hill of a man called Wynsige'. OE pers. name + mǣre + hyll.

Wincle Ches. Winchul c.1190. 'Hill of a man called *Wineca or by a bend'. OE pers. name or wince + hyll.

Windermere Cumbria. Winandermere 12th cent. 'Lake of a man called Vinandr'. OScand. pers. name (genitive -ar) + OE mere.

Winderton Warwicks. Winterton 1166. 'Farmstead used in winter'. OE winter + tūn.

Windlesham Surrey. Windesham 1178, Windlesham 1227. Probably 'homestead of a man called *Windel'. OE pers. name + hām. Alternatively the first element may be OE *windels 'a windlass'.

Windley Derbys. Winleg 12th cent. 'Meadow clearing'. OE *winn + lēah.

Windrush Glos. Wenric 1086 (DB). Named from the River Windrush, a Celtic river-name possibly meaning 'white fen'.

Windsor Berks. Windlesoran c.1060, Windesores 1086 (DB). 'Bank or slope with a windlass'. OE *windels + ōra.

Winestead E. R. Yorks. Wifestede 1086 (DB). 'Homestead of the women, or of a woman called *Wīfe'. OE wīf or pers. name + stede.

Winfarthing Norfolk. Wineferthinc 1086 (DB). 'Quarter of an estate belonging to a man called Wina'. OE pers. name + feorthung.

Winford N. Som. Wunfrod c.1000, Wenfrod 1086 (DB). A Celtic river-name meaning 'white or bright stream'. Celtic *winn + *frud.

Winforton Heref. & Worcs. Widferdestune |sic| 1086 (DB), Wynfreton 1265. Probably 'farmstead or estate of a man called Winefrith'. OE pers. name + tūn.

Winfrith Newburgh Dorset. Winfrode 1086 (DB). Identical in origin with WINFORD. Manorial affix from the Newburgh family, here from the 12th cent.

Wing Bucks. Weowungum |sic| 966–75, Witehunge 1086 (DB). Possibly '(settlement of) the family or followers of a man called *Wiwa', OE pers. name + -ingas. Alternatively '(settlement of) the dwellers at, or devotees of, a heathen temple', OE wīg, wēoh + -ingas.

Wing Rutland. Wenge 12th cent. 'The field'. OScand. vengi.

Wingate(s), 'wind-swept gap(s) or pass(es)', OE *windgeat: examples include: **Wingate** Durham. Windegatum 1071–80. **Wingates** Northum. Wyndegates 1208.

Wingerworth Derbys. Wingreurde 1086 (DB). 'Enclosure of a man called *Winegār'. OE pers. name + worth.

Wingfield Beds. Winfeld c.1200. 'Open land used for pasture, or by a nook'. OE *winn or wince + feld.

Wingfield Suffolk. Wingefeld c.1035, Wighefelda 1086 (DB). Probably 'open land of the family or followers of a man called *Wīga'. OE pers. name + -inga- + feld. Alternatively the first element may be OE wīg 'heathen temple'.

Wingfield, North & Wingfield, South Derbys. Wynnefeld 1002, Winnefelt, Winefeld 1086 (DB). 'Open land used for pasture'. OE *winn + feld.

Wingham Kent. Uuigincggaham 834, Wingheham 1086 (DB). 'Homestead of the family or followers of a man called *Wīga'. OE pers. name + -inga- + hām. Alternatively the first element may be OE wīg 'heathen temple'.

Wingrave Bucks. Withungrave |sic| 1086 (DB), Wiungraua 1163. Possibly 'grove of the family or followers of a man called *Wiwa', OE pers. name + -inga- + grāf. Alternatively 'grove of the dwellers at, or devotees of, a heathen temple', OE wīg, wēoh + -inga- + grāf.

Winkburn Notts. Wicheburne |sic| 1086 (DB), Winkeburna c.1150. 'Stream of a man called *Wineca, or with bends in it'. OE pers. name or *wincel (with Scand. -k-) + burna.

Winkfield Berks. Winecanfeld 942, Wenesfelle |sic| 1086 (DB). 'Open land of a man called *Wineca'. OE pers. name + feld.

Winkleigh Devon. Wincheleia 1086 (DB). 'Woodland clearing of a man called *Wineca'. OE pers. name + lēah.

Winksley N. Yorks. Wincheslaie 1086 (DB). 'Woodland clearing of a man called Winuc'. OE pers. name + lēah.

Winmarleigh Lancs. Wynemerislega 1212. 'Woodland clearing of a man called Winemǣr'. OE pers. name + lēah.

Winnersh Berks. *Wenesse* 1190. 'Ploughed field by meadow'. OE **winn + ersc*.

Winscales Cumbria. *Wyndscales* 1227. 'Temporary huts or sheds in a windy place'. OE *wind* + OScand. *skáli*.

Winscombe N. Som. *Winescumbe* c.965, *Winescome* 1086 (DB). 'Valley of a man called Wine'. OE pers. name + *cumb*.

Winsford, 'ford of a man called Wine', OE pers. name + *ford*: **Winsford** Ches. *Wyneford* c.1334. **Winsford** Somerset. *Winesford* 1086 (DB).

Winsham Somerset. *Winesham* 1046, 1086 (DB). 'Homestead or enclosure of a man called Wine'. OE pers. name + *hām* or *hamm*.

Winshill Staffs. *Wineshylle* 1002. 'Hill of a man called Wine'. OE pers. name + *hyll*.

Winskill Cumbria. *Wyndscales* 1292. 'Temporary huts or sheds in a windy place'. OE *wind* + OScand. *skáli*.

Winslade Hants. *Winesflot* 1086 (DB). 'Spring or channel of a man called Wine'. OE pers. name + *flōde*.

Winsley Wilts. *Winesleg* 1242. 'Woodland clearing of a man called Wine'. OE pers. name + *lēah*.

Winslow Bucks. *Wineshlauu* 795, *Weneslai* 1086 (DB). 'Mound of a man called Wine'. OE pers. name + *hlāw*.

Winson Glos. *Winestune* 1086 (DB). 'Farmstead or village of a man called Wine'. OE pers. name + *tūn*.

Winster Cumbria. *Winster* 13th cent. Named from the River Winster, a Celtic river-name meaning 'white stream' or an OScand. river-name meaning 'the left one'.

Winster Derbys. *Winsterne* 1086 (DB). 'Thorn-tree of a man called Wine'. OE pers. name + *thyrne*.

Winston, 'farmstead or village of a man called Wine', OE pers. name + *tūn*: **Winston** Durham. *Winestona* 1091. **Winston** Suffolk. *Winestuna* 1086 (DB).

Winstone Glos. *Winestan* 1086 (DB). '(Boundary) stone of a man called Wynna'. OE pers. name + *stān*.

Winterborne, *Winterbourne*, originally a river-name 'winter stream, i.e. stream flowing most strongly in winter', OE *winter + burna*; examples of places named from their situation on the various rivers so called include: **Winterborne Came** Dorset. *Wintreburne* 1086 (DB), *Winterburn Caam* 1280. Affix from its early possession by the Norman Abbey of Caen. **Winterborne Clenston** Dorset. *Wintreburne* 1086 (DB), *Wynterburn Clencheston* 1303. Affix means 'estate (*tūn*) of the Clench family'. **Winterborne Stickland** Dorset. *Winterburne* 1086 (DB), *Winterburn Stikellane* 1203. Affix means '(with a) steep lane', from OE *sticol + lane*. **Winterborne Whitechurch** Dorset. *Wintreburne* 1086 (DB), *Wynterborn Wytecherch* 1268. Affix means '(with a) white, i.e. stone-built, church', OE *hwīt + cirice*. **Winterborne Zelston** Dorset. *Wintreborne* 1086 (DB), *Wynterbourn Selyston* 1350. Affix means 'estate (*tūn*) of the de Seles family'. **Winterbourne** S. Glos. *Wintreborne* 1086 (DB). **Winterbourne Abbas** Dorset. *Wintreburne* 1086 (DB), *Wynterburn Abbatis* 1244. Latin affix 'of the abbot' refers to early possession by the Abbey of Cerne. **Winterbourne Bassett** & **Winterbourne Monkton** Wilts. *Wintreburn* 950, 1086 (DB), *Winterburn Basset* 1242, *Moneke Wynterburn* 1251. Distinguishing affixes from early possession by the Basset family and by the

monks of Glastonbury Abbey. **Winterbourne Dauntsey, Winterbourne Earls** & **Winterbourne Gunner** Wilts. *Wintreburne* 1086 (DB), *Wynterburne Dauntesie* 1268, *Winterburne Earls* 1250, *Winterburn Gonor* 1267. Distinguishing affixes from early possession by the Danteseye family, by the Earls of Salisbury, and by a lady called Gunnora (here in 1249).

Winteringham N. Lincs. *Wintringeham* 1086 (DB). 'Homestead of the family or followers of a man called Wintra'. OE pers. name + *-inga- + hām*.

Wintersett W. Yorks. *Wintersete* c.1125. 'Fold used in winter'. OE *winter + set*.

Winterslow Wilts. *Wintreslev* 1086 (DB). 'Mound or tumulus of a man called Winter'. OE pers. name + *hlǣw*.

Winterton N. Lincs. *Wintringatun* c.1067, *Wintrintune* 1086 (DB). 'Farmstead of the family or followers of a man called Wintra'. OE pers. name + *-inga- + tūn*.

Winterton-on-Sea Norfolk. *Winttertonne* 1044–7, *Wintretuna* 1086 (DB). 'Farmstead used in winter'. OE *winter + tūn*.

Winthorpe Lincs. *Winetorp* 12th cent. 'Outlying farmstead or hamlet of a man called Wina'. OE pers. name + OScand. *thorp*.

Winthorpe Notts. *Wimuntorp* 1086 (DB). 'Outlying farmstead or hamlet of a man called Wīgmund or Vigmundr'. OE or OScand. pers. name + *thorp*.

Winton Cumbria. *Wyntuna* c.1094. Probably 'pasture farmstead'. OE **winn + tūn*.

Winton Dorset, a suburb of Bournemouth named from the Earl of Eglinton, created also Earl of *Winton* in 1859, a kinsman of the Talbot sisters. (*See* TALBOT VILLAGE).

Wintringham N. Yorks. *Wentrigham* 1086 (DB), *Wintringham* 1169. 'Homestead of the family or followers of a man called Wintra'. OE pers. name + *-inga- + hām*.

Winwick, 'dwelling or (dairy) farm of a man called Wina', OE pers. name + *wīc*: **Winwick** Cambs. *Wineuuiche* 1086 (DB). **Winwick** Northants. *Winewican* 1043, *Winewiche* 1086 (DB).

Winwick Ches. *Winequic* 1170, *Winewich* 1204. 'Dwelling or (dairy) farm of a man called **Wineca*'. OE pers. name + *wīc*.

Wirksworth Derbys. *Wyrcesuuyrthe* 835, *Werchesworde* 1086 (DB). 'Enclosure of a man called **Weorc*'. OE pers. name + *worth*.

Wirral Ches. *Wirhealum, Wirheale* early 10th cent. '(Place at) the nook(s) where bog-myrtle grows'. OE *wīr + halh*.

Wirswall Ches. *Wireswelle* 1086 (DB). 'Spring or stream of a man called Wīghere'. OE pers. name + *wella*.

Wisbech Cambs. *Wisbece* 1086 (DB). Possibly 'marshy-meadow valley or ridge'. OE *wisc* or **wisse + bece* or *bæc* (locative **bece*). Alternatively the first element may be the River Wissey, itself an OE name meaning 'marshy stream'.

Wisborough Green W. Sussex. *Wisebregh* 1227. 'Marshy-meadow hill'. OE *wisc + beorg*.

Wiseton Notts. *Wisetone* 1086 (DB). 'Farmstead of a man called Wīsa', or 'marshy-meadow farmstead'. OE pers. name or *wisc + tūn*.

Wishaw N. Lan. *Witscaga* 1086 (DB). 'Wood'. OE *sceaga*; doubtful first element.

Wishford, Great Wilts. *Wicheford* 1086 (DB). 'Ford where wych-elms grow'. OE *wice* + *ford*.

Wiske (river) N. Yorks., *see* APPLETON WISKE.

Wisley Surrey. *Wiselei* 1086 (DB). 'Marshy-meadow clearing'. OE *wisc* + *lēah*.

Wispington Lincs. *Wispinctune* 1086 (DB). Possibly 'farmstead at the place where brushwood grows'. OE **wisp* + *-ing* + *tūn*.

Wissett Suffolk. *Wisseta* 1086 (DB), *Witseta* 1165. Possibly 'fold of a man called Witta'. OE pers. name + *set*.

Wissington Suffolk. *Wiswythetun* c.1000. 'Farmstead or estate of a woman called Wīgswīth'. OE pers. name + *tūn*.

Wistanstow Shrops. *Wistanestou* 1086 (DB). 'Holy place of St Wīgstān'. OE saint's name (Wīgstān was a Mercian prince murdered in 849 or 850) + *stōw*.

Wistanswick Shrops. *Wistaneswick* 1274. 'Dwelling or (dairy) farm of a man called Wīgstān'. OE pers. name + *wīc*.

Wistaston Ches. *Wistanestune* 1086 (DB). 'Farmstead or village of a man called Wīgstān'. OE pers. name + *tūn*.

Wiston W. Sussex. *Wistanestun* 1086 (DB). 'Farmstead or village of a man called Wīgstān or Winestān'. OE pers. name + *tūn*.

Wiston (*Cas-wis*) Pemb. *Castellum Wiz* 1146, *Wistune* 1319. 'Wizo's farmstead'. OE *tūn*. Wizo came from Flanders to set up a castle here in the 12th cent. Its Welsh name was *Castell Gwis*, 'Wizo's castle', which gave the present Welsh name.

Wiston S. Lan. *Wicestun* c.1155. 'Wice's farm'. OE pers. name + *tūn*.

Wistow, 'the dwelling place', OE *wīcstōw*: **Wistow** Cambs. *Wicstoue* 974, *Wistov* 1086 (DB). **Wistow** N. Yorks. *Wicstow* c.1030.

Wistow Leics. *Wistanestov* 1086 (DB). 'Holy place of St Wīgstān', from OE *stōw*, thus identical with WISTANSTOW Shrops.

Wiswell Lancs. *Wisewell* 1207. Possibly 'spring or stream near a marshy meadow'. OE *wisc* or **wisse* + *wella*.

Witcham Cambs. *Wichamme* 970, *Wiceham* 1086 (DB). 'Promontory where wych-elms grow'. OE *wice* + *hamm*.

Witchampton Dorset. *Wichemetune* 1086 (DB). Probably 'farmstead of the dwellers at a village associated with an earlier Romano-British settlement'. OE *wic* + *hāeme* + *tūn*.

Witchford Cambs. *Wiceford* 1086 (DB). 'Ford where wych-elms grow'. OE *wice* + *ford*.

Witchingham, Great Norfolk. *Wicinghaham* 1086 (DB). 'Homestead of the family or followers of a man called **Wic*', OE pers. name + *-inga-* + *hām*. Alternatively the first element may be OE *wīcinga* 'of the pirates'.

Witcombe, Great Glos. *Wydecomb* 1220. 'Wide valley'. OE *wīd* + *cumb*.

Witham Essex. *Witham* late 9th cent., 1086 (DB). Probably 'homestead near a river-bend'. OE **wiht* + *hām*.

Witham Friary Somerset. *Witeham* 1086 (DB). 'Homestead of a councillor, or of a man called Witta'. OE *wita* or pers. name + *hām*. The affix *Friary*, found from 16th cent., is possibly from Latin *fraeria* 'guild'.

Witham on the Hill Lincs. *Witham* 1086 (DB). Probably 'homestead in a bend'. OE **wiht* + *hām*.

Witham, North & **Witham, South** Lincs. *Widme* 1086 (DB). Named from the River Witham, a Celtic or pre-Celtic river-name of uncertain origin.

Witheridge Devon. *Wiriga* |*sic*| 1086 (DB), *Wytherigge* 1256. 'Willow-tree ridge', or 'ridge where wether-sheep are kept'. OE *wīthig* or *wether* + *hrycg*.

Witherley Leics. *Wytherdele* c.1204. 'Woodland clearing of a woman called Wīgthrȳth'. OE pers. name + *lēah*.

Withern Lincs. *Widerne* 1086 (DB). Probably 'house in the wood'. OE *widu, wudu* + *ærn*.

Withernsea E. R. Yorks. *Widfornessei* 1086 (DB). Possibly 'lake at the place near the thorn-tree'. OE *with* + *thorn* + *sǣ*.

Withernwick E. R. Yorks. *Widforneuuic* 1086 (DB). Possibly 'dairy farm of the place near the thorn-tree'. OE *with* + *thorn* + *wīc*.

Withersdale Street Suffolk. *Weresdel* |*sic*| 1086 (DB), *Wideresdala* 1184. 'Valley where wether-sheep are kept'. OE *wether* + *dæl*.

Withersfield Suffolk. *Wedresfelda* 1086 (DB). 'Open land where wether-sheep are kept.' OE *wether* + *feld*.

Witherslack Cumbria. *Witherslake* c.1190. 'Valley of the wood, or of the willow-tree'. OScand. *vithr* (genitive *vithar*) or *víth* (genitive *víthjar*) + *slakki*.

Withiel Cornwall. *Widie* 1086 (DB). 'Wooded place'. Cornish *gwydh* 'trees' with suffix **-yel*.

Withiel Florey Somerset. *Withiglea* 737, *Wythele Flory* 1305. 'Wood or clearing where willow-trees grow'. OE *wīthig* + *lēah*. Manorial affix from the de Flury family, here in the 13th cent.

Withington, usually 'farmstead with a willow copse', OE **wīthign* + *tūn*; examples include: **Withington** Ches. *Widinton* 1185. **Withington** Heref. & Worcs. *Widingtune* 1086 (DB).

However the following has a different origin: **Withington** Glos. *Wudiandun* 737, *Widindune* 1086 (DB). 'Hill of a man called Widia'. OE pers. name (genitive *-n*) + *dūn*.

Withnell Lancs. *Withinhull* c.1160. 'Hill where willow-trees grow'. OE **wīthigen* + *hyll*.

Withybrook Warwicks. *Wythibroc* 12th cent. 'Willow-tree brook'. OE *wīthig* + *brōc*.

Withycombe, 'valley where willow-trees grow', OE *wīthig* + *cumb*: **Withycombe** Somerset. *Widicumbe* 1086 (DB). **Withycombe Raleigh** Devon. *Widecome* 1086 (DB), *Widecombe Ralegh* 1465. Manorial affix from the de Ralegh family, here in the early 14th cent.

Withyham E. Sussex. *Withiham* 1230. 'Willow-tree enclosure or promontory'. OE *wīthig* + *hamm*.

Withypool Somerset. *Widepolle* 1086 (DB). 'Willow-tree pool'. OE *wīthig* + *pōl*.

Witley Surrey. *Witlei* 1086 (DB). 'Woodland clearing in a bend, or of a man called Witta'. OE **wiht* or pers. name + *lēah*.

Witley, Great & *Witley, Little* Heref. & Worcs. *Wittlæg* 964, *Witlege* 1086 (DB). 'Woodland clearing in a bend'. OE **wiht* + *lēah*.

Witnesham Suffolk. *Witdesham* |sic| 1086 (DB), *Witnesham* 1254. Possibly 'homestead of a man called **Wittīn*'. OE pers. name + *hām*.

Witney Oxon. *Wyttanige* 969, *Witenie* 1086 (DB). 'Island, or dry ground in marsh, of a man called Witta'. OE pers. name (genitive *-n*) + *ēg*.

Wittenham, Little & *Wittenham, Long* Oxon. *Wittanham* c.865, *Witeham* 1086 (DB). 'River-bend land of a man called Witta'. OE pers. name (genitive *-n*) + *hamm*.

Witter (*Uachtar*) Down. 'Upper place'.

Wittering Cambs. *Witheringaeige* 972, *Witheringham* 1086 (DB). *Witeringa* 1167. '(Island or homestead of) the family or followers of a man called Wither'. OE pers. name + *-ingas* (in genitive plural with *ēg* and *hām* in the early forms).

Wittering, East & *Wittering, West* W. Sussex. *Wihttringes* 683, *Westringes* |sic| 1086 (DB). '(Settlement of) the family or followers of a man called Wihthere'. OE pers. name + *-ingas*.

Wittersham Kent. *Wihtriceshamme* 1032. 'Promontory of a man called Wihtrīc'. OE pers. name + *hamm*.

Witton, a common name, usually 'farmstead in or by a wood', OE *wudu* or *widu* + *tūn*; for example: **Witton Bridge** Norfolk. *Widituna* 1086 (DB). **Witton, East** & **Witton, West** N. Yorks. *Witun* 1086 (DB). **Witton Gilbert** Durham. *Wyton* 1195. Manorial affix from its possession by Gilbert de la Ley in the 12th cent. **Witton-le-Wear** Durham. *Wudutun* c.1050. On the River Wear, for which *see* MONKWEARMOUTH.
However some Wittons have a different origin: **Witton** Ches. *Witune* 1086 (DB). 'Estate with a salt-works'. OE *wīc* + *tūn*. **Witton, Upper** W. Mids. *Witone* 1086 (DB). Possibly 'farmstead by an earlier Romano-British settlement'. OE *wīc* + *tūn*.

Wiveliscombe Somerset. *Wifelescumb* 854, *Wivelescome* 1086 (DB). 'Valley of a man called **Wifel*'. OE pers. name + *cumb*, but *see* next name.

Wivelsfield E. Sussex. *Wifelesfeld* c.765. Probably 'open land of a man called **Wifel*', OE pers. name + *feld*. Alternatively the first element in this and the previous name may be the noun *wifel* 'weevil' denoting 'weevil-infested land'.

Wivenhoe Essex. *Wiunhov* 1086 (DB). 'Hillspur of a woman called **Wīfe*'. OE pers. name (genitive *-n*) + *hōh*.

Wiveton Norfolk. *Wiuentona* 1086 (DB). 'Farmstead or village of a woman called **Wīfe*'. OE pers name (genitive *-n*) + *tūn*.

Wix Essex. *Wica* 1086 (DB). 'The dwellings or specialized farm'. OE *wīc* in a ME plural form *wikes*.

Wixford Warwicks. *Wihtlachesforde* 962, *Witelavesford* |sic| 1086 (DB). 'Ford of a man called Wihtlāc'. OE pers. name + *ford*.

Wixoe Suffolk. *Wlteskeou* |sic| 1086 (DB), *Widekeshoo* 1205. 'Hill-spur of a man called Widuc'. OE pers. name + *hōh*.

Woburn Beds. *Woburne* 1086 (DB). '(Place at) the crooked or winding stream'. OE *wōh* + *burna*. It gives name to nearby **Woburn Sands** Bucks.

Wokefield Park Berks. *Weonfelda* c.950, *Hocfelle* 1086 (DB). Probably 'open land of a man called **Weohha*'. OE pers. name + *feld*.

Woking Surrey. *Wocchinges* c.712, *Wochinges* 1086 (DB). '(Settlement of) the family or followers of a man called **Wocc(a)*'. OE pers. name + *-ingas*.

Woldingham Surrey. *Wallingeham* |sic| 1086 (DB), *Waldingham* 1204. Probably 'homestead of the forest dwellers'. OE *weald* + *-inga-* + *hām*. Alternatively 'homestead of the family or followers of a man called **Wealda*', with an OE pers. name as first element.

Wolds, The (upland districts, i. Leics., ii. Lincs., iii. N. Yorks. & E. R. Yorks.), from OE *wald* 'high forest-land, later cleared', *see* FOSTON ON THE WOLDS, GARTON ON THE WOLDS, etc.

Wolferton Norfolk. *Wulferton* 1166. 'Farmstead or village of a man called Wulfhere'. OE pers. name + *tūn*.

Wolford, Great & *Wolford, Little* Warwicks. *Wolwarde* 1086 (DB). 'Place protected against wolves'. OE *wulf* + *weard*.

Wolfsdale Pemb. *Wolvedale* 1312. 'Valley frequented by wolves'. OE *wulf* + *dæl*.

Wollaston Northants. *Wilavestone* |sic| 1086 (DB), *Wullaueston* 1190. 'Farmstead or village of a man called Wulflāf. OE pers. name + *tūn*.

Wollaston Shrops. *Willavestune* 1086 (DB). 'Farmstead or village of a man called Wīglāf'. OE pers. name + *tūn*.

Wollerton Shrops. *Ulvretone* 1086 (DB), *Wluruntona* c.1135. 'Farmstead or village of a woman called Wulfrūn'. OE pers. name + *tūn*.

Wolsingham Durham. *Wlsingham* c.1150. 'Homestead of the family or followers of a man called Wulfsige'. OE pers. name + *-inga-* + *hām*.

Wolstanton Staffs. *Wlstanetone* 1086 (DB). 'Farmstead or village of a man called Wulfstān'. OE pers. name + *tūn*.

Wolston Warwicks. *Ulvricetone* 1086 (DB). 'Farmstead or village of a man called Wulfrīc'. OE pers. name + *tūn*.

Wolvercote Oxon. *Ulfgarcote* 1086 (DB). 'Cottage associated with a man called Wulfgār'. OE pers. name + *-ing-* + *cot*.

Wolverhampton W. Mids. *Heantune* 985, *Wolvrenehamptonia* c.1080. Originally 'high farmstead', from OE *hēah* (dative *hēan*) + *tūn*, later with the addition of the OE pers. name *Wulfrūn*, the lady to whom the manor was given in 985.

Wolverley Heref. & Worcs. *Wulfferdinleh* 866, *Ulwardelei* 1086 (DB). 'Woodland clearing associated with a man called Wulfweard'. OE pers. name + *-ing-* + *lēah*.

Wolverton Bucks. *Wluerintone* 1086 (DB). 'Estate associated with a man called Wulfhere'. OE pers. name + *-ing-* + *tūn*.

Wolvey Warwicks. *Ulveia* 1086 (DB). Probably 'enclosure protected against wolves'. OE *wulf* + *hege* or *hæg*.

Wolviston Stock. on T. *Oluestona* 1091. 'Farmstead or village of a man called Wulf'. OE pers. name + *tūn*.

Wombleton N. Yorks. *Winbeltun* 1086 (DB). 'Farmstead or village of a man called Wynbald or Winebald'. OE pers. name + *tūn*.

Wombourn Staffs. *Wamburne* 1086 (DB). '(Place at) the crooked or winding stream'. OE *wōh* (dative *wōn*) + *burna*.

Wombwell S. Yorks. *Wanbuelle* 1086 (DB). 'Spring or stream in a hollow, or of a man called *Wamba*'. OE *wamb* or pers. name + *wella*.

Womenswold Kent. *Wimlincgawald* 824. Possibly 'forest of the family or followers of a man called *Wīmel*'. OE pers. name + -*inga*- + *weald*.

Wonersh Surrey. *Woghenhers* 1199. 'Crooked ploughed field'. OE *wōh* (dative *wōn*) + *ersc*.

Wonston, South Hants. *Wynsigestune* 901, *Wenesistune* 1086 (DB). 'Farmstead or village of a man called Wynsige'. OE pers. name + *tūn*.

Wooburn Bucks. *Waburna* c.1075, *Waborne* 1086 (DB). Probably 'stream with its banks walled up, or with a dam'. OE *wāg* + *burna*. Alternatively the first element may be OE *wōh* 'crooked, winding'.

Wood as affix, *see* main name, e.g. for **Wood Dalling** (Norfolk) *see* DALLING.

Wood Green Gtr. London. *Wodegrene* 1502. 'Green place near woodland'. OE *wudu* + *grēne*.

Woodale N. Yorks. *Wulvedale* 1223. 'Valley frequented by wolves'. OE *wulf* + *dæl*.

Woodbastwick Norfolk. *Bastwik* 1044–7, *Bastuuic* 1086 (DB), *Wodbastwyk* 1253. 'Farm where bast (the bark of the limetree used for rope-making) is got'. OE *bæst* + *wīc*, with the later addition of *wudu* 'wood'.

Woodborough Notts. *Udeburg* 1086 (DB). 'Fortified place by the wood'. OE *wudu* + *burh*.

Woodborough Wilts. *Wideberghe* 1208. 'Wooded hill'. OE *wudu* + *beorg*.

Woodbridge Suffolk. *Oddebruge* c.1050, *Wudebrige* 1086 (DB). 'Wooden bridge', or 'bridge near the wood'. OE *wudu* + *brycg*.

Woodburn, East Northum. *Wodeburn* 1265. 'Stream in the wood'. OE *wudu* + *burna*.

Woodbury Devon. *Wodeberia* 1086 (DB). 'Fortified place by the wood'. OE *wudu* + *burh* (dative *byrig*).

Woodbury Salterton Devon, *see* SALTERTON.

Woodchester Glos. *Uuduceastir* 716–43, *Widecestre* 1086 (DB). 'Roman camp in the wood'. OE *wudu* + *ceaster*.

Woodchurch Kent. *Wuducirce* c.1100. 'Wooden church', or 'church by the wood'. OE *wudu* + *cirice*.

Woodcote, *Woodcott*, 'cottage(s) in or by a wood', OE *wudu* + *cot*; examples include: **Woodcote** Gtr. London. *Wudecot* 1200. **Woodcote** Oxon. *Wdecote* 1109.

Woodditton Cambs. *Dictune* 1022, *Wodedittone* 1227. 'Farmstead by a ditch or dyke', OE *dīc* + *tūn*, with affix *wudu* 'wood' to distinguish this place from FEN DITTON.

Woodeaton Oxon. *Etone* 1086 (DB), *Wudeetun* 1185. 'Farmstead by a river'. OE *ēa* + *tūn*, with the later affix *wudu* 'wood'.

Woodend, '(place at) the end of the wood', OE *wudu* + *ende*; for example **Woodend** Northants. *Wodende* 1316.

Woodford, 'ford in or by a wood', OE *wudu* + *ford*; examples include: **Woodford** Gtr. London. *Wdefort* 1086 (DB). **Woodford** Gtr. Manch. *Wideforde* 1248. **Woodford** Northants., near Thrapston. *Wodeford* 1086 (DB). **Woodford** Wilts. *Wuduforda* 972. **Woodford Halse** Northants. *Wodeford* 1086 (DB). Affix from the manor of HALSE.

Woodhall, 'hall in or by a wood', OE *wudu* + *h(e)all*; for example **Woodhall Spa** Lincs. *Wudehalle* 12th cent. (with recent affix from its reputation as a watering-place).

Woodham, usually 'homestead or village in or by a wood', OE *wudu* + *hām*; examples include: **Woodham** Surrey. *Wodeham* 672–4. **Woodham Ferrers, Woodham Mortimer**, & **Woodham Walter** Essex. *Wudaham* c.975, *Udeham*, *Odeham*, *Wdeham* 1086 (DB), *Wodeham Ferrers* 1230, *Wodeham Mortimer* 1255, *Wodeham Walter* 1238. Manorial affixes from early possession of estates here by the de Ferrers, Mortimer, and Fitzwalter families.

Woodhay, East (Hants.) & *Woodhay, West* (Berks.) *Wideheia* c.1150. 'Wide enclosure'. OE *wīd* (dative -*an*) + *hæg*.

Woodhorn Northum. *Wudehorn* 1178. 'Wooded horn of land or promontory'. OE *wudu* + *horn*.

Woodhouse, 'house(s) in or near a wood', OE *wudu* + *hūs*; examples include: **Woodhouse** Leics. *Wodehuses* c.1220. **Woodhouse Eaves** has affix from OE *efes* 'edge of a wood' with reference to CHARNWOOD FOREST. **Woodhouse** S. YORKS. *Wdehus* 1200.

Woodhurst Cambs. *Wdeherst* 1209. Originally OE *hyrst* 'wooded hill' with the later addition of *wudu* 'wood'.

Woodland(s), 'cultivated land in or near a wood', OE *wudu* + *land*; examples include: **Woodland** Devon. *Wodelonde* 1328. **Woodlands** Dorset. *Wodelande* 1244.

Woodleigh Devon. *Wuduleage* c.1010, *Odelie* 1086 (DB). 'Clearing in a wood'. OE *wudu* + *lēah*.

Woodlesford W. Yorks. *Wridelesford* 12th cent. 'Ford near a thicket'. OE *wrīdels* + *ford*.

Woodmancote, *Woodmancott*, 'cottage(s) of the woodsmen or foresters', OE *wudu-mann* + *cot*; examples include: **Woodmancote** Glos., near Rendcomb. *Wodemancote* 12th cent. **Woodmancott** Hants. *Woedemancote* 903, *Udemanecote* 1086 (DB).

Woodmansey E. R. Yorks. *Wodemanse* 1289. 'Pool of the woodsman or forester'. OE *wudu-mann* + *sǣ*.

Woodmansterne Surrey. *Odemerestor* |*sic*| 1086 (DB), *Wudemaresthorne* c.1190. 'Thorn-tree by the boundary of the wood'. OE *wudu* + *mǣre* + *thorn*.

Woodnesborough Kent. *Wanesberge* |*sic*| 1086 (DB), *Wodnesbeorge* c.1100. 'Mound associated with the heathen god Wōden'. OE god-name + *beorg*.

Woodnewton Northants. *Niwetone* 1086 (DB), *Wodeneuton* 1255. 'New farmstead (in woodland)'. OE *nīwe* + *tūn* with the later addition of *wudu*.

Woodperry Oxon. *Perie* 1086 (DB), *Wodeperi* 1242. Identical with WATERPERRY, but with ME *wode* 'wood'.

Woodplumpton Lancs. *Pluntun* 1086 (DB), *Wodeplumpton* 1327. 'Farmstead (in woodland) where plum-trees grow'. OE *plūme* + *tūn* with the later addition of *wudu*.

Woodrising Norfolk. *Risinga* 1086 (DB), *Woderisingg* 1291. Probably '(settlement of) the family or followers of a man called *Risa'. OE pers. name + *-ingas*, with the later addition of *wudu*.

Woodsetts S. Yorks. *Wodesete* 1324. 'Folds (for animals) in the wood'. OE *wudu* + *set*.

Woodsford Dorset. *Wardesford* 1086 (DB). 'Ford of a man called *Weard'. OE pers. name + *ford*.

Woodstock Oxon. *Wudestoce* c.1000, *Wodestoch* 1086 (DB). 'Settlement in woodland'. OE *wudu* + *stoc*.

Woodthorpe. 'outlying farmstead or hamlet in woodland', OE *wudu* + OScand. *thorp*: **Woodthorpe** Derbys. *Wodethorpe* 1258. **Woodthorpe** Lincs. *Wdetorp* 12th cent.

Woodton Norfolk. *Wodetuna* 1086 (DB). 'Farmstead in or near a wood'. OE *wudu* + *tūn*.

Woodville Derbys., a modern name dating from 1845, until then known as *Wooden-Box* from the wooden hut here for collecting toll at the turnpike.

Woodyates, East & *Woodyates, West* Dorset. *Wdegeate* 9th cent., *Odiete* 1086 (DB). '(Place at) the gate or gap in the wood'. OE *wudu* + *geat*.

Woofferton Shrops. *Wulfreton* 1221. 'Farmstead of a man called Wulfhere or Wulffrith'. OE pers. name + *tūn*.

Wookey Somerset. *Woky* 1065. '(Place at) the trap or snare for animals'. OE *wōcig*, probably originally with reference to Wookey Hole (*Wokyhole* 1065, with OE *hol* 'ravine').

Wool Dorset. *Welle* 1086 (DB). '(Place at) the spring or springs'. OE *wiella*.

Woolacombe Devon. *Wellecome* 1086 (DB). 'Valley with a spring or stream'. OE *wiella* + *cumb*.

Woolaston Glos. *Odelaweston* 1086 (DB). 'Farmstead of a man called Wulflāf'. OE pers. name + *tūn*.

Woolbeding W. Sussex. *Welbedlinge* 1086 (DB). Probably 'place associated with a man called Wulfbeald'. OE pers. name + *-ing*.

Wooler Northum. *Wulloure* 1187. Probably 'spring promontory'. OE *wella* + **ofer*.

Woolfardisworthy Devon, near Crediton. *Ulfaldeshodes* |*sic*| 1086 (DB), *Wolfardesworthi* 1264. 'Enclosure of a man called Wulfheard'. OE pers. name + *worthig*.

Woolhampton Berks. *Ollavintone* 1086 (DB). 'Estate associated with a man called Wulflāf'. OE pers. name + *-ing-* + *tūn*.

Woolhope Heref. & Worcs. *Hope* 1086 (DB), *Wulvivehop* 1234. '(Place at) the valley'. OE *hop*, with later addition from a woman called Wulfgifu who gave the manor to Hereford Cathedral in the 11th cent.

Woolland Dorset. *Wonlonde* 934, *Winlande* 1086 (DB). 'Estate with pasture or meadow'. OE **wynn* + *land*.

Woolley, usually 'wood or clearing frequented by wolves', OE *wulf* + *lēah*; examples include: **Woolley** Cambs. *Ciluelai* |*sic*| 1086 (DB), *Wulueleia* 1158. **Woolley** W. Yorks. *Wiluelai* 1086 (DB).

Woolpit Suffolk. *Wlpit* 10th cent., *Wlfpeta* 1086 (DB). 'Pit for trapping wolves'. OE *wulf-pytt*.

Woolscott Warwicks. *Wulscote* c.1235. Probably 'cottage(s) of a man called Wulfsige'. OE pers. name + *cot*.

Woolstaston Shrops. *Ulestanestune* 1086 (DB). 'Farmstead of a man called Wulfstān'. OE pers. name + *tūn*.

Woolsthorpe Lincs., near Grantham. *Ulestanestorp* 1086 (DB). 'Outlying farmstead or hamlet of a man called. Wulfstān'. OE pers. name + OScand. *thorp*.

Woolston Ches. *Ulfitona* 1142. 'Farmstead of a man called Wulfsige'. OE pers. name + *tūn*.

Woolston Devon. *Ulsistone* 1086 (DB). Identical in origin with the previous name.

Woolston Hants. *Olvestune* 1086 (DB). 'Farmstead of a man called Wulf'. OE pers. name + *tūn*.

Woolstone Oxon. *Olvricestone* 1086 (DB). 'Estate of a man called Wulfrīc'. OE pers. name + *tūn*. The Wulfrīc in question is named in 10th cent. charters.

Woolstone, Great & *Woolstone, Little* Bucks. *Wlsiestone* 1086 (DB). 'Farmstead of a man called Wulfsige'. OE pers. name + *tūn*.

Woolton Mersey. *Uluentune* 1086 (DB). 'Farmstead of a man called *Wulfa'. OE pers. name (genitive -n) + *tūn*.

Woolverstone Suffolk. *Uluerestuna* 1086 (DB). 'Farmstead of a man called Wulfhere'. OE pers. name + *tūn*.

Woolverton Somerset. *Wulfrinton* 1196. Probably 'estate associated with a man called Wulfhere'. OE pers. name + *-ing-* + *tūn*.

Woolwich Gtr. London. *Uuluuich* 918, *Hulviz* |*sic*| 1086 (DB). 'Port from which wool is shipped'. OE *wull* + *wīc*.

Woore Shrops. *Wavre* 1086 (DB). Possibly '(place by) the swaying tree'. OE *wæfre*.

Wootton, a common name, 'farmstead in or near a wood', OE wudu + *tūn*; examples include: **Wootton** Northants. *Witone* 1086 (DB). **Wootton** Oxon., near Abingdon. *Wuttune* 985. **Wootton Bassett** Wilts. *Wdetun* 680, *Wodetone* 1086 (DB), *Wotton Basset* 1272. Manorial affix from the Basset family, here in the 13th cent. **Wootton Fitzpaine** Dorset. *Wodetone* 1086 (DB), *Wotton Fitz Payn* 1392. Manorial affix from the Fitz Payn family, here in the 14th cent. **Wootton, Glanvilles** Dorset. *Widetone* 1086 (DB), *Wotton Glaunuill* 1288. Manorial affix from the Glanville family, here in the 13th cent. **Wootton, Leek** Warwicks. *Wottona* 1122, *Lecwotton* 1285. Affix presumably OE *lēac* 'leek' from their cultivation here. **Wootton, North & Wootton, South** Norfolk. *Wdetuna* 1086 (DB), *Nordwitton* 1166, *Sudwutton* 1182. **Wootton Rivers** Wilts. *Wdutun* 804,

Otone 1086 (DB), *Wotton Ryvers* 1332. Manorial affix from the de Rivere family, here in the 13th cent. **Wootton St Lawrence** Hants. *Wudatune* 990, *Odetone* 1086 (DB). Affix from the dedication of the church. **Wootton Wawen** Warwicks. *Uuidutuun* 716–37, *Wotone* 1086 (DB), *Wageneswitona* c.1142. Affix from its possession in the 11th cent. by a man called Wagen (OScand. *Vagn*).

Worcester Heref. & Worcs. *Weogorna civitas* 691, *Wigranceastre* 717, *Wirecestre* 1086 (DB). 'Roman town of the Weogora tribe'. Pre-English folk-name (possibly from a Celtic river-name meaning 'winding river') + OE *ceaster*. **Worcestershire** (OE *scīr* 'district') is first referred to in the 11th cent.

Wordsley W. Mids. *Wuluardeslea* 12th cent. 'Woodland clearing of a man called Wulfweard'. OE pers. name + *lēah*.

Worfield Shrops. *Wrfeld* 1086 (DB). 'Open land on the River Worfe'. OE river-name (meaning 'winding') + *feld*.

Workingham Berks. *Wokingeham* 1146. 'Homestead of the family or followers of a man called *Wocca(a)'. OE pers. name + *-inga-* + *hām*.

Workington Cumbria. *Wirkynton* c.1125. 'Estate associated with a man called *Weorc'. OE pers. name + *-ing-* + *tūn*.

Worksop Notts. *Werchesope* 1086 (DB). 'Enclosure or valley of a man called *Weorc'. OE pers. name + *hop*.

Worlaby N. Lincs. *Uluricebi* 1086 (DB). 'Farmstead or village of a man called Wulfrīc'. OE pers. name + OScand. *bȳ*.

Worldham, East & *Worldham, West* Hants. *Werildeham* 1086 (DB). Probably 'homestead of a woman called *Wærhild'. OE pers. name + *hām*.

Worle N. Som. *Worle* 1086 (DB). Probably 'wood or clearing frequented by wood-grouse'. OE *wōr* + *lēah*.

Worleston Ches. *Werblestune* |sic| 1086 (DB), *Weruelestona* c.1100. Possibly 'farmstead at the clearing for cattle'. OE *weorf* + *lēah* (genitive *lēas*) + *tūn*.

Worlingham Suffolk. *Werlingaham* 1086 (DB). Probably 'homestead of the family or followers of a man called *Wērel'. OE pers. name + *-inga-* + *hām*.

Worlington Devon. *Ulvredintone* 1086 (DB). 'Estate associated with a man called Wulfrēd'. OE pers. name + *-ing-* + *tūn*.

Worlington Suffolk. *Wirilintona* 1086 (DB), *Wridelingeton* 1201. 'Farmstead by the winding stream'. OE *wride* + *wella* + *-ing-* + *tūn*.

Worlingworth Suffolk. *Wilrincgawertha* c.1035, *Wyrlingwortha* 1086 (DB). 'Enclosure of the family or followers of a man called Wilhere'. OE pers. name + *-inga-* + *worth*.

Wormbridge Heref. & Worcs. *Wermebrig* 1207. 'Bridge on Worm Brook'. Celtic river-name (meaning 'dark stream') + OE *brycg*.

Wormegay Norfolk. *Wermegai* 1086 (DB). 'Island of the family or followers of a man called *Wyrma'. OE pers. name + *-inga-* + *ēg*.

Wormhill Derbys. *Wruenele* |sic| 1086 (DB), *Wermehull* c.1105. Probably 'hill of a man called *Wyrma'. OE pers. name + *hyll*.

Wormingford Essex. *Widemondefort* 1086 (DB). 'Ford of a man called *Withermund'. OE pers. name + *ford*.

Worminghall Bucks. *Wermelle* |sic| 1086 (DB), *Wirmenhale* c.1218. Probably 'nook of land of a man called *Wyrma'. OE pers. name (genitive *-n*) + *halh*.

Wormington Glos. *Wermetune* 1086 (DB). 'Estate associated with a man called *Wyrma'. OE pers. name + *-ing-* + *tūn*.

Worminster Somerset. *Wormester* 946. 'Rocky hill of the snake or dragon'. OE *wyrm* + *torr*.

Wormleighton Warwicks. *Wilmanlehttune* 956, *Wimelestone* 1086 (DB). 'Herb garden of a man called *Wilma'. OE pers. name + *lēac-tūn*.

Wormley Herts. *Wrmeleia* c.1060, *Wermelai* 1086 (DB). 'Woodland clearing infested with snakes'. OE *wyrm* + *lēah*.

Worms Head (*Penrhyn Gwyr*) Swan. *Wormyshede* 15th cent. 'Snake's head'. OE *wyrm* + *hēafod*. Cp. GREAT ORMES HEAD. The Welsh name means 'Gower promontory' (Welsh *penrhyn*). *See* GOWER.

Wormshill Kent. *Godeselle* |sic| 1086 (DB), *Wotnesell* c.1225, *Worneshelle* 1254. Possibly 'hill of the heathen god Wōden', OE god-name + *hyll*. Alternatively 'shelter for a herd of pigs', OE *weorn* + *(ge)sell*.

Wormsley Heref. & Worcs. *Wermeslai* 1086 (DB). 'Woodland clearing of a man called *Wyrm', or 'one infested with snakes'. OE pers. name or *wyrm* + *lēah*.

Wormwood Scrubs Gtr. London. *Wermeholte* 1200. 'Snake-infested wood'. OE *wyrm* + *holt*, with the later addition of *scrubb* 'scrubland, place overgrown with brushwood'.

Worplesdon Surrey. *Werpesdune* 1086 (DB). 'Hill with a path or track'. OE *werpels* + *dūn*.

Worrall S. Yorks. *Wihale* 1086 (DB), *Wirhal* 1218. Probably 'nook of land where bog-myrtle grows'. OE *wīr* + *halh*.

Worsall, High & *Worsall, Low* N. Yorks. *Wirceshel*, *Wercheshale* 1086 (DB). 'Nook of land of a man called *Weorc'. OE pers. name + *halh*.

Worsbrough S. Yorks. *Wircesburg* 1086 (DB). 'Stronghold of a man called *Wyrc'. OE pers. name + *burh*.

Worsley Gtr. Manch. *Werkesleia* 1196, *Wyrkitheley* 1246. Possibly 'woodland clearing of a woman called *Weorcgȳth or of a man called *Weorchæth'. OE pers. name + *lēah*.

Worstead Norfolk. *Wrthestede* 1044–7, *Wrdestedam* 1086 (DB). 'Site of an enclosure, a farmstead'. OE *worth* + *stede*.

Worsthorne Lancs. *Worthesthorn* 1202. 'Thorn-tree of a man called *Weorth'. OE pers. name + *thorn*.

Worston Lancs. *Wrtheston* 1212. 'Farmstead of a man called *Weorth'. OE pers. name + *tūn*.

Worth, 'the enclosure, the enclosed settlement', OE *worth*; examples include: **Worth** Kent. *Wurth* 1226. **Worth** W. Sussex. *Orde* 1086 (DB). **Worth Matravers** Dorset. *Wirde* 1086

(DB). *Worth Matrauers* 1664. Manorial affix from the Mautravers family, here from the 14th cent.

Wortham Suffolk. *Wrtham* c.950, *Wortham* 1086 (DB). 'Homestead with an enclosure'. OE *worth* + *hām*.

Worthen Shrops. *Wrdine* 1086 (DB). 'The enclosure'. OE *worthign*.

Worthing Norfolk. *Worthing* 1282. Probably identical in origin with the previous name.

Worthing W. Sussex. *Ordinges* 1086 (DB). Probably '(settlement of) the family or followers of a man called *Weorth'. OE pers. name + *-ingas*.

Worthington Leics. *Werditone* 1086 (DB). Probably 'estate associated with a man called *Weorth'. OE pers. name + *-ing-* + *tūn*.

Worthy, Headbourne, *Worthy, Kings*, & *Worthy, Martyr* Hants. *Worthige* 825, *Ordie* 1086 (DB), *Hydeburne Worthy* c.1270, *Chinges Ordia* 1157, *Wordia le Martre* 1243. 'The enclosure(s)'. OE *worthig*. The affix Headbourne is an old stream-name ('stream by the hides of land', OE *hīd* + *burna*), the other affixes being from early possession by the king and the le Martre family.

Worting Hants. *Wyrtingas* 960, *Wortinges* 1086 (DB). Possibly 'the herb gardens', from the plural of an OE word *wyrting*.

Wortley S. Yorks. *Wirtleie* 1086 (DB). 'Woodland clearing used for growing vegetables'. OE *wyrt* + *lēah*.

Worton Wilts. *Wrton* 1173. 'The vegetable garden'. OE *wyrt-tūn*.

Worton, Nether & *Worton, Over* Oxon. *Ortune* 1050–2, *Hortone* 1086 (DB). 'Farmstead by a bank or slope'. OE *ōra* + *tūn*.

Wotherton Shrops. *Udevertune* 1086 (DB). 'Farmstead by the woodland ford'. OE *wudu* + *ford* + *tūn*.

Wotton, 'farmstead in or near a wood', OE *wudu* + *tūn*; examples include: **Wotton** Surrey. *Wodetones* 1086 (DB). **Wotton under Edge** Glos. *Wudutune* 940, *Vutune* 1086 (DB). Affix refers to its situation under the Cotswold escarpment. **Wotton Underwood** Bucks. *Wudotun* 848, *Oltone* |*sic*| 1086 (DB). Affix means 'within the wood'.

Woughton on the Green Bucks. *Ulchetone* |*sic*| 1086 (DB), *Wocheton* 1163. Probably 'farmstead of a man called *Wēoca'. OE pers. name + *tūn*.

Wouldham Kent. *Uuldaham* 811, *Oldeham* 1086 (DB). 'Homestead of a man called *Wulda'. OE pers. name + *hām*.

Wrabness Essex. *Wrabenasa* 1086 (DB). 'Headland of a man called *Wrabba'. OE pers. name + *næss*.

Wrafton Devon. *Wratheton* 1238. Possibly 'farmstead built on piles or timber supports'. OE *wrathu* + *tūn*.

Wragby, 'farmstead or village of a man called Wraggi', OScand. pers. name + *bý*: **Wragby** Lincs. *Waragebi* 1086 (DB). **Wragby** W. Yorks. *Wraggebi* 1160–70.

Wramplingham Norfolk. *Wranplincham* 1086 (DB). OE *hām* 'homestead' with an uncertain first element, probably a pers. name or tribal name.

Wrangle Lincs. *Werangle* 1086 (DB). 'Crooked stream or other feature'. OE *wrengel* or OScand. *vrengill*.

Wrantage Somerset. *Wrentis* 1199. 'Pasture for stallions'. OE *wræna* + *etisc*.

Wrath, Cape. *See* CAPE WRATH.

Wratting, 'place where crosswort or hellebore grows', OE *wrætt* + *-ing*: **Wratting, Great** & **Wratting, Little** Suffolk. *Wratinga* 1086 (DB). **Wratting, West** Cambs. *Wreattinge* 974, *Waratinge* 1086 (DB).

Wrawby N. Lincs. *Waragebi* 1086 (DB). Probably 'farmstead or village of a man called *Wraghi'. OScand. pers. name + *bý*.

Wraxall, 'nook of land frequented by the buzzard or other bird of prey', OE *wrocc* + *halh*: **Wraxall** Dorset. *Brocheshale* |*sic*| 1086 (DB), *Wrokeshal* 1196. **Wraxall** N. Som. *Werocosale* 1086 (DB). **Wraxall, North** Wilts. *Werocheshalle* 1086 (DB). **Wraxall, South** Wilts. *Wroxhal* 1227.

Wray, *Wrea*, *Wreay*, 'secluded nook or corner of land', OScand. *vrá*; examples include: **Wray** Lancs. *Wra* 1227. **Wray, High** Cumbria. *Wraye* c.1535. **Wrea Green** Lancs. *Wra* 1201. **Wreay** Cumbria, near Soulby. *Wra* 1487.

Wraysbury Berks. *Wirecesberie* |*sic*| 1086 (DB), *Wiredesbur* 1195. 'Stronghold of a man called *Wīgrēd'. OE pers. name + *burh* (dative *byrig*).

Wreake (river) Leics., *see* FRISBY ON THE WREAKE.

Wrecclesham Surrey. *Wrecclesham* 1225. Probably 'homestead or enclosure of a man called *Wrecel'. OE pers. name + *hām* or *hamm*.

Wrecsam. *See* WREXHAM.

Wrekin, The Shrops., *see* WROXETER.

Wrelton N. Yorks. *Wereltun* 1086 (DB). Possibly 'farmstead by the hill where criminals are hanged'. OE *wearg* + *hyll* + *tūn*.

Wrenbury Ches. *Wareneberie* 1086 (DB). 'Stronghold of the wren, or of a man called *Wrenna'. OE *wrenna* or pers. name + *burh* (dative *byrig*).

Wreningham Norfolk. *Wreningham* c.1060, *Urnincham* |*sic*| 1086 (DB). Probably 'homestead of the family or followers of a man called *Wrenna'. OE pers. name + *-inga-* + *hām*.

Wrentham Suffolk. *Wretham* |*sic*| 1086 (DB), *Wrentham* 1228. Probably 'homestead of a man called *Wrenta'. OE pers. name + *hām*.

Wressle E. R. Yorks. *Weresa* |*sic*| 1086 (DB), *Wresel* 1183. From OE *wræsel* 'something twisted', perhaps referring to broken ground or a winding river.

Wrestlingworth Beds. *Wrastlingewrd* c.1150. Probably 'enclosure of the family or followers of a man called *Wræstel'. OE pers. name + *-inga-* + *worth*.

Wretham, East Norfolk. *Wretham* 1086 (DB). 'Homestead where crosswort or hellebore grows'. OE *wrætt* + *hām*.

Wretton Norfolk. *Wretton* 1198. 'Farmstead where crosswort or hellebore grows'. OE *wrætt* + *tūn*.

Wrexham (*Wrecsam*) Wrex. *Wristlesham* 1161, *Gwregsam* 1291. 'Wryhtel's water meadow'. OE pers. name + *hamm*.

Wribbenhall Heref. & Worcs. *Gurberhale |sic|* 1086 (DB), *Wrubbenhale c.*1160 'Nook of land of a man called *Wrybba'. OE pers. name (genitive -n) + *halh*.

Wrightington Lancs. *Wrichtington* 1202. Possibly 'farmstead or village of the wrights or carpenters'. OE *wyrhta* (genitive plural -*ena*) + *tūn*.

Wrinehill Staffs. *Wrinehull* 1225. OE *hyll* 'hill' with an uncertain first element, possibly a stream-name or an earlier name for the hill itself.

Wrington N. Som. *Wringtone* 926, *Weritone |sic|* 1086 (DB). 'Farmstead on the river called *Wring'*. Earlier or alternative name (possibly meaning 'winding stream') for the River Yeo + OE *tūn*.

Writtle Essex. *Writele* 1066–76, *Writelam* 1086 (DB). Originally a river-name from OE *writol* 'babbling', an earlier name for the River Wid.

Wrockwardine Shrops. *Recordine* 1086 (DB), *Wrocwurthin* 1196. 'Enclosure by the hill called the Wrekin'. Celtic name (*see* WROXETER) + OE *worthign*.

Wroot N. Lincs. *Wroth* 1157. 'Snout-like spur of land'. OE *wrōt*.

Wrotham Kent. *Uurotaham* 788, *Broteham |sic|* 1086 (DB). 'Homestead of a man called *Wrōta'.* OE pers. name + *hām*.

Wroughton Wilts. *Wervetone* 1086 (DB). 'Farmstead on the river called *Worf'.* Celtic river-name meaning 'winding stream' (an old name of the River Ray) + OE *tūn*.

Wroxall I. of Wight. *Wroccesheale* 1038–44, *Warochesselle* 1086 (DB). 'Nook of land frequented by the buzzard or other bird of prey'. OE *wrocc* + *halh*.

Wroxeter Shrops. *Ouirokōnion c.*150, *Rochecestre* 1086 (DB). 'Roman fort at or near *Uriconio* or the Wrekin'. Ancient Celtic name (possibly 'town of Virico') + OE *ceaster*.

Wroxham Norfolk. *Vrochesham* 1086 (DB). 'Homestead or enclosure of the buzzard, or of a man called *Wrocc'.* OE *wrocc* or pers. name + *hām* or *hamm*.

Wroxton Oxon. *Werochestan* 1086 (DB). Probably 'stone of the buzzards or other birds of prey'. OE *wrocc* + *stān*.

Wyaston Derbys. *Widerdestune |sic|* 1086 (DB), *Wyardestone* 1244. 'Farmstead of a man called *Wīgheard'.* OE pers. name + *tūn*.

Wyberton Lincs. *Wibertune* 1086 (DB). Possibly 'farmstead of a man called *Wīgbeorht* or of a woman called *Wīgburh'.* OE pers. name + *tūn*.

Wyboston Beds. *Wiboldestone* 1086 (DB). 'Farmstead of a man called *Wīgbeald'.* OE pers. name + *tūn*.

Wybunbury Ches. *Wimeberie* 1086 (DB), *Wybbunberi c.*1210. 'Stronghold or manor-house of a man called *Wīgbeorn'.* OE pers. name + *burh* (dative *byrig*).

Wychbold Heref. & Worcs. *Uuicbold* 692, *Wicelbold* 1086 (DB). 'Dwelling near the trading settlement'. OE *wīc* + *bold*.

Wychwood (old forest) Oxon., *see* ASCOTT UNDER WYCHWOOD.

Wycliffe Durham. *Witcliue* 1086 (DB). Probably 'white cliff or bank'. OE *hwīt* + *clif*.

Wycomb Leics. *Wiche* 1086 (DB), *Wicham* 1316. Possibly identical in origin with the next name, but more likely to be from OE *wīc-hām* for which *see* WICKHAM.

Wycombe, High & *Wycombe, West* Bucks. *Wicumun c.*970, *Wicumbe* 1086 (DB). '(Place) at the dwellings or settlements'. OE *wīc* in a dative plural form *wīcum*. The river-name **Wye** here is probably only a 'back-formation' from the place-name.

Wyddfa, Yr. *See* SNOWDON.

Wyddgrug, Yr. *See* MOLD.

Wyddial Herts. *Widihale* 1086 (DB). 'Nook of land where willow-trees grow'. OE *wīthig* + *halh*.

Wye (river) Heref. & Worcs., *see* ROSS ON WYE. The river-name **Wye** in Derbyshire is identical in origin.

Wye Kent. *Uuiæ* 839, *Wi* 1086 (DB). '(Place at) the heathen temple'. OE *wīg*.

Wye. *See* HAY-ON-WYE.

Wyke, 'the dwelling, the specialized farm or trading settlement', OE *wīc*; examples include: **Wyke** Surrey. *Wucha* 1086 (DB). **Wyke Regis** Dorset. *Wike* 984, *Kingeswik* 1242. Anciently a royal manor, hence the Latin affix *Regis* 'of the king'.

Wykeham N. Yorks. *Wicham* 1086 (DB). Probably 'homestead associated with an earlier Romano-British settlement'. OE *wīc-hām*.

Wylam Northum. *Wylum* 12th cent. Probably '(place at) the fish-traps'. OE *wīl* or *wīle* in a dative plural form *wīlum*.

Wylye Wilts. *Wilig* 901, *Wili* 1086 (DB). Named from the River Wylye, a pre-English river-name possibly meaning 'tricky stream', i.e. one liable to flood.

Wymering Hants. *Wimeringes* 1086 (DB). '(Settlement of) the family or followers of a man called *Wīgmǣr'.* OE pers. name + *-ingas*.

Wymeswold Leics. *Wimundeswald* 1086 (DB). 'Forest of a man called *Wīgmund'.* OE pers. name + *wald*.

Wymington Beds. *Wimentone* 1086 (DB). Probably 'farmstead of a man called *Wīdmund'.* OE pers. name + *tūn*.

Wymondham, 'homestead of a man called *Wīgmund',* OE pers. name + *hām*: **Wymondham** Leics. *Wimundesham* 1086 (DB). **Wymondham** Norfolk. *Wimundham* 1086 (DB).

Wymondley, Great & *Wymondley, Little* Herts. *Wilmundeslea* 11th cent., *Wimundeslai* 1086 (DB). 'Woodland clearing of a man called Wilmund'. OE pers. name + *lēah*.

Wynford Eagle Dorset. *Wenfrot* 1086 (DB), *Wynfrod Egle* 1288. A Celtic river-name meaning 'white or bright stream', Celtic *winn* + *frud*. Manorial affix from the del Egle family, here in the 13th cent.

Wyre Forest Heref. & Worcs., Shrops. *Wyre c.*1080. Possibly from a Celtic river-name meaning 'winding river'.

Wyre Piddle Heref. & Worcs., *see* PIDDLE.

Wyrley, Great & *Wyrley, Little* Staffs. *Wereleia* 1086 (DB). 'Woodland clearing where bog-myrtle grows'. OE *wīr* + *lēah*.

Wysall Notts. *Wisoc* 1086 (DB). Possibly 'hill-spur of the heathen temple'. OE *wīg* + *hōh*.

Wytham Oxon. *Wihtham c.*957, *Winteham* |*sic*| 1086 (DB). 'Homestead or village in a river-bend'. OE **wiht* + *hām*.

Wytheford, Great Shrops. *Wicford* |*sic*| 1086 (DB), *Widiford* 1195. 'Ford where willow-trees grow'. OE *wīthig* + *ford*.

Wyton Cambs. *Witune* 1086 (DB), *Wictun* 1253. 'Dwelling place, farmstead with a dwelling'. OE *wīc-tūn*.

Wyverstone Suffolk. *Wiuerthestune* 1086 (DB). 'Farmstead of a man called Wīgferth'. OE pers. name + *tūn*.

Wyvis Forest Highland. 'Forest by Ben Wyvis'. The mountain name means 'high hill' (Gaelic *beinn* + *uais*; locative of *uas*).

Y

Yaddlethorpe N. Lincs. *Iadulfestorp* 1086 (DB). 'Outlying farmstead or hamlet of a man called Ēadwulf'. OE pers. name + OScand. *thorp*.

Yafforth N. Yorks. *Iaforde* 1086 (DB). 'Ford, over the river (Wiske)'. OE *ēa* + *ford*.

Yalding Kent. *Hallinges* 1086 (DB). *Ealding* 1207. '(Settlement of) the family or followers of a man called Ealda'. OE pers. name + *-ingas*.

Yanworth Glos. *Janeworth* c.1050, *Teneurde |sic|* 1086 (DB). 'Enclosure used for lambs, or of a man called *Gæna*'. OE *ēan* or pers. name + *worth*.

Yapham E. R. Yorks. *Iapun* 1086 (DB). '(Place at) the steep slopes'. OE *gēap* in a dative plural form *gēapum*.

Yapton W. Sussex. *Abbiton* c.1187. 'Estate associated with a man called *Eabba*'. OE pers. name + *-ing-* + *tūn*.

Yarburgh Lincs. *Gereburg* 1086 (DB), *Jerdeburc* 12th cent. 'The earthwork, the fortification built of earth'. OE *eorth-burh*.

Yarcombe Devon. *Erececombe* 10th cent., *Erticoma* 1086 (DB). 'Valley of the River Yarty'. Old river-name of uncertain origin + OE *cumb*.

Yardley, 'wood or clearing where rods or spars are obtained', OE *gyrd* + *lēah*: **Yardley** W. Mids. *Gyrdleah* 972, *Gerlei* 1086 (DB). **Yardley Gobion** Northants. *Gerdeslai* 1086 (DB). *Yerdele Gobioun* 1353. Manorial affix from the Gubyun family, here in the 13th cent. **Yardley Hastings** Northants. *Gerdelai* 1086 (DB), *Yerdele Hastinges* 1316. Manorial affix from the de Hastinges family, here in the 13th cent.

Yarkhill Heref. & Worcs. *Geardcylle* 811, *Archel* 1086 (DB). 'Kiln with a yard or enclosure'. OE *geard* + *cyln*.

Yarlet Staffs. *Erlide* 1086 (DB). Possibly 'gravelly slope, or eagle slope'. OE *ēar* or *earn* + *hlith*.

Yarlington Somerset. *Gerlincgetuna* 1086 (DB). 'Farmstead of the family or followers of a man called *Gerla*'. OE pers. name + *-inga-* + *tūn*.

Yarm Stock. on T. *Iarun* 1086 (DB). '(Place at) the fish-weirs'. OE *gear* in a dative plural form *gearum*.

Yarmouth I. of Wight. *Ermud* 1086 (DB), *Ernemuth* 1223. 'Gravelly or muddy estuary'. OE *ēaren* + *mūtha*. The river-name **Yar** is a 'back-formation' from the place-name.

Yarmouth, Great Norfolk. *Gernemwa* 1086 (DB). '(Place at) the mouth of the River Yare'. Celtic river-name (probably 'babbling stream') + OE *mūtha*.

Yarnfield Staffs. *Ernefeld* 1266. 'Open land frequented by eagles'. OE *earn* + *feld*.

Yarnscombe Devon. *Hernescome* 1086 (DB). 'Valley of the eagle'. OE *earn* + *cumb*.

Yarnton Oxon. *Ærdintune* 1005, *Hardintone* 1086 (DB). 'Estate associated with a man called *Earda*'. OE pers. name + *-ing-* + *tūn*.

Yarpole Heref. & Worcs. *Iarpol* 1086 (DB), 'Pool with a weir or dam for catching fish'. OE *gear* + *pōl*.

Yarrow Sc. Bord. *Gierwa* c.1120. '(Place by) Yarrow Water'. The river name means 'rough one' (Welsh *garw*).

Yarty (river) Devon, *see* YARCOMBE.

Yarwell Northants. *Jarwelle* 1166. 'Spring by the dam(s) for catching fish'. OE *gear* + *wella*.

Yate S. Glos. *Geate* 779, *Giete* 1086 (DB). '(Place at) the gate or gap'. OE *geat*.

Yateley Hants. *Yatele* 1248. 'Woodland clearing with or near a gate or gap'. OE *geat* + *lēah*.

Yatesbury Wilts. *Etesberie* 1086 (DB). 'Stronghold of a man called Gēat'. OE pers. name + *burh* (dative *byrig*).

Yattendon Berks. *Etingedene* 1086 (DB). Probably 'valley of the family or followers of a man called Gēat'. OE pers. name + *-inga-* + *denu*.

Yatton N. Som. *Iatune* 1086 (DB). 'Farmstead by a river'. OE *ēa* + *tūn*.

Yatton Heref. & Worcs. *Getune* 1086 (DB). 'Farmstead near a gate or gap'. OE *geat* + *tūn*.

Yatton Keynell Wilts. *Getone* 1086 (DB), *Yatton Kaynel* 1289. Identical in origin with the previous name. Manorial affix from the Caynel family, here in the 13th cent.

Yaverland I. of Wight. *Everelande* 683, *Evreland* 1086 (DB). 'Cultivated land where boars are kept'. OE *eofor* + *land*.

Yaxham Norfolk. *Jachesham* 1086 (DB). 'Homestead or enclosure of the cuckoo or of a man called *Gēac*'. OE *gēac* or pers. name + *hām* or *hamm*.

Yaxley, 'wood or clearing of the cuckoo', OE *gēac* + *lēah*: **Yaxley** Cambs. *Geaceslea* 963–84 *Iacheslei* 1086 (DB). **Yaxley** Suffolk. *Jacheslea* 1086 (DB).

Yazor Heref. & Worcs. *Iavesovre* 1086 (DB), *Iagesoure* 1242. 'Ridge of a man called Iago'. Welsh pers. name + OE *ofer*.

Yeading Gtr. London. *Geddinges* 716–57. '(Settlement of) the family or followers of a man called Geddi'. OE pers. name + *-ingas*.

Yeadon W. Yorks. *Iadun* 1086 (DB). Probably 'steep hill'. OE *gēh* + *dūn*.

Yealand Conyers & *Yealand Redmayne* Lancs. *Jalant* 1086 (DB)., *Yeland Coygners* 1301, *Yeland Redman* 1341. 'High cultivated land. OE *hēah* + *land*. Distinguishing affixes from early possession by the de Conyers and Redeman families.

Yealmpton Devon. *Elintona* 1086 (DB). 'Farmstead on the River Yealm'. Celtic or pre-Celtic river-name (of doubtful meaning) + OE *tūn*.

Yearsley N. Yorks. *Eureslage* 1086 (DB). 'Wood or clearing of the wild boar, or of a man called *Eofor*'. OE *eofor* or pers. name + *lēah*.

Yeaton Shrops. *Aitone* 1086 (DB), *Eton* 1327. 'Farmstead by a river'. OE *ēa* + *tūn*.

Yeaveley Derbys. *Gheveli* 1086 (DB). 'Woodland clearing of a man called *Geofa*'. OE pers. name + *lēah*.

Yedingham N. Yorks. *Edingham* 1170–5. 'Homestead of the family or followers of a man called Ēada'. OE pers. name + *-inga-* + *hām*.

Yelden Beds. *Giveldene* 1086 (DB). 'Valley of the tribe called *Gifle*'. Old tribal name (for which *see* NORTHILL) + OE *denu*.

Yeldham, Great & *Yeldham, Little* Essex. *Geldeham* 1086 (DB). Probably 'homestead liable to pay a certain tax'. OE *gield* + *hām*.

Yelford Oxon. *Aieleforde* 1086 (DB). 'Ford of a man called *Ægel*'. OE pers. name + *ford*.

Yell (island) Shet. *Yala* c.1250. Pre-Scand. name.

Yelling Cambs. *Gillinge* 974, *Gellinge* 1086 (DB). Probably '(settlement of) the family or followers of a man called *Giella*'. OE pers. name + *-ingas*.

Yelvertoft Northants. *Gelvrecote* |*sic*| 1086 (DB), *Gelvertoft* 12th cent. Possibly 'homestead of a man called *Geldfrith*'. OE pers. name + OScand. *toft* (replacing OE *cot* 'cottage'). Alternatively the first part of the name may be 'ford at a pool', from an OE *gēol* + *ford*.

Yelverton Devon. *Elleford* 1291, *Elverton* 1765. Originally 'elder-tree ford', from OE *ellen* + *ford*, with the later addition of *tūn* 'village'.

Yeoford Devon. *Ioweford* 1242. 'Ford on the River Yeo'. OE river-name (possibly 'yew stream') + *ford*.

Yeolmbridge Cornwall. *Yambrigge* 13th cent. Possibly 'bridge by the river meadow'. OE *ēa* + *hamm* + *brycg*.

Yeovil Somerset. *Gifle* c.880, *Givele* 1086 (DB). '(Place on) the River *Gifl*'. Celtic river-name (meaning 'forked river'), an earlier name for the River Yeo (the form of which has been influenced by OE *ēa* 'river').

Yeovilton Somerset. *Geveltone* 1086 (DB). 'Farmstead on the River *Gifl*'. Celtic river-name (*see* YEOVIL) + OE *tūn*.

Yerbeston Pemb. *Jerbardeston* 14th cent. 'Gerbard's farm'. OGerman pers. name + OE *tūn*.

Yetlington Northum. *Yettlinton* 1187. Possibly 'estate associated with a man called *Gēatela*'. OE pers. name + *-ing-* + *tūn*.

Yetminster Dorset. *Etiminstre* 1086 (DB). 'Church of a man called Ēata'. OE pers. name + *mynster*.

Yettington Devon. *Yethemeton* 1242. 'Farmstead of the dwellers by the gate or gap'. OE *geat* + *hǣme* + *tūn*.

Yiewsley Gtr. London. *Wiuesleg* 1235. Probably 'woodland clearing of a man called *Wifel*'. OE pers. name + *lēah*.

Ynys Byr. *See* CALDY ISLAND.

Ynys Cantwr (island) Pemb. 'Precentor's island'. Welsh *ynys* + *cantwr*. The island was formerly owned by the precentor of St David's.

Ynys Deullyn (island) Pemb. 'Island in the two lakes'. Welsh *ynys* + *dau* + *llyn*.

Ynys Dewi. *See* RAMSEY ISLAND.

Ynys Enlli. *See* BARDSEY ISLAND.

Ynys Gybi. *See* HOLY ISLAND.

Ynys Seiriol. *See* PUFFIN ISLAND.

Ynys-ddu Cphy. 'Black island'. Welsh *ynys* + *du*.

Ynysoedd y Moelrhoniaid. *See* SKERRIES.

Yockenthwaite N. Yorks. *Yoghannesthweit* 1241. 'Clearing of a man called Eogan'. OIrish pers. name + OScand. *thveit*.

Yockleton Shrops. *Ioclehuile* 1086 (DB). Possibly 'hill by a small manor or estate'. OE *geocled* + *hyll* (later replaced by *tūn*).

Yokefleet E. R. Yorks. *Iucufled* 1086 (DB). Probably 'creek or stream of a man called Jókell'. OScand. pers. name + *flēot*.

Yoker Glas. *Pont Yochyrr* 1505. '(Place on) low-lying ground'. Gaelic *euchair*.

York *Ebórakon* c.150, *Eboracum, Euruic* 1086 (DB). An ancient Celtic name meaning 'estate of a man called Eburos' or (more probably) 'yew-tree estate'. **Yorkshire** (OE *scīr* 'district') is first referred to in the 11th cent.

York Town Surrey, so named in the early 19th cent. after Frederick, Duke of York, who founded Sandhurst College in 1812.

Yorton Shrops. *Iartune* 1086 (DB). 'Farmstead with a yard'. OE *geard* + *tūn*.

Youghal (*Eochaill*) Cork, Tipperary. 'Yew wood'.

Youlgreave Derbys. *Giolgrave* 1086 (DB). 'Yellow grove or pit'. OE *geolu* + *grǣfe* or *grǣf*.

Youlthorpe E. R. Yorks. *Aiulftorp* 1086 (DB), *Joletorp* 1166. 'Outlying farmstead or hamlet of a man called Eyjulfr or Jól(i)'. OScand. pers. name + *thorp*.

Youlton N. Yorks. *Ioletun* 1086 (DB). 'Farmstead of a man called Jóli'. OScand. pers. name + OE *tūn*.

Yoxall Staffs. *Iocheshale* 1086 (DB). Possibly 'nook comprising a yoke or measure of land'. OE *geoc* + *halh*.

Yoxford Suffolk. *Gokesford* 1086 (DB). 'Ford wide enough for a yoke of oxen'. OE *geoc* + *ford*. The river-name **Yox** is a 'back-formation' from the place-name.

Ysceifiog Flin. *Schiviau* 1086 (DB). '(Place) abounding in elder trees'. Welsh *ysgaw*.

Ystalyfera Neat. *Ynys Tal y Veran* 1582, *Tir Ynystalverran* 1604, *Staleyfera* 1729, *Ystal-y-fera* 1831.

Possibly 'river meadow at the end of the short share (of land)'. Welsh *ynys* + *tâl* + *y* + *ber* + *rhan*.

Ystrad Mynach Cphy. *Ystrad manach* 1635, *Ystrad y Mynach* 1833. 'Valley of the monk'. Welsh *ystrad* + *mynach*.

Ystradgynlais Powys. *Stradgenles* 1372, *Estradgynles* 1493. 'Valley of Cynlais'. Welsh *ystrad*. The identity of Cynlais is unknown.

Ystumllwynarth. *See* OYSTERMOUTH.

Z

Zeal Monachorum Devon. *Seale* 956, *Sele Monachorum* 1275. '(Place at) the sallow-tree'. OE *sealh*. Latin affix 'of the monks' refers to early possession by Buckfast Abbey.

Zeal, South Devon. *La Sele* 1168. 'The hall', or 'the sallow-tree'. OE *sele* or *sealh*.

Zeals Wilts. *Sele* 1086 (DB), *Seles* 1176. 'The sallow-trees'. OE *sealh* in a plural form.

Zennor Cornwall. 'Church of *Sanctus Sinar*' *c*.1170. From the female patron saint of the church.

Zetland. *See* SHETLAND.

GLOSSARY OF SOME COMMON ELEMENTS IN ENGLISH PLACE-NAMES

In this list, OE stands for Old English, ME for Middle English, OFrench for Old French, and OScand. for Old Scandinavian. The OE letters 'thorn' and 'eth' have been rendered *th* throughout. The OE letter æ ('ash') represents a sound between *a* and *e*. Elements with an asterisk are postulated or hypothetical forms, that is they are words not recorded in independent use or only found in use at a later date.

á *OScand.* river
āc *OE* oak-tree
*ācen *OE* made of oak, growing with oak-trees
ād *OE* funeral pyre, beacon
æcer *OE* plot of cultivated or arable land
ǣl, ēl *OE* eel
æppel *OE* apple-tree
ærn *OE* house, building, dwelling
æsc *OE* ash-tree
æspe *OE* aspen-tree, white poplar
ǣwell *OE* river-source
ǣwelm *OE* river-source
akr *OScand.* plot of cultivated or arable land
ald, eald *OE* old, long used
alor *OE* alder-tree
*anger *OE* grassland, pasture
ānstīg *OE* narrow or lonely track, track linking other routes
apuldor *OE* apple-tree
askr *OScand.* ash-tree
austr *OScand.* east
bæc *OE* back, ridge
bæce, bece *OE* stream in a valley
bærnet *OE* land cleared by burning
bæth *OE* bath
*bagga *OE* bag, *probably* badger
banke *OScand.* bank, hill-slope
bār *OE* boar
bēacen *OE* beacon, signal
bēam *OE* tree-trunk, beam of timber
bēan *OE* bean
bearu *OE* grove, wood
beau, bel *OFrench* fine, beautiful
bēce *OE* beech-tree
bekkr *OScand.* stream
bēl *OE* fire, funeral pyre, beacon
*bel *OE* glade, dry ground in marsh
bēo *OE* bee
beofor *OE* beaver
beonet *OE* bent-grass, coarse grass
beorc *OE* birch-tree

beorg, berg *OE* hill, mound, tumulus
*bēos *OE* bent-grass, rough grass
bere *OE* barley
bere-ærn *OE* barn, store-house for barley
bere-tūn, bær-tūn *OE* barley farm, corn farm, *later* outlying grange or demesne farm
bere-wīc *OE* barley farm, *later* outlying grange or dependent farm
berg *OScand.* hill
*bic, *bica *OE* pointed hill or ridge
bīcere *OE* bee-keeper
bigging *ME* a building
birce *OE* birch-tree
blæc *OE* black, dark-coloured
blá(r) *OScand.* dark, cheerless, exposed
bōc *OE* (i) beech-tree, (ii) book, charter
bōc-land *OE* land granted by charter
boga *OE* bow, arch, bend
*boi(a) *OE* boy, servant
bóndi *OScand.* peasant landowner
botm, *bothm *OE*, **botn** *OScand.* broad river valley, valley bottom
bōthl, bōtl, bold *OE* special house or building
box *OE* box-tree
brād *OE* broad, spacious
brēc, brǣ *OE* land broken up for cultivation
bred *OE* board, plank
*breȝ *Celtic* hill
brekka *OScand.* hill-slope
brēmel, brembel *OE* bramble, blackberry bush
brende *ME* burnt, cleared by burning
brēr *OE* briars
Brettas *OE* Britons
brōc *OE* brook, stream
brocc *OE* badger
brōm *OE* thorny bush, broom
brycg *OE* bridge, *sometimes* causeway
bucc *OE* buck, stag
bucca *OE* he-goat
*bula *OE* bull
būr *OE* cottage, dwelling

(ge)būr *OE* peasant holding land for rent or services

burh (*dative* **byrig**) *OE* fortified place, stronghold, *variously applied to Iron-Age hill-forts, Roman and Anglo-Saxon fortifications, and fortified houses, later to manors or manor houses and to towns or boroughs*

burna *OE* stream

bury *ME* (*from dative* byrig *of OE* burh) manor, manor house

búth, bōth *OScand.* booth, temporary shelter

bý *OScand.* farmstead, village, settlement

byden *OE* vessel, tub, hollow

***cadeir** *Celtic* chair, lofty place

cærse *OE* cress, water-cress

calc, cealc *OE* chalk, limestone

cald, ceald *OE* cold

calf, cealf *OE* calf

calu *OE* bald, bare, lacking vegetation, *often* bare hill

camb *OE* hill-crest, ridge

camp *OE* enclosed piece of land, *originally* open uncultivated land on the edge of a Romano-British settlement

cat(t) *OE* cat, wild-cat

cēap *OE* trade, market

ceaster, cæster *OE* Roman station or walled town, old fortification or earthwork

***cēd** *Celtic* forest, wood

ceorl *OE* freeman, peasant

cēping, cīeping *OE* market

cēse, *cīese *OE* cheese

cild *OE* child, youth, younger son, young nobleman

cirice *OE* church

cisel, ceosol *OE* gravel, shingle

clæfre *OE* clover

clæg *OE* clay, clayey soil

clif *OE* cliff, slope, river-bank

***clōh** *OE* ravine, deep valley

***clopp(a)** *OE* lump, hill

cniht *OE* youth, servant, retainer

cnoll *OE* hill-top, *later* hillock

cocc *OE* (i) heap, hillock, (ii) cock of wild bird, woodcock

cofa *OE* chamber, cave, cove

col *OE* coal, charcoal

cōl *OE* cool

copp *OE* hill-top

cot *OE* cottage, hut, shelter

cran, corn *OE* crane, *also probably* heron *or similar bird*

crāwe *OE* crow

croft *OE* enclosure, small enclosed field

cros *OE* cross

***crūg** *Celtic* hill, mound, tumulus

cū *OE* cow

cumb *OE* coomb, valley, *used particularly of relatively short or broad valleys*

***Cumbre** *OE* the Cymry, the Cumbrian Britons

cwēn *OE* queen

cwene *OE* woman

cweorn *OE* quern, hand-mill

cyln *OE* kiln

cyne- *OE* royal

cyning *OE* king

cȳta *OE* kite

dæl *OE* pit, hollow, valley

dalr *OScand.* valley

denn *OE* woodland pasture, especially for swine

denu *OE* valley, *used particularly of relatively long, narrow valleys*

dēop *OE* deep

dēor *OE* animal, *also* deer

derne, dierne *OE* hidden, overgrown with vegetation

dīc *OE* ditch, dyke, *also* embankment

***djúr, dýr** *OScand.* animal, *also* deer

dræg *OE* a portage or slope used for dragging down loads, *also* a dray, a sledge

dūn *OE* hill, down

ēa *OE* river

earn *OE* eagle

ēast *OE* east, eastern

ecg *OE* edge, escarpment

edisc *OE* enclosure, enclosed park

ēg, īeg *OE* island, land partly surrounded by water, dry ground in marsh, well-watered land, promontory

***eglēs** *Celtic* Romano-British Christian church

eik *OScand.* oak-tree

elfitu *OE* swan

elle(r)n *OE* elder-tree

elm *OE* elm-tree

ende *OE*, **endi** *OScand.* end, district of an estate

ened *OE* duck

Engle *OE* the Angles, *later* the English

eofor *OE* wild boar

eorl *OE* nobleman

eowestre *OE* sheep-fold

eowu *OE* ewe

erg, ǽrgi *OScand.* shieling, hill pasture, summer pasture

ersc *OE* ploughed or stubble field

eski *OScand.* place growing with ash-trees

fæger *OE* fair, pleasant

fæsten *OE* stronghold

fāg *OE* variegated, multi-coloured

fald *OE* fold, enclosure for animals

fearn *OE* fern, bracken

feld *OE* open country, tract of land cleared of trees

fenn *OE* fen, marshy ground

fennig *OE* marshy, muddy

ferja *OScand.* ferry

fleax *OE* flax

flēot *OE* estuary, inlet, creek, *also* stream

fola *OE*, **foli** *OScand.* foal

folc *OE* folk, tribe, people

ford *OE* ford, river-crossing

fox *OE* fox

fugol *OE* (wild) fowl, bird

fūl *OE* foul, dirty

*funta *OE* spring (*a loan-word from Latin* fons, fontis *and therefore possibly used of a spring characterized by Roman building work*)

fyrhth(e) *OE* woodland, *often* sparse woodland or scrub

fyrs *OE* furze

gærs *OE*, **gres** *OScand.* grass

gāra *OE* triangular plot of ground, point of land

garthr *OScand.* enclosure

gāt *OE*, **geit** *OScand. goat*

gata *OScand.* road, street

*gē *OE* district, region

gēac *OE* cuckoo

geard *OE* yard, enclosure

geat *OE* gate, gap, pass

gil *OScand.* deep narrow valley, ravine

gōs *OE* goose

græf *OE* pit, trench

græfe *OE* thicket, brushwood, grove

grāf(a) *OE* grove, copse

grēne *OE* (i) green-coloured, (ii) grassy place, village green

grēot *OE* gravel

hæcc *OE* hatch, hatch-gate, flood-gate

hæg, gehæg *OE* enclosure

hǣme *OE* inhabitants, dwellers

*hær *OE* rock, heap of stones

*hǣs, *hǣse *OE* (land overgrown with) brushwood

hæsel *OE* hazel-tree

hēth *OE* heath, heather, uncultivated land overgrown with heather

hafoc *OE* hawk

haga *OE*, **hagi** *OScand.* hedged enclosure

hagu-thorn *OE* hawthorn

halh *OE* nook or corner of land, *often used of land in a hollow or river-bend*

hālig *OE* holy

hām *OE* homestead, village, manor, estate

hamm *OE* enclosure, land hemmed in by water or marsh or higher ground, land in a river-bend, river-meadow, promontory

*hamol, *hamel *OE* mutilated, crooked

hām-stede, hǣm-styde *OE* homestead, site of a dwelling

hām-tūn *OE* home farm or settlement, enclosure in which a homestead stands

hana *OE* cock (of wild bird)

hangra *OE* wood on a steep slope

hār *OE* hoar, grey, *also* boundary

hara *OE* hare

*hāth *OE* heath, heather, uncultivated land

haugr *OScand.* hill, mound, tumulus

hēafod *OE* head, headland, end of a ridge, river-source

hēah *OE* high, *also* chief

hearg *OE* heathen shrine or temple

hecg(e) *OE* hedge

hēg, hīeg *OE* hay

helde, hielde *OE* slope

hengest *OE* stallion

henn *OE* hen (of wild bird)

heorot *OE* hart, stag

here *OE* army

hīd *OE* hide of land, amount of land for the support of one free family and its dependants (*usually about 120 acres*)

hind *OE* hind, doe

hīwan (*genitive* **hīgna**) *OE* household, members of a family or religious community

hīwisc *OE* household, amount of land for the support of a family

hlāw, hlǣw *OE* tumulus, mound, hill

hlinc *OE* ridge, ledge, terrace

hlith *OE*, **hlíth** *OScand.* hill-slope

hlōse *OE* pigsty

hōc *OE* hook or corner of land, land in a bend

hōh *OE* heel of land, projecting hill-spur

hol *OE* (i) *as noun* a hole or hollow, (ii) *as adjective* hollow, deep

holegn *OE* holly

holmr *OScand.* island, raised ground in marsh, river-meadow

holt *OE* wood, thicket

hop *OE* small enclosed valley, enclosure in marsh or moor

horn *OE*, *OScand.*, ***horna** *OE* horn, hornshaped hill or piece of land

hors *OE* horse

horu *OE* filth, dirt

hrēfn *OE*, **hrafn** *OScand.* raven

hramsa *OE* garlic

hrēod *OE* reed, rush

hrīs *OE*, **hrís** *OScand.* brushwood, shrubs

hrīther *OE* ox, cattle

hrōc *OE*, **hrókr** *OScand.* rook

hrycg *OE*, **hryggr** *OScand.* ridge

hund *OE* dog

hunig *OE* honey

hunta *OE* huntsman

hūs *OE*, **hús** *OScand.* house

*hvin *OScand.* gorse

hwǣte *OE* wheat

hwēol *OE* wheel, circular feature

hwerfel, hwyrfel *OE*, **hvirfill** *OScand.* circle, circular feature

hwīt *OE*, **hvítr** *OScand.* white

hyll *OE* hill

hyrst *OE* wooded hill

hȳth *OE* landing-place or harbour, inland port

-ing *OE suffix* place or stream characterized by, place belonging to

-ing- *OE connective particle implying* associated with *or* called after

-inga- *OE genitive (possessive) case of* **-ingas**

-ingas *OE plural suffix* people of, family or followers of, dwellers at

īw, ēow, *īg *OE* yew-tree

kaldr *OScand.* cold

kalfr *OScand.* calf

karl *OScand.* freeman, peasant

kelda *OScand.* spring

kirkja *OScand.* church

kjarr *OScand.* marsh overgrown with brushwood

konungr, kunung *OScand.* king

krók *OScand.* bend, land in a riverbend

kross *OScand.* cross

lacu *OE* stream, water-course

lād *OE* water-course, **gelād** *OE* river-crossing

***læcc, *læce** *OE* stream, bog

læs *OE* pasture, meadow-land

lamb *OE* lamb

land *OE* tract of land, estate, cultivated land

***lann** *Cornish, OWelsh,* **llan** *Welsh* churchyard, church-site, church

lang *OE,* **langr** *OScand.* long

lāwerce *OE* lark

lēac *OE* leek, garlic

lēah *OE* wood, woodland clearing or glade, *later* pasture, meadow

līn *OE,* **lín** *OScand.* flax

lind *OE* lime-tree

loc, loca *OE* lock, fold, enclosure

lundr *OScand.* small wood or grove

lȳtel *OE* little

mǣd *OE* meadow

mǣgden *OE* maiden

mǣl, mēl *OE* cross, crucifix

mǣne, gemǣne *OE* held in common, communal

mǣre, gemǣre *OE* boundary

***mapel, *mapul, mapuldor** *OE* mapletree

marr *OScand.* fen, marsh

mearc *OE* boundary

melr *OScand.* sand-bank, sand-hill

mēos *OE* moss

mere *OE* pond, pool, lake

mersc *OE* marsh, marshland

micel, mycel *OE,* **mikill** *OScand.* great

middel *OE* middle

***mönïth** *Celtic,* **mynydd** *Welsh* mountain, hill

mont *OFrench, ME* mount, hill

mōr *OE,* **mór** *OScand.* moor, marshy ground, barren upland

mos *OE,* **mosi** *OScand.* moss, marsh, bog

munuc *OE* monk

mūs *OE,* **mús** *OScand.* mouse

mūtha *OE* river-mouth, estuary

myln *OE* mill

mynster *OE* monastery, church of a monastery, minster or large church

mýrr *OScand.* mire, bog, swampy ground

mȳthe, gemȳthe *OE* confluence of rivers

nǣss, ness *OE,* **nes** *OScand.* promontory, headland

nīwe, nēowe *OE* new

north *OE* north, northern

ōfer *OE* bank, margin, shore

***ofer, *ufer** *OE* flat-topped ridge, hill, promontory

ōra *OE* (i) shore, hill-slope, flat-topped hill, (ii) ore, iron-ore

oter *OE* otter

oxa *OE* ox

pæth *OE* path, track

***penn** *Celtic* head, end, hill, *also* chief (*adjective*)

penn *OE* pen, fold, enclosure for animals

peru *OE* pear

pirige, pyrige *OE* pear-tree

plega *OE* play, games, sport

plūme *OE* plum, plum-tree

pōl, *pull *OE* pool, pond, creek

port *OE* (i) harbour, (ii) town, market town, market, (iii) gate

prēost *OE* priest

pres, prys *Welsh* brushwood, thicket

pyll *OE* tidal creek, pool, stream

pytt *OE* pit, hollow

rá *OScand.* (i) roe, roebuck, (ii) boundary

rauthr *OScand.* red

rēad *OE* red

rēfa *OE* reeve, bailiff

***ric** *OE* raised straight strip of land, narrow ridge

risc, *rysc *OE* rush

rīth, rīthig *OE* small stream

***rod, *rodu** *OE* clearing

***ros** *Celtic* moor, health, *also* promontory

rūh *OE* rough

ryge *OE,* **rugr** *OScand.* rye

sǣ *OE* **sǣr** *OScand.* sea, inland lake

sǣte *OE plural* dwellers, settlers

sǣtr *OScand.* shieling, hill pasture, summer pasture

salh, sealh *OE* sallow, willow

salt *OE* (i) salt, (ii) salty (*adjective*)

sand *OE,* **sandr** *OScand.* sand

saurr *OScand.* mud, dirt, sour ground

sceaga *OE* small wood, copse

scēap, scēp, scīp, *scīep *OE* sheep

scēat *OE* corner or angle of land, projecting wood or piece of land

***scēla** *OE* temporary hut or shelter

scelf, scielf, scylfe *OE* shelf of level or gently sloping ground, ledge

scēne, scīene *OE* bright, beautiful

scīr *OE* (i) shire, district, (ii) bright, clear

scucca *OE* evil spirit, demon

Seaxe *OE* the Saxons

sele *OE* dwelling, house, hall

***sele, *siele** *OE* sallow or willow copse

seofon *OE* seven

set, geset *OE* dwelling, stable, fold

sīc *OE* small stream

sīd *OE* large, extensive

sīde *OE* hill-side

skáli *OScand.* temporary hut or shed

skógr *OScand.* wood

slæd *OE* valley

*slæp *OE* slippery muddy place

slakki *OScand.* shallow valley

slōh *OE* slough, mire

sol *OE* muddy place

stæth *OE*, **stoth** *OScand.* landing-place

stall, steall *OE* stall for animals, fishing pool

stān *OE*, **steinn** *OScand.* stone, rock, boundary stone

stapol *OE* post, pillar of wood or stone

stede *OE* enclosed pasture, place, site

steort *OE* tail or tongue of land

stīg *OE*, **stígr** *OScand.* path, narrow road

stoc *OE* place, outlying farmstead or hamlet, secondary or dependent settlement

stocc *OE*, **stokkr** *OScand,* tree-trunk, stump, log

stōd *OE* stud, herd of horses

stōw *OE* place, assembly place, holy place

strǣt *OE* Roman road, paved road

strōd *OE* marshy land overgrown with brushwood

sumor *OE*, **sumarr** *OScand.* summer

sūth *OE* south, southern

swan *OE* swan

swān *OE* herdsman, peasant

swīn *OE* **svín** *OScand.* swine, pig

thing *OE*, *OScand.* assembly, meeting

thorn *OE*, *OScand.* thorn-tree

thorp *OScand.* secondary settlement, dependent outlying farmstead or hamlet

throp *OE* dependent outlying farmstead, hamlet

Thunor *OE heathen Saxon god (corresponding to the Scandinavian* Thor)

thveit *OScand.* clearing, meadow, paddock

thyrne *OE*, **thyrnir** *OScand.* thorn-tree

thyrs *OE* giant, demon

ticce(n) *OE* kid, young goat

Tīw, Tig *OE heathen Germanic god*

toft, topt *OScand.* site of a house or building, curtilage, homestead

torr *OE* rock, rocky hill

*tōt(e) *OE* look-out place

toun *ME (from OE* tūn) village, manor, estate

trēo(w) *OE* tree, post, beam

tūn *OE* enclosure, farmstead, village, manor, estate

twī- *OE* double

twisla *OE* fork of a river, junction of streams

upp *OE* higher up

vath *OScand.* ford

vithr *OScand.* wood

vrá, rá *OScand.* nook or corner of land

wād *OE* woad

wæd, gewæd *OE* ford, crossing-place

*wæsse *OE* riverside land liable to flood

wæter *OE* water, river, lake

wald, weald *OE* woodland, forest, high forest land later cleared

walh, wealh *OE* Briton, Welshman

wall, weall *OE* wall, bank

-ware *OE plural* dwellers

weard *OE* watch, ward, protection

weg *OE* way, track, road

wella, wiella, wælla *OE* spring, stream

weorc, geweorc *OE* building, fortification

wer, wær *OE* weir, river-dam, fishing-enclosure in a river

west *OE* west, western

wēt, wæt *OE* wet, damp

wether *OE* wether, ram

wīc *OE* earlier Romano-British settlement; dwelling, specialized farm or building, dairy farm; trading or industrial settlement, harbour

wice *OE* wych-elm

*wīc-hām *OE* homestead associated with an earlier Romano-British settlement

wīd *OE* wide, spacious

wīg, wēoh *OE* heathen shrine or temple

*wilig, welig *OE* willow-tree

wīthig *OE* withy, willow-tree

Wōden *OE heathen Germanic god (corresponding to the Scandinavian* Othin)

wōh *OE* twisted, crooked

worth, worthig, worthign *OE* enclosure, enclosed settlement

wudu, *earlier* **widu** *OE* wood, forest, *also* timber

wulf *OE*, **ulfr** *OScand.* wolf

wyrm, wurm *OE* reptile, snake, *also* dragon

yfer *OE* edge or brow of a hill